DATE			

THE AMERICAN HERITAGE

WORD FREQUENCY BOOK

THE AMERICAN HERITAGE

WORD FREQUENCY BOOK

John B. Carroll
SENIOR RESEARCH PSYCHOLOGIST
EDUCATIONAL TESTING SERVICE

Peter Davies
EDITOR IN CHIEF
DICTIONARY DIVISION
AMERICAN HERITAGE PUBLISHING CO., INC.

Barry Richman
EXECUTIVE EDITOR
DICTIONARY DIVISION
AMERICAN HERITAGE PUBLISHING CO., INC.

Houghton Mifflin Company
BOSTON • NEW YORK • ATLANTA • GENEVA, ILLINOIS • DALLAS • PALO ALTO

American Heritage Publishing Co., Inc.
NEW YORK

Library of Congress Catalog Card Number: 72-181517
ISBN: 0-395-13570-2

Art Director
Terrence J. Gaughan

Copy Editor
Anne D. Steinhardt

Production Supervisor
Mauricio Sola

PE
1691
.C3

Computer composition of word data for publication by
R. R. Donnelley and Sons Company, Electronic Graphics®
Division, Chicago, Illinois.

Foreword

A word-frequency study, such as the one on which this book is based, is essentially an experimental attack on our ignorance of the lexicon. Its purpose is to learn something about the composition and structure of this very large, abstract entity by examining a relatively small, concrete part of it. In the work reported here, the approach taken was to examine textual samples from published materials to which students are exposed in grades 3 through 9. The publications used (the "sampling texts") were named by educator-respondents who participated in a survey of schools performed in November, 1969. Ultimately, more than 5 million words of running text were extracted for analysis from over 1,000 different publications. This book describes the procedures used in the work, presents the data derived from it, and indicates some of the uses to which the data have already been put. The introductory material for this book contains three individually signed articles, one on the development of the American Heritage Intermediate Corpus (AHI Corpus) by Barry Richman, one on the statistical analysis of the data by John B. Carroll, and one on the uses of the Corpus in lexicography by Peter Davies. The work described in these articles, however, is the result of close collaboration of the authors on all aspects of the project. As a preface to this material, a summary of the project's motivation and objectives may be helpful.

It is quite difficult to think about the lexicon. For many purposes it may be regarded as infinite; there is more than one reasonable way to define its elements, and it is not always clear how to distinguish one element from another; the structure of the lexicon is interlaced with the grammar of the language; the lexicon changes with time; and, finally, there are important differences in the way the lexicon is used in speech and in writing. In spite of these difficulties, it is the lexicographer's task to make adequate, or at least useful, representations of the lexicon.

What is needed for any kind of lexical representation at all is evidence of how the lexicon is constituted — really, of how speakers and writers make use of it and, in a sense, create it. Good evidence comes from citations, which are occurrences of words in context. The more citations, the better the evidence. The more diverse the contexts, the better the evidence. Ideal evidence would come from citations drawn from all possible spoken and written sources. Ideal citations would have enough context to exhibit a particular word's meaning and syntactic function; if derived from oral sources, they would have phonetic representations. There would be enough ideal citations for every word so that *all* the meanings, syntactic functions, and pronunciations for each could be determined. The citations would be gathered in proportion to the actual occurrence of words in speech and writing so that lexical attributes could be reliably discriminated according to occurrence frequencies. There would be statistical tables to help interpret the patterns of occurrence.

Needless to say, the ideal citation file does not exist. In recent years, however, it has become economically possible to analyze millions of words of written text with computers. The meaning of this development for lexicography is quite important.[1] It is in fact the single most important circumstance underlying the work described here, virtually all of which was designed to produce a citation base for *The American Heritage School Dictionary*.

The AHSD is a general English dictionary for students in the (approximate) grade range 4 through 8. Broadly speaking, such a dictionary must deal with the vocabulary of several sources: (1) written materials to which the student is exposed; (2) language that the student hears; (3) materials that the student writes; and (4) the student's own spoken language. These lexical components are not mutually exclusive, nor are they equally important from the standpoint of reference value to the student. The partition itself, however, suggests that a useful dictionary word list could be assembled from some combination of existing word-frequency data. One might draw on the work of Horn,[2] Rinsland,[3] Thorndike and Lorge,[4] and Kučera and Francis[5] for the written components and on that of Wepman and Hass,[6] Howes,[7] and Beier *et al.*[8] for the oral portions. The difficulty is that it is hard to see how to integrate such diverse data fairly and simply so that they would be of editorial use in dictionary making. It is also likely that some of the earlier studies would be of limited use in studying contemporary vocabulary, while some of the more recent ones would be inapplicable for the 4-to-8 grade range. Only the Kučera-Francis work is of sufficient size and manipulability to yield a substantial word list and citation base for lexicography. The Brown University Corpus is, however, derived from adult materials, and it was not a purpose of its authors to produce grade-level or curriculum-content discrimination over the lexical ground covered.

From these considerations, it seemed clear that a new study was needed for the AHSD. By extrapolating from data in the Brown University Corpus, it was estimated that about 85,000 different words might be expected in samples of running text amounting to a total of 5 million words. This calculation, which turned out to be quite accurate, made it possible to estimate most of the important costs of the sampling and computer activities anticipated. It was then decided that only the published materials used in schools formed a sufficiently limited, well-defined, reference-relevant, and economically accessible source of the lexical data wanted.

Since the AHSD was to be written primarily for grades 4 through 8, the study was designed to encompass grades 3 through 9, thereby avoiding unnecessarily sharp cutoffs in vocabulary at the high and low ends. The materials themselves include textbooks, periodicals, encyclopedias, novels, student workbooks, kits, and so on, all of which contain vocabulary to which students are exposed by requirement or by recommendation. Some of these publications are normally found in the classroom, others in the school library. In either case, these are circum-stances that support the assumption that the vocabulary they contain is (a) likely to be encountered by students, (b) of some pedagogical significance, and (c) therefore of substantial reference value to the student. The strength of this compound proposition for a particular word-frequency study depends on how good one's information is about the publications students actually encounter. It was somewhat surprising to discover that such information is not easy to come by, at least not for a broad range of content areas in the grades of interest. And, again, it was felt that the most current information available should be used. This was the reason for the national survey of educators, about which more is said in following sections. It is worth noting here, however, that the information respondents provided about the use of materials in their own schools is the information used to code the publications sampled. This means that the grade-level and subject-category assignments for each word are based on the consensus of respondents' reports, not publishers' specifications. This is important because publishers' specifications are not always followed and because many publications (most periodicals, novels, etc.) are not graded by publishers for school use. To some extent, therefore, the survey and the derivative word data are sensitive to deviation in use of materials from publisher-specified norms. In similar fashion, the content-area and broad library-area assignments are based on respondents' reports, so that the categorical assignments of word data along this axis should also be fairly well positioned with respect to actual occurrence.

The stratification of the AHI Corpus, its size, and the tightly focused lexical ground it covers are suggestive of a number of lines of investigation and interpretation. These lines should not be pursued without caution. The Corpus is, in the first place, a body of *graphic* words, that is, words defined for the computer's convenience as strings of characters bounded left and right by space. This definition is insensitive to differences in meaning and function; it treats all words spelled the same way as the same word. Consequently, words like "set," "run," and "table" are treated as undifferentiated units in the major lists in this book. Access to their syntactic and semantic complexity is available only through the citations. To a limited extent, this situation is improved by the capitalization coding in the AHI Corpus. Thus it is possible to distinguish "March" from "march." This is hardly adequate parsing. Further caution is necessary because the Corpus is drawn from written, and edited, published materials. There is no direct oral input. Therefore, the Corpus can support only limited inferences about the spoken language. Finally, at the

risk of belaboring the obvious, the Corpus reflects neither the vocabulary that students *know* nor the vocabulary that the authors imagine they should know, but only the vocabulary to which they are exposed.

Within these limitations, the AHI Corpus is nonetheless a highly informative probe of what might be called the American school lexicon. Its sources, size, and educationally oriented coding make possible a variety of observations that would be quite laborious or even impossible without it. A case in point is the set of word-frequency distributions prepared by John Carroll for grades and subjects. But even the simple exercise of tracing the pattern of occurrence of a single word, or set of related words, across Corpus categories seems to generate special insights. Both the expected patterns and the anomalies (which often appear less anomalous in hindsight) are fascinating. Part of the reason for this is that the sources on which the AHI Corpus is based provide a cultural frame of reference for judgment and comparison. As Peter Davies has put it, the Corpus is a reflection of the culture talking to its children. *Barry Richman*

FOOTNOTES

1. See Henry Kučera, "Computers in Language Analysis and in Lexicography," in *The American Heritage Dictionary of the English Language* (American Heritage Publishing Company, Inc., and Houghton Mifflin Company, Boston, 1969), pp. XXXVIII–XL.

2. Ernest Horn, *A Basic Writing Vocabulary—10,000 Words Most Commonly Used in Writing* (State University of Iowa, Iowa City, 1926).

3. Henry D. Rinsland, *A Basic Vocabulary of Elementary School Children* (The Macmillan Company, New York, 1945).

4. Edward L. Thorndike and Irving Lorge, *The Teacher's Word Book of 30,000 Words* (Teachers College, Columbia University, New York, 1944).

5. Henry Kučera and W. Nelson Francis, *Computational Analysis of Present-Day American English* (Brown University Press, Providence, 1967).

6. Joseph M. Wepman and Wilbur Hass, *A Spoken Word Count (children—ages 5, 6 and 7)* (Language Research Associates, Chicago, 1969).

7. Davis H. Howes, "A Word Count of Spoken English," *Journal of Verbal Learning and Verbal Behavior,* Vol. 5 (1966), pp. 572–606.

8. Ernst G. Beier, John A. Starkweather, and Don E. Miller, "Analysis of Word Frequencies in Spoken Language of Children," *Language and Speech,* Vol. 10 (1967), pp. 217–227.

Acknowledgments

The idea of the American Heritage Intermediate Corpus was the conjunction of a number of influences, the most important of which was probably the existence of the Brown University Corpus. The present work benefits both from the model the Corpus provided and from the early advice and aid of Henry Kučera. A strong inspiration for the work came from James Sledd's advocacy of substantial, well-coded machine-processable data for lexicography. Decision making on many important linguistic and lexicological aspects of the project was based on investigations and recommendations made by David Rattray, Dictionary Division, American Heritage.

The preparation of the AHI Corpus in a commercial environment was a notion that failed to intimidate Andrew Bingham, Vice President, American Heritage Publishing Company, and Wendell Ward, Chairman of the Board, Fulfillment Corporation of America. Their contributions were a series of object lessons in maximizing the yield of available resources — time, equipment, personnel, and enthusiasm.

In the survey performed to establish the publications sampling universe, a questionnaire was used that was designed and tested by Arthur Brieger, Assistant Superintendent, Brentwood School District, Brentwood, New York. His assistance was also essential in selecting survey respondents, structuring the survey to reflect curriculum divisions and publications diversity, and acquiring the sampling texts. Penelope Davoll Gosling typed, mailed, received, tabulated, and helped analyze the survey questionnaires at American Heritage.

The following members of the editorial staff of the American Heritage Dictionary Division counted to five million together: Bruce Bohle, Myrna Breskin, Olga Coren, Jacqueline Dwyer, Vastie Isom, Kenneth Katzner, William King, Elizabeth May, Richard Norton, Harold Rodgers, and Nancy Stein. The meticulous, inquisitive, critical care with which these individuals attacked the demanding and fatiguing job of sampling is deeply appreciated.

The machine work for the AHI Corpus was designed, programmed, and executed at the Fulfillment Corporation of America in Marion, Ohio. The leadership for this enormous, intricately detailed task was provided by Larry Geissler, Vice President, Jim Schemmel, Vice President/Data Systems, Jack Courtney, Executive Vice President, and Al Gentzler, President. Without the efficiency, foresight, and discipline of this group, the project could not have been completed.

Gordon Davis, Scientific Programmer Analyst, Educational Testing Service, programmed the creation of the final tape records from which the major lists in this book were composed.

At a time when the AHI Corpus was envisioned as a purely lexicographic tool, Marilyn Richman suggested that a separate word frequency book might be of some interest for educational purposes. A good suggestion. In Princeton, *ad hoc* card sorting, criticism, encouragement, and hospitality were provided by Mary Carroll. Fran Davies made various graphic designs for this book and for *The American Heritage School Dictionary*. The authors are grateful.

Some aspects of the mathematical analysis of the AHI Corpus were supported in part by the National Institute of Child Health and Human Development, under Research Grant 1-P01-HD01762 to Educational Testing Service.   *J.B.C., P.D., B.R.*

Contents

Foreword v
Barry Richman

Acknowledgments ix

The Development of the Corpus xiii
Barry Richman

Statistical Analysis of the Corpus xxi
John B. Carroll

New Views of Lexicon xli
Peter Davies

Guide to the Alphabetical List 1

Alphabetical List 5

Special Notes 559

Guide to the Rank List 563

Rank List 565

Guide to the Frequency Distributions 753

Frequency Distributions 755

Guide to the Frequency Distribution Graphs 811

Frequency Distribution Graphs 813

Appendix A. Survey Respondents 827

Appendix B. The Sampling Texts 831

Table A-1 Summary of respondent-selection criteria and overall survey response. The survey was performed in November and December of 1969.

School Type	Public school systems with enrollments of at least ten thousand students	Roman Catholic diocesan systems	Independent (private) schools
Target Respondent	Superintendent	Diocesan Superintendent	Headmaster
Source of Mailing List	*Education Directory, Public School Systems 1968-69/Part 2* (National Center for Educational Statistics, Washington, 1968)	*Patterson's American Education* (Educational Directories Inc., Illinois, 1969)	*The Handbook of Private Schools* (Porter Sargent, Boston, 1966)
Sampling and Respondent Selection Criteria	Approximately uniform geographic distribution (fifth-name sampling centered on system of highest enrollment in any given state). Adjustments to achieve spread in enrollments and geographic distribution within states. Classes taught in grades 3 through 9.	Approximately uniform geographic distribution; no more than one respondent per state. Classes taught in grades 3 through 9.	Classes taught in grades 3 through 9; nonspecialized; co-educational; widest possible geographic distribution.
Number of Schools or Systems Asked to Participate	155	44	22
Number That Completed Satisfactory Questionnaires	71	28	8
Number of Questionnaires Actually Used	71	11*	8

*Reduced to bring the ratio of public school and Roman Catholic school questionnaires used into approximate equality with the corresponding ratio of student enrollments at a national level.

The Development of the Corpus

Barry Richman

The American Heritage Intermediate Corpus is a computer-assembled selection of 5,088,721 words (*tokens*) drawn in 500-word samples from 1,045 published materials (*texts*). The AHI Corpus contains 86,741 different words (*types*).[1] A word is defined as a string of graphic characters bounded left and right by space. Graphic characters permitted in the string include letters of the alphabet, numerals, internal punctuation (chiefly hyphen and apostrophe), certain mathematical symbols, and a very few specially coded characters. The AHI Corpus is coded for capitalization. It is not parsed or lemmatized. The texts from which the AHI Corpus was drawn include textbooks, workbooks, kits, novels, poetry, general nonfiction, encyclopedias, and magazines. They were chosen and sampled to represent, as nearly as possible, the range of required and recommended reading to which students are exposed in school grades 3 through 9 in the United States. The survey on which the sampling-text selection was based was conducted in November and December of 1969.

The composition of the AHI Corpus was determined by the need to generate lexical data especially useful for editorial purposes in preparing *The American Heritage School Dictionary*. These data fall into two major categories, citations and descriptive statistics. The citations are occurrences of types, extracted by computer and printed on slips of paper in sufficient context to permit analysis for definitions. The descriptive statistics characterize the type population of the Corpus in terms of occurrence frequency and distribution in coded categories. The categories for which analytic data are presented here are (a) curriculum and library areas and (b) grade levels. The

coding, however, permits every token in the AHI Corpus to be traced to its source text and identifies every source text as having been cited by a particular combination of public, Roman Catholic, and independent schools.

THE SURVEY OF SCHOOLS

The sampling texts used to generate the AHI Corpus were selected from 6,162 different titles cited in the response to a national survey of schools in the United States. The sampling texts used and the survey respondents are listed in the appendices to this book. The survey instrument was a 10-page questionnaire mailed to respondents selected as indicated by Table A-1.

The target respondents were, in general, the highest administrative officers in their systems. They were asked to delegate completion of the questionnaire if necessary. Inspection of the respondent list shows that this was often done. Respondents were invited to communicate their questions by phone, and several did so. From these conversations, and from other telephone spot checks, it is known that some respondents regarded their own schools as representative of the system and completed the questionnaires accordingly. Others had access to centralized information about their systems, performed their own limited surveys by copying questionnaire pages and forwarding them to area specialists, or used a combination of techniques to complete the questionnaires. No effort has been made to reflect these differences in data gathering in the survey summaries. It has in fact been assumed that the overall convergence of responses, as indicated by the relative number of times different

titles were cited or assigned to a particular grade-subject position, would be substantially unaffected by weighting school-system responses differently from individual school responses.

The questionnaire was divided into 22 categories,[2] principally curriculum areas. There were, however, three library categories, a magazine category, and a category for various additional material (see Table

Table A-2 Questionnaire categories.

Reading
Reading Supplementary
English and Grammar
Composition
Literature
Mathematics
Mathematics Supplementary
Social Studies
Social Studies Supplementary
Spelling
Spelling Supplementary
Science
Science Supplementary
Music
Art
Home Economics
Shop
Library Fiction
Library Nonfiction
Library General Reference
Magazines
Additional*

*This category was subsequently renamed "Religion" since most titles placed in it could either be reassigned to other categories or were of a clearly religious nature.

A-2). For descriptive convenience, "subject" will be used hereafter to distinguish any of these categories from "grade" categories. In addition to positioning individual titles within these categories, respondents were asked to assign each title a grade or grade range corresponding to the use of the publication in their own school systems. The degree of actual use was stressed. Respondents were asked to list "the textbooks, individual study and practice materials, library books, and other reading matter most commonly used in your grades 3 through 9." They were also told, "If different texts are used in different schools with which you are associated, please list the one most commonly used, the second most commonly used, and so on." The reason for requesting the most popular titles was to maximize the likelihood that the

titles eventually sampled would contain the vocabulary to which students were actually, and most often, exposed.

Analysis of the survey response was carried out at Educational Testing Service, Princeton, New Jersey, beginning in January, 1970. The first phase of the analysis was designed to identify, count, and systematically list all the titles cited by respondents. In outline, the data reduction followed this sequence:

1. The questionnaires were edited to simplify keypunching and the anticipated sorting. The editing consisted chiefly of abbreviating words used repeatedly in titles (e.g., "Math" for "Mathematics," "Mod" for "Modern," etc.), removing articles from the beginning of titles, abbreviating publishers' names, removing the names of all but the first author of multiauthored texts, and rearranging author-title-publisher-date information when it was out of order. In this phase, too, an alphanumeric subject code was assigned to each questionnaire category.

2. An IBM card was punched for each title appearing in each questionnaire. (There were 19,864 such cards.) This card contained all the characteristic information for the title: author, title, publisher, date, subject, grade, and school. The school code identified both the school respondent type (public, Catholic, or independent—coded as P, C, and I, respectively) and the individual respondent school.

3. The cards were sorted to bring all identical author-title-publisher triplets together and were subsequently tabulated.

4. The tabulation was inspected to insure that all required information was present for each title and that identical titles had indeed been grouped together. Ambiguous titles were checked against the questionnaires and against publishers' catalogs. Titles that could not be unambiguously identified were deleted. Titles of dictionaries, professional journals, nontextual materials (mechanical devices), and other materials either not acceptable for running-text sampling or clearly not intended for students in grades 3 through 9 were also deleted.

5. The changes made on the tabulation were used to correct the card file.

In the second phase of the analysis, the corrected card file was used to generate summary information for each title. The purpose of the summaries was principally to allow each title to be assigned to a single grade and subject, based on the recommendations of the survey respondents. (In the following, "recommendation" is used, rather than "citation," to indicate a single instance in which a survey respondent cited a particular text; "citation" has another technical meaning in this book. It should be remem-

bered, however, that respondents were asked for information about the actual use, not value, of publications.) Unique grade-subject assignments were regarded as an essential simplification for both the word-sampling scheme and the interpretation of word-frequency breakdowns by grade and subject. The assignments involved the following algorithm, which was executed by computer:

1. A title cited just once by a respondent, and by one respondent only, was assigned to the subject and grade specified by that respondent.
2. A title cited more than once was assigned to the modal grade, if a modal grade existed. A modal grade was defined to have at least one more respondent recommendation for the title than any other grade.
3. If no modal grade existed, the title was assigned to the lowest grade in the range of recommendations.
4. A title cited more than once was assigned to the modal subject, if a modal subject existed.
5. If no modal subject existed, the title was assigned to the first-occurring subject in the order given, top to bottom, in Table A-2.

The main effect of this algorithm was to shift grade-level assignments toward the lower grades in the case of texts equally recommended for several grades. To a considerably lesser extent, the algorithm tended to shift texts toward standard or basal curriculum areas. For example, a textbook cited an equal number of times under Mathematics and Mathematics Supplementary would be assigned to the category Mathematics; similarly, a novel cited an equal number of times in Literature and Library Fiction would be assigned to the category Literature. It is important to recognize that these effects carry over to the word-frequency data themselves. In fact, an important reason for using the algorithm adopted rather than one involving an averaging procedure is that the general effects of the algorithm on the word-frequency data are readily accessible to intuitive grasp.

In the third and final phase of the survey analysis, the individual title summaries were used to fill the grade-subject matrix (Table A-3), which is the master summary of the survey response and the structured input data for the full sampling scheme described below. The grade-subject matrix is a rectangular array of cells, each cell being uniquely determined by a particular grade and a particular subject. In each cell of the full matrix, the following quantities are displayed: (1) the total number of different texts that the respondent consensus recommended for that cell; (2) the number of recommendations these texts received in aggregate; (3) the number of texts selected for sampling in that cell; (4) the number of recommendations these sampling texts received; and (5) the

number of samples to be taken from the sampling texts in that cell. Line N in any cell contains the cell summary for the entire survey response; line M, immediately following, contains the cell summary for the intended sample. In cases where the sample eventually taken differs from the line M specification, the actual number is given in parentheses. The row and column summaries display the overall patterns of grade and subject use of publications as determined by the survey.

As an example, consider the cell defined by *Grade 3* and *Reading* in Table A-3. This is the leftmost and topmost cell in the matrix. Line N indicates that 94 different texts were cited by survey respondents for this particular cell. These texts received an aggregate of 540 recommendations (were cited in questionnaires an aggregate of 540 times). Of the 94 texts, 15 were selected for sampling; these 15 accounted for 300 of the 540 recommendations. The sampling scheme (discussed below) called for 270 samples to be taken from the 15 sampling texts selected. Since there are no numbers in parentheses on line M of the cell, the actual sampling followed specifications exactly.

SAMPLING PROCEDURES

The purpose of the sampling scheme was to generate representative lexical data—both citations and descriptive statistics—for every cell in the grade-subject matrix. In particular, it was specifically proposed to choose sampling texts that students were most likely to encounter in each cell, to sample each cell to an extent that represented its pedagogical importance relative to every other cell, and to maximize the diversity of sampling sources within each cell.

One of the first decisions made was to sample at least 1,000 of the 6,162 texts identified by the survey. It was judged that this was the largest number of texts that could be acquired in the time available and kept under sufficient control through sampling. It was also judged that the overall convergence of respondent recommendations on the particular group of texts selected for sampling was adequate. The texts finally selected received approximately 46% of all respondent recommendations while constituting only about 16% of the total number of different titles cited.

It was decided to sample running text rather than individual words because citations were wanted. The amount of running text per sample was set at 500 words (or as near 500 words as could be achieved in complete sentences). In part, this decision was guided by the results of a pilot test undertaken to try out various procedural options for the eventual work on

Table A-3. The grade-subject matrix summarizes the survey response for each cell on line *N*. The sampling objectives for each cell are specified on line *M*. Numbers in parentheses indicate deviations from the formal sampling specifications; when no parenthetical values are given, the actual sampling followed specifications exactly.

QUESTIONNAIRE CATEGORY (SUBJECT)		Grade 3 Texts	Recommendations	Samples	Grade 4 Texts	Recommendations	Samples	Grade 5 Texts	Recommendations	Samples	Grade 6 Texts	Recommendations	Samples
Reading	N	94	540		94	494		27	296		39	312	
	M	15	300	270	15	253	240(248)	4(5)	129(150)	136(149)	6(7)	168(187)	150(157)
Reading Supplementary	N	190	679		91	408		81	316		102	541	
	M	31(36)	279(267)	341(342)	15	158	210(199)	13	154	156	17(18)	160	272
English & Grammar	N	27	128		22	129		23	128		27	128	
	M	4	62	60	4	66	72(71)	4	66	68	4	64	60
Composition	N	9	21		10	23		5	17		6	18	
	M	1	8	7	2	13	14(12)	1	11	11	1	10	9
Literature	N	9	33		19	42		6	30		7	27	
	M	1	16	11(17)	3	23	21	1	12	16	1	11	12
Mathematics	N	29	152		25	150		29	155		27	158	
	M	5	78(68)	80	4	68	76	5	73	85	4	68	72
Mathematics Supplementary	N	29	54		24	47		18	42		24	55	
	M	5	23	30	4	17(13)	24	3	13	21	4	20(16)	28
Social Studies	N	45	148		52	225		79	282		60	263	
	M	7	81	70	8(9)	105(113)	104(113)	13	113	143	10	120	140
Social Studies Supplementary	N	23	56		46	83		31	78		18	37	
	M	4(5)	22(23)	32	7	28(27)	42	5	34	40	3	14	18
Spelling	N	22	132		26	142		25	135		24	139	
	M	4	74	76	4	79	68	4	77	68	4	77	72
Spelling Supplementary	N	4	7		6	9		6	9		7	10	
	M	1	3	5	1	3	5	1	3	5	1	3	4
Science	N	46	219		33	214		40	227		30	197	
	M	7	126	105(110)	5	114	100(108)	6	133	108(114)	5	111	100
Science Supplementary	N	54	81		30	51		24	52		94	166	
	M	9	19	45(42)	5	13	25	4	16	28	15	52	75
Music	N	21	118		18	128		17	120		13	115	
	M	3(5)	62(82)	51(59)	3	71	66	3	63	66(62)	2(3)	50(66)	54(58)
Art	N	18	36		18	35		6	21		10	25	
	M	3	16	18(17)	3	16	18	1(2)	7(10)	11	2	12	16(13)
Home Economics	N	0	0		0	0		0	0		0	0	
	M	0	0	0	0	0	0	0	0	0	0	0	0
Shop	N	0	0		0	0		0	0		0	0	
	M	0	0	0	0	0	0	0	0	0	0	0	0
Library Fiction	N	181	247		99	176		74	161		50	169	
	M	29(33)	85(92)	116(121)	16	83	96	12	77	84	8	78	80
Library Nonfiction	N	226	450		289	489		99	142		60	75	
	M	37(62)	151(178)	222	47(49)	102(106)	235(243)	16(18)	37(41)	64(72)	10	24	40
Library Reference	N	42	113		21	101		9	173		5	37	
	M	7	57	56	3	78	45	1(2)	76(138)	60(87)	1	14	23
Magazines	N	21	105		18	110		6	66		15	175	
	M	3	65	48	3	57	57	1	31	34	2(3)	91(112)	72(88)
Religion	N	10	10		4	4		1	1		3	3	
	M	2	2	6	1	1	3	0	0	0	0	0	0
TOTALS	N	1,100	3,329		945	3,060		606	2,451		621	2,650	
	M	178(215)	1,529(1,562)	1,649(1,670)	153(156)	1,348(1,355)	1,521(1,540)	98(103)	1,125(1,215)	1,204(1,254)	100(104)	1,147(1,199)	1,297(1,321)

the AHI Corpus. The pilot test was based on 100,000 words drawn from arbitrarily selected elementary-level texts in 500- and 2,000-word samples. The results, rendered doubtful by evidence that random sampling had not been achieved, indicated little difference in the expected number of types at the five-million word level, but there was some tendency toward greater diversity of types from 500-word samples. The choice was finally made on the judgment that 500 words provided adequate flexibility for generating citation context and that it was easier to count 500-word samples than 2,000-word samples.

At this point the principal parameters of the sampling scheme were determined: 1,000 sampling texts and 10,000 500-word samples. The formulas used to determine the number of samples to be taken in each cell (n_s) and the number of sampling texts to be selected in each cell (n_t) were defined as follows:

$$n_s = \frac{r}{R} \times N_s \quad \text{and} \quad n_t = \frac{t}{T} \times N_t,$$

$r =$ the number of recommendations received by all the texts in a particular grade-subject cell,

$R =$ the total number of recommendations received by all the texts identified in the survey,

$N_s =$ the total number of samples to be taken,

$t =$ the number of different texts falling in any particular grade-subject cell,

$T =$ the total number of different texts identified in the survey,

$N_t =$ the total number of texts to be sampled.

Grade 7			Grade 8			Grade 9			Ungraded			Totals		
Texts	Recommendations	Samples	Texts	Recommendations	Samples	Texts	Recommendations	Samples	Texts	Recommendations	Samples	Texts	Recommendations	Samples
120	585		57	248		13	23		0	0		444	2,498	
19	212(211)	285	9	108	117(125)	2	7	10	0	0	0	70(72)	1,177(1,216)	1,208(1,244)
46	136		25	69		14	28		7	9		556	2,186	
7	74	63(68)	4	40(25)	36	2	12	12	1	3	4	90(96)	880(853)	1,094(1,089)
56	195		37	172		68	206		21	21		281	1,107	
9	114	99	6	97	84	11(12)	94(100)	99(108)	3	3	9	45(46)	566(572)	551(559)
12	52		12	44		22	66		0	0		76	241	
2	23	26	2	23	22	4(3)	28(22)	36(27)	0	0	0	13(12)	116(110)	125(114)
60	402		51	217		96	306		5	5		253	1,062	
10	170(168)	210	8	129	104(109)	16	180	160	1	1	3	41	542(540)	537(548)
42	192		37	176		38	166		0	0		227	1,149	
7	111	98	6	101	90	6	98	84	0	0	0	37	597(587)	585
30	52		49	90		20	28		10	10		204	378	
5(4)	22(20)	25(20)	8	35	48	3	11(7)	12	2	2	6	34(33)	143(129)	194(189)
69	149		103	245		56	127		1	1		465	1,440	
11	62	77	17	135(132)	119	9	62	63	0	0	0	75(76)	678(683)	716(725)
49	98		69	131		33	42		4	4		273	529	
8	45	48	11	46(43)	66	5	13	20	1	1	3	44(45)	203(200)	269
23	108		21	105		4	7		0	0		145	768	
4	55	60	3	45	48	1	4	5	0	0	0	24	411	397
5	6		3	4		4	5		0	0		35	50	
1	2	4	0	0	0	1	2	4	0	0	0	6	16	27
43	174		41	144		39	184		0	0		272	1,359	
7	73	91(88)	7	58	77	6	91	90	0	0	0	43	706	671(687)
37	87		26	38		11	15		146	153		422	643	
6	36	42	4	8	20	2	5	8	24(23)	31(29)	72(77)	69(68)	180(178)	315(317)
35	133		38	129		24	51		7	7		173	801	
6	82(79)	72	6	81	66	4	22	28	1	1	3	28(31)	432(465)	406(414)
19	23		14	42		9	14		0	0		94	196	
3	6	12	2	22	18	1	4	5(7)	0	0	0	15(16)	83(86)	98(96)
48	77		23	94		34	134		1	1		106	306	
8	37(36)	40	4	56	52	6	67	72	0	0	0	18	160(159)	164
46	76		27	78		41	106		1	1		115	261	
7	31(28)	35	4	27	36	7	57(54)	56	0	0	0	18	115(109)	127
115	284		28	70		28	39		17	17		592	1,163	
19	164	152	5	45	40	5	16	20	3	3	9	97(101)	551(558)	597(602)
143	171		25	43		37	55		31	31		910	1,456	
23	51	92	4	22	20	6	20	30	5	5	15	148(177)	412(447)	718(734)
111	346		15	110		29	152		11	11		243	1,043	
18	176	180	2	50	46(54)	5	48	80	2	2	6	39(40)	501(563)	496(531)
60	334		8	90		16	125		106	197		250	1,202	
10	179	170	1(2)	25(49)	35(45)	3	53	72	17	101(96)	102	40(42)	602(642)	590(616)
2	2		1	1		4	4		1	1		26	26	
0	0	0	0	0	0	1(0)	1(0)	3(0)	0	0	0	4(3)	4(3)	12(9)
1,171	3,682		710	2,340		640	1,883		369	469		6,162	19,864	
190(189)	1,725(1,713)	1,881(1,878)	113(114)	1,153(1,156)	1,144(1,175)	106(105)	895(887)	969(968)	60(59)	153(146)	232(237)	998(1,045)	9,075(9,233)	9,897(10,043)

In these formulas, the two ratios r/R and t/T are regarded, respectively, as measures of the pedagogical significance and textual diversity of any particular cell relative to any other cell. In the first case (r/R), the underlying assumption is that the respondents' collective assessment of the importance of any particular cell varies directly with the *number of recommendations* made for all publications in that cell. On the other hand, the respondents' collective assessment of the diversity of publications available (or necessary) for any particular cell is assumed to vary directly with the *number of different titles* falling in that cell.

Given the number of samples to be taken in each cell[3] and the number of texts from which the samples were to be taken, a procedure was required for select-ing the specific texts to be sampled. The procedure adopted was to select the most frequently recommended text in the cell first, the next most frequently recommended text in the cell second, and so on until n_t texts were selected. The selection program was written so that if it encountered a run of texts with the same number of recommendations at a stage in the selection when not all the texts in the run could be selected without exceeding n_t, it would select the remaining number of texts required at random from those in the run. This algorithm was chosen to be consistent with the objective of selecting texts in each cell that had the highest empirical probability of being encountered by students.

It was decided to take the same number of samples from each text in the cell and to sample at uniform

intervals, beginning with the first page, in each text. Thus, the number of samples (k) taken in any particular text was determined for any cell by $k = n_s/n_t$. Choosing k based on the length of individual texts was rejected as being unacceptably laborious and logistically impossible (all sampling texts would have had to be acquired and the number of words, not pages, in them counted before the weighting factors could be established). Calculations indicated that choosing k in proportion to the number of recommendations that individual texts received was also unworkable. Many texts in the highly convergent cells (cells in which a few texts account for most of the recommendations) would have been required to yield more samples than the number of words in them allowed, while others chosen for sampling would have had so few samples specified as to be virtually unrepresented. Even though k was chosen as a cell constant, some sampling texts could not yield the full number of samples required. When this happened, additional samples were taken from the other sampling texts in the cell, or occasionally from other texts in the cell having the same number of recommendations that were not originally chosen by the selection algorithm. Similar adjustments were made when a text chosen for sampling could not be acquired. Only a few alternative texts had to be used because of the unavailability of first choices. The alternatives were always selected in order of recommendations, consistent with the algorithm for first choices. The texts were subjected to uniform sampling rather than random sampling, chiefly to assure at least minimal coverage of lexically and stylistically segmented texts. These included instructional materials with controlled increases in vocabulary from beginning to end, magazines organized in different "departments" (letters to the editor, editorials, reportage, etc.), and certain library reference materials.

The actual selection of text samples was performed by members of the American Heritage Dictionary Division staff in accordance with two guiding principles: (1) Samples were to be taken at approximately uniform intervals throughout the texts; and (2) equal numbers of samples were to be taken from each volume of a multivolume work (or from each available issue of a magazine). As the sampling texts were acquired, each text was provided with a sampling control card on which the number of samples to be taken (k) was indicated. The sampling interval for the text (i.e., the number of pages between the first pages in successive samples) was determined by dividing the number of pages in the text by k. The first sample began on the first page in the text, with subsequent samples beginning at uniform intervals thereafter. In practice, it was often difficult to maintain absolutely uniform sampling intervals in a given text. Music and Art texts, for example, commonly contained highly irregular amounts of running text at highly irregular intervals. Magazines presented a variety of format problems and often contained ineligible material (discussed below). Encyclopedias, multivolume publications in general, and special reference materials such as atlases created similar problems. Nevertheless, the guiding principles were closely followed throughout the sampling.

The staff was told not to estimate 500 words, but to count them word by word. All running text consisting of complete sentences was eligible for inclusion in the samples. Blank-space exercises that otherwise contained, or constituted, complete sentences were acceptable. Textual material explicitly excluded from the samples included headings, captions, footnotes, glossaries, tables, word lists, indexes, teachers' material (and any other matter obviously not intended for the student), advertisements, phonetic spellings given as glosses, and numbers not in sentences (e.g., paragraph or exercise numbers). Foreign words were permitted in the samples if they occurred in the context of an "essentially English sentence." The responsibility for judging whether or not a textual segment was an essentially English sentence was left to the sampler. Long passages in foreign languages were excluded. In general, the exclusions were based on the citation-oriented objective of sampling complete sentences only. In some instances, however, the exclusions were based on foreseeable input and context-sequencing problems—especially for the headings, captions, and footnotes. Similarly, advertisements were excluded because of the difficulty of marking the usually eccentric textual topography in a coherent input sequence. Sample boundaries were indicated with a pair of right-angle marks, one in a standard orientation to indicate the beginning of a sample and the other oppositely oriented to indicate its end. No editing of any kind other than the deletion of excluded material was performed. Samples began with the first sentence on the first page to be sampled and continued to the end of the last sentence needed to include approximately 500 words.

DATA PROCESSING

All data processing of word samples was performed at the Fulfillment Corporation of America in Marion, Ohio. Sampling texts prepared in the fashion described above were delivered to FCA from May through

July of 1970. Ultimately 1,657 volumes of text (counting each issue of a magazine, each volume of multi-volume reference works, etc., as a single volume of text) were processed. There were 10,043 samples and a total of 33,623 pages of sampling text.

At FCA, every page included in a sample was given an identity code consisting of both source-identification and descriptive elements. The source-identification portion included the text's assigned control number, the sample number, and the page number. The descriptive elements included subject, grade, school-system mix (the combination of public, Catholic, and independent schools that cited the text in which the sample appeared), and text type (textbook, kit, programmed material, nonfiction, general reference, individual study material, fiction, magazine).

After identity codes were posted on the sampled pages, the samples were marked for punctuation. In particular, it was necessary to code each capitalized word so that the capitalized letter, or letters, would be identifiable both in machine processing and final outputs. Initial capitalization was *not* coded if the only reason for the appearance of the capital was its position at the beginning of the sentence. Any punctuation or character unavailable on the IBM 029 keypunch keyboard was encoded as a special "all-other" character. In general, no effort was made to identify the presence of diacritical marks or different typefaces.

The samples were keystroked freeform onto IBM cards using IBM 029 keypunch equipment. The cards were then printed in a continuous listing for visual verification. This verification was performed for all cards and consisted of a continuous reading for errors against the original samples. The cost of total keystroke verification was regarded as unacceptable. Errors found in the visual verification were corrected on the sample cards, and the entire verification was repeated as before. The word types appearing in the lists in this book have been subjected to a further error-detection procedure in which some 11,000 suspicious types selected from the Corpus rank list were checked against citations or the original sources. This procedure resulted in the discovery of 3,700 keystroking errors and a small number of source errors (apparent misspellings in the original texts). The keystroking errors were corrected and the statistics recomputed for presentation in this book. The apparent source errors are listed separately at the end of the Alphabetical List but were not corrected in the lists themselves.

The samples were transferred from cards to magnetic tape in 80-character "card image" form. All subsequent processing was performed on the tape records. The equipment used included two IBM 360 Model 30 computers, each with 65K storage positions, one with eight 9-channel, 800-bpi IBM 2401 tape drives and the other with four 9-channel, 800-bpi IBM 2401 tape drives. The computers shared an IBM 2314A2 disk unit, and each had an 1100-line-per-minute printer. Each computer had a standard card reader and card punch.

The AHI Corpus in running form occupies 15 reels of tape. This file was used to generate two other files containing essentially different kinds of word records: (1) 290-position *citation records* consisting of the token, its control number, its identity code, and 240 positions of context; and (2) 50-position *statistical tag records,* which contain the token, its control number, and its identity code, but no context. The citation records are accessed by a citation-select control deck and were used to produce paper citation slips for editorial use. The statistical tag records were the basis for all counting operations used to generate descriptive statistics. The editorial outputs prepared from the tape files included an alphabetical and statistical list, the forerunner of the Alphabetical List in this book; a rank list, ascending, by raw frequency; approximately 700,000 citations selected for special utility in defining; a microfilm of the AHI Corpus in running form; and a locator list that can be used to determine the source of every token in the Corpus.

FOOTNOTES

1. The distinction between *types* and *tokens*, conventionally used in discussions of word frequency, is frequently employed throughout this work. A *type* is a particular word, counted just once, regardless of how many times it occurs; a *token* is any of the individual occurrences of the type. For example, the type *the* has 373,123 tokens (occurs 373,123 times) in the AHI Corpus.

2. The distribution statistics presented in following sections of this book are, however, based on 17 categories formed by combining the word-frequency data for the five "Supplementary" categories in Table A-2 with the corresponding data for the basal categories.

3. It should be noted that the number of samples called for in the formula for n_s is often somewhat different from the number given in any particular cell of Table A-3. This is ultimately a consequence of requiring that n_s be exactly divisible by n_t (i.e., of requiring that k, the number of samples per text, be an integral constant for any given cell). Meeting this requirement, while maintaining the predetermined values of N_s and N_t, introduced numerical rounding at the cell level. The numbers of samples enclosed in parentheses in Table A-3 frequently reflect increases made during the sampling in order to compensate.

Statistical Analysis of the Corpus

John B. Carroll

As one inspects the data assembled here, many questions come to mind: How representative of the total lexicon of English are the word types that are listed? How accurate and reliable are the frequency data? How do the vocabularies for the various grade levels and subject matters differ? What is the effect of the word-unit chosen to be the basis of the frequency counts?

To some of these questions it is now possible to give answers that are probably correct within fairly narrow limits. Many of these answers can be derived through the analysis of the Corpus on the basis of a powerful statistical model of vocabulary that can be shown to account for the data in a surprisingly precise way. This model, which apparently was first developed by G. Herdan,[1] is called the *lognormal* model, because it postulates that the total vocabulary underlying a corpus is distributed according to the familiar "normal distribution" when the logarithms of the frequencies are used. The model has been further refined and applied to several well-known word-frequency distributions, including the Lorge Magazine Count[2] and the Brown University Corpus assembled by Kučera and Francis.[3] We are gratified to be able to apply it to the data now assembled here.

Although complete understanding of the lognormal model requires considerable mathematical sophistication, we will attempt to give a simplified explanation in order to permit the reader to gain some appreciation of it as it is applied to the various frequency counts presented here. To make this explanation as concrete as possible, we will base it on the data for the complete American Heritage Intermediate Corpus of 5,088,721 tokens and 86,741 types.[4]

THE LOGNORMAL MODEL OF WORD-FREQUENCY DISTRIBUTION

Basic to an understanding of the lognormal model are the following concepts or ideas:

1. Any particular corpus of tokens gathered according to a particular set of procedures can be assumed to constitute only a *finite* sample of a presumptive *infinite* corpus that might be assembled by continuing indefinitely to sample words according to the same procedures. For example, the AHI Corpus, assembled by following certain rules and procedures, is only a small sample of the infinite number of words that might be gathered by following the same procedures indefinitely. Similarly, the 840,857 tokens assigned to grade 3 are only a small sample of the infinite number of tokens that could *in theory* be obtained by sampling grade 3 publications indefinitely. (This is only a theoretical idea, because obviously the number of grade 3 publications is limited; nevertheless, the idea is useful and conceivable from a mathematical standpoint.) Note, however, that the theoretical population of words underlying the total AHI Corpus might have characteristics different from those of the theoretical population of words underlying the grade 3 section of the Corpus.

2. In the theoretical population of tokens giving rise to any particular sample, each word type has a "true" probability, defined as the proportion of the total token population accounted for by that word type. For example, suppose that the word type *the* has a true probability of .07; this means that 7% of all tokens in the population will be examples of the type *the*. Mathematically, the true probability, symbolized as π, is the limit of the ratio of the number of tokens of a given word type to the total number of tokens, as the number of tokens increases without limit. π can take

any value between 0 and 1; many word types will, of course, have extremely small values of π, such as .000000001, or 1 in a billion.

3. The lognormal model assumes that there is a finite number of word types represented in the infinite population of word tokens and that the logarithms of the probabilities of these types are distributed according to the so-called "normal" distribution, with a mean μ_τ and a standard deviation σ. For convenience, we use logarithms to the base 10, so that $\log(.1) = -1$, $\log(.01) = -2$, $\log(.001) = -3$, etc. By computational procedures that we will not explain here, we estimate that the population of word types from which the AHI Corpus was drawn has (approximately) 609,606 word types, distributed as shown in Figure B-1 with a mean logarithmic probability of -8.8784 and standard deviation of 1.6392. The height of the curve at any point represents the relative frequency of types at that point. By virtue of the mathematical properties of the normal distribution, this means that half of the word types have logarithmic probabilities *below* the mean of -8.8784 (corresponding to a probability of .0000000013231), and the other half have logarithmic probabilities *above* this value. The standard deviation is a measure of the spread or dispersion of the distribution, and again by virtue of the mathematical properties of the normal distribution, we can make a table (Table B-1) showing the number of types having given true probabilities (or less) at various points in the distribution, at intervals of one standard deviation.

Table B-1. The theoretical type distribution for the AHI Corpus.

Standard Deviation from the Mean of the Type Distribution	log (π)	True Probability (π)	Cumulative Proportion*	Cumulative Types
-3σ	-13.7960	.000000000000015996	.001350	823
-2σ	-12.1568	.00000000000069695	.02275	13868
-1σ	-10.5176	.000000000030367	.15866	96720
0	-8.8784	.0000000013231	.50000	304803
1σ	-7.2392	.000000057650	.84134	512886
2σ	-5.6000	.0000025119	.97725	595737
3σ	-3.9608	.00010945	.998650	608783
4σ	-2.3216	.0047687	.99996833	609587
5σ	-0.6824	.20778	.999999713	609605.8

*These proportions are given by the properties of the normal distribution, as given in tables of cumulative areas of this distribution.

The first line of this table is to be interpreted as meaning that, starting at the left-hand end of Figure B-1 and running up to 3 standard deviations to the *left* of the mean, where the logarithmic probability is -13.7960 (corresponding to a true probability of .000000000000015996), we encounter .001350 of all the types, i.e., 823 of them. Similarly, the last line means that if we start at the left-hand end of Figure B-1 and go to 5 standard deviations to the *right* of the

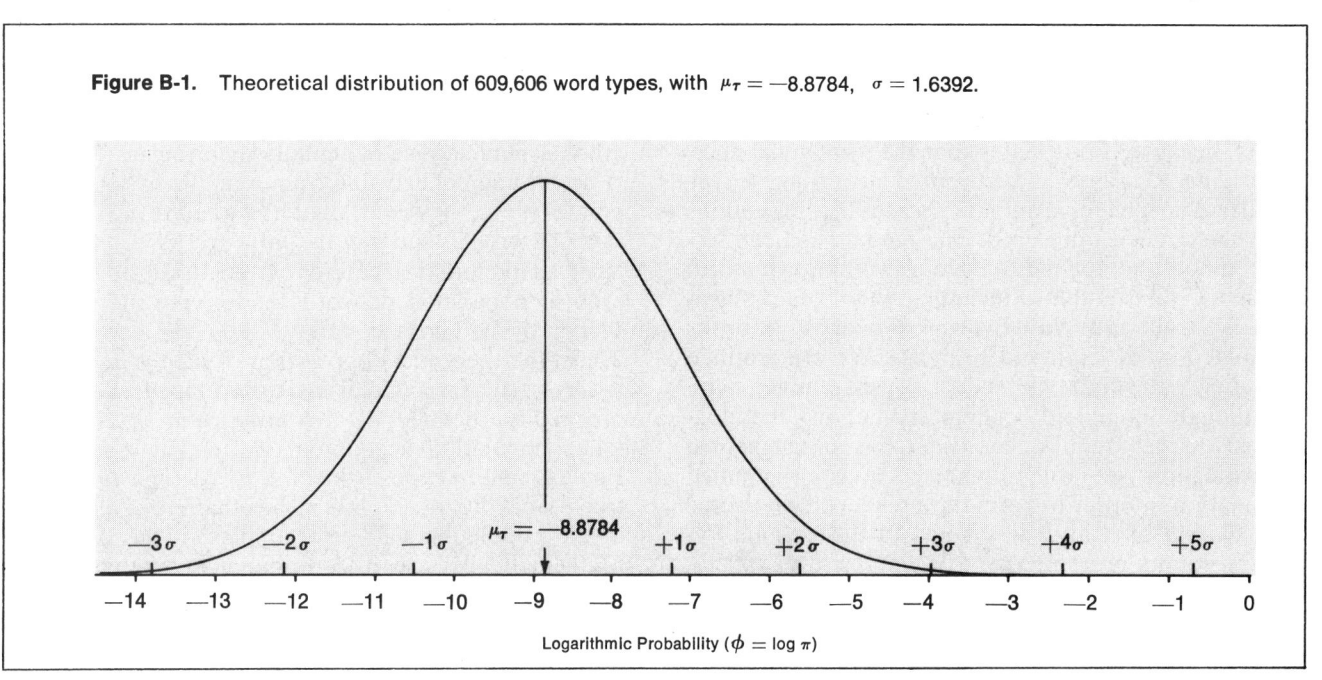

Figure B-1. Theoretical distribution of 609,606 word types, with $\mu_\tau = -8.8784$, $\sigma = 1.6392$.

Logarithmic Probability ($\phi = \log \pi$)

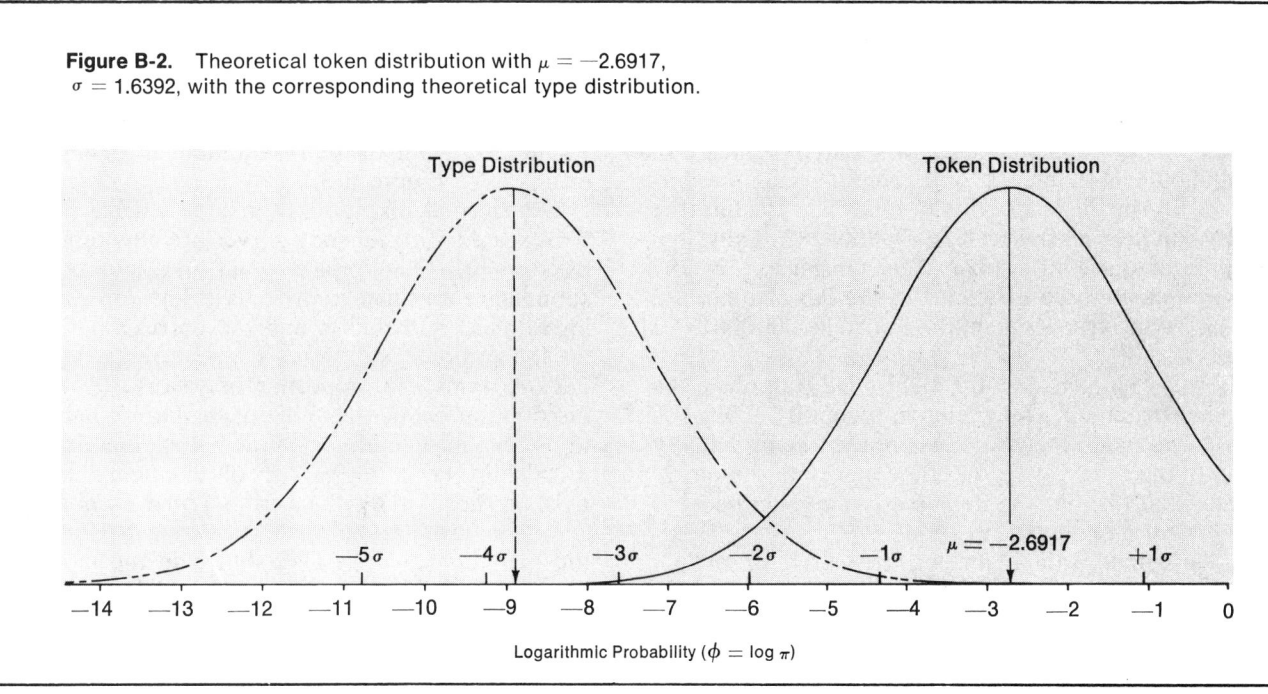

Figure B-2. Theoretical token distribution with $\mu = -2.6917$, $\sigma = 1.6392$, with the corresponding theoretical type distribution.

Type Distribution

Token Distribution

-5σ -4σ -3σ -2σ -1σ $\mu = -2.6917$ $+1\sigma$

−14 −13 −12 −11 −10 −9 −8 −7 −6 −5 −4 −3 −2 −1 0

Logarithmic Probability ($\phi = \log \pi$)

mean, where the logarithmic probability is -0.6824 (corresponding to a true probability of .20778), we encounter .999999713 of all the 609,606 types, i.e., 609,605.8, or practically all of them. It may be a little difficult to think of this theoretical population of types, of which most have extremely small probabilities, but this is what the model specifies. As we shall see, only a relatively small proportion of the types (just the "top of the iceberg," so to speak) is likely to show up even in a sample of 5,088,721 tokens.

4. Generated by the lognormal distribution of types, there is a corresponding theoretical lognormal distribution of *tokens,* with the same standard deviation but with a higher mean. This lognormal distribution of tokens, as it is estimated to exist for the AHI Corpus, is shown in Figure B-2, superimposed on the distribution of types. The logarithmic mean for this token distribution is -2.6917. (If the mean of the token distribution is symbolized as μ, its mathematical relation with the mean of the type distribution is as follows: $\mu = \mu_\tau + 2.3026\,\sigma^2$.)

We will try to explain how the theoretical *token* distribution is generated from the theoretical type distribution. We can think of the theoretical type distribution as being divided into 609,606 vertical slices, one for each type, each slice having the same area. For example (referring to Table B-1), at $+4\sigma$ suppose that there exists a single type with a logarithmic probability of -2.3216, or a true probability of .0047687. By the definition of the true probability, this is the proportion of tokens that would be accounted for by this particular type, and hence it is also the area of

the token distribution accounted for by this type. To represent this area in the token distribution, a relatively high slice is required. As we move up and down in the type distribution, it happens that, by mathematical necessity, the heights of the corresponding slices in the token distribution form the curve of a normal distribution with a mean and a standard deviation that are related to the parameters of the type distribution.

Again using the properties of the normal distribution, we can form a table that shows the proportions of the token distribution that fall below given points. The first line of Table B-2 is to be interpreted as follows: At 5 standard deviations below the mean of the

Table B-2 The theoretical token distribution for the AHI Corpus.

Standard Deviation from the Mean of the Token Distribution	log (π)	True Probability (π)	Cumulative Proportion of Tokens
-5σ	-10.8877	.000000000012951	.000000287
-4σ	-9.2485	.00000000056429	.00003167
-3σ	-7.6093	.000000024587	.001350
-2σ	-5.9701	.0000010713	.02275
-1σ	-4.3309	.000046677	.15866
0σ	-2.6917	.0020338	.50000
$+1\sigma$	-1.0525	.088614	.84134

token distribution, the logarithmic probability is -10.8877 (corresponding to a probability of .000000000013), and in a theoretically infinite corpus of tokens the proportion of tokens having this true probability (or less) would be .000000287. Thus, in a sample of one billion tokens, one might expect 287 of the tokens to be examples of the large number of types having true probabilities of .000000000013 or less.

It will be noted that the right-hand portion of the token distribution, as depicted in Figure B-2, comes to an abrupt end at $\log \pi = 0$, where the true probability is 1. In the refined version of the model, this anomaly is adjusted for, but the details are not given here, as they need not concern the reader.[5]

5. Any finite sample of tokens will represent an upward-biased sample of the types in the underlying theoretical distribution. That is, the more frequent types (those with higher true probabilities) are more likely to appear in the sample. Nearly all the high-probability types are likely to appear in the sample, while only a few of the rarer types will. Of any group of types with approximately similar probabilities, the number of types that will appear once, twice, or any number of times in the sample can be predicted by probability theory. (The Poisson distribution is used for this purpose.) From such considerations, the form of the *sample* type and token distributions can be predicted and compared with the actual distributions. In practice, computations are performed to find the parameters (mean and standard deviation) of the theoretical distribution of types that generates a sample token distribution that best approximates the actual token distribution. The parameters of the theoretical type distribution given here, $\mu_\tau = -8.8784$ and $\sigma = 1.6392$, are in fact the parameters that give the *predicted* token distribution for a sample of 5,088,721 tokens that best fits, according to a certain criterion,[6] the actual token distribution of the total AHI Corpus.

6. While up to this point the theoretical type and token distributions have been represented in the familiar form of frequency curves, there is a more convenient way to depict these distributions, namely, by the graphing of the *cumulative* frequency distribution on lognormal coordinates. The base line for such a graph is still the logarithmic probability, but the ordinate is scaled in terms of the "normal-deviate" values of the cumulative proportions. These normal-deviate values are in effect the number of standard-deviation units above (+) or below (−) the mean of the normal distribution and correspond to cumulative areas up to a given point, measured from the left-hand, or $-\infty$, end of the normal distribution frequency

curve. This can easily be understood by comparing Figure B-2 with its representation in lognormal coordinates in Figure B-3.

The normal distributions that in Figure B-2 were represented by frequency curves are now represented by straight lines. For any point on a line, the corresponding coordinate on the base line represents the logarithmic probability, and the corresponding value on the ordinate, or "Y-axis," represents, in normal deviate terms, the proportion of area in the frequency distribution below the value of ϕ. The actual proportions for the several normal-deviate values are shown in a short table at the top of the figure. (By subtracting these proportions from 1, the proportions of area *above* the given value of ϕ can be found, and these proportions are also shown in the table.) The reason the lines are straight is that the proportions corresponding to the normal-deviate values are precisely those expected by virtue of the mathematical characteristics of the normal distribution, and these distributions are by hypothesis normal distributions. In the figure, the arrows are placed to help the reader find the means of the two distributions on the base line that correspond to a normal-deviate value of 0 and a cumulative proportional area of exactly .5 below each mean. Since the two distributions have the same standard deviation, the two distribution lines have the same slope and are hence exactly parallel. (If the standard deviations were smaller, the slopes would be greater. A limit would be reached if the standard deviations were zero, in which case the distributions would be identical vertical lines, representing a case in which all types would have identical frequencies.)

7. A similar graphical representation can be used to display *sample* type and token distributions, either the actual distributions from raw data or distributions predicted mathematically. Figure B-4 (p. xxvi) is the same as Figure B-3, but the actual type and token distributions for the raw data of the total AHI Corpus have been added. The interpretation of the values of ϕ on the base line for these distributions, however, is somewhat different from the interpretation for the theoretical distributions. The actual distributions do not yield the *true* probabilities of the types, but only estimates of them — and these estimates are on the average biased upward. Consider, for example, the leftmost point in the actual token distribution, plotted for $\phi = -6.5305$ and normal deviate $= -2.4628$. This represents the fact that in the actual distribution 35,079 types appeared just once, accounting, of course, for 35,079 tokens — that is, for .006893 of the total number of 5,088,721 tokens (-2.4628 is the normal deviate corresponding to a cumulative area of .006893). The probability of occurrence of each of these

Figure B-3. Representation of the theoretical type and token distributions of Figure B-2 on lognormal coordinates. The proportions of areas below and above selected values of normal deviates are as follows:

Proportion Below	Normal Deviate	Proportion Above
.9999997133	5	.0000002867
.99996833	4	.00003167
.998650	3	.001350
.97725	2	.02275
.8413	1	.1587
.5000	0	.5000
.1587	—1	.8413
.02275	—2	.97725
.001350	—3	.998650
.00003167	—4	.99996833
.0000002867	—5	.9999997133

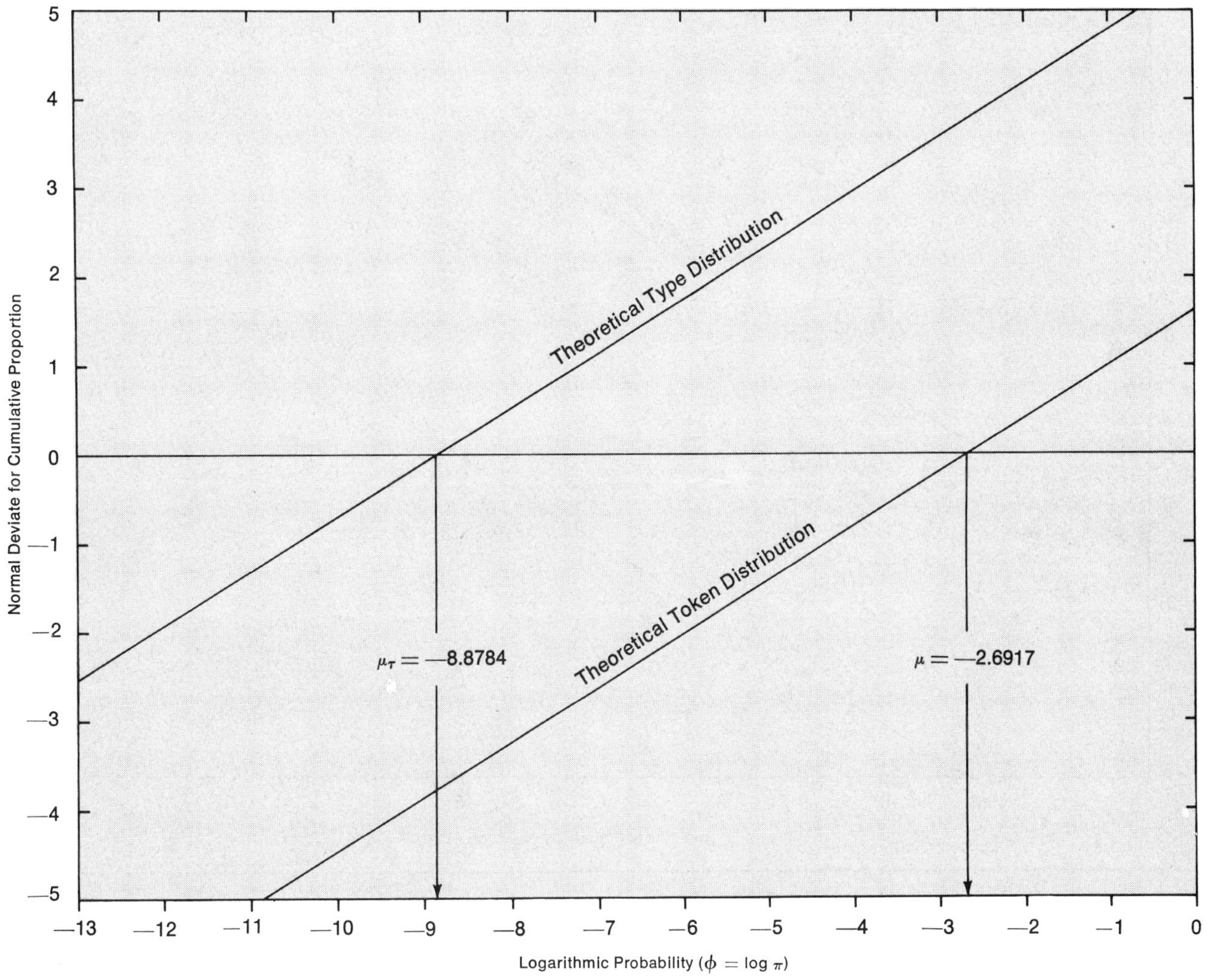

35,079 tokens can be said to be 1/5,088,721, or .00000019651; the corresponding logarithmic probability is —6.7066. The value of —6.5305 that is plotted is derived by regarding the frequency as a continuous variable extending from $\frac{1}{2}$ to $1\frac{1}{2}$; thus, the logarithmic probability for the upper bound $(1\frac{1}{2}/5,088,721)$ is

plotted. A similar consideration applies to the remainder of the points; i.e., logarithmic probabilities are computed from frequencies of $2\frac{1}{2}$, $3\frac{1}{2}$, $4\frac{1}{2}$, etc.

Let us return, however, to the point made above that the actual distributions yield biased estimates of the true probabilities. The 35,079 *hapax legomena* that

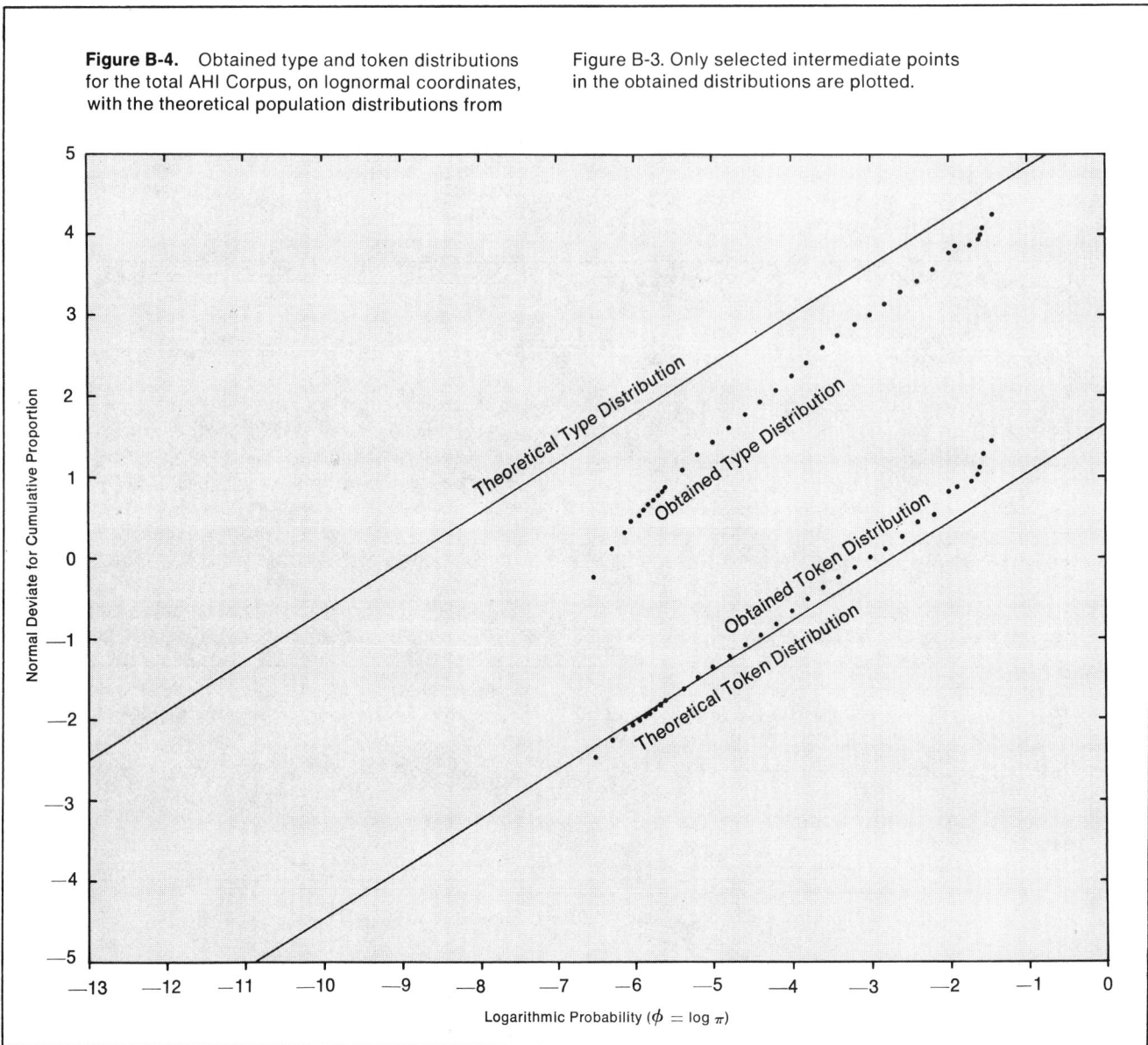

Figure B-4. Obtained type and token distributions for the total AHI Corpus, on lognormal coordinates, with the theoretical population distributions from Figure B-3. Only selected intermediate points in the obtained distributions are plotted.

appeared in the samples undoubtedly have true probabilities over a fairly wide range. Their *empirical* probabilities of .00000019651 each are, therefore, not to be regarded as true probabilities, even though (in logarithmic form) they can be plotted on the same base line as the true probabilities.

In Figure B-4, it will be noticed that the actual type and token distributions do not conform exactly to the theoretical distributions. The fit is fairly close in the case of the token distribution, although there is some tendency for the curve to bend down at the lower end and to curve upward at the upper end. These minor deviations in the token distribution are to be expected, not only because of chance variation, but also because a finite sample tends to include only a small number of the rarer types, and thus the more common types are slightly overrepresented. Furthermore, the points for the types of very high frequency tend to be shifted upward because the frequency curve of the theoretical token distribution is truncated at $\phi = 0$; to compensate for this, the actual token frequency curve descends more rapidly at its right-hand end than is expected from the theoretical distribution.

In the case of the actual *type* distribution, there is a

marked departure from the theoretical type distribution, even though the two curves are roughly parallel. This is mainly because the actual type distribution includes only a relatively small proportion of the types estimated to exist in the theoretical distribution. In the case of the AHI Corpus, a total of 86,741 types actually appeared, as against an estimated 606,906 in the theoretical population. Consider the leftmost point in the actual type distribution, plotted for a frequency of $1\frac{1}{2}$, corresponding to an empirical logarithmic probability of -6.5305, and for a normal deviate of -0.2419, corresponding to a cumulative area of .4044. This represents the fact that the 35,709 types that occurred *once* in the sample constitute .4044 of the 86,741 types that appeared in the sample as a whole. However, the theoretical type distribution curve at $\phi = -6.5305$ has a normal deviate of 1.4320, which corresponds to a cumulative area of about .9239, meaning that in the theoretical type distribution .9239, or 560,720, of the 606,906 tokens would have true probabilities of -6.5305 or less. This leaves about 46,186 types in the theoretical distribution that would have true logarithmic probabilities *greater* than -6.5305. This figure may be compared with 51,662, the number of types in the actual distribution that had *empirical* logarithmic probabilities greater than -6.5305. It is probable that the true logarithmic probabilities of *some* of these 51,662 types are less than -6.5305, for as we have said, the empirical probabilities of types that actually appear in a sample are biased upward.

The apparent discrepancy between the theoretical type distribution and the empirical type distribution is accounted for, therefore, by the fact that they refer to different base figures: The theoretical type distribution shows cumulative areas for the types in the theoretical distribution (estimated at 606,906 for the AHI Corpus), and the empirical type distribution shows cumulative areas for the types actually appearing in the sample (86,741 in the AHI Corpus).

8. The usefulness and probable validity of the lognormal model are supported by the highly satisfactory agreement that can be obtained between empirical data and data predicted from the model. The reader should now compare Figure B-4 with the graph on page 813 for the lognormal representation of the total AHI Corpus. The major difference between these two graphs is that in the latter, lines for *predicted* sample type and token distributions are shown. These predictions are made by elaborate statistical calculations whose details need not be given here.[2] Suffice it to point out that the predicted distributions in Graph 1 on page 813 are very close fits to the empirical distributions, appearing to justify the general validity

of the lognormal model. As is often true in such situations, it is possible that other models would fit the data equally closely, or even better, but it is beyond the present scope to investigate this. However, the model of word frequency proposed by Zipf[7] is, in the opinion of this writer, inferior to the lognormal model. Mandelbrot's[8] modification of Zipf's model has not been investigated for the present data.

There are some minor format differences between Figure B-4 and Graph 1 to which the reader's attention may be called. First, the base line of Graph 1 is scaled, not in terms of ϕ, but in terms of a further transformation of ϕ to the Standard Frequency Index (SFI) used elsewhere in this book. The SFI values are related to ϕ and π in the following way:

$$\text{SFI} = 10(\phi + 10) = 10(\log \pi + 10).$$

(Thus, $\phi = -1.0$ corresponds to SFI = 90; $\phi = -2.0$ corresponds to SFI = 80, etc.) Second, Graph 1 depicts only the portion of Figure B-4 that actually contains the empirical type and token distributions. Since these empirical distributions do not extend down to the extremely low probabilities represented in the left-hand portion of Figure B-4, there is no need to show that portion in Graph 1 and the remaining graphs depicting subsections of the AHI Corpus.

Some interesting observations can be made from lognormal graphs. For example, how many types does one have to "know" to know 95% of the tokens in the population of texts from which a corpus has been derived? This problem can be made somewhat more concrete. Suppose one were making a reading machine for the blind—a machine that would recognize printed words and convert them into their pronunciations. On the assumption that the machine would have a separate pronunciation for every graphic form, how many types would have to be stored in the machine's "memory" to insure that it would have pronunciations for a given proportion of all tokens that it might encounter? To answer this kind of question, it is prudent to use the theoretical, rather than the actual, distribution curves, because the former refer to the population of tokens and types with which one is dealing. Suppose one wants the machine to recognize and pronounce 95% of all tokens. Referring to the theoretical token distribution curve of the AHI Corpus at the normal deviate corresponding to 95% *above* a given point, namely, -1.6448, the value of SFI at this point is 46.286. Directly above this point on the theoretical *type* distribution curve, the normal deviate value is 2.1392, which corresponds to an area of .0162 *above* the point. Applying this proportion to the 609,606 types in the theoretical distribution, we find that the machine must store the

pronunciations of the first 9,876 of highest probability. By similar calculations, it can be found that in order to insure that 99% of the tokens have stored pronunciations, the machine must store the first 43,831 types in frequency. The problem would be, *which* types? The first 9,876 types in the theoretical distribution are not necessarily the first 9,876 types in the actual distribution. In the actual type distribution, the first 9,876 types constitute .1138 of the total types. Reading from the empirical type distribution curve at the normal deviate corresponding to an upper area of .1138, namely, +1.2066, we find SFI = approximately 47. Now referring to the theoretical token curve at SFI = 47 and reading off the normal deviate at that point, −1.6, we see that these final 9,876 types may be expected to include about 94.5% of the tokens, instead of 95%. The slight decrement is apparently due to the bias in the empirical sampling, i.e., to the fact that some types in the sample have probabilities that are overestimated, while others have probabilities that are underestimated.

The above will illustrate the possible uses of the frequency distributions and lognormal graphs to draw conclusions about vocabulary sizes and coverage. The calculations made here utilized statistical tables and formulas – in particular, tables of normal distribution areas such as can be found in various sources. For the reader who wishes to make his own calculations, it may help to know that the formulas for the theoretical distribution lines are as follows, given the parameters μ, μ_τ, and σ in SFI units (as shown, for example, in Table B-9).

The theoretical token distribution:

ξ = normal deviate = $(SFI - \mu_\tau)/\sigma$;

$SFI = \mu_\tau + \sigma\xi$.

The theoretical type distribution:

ξ = normal deviate = $(SFI - \mu)/\sigma$;

$SFI = \mu + \sigma\xi$.

The formula for the total number of types in the theoretical type distribution is

$$N_\tau = \text{antilog}_{10}(.011513\sigma^2 - .1\mu + 10).$$

There are serious limitations in these calculations in that they have been applied to *graphic types* as defined for the AHI Corpus. Thus, in saying that there are 86,741 different graphic types, we have to keep in mind that this number would undoubtedly be reduced considerably if the types were further classified into dictionary entries, or "lemmatized." If a lemmatized frequency distribution were available for the AHI Corpus, the estimate of the number of types in the theoretical distribution would be considerably reduced from the value of 609,606.

SOME ANALYSES OF THE TOTAL AHI CORPUS

In our exposition of the lognormal model, we have already established several facts about the word-frequency distribution of the total AHI Corpus: that its shape implies, according to the lognormal model, that it can be regarded as being derived from a theoretical word-type distribution that has approximately 609,606 types; that in this theoretical word-type distribution half of the types have true probabilities below an SFI value of 11.216 (a probability of about 13 in 10 billion); and that in the underlying *token* distribution, half of the tokens have true probabilities below an SFI value of 73.083 (corresponding to a probability of about 2 in a thousand). In simple terms, this means that the American school lexicon, as defined in the AHI Corpus, contains a large number of rare word types, even though the large majority of running words are fairly common words. (The first 1,000 types in the obtained token distribution, nearly all of them being words that would be considered quite common and familiar, account for about 74% of all tokens in the AHI Corpus; the first 5,000 types account for about 89.4%.) This admixture of large numbers of common words with large numbers of rare words presents a kind of paradox that is the plague of the English teacher. Of course, it is true that many of the "rare" word types are compounds of – or are derived from – common words, but even after these are laid aside, there still remain many rare words whose meanings must be learned if the student is to attain full comprehension of the verbal materials to which he is exposed.

It is interesting to compare the AHI Corpus with two other corpuses that have been subjected to approximately the same kind of analysis and statistical treatment, both based on materials composed primarily for adults rather than for school children. Table B-3 presents relevant data.

The AHI Corpus has a higher proportion of "high probability," or "easy," words than the other two corpuses, as indicated by the fact that μ is higher. Nevertheless, its theoretical type distribution has a broader range and thus extends further into the domain of very rare types; this is indicated by a higher value of σ and a lower value of μ_τ. As a consequence, the theoretical population of types is larger by a factor of about 2. This may be partly due to the fact

that the AHI Corpus definition of a word type pays more attention to capitalization, and certain other details, than the other two counts. (Capitalized and noncapitalized words are not distinguished in the Brown University Count, and they are unreliably distinguished in the Lorge Magazine Count.) For comments on the indices of "diversity" reported in the table, see below.

Thus far we have considered the total AHI Corpus from the standpoint of an analysis of distribution of actual frequencies. In the preparation of the Alphabetical List, however, three additional statistics were given for each word type: D, a measure of the dispersion of the frequencies over 17 subject categories; U, a frequency-per-million adjusted for the value of D in such a way that types that tend to concentrate in few categories would have lower frequencies-per-million than types that are equally likely to be found in all categories; and SFI, an index derived directly from U. In effect, the U and SFI values represent attempts to estimate the true relative frequencies of the types in an infinite corpus. It is useful to study the distribution of the D, U, and SFI values.

The frequency distribution of D over the 86,741 types found in the AHI Corpus is given in Table B-4 (see following page).[9] More than half of the word types, or 54.12%, to be exact, have values of 0.0 (or at least no more than .0099). A D value of 0.0000 is recorded for word types that appear (regardless of their frequency) in only *one* subject category. (For example, the word type *Abrams* appeared only in the Magazines category, and it appeared there ten times.) At the opposite extreme, there are 17 words (*the, one,*

a, on, for, as, and, from, in, that, when, at, another, more, of, to, and *with,* in descending order of D) that have D values in the range .9900 to .9999. These are words that have the greatest tendency to appear with equal likelihood in all subject categories.

The cumulative distribution of D values is represented graphically in Figure B-5 (see p. xxxi). Surprisingly, it was found to be rather precisely described as a derivative of a normal distribution; to be specific, if the normal-deviate value for $(.5 + \frac{1}{2}D)$ is found and multiplied by 1.455, the result will be approximately the normal-deviate value of the cumulative proportional area below that value of D. This novel finding is simply an empirical one that as yet has no theoretical rationale. It is represented by the straight line drawn to fit the points plotted in Figure B-5. The minor deviations of the points from the line that occur at the left-hand end can be explained as reflecting the greater than usual chance deviations that arise from very small and unreliable frequency values. The deviations at the upper right-hand end are probably due to a well-known systematic downward bias in very high values of D. That is, even if a word type had a "true" value of $D = 1.0000$, inevitable sampling variations in its probabilities in different subject categories would cause the obtained value to be less than unity.

One may expect values of D to be rather highly correlated with frequency values (F, U, or SFI), but the correlation is far from perfect. (In a sample of 56 words of widely varying frequency that have been studied, D correlated to the extent of .8538 with the logarithm of F and to the extent of .9105 with SFI values.) D is therefore a highly useful piece of in-

Table B-3. Comparison of the AHI Corpus with two other word-frequency counts. The values of μ, σ, and μ_T are given in SFI units.

Source	N	n	μ	σ	μ_T	N_T	Index of Diversity
AHI Corpus	5088721	86741	73.083	16.392	11.216	609606	1.642
Lorge Magazine Count*	4591122	74677	70.868	14.960	19.336	308886	1.947
Brown University Corpus**	1014232	50406	68.648	14.536	19.997	369611	2.157

*Thorndike and Lorge, *op. cit.* The parameters given here are slightly different from those given by Carroll, in Zale, 1968, *op. cit.*, because of further refinements of the lognormal model since 1968. Specifically, it has been found that better fits to data can be obtained by discarding the area represented by one-half of the top word type in the type distribution.

**Kučera and Francis, *op. cit.* Again, the parameters given here are revised to reflect the methods used in the present compilation. All three distributions in this table have been analyzed by the same algorithm.

Table B-4. The frequency distribution of *D*.

D	Frequency	Cumulative Frequency	Cumulative Proportion	Normal Deviate Value of Cumulative Proportion	D	Frequency	Cumulative Frequency	Cumulative Proportion	Normal Deviate Value of Cumulative Proportion
.00–.0099	46941	46941	0.541163	.1035	.50–.5099	434	72957	0.841090	.9989
.01–.0199	24	46965	0.541439	.1040	.51–.5199	456	73413	0.846347	1.0207
.02–.0299	37	47002	0.541866	.1052	.52–.5299	453	73866	0.851570	1.0432
.03–.0399	48	47050	0.542419	.1065	.53–.5399	543	74409	0.857830	1.0706
.04–.0499	53	47103	0.543030	.1080	.54–.5499	474	74883	0.863294	1.0952
.05–.0599	77	47180	0.543918	.1103	.55–.5599	526	75409	0.869358	1.1233
.06–.0699	124	47304	0.545348	.1138	.56–.5699	448	75857	0.874523	1.1480
.07–.0799	107	47411	0.546581	.1170	.57–.5799	387	76244	0.878985	1.1699
.08–.0899	151	47562	0.548322	.1214	.58–.5899	408	76652	0.883688	1.1936
.09–.0999	220	47782	0.550858	.1279	.59–.5999	461	77113	0.889003	1.2212
.10–.1099	134	47916	0.552403	.1317	.60–.6099	453	77566	0.894225	1.2493
.11–.1199	275	48191	0.555573	.1398	.61–.6199	410	77976	0.898952	1.2755
.12–.1299	316	48507	0.559216	.1489	.62–.6299	398	78374	0.903540	1.3020
.13–.1399	210	48717	0.561637	.1550	.63–.6399	415	78789	0.908325	1.3305
.14–.1499	424	49141	0.566526	.1675	.64–.6499	365	79154	0.912533	1.3565
.15–.1599	237	49378	0.569258	.1743	.65–.6599	416	79570	0.917329	1.3871
.16–.1699	569	49947	0.575818	.1912	.66–.6699	365	79935	0.921537	1.4155
.17–.1799	892	50839	0.586101	.2175	.67–.6799	372	80307	0.925825	1.4353
.18–.1899	768	51607	0.594955	.2404	.68–.6899	340	80647	0.929745	1.4746
.19–.1999	655	52262	0.602506	.2598	.69–.6999	335	80982	0.933607	1.5031
.20–.2099	543	52805	0.608766	.2762	.70–.7099	359	81341	0.937746	1.5360
.21–.2199	875	53680	0.618854	.3026	.71–.7199	307	81648	0.941285	1.5655
.22–.2299	1374	55054	0.634694	.3443	.72–.7299	368	82016	0.945527	1.6030
.23–.2399	1681	56735	0.654074	.3964	.73–.7399	314	82330	0.949147	1.6366
.24–.2499	3401	60136	0.693282	.5052	.74–.7499	359	82689	0.953286	1.6776
.25–.2599	184	60320	0.695404	.5112	.75–.7599	298	82987	0.956722	1.7138
.26–.2699	209	60529	0.697813	.5181	.76–.7699	293	83280	0.960100	1.7518
.27–.2799	220	60749	0.700349	.5253	.77–.7799	265	83545	0.963155	1.7885
.28–.2899	264	61013	0.703393	.5342	.78–.7899	278	83823	0.966360	1.8297
.29–.2999	302	61315	0.706874	.5444	.79–.7999	281	84104	0.969599	1.8749
.30–.3099	349	61664	0.710898	.5560	.80–.8099	266	84370	0.972666	1.9215
.31–.3199	392	62056	0.715417	.5692	.81–.8199	248	84618	0.975525	1.9690
.32–.3299	483	62539	0.720985	.5858	.82–.8299	212	84830	0.977969	2.0131
.33–.3399	763	63302	0.729782	.6122	.83–.8399	259	85089	0.980955	2.0740
.34–.3499	748	64050	0.738405	.6384	.84–.8499	203	85292	0.983295	2.1270
.35–.3599	504	64554	0.744215	.6563	.85–.8599	210	85502	0.985716	2.1892
.36–.3699	679	65233	0.752043	.6808	.86–.8699	159	85661	0.987549	2.2431
.37–.3799	1066	66299	0.764333	.7202	.87–.8799	148	85809	0.989255	2.2999
.38–.3899	997	67296	0.775827	.7581	.88–.8899	177	85986	0.991296	2.3780
.39–.3999	325	67621	0.779574	.7708	.89–.8999	149	86135	0.993014	2.4580
.40–.4099	318	67939	0.783240	.7830	.90–.9099	118	86253	0.994374	2.5350
.41–.4199	398	68337	0.787828	.7988	.91–.9199	115	86368	0.995700	2.6276
.42–.4299	410	68747	0.792555	.8151	.92–.9299	101	86469	0.996864	2.7332
.43–.4399	440	69187	0.797627	.8331	.93–.9399	68	86537	0.997648	2.8266
.44–.4499	536	69723	0.803807	.8553	.94–.9499	57	86594	0.998305	2.9300
.45–.4599	696	70419	0.811831	.8845	.95–.9599	45	86639	0.998824	3.0418
.46–.4699	515	70934	0.817768	.9070	.96–.9699	26	86665	0.999124	3.1293
.47–.4799	624	71558	0.824962	.9345	.97–.9799	39	86704	0.999573	3.3349
.48–.4899	609	72167	0.831983	.9621	.98–.9899	20	86724	0.999804	3.5463
.49–.4999	356	72523	0.836087	.9782	.99–.9999	17	86741	1.000000	+INF.

formation in judging whether a word is equally likely to be used in different kinds of verbal material or, on the contrary, likely to be used only in certain kinds of subject matter. Consider, for example, the *D* values of the following words, all with SFI values of 59.8:

.9107	return	.7668	method
.8954	position	.6628	king
.8586	bear	.5259	missing
.8024	bought	.2784	song

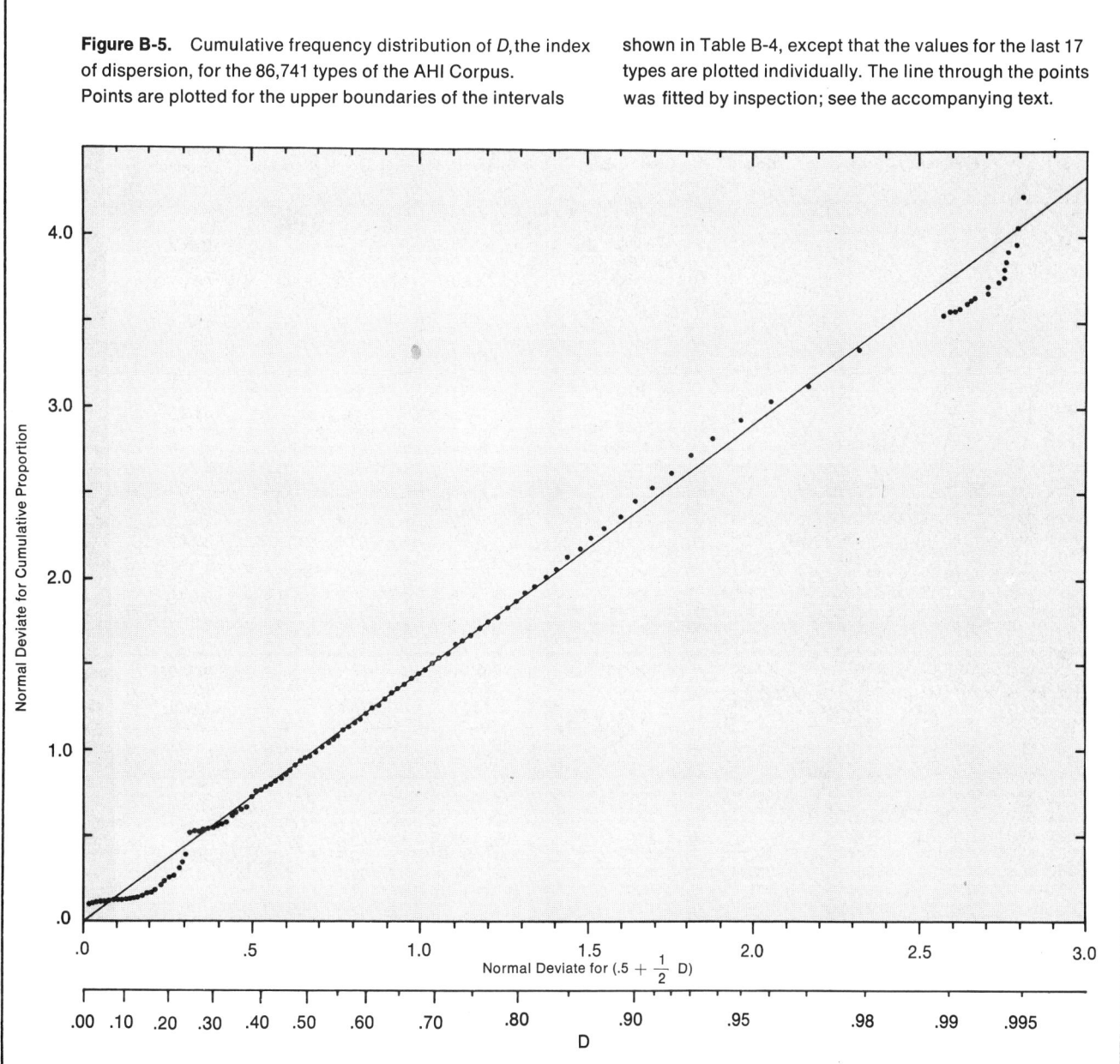

Figure B-5. Cumulative frequency distribution of *D*, the index of dispersion, for the 86,741 types of the AHI Corpus. Points are plotted for the upper boundaries of the intervals shown in Table B-4, except that the values for the last 17 types are plotted individually. The line through the points was fitted by inspection; see the accompanying text.

As mentioned previously, *U* and SFI values are frequency values that have been adjusted for *D*.[10] *U* is scaled in terms of frequency-per-million to provide an index of frequency that parallels those used by Thorndike and Lorge[11] and the frequency values reported by Kučera and Francis.[12]

We should expect the distribution of *U* or of SFI to follow the lognormal model, and this is the case; see Table B-5 (p. xxxii) and Figure B-6 (p. xxxiii). In fact, the distribution is, in general, a more faithful fit to the lognormal model than the distribution of raw frequencies shown in Graph 1, page 813. The points plotted in Figure B-6 may be regarded as analogous to an expected type distribution for a sample of a size comparable to the total AHI Corpus, with true probabilities plotted rather than actual probabilities. Note that the points conform approximately to a straight line over the range SFI = 21 to 83 and do not show the downward curving that is characteristic of the actual type distribution plotted in Graph 1. This suggests

Table B-5. The frequency distribution of U and SFI.*

U at Lower Bound of Interval	SFI	Frequency	Cumulative Frequency	Cumulative Proportion to Upper Bound	Normal Deviate Value of Cumulative Proportion
.00016–	2.0– 2.9	11	11	.000127	−3.6585
.00020–	3.0– 3.9	0	11	.000127	−3.6585
.00025–	4.0– 4.9	0	11	.000127	−3.6585
.00031–	5.0– 5.9	7	18	.000208	−3.5303
.00039–	6.0– 6.9	0	18	.000208	−3.5303
.00050–	7.0– 7.9	1	19	.000219	−3.5160
.00062–	8.0– 8.9	0	19	.000219	−3.5160
.00079–	9.0– 9.9	0	19	.000219	−3.5160
.00099–	10.0–10.9	0	19	.000219	−3.5160
.0012–	11.0–11.9	0	19	.000219	−3.5160
.0016–	12.0–12.9	291	310	.003574	−2.6899
.0020–	13.0–13.9	273	583	.006721	−2.4718
.0025–	14.0–14.9	674	1257	.014491	−2.1836
.0031–	15.0–15.9	543	1800	.020751	−2.0384
.0039–	16.0–16.9	18	1818	.020959	−2.0347
.0050–	17.0–17.9	119	1937	.022331	−2.0078
.0062–	18.0–18.9	152	2089	.024083	−1.9760
.0079–	19.0–19.9	2325	4414	.050887	−1.6363
.0099–	20.0–20.9	16855	21269	.245201	−.6897
.0124–	21.0–21.9	4686	25955	.299224	−.5267
.0157–	22.0–22.9	4779	30734	.354319	−.3737
.0197–	23.0–23.9	2704	33438	.385492	−.2911
.0248–	24.0–24.9	902	34340	.395891	−.2640
.0313–	25.0–25.9	1272	35612	.410556	−.2261
.0394–	26.0–26.9	6503	42115	.485526	−.0362
.0495–	27.0–27.9	722	42837	.493849	−.0153
.0624–	28.0–28.9	868	43705	.503856	.0096
.0785–	29.0–29.9	1864	45569	.525346	.0635
.0989–	30.0–30.9	4894	50463	.581766	.2062
.1244–	31.0–31.9	2216	52679	.607314	.2723
.1567–	32.0–32.9	1996	54675	.630325	.3326
.1972–	33.0–33.9	2310	56985	.656956	.4041
.2483–	34.0–34.9	2398	59383	.684601	.4806
.3126–	35.0–35.9	2006	61389	.707728	.5467
.3936–	36.0–36.9	2265	63654	.733840	.6244
.4954–	37.0–37.9	1919	65573	.755963	.6933
.6237–	38.0–38.9	1938	67511	.778305	.7664
.7852–	39.0–39.9	1859	69370	.799737	.8406
.9886–	40.0–40.9	1674	71044	.819036	.9117
1.2445–	41.0–41.9	1630	72674	.837828	.9855
1.5668–	42.0–42.9	1484	74158	.854936	1.0579
1.9724–	43.0–43.9	1338	75496	.870361	1.1280
2.4831–	44.0–44.9	1273	76769	.885037	1.2005
3.1261–	45.0–45.9	1158	77927	.898387	1.2724
3.9355–	46.0–46.9	1027	78954	.910227	1.3422
4.9545–	47.0–47.9	979	79933	.921513	1.4153
6.2373–	48.0–48.9	894	80827	.931820	1.4895
7.8524–	49.0–49.9	769	81596	.940685	1.5605
9.8855–	50.0–50.9	705	82301	.948813	1.6334
12.445–	51.0–51.9	640	82941	.956191	1.7080
15.668–	52.0–52.9	540	83481	.962417	1.7795
19.724–	53.0–53.9	494	83975	.968112	1.8538
24.831–	54.0–54.9	436	84411	.973138	1.9290
31.261–	55.0–55.9	377	84788	.977485	2.0044
39.355–	56.0–56.9	325	85113	.981231	2.0800
49.545–	57.0–57.9	305	85418	.984748	2.1634
62.373–	58.0–58.9	243	85661	.987549	2.2429
78.524–	59.0–59.9	185	85846	.989682	2.3146
98.855–	60.0–60.9	166	86012	.991596	2.3909
124.45–	61.0–61.9	150	86162	.993325	2.4743
156.68–	62.0–62.9	127	86289	.994789	2.5615
197.24–	63.0–63.9	92	86381	.995850	2.6396
248.31–	64.0–64.9	67	86448	.996622	2.7068
312.61–	65.0–65.9	49	86497	.997187	2.7688
393.55–	66.0–66.9	48	86545	.997740	2.8394
495.45–	67.0–67.9	35	86580	.998144	2.9016
623.73–	68.0–68.9	23	86603	.998409	2.9496
785.24–	69.0–69.9	27	86630	.998720	3.0162
988.55–	70.0–70.9	25	86655	.999009	3.0928
1244.5–	71.0–71.9	15	86670	.999181	3.1492
1566.8–	72.0–72.9	9	86679	.999285	3.1886
1972.4–	73.0–73.9	20	86699	.999516	3.2995
2483.1–	74.0–74.9	8	86707	.999608	3.3584
3126.1–	75.0–75.9	8	86715	.999700	3.4318
3935.5–	76.0–76.9	7	86722	.999781	3.5160
4954.5–	77.0–77.9	3	86725	.999816	3.5613
6237.3–	78.0–78.9	5	86730	.999873	3.6585
7852.4–	79.0–79.9	4	86734	.999919	3.7721
9885.5–	80.0–80.9	1	86735	.999931	3.8110
12445.–	81.0–81.9	0	86735	.999931	3.8110
15668.–	82.0–82.9	1	86736	.999942	3.8557
19724.–	83.0–83.9	2	86738	.999965	3.9788
24831.–	84.0–84.9	2	86740	.999988	4.2323
31261.–	85.0–85.9	0	86740	.999988	4.2323
39355.–	86.0–86.9	0	86740	.999988	4.2323
49545.–	87.0–87.9	0	86740	.999988	4.2323
62373.–	88.0–88.9	1	86741	1.000000	+INF.
78524.–	89.0–89.9	0	86741	1.000000	+INF.

*Since SFI is a logarithmic transform of U, it is efficient to give both frequency distributions in the same table. Since the SFI values given in the Alphabetical and Rank lists are rounded to one decimal, the true bounds of each SFI interval are .05 below and .05 above the bounds given, e.g., the true bounds of the interval given as 2.0–2.9 are actually 1.95–2.95. The U value given for each interval is the value corresponding to the true lower bound. The upper bound of U for each interval is the same as the lower bound for the next higher interval. Since cumulative proportions are given starting from the lowest interval, the cumulative proportion given for each interval must be regarded as relating to the upper bound of the interval. Finally, it should be noted that this table pertains to the frequency distributions of U and SFI over types, not tokens.

The values of U can be used to obtain the corresponding values of π, the word probability. Divide U by 1,000,000; that is, move the decimal point 6 places to the left. For example, the probability at the lower bound of the interval SFI = 41.0–41.9 is .0000012445.

Figure B-6. Cumulative frequency distribution of U and of SFI values for the 86,741 types of the AHI Corpus. Points are plotted for the upper boundaries of the intervals of SFI shown in Table B-5. The line through the points was fitted by inspection; see the accompanying text. The base line is scaled in terms of SFI, with corresponding values of U shown in parentheses.

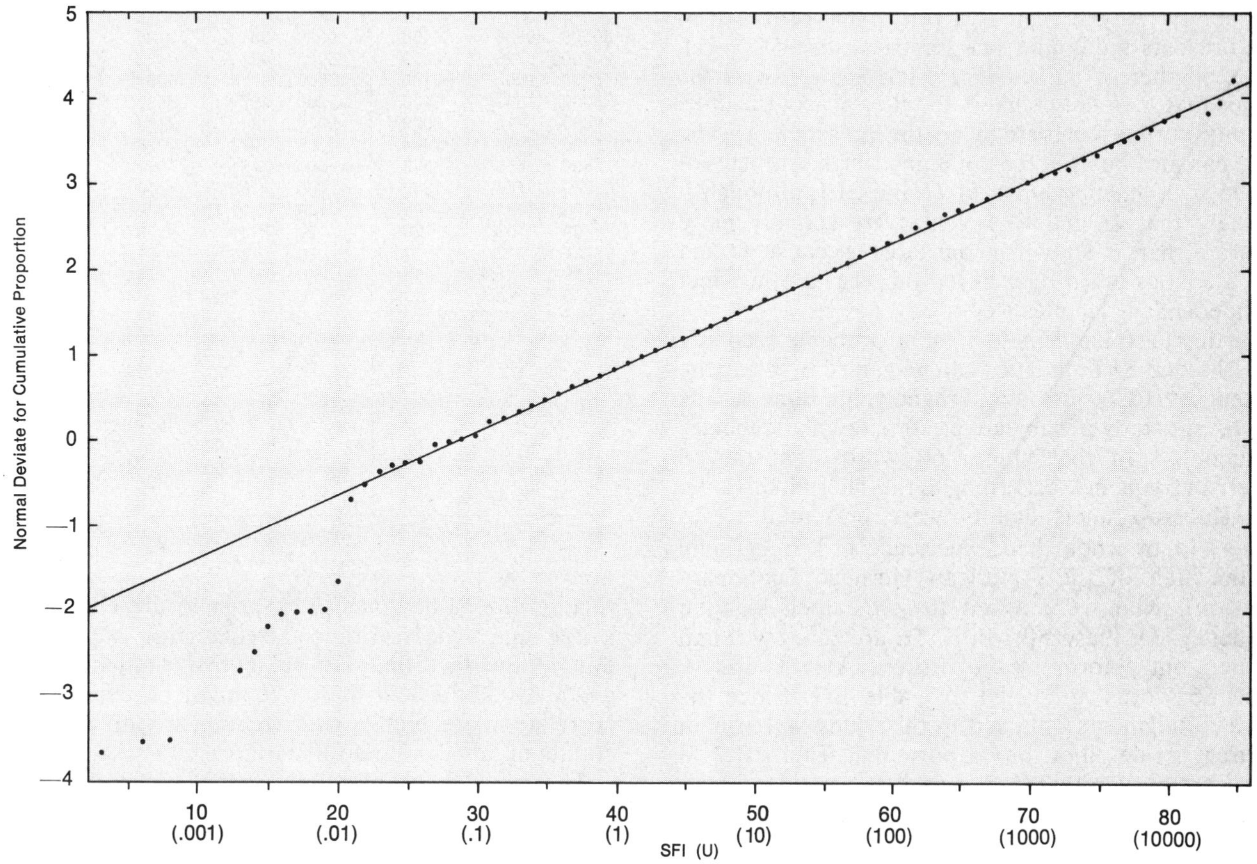

that the correction of the frequencies for dispersion over the categories generally produces U and SFI values that are more accurate reflections of true probabilities than the raw frequency values, down to SFI values of about 21 (where $U = .0126$). It is only for U and SFI values in the extremely low range of SFI $= 0$ to 20 ($U = .0001$ to .01) that the curve shows a marked deviation from the lognormal model. Here, the SFI values are based upon extremely low frequencies in the smaller subject categories (i.e., those containing relatively few tokens); these frequencies are themselves unreliable, and hence the SFI values are also quite unreliable. The deviation of the points from a straight line in this low range can also be interpreted as showing that a much larger corpus than

the AHI Corpus, large as it is, would be necessary in order to provide accurate estimates of the probabilities of extremely rare types. Probably a corpus 100 times larger (i.e., about 500 million words) would be necessary to give accurate SFI values down to SFI $= 0$.

THE RELIABILITY AND ACCURACY OF *F, U,* AND SFI STATISTICS

Suppose a *second* AHI Corpus, comparable to the present one, were to be obtained and analyzed. How much would the *F, U,* and SFI statistics for individual word types differ from those reported here? This

would be one way to estimate how accurate they are. Obviously, the expense of obtaining such a further corpus precludes this kind of analysis. Statistical theory, however, makes possible some estimates of the reliability of these statistics.

For the total corpus, the higher the frequency, the more likely it is to be an accurate estimate of the true probability. At the right is a brief table (Table B-6) that presents the confidence limits, at the 95% level, for a number of values of F. The table shows the ranges that F would be likely to take, 95% of the time, for any corpus comparable to the present one. The table can also be used for obtaining rough estimates of the 95% confidence limits of U and SFI, although it is likely that U and SFI values are actually more accurate than is shown in the table, because U and SFI statistics are in fact based on what are in effect 17 independent samples.[13]

Further useful information on the probable accuracy of F, U, and SFI statistics can be gained by using the present AHI Corpus data in reanalyzing some results of a recent study of subjective estimates of vocabulary frequency.[14] In that study, 60 words that ranged widely in frequency according to the Thorndike-Lorge and Kučera-Francis counts were presented to 28 adults (15 of whom had experience in lexicography on the staff of the American Heritage Dictionary Division), who were asked to judge their relative frequency. Of these 60 words, 56 are actually found in their entry form in the present AHI Corpus[15]; these 56 words are listed in Table B-7. Since the average judgments obtained in this study were on an arbitrary scale, they are reported in Table B-7 in three forms, such that their means and standard deviations are the same as (1) those of the raw F values of the AHI Corpus transformed into SFI units, (2) those of the AHI Corpus SFI values themselves, and (3) those of the raw frequency values derived from the Thorndike-Lorge or Kučera-Francis tables, transformed into SFI units. In each case, the SFI values from the objective frequency counts with which the subjective estimates are to be compared are also listed, together with the algebraic difference between the values in each pair.

The correlations between the subjective estimates and the objective data are very high, being, respectively, .9493 (raw AHI Corpus frequencies), .9517 (AHI Corpus SFI values), and .9661 (Thorndike-Lorge and Kučera-Francis frequencies). The fact that the subjective estimates correlate slightly more highly with the AHI Corpus SFI values as adjusted for D than with the AHI Corpus raw frequency values suggests that this adjustment makes for a slightly more valid index of frequency. The even higher cor-

Table B-6. 95% confidence limits for selected values of F, U, and SFI for the AHI Corpus ($N = 5,088,721$ tokens).

F	Lower	Upper	U	Lower	Upper	SFI	Lower	Upper
50000	49566	50438	50000	49811	50190	80	79.96	80.04
20000	19725	20279	20000	19879	20122	75	74.93	75.07
10000	9806	10198	10000	9914	10087	70	69.88	70.12
5000	4863	5140	5000	4939	5062	65	64.79	65.21
2000	1914	2090	2000	1962	2039	60	59.62	60.38
1000	940	1064	1000	973	1028	55	54.33	55.67
500	458	546	500	481	520	50	48.81	51.19
200	174	230	200	188	213	45	42.90	47.10
100	82	122	100	91.7	109.1	40	36.34	43.66
50	38	66	50	44.2	56.5	35	28.82	41.18
20	13	31	20	16.5	24.3	30	20.25	39.75
10	5.4	18.4	10	7.6	13.2	25	10.88	39.12
5	2.1	11.7	5	3.4	7.4	20	1.11	38.89
2	.55	7.3	2	1.1	3.7	15	−8.82	38.82
1	.18	5.7	1	.43	2.3	10	−18.79	38.79
				.5	.16	1.6	5	−28.78	38.78
			.2	.04	1.1			
			.1	.01	.94			
			.05	.003	.85			
			.02	.0005	.79			
			.01	.0001	.77			

relation that is obtained in the case of the Thorndike-Lorge and Kučera-Francis frequencies is probably due to the fact that the subjective estimates were given by adults and therefore might be expected to correlate more highly with frequencies of words in counts of adult-oriented materials.

The average absolute discrepancies in the three cases are 3.6, 4.0, and 2.6, respectively, but careful inspection of the table shows that for the higher-frequency words, the discrepancies are generally smaller in the case of the AHI Corpus SFI values.

WHERE DO *HAPAX LEGOMENA* COME FROM?

Another way of looking at the reliability of frequency statistics is to consider the question of where *hapax legomena* (types appearing once in a corpus) come from or, put otherwise, how many rare types are likely to appear in a corpus. If one accepts the lognormal model, this kind of question can be examined, because the model enables one to estimate the distribution of rare types in a corpus.

Table B-8 (p. xxxvi) shows the results of such an analysis. Each row gives the expected distribution, in the AHI Corpus, of a particular section or interval

Table B-7. Comparisons of subjective estimates of word frequency with objective word-frequency data.* The subjective estimates are adjusted to have the same mean and standard deviation as the objective data with which they are compared; both subjective and objective data are given in SFI units.

	Word	According to AHI Corpus F Values			According to AHI Corpus SFI Values			According to Thorndike-Lorge and Kučera-Francis F Values		
		Subjective Estimate	AHI Corpus F	Difference	Subjective Estimate	AHI Corpus SFI	Difference	Subjective Estimate	T-L, K-F F	Difference
1	the	86.6	88.7	−2.1	90.0	88.6	1.4	84.4	88.4	−4.0
2	and	83.9	84.2	−0.4	86.7	84.2	2.5	82.0	84.5	−2.5
3	of	81.3	84.6	−3.3	83.6	84.5	−0.9	79.8	85.6	−5.8
4	that	78.5	79.7	−1.2	80.3	79.7	0.6	77.4	80.2	−2.8
5	you	77.4	80.0	−2.6	79.0	79.8	−0.8	76.4	75.1	1.3
6	as	77.2	78.0	−0.8	78.7	78.0	0.7	76.2	78.5	−2.3
7	by	77.0	76.0	1.0	78.5	75.9	2.6	76.1	77.2	−1.1
8	when	73.9	74.9	−1.1	74.7	74.9	−0.2	73.3	73.6	−0.3
9	each	71.7	74.5	−2.8	72.0	73.8	−1.8	71.4	69.4	2.0
10	after	71.4	70.7	0.8	71.7	70.6	1.1	71.2	70.2	1.0
11	other	71.2	73.2	−2.0	71.5	73.2	−1.7	71.0	72.2	−1.2
12	again	70.0	68.8	1.2	70.1	68.5	1.6	70.0	67.6	2.4
13	next	68.5	67.3	1.2	68.2	67.2	1.0	68.6	65.9	2.7
14	few	66.3	67.2	−0.9	65.5	67.1	−1.6	66.7	67.7	−1.0
15	half	65.1	64.7	0.4	64.1	64.5	−0.4	65.7	64.3	1.4
16	night	64.1	66.6	−2.5	62.9	66.0	−3.1	64.8	66.1	−1.3
17	early	63.4	64.5	−1.1	62.0	64.0	−2.0	64.1	65.6	−1.5
18	couple	62.6	56.0	6.6	61.0	55.1	5.9	63.4	60.8	2.6
19	price	62.2	57.5	4.6	60.6	56.6	4.0	63.1	60.3	2.8
20	result	61.9	60.7	1.2	60.2	60.2	0.0	62.8	63.8	−1.0
21	list	60.7	65.4	−4.8	58.7	63.3	−4.6	61.8	61.2	0.6
22	final	60.5	59.6	0.9	58.5	58.4	0.1	61.6	61.9	−0.3
23	music	60.4	66.2	−5.8	58.4	61.8	−3.4	61.5	63.3	−1.8
24	actual	59.9	54.8	5.1	57.8	54.2	3.6	61.1	60.0	1.1
25	suit	59.7	57.6	2.2	57.6	56.9	0.7	61.0	56.7	4.3
26	base	59.1	62.4	−3.3	56.9	61.6	−4.8	60.4	59.5	0.9
27	address	58.8	53.8	4.9	56.5	51.6	4.9	60.1	58.8	1.3
28	spread	57.8	60.2	−2.4	55.3	59.8	−4.5	59.3	59.1	0.2
29	humor	56.4	51.5	4.9	53.6	50.6	0.7	58.0	56.6	1.4
30	scale	55.3	61.6	−6.3	52.2	59.3	−7.1	57.0	57.7	−0.7
31	switch	55.2	53.7	1.5	52.2	52.2	0.0	57.0	51.8	5.2
32	victim	54.4	50.8	3.6	51.2	49.7	1.5	56.3	55.6	0.7
33	swift	54.3	54.1	0.2	51.1	53.0	−1.9	56.2	56.3	−0.1
34	superb	52.7	45.5	7.2	49.2	43.5	5.7	54.8	49.0	5.8
35	dissent	52.0	39.9	12.1	48.3	33.6	14.7	54.2	46.0	8.2
36	convert	51.8	49.2	2.7	48.1	47.7	0.4	54.0	54.0	0.0
37	anchor	49.4	51.7	−2.2	45.2	51.2	−6.0	51.9	54.1	−2.2
38	charter	48.2	46.7	1.4	43.6	44.1	−0.5	50.8	53.0	−2.2
39	stride	47.2	47.6	−0.4	42.4	45.0	−2.6	49.9	52.6	−2.7
40	ignite	46.9	42.5	4.5	42.2	40.4	1.8	49.7	43.0	6.7
41	heritage	46.2	49.6	−3.4	41.3	47.7	−6.4	49.1	49.0	0.1
42	thud	44.9	47.1	−2.2	39.7	45.8	−6.1	47.9	46.0	1.9
43	skirmish	44.9	37.7	7.2	39.7	32.3	7.4	47.9	48.5	−0.6
44	volcano	44.8	52.8	−8.0	39.6	51.9	−12.3	47.9	51.5	−3.6
45	straggle	41.7	32.9	8.8	35.8	22.9	12.9	45.2	44.8	0.4
46	veterinary	41.2	37.7	3.5	35.2	34.0	1.2	44.7	40.0	4.7
47	cryptic	40.1	32.9	7.1	33.9	20.2	13.7	43.7	40.0	3.7
48	modulate	39.6	35.9	3.7	33.4	22.1	11.3	43.4	39.8	3.6
49	cloister	39.4	37.7	1.7	33.0	25.6	7.4	43.1	47.8	−4.7
50	shank	39.3	44.1	−4.8	32.9	41.1	−8.2	43.0	43.0	0.0
51	dill	39.1	40.7	−1.6	32.7	37.8	−5.1	42.9	38.2	4.7
52	vicar	35.6	35.9	−0.4	28.4	30.2	−1.8	39.8	44.8	−5.0
53	ocular	32.7	35.9	−3.3	25.0	26.0	−1.0	37.3	37.9	−0.6
54	torpor	30.1	32.9	−2.8	21.9	20.8	1.1	35.0	38.9	−3.9
55	pachyderm	24.4	32.9	−8.5	15.0	20.7	−5.7	30.0	35.9	−5.9
56	echidna	13.7	32.9	−19.3	2.0	20.2	−18.2	20.6	33.5	−12.9
Mean		55.9	55.9	0.0	53.0	53.0	0.0	57.6	57.6	0.0
Standard deviation		15.3	15.3	4.9	18.5	18.5	5.7	13.4	13.4	3.5
Mean absolute difference				3.6			4.0			2.6

*The values shown were rounded to one decimal place from a computer print-out that showed them to four decimal places. The small discrepancies that occasionally occur in the values of the differences between subjective estimates and objective data are due to this rounding process.

Table B-8. Expected distribution of types in the AHI Corpus, based on a lognormal model.*

Average "True" SFI	Total Number of Types in Population	Number of Types Expected to Appear in Sample a Given Number of Times					
		0	1	2	3	4	5+
(Above 43.8)	14177	0	0	0	0	0	14177
43.0	3704	0	0	2	6	19	3677
41.4	4474	1	9	39	107	222	4096
39.8	5351	18	104	294	558	792	3585
38.1	6335	129	502	977	1269	1236	2222
36.5	7427	513	1372	1832	1632	1090	988
34.8	8620	1379	2528	2316	1414	648	335
33.2	9905	2819	3542	2226	933	293	92
31.6	11268	4759	4102	1768	508	109	22
29.9	12692	7028	4154	1228	242	36	4
28.3	14154	9436	3826	776	105	10	1
26.6	15627	11833	3291	458	42	3	0
25.0	17081	14116	2692	257	15	1	0
23.4	18486	16220	2121	139	6	0	0
21.7	19807	18108	1624	73	2	0	0
20.1	21012	19758	1216	37	1	0	0
18.5	22068	21156	893	19	0	0	0
16.8	22946	22292	645	9	0	0	0
15.2	23623	23159	460	4	0	0	0
13.5	24077	23752	323	2	0	0	0
11.9	24297	24071	225	1	0	0	0
10.3	24275	24121	154	0	0	0	0
8.6	24011	23906	105	0	0	0	0
7.0	23515	23444	71	0	0	0	0
5.4	22800	22753	47	0	0	0	0
3.7	21886	21855	31	0	0	0	0
2.1	20800	20780	20	0	0	0	0
0.4	19572	19559	13	0	0	0	0
−1.2	18233	18225	8	0	0	0	0
−2.8	16817	16812	5	0	0	0	0
−4.5	15357	15354	3	0	0	0	0
−6.1	13884	13882	2	0	0	0	0
−7.7	12427	12426	1	0	0	0	0
(Below −8.6)	69090	69089	1	0	0	0	0
Expected Total	609798	522753	34089	12458	6842	4460	29196
Actual	86741	0	35079	11915	6242	4176	29279

*Small discrepancies in column and row sums are due to rounding errors.

The first row of the table is for all types whose theoretical probabilities represented by an SFI value of 43.8 or above — i.e., any type that would be expected to occur 24 times or more in a million tokens. As indicated in column 2, there are presumably 14,177 such types. The remaining entries in this row are all zeros, except for the last column, which indicates that all those types would be expected to occur *at least* 5 times in a 5,088,721-word corpus, even allowing for chance variation.

Now consider, for example, the row for average SFI = 28.3 (corresponding to a theoretical probability of about 8.3 in 100 million). Column 2 reports that there are 14,154 types in this interval; the remaining entries show that of these, 9,436 would be expected not to appear at all in the AHI Corpus, but that 3,826 would appear once, 776 would appear twice, 105 would appear 3 times, 10 would appear 4 times, and 1 would appear 5 times or more. (These numbers are predicted by the Poisson distribution.)

Near the bottom of the table all these numbers are totaled, and an additional row shows, for comparison, the actual numbers of types that appeared 1, 2, 3, 4, and 5+ times in the Corpus. Of course there is no direct way of telling how many possible types did *not* appear in the Corpus; we can only estimate this number by reference to the lognormal model.

Now consider the spread of the numbers in the columns for frequencies of 1, 2, 3, 4, and 5+. If a type appeared *once* in the Corpus, its true probability (in SFI units) could be anywhere from 41.4 down to below −8.6. The most probable value of the true probability could be taken to be SFI = 29.9, where the number of types for that frequency is highest (4,154). The 95% confidence limits can be determined by counting 2.5% of the types from the bottom and from the top of the distribution, producing confidence limits of upper SFI = about 38.0 and lower SFI = about 14.3. (Compare this with the confidence limits in Table B-6.) Similar considerations apply to the remaining columns.

As far as our original question — where do *hapax legomena* come from? — is concerned, we can only say that they come from almost anywhere in the lower reaches of the theoretical type distribution. Their occurrence in a particular corpus is, in a sense, a matter of chance. Furthermore, the empirical SFI value derived from the raw frequency of a *hapax* is generally an *over*estimation of the true probability. For types that have a frequency of one in the AHI Corpus, the empirical probability is expressed in SFI units as about 37.1. It is evident from the table, however, that nearly all the types expected to appear in a 5,088,721-word sample have SFI values of *less* than 37.1.

of the theoretical type distribution. It will be recalled that it was estimated that there are approximately 609,606 types in the theoretical type population. In the particular computer run that produced this table, the number turned out to be 609,798 (because of problems in the rounding of numbers); this figure appears as the total of column 2. The numbers appearing above this total in column 2 are the numbers of types assumed to exist in given sections of the theoretical type distribution, sections whose average SFI values are given in column 1. The remaining columns of the table give the numbers of these types that may be expected to appear in the 5,088,721-word sample 0 times, 1 time, 2 times, 3 times, 4 times, or 5 or more times.

ANALYSIS OF THE CORPUS BY GRADE AND SUBJECT MATTER

The procedures that were followed in sampling for the various grades resulted in some variation over grades in the number of words available for analysis. As may be seen in Table B-9, the largest numbers of tokens were found at grades 3 and 7. Separate frequency distributions for each grade, and for the "ungraded" texts, may be found on pages 755–779, with lognormal graphs corresponding to these frequency distributions on pages 813–817.

The expectation that the frequency distributions would differ systematically by grade was confirmed by the lognormal analyses of these distributions. In general, the parameters of the estimated underlying theoretical distributions conformed to a pattern revealing increasing difficulty and diversity of the vocabulary with advancing grade. Note, for example, that the parameter μ (in SFI units) decreases progressively from 73.497 at grade 3 to 69.252 at grade 9. These parameters represent (in SFI units) the median word probabilities in the theoretical token populations from which the samples were drawn. Also, the parameters μ_τ, yielding the median probabilities in the type distributions, tend to decrease somewhat by grade.

Table B-9. The number of tokens, types, and *hapaxes* found in the grade and subject subsets of the AHI Corpus, together with the parameters of the estimated theoretical distributions for each. The values of μ, σ, and μ_T are given in SFI units.

		Data from Empirical Distributions			Parameters of Estimated Theoretical Distributions				
		Tokens N	Types n	Hapaxes n_1	μ	σ	μ_τ	Total Types N_τ	Index of Diversity
Total Corpus		5088721	86741	35079	73.083	16.392	11.216	609606	1.642
Grade 3		840857	23477	8963	73.497	14.328	26.226	103234	1.847
Grade 4		776538	25324	9762	72.291	14.079	26.651	112954	1.968
Grade 5		634283	28488	11872	70.656	13.996	25.549	154785	2.096
Grade 6		667896	29736	12225	70.522	14.012	25.317	161441	2.104
Grade 7		957328	42180	18012	69.871	14.529	21.263	277523	2.074
Grade 8		600457	32709	14423	69.714	14.176	23.439	219956	2.136
Grade 9		489527	30693	13854	69.252	14.014	24.033	216651	2.194
Ungraded		121880	15985	8224	68.117	13.316	27.287	169758	2.394
		5088766*							
Reading	(A)	1182971	33296	12712	72.316	14.554	23.543	161088	1.902
English & Grammar	(B)	283367	16183	7459	74.096	15.052	21.999	156760	1.722
Composition	(C)	57776	7423	3774	71.811	13.378	30.598	75784	2.107
Literature	(D)	277907	19987	9188	70.881	14.177	24.603	168186	2.054
Mathematics	(E)	387619	10781	4057	77.351	14.527	28.760	49483	1.559
Social Studies	(F)	503620	21043	8409	71.769	13.710	28.488	97078	2.059
Spelling	(G)	210157	8845	4001	80.201	16.215	19.659	101624	1.221
Science	(H)	510570	18076	6984	72.870	13.694	29.692	74459	1.981
Music	(J)	209364	13850	6176	72.633	14.005	27.473	98789	1.954
Art	(K)	47887	5231	2615	74.771	13.869	30.484	54603	1.819
Home Economics	(L)	83387	7152	3050	71.816	12.006	38.626	30056	2.348
Shop	(M)	65375	6272	2813	72.342	12.255	37.758	31261	2.257
Library Fiction	(N)	303603	18415	8277	72.386	14.480	24.105	149783	1.907
Library Nonfiction	(P)	374885	23737	10724	70.607	14.179	24.313	179473	2.073
Library Reference	(Q)	271040	25545	12294	67.485	13.312	26.681	195757	2.442
Magazines	(R)	314643	29296	14206	67.419	13.684	24.302	259383	2.381
Religion	(S)	4595	863	423	76.958	10.687	50.661	4160	2.156
		5088766*							

*These totals are slightly in excess of the figure given for the total Corpus. The discrepancy was caused by technical problems in making final corrections to type frequencies in the computer tape from which the Alphabetical List was produced. Discrepancies in individual subject categories were so small (never more than about 5) that it was not considered worthwhile to rerun the distributions for the lognormal calculations.

Table B-9 also shows the statistics for the various subject sections of the AHI Corpus. The frequency distributions and graphs for these samples are to be found on pages 780–809 and 817–825, respectively. These samples vary markedly in size, from 1,182,971 tokens in the Reading category down to 4,595 tokens in Religion. In theory, variations in size of sample should make no difference in the lognormal calculations; that is, the same theoretical distributions could be estimated from either small or large samples. In practice, however, size of sample tends to be associated with the parameters of the estimated distributions because the larger the sample, the more likely it is to embrace a greater diversity of content and subject matter and hence vocabulary.

For comparing distributions, it is useful to make a two-dimensional plot of the respective values of μ and σ, the two parameters that describe any given distribution. Such a plot is presented in Figure B-7. The parameters for the total AHI Corpus and for the several grade-level distributions are also represented there and, for comparison, the parameters for the Lorge Magazine Count and the Brown University Corpus.

The curved lines on this graph show the regions where given theoretical vocabulary sizes (N_T) would fall. The various AHI Corpus subject samples appear to be drawn from vocabularies of different sizes, ranging from a theoretical vocabulary of 4,160 types for Religion to a theoretical vocabulary of 259,383 types for Magazines. Of interest is the fact that the

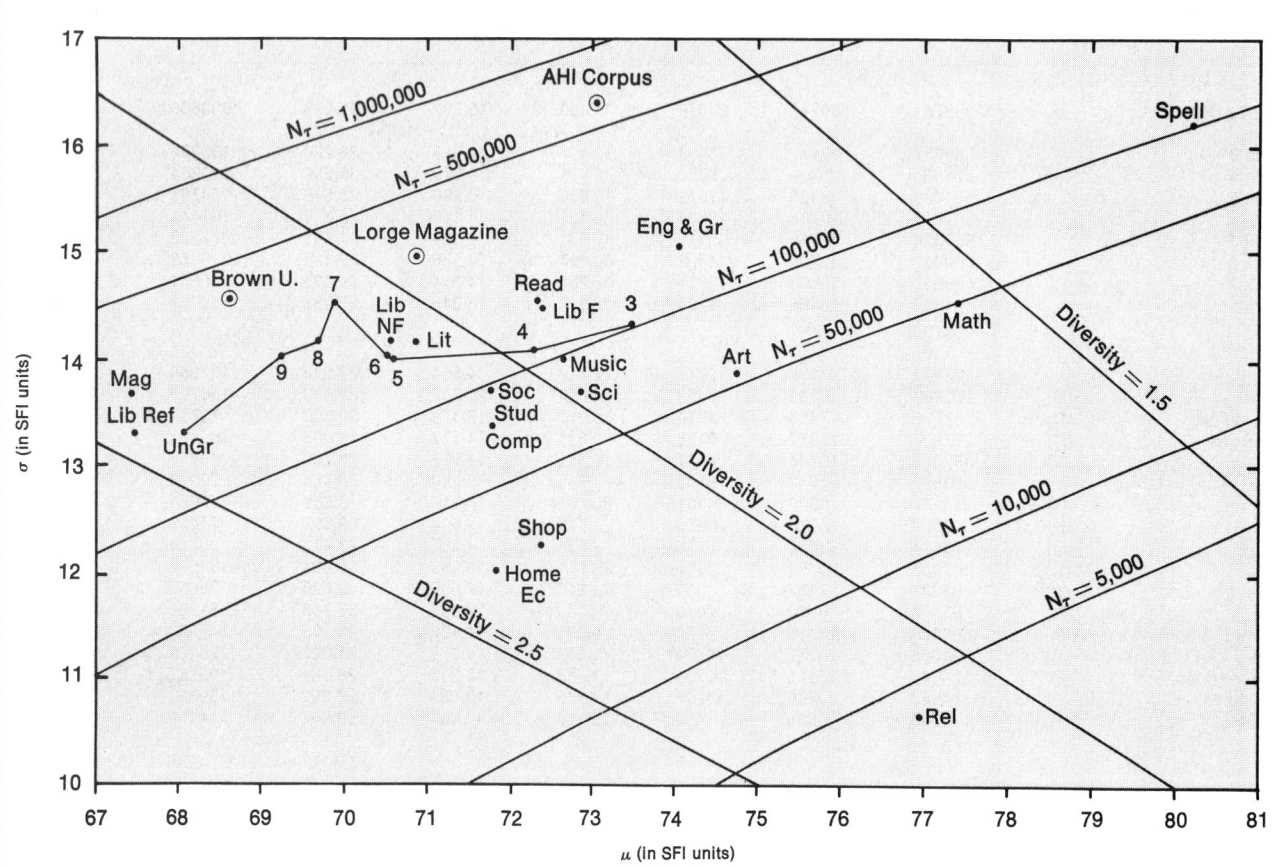

Figure B-7. Locations of the AHI Corpus and subsections thereof in the space defined by the mean (μ) and standard deviation (σ) for theoretical token distributions. μ and σ are scaled in SFI units. Abbreviations are those employed in the headings of the Alphabetical List. The points for the grade-by-grade subsections of the Corpus are connected by a line. For comparison, points are also shown for the Lorge Magazine Count and the Kučera-Francis Brown University Count. See the text for explanations of other lines shown.

theoretical vocabulary underlying the Magazines category is roughly the same as is estimated for the Lorge Magazine Count. Ranking in order after the Magazines category are the following:

Library Reference	195,757
Library Nonfiction	179,473
Literature	168,186
Reading	161,088
English & Grammar	156,760
Library Fiction	149,783
Spelling	101,624
Music	98,789
Social Studies	97,078
Composition	75,784
Science	74,459
Art	54,603
Mathematics	49,483
Shop	31,261
Home Economics	30,056
Religion	4,160

The theoretical distributions for subjects also vary in *diversity*. The indices of diversity reported in Table B-9 are computed as $-\mu/\sigma$, where μ and σ are in the original logarithmic units, and the oblique lines plotted in Figure B-7 show where the parameters for samples of given degrees of diversity would fall. Diversity is a measure of the degree to which the token distribution tends to have *different* words. There would be maximum diversity if all words in the distribution had equal probabilities, whereas diversity is low when most of the words in the token distribution tend to be the same high-frequency words. Most of the samples have indices of diversity that center around 2.0, which is somewhere near the average value found for large samples of adult text such as the Brown University Corpus and the Lorge Magazine Count. An unusually low value of diversity, 1.221, is found for the Spelling sample, a result that is to be interpreted as meaning that spelling materials tend to concentrate their attention on a relatively small number of more or less common words. The samples for English & Grammar and for Mathematics also tend to have somewhat lower diversities than usual. Unusually high diversity indices are found for the Library Reference, Magazines, Shop, and Home Economics samples, indicating that these samples tend to use more different, rare words than normal.

Particularly noteworthy is the relatively low diversity index of 1.642 found for the total AHI Corpus, as compared with values of 1.947 for the Lorge Magazine Count and 2.157 for the Brown University Corpus. Further, this value is distinctly lower than those found for the component samples. The probable interpretation of this result is that despite the diversity of content and subject matter represented in the AHI Corpus, when all samples are considered together, the indication is that the "American school lexicon" has a tendency to emphasize the more common words and to use them more often than is the case in adult materials. This is true, apparently, even though the *total* vocabulary represented by the American school lexicon is somewhat larger than the vocabularies that are estimated to underlie the large samples of adult-oriented materials such as the Lorge Magazine Count and the Brown University Corpus. This result probably reflects the fact that there has been a tendency to simplify the vocabulary of school materials, particularly at the lower grade levels. It may be noted that the indices of diversity tend to increase with grade level, with "ungraded" material showing the highest diversity.

FOOTNOTES

1. Gustav Herdan, *Type-Token Mathematics* (Mouton, The Hague, 1960).

2. John B. Carroll, "Word Frequency Studies and the Lognormal Distribution," in E. M. Zale (Ed.), *Proceedings of the Conference on Language and Language Behavior* (Appleton-Century-Crofts, New York, 1968), pp. 213–235. This article also presents the basic mathematical description of the lognormal model and the computations necessary for it's application to actual data. The Lorge Magazine Count is one of the word-frequency counts presented in *The Teacher's Word Book of 30,000 Words*. See footnote 11.

3. John B. Carroll, "On Sampling from a Lognormal Model of Word-Frequency Distribution," in Henry Kučera and W. Nelson Francis, *Computational Analysis of Present-Day American English* (Brown University Press, Providence, 1967), pp. 406–424.

4. As noted in the preceding article, the definition of a type used in the AHI Corpus is "a string of graphic characters bounded left and right by space," with certain restrictions on the characters permitted in the string. Consequently, *have, has, had,* and *having* are treated as different word types even though they are all forms of the verb *have*. Similarly, *word, Word, word's, worded, wordiness, wording, words, Words,* and *wordy* (all found in the AHI Corpus) are all counted as different. This definition of word type has the effect of considerably increasing the number of types over what would be found if the words were classified according to dictionary entries. Nevertheless, there is good reason to believe that the lognormal model is applicable, in principle, *no matter how* word types are defined. We will consider later what effect a different definition of word type might have on the resulting distributions and their analysis.

5. The problem of effecting the adjustment is discussed on pages 220–222 of the article referred to in footnote 2. It has now been determined that the "alternative procedure" mentioned there, "to delete an area at the upper extreme of the type distribution corresponding to one-half word-type (with a corresponding deletion in the token distribution) and then to cut successive areas $1/N_\tau$ from the word-type distribution . . . , adjusting probabilities for the deleted area," produces more generally satisfactory agreement between observed and predicted frequencies, especially for high-frequency types. This procedure has been used for all computations performed for the present analysis.

6. The criterion used is described on pages 224 and 225 of the article cited in footnote 2. Briefly, one finds the parameters that yield a predicted token distribution that has the same linear regression line of the normal-deviate values on ϕ as the obtained token distribution, the points being weighted by their frequency values.

7. G. K. Zipf, *The Psycho-Biology of Language* (Houghton Mifflin Company, Boston, 1935; reprinted with an introduction by G. A. Miller, M.I.T. Press, Cambridge, 1965).

8. Benoit Mandelbrot, "On the Theory of Word Frequencies and on Related Markovian Models of Discourse," in Roman Jakobson (Ed.), *Structure of Language and its Mathematical Aspects* (American Mathematical Society, Providence, 1961), pp. 190–219.

9. D is a measure of relative entropy based on information-theory statistics. The formula may be given as

$$D = [\log(\Sigma p_i) - (\Sigma p_i \log p_i)/\Sigma p_i]/\log n,$$

where

n = number of categories,

i = category number, $i = 1, 2, . . . , n$,

p_i = probability of a token in the ith category,

and

$$p_i \log p_i = 0 \text{ for } p_i = 0.$$

This is the same quantity D_2 derived in J. B. Carroll, "An Alternative to Juilland's Usage Coefficient for Lexical Frequencies, and a Proposal for a Standard Frequency Index (SFI)," *Computer Studies in the Humanities and Verbal Behavior* (in press). The computation of D is illustrated in Table D-2.

10. The adjustment is made by the following formula:

$$U = (1,000,000/N) [FD + (1 - D)f_{\min}],$$

where

N = total number of tokens in the corpus,

F = frequency of the word in the corpus,

D = index of dispersion,

$f_{\min}$ = $1/N$ times the sum of the products of f_i and s_i, where f_i is the frequency in category i and s_i is the number of tokens in the category.

SFI is computed from U by the formula:

$$SFI = 10(\log_{10} U + 4).$$

U is the same quantity U_m derived in the reference cited in footnote 9. The computation of U is illustrated in Table D-2.

11. Edward L. Thorndike and Irving Lorge, *The Teacher's Word Book of 30,000 Words* (Teachers College, Columbia University, New York, 1944).

12. Henry Kučera and W. Nelson Francis, *Computational Analysis of Present-Day American English* (Brown University Press, Providence, 1967).

13. The statistical theory required for properly estimating the accuracy of U and SFI statistics has not been worked out; therefore, the construction of the table involves the same theory that is used for evaluating F statistics, namely, the confidence-limit formulas to be found in S. S. Wilks, *Elementary Statistical Analysis* (Princeton University Press, Princeton, 1944).

14. John B. Carroll, "Measurement Properties of Subjective Magnitude Estimates of Word Frequency," *Journal of Verbal Learning and Verbal Behavior* (Vol. 10, December, 1971), pp. 135–142.

15. The words not found were *drivel, abduct, spicula,* and *grout,* but *abducted* and *abducting* were each found once.

New Views of Lexicon

Peter Davies

"The amount of information in the lexicon is the amount of information in our memories; the method in which it is stored is the method in which all information is stored; the method in which it is processed and retrieved is the method in which all information is processed and retrieved."

John Macnamara, "Parsimony and the lexicon," *Language,* 47.2 (1971), pp. 389–374.

Macnamara's insistence that linguistic or lexical information is not distinct from general information, his argument that neither "semantic trees" nor dictionary entries are even indirectly models of actual linguistic storage or competence, and finally his assertion that only arbitrary decisions can be made about subdividing the meanings of a polysemic word are both refreshing and daunting to a practical lexicographer. It is clear that the sentence "The child asked the teacher to leave the room" is not likely to be properly interpreted except by access to full knowledge of the usual relationship between child and teacher, and it is also clear that such knowledge is easily stored in and retrieved by the brain, but that it could hardly be stored in any conceivable dictionary unless the dictionary were expanded to be an inventory of the entire culture. And even this would leave unaccounted for vast tracts of local and individual knowledge that only a madman could wish to record. Dictionaries can still usefully stick to their old task of recording in handy format a small canonical set of attributes for a selection of words, without claiming that the attributes are the totality of lexical information or that the selection of words is a complete listing of lexical items.

Defining from citations in one way or another is still the only reliable way in which a lexicographer can identify a reasonable and relevant set of semantic attributes to record. If the citations are gathered in a random way, or if they are gathered in a number of separate judgmentally biased ways, the significance of each citation in the total lexicon must be assessed individually. But if they are gathered in a statistically controlled way so that they represent a section of culture that can be simply and rigorously described, the value of the data is much greater and more systematic. The Corpus that this book reports is derived and structured so that it does adequately represent a very important and distinctive section of our culture, namely, the printed language of the American elementary educational system. This Corpus can be regarded as representing a culturally marked subset of the total lexicon of English.

This is not true of the great historical collections of citations, nor of most existing word counts. If it is true of the Kučera-Francis Corpus,[1] it is so in a limited sense, since a sample of one million tokens is small in relation to the amount of lexicon that exists in the whole of published American English. The AHI Corpus is larger and presumably represents its subset better. It is thus possible to make inferences and generalizations about the American school lexicon from the data with considerably more confidence than has been possible in the past.

The Corpus has in fact enabled us to write a School Dictionary that can claim to describe a truly relevant chunk of the lexicon to which American children are

exposed in the schools. This sublexicon is consciously structured to an unusual extent. It tries hard to practice what it preaches and very often succeeds. Although it is generated by adults—the textbook writers and the classic and other authors approved for reading in the schools—it should not be regarded as a subset of the adult lexicon that adults use to each other, as represented by the Kučera-Francis Corpus. If adults use a special subset of spoken language when they talk to children, this educational subset is its printed counterpart. As an isolated bit of evidence that this assertion may have some validity, there is the fact that the AHI Corpus shows twice as many uses of the set *boy/girl* as it does of the unmarked noun *child/children,* while in the Kučera-Francis Corpus the equivalent ratio is only 1.3 to one. The pedagogical lexicon seems in this respect to have a greater tendency to distinguish children by their sex-marked terms, while the lexicon of adults writing for adults is relatively more likely to use the unmarked noun.

The external parameters and derivation of the Corpus establish the cultural position and relevance of the data in general. The internal structure permits considerable manipulation of the data in ways still directly related to the cultural matrix. The two most interesting axes along which the data can be viewed are grade and subject. The value of these focuses for making a School Dictionary will be immediately apparent.

The editors of *The American Heritage School Dictionary* had easy access to the Alphabetical List through desk-top microfilm readers. Each graphic type in the list could thus be read in summary profile, so that even before looking at citations in order to analyze and define, the editors had an overview of the type's general weight and distribution within the sublexicon.

Citations are the indispensable raw materials of defining. It would have been an inelegant use of our time to try to inspect all of the possible five million citations; there is parsimony even in commercial lexicography. Two hundred high-frequency function words alone account for nearly half of the token population, and many of the other graphic types are obviously not "lexical items" in our traditional sense. Our task was to write a dictionary that would have approximately 35,000 "main entries," which we estimated would be likely to comprise about 55,000 "words," if inflected forms are counted, and about 70,000 separate definitions. We therefore decided to go through the Alphabetical List, using *The American Heritage Dictionary of the English Language* (AHD) as an approximate index of how many different senses each type might have, and to ask for very roughly ten

citations for each expected sense. The citations were selected from those available as a spaced sample; that is, if one in three were selected for a particular type, every third occurrence was taken from the sequence in which the tokens were stored. This resulted in the selection of approximately proportional samples of the tokens in each grade and in each subject category; this is illustrated in Figures C-12 and C-13 below. The greatest number of citations taken for any one word was 1,000 for *take* out of a possible 4,089, with 200 each for *taken, takes, taking,* and *took*—in all 1,800 citations for this basic word, which has about 200 different uses defined in the AHD. At the other end of the scale, many of the fully "lexical" types occurred with frequencies too low to provide ten citations per expected sense; for these we took all the available citations. In this way, about 700,000 citations were printed out.

The practical needs of lexicography were well served by the two kinds of evidence, the summaries and the citations. An example of their utilization (in the analysis of the type *major*) is given later in this article; others appear in the introduction to *The American Heritage School Dictionary* and, of course, in the Dictionary itself.

The experience of working intensively with these materials exposed us to some novel views of the nature of lexicon. The Corpus does not discriminate against proper nouns, numerals, formulas, nonce words, nonsense words, and other real forms not usually considered lexical in a formal sense, nor does it impose the artificial symmetry that linguistic logic tends to impose on sets of words felt to be analogous. On the other hand, it presents other kinds of symmetry that are not readily apparent. There are deep harmonies of frequency and correspondence in the lexicon, of which speakers may unconsciously be aware, but that have never yet been clearly exhibited for analysis.

To a practical lexicographer, and perhaps to others, some of these configurations are surprising and exciting, and they seem to offer possibilities for new kinds of linguistic and nonlinguistic investigation. If lexicon is regarded as a cultural inventory, then a culture can be examined through its use of lexicon. Ancient and even prehistoric cultures have long been investigated from this standpoint in the field of Indo-European studies and elsewhere, and the modern technique of "content analysis" likewise extracts valuable social or other information from textual data. It seems possible that highly structured analysis of text in the form of a corpus can go beyond making cultural descriptions from linguistic evidence and contribute to the understanding of the relationship of

Table C-1 Kinship Terms.
AHI Corpus adjusted frequencies per one million words (U).

mother	418	father	405	parent	8
Mother	166	Father	73		
mothers	22	fathers	12	parents	77
Mothers	0.4	Fathers	1		
wife	103	husband	34	spouse	0.01
wives	9	husbands	3	spouses	0
daughter	47	son	100	child	128
Daughter	0.7	Son	4	Child	5
daughters	4	sons	17	children	466
sister	70	brother	104	sibling	0
Sister	3	Brother	19		
sisters	29	brothers	59	siblings	0.01
Sisters	0.5	Brothers	2		
mother-in-law	0.1	father-in-law	0.02		
sister-in-law	0.1	brother-in-law	1		
daughter-in-law	0.05	son-in-law	1		
aunt	16	uncle	32		
Aunt	40	Uncle	85		
aunts	1	uncles	0.8		
Aunts	2	Uncles	0		
				cousin	16
				Cousin	9
				cousins	8
niece	1	nephew	2		
nieces	0.01	nephews	0.6		
grandmother	23	grandfather	30	grandparent	0.1
Grandmother	12	Grandfather	37	grandparents	5
granddaughter	0.7	grandson	0.6	grandchild	0.1
granddaughters	0.05	grandsons	0.3	grandchildren	2
ma	0.5	pa	1		
Ma	21	Pa	31		
mama	1	papa	3		
Mama	48	Papa	41		
mom	2	(pop	20)		
Mom	18	Pop	7		
Momma	0.2	Poppa	0.05		
mommy	0.9				
Mommy	0.1				
mum	0.05	dad	15		
Mum	0.01	Dad	51		
mummy	2	daddy	1		
Mummy	0.8	Daddy	11		
grandma	0.5	grandpa	0.7		
Grandma	10	Grandpa	8		
granny	0.02	granddad	0.1		
Granny	2	Granddad	0.8		
Auntie	0.1				
Aunty	0.7				
motherhood	0.1	fatherhood	0.1		
sisterhood	0	brotherhood	1		
motherly	0.1	fatherly	0.1		
sisterly	0.01	brotherly	0.3		

language and culture, with insights in both directions.

The graphs and tables that follow present some selected data of miscellaneous interest. The appended observations are offered with diffidence, but the material often speaks clearly for itself.

The figures represented in most of the following sections refer to occurrences of *graphic types* displayed in the Alphabetical List in the main body of this book. Thus, in the section on kinship terms the type *husband* includes some instances of the verb; in the section on numbers *one* includes the pronoun; in the section on color terms the type *green* includes "green with envy," and *orange* includes the fruit. If this fact is clearly borne in mind, the comparisons are valid, and no distortion need result.

Different kinds of frequency statistics are used for different purposes. For the summary comparisons the adjusted frequency figure U is used (see pages 1–4). For most of the comparisons through grades and subjects, unadjusted subfrequencies are used. For one graph of number types, the Standard Frequency Index (SFI) is used (see pages 1–4). All of these statistics can be checked out in the Alphabetical List. Finally, in the case of Figure C-14, the frequencies are based on editorial analysis of citations.

KINSHIP TERMS

The subculture that the Corpus represents is the elementary educational system of the United States. This subculture's attitude toward and use of kinship terms may be expected to be an important aspect of the way in which the culture perpetuates its familial structure. Here comparison with matched data from regional and above all oral sources would be most interesting. But some generalizations can be made from the Corpus data in isolation.

Mother and Father

The formal nouns *father* and *mother* occur about equally often. The upper-case type *Mother,* presumably representing chiefly the formal appellative or proper noun ("Ask Mother"), occurs twice as often as its counterpart. On the other hand, in the informal or hypocoristic types *Ma, Pa,* etc., the paternal side dominates by a similar proportion. In the aggregate of all parental types, formal and informal, the two sides are remarkably equal. The difference seems to be that in representations of speech within the family, and in pedagogical equivalents, the mother often receives a more formal title than the father.

Wife and Husband

This is the only pair of terms in which the sex *of the counterpart* is specified. "My wife" is said only by a man, and "their husbands" has *women* for the underlying subject of discourse. How should the three-to-one disparity between the two terms be interpreted?

Among the female kinship terms, *wife* ranks second to *mother*. *Husband*, on the other hand, ranks eighth among the male terms—coming not only after *father, son, brother, papa,* and *dad,* but even after *uncle* and *grandfather.* A clear inference is that while the female's most important role is as *mother,* her second and only other important role is as *wife,* while the equivalent is not true for the male; his chief role is also as parent, but he has four other roles more important than that of *husband.*

Other Adults

One effect of the above is that in the other two important pairs of adult roles, *grandparent* and *uncle/ aunt,* the male term dominates its partner. The only exception to this is in the hypocoristic terms for *grandparents,* which are quite evenly matched. (The frequencies for the in-laws are so low that they do not seem very significant. This may in part be a sign that it is not considered necessary for children to think about these relationships, but the Kučera-Francis figures are little higher.)

Children

Both as offspring and as siblings, males are much more often mentioned than females. It is interesting that the native unmarked noun *child* is more frequent than the sex-marked terms, while the recently imported *sibling* has yet to make any headway at this level. A group of offspring that includes both sexes can be thought of collectively, but this does not apply to congeners.

MALE/FEMALE PAIRS

Boy dominates *girl* by two to one, but in the Kučera-Francis Corpus, *boy* has only a small margin of superiority. This suggests that while the disparity between males and females at the most general level, as marked by pronouns, is of roughly equal importance in both subsets of the culture, the disparity between boys and girls is important to the adult-to-child (pedagogical) subculture but not to the adult-to-adult culture. It is also true that the AHI Corpus shows twice as many uses of *boy/girl* as of *child/children,* while in Kučera-

Table C-2 Male/Female Pairs.
AHI Corpus adjusted frequencies per one million words (*U*).

female	21	male	20
females	3	males	5
feminine	1	masculine	0.6
femininity	0.1	masculinity	0.01
woman	126	man	972
Woman	3	Man	27
women	100	men	681
womanhood	0.1	manhood	2
womanly	0	manly	1
Mrs.	252	Mr.	612
Miss	166		
queen	36	king	96
Queen	33	King	120
princess	17	prince	16
Princess	14	Prince	26
lady	87	gentleman	20
ladies	20	gentlemen	14
		lord	9
		lords	6
girl	195	boy	455
girls	196	boys	386
she	2275	he	8245
her	1877	him	1762
hers	8	his	5361

Francis the equivalent ratio is only 1.3 to one.

In Figures C-1 and C-2, it can be seen that *boy* dominates *girl* in the reading matter of every grade from 3 to 9 and in every subject except two: In Magazines there is near parity, and in Home Economics the prominence of *girl* marks the future role of *mother* and *wife.* Figures C-3 and C-4 show, however, that even in this last category the masculine pronoun is still used about 1.7 times as often as the feminine.

NUMBERS AND NUMERALS

It was a considerable surprise when we observed (1) that the numbers *one* through *nine* are ranked by total frequency in their ordinal sequence (Figure C-5), (2) that the (Arabic) numerals *1* through *9* follow the same order but with a break at *8* (Figure C-6), and (3) that both of these phenomena are identically represented in the Kučera-Francis Corpus. This is clearly in part mathematicians' territory. Benford's Law states that in some lists of apparently random numbers, lower first digits occur more frequently

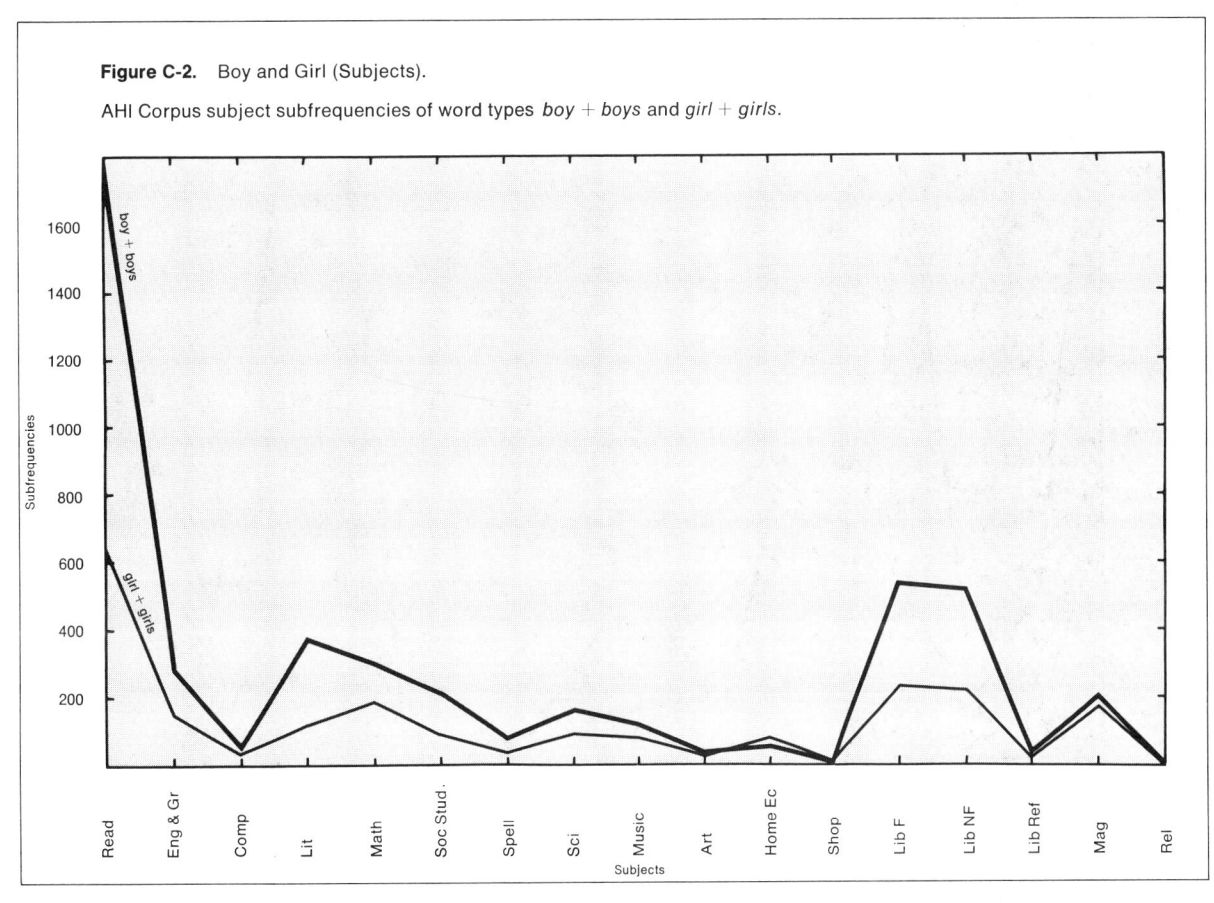

Figure C-1. Boy and Girl (Grades).

AHI Corpus grade subfrequencies of word types *boy* + *boys* and *girl* + *girls*.

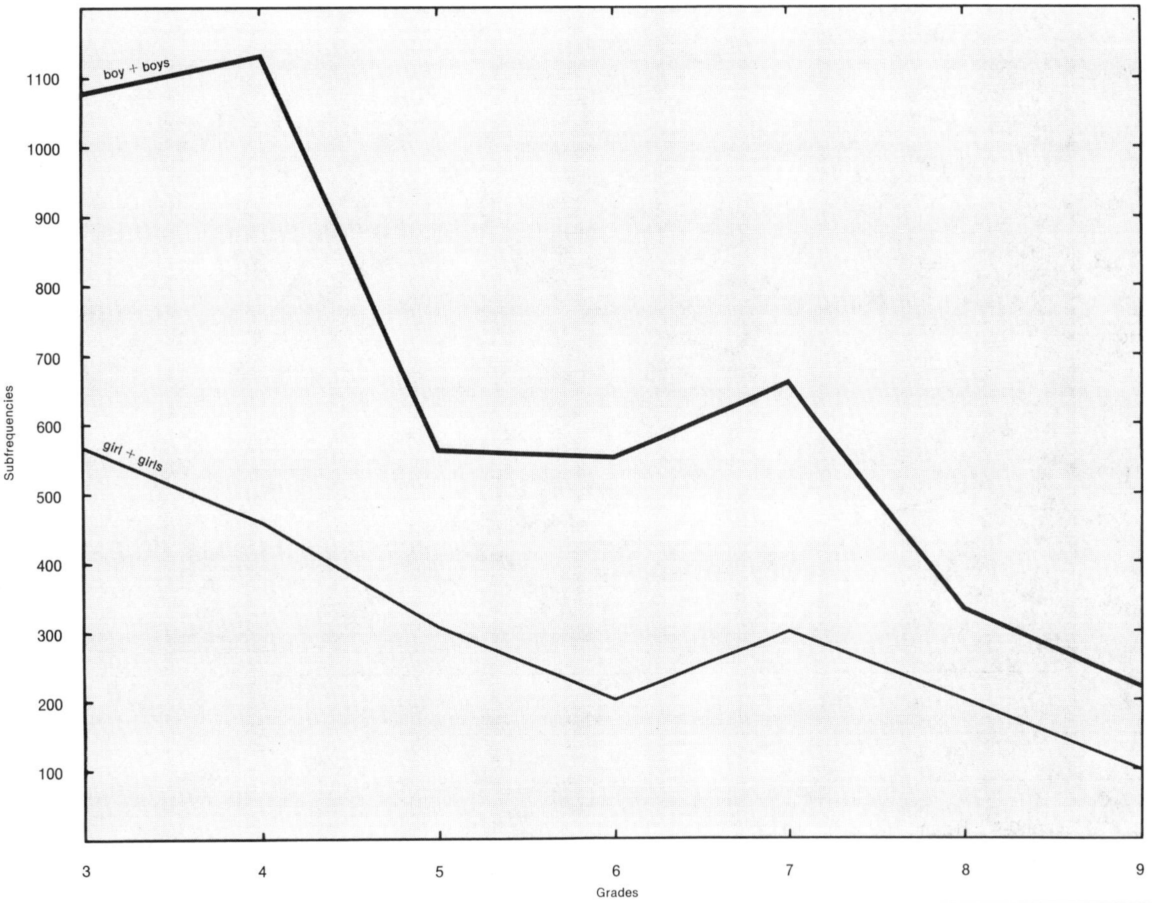

Figure C-2. Boy and Girl (Subjects).

AHI Corpus subject subfrequencies of word types *boy* + *boys* and *girl* + *girls*.

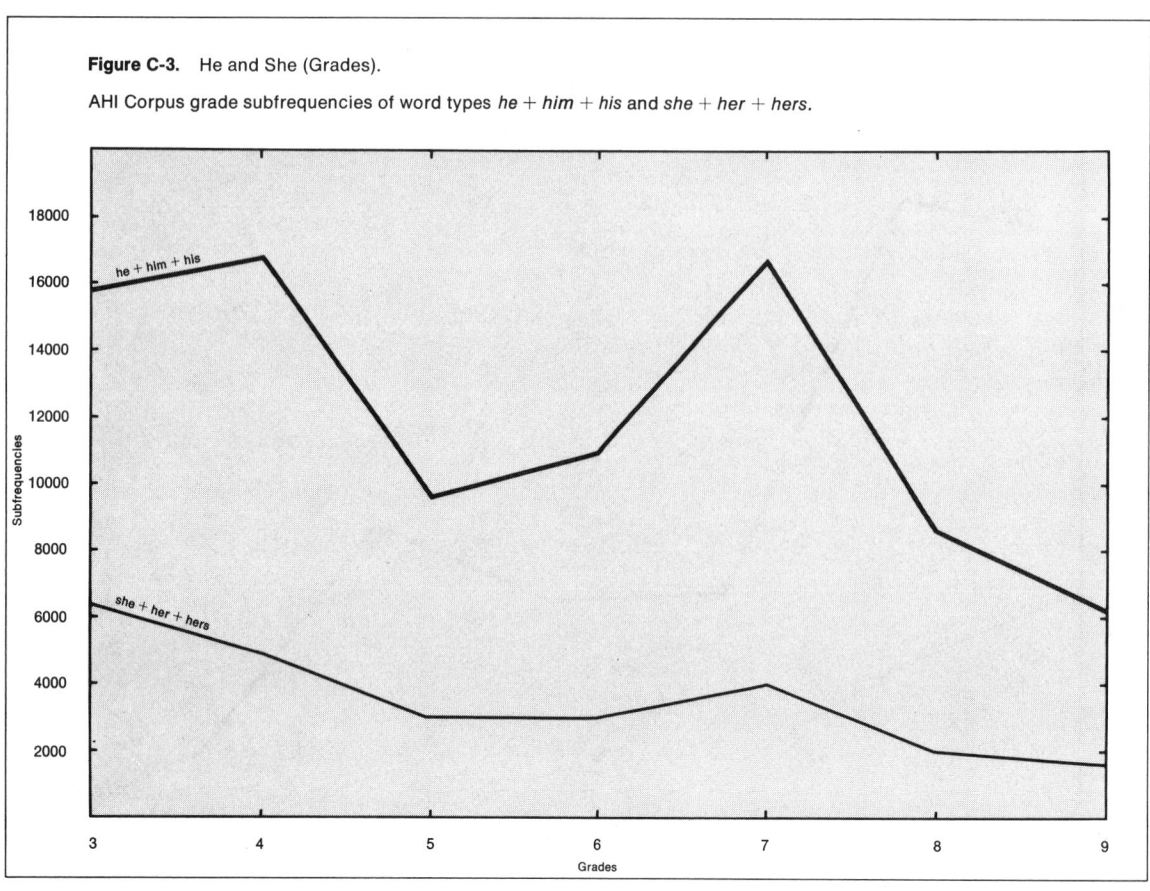

Figure C-3. He and She (Grades).

AHI Corpus grade subfrequencies of word types *he* + *him* + *his* and *she* + *her* + *hers*.

Figure C-4. He and She (Subjects).

AHI Corpus subject subfrequencies of word types *he* + *him* + *his* and *she* + *her* + *hers*.

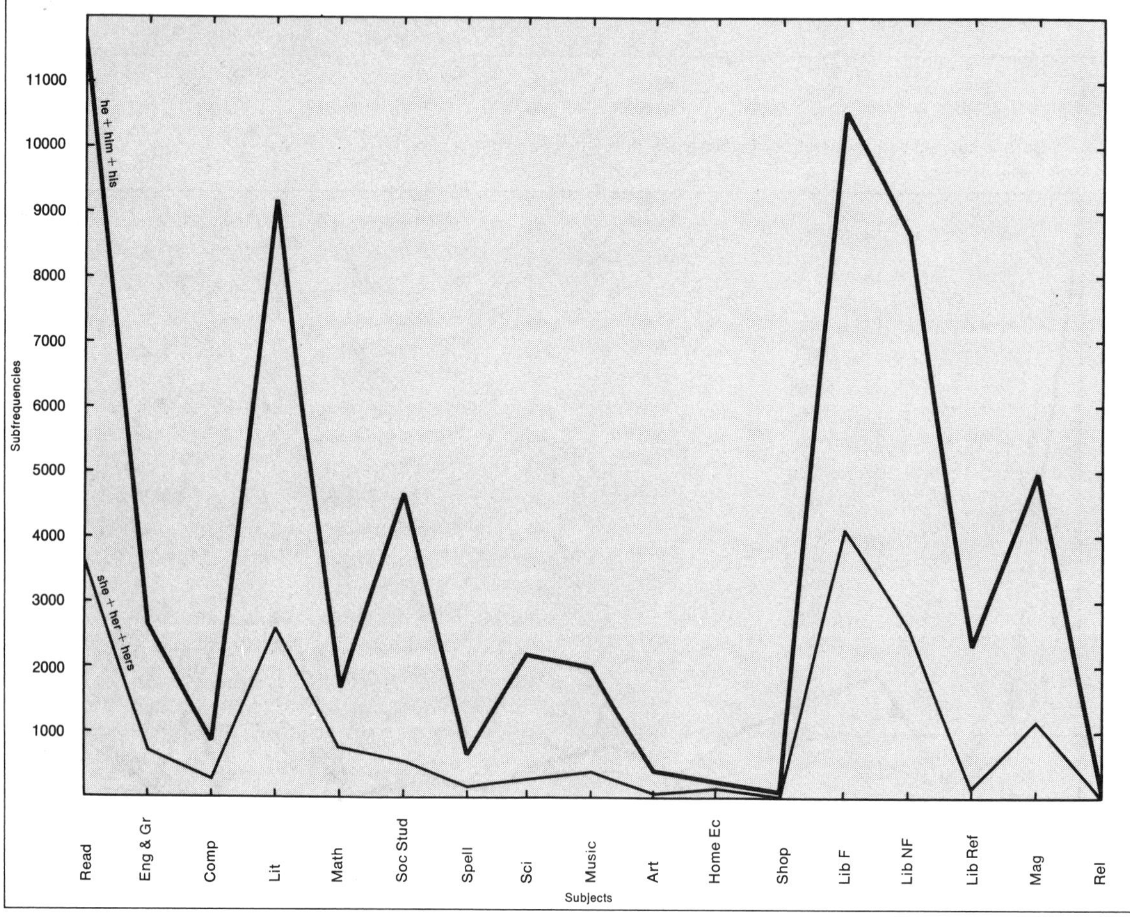

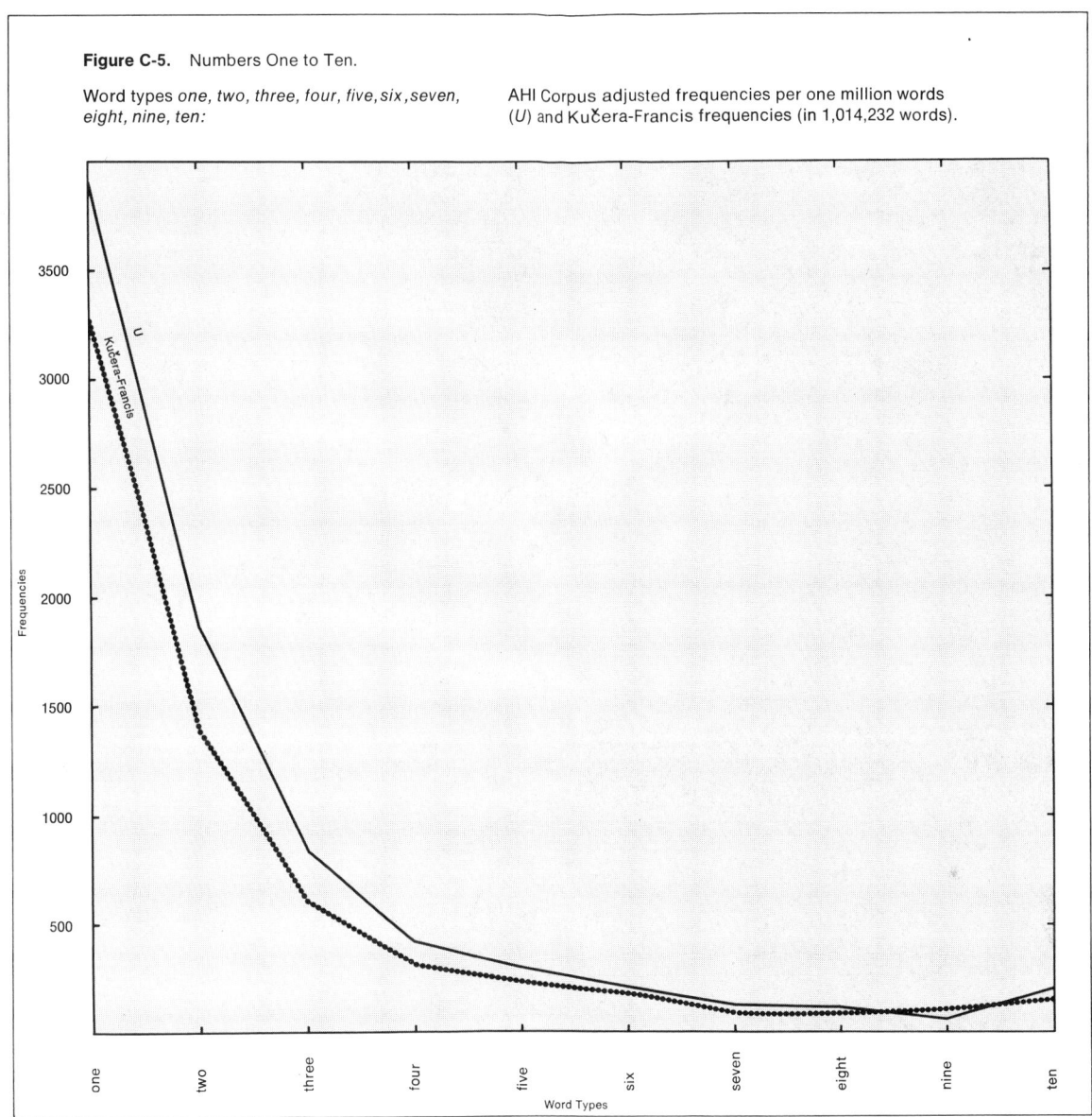

Figure C-5. Numbers One to Ten.

Word types *one, two, three, four, five, six, seven, eight, nine, ten:*

AHI Corpus adjusted frequencies per one million words (*U*) and Kučera-Francis frequencies (in 1,014,232 words).

than higher.[2] The mathematical arguments hinge on the randomness of the data, and since mathematicians have striven to explain the phenomenon either as a universal constant or as a culture-induced bias, it may be acceptable to give a lexicological view.

The two corpuses are not random; they are culturally defined word lists in which cultural world view controls even the numbers. In the first nine numbers and the first seven Arabic numerals, the culture simply prefers lower figures. After, respectively, *nine* and *7*, the culture generally prefers lower figures but is also fond of certain key multiples (chiefly but not exclusively the decimals and pentads) and has a marked dislike for primes. The adult corpus and the pedagogical corpus are extremely consistent in these preferences. (Incidentally, the effects of Benford's Law can also be observed in the type list itself; there are nearly ten times as many numeral types beginning with 1 as with 9 – an even higher ratio than predicted by the law. A large number of these numerals are, of course, dates; clearly, at this particular stage of the Christian era, the most used first digit for dates is 1. But by the late ninth millennium this preference will have changed completely . . .)

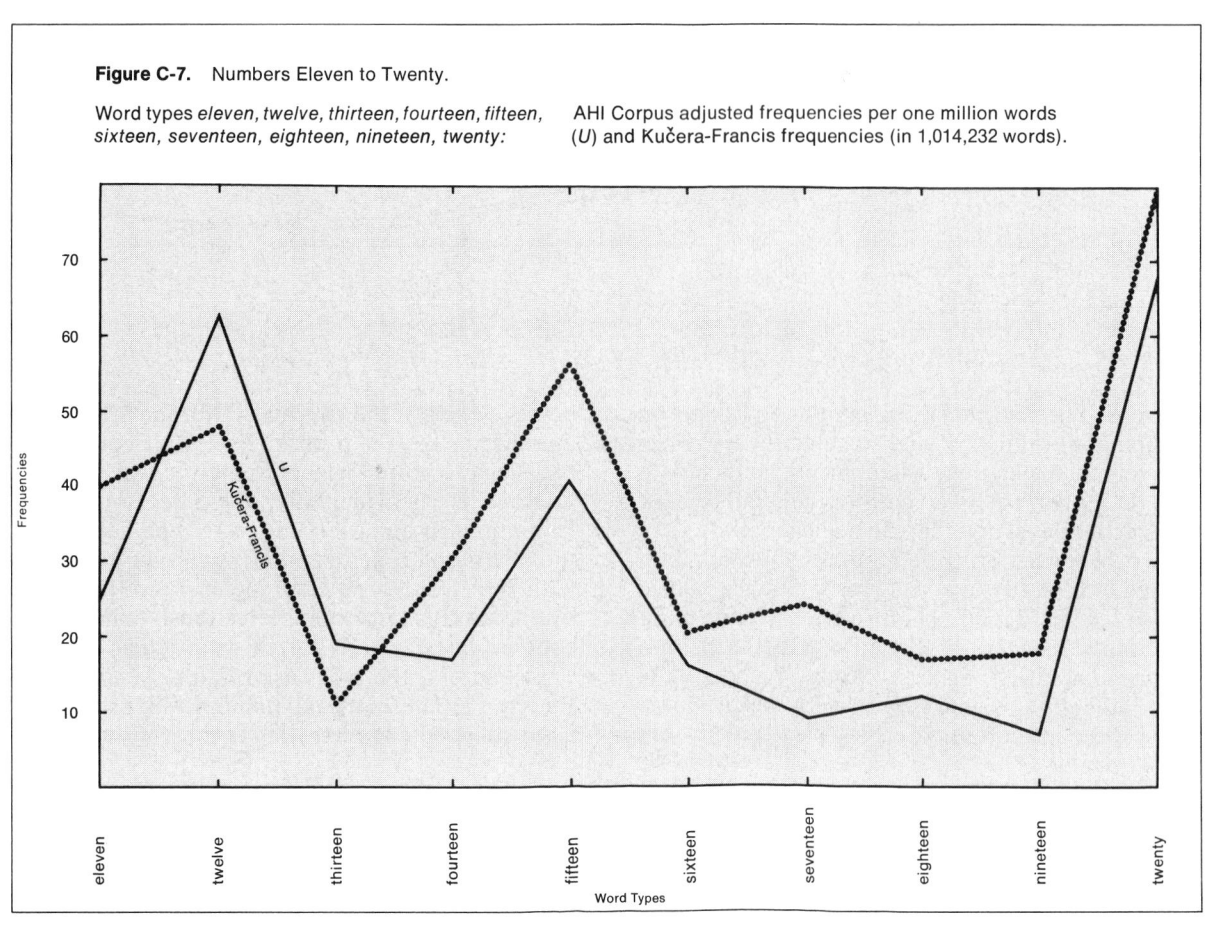

Figure C-6. Numerals 1 to 10.

Arabic numeral types *1, 2, 3, 4, 5, 6, 7, 8, 9, 10:* AHI Corpus adjusted frequencies per one million words (*U*) and Kučera-Francis frequencies (in 1,014,232 words).

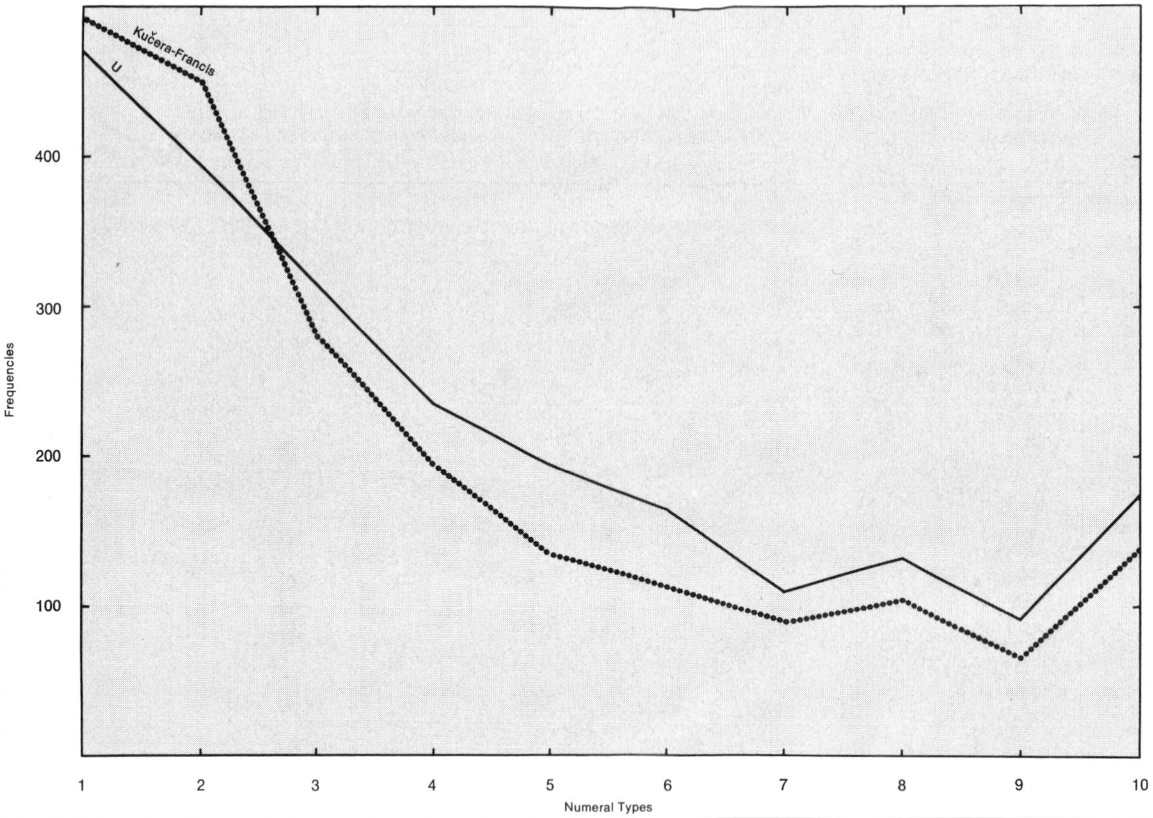

Figure C-7. Numbers Eleven to Twenty.

Word types *eleven, twelve, thirteen, fourteen, fifteen, sixteen, seventeen, eighteen, nineteen, twenty:* AHI Corpus adjusted frequencies per one million words (*U*) and Kučera-Francis frequencies (in 1,014,232 words).

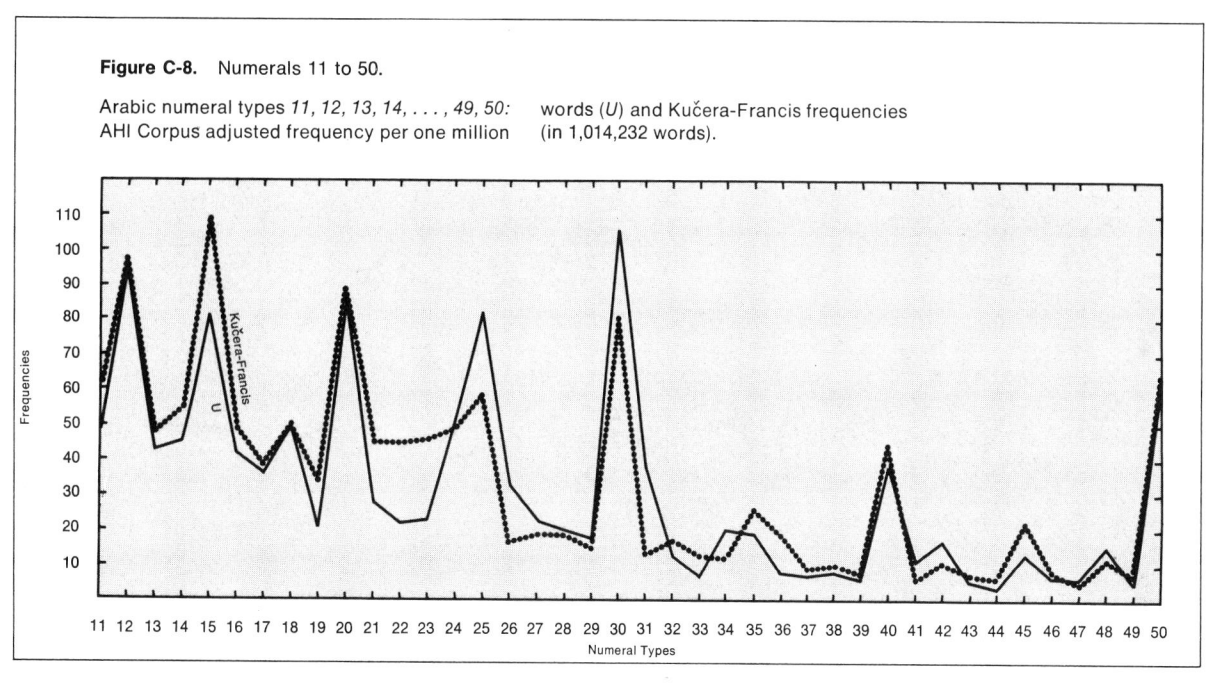

Figure C-8. Numerals 11 to 50.

Arabic numeral types *11, 12, 13, 14, . . . , 49, 50:* AHI Corpus adjusted frequency per one million words (*U*) and Kučera-Francis frequencies (in 1,014,232 words).

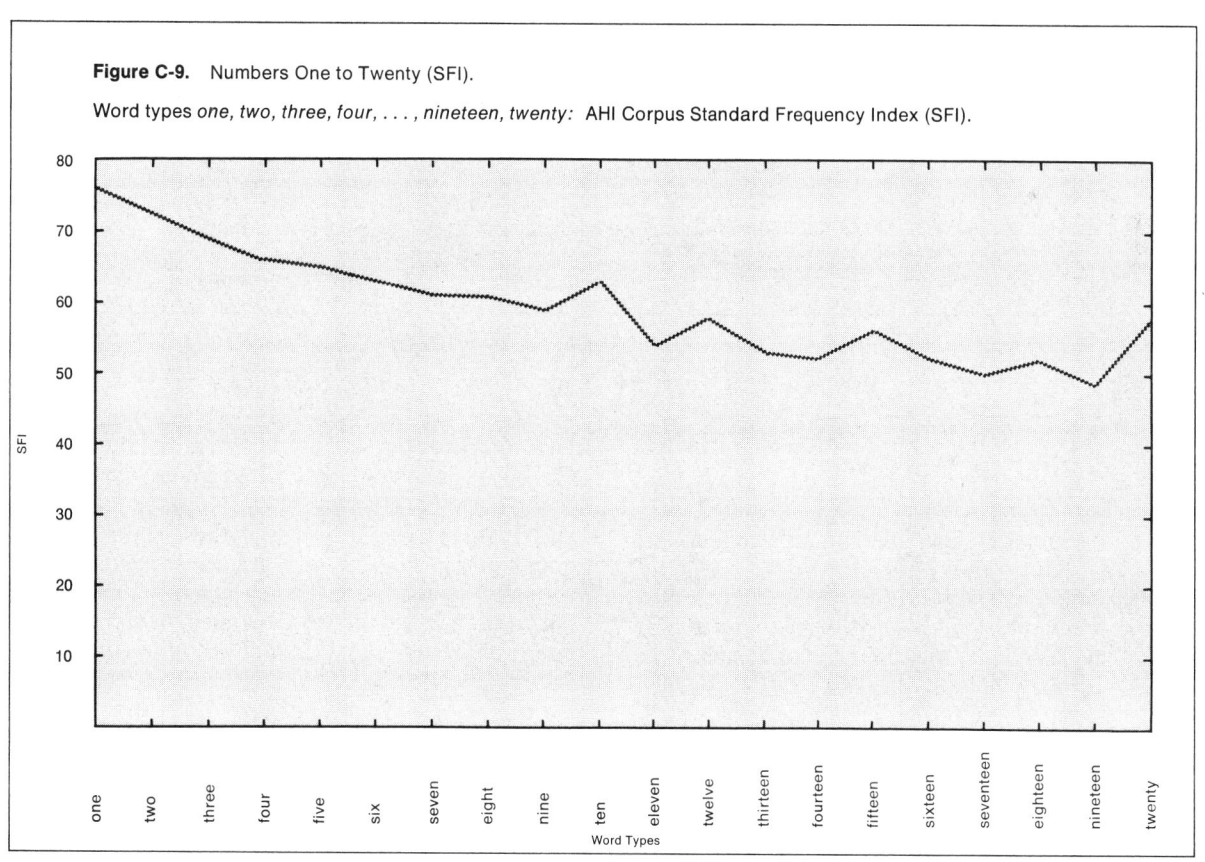

Figure C-9. Numbers One to Twenty (SFI).

Word types *one, two, three, four, . . . , nineteen, twenty:* AHI Corpus Standard Frequency Index (SFI).

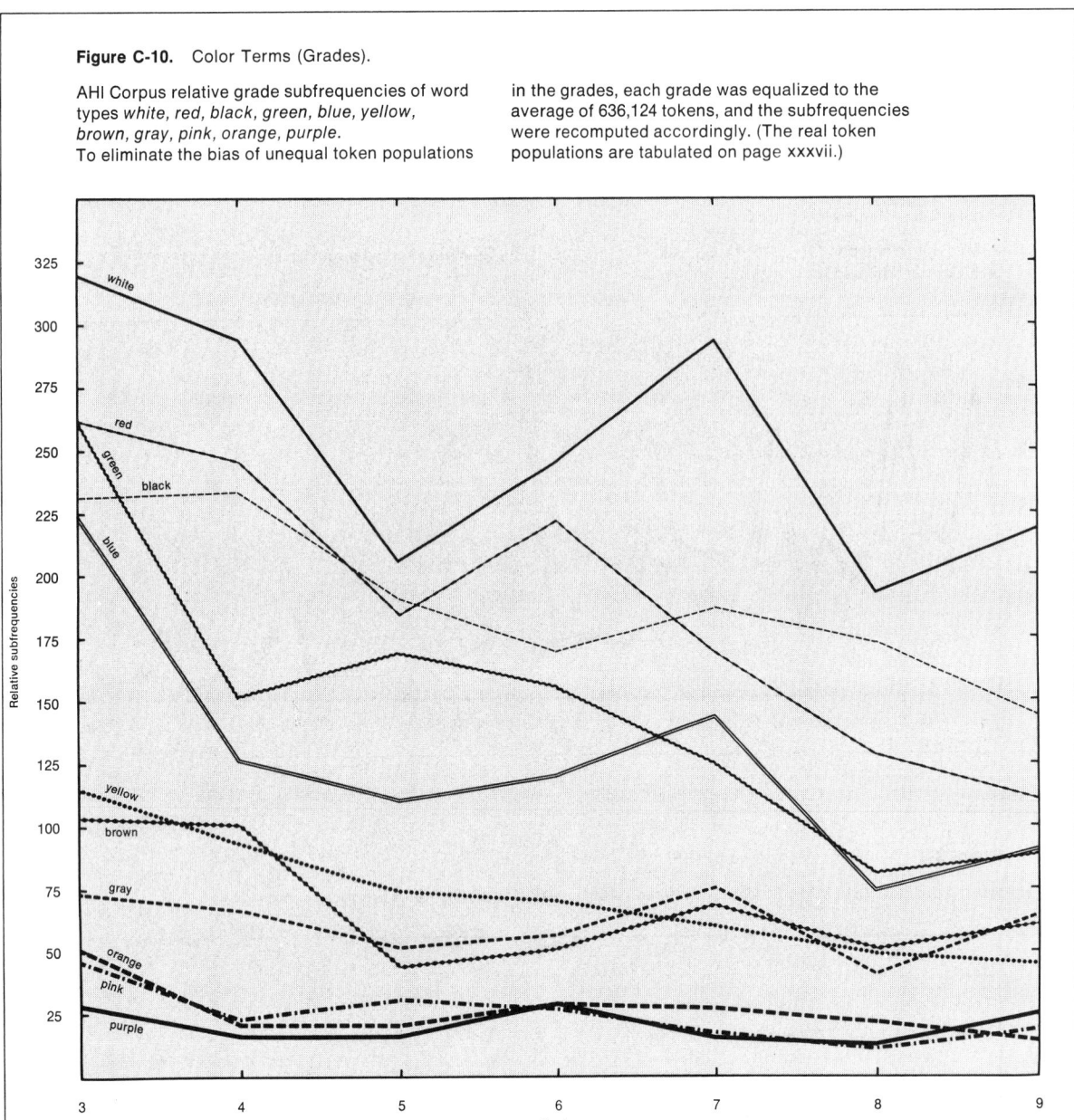

Figure C-10. Color Terms (Grades).

AHI Corpus relative grade subfrequencies of word types *white, red, black, green, blue, yellow, brown, gray, pink, orange, purple.*
To eliminate the bias of unequal token populations in the grades, each grade was equalized to the average of 636,124 tokens, and the subfrequencies were recomputed accordingly. (The real token populations are tabulated on page xxxvii.)

COLOR TERMS

The basic color terms have often been studied as a lexical set, or semantic field. Berlin and Kay[3] assert that there is "a total universal inventory of exactly eleven basic color terms" and that all languages subscribe to this inventory in a consistent manner. All languages that have only five basic color terms have *black, white, red, green,* and *yellow,* and languages that have six terms have these plus *blue,* and so forth. Hays and Perkins[4] have presented evidence that the Berlin-Kay order also corresponds to frequency in English, Spanish, French, German, Russian, and Rumanian. The frequencies in the AHI Corpus do not precisely correspond to those given by Hays and Perkins, but it should be remembered that our Corpus represents only a subset, not a whole language.

A simple visual comparison of Figure C-10 and Figure C-11 shows that the stratification of frequencies is stable in the grades and unstable in the subjects. In the grades, *white* is the unchallenged winner. There are then three zones, which do not impinge on each other but within which there is interchange; *red, green, black,* and *blue* form the high zone; *yellow, brown,* and *gray* form the middle zone; and *orange, pink,* and *purple* form the low zone.

In the subjects, it seemed impossible to show all eleven color terms on a single graph because they are so entangled. The color vocabulary as a whole is far the strongest in Art, as would be expected. *White*

l

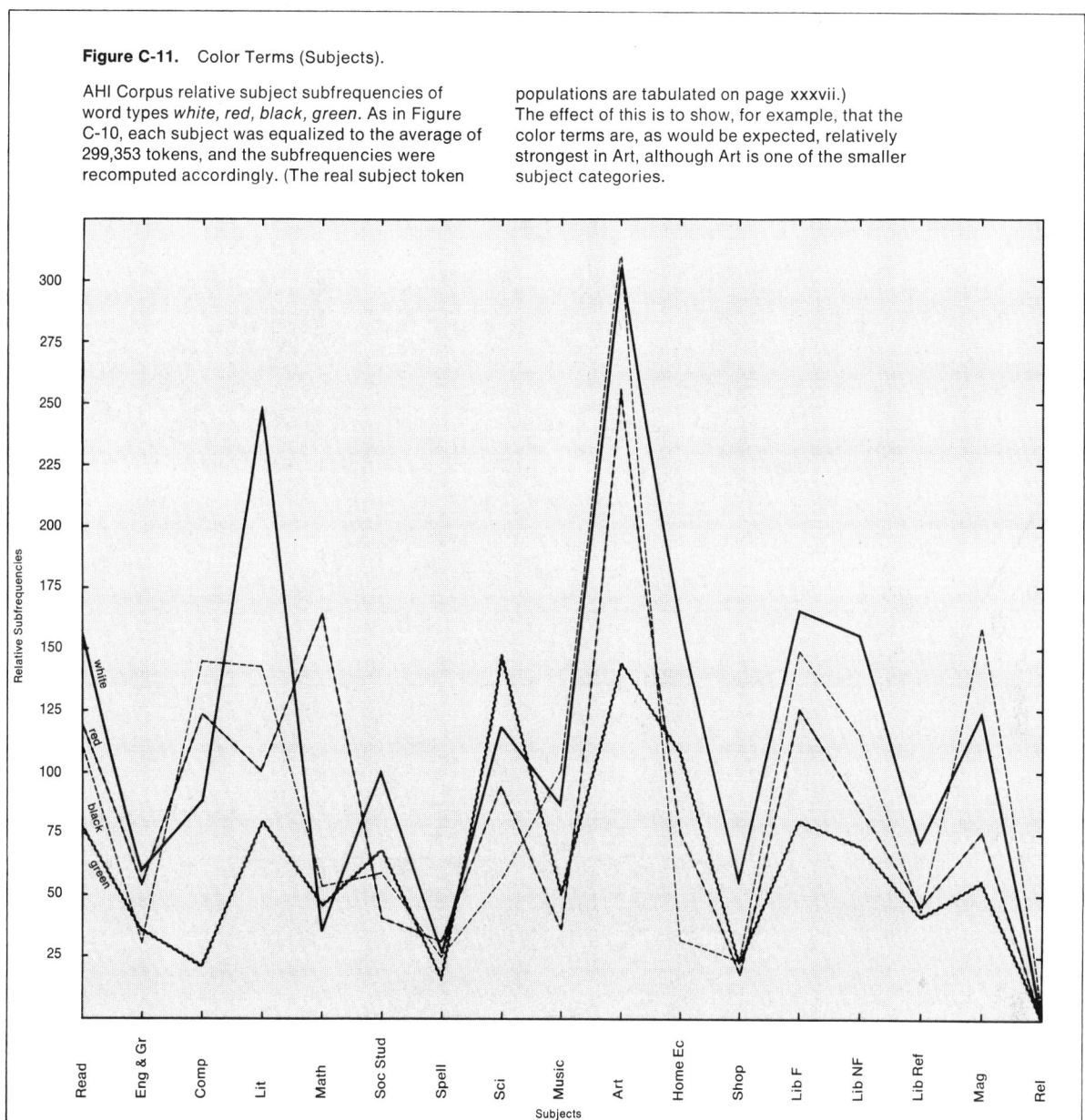

Figure C-11. Color Terms (Subjects).

AHI Corpus relative subject subfrequencies of word types *white, red, black, green.* As in Figure C-10, each subject was equalized to the average of 299,353 tokens, and the subfrequencies were recomputed accordingly. (The real subject token populations are tabulated on page xxxvii.) The effect of this is to show, for example, that the color terms are, as would be expected, relatively strongest in Art, although Art is one of the smaller subject categories.

is no longer unchallenged; it wins only in eight out of 17 categories. *Black* wins in four categories, and *green* in Science (and by a narrow margin *brown* predominates in Home Economics). The basic stratification is notably stable in Reading (the biggest of the Subjects by token population), Literature, and the three Library categories.

MAJOR

The adjective *major* has had an interesting historical development in English. It first appeared in the fifteenth century as a borrowing from Latin *mājor,* "greater" — "chiefly in certain special collocations which originated in medieval or modern Latin" (*The Oxford English Dictionary*). These collocations were virtually taxonomic classifications like *the major prophets* and *the major orders* (of the clergy). Beginning in the sixteenth century, *major* developed three analogous technical uses, in logic, mathematics, and music, that were also limited to specific collocations. It also acquired the generalized meaning "constituting the majority," a meaning found almost entirely with nouns like *part* and *portion.* Aside from these uses, the OED recognizes only one isolated and "obsolete" Shakespearian use, "My major vow lies here," apparently in the meaning "most important." The OED notes at the end of the first sense that "occasional uses (as 'a major poet') are sometimes suggested by antithesis with the recognized collocations

Figure C-12. Major (Grades).

AHI Corpus grade subfrequencies of word type *major,* with distribution of the 200 citations selected for print-out.

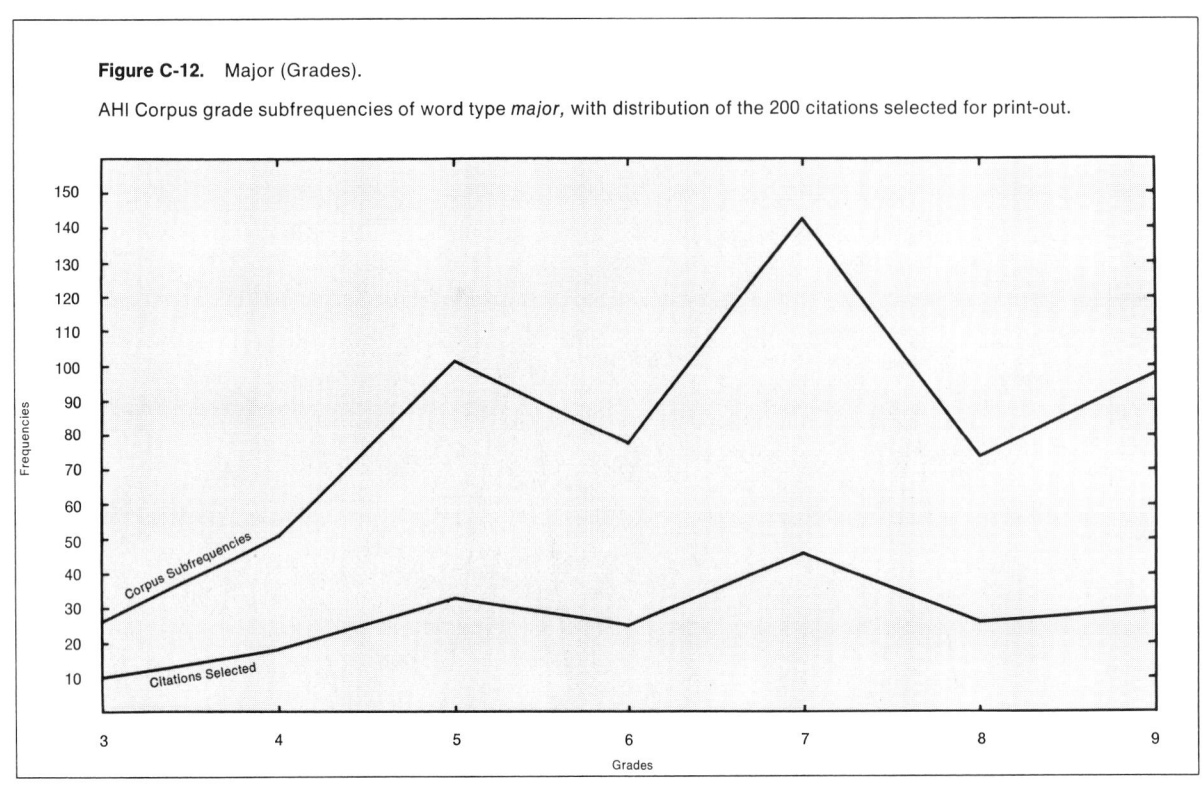

Figure C-13. Major (Subjects).

AHI Corpus subject subfrequencies of word type *major,* with distribution of the 200 citations selected for print-out.

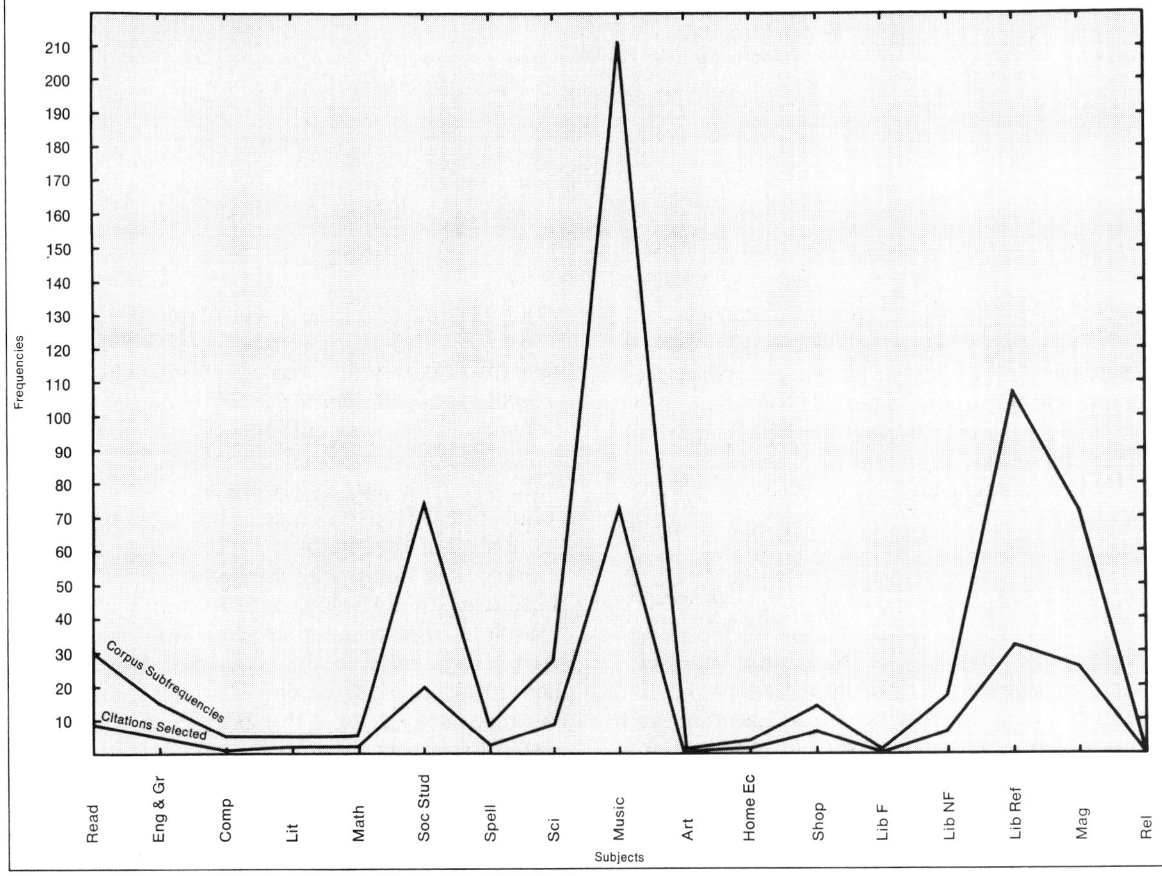

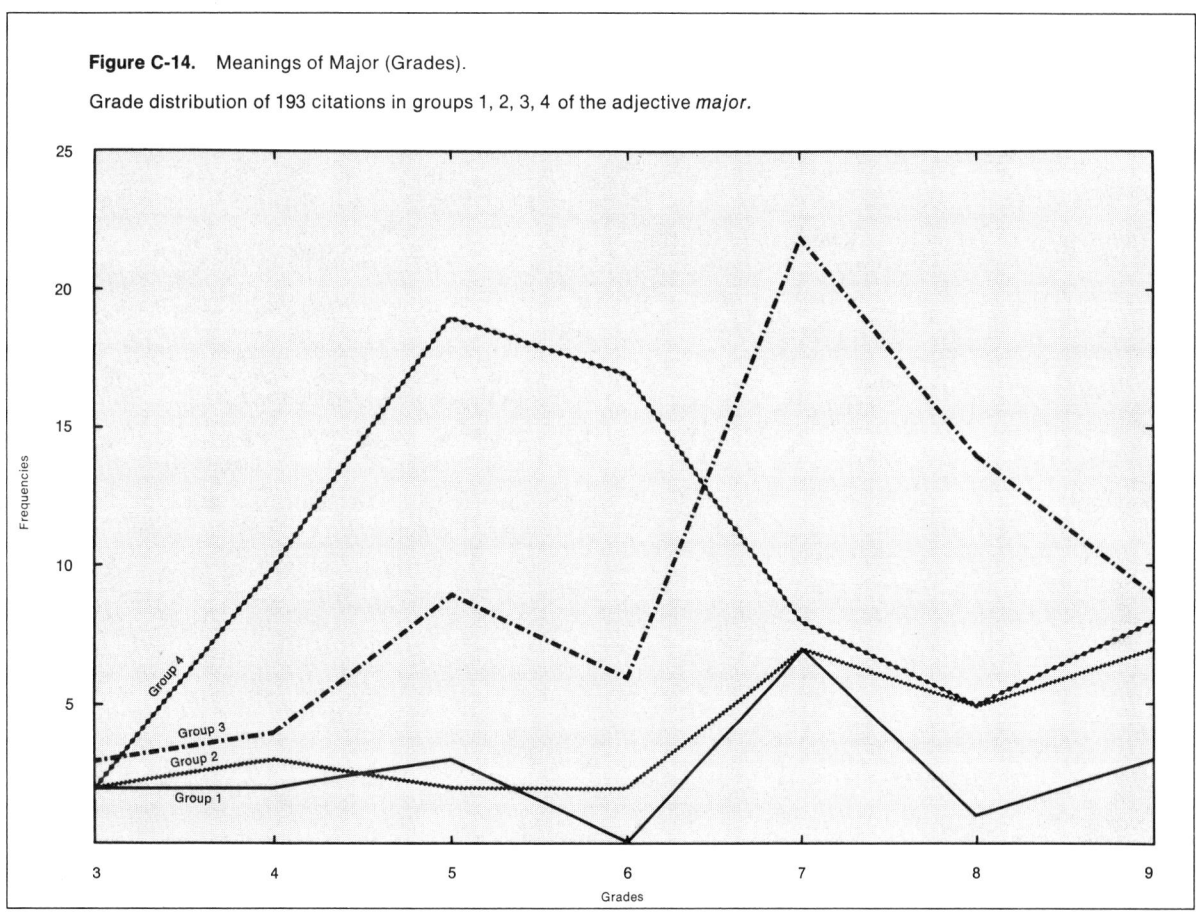

Figure C-14. Meanings of Major (Grades).

Grade distribution of 193 citations in groups 1, 2, 3, 4 of the adjective *major*.

of *minor*." But it has no citations for these.

In the AHI Corpus, the type *major* occurs 597 times. On the basis of the 18 separate definitions in the AHD, 200 citations were printed out—approximately one in three of those available. Figures C-12 and C-13 show the distribution across grades and subjects of the total frequency and of the citation selection; the one-in-three ratio holds approximately good in each subfrequency.

The 200 citations were inspected; 193 of them were adjectival uses. Of these, 69 were in technical musical uses, all of them occurring in the Music category. Of the remaining 124 citations, one was in the phrase *a major general,* in which *major* is technically a noun. Two citations represent the OED's sense "constituting the majority": *the major portion of the liquids* and *the major strength of the bee forces.* It is rather surprising that the remaining 120 citations appear to represent uses that were not recognized by the OED, except possibly in the "obsolete" Shakespearian use and in the note about "a major poet." It seems that only in this century has *major* become a general ad-

jective available for a wide range of uses outside of technical uses and set collocations.

The 120 citations were analyzed into three groups, chiefly by syntactic markings.

1. The first group, with 19 citations, seemed to have a superlative force signaled by the definite article with singular noun phrases. Nine of these had possessive pronouns or phrases specifying the field within which the superlative was to be understood:

The major export of Ethiopia is coffee.

. . . did his major work in Europe.

Turkey's major deposit of coal . . .

The rest had no possessives:

The major problem had been that . . .

This was the major consideration.

2. The second group possibly continues the OED's specific or "taxonomic" sense in a loose way. In this group the nouns are presented as members of specified subdivisions, like *the major prophets,* considered definitively "more important" within their

larger classes. These were marked by the definite article or by numerals, with plural noun phrases:

The major divisions of the foot ruler are inches.

. . . ranking among the South's major industries.

There are four major verb types.

The smallest of the eleven major islands . . .

3. The remaining group, the largest, seems to represent a sense that has lost all comparative and specific force and that can be glossed simply as "important" or "considerable." Most of these are marked by indefinite or negative determiners or by none:

Fishing is a major industry.

. . . to finance major highway improvements.

. . . growing to major importance.

Also apparently to be included here are cases in which the noun phrases are predominantly qualified by an ordinal or other definite adjective:

The only major restraint upon fertility . . .

Germany's third major offensive . . .

A fourth group comprises the 69 citations showing technical musical senses.

Figure C-14 shows the distributions of these groups, with the musical senses, through the grades.

FOOTNOTES

1. Henry Kučera and W. Nelson Francis, *Computational Analysis of Present-Day American English* (Brown University Press, Providence, 1967).

2. Ralph A. Raimi, "The Peculiar Distribution of First Digits," *Scientific American* (December, 1969), p. 109.

3. Brent Berlin and Paul Kay, *Basic Color Terms* (University of California Press, Berkeley, 1969).

4. David G. Hays and Revere Dale Perkins, "Correlation of Frequency With Order of Introduction" (forthcoming).

Guide to the Alphabetical List

The Alphabetical List presents the 86,741 different words (*word types*) found in the 5,088,721 words of running text (*tokens*) sampled to produce the American Heritage Intermediate Corpus. The word types are listed with extensive information about their frequencies (number of occurrences) in the Corpus as a whole and in the grade and subject divisions of the Corpus. Full understanding of this information requires some study of the details below and of the introductory articles in this book. Nevertheless, it is quite easy to understand the overall nature of the data given here. In order of columns, from left to right, the quantities tabulated are *F,* the word type's total frequency in the Corpus; *D, U,* and SFI, statistics devised to help analyze the relationship of a word type's total frequency to its subfrequencies in the subject categories of the Corpus; grade-level breakdowns of the word type's total frequency; and subject-category breakdowns of its total frequency.

The reader should note that the 17 subject categories for which data are presented here, and elsewhere in this book, represent the full 22 categories of the original survey questionnaires. The reduction to 17 categories was achieved by combining the data for five supplementary categories (Reading Supplementary, for example) with the basal categories to which they are related (in this case, Reading).

The list begins with the word types starting with the letter *a.* The word types are alphabetically ordered through *zzz-zzz-zzz,* after which word types beginning with digits, symbols, and punctuation marks are found. Within the alphabetical portion of the list, certain symbols and punctuation marks *within* a word are ordered before the letter *a,* but digits and certain other symbols are ordered after the letter *z.* A capitalized word appears immediately following the corresponding lower-case word. The reader wishing further understanding of the principles of the ordering is advised to examine the list with some care.

On each page of the list, word types that occurred at least twice in the Corpus are printed beginning at the top of the page. To save space, word types that occurred only once are printed in six columns at the bottom of the page (with the number and code letter indicating the grade and subject in which the word type occurred). *All* the word types printed on a page, however, come from the interval specified by the pair of words printed at the top of the page (on the same line and across from the page number). Therefore, if a word type is not found in the upper page listing, it should be sought in the columns at the bottom. The horizontal lines printed across the page are intended only as aids to the eye.

Some word types are printed with the symbol * * immediately following. These are explained in a section of Special Notes at the end of the Alphabetical List. The Special Notes also contain specialized information about misspelled words, apparent errors in the sampling texts, and related matters.

For each word type in the main part of the list on each page, the following information is given:
1. The word type itself. (When the word type is too long for the space allowed on a single line, the extra characters are printed on a new line without hyphenation.)
2. F = the number of times the word type occurred in the total Corpus of 5,088,721 tokens. For the frequency distribution of F, see the Frequency Distributions (pages 755–760) and the Frequency Distribution Graphs (page 813).
3. D = an index of dispersion, which can take values from .0000 to 1.0000, based on the dispersion of the

Table D-1. Key to the headings in the Alphabetical List. This table also gives the values of U and SFI for the *hapax legomena* ($F = 1$) listed at the bottom of each page.

Code	Heading	Meaning	Value of U for a Hapax	Value of SFI for a Hapax
3, 4, . . . , 9	Gr 3, Gr 4, . . . , Gr 9	Grade 3, Grade 4, . . . , Grade 9	—	—
X	UnGr	Ungraded	—	—
A	Read	Reading	.0457	26.6
B	Eng & Gr	English & Grammar	.0109	20.4
C	Comp	Composition	.0022	13.5
D	Lit	Literature	.0107	20.3
E	Math	Mathematics	.0150	21.8
F	Soc Stud	Social Studies	.0194	22.9
G	Spell	Spelling	.0081	19.1
H	Sci	Science	.0197	22.9
J	Music	Music	.0081	19.1
K	Art	Art	.0018	12.7
L	Home Ec	Home Economics	.0032	15.1
M	Shop	Shop	.0025	14.0
N	Lib F	Library Fiction	.0117	20.7
P	Lib NF	Library Nonfiction	.0145	21.6
Q	Lib Ref	Library Reference	.0105	20.2
R	Mag	Magazines	.0122	20.8
S	Rel	Religion	.0002	2.5

frequencies over the 17 subject categories (coded A through S in the heading on the right-hand side of each page). D takes the value .0000 when all occurrences of the word type are found in a single category, regardless of the frequency. It would take the value 1.0000 if the frequencies were distributed over the 17 categories exactly proportionally to the total numbers of tokens in these categories. Values between .0000 and 1.0000 indicate degrees of dispersion between these extremes. For a note on the computation of D, see page xl. For information on the distribution of D over the 86,741 word types in the Corpus, see page xxix, Table B-4, and Figure B-5.

4. U = the estimated frequency-per-million tokens, derived from F with an adjustment for D. U would equal $F/5.088721$ for a word type with $D = 1.0000$, the constant 5.088721 being used to adjust the frequency to a base of 1 million. However, to the extent that D is less than 1.0000, the value of U is adjusted downward; when D is .0000, U will take a certain minimum value reflecting the average weighted probability of the type over the 17 subject categories. In this way it is believed that U better reflects the true frequency-per-million that would be found in a corpus of indefinitely large size. For information on the distribution of U over the 86,741 word types in the Cor-

pus, see page xxxi, Table B-5, and Figure B-6. For further details on the computation of U, see page xl. The scaling of U in terms of frequency-per-million makes possible direct comparison to values given by Thorndike and Lorge and by Kučera and Francis.

5. SFI = Standard Frequency Index = $10(\log_{10}U + 4)$. As can be seen, this is derived directly from U and hence has some of the same characteristics as U. We believe that the reader will find this to be a simple and convenient way of indicating word probabilities, once it is understood. A word type with SFI = 90 would be expected to occur once in every 10 tokens; one with SFI = 80 would be expected to occur once in every 100 tokens, etc. A convenient mental reference point is provided by SFI = 40, the value for a word that would occur once in a million tokens. Each unit of SFI represents an increase of about 25.9% in probability or frequency. See Table B-5 for U values and probabilities corresponding to SFI.

6. The simple frequencies of the word types in the sections of the Corpus assigned to grades 3, 4, 5, 6, 7, 8, 9, and to the ungraded material. The sum of these frequencies is equal to F. It should be borne in mind that the sizes of these subsections of the Corpus vary somewhat; the total number of tokens in each section may be found in Table B-9. The distributions and

Table D-2. An illustration of the computation of F, D, U, and SFI for combined types.*

Subject Category		word	Word	word's	worded	wording	words	Words	Total (f_i)	Total Tokens in Category (s_i)	s_i/N = t_i	f_i/s_i = p_i	−p_i log p_i
Read	A	1518	3	0	0	2	1200	3	2726	1182971	.232467	.002304	.006078
Eng & Gr	B	1281	0	2	1	2	1930	3	3219	283367	.055685	.011360	.022091
Comp	C	105	0	0	0	1	183	0	289	57776	.011354	.005002	.011509
Lit	D	120	2	0	0	0	192	0	314	277907	.054612	.001130	.003330
Math	E	120	0	0	0	0	154	0	274	387619	.076171	.000707	.002227
Soc Stud	F	96	0	0	1	0	93	0	190	503620	.098967	.000377	.001292
Spell	G	3782	266	0	0	0	6680	485	11213	210157	.041298	.053355	.067912
Sci	H	101	0	0	0	0	69	0	170	510570	.100333	.000333	.001158
Music	J	82	0	0	0	0	324	0	406	209364	.041142	.001939	.005260
Art	K	12	0	0	0	0	35	1	48	47887	.009410	.001002	.003006
Home Ec	L	7	0	0	0	0	6	0	13	83387	.016386	.000156	.000594
Shop	M	3	0	0	0	0	12	0	15	65375	.012847	.000229	.000835
Lib F	N	65	0	0	0	2	96	0	163	303603	.059661	.000537	.001756
Lib NF	P	103	0	0	0	0	112	0	215	374885	.073669	.000574	.001859
Lib Ref	Q	63	0	0	0	0	57	0	120	271040	.053262	.000443	.001485
Mag	R	69	0	0	0	0	67	0	136	314643	.061831	.000432	.001454
Relig	S	5	1	0	0	0	5	0	11	4595	.000903	.002394	.006274
Total		7532	272	2	2	7	11215	492	19522 = F	5088766 = N	$\Sigma f_i t_i =$ 1411.13 = f_{min}	.082274 = P	.138120 = $-\Sigma p_i \log p_i$
D		.5197	.1614	.0000	.2306	.4037	.4756	.0312 ‖ .4828					
U		829.53	10.57	.0219	.1140	.6382	1124.2	6.993 ‖ 1995.42					
SFI		69.2	50.2	23.4	30.6	38.0	70.5	48.5 ‖ 73.0					

$\log n = \log 17 = 1.230449$ $\log P = -1.084737$

$$D = [\log P + (-\Sigma p_i \log p_i)/P]/\log n =$$
$$[-1.084737 + .138120/.082274]/1.230449 = .4828$$

$$U = (1000000/N)[FD + (1-D)f_{min}] =$$
$$.196511\,[(19522)(.4828) + (1-.4828)(1411.13)] = 1995.42$$

$$SFI = 10\,(\log U + 4) = 10\,(3.300034 + 4) = 73.0003$$

*In this table, certain conventions are followed. A single-line rule within the table indicates that a sum of a column or row of figures is taken. Numbers printed in boldface are numbers that may be considered as constants that would always be used in computations involving combinations of frequencies over the 17 subject categories of the AHI Corpus; they do not need to be recomputed unless one desires to combine frequencies over fewer than 17 categories. However, the formulas are given in general terms to permit their use in any desired computations.

The type frequencies for the seven types are extracted from the Alphabetical List; in addition, the several values of D, U, and SFI for these types as given in the Alphabetical List are shown at the bottom left for comparison with the values computed here for the seven types combined.

The total frequencies for the seven types are computed by simple addition across the rows and listed in the column headed "Total (f_i)." The next column gives the total number of tokens in each subject category (s_i). From this point on, the calculations are self-explanatory. The final results are shown at the bottom of the column headed "Total (f_i)."

It may be noted that the value of U for the combined types, 1995.42, is approximately equal to the sum of the separate U values, 1972.06. The amount of the discrepancy is a function of the extent to which the frequencies are differently distributed over the subject categories in the several types. Thus, in general it is legitimate to sum U values for separate types if it is kept in mind that the result will be only an approximation.

3

graphs for these data are to be found in the sections of this book containing the Frequency Distributions and the Frequency Distribution Graphs.

7. The simple frequencies of the word types in the 17 subject categories. (See Table D-1 for a listing of the full subject-category titles.) The sum of these frequencies is equal to F. The total number of tokens in the categories varies considerably, a fact that should be taken into account in interpreting these frequencies; see Table B-9. The distributions and lognormal plots for these categories may be found in the sections of this book containing the Frequency Distributions and the Frequency Distribution Graphs.

Types listed at the bottom of each page are those with frequencies of 1. The symbols preceding each word type indicate the grade and subject category in which the word type appeared; for this purpose the symbols are the same as those used in the page heading and are fully explained in Table D-1. Since of necessity these word types appear in only one category, they all have a D value of .0000. The U and SFI values depend on the category in which the type appears. These values are given in Table D-1. The U and SFI values are, however, probably rather unreliable due to the sampling error inherent in a frequency of 1.

By using other tabulations included in this book, it is possible to ascertain the rank of a word type, either in the total Corpus (in terms of either F or U) or in given sections of it (in terms of simple frequency). If the rank is desired in terms of U, determine the U value from the Alphabetical List and look for that value of U in the Rank List, finding the rank by counting from the rank numbers given after every 100 types. If the rank is desired in terms of frequency, determine the frequency (F, for the total Corpus, or the frequency in the given grade or subject section of the Corpus) from the Alphabetical List and find the rank in the appropriate frequency distribution.

Since word types are here defined in terms of graphic forms, for some purposes it may be desirable to combine the data for different graphic forms for the same entry form. Table D-2 illustrates the combination of data for the types *word, Word, word's, worded, wording, words,* and *Words.* It also illustrates the computations involved in determining F, D, U, and SFI for the combination of types. The recomputation of F involves simple additions, but the computations for D, U, and SFI are somewhat more intricate.

Word Type	F	D	U	SFI	3 Gr 3	4 Gr 4	5 Gr 5	6 Gr 6	7 Gr 7	8 Gr 8	9 Gr 9	X UnGr	A Read	B Eng & Gr	C Comp	D Lit	E Math	F Soc Stud	G Spell	H Sci	J Music	K Art	L Home Ec	M Shop	N Lib F	P Lib NF	Q Lib Ref	R Mag	S Rel
a	124959	.9948	24441	83.9	20742	18458	15103	16148	23836	15135	12320	3217	28905	8106	1944	6769	10090	9826	4745	13914	5232	1259	2260	1973	6739	8967	5902	8262	66
A	1535	.7643	236.24	63.7	232	220	192	205	232	211	215	28	138	50	5	37	716	26	112	70	174	4	24	31	9	39	38	62	0
A**	157	.7701	24.306	53.9	6	40	9	27	30	27	13	5	10	15	0	2	21	13	15	8	6	0	0	1	0	35	27	4	0
A-SPREADING	2	.1814	.1187	30.7	0	2	0	0	0	0	0	0	1	0	0	0	0	0	0	0	0	0	0	0	0	0	0	1	0
A-A	2	.0000	.0050	17.0	0	0	0	0	0	0	2	0	0	0	0	0	0	0	0	0	0	0	0	2	0	0	0	0	0
A-B-A	3	.0000	.0243	23.8	3	0	0	0	0	0	0	0	0	0	0	0	0	0	0	0	3	0	0	0	0	0	0	0	0
A-B-A-C-A	2	.0000	.0162	22.1	0	0	0	0	2	0	0	0	0	0	0	0	0	0	0	0	2	0	0	0	0	0	0	0	0
a-bed	2	.0000	.0219	23.4	1	0	0	0	1	0	0	0	0	2	0	0	0	0	0	0	0	0	0	0	0	0	0	0	0
a-blowing	6	.2028	.3977	36.0	2	0	0	1	0	3	0	0	4	0	0	0	0	0	0	0	2	0	0	0	0	0	0	0	0
a-coming	3	.2261	.2131	33.3	0	0	0	2	1	0	0	0	2	0	0	0	0	0	0	0	0	0	0	0	1	0	0	0	0
a-courtin'	2	.0000	.0162	22.1	0	1	1	0	0	0	0	0	0	0	0	0	0	0	0	0	2	0	0	0	0	0	0	0	0
a-courting	2	.0000	.0914	29.6	0	0	0	0	2	0	0	0	2	0	0	0	0	0	0	0	0	0	0	0	0	0	0	0	0
a-d	4	.0000	.0599	27.8	0	0	1	0	2	1	0	0	0	0	0	0	4	0	0	0	0	0	0	0	0	0	0	0	0
a-dabbling	2	.0000	.0215	23.3	0	0	2	0	0	0	0	0	0	0	0	2	0	0	0	0	0	0	0	0	0	0	0	0	0
a-f	3	.2076	.1618	32.1	1	0	0	1	0	0	1	0	0	0	0	0	2	0	0	1	0	0	0	0	0	0	0	0	0
A-flat	2	.0000	.0162	22.1	0	0	0	0	0	0	2	0	0	0	0	0	0	0	0	0	2	0	0	0	0	0	0	0	0
a-giving	2	.0000	.0162	22.1	2	0	0	0	0	0	0	0	0	0	0	0	0	0	0	0	2	0	0	0	0	0	0	0	0
a-goin'	6	.2226	.3457	35.4	4	0	0	1	0	0	1	0	1	0	0	0	0	0	0	0	0	0	0	0	4	1	0	0	0
a-laying	2	.2387	.1089	30.4	0	0	0	1	1	0	0	0	0	0	0	0	0	0	0	0	1	0	0	0	1	0	0	0	0
a-long	5	.0000	.0724	28.6	5	0	0	0	0	0	0	0	0	0	0	0	0	0	0	0	0	0	0	0	0	5	0	0	0
a-lookin'	3	.0000	.0591	27.7	0	3	0	0	0	0	0	0	0	0	0	0	0	0	0	3	0	0	0	0	0	0	0	0	0
a-picking	2	.1494	.1045	30.2	1	0	1	0	0	0	0	0	1	0	0	0	0	0	0	0	1	0	0	0	0	0	0	0	0
a-raking	2	.0000	.0162	22.1	2	0	0	0	0	0	0	0	0	0	0	0	0	0	0	0	2	0	0	0	0	0	0	0	0
a-ridin'	2	.0000	.0162	22.1	0	0	0	0	0	0	2	0	0	0	0	0	0	0	0	0	2	0	0	0	0	0	0	0	0
a-rovin'	2	.0000	.0162	22.1	0	0	0	2	0	0	0	0	0	0	0	0	0	0	0	0	2	0	0	0	0	0	0	0	0
a-roving	4	.0000	.0323	25.1	0	0	0	0	0	4	0	0	0	0	0	0	0	0	0	0	4	0	0	0	0	0	0	0	0
a-rum-a-tee-tum	5	.0000	.2284	33.6	5	0	0	0	0	0	0	0	5	0	0	0	0	0	0	0	0	0	0	0	0	0	0	0	0
a-rum-a-tee-tum-a-tee-tum	2	.0000	.0914	29.6	2	0	0	0	0	0	0	0	2	0	0	0	0	0	0	0	0	0	0	0	0	0	0	0	0
a-running	4	.3799	.3291	35.2	0	3	1	0	0	0	0	0	0	0	0	0	0	0	0	0	1	0	0	0	0	2	0	1	0
a-sailing	9	.3232	.7313	38.6	6	0	3	0	0	0	0	0	4	0	0	0	0	0	0	0	3	0	0	0	0	2	0	0	0
a-singing	2	.0000	.0162	22.1	2	0	0	0	0	0	0	0	0	0	0	0	0	0	0	0	2	0	0	0	0	0	0	0	0
a-stirring	3	.2212	.2099	33.2	0	3	0	0	0	0	0	0	2	0	0	1	0	0	0	0	0	0	0	0	0	0	0	0	0
a-sunning	2	.0000	.0914	29.6	0	2	0	0	0	0	0	0	2	0	0	0	0	0	0	0	0	0	0	0	0	0	0	0	0
a-swimming	2	.1494	.1045	30.2	0	0	0	1	1	0	0	0	1	0	0	0	0	0	0	0	1	0	0	0	0	0	0	0	0
a-wonderin'	2	.2443	.1130	30.5	0	0	0	0	1	1	0	0	0	0	0	1	0	0	0	0	0	0	0	0	1	0	0	0	0
a-workin'	2	.0000	.0389	25.9	0	0	0	0	0	2	0	0	0	0	0	0	0	2	0	0	0	0	0	0	0	0	0	0	0
a/b	27	.0000	.4041	36.1	0	0	1	0	9	6	11	0	0	0	0	0	27	0	0	0	0	0	0	0	0	0	0	0	0
a/c	2	.0000	.0299	24.8	0	0	0	0	0	1	1	0	0	0	0	0	2	0	0	0	0	0	0	0	0	0	0	0	0
a/12	2	.0000	.0299	24.8	0	0	2	0	0	0	0	0	0	0	0	0	2	0	0	0	0	0	0	0	0	0	0	0	0
a/6	2	.0000	.0299	24.8	0	0	2	0	0	0	0	0	0	0	0	0	2	0	0	0	0	0	0	0	0	0	0	0	0
a/8	3	.0000	.0449	26.5	0	0	3	0	0	0	0	0	0	0	0	0	3	0	0	0	0	0	0	0	0	0	0	0	0
a'	7	.2446	.3879	35.9	0	0	3	2	1	1	0	0	0	4	0	0	0	0	0	0	3	0	0	0	0	0	0	0	0
a'right	3	.0000	.0352	25.5	0	0	0	0	3	0	0	0	0	0	0	0	0	0	0	0	0	0	0	0	3	0	0	0	0
a's	19	.1778	.9189	39.6	1	3	5	6	2	1	1	0	4	2	0	0	0	0	13	0	0	0	0	0	0	0	0	0	0
A's	14	.4518	1.3496	41.3	5	0	1	3	1	4	0	0	0	0	0	0	6	0	0	0	1	0	0	0	0	5	0	2	0
AA	2	.2109	.0918	29.6	0	0	0	0	2	0	0	0	0	0	0	0	0	0	0	0	1	0	1	0	0	0	0	0	0
AAA	2	.0000	.0389	25.9	0	0	0	0	0	2	0	0	0	0	0	0	0	2	0	0	0	0	0	0	0	0	0	0	0
AABA	2	.0000	.0162	22.1	0	0	0	0	1	1	0	0	0	0	0	0	0	0	0	0	2	0	0	0	0	0	0	0	0
AABB	3	.0000	.0243	23.8	2	0	1	0	0	0	0	0	0	0	0	0	0	0	0	0	3	0	0	0	0	0	0	0	0
aah	2	.1787	.1174	30.7	0	1	0	1	0	0	0	0	1	0	0	0	0	0	0	0	0	0	0	0	1	0	0	0	0
Aalborg	5	.0000	.0523	27.2	5	0	0	0	0	0	0	0	0	0	0	0	0	0	0	0	0	0	0	0	0	0	5	0	0
aardvark	10	.3707	.9720	39.9	0	0	0	0	9	0	1	0	8	1	0	0	0	0	0	0	0	0	0	0	0	0	1	0	0
aardvarks	5	.0000	.2284	33.6	0	0	0	0	4	1	0	0	5	0	0	0	0	0	0	0	0	0	0	0	0	0	0	0	0
Aarhus	6	.0000	.0628	28.0	6	0	0	0	0	0	0	0	0	0	0	0	0	0	0	0	0	0	0	0	0	0	6	0	0
Aari	7	.0000	.3198	35.0	7	0	0	0	0	0	0	0	7	0	0	0	0	0	0	0	0	0	0	0	0	0	0	0	0
Aaron	16	.2909	1.2032	40.8	0	2	3	3	4	3	1	0	7	1	0	0	0	1	0	0	7	0	0	0	0	0	0	0	0
AAU	5	.0000	.0608	27.8	0	0	0	0	3	2	0	0	0	0	0	0	0	0	0	0	0	0	0	0	0	0	0	5	0
ab	9	.1703	.4072	36.1	0	0	3	0	0	1	5	0	0	0	0	0	8	0	1	0	0	0	0	0	0	0	0	0	0
AB	186	.1587	8.1045	49.1	20	18	22	15	26	53	32	0	0	0	0	0	179	0	0	2	1	0	0	4	0	0	0	0	0
ABA	3	.0000	.0243	23.8	1	1	0	0	0	1	0	0	0	0	0	0	0	0	0	0	3	0	0	0	0	0	0	0	0
Ababa	14	.1931	.7363	38.7	0	0	2	2	10	0	0	0	0	0	0	0	0	12	0	0	0	0	0	0	0	0	2	0	0
abaca	2	.0000	.0209	23.2	2	0	0	0	0	0	0	0	0	0	0	0	0	0	0	0	0	0	0	0	0	0	2	0	0
aback	2	.1814	.1187	30.7	0	0	0	1	1	0	0	0	1	0	0	0	0	0	0	0	0	0	0	0	0	0	0	1	0
abacus	86	.1178	3.2040	45.1	11	8	30	5	5	11	16	0	3	0	0	0	78	0	0	0	0	0	0	0	0	4	0	1	0
Abadan	3	.0000	.0583	27.7	0	0	0	0	1	0	2	0	0	0	0	0	0	3	0	0	0	0	0	0	0	0	0	0	0
abalone	4	.4347	.3897	35.9	0	0	0	2	1	1	0	0	1	0	0	0	0	1	0	0	1	0	0	0	1	0	0	0	0
abandon	20	.7873	3.1660	45.0	1	0	1	1	9	5	2	1	3	1	1	4	0	2	2	1	1	0	0	0	2	1	1	1	0
abandoned	69	.8009	11.152	50.5	5	3	8	8	24	11	5	5	16	2	1	3	0	13	0	3	2	0	0	0	6	8	10	5	0
abandoning	4	.4519	.3985	36.0	0	0	0	1	3	0	0	0	1	0	0	1	0	0	0	0	0	0	0	0	0	0	1	1	0
abandonment	2	.2446	.1122	30.5	0	0	0	0	1	1	0	0	0	0	0	1	0	0	0	0	0	0	0	0	0	0	1	0	0
abated	3	.0000	.0434	26.4	2	0	1	0	0	0	0	0	0	0	0	0	0	0	0	0	0	0	0	0	0	3	0	0	0
abating	3	.3399	.2456	33.9	0	0	2	0	1	0	0	0	1	0	0	1	0	0	0	0	0	0	0	0	0	0	0	1	0
Abba	13	.1953	.6241	38.0	0	10	0	2	0	0	1	0	0	0	0	10	0	1	0	0	0	0	0	0	0	2	0	0	0
Abbas	2	.0000	.0290	24.6	0	0	0	0	2	0	0	0	0	0	0	0	0	0	0	0	0	0	0	0	0	2	0	0	0
Abbe	2	.2401	.1133	30.5	0	0	0	0	2	0	0	0	0	0	0	0	0	0	0	0	0	0	0	0	0	1	1	0	0
abbe's	3	.0000	.0434	26.4	0	0	0	0	3	0	0	0	0	0	0	0	0	0	0	0	0	0	0	0	0	3	0	0	0
abbey	3	.0000	.0314	25.0	0	0	0	0	0	0	3	0	0	0	0	0	0	0	0	0	0	0	0	0	0	0	3	0	0
Abbey	11	.6151	1.4273	41.5	0	4	0	2	3	2	0	0	4	2	0	0	0	0	1	0	1	0	0	0	1	0	2	0	0
Abbie	8	.0000	.3655	35.6	8	0	0	0	0	0	0	0	8	0	0	0	0	0	0	0	0	0	0	0	0	0	0	0	0

4E aDC-9
4J ABA
9E aN
8G a-
4B A-OK
3J A-A-B
3J A-B
9J A-C-sharp-E
4G A-J
8N a-a-ah
4J a-a-all
8D a-all
7R A-arms
5E a-b
4P A-b-c-d-e-f-g
3J a-banging
7N a-barking
7R a-bit-under-$2000
9J a-blazin'
4P a-bo-a-ard
3P a-boar-r-r-rd
9Q A-bomb
9Q A-bombs
7N a-booming
5A a-borning
4N a-borrowing
6R a-building
7N a-buyin'
3A a-buzz
6E a-c
7A a-callin'
9D a-cap'ring
5P a-charging
4J a-chawin'
3A a-choo
7A a-chunkin'
3J a-clanging
7D a-clinking
7A a-comin'
3B a-cooling
5J a-courtin's
4J a-crying
XR a-diorable
7N a-doin'
7N a-doing
4J a-drooping
3J a-drying
5A a-dying
6G a-e
8D a-fighting
7B a-fishing
5J a-flirtin's
5J a-floating
3A a-flutter
4J a-flying
7E a-g
5G a-gainst
7N a-gittin'
5A a-glare
3J a-glow
7N a-going
7B a-groaning
5A a-growing
6R a-h-h-h
3J a-hanging
3J a-hauling
8J a-having
6J a-hoeing
9D a-hold
3J a-holidaying
7N a-hunting
4J a-io-la
8D a-ketchin'
7A a-kinda
6J a-leaping
7J a-leaving
5J a-light
3A a-lightly
7L A-line
3A a-list'nin'
3J a-marketing
6J a-milking
6B a-musing
5J A-natural
7N a-patchin'
8J a-pitching
3R a-plenty
3A a-prickle
6J a-puffing
5D a-quiver
8D a-raiding
5P a-rowing
6N a-rubbishing
XA a-scolding
6J a-scratching
4J a-scurrying
3J a-selling
3A A-shaped**
3J a-shine
4P a-shinin'
8D a-shining
4J a-sickalum
7J a-sitting
7A a-skitin'
4N a-sorrowing
8J a-squealing
8D a-standin'
8D a-standing
5P a-steering
7A A-student
7A a-stumblin'
7A a-swellin'
8J a-takin'
7A a-tall
7A a-tchee
6A a-telling
3J a-tingle
3A a-tipsy
4N a-tou-tou-tou-tou
7N a-tremble
3B a-tumble
8J a-twirling
8J a-waitin'
4J a-wand'ring
7A a-wanderin'
3B a-warming
4J a-wassailing
7A a-watching
7N a-weaving
7J a-whistling
3R a-wonder
5A A-1
3A A-11
3P A/P-22S
8E a/n
3A a
7D A'astonah
7R AA/F
7A aaaaaa
5Q Aarau
7A aardvark's
9E ab/cd
4P AB'S**
4J ABAB
5P abaci
5P Abako
8G abandoner
7A abandons
8D abashed
9A abatement
6N abates
5P abattoir
6P abba
4D Abba's
7J abbe

Word Type	F	D	U	SFI	3 Gr 3	4 Gr 4	5 Gr 5	6 Gr 6	7 Gr 7	8 Gr 8	9 Gr 9	X UnGr	A Read	B Eng & Gr	C Comp	D Lit	E Math	F Soc Stud	G Spell	H Sci	J Music	K Art	L Home Ec	M Shop	N Lib F	P Lib NF	Q Lib Ref	R Mag	S Rel
abbot	3	.2279	.2143	33.3	0	0	2	0	1	0	0	0	2	0	0	0	0	0	0	0	0	0	0	0	0	0	0	1	0
Abbot	5	.2242	.2842	34.5	0	2	3	0	0	0	0	0	0	0	0	0	0	2	0	0	0	0	0	0	0	3	0	0	0
abbots	2	.0000	.0389	25.9	0	0	0	0	0	2	0	0	0	0	0	0	0	2	0	0	0	0	0	0	0	0	0	0	0
Abbott	18	.3115	1.2599	41.0	1	4	11	0	0	1	0	1	1	0	0	0	0	0	0	0	1	0	0	0	0	0	11	5	0
Abbott's	7	.3602	.5451	37.4	0	1	2	0	3	1	0	0	0	0	0	0	0	0	0	0	1	0	0	0	0	0	2	4	0
abbreviate	13	.4934	1.3359	41.3	0	2	5	1	3	0	2	0	0	5	0	0	3	0	3	0	0	0	0	0	0	1	1	0	0
abbreviated	28	.6138	3.4904	45.4	6	7	1	2	1	3	8	0	0	11	1	0	3	0	8	2	1	0	0	1	0	0	1	0	0
abbreviation	55	.4019	4.7010	46.7	10	13	17	6	5	2	2	0	3	11	3	1	1	0	34	1	0	0	0	0	0	0	0	1	0
abbreviations	71	.3503	5.3837	47.3	8	15	18	4	14	0	11	1	2	27	0	1	4	0	35	0	0	0	0	0	0	0	1	1	0
Abby	45	.0880	1.5689	42.0	38	0	0	0	0	7	0	0	10	0	0	0	0	0	0	0	0	0	0	0	35	0	0	0	0
Abby's	2	.0000	.0914	29.6	0	0	0	0	0	2	0	0	2	0	0	0	0	0	0	0	0	0	0	0	0	0	0	0	0
abc	3	.2444	.1728	32.4	1	0	2	0	0	0	0	0	0	0	0	0	2	0	1	0	0	0	0	0	0	0	0	0	0
ABC	78	.1048	2.6385	44.2	1	5	11	4	7	29	21	0	0	0	0	0	74	0	1	0	0	0	0	0	0	0	0	3	0
ABC-tv	2	.0000	.0243	23.9	0	0	0	1	1	0	0	0	0	0	0	0	0	0	0	0	0	0	0	0	0	0	0	2	0
ABC'S	4	.3468	.2972	34.7	2	0	0	0	0	2	0	0	0	1	0	0	0	0	2	0	0	0	0	0	0	0	1	0	0
ABCD	56	.1126	1.9724	42.9	0	6	26	5	2	10	7	0	0	0	0	0	55	0	0	0	0	0	0	1	0	0	0	0	0
ABCDE	3	.0965	.0750	28.7	0	0	0	0	0	0	3	0	0	0	0	0	1	0	0	0	0	0	0	2	0	0	0	0	0
ABD	6	.0000	.0898	29.5	0	0	0	2	0	3	1	0	0	0	0	0	6	0	0	0	0	0	0	0	0	0	0	0	0
Abdel	5	.1990	.2695	34.3	0	0	1	1	1	1	1	0	0	0	0	0	0	4	0	0	0	0	0	0	0	1	0	0	0
abdicated	4	.3498	.3059	34.9	0	0	0	1	3	0	1	0	0	0	0	0	0	0	0	0	0	0	0	0	0	1	2	1	0
abdication	3	.3847	.2494	34.0	0	0	1	0	2	0	0	0	0	0	0	0	0	0	0	0	0	0	0	0	1	1	1	0	0
abdomen	42	.4052	3.7563	45.7	9	0	5	6	8	9	5	0	0	0	0	0	0	0	1	25	0	0	0	0	0	6	10	0	0
abdomens	4	.1737	.1745	32.4	1	0	0	1	2	0	0	0	0	0	0	0	0	0	0	0	0	0	0	0	0	1	3	0	0
abdominal	13	.3611	1.0760	40.3	0	0	1	1	2	3	6	0	1	0	0	0	0	0	0	7	0	0	0	0	0	1	4	0	0
Abdul	3	.2279	.2143	33.3	0	0	0	1	2	0	0	0	2	0	0	0	0	0	0	0	0	0	0	0	0	0	0	1	0
Abdulgani	2	.0000	.0209	23.2	0	0	0	0	0	2	0	0	0	0	0	0	0	0	0	0	0	0	0	0	0	0	2	0	0
Abdulla	2	.0000	.0914	29.6	0	0	0	0	2	0	0	0	2	0	0	0	0	0	0	0	0	0	0	0	0	0	0	0	0
Abdullah	2	.0000	.0215	23.3	0	0	0	2	0	0	0	0	0	0	0	2	0	0	0	0	0	0	0	0	0	0	0	0	0
Abe	63	.6672	8.9811	49.5	21	4	11	7	9	10	1	0	41	1	0	3	0	4	0	1	2	0	0	0	1	5	5	0	0
ABE	5	.0000	.0537	27.3	0	0	0	0	0	5	0	0	0	0	0	5	0	0	0	0	0	0	0	0	0	0	0	0	0
Abe's	5	.4322	.4885	36.9	0	0	4	0	1	0	0	0	1	0	0	0	0	2	0	1	1	0	0	0	0	0	0	0	0
Abel	8	.0978	.2453	33.9	0	8	0	0	0	0	0	0	0	0	0	0	0	1	0	0	0	0	0	0	7	0	0	0	0
Aberbrothok	4	.0000	.0579	27.6	0	0	4	0	0	0	0	0	0	0	0	0	0	0	0	0	0	0	0	0	0	4	0	0	0
Abercrombie	32	.0478	.6581	38.2	31	0	0	0	0	0	0	1	0	0	0	0	0	0	0	0	0	0	0	0	31	0	0	1	0
Abercrombie's	3	.0000	.0352	25.5	3	0	0	0	0	0	0	0	0	0	0	0	0	0	0	0	0	0	0	0	3	0	0	0	0
Aberdeen	3	.3766	.2497	34.0	0	0	1	1	0	1	0	0	0	0	0	0	0	1	0	0	0	0	0	0	0	1	1	0	0
aberrations	2	.0000	.0209	23.2	0	0	0	0	0	0	0	2	0	0	0	0	0	0	0	0	0	0	0	0	0	0	2	0	0
Aberystwyth	2	.0000	.0243	23.9	0	0	0	0	2	0	0	0	0	0	0	0	0	0	0	0	0	0	0	0	0	0	0	2	0
abet	4	.4530	.4014	36.0	0	0	1	0	1	1	1	0	1	0	0	0	0	0	0	0	0	0	0	0	0	1	1	1	0
abeyance	2	.2446	.1142	30.6	0	0	1	0	1	0	0	0	0	0	0	0	0	0	0	0	0	0	0	0	1	0	0	1	0
ABFE	2	.0000	.0299	24.8	0	0	2	0	0	0	0	0	0	0	0	0	2	0	0	0	0	0	0	0	0	0	0	0	0
Abh	2	.0000	.0914	29.6	0	0	2	0	0	0	0	0	2	0	0	0	0	0	0	0	0	0	0	0	0	0	0	0	0
abide	10	.6523	1.3451	41.3	1	2	0	1	1	4	0	1	2	2	0	1	0	0	0	0	1	0	0	0	2	1	0	1	0
abiding	2	.2285	.1129	30.5	0	0	0	0	1	0	1	0	0	0	0	0	0	1	0	0	0	0	0	0	0	0	1	0	0
Abigail	15	.1409	.7358	38.7	0	10	5	0	0	0	0	0	5	0	0	0	0	0	0	0	0	0	0	0	0	10	0	0	0
Abilene	16	.4563	1.5665	41.9	0	0	6	3	5	2	0	0	0	0	0	1	0	7	0	0	0	0	0	0	4	0	0	4	0
abilities	33	.6858	4.6042	46.6	1	3	5	3	5	5	10	1	3	1	0	0	0	2	0	7	0	1	4	3	0	5	3	4	0
ability	250	.8829	43.849	56.4	3	12	26	28	79	43	54	5	30	8	4	15	7	17	9	41	15	3	8	16	1	18	31	27	0
ablaze	4	.4516	.4046	36.1	2	0	0	1	1	0	0	0	1	0	0	1	0	1	0	0	0	0	0	0	0	1	0	0	0
able	1260	.9281	231.75	63.7	171	191	140	178	252	154	141	33	301	88	11	65	64	134	57	206	26	6	27	9	49	95	63	54	5
Able	11	.0000	.1337	31.3	11	0	0	0	0	0	0	0	0	0	0	0	0	0	0	0	0	0	0	0	0	0	0	11	0
able-bodied	6	.3818	.5656	37.5	0	1	0	2	1	0	2	0	3	0	0	1	0	2	0	0	0	0	0	0	0	0	0	0	0
ably	2	.0000	.0290	24.6	0	0	0	1	1	0	0	0	0	0	0	0	0	0	0	0	0	0	0	0	0	2	0	0	0
ABM	2	.0000	.0243	23.9	0	0	0	0	0	2	0	0	0	0	0	0	0	0	0	0	0	0	0	0	0	0	0	2	0
Abner	9	.3336	.7575	38.8	0	0	0	7	0	2	0	0	4	0	0	1	0	0	0	0	0	0	0	0	0	4	0	0	0
abnormal	10	.4147	.9144	39.6	0	0	1	0	5	0	3	1	0	0	0	0	0	0	1	7	0	0	0	0	1	0	0	1	0
abnormalities	4	.3352	.2986	34.8	0	0	0	0	1	1	0	2	0	0	0	0	0	0	0	1	0	0	0	0	0	0	2	1	0
aboard	155	.7903	25.040	54.0	15	56	11	22	30	7	9	5	78	2	3	8	0	11	0	10	3	0	0	0	6	15	5	14	0
Aboard	3	.0000	.1370	31.4	0	0	0	3	0	0	0	0	3	0	0	0	0	0	0	0	0	0	0	0	0	0	0	0	0
abode	5	.4828	.5050	37.0	0	0	0	3	2	0	0	0	0	0	0	0	0	0	0	0	1	0	0	0	1	2	1	0	0
abodes	3	.2043	.1486	31.7	0	0	0	1	1	0	1	0	0	0	0	0	0	0	0	0	0	0	0	0	0	1	2	0	0
abolish	4	.3831	.3408	35.3	1	0	0	0	1	2	0	0	0	1	0	0	0	2	0	0	0	0	0	0	0	1	0	0	0
abolished	14	.4534	1.3709	41.4	3	0	3	0	4	3	1	0	0	1	0	0	0	7	0	0	0	0	0	0	0	4	2	0	0
abolishing	4	.2183	.2285	33.6	0	0	1	0	0	3	0	0	0	0	0	0	0	3	0	0	0	0	0	0	0	1	0	0	0
abolition	5	.2242	.2842	34.5	0	0	1	0	2	2	0	0	0	0	0	0	0	2	0	0	0	0	0	0	0	3	0	0	0
abolitionist	2	.2408	.1204	30.8	0	0	0	0	1	1	0	0	0	0	0	0	0	1	0	0	0	0	0	0	0	1	0	0	0
abolitionists	7	.5288	.7914	39.0	0	0	0	0	4	2	1	0	1	0	0	0	0	2	0	0	0	0	0	0	1	2	1	0	0
Abolitionists	2	.2152	.1357	31.3	0	0	0	0	1	1	0	0	1	0	0	0	0	1	0	0	0	0	0	0	0	0	0	0	0
abominable	2	.2446	.1142	30.6	0	0	0	0	1	0	0	1	0	0	0	0	0	0	0	0	0	0	0	0	1	0	0	1	0
aboriginal	3	.3852	.2500	34.0	0	0	1	1	1	0	0	0	0	0	0	1	0	0	0	0	0	0	0	0	0	1	0	1	0
aborigines	13	.3856	1.1370	40.6	1	0	0	2	1	0	9	0	1	0	1	0	0	9	0	0	0	0	0	0	0	0	0	2	0
abortion	8	.0000	.0972	29.9	0	0	0	0	8	0	0	0	0	0	0	0	0	0	0	0	0	0	0	0	0	0	0	8	0
abortions	5	.1628	.2128	33.3	0	0	1	0	4	0	0	0	0	0	0	0	0	0	0	0	0	0	0	0	0	1	0	4	0
abortive	2	.2440	.1132	30.5	0	0	0	0	0	2	0	0	0	0	0	1	0	0	0	0	0	0	0	0	0	0	0	1	0
Abou	3	.0000	.1370	31.4	3	0	0	0	0	0	0	0	3	0	0	0	0	0	0	0	0	0	0	0	0	0	0	0	0
abound	15	.4612	1.4833	41.7	0	0	0	0	8	3	2	2	1	0	0	0	0	1	1	3	0	0	0	0	0	0	7	2	0
abounded	3	.1639	.1674	32.2	0	0	0	1	0	2	0	0	1	0	0	0	0	2	0	0	0	0	0	0	0	0	0	0	0
abounding	3	.3346	.2478	33.9	0	0	0	0	3	0	0	0	1	0	0	0	0	0	0	1	0	0	0	0	0	0	1	0	0
abounds	5	.4064	.4395	36.4	0	0	0	0	3	0	2	0	0	0	1	0	0	1	0	1	0	0	0	0	1	1	0	0	0
about	12496	.9851	2423.0	73.8	2168	2117	1639	1660	2325	1371	952	264	3100	1003	125	651	924	1433	272	1535	248	137	155	79	732	841	491	756	14
About	8	.2558	.4886	36.9	1	2	1	0	2	2	0	0	1	0	0	0	0	1	5	0	0	0	0	0	0	0	1	0	0
ABOUT	3	.0000	.1370	31.4	0	3	0	0	0	0	0	0	3	0	0	0	0	0	0	0	0	0	0	0	0	0	0	0	0
above	2298	.9659	437.70	66.4	286	336	298	398	452	274	209	45	437	203	33	83	401	197	121	272	118	25	22	20	73	99	101	92	1
Above	2	.1698	.1133	30.5	1	0	0	0	1	0	0	0	1	0	0	0	0	0	0	0	0	0	0	0	0	0	1	0	0
above-mentioned	2	.2446	.1123	30.5	0	0	0	0	0	1	1	0	0	1	0	0	0	0	0	0	0	0	0	0	0	0	1	0	0
abrading	4	.2107	.2095	33.2	0	0	0	0	3	0	1	0	0	0	0	0	0	0	0	0	0	0	0	0	0	3	0	1	0
Abraham	88	.0788	2.6945	44.3	37	16	10	8	7	8	2	0	13	3	0	3	1	19	0	3	2	0	0	0	1	17	4	2	20
Abraham's	2	.0182	.0264	24.2	1	0	1	0	0	0	0	0	0	0	0	0	0	1	0	0	0	0	0	0	0	0	0	0	1
Abram	3	.0000	.0322	25.1	0	0	0	0	0	0	3	0	0	0	0	3	0	0	0	0	0	0	0	0	0	0	0	0	0
Abrams	10	.0000	.1215	30.8	0	0	0	0	10	0	0	0	0	0	0	0	0	0	0	0	0	0	0	0	0	0	0	10	0
Abrams'	2	.2442	.1134	30.5	0	0	0	0	2	0	0	0	0	1	0	0	0	0	0	0	0	0	0	0	0	0	0	1	0
abrasion	3	.1785	.1397	31.5	0	0	0	0	0	2	1	0	0	0	0	0	0	0	0	2	0	0	0	1	0	0	0	0	0
abrasive	31	.1871	1.3388	41.3	0	1	1	0	16	2	10	1	0	0	0	0	0	0	0	2	0	0	0	17	0	8	1	3	0
abrasives	24	.1050	.6399	38.1	0	0	0	0	22	0	2	0	0	0	0	0	0	0	0	1	0	0	0	16	0	7	0	0	0

3A Abbotts
3E ABCDA
9E ABCDEF
7P Abd
7P Abd-el-Kader
9F abdicate
7Q abdicating
7Q abdomen-wagging
XR abducted
7D abducting
7N abduction
8Q Abdullah's
7D abed
7J Abednego
7D Abenakis
7Q Aberdares
7F Aberdeen-Angus
8Q Aberdeenshire
8B Aberdour
7R Abernathy
8Q aberrant
7Q aberrantly
9R abets
9D abetted
4E ABF
8D abhorred
7D abhorrence
4P Abiah
9Q ability-to-pay
7D Abinadab
5R Abington
8D abject
9D ablative
8F ablest
XH Abney
5Q abnormality
7Q abnormally
9B abolish/abolition
7A Abolitionist
7A Abominable
9B abominate
8Q abomination
8B aboone
7D aboot
7R abortionist
7R abortionists
6R about-face
6H abouts
3R above-water
7E ABP
7E ABQ
4F abra
XH abrade
7C abraded
7R Abramses
7R abrazo

Word Type	F	D	U	SFI	3 Gr 3	4 Gr 4	5 Gr 5	6 Gr 6	7 Gr 7	8 Gr 8	9 Gr 9	X UnGr	A Read	B Eng & Gr	C Comp	D Lit	E Math	F Soc Stud	G Spell	H Sci	J Music	K Art	L Home Ec	M Shop	N Lib F	P Lib NF	Q Lib Ref	R Mag	S Rel
abreast	13	.6126	1.6900	42.3	0	0	1	3	7	1	1	0	5	0	0	2	0	0	0	0	0	0	0	0	2	1	1	2	0
abroad	62	.8157	10.127	50.1	4	3	10	7	12	10	16	0	6	6	0	4	1	12	1	1	1	1	0	0	5	7	5	12	0
abrupt	14	.6352	1.8055	42.6	0	2	3	0	3	3	3	0	1	1	2	1	0	0	2	0	1	0	0	1	0	2	3	0	0
abruptly	33	.7163	4.8450	46.9	1	4	3	6	10	4	5	0	9	4	0	5	0	1	0	1	0	0	0	0	3	3	4	3	0
Absalom	2	.0000	.0209	23.2	0	0	0	0	2	0	0	0	0	0	0	0	0	0	0	0	0	0	0	0	0	0	2	0	0
abscess	6	.2278	.3385	35.3	0	0	0	0	3	3	0	0	0	0	0	0	0	0	0	3	0	0	0	0	0	0	3	0	0
absence	48	.7912	7.6367	48.8	0	2	4	9	11	11	10	1	7	3	0	8	0	2	0	5	2	0	1	0	4	4	8	4	0
absences	4	.2855	.2831	34.5	0	1	0	0	1	2	0	0	1	0	0	2	1	0	0	0	0	0	0	0	0	0	0	0	0
absent	36	.7326	5.3215	47.3	4	7	2	2	10	5	5	1	2	2	1	0	9	0	1	1	0	0	1	0	6	8	5	0	0
absent-minded	3	.3394	.2451	33.9	0	1	0	0	1	0	1	0	1	0	0	1	0	0	0	0	0	0	0	0	1	0	0	0	0
absent-mindedly	3	.3394	.2451	33.9	0	0	0	0	2	1	0	0	1	0	0	1	0	0	0	0	0	0	0	0	1	0	0	0	0
absentee	2	.2408	.1204	30.8	0	0	1	0	1	0	0	0	0	0	0	0	0	1	0	0	0	0	0	0	0	1	0	0	0
absently	5	.3377	.3703	35.7	0	4	0	0	0	1	0	0	0	0	0	1	0	0	0	0	0	0	0	0	3	0	0	1	0
absentminded	2	.1787	.1174	30.7	1	0	0	0	1	0	0	0	1	0	0	0	0	0	0	0	0	0	0	0	1	0	0	0	0
absolute	79	.7583	12.051	50.8	1	1	6	3	14	30	23	1	1	3	0	3	24	9	0	12	7	1	0	0	1	1	10	7	0
Absolute	2	.0000	.0162	22.1	0	0	0	0	2	0	0	0	0	0	0	0	0	0	0	0	2	0	0	0	0	0	0	0	0
absolutely	70	.8430	11.795	50.7	5	4	4	10	16	8	16	7	13	1	1	4	0	1	2	4	1	0	3	1	12	11	5	11	0
absolutist	3	.2043	.1486	31.7	0	0	1	0	0	2	0	0	0	0	0	0	0	0	0	0	0	0	0	0	0	1	2	0	0
absorb	52	.6624	7.0693	48.5	4	1	6	10	12	10	8	1	5	2	0	1	1	0	1	20	1	0	4	0	0	1	11	5	0
absorbed	74	.8052	11.956	50.8	6	5	7	10	20	17	7	2	8	1	1	5	0	2	0	24	6	1	3	0	4	5	13	1	0
absorbent	7	.3234	.4874	36.9	0	1	0	0	3	2	1	0	0	1	0	0	0	0	0	1	0	0	3	0	0	0	1	1	0
absorbers	3	.2159	.1532	31.9	1	0	0	0	2	0	0	0	0	0	0	0	0	0	0	0	0	0	0	0	0	0	2	1	0
absorbing	8	.3149	.6132	37.9	1	0	1	1	3	2	0	0	2	0	0	0	0	1	0	1	0	0	0	0	0	0	4	0	0
absorbs	19	.5623	2.2392	43.5	1	0	2	6	4	3	3	0	1	1	0	0	0	2	0	9	1	0	2	0	0	0	3	0	0
absorption	16	.3566	1.3041	41.2	0	0	1	1	2	4	6	2	0	0	0	0	0	0	0	12	0	0	0	0	0	1	2	1	0
abstain	2	.2285	.1129	30.5	0	0	0	0	0	1	1	0	0	0	0	0	0	1	0	0	0	0	0	0	0	0	1	0	0
abstract	28	.4829	2.7941	44.5	0	1	0	5	3	12	6	1	2	3	4	0	0	1	2	0	0	8	0	1	0	1	5	1	0
abstracted	4	.1901	.1843	32.7	0	0	1	3	0	0	0	0	0	0	0	0	0	0	0	0	0	0	0	0	1	0	3	0	0
absurd	22	.6598	3.0359	44.8	8	1	2	1	5	2	1	2	9	4	2	0	0	0	1	1	0	0	1	0	1	1	1	1	0
absurdity	2	.2437	.1129	30.5	0	0	0	0	1	0	0	1	0	0	0	0	0	0	0	0	0	0	0	0	0	0	1	1	0
absurdly	3	.3771	.2489	34.0	0	0	0	0	3	0	0	0	0	0	0	1	0	0	0	1	0	0	0	0	0	0	0	1	0
Abu	2	.0000	.0209	23.2	0	0	0	0	0	0	1	1	0	0	0	0	0	0	0	0	0	0	0	0	0	0	2	0	0
abundance	55	.7271	8.1351	49.1	2	5	4	4	23	3	12	2	8	0	0	1	0	11	0	8	2	1	1	1	1	2	18	1	0
abundant	63	.5738	7.5385	48.8	7	1	7	11	17	8	7	5	2	0	0	1	0	14	1	16	0	0	0	0	1	2	20	6	0
abundantly	5	.4267	.4793	36.8	2	0	0	1	1	0	0	1	1	0	0	0	0	0	0	1	0	0	0	0	0	2	1	0	0
abuse	9	.4989	1.0052	40.0	0	0	1	0	3	3	1	1	4	0	0	0	0	0	0	1	0	0	1	0	0	2	1	0	0
abused	6	.3982	.5348	37.3	0	0	1	1	2	1	1	0	1	2	0	2	0	1	0	0	0	0	0	0	0	0	0	0	0
abuses	7	.4440	.7016	38.5	1	0	1	0	3	2	0	0	2	0	0	0	0	2	0	0	0	0	0	0	0	0	2	1	0
abusing	3	.3400	.2455	33.9	0	0	0	1	1	0	1	0	1	1	0	0	0	0	0	0	0	0	0	0	1	0	0	0	0
abusive	2	.2407	.1138	30.6	0	0	0	0	1	0	1	0	0	0	0	1	0	0	0	0	0	0	0	0	0	1	0	0	0
abyss	5	.4786	.5420	37.3	0	1	2	2	0	0	0	0	2	0	0	0	0	0	0	1	0	0	0	0	0	1	0	1	0
ac	3	.2444	.1728	32.4	0	0	0	0	1	1	1	0	0	0	0	0	2	0	1	0	0	0	0	0	0	0	0	0	0
AC	48	.0936	1.5214	41.8	1	2	8	9	6	13	9	0	0	0	0	0	46	0	0	0	2	0	0	0	0	0	0	0	0
AC'S**	3	.0000	.1370	31.4	0	0	0	3	0	0	0	0	3	0	0	0	0	0	0	0	0	0	0	0	0	0	0	0	0
acacia	4	.4845	.4027	36.0	0	0	0	1	2	1	0	0	0	0	0	0	0	0	0	0	1	0	0	0	1	0	1	1	0
Acacia	2	.0000	.0162	22.1	0	0	0	0	0	2	0	0	0	0	0	0	0	0	0	0	2	0	0	0	0	0	0	0	0
academic	19	.4909	1.9529	42.9	2	1	2	0	4	4	5	1	0	0	1	0	1	3	0	0	0	0	0	0	0	0	6	8	0
Academic	2	.1387	.0689	28.4	1	0	0	0	0	0	1	0	0	0	1	0	0	0	0	0	0	0	0	0	0	1	0	0	0
academically	3	.0000	.0365	25.6	0	0	0	0	3	0	0	0	0	0	0	0	0	0	0	0	0	0	0	0	0	0	0	3	0
academy	13	.4076	1.1401	40.6	0	5	0	1	0	1	1	5	0	1	0	0	0	0	0	0	0	0	0	0	0	5	1	6	0
Academy	67	.6952	9.5060	49.8	6	12	6	13	3	15	9	3	8	1	1	0	0	13	0	1	3	0	1	0	0	14	17	8	0
Acadia	8	.3830	.6751	38.3	2	0	2	4	0	0	0	0	0	0	0	0	0	4	0	0	2	0	0	0	0	0	0	2	0
Acadian	3	.2071	.1434	31.6	0	0	2	0	0	1	0	0	0	0	0	1	0	0	0	0	2	0	0	0	0	0	0	0	0
Acadians	8	.2388	.4679	36.7	0	0	3	5	0	0	0	0	0	0	0	0	0	5	0	0	3	0	0	0	0	0	0	0	0
ACB	3	.0000	.0449	26.5	0	0	0	0	1	2	0	0	0	0	0	0	3	0	0	0	0	0	0	0	0	0	0	0	0
Accardi	2	.0000	.0290	24.6	0	2	0	0	0	0	0	0	0	0	0	0	0	0	0	0	0	0	0	0	0	2	0	0	0
accelerando	3	.0000	.0243	23.8	0	0	0	2	1	0	0	0	0	0	0	0	0	0	0	0	3	0	0	0	0	0	0	0	0
accelerate	8	.5477	.9095	39.6	0	0	1	1	4	1	0	1	0	0	0	0	0	0	0	2	1	0	0	0	0	1	2	2	0
accelerated	12	.3787	.9889	40.0	0	0	1	6	2	1	1	1	0	0	0	0	1	0	0	2	0	0	0	0	0	1	7	1	0
accelerates	2	.2446	.1184	30.7	1	0	0	0	0	0	1	0	0	0	0	0	1	0	0	0	0	0	0	0	0	1	0	0	0
accelerating	6	.3072	.4065	36.1	0	0	0	0	3	1	1	1	0	0	1	0	0	0	0	1	0	0	0	0	0	0	4	0	0
acceleration	19	.6480	2.5276	44.0	1	0	0	9	5	0	2	2	2	0	1	0	2	0	0	2	0	0	0	0	1	3	5	3	0
accelerator	5	.3157	.3891	35.9	1	0	0	2	1	0	1	0	1	0	0	0	0	0	0	3	0	0	0	0	0	0	1	0	0
accelerators	4	.0000	.0789	29.0	0	0	0	3	0	1	0	0	0	0	0	0	0	0	0	4	0	0	0	0	0	0	0	0	0
accent	204	.4534	19.386	52.9	14	45	51	38	29	12	15	0	12	11	0	5	0	2	129	1	24	1	6	0	0	7	2	4	0
accented	124	.3419	9.7785	49.9	23	24	18	20	16	15	7	1	32	1	0	0	0	0	72	0	17	1	1	0	0	0	0	0	0
accenting	4	.2800	.2967	34.7	0	0	0	0	2	1	1	0	2	0	0	0	0	0	0	0	0	0	1	0	1	0	0	0	0
accents	31	.4719	3.0352	44.8	1	7	5	7	7	4	0	0	1	0	0	1	0	1	11	0	14	1	0	0	1	0	0	1	0
accentuate	3	.2196	.1435	31.6	0	0	0	0	2	0	1	0	0	0	0	0	0	0	0	0	2	1	0	0	0	0	0	0	0
accentuated	2	.2433	.1158	30.6	0	0	0	1	0	0	0	1	0	0	0	0	0	0	0	0	0	0	0	0	0	1	0	1	0
accept	159	.8935	28.256	54.5	14	8	17	17	35	32	32	4	32	16	2	7	3	27	4	10	5	0	3	0	7	12	11	20	0
acceptable	45	.6521	5.9286	47.7	0	1	1	0	12	9	20	2	0	21	1	1	0	2	4	0	1	0	4	0	0	2	4	5	0
acceptance	32	.7613	4.9049	46.9	0	1	7	2	8	8	5	1	3	2	2	2	0	4	0	1	1	0	1	0	2	7	6	1	0
accepted	169	.8354	28.287	54.5	9	4	18	22	42	46	22	6	30	11	2	11	5	26	0	20	7	1	1	0	8	11	22	13	1
accepting	22	.7883	3.4867	45.4	0	0	3	5	3	3	7	1	3	2	1	2	0	2	0	2	0	0	1	0	2	1	2	4	0
acceptor	3	.2445	.1818	32.6	0	0	0	0	1	1	1	0	0	0	0	0	0	0	0	2	0	0	0	0	0	0	1	0	0
accepts	9	.4966	.9255	39.7	0	0	0	1	3	3	2	0	0	0	1	0	0	1	0	1	0	0	2	0	0	1	3	0	0
access	34	.6278	4.3584	46.4	1	2	2	4	14	4	5	2	0	1	0	1	0	6	1	0	0	0	0	0	4	3	9	9	0
accessibility	2	.1698	.1133	30.5	0	0	0	0	0	1	0	1	1	0	0	0	0	0	0	0	0	0	0	0	0	0	1	0	0
accessible	7	.4768	.6889	38.4	0	0	0	0	1	0	3	3	0	0	0	0	0	0	0	0	0	0	1	1	0	0	2	3	0
accessories	23	.3019	1.4929	41.7	1	0	1	0	6	6	7	2	1	2	0	0	0	0	0	0	0	0	13	1	0	1	2	3	0
accident	176	.8531	30.030	54.8	15	13	23	13	48	36	24	4	42	10	11	12	0	15	8	22	1	2	4	1	13	6	8	21	0
accidental	17	.6094	2.0998	43.2	0	0	2	3	4	5	3	0	0	0	1	1	0	1	0	1	5	0	2	0	0	0	5	1	0
accidentally	30	.7289	4.4262	46.5	1	1	7	3	9	4	4	1	2	1	0	3	0	2	0	7	2	0	0	0	4	1	6	2	0
accidentals	10	.0000	.0808	29.1	0	0	0	1	2	1	6	0	0	0	0	0	0	0	0	0	10	0	0	0	0	0	0	0	0
accidents	101	.7350	15.021	51.8	5	9	23	5	28	18	12	1	5	2	8	1	7	11	3	35	0	1	1	0	4	1	6	16	0
ACCION	3	.0000	.0365	25.6	0	0	0	0	0	3	0	0	0	0	0	0	0	0	0	0	0	0	0	0	0	0	0	3	0
acclaim	10	.5830	1.2032	40.8	0	1	0	1	2	4	2	0	1	0	1	2	0	1	0	0	2	0	0	0	0	0	2	1	0
acclaimed	7	.4540	.6679	38.2	0	0	2	0	1	1	3	0	0	1	0	0	0	0	0	0	1	0	0	0	0	2	3	0	0
acclimatization	2	.2446	.1122	30.5	0	0	0	0	1	1	0	0	0	0	0	1	0	0	0	0	0	0	0	0	0	0	1	0	0
accommodate	14	.5914	1.6922	42.3	1	0	0	0	5	2	4	2	0	1	0	0	0	2	0	0	2	0	1	0	0	0	4	4	0
accommodated	3	.2540	.1940	32.9	0	0	0	0	2	0	1	0	1	0	0	0	0	0	0	0	0	0	1	0	0	0	1	0	0
accommodating	2	.0000	.0243	23.9	0	0	0	1	0	0	0	1	0	0	0	0	0	0	0	0	0	0	0	0	0	0	0	2	0
accommodation	4	.2011	.1965	32.9	0	0	0	0	2	0	0	2	0	0	0	0	0	0	0	0	0	0	0	0	1	0	0	3	0
accommodations	6	.3873	.5223	37.2	1	0	1	0	1	1	0	2	1	0	0	0	0	0	0	0	0	0	0	0	0	1	1	3	0

XR Abricot
8F abridged
9F abridging
4J Abroad
7P abrogated
4P abruptness
7H abscessed
8E abscissa
9E abscissas
4P Absent
7P absentmindedly
8A absolument
8F absolution
5P absolutism
8F Absolved
9G absorb-achieve
XH absorbable
7R absorber
XH absorptions
5Q Abstract
7D abstractedly
9D abstraction
8Q Abstraction
8K abstractionism
5Q abstractions
7Q abstractly
9Q abstractness
9R Absurd
8D absurdities
7A Abulbul
7R abutment
XQ abutments
8A abutted
7P Abyssinian
7B Abyssinians
9E ac/bc
8R academics
8Q Academie
8F academies
XH Acamar
7R accademies
5P accentless
7B acceptably
5Q Accepted
9Q Access
8F accession
7H accessory
6B accident-free
7B Accidents
7N acclamations
7R acclimated
5P acclimatized
5P acclimatizing

Word Type	F	D	U	SFI	3 Gr 3	4 Gr 4	5 Gr 5	6 Gr 6	7 Gr 7	8 Gr 8	9 Gr 9	X UnGr	A Read	B Eng & Gr	C Comp	D Lit	E Math	F Soc Stud	G Spell	H Sci	J Music	K Art	L Home Ec	M Shop	N Lib F	P Lib NF	Q Lib Ref	R Mag	S Rel
accompanied	76	.6917	10.699	50.3	3	5	10	15	18	14	8	3	10	2	3	3	0	2	0	5	22	0	0	0	4	10	7	8	0
accompanies	9	.2123	.4766	36.8	2	0	0	4	1	1	1	0	1	0	0	0	0	0	0	1	6	0	0	0	0	1	0	0	0
accompaniment	149	.1090	4.3590	46.4	8	28	23	37	16	11	25	1	2	0	0	2	0	0	0	0	138	0	1	0	2	3	1	0	0
accompaniments	15	.2869	.9213	39.6	0	4	1	1	7	2	0	0	0	0	0	0	0	0	0	0	10	0	4	0	0	0	0	1	0
accompanist	4	.3424	.2945	34.7	1	0	1	0	0	0	2	0	0	0	0	1	0	0	0	0	2	0	0	0	1	0	0	0	0
accompany	90	.4185	7.8992	49.0	16	12	14	20	12	6	8	2	2	3	1	3	0	1	3	1	65	0	3	0	1	2	2	3	0
accompanying	23	.5616	2.6569	44.2	0	2	4	2	11	2	2	0	1	0	0	0	0	0	0	1	9	0	1	0	2	2	5	2	0
accomplish	37	.7266	5.4187	47.3	2	0	3	3	9	6	14	0	2	4	0	3	0	6	1	3	2	1	6	0	1	1	3	4	0
accomplished	71	.8525	12.074	50.8	2	0	7	10	25	9	16	2	11	3	1	5	1	6	0	5	6	0	1	2	3	3	14	10	0
accomplishing	4	.3683	.3188	35.0	0	1	0	0	2	0	0	1	0	0	0	1	0	0	0	0	0	0	0	0	2	0	0	1	0
accomplishment	22	.6973	3.1026	44.9	0	2	1	2	9	2	4	2	1	2	0	0	0	2	0	2	2	1	2	0	0	1	2	7	0
accomplishments	29	.5846	3.5676	45.5	0	1	3	3	9	4	9	0	7	0	0	3	1	4	0	1	0	4	1	0	2	1	3	2	0
accord	12	.6442	1.6220	42.1	0	1	3	1	3	2	2	0	4	0	0	0	0	1	1	1	0	0	0	0	2	1	2	0	0
accordance	12	.6376	1.5644	41.9	0	1	0	5	1	2	3	0	1	2	0	0	1	0	3	1	1	0	0	0	0	0	2	1	0
accorded	6	.4518	.5771	37.6	0	0	2	0	1	2	1	0	0	0	0	0	0	1	0	0	0	0	0	0	1	2	2	0	0
according	403	.9478	75.409	58.8	23	32	33	42	107	74	68	24	45	36	11	23	27	35	13	59	13	1	11	10	9	29	38	42	1
accordingly	29	.7878	4.6154	46.6	1	1	3	4	7	4	9	0	7	3	1	2	0	4	0	1	0	0	1	0	2	2	5	1	0
accordion	11	.6818	1.5416	41.9	1	4	2	1	3	0	0	0	2	1	0	1	0	1	0	2	2	0	0	0	0	1	1	0	0
account	206	.8911	36.505	55.6	8	11	18	30	48	40	45	6	36	10	2	14	26	15	4	33	0	1	9	0	17	10	16	13	0
Account	2	.1948	.1250	31.0	1	0	0	0	1	0	0	0	1	0	0	0	0	0	0	0	0	0	0	0	0	1	0	0	0
accountable	3	.2435	.2274	33.6	0	0	0	0	3	0	0	0	2	0	0	0	0	1	0	0	0	0	0	0	0	0	0	0	0
accounted	9	.6767	1.2584	41.0	0	1	0	4	2	1	1	0	2	1	0	0	1	2	0	0	0	0	0	0	1	0	1	1	0
accounting	5	.2424	.2988	34.8	0	0	0	0	3	0	2	0	0	0	0	0	0	0	0	3	0	0	3	0	0	0	2	0	0
accounts	63	.8055	10.173	50.1	4	5	6	10	16	13	6	3	6	1	1	2	2	9	1	6	0	0	0	0	4	6	13	9	0
accredited	3	.2159	.1532	31.9	0	0	0	0	1	1	1	0	0	0	0	0	0	0	0	0	0	0	0	0	0	0	2	1	0
accumulate	11	.5168	1.2030	40.8	0	0	1	1	2	2	2	3	0	0	0	0	0	1	0	5	0	0	0	0	0	1	2	2	0
accumulated	20	.5818	2.4243	43.8	0	0	0	1	6	3	8	2	1	0	0	2	0	1	0	7	0	0	0	0	0	1	4	4	0
accumulates	2	.1892	.0858	29.3	0	0	0	1	0	1	0	0	0	1	0	0	0	0	0	0	0	0	1	0	0	0	0	0	0
accumulating	3	.3365	.2489	34.0	0	0	0	0	1	1	1	0	1	0	0	1	0	0	0	1	0	0	0	0	0	0	0	0	0
accumulation	19	.6577	2.5613	44.1	0	1	0	3	6	4	5	0	1	1	1	0	0	1	0	8	0	1	0	0	0	1	3	2	0
accuracy	50	.8216	8.2061	49.1	0	6	1	1	19	11	7	5	4	3	1	2	9	1	2	8	0	0	4	3	2	3	4	4	0
Accuracy	20	.0000	.2994	34.8	13	7	0	0	0	0	0	0	0	0	0	0	20	0	0	0	0	0	0	0	0	0	0	0	0
accurate	166	.7435	24.926	54.0	0	13	20	11	42	31	40	9	12	17	1	1	17	10	0	47	0	1	7	16	0	7	18	12	0
accurately	78	.7878	12.350	50.9	1	7	4	3	33	6	18	6	10	9	2	1	8	2	1	17	2	0	5	6	0	3	9	3	0
accursed	4	.3715	.3204	35.1	0	0	1	0	2	0	1	0	0	1	0	1	0	0	0	0	0	0	0	0	2	0	0	0	0
accusation	4	.3360	.3283	35.2	0	0	1	0	0	2	1	0	1	0	0	0	0	2	0	0	0	0	0	0	0	0	0	1	0
accusations	2	.2408	.1204	30.8	0	0	0	0	0	1	1	0	0	0	0	0	0	1	0	0	0	0	0	0	0	1	0	0	0
accuse	5	.0760	.1529	31.8	1	0	2	0	1	0	1	0	1	0	0	0	0	0	0	0	0	0	0	0	0	1	0	2	1
accused	49	.4642	4.9805	47.0	2	1	5	1	12	6	22	0	7	2	0	3	0	18	1	1	0	0	0	0	0	7	6	3	1
accusers	3	.3852	.2500	34.0	0	0	0	0	1	0	2	0	0	0	0	1	0	0	0	0	0	0	0	0	0	1	0	1	0
accusing	4	.3677	.3659	35.6	0	0	0	1	3	0	0	0	2	0	0	1	0	1	0	0	0	0	0	0	0	0	0	0	0
accusingly	2	.1787	.1174	30.7	1	0	0	1	0	0	0	0	1	0	0	0	0	0	0	0	0	0	0	0	1	0	0	0	0
accustom	2	.0000	.0290	24.6	0	0	0	2	0	0	0	0	0	0	0	0	0	0	0	0	0	0	0	0	0	2	0	0	0
accustomed	55	.8192	9.0473	49.6	2	6	4	9	16	11	6	1	12	2	2	6	0	6	0	3	7	0	2	0	4	6	3	2	0
ACD	3	.2076	.1618	32.1	0	0	0	0	0	2	1	0	0	0	0	0	2	0	0	1	0	0	0	0	0	0	0	0	0
ace	3	.3427	.2477	33.9	1	0	0	1	1	0	0	0	1	0	0	0	0	0	0	0	0	0	0	0	1	0	0	1	0
Ace	12	.1874	.6137	37.9	0	0	0	2	0	9	1	0	2	0	0	1	0	0	0	0	0	0	0	0	0	0	0	9	0
acephali	2	.0000	.0234	23.7	0	0	0	0	2	0	0	0	0	0	0	0	0	0	0	0	0	0	0	0	2	0	0	0	0
acetate	5	.1610	.1839	32.6	0	0	0	0	1	2	2	0	0	0	0	0	0	0	0	0	0	0	3	0	0	0	2	0	0
acetic	4	.2278	.2257	33.5	0	0	2	0	0	2	0	0	0	0	0	0	0	0	0	2	0	0	0	0	0	0	2	0	0
acetylene	7	.1018	.2691	34.3	0	2	0	0	0	5	0	0	2	0	0	0	0	0	0	0	0	0	0	0	0	0	5	0	0
ach	4	.0919	.1430	31.6	0	4	0	0	0	0	0	0	1	0	0	3	0	0	0	0	0	0	0	0	0	2	0	2	0
ache	13	.6419	1.7206	42.4	0	3	1	1	2	2	3	1	2	2	0	0	0	0	2	1	0	0	0	0	2	1	0	0	0
ached	27	.4701	2.8948	44.6	2	5	5	4	7	2	2	0	13	1	0	4	0	0	0	0	0	0	1	0	8	0	0	1	0
aches	10	.6390	1.3412	41.3	0	0	1	4	3	2	0	0	4	0	0	1	0	0	1	0	1	0	1	0	1	0	0	0	0
achieve	69	.8387	11.516	50.6	2	2	5	8	11	21	19	1	1	3	1	1	1	14	2	7	7	4	3	1	1	6	11	6	0
achieved	86	.8090	13.911	51.4	1	2	8	7	21	22	20	5	6	3	0	6	1	12	1	5	10	2	4	0	0	10	16	10	0
achievement	41	.6878	5.7519	47.6	2	1	6	2	11	9	8	2	5	3	0	2	1	6	0	0	2	0	1	0	0	4	14	3	0
Achievement	3	.0000	.0583	27.7	0	0	0	0	0	0	3	0	0	0	0	0	0	3	0	0	0	0	0	0	0	0	0	0	0
achievements	41	.7642	6.3109	48.0	1	2	1	8	7	7	12	3	2	5	1	0	0	11	0	6	1	1	0	0	2	3	8	1	0
achieves	10	.6071	1.2217	40.9	0	2	0	0	3	2	2	1	0	0	1	1	0	0	0	0	4	1	1	0	0	0	1	1	0
achieving	15	.6506	1.9998	43.0	0	0	1	1	3	6	2	2	1	0	0	1	0	4	1	1	1	1	0	0	0	1	0	4	0
Achilles	3	.3274	.2362	33.7	0	0	1	0	1	1	0	0	1	0	0	0	0	0	1	0	0	0	0	0	0	0	1	0	0
aching	33	.6922	4.6971	46.7	6	4	4	2	8	5	1	3	9	3	0	2	0	1	1	1	7	0	0	0	3	0	1	5	0
Achmet	9	.2292	.4844	36.9	0	0	0	6	3	0	0	0	0	0	0	3	0	0	0	0	0	0	0	0	6	0	0	0	0
Achmet's	4	.2443	.2260	33.5	0	0	0	2	2	0	0	0	0	0	0	2	0	0	0	0	0	0	0	0	2	0	0	0	0
acid	140	.6195	17.891	52.5	3	6	19	13	27	17	47	8	4	0	0	1	6	0	0	74	1	0	9	5	2	3	31	4	0
acid-core	3	.0000	.0076	18.8	0	0	0	0	0	3	0	0	0	0	0	0	0	0	0	0	0	0	0	3	0	0	0	0	0
acidic	3	.0000	.0591	27.7	0	0	0	0	1	0	2	0	0	0	0	0	0	0	0	3	0	0	0	0	0	0	0	0	0
acidity	4	.3402	.3064	34.9	0	0	0	0	1	0	1	2	0	0	0	0	1	0	0	1	0	0	0	0	0	0	0	2	0
acids	59	.5003	6.2641	48.0	0	0	8	8	18	8	12	5	0	0	0	0	0	0	0	39	0	0	7	1	2	0	7	3	0
Ackley	6	.2435	.4680	36.7	0	0	0	0	1	5	0	0	5	0	0	1	0	0	0	0	0	0	0	0	0	0	0	0	0
acknowledge	7	.4549	.6693	38.3	1	1	0	0	3	2	0	0	0	0	0	1	0	0	0	0	0	0	0	0	1	0	2	3	0
acknowledged	17	.6671	2.3057	43.6	0	1	2	1	3	5	4	1	1	0	0	1	0	1	0	0	1	1	0	0	3	2	2	5	0
acknowledges	4	.3641	.3177	35.0	0	0	0	1	2	0	1	0	0	0	0	1	0	0	0	0	0	0	0	0	0	1	0	2	0
acknowledging	3	.0000	.0352	25.5	0	0	0	1	1	1	0	0	0	0	0	0	0	0	0	0	0	0	0	0	3	0	0	0	0
acknowledgment	3	.3427	.2477	33.9	0	0	0	0	0	1	2	0	1	0	0	0	0	0	0	0	0	0	0	0	1	0	0	1	0
acne	5	.2368	.2953	34.7	0	0	0	0	4	0	1	0	0	0	0	0	0	0	0	4	0	0	1	0	0	0	0	0	0
Aconcagua	2	.2285	.1129	30.5	1	0	0	1	0	0	0	0	0	0	0	0	0	1	0	0	0	0	0	0	0	0	1	0	0
acorn	10	.5007	1.0756	40.3	1	4	0	2	0	0	2	1	1	0	1	0	0	0	0	5	0	0	0	0	0	1	1	1	0
acorns	29	.6451	3.9863	46.0	12	4	1	2	4	2	1	3	14	0	0	2	0	3	0	3	0	0	0	0	0	5	1	1	0
acoustical	9	.1052	.2533	34.0	0	0	0	0	7	1	0	1	0	0	0	0	0	0	0	0	8	0	0	0	0	0	1	0	0
acoustics	6	.3826	.4891	36.9	0	0	0	0	1	4	0	1	0	0	0	0	0	0	0	0	2	0	0	0	0	0	2	2	0
acquaint	5	.4244	.4408	36.4	0	0	0	1	1	1	2	0	0	0	0	0	0	0	1	0	2	0	0	1	0	1	0	0	0
acquaintance	21	.6286	2.7258	44.4	0	2	2	2	6	1	6	2	3	1	0	7	0	1	0	1	1	0	0	0	0	1	2	4	0
acquaintances	6	.4552	.5794	37.6	0	1	0	0	5	0	0	0	0	1	0	0	0	0	0	1	0	0	0	0	2	0	0	2	0
acquaintanceship	2	.2303	.1079	30.3	0	0	1	0	0	0	1	0	0	0	0	0	0	0	0	0	1	0	0	0	0	1	0	0	0
acquainted	36	.8998	6.4361	48.1	0	3	2	6	10	10	5	0	8	3	0	5	1	3	1	3	2	1	1	1	1	2	2	2	0
acquiescence	2	.2437	.1129	30.5	0	0	1	0	1	0	0	0	0	0	0	0	0	0	0	0	0	0	0	0	0	0	1	1	0
acquire	33	.8108	5.3584	47.3	0	2	3	3	7	8	8	2	4	4	0	0	0	5	1	1	1	1	2	1	0	5	5	3	0
acquired	48	.8307	7.9656	49.0	2	0	4	7	11	12	9	3	3	5	1	0	0	11	0	7	1	0	2	1	3	4	7	3	0
acquires	4	.2918	.2663	34.3	0	0	0	1	2	0	1	0	0	0	1	0	0	0	0	2	0	0	0	0	0	0	1	0	0
acquiring	6	.4763	.5984	37.8	0	0	0	0	1	3	2	0	0	1	1	0	1	2	0	0	0	0	1	0	0	0	0	0	0
acquisition	4	.3519	.3117	34.9	0	1	0	0	0	1	1	1	0	0	0	0	0	1	0	0	0	0	0	0	0	0	1	2	0
acquit	2	.2285	.1129	30.5	0	0	1	0	0	1	0	0	0	0	0	0	0	1	0	0	0	0	0	0	0	0	1	0	0
acquittal	2	.2437	.1129	30.5	0	0	1	0	0	1	0	0	0	0	0	0	0	0	0	0	0	0	0	0	0	0	1	1	0

7Q accomplishes
6D accordin'
XJ According
9A accost
8F accountants
9Q Accounts
9D accoutered
8D accouterments
7Q accrual
8A accrue
5Q acculturation
5Q Acculturation
XH accumulations
9Q accumulator
7Q accuracies
6A accuser
8A accuses
6A Ace's
5Q Acer
5Q Aceraceae
9Q aces
5E Aces
8L acetates
6E ACF
6J Ach
9D Achaean
6P Achelous
XH Achernar
8F Acheson
9R Achilles'
6R achoo
3A acid-loaded
6A acid-secreting
8M acid-type
9L acidify
8F acidly
XR acidulous
7D Ackley's
7N aclostones
8A acme
9R acoustic
9E acquaints
8F acquiesce
XR acquirable
9K acquirement
8Q acquisitions
7N acquisitiveness

Word Type	F	D	U	SFI	3 Gr 3	4 Gr 4	5 Gr 5	6 Gr 6	7 Gr 7	8 Gr 8	9 Gr 9	X UnGr	A Read	B Eng & Gr	C Comp	D Lit	E Math	F Soc Stud	G Spell	H Sci	J Music	K Art	L Home Ec	M Shop	N Lib F	P Lib NF	Q Lib Ref	R Mag	S Rel
acquitted	9	.3244	.6675	38.2	0	0	5	1	1	1	1	0	1	0	0	2	0	1	0	0	0	0	0	0	0	0	5	0	0
acre	64	.6985	9.1554	49.6	4	8	16	10	13	2	5	6	8	0	0	0	7	24	5	3	1	0	0	0	1	2	8	5	0
acre-feet	2	.0000	.0290	24.6	0	0	2	0	0	0	0	0	0	0	0	0	0	0	0	0	0	0	0	0	0	2	0	0	0
acreage	9	.4506	.8810	39.4	1	0	2	1	2	0	2	1	1	0	0	0	0	1	0	0	0	0	0	0	0	2	1	4	0
acreages	2	.0000	.0243	23.9	0	0	0	0	0	0	0	2	0	0	0	0	0	0	0	0	0	0	0	0	0	0	0	2	0
acres	159	.7249	23.487	53.7	7	20	39	34	26	5	17	11	22	2	2	2	19	48	1	2	0	0	0	0	3	9	23	26	0
Acrilan	3	.0000	.0097	19.8	0	0	0	0	0	1	2	0	0	0	0	0	0	0	0	0	0	0	3	0	0	0	0	0	0
acrobat	4	.3718	.3639	35.6	0	3	1	0	0	0	0	0	2	1	0	0	0	0	0	0	0	0	0	0	1	0	0	0	0
acrobatic	2	.1948	.1250	31.0	0	0	0	1	1	0	0	0	1	0	0	0	0	0	0	0	0	0	0	0	0	1	0	0	0
acrobatics	3	.3394	.2451	33.9	1	0	0	0	1	0	1	0	1	0	0	1	0	0	0	0	0	0	0	0	1	0	0	0	0
acrobats	9	.5042	.9812	39.9	0	4	3	1	0	0	1	0	2	0	1	0	0	0	0	1	0	0	0	0	1	3	0	1	0
Acropolis	4	.3829	.3404	35.3	0	2	0	0	2	0	0	0	0	0	0	0	0	2	0	0	0	0	0	0	0	1	1	0	0
across	1942	.9398	361.27	65.6	340	336	280	313	321	189	123	40	536	51	34	135	53	280	16	183	49	13	20	40	143	178	68	143	0
Acrux	6	.0000	.1183	30.7	0	0	0	0	0	6	0	0	0	0	0	0	0	0	0	6	0	0	0	0	0	0	0	0	0
act	457	.9197	83.348	59.2	65	76	50	52	95	68	38	13	105	26	5	34	2	26	9	67	21	1	10	2	22	44	53	30	0
Act	98	.5393	11.238	50.5	2	2	24	1	14	39	12	4	10	0	0	1	0	45	0	6	3	0	0	0	0	1	23	9	0
acted	83	.8701	14.472	51.6	7	12	12	18	17	9	8	0	33	3	0	4	1	6	3	5	4	1	0	0	7	8	5	3	0
acting	104	.7443	15.792	52.0	18	15	11	8	20	14	14	4	28	11	1	4	2	10	1	11	5	0	4	0	7	5	2	12	1
action	519	.8425	87.210	59.4	21	37	61	68	120	95	97	20	62	91	18	15	0	32	26	66	24	23	0	19	13	26	49	55	0
Action	5	.2849	.3340	35.2	0	0	1	1	1	2	0	0	0	0	0	0	0	1	0	1	0	0	0	0	0	0	0	3	0
actions	128	.8028	20.620	53.1	6	8	10	17	36	30	18	3	17	17	5	8	0	6	2	32	4	5	9	0	0	4	8	11	0
activate	2	.0000	.0243	23.9	0	0	0	0	1	0	0	1	0	0	0	0	0	0	0	0	0	0	0	0	0	0	0	2	0
activated	5	.3461	.3825	35.8	0	0	0	0	2	2	0	1	0	0	0	0	0	0	0	1	0	0	0	0	0	0	2	2	0
activates	4	.2287	.2348	33.7	0	0	0	0	2	1	1	0	0	0	0	0	0	0	0	3	0	0	0	0	0	0	0	1	0
active	178	.8363	29.773	54.7	7	18	30	24	46	23	26	4	23	7	3	3	0	18	1	42	17	0	8	2	1	16	25	12	0
actively	16	.5988	2.0089	43.0	0	1	0	0	8	3	3	1	2	0	0	1	0	2	0	7	0	0	0	1	0	0	2	1	0
activism	4	.0000	.0486	26.9	0	0	0	0	0	1	3	0	0	0	0	0	0	0	0	0	0	0	0	0	0	0	0	4	0
activist	4	.1622	.1743	32.4	0	0	0	0	2	1	1	0	0	0	0	0	0	1	0	0	0	0	0	0	0	0	0	3	0
activists	6	.0000	.0729	28.6	0	0	1	0	0	1	4	0	0	0	0	0	0	0	0	0	0	0	0	0	0	0	0	6	0
activities	263	.8190	43.007	56.3	19	15	35	31	46	42	65	10	10	9	7	4	2	39	17	63	13	5	28	1	2	12	29	22	0
Activities	5	.3814	.4791	36.8	0	0	0	0	3	1	0	1	3	0	0	0	0	1	0	0	0	0	0	0	0	0	0	1	0
activity	164	.8215	26.963	54.3	10	9	10	17	46	21	43	8	17	6	8	6	1	14	4	42	1	0	9	5	2	11	19	19	0
Activity	20	.3900	1.8990	42.8	0	3	0	0	14	1	2	0	10	6	0	0	0	3	0	1	0	0	0	0	0	0	0	0	0
actor	44	.7697	6.9045	48.4	8	8	4	3	11	3	6	1	17	7	1	2	0	1	3	0	0	0	0	0	3	4	3	3	0
actors	51	.7535	7.8251	48.9	8	6	5	5	10	10	2	5	14	8	1	2	0	6	2	0	1	0	0	0	2	5	0	10	0
actress	16	.5292	1.7600	42.5	0	2	3	0	2	5	3	1	1	1	3	3	0	2	1	0	0	0	0	0	0	1	1	3	0
actresses	2	.0000	.0243	23.9	0	1	0	0	0	0	0	1	0	0	0	0	0	0	0	0	0	0	0	0	0	0	0	2	0
acts	168	.8449	28.395	54.5	16	19	23	23	33	25	29	0	24	16	1	4	1	16	2	49	7	0	0	2	4	13	16	13	0
Acts	6	.2062	.3286	35.2	0	0	0	0	0	5	1	0	0	0	0	0	0	5	0	0	0	0	0	0	0	0	1	0	0
actual	152	.8767	26.511	54.2	4	6	13	18	39	30	32	10	21	8	2	8	23	8	2	25	5	4	3	8	0	5	19	11	0
actuality	4	.3688	.3102	34.9	0	0	0	0	1	1	2	0	0	0	0	0	0	0	0	0	1	1	0	0	1	0	1	0	0
actually	462	.9383	85.725	59.3	22	30	40	66	138	65	74	27	77	25	10	21	19	31	8	83	11	4	10	6	17	39	56	45	0
actuation	2	.0000	.0243	23.9	0	0	0	0	2	0	0	0	0	0	0	0	0	0	0	0	0	0	0	0	0	0	0	2	0
acute	38	.6782	5.2490	47.2	0	1	2	1	8	17	9	0	2	1	0	1	17	3	0	1	0	0	1	1	1	1	8	1	0
ad	31	.5822	3.7873	45.8	3	0	7	4	11	4	1	1	7	2	0	0	3	0	9	0	0	0	0	0	5	0	2	3	0
Ad	4	.3771	.3293	35.2	0	2	0	1	0	0	0	1	0	0	0	0	0	0	0	0	0	0	0	0	1	2	0	1	0
AD	29	.1635	1.2847	41.1	1	0	7	7	4	7	3	0	0	0	0	0	28	0	0	0	0	0	0	1	0	0	0	0	0
ad-	6	.0000	.0487	26.9	0	0	0	0	2	4	0	0	0	0	0	0	0	0	6	0	0	0	0	0	0	0	0	0	0
ad-dress	2	.0000	.0219	23.4	0	2	0	0	0	0	0	0	0	2	0	0	0	0	0	0	0	0	0	0	0	0	0	0	0
Ada	3	.0000	.0352	25.5	0	0	0	0	3	0	0	0	0	0	0	0	0	0	0	0	0	0	0	0	3	0	0	0	0
adagio	2	.0000	.0162	22.1	0	0	0	0	0	1	1	0	0	0	0	0	0	0	0	0	2	0	0	0	0	0	0	0	0
Adair	6	.0000	.2741	34.4	0	0	6	0	0	0	0	0	6	0	0	0	0	0	0	0	0	0	0	0	0	0	0	0	0
Adam	50	.3861	4.2600	46.3	2	3	3	6	6	3	3	24	5	4	0	0	0	0	0	0	0	0	0	0	30	5	6	0	0
Adam's	9	.5170	1.0128	40.1	0	1	0	4	1	2	1	0	2	2	0	0	0	1	0	3	0	0	0	0	1	0	0	0	0
adamant	2	.2433	.1158	30.6	0	0	1	0	1	0	0	0	0	0	0	0	0	0	0	0	0	0	0	0	0	1	0	1	0
adamantly	2	.2442	.1134	30.5	0	0	0	0	0	0	2	0	0	1	0	0	0	0	0	0	0	0	0	0	0	0	0	1	0
Adams	89	.7332	13.326	51.2	6	13	7	11	18	25	9	0	20	7	0	3	6	15	0	0	0	0	0	0	10	12	2	14	0
Adams'	7	.5539	.8380	39.2	2	1	0	0	1	3	0	0	2	0	0	1	1	2	0	0	0	0	0	0	0	1	0	0	0
Adamson	2	.0000	.0914	29.6	0	0	0	2	0	0	0	0	2	0	0	0	0	0	0	0	0	0	0	0	0	0	0	0	0
adapt	25	.6139	3.1460	45.0	1	7	2	1	10	1	2	1	0	0	1	0	0	2	2	9	0	0	2	0	1	0	8	0	0
adaptability	3	.3827	.2446	33.9	0	0	0	1	1	0	0	1	0	0	0	0	0	0	1	0	0	0	0	0	0	0	1	1	0
adaptable	4	.3611	.3119	34.9	0	0	0	0	2	0	1	1	0	0	0	1	0	0	0	0	0	0	0	0	0	0	2	1	0
adaptation	27	.4432	2.6091	44.2	1	12	5	2	4	0	3	0	0	0	0	0	0	0	0	19	2	0	0	0	0	1	2	3	0
adaptations	29	.2399	1.7453	42.4	10	4	4	0	10	0	1	0	0	0	0	0	0	0	0	21	0	0	0	0	0	0	8	0	0
adapted	117	.6262	15.150	51.8	11	38	11	12	33	6	5	1	5	0	0	0	0	2	3	66	7	0	3	0	1	5	18	7	0
adapting	7	.3976	.5931	37.7	0	0	1	0	5	1	0	0	0	0	0	0	0	0	0	0	1	0	0	0	0	1	4	1	0
adaptive	2	.2437	.1129	30.5	0	0	0	0	2	0	0	0	0	0	0	0	0	0	0	0	0	0	0	0	0	0	1	1	0
adapts	3	.2254	.1785	32.5	0	2	0	0	0	0	1	0	0	0	0	0	0	1	0	2	0	0	0	0	0	0	0	0	0
ADB	2	.0000	.0299	24.8	0	0	1	1	0	0	0	0	0	0	0	0	2	0	0	0	0	0	0	0	0	0	0	0	0
ADC	5	.0000	.0748	28.7	0	1	2	1	0	1	0	0	0	0	0	0	5	0	0	0	0	0	0	0	0	0	0	0	0
add	1654	.7371	245.42	63.9	378	211	210	232	235	156	205	27	117	145	27	10	473	20	417	100	72	22	152	9	4	35	11	40	0
ADD	2	.0000	.0299	24.8	2	0	0	0	0	0	0	0	0	0	0	0	2	0	0	0	0	0	0	0	0	0	0	0	0
Addams	12	.1642	.8235	39.2	0	11	1	0	0	0	0	0	11	0	0	0	0	1	0	0	0	0	0	0	0	0	0	0	0
added	972	.8923	172.23	62.4	108	166	122	109	150	183	114	20	160	76	12	23	86	70	190	60	39	11	41	24	46	70	25	39	0
addend	65	.0000	.9730	39.9	12	11	11	13	9	4	2	3	0	0	0	0	65	0	0	0	0	0	0	0	0	0	0	0	0
addends	136	.0000	2.0357	43.1	32	26	27	20	19	3	3	6	0	0	0	0	136	0	0	0	0	0	0	0	0	0	0	0	0
adder	2	.0000	.0914	29.6	0	0	0	0	2	0	0	0	2	0	0	0	0	0	0	0	0	0	0	0	0	0	0	0	0
addict	6	.3583	.4874	36.9	0	0	0	0	4	0	2	0	0	0	0	1	0	0	0	4	0	0	0	0	1	0	0	0	0
addicted	9	.3523	.7202	38.6	0	0	0	0	7	0	1	1	0	0	0	1	0	0	0	6	0	0	0	0	0	0	2	0	0
addiction	3	.1927	.1491	31.7	0	0	0	0	2	0	1	0	0	0	0	0	0	0	0	1	0	0	0	0	0	0	0	2	0
addicts	2	.0000	.0243	23.9	0	0	0	0	1	0	0	1	0	0	0	0	0	0	0	0	0	0	0	0	0	0	0	2	0
Addie	2	.0000	.0914	29.6	0	0	0	0	2	0	0	0	2	0	0	0	0	0	0	0	0	0	0	0	0	0	0	0	0
adding	626	.6839	86.651	59.4	66	93	78	116	101	89	74	9	38	83	6	6	137	8	245	27	23	8	16	5	5	1	9	9	0
Addio	2	.0000	.0914	29.6	0	0	2	0	0	0	0	0	2	0	0	0	0	0	0	0	0	0	0	0	0	0	0	0	0
Addis	14	.1931	.7363	38.7	0	0	2	2	10	0	0	0	0	0	0	0	0	12	0	0	0	0	0	0	0	0	2	0	0
addition	695	.7398	103.86	60.2	34	81	76	86	167	122	112	17	31	25	3	2	367	63	14	49	23	2	22	7	5	19	32	31	0
Addition	16	.0970	.5184	37.1	0	4	7	0	2	1	2	0	0	0	0	0	15	0	0	0	0	0	0	0	1	0	0	0	0
additional	169	.8777	29.460	54.7	2	7	23	16	48	29	36	8	12	16	8	0	16	23	8	26	6	2	8	7	2	6	14	15	0
additions	27	.5286	2.9985	44.8	1	1	8	0	9	5	1	2	1	1	0	1	16	3	0	0	0	0	2	0	0	2	1	0	0
additive	32	.2321	1.8196	42.6	0	0	1	2	11	13	5	0	0	0	0	0	27	0	0	1	0	0	0	0	0	0	2	2	0
additives	11	.4803	1.1201	40.5	0	0	0	3	1	5	2	0	0	0	0	0	0	0	0	5	0	0	1	0	0	0	3	2	0
addled	3	.3873	.2485	34.0	0	0	1	0	2	0	0	0	0	0	0	1	0	0	0	0	0	0	0	0	1	0	1	0	0
addlegram	4	.0000	.0325	25.1	0	0	0	0	0	0	4	0	0	0	0	0	0	0	4	0	0	0	0	0	0	0	0	0	0
address	123	.5671	14.556	51.6	23	19	25	11	30	8	6	1	17	61	9	1	2	9	4	1	0	0	0	0	6	4	4	5	0

7Q Acraea
5A acre-and-a-half
XH acre-by-acre
7R acrid
7R acrimonious
7F acropolis
3G Across
4N across't
4N acrost
8G acrylic
XH Actaea
9B acted-upon
7D actin'
5B Acting
8Q actinomycosis
7Q actinopterygians
7F action-packed
9H action-reaction
7A Active
5A Acton
8C actor's
5R actors'
4Q actually-used
9P actuate
5A actuated
7R actuator
5P acumen
XQ acutely
7N acuteness
4B AD-dress
7N Ada's
7R adage
7J Adagissimo
9H adam's
7Q adamanteus
7R Adamowicz
7A Adams-supported
6A Adamsale
6A Adamsons
7R adapter
7R adapters
3H adaptions
5P adazzle
7R add-oil
7E Addam's
7H addicting
7R addictive
8G Adding
5A Addio's
9C Addison's
3E ADDITION
3E addition-subtraction
8E additive-inverse
8H Additives
9G addlegrams

Word Type	F	D	U	SFI	3 Gr 3	4 Gr 4	5 Gr 5	6 Gr 6	7 Gr 7	8 Gr 8	9 Gr 9	X UnGr	A Read	B Eng & Gr	C Comp	D Lit	E Math	F Soc Stud	G Spell	H Sci	J Music	K Art	L Home Ec	M Shop	N Lib F	P Lib NF	Q Lib Ref	R Mag	S Rel
Address	4	.4520	.4002	36.0	0	0	1	1	2	0	0	0	1	1	0	1	0	0	0	0	0	0	0	0	0	1	0	0	0
addressed	49	.6224	6.2898	48.0	5	4	2	5	8	6	19	0	7	6	5	14	0	4	1	0	0	0	0	0	4	5	1	2	0
addresses	22	.5244	2.4159	43.8	4	3	5	1	4	3	2	0	2	11	2	1	0	2	1	0	0	0	0	0	0	1	0	2	0
addressing	13	.5807	1.5766	42.0	0	0	0	2	4	5	2	0	2	3	0	2	0	0	0	0	0	0	0	0	3	2	0	1	0
adds	108	.8429	18.129	52.6	11	5	17	8	22	21	21	3	10	11	2	1	11	3	8	6	12	4	8	0	2	7	6	17	0
Adelaide	4	.0000	.0778	28.9	0	2	0	1	1	0	0	0	0	0	0	0	0	4	0	0	0	0	0	0	0	0	0	0	0
Adele	2	.0000	.0914	29.6	0	0	2	0	0	0	0	0	2	0	0	0	0	0	0	0	0	0	0	0	0	0	0	0	0
Adelina	2	.0000	.0914	29.6	0	0	0	2	0	0	0	0	2	0	0	0	0	0	0	0	0	0	0	0	0	0	0	0	0
Aden	10	.4172	.9238	39.7	1	0	3	4	2	0	0	0	1	0	0	0	0	4	0	0	0	0	0	0	2	0	3	0	0
adenine	2	.0000	.0394	26.0	0	0	0	0	0	0	2	0	0	0	0	0	0	0	0	2	0	0	0	0	0	0	0	0	0
adenosine	3	.2445	.1818	32.6	0	0	0	0	1	0	2	0	0	0	0	0	0	0	0	2	0	0	0	0	0	0	1	0	0
adept	4	.3450	.2950	34.7	0	0	0	0	3	0	1	0	0	0	0	0	0	0	0	0	0	0	1	0	0	0	2	1	0
adequacy	2	.0000	.0243	23.9	0	0	0	0	0	1	1	0	0	0	0	0	0	0	0	0	0	0	0	0	0	0	0	2	0
adequate	44	.5020	4.5757	46.6	1	0	3	1	11	15	9	4	1	1	0	0	0	4	0	4	3	0	13	1	0	1	11	5	0
adequately	11	.5657	1.2745	41.1	0	0	0	1	3	1	4	2	0	1	0	0	1	0	1	0	0	0	1	0	0	0	2	5	0
ADHE	3	.0000	.0449	26.5	0	0	3	0	0	0	0	0	0	0	0	0	3	0	0	0	0	0	0	0	0	0	0	0	0
adhere	7	.5573	.7926	39.0	1	0	0	0	4	0	2	0	0	0	0	0	0	0	0	0	0	1	1	1	1	2	1	0	0
adhered	6	.3948	.5040	37.0	0	0	0	1	1	2	2	0	0	0	0	2	0	1	0	0	0	1	0	0	0	0	2	0	0
adherents	4	.3224	.2764	34.4	0	0	0	0	1	1	2	0	0	0	1	1	0	0	0	0	0	0	0	0	0	0	2	0	0
adheres	2	.2421	.0995	30.0	0	0	0	0	0	0	2	0	0	0	0	0	0	0	0	0	0	0	1	1	0	0	0	0	0
adhering	3	.3099	.1981	33.0	0	0	0	0	2	0	1	0	0	0	0	0	0	0	0	0	1	0	0	1	1	0	0	0	0
adhesive	23	.5705	2.6970	44.3	0	11	1	2	4	2	2	1	1	0	0	2	0	0	0	3	0	2	1	1	0	1	12	0	0
adhesives	9	.1126	.2842	34.5	0	8	0	0	1	0	0	0	0	0	0	0	0	0	0	0	0	0	0	0	0	0	8	1	0
adieu	14	.3566	1.0674	40.3	0	3	1	2	0	0	8	0	0	0	0	8	0	0	2	0	4	0	0	0	0	0	0	0	0
Adirondack	10	.4332	.9221	39.6	0	0	1	0	7	1	0	1	0	0	0	0	0	1	0	1	0	0	0	1	0	0	1	6	0
Adirondacks	7	.5171	.7759	38.9	0	0	2	0	4	0	0	1	1	0	0	0	0	2	0	0	0	0	0	0	0	1	1	2	0
adj	12	.2060	.5722	37.6	0	1	2	3	3	2	1	0	0	4	0	0	0	0	8	0	0	0	0	0	0	0	0	0	0
Adj	9	.0000	.0985	29.9	0	0	2	0	0	0	7	0	0	9	0	0	0	0	0	0	0	0	0	0	0	0	0	0	0
ADJ	2	.0000	.0219	23.4	0	0	0	2	0	0	0	0	0	2	0	0	0	0	0	0	0	0	0	0	0	0	0	0	0
adjacent	42	.6962	5.9246	47.7	1	1	1	3	19	3	12	2	1	0	0	2	17	3	0	1	3	0	0	1	4	0	4	6	0
adjective	337	.4063	28.848	54.6	0	23	41	66	71	78	58	0	3	215	40	3	0	1	69	2	1	0	0	0	0	0	2	1	0
adjective-forming	4	.0000	.0325	25.1	0	0	0	0	0	4	0	0	0	0	0	0	0	0	4	0	0	0	0	0	0	0	0	0	0
adjectives	270	.4168	23.606	53.7	0	20	24	42	75	68	41	0	4	143	33	1	1	0	84	0	4	0	0	0	0	0	0	0	0
Adjectives	4	.1757	.1672	32.2	0	0	2	1	0	0	1	0	0	1	0	0	0	0	3	0	0	0	0	0	0	0	0	0	0
adjoining	21	.7289	3.1034	44.9	1	3	1	1	6	3	6	0	2	0	0	1	0	2	0	3	0	0	1	0	3	4	3	2	0
adjourn	8	.4855	.8103	39.1	1	1	1	0	2	3	0	0	0	1	0	0	1	0	3	0	0	0	0	0	0	2	0	1	0
adjourned	5	.5612	.5815	37.6	1	1	0	0	0	1	1	1	0	0	0	1	0	1	0	0	0	0	0	0	1	1	0	1	0
adjourns	2	.0000	.0290	24.6	2	0	0	0	0	0	0	0	0	0	0	0	0	0	0	0	0	0	0	0	0	2	0	0	0
adjust	74	.4502	6.9975	48.4	1	4	2	5	31	19	10	2	4	1	0	2	3	1	1	9	3	0	3	26	3	6	7	5	0
adjustable	17	.1637	.6536	38.2	0	0	0	1	10	2	3	1	0	0	0	0	0	0	0	1	0	0	0	9	0	0	0	7	0
adjusted	50	.4916	5.2062	47.2	3	2	3	7	12	10	12	1	10	0	3	3	0	1	0	3	1	0	5	16	2	2	0	4	0
adjuster	2	.0000	.0243	23.9	0	0	0	0	2	0	0	0	0	0	0	0	0	0	0	0	0	0	0	0	0	0	0	2	0
adjusting	25	.5481	2.8444	44.5	0	3	1	2	6	9	4	0	3	0	0	2	0	1	0	1	2	0	2	6	1	2	1	4	0
adjustment	32	.3701	2.4619	43.9	0	0	0	0	13	9	9	1	0	3	0	0	0	0	0	2	1	0	5	14	0	0	2	5	0
adjustments	24	.3895	1.9599	42.9	0	0	1	1	9	5	8	0	1	0	0	0	0	2	0	1	1	0	6	9	1	1	2	0	0
adjusts	9	.5155	.9793	39.9	1	1	1	0	4	0	2	0	1	0	0	0	0	1	0	0	0	0	0	1	0	1	2	3	0
Adlai	57	.1203	2.0635	43.1	0	52	0	0	4	0	1	0	0	0	0	1	0	0	0	0	0	0	0	0	0	53	0	3	0
Adm	3	.2321	.1635	32.1	0	0	0	0	1	0	2	0	0	0	0	0	0	0	0	0	0	0	0	0	0	0	1	2	0
admen	2	.0000	.0243	23.9	0	0	0	0	0	0	2	0	0	0	0	0	0	0	0	0	0	0	0	0	0	0	0	2	0
administer	8	.5829	.9753	39.9	0	0	0	1	3	0	3	1	1	2	0	0	0	2	0	0	1	0	0	0	0	1	0	1	0
administered	14	.4602	1.3561	41.3	0	0	1	2	7	3	1	0	0	0	3	1	0	4	0	0	0	0	0	0	1	1	2	2	0
administering	8	.5215	.8714	39.4	0	1	2	0	4	0	1	0	0	0	0	0	0	0	0	1	0	0	0	0	1	3	2	1	0
administers	5	.1285	.1797	32.5	0	1	1	0	2	1	0	0	0	0	0	0	0	1	0	0	0	0	0	0	0	0	4	0	0
administration	57	.4454	5.4618	47.4	3	2	12	3	9	9	12	7	3	0	0	0	0	11	0	0	0	0	0	0	0	5	19	19	0
Administration	51	.3722	4.2234	46.3	0	0	1	5	2	11	31	1	2	1	0	0	0	13	0	1	0	0	0	0	0	1	3	30	0
Administration's	4	.1828	.1857	32.7	0	0	0	0	0	0	4	0	0	0	0	0	1	0	0	0	0	0	0	0	0	0	0	3	0
administrations	5	.2580	.3252	35.1	0	0	0	0	3	0	2	0	1	0	0	0	0	0	0	0	0	0	0	0	0	1	0	3	0
administrative	28	.4396	2.6436	44.2	0	1	3	1	6	11	5	1	1	0	0	0	0	7	1	0	0	0	0	0	0	1	13	5	0
administrator	6	.4600	.5935	37.7	0	1	1	0	2	0	1	1	0	0	0	0	0	2	0	1	0	0	0	0	1	0	0	2	0
Administrator	2	.2278	.1128	30.5	0	0	0	0	1	0	0	1	0	0	0	0	0	0	0	1	0	0	0	0	0	0	1	0	0
administrators	7	.4435	.6659	38.2	0	0	1	0	2	1	2	1	0	0	0	0	0	2	0	0	0	0	0	0	0	1	1	3	0
admirable	9	.5753	1.0796	40.3	0	0	0	0	4	1	2	2	1	1	0	1	0	0	0	0	0	0	0	0	2	3	0	1	0
admirably	2	.1814	.1187	30.7	0	0	0	0	0	1	0	1	1	0	0	0	0	0	0	0	0	0	0	0	0	0	0	1	0
admiral	12	.4063	1.0722	40.3	0	1	0	3	0	2	4	2	1	6	0	0	0	3	0	0	0	0	0	0	0	0	1	1	0
Admiral	69	.5916	9.0223	49.6	0	18	32	4	7	5	3	0	47	0	0	2	0	3	0	0	0	0	0	0	4	9	2	2	0
Admiral's	2	.0000	.0914	29.6	0	2	0	0	0	0	0	0	2	0	0	0	0	0	0	0	0	0	0	0	0	0	0	0	0
admiration	41	.7325	6.1451	47.9	3	4	6	5	7	10	6	0	12	2	0	3	0	3	0	0	0	1	0	0	6	4	2	8	0
admire	54	.8392	9.0683	49.6	3	7	6	9	13	5	10	1	12	8	1	6	0	6	2	0	1	1	4	0	3	3	4	3	0
admired	49	.7914	7.8242	48.9	2	9	9	5	14	5	3	2	11	2	0	6	0	5	0	0	2	0	1	0	6	6	4	6	0
admirer	2	.2417	.1091	30.4	0	0	0	1	0	1	0	0	0	0	0	0	0	0	0	0	1	0	0	0	0	0	1	0	0
ADMIRER	8	.0000	.0859	29.3	0	0	0	0	0	8	0	0	0	0	0	8	0	0	0	0	0	0	0	0	0	0	0	0	0
admirers	7	.3296	.5114	37.1	1	1	1	0	3	0	0	1	0	0	0	0	0	0	0	0	0	0	0	0	2	1	0	4	0
ADMIRERS	11	.0000	.1180	30.7	0	0	0	0	0	11	0	0	0	0	0	11	0	0	0	0	0	0	0	0	0	0	0	0	0
admires	3	.3373	.2136	33.3	0	0	2	0	1	0	0	0	0	1	0	0	0	0	0	0	1	0	1	0	0	0	0	0	0
admiring	27	.6336	3.5896	45.6	3	4	0	6	6	3	5	0	9	1	0	5	0	0	0	0	0	0	1	0	5	5	0	1	0
admiringly	10	.4297	1.0081	40.0	0	3	2	2	1	2	0	0	5	0	0	3	0	0	0	0	0	0	0	0	1	1	0	0	0
admission	25	.7551	3.8283	45.8	1	4	5	3	3	7	2	0	4	2	0	1	3	5	0	0	0	0	0	0	2	4	2	2	0
admissions	3	.2266	.1614	32.1	0	0	0	1	1	0	0	1	0	0	0	0	0	0	0	0	0	0	0	0	1	0	0	2	0
admit	74	.5812	9.2762	49.7	10	7	10	9	20	5	10	3	31	3	1	4	1	5	0	2	0	0	0	0	6	6	3	11	1
admits	9	.3858	.7594	38.8	1	1	1	0	1	5	0	0	0	0	0	1	0	0	0	2	0	0	0	0	0	1	0	5	0
admittance	2	.2443	.1130	30.5	0	1	0	0	1	0	0	0	0	0	0	1	0	0	0	0	0	0	0	0	1	0	0	0	0
admitted	100	.7459	15.182	51.8	8	7	13	16	24	15	10	7	23	0	3	7	2	14	0	2	1	0	0	0	17	7	5	19	0
admittedly	3	.2266	.1614	32.1	0	0	0	0	2	0	1	0	0	0	0	0	0	0	0	0	0	0	0	0	1	0	0	2	0
admitting	5	.3684	.4146	36.2	0	1	0	0	1	3	0	0	0	0	0	0	0	3	0	0	0	0	0	0	0	1	1	0	0
admonished	2	.2152	.1357	31.3	0	0	0	1	0	1	0	0	1	0	0	0	0	1	0	0	0	0	0	0	0	0	0	0	0
ado	4	.3622	.3131	35.0	0	0	0	0	0	2	1	1	0	1	0	2	0	0	0	0	0	0	0	0	0	0	0	1	0
adobe	40	.5296	4.5804	46.6	9	10	2	10	1	3	5	0	8	0	0	5	0	20	1	0	0	0	0	0	0	2	4	0	0
adolescence	6	.2683	.3517	35.5	0	0	0	0	2	4	0	0	0	1	0	0	0	0	0	1	1	0	3	0	0	0	0	0	0
adolescent	5	.4496	.4696	36.7	0	0	1	0	2	1	1	0	0	1	1	1	0	0	0	0	0	0	0	0	0	1	0	1	0
adolescents	2	.0857	.0784	28.9	0	0	0	0	0	2	0	0	1	0	0	0	0	0	0	0	0	0	1	0	0	0	0	0	0
Adolf	11	.3546	.8975	39.5	0	0	1	1	6	2	1	0	1	0	0	0	0	3	0	0	0	0	0	0	0	6	0	1	0
Adolph	4	.4485	.4009	36.0	2	0	0	0	2	0	0	0	1	0	0	0	0	1	0	0	0	0	0	0	0	0	1	1	0
Adolphe	3	.3847	.2448	33.9	0	0	0	0	0	3	0	0	0	0	0	1	0	0	0	0	1	0	0	0	0	0	1	0	0
Adolphus	2	.2401	.1133	30.5	0	0	1	0	0	0	1	0	0	0	0	0	0	0	0	0	0	0	0	0	0	1	1	0	0
Adonais	2	.0000	.0290	24.6	0	0	0	0	2	0	0	0	0	0	0	0	0	0	0	0	0	0	0	0	0	2	0	0	0
Adonis	2	.2160	.1362	31.3	0	0	0	0	0	2	0	0	1	0	0	0	0	0	0	1	0	0	0	0	0	0	0	0	0
adopt	16	.6380	2.0924	43.2	0	1	2	2	5	2	4	0	0	1	0	2	0	6	2	1	0	0	0	0	0	3	1	0	0
adopted	100	.8210	16.444	52.2	5	5	13	14	27	19	12	5	12	7	0	6	1	22	2	6	3	2	0	2	1	10	22	4	0

7P addressee
5Q Aden's
6R Adenauer
XH adenocarcinoma
XH adeptly
8R adeptness
8A ADF
9Q adherence
7R adhesive-backed
3P ADI
9H adiabatic
5Q Adige
XR adipose
9D adjective-happy
5A Adjidaumo
8H adjoin
XR adjoins
3P adjourning
7R adjustable-voltage
7M adjusters
6E Adler
9R Administrations
4R admiral's
5P admirals
5P admixture
5P admixtures
9R admonish
7C admonition
4Q Adobe
4F adobes
7R Adolfo
8R Adolpho

Word Type	F	D	U	SFI	3 Gr 3	4 Gr 4	5 Gr 5	6 Gr 6	7 Gr 7	8 Gr 8	9 Gr 9	X UnGr	A Read	B Eng & Gr	C Comp	D Lit	E Math	F Soc Stud	G Spell	H Sci	J Music	K Art	L Home Ec	M Shop	N Lib F	P Lib NF	Q Lib Ref	R Mag	S Rel
adopting	5	.4732	.5365	37.3	0	1	0	2	1	0	1	0	2	0	0	0	0	1	0	0	0	0	0	0	0	1	1	0	0
adoption	8	.4550	.7876	39.0	0	0	2	0	3	1	2	0	1	0	0	2	0	1	0	0	0	0	0	0	0	1	3	0	0
adorable	2	.1814	.1187	30.7	0	0	1	1	0	0	0	0	1	0	0	0	0	0	0	0	0	0	0	0	0	0	0	1	0
adore	4	.0700	.1127	30.5	0	1	1	0	2	0	0	0	1	0	0	0	0	0	0	0	2	0	0	0	0	0	0	0	1
adored	5	.3607	.3899	35.9	0	0	0	2	0	2	1	0	0	0	0	1	0	1	0	0	0	1	0	0	2	0	0	0	0
adoring	2	.1812	.0838	29.2	0	0	0	0	0	2	0	0	0	0	0	0	0	0	0	0	0	0	1	0	0	0	0	1	0
adorn	6	.3476	.5208	37.2	0	0	0	0	1	1	4	0	3	0	0	0	0	0	0	0	0	0	0	0	0	0	2	1	0
adorned	12	.6200	1.5346	41.9	1	0	0	4	2	3	1	1	1	0	0	0	0	4	1	0	1	1	0	0	0	1	1	2	0
adorning	2	.2437	.1129	30.5	0	0	0	0	1	0	0	1	0	0	0	0	0	0	0	0	0	0	0	0	0	0	1	1	0
adornment	2	.2152	.1357	31.3	0	0	0	0	1	0	1	0	1	0	0	0	0	1	0	0	0	0	0	0	0	0	0	0	0
adown	2	.1717	.1142	30.6	0	0	0	0	2	0	0	0	1	0	0	1	0	0	0	0	0	0	0	0	0	0	0	0	0
ADP	7	.0000	.1380	31.4	0	0	0	0	0	0	7	0	0	0	0	0	0	0	0	7	0	0	0	0	0	0	0	0	0
adrenal	2	.2278	.1128	30.5	0	0	0	0	1	0	1	0	0	0	0	0	0	0	0	1	0	0	0	0	0	0	1	0	0
adrenalin	4	.1611	.1738	32.4	0	0	0	1	1	1	0	1	0	0	0	0	0	0	0	1	0	0	0	0	0	0	0	3	0
adrenaline	4	.2287	.2348	33.7	0	0	0	0	3	1	0	0	0	0	0	0	0	0	0	3	0	0	0	0	0	0	0	1	0
adrenals	3	.0000	.0591	27.7	0	0	0	0	3	0	0	0	0	0	0	0	0	0	0	3	0	0	0	0	0	0	0	0	0
Adrian	4	.2437	.2257	33.5	0	0	0	0	2	0	2	0	0	0	0	0	0	0	0	0	0	0	0	0	0	0	2	2	0
Adriatic	9	.6110	1.1266	40.5	1	0	1	2	2	0	3	0	0	0	0	0	0	2	0	0	1	0	0	0	1	1	2	2	0
adrift	5	.3233	.3595	35.6	3	0	0	0	1	0	1	0	0	0	0	0	0	0	0	0	0	0	0	0	3	1	0	1	0
adroit	2	.2152	.1357	31.3	0	0	0	0	0	1	1	0	1	0	0	0	0	1	0	0	0	0	0	0	0	0	0	0	0
ads	17	.5813	2.1416	43.3	1	3	0	4	6	2	1	0	8	3	0	0	0	1	0	0	0	0	1	0	0	3	0	1	0
adult	152	.7568	23.183	53.7	6	14	19	15	63	14	16	5	8	3	1	5	15	2	1	46	1	1	7	0	0	6	35	21	0
adulterated	2	.2346	.1166	30.7	0	0	0	0	0	1	1	0	0	0	0	0	0	0	0	1	0	0	0	0	0	0	0	1	0
adultery	5	.3687	.4014	36.0	0	0	4	0	1	0	0	0	0	0	0	0	0	0	0	0	0	0	0	0	0	2	2	1	0
adulthood	8	.3498	.6036	37.8	0	0	0	2	1	4	1	0	0	1	0	0	0	0	0	2	0	0	3	0	0	0	1	1	0
adults	111	.7389	16.573	52.2	6	7	20	12	30	16	17	3	8	9	0	4	12	12	1	16	1	0	10	0	0	6	9	23	0
adults'	2	.1972	.1262	31.0	0	0	1	0	1	0	0	0	1	0	0	0	1	0	0	0	0	0	0	0	0	0	0	0	0
adv	8	.2179	.4000	36.0	0	0	2	2	1	2	1	0	0	3	0	0	0	0	5	0	0	0	0	0	0	0	0	0	0
Adv	2	.0000	.0219	23.4	0	0	0	0	0	0	2	0	0	2	0	0	0	0	0	0	0	0	0	0	0	0	0	0	0
Adv-f	5	.0000	.0547	27.4	0	0	0	0	0	0	5	0	0	5	0	0	0	0	0	0	0	0	0	0	0	0	0	0	0
Adv-m	6	.0000	.0657	28.2	0	0	0	0	0	0	6	0	0	6	0	0	0	0	0	0	0	0	0	0	0	0	0	0	0
Adv-p	5	.0000	.0547	27.4	0	0	0	0	0	0	5	0	0	5	0	0	0	0	0	0	0	0	0	0	0	0	0	0	0
Adv-t	4	.0000	.0438	26.4	0	0	0	0	0	0	4	0	0	4	0	0	0	0	0	0	0	0	0	0	0	0	0	0	0
advance	114	.8647	19.615	52.9	4	1	5	12	56	21	10	5	11	7	2	3	1	14	2	9	1	1	5	2	4	7	16	29	0
advanced	116	.8905	20.506	53.1	4	7	13	10	33	22	25	2	10	2	2	10	2	19	0	14	5	1	1	2	9	10	21	8	0
Advanced	2	.2346	.1166	30.7	0	0	0	1	0	1	0	0	0	0	0	0	0	0	0	1	0	0	0	0	0	0	0	1	0
advancement	8	.4536	.7753	38.9	0	1	0	0	1	4	1	1	1	0	0	0	1	0	1	0	0	0	1	0	0	0	4	0	0
Advancement	3	.3766	.2497	34.0	0	0	1	0	0	1	1	0	0	0	0	0	0	1	0	0	0	0	0	0	0	1	1	0	0
advancements	4	.0000	.0789	29.0	0	0	1	0	0	3	0	0	0	0	0	0	0	0	0	4	0	0	0	0	0	0	0	0	0
advances	47	.8348	7.8355	48.9	1	0	8	4	10	14	8	2	3	0	1	3	0	9	1	11	4	0	1	1	1	2	8	2	0
advancing	30	.7434	4.5222	46.6	2	2	2	1	6	8	8	1	4	0	0	3	1	5	0	3	0	0	2	0	3	5	3	1	0
advantage	116	.8657	19.985	53.0	3	4	10	15	36	25	16	7	12	7	0	5	1	14	4	15	2	2	8	2	4	13	18	9	0
advantageous	9	.5591	1.0400	40.2	1	0	0	0	3	2	2	1	0	0	0	0	0	1	1	2	0	0	1	0	0	1	3	0	0
advantages	70	.8775	12.204	50.9	2	8	7	5	15	20	11	2	6	6	2	4	1	17	0	5	4	1	4	2	2	2	9	5	0
advection	3	.0000	.0591	27.7	0	0	0	0	0	0	3	0	0	0	0	0	0	0	0	3	0	0	0	0	0	0	0	0	0
advent	11	.5748	1.2947	41.1	1	0	1	1	2	3	3	0	0	0	0	1	0	0	0	0	1	0	0	0	2	1	4	2	0
adventure	152	.8372	25.589	54.1	25	27	19	31	28	16	5	1	55	13	2	15	0	8	2	3	5	8	4	1	11	14	4	7	0
Adventure	4	.4519	.3985	36.0	0	0	0	0	3	0	1	0	1	0	0	1	0	0	0	0	0	0	0	0	0	0	1	1	0
adventure's	2	.0000	.0914	29.6	0	0	0	2	0	0	0	0	2	0	0	0	0	0	0	0	0	0	0	0	0	0	0	0	0
adventurer	17	.6214	2.2053	43.4	1	0	3	2	6	2	1	2	4	1	0	0	0	1	0	1	1	0	0	0	1	0	5	3	0
adventurers	19	.6429	2.5343	44.0	2	0	5	2	5	2	2	1	3	1	0	1	0	6	0	1	0	0	0	0	2	1	4	0	0
adventures	122	.8249	20.289	53.1	14	26	14	21	28	15	2	2	43	21	1	11	0	10	1	3	5	2	0	0	10	7	2	6	0
Adventures	5	.4308	.4753	36.8	0	0	2	1	2	0	0	0	1	1	0	0	0	0	0	0	0	0	0	0	0	0	1	2	0
adventuresome	3	.3768	.2437	33.9	0	0	1	1	1	0	0	0	0	0	0	0	0	0	0	0	1	0	0	0	0	1	0	1	0
Adventuress	4	.0000	.0486	26.9	0	0	4	0	0	0	0	0	0	0	0	0	0	0	0	0	0	0	0	0	0	0	0	4	0
adventuring	5	.3926	.4468	36.5	2	2	0	0	1	0	0	0	1	0	0	0	0	1	0	0	0	0	0	0	0	1	2	0	0
adventurous	23	.6639	3.1725	45.0	3	4	2	6	5	1	1	1	7	1	0	2	0	0	0	0	0	0	0	0	3	3	3	4	0
adverb	167	.3286	11.760	50.7	0	13	12	29	51	31	31	0	0	108	35	0	0	0	24	0	0	0	0	0	0	0	0	0	0
adverbial	37	.3213	2.5366	44.0	0	2	3	11	0	14	7	0	0	19	10	0	0	0	8	0	0	0	0	0	0	0	0	0	0
adverbials	19	.0000	.2079	33.2	0	3	2	1	1	6	6	0	0	19	0	0	0	0	0	0	0	0	0	0	0	0	0	0	0
adverbs	132	.3629	10.229	50.1	0	13	12	11	55	25	16	0	1	92	15	0	0	0	24	0	0	0	0	0	0	0	0	0	0
adversaries	2	.0000	.0243	23.9	0	0	1	0	0	0	1	0	0	0	0	0	0	0	0	0	0	0	0	0	0	0	0	2	0
adversary	6	.4316	.5935	37.7	0	0	0	1	2	1	1	1	2	0	0	0	0	1	0	0	0	0	0	0	2	1	0	0	0
adverse	8	.6094	1.0006	40.0	0	1	0	0	4	2	1	0	0	0	0	1	0	2	0	0	0	0	0	0	1	1	2	1	0
adversity	2	.2437	.1129	30.5	0	0	0	1	1	0	0	0	0	0	0	0	0	0	0	0	0	0	0	0	0	0	1	1	0
advertise	21	.7621	3.2215	45.1	5	2	5	1	3	4	1	0	1	1	1	0	0	7	1	2	0	1	1	0	2	2	2	0	0
advertised	20	.7267	2.9680	44.7	2	0	2	2	5	2	6	1	5	4	1	1	1	2	1	0	0	0	0	0	1	1	0	3	0
advertisement	28	.5455	3.2062	45.1	2	6	3	1	2	10	4	0	5	7	0	2	1	1	4	0	1	4	0	0	0	2	0	1	0
advertisements	33	.5368	3.6442	45.6	2	2	3	4	3	14	4	1	2	7	0	0	1	3	2	0	1	8	3	1	1	1	2	1	0
advertiser	2	.0000	.0219	23.4	0	0	0	0	0	0	2	0	0	2	0	0	0	0	0	0	0	0	0	0	0	0	0	0	0
advertisers	2	.2351	.1166	30.7	0	0	1	0	0	0	0	1	0	0	0	0	0	1	0	0	0	0	0	0	0	0	0	1	0
advertises	3	.3675	.2410	33.8	0	0	0	1	1	1	0	0	0	1	0	0	0	1	1	0	0	0	0	0	0	0	0	0	0
advertising	45	.8555	7.6638	48.8	4	1	3	3	6	11	15	2	3	6	1	3	4	4	0	5	0	1	1	0	3	2	3	9	0
advice	137	.8880	24.232	53.8	10	20	12	20	36	24	15	0	36	13	4	11	5	12	2	6	1	0	4	1	12	14	3	13	0
advisable	12	.3092	.7725	38.9	0	0	0	0	5	3	4	0	0	1	0	0	1	0	0	0	0	0	3	6	0	0	0	1	0
advise	29	.8134	4.7206	46.7	2	3	5	4	5	7	3	0	3	3	0	3	0	3	1	2	1	0	2	0	3	2	2	4	0
advised	39	.7324	5.8281	47.7	1	7	2	5	7	7	9	1	9	4	0	5	0	3	0	2	0	0	1	0	0	6	2	7	0
adviser	12	.6365	1.5528	41.9	0	1	4	0	2	1	4	0	0	1	0	0	0	2	1	0	0	0	1	0	1	0	2	4	0
advisers	8	.4207	.7558	38.8	1	0	4	0	1	2	0	0	1	0	0	0	0	4	0	0	0	0	0	0	0	2	1	0	0
advises	9	.5091	.9665	39.9	1	1	3	0	1	1	2	0	0	0	0	0	0	5	0	0	0	0	1	0	1	0	1	1	0
advising	2	.2351	.1166	30.7	0	0	0	0	1	0	0	1	0	0	0	0	0	1	0	0	0	0	0	0	0	0	0	1	0
advisor	7	.3879	.6330	38.0	0	0	0	0	6	0	1	0	2	0	0	0	1	0	0	1	0	0	0	0	0	0	0	3	0
Advisor	3	.2279	.2143	33.3	0	0	0	1	2	0	0	0	2	0	0	0	0	0	0	0	0	0	0	0	0	0	0	1	0
advisors	2	.1814	.1187	30.7	0	0	1	0	1	0	0	0	1	0	0	0	0	0	0	0	0	0	0	0	0	0	0	1	0
advisory	6	.3843	.5041	37.0	0	0	1	1	2	0	2	0	0	0	0	0	0	1	0	1	0	0	0	0	0	0	3	1	0
Advisory	4	.2360	.2112	33.2	0	0	1	0	2	0	1	0	0	0	1	0	0	0	0	0	0	0	0	0	0	0	3	0	0
advocate	10	.5462	1.1411	40.6	0	0	1	1	1	5	1	1	1	0	0	0	0	1	1	0	1	0	0	0	0	0	3	3	0
advocated	9	.4168	.8090	39.1	0	0	1	0	1	4	2	1	0	0	0	1	0	3	0	0	0	0	0	0	0	0	4	1	0
advocates	7	.3579	.5531	37.4	0	0	1	0	1	3	1	1	0	0	0	0	0	2	0	0	0	0	0	0	0	0	3	2	0
advocating	2	.0000	.0243	23.9	0	0	0	0	1	0	1	0	0	0	0	0	0	0	0	0	0	0	0	0	0	0	0	2	0
ae	4	.0000	.1827	32.6	0	4	0	0	0	0	0	0	4	0	0	0	0	0	0	0	0	0	0	0	0	0	0	0	0
AE	12	.3265	.8778	39.4	0	0	4	1	0	2	5	0	0	0	0	0	10	0	1	0	0	0	0	1	0	0	0	0	0
Aea	2	.0000	.0914	29.6	0	0	0	2	0	0	0	0	2	0	0	0	0	0	0	0	0	0	0	0	0	0	0	0	0
AEC	9	.1342	.3305	35.2	0	0	0	0	0	8	1	0	0	0	0	0	0	0	0	0	0	0	0	0	0	0	1	8	0
Aeetes	3	.0000	.1370	31.4	0	0	0	1	0	2	0	0	3	0	0	0	0	0	0	0	0	0	0	0	0	0	0	0	0
Aegean	21	.3577	1.7220	42.4	0	1	0	2	13	2	3	0	2	0	0	0	0	13	0	0	0	3	0	0	0	0	2	1	0
Aegisthus	3	.0000	.0434	26.4	0	0	0	0	3	0	0	0	0	0	0	0	0	0	0	0	0	0	0	0	0	3	0	0	0

7Q adopts
7P adoration
6R adorns
6B adress
5P Adriaan
8Q Adriaen
7R Adriana
5P Adrianople
7R Ads
8F adulation
9R adulatory
5H adult's
8D Advance
6A advancin'
7Q advantageously
7N Advantages
9P Adventist
4P adventure-loving
8A adventured
8F Adventurers
7N ADVENTURES
5R Adventuress's
XP Adventuring
6A Adventurous
7A adversary's
7P adversely
6P Advertiser
7B Advice
9G advisability
8B advise/eyes
9R Adviser
8F Advisers
3P Advocate
8D adze
7R AEC'S
7R Aedan's
4E AEF
9Q Aegina
9Q Aegir
8A Aelder

Word Type	F	D	U	SFI	3 Gr 3	4 Gr 4	5 Gr 5	6 Gr 6	7 Gr 7	8 Gr 8	9 Gr 9	X UnGr	A Read	B Eng & Gr	C Comp	D Lit	E Math	F Soc Stud	G Spell	H Sci	J Music	K Art	L Home Ec	M Shop	N Lib F	P Lib NF	Q Lib Ref	R Mag	S Rel
Aelfric	2	.0000	.0209	23.2	0	0	0	0	2	0	0	0	0	0	0	0	0	0	0	0	0	0	0	0	0	0	2	0	0
Aeneas	4	.0000	.0579	27.6	0	0	0	4	0	0	0	0	0	0	0	0	0	0	0	0	0	0	0	0	0	4	0	0	0
Aeolian	4	.0000	.0323	25.1	0	0	0	2	1	1	0	0	0	0	0	0	0	0	0	0	4	0	0	0	0	0	0	0	0
aerated	2	.0000	.0243	23.9	0	0	0	0	1	0	0	1	0	0	0	0	0	0	0	0	0	0	0	0	0	0	0	2	0
aeration	3	.2239	.1775	32.5	0	0	0	0	1	2	0	0	0	0	0	0	0	2	0	1	0	0	0	0	0	0	0	0	0
aerial	17	.5350	1.9272	42.8	0	0	2	4	5	2	2	2	2	1	0	1	0	2	0	5	0	2	0	0	0	0	1	3	0
aerials	4	.1335	.1958	32.9	1	0	0	3	0	0	0	0	1	0	0	0	0	0	0	3	0	0	0	0	0	0	0	0	0
Aernam	3	.0000	.0352	25.5	0	3	0	0	0	0	0	0	0	0	0	0	0	0	0	0	0	0	0	0	3	0	0	0	0
Aerodrome	2	.0000	.0914	29.6	0	2	0	0	0	0	0	0	2	0	0	0	0	0	0	0	0	0	0	0	0	0	0	0	0
aerodynamics	2	.2278	.1128	30.5	0	0	1	0	0	1	0	0	0	0	0	0	0	0	0	1	0	0	0	0	0	0	1	0	0
aeronautical	3	.1813	.1402	31.5	0	0	0	0	0	1	2	0	0	0	0	0	0	0	0	1	0	0	0	0	0	0	2	0	0
aeronautics	6	.4080	.5423	37.3	0	0	1	2	0	1	2	0	1	2	0	0	1	0	0	0	0	0	0	0	0	0	2	0	0
Aeronautics	7	.5474	.7997	39.0	0	0	1	2	1	0	3	0	0	0	0	0	1	2	0	0	0	0	0	0	0	1	1	2	0
aeroplane	3	.0000	.1370	31.4	0	0	0	3	0	0	0	0	3	0	0	0	0	0	0	0	0	0	0	0	0	0	0	0	0
aerospace	10	.3097	.7025	38.5	6	1	0	2	1	0	0	0	0	0	0	0	0	0	0	0	0	0	0	0	0	7	1	2	0
Aerospace	4	.2424	.3036	34.8	0	3	0	1	0	0	0	0	3	0	0	0	0	0	0	0	0	0	0	0	0	0	0	1	0
Aesir	2	.0000	.0209	23.2	0	0	0	0	0	0	2	0	0	0	0	0	0	0	0	0	0	0	0	0	0	0	2	0	0
Aeson	13	.2029	.9639	39.8	0	0	0	12	1	0	0	0	12	0	0	1	0	0	0	0	0	0	0	0	0	0	0	0	0
Aesop	4	.3553	.3095	34.9	0	1	0	0	1	1	0	1	0	1	0	2	0	0	0	0	0	0	0	0	0	1	0	0	0
Aesop's	2	.1717	.1142	30.6	0	0	0	0	1	1	0	0	1	0	0	1	0	0	0	0	0	0	0	0	0	0	0	0	0
aesthetic	5	.4379	.4539	36.6	0	0	0	0	0	0	3	2	0	0	0	0	0	0	0	0	2	0	1	0	0	0	1	1	0
aesthetically	2	.2375	.1088	30.4	0	0	0	0	0	0	2	0	0	0	0	0	0	0	0	0	1	0	0	0	0	0	0	1	0
Aetes	2	.0000	.0914	29.6	0	0	0	2	0	0	0	0	2	0	0	0	0	0	0	0	0	0	0	0	0	0	0	0	0
af	2	.2139	.1057	30.2	0	0	1	0	1	0	0	0	0	0	0	0	0	1	1	0	0	0	0	0	0	0	0	0	0
AF	7	.2267	.4102	36.1	0	0	1	0	0	6	0	0	0	0	0	0	2	5	0	0	0	0	0	0	0	0	0	0	0
afar	14	.4740	1.4921	41.7	4	2	1	3	4	0	0	0	6	0	0	0	0	0	0	0	4	0	0	0	1	2	1	0	0
Afars	2	.0000	.0389	25.9	0	0	0	2	0	0	0	0	0	0	0	0	0	2	0	0	0	0	0	0	0	0	0	0	0
afeared	4	.2417	.3028	34.8	0	0	1	1	0	2	0	0	3	0	0	0	0	0	0	0	0	0	0	0	1	0	0	0	0
affably	2	.1717	.1142	30.6	0	0	0	0	1	1	0	0	1	0	0	1	0	0	0	0	0	0	0	0	0	0	0	0	0
affair	49	.7060	7.1049	48.5	5	4	0	5	12	16	4	3	13	0	0	2	0	2	1	1	1	0	3	0	3	13	1	9	0
affairs	102	.7509	15.457	51.9	5	4	16	10	23	23	20	1	5	5	0	2	0	35	1	2	1	1	3	0	1	16	19	11	0
Affairs	9	.2838	.5994	37.8	0	0	2	2	1	2	2	0	1	0	0	0	0	0	0	0	0	0	0	0	0	0	4	4	0
affect	173	.8637	29.758	54.7	11	18	28	18	29	26	31	12	11	9	2	6	16	20	4	60	4	2	10	1	1	3	14	10	0
AFFECT	2	.0000	.0394	26.0	2	0	0	0	0	0	0	0	0	0	0	0	0	0	0	2	0	0	0	0	0	0	0	0	0
affected	105	.8371	17.536	52.4	2	0	17	9	31	19	23	4	4	12	2	0	2	15	2	30	4	0	3	4	2	6	15	4	0
affecting	20	.7156	2.9122	44.6	0	2	2	1	8	3	4	0	2	3	0	1	2	1	0	6	0	0	1	0	0	0	2	2	0
affection	31	.8061	5.0077	47.0	4	0	4	5	3	7	7	1	4	1	1	4	0	3	0	0	2	0	1	0	2	4	4	5	0
affectionate	18	.6463	2.4314	43.9	2	2	1	1	5	3	2	2	6	0	1	2	0	0	0	0	0	0	0	0	1	3	2	3	0
affectionately	11	.6364	1.4539	41.6	1	0	0	3	2	1	3	1	2	0	0	2	0	1	0	1	0	0	0	0	2	2	1	0	0
affections	7	.4677	.7044	38.5	0	0	0	1	1	1	3	1	1	0	0	3	0	0	0	0	0	0	0	0	1	1	1	0	0
affects	57	.7303	8.4137	49.2	2	4	15	3	11	12	9	1	2	7	0	2	0	4	2	21	6	0	4	0	0	2	5	2	0
affiliated	6	.2966	.3953	36.0	1	0	2	0	1	1	1	0	0	0	0	1	0	0	0	0	0	0	0	0	0	0	4	1	0
affiliates	3	.2159	.1532	31.9	0	0	2	1	0	0	0	0	0	0	0	0	0	0	0	0	0	0	0	0	0	0	2	1	0
affiliation	2	.0000	.0209	23.2	0	0	0	0	0	2	0	0	0	0	0	0	0	0	0	0	0	0	0	0	0	0	2	0	0
affinity	4	.2437	.2257	33.5	0	0	1	1	1	0	1	0	0	0	0	0	0	0	0	0	0	0	0	0	0	0	2	2	0
affirmative	2	.1733	.1149	30.6	0	0	0	1	1	0	0	0	1	1	0	0	0	0	0	0	0	0	0	0	0	0	0	0	0
affirmatively	2	.1814	.1187	30.7	0	0	0	0	0	0	2	0	1	0	0	0	0	0	0	0	0	0	0	0	0	0	0	1	0
affirmed	5	.5386	.5712	37.6	0	0	0	0	0	3	2	0	1	1	0	0	0	0	0	0	0	0	0	0	1	0	1	1	0
affix	5	.2442	.2770	34.4	0	0	0	0	1	4	0	0	0	3	0	0	0	0	2	0	0	0	0	0	0	0	0	0	0
affixes	6	.0000	.0657	28.2	0	0	0	0	0	4	2	0	0	6	0	0	0	0	0	0	0	0	0	0	0	0	0	0	0
afflict	2	.2441	.1127	30.5	0	0	0	1	0	0	1	0	0	0	0	0	0	0	0	0	0	0	0	0	1	0	1	0	0
afflicted	17	.5139	1.8454	42.7	0	0	1	1	2	0	12	1	1	0	0	1	0	1	0	0	0	0	0	0	1	9	1	3	0
afflicting	2	.2437	.1129	30.5	0	0	0	0	1	0	1	0	0	0	0	0	0	0	0	0	0	0	0	0	0	0	1	1	0
affliction	10	.5563	1.1506	40.6	1	0	1	4	0	1	2	1	0	1	0	1	0	0	0	1	0	0	0	0	4	2	0	1	0
afflicts	3	.2159	.1532	31.9	0	0	0	1	1	0	1	0	0	0	0	0	0	0	0	0	0	0	0	0	0	0	2	1	0
affluence	3	.1937	.1495	31.7	0	0	0	0	1	2	0	0	0	0	0	0	0	1	0	0	0	0	0	0	0	0	0	2	0
affluent	3	.1277	.1363	31.3	0	0	0	0	1	2	0	0	1	0	0	0	0	0	0	0	0	0	0	0	0	0	0	2	0
afford	96	.7957	15.418	51.9	10	14	7	17	17	16	11	4	22	2	0	14	0	19	1	2	2	0	4	0	8	9	5	8	0
afforded	8	.5403	.9125	39.6	0	0	0	3	3	1	1	0	1	0	0	0	0	1	0	0	0	0	0	0	3	1	1	1	0
affords	4	.4242	.3545	35.5	0	0	0	0	1	1	1	1	0	0	0	1	0	0	0	0	0	0	1	0	0	0	1	1	0
affrighted	2	.1787	.1174	30.7	0	1	0	1	0	0	0	0	1	0	0	0	0	0	0	0	0	0	0	0	1	0	0	0	0
affronted	3	.2175	.1545	31.9	0	0	0	0	0	2	0	1	0	0	0	2	0	0	0	0	0	0	0	0	0	0	0	1	0
Afghan	2	.2446	.1123	30.5	0	0	0	0	0	2	0	0	0	1	0	0	0	0	0	0	0	0	0	0	0	0	1	0	0
Afghanistan	3	.1639	.1674	32.2	1	0	0	1	0	0	1	0	1	0	0	0	0	2	0	0	0	0	0	0	0	0	0	0	0
aficionados	2	.2437	.1129	30.5	0	0	0	0	1	0	1	0	0	0	0	0	0	0	0	0	0	0	0	0	0	0	1	1	0
afield	6	.4382	.5577	37.5	0	0	1	0	1	0	1	3	0	0	0	0	0	0	0	0	0	0	0	0	1	1	1	3	0
afikomen	4	.0000	.1827	32.6	0	4	0	0	0	0	0	0	4	0	0	0	0	0	0	0	0	0	0	0	0	0	0	0	0
afire	13	.5692	1.5709	42.0	0	1	1	2	5	1	1	2	3	0	0	3	0	0	0	2	0	0	0	0	1	1	0	3	0
AFL	2	.0000	.0243	23.9	0	0	0	1	1	0	0	0	0	0	0	0	0	0	0	0	0	0	0	0	0	0	0	2	0
AFL-CIO's	2	.0000	.0243	23.9	0	0	0	0	0	0	2	0	0	0	0	0	0	0	0	0	0	0	0	0	0	0	0	2	0
AFL-CIO	2	.0000	.0243	23.9	0	0	0	0	0	0	2	0	0	0	0	0	0	0	0	0	0	0	0	0	0	0	0	2	0
aflame	3	.3408	.2477	33.9	0	0	1	0	1	1	0	0	1	0	0	1	0	0	0	0	0	0	0	0	0	1	0	0	0
afloat	19	.6890	2.6798	44.3	2	0	5	4	6	2	0	0	3	0	0	1	0	1	0	1	1	0	1	0	3	6	0	2	0
afoot	14	.6326	1.8554	42.7	2	0	2	4	3	0	2	1	4	0	1	2	0	1	0	1	0	0	0	0	1	3	0	1	0
afore	7	.4077	.6471	38.1	0	0	1	0	1	2	3	0	2	0	0	3	0	0	0	0	0	0	0	0	1	0	1	0	0
aforementioned	3	.2227	.1589	32.0	0	0	0	0	2	0	0	1	0	0	0	0	0	0	0	0	0	0	0	0	2	0	0	1	0
afoul	2	.2285	.1129	30.5	0	0	0	0	1	1	0	0	0	0	0	0	0	1	0	0	0	0	0	0	0	0	1	0	0
afraid	607	.8130	100.45	60.0	171	149	72	72	80	36	24	3	326	13	2	42	0	30	6	17	4	0	5	0	67	64	5	25	1
Afraid	6	.2941	.4210	36.2	0	1	1	3	0	0	1	0	1	0	0	0	0	0	0	0	0	0	0	0	3	0	0	2	0
afresh	2	.2446	.1142	30.6	0	0	0	1	0	0	0	1	0	0	0	0	0	0	0	0	0	0	0	0	1	0	0	1	0
Afric	4	.3713	.3634	35.6	0	0	0	0	0	4	0	0	2	0	0	1	0	0	0	0	0	0	0	0	1	0	0	0	0
Africa	619	.6601	84.198	59.3	37	73	74	141	179	39	74	2	44	12	1	5	6	336	5	17	15	1	0	0	16	62	76	23	0
Africa's	29	.4374	2.7716	44.4	0	0	7	5	14	0	3	0	0	0	0	0	1	18	0	0	0	0	0	0	0	6	3	1	0
African	228	.7236	33.444	55.2	13	9	44	34	83	20	24	1	16	4	2	4	0	67	0	10	14	5	0	0	2	31	61	12	0
Africans	49	.5418	5.6154	47.5	0	1	12	11	19	3	3	0	2	0	0	2	0	29	0	0	3	0	0	0	0	7	4	2	0
Afrikaans	2	.0000	.0209	23.2	0	0	0	0	0	0	2	0	0	0	0	0	0	0	0	0	0	0	0	0	0	0	2	0	0
Afrikaner	3	.2063	.1600	32.0	0	0	2	0	1	0	0	0	0	0	0	0	0	1	0	0	0	0	0	0	0	2	0	0	0
Afrikaners	2	.0000	.0290	24.6	0	0	2	0	0	0	0	0	0	0	0	0	0	0	0	0	0	0	0	0	0	2	0	0	0
Afro	2	.2351	.1166	30.7	0	0	1	0	0	0	0	1	0	0	0	0	0	1	0	0	0	0	0	0	0	0	0	1	0
Afro-American	4	.0000	.0486	26.9	0	0	0	0	3	1	0	0	0	0	0	0	0	0	0	0	0	0	0	0	0	0	0	4	0
AFROTC	3	.0000	.0434	26.4	3	0	0	0	0	0	0	0	0	0	0	0	0	0	0	0	0	0	0	0	0	3	0	0	0
aft	17	.6395	2.2588	43.5	3	0	2	1	6	4	1	0	4	1	0	1	0	0	0	0	1	0	0	0	4	3	0	3	0
after	5915	.9814	1143.1	70.6	991	954	776	776	1092	661	545	120	1615	459	64	304	166	621	343	401	170	26	96	63	410	520	292	362	3
After	2	.1814	.1187	30.7	0	0	0	0	1	0	0	1	1	0	0	0	0	0	0	0	0	0	0	0	0	0	0	1	0
After-Shaving	4	.0000	.1827	32.6	0	0	0	4	0	0	0	0	4	0	0	0	0	0	0	0	0	0	0	0	0	0	0	0	0

8A Aeneas's
7G Aenglisc
6A aerie
6A Aero-Medical
3P aerobatics
XR aerodynamic
9Q aerodynamically
6B aerogram
7H aerometeorograph
7Q aeronauts
5N aeroplanes
8B aerosol
3P Aerosystems
5N aeryoplanes
7F Aeschylus
6A Aeson's
6A Aetes'
7G Aetna
XR AFB
6E AFC
9D afeard
6A affable
5Q Affair
6A affair's
7Q affectation
8F affiliate
7Q affinities
8F affirmation
5Q affirms
8F affixed
7H afflictions
8Q affording
9D affray
8D affront
5Q AFL**
4R aflare
4A aflutter
9D aforesaid
8J African-American
9Q Africana
8F Africanizing
4Q Afrika
5P Afrikaans-speaking
7F Afrikanders
5P Afrikaner-controlled
5P Afrikaner's
9R Afro-Americans
8F Afro-Asian
8J Afro-Cuban
6E AFT

Word Type	F	D	U	SFI	3 Gr 3	4 Gr 4	5 Gr 5	6 Gr 6	7 Gr 7	8 Gr 8	9 Gr 9	X UnGr	A Read	B Eng & Gr	C Comp	D Lit	E Math	F Soc Stud	G Spell	H Sci	J Music	K Art	L Home Ec	M Shop	N Lib F	P Lib NF	Q Lib Ref	R Mag	S Rel
after-dinner	2	.2305	.1080	30.3	1	0	0	0	0	1	0	0	0	0	0	0	0	0	1	0	0	0	0	0	0	1	0	0	0
after-school	8	.4694	.8107	39.1	0	1	1	0	1	1	4	0	0	0	0	0	1	3	0	2	0	0	0	0	0	0	0	2	0
afterburner	2	.0000	.0290	24.6	2	0	0	0	0	0	0	0	0	0	0	0	0	0	0	0	0	0	0	0	0	2	0	0	0
afterburners	2	.0000	.0290	24.6	2	0	0	0	0	0	0	0	0	0	0	0	0	0	0	0	0	0	0	0	0	2	0	0	0
aftereffects	2	.2401	.1133	30.5	0	0	2	0	0	0	0	0	0	0	0	0	0	0	0	0	0	0	0	0	0	1	1	0	0
afterhold	2	.0000	.0162	22.1	2	0	0	0	0	0	0	0	0	0	0	0	0	0	0	0	2	0	0	0	0	0	0	0	0
afterimage	3	.0000	.0591	27.7	0	0	0	0	3	0	0	0	0	0	0	0	0	0	0	3	0	0	0	0	0	0	0	0	0
afterlife	2	.0000	.0389	25.9	0	0	0	0	2	0	0	0	0	0	0	0	0	2	0	0	0	0	0	0	0	0	0	0	0
aftermath	4	.3184	.2823	34.5	0	0	0	0	1	2	1	0	0	0	0	0	0	1	0	0	0	0	1	0	0	0	0	2	0
afternoon	549	.8256	91.597	59.6	119	130	46	70	104	44	31	5	228	19	16	40	19	29	6	14	5	0	2	0	59	63	9	40	0
afternoon's	6	.2411	.4668	36.7	0	0	1	2	1	2	0	0	5	0	0	0	0	0	0	0	0	0	0	0	0	0	0	1	0
afternoons	22	.7005	3.2129	45.1	4	6	1	3	4	1	3	0	10	0	0	1	2	1	0	0	0	0	0	0	2	2	1	3	0
afterthought	5	.0000	.2284	33.6	1	1	0	3	0	0	0	0	5	0	0	0	0	0	0	0	0	0	0	0	0	0	0	0	0
afterward	69	.8015	11.135	50.5	3	6	5	10	23	12	6	4	14	2	0	13	0	7	2	4	1	0	2	0	2	8	5	9	0
afterwards	134	.5298	14.964	51.8	4	30	23	28	35	7	7	0	23	4	2	6	0	4	62	3	1	0	0	0	21	2	2	4	0
Ag	2	.0000	.0394	26.0	0	0	0	0	1	1	0	0	0	0	0	0	0	0	0	2	0	0	0	0	0	0	0	0	0
ag'in	2	.0000	.0234	23.7	0	0	0	0	2	0	0	0	0	0	0	0	0	0	0	0	0	0	0	0	2	0	0	0	0
again	3892	.9197	711.10	68.5	781	716	489	528	703	366	236	73	1400	143	29	318	94	178	233	278	126	16	24	18	457	339	77	162	0
against	1755	.9242	321.54	65.1	206	226	221	224	395	244	194	45	435	45	22	145	3	182	8	153	28	31	21	27	175	183	129	163	5
Against	4	.0000	.0486	26.9	0	0	0	0	0	2	0	2	0	0	0	0	0	0	0	0	0	0	0	0	0	0	0	4	0
Agamemnon	5	.1634	.2733	34.4	0	0	1	0	3	1	0	0	2	0	0	0	0	0	0	0	0	0	0	0	0	3	0	0	0
Agamemnon's	3	.2212	.2099	33.2	0	0	0	0	0	2	1	0	2	0	0	1	0	0	0	0	0	0	0	0	0	0	0	0	0
agar	4	.2353	.2382	33.8	0	0	3	0	1	0	0	0	0	0	0	0	0	0	0	3	0	0	0	0	0	0	1	0	0
Agard	2	.0000	.0914	29.6	0	2	0	0	0	0	0	0	2	0	0	0	0	0	0	0	0	0	0	0	0	0	0	0	0
Agassiz	12	.2338	.8719	39.4	5	0	0	7	0	0	0	0	7	0	0	0	0	0	0	5	0	0	0	0	0	0	0	0	0
Agassiz'	2	.0000	.0394	26.0	2	0	0	0	0	0	0	0	0	0	0	0	0	0	0	2	0	0	0	0	0	0	0	0	0
Agassiz's	4	.0000	.1827	32.6	0	0	0	4	0	0	0	0	4	0	0	0	0	0	0	0	0	0	0	0	0	0	0	0	0
agate	2	.1223	.0628	28.0	1	0	0	0	1	0	0	0	0	0	0	0	1	0	0	0	0	1	0	0	0	0	0	0	0
agates	3	.2390	.1719	32.4	2	0	0	0	1	0	0	0	0	0	0	1	2	0	0	0	0	0	0	0	0	0	0	0	0
Agatha	3	.0000	.1370	31.4	0	0	2	1	0	0	0	0	3	0	0	0	0	0	0	0	0	0	0	0	0	0	0	0	0
Agatha's	2	.0000	.0290	24.6	2	0	0	0	0	0	0	0	0	0	0	0	0	0	0	0	0	0	0	0	0	2	0	0	0
agave	2	.0000	.0389	25.9	0	0	1	0	1	0	0	0	0	0	0	0	0	2	0	0	0	0	0	0	0	0	0	0	0
Agba	48	.1397	1.7967	42.5	0	0	0	42	6	0	0	0	0	0	0	6	0	0	0	0	0	0	0	0	42	0	0	0	0
Agba's	20	.0745	.5090	37.1	0	0	0	19	1	0	0	0	0	0	0	1	0	0	0	0	0	0	0	0	19	0	0	0	0
age	617	.9555	116.36	60.7	57	68	74	62	132	94	100	30	101	30	7	42	31	59	15	79	26	5	18	10	22	58	70	44	0
Age	93	.7128	13.488	51.3	12	10	7	15	20	16	13	0	6	5	0	0	0	27	0	15	5	0	1	0	0	13	15	6	0
age-old	11	.4894	1.1405	40.6	2	2	1	1	4	0	1	0	1	0	0	0	0	1	0	0	1	0	0	0	1	0	5	2	0
aged	39	.6852	5.4541	47.4	2	5	0	2	8	6	16	0	4	2	0	4	2	4	0	2	0	0	0	0	3	1	4	13	0
Agelaos	2	.0000	.0215	23.3	0	0	0	0	0	0	2	0	0	0	0	2	0	0	0	0	0	0	0	0	0	0	0	0	0
agencies	40	.7290	5.9064	47.7	0	0	13	5	3	8	10	1	1	1	0	0	1	11	0	9	0	0	1	1	0	3	5	7	0
agency	37	.5678	4.3763	46.4	0	1	11	2	6	5	11	1	3	2	0	1	2	6	1	1	0	0	0	0	0	0	15	6	0
Agency	8	.5178	.8680	39.4	0	1	2	0	3	1	0	1	0	0	0	0	3	1	0	0	0	0	0	0	0	1	2	1	0
agenda	2	.1621	.0746	28.7	0	0	0	0	0	1	1	0	0	0	1	1	0	0	0	0	0	0	0	0	0	0	0	0	0
agent	79	.8783	13.814	51.4	3	4	9	3	31	9	14	6	13	4	1	11	3	6	2	10	0	0	2	1	1	10	4	11	0
Agent	3	.2279	.2143	33.3	2	1	0	0	0	0	0	0	2	0	0	0	0	0	0	0	0	0	0	0	0	0	0	1	0
agents	44	.6469	5.8485	47.7	1	6	5	2	13	6	7	4	3	1	0	0	0	5	0	8	0	0	0	1	0	8	11	7	0
ages	114	.6632	15.523	51.9	8	12	19	5	33	20	13	4	14	2	1	5	13	9	1	21	3	1	6	1	1	10	15	9	2
Ages	66	.6373	8.6459	49.4	2	7	8	14	11	14	8	2	5	4	0	0	1	20	1	2	6	2	0	0	0	3	22	0	0
aggravating	3	.3870	.2492	34.0	0	0	2	0	1	0	0	0	0	0	0	0	0	0	0	0	0	0	0	0	1	0	1	1	0
aggravation	2	.2440	.1132	30.5	0	0	0	0	0	1	1	0	0	0	0	1	0	0	0	0	0	0	0	0	0	0	0	1	0
aggregate	6	.1813	.2803	34.5	0	0	0	0	3	2	0	1	0	0	0	0	0	0	0	2	0	0	0	0	0	0	4	0	0
aggregates	4	.3864	.3418	35.3	0	0	0	0	1	0	0	3	0	0	0	0	0	0	0	2	0	0	0	0	0	0	1	1	0
aggression	14	.4506	1.3467	41.3	0	0	2	1	6	3	1	1	0	1	0	0	0	3	0	1	0	0	0	0	0	0	2	7	0
aggressive	18	.5490	2.0920	43.2	1	0	1	0	9	3	2	2	3	0	1	0	0	3	0	0	0	0	0	0	0	2	2	7	0
aggressiveness	4	.3359	.2989	34.8	0	0	0	0	2	1	1	0	0	0	0	0	0	1	0	0	0	0	0	0	0	0	2	1	0
aggressors	2	.2285	.1129	30.5	0	0	0	0	1	1	0	0	0	0	0	0	0	1	0	0	0	0	0	0	0	0	1	0	0
aggrieved	2	.1787	.1174	30.7	0	0	1	0	1	0	0	0	1	0	0	0	0	0	0	0	0	0	0	0	1	0	0	0	0
Aggy	5	.0000	.0586	27.7	0	0	5	0	0	0	0	0	0	0	0	0	0	0	0	0	0	0	0	0	5	0	0	0	0
aghast	8	.4845	.8451	39.3	1	0	1	1	5	0	0	0	2	0	0	3	0	0	0	0	0	0	0	0	1	1	0	1	0
agile	11	.5967	1.3805	41.4	0	0	1	4	3	1	1	1	2	0	0	0	0	0	0	3	1	0	0	0	0	3	1	1	0
agilely	2	.0665	.0708	28.5	0	0	0	0	0	2	0	0	1	0	1	0	0	0	0	0	0	0	0	0	0	0	0	0	0
agility	7	.3585	.5686	37.5	0	0	0	5	2	0	0	0	0	0	0	0	0	0	0	4	0	0	0	0	0	1	0	2	0
agin	4	.0974	.1495	31.7	0	0	0	0	2	2	0	0	1	0	0	0	0	0	0	0	0	0	0	0	3	0	0	0	0
Agincourt	2	.0000	.0219	23.4	0	0	0	0	1	0	0	1	0	2	0	0	0	0	0	0	0	0	0	0	0	0	0	0	0
aging	13	.6634	1.7660	42.5	2	1	2	1	1	2	2	2	1	1	0	0	0	1	0	2	0	0	0	0	1	2	3	2	0
agitate	3	.3553	.2609	34.2	0	0	0	1	0	1	1	0	1	0	0	0	0	0	0	1	0	0	0	0	0	1	0	0	0
agitated	16	.6552	2.1164	43.3	1	0	0	0	6	4	5	0	0	0	1	1	0	1	0	1	6	1	0	0	2	1	1	1	0
agitation	10	.5623	1.1742	40.7	0	0	0	2	2	4	2	0	1	0	0	3	0	2	0	0	1	0	0	0	0	0	2	1	0
agitator	6	.0000	.0729	28.6	0	0	0	0	0	0	0	6	0	0	0	0	0	0	0	0	0	0	0	0	0	0	0	6	0
agitators	4	.2281	.2337	33.7	0	0	0	0	0	3	0	1	0	0	0	0	0	3	0	0	0	0	0	0	0	0	0	1	0
aglow	3	.3399	.2456	33.9	0	0	0	1	1	0	0	1	1	0	0	1	0	0	0	0	0	0	0	0	0	0	0	1	0
Agnes	26	.5510	3.1763	45.0	13	0	2	7	1	0	2	1	15	0	1	6	2	0	0	0	0	0	0	0	0	0	1	1	0
Agnew	7	.1564	.2855	34.6	0	0	0	0	6	0	1	0	0	0	0	0	0	0	0	0	0	0	0	0	0	0	1	6	0
agnostic	3	.0000	.0365	25.6	0	0	0	0	3	0	0	0	0	0	0	0	0	0	0	0	0	0	0	0	0	0	0	3	0
ago	1387	.9172	252.45	64.0	274	274	175	193	224	105	91	51	310	61	7	52	53	257	33	146	58	12	2	3	38	114	82	159	0
agonies	3	.2143	.1568	32.0	0	0	0	0	0	0	2	1	0	0	0	0	0	0	0	0	0	0	0	0	0	1	0	2	0
agonized	2	.2443	.1130	30.5	0	0	0	0	1	0	1	0	0	0	0	1	0	0	0	0	0	0	0	0	1	0	0	0	0
agonizing	3	.2309	.1631	32.1	0	0	0	0	0	0	3	0	0	0	0	1	0	0	0	0	0	0	0	0	0	0	0	2	0
agonizingly	2	.2433	.1158	30.6	0	0	0	0	0	1	1	0	0	0	0	0	0	0	0	0	0	0	0	0	0	1	0	1	0
agony	23	.6583	3.1548	45.0	0	2	1	5	1	6	6	2	8	1	2	3	0	0	0	1	1	0	0	0	4	1	1	1	0
Agony	8	.0000	.3655	35.6	0	8	0	0	0	0	0	0	8	0	0	0	0	0	0	0	0	0	0	0	0	0	0	0	0
agootuk	2	.0000	.0162	22.1	0	0	0	2	0	0	0	0	0	0	0	0	0	0	0	0	2	0	0	0	0	0	0	0	0
Agoutis	2	.0000	.0209	23.2	0	0	0	0	2	0	0	0	0	0	0	0	0	0	0	0	0	0	0	0	0	0	2	0	0
Agramonte	8	.2275	.5677	37.5	0	3	0	0	0	5	0	0	5	0	0	0	0	0	0	0	0	0	0	0	0	3	0	0	0
agrarian	3	.3769	.2484	34.0	0	1	0	0	1	1	0	0	0	0	0	0	0	1	0	0	0	0	0	0	0	0	1	1	0
agree	262	.8887	46.325	56.7	27	21	33	32	65	40	39	5	50	39	1	13	36	28	14	18	1	3	3	0	9	10	10	27	0
agreeable	19	.5618	2.2964	43.6	0	2	2	2	9	2	2	0	7	1	0	0	0	0	1	0	1	0	0	0	6	0	0	3	0
agreeably	2	.2442	.1134	30.5	0	0	0	0	1	0	0	1	0	1	0	0	0	0	0	0	0	0	0	0	0	0	0	1	0
agreed	325	.8346	54.620	57.4	45	66	49	49	50	44	17	5	105	5	1	21	10	60	1	9	5	1	0	0	29	34	12	32	0
agreed-on	2	.0000	.0209	23.2	0	0	2	0	0	0	0	0	0	0	0	0	0	0	0	0	0	0	0	0	0	0	2	0	0
agreeing	12	.6303	1.5806	42.0	0	3	1	2	1	2	3	0	3	0	0	1	0	1	1	1	0	0	0	0	2	0	0	3	0
agreement	85	.7929	13.560	51.3	4	5	7	9	22	19	13	6	11	10	0	0	5	21	4	3	3	0	1	0	2	2	12	11	0
Agreement	2	.2437	.1129	30.5	0	1	0	0	0	0	0	1	0	0	0	0	0	0	0	0	0	0	0	0	0	0	1	1	0
agreements	24	.6086	3.0113	44.8	1	0	8	1	1	6	6	1	1	0	0	0	3	4	1	0	0	0	0	0	0	4	5	6	0
agrees	24	.7062	3.4445	45.4	0	1	1	5	9	5	3	0	2	5	1	1	0	4	0	3	0	0	0	1	0	2	0	5	0

7D after-effects
8K after-life
4A after-midnight
9K after-the-storm
5R afterbath
6A aftercabin
7A afterhatch
9D afterhours
7H afterimages
7J Afternoon
3P aftershaft
3P aftershafts
XR ag
9Q Aga
6J Again
8Q again-great
8D againe
8F Agana
8D agape
6Q agar-agar
7A Agate
7Q age-long
6N age-worn
7Q age's
7Q ageless
3P Agencies
7R agency's
9R agendas
9R aggg
9B Aggie
7R aggrandisement
7N aggrandizements
9Q aggravate
4N aggreement
4Q aggregation
9A aggregations
7A aggressions
8B aggressively
8F aggressor
9L Agilon
9R Aging
8N aginst
7D agleam
6J Ago
8F agoing
7Q agouti
7Q agoutis
8F Agrarians
7Q Agricola's

Word Type	F	D	U	SFI	3 Gr 3	4 Gr 4	5 Gr 5	6 Gr 6	7 Gr 7	8 Gr 8	9 Gr 9	X UnGr	A Read	B Eng & Gr	C Comp	D Lit	E Math	F Soc Stud	G Spell	H Sci	J Music	K Art	L Home Ec	M Shop	N Lib F	P Lib NF	Q Lib Ref	R Mag	S Rel
agricultural	86	.5658	10.178	50.1	13	1	15	14	20	9	9	5	3	0	0	1	1	35	2	5	0	0	0	0	0	12	23	4	0
Agricultural	7	.3267	.5083	37.1	0	0	2	0	0	1	2	2	0	0	0	0	0	0	0	1	0	0	0	0	0	0	3	3	0
agriculture	98	.6162	12.456	51.0	11	6	20	17	20	10	9	5	0	3	0	0	0	42	3	10	0	0	1	0	0	11	23	5	0
Agriculture	33	.7233	4.8232	46.8	5	0	6	3	5	3	7	4	1	1	0	2	0	1	0	9	0	0	2	1	0	5	6	5	0
Agriculture's	2	.1432	.0759	28.8	0	0	0	0	0	0	1	1	0	0	0	0	0	0	0	1	0	0	1	0	0	0	0	0	0
AGS	2	.0000	.0209	23.2	0	0	0	0	0	0	2	0	0	0	0	0	0	0	0	0	0	0	0	0	0	0	2	0	0
ague	4	.2969	.2888	34.6	0	0	0	1	1	1	1	0	1	0	0	2	0	0	0	0	0	0	0	0	1	0	0	0	0
ah	116	.6727	16.343	52.1	18	18	21	16	16	18	9	0	52	2	4	23	0	1	0	2	6	0	0	0	17	5	0	4	0
Ah	4	.2741	.2683	34.3	0	0	0	3	0	1	0	0	1	1	0	0	0	0	0	0	2	0	0	0	0	0	0	0	0
Ah-yo-keh	3	.0000	.1370	31.4	0	0	0	3	0	0	0	0	3	0	0	0	0	0	0	0	0	0	0	0	0	0	0	0	0
aha	6	.2435	.4680	36.7	4	2	0	0	0	0	0	0	5	0	0	1	0	0	0	0	0	0	0	0	0	0	0	0	0
Ahasuerus	2	.0000	.0162	22.1	0	0	0	0	0	2	0	0	0	0	0	0	0	0	0	0	2	0	0	0	0	0	0	0	0
ahead	639	.8557	109.92	60.4	103	131	64	73	132	73	52	11	265	21	8	55	10	39	3	35	3	1	3	0	56	71	18	51	0
Ahead	2	.2412	.1141	30.6	0	0	0	1	1	0	0	0	0	1	0	0	0	0	0	0	0	0	0	0	0	1	0	0	0
ahhh	2	.0000	.0914	29.6	0	0	0	0	2	0	0	0	2	0	0	0	0	0	0	0	0	0	0	0	0	0	0	0	0
Ahmadabad	3	.0000	.0365	25.6	0	0	0	0	0	3	0	0	0	0	0	0	0	0	0	0	0	0	0	0	0	0	0	3	0
Ahmed	4	.3351	.3269	35.1	0	0	0	3	0	0	1	0	1	1	0	0	0	2	0	0	0	0	0	0	0	0	0	0	0
Ahmeek	6	.0000	.0644	28.1	0	0	0	0	0	0	6	0	0	0	0	6	0	0	0	0	0	0	0	0	0	0	0	0	0
ahoy	11	.3167	.9138	39.6	0	4	5	2	0	0	0	0	6	0	0	0	0	0	0	0	0	0	0	0	4	1	0	0	0
Ahrirang	2	.0000	.0162	22.1	0	2	0	0	0	0	0	0	0	0	0	0	0	0	0	0	2	0	0	0	0	0	0	0	0
ai	15	.1839	.6495	38.1	2	1	5	5	1	1	0	0	0	1	0	0	0	0	12	0	0	0	0	0	2	0	0	0	0
Ai	4	.0000	.1827	32.6	0	0	0	0	4	0	0	0	4	0	0	0	0	0	0	0	0	0	0	0	0	0	0	0	0
Ai-yani	2	.0000	.0290	24.6	0	2	0	0	0	0	0	0	0	0	0	0	0	0	0	0	0	0	0	0	0	2	0	0	0
aia	3	.0000	.0352	25.5	0	0	0	3	0	0	0	0	0	0	0	0	0	0	0	0	0	0	0	0	3	0	0	0	0
Aiaian	2	.0000	.0215	23.3	0	0	0	0	0	0	2	0	0	0	0	2	0	0	0	0	0	0	0	0	0	0	0	0	0
aid	194	.8619	33.349	55.2	10	7	21	17	51	41	29	18	24	6	1	3	6	37	3	32	4	0	6	2	4	12	29	25	0
Aid	3	.3863	.2513	34.0	1	0	1	0	1	0	0	0	0	0	0	0	0	0	0	0	0	0	0	0	1	1	0	1	0
Aida	6	.0000	.0485	26.9	0	0	0	1	1	2	2	0	0	0	0	0	0	0	0	0	6	0	0	0	0	0	0	0	0
aide	5	.2882	.3474	35.4	0	0	0	0	0	3	2	0	1	0	0	0	0	0	0	0	1	0	0	0	0	0	0	3	0
aide-de-camp	3	.2260	.1580	32.0	0	0	0	0	0	1	2	0	0	0	0	2	0	0	0	0	0	0	0	0	0	0	1	0	0
aided	25	.6707	3.4453	45.4	0	1	4	3	5	8	4	0	3	0	2	0	0	8	0	4	1	0	1	0	1	0	2	3	0
aides	6	.1453	.2356	33.7	0	1	0	0	1	2	2	0	0	0	0	0	0	0	0	0	0	0	0	0	0	1	0	5	0
aiding	7	.5904	.8584	39.3	0	0	1	1	3	2	0	0	1	1	0	0	1	0	0	1	1	0	1	0	0	0	1	0	0
aids	28	.8027	4.4816	46.5	2	4	0	0	10	6	5	1	1	4	1	1	0	4	0	0	1	1	2	2	1	2	6	2	0
Aids	2	.0000	.0162	22.1	0	0	0	0	1	1	0	0	0	0	0	0	0	0	0	0	2	0	0	0	0	0	0	0	0
Aigisthos	5	.0000	.0537	27.3	0	0	0	0	0	0	5	0	0	0	0	5	0	0	0	0	0	0	0	0	0	0	0	0	0
Aiguille	2	.0000	.0209	23.2	0	0	0	0	2	0	0	0	0	0	0	0	0	0	0	0	0	0	0	0	0	0	2	0	0
Aiken	8	.5338	.8896	39.5	2	0	2	0	0	2	2	0	0	1	0	0	0	3	0	0	2	0	0	0	0	0	1	1	0
Aiku	2	.0000	.0389	25.9	0	0	0	0	0	2	0	0	0	0	0	0	0	2	0	0	0	0	0	0	0	0	0	0	0
aileron	5	.2396	.3805	35.8	0	4	1	0	0	0	0	0	4	0	0	0	0	0	1	0	0	0	0	0	0	0	0	0	0
ailerons	2	.0000	.0394	26.0	0	2	0	0	0	0	0	0	0	0	0	0	0	0	0	2	0	0	0	0	0	0	0	0	0
ailing	6	.2765	.4325	36.4	0	0	0	0	3	1	0	2	2	0	0	0	0	1	0	0	0	0	0	0	0	0	0	3	0
ailments	13	.4826	1.3255	41.2	0	0	1	3	2	4	2	1	0	0	0	1	0	0	0	6	0	0	2	0	0	0	3	1	0
ails	2	.2446	.1142	30.6	0	0	0	0	1	0	0	1	0	0	0	0	0	0	0	0	0	0	0	0	1	0	0	1	0
aim	93	.8891	16.436	52.2	6	21	8	8	21	11	15	3	15	6	2	6	1	10	2	3	3	1	2	0	5	23	5	9	0
aimed	45	.7716	7.0646	48.5	3	10	6	6	8	9	1	2	14	1	1	1	0	4	0	2	0	0	0	1	2	9	2	8	0
aiming	13	.6114	1.6845	42.3	2	3	3	0	3	1	1	0	5	1	1	1	0	0	0	0	1	0	0	0	1	3	0	0	0
aimless	6	.5523	.7158	38.5	0	1	0	0	4	0	1	0	2	1	0	0	0	1	0	0	0	0	0	0	0	0	1	1	0
aimlessly	4	.2417	.3028	34.8	0	0	1	1	2	0	0	0	3	0	0	0	0	0	0	0	0	0	0	0	1	0	0	0	0
aims	27	.7940	4.3058	46.3	1	0	5	1	9	7	2	2	4	2	0	0	0	4	0	1	1	1	2	1	1	2	4	4	0
ain	2	.2408	.1091	30.4	0	0	1	0	0	1	0	0	0	1	0	0	0	0	1	0	0	0	0	0	0	0	0	0	0
ain't	187	.5022	20.431	53.1	13	3	16	9	82	42	21	1	54	11	0	54	0	0	0	0	3	0	0	0	57	5	0	3	0
Ainsworth	3	.2401	.1655	32.2	0	0	3	0	0	0	0	0	0	0	0	0	0	0	0	0	1	0	0	0	2	0	0	0	0
Ainus	2	.0000	.0209	23.2	0	0	0	0	2	0	0	0	0	0	0	0	0	0	0	0	0	0	0	0	0	0	2	0	0
air	3673	.7868	585.08	67.7	1058	596	483	408	534	305	203	86	671	54	30	127	14	189	23	1691	71	9	7	16	109	309	159	194	0
Air	126	.6850	17.940	52.5	30	10	11	9	30	16	12	8	44	1	0	4	0	12	0	2	3	1	0	0	0	19	8	32	0
AIR	5	.3359	.3766	35.8	5	0	0	0	0	0	0	0	0	0	0	0	0	0	0	2	2	0	0	0	0	1	0	0	0
air-breathing	4	.1335	.1958	32.9	0	0	0	2	1	0	0	1	1	0	0	0	0	0	0	3	0	0	0	0	0	0	0	0	0
air-conditioned	6	.5511	.7186	38.6	1	0	1	1	1	1	0	1	2	0	0	0	0	1	0	1	0	0	0	0	0	0	1	1	0
Air-conditioned	2	.0000	.0914	29.6	0	0	0	2	0	0	0	0	2	0	0	0	0	0	0	0	0	0	0	0	0	0	0	0	0
air-conditioner	2	.1814	.1187	30.7	0	0	1	1	0	0	0	0	1	0	0	0	0	0	0	0	0	0	0	0	0	0	0	1	0
air-conditioning	8	.5450	.9047	39.6	0	0	1	2	1	0	4	0	0	0	0	1	0	1	0	2	0	0	0	1	0	0	2	1	0
air-cooled	4	.2107	.2095	33.2	0	1	3	0	0	0	0	0	0	0	0	0	0	0	0	0	0	0	0	0	0	3	0	1	0
air-mail	4	.0000	.1827	32.6	0	2	2	0	0	0	0	0	4	0	0	0	0	0	0	0	0	0	0	0	0	0	0	0	0
air-ship	2	.0000	.0234	23.7	0	0	2	0	0	0	0	0	0	0	0	0	0	0	0	0	0	0	0	0	2	0	0	0	0
air-speed	2	.2351	.1166	30.7	0	1	0	0	0	0	0	1	0	0	0	0	0	1	0	0	0	0	0	0	0	0	0	1	0
air-supported	3	.0000	.0314	25.0	0	0	0	0	0	0	3	0	0	0	0	0	0	0	0	0	0	0	0	0	0	0	3	0	0
airborne	4	.3280	.2948	34.7	1	1	1	0	0	0	1	0	0	0	0	0	0	0	0	1	0	0	0	0	0	1	2	0	0
aircraft	81	.6398	10.762	50.3	5	9	6	10	21	7	12	11	15	0	0	3	1	12	0	12	0	0	0	6	0	4	7	21	0
aired	3	.2123	.1792	32.5	0	2	0	0	0	1	0	0	1	0	0	0	0	0	0	1	0	0	1	0	0	0	0	0	0
Airedale	2	.2443	.1130	30.5	0	0	1	0	1	0	0	0	0	0	0	1	0	0	0	0	0	0	0	0	1	0	0	0	0
Aires	28	.2815	1.8758	42.7	7	2	0	8	9	0	1	1	0	0	0	0	0	17	0	1	0	0	0	0	0	0	10	0	0
airfield	11	.6998	1.5578	41.9	0	0	1	1	4	5	0	0	0	1	0	2	0	1	0	2	0	0	0	0	1	1	2	1	0
airfields	10	.4832	1.0453	40.2	0	1	2	2	1	2	0	2	1	0	0	0	0	4	0	0	0	0	0	0	0	1	0	3	0
airfoil	6	.2071	.3307	35.2	0	4	0	0	0	1	1	0	0	0	0	0	0	0	0	5	0	0	0	0	0	0	1	0	0
airily	2	.1717	.1142	30.6	0	1	0	0	0	1	0	0	1	0	0	1	0	0	0	0	0	0	0	0	0	0	0	0	0
airing	4	.4568	.4091	36.1	0	3	0	1	0	0	0	0	1	0	0	0	0	0	0	1	0	0	0	0	0	1	0	1	0
airless	4	.4501	.4035	36.1	0	1	0	1	1	0	1	0	1	0	0	0	0	0	0	1	0	0	0	0	0	1	1	0	0
airline	35	.5917	4.3283	46.4	4	4	4	7	4	5	5	2	5	1	0	0	11	5	0	0	0	0	0	3	0	2	1	7	0
airliner	14	.5125	1.6013	42.0	6	3	0	2	3	0	0	0	6	0	0	0	4	0	0	1	0	0	0	0	0	1	0	2	0
airliners	11	.5969	1.3641	41.3	5	1	1	1	2	1	0	0	1	0	0	1	1	1	0	1	0	0	0	1	0	4	0	1	0
airlines	24	.6398	3.2161	45.1	2	6	5	1	1	4	1	4	6	0	0	1	0	7	0	1	0	0	0	0	0	1	2	5	0
Airlines	8	.4250	.7703	38.9	0	0	0	0	4	0	1	3	2	1	0	0	1	2	0	0	0	0	0	0	0	0	0	3	0
airmail	15	.5152	1.6534	42.2	7	1	0	1	6	0	0	0	2	2	0	0	5	3	0	0	0	0	0	0	0	0	3	0	0
airman	10	.1415	.4912	36.9	0	6	0	1	0	3	0	0	4	6	0	0	0	0	0	0	0	0	0	0	0	0	0	0	0
airmanship	2	.0000	.0914	29.6	0	0	0	0	2	0	0	0	2	0	0	0	0	0	0	0	0	0	0	0	0	0	0	0	0
airmen	19	.4210	1.9642	42.9	1	1	10	2	1	3	1	0	12	0	0	0	0	5	0	1	0	0	0	0	0	0	0	1	0
airplane	298	.8537	50.969	57.1	72	69	31	27	42	34	19	4	65	13	3	6	32	54	4	71	0	7	0	2	6	14	9	12	0
Airplane	2	.0000	.0914	29.6	0	0	0	1	1	0	0	0	2	0	0	0	0	0	0	0	0	0	0	0	0	0	0	0	0
airplanes	168	.8400	28.297	54.5	49	25	31	22	15	15	5	6	30	10	1	1	13	50	0	29	3	4	1	5	1	5	9	6	0
airport	123	.7470	18.802	52.7	45	19	16	17	17	6	2	1	32	6	0	0	7	45	3	7	0	0	0	1	3	7	2	10	0
Airport	16	.6589	2.1857	43.4	2	3	4	4	1	1	1	0	4	1	1	0	1	2	0	0	0	0	0	0	0	2	3	2	0
airports	31	.6850	4.3567	46.4	12	4	3	5	4	1	1	1	6	1	1	0	0	3	0	1	0	0	0	2	0	6	4	7	0

5P agriculturalists
7Q agriculturists
5P agronomists
5Q agronomy
7R aground
XR Agua
7D ague-fit
4P ah-h-h
5E ah-hah
7P Ah'm
3P Ahab
4P ahem
7A ahhhhh
3A ahhhhhh
4P ahhhhhhh
9L ahing
6J ahl-bay-neez
3A ahlan-wa-sahlan
7R Ahmadi
5P Ahmadu
9D Ahmeek's
6R Ahnapee
7R AHRA
8A aht
7D Ahwelab
7R Ahyee-aye-ty-fahve
7R AiResearch
9D Aigisthos'
6A ailed
3B Aileen
5N ailin'
5Q Ainsworth's
XR Air-India
7R Air-Lines
4A air-blast
4A air-borne
3P air-cooling
9Q air-cushion
8F air-defense
7R air-driven
7P air-drying
3F air-filled
7Q air-intake
9B air-line
4Q air-navigation
8B air-raid
9H air-sea
XR air-supply
7R air-to-ground
8A air-traffic
XR air-transport
7H air-vaulted
4F air-view
8R air-weapon
8F airbrakes
XR Aircraft
7Q aircraft's
9P airedale
7R Airheart
7R Airhearts
5N airhole
6A airhose
5J airiness
7P Airing
6A airings
7P airless-spray
7H airlessness
5E Airline
8E airline's
XR airly
3R Airmanship
3P AIRPORTS

Word Type	F	D	U	SFI	3 Gr 3	4 Gr 4	5 Gr 5	6 Gr 6	7 Gr 7	8 Gr 8	9 Gr 9	X UnGr	A Read	B Eng & Gr	C Comp	D Lit	E Math	F Soc Stud	G Spell	H Sci	J Music	K Art	L Home Ec	M Shop	N Lib F	P Lib NF	Q Lib Ref	R Mag	S Rel
airs	7	.5028	.7228	38.6	1	0	3	1	1	1	0	0	0	2	1	1	0	0	0	0	2	0	0	0	1	0	0	0	0
airship	2	.2346	.1166	30.7	1	0	0	0	0	0	0	1	0	0	0	0	0	0	0	1	0	0	0	0	0	0	0	1	0
airstrip	3	.3406	.2461	33.9	0	1	0	1	0	0	1	0	1	1	0	0	0	0	0	0	0	0	0	0	0	0	0	1	0
airtight	11	.5579	1.3054	41.2	2	2	3	2	0	1	1	0	2	1	0	0	0	1	0	4	0	0	1	0	0	0	2	0	0
airways	9	.4698	.9966	40.0	0	1	0	2	2	4	0	0	6	0	0	1	0	0	1	1	0	0	0	0	0	0	0	0	0
airy	20	.6831	2.7960	44.5	2	2	3	2	4	1	4	2	3	1	0	4	0	1	1	3	0	1	0	0	4	0	0	2	0
aisle	15	.5438	1.7197	42.4	0	7	4	0	1	0	3	0	2	2	0	3	0	0	0	0	0	0	0	0	1	6	0	1	0
aisles	10	.6091	1.2973	41.1	2	2	1	1	2	0	2	0	4	0	0	1	0	1	0	0	1	0	0	0	2	0	0	1	0
Akiko	3	.0000	.0583	27.7	0	3	0	0	0	0	0	0	0	0	0	0	0	3	0	0	0	0	0	0	0	0	0	0	0
akin	4	.2412	.2282	33.6	1	2	0	0	1	0	0	0	0	2	0	0	0	0	0	0	0	0	0	0	0	2	0	0	0
Akron	4	.2404	.2283	33.6	0	4	0	0	0	0	0	0	0	2	0	0	2	0	0	0	0	0	0	0	0	0	0	0	0
Aku	10	.0000	.4568	36.6	10	0	0	0	0	0	0	0	10	0	0	0	0	0	0	0	0	0	0	0	0	0	0	0	0
akua	7	.0000	.3198	35.0	0	7	0	0	0	0	0	0	7	0	0	0	0	0	0	0	0	0	0	0	0	0	0	0	0
al	29	.2632	1.6863	42.3	0	1	5	15	6	2	0	0	0	1	0	0	0	0	22	0	3	0	0	0	0	1	0	2	0
Al	142	.5996	18.881	52.8	64	27	12	26	6	1	5	1	108	4	0	2	4	0	2	1	0	0	0	0	9	9	0	3	0
Al's	13	.0000	.5939	37.7	4	5	0	4	0	0	0	0	13	0	0	0	0	0	0	0	0	0	0	0	0	0	0	0	0
Ala	2	.2437	.1129	30.5	0	0	1	0	0	0	0	1	0	0	0	0	0	0	0	0	0	0	0	0	0	0	1	1	0
Alabama	51	.6982	7.2686	48.6	3	8	11	3	7	10	5	4	5	0	0	5	0	14	0	2	2	0	0	0	1	9	7	6	0
alabaster	5	.4154	.4445	36.5	2	0	0	2	0	0	1	0	0	0	0	0	0	0	0	1	2	0	0	0	1	1	0	0	0
alack	6	.3688	.4741	36.8	0	2	0	0	0	1	3	0	0	2	0	3	0	0	0	0	1	0	0	0	0	0	0	0	0
Aladdin	34	.3855	3.2016	45.1	14	5	15	0	0	0	0	0	19	0	3	0	1	0	0	0	0	0	0	0	11	0	0	0	0
Aladdin's	4	.3123	.2986	34.8	0	0	3	0	0	1	0	0	1	0	0	0	0	0	1	0	0	0	0	0	2	0	0	0	0
Alameda	7	.2635	.4293	36.3	0	1	1	4	0	0	1	0	0	0	0	0	0	1	0	0	0	0	0	0	0	0	1	5	0
Alamein	2	.2433	.1158	30.6	0	0	0	0	1	0	1	0	0	0	0	0	0	0	0	0	0	0	0	0	0	1	0	1	0
Alamo	38	.4756	4.1778	46.2	3	16	5	1	5	8	0	0	21	0	0	0	0	2	0	0	3	0	0	0	0	11	0	1	0
Alamosa	3	.2321	.1635	32.1	0	0	0	0	1	0	0	2	0	0	0	0	0	0	0	0	0	0	0	0	0	0	1	2	0
Alan	31	.5391	3.5085	45.5	2	4	10	3	6	3	2	1	2	6	0	0	13	0	0	2	1	0	0	0	0	1	0	6	0
alanine	3	.0000	.0591	27.7	0	0	0	0	3	0	0	0	0	0	0	0	0	0	0	3	0	0	0	0	0	0	0	0	0
Alaric	9	.0000	.1055	30.2	9	0	0	0	0	0	0	0	0	0	0	0	0	0	0	0	0	0	0	0	9	0	0	0	0
alarm	105	.7626	16.495	52.2	25	21	7	18	19	8	7	0	57	5	3	10	0	5	0	4	1	0	0	0	7	5	3	5	0
alarmed	37	.6540	5.0423	47.0	8	7	7	5	4	2	4	0	11	1	3	1	0	5	0	0	0	0	0	0	4	6	3	3	0
alarming	7	.5314	.7802	38.9	0	1	1	0	3	1	1	0	0	0	0	1	0	1	0	2	0	0	0	0	0	1	2	0	0
alarms	9	.4574	.9078	39.6	0	1	0	4	3	0	1	0	2	0	0	0	0	0	0	1	1	0	0	0	0	1	0	4	0
alas	44	.6869	6.2209	47.9	8	8	4	6	7	3	8	0	12	4	1	14	0	1	1	0	3	0	0	0	4	3	0	1	0
Alaska	330	.5482	38.843	55.9	58	59	148	16	18	16	11	4	50	3	0	6	7	203	0	17	7	0	0	0	2	12	6	17	0
Alaska's	20	.3444	1.6405	42.1	1	1	16	1	1	0	0	0	3	0	0	0	0	14	0	0	2	0	0	0	0	0	0	1	0
Alaskan	28	.4900	3.0695	44.9	2	3	15	1	4	2	1	0	9	0	0	2	0	13	0	0	0	0	0	0	0	0	1	3	0
Alaskans	9	.2287	.5541	37.4	0	1	7	0	0	0	0	1	1	0	0	0	0	7	0	0	0	0	0	0	0	0	0	1	0
Alban	3	.3766	.2497	34.0	1	0	0	1	0	0	1	0	0	0	0	0	0	1	0	0	0	0	0	0	0	1	1	0	0
Albania	8	.1363	.2895	34.6	0	6	0	0	1	0	1	0	0	7	0	0	0	0	0	0	0	0	0	0	0	0	1	0	0
Albanians	2	.2351	.1166	30.7	0	0	0	0	1	0	1	0	0	0	0	0	0	1	0	0	0	0	0	0	0	0	0	1	0
Albany	44	.5089	4.7029	46.7	3	2	24	1	3	10	1	0	1	2	0	1	0	12	0	0	1	0	0	0	2	2	21	2	0
albatross	5	.3687	.4522	36.6	1	2	0	1	0	0	0	1	2	0	0	0	0	0	0	2	0	0	0	0	1	0	0	0	0
albatrosses	7	.5000	.7359	38.7	2	0	0	1	3	0	0	1	0	0	0	0	1	0	0	1	0	0	0	0	0	1	1	3	0
Albe	7	.0000	.0821	29.1	0	7	0	0	0	0	0	0	0	0	0	0	0	0	0	0	0	0	0	0	7	0	0	0	0
Albee	2	.0000	.0243	23.9	0	0	0	0	0	0	1	1	0	0	0	0	0	0	0	0	0	0	0	0	0	0	0	2	0
Albee's	4	.0000	.0486	26.9	0	0	0	0	0	0	4	0	0	0	0	0	0	0	0	0	0	0	0	0	0	0	0	4	0
albeit	3	.1927	.1491	31.7	0	0	0	0	1	0	0	2	0	0	0	0	0	0	0	1	0	0	0	0	0	0	0	2	0
Albemarle	2	.2407	.1138	30.6	0	2	0	0	0	0	0	0	0	0	0	1	0	0	0	0	0	0	0	0	0	1	0	0	0
Albers	5	.3550	.4331	36.4	0	1	0	0	4	0	0	0	2	0	0	0	0	0	0	0	0	0	0	0	0	2	1	0	0
Albert	118	.7402	18.016	52.6	10	56	7	20	8	15	2	0	52	3	1	3	4	3	0	6	0	0	0	0	2	26	7	11	0
Albert's	3	.2357	.2199	33.4	0	3	0	0	0	0	0	0	2	0	0	0	0	0	0	0	0	0	0	0	0	1	0	0	0
Alberta	11	.3365	.8406	39.2	0	0	5	1	4	1	0	0	0	0	0	0	0	6	0	0	0	0	0	0	0	0	4	1	0
Albertine	7	.0566	.1818	32.6	1	0	0	0	0	0	6	0	1	0	0	6	0	0	0	0	0	0	0	0	0	0	0	0	0
Alberto	3	.0994	.0714	28.5	0	0	0	0	0	2	1	0	0	0	0	0	0	0	0	0	0	2	0	0	0	0	1	0	0
Albion	2	.0000	.0290	24.6	0	2	0	0	0	0	0	0	0	0	0	0	0	0	0	0	0	0	0	0	0	2	0	0	0
Albon	3	.0000	.0434	26.4	0	3	0	0	0	0	0	0	0	0	0	0	0	0	0	0	0	0	0	0	0	3	0	0	0
Albrecht	4	.2186	.2141	33.3	0	0	3	0	1	0	0	0	0	0	0	1	0	0	0	0	0	0	0	0	0	3	0	0	0
album	11	.5392	1.2221	40.9	1	0	4	0	3	2	1	0	0	3	1	2	2	0	0	0	0	0	0	0	0	0	0	3	0
Album	15	.0000	.1213	30.8	15	0	0	0	0	0	0	0	0	0	0	0	0	0	0	0	15	0	0	0	0	0	0	0	0
albumin	8	.2353	.4765	36.8	0	0	0	2	6	0	0	0	0	0	0	0	0	0	0	6	0	0	0	0	0	0	2	0	0
albums	2	.0000	.0243	23.9	0	0	0	0	1	0	1	0	0	0	0	0	0	0	0	0	0	0	0	0	0	0	0	2	0
Alces	3	.0000	.0314	25.0	0	0	3	0	0	0	0	0	0	0	0	0	0	0	0	0	0	0	0	0	0	0	3	0	0
ALCHEMIST	8	.0000	.0859	29.3	0	0	0	0	0	8	0	0	0	0	0	8	0	0	0	0	0	0	0	0	0	0	0	0	0
alchemists	21	.3718	1.9281	42.9	3	1	8	5	1	0	3	0	11	0	0	0	0	0	0	2	0	0	0	0	1	0	7	0	0
alchemy	11	.2041	.6035	37.8	0	0	0	5	3	0	3	0	2	0	0	0	0	0	0	2	0	0	0	0	0	0	7	0	0
Alcindor	7	.0000	.0851	29.3	0	2	0	1	0	4	0	0	0	0	0	0	0	0	0	0	0	0	0	0	0	0	0	7	0
Alcock	11	.0000	.5025	37.0	0	0	0	11	0	0	0	0	11	0	0	0	0	0	0	0	0	0	0	0	0	0	0	0	0
alcohol	102	.5194	11.176	50.5	1	3	8	24	13	21	29	3	0	0	7	1	4	2	0	57	0	0	0	0	0	2	24	5	0
alcoholic	18	.2220	1.0550	40.2	0	0	0	1	0	15	1	1	0	0	0	0	0	2	0	15	0	0	0	0	0	0	0	1	0
alcoholics	2	.2405	.1205	30.8	0	0	1	0	0	1	0	0	0	0	0	0	0	0	0	1	0	0	0	0	0	1	0	0	0
alcohols	5	.1275	.1790	32.5	0	0	0	4	1	0	0	0	0	0	0	0	0	0	0	1	0	0	0	0	0	0	4	0	0
Alcott	7	.2331	.4206	36.2	0	1	1	5	0	0	0	0	1	0	0	0	0	0	0	0	0	0	0	0	0	5	0	1	0
alcove	5	.2055	.2584	34.1	0	0	0	0	2	3	0	0	0	0	0	3	0	2	0	0	0	0	0	0	0	0	0	0	0
Alden	2	.1494	.1045	30.2	0	0	0	0	0	2	0	0	1	0	0	0	0	0	0	0	1	0	0	0	0	0	0	0	0
alder	8	.4279	.7847	38.9	1	1	1	0	1	4	0	0	2	0	0	0	0	4	0	0	0	0	0	0	0	1	0	1	0
aldermen	2	.2285	.1129	30.5	0	0	0	0	1	0	1	0	0	0	0	0	0	1	0	0	0	0	0	0	0	0	1	0	0
alders	4	.2424	.3036	34.8	0	3	0	1	0	0	0	0	3	0	0	0	0	0	0	0	0	0	0	0	0	0	0	1	0
Aldrich	7	.0000	.0733	28.6	0	0	1	0	0	6	0	0	0	0	0	0	0	0	0	0	0	0	0	0	0	0	7	0	0
Aldrich's	3	.0000	.0314	25.0	0	0	0	0	0	3	0	0	0	0	0	0	0	0	0	0	0	0	0	0	0	0	3	0	0
Aldrin	13	.0695	.3314	35.2	1	0	0	3	4	4	1	0	0	0	0	0	0	1	0	0	0	0	0	0	0	0	0	12	0
ale	8	.3991	.7280	38.6	2	0	0	1	2	2	1	0	2	0	0	3	0	1	0	0	0	0	0	0	0	0	0	2	0
Alec	87	.2450	4.9873	47.0	0	3	9	5	70	0	0	0	0	0	0	1	9	0	0	0	0	0	0	0	69	3	0	5	0
Alec's	6	.2360	.3419	35.3	0	0	4	0	2	0	0	0	0	0	0	0	4	0	0	0	0	0	0	0	2	0	0	0	0
aleck	2	.0000	.0914	29.6	0	0	0	0	2	0	0	0	2	0	0	0	0	0	0	0	0	0	0	0	0	0	0	0	0
Aleda	4	.0000	.0469	26.7	0	0	0	4	0	0	0	0	0	0	0	0	0	0	0	0	0	0	0	0	4	0	0	0	0
Alejandra	7	.0000	.0851	29.3	0	0	7	0	0	0	0	0	0	0	0	0	0	0	0	0	0	0	0	0	0	0	0	7	0
Alemite	3	.0000	.1370	31.4	0	0	0	0	3	0	0	0	3	0	0	0	0	0	0	0	0	0	0	0	0	0	0	0	0
aleph	4	.1757	.1672	32.2	0	1	0	0	3	0	0	0	0	1	0	0	0	0	3	0	0	0	0	0	0	0	0	0	0
alert	63	.8185	10.350	50.1	5	10	6	6	20	6	10	0	15	4	5	7	1	3	2	3	1	0	2	2	6	3	4	5	0
alerted	7	.4625	.7050	38.5	0	1	0	2	3	1	0	0	1	0	0	0	0	0	0	1	0	0	0	0	1	1	0	3	0

3A airships
3P airspeed
9A airstrips
5A airwaves
9F Aix-la-Chapelle
5P ajar
8Q Ajmer
4A Ak
5A Akana
5Q Akasaka
6P AKC
7F Akh-en-Aten
9Q Akhenaton
8A Aklavik
8E AL
9R Al-Fatah
5Q al-Janubiyah
7P Al-Jazair
4E al-Rashid
6R al-Shatti
5Q al-Yaman
5A Al-ay-ek-sa
8Q Alabian
8R Alamogordo
5E Alan's
6A alarm-clock
5A alarm-riders
6R alarmingly
7B alarum
8R alaska
9N albacore
9R Albano
6J Albeniz
6J Alberich
7B ALBERT
6Q Albertus
3P albino
7A albinos
XH Albireo
4P Albon's
8A Albright
7Q albumen
7Q Albuquerque
7A Alcatraz
5Q Alcelaphus
5Q alces
6P alchemist
9Q alchemists'
8Q Alcide
9D Alcides
6A Alcimide
8R Alcindor's
6R Alco
8H Alcohol
9H alcoholism
8H alcometer
4G alcorque
6P Alcott's
6P Alcotts
7M Aldalox
7J Alder
9D alderman
5F Aldermanbury
7N aldermanic
7J Alders
XR Aldolph
8Q Aldrich-Vreeland
8R Aldrin's
8G ale-drinker
8D ale-house
3P Aleck
6A Aleck's
5Q Alegre
8B alehouse
6A Aleid
8R Aleksandr
8Q Aleksandrovich
7Q Alemanni
7D Aleppo
XR alerting

Word Type	F	D	U	SFI	3 Gr 3	4 Gr 4	5 Gr 5	6 Gr 6	7 Gr 7	8 Gr 8	9 Gr 9	X UnGr	A Read	B Eng & Gr	C Comp	D Lit	E Math	F Soc Stud	G Spell	H Sci	J Music	K Art	L Home Ec	M Shop	N Lib F	P Lib NF	Q Lib Ref	R Mag	S Rel
alertly	2	.2446	.1123	30.5	0	0	0	0	1	0	1	0	0	1	0	0	0	0	0	0	0	0	0	0	0	0	1	0	0
alertness	6	.3852	.5198	37.2	1	0	0	2	0	1	2	0	1	0	0	0	0	0	0	1	0	1	0	0	0	2	1	0	0
alerts	2	.2437	.1129	30.5	0	0	1	1	0	0	0	0	0	0	0	0	0	0	0	0	0	0	0	0	0	0	1	1	0
Alessandro	6	.4408	.5894	37.7	0	1	2	1	0	0	1	1	1	0	0	0	0	0	0	2	0	0	0	0	0	2	1	0	0
Aleut	6	.0688	.1783	32.5	1	0	0	5	0	0	0	0	1	0	0	0	0	0	0	0	0	0	0	0	5	0	0	0	0
Aleutian	8	.4789	.8850	39.5	0	0	5	0	0	2	1	0	4	0	0	0	0	2	0	1	0	0	0	0	0	0	0	1	0
Aleutians	2	.2437	.1129	30.5	0	0	0	0	1	1	0	0	0	0	0	0	0	0	0	0	0	0	0	0	0	0	1	1	0
Aleuts	12	.3015	.8545	39.3	1	0	2	9	0	0	0	0	2	0	0	0	0	0	0	0	1	0	0	0	8	0	0	1	0
alewife	4	.0000	.0486	26.9	0	0	0	1	0	3	0	0	0	0	0	0	0	0	0	0	0	0	0	0	0	0	0	4	0
alewives	5	.1794	.2258	33.5	1	0	0	1	0	3	0	0	0	0	0	0	0	0	0	0	0	0	0	0	1	0	0	4	0
Alex	22	.3812	2.1005	43.2	0	14	0	0	0	1	7	0	14	3	0	0	0	0	0	0	0	0	0	0	5	0	0	0	0
Alex'	2	.0000	.0914	29.6	0	2	0	0	0	0	0	0	2	0	0	0	0	0	0	0	0	0	0	0	0	0	0	0	0
Alexander	72	.6949	10.272	50.1	5	9	10	4	16	17	5	6	13	8	0	0	0	12	0	8	2	0	0	0	1	11	14	3	0
Alexander's	4	.2278	.2911	34.6	2	1	0	0	0	1	0	0	3	0	0	0	0	0	0	0	1	0	0	0	0	0	0	0	0
Alexandra	10	.1982	.4712	36.7	0	0	0	0	0	0	10	0	0	0	0	8	0	0	0	0	2	0	0	0	0	0	0	0	0
Alexandre	3	.1169	.1277	31.1	0	1	0	0	1	1	0	0	1	0	0	0	0	0	0	0	0	0	0	0	0	0	2	0	0
Alexandria	13	.3772	1.1056	40.4	0	4	1	0	5	1	2	0	0	0	0	0	0	9	0	1	0	0	0	0	0	0	2	1	0
Alexandrian	3	.2239	.1775	32.5	0	0	0	0	0	1	2	0	0	0	0	0	0	2	0	1	0	0	0	0	0	0	0	0	0
alexandrine	4	.0000	.0438	26.4	0	0	0	0	0	0	0	4	0	4	0	0	0	0	0	0	0	0	0	0	0	0	0	0	0
Alexis	3	.3754	.2470	33.9	0	0	0	0	0	0	2	1	0	1	0	0	0	0	0	1	0	0	0	0	0	0	1	0	0
Alf	17	.0000	.2461	33.9	0	17	0	0	0	0	0	0	0	0	0	0	0	0	0	0	0	0	0	0	0	17	0	0	0
alfalfa	23	.4666	2.4037	43.8	1	1	5	13	1	1	1	0	5	1	0	0	0	12	0	3	0	0	0	0	0	0	2	0	0
Alfonso	5	.2445	.3875	35.9	0	0	4	0	0	1	0	0	4	0	0	0	0	0	0	0	0	0	0	0	0	0	0	1	0
Alfred	33	.6584	4.4815	46.5	2	3	3	6	10	1	5	3	7	5	0	1	0	3	2	0	2	0	0	0	0	1	10	2	0
Alfred's	3	.3766	.2497	34.0	0	1	0	1	1	0	0	0	0	0	0	0	0	1	0	0	0	0	0	0	0	1	1	0	0
alga	3	.2427	.1822	32.6	0	1	0	0	0	0	1	1	0	0	0	0	0	0	0	2	0	0	0	0	0	0	0	1	0
algae	64	.3900	5.5950	47.5	15	4	15	13	7	0	4	6	1	0	0	1	0	0	0	45	0	0	0	0	1	0	11	5	0
algebra	27	.5579	3.1373	45.0	0	0	2	1	4	9	11	0	1	4	0	0	15	1	0	1	0	0	0	1	0	0	2	2	0
algebraic	4	.2220	.2176	33.4	0	0	0	0	0	3	1	0	0	0	0	0	3	0	0	0	0	0	0	0	0	0	1	0	0
Algenib	3	.0000	.0591	27.7	0	0	0	0	0	0	0	3	0	0	0	0	0	0	0	3	0	0	0	0	0	0	0	0	0
Algeria	47	.3207	3.5176	45.5	7	1	1	21	7	0	10	0	0	0	0	0	0	34	0	0	0	0	0	0	0	5	8	0	0
Algeria's	5	.0000	.0972	29.9	0	0	0	1	0	0	4	0	0	0	0	0	0	5	0	0	0	0	0	0	0	0	0	0	0
Algerian	8	.3513	.6420	38.1	0	0	0	2	2	0	4	0	0	0	0	0	0	5	0	0	0	0	0	0	0	2	0	1	0
Algerians	4	.2285	.2258	33.5	2	0	0	0	0	0	2	0	0	0	0	0	0	2	0	0	0	0	0	0	0	0	2	0	0
Algernon	2	.1814	.1187	30.7	0	0	1	0	1	0	0	0	1	0	0	0	0	0	0	0	0	0	0	0	0	0	0	1	0
Algiers	5	.3220	.3933	35.9	1	0	0	1	2	0	1	0	1	0	0	0	0	2	0	0	0	0	0	0	0	2	0	0	0
Algonquian	2	.2401	.1133	30.5	1	0	0	0	1	0	0	0	0	0	0	0	0	0	0	0	0	0	0	0	0	1	1	0	0
Algonquians	2	.0000	.0290	24.6	2	0	0	0	0	0	0	0	0	0	0	0	0	0	0	0	0	0	0	0	0	2	0	0	0
Algonquin	2	.1840	.0808	29.1	1	0	1	0	0	0	0	0	0	0	1	0	0	0	1	0	0	0	0	0	0	0	0	0	0
algorithm	10	.0000	.1497	31.8	0	0	0	0	9	0	1	0	0	0	0	0	10	0	0	0	0	0	0	0	0	0	0	0	0
Algorithm	2	.0000	.0299	24.8	0	0	0	0	0	2	0	0	0	0	0	0	2	0	0	0	0	0	0	0	0	0	0	0	0
Alhambra	4	.1349	.2265	33.6	0	0	0	3	0	0	1	0	3	0	1	0	0	0	0	0	0	0	0	0	0	0	0	0	0
Ali	65	.6078	8.4472	49.3	0	36	8	16	0	2	3	0	29	10	0	10	1	2	0	0	0	0	0	0	8	0	5	0	0
alibi	3	.3875	.2489	34.0	1	0	0	0	0	1	1	0	0	1	0	1	0	0	0	0	0	0	0	0	1	0	0	0	0
Alice	223	.5765	27.260	54.4	14	50	114	4	6	26	5	4	59	36	2	0	15	8	1	0	0	0	0	0	83	16	3	0	0
Alice's	7	.4703	.7109	38.5	1	2	2	1	1	0	0	0	1	0	0	0	1	0	0	0	0	0	0	0	3	1	1	0	0
Alicia	6	.0000	.2741	34.4	0	0	6	0	0	0	0	0	6	0	0	0	0	0	0	0	0	0	0	0	0	0	0	0	0
alien	17	.6476	2.2402	43.5	0	1	2	0	8	3	3	0	0	0	0	4	0	3	1	0	0	0	0	0	1	2	3	3	0
Alien	4	.0000	.0778	28.9	0	0	0	0	0	4	0	0	0	0	0	0	0	4	0	0	0	0	0	0	0	0	0	0	0
alienated	4	.0000	.0486	26.9	0	0	0	0	1	2	1	0	0	0	0	0	0	0	0	0	0	0	0	0	0	0	0	4	0
alienating	2	.1814	.1187	30.7	0	0	0	0	1	1	0	0	1	0	0	0	0	0	0	0	0	0	0	0	0	0	0	1	0
Alighieri	2	.0000	.0209	23.2	0	0	2	0	0	0	0	0	0	0	0	0	0	0	0	0	0	0	0	0	0	0	2	0	0
alight	12	.4516	1.1795	40.7	0	1	5	0	4	1	1	0	2	0	0	3	0	0	0	0	0	0	0	0	5	1	0	1	0
alighted	9	.3672	.8061	39.1	1	1	1	1	3	0	1	1	4	0	0	2	0	0	0	0	0	0	0	0	0	3	0	0	0
alighting	2	.1787	.1174	30.7	0	0	0	1	1	0	0	0	1	0	0	0	0	0	0	0	0	0	0	0	1	0	0	0	0
align	4	.3617	.3238	35.1	0	0	0	2	1	0	1	0	0	0	0	0	2	0	0	1	0	0	0	0	0	0	0	1	0
aligned	5	.4059	.4286	36.3	0	1	0	0	1	0	2	1	0	0	0	0	0	0	0	0	0	0	0	1	0	1	2	1	0
alignment	7	.5485	.7938	39.0	0	0	2	0	3	1	1	0	0	0	0	0	0	0	1	2	0	0	0	1	0	1	1	1	0
alike	463	.9324	85.349	59.3	119	97	37	59	71	55	21	4	51	51	5	18	40	26	62	88	38	4	8	6	18	26	13	8	1
Alioto	6	.0000	.0729	28.6	0	0	0	0	0	0	6	0	0	0	0	0	0	0	0	0	0	0	0	0	0	0	0	6	0
Alioto's	3	.0000	.0365	25.6	0	0	0	0	0	0	3	0	0	0	0	0	0	0	0	0	0	0	0	0	0	0	0	3	0
Alison	2	.2420	.1154	30.6	0	0	0	2	0	0	0	0	0	0	0	0	1	0	0	0	0	0	0	0	1	0	0	0	0
alive	376	.8146	61.778	57.9	73	52	67	43	81	35	14	11	92	9	1	27	1	18	1	120	13	2	0	0	30	22	19	21	0
alkali	12	.4397	1.1654	40.7	1	1	0	0	5	5	0	0	1	0	0	0	0	1	0	6	0	0	0	0	0	1	3	0	0
alkaline	4	.1995	.2197	33.4	0	0	1	0	0	0	1	2	0	0	0	0	0	1	0	3	0	0	0	0	0	0	0	0	0
Alkemade	6	.0000	.2741	34.4	0	0	0	6	0	0	0	0	6	0	0	0	0	0	0	0	0	0	0	0	0	0	0	0	0
Alkemade's	2	.0000	.0914	29.6	0	0	0	2	0	0	0	0	2	0	0	0	0	0	0	0	0	0	0	0	0	0	0	0	0
all	16997	.9797	3280.2	75.2	3493	2778	1891	2197	3023	1826	1392	397	4921	755	177	1143	779	1405	406	1658	599	132	186	152	1502	1428	767	956	31
All	40	.6115	5.1466	47.1	4	6	6	9	5	7	2	1	13	1	0	3	0	1	0	0	10	0	0	0	3	0	4	5	0
ALL	5	.3666	.4171	36.2	0	0	2	0	2	0	1	0	1	0	0	2	0	1	0	0	0	0	1	0	0	0	0	0	0
all-American	3	.2279	.2143	33.3	2	1	0	0	0	0	0	0	2	0	0	0	0	0	0	0	0	0	0	0	0	0	0	1	0
All-American	5	.3285	.3649	35.6	0	1	0	3	0	0	1	0	0	0	0	0	0	0	0	0	0	0	0	0	1	1	0	3	0
All-Star	3	.0000	.0365	25.6	0	0	0	1	0	0	2	0	0	0	0	0	0	0	0	0	0	0	0	0	0	0	0	3	0
All-State	2	.2443	.1130	30.5	0	0	0	0	1	1	0	0	0	0	0	1	0	0	0	0	0	0	0	0	1	0	0	0	0
all-day	6	.5433	.6738	38.3	1	1	3	0	1	0	0	0	0	1	0	1	0	1	0	0	1	0	0	0	2	0	0	0	0
all-fired	4	.2381	.2674	34.3	1	0	0	1	1	1	0	0	2	0	1	0	0	0	0	0	0	0	0	0	1	0	0	0	0
all-important	10	.6633	1.3742	41.4	0	0	1	3	1	2	2	1	2	0	0	0	0	1	0	2	1	0	0	0	0	2	1	1	0
all-inclusive	4	.4803	.4071	36.1	1	0	0	1	1	1	0	0	0	0	0	0	0	0	0	1	0	0	0	0	0	1	1	1	0
all-night	5	.4173	.4622	36.6	0	0	1	0	4	0	0	0	1	0	0	1	0	0	0	0	0	0	0	0	0	0	2	1	0
all-out	10	.3095	.6976	38.4	1	0	0	1	4	1	3	0	0	0	0	0	0	1	0	0	0	0	0	0	0	1	1	7	0
all-over	3	.0000	.0055	17.4	0	0	3	0	0	0	0	0	0	0	0	0	0	0	0	0	0	3	0	0	0	0	0	0	0
all-powerful	2	.0000	.0389	25.9	0	0	1	0	1	0	0	0	0	0	0	0	0	2	0	0	0	0	0	0	0	0	0	0	0
all-purpose	5	.1725	.2593	34.1	1	0	0	0	4	0	0	0	2	0	0	0	0	0	0	0	0	0	0	2	0	0	0	1	0
all-round	6	.4024	.5158	37.1	0	0	0	0	2	0	3	1	0	0	0	1	0	1	0	0	0	0	0	1	0	0	0	3	0
all-star	3	.3380	.2498	34.0	0	0	0	2	1	0	0	0	1	1	0	0	0	0	0	1	0	0	0	0	0	0	0	0	0
all-state	3	.1277	.1363	31.3	0	0	0	2	1	0	0	0	1	0	0	0	0	0	0	0	0	0	0	0	0	0	0	2	0
All-the-Beaver-there-was	2	.0000	.0234	23.7	0	2	0	0	0	0	0	0	0	0	0	0	0	0	0	0	0	0	0	0	2	0	0	0	0
All-the-Cow-there-was	4	.0000	.0469	26.7	0	4	0	0	0	0	0	0	0	0	0	0	0	0	0	0	0	0	0	0	4	0	0	0	0
All-the-Elephant-there**	5	.0000	.0586	27.7	0	5	0	0	0	0	0	0	0	0	0	0	0	0	0	0	0	0	0	0	5	0	0	0	0
All-the-Turtle-there-was	2	.0000	.0234	23.7	0	2	0	0	0	0	0	0	0	0	0	0	0	0	0	0	0	0	0	0	2	0	0	0	0
all-time	9	.0000	.1094	30.4	0	1	0	3	2	1	1	1	0	0	0	0	0	0	0	0	0	0	0	0	0	0	0	9	0
all-water	2	.0000	.0389	25.9	0	1	1	0	0	0	0	0	0	0	0	0	0	2	0	0	0	0	0	0	0	0	0	0	0

8B Alex's
7Q Alexanders
9D Alexandra's
7Q Alexandrians
3A Alexandrova
XR Alfa
7A alfilaria
XH Alfonsine
5A Alfonso's
7A Alfredo
XH Algae
9R algal
9N Alger
7P Algerie
5F Algonkian
8F Algonquins
4E algorism
8Q Ali's
9P aliases
7P alienate
8R alienation
9F aliens
7Q aligning
7G alike-words
3A alikenesses
7H alimentary
4B alimonia
9R Alioto-arranged
5R Alison's
8A Alive
9J aliveness
9D Aljinavich
5Q alkalies
8M alkalis
8Q alkalosis
5F Alki
7F all-Ethiopian
9R all-European
8F all-Negro
8R All-Pro
7N All-Stars
5A all-around
6A all-astronaut
5R all-black
9D all-comprehensive
7B all-dreaded
7Q all-electric
7Q all-embracing
5P all-encompassing
8A all-gifted
3H all-glass
7R all-male
7R all-new
4R all-professional
8F all-steel
9Q all-too-ailing

Word Type	F	D	U	SFI	3 Gr 3	4 Gr 4	5 Gr 5	6 Gr 6	7 Gr 7	8 Gr 8	9 Gr 9	X UnGr	A Read	B Eng & Gr	C Comp	D Lit	E Math	F Soc Stud	G Spell	H Sci	J Music	K Art	L Home Ec	M Shop	N Lib F	P Lib NF	Q Lib Ref	R Mag	S Rel
all's	5	.4543	.4933	36.9	0	1	1	1	1	0	1	0	1	0	0	1	0	0	0	0	0	0	1	0	1	1	0	0	0
alla	2	.0000	.0162	22.1	0	0	1	1	0	0	0	0	0	0	0	0	0	0	0	0	2	0	0	0	0	0	0	0	0
Allah	11	.5574	1.2817	41.1	0	3	0	4	2	1	1	0	1	3	0	1	0	3	0	0	0	1	0	0	1	0	0	1	0
Allan	45	.6280	6.1047	47.9	6	3	1	17	2	13	0	3	26	0	0	0	0	9	1	0	1	0	0	0	0	4	2	2	0
Allan's	3	.2197	.2090	33.2	0	1	0	2	0	0	0	0	2	0	0	0	0	0	0	0	0	0	0	0	0	0	1	0	0
allantois	4	.0000	.0419	26.2	0	0	0	0	4	0	0	0	0	0	0	0	0	0	0	0	0	0	0	0	0	0	4	0	0
allay	2	.0000	.0209	23.2	0	0	0	0	1	0	1	0	0	0	0	0	0	0	0	0	0	0	0	0	0	0	2	0	0
allay-oop	2	.0000	.0914	29.6	2	0	0	0	0	0	0	0	2	0	0	0	0	0	0	0	0	0	0	0	0	0	0	0	0
allegations	2	.0000	.0243	23.9	0	0	0	0	1	0	1	0	0	0	0	0	0	0	0	0	0	0	0	0	0	0	0	2	0
alleged	5	.4311	.4755	36.8	0	0	0	0	3	0	2	0	1	0	0	1	0	0	0	0	0	0	0	0	0	0	1	2	0
allegedly	4	.3519	.3117	34.9	0	0	0	0	2	1	1	0	0	0	0	0	0	1	0	0	0	0	0	0	0	0	1	2	0
Allegheny	19	.4817	2.0603	43.1	2	2	6	3	3	2	0	1	6	0	0	0	0	8	0	1	0	0	0	0	0	3	0	1	0
allegiance	21	.6796	2.9397	44.7	1	2	1	4	4	4	5	0	4	0	0	2	0	7	1	0	2	0	0	0	1	1	3	0	0
Allegiance	7	.3683	.6352	38.0	0	3	0	0	0	1	3	0	3	0	0	0	0	3	0	0	1	0	0	0	0	0	0	0	0
allegorical	2	.2433	.1158	30.6	0	0	0	1	0	0	0	1	0	0	0	0	0	0	0	0	0	0	0	0	0	1	0	1	0
allegory	3	.3863	.2513	34.0	0	0	1	0	1	0	1	0	0	0	0	0	0	0	0	0	0	0	0	0	1	1	0	1	0
allegro	7	.1253	.2239	33.5	0	0	2	1	1	3	0	0	0	0	0	0	0	0	0	0	6	0	0	0	0	0	1	0	0
Allegro	3	.0000	.0243	23.8	0	0	2	0	1	0	0	0	0	0	0	0	0	0	0	0	3	0	0	0	0	0	0	0	0
Alleluia	4	.0000	.0323	25.1	1	0	0	0	2	0	1	0	0	0	0	0	0	0	0	0	4	0	0	0	0	0	0	0	0
allemande	2	.0000	.0162	22.1	0	0	1	0	0	1	0	0	0	0	0	0	0	0	0	0	2	0	0	0	0	0	0	0	0
Allen	86	.6266	11.319	50.5	29	13	6	5	15	3	14	1	24	6	0	0	4	16	0	0	0	1	0	0	5	0	2	28	0
Allen's	3	.3795	.2506	34.0	0	0	0	0	1	1	1	0	0	0	0	0	0	1	0	0	0	0	0	0	1	0	0	1	0
Allens	12	.0562	.3775	35.8	1	10	1	0	0	0	0	0	1	0	0	0	0	11	0	0	0	0	0	0	0	0	0	0	0
Aller	2	.0000	.0914	29.6	0	0	0	0	2	0	0	0	2	0	0	0	0	0	0	0	0	0	0	0	0	0	0	0	0
Allerton	10	.0000	.4568	36.6	10	0	0	0	0	0	0	0	10	0	0	0	0	0	0	0	0	0	0	0	0	0	0	0	0
Allerton's	2	.0000	.0914	29.6	2	0	0	0	0	0	0	0	2	0	0	0	0	0	0	0	0	0	0	0	0	0	0	0	0
alleviate	2	.2433	.1158	30.6	0	0	0	0	1	0	0	1	0	0	0	0	0	0	0	0	0	0	0	0	0	1	0	1	0
alleviated	2	.2433	.1158	30.6	0	0	0	0	2	0	0	0	0	0	0	0	0	0	0	0	0	0	0	0	0	1	0	1	0
alley	43	.5727	5.5057	47.4	20	1	5	4	8	3	2	0	30	1	0	4	2	0	0	4	0	0	0	0	0	1	0	1	0
Alley	12	.2882	.7610	38.8	1	0	0	0	9	1	1	0	0	0	0	1	0	0	0	0	8	0	0	0	0	1	0	2	0
alleys	15	.6184	1.9280	42.9	1	3	1	1	4	4	1	0	2	0	1	1	0	5	0	0	0	0	0	0	0	2	2	2	0
alleyway	2	.0000	.0914	29.6	0	0	0	1	1	0	0	0	2	0	0	0	0	0	0	0	0	0	0	0	0	0	0	0	0
alliance	15	.5213	1.6451	42.2	1	0	1	0	1	8	4	0	0	0	0	0	0	7	0	0	1	0	0	0	0	1	3	3	0
Alliance	8	.2348	.4745	36.8	0	0	0	0	3	4	1	0	0	0	0	0	0	6	0	0	0	0	0	0	0	0	2	0	0
alliances	4	.2348	.2372	33.8	0	0	1	0	0	1	2	0	0	0	0	0	0	3	0	0	0	0	0	0	0	0	1	0	0
allied	23	.6624	3.0955	44.9	4	0	3	1	3	4	7	1	0	0	0	1	1	5	0	0	1	0	0	1	0	3	6	5	0
Allied	21	.4407	2.0353	43.1	0	6	0	3	3	6	3	0	2	0	0	0	0	10	0	0	0	0	0	0	0	1	6	2	0
allies	30	.5610	3.5236	45.5	0	0	2	5	8	5	9	1	1	1	0	0	0	13	0	1	0	0	0	0	1	1	5	7	0
Allies	34	.4009	3.0086	44.8	2	4	3	2	7	11	5	0	0	0	0	0	0	20	0	0	0	0	0	0	0	3	9	2	0
alligator	34	.7172	5.0350	47.0	10	3	2	9	7	2	1	0	14	1	0	3	0	1	1	0	1	0	0	1	8	1	3	0	0
Alligator	25	.3438	2.3469	43.7	3	21	1	0	0	0	0	0	21	0	0	0	0	0	0	0	1	0	0	0	3	0	0	0	0
alligator's	3	.3450	.2505	34.0	2	0	0	1	0	0	0	0	1	0	0	0	0	0	0	0	0	0	0	0	1	1	0	0	0
alligators	33	.5563	4.0725	46.1	21	1	0	3	6	1	0	1	17	0	0	1	0	0	0	10	0	0	0	0	0	2	1	2	0
Alligators	2	.0000	.0234	23.7	2	0	0	0	0	0	0	0	0	0	0	0	0	0	0	0	0	0	0	0	2	0	0	0	0
Allis	2	.0000	.0914	29.6	0	0	0	2	0	0	0	0	2	0	0	0	0	0	0	0	0	0	0	0	0	0	0	0	0
Allison	3	.3465	.2515	34.0	0	1	0	0	1	0	1	0	1	0	0	0	0	0	0	0	0	0	0	0	0	1	0	1	0
allosaurus	3	.0000	.0434	26.4	0	3	0	0	0	0	0	0	0	0	0	0	0	0	0	0	0	0	0	0	0	3	0	0	0
Allosaurus	9	.0000	.1303	31.1	9	0	0	0	0	0	0	0	0	0	0	0	0	0	0	0	0	0	0	0	0	9	0	0	0
allot	3	.3855	.2503	34.0	1	0	0	0	1	0	1	0	0	1	0	0	0	0	0	0	0	0	0	0	0	1	0	1	0
allotted	10	.5400	1.1049	40.4	1	0	2	0	2	1	4	0	0	0	0	1	1	0	0	0	0	0	2	1	0	2	3	0	0
allover	2	.0000	.0037	15.7	0	1	0	1	0	0	0	0	0	0	0	0	0	0	0	0	0	2	0	0	0	0	0	0	0
allow	229	.8229	37.668	55.8	20	24	22	29	46	41	37	10	23	12	2	8	9	16	2	41	1	3	19	18	20	19	14	22	0
allowable	2	.2427	.1159	30.6	0	0	0	0	1	0	1	0	0	0	0	0	1	0	0	0	0	0	0	0	0	0	0	1	0
allowance	64	.4270	5.8445	47.7	1	6	1	6	15	19	15	1	9	9	0	0	5	1	2	1	0	0	26	3	3	1	1	3	0
allowances	27	.3649	2.0753	43.2	0	0	2	0	1	8	16	0	1	0	0	0	3	1	0	0	0	0	13	4	0	0	2	3	0
allowed	278	.9190	50.667	57.0	21	37	31	34	56	60	29	10	59	3	3	16	4	50	3	19	3	4	5	5	25	31	18	30	0
allowing	34	.7442	5.1096	47.1	2	0	3	2	18	2	5	2	4	0	0	1	0	2	0	4	0	2	2	2	3	4	3	7	0
allows	60	.7415	9.0085	49.5	4	7	9	9	13	12	5	1	5	1	0	1	7	6	1	16	0	0	4	0	1	3	10	5	0
alloy	34	.4001	3.1572	45.0	13	1	0	3	3	5	9	0	12	0	0	0	4	1	0	6	0	0	0	7	0	0	3	1	0
alloyed	2	.2278	.1128	30.5	0	1	0	0	0	0	1	0	0	0	0	0	0	0	0	1	0	0	0	0	0	0	1	0	0
alloys	28	.4804	2.9485	44.7	6	5	0	6	2	5	2	2	6	0	0	0	0	0	0	9	0	0	0	1	0	2	10	0	0
allspice	3	.3179	.2054	33.1	0	0	1	0	0	1	0	1	0	1	0	0	0	0	0	0	0	0	1	0	0	0	0	1	0
alluded	4	.3699	.3150	35.0	0	0	0	1	2	0	1	0	0	1	1	1	0	0	0	0	0	0	0	0	0	1	0	0	0
alludes	2	.0000	.0290	24.6	0	0	0	2	0	0	0	0	0	0	0	0	0	0	0	0	0	0	0	0	0	2	0	0	0
alluring	4	.3540	.3119	34.9	0	0	0	1	1	1	0	1	0	0	0	0	0	0	0	1	1	0	0	0	0	0	0	2	0
allus	2	.0000	.0234	23.7	0	0	1	0	1	0	0	0	0	0	0	0	0	0	0	0	0	0	0	0	2	0	0	0	0
allusions	7	.3355	.5015	37.0	0	0	0	0	1	3	3	0	0	3	2	1	0	0	0	0	0	0	0	0	0	0	0	1	0
alluvial	10	.2652	.6590	38.2	0	0	1	0	1	2	5	1	0	0	0	0	0	1	0	8	0	0	0	0	0	0	1	0	0
Alluvial	4	.2353	.2382	33.8	0	0	1	0	0	3	0	0	0	0	0	0	0	0	0	3	0	0	0	0	0	0	1	0	0
ally	20	.6216	2.5444	44.1	1	0	1	1	8	3	5	1	0	0	0	0	0	6	3	0	0	0	1	0	0	4	4	2	0
alma	3	.3781	.2493	34.0	0	0	0	0	1	2	0	0	0	1	0	0	0	1	0	0	0	0	0	0	0	0	0	1	0
Alma	5	.2445	.3875	35.9	0	2	0	0	2	0	1	0	4	0	0	0	0	0	0	0	0	0	0	0	0	0	0	1	0
almanac	6	.3356	.4485	36.5	1	3	0	1	0	1	0	0	0	1	0	1	0	0	0	0	0	0	0	0	0	4	0	0	0
Almanac	11	.4848	1.1239	40.5	0	4	1	0	4	0	2	0	0	4	0	0	0	1	0	1	0	0	0	0	0	3	2	0	0
almanacs	12	.5101	1.3314	41.2	0	1	1	2	0	7	0	1	2	2	0	0	0	5	0	2	0	0	0	0	0	0	0	1	0
almighty	3	.3394	.2451	33.9	0	1	0	0	0	1	1	0	1	0	0	1	0	0	0	0	0	0	0	0	1	0	0	0	0
Almighty	8	.5677	.9912	40.0	0	0	0	1	3	3	1	0	4	1	0	1	0	0	0	0	0	0	0	0	1	0	0	1	0
almirante	2	.0000	.0219	23.4	0	0	0	0	0	0	0	2	0	2	0	0	0	0	0	0	0	0	0	0	0	0	0	0	0
almond	6	.0971	.2435	33.9	1	4	0	1	0	0	0	0	1	0	0	0	0	5	0	0	0	0	0	0	0	0	0	0	0
almonds	6	.4338	.5783	37.6	0	0	1	1	1	0	3	0	1	0	0	0	2	1	0	1	0	0	1	0	0	0	0	0	0
almost	2324	.9390	432.01	66.4	372	364	287	329	450	244	208	70	617	88	26	106	25	380	33	248	58	18	16	15	143	222	162	167	0
alms	2	.2444	.1132	30.5	0	1	0	1	0	0	0	0	0	1	0	0	0	0	0	0	0	0	0	0	1	0	0	0	0
Alnico	3	.0000	.0591	27.7	1	0	0	0	0	0	2	0	0	0	0	0	0	0	0	3	0	0	0	0	0	0	0	0	0
aloft	25	.6657	3.4785	45.4	0	5	1	2	9	6	1	1	9	0	0	2	0	0	0	5	1	1	0	0	5	0	1	1	0
aloha	8	.3876	.7871	39.0	5	1	0	1	0	1	0	0	6	0	0	0	0	0	1	0	1	0	0	0	0	0	0	0	0
Aloha	3	.1621	.1254	31.0	0	0	1	0	2	0	0	0	0	0	0	0	0	1	0	0	2	0	0	0	0	0	0	0	0
Alois	14	.0000	.6396	38.1	0	0	14	0	0	0	0	0	14	0	0	0	0	0	0	0	0	0	0	0	0	0	0	0	0
alone	825	.9533	155.44	61.9	146	128	83	97	180	90	86	15	270	59	7	63	5	50	13	65	32	7	17	2	86	53	37	58	1
Alone	2	.0000	.0215	23.3	0	0	0	0	0	2	0	0	0	0	0	2	0	0	0	0	0	0	0	0	0	0	0	0	0
along	2835	.9675	541.10	67.3	537	506	403	367	520	251	191	60	779	86	29	179	84	476	28	239	91	14	46	25	187	255	148	168	1
alongside	79	.7947	12.712	51.0	11	15	6	13	23	7	4	0	25	5	1	2	0	5	1	1	1	0	0	1	15	14	1	7	0
Alonso	2	.2351	.1166	30.7	0	0	1	0	0	0	1	0	0	0	0	0	0	1	0	0	0	0	0	0	0	0	0	1	0
Alonzo	49	.0000	2.2384	43.5	47	0	2	0	0	0	0	0	49	0	0	0	0	0	0	0	0	0	0	0	0	0	0	0	0
Alonzo's	2	.0000	.0914	29.6	2	0	0	0	0	0	0	0	2	0	0	0	0	0	0	0	0	0	0	0	0	0	0	0	0
aloof	8	.5072	.8616	39.4	0	1	1	1	1	2	2	0	1	0	0	2	0	0	1	0	0	0	0	0	1	3	0	0	0

3A Allard
8R allayed
8Q allaying
4J Alle
8R allegation
7N Alleghany
9R allegories
XQ allele
XQ alleles
6G allelon
7J alleluia
7P allemandes
XR Allendale
4F Allens'
5R Allentown
XB aller
9L allergies
9L allergy
8Q alleviation
6R alleyways
8F Alliances
6P Allie
9Q allies'
6A ALLIGATOR
9P Allisons
5P allocation
5P allocations
4P allosaurs
9B allotment
4Q Alloy
8Q alloy-surface
3A alls
5A Allston
8B allude
7P allures
8B allusion
8F allusive
5Q alluvium
9R Allyson
XH Almach
6F Almaden
8H Almagest
4P Almanacs
4H Almanor
7R almendro
6Q Almon
8F almond-shaped
6A almond-tree
3A almost-eleven
3A almost-forgotten
7H alnico
4A aloes
7R alongshore

Word Type	F	D	U	SFI	3 Gr 3	4 Gr 4	5 Gr 5	6 Gr 6	7 Gr 7	8 Gr 8	9 Gr 9	X UnGr	A Read	B Eng & Gr	C Comp	D Lit	E Math	F Soc Stud	G Spell	H Sci	J Music	K Art	L Home Ec	M Shop	N Lib F	P Lib NF	Q Lib Ref	R Mag	S Rel
aloofness	3	.2060	.1500	31.8	0	0	1	0	2	0	0	0	0	0	0	2	0	0	0	0	0	0	0	0	0	1	0	0	0
aloud	230	.6378	30.273	54.8	40	41	25	47	38	22	16	1	44	98	15	11	4	3	6	0	5	1	0	0	18	14	0	11	0
alp	4	.0000	.1827	32.6	0	4	0	0	0	0	0	0	4	0	0	0	0	0	0	0	0	0	0	0	0	0	0	0	0
alpha	9	.4301	.8318	39.2	0	0	2	4	1	1	1	0	0	1	0	0	0	0	3	4	0	0	0	0	0	0	1	0	0
Alpha	12	.1593	.5316	37.3	0	1	0	0	0	10	0	1	0	0	0	3	1	0	0	7	0	0	0	0	0	0	0	0	1
alphabet	206	.6833	28.676	54.6	50	34	22	12	61	16	4	7	34	47	1	3	12	3	74	1	6	6	2	4	1	8	3	1	0
Alphabet	2	.1948	.1250	31.0	1	1	0	0	0	0	0	0	1	0	0	0	0	0	0	0	0	0	0	0	0	1	0	0	0
alphabetic	7	.3676	.5482	37.4	0	0	1	0	4	1	1	0	0	2	0	0	0	0	3	0	0	0	0	0	0	0	2	0	0
alphabetical	204	.2478	11.937	50.8	63	65	31	28	11	5	1	0	23	36	0	0	1	1	137	1	0	0	0	0	0	0	4	1	0
alphabetically	17	.4105	1.5008	41.8	0	5	2	3	5	2	0	0	1	9	0	0	0	1	3	0	0	0	0	0	0	0	3	0	0
alphabetize	20	.0565	.3779	35.8	4	6	8	1	1	0	0	0	0	1	0	0	0	0	19	0	0	0	0	0	0	0	0	0	0
alphabets	6	.3502	.5164	37.1	1	0	0	2	1	1	1	0	3	0	0	0	0	0	1	0	0	1	0	0	0	0	0	1	0
alphabetum	2	.0000	.0162	22.1	0	0	0	2	0	0	0	0	0	0	0	0	0	0	2	0	0	0	0	0	0	0	0	0	0
Alpheratz	5	.0000	.0986	29.9	0	0	0	0	0	0	0	5	0	0	0	0	0	0	0	5	0	0	0	0	0	0	0	0	0
Alphonso	2	.0000	.0299	24.8	0	0	0	0	2	0	0	0	0	0	0	0	2	0	0	0	0	0	0	0	0	0	0	0	0
alphorn	4	.0000	.1827	32.6	4	0	0	0	0	0	0	0	4	0	0	0	0	0	0	0	0	0	0	0	0	0	0	0	0
alpine	6	.1473	.2287	33.6	0	0	0	0	6	0	0	0	0	0	0	0	0	0	0	0	0	0	0	0	0	0	5	1	0
Alpine	11	.3218	.7856	39.0	2	0	3	0	5	1	0	0	0	0	0	1	0	0	0	1	0	0	0	0	0	2	7	0	0
Alps	54	.6032	6.7753	48.3	11	2	6	12	15	4	3	1	5	2	0	2	0	16	0	2	1	0	0	0	0	10	15	1	0
already	1002	.9533	188.67	62.8	107	155	86	135	249	131	111	28	224	69	10	69	46	103	28	90	17	6	14	4	79	93	49	101	0
ALS	2	.0000	.0209	23.2	0	0	0	0	0	0	2	0	0	0	0	0	0	0	0	0	0	0	0	0	0	0	2	0	0
also	4647	.9550	875.79	69.4	499	605	676	576	929	679	549	134	537	250	44	89	275	965	162	777	192	57	120	95	52	265	500	263	4
Alston	3	.3847	.2496	34.0	1	0	1	0	0	1	0	0	0	0	0	0	0	0	0	0	0	0	0	0	0	1	1	1	0
Alstyne	3	.0000	.0352	25.5	0	3	0	0	0	0	0	0	0	0	0	0	0	0	0	0	0	0	0	0	3	0	0	0	0
alt	7	.0000	.0733	28.6	0	0	7	0	0	0	0	0	0	0	0	0	0	0	0	0	0	0	0	0	0	0	7	0	0
Altai	2	.0000	.0209	23.2	0	0	0	0	0	2	0	0	0	0	0	0	0	0	0	0	0	0	0	0	0	0	2	0	0
altar	24	.6279	3.1406	45.0	2	2	1	4	6	2	5	2	5	2	0	5	0	4	0	0	0	0	0	0	0	2	1	5	0
altars	3	.2379	.1705	32.3	1	0	1	0	1	0	0	0	0	0	0	1	0	0	0	0	0	0	0	0	0	2	0	0	0
Altdorf	3	.0000	.1370	31.4	0	0	0	3	0	0	0	0	3	0	0	0	0	0	0	0	0	0	0	0	0	0	0	0	0
alter	32	.4885	3.2646	45.1	0	2	2	1	9	7	10	1	2	0	0	1	0	3	1	1	4	0	9	0	0	0	4	7	0
alteration	12	.2088	.5707	37.6	0	0	0	0	3	2	6	1	0	0	0	0	0	0	0	2	0	0	7	0	0	1	1	1	0
alterations	14	.2906	.8717	39.4	0	1	1	1	2	1	7	1	0	0	0	0	0	0	0	1	2	0	7	0	0	0	3	1	0
altercation	3	.2196	.1554	31.9	0	0	0	0	0	3	0	0	0	0	0	2	0	0	0	0	0	0	0	0	1	0	0	0	0
altered	38	.7335	5.6142	47.5	0	1	1	3	11	9	5	8	2	5	0	3	0	1	0	5	7	0	2	0	1	1	4	7	0
altering	13	.5197	1.3760	41.4	0	0	1	2	6	1	2	1	0	1	0	0	0	0	1	1	1	2	4	0	0	1	1	1	0
alternate	42	.6339	5.3917	47.3	0	2	4	8	7	10	11	0	0	1	0	1	11	1	0	1	10	0	2	5	0	1	8	1	0
alternated	2	.1698	.1133	30.5	0	0	0	1	0	1	0	0	1	0	0	0	0	0	0	0	0	0	0	0	0	0	1	0	0
alternately	14	.5616	1.5942	42.0	0	0	3	2	3	2	3	1	0	1	0	0	0	0	0	0	5	0	2	2	0	1	1	2	0
alternates	3	.0995	.1144	30.6	0	0	1	1	0	1	0	0	1	0	0	0	0	0	0	0	2	0	0	0	0	0	0	0	0
alternating	27	.6511	3.5616	45.5	0	1	2	3	5	9	6	1	0	1	0	0	1	1	0	7	6	1	1	4	0	2	3	0	0
alternating-current	2	.1738	.0790	29.0	0	0	0	0	0	1	1	0	0	0	0	0	0	0	0	0	0	0	0	1	0	0	1	0	0
alternative	21	.6547	2.7871	44.5	0	1	0	1	3	7	6	3	0	2	0	2	1	1	4	1	0	0	0	0	1	0	2	7	0
alternatives	4	.0000	.0486	26.9	0	0	0	0	1	0	2	1	0	0	0	0	0	0	0	0	0	0	0	0	0	0	0	4	0
alters	6	.3773	.4731	36.7	0	1	1	1	0	1	1	1	0	0	0	0	0	0	0	0	2	0	2	0	0	0	1	1	0
although	937	.9297	172.42	62.4	63	80	103	107	260	169	123	32	157	70	8	34	17	141	18	99	57	12	22	4	30	72	119	77	0
altimeter	15	.1035	.5659	37.5	0	0	14	0	0	0	1	0	0	0	0	0	1	0	0	14	0	0	0	0	0	0	0	0	0
altitude	145	.6603	19.759	53.0	4	31	18	18	22	32	19	1	12	1	0	2	40	45	0	28	0	0	0	3	0	3	6	5	0
altitudes	20	.6116	2.5392	44.0	0	2	0	5	5	4	3	1	2	0	1	0	3	1	0	5	0	0	0	0	0	0	3	5	0
alto	23	.0409	.3695	35.7	0	4	2	4	4	3	6	0	0	0	0	0	0	0	0	0	22	0	0	0	0	1	0	0	0
altogether	113	.7716	17.610	52.5	21	13	9	19	25	11	9	6	16	5	0	8	32	7	4	9	0	0	0	0	15	6	5	6	0
altos	3	.0000	.0243	23.8	0	0	0	0	0	1	2	0	0	0	0	0	0	0	0	0	3	0	0	0	0	0	0	0	0
alum	5	.0000	.0986	29.9	0	3	1	1	0	0	0	0	0	0	0	0	0	0	0	5	0	0	0	0	0	0	0	0	0
alumina	4	.3344	.3261	35.1	0	0	1	1	1	0	1	0	1	0	0	0	0	2	0	0	0	0	0	0	0	0	1	0	0
aluminum	134	.5925	16.631	52.2	19	17	8	20	27	17	22	4	25	2	0	0	1	9	0	33	0	3	1	22	1	7	12	18	0
Aluminum	3	.2197	.2090	33.2	2	0	1	0	0	0	0	0	2	0	0	0	0	0	0	0	0	0	0	0	0	0	1	0	0
alumni	3	.1937	.1495	31.7	0	0	1	0	0	0	0	2	0	0	0	0	0	1	0	0	0	0	0	0	0	0	0	2	0
Alva	4	.1999	.1920	32.8	0	2	0	0	2	0	0	0	0	3	0	1	0	0	0	0	0	0	0	0	0	0	0	0	0
Alvarado	3	.0000	.0365	25.6	0	0	0	1	0	0	2	0	0	0	0	0	0	0	0	0	0	0	0	0	0	0	0	3	0
Alvarez	5	.2326	.3837	35.8	0	0	1	0	0	4	0	0	4	0	0	0	0	1	0	0	0	0	0	0	0	0	0	0	0
Alvaro	32	.0000	1.4618	41.6	8	24	0	0	0	0	0	0	32	0	0	0	0	0	0	0	0	0	0	0	0	0	0	0	0
alveoli	2	.0000	.0243	23.9	0	0	0	0	2	0	0	0	0	0	0	0	0	0	0	0	0	0	0	0	0	0	0	2	0
Alvin	40	.2583	3.2888	45.2	15	0	3	10	8	4	0	0	36	3	0	0	0	1	0	0	0	0	0	0	0	0	0	0	0
Alvin's	4	.0000	.1827	32.6	1	0	0	0	3	0	0	0	4	0	0	0	0	0	0	0	0	0	0	0	0	0	0	0	0
alway	2	.0000	.0162	22.1	0	0	2	0	0	0	0	0	0	0	0	0	0	0	0	0	2	0	0	0	0	0	0	0	0
always	2657	.9667	506.70	67.0	521	459	289	359	467	252	226	84	748	188	30	162	111	180	105	231	67	18	45	40	219	268	98	140	7
am	1294	.7560	199.87	63.0	305	240	129	168	206	110	109	27	478	86	12	196	41	36	70	20	28	12	1	0	138	82	4	80	10
Am	8	.2664	.4797	36.8	0	1	1	0	1	0	4	1	0	0	0	0	0	0	1	0	0	0	0	0	0	0	6	1	0
AM	9	.5052	.9515	39.8	1	0	0	1	3	2	2	0	0	0	0	3	1	0	0	2	2	0	0	0	0	1	0	0	0
Ama	8	.0000	.3655	35.6	0	0	8	0	0	0	0	0	8	0	0	0	0	0	0	0	0	0	0	0	0	0	0	0	0
Amadeus	5	.1563	.1897	32.8	1	2	0	1	0	1	0	0	0	0	0	0	0	0	0	0	4	0	0	0	0	0	1	0	0
Amahl	8	.0000	.0647	28.1	0	0	0	2	0	6	0	0	0	0	0	0	0	0	0	0	8	0	0	0	0	0	0	0	0
Amahl's	3	.0000	.0243	23.8	0	0	0	0	0	3	0	0	0	0	0	0	0	0	0	0	3	0	0	0	0	0	0	0	0
Amal	3	.0000	.0322	25.1	0	0	0	0	0	0	3	0	0	0	0	3	0	0	0	0	0	0	0	0	0	0	0	0	0
AMAL	6	.0000	.0644	28.1	0	0	0	0	0	0	6	0	0	0	0	6	0	0	0	0	0	0	0	0	0	0	0	0	0
Amal's	2	.0000	.0215	23.3	0	0	0	0	0	0	2	0	0	0	0	2	0	0	0	0	0	0	0	0	0	0	0	0	0
amalgam	2	.1948	.1250	31.0	1	0	1	0	0	0	0	0	1	0	0	0	0	0	0	0	0	0	0	0	0	1	0	0	0
amalgamated	2	.2446	.1122	30.5	0	0	0	0	0	2	0	0	0	0	0	1	0	0	0	0	0	0	0	0	0	0	1	0	0
Amanda	10	.3829	.9680	39.9	0	1	0	9	0	0	0	0	7	0	0	2	0	0	0	0	1	0	0	0	0	0	0	0	0
Amarillo	2	.0000	.0389	25.9	0	0	1	0	1	0	0	0	0	0	0	0	0	2	0	0	0	0	0	0	0	0	0	0	0
amass	2	.2331	.1157	30.6	0	0	1	0	1	0	0	0	0	0	0	0	0	0	0	1	0	0	0	0	1	0	0	0	0
amassed	6	.3928	.5018	37.0	0	0	0	0	0	1	5	0	0	0	1	1	0	1	0	0	0	0	0	0	0	0	3	0	0
amateur	39	.7402	5.8687	47.7	1	0	5	11	6	3	7	6	7	2	0	1	1	0	1	7	4	0	0	0	0	9	4	3	0
amateurs	20	.5050	2.1220	43.3	0	0	0	6	7	2	2	3	1	0	0	0	0	1	0	2	7	0	0	0	0	5	3	1	0
amaze	2	.1733	.1149	30.6	1	0	0	1	0	0	0	0	1	1	0	0	0	0	0	0	0	0	0	0	0	0	0	0	0
amazed	49	.7163	7.3212	48.6	8	8	9	7	7	5	5	0	25	1	0	2	0	6	1	2	0	0	0	0	2	5	0	5	0
amazement	43	.6773	6.0832	47.8	3	11	4	3	10	4	8	0	18	0	2	9	1	2	1	0	1	0	0	0	1	6	0	2	0
amazes	4	.1814	.2373	33.8	0	1	0	3	0	0	0	0	2	0	0	0	0	0	0	0	0	0	0	0	0	0	0	2	0
amazing	85	.8862	15.004	51.8	6	15	12	11	20	13	3	5	19	8	1	2	2	9	2	11	4	2	0	0	3	7	5	10	0
amazingly	9	.3976	.7828	38.9	1	0	1	2	2	1	2	0	1	0	0	0	0	1	0	0	0	2	0	0	1	2	1	1	0
Amazon	76	.3046	5.5444	47.4	1	16	17	18	10	1	12	1	1	0	0	1	1	64	0	2	0	0	0	0	1	0	5	1	0
ambassador	10	.5928	1.2245	40.9	0	2	0	1	2	2	3	0	1	1	1	0	0	2	1	0	2	0	0	0	0	0	0	2	0
Ambassador	8	.5238	.8771	39.4	0	1	0	0	1	1	5	0	0	1	0	0	0	2	0	0	0	0	0	0	1	1	0	3	0
ambassadors	4	.3832	.3414	35.3	1	0	1	0	1	0	1	0	0	0	0	0	0	2	0	0	0	0	0	0	1	1	0	0	0

8H alot
7B Aloud
6J Alouette
7M Aloxite
8L alpaca
6R Alpert
5F alphabet-makers
3G alphabetized
6G alphabetizing
XH Alphecca
6A Alphonse
8R Alphonzo
3A alphorns
7E Alphy
8R Alpo
4J Alrang
9B alright
5G als
4A Alsace
7P Alsatians
6R Alselmo
7R ALSEP
8R Alsop
4N Alstyne's
4F Alta
XH Altair
6R Altamaha
XR Altamonte
7A altar's
6F altarpieces
8C Altenbergian
8D alternations
5P alternatively
7R Altgeld
9B Althea
6F Althing
7R altho'
5H altimeters
4F altiplano
4E Altoona
5P altruism
6H aluminum-foil
XR aluminumized
7M Alundum
3A Alvaro's
7R alveolus
7R Alvina
5P Alvsborg
4A ALWAYS
7A Alyse
6H alyssum
3A Alzate
8E am+n**
8E am**
9Q Am's
9D AMAL'S
8D Amalekites
3P Amalfi
XR Amalgamated
7A Amalie
6A Amanda's
8G amare
9D amasses
7R amateur-built
6H amateur's
XR amateurism
9D amazedly
8E Amazon's
6F Amazons

Word Type	F	D	U	SFI	3 Gr 3	4 Gr 4	5 Gr 5	6 Gr 6	7 Gr 7	8 Gr 8	9 Gr 9	X UnGr	A Read	B Eng & Gr	C Comp	D Lit	E Math	F Soc Stud	G Spell	H Sci	J Music	K Art	L Home Ec	M Shop	N Lib F	P Lib NF	Q Lib Ref	R Mag	S Rel
Ambassadors	2	.0000	.0389	25.9	2	0	0	0	0	0	0	0	0	0	0	0	0	2	0	0	0	0	0	0	0	0	0	0	0
Ambato	3	.0000	.1370	31.4	0	3	0	0	0	0	0	0	3	0	0	0	0	0	0	0	0	0	0	0	0	0	0	0	0
amber	14	.5713	1.6764	42.2	0	2	1	0	2	9	0	0	2	1	0	0	0	0	1	5	1	0	0	2	1	0	1	0	0
ambergris	4	.4568	.4091	36.1	1	1	1	0	0	0	0	1	1	0	0	0	0	0	0	1	0	0	0	0	0	1	0	1	0
Amberson	4	.0000	.0579	27.6	0	0	0	0	4	0	0	0	0	0	0	0	0	0	0	0	0	0	0	0	0	4	0	0	0
ambient	2	.0000	.0243	23.9	0	0	0	0	2	0	0	0	0	0	0	0	0	0	0	0	0	0	0	0	0	0	0	2	0
ambiguity	2	.0000	.0243	23.9	0	0	0	0	1	1	0	0	0	0	0	0	0	0	0	0	0	0	0	0	0	0	0	2	0
ambiguous	2	.2433	.1158	30.6	0	0	0	0	0	1	1	0	0	0	0	0	0	0	0	0	0	0	0	0	0	1	0	1	0
ambition	38	.7390	5.7229	47.6	4	2	5	4	9	7	7	0	9	5	0	2	0	4	1	0	0	0	0	0	3	4	3	7	0
ambitions	10	.4382	.9563	39.8	0	0	1	0	5	2	2	0	2	3	0	0	0	0	0	0	0	0	2	0	0	1	0	2	0
Ambitioso	2	.0000	.0290	24.6	0	0	0	0	2	0	0	0	0	0	0	0	0	0	0	0	0	0	0	0	0	2	0	0	0
ambitious	35	.7238	5.1385	47.1	0	2	7	3	13	6	3	1	4	1	1	5	0	5	1	0	0	0	0	0	1	8	7	2	0
ambivalence	3	.2143	.1568	32.0	0	0	0	0	2	0	1	0	0	0	0	0	0	0	0	0	0	0	0	0	0	1	0	2	0
ambled	10	.4639	1.1055	40.4	3	4	1	1	0	1	0	0	7	0	0	1	0	1	0	0	0	0	0	0	1	0	0	0	0
ambles	2	.0000	.0914	29.6	0	0	2	0	0	0	0	0	2	0	0	0	0	0	0	0	0	0	0	0	0	0	0	0	0
ambling	4	.4535	.4020	36.0	0	1	1	0	1	1	0	0	1	1	0	0	1	0	0	0	0	0	0	0	1	0	0	0	0
Ambrose	7	.3665	.5554	37.4	0	5	0	0	1	1	0	0	0	0	1	0	0	0	0	0	0	0	0	0	0	4	2	0	0
ambrosia	5	.3833	.4767	36.8	0	0	0	4	0	0	1	0	3	0	0	1	0	0	0	0	0	0	0	0	0	1	0	0	0
ambulance	15	.6298	2.0250	43.1	6	0	0	0	4	3	1	1	8	1	0	0	0	1	2	1	0	0	0	0	1	0	0	1	0
Ambulance	2	.0000	.0914	29.6	0	0	0	0	0	0	2	0	2	0	0	0	0	0	0	0	0	0	0	0	0	0	0	0	0
ambulances	4	.2386	.2998	34.8	1	0	1	1	0	1	0	0	3	0	0	0	0	0	0	0	0	0	0	0	0	0	1	0	0
ambush	12	.5868	1.4887	41.7	1	2	3	1	3	1	1	0	3	0	0	2	0	1	0	0	0	0	0	0	1	3	2	0	0
ambushed	3	.3390	.2450	33.9	0	1	0	0	1	0	0	1	1	0	0	0	0	0	0	0	0	0	0	0	0	0	1	1	0
ambushing	2	.0000	.0209	23.2	0	0	0	0	2	0	0	0	0	0	0	0	0	0	0	0	0	0	0	0	0	0	2	0	0
AMC	5	.0000	.0608	27.8	0	0	0	0	2	0	3	0	0	0	0	0	0	0	0	0	0	0	0	0	0	0	0	5	0
AMC'S	2	.0000	.0243	23.9	0	0	0	0	0	0	2	0	0	0	0	0	0	0	0	0	0	0	0	0	0	0	0	2	0
Amchitka	5	.0000	.0608	27.8	0	0	0	0	0	5	0	0	0	0	0	0	0	0	0	0	0	0	0	0	0	0	0	5	0
ameba	23	.3195	1.7463	42.4	6	0	2	3	11	1	0	0	1	0	0	0	0	0	0	16	0	0	0	0	0	5	1	0	0
amebas	3	.0000	.0591	27.7	0	0	0	0	3	0	0	0	0	0	0	0	0	0	0	3	0	0	0	0	0	0	0	0	0
Amed	21	.0000	.9593	39.8	0	0	0	0	21	0	0	0	21	0	0	0	0	0	0	0	0	0	0	0	0	0	0	0	0
Amed's	3	.0000	.1370	31.4	0	0	0	0	3	0	0	0	3	0	0	0	0	0	0	0	0	0	0	0	0	0	0	0	0
Amelia	25	.0000	1.1421	40.6	0	25	0	0	0	0	0	0	25	0	0	0	0	0	0	0	0	0	0	0	0	0	0	0	0
amen	7	.1253	.2879	34.6	1	1	2	0	0	0	3	0	2	1	0	2	0	0	0	0	1	0	0	0	0	0	0	0	1
Amen	11	.1239	.3518	35.5	0	3	0	3	3	0	2	0	0	0	0	2	0	0	0	0	3	0	0	0	3	1	0	0	2
amend	2	.2306	.1140	30.6	0	0	0	0	0	1	1	0	0	1	0	0	0	1	0	0	0	0	0	0	0	0	0	0	0
amended	7	.5493	.8006	39.0	1	1	0	0	1	2	1	1	0	0	0	1	0	2	0	0	0	0	0	0	2	1	0	1	0
amending	2	.0000	.0389	25.9	0	0	0	0	0	2	0	0	0	0	0	0	0	2	0	0	0	0	0	0	0	0	0	0	0
amendment	12	.5838	1.4833	41.7	1	0	0	0	0	4	7	0	2	0	0	0	0	4	0	2	0	0	0	0	0	1	2	1	0
Amendment	24	.5129	2.7055	44.3	2	0	1	0	3	8	9	1	6	0	0	0	0	11	0	1	0	0	0	0	0	4	1	1	0
amendments	22	.4237	2.1025	43.2	1	0	0	6	1	10	3	1	2	0	0	0	0	11	0	7	0	0	0	0	0	1	0	1	0
Amenemhet	2	.0000	.0389	25.9	0	0	0	0	2	0	0	0	0	0	0	0	0	2	0	0	0	0	0	0	0	0	0	0	0
Amenhotep	5	.2426	.2985	34.7	0	0	1	0	3	0	1	0	0	0	0	0	0	3	0	0	0	0	0	0	0	0	2	0	0
amenities	5	.4720	.4941	36.9	0	0	0	0	0	3	1	1	0	0	0	0	0	0	0	0	1	0	0	0	0	1	1	2	0
America	1321	.7906	210.59	63.2	150	150	255	216	256	160	125	9	173	38	4	29	17	559	12	59	102	7	7	3	7	93	153	58	0
America's	114	.7799	17.935	52.5	8	11	15	8	20	38	12	2	15	6	0	4	2	37	4	1	7	1	0	0	0	9	9	19	0
american	3	.0000	.0328	25.2	0	0	0	0	0	1	2	0	0	3	0	0	0	0	0	0	0	0	0	0	0	0	0	0	0
American	1575	.8170	257.99	64.1	94	98	287	161	346	386	165	38	192	84	7	39	8	459	25	43	188	4	6	8	11	127	196	178	0
AMERICAN	2	.0000	.0243	23.9	0	0	1	0	1	0	0	0	0	0	0	0	0	0	0	0	0	0	0	0	0	0	0	2	0
American-made	5	.2351	.2880	34.6	0	1	2	0	0	2	0	0	0	0	0	0	0	3	0	0	2	0	0	0	0	0	0	0	0
American's	3	.2187	.1555	31.9	0	0	0	0	2	0	1	0	0	2	0	0	0	0	0	0	0	0	0	0	0	0	0	1	0
Americana	2	.1733	.1149	30.6	0	0	0	0	0	1	1	0	1	1	0	0	0	0	0	0	0	0	0	0	0	0	0	0	0
Americanists	2	.0000	.0209	23.2	0	0	0	0	0	0	2	0	0	0	0	0	0	0	0	0	0	0	0	0	0	0	2	0	0
Americans	527	.7449	79.634	59.0	29	35	129	38	80	160	49	7	53	30	4	13	0	247	32	6	22	0	2	0	2	39	22	55	0
Americans'	4	.3360	.3283	35.2	1	0	0	1	0	2	0	0	1	0	0	0	0	2	0	0	0	0	0	0	0	0	0	1	0
Americas	31	.4831	3.2359	45.1	0	3	9	5	6	5	3	0	3	2	0	0	0	14	0	0	0	0	0	0	0	2	9	1	0
Ames	14	.4009	1.1941	40.8	2	0	0	1	0	0	10	1	0	0	0	9	0	0	0	0	0	0	0	1	0	2	0	2	0
amethyst	2	.2446	.1122	30.5	0	0	1	0	1	0	0	0	0	0	0	1	0	0	0	0	0	0	0	0	0	0	1	0	0
Amhara	2	.0000	.0389	25.9	0	0	0	1	1	0	0	0	0	0	0	0	0	2	0	0	0	0	0	0	0	0	0	0	0
Amharas	5	.0000	.0972	29.9	0	0	0	1	4	0	0	0	0	0	0	0	0	5	0	0	0	0	0	0	0	0	0	0	0
Amharic	2	.2285	.1129	30.5	0	0	0	0	1	0	1	0	0	0	0	0	0	1	0	0	0	0	0	0	0	0	1	0	0
Amherst	5	.3854	.4790	36.8	0	0	2	3	0	0	0	0	3	0	0	0	0	0	0	0	0	0	0	0	1	1	0	0	0
ami	3	.0000	.1370	31.4	0	0	0	0	1	0	2	0	3	0	0	0	0	0	0	0	0	0	0	0	0	0	0	0	0
amiable	7	.2816	.4705	36.7	0	0	0	2	1	1	2	1	1	0	0	2	0	0	0	0	0	0	0	0	0	0	0	4	0
amiably	5	.3306	.3615	35.6	0	0	0	0	1	1	3	0	0	0	0	3	0	0	0	0	0	0	0	0	0	0	1	1	0
amicable	3	.3874	.2487	34.0	0	1	0	0	1	1	0	0	0	1	0	0	0	0	0	0	0	0	0	0	1	0	1	0	0
amid	36	.6712	4.9887	47.0	0	0	6	6	6	11	4	3	8	0	2	5	0	3	0	3	0	0	0	0	5	4	0	6	0
amidst	16	.6652	2.2391	43.5	0	1	5	8	1	0	1	0	7	1	0	0	0	2	0	0	0	0	0	0	1	1	2	2	0
amigo	5	.2445	.3875	35.9	2	0	0	3	0	0	0	0	4	0	0	0	0	0	0	0	0	0	0	0	0	0	0	1	0
amigos	4	.0000	.1827	32.6	4	0	0	0	0	0	0	0	4	0	0	0	0	0	0	0	0	0	0	0	0	0	0	0	0
Amik	9	.2212	.6853	38.4	0	0	8	1	0	0	0	0	8	0	0	0	0	0	0	0	0	0	0	0	0	0	0	1	0
amino	38	.3697	3.1446	45.0	0	0	0	7	19	5	6	1	0	0	0	0	0	0	0	27	0	0	6	0	0	0	2	3	0
Amir	2	.1698	.1133	30.5	0	0	0	0	1	1	0	0	1	0	0	0	0	0	0	0	0	0	0	0	0	0	1	0	0
amir-al-bahr	2	.0000	.0219	23.4	0	0	0	0	0	0	0	2	0	2	0	0	0	0	0	0	0	0	0	0	0	0	0	0	0
amiral	3	.0000	.0328	25.2	0	0	0	0	0	0	0	3	0	3	0	0	0	0	0	0	0	0	0	0	0	0	0	0	0
Amish	6	.0706	.1822	32.6	0	0	0	1	5	0	0	0	1	0	0	0	0	0	0	0	0	0	0	0	0	0	0	5	0
amiss	2	.2446	.1142	30.6	0	0	0	1	0	1	0	0	0	0	0	0	0	0	0	0	0	0	0	0	1	0	0	1	0
ammonia	23	.4910	2.4049	43.8	0	4	5	3	5	2	3	1	1	0	0	2	0	1	0	8	0	0	0	0	0	0	8	3	0
ammonium	15	.2384	.8999	39.5	0	1	7	2	2	0	1	2	0	0	0	0	0	0	0	11	0	0	0	0	0	0	4	0	0
ammunition	39	.6593	5.2607	47.2	0	10	10	0	6	5	4	4	3	1	1	4	0	5	0	0	0	0	0	0	0	12	7	6	0
amniotic	3	.0000	.0314	25.0	0	0	0	0	3	0	0	0	0	0	0	0	0	0	0	0	0	0	0	0	0	0	3	0	0
amoeba	6	.2071	.3307	35.2	0	0	4	1	1	0	0	0	0	0	0	0	0	0	0	5	0	0	0	0	0	0	1	0	0
amoebic	2	.0000	.0394	26.0	0	0	0	2	0	0	0	0	0	0	0	0	0	0	0	2	0	0	0	0	0	0	0	0	0
among	1308	.9182	238.06	63.8	121	117	145	176	355	196	151	47	222	47	22	105	31	187	13	155	39	9	9	3	76	110	164	112	4
amongst	25	.5078	2.8271	44.5	1	2	3	6	8	3	0	2	11	0	0	0	0	1	0	0	1	0	0	0	8	1	0	3	0
Amontons	2	.0000	.0209	23.2	0	0	0	0	2	0	0	0	0	0	0	0	0	0	0	0	0	0	0	0	0	0	2	0	0
amorphous	4	.3280	.2948	34.7	0	0	3	0	0	0	0	1	0	0	0	0	0	0	0	1	0	0	0	0	0	1	2	0	0
Amos	73	.1441	3.1830	45.0	8	5	52	5	0	3	0	0	13	0	0	2	0	1	0	0	0	0	0	0	57	0	0	0	0
Amos'	2	.0000	.0234	23.7	0	0	2	0	0	0	0	0	0	0	0	0	0	0	0	0	0	0	0	0	2	0	0	0	0
amount	701	.7451	105.75	60.2	68	77	70	85	113	129	132	27	72	17	0	7	128	53	3	207	6	4	70	32	7	26	48	21	0
amounted	23	.6264	2.9984	44.8	0	1	3	3	6	3	7	0	4	0	0	0	3	4	0	0	0	0	0	0	1	2	5	4	0
amounting	4	.3827	.3419	35.3	0	0	0	0	1	0	0	3	0	0	0	0	1	0	0	2	0	0	0	0	0	0	0	1	0
amounts	214	.7088	30.898	54.9	28	19	37	18	47	29	30	6	12	2	0	0	43	37	0	70	2	0	14	4	0	9	17	4	0
ampere	2	.1249	.0685	28.4	0	0	0	0	0	2	0	0	0	0	0	0	0	0	0	1	0	0	0	1	0	0	0	0	0
amperes	6	.3287	.4504	36.5	0	0	4	0	1	1	0	0	0	0	0	0	0	0	0	4	0	0	0	1	0	0	0	1	0

8A amber-colored
8D amber-tinted
3P ambidextrous
7R ambience
5B Ambition
9E Ambitious
9Q ambivalent
7A amble
4A Amboseli
9D ambrosial
3P Ambrosiana
7G ambulant
5P ambuscade
9D ambuscadoes
3G ame
3P AMEBA
3P ameba's
8B amelia
7F Amen-Re
5A amercy
7A America'
8F American-born
9R American-controlled
4Q American-designed
7P American-type
5Q americana
XR Americanese
5P Americanism
9Q Americanist
8F Americano
7H americanus
5F Amerigo
7A Amesburg
5Q Amesbury
6N amethysts
7R AMF
6A amicably
7J Amici
9Q amics
6P amidship
7Q amidships
5A Amik's
8Q Amintore
7P amir
7B amity
4N Amma
6J amman
9R Amman
8M ammeter
5H ammoniac
8J Ammunition
9J Amneris
8G amnesty
7H Amoeba
7Q amoebalike
6H amoebas
7A Amon
4P Among
7R amoral
8F Amount

Word Type	F	D	U	SFI	3 Gr 3	4 Gr 4	5 Gr 5	6 Gr 6	7 Gr 7	8 Gr 8	9 Gr 9	X UnGr	A Read	B Eng & Gr	C Comp	D Lit	E Math	F Soc Stud	G Spell	H Sci	J Music	K Art	L Home Ec	M Shop	N Lib F	P Lib NF	Q Lib Ref	R Mag	S Rel
amphetamines	3	.0000	.0365	25.6	0	0	0	0	1	1	1	0	0	0	0	0	0	0	0	0	0	0	0	0	0	0	0	3	0
amphibian	14	.3197	1.0387	40.2	5	1	0	2	5	0	0	1	0	0	0	0	0	0	0	9	0	0	0	0	0	1	4	0	0
amphibians	68	.3768	5.7351	47.6	15	11	2	13	23	0	1	3	0	0	0	0	0	0	0	38	0	0	0	0	0	15	15	0	0
amphibious	7	.4349	.6500	38.1	0	0	1	1	3	0	2	0	0	1	0	1	0	0	0	0	0	0	0	0	0	4	0	1	0
amphibole	2	.0000	.0394	26.0	0	0	0	0	0	0	0	2	0	0	0	0	0	0	0	2	0	0	0	0	0	0	0	0	0
amphiboles	5	.0000	.0986	29.9	0	0	0	0	0	0	1	4	0	0	0	0	0	0	0	5	0	0	0	0	0	0	0	0	0
amphidromic	3	.0000	.0591	27.7	0	0	0	0	0	0	0	3	0	0	0	0	0	0	0	3	0	0	0	0	0	0	0	0	0
amphitheater	5	.2423	.2894	34.6	1	0	1	0	0	1	0	2	0	0	0	0	0	0	0	0	0	0	0	0	0	3	0	2	0
amphitheatre	2	.0000	.0215	23.3	0	0	0	0	1	1	0	0	0	0	0	2	0	0	0	0	0	0	0	0	0	0	0	0	0
AMPI	6	.0000	.0729	28.6	0	0	0	0	0	0	0	6	0	0	0	0	0	0	0	0	0	0	0	0	0	0	0	6	0
ample	18	.6676	2.4209	43.8	1	1	0	3	3	3	6	1	0	1	0	2	0	1	2	1	3	0	3	0	1	0	2	2	0
amplification	2	.1937	.0847	29.3	0	0	0	0	1	1	0	0	0	0	0	0	0	0	0	0	1	0	0	1	0	0	0	0	0
amplified	17	.4544	1.6117	42.1	0	1	1	2	9	3	1	0	0	0	0	0	0	0	0	2	10	0	0	1	1	1	1	1	0
amplifier	15	.3704	1.1985	40.8	1	3	0	0	6	4	1	0	0	0	0	0	0	1	0	2	8	0	0	0	3	0	1	0	0
amplifiers	3	.3553	.2609	34.2	0	0	0	1	1	1	0	0	1	0	0	0	0	0	0	1	0	0	0	0	0	1	0	0	0
amplifies	7	.4500	.6691	38.3	1	0	0	0	5	1	0	0	0	0	0	0	0	0	0	2	2	0	0	0	0	1	2	0	0
amplify	5	.3442	.3827	35.8	0	1	0	0	0	4	0	0	0	0	0	0	0	0	0	2	2	0	0	0	0	0	0	1	0
amplifying	8	.4225	.7975	39.0	0	0	0	4	2	0	2	0	4	0	0	0	0	0	0	1	2	0	0	0	0	0	0	1	0
amplitude	12	.2428	.7252	38.6	0	0	1	0	0	2	3	6	0	0	0	0	0	0	0	9	3	0	0	0	0	0	0	0	0
amplitudes	4	.0000	.0789	29.0	0	0	0	0	0	0	0	4	0	0	0	0	0	0	0	4	0	0	0	0	0	0	0	0	0
amply	2	.0000	.0209	23.2	0	0	0	0	1	0	1	0	0	0	0	0	0	0	0	0	0	0	0	0	0	0	2	0	0
amps	3	.0000	.0076	18.8	0	0	0	0	0	3	0	0	0	0	0	0	0	0	0	0	0	0	0	3	0	0	0	0	0
Amsterdam	35	.6289	4.5412	46.6	1	12	11	2	2	6	1	0	2	1	0	0	0	18	1	0	5	1	0	0	0	1	5	1	0
amuck	2	.1717	.1142	30.6	0	1	1	0	0	0	0	0	1	0	0	1	0	0	0	0	0	0	0	0	0	0	0	0	0
amulet	4	.1717	.2284	33.6	0	0	1	1	2	0	0	0	2	0	0	2	0	0	0	0	0	0	0	0	0	0	0	0	0
Amundsen	10	.0000	.1945	32.9	0	9	0	0	1	0	0	0	0	0	0	0	0	10	0	0	0	0	0	0	0	0	0	0	0
Amur	3	.0000	.0365	25.6	0	0	0	0	3	0	0	0	0	0	0	0	0	0	0	0	0	0	0	0	0	0	0	3	0
amuse	23	.7012	3.3164	45.2	1	5	3	8	1	3	2	0	7	1	0	3	0	0	3	0	2	0	0	0	3	3	1	0	0
amused	34	.7163	5.0340	47.0	3	13	5	4	4	3	2	0	14	1	1	2	0	1	0	0	1	0	0	0	5	5	4	0	0
amusement	34	.8114	5.5606	47.5	4	8	3	3	4	6	6	0	9	0	1	2	0	5	1	1	2	0	0	0	4	4	2	3	0
amusements	8	.5323	.8991	39.5	1	0	1	0	1	4	0	1	1	1	0	0	0	1	0	0	0	0	1	0	0	3	1	0	0
amusing	54	.7136	7.8284	48.9	6	11	4	5	10	12	3	3	10	11	5	4	0	1	1	1	2	4	0	1	1	9	2	2	0
amusingly	2	.0000	.0215	23.3	0	0	0	0	0	2	0	0	0	0	0	2	0	0	0	0	0	0	0	0	0	0	0	0	0
Amy	68	.5184	7.6738	48.9	34	5	0	0	19	5	5	0	25	1	9	10	4	0	0	0	4	0	0	0	14	0	0	1	0
Amy's	10	.3708	.8460	39.3	2	1	0	0	6	0	1	0	2	0	0	2	1	0	0	0	0	0	0	0	5	0	0	0	0
amylase	3	.0000	.0591	27.7	0	0	0	0	2	0	0	1	0	0	0	0	0	0	0	3	0	0	0	0	0	0	0	0	0
an	14696	.9717	2813.9	74.5	1700	1839	1762	1876	3198	2096	1794	431	2640	1215	283	663	1281	1185	478	1926	714	168	203	250	572	963	1061	1093	1
An	10	.6978	1.4193	41.5	0	4	0	0	4	2	0	0	1	2	0	1	0	0	1	2	1	0	0	0	0	1	1	0	0
AN	4	.3295	.2965	34.7	0	0	0	1	0	0	3	0	0	0	0	2	1	1	0	0	0	0	0	0	0	0	0	0	0
an'	142	.5178	16.724	52.2	20	5	0	23	55	37	2	0	91	2	0	23	0	0	0	0	5	0	0	0	19	2	0	0	0
Ana	2	.1698	.1133	30.5	0	0	1	0	0	1	0	0	1	0	0	0	0	0	0	0	0	0	0	0	0	0	1	0	0
Ana's	2	.0000	.0914	29.6	0	0	2	0	0	0	0	0	2	0	0	0	0	0	0	0	0	0	0	0	0	0	0	0	0
Anabaptist	3	.0000	.0365	25.6	0	0	0	0	2	0	1	0	0	0	0	0	0	0	0	0	0	0	0	0	0	0	0	3	0
anabolic	2	.2278	.1128	30.5	0	0	0	1	0	0	1	0	0	0	0	0	0	0	0	1	0	0	0	0	0	0	1	0	0
anacondas	2	.2285	.1129	30.5	0	0	0	1	1	0	0	0	0	0	0	0	0	1	0	0	0	0	0	0	0	0	1	0	0
Anacostia	4	.3603	.3219	35.1	2	0	0	0	1	1	0	0	0	0	0	0	0	1	0	0	0	0	0	0	0	2	0	1	0
anaerobic	3	.2445	.1818	32.6	0	0	0	0	0	1	2	0	0	0	0	0	0	0	0	2	0	0	0	0	0	0	1	0	0
Anagnos	2	.0000	.0914	29.6	0	0	2	0	0	0	0	0	2	0	0	0	0	0	0	0	0	0	0	0	0	0	0	0	0
Anaheim	4	.1622	.1743	32.4	0	0	1	0	0	0	3	0	0	0	0	0	0	1	0	0	0	0	0	0	0	0	0	3	0
anal	3	.2304	.1619	32.1	0	0	0	0	3	0	0	0	0	0	0	0	0	0	0	0	0	0	0	0	2	0	1	0	0
Analdas	8	.2370	.4418	36.5	5	0	3	0	0	0	0	0	0	0	0	3	0	0	0	0	0	0	0	0	5	0	0	0	0
Analdas'	2	.0000	.0234	23.7	2	0	0	0	0	0	0	0	0	0	0	0	0	0	0	0	0	0	0	0	2	0	0	0	0
analogies	2	.0000	.0209	23.2	0	0	0	0	1	1	0	0	0	0	0	0	0	0	0	0	0	0	0	0	0	0	2	0	0
analogy	2	.2437	.1129	30.5	0	0	0	0	1	0	0	1	0	0	0	0	0	0	0	0	0	0	0	0	0	0	1	1	0
analyses	5	.5555	.5782	37.6	0	0	0	0	2	1	1	1	0	1	0	0	0	1	0	1	0	0	0	0	0	0	1	1	0
analysis	54	.7456	8.1153	49.1	0	1	4	7	12	6	11	13	2	1	0	0	0	4	2	13	5	0	1	1	0	3	7	15	0
Analysis	2	.2437	.1129	30.5	0	0	1	0	0	0	0	1	0	0	0	0	0	0	0	0	0	0	0	0	0	0	1	1	0
analyst	3	.3465	.2515	34.0	0	0	1	0	1	0	0	1	1	0	0	0	0	0	0	0	0	0	0	0	0	1	0	1	0
analysts	4	.3540	.3119	34.9	0	0	0	0	0	1	3	0	0	0	0	0	0	0	0	1	1	0	0	0	0	0	0	2	0
analytical	3	.3826	.2445	33.9	0	0	1	0	1	0	1	0	0	0	0	0	0	0	0	0	1	0	0	0	0	0	1	1	0
analyze	37	.7924	5.8491	47.7	0	0	1	5	11	11	9	0	0	7	1	1	1	1	5	8	4	1	3	0	0	0	3	2	0
analyzed	10	.5962	1.2269	40.9	1	0	0	4	3	1	1	0	0	0	0	0	0	0	1	4	1	0	1	0	0	1	0	2	0
analyzes	2	.2300	.1140	30.6	0	0	0	1	0	0	1	0	0	1	0	0	0	0	0	1	0	0	0	0	0	0	0	0	0
analyzing	18	.7037	2.5885	44.1	0	0	5	3	5	4	1	0	3	3	0	0	2	1	1	3	3	0	0	0	0	1	1	0	0
Ananse	9	.0000	.0966	29.8	0	0	0	0	9	0	0	0	0	0	0	9	0	0	0	0	0	0	0	0	0	0	0	0	0
Ananse's	2	.0000	.0215	23.3	0	0	0	0	2	0	0	0	0	0	0	2	0	0	0	0	0	0	0	0	0	0	0	0	0
Anansi	2	.0000	.0290	24.6	0	0	0	0	2	0	0	0	0	0	0	0	0	0	0	0	0	0	0	0	0	2	0	0	0
anaphase	2	.0000	.0209	23.2	0	0	0	2	0	0	0	0	0	0	0	0	0	0	0	0	0	0	0	0	0	0	2	0	0
anarchists	2	.0000	.0243	23.9	0	0	0	0	0	1	1	0	0	0	0	0	0	0	0	0	0	0	0	0	0	0	0	2	0
anarchy	3	.2321	.1635	32.1	0	0	0	0	1	1	1	0	0	0	0	0	0	0	0	0	0	0	0	0	0	0	1	2	0
Anasazi	3	.0000	.0314	25.0	0	3	0	0	0	0	0	0	0	0	0	0	0	0	0	0	0	0	0	0	0	0	3	0	0
Anatolia	11	.2416	.6694	38.3	0	0	4	0	7	0	0	0	0	0	0	0	0	7	0	0	0	0	0	0	0	4	0	0	0
Anatolian	2	.0000	.0389	25.9	0	0	0	0	2	0	0	0	0	0	0	0	0	2	0	0	0	0	0	0	0	0	0	0	0
anatomical	5	.1275	.1790	32.5	0	0	0	0	2	0	2	1	0	0	0	0	0	0	0	1	0	0	0	0	0	0	4	0	0
anatomically	2	.2441	.1127	30.5	0	0	0	0	2	0	0	0	0	0	0	0	0	0	0	0	0	0	0	0	1	0	1	0	0
anatomist	2	.2278	.1128	30.5	0	0	0	0	1	1	0	0	0	0	0	0	0	0	0	1	0	0	0	0	0	0	1	0	0
anatomists	2	.2278	.1128	30.5	0	0	0	0	0	1	1	0	0	0	0	0	0	0	0	1	0	0	0	0	0	0	1	0	0
anatomy	24	.3903	2.0309	43.1	0	1	0	2	8	3	9	1	0	0	0	0	0	1	0	4	0	0	0	0	0	2	13	4	0
Anax	2	.0000	.0290	24.6	2	0	0	0	0	0	0	0	0	0	0	0	0	0	0	0	0	0	0	0	0	2	0	0	0
ance	18	.0613	.3566	35.5	0	0	0	2	13	3	0	0	0	1	0	0	0	0	17	0	0	0	0	0	0	0	0	0	0
ancestor	28	.6177	3.5445	45.5	2	3	3	5	8	4	2	1	2	1	0	0	0	1	2	4	6	3	0	0	0	3	4	2	0
ancestors	123	.7232	18.178	52.6	8	13	25	17	37	11	7	5	23	2	0	3	0	35	0	5	1	1	2	0	2	20	26	3	0
Ancestors	2	.0000	.0389	25.9	0	0	0	0	0	2	0	0	0	0	0	0	0	2	0	0	0	0	0	0	0	0	0	0	0
ancestral	18	.3241	1.3429	41.3	0	1	1	2	11	1	0	2	2	0	0	0	0	3	0	0	0	0	0	0	0	0	10	3	0
ancestry	23	.5380	2.6256	44.2	0	0	4	2	6	9	2	0	2	1	0	0	0	12	0	0	1	0	0	0	1	0	5	1	0
ancha	2	.0000	.0162	22.1	1	1	0	0	0	0	0	0	0	0	0	0	0	0	0	0	2	0	0	0	0	0	0	0	0
anchor	75	.8798	13.157	51.2	3	22	12	12	10	11	4	1	20	1	0	3	0	7	1	4	5	1	3	1	10	6	5	8	0
anchorage	6	.4942	.6392	38.1	0	1	1	0	2	1	1	0	1	0	0	2	0	0	0	1	0	0	0	0	0	1	1	0	0
Anchorage	15	.3763	1.3465	41.3	5	6	3	1	0	0	0	0	4	0	0	0	0	9	0	0	1	0	0	0	0	1	0	0	0
anchorages	2	.0000	.0209	23.2	0	0	0	0	0	0	2	0	0	0	0	0	0	0	0	0	0	0	0	0	0	0	2	0	0
anchored	44	.7582	6.7947	48.3	4	9	4	9	11	4	1	2	12	3	2	0	0	6	0	5	1	0	0	0	5	2	4	4	0
anchoring	5	.5370	.5704	37.6	0	2	0	1	0	1	1	0	1	1	0	1	0	0	0	0	0	0	0	0	0	1	1	0	0
anchors	5	.2222	.2934	34.7	0	0	2	1	2	0	0	0	1	0	0	0	0	1	0	0	0	0	0	0	0	0	3	0	0
anchovies	3	.2445	.1818	32.6	0	2	0	0	1	0	0	0	0	0	0	0	0	0	0	2	0	0	0	0	0	0	1	0	0
ancient	515	.8983	91.858	59.6	33	40	66	102	139	58	63	14	65	25	2	24	19	116	10	48	27	5	1	6	12	44	81	30	0

7H amphibia
7Q Amphibia
4Q Amphibian
4Q Amphibians
9Q Amphibole
XH amphibolite
9H Amphioxus
9D Amphithea
3P amphitheatres
8D Amphitrite
7H Amplification
8J Amplitude
9P amputate
6R amputation
6A Amroo
XQ Amsterdam's
7R AMT
6N amulets
7J amuses
8B amusin'
6A Amycus
7H amylose
9Q amyotrophic
8E an**
5Q AN-FO
6R AN/FSR-2
6J An'
4A anablep
7N anableps
6Q anabolism
7R anachronism
5P anachronistic
5P Anadolu
5A Anagnos'
9Q anagram
9E analogous
XH analytic
8J analytically
8Q anarchism
8F Anastas
9R anathema
4P anatosaurs
4P anatosaurus
8F Ancestor
4G Ancestry
8N anchor-chain
8A anchor's
5J Anchorage's
8D anchorstone
9R ancien

Word Type	F	D	U	SFI	3 Gr 3	4 Gr 4	5 Gr 5	6 Gr 6	7 Gr 7	8 Gr 8	9 Gr 9	X UnGr	A Read	B Eng & Gr	C Comp	D Lit	E Math	F Soc Stud	G Spell	H Sci	J Music	K Art	L Home Ec	M Shop	N Lib F	P Lib NF	Q Lib Ref	R Mag	S Rel
Ancient	7	.5478	.7797	38.9	0	0	2	0	1	1	2	1	0	0	0	0	0	0	0	0	1	1	1	0	1	0	2	1	0
anciently	2	.2442	.1134	30.5	0	0	0	0	1	0	0	1	0	1	0	0	0	0	0	0	0	0	0	0	0	0	0	1	0
ancients	7	.5109	.7608	38.8	2	0	0	1	3	0	0	1	1	0	0	1	0	0	0	0	0	0	0	0	0	2	2	1	0
and	133899	.9940	26172	84.2	20392	18760	16755	17715	26967	16687	13219	3404	31329	5909	1471	9142	7343	13798	4339	10510	5902	1422	2693	1762	10332	10699	8453	8623	172
And	5	.3585	.3857	35.9	0	0	0	3	1	0	1	0	0	0	0	0	0	0	0	0	2	0	0	0	1	0	0	2	0
AND	17	.5524	2.1069	43.2	3	2	4	8	0	0	0	0	11	0	0	0	0	1	0	1	2	0	0	0	0	1	0	1	0
and/or	8	.3225	.5387	37.3	0	0	0	0	3	3	2	0	0	0	0	0	1	0	0	0	0	0	3	3	0	1	0	0	0
and's	2	.0000	.0219	23.4	0	0	0	0	0	1	1	0	0	2	0	0	0	0	0	0	0	0	0	0	0	0	0	0	0
Andalusia	2	.0000	.0162	22.1	0	0	0	2	0	0	0	0	0	0	0	0	0	0	0	0	2	0	0	0	0	0	0	0	0
andante	2	.2417	.1091	30.4	0	0	1	0	1	0	0	0	0	0	0	0	0	0	0	0	1	0	0	0	0	0	1	0	0
Andante	2	.0000	.0162	22.1	0	1	1	0	0	0	0	0	0	0	0	0	0	0	0	0	2	0	0	0	0	0	0	0	0
Andau	4	.0000	.0429	26.3	0	0	0	0	4	0	0	0	0	0	0	4	0	0	0	0	0	0	0	0	0	0	0	0	0
Andean	6	.5303	.6860	38.4	0	0	1	1	4	0	0	0	1	0	0	0	0	2	0	1	0	0	0	0	0	1	1	0	0
Anders	6	.3473	.4886	36.9	0	0	3	1	1	1	0	0	1	0	0	0	0	1	0	1	0	0	0	0	0	0	0	3	0
Andersen	15	.4471	1.5813	42.0	1	5	0	8	0	1	0	0	9	0	0	0	0	0	0	0	1	0	0	0	4	0	1	0	0
Anderson	47	.6152	6.2135	47.9	3	15	0	16	8	3	1	1	25	0	0	1	0	1	0	0	7	0	0	0	2	1	4	6	0
Anderson's	5	.4685	.5252	37.2	0	3	0	0	0	1	0	1	2	0	0	0	0	0	1	0	0	0	0	0	0	0	1	1	0
Andes	59	.4689	6.0148	47.8	7	5	7	16	19	0	5	0	4	2	0	0	0	33	0	3	1	0	0	0	0	2	14	0	0
Andorra	2	.2285	.1129	30.5	0	0	1	1	0	0	0	0	0	0	0	0	0	1	0	0	0	0	0	0	0	0	1	0	0
Andover	3	.2387	.1708	32.3	0	2	0	0	0	0	1	0	0	0	0	0	0	0	0	0	0	0	0	0	0	2	1	0	0
Andre	31	.5208	3.5763	45.5	0	10	6	10	0	3	2	0	14	1	0	0	0	0	0	0	0	0	0	0	10	2	2	2	0
Andrea	14	.4096	1.4188	41.5	0	0	0	0	2	10	2	0	10	0	0	2	0	0	0	0	0	1	0	0	0	1	0	0	0
Andrea's	2	.0000	.0914	29.6	0	0	0	0	0	2	0	0	2	0	0	0	0	0	0	0	0	0	0	0	0	0	0	0	0
Andreas	2	.0000	.0394	26.0	0	0	0	0	0	1	1	0	0	0	0	0	0	0	0	2	0	0	0	0	0	0	0	0	0
Andrei	3	.3769	.2484	34.0	0	0	0	0	2	0	1	0	0	0	0	0	0	1	0	0	0	0	0	0	0	0	1	1	0
Andrew	75	.7571	11.502	50.6	14	8	22	2	6	15	7	1	11	5	1	2	2	21	1	0	0	0	0	0	15	5	4	8	0
Andrew's	4	.0974	.1495	31.7	0	0	3	0	1	0	0	0	1	0	0	0	0	0	0	0	0	0	0	0	3	0	0	0	0
Andrews	14	.5516	1.6377	42.1	1	0	5	1	2	2	1	2	3	2	0	1	0	0	0	1	0	0	0	0	0	0	4	3	0
Andrews'	2	.0000	.0243	23.9	0	0	0	0	0	0	0	2	0	0	0	0	0	0	0	0	0	0	0	0	0	0	0	2	0
Androcles	15	.0000	.6852	38.4	0	4	11	0	0	0	0	0	15	0	0	0	0	0	0	0	0	0	0	0	0	0	0	0	0
Andromeda	8	.4941	.8601	39.3	0	0	0	0	0	2	3	3	1	0	0	1	1	0	0	4	0	0	0	0	0	1	0	0	0
Andros	5	.3779	.4200	36.2	0	1	1	0	0	3	0	0	0	0	0	0	0	3	1	0	0	0	0	0	1	0	0	0	0
Andulko	2	.0000	.0162	22.1	2	0	0	0	0	0	0	0	0	0	0	0	0	0	0	0	2	0	0	0	0	0	0	0	0
Andy	232	.6220	31.692	55.0	27	140	27	21	0	7	9	1	175	6	2	15	5	9	0	12	0	0	0	0	0	5	0	3	0
Andy's	25	.5597	3.1214	44.9	0	16	6	1	0	1	1	0	16	1	0	4	0	0	1	2	0	0	0	0	0	0	0	1	0
anecdote	2	.0000	.0219	23.4	0	0	0	0	0	2	0	0	0	2	0	0	0	0	0	0	0	0	0	0	0	0	0	0	0
anecdotes	6	.2222	.3261	35.1	0	0	0	2	3	0	1	0	1	0	2	3	0	0	0	0	0	0	0	0	0	0	0	0	0
anemia	6	.4101	.5228	37.2	0	0	0	0	1	3	2	0	0	0	0	0	0	0	0	1	0	0	1	0	0	0	3	1	0
anemic	3	.2383	.1815	32.6	0	0	1	0	1	0	1	0	0	0	0	0	0	0	0	2	0	0	0	0	0	1	0	0	0
anemometer	7	.1690	.3428	35.4	1	0	0	0	4	2	0	0	0	0	0	0	0	0	0	6	0	0	0	0	0	1	0	0	0
anemone	6	.2445	.3637	35.6	0	0	0	0	5	0	1	0	0	0	0	0	0	0	0	4	0	0	0	0	0	0	2	0	0
anemones	4	.3362	.3304	35.2	1	0	1	1	0	1	0	0	1	0	0	0	0	0	0	2	0	0	0	0	0	1	0	0	0
aneroid	6	.0000	.1183	30.7	0	0	3	0	0	3	0	0	0	0	0	0	0	0	0	6	0	0	0	0	0	0	0	0	0
anesthetic	8	.0900	.2261	33.5	0	0	4	2	1	1	0	0	0	0	0	0	0	0	0	1	0	0	0	0	0	0	7	0	0
anesthetics	7	.2756	.4520	36.6	0	0	2	0	0	4	1	0	0	0	0	0	0	1	0	2	0	0	0	0	0	0	4	0	0
anew	11	.7326	1.6324	42.1	0	2	1	1	4	0	2	1	1	0	0	1	0	2	0	1	1	0	0	0	1	1	2	1	0
angakok	4	.0000	.1827	32.6	0	4	0	0	0	0	0	0	4	0	0	0	0	0	0	0	0	0	0	0	0	0	0	0	0
angakoks	3	.0000	.1370	31.4	0	3	0	0	0	0	0	0	3	0	0	0	0	0	0	0	0	0	0	0	0	0	0	0	0
angel	45	.5695	5.3923	47.3	13	2	3	6	9	4	8	0	9	4	0	6	2	3	1	0	2	2	0	0	4	7	3	1	1
Angel	12	.3396	1.0379	40.2	2	1	2	5	1	0	1	0	7	0	2	0	0	0	0	0	0	0	0	0	0	0	1	2	0
Angela	5	.2467	.3124	34.9	1	2	0	1	1	0	0	0	1	3	0	0	0	0	0	0	0	0	0	0	0	1	0	0	0
Angeles	5	.2138	.2693	34.3	0	1	0	3	1	0	0	0	0	0	0	0	0	2	0	0	0	0	0	0	0	0	0	3	0
angelfish	2	.1787	.1174	30.7	0	2	0	0	0	0	0	0	1	0	0	0	0	0	0	0	0	0	0	0	1	0	0	0	0
angelic	2	.2375	.1088	30.4	0	0	0	0	1	0	0	1	0	0	0	0	0	0	0	0	1	0	0	0	0	0	0	1	0
Angelo	5	.4753	.5377	37.3	2	1	0	1	1	0	0	0	2	0	0	0	0	1	0	0	0	0	0	0	1	0	0	1	0
angels	36	.4822	3.7502	45.7	5	5	2	8	6	3	2	5	8	1	0	3	0	3	0	0	10	2	0	0	0	3	1	4	1
Angels	9	.3850	.8694	39.4	0	0	0	1	7	0	1	0	6	0	0	0	0	0	0	0	1	0	0	0	0	0	0	2	0
anger	108	.6142	14.020	51.5	16	9	17	10	28	18	9	1	39	7	3	8	0	4	1	5	3	2	2	0	21	5	3	3	2
angered	12	.5817	1.4895	41.7	0	1	4	2	0	4	1	0	3	0	0	1	0	5	0	0	0	0	0	0	1	1	1	0	0
angering	2	.2351	.1166	30.7	0	0	0	0	1	0	1	0	0	0	0	0	0	1	0	0	0	0	0	0	0	0	0	1	0
angers	3	.3875	.2489	34.0	0	1	0	0	0	1	1	0	0	1	0	1	0	0	0	0	0	0	0	0	1	0	0	0	0
Angie	6	.1316	.2597	34.1	2	0	0	0	4	0	0	0	2	0	0	0	0	1	0	0	0	0	3	0	0	0	0	0	0
angiosperms	2	.2278	.1128	30.5	0	0	0	1	0	0	1	0	0	0	0	0	0	0	0	1	0	0	0	0	0	0	1	0	0
Angkor	7	.0000	.1361	31.3	0	0	0	7	0	0	0	0	0	0	0	0	0	7	0	0	0	0	0	0	0	0	0	0	0
angle	462	.5241	50.707	57.1	26	24	44	73	123	90	72	10	5	2	1	9	307	1	1	50	0	2	2	42	2	9	13	16	0
Angle	3	.2610	.1787	32.5	0	1	0	0	0	1	1	0	0	0	0	0	0	1	0	0	0	0	0	1	1	0	0	0	0
Angle-land	2	.0000	.0219	23.4	0	2	0	0	0	0	0	0	0	2	0	0	0	0	0	0	0	0	0	0	0	0	0	0	0
angle-measuring	2	.0000	.0394	26.0	0	0	0	0	2	0	0	0	0	0	0	0	0	0	0	2	0	0	0	0	0	0	0	0	0
angle-worm	3	.2257	.1583	32.0	0	1	0	0	2	0	0	0	0	2	0	1	0	0	0	0	0	0	0	0	0	0	0	0	0
angler	3	.2266	.1614	32.1	0	0	0	0	1	1	0	1	0	0	0	0	0	0	0	0	0	0	0	0	1	0	0	2	0
anglers	3	.0000	.0365	25.6	0	0	0	2	0	0	0	1	0	0	0	0	0	0	0	0	0	0	0	0	0	0	0	3	0
angles	414	.4513	39.922	56.0	19	12	38	39	92	96	104	14	2	0	0	2	332	2	0	21	1	4	4	29	2	3	7	5	0
Angles	22	.5031	2.3242	43.7	0	1	1	7	9	2	1	1	1	7	0	1	0	5	6	0	0	0	0	0	0	0	2	0	0
angleworm	2	.2291	.1135	30.5	0	0	0	1	0	1	0	0	0	0	0	1	0	0	0	1	0	0	0	0	0	0	0	0	0
Anglican	2	.2437	.1129	30.5	0	0	0	0	1	1	0	0	0	0	0	0	0	0	0	0	0	0	0	0	0	0	1	1	0
Anglicized	2	.0000	.0209	23.2	0	1	0	0	0	1	0	0	0	0	0	0	0	0	0	0	0	0	0	0	0	0	2	0	0
Anglo-America	6	.0000	.1167	30.7	0	0	0	0	0	0	6	0	0	0	0	0	0	6	0	0	0	0	0	0	0	0	0	0	0
Anglo-American	2	.2137	.1056	30.2	0	0	1	0	1	0	0	0	0	0	0	0	0	1	0	0	1	0	0	0	0	0	0	0	0
Anglo-French	4	.1622	.1743	32.4	0	0	0	0	1	1	2	0	0	0	0	0	0	1	0	0	0	0	0	0	0	0	0	3	0
Anglo-Saxon	56	.3799	4.5338	46.6	0	5	4	23	15	0	2	7	0	23	0	0	0	3	25	0	0	0	0	0	1	0	2	2	0
Anglo-Saxons	13	.3569	.9954	40.0	0	1	2	4	3	3	0	0	0	3	0	0	0	1	7	0	0	0	0	0	0	0	2	0	0
Angola	7	.0000	.1361	31.3	0	1	0	5	0	0	1	0	0	0	0	0	0	7	0	0	0	0	0	0	0	0	0	0	0
angora	3	.2327	.1564	31.9	0	0	0	0	0	2	1	0	0	2	0	0	0	0	0	0	0	0	1	0	0	0	0	0	0
Angora	4	.2330	.2363	33.7	0	0	1	2	0	0	1	0	0	1	0	0	0	3	0	0	0	0	0	0	0	0	0	0	0
angrier	8	.2284	.6152	37.9	5	2	0	1	0	0	0	0	7	0	0	0	0	0	0	0	0	0	0	0	0	0	0	1	0
angrily	90	.7339	13.636	51.3	12	19	10	16	21	6	6	0	41	7	1	10	0	4	0	1	1	0	0	0	16	4	2	3	0
angry	402	.7619	63.130	58.0	116	85	33	65	59	21	18	5	220	17	11	21	0	24	4	15	1	1	1	0	35	23	3	24	2
angstrom	6	.2445	.3637	35.6	0	0	0	2	0	0	0	4	0	0	0	0	0	0	0	4	0	0	0	0	0	0	2	0	0
anguish	8	.6028	1.0125	40.1	0	0	1	2	2	0	3	0	2	1	0	1	0	0	0	0	0	0	0	0	2	1	0	1	0
anguished	4	.3741	.3191	35.0	0	0	0	0	2	0	1	1	0	0	0	2	0	0	0	0	1	0	0	0	0	0	1	0	0
angular	20	.6084	2.4691	43.9	0	0	0	1	6	5	4	4	0	0	0	1	1	0	0	4	3	3	1	2	0	1	4	0	0
Angus	5	.3265	.3629	35.6	0	0	1	0	2	2	0	0	0	0	1	2	0	2	0	0	0	0	0	0	0	0	0	0	0
Anhalt-Cothen	2	.0000	.0290	24.6	0	0	0	0	2	0	0	0	0	0	0	0	0	0	0	0	0	0	0	0	0	2	0	0	0
anhydrous	2	.2278	.1128	30.5	0	1	0	0	0	1	0	0	0	0	0	0	0	0	0	1	0	0	0	0	0	0	1	0	0
animal	1122	.8210	185.62	62.7	279	165	108	147	269	72	43	39	304	37	5	43	10	42	18	312	7	43	10	2	31	111	98	49	0
Animal	26	.4397	2.4802	43.9	11	4	0	1	3	1	6	0	3	3	0	0	0	1	0	0	0	0	0	0	4	0	1	14	0
animal-like	4	.4804	.4054	36.1	1	0	0	0	2	1	0	0	0	1	0	1	0	0	0	1	0	0	0	0	0	0	0	1	0

7N ancient-looking
8G ancy
8Q ancylostomiasis
7B and-so
6J Andalouse
7F Andaman
4N Andersens
9R Andersons'
7N andiron
8A Andre's
4Q Andrija
4A Androcles'
8B Andys
7H anemometers
8Q anesthesia
9Q anesthetize
XH anesthetized
4A angakok's
7D angel-cake
7H angel's
9D angelical
6A angelically
4A angels'
7A Angels'
8K Anger
8E Angle-Side-Angle
7E angle-measure
8D angled
6F Angleland
7Q anglerfishes
8D Angleworm
8Q Anglicanism
8F Anglicans
XR angling
XB Anglish
7B AngloSaxon
6Q angstroms
4F Anguilla
7Q Anguis
9B Angus'

Word Type	F	D	U	SFI	3 Gr 3	4 Gr 4	5 Gr 5	6 Gr 6	7 Gr 7	8 Gr 8	9 Gr 9	X UnGr	A Read	B Eng & Gr	C Comp	D Lit	E Math	F Soc Stud	G Spell	H Sci	J Music	K Art	L Home Ec	M Shop	N Lib F	P Lib NF	Q Lib Ref	R Mag	S Rel
animal's	41	.5589	4.9574	47.0	9	6	2	5	14	4	0	1	14	1	0	1	0	0	0	14	0	3	0	0	2	0	5	1	0
animals	2625	.8562	450.23	66.5	827	388	285	361	466	130	114	54	606	62	19	62	36	224	40	903	36	64	6	0	71	244	167	82	3
Animals	28	.4960	3.0354	44.8	17	7	3	1	0	0	0	0	8	1	0	1	0	0	0	3	4	0	0	0	11	0	0	0	0
ANIMALS	3	.0000	.0434	26.4	2	0	0	1	0	0	0	0	0	0	0	0	0	0	0	0	0	0	0	0	0	3	0	0	0
animals'	12	.5268	1.3820	41.4	6	1	1	0	2	1	0	1	4	0	0	0	0	0	0	3	0	1	0	0	0	2	1	1	0
animate	3	.3872	.2490	34.0	0	0	0	0	1	1	1	0	0	1	0	1	0	0	0	0	0	0	0	0	0	0	0	1	0
animated	12	.5795	1.4277	41.5	0	0	1	1	3	3	2	2	0	0	0	1	0	1	0	1	2	1	0	0	0	2	0	4	0
animism	3	.1937	.1495	31.7	0	0	0	2	1	0	0	0	0	0	0	0	0	1	0	0	0	0	0	0	0	0	0	2	0
animosities	3	.3465	.2515	34.0	0	0	1	0	1	0	1	0	1	0	0	0	0	0	0	0	0	0	0	0	0	1	0	1	0
animosity	2	.0000	.0243	23.9	0	0	0	1	1	0	0	0	0	0	0	0	0	0	0	0	0	0	0	0	0	0	0	2	0
Anita	18	.2212	1.3706	41.4	0	7	0	0	9	2	0	0	16	0	0	0	0	0	0	0	0	0	0	0	0	0	0	2	0
Anjou	2	.2408	.1204	30.8	0	0	1	0	0	1	0	0	0	0	0	0	0	1	0	0	0	0	0	0	0	1	0	0	0
Ankara	2	.2408	.1204	30.8	0	0	1	0	1	0	0	0	0	0	0	0	0	1	0	0	0	0	0	0	0	1	0	0	0
Ankeny	5	.0000	.2284	33.6	0	0	0	0	5	0	0	0	5	0	0	0	0	0	0	0	0	0	0	0	0	0	0	0	0
ankle	40	.6898	5.7615	47.6	10	10	4	4	7	2	2	1	18	1	3	1	2	0	1	4	0	0	1	0	2	6	0	1	0
ankle-deep	3	.2197	.2090	33.2	1	0	0	0	1	1	0	0	2	0	0	0	0	0	0	0	0	0	0	0	0	0	1	0	0
ankles	23	.5941	2.9061	44.6	3	6	6	2	3	3	0	0	8	0	0	2	0	0	0	3	1	2	0	0	3	1	0	3	0
Ankylosaurus	4	.0000	.0579	27.6	4	0	0	0	0	0	0	0	0	0	0	0	0	0	0	0	0	0	0	0	0	4	0	0	0
Ann	390	.6885	56.693	57.5	221	77	44	21	13	6	7	1	227	16	0	0	43	27	6	0	1	11	1	0	1	49	2	6	0
Ann's	40	.6360	5.4380	47.4	15	11	8	2	3	0	1	0	21	3	0	1	8	0	1	0	0	1	0	0	0	5	0	0	0
Anna	129	.6068	16.583	52.2	66	19	18	3	7	7	9	0	44	10	0	1	0	3	1	0	2	0	0	0	38	14	0	16	0
Annabelle	23	.4237	2.4021	43.8	0	7	0	5	10	0	1	0	17	1	0	1	0	0	0	0	0	0	0	0	4	0	0	0	0
annals	7	.3684	.5862	37.7	0	1	0	1	2	0	3	0	1	0	0	0	0	0	0	1	0	0	0	0	0	2	3	0	0
Annapolis	7	.2537	.4664	36.7	1	0	0	0	0	5	1	0	1	0	0	0	0	5	0	0	0	0	0	0	0	1	0	0	0
annas	4	.0000	.1827	32.6	4	0	0	0	0	0	0	0	4	0	0	0	0	0	0	0	0	0	0	0	0	0	0	0	0
Anne	67	.7352	10.110	50.0	4	6	14	7	21	10	4	1	26	2	2	15	3	0	0	0	0	2	1	0	0	7	7	2	0
Anne's	16	.5017	1.7879	42.5	3	3	1	1	1	5	2	0	7	0	2	1	3	0	0	1	1	0	0	0	0	1	0	0	0
annealed	2	.0000	.0050	17.0	0	0	0	0	1	1	0	0	0	0	0	0	0	0	0	0	0	0	0	2	0	0	0	0	0
annealing	3	.1856	.1648	32.2	1	0	0	0	0	0	1	1	1	0	0	0	0	0	0	1	0	0	0	1	0	0	0	0	0
Annette	14	.0000	.6396	38.1	10	0	0	4	0	0	0	0	14	0	0	0	0	0	0	0	0	0	0	0	0	0	0	0	0
Annette's	2	.0000	.0914	29.6	2	0	0	0	0	0	0	0	2	0	0	0	0	0	0	0	0	0	0	0	0	0	0	0	0
annex	14	.5124	1.5342	41.9	2	0	1	4	3	3	1	0	2	1	0	0	7	0	0	0	0	0	0	0	2	1	1	0	0
annexation	5	.3684	.4146	36.2	0	0	1	0	1	2	1	0	0	0	0	0	0	3	0	0	0	0	0	0	0	1	1	0	0
Annexe	9	.2357	.6596	38.2	0	0	0	0	0	9	0	0	6	0	0	0	0	0	0	0	0	0	0	0	0	3	0	0	0
annexed	12	.4577	1.1738	40.7	0	1	4	1	5	1	0	0	0	0	0	0	3	3	0	0	0	0	0	0	0	2	4	0	0
annexing	2	.2417	.1211	30.8	0	0	0	0	1	0	1	0	0	0	0	0	1	1	0	0	0	0	0	0	0	0	0	0	0
Annie	104	.3987	9.4830	49.8	7	63	9	0	2	1	22	0	26	0	0	22	0	0	0	0	1	0	0	0	2	52	0	1	0
Annie's	9	.3336	.7575	38.8	1	4	3	0	0	0	1	0	4	0	0	1	0	0	0	0	0	0	0	0	0	4	0	0	0
annihilated	2	.1787	.1174	30.7	0	0	0	0	2	0	0	0	1	0	0	0	0	0	0	0	0	0	0	0	1	0	0	0	0
annihilation	3	.3870	.2486	34.0	0	0	0	0	0	2	1	0	0	0	0	1	0	0	0	0	0	0	0	0	0	0	1	1	0
Annika	16	.1787	.9390	39.7	14	2	0	0	0	0	0	0	8	0	0	0	0	0	0	0	0	0	0	0	8	0	0	0	0
anniversary	25	.7359	3.7408	45.7	0	6	2	6	2	5	2	2	5	1	0	0	0	1	2	2	1	0	0	0	3	1	4	5	0
announce	32	.8262	5.2930	47.2	3	3	3	4	10	4	4	1	5	3	1	4	0	3	0	2	3	0	0	1	1	5	1	3	0
announced	162	.8503	27.606	54.4	13	19	18	26	39	29	15	3	44	4	3	7	5	20	1	5	3	0	3	0	15	18	5	29	0
announcement	37	.6228	4.7962	46.8	6	5	2	2	6	14	1	1	8	11	1	0	0	2	0	0	0	0	0	0	2	2	2	9	0
announcements	8	.1918	.3863	35.9	0	0	1	1	1	5	0	0	0	6	0	0	0	1	0	1	0	0	0	0	0	0	0	0	0
announcer	17	.7178	2.5156	44.0	5	1	3	5	3	0	0	0	6	2	0	1	1	2	1	0	0	0	0	0	2	0	0	2	0
Announcer	2	.0000	.0914	29.6	0	0	0	1	1	0	0	0	2	0	0	0	0	0	0	0	0	0	0	0	0	0	0	0	0
ANNOUNCER	9	.0457	.2064	33.1	0	0	0	1	1	7	0	0	1	0	0	8	0	0	0	0	0	0	0	0	0	0	0	0	0
announcers	2	.2446	.1125	30.5	0	1	0	0	0	0	1	0	0	1	0	1	0	0	0	0	0	0	0	0	0	0	0	0	0
announces	16	.6955	2.2714	43.6	1	3	2	1	3	4	2	0	2	1	0	1	1	4	0	0	3	0	0	0	0	1	2	1	0
announcing	14	.2410	.8090	39.1	2	0	0	1	3	5	2	1	1	3	0	1	0	0	0	1	1	0	0	0	0	1	0	5	1
annoy	13	.5154	1.4536	41.6	1	2	0	2	3	3	2	0	4	0	2	0	0	1	1	1	0	0	0	0	2	1	1	0	0
annoyance	13	.5582	1.5371	41.9	2	2	1	1	3	2	1	1	3	1	1	0	0	0	0	1	0	0	0	0	5	0	1	1	0
annoyances	3	.3776	.2504	34.0	0	1	0	0	0	0	2	0	0	0	0	1	0	1	0	0	0	0	0	0	0	1	0	0	0
annoyed	44	.4049	3.9617	46.0	3	5	5	13	7	7	3	1	10	2	10	11	0	1	0	1	0	0	0	0	5	4	0	0	0
annoying	16	.7670	2.4854	44.0	2	1	3	2	1	2	2	3	3	2	0	0	0	2	0	3	1	0	1	0	1	1	1	1	0
annual	85	.8515	14.428	51.6	2	9	8	11	15	17	16	7	6	4	1	2	3	19	1	7	2	0	2	0	4	9	10	15	0
annually	39	.6376	5.1078	47.1	2	1	2	2	14	6	10	2	4	1	0	1	6	3	0	0	1	0	1	0	0	1	14	7	0
annuals	5	.2332	.2712	34.3	2	0	0	2	1	0	0	0	0	0	0	0	0	0	0	0	0	0	0	0	2	0	3	0	0
annular	3	.0986	.0757	28.8	0	1	0	0	0	2	0	0	0	0	0	0	0	0	0	0	0	0	0	2	0	1	0	0	0
annulled	2	.2441	.1127	30.5	0	0	0	0	0	1	1	0	0	0	0	0	0	0	0	0	0	0	0	0	1	0	1	0	0
annum	5	.3625	.3984	36.0	0	0	0	0	3	2	0	0	0	1	0	0	3	0	0	0	0	0	0	0	0	0	1	0	0
anode	4	.0000	.0789	29.0	0	1	0	0	0	0	0	3	0	0	0	0	0	0	0	4	0	0	0	0	0	0	0	0	0
anoint	3	.2245	.1512	31.8	0	0	3	0	0	0	0	0	0	0	0	0	0	0	1	0	2	0	0	0	0	0	0	0	0
anole	3	.0000	.0591	27.7	0	0	0	0	0	0	3	0	0	0	0	0	0	0	0	3	0	0	0	0	0	0	0	0	0
anomaly	2	.1698	.1133	30.5	0	0	0	0	1	1	0	0	1	0	0	0	0	0	0	0	0	0	0	0	0	0	1	0	0
anon	5	.1400	.2438	33.9	0	0	0	1	0	2	2	0	2	0	0	3	0	0	0	0	0	0	0	0	0	0	0	0	0
anonymous	6	.3730	.5104	37.1	0	0	0	1	2	1	1	1	1	0	0	1	0	0	0	1	0	0	0	0	0	0	0	3	0
another	4377	.9920	854.00	69.3	772	700	544	588	815	484	379	95	1033	272	47	186	349	447	149	547	195	51	54	37	233	351	195	229	2
Another	5	.0000	.0608	27.8	5	0	0	0	0	0	0	0	0	0	0	0	0	0	0	0	0	0	0	0	0	0	0	5	0
another's	21	.7033	3.0284	44.8	2	3	0	3	4	3	5	1	5	3	1	5	0	1	0	2	0	0	0	0	1	1	1	1	0
Ansel	3	.0000	.0322	25.1	0	0	0	0	0	0	3	0	0	0	0	3	0	0	0	0	0	0	0	0	0	0	0	0	0
answer	2002	.8179	329.65	65.2	353	320	262	291	361	216	172	27	477	153	12	84	763	85	55	159	40	2	7	10	52	50	14	36	3
Answer	2	.2398	.1138	30.6	0	1	0	0	1	0	0	0	0	0	0	1	1	0	0	0	0	0	0	0	0	0	0	0	0
answered	720	.8180	119.24	60.8	162	182	95	70	111	61	33	6	298	31	7	53	35	54	6	17	8	0	0	0	97	85	4	23	2
answering	81	.8516	13.813	51.4	7	16	10	8	19	13	5	3	21	10	0	5	8	4	1	7	4	2	0	0	7	7	2	3	0
answers	708	.7399	106.50	60.3	198	107	88	82	115	73	39	6	109	57	6	7	297	51	35	85	8	0	12	1	2	9	10	19	0
ant	146	.6657	20.303	53.1	78	15	1	9	26	13	3	1	46	9	0	2	4	3	19	48	1	0	0	0	0	0	9	5	0
ant's	7	.0000	.1380	31.4	7	0	0	0	0	0	0	0	0	0	0	0	0	0	0	7	0	0	0	0	0	0	0	0	0
Antaeus	2	.0000	.0914	29.6	0	0	0	0	2	0	0	0	2	0	0	0	0	0	0	0	0	0	0	0	0	0	0	0	0
antagonism	7	.4842	.7294	38.6	0	0	1	0	1	0	3	2	1	2	0	2	0	1	0	0	0	0	0	0	0	1	0	0	0
antagonist	2	.0000	.0215	23.3	0	0	0	0	0	1	1	0	0	0	0	2	0	0	0	0	0	0	0	0	0	0	0	0	0
antagonists	3	.2357	.2199	33.4	0	0	0	0	3	0	0	0	2	0	0	0	0	0	0	0	0	0	0	0	0	1	0	0	0
antagonize	2	.2351	.1166	30.7	0	0	0	0	1	0	1	0	0	0	0	0	0	1	0	0	0	0	0	0	0	0	0	1	0
Antalya	2	.0000	.0389	25.9	0	0	0	0	2	0	0	0	0	0	0	0	0	2	0	0	0	0	0	0	0	0	0	0	0
antarctic	5	.4710	.5332	37.3	0	0	1	3	1	0	0	0	2	0	0	0	0	0	0	1	0	0	0	0	1	0	1	0	0
Antarctic	49	.5035	5.4822	47.4	1	25	3	12	3	3	2	0	14	0	0	3	0	5	0	24	0	0	0	0	2	0	1	0	0
Antarctica	58	.5399	6.8037	48.3	3	23	4	12	9	3	3	1	13	0	0	3	2	27	0	10	0	0	0	0	0	1	2	0	0
Antares	4	.0000	.0789	29.0	0	0	0	0	0	0	1	3	0	0	0	0	0	0	0	4	0	0	0	0	0	0	0	0	0
ante	3	.2060	.1430	31.6	0	0	0	0	2	0	1	0	0	1	0	0	0	0	2	0	0	0	0	0	0	0	0	0	0
anteater	26	.3043	2.3015	43.6	23	0	0	0	2	0	0	1	22	0	0	0	0	0	0	2	0	0	0	0	0	2	0	0	0
Anteater	3	.0000	.1370	31.4	3	0	0	0	0	0	0	0	3	0	0	0	0	0	0	0	0	0	0	0	0	0	0	0	0
anteater's	2	.0000	.0914	29.6	1	0	0	0	1	0	0	0	2	0	0	0	0	0	0	0	0	0	0	0	0	0	0	0	0

9H animalcule
4A animalports
5A animals's
XH Animas
6R animated-live-action
XR animation
9Q Anio
XR anis
7Q anise
4P ankylosaurs
4P ankylosaurus
6R AnnArbor
9R Ann-Margret
5R Ann-Margret's
5J Anna's
7A Annabelle's
XH annabergite
XR Annahoj
5Q AnnalenderPhysik
5Q Annals
XR Anne-Marie
8F Anne-style
8M anneal
7P annexes
7Q annihilate
7Q annihilating
5A anniversaries
7Q Anniversary
9B anno
XR annotated
6A announcer's
4B annoyingly
XR annoys
5P annuities
5Q annul
7R anodized
3S anointed
8D anointest
5P anonymity
7N anonymously
7H Anopheles
7A anosmics
9D another'n
9R ans
5A anser
3Q Ansgar
7P answer'd
9P answerable
7D answerer
6B Answering
4B Ant
3P ANT
7G ant-
3A ant-eating
3A ant-sniffer
7A antagonisms
8F antagonistic
XR ante-bellum

Word Type	F	D	U	SFI	3 Gr 3	4 Gr 4	5 Gr 5	6 Gr 6	7 Gr 7	8 Gr 8	9 Gr 9	X UnGr	A Read	B Eng & Gr	C Comp	D Lit	E Math	F Soc Stud	G Spell	H Sci	J Music	K Art	L Home Ec	M Shop	N Lib F	P Lib NF	Q Lib Ref	R Mag	S Rel
anteaters	7	.3835	.6734	38.3	5	1	0	0	0	0	0	1	4	0	0	0	0	0	0	2	0	0	0	0	0	1	0	0	0
antebellum	2	.2376	.1088	30.4	0	0	0	0	1	1	0	0	0	0	0	0	0	0	1	0	0	0	0	0	0	0	0	1	0
antecedent	15	.2255	.7345	38.7	0	0	0	0	11	0	4	0	0	4	8	0	0	0	1	0	1	0	0	0	0	0	0	1	0
antechamber	2	.0000	.0914	29.6	0	0	0	0	0	2	0	0	2	0	0	0	0	0	0	0	0	0	0	0	0	0	0	0	0
antelope	22	.6480	2.9867	44.8	0	3	4	3	10	0	2	0	7	0	0	0	0	5	0	1	1	0	1	0	1	1	5	0	0
Antelope	2	.1458	.0682	28.3	1	1	0	0	0	0	0	0	0	1	0	0	0	0	0	0	0	1	0	0	0	0	0	0	0
antelopes	17	.5111	1.8568	42.7	6	1	0	2	8	0	0	0	2	0	0	0	0	3	0	1	0	0	0	0	1	5	5	0	0
antenna	31	.6260	4.0028	46.0	0	1	2	6	7	7	5	3	2	1	0	1	0	1	0	11	0	0	0	2	0	1	5	7	0
antennae	36	.5460	4.1180	46.1	24	0	3	3	5	0	1	0	0	1	0	0	0	0	0	16	0	0	0	1	0	11	6	1	0
antennas	9	.6089	1.1546	40.6	1	0	1	1	5	0	1	0	2	1	0	0	0	0	0	3	0	0	0	0	0	1	1	1	0
anteroom	2	.1473	.0686	28.4	0	0	0	0	1	1	0	0	0	0	0	1	0	0	0	0	0	1	0	0	0	0	0	0	0
anthem	12	.2021	.5891	37.7	0	3	5	2	1	1	0	0	1	0	0	0	0	0	0	0	9	0	0	0	0	0	1	1	0
Anthem	4	.0759	.1243	30.9	0	4	0	0	0	0	0	0	1	0	0	0	0	0	0	0	3	0	0	0	0	0	0	0	0
anthems	3	.1852	.1342	31.3	0	1	0	0	1	0	1	0	0	0	0	0	0	0	0	0	2	0	0	0	0	1	0	0	0
anther	2	.0000	.0394	26.0	0	0	0	0	0	0	2	0	0	0	0	0	0	0	0	2	0	0	0	0	0	0	0	0	0
anthill	8	.6173	1.0409	40.2	1	3	0	2	1	1	0	0	2	1	0	1	0	1	0	2	0	0	0	0	0	0	0	1	0
Anthill	2	.0000	.0219	23.4	0	2	0	0	0	0	0	0	0	2	0	0	0	0	0	0	0	0	0	0	0	0	0	0	0
anthologies	2	.0000	.0243	23.9	0	0	0	0	0	0	0	2	0	0	0	0	0	0	0	0	0	0	0	0	0	0	0	2	0
anthology	2	.2412	.1141	30.6	0	0	0	0	1	0	1	0	0	1	0	0	0	0	0	0	0	0	0	0	0	1	0	0	0
Anthony	8	.5505	.9130	39.6	0	2	1	0	1	2	2	0	0	1	0	1	0	2	0	0	0	0	0	0	0	0	2	2	0
Anthony's	2	.0000	.0219	23.4	0	2	0	0	0	0	0	0	0	2	0	0	0	0	0	0	0	0	0	0	0	0	0	0	0
anthracite	3	.3553	.2609	34.2	1	0	0	1	0	1	0	0	1	0	0	0	0	0	0	1	0	0	0	0	0	1	0	0	0
anthrax	17	.0429	.4889	36.9	0	0	1	13	0	0	0	3	1	0	0	0	0	0	0	16	0	0	0	0	0	0	0	0	0
anthropoid	3	.1169	.1277	31.1	0	0	0	0	2	1	0	0	1	0	0	0	0	0	0	0	0	0	0	0	0	0	2	0	0
anthropological	5	.3116	.3461	35.4	0	0	1	0	0	1	2	1	0	0	0	0	0	0	0	0	0	0	0	0	0	1	3	1	0
anthropologist	7	.5365	.7850	38.9	1	0	0	0	2	1	2	1	0	0	0	0	1	2	0	0	0	0	0	0	0	1	2	1	0
anthropologists	21	.1797	.9551	39.8	0	0	5	0	7	6	3	0	0	0	0	0	1	4	0	0	0	0	0	0	0	0	16	0	0
anthropology	5	.0000	.0523	27.2	0	0	1	0	0	1	3	0	0	0	0	0	0	0	0	0	0	0	0	0	0	0	5	0	0
anthropomorphism	2	.0000	.0243	23.9	0	0	0	0	2	0	0	0	0	0	0	0	0	0	0	0	0	0	0	0	0	0	0	2	0
anti	2	.1814	.1187	30.7	0	0	0	1	0	0	0	1	1	0	0	0	0	0	0	0	0	0	0	0	0	0	0	1	0
anti-	2	.2376	.1088	30.4	0	0	0	0	2	0	0	0	0	0	0	0	0	0	1	0	0	0	0	0	0	0	0	1	0
anti-American	3	.2425	.1816	32.6	0	0	0	0	1	2	0	0	0	0	0	0	0	2	0	0	0	0	0	0	0	0	0	1	0
anti-Chinese	2	.0000	.0389	25.9	0	0	0	0	0	2	0	0	0	0	0	0	0	2	0	0	0	0	0	0	0	0	0	0	0
anti-Semitic	2	.2405	.1205	30.8	0	0	0	0	2	0	0	0	0	0	0	0	0	0	0	1	0	0	0	0	0	1	0	0	0
anti-aircraft	6	.5189	.6680	38.2	0	1	0	1	4	0	0	0	1	0	0	0	0	1	0	0	0	0	0	0	0	2	1	1	0
anti-freeze	3	.3553	.2608	34.2	1	1	0	1	0	0	0	0	1	0	0	0	0	1	0	0	0	0	0	0	0	1	0	0	0
anti-matter	3	.0000	.0591	27.7	0	0	0	0	0	0	0	3	0	0	0	0	0	0	0	3	0	0	0	0	0	0	0	0	0
anti-particles	2	.0000	.0394	26.0	0	0	0	0	0	0	0	2	0	0	0	0	0	0	0	2	0	0	0	0	0	0	0	0	0
anti-slavery	2	.0000	.0389	25.9	0	0	0	0	0	1	1	0	0	0	0	0	0	2	0	0	0	0	0	0	0	0	0	0	0
antiaircraft	3	.2332	.1690	32.3	0	0	2	0	0	0	1	0	0	0	0	0	0	0	0	0	0	0	0	0	0	2	0	1	0
antibacterial	2	.0000	.0394	26.0	0	0	0	0	0	0	2	0	0	0	0	0	0	0	0	2	0	0	0	0	0	0	0	0	0
antibiotic	7	.2740	.4893	36.9	1	0	0	2	2	2	0	0	1	0	0	0	0	0	0	5	0	0	0	0	0	0	1	0	0
antibiotics	24	.4857	2.5040	44.0	0	3	1	5	3	4	8	0	0	0	0	0	1	0	1	16	0	0	0	0	0	3	2	1	0
antibodies	14	.1230	.5739	37.6	0	2	0	6	5	0	0	1	0	0	0	0	0	0	0	13	0	0	0	0	0	0	0	1	0
antibody	2	.0000	.0394	26.0	0	0	0	2	0	0	0	0	0	0	0	0	0	0	0	2	0	0	0	0	0	0	0	0	0
antic	2	.2440	.1132	30.5	0	0	0	0	1	0	1	0	0	0	0	1	0	0	0	0	0	0	0	0	0	0	0	1	0
anticipate	8	.4399	.7671	38.8	0	0	0	0	3	0	4	1	1	0	0	1	0	1	0	0	0	0	0	0	0	0	1	4	0
anticipated	11	.3503	.8245	39.2	1	0	0	1	4	2	1	2	0	1	3	1	0	0	0	0	0	0	0	0	0	1	0	5	0
anticipates	4	.2442	.2268	33.6	0	0	0	0	0	3	0	1	0	2	0	0	0	0	0	0	0	0	0	0	0	0	0	2	0
anticipating	3	.3795	.2506	34.0	0	0	0	1	0	1	1	0	0	0	0	0	0	1	0	0	0	0	0	0	1	0	0	1	0
anticipation	13	.5908	1.6272	42.1	1	0	1	3	5	2	1	0	4	1	0	3	0	0	0	0	0	0	0	0	2	1	0	2	0
Anticipations	2	.0000	.0243	23.9	0	0	0	0	0	2	0	0	0	0	0	0	0	0	0	0	0	0	0	0	0	0	0	2	0
antics	10	.5802	1.2027	40.8	1	3	1	0	3	2	0	0	1	0	0	0	0	0	0	0	2	0	0	0	2	2	1	2	0
antidemocratic	2	.2297	.1135	30.6	0	0	0	0	0	1	1	0	0	0	0	1	0	1	0	0	0	0	0	0	0	0	0	0	0
antifreeze	2	.0000	.0209	23.2	0	0	0	1	0	1	0	0	0	0	0	0	0	0	0	0	0	0	0	0	0	0	2	0	0
antigen	2	.0000	.0394	26.0	0	0	0	0	0	0	0	2	0	0	0	0	0	0	0	2	0	0	0	0	0	0	0	0	0
Antigone	2	.0000	.0209	23.2	0	0	0	0	0	2	0	0	0	0	0	0	0	0	0	0	0	0	0	0	0	0	2	0	0
antiknock	2	.0000	.0209	23.2	0	0	0	2	0	0	0	0	0	0	0	0	0	0	0	0	0	0	0	0	0	0	2	0	0
Antilles	4	.3730	.3365	35.3	0	0	0	2	0	1	1	0	0	0	0	0	0	2	0	1	0	0	0	0	0	0	1	0	0
antimony	6	.4017	.5486	37.4	2	0	2	0	1	1	0	0	1	0	0	0	0	2	0	1	0	0	0	0	0	0	2	0	0
Antinous	3	.0000	.1370	31.4	0	0	0	0	3	0	0	0	3	0	0	0	0	0	0	0	0	0	0	0	0	0	0	0	0
Antioch	2	.2437	.1129	30.5	0	1	0	1	0	0	0	0	0	0	0	0	0	0	0	0	0	0	0	0	0	0	1	1	0
Antiochus	3	.0000	.0243	23.8	0	0	0	0	0	3	0	0	0	0	0	0	0	0	0	0	3	0	0	0	0	0	0	0	0
Antioquia	2	.0000	.0290	24.6	0	0	2	0	0	0	0	0	0	0	0	0	0	0	0	0	0	0	0	0	0	2	0	0	0
antipathies	2	.2446	.1142	30.6	0	0	0	0	2	0	0	0	0	0	0	0	0	0	0	0	0	0	0	0	1	0	0	1	0
antiperspirant	2	.0000	.0243	23.9	0	0	0	0	2	0	0	0	0	0	0	0	0	0	0	0	0	0	0	0	0	0	0	2	0
antiphonal	8	.0000	.0647	28.1	0	0	0	6	1	1	0	0	0	0	0	0	0	0	0	0	8	0	0	0	0	0	0	0	0
antiphony	2	.2411	.1091	30.4	0	0	0	0	1	1	0	0	0	0	0	1	0	0	0	0	1	0	0	0	0	0	0	0	0
antique	17	.5846	2.0903	43.2	0	0	1	8	4	1	2	1	4	4	0	1	0	0	0	0	0	0	0	0	2	0	2	4	0
antiques	3	.3781	.2493	34.0	0	0	0	0	1	1	1	0	0	1	0	0	0	1	0	0	0	0	0	0	0	0	0	1	0
antiquity	8	.3434	.6020	37.8	0	0	0	0	2	1	4	1	0	0	0	1	0	1	0	0	0	0	0	0	0	0	5	1	0
antiseptic	14	.3791	1.1981	40.8	0	0	1	3	2	6	2	0	0	0	0	0	2	0	0	10	0	0	0	0	0	0	1	1	0
antiseptics	6	.0000	.1183	30.7	0	0	0	2	0	4	0	0	0	0	0	0	0	0	0	6	0	0	0	0	0	0	0	0	0
antislavery	4	.1505	.1615	32.1	0	1	2	0	0	1	0	0	0	0	0	0	0	1	0	0	0	0	0	0	0	0	3	0	0
antisocial	2	.2437	.1129	30.5	0	0	0	0	1	0	1	0	0	0	0	0	0	0	0	0	0	0	0	0	0	0	1	1	0
antitank	2	.0000	.0290	24.6	0	0	2	0	0	0	0	0	0	0	0	0	0	0	0	0	0	0	0	0	0	2	0	0	0
antitoxin	21	.2317	1.5136	41.8	0	8	4	0	0	1	0	8	12	0	0	0	0	0	0	9	0	0	0	0	0	0	0	0	0
antitrust	2	.2437	.1129	30.5	0	0	1	0	0	0	1	0	0	0	0	0	0	0	0	0	0	0	0	0	0	0	1	1	0
antiwar	2	.0000	.0243	23.9	0	0	0	0	0	1	1	0	0	0	0	0	0	0	0	0	0	0	0	0	0	0	0	2	0
Antje	13	.0000	.1882	32.7	0	13	0	0	0	0	0	0	0	0	0	0	0	0	0	0	0	0	0	0	0	13	0	0	0
antlered	2	.2297	.1135	30.6	0	0	1	0	0	1	0	0	0	0	0	1	0	1	0	0	0	0	0	0	0	0	0	0	0
antlers	20	.6688	2.7697	44.4	2	2	6	7	1	1	0	1	4	0	0	1	0	2	0	5	0	0	0	0	1	2	4	1	0
Antoine	20	.4319	1.8436	42.7	0	0	0	1	4	1	14	0	1	0	0	11	0	0	0	2	0	1	0	0	0	0	5	0	0
Antoinette	5	.3114	.3665	35.6	1	0	1	1	0	0	2	0	1	0	0	0	0	1	0	0	0	1	0	0	0	0	2	0	0
Anton	13	.1892	.6579	38.2	2	1	3	1	2	0	4	0	2	0	0	0	0	0	0	3	8	0	0	0	0	0	0	0	0
Antonin	2	.2375	.1088	30.4	0	0	0	0	2	0	0	0	0	0	0	0	0	0	0	0	1	0	0	0	0	0	0	1	0
Antonio	40	.5501	4.7906	46.8	12	6	2	2	1	2	15	0	17	0	0	14	1	1	0	0	2	0	0	0	1	1	2	1	0
Antonio's	2	.1717	.1142	30.6	1	0	0	0	0	0	1	0	1	0	0	1	0	0	0	0	0	0	0	0	0	0	0	0	0
Antony	5	.3775	.4753	36.8	0	0	0	0	0	3	1	1	3	1	0	0	0	0	0	1	0	0	0	0	0	0	0	0	0
antonym	37	.1855	1.6732	42.2	1	2	4	8	7	9	4	2	2	8	0	0	0	0	27	0	0	0	0	0	0	0	0	0	0
antonyms	52	.1616	2.1499	43.3	7	4	5	12	19	4	0	1	4	8	0	0	0	0	40	0	0	0	0	0	0	0	0	0	0

7A anteating
9B antecedents
6A antediluvian
9E antelope's
6R Antenna
8A Antenor
XH anterior
5J Antes
9H antheridia
7A anthills
7N anthropophagy
6F Anti-Atlas
7R anti-Castro
8Q anti-Communist
5Q anti-Federalist
7Q Anti-Injunction
XR anti-Irish
XR anti-Know-Nothing
6R Anti-Locust
8F Anti-Nebraska
7P Anti-Slavery
8R anti-U
5P anti-West
9F anti-ballistic
8R anti-ballistic-missile
XR anti-blemish
7R anti-cavity
5P anti-church
3H anti-cyclones
7R anti-doping
8C anti-gun
8C anti-hunting
7A anti-impeaching
7R anti-inflammants
9R anti-inflation
9R anti-inflationary
7R anti-insomnia
7R anti-intellectualism
8Q anti-masque
XH anti-matter-galaxies
7R anti-religious
9F anti-segregation
7R anti-tension
7R anti-trust
8F anti-union
XH anti-universe
7Q anti-war
5P anti-white
5P anticapitalist
9B anticipate/anticipation
8Q Anticleia
9Q anticlimactic
5Q anticlimax
5P anticommunist
5A anticontact
9H anticyclones
8B antidisestablishmentari**
5A antidotes
6A antigravity
8F antilynching
8F antimonopoly
6A Antin
XH antiparticles
7B antipasto
4Q Antipater
7N antipathy
8E antipodal
9R antipollution
5Q antipope
XR antiquarian
9Q Antiquaries
XR antiquated
7P Antique
6R antique-car
6A antiquities
9Q Antiquities
9R antisubmarine
XR antisway
6H antitetanus
7R antithesis
6A Antone
8B Antonia
8G Antonyms
8G antonyms-words

Word Type	F	D	U	SFI	3 Gr 3	4 Gr 4	5 Gr 5	6 Gr 6	7 Gr 7	8 Gr 8	9 Gr 9	X UnGr	A Read	B Eng & Gr	C Comp	D Lit	E Math	F Soc Stud	G Spell	H Sci	J Music	K Art	L Home Ec	M Shop	N Lib F	P Lib NF	Q Lib Ref	R Mag	S Rel
ants	325	.6503	44.388	56.5	191	38	6	28	47	4	9	2	96	22	2	3	1	3	1	137	0	0	0	0	1	17	30	12	0
ants'	4	.2386	.2998	34.8	1	1	0	0	2	0	0	0	3	0	0	0	0	0	0	0	0	0	0	0	0	0	1	0	0
Antwerp	3	.3766	.2497	34.0	0	0	1	1	0	0	1	0	0	0	0	0	0	1	0	0	0	0	0	0	0	1	1	0	0
anus	4	.0000	.0789	29.0	0	0	1	0	1	0	1	1	0	0	0	0	0	0	0	4	0	0	0	0	0	0	0	0	0
anvil	33	.2690	2.0123	43.0	0	0	0	6	11	12	4	0	2	0	0	0	0	0	1	6	1	0	0	15	0	3	1	4	0
anvils	3	.1397	.0937	29.7	0	0	0	0	1	0	2	0	0	0	0	0	0	0	0	0	1	0	0	2	0	0	0	0	0
anxiety	27	.7782	4.2257	46.3	0	1	2	2	12	6	4	0	4	1	1	6	0	1	3	1	0	0	1	0	3	1	1	4	0
anxious	88	.8147	14.452	51.6	12	14	10	12	15	11	14	0	27	7	3	6	0	4	1	1	2	0	1	0	12	12	2	10	0
anxiously	75	.7231	11.233	50.5	13	16	13	10	12	9	1	1	34	3	1	6	0	5	0	1	1	0	0	0	14	7	0	3	0
any	5023	.9705	960.91	69.8	672	718	534	664	1065	699	568	103	1035	297	61	302	585	385	319	482	143	38	99	66	293	343	279	296	0
Any	3	.0000	.0365	25.6	0	0	0	0	3	0	0	0	0	0	0	0	0	0	0	0	0	0	0	0	0	0	0	3	0
anybody	192	.7083	28.010	54.5	23	32	14	19	51	23	26	4	63	16	1	40	0	5	3	1	0	0	0	0	31	15	4	13	0
anybody's	7	.3403	.5307	37.2	0	0	1	1	1	1	3	0	1	2	2	1	0	0	0	0	0	0	0	0	0	0	0	1	0
anyhow	40	.6245	5.3206	47.3	4	5	2	6	18	3	1	1	18	2	0	5	0	1	0	0	0	0	0	0	7	5	0	2	0
anymore	25	.5499	2.9693	44.7	7	4	5	1	3	2	1	2	9	1	0	0	0	0	0	0	0	0	1	0	6	1	0	7	0
anyone	552	.9219	101.07	60.0	100	95	61	76	93	65	46	16	199	33	10	28	9	46	8	33	13	1	5	6	49	56	10	46	0
anyone's	12	.5629	1.4470	41.6	3	0	0	1	3	3	2	0	4	1	0	1	0	1	0	0	0	1	0	0	1	0	0	3	0
anyplace	2	.2437	.1129	30.5	0	0	0	0	1	0	0	1	0	0	0	0	0	0	0	0	0	0	0	0	0	0	1	1	0
anything	1214	.8985	217.41	63.4	226	236	128	144	219	116	120	25	449	67	6	123	7	33	14	96	13	5	10	4	171	107	32	75	2
anytime	6	.4737	.6426	38.1	2	1	0	1	1	1	0	0	2	0	0	0	1	2	0	0	0	0	0	0	0	1	0	0	0
anyway	217	.7097	31.977	55.0	40	47	19	23	51	8	26	3	96	7	2	21	0	6	0	4	1	0	0	0	40	25	1	14	0
anyways	2	.1733	.1149	30.6	0	0	0	0	2	0	0	0	1	1	0	0	0	0	0	0	0	0	0	0	0	0	0	0	0
anywhere	200	.8393	33.673	55.3	47	31	17	24	42	16	13	10	50	13	3	14	2	15	0	18	7	0	0	0	14	19	15	30	0
anywheres	2	.2443	.1130	30.5	0	1	0	0	0	1	0	0	0	0	0	1	0	0	0	0	0	0	0	0	1	0	0	0	0
AOB	12	.0000	.1796	32.5	0	1	4	2	1	2	2	0	0	0	0	0	12	0	0	0	0	0	0	0	0	0	0	0	0
AOC	5	.0000	.0748	28.7	0	0	3	0	0	0	2	0	0	0	0	0	5	0	0	0	0	0	0	0	0	0	0	0	0
AOE	3	.0000	.0449	26.5	0	0	3	0	0	0	0	0	0	0	0	0	3	0	0	0	0	0	0	0	0	0	0	0	0
aorta	5	.2213	.2870	34.6	0	0	0	1	0	2	2	0	0	0	0	0	0	0	0	4	0	0	0	0	0	0	1	0	0
Aouda	12	.0000	.1407	31.5	0	0	0	0	12	0	0	0	0	0	0	0	0	0	0	0	0	0	0	0	12	0	0	0	0
AP	2	.0000	.0299	24.8	0	1	0	0	0	1	0	0	0	0	0	0	2	0	0	0	0	0	0	0	0	0	0	0	0
apace	2	.2427	.1152	30.6	0	0	0	1	1	0	0	0	0	0	0	0	0	0	0	0	0	0	0	0	1	1	0	0	0
Apache	20	.4255	1.9611	42.9	0	0	8	2	6	0	0	4	8	1	0	5	0	0	0	0	0	0	0	0	0	0	0	6	0
Apaches	7	.3022	.5439	37.4	0	0	1	0	6	0	0	0	3	0	0	3	0	0	0	0	0	0	0	0	0	1	0	0	0
apart	414	.9308	76.231	58.8	51	66	57	51	71	51	51	16	49	14	6	18	32	29	2	100	31	4	7	10	17	28	31	36	0
apartheid	5	.1649	.2071	33.2	0	0	0	0	1	0	4	0	0	0	0	0	0	0	0	0	0	0	0	0	0	0	4	1	0
apartment	183	.6971	26.612	54.3	90	9	8	21	28	12	13	2	76	5	0	4	0	50	0	1	0	0	4	0	8	5	5	25	0
Apartment	5	.0000	.0608	27.8	5	0	0	0	0	0	0	0	0	0	0	0	0	0	0	0	0	0	0	0	0	0	0	5	0
apartments	30	.6744	4.1214	46.2	11	1	3	1	2	2	8	2	1	1	1	0	0	11	0	0	0	0	2	0	1	2	4	7	0
apathetic	2	.2376	.1088	30.4	0	0	0	0	0	1	1	0	0	0	0	0	0	0	1	0	0	0	0	0	0	0	0	1	0
apathy	3	.3465	.2515	34.0	0	0	1	0	1	1	0	0	1	0	0	0	0	0	0	0	0	0	0	0	0	1	0	1	0
apatite	2	.0000	.0394	26.0	0	0	0	0	0	0	2	0	0	0	0	0	0	0	0	2	0	0	0	0	0	0	0	0	0
APBA	2	.0000	.0243	23.9	0	0	0	0	0	2	0	0	0	0	0	0	0	0	0	0	0	0	0	0	0	0	0	2	0
ape	17	.2480	1.0952	40.4	2	0	0	0	13	2	0	0	5	0	0	2	0	0	0	0	0	0	0	0	0	0	10	0	0
apelike	4	.0904	.1412	31.5	0	0	0	1	3	0	0	0	1	0	0	0	0	0	0	0	0	0	0	0	0	0	3	0	0
Apennine	4	.2348	.2372	33.8	0	1	0	3	0	0	0	0	0	0	0	0	0	3	0	0	0	0	0	0	0	0	1	0	0
Apennines	5	.3830	.4247	36.3	3	0	0	2	0	0	0	0	0	0	0	0	0	2	0	0	0	0	0	0	0	2	1	0	0
aperture	4	.3065	.2965	34.7	0	0	0	1	1	1	0	1	1	1	0	0	0	0	0	0	0	0	0	0	2	0	0	0	0
apertures	2	.0000	.0394	26.0	0	0	0	0	0	0	0	2	0	0	0	0	0	0	0	2	0	0	0	0	0	0	0	0	0
apes	25	.3416	1.9875	43.0	1	2	0	1	19	1	1	0	4	0	0	0	0	5	0	2	0	0	0	0	0	1	13	0	0
apex	5	.4352	.4670	36.7	0	0	0	0	1	4	0	0	0	0	0	0	1	1	0	0	0	0	0	0	0	1	2	0	0
aphid	4	.2353	.2382	33.8	2	0	0	0	2	0	0	0	0	0	0	0	0	0	0	3	0	0	0	0	0	0	1	0	0
aphids	35	.3492	2.9949	44.8	15	1	0	4	15	0	0	0	11	0	0	0	0	0	0	17	0	0	0	0	0	0	7	0	0
aphrodisiac	3	.0000	.0365	25.6	0	0	0	1	0	0	0	2	0	0	0	0	0	0	0	0	0	0	0	0	0	0	0	3	0
Aphrodite	4	.0000	.1827	32.6	0	0	0	0	0	4	0	0	4	0	0	0	0	0	0	0	0	0	0	0	0	0	0	0	0
apiece	27	.6222	3.5370	45.5	5	3	3	2	6	1	2	5	8	0	0	1	10	1	1	0	0	0	0	0	3	0	1	2	0
apocalyptic	2	.0000	.0243	23.9	0	0	0	0	1	1	0	0	0	0	0	0	0	0	0	0	0	0	0	0	0	0	0	2	0
apocryphal	2	.2446	.1122	30.5	0	0	0	0	1	0	1	0	0	0	0	1	0	0	0	0	0	0	0	0	0	0	1	0	0
apogee	5	.0000	.0986	29.9	3	0	0	0	0	2	0	0	0	0	0	0	0	0	0	5	0	0	0	0	0	0	0	0	0
Apollo	108	.7183	15.718	52.0	10	24	9	15	29	11	10	0	10	14	0	5	3	8	1	8	1	3	0	2	0	1	9	43	0
apologetic	2	.1787	.1174	30.7	0	0	0	0	1	1	0	0	1	0	0	0	0	0	0	0	0	0	0	0	1	0	0	0	0
apologetically	6	.0000	.0644	28.1	0	0	0	1	5	0	0	0	0	0	0	6	0	0	0	0	0	0	0	0	0	0	0	0	0
apologies	5	.4592	.4871	36.9	0	0	0	1	2	0	2	0	0	0	0	1	0	0	0	1	0	0	0	0	1	0	0	2	0
apologize	11	.4673	1.2066	40.8	4	3	0	3	1	0	0	0	7	1	0	0	0	0	0	0	0	0	0	0	2	1	0	0	0
apologized	4	.4522	.3988	36.0	0	0	2	0	0	1	1	0	1	1	0	0	0	0	0	0	0	0	0	0	0	0	1	1	0
apology	11	.4734	1.1627	40.7	3	0	1	1	2	2	2	0	4	4	0	0	0	0	0	0	0	0	0	0	1	1	0	1	0
Apolonia	3	.0000	.0322	25.1	0	0	0	0	3	0	0	0	0	0	0	3	0	0	0	0	0	0	0	0	0	0	0	0	0
apostle	2	.2408	.1091	30.4	0	0	0	1	1	0	0	0	0	1	0	0	0	0	1	0	0	0	0	0	0	0	0	0	0
apostolic	2	.0000	.0290	24.6	0	0	2	0	0	0	0	0	0	0	0	0	0	0	0	0	0	0	0	0	0	2	0	0	0
apostrophe	98	.3397	7.2698	48.6	16	27	19	22	2	4	8	0	5	46	2	0	0	0	45	0	0	0	0	0	0	0	0	0	0
apostrophes	12	.3200	.8223	39.2	0	1	3	1	3	3	1	0	0	7	3	0	0	0	2	0	0	0	0	0	0	0	0	0	0
Appalachian	56	.5861	6.8240	48.3	6	1	21	8	6	8	4	2	2	0	0	1	0	25	0	2	8	0	0	0	0	4	10	4	0
Appalachians	36	.5733	4.2822	46.3	6	1	10	0	6	12	1	0	0	0	0	0	0	12	0	3	3	0	0	0	0	5	10	3	0
appalled	10	.6096	1.2971	41.1	0	0	0	1	6	2	0	1	4	0	0	0	0	1	1	0	1	0	0	0	2	0	0	1	0
appalling	8	.4752	.8145	39.1	0	0	0	1	3	3	1	0	1	0	0	3	0	0	0	0	0	0	0	0	1	1	0	2	0
appalls	2	.0000	.0209	23.2	0	0	0	0	1	0	1	0	0	0	0	0	0	0	0	0	0	0	0	0	0	0	2	0	0
Appam	3	.0000	.0314	25.0	0	0	0	0	0	3	0	0	0	0	0	0	0	0	0	0	0	0	0	0	0	0	3	0	0
apparatus	51	.7464	7.7177	48.9	0	4	3	8	8	14	9	5	7	2	2	2	0	0	0	17	1	0	1	0	4	3	10	2	0
apparel	6	.4148	.5648	37.5	0	0	0	1	3	0	2	0	2	0	0	0	0	0	0	0	0	0	1	0	0	0	1	2	0
apparent	71	.8347	11.852	50.7	0	2	0	4	33	14	13	5	10	3	1	5	3	3	0	14	4	0	2	1	1	1	16	7	0
apparently	126	.7908	20.092	53.0	6	3	12	12	43	17	24	9	25	4	1	14	1	5	0	16	1	0	2	0	6	8	26	17	0
apparition	9	.4598	.8887	39.5	0	1	0	0	4	2	2	0	1	2	0	1	0	0	0	0	0	0	0	0	4	1	0	0	0
appeal	79	.7105	11.344	50.5	3	6	10	1	19	17	20	3	7	7	9	8	0	4	0	1	5	0	1	1	3	7	7	19	0
appealed	25	.7370	3.7756	45.8	2	1	4	2	6	6	4	0	7	1	0	2	0	6	0	1	0	0	0	0	2	3	2	1	0
appealing	33	.6784	4.5512	46.6	1	0	1	5	9	9	8	0	4	3	3	3	0	2	0	1	9	0	0	1	0	1	2	4	0
appeals	29	.6822	4.0559	46.1	0	0	4	3	4	4	13	1	6	4	2	3	0	4	0	0	0	0	3	0	0	2	2	3	0
Appeals	5	.0000	.0972	29.9	0	0	0	0	2	1	2	0	0	0	0	0	0	5	0	0	0	0	0	0	0	0	0	0	0
appear	413	.9146	74.867	58.7	18	53	44	60	93	66	53	26	69	41	8	13	26	29	17	69	21	16	9	8	11	16	41	19	0
appearance	247	.8180	40.361	56.1	5	14	10	27	73	56	48	14	24	11	6	14	1	10	2	50	11	8	28	15	10	15	30	12	0
appearances	16	.5836	1.9501	42.9	1	0	4	2	7	2	0	0	2	2	0	0	0	0	0	2	0	0	0	0	1	2	1	6	0
appeared	347	.8334	58.107	57.6	34	35	61	53	78	47	31	8	96	10	10	29	6	31	2	23	10	0	0	0	47	33	30	20	0
appearing	36	.7860	5.6834	47.5	3	7	2	1	12	4	4	3	4	2	0	1	2	1	0	4	4	0	0	1	3	2	8	4	0
appears	241	.9068	43.281	56.4	12	17	26	32	62	42	35	15	19	34	5	15	18	14	17	38	21	2	3	9	0	11	20	15	0
appease	7	.4671	.6794	38.3	0	0	2	2	1	1	1	0	0	1	0	1	0	0	0	0	0	1	0	0	3	0	1	0	0
appeasement	4	.1325	.1944	32.9	0	0	0	0	1	2	1	0	1	0	0	0	0	3	0	0	0	0	0	0	0	0	0	0	0

7B Ants
8Q Antun
8L anxieties
5P anxiety-ridden
3Q Anxious
7R Anyone
3A anythin'
5R Anything
4N anything-land
6P anything's
7A Anza-Borrego
8F Anzio
9E AO
9F AO-wnr
9E AOD
5E AOG
7G ap
9Q APARTHEID
3R apartment-sized
4Q apartment-type
3A apartment's
9E Apartments
9Q apartness
7D apathetically
7Q Ape
8D ape's
8A apeak
7R aperitifs
7Q aphid-tenders
4A aphids'
3N aphis
8A Aphrodite's
3P apiary
8A aplenty
9D APLEY
8Q Apo
7Q APO
9R Apollo's
XH Apollonius
XR Apollos
9R apologizing
7B Apostate
7A apostates
7P apostles
4S Apostles
4P apothecary
9P apothecary's
9B APP
6R Appalachicola
7G appall
7R Appalled
3P Appaloosa
6A Appaloosas
8Q appanage
7N appareled
8C apparels
9Q apparitions
7D Appassionata
7P appear'd
4R appeased

Word Type	F	D	U	SFI	3 Gr 3	4 Gr 4	5 Gr 5	6 Gr 6	7 Gr 7	8 Gr 8	9 Gr 9	X UnGr	A Read	B Eng & Gr	C Comp	D Lit	E Math	F Soc Stud	G Spell	H Sci	J Music	K Art	L Home Ec	M Shop	N Lib F	P Lib NF	Q Lib Ref	R Mag	S Rel
appellate	6	.1955	.3185	35.0	0	0	0	0	2	0	4	0	0	0	0	0	0	5	0	0	0	0	0	0	0	0	0	1	0
appendage	4	.0867	.0858	29.3	0	0	0	0	1	0	3	0	0	0	0	0	0	0	0	0	0	0	0	3	1	0	0	0	0
appendages	7	.2416	.4240	36.3	0	0	0	0	5	1	1	0	0	0	0	0	0	0	0	6	0	0	0	1	0	0	0	0	0
Appendix	6	.4180	.5469	37.4	0	0	1	0	1	0	4	0	0	1	0	0	0	1	0	3	0	0	1	0	0	0	0	0	0
Appenzell	2	.0000	.0290	24.6	0	0	2	0	0	0	0	0	0	0	0	0	0	0	0	0	0	0	0	0	0	2	0	0	0
appetite	48	.5486	5.5652	47.5	5	6	3	5	9	8	12	0	10	0	1	3	0	2	0	7	1	0	12	0	4	3	1	4	0
appetites	15	.6958	2.1149	43.3	2	3	0	3	4	0	3	0	0	0	0	0	0	1	0	4	1	0	1	0	1	3	2	2	0
appetizer	2	.1812	.0838	29.2	0	0	0	0	2	0	0	0	0	0	0	0	0	0	0	0	0	0	1	0	0	0	0	1	0
appetizing	7	.4206	.6237	38.0	0	0	3	0	1	0	3	0	0	1	0	1	0	0	0	2	0	0	2	0	0	0	1	0	0
Appian	2	.2401	.1133	30.5	1	0	0	0	0	0	1	0	0	0	0	0	0	0	0	0	0	0	0	0	0	1	1	0	0
applaud	5	.4740	.5375	37.3	1	1	0	1	1	0	1	0	2	0	0	1	0	0	0	1	0	0	0	0	0	1	0	0	0
applauded	11	.5887	1.3511	41.3	0	1	0	1	2	5	1	1	2	2	1	0	0	1	0	0	1	0	0	0	1	0	0	3	0
applauding	2	.1717	.1142	30.6	0	0	0	1	0	0	1	0	1	0	0	1	0	0	0	0	0	0	0	0	0	0	0	0	0
applauds	2	.2411	.1091	30.4	0	0	0	0	0	0	2	0	0	0	0	1	0	0	0	0	1	0	0	0	0	0	0	0	0
applause	31	.7790	4.9068	46.9	2	2	3	5	8	2	6	3	11	0	1	4	0	1	1	1	1	0	1	0	5	2	0	3	0
apple	294	.9018	52.856	57.2	94	47	27	37	46	26	14	3	117	18	7	16	27	10	12	40	7	2	4	0	15	8	3	8	0
Apple	4	.2280	.2913	34.6	3	0	0	1	0	0	0	0	3	0	0	0	0	0	1	0	0	0	0	0	0	0	0	0	0
apple-pie	2	.2407	.1138	30.6	0	0	1	0	1	0	0	0	0	0	0	1	0	0	0	0	0	0	0	0	0	1	0	0	0
Applegate	2	.1717	.1142	30.6	0	1	0	1	0	0	0	0	1	0	0	1	0	0	0	0	0	0	0	0	0	0	0	0	0
apples	284	.7377	43.052	56.3	115	72	17	24	25	13	10	8	103	8	3	1	98	9	9	7	0	0	8	0	11	14	3	10	0
applesauce	5	.2803	.3054	34.8	2	0	1	0	0	0	2	0	0	1	0	0	0	0	0	0	0	0	2	0	0	0	0	2	0
Appleseed	9	.0000	.4111	36.1	6	0	0	1	2	0	0	0	9	0	0	0	0	0	0	0	0	0	0	0	0	0	0	0	0
appliance	14	.5663	1.6293	42.1	0	0	2	0	2	4	3	3	0	0	1	0	0	1	0	2	0	0	0	1	0	0	5	4	0
appliances	31	.3597	2.4560	43.9	2	0	0	3	6	16	3	1	2	0	0	0	0	5	0	4	0	0	0	9	0	0	6	5	0
applicable	3	.3109	.2027	33.1	0	0	0	0	2	1	0	0	0	0	0	0	0	0	0	0	0	0	1	0	0	1	1	0	0
applicant	8	.4949	.8414	39.3	0	1	0	0	5	1	1	0	1	1	1	0	0	0	0	1	0	0	0	0	0	0	1	3	0
applicants	2	.0000	.0243	23.9	0	0	0	0	2	0	0	0	0	0	0	0	0	0	0	0	0	0	0	0	0	0	0	2	0
application	58	.7593	8.8835	49.5	0	5	0	6	11	18	16	2	8	7	0	4	9	0	0	7	1	0	4	3	1	0	9	5	0
applications	33	.4157	2.9360	44.7	0	1	2	1	11	12	4	2	2	0	0	1	7	0	0	2	0	0	0	9	0	2	5	5	0
applied	178	.7048	25.294	54.0	6	14	13	14	46	44	32	9	4	9	1	3	22	6	0	26	6	1	9	27	3	14	34	13	0
applies	37	.7665	5.7063	47.6	0	0	8	3	10	3	10	3	4	6	1	1	8	0	2	2	0	0	2	0	0	1	6	4	0
apply	192	.4909	19.672	52.9	6	6	7	16	46	54	50	7	13	22	1	2	9	8	5	28	2	2	10	65	0	5	8	12	0
applying	47	.6343	6.0345	47.8	0	1	2	0	19	10	11	4	1	8	0	1	6	2	1	2	1	1	5	10	0	2	3	4	0
appoint	11	.4740	1.1208	40.5	0	0	0	2	1	2	6	0	1	1	0	0	0	5	1	0	0	0	2	0	0	1	0	0	0
appointed	102	.7096	14.713	51.7	6	8	21	9	22	24	11	1	9	7	2	0	0	28	1	1	4	0	0	0	3	12	27	8	0
appointee	2	.0000	.0389	25.9	0	0	0	0	1	1	0	0	0	0	0	0	0	2	0	0	0	0	0	0	0	0	0	0	0
appointing	8	.5554	.9275	39.7	0	0	0	1	4	2	1	0	0	1	0	0	0	3	0	0	0	0	0	0	1	2	0	1	0
appointment	24	.6521	3.2081	45.1	0	1	1	0	12	5	4	1	2	2	0	3	0	5	0	0	1	0	0	0	0	1	3	7	0
appointments	14	.4758	1.4082	41.5	0	0	1	0	5	3	5	0	0	0	0	0	0	5	0	0	0	0	1	0	0	0	5	3	0
appoints	4	.2401	.2266	33.6	0	0	1	0	2	1	0	0	0	0	0	0	0	0	0	0	0	0	0	0	0	2	2	0	0
Appomattox	7	.4224	.6698	38.3	0	0	0	2	1	2	2	0	2	2	0	0	0	1	0	0	0	0	0	0	0	0	2	0	0
apposition	2	.0000	.0219	23.4	0	0	0	0	0	0	2	0	0	2	0	0	0	0	0	0	0	0	0	0	0	0	0	0	0
appositive	38	.1274	1.3067	41.2	0	0	0	13	0	4	21	0	0	37	1	0	0	0	0	0	0	0	0	0	0	0	0	0	0
appositives	8	.0000	.0875	29.4	0	0	0	5	0	1	2	0	0	8	0	0	0	0	0	0	0	0	0	0	0	0	0	0	0
appraisal	4	.2680	.2737	34.4	0	0	0	0	2	1	1	0	1	0	0	0	0	1	0	0	0	0	0	0	0	0	2	0	0
appraised	3	.3852	.2500	34.0	0	0	0	0	0	0	3	0	0	0	0	1	0	0	0	0	0	0	0	0	0	1	0	1	0
appreciable	2	.1718	.0785	28.9	0	0	0	0	0	1	1	0	0	0	0	1	0	0	0	0	0	0	0	1	0	0	0	0	0
appreciably	4	.3503	.3110	34.9	0	0	0	0	1	1	1	1	0	1	0	0	0	0	0	1	0	0	0	0	0	0	0	2	0
appreciate	47	.7570	7.1413	48.5	1	1	3	4	22	10	6	0	5	5	4	7	1	2	0	2	2	4	3	3	3	2	0	4	0
appreciated	20	.7784	3.1183	44.9	1	2	1	3	6	2	4	1	2	2	1	2	0	0	0	0	1	1	1	0	2	1	4	3	0
appreciates	3	.3452	.2543	34.1	0	1	0	1	0	1	0	0	1	0	0	0	0	0	0	1	0	0	0	0	0	0	0	1	0
appreciating	2	.1717	.1142	30.6	0	0	0	0	2	0	0	0	1	0	0	1	0	0	0	0	0	0	0	0	0	0	0	0	0
appreciation	39	.7616	5.9890	47.8	4	0	1	2	13	10	5	4	6	5	0	0	1	0	2	3	4	1	0	3	1	4	1	8	0
appreciative	5	.5305	.5641	37.5	0	1	1	0	0	1	1	1	1	1	0	0	0	0	0	0	1	0	0	0	0	1	0	1	0
appreciatively	3	.3399	.2456	33.9	1	0	0	0	1	0	0	1	1	0	0	1	0	0	0	0	0	0	0	0	0	0	0	1	0
apprehend	3	.0000	.0243	23.9	0	0	0	0	0	0	3	0	0	0	0	0	0	0	3	0	0	0	0	0	0	0	0	0	0
apprehension	10	.6117	1.2939	41.1	0	0	1	3	4	2	0	0	3	0	0	1	0	2	0	0	0	0	0	0	2	1	0	1	0
apprehensions	2	.2441	.1127	30.5	0	0	0	1	0	0	1	0	0	0	0	0	0	0	0	0	0	0	0	0	1	0	1	0	0
apprehensive	6	.4005	.5382	37.3	0	0	0	0	3	2	1	0	1	0	0	2	0	1	0	0	0	0	0	0	2	0	0	0	0
apprehensively	2	.2443	.1130	30.5	0	0	0	0	1	1	0	0	0	0	0	1	0	0	0	0	0	0	0	0	1	0	0	0	0
apprentice	27	.7669	4.2213	46.3	0	5	9	5	5	2	1	0	9	2	0	1	0	2	0	1	1	0	0	0	3	5	1	2	0
Apprentice	5	.3221	.3809	35.8	0	0	0	1	3	1	0	0	1	0	0	0	0	0	0	2	1	1	0	0	0	0	0	0	0
apprenticed	8	.3820	.7351	38.7	0	1	3	0	2	1	1	0	4	0	0	2	0	0	0	0	0	1	0	0	1	0	0	0	0
apprentices	5	.4242	.4679	36.7	0	0	2	0	2	0	1	0	1	2	0	1	0	0	0	0	0	0	0	0	0	0	1	0	0
apprenticeship	6	.4299	.5446	37.4	0	0	0	1	5	0	0	0	0	0	0	0	0	0	0	0	1	0	0	1	0	3	0	1	0
approach	114	.8405	19.153	52.8	4	6	7	16	29	18	30	4	21	2	0	16	2	2	2	9	8	3	3	0	9	6	14	17	0
approached	115	.7205	17.063	52.3	14	13	12	15	32	18	10	1	42	6	6	9	0	6	0	1	0	0	0	0	15	15	7	8	0
approaches	50	.8722	8.6685	49.4	0	2	5	9	12	10	11	1	3	2	0	2	7	3	0	10	2	1	2	1	1	4	7	5	0
approaching	93	.7995	15.004	51.8	4	7	14	15	22	18	13	0	24	4	6	7	1	4	2	14	1	0	3	0	10	4	4	9	0
Approaching	4	.0000	.0325	25.1	0	0	0	0	1	3	0	0	0	0	0	0	0	0	4	0	0	0	0	0	0	0	0	0	0
approbation	2	.2137	.1056	30.2	0	0	0	0	0	1	1	0	0	0	0	0	0	1	0	0	1	0	0	0	0	0	0	0	0
appropriate	167	.7358	24.586	53.9	3	7	14	14	46	43	35	5	6	32	17	6	5	6	22	2	26	1	21	4	0	4	6	9	0
appropriately	11	.5639	1.2827	41.1	0	0	0	3	2	2	3	1	1	2	0	0	0	0	0	0	2	0	1	0	0	0	1	4	0
appropriation	4	.4526	.3993	36.0	0	0	0	0	2	0	1	1	1	1	0	1	0	0	0	0	0	0	0	0	0	0	0	1	0
appropriations	2	.0000	.0209	23.2	0	0	0	0	2	0	0	0	0	0	0	0	0	0	0	0	0	0	0	0	0	0	2	0	0
Appropriations	2	.0000	.0243	23.9	0	0	0	0	1	0	1	0	0	0	0	0	0	0	0	0	0	0	0	0	0	0	0	2	0
approval	51	.7069	7.3566	48.7	3	5	3	6	10	10	13	1	9	6	0	3	0	9	0	1	1	0	6	0	3	5	4	4	0
approve	27	.5517	3.1132	44.9	0	5	3	1	6	7	4	1	3	1	0	2	0	5	1	1	0	0	6	0	0	4	3	1	0
approved	36	.6863	5.0430	47.0	2	2	2	3	6	14	7	0	4	3	0	0	0	10	0	1	0	0	4	1	2	1	4	6	0
approves	8	.4552	.7767	38.9	1	0	1	1	2	0	2	1	1	0	0	1	0	0	0	0	0	0	2	0	0	1	1	2	0
approving	2	.2444	.1132	30.5	0	0	0	1	1	0	0	0	0	1	0	0	0	0	0	0	0	0	0	0	1	0	0	0	0
approvingly	8	.2528	.4688	36.7	1	1	0	2	3	1	0	0	0	0	0	1	0	0	0	0	0	0	0	0	6	1	0	0	0
approximate	67	.5686	7.9315	49.0	0	14	9	6	9	14	13	2	0	0	0	0	36	14	2	7	2	0	2	0	0	0	3	1	0
approximated	8	.4740	.8122	39.1	0	1	0	0	2	2	2	1	1	1	0	0	1	0	0	0	0	0	0	0	0	0	3	2	0
approximately	139	.7397	20.727	53.2	1	7	13	7	32	37	27	15	3	3	4	1	55	6	1	24	0	0	4	6	0	4	20	8	0
approximation	20	.0575	.5126	37.1	0	0	0	1	4	12	2	1	0	0	0	0	19	0	0	1	0	0	0	0	0	0	0	0	0
approximations	13	.1197	.4731	36.7	0	0	1	0	3	9	0	0	0	0	0	0	12	0	0	0	0	0	0	0	0	0	1	0	0
Apr	4	.0000	.0419	26.2	0	0	0	0	0	1	3	0	0	0	0	0	0	0	0	0	0	0	0	0	0	0	4	0	0
apricot	6	.4828	.6322	38.0	0	1	1	0	2	2	0	0	1	2	0	0	1	1	0	1	0	0	0	0	0	0	0	0	0
apricots	11	.4595	1.1117	40.5	2	1	1	2	2	0	2	1	2	0	0	0	0	4	0	1	0	0	2	0	1	0	0	1	0
April	164	.8549	27.990	54.5	36	23	17	20	25	21	20	2	27	13	1	9	5	21	9	4	2	0	0	1	5	24	20	23	0
April's	2	.1733	.1149	30.6	0	0	0	1	1	0	0	0	1	1	0	0	0	0	0	0	0	0	0	0	0	0	0	0	0
apron	96	.5895	11.928	50.8	21	11	12	15	8	26	2	1	31	6	0	5	4	0	4	0	0	1	22	1	13	4	3	2	0
aprons	16	.5448	1.8809	42.7	2	2	1	4	2	2	2	1	5	0	0	2	3	2	0	0	0	0	2	0	0	2	0	0	0
apt	33	.8114	5.3762	47.3	0	3	4	7	9	6	2	2	5	3	0	2	0	2	2	5	0	0	1	0	2	5	1	5	0
aptitude	4	.3675	.3150	35.0	0	0	1	0	0	0	2	1	0	0	0	0	0	0	1	0	0	0	0	0	0	0	2	1	0

7N appellation
9Q appended
8A appendicitis
8F appending
8H appendix
7N appertain
8A appertaining
3A appetite-satisfying
9L Appetizers
5P apple-cheeked
8F apple-growing
8D apple-orchard
3A apple-tart
6K Apples
4F APPLES
9R Appliance
XR appliance's
XH Applicator
8M Applied
9Q applied-research
6K applique
XP appliqued
8L appliques
6B apply-application
9L Applying
9Q appointees
5Q apportioning
5Q appraisals
7R Appreciation
9G apprehended
6A apprenticing
7D appropiate
8F appropriated
7Q appropriating
XR approximates
8E approximating
5P appurtenances
9D apricocks
8D Aprils
7R APRO
9R apropos
6A Apsyrtus
7N apteronotes
7Q apteryx

Word Type	F	D	U	SFI	3 Gr 3	4 Gr 4	5 Gr 5	6 Gr 6	7 Gr 7	8 Gr 8	9 Gr 9	X UnGr	A Read	B Eng & Gr	C Comp	D Lit	E Math	F Soc Stud	G Spell	H Sci	J Music	K Art	L Home Ec	M Shop	N Lib F	P Lib NF	Q Lib Ref	R Mag	S Rel
aptly	5	.3608	.3926	35.9	0	0	0	0	3	1	0	1	0	0	0	0	0	0	0	0	0	0	0	0	0	1	2	2	0
Apuane	2	.0000	.0290	24.6	2	0	0	0	0	0	0	0	0	0	0	0	0	0	0	0	0	0	0	0	0	2	0	0	0
aqualung	4	.2197	.2408	33.8	0	2	0	1	0	1	0	0	1	0	1	0	0	0	0	2	0	0	0	0	0	0	0	0	0
aquanauts	2	.1814	.1187	30.7	0	1	0	1	0	0	0	0	1	0	0	0	0	0	0	0	0	0	0	0	0	0	0	1	0
aquarium	70	.6686	9.6210	49.8	25	13	12	6	10	4	0	0	5	2	3	1	6	1	0	39	1	2	0	0	1	0	1	8	0
Aquarium	3	.2437	.2277	33.6	1	0	2	0	0	0	0	0	2	0	0	0	0	0	0	1	0	0	0	0	0	0	0	0	0
aquariums	4	.1998	.2062	33.1	1	0	0	2	0	1	0	0	0	0	1	0	0	0	0	3	0	0	0	0	0	0	0	0	0
aquatic	21	.3502	1.6209	42.1	0	1	0	0	18	1	0	1	0	1	0	0	0	0	0	5	0	0	0	0	3	0	12	0	0
aqueduct	4	.2285	.2258	33.5	0	2	0	0	1	1	0	0	0	0	0	0	0	2	0	0	0	0	0	0	0	0	2	0	0
Aqueduct	2	.0000	.0389	25.9	0	0	2	0	0	0	0	0	0	0	0	0	0	2	0	0	0	0	0	0	0	0	0	0	0
aqueducts	17	.5480	1.9859	43.0	1	0	3	3	3	1	4	2	3	0	0	0	0	4	0	3	0	0	0	1	0	1	5	0	0
Aquitaine	2	.2285	.1129	30.5	0	0	0	0	1	1	0	0	0	0	0	0	0	1	0	0	0	0	0	0	0	0	1	0	0
ar	18	.0203	.2518	34.0	4	4	5	1	4	0	0	0	1	0	0	0	0	0	17	0	0	0	0	0	0	0	0	0	0
AR	4	.0000	.0599	27.8	0	0	4	0	0	0	0	0	0	0	0	0	4	0	0	0	0	0	0	0	0	0	0	0	0
Ar-luk	2	.0000	.0389	25.9	0	2	0	0	0	0	0	0	0	0	0	0	0	2	0	0	0	0	0	0	0	0	0	0	0
Ara	2	.0000	.0243	23.9	0	0	0	2	0	0	0	0	0	0	0	0	0	0	0	0	0	0	0	0	0	0	0	2	0
Arab	81	.5254	9.0642	49.6	3	4	17	28	13	2	14	0	6	0	0	0	0	38	0	0	1	0	0	0	0	14	8	14	0
Arab's	2	.0000	.0243	23.9	0	0	0	2	0	0	0	0	0	0	0	0	0	0	0	0	0	0	0	0	0	0	0	2	0
Arabelle	18	.0000	.8223	39.2	18	0	0	0	0	0	0	0	18	0	0	0	0	0	0	0	0	0	0	0	0	0	0	0	0
Arabelle's	6	.0000	.2741	34.4	6	0	0	0	0	0	0	0	6	0	0	0	0	0	0	0	0	0	0	0	0	0	0	0	0
Arabia	51	.6300	6.6578	48.2	4	9	1	13	13	2	8	1	4	2	0	2	0	26	1	0	5	0	0	0	0	7	1	3	0
Arabian	48	.7657	7.4106	48.7	6	12	3	16	5	2	4	0	5	2	0	1	1	10	2	0	4	0	0	0	2	6	6	9	0
Arabian's	3	.0000	.0365	25.6	0	0	0	3	0	0	0	0	0	0	0	0	0	0	0	0	0	0	0	0	0	0	0	3	0
Arabic	37	.7161	5.3614	47.3	2	9	7	4	7	2	6	0	2	4	0	0	2	5	3	2	3	0	0	0	0	6	9	1	0
Arable	17	.0000	.1993	33.0	0	17	0	0	0	0	0	0	0	0	0	0	0	0	0	0	0	0	0	0	17	0	0	0	0
Arables	2	.0000	.0234	23.7	0	2	0	0	0	0	0	0	0	0	0	0	0	0	0	0	0	0	0	0	2	0	0	0	0
Arabs	81	.6399	10.706	50.3	0	1	9	24	24	5	16	2	5	4	0	1	3	43	1	0	3	0	0	0	0	4	8	9	0
Arachne	14	.1906	1.0145	40.1	0	3	0	4	1	6	0	0	13	0	0	0	0	0	0	0	0	0	0	0	1	0	0	0	0
Aragon	4	.3603	.3110	34.9	0	0	3	1	0	0	0	0	0	0	0	0	0	0	0	0	1	0	0	0	0	1	2	0	0
Aragonaise	2	.0000	.0162	22.1	0	0	0	2	0	0	0	0	0	0	0	0	0	0	0	0	2	0	0	0	0	0	0	0	0
aragonite	3	.3346	.2478	33.9	0	0	0	0	0	2	0	1	1	0	0	0	0	0	0	1	0	0	0	0	0	0	1	0	0
arahkun	2	.0000	.0162	22.1	0	0	2	0	0	0	0	0	0	0	0	0	0	0	2	0	0	0	0	0	0	0	0	0	0
Aram	4	.3141	.3005	34.8	0	0	0	1	3	0	0	0	1	0	0	0	0	0	0	0	1	0	0	0	0	0	0	2	0
arapaima	4	.0000	.0419	26.2	0	0	0	0	4	0	0	0	0	0	0	0	0	0	0	0	0	0	0	0	0	0	4	0	0
Ararat	7	.2267	.3940	36.0	0	1	0	0	6	0	0	0	1	0	0	0	0	0	0	0	1	0	0	0	0	0	5	0	0
Arata	4	.0000	.0429	26.3	0	0	0	0	0	0	4	0	0	0	0	4	0	0	0	0	0	0	0	0	0	0	0	0	0
Arata's	2	.0000	.0215	23.3	0	0	0	0	0	0	2	0	0	0	0	2	0	0	0	0	0	0	0	0	0	0	0	0	0
Araucanian	5	.2205	.2855	34.6	0	3	0	1	1	0	0	0	0	0	0	0	0	4	0	0	0	0	0	0	0	0	1	0	0
Araucanians	7	.2408	.4210	36.2	0	4	1	1	1	0	0	0	0	0	0	0	0	5	0	0	0	0	0	0	0	0	2	0	0
Arbigland	2	.0000	.0290	24.6	0	2	0	0	0	0	0	0	0	0	0	0	0	0	0	0	0	0	0	0	0	2	0	0	0
arbitrarily	6	.5282	.6597	38.2	0	0	0	1	2	1	1	1	0	1	0	0	0	0	0	1	0	0	0	0	0	1	2	1	0
arbitrary	6	.5324	.6644	38.2	0	0	1	2	1	2	0	0	0	2	0	0	0	1	0	0	0	0	0	0	0	1	1	1	0
arbitration	5	.1649	.2071	33.2	0	0	1	0	2	0	2	0	0	0	0	0	0	0	0	0	0	0	0	0	0	0	4	1	0
arbor	7	.4049	.6598	38.2	0	2	0	0	4	0	1	0	3	0	0	2	0	0	0	0	0	0	0	1	1	0	0	0	0
Arbor	5	.3706	.4041	36.1	3	0	0	1	0	1	0	0	0	0	0	0	3	0	0	0	1	0	0	0	0	0	1	0	0
arboreal	2	.0000	.0209	23.2	0	0	0	0	2	0	0	0	0	0	0	0	0	0	0	0	0	0	0	0	0	0	2	0	0
Arbuthnot	2	.0000	.0215	23.3	0	0	0	0	0	0	2	0	0	0	0	2	0	0	0	0	0	0	0	0	0	0	0	0	0
arc	93	.4760	9.4019	49.7	1	2	6	24	21	18	18	3	5	0	0	2	49	2	0	6	1	0	0	15	1	3	6	3	0
Arc	6	.4218	.5647	37.5	1	1	1	0	1	0	1	1	1	1	0	0	0	2	0	0	0	0	0	0	0	0	2	0	0
Arcade	2	.0000	.0243	23.9	0	0	0	0	2	0	0	0	0	0	0	0	0	0	0	0	0	0	0	0	0	0	0	2	0
arch	26	.7484	3.9306	45.9	5	3	3	2	7	2	3	1	3	1	0	2	1	3	2	2	1	2	0	0	1	3	1	4	0
Arch	5	.2178	.2834	34.5	4	0	0	0	1	0	0	0	0	1	0	0	0	4	0	0	0	0	0	0	0	0	0	0	0
archaeological	7	.4361	.6887	38.4	0	0	3	0	0	3	1	0	2	0	0	0	0	0	0	0	0	0	0	0	0	3	1	1	0
archaeologist	9	.4365	.8318	39.2	0	0	5	0	0	2	1	1	0	1	0	0	0	0	0	0	0	0	0	0	0	2	4	2	0
archaeologists	31	.6093	3.9057	45.9	0	6	6	7	6	4	2	0	2	5	0	0	0	11	4	0	0	0	0	0	0	1	5	3	0
archaeology	10	.5280	1.0984	40.4	0	0	6	2	0	2	0	0	0	1	0	0	1	0	0	0	0	0	0	0	0	4	2	2	0
Archaeology	4	.2017	.1931	32.9	0	0	4	0	0	0	0	0	0	3	0	0	0	0	0	0	0	0	0	0	0	0	1	0	0
Archaeopteryx	3	.0000	.0314	25.0	0	0	0	0	3	0	0	0	0	0	0	0	0	0	0	0	0	0	0	0	0	0	3	0	0
archaic	8	.4693	.7969	39.0	0	0	2	0	2	0	1	3	0	1	0	0	0	0	0	3	0	1	0	0	0	2	1	0	0
archbishop	2	.2408	.1204	30.8	0	0	1	0	0	1	0	0	0	0	0	0	0	1	0	0	0	0	0	0	0	1	0	0	0
Archbishop	14	.5820	1.7114	42.3	0	3	2	3	5	1	0	0	3	0	0	0	0	0	0	0	1	0	0	0	2	2	4	2	0
archbishop's	2	.0000	.0914	29.6	0	0	2	0	0	0	0	0	2	0	0	0	0	0	0	0	0	0	0	0	0	0	0	0	0
archbishops	2	.0000	.0389	25.9	0	0	0	0	0	2	0	0	0	0	0	0	0	2	0	0	0	0	0	0	0	0	0	0	0
arched	13	.5810	1.6338	42.1	1	2	2	3	4	0	1	0	6	0	0	3	0	0	0	1	1	0	0	0	0	0	1	1	0
archeological	4	.2437	.2257	33.5	0	1	0	0	2	1	0	0	0	0	0	0	0	0	0	0	0	0	0	0	0	0	2	2	0
archeologist	4	.0904	.1412	31.5	0	1	1	0	1	0	1	0	1	0	0	0	0	0	0	0	0	0	0	0	0	0	3	0	0
archeologists	7	.3675	.5664	37.5	0	1	0	3	1	1	1	0	0	0	0	0	0	2	0	0	0	0	0	0	0	0	2	3	0
archeology	2	.2437	.1129	30.5	0	0	0	0	1	0	1	0	0	0	0	0	0	0	0	0	0	0	0	0	0	0	1	1	0
Archeozoic	2	.0000	.0394	26.0	0	0	0	0	0	0	2	0	0	0	0	0	0	0	0	2	0	0	0	0	0	0	0	0	0
archer	6	.4962	.6387	38.1	0	1	0	2	2	0	0	1	1	0	0	0	0	0	0	1	1	0	0	0	0	0	2	1	0
archers	6	.3599	.4934	36.9	0	0	2	3	1	0	0	0	1	0	0	3	0	1	0	0	0	0	0	0	0	0	1	0	0
archery	3	.2435	.2274	33.6	0	0	1	1	0	0	1	0	2	0	0	0	0	1	0	0	0	0	0	0	0	0	0	0	0
arches	17	.6157	2.1519	43.3	5	1	2	2	4	0	2	1	1	0	0	0	0	3	0	0	0	1	0	1	0	5	4	2	0
Archibald	6	.4422	.5690	37.6	0	0	1	3	0	1	1	0	0	0	0	0	0	1	0	0	0	0	0	0	0	3	1	1	0
Archie	7	.0000	.3198	35.0	0	5	1	1	0	0	0	0	7	0	0	0	0	0	0	0	0	0	0	0	0	0	0	0	0
Archimedes	36	.3712	3.0903	44.9	0	7	0	1	3	2	1	22	7	0	0	0	2	1	0	1	0	0	0	0	0	22	3	0	0
arching	7	.5319	.8017	39.0	0	1	1	0	3	1	1	0	2	0	0	0	0	0	0	0	1	0	0	0	2	1	0	1	0
Archipelago	9	.0917	.2682	34.3	8	0	0	1	0	0	0	0	0	0	0	0	0	1	0	0	0	0	0	0	0	0	0	8	0
architect	31	.5457	3.5048	45.4	1	2	4	3	3	5	9	4	2	0	0	0	7	2	1	0	3	5	0	1	0	0	2	8	0
architect's	2	.0000	.0162	22.1	0	2	0	0	0	0	0	0	0	0	0	0	0	0	0	0	2	0	0	0	0	0	0	0	0
architects	34	.5845	4.0598	46.1	3	1	0	4	8	10	4	4	1	1	0	0	2	4	0	0	2	4	0	5	0	2	9	4	0
architectural	23	.5781	2.7375	44.4	0	0	0	3	6	9	4	1	2	1	0	0	0	4	0	0	1	1	1	5	0	1	6	1	0
architecture	60	.7087	8.5808	49.3	4	1	4	4	12	14	10	11	2	0	2	0	3	10	0	1	8	2	0	1	0	3	22	6	0
Archive	2	.0000	.0290	24.6	0	0	0	0	2	0	0	0	0	0	0	0	0	0	0	0	0	0	0	0	0	2	0	0	0
archives	3	.2411	.1667	32.2	0	0	0	2	1	0	0	0	0	0	0	0	0	0	0	0	1	0	0	0	0	0	0	2	0
archy	3	.0000	.0322	25.1	0	0	0	0	0	3	0	0	0	0	0	3	0	0	0	0	0	0	0	0	0	0	0	0	0
archy's	2	.0000	.0215	23.3	0	0	0	0	0	2	0	0	0	0	0	2	0	0	0	0	0	0	0	0	0	0	0	0	0
arco	2	.0000	.0162	22.1	0	0	0	1	1	0	0	0	0	0	0	0	0	0	0	0	2	0	0	0	0	0	0	0	0
arcs	44	.3553	3.4717	45.4	1	0	3	8	9	10	13	0	1	0	0	0	29	0	0	5	0	0	0	7	1	0	0	1	0
arctic	36	.6028	4.6173	46.6	0	1	3	17	8	5	2	0	10	0	1	0	0	2	1	16	0	0	0	0	0	0	4	2	0
Arctic	109	.7101	15.853	52.0	14	18	21	20	19	6	9	2	14	4	0	4	0	47	2	12	1	0	0	0	2	12	7	4	0

7Q Aptonga
9D aqua
5B Aqua-Lung
5H aquaculture
5H aqualungs
9H aquamarine
XH aquaria
8R Aquarian
9R Aquarius
3H Aquatic
XR aquatint
3Q Aquavit
8Q aqueous
XH Aquilegia

6P Aquilo
4F Ar-luk's
9D ar-r
9R Arab-Israeli
5P Araba
8J arabeske
8J Arabeske
6R arabesque
6F Arabia's
8D Arabians
6F Arabic-speaking
8F arable
4N Arable's
8Q Arabshah

4A Araby
7H arachnid
7H arachnids
8D Arak
7F Arakan
6F Aral
5P Aramaeans
9D Aramco
9R Aramco's
3P Araminta
7R Arantes
7Q Arapaima
7Q Araucana
8Q Araucania

4F Araucanians'
4A arbis
4A arbislach
9R arbiter
8Q arbitrate
9D arbitrating
5Q Arbitration
8Q arbitrator
7Q arborealists
7R arboretum
9Q Arboretum
8B arborous
8N arbors
9D arc-light

7G arcade
5P Arcadia
4Q Arcangelo
7R arch-Stalinist
8Q arch-rival
5B archaeologist's
8K Archaic
7N archangel
5Q Archbald
8F Archduke
9H archegonia
4A Archie's
XP Archimedes'
XH archipelago

9R Architect
9Q architect-engineer
8Q Architects
9K architects'
9Q Architecture
3P Archives
7Q archpredator
9D Archuleta
3N archway
6N archways
7A Arcola
4R Arctic's

Word Type	F	D	U	SFI	3 Gr 3	4 Gr 4	5 Gr 5	6 Gr 6	7 Gr 7	8 Gr 8	9 Gr 9	X UnGr	A Read	B Eng & Gr	C Comp	D Lit	E Math	F Soc Stud	G Spell	H Sci	J Music	K Art	L Home Ec	M Shop	N Lib F	P Lib NF	Q Lib Ref	R Mag	S Rel
Arcturus	6	.0000	.1183	30.7	0	0	0	0	1	0	0	5	0	0	0	0	0	0	0	6	0	0	0	0	0	0	0	0	0
Ardennes	3	.2425	.1816	32.6	0	0	0	2	1	0	0	0	0	0	0	0	0	2	0	0	0	0	0	0	0	0	0	1	0
ardent	13	.6473	1.7202	42.4	1	0	1	2	2	3	4	0	1	0	0	0	0	2	2	0	3	0	0	0	1	2	1	1	0
Ardeth	2	.0000	.0215	23.3	0	2	0	0	0	0	0	0	0	0	0	2	0	0	0	0	0	0	0	0	0	0	0	0	0
ardor	3	.3768	.2437	33.9	0	0	0	0	0	0	2	1	0	0	0	0	0	0	0	0	1	0	0	0	0	1	0	1	0
arduous	4	.4504	.4035	36.1	0	0	1	0	0	1	2	0	1	0	0	0	0	1	0	0	0	0	0	0	0	1	1	0	0
are	35454	.9647	6743.4	78.3	6056	4871	4690	4805	6614	3852	3714	852	4484	2803	363	823	3967	4715	1807	6526	1385	407	984	818	502	1968	2213	1667	22
Are	47	.4061	4.1523	46.2	37	1	1	2	5	0	0	1	1	0	0	1	37	0	0	0	3	0	2	0	0	0	1	2	0
ARE	3	.0000	.0591	27.7	3	0	0	0	0	0	0	0	0	0	0	0	0	0	0	3	0	0	0	0	0	0	0	0	0
area	1403	.7329	208.36	63.2	62	101	272	232	257	253	175	51	66	21	2	8	475	361	5	113	4	1	18	13	3	48	153	112	0
Area	7	.2919	.4777	36.8	0	0	1	2	2	0	1	1	0	0	0	0	0	1	0	2	0	0	0	0	0	0	0	4	0
area's	9	.4513	.8687	39.4	0	1	1	1	5	0	0	1	0	0	0	0	0	3	0	0	0	0	0	0	0	1	3	2	0
areas	689	.7840	108.68	60.4	25	55	125	102	157	79	121	25	34	8	0	6	38	265	2	109	11	17	14	15	0	21	102	47	0
Areas	2	.0000	.0064	18.1	0	0	0	0	0	0	2	0	0	0	0	0	0	0	0	0	0	0	2	0	0	0	0	0	0
Arecibo	2	.0000	.0243	23.9	0	0	0	0	2	0	0	0	0	0	0	0	0	0	0	0	0	0	0	0	0	0	0	2	0
aren'	3	.0000	.1370	31.4	3	0	0	0	0	0	0	0	3	0	0	0	0	0	0	0	0	0	0	0	0	0	0	0	0
aren't	239	.8469	40.597	56.1	57	64	16	32	21	25	20	4	73	31	4	24	1	4	2	9	0	2	2	2	23	40	2	20	0
arena	26	.5610	3.2291	45.1	1	4	1	2	11	4	3	0	16	2	2	2	0	1	0	0	2	0	0	0	0	0	0	1	0
arenas	2	.1698	.1133	30.5	1	0	1	0	0	0	0	0	1	0	0	0	0	0	0	0	0	0	0	0	0	0	1	0	0
Arenas	2	.2351	.1166	30.7	0	0	0	1	1	0	0	0	0	0	0	0	0	1	0	0	0	0	0	0	0	0	0	1	0
Areopagitica	2	.0000	.0209	23.2	0	0	0	0	0	0	2	0	0	0	0	0	0	0	0	0	0	0	0	0	0	0	2	0	0
Arequipa	2	.0000	.0389	25.9	0	0	0	0	2	0	0	0	0	0	0	0	0	2	0	0	0	0	0	0	0	0	0	0	0
Argentina	94	.3295	7.0951	48.5	38	3	5	27	16	0	5	0	4	0	0	0	0	40	0	2	1	0	0	0	0	0	45	2	0
Argentina's	15	.1824	.7026	38.5	10	0	0	1	4	0	0	0	0	0	0	0	0	5	0	0	0	0	0	0	0	0	10	0	0
Argentine	16	.2292	.8786	39.4	9	0	0	2	3	0	1	1	0	0	0	0	0	4	0	0	0	0	0	0	0	0	11	1	0
Argentines	7	.2118	.3703	35.7	4	0	0	2	1	0	0	0	0	0	0	0	0	3	0	0	0	0	0	0	0	0	4	0	0
Argentinian	3	.0000	.0314	25.0	0	0	0	0	2	0	1	0	0	0	0	0	0	0	0	0	0	0	0	0	0	0	3	0	0
Argess	5	.0000	.0586	27.7	0	5	0	0	0	0	0	0	0	0	0	0	0	0	0	0	0	0	0	0	5	0	0	0	0
arginine	2	.0000	.0394	26.0	0	0	0	0	0	0	2	0	0	0	0	0	0	0	0	2	0	0	0	0	0	0	0	0	0
Argo	10	.2215	.7638	38.8	0	0	0	9	1	0	0	0	9	0	0	1	0	0	0	0	0	0	0	0	0	0	0	0	0
argon	15	.2213	.8610	39.4	0	1	1	0	6	2	4	1	0	0	0	0	0	0	0	12	0	0	0	0	0	0	3	0	0
Argonauts	13	.0000	.5939	37.7	0	0	0	13	0	0	0	0	13	0	0	0	0	0	0	0	0	0	0	0	0	0	0	0	0
Argonne	2	.2437	.1129	30.5	0	0	0	0	2	0	0	0	0	0	0	0	0	0	0	0	0	0	0	0	0	0	1	1	0
Argos	2	.0000	.0215	23.3	0	0	0	0	0	0	2	0	0	0	0	2	0	0	0	0	0	0	0	0	0	0	0	0	0
argue	49	.7364	7.3230	48.6	4	4	4	8	12	11	6	0	8	10	0	0	2	6	2	0	1	0	0	0	5	2	6	7	0
argued	52	.7222	7.7140	48.9	4	5	9	3	12	12	7	0	15	2	0	6	0	12	0	0	1	0	0	0	3	4	7	2	0
argues	6	.3982	.5348	37.3	0	1	0	0	3	0	2	0	1	2	0	2	0	1	0	0	0	0	0	0	0	0	0	0	0
arguing	22	.7826	3.5084	45.5	1	2	6	2	5	3	2	1	9	2	0	2	0	1	1	1	1	0	0	0	1	2	0	2	0
argument	85	.8516	14.469	51.6	6	4	9	4	25	24	12	1	17	15	1	8	9	12	2	0	1	0	2	0	3	5	5	5	0
arguments	42	.7998	6.7303	48.3	0	2	3	3	8	7	15	4	2	3	0	7	3	10	1	2	2	0	0	0	3	1	3	5	0
Argus	8	.2393	.6011	37.8	0	0	4	1	3	0	0	0	6	0	0	2	0	0	0	0	0	0	0	0	0	0	0	0	0
Argyle	2	.2427	.1152	30.6	0	1	0	0	1	0	0	0	0	0	0	0	0	0	0	0	0	0	0	0	1	1	0	0	0
argyrol	3	.0000	.0449	26.5	0	0	0	0	0	0	3	0	0	0	0	0	3	0	0	0	0	0	0	0	0	0	0	0	0
aria	15	.0574	.2896	34.6	0	0	0	4	3	8	0	0	0	0	0	0	0	0	0	0	14	0	0	0	0	1	0	0	0
arias	9	.0956	.2386	33.8	0	0	0	2	1	4	2	0	0	0	0	0	0	0	0	0	8	0	0	0	0	0	0	1	0
arid	20	.4590	1.9944	43.0	4	0	0	3	10	1	0	2	3	0	0	0	0	1	0	2	0	0	0	0	1	0	8	5	0
Aries	6	.2430	.3585	35.5	0	0	0	2	0	0	0	4	0	0	0	0	0	0	2	4	0	0	0	0	0	0	0	0	0
Arikara	2	.0000	.0914	29.6	0	2	0	0	0	0	0	0	2	0	0	0	0	0	0	0	0	0	0	0	0	0	0	0	0
Arirang	5	.0000	.0404	26.1	0	0	0	5	0	0	0	0	0	0	0	0	0	0	0	0	5	0	0	0	0	0	0	0	0
arise	52	.7536	7.8820	49.0	0	2	7	6	16	5	12	4	2	2	0	6	1	3	0	10	3	0	4	0	1	6	10	4	0
arisen	5	.3564	.3984	36.0	1	0	0	1	0	1	2	0	0	0	0	0	0	0	0	2	0	0	0	0	0	1	2	0	0
arises	12	.6498	1.6161	42.1	0	1	1	1	3	0	4	2	2	1	0	1	1	0	0	4	1	0	0	0	0	0	0	2	0
ariseth	2	.0000	.0290	24.6	1	0	1	0	0	0	0	0	0	0	0	0	0	0	0	0	0	0	0	0	0	2	0	0	0
arising	13	.5767	1.5470	41.9	0	0	1	1	2	7	0	2	0	0	0	1	3	0	0	3	0	0	1	0	0	1	4	0	0
Aristarchus	3	.3781	.2548	34.1	0	0	0	1	0	1	1	0	0	0	0	0	0	1	0	1	0	0	0	0	0	0	0	1	0
Aristide	2	.1493	.0692	28.4	0	0	1	0	0	0	1	0	0	0	0	0	0	0	0	0	0	1	0	0	0	0	1	0	0
aristocracy	8	.4261	.7125	38.5	0	0	1	0	0	4	3	0	0	0	0	0	0	0	0	0	2	1	0	0	0	1	4	0	0
aristocrat	2	.2401	.1133	30.5	1	0	0	1	0	0	0	0	0	0	0	0	0	0	0	0	0	0	0	0	0	1	1	0	0
aristocratic	13	.5670	1.5356	41.9	0	1	1	1	1	6	2	1	1	0	0	3	0	2	0	0	0	0	0	0	0	2	3	2	0
aristocrats	3	.1639	.1674	32.2	0	0	0	1	0	2	0	0	1	0	0	0	0	2	0	0	0	0	0	0	0	0	0	0	0
Aristotle	23	.5739	2.7785	44.4	3	0	1	7	5	1	3	3	2	0	0	0	0	8	0	4	0	0	0	0	0	2	4	3	0
Aristotle's	2	.1698	.1133	30.5	0	0	2	0	0	0	0	0	1	0	0	0	0	0	0	0	0	0	0	0	0	0	1	0	0
arithmetic	212	.5283	24.223	53.8	22	26	21	14	69	28	28	4	52	4	1	2	120	6	4	3	0	0	0	0	7	5	5	3	0
Arithmetic	2	.1733	.1149	30.6	1	0	1	0	0	0	0	0	1	1	0	0	0	0	0	0	0	0	0	0	0	0	0	0	0
Ariz	2	.0000	.0243	23.9	0	0	0	1	0	0	1	0	0	0	0	0	0	0	0	0	0	0	0	0	0	0	0	2	0
Arizona	87	.6564	11.766	50.7	6	10	15	10	22	4	3	17	11	3	0	1	2	18	0	7	1	0	1	0	1	1	10	31	0
Arizona's	3	.1937	.1495	31.7	0	1	2	0	0	0	0	0	0	0	0	0	0	1	0	0	0	0	0	0	0	0	0	2	0
ark	19	.1066	.5483	37.4	10	7	0	1	0	0	0	1	0	0	0	1	0	0	1	1	7	0	0	0	0	5	0	0	4
Ark	12	.5482	1.4783	41.7	0	1	1	0	9	0	1	0	8	0	0	0	0	0	0	0	1	0	0	0	0	1	1	1	0
Arkansas	49	.6484	6.5284	48.1	4	5	16	4	8	8	4	0	1	1	0	1	2	28	0	0	1	0	0	2	1	2	4	6	0
Arkwright's	2	.1698	.1133	30.5	0	0	0	0	2	0	0	0	1	0	0	0	0	0	0	0	0	0	0	0	0	0	1	0	0
Arlee	3	.0000	.1370	31.4	0	0	0	0	3	0	0	0	3	0	0	0	0	0	0	0	0	0	0	0	0	0	0	0	0
Arlene	3	.2384	.1717	32.3	0	0	2	0	0	0	1	0	0	1	0	0	2	0	0	0	0	0	0	0	0	0	0	0	0
Arlington	7	.4005	.6105	37.9	2	2	1	0	0	2	0	0	0	0	0	0	0	1	0	1	0	0	0	0	0	2	3	0	0
Arliss	14	.2340	.7657	38.8	0	0	0	0	9	5	0	0	0	0	0	5	0	0	0	0	0	0	0	0	9	0	0	0	0
arm	491	.8399	82.924	59.2	106	80	45	70	82	42	43	23	164	11	7	47	9	18	7	65	15	2	6	2	50	38	16	31	3
Arm	4	.0000	.1827	32.6	3	0	0	0	1	0	0	0	4	0	0	0	0	0	0	0	0	0	0	0	0	0	0	0	0
arm's	8	.5308	.8841	39.5	0	2	1	0	3	2	0	0	0	0	0	1	0	0	0	2	0	0	1	0	2	2	0	0	0
armada	3	.3383	.2498	34.0	0	0	1	0	0	1	0	1	1	1	0	0	0	1	0	0	0	0	0	0	0	0	0	0	0
Armada	3	.2143	.1568	32.0	0	0	0	2	1	0	0	0	0	0	0	0	0	0	0	0	0	0	0	0	0	1	0	2	0
armadillo	12	.6121	1.5935	42.0	7	1	1	0	1	0	2	0	7	1	0	0	0	0	0	1	0	0	0	0	1	1	1	0	0
Armadillo	3	.0000	.1370	31.4	3	0	0	0	0	0	0	0	3	0	0	0	0	0	0	0	0	0	0	0	0	0	0	0	0
armadillos	2	.1698	.1133	30.5	1	0	0	0	1	0	0	0	1	0	0	0	0	0	0	0	0	0	0	0	0	0	1	0	0
Armageddon	3	.0000	.0365	25.6	0	0	0	0	3	0	0	0	0	0	0	0	0	0	0	0	0	0	0	0	0	0	0	3	0
armament	4	.3740	.3226	35.1	0	1	0	0	1	1	1	0	0	1	0	0	0	0	0	0	0	0	0	0	0	0	1	2	0
armaments	2	.2306	.1140	30.6	0	0	0	0	0	0	2	0	0	1	0	0	0	1	0	0	0	0	0	0	0	0	0	0	0
Armand	4	.0000	.1827	32.6	4	0	0	0	0	0	0	0	4	0	0	0	0	0	0	0	0	0	0	0	0	0	0	0	0
armature	17	.0081	.1125	30.5	0	0	0	0	1	16	0	0	1	0	0	0	0	0	0	0	0	0	0	16	0	0	0	0	0
armchair	8	.3719	.6610	38.2	0	0	2	0	3	2	1	0	1	0	0	4	0	0	0	0	0	0	0	0	0	0	2	1	0
armchairs	2	.1717	.1142	30.6	0	0	0	1	0	0	1	0	1	0	0	1	0	0	0	0	0	0	0	0	0	0	0	0	0
armed	103	.7518	15.677	52.0	9	9	5	15	26	24	15	0	14	3	0	10	0	22	0	1	1	0	1	0	10	12	17	12	0
Armed	12	.4458	1.2240	40.9	0	0	0	2	7	3	0	0	5	0	1	0	0	1	0	1	0	0	0	0	0	0	4	0	0
Armenia	3	.0000	.0314	25.0	0	0	0	0	0	3	0	0	0	0	0	0	0	0	0	0	0	0	0	0	0	0	3	0	0
Armenian	8	.4028	.7419	38.7	0	0	0	1	4	3	0	0	3	0	1	3	0	0	0	0	0	0	0	0	0	0	1	0	0
armful	4	.1787	.2347	33.7	1	0	2	0	0	1	0	0	2	0	0	0	0	0	0	0	0	0	0	0	2	0	0	0	0

3G ard
5P Ard
XH Ardan
7R ardderchag
9R ardently
3E AREA
4Q areal
3E AREAS
7R Arecibo's
5P Arendt
6A Ares
8R Aretha
7N arf-arf
5Q Argenteuil
7F Argentina-Brazil
7A Argentinean
7H argentum
4N Argess'
9D Argives
6A Argonaut
6P Argonautic
9D argosies
6A argufying
9F ARGUMENT
9R argumentative
XR Argyllshire
7Q aridity
3K Ariel
7A aright
4A Arikara's
8A Aristides
5P aristocracies
7F Aristophanes
7P Aristophanes'
7Q Aristotelian
8E arithemtic
9Q Arithmetick
4Q Arius
7Q Arizona-Mexico
5F Arkansas's
7N Arliss's
8B Arlo's
3A armadillo's
7Q Armagh
9B armbands
8R Armchair
8B arme
9Q Armenians
XR armes
8F armfuls

Word Type	F	D	U	SFI	3 Gr 3	4 Gr 4	5 Gr 5	6 Gr 6	7 Gr 7	8 Gr 8	9 Gr 9	X UnGr	A Read	B Eng & Gr	C Comp	D Lit	E Math	F Soc Stud	G Spell	H Sci	J Music	K Art	L Home Ec	M Shop	N Lib F	P Lib NF	Q Lib Ref	R Mag	S Rel
armhole	9	.0000	.0290	24.6	0	0	0	0	5	0	4	0	0	0	0	0	0	0	0	0	0	0	9	0	0	0	0	0	0
armholes	3	.0000	.0097	19.8	0	0	0	0	2	1	0	0	0	0	0	0	0	0	0	0	0	0	3	0	0	0	0	0	0
armies	110	.5950	13.683	51.4	8	6	12	18	22	37	7	0	8	2	0	5	0	62	1	0	2	0	0	0	2	8	16	4	0
Arminian	2	.0000	.0209	23.2	0	0	0	0	0	2	0	0	0	0	0	0	0	0	0	0	0	0	0	0	0	0	2	0	0
Arminianism	3	.0000	.0314	25.0	0	0	0	0	0	3	0	0	0	0	0	0	0	0	0	0	0	0	0	0	0	0	3	0	0
Arminius	8	.0000	.0837	29.2	0	0	0	0	0	8	0	0	0	0	0	0	0	0	0	0	0	0	0	0	0	0	8	0	0
armistice	9	.2084	.4993	37.0	0	0	2	0	0	1	6	0	0	0	0	0	0	7	0	0	0	0	0	0	0	2	0	0	0
Armistice	3	.1169	.1277	31.1	0	2	0	0	1	0	0	0	1	0	0	0	0	0	0	0	0	0	0	0	0	0	2	0	0
armload	2	.0000	.0914	29.6	0	1	0	0	0	1	0	0	2	0	0	0	0	0	0	0	0	0	0	0	0	0	0	0	0
armloads	3	.3431	.2528	34.0	0	0	1	1	1	0	0	0	1	0	0	0	0	1	0	0	0	0	0	0	1	0	0	0	0
armonica	2	.0000	.0290	24.6	2	0	0	0	0	0	0	0	0	0	0	0	0	0	0	0	0	0	0	0	0	2	0	0	0
armor	60	.7893	9.6048	49.8	7	8	6	14	17	4	3	1	18	1	0	5	0	10	1	6	0	2	0	1	1	8	6	1	0
armored	13	.5692	1.5383	41.9	2	2	2	1	2	4	0	0	1	0	0	0	0	1	0	0	1	0	0	1	0	6	2	1	0
armories	2	.2351	.1166	30.7	0	0	0	0	1	1	0	0	0	0	0	0	0	1	0	0	0	0	0	0	0	0	0	1	0
armory	7	.3728	.6492	38.1	0	0	0	4	0	2	1	0	4	0	0	0	0	0	0	0	0	0	0	0	0	0	1	2	0
Armory	2	.0000	.0209	23.2	0	0	2	0	0	0	0	0	0	0	0	0	0	0	0	0	0	0	0	0	0	0	2	0	0
armour	6	.2419	.4673	36.7	0	1	1	4	0	0	0	0	5	0	0	0	0	0	0	0	0	0	0	0	1	0	0	0	0
Armour	2	.0000	.0243	23.9	0	0	0	0	0	0	0	2	0	0	0	0	0	0	0	0	0	0	0	0	0	0	0	2	0
arms	630	.8846	111.24	60.5	118	121	81	88	116	54	44	8	210	10	8	48	11	30	1	53	26	15	5	1	70	71	22	49	0
Arms	2	.2408	.1204	30.8	0	1	0	0	0	1	0	0	0	0	0	0	0	1	0	0	0	0	0	0	0	1	0	0	0
Armstrong	30	.6444	3.9316	45.9	5	3	0	7	7	6	2	0	0	4	0	3	0	4	0	0	3	0	0	1	0	4	0	11	0
army	412	.7681	64.172	58.1	47	62	66	40	68	85	35	9	76	15	2	25	2	135	7	6	5	0	0	0	15	69	39	16	0
Army	148	.6934	21.065	53.2	12	19	21	22	19	25	22	8	29	0	0	10	1	21	0	4	4	0	0	0	3	22	26	28	0
army's	6	.3537	.4878	36.9	0	0	1	0	1	3	1	0	1	0	0	3	0	1	0	0	0	0	0	0	0	0	0	1	0
Army's	5	.2753	.3378	35.3	1	0	2	0	1	1	0	0	1	0	0	1	0	0	0	0	0	0	0	0	0	0	0	3	0
Arne	5	.0000	.2284	33.6	0	0	0	0	5	0	0	0	5	0	0	0	0	0	0	0	0	0	0	0	0	0	0	0	0
Arnhem	2	.1948	.1250	31.0	0	0	0	0	2	0	0	0	1	0	0	0	0	0	0	0	0	0	0	0	0	1	0	0	0
Arnie	41	.0903	2.4037	43.8	23	17	0	0	1	0	0	0	40	0	0	0	1	0	0	0	0	0	0	0	0	0	0	0	0
Arnie's	5	.0000	.2284	33.6	2	3	0	0	0	0	0	0	5	0	0	0	0	0	0	0	0	0	0	0	0	0	0	0	0
Arno	4	.2437	.2257	33.5	0	0	0	0	2	2	0	0	0	0	0	0	0	0	0	0	0	0	0	0	0	0	2	2	0
Arnold	16	.6868	2.2516	43.5	1	1	1	0	2	6	5	0	3	3	0	2	1	2	0	0	2	0	0	0	0	0	2	1	0
Arnulf	11	.0000	.5025	37.0	0	0	0	11	0	0	0	0	11	0	0	0	0	0	0	0	0	0	0	0	0	0	0	0	0
aroma	9	.5504	1.0127	40.1	0	1	0	2	1	2	3	0	0	1	1	0	0	1	0	0	0	0	2	0	2	1	1	0	0
Aroma	31	.2406	2.3349	43.7	0	0	8	23	0	0	0	0	23	0	0	0	0	0	0	0	0	0	0	0	8	0	0	0	0
Aroma's	4	.2417	.3028	34.8	0	0	1	3	0	0	0	0	3	0	0	0	0	0	0	0	0	0	0	0	1	0	0	0	0
aromatic	5	.3436	.4206	36.2	0	0	0	0	3	0	0	2	2	0	0	1	0	0	0	0	0	0	0	0	0	0	0	2	0
aroo-oo-h	2	.0000	.0914	29.6	0	2	0	0	0	0	0	0	2	0	0	0	0	0	0	0	0	0	0	0	0	0	0	0	0
Aroon	3	.0000	.0243	23.8	0	0	0	3	0	0	0	0	0	0	0	0	0	0	0	0	3	0	0	0	0	0	0	0	0
arose	77	.7614	11.968	50.8	10	4	10	9	19	11	8	6	26	4	0	7	0	8	0	5	1	0	0	0	8	6	10	2	0
around	4632	.9514	871.48	69.4	1119	893	566	542	752	378	296	86	1501	139	36	248	110	388	83	625	117	45	53	46	401	419	152	269	0
Around	2	.2160	.1362	31.3	0	0	1	1	0	0	0	0	1	0	0	0	0	0	0	1	0	0	0	0	0	0	0	0	0
arouse	25	.5999	3.1186	44.9	0	1	1	2	5	6	10	0	5	3	4	1	0	1	0	2	1	2	0	0	0	3	2	1	0
aroused	35	.6699	4.8222	46.8	0	2	3	5	10	7	7	1	5	0	0	4	0	9	0	1	0	1	0	0	0	5	7	3	0
arouses	3	.3271	.2364	33.7	0	0	0	0	2	1	0	0	1	1	0	0	0	0	0	0	1	0	0	0	0	0	0	0	0
arousing	5	.5305	.5641	37.5	0	0	2	1	0	1	1	0	1	0	0	1	0	0	1	0	0	0	0	0	0	1	0	1	0
arrange	184	.7930	29.197	54.7	19	28	16	38	23	20	34	6	14	22	2	8	52	6	18	8	5	5	23	3	3	7	3	5	0
arranged	240	.8674	41.435	56.2	10	33	29	32	51	35	39	11	35	39	3	7	22	12	7	28	20	4	22	4	5	9	15	8	0
arrangement	145	.8232	23.831	53.8	3	10	21	19	33	26	26	7	13	4	1	7	5	16	3	16	28	5	5	5	0	2	29	6	0
Arrangement	5	.0000	.0608	27.8	0	0	0	0	0	0	5	0	0	0	0	0	0	0	0	0	0	0	0	0	0	0	0	5	0
arrangements	38	.7767	5.9312	47.7	1	1	5	5	6	6	13	1	6	5	0	1	0	3	1	1	5	1	4	3	1	3	2	2	0
arranger	4	.0000	.0323	25.1	0	0	0	0	0	4	0	0	0	0	0	0	0	0	0	0	4	0	0	0	0	0	0	0	0
arranges	14	.7090	1.9967	43.0	1	3	1	2	1	4	2	0	0	1	0	1	0	2	0	1	2	1	0	1	0	1	3	1	0
arranging	30	.7582	4.5766	46.6	3	5	2	3	6	5	6	0	4	5	0	4	0	3	2	0	1	2	3	1	2	2	1	0	0
array	57	.6699	7.7926	48.9	1	9	2	3	24	12	6	0	3	2	1	5	31	3	0	1	0	0	1	0	2	1	4	3	0
arrayed	4	.1594	.1712	32.3	0	0	1	0	2	1	0	0	0	0	0	0	0	1	0	0	0	0	0	0	3	0	0	0	0
arrays	5	.0000	.0748	28.7	1	2	0	0	1	0	1	0	0	0	0	0	5	0	0	0	0	0	0	0	0	0	0	0	0
arreh	2	.0000	.0914	29.6	0	2	0	0	0	0	0	0	2	0	0	0	0	0	0	0	0	0	0	0	0	0	0	0	0
arrest	23	.7236	3.4136	45.3	6	2	3	1	6	3	2	0	7	1	0	2	0	2	1	0	0	0	0	0	5	1	2	2	0
arrested	39	.7086	5.6320	47.5	5	1	8	1	10	8	6	0	6	2	0	2	0	4	1	0	0	0	0	0	5	4	7	8	0
arresting	3	.3385	.2445	33.9	1	0	1	0	1	0	0	0	1	0	0	0	0	0	0	0	0	0	0	0	1	0	1	0	0
arrests	12	.4838	1.2358	40.9	0	0	0	1	5	3	2	1	0	0	0	1	0	2	0	3	0	0	0	0	0	1	0	5	0
Arrietty	50	.0000	.5862	37.7	0	0	50	0	0	0	0	0	0	0	0	0	0	0	0	0	0	0	0	0	50	0	0	0	0
Arrietty's	2	.0000	.0234	23.7	0	0	2	0	0	0	0	0	0	0	0	0	0	0	0	0	0	0	0	0	2	0	0	0	0
arris	4	.0000	.0101	20.0	0	0	0	0	0	0	4	0	0	0	0	0	0	0	0	0	0	0	0	4	0	0	0	0	0
arrival	62	.7657	9.6649	49.9	4	4	4	10	21	13	4	2	21	0	3	6	0	4	1	1	4	0	0	0	5	5	6	6	0
arrivals	8	.4427	.7688	38.9	0	1	0	0	4	3	0	0	0	0	0	2	0	4	0	1	0	0	0	0	1	0	0	0	0
arrive	136	.9094	24.566	53.9	20	15	20	15	18	23	23	2	32	16	3	6	8	24	4	11	2	1	4	0	6	6	3	10	0
arrived	355	.8500	60.573	57.8	54	56	52	52	65	39	28	9	117	23	3	20	7	44	5	6	6	0	0	0	33	33	21	37	0
arrives	42	.8365	7.0296	48.5	5	3	4	6	9	6	7	2	7	2	1	4	3	6	0	3	5	0	0	1	2	0	2	6	0
arriving	44	.8839	7.7354	48.9	9	5	5	2	3	9	7	4	7	3	1	3	1	6	2	2	1	1	0	0	6	5	2	4	0
arrogance	2	.0000	.0243	23.9	0	0	0	1	0	1	0	0	0	0	0	0	0	0	0	0	0	0	0	0	0	0	0	2	0
arrogant	7	.4676	.7159	38.5	0	0	0	0	3	3	1	0	2	0	1	0	0	0	0	0	1	0	0	0	0	0	1	2	0
arrow	193	.8462	32.743	55.2	41	60	20	15	20	25	12	0	47	12	2	8	49	10	3	21	4	0	0	3	3	22	4	5	0
Arrow	47	.2694	3.2589	45.1	9	10	0	0	28	0	0	0	15	0	0	27	0	2	0	0	0	0	0	0	1	2	0	0	0
Arrow's	2	.0000	.0215	23.3	0	0	0	0	2	0	0	0	0	0	0	2	0	0	0	0	0	0	0	0	0	0	0	0	0
arrowhead	8	.5417	.9093	39.6	1	2	0	0	1	1	2	1	1	0	1	0	1	0	0	1	0	0	0	1	1	2	0	0	0
Arrowhead	3	.0000	.1370	31.4	3	0	0	0	0	0	0	0	3	0	0	0	0	0	0	0	0	0	0	0	0	0	0	0	0
arrowheads	14	.3109	.9845	39.9	1	2	1	1	1	2	5	1	1	0	0	0	1	2	0	2	0	0	0	5	2	0	0	1	0
arrows	166	.8553	28.404	54.5	32	37	20	22	26	17	12	0	41	8	1	8	37	15	3	6	4	0	6	7	13	11	5	1	0
arsenal	9	.4582	.9341	39.7	0	0	3	3	3	0	0	0	3	0	0	0	0	3	0	0	0	0	0	0	0	0	2	1	0
Arsenal	2	.2437	.1129	30.5	0	0	0	0	2	0	0	0	0	0	0	0	0	0	0	0	0	0	0	0	0	0	1	1	0
arsenals	3	.2444	.1814	32.6	0	1	0	0	0	2	0	0	0	0	0	0	0	2	0	0	0	0	0	0	0	0	1	0	0
arsenic	4	.2353	.2382	33.8	0	0	0	0	0	1	2	1	0	0	0	0	0	0	0	3	0	0	0	0	0	0	1	0	0
arson	2	.2440	.1132	30.5	0	0	0	0	2	0	0	0	0	0	0	1	0	0	0	0	0	0	0	0	0	0	0	1	0
art	592	.4567	56.431	57.5	93	68	56	63	74	110	78	50	26	19	3	39	5	53	4	16	83	186	3	2	4	27	76	45	1
Art	63	.6447	8.3455	49.2	2	0	11	21	6	8	8	7	10	4	0	0	0	3	0	0	3	2	0	5	0	2	10	24	0
art's	2	.2437	.1129	30.5	0	0	1	0	0	1	0	0	0	0	0	0	0	0	0	0	0	0	0	0	0	0	1	1	0
Art's	5	.0824	.1675	32.2	0	0	0	5	0	0	0	0	1	0	0	0	0	0	0	0	0	0	0	0	0	0	0	4	0
Artash	2	.0000	.0219	23.4	0	0	0	0	0	0	2	0	0	2	0	0	0	0	0	0	0	0	0	0	0	0	0	0	0
arteries	42	.3034	3.0242	44.8	2	5	10	9	0	11	5	0	0	0	0	0	0	0	3	34	0	0	0	0	0	0	5	0	0
arteriosclerosis	2	.0000	.0394	26.0	0	0	2	0	0	0	0	0	0	0	0	0	0	0	0	2	0	0	0	0	0	0	0	0	0
artery	15	.4128	1.3683	41.4	2	1	2	3	0	1	6	0	0	0	0	1	0	0	0	10	0	0	0	0	0	2	2	0	0
artesian	4	.2305	.2357	33.7	0	0	2	1	0	1	0	0	0	0	0	0	0	0	0	3	0	0	0	0	1	0	0	0	0
Artesian	2	.2351	.1166	30.7	0	0	0	1	0	0	0	1	0	0	0	0	0	1	0	0	0	0	0	0	0	0	0	1	0
artful	2	.1717	.1142	30.6	0	0	0	0	2	0	0	0	1	0	0	1	0	0	0	0	0	0	0	0	0	0	0	0	0

7F Armies
8F arming
8Q Arminius'
8K Armitage's
7P armor-bearer
7F armor-covered
5P armor-piercing
7A armorer
9Q Armorial
3P ARMOURED
8F armpit
8R Army-McCarthy
9D Army-type
3N Arnaud's
9L Arnel
8F Arnold's
8Q Arnoldus
XR aroma-chemicals
XR aromatherapy
5F Aroostook
9R Arouet
9R aroun-
XR around-town
5Q Arp
8K Arp's
9J arpeggio
9J arpeggios
9Q Arpi
7A arrears
7Q arribadas
9Q Arrigo
9D Arrivederci
9R arrogantly
7A arrogating
7Q arrow-fire
4H arrow-like
7Q arrow-swift
7R arrow's
5N arrowless
8F arrowpoint
3A arroz
4A ARRS
XH arsenate
XH arsenical
9Q art-collecting
7M art-object
6P art-song
8Q art-work
5Q Artaphernes
8Q Artemis
9Q arteriole
9Q arterioles
XR Artes
6H artesian-well

Word Type	F	D	U	SFI	3 Gr 3	4 Gr 4	5 Gr 5	6 Gr 6	7 Gr 7	8 Gr 8	9 Gr 9	X UnGr	A Read	B Eng & Gr	C Comp	D Lit	E Math	F Soc Stud	G Spell	H Sci	J Music	K Art	L Home Ec	M Shop	N Lib F	P Lib NF	Q Lib Ref	R Mag	S Rel
arthritis	2	.2412	.1091	30.4	0	0	0	0	1	1	0	0	0	0	0	1	0	0	1	0	0	0	0	0	0	0	0	0	0
arthropod	6	.2071	.3307	35.2	0	0	0	0	2	3	1	0	0	0	0	0	0	0	0	5	0	0	0	0	0	0	1	0	0
arthropods	25	.0920	.8913	39.5	0	0	1	2	9	11	2	0	0	0	0	0	0	0	0	24	0	0	0	0	0	0	1	0	0
Arthur	117	.7612	18.323	52.6	2	15	5	37	29	19	8	2	60	4	0	12	5	3	2	2	2	0	0	0	2	4	5	16	0
ARTHUR	22	.0597	.4814	36.8	0	1	0	0	0	21	0	0	0	0	0	21	0	0	0	0	0	0	0	0	0	0	0	1	0
Arthur's	11	.2395	.8234	39.2	0	3	0	7	1	0	0	0	8	0	0	0	0	0	0	0	0	0	0	0	0	0	0	3	0
Artic	21	.6088	2.6336	44.2	1	7	4	3	0	1	5	0	0	1	0	2	1	7	0	0	0	0	0	0	0	3	1	6	0
artichoke	2	.1497	.1046	30.2	0	1	0	1	0	0	0	0	1	0	0	0	0	0	1	0	0	0	0	0	0	0	0	0	0
artichokes	5	.2445	.3864	35.9	0	0	0	4	0	0	0	1	4	0	0	1	0	0	0	0	0	0	0	0	0	0	0	0	0
article	253	.8135	41.963	56.2	6	21	25	30	130	30	9	2	153	22	3	6	3	9	1	2	3	0	5	5	1	10	6	24	0
Article	8	.3606	.6494	38.1	0	1	1	0	0	3	3	0	0	1	0	0	0	5	0	0	0	0	0	0	0	0	2	0	0
articles	165	.8017	26.567	54.2	1	23	25	16	40	27	25	8	31	25	4	5	2	26	1	4	0	8	12	9	2	5	17	14	0
Articles	15	.2444	.9069	39.6	0	0	5	0	0	10	0	0	0	0	0	0	0	10	0	0	0	0	0	0	0	0	5	0	0
articulate	7	.5891	.8587	39.3	0	0	1	0	4	1	1	0	1	1	0	0	0	0	0	0	0	0	0	0	1	1	1	2	0
articulated	2	.2375	.1088	30.4	0	0	0	1	1	0	0	0	0	0	0	0	0	0	0	0	1	0	0	0	0	0	0	1	0
articulation	2	.2417	.1091	30.4	0	0	0	0	0	1	0	1	0	0	0	0	0	0	0	0	1	0	0	0	0	0	1	0	0
Artie	20	.1582	1.3626	41.3	0	0	0	0	20	0	0	0	19	0	0	0	0	0	0	0	0	0	0	0	0	0	0	1	0
artifacts	3	.3769	.2484	34.0	0	0	0	1	1	0	0	1	0	0	0	0	0	1	0	0	0	0	0	0	0	0	1	1	0
artifical	2	.1378	.0662	28.2	1	0	0	0	1	0	0	0	0	0	0	0	0	0	0	0	0	1	0	0	0	0	0	1	0
artifice	2	.1733	.1149	30.6	0	0	0	1	0	0	1	0	1	1	0	0	0	0	0	0	0	0	0	0	0	0	0	0	0
artificial	79	.7081	11.411	50.6	3	2	12	16	19	16	8	3	6	0	0	1	5	4	0	35	1	1	1	0	0	5	13	7	0
artificially	6	.2942	.4422	36.5	0	0	1	3	0	1	1	0	1	0	0	0	0	0	0	4	0	0	0	0	0	0	1	0	0
artillery	25	.6399	3.3011	45.2	1	2	1	2	7	8	3	1	3	0	0	3	0	4	0	0	0	0	0	0	2	5	2	6	0
Artillery	4	.3832	.3414	35.3	0	0	0	1	1	1	1	0	0	0	0	0	0	2	0	0	0	0	0	0	1	1	0	0	0
artillerymen	3	.3756	.2468	33.9	0	0	0	0	1	2	0	0	0	0	0	1	0	1	0	0	0	0	0	0	0	0	1	0	0
artisan	2	.2408	.1204	30.8	0	0	1	0	0	1	0	0	0	0	0	0	0	1	0	0	0	0	0	0	0	1	0	0	0
artisans	7	.4548	.6881	38.4	1	0	0	3	2	1	0	0	1	0	0	0	0	1	0	0	0	1	0	0	0	1	2	1	0
artist	213	.3324	15.630	51.9	38	53	7	21	49	24	12	9	28	14	1	7	1	4	5	3	37	79	0	0	2	12	10	10	0
Artist	4	.0000	.1827	32.6	3	0	0	1	1	0	0	0	4	0	0	0	0	0	0	0	0	0	0	0	0	0	0	0	0
artist's	21	.3747	1.6787	42.2	1	6	1	1	5	4	0	3	1	0	0	0	0	0	1	1	5	6	0	0	2	1	0	4	0
artistic	47	.6072	5.8212	47.7	8	1	1	1	4	13	14	5	3	1	0	0	2	1	0	0	16	0	3	3	0	1	14	3	0
artistry	4	.3334	.2895	34.6	1	1	0	0	1	0	1	0	0	0	0	0	0	0	0	0	2	0	0	0	0	1	1	0	0
artists	149	.4364	13.840	51.4	19	30	17	14	37	20	6	6	15	5	0	9	1	13	0	0	22	39	2	0	0	13	16	14	0
artists'	2	.1693	.0748	28.7	0	1	0	1	0	0	0	0	0	0	0	0	0	0	1	0	0	1	0	0	0	0	0	0	0
arts	95	.7175	13.715	51.4	0	8	18	8	13	19	11	18	3	1	1	2	0	11	1	1	21	4	0	2	2	5	31	10	0
Arts	19	.5698	2.2484	43.5	0	2	6	1	4	4	1	1	2	1	0	1	0	0	0	1	2	0	0	0	1	0	8	3	0
Arturo	8	.0000	.3655	35.6	8	0	0	0	0	0	0	0	8	0	0	0	0	0	0	0	0	0	0	0	0	0	0	0	0
artwork	2	.1814	.1187	30.7	0	1	0	0	1	0	0	0	1	0	0	0	0	0	0	0	0	0	0	0	0	0	0	0	0
ary	7	.2444	.3900	35.9	0	0	1	0	3	3	0	0	0	0	0	0	0	0	3	0	0	0	0	0	4	0	0	1	0
Aryan	2	.0000	.0219	23.4	0	0	0	0	2	0	0	0	0	2	0	0	0	0	0	0	0	0	0	0	0	0	0	0	0
Aryans	4	.0000	.0778	28.9	0	0	0	0	4	0	0	0	0	0	0	0	0	4	0	0	0	0	0	0	0	0	0	0	0
as	32208	.9941	6295.5	78.0	4221	4301	3914	4471	6532	4254	3699	816	7003	1766	380	1678	2265	3023	1113	3551	1618	312	596	515	1857	2289	2173	2055	14
As	10	.5305	1.1004	40.4	1	0	0	1	4	2	0	2	0	2	0	0	0	0	0	1	2	0	0	0	0	2	0	3	0
Asa	7	.3450	.5885	37.7	0	0	1	0	1	4	1	0	2	0	0	0	0	3	0	0	0	0	0	0	0	0	0	2	0
ASA	3	.1993	.1435	31.6	0	0	0	0	0	2	1	0	0	0	0	0	2	0	0	0	0	0	0	1	0	0	0	0	0
Asakusa	3	.2444	.1814	32.6	0	2	1	0	0	0	0	0	0	0	0	0	0	2	0	0	0	0	0	0	0	0	1	0	0
asbestos	8	.5043	.8586	39.3	1	0	2	0	1	2	1	1	1	0	0	0	0	1	0	1	0	0	0	1	0	0	2	2	0
ascend	5	.4860	.5175	37.1	1	1	0	0	1	2	0	0	0	0	0	0	0	0	0	2	0	0	0	0	1	1	0	1	0
ascendancy	2	.2137	.1056	30.2	0	0	0	0	0	2	0	0	0	0	0	0	0	1	0	0	1	0	0	0	0	0	0	0	0
ascended	10	.4722	1.0957	40.4	0	0	0	3	2	4	1	0	6	0	0	2	0	0	0	0	0	0	0	0	1	0	1	0	0
ascending	9	.3266	.6667	38.2	0	0	0	0	4	3	2	0	1	0	0	0	1	1	0	0	5	0	0	0	1	0	0	0	0
Ascension	3	.3848	.2449	33.9	0	0	1	0	1	0	1	0	0	0	0	1	0	0	1	0	0	0	0	0	0	0	1	0	0
ascent	22	.5680	2.6067	44.2	0	1	2	3	13	1	1	1	2	0	0	3	0	1	1	3	0	0	0	0	0	0	4	8	0
ascents	3	.1832	.1417	31.5	0	0	0	0	0	3	0	0	0	0	0	2	0	0	0	1	0	0	0	0	0	0	0	0	0
ascertain	5	.4119	.4587	36.6	0	1	0	0	3	0	1	0	1	0	0	1	0	0	0	0	0	0	0	0	0	1	2	0	0
ascertained	2	.2443	.1130	30.5	0	0	0	0	1	0	1	0	0	0	0	1	0	0	0	0	0	0	0	0	1	0	0	0	0
ascorbic	4	.1432	.1519	31.8	0	0	0	0	2	2	0	0	0	0	0	0	0	0	0	2	0	0	2	0	0	0	0	0	0
ascribed	3	.2427	.1822	32.6	0	0	0	0	1	0	0	2	0	0	0	0	0	0	0	2	0	0	0	0	0	0	0	1	0
aseptic	4	.2287	.2348	33.7	0	0	0	0	1	3	0	0	0	0	0	0	0	0	0	3	0	0	0	0	0	0	0	1	0
asexual	2	.0000	.0394	26.0	0	0	0	0	2	0	0	0	0	0	0	0	0	0	0	2	0	0	0	0	0	0	0	0	0
Asgard	2	.1698	.1133	30.5	0	0	2	0	0	0	0	0	1	0	0	0	0	0	0	0	0	0	0	0	0	0	1	0	0
ash	36	.7582	5.5475	47.4	4	6	5	5	7	5	3	1	9	1	0	3	0	1	1	5	0	0	0	2	4	5	4	1	0
Ash	4	.2206	.2167	33.4	0	0	0	0	1	3	0	0	0	0	0	1	3	0	0	0	0	0	0	0	0	0	0	0	0
ashamed	51	.6155	6.7202	48.3	6	8	6	7	12	5	7	0	25	1	0	13	0	0	0	1	1	0	1	0	6	2	0	1	0
Ashanti	2	.0000	.0290	24.6	0	0	0	0	2	0	0	0	0	0	0	0	0	0	0	0	0	0	0	0	0	2	0	0	0
Ashby's	2	.0000	.0290	24.6	0	2	0	0	0	0	0	0	0	0	0	0	0	0	0	0	0	0	0	0	0	2	0	0	0
ashcan	2	.1733	.1149	30.6	0	0	0	1	0	1	0	0	1	1	0	0	0	0	0	0	0	0	0	0	0	0	0	0	0
ashen	2	.1814	.1187	30.7	0	1	0	0	1	0	0	0	1	0	0	0	0	0	0	0	0	0	0	0	0	0	0	1	0
ashes	87	.7395	13.235	51.2	17	22	15	9	7	9	3	5	32	2	0	10	0	6	2	13	0	0	0	0	2	13	1	6	0
Ashland	4	.2107	.2095	33.2	1	2	0	0	0	0	0	1	0	0	0	0	0	0	0	0	0	0	0	0	0	3	0	1	0
Ashley	4	.2183	.2285	33.6	0	1	0	0	0	3	0	0	0	0	0	0	0	3	0	0	0	0	0	0	0	1	0	0	0
Ashley's	2	.2408	.1204	30.8	0	1	0	0	0	1	0	0	0	0	0	0	0	1	0	0	0	0	0	0	0	1	0	0	0
ashore	79	.7995	12.779	51.1	6	11	10	14	27	6	4	1	24	3	1	4	0	11	0	3	1	0	0	0	10	5	8	9	0
Ashur	2	.2444	.1132	30.5	0	0	0	2	0	0	0	0	0	1	0	0	0	0	0	0	0	0	0	0	1	0	0	0	0
Asia	381	.5555	44.790	56.5	25	36	67	87	93	45	23	5	22	6	0	2	2	246	4	11	4	1	0	0	1	32	40	10	0
Asia's	3	.2366	.1806	32.6	0	0	1	0	1	0	1	0	0	0	0	0	1	2	0	0	0	0	0	0	0	0	0	0	0
Asian	34	.5892	4.1662	46.2	0	1	5	4	12	10	2	0	1	2	0	0	0	15	0	0	1	0	0	0	0	6	3	6	0
Asians	11	.0602	.3559	35.5	0	0	0	4	6	1	0	0	1	0	0	0	0	10	0	0	0	0	0	0	0	0	0	0	0
Asiatic	12	.4798	1.2197	40.9	0	1	2	0	5	3	1	0	0	0	0	0	0	4	0	0	0	0	0	1	0	4	3	0	0
aside	182	.8698	31.606	55.0	18	26	17	22	47	18	27	7	48	8	4	18	3	13	2	9	5	0	7	0	14	13	14	24	0
ask	900	.8271	150.04	61.8	176	166	109	104	160	100	73	12	309	82	6	78	37	69	11	65	17	5	24	5	68	65	2	51	6
asked	2924	.8412	496.85	67.0	752	680	310	347	422	238	154	21	1436	103	22	189	55	185	21	38	22	3	5	2	388	310	16	126	3
askew	2	.0000	.0914	29.6	1	0	0	1	0	0	0	0	2	0	0	0	0	0	0	0	0	0	0	0	0	0	0	0	0
askin'	3	.3873	.2495	34.0	0	0	0	0	3	0	0	0	0	0	0	1	0	0	0	0	0	0	0	0	1	0	0	1	0
asking	155	.6551	21.344	53.3	22	24	19	19	29	18	22	2	63	12	0	13	3	11	1	4	3	1	2	1	10	15	2	12	2
asks	167	.6212	22.200	53.5	80	14	15	8	22	10	15	3	79	17	3	4	10	13	1	12	4	0	1	0	4	3	0	14	2
aslant	2	.1787	.1174	30.7	0	1	0	1	0	0	0	0	1	0	0	0	0	0	0	0	0	0	0	0	1	0	0	0	0
asleep	293	.7628	45.799	56.6	71	65	28	43	41	20	21	4	131	5	9	36	1	8	7	7	5	0	1	0	39	36	1	7	0
asparagus	7	.5113	.7457	38.7	0	0	1	1	1	0	1	3	0	0	0	0	0	0	0	1	0	0	1	0	0	2	1	2	0
aspect	53	.6504	7.0236	48.5	1	2	3	2	14	10	17	4	5	1	7	3	0	2	1	2	4	0	1	0	4	1	14	8	0
aspects	46	.8040	7.3734	48.7	0	0	2	0	17	11	10	6	1	2	2	2	2	2	1	2	8	1	0	1	0	3	9	10	0
aspen	9	.3605	.7915	39.0	0	3	0	2	2	0	1	1	4	0	0	2	0	0	0	0	0	0	0	0	0	0	0	3	0
Aspen	3	.0939	.1398	31.5	0	1	0	0	2	0	0	0	2	0	0	0	0	0	0	0	0	1	0	0	0	0	0	0	0

6R Artful
6A artfully
8Q Artibonite
5P articals
6N artichoke-boilers
7A articulating
7A Artie's
7Q artifact
7N artifices
9Q Artificial
8A artillerists
8R Artinish
4Q artisan-cultivator
XR artist-producer
6A Artist's
9J Artistic
8K artistically
5Q Artists
5P Artois
8Q Arundel
7E Arwell
7E Arwells
XR asafoetida
5Q Asahi
9R Asan
7A Asaph
6J Asar
5Q Asbestos
4A asbestoslike
5A Asbury
8G Ascalon
7H ascaris
9R ascendant
9E ascends
XH ascension
8F ascensions
9Q ascetic
6R Asclepius
6B ascribe
8A ascribes
6R Ase-bun
5Q ash-Sha'biyah
7R ash-blond
7N ash-hopper
4P ash-wood
5A Ashbellows
4P Ashburn
7D ashcake
5Q Ashcan
5R Ashford
7N ashhopper
4P Ashtabula
8Q Ashtead
9R ashtray
7D ashwood
3P ashy
9D Asiatics
3Q Asid
3P Asil
9B asinine/asininity
7B Askew
7B Askew's
6P Asleep
9P Asmodeus
8Q Asoka
6A asparkle
8G aspectus

Word Type	F	D	U	SFI	3 Gr 3	4 Gr 4	5 Gr 5	6 Gr 6	7 Gr 7	8 Gr 8	9 Gr 9	X UnGr	A Read	B Eng & Gr	C Comp	D Lit	E Math	F Soc Stud	G Spell	H Sci	J Music	K Art	L Home Ec	M Shop	N Lib F	P Lib NF	Q Lib Ref	R Mag	S Rel
aspens	2	.0000	.0215	23.3	0	0	0	0	1	1	0	0	0	0	0	2	0	0	0	0	0	0	0	0	0	0	0	0	0
asphalt	10	.5072	1.1023	40.4	2	2	0	1	2	2	0	1	2	0	0	0	0	2	0	1	0	0	0	0	0	3	2	0	0
aspirations	4	.4804	.4052	36.1	0	0	0	0	2	1	1	0	0	1	0	0	0	1	0	0	0	0	0	0	0	0	1	1	0
aspire	2	.1718	.0785	28.9	0	0	0	0	2	0	0	0	0	0	0	1	0	0	0	0	0	0	0	1	0	0	0	0	0
aspirin	3	.1434	.1493	31.7	1	0	0	0	0	0	2	0	1	0	0	0	2	0	0	0	0	0	0	0	0	0	0	0	0
aspirins	2	.2160	.1362	31.3	0	0	0	0	1	1	0	0	1	0	0	0	0	0	0	1	0	0	0	0	0	0	0	0	0
ass	24	.3148	1.8878	42.8	12	0	1	9	1	1	0	0	9	0	0	0	0	0	0	0	0	0	0	0	0	5	10	0	0
assailed	3	.2279	.2143	33.3	0	0	0	1	1	0	0	1	2	0	0	0	0	0	0	0	0	0	0	0	0	0	0	1	0
assassin	3	.2427	.1822	32.6	0	0	0	0	0	1	0	2	0	0	0	0	0	0	0	2	0	0	0	0	0	0	0	1	0
assassinated	10	.4560	.9640	39.8	0	0	1	0	6	2	0	1	0	1	0	1	0	2	0	0	0	0	0	0	1	0	5	0	0
assassination	2	.1814	.1187	30.7	0	0	0	1	1	0	0	0	1	0	0	0	0	0	0	0	0	0	0	0	0	0	0	1	0
assassins	9	.3331	.6645	38.2	0	0	0	7	0	1	0	1	0	0	0	1	0	0	0	1	0	0	0	0	6	0	0	1	0
Assateague	6	.1250	.2684	34.3	0	2	4	0	0	0	0	0	2	0	0	0	0	0	0	0	0	0	0	0	4	0	0	0	0
assault	21	.5426	2.4004	43.8	0	0	1	0	8	8	4	0	2	1	0	0	0	5	0	1	0	0	0	0	1	0	7	4	0
assaulted	3	.3776	.2493	34.0	0	0	0	0	1	0	1	1	0	1	0	0	0	0	0	1	0	0	0	0	0	0	0	1	0
assaulting	3	.2444	.1814	32.6	0	0	0	0	1	2	0	0	0	0	0	0	0	2	0	0	0	0	0	0	0	0	1	0	0
assaults	7	.2205	.3670	35.6	0	0	0	0	3	0	1	3	0	0	0	0	0	0	0	0	0	0	0	0	0	0	2	5	0
assayed	2	.1814	.1187	30.7	0	0	0	0	0	2	0	0	1	0	0	0	0	0	0	0	0	0	0	0	0	0	0	1	0
assemblage	3	.3394	.2451	33.9	0	0	0	1	1	1	0	0	1	0	0	1	0	0	0	0	0	0	0	0	1	0	0	0	0
assemble	38	.6732	5.2551	47.2	0	1	2	4	12	15	3	1	9	0	2	1	1	2	1	4	1	0	3	6	0	2	3	3	0
assembled	58	.6773	7.9978	49.0	3	5	7	1	15	11	13	3	6	0	4	4	1	9	0	3	2	0	1	9	3	8	3	5	0
assemblies	22	.6414	2.9217	44.7	0	0	1	0	5	9	7	0	4	1	0	3	0	5	0	0	0	0	0	2	0	2	2	3	0
assembling	11	.6145	1.3839	41.4	0	0	0	1	2	5	3	0	1	0	0	1	1	1	0	0	1	0	1	2	0	1	1	1	0
assembly	124	.5501	14.322	51.6	8	4	8	8	28	42	25	1	22	6	1	4	3	20	2	1	5	0	2	30	1	4	12	11	0
Assembly	54	.5134	6.0297	47.8	2	0	2	14	14	15	7	0	13	0	1	1	0	20	0	0	1	0	0	0	0	1	17	0	0
assembly-line	3	.1639	.1674	32.2	0	0	2	0	0	0	1	0	1	0	0	0	0	2	0	0	0	0	0	0	0	0	0	0	0
assemblyman	3	.0000	.0322	25.1	0	0	0	0	3	0	0	0	0	0	0	3	0	0	0	0	0	0	0	0	0	0	0	0	0
assent	4	.4846	.4028	36.1	0	0	1	0	3	0	0	0	0	0	0	0	0	0	1	0	0	0	0	0	1	0	1	1	0
assented	2	.0000	.0234	23.7	0	0	0	0	1	1	0	0	0	0	0	0	0	0	0	0	0	0	0	0	2	0	0	0	0
assert	6	.3648	.4921	36.9	0	0	1	0	1	3	1	0	0	0	0	0	1	3	0	0	0	0	0	0	0	0	0	2	0
asserted	7	.3721	.5877	37.7	0	0	1	0	3	2	1	0	1	0	0	0	0	1	0	0	0	0	0	0	0	0	3	2	0
assertions	2	.2417	.1211	30.8	0	0	0	0	0	1	1	0	0	0	0	0	1	1	0	0	0	0	0	0	0	0	0	0	0
asserts	6	.3571	.4726	36.7	0	0	0	0	2	3	1	0	0	0	0	0	3	0	0	0	0	0	0	0	0	1	2	0	0
asses	6	.2357	.4397	36.4	2	0	0	3	0	1	0	0	4	0	0	0	0	0	0	0	0	0	0	0	0	2	0	0	0
assess	3	.3847	.2496	34.0	0	0	1	0	0	0	1	1	0	0	0	0	0	0	0	0	0	0	0	0	0	1	1	1	0
assessed	5	.0000	.0748	28.7	0	0	0	0	2	0	3	0	0	0	0	0	5	0	0	0	0	0	0	0	0	0	0	0	0
assessing	2	.2405	.1205	30.8	0	0	1	0	0	1	0	0	0	0	0	0	0	0	0	1	0	0	0	0	0	1	0	0	0
assessor	2	.0000	.0389	25.9	0	0	0	0	0	1	1	0	0	0	0	0	0	2	0	0	0	0	0	0	0	0	0	0	0
asset	13	.5021	1.3405	41.3	0	0	0	0	5	5	3	0	0	0	3	1	1	1	0	0	0	0	2	0	1	1	3	0	0
assets	7	.3579	.5531	37.4	0	0	3	1	0	3	0	0	0	0	0	0	0	2	0	0	0	0	0	0	0	0	3	2	0
assiduously	2	.2446	.1122	30.5	0	0	0	0	1	1	0	0	0	0	0	1	0	0	0	0	0	0	0	0	0	0	1	0	0
assign	12	.5610	1.4100	41.5	0	2	3	1	3	2	0	1	1	1	0	0	6	0	1	1	0	0	0	0	1	0	0	1	0
assigned	65	.7495	9.8516	49.9	2	8	4	8	16	13	8	6	9	1	5	1	17	4	1	3	3	0	0	1	4	2	3	11	0
assigning	4	.3229	.3125	34.9	0	0	0	0	1	2	1	0	1	1	0	0	2	0	0	0	0	0	0	0	0	0	0	0	0
assignment	71	.5411	8.1961	49.1	1	0	4	12	21	13	19	1	19	29	5	2	1	0	2	0	0	0	0	0	1	1	0	11	0
assignments	30	.6418	3.9535	46.0	2	0	3	0	6	6	12	1	4	11	2	2	3	0	0	1	0	0	1	0	0	2	0	4	0
assigns	9	.3026	.6260	38.0	0	0	2	1	1	0	5	0	0	0	0	0	6	1	0	0	0	0	0	0	0	0	2	0	0
assimilated	2	.2407	.1090	30.4	0	0	0	0	0	1	1	0	0	1	0	0	0	0	0	0	1	0	0	0	0	0	0	0	0
assimilation	13	.4942	1.3487	41.3	0	0	2	1	3	3	2	2	0	4	0	0	0	1	0	0	0	0	0	0	0	5	1	2	0
Assisi	4	.3778	.3231	35.1	2	0	1	1	0	0	0	0	0	0	0	0	0	0	0	0	1	0	0	0	2	0	1	0	0
assist	33	.7640	5.0905	47.1	1	0	3	4	10	7	6	2	5	0	3	0	1	4	3	6	1	0	1	1	1	1	4	2	0
assistance	39	.8339	6.4939	48.1	2	2	2	6	8	9	6	4	5	1	1	3	0	2	1	3	1	0	3	1	1	5	6	6	0
assistant	50	.7449	7.5628	48.8	3	3	4	11	5	14	8	2	10	1	0	2	1	4	4	1	1	0	0	0	2	4	7	13	0
Assistant	6	.4456	.5715	37.6	0	0	1	0	0	1	4	0	0	0	0	0	0	1	0	0	1	0	0	0	0	3	0	1	0
assistants	23	.6919	3.2355	45.1	5	1	0	2	6	3	4	2	1	0	0	1	0	1	0	4	1	0	0	0	5	5	2	3	0
assisted	24	.6663	3.2578	45.1	1	0	2	5	7	3	6	0	2	2	0	4	0	1	0	0	1	0	0	0	5	2	6	1	0
assisting	3	.3390	.2450	33.9	0	0	0	1	0	1	1	0	1	0	0	0	0	0	0	0	0	0	0	0	0	0	1	1	0
assists	5	.4424	.4787	36.8	0	0	3	0	0	1	1	0	1	0	0	0	0	0	1	0	0	0	0	1	0	0	1	1	0
associate	34	.7630	5.2264	47.2	0	1	4	5	7	8	7	2	3	1	1	2	2	3	0	4	3	0	0	0	0	2	4	9	0
Associate	4	.4818	.4128	36.2	1	0	0	0	2	0	0	1	0	0	0	0	0	1	0	1	0	0	0	0	0	1	0	1	0
associated	98	.8043	15.744	52.0	1	3	15	4	31	16	23	5	4	6	0	5	9	2	2	11	12	0	3	2	0	6	24	12	0
Associated	6	.2480	.3712	35.7	0	0	0	1	0	1	0	4	1	0	0	0	0	0	0	0	0	0	0	0	0	0	1	4	0
associates	13	.4711	1.2773	41.1	0	0	0	0	8	2	2	1	0	0	2	0	1	0	0	1	0	0	0	0	1	0	5	3	0
Associates	6	.3627	.5371	37.3	0	0	0	3	1	0	1	1	3	0	0	0	0	0	0	0	0	0	0	0	0	0	1	2	0
associating	5	.4303	.4516	36.5	0	0	0	0	1	2	2	0	0	1	0	2	1	0	0	0	0	0	1	0	0	0	0	0	0
association	40	.7676	6.1599	47.9	1	1	5	0	13	7	13	0	0	3	0	1	0	8	3	5	1	0	1	0	1	4	10	3	0
Association	57	.6262	7.3435	48.7	1	4	4	5	6	17	11	9	3	0	0	0	0	9	0	6	1	0	1	1	2	3	4	27	0
associations	26	.6426	3.4474	45.4	0	0	6	4	6	5	4	1	4	0	0	0	1	2	0	2	1	0	1	0	1	3	10	1	0
Associations	3	.0000	.0365	25.6	0	0	0	0	0	0	2	1	0	0	0	0	0	0	0	0	0	0	0	0	0	0	0	3	0
associative	66	.0389	1.4629	41.7	1	7	13	10	23	9	3	0	0	0	0	0	64	0	0	2	0	0	0	0	0	0	0	0	0
Associative	5	.0000	.0748	28.7	1	2	1	0	1	0	0	0	0	0	0	0	5	0	0	0	0	0	0	0	0	0	0	0	0
assorted	8	.4725	.8475	39.3	1	0	2	2	0	0	2	1	3	0	0	0	0	0	0	0	1	0	0	0	0	2	0	2	0
assortment	17	.6050	2.1267	43.3	1	0	0	1	6	2	5	2	2	2	2	0	2	1	0	0	0	0	0	0	1	2	1	4	0
assume	99	.8347	16.491	52.2	4	0	4	7	28	26	24	6	5	6	1	3	24	6	1	17	1	0	1	4	1	7	14	8	0
assumed	75	.8192	12.267	50.9	1	1	8	6	19	19	19	2	3	1	0	7	6	8	1	9	0	1	1	2	5	5	21	5	0
assumes	12	.7831	1.8876	42.8	0	0	0	1	3	2	4	2	1	1	0	0	1	0	1	2	1	0	0	0	1	1	1	2	0
assuming	26	.6572	3.4813	45.4	1	0	1	0	7	5	9	3	0	2	0	0	11	1	0	2	0	0	0	1	1	2	1	5	0
assumption	26	.6440	3.4262	45.3	0	0	3	1	6	8	7	1	0	0	0	1	9	1	0	6	0	0	0	1	0	1	2	5	0
assumptions	14	.4201	1.2775	41.1	0	0	3	2	2	3	3	1	0	0	0	0	1	0	0	6	0	0	0	0	0	0	5	2	0
assurance	12	.6484	1.6081	42.1	0	1	0	0	3	4	1	3	2	0	0	1	0	2	1	0	0	0	0	0	0	2	1	3	0
assurances	2	.2442	.1134	30.5	0	0	0	0	1	1	0	0	0	1	0	0	0	0	0	0	0	0	0	0	0	0	0	1	0
assure	23	.7060	3.2956	45.2	0	0	3	5	7	3	5	0	2	0	0	2	0	4	1	0	0	0	0	1	5	1	2	5	0
assured	59	.7749	9.2371	49.7	0	6	9	7	12	11	14	0	13	4	3	7	0	4	1	0	0	0	2	0	10	7	2	6	0
assures	7	.4878	.7194	38.6	0	0	2	0	1	2	2	0	0	0	0	0	3	0	0	1	0	0	1	0	0	1	0	1	0
assuring	3	.2468	.1912	32.8	0	0	0	2	0	0	1	0	1	0	0	0	0	0	0	0	0	0	1	0	1	0	0	0	0
Assyria	2	.2446	.1123	30.5	0	0	1	0	0	0	0	1	0	1	0	0	0	0	0	0	0	0	0	0	0	0	1	0	0
Assyrian	7	.3380	.5043	37.0	0	0	0	3	2	0	2	0	0	3	2	0	0	0	0	0	0	0	0	0	1	0	1	0	0
Assyrians	6	.3943	.5126	37.1	0	0	0	2	1	2	1	0	0	0	0	0	0	3	1	0	0	1	0	0	0	0	1	0	0
aster	3	.2365	.1616	32.1	0	0	1	1	0	0	1	0	0	0	0	0	0	0	0	0	1	0	0	0	0	0	2	0	0
Aster	9	.0000	.1303	31.1	9	0	0	0	0	0	0	0	0	0	0	0	0	0	0	0	0	0	0	0	0	9	0	0	0
Aster's	3	.0000	.0434	26.4	3	0	0	0	0	0	0	0	0	0	0	0	0	0	0	0	0	0	0	0	0	3	0	0	0
asterisks	2	.0000	.0299	24.8	0	0	0	0	2	0	0	0	0	0	0	0	2	0	0	0	0	0	0	0	0	0	0	0	0
astern	9	.4543	.9216	39.6	0	0	0	2	2	3	1	1	3	0	0	0	0	0	0	0	0	0	0	0	1	3	0	2	0
asteroid	5	.3152	.3888	35.9	0	1	1	0	1	2	0	0	1	0	0	1	0	0	0	3	0	0	0	0	0	0	0	0	0
asteroids	22	.3649	1.8238	42.6	0	3	2	2	3	12	0	0	0	0	0	3	0	1	0	16	0	0	0	0	0	0	2	0	0
asters	11	.6008	1.3591	41.3	1	0	1	6	1	0	2	0	1	1	1	1	0	0	0	1	1	0	0	0	1	0	4	0	0
asthma	4	.1349	.2265	33.6	0	0	2	0	1	0	1	0	3	0	1	0	0	0	0	0	0	0	0	0	0	0	0	0	0

8D asperity
3J asphalt's
4J aspic
7N aspirant
9J aspirate
9D aspired
6N aspiring
8D asquealing
7A assail
9D assailant
8R assailing
6A Assam
6R Assassin
6R assassin-turned-informer
7D assassin's
8R assassinate
7Q Assassinations
7H assault-and-battery
8B assaying
7Q assemblages
8F Assembled
7P assembles
6A Assen
5Q asserting
9Q assertion
8R assertive
7Q assessments
8Q assessors
7C assiduity
7C assiduous
9J assimilate
9Q assimilating
7Q association's
8C Association's
7Q assortments
5A assukiak
XR assuredly
7N ast
6R asterisk

Word Type	F	D	U	SFI	3 Gr 3	4 Gr 4	5 Gr 5	6 Gr 6	7 Gr 7	8 Gr 8	9 Gr 9	X UnGr	A Read	B Eng & Gr	C Comp	D Lit	E Math	F Soc Stud	G Spell	H Sci	J Music	K Art	L Home Ec	M Shop	N Lib F	P Lib NF	Q Lib Ref	R Mag	S Rel
astigmatic	3	.2427	.1822	32.6	0	0	0	0	0	2	1	0	0	0	0	0	0	0	0	2	0	0	0	0	0	0	0	1	0
astir	7	.4589	.7058	38.5	0	0	2	1	1	2	1	0	2	0	1	2	0	0	0	0	1	0	0	0	0	1	0	0	0
astonish	5	.2682	.3044	34.8	0	1	0	0	2	1	0	1	0	0	0	0	0	0	3	1	0	0	0	0	1	0	0	0	0
astonished	49	.7043	7.1483	48.5	9	6	11	6	7	5	2	3	18	1	1	4	1	2	0	5	0	0	0	0	12	3	0	2	0
astonishing	34	.7598	5.2146	47.2	3	4	1	3	15	3	4	1	5	1	1	2	1	0	0	2	0	1	0	0	3	6	8	4	0
astonishingly	5	.4599	.4875	36.9	0	0	0	1	1	1	1	1	0	0	0	0	0	1	0	0	0	0	0	0	1	0	1	2	0
astonishment	34	.6281	4.4705	46.5	7	4	2	8	8	4	0	1	10	0	1	4	0	1	0	0	0	0	0	0	9	1	1	7	0
Astor	10	.3820	.8527	39.3	0	0	3	0	1	3	3	0	0	0	0	0	0	5	0	0	0	0	0	0	0	3	0	2	0
Astoria	6	.0971	.2435	33.9	0	0	2	0	0	3	1	0	1	0	0	0	0	5	0	0	0	0	0	0	0	0	0	0	0
astounded	8	.4083	.7702	38.9	0	1	0	2	2	3	0	0	4	0	1	2	0	0	0	0	0	0	0	0	0	0	1	0	0
astounding	5	.3713	.3959	36.0	1	0	0	0	3	1	0	0	0	0	0	0	0	0	0	0	0	1	0	0	0	1	2	1	0
astray	5	.4738	.4923	36.9	1	0	0	0	3	0	1	0	0	1	0	2	0	0	0	0	1	0	0	0	0	0	1	0	0
Astrea	3	.0000	.0434	26.4	0	0	0	3	0	0	0	0	0	0	0	0	0	0	0	0	0	0	0	0	0	3	0	0	0
astride	6	.3252	.4817	36.8	0	4	1	1	0	0	0	0	2	0	0	1	0	0	0	0	0	0	0	0	0	3	0	0	0
astrocytoma	2	.0000	.0290	24.6	0	0	0	0	0	0	2	0	0	0	0	0	0	0	0	0	0	0	0	0	0	2	0	0	0
ASTROGATOR	4	.0000	.0469	26.7	4	0	0	0	0	0	0	0	0	0	0	0	0	0	0	0	0	0	0	0	4	0	0	0	0
astrolabe	2	.2297	.1135	30.6	0	0	0	0	1	1	0	0	0	0	0	1	0	1	0	0	0	0	0	0	0	0	0	0	0
astrologer	4	.3477	.3086	34.9	0	2	0	0	0	1	0	1	0	1	0	0	0	0	0	1	0	0	0	0	2	0	0	0	0
astrologers	3	.0000	.0591	27.7	0	0	0	0	0	0	0	3	0	0	0	0	0	0	0	3	0	0	0	0	0	0	0	0	0
astrology	9	.4561	.8878	39.5	0	0	0	1	2	1	0	5	0	1	0	0	0	0	0	5	0	0	0	0	0	2	1	0	0
astronaut	83	.7444	12.676	51.0	7	11	7	31	7	17	2	1	27	11	0	1	3	7	3	19	0	0	0	0	0	4	3	5	0
Astronaut	4	.1622	.1743	32.4	1	0	0	2	0	1	0	0	0	0	0	0	0	1	0	0	0	0	0	0	0	0	0	3	0
astronaut's	3	.1650	.1684	32.3	0	1	0	1	1	0	0	0	1	0	0	0	0	0	0	2	0	0	0	0	0	0	0	0	0
astronautics	3	.3346	.2478	33.9	0	0	0	1	0	0	2	0	1	0	0	0	0	0	0	1	0	0	0	0	0	0	1	0	0
astronauts	109	.6718	14.944	51.7	19	16	33	14	14	6	6	1	3	6	0	0	3	12	0	27	0	1	1	0	0	6	14	36	0
Astronauts	2	.2285	.1129	30.5	0	0	1	0	0	0	1	0	0	0	0	0	0	1	0	0	0	0	0	0	0	0	1	0	0
astronauts'	3	.1277	.1363	31.3	0	0	0	1	1	1	0	0	1	0	0	0	0	0	0	0	0	0	0	0	0	0	0	2	0
astronomer	49	.5967	6.1135	47.9	1	6	3	5	8	11	5	10	3	2	0	0	3	1	0	27	0	0	0	0	1	3	5	4	0
astronomers	125	.4716	13.018	51.1	0	25	16	19	26	18	10	11	19	2	0	1	2	1	0	76	0	0	0	0	0	1	17	6	0
astronomical	12	.2969	.8545	39.3	0	0	0	1	3	4	2	2	0	0	0	0	2	0	0	9	0	0	0	0	0	0	0	1	0
astronomy	48	.6294	6.2785	48.0	0	3	10	8	11	7	5	4	7	4	0	0	2	2	0	13	0	0	0	0	0	4	12	4	0
Astronomy	4	.2437	.2257	33.5	0	0	1	0	2	0	1	0	0	0	0	0	0	0	0	0	0	0	0	0	0	0	2	2	0
astrophysicists	3	.2427	.1822	32.6	0	0	0	0	2	0	0	1	0	0	0	0	0	0	0	2	0	0	0	0	0	0	0	1	0
astute	9	.5505	1.0374	40.2	0	0	0	1	2	2	4	0	1	2	0	0	0	1	2	0	0	0	0	0	0	1	0	2	0
asu	2	.0000	.0389	25.9	0	0	0	2	0	0	0	0	0	0	0	0	0	2	0	0	0	0	0	0	0	0	0	0	0
Asuncion	11	.0000	.2139	33.3	0	0	0	4	7	0	0	0	0	0	0	0	0	11	0	0	0	0	0	0	0	0	0	0	0
asunder	6	.4045	.5335	37.3	0	1	0	1	0	2	2	0	1	0	0	2	0	0	0	0	2	0	0	0	1	0	0	0	0
Aswan	7	.2432	.4210	36.2	0	0	0	1	1	2	3	0	0	0	0	0	0	4	0	0	0	0	0	0	0	0	0	3	0
at	23975	.9921	4678.3	76.7	4415	3988	2833	3020	4531	2515	2053	620	7051	1064	255	1583	1361	1850	606	2175	719	205	358	240	1925	1830	1033	1701	19
At	5	.3577	.3868	35.9	1	0	0	0	2	1	1	0	0	0	0	0	0	0	0	0	1	0	0	0	0	0	1	3	0
AT	4	.1135	.1696	32.3	0	1	2	1	0	0	0	0	1	0	0	0	3	0	0	0	0	0	0	0	0	0	0	0	0
at-home	2	.0000	.0243	23.9	0	0	0	0	0	0	0	2	0	0	0	0	0	0	0	0	0	0	0	0	0	0	0	2	0
At-mun	2	.0000	.0234	23.7	0	0	2	0	0	0	0	0	0	0	0	0	0	0	0	0	0	0	0	0	2	0	0	0	0
At-mun-shi	4	.0000	.0469	26.7	0	0	4	0	0	0	0	0	0	0	0	0	0	0	0	0	0	0	0	0	4	0	0	0	0
Atacama	2	.2285	.1129	30.5	0	0	1	1	0	0	0	0	0	0	0	0	0	1	0	0	0	0	0	0	0	0	1	0	0
Atalanta	4	.0000	.1827	32.6	0	0	0	4	0	0	0	0	4	0	0	0	0	0	0	0	0	0	0	0	0	0	0	0	0
Ataturk	11	.2349	.6486	38.1	0	0	6	0	5	0	0	0	0	0	0	0	0	5	0	0	0	0	0	0	0	6	0	0	0
Ataturk's	3	.0000	.0434	26.4	0	0	3	0	0	0	0	0	0	0	0	0	0	0	0	0	0	0	0	0	0	3	0	0	0
ate	440	.8435	74.618	58.7	149	75	63	49	51	21	26	6	159	47	2	35	42	13	29	17	3	0	0	0	46	28	6	12	1
Aten	3	.0000	.0583	27.7	0	0	0	0	3	0	0	0	0	0	0	0	0	3	0	0	0	0	0	0	0	0	0	0	0
Ateoord	2	.0000	.0234	23.7	0	2	0	0	0	0	0	0	0	0	0	0	0	0	0	0	0	0	0	0	2	0	0	0	0
ATEOORD	3	.0000	.0352	25.5	0	3	0	0	0	0	0	0	0	0	0	0	0	0	0	0	0	0	0	0	3	0	0	0	0
Ath-mun	3	.0000	.0352	25.5	0	0	3	0	0	0	0	0	0	0	0	0	0	0	0	0	0	0	0	0	3	0	0	0	0
Athabasca	2	.0000	.0243	23.9	0	0	0	0	2	0	0	0	0	0	0	0	0	0	0	0	0	0	0	0	0	0	0	2	0
Athamas	2	.0000	.0914	29.6	0	0	0	0	0	2	0	0	2	0	0	0	0	0	0	0	0	0	0	0	0	0	0	0	0
atheist	5	.3163	.3514	35.5	0	0	1	0	1	0	3	0	0	3	0	0	0	0	0	0	0	0	0	0	0	1	0	1	0
atheists	2	.0000	.0209	23.2	0	0	0	0	0	1	1	0	0	0	0	0	0	0	0	0	0	0	0	0	0	0	2	0	0
Athena	22	.2286	1.4938	41.7	1	2	0	7	0	11	1	0	13	3	0	0	0	1	0	0	0	5	0	0	0	0	0	0	0
Athena's	4	.2399	.3011	34.8	0	0	0	1	0	3	0	0	3	1	0	0	0	0	0	0	0	0	0	0	0	0	0	0	0
Athene	12	.1717	.6853	38.4	0	0	0	0	1	7	4	0	6	0	0	6	0	0	0	0	0	0	0	0	0	0	0	0	0
Atheneum	2	.2278	.1128	30.5	0	0	1	1	0	0	0	0	0	0	0	0	0	0	0	1	0	0	0	0	0	0	1	0	0
Athenian	20	.4836	2.0474	43.1	2	0	3	1	6	6	2	0	0	0	0	1	0	8	1	0	0	0	0	0	1	1	8	0	0
Athenians	15	.3869	1.2811	41.1	7	1	3	2	0	2	0	0	0	0	0	0	0	9	0	0	0	1	0	0	0	0	5	0	0
Athens	71	.5831	8.6899	49.4	9	6	3	21	14	10	8	0	8	1	0	7	0	37	0	0	1	4	0	0	1	1	10	1	0
athlete	33	.7702	5.1334	47.1	2	1	2	3	12	6	7	0	6	3	1	3	0	1	0	3	2	0	1	0	1	3	0	9	0
athlete's	3	.3771	.2489	34.0	0	0	0	0	2	0	1	0	0	0	0	1	0	0	0	1	0	0	0	0	0	0	0	1	0
athletes	42	.7036	6.0476	47.8	2	6	8	7	10	3	6	0	8	7	0	1	2	3	0	3	0	1	0	0	0	3	2	12	0
athletic	42	.8443	7.0912	48.5	2	5	2	2	11	11	9	0	8	1	0	7	0	2	1	4	2	1	0	1	2	6	2	5	0
Athletic	6	.3521	.4792	36.8	0	1	0	3	0	1	1	0	1	0	1	0	0	0	0	0	0	0	0	0	0	1	0	3	0
athletics	14	.5531	1.6330	42.1	0	0	1	3	0	1	9	0	2	4	0	3	0	0	0	3	0	0	0	0	0	0	1	1	0
Athletics	7	.2988	.5230	37.2	1	3	1	2	0	0	0	0	2	0	0	0	0	0	0	0	0	0	0	0	0	4	1	0	0
ation	2	.0000	.0162	22.1	0	0	0	1	1	0	0	0	0	0	0	0	0	0	2	0	0	0	0	0	0	0	0	0	0
Atlanta	31	.5166	3.3552	45.3	7	1	5	7	5	4	2	0	0	0	0	0	6	6	0	0	0	0	0	1	0	2	1	15	0
Atlanta's	2	.0000	.0243	23.9	0	0	0	1	0	1	0	0	0	0	0	0	0	0	0	0	0	0	0	0	0	0	0	2	0
Atlantic	399	.6488	53.524	57.3	50	50	83	66	68	32	38	12	30	3	1	3	2	188	0	47	4	0	0	0	9	41	50	21	0
atlas	39	.2556	2.3243	43.7	1	28	3	0	4	2	1	0	1	5	0	0	0	4	0	1	0	0	0	0	0	0	28	0	0
Atlas	37	.2971	2.6584	44.2	1	4	2	21	6	0	3	0	1	0	0	0	2	30	0	0	0	0	0	0	0	2	2	0	0
atlases	13	.3094	.9109	39.6	0	7	0	1	1	1	2	1	1	3	0	0	0	0	0	0	0	0	0	0	0	0	8	1	0
Atlases	3	.0000	.0314	25.0	0	3	0	0	0	0	0	0	0	0	0	0	0	0	0	0	0	0	0	0	0	0	3	0	0
atmosphere	395	.6168	50.807	57.1	80	36	36	50	78	49	56	10	26	3	3	7	1	10	2	268	4	1	3	0	5	9	30	23	0
atmospheres	5	.2144	.2818	34.5	0	0	0	0	1	0	4	0	0	0	0	0	0	0	0	4	0	0	0	0	1	0	0	0	0
atmospheric	42	.5766	5.0832	47.1	3	3	4	2	12	10	6	2	2	0	0	0	0	0	1	26	0	1	0	0	1	4	2	5	0
atole	4	.0000	.0778	28.9	0	4	0	0	0	0	0	0	0	0	0	0	0	4	0	0	0	0	0	0	0	0	0	0	0
atoll	6	.4723	.6072	37.8	0	0	0	1	3	1	1	0	0	0	0	1	0	3	0	0	0	0	0	0	1	1	0	0	0
atolls	2	.2437	.1129	30.5	0	1	0	0	1	0	0	0	0	0	0	0	0	0	0	0	0	0	0	0	0	0	1	1	0
atom	225	.5495	26.009	54.2	9	8	44	32	57	53	19	3	1	0	0	0	5	9	2	143	3	0	0	5	1	7	43	6	0
atom's	2	.0000	.0394	26.0	0	0	0	0	1	1	0	0	0	0	0	0	0	0	0	2	0	0	0	0	0	0	0	0	0
atomic	213	.6957	30.545	54.8	6	11	40	62	31	43	18	2	40	1	0	1	15	31	3	73	1	0	0	1	0	6	32	9	0
Atomic	11	.5050	1.1713	40.7	0	0	2	1	1	4	2	1	0	0	0	0	0	1	0	3	0	0	0	0	0	1	3	3	0
atomic-energy	4	.3863	.3414	35.3	0	0	1	0	1	1	1	0	0	0	0	0	0	2	0	0	0	0	0	0	0	0	1	1	0
atomic-powered	2	.1814	.1187	30.7	0	1	0	0	0	0	1	0	1	0	0	0	0	0	0	0	0	0	0	0	0	0	0	1	0
atoms	332	.4786	34.381	55.4	31	20	98	46	58	40	34	5	6	1	1	0	2	1	1	253	0	0	0	11	0	24	26	6	0
atonal	2	.0000	.0162	22.1	0	0	0	0	0	2	0	0	0	0	0	0	0	0	0	0	2	0	0	0	0	0	0	0	0
atonement	2	.0000	.0209	23.2	0	0	0	0	0	2	0	0	0	0	0	0	0	0	0	0	0	0	0	0	0	0	2	0	0
Atonement	2	.1814	.1187	30.7	0	1	0	0	0	0	1	0	1	0	0	0	0	0	0	0	0	0	0	0	0	0	0	1	0

XN astonishments
5F Astor's
9P Astors
7Q astounds
5A astraddle
8G astro
9P astroblastoma
7H astrobleme
9Q astrolabes
6B astron
9Q astronautical
6P Astronautical
XH astronomer's
8B astronomers'
7H astronomy's
9H astrophysics
8R Astros
7H astutely
XP asura
7D asymmetrical
7D asymmetrically
8Q Asyut
9R AT&T
4N at-at-at
6G at-tic
5F Atahualpa
7A Atchafalaya
7A Atchison
5G atchitamon
8R Atco
5P Ath
4R Athalie
6F Athenians'
9D Athens'
6A Athlete
9R athwart
3J Atira
5Q Atkins
6R Atlantans
7R Atlantic-salmon
8Q Atlantis
3H ATMOSPHERE
6R atmospherically
8H atmospherics
XR Atoll
7H atom-smashing
8Q atomic-scale
9D atomies
XR atomized
7Q atomoi
9Q Aton
8R atonality

Word Type	F	D	U	SFI	3 Gr 3	4 Gr 4	5 Gr 5	6 Gr 6	7 Gr 7	8 Gr 8	9 Gr 9	X UnGr	A Read	B Eng & Gr	C Comp	D Lit	E Math	F Soc Stud	G Spell	H Sci	J Music	K Art	L Home Ec	M Shop	N Lib F	P Lib NF	Q Lib Ref	R Mag	S Rel
atop	14	.4060	1.3213	41.2	1	0	3	3	4	1	2	0	5	0	0	0	0	1	0	0	0	0	0	0	3	0	0	5	0
ATP	12	.2353	.7147	38.5	0	0	0	0	3	0	9	0	0	0	0	0	0	0	0	9	0	0	0	0	0	0	3	0	0
Atreus	2	.0000	.0215	23.3	0	0	0	0	0	0	2	0	0	0	0	2	0	0	0	0	0	0	0	0	0	0	0	0	0
Atri	5	.0000	.2284	33.6	0	1	0	4	0	0	0	0	5	0	0	0	0	0	0	0	0	0	0	0	0	0	0	0	0
atrium	2	.2278	.1128	30.5	0	0	1	0	0	0	1	0	0	0	0	0	0	0	0	1	0	0	0	0	0	0	1	0	0
atrophy	2	.2437	.1129	30.5	0	0	0	0	0	1	1	0	0	0	0	0	0	0	0	0	0	0	0	0	0	0	1	1	0
attach	48	.5982	5.9636	47.8	2	2	11	3	15	6	7	2	5	1	0	1	3	1	1	20	1	0	8	4	0	1	1	1	0
attached	201	.8981	35.832	55.5	12	19	30	35	54	30	17	4	26	11	2	2	5	10	10	52	10	1	10	5	8	15	24	10	0
attaches	10	.4238	.9708	39.9	0	0	2	1	7	0	0	0	2	0	0	0	0	2	0	5	0	0	0	0	0	0	1	0	0
attaching	10	.2487	.5577	37.5	0	0	0	0	3	2	4	1	0	0	0	0	1	0	0	1	0	0	5	0	0	2	0	1	0
attachment	17	.3987	1.5061	41.8	0	1	1	3	5	3	4	0	3	0	0	0	0	2	0	2	0	0	5	0	0	1	3	1	0
attachments	2	.2437	.1129	30.5	0	0	0	0	2	0	0	0	0	0	0	0	0	0	0	0	0	0	0	0	0	0	1	1	0
attack	273	.7838	43.477	56.4	25	40	42	27	57	46	28	8	84	5	2	20	0	53	2	20	1	0	0	0	6	27	35	18	0
attacked	104	.7611	16.147	52.1	7	9	17	19	16	23	10	3	29	4	0	4	0	32	1	3	2	0	0	0	4	10	6	9	0
attackers	9	.5030	1.0097	40.0	1	0	1	1	4	1	1	0	4	0	1	0	0	1	0	0	0	0	0	0	0	1	1	1	0
attacking	41	.7180	6.1006	47.9	6	4	8	5	10	6	1	1	17	2	0	2	0	8	0	0	2	0	0	0	0	4	2	4	0
attacks	71	.6673	9.7225	49.9	4	5	10	8	21	7	12	4	7	2	0	1	0	12	0	9	2	0	0	0	0	9	15	14	0
attain	20	.8140	3.2495	45.1	0	2	0	1	10	4	3	0	1	1	0	2	3	0	1	2	3	0	1	0	2	1	1	2	0
attainable	2	.2152	.1357	31.3	0	0	0	0	0	2	0	0	1	0	0	0	0	1	0	0	0	0	0	0	0	0	0	0	0
attainder	2	.0000	.0389	25.9	0	0	0	0	0	2	0	0	0	0	0	0	0	2	0	0	0	0	0	0	0	0	0	0	0
attained	20	.6917	2.8028	44.5	0	0	2	4	5	7	2	0	0	1	0	2	0	2	0	5	3	0	0	0	1	0	3	3	0
attaining	5	.4638	.4849	36.9	0	0	0	0	2	0	2	1	0	1	0	0	0	0	0	0	1	0	0	0	0	1	2	0	0
attainment	4	.3210	.3104	34.9	0	0	0	1	3	0	0	0	1	1	0	0	0	0	0	0	0	0	0	0	0	2	0	0	0
attains	4	.3465	.3040	34.8	0	0	0	0	1	3	0	0	0	0	0	0	0	1	0	0	1	0	0	0	0	0	2	0	0
attempt	138	.8903	24.405	53.9	3	5	16	17	37	20	32	8	22	10	4	10	2	12	4	10	1	1	5	7	4	15	16	15	0
attempted	67	.7784	10.495	50.2	0	4	6	8	19	14	11	5	9	5	0	1	1	5	1	2	4	0	0	1	9	7	17	5	0
attempting	33	.6935	4.6433	46.7	2	2	2	2	12	4	7	2	2	3	0	1	1	2	0	4	0	0	0	2	5	0	8	5	0
attempts	81	.8397	13.591	51.3	2	3	7	12	24	17	14	2	11	6	3	1	2	12	3	8	0	0	2	2	1	5	15	10	0
attend	105	.9030	18.811	52.7	3	16	15	15	25	8	19	4	15	10	1	9	2	21	4	2	3	1	2	0	11	4	10	10	0
attendance	10	.6521	1.3405	41.3	0	1	2	1	2	1	3	0	1	1	0	0	2	2	1	0	0	0	0	0	1	0	0	2	0
attendant	10	.3893	.8381	39.2	0	0	3	0	6	1	0	0	1	1	3	0	1	0	1	0	0	0	0	0	0	0	2	1	0
attendants	10	.5903	1.2373	40.9	0	1	0	4	2	0	3	0	2	2	0	0	0	1	0	0	1	0	0	0	2	0	0	2	0
attended	80	.8589	13.684	51.4	2	7	13	9	13	22	12	2	8	5	1	1	10	12	1	2	8	0	2	0	6	4	11	9	0
attending	33	.7329	4.9095	46.9	1	3	3	3	8	4	11	0	6	2	0	2	0	3	0	0	2	0	2	0	2	1	5	8	0
attends	3	.2431	.1816	32.6	0	0	1	0	2	0	0	0	0	0	0	0	0	2	0	0	0	0	0	0	1	0	0	0	0
attention	471	.9244	86.237	59.4	41	53	52	42	122	79	70	12	104	49	14	32	4	35	21	20	27	11	17	4	32	42	22	37	0
attentions	5	.5559	.5727	37.6	0	0	1	0	2	1	1	0	0	1	0	1	0	1	0	0	1	0	0	0	0	0	1	0	0
attentive	10	.4460	.9543	39.8	0	0	1	4	0	2	1	2	1	0	2	3	0	0	0	1	0	0	0	0	1	1	0	1	0
attentively	11	.5794	1.3475	41.3	2	0	1	1	3	1	3	0	3	2	0	3	0	0	0	0	1	0	0	0	0	1	0	1	0
Atterdag	2	.0000	.0290	24.6	0	0	2	0	0	0	0	0	0	0	0	0	0	0	0	0	0	0	0	0	0	2	0	0	0
attested	3	.3766	.2480	33.9	0	0	0	0	1	2	0	0	0	0	0	0	0	1	0	0	0	0	0	0	1	0	1	0	0
Atti	8	.0000	.3655	35.6	0	8	0	0	0	0	0	0	8	0	0	0	0	0	0	0	0	0	0	0	0	0	0	0	0
attic	45	.6791	6.2805	48.0	4	10	6	8	7	8	1	1	9	2	3	1	1	4	1	0	1	0	0	0	11	10	0	2	0
Attica	4	.2348	.2372	33.8	0	0	0	0	3	1	0	0	0	0	0	0	0	3	0	0	0	0	0	0	0	0	1	0	0
attics	2	.0725	.0732	28.6	1	0	0	0	0	0	1	0	1	0	0	0	0	0	0	0	0	0	0	1	0	0	0	0	0
Atticus	31	.0000	.3327	35.2	0	0	0	0	0	0	31	0	0	0	0	31	0	0	0	0	0	0	0	0	0	0	0	0	0
Atticus's	2	.0000	.0215	23.3	0	0	0	0	0	0	2	0	0	0	0	2	0	0	0	0	0	0	0	0	0	0	0	0	0
Attila	4	.1494	.1609	32.1	0	0	0	0	2	0	1	1	0	0	0	0	0	0	0	1	0	0	0	0	0	0	3	0	0
attire	5	.3048	.3825	35.8	0	4	0	0	1	0	0	0	2	0	0	0	0	0	2	0	0	0	0	0	1	0	0	0	0
attired	2	.2375	.1088	30.4	0	0	0	0	1	0	1	0	0	0	0	0	0	0	0	0	1	0	0	0	0	0	0	1	0
attitude	102	.7633	15.698	52.0	1	4	7	4	27	27	30	2	17	8	11	10	0	10	2	2	4	1	6	0	7	9	7	8	0
attitudes	69	.7697	10.719	50.3	1	0	26	3	15	10	13	1	5	3	0	4	0	21	1	13	4	0	0	0	1	5	6	6	0
attorney	14	.5003	1.4639	41.7	0	0	0	0	4	8	2	0	0	6	0	0	0	3	2	0	0	0	0	0	0	0	1	2	0
Attorney	15	.3129	1.0992	40.4	0	1	1	0	3	5	4	1	0	0	0	0	0	10	0	0	0	0	0	0	0	1	0	4	0
attorneys	5	.0000	.0972	29.9	0	0	0	0	2	1	2	0	0	0	0	0	0	5	0	0	0	0	0	0	0	0	0	0	0
attract	101	.7740	15.773	52.0	16	4	16	14	19	16	14	2	14	3	0	2	0	12	0	26	4	6	3	5	1	7	10	8	0
attracted	107	.7918	17.052	52.3	8	14	16	13	25	18	10	3	12	1	0	5	0	13	0	31	8	0	1	4	3	7	14	8	0
attracting	8	.5450	.9160	39.6	0	1	2	0	1	1	2	1	0	0	0	0	0	1	0	3	0	0	0	0	0	2	1	1	0
attraction	73	.6179	9.4080	49.7	4	16	15	6	11	13	5	3	7	1	0	1	0	3	0	42	1	0	0	2	1	1	9	5	0
attractions	20	.5524	2.3158	43.6	2	0	5	1	0	1	5	6	2	0	0	0	0	1	0	1	1	0	0	0	0	4	4	7	0
attractive	128	.5742	14.958	51.7	5	7	11	5	27	41	29	3	5	4	1	2	0	7	0	5	5	7	47	8	4	12	11	10	0
attractively	10	.2564	.5408	37.3	0	1	1	0	3	2	3	0	0	0	0	1	0	0	0	0	0	1	7	0	0	1	0	0	0
attractiveness	7	.3538	.5269	37.2	0	0	0	0	1	3	2	1	0	0	0	1	0	0	0	2	0	0	3	1	0	0	0	0	0
attracts	21	.6713	2.8707	44.6	1	0	5	2	5	4	2	2	0	3	0	0	0	3	0	7	2	0	0	1	0	0	2	3	0
attributable	2	.1926	.0867	29.4	0	0	0	0	1	1	0	0	0	0	0	0	0	0	0	0	0	0	1	0	0	0	1	0	0
attributed	14	.5693	1.6544	42.2	0	0	2	2	2	3	2	3	1	1	0	0	0	0	0	1	1	0	0	0	0	3	5	2	0
attributes	10	.3422	.7553	38.8	0	1	1	1	5	0	2	0	1	1	0	0	0	0	0	0	0	0	2	0	0	0	6	0	0
attributing	2	.2285	.1129	30.5	0	0	0	0	1	1	0	0	0	0	0	0	0	1	0	0	0	0	0	0	0	0	1	0	0
attrition	5	.4409	.4707	36.7	1	0	0	0	0	2	2	0	0	0	0	0	0	1	0	0	0	0	0	0	0	1	2	1	0
Attucks	12	.2175	.6180	37.9	0	0	0	0	12	0	0	0	0	0	0	8	0	0	0	0	0	0	0	0	0	0	0	4	0
ATTUCKS	35	.0000	.3756	35.7	0	0	0	0	35	0	0	0	0	0	0	35	0	0	0	0	0	0	0	0	0	0	0	0	0
attuned	4	.3097	.2992	34.8	0	2	0	0	0	0	0	2	1	0	0	1	0	0	0	0	0	0	0	0	0	0	0	2	0
Atuk	3	.0000	.0243	23.9	0	3	0	0	0	0	0	0	0	0	0	0	0	0	3	0	0	0	0	0	0	0	0	0	0
Atuk's	2	.0000	.0162	22.1	0	2	0	0	0	0	0	0	0	0	0	0	0	0	2	0	0	0	0	0	0	0	0	0	0
au	14	.2573	.8552	39.3	3	3	2	5	1	0	0	0	2	2	0	0	0	0	9	0	0	0	0	0	0	0	0	1	0
Au	2	.2405	.1205	30.8	1	0	0	0	0	1	0	0	0	0	0	0	0	0	0	1	0	0	0	0	0	1	0	0	0
Aubrey	2	.0000	.0209	23.2	0	0	2	0	0	0	0	0	0	0	0	0	0	0	0	0	0	0	0	0	0	0	2	0	0
Auburn	2	.0000	.0914	29.6	0	0	0	0	0	2	0	0	2	0	0	0	0	0	0	0	0	0	0	0	0	0	0	0	0
Auckland	5	.0000	.0972	29.9	0	5	0	0	0	0	0	0	0	0	0	0	0	5	0	0	0	0	0	0	0	0	0	0	0
auction	18	.6473	2.3753	43.8	1	0	2	4	2	4	5	0	1	6	1	3	0	1	0	0	0	0	0	0	1	3	1	1	0
auctions	4	.3509	.3113	34.9	0	1	0	0	0	0	1	2	0	1	0	0	0	1	0	0	0	0	0	0	0	0	0	2	0
audacious	4	.3874	.3414	35.3	0	0	0	0	1	3	0	0	0	0	0	1	0	2	0	0	0	0	0	0	0	0	1	0	0
audible	9	.6011	1.1199	40.5	0	0	0	1	5	2	1	0	1	0	0	3	0	0	0	1	1	0	0	0	1	1	1	0	0
audience	209	.8000	33.777	55.3	25	22	12	29	35	30	48	8	66	33	8	10	0	7	6	1	20	0	3	0	10	25	2	18	0
audiences	30	.5074	3.2322	45.1	1	0	3	6	4	7	6	3	5	1	0	2	0	1	0	1	12	0	0	0	0	0	3	5	0
audio	9	.3216	.6245	38.0	0	0	0	0	2	4	3	0	0	1	0	0	0	0	0	2	3	0	0	3	0	0	0	0	0
audio-frequency	2	.0000	.0394	26.0	0	0	0	0	0	0	2	0	0	0	0	0	0	0	0	2	0	0	0	0	0	0	0	0	0
auditorium	32	.6330	4.1406	46.2	6	3	1	6	5	4	7	0	2	5	4	3	7	2	0	0	2	0	0	0	3	2	0	2	0
auditory	9	.4499	.8676	39.4	0	3	0	2	1	1	2	0	0	2	1	0	0	0	0	5	1	0	0	0	0	0	0	0	0
Audubon	13	.4917	1.3903	41.4	1	1	1	6	3	0	0	1	3	0	0	3	0	0	0	0	0	0	0	0	0	5	1	1	0
aue	2	.0000	.0234	23.7	0	0	0	2	0	0	0	0	0	0	0	0	0	0	0	0	0	0	0	0	2	0	0	0	0
Auenbrugger	3	.0000	.1370	31.4	0	0	3	0	0	0	0	0	3	0	0	0	0	0	0	0	0	0	0	0	0	0	0	0	0
Aug	12	.0000	.1256	31.0	0	0	3	0	3	6	0	0	0	0	0	0	0	0	0	0	0	0	0	0	0	0	12	0	0
auger	13	.1159	.4393	36.4	0	0	0	0	1	10	0	2	1	0	0	0	0	0	0	5	0	0	0	7	0	0	0	0	0
Auggie	14	.0000	.0312	24.9	0	0	0	0	0	14	0	0	0	0	14	0	0	0	0	0	0	0	0	0	0	0	0	0	0
aught	4	.4445	.3917	35.9	0	0	0	2	0	1	1	0	1	0	0	1	0	0	0	0	1	0	0	0	1	0	0	0	0

9D Atreus'
9D atrocious
7R ATS-3
7D attaboy
5P attache
9B Attack
7Q attacker
6Q attars
9D attendeth
7H attest
9E attesting
9R attests
4A Atti's
6A Attic
XR Attitudes
8J Attorney-General
9D Attorney-at-Law
9D attorney's
8F Attorney's
7F attorneys'
7R Attuck's
7D Attucks'
5A Atupaluk
6J aubade
6J Aubade
7R auburn
9D auctioned
XR auctioneer
7R audacity
9A Auden
9R audibles
7D audibly
6R Audience
9Q audio-visual
9A audition
4R auditor
5Q Auditorium
5Q auditorium's
7A auditoriums
9J auditors
5R Audrey
5C Audrey's
XR Audubon's
5A Auenbrugger's
7R Auerswald
6A auf
8A Augeas
3P AUGER

Word Type	F	D	U	SFI	3 Gr 3	4 Gr 4	5 Gr 5	6 Gr 6	7 Gr 7	8 Gr 8	9 Gr 9	X UnGr	A Read	B Eng & Gr	C Comp	D Lit	E Math	F Soc Stud	G Spell	H Sci	J Music	K Art	L Home Ec	M Shop	N Lib F	P Lib NF	Q Lib Ref	R Mag	S Rel
augmentation	4	.0000	.0323	25.1	0	0	0	0	3	1	0	0	0	0	0	0	0	0	0	0	4	0	0	0	0	0	0	0	0
augmented	4	.4819	.4016	36.0	0	0	1	0	1	2	0	0	0	1	0	0	0	0	0	0	1	0	0	0	0	1	1	0	0
august	6	.6037	.7567	38.8	0	0	1	0	1	1	3	0	1	1	0	0	0	1	0	0	0	0	0	0	0	1	1	1	0
August	137	.8577	23.491	53.7	10	23	20	12	27	22	21	2	27	3	3	6	6	36	2	4	1	0	1	1	4	12	11	20	0
AUGUST	13	.0000	.1395	31.4	0	0	0	0	13	0	0	0	0	0	0	13	0	0	0	0	0	0	0	0	0	0	0	0	0
Augusta	3	.2387	.1708	32.3	0	2	1	0	0	0	0	0	0	0	0	0	0	0	0	0	0	0	0	0	0	2	1	0	0
Auguste	7	.4100	.6501	38.1	0	1	1	1	1	2	1	0	2	0	0	0	0	0	0	1	0	1	0	0	0	0	2	1	0
Augustin	2	.2417	.1091	30.4	0	0	0	1	0	1	0	0	0	0	0	0	0	0	0	0	1	0	0	0	0	0	1	0	0
Augustine	12	.5174	1.3113	41.2	0	1	4	1	5	0	0	1	0	1	0	0	0	5	0	0	0	0	0	0	0	4	1	1	0
Augustinian	2	.0000	.0209	23.2	1	0	0	0	0	0	1	0	0	0	0	0	0	0	0	0	0	0	0	0	0	0	2	0	0
Augustus	35	.4848	3.9087	45.9	0	11	6	2	12	0	3	1	18	0	0	0	0	12	1	0	0	0	0	0	0	1	0	3	0
Augustus'	5	.2326	.3837	35.8	0	2	2	0	1	0	0	0	4	0	0	0	0	1	0	0	0	0	0	0	0	0	0	0	0
auk	4	.2348	.2372	33.8	0	0	0	0	1	0	3	0	0	0	0	0	0	3	0	0	0	0	0	0	0	0	1	0	0
Auka	10	.0000	.1172	30.7	0	0	10	0	0	0	0	0	0	0	0	0	0	0	0	0	0	0	0	0	10	0	0	0	0
auld	2	.2412	.1141	30.6	0	1	0	0	0	1	0	0	0	1	0	0	0	0	0	0	0	0	0	0	0	1	0	0	0
Auld	5	.3812	.4221	36.3	0	0	4	0	1	0	0	0	0	0	0	0	0	3	0	0	1	0	0	0	0	0	1	0	0
aunt	109	.7147	15.877	52.0	20	18	11	4	35	17	4	0	24	4	2	38	2	0	7	1	10	0	2	0	10	8	0	1	0
Aunt	287	.6779	40.303	56.1	83	36	29	36	54	25	24	0	88	16	0	43	1	2	2	4	7	0	1	0	70	41	0	12	0
aunt's	10	.5522	1.1711	40.7	0	2	1	0	5	2	0	0	2	1	0	3	0	0	0	1	0	0	0	0	2	1	0	0	0
Auntie	2	.2433	.1158	30.6	0	1	0	0	1	0	0	0	0	0	0	0	0	0	0	0	0	0	0	0	0	1	0	1	0
aunts	26	.3537	2.1132	43.2	6	5	1	1	3	3	7	0	5	5	0	4	0	0	0	1	1	0	0	0	1	6	2	0	1
Aunts	4	.2313	.2106	33.2	0	0	0	0	0	4	0	0	0	0	1	0	0	0	0	0	0	0	0	0	3	0	0	0	0
Aunty	9	.2860	.6773	38.3	0	1	0	0	4	0	4	0	4	0	0	4	0	0	0	0	0	0	0	0	0	1	0	0	0
aura	2	.1160	.0650	28.1	0	0	0	0	1	0	1	0	0	0	1	0	0	0	0	1	0	0	0	0	0	0	0	0	0
Aurelius	3	.2043	.1486	31.7	0	0	0	0	0	0	1	2	0	0	0	0	0	0	0	0	0	0	0	0	0	1	2	0	0
aureomycin	3	.2430	.1792	32.5	0	0	0	0	0	2	0	1	0	0	0	0	0	0	1	2	0	0	0	0	0	0	0	0	0
auricle	5	.0000	.0986	29.9	0	1	2	0	0	2	0	0	0	0	0	0	0	0	0	5	0	0	0	0	0	0	0	0	0
auricles	4	.0000	.0789	29.0	0	0	1	0	0	3	0	0	0	0	0	0	0	0	0	4	0	0	0	0	0	0	0	0	0
aurora	4	.1494	.1609	32.1	3	0	0	0	1	0	0	0	0	0	0	0	0	0	0	1	0	0	0	0	0	0	3	0	0
auspices	2	.0000	.0290	24.6	0	0	0	1	1	0	0	0	0	0	0	0	0	0	0	0	0	0	0	0	0	2	0	0	0
auspicious	2	.1948	.1250	31.0	0	0	0	0	1	0	1	0	1	0	0	0	0	0	0	0	0	0	0	0	0	1	0	0	0
austere	9	.6081	1.1231	40.5	0	0	1	2	2	2	2	0	0	1	0	0	0	2	0	0	0	0	0	0	1	1	2	2	0
Austerfield	6	.0000	.0869	29.4	0	6	0	0	0	0	0	0	0	0	0	0	0	0	0	0	0	0	0	0	0	6	0	0	0
austerity	2	.1814	.1187	30.7	0	0	0	1	1	0	0	0	1	0	0	0	0	0	0	0	0	0	0	0	0	0	0	1	0
Austin	11	.5182	1.2038	40.8	2	1	1	0	2	5	0	0	0	0	0	0	1	6	0	0	1	0	0	0	2	0	1	0	0
Austine	20	.1787	1.1737	40.7	10	10	0	0	0	0	0	0	10	0	0	0	0	0	0	0	0	0	0	0	10	0	0	0	0
Austine's	2	.0000	.0234	23.7	2	0	0	0	0	0	0	0	0	0	0	0	0	0	0	0	0	0	0	0	2	0	0	0	0
Australia	206	.6701	28.534	54.6	12	47	31	66	25	6	17	2	24	3	2	5	5	110	1	23	1	0	0	0	2	13	12	5	0
Australia's	11	.4108	1.0300	40.1	0	1	1	5	2	1	1	0	2	0	0	0	0	6	0	0	0	0	0	0	0	0	2	1	0
Australian	23	.6254	2.9977	44.8	0	9	4	4	3	1	2	0	3	1	0	0	0	9	1	2	0	0	0	0	0	1	1	5	0
Australians	15	.2731	1.0033	40.0	0	1	6	6	1	1	0	0	0	0	0	0	0	12	0	0	0	0	0	0	0	2	1	0	0
australis	2	.2401	.1133	30.5	1	0	1	0	0	0	0	0	0	0	0	0	0	0	0	0	0	0	0	0	0	1	1	0	0
australopithecine	2	.0000	.0209	23.2	0	0	0	0	2	0	0	0	0	0	0	0	0	0	0	0	0	0	0	0	0	0	2	0	0
australopithecines	2	.0000	.0209	23.2	0	0	0	0	2	0	0	0	0	0	0	0	0	0	0	0	0	0	0	0	0	0	2	0	0
Australopithecus	4	.2278	.2257	33.5	0	0	0	0	4	0	0	0	0	0	0	0	0	0	0	2	0	0	0	0	0	0	2	0	0
Austria	83	.6910	11.681	50.7	6	1	10	6	31	7	21	1	4	0	0	8	4	32	0	0	9	1	0	0	0	9	13	3	0
Austria-Hungary	9	.2387	.5685	37.5	0	0	0	2	1	5	1	0	1	0	0	0	0	7	0	0	0	0	0	0	0	0	1	0	0
Austria's	3	.3222	.2365	33.7	0	0	1	1	0	1	0	0	1	0	0	0	1	0	0	0	1	0	0	0	0	0	0	0	0
Austrian	35	.6050	4.3649	46.4	4	2	10	3	5	2	9	0	1	0	0	1	2	8	0	3	8	0	0	0	0	6	6	0	0
Austrians	3	.3674	.2406	33.8	0	0	1	0	1	0	1	0	0	0	0	0	0	1	0	0	1	0	0	0	0	0	1	0	0
Austro-Hungarian	3	.3665	.2412	33.8	0	0	0	0	1	1	1	0	0	0	0	0	0	1	0	0	1	0	0	0	0	0	0	1	0
authentic	20	.4790	2.0434	43.1	1	0	1	1	7	5	1	4	2	0	0	0	0	2	0	1	5	0	0	0	0	0	2	8	0
authenticated	3	.2444	.1814	32.6	0	1	0	0	1	1	0	0	0	0	0	0	0	2	0	0	0	0	0	0	0	0	1	0	0
author	216	.7450	33.097	55.2	6	36	31	39	43	33	18	10	96	42	2	16	1	7	3	3	7	0	0	0	0	7	12	20	0
Author	3	.3842	.2448	33.9	0	1	0	1	0	0	1	0	0	1	0	1	0	0	0	0	1	0	0	0	0	0	0	0	0
author's	41	.6291	5.5044	47.4	0	13	5	4	7	7	4	1	21	10	1	2	0	0	0	0	1	0	0	0	0	1	1	4	0
authoritative	3	.1937	.1495	31.7	0	0	0	0	0	1	0	2	0	0	0	0	0	1	0	0	0	0	0	0	0	0	0	2	0
authorities	47	.7073	6.7707	48.3	1	1	4	5	16	11	7	2	6	3	0	3	0	7	3	1	0	0	0	0	0	8	9	7	0
authority	110	.7392	16.453	52.2	5	5	15	4	28	28	19	6	9	6	1	5	0	25	0	4	1	0	0	0	4	15	19	21	0
Authority	10	.4855	1.0323	40.1	1	0	2	1	2	1	0	3	0	1	0	0	0	3	0	1	0	0	0	0	0	1	0	4	0
authorized	14	.4257	1.2965	41.1	1	0	0	0	7	2	3	1	1	0	0	0	1	3	0	0	0	0	0	0	0	0	6	3	0
authorizing	2	.2408	.1204	30.8	0	0	0	0	0	1	1	0	0	0	0	0	0	1	0	0	0	0	0	0	0	1	0	0	0
authors	45	.7964	7.2015	48.6	1	5	12	4	8	4	9	2	7	12	1	2	2	5	0	1	2	1	0	0	1	3	6	2	0
authors'	4	.0931	.1444	31.6	0	0	0	4	0	0	0	0	1	3	0	0	0	0	0	0	0	0	0	0	0	0	0	0	0
authorship	2	.2446	.1123	30.5	0	0	0	0	0	1	1	0	0	1	0	0	0	0	0	0	0	0	0	0	0	0	1	0	0
auto	39	.6012	4.8706	46.9	4	3	6	3	11	3	6	3	3	0	0	0	2	9	3	3	0	0	0	0	1	2	1	15	0
Auto	2	.0000	.0243	23.9	0	0	0	0	0	0	2	0	0	0	0	0	0	0	0	0	0	0	0	0	0	0	0	2	0
Auto-Union	2	.0000	.0290	24.6	0	0	0	0	0	0	0	2	0	0	0	0	0	0	0	0	0	0	0	0	0	2	0	0	0
autobiographical	7	.5127	.7576	38.8	0	0	1	0	5	1	0	0	1	2	0	1	0	0	1	0	0	0	0	0	0	0	2	0	0
autobiographies	2	.2398	.1138	30.6	0	0	0	0	1	0	1	0	0	0	0	1	1	0	0	0	0	0	0	0	0	0	0	0	0
autobiography	9	.4354	.9045	39.6	0	2	2	0	2	2	1	0	4	3	0	0	0	0	1	0	0	0	0	0	0	1	0	0	0
Autobiography	4	.3519	.3117	34.9	0	0	1	0	1	1	1	0	0	0	0	0	0	1	0	0	0	0	0	0	0	0	1	2	0
autocratic	3	.2159	.1532	31.9	0	0	1	0	0	0	2	0	0	0	0	0	0	0	0	0	0	0	0	0	0	0	2	1	0
autograph	13	.4560	1.3960	41.4	6	1	0	1	3	2	0	0	8	0	0	0	0	0	1	0	0	0	0	0	0	1	0	3	0
autographed	2	.2433	.1158	30.6	0	0	0	0	2	0	0	0	0	0	0	0	0	0	0	0	0	0	0	0	0	1	0	1	0
autoharp	100	.0000	.8085	39.1	16	35	26	19	3	1	0	0	0	0	0	0	0	0	0	0	100	0	0	0	0	0	0	0	0
Autoharp	3	.0000	.0243	23.8	0	0	0	0	2	1	0	0	0	0	0	0	0	0	0	0	3	0	0	0	0	0	0	0	0
Autolycos	7	.0000	.0751	28.8	0	0	0	0	0	0	7	0	0	0	0	7	0	0	0	0	0	0	0	0	0	0	0	0	0
automated	17	.4737	1.7087	42.3	4	0	0	3	5	3	2	0	0	0	0	0	0	0	0	7	0	0	0	1	0	0	6	3	0
automatic	84	.7704	13.042	51.2	1	0	12	20	23	16	11	1	10	1	0	12	3	2	1	19	1	0	3	6	1	7	7	11	0
Automatic	3	.3263	.2368	33.7	0	0	0	0	2	1	0	0	1	0	0	0	0	0	0	0	1	0	0	0	0	0	0	1	0
automatically	61	.8034	9.8405	49.9	2	2	8	7	16	15	9	2	7	9	0	3	3	0	1	18	1	0	1	1	1	1	7	8	0
automation	26	.3842	2.1920	43.4	0	0	0	1	10	4	11	0	2	0	0	2	0	1	0	3	0	0	0	1	0	0	17	0	0
automobile	244	.8581	41.738	56.2	23	41	35	20	61	32	28	4	20	10	3	13	15	55	3	39	2	1	0	11	5	27	27	13	0
Automobile	4	.3637	.3175	35.0	0	1	1	1	0	0	1	0	0	1	0	0	0	0	0	0	0	0	0	0	0	1	0	2	0
automobile-assembly	2	.0000	.0389	25.9	0	0	1	0	1	0	0	0	0	0	0	0	0	2	0	0	0	0	0	0	0	0	0	0	0
automobiles	181	.7630	27.957	54.5	19	34	38	24	22	28	13	3	18	7	3	0	3	94	1	13	1	2	1	8	3	12	10	5	0
automotive	6	.1473	.2287	33.6	0	0	0	1	2	0	3	0	0	0	0	0	0	0	0	0	0	0	0	0	0	0	5	1	0
autonomic	11	.2359	.6403	38.1	0	0	0	6	0	1	4	0	0	0	0	0	0	0	0	6	0	0	0	0	0	0	5	0	0
autonomous	8	.4355	.7425	38.7	0	0	4	1	1	1	1	0	0	0	0	0	0	0	1	1	0	0	0	0	0	3	3	0	0
autonomy	3	.3769	.2484	34.0	0	0	0	0	0	2	1	0	0	0	0	0	0	1	0	0	0	0	0	0	0	0	1	1	0
autos	8	.3715	.6655	38.2	1	0	5	0	0	0	2	0	0	0	0	0	0	5	0	0	1	0	0	0	0	0	0	2	0
autostrada	2	.0000	.0290	24.6	2	0	0	0	0	0	0	0	0	0	0	0	0	0	0	0	0	0	0	0	0	2	0	0	0
autumn	139	.7956	22.307	53.5	26	14	19	24	27	11	9	9	34	5	10	7	0	9	3	15	14	2	0	0	9	12	6	13	0

XH augite
9D augments
4P Augsbury
8Q augurs
7F August's
4R Auguste's
8Q Augustinians
3A Augusto
8Q Augustulus
5H auks
8A Aulis
3P Auntie's
9D Aunty's
9J aural
3P Aurelian
8G aureus
5J Aurora
3P aurum
8A Auslander
5Q Austen
6P Auster
8N austere-looking
8F Austin's
6R Australasia
7B Australian's
XH Australis
7Q Austrasia
7Q Austrasians
9Q Austrian-Hungarian
5R authentically
4Q authenticity
XR author-director
6J authored
7R authoritarian
9Q authoritatively
7R authorization
4Q Authorized
7Q authorizes
9Q autics
XP Auto-Unions
7R auto-racing's
8F auto-suggestion
5F auto-tag
7G autobiographical**
7R autoclavable
7R autoclaving
3A autographing
4R autoharps
7G autoloading
7Q automa-
9Q automate
7Q automatization
8D automatons
7R Automotive
8A autopsies
3Q Autostrada
XH autotrophic

Word Type	F	D	U	SFI	3 Gr 3	4 Gr 4	5 Gr 5	6 Gr 6	7 Gr 7	8 Gr 8	9 Gr 9	X UnGr	A Read	B Eng & Gr	C Comp	D Lit	E Math	F Soc Stud	G Spell	H Sci	J Music	K Art	L Home Ec	M Shop	N Lib F	P Lib NF	Q Lib Ref	R Mag	S Rel
Autumn	8	.4263	.7720	38.9	2	0	4	2	0	0	0	0	3	2	1	0	0	0	0	0	2	0	0	0	0	0	0	0	0
aux	2	.0000	.0219	23.4	0	1	0	0	0	0	1	0	0	2	0	0	0	0	0	0	0	0	0	0	0	0	0	0	0
Aux	6	.0000	.0657	28.2	0	0	0	0	2	3	1	0	0	6	0	0	0	0	0	0	0	0	0	0	0	0	0	0	0
auxiliaries	39	.0000	.4268	36.3	7	3	1	5	4	12	7	0	0	39	0	0	0	0	0	0	0	0	0	0	0	0	0	0	0
auxiliary	83	.4610	7.9073	49.0	9	10	16	9	7	13	19	0	0	52	9	0	0	0	0	0	1	0	0	13	0	0	4	4	0
av	3	.0000	.1370	31.4	0	0	0	0	0	3	0	0	3	0	0	0	0	0	0	0	0	0	0	0	0	0	0	0	0
avail	9	.6331	1.1747	40.7	2	0	1	1	1	1	2	1	1	0	0	1	0	0	0	1	0	0	0	0	1	2	2	1	0
availability	3	.3395	.2468	33.9	0	0	1	0	1	0	0	1	1	0	0	0	0	0	0	0	0	0	0	0	0	1	1	0	0
available	240	.7451	35.947	55.6	3	8	14	19	89	36	50	21	12	11	1	2	3	27	1	28	20	1	20	24	2	8	36	44	0
Avakian	4	.0000	.0486	26.9	0	0	0	0	4	0	0	0	0	0	0	0	0	0	0	0	0	0	0	0	0	0	0	4	0
avalanche	10	.3594	.9119	39.6	0	0	1	3	5	1	0	0	6	0	0	0	0	0	0	0	0	0	0	0	0	0	1	3	0
avalanches	4	.0000	.0419	26.2	0	0	0	0	4	0	0	0	0	0	0	0	0	0	0	0	0	0	0	0	0	0	4	0	0
avant	4	.2376	.2177	33.4	0	0	0	0	2	0	0	2	0	0	0	0	0	0	2	0	0	0	0	0	0	0	0	2	0
avant-garde	9	.4318	.8212	39.1	0	0	0	0	0	5	2	2	0	0	0	0	0	1	0	0	3	0	0	0	0	0	2	3	0
avarice	2	.2285	.1129	30.5	0	0	0	0	0	2	0	0	0	0	0	0	0	1	0	0	0	0	0	0	0	0	1	0	0
avariciously	2	.1787	.1174	30.7	0	0	0	0	2	0	0	0	1	0	0	0	0	0	0	0	0	0	0	0	1	0	0	0	0
avast	3	.2441	.1719	32.4	1	1	0	1	0	0	0	0	0	0	0	0	0	0	1	0	0	0	0	0	0	2	0	0	0
Ave	5	.2436	.2754	34.4	0	0	3	1	1	0	0	0	0	0	0	0	0	0	2	0	0	0	0	0	0	0	3	0	0
avenge	2	.2337	.1157	30.6	0	0	1	0	0	1	0	0	0	0	0	0	0	1	0	0	0	0	0	0	1	0	0	0	0
avenged	2	.0000	.0914	29.6	0	0	1	1	0	0	0	0	2	0	0	0	0	0	0	0	0	0	0	0	0	0	0	0	0
Avenger	2	.1814	.1187	30.7	0	0	0	1	1	0	0	0	1	0	0	0	0	0	0	0	0	0	0	0	0	0	0	1	0
avenging	3	.2053	.1597	32.0	0	0	0	1	2	0	0	0	0	0	0	0	0	0	0	1	0	0	0	0	0	2	0	0	0
avenue	15	.5673	1.7889	42.5	1	2	1	0	6	2	3	0	3	1	2	2	2	0	0	0	0	0	0	0	0	3	1	1	0
Avenue	59	.8123	9.6669	49.9	9	14	1	5	13	13	4	0	17	9	1	5	2	9	1	0	1	0	0	0	4	3	1	6	0
avenues	11	.5440	1.2565	41.0	4	0	1	0	3	3	0	0	1	0	0	0	4	1	0	0	2	0	0	0	2	0	0	1	0
average	413	.7426	61.984	57.9	15	21	50	64	92	77	78	16	16	4	2	5	156	45	4	65	1	0	6	2	1	19	43	44	0
average-sized	2	.2285	.1129	30.5	0	0	0	0	0	0	2	0	0	0	0	0	0	1	0	0	0	0	0	0	0	0	1	0	0
averaged	9	.4379	.8635	39.4	0	0	0	3	1	0	3	2	1	0	0	0	2	0	0	1	0	0	0	0	0	1	0	4	0
averages	28	.6220	3.5955	45.6	0	1	7	4	9	4	3	0	1	2	0	0	10	6	0	2	0	0	0	0	0	1	2	4	0
averaging	19	.5963	2.3481	43.7	0	0	2	4	1	7	2	3	1	0	0	0	5	1	0	2	0	0	0	0	0	3	4	3	0
aversion	4	.1551	.1455	31.6	0	0	1	1	1	1	0	0	0	0	2	0	0	0	0	0	0	0	0	0	2	0	0	0	0
avert	6	.4313	.5709	37.6	0	0	1	0	2	0	2	1	1	0	0	1	0	0	0	0	0	0	0	0	0	2	0	2	0
averted	2	.2407	.1138	30.6	0	0	1	0	1	0	0	0	0	0	0	1	0	0	0	0	0	0	0	0	0	1	0	0	0
Avery	9	.0880	.3138	35.0	0	8	1	0	0	0	0	0	2	0	0	0	0	0	0	0	0	0	0	0	7	0	0	0	0
Aviak	4	.0000	.1827	32.6	0	0	4	0	0	0	0	0	4	0	0	0	0	0	0	0	0	0	0	0	0	0	0	0	0
aviary	2	.2446	.1084	30.3	1	0	0	0	1	0	0	0	0	0	0	0	0	0	1	0	1	0	0	0	0	0	0	0	0
aviation	26	.6274	3.4646	45.4	0	0	1	5	12	2	4	2	11	0	0	1	0	0	4	4	0	0	0	0	0	1	3	2	0
Aviation	3	.1650	.1684	32.3	0	0	1	0	0	0	0	2	1	0	0	0	0	0	0	2	0	0	0	0	0	0	0	0	0
aviator	2	.2418	.1091	30.4	0	0	1	0	1	0	0	0	0	0	0	0	0	0	1	0	0	0	0	0	0	0	1	0	0
aviators	4	.2386	.2998	34.8	1	0	0	2	1	0	0	0	3	0	0	0	0	0	0	0	0	0	0	0	0	0	1	0	0
avid	5	.2418	.2811	34.5	0	0	0	0	1	0	3	1	0	0	0	0	0	0	0	0	0	0	0	0	0	0	2	3	0
avidly	2	.2437	.1129	30.5	0	0	0	0	2	0	0	0	0	0	0	0	0	0	0	0	0	0	0	0	0	0	1	1	0
Avignon	2	.0000	.0389	25.9	0	0	0	0	0	0	2	0	0	0	0	0	0	2	0	0	0	0	0	0	0	0	0	0	0
Aviv	9	.2444	.5495	37.4	0	0	4	1	4	0	0	0	0	0	0	0	0	5	0	0	0	0	0	0	0	4	0	0	0
AVO	3	.0000	.0322	25.1	0	0	0	0	3	0	0	0	0	0	0	3	0	0	0	0	0	0	0	0	0	0	0	0	0
avocat	2	.0000	.0162	22.1	0	0	2	0	0	0	0	0	0	0	0	0	0	0	0	0	2	0	0	0	0	0	0	0	0
avoid	246	.8075	39.757	56.0	10	23	30	30	50	42	52	9	22	42	1	7	10	13	8	43	1	2	28	6	9	11	13	30	0
avoided	51	.8186	8.3661	49.2	3	1	5	10	11	6	13	2	8	6	0	2	3	3	0	5	1	0	4	2	3	5	4	5	0
avoiding	16	.5263	1.7456	42.4	0	1	2	0	5	4	2	2	1	3	0	0	0	0	1	1	0	0	4	0	3	1	1	1	0
avoids	6	.5357	.6878	38.4	1	0	2	0	1	0	2	0	1	1	0	0	0	0	0	2	0	0	0	0	0	1	1	0	0
Avoirdupois	2	.0000	.0299	24.8	0	0	0	2	0	0	0	0	0	0	0	0	2	0	0	0	0	0	0	0	0	0	0	0	0
Avon	3	.2121	.1560	31.9	1	0	0	0	2	0	0	0	0	0	0	0	1	0	0	0	0	0	0	0	0	0	0	2	0
Avondale	5	.1468	.2522	34.0	0	0	0	0	3	2	0	0	2	0	0	0	0	0	0	0	0	0	0	0	3	0	0	0	0
aw	35	.6296	4.6416	46.7	3	10	4	3	8	6	1	0	13	3	0	2	0	0	6	0	0	0	0	0	5	5	0	1	0
await	19	.6736	2.6350	44.2	2	2	3	2	3	3	2	2	3	1	0	0	0	4	0	2	1	0	0	0	0	1	3	4	0
awaited	28	.6607	3.9090	45.9	3	3	5	11	4	1	0	1	14	0	2	1	0	2	0	1	1	0	0	0	3	1	1	2	0
awaiting	22	.7479	3.3687	45.3	1	1	6	5	4	4	1	0	8	1	1	2	0	3	0	0	1	0	0	0	1	1	3	1	0
awaits	7	.4285	.6930	38.4	0	1	2	2	1	0	1	0	3	0	1	0	0	0	0	1	0	0	0	0	1	0	1	0	0
awake	134	.7871	21.522	53.3	41	31	17	12	16	5	12	0	62	2	2	10	0	8	3	1	5	0	2	0	13	24	0	2	0
awaken	19	.5087	2.1432	43.3	2	2	2	7	3	2	1	0	9	1	0	1	0	0	0	0	6	0	1	0	1	0	0	0	0
awakened	70	.7921	11.227	50.5	4	10	5	10	26	7	8	0	22	3	3	11	0	5	0	2	1	1	1	0	7	11	0	3	0
awakening	12	.5523	1.4500	41.6	0	0	2	2	4	3	0	1	5	1	0	1	0	3	0	0	0	0	0	0	0	0	2	0	0
awakenings	4	.0000	.0789	29.0	0	0	0	0	4	0	0	0	0	0	0	0	0	0	0	4	0	0	0	0	0	0	0	0	0
awakens	3	.3231	.2367	33.7	1	0	0	1	1	0	0	0	1	0	0	0	0	0	0	0	1	0	0	0	0	1	0	0	0
awakes	2	.2411	.1091	30.4	0	0	1	0	1	0	0	0	0	0	0	1	0	0	0	0	1	0	0	0	0	0	0	0	0
awaking	2	.2411	.1091	30.4	0	1	0	0	0	0	1	0	0	0	0	1	0	0	0	0	1	0	0	0	0	0	0	0	0
award	30	.6538	4.0955	46.1	0	1	10	2	5	1	9	2	10	4	0	1	0	2	0	0	1	0	0	0	1	0	4	7	0
Award	9	.5469	1.0682	40.3	0	2	2	0	0	3	1	1	3	0	0	0	0	2	0	0	1	0	0	0	0	1	0	2	0
award-winning	2	.2440	.1132	30.5	0	0	0	0	1	0	1	0	0	0	0	1	0	0	0	0	0	0	0	0	0	0	0	1	0
awarded	41	.7006	5.8528	47.7	1	2	7	5	12	9	2	3	6	3	1	3	0	3	0	1	1	0	0	0	1	5	14	3	0
awards	16	.6027	2.0498	43.1	0	1	1	2	6	4	1	1	6	0	1	3	0	0	0	1	0	0	0	0	0	1	1	3	0
Awards	2	.2446	.1125	30.5	0	0	0	0	1	0	1	0	0	1	0	1	0	0	0	0	0	0	0	0	0	0	0	0	0
aware	172	.8467	29.040	54.6	13	9	20	20	44	30	32	4	21	17	7	15	2	11	3	21	8	9	3	0	17	8	11	19	0
awareness	36	.7835	5.6445	47.5	1	2	1	2	10	5	8	7	2	5	1	3	0	1	0	2	4	1	0	0	2	1	7	7	0
awash	3	.3824	.2446	33.9	0	0	0	2	1	0	0	0	0	0	0	1	0	0	0	0	1	0	0	0	0	0	0	1	0
away	3814	.9429	712.19	68.5	881	789	423	479	649	313	219	61	1382	104	41	291	44	264	24	413	100	26	24	31	389	370	87	222	2
Away	3	.2332	.1690	32.3	0	0	1	0	2	0	0	0	0	0	0	0	0	0	0	0	0	0	0	0	0	2	0	1	0
aways	2	.1717	.1142	30.6	0	0	0	0	1	1	0	0	1	0	0	1	0	0	0	0	0	0	0	0	0	0	0	0	0
awe	33	.7088	4.7757	46.8	3	4	5	8	9	1	3	0	6	0	0	4	0	2	0	1	1	0	0	0	5	4	4	6	0
awe-inspiring	3	.3776	.2504	34.0	0	1	1	0	0	1	0	0	0	0	0	1	0	1	0	0	0	0	0	0	0	1	0	0	0
awed	14	.6086	1.8341	42.6	1	1	1	5	4	2	0	0	7	0	0	1	0	0	0	0	0	0	0	0	1	3	1	1	0
awesome	21	.5283	2.4003	43.8	0	0	3	5	5	3	2	3	6	0	0	0	0	1	0	2	0	1	0	0	1	0	1	9	0
awful	106	.6169	13.970	51.5	19	26	16	15	14	8	5	3	49	3	0	10	0	1	1	0	0	0	0	0	26	9	1	6	0
Awful	4	.0000	.0486	26.9	4	0	0	0	0	0	0	0	0	0	0	0	0	0	0	0	0	0	0	0	0	0	0	4	0
awfullest	2	.0000	.0914	29.6	1	1	0	0	0	0	0	0	2	0	0	0	0	0	0	0	0	0	0	0	0	0	0	0	0
awfully	45	.7215	6.7641	48.3	10	4	8	15	3	1	4	0	25	2	0	4	0	0	1	0	1	0	0	0	2	5	1	4	0
awfulness	2	.1717	.1142	30.6	0	0	0	0	1	1	0	0	1	0	0	1	0	0	0	0	0	0	0	0	0	0	0	0	0
awhile	47	.7687	7.3121	48.6	10	10	7	7	4	7	2	0	10	1	0	3	0	4	3	2	5	1	0	0	9	8	0	1	0
awkward	62	.8704	10.748	50.3	2	7	5	3	17	18	8	2	12	6	1	7	2	0	4	2	1	2	1	0	8	6	3	7	0
awkwardly	8	.4352	.7594	38.8	0	1	3	1	1	0	2	0	1	0	0	1	0	1	0	0	0	0	0	0	4	0	1	0	0
awkwardness	2	.2388	.0980	29.9	0	0	0	0	0	1	1	0	0	0	1	0	0	0	0	0	0	0	1	0	0	0	0	0	0
awl	6	.2890	.4811	36.8	4	0	0	0	1	1	0	0	4	0	0	0	0	0	0	0	0	0	0	1	0	0	0	1	0
awning	2	.1814	.1187	30.7	0	1	0	0	1	0	0	0	1	0	0	0	0	0	0	0	0	0	0	0	0	0	0	1	0
awoke	54	.7100	7.9574	49.0	3	15	5	11	8	6	5	1	23	2	0	7	1	4	0	1	0	0	0	0	8	5	2	1	0
awry	3	.2292	.1615	32.1	0	0	0	1	2	0	0	0	0	0	0	1	0	0	0	0	0	0	0	0	2	0	0	0	0
ax	83	.7211	12.473	51.0	3	18	9	12	28	5	7	1	45	1	0	8	4	4	1	2	0	0	0	0	11	2	2	3	0
AX	2	.0000	.0299	24.8	0	0	0	0	2	0	0	0	0	0	0	0	2	0	0	0	0	0	0	0	0	0	0	0	0

9C autumn-tired
7D Autumn's
6N autumnal
9B AUXILIARIES
3B auxuliaries
7R Avakian's
9A avance
7H avaricious
4E Avenues
9B aver
7R average-size
6P Avernus
7Q averse
7H Aves
8Q Avgustincic
7G aviatress
7G aviatrix
7Q aviculturists
8F avidity
7G avis
9R avocado
7F avocados
8G avocation
8J avoidance
8Q avowed
8F avowedly
XP Avusrennen
4A aw-w-w-w
8J awa'
7A awarding
6F Awash
9D awe-struck
5F awela
3A awk
6A awkward-looking
4F awnings
7P awqaf
4A ax-handle

Word Type	F	D	U	SFI	3 Gr 3	4 Gr 4	5 Gr 5	6 Gr 6	7 Gr 7	8 Gr 8	9 Gr 9	X UnGr	A Read	B Eng & Gr	C Comp	D Lit	E Math	F Soc Stud	G Spell	H Sci	J Music	K Art	L Home Ec	M Shop	N Lib F	P Lib NF	Q Lib Ref	R Mag	S Rel
ax-handles	3	.0000	.1370	31.4	0	3	0	0	0	0	0	0	3	0	0	0	0	0	0	0	0	0	0	0	0	0	0	0	0
axe	27	.5522	3.2508	45.1	0	9	4	2	8	3	1	0	12	0	1	5	0	1	0	0	0	0	0	0	7	0	1	0	0
Axe	2	.0000	.0234	23.7	0	2	0	0	0	0	0	0	0	0	0	0	0	0	0	0	0	0	0	0	2	0	0	0	0
Axelrod	2	.0000	.0394	26.0	0	0	0	0	0	2	0	0	0	0	0	0	0	0	0	2	0	0	0	0	0	0	0	0	0
axes	49	.7389	7.4228	48.7	6	5	9	2	7	11	8	1	14	0	0	3	12	12	0	2	0	0	1	1	1	1	1	1	0
axhead	3	.0000	.1370	31.4	3	0	0	0	0	0	0	0	3	0	0	0	0	0	0	0	0	0	0	0	0	0	0	0	0
axial	2	.1249	.0685	28.4	0	0	0	0	0	0	1	1	0	0	0	0	0	0	0	1	0	0	0	1	0	0	0	0	0
axiom	10	.1610	.4361	36.4	0	0	0	0	0	0	10	0	0	0	0	0	9	0	1	0	0	0	0	0	0	0	0	0	0
axioms	5	.2207	.2647	34.2	0	0	0	3	1	0	1	0	0	0	0	0	2	0	0	0	0	0	0	0	0	0	3	0	0
axis	101	.6377	13.320	51.2	21	15	16	7	9	15	8	10	5	0	0	0	19	27	1	34	0	0	1	4	0	0	10	0	0
Axis	6	.1823	.2810	34.5	0	4	0	0	0	2	0	0	0	0	0	0	0	2	0	0	0	0	0	0	0	0	4	0	0
axle	41	.7168	5.9729	47.8	3	16	2	1	10	1	4	4	2	2	1	0	0	6	0	14	2	0	0	0	0	4	3	7	0
axles	7	.3008	.4736	36.8	0	1	3	0	2	1	0	0	0	0	0	0	0	1	0	0	0	0	0	0	0	0	4	2	0
Axley	6	.0000	.2741	34.4	0	0	0	0	0	6	0	0	6	0	0	0	0	0	0	0	0	0	0	0	0	0	0	0	0
axon	7	.0000	.1380	31.4	0	0	0	7	0	0	0	0	0	0	0	0	0	0	0	7	0	0	0	0	0	0	0	0	0
axons	2	.0000	.0394	26.0	0	0	0	2	0	0	0	0	0	0	0	0	0	0	0	2	0	0	0	0	0	0	0	0	0
ay	72	.5069	7.8282	48.9	7	4	6	34	3	2	16	0	18	0	0	16	0	1	12	0	21	0	0	0	3	1	0	0	0
Ay	7	.0000	.0821	29.1	0	0	7	0	0	0	0	0	0	0	0	0	0	0	0	0	0	0	0	0	7	0	0	0	0
AY	5	.0000	.0748	28.7	0	0	1	0	3	1	0	0	0	0	0	0	5	0	0	0	0	0	0	0	0	0	0	0	0
Ayd	3	.0000	.0365	25.6	0	0	0	0	0	0	0	3	0	0	0	0	0	0	0	0	0	0	0	0	0	0	0	3	0
aye	51	.5340	5.9102	47.7	3	1	0	22	15	8	2	0	17	3	0	10	0	0	0	0	0	0	0	0	8	13	0	0	0
ayes	2	.1733	.1149	30.6	0	0	1	0	1	0	0	0	1	1	0	0	0	0	0	0	0	0	0	0	0	0	0	0	0
Aymara	12	.0000	.2334	33.7	0	12	0	0	0	0	0	0	0	0	0	0	0	12	0	0	0	0	0	0	0	0	0	0	0
Ayr	3	.0000	.0314	25.0	0	0	3	0	0	0	0	0	0	0	0	0	0	0	0	0	0	0	0	0	0	0	3	0	0
Azalea	6	.0000	.1183	30.7	0	0	0	0	0	0	0	6	0	0	0	0	0	0	0	6	0	0	0	0	0	0	0	0	0
azaleas	4	.4806	.4072	36.1	1	0	0	1	0	2	0	0	0	0	0	0	0	1	0	0	0	0	0	0	0	1	1	1	0
Azaleas	2	.0000	.0394	26.0	0	0	0	0	0	0	0	2	0	0	0	0	0	0	0	2	0	0	0	0	0	0	0	0	0
Azores	7	.5440	.8011	39.0	0	2	0	1	2	0	2	0	0	0	0	0	0	1	0	3	0	0	0	0	0	1	1	1	0
Aztec	21	.4766	2.1487	43.3	0	1	9	8	1	0	2	0	0	2	0	0	0	14	0	0	1	0	0	0	0	0	2	2	0
Aztecs	17	.4862	1.7588	42.5	0	1	7	6	1	1	1	0	0	0	0	0	0	9	0	1	3	0	0	0	1	0	3	0	0
Azuloy	2	.0000	.0234	23.7	0	0	2	0	0	0	0	0	0	0	0	0	0	0	0	0	0	0	0	0	2	0	0	0	0
azure	8	.4540	.7790	38.9	3	1	1	0	0	1	0	2	1	3	1	0	0	0	0	0	0	0	0	0	0	1	0	2	0
A1	2	.2287	.1077	30.3	0	0	0	1	1	0	0	0	0	0	0	0	1	0	0	0	1	0	0	0	0	0	0	0	0
a2	6	.0000	.0898	29.5	0	0	0	0	0	6	0	0	0	0	0	0	6	0	0	0	0	0	0	0	0	0	0	0	0
A2	3	.2444	.1728	32.4	0	0	0	2	1	0	0	0	0	0	0	0	2	0	0	0	1	0	0	0	0	0	0	0	0
a3	3	.0000	.0449	26.5	0	0	0	0	0	3	0	0	0	0	0	0	3	0	0	0	0	0	0	0	0	0	0	0	0
a3/a3**	2	.0000	.0299	24.8	0	0	0	0	0	0	2	0	0	0	0	0	2	0	0	0	0	0	0	0	0	0	0	0	0
b	900	.6231	116.14	60.6	79	84	107	124	145	203	153	5	111	33	2	3	483	3	121	59	8	0	7	15	2	34	18	1	0
B	1095	.7140	158.76	62.0	184	187	140	141	153	148	129	13	112	25	5	6	563	22	65	62	136	5	14	30	7	14	15	14	0
B**	132	.6918	18.509	52.7	6	5	5	18	36	36	16	10	6	16	0	1	11	19	3	7	1	6	0	2	0	4	50	6	0
B&M	6	.0000	.0729	28.6	0	0	0	0	6	0	0	0	0	0	0	0	0	0	0	0	0	0	0	0	0	0	0	6	0
B-complex	2	.0000	.0394	26.0	0	0	1	0	0	0	1	0	0	0	0	0	0	0	0	2	0	0	0	0	0	0	0	0	0
B-flat	3	.0000	.0243	23.8	0	0	0	0	0	0	3	0	0	0	0	0	0	0	0	0	3	0	0	0	0	0	0	0	0
b-r-rrm	6	.0000	.2741	34.4	6	0	0	0	0	0	0	0	6	0	0	0	0	0	0	0	0	0	0	0	0	0	0	0	0
B-52	3	.2321	.1635	32.1	0	0	0	0	2	1	0	0	0	0	0	0	0	0	0	0	0	0	0	0	0	0	1	2	0
b/12	2	.0000	.0299	24.8	0	0	2	0	0	0	0	0	0	0	0	0	2	0	0	0	0	0	0	0	0	0	0	0	0
b/6	2	.0000	.0299	24.8	0	0	2	0	0	0	0	0	0	0	0	0	2	0	0	0	0	0	0	0	0	0	0	0	0
b/8	3	.0000	.0449	26.5	0	0	3	0	0	0	0	0	0	0	0	0	3	0	0	0	0	0	0	0	0	0	0	0	0
b	2	.0000	.0914	29.6	2	0	0	0	0	0	0	0	2	0	0	0	0	0	0	0	0	0	0	0	0	0	0	0	0
b'long	2	.0000	.0234	23.7	0	0	0	0	2	0	0	0	0	0	0	0	0	0	0	0	0	0	0	0	2	0	0	0	0
B's	6	.3710	.4879	36.9	1	0	1	0	1	2	1	0	0	1	0	0	3	0	0	0	0	0	0	0	0	0	0	2	0
ba	12	.4356	1.1044	40.4	4	0	0	0	5	0	3	0	0	1	0	0	3	0	0	0	4	0	0	0	0	0	0	4	0
BA	7	.1694	.3167	35.0	0	0	1	1	2	1	2	0	0	1	0	0	6	0	0	0	0	0	0	0	0	0	0	0	0
Ba-boo	10	.0000	.4568	36.6	10	0	0	0	0	0	0	0	10	0	0	0	0	0	0	0	0	0	0	0	0	0	0	0	0
baa	2	.0000	.0914	29.6	2	0	0	0	0	0	0	0	2	0	0	0	0	0	0	0	0	0	0	0	0	0	0	0	0
Baade	4	.0000	.0789	29.0	0	0	0	0	4	0	0	0	0	0	0	0	0	0	0	4	0	0	0	0	0	0	0	0	0
Baal	3	.2058	.1429	31.5	0	0	0	1	0	2	0	0	0	1	0	0	0	0	0	0	2	0	0	0	0	0	0	0	0
Baba	46	.4978	5.0718	47.1	7	25	0	14	0	0	0	0	18	10	0	10	1	0	0	0	0	0	0	0	0	0	0	7	0
Baba's	2	.0000	.0914	29.6	0	1	0	1	0	0	0	0	2	0	0	0	0	0	0	0	0	0	0	0	0	0	0	0	0
Babbage	3	.0000	.0449	26.5	0	0	0	0	0	3	0	0	0	0	0	0	3	0	0	0	0	0	0	0	0	0	0	0	0
Babbitt	2	.0000	.0162	22.1	0	1	0	1	0	0	0	0	0	0	0	0	0	0	0	0	2	0	0	0	0	0	0	0	0
babble	7	.4384	.6849	38.4	3	1	0	2	1	0	0	0	2	2	1	1	0	1	0	0	0	0	0	0	0	0	0	0	0
babbling	3	.3399	.2456	33.9	0	0	1	0	0	1	1	0	1	0	0	1	0	0	0	0	0	0	0	0	0	0	0	1	0
babe	5	.3822	.4117	36.1	0	0	1	0	2	1	1	0	0	0	0	2	0	0	0	0	1	0	0	0	0	2	0	0	0
Babe	69	.5525	8.4212	49.3	12	12	9	3	8	18	6	1	36	0	0	9	4	0	0	0	1	0	0	0	0	16	0	3	0
Babe's	5	.3833	.4767	36.8	1	0	0	0	1	2	1	0	3	0	0	1	0	0	0	0	0	0	0	0	0	1	0	0	0
Babel	2	.1378	.0662	28.2	0	0	0	0	0	2	0	0	0	0	0	0	0	0	0	0	0	1	0	0	0	0	0	1	0
Babenberg	3	.0000	.0314	25.0	0	0	0	0	0	0	3	0	0	0	0	0	0	0	0	0	0	0	0	0	0	0	3	0	0
Babi	3	.0000	.1370	31.4	0	0	0	0	3	0	0	0	3	0	0	0	0	0	0	0	0	0	0	0	0	0	0	0	0
babies	198	.7910	31.921	55.0	80	29	31	22	16	9	7	4	82	2	1	8	0	4	3	38	2	0	1	0	8	34	9	6	0
babies'	4	.4339	.3887	35.9	0	1	0	0	0	1	1	1	1	0	0	1	0	0	1	1	0	0	0	0	0	0	0	0	0
baboon	12	.2928	.8049	39.1	8	0	0	0	0	4	0	0	1	0	3	0	0	0	0	0	1	0	0	0	0	7	0	0	0
Baboon	5	.3377	.3703	35.7	1	3	1	0	0	0	0	0	0	0	0	1	0	0	0	0	0	0	0	0	3	0	0	1	0
baboons	23	.3392	1.8501	42.7	8	1	1	0	2	11	0	0	7	0	5	0	0	0	0	0	0	0	0	0	0	8	2	1	0
baboons'	3	.0000	.0434	26.4	2	0	0	0	1	0	0	0	0	0	0	0	0	0	0	0	0	0	0	0	0	3	0	0	0
Babworth	2	.0000	.0290	24.6	0	2	0	0	0	0	0	0	0	0	0	0	0	0	0	0	0	0	0	0	0	2	0	0	0
baby	751	.8867	132.97	61.2	288	134	86	77	101	30	27	8	275	22	12	52	19	5	16	83	14	3	24	0	51	111	30	34	0
Baby	62	.5160	6.9648	48.4	6	17	10	0	17	2	10	0	19	0	0	1	0	2	1	0	3	0	0	0	25	10	0	1	0
baby-o	3	.0000	.0243	23.8	3	0	0	0	0	0	0	0	0	0	0	0	0	0	0	0	3	0	0	0	0	0	0	0	0
baby-sit	2	.2408	.1091	30.4	0	0	0	2	0	0	0	0	0	1	0	0	0	0	1	0	0	0	0	0	0	0	0	0	0
baby-sitting	16	.3571	1.2393	40.9	0	1	1	0	9	0	5	0	1	1	0	0	0	1	0	0	0	0	6	0	4	1	0	2	0
baby's	39	.7053	5.6270	47.5	14	3	1	2	12	3	3	1	7	0	1	8	0	1	1	9	0	0	2	0	0	7	3	0	0
babying	2	.1717	.1142	30.6	0	0	1	0	1	0	0	0	1	0	0	1	0	0	0	0	0	0	0	0	0	0	0	0	0
Babylon	31	.5249	3.5313	45.5	9	3	1	7	11	0	0	0	9	0	0	0	1	7	0	0	8	0	0	0	0	3	3	0	0
Babylonia	4	.3873	.3414	35.3	0	1	0	1	0	1	1	0	0	1	0	0	0	2	0	0	0	0	0	0	0	0	1	0	0
Babylonian	13	.5318	1.4625	41.7	0	0	0	1	9	2	1	0	1	0	0	0	6	2	0	0	1	0	0	0	0	2	1	0	0
Babylonians	13	.5100	1.4088	41.5	0	0	1	0	5	5	2	0	1	0	0	0	7	2	1	0	1	0	0	0	0	0	1	0	0
babysitting	3	.0000	.0449	26.5	0	1	0	2	0	0	0	0	0	0	0	0	3	0	0	0	0	0	0	0	0	0	0	0	0
Bac	2	.0000	.0290	24.6	0	0	0	0	2	0	0	0	0	0	0	0	0	0	0	0	0	0	0	0	0	2	0	0	0

8H Axelrod's
5Q Axes
3A axheads
4Q Axis-held
4P axle-deep
5D axle's
3A axlike
8F axmen
8R Ayala
4F Ayamra
XR AYC
8H Aycock
5P Ayin
9R Ayllon
4A ayoung
9Q Ayyubid
3N Azalie
7Q azarae
5A Azaz
7R Azerbaijan
4Q azimuth
5F azimuthal
4F Azimuthal
4Q azimuths
6Q azote
9R Azrin
6J Azul
5N Azuloy's
3A azurite
7N azurors
8E a0
9G A1**
9E a2/b2**
9E a3**
9G A3d**
9G A4ly**
7J A7
9E bN
9M B-B
3J B-I-N-G-O
4P B-a-b-y
6N b-b-bless
6N b-b-breed
6N b-b-bullet
4A b-beads
5H B-group
5J B-line
6A b-r-r-ring
3D B-u-s
XH B-vitamin
5B B-130
5Q B-17
5Q B-25
8R B-52s
9C B-58
5E b/a
8E b/c
9E b/d
3A bll
3A bts
8D b'jiminey
9R B'nai
9R B'rith
4J B'y
6J Ba-o
4A baa-aa-aa
XH baa-ing
7H Baade's
6R baaing
4G baas
9Q Babb
8D babbled
4D babby
7A Babel's
5A babes
6J Babes
3D babied
8Q Babington
5A Babis
7R Babler
7R Babler's
7Q baboon's
4P Babworth's
7A baby-round
3A baby-sat
6B baby-sits
7R baby-sitter
7L baby-sitters
9N Baby's
7R babyhood
3Q babyish

Word Type	F	D	U	SFI	3 Gr 3	4 Gr 4	5 Gr 5	6 Gr 6	7 Gr 7	8 Gr 8	9 Gr 9	X UnGr	A Read	B Eng & Gr	C Comp	D Lit	E Math	F Soc Stud	G Spell	H Sci	J Music	K Art	L Home Ec	M Shop	N Lib F	P Lib NF	Q Lib Ref	R Mag	S Rel
BAC	10	.0000	.1497	31.8	0	0	0	0	7	0	3	0	0	0	0	0	10	0	0	0	0	0	0	0	0	0	0	0	0
Baca	2	.0000	.0914	29.6	0	0	0	2	0	0	0	0	2	0	0	0	0	0	0	0	0	0	0	0	0	0	0	0	0
baccalaureate	2	.0000	.0209	23.2	0	0	0	0	2	0	0	0	0	0	0	0	0	0	0	0	0	0	0	0	0	0	2	0	0
Bach	70	.1712	2.9021	44.6	3	9	4	12	21	11	10	0	0	0	0	0	0	0	0	0	54	0	0	0	0	14	2	0	0
Bach's	25	.1491	.9374	39.7	0	3	2	3	10	4	1	2	0	0	0	0	0	0	0	0	19	0	0	0	0	6	0	0	0
bachelor	9	.3067	.6328	38.0	1	0	0	0	6	1	1	0	1	0	0	6	0	0	1	0	0	0	0	0	0	0	0	1	0
bachelor's	6	.5302	.6620	38.2	0	0	1	0	3	1	1	0	0	0	0	2	1	1	0	0	0	0	0	0	0	0	1	1	0
bachelors	2	.2297	.1135	30.6	0	0	0	0	1	0	1	0	0	0	0	1	0	1	0	0	0	0	0	0	0	0	0	0	0
Bachelors	4	.0000	.0486	26.9	0	0	0	0	3	1	0	0	0	0	0	0	0	0	0	0	0	0	0	0	0	0	0	4	0
Bachianas	2	.0000	.0162	22.1	0	0	0	2	0	0	0	0	0	0	0	0	0	0	0	0	2	0	0	0	0	0	0	0	0
bacilli	6	.0000	.1183	30.7	0	0	0	2	1	0	0	3	0	0	0	0	0	0	0	6	0	0	0	0	0	0	0	0	0
bacillus	2	.2278	.1128	30.5	0	0	0	1	0	1	0	0	0	0	0	0	0	0	0	1	0	0	0	0	0	0	1	0	0
back	5862	.9039	1055.6	70.2	1279	1137	565	731	1099	572	374	105	2270	135	33	479	62	290	73	385	137	19	74	38	734	582	160	391	0
Back	9	.5252	.9710	39.9	0	3	3	0	0	1	0	2	0	1	0	0	0	0	1	0	3	0	0	0	0	0	2	2	0
back-and-forth	2	.2421	.0995	30.0	0	0	0	0	0	0	2	0	0	0	0	0	0	0	0	0	0	0	1	1	0	0	0	0	0
back-bedroom	2	.1948	.1250	31.0	2	0	0	0	0	0	0	0	1	0	0	0	0	0	0	0	0	0	0	0	0	1	0	0	0
back-breaking	4	.3354	.3295	35.2	1	1	0	1	1	0	0	0	1	0	0	0	0	2	0	0	0	0	0	0	0	1	0	0	0
back-pocket	2	.0000	.0243	23.9	2	0	0	0	0	0	0	0	0	0	0	0	0	0	0	0	0	0	0	0	0	0	0	2	0
back-scratcher	2	.0000	.0234	23.7	0	0	0	0	2	0	0	0	0	0	0	0	0	0	0	0	0	0	0	0	2	0	0	0	0
back-seat	2	.0000	.0209	23.2	0	0	2	0	0	0	0	0	0	0	0	0	0	0	0	0	0	0	0	0	0	0	2	0	0
back-to-back	2	.0000	.0162	22.1	0	0	2	0	0	0	0	0	0	0	0	0	0	0	0	0	2	0	0	0	0	0	0	0	0
backbone	29	.5145	3.2187	45.1	4	2	7	2	8	2	2	2	3	0	0	0	0	2	1	18	1	0	0	0	0	0	3	1	0
backboned	7	.3578	.5498	37.4	0	5	0	0	2	0	0	0	0	0	0	1	0	0	0	0	0	0	0	0	0	4	2	0	0
backbones	21	.3263	1.6101	42.1	1	2	3	12	3	0	0	0	0	0	0	0	0	1	0	17	0	0	0	0	1	1	1	0	0
backbreaking	3	.3395	.2468	33.9	1	0	2	0	0	0	0	0	1	0	0	0	0	0	0	0	0	0	0	0	0	1	1	0	0
backed	79	.7223	11.786	50.7	20	4	8	8	16	18	5	0	32	5	1	2	0	7	0	0	0	0	0	0	15	4	4	9	0
backer	2	.1814	.1187	30.7	0	0	0	1	0	1	0	0	1	0	0	0	0	0	0	0	0	0	0	0	0	0	0	1	0
backers	7	.4656	.7081	38.5	0	0	1	1	2	3	0	0	1	0	0	0	0	1	0	0	0	0	0	0	0	1	1	3	0
backfield	2	.0000	.0243	23.9	0	0	0	0	0	0	2	0	0	0	0	0	0	0	0	0	0	0	0	0	0	0	0	2	0
background	166	.6488	21.970	53.4	17	20	22	10	39	31	19	8	20	3	5	9	0	18	2	13	16	31	7	11	4	9	9	9	0
backgrounds	23	.2836	1.4604	41.6	3	3	2	2	4	5	4	0	1	0	0	1	0	5	1	1	2	9	0	0	0	0	1	2	0
backhand	2	.0000	.0914	29.6	0	0	1	0	1	0	0	0	2	0	0	0	0	0	0	0	0	0	0	0	0	0	0	0	0
backing	37	.5281	4.2367	46.3	4	0	4	4	14	4	6	1	12	1	1	0	0	6	0	3	0	0	0	7	1	2	2	2	0
backpack	2	.0000	.0243	23.9	0	0	0	0	2	0	0	0	0	0	0	0	0	0	0	0	0	0	0	0	0	0	0	2	0
backpacks	2	.0000	.0243	23.9	0	0	0	0	2	0	0	0	0	0	0	0	0	0	0	0	0	0	0	0	0	0	0	2	0
backs	99	.8362	16.673	52.2	28	15	12	13	13	12	5	1	36	2	4	5	1	14	0	3	2	1	1	0	10	12	5	3	0
backsaw	2	.0000	.0050	17.0	0	0	0	0	1	0	1	0	0	0	0	0	0	0	0	0	0	0	0	2	0	0	0	0	0
backside	4	.0996	.1523	31.8	0	0	0	0	3	0	1	0	1	0	0	0	0	0	0	0	0	0	0	0	0	0	0	3	0
backslaps	2	.0000	.0914	29.6	0	0	0	2	0	0	0	0	2	0	0	0	0	0	0	0	0	0	0	0	0	0	0	0	0
backstage	7	.3953	.6343	38.0	0	2	0	1	1	0	3	0	2	0	0	3	0	0	0	0	0	0	0	0	1	1	0	0	0
backstop	4	.4538	.4020	36.0	0	1	0	1	2	0	0	0	1	0	0	1	0	0	0	0	0	0	0	0	0	1	0	1	0
backup	4	.2346	.2332	33.7	0	0	0	1	1	0	0	2	0	0	0	0	0	0	0	2	0	0	0	0	0	0	0	2	0
backward	121	.8838	21.310	53.3	14	12	18	21	27	11	14	4	28	3	1	10	1	9	5	21	8	0	1	0	10	8	11	5	0
backwards	44	.7852	7.0326	48.5	5	3	1	13	9	8	2	3	17	2	0	3	5	0	0	4	2	0	0	0	1	2	4	4	0
backwater	2	.2440	.1132	30.5	0	0	1	1	0	0	0	0	0	0	0	1	0	0	0	0	0	0	0	0	0	0	0	1	0
backwoods	5	.4662	.5254	37.2	1	0	0	1	3	0	0	0	2	0	0	0	0	0	0	0	1	0	0	0	0	1	0	1	0
backyard	41	.6873	5.8046	47.6	7	10	3	7	2	3	4	5	10	2	3	2	3	1	0	4	0	0	0	0	1	5	1	9	0
backyards	6	.4292	.5502	37.4	3	0	0	0	1	1	1	0	0	1	0	0	0	1	0	0	0	0	0	0	0	0	1	3	0
bacon	99	.5656	11.667	50.7	13	10	4	13	18	22	17	2	16	3	3	11	1	10	3	1	1	0	27	0	11	7	1	4	0
Bacon	7	.2635	.4293	36.3	0	0	0	2	5	0	0	0	0	0	0	0	0	1	0	0	0	0	0	0	0	0	1	5	0
bacteria	231	.3137	17.444	52.4	10	17	25	88	37	17	16	21	13	1	0	0	0	3	1	191	0	0	1	0	1	0	17	3	0
bacterial	10	.1626	.4769	36.8	0	0	0	3	4	1	2	0	0	0	0	0	0	0	0	9	0	0	0	0	0	0	1	0	0
bacteriology	2	.2278	.1128	30.5	0	0	0	0	0	0	2	0	0	0	0	0	0	0	0	1	0	0	0	0	0	0	1	0	0
bacterium	12	.1669	.5809	37.6	0	0	3	4	4	0	0	1	0	0	0	0	0	0	1	11	0	0	0	0	0	0	0	0	0
bad	660	.8280	110.23	60.4	142	109	65	84	136	60	52	12	251	37	3	62	1	26	10	16	9	0	7	1	95	61	10	71	0
Bad	4	.3706	.3628	35.6	0	1	0	0	2	1	0	0	2	0	0	0	0	0	0	0	0	0	0	0	1	0	1	0	0
BAD	4	.0000	.0599	27.8	0	0	0	0	0	0	4	0	0	0	0	0	4	0	0	0	0	0	0	0	0	0	0	0	0
bad-smelling	3	.2435	.2274	33.6	1	1	1	0	0	0	0	0	2	0	0	0	0	1	0	0	0	0	0	0	0	0	0	0	0
bad-tempered	7	.3853	.6846	38.4	1	1	2	1	1	0	1	0	5	1	0	0	0	0	0	0	0	0	0	0	0	0	0	1	0
bade	26	.5705	3.2514	45.1	4	2	1	10	5	3	1	0	14	0	0	4	0	1	0	0	0	0	0	0	4	0	1	2	0
badge	12	.6186	1.5775	42.0	6	0	1	2	2	0	0	1	5	2	0	0	0	0	1	0	0	0	0	0	1	2	0	1	0
Badge	5	.4656	.4901	36.9	1	2	0	1	0	1	0	0	0	1	0	0	0	0	0	0	0	0	0	0	2	1	0	1	0
badger	7	.3908	.6286	38.0	0	1	1	1	3	0	1	0	2	0	0	0	0	0	0	0	0	0	0	0	0	1	3	1	0
Badger	12	.1657	.5493	37.4	1	9	0	0	0	2	0	0	1	0	0	0	0	2	0	0	0	0	0	0	9	0	0	0	0
badger's	5	.0000	.0586	27.7	0	1	4	0	0	0	0	0	0	0	0	0	0	0	0	0	0	0	0	0	5	0	0	0	0
badgers	3	.3811	.2534	34.0	2	0	0	1	0	0	0	0	0	0	0	0	0	0	0	1	0	0	0	0	0	1	0	1	0
badges	15	.6135	1.9232	42.8	2	2	6	1	2	1	1	0	3	1	0	0	5	1	1	0	0	0	0	0	0	0	1	3	0
Badinerie	4	.0000	.0323	25.1	0	0	4	0	0	0	0	0	0	0	0	0	0	0	0	0	4	0	0	0	0	0	0	0	0
badly	159	.8507	27.164	54.3	26	27	14	23	29	22	16	2	54	5	2	10	0	25	2	5	5	0	1	0	13	17	3	17	0
badmen	3	.0000	.0352	25.5	3	0	0	0	0	0	0	0	0	0	0	0	0	0	0	0	0	0	0	0	3	0	0	0	0
badminton	4	.2017	.1931	32.9	0	0	1	0	2	1	0	0	0	3	0	0	0	0	0	0	0	0	0	0	0	0	1	0	0
badness	3	.2236	.1570	32.0	0	0	0	0	1	2	0	0	0	1	0	2	0	0	0	0	0	0	0	0	0	0	0	0	0
BAE	3	.0000	.0449	26.5	0	0	0	0	3	0	0	0	0	0	0	0	3	0	0	0	0	0	0	0	0	0	0	0	0
baffle	6	.5013	.6186	37.9	0	0	0	1	3	0	2	0	0	1	0	2	0	0	1	0	0	0	0	1	0	0	0	1	0
baffled	16	.4895	1.7771	42.5	1	0	3	2	4	2	4	0	8	0	0	4	0	0	0	1	0	0	0	0	2	1	0	0	0
baffling	3	.3395	.2468	33.9	0	0	1	0	0	1	1	0	1	0	0	0	0	0	0	0	0	0	0	0	0	1	1	0	0
bag	371	.8450	63.031	58.0	110	62	31	54	70	32	11	1	134	21	10	24	32	15	8	23	0	0	4	0	42	33	2	23	0
Bag-jagderags	2	.0000	.0234	23.7	0	2	0	0	0	0	0	0	0	0	0	0	0	0	0	0	0	0	0	0	2	0	0	0	0
Bagasset	3	.0000	.1370	31.4	0	0	0	3	0	0	0	0	3	0	0	0	0	0	0	0	0	0	0	0	0	0	0	0	0
Bagby	3	.0000	.1370	31.4	0	0	3	0	0	0	0	0	3	0	0	0	0	0	0	0	0	0	0	0	0	0	0	0	0
Bagdad	3	.3431	.2528	34.0	0	2	1	0	0	0	0	0	1	0	0	0	0	1	0	0	0	0	0	0	1	0	0	0	0
bagful	2	.1787	.1174	30.7	0	0	1	1	0	0	0	0	1	0	0	0	0	0	0	0	0	0	0	0	1	0	0	0	0
baggage	21	.7002	3.0055	44.8	5	4	1	0	7	3	1	0	3	1	0	3	1	3	0	0	0	0	0	0	2	6	1	1	0
bagged	4	.4835	.4115	36.1	0	1	0	1	1	1	0	0	0	0	0	0	1	0	0	1	0	0	0	0	1	1	0	0	0
baggitaway	3	.0000	.0434	26.4	0	3	0	0	0	0	0	0	0	0	0	0	0	0	0	0	0	0	0	0	0	3	0	0	0
baggy	11	.5997	1.3906	41.4	1	3	2	1	1	0	1	2	3	2	0	1	0	0	0	0	0	0	0	0	0	3	1	1	0
Baghdad	11	.5984	1.4177	41.5	0	0	1	5	2	2	1	0	5	0	0	2	1	1	0	0	0	0	0	0	0	1	1	0	0
bagpipe	12	.2119	.6125	37.9	1	0	8	2	0	1	0	0	1	3	0	0	0	0	0	0	8	0	0	0	0	0	0	0	0
Bagpipe	2	.0000	.0219	23.4	0	0	2	0	0	0	0	0	0	2	0	0	0	0	0	0	0	0	0	0	0	0	0	0	0
bagpipes	9	.2394	.7075	38.5	7	0	2	0	0	0	0	0	8	0	0	0	0	0	0	0	1	0	0	0	0	0	0	0	0
bags	143	.8158	23.540	53.7	49	25	13	16	18	13	9	0	43	1	2	9	30	16	0	3	0	1	6	0	6	18	2	6	0
Baguio	4	.1505	.1615	32.1	3	1	0	0	0	0	0	0	0	0	0	0	0	1	0	0	0	0	0	0	0	0	3	0	0
bah	4	.3231	.3016	34.8	0	0	1	1	0	1	0	1	1	0	1	1	0	0	0	0	0	0	0	0	1	0	0	0	0

6Q Bacchus
6A baccy
9R Bach-rock
6R Bachelor
7Q Bachman's
7P Bachs
XH bacillus-swarming
3P BACK
7R back-alley
XH back-boned
9F back-country
7N back-fired
4N back-garden
7D back-somersault
9L back-to-school
4Q back-to-the-wall
7R back-up
5P back-yard
8A backache
8A backboard
8A backboards
5Q backcountry
7R backdoor
6N backdrop
XR Background
7M backings
5F backlands
8R backlash
9R backlog
7R backpackers
XR Backstairs
6A Backstroke
7Q backtracking
XH backups
9D backward-facing
8A backwash
7P backwoodsman
8F backwoodsmen
7R backwoodsy
6A Backyard
7Q Bacon's
4G baconburger
3N bacons
6H Bacteria
9H bacteriologist
7H bacteriophages
3N bad-
8R bad-dream
5R bad-looking
6A bad-mannered
4N Badger's
7A badgered
5E Badgers
9H Badlands
5D badman
7R Badminton
6J Baffin's
6R bag-dir
6A bag's
5A Bagby's
4F baggage-car
3P baggage-smashers
4A Baggott
4A Baggott's
9D bagpiper
6J Bagpiper
6J Bagpipes

Word Type	F	D	U	SFI	3 Gr 3	4 Gr 4	5 Gr 5	6 Gr 6	7 Gr 7	8 Gr 8	9 Gr 9	X UnGr	A Read	B Eng & Gr	C Comp	D Lit	E Math	F Soc Stud	G Spell	H Sci	J Music	K Art	L Home Ec	M Shop	N Lib F	P Lib NF	Q Lib Ref	R Mag	S Rel
Bahama	2	.2446	.1257	31.0	0	0	0	1	0	0	0	1	0	0	0	0	0	1	0	1	0	0	0	0	0	0	0	0	0
Bahamas	4	.3730	.3365	35.3	0	0	3	0	0	0	0	1	0	0	0	0	0	2	0	1	0	0	0	0	0	0	1	0	0
Bahrein	2	.0000	.0389	25.9	0	0	0	1	0	0	1	0	0	0	0	0	0	2	0	0	0	0	0	0	0	0	0	0	0
bail	10	.5156	1.0830	40.3	0	0	1	1	5	2	1	0	1	0	1	0	0	0	0	0	0	0	0	0	4	1	1	2	0
bailey	2	.0000	.0234	23.7	0	0	0	2	0	0	0	0	0	0	0	0	0	0	0	0	0	0	0	0	2	0	0	0	0
Bailey	11	.4182	1.0028	40.0	0	4	1	1	2	1	0	2	1	0	0	0	0	0	0	0	0	0	0	0	1	2	1	6	0
bailiff	2	.2285	.1129	30.5	0	0	0	0	1	1	0	0	0	0	0	0	0	1	0	0	0	0	0	0	0	0	1	0	0
bailing	3	.3394	.2451	33.9	0	1	0	0	1	0	1	0	1	0	0	1	0	0	0	0	0	0	0	0	1	0	0	0	0
Bairn	2	.0000	.0914	29.6	0	0	2	0	0	0	0	0	2	0	0	0	0	0	0	0	0	0	0	0	0	0	0	0	0
bait	43	.7085	6.3527	48.0	19	8	0	4	4	6	1	1	22	2	2	2	0	2	0	0	1	0	0	0	1	5	1	5	0
baited	5	.3790	.4128	36.2	1	1	1	2	0	0	0	0	0	0	1	0	0	2	0	0	0	0	0	0	1	0	0	1	0
bake	93	.4415	8.7264	49.4	16	20	5	0	19	6	23	4	10	7	0	1	4	6	4	1	3	0	36	1	1	9	1	9	0
baked	93	.7094	13.448	51.3	20	18	10	9	14	7	10	5	19	11	1	1	5	5	2	6	2	0	17	2	7	8	3	4	0
baker	19	.6977	2.7078	44.3	11	3	3	0	1	1	0	0	3	2	0	2	4	1	0	0	2	0	0	0	0	3	2	0	0
Baker	49	.7148	7.2286	48.6	24	2	3	4	5	4	7	0	18	4	3	1	2	6	0	1	0	0	0	0	5	1	5	3	0
baker's	8	.3406	.6862	38.4	5	0	0	2	1	0	0	0	4	0	0	1	0	0	0	0	0	0	0	0	3	0	0	0	0
Baker's	6	.1020	.2258	33.5	2	0	0	1	0	0	3	0	2	0	3	0	0	1	0	0	0	0	0	0	0	0	0	0	0
bakeries	5	.5353	.5770	37.6	2	1	1	0	0	1	0	0	1	0	0	0	0	1	0	1	0	0	0	0	0	1	1	0	0
bakers	3	.3759	.2471	33.9	0	0	2	0	0	0	0	1	0	1	0	0	0	1	0	0	0	0	0	0	0	0	1	0	0
Bakers	6	.3485	.5152	37.1	4	0	0	1	1	0	0	0	2	0	0	0	0	3	0	0	0	0	0	0	0	0	1	0	0
Bakers'	2	.2152	.1357	31.3	1	1	0	0	0	0	0	0	1	0	0	0	0	1	0	0	0	0	0	0	0	0	0	0	0
Bakersville	2	.0000	.0914	29.6	0	0	0	0	2	0	0	0	2	0	0	0	0	0	0	0	0	0	0	0	0	0	0	0	0
Bakerville	3	.0000	.1370	31.4	0	3	0	0	0	0	0	0	3	0	0	0	0	0	0	0	0	0	0	0	0	0	0	0	0
bakery	29	.7267	4.3502	46.4	8	2	3	3	8	3	2	0	12	1	0	1	1	3	3	1	0	0	1	0	5	1	0	0	0
Bakery	2	.0000	.0914	29.6	0	2	0	0	0	0	0	0	2	0	0	0	0	0	0	0	0	0	0	0	0	0	0	0	0
bakes	10	.5633	1.1806	40.7	0	5	1	1	1	0	2	0	1	3	0	1	2	2	0	0	0	0	0	0	0	0	1	0	0
baking	128	.4493	12.254	50.9	12	28	12	11	14	13	37	1	12	3	1	2	1	12	2	17	0	0	48	3	1	18	4	4	0
baking-soda	2	.0000	.0394	26.0	0	0	0	0	0	2	0	0	0	0	0	0	0	0	0	2	0	0	0	0	0	0	0	0	0
Bakito	4	.0000	.1827	32.6	4	0	0	0	0	0	0	0	4	0	0	0	0	0	0	0	0	0	0	0	0	0	0	0	0
Balaam	3	.2357	.2199	33.4	1	0	2	0	0	0	0	0	2	0	0	0	0	0	0	0	0	0	0	0	0	1	0	0	0
balalaika	12	.1983	.5585	37.5	4	2	2	4	0	0	0	0	0	0	0	0	0	0	0	0	8	0	0	0	0	0	0	4	0
balance	263	.8323	43.809	56.4	14	26	27	27	44	53	62	10	35	5	0	12	18	13	5	75	10	4	22	3	2	21	21	17	0
Balance	4	.3678	.3187	35.0	0	0	1	0	0	0	2	1	0	0	0	0	0	0	0	0	1	0	0	0	0	1	0	2	0
balanced	60	.8414	10.073	50.0	4	11	6	4	15	10	8	2	6	1	2	4	0	3	0	15	1	2	4	2	4	5	3	8	0
balances	18	.6596	2.4399	43.9	4	3	2	0	3	2	4	0	2	0	0	0	0	3	0	3	2	1	0	0	0	3	3	1	0
balancing	11	.6248	1.4208	41.5	2	3	1	0	3	1	1	0	2	0	0	1	0	0	0	0	1	1	0	0	2	2	1	1	0
Balboa	4	.3396	.3008	34.8	0	0	3	0	0	0	1	0	0	1	0	0	0	1	0	0	0	0	0	0	0	0	2	0	0
balconies	10	.4815	1.0675	40.3	1	2	1	2	2	2	0	0	3	0	1	0	0	4	0	0	0	0	0	1	0	1	0	0	0
balcony	39	.7502	5.9721	47.8	16	5	5	3	4	3	2	1	12	4	0	3	2	3	0	0	2	0	0	0	4	3	0	6	0
bald	33	.5929	4.3103	46.3	10	1	1	9	6	1	4	1	22	0	0	4	0	1	0	0	0	0	0	0	1	2	1	2	0
Bald	7	.3895	.6135	37.9	0	0	0	1	6	0	0	0	1	0	0	3	0	2	0	0	0	0	0	0	0	0	1	0	0
Balder	10	.1332	.3505	35.4	0	0	10	0	0	0	0	0	0	0	0	0	0	0	1	0	0	0	0	0	0	0	9	0	0
Baldwin	5	.3226	.3545	35.5	0	0	4	1	0	0	0	0	0	0	0	0	0	0	0	0	0	0	0	0	1	0	3	1	0
Baldy	10	.3080	.8058	39.1	4	5	0	0	0	0	1	0	5	0	0	0	0	0	0	0	0	0	0	0	4	1	0	0	0
bale	8	.4793	.8269	39.2	0	1	5	0	2	0	0	0	1	0	0	0	0	1	0	0	0	0	0	0	0	2	1	3	0
baled	3	.2432	.1789	32.5	1	1	0	1	0	0	0	0	0	0	0	0	0	2	0	0	1	0	0	0	0	0	0	0	0
baleen	17	.2317	.9479	39.8	12	0	0	0	5	0	0	0	0	0	0	0	0	0	0	0	0	0	0	0	0	12	5	0	0
baleful	4	.3706	.3628	35.6	1	0	0	1	2	0	0	0	2	0	0	0	0	0	0	0	0	0	0	0	1	0	1	0	0
bales	21	.4624	2.2243	43.5	2	8	3	1	4	3	0	0	8	0	0	0	0	8	0	0	0	0	0	0	2	3	0	0	0
Balfour	4	.0000	.0778	28.9	0	0	0	0	2	2	0	0	0	0	0	0	0	4	0	0	0	0	0	0	0	0	0	0	0
Bali	4	.0000	.0486	26.9	0	0	0	4	0	0	0	0	0	0	0	0	0	0	0	0	0	0	0	0	0	0	0	4	0
Bali's	2	.0000	.0243	23.9	0	0	0	2	0	0	0	0	0	0	0	0	0	0	0	0	0	0	0	0	0	0	0	2	0
Balinese	2	.0000	.0243	23.9	0	0	0	2	0	0	0	0	0	0	0	0	0	0	0	0	0	0	0	0	0	0	0	2	0
balk	2	.2417	.1091	30.4	1	0	0	0	1	0	0	0	0	0	0	0	0	0	0	0	1	0	0	0	0	0	1	0	0
Balkan	10	.5263	1.0990	40.4	0	0	2	1	3	4	0	0	0	0	0	0	0	4	2	0	2	0	0	0	0	1	0	1	0
Balkans	5	.3684	.4146	36.2	0	1	1	0	2	0	1	0	0	0	0	0	0	3	0	0	0	0	0	0	0	1	1	0	0
balked	4	.3584	.3139	35.0	0	1	0	1	2	0	0	0	0	0	0	0	0	0	0	0	0	0	0	0	2	1	0	1	0
ball	1061	.9310	195.83	62.9	276	231	121	112	165	91	50	15	325	59	25	34	33	51	23	174	15	11	10	15	68	134	27	57	0
Ball	33	.6016	4.2553	46.3	9	6	5	2	10	1	0	0	14	0	0	0	1	3	0	2	7	0	0	0	1	3	0	2	0
ball-and-socket	5	.0000	.0986	29.9	0	0	5	0	0	0	0	0	0	0	0	0	0	0	0	5	0	0	0	0	0	0	0	0	0
ball-peen	7	.0454	.0907	29.6	0	0	0	0	3	4	0	0	0	0	0	0	0	0	0	0	0	0	0	6	0	1	0	0	0
ball-point	5	.3085	.3479	35.4	0	1	0	2	1	0	1	0	1	0	2	0	0	0	0	0	0	0	0	1	0	0	0	1	0
ball-shaped	2	.1698	.1133	30.5	1	0	0	0	1	0	0	0	1	0	0	0	0	0	0	0	0	0	0	0	0	0	1	0	0
Ball's	3	.1169	.1277	31.1	1	1	0	0	0	1	0	0	1	0	0	0	0	0	0	0	0	0	0	0	0	0	2	0	0
ballad	41	.3361	2.9674	44.7	2	6	13	6	6	4	4	0	0	6	0	7	0	1	0	0	25	0	0	0	0	2	0	0	0
ballads	32	.4359	2.9407	44.7	0	1	9	9	6	5	2	0	1	11	0	3	0	0	0	0	13	0	0	0	0	1	0	3	0
Ballard	8	.0000	.0972	29.9	0	0	0	0	8	0	0	0	0	0	0	0	0	0	0	0	0	0	0	0	0	0	0	8	0
ballast	8	.4882	.8927	39.5	0	2	2	0	2	0	1	1	4	0	0	0	0	0	0	2	0	0	0	0	0	0	1	1	0
ballerina	4	.3757	.3228	35.1	1	1	1	0	1	0	0	0	0	0	0	0	0	0	0	0	1	0	0	0	1	0	0	2	0
Ballerina	9	.0000	.0728	28.6	0	1	0	0	4	0	4	0	0	0	0	0	0	0	0	0	9	0	0	0	0	0	0	0	0
ballerinas	2	.2417	.1091	30.4	0	0	0	0	1	1	0	0	0	0	0	0	0	0	0	0	1	0	0	0	0	0	1	0	0
ballet	89	.4696	8.7825	49.4	6	18	3	10	23	21	8	0	7	0	1	0	0	1	1	0	52	1	0	0	5	4	13	4	0
Ballet	10	.2463	.5516	37.4	0	1	1	0	3	1	4	0	0	0	0	0	0	0	0	0	7	0	0	0	0	0	2	1	0
ballets	17	.1959	.7746	38.9	1	2	0	0	6	5	3	0	0	0	0	0	0	0	0	0	12	0	0	0	0	0	5	0	0
Ballinascarthy	2	.0000	.0243	23.9	0	0	0	2	0	0	0	0	0	0	0	0	0	0	0	0	0	0	0	0	0	0	0	2	0
ballista	2	.0000	.0209	23.2	0	0	0	0	2	0	0	0	0	0	0	0	0	0	0	0	0	0	0	0	0	0	2	0	0
ballistic	4	.3790	.3299	35.2	2	0	0	0	2	0	0	0	0	0	0	0	0	0	0	0	0	0	0	0	0	2	1	1	0
Ballistic	2	.0000	.0209	23.2	0	0	0	0	0	0	2	0	0	0	0	0	0	0	0	0	0	0	0	0	0	0	2	0	0
balloon	233	.7241	34.490	55.4	98	34	40	23	16	9	2	11	37	8	5	0	5	1	5	116	1	2	0	1	7	3	7	35	0
ballooned	3	.3811	.2534	34.0	1	0	1	1	0	0	0	0	0	0	0	0	0	0	0	1	0	0	0	0	0	1	0	1	0
ballooning	5	.3117	.3816	35.8	2	0	0	3	0	0	0	0	1	0	0	0	0	0	0	2	0	0	0	0	0	0	0	2	0
balloonist	5	.3733	.4141	36.2	2	1	1	0	1	0	0	0	0	0	0	0	0	0	0	2	0	0	0	0	1	0	0	2	0
balloons	98	.6590	13.292	51.2	16	20	31	8	9	7	5	2	5	5	1	2	12	1	0	53	1	0	0	1	0	0	3	14	0
ballot	11	.6159	1.4019	41.5	0	0	2	1	2	5	1	0	1	3	0	0	1	2	0	0	0	0	0	0	0	2	1	1	0
balloting	2	.1698	.1133	30.5	0	0	0	0	1	1	0	0	1	0	0	0	0	0	0	0	0	0	0	0	0	0	1	0	0
ballots	6	.4406	.5903	37.7	0	0	0	1	3	1	1	0	1	0	0	0	2	2	0	0	0	0	0	0	0	0	0	1	0
ballplayer	12	.5212	1.3808	41.4	1	0	0	1	5	3	2	0	5	1	0	2	0	0	0	1	0	0	0	0	0	0	0	3	0
ballplayers	6	.3089	.4599	36.6	1	0	0	0	2	1	2	0	2	0	0	1	0	0	0	0	0	0	0	0	0	0	0	3	0
ballroom	12	.4491	1.2829	41.1	2	1	8	1	0	0	0	0	8	0	0	0	0	0	0	0	2	0	0	0	0	1	1	0	0
balls	170	.9274	31.250	54.9	49	36	23	27	15	8	11	1	42	3	1	5	28	9	4	21	5	1	1	1	7	20	10	12	0
Balmat	2	.0000	.0209	23.2	0	0	0	0	2	0	0	0	0	0	0	0	0	0	0	0	0	0	0	0	0	0	2	0	0
balmy	3	.3390	.2450	33.9	0	0	0	1	1	0	0	1	1	0	0	0	0	0	0	0	0	0	0	0	0	0	1	1	0

8Q Bahawalpur
5N Bahman
4P Baikal
7N bailed
8B bailer
8F bailiffs
6A bailin'
7A bailiwick
XR Bain
6A bain't
5R Baines
7P Baire
7P Bait

4F baiting
9N baits
8D Bakebe
6J Baked
3A baked-mud
8M bakelite
7R Bakersfield
6H bakterion
5A Balahait
6J Balalyka
7R balance-vote
4A balance-weight
8J Balanchine

7Q Balanchine's
5Q balata
9D Balboni
3A balconied
5P balcony-festooned
5Q Balder's
XH balderdash
7D Baleful
XR Balenciaga
8N baler
5H baling
7N balistae
6F Balkash

8Q Balkh
7R Balkhash
5N balking
6C balky
3P BALL
6A ball-carrying
7P ball-handler
8M ball-type
7D ball's
8J Ballade
3A Ballaghadereen
3A Ballarat
7R ballclub

5P Balle
5N balled
7R baller
5J Baller
9J Ballet-Russe
9J ballet-drama
6R ballet-like
7J ballet's
7Q Ballets
6C ballfield
4E ballgame
4N ballgames
XH Ballinger

4Q ballistas
3B Balloon
4A balloon-shaped
4Q balloon-tire
3R balloonists
7R ballplayer's
5J Ballroom
6J ballrooms
7R Balls
3A bally
9B baloney

Word Type	F	D	U	SFI	3 Gr 3	4 Gr 4	5 Gr 5	6 Gr 6	7 Gr 7	8 Gr 8	9 Gr 9	X UnGr	A Read	B Eng & Gr	C Comp	D Lit	E Math	F Soc Stud	G Spell	H Sci	J Music	K Art	L Home Ec	M Shop	N Lib F	P Lib NF	Q Lib Ref	R Mag	S Rel
balsa	6	.1475	.2212	33.4	0	3	0	0	2	1	0	0	0	0	0	0	0	0	0	2	0	3	0	0	0	0	1	0	0
balsa-wood	3	.2076	.1618	32.1	0	1	2	0	0	0	0	0	0	0	0	0	2	0	0	1	0	0	0	0	0	0	0	0	0
balsam	6	.5566	.7181	38.6	1	1	0	1	1	1	1	0	2	1	0	0	0	0	0	0	0	0	0	0	0	1	1	1	0
Balser	5	.0000	.2284	33.6	5	0	0	0	0	0	0	0	5	0	0	0	0	0	0	0	0	0	0	0	0	0	0	0	0
Balthasar	3	.2374	.1625	32.1	0	0	1	0	0	0	2	0	0	0	0	2	0	0	0	0	1	0	0	0	0	0	0	0	0
Baltic	19	.3500	1.4826	41.7	6	0	4	3	1	4	1	0	0	0	0	0	0	5	0	2	0	0	0	0	0	2	10	0	0
Baltimore	60	.7205	8.8660	49.5	14	11	2	7	6	14	6	0	14	5	0	2	0	16	0	2	2	0	0	0	0	8	3	8	0
Balto	4	.0000	.1827	32.6	0	4	0	0	0	0	0	0	4	0	0	0	0	0	0	0	0	0	0	0	0	0	0	0	0
Balto's	2	.0000	.0914	29.6	0	2	0	0	0	0	0	0	2	0	0	0	0	0	0	0	0	0	0	0	0	0	0	0	0
Balzac	4	.3473	.2990	34.8	0	0	1	0	0	0	2	1	0	0	0	0	0	1	0	0	1	1	0	0	0	0	1	0	0
Bamberg	2	.0000	.0209	23.2	0	0	2	0	0	0	0	0	0	0	0	0	0	0	0	0	0	0	0	0	0	0	2	0	0
Bambi	15	.0000	.6852	38.4	6	0	0	9	0	0	0	0	15	0	0	0	0	0	0	0	0	0	0	0	0	0	0	0	0
bambino	3	.0000	.0352	25.5	0	0	0	3	0	0	0	0	0	0	0	0	0	0	0	0	0	0	0	0	3	0	0	0	0
bamboo	69	.7172	10.051	50.0	9	10	3	18	14	11	3	1	8	0	0	3	0	11	0	0	9	1	1	0	2	20	12	2	0
Bamboo	2	.0000	.0389	25.9	0	0	0	0	0	2	0	0	0	0	0	0	0	2	0	0	0	0	0	0	0	0	0	0	0
bamboos	11	.5007	1.1590	40.6	1	0	0	2	7	1	0	0	1	0	0	2	0	0	0	0	1	0	0	0	1	1	5	0	0
bamboula	5	.0000	.0404	26.1	0	0	4	1	0	0	0	0	0	0	0	0	0	0	0	0	5	0	0	0	0	0	0	0	0
Bamboula	4	.0000	.0323	25.1	0	0	4	0	0	0	0	0	0	0	0	0	0	0	0	0	4	0	0	0	0	0	0	0	0
ban	19	.4132	1.7397	42.4	0	0	1	1	9	4	4	0	3	1	0	0	0	0	1	0	0	0	0	0	0	4	0	10	0
Ban	6	.0000	.0869	29.4	0	0	0	1	0	0	5	0	0	0	0	0	0	0	0	0	0	0	0	0	0	6	0	0	0
banana	59	.7695	9.2952	49.7	9	12	2	16	12	3	5	0	26	2	1	2	2	10	3	2	0	0	4	0	2	1	0	4	0
Banana	4	.2954	.2881	34.6	1	0	0	0	2	0	1	0	1	0	0	2	0	0	0	0	0	0	0	0	0	0	0	1	0
bananas	133	.7770	20.964	53.2	36	15	8	35	32	4	3	0	33	0	1	3	2	41	1	1	11	0	6	0	4	17	8	5	0
Bananas	2	.2446	.1142	30.6	0	1	0	0	1	0	0	0	0	0	0	0	0	0	0	0	0	0	0	0	1	0	0	1	0
Bancroft	3	.2137	.1446	31.6	0	1	0	0	0	0	2	0	0	0	1	2	0	0	0	0	0	0	0	0	0	0	0	0	0
band	403	.8162	66.117	58.2	59	82	62	39	63	69	28	1	95	15	5	13	2	17	11	61	94	0	10	7	13	31	8	21	0
Band	13	.2277	.6651	38.2	0	0	2	5	0	5	1	0	0	1	0	0	0	0	2	0	10	0	0	0	0	0	0	0	0
BAND	2	.0000	.0290	24.6	0	2	0	0	0	0	0	0	0	0	0	0	0	0	0	0	0	0	0	0	0	2	0	0	0
band's	4	.3267	.2856	34.6	0	1	0	0	1	2	0	0	0	0	0	0	0	0	0	0	2	0	0	0	0	1	0	1	0
bandage	16	.6746	2.2766	43.6	2	1	5	1	1	4	0	2	8	1	0	1	0	0	0	2	0	0	0	0	1	2	1	0	0
bandaged	4	.3755	.3686	35.7	0	1	0	2	0	0	1	0	2	0	0	0	0	0	0	0	0	0	0	0	1	1	0	0	0
bandages	14	.7163	2.0636	43.1	1	1	6	0	1	1	3	1	4	0	0	1	0	2	0	1	0	0	0	0	1	2	1	2	0
bandaging	2	.2407	.1138	30.6	0	0	0	0	1	0	0	1	0	0	0	1	0	0	0	0	0	0	0	0	0	1	0	0	0
Bandana	2	.0000	.0243	23.9	0	0	0	0	2	0	0	0	0	0	0	0	0	0	0	0	0	0	0	0	0	0	0	2	0
bandanna	8	.5662	.9903	40.0	5	0	0	0	2	0	1	0	4	1	0	1	0	0	0	0	0	0	0	0	0	1	0	1	0
bandannas	2	.1814	.1187	30.7	1	0	0	0	0	1	0	0	1	0	0	0	0	0	0	0	0	0	0	0	0	0	0	1	0
banded	20	.7050	2.8794	44.6	2	5	0	0	9	1	3	0	3	0	0	0	0	3	1	2	1	0	0	0	2	2	5	1	0
bandit	9	.4790	1.0094	40.0	1	4	0	1	3	0	0	0	6	0	0	1	0	0	0	0	0	0	0	0	0	1	0	1	0
bandits	10	.3422	.8942	39.5	0	4	3	1	1	1	0	0	6	0	0	0	0	1	0	0	0	0	0	0	0	3	0	0	0
bandlike	2	.2278	.1128	30.5	0	0	0	0	2	0	0	0	0	0	0	0	0	0	0	1	0	0	0	0	0	0	1	0	0
bands	142	.7417	21.324	53.3	16	28	25	18	12	32	8	3	20	2	1	2	2	12	0	26	45	3	2	1	3	7	11	5	0
bandstand	3	.0995	.1144	30.6	1	0	1	0	0	1	0	0	1	0	0	0	0	0	0	0	2	0	0	0	0	0	0	0	0
bandwagon	2	.0000	.0243	23.9	0	0	0	0	1	1	0	0	0	0	0	0	0	0	0	0	0	0	0	0	0	0	0	2	0
bandwagons	4	.0000	.0089	19.5	0	0	0	0	0	0	4	0	0	0	4	0	0	0	0	0	0	0	0	0	0	0	0	0	0
bandy	3	.2236	.1570	32.0	0	2	0	0	0	1	0	0	0	1	0	2	0	0	0	0	0	0	0	0	0	0	0	0	0
Baneberry	4	.0000	.0789	29.0	0	0	0	0	0	0	0	4	0	0	0	0	0	0	0	4	0	0	0	0	0	0	0	0	0
baneful	2	.1698	.1133	30.5	0	0	1	1	0	0	0	0	1	0	0	0	0	0	0	0	0	0	0	0	0	0	1	0	0
bang	75	.7967	12.133	50.8	25	13	13	7	10	3	3	1	30	7	1	7	0	3	0	2	1	0	2	0	7	10	0	5	0
Bang	2	.0000	.0243	23.9	0	0	0	2	0	0	0	0	0	0	0	0	0	0	0	0	0	0	0	0	0	0	0	2	0
banged	33	.5641	4.0684	46.1	8	6	4	1	10	3	1	0	16	0	0	2	0	0	0	0	1	0	0	0	7	6	0	1	0
banging	33	.6195	4.4050	46.4	5	8	3	7	6	1	2	1	19	1	0	2	0	0	0	0	0	0	2	0	5	2	0	2	0
Bangkok	5	.2924	.3577	35.5	0	0	1	0	1	0	3	0	1	0	0	0	0	0	0	0	0	0	0	0	0	3	1	0	0
bangs	10	.4447	.9444	39.8	3	0	0	1	0	2	3	1	1	0	0	1	0	0	0	0	0	0	3	0	1	1	1	2	0
Bangs	19	.2051	1.2424	40.9	6	0	5	0	0	0	0	8	11	0	0	0	0	0	0	0	0	0	0	0	0	0	0	8	0
banish	4	.4450	.3914	35.9	0	0	1	1	1	0	1	0	1	0	0	1	0	0	1	0	0	0	0	0	0	0	1	0	0
banished	15	.6569	2.0517	43.1	0	0	1	5	0	2	6	1	5	1	0	3	0	0	0	0	1	0	0	0	1	0	2	2	0
banishment	2	.2427	.1152	30.6	0	0	0	0	2	0	0	0	0	0	0	0	0	0	0	0	0	0	0	0	1	1	0	0	0
banister	9	.6067	1.1548	40.6	1	1	1	0	3	1	2	0	3	2	0	1	0	0	0	0	0	0	0	0	1	1	0	1	0
banisters	2	.0000	.0914	29.6	2	0	0	0	0	0	0	0	2	0	0	0	0	0	0	0	0	0	0	0	0	0	0	0	0
banjo	32	.3617	2.5558	44.1	2	6	11	7	3	1	2	0	4	4	0	0	0	0	1	0	19	0	0	0	1	2	0	1	0
Banjo	9	.0000	.0728	28.6	8	0	1	0	0	0	0	0	0	0	0	0	0	0	0	0	9	0	0	0	0	0	0	0	0
banjos	2	.1494	.1045	30.2	0	0	1	1	0	0	0	0	1	0	0	0	0	0	0	0	1	0	0	0	0	0	0	0	0
bank	465	.8428	78.860	59.0	114	70	47	60	82	46	36	10	168	8	1	37	53	38	8	10	5	0	1	0	23	61	20	32	0
Bank	59	.5384	6.8313	48.3	2	2	4	3	32	4	12	0	16	0	0	4	0	8	0	0	0	0	0	0	2	0	17	12	0
Bank's	2	.0000	.0209	23.2	0	0	0	0	2	0	0	0	0	0	0	0	0	0	0	0	0	0	0	0	0	0	2	0	0
banked	8	.4775	.8919	39.5	1	2	0	2	0	2	1	0	5	0	0	1	0	1	0	0	0	0	0	0	1	0	0	0	0
banker	14	.6810	1.9529	42.9	0	1	0	0	6	3	4	0	2	0	0	4	2	1	1	1	0	0	0	0	0	1	1	1	0
bankers	9	.3950	.7902	39.0	1	0	0	0	1	0	5	2	1	1	0	0	0	1	0	0	0	0	0	0	0	1	0	5	0
banking	20	.4213	1.8052	42.6	0	2	2	2	9	3	2	0	0	0	0	0	1	4	0	0	0	0	0	0	1	1	11	2	0
bankrout	3	.0000	.0322	25.1	0	0	0	0	0	0	3	0	0	0	0	3	0	0	0	0	0	0	0	0	0	0	0	0	0
bankrupt	3	.3827	.2446	33.9	0	1	0	1	0	0	1	0	0	0	0	0	0	0	1	0	0	0	0	0	0	0	1	1	0
bankruptcy	2	.0000	.0389	25.9	0	0	0	0	0	1	1	0	0	0	0	0	0	2	0	0	0	0	0	0	0	0	0	0	0
banks	219	.7799	34.520	55.4	32	32	36	31	47	17	19	5	35	6	3	12	2	63	1	15	0	0	0	0	11	21	30	20	0
Banks	33	.6165	4.2372	46.3	4	6	12	1	6	3	1	0	7	2	0	1	0	0	0	1	1	0	0	0	12	1	5	3	0
banned	11	.5294	1.2082	40.8	0	0	1	3	0	4	2	1	0	1	0	0	0	2	0	0	2	0	0	0	0	0	2	4	0
Banneker	3	.2435	.2274	33.6	0	2	1	0	0	0	0	0	2	0	0	0	0	1	0	0	0	0	0	0	0	0	0	0	0
banner	16	.6945	2.2831	43.6	3	3	1	1	3	2	3	0	4	0	0	0	0	1	2	0	1	0	0	0	3	2	1	2	0
Banner	13	.2562	.8205	39.1	1	5	1	1	0	4	1	0	3	1	0	0	0	0	0	0	8	0	0	0	0	0	1	0	0
banners	12	.4857	1.2567	41.0	0	1	0	4	6	0	1	0	2	2	0	0	0	1	0	0	0	0	0	0	3	0	0	4	0
Banning	2	.0000	.0037	15.7	0	0	0	0	0	2	0	0	0	0	0	0	0	0	0	0	0	2	0	0	0	0	0	0	0
banquet	21	.6948	3.0264	44.8	0	3	5	5	5	2	1	0	8	1	0	0	0	2	1	0	1	1	0	0	4	2	0	1	0
banquets	5	.3546	.4331	36.4	0	0	1	3	0	0	1	0	2	1	0	0	0	0	0	0	0	0	0	0	0	2	0	0	0
banshee	4	.3369	.2914	34.6	2	0	0	1	1	0	0	0	0	0	0	0	0	0	0	0	2	0	0	0	1	0	0	1	0
Bantu	26	.4791	2.7417	44.4	4	9	1	4	1	0	7	0	5	0	0	0	0	12	0	0	0	0	0	0	3	1	5	0	0
Banya	5	.0000	.0972	29.9	0	0	0	0	0	5	0	0	0	0	0	0	0	5	0	0	0	0	0	0	0	0	0	0	0
banyan	3	.0966	.0702	28.5	0	0	0	0	0	2	1	0	0	1	0	0	0	0	0	0	0	2	0	0	0	0	0	0	0
baptism	6	.0493	.1334	31.3	2	0	0	1	3	0	0	0	1	0	0	2	0	0	0	0	0	0	0	0	1	0	0	0	2
Baptism	3	.0000	.0005	7.3	0	3	0	0	0	0	0	0	0	0	0	0	0	0	0	0	0	0	0	0	0	0	0	0	3
Baptist	13	.4825	1.3081	41.2	0	0	2	0	5	1	4	1	0	0	0	5	0	0	0	0	0	0	0	0	1	1	4	2	0
Baptiste	4	.1873	.1827	32.6	0	1	1	0	1	1	0	0	0	0	0	0	0	0	0	0	0	0	0	0	0	0	3	1	0
baptize	4	.3874	.3414	35.3	0	2	0	0	2	0	0	0	0	0	0	1	0	2	0	0	0	0	0	0	0	0	1	0	0
baptized	13	.1260	.4743	36.8	2	4	1	1	1	2	2	0	1	0	0	2	0	2	0	0	0	0	0	0	1	1	4	0	2
bar	325	.7979	52.051	57.2	55	51	36	30	69	40	36	8	39	2	2	22	101	8	1	29	32	0	8	19	9	22	13	18	0

4A Balsora
8F Baltimores
7B Balto-Slavic
8Q Baluchistan
5Q Balzac's
3P bam
7P Bamayassi
9Q Bambara-Maninka
6N bambinos
6A bamboo-matted
8Q Bampton
9L Ban-Lon

9R banal
XR banality
6F banana-shipping
4P Banat
8F Bancroft's
3N band-concert
7M band-iron
7P Banda
5K Bandersnatch
7R bandied
7R banding
5A Bandit

5P bandoleers
6R Bandon
8N bandy-legged
7Q bane
8C Bang-All
7B bang-up
9R banged-up
7A Bangkok's
5P bangles
8R Bangor
7F Bangui
6F Banias

8D banishing
6J banjo-like
7D BANK
7N bank-notes
9R bank's
7A bankbook
4A Banker
4A banker's
9D banking-house
9D Banking-house
9D banknotes
7Q banks'

7B bannanner
4A Bannekers
8D bannerlike
8R banning
7D bannister
5A Banquet
3J Banshee
7R banshees
9D bantam
6A Bantam
6A banter
7H Banting

9N Bantu's
8Q Bao
7Q baobab
4J bap
3B bapples
7D baptismal
9B baptist
5J Baptiste's
9K Baptistry
8F Baptists

Word Type	F	D	U	SFI	3 Gr 3	4 Gr 4	5 Gr 5	6 Gr 6	7 Gr 7	8 Gr 8	9 Gr 9	X UnGr	A Read	B Eng & Gr	C Comp	D Lit	E Math	F Soc Stud	G Spell	H Sci	J Music	K Art	L Home Ec	M Shop	N Lib F	P Lib NF	Q Lib Ref	R Mag	S Rel
Bar	14	.6221	1.7845	42.5	3	3	1	0	3	3	1	0	1	0	0	2	0	0	0	0	0	0	1	0	4	2	1	3	0
BAR	2	.0000	.0290	24.6	0	0	1	1	0	0	0	0	0	0	0	0	0	0	0	0	0	0	0	0	0	2	0	0	0
bar'	2	.0000	.0234	23.7	0	0	0	0	2	0	0	0	0	0	0	0	0	0	0	0	0	0	0	0	2	0	0	0	0
Baraboo	2	.0000	.0290	24.6	0	2	0	0	0	0	0	0	0	0	0	0	0	0	0	0	0	0	0	0	0	2	0	0	0
barb	4	.3280	.2948	34.7	2	0	0	0	2	0	0	0	0	0	0	0	0	0	0	1	0	0	0	0	0	1	2	0	0
Barbados	2	.0000	.0243	23.9	0	0	1	0	1	0	0	0	0	0	0	0	0	0	0	0	0	0	0	0	0	0	0	2	0
Barbara	46	.6675	6.3289	48.0	7	4	6	11	12	3	3	0	9	14	1	0	7	5	0	0	0	0	0	0	2	1	2	5	0
Barbara's	2	.2404	.1142	30.6	0	0	0	2	0	0	0	0	0	1	0	0	1	0	0	0	0	0	0	0	0	0	0	0	0
barbarian	14	.5553	1.5973	42.0	4	0	0	0	2	3	1	4	0	1	1	1	0	2	0	0	1	0	0	0	0	0	7	1	0
barbarians	17	.5723	2.0178	43.0	0	0	2	3	4	5	1	2	0	1	0	2	0	8	0	0	0	0	1	0	0	1	4	0	0
barbarism	2	.1948	.1250	31.0	0	0	1	0	1	0	0	0	1	0	0	0	0	0	0	0	0	0	0	0	0	1	0	0	0
barbarous	6	.3690	.4829	36.8	0	0	0	0	4	1	1	0	0	1	0	2	0	0	0	0	0	0	0	0	0	3	0	0	0
Barbary	12	.4162	1.0702	40.3	0	4	4	0	1	3	0	0	0	0	0	0	0	3	0	0	4	0	0	0	4	1	0	0	0
Barbe	15	.0000	.6852	38.4	15	0	0	0	0	0	0	0	15	0	0	0	0	0	0	0	0	0	0	0	0	0	0	0	0
barbecue	11	.3542	.9445	39.8	2	1	1	0	3	0	1	3	4	0	0	0	0	0	0	0	0	0	0	0	0	4	0	3	0
Barbecue	4	.1787	.2347	33.7	0	0	0	2	2	0	0	0	2	0	0	0	0	0	0	0	0	0	0	0	2	0	0	0	0
barbed	18	.5477	2.1320	43.3	0	1	3	5	2	2	0	5	6	0	0	1	0	2	0	0	0	0	0	0	2	0	1	6	0
barbed-wire	7	.3812	.6203	37.9	0	1	0	1	4	0	0	1	2	0	0	3	0	1	0	0	0	0	0	0	0	0	0	1	0
barbels	2	.1551	.0728	28.6	0	1	0	0	0	0	1	0	0	0	1	0	0	0	0	0	0	0	0	0	1	0	0	0	0
barber	49	.5502	5.7211	47.6	1	0	13	11	3	19	2	0	10	2	0	18	0	4	0	1	1	0	0	0	9	4	0	0	0
Barber	11	.0310	.1895	32.8	1	0	3	4	1	2	0	0	1	0	0	0	0	0	0	0	10	0	0	0	0	0	0	0	0
barber's	3	.0000	.0322	25.1	0	0	0	0	0	3	0	0	0	0	0	3	0	0	0	0	0	0	0	0	0	0	0	0	0
barbers	13	.5555	1.5957	42.0	1	1	5	3	0	3	0	0	6	0	0	1	0	2	0	3	0	0	0	0	0	1	0	0	0
barbershop	9	.2438	.5215	37.2	0	0	1	3	1	4	0	0	1	0	0	1	0	0	0	0	6	0	0	0	0	1	0	0	0
Barbicane	3	.2239	.1775	32.5	0	0	2	0	0	0	0	1	0	0	0	0	0	2	0	1	0	0	0	0	0	0	0	0	0
barbicels	2	.0000	.0209	23.2	0	0	0	0	2	0	0	0	0	0	0	0	0	0	0	0	0	0	0	0	0	0	2	0	0
Barbier	5	.1786	.2193	33.4	0	0	0	0	4	0	1	0	0	0	0	4	0	0	0	0	0	0	0	0	0	0	1	0	0
Barbier's	3	.0000	.0322	25.1	0	0	0	0	3	0	0	0	0	0	0	3	0	0	0	0	0	0	0	0	0	0	0	0	0
barbiturates	2	.0000	.0243	23.9	0	0	0	0	1	0	1	0	0	0	0	0	0	0	0	0	0	0	0	0	0	0	0	2	0
Barbizon	4	.1493	.1383	31.4	0	0	2	0	0	0	2	0	0	0	0	0	0	0	0	0	0	2	0	0	0	0	2	0	0
barbs	16	.4883	1.6602	42.2	10	0	0	0	3	0	0	3	0	0	0	0	0	0	0	6	0	0	0	0	0	4	3	3	0
barbules	2	.0000	.0209	23.2	0	0	0	0	2	0	0	0	0	0	0	0	0	0	0	0	0	0	0	0	0	0	2	0	0
Barby	8	.0000	.3655	35.6	8	0	0	0	0	0	0	0	8	0	0	0	0	0	0	0	0	0	0	0	0	0	0	0	0
Bard	3	.0000	.1370	31.4	0	0	0	3	0	0	0	0	3	0	0	0	0	0	0	0	0	0	0	0	0	0	0	0	0
bards	2	.0000	.0209	23.2	0	0	0	0	2	0	0	0	0	0	0	0	0	0	0	0	0	0	0	0	0	0	2	0	0
bare	198	.8911	35.142	55.5	34	32	34	28	38	19	10	3	51	4	2	17	0	22	4	21	10	1	0	2	28	19	11	6	0
bare-knuckle	3	.0000	.0434	26.4	0	0	0	3	0	0	0	0	0	0	0	0	0	0	0	0	0	0	0	0	0	3	0	0	0
bareback	12	.4367	1.1903	40.8	1	4	1	5	1	0	0	0	4	0	0	3	0	0	0	0	0	0	0	0	0	4	0	1	0
bareback-riding	2	.0000	.0914	29.6	0	0	0	2	0	0	0	0	2	0	0	0	0	0	0	0	0	0	0	0	0	0	0	0	0
bared	14	.4907	1.4863	41.7	0	1	3	0	9	1	0	0	3	1	0	3	0	0	0	0	0	0	0	0	5	2	0	0	0
barefaced	2	.1717	.1142	30.6	0	0	0	1	0	0	1	0	1	0	0	1	0	0	0	0	0	0	0	0	0	0	0	0	0
barefoot	17	.7345	2.5375	44.0	3	3	1	3	4	2	1	0	3	1	0	3	0	2	0	0	1	0	0	0	1	3	2	1	0
Barefoot	2	.0000	.0215	23.3	2	0	0	0	0	0	0	0	0	0	0	2	0	0	0	0	0	0	0	0	0	0	0	0	0
bareheaded	3	.2292	.1615	32.1	0	0	0	1	2	0	0	0	0	0	0	1	0	0	0	0	0	0	0	0	2	0	0	0	0
barely	75	.7643	11.708	50.7	3	10	8	7	23	10	10	4	28	4	2	8	0	4	0	5	0	0	0	0	9	4	2	9	0
bargain	47	.7542	7.2066	48.6	5	10	5	6	1	13	6	1	12	1	0	4	0	6	2	0	5	0	1	0	10	4	0	2	0
bargained	7	.3722	.6487	38.1	0	0	1	2	3	0	1	0	4	0	0	1	0	0	0	0	0	0	0	0	0	0	0	2	0
bargaining	21	.3176	1.4960	41.7	0	0	11	0	2	0	7	1	1	0	0	0	0	0	0	0	0	0	0	0	1	0	10	9	0
bargains	5	.5306	.5639	37.5	1	0	0	1	1	0	2	0	1	0	0	1	0	0	1	0	0	0	0	0	1	1	0	0	0
barge	35	.5788	4.2240	46.3	3	1	1	4	13	0	12	1	5	0	0	0	0	2	0	1	6	0	0	0	2	3	12	4	0
Barge	5	.4599	.4875	36.9	0	0	2	0	1	0	0	2	0	0	0	0	0	1	0	0	0	0	0	0	1	0	1	2	0
Bargello	2	.0000	.0209	23.2	0	0	0	0	2	0	0	0	0	0	0	0	0	0	0	0	0	0	0	0	0	0	2	0	0
barges	52	.6226	6.7671	48.3	14	9	8	4	8	1	6	2	9	3	0	0	0	22	0	1	5	0	0	0	0	3	7	2	0
bari	7	.0000	.0851	29.3	0	0	0	0	0	0	0	7	0	0	0	0	0	0	0	0	0	0	0	0	0	0	0	7	0
baring	2	.1814	.1187	30.7	0	0	0	1	0	0	0	1	1	0	0	0	0	0	0	0	0	0	0	0	0	0	0	1	0
barite	2	.0000	.0389	25.9	0	0	1	0	1	0	0	0	0	0	0	0	0	2	0	0	0	0	0	0	0	0	0	0	0
baritone	12	.1641	.4735	36.8	0	1	0	0	5	6	0	0	0	0	0	0	0	0	0	0	10	0	0	0	0	0	1	1	0
barium	4	.2085	.2127	33.3	0	0	0	0	2	1	0	1	0	0	0	0	0	0	0	3	0	0	0	1	0	0	0	0	0
bark	204	.8753	35.704	55.5	40	41	33	46	32	5	4	3	73	12	7	17	1	14	10	19	4	4	0	2	13	11	16	1	0
barked	58	.5821	7.3133	48.6	19	12	9	8	8	2	0	0	28	5	2	2	0	2	0	0	0	0	0	0	17	1	0	1	0
barker	2	.1494	.1045	30.2	1	0	0	0	1	0	0	0	1	0	0	0	0	0	0	0	1	0	0	0	0	0	0	0	0
Barker	7	.3603	.6367	38.0	1	0	0	3	2	0	1	0	4	0	0	0	0	0	0	0	0	0	0	0	2	1	0	0	0
Barker's	2	.2412	.1091	30.4	1	0	0	0	0	0	1	0	0	0	0	1	0	0	1	0	0	0	0	0	0	0	0	0	0
Barkham	2	.0000	.0234	23.7	0	2	0	0	0	0	0	0	0	0	0	0	0	0	0	0	0	0	0	0	2	0	0	0	0
barking	68	.5277	8.0059	49.0	16	15	12	13	7	4	1	0	37	0	5	3	0	0	0	0	0	0	0	0	14	6	0	3	0
barks	19	.6445	2.5345	44.0	3	3	2	2	4	1	2	2	4	2	2	1	0	1	1	1	0	0	0	0	2	4	0	1	0
barley	59	.5525	6.9031	48.4	4	10	5	19	14	2	5	0	4	0	0	4	0	35	0	4	0	0	1	0	0	1	8	2	0
Barlow	2	.1494	.1045	30.2	0	1	0	0	0	1	0	0	1	0	0	0	0	0	0	0	1	0	0	0	0	0	0	0	0
Barlowe	4	.0000	.0419	26.2	0	0	0	0	4	0	0	0	0	0	0	0	0	0	0	0	0	0	0	0	0	0	4	0	0
Barlowe's	2	.0000	.0209	23.2	0	0	0	0	2	0	0	0	0	0	0	0	0	0	0	0	0	0	0	0	0	0	2	0	0
barman	2	.0000	.0243	23.9	0	0	0	0	0	0	0	2	0	0	0	0	0	0	0	0	0	0	0	0	0	0	0	2	0
barn	362	.7368	54.841	57.4	103	90	36	32	34	42	19	6	147	7	21	35	1	16	6	9	4	3	0	0	66	32	3	12	0
Barn-Owl	3	.2257	.1583	32.0	0	1	0	0	2	0	0	0	0	2	0	1	0	0	0	0	0	0	0	0	0	0	0	0	0
Barnabe	4	.0000	.1827	32.6	4	0	0	0	0	0	0	0	4	0	0	0	0	0	0	0	0	0	0	0	0	0	0	0	0
barnacle	4	.0000	.0789	29.0	0	0	0	0	4	0	0	0	0	0	0	0	0	0	0	4	0	0	0	0	0	0	0	0	0
barnacles	9	.5052	.9763	39.9	1	1	0	1	4	2	0	0	1	1	0	2	0	0	0	4	0	0	0	0	0	0	1	0	0
Barnard	3	.0000	.0365	25.6	0	0	0	0	3	0	0	0	0	0	0	0	0	0	0	0	0	0	0	0	0	0	0	3	0
Barnes	8	.4764	.8926	39.5	2	1	0	0	4	1	0	0	5	0	0	0	0	1	0	0	0	0	0	0	0	1	0	1	0
Barney	19	.3178	1.6070	42.1	11	5	1	0	2	0	0	0	11	0	0	0	0	0	0	0	0	0	0	0	0	7	0	1	0
barns	44	.7992	7.0810	48.5	14	2	11	3	10	4	0	0	7	0	1	7	1	12	0	3	1	1	0	0	4	3	3	1	0
Barnum	23	.2351	1.3155	41.2	0	20	0	2	0	1	0	0	0	0	0	0	0	1	0	0	0	0	0	0	1	19	0	2	0
barnyard	20	.5238	2.3404	43.7	4	7	2	2	0	4	1	0	11	0	2	3	0	1	0	0	1	0	0	0	0	1	1	0	0
Barnyard	2	.0000	.0215	23.3	0	2	0	0	0	0	0	0	0	0	0	2	0	0	0	0	0	0	0	0	0	0	0	0	0
barometer	42	.2774	2.9024	44.6	5	0	18	1	4	13	0	1	2	1	0	0	1	0	0	35	0	0	0	0	0	2	0	1	0
barometers	8	.1804	.4055	36.1	1	0	1	0	2	4	0	0	0	0	0	1	0	0	0	7	0	0	0	0	0	0	0	0	0
barometric	2	.0000	.0394	26.0	0	0	0	0	0	1	1	0	0	0	0	0	0	0	0	2	0	0	0	0	0	0	0	0	0
baron	13	.4578	1.4350	41.6	0	0	1	0	11	0	1	0	10	0	0	1	0	0	0	0	0	0	0	0	1	0	1	0	0
Baron	22	.5460	2.6142	44.2	0	6	0	1	5	9	1	0	9	2	0	1	0	0	0	0	0	0	0	0	7	0	2	1	0
barons	12	.5337	1.3786	41.4	0	0	0	3	4	4	1	0	3	2	0	3	0	3	1	0	0	0	0	0	0	0	0	0	0
Baroque	33	.3198	2.2584	43.5	0	0	3	0	5	20	0	5	0	0	0	0	0	0	0	0	24	2	0	0	0	0	7	0	0
barque	2	.0000	.0914	29.6	0	0	0	2	0	0	0	0	2	0	0	0	0	0	0	0	0	0	0	0	0	0	0	0	0
barracks	10	.5432	1.1889	40.8	1	2	3	0	1	3	0	0	4	0	0	0	0	1	0	0	0	0	0	0	0	2	1	2	0

3A Bar-K
3K Bar-Tal
4J bar-ley
9M bar-tap
6J Bar-tock
7R Bara
9B Barabino
7K Baranoff
XR Barb-arians
7A barb-wire
5A barba
8F barbaric
9F Barbarossa
9L barbecued
7R BARBECUED
4P barbecues
9D barbell
9N barbeque
5J Barber's
8A barbered
5P barbering
8F barbershops
8Q barbican
3E Barbie
8R Barbra
7Q barbtailed
XR Barcelona
4P Barclay
6R bardic
XH Bare
XR bare-assed
9R bare-knuckled
3H bare-looking
6A bare-sandaled
4P barefooted
7B bares
3A bargain's
9R Bargaining
9Q barge's
XR barged
3P BARGES
9R Barillet
7N Baring
8J baritone-horn
8J baritones
4P bark-covered
4A bark-stickers
8A barkeeper
9J barkers
7N barkin'
6N barley-cakes
XR barley-planting
6E barleycorn
6E barleycorns
7A barlow
XR barman's
4D barn-door
5J barn-raising
9D Barnabas
6R barnacle-encrusted
5P Barnato
9Q Barnave
3J Barnby
4A Barneses
9D Barnett
3A Barney's
5N barnyards
7A baron's
6A Baron's
8Q baroness
7R baroque
3A Barpur
4A Barr

Word Type	F	D	U	SFI	3 Gr 3	4 Gr 4	5 Gr 5	6 Gr 6	7 Gr 7	8 Gr 8	9 Gr 9	X UnGr	A Read	B Eng & Gr	C Comp	D Lit	E Math	F Soc Stud	G Spell	H Sci	J Music	K Art	L Home Ec	M Shop	N Lib F	P Lib NF	Q Lib Ref	R Mag	S Rel
Barracombie	5	.0000	.0537	27.3	0	0	0	0	0	0	5	0	0	0	0	5	0	0	0	0	0	0	0	0	0	0	0	0	0
barracuda	3	.3759	.2471	33.9	0	0	1	0	1	0	1	0	0	1	0	0	0	1	0	0	0	0	0	0	0	0	1	0	0
barrage	6	.5530	.7178	38.6	0	0	0	0	2	2	1	1	2	1	0	1	0	1	0	0	0	0	0	0	0	1	0	0	0
Barrage	2	.0000	.0209	23.2	0	0	0	0	0	2	0	0	0	0	0	0	0	0	0	0	0	0	0	0	0	0	2	0	0
barred	26	.7146	3.8043	45.8	0	3	3	4	6	7	3	0	6	0	1	4	0	4	0	1	0	0	0	0	1	2	3	4	0
barrel	86	.8195	14.181	51.5	11	32	16	6	8	7	6	0	21	3	1	8	1	3	3	8	1	1	0	0	5	26	3	2	0
Barrell	2	.0000	.0290	24.6	0	2	0	0	0	0	0	0	0	0	0	0	0	0	0	0	0	0	0	0	0	2	0	0	0
barrels	54	.8115	8.8007	49.4	9	18	8	8	7	2	2	0	9	7	2	4	3	5	0	3	2	0	0	0	3	11	2	3	0
barren	61	.8207	10.062	50.0	4	7	6	14	17	3	6	4	14	3	2	5	0	10	0	4	3	1	0	0	1	4	10	4	0
barrenness	2	.2441	.1127	30.5	0	0	0	0	2	0	0	0	0	0	0	0	0	0	0	0	0	0	0	0	1	0	1	0	0
Barrett	10	.2763	.7220	38.6	0	0	4	0	0	0	6	0	4	1	0	5	0	0	0	0	0	0	0	0	0	0	0	0	0
barriadas	2	.0000	.0243	23.9	0	0	0	2	0	0	0	0	0	0	0	0	0	0	0	0	0	0	0	0	0	0	0	2	0
barricade	3	.3380	.2439	33.9	0	0	1	0	0	2	0	0	1	1	0	1	0	0	0	0	0	0	0	0	0	0	0	0	0
Barricune	10	.0000	.1073	30.3	0	0	0	0	10	0	0	0	0	0	0	10	0	0	0	0	0	0	0	0	0	0	0	0	0
barrier	47	.7426	7.0305	48.5	5	0	4	7	15	7	8	1	1	1	0	1	1	3	1	8	2	0	0	0	7	6	11	5	0
barrier-reef	3	.0000	.0352	25.5	0	0	0	3	0	0	0	0	0	0	0	0	0	0	0	0	0	0	0	0	3	0	0	0	0
barriers	43	.6381	5.6330	47.5	2	3	9	2	14	2	11	0	1	1	0	2	0	15	0	3	0	1	0	0	2	6	12	0	0
barring	7	.5251	.7942	39.0	0	0	0	3	2	2	0	0	2	0	0	2	0	0	0	0	0	0	0	0	1	1	0	1	0
barrister	2	.2437	.1129	30.5	0	0	1	0	0	1	0	0	0	0	0	0	0	0	0	0	0	0	0	0	0	0	1	1	0
barrow	5	.2542	.3208	35.1	1	1	0	0	3	0	0	0	1	0	0	0	0	0	0	0	0	0	0	0	3	1	0	0	0
Barrow	7	.2334	.5130	37.1	0	0	4	0	0	1	2	0	5	2	0	0	0	0	0	0	0	0	0	0	0	0	0	0	0
Barry	13	.4180	1.2227	40.9	0	1	1	0	11	0	0	0	4	0	2	0	0	0	1	0	0	0	0	0	5	0	0	1	0
bars	187	.8204	30.754	54.9	35	38	35	14	35	13	11	6	33	3	0	10	41	4	2	7	28	0	2	3	17	7	13	17	0
Barsad	8	.0000	.0859	29.3	0	0	0	0	0	0	8	0	0	0	0	8	0	0	0	0	0	0	0	0	0	0	0	0	0
Barske	2	.0000	.0243	23.9	0	0	0	0	0	0	0	2	0	0	0	0	0	0	0	0	0	0	0	0	0	0	0	2	0
Bart	143	.2653	11.995	50.8	10	126	2	1	4	0	0	0	132	0	0	0	2	0	0	0	0	0	0	0	0	4	0	5	0
Bart's	23	.1333	1.4860	41.7	0	23	0	0	0	0	0	0	22	0	0	0	0	0	0	0	0	0	0	0	0	1	0	0	0
Barten	3	.0000	.0583	27.7	0	0	3	0	0	0	0	0	0	0	0	0	0	3	0	0	0	0	0	0	0	0	0	0	0
barter	17	.1414	.6964	38.4	12	0	1	0	1	0	3	0	0	0	0	0	0	3	0	0	0	0	0	0	0	14	0	0	0
bartered	4	.2348	.2372	33.8	0	0	0	0	2	2	0	0	0	0	0	0	0	3	0	0	0	0	0	0	0	0	1	0	0
bartering	2	.1717	.1142	30.6	1	0	0	0	1	0	0	0	1	0	0	1	0	0	0	0	0	0	0	0	0	0	0	0	0
Barth	19	.1625	1.3055	41.2	18	0	0	0	1	0	0	0	18	0	0	0	0	0	0	0	0	0	0	0	0	0	0	1	0
Bartholdi	2	.0000	.0914	29.6	0	0	2	0	0	0	0	0	2	0	0	0	0	0	0	0	0	0	0	0	0	0	0	0	0
Bartholomew	56	.2699	3.4588	45.4	45	4	3	0	0	0	1	3	0	2	0	0	0	1	0	0	0	0	0	0	45	3	2	3	0
Bartholomew's	3	.0000	.0352	25.5	3	0	0	0	0	0	0	0	0	0	0	0	0	0	0	0	0	0	0	0	3	0	0	0	0
Bartlett	5	.3676	.3963	36.0	0	0	0	1	4	0	0	0	0	2	0	2	0	0	0	0	0	0	0	0	0	0	0	1	0
Bartok	12	.0000	.0970	29.9	1	0	2	2	2	5	0	0	0	0	0	0	0	0	0	0	12	0	0	0	0	0	0	0	0
Barton	30	.4752	3.2673	45.1	0	4	9	15	1	1	0	0	14	0	0	0	0	7	0	1	0	0	0	0	7	0	1	0	0
Barton's	3	.2261	.2131	33.3	2	0	0	1	0	0	0	0	2	0	0	0	0	0	0	0	0	0	0	0	1	0	0	0	0
bas-relief	3	.3395	.2468	33.9	0	0	0	0	1	0	1	1	1	0	0	0	0	0	0	0	0	0	0	0	0	1	1	0	0
basal	3	.2445	.1818	32.6	0	0	0	0	0	1	0	2	0	0	0	0	0	0	0	2	0	0	0	0	0	0	1	0	0
basalt	15	.3957	1.3147	41.2	0	0	1	7	4	1	2	0	0	0	0	0	0	0	0	9	0	0	0	0	1	1	4	0	0
Bascom	7	.2326	.5117	37.1	0	0	5	0	2	0	0	0	5	0	0	2	0	0	0	0	0	0	0	0	0	0	0	0	0
base	881	.8170	144.46	61.6	68	145	85	109	174	139	96	65	158	46	44	18	304	22	59	72	5	5	8	16	13	39	35	37	0
Base	19	.5578	2.2956	43.6	5	3	1	2	5	2	0	1	7	0	0	1	0	0	0	1	0	0	0	0	0	5	1	4	0
base-	2	.0000	.0299	24.8	0	1	0	0	0	0	1	0	0	0	0	0	2	0	0	0	0	0	0	0	0	0	0	0	0
base-five	5	.0000	.0748	28.7	0	0	0	3	2	0	0	0	0	0	0	0	5	0	0	0	0	0	0	0	0	0	0	0	0
base-seven	4	.0000	.0599	27.8	0	0	0	0	0	0	4	0	0	0	0	0	4	0	0	0	0	0	0	0	0	0	0	0	0
base-six	2	.0000	.0299	24.8	0	1	0	0	1	0	0	0	0	0	0	0	2	0	0	0	0	0	0	0	0	0	0	0	0
base-ten	17	.0000	.2545	34.1	0	0	0	7	3	0	7	0	0	0	0	0	17	0	0	0	0	0	0	0	0	0	0	0	0
base-twelve	2	.0000	.0299	24.8	0	0	0	0	2	0	0	0	0	0	0	0	2	0	0	0	0	0	0	0	0	0	0	0	0
baseball	322	.9049	57.956	57.6	62	68	34	56	44	28	26	4	97	34	4	16	36	13	6	12	1	1	3	2	12	41	10	34	0
Baseball	8	.4535	.8232	39.2	0	2	2	4	0	0	0	0	3	1	0	0	0	0	0	0	0	0	0	0	0	3	1	0	0
baseball's	8	.3128	.6341	38.0	2	0	1	2	1	0	2	0	3	0	0	0	0	0	0	0	0	0	0	0	0	4	0	1	0
baseballs	9	.4469	.9082	39.6	4	3	1	1	0	0	0	0	3	0	0	0	0	0	0	0	0	0	0	0	0	2	1	3	0
baseboard	9	.1361	.3513	35.5	0	0	0	0	9	0	0	0	0	0	0	0	0	0	0	0	0	0	0	0	0	8	0	1	0
based	361	.7695	55.663	57.5	3	21	52	59	87	72	53	14	18	18	18	7	26	32	2	28	119	4	7	4	0	22	31	25	0
Basel	6	.3871	.5823	37.7	0	0	4	1	0	1	0	0	4	0	0	0	0	0	0	0	0	0	0	0	0	0	1	1	0
baseman	27	.6479	3.6467	45.6	7	1	11	5	1	1	1	0	8	1	1	0	0	0	0	1	0	0	0	0	1	5	6	4	0
basemen	2	.2442	.1134	30.5	0	0	0	2	0	0	0	0	0	1	0	0	0	0	0	0	0	0	0	0	0	0	0	1	0
basement	41	.7291	6.2297	47.9	13	9	5	4	5	3	2	0	23	1	0	1	1	2	3	5	0	0	0	0	2	1	0	2	0
basements	5	.3417	.4014	36.0	1	0	0	2	0	1	1	0	1	0	0	0	0	0	0	2	0	0	0	1	0	0	0	1	0
bases	131	.7694	20.420	53.1	12	16	16	14	18	24	19	12	24	11	1	2	40	4	0	21	0	0	1	0	5	5	9	8	0
Bashar	4	.0000	.0486	26.9	0	0	0	4	0	0	0	0	0	0	0	0	0	0	0	0	0	0	0	0	0	0	0	4	0
basic	517	.8256	84.996	59.3	13	21	59	41	138	86	141	18	11	46	23	8	88	33	8	65	36	2	41	27	1	10	74	44	0
Basic	13	.2897	.8846	39.5	0	3	0	0	3	0	7	0	3	0	0	0	0	0	7	0	0	0	3	0	0	0	0	0	0
basically	54	.8206	8.8312	49.5	1	2	1	4	24	7	12	3	1	4	2	1	0	1	1	10	4	1	1	1	0	3	11	13	0
basil	5	.1610	.1839	32.6	0	0	0	1	1	0	3	0	0	0	0	0	0	0	0	0	0	0	3	0	0	0	2	0	0
Basil	2	.1717	.1142	30.6	0	1	0	0	0	1	0	0	1	0	0	1	0	0	0	0	0	0	0	0	0	0	0	0	0
Basilica	2	.2285	.1129	30.5	0	1	0	0	1	0	0	0	0	0	0	0	0	1	0	0	0	0	0	0	0	0	1	0	0
basin	62	.6440	8.2423	49.2	2	11	13	13	12	2	9	0	3	0	0	6	0	21	0	15	0	0	0	0	9	3	2	3	0
Basin	28	.4047	2.5524	44.1	0	1	6	5	4	2	10	0	1	0	0	1	0	19	0	5	0	0	0	0	0	0	1	1	0
basins	19	.4810	1.9836	43.0	1	3	2	3	5	0	5	0	1	0	0	1	0	7	0	7	0	0	0	0	0	0	3	0	0
Basins	2	.0000	.0389	25.9	0	0	0	2	0	0	0	0	0	0	0	0	0	2	0	0	0	0	0	0	0	0	0	0	0
basis	189	.8791	32.966	55.2	5	5	16	14	56	42	39	12	9	11	5	5	8	19	3	26	17	3	8	4	0	10	39	22	0
bask	4	.3829	.3404	35.3	0	0	0	2	1	1	0	0	0	0	0	0	0	2	0	0	0	0	0	0	0	1	1	0	0
basket	227	.8604	39.209	55.9	90	31	22	27	25	19	7	6	93	10	2	17	9	14	7	4	2	2	1	0	37	19	2	8	0
Basket	4	.0000	.0419	26.2	0	4	0	0	0	0	0	0	0	0	0	0	0	0	0	0	0	0	0	0	0	0	4	0	0
basketball	121	.7683	18.836	52.8	12	17	14	10	29	26	12	1	28	26	3	2	17	5	0	6	0	0	3	0	7	5	1	18	0
Basketball	2	.0000	.0243	23.9	0	0	0	0	0	2	0	0	0	0	0	0	0	0	0	0	0	0	0	0	0	0	0	2	0
basketball's	2	.0000	.0243	23.9	0	1	0	0	0	1	0	0	0	0	0	0	0	0	0	0	0	0	0	0	0	0	0	2	0
basketballs	8	.2890	.5608	37.5	2	4	1	0	1	0	0	0	0	0	0	0	0	1	0	6	0	0	0	0	0	0	0	1	0
basketful	2	.2412	.1141	30.6	1	0	0	0	1	0	0	0	0	1	0	0	0	0	0	0	0	0	0	0	0	1	0	0	0
basketmaker	3	.0000	.0322	25.1	0	0	0	0	3	0	0	0	0	0	0	3	0	0	0	0	0	0	0	0	0	0	0	0	0
basketry	3	.2043	.1486	31.7	1	0	1	0	1	0	0	0	0	0	0	0	0	0	0	0	0	0	0	0	0	1	2	0	0
baskets	113	.8072	18.610	52.7	51	21	9	13	12	6	1	0	61	1	1	5	3	15	1	4	0	1	0	0	5	12	3	1	0
basking	7	.5304	.7988	39.0	0	2	0	0	4	0	1	0	2	0	0	2	0	0	0	0	0	0	0	0	1	0	1	1	0
Basque	3	.2387	.1708	32.3	0	0	1	0	2	0	0	0	0	0	0	0	0	0	0	0	0	0	0	0	0	2	0	0	0
Basra	3	.1639	.1674	32.2	0	0	0	2	1	0	0	0	1	0	0	0	0	2	0	0	0	0	0	0	0	0	0	0	0
bass	157	.4196	14.086	51.5	15	14	9	23	60	21	3	12	12	1	1	11	0	2	0	7	95	0	0	1	0	6	3	18	0
Bass	2	.0000	.0243	23.9	0	0	0	1	0	0	1	0	0	0	0	0	0	0	0	0	0	0	0	0	0	0	0	2	0
Bassanio	12	.0000	.1288	31.1	0	0	0	0	0	0	12	0	0	0	0	12	0	0	0	0	0	0	0	0	0	0	0	0	0
basses	10	.0000	.0808	29.1	0	2	1	1	3	2	1	0	0	0	0	0	0	0	0	0	10	0	0	0	0	0	0	0	0
bassoon	29	.1972	1.3148	41.2	5	7	2	1	10	3	1	0	0	1	1	0	0	0	0	0	26	0	0	0	0	1	0	0	0

7R Barracuda
8R barrages
6F Barranquilla
6G Barrel
7D barrel-flash
6A barrel-making
4H barrelchested
7D Barrens
5A Barrett's
5A Barretts
7A barricaded
6R barricading
7D Barricune's
8G Barrie's
7F Barrier
7H Barringer
6A Barrinish
3Q barrios
5R Barrios
7Q Barro
3P barrowload
6N barrows
9A Bars
6A Bartholdi's
9B Bartholomovich
4J Bartica
7D Bartlett's
9B Barto
7J Bartok's
6F Bartolome
8Q Barulas
9Q Barwalde
7G bas
5P Bas-Ixelles
5A Bascom's
7P baseboards
4N baser
8R bases-loaded
7A basest
7R bash
7P bashful
6A bashfully
7P bashfulness
9L basic-type
XR basics
9K basilica
9B basinet
7N Basinghall
4A basked
4E basket-ball
XH basket-makers
5A basket's
7R basketweave
8D basketwork
6A basques
9D bass-baritone
9D Bassanio's
6P Basses-Pyrenees
9B bassinet
7Q basslike
6P basso
8J bassoon's

Word Type	F	D	U	SFI	3 Gr 3	4 Gr 4	5 Gr 5	6 Gr 6	7 Gr 7	8 Gr 8	9 Gr 9	X UnGr	A Read	B Eng & Gr	C Comp	D Lit	E Math	F Soc Stud	G Spell	H Sci	J Music	K Art	L Home Ec	M Shop	N Lib F	P Lib NF	Q Lib Ref	R Mag	S Rel
bassoonist	2	.0000	.0162	22.1	2	0	0	0	0	0	0	0	0	0	0	0	0	0	0	0	2	0	0	0	0	0	0	0	0
bassoons	12	.0855	.2924	34.7	0	2	2	1	1	3	3	0	0	0	0	0	0	0	0	0	11	0	0	0	0	0	1	0	0
basswood	5	.2727	.3346	35.2	0	2	0	1	0	0	1	1	1	0	0	0	0	0	0	0	0	0	0	1	0	3	0	0	0
bastard	9	.5204	.9680	39.9	0	0	0	0	5	1	2	1	0	0	0	3	0	0	0	0	0	0	0	1	2	2	0	1	0
baste	5	.0908	.1105	30.4	1	0	0	0	1	0	3	0	0	0	0	0	0	0	0	0	0	0	4	0	0	0	1	0	0
basted	3	.2540	.1940	32.9	2	0	0	0	0	0	1	0	1	0	0	0	0	0	0	0	0	0	1	0	0	0	1	0	0
Bastille	7	.2070	.3710	35.7	1	4	0	1	0	0	1	0	1	0	0	1	0	0	0	0	0	0	0	0	0	0	5	0	0
basting	20	.0877	.4252	36.3	1	0	0	1	1	1	16	0	0	0	0	1	0	0	0	0	0	0	17	0	0	0	1	1	0
bastings	4	.0000	.0129	21.1	0	0	0	0	0	0	4	0	0	0	0	0	0	0	0	0	0	0	4	0	0	0	0	0	0
bastnaesite	2	.0000	.0209	23.2	0	0	0	0	2	0	0	0	0	0	0	0	0	0	0	0	0	0	0	0	0	0	2	0	0
bat	264	.8188	43.450	56.4	68	46	30	28	80	5	5	2	61	8	1	31	21	0	11	13	1	0	0	3	32	51	5	26	0
Bat	21	.5618	2.5858	44.1	11	2	0	1	7	0	0	0	11	2	0	5	0	0	0	0	1	0	0	0	1	0	0	1	0
Bat-Poet	2	.0000	.0215	23.3	0	0	0	0	2	0	0	0	0	0	0	2	0	0	0	0	0	0	0	0	0	0	0	0	0
bat's	7	.3157	.4983	37.0	0	0	0	0	6	0	1	0	0	0	0	1	0	0	0	0	0	0	0	0	0	5	1	0	0
Bataan	2	.0000	.0914	29.6	2	0	0	0	0	0	0	0	2	0	0	0	0	0	0	0	0	0	0	0	0	0	0	0	0
batboy	3	.0000	.0583	27.7	3	0	0	0	0	0	0	0	0	0	0	0	0	3	0	0	0	0	0	0	0	0	0	0	0
batch	9	.6206	1.1787	40.7	1	2	1	1	1	1	2	0	3	0	0	1	1	0	0	0	0	0	0	0	1	2	1	0	0
bated	2	.1787	.1174	30.7	0	0	0	2	0	0	0	0	1	0	0	0	0	0	0	0	0	0	0	0	1	0	0	0	0
Bates	36	.4589	3.9835	46.0	27	5	1	0	1	2	0	0	28	0	2	0	0	0	0	0	1	0	0	0	0	4	0	1	0
bath	95	.7610	14.769	51.7	22	14	23	7	14	5	8	2	33	0	0	4	0	1	5	17	0	1	2	0	8	7	0	17	0
bathe	22	.7218	3.2223	45.1	4	1	2	3	6	2	3	1	3	1	0	4	0	1	2	3	0	0	2	0	2	2	2	0	0
bathed	14	.5501	1.7232	42.4	2	2	4	0	5	0	1	0	9	0	0	1	0	0	0	0	1	0	0	0	1	0	0	2	0
bathes	5	.3921	.4234	36.3	0	0	0	1	2	0	2	0	0	1	0	1	0	1	0	1	0	1	0	0	0	0	0	0	0
bathhouse	7	.0000	.1013	30.1	7	0	0	0	0	0	0	0	0	0	0	0	0	0	0	0	0	0	0	0	0	7	0	0	0
bathing	32	.7610	4.9387	46.9	2	1	7	6	7	7	2	0	7	2	1	1	0	4	0	3	0	0	3	0	2	4	2	3	0
batholiths	2	.0000	.0394	26.0	0	0	0	0	0	0	2	0	0	0	0	0	0	0	0	2	0	0	0	0	0	0	0	0	0
bathrobe	8	.3264	.6662	38.2	1	0	0	3	1	1	2	0	4	0	0	3	0	0	0	0	0	0	0	0	0	0	0	1	0
bathroom	42	.7164	6.2194	47.9	12	9	4	5	7	2	2	1	16	0	0	4	0	4	0	3	0	0	0	1	7	1	1	5	0
bathrooms	5	.5365	.5781	37.6	0	1	1	0	2	1	0	0	1	0	0	1	0	1	0	1	0	0	0	0	0	1	0	0	0
baths	18	.6088	2.3176	43.7	7	1	3	0	5	0	1	1	6	1	0	0	0	0	0	0	0	0	0	0	3	3	3	2	0
Bathsheba	2	.0000	.0234	23.7	0	2	0	0	0	0	0	0	0	0	0	0	0	0	0	0	0	0	0	0	2	0	0	0	0
bathtub	28	.7108	4.1618	46.2	4	7	6	3	3	1	3	1	14	1	0	1	0	2	0	6	0	0	0	0	1	1	1	1	0
bathtubs	4	.2390	.2703	34.3	1	0	1	0	1	0	1	0	2	0	0	0	0	0	0	0	0	0	0	1	0	1	0	0	0
Bathurst	4	.3352	.2986	34.8	0	2	0	1	0	0	1	0	0	0	0	0	0	0	0	1	0	0	0	0	0	0	2	1	0
bathyscaphe	12	.0567	.3815	35.8	0	0	9	2	1	0	0	0	1	0	0	0	0	0	0	11	0	0	0	0	0	0	0	0	0
bathysphere	16	.1335	.7831	38.9	4	0	6	6	0	0	0	0	4	0	0	0	0	0	0	12	0	0	0	0	0	0	0	0	0
Batista	3	.1937	.1495	31.7	0	0	0	0	2	1	0	0	0	0	0	0	0	1	0	0	0	0	0	0	0	0	0	2	0
batiste	2	.0000	.0064	18.1	0	0	0	0	0	2	0	0	0	0	0	0	0	0	0	0	0	0	2	0	0	0	0	0	0
baton	11	.3968	.9921	40.0	0	2	0	3	3	3	0	0	3	0	0	0	0	0	0	0	4	0	0	0	0	2	0	2	0
BatonRouge	5	.0000	.0972	29.9	0	0	5	0	0	0	0	0	0	0	0	0	0	5	0	0	0	0	0	0	0	0	0	0	0
batons	3	.2279	.2143	33.3	0	2	0	0	1	0	0	0	2	0	0	0	0	0	0	0	0	0	0	0	0	0	0	1	0
Batouala	2	.0000	.0290	24.6	0	0	0	0	2	0	0	0	0	0	0	0	0	0	0	0	0	0	0	0	0	2	0	0	0
bats	110	.6205	14.146	51.5	13	11	1	25	51	5	0	4	12	2	0	5	0	1	0	14	1	0	0	0	4	46	8	17	0
bats'	2	.1814	.1187	30.7	0	0	0	2	0	0	0	0	1	0	0	0	0	0	0	0	0	0	0	0	0	0	0	1	0
batsman	4	.0919	.1430	31.6	0	0	0	0	1	0	3	0	1	0	0	3	0	0	0	0	0	0	0	0	0	0	0	0	0
Batt's	4	.0000	.0486	26.9	0	0	0	0	0	4	0	0	0	0	0	0	0	0	0	0	0	0	0	0	0	0	0	4	0
battalion	4	.3677	.3659	35.6	0	0	1	0	0	3	0	0	2	0	0	1	0	1	0	0	0	0	0	0	0	0	0	0	0
Battalion	2	.0000	.0389	25.9	0	0	0	0	0	2	0	0	0	0	0	0	0	2	0	0	0	0	0	0	0	0	0	0	0
battalions	3	.2425	.1816	32.6	0	0	0	0	0	1	2	0	0	0	0	0	0	2	0	0	0	0	0	0	0	0	0	1	0
batted	11	.6212	1.4438	41.6	5	1	0	2	3	0	0	0	4	0	0	1	0	0	0	0	1	0	0	0	1	2	0	2	0
Batten	6	.1810	.2817	34.5	0	5	0	0	0	0	1	0	0	1	0	0	0	0	0	0	0	0	0	0	0	5	0	0	0
batter	81	.4823	8.4337	49.3	21	6	11	4	11	5	22	1	21	5	2	4	0	0	0	3	0	0	25	0	5	7	6	3	0
batter's	5	.4161	.4629	36.7	1	1	0	2	0	0	1	0	1	2	0	0	0	0	0	0	0	0	0	0	0	1	1	0	0
battered	33	.7466	5.0806	47.1	3	1	6	5	8	5	4	1	16	3	1	3	0	1	0	2	0	0	0	0	3	2	1	1	0
batteries	39	.6765	5.4278	47.3	8	11	2	5	6	2	0	5	5	0	0	1	2	2	0	11	0	0	0	0	1	6	3	8	0
battering	11	.4862	1.1975	40.8	0	0	1	2	3	2	3	0	5	1	1	0	0	0	0	0	0	0	0	0	0	0	3	1	0
batters	14	.4652	1.4698	41.7	6	2	2	1	1	2	0	0	5	0	0	0	0	0	1	1	0	0	0	0	0	6	0	1	0
battery	91	.6856	12.794	51.1	13	22	7	9	11	11	4	14	12	0	0	4	1	2	2	26	0	0	0	6	5	22	2	9	0
Battery	3	.0000	.0434	26.4	1	0	0	2	0	0	0	0	0	0	0	0	0	0	0	0	0	0	0	0	0	3	0	0	0
battery-operated	2	.2285	.1129	30.5	1	0	0	0	0	0	1	0	0	0	0	0	0	1	0	0	0	0	0	0	0	0	1	0	0
battery-powered	3	.2159	.1532	31.9	0	0	0	1	0	0	2	0	0	0	0	0	0	0	0	0	0	0	0	0	0	0	2	1	0
batting	50	.6888	7.0981	48.5	13	9	2	11	14	0	1	0	12	1	0	1	8	0	0	2	0	1	0	0	4	12	0	9	0
battle	285	.7893	45.564	56.6	24	40	43	43	65	42	22	6	80	12	0	30	0	47	1	5	9	0	0	0	17	37	23	23	1
Battle	49	.7225	7.2124	48.6	0	6	8	6	8	15	3	3	9	5	0	1	0	10	0	1	5	1	0	0	4	0	11	2	0
battle-ax	2	.0000	.0914	29.6	0	0	0	2	0	0	0	0	2	0	0	0	0	0	0	0	0	0	0	0	0	0	0	0	0
battled	19	.6370	2.5513	44.1	1	3	6	2	2	4	1	0	6	0	0	1	0	5	0	1	0	0	0	0	2	1	0	3	0
battlefield	19	.6107	2.4521	43.9	0	2	1	4	4	6	2	0	6	1	0	4	0	2	0	0	0	0	0	0	1	1	0	4	0
battlefields	8	.5390	.9335	39.7	0	1	2	0	3	2	0	0	2	0	0	0	0	3	0	0	0	0	0	0	0	1	1	1	0
Battlefields	2	.0000	.0914	29.6	0	1	1	0	0	0	0	0	2	0	0	0	0	0	0	0	0	0	0	0	0	0	0	0	0
battleground	6	.2773	.4266	36.3	0	0	1	3	2	0	0	0	1	0	0	0	0	4	0	0	0	0	0	0	0	1	0	0	0
battlements	5	.4483	.4754	36.8	0	0	0	1	2	1	1	0	0	0	0	1	0	1	0	0	0	0	0	0	0	0	2	1	0
battler	2	.2433	.1158	30.6	1	0	0	0	0	0	0	1	0	0	0	0	0	0	0	0	0	0	0	0	0	1	0	1	0
battles	71	.7928	11.398	50.6	4	8	19	13	12	15	0	0	19	3	1	2	0	19	0	1	1	1	0	0	2	10	9	3	0
Battles	3	.2425	.1816	32.6	0	0	0	0	1	2	0	0	0	0	0	0	0	2	0	0	0	0	0	0	0	0	0	1	0
battleship	9	.4991	.9694	39.9	0	0	1	2	2	2	2	0	1	1	0	0	0	4	0	0	0	0	0	0	0	1	0	2	0
battleships	7	.5596	.8579	39.3	0	1	1	2	0	1	1	1	3	0	0	0	0	1	0	1	0	0	0	0	1	0	0	1	0
battling	9	.4510	.8684	39.4	0	1	1	1	3	2	1	0	1	0	1	4	0	0	0	0	0	0	0	0	2	1	0	0	0
Bauer	2	.2412	.1091	30.4	0	0	1	0	0	0	1	0	0	0	0	1	0	0	1	0	0	0	0	0	0	0	0	0	0
Baugh	4	.0000	.0486	26.9	0	0	0	4	0	0	0	0	0	0	0	0	0	0	0	0	0	0	0	0	0	0	0	4	0
Baumer	8	.0000	.0859	29.3	0	0	0	0	0	0	8	0	0	0	0	8	0	0	0	0	0	0	0	0	0	0	0	0	0
Baumer's	2	.0000	.0215	23.3	0	0	0	0	0	0	2	0	0	0	0	2	0	0	0	0	0	0	0	0	0	0	0	0	0
Bautista	2	.0000	.0389	25.9	0	0	0	0	1	1	0	0	0	0	0	0	0	2	0	0	0	0	0	0	0	0	0	0	0
bauxite	19	.3800	1.6266	42.1	3	0	5	2	7	2	0	0	1	0	0	0	0	13	0	0	0	0	0	2	0	0	3	0	0
Bavaria	3	.2444	.1814	32.6	0	0	0	0	1	0	2	0	0	0	0	0	0	2	0	0	0	0	0	0	0	0	1	0	0
Bavarian	5	.4391	.4860	36.9	0	0	1	0	2	1	0	1	1	0	0	0	0	0	0	0	0	0	0	0	0	2	1	1	0
bawl	7	.5460	.8195	39.1	3	2	0	0	1	1	0	0	2	0	0	1	0	0	0	0	1	0	0	0	1	2	0	0	0
bawled	5	.3410	.4178	36.2	0	2	0	0	3	0	0	0	2	0	0	1	0	0	0	0	0	0	0	0	2	0	0	0	0
bawling	4	.3071	.2967	34.7	0	0	0	1	2	1	0	0	1	0	0	1	0	0	0	0	0	0	0	0	2	0	0	0	0
Bawtry	4	.0000	.0579	27.6	0	4	0	0	0	0	0	0	0	0	0	0	0	0	0	0	0	0	0	0	0	4	0	0	0
Baxter	11	.0939	.3224	35.1	0	1	0	0	10	0	0	0	0	0	0	0	0	0	0	0	0	0	0	0	10	1	0	0	0
Baxters	4	.1826	.1841	32.7	0	1	0	0	3	0	0	0	0	0	0	0	0	0	0	0	0	0	0	0	3	1	0	0	0
bay	121	.7701	18.847	52.8	13	23	21	25	17	13	5	4	20	3	1	7	0	24	1	2	1	0	0	0	16	21	6	19	0
Bay	169	.7444	25.659	54.1	18	7	55	25	27	21	12	4	35	2	1	1	6	54	0	8	5	0	0	0	3	13	14	27	0
Bay's	2	.0000	.0243	23.9	0	0	0	0	1	0	1	0	0	0	0	0	0	0	0	0	0	0	0	0	0	0	0	2	0

6R Basswood
6A basta
9R Bastile
7P bastions
6F Basutoland
6P BAT
7Q bat-eared
XD batata
7R batches
7L bateau
3J Bateau
7R bath's
9H batholith
7R bathos
9L bathrobes
5H bathy
7A bathyscaphes
9H bathyscaphs
5H bathyspheres
6H bathythermographs
9R Batman
7R Baton
XH Batrachium
7N batten
3A battened
9B battercakes
6A batterings
8D battery's
7Q batterylike
7R Battey
4J battin'
8R Battista
8F battle-field
9R battle-hardened
3A battle-lit
7N battle-scarred
8N battle-viewing
3A battle's
9R battlefronts
8F battlegrounds
6A battleships'
6A battlewise
7R Batts
9F Batu
7N Batulcar's
4Q bauble
5Q Baudelaire
7J Baum
5F Bauxite
4N Baviaan
9R bawdiness
7N bawdkin
7N bawdricks
7R bawdy
7N Baxter's
4E BayCity
7Q bay-breasted
7N bay-head
6R bay's

Word Type	F	D	U	SFI	3 Gr 3	4 Gr 4	5 Gr 5	6 Gr 6	7 Gr 7	8 Gr 8	9 Gr 9	X UnGr	A Read	B Eng & Gr	C Comp	D Lit	E Math	F Soc Stud	G Spell	H Sci	J Music	K Art	L Home Ec	M Shop	N Lib F	P Lib NF	Q Lib Ref	R Mag	S Rel
Baya	11	.0000	.2139	33.3	0	11	0	0	0	0	0	0	0	0	0	0	0	11	0	0	0	0	0	0	0	0	0	0	0
Bayard	3	.0000	.1370	31.4	0	0	0	3	0	0	0	0	3	0	0	0	0	0	0	0	0	0	0	0	0	0	0	0	0
bayberry	2	.0000	.0914	29.6	0	0	1	0	1	0	0	0	2	0	0	0	0	0	0	0	0	0	0	0	0	0	0	0	0
Bayeux	2	.0000	.0037	15.7	0	0	0	0	0	2	0	0	0	0	0	0	0	0	0	0	0	2	0	0	0	0	0	0	0
Bayezit	2	.0000	.0290	24.6	0	0	2	0	0	0	0	0	0	0	0	0	0	0	0	0	0	0	0	0	0	2	0	0	0
baying	3	.2076	.1697	32.3	1	0	0	0	1	0	1	0	1	0	1	0	0	0	0	0	0	0	0	0	1	0	0	0	0
Baylor	2	.0000	.0243	23.9	0	0	0	0	0	2	0	0	0	0	0	0	0	0	0	0	0	0	0	0	0	0	0	2	0
bayonet	5	.3530	.4326	36.4	0	0	4	0	1	0	0	0	2	0	0	0	0	0	0	0	0	0	0	0	0	2	0	1	0
bayonets	7	.5061	.7599	38.8	1	0	2	0	1	2	1	0	1	0	0	1	0	1	0	0	0	0	0	0	0	2	0	2	0
Bayonne	4	.2420	.3089	34.9	0	3	1	0	0	0	0	0	3	0	0	0	0	1	0	0	0	0	0	0	0	0	0	0	0
bayou	3	.2261	.2131	33.3	1	0	0	1	0	1	0	0	2	0	0	0	0	0	0	0	0	0	0	0	1	0	0	0	0
bays	23	.6661	3.1494	45.0	8	4	2	5	0	1	2	1	2	1	1	0	0	8	0	3	0	0	0	0	0	2	3	3	0
Bayside	2	.0000	.0243	23.9	0	0	0	2	0	0	0	0	0	0	0	0	0	0	0	0	0	0	0	0	0	0	0	2	0
bazaar	4	.3688	.3668	35.6	0	3	0	0	0	0	1	0	2	1	0	0	0	1	0	0	0	0	0	0	0	0	0	0	0
bazaars	3	.2279	.2143	33.3	0	0	0	2	1	0	0	0	2	0	0	0	0	0	0	0	0	0	0	0	0	0	0	1	0
bb	2	.0000	.0162	22.1	0	0	0	0	1	1	0	0	0	0	0	0	0	0	2	0	0	0	0	0	0	0	0	0	0
BB	2	.2398	.1138	30.6	0	0	0	0	0	1	1	0	0	0	0	1	1	0	0	0	0	0	0	0	0	0	0	0	0
bbl	3	.0000	.0365	25.6	0	0	0	0	0	0	3	0	0	0	0	0	0	0	0	0	0	0	0	0	0	0	0	3	0
bc	6	.0000	.0898	29.5	0	0	2	0	2	2	0	0	0	0	0	0	6	0	0	0	0	0	0	0	0	0	0	0	0
BC	53	.2189	2.8795	44.6	2	3	10	10	7	14	7	0	0	1	0	0	49	0	0	0	0	0	0	1	0	0	2	0	0
BD	12	.2286	.6680	38.2	0	0	2	5	1	2	2	0	0	0	0	0	11	0	0	0	0	0	0	1	0	0	0	0	0
be	23746	.9732	4554.0	76.6	3331	3370	2737	2950	4657	3211	2863	627	5144	1674	240	1203	1668	1996	671	2604	864	223	964	728	1322	1774	1128	1521	22
Be	9	.4411	.8345	39.2	1	0	0	4	1	3	0	0	0	2	0	0	0	0	0	0	3	0	0	0	0	1	0	3	0
BE	7	.1213	.2377	33.8	0	0	0	0	3	4	0	0	0	6	0	0	1	0	0	0	0	0	0	0	0	0	0	0	0
beach	308	.8508	52.711	57.2	67	43	31	57	58	39	5	8	130	14	5	24	6	18	6	15	0	10	1	1	28	18	5	27	0
Beach	49	.5859	6.3845	48.1	19	0	6	0	1	21	2	0	35	0	0	2	0	3	0	0	0	0	0	0	1	3	1	4	0
beached	5	.3833	.4767	36.8	1	0	0	2	2	0	0	0	3	0	0	1	0	0	0	0	0	0	0	0	0	1	0	0	0
beaches	63	.7070	9.0991	49.6	10	6	15	7	15	6	3	1	8	5	0	2	0	16	1	4	0	0	0	0	0	11	8	8	0
beachhead	3	.3815	.2534	34.0	0	0	0	0	2	1	0	0	0	0	0	0	0	1	0	0	0	0	0	0	0	1	0	1	0
beacon	15	.5432	1.7416	42.4	2	0	0	2	5	4	1	1	4	0	2	0	0	1	0	2	0	1	0	0	3	0	0	2	0
beacons	2	.1814	.1187	30.7	0	0	0	0	1	0	0	1	1	0	0	0	0	0	0	0	0	0	0	0	0	0	0	1	0
bead	24	.4105	2.3231	43.7	5	0	0	0	5	3	10	1	8	0	0	0	2	0	0	12	0	0	0	0	0	0	0	2	0
Bead	7	.0000	.1380	31.4	0	7	0	0	0	0	0	0	0	0	0	0	0	0	0	7	0	0	0	0	0	0	0	0	0
beaded	3	.3870	.2492	34.0	0	1	0	1	1	0	0	0	0	0	0	0	0	0	0	0	0	0	0	0	1	0	1	1	0
beading	2	.1483	.0728	28.6	0	0	0	0	0	1	0	1	0	0	0	0	0	0	0	0	0	0	0	1	0	1	0	0	0
Beadle	3	.0000	.0591	27.7	0	0	0	0	0	0	3	0	0	0	0	0	0	0	0	3	0	0	0	0	0	0	0	0	0
beads	143	.7483	21.896	53.4	41	16	30	7	11	9	26	3	44	4	0	0	41	6	1	14	0	2	0	2	13	13	0	3	0
beadwork	3	.3553	.2608	34.2	0	0	1	0	1	0	0	1	1	0	0	0	0	1	0	0	0	0	0	0	0	1	0	0	0
beady	7	.5039	.7569	38.8	2	2	1	1	1	0	0	0	1	0	0	1	0	0	0	1	0	0	0	0	2	2	0	0	0
beagle	7	.3622	.6365	38.0	4	1	1	0	0	1	0	0	4	2	0	0	0	0	0	0	0	0	0	0	0	0	0	1	0
Beagle	12	.1673	.5139	37.1	0	0	0	10	0	0	2	0	0	2	0	0	0	0	0	0	0	0	0	0	0	0	0	10	0
beak	48	.6350	6.4867	48.1	22	10	6	2	4	1	0	3	21	2	0	3	0	0	0	8	0	0	0	0	3	10	1	0	0
beaker	27	.1105	1.0760	40.3	1	2	1	0	6	10	4	3	1	0	0	0	0	0	0	25	0	0	0	0	1	0	0	0	0
beakers	4	.0000	.0789	29.0	1	1	0	0	0	2	0	0	0	0	0	0	0	0	0	4	0	0	0	0	0	0	0	0	0
beaks	29	.4235	2.7302	44.4	16	4	3	2	4	0	0	0	5	0	0	0	0	1	0	6	0	4	0	0	0	10	3	0	0
Beale	2	.0000	.0914	29.6	0	0	0	2	0	0	0	0	2	0	0	0	0	0	0	0	0	0	0	0	0	0	0	0	0
Beall	2	.0000	.0914	29.6	0	0	0	0	2	0	0	0	2	0	0	0	0	0	0	0	0	0	0	0	0	0	0	0	0
beam	135	.7458	20.513	53.1	12	7	26	36	12	26	9	7	25	0	3	2	2	2	0	58	3	0	0	2	10	4	11	13	0
beamed	24	.5542	2.8939	44.6	5	5	3	5	4	1	0	1	10	2	0	1	0	0	0	1	0	0	0	0	6	0	0	4	0
beaming	11	.2320	.7110	38.5	2	2	1	2	0	1	2	1	4	0	0	0	0	0	0	1	0	0	0	0	6	0	0	0	0
beamish	2	.1458	.0682	28.3	0	0	1	1	0	0	0	0	0	1	0	0	0	0	0	0	0	1	0	0	0	0	0	0	0
beams	66	.6365	8.6898	49.4	8	2	3	24	8	5	13	3	12	3	2	5	0	0	0	12	0	0	0	7	0	2	4	19	0
bean	88	.5987	11.162	50.5	47	12	6	6	7	6	1	3	18	1	0	1	1	2	1	40	2	0	0	0	3	18	0	1	0
Bean	12	.4573	1.2745	41.1	3	5	0	2	2	0	0	0	6	0	0	0	0	2	0	0	0	0	0	0	1	0	0	3	0
beanbag	6	.2437	.4554	36.6	0	1	1	4	0	0	0	0	4	0	0	0	0	0	0	2	0	0	0	0	0	0	0	0	0
Beanery	2	.0000	.0037	15.7	0	0	0	0	0	2	0	0	0	0	0	0	0	0	0	0	0	2	0	0	0	0	0	0	0
beans	199	.7787	31.459	55.0	70	31	21	20	28	12	14	3	55	8	0	9	5	33	2	25	0	0	13	0	24	9	10	6	0
beanstalk	2	.1698	.1133	30.5	1	0	1	0	0	0	0	0	1	0	0	0	0	0	0	0	0	0	0	0	0	0	1	0	0
Beanstalk	2	.1733	.1149	30.6	1	0	1	0	0	0	0	0	1	1	0	0	0	0	0	0	0	0	0	0	0	0	0	0	0
bear	557	.8586	96.009	59.8	116	85	108	71	109	35	24	9	225	25	7	69	3	20	9	23	8	2	2	0	65	46	28	25	0
Bear	130	.6075	17.243	52.4	53	38	11	4	4	18	0	2	84	0	0	21	2	3	1	2	3	0	0	0	4	1	0	9	0
bear's	21	.5830	2.6336	44.2	3	3	6	0	8	0	0	1	9	0	0	2	0	0	0	0	0	1	0	0	5	2	0	2	0
Bear's	4	.0919	.1430	31.6	1	0	0	0	2	1	0	0	1	0	0	3	0	0	0	0	0	0	0	0	0	0	0	0	0
bearable	3	.3369	.2489	34.0	0	0	2	0	1	0	0	0	1	0	0	1	0	1	0	0	0	0	0	0	0	0	0	0	0
Bearcat	49	.0000	2.2384	43.5	0	0	0	0	0	49	0	0	49	0	0	0	0	0	0	0	0	0	0	0	0	0	0	0	0
Bearcats	2	.0000	.0914	29.6	0	0	0	0	0	2	0	0	2	0	0	0	0	0	0	0	0	0	0	0	0	0	0	0	0
beard	89	.7173	13.217	51.2	20	12	13	8	15	8	12	1	39	4	2	14	0	2	0	0	1	0	0	0	9	13	1	4	0
bearded	22	.5781	2.6386	44.2	0	2	4	3	1	8	2	2	1	1	0	5	0	3	0	0	0	0	0	0	1	7	0	4	0
beards	12	.5352	1.4584	41.6	0	1	1	3	2	4	1	0	8	0	0	1	0	1	0	0	0	0	0	0	0	1	0	1	0
bearer	6	.3708	.4846	36.9	0	1	1	0	3	1	0	0	0	0	0	2	0	0	0	0	0	0	0	0	0	3	1	0	0
bearers	11	.5199	1.1851	40.7	0	0	0	3	3	2	3	0	0	1	0	2	0	0	0	2	3	0	0	0	0	0	3	0	0
bearing	57	.8023	9.1797	49.6	2	3	7	9	19	7	8	2	7	3	1	3	0	4	0	5	0	0	0	1	9	9	5	10	0
bearings	23	.7331	3.4132	45.3	0	1	3	2	14	0	3	0	2	1	0	0	1	1	1	4	0	0	0	1	1	2	2	7	0
bears	195	.8288	32.582	55.1	57	22	32	25	31	8	10	10	69	8	3	6	1	20	5	9	4	1	0	0	13	19	16	20	1
Bears	23	.4613	2.3070	43.6	12	4	2	1	2	0	2	0	4	1	0	2	0	1	0	0	0	0	0	0	11	0	0	4	0
bears'	4	.3057	.2921	34.7	1	1	0	0	1	1	0	0	1	0	1	0	1	0	0	0	0	0	0	0	1	0	0	0	0
Bears'	3	.2227	.1589	32.0	2	0	0	0	1	0	0	0	0	0	0	0	0	0	0	0	0	0	0	0	2	0	0	1	0
bearskin	9	.4675	.9391	39.7	2	2	1	2	2	0	0	0	3	0	0	2	0	0	0	0	0	0	0	0	2	2	0	0	0
beast	103	.8170	17.056	52.3	17	16	8	28	18	8	6	2	48	3	2	12	0	1	2	3	2	1	0	0	11	12	3	3	0
Beast	2	.2375	.1088	30.4	0	0	0	0	1	0	0	1	0	0	0	0	0	0	0	0	1	0	0	0	0	0	0	1	0
beast's	2	.0000	.0914	29.6	0	0	0	2	0	0	0	0	2	0	0	0	0	0	0	0	0	0	0	0	0	0	0	0	0
beastly	3	.0000	.1370	31.4	0	0	0	2	0	1	0	0	3	0	0	0	0	0	0	0	0	0	0	0	0	0	0	0	0
beasts	70	.7673	10.960	50.4	11	15	15	11	9	2	1	6	24	0	0	5	0	6	0	6	1	1	0	0	9	12	2	4	0
Beasts	3	.2028	.1988	33.0	1	0	0	0	1	0	1	0	2	0	0	0	0	0	0	0	1	0	0	0	0	0	0	0	0
beat	540	.7272	79.587	59.0	80	88	85	68	96	53	63	7	97	18	2	42	6	8	5	28	190	3	31	6	34	28	9	33	0
beaten	71	.7314	10.643	50.3	7	13	8	9	14	6	12	2	23	1	1	7	0	8	0	0	0	0	6	0	7	10	4	4	0
beater	18	.1073	.4895	36.9	1	0	0	0	5	1	11	0	1	0	0	0	0	0	0	0	1	0	14	0	0	0	0	2	0
beaters	9	.5639	1.0678	40.3	0	0	1	2	4	1	1	0	2	0	0	1	0	0	0	0	1	0	1	0	1	0	0	3	0
beating	127	.7899	20.311	53.1	19	18	20	26	20	7	13	4	37	2	2	12	0	3	0	21	6	0	8	0	17	12	3	4	0
beatings	5	.0824	.1675	32.2	0	0	0	0	2	1	2	0	1	0	0	0	0	0	0	0	0	0	0	0	0	0	0	4	0
Beatle	3	.0000	.0365	25.6	0	0	1	0	0	1	1	0	0	0	0	0	0	0	0	0	0	0	0	0	0	0	0	3	0
Beatles	2	.0000	.0243	23.9	0	0	2	0	0	0	0	0	0	0	0	0	0	0	0	0	0	0	0	0	0	0	0	2	0
Beatrice	10	.5812	1.1970	40.8	1	1	1	0	4	1	2	0	0	0	0	3	1	2	0	0	0	0	0	0	1	0	2	1	0
beats	210	.3498	15.901	52.0	62	28	35	19	30	7	28	1	4	0	1	3	5	0	0	28	148	0	6	0	3	7	2	3	0

4F Baya's
7N bayed
9Q Bayliss
8R Baylor's
6A bayous
7J Bayreuth
8C Bazaar
5P bazooka
7E BCA
5E BCD
5E BCGF
8R BCS**
8R BCS'**
7R BD-1
7R BD-4
7R BD-4's
8E BDC
8R be-in
9D be'st
9B Beachcombers
8R beachfront
7P beachheads
6R beachside
9B Beacon
7N bead-rings
9D beadbonny
8D Beads
3A Beady
3A Beady-Eyes
3A beady-eyed
8R beadyeyed
6R Beagle's
8B beagles
4J beaked
3P beakfuls
9M beakhorn
8B beaklike
8B beal
6A Beale's
9M Beam
3A BEAN
3A bean-bag
XP bean-hole
7A bean-picker
9Q bean-root
6H bean-shooters
3A Bean's
9A beanburgers
7A beanings
6Q bear-berry
4A bear-fighting
6J Bearer
5Q Bearers
9M Bearing
7D bearlike
4A bearskins
7A Beaseley
4H beat-beat-beat
9N beat-up
9D beatified
9D beatifying
6R Beatles'
7D Beatrice's

Word Type	F	D	U	SFI	Gr 3	Gr 4	Gr 5	Gr 6	Gr 7	Gr 8	Gr 9	UnGr	A Read	B Eng & Gr	C Comp	D Lit	E Math	F Soc Stud	G Spell	H Sci	J Music	K Art	L Home Ec	M Shop	N Lib F	P Lib NF	Q Lib Ref	R Mag	S Rel
beau	3	.3824	.2446	33.9	0	0	0	1	2	0	0	0	0	0	0	1	0	0	0	0	1	0	0	0	0	0	0	1	0
Beau	4	.2424	.3036	34.8	0	0	0	1	1	2	0	0	3	0	0	0	0	0	0	0	0	0	0	0	0	0	0	1	0
Beaubrun	2	.0000	.0243	23.9	0	0	2	0	0	0	0	0	0	0	0	0	0	0	0	0	0	0	0	0	0	0	0	2	0
Beaufort	2	.2401	.1133	30.5	1	0	0	0	0	1	0	0	0	0	0	0	0	0	0	0	0	0	0	0	0	1	1	0	0
Beaujeu	3	.0000	.0434	26.4	0	3	0	0	0	0	0	0	0	0	0	0	0	0	0	0	0	0	0	0	0	3	0	0	0
Beaumont	12	.4043	1.0570	40.2	0	0	0	0	0	0	7	5	0	0	0	1	0	0	0	5	0	0	0	0	0	0	5	1	0
Beauregard	10	.0000	.1945	32.9	0	0	0	0	0	10	0	0	0	0	0	0	0	10	0	0	0	0	0	0	0	0	0	0	0
beauties	13	.5879	1.5941	42.0	0	2	3	1	2	2	0	3	2	0	1	0	0	1	0	0	1	0	0	0	0	3	1	4	0
beautified	2	.1840	.0808	29.1	0	0	0	0	1	0	1	0	0	0	1	0	0	0	1	0	0	0	0	0	0	0	0	0	0
beautiful	1048	.8585	180.38	62.6	288	161	132	158	135	91	54	29	368	37	7	52	1	147	9	42	90	45	10	9	57	82	30	58	4
Beautiful	17	.5121	1.8426	42.7	5	2	1	2	1	3	2	1	2	1	0	0	0	3	1	0	5	0	0	0	0	0	0	5	0
beautifully	56	.8379	9.4271	49.7	3	9	8	9	11	4	11	1	20	3	2	3	0	2	0	0	3	2	2	1	4	5	8	1	0
beautify	4	.3491	.3066	34.9	0	0	2	1	1	0	0	0	0	2	0	0	0	1	1	0	0	0	0	0	0	0	0	0	0
beauty	330	.8289	54.815	57.4	43	37	46	44	51	65	32	12	71	13	3	24	3	42	1	11	46	20	8	6	9	25	20	28	0
Beauty	106	.2163	5.6249	47.5	2	3	3	2	91	0	4	1	6	0	0	3	0	0	0	0	4	0	0	0	89	0	1	3	0
Beauty's	6	.2445	.3343	35.2	0	0	0	0	5	0	1	0	0	0	1	0	0	0	0	0	0	0	0	0	5	0	0	0	0
beaver	96	.7814	15.393	51.9	26	12	15	15	16	8	4	0	51	1	2	4	0	7	0	12	3	0	0	0	3	5	2	6	0
Beaver	34	.4788	3.5421	45.5	13	7	0	4	9	1	0	0	7	1	0	0	0	0	0	0	0	0	0	0	11	7	0	8	0
beaver-swamp	2	.0000	.0234	23.7	0	2	0	0	0	0	0	0	0	0	0	0	0	0	0	0	0	0	0	0	2	0	0	0	0
beaver's	5	.1496	.2557	34.1	2	1	0	2	0	0	0	0	2	0	0	0	0	0	0	0	0	0	0	0	0	0	0	3	0
Beaver's	7	.1288	.2510	34.0	1	0	0	0	6	0	0	0	0	0	0	0	0	0	0	0	0	0	0	0	6	1	0	0	0
beavers	43	.6618	5.9657	47.8	6	11	4	14	2	4	2	0	15	0	0	0	0	3	3	7	0	0	0	0	0	8	2	5	0
Beavers	24	.0000	.3474	35.4	24	0	0	0	0	0	0	0	0	0	0	0	0	0	0	0	0	0	0	0	0	24	0	0	0
Beavers'	5	.0000	.0724	28.6	5	0	0	0	0	0	0	0	0	0	0	0	0	0	0	0	0	0	0	0	0	5	0	0	0
Beban	2	.0000	.0243	23.9	0	0	0	0	2	0	0	0	0	0	0	0	0	0	0	0	0	0	0	0	0	0	0	2	0
Bebrycians	3	.0000	.1370	31.4	0	0	0	3	0	0	0	0	3	0	0	0	0	0	0	0	0	0	0	0	0	0	0	0	0
became	1501	.8155	246.38	63.9	153	182	271	228	285	241	111	30	342	46	12	50	19	318	29	82	110	8	2	3	50	128	206	87	9
because	4207	.9833	814.42	69.1	634	657	498	502	801	522	458	135	977	231	54	191	181	522	95	525	129	37	134	49	251	318	217	290	6
Beck	2	.1787	.1174	30.7	1	0	1	0	0	0	0	0	1	0	0	0	0	0	0	0	0	0	0	0	1	0	0	0	0
Becker	17	.3114	1.4090	41.5	9	8	0	0	0	0	0	0	8	0	0	0	0	8	0	0	0	0	0	0	0	1	0	0	0
Beckers	2	.2152	.1357	31.3	1	1	0	0	0	0	0	0	1	0	0	0	0	1	0	0	0	0	0	0	0	0	0	0	0
Becket's	2	.2375	.1088	30.4	0	1	1	0	0	0	0	0	0	0	0	0	0	0	0	0	1	0	0	0	0	0	0	1	0
Beckett	7	.1420	.2661	34.3	6	0	0	0	0	0	0	1	0	0	0	0	0	0	0	0	0	0	0	0	6	0	0	1	0
Beckie	5	.0000	.2284	33.6	5	0	0	0	0	0	0	0	5	0	0	0	0	0	0	0	0	0	0	0	0	0	0	0	0
Beckmesser	5	.0000	.0404	26.1	0	0	0	5	0	0	0	0	0	0	0	0	0	0	0	0	5	0	0	0	0	0	0	0	0
beckoned	11	.6772	1.5438	41.9	1	2	0	5	1	2	0	0	3	1	0	0	0	2	1	0	0	0	0	0	1	2	0	1	0
beckoning	8	.5496	.9497	39.8	0	0	2	2	2	2	0	0	3	1	0	1	0	0	0	0	1	0	0	0	2	0	0	0	0
Becky	29	.4405	2.9183	44.7	8	5	0	1	14	1	0	0	11	1	0	0	0	0	0	1	0	0	0	0	12	3	0	1	0
Becky's	3	.3380	.2498	34.0	1	0	0	1	1	0	0	0	1	1	0	0	0	0	0	1	0	0	0	0	0	0	0	0	0
become	1304	.9476	244.10	63.9	133	166	159	170	278	178	176	44	197	70	11	53	14	190	28	250	56	17	45	16	31	103	111	109	3
becomes	475	.8727	82.481	59.2	74	49	45	44	117	69	59	18	36	8	10	7	15	45	13	166	36	3	13	17	2	41	25	38	0
Becomes	2	.0000	.0914	29.6	0	0	0	2	0	0	0	0	2	0	0	0	0	0	0	0	0	0	0	0	0	0	0	0	0
becoming	194	.7804	30.547	54.8	16	11	23	22	55	34	27	6	38	6	4	6	0	20	2	23	6	2	24	0	5	18	21	19	0
Becquerel	5	.0000	.0986	29.9	0	0	0	0	0	3	2	0	0	0	0	0	0	0	0	5	0	0	0	0	0	0	0	0	0
bed	841	.8623	145.50	61.6	214	152	92	98	136	66	68	15	349	30	18	95	9	24	11	19	13	0	22	1	111	89	8	41	1
bed's	2	.2443	.1130	30.5	0	0	0	0	2	0	0	0	0	0	0	1	0	0	0	0	0	0	0	0	1	0	0	0	0
bedbugs	2	.2433	.1158	30.6	1	0	1	0	0	0	0	0	0	0	0	0	0	0	0	0	0	0	0	0	0	1	0	1	0
BEDC	5	.0000	.0608	27.8	0	0	0	0	0	5	0	0	0	0	0	0	0	0	0	0	0	0	0	0	0	0	0	5	0
bedclothes	6	.4143	.5639	37.5	1	1	1	1	1	0	1	0	2	0	0	1	0	0	0	0	0	0	1	0	2	0	0	0	0
bedded	4	.3713	.3634	35.6	0	1	0	1	0	1	1	0	2	0	0	1	0	0	0	0	0	0	0	0	1	0	0	0	0
bedding	23	.6837	3.2518	45.1	3	4	3	4	6	3	0	0	7	0	1	3	0	0	1	1	0	0	0	0	3	5	2	0	0
Bede	10	.1882	.4657	36.7	0	0	0	0	10	0	0	0	0	0	0	0	0	0	0	0	0	0	0	0	0	0	2	8	0
bedecked	6	.4673	.6058	37.8	1	2	0	1	0	1	1	0	1	0	1	1	0	1	0	0	0	0	0	0	0	1	1	0	0
Bedelia	25	.0000	1.1421	40.6	0	25	0	0	0	0	0	0	25	0	0	0	0	0	0	0	0	0	0	0	0	0	0	0	0
Bedell	4	.2708	.2760	34.4	0	0	2	1	0	1	0	0	1	0	0	2	0	1	0	0	0	0	0	0	0	0	0	0	0
Bedells	2	.0000	.0215	23.3	0	0	2	0	0	0	0	0	0	0	0	2	0	0	0	0	0	0	0	0	0	0	0	0	0
Bedford	2	.2412	.1141	30.6	0	1	0	0	1	0	0	0	0	1	0	0	0	0	0	0	0	0	0	0	0	1	0	0	0
bedlam	8	.2848	.5783	37.6	0	0	1	1	2	1	3	0	3	0	2	0	0	0	0	0	0	0	0	0	0	2	0	1	0
Bedloe's	3	.2357	.2199	33.4	0	0	1	2	0	0	0	0	2	0	0	0	0	0	0	0	0	0	0	0	0	1	0	0	0
Bedlow	2	.0000	.0914	29.6	0	0	0	2	0	0	0	0	2	0	0	0	0	0	0	0	0	0	0	0	0	0	0	0	0
bedpost	2	.1787	.1174	30.7	0	1	1	0	0	0	0	0	1	0	0	0	0	0	0	0	0	0	0	0	1	0	0	0	0
bedraggled	5	.2655	.3711	35.7	0	2	0	2	0	1	0	0	3	0	1	1	0	0	0	0	0	0	0	0	0	0	0	0	0
bedrock	14	.4128	1.3085	41.2	3	0	1	2	1	1	5	1	2	0	0	0	0	0	0	8	0	0	0	0	0	0	2	2	0
bedroll	3	.3427	.2477	33.9	0	0	0	1	2	0	0	0	1	0	0	0	0	0	0	0	0	0	0	0	1	0	0	1	0
bedroom	125	.7425	19.108	52.8	27	32	17	8	33	4	4	0	58	2	0	11	1	2	4	0	0	2	6	0	15	5	0	19	0
bedrooms	15	.6092	1.8876	42.8	4	1	2	1	2	2	1	2	2	0	0	2	0	1	0	0	0	0	2	0	3	1	1	3	0
beds	119	.8626	20.525	53.1	21	17	19	18	12	13	15	4	29	4	0	4	1	9	2	18	6	0	2	1	20	14	4	5	0
bedside	10	.5796	1.2418	40.9	0	3	0	1	4	1	1	0	4	0	0	0	0	0	0	0	1	0	1	0	1	1	0	2	0
bedspread	5	.4403	.4883	36.9	1	1	0	2	1	0	0	0	1	0	0	0	2	0	0	0	0	0	0	0	1	0	0	1	0
bedspreads	2	.1698	.1133	30.5	0	0	1	0	1	0	0	0	1	0	0	0	0	0	0	0	0	0	0	0	0	0	1	0	0
bedsprings	2	.0000	.0914	29.6	2	0	0	0	0	0	0	0	2	0	0	0	0	0	0	0	0	0	0	0	0	0	0	0	0
bedstead	2	.0000	.0234	23.7	0	2	0	0	0	0	0	0	0	0	0	0	0	0	0	0	0	0	0	0	2	0	0	0	0
bedtime	30	.6871	4.3058	46.3	8	6	7	2	3	3	1	0	13	1	2	2	0	2	0	3	0	0	0	0	3	2	1	1	0
bee	128	.7022	18.467	52.7	51	22	10	15	20	6	3	1	29	5	0	4	3	0	9	17	0	0	0	0	5	43	8	5	0
Bee	6	.2471	.3894	35.9	3	2	1	0	0	0	0	0	2	0	0	0	0	0	3	0	0	0	0	0	0	1	0	0	0
bee-flower	2	.0000	.0394	26.0	0	0	0	2	0	0	0	0	0	0	0	0	0	0	0	2	0	0	0	0	0	0	0	0	0
bee-sting	3	.0000	.1370	31.4	0	0	0	3	0	0	0	0	3	0	0	0	0	0	0	0	0	0	0	0	0	0	0	0	0
bee-tree	3	.0000	.0352	25.5	0	0	0	0	3	0	0	0	0	0	0	0	0	0	0	0	0	0	0	0	3	0	0	0	0
bee's	11	.3735	.9620	39.8	6	1	1	1	1	0	1	0	3	0	0	1	0	0	0	0	0	0	0	0	0	6	0	1	0
Beebe	20	.4342	2.0099	43.0	5	2	6	6	1	0	0	0	7	0	0	0	0	0	0	8	0	0	0	0	4	0	0	1	0
beech	19	.5456	2.2210	43.5	1	1	2	8	5	2	0	0	4	1	0	0	0	0	0	6	0	0	0	0	1	2	5	0	0
beechdrops	3	.0000	.0591	27.7	0	0	0	3	0	0	0	0	0	0	0	0	0	0	0	3	0	0	0	0	0	0	0	0	0
Beecher	3	.2378	.1809	32.6	1	0	1	0	0	1	0	0	0	0	0	0	0	2	0	0	0	0	0	0	0	1	0	0	0
beeches	5	.0000	.0586	27.7	0	0	0	0	5	0	0	0	0	0	0	0	0	0	0	0	0	0	0	0	5	0	0	0	0
beechnuts	3	.3801	.2525	34.0	0	1	0	1	1	0	0	0	0	0	0	0	0	0	0	1	0	0	0	0	1	1	0	0	0
beef	125	.7399	18.742	52.7	14	15	20	23	26	5	20	2	17	4	1	5	4	26	6	9	0	0	16	0	9	9	5	14	0
beef-bone	2	.0000	.0914	29.6	0	0	2	0	0	0	0	0	2	0	0	0	0	0	0	0	0	0	0	0	0	0	0	0	0
beefeaters	2	.1814	.1187	30.7	0	0	0	2	0	0	0	0	1	0	0	0	0	0	0	0	0	0	0	0	0	0	0	1	0
beefsteak	4	.3743	.3712	35.7	2	0	0	2	0	0	0	0	2	0	0	0	0	1	0	0	0	0	0	0	0	0	0	1	0
beehive	12	.3608	1.1349	40.5	0	3	2	6	0	0	1	0	9	0	0	0	0	1	0	0	0	1	0	0	0	0	0	1	0
Beehive	5	.1425	.2983	34.7	4	0	1	0	0	0	0	0	4	0	0	0	0	0	0	0	0	1	0	0	0	0	0	0	0
beehives	3	.1832	.1417	31.5	0	1	0	0	0	2	0	0	0	0	0	2	0	0	0	1	0	0	0	0	0	0	0	0	0
beeline	4	.3693	.3613	35.6	0	1	1	0	2	0	0	0	2	0	0	1	0	0	0	0	0	0	0	0	0	0	1	0	0
been	7645	.9582	1446.6	71.6	904	1021	899	1110	1731	984	786	210	2069	332	77	479	190	960	151	612	194	63	95	68	589	611	548	607	0

9B Beau-Dur
3G beau-ti-ful
8Q Beauchamps
XN Beauregarde
7R beaut
7A beauteous
6R beautification
8B beautifulest
7H beautifying
9J beauty's
8A beaver-talk
6P becalmed
8J Because
3A because-why
9D bechanced
9B Bechtelsville
6F Bechuanaland
7P beck
6J Beckmesser's
3N beckon
XR beckons
6D becometh
9L becomingness
4N bed-maker
4N bed-maker's
6N bed-time
8R bed-wetting
8Q Bedarieux
9D bedaubed
7R bedazzlements
6J bedbug
8R BEDC-presiding
8R BEDC'S
5G bede
7R Bede's
5P bedevil
5P bedeviled
7N bedewed
7N bedfellow
8B bedford
5A bedknob
7A Bedlam
7F Bedouin
3Q Bedouins
3A bedposts
8J Bedrich
6A bedroom's
6J bee-ee-ee
3P bee-keeper
7D bee-taming
4N bee's-wax
4P beech-tree
8A Beechcraft
4P Beechland
7N Beef
6A Beekman

Word Type	F	D	U	SFI	3 Gr 3	4 Gr 4	5 Gr 5	6 Gr 6	7 Gr 7	8 Gr 8	9 Gr 9	X UnGr	A Read	B Eng & Gr	C Comp	D Lit	E Math	F Soc Stud	G Spell	H Sci	J Music	K Art	L Home Ec	M Shop	N Lib F	P Lib NF	Q Lib Ref	R Mag	S Rel
Been	6	.1947	.3022	34.8	0	0	0	1	0	5	0	0	1	0	0	0	0	0	0	0	4	0	0	0	0	0	0	1	0
beep	2	.2433	.1158	30.6	1	0	0	1	0	0	0	0	0	0	0	0	0	0	0	0	0	0	0	0	0	1	0	1	0
Beep	2	.0000	.0243	23.9	2	0	0	0	0	0	0	0	0	0	0	0	0	0	0	0	0	0	0	0	0	0	0	2	0
beep-beep	2	.0000	.0290	24.6	0	1	0	1	0	0	0	0	0	0	0	0	0	0	0	0	0	0	0	0	0	2	0	0	0
beeps	5	.2395	.3804	35.8	0	0	4	0	1	0	0	0	4	0	0	0	0	0	0	0	1	0	0	0	0	0	0	0	0
beer	24	.6415	3.1966	45.0	3	1	1	4	11	1	2	1	5	0	0	1	1	2	0	0	0	0	0	0	1	4	4	6	0
Beersheba	12	.2851	.8436	39.3	1	0	4	0	7	0	0	0	1	0	0	0	0	7	0	0	0	0	0	0	0	4	0	0	0
bees	183	.7257	27.180	54.3	68	27	4	41	34	5	3	1	45	4	2	8	0	1	12	25	1	0	0	0	4	59	18	4	0
Bees	4	.2424	.3036	34.8	3	0	0	0	0	0	1	0	3	0	0	0	0	0	0	0	0	0	0	0	0	0	0	1	0
bees'	3	.3370	.2430	33.9	0	0	1	0	2	0	0	0	1	0	0	1	0	0	0	0	0	0	0	0	0	0	1	0	0
beeswax	10	.6475	1.3201	41.2	2	2	0	2	2	2	0	0	0	0	0	1	0	1	0	1	0	0	0	0	2	2	2	1	0
beet	6	.3416	.4741	36.8	2	1	2	1	0	0	0	0	1	2	0	0	0	2	0	0	0	1	0	0	0	0	0	0	0
beet-sugar	2	.0000	.0389	25.9	0	0	1	1	0	0	0	0	0	0	0	0	0	2	0	0	0	0	0	0	0	0	0	0	0
Beethoven	44	.1707	2.0584	43.1	0	3	6	9	5	16	5	0	9	1	0	1	0	0	0	0	32	0	0	0	0	0	1	0	0
Beethoven's	6	.2034	.3105	34.9	0	0	1	0	3	2	0	0	1	0	0	1	0	0	0	0	4	0	0	0	0	0	0	0	0
beetle	41	.7351	6.1008	47.9	11	14	1	7	5	0	3	0	3	2	0	3	8	1	0	7	0	0	0	0	8	3	4	2	0
Beetle	8	.3571	.6290	38.0	3	2	0	0	2	1	0	0	0	0	0	1	0	0	0	0	0	0	0	0	0	4	0	3	0
beetle-car	2	.0000	.0914	29.6	0	0	0	2	0	0	0	0	2	0	0	0	0	0	0	0	0	0	0	0	0	0	0	0	0
beetles	43	.6274	5.5826	47.5	19	4	1	10	6	0	1	2	3	1	0	2	2	1	0	13	0	0	0	0	2	14	5	0	0
beets	44	.6972	6.2919	48.0	9	6	8	11	6	0	4	0	5	0	1	1	1	22	0	5	1	0	1	0	1	0	5	1	0
beeves	2	.0000	.0215	23.3	0	0	0	0	0	0	2	0	0	0	0	2	0	0	0	0	0	0	0	0	0	0	0	0	0
Beezus	15	.1250	.6710	38.3	13	2	0	0	0	0	0	0	5	0	0	0	0	0	0	0	0	0	0	0	10	0	0	0	0
befall	5	.3536	.4328	36.4	0	0	3	2	0	0	0	0	2	0	0	0	0	0	0	0	0	0	0	0	1	2	0	0	0
befallen	5	.2086	.3320	35.2	0	1	0	2	2	0	0	0	3	0	0	0	0	0	0	0	0	0	0	0	2	0	0	0	0
befell	3	.1879	.1589	32.0	0	0	0	2	0	1	0	0	1	0	0	0	0	0	0	0	0	1	0	0	1	0	0	0	0
befits	2	.1814	.1187	30.7	0	0	0	1	1	0	0	0	1	0	0	0	0	0	0	0	0	0	0	0	0	0	0	1	0
befitted	2	.1787	.1174	30.7	0	0	1	0	1	0	0	0	1	0	0	0	0	0	0	0	0	0	0	0	1	0	0	0	0
before	5275	.9732	1011.9	70.1	793	902	618	801	947	608	497	109	1551	356	50	323	123	471	417	305	175	23	124	58	346	439	170	340	4
before-mentioned	2	.2411	.1091	30.4	0	0	0	0	1	0	1	0	0	0	0	1	0	0	0	0	1	0	0	0	0	0	0	0	0
beforehand	15	.6442	2.0023	43.0	0	2	1	2	5	3	2	0	4	0	0	2	1	1	0	0	1	1	2	0	2	0	0	1	0
befriended	3	.2435	.2274	33.6	0	0	2	1	0	0	0	0	2	0	0	0	0	1	0	0	0	0	0	0	0	0	0	0	0
beg	42	.6817	5.9059	47.7	5	8	4	9	9	0	7	0	12	2	0	10	0	0	4	0	2	0	0	0	5	4	0	3	0
began	2491	.8683	433.46	66.4	511	457	343	328	405	263	143	41	929	71	12	148	17	334	22	101	63	13	1	4	247	245	136	140	8
beggar	34	.6909	4.9365	46.9	5	2	8	3	8	3	4	1	19	3	1	5	0	0	1	1	0	0	0	0	1	2	1	0	0
beggar's	2	.2152	.1357	31.3	0	0	1	1	0	0	0	0	1	0	0	0	0	1	0	0	0	0	0	0	0	0	0	0	0
beggarly	3	.0000	.0328	25.2	3	0	0	0	0	0	0	0	0	3	0	0	0	0	0	0	0	0	0	0	0	0	0	0	0
beggars	14	.5548	1.6609	42.2	0	2	2	6	2	1	1	0	4	0	0	4	0	0	0	1	2	0	0	0	1	2	0	0	0
begged	97	.5239	11.377	50.6	20	23	20	14	13	3	3	1	51	0	0	7	0	6	0	0	0	0	0	0	16	10	2	4	1
begging	38	.6986	5.5019	47.4	4	7	3	7	10	4	1	2	14	0	0	3	0	1	0	2	2	0	0	0	8	4	1	3	0
begin	976	.8970	173.67	62.4	180	208	132	125	149	79	80	23	134	144	25	37	36	80	190	99	55	11	30	4	42	35	23	30	1
beginner	12	.4658	1.1479	40.6	0	0	1	0	2	1	6	2	0	0	2	0	0	0	0	3	0	0	3	3	1	0	0	0	0
beginner's	3	.2784	.1822	32.6	0	0	1	0	1	1	0	0	0	0	1	1	0	0	0	0	0	0	0	0	0	0	0	1	0
beginners	13	.4150	1.1369	40.6	0	0	0	1	3	1	5	3	0	0	0	1	0	0	0	4	0	0	2	4	0	1	1	0	0
beginning	1005	.9049	180.31	62.6	138	140	138	138	223	125	86	17	162	122	31	37	36	87	182	44	100	8	11	12	35	36	52	49	1
Beginning	2	.2331	.1157	30.6	0	1	0	0	1	0	0	0	0	0	0	0	0	0	0	1	0	0	0	0	1	0	0	0	0
beginnings	50	.7477	7.5559	48.8	5	3	4	5	15	5	7	6	5	5	2	0	0	11	6	6	4	0	0	0	0	3	7	1	0
begins	638	.8462	107.68	60.3	142	109	81	80	97	58	55	16	89	64	32	17	9	45	124	86	77	3	9	3	3	18	25	33	1
begone	6	.4004	.5546	37.4	1	0	0	3	2	0	0	0	2	0	0	1	0	1	0	0	2	0	0	0	0	0	0	0	0
begonias	2	.0000	.0234	23.7	0	0	0	0	2	0	0	0	0	0	0	0	0	0	0	0	0	0	0	0	2	0	0	0	0
begorra	2	.1948	.1250	31.0	0	1	1	0	0	0	0	0	1	0	0	0	0	0	0	0	0	0	0	0	0	1	0	0	0
begot	2	.2443	.1130	30.5	0	0	0	0	1	0	1	0	0	0	0	1	0	0	0	0	0	0	0	0	1	0	0	0	0
begrudged	3	.3380	.2439	33.9	0	0	0	1	0	1	1	0	1	1	0	1	0	0	0	0	0	0	0	0	0	0	0	0	0
begs	6	.2355	.4634	36.7	2	0	1	2	1	0	0	0	5	0	0	0	0	0	0	0	0	0	0	0	0	1	0	0	0
beguile	2	.2446	.1125	30.5	0	0	0	0	0	0	2	0	0	1	0	1	0	0	0	0	0	0	0	0	0	0	0	0	0
beguiled	2	.0000	.0215	23.3	0	0	0	0	0	0	2	0	0	0	0	2	0	0	0	0	0	0	0	0	0	0	0	0	0
begun	205	.8969	36.542	55.6	15	28	30	28	49	31	17	7	39	12	1	15	2	20	3	19	9	1	1	0	19	20	21	23	0
behalf	11	.6232	1.4243	41.5	1	0	0	1	3	4	1	1	2	1	0	2	0	1	0	0	0	0	0	0	0	1	1	3	0
behave	96	.8956	17.078	52.3	12	26	9	12	15	12	9	1	13	3	1	6	4	2	3	32	3	3	3	2	7	5	5	4	0
behaved	17	.7008	2.4699	43.9	1	4	0	4	2	6	0	0	7	1	0	3	0	0	1	0	1	0	0	0	1	1	0	2	0
behaves	17	.5198	1.8835	42.7	0	7	3	0	3	3	0	1	1	2	0	0	0	0	1	10	0	0	0	0	0	0	2	1	0
behaving	15	.6413	2.0318	43.1	1	5	1	2	4	1	1	0	6	0	0	0	0	0	0	2	0	0	1	0	1	3	1	1	0
behavior	172	.7685	26.649	54.3	1	17	8	23	60	22	35	6	17	11	1	9	0	6	0	57	0	1	12	2	3	5	33	15	0
behavioral	3	.0000	.0314	25.0	0	0	0	0	3	0	0	0	0	0	0	0	0	0	0	0	0	0	0	0	0	0	3	0	0
beheaded	7	.1004	.2121	33.3	2	0	3	2	0	0	0	0	0	0	0	0	0	1	0	0	0	0	0	0	0	0	6	0	0
beheading	2	.2441	.1127	30.5	0	0	1	0	0	0	1	0	0	0	0	0	0	0	0	0	0	0	0	0	1	0	1	0	0
beheld	15	.6022	1.9386	42.9	1	2	1	2	3	3	3	0	7	0	0	3	0	0	0	0	1	0	0	0	1	2	1	0	0
behind	1376	.8705	240.18	63.8	251	276	161	156	296	123	88	25	591	38	18	117	4	90	3	55	24	7	9	2	169	110	46	93	0
behold	34	.5389	3.8997	45.9	7	2	1	6	6	1	11	0	8	1	0	13	0	0	0	0	5	0	0	0	1	3	0	3	0
beholden	3	.3847	.2448	33.9	0	1	0	0	1	0	1	0	0	0	0	1	0	0	0	0	1	0	0	0	0	0	1	0	0
beholding	2	.2446	.1125	30.5	0	0	0	0	1	1	0	0	0	1	0	1	0	0	0	0	0	0	0	0	0	0	0	0	0
Behrman	2	.0000	.0243	23.9	0	0	0	0	0	0	0	2	0	0	0	0	0	0	0	0	0	0	0	0	0	0	0	2	0
beige	15	.0990	.3584	35.5	0	0	1	0	1	4	8	1	0	1	0	0	0	0	0	0	0	0	12	0	0	0	0	2	0
Beijerinck	2	.0000	.0394	26.0	0	0	2	0	0	0	0	0	0	0	0	0	0	0	0	2	0	0	0	0	0	0	0	0	0
bein'	9	.3024	.6084	37.8	1	0	0	3	3	1	1	0	0	0	0	1	0	0	0	0	0	0	0	0	6	0	0	2	0
being	2092	.9497	392.50	65.9	228	274	258	267	457	292	245	71	422	106	24	160	51	193	27	284	72	9	54	31	162	158	137	202	0
Being	4	.2003	.1916	32.8	0	0	0	0	3	1	0	0	0	0	0	3	0	0	0	0	0	0	0	0	0	0	1	0	0
beings	123	.8500	20.874	53.2	11	5	21	12	36	16	17	5	18	15	1	12	1	5	3	23	0	4	5	0	8	16	7	5	0
Beirut	5	.3779	.4755	36.8	3	0	0	1	0	0	1	0	3	1	0	0	0	1	0	0	0	0	0	0	0	0	0	0	0
Bel	2	.1812	.0838	29.2	0	0	0	0	2	0	0	0	0	0	0	0	0	0	0	0	0	0	1	0	0	0	0	1	0
bela	5	.0000	.0404	26.1	0	0	0	5	0	0	0	0	0	0	0	0	0	0	0	0	5	0	0	0	0	0	0	0	0
Bela	7	.0000	.0566	27.5	0	0	1	2	2	2	0	0	0	0	0	0	0	0	0	0	7	0	0	0	0	0	0	0	0
belay	2	.2412	.1141	30.6	1	0	0	0	1	0	0	0	0	1	0	0	0	0	0	0	0	0	0	0	0	1	0	0	0
belched	2	.2291	.1135	30.5	0	0	0	0	0	1	0	1	0	0	0	1	0	0	0	1	0	0	0	0	0	0	0	0	0
belching	4	.3813	.3772	35.8	0	1	1	0	1	1	0	0	2	0	0	0	0	1	0	0	0	0	0	0	0	1	0	0	0
Belden	5	.0000	.2284	33.6	0	0	0	5	0	0	0	0	5	0	0	0	0	0	0	0	0	0	0	0	0	0	0	0	0
beleaguered	4	.3766	.3696	35.7	1	0	1	0	0	1	1	0	2	0	0	0	0	0	0	0	0	0	0	0	0	1	0	1	0
Belem	8	.1813	.4050	36.1	0	0	7	1	0	0	0	0	0	0	0	0	0	7	0	0	0	0	0	0	0	0	1	0	0
belfry	10	.5637	1.2449	41.0	0	1	2	4	2	1	0	0	6	1	0	1	0	0	0	0	1	0	0	0	0	0	1	0	0
Belgian	28	.5336	3.1675	45.0	1	1	12	3	4	5	2	0	2	0	0	0	0	6	0	3	1	0	0	0	0	13	2	1	0
Belgians	21	.2382	1.2650	41.0	0	2	11	7	1	0	0	0	1	0	0	0	0	7	0	0	0	0	0	0	0	13	0	0	0
Belgium	60	.6237	7.7751	48.9	4	2	9	21	6	8	9	1	6	0	0	0	0	29	1	0	0	1	2	0	0	11	9	1	0
Belgrade	9	.4781	.9010	39.5	0	0	2	0	2	4	1	0	0	2	0	1	0	1	0	0	0	0	0	0	0	0	4	1	0
belied	2	.2152	.1357	31.3	0	0	0	0	0	2	0	0	1	0	0	0	0	1	0	0	0	0	0	0	0	0	0	0	0
belief	82	.5189	9.1081	49.6	2	5	14	4	22	13	20	2	15	2	0	6	0	15	2	5	1	1	2	0	1	6	19	5	2

3N BEEN
5A beeped
6Q beers
6N bees'-wax
7Q beetle-browed
4N beetle's
7P Beetle's
5A beetlelike
7Q beetling
8F befit
6R befitting

8B befooled
6J Before
7D before-death
5G beforehead
4A befriends
XR befuddle
7R befuddled
9R begat
7R beget
8A begets
9J begetteth

4J Beggar-man
3P beggar-priests
6A beggin'
3G begining
8N beginnin'
4N Beginnings
3A begonia
XR begotten
7D begrudge
9D beguil'd
9D beguiling

9B Beh-eh
9B Beh-eh-h'
7R Behavior
7Q behaviorally
9R behaviorism
6H behaviors
5N behaviour
6R behead
3Q beheadings
XR behemoths
7A behests

7A Behind
8D behinde
7N behine
8D behint
6A beholder
3P beholdeth
5P behooves
XH Behring
7A being-dragged
4P bejabers
7D Bejance

5A bejeepers
8R bejeweled
9D belated
7Q belatedly
6F belch
5A belches
7N beldame
7J belfries
8Q Belgaum
6F Belgium's

Word Type	F	D	U	SFI	3 Gr 3	4 Gr 4	5 Gr 5	6 Gr 6	7 Gr 7	8 Gr 8	9 Gr 9	X UnGr	A Read	B Eng & Gr	C Comp	D Lit	E Math	F Soc Stud	G Spell	H Sci	J Music	K Art	L Home Ec	M Shop	N Lib F	P Lib NF	Q Lib Ref	R Mag	S Rel
beliefs	63	.6576	8.5203	49.3	1	1	4	10	16	11	18	2	3	0	0	4	1	33	0	3	1	1	0	0	0	4	8	5	0
believable	7	.4562	.7078	38.5	0	0	1	0	1	3	0	2	2	1	0	0	0	1	0	0	0	1	0	0	1	0	0	1	0
believe	685	.5586	82.686	59.2	102	105	76	102	147	72	63	18	244	39	1	67	1	48	7	67	17	2	2	0	44	48	26	60	12
believed	412	.6695	57.121	57.6	29	44	80	52	88	56	48	15	89	11	1	19	1	90	3	55	9	3	1	2	14	33	56	20	5
believer	6	.2977	.4237	36.3	0	0	0	0	4	0	2	0	1	0	0	2	0	0	0	0	0	0	0	0	0	0	0	3	0
believers	7	.5084	.7445	38.7	0	0	0	2	1	1	2	1	0	1	0	0	0	1	0	0	0	0	0	0	0	1	1	3	0
believes	52	.5080	5.6613	47.5	8	3	4	8	7	8	8	6	9	1	0	4	0	1	1	4	1	0	0	0	2	8	4	16	1
believing	28	.7854	4.4809	46.5	2	1	5	3	4	8	4	1	11	1	0	2	0	4	2	2	1	0	0	0	1	3	1	0	0
Belinda	31	.4329	3.1765	45.0	9	1	7	0	4	10	0	0	17	0	0	0	0	0	0	0	4	0	0	0	0	9	0	1	0
Belinda's	2	.1948	.1250	31.0	1	0	1	0	0	0	0	0	1	0	0	0	0	0	0	0	0	0	0	0	0	1	0	0	0
Belindy	4	.0000	.1827	32.6	4	0	0	0	0	0	0	0	4	0	0	0	0	0	0	0	0	0	0	0	0	0	0	0	0
Belinsky	8	.2059	.3990	36.0	0	0	0	0	6	0	2	0	0	2	0	0	0	0	0	0	0	0	0	0	0	0	0	6	0
Belknap	3	.2321	.1635	32.1	0	0	1	2	0	0	0	0	0	0	0	0	0	0	0	0	0	0	0	0	0	0	1	2	0
bell	321	.8475	54.788	57.4	85	58	50	46	33	30	17	2	137	17	7	17	1	12	6	46	22	0	0	5	19	23	1	8	0
Bell	79	.7647	12.404	50.9	20	6	9	15	11	14	2	2	38	2	0	2	2	5	1	2	6	0	0	0	0	8	7	6	0
bell-like	3	.3272	.2361	33.7	1	1	0	1	0	0	0	0	1	0	0	0	0	0	0	0	1	0	0	0	0	0	1	0	0
bell-shaped	5	.3736	.4248	36.3	1	1	0	2	0	0	0	1	1	0	0	0	0	0	0	1	2	0	0	0	0	0	1	0	0
Bell's	7	.5365	.8125	39.1	1	2	2	0	1	1	0	0	2	0	0	0	2	1	1	0	0	0	0	0	1	0	0	0	0
Bellario	3	.0000	.0322	25.1	0	0	0	0	0	0	3	0	0	0	0	3	0	0	0	0	0	0	0	0	0	0	0	0	0
belle	3	.0000	.0434	26.4	0	2	0	0	1	0	0	0	0	0	0	0	0	0	0	0	0	0	0	0	0	3	0	0	0
Belle	13	.3166	.9887	40.0	5	3	0	0	2	0	3	0	3	0	0	5	0	0	0	0	0	0	0	0	0	5	0	0	0
Belleau	6	.1955	.3185	35.0	0	0	0	0	1	5	0	0	0	0	0	0	0	5	0	0	0	0	0	0	0	0	0	1	0
Bellerophon	2	.1698	.1133	30.5	0	0	0	0	0	1	1	0	1	0	0	0	0	0	0	0	0	0	0	0	0	0	1	0	0
bellies	3	.2120	.1548	31.9	0	0	1	0	2	0	0	0	0	0	0	0	0	0	0	0	0	0	0	0	2	1	0	0	0
belligerent	3	.3769	.2484	34.0	0	0	0	0	1	2	0	0	0	0	0	0	0	1	0	0	0	0	0	0	0	0	1	1	0
belligerently	3	.2279	.2143	33.3	0	0	0	1	1	1	0	0	2	0	0	0	0	0	0	0	0	0	0	0	0	0	0	1	0
belligerents	6	.0000	.0628	28.0	0	0	4	0	0	2	0	0	0	0	0	0	0	0	0	0	0	0	0	0	0	0	6	0	0
Bellini	3	.0995	.1144	30.6	0	0	0	1	0	2	0	0	1	0	0	0	0	0	0	0	2	0	0	0	0	0	0	0	0
Bellinis	2	.0000	.0914	29.6	0	2	0	0	0	0	0	0	2	0	0	0	0	0	0	0	0	0	0	0	0	0	0	0	0
Bello	4	.3609	.3221	35.1	0	0	3	1	0	0	0	0	0	0	0	0	0	1	0	0	0	0	0	0	1	2	0	0	0
bellow	11	.5387	1.2894	41.1	1	1	2	4	1	1	1	0	4	1	0	2	0	0	0	0	0	0	0	0	0	3	0	1	0
bellowed	12	.4471	1.2245	40.9	0	2	6	2	0	2	0	0	5	0	0	3	0	0	0	0	0	0	0	0	3	0	0	1	0
bellowing	4	.1787	.2347	33.7	0	1	1	1	1	0	0	0	2	0	0	0	0	0	0	0	0	0	0	0	2	0	0	0	0
bellows	12	.6510	1.6298	42.1	0	2	4	0	0	4	2	0	4	0	0	1	0	0	1	1	0	0	0	1	1	1	2	0	0
Bellrose	3	.0000	.0365	25.6	0	0	0	0	3	0	0	0	0	0	0	0	0	0	0	0	0	0	0	0	0	0	0	3	0
bells	303	.4322	28.514	54.6	85	98	38	44	19	8	9	2	55	9	2	9	0	17	1	1	174	1	0	0	15	8	6	5	0
Bells	6	.4549	.5694	37.6	1	0	2	1	1	1	0	0	0	2	0	0	0	0	0	0	2	0	0	0	0	0	1	1	0
belly	46	.6762	6.3811	48.0	8	3	1	6	16	5	5	2	8	0	2	4	0	2	0	0	0	0	0	0	9	11	5	5	0
belly-deep	2	.2440	.1132	30.5	0	0	0	1	1	0	0	0	0	0	0	1	0	0	0	0	0	0	0	0	0	0	0	1	0
Belmont	2	.0000	.0234	23.7	0	0	0	1	1	0	0	0	0	0	0	0	0	0	0	0	0	0	0	0	2	0	0	0	0
Belond	2	.0000	.0290	24.6	0	0	0	0	0	0	0	2	0	0	0	0	0	0	0	0	0	0	0	0	0	2	0	0	0
belong	320	.8694	55.471	57.4	50	45	40	47	77	40	15	6	62	57	7	3	27	26	30	42	10	8	6	0	5	15	16	6	0
belonged	165	.7514	25.345	54.0	36	29	25	20	29	14	10	2	51	4	1	15	0	28	0	3	1	0	0	0	22	28	5	7	0
belonging	63	.8431	10.608	50.3	1	4	9	14	16	5	11	3	7	1	0	6	1	10	1	6	0	0	2	1	6	8	8	6	0
belongings	24	.7249	3.5622	45.5	8	2	6	2	5	1	0	0	6	1	0	2	0	4	0	0	0	0	1	0	2	6	1	1	0
belongs	190	.8971	33.922	55.3	41	40	21	28	32	16	11	1	53	17	1	2	13	11	12	17	9	5	0	1	7	15	17	10	0
beloved	48	.5054	5.3469	47.3	3	9	4	11	8	5	5	3	18	1	0	3	0	3	0	1	6	0	1	0	3	4	1	6	1
Beloved	13	.1013	.3949	36.0	0	12	1	0	0	0	0	0	0	0	0	1	0	0	0	0	0	0	0	0	12	0	0	0	0
below	3276	.7907	521.90	67.2	505	629	470	540	572	320	212	28	626	498	27	40	772	134	585	221	116	23	19	9	24	53	63	66	0
below-zero	2	.1948	.1250	31.0	1	0	1	0	0	0	0	0	1	0	0	0	0	0	0	0	0	0	0	0	0	1	0	0	0
Belshazzar	6	.0000	.0485	26.9	0	0	0	0	6	0	0	0	0	0	0	0	0	0	0	0	6	0	0	0	0	0	0	0	0
Belshazzar's	2	.0000	.0162	22.1	0	0	0	0	2	0	0	0	0	0	0	0	0	0	0	0	2	0	0	0	0	0	0	0	0
belt	174	.8316	29.103	54.6	22	21	30	22	40	27	6	6	47	5	1	10	0	30	0	26	0	0	8	5	12	14	10	6	0
Belt	17	.1602	.8274	39.2	0	2	13	0	1	1	0	0	1	0	0	0	0	15	0	0	0	0	0	0	0	0	1	0	0
belted	3	.3465	.2515	34.0	2	0	0	0	0	0	0	1	1	0	0	0	0	0	0	0	0	0	0	0	0	1	0	1	0
belting	6	.1637	.2227	33.5	0	0	1	1	0	4	0	0	0	0	0	0	0	0	0	0	0	0	4	0	0	0	1	1	0
belts	86	.8354	14.416	51.6	19	11	8	4	9	22	12	1	17	10	1	3	0	20	2	16	0	1	3	0	0	5	4	4	0
Beltsville	7	.0000	.3198	35.0	0	7	0	0	0	0	0	0	7	0	0	0	0	0	0	0	0	0	0	0	0	0	0	0	0
Belvedere	2	.0000	.0215	23.3	0	0	0	0	0	0	2	0	0	0	0	2	0	0	0	0	0	0	0	0	0	0	0	0	0
Bemba	3	.0000	.0434	26.4	0	0	0	0	3	0	0	0	0	0	0	0	0	0	0	0	0	0	0	0	0	3	0	0	0
ben	7	.1093	.2839	34.5	1	0	0	0	5	1	0	0	2	0	0	0	0	0	0	0	0	0	0	0	5	0	0	0	0
Ben	332	.6375	45.255	56.6	125	132	18	18	26	11	2	0	180	4	0	18	11	12	2	0	0	1	2	1	87	13	1	0	0
Ben-Gurion	3	.0000	.0434	26.4	0	0	3	0	0	0	0	0	0	0	0	0	0	0	0	0	0	0	0	0	0	3	0	0	0
Ben-Gurion's	2	.0000	.0290	24.6	0	0	2	0	0	0	0	0	0	0	0	0	0	0	0	0	0	0	0	0	0	2	0	0	0
Ben's	25	.3720	2.2749	43.6	5	14	0	4	2	0	0	0	12	0	0	0	1	1	0	0	0	0	0	0	10	0	0	1	0
Benbow	2	.2443	.1130	30.5	0	0	0	0	1	0	1	0	0	0	0	1	0	0	0	0	0	0	0	0	1	0	0	0	0
bench	140	.6236	18.122	52.6	21	26	10	18	30	15	19	1	33	3	2	15	0	1	1	0	1	1	0	23	20	21	4	15	0
Bench	2	.2446	.1142	30.6	0	0	0	0	2	0	0	0	0	0	0	0	0	0	0	0	0	0	0	0	1	0	0	1	0
benches	38	.6684	5.1790	47.1	9	7	4	6	4	6	2	0	3	0	0	7	0	4	0	0	1	1	0	0	13	4	3	2	0
Benchly	6	.0000	.2741	34.4	6	0	0	0	0	0	0	0	6	0	0	0	0	0	0	0	0	0	0	0	0	0	0	0	0
bend	180	.7166	26.295	54.2	31	33	23	18	33	21	14	7	39	2	2	6	2	8	3	34	3	15	1	26	8	11	8	11	1
Bend	21	.4594	2.2314	43.5	1	6	1	10	2	1	0	0	11	0	0	0	0	0	0	0	1	0	0	0	0	1	1	7	0
Bender	3	.2357	.2199	33.4	0	2	0	1	0	0	0	0	2	0	0	0	0	0	0	0	0	0	0	0	0	1	0	0	0
Bendigeid	3	.0000	.0434	26.4	0	0	0	0	3	0	0	0	0	0	0	0	0	0	0	0	0	0	0	0	0	3	0	0	0
bending	81	.5091	8.7119	49.4	6	6	5	10	19	16	18	1	13	2	1	4	2	1	0	11	1	3	0	24	8	5	1	5	0
Bendix	2	.0000	.0243	23.9	0	0	0	2	0	0	0	0	0	0	0	0	0	0	0	0	0	0	0	0	0	0	0	2	0
bends	73	.5294	8.2011	49.1	6	13	3	12	12	12	14	1	15	1	1	2	0	0	0	22	1	8	1	16	0	1	4	1	0
Bendy	4	.0000	.1827	32.6	0	0	0	4	0	0	0	0	4	0	0	0	0	0	0	0	0	0	0	0	0	0	0	0	0
beneath	321	.8964	57.269	57.6	35	50	41	43	72	29	40	11	80	12	3	22	1	19	1	63	9	3	6	0	23	26	30	23	0
Benedek	6	.0000	.2741	34.4	6	0	0	0	0	0	0	0	6	0	0	0	0	0	0	0	0	0	0	0	0	0	0	0	0
Benedict	11	.5424	1.2862	41.1	0	0	1	0	3	5	2	0	3	1	0	2	0	3	0	0	0	0	0	0	0	0	2	0	0
benediction	3	.3873	.2485	34.0	0	1	0	0	1	0	1	0	0	0	0	1	0	0	0	0	0	0	0	0	1	0	1	0	0
benefactor	3	.2732	.1800	32.6	0	0	0	1	2	0	0	0	0	0	1	0	0	0	0	0	0	0	0	0	1	0	0	1	0
beneficial	7	.4358	.6521	38.1	1	0	0	2	1	1	1	1	0	0	0	1	0	0	0	2	0	0	0	0	1	0	3	0	0
beneficiaries	3	.2321	.1635	32.1	0	0	0	0	1	0	1	1	0	0	0	0	0	0	0	0	0	0	0	0	0	0	1	2	0
benefit	75	.7374	11.147	50.5	4	2	6	4	19	14	16	10	2	4	0	3	1	14	5	8	0	0	4	0	0	4	14	16	0
benefited	7	.4116	.6522	38.1	1	0	0	3	0	2	1	0	1	0	0	0	0	4	0	0	0	0	0	0	0	0	1	1	0
benefits	60	.6513	8.0254	49.0	5	0	4	5	18	14	5	9	5	1	0	5	0	13	0	4	1	0	0	0	1	2	12	16	0
benevolence	2	.2407	.1138	30.6	0	0	1	0	1	0	0	0	0	0	0	1	0	0	0	0	0	0	0	0	0	1	0	0	0
benevolent	6	.6052	.7586	38.8	0	0	1	1	1	1	2	0	1	0	0	1	0	1	0	0	0	0	0	0	1	1	0	1	0
Bengal	4	.3271	.3195	35.0	0	1	1	0	0	1	1	0	1	0	0	0	0	2	1	0	0	0	0	0	0	0	0	0	0
Bengt	3	.2379	.1705	32.3	0	0	0	0	0	2	1	0	0	0	0	1	0	0	0	0	0	0	0	0	0	2	0	0	0

5A Believable
7J Believe
8A believingly
5P Beline
8A belittle
9R bell-bottoms
4B bell-wether
5A bell's
9R bella
7D Bellacoola
3P Bellagio
9D Bellario's
XR Bellas
8R bellbottoms
7N bellerin'
6A belles
9R belli
6D bellied
5P belligerence
7R belling
3R Bellingham
8J Bellini's
8B Belloc's
4F bellowings
8A Bellows
5A bellshaped
7R bellwether
7A belly-landing
5B bellying
9R Belmondo
7N Belmont's
3P Belmore
XR Beloit
XP Belond-AP**
XP Belond-owned
8N belongin'
7R below-the-front-bumper
7H below-the-surface
3P belowworm
4A Belted
9Q beltlike
7P Bembe
7Q bembecids
9H Bemberg
7Q Bembex
8F Bemis
7A bemoaned
9Q BEMS
7N ben'
6N Benamuckee
6R Benane
4Q Benavente
8N Benches
3A Benchly's
7R benchtop
7R bender
4A Benders
5N bendin'
6A Bendy's
3A Benedek's
6N Benedicite
8D Benedict's
7J Benedictine
6R benefactors
9D benefice
7Q beneficiary
7R benefiting
9Q Benet
9B Benet's
4N Beneteau
XR benevolents
7B Bengali
6R Bengals

Word Type	F	D	U	SFI	3 Gr 3	4 Gr 4	5 Gr 5	6 Gr 6	7 Gr 7	8 Gr 8	9 Gr 9	X UnGr	A Read	B Eng & Gr	C Comp	D Lit	E Math	F Soc Stud	G Spell	H Sci	J Music	K Art	L Home Ec	M Shop	N Lib F	P Lib NF	Q Lib Ref	R Mag	S Rel
Bengtson	2	.0000	.0243	23.9	0	0	0	2	0	0	0	0	0	0	0	0	0	0	0	0	0	0	0	0	0	0	0	2	0
benighted	2	.2443	.1130	30.5	0	0	0	0	1	0	1	0	0	0	0	1	0	0	0	0	0	0	0	0	1	0	0	0	0
benign	6	.3695	.5002	37.0	0	0	0	0	1	2	3	0	1	0	0	1	0	0	0	0	0	0	0	0	0	1	3	0	0
Benin	2	.1814	.1187	30.7	1	0	0	0	0	1	0	0	1	0	0	0	0	0	0	0	0	0	0	0	0	0	0	1	0
Benito	7	.3665	.6345	38.0	1	2	0	1	2	1	0	0	3	0	0	0	0	3	0	0	0	0	0	0	0	0	1	0	0
Benjamin	129	.7415	19.540	52.9	39	26	8	19	14	15	6	2	37	4	0	7	1	16	0	4	11	0	0	1	33	5	8	2	0
Benjamin's	6	.1787	.3521	35.5	3	2	0	1	0	0	0	0	3	0	0	0	0	0	0	0	0	0	0	0	3	0	0	0	0
Benji	14	.0000	.6396	38.1	0	14	0	0	0	0	0	0	14	0	0	0	0	0	0	0	0	0	0	0	0	0	0	0	0
Benjie	27	.0000	1.2334	40.9	11	16	0	0	0	0	0	0	27	0	0	0	0	0	0	0	0	0	0	0	0	0	0	0	0
Benjy	4	.1948	.2500	34.0	0	2	0	2	0	0	0	0	2	0	0	0	0	0	0	0	0	0	0	0	0	2	0	0	0
Benn	11	.0000	.5025	37.0	11	0	0	0	0	0	0	0	11	0	0	0	0	0	0	0	0	0	0	0	0	0	0	0	0
Bennett	11	.6422	1.4619	41.6	0	0	2	0	2	0	4	3	2	2	0	1	0	0	0	1	0	0	0	0	0	2	2	1	0
Benning	2	.1814	.1187	30.7	1	0	0	1	0	0	0	0	1	0	0	0	0	0	0	0	0	0	0	0	0	0	0	1	0
Bennington	2	.2137	.1056	30.2	0	0	1	0	0	1	0	0	0	0	0	0	0	1	0	0	1	0	0	0	0	0	0	0	0
Benny	52	.3132	3.6275	45.6	39	0	0	1	12	0	0	0	1	0	0	19	0	0	0	0	1	0	0	0	30	0	0	1	0
Benny's	2	.2427	.1152	30.6	2	0	0	0	0	0	0	0	0	0	0	0	0	0	0	0	0	0	0	0	1	1	0	0	0
Benoit	3	.2304	.1619	32.1	2	0	0	0	1	0	0	0	0	0	0	0	0	0	0	0	0	0	0	0	2	0	1	0	0
Benson	9	.3231	.6946	38.4	0	6	0	0	1	1	0	1	2	0	0	0	0	0	0	1	0	0	0	0	5	0	0	1	0
bent	244	.7631	38.022	55.8	41	29	24	39	55	31	18	7	96	1	2	19	4	4	1	19	4	7	0	20	28	16	8	15	0
Bentham	2	.0000	.0209	23.2	0	0	2	0	0	0	0	0	0	0	0	0	0	0	0	0	0	0	0	0	0	0	2	0	0
benthos	2	.0000	.0243	23.9	0	0	0	0	0	0	0	2	0	0	0	0	0	0	0	0	0	0	0	0	0	0	0	2	0
Bentley	3	.2054	.1422	31.5	0	0	0	1	0	0	0	2	0	0	1	0	0	0	0	0	0	0	0	0	0	0	0	2	0
Benton	13	.3390	1.2005	40.8	0	2	0	0	10	1	0	0	10	0	0	0	2	1	0	0	0	0	0	0	0	0	0	0	0
Benton's	2	.1733	.1149	30.6	0	0	0	0	2	0	0	0	1	1	0	0	0	0	0	0	0	0	0	0	0	0	0	0	0
benumbed	2	.0000	.0219	23.4	0	0	1	0	0	0	0	1	0	2	0	0	0	0	0	0	0	0	0	0	0	0	0	0	0
Benvolio	17	.0679	.4946	36.9	0	0	0	0	0	3	14	0	3	0	0	14	0	0	0	0	0	0	0	0	0	0	0	0	0
benzine	2	.1948	.1250	31.0	0	0	0	1	1	0	0	0	1	0	0	0	0	0	0	0	0	0	0	0	0	1	0	0	0
Beowulf	2	.0000	.0209	23.2	0	0	0	0	2	0	0	0	0	0	0	0	0	0	0	0	0	0	0	0	0	0	2	0	0
bequeathed	2	.2446	.1123	30.5	0	0	0	0	0	1	0	1	0	1	0	0	0	0	0	0	0	0	0	0	0	0	1	0	0
bequests	3	.0000	.0314	25.0	0	0	0	0	0	3	0	0	0	0	0	0	0	0	0	0	0	0	0	0	0	0	3	0	0
Beraha	2	.0000	.0914	29.6	0	0	0	0	2	0	0	0	2	0	0	0	0	0	0	0	0	0	0	0	0	0	0	0	0
Berber	4	.2183	.2285	33.6	0	0	1	0	2	0	1	0	0	0	0	0	0	3	0	0	0	0	0	0	0	1	0	0	0
Berbers	15	.2441	.9485	39.8	0	0	2	6	6	0	1	0	1	0	0	0	0	11	0	0	0	0	0	0	0	3	0	0	0
bereft	3	.1187	.1291	31.1	0	0	0	1	1	0	1	0	1	0	0	2	0	0	0	0	0	0	0	0	0	0	0	0	0
beret	4	.2827	.2741	34.4	1	2	0	0	0	0	1	0	1	0	0	0	0	0	0	0	0	0	1	0	2	0	0	0	0
bergamot	2	.1698	.1133	30.5	0	0	0	1	0	0	1	0	1	0	0	0	0	0	0	0	0	0	0	0	0	0	1	0	0
Bergen	14	.3192	1.1452	40.6	5	5	0	4	0	0	0	0	5	0	0	0	0	8	0	0	1	0	0	0	0	0	0	0	0
Berger	3	.0000	.0365	25.6	0	3	0	0	0	0	0	0	0	0	0	0	0	0	0	0	0	0	0	0	0	0	0	3	0
Bergitta	2	.0000	.0290	24.6	0	0	0	0	2	0	0	0	0	0	0	0	0	0	0	0	0	0	0	0	0	2	0	0	0
Bergom	2	.0000	.0234	23.7	0	2	0	0	0	0	0	0	0	0	0	0	0	0	0	0	0	0	0	0	2	0	0	0	0
beribboned	2	.2407	.1138	30.6	0	0	1	0	0	0	0	1	0	0	0	1	0	0	0	0	0	0	0	0	0	1	0	0	0
beriberi	6	.0000	.1183	30.7	0	0	4	0	2	0	0	0	0	0	0	0	0	0	0	6	0	0	0	0	0	0	0	0	0
Bering	25	.3116	1.9824	43.0	0	1	10	1	2	10	1	0	7	0	0	0	0	16	0	0	0	0	0	0	0	1	1	0	0
Berkeley	16	.2155	.8872	39.5	0	0	1	0	2	6	2	5	2	0	0	0	0	1	0	0	0	0	0	0	0	0	1	12	0
Berkey	6	.0000	.0869	29.4	0	0	6	0	0	0	0	0	0	0	0	0	0	0	0	0	0	0	0	0	0	6	0	0	0
Berlin	51	.5391	5.7571	47.6	0	3	0	13	9	13	10	3	2	0	0	0	0	13	0	2	7	0	0	0	0	3	4	20	0
Berliner	17	.2560	.9693	39.9	0	0	0	0	11	6	0	0	0	0	0	0	0	0	0	0	11	0	0	0	0	0	5	1	0
Berliner's	4	.0000	.0323	25.1	0	0	0	0	4	0	0	0	0	0	0	0	0	0	0	0	4	0	0	0	0	0	0	0	0
Berlioz	10	.4277	.8953	39.5	0	0	0	0	2	4	4	0	0	0	1	0	0	1	0	0	4	0	0	0	0	0	4	0	0
Bermuda	9	.4156	.7957	39.0	1	0	1	0	3	2	2	0	0	1	0	0	0	0	0	0	0	0	0	0	0	1	4	3	0
Bern	6	.3419	.4583	36.6	0	1	4	0	0	1	0	0	0	0	0	0	0	1	0	0	0	0	0	0	0	3	2	0	0
Bernard	10	.5978	1.2635	41.0	0	1	3	0	2	2	2	0	3	0	0	1	0	1	1	0	0	0	0	0	0	0	2	2	0
Bernard's	2	.0000	.0299	24.8	0	0	0	0	0	0	2	0	0	0	0	0	2	0	0	0	0	0	0	0	0	0	0	0	0
Bernardo	6	.0000	.1167	30.7	0	0	0	6	0	0	0	0	0	0	0	0	0	6	0	0	0	0	0	0	0	0	0	0	0
Berne	3	.2019	.1477	31.7	0	0	0	0	1	2	0	0	0	0	0	0	1	0	0	0	0	0	0	0	0	0	2	0	0
Bernhard	2	.2446	.1184	30.7	0	0	1	0	0	1	0	0	0	0	0	0	1	0	0	0	0	0	0	0	0	1	0	0	0
Bernissart	2	.0000	.0290	24.6	0	0	2	0	0	0	0	0	0	0	0	0	0	0	0	0	0	0	0	0	0	2	0	0	0
Bernoulli's	5	.0000	.0986	29.9	0	2	0	2	0	1	0	0	0	0	0	0	0	0	0	5	0	0	0	0	0	0	0	0	0
Bernstein	12	.2149	.5905	37.7	0	0	0	0	2	10	0	0	0	2	0	0	0	0	0	0	9	0	0	0	0	0	0	1	0
Berra	2	.0000	.0290	24.6	1	0	0	1	0	0	0	0	0	0	0	0	0	0	0	0	0	0	0	0	0	2	0	0	0
Berri	2	.0000	.0243	23.9	0	0	0	0	0	0	0	2	0	0	0	0	0	0	0	0	0	0	0	0	0	0	0	2	0
berries	104	.7358	15.618	51.9	31	10	19	8	15	11	6	4	24	6	0	6	0	19	2	8	3	1	2	0	15	9	4	4	1
Berrigan	9	.0000	.1094	30.4	0	0	0	0	0	0	9	0	0	0	0	0	0	0	0	0	0	0	0	0	0	0	0	9	0
berry	16	.6713	2.2192	43.5	1	4	2	4	1	2	1	1	4	0	0	0	0	1	1	1	1	0	0	0	4	0	2	2	0
Berry	19	.1160	.8143	39.1	1	18	0	0	0	0	0	0	5	0	0	0	0	0	0	0	0	0	0	0	0	14	0	0	0
berry's	3	.3272	.2363	33.7	1	0	2	0	0	0	0	0	1	0	0	1	0	0	0	0	1	0	0	0	0	0	0	0	0
berrytime	2	.2446	.1122	30.5	0	0	0	0	1	1	0	0	0	0	0	1	0	0	0	0	0	0	0	0	0	0	1	0	0
Bert	143	.4191	14.907	51.7	23	0	0	0	12	108	0	0	109	1	0	5	5	0	0	0	0	0	0	0	23	0	0	0	0
Bert's	3	.0000	.1370	31.4	0	0	0	0	0	3	0	0	3	0	0	0	0	0	0	0	0	0	0	0	0	0	0	0	0
berth	14	.7150	2.0480	43.1	3	0	0	6	2	2	1	0	3	2	0	1	0	2	0	0	0	0	0	0	1	2	1	2	0
Bertha	13	.2898	1.0246	40.1	0	5	0	7	0	1	0	0	7	0	0	0	0	0	0	1	0	0	0	0	0	0	0	5	0
Berthe	6	.2355	.4634	36.7	5	1	0	0	0	0	0	0	5	0	0	0	0	0	0	0	0	0	0	0	0	1	0	0	0
berths	2	.1948	.1250	31.0	0	1	0	0	0	1	0	0	1	0	0	0	0	0	0	0	0	0	0	0	0	1	0	0	0
Bertie	12	.3596	1.1362	40.6	2	1	0	8	1	0	0	0	9	0	0	0	0	0	0	0	0	0	0	0	0	1	0	2	0
Bertillon	2	.0000	.0914	29.6	0	0	0	2	0	0	0	0	2	0	0	0	0	0	0	0	0	0	0	0	0	0	0	0	0
Bertrand	9	.0000	.4111	36.1	0	0	0	0	9	0	0	0	9	0	0	0	0	0	0	0	0	0	0	0	0	0	0	0	0
beryl	6	.0000	.1183	30.7	0	0	0	0	0	0	5	1	0	0	0	0	0	0	0	6	0	0	0	0	0	0	0	0	0
beryllium	3	.2445	.1818	32.6	0	1	0	0	0	0	2	0	0	0	0	0	0	0	0	2	0	0	0	0	0	0	1	0	0
Berzelius	4	.0000	.0789	29.0	0	0	0	0	3	0	0	1	0	0	0	0	0	0	0	4	0	0	0	0	0	0	0	0	0
bescreened	2	.0000	.0215	23.3	0	0	0	0	0	0	2	0	0	0	0	2	0	0	0	0	0	0	0	0	0	0	0	0	0
beseech	11	.1854	.5541	37.4	0	0	1	0	3	0	7	0	2	1	0	8	0	0	0	0	0	0	0	0	0	0	0	0	0
beseeching	3	.1187	.1291	31.1	0	0	1	0	0	1	1	0	1	0	0	2	0	0	0	0	0	0	0	0	0	0	0	0	0
beset	6	.5066	.6515	38.1	0	1	0	0	0	5	0	0	1	0	0	1	0	1	0	0	0	0	0	0	2	0	1	0	0
beside	725	.8371	122.34	60.9	132	161	89	117	123	53	41	9	301	33	7	88	8	36	53	11	8	2	2	0	73	71	8	24	0
besides	368	.8969	65.724	58.2	40	67	49	58	72	42	33	7	104	34	5	29	6	36	2	40	5	1	3	0	32	34	15	22	0
besieged	10	.4676	1.0032	40.0	0	0	0	4	3	1	1	1	1	3	0	0	0	1	0	0	0	0	0	0	0	2	3	0	0
besieging	3	.1823	.1405	31.5	0	0	0	0	0	0	3	0	0	0	0	0	0	1	0	0	0	0	0	0	0	0	2	0	0
besought	2	.1948	.1250	31.0	1	0	0	0	0	1	0	0	1	0	0	0	0	0	0	0	0	0	0	0	0	1	0	0	0
Bess	24	.6016	3.1221	44.9	0	6	1	0	5	10	2	0	13	0	0	1	0	0	0	0	4	0	0	0	1	3	1	1	0
Bessel	2	.0000	.0394	26.0	0	0	0	0	2	0	0	0	0	0	0	0	0	0	0	2	0	0	0	0	0	0	0	0	0
Bessie	75	.2981	5.1622	47.1	2	58	0	1	10	4	0	0	2	0	0	8	0	0	0	0	1	0	0	0	6	58	0	0	0
Bessie's	5	.1993	.2508	34.0	0	4	0	0	1	0	0	0	0	0	0	1	0	0	0	0	0	0	0	0	0	4	0	0	0
Besso	8	.0000	.0875	29.4	0	0	0	0	0	0	8	0	0	8	0	0	0	0	0	0	0	0	0	0	0	0	0	0	0
best	1884	.9738	361.60	65.6	347	330	214	226	336	183	191	57	512	130	23	109	48	164	55	131	56	18	65	36	120	177	74	165	1

6A Benito's
4A Benji's
3A Benjie's
XR Bensen
4A Bent
7L bent-handled
7Q bent-kneed
9D bent-over
5Q Bentham's
4F Benue
5G benz
5Q benzene
7Q bequeath
9K bequeaths
8Q Berain
6C berated
7D berating
4D berberris
7P Berchtesgaden
9P berg
8J Berg
8A Bergen-Belsen
8B Bergman's
9A Bergson
9D berhyme
3Q beri-beri
6F Beria
8J Berkshire
5R Berkshires
7P berl
6R Berliners
XR Berlitz
5P Bernadotte
5P Bernadottes
5P Bernhard's
3A Bernice
8H Bernoulli
8J Bernstein's
6R Berries
8D berry-picking
4A Berry's
7Q berrypickers
4P Berrys
6H Berta
6A Bertini
4A Berton
7N beruffled
8D besett
8Q Beslic
9R beslime
6N besom
9D bespattered
9R bespectacled
8D besplashed
7D bespoke
6J bespoken
6G Bess's
9B Besso's

Word Type	F	D	U	SFI	3 Gr 3	4 Gr 4	5 Gr 5	6 Gr 6	7 Gr 7	8 Gr 8	9 Gr 9	X UnGr	A Read	B Eng & Gr	C Comp	D Lit	E Math	F Soc Stud	G Spell	H Sci	J Music	K Art	L Home Ec	M Shop	N Lib F	P Lib NF	Q Lib Ref	R Mag	S Rel
Best	30	.5289	3.3655	45.3	8	12	4	3	1	1	1	0	4	0	0	1	0	7	0	0	2	0	1	0	14	0	0	1	0
best-	2	.1733	.1149	30.6	0	1	1	0	0	0	0	0	1	1	0	0	0	0	0	0	0	0	0	0	0	0	0	0	0
best-dressed	2	.1733	.1149	30.6	0	0	0	1	0	1	0	0	1	1	0	0	0	0	0	0	0	0	0	0	0	0	0	0	0
best-known	40	.6599	5.4140	47.3	3	9	9	7	5	4	3	0	6	0	0	2	0	4	0	2	8	2	0	0	0	3	9	4	0
best-liked	4	.4641	.3966	36.0	0	1	0	1	1	1	0	0	0	0	0	0	0	1	0	1	1	0	0	0	0	0	0	1	0
best-looking	3	.0000	.1370	31.4	2	1	0	0	0	0	0	0	3	0	0	0	0	0	0	0	0	0	0	0	0	0	0	0	0
best-loved	8	.3867	.7009	38.5	1	0	0	1	3	1	2	0	2	0	0	2	0	0	0	0	3	0	0	0	0	1	0	0	0
best-protected	2	.0000	.0914	29.6	0	1	0	0	1	0	0	0	2	0	0	0	0	0	0	0	0	0	0	0	0	0	0	0	0
best-selling	4	.0000	.0486	26.9	0	1	0	0	1	1	1	0	0	0	0	0	0	0	0	0	0	0	0	0	0	0	0	4	0
best-trained	3	.2357	.2199	33.4	0	1	0	0	0	1	0	1	2	0	0	0	0	0	0	0	0	0	0	0	0	1	0	0	0
Besterman	3	.0000	.0365	25.6	0	0	0	0	0	0	3	0	0	0	0	0	0	0	0	0	0	0	0	0	0	0	0	3	0
Besterman's	2	.0000	.0243	23.9	0	0	0	0	0	0	2	0	0	0	0	0	0	0	0	0	0	0	0	0	0	0	0	2	0
besting	2	.2405	.1205	30.8	0	0	0	0	2	0	0	0	0	0	0	0	0	0	0	1	0	0	0	0	0	1	0	0	0
bestow	4	.2685	.2438	33.9	0	1	0	1	0	1	1	0	0	0	0	0	0	1	0	0	0	1	0	0	2	0	0	0	0
bestowed	14	.5380	1.6015	42.0	0	1	0	3	3	1	3	3	3	2	0	3	0	0	0	0	0	0	0	0	3	0	0	3	0
bestowing	2	.1698	.1133	30.5	0	0	1	0	0	0	1	0	1	0	0	0	0	0	0	0	0	0	0	0	0	0	1	0	0
bestride	3	.2257	.1583	32.0	0	2	0	0	0	0	1	0	0	2	0	1	0	0	0	0	0	0	0	0	0	0	0	0	0
bestrides	2	.0000	.0215	23.3	0	0	0	0	0	0	2	0	0	0	0	2	0	0	0	0	0	0	0	0	0	0	0	0	0
bet	157	.7659	24.535	53.9	24	44	17	10	36	19	5	2	60	12	2	22	2	1	3	1	4	0	0	0	22	15	0	13	0
Bet	9	.0000	.4111	36.1	0	0	0	9	0	0	0	0	9	0	0	0	0	0	0	0	0	0	0	0	0	0	0	0	0
beta	13	.3330	.9925	40.0	0	0	2	3	1	0	1	6	0	1	0	0	0	0	3	9	0	0	0	0	0	0	0	0	0
Beta	3	.0000	.0591	27.7	0	0	0	0	0	3	0	0	0	0	0	0	0	0	0	3	0	0	0	0	0	0	0	0	0
betcha	2	.2407	.1138	30.6	1	0	0	0	0	1	0	0	0	0	0	1	0	0	0	0	0	0	0	0	0	1	0	0	0
Betelgeuse	3	.2383	.1815	32.6	0	0	2	0	1	0	0	0	0	0	0	0	0	0	0	2	0	0	0	0	0	1	0	0	0
Beth	58	.2667	3.7314	45.7	8	1	1	1	22	0	25	0	7	1	0	0	7	0	0	0	0	0	0	0	41	1	0	1	0
Beth's	4	.2034	.1966	32.9	1	0	0	0	2	0	1	0	0	1	0	0	0	0	0	0	0	0	0	0	3	0	0	0	0
Bethel	6	.0000	.0869	29.4	0	6	0	0	0	0	0	0	0	0	0	0	0	0	0	0	0	0	0	0	0	6	0	0	0
Bethenia	6	.0000	.2741	34.4	0	0	6	0	0	0	0	0	6	0	0	0	0	0	0	0	0	0	0	0	0	0	0	0	0
Bethenia's	2	.0000	.0914	29.6	0	0	2	0	0	0	0	0	2	0	0	0	0	0	0	0	0	0	0	0	0	0	0	0	0
bethink	2	.0000	.0215	23.3	0	0	0	0	0	0	2	0	0	0	0	2	0	0	0	0	0	0	0	0	0	0	0	0	0
Bethlehem	31	.4162	2.7320	44.4	6	1	5	3	3	4	6	3	0	6	0	3	0	2	0	0	10	0	0	0	0	5	1	3	1
Bethlehemovich	2	.0000	.0219	23.4	0	0	0	0	0	0	2	0	0	2	0	0	0	0	0	0	0	0	0	0	0	0	0	0	0
Bethune	2	.2285	.1129	30.5	0	0	2	0	0	0	0	0	0	0	0	0	0	1	0	0	0	0	0	0	0	0	1	0	0
betimes	2	.2446	.1122	30.5	0	0	0	0	1	0	1	0	0	0	0	1	0	0	0	0	0	0	0	0	0	0	1	0	0
Beto	11	.0000	.5025	37.0	11	0	0	0	0	0	0	0	11	0	0	0	0	0	0	0	0	0	0	0	0	0	0	0	0
betray	13	.6997	1.8615	42.7	1	0	2	2	4	3	1	0	3	1	0	0	0	0	1	0	2	0	0	0	1	2	2	1	0
betrayal	3	.3847	.2494	34.0	0	0	0	0	1	1	1	0	0	0	0	0	0	0	0	0	0	0	0	0	1	1	1	0	0
betrayed	15	.5946	1.8783	42.7	0	0	0	1	8	2	3	1	4	0	0	3	0	0	0	0	0	0	0	0	3	1	2	2	0
betraying	3	.2261	.2131	33.3	0	1	0	0	1	1	0	0	2	0	0	0	0	0	0	0	0	0	0	0	1	0	0	0	0
betrothal	2	.1717	.1142	30.6	0	0	0	0	0	1	1	0	1	0	0	1	0	0	0	0	0	0	0	0	0	0	0	0	0
betrothed	3	.3263	.2368	33.7	0	0	0	1	0	2	0	0	1	0	0	0	0	0	0	0	1	0	0	0	0	0	0	1	0
bets	4	.3212	.3104	34.9	1	0	0	2	1	0	0	0	1	0	0	1	0	0	0	0	0	0	0	0	0	2	0	0	0
Betsy	320	.4646	31.980	55.0	186	101	6	9	2	16	0	0	32	7	0	11	2	16	0	0	2	0	0	0	158	83	9	0	0
Betsy's	21	.1645	.9463	39.8	17	3	0	1	0	0	0	0	2	0	0	0	1	0	0	0	0	0	0	0	17	1	0	0	0
better	1911	.9580	361.65	65.6	375	292	229	230	355	207	174	49	596	99	9	135	32	212	26	162	35	12	52	25	170	167	51	127	1
Better	4	.0000	.1827	32.6	4	0	0	0	0	0	0	0	4	0	0	0	0	0	0	0	0	0	0	0	0	0	0	0	0
bettered	3	.3394	.2451	33.9	0	0	2	0	0	0	1	0	1	0	0	1	0	0	0	0	0	0	0	0	1	0	0	0	0
betters	2	.0000	.0914	29.6	0	0	1	1	0	0	0	0	2	0	0	0	0	0	0	0	0	0	0	0	0	0	0	0	0
Bettina	3	.0000	.0434	26.4	0	0	0	0	3	0	0	0	0	0	0	0	0	0	0	0	0	0	0	0	0	3	0	0	0
betting	7	.3439	.6106	37.9	0	2	0	3	2	0	0	0	4	0	0	1	0	0	2	0	0	0	0	0	0	0	0	0	0
Betty	109	.7541	16.708	52.2	34	22	17	11	16	3	5	1	28	18	2	0	28	2	8	1	0	3	1	0	1	4	0	13	0
Betty's	12	.2321	.6625	38.2	7	2	1	0	0	0	0	2	1	2	0	0	5	0	0	0	0	4	0	0	0	0	0	0	0
between	3324	.9660	632.93	68.0	315	376	434	484	698	557	366	94	413	236	35	108	407	409	276	402	149	22	49	76	104	177	263	197	1
Between	20	.3667	1.6596	42.2	0	5	4	2	5	2	2	0	2	2	0	0	0	9	0	0	7	0	0	0	0	0	0	0	0
between-meal	2	.2346	.1166	30.7	0	0	0	0	2	0	0	0	0	0	0	0	0	0	0	1	0	0	0	0	0	0	0	1	0
Between-the-Logs	3	.0000	.0322	25.1	0	0	0	0	3	0	0	0	0	0	0	3	0	0	0	0	0	0	0	0	0	0	0	0	0
betweenness	2	.0000	.0299	24.8	0	0	0	0	0	2	0	0	0	0	0	0	2	0	0	0	0	0	0	0	0	0	0	0	0
Beulah	3	.2236	.1570	32.0	0	0	0	0	0	0	3	0	0	1	0	2	0	0	0	0	0	0	0	0	0	0	0	0	0
bevel	27	.0256	.2257	33.5	0	0	0	0	16	8	3	0	0	0	0	0	0	0	0	0	0	0	0	25	0	2	0	0	0
beveled	5	.0000	.0126	21.0	0	0	0	0	3	1	1	0	0	0	0	0	0	0	0	0	0	0	0	5	0	0	0	0	0
Bevens	2	.0000	.0290	24.6	2	0	0	0	0	0	0	0	0	0	0	0	0	0	0	0	0	0	0	0	0	2	0	0	0
Bevens'	2	.0000	.0290	24.6	2	0	0	0	0	0	0	0	0	0	0	0	0	0	0	0	0	0	0	0	0	2	0	0	0
beverage	15	.1560	.5991	37.8	0	0	0	1	2	5	6	1	1	0	0	0	0	3	0	1	0	0	9	0	0	0	0	1	0
beverages	23	.3286	1.6908	42.3	3	0	1	1	2	9	7	0	1	0	0	0	0	1	0	8	0	0	8	0	0	0	2	3	0
Beverly	4	.2780	.2502	34.0	0	3	0	0	1	0	0	0	1	0	0	0	2	0	0	0	0	1	0	0	0	0	0	1	0
beware	16	.5753	1.8987	42.8	1	0	2	1	7	3	2	0	2	2	0	2	0	1	0	0	1	2	3	0	1	0	0	2	0
bewildered	21	.5965	2.6974	44.3	0	4	2	3	7	3	2	0	10	1	1	2	0	1	0	0	0	0	0	0	5	1	0	0	0
bewildering	12	.4727	1.2323	40.9	0	0	1	1	7	2	0	1	2	0	0	1	0	0	0	2	0	0	0	0	0	0	2	5	0
bewilderment	8	.5601	.9858	39.9	0	1	1	1	2	1	1	1	4	0	0	0	0	0	0	1	0	0	0	0	1	1	1	0	0
bewitch	4	.3832	.3307	35.2	1	1	0	0	0	1	1	0	0	0	0	1	0	0	0	0	1	0	0	0	0	2	0	0	0
bewitched	9	.4050	.8275	39.2	1	3	1	2	2	0	0	0	3	0	2	1	0	0	0	0	1	0	0	0	0	1	0	1	0
Bey	3	.0000	.1370	31.4	0	3	0	0	0	0	0	0	3	0	0	0	0	0	0	0	0	0	0	0	0	0	0	0	0
beyond	485	.9219	88.673	59.5	38	60	58	66	118	69	59	17	122	15	9	53	6	63	3	39	5	6	8	5	31	33	43	44	0
BF	4	.0000	.0599	27.8	0	0	0	0	4	0	0	0	0	0	0	0	4	0	0	0	0	0	0	0	0	0	0	0	0
BFGC	2	.0000	.0299	24.8	0	0	2	0	0	0	0	0	0	0	0	0	2	0	0	0	0	0	0	0	0	0	0	0	0
Bh	4	.0000	.0599	27.8	0	0	0	0	0	4	0	0	0	0	0	0	4	0	0	0	0	0	0	0	0	0	0	0	0
BHN	6	.0000	.0151	21.8	0	0	0	0	0	0	6	0	0	0	0	0	0	0	0	0	0	0	0	6	0	0	0	0	0
bi	7	.4968	.7404	38.7	1	1	0	0	4	1	0	0	1	1	0	0	2	0	2	0	0	0	0	0	0	0	1	0	0
Biafra	4	.3134	.2876	34.6	0	1	0	0	3	0	0	0	0	0	0	0	0	1	0	1	0	0	0	0	0	0	2	0	0
Biafran	3	.0000	.0365	25.6	0	0	0	0	0	3	0	0	0	0	0	0	0	0	0	0	0	0	0	0	0	0	0	3	0
Biafu	9	.0000	.4111	36.1	0	9	0	0	0	0	0	0	9	0	0	0	0	0	0	0	0	0	0	0	0	0	0	0	0
Bianca	9	.0000	.4111	36.1	0	0	9	0	0	0	0	0	9	0	0	0	0	0	0	0	0	0	0	0	0	0	0	0	0
Bianca's	2	.0000	.0914	29.6	0	0	2	0	0	0	0	0	2	0	0	0	0	0	0	0	0	0	0	0	0	0	0	0	0
bias	37	.1193	1.1341	40.5	0	0	1	0	13	5	18	0	1	0	0	0	0	0	0	7	0	0	26	0	0	1	2	0	0
biased	2	.1733	.1149	30.6	0	0	0	1	0	1	0	0	1	1	0	0	0	0	0	0	0	0	0	0	0	0	0	0	0
bib	6	.3877	.5211	37.2	0	4	0	0	0	1	1	0	1	0	0	0	0	0	0	0	0	0	1	0	0	3	0	1	0
Bibby	2	.0000	.0234	23.7	0	0	0	0	2	0	0	0	0	0	0	0	0	0	0	0	0	0	0	0	2	0	0	0	0
Bible	130	.5571	15.213	51.8	13	19	17	18	34	17	10	2	20	9	0	6	0	16	12	1	6	1	1	1	6	19	27	2	3
Bibles	10	.4275	.8957	39.5	0	2	1	3	1	0	3	0	0	1	0	0	0	1	1	0	0	0	0	3	1	2	1	0	0
Biblical	18	.6167	2.2714	43.6	0	0	3	1	8	0	4	2	0	3	0	2	0	3	0	0	0	0	0	0	0	3	4	3	0
bibliography	4	.3503	.3110	34.9	0	0	0	0	0	0	1	3	0	1	0	0	0	0	0	1	0	0	0	0	0	0	0	2	0

3R BEST
5P best-adjusted
5A best-beloved
9F best-developed
9Q best-informed
6R best-kept
9B best-laid
7R best-named
5Q best-prepared
9D best-regarded
XR best-seller
3F Best's
7R bested
7A bestest
8F bestial
7Q bestiary
7D bestir
4B bestraddle
5N bestrewn
8D bestrode
9F Betancourt
6H betatron
8H betatrons
9B bete
7P betel
7B beth
9B Beth-le-hem
7H Bethe
3A Beto's
6A betook
9P Betrand
7A betrayals
7P betrayer
9R betrays
9D betroth'd
5Q Betrothed
3D BETSY
6A better-behaved
6F better-drained
3P better-educated
5P better-known
6J better-organized
7P better-quality
6P better-than-average
6A better'n
XH bettering
3A Bettine
7P Bettys
7H between-meals
7P betwixt
9M bevel-edged
9M beveling
8R Beverage
4R Beverley
3A Bevis
8A bevy
6A bewailing
9Q bewilderingly
3Q bewitching
7A bewteen
4A Bey's
5P Beyoglu
9D Beyond
6E BG
7B bh
6E BH
7F Bhutan
3A Bi
6J BiSHvet
4N Bi-Coloured-Python-R**
7A bi-cycle
XR bi-monthly
3A bi
6R BIA'S**
8R Biafra's
8R Biafrans
4A Biafu's
5P Biagio
8L bias-binding
9D Bibb
4J bibble
7A Bibbs
9Q bible
XH biblical

Word Type	F	D	U	SFI	3 Gr 3	4 Gr 4	5 Gr 5	6 Gr 6	7 Gr 7	8 Gr 8	9 Gr 9	X UnGr	A Read	B Eng & Gr	C Comp	D Lit	E Math	F Soc Stud	G Spell	H Sci	J Music	K Art	L Home Ec	M Shop	N Lib F	P Lib NF	Q Lib Ref	R Mag	S Rel
bicarbonate	5	.2926	.3754	35.7	0	0	3	1	0	0	1	0	1	0	0	0	0	1	0	3	0	0	0	0	0	0	0	0	0
biceps	11	.1543	.5092	37.1	0	0	0	0	0	0	1	10	0	0	0	0	0	0	0	10	0	0	0	0	0	0	1	0	0
bicker	2	.1698	.1133	30.5	0	0	0	0	2	0	0	0	1	0	0	0	0	0	0	0	0	0	0	0	0	0	1	0	0
bickered	2	.0000	.0290	24.6	2	0	0	0	0	0	0	0	0	0	0	0	0	0	0	0	0	0	0	0	0	2	0	0	0
bickering	4	.3696	.3616	35.6	0	0	0	1	1	1	1	0	2	1	0	0	0	0	0	0	0	0	0	0	0	0	1	0	0
bicuspids	2	.0000	.0394	26.0	0	0	2	0	0	0	0	0	0	0	0	0	0	0	0	2	0	0	0	0	0	0	0	0	0
bicycle	182	.8307	30.422	54.8	54	40	20	15	22	16	11	4	57	25	8	3	21	10	9	22	0	0	2	4	5	1	7	8	0
Bicycle	2	.1733	.1149	30.6	1	0	0	0	0	0	1	0	1	1	0	0	0	0	0	0	0	0	0	0	0	0	0	0	0
bicycles	52	.7280	7.8005	48.9	17	17	3	5	6	4	0	0	17	3	0	0	2	18	0	1	1	1	0	0	2	1	1	5	0
bicycling	4	.2424	.3036	34.8	1	0	1	0	0	1	0	1	3	0	0	0	0	0	0	0	0	0	0	0	0	0	0	1	0
bid	38	.6769	5.2552	47.2	6	3	4	6	3	1	13	2	5	0	0	10	0	4	1	0	4	0	0	0	6	1	2	5	0
bidden	3	.2196	.1554	31.9	0	1	0	0	1	0	1	0	0	0	0	2	0	0	0	0	0	0	0	0	1	0	0	0	0
bidder	4	.4791	.4053	36.1	0	1	0	1	2	0	0	0	0	0	0	1	0	1	0	0	0	0	0	0	0	1	1	0	0
bidders	2	.0000	.0215	23.3	0	0	0	0	0	1	1	0	0	0	0	2	0	0	0	0	0	0	0	0	0	0	0	0	0
Biddie	8	.0000	.3655	35.6	0	0	8	0	0	0	0	0	8	0	0	0	0	0	0	0	0	0	0	0	0	0	0	0	0
Biddie's	3	.0000	.1370	31.4	0	0	3	0	0	0	0	0	3	0	0	0	0	0	0	0	0	0	0	0	0	0	0	0	0
bidding	9	.4763	.9710	39.9	1	2	2	1	1	2	0	0	4	0	0	0	0	0	0	0	0	0	0	0	2	2	1	0	0
Biddlewee	3	.0000	.1370	31.4	0	0	3	0	0	0	0	0	3	0	0	0	0	0	0	0	0	0	0	0	0	0	0	0	0
Biddlewees	5	.0000	.2284	33.6	0	0	5	0	0	0	0	0	5	0	0	0	0	0	0	0	0	0	0	0	0	0	0	0	0
Biddy	11	.0724	.2742	34.4	0	0	0	0	0	1	10	0	0	0	0	10	0	1	0	0	0	0	0	0	0	0	0	0	0
bide	2	.2412	.1141	30.6	1	0	0	1	0	0	0	0	0	1	0	0	0	0	0	0	0	0	0	0	0	1	0	0	0
biding	2	.1787	.1174	30.7	0	1	0	1	0	0	0	0	1	0	0	0	0	0	0	0	0	0	0	0	1	0	0	0	0
bids	11	.5170	1.1926	40.8	1	0	0	0	3	2	5	0	1	0	0	5	0	1	0	0	1	1	0	0	0	1	0	1	0
Bidwell	5	.0000	.0724	28.6	0	5	0	0	0	0	0	0	0	0	0	0	0	0	0	0	0	0	0	0	0	5	0	0	0
bien	3	.2279	.2143	33.3	0	0	0	0	0	2	0	1	2	0	0	0	0	0	0	0	0	0	0	0	0	0	0	1	0
biennial	2	.2437	.1129	30.5	0	0	0	1	0	0	1	0	0	0	0	0	0	0	0	0	0	0	0	0	0	0	1	1	0
bier	3	.2292	.1615	32.1	0	0	2	0	0	0	1	0	0	0	0	1	0	0	0	0	0	0	0	0	2	0	0	0	0
bifocals	2	.2446	.1125	30.5	0	0	0	0	1	0	1	0	0	1	0	1	0	0	0	0	0	0	0	0	0	0	0	0	0
big	3476	.8792	611.96	67.9	1297	714	334	337	412	206	133	43	1440	88	15	169	13	329	28	277	54	46	11	10	290	426	46	234	0
Big	230	.7002	33.713	55.3	69	44	27	41	28	15	2	4	117	2	0	15	2	6	1	20	1	0	0	0	34	11	1	20	0
BIG	6	.2355	.4634	36.7	1	0	0	0	5	0	0	0	5	0	0	0	0	0	0	0	0	0	0	0	0	1	0	0	0
big-city	2	.0000	.0243	23.9	0	0	0	0	0	1	1	0	0	0	0	0	0	0	0	0	0	0	0	0	0	0	0	2	0
big-eared	5	.4395	.4863	36.9	1	0	0	2	2	0	0	0	1	0	0	1	0	0	0	0	0	0	0	0	1	2	0	0	0
big-game	11	.6210	1.4201	41.5	0	3	1	1	3	1	0	2	2	0	0	1	0	1	0	0	0	0	0	0	1	1	2	3	0
big-league	5	.2445	.3864	35.9	0	0	0	1	1	2	1	0	4	0	0	1	0	0	0	0	0	0	0	0	0	0	0	0	0
big-mouthed	3	.0000	.0352	25.5	0	0	0	3	0	0	0	0	0	0	0	0	0	0	0	0	0	0	0	0	3	0	0	0	0
big-nosed	4	.1668	.1611	32.1	0	0	0	0	1	3	0	0	0	0	2	0	0	1	0	0	0	0	0	0	0	0	0	1	0
big-time	3	.0000	.0365	25.6	0	0	0	0	2	0	0	1	0	0	0	0	0	0	0	0	0	0	0	0	0	0	0	3	0
Big's	6	.0000	.2741	34.4	0	0	0	6	0	0	0	0	6	0	0	0	0	0	0	0	0	0	0	0	0	0	0	0	0
Bigfoot	12	.0000	.5482	37.4	0	0	12	0	0	0	0	0	12	0	0	0	0	0	0	0	0	0	0	0	0	0	0	0	0
bigger	336	.8207	55.695	57.5	150	68	29	24	28	22	10	5	107	12	4	13	1	27	5	70	4	0	0	0	21	49	5	18	0
bigger'n	2	.1787	.1174	30.7	0	0	1	0	0	1	0	0	1	0	0	0	0	0	0	0	0	0	0	0	1	0	0	0	0
biggest	206	.8524	35.245	55.5	57	38	20	24	36	18	12	1	69	2	3	9	0	21	3	10	2	0	1	2	10	35	13	26	0
bigness	3	.2143	.1568	32.0	0	0	1	0	1	0	0	1	0	0	0	0	0	0	0	0	0	0	0	0	0	1	0	2	0
bigotry	2	.2408	.1204	30.8	0	0	1	0	0	1	0	0	0	0	0	0	0	1	0	0	0	0	0	0	0	1	0	0	0
Bijo	2	.0000	.0219	23.4	0	0	0	0	0	0	2	0	0	2	0	0	0	0	0	0	0	0	0	0	0	0	0	0	0
bike	105	.6700	15.017	51.8	64	11	6	3	20	1	0	0	71	13	0	3	3	0	2	0	1	1	1	0	0	0	0	10	0
bikes	19	.3626	1.7059	42.3	8	0	4	0	7	0	0	0	9	0	0	0	7	0	0	0	0	0	0	0	0	0	0	3	0
bikini	2	.2433	.1158	30.6	0	0	1	0	0	0	0	1	0	0	0	0	0	0	0	0	0	0	0	0	0	1	0	1	0
bilateral	2	.0000	.0394	26.0	0	0	0	0	2	0	0	0	0	0	0	0	0	0	0	2	0	0	0	0	0	0	0	0	0
bilaterally	2	.0000	.0209	23.2	0	0	1	0	1	0	0	0	0	0	0	0	0	0	0	0	0	0	0	0	0	0	2	0	0
bile	5	.4587	.4821	36.8	0	0	0	0	2	0	2	1	0	1	0	0	0	0	0	0	0	0	0	0	1	1	2	0	0
bilingual	5	.1820	.2261	33.5	0	0	4	0	0	0	1	0	0	1	0	0	0	0	0	0	0	0	0	0	4	0	0	0	0
bill	221	.8606	38.039	55.8	82	29	21	13	29	17	20	10	55	10	1	7	31	13	3	6	0	1	2	2	6	55	10	19	0
Bill	1075	.7911	174.02	62.4	268	303	125	79	132	134	27	7	580	82	1	57	93	43	16	5	3	3	0	0	51	89	5	47	0
bill's	2	.1814	.1187	30.7	0	0	0	0	1	0	0	1	1	0	0	0	0	0	0	0	0	0	0	0	0	0	0	1	0
Bill's	84	.7343	12.826	51.1	24	15	9	6	13	16	1	0	48	6	0	3	5	4	4	0	0	0	0	0	4	5	0	5	0
billboard	2	.2306	.1140	30.6	0	0	0	0	0	2	0	0	0	1	0	0	0	1	0	0	0	0	0	0	0	0	0	0	0
billboards	6	.3427	.4581	36.6	0	1	0	0	1	0	4	0	0	3	0	0	0	2	0	0	0	0	0	0	0	0	1	0	0
billed	4	.3597	.3542	35.5	2	0	1	0	0	1	0	0	2	0	0	0	0	0	0	0	1	0	0	0	0	0	0	1	0
Billiam	5	.0000	.2284	33.6	0	0	5	0	0	0	0	0	5	0	0	0	0	0	0	0	0	0	0	0	0	0	0	0	0
billiard	7	.3836	.5703	37.6	0	0	2	0	0	3	2	0	0	0	0	3	0	0	0	0	2	0	0	0	0	0	2	0	0
Billie	2	.2443	.1130	30.5	0	0	1	0	0	1	0	0	0	0	0	1	0	0	0	0	0	0	0	0	1	0	0	0	0
billies	2	.0000	.0914	29.6	0	2	0	0	0	0	0	0	2	0	0	0	0	0	0	0	0	0	0	0	0	0	0	0	0
billing	5	.2316	.2703	34.3	0	0	1	0	2	0	2	0	0	0	0	0	0	0	0	0	0	0	0	0	0	0	3	2	0
Billings	18	.2561	1.1861	40.7	1	2	5	4	4	2	0	0	6	1	0	1	0	0	0	0	10	0	0	0	0	0	0	0	0
Billings'	6	.2028	.3977	36.0	1	0	0	3	2	0	0	0	4	0	0	0	0	0	0	0	2	0	0	0	0	0	0	0	0
billion	147	.6174	18.714	52.7	5	11	26	8	43	17	31	6	3	0	0	6	19	28	0	29	0	0	0	0	0	5	40	17	0
billion-dollar	3	.2425	.1816	32.6	0	0	0	0	1	1	1	0	0	0	0	0	0	2	0	0	0	0	0	0	0	0	0	1	0
billions	67	.5081	7.3131	48.6	11	16	11	7	13	2	7	0	4	1	0	0	3	5	0	38	0	0	0	0	0	3	12	1	0
billitch	2	.0000	.0219	23.4	0	0	0	2	0	0	0	0	0	2	0	0	0	0	0	0	0	0	0	0	0	0	0	0	0
billowed	4	.3212	.3104	34.9	0	2	0	1	0	0	1	0	1	0	0	1	0	0	0	0	0	0	0	0	0	2	0	0	0
billowing	10	.6505	1.3465	41.3	0	2	1	1	2	2	0	2	2	2	0	1	0	0	0	1	0	0	0	0	0	2	1	1	0
billows	14	.5968	1.7767	42.5	2	2	4	2	3	1	0	0	5	3	0	1	0	0	0	0	0	0	0	0	2	1	0	2	0
billowy	6	.2252	.3635	35.6	0	0	1	2	3	0	0	0	2	1	2	0	0	0	0	1	0	0	0	0	0	0	0	0	0
bills	96	.7780	15.161	51.8	28	17	14	9	11	6	8	3	27	2	0	6	10	7	1	3	0	0	0	0	5	19	9	7	0
billy	15	.4669	1.6672	42.2	1	7	1	0	4	1	1	0	11	1	0	0	0	0	1	0	0	0	0	0	0	0	0	2	0
Billy	450	.7466	69.138	58.4	182	86	32	18	66	54	11	1	199	9	2	25	6	45	6	3	27	0	0	0	81	10	0	37	0
BILLY	3	.0000	.0322	25.1	0	0	0	0	1	2	0	0	0	0	0	3	0	0	0	0	0	0	0	0	0	0	0	0	0
Billy's	40	.6983	5.8122	47.6	15	10	2	4	3	5	1	0	17	1	0	4	4	3	0	0	2	0	0	0	6	0	0	3	0
Bilsen	2	.0000	.0290	24.6	0	0	2	0	0	0	0	0	0	0	0	0	0	0	0	0	0	0	0	0	0	2	0	0	0
biltong	2	.0000	.0209	23.2	0	0	0	0	2	0	0	0	0	0	0	0	0	0	0	0	0	0	0	0	0	0	2	0	0
bimba	6	.0000	.0485	26.9	0	0	0	6	0	0	0	0	0	0	0	0	0	0	0	0	6	0	0	0	0	0	0	0	0
bimetal	13	.1139	.4114	36.1	0	0	0	3	0	7	3	0	0	0	0	0	0	0	0	6	0	0	0	7	0	0	0	0	0
bimetal-strip	3	.0000	.0076	18.8	0	0	0	0	0	3	0	0	0	0	0	0	0	0	0	0	0	0	0	3	0	0	0	0	0
bimonthly	2	.0000	.0299	24.8	0	0	0	2	0	0	0	0	0	0	0	0	2	0	0	0	0	0	0	0	0	0	0	0	0
bin	27	.6868	3.8564	45.9	0	3	2	3	9	6	4	0	10	2	1	2	6	2	0	0	0	0	0	0	3	0	0	1	0
binaries	2	.2346	.1166	30.7	0	0	0	0	1	0	1	0	0	0	0	0	0	0	0	1	0	0	0	0	0	0	0	1	0
binary	30	.3406	2.2954	43.6	0	1	6	1	3	13	6	0	0	0	0	0	22	0	0	3	2	0	0	0	0	0	3	0	0
Binary	2	.0000	.0299	24.8	0	0	2	0	0	0	0	0	0	0	0	0	2	0	0	0	0	0	0	0	0	0	0	0	0
bind	27	.7072	3.8764	45.9	1	1	3	4	5	3	9	1	5	1	1	1	0	2	0	1	2	1	6	1	3	1	1	1	0
binder	3	.3421	.2123	33.3	0	0	0	0	1	0	2	0	0	0	0	0	0	0	0	0	0	0	1	1	0	0	1	0	0
Bindibu	5	.0000	.0972	29.9	0	5	0	0	0	0	0	0	0	0	0	0	0	5	0	0	0	0	0	0	0	0	0	0	0

5A bibs
7Q bichir
7Q bichirs
9M bichromate
4Q Bickell
5H bicuspid
8H bicycle-safety
5G biddan
5A Biddlewee's
7A Biddlewhite
7A Biddlewhite's
5Q biennially
6Q biennials
9R Biff
6A Bifrost
8R BigSur
8F Big-Foot
XR big-bass
9N big-deal
7R big-displacement
5A big-eyed
8R big-government
6F big-headed
7R big-inch
8A big-leaguers
4N big-starred
8R big-university
9R bigger-than-ever
6R biggies
5B Biggs
7Q bighorn
9N bight
7A Bigmouth
6A Bigsy's
5P bij
8C Bijou
4A bike's
7R bikemakers
9R bikini-clad
5A Bikle
5A bild
8B bilge
XR bilious
5N Billerica
8F billeted
8R billets
7P billetted
7M billfold
3F billfolds
9D billiards
5J Billing's
XH Billingham
7N Billingsgate
8J Billion
7H billion-odd
6P billow
4P Bills
6A Billy-goat
4A billy's
7P billygoat
8B Billys
7N bilobed
7F Biloxi
5P Bilsen's
9Q Bilskilnir
5P Binche
9M bindery

Word Type	F	D	U	SFI	3 Gr 3	4 Gr 4	5 Gr 5	6 Gr 6	7 Gr 7	8 Gr 8	9 Gr 9	X UnGr	A Read	B Eng & Gr	C Comp	D Lit	E Math	F Soc Stud	G Spell	H Sci	J Music	K Art	L Home Ec	M Shop	N Lib F	P Lib NF	Q Lib Ref	R Mag	S Rel
binding	46	.6048	5.7589	47.6	0	0	7	8	5	8	12	6	3	2	0	0	0	3	0	21	0	1	8	1	2	0	4	1	0
bindings	8	.3431	.6047	37.8	0	1	1	0	2	1	3	0	1	0	0	0	0	0	1	0	0	0	3	0	1	0	0	2	0
binds	4	.3833	.3412	35.3	0	0	0	1	1	1	1	0	0	0	0	1	0	0	0	2	0	0	0	0	0	1	0	0	0
Bing	12	.4792	1.3427	41.3	0	9	0	1	1	0	0	1	8	0	0	1	0	0	0	0	1	0	0	0	0	0	0	2	0
Bingham	3	.3840	.2594	34.1	1	0	1	0	0	0	0	1	0	0	0	0	0	1	0	1	0	0	0	0	0	1	0	0	0
Binghamton	2	.0000	.0290	24.6	0	2	0	0	0	0	0	0	0	0	0	0	0	0	0	0	0	0	0	0	0	2	0	0	0
Binney	12	.0000	.1407	31.5	12	0	0	0	0	0	0	0	0	0	0	0	0	0	0	0	0	0	0	0	12	0	0	0	0
binoculars	20	.5562	2.3976	43.8	5	2	1	5	4	0	2	1	6	1	0	1	0	0	0	4	0	0	0	0	0	2	0	6	0
binomial	3	.2371	.1813	32.6	0	0	1	0	0	0	2	0	0	0	0	0	1	0	0	2	0	0	0	0	0	0	0	0	0
bins	4	.3545	.3102	34.9	1	0	0	0	0	2	1	0	0	0	0	0	0	0	0	1	0	0	0	1	0	1	0	1	0
bio	2	.2376	.1088	30.4	0	0	0	0	2	0	0	0	0	0	0	0	0	0	1	0	0	0	0	0	0	0	0	1	0
biochemical	2	.0000	.0394	26.0	0	0	0	0	1	0	1	0	0	0	0	0	0	0	0	2	0	0	0	0	0	0	0	0	0
biochemist	3	.2159	.1532	31.9	0	0	0	0	0	0	2	1	0	0	0	0	0	0	0	0	0	0	0	0	0	0	2	1	0
biochemistry	2	.0000	.0209	23.2	0	0	0	0	1	0	1	0	0	0	0	0	0	0	0	0	0	0	0	0	0	0	2	0	0
biochemists	3	.2427	.1822	32.6	0	0	0	1	1	0	1	0	0	0	0	0	0	0	0	2	0	0	0	0	0	0	0	1	0
bioengineers	2	.0000	.0209	23.2	0	0	0	0	0	0	2	0	0	0	0	0	0	0	0	0	0	0	0	0	0	0	2	0	0
biographer	4	.2337	.2387	33.8	0	0	1	0	1	0	2	0	1	0	0	0	0	0	0	0	0	1	0	0	0	0	0	2	0
biographical	7	.1422	.2638	34.2	0	0	0	0	1	2	4	0	1	0	4	0	0	0	0	0	0	0	0	0	0	1	1	0	0
biographies	18	.4429	1.7090	42.3	0	3	2	6	5	0	1	1	2	10	2	1	0	0	0	0	0	0	0	0	0	2	1	0	0
biography	26	.6083	3.3357	45.2	0	1	5	4	7	5	4	0	9	7	2	3	0	0	1	0	0	0	0	0	0	1	1	2	0
Biography	3	.1200	.1302	31.1	0	0	0	0	2	0	1	0	1	2	0	0	0	0	0	0	0	0	0	0	0	0	0	0	0
biologic	3	.2445	.1818	32.6	0	0	0	0	1	0	0	2	0	0	0	0	0	0	0	2	0	0	0	0	0	0	1	0	0
biological	25	.4025	2.1962	43.4	0	0	2	0	13	1	6	3	1	0	0	0	0	0	0	6	0	0	0	0	0	1	11	6	0
biologist	14	.5019	1.4975	41.8	0	0	1	2	7	0	3	1	1	0	1	0	0	0	0	6	0	0	0	0	0	0	3	3	0
biologists	36	.4256	3.4116	45.3	0	0	4	2	18	5	5	2	3	0	0	1	0	0	0	22	0	0	0	0	0	0	3	7	0
biology	36	.5726	4.2910	46.3	0	0	6	3	7	5	11	4	0	2	0	3	1	0	1	19	0	0	0	0	0	0	7	3	0
bionics	5	.0000	.0523	27.2	0	0	0	0	0	0	5	0	0	0	0	0	0	0	0	0	0	0	0	0	0	0	5	0	0
biophysicist	2	.0000	.0209	23.2	0	0	0	0	0	0	2	0	0	0	0	0	0	0	0	0	0	0	0	0	0	0	2	0	0
biosphere	12	.0000	.2366	33.7	0	0	0	0	11	1	0	0	0	0	0	0	0	0	0	12	0	0	0	0	0	0	0	0	0
biotic	5	.2121	.2801	34.5	0	0	0	0	3	0	2	0	0	0	0	0	0	0	0	4	0	0	0	0	0	0	0	1	0
biplane	2	.0000	.0914	29.6	0	0	0	2	0	0	0	0	2	0	0	0	0	0	0	0	0	0	0	0	0	0	0	0	0
birch	33	.8202	5.4490	47.4	5	2	6	8	3	5	3	1	9	1	0	3	0	4	1	1	1	0	0	1	2	6	3	1	0
Birch	3	.3272	.2363	33.7	0	2	0	0	0	1	0	0	1	0	0	1	0	0	0	0	1	0	0	0	0	0	0	0	0
birch-bark	6	.4375	.5551	37.4	1	0	1	1	2	0	0	1	0	0	0	1	0	1	0	0	2	0	0	0	2	0	0	0	0
Birchers	4	.0000	.0486	26.9	0	0	0	0	0	0	4	0	0	0	0	0	0	0	0	0	0	0	0	0	0	0	0	4	0
birches	6	.3365	.5101	37.1	0	2	1	1	2	0	0	0	3	0	1	0	0	0	0	1	0	0	0	0	1	0	0	0	0
bird	812	.8863	143.81	61.6	284	116	81	125	119	31	20	36	323	59	4	28	8	10	18	93	31	18	3	3	20	85	67	42	0
Bird	46	.5442	5.4395	47.4	6	9	7	1	15	3	3	2	18	0	0	16	0	0	0	1	1	0	0	0	1	2	4	3	0
bird-aircraft	2	.0000	.0243	23.9	0	0	0	0	0	0	0	2	0	0	0	0	0	0	0	0	0	0	0	0	0	0	0	2	0
bird-lovers	2	.2407	.1138	30.6	0	0	1	0	1	0	0	0	0	0	0	1	0	0	0	0	0	0	0	0	0	1	0	0	0
bird-walker	2	.0000	.0215	23.3	0	0	0	0	2	0	0	0	0	0	0	2	0	0	0	0	0	0	0	0	0	0	0	0	0
bird-walkers	5	.0000	.0537	27.3	0	0	0	0	5	0	0	0	0	0	0	5	0	0	0	0	0	0	0	0	0	0	0	0	0
bird's	64	.6869	9.0783	49.6	23	14	6	11	5	1	3	1	15	4	0	1	0	0	0	21	2	3	0	0	1	9	6	2	0
bird's-eye	2	.2152	.1357	31.3	0	2	0	0	0	0	0	0	1	0	0	0	0	1	0	0	0	0	0	0	0	0	0	0	0
birdbath	3	.0646	.0600	27.8	2	0	0	1	0	0	0	0	0	0	0	0	0	0	0	1	0	2	0	0	0	0	0	0	0
birdhouse	4	.2417	.3028	34.8	1	2	0	0	1	0	0	0	3	0	0	0	0	0	0	0	0	0	0	0	1	0	0	0	0
birdie	2	.1494	.1045	30.2	0	1	0	1	0	0	0	0	1	0	0	0	0	0	0	0	1	0	0	0	0	0	0	0	0
Birdie	50	.0578	1.1206	40.5	0	0	49	0	1	0	0	0	0	0	0	0	0	0	0	0	0	0	0	0	48	0	0	2	0
birdlike	5	.2433	.2841	34.5	1	2	0	0	1	1	0	0	0	0	0	0	0	0	0	0	2	0	0	0	0	3	0	0	0
birds	1203	.8690	209.02	63.2	435	150	100	169	233	43	30	43	337	44	10	30	33	39	14	245	24	41	1	4	26	127	157	70	1
Birds	10	.4014	.9152	39.6	5	0	0	2	1	1	1	0	3	0	0	1	0	0	0	0	0	0	0	1	0	0	0	5	0
birds'	29	.7463	4.4067	46.4	12	5	2	2	4	1	1	2	6	3	0	2	0	2	0	5	0	0	0	0	1	4	2	4	0
birdseed	4	.0000	.1827	32.6	4	0	0	0	0	0	0	0	4	0	0	0	0	0	0	0	0	0	0	0	0	0	0	0	0
Birk	14	.0000	.6396	38.1	14	0	0	0	0	0	0	0	14	0	0	0	0	0	0	0	0	0	0	0	0	0	0	0	0
Birmingham	10	.3539	.8276	39.2	1	0	5	1	2	1	0	0	1	0	0	0	0	7	0	0	1	0	0	0	0	1	0	0	0
birth	147	.8744	25.574	54.1	9	17	14	18	42	22	11	14	19	5	3	6	1	13	3	18	3	1	5	1	5	21	33	10	0
birthday	241	.8803	42.375	56.3	100	49	15	29	17	16	11	4	84	27	6	9	17	9	9	2	6	1	3	0	18	24	2	24	0
Birthday	9	.4927	.9633	39.8	2	2	1	2	1	0	1	0	2	1	0	0	0	1	0	0	2	0	0	0	0	3	0	0	0
birthdays	17	.5860	2.1331	43.3	7	6	3	0	0	0	1	0	6	1	0	0	0	2	0	0	0	0	1	0	0	5	0	2	0
birthmark	5	.0000	.0608	27.8	2	0	3	0	0	0	0	0	0	0	0	0	0	0	0	0	0	0	0	0	0	0	0	5	0
birthplace	14	.5073	1.5031	41.8	1	0	1	2	5	3	0	2	1	0	2	0	0	3	0	2	0	0	0	0	0	1	3	2	0
birthrate	3	.1937	.1495	31.7	0	0	0	0	3	0	0	0	0	0	0	0	0	1	0	0	0	0	0	0	0	0	0	2	0
birthrates	3	.0000	.0365	25.6	0	0	0	0	3	0	0	0	0	0	0	0	0	0	0	0	0	0	0	0	0	0	0	3	0
birthright	2	.2411	.1091	30.4	0	1	1	0	0	0	0	0	0	0	0	1	0	0	0	0	1	0	0	0	0	0	0	0	0
births	5	.4547	.4844	36.9	0	0	1	0	2	2	0	0	0	0	0	0	0	0	0	1	0	0	0	0	0	1	1	2	0
birthstone	4	.0000	.0599	27.8	0	4	0	0	0	0	0	0	0	0	0	0	4	0	0	0	0	0	0	0	0	0	0	0	0
Birtwick	4	.0000	.0469	26.7	0	0	0	0	4	0	0	0	0	0	0	0	0	0	0	0	0	0	0	0	4	0	0	0	0
Biscay	4	.3396	.3008	34.8	1	0	1	0	1	0	1	0	0	1	0	0	0	1	0	0	0	0	0	0	0	0	2	0	0
biscuit	17	.5824	2.0382	43.1	1	0	4	3	4	0	5	0	2	2	0	3	0	0	0	0	0	0	4	1	2	1	1	1	0
biscuits	45	.4986	4.7842	46.8	5	3	2	12	10	5	8	0	9	10	0	3	0	0	0	0	0	0	10	0	7	4	1	1	0
bisect	17	.1518	.7161	38.5	0	0	0	4	4	7	2	0	0	2	0	0	15	0	0	0	0	0	0	0	0	0	0	0	0
bisected	2	.2427	.1159	30.6	0	0	0	0	1	1	0	0	0	0	0	0	1	0	0	0	0	0	0	0	0	0	0	1	0
bisector	10	.0000	.1497	31.8	0	0	0	1	1	7	1	0	0	0	0	0	10	0	0	0	0	0	0	0	0	0	0	0	0
bisectors	4	.1776	.1927	32.8	0	0	0	1	0	1	1	1	0	0	0	0	3	0	0	1	0	0	0	0	0	0	0	0	0
bisects	4	.0000	.0599	27.8	0	0	0	0	0	2	2	0	0	0	0	0	4	0	0	0	0	0	0	0	0	0	0	0	0
bishop	31	.4903	3.5688	45.5	1	12	10	4	2	2	0	0	23	0	0	0	0	0	1	0	0	0	0	0	1	2	4	0	0
Bishop	25	.6119	3.1697	45.0	2	4	0	6	8	4	1	0	4	0	0	1	0	0	0	0	0	1	0	0	6	2	4	7	0
bishop's	3	.3394	.2451	33.9	0	0	1	0	1	1	0	0	1	0	0	1	0	0	0	0	0	0	0	0	1	0	0	0	0
bishops	12	.4191	1.1250	40.5	2	2	0	0	5	2	1	0	2	0	0	0	0	4	0	0	0	0	0	0	0	0	4	2	0
Bismarck	2	.0000	.0389	25.9	0	0	0	0	2	0	0	0	0	0	0	0	0	2	0	0	0	0	0	0	0	0	0	0	0
bismuth	3	.2286	.1800	32.6	1	0	0	0	0	2	0	0	1	0	0	0	0	0	0	0	0	0	0	1	0	0	1	0	0
bison	18	.5254	2.0206	43.1	1	0	1	3	10	1	1	1	3	0	0	1	0	1	1	4	0	0	0	0	0	1	7	0	0
bit	600	.8747	105.03	60.2	115	95	76	83	114	62	42	13	235	28	6	61	3	11	2	41	8	3	4	19	58	51	16	54	0
BIT	3	.1409	.1472	31.7	2	1	0	0	0	0	0	0	1	0	0	0	0	0	0	0	0	0	0	0	0	2	0	0	0
bitch	4	.4886	.4071	36.1	0	0	0	0	3	0	0	1	0	0	0	1	0	0	0	0	0	0	0	0	1	0	1	1	0
bite	172	.8482	29.364	54.7	47	23	25	22	29	11	12	3	72	6	2	20	0	1	3	24	3	1	5	0	13	16	4	2	0
bite-size	2	.0000	.0394	26.0	0	0	2	0	0	0	0	0	0	0	0	0	0	0	0	2	0	0	0	0	0	0	0	0	0
bite-sized	2	.2412	.1141	30.6	0	1	0	0	0	1	0	0	0	1	0	0	0	0	0	0	0	0	0	0	0	1	0	0	0
bites	41	.7815	6.4892	48.1	11	5	2	4	11	4	3	1	10	2	0	4	0	0	1	8	0	0	1	0	5	5	1	4	0
biting	44	.7925	7.0267	48.5	6	6	11	6	6	4	5	0	8	4	0	2	0	0	2	7	0	0	1	0	5	8	4	3	0
bits	196	.8986	35.040	55.4	45	39	23	27	31	19	12	0	44	8	3	9	6	10	0	56	2	4	3	3	11	18	11	8	0
bitsy	2	.1787	.1174	30.7	0	0	0	1	1	0	0	0	1	0	0	0	0	0	0	0	0	0	0	0	1	0	0	0	0
Bitsy	66	.2094	4.9387	46.9	0	0	0	60	6	0	0	0	60	0	0	0	0	0	0	0	0	0	0	0	6	0	0	0	0
bitten	33	.7259	4.9162	46.9	4	3	7	2	9	1	6	1	10	1	0	4	0	0	0	4	2	0	0	0	4	6	1	1	0

7N bindweed
8F binge
3N bingo
3N Binney's
6B binning
9Q bioastronautics
9Q bioengineer
9D biogen
5A biographers
7B biography's
5Q Biological
7Q biologically
9H biologist's
9R Biologists
7Q biome
7Q biomes
7Q biophysicists
9H bios
XH Biot
9H biotin
9R bipartisan
5P bipod
7A birchbark
4A bird-banding
7Q bird-borne
5J bird-catcher
3R bird-eating
3G bird-feeding
3P bird-hip
4P bird-hipped
5Q bird-hunting
5N bird-like
9E bird-powered
9D bird-waking
9D bird's-nest
5Q birdbander
3K birdbaths
6A birdcage
4A birdcall
5A birdcalls
4A birdland
9Q birdlife
3A Birds'
7N Birdsong
XR birdsongs
9R biretta
4A Birora
7H Birr
7Q Birth
9R birth-control
4Q Birthplace
4F birthplaces
9D bis-
9R Biscayne
4N Biscuits
6B bisecting
7R bisexual
7Q bishoprics
7F Bismarck's
XP bison's
8K bisons
7E Bisons
XR bisque
3A Bit
7D bit-roller

Word Type	F	D	U	SFI	3 Gr 3	4 Gr 4	5 Gr 5	6 Gr 6	7 Gr 7	8 Gr 8	9 Gr 9	X UnGr	A Read	B Eng & Gr	C Comp	D Lit	E Math	F Soc Stud	G Spell	H Sci	J Music	K Art	L Home Ec	M Shop	N Lib F	P Lib NF	Q Lib Ref	R Mag	S Rel
bitter	103	.8530	17.615	52.5	6	11	12	12	34	18	6	4	30	5	2	8	0	20	1	2	2	0	1	0	8	11	5	8	0
Bitter	2	.0000	.0243	23.9	0	0	0	0	1	1	0	0	0	0	0	0	0	0	0	0	0	0	0	0	0	0	0	2	0
bitter-cold	2	.2408	.1204	30.8	0	0	0	1	0	0	1	0	0	0	0	0	0	1	0	0	0	0	0	0	0	1	0	0	0
bitterest	3	.2357	.2199	33.4	0	0	1	0	1	0	0	1	2	0	0	0	0	0	0	0	0	0	0	0	0	1	0	0	0
bitterly	43	.7020	6.2897	48.0	2	10	5	10	7	3	6	0	20	2	0	4	0	2	0	0	0	0	0	0	2	4	4	5	0
bittern	2	.2446	.1125	30.5	0	0	0	1	1	0	0	0	0	1	0	1	0	0	0	0	0	0	0	0	0	0	0	0	0
bitterness	11	.4971	1.1993	40.8	2	0	2	0	5	0	2	0	3	0	0	2	0	1	0	0	0	0	0	0	0	4	0	1	0
bitterns	2	.1698	.1133	30.5	0	0	0	1	1	0	0	0	1	0	0	0	0	0	0	0	0	0	0	0	0	0	1	0	0
bitterroot	3	.0000	.1370	31.4	0	0	0	0	3	0	0	0	3	0	0	0	0	0	0	0	0	0	0	0	0	0	0	0	0
bittersweet	2	.0000	.0243	23.9	0	0	0	0	0	1	0	1	0	0	0	0	0	0	0	0	0	0	0	0	0	0	0	2	0
bitty	3	.2009	.1407	31.5	0	1	1	0	1	0	0	0	0	0	0	0	0	0	0	0	2	0	0	0	1	0	0	0	0
bitumen	3	.1858	.1432	31.6	0	0	0	0	1	2	0	0	0	2	0	0	0	1	0	0	0	0	0	0	0	0	0	0	0
bituminous	4	.3750	.3392	35.3	0	0	0	0	1	2	1	0	0	0	0	0	0	1	0	2	0	0	0	0	0	0	0	1	0
bivalve	2	.2278	.1128	30.5	0	0	0	0	1	0	1	0	0	0	0	0	0	0	0	1	0	0	0	0	0	0	1	0	0
bivalves	5	.3749	.4195	36.2	0	0	0	1	1	0	3	0	0	0	0	0	0	0	0	3	0	0	0	0	0	0	1	1	0
Bixby	4	.0000	.1827	32.6	0	0	0	0	0	4	0	0	4	0	0	0	0	0	0	0	0	0	0	0	0	0	0	0	0
bizarre	13	.2682	.7888	39.0	0	0	0	1	9	2	1	0	0	1	0	0	0	0	0	0	0	0	0	0	0	0	9	3	0
Bizet	9	.1052	.2533	34.0	2	0	0	1	3	3	0	0	0	0	0	0	0	0	0	0	8	0	0	0	0	0	1	0	0
Bjarni	4	.0000	.0438	26.4	0	0	0	4	0	0	0	0	0	4	0	0	0	0	0	0	0	0	0	0	0	0	0	0	0
bl	7	.0000	.0568	27.5	2	0	4	1	0	0	0	0	0	0	0	0	0	0	7	0	0	0	0	0	0	0	0	0	0
black	1556	.8892	275.67	64.4	307	285	189	177	281	163	111	43	445	28	28	133	68	100	18	97	71	51	9	5	153	144	40	166	0
Black	283	.6147	36.278	55.6	31	17	30	27	146	17	11	4	55	5	1	10	1	30	1	3	6	0	0	0	125	18	15	13	0
black-and-blue	3	.0000	.1370	31.4	2	0	0	0	1	0	0	0	3	0	0	0	0	0	0	0	0	0	0	0	0	0	0	0	0
black-and-silver-striped	2	.1787	.1174	30.7	1	1	0	0	0	0	0	0	1	0	0	0	0	0	0	0	0	0	0	0	1	0	0	0	0
black-and-white	15	.4271	1.5783	42.0	3	3	2	1	4	2	0	0	11	0	0	0	0	1	0	0	0	0	0	0	0	1	2	0	0
black-box	4	.0000	.0789	29.0	0	0	4	0	0	0	0	0	0	0	0	0	0	0	0	4	0	0	0	0	0	0	0	0	0
black-eyed	10	.3660	.9054	39.6	2	0	0	2	3	3	0	0	5	0	0	0	0	0	0	0	0	0	0	0	0	2	0	3	0
black-haired	3	.3465	.2515	34.0	1	0	0	1	1	0	0	0	1	0	0	0	0	0	0	0	0	0	0	0	0	1	0	1	0
black-iron	2	.0000	.0050	17.0	0	0	0	0	0	0	2	0	0	0	0	0	0	0	0	0	0	0	0	2	0	0	0	0	0
black-top	2	.0000	.0914	29.6	0	2	0	0	0	0	0	0	2	0	0	0	0	0	0	0	0	0	0	0	0	0	0	0	0
black-walnut	3	.1277	.1363	31.3	0	1	0	0	2	0	0	0	1	0	0	0	0	0	0	0	0	0	0	0	0	0	0	2	0
Black's	15	.2345	.8588	39.3	0	3	0	1	11	0	0	0	1	0	0	0	2	0	0	0	0	0	0	0	11	1	0	0	0
Blackbeard	4	.0000	.1827	32.6	4	0	0	0	0	0	0	0	4	0	0	0	0	0	0	0	0	0	0	0	0	0	0	0	0
Blackbeard's	2	.1814	.1187	30.7	0	1	0	1	0	0	0	0	1	0	0	0	0	0	0	0	0	0	0	0	0	0	0	1	0
blackberries	14	.5339	1.5882	42.0	2	1	5	1	2	2	0	1	2	0	0	1	0	1	0	2	0	0	0	0	6	1	1	0	0
blackberry	9	.4609	.9585	39.8	4	0	0	2	2	1	0	0	4	0	0	0	0	1	0	2	0	0	0	0	0	0	0	2	0
blackbird	4	.2278	.2911	34.6	1	1	1	0	0	1	0	0	3	0	0	0	0	0	0	0	1	0	0	0	0	0	0	0	0
blackbirds	12	.5966	1.4879	41.7	10	0	1	0	0	1	0	0	1	0	1	0	3	0	0	3	1	0	0	0	1	2	0	0	0
Blackbirds	7	.0000	.0751	28.8	0	7	0	0	0	0	0	0	0	0	0	7	0	0	0	0	0	0	0	0	0	0	0	0	0
blackboard	39	.6494	5.2955	47.2	17	5	1	3	5	6	2	0	13	3	2	0	4	2	0	0	1	0	0	0	11	2	0	1	0
blackboards	3	.3450	.2505	34.0	1	1	0	1	0	0	0	0	1	0	0	0	0	0	0	0	0	0	0	0	1	1	0	0	0
blacked	6	.2279	.4286	36.3	0	2	0	0	2	1	1	0	4	0	0	0	0	0	0	0	0	0	0	0	0	0	0	2	0
blacken	3	.2261	.2131	33.3	1	0	0	1	0	0	1	0	2	0	0	0	0	0	0	0	0	0	0	0	1	0	0	0	0
blackened	21	.5692	2.5196	44.0	1	4	0	4	6	3	3	0	5	0	2	6	0	0	0	0	0	0	0	0	2	2	1	3	0
blackening	3	.3394	.2451	33.9	0	1	0	0	2	0	0	0	1	0	0	1	0	0	0	0	0	0	0	0	1	0	0	0	0
blacker	8	.2341	.6211	37.9	1	1	1	2	3	0	0	0	7	0	0	1	0	0	0	0	0	0	0	0	0	0	0	0	0
Blackfeet	7	.0000	.3198	35.0	1	0	3	0	3	0	0	0	7	0	0	0	0	0	0	0	0	0	0	0	0	0	0	0	0
Blackfoot	6	.2357	.4397	36.4	2	0	4	0	0	0	0	0	4	0	0	0	0	0	0	0	0	0	0	0	0	2	0	0	0
blackheads	3	.0000	.0097	19.8	0	0	0	0	1	2	0	0	0	0	0	0	0	0	0	0	0	0	3	0	0	0	0	0	0
Blackie's	2	.0000	.0290	24.6	0	2	0	0	0	0	0	0	0	0	0	0	0	0	0	0	0	0	0	0	0	2	0	0	0
blackish	4	.3869	.3419	35.3	1	0	0	0	2	0	1	0	0	0	0	0	0	0	0	2	0	0	0	0	1	0	1	0	0
blackly	3	.2804	.1831	32.6	0	0	0	0	2	0	1	0	0	0	1	1	0	0	0	0	0	0	0	0	1	0	0	0	0
blackness	26	.6089	3.3230	45.2	3	1	6	4	4	3	3	2	7	0	1	7	0	0	0	1	0	0	0	0	3	2	0	5	0
blackout	5	.2557	.3182	35.0	0	0	0	0	4	0	1	0	1	0	0	3	0	0	0	0	0	0	0	0	0	0	0	1	0
BLACKOUT	4	.0000	.0469	26.7	0	0	0	4	0	0	0	0	0	0	0	0	0	0	0	0	0	0	0	0	4	0	0	0	0
blacks	22	.5422	2.4711	43.9	0	1	3	0	6	4	5	3	0	1	0	0	0	4	0	0	0	1	0	1	1	1	0	13	0
blacksmith	35	.6738	4.8857	46.9	5	11	8	3	3	3	2	0	10	0	3	1	0	6	0	0	2	0	0	1	1	8	2	1	0
blacksmith's	5	.3601	.4423	36.5	0	1	2	1	1	0	0	0	2	0	0	0	0	2	0	0	1	0	0	0	0	0	0	0	0
blacksmiths	8	.3821	.7045	38.5	2	0	4	0	0	2	0	0	1	0	0	1	0	5	0	0	0	0	0	0	0	1	0	0	0
blacktop	3	.3399	.2456	33.9	1	0	0	0	0	0	2	0	1	0	0	1	0	0	0	0	0	0	0	0	0	0	0	1	0
Blackwell	4	.3813	.3309	35.2	0	2	0	1	0	0	1	0	0	1	0	0	0	0	0	0	0	0	0	0	0	2	1	0	0
Blacky	4	.0000	.0325	25.1	0	4	0	0	0	0	0	0	0	0	0	0	0	0	4	0	0	0	0	0	0	0	0	0	0
bladder	33	.3721	2.6827	44.3	0	3	5	0	7	14	4	0	0	0	0	0	0	0	0	10	1	0	1	0	0	0	20	1	0
blade	137	.4059	12.078	50.8	5	10	9	11	56	27	17	2	21	5	0	7	4	3	1	8	1	3	1	52	4	17	1	9	0
Blade	4	.0000	.0429	26.3	0	0	0	0	4	0	0	0	0	0	0	4	0	0	0	0	0	0	0	0	0	0	0	0	0
blades	57	.7080	8.2485	49.2	5	11	7	5	17	4	7	1	11	0	1	2	3	5	0	11	0	0	2	7	2	3	5	5	0
Blades	2	.0000	.0243	23.9	0	0	0	0	2	0	0	0	0	0	0	0	0	0	0	0	0	0	0	0	0	0	0	2	0
Blaine	8	.3079	.5787	37.6	0	0	0	0	6	2	0	0	1	1	0	0	0	1	0	0	0	0	0	0	0	0	0	5	0
Blair's	3	.0000	.0067	18.3	0	0	0	0	3	0	0	0	0	0	3	0	0	0	0	0	0	0	0	0	0	0	0	0	0
Blake	33	.6462	4.5478	46.6	26	4	0	0	1	1	1	0	17	1	0	0	0	5	0	0	0	0	0	0	4	3	1	2	0
Blake's	3	.2411	.1667	32.2	2	1	0	0	0	0	0	0	0	0	0	0	0	0	0	0	1	0	0	0	0	0	0	2	0
blame	79	.8277	13.100	51.2	10	10	5	8	18	7	19	2	12	0	1	12	1	8	1	8	3	0	2	0	8	14	1	8	0
blamed	23	.6359	3.0295	44.8	0	4	4	1	5	7	2	0	2	0	0	0	0	7	0	3	0	0	0	0	3	4	1	3	0
blameless	3	.1187	.1291	31.1	0	0	0	1	0	0	2	0	1	0	0	2	0	0	0	0	0	0	0	0	0	0	0	0	0
blames	2	.1698	.1133	30.5	0	0	0	0	1	0	1	0	1	0	0	0	0	0	0	0	0	0	0	0	0	0	1	0	0
blaming	6	.3820	.5664	37.5	0	1	0	2	1	0	2	0	3	0	0	0	0	2	0	0	0	0	0	0	1	0	0	0	0
Blanc	5	.3423	.3887	35.9	0	0	0	2	2	0	0	1	0	0	0	0	0	2	0	1	0	0	0	0	0	0	2	0	0
Blanchard	4	.0000	.1827	32.6	4	0	0	0	0	0	0	0	4	0	0	0	0	0	0	0	0	0	0	0	0	0	0	0	0
Blanche	59	.2286	4.6528	46.7	1	56	0	0	1	0	1	0	56	0	0	0	1	0	0	0	1	0	0	0	0	1	0	0	0
Blanche's	7	.0000	.3198	35.0	0	7	0	0	0	0	0	0	7	0	0	0	0	0	0	0	0	0	0	0	0	0	0	0	0
bland	6	.2949	.4336	36.4	0	0	0	0	3	1	2	0	2	0	0	0	0	0	0	0	0	0	2	0	1	0	0	1	0
Bland	3	.0995	.1144	30.6	0	0	2	0	1	0	0	0	1	0	0	0	0	0	0	0	2	0	0	0	0	0	0	0	0
Blandina	4	.0000	.1827	32.6	0	4	0	0	0	0	0	0	4	0	0	0	0	0	0	0	0	0	0	0	0	0	0	0	0
blandly	2	.1814	.1187	30.7	0	0	0	0	2	0	0	0	1	0	0	0	0	0	0	0	0	0	0	0	0	0	0	1	0
blank	255	.6951	36.434	55.6	49	50	24	34	45	19	32	2	70	48	9	5	43	6	52	2	0	0	0	2	3	8	1	6	0
blanked	2	.2440	.1132	30.5	0	0	0	0	0	2	0	0	0	0	0	1	0	0	0	0	0	0	0	0	0	0	0	1	0
blanket	188	.8313	31.610	55.0	58	28	21	13	52	6	7	3	87	4	2	30	0	9	2	24	3	1	3	0	8	8	3	4	0
blanket's	2	.1717	.1142	30.6	0	0	0	0	2	0	0	0	1	0	0	1	0	0	0	0	0	0	0	0	0	0	0	0	0
blanketed	12	.5560	1.4544	41.6	1	2	1	2	4	2	0	0	5	0	0	0	0	1	0	1	0	0	0	0	1	0	3	1	0
blanketing	2	.1948	.1250	31.0	1	0	0	1	0	0	0	0	1	0	0	0	0	0	0	0	0	0	0	0	0	1	0	0	0

4N bitterer
6R Bitterroot
8D Bixler
9R biz
4Q Bizerte
4J Bizet's
6E BK
3A bl
3P bla-bla-bla-bla-bla
3P blab
7N blabber
8R black-
7R black-and-gold
7C black-and-tan
5A black-and-yellow
7N Black-boy
9J black-brow'd
4A Black-capped
7N black-coated
6N black-dotted
7R black-elastic
5B black-feathered
7D black-footed
7R black-fringed
6R black-gloved
XR black-green
7A black-hand
9R black-leather
3A black-looking
3P black-maned
7Q black-necked
7B black-penciled
XH black-skinned
8A black-smudged
9C black-stump
8R black-tinted
8A black-tipped
7R blackballed
8B blackbeard
4P blackberrying
4D Blackbird
7F Blackburn
6F blackens
7N blacker-than-night
7B blackest
5A Blackfish
3P Blackfoot's
7R Blackfooted
7A blackguard
7D blackguards
4C Blackie
9C blacking
7N blackjack
7D blackline
7D blacklisted
7A blackmail
3A Blacks
9H blacksmithing
4P Blackstone
7R blacktails
4D blackthorn
8E Blackton
XH blacktongue
7R blacktopped
XR blacktopping
6N Blackwell's
3A Blackwood
7Q bladders
7Q bladderwort's
4N blade-bone
5P blade-wielding
9D bladed
3P bladelike
XR blah
XR Blaiberg
4G Blair
8E Blaise
5D Blaiseville
6B blanca
7A Blanca
4N Blancas

Word Type	F	D	U	SFI	3 Gr 3	4 Gr 4	5 Gr 5	6 Gr 6	7 Gr 7	8 Gr 8	9 Gr 9	X UnGr	A Read	B Eng & Gr	C Comp	D Lit	E Math	F Soc Stud	G Spell	H Sci	J Music	K Art	L Home Ec	M Shop	N Lib F	P Lib NF	Q Lib Ref	R Mag	S Rel
blankets	116	.8384	19.619	52.9	20	25	13	12	21	14	3	8	48	1	3	8	0	19	1	6	1	1	1	0	13	8	3	3	0
blankly	5	.3313	.4088	36.1	0	0	0	2	1	2	0	0	2	0	0	2	0	0	0	0	0	0	0	0	1	0	0	0	0
blanks	154	.6242	19.804	53.0	52	42	13	13	16	6	12	0	18	10	9	0	75	3	28	0	0	0	1	5	0	1	2	2	0
blare	5	.3753	.4670	36.7	1	0	1	2	1	0	0	0	3	0	0	0	0	0	0	0	1	0	0	0	0	0	0	1	0
blared	3	.1409	.1472	31.7	0	1	0	1	0	0	1	0	1	0	0	0	0	0	0	0	0	0	0	0	0	2	0	0	0
blares	3	.3390	.2450	33.9	1	0	1	0	0	0	1	0	1	0	0	0	0	0	0	0	0	0	0	0	0	0	1	1	0
blaring	5	.4100	.4422	36.5	0	0	1	0	1	3	0	0	0	0	1	1	0	1	0	1	0	0	0	0	0	1	0	0	0
Blarney	3	.0000	.0365	25.6	0	0	0	3	0	0	0	0	0	0	0	0	0	0	0	0	0	0	0	0	0	0	0	3	0
blasphemy	2	.2446	.1122	30.5	0	0	0	0	1	1	0	0	0	0	0	1	0	0	0	0	0	0	0	0	0	0	1	0	0
Blass	2	.0000	.0914	29.6	0	2	0	0	0	0	0	0	2	0	0	0	0	0	0	0	0	0	0	0	0	0	0	0	0
blast	74	.8225	12.233	50.9	11	10	12	8	12	12	9	0	17	10	2	3	0	11	0	8	6	0	0	1	4	1	2	9	0
blast-off	16	.4169	1.4826	41.7	8	1	2	4	1	0	0	0	2	0	0	0	10	0	0	2	0	1	0	0	0	0	0	1	0
blasted	17	.6073	2.1962	43.4	0	1	3	4	4	4	1	0	6	0	0	2	0	3	0	0	0	0	0	0	0	2	3	1	0
blastholes	3	.0000	.0314	25.0	0	0	2	0	0	0	1	0	0	0	0	0	0	0	0	0	0	0	0	0	0	0	3	0	0
blasting	14	.6992	2.0015	43.0	2	1	4	3	3	0	1	0	2	2	0	0	0	1	0	2	0	0	0	0	2	2	1	2	0
blastoff	2	.2391	.1133	30.5	0	0	1	0	0	1	0	0	0	0	0	0	1	0	0	0	0	0	0	0	0	0	1	0	0
blasts	18	.6292	2.3699	43.7	3	2	2	4	3	2	0	2	4	0	0	1	0	3	0	2	0	0	0	0	4	1	0	3	0
blatant	4	.0996	.1523	31.8	0	0	0	0	2	1	1	0	1	0	0	0	0	0	0	0	0	0	0	0	0	0	0	3	0
Blatchford	4	.0000	.0486	26.9	0	0	0	0	0	4	0	0	0	0	0	0	0	0	0	0	0	0	0	0	0	0	0	4	0
Blatchford's	4	.0000	.0486	26.9	0	0	0	0	0	4	0	0	0	0	0	0	0	0	0	0	0	0	0	0	0	0	0	4	0
blaze	34	.7238	5.0434	47.0	2	2	4	9	8	5	1	3	10	0	2	6	0	3	1	2	1	0	0	0	5	2	1	1	0
Blaze	25	.3703	2.3071	43.6	17	8	0	0	0	0	0	0	13	0	0	6	0	6	0	0	0	0	0	0	0	0	0	0	0
Blaze's	4	.0000	.0778	28.9	0	4	0	0	0	0	0	0	0	0	0	0	0	4	0	0	0	0	0	0	0	0	0	0	0
blazed	21	.6081	2.7476	44.4	0	4	1	6	5	1	2	2	10	0	0	2	0	2	0	0	0	0	0	0	3	3	0	1	0
blazer	2	.2433	.1158	30.6	1	0	0	1	0	0	0	0	0	0	0	0	0	0	0	0	0	0	0	0	0	1	0	1	0
blazes	3	.3722	.2508	34.0	1	0	1	0	1	0	0	0	0	0	0	1	0	1	0	1	0	0	0	0	0	0	0	0	0
blazing	44	.7287	6.6083	48.2	3	4	3	7	11	8	6	2	18	0	0	3	0	2	0	3	1	2	1	0	8	1	1	4	0
blazon	2	.1717	.1142	30.6	0	0	0	1	0	0	1	0	1	0	0	1	0	0	0	0	0	0	0	0	0	0	0	0	0
bleach	6	.3793	.5819	37.6	1	0	0	4	1	0	0	0	4	0	0	0	0	0	0	1	0	0	0	0	0	1	0	0	0
bleached	15	.5976	1.8541	42.7	0	1	1	1	4	5	3	0	2	0	0	2	0	1	0	2	0	0	3	1	2	0	1	1	0
bleachers	6	.3117	.4833	36.8	3	1	0	2	0	0	0	0	3	0	0	0	1	0	0	0	0	1	0	0	0	1	0	0	0
bleaching	5	.3159	.3664	35.6	0	0	1	0	3	0	1	0	0	0	0	0	0	1	0	3	0	0	1	0	0	0	0	0	0
bleak	19	.7350	2.8214	44.5	1	1	1	2	8	2	4	0	2	2	1	4	0	3	1	0	1	0	0	0	1	1	3	0	0
bleat	8	.2301	.6170	37.9	5	2	1	0	0	0	0	0	7	0	0	0	0	0	0	0	0	0	0	0	1	0	0	0	0
bleated	2	.1787	.1174	30.7	0	0	0	2	0	0	0	0	1	0	0	0	0	0	0	0	0	0	0	0	1	0	0	0	0
bleating	15	.6515	2.0116	43.0	2	4	3	2	1	1	2	0	2	3	0	2	0	2	0	0	0	0	0	0	2	2	0	2	0
bled	7	.4937	.7405	38.7	0	0	0	1	4	2	0	0	1	1	0	2	0	0	0	1	0	0	0	0	2	0	0	0	0
bleed	13	.5340	1.4622	41.6	1	1	1	2	6	1	1	0	1	0	0	4	0	0	2	4	0	0	0	0	0	1	0	1	0
bleeding	33	.7649	5.1371	47.1	2	1	11	3	8	5	3	0	10	1	0	3	0	1	0	3	1	0	1	0	7	4	1	1	0
Bleeding	3	.0000	.0583	27.7	0	0	0	0	0	3	0	0	0	0	0	0	0	3	0	0	0	0	0	0	0	0	0	0	0
bleeds	2	.2291	.1135	30.5	0	0	1	0	1	0	0	0	0	0	0	1	0	0	0	1	0	0	0	0	0	0	0	0	0
blemish	3	.3319	.2114	33.3	0	0	1	0	1	1	0	0	0	0	0	0	0	0	1	0	0	0	1	0	0	0	0	1	0
blemishes	7	.1419	.2284	33.6	0	0	1	0	1	5	0	0	0	0	0	0	0	0	0	0	0	0	5	0	0	0	1	1	0
blend	175	.5700	20.533	53.1	36	24	23	21	36	12	19	4	20	3	0	0	0	4	88	1	12	2	22	4	2	0	4	13	0
Blend	2	.0000	.0243	23.9	0	0	0	0	0	0	0	2	0	0	0	0	0	0	0	0	0	0	0	0	0	0	0	2	0
blend-vowel	4	.0000	.0325	25.1	0	0	0	0	4	0	0	0	0	0	0	0	0	0	4	0	0	0	0	0	0	0	0	0	0
blended	29	.3280	2.0030	43.0	1	1	2	5	4	0	14	2	0	0	0	1	0	0	2	0	2	0	15	0	1	1	2	5	0
blender	8	.2423	.4411	36.4	4	0	0	0	0	0	2	2	0	0	0	0	0	0	0	0	0	0	2	0	0	0	0	6	0
blenders	2	.2437	.1129	30.5	1	0	0	0	1	0	0	0	0	0	0	0	0	0	0	0	0	0	0	0	0	0	1	1	0
blending	23	.5974	2.7920	44.5	0	1	6	3	0	3	7	3	1	0	2	0	0	1	7	1	3	0	4	0	0	0	2	2	0
blends	64	.4998	6.6258	48.2	14	7	6	9	15	4	9	0	5	1	0	0	0	1	38	2	3	2	10	1	0	0	1	0	0
bless	36	.2814	2.5040	44.0	13	3	2	7	1	1	3	6	9	1	0	3	0	2	0	0	5	0	0	0	3	5	0	6	2
Bless	2	.2306	.1140	30.6	1	0	1	0	0	0	0	0	0	1	0	0	0	1	0	0	0	0	0	0	0	0	0	0	0
blessed	38	.4423	3.7118	45.7	2	1	6	3	11	5	9	1	8	2	0	10	0	4	0	1	3	0	0	0	1	4	1	3	1
Blessed	2	.0182	.0264	24.2	0	1	0	0	0	1	0	0	0	0	0	0	0	1	0	0	0	0	0	0	0	0	0	0	1
blessing	23	.7569	3.5212	45.5	1	2	0	6	4	5	3	2	3	2	1	3	0	5	0	2	1	0	0	0	2	1	0	3	0
blessings	15	.6592	2.0665	43.2	0	3	2	4	2	2	1	1	5	0	0	0	0	3	2	0	1	0	0	0	1	1	0	2	0
Blessings	2	.0000	.0389	25.9	0	0	0	0	0	2	0	0	0	0	0	0	0	2	0	0	0	0	0	0	0	0	0	0	0
blest	6	.3373	.4608	36.6	0	3	1	1	0	0	1	0	1	0	0	1	0	0	0	0	3	0	0	0	0	1	0	0	0
blew	222	.7565	34.376	55.4	63	45	21	28	37	16	10	2	86	18	0	20	1	12	3	5	11	0	0	0	34	21	0	11	0
bliggens	8	.0000	.0859	29.3	0	0	0	0	0	8	0	0	0	0	0	8	0	0	0	0	0	0	0	0	0	0	0	0	0
Bligh	2	.0000	.0914	29.6	0	0	0	0	0	2	0	0	2	0	0	0	0	0	0	0	0	0	0	0	0	0	0	0	0
blight	8	.2424	.6072	37.8	0	0	1	5	1	0	1	0	6	0	0	0	0	0	0	0	0	0	0	0	0	0	0	2	0
blighted	2	.2351	.1166	30.7	0	0	0	0	0	1	0	1	0	0	0	0	0	1	0	0	0	0	0	0	0	0	0	1	0
blimey	2	.0000	.0914	29.6	0	0	0	0	0	2	0	0	2	0	0	0	0	0	0	0	0	0	0	0	0	0	0	0	0
blind	181	.7739	28.257	54.5	22	14	23	20	59	17	24	2	32	14	1	49	0	3	4	12	3	0	0	1	14	13	21	14	0
Blind	10	.3407	.7441	38.7	0	0	0	0	3	5	2	0	0	0	0	3	0	0	0	0	1	0	0	0	0	0	0	6	0
blinded	23	.6592	3.1590	45.0	1	4	1	4	6	2	4	1	8	3	1	4	0	0	0	0	0	0	0	0	2	2	3	0	0
blindfold	3	.3779	.2436	33.9	0	0	1	1	0	1	0	0	0	1	0	0	0	0	0	0	1	0	0	0	0	1	0	0	0
blindfolded	8	.5156	.8594	39.3	1	0	2	1	0	3	1	0	0	1	0	0	0	0	0	1	2	0	0	0	0	3	1	0	0
blinding	16	.5928	2.0590	43.1	1	3	3	3	4	1	1	0	8	0	0	0	0	1	0	1	0	0	0	0	0	2	2	2	0
blindingly	3	.3768	.2484	34.0	0	1	0	0	1	0	0	1	0	0	0	1	0	0	0	1	0	0	0	0	1	0	0	0	0
blindly	9	.5354	1.0490	40.2	1	1	1	0	5	1	0	0	3	0	0	1	0	1	0	0	0	0	0	0	2	2	0	0	0
blindman's	4	.3755	.3686	35.7	1	1	0	1	1	0	0	0	2	0	0	0	0	0	0	0	0	0	0	0	1	1	0	0	0
blindness	18	.6182	2.3230	43.7	0	0	1	3	6	6	1	1	3	1	0	5	1	1	0	5	0	0	0	0	1	0	1	0	0
blinds	10	.5867	1.2283	40.9	1	0	3	0	4	1	1	0	2	0	1	1	1	0	0	0	0	0	0	0	2	2	1	0	0
blink	16	.5257	1.8127	42.6	3	2	3	3	2	1	0	2	3	0	0	0	0	0	0	5	0	0	0	0	2	2	0	4	0
Blink	12	.1688	.6722	38.3	7	0	5	0	0	0	0	0	5	0	0	0	0	0	0	0	0	0	0	0	0	7	0	0	0
blinked	22	.5969	2.8638	44.6	3	6	4	2	3	3	1	0	13	1	0	2	0	0	0	0	0	0	0	0	3	2	0	1	0
blinking	26	.7036	3.8088	45.8	4	0	6	6	5	3	2	0	11	1	0	1	0	0	0	5	0	0	0	0	3	2	1	2	0
blinks	3	.3418	.2483	33.9	1	1	0	0	0	1	0	0	1	1	0	0	0	0	0	0	0	0	0	0	0	1	0	0	0
blip	3	.0000	.0591	27.7	0	3	0	0	0	0	0	0	0	0	0	0	0	0	0	3	0	0	0	0	0	0	0	0	0
bliss	6	.3041	.4355	36.4	1	0	0	2	1	2	0	0	1	0	0	2	0	0	0	0	0	0	0	0	0	3	0	0	0
Bliss	3	.1277	.1363	31.3	0	0	0	0	1	1	1	0	1	0	0	0	0	0	0	0	0	0	0	0	0	0	0	2	0
blissfully	3	.2227	.1589	32.0	0	1	0	1	1	0	0	0	0	0	0	0	0	0	0	0	0	0	0	0	2	0	0	1	0
blister	3	.1650	.1684	32.3	0	0	1	0	1	0	0	1	1	0	0	0	0	0	0	2	0	0	0	0	0	0	0	0	0
blistered	12	.5419	1.4063	41.5	1	1	4	2	2	1	1	0	4	0	1	3	0	0	0	2	0	0	0	0	1	0	0	1	0
blistering	8	.5555	.9816	39.9	1	0	4	0	1	1	1	0	4	1	0	1	0	1	0	1	0	0	0	0	0	0	0	0	0
blisters	8	.4811	.8580	39.3	0	0	0	2	3	1	1	1	3	0	0	2	0	0	0	1	0	0	1	0	0	1	0	0	0
blithe	3	.3272	.2363	33.7	0	0	1	0	1	1	0	0	1	0	0	1	0	0	0	0	1	0	0	0	0	0	0	0	0
blizzard	22	.5335	2.5577	44.1	3	3	0	5	6	2	2	1	8	0	3	2	0	1	1	4	0	0	0	0	1	1	0	1	0
Blizzard	2	.0000	.0394	26.0	0	0	0	0	2	0	0	0	0	0	0	0	0	0	0	2	0	0	0	0	0	0	0	0	0
blizzards	8	.5210	.9072	39.6	1	2	0	1	2	1	1	0	3	0	1	0	0	0	0	0	1	0	0	0	1	1	1	0	0
bloat	2	.2444	.1132	30.5	0	0	0	0	1	0	1	0	0	1	0	0	0	0	0	0	0	0	0	0	1	0	0	0	0
bloated	5	.3982	.4204	36.2	0	0	0	0	3	0	2	0	0	0	1	1	0	0	0	0	0	0	0	0	0	1	2	0	0
blob	7	.4307	.6605	38.2	2	0	0	2	2	0	1	0	1	0	0	2	0	0	0	0	0	0	0	0	2	2	0	0	0
blobs	2	.1733	.1149	30.6	0	0	0	1	0	0	1	0	1	1	0	0	0	0	0	0	0	0	0	0	0	0	0	0	0
bloc	6	.5050	.6520	38.1	0	0	1	1	0	3	1	0	1	0	0	0	0	1	0	0	0	0	0	0	0	1	1	2	0

7R Blanton
6R blarney
6R Blarney's
6R blase
6H Blast
4H BLAST
7A blaster
6J blaws
5F blazers
5F BLAZERS
9D bleakest
8B Blear
9B bleary
6N bleatings
9Q Bleek
7A Blefuscu
4N blenched
8F Blended
XB Blenheim
7Q blenny
9D blent
XR blesses
7N blessin'
3R Blimp
5H blimplike
9P blind-man's
7Q blindfolds
8R Blindness
7N blissful
7N blithely
6J Blitzen
4Q Blitzkrieg
8F Bliven
9A blizzard-swept
4A blizzard's
7A blizzardy

Word Type	F	D	U	SFI	3 Gr 3	4 Gr 4	5 Gr 5	6 Gr 6	7 Gr 7	8 Gr 8	9 Gr 9	X UnGr	A Read	B Eng & Gr	C Comp	D Lit	E Math	F Soc Stud	G Spell	H Sci	J Music	K Art	L Home Ec	M Shop	N Lib F	P Lib NF	Q Lib Ref	R Mag	S Rel
block	328	.6934	46.513	56.7	70	23	29	34	75	32	61	4	65	15	3	12	30	13	5	52	3	15	5	55	7	15	12	21	0
Block	13	.4416	1.4054	41.5	10	2	0	0	0	0	0	1	10	0	0	0	0	1	0	0	1	0	0	0	0	0	0	1	0
blockade	5	.2037	.2562	34.1	0	2	0	0	0	2	1	0	0	0	0	0	0	2	0	0	0	0	0	0	0	0	3	0	0
blockaded	2	.2285	.1129	30.5	0	0	0	0	0	1	1	0	0	0	0	0	0	1	0	0	0	0	0	0	0	0	1	0	0
blockades	3	.0000	.0583	27.7	0	0	0	0	0	3	0	0	0	0	0	0	0	3	0	0	0	0	0	0	0	0	0	0	0
blockading	2	.2446	.1123	30.5	0	1	0	0	0	1	0	0	0	1	0	0	0	0	0	0	0	0	0	0	0	0	1	0	0
blocked	43	.7699	6.7565	48.3	5	10	6	2	10	5	5	0	15	0	0	4	0	9	0	3	2	0	0	1	4	1	1	3	0
blocker	3	.2300	.1627	32.1	0	0	0	1	0	0	2	0	0	1	0	0	0	0	0	0	0	0	0	0	0	0	0	2	0
blockhead	2	.0665	.0708	28.5	0	0	1	0	1	0	0	0	1	0	1	0	0	0	0	0	0	0	0	0	0	0	0	0	0
blockhouse	5	.2445	.3864	35.9	2	0	3	0	0	0	0	0	4	0	0	1	0	0	0	0	0	0	0	0	0	0	0	0	0
blocking	12	.5942	1.5318	41.9	0	0	1	1	5	3	1	1	5	1	0	0	0	0	2	2	0	0	0	0	0	1	0	1	0
blocklike	2	.1483	.0728	28.6	0	0	0	0	2	0	0	0	0	0	0	0	0	0	0	0	0	0	0	1	0	1	0	0	0
blocks	260	.9012	46.522	56.7	52	48	34	32	35	33	23	3	44	12	2	9	41	23	15	31	10	11	2	7	10	16	12	15	0
blocs	2	.1698	.1133	30.5	0	0	1	0	1	0	0	0	1	0	0	0	0	0	0	0	0	0	0	0	0	0	1	0	0
Blodeuwedd	2	.0000	.0290	24.6	0	0	0	0	2	0	0	0	0	0	0	0	0	0	0	0	0	0	0	0	0	2	0	0	0
Bloemfontein	5	.0000	.2284	33.6	0	0	0	0	5	0	0	0	5	0	0	0	0	0	0	0	0	0	0	0	0	0	0	0	0
blond	22	.5736	2.6748	44.3	3	1	5	6	2	2	3	0	5	0	0	2	0	2	0	0	0	0	0	0	2	5	0	6	0
blonde	9	.4582	.9142	39.6	1	1	0	1	1	2	2	1	3	1	0	1	0	0	0	0	0	0	2	0	0	1	0	1	0
blonds	3	.2366	.1806	32.6	0	0	0	2	0	0	1	0	0	0	0	0	1	2	0	0	0	0	0	0	0	0	0	0	0
blood	705	.7422	106.38	60.3	58	89	107	97	146	99	78	31	79	13	4	57	4	13	4	369	7	1	7	1	27	28	57	34	0
Blood	3	.3847	.2496	34.0	0	0	1	0	2	0	0	0	0	0	0	0	0	0	0	0	0	0	0	0	0	1	1	1	0
blood-red	5	.3844	.4760	36.8	2	2	0	0	0	1	0	0	3	1	0	0	0	0	0	0	0	0	0	0	1	0	0	0	0
blood-soaked	2	.1717	.1142	30.6	0	0	0	1	0	1	0	0	1	0	0	1	0	0	0	0	0	0	0	0	0	0	0	0	0
blood-sucking	2	.2405	.1205	30.8	0	0	0	0	1	0	0	1	0	0	0	0	0	0	0	1	0	0	0	0	0	1	0	0	0
blood-thirsty	2	.1717	.1142	30.6	0	0	0	1	0	1	0	0	1	0	0	1	0	0	0	0	0	0	0	0	0	0	0	0	0
blood-vessel	6	.2445	.3637	35.6	0	0	0	0	2	0	4	0	0	0	0	0	0	0	0	4	0	0	0	0	0	0	2	0	0
blooded	12	.4309	1.1505	40.6	6	0	0	0	5	1	0	0	1	0	0	1	0	0	0	8	0	0	0	0	1	0	1	0	0
bloodhound	2	.0000	.0914	29.6	0	0	1	0	0	1	0	0	2	0	0	0	0	0	0	0	0	0	0	0	0	0	0	0	0
bloodhounds	6	.2129	.3322	35.2	0	1	0	0	3	0	2	0	1	0	0	4	0	0	0	0	0	0	0	0	0	1	0	0	0
bloodiest	3	.3776	.2504	34.0	0	0	0	0	1	2	0	0	0	0	0	1	0	1	0	0	0	0	0	0	0	1	0	0	0
bloodletting	5	.1777	.2554	34.1	0	0	0	0	0	5	0	0	0	0	0	0	0	1	0	4	0	0	0	0	0	0	0	0	0
bloods	2	.1717	.1142	30.6	0	1	0	0	0	0	1	0	1	0	0	1	0	0	0	0	0	0	0	0	0	0	0	0	0
bloodshed	9	.4968	.9642	39.8	1	1	0	2	3	2	0	0	1	0	0	2	0	4	0	0	0	0	0	0	0	1	1	0	0
bloodshot	5	.3313	.4088	36.1	0	0	0	0	2	0	3	0	2	0	0	2	0	0	0	0	0	0	0	0	1	0	0	0	0
bloodstained	3	.2261	.2131	33.3	0	0	0	0	2	1	0	0	2	0	0	0	0	0	0	0	0	0	0	0	1	0	0	0	0
bloodstream	9	.1940	.4623	36.6	0	0	1	1	1	0	6	0	1	0	0	0	0	0	0	2	0	0	0	0	0	0	6	0	0
bloodthirsty	5	.4270	.4804	36.8	2	0	0	0	2	0	1	0	1	0	0	0	0	1	0	0	0	0	0	0	0	2	0	1	0
bloody	49	.6945	6.9986	48.5	4	3	6	7	13	9	5	2	11	0	0	8	0	10	0	0	1	0	0	0	4	4	6	5	0
Bloody	3	.3815	.2534	34.0	0	1	0	1	0	1	0	0	0	0	0	0	0	1	0	0	0	0	0	0	0	1	0	1	0
bloom	63	.8562	10.784	50.3	13	7	9	12	15	4	0	3	12	5	0	4	0	7	2	13	3	1	0	0	4	7	2	3	0
Bloom	2	.0000	.0243	23.9	0	0	1	0	0	0	1	0	0	0	0	0	0	0	0	0	0	0	0	0	0	0	0	2	0
bloomed	11	.6489	1.4769	41.7	0	0	0	3	4	1	1	2	2	2	0	2	0	0	0	2	0	0	0	0	0	1	1	1	0
Bloomfield	4	.1873	.1827	32.6	0	0	0	0	1	0	3	0	0	0	0	0	0	0	0	0	0	0	0	0	0	0	3	1	0
blooming	21	.7002	3.0096	44.8	3	5	2	2	5	3	0	1	5	0	2	2	0	1	0	2	2	1	0	0	1	1	3	1	0
Bloomington	11	.2182	.5907	37.7	0	8	0	0	3	0	0	0	0	0	0	0	0	0	0	0	0	0	0	0	0	8	0	3	0
blooms	7	.5618	.8293	39.2	2	0	0	2	2	0	0	1	1	1	0	0	0	1	0	1	0	0	0	0	0	0	2	1	0
blossom	40	.6424	5.4420	47.4	9	4	2	13	7	2	1	2	16	0	0	2	0	0	4	14	1	1	0	0	0	1	0	1	0
Blossom	4	.4525	.4044	36.1	2	0	0	0	1	0	0	1	1	0	0	0	0	1	0	0	0	0	0	0	1	0	0	1	0
blossomed	8	.4145	.7656	38.8	1	1	2	0	1	2	1	0	3	0	0	3	1	0	0	0	0	0	0	0	0	0	1	0	0
blossoming	4	.3362	.3304	35.2	2	1	0	0	1	0	0	0	1	0	0	0	0	0	0	2	0	0	0	0	0	1	0	0	0
blossoms	76	.7559	11.801	50.7	30	11	4	17	9	2	2	1	33	1	3	6	0	4	1	14	6	0	0	0	2	1	2	3	0
blot	6	.5483	.7103	38.5	1	2	0	0	1	1	0	1	2	0	0	0	1	0	1	0	0	0	0	0	0	1	0	1	0
Blot	2	.0000	.0914	29.6	0	0	0	2	0	0	0	0	2	0	0	0	0	0	0	0	0	0	0	0	0	0	0	0	0
blotches	2	.0000	.0234	23.7	0	0	0	0	0	0	2	0	0	0	0	0	0	0	0	0	0	0	0	0	2	0	0	0	0
blotted	3	.0000	.1370	31.4	0	1	0	1	1	0	0	0	3	0	0	0	0	0	0	0	0	0	0	0	0	0	0	0	0
blotter	11	.5960	1.3516	41.3	2	0	5	0	2	1	1	0	0	1	0	0	0	4	0	0	0	0	1	0	2	2	0	1	0
blotting	17	.5355	1.9368	42.9	5	0	2	1	8	1	0	0	3	1	2	1	0	0	0	3	0	0	0	0	2	5	0	0	0
Blotto	14	.1972	1.0279	40.1	0	0	13	1	0	0	0	0	13	0	0	1	0	0	0	0	0	0	0	0	0	0	0	0	0
blouse	64	.2752	3.9638	46.0	7	6	2	2	7	15	25	0	9	4	2	1	3	0	0	0	0	1	40	0	3	0	0	1	0
Blouse	9	.0177	.1015	30.1	0	0	0	0	0	1	8	0	1	0	0	0	0	0	0	0	0	0	8	0	0	0	0	0	0
blouses	14	.1323	.4657	36.7	3	0	0	1	2	4	4	0	0	0	0	0	2	3	0	0	0	0	9	0	0	0	0	0	0
blow	411	.8495	70.076	58.5	94	58	71	60	72	29	23	4	128	7	2	24	1	35	3	57	45	0	0	4	25	38	19	23	0
Blow	2	.0000	.0162	22.1	0	0	2	0	0	0	0	0	0	0	0	0	0	0	0	0	2	0	0	0	0	0	0	0	0
Blow-Up	3	.0000	.0365	25.6	0	0	0	0	0	0	0	3	0	0	0	0	0	0	0	0	0	0	0	0	0	0	0	3	0
blow-holes	2	.2427	.1152	30.6	1	0	0	0	1	0	0	0	0	0	0	0	0	0	0	0	0	0	0	0	1	1	0	0	0
blowed	2	.2442	.1134	30.5	0	0	0	0	1	0	1	0	0	1	0	0	0	0	0	0	0	0	0	0	0	0	0	1	0
blower	9	.3841	.8609	39.3	0	0	5	2	1	1	0	0	5	0	0	0	0	3	0	0	1	0	0	0	0	0	0	0	0
blowers	5	.3184	.3581	35.5	0	1	0	0	2	0	2	0	0	0	0	0	0	1	0	0	0	0	0	0	0	0	1	3	0
blowhole	4	.0000	.1827	32.6	0	4	0	0	0	0	0	0	4	0	0	0	0	0	0	0	0	0	0	0	0	0	0	0	0
blowholes	3	.0000	.0434	26.4	3	0	0	0	0	0	0	0	0	0	0	0	0	0	0	0	0	0	0	0	0	3	0	0	0
blowing	182	.8206	30.081	54.8	46	39	29	25	19	7	12	5	51	3	5	12	0	14	0	29	16	2	0	1	20	16	4	8	1
blown	88	.8418	14.850	51.7	23	6	13	21	9	10	4	2	19	3	0	3	1	3	0	21	5	1	0	1	12	9	3	7	0
blowout	2	.0000	.0394	26.0	0	0	2	0	0	0	0	0	0	0	0	0	0	0	0	2	0	0	0	0	0	0	0	0	0
blowpipe	2	.0000	.0389	25.9	0	0	0	0	2	0	0	0	0	0	0	0	0	2	0	0	0	0	0	0	0	0	0	0	0
blows	124	.7235	18.304	52.6	29	11	17	23	18	15	6	5	24	6	0	6	0	11	2	28	11	0	0	11	10	10	3	2	0
blowtorch	4	.3439	.3160	35.0	0	0	0	1	0	2	1	0	1	1	0	0	0	0	0	0	0	0	0	1	0	0	1	0	0
BLT	2	.0000	.0064	18.1	0	0	0	0	2	0	0	0	0	0	0	0	0	0	0	0	0	0	2	0	0	0	0	0	0
blub	4	.0000	.0579	27.6	0	0	0	0	0	4	0	0	0	0	0	0	0	0	0	0	0	0	0	0	0	4	0	0	0
blubber	20	.5401	2.4042	43.8	4	3	10	1	2	0	0	0	11	0	0	0	0	0	1	0	1	0	0	0	0	5	2	0	0
blude-reid	2	.0000	.0219	23.4	0	0	0	0	0	2	0	0	0	2	0	0	0	0	0	0	0	0	0	0	0	0	0	0	0
bludgeon	3	.2060	.1500	31.8	1	0	0	0	0	0	2	0	0	0	0	2	0	0	0	0	0	0	0	0	0	1	0	0	0
blue	1071	.9101	193.67	62.9	294	156	110	126	215	70	69	31	306	58	7	72	125	57	36	86	31	39	19	4	73	68	33	57	0
Blue	93	.7261	13.873	51.4	17	9	12	11	35	7	0	2	30	1	0	22	1	15	1	0	2	1	0	0	2	6	2	10	0
blue-and-white	4	.3071	.2967	34.7	1	0	1	1	0	1	0	0	1	0	0	1	0	0	0	0	0	0	0	0	2	0	0	0	0
blue-black	6	.4740	.6389	38.1	1	0	1	1	2	0	1	0	2	1	0	0	0	0	0	2	0	0	0	0	0	0	1	0	0
blue-eyed	7	.3854	.6446	38.1	0	1	0	2	2	2	0	0	3	0	1	0	0	2	0	0	1	0	0	0	0	0	0	0	0
blue-gray	5	.4688	.4985	37.0	1	1	0	1	1	1	0	0	0	0	0	1	0	1	0	0	0	0	0	0	0	2	0	1	0
blue-green	15	.5561	1.7979	42.5	0	3	2	1	3	2	1	3	5	0	0	0	0	1	0	4	0	1	2	0	0	0	1	1	0
blue-tail	3	.0000	.0243	23.8	3	0	0	0	0	0	0	0	0	0	0	0	0	0	0	0	3	0	0	0	0	0	0	0	0
blue-ticked	2	.0000	.0234	23.7	0	0	0	0	2	0	0	0	0	0	0	0	0	0	0	0	0	0	0	0	2	0	0	0	0
blue-white	10	.4986	1.0936	40.4	0	0	6	0	2	2	0	0	2	0	0	1	0	0	0	5	0	0	0	0	1	1	0	0	0

7J Bloch
6A block-and-tackle
7N block-house
XH block-mounted
5Q block-signal
3A Block's
XR blocked-off
6J Blockflote
7A blockheaded
6N Blockheads
4A blockhouses
4K blockiness
9M blocking-in
4N blocky
XR blokes
3P blond-haired
7M blonded
7P blondes
7R blood-and-guts
8B blood-curdling
8Q blood-group
9C blood-swollen
8H blood's
4N bloodcurdling
6F bloodily
9Q bloodless
7Q bloodlines
6R BLOODSTOCK
7R bloody-mindedness
5A bloody-nosed
3P bloomer
4P Bloomer
9Q Bloomfield's
5A bloomin'
5A Bloomingdale
6R Blossom's
7A blotch
4N blotchy
6A Blott
5A Blotto's
9L blouse-and-skirt
3E blouse-skirt
8L bloused
4A blow-down
3P blow-hole
4A blow-outs
XR blowdowns
5Q blowflies
9M blowhorn
7A blowin'
3Q blowouts
8A blowy
9R BLS
7R bludgeoned
9D blue-
3A Blue-Backed
3J Blue-Tail
4R blue-and-yellow
3A blue-bonneted
8A blue-checked
8D blue-clothed
8R blue-collar
5Q blue-domed
7R Blue-footed
XH Blue-green
XR blue-grey
4A blue-gums
5A blue-jay
3R blue-lined
4P blue-painted
7R blue-pencil
9D blue-prowed
7L blue-purple
9Q blue-red
4P blue-ribbon
7H blue-sensitive
9B blue-speckled
7L blue-violet

Word Type	F	D	U	SFI	3 Gr 3	4 Gr 4	5 Gr 5	6 Gr 6	7 Gr 7	8 Gr 8	9 Gr 9	X UnGr	A Read	B Eng & Gr	C Comp	D Lit	E Math	F Soc Stud	G Spell	H Sci	J Music	K Art	L Home Ec	M Shop	N Lib F	P Lib NF	Q Lib Ref	R Mag	S Rel
Bluebeard	2	.1497	.1046	30.2	1	0	0	0	0	1	0	0	1	0	0	0	0	0	1	0	0	0	0	0	0	0	0	0	0
Bluebell	2	.0000	.0234	23.7	0	0	0	0	0	0	2	0	0	0	0	0	0	0	0	0	0	0	0	0	2	0	0	0	0
blueberries	16	.5216	1.8494	42.7	1	9	3	0	0	3	0	0	7	1	0	0	2	3	0	0	0	0	2	0	0	0	0	1	0
blueberry	8	.4164	.7736	38.9	2	2	1	1	1	0	1	0	3	1	0	0	0	1	0	0	0	0	0	0	0	0	0	3	0
Blueberry	8	.2155	.5456	37.4	5	0	0	0	0	0	0	3	5	0	0	0	0	0	0	0	0	0	0	0	3	0	0	0	0
bluebird	10	.4019	.8999	39.5	3	4	0	2	0	1	0	0	2	0	0	0	0	0	0	0	3	0	0	0	0	4	1	0	0
Bluebird	3	.2223	.2106	33.2	1	2	0	0	0	0	0	0	2	1	0	0	0	0	0	0	0	0	0	0	0	0	0	0	0
bluebirds	14	.5575	1.6389	42.1	8	0	0	1	4	0	0	1	2	0	0	0	5	0	0	0	2	0	0	0	1	0	3	1	0
Bluegrass	3	.2227	.1589	32.0	2	0	0	0	0	0	0	1	0	0	0	0	0	0	0	0	0	0	0	0	2	0	0	1	0
bluejay	4	.3729	.3664	35.6	1	1	1	0	0	1	0	0	2	1	0	0	0	0	0	0	0	0	0	0	0	1	0	0	0
Bluejay	2	.0000	.0914	29.6	0	0	2	0	0	0	0	0	2	0	0	0	0	0	0	0	0	0	0	0	0	0	0	0	0
bluejay's	2	.1948	.1250	31.0	1	0	0	0	0	1	0	0	1	0	0	0	0	0	0	0	0	0	0	0	0	1	0	0	0
bluejays	3	.2369	.2208	33.4	0	0	1	0	0	1	0	1	2	0	0	0	1	0	0	0	0	0	0	0	0	0	0	0	0
blueprint	12	.5966	1.4939	41.7	1	0	0	0	2	4	2	3	1	1	0	0	1	3	0	3	0	0	0	1	0	0	0	2	0
blueprints	6	.1660	.2667	34.3	0	0	0	0	4	1	0	1	1	0	0	0	0	0	0	1	0	0	0	3	0	0	0	1	0
blues	35	.4469	3.2677	45.1	3	2	6	13	1	5	3	2	1	0	0	0	0	0	2	2	21	3	0	0	0	1	1	4	0
Blues	11	.0730	.2463	33.9	0	0	1	8	1	1	0	0	0	0	0	0	0	0	0	0	10	0	0	0	0	1	0	0	0
Bluey	27	.0000	1.2334	40.9	0	0	0	27	0	0	0	0	27	0	0	0	0	0	0	0	0	0	0	0	0	0	0	0	0
Bluey's	2	.0000	.0914	29.6	0	0	0	2	0	0	0	0	2	0	0	0	0	0	0	0	0	0	0	0	0	0	0	0	0
bluff	27	.6858	3.8449	45.8	6	2	7	4	3	2	2	1	9	1	1	1	0	3	0	0	0	0	0	0	1	8	1	2	0
Bluff	6	.3263	.5043	37.0	2	2	0	0	0	2	0	0	3	0	0	0	0	1	0	0	0	0	0	0	0	0	2	0	0
bluffs	6	.3723	.5618	37.5	0	1	2	2	0	0	0	1	3	0	0	0	0	2	0	1	0	0	0	0	0	0	0	0	0
bluish	14	.6506	1.8665	42.7	1	1	1	1	4	0	4	2	0	0	0	1	0	2	0	5	0	0	0	0	2	1	2	1	0
Blumberg	2	.0000	.0914	29.6	0	2	0	0	0	0	0	0	2	0	0	0	0	0	0	0	0	0	0	0	0	0	0	0	0
blunder	8	.4740	.7943	39.0	0	0	0	1	4	1	1	1	0	1	0	4	0	0	1	1	0	0	0	0	1	0	0	0	0
blunderbuss	2	.0000	.0219	23.4	0	0	0	0	1	1	0	0	0	2	0	0	0	0	0	0	0	0	0	0	0	0	0	0	0
blundered	3	.2261	.2131	33.3	0	0	1	0	2	0	0	0	2	0	0	0	0	0	0	0	0	0	0	0	1	0	0	0	0
blundering	6	.3548	.5005	37.0	0	2	1	0	1	2	0	0	2	0	0	1	0	0	0	0	0	1	0	0	2	0	0	0	0
blunders	4	.3874	.3419	35.3	0	1	0	0	1	2	0	0	0	1	0	1	0	0	0	2	0	0	0	0	0	0	0	0	0
blunt	25	.7978	4.0141	46.0	3	3	1	4	4	6	3	1	5	0	0	2	0	1	0	3	2	1	1	1	3	3	0	3	0
blunted	2	.2285	.1129	30.5	0	0	0	0	1	1	0	0	0	0	0	0	0	1	0	0	0	0	0	0	0	0	1	0	0
bluntly	3	.3863	.2513	34.0	0	0	1	0	1	1	0	0	0	0	0	0	0	0	0	0	0	0	0	0	1	1	0	1	0
bluntness	3	.1277	.1363	31.3	0	0	0	0	2	0	1	0	1	0	0	0	0	0	0	0	0	0	0	0	0	0	0	2	0
blur	11	.5524	1.3366	41.3	3	2	2	3	1	0	0	0	5	0	0	0	0	0	0	2	0	0	0	0	1	1	0	2	0
blurred	16	.7033	2.2841	43.6	2	1	2	1	5	1	4	0	2	2	0	1	0	0	2	1	2	0	0	0	4	0	1	1	0
blurring	2	.0580	.0676	28.3	1	0	0	1	0	0	0	0	1	0	0	0	0	0	0	0	0	1	0	0	0	0	0	0	0
blurry	2	.1698	.1133	30.5	1	0	1	0	0	0	0	0	1	0	0	0	0	0	0	0	0	0	0	0	0	0	1	0	0
blurted	12	.5270	1.4071	41.5	1	2	3	0	5	0	1	0	6	0	0	1	0	0	0	0	0	0	0	0	1	1	0	3	0
blurting	4	.1892	.1847	32.7	0	0	0	0	3	1	0	0	0	0	0	3	0	0	0	0	0	0	0	0	0	0	0	1	0
blush	13	.6294	1.6997	42.3	1	3	1	0	4	1	2	1	2	0	0	2	0	1	0	2	0	0	0	0	3	2	0	1	0
blushed	12	.5605	1.4557	41.6	1	4	3	0	3	1	0	0	5	1	1	1	0	0	0	0	0	0	0	0	2	2	0	0	0
blushes	3	.3400	.2455	33.9	0	0	1	0	0	2	0	0	1	1	0	0	0	0	0	0	0	0	0	0	1	0	0	0	0
blushing	10	.3746	.8549	39.3	1	3	4	0	0	1	1	0	2	1	0	0	0	0	0	0	0	0	0	0	5	2	0	0	0
bluster	5	.3436	.4206	36.2	0	0	0	0	1	3	1	0	2	0	0	1	0	0	0	0	0	0	0	0	0	0	0	2	0
blustered	3	.1187	.1291	31.1	0	0	0	0	2	1	0	0	1	0	0	2	0	0	0	0	0	0	0	0	0	0	0	0	0
Blvd	2	.0000	.0243	23.9	0	0	0	0	2	0	0	0	0	0	0	0	0	0	0	0	0	0	0	0	0	0	0	2	0
BMW	6	.0000	.0729	28.6	0	0	0	0	0	0	0	6	0	0	0	0	0	0	0	0	0	0	0	0	0	0	0	6	0
Bo	10	.3462	.7681	38.9	5	0	0	0	4	1	0	0	0	0	0	1	5	0	0	0	0	0	0	0	0	0	0	4	0
Bo-o-o-n-e	5	.0000	.2284	33.6	0	5	0	0	0	0	0	0	5	0	0	0	0	0	0	0	0	0	0	0	0	0	0	0	0
Bo-o-o-o-n-e	2	.0000	.0914	29.6	0	2	0	0	0	0	0	0	2	0	0	0	0	0	0	0	0	0	0	0	0	0	0	0	0
boa	2	.0000	.0243	23.9	0	0	0	0	2	0	0	0	0	0	0	0	0	0	0	0	0	0	0	0	0	0	0	2	0
boar	19	.4992	2.1426	43.3	1	0	1	2	11	2	2	0	10	0	0	5	0	0	0	0	1	0	0	0	2	1	0	0	0
boar's	2	.2443	.1130	30.5	0	0	0	0	1	0	1	0	0	0	0	1	0	0	0	0	0	0	0	0	1	0	0	0	0
board	536	.8918	95.003	59.8	77	99	62	59	104	68	56	11	95	34	4	18	68	45	26	45	8	1	24	28	29	61	22	28	0
Board	41	.5118	4.4345	46.5	5	1	4	2	15	2	11	1	3	1	0	1	1	8	0	0	0	0	0	0	0	1	14	12	0
Board's	3	.2159	.1532	31.9	0	0	0	0	2	0	1	0	0	0	0	0	0	0	0	0	0	0	0	0	0	0	2	1	0
boarded	23	.7356	3.4323	45.4	0	6	3	5	4	3	1	1	3	4	0	2	0	5	1	0	0	0	0	0	2	2	1	3	0
boarder	5	.3451	.4196	36.2	0	1	0	0	0	4	0	0	2	0	0	0	0	0	0	0	1	0	0	0	2	0	0	0	0
boarders	2	.0000	.0234	23.7	0	0	0	0	0	2	0	0	0	0	0	0	0	0	0	0	0	0	0	0	2	0	0	0	0
boarding	15	.4427	1.5204	41.8	1	4	1	0	3	3	3	0	6	4	0	1	0	0	0	0	0	0	0	0	0	4	0	0	0
Boarding-House	3	.0000	.0067	18.3	0	0	0	0	3	0	0	0	0	0	3	0	0	0	0	0	0	0	0	0	0	0	0	0	0
boardinghouse	4	.3394	.3015	34.8	0	0	0	0	0	2	2	0	0	0	0	2	0	1	0	0	0	0	0	0	1	0	0	0	0
boards	132	.7705	20.610	53.1	17	20	19	8	37	23	8	0	35	1	4	9	13	8	1	9	1	1	2	15	9	14	7	3	0
boardwalk	3	.0000	.1370	31.4	0	3	0	0	0	0	0	0	3	0	0	0	0	0	0	0	0	0	0	0	0	0	0	0	0
boars	2	.1733	.1149	30.6	0	0	0	1	1	0	0	0	1	1	0	0	0	0	0	0	0	0	0	0	0	0	0	0	0
Boas	4	.0000	.0419	26.2	0	0	1	0	0	0	3	0	0	0	0	0	0	0	0	0	0	0	0	0	0	0	4	0	0
boast	18	.6954	2.5828	44.1	0	2	1	5	3	2	5	0	6	3	0	2	0	0	0	0	2	0	0	0	1	1	2	1	0
boasted	24	.5976	3.0860	44.9	5	5	1	1	4	6	1	1	10	0	0	1	0	4	0	0	0	0	0	0	0	5	1	3	0
boastful	8	.3782	.7184	38.6	2	0	1	0	2	2	1	0	3	0	0	2	0	2	0	0	0	1	0	0	0	0	0	0	0
boasting	14	.4433	1.4708	41.7	0	1	2	3	3	4	1	0	8	0	0	3	0	2	0	0	0	0	0	0	0	1	0	0	0
boasts	6	.2266	.3513	35.5	0	0	0	1	2	1	0	2	1	0	0	0	0	0	0	0	0	0	0	0	0	1	0	4	0
boat	933	.8654	162.11	62.1	160	294	109	121	149	34	44	22	407	37	21	56	17	89	9	29	14	6	0	2	77	88	8	73	0
Boat	26	.3325	1.9632	42.9	5	1	4	0	5	3	8	0	3	0	0	0	0	1	0	0	12	0	0	0	0	9	0	1	0
boat-in-the-bottle	3	.0000	.1370	31.4	3	0	0	0	0	0	0	0	3	0	0	0	0	0	0	0	0	0	0	0	0	0	0	0	0
boat-shaped	2	.2300	.1140	30.6	0	0	1	1	0	0	0	0	0	1	0	0	0	0	0	1	0	0	0	0	0	0	0	0	0
boat's	10	.4637	1.1051	40.4	0	5	1	3	0	0	1	0	7	0	0	0	0	0	0	1	0	0	0	0	1	0	1	0	0
boathouse	5	.2038	.3268	35.1	0	2	2	1	0	0	0	0	3	2	0	0	0	0	0	0	0	0	0	0	0	0	0	0	0
boating	17	.5606	1.9770	43.0	1	2	1	4	3	4	1	1	0	2	2	0	2	6	0	1	1	0	0	0	0	0	0	3	0
boatloads	3	.3465	.2515	34.0	1	0	0	0	0	1	1	0	1	0	0	0	0	0	0	0	0	0	0	0	0	1	0	1	0
boatman	13	.4948	1.3527	41.3	7	2	1	1	0	2	0	0	0	0	2	0	0	0	0	5	1	0	0	0	2	2	0	1	0
boatman's	2	.2303	.1079	30.3	1	0	0	1	0	0	0	0	0	0	0	0	0	0	0	0	1	0	0	0	0	1	0	0	0
boatmen	10	.4442	.9995	40.0	2	0	3	0	3	0	0	2	3	0	0	1	0	0	0	0	0	0	0	0	0	3	0	3	0
boats	391	.8483	66.503	58.2	111	82	59	45	66	13	12	3	92	12	5	8	6	112	5	16	8	6	0	1	16	68	11	25	0
Boats	2	.2412	.1141	30.6	1	0	0	0	0	0	1	0	0	1	0	0	0	0	0	0	0	0	0	0	0	1	0	0	0
bob	13	.6861	1.8246	42.6	2	4	3	0	2	0	2	0	2	1	1	1	0	0	0	4	1	0	1	0	1	0	0	1	0
Bob	535	.8149	88.611	59.5	165	98	41	58	127	22	20	4	272	32	2	17	69	34	28	8	0	8	1	0	10	22	0	32	0
Bob's	49	.7112	7.2271	48.6	7	13	2	4	19	4	0	0	21	4	0	3	9	3	4	0	0	1	0	0	0	0	0	4	0
bobbed	22	.4969	2.3992	43.8	5	4	1	6	4	2	0	0	7	1	0	2	0	0	0	0	0	0	0	0	9	2	0	1	0
bobber	4	.2174	.2134	33.3	0	3	0	0	1	0	0	0	0	1	0	0	0	0	0	0	0	0	0	0	0	3	0	0	0
bobbin	17	.0099	.1295	31.1	1	0	0	0	0	7	9	0	1	0	0	0	0	0	0	0	0	0	16	0	0	0	0	0	0
bobbing	25	.5980	3.1832	45.0	8	2	2	7	4	0	2	0	9	0	0	2	0	1	0	0	0	0	0	0	7	2	1	3	0
bobbins	4	.3138	.2609	34.2	0	0	0	0	1	2	1	0	0	0	0	0	0	0	0	0	0	0	2	1	1	0	0	0	0
bobby	7	.1034	.3147	35.0	1	0	1	0	2	3	0	0	4	0	0	0	0	0	0	0	0	0	3	0	0	0	0	0	0
Bobby	90	.5991	11.784	50.7	14	19	20	23	10	4	0	0	54	3	0	1	5	8	0	0	1	0	0	0	2	0	0	16	0

3J blue-wing
8A blue-wrappered
4N bluebells
XN blueberry-pickers
4A Bluebird's
5R Bluebirds
8A bluebottles
9D bluecoat
7M blued
7R Bluefaced
7Q bluefish
3N bluegrass
6E Bluejays
6A blueness
XR Blueprint
9F blueprinted
8D bluer
8F bluff'd
9R bluffed
3A bluffer
3A bluffers
5A bluffing
8B Bluffs
3Q bluish-green
8D bluish-white
4A Blumberg's
7M blunger
7M blungering
6P Blunt
9D blunt-nosed
8K blurriness
8C blurs
5A blustering
6N blusterous
7B bo
8R Bo's
6A bo'sun
7E BOA
6D Boar
3A board-an'-keep
8A boarding-house
7Q boas
5A boaster
4P boastingly
4N boat-racing
6A boat-steerer
XR boated
XR boaters
4R boathook
3J Boating
4P boatlike
3A boatload
7J boatmen's
6J Boatmen's
7N boatswain
9R boatyard
3A bob-tail
9D bob-white
9L Bobbin
6A bobbled

Word Type	F	D	U	SFI	3 Gr 3	4 Gr 4	5 Gr 5	6 Gr 6	7 Gr 7	8 Gr 8	9 Gr 9	X UnGr	A Read	B Eng & Gr	C Comp	D Lit	E Math	F Soc Stud	G Spell	H Sci	J Music	K Art	L Home Ec	M Shop	N Lib F	P Lib NF	Q Lib Ref	R Mag	S Rel
Bobby's	10	.1800	.7068	38.5	1	4	3	2	0	0	0	0	9	0	0	0	0	1	0	0	0	0	0	0	0	0	0	0	0
bobcat	5	.2664	.3459	35.4	2	1	0	0	2	0	0	0	2	0	0	2	0	0	0	0	0	1	0	0	0	0	0	0	0
bobcats	4	.3727	.3210	35.1	0	0	0	0	3	0	1	0	0	0	0	1	0	0	0	0	0	0	0	0	2	0	1	0	0
bobolink	4	.1497	.2092	33.2	0	0	4	0	0	0	0	0	2	0	0	0	0	0	2	0	0	0	0	0	0	0	0	0	0
bobs	2	.0000	.0234	23.7	0	0	0	2	0	0	0	0	0	0	0	0	0	0	0	0	0	0	0	0	2	0	0	0	0
bobsled	8	.2097	.5357	37.3	0	0	1	4	0	3	0	0	5	0	0	3	0	0	0	0	0	0	0	0	0	0	0	0	0
bobtail	2	.1494	.1045	30.2	0	0	0	1	1	0	0	0	1	0	0	0	0	0	0	0	1	0	0	0	0	0	0	0	0
bobtailed	2	.0000	.0914	29.6	0	0	1	0	1	0	0	0	2	0	0	0	0	0	0	0	0	0	0	0	0	0	0	0	0
bobwhite	3	.2091	.1444	31.6	0	0	2	0	1	0	0	0	0	0	0	0	0	0	2	0	0	0	0	0	0	0	1	0	0
Boccaccio	2	.0000	.0209	23.2	0	0	2	0	0	0	0	0	0	0	0	0	0	0	0	0	0	0	0	0	0	0	2	0	0
BOD	5	.0000	.0748	28.7	0	0	4	0	0	0	1	0	0	0	0	0	5	0	0	0	0	0	0	0	0	0	0	0	0
bode	2	.0000	.0234	23.7	0	0	0	0	2	0	0	0	0	0	0	0	0	0	0	0	0	0	0	0	2	0	0	0	0
Bode	2	.2278	.1128	30.5	0	0	0	0	0	2	0	0	0	0	0	0	0	0	0	1	0	0	0	0	0	0	1	0	0
Bode's	5	.0000	.0986	29.9	0	0	0	0	0	5	0	0	0	0	0	0	0	0	0	5	0	0	0	0	0	0	0	0	0
Bodger	2	.0000	.0234	23.7	0	0	0	0	2	0	0	0	0	0	0	0	0	0	0	0	0	0	0	0	2	0	0	0	0
bodguts	3	.0000	.0328	25.2	0	0	0	0	0	0	3	0	0	3	0	0	0	0	0	0	0	0	0	0	0	0	0	0	0
bodice	19	.0295	.1769	32.5	0	0	0	1	1	6	11	0	0	0	0	1	0	0	0	0	0	0	18	0	0	0	0	0	0
bodies	387	.7904	61.715	57.9	85	42	34	66	83	38	28	11	51	3	0	9	3	35	2	147	3	8	3	2	13	47	45	16	0
bodily	14	.4946	1.4397	41.6	0	0	0	2	3	3	6	0	0	2	0	1	0	0	0	1	2	0	0	0	0	1	7	0	0
body	1783	.8274	295.73	64.7	297	224	248	251	339	175	198	51	224	43	14	58	32	60	17	753	22	46	77	9	60	131	172	65	0
Body	3	.2445	.1903	32.8	0	0	0	1	1	0	0	1	1	0	0	0	0	0	0	0	0	0	1	0	0	0	0	1	0
body-building	6	.0000	.1183	30.7	0	0	0	6	0	0	0	0	0	0	0	0	0	0	0	6	0	0	0	0	0	0	0	0	0
body's	32	.3994	2.7431	44.4	0	0	1	2	6	3	20	0	0	0	0	0	0	0	0	8	0	0	4	0	0	1	18	1	0
bodyguard	5	.3574	.3845	35.8	0	0	0	1	2	0	1	1	0	0	0	0	0	0	2	0	0	0	0	0	2	0	0	1	0
Boers	5	.1285	.1797	32.5	0	0	0	0	4	1	0	0	0	0	0	0	0	1	0	0	0	0	0	0	0	0	4	0	0
bog	14	.5895	1.7289	42.4	2	5	0	2	2	2	0	1	3	1	0	2	0	0	1	2	4	0	0	0	1	0	0	0	0
Bogana	4	.0000	.0778	28.9	0	4	0	0	0	0	0	0	0	0	0	0	0	4	0	0	0	0	0	0	0	0	0	0	0
Bogana's	2	.0000	.0389	25.9	0	2	0	0	0	0	0	0	0	0	0	0	0	2	0	0	0	0	0	0	0	0	0	0	0
boggy	2	.2441	.1127	30.5	0	2	0	0	0	0	0	0	0	0	0	0	0	0	0	0	0	0	0	0	1	0	1	0	0
Bogota	8	.3093	.5844	37.7	0	0	1	6	0	0	1	0	0	1	0	0	0	6	0	0	0	0	0	0	0	1	0	0	0
bogs	17	.5840	2.1201	43.3	6	0	3	2	6	0	0	0	5	0	0	1	0	3	0	3	1	0	0	0	0	0	4	0	0
Bogus	3	.0000	.1370	31.4	0	0	0	3	0	0	0	0	3	0	0	0	0	0	0	0	0	0	0	0	0	0	0	0	0
Bohemia	16	.3896	1.3565	41.3	0	0	0	6	1	8	0	1	0	0	0	0	0	6	0	1	7	0	0	0	1	0	1	0	0
Bohemian	6	.4016	.5400	37.3	0	0	0	4	1	1	0	0	1	0	0	0	0	2	0	0	2	0	0	0	0	0	1	0	0
Bohr	8	.0900	.2261	33.5	0	0	0	0	5	3	0	0	0	0	0	0	0	0	0	1	0	0	0	0	0	0	7	0	0
Bohr's	2	.2278	.1128	30.5	0	0	0	0	2	0	0	0	0	0	0	0	0	0	0	1	0	0	0	0	0	0	1	0	0
bohte	2	.0000	.0162	22.1	0	0	0	0	0	2	0	0	0	0	0	0	0	0	2	0	0	0	0	0	0	0	0	0	0
boil	81	.6083	10.275	50.1	6	10	14	13	21	5	9	3	10	2	0	2	0	3	3	35	0	0	10	0	5	7	0	4	0
boiled	64	.8555	10.959	50.4	5	7	9	14	12	2	6	9	16	2	1	3	1	2	1	14	0	0	3	1	8	4	2	6	0
boiled-sweet	2	.0000	.0234	23.7	0	0	0	0	0	0	0	2	0	0	0	0	0	0	0	0	0	0	0	0	2	0	0	0	0
boiler	37	.5894	4.6780	46.7	1	11	11	1	6	5	2	0	14	2	0	6	0	0	0	10	0	0	3	0	0	0	1	1	0
boilers	9	.3983	.8367	39.2	1	3	2	0	1	2	0	0	2	0	0	0	0	1	0	5	0	0	0	0	0	0	1	0	0
boiling	124	.6961	17.636	52.5	10	12	10	19	25	15	23	10	14	6	2	1	12	1	0	47	1	0	14	0	5	6	4	11	0
boils	23	.7555	3.5175	45.5	2	2	3	7	3	1	5	0	3	1	0	0	5	2	1	5	0	0	1	1	0	0	1	3	0
boisterous	4	.3182	.2816	34.5	0	0	0	0	0	1	3	0	0	0	0	0	0	1	0	0	2	0	0	0	0	0	1	0	0
Bok	12	.0000	.1737	32.4	0	12	0	0	0	0	0	0	0	0	0	0	0	0	0	0	0	0	0	0	0	12	0	0	0
bola	10	.0000	.4568	36.6	10	0	0	0	0	0	0	0	10	0	0	0	0	0	0	0	0	0	0	0	0	0	0	0	0
bolas	2	.1814	.1187	30.7	0	0	0	0	2	0	0	0	1	0	0	0	0	0	0	0	0	0	0	0	0	0	0	1	0
bold	87	.8131	14.182	51.5	12	7	10	12	17	13	10	6	14	3	1	16	0	9	0	4	8	4	1	0	7	5	5	10	0
bold-face	2	.2289	.1077	30.3	0	0	0	0	1	1	0	0	0	0	0	0	1	0	1	0	0	0	0	0	0	0	0	0	0
bold-faced	4	.2408	.2182	33.4	0	0	0	0	2	0	2	0	0	2	0	0	0	0	2	0	0	0	0	0	0	0	0	0	0
bolder	3	.2292	.1615	32.1	0	0	0	2	0	1	0	0	0	0	0	1	0	0	0	0	0	0	0	0	2	0	0	0	0
boldest	6	.5047	.6464	38.1	1	0	1	0	1	1	2	0	1	0	0	1	0	0	0	0	0	0	0	0	1	1	2	0	0
boldface	43	.3043	3.7312	45.7	1	14	0	6	21	1	0	0	35	1	0	0	0	0	7	0	0	0	0	0	0	0	0	0	0
boldly	37	.7496	5.6829	47.5	3	3	5	3	12	6	5	0	14	0	0	5	0	3	0	1	2	0	0	1	5	4	1	1	0
boldness	5	.4732	.5365	37.3	1	0	0	1	1	2	0	0	2	0	0	0	0	1	0	0	0	0	0	0	0	1	1	0	0
Bolero	2	.2401	.1133	30.5	1	0	0	1	0	0	0	0	0	0	0	0	0	0	0	0	0	0	0	0	0	1	1	0	0
Boleyn	3	.0000	.0314	25.0	0	0	3	0	0	0	0	0	0	0	0	0	0	0	0	0	0	0	0	0	0	0	3	0	0
Bolingbroke	2	.0000	.0209	23.2	0	0	2	0	0	0	0	0	0	0	0	0	0	0	0	0	0	0	0	0	0	0	2	0	0
Bolivar	17	.3093	1.2418	40.9	3	1	2	11	0	0	0	0	0	0	0	0	0	12	0	0	0	0	0	0	0	4	1	0	0
Bolivar's	4	.0000	.0778	28.9	0	0	0	4	0	0	0	0	0	0	0	0	0	4	0	0	0	0	0	0	0	0	0	0	0
Bolivia	22	.3089	1.6184	42.1	2	0	3	11	4	0	2	0	1	0	0	0	0	15	0	1	0	0	0	0	0	0	5	0	0
Bolivian	3	.2254	.1785	32.5	0	0	0	1	0	0	0	2	0	0	0	0	0	1	0	2	0	0	0	0	0	0	0	0	0
boll	16	.3853	1.5484	41.9	5	3	7	0	0	1	0	0	9	0	0	0	0	3	0	4	0	0	0	0	0	0	0	0	0
bolls	9	.3947	.8104	39.1	2	6	0	0	0	0	1	0	1	0	0	0	0	5	0	2	0	0	1	0	0	0	0	0	0
bologna	4	.3501	.2980	34.7	0	0	0	0	2	1	1	0	0	1	0	0	0	0	0	0	0	0	1	0	0	0	2	0	0
Bologna	4	.3406	.2870	34.6	1	0	0	0	0	2	1	0	0	0	0	0	0	0	2	0	0	0	0	1	0	0	1	0	0
Bolshoi	2	.2297	.1135	30.6	0	0	0	1	0	0	1	0	0	0	0	1	0	1	0	0	0	0	0	0	0	0	0	0	0
bolster	3	.3756	.2468	33.9	1	0	0	0	1	0	1	0	0	0	0	1	0	1	0	0	0	0	0	0	0	0	1	0	0
bolstered	2	.0000	.0389	25.9	0	0	0	0	1	1	0	0	0	0	0	0	0	2	0	0	0	0	0	0	0	0	0	0	0
Bolsun	15	.0000	.2171	33.4	15	0	0	0	0	0	0	0	0	0	0	0	0	0	0	0	0	0	0	0	0	15	0	0	0
bolt	60	.5366	6.8586	48.4	12	4	6	10	13	4	11	0	14	1	1	4	0	0	0	8	0	0	1	12	2	13	0	4	0
Bolt	2	.0000	.0050	17.0	0	0	0	0	0	0	2	0	0	0	0	0	0	0	0	0	0	0	0	2	0	0	0	0	0
bolt-on	2	.0000	.0243	23.9	0	0	0	0	2	0	0	0	0	0	0	0	0	0	0	0	0	0	0	0	0	0	0	2	0
bolted	26	.7188	3.8277	45.8	3	3	3	4	6	5	1	1	7	4	0	1	0	2	0	0	0	0	0	1	5	3	1	2	0
bolts	37	.1969	1.6947	42.3	3	1	1	5	5	5	16	1	2	0	0	0	2	0	1	1	0	0	0	21	1	2	0	7	0
Bomar	3	.0000	.0055	17.4	0	1	0	0	2	0	0	0	0	0	0	0	0	0	0	0	0	3	0	0	0	0	0	0	0
bomb	58	.7555	8.8855	49.5	1	1	13	8	8	17	9	1	8	1	1	0	1	9	0	14	0	0	0	1	2	3	5	13	0
Bomb	2	.2437	.1129	30.5	0	0	1	1	0	0	0	0	0	0	0	0	0	0	0	0	0	0	0	0	0	0	1	1	0
bombarded	7	.4688	.6995	38.4	0	0	1	3	2	1	0	0	0	0	0	1	0	0	0	3	0	0	0	0	0	0	2	1	0
bombarding	4	.3496	.3058	34.9	0	0	0	1	1	1	1	0	0	0	0	0	1	0	0	0	0	0	0	0	1	0	2	0	0
bombardment	10	.4999	1.0883	40.4	0	0	0	0	2	6	2	0	2	1	0	0	0	2	0	2	0	0	0	0	0	0	3	0	0
Bombay	10	.3442	.8455	39.3	1	4	0	3	2	0	0	0	3	0	0	0	0	5	0	0	0	0	0	0	2	0	0	0	0
bombed	10	.4770	1.0309	40.1	1	3	1	2	0	2	1	0	1	0	0	0	0	4	0	0	0	0	0	0	1	0	3	1	0
bomber	12	.5048	1.3544	41.3	0	1	1	3	1	4	1	1	5	0	0	0	0	3	0	1	0	1	0	0	0	0	1	1	0
bomberos	5	.0000	.2284	33.6	0	5	0	0	0	0	0	0	5	0	0	0	0	0	0	0	0	0	0	0	0	0	0	0	0
bombers	16	.5606	1.9729	43.0	0	3	2	5	2	0	4	0	8	0	0	0	0	2	0	0	0	0	0	0	0	2	2	2	0
Bombers	2	.0000	.0243	23.9	0	0	0	0	2	0	0	0	0	0	0	0	0	0	0	0	0	0	0	0	0	0	0	2	0
bombing	19	.4843	1.9886	43.0	2	2	3	3	1	2	6	0	3	0	0	0	0	4	1	0	0	0	0	0	0	0	4	7	0
bombings	5	.2392	.3123	34.9	0	0	0	2	1	1	1	0	1	0	0	0	0	1	0	0	0	0	0	0	0	0	0	3	0
Bombolini	3	.0000	.0365	25.6	0	0	0	0	0	0	3	0	0	0	0	0	0	0	0	0	0	0	0	0	0	0	0	3	0
bombs	38	.6895	5.4968	47.4	0	6	3	13	6	4	6	0	17	2	0	1	0	8	0	4	0	0	0	0	0	3	2	1	0
bombshell	3	.1169	.1277	31.1	0	1	0	0	2	0	0	0	1	0	0	0	0	0	0	0	0	0	0	0	0	0	2	0	0
Bomex	3	.0000	.0365	25.6	0	0	0	0	3	0	0	0	0	0	0	0	0	0	0	0	0	0	0	0	0	0	0	3	0

7R bobby-soxer
3A Bobo
6F bobsledding
3P bobwhites
5B boc
5Q Boccaccio's
5J Boccherini
7N Boco
8D bodde
8D boddee
6A boded
9D bodes
9L bodkin
6F Bodo
XR Bodrugan
XR Bodrugan's
8R body-builder
6N body-coat
3K body-like
9Q body-nourishing
XR bodyguards
XR Boeing
XH Boer
8F Boeuf
4J Bog
9D Bogart
9L bogey
6R bogeymen
7A bogged
XR boggles
9Q Bogislav
5A bogle
5A bogle's
6A bogus
8J Boheme
8J Bohemia's
9B Bohemians
9J Bohm
6R Bohnson
3Q Bohol
7Q boids
6A bois
8F Boise
5A boisterously
9Q Boito
4P Boks'
7J bolero
8P Bolkestein
6R bollixed
7H bollworm
6A bolognas
7R Bolshevik
7N Bolshie
XR bolstering
6R bolsters
3P Bolsun's
8D bolt-action
6R bolting
7J Bolton
7E Bolyai
7Q bombard
7B bombards
7A bombastic
4A bombero
4A Bomberos'
7Q bombsight

Word Type	F	D	U	SFI	3 Gr 3	4 Gr 4	5 Gr 5	6 Gr 6	7 Gr 7	8 Gr 8	9 Gr 9	X UnGr	A Read	B Eng & Gr	C Comp	D Lit	E Math	F Soc Stud	G Spell	H Sci	J Music	K Art	L Home Ec	M Shop	N Lib F	P Lib NF	Q Lib Ref	R Mag	S Rel
BOMEX	2	.0000	.0394	26.0	0	0	0	0	2	0	0	0	0	0	0	0	0	0	0	2	0	0	0	0	0	0	0	0	0
bon	3	.3427	.2477	33.9	0	0	1	0	0	0	2	0	1	0	0	0	0	0	0	0	0	0	0	0	1	0	0	1	0
Bon	6	.5372	.6886	38.4	0	1	1	2	2	0	0	0	1	0	0	1	0	2	0	0	0	0	0	0	1	0	0	1	0
Bonanza	2	.1948	.1250	31.0	1	0	0	0	0	1	0	0	1	0	0	0	0	0	0	0	0	0	0	0	0	1	0	0	0
Bonaparte	5	.2441	.3058	34.9	0	0	1	2	1	1	0	0	0	0	0	0	0	3	0	0	0	0	0	0	0	2	0	0	0
Bonatti	2	.0000	.0914	29.6	0	2	0	0	0	0	0	0	2	0	0	0	0	0	0	0	0	0	0	0	0	0	0	0	0
bonbon	2	.1787	.1174	30.7	1	0	0	1	0	0	0	0	1	0	0	0	0	0	0	0	0	0	0	0	1	0	0	0	0
bond	40	.6732	5.4803	47.4	3	3	9	6	6	2	9	2	2	0	0	4	1	3	0	6	0	1	0	1	0	1	14	7	0
Bond	3	.3553	.2608	34.2	1	0	0	1	0	1	0	0	1	0	0	0	0	1	0	0	0	0	0	0	0	1	0	0	0
bondage	3	.1910	.1473	31.7	0	0	1	0	1	1	0	0	0	0	0	0	0	1	0	0	0	0	0	0	2	0	0	0	0
bonded	9	.2203	.4433	36.5	0	0	0	0	2	0	7	0	0	0	0	0	0	0	0	1	0	0	5	0	0	0	2	1	0
bondholder	3	.0000	.0314	25.0	0	0	3	0	0	0	0	0	0	0	0	0	0	0	0	0	0	0	0	0	0	0	3	0	0
bonding	13	.3139	.8828	39.5	0	3	0	0	2	1	7	0	0	0	0	0	0	0	0	1	0	0	4	0	0	0	7	1	0
bonds	50	.4668	5.0137	47.0	0	0	20	11	11	0	8	0	1	0	0	1	2	5	0	20	0	0	0	0	1	0	19	1	0
Bonds	6	.3633	.4717	36.7	0	0	2	0	0	4	0	0	1	0	0	1	0	0	0	0	0	0	0	0	0	0	2	3	0
bondsmen	2	.0000	.0389	25.9	0	0	0	0	0	2	0	0	0	0	0	0	0	2	0	0	0	0	0	0	0	0	0	0	0
bone	258	.8183	42.471	56.3	43	33	53	28	34	26	30	11	53	3	2	6	9	7	8	65	0	0	3	0	9	35	26	32	0
Bone	2	.0000	.0914	29.6	0	2	0	0	0	0	0	0	2	0	0	0	0	0	0	0	0	0	0	0	0	0	0	0	0
bones	491	.8328	81.934	59.1	114	66	103	47	74	42	31	14	62	10	2	22	31	11	4	178	7	2	9	0	19	72	43	19	0
Bones	2	.2446	.1125	30.5	1	0	0	0	0	0	1	0	0	1	0	1	0	0	0	0	0	0	0	0	0	0	0	0	0
Bonfiglio	5	.0000	.0608	27.8	0	0	0	0	5	0	0	0	0	0	0	0	0	0	0	0	0	0	0	0	0	0	0	5	0
bonfire	13	.5756	1.5479	41.9	1	5	2	1	2	1	0	1	1	0	2	0	0	1	1	1	1	0	0	0	2	2	0	2	0
bonfires	4	.3199	.3102	34.9	1	1	1	0	1	0	0	0	1	0	0	0	0	0	0	0	0	0	0	0	1	2	0	0	0
bong	3	.2196	.1554	31.9	0	0	1	0	2	0	0	0	0	0	0	2	0	0	0	0	0	0	0	0	1	0	0	0	0
BONG	2	.0000	.0234	23.7	0	0	0	2	0	0	0	0	0	0	0	0	0	0	0	0	0	0	0	0	2	0	0	0	0
bongo	4	.1672	.1617	32.1	0	1	0	0	2	0	1	0	0	0	0	0	0	0	0	0	3	0	0	0	0	0	0	1	0
bongos	2	.2375	.1088	30.4	0	0	0	0	1	0	1	0	0	0	0	0	0	0	0	0	1	0	0	0	0	0	0	1	0
Bonheur	2	.1698	.1133	30.5	0	0	1	1	0	0	0	0	1	0	0	0	0	0	0	0	0	0	0	0	0	0	1	0	0
Bonhomme	6	.0000	.2741	34.4	0	0	0	6	0	0	0	0	6	0	0	0	0	0	0	0	0	0	0	0	0	0	0	0	0
Boniface	10	.1518	.5300	37.2	0	3	0	0	0	0	7	0	3	0	0	0	0	7	0	0	0	0	0	0	0	0	0	0	0
Boniface's	3	.0000	.0583	27.7	0	0	0	0	0	0	3	0	0	0	0	0	0	3	0	0	0	0	0	0	0	0	0	0	0
bonjour	2	.1717	.1142	30.6	0	0	0	0	1	0	1	0	1	0	0	1	0	0	0	0	0	0	0	0	0	0	0	0	0
Bonkey	6	.0000	.0485	26.9	6	0	0	0	0	0	0	0	0	0	0	0	0	0	0	0	6	0	0	0	0	0	0	0	0
Bonn	4	.3409	.3067	34.9	0	0	0	1	1	1	1	0	0	0	0	0	1	1	0	0	0	0	0	0	0	0	0	2	0
bonnet	16	.4504	1.6749	42.2	5	6	0	1	2	1	1	0	8	0	0	2	0	0	0	0	0	0	0	0	1	5	0	0	0
bonnets	7	.5158	.7454	38.7	1	2	0	1	0	2	1	0	0	0	0	1	1	0	0	0	2	0	1	0	0	2	0	0	0
bonnie	8	.4007	.7290	38.6	0	1	5	0	0	0	2	0	2	3	0	2	0	1	0	0	0	0	0	0	0	0	0	0	0
Bonnie	14	.6468	1.8734	42.7	0	4	4	3	1	1	1	0	2	0	0	1	1	3	0	2	3	0	0	0	0	1	0	1	0
bonny	8	.3526	.7196	38.6	4	0	1	0	1	1	1	0	5	0	0	1	0	0	0	0	2	0	0	0	0	0	0	0	0
Bonny	2	.0000	.0162	22.1	0	2	0	0	0	0	0	0	0	0	0	0	0	0	0	0	2	0	0	0	0	0	0	0	0
bonus	21	.3952	1.8244	42.6	0	2	3	3	8	1	2	2	3	1	0	0	0	1	10	0	0	0	0	0	0	0	1	5	0
Bonus	2	.0000	.0389	25.9	0	0	0	0	0	2	0	0	0	0	0	0	0	2	0	0	0	0	0	0	0	0	0	0	0
bonuses	3	.1986	.1398	31.5	0	0	1	0	2	0	0	0	0	0	0	0	0	0	2	0	0	0	0	0	0	0	1	0	0
bony	48	.7179	6.9796	48.4	7	11	2	8	10	4	4	2	3	1	0	4	0	3	1	8	0	3	0	0	6	10	5	4	0
boo	4	.3518	.3077	34.9	0	0	0	0	2	2	0	0	0	0	0	2	0	0	0	0	0	0	0	0	0	1	0	1	0
boo-oo	2	.2407	.1090	30.4	2	0	0	0	0	0	0	0	0	1	0	0	0	0	0	0	1	0	0	0	0	0	0	0	0
boo-oo-oom	2	.2407	.1090	30.4	2	0	0	0	0	0	0	0	0	1	0	0	0	0	0	0	1	0	0	0	0	0	0	0	0
boobies	4	.0000	.0486	26.9	0	0	0	0	4	0	0	0	0	0	0	0	0	0	0	0	0	0	0	0	0	0	0	4	0
booby	7	.3698	.6466	38.1	2	3	0	0	2	0	0	0	4	0	0	0	0	0	0	0	0	0	0	0	1	0	0	2	0
Boodles	29	.0000	.3400	35.3	29	0	0	0	0	0	0	0	0	0	0	0	0	0	0	0	0	0	0	0	29	0	0	0	0
Boodles'	2	.0000	.0234	23.7	2	0	0	0	0	0	0	0	0	0	0	0	0	0	0	0	0	0	0	0	2	0	0	0	0
booed	4	.2107	.2095	33.2	0	1	0	0	2	0	1	0	0	0	0	0	0	0	0	0	0	0	0	0	0	3	0	1	0
boogaloo	2	.0000	.0243	23.9	0	0	0	0	0	0	2	0	0	0	0	0	0	0	0	0	0	0	0	0	0	0	0	2	0
boogie-woogie	4	.0000	.0323	25.1	0	0	0	3	0	1	0	0	0	0	0	0	0	0	0	0	4	0	0	0	0	0	0	0	0
booing	2	.0000	.0243	23.9	0	0	0	0	2	0	0	0	0	0	0	0	0	0	0	0	0	0	0	0	0	0	0	2	0
book	1453	.9457	271.65	64.3	249	267	175	190	256	165	114	37	345	272	14	50	116	111	94	137	61	10	23	17	34	66	33	68	2
Book	64	.7542	9.9100	50.0	4	16	15	12	11	2	3	1	29	13	1	2	0	3	2	0	4	0	0	0	3	4	1	2	0
book-learning	2	.0000	.0914	29.6	0	0	0	2	0	0	0	0	2	0	0	0	0	0	0	0	0	0	0	0	0	0	0	0	0
book's	2	.1814	.1187	30.7	0	0	0	1	1	0	0	0	1	0	0	0	0	0	0	0	0	0	0	0	0	0	0	1	0
bookcase	17	.3042	1.1160	40.5	0	1	3	0	2	10	1	0	1	1	1	1	1	0	0	0	0	0	10	0	0	1	0	1	0
bookcases	3	.2672	.1815	32.6	1	0	0	1	0	1	0	0	0	0	0	0	0	0	0	1	0	0	0	1	0	0	1	0	0
bookend	2	.0000	.0050	17.0	0	0	0	0	0	0	2	0	0	0	0	0	0	0	0	0	0	0	0	2	0	0	0	0	0
Booker	7	.2445	.5383	37.3	0	4	1	1	0	1	0	0	5	0	0	0	0	2	0	0	0	0	0	0	0	0	0	0	0
bookish	2	.1494	.1045	30.2	0	0	0	0	1	1	0	0	1	0	0	0	0	0	0	0	1	0	0	0	0	0	0	0	0
bookkeeping	4	.4742	.3984	36.0	0	0	0	0	1	2	1	0	0	0	0	1	0	1	1	0	0	0	0	0	0	0	1	0	0
booklet	18	.5957	2.2341	43.5	0	3	1	1	3	6	1	3	3	3	0	0	2	2	0	2	0	1	3	0	0	0	0	2	0
booklets	5	.2028	.2557	34.1	0	0	2	0	2	0	0	1	0	0	0	0	0	0	0	2	0	0	0	0	0	0	3	0	0
bookmakers	5	.0000	.0724	28.6	0	0	0	5	0	0	0	0	0	0	0	0	0	0	0	0	0	0	0	0	0	5	0	0	0
bookmaking	5	.0000	.0724	28.6	0	0	0	5	0	0	0	0	0	0	0	0	0	0	0	0	0	0	0	0	0	5	0	0	0
bookmark	3	.1200	.1302	31.1	0	0	0	0	1	2	0	0	1	2	0	0	0	0	0	0	0	0	0	0	0	0	0	0	0
books	902	.8930	160.23	62.0	165	162	117	113	162	103	55	25	201	201	5	37	105	90	33	32	14	6	12	9	43	41	25	48	0
Books	7	.3921	.5886	37.7	0	0	1	0	3	1	2	0	0	4	0	1	0	0	0	0	0	0	0	0	0	1	0	1	0
bookseller	2	.2408	.1204	30.8	0	1	0	0	0	1	0	0	0	0	0	0	0	1	0	0	0	0	0	0	0	1	0	0	0
bookshelves	4	.3726	.3697	35.7	2	1	0	1	0	0	0	0	2	0	0	0	0	1	0	0	0	0	0	0	1	0	0	0	0
bookworm	2	.2427	.1152	30.6	0	0	0	1	1	0	0	0	0	0	0	0	0	0	0	0	0	0	0	0	1	1	0	0	0
boom	61	.7494	9.2887	49.7	8	3	8	9	16	11	3	3	13	0	2	2	0	10	2	2	1	0	0	0	5	2	9	13	0
Boom	3	.0000	.0365	25.6	0	0	0	0	0	0	0	3	0	0	0	0	0	0	0	0	0	0	0	0	0	0	0	3	0
BOOM	2	.1814	.1187	30.7	1	1	0	0	0	0	0	0	1	0	0	0	0	0	0	0	0	0	0	0	0	0	0	1	0
boomed	16	.5798	2.0138	43.0	9	2	1	1	2	1	0	0	8	0	0	1	0	0	0	0	1	0	0	0	4	0	1	1	0
boomer	2	.0000	.0914	29.6	2	0	0	0	0	0	0	0	2	0	0	0	0	0	0	0	0	0	0	0	0	0	0	0	0
Boomer	26	.2446	2.0160	43.0	12	0	5	0	9	0	0	0	21	5	0	0	0	0	0	0	0	0	0	0	0	0	0	0	0
boomerang	20	.3544	1.8814	42.7	8	9	3	0	0	0	0	0	15	3	0	0	0	2	0	0	0	0	0	0	0	0	0	0	0
booming	37	.6602	5.1202	47.1	3	6	5	9	5	5	4	0	14	0	0	1	0	6	0	0	3	0	0	0	6	0	3	4	0
booms	9	.6094	1.1305	40.5	1	0	1	0	2	2	1	2	0	1	0	1	0	1	0	3	0	0	0	0	0	0	1	2	0
boon	11	.6602	1.4813	41.7	1	0	2	0	6	0	2	0	1	2	0	1	0	1	1	0	1	0	0	0	0	1	3	0	0
boondocks	2	.0000	.0243	23.9	0	0	0	0	1	0	1	0	0	0	0	0	0	0	0	0	0	0	0	0	0	0	0	2	0
Boone	44	.6262	5.8647	47.7	2	17	19	3	2	0	1	0	18	3	0	2	0	7	0	0	1	0	0	0	0	11	0	2	0
Boone's	8	.4858	.8908	39.5	0	4	3	0	1	0	0	0	4	1	0	0	0	2	0	0	0	0	0	0	0	1	0	0	0
Boones	2	.0000	.0290	24.6	0	0	2	0	0	0	0	0	0	0	0	0	0	0	0	0	0	0	0	0	0	2	0	0	0
Boonesborough	20	.3136	1.6522	42.2	0	3	15	0	2	0	0	0	10	0	0	0	0	2	0	0	0	0	0	0	0	8	0	0	0
Boonie-Bike	2	.0000	.0243	23.9	0	0	0	0	2	0	0	0	0	0	0	0	0	0	0	0	0	0	0	0	0	0	0	2	0
boos	2	.2303	.1079	30.3	1	0	0	0	0	1	0	0	0	0	0	0	0	0	0	0	1	0	0	0	0	1	0	0	0
boost	12	.2604	.7455	38.7	2	1	1	1	3	0	3	1	1	0	0	0	0	0	1	0	0	0	0	0	0	1	0	9	0

9R Bompensiero
3E Bona
6R bonanza
9Q Bonapartists
4A Bonatti's
XR bonbons
4Q bone-chilling
3P bone-digger
7Q bone-dry
6A bone-hard
XP bone-jarring
7R bone-rattling
4P Bone's
XR boned
XR boneless
3J bones-O
4N boneset
6P bong-bonged
3A Bong-tree
6N BONGGGG
3F bongs
4A Bonham
6N bonitos
4J bonked
6E Bonnard
XR Bonne
6A Bonneville
7R Bonnier
5A bonsoir
4N Bonte-Buck
3A Bonwit's
XP bonze
9D Boo
4J boo-shy-lo-ree
7R Boobies
9R booby-bomb
3N Bood
3N boodles
9R boogie
8J Boogie-Woogie
8A boohooing
8F book-burning
6E book-case
3B book-file
5A book-lined
3Q book-loving
XR book-movie
6P book-seller
5N book-shelves
9M bookbinders
8M bookends
7A bookkeeper
9A bookkeepers
XF Booklet
3P booklice
9B booklovers
6P bookmakers'
XR bookmobile
9M bookracks
8B bookseller's
7R bookshelf
7Q Bookshelf
4A bookside
9E bookstore
4A bookstores
4J boom--m--m
6A boom-boom-boom
5N Boom's
3A boomerangs
6A Boopfaddle
7D boorish

Word Type	F	D	U	SFI	3 Gr 3	4 Gr 4	5 Gr 5	6 Gr 6	7 Gr 7	8 Gr 8	9 Gr 9	X UnGr	A Read	B Eng & Gr	C Comp	D Lit	E Math	F Soc Stud	G Spell	H Sci	J Music	K Art	L Home Ec	M Shop	N Lib F	P Lib NF	Q Lib Ref	R Mag	S Rel
boosted	10	.4903	1.0878	40.4	4	3	1	0	1	0	1	0	4	0	1	0	0	0	0	0	0	0	0	0	2	1	2	0	0
booster	9	.4620	.9066	39.6	0	2	0	2	3	0	1	1	1	0	0	0	1	0	0	4	0	0	0	1	0	0	0	2	0
boosts	3	.0000	.0365	25.6	0	0	0	0	0	0	3	0	0	0	0	0	0	0	0	0	0	0	0	0	0	0	0	3	0
boot	33	.8522	5.6262	47.5	8	5	6	7	3	2	1	1	8	2	1	1	1	3	2	1	1	0	0	0	3	3	4	3	0
boot-shaped	2	.0000	.0389	25.9	0	0	1	1	0	0	0	0	0	0	0	0	0	2	0	0	0	0	0	0	0	0	0	0	0
bootblack	2	.0000	.0914	29.6	0	0	0	2	0	0	0	0	2	0	0	0	0	0	0	0	0	0	0	0	0	0	0	0	0
booted	2	.1717	.1142	30.6	0	0	0	1	1	0	0	0	1	0	0	1	0	0	0	0	0	0	0	0	0	0	0	0	0
booth	32	.6508	4.3641	46.4	8	10	0	1	6	2	4	1	12	1	0	5	0	0	0	0	3	0	0	0	5	4	0	2	0
Booth	3	.3764	.2475	33.9	0	0	0	0	0	1	2	0	0	1	0	1	0	1	0	0	0	0	0	0	0	0	0	0	0
Boothbay	3	.2427	.1822	32.6	0	0	0	0	1	2	0	0	0	0	0	0	0	0	0	2	0	0	0	0	0	0	0	1	0
booths	12	.5101	1.3348	41.3	0	6	0	1	1	0	4	0	4	0	0	2	0	0	0	0	3	0	0	0	1	2	0	0	0
bootjack	2	.2387	.1089	30.4	0	0	0	2	0	0	0	0	0	0	0	0	0	0	0	0	1	0	0	0	1	0	0	0	0
boots	176	.8182	29.127	54.6	47	43	20	15	31	11	7	2	71	6	1	14	3	7	2	5	7	0	0	0	22	16	3	19	0
Boots	31	.2429	2.4196	43.8	14	17	0	0	0	0	0	0	26	0	0	5	0	0	0	0	0	0	0	0	0	0	0	0	0
booty	5	.4029	.4540	36.6	1	1	0	0	2	1	0	0	1	0	0	2	0	0	0	1	0	0	0	0	0	0	1	0	0
bop	2	.2411	.1091	30.4	0	0	0	1	0	0	1	0	0	0	0	1	0	0	0	0	1	0	0	0	0	0	0	0	0
Bopsulai	2	.0000	.0234	23.7	0	2	0	0	0	0	0	0	0	0	0	0	0	0	0	0	0	0	0	0	2	0	0	0	0
Boran	2	.0000	.0290	24.6	0	0	0	0	2	0	0	0	0	0	0	0	0	0	0	0	0	0	0	0	0	2	0	0	0
borax	14	.3047	1.0600	40.3	1	0	3	3	0	3	2	2	2	1	0	0	0	1	0	10	0	0	0	0	0	0	0	0	0
Borch	2	.0000	.0243	23.9	0	0	0	0	0	0	2	0	0	0	0	0	0	0	0	0	0	0	0	0	0	0	0	2	0
Bordeaux	12	.2709	.7594	38.8	6	0	0	0	1	0	4	1	0	0	0	0	0	4	0	0	0	0	0	0	0	1	7	0	0
border	155	.7214	22.724	53.6	10	11	27	32	38	19	14	4	10	1	0	2	2	68	4	4	1	1	0	2	1	16	25	18	0
Border	2	.1814	.1187	30.7	0	0	1	1	0	0	0	0	1	0	0	0	0	0	0	0	0	0	0	0	0	0	0	1	0
bordered	16	.5937	1.9913	43.0	2	1	1	1	5	4	0	2	2	0	1	0	0	6	0	1	0	0	0	0	0	3	2	1	0
bordering	19	.7056	2.7567	44.4	1	2	4	3	5	0	3	1	4	1	0	1	1	7	0	0	0	0	0	0	1	1	2	1	0
borderland	2	.2137	.1056	30.2	0	0	0	0	0	1	1	0	0	0	0	0	0	1	0	0	1	0	0	0	0	0	0	0	0
borderline	3	.3771	.2489	34.0	0	0	0	0	1	1	1	0	0	0	0	1	0	0	0	1	0	0	0	0	0	0	0	1	0
borders	66	.7363	9.8128	49.9	10	5	13	2	19	11	5	1	1	2	1	0	0	29	0	2	1	1	2	0	5	4	15	3	0
bore	89	.7792	14.016	51.5	4	6	7	12	27	17	13	3	21	1	2	10	0	6	1	8	3	0	0	7	5	5	11	9	0
borealis	2	.2278	.1128	30.5	1	0	0	0	1	0	0	0	0	0	0	0	0	0	0	1	0	0	0	0	0	0	1	0	0
Borealis	2	.0000	.0394	26.0	0	0	0	0	1	0	0	1	0	0	0	0	0	0	0	2	0	0	0	0	0	0	0	0	0
Boreas	3	.1409	.1472	31.7	0	0	0	3	0	0	0	0	1	0	0	0	0	0	0	0	0	0	0	0	0	2	0	0	0
bored	48	.8196	7.9102	49.0	0	4	4	10	18	7	3	2	14	1	2	5	0	1	1	2	2	0	1	3	5	2	3	6	0
boredom	5	.4721	.4941	36.9	0	0	0	0	4	0	1	0	0	0	0	0	0	0	1	0	0	0	0	0	0	1	1	2	0
borer	2	.2278	.1128	30.5	0	1	0	0	1	0	0	0	0	0	0	0	0	0	0	1	0	0	0	0	0	0	1	0	0
borers	4	.3739	.3373	35.3	0	2	1	0	1	0	0	0	0	0	0	0	0	1	0	2	0	0	0	0	0	0	1	0	0
bores	2	.2412	.1141	30.6	0	0	0	0	1	0	1	0	0	1	0	0	0	0	0	0	0	0	0	0	0	1	0	0	0
boric	4	.2344	.2377	33.8	0	0	0	3	1	0	0	0	0	0	0	1	0	0	0	3	0	0	0	0	0	0	0	0	0
boring	36	.5485	4.1059	46.1	0	3	3	4	9	10	5	2	5	2	1	2	1	0	1	2	0	0	1	10	1	3	3	4	0
Boris	6	.1389	.2076	33.2	0	0	0	5	0	1	0	0	0	0	0	0	0	0	0	0	5	0	0	0	0	0	1	0	0
Borman	7	.1103	.2338	33.7	1	0	1	4	1	0	0	0	0	0	0	0	0	1	0	0	0	0	0	0	0	0	0	6	0
born	637	.7870	101.37	60.1	107	70	115	104	114	61	46	20	147	23	7	41	9	81	6	80	43	1	3	1	23	58	70	39	5
Born	3	.2321	.1635	32.1	0	0	0	0	0	1	1	1	0	0	0	0	0	0	0	0	0	0	0	0	0	0	1	2	0
borne	25	.6717	3.4681	45.4	3	0	0	4	9	4	2	3	6	2	0	2	0	1	0	2	0	0	0	0	4	0	5	3	0
Borneo	11	.3310	.8373	39.2	0	0	3	2	4	2	0	0	0	0	0	0	0	7	0	0	0	0	0	0	0	1	3	0	0
Bornholm	2	.0000	.0209	23.2	2	0	0	0	0	0	0	0	0	0	0	0	0	0	0	0	0	0	0	0	0	0	2	0	0
Bornstein	3	.0000	.0365	25.6	0	0	3	0	0	0	0	0	0	0	0	0	0	0	0	0	0	0	0	0	0	0	0	3	0
Borodin	2	.0000	.0162	22.1	0	0	0	0	0	1	1	0	0	0	0	0	0	0	0	0	2	0	0	0	0	0	0	0	0
borogoves	2	.1458	.0682	28.3	0	0	1	1	0	0	0	0	0	1	0	0	0	0	0	0	0	1	0	0	0	0	0	0	0
boron	6	.2278	.3385	35.3	0	1	1	2	0	0	2	0	0	0	0	0	0	0	0	3	0	0	0	0	0	0	3	0	0
borough	2	.2408	.1204	30.8	1	0	0	0	0	0	1	0	0	0	0	0	0	1	0	0	0	0	0	0	0	1	0	0	0
Boroughcastle	2	.0000	.0234	23.7	0	0	0	0	2	0	0	0	0	0	0	0	0	0	0	0	0	0	0	0	2	0	0	0	0
boroughs	3	.0000	.0434	26.4	3	0	0	0	0	0	0	0	0	0	0	0	0	0	0	0	0	0	0	0	0	3	0	0	0
Borre	3	.0000	.1370	31.4	0	0	0	0	3	0	0	0	3	0	0	0	0	0	0	0	0	0	0	0	0	0	0	0	0
borrow	80	.8155	13.096	51.2	13	16	8	15	15	9	4	0	15	14	1	2	2	9	6	1	2	0	0	0	13	7	3	5	0
borrowed	145	.7541	22.074	53.4	14	15	19	26	47	15	8	1	21	35	1	10	25	3	21	2	8	0	0	0	3	5	7	4	0
Borrowed	2	.0000	.0914	29.6	0	0	0	0	0	2	0	0	2	0	0	0	0	0	0	0	0	0	0	0	0	0	0	0	0
borrower	2	.0000	.0209	23.2	0	0	2	0	0	0	0	0	0	0	0	0	0	0	0	0	0	0	0	0	0	0	2	0	0
borrowers	3	.0000	.0365	25.6	0	0	C	0	0	0	3	0	0	0	0	0	0	0	0	0	0	0	0	0	0	0	0	3	0
Borrowers	4	.0000	.0469	26.7	0	0	4	0	0	0	0	0	0	0	0	0	0	0	0	0	0	0	0	0	4	0	0	0	0
borrowing	25	.6532	3.3413	45.2	1	3	7	3	8	0	0	3	3	6	0	0	3	0	2	0	0	1	0	0	7	0	2	1	0
borrowings	7	.2484	.3884	35.9	0	0	2	0	2	3	0	0	0	1	0	0	0	0	5	0	0	0	0	0	0	0	1	0	0
bos'n	2	.0000	.0243	23.9	0	0	2	0	0	0	0	0	0	0	0	0	0	0	0	0	0	0	0	0	0	0	0	2	0
bos'n's	2	.0000	.0243	23.9	0	0	2	0	0	0	0	0	0	0	0	0	0	0	0	0	0	0	0	0	0	0	0	2	0
Boscoe	2	.0000	.0215	23.3	0	0	0	0	2	0	0	0	0	0	0	2	0	0	0	0	0	0	0	0	0	0	0	0	0
bosom	16	.4591	1.5805	42.0	1	0	1	2	5	1	6	0	2	0	0	7	0	0	0	0	1	0	0	0	3	3	0	0	0
bosoms	2	.0000	.0215	23.3	0	0	0	0	1	0	1	0	0	0	0	2	0	0	0	0	0	0	0	0	0	0	0	0	0
Bosporus	12	.3221	.8996	39.5	0	0	1	0	8	2	0	1	0	0	0	0	0	8	0	0	0	0	0	0	0	1	0	3	0
boss	80	.7675	12.595	51.0	25	13	6	8	15	7	5	1	40	1	0	6	0	1	7	1	3	0	0	2	1	10	2	6	0
Boss	6	.4372	.5940	37.7	0	1	0	2	1	2	0	0	2	0	0	2	0	0	0	0	0	0	0	0	0	1	0	1	0
boss's	2	.1814	.1187	30.7	0	0	0	0	1	1	0	0	1	0	0	0	0	0	0	0	0	0	0	0	0	0	0	1	0
bossed	2	.1698	.1133	30.5	0	0	0	0	1	0	1	0	1	0	0	0	0	0	0	0	0	0	0	0	0	0	1	0	0
bosses	10	.5432	1.1754	40.7	0	1	0	0	5	3	1	0	3	0	0	0	0	3	1	0	0	0	0	0	0	0	2	1	0
bossy	8	.3383	.6599	38.2	2	1	0	0	3	0	0	2	3	0	0	3	0	0	0	0	0	0	0	0	0	0	0	2	0
Boston	255	.8095	41.625	56.2	41	41	54	21	38	45	13	2	57	5	0	3	3	72	1	10	12	1	1	0	22	34	17	17	0
Boston's	6	.5442	.6754	38.3	0	0	2	0	3	1	0	0	0	0	0	0	0	1	0	0	1	0	0	0	1	0	1	2	0
Bostonians	2	.2401	.1133	30.5	1	0	0	0	1	0	0	0	0	0	0	0	0	0	0	0	0	0	0	0	0	1	1	0	0
bosun's	4	.1717	.2284	33.6	0	0	2	0	0	0	2	0	2	0	0	2	0	0	0	0	0	0	0	0	0	0	0	0	0
Boswell	3	.3870	.2492	34.0	0	0	0	0	0	0	2	1	0	0	0	0	0	0	0	0	0	0	0	0	1	0	1	1	0
botanical	11	.4493	1.0554	40.2	1	0	0	0	6	1	2	1	1	0	0	1	0	0	0	1	0	1	0	0	0	0	6	1	0
botanically	2	.0000	.0394	26.0	0	0	0	0	2	0	0	0	0	0	0	0	0	0	0	2	0	0	0	0	0	0	0	0	0
botanist	7	.3280	.5726	37.6	0	0	3	1	2	1	0	0	2	0	0	0	0	0	0	4	0	0	0	0	0	0	1	0	0
botanists	9	.1719	.4433	36.5	0	0	7	0	1	1	0	0	0	0	0	0	0	0	0	8	0	0	0	0	0	0	1	0	0
botany	9	.1351	.3586	35.5	0	0	0	2	7	0	0	0	1	0	0	0	0	1	0	0	0	0	0	0	0	0	7	0	0
both	2646	.9829	511.92	67.1	331	349	290	333	517	397	350	79	433	131	25	120	318	254	144	291	134	37	57	53	105	173	186	184	1
Both	2	.0000	.0914	29.6	0	0	0	0	2	0	0	0	2	0	0	0	0	0	0	0	0	0	0	0	0	0	0	0	0
bother	100	.6567	13.712	51.4	24	17	12	14	17	12	4	0	34	3	2	14	0	2	2	3	2	0	0	0	14	17	0	6	1
bothered	32	.7575	4.9424	46.9	6	2	5	2	7	4	5	1	10	1	0	5	0	1	0	2	1	0	0	0	3	4	2	3	0
botherin'	2	.1787	.1174	30.7	0	0	0	1	0	1	0	0	1	0	0	0	0	0	0	0	0	0	0	0	1	0	0	0	0
bothering	21	.6061	2.7574	44.4	3	4	1	0	8	1	4	0	12	2	1	3	0	1	0	0	0	0	0	0	1	1	0	0	0
bothers	7	.5393	.8093	39.1	0	2	1	1	0	2	1	0	2	1	0	0	0	0	1	0	0	0	0	0	1	0	0	2	0
Botticelli	4	.0683	.0702	28.5	0	0	0	0	3	1	0	0	0	0	0	0	0	0	0	0	0	3	0	0	0	0	0	1	0
bottle	346	.8057	56.397	57.5	91	59	55	39	48	19	30	5	93	6	2	18	13	1	4	142	5	4	4	0	18	18	3	15	0
bottle-brush	2	.0000	.0914	29.6	0	2	0	0	0	0	0	0	2	0	0	0	0	0	0	0	0	0	0	0	0	0	0	0	0

8F booster's
XR boosting
XR Boot
7N boot-box
7R boot-sole
7M boot-strap
7H Bootes
9B Boothe
6H Boothia
5N bootlaces
3P bootshaped
3B boppling
4N Bopsulai's
7F bora
8Q Borba
7R border-to-border
8F borderlands
7Q Bordes
7Q boreal
7A boreen
5Q borehole
5Q boreholes
5Q boresomely
7R Borg-Warner
5P Borgese
8B Boring
XR borning
3A bornite
9J Borodin's
7B Borough
8F borrower's
7B borrowers'
8E borrows
7A borryed
5P Borsalino
7D Borup's
8Q Bosanquet
8Q Bosnia-Hercegovina
9R Bosnia-Herzegovina
3P boss-giraffe
7Q boss'
8J bossa
5A bossier
7D bossin'
8N bossing
8B Bostonian
8B bot
9Q Botanic
8Q Botanical
7R botched
6A BOTH
4A botheration
9L bothersome
6F Bothnia
7P Botkin's
XH botryoidal
3A Botte
7F bottle-makers
3A bottle-nosed
3R bottle-top

Word Type	F	D	U	SFI	3 Gr 3	4 Gr 4	5 Gr 5	6 Gr 6	7 Gr 7	8 Gr 8	9 Gr 9	X UnGr	A Read	B Eng & Gr	C Comp	D Lit	E Math	F Soc Stud	G Spell	H Sci	J Music	K Art	L Home Ec	M Shop	N Lib F	P Lib NF	Q Lib Ref	R Mag	S Rel
bottled	7	.5239	.7772	38.9	2	1	0	1	1	0	2	0	1	0	0	0	0	1	0	0	0	0	1	0	1	1	0	2	0
bottleneck	2	.2285	.1129	30.5	0	1	0	0	0	0	1	0	0	0	0	0	0	1	0	0	0	0	0	0	0	0	1	0	0
bottlenecks	2	.1814	.1187	30.7	0	0	0	1	0	0	1	0	1	0	0	0	0	0	0	0	0	0	0	0	0	0	0	1	0
bottles	114	.8374	19.166	52.8	29	17	7	21	12	8	10	10	25	3	0	7	16	5	1	33	3	1	1	0	10	3	5	1	0
bottom	858	.9112	155.27	61.9	168	135	116	109	151	71	87	21	204	18	10	32	51	46	11	216	17	5	26	30	41	61	41	49	0
Bottom	2	.2440	.1132	30.5	0	0	0	0	1	0	1	0	0	0	0	1	0	0	0	0	0	0	0	0	0	0	0	1	0
BOTTOM	9	.0000	.0966	29.8	0	0	0	0	0	0	9	0	0	0	0	9	0	0	0	0	0	0	0	0	0	0	0	0	0
bottoming	2	.1620	.0760	28.8	0	0	0	0	1	1	0	0	0	0	0	0	0	0	0	0	0	0	0	1	0	0	0	1	0
bottomlands	2	.0000	.0209	23.2	0	0	0	0	1	0	1	0	0	0	0	0	0	0	0	0	0	0	0	0	0	0	2	0	0
bottomless	8	.4698	.8504	39.3	0	1	1	2	1	2	1	0	3	0	0	1	0	2	0	0	0	0	0	0	0	0	0	2	0
bottoms	24	.5927	3.0047	44.8	4	3	6	2	5	2	2	0	5	0	0	2	0	3	0	6	0	0	0	0	3	0	5	0	0
Boucher	3	.2027	.1376	31.4	0	0	2	0	0	0	1	0	0	0	0	0	0	0	0	0	0	1	0	0	0	0	2	0	0
bough	20	.5118	2.1768	43.4	4	5	1	4	3	3	0	0	4	2	0	2	0	0	0	0	8	0	0	0	0	1	2	1	0
boughs	18	.6535	2.4908	44.0	2	2	0	5	6	2	1	0	9	0	1	1	0	2	0	0	2	0	0	0	1	1	0	1	0
bought	598	.8024	96.824	59.9	169	107	95	65	74	43	38	7	140	42	4	24	210	67	18	6	7	2	7	0	26	21	5	19	0
bouillon	3	.1125	.0853	29.3	0	0	1	0	2	0	0	0	0	0	0	0	1	0	0	0	0	0	2	0	0	0	0	0	0
Boula	3	.0000	.0434	26.4	0	0	0	0	3	0	0	0	0	0	0	0	0	0	0	0	0	0	0	0	0	3	0	0	0
boulder	23	.5337	2.6404	44.2	1	0	2	5	4	2	8	1	5	1	2	0	0	0	0	9	0	0	0	0	0	0	3	3	0
Boulder	4	.3540	.3119	34.9	0	1	0	0	0	0	0	3	0	0	0	0	0	0	0	1	1	0	0	0	0	0	0	2	0
boulders	34	.6394	4.5282	46.6	3	3	2	6	5	6	9	0	5	0	0	4	0	4	0	14	0	0	0	0	2	1	1	3	0
boulevard	6	.5050	.6520	38.1	0	0	1	1	3	0	1	0	1	0	0	0	0	1	0	0	0	0	0	0	0	1	1	2	0
Boulevard	4	.2298	.2346	33.7	0	3	0	1	0	0	0	0	0	0	0	0	0	3	0	0	0	0	0	0	1	0	0	0	0
boulevards	10	.3743	.8368	39.2	2	0	1	3	2	2	0	0	0	0	0	0	0	6	0	0	0	0	0	0	0	0	2	2	0
bounce	53	.6721	7.3155	48.6	10	14	7	9	8	2	1	2	7	1	1	0	0	0	0	14	9	0	0	0	2	12	1	6	0
Bounce	11	.0000	.5025	37.0	0	0	0	11	0	0	0	0	11	0	0	0	0	0	0	0	0	0	0	0	0	0	0	0	0
bounced	40	.6904	5.7239	47.6	7	9	5	4	2	6	7	0	14	0	2	10	0	1	0	5	1	0	0	1	1	3	0	2	0
bounces	19	.3933	1.6713	42.2	5	7	0	5	1	1	0	0	0	1	0	0	0	0	0	13	0	0	0	0	2	3	0	0	0
bouncing	39	.6492	5.2622	47.2	6	3	7	5	8	5	5	0	8	3	0	0	0	2	0	7	0	0	0	0	2	6	1	10	0
bouncy	5	.3541	.4015	36.0	2	0	1	1	0	1	0	0	1	0	1	1	0	0	0	0	0	0	0	0	0	0	0	2	0
bound	170	.8771	29.732	54.7	8	21	20	33	36	27	23	2	42	10	0	24	5	13	2	8	10	0	3	1	18	10	11	13	0
Bound	6	.2962	.4185	36.2	0	1	2	0	3	0	0	0	1	0	0	0	0	0	0	0	2	0	0	0	0	0	0	3	0
boundaries	69	.6105	8.7451	49.4	6	5	5	19	10	13	9	2	2	2	0	0	4	34	0	9	0	1	0	0	0	1	13	3	0
Boundaries	2	.0000	.0389	25.9	0	2	0	0	0	0	0	0	0	0	0	0	0	2	0	0	0	0	0	0	0	0	0	0	0
boundary	79	.6487	10.523	50.2	10	10	8	9	26	8	8	0	1	1	0	3	9	32	0	7	0	0	0	0	1	6	15	4	0
bounded	31	.7085	4.5023	46.5	4	2	9	3	5	4	2	2	7	0	0	2	5	2	0	1	0	0	0	0	5	2	5	2	0
bounding	11	.4448	1.0909	40.4	1	1	3	1	3	0	1	1	3	0	0	1	0	0	0	0	0	0	0	0	5	1	0	1	0
boundless	8	.5909	.9687	39.9	0	1	1	3	1	1	1	0	0	1	1	1	0	2	0	0	0	0	0	0	1	0	1	1	0
bounds	20	.7286	2.9975	44.8	1	2	1	5	4	6	0	1	7	0	0	0	1	2	0	1	1	0	1	0	3	2	0	2	0
bounteous	2	.1494	.1045	30.2	0	0	0	1	0	1	0	0	1	0	0	0	0	0	0	0	1	0	0	0	0	0	0	0	0
bounties	2	.1814	.1187	30.7	0	0	0	0	1	0	0	1	1	0	0	0	0	0	0	0	0	0	0	0	0	0	0	1	0
bountiful	6	.4476	.5688	37.5	0	0	1	1	1	0	3	0	0	2	0	0	0	2	0	0	0	0	1	0	0	0	1	0	0
bounty	9	.5250	.9753	39.9	0	2	0	2	2	1	0	2	0	0	0	1	0	0	0	0	1	0	0	0	1	0	3	3	0
bouquet	13	.5841	1.6324	42.1	0	4	0	4	3	0	2	0	5	1	0	3	0	0	0	2	0	0	0	0	1	1	0	0	0
bouquets	24	.3678	2.1778	43.4	3	5	0	14	1	1	0	0	9	0	0	0	0	2	0	12	0	0	0	0	0	1	0	0	0
bourbon	4	.3641	.3177	35.0	0	0	1	0	0	1	2	0	0	0	0	1	0	0	0	0	0	0	0	0	0	1	0	2	0
Bourbon	2	.2437	.1129	30.5	0	0	0	0	1	0	1	0	0	0	0	0	0	0	0	0	0	0	0	0	0	0	1	1	0
Bourbons	4	.2433	.2315	33.6	0	0	2	0	2	0	0	0	0	0	0	0	0	0	0	0	0	0	0	0	0	2	0	2	0
bourgeois	4	.3678	.3187	35.0	0	0	1	0	0	0	3	0	0	0	0	0	0	0	0	0	1	0	0	0	0	1	0	2	0
bourgeoisie	4	.1737	.1745	32.4	0	0	1	0	0	3	0	0	0	0	0	0	0	0	0	0	0	0	0	0	0	1	3	0	0
bourne	2	.0665	.0708	28.5	0	0	0	1	0	0	1	0	1	0	1	0	0	0	0	0	0	0	0	0	0	0	0	0	0
bourree	2	.0000	.0162	22.1	0	0	1	0	0	1	0	0	0	0	0	0	0	0	0	0	2	0	0	0	0	0	0	0	0
Bourree	5	.0000	.0404	26.1	0	3	2	0	0	0	0	0	0	0	0	0	0	0	0	0	5	0	0	0	0	0	0	0	0
bouts	6	.3704	.5175	37.1	0	0	0	3	1	1	0	1	1	0	0	0	0	1	0	1	0	0	0	0	0	3	0	0	0
bow	281	.8167	46.265	56.7	47	85	18	42	50	22	15	2	93	7	3	27	0	10	9	1	38	0	0	6	25	40	7	15	0
bow-wow-wow	2	.0000	.0914	29.6	1	1	0	0	0	0	0	0	2	0	0	0	0	0	0	0	0	0	0	0	0	0	0	0	0
Bowditch	5	.1979	.2497	34.0	0	0	1	4	0	0	0	0	0	1	0	0	0	0	0	0	0	0	0	0	0	4	0	0	0
bowed	66	.6343	8.8781	49.5	12	11	8	9	18	8	0	0	30	0	0	6	0	1	1	2	10	0	0	0	11	4	1	0	0
bowels	5	.4326	.4543	36.6	0	0	0	1	3	0	1	0	0	0	0	0	0	0	0	0	0	0	1	0	2	1	1	0	0
Bowen	4	.3790	.3299	35.2	0	2	0	0	0	1	1	0	0	0	0	0	0	0	0	0	0	0	0	0	0	2	1	1	0
bower	4	.3011	.2909	34.6	0	0	1	0	0	1	2	0	1	0	0	2	0	0	0	0	0	0	0	0	0	0	1	0	0
Bower	15	.1167	.5953	37.7	0	0	14	0	1	0	0	0	0	0	0	0	0	14	0	0	0	0	0	0	0	0	0	1	0
Bowers	5	.0000	.0112	20.5	0	0	0	0	0	0	5	0	0	0	5	0	0	0	0	0	0	0	0	0	0	0	0	0	0
Bowie	14	.0000	.6396	38.1	0	2	2	8	0	2	0	0	14	0	0	0	0	0	0	0	0	0	0	0	0	0	0	0	0
Bowie's	2	.0000	.0914	29.6	0	0	1	1	0	0	0	0	2	0	0	0	0	0	0	0	0	0	0	0	0	0	0	0	0
bowing	17	.7388	2.5648	44.1	0	1	2	1	6	4	3	0	5	1	0	2	0	1	0	0	2	0	0	0	1	2	2	1	0
bowl	325	.7833	51.753	57.1	120	55	29	30	50	10	24	7	116	8	1	14	5	16	2	57	4	2	34	6	29	14	7	10	0
Bowl	12	.2850	.8266	39.2	0	0	1	0	7	2	2	0	2	0	0	0	0	1	0	0	1	0	0	0	0	0	0	8	0
bowl-like	3	.0000	.1370	31.4	1	2	0	0	0	0	0	0	3	0	0	0	0	0	0	0	0	0	0	0	0	0	0	0	0
bowl-shaped	2	.2278	.1128	30.5	1	0	0	1	0	0	0	0	0	0	0	0	0	0	0	1	0	0	0	0	0	0	1	0	0
bowl's	2	.0000	.0290	24.6	2	0	0	0	0	0	0	0	0	0	0	0	0	0	0	0	0	0	0	0	0	2	0	0	0
bowled	3	.2435	.2274	33.6	2	0	1	0	0	0	0	0	2	0	0	0	0	1	0	0	0	0	0	0	0	0	0	0	0
bowler	9	.3792	.8521	39.3	7	2	0	0	0	0	0	0	5	0	0	0	0	0	0	2	0	0	0	0	0	0	0	2	0
bowlers	3	.2279	.2143	33.3	2	1	0	0	0	0	0	0	2	0	0	0	0	0	0	0	0	0	0	0	0	0	0	1	0
bowling	36	.7467	5.5515	47.4	14	5	5	3	4	3	2	0	18	2	1	0	4	1	1	2	0	0	0	0	0	2	1	4	0
Bowling	3	.2043	.1486	31.7	0	0	2	0	1	0	0	0	0	0	0	0	0	0	0	0	0	0	0	0	0	1	2	0	0
bowls	53	.8297	8.8935	49.5	21	10	6	3	11	0	2	0	23	0	0	2	0	5	0	9	1	1	2	1	2	3	2	2	0
bowman	5	.4686	.5251	37.2	0	0	0	3	2	0	0	0	2	0	0	0	0	0	0	0	1	0	0	0	1	0	1	0	0
Bowman	11	.4147	1.0581	40.2	4	5	1	0	0	0	1	0	4	0	0	1	0	0	0	0	0	0	0	0	0	5	1	0	0
bows	41	.7041	5.9240	47.7	8	11	4	8	4	3	3	0	9	0	0	4	1	12	0	0	5	0	1	0	6	0	2	1	0
bowsprit	4	.3189	.2753	34.4	0	0	0	0	3	0	1	0	0	0	1	0	0	0	0	0	0	0	0	0	2	0	1	0	0
bowstring	6	.5303	.6603	38.2	0	1	0	1	3	1	0	0	0	0	0	0	0	1	0	0	1	0	0	0	1	1	2	0	0
bowstrings	2	.2152	.1357	31.3	0	0	1	1	0	0	0	0	1	0	0	0	0	1	0	0	0	0	0	0	0	0	0	0	0
box	1145	.9100	207.12	63.2	366	161	182	140	118	99	65	14	362	54	7	43	215	26	91	85	11	14	18	27	74	59	18	41	0
Box	30	.5753	3.5656	45.5	12	9	1	4	2	0	1	1	2	2	0	0	4	1	8	0	0	0	0	0	9	0	1	3	0
boxcar	9	.3621	.7258	38.6	3	5	0	0	0	1	0	0	0	0	0	0	4	2	0	0	0	0	0	0	3	0	0	0	0
boxcars	8	.4440	.8133	39.1	1	3	2	2	0	0	0	0	3	0	0	0	2	1	0	0	0	0	0	0	0	0	2	0	0
boxed	11	.5597	1.3162	41.2	2	1	2	3	1	0	2	0	3	0	0	0	0	2	0	0	1	0	0	1	1	3	0	0	0
boxer	23	.6414	3.1378	45.0	12	1	4	0	2	2	1	1	12	1	0	1	0	0	0	0	0	1	0	0	1	2	4	1	0
Boxer	17	.4749	1.7167	42.3	0	3	2	0	1	6	5	0	0	0	0	3	0	7	0	0	0	0	0	0	5	0	2	0	0
Boxer's	2	.0000	.0234	23.7	0	0	0	0	0	0	2	0	0	0	0	0	0	0	0	0	0	0	0	0	2	0	0	0	0
boxers	3	.0000	.1370	31.4	2	0	0	0	1	0	0	0	3	0	0	0	0	0	0	0	0	0	0	0	0	0	0	0	0
Boxers	3	.0000	.0583	27.7	0	0	0	0	1	2	0	0	0	0	0	0	0	3	0	0	0	0	0	0	0	0	0	0	0
boxes	331	.8010	53.454	57.3	136	64	34	24	33	14	21	5	73	10	3	12	140	14	13	13	1	7	7	2	12	7	4	13	0
Boxhall	3	.0000	.0434	26.4	0	0	0	0	0	0	3	0	0	0	0	0	0	0	0	0	0	0	0	0	0	3	0	0	0

8H bottling
4R Bottom-Fix
7Q bottomland
5J Bottoms
XR boudoirs
5Q Boudry
7P Bougainville
8G boughte
8Q Bouguereau
XR bouillabaisse
9Q Boulanger
XR boulder-paved
7Q boulder's
7Q Boulton
4D bounceful
8B bouncer
5A Bouncer
7D Bour-the-King
XN Bourbonnais
6J bourdon
9R Bournemouth
8D bout
XR Bouvet
XR Bouvier
5Q Bovary
5Q Bovidae
4N bow-and-arrow
9D bow-boy's
5A bow-legged
9Q bow-sprit
3G bow-wow
3A bow-wow-ow-ow
3A bow-wow-ow-ow-ow
4P bow's
5H bowel
3J bowers
9C Bowers'
4A bowhead
3P bowheads
3R Bowhemia
8A bowie
8A bowie-knife
7A bowin'
8D bowlders
3P bowlegged
5H bowlegs
4R Bowler
4R Bowlers
7R Bowles
4R bowling's
6P bowsed
3N bowser-hound
8E box-car
8E box-cars
7R box's
7P boxer's
7P boxful

Word Type	F	D	U	SFI	3 Gr 3	4 Gr 4	5 Gr 5	6 Gr 6	7 Gr 7	8 Gr 8	9 Gr 9	X UnGr	A Read	B Eng & Gr	C Comp	D Lit	E Math	F Soc Stud	G Spell	H Sci	J Music	K Art	L Home Ec	M Shop	N Lib F	P Lib NF	Q Lib Ref	R Mag	S Rel
boxing	26	.5658	3.2392	45.1	10	3	1	6	4	2	0	0	14	0	0	0	0	1	1	1	0	1	0	0	1	7	0	0	0
boxing's	2	.0000	.0914	29.6	2	0	0	0	0	0	0	0	2	0	0	0	0	0	0	0	0	0	0	0	0	0	0	0	0
boxlike	7	.5055	.7528	38.8	1	2	1	1	0	1	1	0	1	1	0	0	0	1	1	1	0	1	0	0	0	0	1	0	0
boxwood	4	.0000	.0419	26.2	0	0	4	0	0	0	0	0	0	0	0	0	0	0	0	0	0	0	0	0	0	0	4	0	0
boy	2529	.9021	454.92	66.6	578	543	303	363	433	160	125	24	1080	124	24	246	99	95	60	81	44	17	18	0	313	217	24	86	1
Boy	207	.6646	29.422	54.7	46	10	16	92	33	4	2	4	139	4	0	0	6	2	1	4	25	1	0	0	11	5	1	8	0
BOY	15	.0000	.1610	32.1	0	0	0	0	0	15	0	0	0	0	0	15	0	0	0	0	0	0	0	0	0	0	0	0	0
boy's	181	.8190	30.044	54.8	34	24	16	44	37	17	8	1	86	18	2	16	4	2	3	6	5	0	1	0	22	8	1	7	0
Boy's	9	.4808	.9770	39.9	2	0	0	6	0	0	0	1	4	0	0	0	0	0	0	0	1	0	0	0	0	2	0	2	0
boycott	9	.3832	.7492	38.7	0	0	4	0	4	0	1	0	0	0	0	2	0	0	0	0	0	0	0	0	0	4	0	3	0
boycotted	2	.0000	.0243	23.9	0	0	0	0	0	0	1	1	0	0	0	0	0	0	0	0	0	0	0	0	0	0	0	2	0
boycotts	2	.0000	.0209	23.2	0	0	0	0	2	0	0	0	0	0	0	0	0	0	0	0	0	0	0	0	0	0	2	0	0
Boyd	27	.1963	1.3075	41.2	0	0	0	1	3	22	0	1	1	22	0	3	0	0	0	0	0	0	0	0	0	0	0	1	0
Boyd's	5	.0000	.0547	27.4	0	0	0	0	0	5	0	0	0	5	0	0	0	0	0	0	0	0	0	0	0	0	0	0	0
Boyer	9	.1282	.3180	35.0	0	0	8	1	0	0	0	0	0	1	0	0	0	0	0	0	0	0	0	0	8	0	0	0	0
boyfriend	7	.2735	.4864	36.9	0	0	4	0	2	0	1	0	2	0	0	0	0	0	0	0	0	0	0	0	1	0	0	4	0
boyhood	28	.7038	4.0375	46.1	0	4	3	4	6	8	1	2	7	1	2	3	0	3	0	0	1	0	0	1	0	1	2	7	0
boyish	5	.3846	.4764	36.8	0	0	1	1	2	1	0	0	3	1	0	0	0	0	0	0	0	0	0	0	0	0	0	1	0
Boyle	4	.4800	.4071	36.1	1	0	1	0	1	0	1	0	0	0	0	0	1	0	0	1	0	0	0	0	0	0	1	1	0
Boyle's	6	.0000	.1183	30.7	0	3	0	0	0	0	3	0	0	0	0	0	0	0	0	6	0	0	0	0	0	0	0	0	0
Boyles	2	.2420	.1154	30.6	0	0	1	0	1	0	0	0	0	0	0	0	1	0	0	0	0	0	0	0	1	0	0	0	0
boys	2155	.9004	386.31	65.9	501	591	261	291	228	168	94	21	682	167	23	125	194	118	19	77	63	17	32	0	216	298	12	112	0
Boys	29	.6845	4.0923	46.1	7	3	6	5	4	2	0	2	8	1	0	1	1	1	0	0	6	0	0	0	1	3	2	5	0
boys'	37	.7676	5.7805	47.6	1	8	8	8	7	4	1	0	13	1	2	4	3	0	0	1	3	0	1	0	4	3	0	2	0
Boys'	14	.4345	1.3875	41.4	1	8	1	3	0	1	0	0	4	1	0	0	0	5	0	0	0	0	0	0	0	0	0	4	0
Bozo	14	.1879	1.0091	40.0	7	0	6	0	0	0	0	1	13	0	0	0	0	0	0	0	0	0	0	0	0	0	0	1	0
br	9	.0000	.0730	28.6	1	2	5	1	0	0	0	0	0	0	0	0	0	0	9	0	0	0	0	0	0	0	0	0	0
Br'er	3	.0000	.0243	23.8	3	0	0	0	0	0	0	0	0	0	0	0	0	0	0	0	3	0	0	0	0	0	0	0	0
brace	20	.6247	2.5928	44.1	3	1	0	3	7	5	0	1	4	1	0	3	1	0	0	1	0	0	0	2	1	2	0	5	0
Brace	2	.2346	.1166	30.7	0	0	0	1	0	0	0	1	0	0	0	0	0	0	0	1	0	0	0	0	0	0	0	1	0
braced	23	.4969	2.5852	44.1	0	1	1	6	8	2	5	0	12	1	0	5	0	0	0	0	0	0	0	0	4	1	0	0	0
bracelet	19	.5838	2.2865	43.6	4	1	0	2	7	0	5	0	1	5	0	1	0	0	1	0	0	0	0	0	3	2	0	6	0
bracelets	11	.6089	1.3858	41.4	1	1	1	1	4	3	0	0	1	0	0	0	0	3	1	0	0	0	1	0	1	1	0	3	0
braces	40	.4200	3.6849	45.7	6	8	6	2	9	7	0	2	3	1	0	3	29	0	0	1	0	0	0	1	0	0	0	2	0
brachiopods	2	.2278	.1128	30.5	0	0	0	0	1	0	1	0	0	0	0	0	0	0	0	1	0	0	0	0	0	0	1	0	0
brachiosaurus	2	.0000	.0290	24.6	0	2	0	0	0	0	0	0	0	0	0	0	0	0	0	0	0	0	0	0	0	2	0	0	0
bracing	5	.4695	.5316	37.3	0	0	0	1	2	0	1	1	2	1	0	0	0	0	0	1	0	0	0	0	0	0	1	0	0
bracken	3	.2212	.2099	33.2	0	0	1	0	2	0	0	0	2	0	0	1	0	0	0	0	0	0	0	0	0	0	0	0	0
bracket	20	.3809	1.6087	42.1	2	0	1	1	7	8	1	0	0	1	0	1	0	0	0	1	1	0	0	7	2	2	0	5	0
brackets	14	.6124	1.7679	42.5	0	1	0	0	5	6	1	1	1	2	0	0	6	0	1	1	0	0	0	1	0	1	0	1	0
Brackett	8	.0000	.0938	29.7	0	0	0	8	0	0	0	0	0	0	0	0	0	0	0	0	0	0	0	0	8	0	0	0	0
brackish	3	.2254	.1785	32.5	0	0	1	0	0	2	0	0	0	0	0	0	0	1	0	2	0	0	0	0	0	0	0	0	0
brad	3	.0000	.0591	27.7	0	0	3	0	0	0	0	0	0	0	0	0	0	0	0	3	0	0	0	0	0	0	0	0	0
Brad	3	.0000	.1370	31.4	2	0	1	0	0	0	0	0	3	0	0	0	0	0	0	0	0	0	0	0	0	0	0	0	0
Bradburn	2	.0000	.0914	29.6	0	0	0	2	0	0	0	0	2	0	0	0	0	0	0	0	0	0	0	0	0	0	0	0	0
Bradbury	4	.0000	.0089	19.5	0	0	0	0	0	0	4	0	0	0	4	0	0	0	0	0	0	0	0	0	0	0	0	0	0
Braddledum	4	.0000	.0323	25.1	4	0	0	0	0	0	0	0	0	0	0	0	0	0	0	0	4	0	0	0	0	0	0	0	0
Braddock	12	.3053	.8689	39.4	2	0	0	0	0	8	2	0	0	0	0	0	0	9	0	0	0	0	0	0	0	2	1	0	0
Bradford	48	.4115	4.9637	47.0	5	8	4	24	2	5	0	0	36	0	0	0	0	5	0	0	0	0	0	0	0	6	1	0	0
Bradford's	3	.0000	.1370	31.4	0	0	0	1	0	2	0	0	3	0	0	0	0	0	0	0	0	0	0	0	0	0	0	0	0
Bradley	11	.3314	.8014	39.0	0	0	0	2	0	8	1	0	0	4	0	0	0	0	0	0	0	0	0	0	0	0	1	6	0
brads	2	.1249	.0685	28.4	0	0	0	0	0	2	0	0	0	0	0	0	0	0	0	1	0	0	0	1	0	0	0	0	0
Brady	15	.0000	.6852	38.4	0	0	15	0	0	0	0	0	15	0	0	0	0	0	0	0	0	0	0	0	0	0	0	0	0
Brady's	5	.2025	.3254	35.1	0	0	1	0	4	0	0	0	3	0	0	2	0	0	0	0	0	0	0	0	0	0	0	0	0
brag	8	.4474	.8263	39.2	0	2	1	3	0	2	0	0	4	1	1	0	0	0	0	0	0	0	0	0	0	1	0	1	0
Brag	4	.2393	.3005	34.8	3	0	0	0	0	1	0	0	3	0	0	1	0	0	0	0	0	0	0	0	0	0	0	0	0
Bragg	10	.2297	.5459	37.4	0	0	2	0	5	1	2	0	0	0	0	0	2	1	0	0	0	0	0	0	0	0	7	0	0
braggart	2	.1814	.1187	30.7	1	0	0	0	1	0	0	0	1	0	0	0	0	0	0	0	0	0	0	0	0	0	0	1	0
bragged	11	.4373	1.1198	40.5	2	5	3	1	0	0	0	0	5	0	0	0	0	0	0	0	0	0	0	0	1	4	0	1	0
bragging	14	.5295	1.5594	41.9	1	5	0	3	1	2	2	0	1	0	0	3	0	1	0	0	0	0	0	0	1	5	0	3	0
brags	4	.4538	.4020	36.0	0	0	0	0	1	1	2	0	1	0	0	1	0	0	0	0	0	0	0	0	0	1	0	1	0
Brahe	7	.0000	.1380	31.4	0	5	0	0	0	0	0	2	0	0	0	0	0	0	0	7	0	0	0	0	0	0	0	0	0
Brahe's	3	.0000	.0591	27.7	0	2	0	0	1	0	0	0	0	0	0	0	0	0	0	3	0	0	0	0	0	0	0	0	0
Brahma	2	.2440	.1132	30.5	0	0	2	0	0	0	0	0	0	0	0	1	0	0	0	0	0	0	0	0	0	0	0	1	0
Brahman	10	.1755	.5058	37.0	0	0	0	2	1	7	0	0	0	0	0	0	0	8	0	2	0	0	0	0	0	0	0	0	0
Brahmans	3	.2444	.1814	32.6	0	1	0	0	0	2	0	0	0	0	0	0	0	2	0	0	0	0	0	0	0	0	1	0	0
Brahms	27	.0000	.2183	33.4	1	8	3	3	3	7	2	0	0	0	0	0	0	0	0	0	27	0	0	0	0	0	0	0	0
Brahms'	3	.0000	.0243	23.8	0	2	1	0	0	0	0	0	0	0	0	0	0	0	0	0	3	0	0	0	0	0	0	0	0
braid	20	.5599	2.4449	43.9	9	1	1	3	3	3	0	0	10	1	0	0	0	1	0	0	0	1	0	2	4	1	0	0	0
braided	17	.6372	2.2722	43.6	6	1	1	1	4	2	2	0	6	0	0	1	0	0	0	1	0	0	1	1	5	1	0	1	0
braiding	6	.3876	.5836	37.7	5	0	0	0	1	0	0	0	4	0	0	0	0	0	0	0	0	0	0	0	1	0	0	1	0
braids	25	.3053	2.1301	43.3	9	4	0	4	3	1	4	0	19	0	0	0	0	0	0	0	0	0	4	0	1	1	0	0	0
braille	2	.0000	.0914	29.6	0	0	2	0	0	0	0	0	2	0	0	0	0	0	0	0	0	0	0	0	0	0	0	0	0
Braille	13	.4629	1.2936	41.1	2	2	0	4	5	0	0	0	2	1	0	4	0	0	4	0	0	0	0	0	0	2	0	0	0
brain	330	.6729	45.860	56.6	17	27	56	56	87	34	43	10	44	3	0	16	12	2	4	171	7	0	0	0	10	31	18	12	0
Brainard	2	.0000	.0914	29.6	0	0	0	0	0	2	0	0	2	0	0	0	0	0	0	0	0	0	0	0	0	0	0	0	0
brainchild	3	.0000	.0365	25.6	0	0	0	0	2	1	0	0	0	0	0	0	0	0	0	0	0	0	0	0	0	0	0	3	0
brains	52	.7374	7.8369	48.9	3	7	2	5	16	8	10	1	14	2	0	8	2	0	0	7	0	0	0	0	5	6	5	3	0
brainstem	2	.0000	.0209	23.2	0	0	0	0	0	0	2	0	0	0	0	0	0	0	0	0	0	0	0	0	0	0	2	0	0
brainwashed	2	.0000	.0243	23.9	0	0	1	0	1	0	0	0	0	0	0	0	0	0	0	0	0	0	0	0	0	0	0	2	0
brainwork	2	.2441	.1127	30.5	0	0	0	0	1	0	1	0	0	0	0	0	0	0	0	0	0	0	0	0	1	0	1	0	0
braising	2	.0000	.0064	18.1	0	0	0	0	0	0	2	0	0	0	0	0	0	0	0	0	0	0	2	0	0	0	0	0	0
brake	73	.6652	10.047	50.0	16	12	6	0	25	6	8	0	20	4	0	2	1	0	2	1	0	0	0	6	11	9	1	16	0
braked	3	.2212	.2099	33.2	0	0	0	0	1	2	0	0	2	0	0	1	0	0	0	0	0	0	0	0	0	0	0	0	0
brakeman	8	.3024	.6067	37.8	6	0	0	1	0	0	1	0	2	0	0	0	0	2	0	0	0	0	0	0	0	4	0	0	0
brakes	67	.7655	10.446	50.2	14	10	3	2	23	8	5	2	22	3	1	3	0	2	0	4	1	0	0	0	8	3	6	14	0
braking	5	.4137	.4652	36.7	0	0	0	0	3	0	1	1	1	0	0	0	0	0	0	1	0	0	0	0	0	0	1	2	0
bramble	4	.3709	.3633	35.6	1	0	1	1	1	0	0	0	2	0	0	0	0	0	0	0	0	0	0	0	0	0	1	1	0
brambles	10	.5511	1.2320	40.9	2	3	1	0	1	2	0	1	6	0	0	0	0	1	0	0	0	0	0	0	1	1	0	1	0
bran	16	.2175	.8211	39.1	1	0	3	1	2	4	5	0	2	0	0	1	0	0	0	0	0	0	9	0	2	0	2	0	0
branch	233	.8927	41.416	56.2	44	36	26	30	54	19	19	5	54	12	0	11	4	33	4	40	12	4	0	2	12	18	19	8	0
Branch	10	.4442	1.0342	40.1	2	0	0	0	0	2	6	0	5	0	0	1	0	0	0	0	0	0	0	0	0	1	0	3	0
branched	8	.4837	.8251	39.2	3	2	0	0	1	1	0	1	1	0	0	0	0	0	0	0	0	1	0	0	1	3	1	1	0
branches	345	.8684	59.903	57.8	68	59	35	64	65	31	18	5	99	12	3	11	4	37	0	41	11	13	0	5	33	37	30	8	1
branching	16	.6367	2.0786	43.2	3	1	1	1	7	1	0	2	0	1	0	2	0	0	0	5	0	0	0	1	2	0	4	1	0

6A Boxing
9B boxtop
5Q Boxwood
7R boxy
5B boy-oh-boy
5J boy-wonder
6A Boy'll
6R BOY'S
5P Boycott
8Q Boydell's
6B Boyds
6D boylike
4E BOYS
XR Bozeman
8H Br
3A BR-RAT-TA-TAT-TAT
5F br-r-r
3N br-r-r-r-r-r
3A br-r-r-ring
9R bra-less
3P BRACE
9C Bracebridge
XH brachii
6N Brackett's
9H brackish-water
3A Brad's
9P bradded
9M Braddock-Rowe
8F Braddock's
8R Bradley's
7N Bradshaw
XH Brah
XR Brahm's
9J Brahmin
7F braid-trimmed
7D Brailles
5F brain-
7N brain-racking
XR brain-scratching
7H brain-twisting
6A brain's
XN brainstorms
9N brainworkers
4P brainy
5Q brakemen
3J Bran
3A branch-shaped
3A branch
3P branchlets

Word Type	F	D	U	SFI	3 Gr 3	4 Gr 4	5 Gr 5	6 Gr 6	7 Gr 7	8 Gr 8	9 Gr 9	X UnGr	A Read	B Eng & Gr	C Comp	D Lit	E Math	F Soc Stud	G Spell	H Sci	J Music	K Art	L Home Ec	M Shop	N Lib F	P Lib NF	Q Lib Ref	R Mag	S Rel
branchlike	2	.0000	.0394	26.0	0	0	0	2	0	0	0	0	0	0	0	0	0	0	0	2	0	0	0	0	0	0	0	0	0
brand	52	.7941	8.2824	49.2	2	5	18	2	13	2	7	3	5	10	1	5	8	5	0	0	1	0	1	0	3	1	2	10	0
Brand	3	.3225	.2367	33.7	1	0	0	1	0	1	0	0	1	0	0	0	1	0	1	0	0	0	0	0	0	0	0	0	0
brand-new	18	.6634	2.4801	43.9	3	4	3	3	3	0	1	1	5	1	1	0	0	2	0	0	0	0	0	0	1	4	1	3	0
branded	6	.5361	.6885	38.4	0	1	1	1	2	0	1	0	1	0	0	1	0	2	0	0	0	0	0	0	1	1	0	0	0
Brandenburg	6	.3608	.4692	36.7	0	1	0	0	2	1	2	0	0	0	0	0	0	0	0	0	1	0	0	0	0	2	3	0	0
brandished	3	.3399	.2456	33.9	0	0	0	0	0	2	1	0	1	0	0	1	0	0	0	0	0	0	0	0	0	0	0	1	0
brandishing	3	.3873	.2495	34.0	0	0	1	0	0	0	1	1	0	0	0	1	0	0	0	0	0	0	0	0	1	0	0	1	0
Brandle	2	.0000	.0243	23.9	0	0	0	0	2	0	0	0	0	0	0	0	0	0	0	0	0	0	0	0	0	0	0	2	0
Brando's	2	.0000	.0243	23.9	0	0	0	0	1	0	1	0	0	0	0	0	0	0	0	0	0	0	0	0	0	0	0	2	0
brands	14	.5258	1.5698	42.0	0	3	7	0	4	0	0	0	2	5	0	0	0	2	0	2	0	0	0	0	2	0	0	1	0
Brandt	6	.2279	.4286	36.3	4	0	0	0	2	0	0	0	4	0	0	0	0	0	0	0	0	0	0	0	0	0	0	2	0
brandy	16	.5201	1.7642	42.5	6	1	1	0	2	4	2	0	1	0	0	2	0	4	0	0	0	0	0	0	1	7	1	0	0
Brandywine	16	.1813	.8101	39.1	12	0	2	0	0	2	0	0	0	0	0	0	0	14	0	0	0	0	0	0	0	0	2	0	0
Brant	14	.0000	.6396	38.1	0	0	0	14	0	0	0	0	14	0	0	0	0	0	0	0	0	0	0	0	0	0	0	0	0
Brant's	2	.0000	.0914	29.6	0	0	0	2	0	0	0	0	2	0	0	0	0	0	0	0	0	0	0	0	0	0	0	0	0
Branwen	2	.0000	.0290	24.6	0	0	0	0	2	0	0	0	0	0	0	0	0	0	0	0	0	0	0	0	0	2	0	0	0
Braque	5	.2394	.2685	34.3	0	0	4	0	0	1	0	0	0	0	0	0	0	0	0	0	0	1	0	0	0	0	4	0	0
braseros	2	.0000	.0389	25.9	0	0	0	2	0	0	0	0	0	0	0	0	0	2	0	0	0	0	0	0	0	0	0	0	0
brash	2	.1948	.1250	31.0	0	0	0	1	0	1	0	0	1	0	0	0	0	0	0	0	0	0	0	0	0	1	0	0	0
Brasileiras	2	.0000	.0162	22.1	0	0	0	2	0	0	0	0	0	0	0	0	0	0	0	0	2	0	0	0	0	0	0	0	0
Brasilia	13	.2302	.7620	38.8	1	0	3	9	0	0	0	0	0	0	0	0	0	10	0	0	0	0	0	0	0	0	3	0	0
brass	191	.6442	25.269	54.0	31	29	19	18	46	38	8	2	32	2	1	12	0	6	0	12	71	1	0	15	16	11	5	7	0
Brass	7	.1146	.2114	33.3	5	0	0	1	0	1	0	0	0	0	0	0	0	0	0	0	6	0	0	0	0	0	0	1	0
brasses	6	.1852	.2683	34.3	1	0	0	0	3	2	0	0	0	0	0	0	0	0	0	0	4	0	0	0	0	2	0	0	0
brassy	3	.3824	.2446	33.9	0	0	0	0	0	0	2	1	0	0	0	1	0	0	0	0	1	0	0	0	0	0	0	1	0
bravado	2	.1787	.1174	30.7	0	0	0	0	2	0	0	0	1	0	0	0	0	0	0	0	0	0	0	0	1	0	0	0	0
brave	282	.7675	44.473	56.5	58	79	44	44	29	16	11	1	142	12	1	16	0	24	6	1	7	0	0	0	23	42	2	6	0
Brave	26	.2494	1.6175	42.1	11	15	0	0	0	0	0	0	4	0	0	0	0	0	0	0	0	0	0	0	16	6	0	0	0
braved	4	.3597	.3542	35.5	0	0	0	1	1	2	0	0	2	0	0	0	0	0	0	0	1	0	0	0	0	0	0	1	0
bravely	43	.7128	6.3569	48.0	9	9	10	5	5	4	1	0	17	1	1	2	0	11	0	0	1	0	0	0	5	4	0	1	0
braver	6	.3598	.5339	37.3	1	1	0	2	1	0	1	0	3	0	0	1	0	0	0	0	0	0	0	0	2	0	0	0	0
bravery	24	.7008	3.4899	45.4	5	3	4	3	2	5	1	1	9	1	0	0	0	4	1	0	1	0	0	0	0	4	3	1	0
braves	35	.3124	3.1168	44.9	8	14	8	2	3	0	0	0	29	1	0	0	0	0	0	0	0	0	0	0	0	5	0	0	0
Braves	9	.2113	.5151	37.1	1	0	1	0	3	4	0	0	2	0	0	0	1	0	0	0	0	0	0	0	0	0	0	6	0
bravest	16	.4332	1.7024	42.3	0	2	6	3	3	1	1	0	12	2	0	1	0	1	0	0	0	0	0	0	0	0	0	0	0
braving	2	.1717	.1142	30.6	0	0	1	0	0	1	0	0	1	0	0	1	0	0	0	0	0	0	0	0	0	0	0	0	0
bravo	7	.1939	.4400	36.4	4	0	0	1	0	2	0	0	4	0	0	3	0	0	0	0	0	0	0	0	0	0	0	0	0
Bravo	3	.1823	.1405	31.5	0	1	0	0	2	0	0	0	0	0	0	0	0	1	0	0	0	0	0	0	0	0	2	0	0
brawl	3	.3394	.2451	33.9	0	0	0	0	1	1	1	0	1	0	0	1	0	0	0	0	0	0	0	0	1	0	0	0	0
brawls	2	.0000	.0215	23.3	0	0	0	0	0	0	2	0	0	0	0	2	0	0	0	0	0	0	0	0	0	0	0	0	0
brawn	2	.2407	.1138	30.6	0	0	0	1	1	0	0	0	0	0	0	1	0	0	0	0	0	0	0	0	0	1	0	0	0
Braxton	2	.2285	.1129	30.5	0	0	0	0	1	1	0	0	0	0	0	0	0	1	0	0	0	0	0	0	0	0	1	0	0
brayer	13	.0000	.0240	23.8	2	1	1	5	3	1	0	0	0	0	0	0	0	0	0	0	0	13	0	0	0	0	0	0	0
braying	5	.3761	.4737	36.8	3	0	1	1	0	0	0	0	3	0	0	0	0	1	0	0	0	0	0	0	0	0	1	0	0
brazen	3	.2844	.1848	32.7	0	0	0	0	2	1	0	0	0	1	1	1	0	0	0	0	0	0	0	0	0	0	0	0	0
brazenly	3	.0000	.1370	31.4	1	0	0	0	1	1	0	0	3	0	0	0	0	0	0	0	0	0	0	0	0	0	0	0	0
Brazil	126	.5078	13.610	51.3	5	8	53	21	17	13	9	0	1	0	0	2	0	82	0	2	10	0	0	0	3	3	19	4	0
Brazil's	9	.1908	.4700	36.7	0	0	5	1	2	0	1	0	0	0	0	0	0	8	0	0	1	0	0	0	0	0	0	0	0
Brazilian	29	.5492	3.3125	45.2	0	0	10	8	7	3	1	0	0	0	1	0	0	13	0	0	5	0	0	0	0	0	7	3	0
Brazils	3	.0000	.0352	25.5	0	0	0	3	0	0	0	0	0	0	0	0	0	0	0	0	0	0	0	0	3	0	0	0	0
Brazos	4	.1325	.1944	32.9	0	0	0	1	3	0	0	0	1	0	0	0	0	3	0	0	0	0	0	0	0	0	0	0	0
breach	8	.4254	.7406	38.7	0	0	0	0	1	3	3	1	1	0	0	1	0	0	0	0	0	0	0	0	0	1	4	1	0
breached	2	.1787	.1174	30.7	0	0	0	1	0	1	0	0	1	0	0	0	0	0	0	0	0	0	0	0	1	0	0	0	0
bread	515	.7300	76.905	58.9	140	81	63	65	69	30	56	11	138	17	0	31	35	33	10	79	12	1	53	0	33	49	12	8	4
Bread	3	.2757	.1896	32.8	1	0	1	0	0	0	1	0	0	0	0	0	0	0	0	1	0	0	1	0	0	1	0	0	0
Bread-Cereal	4	.0000	.0129	21.1	0	0	0	0	3	1	0	0	0	0	0	0	0	0	0	0	0	0	4	0	0	0	0	0	0
bread-and-butter	6	.3708	.4902	36.9	0	1	0	0	1	0	4	0	1	1	0	1	0	0	0	0	0	0	2	0	0	0	1	0	0
breadfruit	6	.4316	.5935	37.7	0	0	0	3	0	3	0	0	2	0	0	0	0	1	0	0	0	0	0	0	2	1	0	0	0
breads	14	.0236	.1250	31.0	0	0	1	0	1	8	4	0	0	0	0	0	0	0	0	1	0	0	13	0	0	0	0	0	0
breadth	13	.4825	1.3408	41.3	0	1	0	3	5	1	2	1	2	0	0	1	0	0	0	2	3	2	0	0	0	2	1	0	0
break	516	.9508	96.973	59.9	89	69	73	76	96	50	53	10	137	18	5	32	15	27	15	102	12	7	12	5	29	40	25	35	0
breakable	2	.0000	.0215	23.3	0	0	0	0	0	0	2	0	0	0	0	2	0	0	0	0	0	0	0	0	0	0	0	0	0
breakage	2	.2437	.1129	30.5	0	0	0	0	1	0	0	1	0	0	0	0	0	0	0	0	0	0	0	0	0	0	1	1	0
breakaway	2	.0000	.0243	23.9	1	0	0	1	0	0	0	0	0	0	0	0	0	0	0	0	0	0	0	0	0	0	0	2	0
breakdown	12	.5609	1.4022	41.5	0	1	0	1	3	3	3	1	0	1	0	0	0	0	0	6	0	0	0	1	0	1	1	2	0
breakdowns	3	.0000	.0314	25.0	0	0	0	0	1	0	2	0	0	0	0	0	0	0	0	0	0	0	0	0	0	0	3	0	0
breaker	9	.5286	1.0067	40.0	2	0	3	0	2	1	1	0	1	1	0	1	0	2	0	0	0	0	0	1	0	3	0	0	0
breakers	17	.5962	2.1938	43.4	2	1	7	2	5	0	0	0	8	0	0	0	0	2	0	1	0	0	0	0	0	3	2	1	0
breakfast	386	.8181	63.761	58.0	96	74	33	35	70	40	33	5	143	30	3	29	2	24	9	11	4	2	28	0	42	37	3	19	0
Breakfast	3	.3429	.2528	34.0	1	2	0	0	0	0	0	0	1	0	0	0	0	0	0	1	0	0	0	0	1	0	0	0	0
breakfasts	9	.3283	.7025	38.5	0	3	1	0	1	3	1	0	3	0	0	1	0	0	0	0	0	0	3	0	1	0	0	1	0
breaking	151	.8126	24.735	53.9	14	17	22	20	44	13	19	2	41	7	0	12	3	9	1	25	4	1	2	8	13	11	4	9	1
breakneck	4	.4813	.4077	36.1	0	0	1	2	0	1	0	0	0	1	0	0	0	1	0	0	0	0	0	0	1	1	0	0	0
breaks	110	.8854	19.373	52.9	13	14	19	18	17	11	15	3	17	5	1	4	2	5	2	32	4	3	2	4	2	5	10	12	0
breakthrough	12	.5025	1.2692	41.0	0	0	1	0	8	0	3	0	0	1	0	0	0	1	0	3	0	0	0	0	0	0	3	4	0
breakup	6	.2622	.3635	35.6	0	0	0	0	4	1	1	0	0	0	0	0	0	0	0	1	0	0	0	0	0	0	4	1	0
breakwater	3	.3553	.2608	34.2	0	0	0	2	1	0	0	0	1	0	0	0	0	1	0	0	0	0	0	0	0	1	0	0	0
breakwaters	2	.2285	.1129	30.5	0	0	0	1	1	0	0	0	0	0	0	0	0	1	0	0	0	0	0	0	0	0	1	0	0
breast	63	.5987	7.9570	49.0	3	5	5	6	19	9	13	3	19	0	0	26	0	0	0	3	3	1	2	0	4	5	0	0	0
breastbone	15	.2909	1.0478	40.2	2	0	7	0	1	3	2	0	0	1	0	0	0	0	0	12	0	0	0	0	0	0	2	0	0
breastplate	3	.0000	.1370	31.4	0	0	3	0	0	0	0	0	3	0	0	0	0	0	0	0	0	0	0	0	0	0	0	0	0
breasts	12	.5989	1.4868	41.7	3	3	0	2	3	0	0	1	1	1	0	1	0	0	0	0	0	0	0	0	2	5	1	1	0
breath	379	.8226	62.879	58.0	56	79	39	50	76	40	31	8	128	16	3	46	1	7	8	43	10	0	3	0	55	32	1	26	0
breath-taking	2	.2337	.1157	30.6	0	1	1	0	0	0	0	0	0	0	0	0	0	1	0	0	0	0	0	0	1	0	0	0	0
breathable	3	.3465	.2515	34.0	1	0	0	1	1	0	0	0	1	0	0	0	0	0	0	0	0	0	0	0	0	1	0	1	0
breathe	204	.6288	26.855	54.3	71	29	24	26	30	18	2	4	32	2	0	8	0	5	1	117	7	0	1	0	4	15	7	5	0
breathed	55	.5949	6.9544	48.4	1	10	13	8	8	10	3	2	18	4	0	9	0	0	0	6	0	0	0	0	14	1	0	3	0
breathes	34	.7299	5.0356	47.0	7	2	4	5	9	2	4	1	3	1	0	0	0	1	0	11	2	1	1	0	0	8	4	2	0
breathing	204	.8537	34.935	55.4	21	28	16	39	52	24	21	3	62	4	2	17	0	2	2	54	4	1	3	0	17	10	13	13	0
breathless	33	.6638	4.5758	46.6	3	4	10	8	4	0	2	2	12	1	0	1	0	1	0	0	1	0	0	0	8	3	1	5	0
breathlessly	25	.5712	3.0882	44.9	0	6	4	9	4	0	1	1	11	1	0	2	0	0	0	0	2	0	0	0	7	0	0	2	0

3A branchy
3A Brand's
6R brandaris
6P Brandel
3D branding
8F Brando
8J Brandon
8F Brangus
9R Braniff
XR Braniff's
7K Brants
7P Branwen's
8K Braque's
XR Braquette
9L bras
6F brasero
7P brashly
6F Brasilia's
4A brass-buttoned
4N brass-heeled
8D brass-mounted
8D brass-tack
8D brat
4A brave's
4N Brave's
7Q Bravery
7R Braves'
7J Bravest
8D bravos
8A brawling
5Q brawny
7A bray
3A brayed
5P brays
7R braze
6N brazier
5F Brazilians
5F brazilwood
7R brazing
7F Brazzaville
9D breaches
4N bread-and-jam
7F bread-basket
4A bread-box
3H bread-cereal
9L bread-crumb
5F breadbasket
9L breadboard
XR breaded
8A Breadfruit
8A breadman's
8M breadraising
7P breadthwise
7A breadwinner
5R Break
7F break-through
9R breakeven
8N breakfast's
8P Breakfast's
9B breakfasted
8N breakin'
XH breaking-up
7R breakout
7A Breakthrough
7Q breakthroughs
7R bream
8N breast-bands
XR breasted
6A breasting
8B breastplates
8R breather
7R breathing-grade
7N breathings

Word Type	F	D	U	SFI	3 Gr 3	4 Gr 4	5 Gr 5	6 Gr 6	7 Gr 7	8 Gr 8	9 Gr 9	X UnGr	A Read	B Eng & Gr	C Comp	D Lit	E Math	F Soc Stud	G Spell	H Sci	J Music	K Art	L Home Ec	M Shop	N Lib F	P Lib NF	Q Lib Ref	R Mag	S Rel
breaths	9	.6025	1.1353	40.6	2	1	1	0	2	2	1	0	2	0	0	1	1	0	0	1	0	0	1	0	2	0	0	1	0
breathtaking	9	.4773	.8916	39.5	1	2	0	3	0	0	2	1	0	1	2	1	0	0	0	1	0	0	0	0	1	0	2	1	0
breathy	3	.2088	.1442	31.6	0	0	0	0	0	2	0	1	0	0	0	0	0	0	0	0	2	0	0	0	0	0	1	0	0
bred	22	.5543	2.5840	44.1	3	4	0	3	5	0	2	5	4	0	0	2	0	0	0	1	0	0	0	0	3	7	0	5	0
Bredo	3	.0000	.1370	31.4	0	3	0	0	0	0	0	0	3	0	0	0	0	0	0	0	0	0	0	0	0	0	0	0	0
Bredo's	3	.0000	.1370	31.4	0	3	0	0	0	0	0	0	3	0	0	0	0	0	0	0	0	0	0	0	0	0	0	0	0
breech	3	.2292	.1615	32.1	0	0	0	0	1	0	0	2	0	0	0	1	0	0	0	0	0	0	0	0	2	0	0	0	0
breeches	23	.5397	2.6798	44.3	1	7	3	4	7	1	0	0	7	1	0	3	0	1	0	0	0	0	0	0	7	4	0	0	0
breed	47	.6506	6.3018	48.0	1	3	6	10	14	6	6	1	6	1	0	3	0	8	0	3	0	0	0	0	2	6	14	4	0
breeders	5	.2530	.3153	35.0	0	0	1	1	3	0	0	0	1	0	0	0	0	0	0	0	0	0	0	0	0	0	3	1	0
breeding	40	.5647	4.6848	46.7	2	1	6	6	16	2	1	6	1	0	0	1	0	3	0	5	0	0	0	0	2	5	14	9	0
breeds	20	.6510	2.6674	44.3	1	0	4	5	2	5	3	0	1	1	0	1	0	6	0	0	0	1	0	0	0	4	3	3	0
Breese	2	.1948	.1250	31.0	0	2	0	0	0	0	0	0	1	0	0	0	0	0	0	0	0	0	0	0	0	1	0	0	0
breeze	147	.7609	22.802	53.6	25	38	22	14	25	12	8	3	46	6	7	14	0	3	2	29	9	0	0	0	12	9	0	10	0
breezed	2	.0665	.0708	28.5	0	0	0	1	1	0	0	0	1	0	1	0	0	0	0	0	0	0	0	0	0	0	0	0	0
breezes	32	.7479	4.8847	46.9	8	3	4	3	9	1	2	2	9	1	2	1	0	7	0	3	2	1	0	0	1	0	2	3	0
breezy	5	.5357	.5727	37.6	2	1	0	0	1	1	0	0	1	1	0	0	0	1	0	0	0	0	0	0	1	0	0	1	0
Breezy	3	.0000	.0434	26.4	3	0	0	0	0	0	0	0	0	0	0	0	0	0	0	0	0	0	0	0	0	3	0	0	0
Bremen	12	.4548	1.2194	40.9	1	0	1	5	0	5	0	0	4	1	0	5	0	0	0	0	0	0	0	0	1	0	1	0	0
Brenda	9	.3115	.6781	38.3	5	0	0	0	4	0	0	0	2	0	0	0	3	0	0	0	0	0	0	0	0	0	0	4	0
Brent	3	.2031	.1990	33.0	2	0	0	0	1	0	0	0	2	0	0	0	0	0	1	0	0	0	0	0	0	0	0	0	0
Brentwood	2	.2442	.1134	30.5	1	0	0	0	1	0	0	0	0	1	0	0	0	0	0	0	0	0	0	0	0	0	0	1	0
Brer	6	.2432	.4679	36.7	0	1	0	0	5	0	0	0	5	1	0	0	0	0	0	0	0	0	0	0	0	0	0	0	0
Breslau	2	.2160	.1362	31.3	0	0	0	1	0	0	0	1	1	0	0	0	0	0	0	1	0	0	0	0	0	0	0	0	0
Brest	3	.2043	.1486	31.7	0	0	2	1	0	0	0	0	0	0	0	0	0	0	0	0	0	0	0	0	0	1	2	0	0
brethren	6	.4741	.6395	38.1	0	1	0	1	1	2	1	0	2	0	0	1	0	2	0	0	0	0	0	0	0	0	0	1	0
Brethren	2	.2297	.1135	30.6	0	0	0	0	1	1	0	0	0	0	0	1	0	1	0	0	0	0	0	0	0	0	0	0	0
Breton	3	.3272	.2361	33.7	1	0	1	0	0	1	0	0	1	0	0	0	0	0	0	0	1	0	0	0	0	0	1	0	0
breve	2	.0000	.0162	22.1	0	0	1	1	0	0	0	0	0	0	0	0	0	0	0	0	2	0	0	0	0	0	0	0	0
brevity	3	.2384	.1717	32.3	0	0	0	1	0	1	1	0	0	1	0	0	2	0	0	0	0	0	0	0	0	0	0	0	0
brew	4	.2843	.2875	34.6	0	1	1	0	0	0	1	1	1	0	0	0	0	1	0	0	0	0	0	0	0	0	0	2	0
brewers	2	.0000	.0394	26.0	0	0	0	0	0	0	0	2	0	0	0	0	0	0	0	2	0	0	0	0	0	0	0	0	0
brewery	3	.3395	.2468	33.9	1	0	0	1	0	1	0	0	1	0	0	0	0	0	0	0	0	0	0	0	0	1	1	0	0
brewing	7	.3698	.6466	38.1	0	0	0	2	1	2	0	2	4	0	0	0	0	0	0	0	0	0	0	0	1	0	0	2	0
brews	3	.3874	.2497	34.0	0	1	1	0	1	0	0	0	0	1	0	0	0	0	0	0	0	0	0	0	1	0	0	1	0
Brewster	26	.6125	3.3826	45.3	3	7	2	9	0	0	1	4	9	1	0	0	0	2	0	1	0	0	0	0	3	7	0	3	0
Brian	37	.3571	3.1354	45.0	0	8	4	0	25	0	0	0	12	0	0	18	0	1	0	0	0	0	0	0	0	2	0	4	0
briar	2	.0000	.0215	23.3	0	0	1	0	0	1	0	0	0	0	0	2	0	0	0	0	0	0	0	0	0	0	0	0	0
bribe	6	.4406	.5890	37.7	0	0	0	0	2	2	2	0	1	0	0	1	0	2	0	0	0	0	0	0	0	2	0	0	0
bribed	4	.4520	.4002	36.0	0	0	0	0	0	2	1	1	1	1	0	1	0	0	0	0	0	0	0	0	0	1	0	0	0
bribes	3	.3350	.2478	33.9	0	0	2	0	0	1	0	0	1	0	0	0	0	1	0	0	0	0	0	0	0	0	1	0	0
bric-a-brac	2	.1814	.1187	30.7	0	0	1	0	1	0	0	0	1	0	0	0	0	0	0	0	0	0	0	0	0	0	0	1	0
brick	132	.8539	22.566	53.5	26	41	7	19	15	4	16	4	33	2	1	5	3	15	3	14	0	3	1	0	7	8	19	18	0
bricklayer	2	.0000	.0394	26.0	0	0	2	0	0	0	0	0	0	0	0	0	0	0	0	2	0	0	0	0	0	0	0	0	0
bricklayers	3	.2445	.1818	32.6	0	2	1	0	0	0	0	0	0	0	0	0	0	0	0	2	0	0	0	0	0	0	1	0	0
brickmaker	3	.1409	.1472	31.7	2	0	0	1	0	0	0	0	1	0	0	0	0	0	0	0	0	0	0	0	0	2	0	0	0
bricks	89	.8698	15.422	51.9	25	22	5	5	8	6	18	0	13	3	0	8	10	14	2	7	0	2	2	3	1	10	11	3	0
brickwork	7	.1670	.3276	35.2	0	0	0	1	0	0	6	0	1	0	0	0	0	1	0	0	0	0	0	0	0	0	5	0	0
brickyard	4	.1112	.1666	32.2	0	4	0	0	0	0	0	0	1	0	0	0	0	0	0	0	0	0	0	0	0	3	0	0	0
brickyards	2	.0000	.0290	24.6	0	2	0	0	0	0	0	0	0	0	0	0	0	0	0	0	0	0	0	0	0	2	0	0	0
bridal	7	.3608	.6347	38.0	2	0	0	1	2	0	2	0	4	0	0	2	0	0	0	0	0	0	0	0	0	0	0	1	0
bride	53	.7252	7.8917	49.0	14	10	2	3	7	8	9	0	17	3	0	10	0	5	0	0	3	0	0	0	4	6	1	4	0
Bride	2	.2408	.1204	30.8	0	0	0	0	0	1	1	0	0	0	0	0	0	1	0	0	0	0	0	0	0	1	0	0	0
bride's	2	.2306	.1140	30.6	0	1	1	0	0	0	0	0	0	1	0	0	0	1	0	0	0	0	0	0	0	0	0	0	0
bridegroom	3	.3380	.2439	33.9	0	0	1	1	0	1	0	0	1	1	0	1	0	0	0	0	0	0	0	0	0	0	0	0	0
brides	3	.2431	.1816	32.6	0	0	1	0	0	2	0	0	0	0	0	0	0	2	0	0	0	0	0	0	1	0	0	0	0
bridesmaid	2	.1907	.0862	29.4	0	0	0	0	0	0	2	0	0	0	0	1	0	0	0	0	0	0	1	0	0	0	0	0	0
bridge	270	.8464	45.852	56.6	58	35	36	45	48	19	28	1	84	16	8	10	11	25	4	5	6	1	0	14	10	46	11	19	0
Bridge	39	.7297	5.8232	47.7	7	4	7	12	6	2	1	0	9	0	0	1	7	9	0	0	1	0	0	0	3	3	4	2	0
bridged	4	.2932	.2861	34.6	0	0	1	1	0	0	2	0	1	0	0	0	0	0	0	0	0	0	0	0	0	0	2	1	0
Bridgeport	5	.4505	.5018	37.0	0	0	2	0	1	1	1	0	1	1	0	0	0	2	0	0	0	0	0	0	0	0	0	1	0
Bridger	8	.2301	.6170	37.9	0	0	7	0	1	0	0	0	7	0	0	0	0	0	0	0	0	0	0	0	1	0	0	0	0
bridges	119	.7090	17.193	52.4	40	6	13	12	13	22	11	2	14	1	1	1	12	24	0	4	1	0	0	9	1	31	11	9	0
Bridges	2	.1717	.1142	30.6	0	0	1	0	0	1	0	0	1	0	0	1	0	0	0	0	0	0	0	0	0	0	0	0	0
Bridget	2	.0000	.0219	23.4	0	2	0	0	0	0	0	0	0	2	0	0	0	0	0	0	0	0	0	0	0	0	0	0	0
bridging	3	.3845	.2448	33.9	0	0	0	0	0	1	2	0	0	1	0	0	0	0	0	0	1	0	0	0	0	0	1	0	0
bridle	39	.5950	4.8765	46.9	4	12	3	3	11	4	2	0	10	0	3	4	0	0	0	0	1	0	0	0	11	8	1	1	0
bridled	6	.2196	.3108	34.9	1	0	0	1	1	0	3	0	0	0	0	4	0	0	0	0	0	0	0	0	2	0	0	0	0
bridles	2	.2297	.1135	30.6	0	0	0	1	0	1	0	0	0	0	0	1	0	1	0	0	0	0	0	0	0	0	0	0	0
brief	160	.7655	24.634	53.9	6	8	18	17	32	47	28	4	21	34	14	10	1	8	18	4	13	0	2	1	7	15	8	4	0
briefcase	3	.1858	.1432	31.6	0	0	0	0	2	0	1	0	0	2	0	0	0	1	0	0	0	0	0	0	0	0	0	0	0
briefed	2	.2351	.1166	30.7	0	0	0	0	0	2	0	0	0	0	0	0	0	1	0	0	0	0	0	0	0	0	0	1	0
briefing	6	.0000	.0729	28.6	0	0	1	0	0	0	5	0	0	0	0	0	0	0	0	0	0	0	0	0	0	0	0	6	0
briefly	62	.8647	10.676	50.3	1	3	6	5	17	14	14	2	7	6	3	3	7	8	1	5	2	0	0	1	5	5	6	3	0
briefs	2	.0000	.0389	25.9	0	0	0	0	2	0	0	0	0	0	0	0	0	2	0	0	0	0	0	0	0	0	0	0	0
brier	6	.4866	.6618	38.2	1	0	1	0	2	0	1	1	3	0	0	1	0	0	0	0	0	0	0	0	1	0	0	1	0
briers	4	.3755	.3686	35.7	0	3	1	0	0	0	0	0	2	0	0	0	0	0	0	0	0	0	0	0	1	1	0	0	0
Brig	10	.0000	.1047	30.2	0	0	1	0	2	7	0	0	0	0	0	0	0	0	0	0	0	0	0	0	0	0	10	0	0
brigade	9	.4437	.8822	39.5	0	0	0	1	2	6	0	0	2	1	0	4	0	1	0	0	0	0	0	0	0	0	1	0	0
Brigade	7	.5609	.8498	39.3	0	0	0	1	4	2	0	0	3	1	0	0	0	0	0	0	1	0	0	0	1	0	1	0	0
brigadier	4	.4495	.4018	36.0	0	0	0	0	1	2	0	1	1	0	0	1	0	1	0	0	0	0	0	0	0	0	0	1	0
Brigadier	4	.4560	.4041	36.1	1	1	0	1	1	0	0	0	1	0	0	0	0	0	0	0	0	0	0	0	1	1	0	1	0
Briggs	8	.2167	.6029	37.8	0	0	5	0	2	1	0	0	7	0	0	0	1	0	0	0	0	0	0	0	0	0	0	0	0
Brigham	4	.3546	.3122	34.9	0	0	1	0	2	1	0	0	0	0	0	0	0	1	0	0	1	0	0	0	0	0	0	2	0
bright	741	.9420	138.13	61.4	205	122	67	93	112	53	47	42	209	26	14	59	3	54	13	97	33	19	11	4	52	79	20	47	1
Bright	35	.4374	3.7723	45.8	14	0	1	5	13	0	1	1	28	1	2	0	0	0	2	0	0	0	0	0	0	0	0	2	0
bright-blue	2	.2408	.1204	30.8	0	1	0	0	1	0	0	0	0	0	0	0	0	1	0	0	0	0	0	0	0	1	0	0	0
bright-colored	27	.6887	3.8643	45.9	8	3	2	7	3	4	0	0	8	0	0	1	0	3	0	8	1	0	0	0	3	2	1	0	0
bright-eyed	12	.4368	1.2028	40.8	3	1	1	1	2	0	4	0	5	0	0	3	0	0	0	0	0	0	0	0	0	1	3	0	0
bright-line	4	.0000	.0789	29.0	0	0	0	0	0	0	4	0	0	0	0	0	0	0	0	4	0	0	0	0	0	0	0	0	0
bright-red	7	.4767	.7637	38.8	1	0	2	2	1	1	0	0	3	0	0	0	0	1	0	2	0	0	0	0	0	0	1	0	0
bright-yellow	2	.2160	.1362	31.3	0	0	0	1	1	0	0	0	1	0	0	0	0	0	0	1	0	0	0	0	0	0	0	0	0
brighten	6	.4502	.5748	37.6	2	0	0	0	0	0	2	2	0	0	1	0	0	0	0	2	0	0	0	0	1	1	0	1	0

7Q breccia
9R Brecht's
3P Breckinridge
7B Bree
8F breech-loading
7A breechclout
6A breed's
7Q breeder
4P breeder-trainer-driver
6H breeder's
7A breeders'
9Q Breeding
4A breeks
7R breeze-rippled
8A breeze-tossed
5A breezeway
4G brek'fast**
7R Brenda's
5R Brendan
6B brendly
7J Brennan
5Q Brenner
8E Brescia
6P Bresnahan
5E Bret's
5Q Breton-speaking
5Q Bretons
7Q Bretton
6A Breukelen
4J Breve
XR brevet
8Q brevetted
8Q Brevoortia
7H brewed
6A brewer
6F breweries
7A Brewing
4P Brewsters
8R Brezhnev
5Q Briand
6P Briareus
6F brick-lined
9D brick-red
6P brick's
4P brickmaking
5D Bricktop
5Q Bridalveil
9B bridesmaids
6A BRIDGE
5P bridgehead
5A Bridger's
8P Bridgman's
9D bridle-rein
7L Brie
7B Brief
6R briefcases
6B briefer
7R briefings
5N brier-patches
4Q Brieux
4P brig
8P brigadier-general
7N Brigadier's
8Q brigand-warrior
3A bright-cheeked
8F bright-green
9D bright-russet
5D bright-veined
7Q bright-winged

Word Type	F	D	U	SFI	3 Gr 3	4 Gr 4	5 Gr 5	6 Gr 6	7 Gr 7	8 Gr 8	9 Gr 9	X UnGr	A Read	B Eng & Gr	C Comp	D Lit	E Math	F Soc Stud	G Spell	H Sci	J Music	K Art	L Home Ec	M Shop	N Lib F	P Lib NF	Q Lib Ref	R Mag	S Rel
brightened	23	.5958	2.8728	44.6	0	8	3	1	5	1	4	1	5	0	0	4	0	0	0	0	1	0	0	0	4	4	0	5	0
brightening	3	.3427	.2477	33.9	0	0	0	1	1	1	0	0	1	0	0	0	0	0	0	0	0	0	0	0	1	0	0	1	0
brightens	4	.0818	.0868	29.4	0	2	1	0	1	0	0	0	0	0	0	0	0	0	0	0	3	0	0	0	0	0	0	0	1
brighter	55	.7110	8.0246	49.0	19	7	4	5	10	7	3	0	11	0	0	5	0	4	0	19	1	0	0	3	2	4	2	4	0
brightest	25	.6652	3.4509	45.4	7	4	2	2	4	3	2	1	5	0	1	0	0	1	0	11	2	0	0	0	1	2	1	1	0
brightly	102	.8244	17.003	52.3	22	31	9	12	17	5	4	2	41	2	1	2	0	9	1	15	2	4	1	0	3	9	5	7	0
brightness	52	.5027	5.6659	47.5	1	6	3	4	19	3	14	2	8	0	0	3	0	0	0	26	0	1	1	0	3	4	3	2	1
Brighty	5	.2395	.3804	35.8	0	0	1	4	0	0	0	0	4	0	0	0	0	0	0	0	1	0	0	0	0	0	0	0	0
Briley	2	.0000	.0243	23.9	0	0	0	0	0	0	2	0	0	0	0	0	0	0	0	0	0	0	0	0	0	0	0	2	0
Brill	7	.0000	.0821	29.1	0	0	7	0	0	0	0	0	0	0	0	0	0	0	0	0	0	0	0	0	7	0	0	0	0
brilliance	11	.6237	1.3902	41.4	0	0	0	0	3	5	2	1	0	0	1	0	0	1	1	1	3	1	0	0	1	0	0	2	0
brilliancy	2	.1948	.1250	31.0	0	0	0	1	0	1	0	0	1	0	0	0	0	0	0	0	0	0	0	0	0	1	0	0	0
brilliant	140	.7019	20.003	53.0	6	12	7	20	35	36	10	14	22	5	0	5	2	8	3	11	16	14	1	0	12	7	15	19	0
brilliantly	19	.6278	2.4673	43.9	1	0	1	1	3	4	3	6	1	1	0	1	0	3	0	6	0	0	0	0	1	1	0	5	0
brillig	9	.2407	.4936	36.9	0	0	1	8	0	0	0	0	0	8	0	0	0	0	0	0	0	1	0	0	0	0	0	0	0
Brillig	3	.2384	.1717	32.3	0	0	0	1	0	2	0	0	0	1	0	0	2	0	0	0	0	0	0	0	0	0	0	0	0
brim	21	.6191	2.6952	44.3	5	4	2	3	3	1	3	0	5	0	3	3	0	0	1	0	2	0	1	0	3	1	0	2	0
Brim	5	.0000	.0586	27.7	5	0	0	0	0	0	0	0	0	0	0	0	0	0	0	0	0	0	0	0	5	0	0	0	0
Brimmer	8	.0000	.3655	35.6	0	0	0	0	0	8	0	0	8	0	0	0	0	0	0	0	0	0	0	0	0	0	0	0	0
brimming	6	.4646	.6237	37.9	1	0	1	1	2	0	1	0	2	1	0	0	0	0	0	0	0	0	0	0	0	2	1	0	0
brimstone	2	.2337	.1157	30.6	0	0	0	0	1	1	0	0	0	0	0	0	0	1	0	0	0	0	0	0	1	0	0	0	0
brindle	6	.2076	.3393	35.3	0	1	2	0	3	0	0	0	2	0	2	0	0	0	0	0	0	0	0	0	2	0	0	0	0
brine	14	.5584	1.6689	42.2	0	5	2	2	5	0	0	0	3	0	1	0	0	0	0	6	1	0	0	0	0	0	1	2	0
Brinell	7	.0000	.0177	22.5	0	0	0	0	0	0	7	0	0	0	0	0	0	0	0	0	0	0	0	7	0	0	0	0	0
bring	1016	.8788	178.23	62.5	202	171	137	131	159	100	95	21	290	47	9	60	7	136	6	82	33	8	39	4	90	97	40	63	5
bringin'	2	.1787	.1174	30.7	0	0	0	2	0	0	0	0	1	0	0	0	0	0	0	0	0	0	0	0	1	0	0	0	0
bringing	165	.8708	28.729	54.6	33	25	15	24	30	19	16	3	50	10	0	11	0	20	1	10	9	0	2	1	16	17	7	11	0
brings	169	.7419	25.443	54.1	35	18	24	21	39	7	18	7	25	8	4	4	2	31	4	25	17	1	4	0	6	17	10	9	2
brink	13	.5707	1.5986	42.0	2	0	3	0	4	2	2	0	5	0	0	3	0	1	0	0	0	0	0	0	0	1	2	1	0
Brink	5	.2038	.3268	35.1	0	0	5	0	0	0	0	0	3	2	0	0	0	0	0	0	0	0	0	0	0	0	0	0	0
Brinker	5	.3547	.4331	36.4	0	3	1	1	0	0	0	0	2	0	0	1	0	0	0	0	0	0	0	0	0	2	0	0	0
briny	3	.1200	.1302	31.1	0	0	1	0	2	0	0	0	1	2	0	0	0	0	0	0	0	0	0	0	0	0	0	0	0
Brisbane	3	.2378	.1809	32.6	0	0	1	1	1	0	0	0	0	0	0	0	0	2	0	0	0	0	0	0	0	1	0	0	0
brisk	26	.7443	3.9270	45.9	1	5	4	4	4	1	2	5	5	0	1	2	0	1	0	1	1	0	0	0	3	4	3	5	0
briskly	27	.6560	3.6721	45.6	2	3	3	3	6	5	4	1	7	1	0	7	0	1	0	1	0	0	0	1	5	1	0	3	0
bristle	3	.1250	.1342	31.3	0	0	1	0	2	0	0	0	1	0	0	0	0	0	0	0	0	0	0	0	2	0	0	0	0
bristled	9	.4654	.8964	39.5	0	0	1	0	6	1	1	0	1	1	0	2	0	0	0	0	0	0	0	0	4	0	0	1	0
bristles	11	.4813	1.1586	40.6	4	1	4	0	2	0	0	0	3	0	0	0	0	0	0	0	0	1	0	0	3	3	1	0	0
bristling	12	.5962	1.5057	41.8	0	1	2	2	5	1	1	0	3	1	0	1	0	0	0	0	0	0	0	0	3	2	0	2	0
bristly	2	.2441	.1127	30.5	0	0	0	0	2	0	0	0	0	0	0	0	0	0	0	0	0	0	0	0	1	0	1	0	0
Bristol	8	.2782	.5199	37.2	1	6	0	0	1	0	0	0	0	0	0	0	0	1	0	0	1	0	0	0	0	6	0	0	0
Britain	149	.6448	19.720	52.9	4	14	33	24	36	16	22	0	5	18	0	4	0	60	3	0	0	0	0	0	2	14	25	18	0
Britain's	14	.4645	1.4059	41.5	0	1	4	0	1	3	5	0	1	0	0	0	0	5	0	0	0	0	0	0	0	1	2	5	0
Britannica	3	.2270	.1588	32.0	0	0	1	0	0	0	2	0	0	2	0	0	0	0	0	0	0	0	0	0	0	0	1	0	0
britches	5	.5332	.5699	37.6	0	0	0	0	3	1	1	0	1	0	0	1	0	1	0	0	0	0	0	0	0	0	1	1	0
Britches	4	.1971	.1895	32.8	0	0	0	0	1	3	0	0	0	1	0	3	0	0	0	0	0	0	0	0	0	0	0	0	0
British	593	.7204	87.256	59.4	26	47	129	81	121	128	51	10	85	18	1	15	2	256	5	15	18	1	0	0	10	37	84	46	0
British-American	3	.2076	.1618	32.1	0	0	1	1	1	0	0	0	0	0	0	0	2	0	0	1	0	0	0	0	0	0	0	0	0
Britisher	2	.1814	.1187	30.7	0	0	0	1	0	0	0	1	1	0	0	0	0	0	0	0	0	0	0	0	0	0	0	1	0
Britons	2	.2152	.1357	31.3	0	0	0	1	0	0	1	0	1	0	0	0	0	1	0	0	0	0	0	0	0	0	0	0	0
Brittany	26	.1993	1.2573	41.0	3	0	17	4	2	0	0	0	0	0	0	1	0	2	0	0	0	0	0	0	0	2	21	0	0
Britten	12	.1389	.4152	36.2	0	1	2	7	2	0	0	0	0	0	0	0	0	0	0	0	10	0	0	0	0	0	2	0	0
brittle	32	.6399	4.2473	46.3	3	2	3	1	11	7	3	2	7	0	0	5	0	1	0	6	0	0	1	4	2	1	2	3	0
brittleness	5	.0000	.0126	21.0	0	0	0	0	0	0	5	0	0	0	0	0	0	0	0	0	0	0	0	5	0	0	0	0	0
broach	2	.1814	.1187	30.7	0	0	0	2	0	0	0	0	1	0	0	0	0	0	0	0	0	0	0	0	0	0	0	1	0
broad	292	.8779	51.040	57.1	39	26	37	60	62	33	27	8	51	17	11	25	1	40	3	18	7	5	0	3	20	40	33	18	0
Broad	5	.0000	.0586	27.7	5	0	0	0	0	0	0	0	0	0	0	0	0	0	0	0	0	0	0	0	5	0	0	0	0
broad-brimmed	4	.4814	.4064	36.1	0	0	1	2	1	0	0	0	0	0	0	1	0	1	0	0	0	0	0	0	1	0	0	1	0
broad-leafed	2	.2446	.1123	30.5	0	0	0	0	2	0	0	0	0	1	0	0	0	0	0	0	0	0	0	0	0	0	1	0	0
broad-leaved	3	.2387	.1708	32.3	2	0	0	0	1	0	0	0	0	0	0	0	0	0	0	0	0	0	0	0	0	2	1	0	0
broad-shouldered	7	.5775	.8477	39.3	1	1	0	1	3	1	0	0	1	0	0	1	0	1	0	0	0	0	0	0	2	1	0	1	0
broadcast	41	.8223	6.7458	48.3	4	8	5	1	10	8	4	1	3	4	1	3	0	7	1	7	3	0	0	0	1	7	3	1	0
broadcaster	3	.3528	.2566	34.1	0	1	0	2	0	0	0	0	1	0	0	0	1	0	0	0	0	0	0	0	0	1	0	0	0
broadcasters	2	.0000	.0914	29.6	0	0	0	0	0	0	2	0	2	0	0	0	0	0	0	0	0	0	0	0	0	0	0	0	0
broadcasting	38	.6488	5.0566	47.0	3	1	0	10	5	12	6	1	2	1	0	1	0	5	0	13	8	0	0	2	0	0	4	2	0
Broadcasting	4	.4448	.3914	35.9	0	0	1	0	1	0	2	0	1	1	0	0	0	0	0	0	1	0	0	0	0	0	1	0	0
broadcasts	16	.5919	1.9584	42.9	1	3	2	0	5	4	1	0	0	0	0	0	0	2	0	5	3	0	0	0	0	3	2	1	0
broadcloth	3	.0000	.0097	19.8	0	0	0	0	0	1	2	0	0	0	0	0	0	0	0	0	0	0	3	0	0	0	0	0	0
broaden	7	.4919	.7101	38.5	0	0	1	2	1	1	2	0	0	3	1	0	0	0	0	0	1	0	0	0	0	0	1	1	0
broadened	7	.4049	.6192	37.9	1	0	1	0	1	0	4	0	0	0	0	0	0	2	0	1	0	0	0	0	0	1	3	0	0
broadening	4	.1789	.1692	32.3	0	0	0	0	2	1	0	1	0	0	0	0	0	0	0	0	3	0	0	0	0	0	1	0	0
broadens	2	.2291	.1135	30.5	0	0	0	0	0	1	1	0	0	0	0	1	0	0	0	1	0	0	0	0	0	0	0	0	0
broader	15	.6316	1.9734	43.0	0	1	2	2	3	3	4	0	3	3	0	1	0	3	0	2	0	1	0	0	0	0	1	1	0
broadest	9	.2449	.5411	37.3	1	2	2	0	2	0	2	0	1	0	0	0	1	1	0	0	0	0	0	0	0	0	6	0	0
broadleaf	2	.2285	.1129	30.5	0	1	0	1	0	0	0	0	0	0	0	0	0	1	0	0	0	0	0	0	0	0	1	0	0
broadly	14	.6727	1.9230	42.8	0	2	1	1	2	3	2	3	1	0	0	0	0	1	0	2	1	0	0	0	2	2	3	2	0
broadside	11	.3414	.8575	39.3	0	1	3	2	5	0	0	0	2	0	0	0	0	0	0	0	5	0	0	0	3	1	0	0	0
Broadway	42	.6131	5.3297	47.3	1	6	3	1	8	18	1	4	6	0	0	1	0	6	0	0	12	1	0	0	2	2	1	11	0
brocade	2	.2152	.1357	31.3	1	0	0	1	0	0	0	0	1	0	0	0	0	1	0	0	0	0	0	0	0	0	0	0	0
broccoli	20	.1970	1.3167	41.2	14	0	0	1	0	0	5	0	14	0	0	0	0	0	0	1	0	0	5	0	0	0	0	0	0
brochure	4	.1892	.1847	32.7	0	0	0	0	0	0	4	0	0	0	0	3	0	0	0	0	0	0	0	0	0	0	0	1	0
brochures	2	.2412	.1141	30.6	1	0	0	1	0	0	0	0	0	1	0	0	0	0	0	0	0	0	0	0	0	1	0	0	0
Brockden	2	.0000	.0219	23.4	0	0	0	0	0	2	0	0	0	2	0	0	0	0	0	0	0	0	0	0	0	0	0	0	0
Brockett	13	.0000	.5939	37.7	0	13	0	0	0	0	0	0	13	0	0	0	0	0	0	0	0	0	0	0	0	0	0	0	0
Brocklin	7	.0000	.0851	29.3	0	0	0	6	0	1	0	0	0	0	0	0	0	0	0	0	0	0	0	0	0	0	0	7	0
Brodas	2	.0000	.0290	24.6	2	0	0	0	0	0	0	0	0	0	0	0	0	0	0	0	0	0	0	0	0	2	0	0	0
Brodhead	2	.0000	.0243	23.9	0	0	0	0	2	0	0	0	0	0	0	0	0	0	0	0	0	0	0	0	0	0	0	2	0
Brodie	3	.2187	.1555	31.9	0	0	0	1	2	0	0	0	0	2	0	0	0	0	0	0	0	0	0	0	0	0	0	1	0
broil	9	.2352	.4740	36.8	0	1	0	2	1	0	4	1	0	0	0	0	0	0	0	0	0	0	4	0	0	1	0	4	0
broiled	8	.4958	.8367	39.2	1	0	0	2	1	2	2	0	1	1	0	1	0	1	1	0	0	0	2	0	0	0	0	1	0
broiler	5	.0000	.0161	22.1	0	0	0	0	0	0	5	0	0	0	0	0	0	0	0	0	0	0	5	0	0	0	0	0	0
broiling	8	.0886	.1833	32.6	1	1	0	0	0	0	6	0	0	0	0	0	0	0	0	0	0	0	6	0	0	2	0	0	0
Brok	9	.0000	.4111	36.1	0	0	9	0	0	0	0	0	9	0	0	0	0	0	0	0	0	0	0	0	0	0	0	0	0
broke	396	.8530	67.748	58.3	60	66	54	59	89	37	25	6	131	27	5	36	7	28	10	8	11	0	0	0	52	33	18	30	0

7D Brightest
7R brightly-colored
7F brightly-dyed
7A brightly-painted
6A Brighty's
9R Briley's
4A Brilliant
XH brilliantly-colored
4N Brillon
7F brimless
4P brims
5P brinded
5Q brindle-colored
6A brindled
3P BRINE
7L brine-cured
8G bringer
7K brinish
7Q brinks
9A brisker
5F bristlecone
XB bristler
4P Bristol's
5J Britannia
5F BRITISH
8F British-born
7R British-made
3P Briton
5Q Brittany's
6J Britten's
7P brittled
8E BRL
7R broached
3P BROAD-LEAVED
6A broad-backed
8H broad-based
9D broad-browed
9Q broad-gauge
6E broad-jump
3P broad-winged
4A broadax
8R Broadcasters
5Q broadhorn
7R broadies
7C broadness
6D broadsword
7R brocaded
8J brocades
3A brocket
7D brogue
7D brogues
7P broidered
9L Broil
8A brok-
5A Brok's

Word Type	F	D	U	SFI	3 Gr 3	4 Gr 4	5 Gr 5	6 Gr 6	7 Gr 7	8 Gr 8	9 Gr 9	X UnGr	A Read	B Eng & Gr	C Comp	D Lit	E Math	F Soc Stud	G Spell	H Sci	J Music	K Art	L Home Ec	M Shop	N Lib F	P Lib NF	Q Lib Ref	R Mag	S Rel
broken	535	.9430	99.853	60.0	101	80	65	71	124	40	44	10	170	32	6	43	21	27	7	56	9	3	5	11	40	54	17	34	0
Broken	3	.2425	.1816	32.6	0	2	0	1	0	0	0	0	0	0	0	0	0	2	0	0	0	0	0	0	0	0	0	1	0
broken-down	6	.4138	.5828	37.7	0	0	1	1	0	3	1	0	3	1	0	1	0	0	0	0	0	0	1	0	0	0	0	0	0
broken-hearted	5	.4216	.4687	36.7	2	1	0	0	1	0	1	0	1	0	0	0	0	0	0	0	0	0	0	0	2	1	1	0	0
broken-line	5	.0000	.0748	28.7	0	0	4	0	0	0	1	0	0	0	0	0	5	0	0	0	0	0	0	0	0	0	0	0	0
broken-winged	2	.1621	.0746	28.7	0	0	0	0	1	0	1	0	0	0	1	1	0	0	0	0	0	0	0	0	0	0	0	0	0
brokenhearted	2	.2387	.1089	30.4	0	1	0	0	0	0	1	0	0	0	0	0	0	0	0	0	1	0	0	0	1	0	0	0	0
broker	4	.0000	.0778	28.9	1	0	0	0	0	0	3	0	0	0	0	0	0	4	0	0	0	0	0	0	0	0	0	0	0
brokers	5	.3775	.4204	36.2	0	1	0	0	1	1	2	0	0	0	0	1	0	3	0	0	0	0	0	0	0	0	1	0	0
Brom	2	.0000	.0914	29.6	0	0	0	0	2	0	0	0	2	0	0	0	0	0	0	0	0	0	0	0	0	0	0	0	0
bromine	9	.2285	.5268	37.2	0	1	1	1	1	3	2	0	0	0	0	0	0	0	0	7	0	0	0	0	0	0	2	0	0
bromthymol	2	.0000	.0394	26.0	0	0	0	0	2	0	0	0	0	0	0	0	0	0	0	2	0	0	0	0	0	0	0	0	0
Bromwell	6	.0000	.0703	28.5	6	0	0	0	0	0	0	0	0	0	0	0	0	0	0	0	0	0	0	0	6	0	0	0	0
bronchi	4	.3352	.2986	34.8	0	0	0	0	1	2	1	0	0	0	0	0	0	0	0	1	0	0	0	0	0	0	2	1	0
bronchial	4	.3864	.3418	35.3	0	0	1	0	1	1	1	0	0	0	0	0	0	0	0	2	0	0	0	0	0	0	1	1	0
bronchitis	2	.2441	.1127	30.5	0	0	1	0	0	0	1	0	0	0	0	0	0	0	0	0	0	0	0	0	1	0	1	0	0
broncho	2	.2297	.1135	30.6	0	0	1	0	1	0	0	0	0	0	0	1	0	1	0	0	0	0	0	0	0	0	0	0	0
broncho's	2	.2411	.1091	30.4	0	1	0	0	1	0	0	0	0	0	0	1	0	0	0	0	1	0	0	0	0	0	0	0	0
bronco	10	.4738	1.0273	40.1	2	3	0	3	2	0	0	0	2	0	0	0	0	0	0	0	3	0	0	0	1	3	0	1	0
Bronson	6	.0797	.2027	33.1	0	0	0	6	0	0	0	0	1	0	0	0	0	0	0	0	0	0	0	0	0	5	0	0	0
brontosaur	2	.0000	.0914	29.6	2	0	0	0	0	0	0	0	2	0	0	0	0	0	0	0	0	0	0	0	0	0	0	0	0
brontosaurus	4	.1112	.1666	32.2	0	3	0	1	0	0	0	0	1	0	0	0	0	0	0	0	0	0	0	0	0	3	0	0	0
Brontosaurus	16	.0629	.4734	36.8	14	0	2	0	0	0	0	0	2	0	0	0	0	0	0	0	0	0	0	0	0	14	0	0	0
Bronx	11	.4537	1.1086	40.4	1	2	3	0	4	0	0	1	3	1	0	1	0	0	0	0	0	0	0	0	0	1	0	5	0
Bronya	3	.0000	.0434	26.4	0	0	0	0	0	0	0	3	0	0	0	0	0	0	0	0	0	0	0	0	0	3	0	0	0
bronze	66	.7120	9.6122	49.8	10	3	6	7	18	5	11	6	16	0	1	7	0	7	0	4	1	6	0	2	2	4	7	9	0
Bronze	6	.1169	.2555	34.1	2	1	0	0	1	1	1	0	2	0	0	0	0	0	0	0	0	0	0	0	0	0	4	0	0
bronze-fitted	2	.0000	.0215	23.3	0	0	0	0	0	0	2	0	0	0	0	2	0	0	0	0	0	0	0	0	0	0	0	0	0
bronzed	5	.3954	.4496	36.5	0	1	0	0	3	0	1	0	1	0	0	2	0	1	0	0	0	0	0	0	0	1	0	0	0
bronzite	2	.0000	.0394	26.0	0	0	0	0	0	0	0	2	0	0	0	0	0	0	0	2	0	0	0	0	0	0	0	0	0
brooch	14	.3425	1.0450	40.2	0	0	3	0	0	10	1	0	0	0	1	1	0	0	0	0	0	0	0	0	11	1	0	0	0
brood	20	.5913	2.4554	43.9	2	1	0	4	5	6	2	0	2	0	0	5	0	0	0	3	0	0	0	0	2	2	5	1	0
brooded	4	.4533	.4015	36.0	1	0	0	0	2	0	1	0	1	0	0	1	0	0	0	0	0	0	0	0	1	1	0	0	0
brooder	2	.0000	.0243	23.9	0	0	0	2	0	0	0	0	0	0	0	0	0	0	0	0	0	0	0	0	0	0	0	2	0
brooding	13	.5854	1.5846	42.0	1	1	0	5	3	1	1	1	2	3	0	2	0	0	0	0	0	0	0	0	1	0	2	3	0
broods	11	.4574	1.1012	40.4	2	2	0	0	5	1	0	1	2	0	0	1	0	0	0	1	0	0	0	0	0	3	4	0	0
brook	76	.5761	9.3569	49.7	24	15	9	7	3	11	3	4	28	11	9	3	0	0	0	3	5	0	0	0	7	9	0	1	0
Brook	6	.3317	.4449	36.5	4	1	0	1	0	0	0	0	0	0	0	0	0	0	0	0	0	0	0	0	0	4	1	1	0
Brook's	2	.0000	.0219	23.4	2	0	0	0	0	0	0	0	0	2	0	0	0	0	0	0	0	0	0	0	0	0	0	0	0
Brooke	2	.2441	.1127	30.5	0	0	0	0	1	1	0	0	0	0	0	0	0	0	0	0	0	0	0	0	1	0	1	0	0
Brookhaven	8	.3866	.6693	38.3	1	0	0	0	3	0	4	0	0	0	0	0	0	0	0	1	0	0	0	0	0	1	4	2	0
Brookline	2	.1733	.1149	30.6	0	0	0	0	0	1	1	0	1	1	0	0	0	0	0	0	0	0	0	0	0	0	0	0	0
Brooklyn	41	.6911	5.8571	47.7	9	1	2	4	10	5	10	0	12	0	0	5	0	6	0	1	2	0	0	0	0	4	6	5	0
Brooklyn's	3	.2332	.1690	32.3	2	0	0	0	0	1	0	0	0	0	0	0	0	0	0	0	0	0	0	0	0	2	0	1	0
brooks	17	.6992	2.4273	43.9	5	5	2	3	1	0	0	1	1	1	0	0	0	7	0	2	1	0	0	0	1	2	1	1	0
Brooks	9	.3750	.7780	38.9	0	1	1	0	5	1	1	0	1	0	0	1	0	6	0	0	0	0	0	0	0	0	1	0	0
Brookville	3	.1409	.1472	31.7	1	2	0	0	0	0	0	0	1	0	0	0	0	0	0	0	0	0	0	0	0	2	0	0	0
broom	78	.7570	12.107	50.8	8	28	16	7	9	8	0	2	35	7	1	10	0	0	5	0	3	0	0	0	5	8	0	4	0
Broom	4	.2446	.2243	33.5	0	2	0	0	2	0	0	0	0	0	0	2	0	0	0	0	0	0	0	0	0	0	2	0	0
broomrape	3	.0000	.0591	27.7	0	0	0	3	0	0	0	0	0	0	0	0	0	0	0	3	0	0	0	0	0	0	0	0	0
brooms	14	.6651	1.8936	42.8	3	3	2	1	0	4	1	0	1	4	1	2	0	1	0	0	1	0	0	0	2	1	0	1	0
broomstick	7	.3238	.5616	37.5	0	1	1	0	1	2	2	0	3	0	0	3	0	0	0	0	0	0	0	1	0	0	0	0	0
broomsticks	2	.1948	.1250	31.0	0	1	1	0	0	0	0	0	1	0	0	0	0	0	0	0	0	0	0	0	0	1	0	0	0
Bror	2	.0000	.0037	15.7	1	0	0	0	1	0	0	0	0	0	0	0	0	0	0	0	0	2	0	0	0	0	0	0	0
Bros	2	.0000	.0243	23.9	0	0	0	0	2	0	0	0	0	0	0	0	0	0	0	0	0	0	0	0	0	0	0	2	0
broth	16	.5507	1.9010	42.8	0	0	5	2	3	1	4	1	6	0	0	4	0	0	0	1	0	0	2	0	1	0	1	1	0
brother	586	.8874	103.87	60.2	103	144	91	71	92	49	27	9	232	44	15	44	42	23	6	4	12	0	8	0	35	71	20	29	1
Brother	183	.4711	18.795	52.7	58	41	6	72	2	3	1	0	37	2	0	2	0	3	0	0	1	0	0	0	100	35	0	2	1
brother-in-law	9	.5329	.9919	40.0	0	1	0	0	4	3	1	0	0	2	0	3	0	0	0	0	0	0	0	0	0	2	1	1	0
brother's	40	.7406	6.0711	47.8	5	9	7	4	8	3	3	1	14	8	0	3	3	2	1	0	0	0	0	0	2	3	3	1	0
brotherhood	11	.5985	1.3591	41.3	1	0	0	2	6	2	0	0	1	0	0	3	0	1	0	0	2	0	0	0	0	1	1	2	0
Brotherhood	3	.2365	.1616	32.1	1	0	1	0	0	1	0	0	0	0	0	0	0	0	0	0	1	0	0	0	0	0	2	0	0
brotherly	4	.3030	.2949	34.7	1	1	0	0	0	1	0	1	1	0	0	0	0	0	0	0	0	0	0	0	2	0	0	1	0
brothers	338	.8676	58.775	57.7	80	114	34	24	48	19	11	8	134	23	4	29	1	16	4	11	7	1	7	0	23	57	5	15	1
Brothers	17	.6305	2.2143	43.5	2	5	1	0	7	1	1	0	2	0	0	4	0	3	0	0	0	0	0	0	2	2	1	3	0
brothers'	7	.4683	.7254	38.6	1	1	0	1	3	1	0	0	2	0	0	0	0	1	0	0	0	0	1	0	0	1	0	2	0
Brothers'	4	.3766	.3696	35.7	0	3	0	0	0	0	1	0	2	0	0	0	0	0	0	0	0	0	0	0	0	1	0	1	0
brought	1357	.9236	248.69	64.0	201	211	209	198	258	169	87	24	397	29	11	84	12	262	15	54	66	9	7	2	128	136	80	63	2
brow	35	.7281	5.2338	47.2	2	4	4	6	7	4	5	3	13	3	1	6	0	0	0	0	1	0	1	0	6	3	0	1	0
Browdowski	5	.0000	.0586	27.7	0	0	0	5	0	0	0	0	0	0	0	0	0	0	0	0	0	0	0	0	5	0	0	0	0
brown	557	.8429	94.148	59.7	136	123	43	54	95	47	47	12	158	26	2	53	14	42	5	26	9	10	46	3	56	63	8	36	0
Brown	227	.8097	37.363	55.7	53	42	13	54	36	15	14	0	104	8	3	1	17	23	2	18	4	0	0	0	28	11	2	6	0
brown-eyed	2	.2387	.1089	30.4	1	1	0	0	0	0	0	0	0	0	0	0	0	0	0	0	1	0	0	0	1	0	0	0	0
brown-skinned	5	.4505	.5037	37.0	0	0	3	0	0	1	0	1	1	0	0	0	0	2	0	0	0	0	0	0	0	1	0	1	0
brown-sounding	2	.1621	.0746	28.7	0	0	0	0	1	1	0	0	0	0	1	1	0	0	0	0	0	0	0	0	0	0	0	0	0
Brown's	18	.6822	2.5439	44.1	7	1	1	3	4	0	2	0	5	1	0	0	2	2	1	1	0	0	0	0	4	2	0	0	0
Browne	9	.3326	.6649	38.2	3	0	0	0	0	6	0	0	0	0	0	1	0	0	0	0	0	0	0	0	0	3	0	5	0
browned	13	.3759	1.0520	40.2	0	7	1	0	3	0	1	1	0	0	0	0	0	0	0	0	0	0	3	0	1	7	0	2	0
Brownell	2	.0000	.0243	23.9	0	0	0	0	2	0	0	0	0	0	0	0	0	0	0	0	0	0	0	0	0	0	0	2	0
browner	2	.0000	.0219	23.4	0	0	0	0	0	0	2	0	0	2	0	0	0	0	0	0	0	0	0	0	0	0	0	0	0
brownest	2	.1787	.1174	30.7	1	1	0	0	0	0	0	0	1	0	0	0	0	0	0	0	0	0	0	0	1	0	0	0	0
brownie	3	.2347	.1695	32.3	0	3	0	0	0	0	0	0	0	0	0	0	0	0	0	0	0	0	0	0	1	2	0	0	0
Brownie	10	.4745	1.0490	40.2	6	3	0	0	0	1	0	0	3	0	0	1	1	0	0	0	0	0	0	0	4	0	0	1	0
brownies	8	.3297	.5817	37.6	0	1	2	2	1	1	1	0	0	4	0	0	0	0	0	0	0	0	0	0	0	1	0	3	0
Brownies	3	.3852	.2500	34.0	0	3	0	0	0	0	0	0	0	0	0	1	0	0	0	0	0	0	0	0	0	1	0	1	0
browning	4	.1812	.1676	32.2	0	0	0	0	1	0	2	1	0	0	0	0	0	0	0	0	0	0	2	0	0	0	0	2	0
Browning	15	.3587	1.3677	41.4	1	0	2	0	9	0	3	0	9	4	0	0	0	0	0	0	0	0	0	0	0	2	0	0	0
brownish	12	.5439	1.3790	41.4	2	0	1	2	4	0	1	2	1	0	0	0	0	1	0	3	0	0	0	0	0	3	3	1	0
browns	5	.4358	.4591	36.6	0	1	0	1	3	0	0	0	0	0	0	0	0	0	0	0	0	0	1	0	0	2	1	1	0
Browns	16	.4030	1.4102	41.5	0	0	0	1	12	0	3	0	1	2	0	0	0	0	0	2	0	0	0	0	2	0	0	9	0
Browns'	2	.1497	.1046	30.2	1	0	0	1	0	0	0	0	1	0	0	0	0	0	1	0	0	0	0	0	0	0	0	0	0
Brownsville	17	.3573	1.3843	41.4	0	11	0	0	5	0	0	1	0	0	0	1	0	13	0	0	0	0	0	0	0	0	2	1	0
brows	12	.6218	1.5346	41.9	1	0	1	0	3	4	2	1	1	0	0	4	0	1	0	1	1	0	0	0	1	0	2	1	0
browse	6	.3535	.4598	36.6	0	0	0	1	4	0	0	1	0	0	0	1	0	0	0	0	0	0	0	0	0	0	3	2	0

7D broken-legged
9M broken-out
7A broken-up
9J brokenheartedly
9F brokerage
7Q bromeliads
3N Bromwell's
4N bronc
7R bronchioles
8Q bronchoscope
7A bronco-busters
3P bronco-bustin'
3D broncobuster
4A broncobusters
6D broncos
5Q Bronislaw
9Q Bronk
6P Bronson's
3P Bronto
8B bronx
5A BRONX
XH bronze-brown
6A bronze-topped
8R bronzes
5R brooders
XR brook-and-brown
8D brook-bottom
7D BROOKLYN
3P Brooklyn-born
7P Brooklynite
5N Broom-Cupboard
5N broom-handle
XP broomhandles
6B brosket
XH brother-sister
5Q brotherhoods
7B brothers-in-law
4B broths
XR Broudy
7P broughtest
7P browbeating
9F BROWN
7H brown-and-white
9P brown-black
7A brown-haired
7C brown-painted
7N brown-paper
8B browne
7R Brownell's
4N brownie's
8D Browning's
3P brownish-gray
9R Brownmiller
8F Brownshirt
7A brownstone
5F Brownville

Word Type	F	D	U	SFI	3 Gr 3	4 Gr 4	5 Gr 5	6 Gr 6	7 Gr 7	8 Gr 8	9 Gr 9	X UnGr	A Read	B Eng & Gr	C Comp	D Lit	E Math	F Soc Stud	G Spell	H Sci	J Music	K Art	L Home Ec	M Shop	N Lib F	P Lib NF	Q Lib Ref	R Mag	S Rel
browsed	5	.3075	.3683	35.7	0	2	0	1	2	0	0	0	1	0	0	0	0	0	0	0	0	0	0	0	0	2	2	0	0
browsing	6	.5378	.6708	38.3	0	0	1	1	3	0	1	0	0	1	0	1	0	0	0	1	0	0	0	0	2	1	0	0	0
Bruce	62	.4655	6.6777	48.2	23	5	1	1	23	8	1	0	34	2	0	19	2	1	0	0	0	0	0	0	0	2	0	2	0
Bruce's	6	.3702	.5019	37.0	1	0	1	0	3	1	0	0	1	1	0	3	1	0	0	0	0	0	0	0	0	0	0	0	0
Brucie	33	.0000	1.5075	41.8	0	0	33	0	0	0	0	0	33	0	0	0	0	0	0	0	0	0	0	0	0	0	0	0	0
Bruegel	3	.2060	.1500	31.8	0	0	0	0	3	0	0	0	0	0	0	2	0	0	0	0	0	0	0	0	0	1	0	0	0
Bruges	4	.1826	.1841	32.7	0	3	1	0	0	0	0	0	0	0	0	0	0	0	0	0	0	0	0	0	3	1	0	0	0
Brugge	2	.0000	.0389	25.9	0	2	0	0	0	0	0	0	0	0	0	0	0	2	0	0	0	0	0	0	0	0	0	0	0
bruise	5	.5329	.5697	37.6	1	1	0	0	2	0	0	1	1	0	0	1	0	0	0	1	0	0	0	0	0	0	1	1	0
bruised	24	.7361	3.5624	45.5	3	1	2	1	11	0	5	1	2	2	1	7	0	1	0	1	0	0	1	0	2	2	1	4	0
bruises	9	.5376	1.0024	40.0	1	0	1	0	3	3	1	0	1	1	1	2	0	0	0	0	0	0	2	0	0	1	1	0	0
Brunei	2	.0000	.0389	25.9	0	0	1	0	1	0	0	0	0	0	0	0	0	2	0	0	0	0	0	0	0	0	0	0	0
Brunet	2	.0000	.0914	29.6	0	0	0	0	0	2	0	0	2	0	0	0	0	0	0	0	0	0	0	0	0	0	0	0	0
brunette	3	.2687	.2001	33.0	0	0	0	1	0	2	0	0	1	0	0	0	0	0	0	0	1	0	1	0	0	0	0	0	0
brunettes	2	.0000	.0299	24.8	0	0	0	2	0	0	0	0	0	0	0	0	2	0	0	0	0	0	0	0	0	0	0	0	0
brung	4	.0000	.0469	26.7	0	0	2	0	2	0	0	0	0	0	0	0	0	0	0	0	0	0	0	0	4	0	0	0	0
Brunnhilde	2	.2387	.1089	30.4	1	0	0	1	0	0	0	0	0	0	0	0	0	0	0	0	1	0	0	0	1	0	0	0	0
Bruno	10	.2881	.8419	39.3	8	0	0	0	0	1	0	1	8	0	1	0	0	0	0	1	0	0	0	0	0	0	0	0	0
Brunswick	10	.4427	.9375	39.7	0	1	0	2	6	0	1	0	0	0	0	4	0	2	0	0	1	0	0	0	0	0	3	0	0
brunt	2	.0000	.0209	23.2	0	0	0	0	1	1	0	0	0	0	0	0	0	0	0	0	0	0	0	0	0	0	2	0	0
brush	251	.5979	31.255	54.9	42	44	22	37	54	36	10	6	58	2	2	26	2	13	3	8	5	46	4	17	30	13	11	11	0
Brush	13	.5516	1.6015	42.0	7	2	0	2	1	0	0	1	8	0	0	0	0	0	0	0	0	0	0	0	1	2	1	1	0
brush-ins	2	.0000	.0243	23.9	0	0	0	0	2	0	0	0	0	0	0	0	0	0	0	0	0	0	0	0	0	0	0	2	0
brushed	75	.8171	12.373	50.9	13	14	7	7	18	8	6	2	28	1	0	9	0	1	1	3	1	2	3	1	13	5	2	5	0
brushes	39	.6085	4.9552	47.0	7	16	1	3	4	4	4	0	10	1	0	3	5	2	0	0	0	6	1	2	2	3	2	2	0
brushing	34	.7444	5.1653	47.1	5	6	4	4	8	4	3	0	10	1	2	5	1	1	0	3	0	0	0	1	4	3	0	3	0
brushland	2	.2440	.1132	30.5	0	1	0	0	1	0	0	0	0	0	0	1	0	0	0	0	0	0	0	0	0	0	0	1	0
brushwood	2	.2440	.1132	30.5	0	0	0	1	0	0	1	0	0	0	0	1	0	0	0	0	0	0	0	0	0	0	0	1	0
brusque	3	.2784	.1822	32.6	0	0	0	0	2	1	0	0	0	0	1	1	0	0	0	0	0	0	0	0	0	0	0	1	0
brusquely	2	.1814	.1187	30.7	0	0	0	0	1	0	1	0	1	0	0	0	0	0	0	0	0	0	0	0	0	0	0	1	0
Brussels	12	.5006	1.3201	41.2	0	0	5	3	1	1	2	0	4	1	0	0	0	0	0	0	0	0	1	0	0	5	1	0	0
brutal	16	.6335	2.0784	43.2	0	1	1	0	6	5	3	0	1	1	0	4	0	4	1	0	3	0	0	0	0	1	0	1	0
brutality	2	.2306	.1140	30.6	0	0	0	0	2	0	0	0	0	1	0	0	0	1	0	0	0	0	0	0	0	0	0	0	0
brutally	4	.3635	.3138	35.0	0	0	1	0	1	1	1	0	0	0	0	2	0	0	0	0	0	0	0	0	0	0	1	1	0
brute	11	.5591	1.3265	41.2	4	1	0	2	1	1	1	1	4	0	0	0	0	0	1	0	0	0	0	0	2	2	0	2	0
brutes	6	.2960	.4211	36.2	0	1	0	0	2	2	1	0	1	0	0	2	0	0	0	0	0	0	0	0	3	0	0	0	0
Brutus	14	.1879	1.0091	40.0	0	0	0	0	0	13	0	1	13	0	0	0	0	0	0	0	0	0	0	0	0	0	0	1	0
Bryan	13	.1241	.5135	37.1	0	6	0	0	1	1	0	5	1	0	0	0	0	1	0	0	0	0	0	0	0	11	0	0	0
Bryan's	2	.0000	.0290	24.6	0	1	1	0	0	0	0	0	0	0	0	0	0	0	0	0	0	0	0	0	0	2	0	0	0
Bryans	2	.0000	.0290	24.6	0	0	2	0	0	0	0	0	0	0	0	0	0	0	0	0	0	0	0	0	0	2	0	0	0
Bryant	6	.5176	.6598	38.2	0	0	0	2	3	0	1	0	1	1	0	0	0	0	0	0	0	0	0	0	2	0	1	1	0
Bryce	3	.3781	.2548	34.1	0	0	1	0	0	0	2	0	0	0	0	0	0	1	0	1	0	0	0	0	0	0	0	1	0
Bryn	3	.2357	.2199	33.4	1	2	0	0	0	0	0	0	2	0	0	0	0	0	0	0	0	0	0	0	0	1	0	0	0
Bs	2	.2442	.1134	30.5	0	0	0	0	1	1	0	0	0	1	0	0	0	0	0	0	0	0	0	0	0	0	0	1	0
bub	5	.3325	.3679	35.7	0	2	0	2	1	0	0	0	0	0	0	1	0	0	0	0	0	0	0	0	0	1	0	3	0
Bub	3	.3847	.2490	34.0	0	1	1	1	0	0	0	0	0	1	0	1	0	0	0	0	0	0	0	0	0	1	0	0	0
bubble	60	.7040	8.8067	49.4	13	1	16	5	16	2	7	0	28	3	2	1	0	3	1	8	0	0	0	0	0	2	10	2	0
bubbled	10	.5021	1.0892	40.4	0	0	3	1	4	0	1	1	2	1	0	3	0	0	0	3	0	0	0	0	0	0	0	1	0
bubbles	94	.7217	13.973	51.5	28	17	20	5	14	6	4	0	26	3	0	2	0	0	1	44	1	0	2	1	2	3	4	5	0
Bubbles	4	.3597	.3542	35.5	4	0	0	0	0	0	0	0	2	0	0	0	0	0	0	0	1	0	0	0	0	0	0	1	0
bubbling	24	.8221	3.9523	46.0	3	5	3	1	7	2	1	2	4	2	1	3	0	2	0	1	1	0	1	0	2	3	1	3	0
bubbly	6	.3654	.4976	37.0	0	0	3	0	3	0	0	0	1	0	0	0	0	0	0	1	0	0	1	0	0	0	0	3	0
bubonic	2	.2278	.1128	30.5	1	0	0	0	0	0	1	0	0	0	0	0	0	0	0	1	0	0	0	0	0	0	1	0	0
buccaneering	2	.2446	.1125	30.5	1	0	1	0	0	0	0	0	0	1	0	1	0	0	0	0	0	0	0	0	0	0	0	0	0
buccaneers	3	.1250	.1342	31.3	0	0	0	1	2	0	0	0	1	0	0	0	0	0	0	0	0	0	0	0	2	0	0	0	0
Buchanan	15	.4415	1.4506	41.6	0	1	1	0	5	8	0	0	1	0	0	4	0	8	0	0	0	0	0	0	0	0	1	1	0
Buchanan's	2	.0000	.0389	25.9	0	0	0	0	0	2	0	0	0	0	0	0	0	2	0	0	0	0	0	0	0	0	0	0	0
Bucharest	4	.1622	.1743	32.4	0	0	0	3	0	1	0	0	0	0	0	0	0	1	0	0	0	0	0	0	0	0	0	3	0
Bucher	4	.0000	.0486	26.9	0	0	0	0	0	0	4	0	0	0	0	0	0	0	0	0	0	0	0	0	0	0	0	4	0
Buchwald	2	.0000	.0215	23.3	0	0	0	0	0	2	0	0	0	0	0	2	0	0	0	0	0	0	0	0	0	0	0	0	0
buck	35	.5181	3.8147	45.8	2	10	1	1	10	8	3	0	4	0	2	9	0	0	0	0	0	0	0	0	16	1	1	2	0
Buck	92	.3447	7.9753	49.0	1	1	11	1	39	38	1	0	46	0	0	2	0	1	0	1	0	0	0	0	39	2	0	1	0
Buck's	7	.2362	.5173	37.1	0	0	0	0	5	2	0	0	5	0	0	0	0	0	0	0	0	0	0	0	2	0	0	0	0
buckboard	2	.1717	.1142	30.6	0	0	0	0	1	0	1	0	1	0	0	1	0	0	0	0	0	0	0	0	0	0	0	0	0
buckbrush	2	.1717	.1142	30.6	0	0	0	0	1	1	0	0	1	0	0	1	0	0	0	0	0	0	0	0	0	0	0	0	0
bucked	5	.3855	.4777	36.8	1	0	0	3	1	0	0	0	3	0	0	0	0	0	0	0	0	0	0	0	1	0	0	1	0
bucket	107	.8435	18.118	52.6	21	19	13	19	15	8	10	2	31	3	1	16	3	7	2	12	3	0	0	0	10	10	2	7	0
Bucket	5	.2045	.2446	33.9	0	0	0	0	0	1	0	4	0	0	0	0	0	0	0	0	1	0	0	0	4	0	0	0	0
bucketfuls	2	.1948	.1250	31.0	1	1	0	0	0	0	0	0	1	0	0	0	0	0	0	0	0	0	0	0	0	1	0	0	0
buckets	45	.7343	6.8382	48.3	5	11	5	16	2	3	3	0	22	1	0	2	0	2	0	0	1	0	0	1	4	9	2	1	0
bucking	13	.5604	1.5672	42.0	3	4	1	2	3	0	0	0	5	0	0	0	0	0	0	0	1	0	0	1	4	0	1	1	0
Buckingham	4	.0000	.1827	32.6	0	0	4	0	0	0	0	0	4	0	0	0	0	0	0	0	0	0	0	0	0	0	0	0	0
buckle	21	.5652	2.5303	44.0	3	11	0	2	1	4	0	0	7	0	0	5	0	1	0	0	0	0	3	1	3	1	0	0	0
Buckle	3	.0000	.1370	31.4	0	0	0	3	0	0	0	0	3	0	0	0	0	0	0	0	0	0	0	0	0	0	0	0	0
buckled	12	.5575	1.4837	41.7	2	2	1	2	3	1	1	0	7	1	0	1	0	0	0	0	0	0	0	0	1	2	0	0	0
buckles	19	.5731	2.3262	43.7	5	4	1	1	3	4	1	0	7	1	0	2	0	1	0	0	1	0	3	0	0	0	1	3	0
Buckles	5	.0000	.0537	27.3	0	0	0	0	5	0	0	0	0	0	0	5	0	0	0	0	0	0	0	0	0	0	0	0	0
buckling	3	.2672	.1815	32.6	0	0	0	0	1	0	2	0	0	0	0	0	0	0	0	1	0	0	0	1	0	0	1	0	0
bucks	10	.6119	1.3004	41.1	0	2	1	0	1	3	3	0	4	2	0	1	0	0	0	0	0	0	0	0	0	1	1	1	0
Bucks	3	.0000	.0365	25.6	0	0	0	0	0	3	0	0	0	0	0	0	0	0	0	0	0	0	0	0	0	0	0	3	0
buckskin	24	.6385	3.2339	45.1	7	8	4	1	3	1	0	0	9	1	0	0	0	1	1	1	0	0	0	0	4	6	0	1	0
buckskin-clad	2	.0000	.0290	24.6	0	1	1	0	0	0	0	0	0	0	0	0	0	0	0	0	0	0	0	0	0	2	0	0	0
buckskins	3	.3852	.2500	34.0	1	0	1	1	0	0	0	0	0	0	0	1	0	0	0	0	0	0	0	0	0	1	0	1	0
bucktail	2	.0000	.0243	23.9	0	0	0	0	2	0	0	0	0	0	0	0	0	0	0	0	0	0	0	0	0	0	0	2	0
buckwheat	20	.4277	2.0137	43.0	7	10	0	2	0	1	0	0	10	0	0	0	0	0	0	2	0	0	1	0	7	0	0	0	0
Bucky	225	.0327	4.0021	46.0	222	0	0	0	3	0	0	0	0	0	0	0	0	0	0	0	0	0	0	0	221	1	0	3	0
Bucky's	6	.0000	.0703	28.5	6	0	0	0	0	0	0	0	0	0	0	0	0	0	0	0	0	0	0	0	6	0	0	0	0
bud	15	.4258	1.4666	41.7	0	1	4	3	3	0	3	1	4	0	0	0	0	0	0	7	0	0	0	0	3	0	0	1	0
Bud	198	.3044	14.176	51.5	5	33	9	5	129	13	2	2	28	1	0	6	0	0	0	0	0	0	0	0	128	32	0	3	0
Bud's	11	.3699	.9087	39.6	0	4	1	1	5	0	0	0	1	1	0	0	0	0	0	0	0	0	0	0	5	4	0	0	0
Buda	2	.0000	.0389	25.9	0	0	0	2	0	0	0	0	0	0	0	0	0	2	0	0	0	0	0	0	0	0	0	0	0
Buda-Pesth	3	.0000	.0591	27.7	0	0	0	0	0	0	0	3	0	0	0	0	0	0	0	3	0	0	0	0	0	0	0	0	0
Budapest	5	.3684	.4519	36.6	0	0	2	2	0	1	0	0	2	0	0	0	0	2	0	0	0	0	0	0	0	0	0	1	0
Budd's	2	.0000	.0389	25.9	0	0	0	0	0	0	2	0	0	0	0	0	0	2	0	0	0	0	0	0	0	0	0	0	0

7Q browsers
4H brr-rr-r-r
9R brrr
6A brrrooom
9B Brubaker
9B Bruces
5A Brucie's
5P Bruin
6P bruisers
3P bruising

6J Bruley
8N brumal
7A Brummell
9F brunets
7D brush-house
7R brush-in
9D brush-scrubbing
XR brushed-on
3P brushless
XQ brushstroke

4K brushstrokes
7A brushwood-fire
XQ brushwork
7R brushy-limbed
8F brutalities
9R brutalized
8A Brute
4N brute's
7D brutish
7R bruuummpphh

5J Bryant's
7H Bryophyllum
4H bryophyte
4H bryophytes
9R BSU
7B bu
8R Bubba
7N buccaneer
XH buccinator
8D Buchwald's

7A Buck'll
7N buck's
7A buckboards
7R bucket-seat
3P Bucketfoot
XN Buckets
8B Buckfield
6A buckler
7N Bucklersbury
7R Buckminster

7R Bucknum
6A buckoes
6R buckshot
7R bucktails
3P Bucktown
5P bucolic
7N bud's
9F Budd
8R Buddah
3A budded

Word Type	F	D	U	SFI	3 Gr 3	4 Gr 4	5 Gr 5	6 Gr 6	7 Gr 7	8 Gr 8	9 Gr 9	X UnGr	A Read	B Eng & Gr	C Comp	D Lit	E Math	F Soc Stud	G Spell	H Sci	J Music	K Art	L Home Ec	M Shop	N Lib F	P Lib NF	Q Lib Ref	R Mag	S Rel
Buddha	8	.1558	.3721	35.7	0	1	0	4	1	1	0	1	0	0	0	0	0	7	0	0	0	0	0	0	0	1	0	0	0
Buddha's	3	.2444	.1814	32.6	0	0	0	1	1	0	1	0	0	0	0	0	0	2	0	0	0	0	0	0	0	0	1	0	0
Buddhism	14	.2422	.8602	39.3	0	0	0	4	3	6	0	1	0	0	0	0	0	12	0	0	0	0	0	0	0	0	1	1	0
Buddhist	17	.4412	1.6298	42.1	0	3	6	3	2	2	1	0	0	0	0	0	0	10	0	0	0	0	0	0	0	2	3	2	0
Buddhists	6	.3437	.4738	36.8	0	0	0	3	2	0	0	1	0	0	0	0	0	4	0	0	0	0	0	0	0	1	0	1	0
buddies	7	.1117	.2888	34.6	0	0	0	6	1	0	0	0	2	0	0	0	0	0	0	0	0	0	0	0	0	0	0	5	0
budding	6	.4711	.6025	37.8	0	0	2	2	1	0	0	1	0	0	0	1	0	0	0	2	0	0	0	0	0	1	0	2	0
buddy	9	.4769	.9874	39.9	2	0	2	2	1	1	1	0	5	0	0	1	0	0	0	0	0	0	0	0	1	0	0	2	0
Buddy	3	.2300	.1627	32.1	0	1	1	1	0	0	0	0	0	1	0	0	0	0	0	0	0	0	0	0	0	0	0	2	0
budge	21	.6601	2.9039	44.6	3	5	3	1	3	2	4	0	8	0	1	5	0	2	0	1	0	0	0	0	1	1	1	1	0
budget	42	.4035	3.6734	45.7	3	1	1	4	3	7	23	0	5	0	0	1	7	1	1	1	0	0	14	0	0	0	4	8	0
Budget	5	.4418	.4846	36.9	1	0	0	0	1	0	3	0	1	0	0	0	1	0	0	0	0	0	1	0	0	1	0	1	0
budgeted	2	.2442	.1134	30.5	0	0	0	0	0	0	2	0	0	1	0	0	0	0	0	0	0	0	0	0	0	0	0	1	0
budgets	2	.2427	.1159	30.6	0	0	0	0	1	1	0	0	0	0	0	0	1	0	0	0	0	0	0	0	0	0	0	1	0
buds	59	.7028	8.5915	49.3	11	11	8	2	19	2	2	4	19	2	0	4	0	2	0	18	0	0	0	0	3	3	6	2	0
Buena	3	.1409	.1472	31.7	1	2	0	0	0	0	0	0	1	0	0	0	0	0	0	0	0	0	0	0	0	2	0	0	0
Buenaventura	2	.0000	.0389	25.9	0	0	0	2	0	0	0	0	0	0	0	0	0	2	0	0	0	0	0	0	0	0	0	0	0
Buenos	27	.2443	1.6252	42.1	7	2	0	8	9	0	1	0	0	0	0	0	0	17	0	0	0	0	0	0	0	0	10	0	0
BuenosAires	2	.2437	.1129	30.5	1	0	0	0	0	0	0	1	0	0	0	0	0	0	0	0	0	0	0	0	0	0	1	1	0
buff	8	.3141	.5972	37.8	1	0	0	1	3	3	0	0	2	1	0	0	0	0	0	0	0	0	0	2	0	3	0	0	0
Buff	7	.4044	.6475	38.1	3	3	1	0	0	0	0	0	2	0	0	0	0	0	0	0	0	0	0	0	3	1	0	1	0
buffalo	188	.7933	30.396	54.8	50	71	19	16	17	2	10	3	81	4	4	7	0	33	2	6	2	1	0	0	6	34	5	3	0
Buffalo	55	.6563	7.5007	48.8	3	27	3	7	12	2	1	0	14	3	0	7	1	9	0	0	8	0	0	0	0	11	0	2	0
buffalo's	3	.2357	.2199	33.4	1	0	0	0	2	0	0	0	2	0	0	0	0	0	0	0	0	0	0	0	0	1	0	0	0
buffaloes	59	.7244	8.7616	49.4	16	16	4	12	8	1	2	0	13	1	1	5	0	12	0	12	0	2	0	0	1	11	1	0	0
buffer	7	.5403	.7931	39.0	0	0	0	1	2	1	3	0	0	1	0	0	0	2	0	1	0	0	0	0	0	1	0	2	0
buffers	2	.1620	.0760	28.8	0	0	0	1	0	1	0	0	0	0	0	0	0	0	0	0	0	0	0	1	0	0	0	1	0
buffet	8	.1765	.3197	35.0	0	0	0	0	1	0	6	1	0	1	0	0	0	0	0	0	0	0	5	0	0	0	0	2	0
buffeting	3	.3805	.2526	34.0	1	0	0	0	2	0	0	0	0	0	0	0	0	1	0	0	0	0	0	0	1	1	0	0	0
Buffie	19	.0000	.2751	34.4	0	19	0	0	0	0	0	0	0	0	0	0	0	0	0	0	0	0	0	0	0	19	0	0	0
buffing	5	.1634	.2733	34.4	0	2	0	0	3	0	0	0	2	0	0	0	0	0	0	0	0	0	0	0	0	3	0	0	0
Buffon	3	.1813	.1402	31.5	0	0	0	0	2	0	0	1	0	0	0	0	0	0	0	1	0	0	0	0	0	0	2	0	0
buffoons	2	.0665	.0708	28.5	0	0	0	0	1	0	1	0	1	0	1	0	0	0	0	0	0	0	0	0	0	0	0	0	0
buffs	2	.0000	.0243	23.9	0	0	0	0	0	1	0	1	0	0	0	0	0	0	0	0	0	0	0	0	0	0	0	2	0
Buffy	5	.0000	.0608	27.8	0	5	0	0	0	0	0	0	0	0	0	0	0	0	0	0	0	0	0	0	0	0	0	5	0
bug	49	.6790	6.8292	48.3	15	9	0	3	20	0	1	1	8	1	0	0	5	0	3	10	4	2	0	0	0	2	0	14	0
Bug	6	.3175	.4229	36.3	2	0	0	4	0	0	0	0	0	0	0	0	0	0	0	0	1	0	0	0	0	1	0	4	0
bugaboo	2	.0000	.0243	23.9	0	0	0	1	0	1	0	0	0	0	0	0	0	0	0	0	0	0	0	0	0	0	0	2	0
buggies	13	.4685	1.4117	41.5	2	1	0	1	3	2	0	4	6	0	0	0	0	2	0	4	0	0	0	0	0	0	0	1	0
buggy	51	.5272	5.9563	47.7	12	19	6	0	7	3	0	4	22	2	0	2	0	0	0	4	1	0	0	0	1	19	0	0	0
bugle	48	.5807	6.0275	47.8	2	9	15	8	3	4	7	0	23	2	0	9	0	0	0	0	6	0	0	0	6	0	0	2	0
Bugle	2	.0000	.0234	23.7	0	0	2	0	0	0	0	0	0	0	0	0	0	0	0	0	0	0	0	0	2	0	0	0	0
bugler	7	.2366	.5437	37.4	0	1	6	0	0	0	0	0	6	0	0	0	0	0	0	0	0	0	0	0	1	0	0	0	0
bugles	11	.4445	1.1143	40.5	2	2	1	3	0	1	2	0	5	0	1	2	0	0	0	0	3	0	0	0	0	0	0	0	0
bugs	59	.6372	7.9698	49.0	29	8	4	0	9	3	3	3	25	1	0	2	0	0	0	9	0	3	0	0	7	8	0	4	0
Bugs	8	.2675	.6332	38.0	1	0	6	0	0	1	0	0	6	0	0	0	0	0	0	0	0	1	0	0	0	1	0	0	0
Buh	23	.0000	.2468	33.9	0	0	0	0	0	23	0	0	0	0	0	23	0	0	0	0	0	0	0	0	0	0	0	0	0
Buick	5	.3211	.4073	36.1	0	0	0	1	3	1	0	0	2	0	0	0	0	1	0	0	0	0	0	0	0	0	0	2	0
build	857	.9261	157.18	62.0	195	149	117	122	99	85	66	24	148	41	6	14	23	188	57	83	40	7	26	25	26	74	34	62	3
build-up	3	.3811	.2534	34.0	0	0	0	0	2	1	0	0	0	0	0	0	0	0	0	1	0	0	0	0	0	1	0	1	0
builded	2	.0000	.0215	23.3	0	0	0	0	2	0	0	0	0	0	0	2	0	0	0	0	0	0	0	0	0	0	0	0	0
builder	26	.6688	3.6249	45.6	1	4	7	4	5	2	3	0	8	1	0	1	0	4	0	3	0	0	0	0	0	1	5	3	0
Builder	2	.0000	.0162	22.1	2	0	0	0	0	0	0	0	0	0	0	0	0	0	2	0	0	0	0	0	0	0	0	0	0
builders	44	.6901	6.2252	47.9	5	8	8	2	3	8	7	3	8	0	0	2	2	10	0	1	0	2	0	2	0	1	10	6	0
Builders	5	.0000	.0724	28.6	5	0	0	0	0	0	0	0	0	0	0	0	0	0	0	0	0	0	0	0	0	5	0	0	0
building	886	.9195	161.52	62.1	165	155	112	124	118	111	84	17	171	44	7	26	40	160	11	106	21	24	11	20	20	71	65	89	0
Building	45	.7330	6.7396	48.3	6	1	9	8	6	4	9	2	11	0	0	0	9	5	4	2	1	0	0	0	1	2	7	3	0
building-up	2	.1493	.0692	28.4	0	0	0	0	1	1	0	0	0	0	0	0	0	0	0	0	0	1	0	0	0	0	1	0	0
building's	2	.2441	.1127	30.5	0	1	0	0	0	0	1	0	0	0	0	0	0	0	0	0	0	0	0	0	1	0	1	0	0
buildings	495	.7502	75.473	58.8	113	94	64	77	59	36	44	8	74	14	2	7	6	223	3	31	5	21	0	8	6	24	31	40	0
builds	59	.7447	8.9534	49.5	11	9	5	11	7	6	5	5	11	4	0	0	1	6	1	19	5	0	1	0	0	6	0	5	0
buildup	3	.2143	.1568	32.0	1	0	0	0	0	0	1	1	0	0	0	0	0	0	0	0	0	0	0	0	0	1	0	2	0
built	1249	.8909	221.36	63.5	221	207	218	230	150	109	81	33	186	38	5	33	26	460	16	85	80	9	3	10	26	114	80	77	1
built-in	25	.5932	3.1337	45.0	3	0	4	4	5	4	4	1	7	3	2	0	0	0	0	4	0	0	0	0	0	1	5	3	0
built-ins	2	.0000	.0290	24.6	0	0	0	0	2	0	0	0	0	0	0	0	0	0	0	0	0	0	0	0	0	2	0	0	0
bulb	141	.6687	19.492	52.9	37	25	23	20	8	19	7	2	18	2	0	1	3	0	1	87	0	3	3	1	2	7	10	3	0
bulbar	2	.2441	.1127	30.5	0	0	0	0	1	0	1	0	0	0	0	0	0	0	0	0	0	0	0	0	1	0	1	0	0
bulbs	40	.6135	5.1087	47.1	11	4	8	6	5	0	5	1	3	0	0	0	9	4	0	14	0	0	0	0	1	2	6	1	0
Bulgaria	15	.4146	1.4166	41.5	1	0	2	2	2	4	3	1	3	0	0	0	0	7	0	0	0	0	0	0	0	0	1	4	0
Bulgarian	4	.3740	.3226	35.1	0	0	0	0	2	2	0	0	0	1	0	0	0	0	0	0	0	0	0	0	0	0	1	2	0
Bulgarians	5	.3184	.3581	35.5	0	0	0	0	1	4	0	0	0	0	0	0	0	1	0	0	0	0	0	0	0	0	1	3	0
bulge	14	.6377	1.8416	42.7	0	3	1	4	5	0	1	0	1	0	0	2	0	3	0	2	0	0	0	0	0	2	1	3	0
bulged	10	.5472	1.2240	40.9	4	1	1	1	2	1	0	0	6	0	0	0	0	0	0	1	1	0	0	0	0	1	0	1	0
bulges	8	.4590	.8439	39.3	0	3	0	3	2	0	0	0	3	0	0	0	0	1	0	3	0	0	0	0	0	0	1	0	0
bulging	11	.4860	1.1148	40.5	2	0	0	1	5	1	1	1	0	0	0	3	0	0	0	0	0	0	0	0	3	0	2	3	0
bulk	46	.4044	3.9625	46.0	1	1	3	3	17	10	10	1	1	0	0	0	0	2	0	7	0	0	14	0	1	2	14	5	0
bulkhead	7	.2594	.4649	36.7	0	0	0	1	2	3	1	0	2	0	0	4	0	0	0	0	0	0	0	0	1	0	0	0	0
bulkheads	5	.1926	.2474	33.9	0	0	0	0	1	0	4	0	0	0	0	0	4	0	0	0	0	0	0	0	0	0	0	1	0
bulkier	2	.0857	.0784	28.9	0	0	1	0	0	0	1	0	1	0	0	0	0	0	0	0	0	0	1	0	0	0	0	0	0
bulks	2	.1551	.0728	28.6	0	0	0	0	1	0	1	0	0	0	1	0	0	0	0	0	0	0	0	0	1	0	0	0	0
bulky	25	.6152	3.1602	45.0	4	2	1	5	5	4	4	0	2	0	1	0	0	5	1	1	0	0	5	0	1	3	3	3	0
bull	84	.7236	12.507	51.0	13	8	7	17	32	5	2	0	30	3	2	2	0	5	0	1	2	0	0	0	22	9	5	3	0
Bull	29	.6361	3.8004	45.8	2	7	1	3	11	5	0	0	4	1	0	9	0	1	0	0	1	0	0	0	1	6	4	2	0
bull-riding	2	.0000	.0914	29.6	0	0	0	2	0	0	0	0	2	0	0	0	0	0	0	0	0	0	0	0	0	0	0	0	0
bull-teams	2	.0000	.0914	29.6	0	0	2	0	0	0	0	0	2	0	0	0	0	0	0	0	0	0	0	0	0	0	0	0	0
bull's	10	.4380	.9888	40.0	0	1	0	2	5	0	0	2	3	0	0	0	0	0	0	0	0	0	0	0	3	3	0	1	0
Bull's	2	.2446	.1122	30.5	1	0	0	0	1	0	0	0	0	0	0	1	0	0	0	0	0	0	0	0	0	0	1	0	0
bull's-eye	5	.3325	.3637	35.6	0	0	1	0	2	2	0	0	0	3	0	0	0	0	0	0	0	0	0	0	0	0	1	1	0
bulldog	13	.5241	1.5255	41.8	2	1	7	0	2	0	1	0	7	0	0	0	0	0	0	0	0	0	0	0	3	1	1	1	0
Bulldog	2	.1717	.1142	30.6	0	1	1	0	0	0	0	0	1	0	0	1	0	0	0	0	0	0	0	0	0	0	0	0	0
bulldogged	2	.0000	.0914	29.6	0	2	0	0	0	0	0	0	2	0	0	0	0	0	0	0	0	0	0	0	0	0	0	0	0
bulldogger	3	.0000	.1370	31.4	0	3	0	0	0	0	0	0	3	0	0	0	0	0	0	0	0	0	0	0	0	0	0	0	0
bulldogging	2	.0000	.0914	29.6	0	2	0	0	0	0	0	0	2	0	0	0	0	0	0	0	0	0	0	0	0	0	0	0	0

8R buddy-bodyguards
7N budged
3Q budgereegahs
7Q budgerigar
XR budgerigars
7N budges
9R budget-battered
XR budgeting
9L budgetmaking
7Q budworm
5J BuenaVista
4J bueno
8J buffa
6R buffalo-drawn
3F buffalo-skin
7Q buffaloe
7Q buffbreasted
5H buffed
4R Buffern
6K buffeted
6A buffetings
4P Buffie's
7A Bufflao
7Q Buffon's
7Q Bufo
7Q Buford
9Q bug-eyed
7R bugaboos
7R bugaloo
6R bugged
7A bugging
7N bugle-blast
8A buglers
8B bugling
3P BUGS
7B Build
XR builder-architect
5R builder's
5F Builders-of-America
3P Builders'
3H building-materials
9R building-trade
7R buildups
XR Built
6F built-up
6A bujeni
7R Bukich
8Q Bukidnon
8Q Bulan
6Q bulblike
7J bulbous
4F Bulbul
7J Bulfinch
8R Bulgarian-Soviet
8Q Bulgars
7R Bulge
6N bulgy
8N bulked
7Q bulkiest
XB bulkily
9L bulkiness
9D bulky-looking
8D bull-pen
6P bull-shouldered
6A bull-voiced
3A BULL'S-eye
7A bull's-eyes
9M bullchain

Word Type	F	D	U	SFI	3 Gr 3	4 Gr 4	5 Gr 5	6 Gr 6	7 Gr 7	8 Gr 8	9 Gr 9	X UnGr	A Read	B Eng & Gr	C Comp	D Lit	E Math	F Soc Stud	G Spell	H Sci	J Music	K Art	L Home Ec	M Shop	N Lib F	P Lib NF	Q Lib Ref	R Mag	S Rel
bulldogs	3	.0000	.1370	31.4	0	1	1	0	1	0	0	0	3	0	0	0	0	0	0	0	0	0	0	0	0	0	0	0	0
Bulldogs	2	.0000	.0299	24.8	0	1	0	0	1	0	0	0	0	0	0	0	2	0	0	0	0	0	0	0	0	0	0	0	0
bulldozer	15	.3898	1.3121	41.2	8	2	0	1	3	1	0	0	2	1	0	0	0	0	0	3	0	0	0	0	8	0	0	1	0
bulldozers	8	.2744	.5421	37.3	2	2	0	3	0	0	1	0	1	0	0	0	0	3	0	0	0	0	0	0	0	0	0	4	0
bulldozing	3	.1277	.1363	31.3	0	0	0	0	1	1	0	1	1	0	0	0	0	0	0	0	0	0	0	0	0	0	0	2	0
bullet	57	.7826	9.0260	49.6	4	14	1	11	15	7	4	1	13	0	1	10	2	0	1	12	1	0	0	0	5	5	4	3	0
Bullet	3	.0000	.0365	25.6	0	0	0	0	1	0	0	2	0	0	0	0	0	0	0	0	0	0	0	0	0	0	0	3	0
bulletin	49	.5797	5.9238	47.7	8	7	5	5	10	1	12	1	6	4	0	1	7	5	2	8	0	0	10	0	0	3	2	1	0
bulletins	10	.4263	.9873	39.9	0	0	0	6	2	0	1	1	3	0	0	0	0	0	0	5	0	0	0	0	0	1	1	0	0
bullets	38	.7473	5.8077	47.6	4	8	4	6	11	1	2	2	12	1	0	5	0	2	1	3	0	0	0	0	5	6	1	2	0
bullfight	8	.4941	.8591	39.3	0	2	0	1	5	0	0	0	2	0	0	0	0	1	0	0	2	0	0	0	2	0	0	1	0
bullfighter	3	.2223	.2106	33.2	0	0	0	1	2	0	0	0	2	1	0	0	0	0	0	0	0	0	0	0	0	0	0	0	0
bullfighting	2	.2337	.1157	30.6	0	1	0	1	0	0	0	0	0	0	0	0	0	1	0	0	0	0	0	0	1	0	0	0	0
bullfights	4	.3344	.3261	35.1	1	0	0	2	0	1	0	0	1	0	0	0	0	2	0	0	0	0	0	0	0	0	1	0	0
Bullfinch	14	.1787	.8216	39.1	5	7	2	0	0	0	0	0	7	0	0	0	0	0	0	0	0	0	0	0	7	0	0	0	0
bullfrog	18	.5148	1.9952	43.0	1	0	0	12	1	3	1	0	2	0	1	1	2	0	0	11	1	0	0	0	0	0	0	0	0
bullfrogs	7	.3492	.5577	37.5	2	0	0	5	0	0	0	0	0	0	0	0	0	0	0	5	1	0	0	0	0	0	0	1	0
bullhead	12	.0000	.2366	33.7	6	0	0	0	6	0	0	0	0	0	0	0	0	0	0	12	0	0	0	0	0	0	0	0	0
bullheads	3	.0000	.0591	27.7	3	0	0	0	0	0	0	0	0	0	0	0	0	0	0	3	0	0	0	0	0	0	0	0	0
bullies	5	.3075	.3904	35.9	0	0	0	1	3	1	0	0	2	0	1	0	0	1	0	0	0	0	0	0	0	1	0	0	0
bullocks	4	.2393	.3005	34.8	0	0	0	2	1	1	0	0	3	0	0	1	0	0	0	0	0	0	0	0	0	0	0	0	0
bullpen	2	.2444	.1132	30.5	0	0	1	0	1	0	0	0	0	1	0	0	0	0	0	0	0	0	0	0	1	0	0	0	0
bullring	2	.0000	.0162	22.1	0	0	0	0	2	0	0	0	0	0	0	0	0	0	0	0	2	0	0	0	0	0	0	0	0
bulls	20	.6122	2.5694	44.1	6	3	0	6	2	1	1	1	5	0	0	1	0	2	0	1	1	0	0	0	7	0	2	1	0
Bulltop	4	.2445	.3067	34.9	1	0	0	2	1	0	0	0	3	0	0	0	0	0	0	0	0	0	0	0	0	1	0	0	0
bullwhackers	3	.0000	.0434	26.4	0	3	0	0	0	0	0	0	0	0	0	0	0	0	0	0	0	0	0	0	0	3	0	0	0
bully	16	.5161	1.8422	42.7	1	5	3	2	5	0	0	0	8	0	0	0	0	0	0	0	2	0	0	0	4	1	1	0	0
bullying	4	.4829	.4095	36.1	0	1	1	0	2	0	0	0	0	0	0	0	0	1	0	0	0	0	0	0	1	1	0	1	0
bulrushes	3	.2236	.1570	32.0	0	1	0	0	2	0	0	0	0	1	0	2	0	0	0	0	0	0	0	0	0	0	0	0	0
bulwark	3	.2212	.2099	33.2	0	0	0	0	2	1	0	0	2	0	0	1	0	0	0	0	0	0	0	0	0	0	0	0	0
bulwarks	2	.2446	.1123	30.5	0	0	0	0	0	1	1	0	0	1	0	0	0	0	0	0	0	0	0	0	0	0	1	0	0
bum	5	.3343	.4151	36.2	1	0	0	0	2	0	1	1	2	0	0	0	0	0	0	0	0	0	0	0	0	1	0	2	0
Bum	5	.0000	.0537	27.3	0	0	0	0	5	0	0	0	0	0	0	5	0	0	0	0	0	0	0	0	0	0	0	0	0
Bumble	2	.0000	.0045	16.5	0	0	0	0	2	0	0	0	0	0	2	0	0	0	0	0	0	0	0	0	0	0	0	0	0
bumblebee	7	.5487	.8378	39.2	0	2	1	1	2	1	0	0	3	1	0	0	0	0	1	1	1	0	0	0	0	0	0	0	0
Bumblebee	3	.0000	.1370	31.4	3	0	0	0	0	0	0	0	3	0	0	0	0	0	0	0	0	0	0	0	0	0	0	0	0
bumblebees	7	.3583	.5583	37.5	0	3	0	3	0	1	0	0	0	0	1	0	0	0	0	4	0	0	0	0	0	0	2	0	0
bumbling	4	.2904	.2847	34.5	0	0	0	0	1	1	2	0	1	0	1	0	0	1	0	0	0	0	0	0	0	0	0	1	0
bumming	3	.0000	.0352	25.5	0	2	0	0	0	0	1	0	0	0	0	0	0	0	0	0	0	0	0	0	3	0	0	0	0
bump	40	.7025	5.8548	47.7	19	4	6	3	1	4	1	2	17	0	1	2	0	0	0	9	1	0	0	0	3	5	0	2	0
bump	2	.0000	.0914	29.6	2	0	0	0	0	0	0	0	2	0	0	0	0	0	0	0	0	0	0	0	0	0	0	0	0
bumped	49	.6571	6.8448	48.4	16	11	8	4	6	3	0	1	27	1	2	0	0	1	0	2	3	0	0	0	2	9	0	2	0
bumper	17	.6790	2.4037	43.8	4	0	2	0	4	2	2	3	5	0	0	0	2	2	0	3	0	0	0	0	1	2	0	2	0
bumpers	3	.2357	.2199	33.4	3	0	0	0	0	0	0	0	2	0	0	0	0	0	0	0	0	0	0	0	0	1	0	0	0
bumping	27	.5930	3.4672	45.4	4	3	4	8	4	1	3	0	13	0	0	3	0	1	0	3	0	0	0	0	4	0	0	3	0
bumpkin	3	.1250	.1342	31.3	1	1	0	1	0	0	0	0	1	0	0	0	0	0	0	0	0	0	0	0	2	0	0	0	0
Bumpo	6	.0000	.0703	28.5	0	6	0	0	0	0	0	0	0	0	0	0	0	0	0	0	0	0	0	0	6	0	0	0	0
Bumppo	2	.0000	.0219	23.4	0	0	0	0	2	0	0	0	0	2	0	0	0	0	0	0	0	0	0	0	0	0	0	0	0
bumps	24	.7183	3.5329	45.5	11	2	0	4	2	3	0	2	6	1	0	1	0	0	0	5	1	1	0	0	0	3	3	3	0
Bumps	51	.0000	.5979	37.8	51	0	0	0	0	0	0	0	0	0	0	0	0	0	0	0	0	0	0	0	51	0	0	0	0
Bumps'	2	.0000	.0234	23.7	2	0	0	0	0	0	0	0	0	0	0	0	0	0	0	0	0	0	0	0	2	0	0	0	0
bumpy	17	.6798	2.3852	43.8	3	5	1	3	3	1	0	1	4	1	1	1	0	2	1	1	0	0	0	0	0	5	1	0	0
bums	2	.2446	.1142	30.6	0	0	0	0	1	0	1	0	0	0	0	0	0	0	0	0	0	0	0	0	1	0	0	1	0
bun	4	.4398	.3923	35.9	0	3	1	0	0	0	0	0	1	0	0	0	1	0	0	0	1	0	0	0	0	1	0	0	0
Bun	2	.0000	.0215	23.3	0	0	0	0	0	0	2	0	0	0	0	2	0	0	0	0	0	0	0	0	0	0	0	0	0
bunch	105	.7435	16.027	52.0	16	14	19	13	22	10	6	5	42	4	4	5	1	2	1	6	4	0	0	0	24	4	1	7	0
Bunche	8	.1990	.5845	37.7	0	0	7	0	0	0	1	0	7	0	0	0	0	1	0	0	0	0	0	0	0	0	0	0	0
bunched	8	.5373	.9352	39.7	0	2	1	2	3	0	0	0	3	0	0	2	0	0	0	0	0	0	0	0	0	1	1	1	0
bunches	32	.7407	4.8222	46.8	9	6	4	3	7	3	0	0	6	1	0	3	3	7	0	1	1	1	0	0	6	0	0	3	0
bunching	2	.0000	.0234	23.7	1	0	1	0	0	0	0	0	0	0	0	0	0	0	0	0	0	0	0	0	2	0	0	0	0
bundle	97	.7189	14.535	51.6	35	16	5	14	22	4	1	0	52	1	2	8	6	3	0	2	0	0	0	0	12	8	0	3	0
bundled	5	.3530	.4326	36.4	1	3	0	1	0	0	0	0	2	0	0	0	0	0	0	0	0	0	0	0	0	2	0	1	0
bundles	83	.7448	12.681	51.0	28	15	9	7	9	11	3	1	26	0	0	1	15	15	0	8	1	0	1	0	6	8	2	0	0
bundling	2	.1814	.1187	30.7	1	0	0	0	1	0	0	0	1	0	0	0	0	0	0	0	0	0	0	0	0	0	0	1	0
bung	2	.0000	.0914	29.6	1	0	0	1	0	0	0	0	2	0	0	0	0	0	0	0	0	0	0	0	0	0	0	0	0
bungalow	11	.5267	1.2489	41.0	0	3	0	1	3	3	0	1	3	0	0	3	0	0	0	0	0	0	0	0	0	2	1	2	0
bungalows	3	.1823	.1405	31.5	0	0	0	0	1	2	0	0	0	0	0	0	0	1	0	0	0	0	0	0	0	0	2	0	0
Bunge	2	.0000	.0209	23.2	0	0	0	0	0	2	0	0	0	0	0	0	0	0	0	0	0	0	0	0	0	0	2	0	0
bungled	3	.3801	.2525	34.0	0	0	1	0	1	0	0	1	0	0	0	0	0	0	0	1	0	0	0	0	1	1	0	0	0
bunions	2	.2446	.1142	30.6	0	1	0	0	1	0	0	0	0	0	0	0	0	0	0	0	0	0	0	0	1	0	0	1	0
bunk	16	.5403	1.9574	42.9	3	2	3	2	1	3	2	0	11	0	0	1	0	0	0	0	1	0	0	0	0	2	0	1	0
Bunker	7	.3945	.6323	38.0	0	3	1	0	1	0	2	0	1	0	0	0	0	1	0	2	0	0	0	0	0	3	0	0	0
bunkers	2	.2437	.1129	30.5	0	0	1	0	0	0	1	0	0	0	0	0	0	0	0	0	0	0	0	0	0	0	1	1	0
bunkhouse	13	.5148	1.4703	41.7	3	1	1	2	2	4	0	0	5	2	0	0	0	0	0	0	1	0	0	0	4	1	0	0	0
bunkhouses	4	.2424	.3036	34.8	1	0	3	0	0	0	0	0	3	0	0	0	0	0	0	0	0	0	0	0	0	0	0	1	0
bunks	11	.5627	1.3684	41.4	2	2	4	2	0	1	0	0	6	0	0	1	0	2	0	0	0	0	0	0	1	0	0	1	0
bunnies	2	.2446	.1142	30.6	0	0	0	0	0	0	2	0	0	0	0	0	0	0	0	0	0	0	0	0	1	0	0	1	0
bunny	5	.3747	.4640	36.7	5	0	0	0	0	0	0	0	3	0	0	0	0	0	1	0	1	0	0	0	0	0	0	0	0
Bunny	24	.2444	1.9481	42.9	23	0	0	0	0	1	0	0	23	0	0	0	0	0	0	0	0	1	0	0	0	0	0	0	0
buns	8	.5209	.8655	39.4	1	5	0	1	0	0	1	0	0	1	0	0	1	0	0	0	2	0	0	0	1	3	0	0	0
bunsen	2	.0000	.0050	17.0	0	0	0	0	0	0	2	0	0	0	0	0	0	0	0	0	0	0	0	2	0	0	0	0	0
Bunsen	6	.3486	.5162	37.1	0	0	0	2	1	2	1	0	2	1	0	0	0	0	0	3	0	0	0	0	0	0	0	0	0
Bunsuru	6	.0000	.2741	34.4	0	0	0	6	0	0	0	0	6	0	0	0	0	0	0	0	0	0	0	0	0	0	0	0	0
bunt	9	.2442	.6954	38.4	6	0	0	2	1	0	0	0	7	0	0	0	0	0	0	0	0	0	0	0	0	2	0	0	0
bunting	6	.2977	.4237	36.3	0	0	2	3	0	0	0	1	1	0	0	2	0	0	0	0	0	0	0	0	0	0	0	3	0
buntings	2	.2441	.1127	30.5	0	0	0	0	2	0	0	0	0	0	0	0	0	0	0	0	0	0	0	0	1	0	1	0	0
Bunyan	29	.5172	3.4144	45.3	1	4	10	3	9	2	0	0	19	0	0	5	0	1	3	0	0	1	0	0	0	0	0	0	0
Bunyan's	2	.0000	.0215	23.3	0	0	0	0	2	0	0	0	0	0	0	2	0	0	0	0	0	0	0	0	0	0	0	0	0
buoy	31	.6168	4.1718	46.2	0	17	3	1	9	1	0	0	20	0	0	1	0	5	1	0	0	0	0	0	0	2	1	1	0
buoyancy	12	.6202	1.5904	42.0	0	2	2	3	4	0	1	0	5	0	0	1	0	0	0	3	0	0	0	0	1	1	0	1	0
buoyant	6	.5068	.6479	38.1	0	0	1	1	1	2	0	1	1	0	0	2	0	0	1	0	0	0	0	0	0	1	0	1	0
buoys	7	.3751	.5969	37.8	0	2	0	0	5	0	0	0	0	0	0	0	0	3	0	3	0	0	0	0	0	0	0	1	0
buraku-min	2	.0000	.0389	25.9	0	0	0	0	0	2	0	0	0	0	0	0	0	2	0	0	0	0	0	0	0	0	0	0	0
Burbank	6	.2187	.3110	34.9	0	3	1	0	2	0	0	0	0	4	0	0	0	0	0	0	0	0	0	0	0	0	0	2	0
burbled	2	.1378	.0662	28.2	1	0	1	0	0	0	0	0	0	0	0	0	0	0	0	0	0	1	0	0	0	0	0	1	0
Burd	11	.0000	.1337	31.3	0	0	0	0	0	0	0	11	0	0	0	0	0	0	0	0	0	0	0	0	0	0	0	11	0
burden	44	.6832	6.1493	47.9	5	2	7	1	12	7	6	4	7	4	0	5	0	2	0	2	1	0	0	0	9	0	9	5	0

6R Bulletin
5B bulletin-board
5R Bulletins
8F bulletproof
3A Bullfinch's
8B Bullfrog
6H bullfrog's
XR Bullitt
4N Bullivant
4P Bulloch
6A bullock
4J bullock's
6A bullocks'
9R Bulls
4P bullwhacker
3A bullwhip
7N bullyrag
7N Bulrushers
8A bumblings
7A bummed
6J bummer
4R bumpity-bump
4N Bumpo's
8Q Buna
3A Bunch
8Q Bundi
6A bundled-up
9Q Bundy
8Q Bungay
8B bungle
8B bunked
7D bunker
4P Bunker's
3A bunkyojo
4J bunny's
4J Bunny's
3A bunnykin
7N Bunsby
3A bunted

Word Type	F	D	U	SFI	3 Gr 3	4 Gr 4	5 Gr 5	6 Gr 6	7 Gr 7	8 Gr 8	9 Gr 9	X UnGr	A Read	B Eng & Gr	C Comp	D Lit	E Math	F Soc Stud	G Spell	H Sci	J Music	K Art	L Home Ec	M Shop	N Lib F	P Lib NF	Q Lib Ref	R Mag	S Rel
Burden	7	.0000	.1013	30.1	6	0	0	0	1	0	0	0	0	0	0	0	0	0	0	0	0	0	0	0	0	7	0	0	0
burdened	2	.1814	.1187	30.7	0	0	0	0	0	0	2	0	1	0	0	0	0	0	0	0	0	0	0	0	0	0	0	1	0
burdens	15	.5755	1.8283	42.6	0	1	1	2	5	3	2	1	3	0	0	0	0	4	0	1	1	0	0	0	0	0	3	3	0
burdensome	4	.2976	.2936	34.7	0	0	0	1	1	1	0	1	1	0	0	0	1	0	0	0	0	0	0	0	0	0	0	2	0
Burdett	4	.1494	.2089	33.2	0	0	2	0	0	1	1	0	2	0	0	0	0	0	0	0	2	0	0	0	0	0	0	0	0
Burdick	10	.2128	.4844	36.9	0	1	5	0	0	0	4	0	0	0	4	0	0	0	0	0	0	0	0	0	0	1	0	5	0
burdock	2	.0000	.0394	26.0	0	1	0	0	1	0	0	0	0	0	0	0	0	0	0	2	0	0	0	0	0	0	0	0	0
Burdoo	2	.0000	.0234	23.7	0	0	2	0	0	0	0	0	0	0	0	0	0	0	0	0	0	0	0	0	2	0	0	0	0
Burdow	5	.0000	.0586	27.7	0	0	0	0	0	5	0	0	0	0	0	0	0	0	0	0	0	0	0	0	5	0	0	0	0
bureau	25	.6575	3.4016	45.3	2	3	4	8	3	3	1	1	4	0	1	3	0	0	1	12	0	0	0	1	1	0	0	2	0
Bureau	60	.7291	8.9088	49.5	7	1	6	9	22	8	6	1	7	1	0	0	2	5	0	21	0	0	1	1	0	7	5	10	0
Bureau's	2	.2346	.1166	30.7	0	0	0	1	1	0	0	0	0	0	0	0	0	0	0	1	0	0	0	0	0	0	0	1	0
bureaucracy	7	.2771	.4435	36.5	0	0	1	0	2	2	2	0	0	1	0	0	0	0	0	0	0	0	0	0	0	1	0	5	0
bureaucrats	3	.2332	.1690	32.3	0	0	2	0	0	0	1	0	0	0	0	0	0	0	0	0	0	0	0	0	0	2	0	1	0
bureaus	5	.4321	.4605	36.6	0	0	0	0	1	0	4	0	0	0	0	1	0	2	0	0	0	0	1	0	0	0	1	0	0
burgeoning	4	.3720	.3216	35.1	1	0	0	0	1	1	1	0	0	0	0	0	0	0	0	0	0	0	0	0	1	0	1	2	0
Burger	9	.3227	.6585	38.2	0	0	0	0	7	1	1	0	0	0	0	0	0	3	0	0	0	0	0	0	0	0	1	5	0
Burger's	2	.0000	.0389	25.9	0	0	0	0	0	0	2	0	0	0	0	0	0	2	0	0	0	0	0	0	0	0	0	0	0
Burgess	3	.0000	.1370	31.4	0	0	3	0	0	0	0	0	3	0	0	0	0	0	0	0	0	0	0	0	0	0	0	0	0
burgesses	2	.2285	.1129	30.5	0	0	0	0	1	0	1	0	0	0	0	0	0	1	0	0	0	0	0	0	0	0	1	0	0
Burgesses	6	.2378	.3617	35.6	2	0	0	0	0	4	0	0	0	0	0	0	0	4	0	0	0	0	0	0	0	2	0	0	0
Burgher	2	.0000	.0914	29.6	0	0	0	0	2	0	0	0	2	0	0	0	0	0	0	0	0	0	0	0	0	0	0	0	0
burghers	3	.1832	.1417	31.5	0	0	0	1	0	0	1	1	0	0	0	2	0	0	0	1	0	0	0	0	0	0	0	0	0
burglar	12	.5128	1.3822	41.4	5	0	0	2	2	3	0	0	6	0	0	1	0	1	0	0	0	0	0	0	0	1	0	3	0
burglars	6	.0000	.2741	34.4	1	2	1	0	2	0	0	0	6	0	0	0	0	0	0	0	0	0	0	0	0	0	0	0	0
burglary	2	.1170	.0651	28.1	0	0	0	0	1	0	1	0	0	0	1	0	0	1	0	0	0	0	0	0	0	0	0	0	0
Burgoyne	6	.3692	.4961	37.0	0	0	0	0	2	4	0	0	0	0	0	0	0	4	0	0	1	0	0	0	0	0	1	0	0
Burgundy	4	.3464	.3040	34.8	2	0	0	0	1	1	0	0	0	0	0	0	0	1	1	0	0	0	0	0	0	0	2	0	0
burial	14	.6302	1.8311	42.6	4	0	0	2	4	1	3	0	3	1	0	2	0	0	0	0	1	0	0	0	4	1	0	2	0
burials	2	.2401	.1133	30.5	0	0	1	0	0	0	0	1	0	0	0	0	0	0	0	0	0	0	0	0	0	1	1	0	0
buried	162	.7781	25.536	54.1	21	22	23	23	35	15	18	5	40	5	1	14	2	12	2	13	7	0	0	0	14	27	18	6	1
buries	4	.3362	.3304	35.2	2	0	1	1	0	0	0	0	1	0	0	0	0	0	0	2	0	0	0	0	0	1	0	0	0
Burk	3	.2009	.1407	31.5	1	0	0	2	0	0	0	0	0	0	0	0	0	0	0	0	2	0	0	0	1	0	0	0	0
Burke	21	.3580	1.8514	42.7	0	4	1	0	10	6	0	0	10	0	0	0	0	0	0	0	1	0	0	0	9	0	0	1	0
Burke's	4	.1112	.1666	32.2	0	0	0	0	0	4	0	0	1	0	0	0	0	0	0	0	0	0	0	0	0	3	0	0	0
Burl	2	.0000	.0243	23.9	0	0	0	0	0	0	2	0	0	0	0	0	0	0	0	0	0	0	0	0	0	0	0	2	0
burlap	19	.3079	1.2956	41.1	2	1	4	5	4	1	0	2	0	0	0	0	0	5	1	1	0	6	0	0	1	1	0	4	0
burlesque	3	.2088	.1442	31.6	0	0	0	0	2	1	0	0	0	0	0	0	0	0	0	0	2	0	0	0	0	0	1	0	0
Burlington	3	.2732	.1800	32.6	0	1	0	0	1	0	0	1	0	0	1	0	0	0	0	0	0	0	0	0	1	0	0	1	0
burly	10	.4172	.9166	39.6	0	0	0	0	9	1	0	0	2	0	0	2	0	0	0	0	0	0	0	2	1	0	0	3	0
Burma	25	.4801	2.5865	44.1	1	0	1	8	10	2	2	1	1	0	0	0	0	14	0	0	1	0	0	0	0	2	1	6	0
Burma's	3	.1937	.1495	31.7	0	0	0	2	1	0	0	0	0	0	0	0	0	1	0	0	0	0	0	0	0	0	0	2	0
Burmese	9	.1501	.3708	35.7	0	0	0	7	2	0	0	0	0	0	0	0	0	2	0	0	0	0	0	0	0	0	0	7	0
burn	190	.7922	30.471	54.8	35	37	36	25	33	9	13	2	46	4	0	16	1	15	0	54	2	0	0	5	10	13	14	10	0
Burn	4	.0974	.1495	31.7	0	0	1	0	3	0	0	0	1	0	0	0	0	0	0	0	0	0	0	0	3	0	0	0	0
burned	264	.8354	44.431	56.5	51	46	37	29	37	34	28	2	89	15	1	23	0	26	0	42	5	0	0	2	24	19	5	13	0
burned-out	4	.4568	.4091	36.1	0	1	0	1	0	0	1	1	1	0	0	0	0	0	0	1	0	0	0	0	0	1	0	1	0
burner	20	.4465	2.0749	43.2	6	1	2	4	0	3	4	0	9	0	0	0	0	0	0	7	0	0	0	2	1	0	0	1	0
burners	9	.3444	.7089	38.5	0	0	0	0	4	3	2	0	0	1	0	0	0	0	0	7	0	0	1	0	0	0	0	0	0
burning	280	.8970	49.989	57.0	42	53	49	32	53	28	21	2	66	7	7	18	1	27	1	68	6	1	3	4	21	19	18	13	0
Burning	8	.4727	.8843	39.5	1	4	1	0	1	1	0	0	5	0	0	0	0	1	0	0	1	0	0	0	1	0	0	0	0
burnished	12	.5326	1.3384	41.3	2	1	0	1	4	0	4	0	1	2	0	3	0	1	0	0	0	0	0	0	4	0	1	0	0
burnout	3	.3815	.2534	34.0	1	1	0	0	1	0	0	0	0	0	0	0	0	1	0	0	0	0	0	0	0	1	0	1	0
burns	91	.7860	14.402	51.6	9	17	16	6	10	23	10	0	5	2	2	4	4	5	3	47	0	0	2	1	1	8	5	2	0
Burns	27	.5260	3.2118	45.1	16	2	6	0	0	1	2	0	17	4	0	2	0	0	0	0	0	0	0	0	0	1	3	0	0
Burns's	2	.0000	.0914	29.6	1	1	0	0	0	0	0	0	2	0	0	0	0	0	0	0	0	0	0	0	0	0	0	0	0
Burnside	6	.2445	.3295	35.2	0	3	0	0	1	1	1	0	0	0	1	0	0	0	0	0	0	0	0	0	0	0	5	0	0
burnt	43	.7157	6.2806	48.0	7	8	0	8	13	0	6	1	9	3	0	4	0	1	3	0	1	0	0	0	10	9	2	1	0
Burnt	3	.0000	.0352	25.5	0	3	0	0	0	0	0	0	0	0	0	0	0	0	0	0	0	0	0	0	3	0	0	0	0
burp	2	.1948	.1250	31.0	0	0	1	0	1	0	0	0	1	0	0	0	0	0	0	0	0	0	0	0	0	1	0	0	0
burr	8	.4577	.8477	39.3	2	2	0	0	4	0	0	0	4	0	0	0	0	0	0	1	0	0	0	0	2	0	1	0	0
Burr	15	.0000	.6852	38.4	0	0	12	0	1	2	0	0	15	0	0	0	0	0	0	0	0	0	0	0	0	0	0	0	0
Burr's	4	.2420	.3089	34.9	0	0	3	0	0	1	0	0	3	0	0	0	0	1	0	0	0	0	0	0	0	0	0	0	0
burred	2	.0000	.0050	17.0	0	0	0	0	2	0	0	0	0	0	0	0	0	0	0	0	0	0	0	2	0	0	0	0	0
burro	55	.6013	7.2085	48.6	24	14	9	4	4	0	0	0	33	0	0	4	0	6	0	0	7	0	0	0	2	0	2	1	0
burro's	2	.0000	.0914	29.6	1	0	0	1	0	0	0	0	2	0	0	0	0	0	0	0	0	0	0	0	0	0	0	0	0
burros	23	.1778	1.2286	40.9	18	0	2	1	2	0	0	0	3	0	0	0	0	19	0	0	0	0	0	0	0	0	1	0	0
Burroughs	4	.0000	.0325	25.1	0	0	0	0	0	0	4	0	0	0	0	0	0	0	4	0	0	0	0	0	0	0	0	0	0
Burroughs'	2	.0000	.0162	22.1	0	0	0	0	0	0	2	0	0	0	0	0	0	0	2	0	0	0	0	0	0	0	0	0	0
burrow	49	.6749	6.8538	48.4	18	3	5	8	11	1	3	0	13	0	0	2	0	0	2	8	0	0	0	0	5	11	7	1	0
burrowed	6	.4804	.6594	38.2	0	0	1	1	3	1	0	0	3	0	0	1	0	1	0	0	0	0	0	0	1	0	0	0	0
burrowers	2	.0000	.0209	23.2	0	0	0	0	2	0	0	0	0	0	0	0	0	0	0	0	0	0	0	0	0	0	2	0	0
burrowing	17	.6471	2.3142	43.6	6	1	1	0	5	1	3	0	6	0	0	3	0	2	0	2	0	0	0	0	1	1	2	0	0
Burrowing	2	.0000	.0914	29.6	2	0	0	0	0	0	0	0	2	0	0	0	0	0	0	0	0	0	0	0	0	0	0	0	0
burrows	26	.4776	2.6535	44.2	7	3	1	3	11	0	0	1	1	0	0	0	0	0	0	8	0	0	0	0	1	6	9	1	0
burrs	8	.5214	.8910	39.5	3	1	0	0	3	1	0	0	1	0	0	1	0	0	0	2	0	0	0	0	0	2	0	2	0
burst	194	.8229	32.245	55.1	30	40	27	33	35	19	6	4	74	1	4	16	0	13	1	10	2	1	1	0	32	19	6	14	0
bursting	36	.7048	5.2107	47.2	5	4	5	6	7	5	3	1	10	2	2	5	0	0	0	2	0	0	0	0	6	4	3	2	0
bursts	19	.6743	2.6300	44.2	0	2	4	1	6	2	3	1	3	0	0	0	0	0	0	5	3	0	1	0	1	1	3	2	0
Burt	3	.3835	.2484	34.0	0	1	1	0	0	1	0	0	0	0	0	1	1	0	0	0	0	0	0	0	0	0	1	0	0
Burton	3	.2236	.1570	32.0	0	0	0	0	0	2	1	0	0	1	0	2	0	0	0	0	0	0	0	0	0	0	0	0	0
bury	52	.6207	6.7017	48.3	6	1	2	11	24	5	3	0	10	1	0	18	0	1	5	2	0	0	0	0	8	4	1	2	0
burying	12	.6139	1.5557	41.9	1	2	2	2	3	2	0	0	4	1	0	0	0	0	0	0	0	0	0	0	1	2	2	2	0
bus	345	.8491	58.869	57.7	112	76	43	44	26	11	29	4	120	31	6	9	31	62	15	9	3	0	2	0	21	7	2	27	0
Bus	7	.5718	.8383	39.2	2	2	3	0	0	0	0	0	1	2	0	1	1	1	0	0	1	0	0	0	0	0	0	0	0
Buscerck	4	.0000	.0429	26.3	0	0	0	0	0	0	4	0	0	0	0	4	0	0	0	0	0	0	0	0	0	0	0	0	0
Busch	8	.0000	.3655	35.6	0	0	0	8	0	0	0	0	8	0	0	0	0	0	0	0	0	0	0	0	0	0	0	0	0
Buselapi	2	.0000	.0914	29.6	0	0	0	2	0	0	0	0	2	0	0	0	0	0	0	0	0	0	0	0	0	0	0	0	0
buses	61	.7092	8.8786	49.5	14	12	8	11	7	4	5	0	12	1	3	1	5	23	1	2	1	0	0	0	0	1	4	7	0
bush	111	.8544	19.017	52.8	22	23	21	22	18	3	1	1	37	2	3	8	0	6	8	7	3	1	0	0	14	13	4	5	0
Bush	25	.5032	2.9555	44.7	11	5	0	6	1	1	0	1	20	0	1	1	0	0	0	1	0	0	0	0	1	1	0	0	0
bushed	2	.2440	.1132	30.5	0	0	0	2	0	0	0	0	0	0	0	1	0	0	0	0	0	0	0	0	0	0	0	1	0
bushel	21	.5882	2.6353	44.2	2	8	2	0	3	4	1	1	7	0	1	3	7	0	0	1	0	0	0	0	1	1	0	0	0
bushels	30	.6819	4.2287	46.3	8	5	5	2	5	1	3	1	7	0	1	0	11	4	1	2	0	0	0	1	0	2	1	0	0
bushes	196	.8405	33.195	55.2	63	43	15	17	40	10	6	2	75	8	2	14	7	19	1	18	1	1	0	0	24	21	2	3	0
bushing	2	.0000	.0243	23.9	0	0	0	0	2	0	0	0	0	0	0	0	0	0	0	0	0	0	0	0	0	0	0	2	0

7D burdening
XH Burdette
9R bureaucracies
8R bureaucrat's
7R bureaucratic
4G burger
7D burgher's
9D burglaries
8D burglarizing
XR burgling
9Q burgomaster
7Q Burgundians
9D burial-ground
5A Burica
8R Burkhart
7R burl
6F burlap-like
9R Burma-Shave
6R Burmans
7R burn-outs
5J burn'd
9H burnable
7N Burnach
5A burned-over
XH Burnet
XR Burnham
7D burnin'
7A burnishing
8B Burns'
8F Burnside's
4Q burnsides
9B Burnsville
7L burping
8M burring
9D Burris
6R Burros
5P Bursa
9B bursted
6R Burwood
9D buryin'
7J Busch-Reisinger
4N Bush-Buck
4R bush-jacket
XH bush-leaguer
4A Bush's
3N Bushes
7J Bushi

Word Type	F	D	U	SFI	3 Gr 3	4 Gr 4	5 Gr 5	6 Gr 6	7 Gr 7	8 Gr 8	9 Gr 9	X UnGr	A Read	B Eng & Gr	C Comp	D Lit	E Math	F Soc Stud	G Spell	H Sci	J Music	K Art	L Home Ec	M Shop	N Lib F	P Lib NF	Q Lib Ref	R Mag	S Rel
bushings	5	.0000	.0608	27.8	0	0	0	0	5	0	0	0	0	0	0	0	0	0	0	0	0	0	0	0	0	0	0	5	0
bushman	3	.0000	.1370	31.4	0	0	0	3	0	0	0	0	3	0	0	0	0	0	0	0	0	0	0	0	0	0	0	0	0
Bushman	8	.3071	.5349	37.3	0	0	2	0	3	0	3	0	0	0	2	0	0	0	0	0	0	0	0	0	0	2	4	0	0
bushmaster	2	.2412	.1141	30.6	1	0	0	0	0	1	0	0	0	1	0	0	0	0	0	0	0	0	0	0	0	1	0	0	0
bushmen	3	.0000	.1370	31.4	0	0	0	3	0	0	0	0	3	0	0	0	0	0	0	0	0	0	0	0	0	0	0	0	0
Bushmen	11	.3066	.8227	39.2	1	0	0	2	8	0	0	0	2	0	0	0	0	5	0	0	0	0	0	0	0	0	4	0	0
Bushnell	2	.0000	.0209	23.2	0	0	1	0	0	0	1	0	0	0	0	0	0	0	0	0	0	0	0	0	0	0	2	0	0
bushy	25	.7048	3.6576	45.6	7	5	2	4	3	1	2	1	11	0	1	1	0	0	0	1	1	1	0	0	2	3	0	4	0
Bushy	3	.0000	.1370	31.4	0	3	0	0	0	0	0	0	3	0	0	0	0	0	0	0	0	0	0	0	0	0	0	0	0
Bushytail	3	.0000	.0365	25.6	3	0	0	0	0	0	0	0	0	0	0	0	0	0	0	0	0	0	0	0	0	0	0	3	0
busied	5	.2086	.3320	35.2	1	1	0	0	2	1	0	0	3	0	0	0	0	0	0	0	0	0	0	0	2	0	0	0	0
busier	5	.2422	.3874	35.9	2	1	1	1	0	0	0	0	4	0	0	0	0	0	0	0	0	0	0	0	0	1	0	0	0
busiest	20	.5912	2.5125	44.0	3	5	5	3	2	0	2	0	5	0	0	0	0	7	0	0	0	0	0	0	1	2	2	3	0
busily	27	.6558	3.7031	45.7	5	6	2	5	4	5	0	0	9	0	0	4	0	0	0	4	0	1	0	0	4	3	0	2	0
business	705	.8596	121.08	60.8	81	76	104	67	144	107	112	14	133	78	4	55	13	174	7	13	9	2	0	4	34	65	49	65	0
Business	8	.4969	.8567	39.3	1	0	2	0	2	1	2	0	1	0	0	2	0	2	0	1	0	0	0	0	0	0	0	2	0
business-like	2	.1814	.1187	30.7	0	0	0	1	1	0	0	0	1	0	0	0	0	0	0	0	0	0	0	0	0	0	0	1	0
businesses	65	.5265	7.2917	48.6	7	7	9	8	7	11	16	0	4	2	0	0	2	37	0	1	0	0	0	0	0	2	8	9	0
businesslike	8	.5610	.9645	39.8	0	2	1	2	0	2	1	0	3	1	0	1	0	0	0	0	0	0	1	0	1	1	0	0	0
businessman	31	.6409	4.1751	46.2	1	3	7	3	5	8	4	0	9	2	0	0	0	11	1	0	0	0	0	0	0	3	3	2	0
businessman's	2	.0000	.0389	25.9	1	0	0	0	0	1	0	0	0	0	0	0	0	2	0	0	0	0	0	0	0	0	0	0	0
businessmen	50	.6422	6.6539	48.2	10	0	12	4	6	13	5	0	6	2	1	0	0	22	1	0	0	0	0	0	0	6	3	9	0
buskin	2	.0000	.0162	22.1	0	2	0	0	0	0	0	0	0	0	0	0	0	0	2	0	0	0	0	0	0	0	0	0	0
BUSMAN	7	.0000	.0751	28.8	0	0	0	0	0	0	7	0	0	0	0	7	0	0	0	0	0	0	0	0	0	0	0	0	0
busses	6	.3191	.4528	36.6	2	1	1	1	0	1	0	0	0	0	0	0	1	4	0	1	0	0	0	0	0	0	0	0	0
bust	20	.5062	2.1151	43.3	0	1	0	2	4	4	8	1	2	0	1	9	0	0	0	0	0	0	4	0	0	2	1	1	0
busted	3	.3875	.2489	34.0	0	0	0	0	1	0	2	0	0	1	0	1	0	0	0	0	0	0	0	0	1	0	0	0	0
Buster	27	.2212	2.0558	43.1	27	0	0	0	0	0	0	0	24	0	0	0	0	0	0	0	0	0	0	0	0	0	0	3	0
bustle	18	.6086	2.2977	43.6	2	5	2	2	2	2	3	0	5	0	0	3	0	0	0	0	3	0	1	0	0	4	0	2	0
bustled	5	.3841	.4756	36.8	0	1	0	2	1	1	0	0	3	0	0	1	0	0	0	0	0	0	0	0	1	0	0	0	0
bustling	23	.6166	2.9612	44.7	5	5	2	4	3	2	1	1	4	0	0	2	0	4	0	0	0	0	0	0	1	7	1	4	0
busy	495	.8984	88.695	59.5	133	123	55	77	43	36	22	6	187	13	6	28	0	85	10	19	13	2	7	1	48	40	10	26	0
but	19196	.9542	3620.2	75.6	3323	2940	2176	2544	3840	2137	1708	528	6175	767	197	1532	293	1532	249	1431	437	102	183	77	1936	1863	910	1501	11
But	4	.3567	.3537	35.5	1	1	0	2	0	0	0	0	2	0	0	0	0	0	0	0	1	0	0	0	0	1	0	0	0
BUT	2	.0000	.0914	29.6	1	1	0	0	0	0	0	0	2	0	0	0	0	0	0	0	0	0	0	0	0	0	0	0	0
Butch	10	.3668	.9666	39.9	0	5	4	0	0	1	0	0	8	0	0	1	0	0	0	0	0	0	0	0	0	0	0	1	0
butcher	32	.7164	4.7244	46.7	6	2	3	11	6	2	2	0	11	2	0	5	0	4	1	0	0	0	0	0	5	2	1	1	0
Butcher	7	.2401	.3936	36.0	0	0	4	0	3	0	0	0	0	0	0	0	0	0	0	0	0	0	0	0	4	0	0	3	0
butcher's	3	.3851	.2497	34.0	0	0	2	0	1	0	0	0	0	0	0	1	0	0	0	0	0	0	0	0	1	1	0	0	0
butchered	6	.3526	.4816	36.8	3	0	0	0	1	1	1	0	0	0	0	0	0	4	0	0	0	0	0	0	1	0	0	1	0
butchering	2	.2351	.1166	30.7	0	0	0	0	0	1	0	1	0	0	0	0	0	1	0	0	0	0	0	0	0	0	0	1	0
butchers	4	.1325	.1944	32.9	2	0	1	1	0	0	0	0	1	0	0	0	0	3	0	0	0	0	0	0	0	0	0	0	0
butchery	2	.2427	.1152	30.6	0	0	1	0	1	0	0	0	0	0	0	0	0	0	0	0	0	0	0	0	1	1	0	0	0
butler	11	.4507	1.1567	40.6	5	0	0	1	3	2	0	0	6	0	0	1	0	0	0	0	0	0	0	0	3	0	0	1	0
Butler	24	.5142	2.6188	44.2	0	2	2	1	13	3	3	0	4	0	0	12	0	0	0	0	0	0	1	0	1	2	3	1	0
Butler's	2	.0000	.0914	29.6	0	1	1	0	0	0	0	0	2	0	0	0	0	0	0	0	0	0	0	0	0	0	0	0	0
buts	4	.3755	.3686	35.7	0	2	1	1	0	0	0	0	2	0	0	0	0	0	0	0	0	0	0	0	1	1	0	0	0
butt	24	.4887	2.6086	44.2	1	3	1	3	13	3	0	0	9	0	0	0	0	0	0	0	0	0	0	2	2	9	0	2	0
butte	4	.3838	.3379	35.3	0	3	1	0	0	0	0	0	0	0	0	0	0	2	1	0	0	0	0	0	1	0	0	0	0
Butte	10	.4943	1.0666	40.3	1	5	0	2	1	1	0	0	1	0	0	1	0	5	0	0	0	0	0	0	0	0	1	2	0
butted	4	.3074	.2706	34.3	0	0	0	1	2	0	1	0	0	0	1	1	0	0	0	0	0	0	0	0	0	2	0	0	0
butter	275	.6474	37.172	55.7	76	45	34	20	56	13	24	7	86	11	0	7	11	30	7	19	0	0	43	0	15	21	13	12	0
Butter	9	.3028	.7169	38.6	4	0	4	1	0	0	0	0	4	0	0	0	0	1	0	0	0	0	0	0	0	4	0	0	0
buttercup	4	.4710	.3950	36.0	0	0	1	2	1	0	0	0	0	1	0	0	0	0	1	1	1	0	0	0	0	0	0	0	0
Buttercup	4	.0000	.1827	32.6	0	4	0	0	0	0	0	0	4	0	0	0	0	0	0	0	0	0	0	0	0	0	0	0	0
buttercups	2	.1387	.0689	28.4	1	0	0	0	0	1	0	0	0	0	1	0	0	0	0	0	0	0	0	0	0	1	0	0	0
buttered	20	.4942	2.0793	43.2	0	2	1	0	7	3	5	2	2	3	0	2	0	0	0	1	0	0	5	0	1	2	0	4	0
butterfat	5	.1070	.1239	30.9	0	0	0	0	4	1	0	0	0	0	0	0	0	0	1	0	0	0	4	0	0	0	0	0	0
Butterfield	2	.2152	.1357	31.3	0	0	0	1	0	1	0	0	1	0	0	0	0	1	0	0	0	0	0	0	0	0	0	0	0
butterflies	81	.7470	12.314	50.9	31	14	5	9	20	1	1	0	18	1	0	2	6	1	0	17	6	1	0	0	2	4	19	4	0
Butterflies	2	.2411	.1091	30.4	1	0	0	0	0	1	0	0	0	0	0	1	0	0	0	0	1	0	0	0	0	0	0	0	0
butterfly	77	.7604	11.922	50.8	26	13	17	6	14	0	1	0	21	1	2	3	1	0	0	17	2	0	0	0	6	9	12	3	0
Butterfly	4	.3827	.3305	35.2	2	0	0	0	1	1	0	0	0	1	0	0	0	0	0	0	1	0	0	0	0	2	0	0	0
butterfly's	5	.3306	.3863	35.9	4	0	0	0	0	1	0	0	1	0	1	0	1	0	0	0	0	0	0	0	0	2	0	0	0
buttering	2	.0000	.0064	18.1	0	0	0	0	0	2	0	0	0	0	0	0	0	0	0	0	0	0	2	0	0	0	0	0	0
buttermilk	24	.4990	2.4804	43.9	0	14	0	0	4	2	3	1	0	0	0	0	2	0	0	0	4	0	5	0	4	8	0	1	0
butternuts	2	.2331	.1157	30.6	0	0	0	2	0	0	0	0	0	0	0	0	0	0	0	1	0	0	0	0	1	0	0	0	0
buttery	2	.2441	.1127	30.5	0	1	0	0	0	1	0	0	0	0	0	0	0	0	0	0	0	0	0	0	1	0	1	0	0
buttocks	2	.0000	.0209	23.2	0	0	0	0	0	0	2	0	0	0	0	0	0	0	0	0	0	0	0	0	0	0	2	0	0
button	130	.8090	21.186	53.3	44	22	22	17	7	8	8	2	35	1	1	5	8	3	0	19	29	1	5	3	4	3	2	11	0
Button	75	.0318	1.4847	41.7	70	5	0	0	0	0	0	0	5	0	0	0	0	0	0	0	0	0	0	0	70	0	0	0	0
Button's	2	.0000	.0234	23.7	2	0	0	0	0	0	0	0	0	0	0	0	0	0	0	0	0	0	0	0	2	0	0	0	0
buttoned	15	.4833	1.6415	42.2	5	3	1	2	3	1	0	0	7	0	0	2	0	0	0	0	0	0	0	0	3	3	0	0	0
buttonhole	8	.2509	.4308	36.3	0	0	0	0	1	5	2	0	0	0	0	0	2	0	0	0	0	0	5	1	0	0	0	0	0
buttonholes	8	.1075	.2055	33.1	0	0	2	0	1	1	4	0	0	0	0	2	0	0	0	0	0	0	6	0	0	0	0	0	0
buttoning	2	.1674	.0805	29.1	0	1	0	0	1	0	0	0	0	0	0	0	0	0	0	0	0	0	1	0	0	1	0	0	0
buttons	113	.7932	18.102	52.6	27	31	15	11	8	7	13	1	31	2	1	2	23	3	0	5	16	2	8	0	7	3	2	8	0
Buttons	25	.1074	1.0014	40.0	16	0	0	9	0	0	0	0	7	0	0	0	0	0	0	0	0	0	0	0	18	0	0	0	0
buttress	4	.3662	.3647	35.6	0	0	0	1	0	2	0	1	2	0	0	0	0	1	0	0	0	0	0	0	0	0	1	0	0
buttresses	2	.1473	.0686	28.4	0	0	0	0	0	0	2	0	0	0	0	1	0	0	0	0	0	1	0	0	0	0	0	0	0
butts	3	.2309	.1631	32.1	0	0	0	0	1	0	0	2	0	0	0	1	0	0	0	0	0	0	0	0	0	0	0	2	0
Buxton	3	.0000	.0365	25.6	0	0	0	3	0	0	0	0	0	0	0	0	0	0	0	0	0	0	0	0	0	0	0	3	0
buy	872	.8634	150.84	61.8	235	170	94	91	125	74	64	19	276	32	2	24	117	180	13	17	8	2	37	4	41	59	13	47	0
buyer	30	.6474	3.9951	46.0	3	7	1	0	11	1	4	3	3	0	0	5	2	7	1	0	0	0	0	0	0	1	4	7	0
buyer's	3	.3764	.2475	33.9	0	1	0	0	1	1	0	0	0	1	0	1	0	1	0	0	0	0	0	0	0	0	0	0	0
buyers	19	.5726	2.2942	43.6	6	3	1	2	7	0	0	0	3	0	1	2	0	7	1	0	0	0	0	0	0	0	0	5	0
buyin'	2	.0000	.0234	23.7	0	0	2	0	0	0	0	0	0	0	0	0	0	0	0	0	0	0	0	0	2	0	0	0	0
buying	97	.6444	12.980	51.1	13	4	14	8	25	10	21	2	25	0	1	2	9	13	2	3	2	0	19	1	2	6	3	9	0
buys	41	.7807	6.4523	48.1	16	2	5	4	7	1	5	1	4	0	0	2	8	9	0	5	1	0	2	0	1	4	2	3	0
Buz	2	.0000	.0914	29.6	0	0	0	0	0	2	0	0	2	0	0	0	0	0	0	0	0	0	0	0	0	0	0	0	0
buzz	28	.7782	4.4208	46.5	8	3	4	0	6	4	2	1	9	2	1	2	0	0	3	2	1	0	0	1	0	4	0	3	0
Buzz	39	.5338	4.5917	46.6	20	0	3	2	3	0	11	0	18	1	0	10	0	2	0	0	0	0	0	0	5	0	0	3	0
Buzzard	6	.2227	.3179	35.0	3	2	1	0	0	0	0	0	0	0	0	0	0	0	0	0	0	0	0	0	4	0	0	2	0
buzzards	2	.1948	.1250	31.0	0	0	2	0	0	0	0	0	1	0	0	0	0	0	0	0	0	0	0	0	0	1	0	0	0
buzzed	21	.7103	3.1138	44.9	10	3	2	1	3	1	1	0	11	0	0	1	0	2	1	0	1	0	0	0	2	1	0	2	0

6A Bushiya
8F Bushki
6A bushland
6A bushman's
7Q bushmasters
7C bushmeat
6J Bushvelt
6P Bushyhead
8R businessmen's
9D Busman
9Q Busoni
6R Buss
7R Bussell
7R bussing
6A buster
3A Buster's
4P busting
6J busybody
8D busying
7B but-ur
9B but's
8G butane
5D butch
4A Butch's
5N Butcher's
5N Butchers
XR butlers
9P Butt
9R butt-of-jokes
9D butt-shaft
3A BUTTER
7D butter's
8F ButterfieldOverland
4A Butterfields
3A butterfish
6A buttermaking
5N Butters
4R Butterscotch
4P butterwoman
6R buttes
7Q butting
XR Button-Eyes
8R button-down
7D button-down-the-front
9Q button-pushing
4N buttonhook
4P buttonless
6R Butts
7R buttstock
5Q Buxaceae
5Q Buxus
7D buyers'
6D buzz-saw
8B buzzard

Word Type	F	D	U	SFI	3 Gr 3	4 Gr 4	5 Gr 5	6 Gr 6	7 Gr 7	8 Gr 8	9 Gr 9	X UnGr	A Read	B Eng & Gr	C Comp	D Lit	E Math	F Soc Stud	G Spell	H Sci	J Music	K Art	L Home Ec	M Shop	N Lib F	P Lib NF	Q Lib Ref	R Mag	S Rel
buzzer	13	.1172	.4206	36.2	0	0	0	1	2	8	1	1	1	0	0	0	0	0	0	3	0	0	0	8	0	0	0	1	0
buzzes	6	.4799	.6059	37.8	0	1	0	2	2	1	0	0	0	0	0	2	0	0	1	2	1	0	0	0	0	0	0	0	0
buzzing	48	.7701	7.5520	48.8	13	8	7	6	7	5	1	1	20	7	1	4	0	1	1	2	0	0	0	0	5	4	1	2	0
BW	2	.0000	.0299	24.8	0	0	0	1	0	1	0	0	0	0	0	0	2	0	0	0	0	0	0	0	0	0	0	0	0
bx	5	.0000	.0748	28.7	0	0	0	0	0	0	5	0	0	0	0	0	5	0	0	0	0	0	0	0	0	0	0	0	0
BX	2	.2446	.1184	30.7	1	0	0	1	0	0	0	0	0	0	0	0	1	0	0	0	0	0	0	0	0	1	0	0	0
by	20189	.9879	3923.8	75.9	2121	2316	2500	2648	4355	2981	2660	608	3275	1085	236	787	2054	2282	843	2052	1171	228	327	372	843	1349	1942	1328	15
BY	2	.2413	.1212	30.8	0	0	0	2	0	0	0	0	0	0	0	0	1	0	0	1	0	0	0	0	0	0	0	0	0
by-line	2	.1948	.1250	31.0	0	1	0	0	1	0	0	0	1	0	0	0	0	0	0	0	0	0	0	0	0	1	0	0	0
by-product	11	.5181	1.2415	40.9	3	0	4	1	1	0	2	0	3	0	0	0	0	0	0	4	0	0	1	0	0	0	2	1	0
by-products	8	.4830	.8193	39.1	1	1	1	0	1	1	3	0	0	0	0	0	0	3	0	1	0	0	0	1	0	1	2	0	0
by-ways	2	.1621	.0746	28.7	0	0	0	0	1	0	1	0	0	0	1	1	0	0	0	0	0	0	0	0	0	0	0	0	0
Bye	2	.0000	.0243	23.9	0	0	2	0	0	0	0	0	0	0	0	0	0	0	0	0	0	0	0	0	0	0	0	2	0
bye-bye	2	.2305	.1080	30.3	0	0	0	0	0	2	0	0	0	0	0	0	0	0	1	0	0	0	0	0	0	1	0	0	0
bygone	7	.4572	.6932	38.4	0	2	0	0	1	2	2	0	1	0	0	0	0	1	0	0	0	1	0	0	0	2	1	1	0
bypass	4	.3366	.3291	35.2	0	0	0	0	2	1	1	0	1	0	0	0	0	0	0	2	0	0	0	0	0	0	0	1	0
byplay	2	.2446	.1142	30.6	0	0	0	0	1	0	1	0	0	0	0	0	0	0	0	0	0	0	0	0	1	0	0	1	0
Byrd	8	.4853	.8464	39.3	0	0	1	2	1	4	0	0	2	1	0	3	0	0	0	1	1	0	0	0	0	0	0	0	0
byre	2	.1948	.1250	31.0	0	1	0	0	1	0	0	0	1	0	0	0	0	0	0	0	0	0	0	0	0	1	0	0	0
Byron	9	.3228	.6456	38.1	0	0	0	1	6	0	2	0	0	0	0	0	0	0	0	0	0	0	0	0	3	1	0	5	0
Bysshe	2	.2446	.1123	30.5	0	0	0	1	0	0	1	0	0	1	0	0	0	0	0	0	0	0	0	0	0	0	1	0	0
bystander	2	.1551	.0728	28.6	1	1	0	0	0	0	0	0	0	0	1	0	0	0	0	0	0	0	0	0	1	0	0	0	0
bystanders	5	.3861	.4798	36.8	0	1	1	2	0	1	0	0	3	0	0	0	0	0	0	0	0	0	0	0	0	1	0	1	0
Byzantine	21	.5563	2.4241	43.8	0	0	6	2	4	3	3	3	1	1	0	0	0	4	0	0	1	2	0	0	0	4	7	1	0
Byzantines	4	.3813	.3309	35.2	0	0	2	0	0	1	0	1	0	1	0	0	0	0	0	0	0	0	0	0	0	2	1	0	0
Byzantium	4	.2348	.2372	33.8	0	1	0	0	3	0	0	0	0	0	0	0	0	3	0	0	0	0	0	0	0	0	1	0	0
bz-z-z	2	.0000	.0162	22.1	2	0	0	0	0	0	0	0	0	0	0	0	0	0	0	0	2	0	0	0	0	0	0	0	0
B1	6	.4298	.5568	37.5	0	0	4	1	0	0	1	0	0	0	0	0	1	0	0	3	0	0	1	0	0	0	1	0	0
b2	4	.0000	.0599	27.8	0	0	0	0	0	4	0	0	0	0	0	0	4	0	0	0	0	0	0	0	0	0	0	0	0
B2	7	.3364	.5402	37.3	0	0	4	1	1	0	1	0	0	0	0	0	1	0	0	5	0	0	1	0	0	0	0	0	0
B5	2	.1738	.0790	29.0	0	0	1	0	0	0	1	0	0	0	0	0	0	0	0	0	0	0	0	1	0	0	1	0	0
c	1005	.7476	152.04	61.8	123	101	130	129	194	183	131	14	160	71	2	2	284	45	240	38	11	6	15	18	3	9	75	26	0
C	945	.7206	138.18	61.4	202	125	122	114	132	107	124	19	115	20	6	3	313	20	26	94	241	3	14	12	0	18	28	32	0
C**	31	.3252	2.8438	44.5	24	0	0	0	5	0	0	2	27	0	0	0	0	0	0	0	0	0	0	0	0	0	2	2	0
C-C	2	.1937	.0847	29.3	0	0	1	0	0	0	1	0	0	0	0	0	0	0	0	0	1	0	0	1	0	0	0	0	0
c-c-come	2	.0000	.0234	23.7	0	0	0	2	0	0	0	0	0	0	0	0	0	0	0	0	0	0	0	0	2	0	0	0	0
C-major	9	.0000	.0728	28.6	0	0	4	5	0	0	0	0	0	0	0	0	0	0	0	0	9	0	0	0	0	0	0	0	0
C-5A	9	.0000	.1094	30.4	0	0	0	0	9	0	0	0	0	0	0	0	0	0	0	0	0	0	0	0	0	0	0	9	0
c/d	8	.0000	.1197	30.8	0	0	1	0	5	0	2	0	0	0	0	0	8	0	0	0	0	0	0	0	0	0	0	0	0
c/12	2	.0000	.0299	24.8	0	0	2	0	0	0	0	0	0	0	0	0	2	0	0	0	0	0	0	0	0	0	0	0	0
c/6	2	.0000	.0299	24.8	0	0	2	0	0	0	0	0	0	0	0	0	2	0	0	0	0	0	0	0	0	0	0	0	0
c/8	3	.0000	.0449	26.5	0	0	3	0	0	0	0	0	0	0	0	0	3	0	0	0	0	0	0	0	0	0	0	0	0
c's	2	.0000	.0219	23.4	0	0	0	0	0	0	2	0	0	2	0	0	0	0	0	0	0	0	0	0	0	0	0	0	0
C's	4	.3732	.3288	35.2	0	1	0	0	1	2	0	0	0	0	0	0	2	0	0	0	0	0	0	0	0	1	0	1	0
ca	4	.0996	.1523	31.8	1	0	0	1	0	0	2	0	1	0	0	0	0	0	0	0	0	0	0	0	0	0	0	3	0
Ca	2	.0000	.0394	26.0	0	0	0	0	0	1	1	0	0	0	0	0	0	0	0	2	0	0	0	0	0	0	0	0	0
CA	6	.0000	.0898	29.5	2	2	0	1	1	0	0	0	0	0	0	0	6	0	0	0	0	0	0	0	0	0	0	0	0
CaO	2	.0000	.0394	26.0	0	0	0	0	0	2	0	0	0	0	0	0	0	0	0	2	0	0	0	0	0	0	0	0	0
ca'n't	6	.0000	.0703	28.5	0	0	6	0	0	0	0	0	0	0	0	0	0	0	0	0	0	0	0	0	6	0	0	0	0
cab	61	.5878	7.9405	49.0	20	14	5	7	13	1	1	0	43	3	1	0	0	0	1	0	0	0	0	0	9	3	0	1	0
cabbage	139	.6694	19.957	53.0	95	8	8	6	5	6	6	5	100	1	1	1	2	5	2	7	0	0	7	0	7	5	1	0	0
cabbages	21	.6102	2.7804	44.4	4	5	6	3	3	0	0	0	12	2	0	1	0	0	0	2	0	0	0	0	2	2	0	0	0
Cabildo	4	.0000	.0778	28.9	0	4	0	0	0	0	0	0	0	0	0	0	0	4	0	0	0	0	0	0	0	0	0	0	0
cabin	404	.7729	64.140	58.1	48	138	35	45	81	34	17	6	213	7	3	24	6	18	9	7	1	0	0	0	38	52	2	24	0
Cabin	12	.5252	1.3287	41.2	2	0	2	0	2	4	2	0	0	1	0	2	0	6	0	0	0	0	0	0	0	2	0	1	0
cabinet	63	.5506	7.1754	48.6	4	0	5	3	17	19	15	0	8	2	0	4	0	4	0	0	4	0	13	12	1	3	9	3	0
Cabinet	32	.4343	3.1095	44.9	2	0	1	0	4	11	14	0	4	0	0	0	0	20	0	0	0	0	0	0	0	2	3	3	0
cabinetmaker	4	.0000	.0579	27.6	0	0	0	0	4	0	0	0	0	0	0	0	0	0	0	0	0	0	0	0	0	4	0	0	0
cabinetmakers	2	.1948	.1250	31.0	0	0	0	1	1	0	0	0	1	0	0	0	0	0	0	0	0	0	0	0	0	1	0	0	0
cabinetmaking	6	.0000	.0869	29.4	0	1	0	0	5	0	0	0	0	0	0	0	0	0	0	0	0	0	0	0	0	6	0	0	0
cabinets	11	.4002	.9194	39.6	0	1	0	0	4	3	3	0	0	0	0	0	0	1	0	0	0	0	3	3	0	3	1	0	0
cabinetwork	2	.1483	.0728	28.6	0	0	0	0	1	0	1	0	0	0	0	0	0	0	0	0	0	0	0	1	0	1	0	0	0
cabins	56	.7594	8.6790	49.4	12	9	14	3	14	2	1	1	16	0	0	6	2	12	1	4	0	0	0	0	4	6	1	4	0
cable	66	.4675	6.7739	48.3	3	12	3	6	19	14	7	2	19	3	1	1	0	2	0	5	0	0	0	15	0	3	3	14	0
cables	60	.6181	7.7543	48.9	8	5	14	4	15	0	12	2	12	0	0	0	0	9	0	6	0	0	0	1	0	5	14	13	0
cabman	2	.1787	.1174	30.7	0	0	0	2	0	0	0	0	1	0	0	0	0	0	0	0	0	0	0	0	1	0	0	0	0
caboose	15	.5396	1.7926	42.5	8	0	5	1	0	0	0	1	8	2	0	0	0	0	0	0	1	0	0	0	0	0	3	1	0
Cabot	10	.3416	.7996	39.0	5	0	3	1	0	0	1	0	2	0	0	0	0	2	0	0	0	0	0	0	0	0	5	1	0
Cabot's	2	.2285	.1129	30.5	1	0	1	0	0	0	0	0	0	0	0	0	0	1	0	0	0	0	0	0	0	0	1	0	0
Cabral	5	.0000	.0972	29.9	0	0	3	2	0	0	0	0	0	0	0	0	0	5	0	0	0	0	0	0	0	0	0	0	0
Cabrillo	11	.0000	.2139	33.3	0	11	0	0	0	0	0	0	0	0	0	0	0	11	0	0	0	0	0	0	0	0	0	0	0
cacao	26	.4211	2.5322	44.0	5	2	4	6	5	0	4	0	7	0	0	0	0	15	2	1	0	0	0	0	0	0	1	0	0
Caccini	2	.0000	.0290	24.6	0	0	0	2	0	0	0	0	0	0	0	0	0	0	0	0	0	0	0	0	0	2	0	0	0
cachalots	3	.0000	.0352	25.5	0	0	0	0	3	0	0	0	0	0	0	0	0	0	0	0	0	0	0	0	3	0	0	0	0
cache	5	.3698	.4028	36.1	2	0	0	0	1	0	2	0	0	0	0	2	0	0	0	0	0	0	0	0	0	2	0	1	0
cackled	4	.0000	.1827	32.6	2	1	0	1	0	0	0	0	4	0	0	0	0	0	0	0	0	0	0	0	0	0	0	0	0
cackling	6	.4312	.5883	37.7	2	2	0	1	0	0	1	0	2	0	0	2	0	1	0	0	1	0	0	0	0	0	0	0	0
cacophony	2	.2433	.1158	30.6	0	0	1	1	0	0	0	0	0	0	0	0	0	0	0	0	0	0	0	0	0	1	0	1	0
cacti	16	.3667	1.4171	41.5	6	2	5	0	2	0	1	0	6	0	0	0	0	0	0	6	0	2	0	0	0	0	2	0	0
cactus	74	.7385	11.325	50.5	39	15	6	3	6	0	3	2	37	2	0	1	0	3	0	9	0	1	0	0	3	12	2	4	0
cactuses	3	.0000	.0591	27.7	0	3	0	0	0	0	0	0	0	0	0	0	0	0	0	3	0	0	0	0	0	0	0	0	0
CAD	6	.0000	.0898	29.5	0	0	0	0	6	0	0	0	0	0	0	0	6	0	0	0	0	0	0	0	0	0	0	0	0
cadaver	4	.0904	.1412	31.5	0	0	0	0	1	0	3	0	1	0	0	0	0	0	0	0	0	0	0	0	0	0	3	0	0
Caddie	76	.2335	4.5531	46.6	0	0	10	61	5	0	0	0	15	0	0	10	0	0	0	0	0	0	0	0	51	0	0	0	0
Caddie's	8	.1397	.2994	34.8	0	0	0	8	0	0	0	0	0	0	0	1	0	0	0	0	0	0	0	0	7	0	0	0	0
caddis	2	.0000	.0243	23.9	0	0	0	0	0	0	0	2	0	0	0	0	0	0	0	0	0	0	0	0	0	0	0	2	0
Caddy	4	.0000	.1827	32.6	0	0	0	0	4	0	0	0	4	0	0	0	0	0	0	0	0	0	0	0	0	0	0	0	0
cadence	6	.2568	.3455	35.4	0	0	0	0	4	0	1	1	0	0	0	1	0	0	0	0	4	0	0	0	0	1	0	0	0
cadences	6	.1370	.2057	33.1	0	0	0	0	4	2	0	0	0	0	0	1	0	0	0	0	5	0	0	0	0	0	0	0	0
cadenza	7	.0000	.0566	27.5	0	4	0	0	0	1	2	0	0	0	0	0	0	0	0	0	7	0	0	0	0	0	0	0	0
cadet	6	.1277	.2726	34.4	4	0	1	1	0	0	0	0	2	0	0	0	0	0	0	0	0	0	0	0	0	0	0	4	0
Cadet	4	.0996	.1523	31.8	2	0	0	1	1	0	0	0	1	0	0	0	0	0	0	0	0	0	0	0	0	0	0	3	0

4H buzzers
6R BVD'S**
7J By
5F By-and-By
9D by-and-by
9D by-street
5R by-your-leave
5E BYC
9E Byer
8A Byfield
6A Byoo
7R bypassing
8F byproduct
8D Byrd's
7R Byrnes
9A Byron's
9Q bytownite
3A byway
7G byways
7F Byzas
9M B3
6Q C-OH
9E c-c
6N c-c-colt
6N c-come
9D c-o-c-a-c-o-l-a
6A c-r-onk
7P C-ration
3B C-100
7R C-141
3F c-4
7R C-4
7R C-5A's
7E c/**
8E c/-3
7E c/a
7E c/b
3A cll
3A crds
6R c'est
5Q C'lina
8A c'mon
8H CaCO3
9H CaF
5Q CaF2
9H CaSO
7N ca'm
7R Caaale
5Q caama
7E CAB
4G cab-in
5J cabacas
8F caballeros
7Q Caballo
8Q Cabanel
3P Cabbage
7B cabin-boy
6A cabinboy
7A cable's
5H cablegrams
5Q cabooses
3A Cabots
4F Cabrillo's
8F cabs
XD cacahuatl
7N cachalot's
9R caches
4A cackle
3A cacklings
9R Cactus
6F cactus-like
7Q cactuslike
6A caddie
7A caddied
6C caddies
9J cadenzas

Word Type	F	D	U	SFI	3 Gr 3	4 Gr 4	5 Gr 5	6 Gr 6	7 Gr 7	8 Gr 8	9 Gr 9	X UnGr	A Read	B Eng & Gr	C Comp	D Lit	E Math	F Soc Stud	G Spell	H Sci	J Music	K Art	L Home Ec	M Shop	N Lib F	P Lib NF	Q Lib Ref	R Mag	S Rel
cadets	23	.2774	1.7456	42.4	10	0	11	0	0	1	1	0	12	0	0	1	0	0	0	0	0	0	0	0	0	0	0	10	0
Cadets	4	.3597	.3542	35.5	1	0	1	1	0	1	0	0	2	0	0	0	0	0	0	0	1	0	0	0	0	0	0	1	0
cadets'	2	.0000	.0914	29.6	0	0	1	1	0	0	0	0	2	0	0	0	0	0	0	0	0	0	0	0	0	0	0	0	0
Cadi	10	.0000	.1172	30.7	0	0	10	0	0	0	0	0	0	0	0	0	0	0	0	0	0	0	0	0	10	0	0	0	0
Cadillac	68	.2707	5.7863	47.6	0	0	0	0	64	2	2	0	64	1	0	0	0	1	0	0	1	0	0	0	0	0	0	1	0
Cadillacs	4	.0000	.1827	32.6	0	0	0	0	3	0	1	0	4	0	0	0	0	0	0	0	0	0	0	0	0	0	0	0	0
Cadiz	2	.2408	.1204	30.8	0	1	0	0	1	0	0	0	0	0	0	0	0	1	0	0	0	0	0	0	0	1	0	0	0
cadmium	17	.4189	1.6703	42.2	6	0	0	7	2	2	0	0	6	0	0	0	0	0	0	9	0	0	0	1	0	0	0	1	0
Cadore	2	.0000	.0914	29.6	0	0	0	2	0	0	0	0	2	0	0	0	0	0	0	0	0	0	0	0	0	0	0	0	0
cadres	3	.0000	.0434	26.4	0	0	3	0	0	0	0	0	0	0	0	0	0	0	0	0	0	0	0	0	0	3	0	0	0
Caecilian	2	.0000	.0209	23.2	0	0	0	0	2	0	0	0	0	0	0	0	0	0	0	0	0	0	0	0	0	0	2	0	0
Caernarvon	2	.0000	.0243	23.9	0	0	0	1	1	0	0	0	0	0	0	0	0	0	0	0	0	0	0	0	0	0	0	2	0
Caesar	33	.7661	5.1396	47.1	2	1	1	2	12	10	5	0	9	3	0	0	0	2	1	3	1	0	0	0	5	5	3	1	0
Caesar's	4	.2446	.2243	33.5	0	0	0	0	1	1	2	0	0	0	0	2	0	0	0	0	0	0	0	0	0	0	2	0	0
cafe	15	.6337	1.9862	43.0	0	0	0	4	1	4	6	0	4	1	0	1	0	2	1	0	0	1	0	0	1	4	0	0	0
Cafe	3	.0000	.0434	26.4	2	0	1	0	0	0	0	0	0	0	0	0	0	0	0	0	0	0	0	0	0	3	0	0	0
cafes	9	.4097	.8217	39.1	2	0	2	0	3	0	2	0	1	0	0	0	0	3	0	0	0	0	0	0	0	2	3	0	0
cafeteria	28	.4022	2.4178	43.8	2	2	0	1	8	6	9	0	3	4	0	0	2	0	2	0	0	0	10	0	3	0	0	4	0
caffeine	4	.3450	.2950	34.7	0	0	2	0	1	0	1	0	0	0	0	0	0	0	0	0	0	0	1	0	0	0	2	1	0
cage	232	.8169	38.407	55.8	111	49	22	13	24	4	6	3	102	3	5	12	9	0	4	23	1	3	0	0	28	31	5	6	0
caged	7	.5170	.7095	38.9	2	3	0	0	0	2	0	0	1	0	0	0	0	0	0	0	0	0	0	0	2	2	1	1	0
cages	42	.7319	6.4205	48.1	27	4	2	6	2	0	1	0	27	0	1	0	1	0	1	3	1	1	0	0	2	2	0	3	0
Cahokia	2	.2297	.1135	30.6	0	0	1	0	0	0	1	0	0	0	0	1	0	1	0	0	0	0	0	0	0	0	0	0	0
caimans	2	.0000	.0209	23.2	0	0	0	0	2	0	0	0	0	0	0	0	0	0	0	0	0	0	0	0	0	0	2	0	0
Caipira	2	.0000	.0162	22.1	0	0	0	0	2	0	0	0	0	0	0	0	0	0	0	0	2	0	0	0	0	0	0	0	0
cairns	2	.0000	.0914	29.6	0	1	0	1	0	0	0	0	2	0	0	0	0	0	0	0	0	0	0	0	0	0	0	0	0
Cairo	29	.4981	3.1255	44.9	1	9	2	0	8	3	6	0	3	1	0	0	1	16	0	0	0	0	0	0	0	1	1	6	0
caisson	10	.0000	.4568	36.6	0	0	0	10	0	0	0	0	10	0	0	0	0	0	0	0	0	0	0	0	0	0	0	0	0
caissons	2	.0000	.0914	29.6	0	0	0	2	0	0	0	0	2	0	0	0	0	0	0	0	0	0	0	0	0	0	0	0	0
cajoled	3	.2427	.1822	32.6	0	0	0	0	2	0	0	1	0	0	0	0	0	0	0	2	0	0	0	0	0	0	0	1	0
Cajun	5	.0619	.1340	31.3	0	0	4	0	1	0	0	0	1	0	0	0	0	0	0	0	4	0	0	0	0	0	0	0	0
Cajuns	2	.0000	.0162	22.1	0	0	2	0	0	0	0	0	0	0	0	0	0	0	0	0	2	0	0	0	0	0	0	0	0
cake	244	.8744	42.621	56.3	84	37	34	21	25	23	18	2	78	29	2	12	29	7	12	7	2	1	10	0	21	8	5	21	0
caked	11	.5402	1.3225	41.2	2	1	4	2	0	2	0	0	6	2	0	1	0	1	0	0	0	0	0	0	0	0	1	0	0
cakes	133	.7550	20.392	53.1	34	27	21	17	8	11	12	3	34	7	0	6	11	8	2	5	6	0	15	0	11	10	14	4	0
Cakewalk	2	.2303	.1079	30.3	1	0	0	0	1	0	0	0	0	0	0	0	0	0	0	0	1	0	0	0	0	1	0	0	0
Cal	10	.4138	.9431	39.7	0	0	2	0	3	3	2	0	3	0	0	2	0	0	0	0	0	0	0	0	0	1	0	4	0
Cal's	2	.2442	.1134	30.5	0	0	0	1	0	1	0	0	0	1	0	0	0	0	0	0	0	0	0	0	0	0	0	1	0
calabashes	2	.1717	.1142	30.6	1	0	0	0	1	0	0	0	1	0	0	1	0	0	0	0	0	0	0	0	0	0	0	0	0
calamity	3	.2304	.1619	32.1	0	0	0	0	3	0	0	0	0	0	0	0	0	0	0	0	0	0	0	0	2	0	1	0	0
calamus	3	.0000	.0434	26.4	3	0	0	0	0	0	0	0	0	0	0	0	0	0	0	0	0	0	0	0	0	3	0	0	0
Calchas	4	.0000	.1827	32.6	0	0	0	0	0	4	0	0	4	0	0	0	0	0	0	0	0	0	0	0	0	0	0	0	0
calcite	5	.0000	.0986	29.9	0	0	1	0	0	1	0	3	0	0	0	0	0	0	0	5	0	0	0	0	0	0	0	0	0
calcium	60	.4266	5.6492	47.5	1	3	5	7	13	12	18	1	3	0	0	0	0	1	1	42	0	0	7	0	0	0	5	1	0
calculate	36	.6038	4.4988	46.5	0	0	1	5	10	7	10	3	2	0	0	1	5	1	0	12	0	0	0	4	1	3	6	1	0
calculated	35	.7688	5.4464	47.4	0	0	0	2	10	5	11	7	5	1	0	1	2	3	0	11	0	0	0	1	2	1	4	4	0
calculating	18	.4526	1.7997	42.6	0	0	0	2	3	8	5	0	3	1	0	0	9	0	0	3	0	0	0	0	0	0	2	0	0
calculation	13	.4434	1.2531	41.0	1	0	1	0	4	5	1	1	1	0	0	0	7	0	0	1	0	0	0	1	0	3	0	0	0
calculations	23	.6227	2.9518	44.7	0	0	2	1	6	8	3	3	1	1	0	1	8	1	0	4	0	0	0	0	0	1	5	1	0
calculator	4	.1960	.2010	33.0	1	0	0	0	2	1	0	0	0	0	0	0	1	0	0	0	0	0	0	0	0	3	0	0	0
calculators	5	.3459	.3867	35.9	0	0	0	1	1	3	0	0	0	0	0	0	3	0	0	0	0	0	0	0	0	1	0	1	0
calculi	3	.0000	.0314	25.0	0	0	0	0	0	3	0	0	0	0	0	0	0	0	0	0	0	0	0	0	0	0	3	0	0
calculus	7	.2863	.4688	36.7	0	0	0	0	0	5	1	1	0	0	0	0	5	0	0	1	0	0	0	0	0	0	1	0	0
Calculus	2	.0000	.0243	23.9	0	0	0	0	0	0	0	2	0	0	0	0	0	0	0	0	0	0	0	0	0	0	0	2	0
Calcutta	7	.3875	.5980	37.8	0	2	0	0	2	0	1	2	0	0	0	0	0	3	0	0	0	0	0	0	2	0	0	2	0
Calder	2	.2160	.1362	31.3	0	1	0	1	0	0	0	0	1	0	0	0	0	0	0	1	0	0	0	0	0	0	0	0	0
Calderon	3	.0000	.0314	25.0	0	3	0	0	0	0	0	0	0	0	0	0	0	0	0	0	0	0	0	0	0	0	3	0	0
caldron	4	.4519	.3985	36.0	0	0	0	1	3	0	0	0	1	0	0	1	0	0	0	0	0	0	0	0	0	0	1	1	0
Caldwell	6	.3627	.4704	36.7	0	0	1	3	2	0	0	0	0	0	0	2	0	0	0	0	0	0	0	0	3	0	1	0	0
CALDWELL	20	.0000	.2146	33.3	0	0	0	0	20	0	0	0	0	0	0	20	0	0	0	0	0	0	0	0	0	0	0	0	0
Cale	12	.1277	.5452	37.4	0	0	4	0	8	0	0	0	4	0	0	0	0	0	0	0	0	0	0	0	0	0	0	8	0
Cale's	3	.1277	.1363	31.3	0	0	1	0	2	0	0	0	1	0	0	0	0	0	0	0	0	0	0	0	0	0	0	2	0
Caleb	10	.2831	.6589	38.2	1	0	9	0	0	0	0	0	0	0	0	0	0	3	0	0	0	0	0	0	6	1	0	0	0
Caledonia	7	.0000	.1361	31.3	0	0	0	0	7	0	0	0	0	0	0	0	0	7	0	0	0	0	0	0	0	0	0	0	0
calendar	66	.6776	9.2534	49.7	8	11	9	8	7	2	18	3	11	0	0	0	5	15	0	20	0	0	0	0	3	3	5	4	0
Calendar	2	.2418	.1091	30.4	0	0	2	0	0	0	0	0	0	0	0	0	0	0	1	0	0	0	0	0	0	0	1	0	0
calendars	14	.6613	1.9374	42.9	3	2	3	3	2	0	1	0	4	0	0	0	1	2	1	4	0	0	0	0	0	1	1	0	0
calendering	2	.0000	.0209	23.2	0	0	2	0	0	0	0	0	0	0	0	0	0	0	0	0	0	0	0	0	0	0	2	0	0
calf	125	.8310	20.836	53.2	37	27	22	20	9	1	5	4	31	6	6	5	0	5	12	8	3	1	1	0	23	14	5	5	0
Calf	5	.0000	.2284	33.6	2	0	0	3	0	0	0	0	5	0	0	0	0	0	0	0	0	0	0	0	0	0	0	0	0
calf-roping	2	.1787	.1174	30.7	1	0	0	1	0	0	0	0	1	0	0	0	0	0	0	0	0	0	0	0	1	0	0	0	0
calf's	6	.5140	.6572	38.2	4	0	2	0	0	0	0	0	1	1	0	1	0	0	0	0	0	0	0	0	2	1	0	0	0
calfskin	2	.0000	.0914	29.6	0	0	0	0	2	0	0	0	2	0	0	0	0	0	0	0	0	0	0	0	0	0	0	0	0
Calgary	5	.0000	.0972	29.9	0	0	5	0	0	0	0	0	0	0	0	0	0	5	0	0	0	0	0	0	0	0	0	0	0
Calhoun	6	.2212	.4538	36.6	0	0	0	0	5	1	0	0	5	0	0	0	0	1	0	0	0	0	0	0	0	0	0	0	0
Calhoun's	6	.0000	.2741	34.4	0	0	0	0	6	0	0	0	6	0	0	0	0	0	0	0	0	0	0	0	0	0	0	0	0
Cali	6	.0000	.1167	30.7	0	0	0	6	0	0	0	0	0	0	0	0	0	6	0	0	0	0	0	0	0	0	0	0	0
caliber	8	.0629	.2367	33.7	0	0	8	0	0	0	0	0	1	0	0	0	0	0	0	0	0	0	0	0	0	7	0	0	0
calibrated	7	.2298	.3732	35.7	0	0	1	0	2	2	2	0	0	0	0	0	1	0	0	2	0	0	0	3	0	0	0	1	0
calico	30	.5195	3.5935	45.6	5	15	3	3	2	2	0	0	22	0	0	1	0	1	1	0	0	0	0	0	4	1	0	0	0
Calico	2	.2405	.1205	30.8	0	1	0	0	0	0	0	1	0	0	0	0	0	0	0	1	0	0	0	0	0	1	0	0	0
caliente	2	.0000	.0389	25.9	0	0	0	1	0	0	1	0	0	0	0	0	0	2	0	0	0	0	0	0	0	0	0	0	0
Calif	17	.3237	1.2638	41.0	0	0	3	3	4	1	2	4	2	0	0	0	1	0	0	0	0	0	0	0	0	0	4	10	0
California	432	.7290	64.217	58.1	65	73	66	40	65	69	33	21	58	8	1	4	6	173	3	32	14	0	1	1	3	22	25	81	0
California's	18	.4989	1.9130	42.8	5	1	0	2	1	3	4	2	1	1	0	0	0	5	0	1	0	0	0	0	0	1	1	8	0
Californian	4	.3799	.3291	35.2	0	0	0	1	1	0	2	0	0	0	0	0	0	0	0	0	1	0	0	0	0	2	0	1	0
Californians	6	.4323	.5775	37.6	0	0	0	3	1	2	0	0	1	0	0	0	0	2	0	0	0	0	0	0	0	0	1	2	0
calipee	6	.0000	.0628	28.0	0	0	0	0	6	0	0	0	0	0	0	0	0	0	0	0	0	0	0	0	0	0	6	0	0
caliper	3	.2136	.1470	31.7	0	0	0	0	2	0	1	0	0	0	0	0	0	0	0	0	0	0	0	1	0	0	0	2	0
calipers	6	.1101	.1604	32.1	0	0	0	0	6	0	0	0	0	0	0	0	0	0	0	0	0	0	0	4	0	0	0	2	0
caliph	2	.1698	.1133	30.5	0	1	0	1	0	0	0	0	1	0	0	0	0	0	0	0	0	0	0	0	0	0	1	0	0
Caliph	15	.3193	1.1779	40.7	0	4	8	1	0	1	1	0	5	0	0	0	1	0	0	0	0	0	0	0	8	0	1	0	0
Caliph's	5	.1953	.2495	34.0	0	0	1	0	0	4	0	0	0	0	0	0	4	0	0	0	0	0	0	0	1	0	0	0	0
caliphate	2	.2401	.1133	30.5	0	0	1	0	0	0	1	0	0	0	0	0	0	0	0	0	0	0	0	0	0	1	1	0	0
Caliphs	3	.0000	.0314	25.0	0	0	0	0	0	0	3	0	0	0	0	0	0	0	0	0	0	0	0	0	0	0	3	0	0
calked	3	.1187	.1291	31.1	0	0	0	0	2	1	0	0	1	0	0	2	0	0	0	0	0	0	0	0	0	0	0	0	0

7Q caecilians
7Q Caedmon's
8H cafeterias
7Q caffra
4R cage-like
7R Cager
3A Cages
3B cah
5J Caillet
7A Cain
7N cain't
5B caique
3P Cairns
7F Cairo's
7Q Cajamarca
5F Cajon
9L Cake
3A cake-baking
8J cakewalk
5Q Cakste
6P Calais
7R calamities
9R Calas
7Q Calaveras
6H calcaneus
9Q calcic
9P calcified
4N calcimine
8L calcium-poor
8D calculatingly
8E Calculator
4J Caldara
9H Caldera
9H calderas
3P caldrons
7F Caledonian
3A calf-like
6N Caliban
8R calibration
8G Calicut
4N CALIFORNIA
6Q Californium
5R calisthenics
8F calking

Word Type	F	D	U	SFI	3 Gr 3	4 Gr 4	5 Gr 5	6 Gr 6	7 Gr 7	8 Gr 8	9 Gr 9	X UnGr	A Read	B Eng & Gr	C Comp	D Lit	E Math	F Soc Stud	G Spell	H Sci	J Music	K Art	L Home Ec	M Shop	N Lib F	P Lib NF	Q Lib Ref	R Mag	S Rel
call	1374	.9053	247.24	63.9	280	251	176	168	218	128	115	38	348	118	13	80	106	126	57	119	57	3	10	5	87	107	31	101	6
Call	10	.4409	.9666	39.9	5	2	0	0	1	1	1	0	1	1	0	0	0	1	0	4	3	0	0	0	0	0	0	0	0
callable	3	.0000	.0314	25.0	0	0	0	0	3	0	0	0	0	0	0	0	0	0	0	0	0	0	0	0	0	0	3	0	0
Callahan	5	.3415	.3820	35.8	1	3	0	0	0	0	1	0	0	0	0	0	1	0	0	0	0	0	0	0	0	3	0	1	0
Callao	3	.2378	.1809	32.6	0	0	0	0	2	1	0	0	0	0	0	0	0	2	0	0	0	0	0	0	0	1	0	0	0
calle	2	.0000	.0162	22.1	0	1	0	0	1	0	0	0	0	0	0	0	0	0	0	0	2	0	0	0	0	0	0	0	0
called	5789	.9733	1110.4	70.5	1179	897	825	780	951	602	459	96	1200	377	30	132	589	778	211	886	315	36	38	89	238	403	285	177	5
caller	9	.5146	.9525	39.8	0	2	3	0	1	0	3	0	0	2	0	2	1	0	0	0	1	0	2	0	0	1	0	0	0
caller's	2	.2417	.1091	30.4	0	0	1	0	0	0	1	0	0	0	0	0	0	0	0	0	1	0	0	0	0	0	1	0	0
callers	4	.3470	.3242	35.1	0	0	0	0	2	1	1	0	1	0	0	0	0	1	0	0	0	0	1	0	0	0	1	0	0
Calles	2	.0000	.0914	29.6	2	0	0	0	0	0	0	0	2	0	0	0	0	0	0	0	0	0	0	0	0	0	0	0	0
calligraphy	3	.1551	.1258	31.0	0	1	0	0	1	1	0	0	0	0	0	0	0	2	0	0	0	1	0	0	0	0	0	0	0
callin'	2	.0000	.0914	29.6	0	0	1	0	1	0	0	0	2	0	0	0	0	0	0	0	0	0	0	0	0	0	0	0	0
calling	230	.7987	37.395	55.7	50	46	20	35	44	17	16	2	106	6	1	19	1	14	4	5	3	0	0	0	32	16	8	15	0
callings	2	.0000	.0209	23.2	0	0	0	0	0	0	2	0	0	0	0	0	0	0	0	0	0	0	0	0	0	0	2	0	0
calloused	3	.3406	.2461	33.9	0	0	0	2	0	0	1	0	1	1	0	0	0	0	0	0	0	0	0	0	0	0	0	1	0
calls	216	.9028	38.709	55.9	37	19	28	22	48	27	33	2	39	26	3	18	10	20	4	17	27	2	2	1	4	10	6	27	0
callus	2	.0000	.0914	29.6	2	0	0	0	0	0	0	0	2	0	0	0	0	0	0	0	0	0	0	0	0	0	0	0	0
calluses	3	.2279	.2143	33.3	2	0	1	0	0	0	0	0	2	0	0	0	0	0	0	0	0	0	0	0	0	0	0	1	0
calm	137	.8697	23.822	53.8	17	17	18	13	34	21	14	3	45	4	3	21	0	2	3	10	7	2	2	0	12	10	3	13	0
calmed	10	.5565	1.1804	40.7	0	0	2	2	5	0	1	0	2	0	0	3	0	1	0	0	0	0	0	0	1	2	0	1	0
calmer	6	.3975	.5522	37.4	0	1	2	0	2	1	0	0	2	0	0	0	0	1	0	0	2	0	0	0	1	0	0	0	0
calmest	2	.0000	.0914	29.6	1	0	0	1	0	0	0	0	2	0	0	0	0	0	0	0	0	0	0	0	0	0	0	0	0
calming	2	.2291	.1135	30.5	0	0	0	0	0	1	1	0	0	0	0	1	0	0	0	1	0	0	0	0	0	0	0	0	0
calmly	44	.7266	6.5735	48.2	3	3	7	9	7	10	5	0	16	1	0	5	0	3	0	0	2	0	2	0	7	3	0	5	0
calmness	7	.4111	.6514	38.1	0	0	0	1	3	3	0	0	2	0	0	2	0	1	0	0	0	1	0	0	1	0	0	0	0
calms	7	.5233	.7863	39.0	0	0	3	0	3	0	0	1	1	0	0	1	0	0	0	3	0	0	0	0	1	0	0	1	0
caloric	18	.2071	.9921	40.0	0	0	3	12	2	1	0	0	0	0	0	0	0	0	0	15	0	0	0	0	0	0	3	0	0
calorie	13	.2607	.8482	39.3	0	2	0	3	1	6	1	0	0	0	0	0	2	1	0	10	0	0	0	0	0	0	0	0	0
Calorie	8	.0000	.1577	32.0	0	0	0	0	0	8	0	0	0	0	0	0	0	0	0	8	0	0	0	0	0	0	0	0	0
calories	49	.4742	4.9614	47.0	1	11	0	6	5	7	19	0	0	0	0	0	24	9	0	9	0	0	5	0	0	0	0	2	0
Calories	12	.0000	.2366	33.7	0	0	0	0	0	12	0	0	0	0	0	0	0	0	0	12	0	0	0	0	0	0	0	0	0
Calpurnia	13	.0000	.1395	31.4	0	0	0	0	0	0	13	0	0	0	0	13	0	0	0	0	0	0	0	0	0	0	0	0	0
Caltech	4	.1873	.1827	32.6	0	0	0	1	0	0	3	0	0	0	0	0	0	0	0	0	0	0	0	0	0	0	3	1	0
calugas	2	.0000	.0914	29.6	0	0	2	0	0	0	0	0	2	0	0	0	0	0	0	0	0	0	0	0	0	0	0	0	0
Calverts	2	.0000	.0389	25.9	0	0	0	0	0	2	0	0	0	0	0	0	0	2	0	0	0	0	0	0	0	0	0	0	0
calves	53	.6723	7.3792	48.7	23	13	9	1	3	1	1	2	13	2	0	1	0	6	0	4	0	1	0	0	15	9	2	0	0
Calvin	5	.4391	.4861	36.9	1	0	1	0	2	1	0	0	1	0	0	1	0	0	0	0	0	0	0	0	0	2	0	1	0
Calvin's	3	.0000	.0314	25.0	0	0	0	0	0	3	0	0	0	0	0	0	0	0	0	0	0	0	0	0	0	0	3	0	0
Calvinism	7	.1361	.2515	34.0	0	0	0	0	0	7	0	0	0	0	0	0	0	0	0	0	0	0	0	0	1	0	6	0	0
calypso	4	.1770	.1679	32.3	0	2	0	0	0	1	1	0	0	0	0	1	0	0	0	0	3	0	0	0	0	0	0	0	0
Calypso	4	.2440	.2264	33.5	0	0	0	0	2	0	2	0	0	0	0	2	0	0	0	0	0	0	0	0	0	0	0	2	0
calyx	5	.0000	.0986	29.9	0	0	0	0	0	0	4	1	0	0	0	0	0	0	0	5	0	0	0	0	0	0	0	0	0
cam	5	.1962	.2531	34.0	0	0	0	0	4	1	0	0	1	0	0	0	0	0	0	0	0	0	0	2	0	0	0	2	0
camaraderie	2	.2351	.1166	30.7	0	0	0	1	0	1	0	0	0	0	0	0	0	1	0	0	0	0	0	0	0	0	0	1	0
Camaralzaman's	3	.0000	.0352	25.5	0	0	3	0	0	0	0	0	0	0	0	0	0	0	0	0	0	0	0	0	3	0	0	0	0
camber	3	.0000	.0365	25.6	0	0	0	0	3	0	0	0	0	0	0	0	0	0	0	0	0	0	0	0	0	0	0	3	0
cambio	5	.0000	.2284	33.6	5	0	0	0	0	0	0	0	5	0	0	0	0	0	0	0	0	0	0	0	0	0	0	0	0
Cambodia	19	.2504	1.1941	40.8	0	0	2	12	3	0	2	0	0	0	0	0	0	16	0	0	0	0	0	0	0	0	1	2	0
Cambodian	4	.2352	.2332	33.7	0	0	0	2	1	1	0	0	0	0	0	0	0	2	0	0	0	0	0	0	0	0	0	2	0
Cambodians	2	.0000	.0389	25.9	0	0	0	2	0	0	0	0	0	0	0	0	0	2	0	0	0	0	0	0	0	0	0	0	0
Cambrian	5	.2424	.2988	34.8	0	0	0	0	2	0	3	0	0	0	0	0	0	0	0	3	0	0	0	0	0	0	2	0	0
Cambridge	16	.4995	1.6967	42.3	0	1	3	2	2	3	5	0	2	0	0	0	0	0	0	0	1	0	0	0	1	3	7	2	0
Camden	4	.3832	.3307	35.2	1	1	0	0	2	0	0	0	0	0	0	1	0	0	0	0	1	0	0	0	0	2	0	0	0
came	4914	.8655	853.23	69.3	1067	942	621	731	783	449	254	67	2016	184	25	423	34	463	77	114	154	7	5	1	603	463	104	231	10
Came	3	.3669	.2412	33.8	0	0	2	0	1	0	0	0	0	0	0	0	0	1	0	0	1	0	0	0	1	0	0	0	0
camel	72	.7803	11.481	50.6	19	14	7	14	13	2	3	0	30	7	0	1	1	12	1	6	1	1	0	0	0	9	1	2	0
Camel	2	.1733	.1149	30.6	1	0	0	1	0	0	0	0	1	1	0	0	0	0	0	0	0	0	0	0	0	0	0	0	0
camel's	10	.5476	1.1903	40.8	3	1	1	1	2	2	0	0	4	1	0	0	0	1	0	0	1	0	0	1	0	2	0	0	0
camellias	3	.3852	.2500	34.0	1	0	0	1	0	0	1	0	0	0	0	1	0	0	0	0	0	0	0	0	0	1	0	1	0
Camelot	5	.0000	.2284	33.6	0	0	0	5	0	0	0	0	5	0	0	0	0	0	0	0	0	0	0	0	0	0	0	0	0
camels	64	.7509	9.8416	49.9	5	18	5	19	11	2	3	1	21	5	3	1	0	19	1	3	1	0	1	0	0	5	2	2	0
Camembert	2	.2106	.0917	29.6	0	0	0	0	1	1	0	0	0	0	0	0	0	0	1	0	0	0	1	0	0	0	0	0	0
cameo	3	.0000	.0328	25.2	0	0	0	0	1	0	2	0	0	3	0	0	0	0	0	0	0	0	0	0	0	0	0	0	0
camera	166	.7288	24.694	53.9	17	22	15	28	34	28	16	6	43	5	2	16	2	6	8	31	1	13	0	13	6	2	5	13	0
Camera	4	.2445	.3067	34.9	0	0	0	3	0	1	0	0	3	0	0	0	0	0	0	0	0	0	0	0	0	1	0	0	0
camera's	2	.1948	.1250	31.0	0	0	0	0	2	0	0	0	1	0	0	0	0	0	0	0	0	0	0	0	0	1	0	0	0
cameraman	7	.2455	.4379	36.4	0	2	0	0	0	2	3	0	2	0	0	0	0	0	0	0	0	0	0	2	0	0	0	3	0
cameramen	3	.2233	.1562	31.9	0	1	0	0	2	0	0	0	0	0	0	1	0	0	0	0	0	0	0	0	0	0	2	0	0
cameras	77	.6271	10.264	50.1	16	26	3	14	6	6	4	2	29	0	0	1	2	5	0	18	0	0	0	1	1	2	0	18	0
Cameron	2	.2442	.1134	30.5	0	1	0	0	0	0	1	0	0	1	0	0	0	0	0	0	0	0	0	0	0	0	0	1	0
Cameroons	2	.0000	.0209	23.2	0	0	0	0	2	0	0	0	0	0	0	0	0	0	0	0	0	0	0	0	0	0	2	0	0
Camille	6	.2789	.3689	35.7	3	1	0	0	0	1	1	0	0	0	0	0	0	1	0	0	1	2	0	0	0	0	0	2	0
camomile	2	.0000	.0234	23.7	1	1	0	0	0	0	0	0	0	0	0	0	0	0	0	0	0	0	0	0	2	0	0	0	0
camouflage	10	.3902	.8803	39.4	0	1	1	4	2	1	1	0	2	4	0	0	0	0	0	0	0	0	0	0	0	1	0	3	0
camouflaged	5	.2766	.3388	35.3	0	0	0	0	3	0	2	0	1	0	0	0	0	0	0	0	0	0	0	0	0	0	1	3	0
camp	378	.8423	64.120	58.1	52	62	74	61	64	38	18	9	151	20	4	22	3	40	16	2	6	0	0	1	31	38	4	40	0
Camp	40	.6994	5.7793	47.6	10	1	5	5	13	2	2	2	12	2	0	3	13	3	1	0	0	0	0	0	1	1	1	3	0
camp's	2	.1948	.1250	31.0	0	1	0	1	0	0	0	0	1	0	0	0	0	0	0	0	0	0	0	0	0	1	0	0	0
campaign	92	.6587	12.463	51.0	5	3	6	6	20	38	13	1	10	7	0	3	0	29	2	1	2	0	0	0	0	2	13	23	0
campaigned	2	.2351	.1166	30.7	0	0	1	0	0	0	1	0	0	0	0	0	0	1	0	0	0	0	0	0	0	0	0	1	0
campaigner	2	.2446	.1122	30.5	0	0	0	0	0	1	1	0	0	0	0	1	0	0	0	0	0	0	0	0	0	0	1	0	0
campaigning	7	.4575	.7229	38.6	0	0	0	2	1	3	1	0	2	0	0	1	0	3	0	0	0	0	0	0	0	0	0	1	0
campaigns	17	.5683	2.0119	43.0	1	1	2	0	4	7	2	0	1	0	0	0	0	2	0	2	1	0	0	0	0	3	6	2	0
Campbell	7	.3858	.6002	37.8	0	0	1	1	2	1	2	0	1	0	0	2	0	0	0	0	0	0	0	0	0	1	3	0	0
camped	25	.6557	3.4509	45.4	4	7	2	4	4	4	0	0	9	1	0	1	0	9	1	0	0	0	0	0	1	1	0	2	0
camper	7	.3645	.5641	37.5	0	1	1	2	3	0	0	0	1	1	2	0	1	0	0	0	0	0	0	0	0	0	1	1	0
campers	18	.3264	1.3426	41.3	1	5	2	4	4	1	1	0	3	0	6	0	1	2	2	1	0	0	0	0	0	1	0	2	0
Campers	2	.0000	.0914	29.6	2	0	0	0	0	0	0	0	2	0	0	0	0	0	0	0	0	0	0	0	0	0	0	0	0
campfire	41	.8103	6.7079	48.3	8	8	5	6	7	5	1	1	13	3	2	5	1	3	0	5	2	1	1	0	0	3	0	2	0
Campfire	2	.1814	.1187	30.7	0	1	0	0	0	1	0	0	1	0	0	0	0	0	0	0	0	0	0	0	0	0	0	1	0
campfires	10	.4703	1.0327	40.1	1	3	3	3	0	0	0	0	2	1	0	0	0	2	0	2	3	0	0	0	0	0	0	0	0
campground	2	.1972	.1262	31.0	0	1	0	0	0	1	0	0	1	0	0	0	1	0	0	0	0	0	0	0	0	0	0	0	0
campgrounds	3	.2279	.2143	33.3	1	0	0	0	1	0	0	1	2	0	0	0	0	0	0	0	0	0	0	0	0	0	0	1	0

7J call-and-response
7R call-up
7B call'd
3R Callahan's
5K Callay
XR Calle
9E called-for
6R Callender
7R Calley
8R Calling
5N calling-like
9C calliope
9K Callister
5K Callooh
5P Calloways
6R Callville
3P calm-spoken
6A calomel
XR Caloosahatchee
9D Calpurnia's
9Q Caltech's
9Q Calton
7A calumnies
7P calumny
4A calving
9R Calvinist
8Q Calvinistic
8F Calvinists
4J Calypso-style
8J cam'
6N cam'st
8Q Camargo
7R Camaro
7R Camaros
7C camatutpeg
7C camatutpegged
6J Camayos
8R Cambay
3A CAMBIO
7H cambium
5Q Cambrai
9R camel-colored
6N camel-necked
6A camel-thorn
4B Camel's
6A camel's-hair
6R camelback
9D camellia
6R camera-like
6P Camerata
7Q Cameroon
7A Camilla
7Q Camillo
8F Camino
7Q camouflages
5P camouflaging
7N camp-fire
6R camp-out
5R camp-outs
9C camp-stools
4Q Campaign
9Q Campania
5R camper's
5A Campers'
7R campesinos
4A camphire

Word Type	F	D	U	SFI	3 Gr 3	4 Gr 4	5 Gr 5	6 Gr 6	7 Gr 7	8 Gr 8	9 Gr 9	X UnGr	A Read	B Eng & Gr	C Comp	D Lit	E Math	F Soc Stud	G Spell	H Sci	J Music	K Art	L Home Ec	M Shop	N Lib F	P Lib NF	Q Lib Ref	R Mag	S Rel
camphor	7	.2315	.5100	37.1	0	2	2	1	2	0	0	0	5	0	0	0	0	0	0	0	0	0	0	0	0	0	2	0	0
camping	70	.7954	11.247	50.5	16	20	7	5	9	5	2	6	18	10	4	3	3	12	1	2	1	0	1	0	3	4	1	7	0
camps	49	.7877	7.8041	48.9	7	7	8	5	11	5	5	1	11	0	0	3	0	9	1	1	1	0	0	1	3	10	4	5	0
campsite	8	.4658	.8537	39.3	0	2	1	1	1	2	1	0	4	1	0	2	0	0	0	0	0	0	0	0	0	0	0	1	0
campsites	2	.0000	.0243	23.9	0	0	1	0	0	0	0	1	0	0	0	0	0	0	0	0	0	0	0	0	0	0	0	2	0
camptown	2	.0000	.0162	22.1	0	0	0	2	0	0	0	0	0	0	0	0	0	0	0	0	2	0	0	0	0	0	0	0	0
Camptown	3	.0000	.0243	23.8	0	0	1	2	0	0	0	0	0	0	0	0	0	0	0	0	3	0	0	0	0	0	0	0	0
campus	38	.3405	2.8390	44.5	0	0	1	2	13	13	5	4	0	1	0	0	0	1	2	0	1	0	0	0	0	0	4	29	0
Campus	3	.2212	.2099	33.2	0	0	0	0	0	3	0	0	2	0	0	1	0	0	0	0	0	0	0	0	0	0	0	0	0
campuses	12	.2324	.6556	38.2	1	0	0	1	1	6	3	0	0	0	0	0	0	0	0	0	1	0	0	0	0	0	1	10	0
camshaft	2	.0000	.0243	23.9	0	0	0	0	2	0	0	0	0	0	0	0	0	0	0	0	0	0	0	0	0	0	0	2	0
can	15247	.9563	2877.8	74.6	3328	2500	1852	2057	2434	1606	1166	304	2594	1052	212	425	1883	1248	727	2815	873	357	342	265	435	846	448	721	4
Can	6	.4456	.5639	37.5	0	2	0	2	2	0	0	0	0	0	0	0	0	0	2	2	0	0	1	0	0	0	1	0	0
CAN	3	.2254	.1785	32.5	0	0	0	2	0	0	1	0	0	0	0	0	0	1	0	2	0	0	0	0	0	0	0	0	0
can'st	2	.2443	.1130	30.5	0	0	0	1	0	0	1	0	0	0	0	1	0	0	0	0	0	0	0	0	1	0	0	0	0
can't	1240	.8405	210.05	63.2	334	269	125	141	190	86	68	27	525	58	9	112	7	40	17	39	16	1	11	5	146	143	0	111	0
Can't	3	.2411	.1667	32.2	0	0	1	1	0	1	0	0	0	0	0	0	0	0	0	0	1	0	0	0	0	0	0	2	0
Canaan	3	.3844	.2487	34.0	1	0	1	0	0	0	0	1	0	1	0	0	0	0	0	0	0	0	0	0	0	1	1	0	0
Canada	271	.7417	40.755	56.1	22	27	71	29	57	25	35	5	28	7	2	7	2	93	2	18	15	0	0	0	7	11	56	23	0
Canada's	12	.4644	1.2049	40.8	0	1	4	0	4	2	1	0	1	0	0	0	0	5	0	0	1	0	0	0	0	0	4	1	0
Canadian	77	.7731	11.963	50.8	3	6	17	9	30	4	3	5	6	2	2	5	2	14	1	0	4	0	0	0	15	2	13	11	0
Canadians	8	.4863	.8482	39.3	0	1	3	0	2	1	0	1	2	0	0	0	0	0	2	1	0	0	0	0	0	1	2	0	0
canal	153	.7538	23.440	53.7	16	23	32	34	21	15	3	9	24	2	1	6	0	68	3	7	6	0	0	0	11	7	8	10	0
Canal	102	.6386	13.485	51.3	2	11	16	23	21	21	5	3	10	13	1	0	4	52	0	0	8	0	0	0	0	1	7	6	0
canalboats	2	.0000	.0389	25.9	0	0	0	0	0	2	0	0	0	0	0	0	0	2	0	0	0	0	0	0	0	0	0	0	0
canals	84	.5945	10.534	50.2	7	13	7	23	11	12	4	7	12	2	0	0	0	44	0	5	1	0	0	0	1	6	5	8	0
canapes	2	.0000	.0914	29.6	0	0	2	0	0	0	0	0	2	0	0	0	0	0	0	0	0	0	0	0	0	0	0	0	0
canaries	13	.6107	1.6968	42.3	4	4	0	1	1	2	0	1	6	2	0	0	0	0	1	0	0	0	0	0	1	1	2	0	0
Canarsies	2	.0000	.0914	29.6	0	1	0	1	0	0	0	0	2	0	0	0	0	0	0	0	0	0	0	0	0	0	0	0	0
canary	24	.7311	3.5708	45.5	3	3	5	5	6	1	0	1	5	5	0	1	0	1	2	1	0	0	0	0	3	2	3	1	0
Canary	13	.6132	1.7010	42.3	2	0	1	3	6	0	0	1	5	1	0	0	0	4	0	0	1	0	0	0	0	0	1	1	0
canary's	2	.0000	.0290	24.6	1	0	0	1	0	0	0	0	0	0	0	0	0	0	0	0	0	0	0	0	0	2	0	0	0
Canaveral	2	.0000	.0394	26.0	0	0	1	0	0	0	0	1	0	0	0	0	0	0	0	2	0	0	0	0	0	0	0	0	0
Canberra	6	.2378	.3617	35.6	0	0	2	4	0	0	0	0	0	0	0	0	0	4	0	0	0	0	0	0	0	2	0	0	0
cancel	10	.6547	1.3508	41.3	0	1	0	1	1	2	4	1	1	1	0	1	0	2	1	3	0	0	0	0	0	0	0	1	0
canceled	5	.3974	.4216	36.2	0	0	0	1	0	3	1	0	0	2	1	0	0	1	0	0	1	0	0	0	0	0	0	0	0
cancelled	4	.3830	.3375	35.3	1	0	1	1	0	0	0	1	0	0	0	0	0	2	0	0	1	0	0	0	0	0	0	1	0
cancels	4	.3445	.3016	34.8	1	1	1	0	1	0	0	0	0	0	1	0	0	0	0	1	0	0	0	0	0	1	1	0	0
cancer	39	.5113	4.2592	46.3	0	0	15	0	4	4	6	10	1	0	0	0	0	0	0	25	0	0	1	0	1	5	1	5	0
Cancer	14	.1823	.7249	38.6	0	4	5	3	1	1	0	0	0	0	0	0	0	11	0	3	0	0	0	0	0	0	0	0	0
cancers	6	.1833	.3085	34.9	0	0	2	0	0	1	1	2	0	0	0	0	0	0	0	5	0	0	0	0	0	1	0	0	0
candelabra	2	.0000	.0162	22.1	0	0	1	0	0	1	0	0	0	0	0	0	0	0	0	0	2	0	0	0	0	0	0	0	0
candid	6	.5080	.6523	38.1	0	0	0	1	2	0	2	1	1	0	0	1	0	1	1	0	0	0	0	0	0	0	0	2	0
candidacy	4	.3092	.2990	34.8	0	0	0	0	1	2	0	1	1	1	0	0	0	0	0	0	0	0	0	0	0	0	0	2	0
candidate	59	.7248	8.6302	49.4	3	0	10	4	11	18	11	2	2	6	0	1	0	11	6	0	0	1	0	0	1	9	11	11	0
candidates	39	.5734	4.7080	46.7	1	0	8	2	4	8	16	0	3	2	0	0	1	23	2	0	0	0	0	0	0	2	3	3	0
candied	3	.2330	.1860	32.7	0	0	0	0	1	1	1	0	1	0	0	0	0	0	0	0	0	0	1	0	0	1	0	0	0
candies	17	.6326	2.1818	43.4	1	7	2	1	4	0	2	0	0	2	2	1	5	1	0	0	1	0	2	0	1	2	0	0	0
Candita	131	.0000	5.9844	47.8	124	7	0	0	0	0	0	0	131	0	0	0	0	0	0	0	0	0	0	0	0	0	0	0	0
Candita's	7	.0000	.3198	35.0	7	0	0	0	0	0	0	0	7	0	0	0	0	0	0	0	0	0	0	0	0	0	0	0	0
candle	165	.5901	20.948	53.2	32	53	26	22	20	3	8	1	65	2	0	11	1	1	0	39	6	2	0	0	15	15	3	3	2
Candle	4	.1814	.2373	33.8	0	1	0	0	0	2	0	1	2	0	0	0	0	0	0	0	0	0	0	0	0	0	0	2	0
candle-lit	2	.0000	.0162	22.1	0	0	0	1	0	0	1	0	0	0	0	0	0	0	0	0	2	0	0	0	0	0	0	0	0
candlelight	16	.5761	1.9308	42.9	0	3	6	1	1	2	1	2	3	0	1	3	0	0	0	1	1	0	0	0	6	0	0	1	0
candlemaker	3	.3553	.2608	34.2	0	2	0	0	1	0	0	0	1	0	0	0	0	1	0	0	0	0	0	0	0	1	0	0	0
candles	87	.7438	13.307	51.2	20	15	16	15	5	5	10	1	36	1	0	6	0	6	0	5	7	0	4	0	4	14	0	4	0
candlestick	9	.3219	.6416	38.1	0	0	0	0	7	2	0	0	0	1	0	6	0	1	0	0	0	0	0	0	1	0	0	0	0
candlesticks	10	.4838	1.1174	40.5	3	2	3	1	0	1	0	0	6	0	0	0	0	0	0	0	1	0	0	0	1	2	0	0	0
candor	2	.0000	.0243	23.9	0	0	0	0	1	1	0	0	0	0	0	0	0	0	0	0	0	0	0	0	0	0	0	2	0
candy	256	.8225	42.289	56.3	87	53	34	22	31	9	12	8	57	24	3	7	86	3	14	10	3	1	8	1	23	4	1	11	0
Candy	28	.3307	2.2216	43.5	21	0	0	0	5	1	1	0	8	0	0	1	0	0	0	0	0	0	0	0	15	0	0	4	0
candy-making	2	.2444	.1132	30.5	0	0	0	0	0	0	1	1	0	1	0	0	0	0	0	0	0	0	0	0	1	0	0	0	0
candystick	2	.0000	.0209	23.2	0	0	0	0	2	0	0	0	0	0	0	0	0	0	0	0	0	0	0	0	0	0	2	0	0
cane	118	.7103	17.360	52.4	20	22	30	12	25	5	4	0	42	1	6	4	0	43	2	2	3	0	1	0	5	2	4	3	0
cane-break	2	.0000	.0162	22.1	2	0	0	0	0	0	0	0	0	0	0	0	0	0	0	0	2	0	0	0	0	0	0	0	0
canes	7	.3452	.5472	37.4	3	0	0	4	0	0	0	0	1	0	0	0	1	0	0	0	1	0	0	0	0	0	4	0	0
Canetto	2	.0000	.0914	29.6	0	0	0	0	2	0	0	0	2	0	0	0	0	0	0	0	0	0	0	0	0	0	0	0	0
canine	3	.1169	.1277	31.1	0	0	0	0	3	0	0	0	1	0	0	0	0	0	0	0	0	0	0	0	0	0	2	0	0
canines	9	.1422	.3303	35.2	0	0	0	1	8	0	0	0	0	0	0	0	0	0	1	0	0	0	0	0	0	0	8	0	0
Canis	4	.2353	.2382	33.8	0	0	0	0	4	0	0	0	0	0	0	0	0	0	0	3	0	0	0	0	0	0	1	0	0
canister	3	.3427	.2477	33.9	0	0	0	0	2	1	0	0	1	0	0	0	0	0	0	0	0	0	0	0	1	0	0	1	0
canisters	2	.0000	.0243	23.9	0	0	0	0	1	1	0	0	0	0	0	0	0	0	0	0	0	0	0	0	0	0	0	2	0
cannabis	4	.0000	.0486	26.9	0	0	0	0	0	0	4	0	0	0	0	0	0	0	0	0	0	0	0	0	0	0	0	4	0
canned	84	.4398	7.9751	49.0	25	12	6	5	11	4	20	1	8	0	0	1	3	24	1	4	0	0	25	0	4	5	5	4	0
canneries	7	.1437	.3145	35.0	0	1	3	0	2	1	0	0	0	0	0	0	0	6	0	1	0	0	0	0	0	0	0	0	0
cannery	5	.4510	.5027	37.0	0	1	3	1	0	0	0	0	1	0	0	0	0	2	0	0	0	0	0	0	1	0	0	1	0
Cannes	2	.2437	.1129	30.5	1	0	0	0	0	0	1	0	0	0	0	0	0	0	0	0	0	0	0	0	0	0	1	1	0
cannibal	4	.0000	.0469	26.7	3	0	0	0	1	0	0	0	0	0	0	0	0	0	0	0	0	0	0	0	4	0	0	0	0
Cannibal	2	.0000	.0162	22.1	0	2	0	0	0	0	0	0	0	0	0	0	0	0	0	0	2	0	0	0	0	0	0	0	0
cannibals	9	.3818	.7862	39.0	4	0	1	1	1	0	0	2	2	0	0	2	0	0	0	1	0	0	0	0	4	0	0	0	0
canning	23	.5836	2.8068	44.5	5	3	6	5	0	1	2	1	1	0	1	0	1	13	0	1	0	0	0	0	2	0	1	3	0
Canning	2	.0000	.0243	23.9	0	0	0	0	0	0	0	2	0	0	0	0	0	0	0	0	0	0	0	0	0	0	0	2	0
cannon	89	.8194	14.721	51.7	2	14	18	12	26	8	3	6	31	0	2	7	0	5	0	9	6	2	0	0	9	9	6	3	0
Cannon	18	.2444	1.3845	41.4	5	0	0	1	11	1	0	0	14	0	0	0	0	0	0	0	0	0	0	0	0	0	0	4	0
cannon's	3	.3450	.2505	34.0	0	0	1	0	0	1	0	1	1	0	0	0	0	0	0	0	0	0	0	0	1	1	0	0	0
Cannonball	2	.0000	.0914	29.6	0	0	2	0	0	0	0	0	2	0	0	0	0	0	0	0	0	0	0	0	0	0	0	0	0
cannonballs	2	.0000	.0914	29.6	0	0	0	0	2	0	0	0	2	0	0	0	0	0	0	0	0	0	0	0	0	0	0	0	0
cannons	7	.5333	.7992	39.0	2	1	2	2	0	0	0	0	2	0	0	0	0	0	1	0	1	0	0	0	0	0	2	1	0
cannot	1279	.9453	239.08	63.8	283	171	136	173	212	135	148	21	263	66	10	61	72	131	39	361	15	6	35	12	21	76	58	52	1
canny	2	.0000	.0243	23.9	0	0	0	0	0	1	0	1	0	0	0	0	0	0	0	0	0	0	0	0	0	0	0	2	0
canoe	164	.7784	26.061	54.2	24	25	17	41	42	3	9	3	71	7	2	18	4	8	2	3	1	0	0	1	33	9	1	4	0
canoeists	2	.2440	.1132	30.5	0	0	0	1	0	0	0	1	0	0	0	1	0	0	0	0	0	0	0	0	0	0	0	1	0
canoemen	2	.0000	.0914	29.6	0	0	1	0	1	0	0	0	2	0	0	0	0	0	0	0	0	0	0	0	0	0	0	0	0

9D Campo
9D campstool
7R Can-Am
9H can's
9R Cana
XB Canaanite
7N Canadas
6R Canadensis
9H Canadian-American
7B Canadian's
7D Canai
6P CANAL
5Q Canal's
6A canali
XQ canalization
5J canaller
3A canalman
7A Canaria
7A Canaries
8F Canarsie
6A canary-coloured
6A canary-yellow
8H canceling
6A cancellation
3F cancelling
9R cancer-causing
9R cancer-like
9Q cancerous
8Q Cancionero
7J candelabrum
8G candidate's
5R CANDIDATES
7R candidly
7Q candiru
3A CANDITA
7P candle-light
4A candle-lighted
6J candle-lighting
3P candle's
5A candleberry
XR candlelighted
6A candlelit
4P candlemaking
4P Candlemas
XR candour
4K candy-filled
3R Candy's
6H candytuft
7Q Cane
4A cane-seated
5A canebrake
7Q canebrakes
8D caned
3F Canfield
3A Cani
7H Canidae
7A canis
4J Cannab'lic
9Q Cannae
9L canned-heat
8R Cannery
4A cannon-balls
5A cannon-sized
6A Cannon's
8A cannonading
5A cannoneer
8K cannoneers
4R cannons'
4F Canoe
5F canoeing
6R canoeloads

Word Type	F	D	U	SFI	3 Gr 3	4 Gr 4	5 Gr 5	6 Gr 6	7 Gr 7	8 Gr 8	9 Gr 9	X UnGr	A Read	B Eng & Gr	C Comp	D Lit	E Math	F Soc Stud	G Spell	H Sci	J Music	K Art	L Home Ec	M Shop	N Lib F	P Lib NF	Q Lib Ref	R Mag	S Rel
canoes	69	.6841	9.7668	49.9	7	8	20	17	9	5	3	0	17	1	0	5	1	20	0	0	2	0	0	0	11	9	3	0	0
canon	21	.0440	.3501	35.4	0	5	0	9	0	2	5	0	0	0	0	0	0	0	0	0	20	0	0	0	0	1	0	0	0
canons	5	.1446	.1801	32.6	0	0	0	2	2	0	1	0	0	0	0	0	0	0	0	0	4	0	0	0	0	0	0	1	0
canopy	15	.5550	1.7710	42.5	3	1	1	2	7	1	0	0	3	0	0	0	0	2	0	0	0	0	0	0	1	5	3	1	0
Canossa	2	.0000	.0209	23.2	0	0	0	0	0	2	0	0	0	0	0	0	0	0	0	0	0	0	0	0	0	0	2	0	0
cans	123	.7819	19.395	52.9	34	19	6	15	21	8	15	5	18	2	0	4	38	9	1	17	1	0	7	5	5	5	4	7	0
canst	6	.3450	.4548	36.6	1	0	1	0	0	0	3	1	0	0	0	3	0	0	0	0	0	0	0	0	0	2	0	1	0
cant	4	.3726	.3183	35.0	1	0	0	0	0	3	0	0	0	1	0	2	0	0	1	0	0	0	0	0	0	0	0	0	0
Cantabrian	2	.0000	.0389	25.9	0	0	0	0	2	0	0	0	0	0	0	0	0	2	0	0	0	0	0	0	0	0	0	0	0
Cantabrians	2	.0000	.0389	25.9	0	0	0	0	2	0	0	0	0	0	0	0	0	2	0	0	0	0	0	0	0	0	0	0	0
cantaloupe	2	.0000	.0243	23.9	0	0	0	0	2	0	0	0	0	0	0	0	0	0	0	0	0	0	0	0	0	0	0	2	0
cantaloupes	6	.3795	.4880	36.9	1	0	1	0	1	1	2	0	0	0	0	0	0	1	1	1	0	0	2	0	1	0	0	0	0
cantankerous	4	.3635	.3138	35.0	0	0	0	1	2	0	1	0	0	0	0	2	0	0	0	0	0	0	0	0	0	0	1	1	0
cantata	4	.0000	.0323	25.1	0	0	1	2	0	0	1	0	0	0	0	0	0	0	0	0	4	0	0	0	0	0	0	0	0
Cantata	3	.0000	.0243	23.8	0	0	1	1	0	0	1	0	0	0	0	0	0	0	0	0	3	0	0	0	0	0	0	0	0
canteen	14	.5564	1.6513	42.2	2	1	2	0	2	3	4	0	3	1	0	4	2	0	0	0	0	0	0	0	0	1	0	3	0
canteens	3	.3553	.2608	34.2	0	0	1	0	2	0	0	0	1	0	0	0	0	1	0	0	0	0	0	0	0	1	0	0	0
Cantello	3	.0000	.1370	31.4	3	0	0	0	0	0	0	0	3	0	0	0	0	0	0	0	0	0	0	0	0	0	0	0	0
Cantellos	2	.0000	.0914	29.6	2	0	0	0	0	0	0	0	2	0	0	0	0	0	0	0	0	0	0	0	0	0	0	0	0
CANTELLOS	3	.0000	.1370	31.4	3	0	0	0	0	0	0	0	3	0	0	0	0	0	0	0	0	0	0	0	0	0	0	0	0
canter	3	.3399	.2456	33.9	0	0	1	1	1	0	0	0	1	0	0	1	0	0	0	0	0	0	0	0	0	0	0	1	0
Canterbury	10	.4912	1.0382	40.2	0	0	2	1	6	1	0	0	1	0	0	0	0	0	3	0	0	0	0	0	2	2	2	0	0
cantered	5	.2579	.3199	35.0	0	2	1	1	1	0	0	0	1	0	0	3	0	0	0	0	0	0	0	0	1	0	0	0	0
cantering	2	.2427	.1152	30.6	0	1	0	0	1	0	0	0	0	0	0	0	0	0	0	0	0	0	0	0	1	1	0	0	0
Cantigny	4	.0000	.0778	28.9	0	0	0	0	0	4	0	0	0	0	0	0	0	4	0	0	0	0	0	0	0	0	0	0	0
cantilever	7	.3556	.6037	37.8	1	0	0	0	2	3	1	0	3	0	0	0	0	0	0	0	0	1	0	0	0	1	0	2	0
cantle	2	.1787	.1174	30.7	0	0	0	0	2	0	0	0	1	0	0	0	0	0	0	0	0	0	0	0	1	0	0	0	0
canton	3	.2387	.1708	32.3	0	0	2	0	1	0	0	0	0	0	0	0	0	0	0	0	0	0	0	0	0	2	1	0	0
Canton	10	.4296	.9838	39.9	0	1	5	1	0	2	1	0	3	1	0	0	0	2	0	0	0	0	0	0	0	4	0	0	0
cantons	6	.1845	.2851	34.5	0	0	5	0	1	0	0	0	0	0	0	0	0	0	0	0	0	0	0	0	0	5	1	0	0
cantos	3	.0000	.0314	25.0	0	0	0	0	0	3	0	0	0	0	0	0	0	0	0	0	0	0	0	0	0	0	3	0	0
Canty	5	.1820	.2261	33.5	0	0	0	0	4	1	0	0	0	1	0	0	0	0	0	0	0	0	0	0	4	0	0	0	0
Canute	11	.2167	.8345	39.2	1	0	10	0	0	0	0	0	10	0	0	0	0	0	0	0	0	0	0	0	0	0	1	0	0
canvas	70	.8004	11.297	50.5	10	8	5	9	20	10	4	4	19	2	0	8	0	3	0	0	4	3	1	1	12	9	3	5	0
canvas-covered	2	.2152	.1357	31.3	0	0	1	1	0	0	0	0	1	0	0	0	0	1	0	0	0	0	0	0	0	0	0	0	0
canvass	3	.1639	.1674	32.2	1	0	0	0	0	0	2	0	1	0	0	0	0	2	0	0	0	0	0	0	0	0	0	0	0
canyon	80	.7304	11.924	50.8	7	7	25	19	6	8	5	3	15	1	0	7	0	18	1	7	1	0	0	0	2	5	5	18	0
Canyon	57	.6588	7.6876	48.9	3	14	12	7	7	7	5	2	1	0	1	1	2	20	0	7	3	0	0	0	4	0	1	17	0
canyons	39	.6589	5.3790	47.3	2	4	7	2	12	4	5	3	11	1	0	2	0	9	0	8	0	0	0	0	0	1	1	6	0
cap	235	.7900	37.555	55.7	77	43	23	11	43	21	16	1	72	13	5	18	2	5	8	26	7	1	3	24	23	13	2	13	0
Cap	68	.1890	4.9614	47.0	0	52	11	4	1	0	0	0	65	0	0	2	0	0	0	0	0	0	0	0	0	0	0	1	0
CAP	12	.0000	.5482	37.4	0	0	0	0	12	0	0	0	12	0	0	0	0	0	0	0	0	0	0	0	0	0	0	0	0
cap'n	10	.2287	.5483	37.4	4	0	0	0	6	0	0	0	0	0	0	0	0	0	0	0	0	0	0	0	6	4	0	0	0
Cap'n	10	.3120	.7499	38.8	5	0	0	0	3	2	0	0	2	0	0	0	0	0	0	0	0	0	0	0	3	5	0	0	0
capabilities	8	.5477	.9095	39.6	0	1	0	0	2	1	2	2	0	0	0	0	0	0	0	2	1	0	0	0	0	1	2	2	0
capability	5	.4689	.4984	37.0	0	0	0	0	4	0	1	0	0	0	0	0	0	1	0	0	0	0	0	0	0	2	1	1	0
capable	86	.8416	14.464	51.6	0	5	4	8	35	15	11	8	13	3	2	3	1	4	2	13	7	0	0	1	3	7	17	10	0
capacitance	9	.0000	.0227	23.6	0	0	0	0	0	9	0	0	0	0	0	0	0	0	0	0	0	0	0	9	0	0	0	0	0
capacities	9	.5570	1.0559	40.2	0	0	1	0	2	4	0	2	1	0	0	0	0	1	0	2	1	0	0	0	0	0	1	3	0
capacitor	15	.0269	.1256	31.0	0	0	0	0	1	14	0	0	0	0	0	0	0	0	0	0	0	0	0	14	0	0	0	1	0
capacitors	9	.0145	.0905	29.6	0	0	0	1	0	8	0	0	1	0	0	0	0	0	0	0	0	0	0	8	0	0	0	0	0
capacity	63	.7587	9.6172	49.8	1	0	5	5	19	11	15	7	3	1	0	1	5	8	0	5	1	0	1	3	1	7	12	15	0
cape	22	.6743	3.1042	44.9	2	2	4	4	9	1	0	0	10	1	1	0	0	1	4	0	1	0	0	0	1	1	0	2	0
Cape	88	.8169	14.440	51.6	2	7	27	15	30	4	0	3	14	0	1	1	6	18	0	9	2	0	0	2	4	8	14	9	0
caped	2	.1948	.1250	31.0	0	0	0	2	0	0	0	0	1	0	0	0	0	0	0	0	0	0	0	0	0	1	0	0	0
Capella	4	.0000	.0789	29.0	0	0	2	0	0	0	0	2	0	0	0	0	0	0	0	4	0	0	0	0	0	0	0	0	0
caper	3	.3450	.2505	34.0	1	1	0	0	0	0	1	0	1	0	0	0	0	0	0	0	0	0	0	0	1	1	0	0	0
capered	3	.2227	.1589	32.0	0	1	0	2	0	0	0	0	0	0	0	0	0	0	0	0	0	0	0	0	2	0	0	1	0
capering	2	.2303	.1079	30.3	1	1	0	0	0	0	0	0	0	0	0	0	0	0	0	0	1	0	0	0	0	1	0	0	0
capers	2	.2128	.1055	30.2	0	0	0	1	0	0	0	1	0	0	0	0	0	0	0	1	1	0	0	0	0	0	0	0	0
capes	6	.3791	.5142	37.1	2	1	2	0	0	1	0	0	0	0	0	0	0	3	0	2	0	0	0	0	0	0	1	0	0
Capes	2	.0000	.0914	29.6	0	0	0	1	1	0	0	0	2	0	0	0	0	0	0	0	0	0	0	0	0	0	0	0	0
Capetian	2	.0000	.0209	23.2	0	0	2	0	0	0	0	0	0	0	0	0	0	0	0	0	0	0	0	0	0	0	2	0	0
Capetown	4	.0000	.0778	28.9	0	1	0	2	0	0	1	0	0	0	0	0	0	4	0	0	0	0	0	0	0	0	0	0	0
capillaries	39	.2622	2.5419	44.1	0	8	2	7	5	11	6	0	0	0	0	0	0	0	1	34	0	0	0	0	0	0	3	1	0
capillary	7	.3669	.5660	37.5	0	1	0	0	5	0	1	0	0	0	0	0	0	0	0	2	0	0	0	0	0	0	2	3	0
capita	7	.4372	.6471	38.1	1	0	1	0	2	0	2	1	0	1	0	0	0	0	0	0	0	0	0	0	0	1	3	2	0
capital	597	.7433	89.431	59.5	111	85	123	102	84	40	43	9	27	147	19	6	9	175	76	5	4	2	0	3	3	25	67	29	0
Capital	10	.5071	1.0927	40.4	1	0	1	1	6	0	1	0	2	1	0	0	0	0	0	0	0	0	0	0	0	4	1	2	0
capitalist	4	.1760	.1902	32.8	0	0	3	0	0	1	0	0	0	0	0	0	0	1	0	0	0	0	0	0	0	3	0	0	0
capitalization	19	.1656	.8254	39.2	0	2	5	2	2	2	6	0	1	16	0	0	0	1	1	0	0	0	0	0	0	0	0	0	0
capitalize	44	.2570	2.4519	43.9	2	2	1	7	19	4	9	0	0	19	18	0	0	0	6	0	0	0	0	0	0	0	0	1	0
capitalized	33	.5229	3.5854	45.5	3	2	4	5	6	8	5	0	2	18	3	1	0	2	5	1	0	0	1	0	0	0	0	0	0
capitalizing	2	.2408	.1091	30.4	0	0	0	1	1	0	0	0	0	1	0	0	0	0	1	0	0	0	0	0	0	0	0	0	0
capitals	45	.3598	3.4582	45.4	3	4	10	5	7	6	10	0	1	10	17	1	0	6	1	0	0	0	0	1	0	3	2	3	0
Capitan	2	.2417	.1091	30.4	0	0	1	0	0	1	0	0	0	0	0	0	0	0	0	0	1	0	0	0	0	0	1	0	0
capitol	14	.5015	1.4711	41.7	1	6	1	5	0	0	1	0	0	4	0	1	0	2	0	0	0	0	0	0	0	2	0	5	0
Capitol	37	.5974	4.5743	46.6	14	3	10	1	6	2	1	0	2	0	0	0	1	5	2	0	1	0	0	0	0	16	5	5	0
capitulate	2	.2433	.1158	30.6	0	0	0	0	1	0	1	0	0	0	0	0	0	0	0	0	0	0	0	0	0	1	0	1	0
capitulated	2	.0000	.0243	23.9	0	0	0	1	0	1	0	0	0	0	0	0	0	0	0	0	0	0	0	0	0	0	0	2	0
cappa	2	.0000	.0162	22.1	0	0	0	0	2	0	0	0	0	0	0	0	0	0	2	0	0	0	0	0	0	0	0	0	0
capped	7	.5300	.7776	38.9	1	1	1	0	2	1	1	0	0	1	0	0	0	1	0	1	0	0	0	0	0	2	0	2	0
Capri	3	.2387	.1708	32.3	2	0	1	0	0	0	0	0	0	0	0	0	0	0	0	0	0	0	0	0	0	2	1	0	0
capricious	5	.5551	.5726	37.6	0	0	0	1	2	1	1	0	0	0	0	1	0	0	0	1	1	0	0	0	0	0	1	1	0
Capricorn	12	.3343	.9320	39.7	0	2	4	5	1	0	0	0	0	0	0	0	0	8	0	2	0	0	0	0	0	0	2	0	0
Capricornus	2	.0000	.0209	23.2	0	0	0	2	0	0	0	0	0	0	0	0	0	0	0	0	0	0	0	0	0	0	2	0	0
caps	69	.8376	11.566	50.6	13	23	11	2	4	5	9	2	11	4	0	6	2	10	0	5	4	0	2	0	4	9	2	10	0
Caps	3	.0000	.1370	31.4	0	3	0	0	0	0	0	0	3	0	0	0	0	0	0	0	0	0	0	0	0	0	0	0	0
Capshaw	4	.0000	.0429	26.3	0	0	0	4	0	0	0	0	0	0	0	4	0	0	0	0	0	0	0	0	0	0	0	0	0
capsize	2	.0665	.0708	28.5	0	0	0	0	1	1	0	0	1	0	1	0	0	0	0	0	0	0	0	0	0	0	0	0	0
capsized	3	.2283	.1611	32.1	0	0	0	1	0	2	0	0	0	1	0	0	0	0	0	0	0	0	0	0	2	0	0	0	0
capstan	7	.1171	.2143	33.3	0	3	0	3	1	0	0	0	0	0	0	0	0	0	0	0	6	0	0	0	1	0	0	0	0
capstone	2	.0000	.0299	24.8	0	0	0	1	0	0	1	0	0	0	0	0	2	0	0	0	0	0	0	0	0	0	0	0	0
capsule	78	.5377	9.1382	49.6	14	5	25	13	8	8	1	4	20	4	0	0	2	2	0	41	0	0	0	0	0	2	5	2	0

8J Canon
8J canonic
8Q Canons
6R cantaloup-size
8G Cantalupo
7J cantatas
5Q cantcher
6R canted
7H cantelopes
5Q Canticles
6P Canto
8F Cantonese
4A cantonment
3A Cantor's
7N Canty's
9N cantyoucantyoucant
7D Canukiesung
5A Canute's
4P canvas-top
7R canvasback
8R canvases
7Q canvassed
7F canyon-like
4J Canzonetta
7F Cao
6R CapCom
XN cap-screwer
4A Cap's
4N Capa
8R Capability
9B capaciosity
9B capacious
9B capacious/capacity
8M capacitive
7A Cape's
9R Capek
9D Capels
3N Capernaum
5Q Capet
XH Caph
7D capitalists
7Q capitalizes
9R capitivity
4R capitol's
7R Capitoline
7Q capitulation
5P capon
7F Capon
8R Capone
4Q capping
7H caprice
4J Caprice
7Q capriciousness
7N capriscus
7M capscrews
6D capsizing
5H capsule's

Word Type	F	D	U	SFI	3 Gr 3	4 Gr 4	5 Gr 5	6 Gr 6	7 Gr 7	8 Gr 8	9 Gr 9	X UnGr	A Read	B Eng & Gr	C Comp	D Lit	E Math	F Soc Stud	G Spell	H Sci	J Music	K Art	L Home Ec	M Shop	N Lib F	P Lib NF	Q Lib Ref	R Mag	S Rel
capsules	10	.5476	1.1603	40.6	0	0	1	3	4	1	1	0	1	0	0	0	1	1	0	3	0	0	0	0	0	0	1	3	0
Capt	11	.3381	.8735	39.4	0	1	0	1	7	0	0	2	2	0	0	0	0	0	0	2	0	0	0	0	1	0	0	6	0
captain	367	.7814	58.892	57.7	54	116	44	49	57	34	13	0	208	9	3	21	1	28	4	1	6	0	0	0	26	41	8	11	0
Captain	392	.6662	55.239	57.4	108	120	33	65	35	21	7	3	201	1	0	12	0	22	2	0	9	1	0	0	52	80	4	8	0
captain's	21	.6876	3.0260	44.8	3	11	4	1	1	0	1	0	10	0	0	1	0	1	1	1	0	0	0	0	3	2	0	2	0
Captain's	8	.3746	.7768	38.9	3	2	1	1	0	1	0	0	6	0	0	0	0	0	0	0	0	0	0	0	1	1	0	0	0
captains	24	.6406	3.1925	45.0	1	3	7	4	2	6	1	0	3	1	0	0	0	9	0	3	0	0	0	0	1	2	4	1	0
Captains	3	.0000	.1370	31.4	0	0	3	0	0	0	0	0	3	0	0	0	0	0	0	0	0	0	0	0	0	0	0	0	0
captions	2	.0000	.0914	29.6	0	0	0	0	2	0	0	0	2	0	0	0	0	0	0	0	0	0	0	0	0	0	0	0	0
captive	21	.6873	2.9800	44.7	2	4	4	1	8	1	1	0	6	0	0	3	0	1	0	0	1	0	0	0	1	4	3	2	0
captives	16	.5229	1.8336	42.6	0	1	5	2	7	1	0	0	6	0	0	5	0	1	0	0	0	0	0	0	2	1	0	1	0
captivity	16	.5470	1.8239	42.6	0	2	1	1	7	0	4	1	1	0	0	3	0	1	0	1	0	0	0	0	1	0	5	4	0
captors	8	.6091	.9979	40.0	1	1	1	0	1	2	2	0	0	1	0	0	0	1	1	0	0	0	0	0	2	2	0	1	0
capture	94	.8094	15.353	51.9	4	14	22	20	16	10	6	2	26	12	1	5	0	13	3	5	2	0	0	0	0	13	9	5	0
captured	153	.8107	25.024	54.0	9	19	25	26	22	36	11	5	41	8	1	8	0	31	1	5	2	1	0	0	3	14	25	13	0
captures	10	.5858	1.2082	40.8	0	2	2	1	1	3	1	0	1	2	1	2	0	0	0	1	2	0	0	0	0	0	1	0	0
capturing	17	.6739	2.3570	43.7	0	1	1	3	7	3	1	1	3	0	0	2	0	4	0	1	1	1	0	0	0	1	3	1	0
Capua	2	.0000	.0209	23.2	0	0	0	0	0	0	2	0	0	0	0	0	0	0	0	0	0	0	0	0	0	0	2	0	0
Capulet	26	.0731	.7942	39.0	0	0	0	0	0	5	21	0	5	0	0	21	0	0	0	0	0	0	0	0	0	0	0	0	0
Capulet's	2	.0000	.0914	29.6	0	0	0	0	0	2	0	0	2	0	0	0	0	0	0	0	0	0	0	0	0	0	0	0	0
Capulets	2	.0000	.0162	22.1	0	0	0	0	0	0	2	0	0	0	0	0	0	0	0	0	2	0	0	0	0	0	0	0	0
Capybara	13	.0000	.5939	37.7	13	0	0	0	0	0	0	0	13	0	0	0	0	0	0	0	0	0	0	0	0	0	0	0	0
car	1752	.8575	302.74	64.8	406	203	97	125	511	295	90	25	909	94	18	69	101	98	20	58	4	5	3	1	145	96	15	116	0
Car	10	.2445	.7749	38.9	0	1	0	0	2	6	0	1	8	0	0	0	0	0	0	0	0	0	0	0	0	0	0	2	0
car's	16	.6348	2.1299	43.3	2	1	1	0	5	2	4	1	5	1	0	0	2	0	0	1	1	0	0	0	0	0	2	4	0
carabao	6	.3405	.5152	37.1	6	0	0	0	0	0	0	0	3	0	0	0	0	0	0	0	0	0	0	0	0	1	2	0	0
carabinieri	3	.0000	.0365	25.6	0	0	0	0	0	0	3	0	0	0	0	0	0	0	0	0	0	0	0	0	0	0	0	3	0
caracal	2	.0000	.0209	23.2	0	0	0	0	2	0	0	0	0	0	0	0	0	0	0	0	0	0	0	0	0	0	2	0	0
Caracas	20	.2809	1.3642	41.3	0	0	5	12	0	2	0	1	0	0	0	0	0	15	0	0	0	0	0	0	0	4	0	1	0
caramel	3	.3400	.2455	33.9	1	1	1	0	0	0	0	0	1	1	0	0	0	0	0	0	0	0	0	0	1	0	0	0	0
carapace	2	.0000	.0209	23.2	0	0	0	1	1	0	0	0	0	0	0	0	0	0	0	0	0	0	0	0	0	0	2	0	0
carat	5	.1485	.1943	32.9	0	0	0	4	0	0	1	0	0	0	0	0	1	0	0	0	0	0	0	0	0	0	4	0	0
carats	4	.0000	.0599	27.8	0	0	0	0	0	0	4	0	0	0	0	0	4	0	0	0	0	0	0	0	0	0	0	0	0
caravan	20	.5555	2.3909	43.8	0	2	0	5	8	2	3	0	5	3	0	0	0	9	1	0	1	0	0	0	0	1	0	0	0
caravans	12	.4159	1.1701	40.7	3	0	2	4	2	1	0	0	4	0	0	0	0	6	0	0	0	0	0	0	0	1	1	0	0
caravels	3	.3350	.2478	33.9	0	0	1	0	2	0	0	0	1	0	0	0	0	1	0	0	0	0	0	0	0	0	1	0	0
caraway	5	.1649	.2071	33.2	0	0	0	4	0	0	0	1	0	0	0	0	0	0	0	0	0	0	0	0	0	0	4	1	0
carb	6	.0000	.0729	28.6	0	0	0	0	6	0	0	0	0	0	0	0	0	0	0	0	0	0	0	0	0	0	0	6	0
carbide	12	.1380	.4528	36.6	0	2	0	0	6	2	2	0	2	0	0	0	0	0	0	0	0	0	0	7	0	1	0	2	0
carbine	2	.2443	.1130	30.5	0	0	0	0	2	0	0	0	0	0	0	1	0	0	0	0	0	0	0	0	1	0	0	0	0
carbines	2	.1814	.1187	30.7	0	0	0	0	1	1	0	0	1	0	0	0	0	0	0	0	0	0	0	0	0	0	0	1	0
carbohydrate	17	.3924	1.4584	41.6	3	0	3	4	2	2	3	0	0	0	0	0	0	0	0	11	0	0	4	1	0	0	1	0	0
carbohydrates	66	.2828	4.4575	46.5	6	3	28	3	12	4	9	1	0	0	0	0	0	0	0	53	0	0	11	0	0	0	2	0	0
carbolic	3	.2433	.1822	32.6	0	0	0	0	0	3	0	0	0	0	0	0	0	0	0	2	0	0	0	0	1	0	0	0	0
carbon	374	.4624	37.715	55.8	52	12	61	56	85	67	36	5	11	1	1	0	8	6	1	290	0	0	0	20	0	5	25	6	0
carbon-dioxide	2	.1814	.1187	30.7	0	0	0	1	0	0	1	0	1	0	0	0	0	0	0	0	0	0	0	0	0	0	0	1	0
carbonate	21	.2729	1.4001	41.5	0	1	0	4	0	9	7	0	0	0	0	0	0	1	0	16	0	0	0	0	0	0	4	0	0
carbonated	11	.2669	.6819	38.3	1	2	0	0	2	2	4	0	0	0	0	0	0	1	0	5	0	0	4	0	0	0	0	1	0
carbonates	2	.2160	.1362	31.3	1	0	0	0	0	1	0	0	1	0	0	0	0	0	0	1	0	0	0	0	0	0	0	0	0
Carboniferous	3	.0000	.0591	27.7	0	0	0	0	0	0	0	3	0	0	0	0	0	0	0	3	0	0	0	0	0	0	0	0	0
carbons	5	.2260	.2850	34.5	0	0	0	4	0	1	0	0	0	0	0	0	0	0	0	4	0	0	0	1	0	0	0	0	0
carburetor	14	.4806	1.4297	41.6	2	0	3	0	9	0	0	0	2	0	1	1	0	0	0	1	0	0	0	3	0	1	0	5	0
carburetors	4	.3706	.3628	35.6	0	0	0	1	2	0	1	0	2	0	0	0	0	0	0	0	0	0	0	0	1	0	1	0	0
carburizing	2	.0000	.0050	17.0	0	0	0	0	0	0	2	0	0	0	0	0	0	0	0	0	0	0	0	2	0	0	0	0	0
carcass	12	.5569	1.4477	41.6	0	0	3	3	3	0	1	2	5	0	1	0	0	0	0	0	0	0	0	0	2	1	1	2	0
carcasses	3	.3399	.2456	33.9	0	0	0	0	1	0	2	0	1	0	0	1	0	0	0	0	0	0	0	0	0	0	0	1	0
card	223	.8528	38.091	55.8	37	36	18	23	55	18	24	12	58	40	1	4	40	16	11	20	0	2	4	1	5	9	1	11	0
Card	16	.4348	1.4873	41.7	1	2	0	0	5	0	3	5	0	3	0	0	7	0	0	0	0	0	0	0	0	1	0	5	0
cardboard	181	.5604	21.393	53.3	57	25	19	18	28	17	8	9	28	0	1	3	37	1	0	56	1	27	3	4	5	7	2	6	0
cardboard-covered	2	.1948	.1250	31.0	0	0	0	0	0	2	0	0	1	0	0	0	0	0	0	0	0	0	0	0	0	1	0	0	0
cardboards	2	.1033	.0599	27.8	0	0	0	1	1	0	0	0	0	0	0	0	0	0	0	1	0	1	0	0	0	0	0	0	0
cardiac	6	.1116	.1956	32.9	0	0	0	0	1	2	3	0	0	0	0	0	0	0	0	1	0	0	0	0	0	0	5	0	0
Cardiff	4	.3730	.3206	35.1	2	0	0	1	1	0	0	0	0	0	0	0	0	0	0	0	1	0	0	0	2	0	0	1	0
cardinal	66	.2881	4.4649	46.5	13	19	19	8	6	0	1	0	1	0	0	0	53	3	1	2	0	0	0	0	0	4	2	0	0
Cardinal	7	.2438	.3959	36.0	0	0	3	0	2	2	0	0	0	0	0	0	0	0	0	0	0	0	0	0	0	0	3	4	0
cardinals	4	.3864	.3418	35.3	2	0	0	0	1	0	0	1	0	0	0	0	0	0	0	2	0	0	0	0	0	0	1	1	0
Cardinals	2	.2433	.1158	30.6	0	0	0	1	1	0	0	0	0	0	0	0	0	0	0	0	0	0	0	0	0	1	0	1	0
cards	186	.8464	31.446	55.0	34	17	26	17	48	22	10	12	28	16	1	4	57	17	18	4	2	3	4	0	6	6	10	10	0
Cards	4	.3732	.3288	35.2	1	0	0	2	1	0	0	0	0	0	0	0	2	0	0	0	0	0	0	0	0	1	0	1	0
care	886	.8942	157.87	62.0	222	153	85	88	141	111	73	13	287	36	6	49	0	69	17	66	21	4	46	13	95	103	19	52	3
cared	68	.7838	10.839	50.4	12	10	7	12	9	7	5	6	23	2	0	4	0	8	0	6	0	0	1	0	9	7	2	6	0
career	108	.7927	17.286	52.4	3	6	10	5	42	19	19	4	27	5	0	6	1	10	1	2	6	0	3	0	3	6	14	24	0
careering	4	.2954	.2881	34.6	0	1	0	1	0	1	1	0	1	0	0	2	0	0	0	0	0	0	0	0	0	0	0	1	0
careers	21	.6431	2.7880	44.5	0	4	3	0	6	4	4	0	3	0	0	0	1	3	0	1	2	0	0	0	0	2	5	4	0
carefree	17	.7313	2.5465	44.1	3	3	4	0	1	5	1	0	5	1	0	2	0	1	0	1	1	0	0	0	3	2	0	1	0
careful	424	.9018	76.005	58.8	54	98	52	40	81	39	49	11	109	31	17	15	10	29	31	47	3	4	19	10	18	46	20	15	0
carefully	993	.9180	180.75	62.6	180	170	129	115	187	96	97	19	245	106	29	43	44	49	111	102	35	12	34	26	45	60	16	36	0
Carel	2	.2446	.1122	30.5	0	0	0	0	1	1	0	0	0	0	0	1	0	0	0	0	0	0	0	0	0	0	1	0	0
careless	65	.7815	10.271	50.1	1	8	7	8	18	11	12	0	16	10	3	5	1	5	4	10	0	0	5	1	3	1	0	1	0
carelessly	25	.7222	3.6863	45.7	4	2	1	1	10	3	4	0	6	3	1	3	0	1	1	1	0	0	0	0	6	2	1	0	0
carelessness	11	.6469	1.4616	41.6	1	0	2	1	3	1	3	0	1	2	0	1	0	2	1	2	0	0	0	1	1	0	0	0	0
cares	35	.7774	5.5450	47.4	1	6	11	3	5	4	4	1	13	1	0	2	0	1	0	5	1	0	1	0	3	1	1	6	0
caress	3	.2304	.1619	32.1	0	0	0	0	3	0	0	0	0	0	0	0	0	0	0	0	0	0	0	0	2	0	1	0	0
caressing	4	.3718	.3639	35.6	0	0	0	0	2	1	1	0	2	1	0	0	0	0	0	0	0	0	0	0	1	0	0	0	0
caressingly	2	.2443	.1130	30.5	0	0	0	0	1	0	1	0	0	0	0	1	0	0	0	0	0	0	0	0	1	0	0	0	0
caretakers	3	.2197	.2090	33.2	0	1	0	1	1	0	0	0	2	0	0	0	0	0	0	0	0	0	0	0	0	0	1	0	0
Carew	6	.0000	.0729	28.6	0	0	0	0	6	0	0	0	0	0	0	0	0	0	0	0	0	0	0	0	0	0	0	6	0
careworn	2	.1717	.1142	30.6	0	0	0	0	1	1	0	0	1	0	0	1	0	0	0	0	0	0	0	0	0	0	0	0	0
carey	4	.0000	.0419	26.2	0	0	0	0	4	0	0	0	0	0	0	0	0	0	0	0	0	0	0	0	0	0	4	0	0
Carey	14	.4519	1.5201	41.8	1	0	10	0	2	0	1	0	10	0	1	0	0	1	0	0	0	0	0	0	0	1	0	1	0
cargo	106	.7009	15.339	51.9	17	21	9	24	29	2	2	2	32	2	0	0	0	13	0	1	4	0	0	0	11	18	7	18	0
cargoes	32	.5297	3.7141	45.7	2	2	6	12	3	4	2	1	9	0	0	1	0	16	0	1	0	0	0	0	0	2	2	1	0
Caribbean	55	.5319	6.2119	47.9	2	2	10	18	14	6	2	1	4	0	0	1	0	27	0	2	4	0	0	0	0	5	12	0	0
caribou	37	.6072	4.8170	46.8	2	3	20	4	6	1	0	1	16	0	0	0	0	8	1	0	2	0	0	0	0	0	5	5	0

5P captain-general
XR Captaine
6R captained
6A captainy
7N capting
5F caption
XR captioned
7R captious
8Q Captiva
9J captivated
7R captivating
8F Captive
9F Captivity
4A captor
8Q Capture
6A Captured
6Q capybara
7Q capybaras
5H car-hour
7R car-pool
7R car-trunk
3A carabao's
7N Carabine
9R carabiniere
6A Carakters
9L caramelizes
5A caramels
9R Carats
5Q Caravaggio
8F caravel
9D carbarn
7P carbide-tipped
8Q Carbon
8H carbon-containing
9M carbon-paper
8E carbon-14
7H carbonic
5Q carbonic-acid
7H carboniferous
9Q carbonized
6Q carbonol
7R carbs
7A card-house
XR cardamom
6A cardamons
7N cardigan
4K carding
9Q cardiovascular
7Q Cardorna
3Q care-free
9D careen
4P careening
7A Carefully
5A carefulness
6G carelesly
6P Cares
9D caressed
6E caret
4A caretaker
7E carets
7Q careyeros
7A carfare
3P CARGO
7R cargo-carrying

Word Type	F	D	U	SFI	3 Gr 3	4 Gr 4	5 Gr 5	6 Gr 6	7 Gr 7	8 Gr 8	9 Gr 9	X UnGr	A Read	B Eng & Gr	C Comp	D Lit	E Math	F Soc Stud	G Spell	H Sci	J Music	K Art	L Home Ec	M Shop	N Lib F	P Lib NF	Q Lib Ref	R Mag	S Rel
caricature	2	.2303	.1079	30.3	0	0	1	0	1	0	0	0	0	0	0	0	0	0	0	0	1	0	0	0	0	1	0	0	0
caricatured	2	.0000	.0243	23.9	0	0	0	0	0	0	1	1	0	0	0	0	0	0	0	0	0	0	0	0	0	0	0	2	0
caries	10	.1626	.4769	36.8	0	0	0	0	9	1	0	0	0	0	0	0	0	0	0	9	0	0	0	0	0	0	1	0	0
carillon	3	.2088	.1442	31.6	0	2	1	0	0	0	0	0	0	0	0	0	0	0	0	0	2	0	0	0	0	0	1	0	0
Carillon	2	.0000	.0162	22.1	0	2	0	0	0	0	0	0	0	0	0	0	0	0	0	0	2	0	0	0	0	0	0	0	0
caring	26	.7162	3.8029	45.8	4	3	4	3	4	3	4	1	5	0	1	1	0	4	0	3	0	0	2	0	6	2	1	1	0
Caring	2	.0000	.0050	17.0	0	0	0	0	2	0	0	0	0	0	0	0	0	0	0	0	0	0	0	2	0	0	0	0	0
Carl	74	.7852	11.705	50.7	11	9	6	2	17	18	5	6	13	15	0	8	2	5	0	1	3	2	0	0	7	8	2	8	0
Carl's	2	.2444	.1132	30.5	0	1	0	0	0	1	0	0	0	1	0	0	0	0	0	0	0	0	0	0	1	0	0	0	0
Carla	3	.3380	.2498	34.0	0	1	0	0	0	1	1	0	1	1	0	0	0	0	0	1	0	0	0	0	0	0	0	0	0
Carlin	2	.0000	.0215	23.3	0	0	0	0	0	0	2	0	0	0	0	2	0	0	0	0	0	0	0	0	0	0	0	0	0
Carlisle	7	.2414	.4297	36.3	0	5	1	0	1	0	0	0	1	0	0	1	0	0	0	0	0	0	0	0	0	5	0	0	0
Carlo	24	.4587	2.5845	44.1	0	14	2	5	2	1	0	0	15	0	0	0	0	0	0	0	4	0	0	0	0	2	3	0	0
Carlo's	2	.0000	.0914	29.6	0	2	0	0	0	0	0	0	2	0	0	0	0	0	0	0	0	0	0	0	0	0	0	0	0
carload	2	.2291	.1135	30.5	0	0	0	0	1	0	1	0	0	0	0	1	0	0	0	1	0	0	0	0	0	0	0	0	0
carloads	5	.4460	.5043	37.0	0	2	0	1	1	0	1	0	1	0	0	0	1	2	0	1	0	0	0	0	0	0	0	0	0
Carlos	318	.3394	30.253	54.8	24	280	2	6	3	1	1	1	292	3	0	0	0	7	0	0	3	0	0	0	0	1	3	9	0
Carlos'	3	.3406	.2461	33.9	0	1	0	1	1	0	0	0	1	1	0	0	0	0	0	0	0	0	0	0	0	0	0	1	0
Carlotta	4	.0000	.0789	29.0	0	0	0	0	4	0	0	0	0	0	0	0	0	0	0	4	0	0	0	0	0	0	0	0	0
Carlson	5	.0000	.0547	27.4	0	1	0	1	0	0	3	0	0	5	0	0	0	0	0	0	0	0	0	0	0	0	0	0	0
Carlyle	6	.2748	.3769	35.8	0	0	0	0	4	1	1	0	0	0	0	4	0	1	0	0	0	0	0	0	0	0	1	0	0
Carman	2	.0000	.0914	29.6	0	0	0	0	0	2	0	0	2	0	0	0	0	0	0	0	0	0	0	0	0	0	0	0	0
Carmelita	3	.0000	.0352	25.5	0	0	0	0	0	3	0	0	0	0	0	0	0	0	0	0	0	0	0	0	3	0	0	0	0
Carmen	43	.1864	2.3211	43.7	4	0	0	1	25	13	0	0	15	0	0	1	0	0	0	0	26	0	0	0	0	0	1	0	0
Carmichael	3	.2175	.1545	31.9	0	0	0	0	0	1	2	0	0	0	0	2	0	0	0	0	0	0	0	0	0	0	0	1	0
CARMICHAEL	4	.0000	.0429	26.3	0	0	0	0	0	0	4	0	0	0	0	4	0	0	0	0	0	0	0	0	0	0	0	0	0
Carminowe	2	.0000	.0243	23.9	0	0	0	0	0	0	0	2	0	0	0	0	0	0	0	0	0	0	0	0	0	0	0	2	0
Carmita	6	.0000	.1167	30.7	0	6	0	0	0	0	0	0	0	0	0	0	0	6	0	0	0	0	0	0	0	0	0	0	0
carnage	3	.2051	.1687	32.3	0	0	0	1	1	1	0	0	1	0	1	0	0	0	0	0	0	0	0	0	0	0	0	1	0
Carnarvon	4	.1112	.1666	32.2	3	0	0	0	0	1	0	0	1	0	0	0	0	0	0	0	0	0	0	0	0	3	0	0	0
Carnatic	6	.0000	.0703	28.5	0	0	0	0	6	0	0	0	0	0	0	0	0	0	0	0	0	0	0	0	6	0	0	0	0
carnation	5	.1127	.2213	33.4	5	0	0	0	0	0	0	0	1	0	0	0	0	0	0	4	0	0	0	0	0	0	0	0	0
carnations	5	.4047	.4558	36.6	1	0	0	4	0	0	0	0	1	2	0	0	0	0	0	1	0	0	0	0	0	0	1	0	0
carne	3	.1584	.1056	30.2	0	0	0	1	0	0	2	0	0	0	0	0	0	0	1	0	0	0	2	0	0	0	0	0	0
Carnegie	15	.4414	1.4574	41.6	1	0	2	1	3	7	1	0	1	0	0	0	0	9	0	0	1	0	0	0	0	1	0	3	0
carnival	43	.6845	6.0551	47.8	17	6	2	7	5	1	3	2	12	2	1	3	1	0	3	0	11	0	0	0	1	2	0	7	0
Carnival	7	.4003	.5970	37.8	3	1	0	0	0	2	0	1	0	0	0	2	0	1	0	0	3	0	0	0	0	0	0	1	0
carnivals	3	.3231	.2367	33.7	1	0	1	0	0	1	0	0	1	0	0	0	0	0	0	0	1	0	0	0	0	1	0	0	0
carnivore	4	.2353	.2382	33.8	0	0	0	0	1	3	0	0	0	0	0	0	0	0	0	3	0	0	0	0	0	0	1	0	0
carnivores	16	.2278	.9027	39.6	0	0	0	0	8	7	0	1	0	0	0	0	0	0	0	8	0	0	0	0	0	0	8	0	0
carnivorous	8	.1484	.3424	35.3	0	0	0	1	6	1	0	0	1	0	0	0	0	0	0	1	0	0	0	0	0	0	6	0	0
carnotite	5	.0000	.2284	33.6	0	0	1	4	0	0	0	0	5	0	0	0	0	0	0	0	0	0	0	0	0	0	0	0	0
carol	22	.0839	.5601	37.5	2	4	4	8	1	1	2	0	1	0	0	0	0	0	1	0	20	0	0	0	0	0	0	0	0
Carol	77	.6291	10.017	50.0	25	9	7	2	0	18	16	0	13	13	0	1	21	6	5	0	3	0	10	0	0	4	0	1	0
Carol's	20	.5950	2.4982	44.0	9	2	1	1	1	6	0	0	5	3	1	1	4	1	5	0	0	0	0	0	0	0	0	0	0
Carole	2	.0000	.0299	24.8	0	0	0	0	2	0	0	0	0	0	0	0	2	0	0	0	0	0	0	0	0	0	0	0	0
carolers	9	.1888	.4558	36.6	6	2	0	1	0	0	0	0	2	0	0	0	0	0	0	0	6	0	0	0	0	0	1	0	0
Carolina	17	.5168	1.9029	42.8	0	4	1	2	5	1	0	4	5	0	0	1	0	0	0	0	2	0	0	0	0	1	1	7	0
Carolinas	11	.6076	1.3712	41.4	2	2	3	0	0	4	0	0	0	1	0	0	0	3	0	0	2	0	0	0	0	2	2	1	0
Caroline	19	.5724	2.3057	43.6	0	1	10	5	2	0	0	1	3	0	0	1	0	6	0	2	0	0	0	0	4	3	0	0	0
Carolines	2	.0000	.0389	25.9	0	0	0	2	0	0	0	0	0	0	0	0	0	2	0	0	0	0	0	0	0	0	0	0	0
caroling	9	.2348	.6724	38.3	7	1	1	0	0	0	0	0	7	0	0	0	0	0	0	0	2	0	0	0	0	0	0	0	0
carols	18	.3827	1.5332	41.9	4	1	3	5	1	1	3	0	4	0	2	0	0	0	1	0	10	0	0	0	0	1	0	0	0
Carols	3	.2833	.1851	32.7	0	1	0	1	0	0	1	0	0	0	1	0	1	0	0	0	1	0	0	0	0	0	0	0	0
Carolyn	2	.2404	.1142	30.6	0	0	0	2	0	0	0	0	0	1	0	0	1	0	0	0	0	0	0	0	0	0	0	0	0
Carothers	3	.0000	.0591	27.7	0	0	0	0	3	0	0	0	0	0	0	0	0	0	0	3	0	0	0	0	0	0	0	0	0
carp	16	.4371	1.4948	41.7	6	4	0	0	2	1	3	0	0	0	0	4	0	4	0	0	1	0	0	0	0	0	0	7	0
Carpathia's	3	.0000	.0434	26.4	0	0	0	0	0	0	3	0	0	0	0	0	0	0	0	0	0	0	0	0	0	3	0	0	0
carpenter	55	.7325	8.2502	49.2	8	16	3	6	15	3	4	0	18	2	5	2	5	4	3	2	3	0	0	2	1	7	1	0	0
Carpenter	16	.4613	1.5654	41.9	0	0	1	1	10	4	0	0	2	5	3	3	0	0	0	0	2	0	0	0	0	0	0	1	0
carpenter's	17	.3794	1.5680	42.0	0	7	1	3	2	4	0	0	9	0	0	0	2	0	0	0	0	0	0	3	2	0	0	1	0
carpenters	22	.7282	3.2593	45.1	0	4	3	6	2	6	1	0	2	1	0	1	1	7	1	5	0	0	0	1	0	1	2	0	0
carpenters'	2	.0580	.0676	28.3	1	0	0	0	0	1	0	0	1	0	0	0	0	0	0	0	0	1	0	0	0	0	0	0	0
carpentry	11	.3506	.8751	39.4	0	0	0	1	5	0	5	0	1	0	0	4	0	1	0	0	0	0	0	0	0	5	0	0	0
carpet	51	.8537	8.7430	49.4	9	12	7	7	8	4	3	1	19	3	1	2	1	4	2	2	0	1	0	0	4	5	1	6	0
carpetbag	2	.2337	.1157	30.6	0	0	0	0	1	1	0	0	0	0	0	0	0	1	0	0	0	0	0	0	1	0	0	0	0
carpeted	4	.3393	.3134	35.0	0	0	0	1	1	1	1	0	1	0	0	1	0	0	0	0	0	0	0	1	1	0	0	0	0
carpeting	3	.3769	.2484	34.0	1	0	1	0	1	0	0	0	0	0	0	0	0	1	0	0	0	0	0	0	0	0	1	1	0
carpets	18	.7227	2.6734	44.3	4	4	1	3	2	3	0	1	5	0	0	2	0	3	1	3	0	0	0	0	1	0	1	2	0
Carr	14	.3570	1.1272	40.5	0	0	2	5	7	0	0	0	2	0	0	7	0	0	0	0	0	0	0	0	0	0	1	4	0
CARR	32	.0000	.3434	35.4	0	0	0	0	32	0	0	0	0	0	0	32	0	0	0	0	0	0	0	0	0	0	0	0	0
Carr's	2	.0000	.0215	23.3	0	0	0	0	2	0	0	0	0	0	0	2	0	0	0	0	0	0	0	0	0	0	0	0	0
Carranza	2	.0000	.0243	23.9	0	0	0	0	2	0	0	0	0	0	0	0	0	0	0	0	0	0	0	0	0	0	0	2	0
Carrara	2	.0000	.0290	24.6	2	0	0	0	0	0	0	0	0	0	0	0	0	0	0	0	0	0	0	0	0	2	0	0	0
carriage	135	.6846	18.972	52.8	27	38	19	11	19	6	13	2	30	1	0	10	0	13	3	1	8	1	0	15	24	23	5	1	0
carriage-door	2	.0000	.0215	23.3	0	0	0	0	0	0	2	0	0	0	0	2	0	0	0	0	0	0	0	0	0	0	0	0	0
carriages	28	.7292	4.1931	46.2	8	4	6	4	5	0	0	1	8	1	1	2	0	9	0	1	0	0	0	0	2	1	1	2	0
Carrie	29	.3451	2.4115	43.8	0	2	21	6	0	0	0	0	10	0	0	4	1	0	0	0	0	0	0	0	14	0	0	0	0
Carrie's	2	.0000	.0234	23.7	0	0	2	0	0	0	0	0	0	0	0	0	0	0	0	0	0	0	0	0	2	0	0	0	0
carried	909	.9182	165.75	62.2	154	147	125	151	145	96	82	9	263	28	5	55	16	125	10	106	21	1	5	7	69	102	54	42	0
carrier	46	.6931	6.5796	48.2	6	2	5	5	4	10	11	3	11	0	0	1	0	2	2	17	7	0	0	1	0	2	2	1	0
carriers	20	.5576	2.3645	43.7	3	1	1	4	3	3	2	3	3	0	0	0	0	4	0	3	0	0	0	0	0	1	4	5	0
carries	184	.8935	32.692	55.1	25	20	22	26	34	28	22	7	27	12	2	7	4	26	2	51	8	0	2	2	3	11	13	14	0
Carrington	2	.0000	.0914	29.6	0	0	0	0	2	0	0	0	2	0	0	0	0	0	0	0	0	0	0	0	0	0	0	0	0
carrion	9	.3297	.6628	38.2	6	0	0	0	1	0	2	0	0	0	0	2	0	0	0	0	0	0	0	0	0	6	1	0	0
Carroll	28	.5910	3.5447	45.5	0	5	7	7	2	5	0	2	10	2	0	0	0	4	1	2	0	0	0	0	0	1	0	8	0
Carroll's	4	.2442	.2268	33.6	0	0	1	3	0	0	0	0	0	2	0	0	0	0	0	0	0	0	0	0	0	0	0	2	0
carrot	44	.7244	6.5917	48.2	30	2	0	4	6	0	1	1	20	2	0	2	0	0	0	2	0	1	2	0	9	4	1	1	0
carrots	52	.4768	5.3700	47.3	23	4	6	2	3	3	11	0	13	3	1	0	0	3	1	3	1	0	16	0	6	3	0	2	0
carrousel	3	.0000	.0365	25.6	0	3	0	0	0	0	0	0	0	0	0	0	0	0	0	0	0	0	0	0	0	0	0	3	0
carry	940	.9284	173.01	62.4	213	135	127	118	154	95	74	24	232	28	9	36	29	135	20	178	14	6	13	2	31	111	44	52	0
Carry	2	.0000	.0162	22.1	0	0	2	0	0	0	0	0	0	0	0	0	0	0	0	0	2	0	0	0	0	0	0	0	0
carrying	421	.8963	75.269	58.8	85	79	46	69	72	39	25	6	150	7	2	26	8	57	2	47	6	3	9	0	24	43	13	24	0
carryings	2	.0000	.0234	23.7	0	0	2	0	0	0	0	0	0	0	0	0	0	0	0	0	0	0	0	0	2	0	0	0	0

4J carillons
XR Carilo
8H Carla's
8R Carlen
5A Carleton
7A Carlito
7Q Carloman
5F Carlsbad
7A Carlton
8Q Carlyle's
6A Carmela
8N Carmelita's
9R Carmelite
8J Carmen's
9Q Carmina
9R carminative
7H carmine
7D Carmon
6Q carnauba
9Q Carnot
4A Caroline's
8Q Carolingian
5N Caroliny
8L carotene
4A carousel
4N carp-fish
9P Carpathia
6R Carpathian
XH carped
6F Carpentaria
8C Carpenter's
8F Carpentier
8F carpetbaggers
6A carpetmaking
9J carping
XR carport
7D carr
7D CARR'S
5F Carrabelle
5Q Carraccis
7N carragheen
3J carramba
9Q Carre
8A Carreno
5R Carriacou
XR Carriage
3P CARRIAGES
6B Carriageway
6R Carrick
5R Carried
7N Carrol
4R Carrousel
4R carrousels
4J carroway
6N carry-all

Word Type	F	D	U	SFI	3 Gr 3	4 Gr 4	5 Gr 5	6 Gr 6	7 Gr 7	8 Gr 8	9 Gr 9	X UnGr	A Read	B Eng & Gr	C Comp	D Lit	E Math	F Soc Stud	G Spell	H Sci	J Music	K Art	L Home Ec	M Shop	N Lib F	P Lib NF	Q Lib Ref	R Mag	S Rel
cars	762	.8359	128.39	61.1	205	108	86	43	153	111	48	8	276	24	7	16	77	128	2	16	1	0	0	11	18	67	33	86	0
Carson	22	.6040	2.7832	44.4	3	7	6	1	3	0	2	0	5	4	2	0	4	1	1	0	0	0	0	0	0	4	0	1	0
cart	136	.7288	20.533	53.1	34	23	11	33	26	7	1	1	66	0	2	8	1	4	1	2	3	0	0	0	24	17	1	7	0
cart-horses	2	.0000	.0914	29.6	0	0	0	2	0	0	0	0	2	0	0	0	0	0	0	0	0	0	0	0	0	0	0	0	0
Cartagena	5	.0000	.0972	29.9	0	0	0	5	0	0	0	0	0	0	0	0	0	5	0	0	0	0	0	0	0	0	0	0	0
carted	2	.2440	.1132	30.5	0	1	0	0	1	0	0	0	0	0	0	1	0	0	0	0	0	0	0	0	0	0	0	1	0
carter	7	.0604	.1921	32.8	0	0	0	7	0	0	0	0	1	0	0	0	0	0	0	0	0	0	0	0	6	0	0	0	0
Carter	77	.5497	9.2738	49.7	42	9	7	7	7	3	2	0	33	2	0	0	1	6	1	0	0	0	0	0	0	18	0	16	0
Carter's	6	.4524	.5814	37.6	1	2	1	0	2	0	0	0	0	0	0	0	1	1	0	0	0	0	0	0	0	2	0	2	0
Carters	5	.4373	.4872	36.9	1	0	0	2	1	0	1	0	1	0	0	0	2	0	0	0	0	0	0	0	0	1	0	1	0
Carterville	2	.0000	.0219	23.4	0	0	0	0	0	2	0	0	0	2	0	0	0	0	0	0	0	0	0	0	0	0	0	0	0
Carthage	11	.4352	1.0302	40.1	0	0	1	4	5	0	1	0	0	0	0	0	0	4	0	0	0	0	0	0	0	1	4	2	0
Carthaginian	2	.2285	.1129	30.5	0	0	0	0	0	1	1	0	0	0	0	0	0	1	0	0	0	0	0	0	0	0	1	0	0
Carthaginians	2	.2285	.1129	30.5	0	0	0	1	0	0	1	0	0	0	0	0	0	1	0	0	0	0	0	0	0	0	1	0	0
Cartier	22	.0000	.4279	36.3	0	0	22	0	0	0	0	0	0	0	0	0	0	22	0	0	0	0	0	0	0	0	0	0	0
cartilage	18	.2401	1.0839	40.3	0	0	2	1	3	7	5	0	0	0	0	0	0	0	0	13	0	0	0	0	0	0	5	0	0
cartilaginous	2	.2331	.1157	30.6	0	0	0	0	1	0	1	0	0	0	0	0	0	0	0	1	0	0	0	0	1	0	0	0	0
cartload	3	.3776	.2504	34.0	0	2	0	0	0	1	0	0	0	0	0	1	0	1	0	0	0	0	0	0	0	1	0	0	0
cartographer	3	.2187	.1555	31.9	0	0	0	0	1	0	2	0	0	2	0	0	0	0	0	0	0	0	0	0	0	0	0	1	0
cartographers	3	.2159	.1532	31.9	0	2	0	1	0	0	0	0	0	0	0	0	0	0	0	0	0	0	0	0	0	0	2	1	0
carton	66	.6584	8.9550	49.5	17	17	1	14	7	3	6	1	9	1	0	0	14	1	1	22	0	1	8	1	7	0	0	1	0
Carton	4	.0000	.0429	26.3	0	0	0	0	0	0	4	0	0	0	0	4	0	0	0	0	0	0	0	0	0	0	0	0	0
cartons	43	.3898	3.7027	45.7	20	3	0	2	15	1	2	0	2	0	0	0	35	0	0	1	0	0	2	1	1	1	0	0	0
cartoon	26	.3768	2.2201	43.5	0	11	1	3	1	8	2	0	4	1	0	0	0	11	3	1	0	5	0	0	0	0	0	1	0
Cartoon	3	.0000	.0365	25.6	0	0	0	3	0	0	0	0	0	0	0	0	0	0	0	0	0	0	0	0	0	0	0	3	0
cartoonist	4	.0484	.0619	27.9	0	0	0	0	0	4	0	0	0	0	0	0	0	1	0	0	0	3	0	0	0	0	0	0	0
cartoonists	5	.2211	.2458	33.9	1	0	0	0	0	2	2	0	0	0	0	0	0	0	0	0	0	2	0	0	0	0	2	1	0
cartoons	32	.4274	3.0310	44.8	5	8	1	7	1	7	3	0	6	1	0	0	1	11	0	0	0	6	1	0	0	0	1	5	0
cartopper	2	.0000	.0243	23.9	0	0	0	0	2	0	0	0	0	0	0	0	0	0	0	0	0	0	0	0	0	0	0	2	0
cartridge	11	.5902	1.3742	41.4	1	3	1	2	2	1	1	0	3	0	0	1	0	0	1	1	0	0	0	0	0	3	2	0	0
cartridges	5	.4784	.5050	37.0	0	1	0	2	2	0	0	0	0	0	0	0	2	0	0	0	0	0	0	0	0	1	1	1	0
carts	40	.7632	6.1987	47.9	11	7	3	7	6	1	3	2	9	0	1	3	2	9	0	2	1	0	0	0	4	0	6	3	0
cartwheel	4	.2389	.2497	34.0	0	2	1	0	1	0	0	0	1	0	0	0	0	1	0	0	2	0	0	0	0	0	0	0	0
cartwheels	3	.3465	.2515	34.0	0	2	0	0	1	0	0	0	1	0	0	0	0	0	0	0	0	0	0	0	0	1	0	1	0
Cartwright	4	.0000	.0486	26.9	0	0	4	0	0	0	0	0	0	0	0	0	0	0	0	0	0	0	0	0	0	0	0	4	0
Cartwright's	2	.1698	.1133	30.5	0	0	0	0	2	0	0	0	1	0	0	0	0	0	0	0	0	0	0	0	0	0	1	0	0
Caruso	7	.2320	.3693	35.7	2	0	0	0	5	0	0	0	0	0	0	0	0	0	0	0	5	0	0	0	0	1	1	0	0
carve	30	.5910	3.8016	45.8	5	7	1	5	5	2	4	1	13	2	0	2	0	1	1	1	0	3	0	0	0	2	2	3	0
carved	123	.6049	15.529	51.9	13	24	14	24	16	15	12	5	26	3	3	6	2	24	3	4	1	20	0	2	5	7	5	12	0
Carver	42	.1101	2.5848	44.1	11	1	0	23	6	0	1	0	41	0	0	1	0	0	0	0	0	0	0	0	0	0	0	0	0
Carver's	2	.0000	.0914	29.6	0	0	0	1	1	0	0	0	2	0	0	0	0	0	0	0	0	0	0	0	0	0	0	0	0
carvers	3	.2184	.1759	32.5	2	0	0	0	0	0	1	0	1	0	0	0	0	0	0	0	0	0	0	1	0	0	0	1	0
Carvers	3	.0000	.1370	31.4	3	0	0	0	0	0	0	0	3	0	0	0	0	0	0	0	0	0	0	0	0	0	0	0	0
carves	10	.2446	.7670	38.8	0	3	7	0	0	0	0	0	7	0	0	0	0	0	0	3	0	0	0	0	0	0	0	0	0
carving	40	.4309	3.7615	45.8	7	5	2	10	9	3	4	0	10	1	1	0	0	3	1	0	0	12	0	5	3	2	1	1	0
carvings	13	.4978	1.4182	41.5	3	0	2	3	3	0	1	1	3	1	0	0	1	5	0	0	0	0	0	0	0	0	3	0	0
Cary	7	.1585	.3013	34.8	0	0	0	0	0	0	6	1	0	0	0	0	0	0	0	0	0	0	0	0	0	6	0	1	0
Carys	3	.0000	.0434	26.4	0	0	0	0	0	0	3	0	0	0	0	0	0	0	0	0	0	0	0	0	0	3	0	0	0
Casa	2	.1698	.1133	30.5	0	0	0	0	2	0	0	0	1	0	0	0	0	0	0	0	0	0	0	0	0	0	1	0	0
Casablanca	2	.2285	.1129	30.5	0	1	0	1	0	0	0	0	0	0	0	0	0	1	0	0	0	0	0	0	0	0	1	0	0
Casas	8	.0775	.2896	34.6	1	0	0	7	0	0	0	0	1	0	0	0	0	7	0	0	0	0	0	0	0	0	0	0	0
cascade	5	.4110	.4623	36.6	0	0	0	3	0	0	2	0	1	0	0	1	0	1	0	0	0	0	0	0	2	0	0	0	0
Cascade	6	.4639	.6013	37.8	0	0	1	0	1	0	3	1	0	0	0	0	0	1	0	3	0	0	0	0	0	0	1	1	0
cascades	4	.1873	.1827	32.6	0	0	2	0	2	0	0	0	0	0	0	0	0	0	0	0	0	0	0	0	0	0	3	1	0
Cascades	6	.4784	.6081	37.8	0	0	2	1	1	1	1	0	0	0	0	1	0	2	0	0	0	0	0	0	0	0	1	2	0
cascading	2	.2437	.1129	30.5	0	0	1	1	0	0	0	0	0	0	0	0	0	0	0	0	0	0	0	0	0	0	1	1	0
Caschcasch	2	.0000	.0234	23.7	0	0	2	0	0	0	0	0	0	0	0	0	0	0	0	0	0	0	0	0	2	0	0	0	0
case	646	.9328	119.21	60.8	52	72	45	63	151	117	119	27	110	32	16	33	75	57	13	60	10	3	15	21	30	47	63	61	0
Case	13	.5786	1.5852	42.0	4	0	0	1	2	3	2	1	3	3	0	0	0	0	0	0	0	0	0	0	3	1	1	2	0
case-hardened	2	.2411	.1091	30.4	0	0	0	1	0	0	1	0	0	0	0	1	0	0	0	0	1	0	0	0	0	0	0	0	0
casehardening	4	.0000	.0101	20.0	0	0	0	0	0	0	4	0	0	0	0	0	0	0	0	0	0	0	0	4	0	0	0	0	0
casein	5	.2068	.2673	34.3	0	1	0	0	4	0	0	0	0	0	0	0	0	0	0	4	0	1	0	0	0	0	0	0	0
casement	5	.2811	.3340	35.2	0	0	0	1	1	0	3	0	1	0	0	3	0	0	0	0	0	0	0	1	0	0	0	0	0
casements	2	.1733	.1149	30.6	0	0	0	2	0	0	0	0	1	1	0	0	0	0	0	0	0	0	0	0	0	0	0	0	0
cases	307	.8460	51.840	57.1	16	17	19	13	80	67	88	7	24	17	3	5	29	80	5	35	1	0	9	7	1	13	47	31	0
Casey	279	.2810	23.373	53.7	45	4	4	205	10	0	11	0	226	3	0	0	0	0	0	0	0	0	0	0	0	50	0	0	0
Casey's	11	.1945	.8000	39.0	1	0	0	2	8	0	0	0	10	0	0	0	0	0	0	0	0	0	0	0	0	1	0	0	0
cash	111	.6640	15.469	51.9	41	6	7	10	15	20	7	5	48	5	0	2	2	12	2	1	0	0	13	0	3	8	7	8	0
Cash	7	.0000	.3198	35.0	7	0	0	0	0	0	0	0	7	0	0	0	0	0	0	0	0	0	0	0	0	0	0	0	0
cashed	3	.3834	.2447	33.9	0	1	1	0	1	0	0	0	0	0	0	0	0	0	1	0	0	0	0	0	1	0	1	0	0
cashes	2	.0000	.0290	24.6	2	0	0	0	0	0	0	0	0	0	0	0	0	0	0	0	0	0	0	0	0	2	0	0	0
cashier	7	.2409	.3975	36.0	1	0	1	0	2	3	0	0	1	1	3	0	0	0	0	0	0	0	0	0	1	0	0	1	0
cashier's	5	.4290	.4744	36.8	1	0	1	0	1	0	2	0	1	1	0	0	0	0	0	0	0	0	0	0	1	0	0	2	0
Cashman	7	.0000	.0851	29.3	0	0	7	0	0	0	0	0	0	0	0	0	0	0	0	0	0	0	0	0	0	0	0	7	0
casing	10	.4571	1.0245	40.1	3	0	0	2	3	2	0	0	4	0	0	0	0	0	0	1	0	0	2	1	0	0	2	0	0
casings	3	.1386	.0963	29.8	0	0	0	0	1	1	1	0	0	0	0	0	0	0	0	0	0	0	2	0	0	0	1	0	0
cask	12	.3610	1.1560	40.6	4	1	3	4	0	0	0	0	10	0	0	0	0	0	1	0	0	0	0	0	1	0	0	0	0
casket	7	.2594	.4649	36.7	0	0	0	0	1	1	5	0	2	0	0	4	0	0	0	0	0	0	0	0	1	0	0	0	0
caskets	6	.1717	.3427	35.3	0	2	0	0	0	0	4	0	3	0	0	3	0	0	0	0	0	0	0	0	0	0	0	0	0
casks	4	.4525	.4044	36.1	0	0	1	0	1	2	0	0	1	0	0	0	0	1	0	0	0	0	0	0	1	0	0	1	0
Caspar	9	.3232	.7313	38.6	3	0	0	4	0	2	0	0	4	0	0	0	0	0	0	0	3	0	0	0	0	2	0	0	0
Caspian	13	.3204	.9753	39.9	0	0	0	6	4	3	0	0	0	1	0	0	3	9	0	0	0	0	0	0	0	0	0	0	0
cassava	2	.2285	.1129	30.5	0	0	0	1	0	1	0	0	0	0	0	0	0	1	0	0	0	0	0	0	0	0	1	0	0
casserole	14	.0000	.0451	26.5	0	0	0	0	6	0	8	0	0	0	0	0	0	0	0	0	0	0	14	0	0	0	0	0	0
casseroles	2	.0000	.0064	18.1	0	0	0	0	1	0	1	0	0	0	0	0	0	0	0	0	0	0	2	0	0	0	0	0	0
Cassim	4	.0000	.1827	32.6	0	4	0	0	0	0	0	0	4	0	0	0	0	0	0	0	0	0	0	0	0	0	0	0	0
Cassiopeia	2	.2291	.1135	30.5	0	0	0	0	0	0	1	1	0	0	0	1	0	0	0	1	0	0	0	0	0	0	0	0	0
Cassius	7	.0000	.3198	35.0	0	0	0	0	0	7	0	0	7	0	0	0	0	0	0	0	0	0	0	0	0	0	0	0	0
cassowary	3	.1200	.1302	31.1	2	0	0	1	0	0	0	0	1	2	0	0	0	0	0	0	0	0	0	0	0	0	0	0	0
cast	145	.8427	24.476	53.9	13	18	12	16	41	21	20	4	38	7	2	16	2	8	0	2	5	2	1	9	12	12	5	24	0
cast-iron	3	.3842	.2485	34.0	0	0	1	0	1	1	0	0	0	0	0	1	0	0	0	0	0	0	0	0	0	1	1	0	0
castanets	11	.3151	.7515	38.8	0	1	1	2	5	1	1	0	0	0	0	1	0	0	0	0	7	0	0	0	0	1	2	0	0
castaways	2	.2433	.1158	30.6	0	1	0	1	0	0	0	0	0	0	0	0	0	0	0	0	0	0	0	0	0	1	0	1	0
caste	16	.4285	1.4647	41.7	0	9	1	3	0	0	2	1	0	0	0	1	0	3	0	1	1	0	0	0	0	1	9	0	0
Castelli	2	.0000	.0243	23.9	0	0	0	0	0	0	1	1	0	0	0	0	0	0	0	0	0	0	0	0	0	0	0	2	0
castes	4	.1505	.1615	32.1	0	3	0	1	0	0	0	0	0	0	0	0	0	1	0	0	0	0	0	0	0	0	3	0	0

9R Cars
4E Carson's
3A Carstairs
7B cart-wheel
6A cart-whip
8F Carta
5P cartel
6N carter's
6N carthorse
7Q Carthusian
5F Cartier's
6A carting
XH cartographic
7R cartopper's
7D cartway
7R cartwheeling
7J Caruso's
9D carver
9P Cary's
XQ caryatid
6B casa
3J Cascabel
9P cascaded
7P casework
8F cash-starved
6H cashew
7D cashing
5R Cashman's
9L cashmere
7N cashmere-sweater
9Q Casilinum
4Q casing-stones
4R Caslavska
4P Cassadaga
8A Cassandra
XR Cassatt
7R Cassell
5P Cassidy
3A Cassiterides
XH cassiterite
9R cassock
7Q cassowaries
9M cast-metal
6A cast-off
6F caster

Word Type	F	D	U	SFI	3 Gr 3	4 Gr 4	5 Gr 5	6 Gr 6	7 Gr 7	8 Gr 8	9 Gr 9	X UnGr	A Read	B Eng & Gr	C Comp	D Lit	E Math	F Soc Stud	G Spell	H Sci	J Music	K Art	L Home Ec	M Shop	N Lib F	P Lib NF	Q Lib Ref	R Mag	S Rel
castigated	2	.2285	.1129	30.5	0	0	0	0	0	2	0	0	0	0	0	0	0	1	0	0	0	0	0	0	0	0	1	0	0
Castile	4	.1737	.1745	32.4	0	0	2	0	0	2	0	0	0	0	0	0	0	0	0	0	0	0	0	0	0	1	3	0	0
casting	40	.4768	4.0193	46.0	2	2	4	1	12	9	9	1	5	0	1	1	1	0	1	0	1	0	0	12	3	3	5	7	0
castings	6	.1215	.1786	32.5	0	0	1	0	0	1	4	0	0	0	0	0	0	0	0	1	0	0	0	4	0	0	1	0	0
Castiza	2	.0000	.0290	24.6	0	0	0	0	2	0	0	0	0	0	0	0	0	0	0	0	0	0	0	0	0	2	0	0	0
castle	191	.7574	29.897	54.8	51	39	29	46	8	13	5	0	111	1	0	14	0	14	2	0	9	4	0	0	9	14	9	4	0
Castle	55	.6521	7.6602	48.8	3	2	28	8	5	6	1	2	32	0	0	2	0	1	0	3	0	0	0	0	5	2	6	4	0
Castle's	2	.1497	.1046	30.2	1	0	1	0	0	0	0	0	1	0	0	0	0	0	1	0	0	0	0	0	0	0	0	0	0
castles	38	.6995	5.4408	47.4	10	7	2	12	4	2	0	1	7	5	0	1	0	5	1	1	6	0	0	0	2	9	1	0	0
castor	4	.0000	.0579	27.6	0	4	0	0	0	0	0	0	0	0	0	0	0	0	0	0	0	0	0	0	0	4	0	0	0
Castor	4	.1854	.1872	32.7	0	0	0	3	1	0	0	0	0	0	0	0	0	0	0	0	0	0	0	0	0	1	0	3	0
Castro	13	.4036	1.1743	40.7	0	0	4	0	5	3	0	1	1	0	1	0	0	8	0	0	0	0	0	0	0	0	0	3	0
Castro's	4	.2352	.2332	33.7	0	0	0	0	2	2	0	0	0	0	0	0	0	2	0	0	0	0	0	0	0	0	0	2	0
casts	23	.6520	3.0727	44.9	0	0	2	2	6	3	7	3	1	2	0	0	8	1	0	4	0	1	0	0	0	1	1	4	0
casual	29	.7019	4.1152	46.1	0	1	5	1	14	3	5	0	1	4	0	4	0	3	0	0	0	0	2	0	1	5	3	6	0
casually	19	.7153	2.7774	44.4	3	1	4	2	4	2	3	0	5	2	1	2	0	0	0	0	0	1	0	0	2	2	1	3	0
casualties	11	.3820	.9306	39.7	0	0	0	0	3	7	1	0	0	0	1	0	0	7	0	0	0	0	0	0	0	0	3	0	0
casualty	3	.1119	.0792	29.0	0	1	0	0	0	2	0	0	0	0	2	0	0	0	0	0	0	0	0	0	0	0	1	0	0
cat	620	.8483	105.85	60.2	265	121	23	34	124	29	17	7	273	68	12	34	8	0	16	32	25	7	0	0	70	23	17	35	0
Cat	66	.5764	8.2800	49.2	31	14	2	8	11	0	0	0	33	3	0	1	0	1	0	0	2	0	0	0	16	1	0	9	0
CAT	8	.2375	.4448	36.5	0	3	0	0	5	0	0	0	0	3	0	0	0	0	0	0	0	0	0	0	0	0	0	5	0
cat's	27	.7238	3.9841	46.0	3	9	0	2	9	1	3	0	6	5	0	5	0	0	2	4	1	0	0	1	1	0	2	0	0
Cat's	5	.3939	.4383	36.4	2	1	0	1	1	0	0	0	1	1	0	0	0	0	0	0	2	0	0	0	1	0	0	0	0
Cat's-meat-Man	2	.0000	.0234	23.7	0	2	0	0	0	0	0	0	0	0	0	0	0	0	0	0	0	0	0	0	2	0	0	0	0
catabolic	2	.2278	.1128	30.5	0	0	0	1	0	0	1	0	0	0	0	0	0	0	0	1	0	0	0	0	0	0	1	0	0
Catala	2	.0000	.0389	25.9	0	2	0	0	0	0	0	0	0	0	0	0	0	2	0	0	0	0	0	0	0	0	0	0	0
catalog	22	.5312	2.5401	44.0	0	5	1	0	12	2	1	1	8	8	0	0	0	0	1	1	0	0	0	1	0	0	0	3	0
cataloged	2	.0000	.0394	26.0	0	0	0	0	2	0	0	0	0	0	0	0	0	0	0	2	0	0	0	0	0	0	0	0	0
catalogs	6	.4291	.5636	37.5	1	0	1	0	3	0	1	0	1	0	0	0	0	0	0	1	0	0	0	1	0	0	2	1	0
catalogue	12	.4529	1.2169	40.9	0	0	2	0	9	0	0	1	4	5	0	1	0	0	0	0	0	0	0	0	1	0	0	1	0
catalogued	2	.2437	.1129	30.5	0	1	0	0	1	0	0	0	0	0	0	0	0	0	0	0	0	0	0	0	0	0	1	1	0
catalogues	3	.2159	.1532	31.9	0	0	0	0	1	2	0	0	0	0	0	0	0	0	0	0	0	0	0	0	0	0	2	1	0
cataloguing	3	.2321	.1635	32.1	0	0	0	0	2	0	0	1	0	0	0	0	0	0	0	0	0	0	0	0	0	0	1	2	0
catalyst	3	.2672	.1815	32.6	0	0	0	0	0	2	1	0	0	0	0	0	0	0	0	1	0	0	0	1	0	0	1	0	0
catalysts	2	.2278	.1128	30.5	0	0	1	0	1	0	0	0	0	0	0	0	0	0	0	1	0	0	0	0	0	0	1	0	0
catapult	3	.3346	.2478	33.9	0	0	0	1	2	0	0	0	1	0	0	0	0	0	0	1	0	0	0	0	0	0	1	0	0
catapulted	2	.1948	.1250	31.0	0	0	1	0	0	0	1	0	1	0	0	0	0	0	0	0	0	0	0	0	0	1	0	0	0
catapults	3	.0000	.0314	25.0	0	1	0	0	1	0	1	0	0	0	0	0	0	0	0	0	0	0	0	0	0	0	3	0	0
cataract	6	.5514	.7097	38.5	0	0	1	1	1	1	1	1	2	0	0	1	0	0	0	0	1	0	0	0	0	0	1	1	0
Catarina	4	.0000	.1827	32.6	0	0	0	4	0	0	0	0	4	0	0	0	0	0	0	0	0	0	0	0	0	0	0	0	0
catastrophe	9	.5891	1.1220	40.5	0	1	0	1	5	1	0	1	2	0	0	0	0	1	0	2	0	0	0	0	1	0	2	1	0
catastrophes	2	.1033	.0599	27.8	0	0	0	0	0	1	0	1	0	0	0	0	0	0	0	1	0	1	0	0	0	0	0	0	0
catastrophic	5	.1285	.1797	32.5	0	1	0	0	2	0	2	0	0	0	0	0	0	1	0	0	0	0	0	0	0	0	4	0	0
catatonic	3	.2321	.1635	32.1	0	0	0	0	2	0	1	0	0	0	0	0	0	0	0	0	0	0	0	0	0	0	1	2	0
catbird	7	.3169	.5590	37.5	0	0	0	0	2	2	1	2	3	1	0	3	0	0	0	0	0	0	0	0	0	0	0	0	0
catbird's	3	.2175	.1545	31.9	0	0	0	0	2	0	0	1	0	0	0	2	0	0	0	0	0	0	0	0	0	0	0	1	0
catboat	2	.1733	.1149	30.6	0	0	0	1	1	0	0	0	1	1	0	0	0	0	0	0	0	0	0	0	0	0	0	0	0
catboats	3	.2223	.2106	33.2	0	0	0	2	1	0	0	0	2	1	0	0	0	0	0	0	0	0	0	0	0	0	0	0	0
catch	679	.8951	121.28	60.8	234	126	69	84	79	57	24	6	268	22	21	40	8	53	14	60	16	8	4	1	52	65	12	35	0
Catch	2	.0000	.0243	23.9	0	0	0	0	0	0	0	2	0	0	0	0	0	0	0	0	0	0	0	0	0	0	0	2	0
catched	4	.3793	.3203	35.1	0	0	0	0	1	0	3	0	0	1	1	1	0	0	0	0	0	0	0	0	1	0	0	0	0
catcher	58	.4463	6.1832	47.9	7	37	5	9	0	0	0	0	37	3	0	0	0	0	0	1	0	0	0	0	0	15	2	0	0
catcher's	9	.4520	.9376	39.7	2	1	2	0	2	1	1	0	4	1	0	0	1	0	0	0	0	0	0	0	0	3	0	0	0
catchers	6	.2569	.3889	35.9	1	1	0	1	3	0	0	0	1	0	0	0	0	0	0	0	0	0	0	0	0	4	0	1	0
catches	88	.8033	14.267	51.5	19	11	8	18	17	9	4	2	20	5	0	12	2	4	0	25	3	2	0	1	3	7	0	4	0
catching	108	.8085	17.656	52.5	20	14	14	14	29	8	6	3	35	4	0	14	1	7	1	10	0	0	1	0	6	13	6	10	0
catchup	3	.1274	.0913	29.6	0	0	1	0	1	0	2	0	0	0	0	0	0	0	0	0	0	0	2	0	0	0	0	1	0
catchy	2	.2407	.1090	30.4	0	0	1	0	0	0	1	0	0	1	0	0	0	0	0	0	1	0	0	0	0	0	0	0	0
categories	29	.5897	3.4837	45.4	0	1	1	1	12	7	6	1	0	11	3	0	1	0	0	1	1	0	1	0	0	0	4	7	0
category	41	.4448	3.8447	45.8	0	0	1	4	7	22	4	3	1	28	2	0	0	0	0	0	0	0	1	0	0	1	1	7	0
catered	2	.2433	.1158	30.6	0	0	0	0	1	1	0	0	0	0	0	0	0	0	0	0	0	0	0	0	0	1	0	1	0
catering	2	.0000	.0243	23.9	0	0	0	0	2	0	0	0	0	0	0	0	0	0	0	0	0	0	0	0	0	0	0	2	0
caterpillar	66	.5139	7.2931	48.6	34	7	4	4	11	2	4	0	7	1	0	4	0	0	0	33	0	0	0	0	0	12	9	0	0
Caterpillar	16	.2065	.7942	39.0	0	0	12	0	4	0	0	0	0	0	0	0	0	0	0	0	0	0	0	0	12	0	4	0	0
caterpillars	33	.5253	3.7121	45.7	20	0	3	4	3	1	1	1	5	1	0	0	0	1	0	6	0	0	0	0	1	14	5	0	0
caterwauling	3	.3465	.2515	34.0	0	2	0	0	1	0	0	0	1	0	0	0	0	0	0	0	0	0	0	0	0	1	0	1	0
catfish	34	.5047	3.6594	45.6	12	4	0	1	11	5	0	1	5	1	0	0	0	1	1	1	0	0	0	0	3	0	5	17	0
catgut	2	.1948	.1250	31.0	1	0	0	0	1	0	0	0	1	0	0	0	0	0	0	0	0	0	0	0	0	1	0	0	0
Cathcart	2	.0000	.0914	29.6	0	0	0	0	2	0	0	0	2	0	0	0	0	0	0	0	0	0	0	0	0	0	0	0	0
cathedral	39	.5179	4.1737	46.2	2	7	8	5	4	5	7	1	0	1	0	0	0	7	0	0	10	5	0	0	0	4	10	2	0
Cathedral	18	.4448	1.7659	42.5	0	3	6	1	1	4	2	1	5	0	0	0	1	1	0	0	3	3	0	0	0	0	4	1	0
cathedrals	12	.3753	.9607	39.8	0	1	0	1	3	0	6	1	0	0	0	0	0	2	0	0	1	3	0	0	0	1	4	1	0
Catherine	26	.3148	1.8877	42.8	2	15	7	0	0	1	1	0	3	0	0	0	1	0	0	0	0	0	0	0	0	0	7	15	0
catheter	3	.0000	.0314	25.0	0	0	0	0	0	1	2	0	0	0	0	0	0	0	0	0	0	0	0	0	0	0	3	0	0
Cathie	5	.1496	.2557	34.1	0	0	5	0	0	0	0	0	2	0	0	0	0	0	0	0	0	0	0	0	0	0	0	3	0
cathode	14	.0000	.2760	34.4	0	0	0	0	0	2	0	12	0	0	0	0	0	0	0	14	0	0	0	0	0	0	0	0	0
Catholic	67	.4881	6.9338	48.4	10	6	12	5	12	11	10	1	5	0	0	3	0	7	0	0	1	0	0	0	0	7	30	14	0
Catholicism	6	.4598	.5888	37.7	1	0	1	0	1	2	1	0	0	0	0	0	0	2	0	0	0	0	0	0	0	1	2	1	0
Catholics	26	.4709	2.5915	44.1	1	3	4	0	3	8	7	0	0	0	0	1	0	7	1	0	0	0	0	0	0	4	12	1	0
Cathy	25	.2814	1.9130	42.8	12	12	0	0	1	0	0	0	12	0	0	0	12	0	0	0	0	0	0	0	0	0	1	0	0
Catlin	10	.0000	.4568	36.6	10	0	0	0	0	0	0	0	10	0	0	0	0	0	0	0	0	0	0	0	0	0	0	0	0
catnip	4	.1494	.2089	33.2	2	0	0	2	0	0	0	0	2	0	0	0	0	0	0	0	2	0	0	0	0	0	0	0	0
cats	211	.8435	35.741	55.5	80	31	9	16	52	10	10	3	69	18	2	19	23	3	5	14	1	7	0	0	19	9	13	9	0
Cats	6	.4862	.6608	38.2	4	1	0	0	0	0	1	0	3	1	0	1	0	0	0	0	1	0	0	0	1	0	0	0	0
Catskill	4	.4470	.3993	36.0	0	0	2	1	1	0	0	0	1	1	0	1	0	1	0	0	0	0	0	0	0	0	0	0	0
Catskills	5	.4511	.4766	36.8	0	0	1	0	1	2	1	0	0	0	0	0	0	1	1	0	0	0	0	0	0	0	2	0	0
catsup	4	.1750	.1896	32.8	0	3	0	0	0	1	0	0	0	0	0	0	0	0	0	1	0	0	0	0	0	3	0	1	0
cattail	4	.3614	.3220	35.1	1	1	0	0	1	0	0	1	0	0	0	1	0	0	0	1	0	0	0	0	0	2	0	0	0
cattails	4	.2344	.2377	33.8	1	0	1	1	1	0	0	0	0	0	0	1	0	0	0	3	0	0	0	0	0	0	0	0	0
cattle	658	.7562	101.11	60.0	111	89	159	100	99	56	23	21	102	11	4	44	0	300	10	37	12	1	0	0	42	34	28	33	0
Cattle-Fax	2	.0000	.0243	23.9	0	0	0	0	0	0	0	2	0	0	0	0	0	0	0	0	0	0	0	0	0	0	0	2	0
cattle-raising	2	.2285	.1129	30.5	1	0	0	1	0	0	0	0	0	0	0	0	0	1	0	0	0	0	0	0	0	0	1	0	0

9R castigates
6R Castilian
8B Castillo
7R Castillon
XR castle-like
6A castle-yard
6R Castor's
6F castra
9Q castrum
8C Casualty
7N casuarinae
9R casus
5R Caswell
7R CAT-clawed
7B cat-danger
3P cat-like
4A cat's-claw
5A cat's-meat-man
6Q catabolism
9R cataclysm
4Q cataclysmic
7E catacombs
6R catafalque
5P Catalans
7A Cataline
6F Catalogue
5P Catalonia
7A catalpa
4H catamaran
7R Catamaran
4Q Catapult
9N catapulting
5Q cataracts
9R catatonia
5D Catawba
7D Catawbas
3H catbirds
3N catcalls
7N catch-as-catch-can
5Q Catcher
4P catching's
8F catchwords
8Q catechism
7R cater
8N caterer
4J caterpillar's
5N Caterpillar's
XR caters
8B Cates
6A Catfish
8F Cathay
XB cathedra
XR cathedral-like
8C Cather
4R Catherine's
9Q catheter's
7R Cathlamet
8Q Catholepistemiad
5Q Catholican
8Q Catholicizing
3A Cathy's
7G cation
3J catkin
6H catkins
8F Catlett
9B catlike
8R catnapped
5E Catnips
5P Cato
9R Catoctin
8Q catolicos
3R CATS
6G cats'
4P Cattaraugus
4A catties
7N cattiness
6D cattle-brands
6A cattle's

Word Type	F	D	U	SFI	3 Gr 3	4 Gr 4	5 Gr 5	6 Gr 6	7 Gr 7	8 Gr 8	9 Gr 9	X UnGr	A Read	B Eng & Gr	C Comp	D Lit	E Math	F Soc Stud	G Spell	H Sci	J Music	K Art	L Home Ec	M Shop	N Lib F	P Lib NF	Q Lib Ref	R Mag	S Rel
cattlemen	18	.2614	1.2289	40.9	0	0	12	1	0	3	2	0	3	2	0	0	0	13	0	0	0	0	0	0	0	0	0	0	0
catwalk	5	.2445	.3864	35.9	0	0	0	0	4	0	1	0	4	0	0	1	0	0	0	0	0	0	0	0	0	0	0	0	0
catwalks	3	.1277	.1363	31.3	0	0	0	0	3	0	0	0	1	0	0	0	0	0	0	0	0	0	0	0	0	0	0	2	0
Cauca	5	.0000	.0972	29.9	0	0	0	5	0	0	0	0	0	0	0	0	0	5	0	0	0	0	0	0	0	0	0	0	0
Caucasian	4	.0000	.0778	28.9	0	0	0	2	0	2	0	0	0	0	0	0	0	4	0	0	0	0	0	0	0	0	0	0	0
Caucasoid	2	.0000	.0290	24.6	0	0	2	0	0	0	0	0	0	0	0	0	0	0	0	0	0	0	0	0	0	2	0	0	0
Caucasoids	2	.0000	.0290	24.6	0	0	2	0	0	0	0	0	0	0	0	0	0	0	0	0	0	0	0	0	0	2	0	0	0
Caucasus	12	.3153	.9026	39.6	0	3	0	5	1	2	1	0	2	0	0	0	0	3	0	1	0	0	0	0	0	0	6	0	0
caudal	2	.2441	.1127	30.5	0	0	0	0	2	0	0	0	0	0	0	0	0	0	0	0	0	0	0	0	1	0	1	0	0
caught	793	.9142	144.22	61.6	137	145	123	109	131	82	56	10	311	35	11	63	20	64	5	32	11	8	4	0	95	70	21	42	1
cauldron	2	.0000	.0290	24.6	0	0	0	0	1	0	0	1	0	0	0	0	0	0	0	0	0	0	0	0	0	2	0	0	0
cauldrons	2	.2351	.1166	30.7	0	0	0	0	1	0	1	0	0	0	0	0	0	1	0	0	0	0	0	0	0	0	0	1	0
cauliflower	10	.2504	.6206	37.9	2	0	1	2	2	0	3	0	2	0	0	0	0	0	1	3	0	0	4	0	0	0	0	0	0
caulking	2	.2442	.1134	30.5	0	0	0	0	1	1	0	0	0	1	0	0	0	0	0	0	0	0	0	0	0	0	0	1	0
cause	502	.8797	87.930	59.4	27	59	51	76	108	89	74	18	73	19	4	25	2	37	14	170	12	3	24	10	11	24	43	31	0
Cause	5	.3717	.4169	36.2	0	0	0	1	1	3	0	0	0	0	0	0	0	3	0	0	0	0	0	0	1	0	0	1	0
caused	346	.8983	61.785	57.9	23	45	47	48	58	65	44	16	53	14	2	8	2	59	7	97	10	1	5	4	13	16	27	28	0
causes	252	.7926	40.248	56.0	16	22	39	36	51	48	31	9	29	6	3	3	2	21	3	122	9	0	10	10	1	6	15	11	1
causeways	4	.0000	.0778	28.9	0	0	3	1	0	0	0	0	0	0	0	0	0	4	0	0	0	0	0	0	0	0	0	0	0
causing	80	.8233	13.187	51.2	4	8	14	12	17	12	9	4	8	4	1	0	0	4	1	24	2	1	0	2	4	6	15	8	0
caustic	5	.3122	.3872	35.9	0	0	0	0	0	2	0	3	1	0	0	0	0	0	0	3	0	0	0	0	0	0	0	1	0
caution	40	.7338	5.9666	47.8	3	0	3	5	13	6	8	2	7	0	0	5	0	1	1	7	0	0	0	2	7	2	3	5	0
Caution	2	.2346	.1166	30.7	1	0	0	0	0	0	1	0	0	0	0	0	0	0	0	1	0	0	0	0	0	0	0	1	0
cautioned	14	.6157	1.8481	42.7	0	3	4	0	4	0	3	0	7	0	0	1	1	0	0	0	1	0	0	0	2	0	0	2	0
cautions	4	.2065	.1925	32.8	0	0	0	0	0	3	0	1	0	0	0	0	0	1	0	0	0	0	2	0	0	0	0	1	0
cautious	18	.7031	2.5829	44.1	0	2	1	2	6	4	3	0	3	2	0	1	0	1	1	2	0	0	0	1	3	0	0	4	0
cautiously	54	.6310	7.2955	48.6	6	2	5	12	18	6	5	0	30	1	2	10	0	0	0	0	0	0	0	0	5	1	2	3	0
cavalcade	4	.3212	.3104	34.9	0	2	1	0	0	1	0	0	1	0	0	1	0	0	0	0	0	0	0	0	0	2	0	0	0
Cavalcades	2	.0000	.0914	29.6	0	0	0	2	0	0	0	0	2	0	0	0	0	0	0	0	0	0	0	0	0	0	0	0	0
cavalier	8	.2583	.4796	36.8	0	2	0	0	1	2	3	0	1	0	0	1	0	0	0	0	0	0	0	3	3	0	0	0	0
Cavaliers	3	.3822	.2446	33.9	0	0	0	1	0	0	1	1	0	1	0	0	0	0	0	0	1	0	0	0	0	0	0	1	0
cavalry	18	.4957	1.9228	42.8	0	0	1	3	5	6	2	1	3	0	0	2	0	4	0	0	0	0	0	0	0	0	6	3	0
Cavalry	7	.4680	.6912	38.4	0	3	0	1	1	0	0	2	0	1	0	0	0	0	0	0	0	0	0	0	0	3	1	2	0
cavalryman	3	.2257	.1583	32.0	0	0	0	2	0	1	0	0	0	2	0	1	0	0	0	0	0	0	0	0	0	0	0	0	0
cavalrymen	4	.4343	.3890	35.9	0	0	0	2	1	1	0	0	1	1	0	0	0	1	0	0	1	0	0	0	0	0	0	0	0
cave	264	.8528	45.285	56.6	38	52	11	82	43	11	22	5	112	8	4	16	6	3	6	27	0	4	0	0	28	21	13	16	0
Cave	20	.4832	2.0394	43.1	0	10	1	3	2	2	1	1	1	2	0	1	0	1	0	0	1	0	0	0	11	0	0	3	0
caved	4	.4341	.3887	35.9	0	1	0	1	1	0	1	0	1	0	0	1	0	1	0	0	1	0	0	0	0	0	0	0	0
caveman	14	.4000	1.2204	40.9	2	0	2	0	3	2	5	0	0	0	0	0	9	0	0	1	0	1	0	0	0	3	0	0	0
Cavendish	5	.0000	.0523	27.2	0	0	0	0	1	1	3	0	0	0	0	0	0	0	0	0	0	0	0	0	0	0	5	0	0
cavern	25	.6748	3.5424	45.5	1	2	7	3	9	1	1	1	12	2	0	1	0	0	0	0	1	0	0	0	5	2	1	1	0
cavernous	2	.2433	.1158	30.6	1	0	0	0	1	0	0	0	0	0	0	0	0	0	0	0	0	0	0	0	0	1	0	1	0
caverns	7	.4639	.7015	38.5	0	0	1	1	2	0	3	0	0	0	0	1	0	1	0	3	0	0	0	0	0	2	0	0	0
cavers	2	.0000	.0243	23.9	0	0	0	0	0	2	0	0	0	0	0	0	0	0	0	0	0	0	0	0	0	0	0	2	0
caves	75	.6085	9.5830	49.8	10	17	5	16	12	12	2	1	15	4	0	1	0	11	1	13	0	1	0	0	1	9	7	11	1
caviar	4	.4800	.4050	36.1	0	1	1	0	0	1	1	0	0	1	0	0	0	0	0	1	0	0	0	0	0	0	1	1	0
caving	4	.3513	.3115	34.9	0	0	0	1	1	2	0	0	0	0	0	1	0	1	0	0	0	0	0	0	0	0	0	2	0
cavitation	2	.0000	.0209	23.2	0	0	0	0	0	2	0	0	0	0	0	0	0	0	0	0	0	0	0	0	0	0	2	0	0
Cavite	2	.0000	.0209	23.2	2	0	0	0	0	0	0	0	0	0	0	0	0	0	0	0	0	0	0	0	0	0	2	0	0
cavities	19	.5467	2.1729	43.4	0	1	2	2	7	0	4	3	0	1	0	0	2	0	1	8	0	0	0	0	0	0	1	6	0
cavity	48	.3630	3.9084	45.9	0	1	10	2	15	5	13	2	1	0	0	0	0	0	0	31	0	0	0	9	1	1	4	1	0
caw	8	.5605	.9864	39.9	1	3	0	3	1	0	0	0	4	0	0	1	0	0	0	1	0	0	0	0	1	1	0	0	0
cawed	3	.3450	.2505	34.0	0	1	0	1	0	1	0	0	1	0	0	0	0	0	0	0	0	0	0	0	1	1	0	0	0
cawing	3	.1187	.1291	31.1	1	0	0	0	1	1	0	0	1	0	0	2	0	0	0	0	0	0	0	0	0	0	0	0	0
Caxton	7	.2488	.4174	36.2	0	0	2	1	2	2	0	0	1	2	0	0	0	0	4	0	0	0	0	0	0	0	0	0	0
Caxton's	4	.2399	.3011	34.8	0	0	1	3	0	0	0	0	3	1	0	0	0	0	0	0	0	0	0	0	0	0	0	0	0
cayenne	2	.0000	.0243	23.9	0	0	0	0	0	0	0	2	0	0	0	0	0	0	0	0	0	0	0	0	0	0	0	2	0
Cayenne	3	.0000	.0434	26.4	0	0	3	0	0	0	0	0	0	0	0	0	0	0	0	0	0	0	0	0	0	3	0	0	0
Cayne's	2	.0000	.0299	24.8	0	0	0	0	0	0	2	0	0	0	0	0	2	0	0	0	0	0	0	0	0	0	0	0	0
Cayuga	2	.0000	.0290	24.6	2	0	0	0	0	0	0	0	0	0	0	0	0	0	0	0	0	0	0	0	0	2	0	0	0
CB	4	.0000	.0599	27.8	1	0	0	1	1	0	1	0	0	0	0	0	4	0	0	0	0	0	0	0	0	0	0	0	0
CBS	10	.2928	.6833	38.3	0	0	0	2	2	0	6	0	1	1	0	1	0	0	0	0	0	0	0	0	0	0	0	7	0
cc	6	.3343	.4479	36.5	0	0	0	0	2	2	1	1	0	0	0	0	3	0	2	1	0	0	0	0	0	0	0	0	0
CC'S**	6	.0000	.2741	34.4	6	0	0	0	0	0	0	0	6	0	0	0	0	0	0	0	0	0	0	0	0	0	0	0	0
CD	74	.0941	2.3610	43.7	7	2	5	8	12	27	13	0	0	0	0	0	73	0	0	0	0	0	0	1	0	0	0	0	0
ce	6	.2408	.3273	35.1	0	1	2	0	2	1	0	0	0	3	0	0	0	0	3	0	0	0	0	0	0	0	0	0	0
cease	27	.7460	4.0656	46.1	0	0	3	9	7	4	3	1	2	4	0	5	1	1	0	5	3	0	0	0	1	3	1	1	0
cease-fire	4	.2281	.2337	33.7	0	0	0	0	0	4	0	0	0	0	0	0	0	3	0	0	0	0	0	0	0	0	0	1	0
ceased	48	.6527	6.5155	48.1	6	3	2	8	8	16	2	3	13	2	0	2	0	1	1	1	1	0	0	0	14	10	3	0	0
ceaseless	10	.5647	1.1599	40.6	0	0	0	0	6	2	2	0	0	0	0	3	0	1	0	0	1	0	0	0	1	0	3	1	0
ceaselessly	2	.2297	.1135	30.6	0	0	1	0	1	0	0	0	0	0	0	1	0	1	0	0	0	0	0	0	0	0	0	0	0
ceases	5	.2897	.3417	35.3	0	1	0	0	1	3	0	0	1	0	0	0	0	0	0	0	0	0	1	0	0	0	3	0	0
ceasing	2	.1787	.1174	30.7	0	0	0	0	1	1	0	0	1	0	0	0	0	0	0	0	0	0	0	0	1	0	0	0	0
Cebu	8	.0000	.0837	29.2	8	0	0	0	0	0	0	0	0	0	0	0	0	0	0	0	0	0	0	0	0	0	8	0	0
Cecil	19	.5385	2.1275	43.3	2	0	3	1	0	1	10	2	1	2	1	9	0	1	0	0	0	0	0	0	0	3	0	2	0
Cecilia	2	.1641	.0751	28.8	0	0	0	0	0	2	0	0	0	0	1	0	0	0	0	0	0	0	0	0	0	0	1	0	0
cecropia	3	.2053	.1597	32.0	3	0	0	0	0	0	0	0	0	0	0	0	0	0	0	1	0	0	0	0	0	2	0	0	0
cedar	31	.7410	4.6987	46.7	5	3	6	7	4	3	2	1	8	0	1	1	2	9	0	1	0	0	0	0	2	3	3	1	0
Cedar	12	.5204	1.3697	41.4	0	3	1	1	0	7	0	0	3	0	0	1	0	2	0	5	0	0	0	0	1	0	0	0	0
cedars	8	.3443	.6093	37.8	1	0	2	0	5	0	0	0	0	0	0	0	0	0	0	0	0	0	0	0	1	3	0	4	0
cede	3	.2387	.1708	32.3	0	0	2	0	1	0	0	0	0	0	0	0	0	0	0	0	0	0	0	0	0	2	1	0	0
CEG	2	.0000	.0162	22.1	0	0	1	1	0	0	0	0	0	0	0	0	0	0	0	0	2	0	0	0	0	0	0	0	0
ceiling	113	.9125	20.489	53.1	20	16	13	13	26	15	5	5	33	4	0	5	9	2	2	19	3	1	2	2	14	7	3	7	0
ceilings	19	.4988	1.9960	43.0	2	2	8	1	1	1	3	1	1	0	0	0	0	0	0	3	0	1	0	0	0	2	9	3	0
ceive	4	.0000	.0438	26.4	0	0	0	0	0	4	0	0	0	4	0	0	0	0	0	0	0	0	0	0	0	0	0	0	0
Celebes	5	.1285	.1797	32.5	1	0	0	1	2	1	0	0	0	0	0	0	0	1	0	0	0	0	0	0	0	0	4	0	0
celebrate	73	.3766	6.3655	48.0	10	19	8	15	10	6	4	1	19	3	0	2	0	15	5	1	9	1	0	0	1	7	2	5	3
celebrated	55	.5945	6.8150	48.3	8	6	5	6	11	9	6	4	9	2	1	1	0	5	0	2	6	0	1	0	1	7	11	8	1
celebrates	6	.3665	.4825	36.8	1	1	1	0	1	2	0	0	0	0	0	0	0	2	0	0	2	0	0	0	0	0	0	2	0
celebrating	20	.6717	2.7930	44.5	6	2	2	2	3	2	3	0	7	0	0	0	0	2	1	0	4	0	1	0	0	2	1	2	0
celebration	63	.7216	9.2969	49.7	5	24	14	11	4	3	1	1	14	0	0	1	0	13	1	0	7	0	0	0	7	9	5	6	0
Celebration	3	.0000	.1370	31.4	2	1	0	0	0	0	0	0	3	0	0	0	0	0	0	0	0	0	0	0	0	0	0	0	0
celebrations	22	.5745	2.6244	44.2	3	5	3	5	4	1	1	0	2	0	0	0	0	5	0	0	7	0	1	0	0	1	3	3	0
celebrities	3	.0000	.0365	25.6	0	0	1	0	1	1	0	0	0	0	0	0	0	0	0	0	0	0	0	0	0	0	0	3	0

8A cattleman
XR Cattlemen's
4N catty-shaped
7Q catus
6F cauc
7A caucus
6J cauld
9H cauliflower-like
6A cauliflowers
8Q causal
9C cause-and-effect
7R Causes
8F causeway
8H CAUTION
XR cautionary
8N cautioning
8D Cautious
5Q Cavalcanti
5P Cavalleria
8R Cavanagh
7Q cave-bear
7N cave-life
4A cave-like
4D cave-mouth
7N cave-wall
9B caveat
3F caved-in
7P cavelike
8K Caveman
6A cavemen
5A Cavern
5F Caverns
7R cavier
4N cavily
7R cavitate
8Q Cavitation
3N cavorted
3P caws
3P cawses
6G cawtion
8Q Caxias
7D Cayugas
8N cayuse
8E CBD
9H CCL4
8R CCNY
6E CE
7G ceable
8Q Ceara
6R ceasefire
6A Cecco
3A Cecie
9J Cecile
3P Cecropia
7Q Cedars
6F cedarwood
7R ceded
7N ceilinged
8J Celebrate

Word Type	F	D	U	SFI	3 Gr 3	4 Gr 4	5 Gr 5	6 Gr 6	7 Gr 7	8 Gr 8	9 Gr 9	X UnGr	A Read	B Eng & Gr	C Comp	D Lit	E Math	F Soc Stud	G Spell	H Sci	J Music	K Art	L Home Ec	M Shop	N Lib F	P Lib NF	Q Lib Ref	R Mag	S Rel
celebrity	4	.3756	.3228	35.1	0	0	2	0	1	0	0	1	0	0	0	0	0	0	1	0	0	0	0	0	1	0	0	2	0
celery	48	.3945	4.1550	46.2	7	6	8	1	13	6	7	0	5	0	0	0	0	4	4	12	0	0	16	0	2	3	1	1	0
celesta	9	.1052	.2533	34.0	1	2	0	0	3	0	3	0	0	0	0	0	0	0	0	0	8	0	0	0	0	0	1	0	0
Celeste	2	.0000	.0215	23.3	0	0	0	0	0	0	2	0	0	0	0	2	0	0	0	0	0	0	0	0	0	0	0	0	0
celestial	17	.6599	2.3218	43.7	0	0	0	2	6	2	3	4	2	1	Q	0	1	3	0	7	1	0	0	0	0	0	1	1	0
Celia	7	.1501	.2756	34.4	0	0	6	0	0	1	0	0	0	1	0	0	0	0	0	0	0	0	0	0	6	0	0	0	0
cell	446	.4056	40.452	56.1	49	17	100	82	126	15	31	26	10	1	0	4	0	0	2	336	0	0	2	0	1	32	52	6	0
cell's	2	.2278	.1128	30.5	0	0	1	0	1	0	0	0	0	0	0	0	0	0	0	1	0	0	0	0	0	0	1	0	0
cellar	77	.7788	12.246	50.9	4	24	11	15	7	6	8	2	35	4	2	9	0	2	5	3	1	0	0	0	7	4	0	5	0
cellars	13	.6426	1.7384	42.4	1	4	1	0	4	0	1	2	3	0	0	1	0	0	0	2	0	0	0	0	1	1	2	3	0
cellists	2	.2407	.1090	30.4	0	1	0	0	0	1	0	0	0	1	0	0	0	0	0	0	1	0	0	0	0	0	0	0	0
cello	28	.0000	.2264	33.5	1	6	6	5	5	5	0	0	0	0	0	0	0	0	0	0	28	0	0	0	0	0	0	0	0
cellophane	20	.4469	2.0307	43.1	7	2	1	6	1	0	3	0	6	1	0	0	2	1	0	8	0	2	0	0	0	0	0	0	0
cellos	7	.0000	.0566	27.5	0	2	1	2	1	1	0	0	0	0	0	0	0	0	0	0	7	0	0	0	0	0	0	0	0
cells	747	.4006	67.101	58.3	122	68	158	105	185	44	38	27	12	0	0	2	5	0	1	602	0	0	10	3	0	20	81	11	0
cellular	5	.2424	.2988	34.8	0	0	0	0	5	0	0	0	0	0	0	0	0	0	0	3	0	0	0	0	0	0	2	0	0
celluloid	4	.1873	.1827	32.6	0	0	3	0	0	0	0	1	0	0	0	0	0	0	0	0	0	0	0	0	0	0	3	1	0
Celluloid	5	.0000	.0523	27.2	0	0	5	0	0	0	0	0	0	0	0	0	0	0	0	0	0	0	0	0	0	0	5	0	0
cellulose	47	.3185	3.4376	45.4	0	0	10	2	14	1	18	2	0	0	0	0	0	0	0	33	0	0	10	0	0	0	2	2	0
Celsius	5	.0000	.0986	29.9	0	0	1	0	0	4	0	0	0	0	0	0	0	0	0	5	0	0	0	0	0	0	0	0	0
Celtic	18	.4168	1.5976	42.0	0	1	4	6	4	0	2	1	0	9	0	0	0	1	0	0	0	0	0	0	0	2	5	1	0
Celts	12	.3992	1.0194	40.1	1	0	1	4	3	0	0	3	0	6	0	0	0	0	1	0	0	0	0	0	0	1	4	0	0
Celyndia	7	.0000	.0821	29.1	0	0	7	0	0	0	0	0	0	0	0	0	0	0	0	0	0	0	0	0	7	0	0	0	0
Celynida	5	.0000	.0586	27.7	0	0	5	0	0	0	0	0	0	0	0	0	0	0	0	0	0	0	0	0	5	0	0	0	0
cement	83	.7962	13.289	51.2	18	10	12	8	18	7	7	3	12	4	1	3	5	19	2	6	0	2	0	7	2	2	9	9	0
cemented	10	.5756	1.1882	40.7	0	0	1	2	4	1	0	2	0	0	0	0	0	1	0	3	1	0	0	1	0	0	2	2	0
cementing	3	.3764	.2483	33.9	0	1	0	0	0	1	0	1	0	0	0	0	0	0	0	1	0	0	0	0	0	0	1	1	0
cemeteries	2	.2437	.1129	30.5	0	1	0	0	0	0	1	0	0	0	0	0	0	0	0	0	0	0	0	0	0	0	1	1	0
cemetery	14	.7029	2.0311	43.1	4	2	2	1	1	1	2	1	5	0	0	1	0	0	1	0	1	0	0	0	3	1	1	1	0
Cemetery	9	.5440	1.0240	40.1	2	1	1	1	1	2	1	0	1	0	1	1	0	1	0	0	0	0	0	0	1	1	3	0	0
Cenozoic	2	.2278	.1128	30.5	0	0	0	1	1	0	0	0	0	0	0	0	0	0	0	1	0	0	0	0	0	0	1	0	0
censor	2	.2437	.1129	30.5	0	0	1	0	1	0	0	0	0	0	0	0	0	0	0	0	0	0	0	0	0	0	1	1	0
censored	2	.2351	.1166	30.7	0	0	0	0	1	1	0	0	0	0	0	0	0	1	0	0	0	0	0	0	0	0	0	1	0
censors	4	.0996	.1523	31.8	0	0	0	0	3	1	0	0	1	0	0	0	0	0	0	0	0	0	0	0	0	0	0	3	0
censorship	9	.3641	.7137	38.5	0	0	3	0	2	0	4	0	0	0	0	0	0	0	0	0	0	0	0	0	0	3	4	2	0
censure	3	.3406	.2461	33.9	0	0	0	0	3	0	0	0	1	1	0	0	0	0	0	0	0	0	0	0	0	0	0	1	0
census	29	.4510	2.8159	44.5	6	6	4	3	6	3	0	1	2	0	0	0	1	4	0	1	0	0	0	0	0	5	14	2	0
Census	2	.2417	.1211	30.8	0	0	0	0	0	1	1	0	0	0	0	0	1	1	0	0	0	0	0	0	0	0	0	0	0
censuses	3	.2159	.1532	31.9	0	2	0	0	1	0	0	0	0	0	0	0	0	0	0	0	0	0	0	0	0	0	2	1	0
cent	364	.8190	59.649	57.8	20	9	29	35	120	39	104	8	25	10	4	3	69	44	6	45	0	0	6	5	6	14	50	77	0
centaur	8	.2789	.6460	38.1	0	0	0	3	2	3	0	0	6	0	0	0	0	0	0	0	0	1	0	0	1	0	0	0	0
Centauri	10	.3360	.7702	38.9	0	0	0	0	0	10	0	0	0	0	0	3	1	0	0	6	0	0	0	0	0	0	0	0	0
centaurs	5	.2445	.3864	35.9	0	0	0	0	1	4	0	0	4	0	0	1	0	0	0	0	0	0	0	0	0	0	0	0	0
centavo	6	.0000	.2741	34.4	6	0	0	0	0	0	0	0	6	0	0	0	0	0	0	0	0	0	0	0	0	0	0	0	0
centavos	10	.2326	.7674	38.8	6	0	3	0	1	0	0	0	8	0	0	0	0	2	0	0	0	0	0	0	0	0	0	0	0
centennial	2	.0000	.0243	23.9	0	0	0	0	1	0	0	1	0	0	0	0	0	0	0	0	0	0	0	0	0	0	0	2	0
Centennial	3	.2444	.1814	32.6	0	0	1	0	0	1	1	0	0	0	0	0	0	2	0	0	0	0	0	0	0	0	1	0	0
center	984	.8349	164.05	62.1	124	141	143	122	166	139	134	15	97	16	5	30	73	176	11	132	102	6	73	59	15	53	87	49	0
Center	67	.7053	9.6269	49.8	4	18	10	16	10	5	3	1	7	2	0	0	4	13	0	4	4	0	0	0	7	1	7	18	0
center-point	2	.0000	.0299	24.8	0	0	0	0	2	0	0	0	0	0	0	0	2	0	0	0	0	0	0	0	0	0	0	0	0
Centerberg	2	.0000	.0219	23.4	0	0	0	0	0	0	2	0	0	2	0	0	0	0	0	0	0	0	0	0	0	0	0	0	0
centerboards	2	.0000	.0290	24.6	0	0	0	0	0	2	0	0	0	0	0	0	0	0	0	0	0	0	0	0	0	2	0	0	0
Centerburg	19	.2549	1.2167	40.9	0	0	12	7	0	0	0	0	4	0	0	3	0	0	0	0	0	0	0	0	12	0	0	0	0
centered	26	.7984	4.1563	46.2	2	3	1	2	8	8	2	0	1	2	0	1	0	8	0	1	1	1	1	1	0	4	3	2	0
centering	2	.1892	.0858	29.3	0	0	0	0	1	0	1	0	0	1	0	0	0	0	0	0	0	0	1	0	0	0	0	0	0
centerpiece	5	.2909	.3230	35.1	0	2	1	0	0	0	2	0	0	0	0	0	0	1	0	0	0	0	2	0	0	1	0	1	0
centerpieces	2	.0000	.0064	18.1	0	0	0	0	0	0	2	0	0	0	0	0	0	0	0	0	0	0	2	0	0	0	0	0	0
centers	140	.7928	22.255	53.5	14	8	28	24	19	15	30	2	6	2	1	0	3	51	0	10	14	1	7	6	1	6	20	12	0
Centerville	10	.3660	.8911	39.5	4	3	0	0	0	3	0	0	4	0	0	0	3	0	0	0	0	0	0	0	0	3	0	0	0
centigrade	15	.2438	.9171	39.6	0	0	7	3	0	5	0	0	0	0	0	0	7	0	0	8	0	0	0	0	0	0	0	0	0
Centigrade	2	.0000	.0914	29.6	2	0	0	0	0	0	0	0	2	0	0	0	0	0	0	0	0	0	0	0	0	0	0	0	0
centimeter	43	.2047	2.2573	43.5	2	8	3	3	8	4	15	0	0	0	0	0	35	0	0	6	0	0	0	0	0	0	2	0	0
centimeters	66	.1030	2.2351	43.5	0	3	19	14	8	9	13	0	0	0	0	0	61	0	0	4	0	0	0	0	0	0	1	0	0
centipede	5	.4025	.4443	36.5	0	1	0	3	1	0	0	0	1	0	0	0	0	0	2	0	1	0	0	0	1	0	0	0	0
centipedes	4	.3862	.3425	35.3	0	1	0	0	0	2	0	1	0	0	0	0	0	0	0	2	0	0	0	0	1	0	0	1	0
central	284	.7264	41.842	56.2	14	26	40	49	66	49	23	17	13	6	5	0	3	116	3	25	5	1	0	1	1	21	60	24	0
Central	187	.7053	26.961	54.3	14	14	38	37	48	19	12	5	18	7	1	3	5	93	0	7	5	0	1	0	2	5	23	17	0
centralized	4	.2437	.2257	33.5	0	0	0	0	0	1	2	1	0	0	0	0	0	0	0	0	0	0	0	0	0	0	2	2	0
centre	6	.1878	.2757	34.4	0	0	2	0	4	0	0	0	0	0	0	0	0	0	1	0	0	0	0	0	5	0	0	0	0
Centre	2	.2433	.1158	30.6	0	0	1	1	0	0	0	0	0	0	0	0	0	0	0	0	0	0	0	0	0	1	0	1	0
centrifugal	9	.3791	.7876	39.0	1	0	1	2	4	1	0	0	2	0	0	0	0	0	0	1	0	0	0	0	0	2	0	4	0
centrifuge	5	.2444	.2887	34.6	0	0	2	3	0	0	0	0	0	0	0	0	0	0	0	0	0	0	0	0	0	3	2	0	0
cents	479	.4681	48.715	56.9	194	82	40	26	44	30	38	25	58	6	1	10	326	14	3	3	0	0	2	0	26	10	6	14	0
cents'	4	.3514	.3043	34.8	1	0	0	1	2	0	0	0	0	0	1	0	1	0	0	0	0	0	0	0	1	1	0	0	0
centum	2	.2289	.1077	30.3	0	0	0	0	2	0	0	0	0	0	0	0	1	0	1	0	0	0	0	0	0	0	0	0	0
centuries	329	.8698	56.930	57.6	26	16	36	60	91	48	34	18	23	25	3	5	15	81	7	29	12	4	2	2	2	31	64	24	0
Centuries	4	.2401	.2266	33.6	0	0	2	0	0	0	2	0	0	0	0	0	0	0	0	0	0	0	0	0	0	2	2	0	0
centuries-old	2	.2285	.1129	30.5	0	0	0	0	1	0	1	0	0	0	0	0	0	1	0	0	0	0	0	0	0	0	1	0	0
century	572	.7981	91.324	59.6	19	22	42	63	159	145	90	32	32	31	2	5	10	71	17	43	95	14	1	10	2	46	149	44	0
Century	103	.3971	8.8302	49.5	0	0	25	1	41	10	26	0	0	0	0	0	0	8	0	6	1	0	0	0	0	25	56	7	0
century's	3	.1621	.1254	31.0	0	0	0	0	0	2	1	0	0	0	0	0	0	1	0	0	2	0	0	0	0	0	0	0	0
cephalothorax	2	.0000	.0394	26.0	0	0	0	0	2	0	0	0	0	0	0	0	0	0	0	2	0	0	0	0	0	0	0	0	0
Cephei	4	.0000	.0789	29.0	0	0	0	0	0	0	2	2	0	0	0	0	0	0	0	4	0	0	0	0	0	0	0	0	0
Cepheid	9	.2204	.5163	37.1	0	0	0	0	2	0	7	0	0	0	0	0	0	0	0	7	0	0	0	0	0	0	0	2	0
Cepheids	2	.0000	.0243	23.9	0	0	0	0	2	0	0	0	0	0	0	0	0	0	0	0	0	0	0	0	0	0	0	2	0
Cepheus	3	.1832	.1417	31.5	0	0	0	0	1	0	2	0	0	0	0	2	0	0	0	1	0	0	0	0	0	0	0	0	0
ceramic	11	.2374	.5950	37.7	0	0	1	0	8	2	0	0	0	0	0	0	0	0	0	0	0	0	0	4	0	6	1	0	0
ceramics	11	.2881	.6781	38.3	0	0	0	0	9	1	0	1	0	0	0	0	0	0	0	1	0	1	0	6	0	2	0	1	0
cereal	66	.4670	6.5137	48.1	15	7	8	0	6	15	14	1	5	5	1	0	4	6	4	10	0	0	23	0	2	0	3	3	0
cereals	46	.2864	2.9940	44.8	4	1	6	5	11	13	5	1	1	2	0	0	0	5	0	15	0	0	19	0	0	1	3	0	0
Cereals	3	.2942	.1970	32.9	2	0	0	0	0	0	1	0	0	0	0	0	0	0	0	1	0	0	1	0	0	0	1	0	0
cerebellum	12	.2071	.6614	38.2	0	0	0	7	1	2	2	0	0	0	0	0	0	0	0	10	0	0	0	0	0	0	2	0	0
cerebral	10	.2426	.6051	37.8	0	0	0	0	8	0	2	0	0	0	0	0	0	0	0	7	0	0	0	0	0	0	3	0	0
cerebrum	26	.2614	1.6872	42.3	0	0	2	6	9	7	2	0	0	0	0	2	0	0	0	22	0	0	0	0	0	0	2	0	0
Cerelle	2	.0000	.0215	23.3	0	0	0	0	2	0	0	0	0	0	0	2	0	0	0	0	0	0	0	0	0	0	0	0	0

7N celerity
7J Celesta
8Q Celestina
3A Celine
XH cell-wall
9Q Cellach
5B cellar-dwellers
7H celled
7N Cellini
7R cello-like
5N Celyndia's
3A Cement
3A cementite
9H cements
5H cementum
5B cemetary
4G cen
5Q Censorship
8Q censured
7F census-takers
8A Centaur
8A centaur's
7R Centauro
8H CENTAURUS
3P center-field
9L center-front
9M center-punch
9P centerboard
8N centerboard-case
7R centerfield
9M centerless
7R centerline
8H Centers
8D centerstage
6E centi-
8P centimeter's
8F central-station
8F centralism
9Q centralization
5P centralize
XH centrally
8P centred
9Q centres
6Q centrioles
9B centripetal
7N centronotes
5G centrum
4N centses
7J century-old
5G cept
5P Cercle
9L Cerealia
7H cerebrospinal
9D cerecloth

Word Type	F	D	U	SFI	3 Gr 3	4 Gr 4	5 Gr 5	6 Gr 6	7 Gr 7	8 Gr 8	9 Gr 9	X UnGr	A Read	B Eng & Gr	C Comp	D Lit	E Math	F Soc Stud	G Spell	H Sci	J Music	K Art	L Home Ec	M Shop	N Lib F	P Lib NF	Q Lib Ref	R Mag	S Rel
ceremonial	11	.5846	1.3595	41.3	1	2	1	0	5	1	1	0	3	1	0	1	0	0	0	0	0	0	0	0	0	1	2	3	0
ceremonies	36	.6122	4.5727	46.6	7	5	2	11	5	2	3	1	5	0	0	0	0	9	0	0	5	3	0	0	1	5	4	4	0
ceremonious	2	.2297	.1135	30.6	0	0	0	0	1	1	0	0	0	0	0	1	0	1	0	0	0	0	0	0	0	0	0	0	0
ceremony	52	.7401	7.8323	48.9	2	2	5	12	17	9	5	0	11	2	0	3	0	11	1	0	8	0	0	0	2	3	4	7	0
Ceres	12	.5856	1.5254	41.8	0	0	1	0	0	9	1	1	6	1	0	1	0	0	0	2	0	0	1	0	0	0	1	0	0
Cerf	2	.0000	.0219	23.4	0	0	0	0	0	0	2	0	0	2	0	0	0	0	0	0	0	0	0	0	0	0	0	0	0
cermets	3	.0000	.0434	26.4	0	0	0	0	3	0	0	0	0	0	0	0	0	0	0	0	0	0	0	0	0	3	0	0	0
Cerro	2	.0000	.0389	25.9	0	0	0	0	2	0	0	0	0	0	0	0	0	2	0	0	0	0	0	0	0	0	0	0	0
certain	1198	.9620	227.26	63.6	82	136	160	133	270	192	192	33	127	99	15	39	96	154	27	237	43	17	34	23	30	58	138	60	1
certainly	391	.8879	69.202	58.4	48	63	47	47	87	46	40	13	116	29	11	36	8	15	1	28	2	3	4	1	38	38	31	30	0
certainty	15	.6877	2.0899	43.2	0	0	1	2	6	2	3	1	0	2	0	3	0	1	0	2	0	0	0	0	1	2	1	3	0
certificate	2	.2285	.1129	30.5	0	0	1	0	0	1	0	0	0	0	0	0	0	1	0	0	0	0	0	0	0	0	1	0	0
Certificate	2	.2351	.1166	30.7	0	0	1	0	0	0	1	0	0	0	0	0	0	1	0	0	0	0	0	0	0	0	0	1	0
certificates	2	.1160	.0650	28.1	0	1	0	0	0	1	0	0	0	0	1	0	0	0	0	1	0	0	0	0	0	0	0	0	0
certified	3	.3202	.2063	33.1	0	0	0	0	1	0	1	1	0	0	0	0	0	0	0	0	0	0	1	0	0	0	1	1	0
certifies	2	.2433	.1158	30.6	1	0	0	0	1	0	0	0	0	0	0	0	0	0	0	0	0	0	0	0	0	1	0	1	0
Cesare	2	.0000	.0243	23.9	0	0	0	0	2	0	0	0	0	0	0	0	0	0	0	0	0	0	0	0	0	0	0	2	0
cessation	2	.2441	.1127	30.5	0	0	0	0	2	0	0	0	0	0	0	0	0	0	0	0	0	0	0	0	1	0	1	0	0
cession	2	.2285	.1129	30.5	0	0	1	0	0	1	0	0	0	0	0	0	0	1	0	0	0	0	0	0	0	0	1	0	0
cetacean	2	.0000	.0234	23.7	0	0	0	0	2	0	0	0	0	0	0	0	0	0	0	0	0	0	0	0	2	0	0	0	0
cetera	2	.0000	.0162	22.1	0	0	0	0	2	0	0	0	0	0	0	0	0	0	2	0	0	0	0	0	0	0	0	0	0
Ceylon	11	.4477	1.0600	40.3	0	1	0	4	4	1	1	0	0	1	0	0	0	6	0	0	1	0	0	0	0	0	3	0	0
Cezanne	11	.1332	.3391	35.3	1	0	1	0	6	3	0	0	0	0	0	1	0	0	0	0	0	7	0	0	0	1	2	0	0
Cezanne's	2	.1378	.0662	28.2	0	0	0	0	0	1	0	1	0	0	0	0	0	0	0	0	0	1	0	0	0	0	0	1	0
CF	3	.0000	.0449	26.5	0	0	0	1	0	0	2	0	0	0	0	0	3	0	0	0	0	0	0	0	0	0	0	0	0
CG	2	.0000	.0299	24.8	0	0	0	0	2	0	0	0	0	0	0	0	2	0	0	0	0	0	0	0	0	0	0	0	0
ch	122	.0981	3.4397	45.4	21	20	26	18	27	9	1	0	5	8	0	0	0	0	108	0	0	0	0	0	0	1	0	0	0
CH	3	.2398	.1721	32.4	0	0	0	1	2	0	0	0	0	0	0	0	2	0	0	0	0	0	0	0	0	0	1	0	0
Ch'en	2	.0000	.0290	24.6	2	0	0	0	0	0	0	0	0	0	0	0	0	0	0	0	0	0	0	0	0	2	0	0	0
Ch'in	5	.1990	.2695	34.3	0	0	0	2	0	2	0	1	0	0	0	0	0	4	0	0	0	0	0	0	0	1	0	0	0
Ch'ing	6	.1955	.3185	35.0	0	0	0	0	1	5	0	0	0	0	0	0	0	5	0	0	0	0	0	0	0	0	0	1	0
cha	2	.0000	.0162	22.1	2	0	0	0	0	0	0	0	0	0	0	0	0	0	0	0	2	0	0	0	0	0	0	0	0
Cha	2	.0000	.0914	29.6	0	2	0	0	0	0	0	0	2	0	0	0	0	0	0	0	0	0	0	0	0	0	0	0	0
Chad	39	.1993	2.9012	44.6	0	0	0	38	1	0	0	0	37	0	0	1	0	0	0	0	0	0	0	0	0	1	0	0	0
Chad's	3	.0000	.1370	31.4	0	0	0	3	0	0	0	0	3	0	0	0	0	0	0	0	0	0	0	0	0	0	0	0	0
Chadwick	4	.0000	.0579	27.6	0	0	0	4	0	0	0	0	0	0	0	0	0	0	0	0	0	0	0	0	0	4	0	0	0
chafed	3	.2321	.1635	32.1	1	0	0	1	1	0	0	0	0	0	0	0	0	0	0	0	0	0	0	0	0	0	1	2	0
chaff	2	.2408	.1204	30.8	1	0	0	0	0	1	0	0	0	0	0	0	0	1	0	0	0	0	0	0	0	1	0	0	0
Chaffray	2	.0000	.0290	24.6	0	2	0	0	0	0	0	0	0	0	0	0	0	0	0	0	0	0	0	0	0	2	0	0	0
Chaffy	6	.0000	.2741	34.4	0	0	0	0	6	0	0	0	6	0	0	0	0	0	0	0	0	0	0	0	0	0	0	0	0
chafing	4	.3641	.3324	35.2	0	0	0	1	1	1	1	0	1	0	0	0	0	0	0	0	0	0	1	0	1	0	0	1	0
Chagres	2	.0000	.0389	25.9	0	0	1	1	0	0	0	0	0	0	0	0	0	2	0	0	0	0	0	0	0	0	0	0	0
chagrin	3	.3852	.2500	34.0	0	0	0	0	2	0	1	0	0	0	0	1	0	0	0	0	0	0	0	0	0	1	0	1	0
chagrined	3	.2054	.1422	31.5	0	0	0	0	0	1	2	0	0	0	1	0	0	0	0	0	0	0	0	0	0	0	0	2	0
Chai	2	.0000	.0290	24.6	0	0	0	0	0	0	2	0	0	0	0	0	0	0	0	0	0	0	0	0	0	2	0	0	0
chain	204	.8612	35.084	55.5	15	34	20	42	54	25	12	2	39	4	6	14	4	16	4	37	3	2	0	0	22	11	25	17	0
Chain	7	.5641	.8190	39.1	0	1	3	1	0	2	0	0	0	1	0	0	2	0	0	2	1	0	0	0	0	0	1	0	0
chained	11	.5492	1.3041	41.2	2	1	0	2	2	3	1	0	4	1	0	2	0	0	0	0	0	0	0	0	2	0	2	0	0
chains	64	.7848	10.138	50.1	4	3	9	13	19	5	9	2	9	0	2	3	0	5	2	22	2	0	0	0	4	6	5	4	0
chair	421	.8777	73.816	58.7	78	73	48	43	73	57	48	1	146	39	3	54	2	10	11	16	8	3	14	2	61	25	11	16	0
Chair	4	.1540	.1653	32.2	0	3	0	0	0	1	0	0	0	3	0	0	0	1	0	0	0	0	0	0	0	0	0	0	0
chairman	73	.5211	8.0003	49.0	12	2	3	4	11	20	19	2	5	28	0	1	0	11	1	0	0	0	0	0	0	3	4	20	0
Chairman	12	.2339	.6568	38.2	0	0	1	0	0	10	1	0	0	9	0	0	0	0	0	0	0	0	0	0	0	1	0	2	0
CHAIRMAN	2	.0000	.0219	23.4	0	0	0	0	2	0	0	0	0	2	0	0	0	0	0	0	0	0	0	0	0	0	0	0	0
chairmen	3	.2425	.1816	32.6	0	1	0	0	0	1	0	1	0	0	0	0	0	2	0	0	0	0	0	0	0	0	0	1	0
chairs	140	.8421	23.648	53.7	32	20	15	12	28	17	11	5	38	12	0	11	30	7	1	7	0	1	7	3	6	10	2	5	0
chaise	8	.3106	.5535	37.4	0	0	0	0	1	7	0	0	0	0	0	2	0	0	0	0	0	0	0	0	5	1	0	0	0
Chalciope	3	.0000	.1370	31.4	0	0	0	3	0	0	0	0	3	0	0	0	0	0	0	0	0	0	0	0	0	0	0	0	0
chalcopyrite	8	.1794	.4754	36.8	3	0	0	0	0	5	0	0	3	0	0	0	0	0	0	5	0	0	0	0	0	0	0	0	0
chalet	2	.0000	.0914	29.6	2	0	0	0	0	0	0	0	2	0	0	0	0	0	0	0	0	0	0	0	0	0	0	0	0
chalets	2	.1948	.1250	31.0	1	0	1	0	0	0	0	0	1	0	0	0	0	0	0	0	0	0	0	0	0	1	0	0	0
chalk	109	.3230	7.8265	48.9	23	35	15	13	13	6	4	0	12	3	4	2	4	3	2	18	0	46	3	0	4	4	4	0	0
chalkboard	64	.6475	8.4983	49.3	16	16	11	10	5	2	4	0	4	13	2	0	20	1	5	14	5	0	0	0	0	0	0	0	0
chalked	6	.3979	.5696	37.6	0	1	0	2	1	1	1	0	3	0	0	0	0	0	0	0	0	0	1	0	0	1	0	1	0
chalking	3	.0000	.1370	31.4	2	0	0	1	0	0	0	0	3	0	0	0	0	0	0	0	0	0	0	0	0	0	0	0	0
chalky	3	.3399	.2456	33.9	0	1	0	1	1	0	0	0	1	0	0	1	0	0	0	0	0	0	0	0	0	0	0	1	0
challenge	106	.8322	17.628	52.5	7	6	10	11	38	15	16	3	15	2	0	12	1	10	15	6	6	1	4	0	3	3	11	17	0
Challenge	4	.0761	.1245	31.0	0	0	1	3	0	0	0	0	1	0	0	0	0	0	3	0	0	0	0	0	0	0	0	0	0
challenged	33	.7602	5.0684	47.0	0	2	2	0	8	11	4	6	4	3	1	2	1	5	0	3	1	0	0	0	0	2	2	9	0
Challenger	3	.3769	.2484	34.0	0	0	0	0	1	0	1	1	0	0	0	0	0	1	0	0	0	0	0	0	0	0	1	1	0
challenges	12	.5912	1.5174	41.8	1	0	3	1	3	2	2	0	5	0	1	0	1	0	0	1	0	0	1	0	0	0	2	1	0
challenging	27	.7701	4.1964	46.2	0	2	6	2	8	5	4	0	4	2	0	3	0	3	2	1	1	0	0	0	0	5	2	4	0
Challico	5	.0000	.0547	27.4	0	0	0	0	0	0	5	0	0	5	0	0	0	0	0	0	0	0	0	0	0	0	0	0	0
Chalvah	4	.0000	.0438	26.4	0	0	0	0	0	0	4	0	0	4	0	0	0	0	0	0	0	0	0	0	0	0	0	0	0
chamber	157	.8022	25.401	54.0	4	33	13	27	37	16	26	1	41	1	3	17	0	1	2	27	22	0	0	3	5	7	18	10	0
Chamber	18	.5235	2.0178	43.0	0	0	1	1	6	3	4	3	3	2	0	0	0	5	0	0	0	0	0	0	0	0	3	5	0
chamber-music	2	.0000	.0162	22.1	0	0	0	0	0	1	1	0	0	0	0	0	0	0	0	0	2	0	0	0	0	0	0	0	0
chambered	3	.3877	.2482	33.9	0	1	0	0	2	0	0	0	0	1	0	1	0	0	0	0	0	0	0	0	0	0	1	0	0
Chamberlain	18	.6472	2.4895	44.0	0	8	0	1	3	4	2	0	10	0	0	0	0	1	0	1	1	0	0	0	0	2	1	2	0
Chamberlain's	3	.1409	.1472	31.7	0	0	0	1	2	0	0	0	1	0	0	0	0	0	0	0	0	0	0	0	0	2	0	0	0
Chamberland	3	.0000	.0591	27.7	0	0	0	0	0	0	0	3	0	0	0	0	0	0	0	3	0	0	0	0	0	0	0	0	0
chambers	26	.6821	3.6258	45.6	1	2	3	1	11	3	5	0	2	0	0	2	1	0	0	9	1	0	0	0	1	2	5	3	0
chambray	2	.1839	.0845	29.3	0	0	0	0	0	2	0	0	0	0	0	0	0	0	0	0	0	0	1	0	1	0	0	0	0
chameleon	2	.2331	.1157	30.6	0	0	0	1	0	0	1	0	0	0	0	0	0	0	0	1	0	0	0	0	1	0	0	0	0
chameleons	3	.3346	.2478	33.9	0	0	0	0	2	0	0	1	1	0	0	0	0	0	0	1	0	0	0	0	0	0	1	0	0
chamfer	16	.0000	.0404	26.1	0	0	0	0	11	3	2	0	0	0	0	0	0	0	0	0	0	0	0	16	0	0	0	0	0
chamfered	2	.0000	.0050	17.0	0	0	0	0	0	1	1	0	0	0	0	0	0	0	0	0	0	0	0	2	0	0	0	0	0
chamois	4	.4530	.4014	36.0	0	0	0	2	1	0	0	1	1	0	0	0	0	0	0	0	0	0	0	0	0	1	1	1	0
champ	11	.3478	.9893	40.0	0	0	0	1	1	9	0	0	7	0	0	3	0	0	0	0	0	0	0	0	0	0	0	1	0
champagne	11	.1641	.4931	36.9	0	0	0	1	6	0	2	2	1	0	0	0	0	0	0	0	0	0	0	0	0	0	1	9	0
Champagne	2	.0000	.0209	23.2	1	0	1	0	0	0	0	0	0	0	0	0	0	0	0	0	0	0	0	0	0	0	2	0	0
champing	2	.2291	.1135	30.5	0	1	0	0	0	0	0	1	0	0	0	1	0	0	0	1	0	0	0	0	0	0	0	0	0

7Q cerements
9Q ceremonially
3J ceremonials
7A Ceremonies
9R ceremoniously
4J Ceremony
7G cerise
3A cerium
7P cermet
8H certain-sized
7R certify
XR certifying
8R certitude
7G cerulean
8G Cervantes'
7N cervical
9H cervix
7J Cesar
4Q cesium
7P Cespedes
9A Cessna
7H cesspool
6F cester
9B cestus
4N Cetacean
7N cetaceous
7N Ceuta
7R cfm
5E CFR
7N Ch
8F Ch'ien
8F Ch'ien-lung
8J cha-cha
7R chaco
7F Chaco
7N chafe
9D chaffed
4J Chaffey
7Q chaffinch
5P chaffinches
4P Chaffray's
8K Chagall
8Q Chagatai
5P Chaim
9F chain-driven
9F chain-gang
XH chain-links
8R chain-smokes
9R chain's
3A chaining
7D chainlets
7N CHAIR
7R chairmanship
6A Chaka
7F Chalcidice
3A chalcocite
8K Chaldeans
7B chalice
7A Chalk
6H chalk-filled
6B chalkboards
9D chalks
7A challengers
4Q Challoner
4P Chalmers
7Q Chalons-sur-Marne
8Q Chambal
4D chamberlain
6A chambermaids
4P Chambersburg
6J Chameleon
9M chamfering
9J Chaminade
7Q Chamonix
8R Champaign-Urbana
5A champed
XR Champernoune

Word Type	F	D	U	SFI	3 Gr 3	4 Gr 4	5 Gr 5	6 Gr 6	7 Gr 7	8 Gr 8	9 Gr 9	X UnGr	A Read	B Eng & Gr	C Comp	D Lit	E Math	F Soc Stud	G Spell	H Sci	J Music	K Art	L Home Ec	M Shop	N Lib F	P Lib NF	Q Lib Ref	R Mag	S Rel
champion	90	.6887	12.951	51.1	16	6	9	24	24	6	4	1	40	2	0	9	0	3	0	2	0	0	0	0	13	13	3	5	0
Champion	17	.3462	1.4217	41.5	9	2	0	0	3	3	0	0	6	0	0	0	0	0	0	0	0	0	0	0	5	0	0	6	0
championed	3	.3350	.2478	33.9	0	0	1	0	0	2	0	0	1	0	0	0	0	1	0	0	0	0	0	0	0	0	1	0	0
champions	16	.3702	1.4767	41.7	4	4	1	2	3	2	0	0	9	0	0	0	0	0	0	0	0	0	0	0	0	3	4	0	0
championship	22	.5981	2.8571	44.6	0	2	6	4	4	5	1	0	12	1	0	2	1	0	0	0	0	0	0	0	0	3	0	3	0
Championship	5	.3343	.4151	36.2	0	1	0	2	0	1	1	0	2	0	0	0	0	0	0	0	0	0	0	0	0	1	0	2	0
championships	9	.4713	.9806	39.9	0	1	0	1	1	5	0	1	5	1	0	0	0	0	0	0	0	0	0	0	0	1	0	2	0
Championships	2	.2351	.1166	30.7	0	0	1	1	0	0	0	0	0	0	0	0	0	1	0	0	0	0	0	0	0	0	0	1	0
Champlain	26	.6310	3.3994	45.3	2	2	11	3	3	4	0	1	2	0	0	0	0	12	0	1	1	0	0	0	2	3	3	2	0
champs	3	.2279	.2143	33.3	1	1	0	1	0	0	0	0	2	0	0	0	0	0	0	0	0	0	0	0	0	0	0	1	0
chance	548	.9059	98.881	60.0	79	109	67	66	123	58	35	11	217	27	2	45	3	28	7	33	7	2	13	4	49	52	17	42	0
Chance	3	.3454	.2542	34.1	1	0	1	1	0	0	0	0	1	0	0	0	0	1	0	0	0	0	0	0	0	0	0	1	0
chanced	10	.6563	1.3661	41.4	4	0	0	1	2	2	1	0	3	1	0	2	0	1	0	0	1	0	0	0	0	1	1	0	0
chancellor	3	.2444	.1814	32.6	0	0	1	0	0	1	1	0	0	0	0	0	0	2	0	0	0	0	0	0	0	0	1	0	0
Chancellor	10	.3368	.7251	38.6	0	0	2	1	1	5	0	1	0	1	0	0	0	0	0	0	6	0	0	0	1	0	0	2	0
Chancellorsville	5	.5598	.5795	37.6	1	0	0	0	1	2	1	0	0	0	0	1	0	1	0	0	0	0	0	0	1	1	1	0	0
chances	80	.8551	13.695	51.4	5	20	8	10	16	12	9	0	20	5	0	5	3	8	1	8	0	0	2	1	6	7	1	13	0
chancet	2	.0000	.0234	23.7	0	0	0	0	1	1	0	0	0	0	0	0	0	0	0	0	0	0	0	0	2	0	0	0	0
Chancho	6	.0000	.0657	28.2	0	0	0	0	0	0	6	0	0	6	0	0	0	0	0	0	0	0	0	0	0	0	0	0	0
Chanco	21	.0000	.3040	34.8	0	21	0	0	0	0	0	0	0	0	0	0	0	0	0	0	0	0	0	0	0	21	0	0	0
Chand	8	.0000	.3655	35.6	8	0	0	0	0	0	0	0	8	0	0	0	0	0	0	0	0	0	0	0	0	0	0	0	0
chandelier	9	.3276	.7494	38.7	0	4	3	2	0	0	0	0	4	0	0	0	0	0	0	0	0	0	0	0	0	4	0	1	0
chandeliers	3	.2357	.2199	33.4	0	1	1	0	0	1	0	0	2	0	0	0	0	0	0	0	0	0	0	0	0	1	0	0	0
Chandler	2	.1814	.1187	30.7	0	0	0	1	1	0	0	0	1	0	0	0	0	0	0	0	0	0	0	0	0	0	0	1	0
Chandrasekhar	2	.0000	.0394	26.0	0	0	0	0	1	0	0	1	0	0	0	0	0	0	0	2	0	0	0	0	0	0	0	0	0
Chang	21	.2789	1.3406	41.3	1	0	0	5	4	1	0	10	0	0	0	0	0	1	0	0	0	0	0	0	4	1	0	15	0
change	1854	.9138	335.64	65.3	333	259	258	281	319	197	164	43	215	152	8	44	219	113	310	363	72	20	28	25	36	87	77	84	1
change-over	2	.1698	.1133	30.5	0	0	0	0	1	1	0	0	1	0	0	0	0	0	0	0	0	0	0	0	0	0	1	0	0
changeable	9	.5315	1.0454	40.2	0	1	4	0	1	3	0	0	3	0	0	0	0	1	1	2	0	0	0	0	0	0	2	0	0
changed	770	.9076	138.67	61.4	97	101	141	117	163	97	42	12	124	41	1	28	28	94	87	149	33	8	7	13	29	51	45	29	3
changes	859	.8766	149.78	61.8	93	109	132	108	149	145	98	25	56	62	6	11	21	106	36	315	61	5	24	8	6	38	64	40	0
changing	383	.8479	64.705	58.1	42	61	66	68	58	51	25	12	27	33	6	10	29	39	85	77	15	8	3	2	5	12	14	18	0
Changing	2	.0000	.0389	25.9	0	0	0	1	1	0	0	0	0	0	0	0	0	2	0	0	0	0	0	0	0	0	0	0	0
channel	65	.7863	10.333	50.1	3	14	2	11	23	2	2	8	16	1	0	8	0	7	1	3	2	0	0	1	2	3	9	12	0
Channel	36	.6587	4.9093	46.9	4	0	7	5	10	2	6	2	7	3	0	3	0	11	1	0	0	0	0	0	0	1	7	3	0
channeled	3	.2239	.1775	32.5	0	0	0	0	1	2	0	0	0	0	0	0	0	2	0	1	0	0	0	0	0	0	0	0	0
channels	39	.6325	5.1020	47.1	2	1	4	7	10	4	7	4	5	1	0	0	0	3	0	8	0	0	0	1	2	1	13	5	0
Chanson	3	.2088	.1442	31.6	0	1	0	1	1	0	0	0	0	0	0	0	0	0	0	0	2	0	0	0	0	0	1	0	0
chant	61	.2251	3.3571	45.3	14	13	4	9	10	6	5	0	8	0	0	5	0	3	0	0	43	0	0	0	0	1	1	0	0
Chant	2	.0000	.0162	22.1	1	0	0	0	0	1	0	0	0	0	0	0	0	0	0	0	2	0	0	0	0	0	0	0	0
chanted	15	.6294	1.9541	42.9	2	5	2	3	0	2	1	0	2	2	0	1	0	2	0	0	1	0	0	0	2	5	0	0	0
chantey	10	.2847	.6526	38.1	2	5	1	0	2	0	0	0	1	0	0	2	0	0	0	0	6	0	0	0	0	1	0	0	0
Chanticleer	15	.1685	1.0405	40.2	0	8	6	1	0	0	0	0	14	0	0	0	0	0	0	0	0	0	0	0	0	1	0	0	0
Chanticleer's	2	.0000	.0914	29.6	0	2	0	0	0	0	0	0	2	0	0	0	0	0	0	0	0	0	0	0	0	0	0	0	0
chanting	18	.5498	2.1566	43.3	2	6	0	5	2	2	1	0	8	0	0	2	0	0	0	0	3	0	0	0	3	0	0	2	0
chants	15	.4309	1.3648	41.4	1	2	3	6	2	0	1	0	0	0	0	1	0	2	0	0	7	0	0	0	2	0	0	3	0
chanty	3	.2223	.2106	33.2	1	0	1	0	0	1	0	0	2	1	0	0	0	0	0	0	0	0	0	0	0	0	0	0	0
Chanuka	7	.0000	.3198	35.0	0	0	0	0	7	0	0	0	7	0	0	0	0	0	0	0	0	0	0	0	0	0	0	0	0
Chanuka's	2	.0000	.0914	29.6	0	0	0	0	2	0	0	0	2	0	0	0	0	0	0	0	0	0	0	0	0	0	0	0	0
Chanukah	9	.0000	.0728	28.6	0	0	6	3	0	0	0	0	0	0	0	0	0	0	0	0	9	0	0	0	0	0	0	0	0
chaos	16	.7663	2.4796	43.9	0	1	2	3	3	4	3	0	3	1	1	1	0	2	1	1	0	0	0	0	2	1	1	2	0
Chaos	5	.0000	.0724	28.6	4	0	0	0	0	0	0	1	0	0	0	0	0	0	0	0	0	0	0	0	0	5	0	0	0
chaotic	2	.0857	.0784	28.9	0	0	0	0	0	1	1	0	1	0	0	0	0	0	0	0	0	0	1	0	0	0	0	0	0
chap	17	.4589	1.7985	42.5	0	3	0	2	10	0	2	0	9	0	0	5	0	0	0	0	0	0	0	1	2	0	0	0	0
Chap	5	.0488	.0763	28.8	0	0	0	0	0	0	5	0	0	0	0	0	0	0	0	1	0	0	0	4	0	0	0	0	0
chaparral	6	.4031	.5322	37.3	0	0	1	3	1	1	0	0	1	0	0	2	0	0	0	0	2	0	0	0	0	0	0	1	0
chapel	26	.6054	3.2422	45.1	3	12	1	5	1	2	2	0	1	0	0	2	0	3	0	0	1	0	0	0	2	7	1	9	0
Chapel	5	.3211	.4073	36.1	0	1	0	2	1	0	1	0	2	0	0	0	0	1	0	0	0	0	0	0	0	0	0	2	0
chapels	3	.0000	.0314	25.0	1	1	1	0	0	0	0	0	0	0	0	0	0	0	0	0	0	0	0	0	0	0	3	0	0
chaperone	3	.0000	.0243	23.8	0	0	0	0	0	3	0	0	0	0	0	0	0	0	0	0	3	0	0	0	0	0	0	0	0
chaperons	4	.0000	.0579	27.6	0	0	0	0	4	0	0	0	0	0	0	0	0	0	0	0	0	0	0	0	0	4	0	0	0
Chapin	3	.2300	.1627	32.1	0	1	0	0	0	0	2	0	0	1	0	0	0	0	0	0	0	0	0	0	0	0	0	2	0
chaplain	4	.0000	.0486	26.9	0	0	0	0	3	1	0	0	0	0	0	0	0	0	0	0	0	0	0	0	0	0	0	4	0
chaplains	2	.2433	.1158	30.6	1	0	0	0	1	0	0	0	0	0	0	0	0	0	0	0	0	0	0	0	0	1	0	1	0
Chapman	3	.0000	.1370	31.4	0	0	0	1	2	0	0	0	3	0	0	0	0	0	0	0	0	0	0	0	0	0	0	0	0
chapped	5	.1877	.2757	34.4	0	2	0	1	0	2	0	0	2	0	0	0	0	0	0	0	0	0	2	0	0	1	0	0	0
chaps	12	.5107	1.3786	41.4	0	2	6	0	0	1	0	3	6	0	0	0	0	1	0	0	0	0	0	0	1	1	0	3	0
chapter	344	.7650	53.165	57.3	34	23	36	28	98	54	58	13	40	78	20	0	39	63	2	63	2	3	2	4	3	6	12	7	0
Chapter	107	.6479	14.262	51.5	7	3	15	3	34	16	27	2	7	18	0	0	6	26	0	29	2	0	12	1	0	3	2	1	0
chapters	62	.6526	8.3392	49.2	3	4	11	10	23	5	5	1	9	11	6	0	2	17	0	6	1	0	4	0	1	2	3	0	0
Chapters	12	.4410	1.1211	40.5	0	0	1	1	1	5	4	0	0	5	0	0	3	1	0	1	0	0	2	0	0	0	0	0	0
character	242	.8400	40.584	56.1	14	27	34	22	58	44	35	8	37	43	2	30	1	13	7	6	34	6	0	2	6	23	21	11	0
character's	5	.2620	.3230	35.1	0	1	0	0	0	3	1	0	1	1	0	3	0	0	0	0	0	0	0	0	0	0	0	0	0
characteristic	147	.7167	21.267	53.3	1	5	8	17	41	36	29	10	4	7	1	3	0	5	1	46	36	7	3	1	0	4	27	2	0
characteristically	5	.3734	.4019	36.0	0	0	0	0	3	2	0	0	0	0	0	1	0	0	0	0	0	0	0	0	0	0	2	2	0
characteristics	189	.7524	28.574	54.6	1	10	10	29	47	51	29	12	4	6	1	3	2	6	2	69	38	3	16	8	0	3	22	6	0
characterize	6	.5161	.6630	38.2	1	0	1	0	0	2	2	0	1	0	0	0	0	1	0	0	1	0	0	0	0	2	1	0	0
characterized	34	.6359	4.3950	46.4	0	2	3	2	11	8	5	3	1	1	0	0	0	0	0	3	9	0	1	1	0	3	11	4	0
characterizes	5	.4612	.4831	36.8	1	0	1	0	0	1	2	0	0	0	0	0	0	0	0	0	1	0	0	0	0	1	2	1	0
characters	157	.7810	24.684	53.9	13	17	21	13	24	30	33	6	32	31	11	21	0	7	3	0	13	4	0	8	2	10	6	9	0
characters'	2	.0000	.0914	29.6	0	0	0	0	0	2	0	0	2	0	0	0	0	0	0	0	0	0	0	0	0	0	0	0	0
Charan	4	.0000	.1827	32.6	4	0	0	0	0	0	0	0	4	0	0	0	0	0	0	0	0	0	0	0	0	0	0	0	0
Charbonneau	6	.0000	.2741	34.4	0	0	6	0	0	0	0	0	6	0	0	0	0	0	0	0	0	0	0	0	0	0	0	0	0
charcoal	42	.7270	6.2636	48.0	3	9	3	8	7	9	3	0	12	1	0	2	0	4	0	9	0	3	1	1	1	5	2	1	0
Charcoal	3	.0000	.1370	31.4	0	0	0	3	0	0	0	0	3	0	0	0	0	0	0	0	0	0	0	0	0	0	0	0	0
Chardin	2	.0000	.0037	15.7	0	0	0	0	0	0	2	0	0	0	0	0	0	0	0	0	0	2	0	0	0	0	0	0	0
Chardin's	2	.0000	.0037	15.7	0	0	0	0	0	0	2	0	0	0	0	0	0	0	0	0	0	2	0	0	0	0	0	0	0
Charette	2	.0000	.0914	29.6	0	0	2	0	0	0	0	0	2	0	0	0	0	0	0	0	0	0	0	0	0	0	0	0	0
charge	278	.8689	48.179	56.8	38	23	34	31	60	57	27	8	55	7	0	16	14	32	2	34	3	3	14	11	7	19	27	34	0
charge-account	2	.0000	.0064	18.1	0	0	0	0	0	2	0	0	0	0	0	0	0	0	0	0	0	0	2	0	0	0	0	0	0
charged	150	.7957	24.034	53.8	7	15	32	17	38	23	14	4	21	3	1	4	2	10	0	45	1	0	1	5	7	6	23	21	0
Chargers	2	.0000	.0243	23.9	0	0	0	1	1	0	0	0	0	0	0	0	0	0	0	0	0	0	0	0	0	0	0	2	0
charges	98	.7057	14.064	51.5	2	3	19	8	21	33	9	3	6	0	0	1	6	14	0	27	0	0	1	7	7	2	15	12	0
charging	24	.3840	2.1214	43.3	4	4	1	3	3	6	2	1	7	2	0	2	0	1	0	0	0	0	0	2	3	4	1	1	1
chariot	28	.6868	3.9241	45.9	3	0	0	2	9	6	5	3	4	1	0	6	1	3	0	1	2	2	0	0	0	1	4	3	0
Chariot	6	.3247	.4132	36.2	0	0	2	1	1	1	1	0	0	0	0	1	0	0	0	0	4	1	0	0	0	0	0	0	0

3N champion's
7Q Champion's
7R Champions
7P Chancellery
7N Chancery
7A chanct
9Q chancy
3A Chand's
7A chandelled
6A chandlers
6P chandlery
9P Chandralekha
3Q changeover
8J changers
XR channelled
8Q Channing
7N chanst
9D chanter
6J chantey-man
7D chanteys
5A chaparreras
7R chape
6F Chapelle
7P chaperoned
5R chaperones
7R chapes
8A Chaplains
XR Chaplin
5P Chaplinesque
8L chapping
4J Char-ley
7Q characin
7Q characins
7B character-sketching
6A character'll
9B characterization
XR charade
XP Charente
7J Charge
8D charger
7R Charger
8D charger's
3P chargers
7Q chariot's

Word Type	F	D	U	SFI	3 Gr 3	4 Gr 4	5 Gr 5	6 Gr 6	7 Gr 7	8 Gr 8	9 Gr 9	X UnGr	A Read	B Eng & Gr	C Comp	D Lit	E Math	F Soc Stud	G Spell	H Sci	J Music	K Art	L Home Ec	M Shop	N Lib F	P Lib NF	Q Lib Ref	R Mag	S Rel
chariots	9	.1526	.3830	35.8	0	1	1	0	6	0	0	1	1	0	0	0	0	0	0	0	0	0	0	0	0	1	7	0	0
charisma	2	.2433	.1158	30.6	0	0	1	0	1	0	0	0	0	0	0	0	0	0	0	0	0	0	0	0	0	1	0	1	0
charismatic	2	.0000	.0243	23.9	0	0	0	0	1	1	0	0	0	0	0	0	0	0	0	0	0	0	0	0	0	0	0	2	0
charitable	11	.5455	1.2979	41.1	0	0	1	2	5	2	0	1	4	0	1	1	0	0	0	0	0	0	0	0	1	3	1	0	0
charities	3	.3877	.2482	33.9	1	0	0	0	1	0	1	0	0	1	0	1	0	0	0	0	0	0	0	0	0	0	1	0	0
charity	19	.7075	2.7233	44.4	3	1	5	1	3	4	2	0	2	0	1	3	1	0	3	0	0	0	0	0	2	3	1	3	0
Charlatan	4	.0000	.0323	25.1	0	0	0	0	4	0	0	0	0	0	0	0	0	0	0	0	4	0	0	0	0	0	0	0	0
Charlemagne	15	.3450	1.2413	40.9	0	0	1	5	5	0	4	0	5	0	0	2	0	1	0	0	0	0	0	0	0	0	7	0	0
Charlemagne's	3	.1169	.1277	31.1	0	0	0	1	2	0	0	0	1	0	0	0	0	0	0	0	0	0	0	0	0	0	2	0	0
Charles	237	.8399	39.892	56.0	30	34	32	33	43	36	28	1	55	11	2	6	6	10	1	10	9	1	1	0	11	45	30	39	0
Charles'	8	.3530	.7092	38.5	4	3	0	0	0	0	1	0	4	0	0	0	0	0	0	0	0	0	0	0	0	3	0	1	0
Charleston	19	.6657	2.5890	44.1	3	4	5	1	1	3	2	0	1	1	0	0	0	6	0	1	2	0	0	0	0	3	2	3	0
Charlestown	11	.3017	.8011	39.0	0	5	0	0	0	4	2	0	2	0	0	0	0	0	0	0	0	0	0	0	3	6	0	0	0
Charley	43	.5719	5.1487	47.1	7	14	0	0	0	19	3	0	7	0	1	2	0	5	0	0	15	0	0	0	3	9	1	0	0
Charley's	11	.3188	.7504	38.8	0	1	0	0	1	9	0	0	0	0	2	0	0	0	0	0	7	0	0	0	0	2	0	0	0
Charlie	115	.7385	17.310	52.4	13	39	7	14	8	6	7	21	28	8	1	11	0	10	0	0	7	0	0	0	23	18	0	9	0
Charlie's	10	.4495	.9749	39.9	1	3	0	1	1	0	0	4	1	0	0	1	0	1	0	0	0	0	0	0	4	3	0	0	0
charlotte	2	.0000	.0215	23.3	0	0	0	0	0	0	2	0	0	0	0	2	0	0	0	0	0	0	0	0	0	0	0	0	0
Charlotte	63	.3856	5.9224	47.7	1	50	7	4	0	0	1	0	33	1	0	0	0	1	0	0	0	0	0	0	24	2	2	0	0
Charlotte's	3	.1250	.1342	31.3	0	3	0	0	0	0	0	0	1	0	0	0	0	0	0	0	0	0	0	0	2	0	0	0	0
Charlottesville	5	.3286	.3733	35.7	0	3	0	0	0	2	0	0	0	0	0	0	0	1	0	0	0	0	0	0	0	3	0	1	0
Charly	4	.0000	.0486	26.9	0	0	4	0	0	0	0	0	0	0	0	0	0	0	0	0	0	0	0	0	0	0	0	4	0
charm	54	.8306	8.9679	49.5	4	6	6	10	10	9	3	6	10	2	3	3	0	3	0	0	7	1	2	1	4	3	4	11	0
charmed	10	.5395	1.1772	40.7	0	1	3	3	1	1	0	1	4	0	0	0	0	0	0	0	0	0	0	0	1	1	2	2	0
charming	65	.7724	10.274	50.1	9	6	7	10	20	4	6	3	31	6	3	2	0	2	0	0	2	1	0	0	4	7	4	3	0
charmingly	3	.3452	.2543	34.1	1	0	0	0	0	0	0	2	1	0	0	0	0	0	0	1	0	0	0	0	0	0	0	1	0
charms	20	.7305	2.9575	44.7	2	8	2	2	3	1	1	1	2	1	1	1	0	5	0	0	3	0	0	0	3	1	1	2	0
charnel	2	.2407	.1138	30.6	0	0	0	0	1	1	0	0	0	0	0	1	0	0	0	0	0	0	0	0	0	1	0	0	0
Charrasse	2	.0000	.0243	23.9	0	0	0	0	0	0	0	2	0	0	0	0	0	0	0	0	0	0	0	0	0	0	0	2	0
charred	9	.5397	1.0142	40.1	0	1	0	3	1	3	1	0	1	0	1	1	0	1	0	0	0	1	0	0	3	1	0	0	0
chart	393	.7112	56.733	57.5	109	58	58	52	44	47	23	2	20	18	0	5	190	21	30	66	12	1	13	4	1	2	6	4	0
Chart	136	.1160	4.1027	46.1	4	34	26	19	51	2	0	0	0	0	0	0	5	0	127	1	0	0	3	0	0	0	0	0	0
Charta	7	.2445	.5495	37.4	0	0	0	6	0	1	0	0	6	0	0	0	0	0	1	0	0	0	0	0	0	0	0	0	0
charted	6	.4144	.5696	37.6	1	0	1	0	1	3	0	0	1	0	0	0	0	3	0	1	0	0	0	0	0	1	0	0	0
charter	24	.5012	2.5836	44.1	0	0	7	2	3	10	2	0	4	1	0	0	0	6	3	0	0	0	0	0	0	0	9	1	0
Charter	15	.4780	1.5684	42.0	0	0	2	3	2	6	2	0	3	0	0	1	0	5	1	0	0	0	0	0	0	0	5	0	0
chartered	6	.1339	.2157	33.3	0	0	5	0	1	0	0	0	0	0	0	0	0	0	0	0	0	0	0	0	0	1	5	0	0
charters	3	.1823	.1405	31.5	0	0	0	0	0	3	0	0	0	0	0	0	0	1	0	0	0	0	0	0	0	0	2	0	0
charting	4	.4484	.4050	36.1	0	1	1	1	1	0	0	0	1	0	0	0	0	1	0	1	0	0	0	0	0	0	1	0	0
Chartres	3	.0978	.0707	28.5	0	0	0	0	0	0	3	0	0	0	0	1	0	0	0	0	0	2	0	0	0	0	0	0	0
charts	85	.8416	14.301	51.6	8	9	18	7	23	6	11	3	9	2	0	9	20	17	0	11	1	1	1	2	1	5	4	2	0
Charts	2	.0000	.0914	29.6	0	0	0	2	0	0	0	0	2	0	0	0	0	0	0	0	0	0	0	0	0	0	0	0	0
Charybdis	3	.0000	.0322	25.1	0	0	0	0	0	0	3	0	0	0	0	3	0	0	0	0	0	0	0	0	0	0	0	0	0
chase	88	.7930	14.214	51.5	20	23	11	7	11	7	5	4	40	4	1	3	2	1	2	2	1	0	0	0	12	9	1	10	0
Chase	13	.5223	1.4647	41.7	5	0	3	0	0	4	1	0	3	0	0	0	0	2	0	0	0	0	0	0	0	2	3	3	0
chased	72	.7390	10.984	50.4	18	20	7	5	12	7	2	1	34	8	0	7	0	3	0	1	3	0	0	0	4	7	1	4	0
chases	9	.5363	1.0381	40.2	1	1	2	2	0	2	1	0	2	2	0	1	2	0	0	2	0	0	0	0	0	0	0	0	0
chasing	62	.7196	9.1941	49.6	20	17	7	4	5	4	5	0	23	6	2	4	0	1	0	1	0	0	0	0	5	8	1	11	0
chasm	2	.0000	.0914	29.6	0	1	0	0	1	0	0	0	2	0	0	0	0	0	0	0	0	0	0	0	0	0	0	0	0
chasms	2	.2433	.1158	30.6	0	0	0	1	1	0	0	0	0	0	0	0	0	0	0	0	0	0	0	0	0	1	0	1	0
chassis	8	.4654	.7843	38.9	0	1	0	0	3	1	1	2	0	0	0	0	0	0	1	0	0	0	0	0	0	3	1	3	0
chaste	6	.4522	.5781	37.6	0	0	1	0	2	1	2	0	0	0	0	2	0	1	0	0	0	0	0	0	0	2	0	1	0
chat	9	.6606	1.2125	40.8	0	1	2	2	1	0	2	1	0	2	0	1	0	1	0	2	0	0	0	0	1	1	0	1	0
chateau	4	.3786	.3298	35.2	0	0	0	0	2	1	1	0	0	0	0	1	0	0	0	0	0	0	0	0	0	2	0	1	0
Chateau	2	.2408	.1204	30.8	0	0	0	0	1	1	0	0	0	0	0	0	0	1	0	0	0	0	0	0	0	1	0	0	0
Chateau-Thierry	2	.0000	.0389	25.9	0	0	0	0	0	2	0	0	0	0	0	0	0	2	0	0	0	0	0	0	0	0	0	0	0
Chatham	3	.1169	.1277	31.1	0	0	1	0	0	0	2	0	1	0	0	0	0	0	0	0	0	0	0	0	0	0	2	0	0
Chattahoochee	2	.2437	.1129	30.5	0	0	0	1	1	0	0	0	0	0	0	0	0	0	0	0	0	0	0	0	0	0	1	1	0
Chattanooga	4	.3344	.3261	35.1	0	0	2	1	1	0	0	0	1	0	0	0	0	2	0	0	0	0	0	0	0	0	1	0	0
chatted	6	.2991	.4499	36.5	1	3	1	0	1	0	0	0	2	0	0	0	0	0	0	0	0	0	0	0	3	0	0	1	0
chattel	3	.2196	.1554	31.9	0	0	1	0	2	0	0	0	0	0	0	2	0	0	0	0	0	0	0	0	1	0	0	0	0
chatter	41	.6784	5.7380	47.6	18	1	3	8	5	4	0	2	11	9	3	1	0	3	0	0	2	0	0	0	2	4	1	5	0
chatterbox	2	.0000	.0219	23.4	0	0	0	0	0	1	1	0	0	2	0	0	0	0	0	0	0	0	0	0	0	0	0	0	0
chattered	21	.5900	2.6883	44.3	3	4	3	4	2	2	2	1	11	0	0	4	0	0	0	0	1	0	0	0	2	2	0	1	0
chattering	39	.7067	5.6891	47.6	9	6	4	9	8	1	1	1	14	2	2	3	0	2	0	0	0	0	0	0	7	3	3	3	0
chatters	3	.2327	.1564	31.9	2	0	0	0	0	1	0	0	0	2	0	0	0	0	0	0	0	0	1	0	0	0	0	0	0
chatting	5	.4727	.5348	37.3	0	2	0	0	2	1	0	0	2	1	0	0	0	1	0	0	0	0	0	0	1	0	0	0	0
Chaucer	4	.0000	.0325	25.1	0	0	0	0	3	1	0	0	0	0	0	0	0	0	4	0	0	0	0	0	0	0	0	0	0
Chaucer's	3	.0000	.0243	23.9	0	0	0	0	1	2	0	0	0	0	0	0	0	0	3	0	0	0	0	0	0	0	0	0	0
chauffeur	6	.4209	.5412	37.3	0	0	2	1	2	0	1	0	0	1	0	0	0	1	0	0	0	0	0	0	3	0	0	1	0
chauffeur-driven	2	.1698	.1133	30.5	0	0	0	0	0	0	2	0	1	0	0	0	0	0	0	0	0	0	0	0	0	0	1	0	0
Chauncey	2	.0000	.0219	23.4	0	0	0	0	0	0	2	0	0	2	0	0	0	0	0	0	0	0	0	0	0	0	0	0	0
Chaverim	4	.0000	.0323	25.1	0	0	3	1	0	0	0	0	0	0	0	0	0	0	0	0	4	0	0	0	0	0	0	0	0
Chavez	5	.0619	.1340	31.3	1	0	2	2	0	0	0	0	1	0	0	0	0	0	0	0	4	0	0	0	0	0	0	0	0
cheap	60	.7934	9.5907	49.8	9	6	7	10	13	10	4	1	9	2	0	2	0	16	5	3	2	0	0	0	6	7	5	3	0
cheaper	28	.6934	4.0097	46.0	2	4	4	7	7	2	1	1	6	0	0	0	2	8	0	5	2	0	0	0	0	1	2	2	0
cheapest	6	.5116	.6648	38.2	0	2	0	0	2	0	1	1	1	0	0	0	0	1	0	1	0	0	0	0	0	2	0	1	0
cheaply	18	.6299	2.3381	43.7	2	1	5	1	2	3	4	0	1	1	1	1	0	8	0	0	0	0	0	0	0	1	2	3	0
cheat	12	.3988	1.0856	40.4	1	0	2	2	2	5	0	0	3	0	0	4	0	0	0	0	0	0	0	0	4	1	0	0	0
cheated	19	.5966	2.3458	43.7	2	1	0	1	7	6	2	0	2	0	0	6	0	1	0	0	0	0	1	0	4	3	0	2	0
cheater	3	.0000	.0322	25.1	0	0	0	0	0	3	0	0	0	0	0	3	0	0	0	0	0	0	0	0	0	0	0	0	0
cheating	8	.4905	.8574	39.3	0	1	2	0	1	3	1	0	2	0	0	2	0	2	0	0	0	0	1	0	0	1	0	0	0
Cheboygan	5	.0000	.0724	28.6	0	5	0	0	0	0	0	0	0	0	0	0	0	0	0	0	0	0	0	0	0	5	0	0	0
check	1024	.7363	152.79	61.8	194	115	131	129	207	147	90	11	161	51	5	19	299	25	250	69	4	1	42	31	10	17	10	30	0
check-out	2	.1698	.1133	30.5	0	0	0	0	2	0	0	0	1	0	0	0	0	0	0	0	0	0	0	0	0	0	1	0	0
check-up	2	.1674	.0805	29.1	0	0	0	0	1	0	1	0	0	0	0	0	0	0	0	0	0	0	1	0	0	1	0	0	0
checked	170	.7164	24.839	54.0	42	27	17	21	34	13	14	2	37	9	0	7	18	4	51	8	0	0	3	1	8	11	4	9	0
checker	15	.6088	1.9035	42.8	8	2	0	0	4	0	1	0	3	0	0	0	0	0	1	0	1	0	0	1	2	6	0	1	0
checkered	2	.1948	.1250	31.0	0	0	1	0	0	0	0	1	1	0	0	0	0	0	0	0	0	0	0	0	0	1	0	0	0
checkers	21	.7109	3.0592	44.9	12	3	2	2	1	0	1	0	5	1	1	2	4	1	0	0	0	0	0	0	2	4	1	0	0
checking	64	.9025	11.478	50.6	14	6	9	6	12	4	10	3	15	4	1	2	7	2	3	4	1	0	2	1	3	10	1	8	0
checklists	2	.0000	.0243	23.9	0	0	0	2	0	0	0	0	0	0	0	0	0	0	0	0	0	0	0	0	0	0	0	2	0
checkout	3	.1937	.1495	31.7	1	0	0	0	2	0	0	0	0	0	0	0	0	1	0	0	0	0	0	0	0	0	0	2	0
checks	56	.8434	9.4251	49.7	16	5	9	3	9	3	10	1	6	1	0	2	13	2	3	4	1	1	3	0	3	9	3	5	0
checkup	6	.1965	.3207	35.1	5	0	0	0	0	0	1	0	0	0	0	0	0	0	0	5	0	0	0	0	0	0	0	1	0
checkups	6	.4634	.5954	37.7	1	2	2	1	0	0	0	0	0	0	0	0	0	1	1	2	0	0	0	0	0	0	0	2	0

7R charitably
8F Charity
7A charlatan
6R Charles's
9B Charleses
4Q Charleston's
7G Charleton's
8B charley
7D CHARLEY
6A Charlton
5R Charly's
XR charmer
8G Charming
7P charnel-roof
6P Charon
XR Charpentier
XP Charron
5Q charterers
3A Chase's
3A chaser
7A chasers
4J Chasse
6J chastens
7R chastise
7J chastised
8A chastising
3A Chat
6N chatelaine
9R Chatelet
8D Chatfield
7N chats
8A chatterin'
XR chatty
4P Chautauqua
9R chaw
7P chawklut
7J Che
9C Cheaper
7N Cheapside
6A Cheat
7P cheats
8G CHECK
3Q check-ups
9Q check-writing
9P checkerboard
8C checklist
7D checkmate
9R checkpoints

Word Type	F	D	U	SFI	3 Gr 3	4 Gr 4	5 Gr 5	6 Gr 6	7 Gr 7	8 Gr 8	9 Gr 9	X UnGr	A Read	B Eng & Gr	C Comp	D Lit	E Math	F Soc Stud	G Spell	H Sci	J Music	K Art	L Home Ec	M Shop	N Lib F	P Lib NF	Q Lib Ref	R Mag	S Rel
Cheddar	3	.1584	.1056	30.2	0	0	0	0	2	1	0	0	0	0	0	0	0	0	1	0	0	0	2	0	0	0	0	0	0
Chee-Chee	9	.1936	.4260	36.3	0	7	2	0	0	0	0	0	0	0	0	2	0	0	0	0	0	0	0	0	7	0	0	0	0
cheek	87	.6623	11.954	50.8	15	11	8	13	21	6	10	3	24	2	1	23	0	1	0	7	3	0	0	0	18	5	0	3	0
cheekbones	5	.2010	.2850	34.5	1	1	0	0	0	1	2	0	2	0	0	0	0	0	0	0	0	0	2	0	1	0	0	0	0
cheeks	94	.7573	14.524	51.6	13	21	10	11	17	12	9	1	32	3	0	11	0	1	0	3	5	1	1	0	19	15	1	2	0
cheeky	2	.0665	.0708	28.5	0	0	0	0	0	1	1	0	1	0	1	0	0	0	0	0	0	0	0	0	0	0	0	0	0
cheep	6	.0000	.2741	34.4	6	0	0	0	0	0	0	0	6	0	0	0	0	0	0	0	0	0	0	0	0	0	0	0	0
cheer	88	.7684	13.897	51.4	29	19	10	7	10	6	4	3	47	2	1	7	0	1	1	1	6	0	0	0	4	11	1	6	0
cheer-cheer	2	.0000	.0914	29.6	2	0	0	0	0	0	0	0	2	0	0	0	0	0	0	0	0	0	0	0	0	0	0	0	0
cheer-up	2	.0000	.0914	29.6	2	0	0	0	0	0	0	0	2	0	0	0	0	0	0	0	0	0	0	0	0	0	0	0	0
cheered	46	.5915	5.9872	47.8	11	14	4	5	4	4	2	2	29	2	0	1	0	1	0	2	1	0	0	0	0	9	0	1	0
cheerful	87	.8178	14.307	51.6	12	10	7	19	16	14	8	1	25	4	4	8	0	3	2	1	3	1	6	0	14	7	2	7	0
Cheerful	7	.0000	.3198	35.0	7	0	0	0	0	0	0	0	7	0	0	0	0	0	0	0	0	0	0	0	0	0	0	0	0
Cheerful's	2	.0000	.0914	29.6	2	0	0	0	0	0	0	0	2	0	0	0	0	0	0	0	0	0	0	0	0	0	0	0	0
cheerfully	54	.6648	7.4821	48.7	6	12	5	7	17	1	5	1	18	1	0	6	0	0	0	2	1	0	0	0	12	9	1	4	0
cheerfulness	5	.4122	.4599	36.6	0	1	1	0	3	0	0	0	1	0	0	2	0	0	0	0	0	0	0	0	1	1	0	0	0
cheerily	7	.3588	.6102	37.9	0	0	0	2	3	1	1	0	3	0	0	2	0	0	0	0	0	0	0	0	2	0	0	0	0
cheering	56	.7091	8.2651	49.2	4	14	2	14	9	9	4	0	26	1	0	3	3	4	0	0	1	0	0	0	9	5	0	4	0
cheerleaders	2	.1223	.0628	28.0	1	0	0	0	1	0	0	0	0	0	0	0	1	0	0	0	0	1	0	0	0	0	0	0	0
cheerless	6	.2330	.3044	34.8	0	3	0	2	1	0	0	0	0	0	3	0	0	0	1	0	0	0	0	0	1	0	0	1	0
cheers	30	.5611	3.7129	45.7	1	9	3	4	8	2	3	0	16	0	0	1	0	3	0	0	0	0	0	0	3	1	0	6	0
cheery	17	.6359	2.2962	43.6	4	2	2	2	4	1	0	2	8	0	1	0	0	1	0	1	0	0	1	0	3	1	0	1	0
cheese	236	.7120	34.447	55.4	55	37	42	23	36	11	26	6	63	5	1	16	6	29	5	18	1	2	36	0	18	20	11	5	0
cheeseburgers	2	.1948	.1250	31.0	0	1	0	0	0	0	1	0	1	0	0	0	0	0	0	0	0	0	0	0	0	1	0	0	0
cheesecloth	5	.2938	.3460	35.4	0	3	0	1	1	0	0	0	0	0	0	0	0	1	0	3	0	0	0	1	0	0	0	0	0
cheeses	22	.4549	2.1349	43.3	1	0	4	0	14	1	1	1	1	0	0	2	0	5	1	4	0	0	6	0	2	1	0	0	0
cheetah	22	.4723	2.4148	43.8	2	12	0	0	4	4	0	0	13	0	1	0	6	0	0	0	0	0	0	0	0	0	2	0	0
cheetahs	9	.2292	.6951	38.4	1	8	0	0	0	0	0	0	8	0	0	0	0	0	0	0	0	0	0	0	0	0	1	0	0
Cheever	3	.0000	.0365	25.6	0	0	0	0	0	0	0	3	0	0	0	0	0	0	0	0	0	0	0	0	0	0	0	3	0
chef	2	.2437	.1129	30.5	0	0	0	0	1	0	0	1	0	0	0	0	0	0	0	0	0	0	0	0	0	0	1	1	0
Chef	2	.0000	.0243	23.9	0	0	0	0	0	0	0	2	0	0	0	0	0	0	0	0	0	0	0	0	0	0	0	2	0
Chef's	2	.0000	.0219	23.4	0	0	0	0	0	2	0	0	0	2	0	0	0	0	0	0	0	0	0	0	0	0	0	0	0
Chelsea	2	.1948	.1250	31.0	0	1	0	1	0	0	0	0	1	0	0	0	0	0	0	0	0	0	0	0	0	1	0	0	0
Chem	6	.0000	.2741	34.4	0	0	0	6	0	0	0	0	6	0	0	0	0	0	0	0	0	0	0	0	0	0	0	0	0
chemical	376	.6381	49.451	56.9	33	16	97	53	61	57	47	12	8	1	2	1	3	19	1	214	1	0	5	12	0	28	70	11	0
Chemical	6	.1618	.2516	34.0	0	1	0	1	1	2	1	0	0	0	0	0	0	0	0	0	0	0	0	0	1	0	0	5	0
chemically	23	.5408	2.6053	44.2	0	2	5	4	4	6	2	0	1	0	0	0	0	0	0	11	0	1	3	0	0	0	5	2	0
chemicals	122	.6617	16.633	52.2	9	14	35	22	24	9	8	1	10	0	0	0	2	27	0	42	0	0	1	5	0	11	20	4	0
chemist	33	.6669	4.5257	46.6	1	2	2	7	4	10	6	1	3	2	0	1	4	0	0	15	1	0	0	1	0	1	5	0	0
chemist's	5	.3775	.4753	36.8	0	0	0	2	0	1	2	0	3	1	0	0	0	0	0	1	0	0	0	0	0	0	0	0	0
chemistry	72	.6088	9.0632	49.6	4	4	16	12	6	8	17	5	4	1	0	0	2	0	1	27	0	0	1	2	0	2	25	7	0
chemists	54	.3921	4.7860	46.8	10	1	10	11	8	7	5	2	3	0	0	1	0	0	0	36	0	0	0	0	0	6	8	0	0
chemosynthetic	2	.0000	.0394	26.0	0	0	0	0	1	0	0	1	0	0	0	0	0	0	0	2	0	0	0	0	0	0	0	0	0
chemotherapy	3	.0000	.0591	27.7	0	0	0	0	1	0	2	0	0	0	0	0	0	0	0	3	0	0	0	0	0	0	0	0	0
Cheops	6	.3182	.4303	36.3	0	2	0	2	0	0	2	0	0	0	0	0	2	1	0	0	0	0	0	0	0	0	3	0	0
cheque-book	2	.0000	.0914	29.6	0	0	0	2	0	0	0	0	2	0	0	0	0	0	0	0	0	0	0	0	0	0	0	0	0
cheques	2	.2444	.1132	30.5	0	0	0	1	1	0	0	0	0	1	0	0	0	0	0	0	0	0	0	0	1	0	0	0	0
cherish	8	.4629	.7982	39.0	0	0	0	0	3	2	1	2	0	0	0	0	0	3	0	1	0	0	0	0	0	2	0	2	0
cherished	23	.7577	3.5260	45.5	0	1	4	3	7	4	3	1	4	0	0	1	0	4	0	0	2	1	1	0	1	4	3	2	0
cherishes	2	.0000	.0243	23.9	0	0	0	1	1	0	0	0	0	0	0	0	0	0	0	0	0	0	0	0	0	0	0	2	0
cherishing	2	.1698	.1133	30.5	0	0	0	0	1	1	0	0	1	0	0	0	0	0	0	0	0	0	0	0	0	0	1	0	0
Cherith	2	.0000	.0290	24.6	2	0	0	0	0	0	0	0	0	0	0	0	0	0	0	0	0	0	0	0	0	2	0	0	0
chernozems	2	.0000	.0394	26.0	0	0	0	0	0	0	2	0	0	0	0	0	0	0	0	2	0	0	0	0	0	0	0	0	0
Cherokee	16	.4689	1.7753	42.5	7	0	2	2	3	0	0	2	11	1	0	0	0	0	0	0	0	0	0	0	0	2	0	2	0
Cherokees	17	.3080	1.2803	41.1	10	4	0	0	3	0	0	0	4	0	0	1	0	0	0	0	0	0	0	0	0	11	1	0	0
Cherrapunji	2	.0000	.0389	25.9	0	2	0	0	0	0	0	0	0	0	0	0	0	2	0	0	0	0	0	0	0	0	0	0	0
cherries	55	.7708	8.6629	49.4	28	13	1	4	3	3	3	0	23	3	0	4	9	0	0	2	1	0	2	0	6	1	1	3	0
cherry	71	.9267	13.050	51.2	19	11	6	12	9	8	6	0	24	4	1	7	2	2	3	6	4	0	1	1	5	3	3	5	0
Cherry	9	.3057	.7085	38.5	2	1	1	5	0	0	0	0	4	0	0	0	0	0	0	0	0	0	0	0	4	0	0	1	0
Cherry-Tree	2	.0000	.0234	23.7	0	0	2	0	0	0	0	0	0	0	0	0	0	0	0	0	0	0	0	0	2	0	0	0	0
Cheryll	3	.0000	.0328	25.2	0	0	0	0	0	0	3	0	0	3	0	0	0	0	0	0	0	0	0	0	0	0	0	0	0
Chesapeake	18	.5809	2.2195	43.5	4	1	5	0	4	3	1	0	4	0	0	0	0	5	0	0	0	0	0	0	1	4	3	1	0
Chesbro	3	.0000	.0434	26.4	0	0	0	3	0	0	0	0	0	0	0	0	0	0	0	0	0	0	0	0	0	3	0	0	0
chess	21	.5824	2.5517	44.1	0	3	3	4	4	1	3	3	3	8	0	2	1	1	0	0	0	0	0	0	2	1	0	3	0
Chess	2	.1814	.1187	30.7	0	0	0	0	0	1	0	1	1	0	0	0	0	0	0	0	0	0	0	0	0	0	0	1	0
chessboard	4	.1733	.2298	33.6	0	2	2	0	0	0	0	0	2	2	0	0	0	0	0	0	0	0	0	0	0	0	0	0	0
chessmen	3	.0000	.0328	25.2	0	3	0	0	0	0	0	0	0	3	0	0	0	0	0	0	0	0	0	0	0	0	0	0	0
chest	231	.7928	37.088	55.7	27	28	47	33	41	36	18	1	64	1	2	26	0	1	1	62	1	1	6	0	32	16	8	10	0
Chest	5	.2264	.2984	34.7	0	3	1	1	0	0	0	0	1	3	0	0	0	0	0	1	0	0	0	0	0	0	0	0	0
chest-deep	2	.2441	.1127	30.5	0	0	0	0	2	0	0	0	0	0	0	0	0	0	0	0	0	0	0	0	1	0	1	0	0
chesten	4	.0000	.1827	32.6	0	0	0	4	0	0	0	0	4	0	0	0	0	0	0	0	0	0	0	0	0	0	0	0	0
Chester	50	.4276	5.0855	47.1	5	10	10	21	3	1	0	0	29	1	0	0	0	2	0	0	12	0	0	0	0	0	0	6	0
Chester's	2	.0000	.0914	29.6	0	0	0	2	0	0	0	0	2	0	0	0	0	0	0	0	0	0	0	0	0	0	0	0	0
Chesterton	2	.0000	.0290	24.6	0	1	1	0	0	0	0	0	0	0	0	0	0	0	0	0	0	0	0	0	0	2	0	0	0
chestnut	24	.5187	2.6574	44.2	5	3	0	5	10	0	0	1	4	0	0	4	0	0	0	2	0	0	0	0	9	4	1	0	0
Chestnut	3	.2120	.1548	31.9	0	2	0	0	1	0	0	0	0	0	0	0	0	0	0	0	0	0	0	0	2	1	0	0	0
chestnut-colored	2	.1717	.1142	30.6	0	0	1	0	0	1	0	0	1	0	0	1	0	0	0	0	0	0	0	0	0	0	0	0	0
chestnuts	13	.2193	.7336	38.7	6	0	2	3	1	1	0	0	2	0	0	9	0	0	0	1	0	0	0	0	0	1	0	0	0
chests	27	.7232	4.0073	46.0	3	5	7	4	0	6	1	1	9	0	0	1	0	3	0	0	2	1	0	2	4	2	1	2	0
Chet	61	.2344	4.4753	46.5	0	0	18	5	18	20	0	0	43	0	0	0	0	0	0	0	0	0	0	0	18	0	0	0	0
Chet's	2	.0000	.0914	29.6	0	0	0	1	0	1	0	0	2	0	0	0	0	0	0	0	0	0	0	0	0	0	0	0	0
chevalier	2	.0000	.0162	22.1	0	0	0	2	0	0	0	0	0	0	0	0	0	0	0	0	2	0	0	0	0	0	0	0	0
Chevalier	5	.3341	.3682	35.7	0	0	0	0	0	5	0	0	0	0	0	0	0	1	0	0	2	0	0	0	0	0	0	2	0
Chevrolet	4	.3409	.3067	34.9	0	0	0	1	2	1	0	0	0	0	0	0	1	1	0	0	0	0	0	0	0	0	0	2	0
Chevy	13	.0000	.1580	32.0	0	0	0	0	13	0	0	0	0	0	0	0	0	0	0	0	0	0	0	0	0	0	0	13	0
chew	49	.7416	7.4140	48.7	14	7	12	5	3	2	6	0	12	4	0	2	0	0	4	10	0	0	0	0	4	7	5	1	0
chewed	34	.7712	5.3161	47.3	4	7	1	7	3	2	7	3	8	1	0	7	0	2	0	6	2	0	1	0	3	2	1	1	0
chewing	68	.8353	11.394	50.6	9	9	8	12	15	4	7	4	14	5	1	8	0	5	2	16	1	0	0	0	4	4	5	3	0
chews	8	.4777	.8251	39.2	2	0	1	3	0	0	2	0	1	1	0	0	0	0	0	1	0	0	0	0	0	2	0	3	0
chewy	2	.1733	.1149	30.6	0	1	0	0	0	0	1	0	1	1	0	0	0	0	0	0	0	0	0	0	0	0	0	0	0
Cheyenne	11	.3767	1.0203	40.1	0	2	2	1	2	4	0	0	5	0	0	0	0	4	0	0	0	0	0	0	0	0	0	2	0
Chi	5	.3812	.4221	36.3	0	0	1	0	2	1	1	0	0	0	0	0	0	3	0	0	1	0	0	0	0	0	1	0	0
Chi-Wee	22	.0000	1.0050	40.0	15	7	0	0	0	0	0	0	22	0	0	0	0	0	0	0	0	0	0	0	0	0	0	0	0
Chi-Wee's	4	.0000	.1827	32.6	2	2	0	0	0	0	0	0	4	0	0	0	0	0	0	0	0	0	0	0	0	0	0	0	0

4N Chee-Chee's
3A cheecha
3A cheep-eep-eep
4A cheeped
3A cheeping
3A cheeriest
7N cheeriness
8A cheerleader
9J cheerly
5B Cheers
4P cheese-butter
5N cheese-making
4G cheeseburger
XH cheeselike
XR Cheever's
8E Chefalo
9P chefs
7G chek-r
7G chek-rz
5P Chekiang
8A Chelmbury
5A Chelmsford
9F Chelyabinsk
XH chemical-coated
8F CheminDesDames
6A chemise
7L Chemistry
4P Chemung
5R Chen
8A Cheney
3P Chengchou
7R Chequamegon
8G cher
9F Chernigov
7R cherry-red
3P cherry-tree
5N cherry-trees
3P cherubs
8Q Cheselden
5N Cheshire-Cat
5N chess-board
7N chest-level
6F chester
7B Chesterfield
8A chestful
7N chestnut-burrs
5P chestnut-falls
7N chestnut's
9B chetireh
3A chetyre
7R Chevette
7F Cheviot
3N Chevrolet's
7N Chevvy
7R Chevy-Ford
9R Chevys
4F chewed-up
8A chewers
9B chewing-gum
7A Cheyennes'

Word Type	F	D	U	SFI	3 Gr 3	4 Gr 4	5 Gr 5	6 Gr 6	7 Gr 7	8 Gr 8	9 Gr 9	X UnGr	A Read	B Eng & Gr	C Comp	D Lit	E Math	F Soc Stud	G Spell	H Sci	J Music	K Art	L Home Ec	M Shop	N Lib F	P Lib NF	Q Lib Ref	R Mag	S Rel
Chiang	16	.2999	1.0820	40.3	0	0	12	2	0	2	0	0	0	0	0	0	0	4	0	0	2	0	0	0	0	0	10	0	0
Chiang's	2	.2285	.1129	30.5	0	0	1	0	0	1	0	0	0	0	0	0	0	1	0	0	0	0	0	0	0	0	1	0	0
Chianti	2	.0000	.0162	22.1	0	0	0	0	0	2	0	0	0	0	0	0	0	0	2	0	0	0	0	0	0	0	0	0	0
Chiapas	5	.0000	.0523	27.2	0	0	5	0	0	0	0	0	0	0	0	0	0	0	0	0	0	0	0	0	0	0	5	0	0
Chibcha	3	.0000	.0314	25.0	0	0	3	0	0	0	0	0	0	0	0	0	0	0	0	0	0	0	0	0	0	0	3	0	0
Chica	5	.0000	.2284	33.6	0	0	5	0	0	0	0	0	5	0	0	0	0	0	0	0	0	0	0	0	0	0	0	0	0
Chica's	2	.0000	.0914	29.6	0	0	2	0	0	0	0	0	2	0	0	0	0	0	0	0	0	0	0	0	0	0	0	0	0
Chicago	236	.8031	38.100	55.8	36	46	24	25	47	32	24	2	31	12	0	4	31	49	1	10	6	1	0	1	3	13	32	42	0
Chicago's	10	.3308	.7355	38.7	1	1	1	0	5	2	0	0	0	0	0	0	0	2	0	0	0	0	0	0	0	0	5	3	0
Chicagoan	2	.2408	.1204	30.8	1	0	0	0	1	0	0	0	0	0	0	0	0	1	0	0	0	0	0	0	0	1	0	0	0
Chicagoans	2	.2401	.1133	30.5	0	1	0	0	1	0	0	0	0	0	0	0	0	0	0	0	0	0	0	0	0	1	1	0	0
Chichen-Itza	5	.0000	.0972	29.9	0	0	0	5	0	0	0	0	0	0	0	0	0	5	0	0	0	0	0	0	0	0	0	0	0
Chichester	2	.2411	.1091	30.4	0	0	1	0	1	0	0	0	0	0	0	1	0	0	0	0	1	0	0	0	0	0	0	0	0
chick	21	.5407	2.4446	43.9	4	1	6	0	2	3	0	5	4	0	0	0	0	0	0	10	0	0	0	0	3	1	1	2	0
Chick	21	.0000	.9593	39.8	3	0	10	0	0	8	0	0	21	0	0	0	0	0	0	0	0	0	0	0	0	0	0	0	0
chick-a-la-bye	2	.0000	.0234	23.7	2	0	0	0	0	0	0	0	0	0	0	0	0	0	0	0	0	0	0	0	2	0	0	0	0
Chick's	2	.0000	.0914	29.6	2	0	0	0	0	0	0	0	2	0	0	0	0	0	0	0	0	0	0	0	0	0	0	0	0
chickadee	4	.2385	.2496	34.0	2	0	2	0	0	0	0	0	1	0	0	0	0	0	2	1	0	0	0	0	0	0	0	0	0
Chickadee	2	.0000	.0914	29.6	0	2	0	0	0	0	0	0	2	0	0	0	0	0	0	0	0	0	0	0	0	0	0	0	0
chickadees	4	.2386	.2998	34.8	3	0	0	1	0	0	0	0	3	0	0	0	0	0	0	0	0	0	0	0	0	0	1	0	0
Chickamauga	2	.0000	.0209	23.2	0	0	0	0	2	0	0	0	0	0	0	0	0	0	0	0	0	0	0	0	0	0	2	0	0
chicken	229	.7920	36.778	55.7	73	35	30	10	41	8	24	8	79	3	0	19	7	3	10	33	2	3	19	0	12	13	4	22	0
Chicken	10	.3697	.8642	39.4	3	0	0	0	5	1	1	0	3	0	0	1	0	0	0	0	0	0	0	0	5	0	0	1	0
chicken-corn	2	.0000	.0914	29.6	0	2	0	0	0	0	0	0	2	0	0	0	0	0	0	0	0	0	0	0	0	0	0	0	0
chicken-wire	2	.2440	.1132	30.5	0	0	0	1	1	0	0	0	0	0	0	1	0	0	0	0	0	0	0	0	0	0	0	1	0
chicken's	3	.3840	.2594	34.1	0	1	1	0	0	0	1	0	0	0	0	0	0	1	0	1	0	0	0	0	0	1	0	0	0
chickens	229	.8353	38.658	55.9	96	48	25	28	16	9	7	0	104	9	2	9	6	28	3	13	1	6	0	0	16	19	2	11	0
chicks	26	.6633	3.6153	45.6	11	5	4	5	0	0	1	0	11	1	0	6	1	0	0	1	2	1	0	0	0	2	0	1	0
chicle	8	.4887	.8925	39.5	0	0	1	2	4	0	1	0	4	1	0	0	0	2	0	0	0	0	0	0	0	0	1	0	0
Chico	16	.0000	.7309	38.6	7	0	1	8	0	0	0	0	16	0	0	0	0	0	0	0	0	0	0	0	0	0	0	0	0
Chico's	5	.0000	.2284	33.6	0	0	0	5	0	0	0	0	5	0	0	0	0	0	0	0	0	0	0	0	0	0	0	0	0
chicory	3	.1587	.1058	30.2	0	0	1	0	2	0	0	0	0	0	0	0	0	0	0	0	1	0	2	0	0	0	0	0	0
chide	2	.0000	.0215	23.3	0	0	0	0	0	0	2	0	0	0	0	2	0	0	0	0	0	0	0	0	0	0	0	0	0
chief	428	.8335	71.644	58.6	49	58	72	62	95	47	40	5	102	9	3	22	5	92	11	25	5	2	4	0	18	35	69	24	2
Chief	105	.7161	15.575	51.9	11	28	14	18	15	12	6	1	44	12	0	5	0	8	0	0	1	0	0	0	7	16	2	10	0
chief's	6	.3850	.5818	37.6	0	1	2	1	2	0	0	0	4	0	0	1	0	0	0	0	0	0	0	0	0	1	0	0	0
chiefest	2	.2427	.1152	30.6	0	0	0	0	2	0	0	0	0	0	0	0	0	0	0	0	0	0	0	0	1	1	0	0	0
chiefly	113	.8270	18.686	52.7	3	2	27	22	32	15	9	3	7	7	1	2	0	33	2	16	5	1	2	1	0	6	25	5	0
Chiefmother	7	.0000	.0751	28.8	0	0	0	0	0	7	0	0	0	0	0	7	0	0	0	0	0	0	0	0	0	0	0	0	0
chiefs	42	.6879	6.0453	47.8	4	5	3	13	11	2	4	0	18	1	0	3	0	10	0	0	2	0	0	0	0	4	3	1	0
Chiefs	3	.3665	.2412	33.8	1	0	0	1	0	0	1	0	0	0	0	0	0	1	0	0	1	0	0	0	0	0	0	1	0
chieftain	14	.4370	1.3268	41.2	3	1	0	3	2	5	0	0	1	1	0	0	0	0	0	0	0	0	0	0	1	9	1	1	0
Chieftain's	2	.0000	.0914	29.6	0	0	0	0	2	0	0	0	2	0	0	0	0	0	0	0	0	0	0	0	0	0	0	0	0
chieftains	6	.1823	.2810	34.5	2	0	0	0	0	1	1	2	0	0	0	0	0	2	0	0	0	0	0	0	0	0	4	0	0
Chieh-hsiu	5	.0000	.0724	28.6	5	0	0	0	0	0	0	0	0	0	0	0	0	0	0	0	0	0	0	0	0	5	0	0	0
Chien	3	.0000	.0434	26.4	0	3	0	0	0	0	0	0	0	0	0	0	0	0	0	0	0	0	0	0	0	3	0	0	0
chiffarobe	2	.0000	.0215	23.3	0	0	0	0	0	0	2	0	0	0	0	2	0	0	0	0	0	0	0	0	0	0	0	0	0
chiffon	5	.0000	.0161	22.1	0	0	0	0	0	0	5	0	0	0	0	0	0	0	0	0	0	0	5	0	0	0	0	0	0
Chigwell	2	.0000	.0290	24.6	0	2	0	0	0	0	0	0	0	0	0	0	0	0	0	0	0	0	0	0	0	2	0	0	0
Chihuahua	3	.3467	.2520	34.0	1	1	0	0	1	0	0	0	1	0	0	0	1	0	0	0	0	0	0	0	0	0	0	1	0
Chihuahuan	2	.1698	.1133	30.5	0	0	0	0	2	0	0	0	1	0	0	0	0	0	0	0	0	0	0	0	0	0	1	0	0
chilblains	3	.0000	.0328	25.2	0	3	0	0	0	0	0	0	0	3	0	0	0	0	0	0	0	0	0	0	0	0	0	0	0
child	730	.8810	128.16	61.1	149	109	82	83	133	77	82	15	197	45	21	81	35	34	15	35	35	9	50	0	40	54	37	42	0
Child	37	.6542	4.9004	46.9	3	10	10	4	1	5	2	2	1	0	1	9	0	1	0	0	9	2	0	0	8	4	0	2	0
CHILD	15	.0000	.1610	32.1	0	0	0	0	15	0	0	0	0	0	0	15	0	0	0	0	0	0	0	0	0	0	0	0	0
child's	73	.7958	11.668	50.7	12	11	4	7	17	16	5	1	11	1	1	7	3	6	0	6	4	1	9	0	4	8	4	8	0
Child's	8	.5975	1.0029	40.0	2	1	2	1	1	0	0	1	2	0	0	2	0	0	0	0	1	0	0	0	0	1	1	1	0
childbearing	5	.1882	.2328	33.7	0	0	0	0	4	0	1	0	0	0	0	0	0	0	0	0	0	0	0	0	0	0	1	4	0
childbirth	2	.2291	.1135	30.5	0	0	0	0	2	0	0	0	0	0	0	1	0	0	0	1	0	0	0	0	0	0	0	0	0
Childe	2	.2433	.1158	30.6	0	0	0	1	0	0	0	1	0	0	0	0	0	0	0	0	0	0	0	0	0	1	0	1	0
childer	4	.0000	.1827	32.6	0	0	0	0	3	1	0	0	4	0	0	0	0	0	0	0	0	0	0	0	0	0	0	0	0
Childeric	3	.0000	.0314	25.0	0	0	0	0	3	0	0	0	0	0	0	0	0	0	0	0	0	0	0	0	0	0	3	0	0
childhood	61	.8539	10.434	50.2	3	7	9	11	5	14	10	2	19	7	2	6	1	3	1	1	3	0	1	0	2	7	3	5	0
Childhood	2	.0000	.0162	22.1	1	0	0	1	0	0	0	0	0	0	0	0	0	0	0	0	2	0	0	0	0	0	0	0	0
childish	15	.5996	1.8564	42.7	0	2	2	0	6	3	1	1	2	1	2	2	0	0	0	0	0	0	1	0	3	3	0	1	0
childless	3	.3759	.2471	33.9	0	0	0	0	1	1	0	1	0	1	0	0	0	1	0	0	0	0	0	0	0	0	1	0	0
childlike	3	.2510	.1672	32.2	0	0	0	0	1	2	0	0	0	0	0	0	0	0	0	0	0	1	0	0	1	0	0	1	0
children	2575	.9094	465.71	66.7	865	580	275	282	269	138	122	44	843	133	16	133	193	281	26	98	99	56	54	3	198	202	46	185	9
Children	12	.6338	1.5402	41.9	4	2	2	1	2	0	1	0	0	2	0	1	0	1	0	0	3	1	0	0	1	0	1	2	0
children's	92	.7404	13.977	51.5	17	24	11	10	17	4	5	4	36	3	1	8	5	2	2	2	4	1	3	0	4	7	3	10	1
Children's	21	.5966	2.5886	44.1	5	9	1	2	4	0	0	0	2	2	0	3	0	1	0	0	4	0	0	0	0	3	0	6	0
childrens	4	.0000	.0438	26.4	0	0	0	0	0	0	4	0	0	4	0	0	0	0	0	0	0	0	0	0	0	0	0	0	0
Childreth	5	.0000	.2284	33.6	5	0	0	0	0	0	0	0	5	0	0	0	0	0	0	0	0	0	0	0	0	0	0	0	0
Childreth's	2	.0000	.0914	29.6	2	0	0	0	0	0	0	0	2	0	0	0	0	0	0	0	0	0	0	0	0	0	0	0	0
Chile	104	.3380	8.2188	49.1	6	15	4	44	30	1	4	0	4	0	0	0	0	82	0	2	0	0	1	0	0	0	13	2	0
Chile's	7	.0000	.1361	31.3	0	2	0	2	3	0	0	0	0	0	0	0	0	7	0	0	0	0	0	0	0	0	0	0	0
Chilean	8	.4751	.8103	39.1	0	0	0	1	5	0	2	0	0	0	0	0	0	4	0	0	1	0	0	0	0	0	1	2	0
Chileans	4	.2281	.2337	33.7	0	0	0	1	2	0	1	0	0	0	0	0	0	3	0	0	0	0	0	0	0	0	0	1	0
chili	12	.4858	1.2049	40.8	1	6	1	0	2	0	2	0	0	2	0	3	0	0	0	0	0	0	3	0	0	2	1	1	0
chill	57	.6209	7.2903	48.6	6	10	2	7	18	2	8	4	9	5	1	5	0	1	0	0	0	0	11	0	7	6	3	9	0
chilled	27	.5001	2.8237	44.5	6	7	0	3	3	2	6	0	1	0	0	2	0	1	1	5	0	0	7	0	4	2	0	4	0
Chillicothe	5	.0000	.0724	28.6	0	3	2	0	0	0	0	0	0	0	0	0	0	0	0	0	0	0	0	0	0	5	0	0	0
chilling	10	.5638	1.2061	40.8	0	1	0	3	2	2	2	0	3	0	1	0	0	1	0	1	0	0	0	0	1	0	1	2	0
chills	7	.3412	.6171	37.9	0	3	1	2	1	0	0	0	4	2	0	0	0	0	0	1	0	0	0	0	0	0	0	0	0
chilly	33	.6180	4.2197	46.3	8	11	1	3	5	2	3	0	5	2	4	3	0	3	0	0	2	0	0	0	1	9	1	3	0
chime	3	.2028	.1988	33.0	1	0	0	0	2	0	0	0	2	0	0	0	0	0	0	0	1	0	0	0	0	0	0	0	0
chimed	7	.3354	.5666	37.5	0	3	1	1	1	1	0	0	2	2	0	0	0	0	0	0	0	0	0	0	2	3	0	0	0
chimes	9	.3694	.7517	38.8	0	3	1	1	3	0	1	0	2	2	0	0	0	0	0	0	4	0	0	0	0	0	1	0	0
chiming	2	.1843	.0808	29.1	2	0	0	0	0	0	0	0	0	0	1	0	0	0	0	0	1	0	0	0	0	0	0	0	0
chimney	76	.7625	11.815	50.7	11	26	12	7	11	3	4	2	25	1	0	8	0	1	4	8	2	0	0	0	11	6	1	9	0
Chimney	2	.1948	.1250	31.0	0	0	1	0	1	0	0	0	1	0	0	0	0	0	0	0	0	0	0	0	0	1	0	0	0
chimney-place	2	.0000	.0914	29.6	1	1	0	0	0	0	0	0	2	0	0	0	0	0	0	0	0	0	0	0	0	0	0	0	0
chimneys	28	.7103	4.1215	46.2	3	11	2	5	3	3	0	1	10	2	0	2	0	6	0	2	0	0	0	0	2	3	0	1	0
chimp	5	.3322	.4085	36.1	0	0	0	0	4	1	0	0	2	0	0	1	0	0	0	0	0	0	0	0	0	0	2	0	0
Chimp	2	.0000	.0914	29.6	2	0	0	0	0	0	0	0	2	0	0	0	0	0	0	0	0	0	0	0	0	0	0	0	0

5B chiang
8F chiao-tzu
5Q chiaro
5Q chiaroscuro
9Q Chiba
8R chic
7Q Chichen
8N Chickahominy
7Q chickarees
7Q Chickasaws
7R CHICKEN
7R Chicken-Hearted
3A chicken-from-outer-space
5F chicken-raising
8D chickenheads
6A Chickey
5D Chicky
7R CHIDE
6A chiding
4P Chief's
9D Chiefly
8D Chiefmother's
7P chieftain's
9P chieftan
7B chien
5F Chigago
7H chiggers
8R Chigi
9L chignon
4E Chihuahuas
4B chilblain
8A child-face
8H child-guidance
7A child-voice
8R child's-eye-view
5P childishness
4P Childs
7D Childsley
7A chile
4G chiliburger
XR chilis
XR chiller
7N chillier
3A chilliness
4R chilly-wonderful
6P Chimaeras
4A chimbley
3A chimbly
9F Chimel
8A Chimera
4P chimmey
7B chimney-sweepers

Word Type	F	D	U	SFI	3 Gr 3	4 Gr 4	5 Gr 5	6 Gr 6	7 Gr 7	8 Gr 8	9 Gr 9	X UnGr	A Read	B Eng & Gr	C Comp	D Lit	E Math	F Soc Stud	G Spell	H Sci	J Music	K Art	L Home Ec	M Shop	N Lib F	P Lib NF	Q Lib Ref	R Mag	S Rel
chimpanzee	15	.5768	1.8594	42.7	5	1	0	0	6	3	0	0	6	1	0	3	0	1	1	0	0	0	0	0	0	0	3	0	0
chimpanzees	4	.2348	.2372	33.8	0	0	0	1	3	0	0	0	0	0	0	0	0	3	0	0	0	0	0	0	0	0	1	0	0
chimps	2	.1814	.1187	30.7	1	0	0	1	0	0	0	0	1	0	0	0	0	0	0	0	0	0	0	0	0	0	0	1	0
chin	118	.7354	17.910	52.5	28	29	11	13	22	9	5	1	55	0	0	7	0	0	2	2	3	2	2	0	26	13	1	5	0
china	34	.7372	5.0980	47.1	2	11	4	5	6	2	4	0	8	2	0	6	0	4	1	0	0	0	2	1	2	0	7	1	0
China	332	.7472	50.417	57.0	22	22	71	50	40	98	24	5	43	2	0	13	1	154	1	10	7	1	1	4	7	37	30	21	0
china-store	2	.0000	.0215	23.3	0	0	0	0	0	2	0	0	0	0	0	2	0	0	0	0	0	0	0	0	0	0	0	0	0
China's	25	.4610	2.5199	44.0	0	2	7	2	3	11	0	0	2	0	0	0	0	13	0	0	0	0	0	0	0	4	1	5	0
chinaberry	3	.2227	.1589	32.0	1	0	0	0	2	0	0	0	0	0	0	0	0	0	0	0	0	0	0	0	2	0	0	1	0
Chinaman	2	.1717	.1142	30.6	0	1	0	0	1	0	0	0	1	0	0	1	0	0	0	0	0	0	0	0	0	0	0	0	0
Chinatown	14	.4442	1.3838	41.4	0	1	0	1	1	10	1	0	2	0	1	1	0	9	0	0	0	0	0	0	1	0	0	0	0
chinaware	2	.0000	.0389	25.9	1	0	0	0	1	0	0	0	0	0	0	0	0	2	0	0	0	0	0	0	0	0	0	0	0
Chincoteague	4	.2417	.3028	34.8	0	3	1	0	0	0	0	0	3	0	0	0	0	0	0	0	0	0	0	0	1	0	0	0	0
Chinese	343	.8403	57.707	57.6	49	15	51	46	36	130	11	5	47	10	5	8	6	145	12	9	8	4	2	0	30	24	13	20	0
Chinese-Americans	6	.0000	.2741	34.4	6	0	0	0	0	0	0	0	6	0	0	0	0	0	0	0	0	0	0	0	0	0	0	0	0
Ching	2	.0000	.0914	29.6	0	2	0	0	0	0	0	0	2	0	0	0	0	0	0	0	0	0	0	0	0	0	0	0	0
Chingachgook	2	.2337	.1157	30.6	0	0	0	0	1	1	0	0	0	0	0	0	0	1	0	0	0	0	0	0	1	0	0	0	0
chink	10	.5793	1.2159	40.8	1	3	1	0	2	2	0	1	2	0	0	1	0	0	0	0	1	0	0	0	3	1	0	2	0
chinked	4	.4814	.4064	36.1	0	0	2	0	2	0	0	0	0	0	0	1	0	1	0	0	0	0	0	0	1	0	0	1	0
chinks	4	.4487	.4010	36.0	0	1	0	0	3	0	0	0	1	0	0	1	0	1	0	0	0	0	0	0	1	0	0	0	0
Chinook	5	.3810	.4789	36.8	0	2	3	0	0	0	0	0	3	0	0	0	0	0	0	1	0	0	0	0	0	0	0	1	0
chinooks	3	.0000	.0583	27.7	0	0	0	3	0	0	0	0	0	0	0	0	0	3	0	0	0	0	0	0	0	0	0	0	0
chins	5	.5326	.5693	37.6	1	0	1	1	1	0	1	0	1	0	0	1	0	0	0	1	0	0	0	0	1	0	1	0	0
Chinwa	3	.0000	.1370	31.4	0	0	0	3	0	0	0	0	3	0	0	0	0	0	0	0	0	0	0	0	0	0	0	0	0
chip	16	.5001	1.7057	42.3	1	2	1	1	4	3	3	1	3	0	0	0	1	0	0	2	0	1	0	4	1	2	1	1	0
Chip	16	.1396	.6592	38.2	0	2	0	0	1	0	13	0	2	0	0	0	0	0	0	0	0	0	0	0	13	0	0	1	0
Chipewyan	2	.0000	.0243	23.9	0	0	0	0	2	0	0	0	0	0	0	0	0	0	0	0	0	0	0	0	0	0	0	2	0
chipmunk	28	.4508	2.8836	44.6	14	3	1	2	6	1	0	1	13	2	0	4	0	0	2	2	0	4	0	0	0	0	0	1	0
Chipmunk	6	.2782	.4458	36.5	4	2	0	0	0	0	0	0	3	0	0	0	0	0	0	0	0	1	0	0	0	0	0	2	0
chipmunks	17	.4880	1.8189	42.6	4	4	0	4	5	0	0	0	5	0	0	3	0	0	0	2	0	2	0	0	0	3	2	0	0
chipped	20	.6780	2.8225	44.5	3	1	5	1	3	1	5	1	8	1	0	0	0	0	0	1	0	0	2	1	2	2	2	1	0
chipper	2	.2152	.1357	31.3	1	0	1	0	0	0	0	0	1	0	0	0	0	1	0	0	0	0	0	0	0	0	0	0	0
Chippewa	3	.2028	.1988	33.0	0	1	0	1	1	0	0	0	2	0	0	0	0	0	0	0	1	0	0	0	0	0	0	0	0
chipping	4	.3726	.3697	35.7	0	0	2	1	1	0	0	0	2	0	0	0	0	1	0	0	0	0	0	0	1	0	0	0	0
Chipping	2	.0000	.0243	23.9	0	0	0	2	0	0	0	0	0	0	0	0	0	0	0	0	0	0	0	0	0	0	0	2	0
Chippy	18	.0000	.8223	39.2	18	0	0	0	0	0	0	0	18	0	0	0	0	0	0	0	0	0	0	0	0	0	0	0	0
Chippy's	3	.0000	.1370	31.4	3	0	0	0	0	0	0	0	3	0	0	0	0	0	0	0	0	0	0	0	0	0	0	0	0
chips	42	.7175	6.1305	47.9	3	6	6	8	7	5	7	0	8	3	1	1	5	5	0	2	0	1	3	6	4	2	0	1	0
Chips	7	.0000	.0851	29.3	0	0	0	7	0	0	0	0	0	0	0	0	0	0	0	0	0	0	0	0	0	0	0	7	0
Chips'	3	.0000	.0365	25.6	0	0	0	3	0	0	0	0	0	0	0	0	0	0	0	0	0	0	0	0	0	0	0	3	0
Chira	3	.0000	.1370	31.4	0	0	0	0	3	0	0	0	3	0	0	0	0	0	0	0	0	0	0	0	0	0	0	0	0
Chira's	7	.0000	.3198	35.0	0	0	0	0	7	0	0	0	7	0	0	0	0	0	0	0	0	0	0	0	0	0	0	0	0
Chiricahua	2	.0000	.0215	23.3	0	0	0	0	2	0	0	0	0	0	0	2	0	0	0	0	0	0	0	0	0	0	0	0	0
Chiricahuas	2	.0000	.0243	23.9	0	0	0	0	2	0	0	0	0	0	0	0	0	0	0	0	0	0	0	0	0	0	0	2	0
Chiron	10	.0000	.4568	36.6	0	0	0	7	0	3	0	0	10	0	0	0	0	0	0	0	0	0	0	0	0	0	0	0	0
chirp	12	.6046	1.5643	41.9	2	0	1	3	3	2	0	1	6	2	0	1	0	0	0	1	0	0	0	0	1	0	0	1	0
chirped	7	.4388	.7025	38.5	0	3	0	0	1	3	0	0	3	0	1	1	0	0	0	0	0	0	0	0	1	1	0	0	0
chirping	12	.4068	1.1495	40.6	3	2	2	2	0	2	1	0	6	2	2	0	0	0	0	0	1	0	0	0	0	0	0	1	0
chirpings	2	.1787	.1174	30.7	0	0	1	1	0	0	0	0	1	0	0	0	0	0	0	0	0	0	0	0	1	0	0	0	0
chirps	4	.2417	.3089	34.9	0	1	2	1	0	0	0	0	3	0	0	0	0	0	0	1	0	0	0	0	0	0	0	0	0
chirr	2	.2427	.1152	30.6	1	0	0	1	0	0	0	0	0	0	0	0	0	0	0	0	0	0	0	0	1	1	0	0	0
chisel	55	.1892	2.4119	43.8	1	0	0	6	24	16	8	0	5	0	0	1	0	0	0	0	0	2	0	38	2	3	1	3	0
chiseled	6	.4401	.5624	37.5	0	0	1	0	1	0	2	2	0	2	0	2	0	0	0	1	0	0	0	0	0	1	0	0	0
chisellike	2	.1698	.1133	30.5	0	1	1	0	0	0	0	0	1	0	0	0	0	0	0	0	0	0	0	0	0	0	1	0	0
chisels	14	.1253	.4259	36.3	2	0	0	0	10	1	1	0	0	0	0	0	0	0	0	0	0	0	0	9	0	4	0	1	0
Chisholm	2	.2351	.1166	30.7	0	0	1	1	0	0	0	0	0	0	0	0	0	1	0	0	0	0	0	0	0	0	0	1	0
Chistiansen	2	.0000	.0290	24.6	0	0	0	0	2	0	0	0	0	0	0	0	0	0	0	0	0	0	0	0	0	2	0	0	0
Chita	2	.0000	.0290	24.6	0	2	0	0	0	0	0	0	0	0	0	0	0	0	0	0	0	0	0	0	0	2	0	0	0
chitin	4	.0000	.0789	29.0	0	0	0	2	2	0	0	0	0	0	0	0	0	0	0	4	0	0	0	0	0	0	0	0	0
chiton	7	.0000	.3198	35.0	0	0	0	7	0	0	0	0	7	0	0	0	0	0	0	0	0	0	0	0	0	0	0	0	0
chittering	3	.3668	.2407	33.8	0	0	0	1	1	0	0	1	0	0	0	1	0	0	0	1	1	0	0	0	0	0	0	0	0
Chitty	2	.0000	.0243	23.9	0	0	0	2	0	0	0	0	0	0	0	0	0	0	0	0	0	0	0	0	0	0	0	2	0
chivalrous	5	.4882	.5167	37.1	0	0	0	0	3	2	0	0	0	0	0	1	0	2	0	0	0	0	0	0	0	0	1	1	0
chivalry	3	.0000	.0434	26.4	1	0	2	0	0	0	0	0	0	0	0	0	0	0	0	0	0	0	0	0	0	3	0	0	0
chives	3	.0000	.0097	19.8	0	0	0	0	2	0	1	0	0	0	0	0	0	0	0	0	0	0	3	0	0	0	0	0	0
chlorate	6	.0000	.1183	30.7	0	0	0	0	1	0	5	0	0	0	0	0	0	0	0	6	0	0	0	0	0	0	0	0	0
chloride	25	.3183	1.8893	42.8	1	4	10	1	1	4	4	0	1	0	0	0	0	0	0	19	0	0	0	0	0	0	2	3	0
chlorides	2	.0000	.0394	26.0	0	0	0	0	0	1	0	1	0	0	0	0	0	0	0	2	0	0	0	0	0	0	0	0	0
chlorination	2	.0000	.0394	26.0	0	0	1	1	0	0	0	0	0	0	0	0	0	0	0	2	0	0	0	0	0	0	0	0	0
chlorine	36	.4824	3.7271	45.7	7	4	13	3	2	2	4	1	0	0	0	0	0	0	2	22	0	0	0	0	0	7	3	2	0
chloroform	8	.3698	.7453	38.7	0	0	2	0	6	0	0	0	5	0	0	1	0	0	0	0	0	0	0	0	0	0	2	0	0
chlorophyll	55	.3022	3.9468	46.0	7	0	17	11	14	0	3	3	0	0	0	0	0	0	0	44	0	0	1	0	0	0	10	0	0
chloroplast	3	.0000	.0591	27.7	0	0	0	0	3	0	0	0	0	0	0	0	0	0	0	3	0	0	0	0	0	0	0	0	0
chloroplasts	10	.1626	.4769	36.8	0	0	8	0	2	0	0	0	0	0	0	0	0	0	0	9	0	0	0	0	0	0	1	0	0
chloroprene	3	.0000	.0591	27.7	0	0	0	0	3	0	0	0	0	0	0	0	0	0	0	3	0	0	0	0	0	0	0	0	0
cho-co-late	2	.0000	.0215	23.3	0	0	0	0	0	0	2	0	0	0	0	2	0	0	0	0	0	0	0	0	0	0	0	0	0
Choate	9	.0000	.1303	31.1	0	9	0	0	0	0	0	0	0	0	0	0	0	0	0	0	0	0	0	0	0	9	0	0	0
chock-full	3	.2443	.1696	32.3	0	0	0	0	1	2	0	0	0	0	1	0	0	1	0	0	0	0	0	0	0	0	0	1	0
chocolate	143	.7429	21.543	53.3	24	35	16	14	14	2	26	12	26	11	2	12	12	20	5	4	0	0	17	0	22	4	1	7	0
chocolate-covered	3	.2437	.2277	33.6	1	1	0	0	0	1	0	0	2	0	0	0	0	0	0	1	0	0	0	0	0	0	0	0	0
choice	207	.8413	34.752	55.4	10	12	33	19	50	33	43	7	27	28	8	7	7	30	2	6	9	2	19	1	5	13	20	23	0
Choice	4	.0000	.0486	26.9	0	0	0	0	0	0	0	4	0	0	0	0	0	0	0	0	0	0	0	0	0	0	0	4	0
choices	50	.5554	5.7917	47.6	2	8	3	5	7	18	6	1	6	16	0	0	9	0	2	4	3	0	8	0	0	0	0	2	0
choir	30	.6367	3.8737	45.9	0	3	9	5	6	2	5	0	1	5	3	1	1	2	3	0	9	0	0	0	0	1	1	3	0
Choir	5	.2069	.2483	33.9	0	4	0	0	1	0	0	0	0	0	0	0	0	0	0	0	1	0	0	0	0	0	0	4	0
choirs	10	.0885	.2512	34.0	1	1	2	1	0	2	3	0	0	0	0	0	0	0	0	0	9	0	0	0	0	0	0	1	0
chok'd	2	.0000	.0290	24.6	0	0	0	0	2	0	0	0	0	0	0	0	0	0	0	0	0	0	0	0	0	2	0	0	0
choke	12	.4115	1.0933	40.4	1	3	2	0	4	1	1	0	3	2	0	0	0	0	2	0	0	0	0	3	1	1	0	0	0
choked	25	.6016	3.1993	45.1	1	4	2	7	8	2	1	0	9	0	0	6	0	2	0	0	0	0	0	0	2	1	1	4	0
choking	26	.6266	3.4491	45.4	2	4	2	5	7	2	3	1	10	0	0	3	0	0	0	2	0	0	0	0	6	2	1	2	0
cholera	13	.4773	1.3250	41.2	1	0	1	3	1	3	4	0	0	0	0	0	0	1	0	6	1	0	0	0	0	1	4	0	0
Cholly	11	.0000	.1337	31.3	0	0	11	0	0	0	0	0	0	0	0	0	0	0	0	0	0	0	0	0	0	0	0	11	0
Cholmondeley	2	.0000	.0215	23.3	0	0	0	0	0	2	0	0	0	0	0	2	0	0	0	0	0	0	0	0	0	0	0	0	0
Chombo	15	.0000	.6852	38.4	0	15	0	0	0	0	0	0	15	0	0	0	0	0	0	0	0	0	0	0	0	0	0	0	0

5Q Chin	5Q Chinese-Japanese	3A Chiquita	7R chit'lins	XH chlorella	XB Choctaw
6N chin-up	5R Ching-ling	3A chirp-chirp-chirp	6P chitarrone	6H chlorinated	7Q Choctaws
3A chin-ups	4A Ching's	3R Chirpie	XH chitin-like	5H chloro	6A choicest
6F China-Japan	7D Chingokhos	3P chirpy	6A chitons	8H chloromycetin	8D chokecherries
6A china-headed	7H chinook	7D chirred	3A chitter-chatter	7G chloros	9Q chokecherry
3A china-rimmed	4P chinquapins	4A Chirrup	7D chittered	3J choc'late	6A Choko-Krunch
8F Chinamen	4A chip-off-the-old-block	4A chirruping	6Q chive	6J chocallo	9D choler
8F Chinatowns	4A Chip's	7N chirrups	7N chivvied	6A chocks	8D choleric
4A Chinee	3A chipmunk's	7P chisel-like	7N chivvying	XN CHOCOLATE	8Q cholesterol
7J chinese	4A Chipmunk's	8M chisel's	7Q Chlodwig	7A chocolate-brown	7R chomped
8F Chinese-American	XR Chippendale	7P chiseling	6P Chloe	8P chocolates	7Q chomping

Word Type	F	D	U	SFI	3 Gr 3	4 Gr 4	5 Gr 5	6 Gr 6	7 Gr 7	8 Gr 8	9 Gr 9	X UnGr	A Read	B Eng & Gr	C Comp	D Lit	E Math	F Soc Stud	G Spell	H Sci	J Music	K Art	L Home Ec	M Shop	N Lib F	P Lib NF	Q Lib Ref	R Mag	S Rel
Chongo	4	.0000	.0469	26.7	0	0	0	0	4	0	0	0	0	0	0	0	0	0	0	0	0	0	0	0	4	0	0	0	0
choo	2	.0000	.0914	29.6	0	1	0	1	0	0	0	0	2	0	0	0	0	0	0	0	0	0	0	0	0	0	0	0	0
Choo	2	.0000	.0914	29.6	0	0	0	2	0	0	0	0	2	0	0	0	0	0	0	0	0	0	0	0	0	0	0	0	0
choose	731	.8595	125.17	61.0	122	95	109	132	111	64	92	6	112	139	37	23	106	50	50	48	47	17	35	11	7	23	8	14	4
Choose	2	.1812	.0838	29.2	0	0	1	0	1	0	0	0	0	0	0	0	0	0	0	0	0	0	1	0	0	0	0	1	0
chooses	24	.6645	3.2698	45.1	2	6	2	3	8	0	3	0	3	4	2	1	1	4	0	3	4	0	0	0	0	1	1	0	0
chooseth	3	.0000	.0322	25.1	0	0	0	0	0	0	3	0	0	0	0	3	0	0	0	0	0	0	0	0	0	0	0	0	0
choosing	69	.8264	11.406	50.6	3	13	5	9	12	12	14	1	12	8	2	1	7	3	1	4	5	1	9	2	2	5	3	4	0
choosy	3	.0000	.1370	31.4	0	0	1	0	0	0	2	0	3	0	0	0	0	0	0	0	0	0	0	0	0	0	0	0	0
chop	28	.7502	4.2521	46.3	5	4	4	3	8	2	2	0	5	2	2	2	0	3	1	0	3	0	0	0	2	5	1	2	0
Chopin	18	.0398	.2914	34.6	0	0	1	1	3	12	0	1	0	0	0	0	0	1	0	0	17	0	0	0	0	0	0	0	0
Chopin's	6	.0000	.0485	26.9	0	0	0	0	0	6	0	0	0	0	0	0	0	0	0	0	6	0	0	0	0	0	0	0	0
chopped	42	.4057	3.8846	45.9	4	5	8	7	6	6	5	1	14	0	0	1	0	3	0	1	0	0	12	0	4	2	1	4	0
chopped-up	2	.0000	.0914	29.6	0	0	1	0	1	0	0	0	2	0	0	0	0	0	0	0	0	0	0	0	0	0	0	0	0
chopping	21	.6419	2.8747	44.6	1	7	2	4	4	3	0	0	11	0	0	1	0	1	0	0	0	0	0	0	3	2	2	1	0
chopping-block	2	.0000	.0234	23.7	0	0	2	0	0	0	0	0	0	0	0	0	0	0	0	0	0	0	0	0	2	0	0	0	0
choppy	12	.6749	1.6549	42.2	1	1	1	2	5	1	0	1	1	1	0	0	0	2	2	1	0	0	0	0	0	2	1	2	0
chops	22	.3965	1.9697	42.9	0	1	4	3	6	0	6	2	6	1	0	1	2	1	0	1	0	0	7	0	1	0	0	2	0
chopsticks	9	.3701	.8443	39.3	1	3	3	2	0	0	0	0	5	0	0	0	0	3	0	0	0	0	0	0	0	1	0	0	0
choral	37	.2596	2.1214	43.3	0	2	5	1	12	1	16	0	0	8	1	0	0	0	0	0	28	0	0	0	0	0	0	0	0
Choral	4	.0000	.0323	25.1	0	0	0	0	0	0	4	0	0	0	0	0	0	0	0	0	4	0	0	0	0	0	0	0	0
chorale	7	.0000	.0566	27.5	0	0	2	0	0	2	3	0	0	0	0	0	0	0	0	0	7	0	0	0	0	0	0	0	0
chord	303	.1195	9.4004	49.7	33	73	85	65	15	22	10	0	0	1	0	0	22	0	0	0	276	0	0	3	0	1	0	0	0
chordal	8	.0000	.0647	28.1	0	0	1	3	2	0	0	2	0	0	0	0	0	0	0	0	8	0	0	0	0	0	0	0	0
Chordata	5	.0000	.0986	29.9	0	0	0	0	3	0	2	0	0	0	0	0	0	0	0	5	0	0	0	0	0	0	0	0	0
chordates	6	.2071	.3307	35.2	0	0	0	0	4	0	2	0	0	0	0	0	0	0	0	5	0	0	0	0	0	0	1	0	0
chording	5	.0000	.0404	26.1	0	0	0	2	1	2	0	0	0	0	0	0	0	0	0	0	5	0	0	0	0	0	0	0	0
chords	257	.1525	9.5224	49.8	30	42	36	71	26	18	34	0	0	1	0	0	11	0	0	0	238	2	0	2	1	2	0	0	0
chore	13	.5908	1.6461	42.2	0	2	2	3	2	2	2	0	5	3	0	0	0	2	0	0	0	0	0	0	1	0	1	1	0
chorea	3	.0000	.0314	25.0	0	3	0	0	0	0	0	0	0	0	0	0	0	0	0	0	0	0	0	0	0	0	3	0	0
choreographer	7	.2419	.3805	35.8	0	4	0	0	1	1	1	0	0	0	0	0	0	0	0	0	5	0	0	0	0	0	1	1	0
choreography	3	.0000	.0243	23.8	0	0	0	0	2	1	0	0	0	0	0	0	0	0	0	0	3	0	0	0	0	0	0	0	0
chores	53	.8049	8.6279	49.4	7	14	9	5	3	3	8	4	17	2	1	5	0	6	0	2	0	0	1	0	2	7	2	8	0
chorion	3	.0000	.0314	25.0	0	0	0	0	3	0	0	0	0	0	0	0	0	0	0	0	0	0	0	0	0	0	3	0	0
choros	2	.2446	.1084	30.3	0	0	0	1	1	0	0	0	0	0	0	0	0	0	1	0	1	0	0	0	0	0	0	0	0
chortle	2	.1497	.1046	30.2	0	0	0	0	0	2	0	0	1	0	0	0	0	0	1	0	0	0	0	0	0	0	0	0	0
chortled	4	.2797	.2732	34.4	0	1	2	0	0	0	1	0	1	0	0	0	0	0	0	0	0	1	0	0	0	1	0	1	0
chortling	2	.1497	.1046	30.2	0	0	1	0	0	1	0	0	1	0	0	0	0	0	1	0	0	0	0	0	0	0	0	0	0
chorus	87	.5455	9.8005	49.9	6	10	5	14	22	15	15	0	6	3	1	12	1	0	1	0	45	0	1	0	2	7	3	5	0
Chorus	11	.4277	1.0919	40.4	0	5	0	0	5	0	1	0	5	0	0	1	0	0	0	0	3	0	0	0	0	2	0	0	0
chorused	7	.4072	.6281	38.0	1	1	0	0	1	2	2	0	1	1	0	2	0	0	0	0	0	0	0	0	0	0	0	3	0
choruses	10	.0976	.2668	34.3	0	0	1	3	1	3	2	0	0	0	0	0	0	0	0	0	9	0	0	0	0	0	1	0	0
chose	171	.6337	22.522	53.5	30	30	29	23	22	20	12	5	35	16	2	9	24	28	4	0	12	4	0	0	5	14	6	9	3
chosen	222	.9179	40.418	56.1	21	39	29	30	43	33	25	2	53	17	9	11	16	35	2	9	8	3	6	6	8	13	11	15	0
choses	2	.0000	.0219	23.4	0	0	0	0	0	0	0	2	0	2	0	0	0	0	0	0	0	0	0	0	0	0	0	0	0
Chou	6	.0000	.1167	30.7	0	0	0	6	0	0	0	0	0	0	0	0	0	6	0	0	0	0	0	0	0	0	0	0	0
Chouchou	13	.1905	.8025	39.0	0	13	0	0	0	0	0	0	7	0	0	0	0	0	0	0	0	0	0	0	6	0	0	0	0
chow	9	.5222	1.0263	40.1	3	1	0	1	0	2	2	0	3	0	0	1	0	2	2	0	0	0	0	0	0	0	0	1	0
Chowanoc	3	.0000	.0434	26.4	0	3	0	0	0	0	0	0	0	0	0	0	0	0	0	0	0	0	0	0	0	3	0	0	0
Chowanocs	2	.0000	.0290	24.6	0	2	0	0	0	0	0	0	0	0	0	0	0	0	0	0	0	0	0	0	0	2	0	0	0
chowder	15	.0000	.6852	38.4	0	0	14	1	0	0	0	0	15	0	0	0	0	0	0	0	0	0	0	0	0	0	0	0	0
Chris	53	.4414	5.5832	47.5	3	4	16	25	4	0	0	1	33	6	0	0	0	3	0	0	0	0	0	0	0	0	0	11	0
Chris'	2	.0000	.0914	29.6	0	0	2	0	0	0	0	0	2	0	0	0	0	0	0	0	0	0	0	0	0	0	0	0	0
Chris's	2	.1814	.1187	30.7	0	0	0	2	0	0	0	0	1	0	0	0	0	0	0	0	0	0	0	0	0	0	0	1	0
Christ	104	.1245	3.4458	45.4	13	28	9	12	18	8	12	4	1	7	1	2	0	13	3	0	8	2	0	1	2	18	12	10	24
Christ's	2	.1787	.1174	30.7	0	0	0	1	0	1	0	0	1	0	0	0	0	0	0	0	0	0	0	0	1	0	0	0	0
Christendom	5	.3814	.4107	36.1	0	0	3	0	1	1	0	0	0	0	0	0	0	0	0	0	1	0	0	0	0	2	2	0	0
christened	4	.2393	.3005	34.8	0	0	0	2	1	0	1	0	3	0	0	1	0	0	0	0	0	0	0	0	0	0	0	0	0
christening	3	.0000	.1370	31.4	0	2	1	0	0	0	0	0	3	0	0	0	0	0	0	0	0	0	0	0	0	0	0	0	0
Christian	154	.5562	17.922	52.5	10	11	22	23	35	27	19	7	17	2	0	17	0	24	2	1	5	4	0	0	5	19	47	8	3
Christianity	50	.6279	6.4396	48.1	5	4	9	13	11	4	3	1	1	4	0	0	0	16	3	0	2	0	0	0	0	7	14	3	0
Christians	56	.5299	6.2265	47.9	5	5	6	4	16	15	5	0	1	0	0	6	1	24	2	0	0	1	0	0	1	4	13	2	1
Christine	32	.1508	1.3518	41.3	0	0	0	0	4	28	0	0	3	1	0	1	0	0	0	0	0	0	0	0	27	0	0	0	0
Christine's	7	.0604	.1921	32.8	0	0	0	0	1	6	0	0	1	0	0	0	0	0	0	0	0	0	0	0	6	0	0	0	0
Christmas	469	.8010	75.836	58.8	162	96	36	55	34	35	31	20	148	14	7	25	8	26	19	3	96	14	2	1	34	26	14	29	3
Christmas-tree	2	.2337	.1157	30.6	1	0	1	0	0	0	0	0	0	0	0	0	0	1	0	0	0	0	0	0	1	0	0	0	0
Christmastime	4	.0996	.1523	31.8	1	0	0	1	0	0	0	2	1	0	0	0	0	0	0	0	0	0	0	0	0	0	0	3	0
Christopher	76	.5739	9.1770	49.6	36	14	11	3	5	5	2	0	12	2	0	0	0	16	0	0	0	0	1	0	31	5	5	4	0
Christopher's	5	.1370	.1919	32.8	4	0	1	0	0	0	0	0	0	0	0	0	0	1	0	0	0	0	0	0	4	0	0	0	0
Christophilos	5	.0000	.2284	33.6	0	5	0	0	0	0	0	0	5	0	0	0	0	0	0	0	0	0	0	0	0	0	0	0	0
Christos	2	.0000	.0219	23.4	0	0	0	0	0	0	2	0	0	2	0	0	0	0	0	0	0	0	0	0	0	0	0	0	0
chromatic	11	.0000	.0889	29.5	0	0	1	1	1	6	2	0	0	0	0	0	0	0	0	0	11	0	0	0	0	0	0	0	0
chromaticism	4	.0000	.0323	25.1	0	0	0	0	1	3	0	0	0	0	0	0	0	0	0	0	4	0	0	0	0	0	0	0	0
chromatin	3	.0000	.0314	25.0	0	0	0	2	0	0	0	1	0	0	0	0	0	0	0	0	0	0	0	0	0	0	3	0	0
chrome	13	.6753	1.8462	42.7	0	0	1	1	8	2	1	0	6	1	0	1	0	2	1	1	0	0	0	0	0	0	1	0	0
chromium	11	.3346	.8720	39.4	1	0	1	2	4	2	1	0	2	0	0	0	0	6	0	0	0	0	0	2	0	0	1	0	0
chromosomal	3	.0000	.0314	25.0	0	0	0	0	1	0	0	2	0	0	0	0	0	0	0	0	0	0	0	0	0	0	3	0	0
chromosome	27	.1813	1.2614	41.0	0	0	0	5	3	0	0	19	0	0	0	0	0	0	0	9	0	0	0	0	0	0	18	0	0
chromosomes	81	.2423	4.8986	46.9	0	0	1	22	23	0	0	35	0	0	0	0	0	0	0	57	0	0	0	0	0	0	24	0	0
chronic	10	.5005	1.0394	40.2	0	0	0	0	2	4	3	1	0	0	0	1	0	1	0	0	0	0	1	0	0	0	4	3	0
chronically	2	.1674	.0805	29.1	0	0	0	0	1	0	1	0	0	0	0	0	0	0	0	0	0	0	1	0	0	1	0	0	0
chronicle	3	.3759	.2471	33.9	0	0	1	0	1	1	0	0	0	1	0	0	0	1	0	0	0	0	0	0	0	0	1	0	0
Chronicle	6	.4391	.5529	37.4	0	0	1	0	4	1	0	0	0	1	0	0	0	0	1	0	0	0	0	0	0	0	3	1	0
chronicler	3	.2304	.1619	32.1	0	0	0	0	3	0	0	0	0	0	0	0	0	0	0	0	0	0	0	0	2	0	1	0	0
chronicles	4	.3618	.3122	34.9	0	0	1	0	2	1	0	0	0	1	0	0	0	0	0	0	0	0	0	0	1	0	2	0	0
Chronicles	2	.0000	.0209	23.2	0	0	1	0	1	0	0	0	0	0	0	0	0	0	0	0	0	0	0	0	0	0	2	0	0
chronological	12	.2965	.7654	38.8	0	0	0	1	3	1	7	0	0	3	5	0	0	1	0	0	1	0	0	0	0	0	1	1	0
chronologically	3	.2187	.1555	31.9	0	0	0	0	0	0	2	1	0	2	0	0	0	0	0	0	0	0	0	0	0	0	0	1	0
chronology	4	.0000	.0419	26.2	0	1	0	0	3	0	0	0	0	0	0	0	0	0	0	0	0	0	0	0	0	0	4	0	0
chronometers	2	.2351	.1166	30.7	0	0	0	1	0	1	0	0	0	0	0	0	0	1	0	0	0	0	0	0	0	0	0	1	0
chronovision	4	.0000	.0438	26.4	0	4	0	0	0	0	0	0	0	4	0	0	0	0	0	0	0	0	0	0	0	0	0	0	0
chrysalis	13	.4076	1.1689	40.7	6	0	3	2	2	0	0	0	0	0	0	0	0	0	0	8	0	0	0	0	1	1	3	0	0
chrysanthemums	6	.4608	.5845	37.7	1	0	0	0	3	1	0	1	0	0	1	1	0	0	0	2	0	0	0	0	1	0	0	1	0
Chrysler	15	.3212	1.0964	40.4	0	0	0	2	8	2	3	0	1	0	1	0	0	2	0	0	0	0	0	0	0	0	0	11	0
Chrysler's	3	.0000	.0365	25.6	0	0	0	0	3	0	0	0	0	0	0	0	0	0	0	0	0	0	0	0	0	0	0	3	0
Chub	9	.0000	.4111	36.1	2	0	0	0	7	0	0	0	9	0	0	0	0	0	0	0	0	0	0	0	0	0	0	0	0

7B chonan
4A choo-choo
4A choos
7Q choosiness
6N chop-whiskers
9D choppin'
7P chorales
7H chordata
9H chordate
5R choreful
8Q choreodrame
8J choreographers
7Q chorister
9R chortles
7D chounce
6A Chow
4P Chowan
4P Chris'mus
9D christ'ning
5P Christianity's
8Q Christianized
8Q Christianizing
7P Christiansen
9R Christie
XR Christina
7D CHRISTINE
4N Christmas-time
XR Christmases
5A Christmasy
8J Christoph
8B christopher
4A Christophilos's
5A Christowe
4P Christy
7J chromatically
6H chromatography
7R Chrome
7R chromed
7F chromite
XH chromosphere
8D chronicled
3A chrysocolla
7N chrysontera
9Q Chrysostom
4F Chu's
6R Chuar

Word Type	F	D	U	SFI	3 Gr 3	4 Gr 4	5 Gr 5	6 Gr 6	7 Gr 7	8 Gr 8	9 Gr 9	X UnGr	A Read	B Eng & Gr	C Comp	D Lit	E Math	F Soc Stud	G Spell	H Sci	J Music	K Art	L Home Ec	M Shop	N Lib F	P Lib NF	Q Lib Ref	R Mag	S Rel
chubby	6	.4103	.5499	37.4	2	2	0	0	0	0	2	0	1	0	0	1	0	0	0	0	0	0	0	0	0	3	0	1	0
Chuchundra	5	.0000	.2284	33.6	0	1	0	4	0	0	0	0	5	0	0	0	0	0	0	0	0	0	0	0	0	0	0	0	0
chuck	21	.5152	2.3334	43.7	3	1	7	0	8	2	0	0	6	0	0	1	0	1	0	0	1	0	0	3	4	0	0	5	0
Chuck	48	.4641	5.0616	47.0	18	3	2	5	17	1	1	1	21	5	0	0	0	0	0	0	0	0	0	0	13	0	0	9	0
chuck-a-luck	3	.0000	.0434	26.4	3	0	0	0	0	0	0	0	0	0	0	0	0	0	0	0	0	0	0	0	0	3	0	0	0
chuck's	3	.0000	.0365	25.6	0	0	0	0	3	0	0	0	0	0	0	0	0	0	0	0	0	0	0	0	0	0	0	3	0
Chuck's	4	.0000	.1827	32.6	4	0	0	0	0	0	0	0	4	0	0	0	0	0	0	0	0	0	0	0	0	0	0	0	0
chucked	2	.1620	.0760	28.8	0	0	0	0	1	1	0	0	0	0	0	0	0	0	0	0	0	0	0	1	0	0	0	1	0
chuckle	19	.5181	2.1678	43.4	1	2	2	6	3	3	1	1	8	0	0	0	0	0	2	0	1	0	0	0	6	0	0	2	0
chuckled	44	.6532	6.0780	47.8	6	15	4	5	5	7	2	0	21	2	1	3	0	0	0	0	0	0	0	0	6	9	0	2	0
chuckles	4	.2424	.3036	34.8	1	1	1	0	1	0	0	0	3	0	0	0	0	0	0	0	0	0	0	0	0	0	0	1	0
chuckling	10	.4362	1.0175	40.1	1	2	1	1	4	1	0	0	5	0	0	3	0	0	0	0	0	0	0	0	1	0	0	1	0
chug	5	.5306	.5646	37.5	1	2	0	1	0	1	0	0	1	0	0	0	0	0	0	0	1	0	0	0	1	1	0	1	0
chug-a-chug	2	.2407	.1090	30.4	2	0	0	0	0	0	0	0	0	1	0	0	0	0	0	0	1	0	0	0	0	0	0	0	0
chugged	9	.5306	1.0266	40.1	4	4	0	1	0	0	0	0	2	0	0	2	0	2	0	0	0	0	0	0	1	0	0	2	0
chugging	2	.0665	.0708	28.5	0	0	2	0	0	0	0	0	1	0	1	0	0	0	0	0	0	0	0	0	0	0	0	0	0
chugs	4	.3730	.3206	35.1	1	1	0	2	0	0	0	0	0	0	0	0	0	0	0	0	1	0	0	0	2	0	0	1	0
Chuka	13	.0000	.5939	37.7	13	0	0	0	0	0	0	0	13	0	0	0	0	0	0	0	0	0	0	0	0	0	0	0	0
chum	8	.3771	.7570	38.8	0	1	0	2	4	1	0	0	5	0	0	1	0	0	0	0	0	0	0	0	0	0	0	2	0
Chumley	14	.0000	.1502	31.8	0	0	0	0	0	14	0	0	0	0	0	14	0	0	0	0	0	0	0	0	0	0	0	0	0
chummy	3	.2445	.1903	32.8	0	1	1	0	1	0	0	0	1	0	0	0	0	0	0	0	0	0	1	0	0	0	0	1	0
chums	3	.1277	.1363	31.3	0	0	2	0	0	0	0	1	1	0	0	0	0	0	0	0	0	0	0	0	0	0	0	2	0
chun	2	.0000	.0162	22.1	0	0	0	0	0	2	0	0	0	0	0	0	0	0	2	0	0	0	0	0	0	0	0	0	0
Chung	2	.0000	.0243	23.9	0	0	0	2	0	0	0	0	0	0	0	0	0	0	0	0	0	0	0	0	0	0	0	2	0
chunk	21	.6691	2.9347	44.7	3	3	2	4	4	2	1	2	8	1	0	2	0	0	0	1	0	0	0	0	1	1	3	4	0
chunks	51	.7710	8.0071	49.0	6	19	6	3	3	5	6	3	16	1	1	1	2	0	0	10	0	0	2	0	1	8	2	7	0
chunky	6	.5191	.6680	38.2	1	2	0	1	1	1	0	0	1	0	0	0	0	0	0	0	0	0	0	0	1	2	1	0	0
church	409	.8681	70.792	58.5	66	59	56	44	70	55	43	16	82	15	1	32	3	64	15	3	53	8	11	0	16	44	26	36	0
Cnurch	118	.3685	9.6630	49.9	8	9	28	5	29	23	12	4	9	0	0	8	0	21	0	0	3	0	0	0	3	14	46	10	4
church's	4	.3360	.3283	35.2	1	0	1	0	0	1	1	0	1	0	0	0	0	2	0	0	0	0	0	0	0	0	0	1	0
churches	96	.6762	13.202	51.2	15	6	18	17	13	19	6	2	3	1	1	0	0	35	1	2	11	8	0	1	1	8	17	7	0
Churches	3	.0000	.0314	25.0	0	0	0	0	2	1	0	0	0	0	0	0	0	0	0	0	0	0	0	0	0	0	3	0	0
Churchill	24	.5654	2.8692	44.6	2	2	7	3	2	5	3	0	3	3	0	0	0	10	0	0	0	0	0	0	0	4	3	1	0
Churchill's	3	.2425	.1816	32.6	0	0	2	0	0	0	1	0	0	0	0	0	0	2	0	0	0	0	0	0	0	0	0	1	0
churchman	2	.2346	.1166	30.7	0	0	0	0	1	0	1	0	0	0	0	0	0	0	0	1	0	0	0	0	0	0	0	1	0
churchmen	4	.2010	.2271	33.6	0	0	0	1	2	0	1	0	1	0	0	0	0	2	0	0	0	1	0	0	0	0	0	0	0
Churchmen	2	.2351	.1166	30.7	0	0	0	0	1	1	0	0	0	0	0	0	0	1	0	0	0	0	0	0	0	0	0	1	0
churchyard	7	.5082	.7575	38.8	0	2	1	0	2	0	0	2	1	0	0	1	0	0	0	0	0	0	0	0	2	1	0	2	0
churlish	2	.1814	.1187	30.7	0	0	1	1	0	0	0	0	1	0	0	0	0	0	0	0	0	0	0	0	0	0	0	1	0
churn	21	.5166	2.3568	43.7	8	0	1	6	1	1	0	4	6	0	1	0	0	3	0	0	0	0	0	0	7	0	0	4	0
churned	12	.5959	1.5213	41.8	1	0	3	3	2	2	0	1	4	0	1	1	0	1	0	2	1	0	0	0	0	0	0	2	0
churning	19	.6752	2.6593	44.2	2	4	4	5	4	0	0	0	5	0	1	0	0	1	1	4	0	0	0	0	2	2	0	3	0
churns	6	.3873	.5822	37.7	3	1	1	1	0	0	0	0	4	0	0	0	0	0	0	0	0	0	0	0	1	0	1	0	0
chute	17	.3509	1.6093	42.1	6	5	6	0	0	0	0	0	14	0	0	0	0	0	0	0	0	0	0	0	2	0	1	0	0
chutes	3	.2309	.1631	32.1	0	0	0	0	0	0	1	2	0	0	0	1	0	0	0	0	0	0	0	0	0	0	0	2	0
ci	9	.1025	.2494	34.0	0	0	0	0	5	3	1	0	0	1	0	0	0	0	8	0	0	0	0	0	0	0	0	0	0
cial	3	.0000	.0243	23.9	0	0	0	0	3	0	0	0	0	0	0	0	0	0	3	0	0	0	0	0	0	0	0	0	0
Cibola	4	.3790	.3299	35.2	2	0	0	1	1	0	0	0	0	0	0	0	0	0	0	0	0	0	0	0	0	2	1	1	0
cicada	4	.0904	.1412	31.5	1	0	0	0	3	0	0	0	1	0	0	0	0	0	0	0	0	0	0	0	0	0	3	0	0
cicadas	3	.3370	.2430	33.9	1	0	0	0	2	0	0	0	1	0	0	1	0	0	0	0	0	0	0	0	0	0	1	0	0
Cicero	3	.0000	.0352	25.5	3	0	0	0	0	0	0	0	0	0	0	0	0	0	0	0	0	0	0	0	3	0	0	0	0
Cichla	2	.0000	.0209	23.2	0	0	0	0	2	0	0	0	0	0	0	0	0	0	0	0	0	0	0	0	0	0	2	0	0
cider	19	.6262	2.4943	44.0	2	3	2	0	4	3	5	0	6	1	0	6	1	0	0	0	0	0	1	0	2	1	0	1	0
Cider	4	.0000	.1827	32.6	0	4	0	0	0	0	0	0	4	0	0	0	0	0	0	0	0	0	0	0	0	0	0	0	0
cigar	30	.7230	4.4215	46.5	4	0	2	2	11	6	4	1	6	2	1	9	0	2	1	3	0	0	0	0	1	1	1	3	0
cigarette	45	.6460	6.0408	47.8	2	1	2	4	24	7	3	2	10	0	2	14	0	3	1	9	0	0	0	0	3	1	1	1	0
cigarettes	25	.6215	3.2221	45.1	2	1	2	2	11	4	1	2	2	0	0	4	0	3	0	7	0	0	0	0	0	3	1	5	0
cigars	11	.5965	1.3476	41.3	1	0	2	1	2	2	2	1	0	1	0	3	0	2	0	0	0	0	0	0	0	2	2	1	0
cilia	22	.1648	1.0615	40.3	3	7	0	0	8	0	4	0	0	0	0	0	0	0	0	19	0	0	0	0	0	3	0	0	0
ciliated	2	.0000	.0394	26.0	0	0	0	0	0	0	2	0	0	0	0	0	0	0	0	2	0	0	0	0	0	0	0	0	0
Cilla	6	.0000	.0703	28.5	0	0	0	0	0	6	0	0	0	0	0	0	0	0	0	0	0	0	0	0	6	0	0	0	0
Cimarron	3	.1187	.1291	31.1	0	0	0	1	2	0	0	0	1	0	0	2	0	0	0	0	0	0	0	0	0	0	0	0	0
cinch	6	.5102	.6515	38.1	0	2	0	0	1	3	0	0	1	1	0	2	0	0	0	0	0	0	0	0	1	0	0	1	0
Cincinnati	25	.4767	2.5178	44.0	2	5	1	3	6	2	2	4	0	1	0	1	0	1	0	2	0	0	0	0	0	6	1	13	0
cinder	11	.5571	1.3069	41.2	1	4	0	2	2	1	1	0	3	0	0	0	0	0	0	1	1	0	0	1	0	3	2	0	0
cinder-block	2	.0000	.0243	23.9	0	0	0	0	2	0	0	0	0	0	0	0	0	0	0	0	0	0	0	0	0	0	0	2	0
Cinderella	21	.3612	1.6914	42.3	14	2	0	4	0	1	0	0	4	0	0	0	0	0	1	0	13	2	0	0	0	1	0	0	0
cinders	17	.4405	1.7969	42.5	4	4	5	1	2	1	0	0	10	0	0	0	0	0	0	5	0	0	0	0	1	1	0	0	0
Cindy	13	.2489	.8460	39.3	0	12	0	0	1	0	0	0	3	0	0	0	9	0	0	0	1	0	0	0	0	0	0	0	0
cinema	5	.3157	.3561	35.5	0	0	0	1	1	0	2	1	0	1	0	0	0	0	0	1	0	0	0	0	0	0	0	3	0
Cinesias	2	.0000	.0290	24.6	0	0	0	0	2	0	0	0	0	0	0	0	0	0	0	0	0	0	0	0	0	2	0	0	0
cinnabar	4	.1335	.1958	32.9	1	0	0	0	0	0	3	0	1	0	0	0	0	0	0	3	0	0	0	0	0	0	0	0	0
cinnamon	30	.4893	3.0505	44.8	3	3	1	3	10	4	3	3	1	2	1	1	0	5	1	1	1	0	11	0	0	2	1	3	0
cious	2	.0000	.0162	22.1	0	0	0	0	2	0	0	0	0	0	0	0	0	0	2	0	0	0	0	0	0	0	0	0	0
cipher	3	.1187	.1291	31.1	0	0	0	1	0	0	2	0	1	0	0	2	0	0	0	0	0	0	0	0	0	0	0	0	0
Circe	4	.2003	.1916	32.8	0	0	0	0	0	1	3	0	0	0	0	3	0	0	0	0	0	0	0	0	0	0	1	0	0
circle	945	.7691	146.45	61.7	140	154	147	140	154	116	80	14	108	20	6	12	382	25	142	66	59	3	4	26	27	31	10	24	0
Circle	27	.7172	3.9806	46.0	2	3	3	12	4	1	2	0	7	0	1	2	0	8	0	2	1	0	0	0	0	2	3	1	0
circled	66	.7167	9.7452	49.9	2	21	10	6	16	7	3	1	22	1	3	5	15	2	0	4	0	0	0	0	8	2	1	3	0
circles	169	.7467	25.564	54.1	28	29	19	15	25	27	22	4	22	3	1	5	66	4	1	26	3	1	1	12	4	4	6	10	0
circlet	3	.3385	.2445	33.9	1	0	1	1	0	0	0	0	1	0	0	0	0	0	0	0	0	0	0	0	1	0	1	0	0
circling	44	.7639	6.8357	48.3	3	9	5	10	11	3	2	1	12	1	0	4	0	5	0	5	1	1	0	0	5	0	7	3	0
circuit	197	.3749	16.243	52.1	23	21	34	21	16	65	10	7	4	0	0	3	1	6	1	93	4	0	0	53	1	15	7	9	0
Circuit	7	.1420	.2661	34.3	0	0	0	6	1	0	0	0	0	0	0	0	0	0	0	0	0	0	0	0	6	0	0	1	0
circuits	30	.3745	2.4816	43.9	2	1	6	3	4	11	3	0	2	0	0	0	0	1	0	10	0	0	0	8	0	3	4	2	0
circular	92	.6411	12.035	50.8	7	3	8	10	18	24	17	5	5	2	1	3	25	1	1	14	0	3	2	18	3	8	3	3	0
circulate	6	.5357	.6878	38.4	0	0	0	0	2	1	3	0	1	1	0	0	0	0	0	2	0	0	0	0	0	1	1	0	0
circulated	11	.4503	1.0519	40.2	0	0	0	0	2	1	5	3	0	0	0	0	0	1	0	1	0	0	0	0	1	0	3	5	0
circulates	8	.4371	.7630	38.8	0	0	0	2	2	2	1	1	0	2	0	0	0	1	0	4	0	0	0	0	0	1	0	0	0
circulating	5	.2129	.2689	34.3	0	0	0	2	1	0	1	1	0	0	0	0	0	0	0	2	0	0	0	0	0	0	0	3	0
circulation	44	.5777	5.3141	47.3	2	1	4	2	8	11	12	4	2	0	0	0	0	0	3	24	0	0	1	0	0	2	7	5	0
circulatory	16	.2436	.9695	39.9	0	1	0	0	5	3	6	1	0	0	0	0	0	0	0	11	0	0	0	0	0	0	5	0	0

6A Chucaro
6A Chucaro's
3P Chuckawalla
7R chucking
5J chuckle-head
3B Chug
3P chug-chug
3P chug-chug-chug
3A Chuka's
7R Chula
7R chumming
8F Chung-kuo
6F Chungking
6R Chungshan
6A church-bells
5P Church-countenanced
7P church-man
4N church-mice
8R church-state
4N church-tower
8D churchlike
4N Churchyard
6A churnin'
5D churring
XR chutney
9B Chutney's
XR chutneys
5A Chuto
6J Chy-kof-skih
8R CIA
7G cible
6P Ciboure
7Q cichlid
7Q Cichlidae
7Q cichlids
4Q Cid
7R CIE
XP cigar-chewing
5H cigarette-smoking
8F cigarmakers
XR cilantro
7H ciliar
7D cinched
6J cinches
7D cinching
XD cinchona
7A Cincinnatus
5A Cinder
XH Cinderella-like
6A Cinderella's
3P cinderman
4A Cinders
9R Cinema
9R cinematically
7R cinematographer
9R cinematographers
7N cineraria
7N cinerarias
7Q cinnamic
XR cinnamon-colored
3P Cinque
6A cinquefoil
7R Cinzano
5Q CIO**
7G cion
6A ciphering
7R cir-cum-stan-ces
9R circ
9E circle's
5F Circles
4R Circraft
5H circuit-closer
7N circuitous
7R circularizes
8Q circularly
7Q circulars

Word Type	F	D	U	SFI	3 Gr 3	4 Gr 4	5 Gr 5	6 Gr 6	7 Gr 7	8 Gr 8	9 Gr 9	X UnGr	A Read	B Eng & Gr	C Comp	D Lit	E Math	F Soc Stud	G Spell	H Sci	J Music	K Art	L Home Ec	M Shop	N Lib F	P Lib NF	Q Lib Ref	R Mag	S Rel
circumcision	2	.0000	.0209	23.2	0	0	0	0	0	0	2	0	0	0	0	0	0	0	0	0	0	0	0	0	0	0	2	0	0
circumference	68	.4829	6.9579	48.4	0	3	2	17	12	15	19	0	0	1	3	0	51	4	0	4	0	0	0	2	0	0	2	1	0
circumferences	3	.0000	.0449	26.5	0	0	0	0	1	1	1	0	0	0	0	0	3	0	0	0	0	0	0	0	0	0	0	0	0
circumnavigation	2	.2346	.1166	30.7	0	0	0	1	0	0	1	0	0	0	0	0	0	0	0	1	0	0	0	0	0	0	0	1	0
circumscribed	6	.3207	.4366	36.4	0	4	0	1	0	0	1	0	0	0	0	0	4	0	0	0	0	0	0	0	1	1	0	0	0
circumscribes	2	.0000	.0299	24.8	0	2	0	0	0	0	0	0	0	0	0	0	2	0	0	0	0	0	0	0	0	0	0	0	0
circumstance	9	.5255	.9785	39.9	0	0	0	1	7	0	1	0	0	0	0	3	0	0	0	0	0	0	0	0	2	1	2	1	0
circumstances	83	.7018	11.825	50.7	4	4	8	4	25	19	17	2	7	6	0	3	0	8	1	6	0	0	3	0	7	6	29	7	0
circumvallation	2	.0000	.0209	23.2	0	0	0	0	0	0	2	0	0	0	0	0	0	0	0	0	0	0	0	0	0	0	2	0	0
circus	216	.7713	33.805	55.3	94	72	6	14	12	8	9	1	64	6	11	5	7	3	12	2	3	8	1	0	29	52	2	11	0
Circus	19	.6007	2.4398	43.9	11	6	0	0	0	1	1	0	8	0	1	0	0	0	0	0	1	0	0	0	2	4	0	3	0
circuses	6	.3723	.5098	37.1	1	3	1	0	0	0	1	0	1	1	0	0	0	0	0	1	0	0	0	0	0	0	0	3	0
Cirque	4	.0000	.1827	32.6	4	0	0	0	0	0	0	0	4	0	0	0	0	0	0	0	0	0	0	0	0	0	0	0	0
cirrus	15	.2664	.9890	40.0	5	1	0	5	3	0	1	0	0	0	0	0	0	0	0	12	0	0	0	0	0	2	0	1	0
cistern	2	.0000	.0914	29.6	0	2	0	0	0	0	0	0	2	0	0	0	0	0	0	0	0	0	0	0	0	0	0	0	0
citadel	5	.5599	.5798	37.6	0	0	0	0	1	0	3	1	0	0	0	1	0	1	0	0	0	0	0	0	0	1	1	1	0
Citadel	3	.0000	.1370	31.4	0	0	0	0	0	3	0	0	3	0	0	0	0	0	0	0	0	0	0	0	0	0	0	0	0
Citation	3	.1639	.1674	32.2	0	0	0	1	0	2	0	0	1	0	0	0	0	2	0	0	0	0	0	0	0	0	0	0	0
citations	3	.1937	.1495	31.7	0	0	0	0	2	1	0	0	0	0	0	0	0	1	0	0	0	0	0	0	0	0	0	2	0
cite	9	.5627	1.0361	40.2	0	1	0	0	3	1	3	1	0	1	1	2	0	0	1	0	0	0	0	0	0	1	0	3	0
cited	7	.3234	.5317	37.3	0	0	1	1	1	0	4	0	1	0	0	0	0	1	0	0	0	0	0	0	0	1	0	4	0
cites	4	.3306	.2831	34.5	0	0	0	0	0	1	2	1	0	0	1	0	0	0	0	0	1	0	0	0	0	0	0	2	0
cities	1043	.6855	146.67	61.7	185	148	213	158	147	114	71	7	72	17	0	9	18	613	11	46	21	9	0	8	5	69	96	49	0
Cities	4	.3498	.3059	34.9	1	0	0	1	2	0	0	0	0	0	0	0	0	0	0	0	0	0	0	0	0	1	2	1	0
citizen	110	.7490	16.693	52.2	2	3	12	11	15	25	41	1	10	7	3	5	3	54	5	3	5	0	0	0	1	2	8	4	0
citizens	230	.7242	33.873	55.3	19	16	33	12	39	68	39	4	19	5	3	11	0	107	3	2	7	0	0	0	5	18	27	23	0
Citizens	7	.2526	.4470	36.5	0	0	0	1	0	2	0	4	1	0	0	0	0	2	0	0	0	0	0	0	0	0	0	4	0
citizens'	2	.2351	.1166	30.7	0	0	0	0	0	0	2	0	0	0	0	0	0	1	0	0	0	0	0	0	0	0	0	1	0
citizenship	33	.4046	2.9817	44.7	0	0	1	0	4	9	19	0	1	0	2	2	0	25	0	0	0	0	0	0	0	3	0	0	0
citric	2	.2346	.1166	30.7	0	0	0	0	0	0	1	1	0	0	0	0	0	0	0	1	0	0	0	0	0	0	0	1	0
Citronella	10	.1697	.4242	36.3	2	0	8	0	0	0	0	0	0	0	0	8	0	0	0	0	0	0	0	0	2	0	0	0	0
citrus	34	.4327	3.2030	45.1	4	0	8	5	6	3	6	2	1	0	0	0	0	20	0	2	0	0	6	0	1	0	2	2	0
city	1843	.8417	310.95	64.9	403	225	301	281	283	191	135	24	329	61	16	74	29	776	26	50	32	10	1	4	35	96	172	129	3
City	226	.7680	35.316	55.5	37	25	28	30	37	53	12	4	62	8	0	4	25	51	0	1	10	0	0	0	7	11	22	25	0
city-dwellers	2	.0000	.0389	25.9	0	0	0	0	0	2	0	0	0	0	0	0	0	2	0	0	0	0	0	0	0	0	0	0	0
city-state	8	.1813	.4050	36.1	0	1	0	4	3	0	0	0	0	0	0	0	0	7	0	0	0	0	0	0	0	0	1	0	0
city-states	12	.3806	1.0237	40.1	0	0	1	5	3	2	1	0	0	0	0	0	0	9	0	0	0	1	0	0	0	1	0	1	0
city's	50	.5254	5.5803	47.5	8	3	15	5	4	2	13	0	4	2	0	0	0	21	0	0	0	0	0	0	0	3	11	9	0
City's	6	.5082	.6524	38.1	0	0	1	2	1	2	0	0	1	0	0	0	0	1	0	0	1	0	0	0	0	0	1	2	0
Ciudad	3	.1823	.1405	31.5	0	0	1	0	2	0	0	0	0	0	0	0	0	1	0	0	0	0	0	0	0	0	2	0	0
civet	2	.2437	.1129	30.5	0	0	0	0	1	0	0	1	0	0	0	0	0	0	0	0	0	0	0	0	0	0	1	1	0
civic	12	.4849	1.2104	40.8	0	0	1	2	2	2	4	1	0	0	0	0	0	1	1	1	1	2	0	0	0	2	4	0	0
Civic	2	.2446	.1123	30.5	0	0	1	0	0	0	1	0	0	1	0	0	0	0	0	0	0	0	0	0	0	0	1	0	0
civics	2	.2152	.1357	31.3	0	0	0	1	0	0	1	0	1	0	0	0	0	1	0	0	0	0	0	0	0	0	0	0	0
Civics	2	.0000	.0389	25.9	0	0	0	0	0	2	0	0	0	0	0	0	0	2	0	0	0	0	0	0	0	0	0	0	0
civil	81	.6858	11.324	50.5	3	0	9	3	16	18	29	3	3	2	0	6	0	35	2	2	0	0	0	2	1	2	13	13	0
Civil	76	.7000	10.841	50.4	4	7	23	0	10	19	9	4	5	2	1	1	2	28	0	0	2	0	0	0	1	14	13	7	0
civil-rights	3	.0000	.0365	25.6	0	0	0	0	0	2	0	1	0	0	0	0	0	0	0	0	0	0	0	0	0	0	0	3	0
civilian	17	.5411	1.9120	42.8	1	1	2	1	4	4	3	1	0	0	0	1	0	4	0	0	1	0	0	0	0	1	3	7	0
civilians	8	.3422	.6146	37.9	1	0	1	0	2	3	1	0	0	0	0	0	0	2	0	0	0	0	0	0	0	2	0	4	0
civilization	124	.7234	18.210	52.6	10	5	13	16	31	29	14	6	10	2	0	1	5	44	2	2	4	0	2	1	0	10	31	10	0
Civilization	2	.2446	.1257	31.0	0	0	0	0	2	0	0	0	0	0	0	0	0	1	0	1	0	0	0	0	0	0	0	0	0
civilizations	23	.6853	3.2357	45.1	1	1	7	1	4	3	5	1	3	2	0	0	3	6	1	2	0	0	0	0	0	2	4	0	0
civilize	4	.3860	.3420	35.3	0	0	1	0	1	2	0	0	0	0	0	0	0	2	0	0	0	0	0	0	1	0	0	1	0
civilized	48	.7563	7.3131	48.6	2	6	3	6	20	2	5	4	3	3	0	12	1	9	1	2	0	0	0	1	1	6	6	3	0
Civilized	3	.2264	.1679	32.2	1	0	0	0	2	0	0	0	0	0	0	0	2	0	0	0	0	0	0	0	0	1	0	0	0
civilizing	3	.3776	.2504	34.0	0	0	1	0	0	1	1	0	0	0	0	1	0	1	0	0	0	0	0	0	0	1	0	0	0
ck	25	.0278	.4069	36.1	7	10	1	1	6	0	0	0	2	0	0	0	0	0	23	0	0	0	0	0	0	0	0	0	0
cl	8	.0000	.0649	28.1	0	3	3	1	1	0	0	0	0	0	0	0	0	0	8	0	0	0	0	0	0	0	0	0	0
Cl	3	.2332	.1690	32.3	2	1	0	0	0	0	0	0	0	0	0	0	0	0	0	0	0	0	0	0	0	2	0	1	0
Cl-	3	.0000	.0365	25.6	0	3	0	0	0	0	0	0	0	0	0	0	0	0	0	0	0	0	0	0	0	0	0	3	0
clacking	6	.5497	.7102	38.5	1	0	1	1	3	0	0	0	2	0	0	0	0	0	0	0	1	0	0	0	1	1	0	1	0
clad	18	.6179	2.3815	43.8	1	0	2	4	7	2	1	1	8	0	0	1	0	4	0	0	0	0	0	0	2	0	1	2	0
Claesz	3	.0000	.0322	25.1	0	0	0	0	3	0	0	0	0	0	0	3	0	0	0	0	0	0	0	0	0	0	0	0	0
claim	125	.8031	20.156	53.0	7	12	17	17	27	20	22	3	14	6	3	2	6	33	1	3	6	0	0	0	10	5	18	18	0
claimed	103	.6520	13.840	51.4	7	6	25	16	17	18	11	3	10	1	0	5	1	39	0	0	4	0	0	0	1	8	13	21	0
claiming	11	.5481	1.2604	41.0	3	0	3	0	1	3	0	1	0	0	0	0	2	4	0	0	0	0	0	0	0	1	2	2	0
claims	53	.6823	7.4340	48.7	1	5	5	1	18	11	11	1	9	0	3	3	0	16	0	3	0	0	1	0	0	3	10	5	0
Claims	2	.2285	.1129	30.5	0	0	0	0	0	0	2	0	0	0	0	0	0	1	0	0	0	0	0	0	0	0	1	0	0
Clair	4	.4839	.4006	36.0	1	1	1	0	0	0	1	0	0	0	0	1	0	0	1	0	1	0	0	0	0	0	0	1	0
Claire	4	.2875	.2848	34.5	0	0	0	2	0	1	1	0	1	2	0	0	1	0	0	0	0	0	0	0	0	0	0	0	0
clam	42	.7019	6.0931	47.8	6	5	7	7	8	3	5	1	13	0	0	0	0	0	0	11	3	0	1	0	2	4	6	2	0
Clam	2	.0000	.0243	23.9	0	0	0	0	2	0	0	0	0	0	0	0	0	0	0	0	0	0	0	0	0	0	0	2	0
clam's	2	.2437	.1129	30.5	0	0	0	1	0	1	0	0	0	0	0	0	0	0	0	0	0	0	0	0	0	0	1	1	0
clambake	2	.0000	.0914	29.6	0	0	2	0	0	0	0	0	2	0	0	0	0	0	0	0	0	0	0	0	0	0	0	0	0
clambered	19	.5912	2.3654	43.7	2	4	1	4	7	0	0	1	5	1	0	4	0	0	0	0	0	0	0	0	4	0	2	3	0
clambering	4	.2991	.2943	34.7	2	0	0	0	1	1	0	0	1	0	0	0	0	0	0	0	0	0	0	0	0	1	0	2	0
clammy	3	.3086	.2017	33.0	0	1	0	0	0	0	2	0	0	1	0	0	0	0	0	0	0	0	1	0	0	1	0	0	0
clamor	9	.5288	.9958	40.0	1	0	0	1	3	2	1	1	1	0	1	1	0	0	0	0	0	0	0	0	3	0	1	2	0
clamored	4	.4518	.3982	36.0	2	1	0	0	0	1	0	0	1	0	0	1	0	0	0	0	0	0	0	0	1	0	1	0	0
clamoring	3	.2465	.1705	32.3	1	0	0	0	0	1	1	0	0	0	1	0	0	1	0	0	0	0	0	0	1	0	0	0	0
clamorous	3	.3870	.2486	34.0	0	0	0	0	1	2	0	0	0	0	0	1	0	0	0	0	0	0	0	0	0	0	1	1	0
clamp	41	.1470	1.6909	42.3	11	1	0	1	7	12	5	4	9	0	0	0	0	0	0	2	0	0	0	23	5	1	0	1	0
clamped	21	.2312	1.1564	40.6	1	1	2	0	4	5	6	2	3	0	0	2	0	1	0	0	0	0	0	10	2	0	0	3	0
clamping	4	.0000	.0101	20.0	0	0	0	0	0	3	1	0	0	0	0	0	0	0	0	0	0	0	0	4	0	0	0	0	0
clamps	22	.2333	1.1986	40.8	2	0	1	2	9	7	1	0	3	0	0	0	0	1	0	1	0	1	0	13	0	1	1	1	0
clams	50	.7036	7.2862	48.6	11	8	11	7	5	4	3	1	16	0	0	2	0	3	0	12	0	0	1	0	0	8	4	4	0
clan	13	.5718	1.5253	41.8	1	2	0	0	4	3	2	1	0	0	0	4	0	0	1	0	0	0	0	0	1	2	1	4	0
Clancy	7	.0000	.3198	35.0	4	0	0	0	0	3	0	0	7	0	0	0	0	0	0	0	0	0	0	0	0	0	0	0	0
clang	9	.5044	.9876	39.9	2	0	5	1	0	1	0	0	2	0	0	0	0	3	0	0	2	0	0	0	0	1	0	1	0
clanged	6	.4510	.6073	37.8	1	1	1	1	1	0	1	0	2	0	0	1	0	0	0	0	0	0	0	0	2	0	0	1	0
clanging	9	.5391	1.0255	40.1	4	0	2	1	2	0	0	0	2	1	1	0	0	0	0	0	2	0	0	0	2	0	0	1	0
clangs	2	.0000	.0914	29.6	0	0	0	0	1	1	0	0	2	0	0	0	0	0	0	0	0	0	0	0	0	0	0	0	0
clank	6	.5495	.7095	38.5	1	1	2	0	1	1	0	0	2	0	0	1	0	0	0	0	1	0	0	0	0	1	0	1	0
clanking	7	.4624	.7365	38.7	2	0	1	1	0	1	1	1	3	1	0	0	0	0	0	0	0	0	0	0	0	1	0	2	0

9B circumspect
6A circumspection
7Q circumvent
9R Cirey
XR cirrhosis
7H cirrostratus
XQ cis
7A citation
8Q Cithaeron
4R citified
9Q Citizen
4P citizen's
XR citizenry
5Q Citizenship
7R Citoyen
5B citron
6R citronella
9H citrulline
3F City-County
5A city-dweller
6A city-lovers
9Q city-sized
9Q city-suburbs
XP city-to-city
7R city-wide
7R civil-engineering
7A Civilian
6A civilised
9Q civitas
9B Ck
3A ckers
3A cl
3A clss
5A clacked
9F Claggart
9Q clairvoyance
8A clamber
3P clambers
7H clamitans
4H clamlike
7N clammed
3R clamming
6A clamoured
6R clams'
7R clamshell-type
8D Clan
7A clandestinely
3J clang-a-clang-a-clang
7P clank'd
5F clanks
5P clannish

Word Type	F	D	U	SFI	3 Gr 3	4 Gr 4	5 Gr 5	6 Gr 6	7 Gr 7	8 Gr 8	9 Gr 9	X UnGr	A Read	B Eng & Gr	C Comp	D Lit	E Math	F Soc Stud	G Spell	H Sci	J Music	K Art	L Home Ec	M Shop	N Lib F	P Lib NF	Q Lib Ref	R Mag	S Rel
clansmen	2	.2297	.1135	30.6	0	0	0	0	1	1	0	0	0	0	0	1	0	1	0	0	0	0	0	0	0	0	0	0	0
clap	89	.1479	3.4162	45.3	41	14	11	10	11	1	1	0	5	0	0	0	0	0	1	4	74	0	0	0	4	0	0	1	0
clapboard	2	.0000	.0243	23.9	0	0	0	2	0	0	0	0	0	0	0	0	0	0	0	0	0	0	0	0	0	0	0	2	0
clapped	55	.5718	6.8073	48.3	16	15	6	9	5	2	2	0	24	1	0	4	0	0	0	0	4	0	0	0	13	9	0	0	0
clapper	4	.2346	.2332	33.7	0	0	1	2	0	1	0	0	0	0	0	0	0	0	0	2	0	0	0	0	0	0	0	2	0
clappers	3	.0995	.1144	30.6	0	0	0	2	1	0	0	0	1	0	0	0	0	0	0	0	2	0	0	0	0	0	0	0	0
clapping	39	.4379	3.8164	45.8	7	3	5	9	12	2	1	0	13	0	1	3	0	0	0	0	18	0	0	0	3	0	1	0	0
Clapping	2	.0000	.0914	29.6	0	2	0	0	0	0	0	0	2	0	0	0	0	0	0	0	0	0	0	0	0	0	0	0	0
claps	9	.3902	.8137	39.1	3	2	0	0	2	0	2	0	3	0	0	2	0	0	0	1	3	0	0	0	0	0	0	0	0
clapt	2	.0000	.0219	23.4	0	0	0	0	0	2	0	0	0	2	0	0	0	0	0	0	0	0	0	0	0	0	0	0	0
Clapton	2	.0000	.0243	23.9	0	0	0	0	0	2	0	0	0	0	0	0	0	0	0	0	0	0	0	0	0	0	0	2	0
Clara	65	.6507	8.9427	49.5	2	22	18	16	6	1	0	0	28	0	1	3	0	14	0	1	3	0	0	0	13	0	0	2	0
Clare	2	.2442	.1134	30.5	0	0	0	0	1	0	1	0	0	1	0	0	0	0	0	0	0	0	0	0	0	0	0	1	0
Clarence	40	.6395	5.4510	47.4	3	15	9	0	2	10	1	0	21	0	1	9	2	0	0	1	0	0	0	0	1	1	3	1	0
Clarence's	2	.0000	.0914	29.6	0	2	0	0	0	0	0	0	2	0	0	0	0	0	0	0	0	0	0	0	0	0	0	0	0
Clarice	3	.1200	.1302	31.1	0	0	0	1	0	0	2	0	1	2	0	0	0	0	0	0	0	0	0	0	0	0	0	0	0
clarified	3	.2123	.1792	32.5	0	0	0	1	1	1	0	0	1	0	0	0	0	0	0	1	0	0	1	0	0	0	0	0	0
clarify	11	.4058	.9402	39.7	0	0	2	0	3	2	4	0	0	1	3	0	3	0	0	0	1	0	0	0	0	1	2	0	0
clarinet	38	.1202	1.2172	40.9	1	9	2	3	11	11	1	0	1	2	0	0	0	0	0	0	33	0	0	0	0	2	0	0	0
clarinets	16	.0690	.3396	35.3	0	2	4	3	0	1	6	0	0	0	0	0	0	0	0	0	15	0	0	0	0	0	1	0	0
Clarissa	8	.2351	.6222	37.9	0	0	1	7	0	0	0	0	7	0	0	0	0	0	0	0	0	0	0	0	0	0	1	0	0
Clarissa's	2	.0000	.0914	29.6	0	0	0	2	0	0	0	0	2	0	0	0	0	0	0	0	0	0	0	0	0	0	0	0	0
clarity	26	.7009	3.6524	45.6	0	0	1	1	12	5	6	1	0	3	4	1	1	0	2	1	5	1	1	0	0	3	2	2	0
Clark	100	.7084	14.492	51.6	2	18	40	10	10	11	8	1	13	1	0	8	5	41	1	2	2	0	0	0	1	6	5	15	0
Clark's	8	.4057	.7325	38.6	0	1	5	0	0	0	2	0	1	0	0	2	0	4	0	0	0	0	0	0	0	1	0	0	0
Clarke	5	.2691	.2967	34.7	0	0	5	0	0	0	0	0	0	0	2	0	0	1	0	0	1	0	0	0	0	0	0	1	0
Clarks'	3	.0000	.0434	26.4	0	3	0	0	0	0	0	0	0	0	0	0	0	0	0	0	0	0	0	0	0	3	0	0	0
Clarkson	2	.0000	.0914	29.6	0	2	0	0	0	0	0	0	2	0	0	0	0	0	0	0	0	0	0	0	0	0	0	0	0
Clarksville	2	.0000	.0914	29.6	0	0	0	1	1	0	0	0	2	0	0	0	0	0	0	0	0	0	0	0	0	0	0	0	0
clash	11	.5336	1.2304	40.9	0	0	2	0	2	2	5	0	1	0	0	1	0	3	0	0	1	0	0	2	0	1	1	1	0
clashed	8	.5822	.9749	39.9	1	1	2	0	1	1	2	0	1	0	0	2	0	2	0	0	0	0	0	0	1	1	1	0	0
clashes	4	.3829	.3404	35.3	0	1	1	0	1	1	0	0	0	0	0	0	0	2	0	0	0	0	0	0	0	1	1	0	0
clashing	4	.2223	.2556	34.1	0	1	0	1	1	1	0	0	2	0	0	1	0	0	0	0	0	1	0	0	0	0	0	0	0
clasp	6	.5567	.7226	38.6	1	2	1	1	0	1	0	0	2	0	0	0	0	0	0	1	0	0	0	0	1	1	0	1	0
clasped	19	.5186	2.1076	43.2	0	4	4	2	5	1	3	0	4	0	0	3	0	0	0	0	1	0	0	0	8	2	1	0	0
clasps	8	.4910	.8345	39.2	2	1	2	2	0	0	1	0	1	3	1	1	0	0	0	1	0	0	0	0	1	0	0	0	0
class	1211	.8533	206.01	63.1	216	204	171	142	163	150	154	11	159	315	11	23	170	104	42	81	111	17	44	4	38	34	22	36	0
Class	41	.6154	5.2145	47.2	9	3	1	6	8	8	5	1	5	12	0	0	4	0	0	0	0	0	0	0	7	5	3	5	0
classed	13	.5003	1.3828	41.4	0	0	1	2	3	1	3	3	0	1	0	0	0	0	1	8	0	0	0	0	1	0	2	0	0
classes	159	.8935	28.197	54.5	15	23	13	15	34	27	24	8	15	20	3	4	8	22	2	15	5	1	0	3	4	17	16	24	0
classic	45	.6494	5.9291	47.7	1	2	3	1	16	10	7	5	1	0	0	1	0	1	0	2	7	1	1	0	1	2	16	12	0
Classic	5	.4244	.4508	36.5	0	0	0	1	0	2	2	0	0	1	0	0	0	1	0	0	2	0	0	0	0	0	0	1	0
classical	63	.3942	5.3242	47.3	0	4	8	2	12	31	3	3	4	0	0	0	0	0	0	1	35	1	0	0	0	3	17	2	0
Classical	28	.2946	1.7849	42.5	0	0	2	1	3	20	0	2	0	1	0	0	0	0	0	0	22	1	0	0	0	0	4	0	0
classicism	2	.2417	.1091	30.4	0	0	0	0	0	1	1	0	0	0	0	0	0	0	0	0	1	0	0	0	0	0	1	0	0
Classicist	2	.0000	.0162	22.1	0	0	0	0	0	2	0	0	0	0	0	0	0	0	0	0	2	0	0	0	0	0	0	0	0
classics	7	.4903	.7284	38.6	1	0	0	1	0	3	1	1	1	1	0	0	0	0	0	0	2	0	0	0	0	0	2	1	0
classification	40	.5661	4.7509	46.8	0	6	4	1	15	3	11	0	5	2	6	0	4	1	0	13	0	0	1	0	1	1	5	1	0
classifications	25	.5783	3.0352	44.8	0	7	1	0	11	3	2	1	4	0	1	1	1	1	1	9	0	0	0	4	0	0	1	2	0
classified	82	.7411	12.264	50.9	3	9	13	5	25	11	14	2	2	6	0	0	8	3	2	31	1	0	3	2	2	1	19	2	0
classifies	11	.5343	1.2435	40.9	0	3	3	0	2	2	1	0	0	0	0	0	2	2	0	5	0	0	0	0	0	0	1	1	0
classify	61	.6999	8.6956	49.4	6	10	8	8	10	11	8	0	2	5	3	0	7	3	0	30	2	0	1	0	0	1	4	3	0
classifying	19	.4144	1.7396	42.4	2	5	6	0	1	4	1	0	0	1	0	0	4	0	0	12	0	0	0	0	0	0	2	0	0
classing	2	.2446	.1142	30.6	0	0	1	0	1	0	0	0	0	0	0	0	0	0	0	0	0	0	0	0	1	0	0	1	0
classmate	30	.4730	3.0010	44.8	4	5	6	4	8	2	1	0	1	16	0	0	0	0	3	5	1	0	0	0	0	1	0	3	0
Classmate	2	.0000	.0162	22.1	2	0	0	0	0	0	0	0	0	0	0	0	0	0	0	0	2	0	0	0	0	0	0	0	0
classmate's	3	.2074	.1511	31.8	0	3	0	0	0	0	0	0	0	2	0	0	0	0	0	0	0	0	0	0	0	1	0	0	0
classmates	124	.7560	18.887	52.8	15	23	16	19	18	12	19	2	13	48	1	8	11	6	9	11	5	2	4	0	2	0	0	4	0
classmates'	3	.1858	.1432	31.6	0	0	1	0	1	0	1	0	0	2	0	0	0	1	0	0	0	0	0	0	0	0	0	0	0
classroom	213	.8220	35.124	55.5	55	48	24	16	42	13	11	4	30	21	5	3	55	15	1	43	8	3	0	0	3	6	6	14	0
classrooms	19	.7313	2.8338	44.5	5	4	1	1	4	1	2	1	4	2	0	0	1	1	0	2	1	0	0	0	1	1	1	5	0
clatter	27	.6342	3.6050	45.6	6	8	4	1	4	2	2	0	10	1	0	5	0	0	0	0	1	0	0	0	5	3	0	2	0
clattered	14	.5741	1.6802	42.3	3	3	2	2	2	0	2	0	2	2	0	1	0	0	0	0	0	0	0	0	4	2	0	3	0
clattering	15	.5563	1.8043	42.6	0	4	2	4	2	2	0	1	6	0	1	4	0	0	0	0	0	0	0	0	0	2	1	1	0
clatters	3	.1144	.1506	31.8	0	0	0	1	0	1	1	0	2	0	0	0	0	0	0	0	0	0	0	1	0	0	0	0	0
Claude	21	.6782	2.8660	44.6	2	2	2	0	1	8	1	5	0	1	1	2	0	1	0	0	4	2	0	0	1	1	3	5	0
Claudia	2	.1605	.0742	28.7	0	0	0	0	1	1	0	0	0	1	1	0	0	0	0	0	0	0	0	0	0	0	0	0	0
Claudio	3	.2088	.1442	31.6	0	1	0	0	0	2	0	0	0	0	0	0	0	0	0	0	2	0	0	0	0	0	1	0	0
Claus	38	.6209	5.0705	47.1	17	9	5	1	1	1	4	0	21	1	0	4	0	0	4	0	0	0	0	0	5	2	0	1	0
clause	91	.3839	7.4123	48.7	0	0	4	1	21	34	30	1	0	45	21	0	11	4	1	0	0	0	0	0	1	0	7	1	0
clauses	55	.4167	4.8532	46.9	0	0	0	0	4	24	27	0	0	32	6	0	14	0	2	0	0	0	0	0	0	0	1	0	0
Clauses	3	.0000	.0328	25.2	0	0	0	3	0	0	0	0	0	3	0	0	0	0	0	0	0	0	0	0	0	0	0	0	0
clave	3	.1852	.1342	31.3	1	0	0	2	0	0	0	0	0	0	0	0	0	0	0	0	2	0	0	0	0	1	0	0	0
Clavel	7	.0000	.0821	29.1	7	0	0	0	0	0	0	0	0	0	0	0	0	0	0	0	0	0	0	0	7	0	0	0	0
claves	14	.0000	.1132	30.5	0	1	6	0	7	0	0	0	0	0	0	0	0	0	0	0	14	0	0	0	0	0	0	0	0
clavichord	2	.0000	.0162	22.1	0	0	1	0	0	0	1	0	0	0	0	0	0	0	0	0	2	0	0	0	0	0	0	0	0
claw	25	.6489	3.4406	45.4	8	6	2	4	4	0	1	0	11	1	0	2	0	0	0	6	0	0	0	0	0	3	1	1	0
clawed	15	.5822	1.8919	42.8	5	1	1	2	4	1	0	1	7	0	0	1	0	0	0	1	0	0	0	0	3	1	2	0	0
clawing	8	.4563	.8202	39.1	0	2	1	1	3	0	1	0	3	0	1	0	0	0	1	0	0	0	0	0	2	1	0	1	0
claws	146	.7663	23.082	53.6	45	34	13	22	22	7	2	1	83	5	1	8	0	1	0	18	0	1	0	0	5	16	4	4	0
clay	330	.6467	44.291	56.5	106	51	26	28	64	24	16	15	82	3	2	5	14	26	5	58	3	40	3	29	1	17	18	24	0
Clay	27	.5589	3.3464	45.2	7	7	3	0	8	2	0	0	15	0	0	0	2	2	0	0	0	0	0	0	0	6	1	1	0
Clay's	3	.0000	.1370	31.4	0	0	0	0	3	0	0	0	3	0	0	0	0	0	0	0	0	0	0	0	0	0	0	0	0
claymores	2	.0000	.0162	22.1	0	0	0	1	0	1	0	0	0	0	0	0	0	0	0	0	2	0	0	0	0	0	0	0	0
clays	5	.0000	.0986	29.9	1	0	0	0	0	0	3	1	0	0	0	0	0	0	0	5	0	0	0	0	0	0	0	0	0
Clayte	2	.0000	.0914	29.6	0	2	0	0	0	0	0	0	2	0	0	0	0	0	0	0	0	0	0	0	0	0	0	0	0
Clayton	4	.3856	.3384	35.3	2	0	1	0	1	0	0	0	0	0	0	0	0	2	0	0	1	0	0	0	0	0	1	0	0
clean	521	.9090	94.020	59.7	118	89	57	56	84	75	32	10	121	13	5	31	0	42	19	78	11	9	31	24	50	38	15	33	1
clean-cut	4	.4111	.3368	35.3	0	0	0	0	1	0	3	0	0	0	0	1	0	0	0	0	1	1	0	1	0	0	0	0	0
cleaned	112	.8117	18.351	52.6	34	20	15	5	11	15	12	0	36	6	1	2	1	16	1	8	0	1	8	7	8	8	6	3	0
cleaner	32	.6999	4.6436	46.7	13	7	0	0	7	4	1	0	12	0	2	3	0	4	0	3	0	0	1	0	2	0	1	4	0
cleaner-upper	2	.0000	.0914	29.6	2	0	0	0	0	0	0	0	2	0	0	0	0	0	0	0	0	0	0	0	0	0	0	0	0
cleaners	24	.7814	3.7768	45.8	4	4	5	0	4	3	4	0	3	1	1	0	2	5	0	4	0	1	1	1	0	0	4	1	0
cleaning	100	.7215	14.774	51.7	24	12	7	9	12	18	16	2	29	5	1	12	0	4	3	12	1	0	14	1	2	8	1	7	0
cleanliness	21	.3636	1.6898	42.3	3	1	3	0	3	5	6	0	3	0	0	2	0	1	0	1	0	0	8	0	0	2	2	2	0

9R clap-and-stomp
7J clap-snap
6C clapboarding
5Q clapboards
7N clapperdogeons
7A claps'd
8R Clapton's
4A Clara's
8D Clarences

4A Claribel
7L clarification
9F clarifying
7J Clarinet
8J clarinet's
8J clarinetist
6E Clarks
3P claspers
4H clasping

8N claspknife
9Q Class-J
8J Classicism
8Q classicists
9K Classicists
XR Classified
5P classless
7R Classroom
6A classroom-offices

8B classwork
8A Claude's
7Q Claudian
6B Claudine
8H Claudius
4A Claus'
4N Claus's
5Q Clause
7P clavier

8J Clavier
3P CLAW
3A Claws
6F clay-brick
8P claybank
3P claybanks
9H claylike
5J claymore
4P Claypoole

9L clean-finish
4N clean-looking
9D clean-out
8R clean-shaven
4R clean-up
5D cleaner's

Word Type	F	D	U	SFI	3 Gr 3	4 Gr 4	5 Gr 5	6 Gr 6	7 Gr 7	8 Gr 8	9 Gr 9	X UnGr	A Read	B Eng & Gr	C Comp	D Lit	E Math	F Soc Stud	G Spell	H Sci	J Music	K Art	L Home Ec	M Shop	N Lib F	P Lib NF	Q Lib Ref	R Mag	S Rel
cleanly	9	.6258	1.1602	40.6	1	1	0	1	4	0	2	0	1	2	0	1	0	1	0	0	0	0	0	0	1	0	2	1	0
cleans	12	.6058	1.5384	41.9	6	2	0	1	3	0	0	0	3	1	0	1	0	0	0	4	0	0	0	0	1	2	0	0	0
cleanse	3	.2887	.1947	32.9	0	0	1	1	0	1	0	0	0	0	0	0	0	1	0	0	0	0	1	0	1	0	0	0	0
cleansed	4	.4452	.3980	36.0	0	0	0	0	3	0	0	1	1	0	0	1	0	0	0	1	0	0	0	0	0	0	1	0	0
cleansers	2	.0000	.0219	23.4	0	0	0	0	0	0	2	0	0	2	0	0	0	0	0	0	0	0	0	0	0	0	0	0	0
cleansing	9	.4794	.9377	39.7	0	0	0	0	3	3	3	0	2	0	0	1	0	1	0	1	0	0	2	0	0	1	1	0	0
cleanup	15	.3748	1.2344	40.9	2	0	2	3	7	0	1	0	0	1	0	0	0	0	0	1	0	0	0	0	0	8	0	5	0
clear	811	.9266	148.94	61.7	91	115	82	117	179	100	104	23	203	74	25	59	12	71	12	91	21	12	9	6	42	72	31	71	0
Clear	2	.1814	.1187	30.7	0	1	0	1	0	0	0	0	1	0	0	0	0	0	0	0	0	0	0	0	0	0	0	1	0
clear-air	3	.2427	.1822	32.6	0	0	0	0	3	0	0	0	0	0	0	0	0	0	0	2	0	0	0	0	0	0	0	1	0
clear-cut	8	.4707	.7833	38.9	0	0	0	0	4	1	3	0	0	2	0	0	0	0	0	0	0	0	0	1	0	0	2	3	0
clear-headed	2	.1717	.1142	30.6	0	0	0	1	0	0	1	0	1	0	0	1	0	0	0	0	0	0	0	0	0	0	0	0	0
clearance	11	.5604	1.2986	41.1	0	0	1	4	4	2	0	0	2	0	0	0	3	0	0	0	0	0	0	1	0	1	2	2	0
cleared	152	.7956	24.517	53.9	23	18	19	31	38	13	9	1	49	2	3	16	1	30	1	4	1	0	0	0	16	10	6	13	0
clearer	38	.7403	5.7090	47.6	3	3	8	4	4	3	12	1	7	11	0	5	3	2	0	2	0	0	1	1	2	1	0	3	0
clearest	8	.5114	.8587	39.3	0	0	2	0	2	3	1	0	1	0	1	1	0	1	0	0	0	0	0	1	0	0	3	0	0
clearing	113	.7158	16.711	52.2	21	20	19	20	24	3	3	3	42	1	1	4	0	14	0	0	1	0	0	0	24	12	5	9	0
clearinghouse	2	.2285	.1129	30.5	0	0	0	0	0	1	1	0	0	0	0	0	0	1	0	0	0	0	0	0	0	0	1	0	0
clearings	9	.3932	.8037	39.1	1	1	1	3	2	1	0	0	1	0	0	0	0	5	0	0	0	0	0	0	0	1	2	0	0
clearly	305	.9319	56.226	57.5	22	34	38	39	73	37	50	12	48	43	11	16	18	29	13	37	15	5	2	4	7	19	19	18	1
clearness	3	.2227	.1495	31.7	1	0	1	0	1	0	0	0	0	0	0	0	0	0	0	0	0	0	0	1	0	0	2	0	0
clears	8	.6162	1.0401	40.2	1	1	2	0	1	3	0	0	2	0	0	1	0	1	0	2	0	0	0	0	0	1	1	0	0
Clearwater	23	.0615	.5315	37.3	0	22	0	1	0	0	0	0	0	0	0	0	0	0	0	0	0	0	0	0	22	0	0	1	0
cleats	4	.0000	.0101	20.0	0	0	0	0	0	4	0	0	0	0	0	0	0	0	0	0	0	0	0	4	0	0	0	0	0
cleavage	12	.2554	.7676	38.9	0	0	0	2	0	1	1	8	0	0	0	0	0	0	0	10	0	0	0	0	0	1	1	0	0
cleavages	2	.2446	.1257	31.0	0	0	0	0	0	1	0	1	0	0	0	0	0	1	0	1	0	0	0	0	0	0	0	0	0
cleave	2	.1717	.1142	30.6	0	1	0	0	0	1	0	0	1	0	0	1	0	0	0	0	0	0	0	0	0	0	0	0	0
Cleevendon	5	.0000	.0547	27.4	0	0	0	0	0	0	5	0	0	5	0	0	0	0	0	0	0	0	0	0	0	0	0	0	0
clef	19	.0000	.1536	31.9	1	2	4	3	9	0	0	0	0	0	0	0	0	0	0	0	19	0	0	0	0	0	0	0	0
clefs	3	.0000	.0243	23.8	0	0	1	0	2	0	0	0	0	0	0	0	0	0	0	0	3	0	0	0	0	0	0	0	0
cleft	12	.3382	.9384	39.7	1	0	1	2	6	0	2	0	2	0	0	7	0	0	0	1	0	0	0	0	0	1	0	1	0
Cleges	2	.0000	.0914	29.6	0	0	0	2	0	0	0	0	2	0	0	0	0	0	0	0	0	0	0	0	0	0	0	0	0
Cleland	2	.0000	.0290	24.6	0	2	0	0	0	0	0	0	0	0	0	0	0	0	0	0	0	0	0	0	0	2	0	0	0
Clem	5	.0000	.0724	28.6	0	5	0	0	0	0	0	0	0	0	0	0	0	0	0	0	0	0	0	0	0	5	0	0	0
Clemens	7	.4671	.7406	38.7	0	2	1	1	2	1	0	0	3	1	0	0	0	0	0	0	0	0	0	0	1	0	0	2	0
Clement	14	.3076	1.1733	40.7	1	8	4	0	1	0	0	0	9	0	0	0	0	1	0	0	0	0	0	0	0	0	4	0	0
Clement's	2	.0000	.0914	29.6	0	2	0	0	0	0	0	0	2	0	0	0	0	0	0	0	0	0	0	0	0	0	0	0	0
Clementine	12	.0000	.0970	29.9	0	7	2	2	1	0	0	0	0	0	0	0	0	0	0	0	12	0	0	0	0	0	0	0	0
clench	2	.2446	.1257	31.0	0	1	1	0	0	0	0	0	0	0	0	0	0	1	0	1	0	0	0	0	0	0	0	0	0
clenched	13	.5357	1.5055	41.8	1	2	3	2	4	0	0	1	4	0	0	2	0	0	0	0	0	0	0	0	3	3	0	1	0
clenching	3	.2261	.2131	33.3	0	2	1	0	0	0	0	0	2	0	0	0	0	0	0	0	0	0	0	0	1	0	0	0	0
Cleng	7	.0000	.3198	35.0	0	0	0	7	0	0	0	0	7	0	0	0	0	0	0	0	0	0	0	0	0	0	0	0	0
Cleopatra	2	.1473	.0686	28.4	0	0	1	0	0	0	1	0	0	0	0	1	0	0	0	0	0	1	0	0	0	0	0	0	0
clergy	13	.5763	1.5532	41.9	0	0	1	1	1	1	9	0	0	0	1	1	0	6	0	0	1	0	0	0	0	2	0	2	0
clergyman	12	.5230	1.3140	41.2	1	1	1	1	4	0	3	1	1	1	0	5	0	0	0	0	0	0	1	0	0	3	0	1	0
clergymen	2	.2351	.1166	30.7	0	0	1	0	1	0	0	0	0	0	0	0	0	1	0	0	0	0	0	0	0	0	0	1	0
clerical	7	.1334	.2484	34.0	0	0	0	0	5	0	2	0	0	0	0	0	0	0	0	0	0	0	0	0	0	0	6	1	0
clerics	2	.2433	.1158	30.6	0	0	1	0	0	1	0	0	0	0	0	0	0	0	0	0	0	0	0	0	0	1	0	1	0
clerk	104	.8125	16.985	52.3	32	15	9	7	21	10	8	2	21	6	2	6	35	5	5	1	1	0	2	0	2	5	9	4	0
Clerk	17	.5023	1.8998	42.8	8	0	0	0	6	1	2	0	7	0	0	1	0	0	0	1	0	0	0	0	6	1	1	0	0
CLERK	3	.0000	.0322	25.1	0	0	0	0	3	0	0	0	0	0	0	3	0	0	0	0	0	0	0	0	0	0	0	0	0
clerk's	4	.3695	.3354	35.3	0	0	0	0	1	1	2	0	1	0	0	1	0	0	0	0	0	0	1	0	1	0	0	0	0
Clerk's	2	.2427	.1152	30.6	1	0	0	0	1	0	0	0	0	0	0	0	0	0	0	0	0	0	0	0	1	1	0	0	0
clerks	20	.6666	2.7719	44.4	1	0	5	1	4	7	1	1	5	0	0	0	3	5	0	0	0	0	0	0	2	2	2	1	0
Clermont	5	.3926	.4468	36.5	1	2	2	0	0	0	0	0	1	0	0	0	0	1	0	0	0	0	0	0	0	1	2	0	0
Cleveland	39	.7455	5.9115	47.7	4	6	5	5	5	6	8	0	8	2	0	3	6	5	0	0	1	0	0	0	1	1	5	7	0
Cleveland's	2	.0000	.0243	23.9	0	0	0	0	1	1	0	0	0	0	0	0	0	0	0	0	0	0	0	0	0	0	0	2	0
clever	128	.8328	21.551	53.3	23	30	22	17	13	16	5	2	63	5	3	8	0	5	3	2	6	3	1	0	15	11	2	1	0
cleverer	2	.2444	.1132	30.5	0	1	0	1	0	0	0	0	0	1	0	0	0	0	0	0	0	0	0	0	1	0	0	0	0
cleverest	6	.3531	.5259	37.2	1	0	2	2	1	0	0	0	3	1	0	2	0	0	0	0	0	0	0	0	0	0	0	0	0
cleverly	9	.5158	1.0117	40.1	2	1	0	3	0	2	1	0	3	0	0	0	0	0	0	0	0	0	1	0	1	2	0	2	0
cleverness	9	.4691	.9599	39.8	1	1	2	3	1	0	1	0	4	0	0	2	0	0	0	0	0	0	0	0	0	2	0	1	0
Cleves	2	.0000	.0209	23.2	0	0	2	0	0	0	0	0	0	0	0	0	0	0	0	0	0	0	0	0	0	0	2	0	0
cliche	4	.2073	.2003	33.0	0	0	0	0	0	1	1	2	0	0	0	1	0	0	0	0	0	0	0	0	0	0	0	3	0
cliches	3	.2270	.1588	32.0	0	0	0	2	0	1	0	0	0	2	0	0	0	0	0	0	0	0	0	0	0	0	1	0	0
click	31	.7294	4.6336	46.7	3	7	7	4	7	2	0	1	9	1	0	4	0	1	0	4	3	0	0	0	2	3	0	4	0
clicked	12	.6164	1.5624	41.9	2	1	4	1	1	3	0	0	4	0	1	2	0	1	0	1	0	0	0	0	1	1	0	1	0
clicket	4	.0000	.1827	32.6	0	4	0	0	0	0	0	0	4	0	0	0	0	0	0	0	0	0	0	0	0	0	0	0	0
clickety-clack	2	.0000	.0914	29.6	1	0	1	0	0	0	0	0	2	0	0	0	0	0	0	0	0	0	0	0	0	0	0	0	0
clicking	22	.6786	3.0634	44.9	4	4	2	3	5	1	2	1	4	1	2	0	0	2	0	2	2	0	0	0	4	2	1	2	0
clicks	13	.2284	.8145	39.1	0	1	1	3	2	5	1	0	2	1	0	0	0	0	0	10	0	0	0	0	0	0	0	0	0
client	14	.5378	1.5564	41.9	0	2	0	0	2	3	4	3	0	1	0	5	1	0	0	0	0	0	0	0	2	1	0	4	0
clients	4	.4538	.4020	36.0	0	0	1	0	1	1	1	0	1	0	0	1	0	0	0	0	0	0	0	0	0	1	0	1	0
cliff	94	.8146	15.483	51.9	12	10	14	25	12	12	9	0	34	5	1	10	2	7	0	6	1	0	0	0	9	3	4	12	0
Cliff	62	.4840	7.1687	48.6	0	4	4	1	2	51	0	0	51	2	0	0	2	0	0	0	0	0	0	0	0	1	3	3	0
cliff-dwelling	2	.0000	.0389	25.9	0	0	0	0	0	2	0	0	0	0	0	0	0	2	0	0	0	0	0	0	0	0	0	0	0
cliff-top	2	.2401	.1133	30.5	0	0	0	0	2	0	0	0	0	0	0	0	0	0	0	0	0	0	0	0	0	1	1	0	0
Cliff's	8	.0000	.3655	35.6	0	0	0	0	0	8	0	0	8	0	0	0	0	0	0	0	0	0	0	0	0	0	0	0	0
Clifford	6	.4540	.5766	37.6	0	2	0	1	0	0	2	1	0	2	0	0	1	0	0	0	0	0	0	0	0	1	0	2	0
cliffs	56	.7456	8.5083	49.3	6	8	12	8	9	5	6	2	12	1	0	5	0	11	0	6	2	0	0	0	1	3	5	10	0
Cliffs	4	.0000	.0579	27.6	2	0	2	0	0	0	0	0	0	0	0	0	0	0	0	0	0	0	0	0	0	4	0	0	0
climactic	3	.2071	.1434	31.6	0	0	0	0	1	0	2	0	0	0	0	1	0	0	0	0	2	0	0	0	0	0	0	0	0
climate	451	.5342	51.332	57.1	35	61	120	70	80	33	47	5	21	4	0	2	0	255	3	83	2	0	0	1	0	12	58	10	0
Climate	5	.3554	.4063	36.1	0	0	1	0	4	0	0	0	0	0	0	0	0	3	0	1	0	0	0	0	0	0	1	0	0
climates	72	.5952	8.9293	49.5	10	12	13	3	19	6	8	1	3	0	0	1	0	19	0	25	2	0	0	1	0	1	18	2	0
climatic	19	.4610	1.9085	42.8	0	1	1	1	7	2	7	0	1	0	0	0	0	6	0	6	0	0	0	0	0	1	5	0	0
climax	44	.4403	4.0423	46.1	0	4	9	2	15	4	9	1	2	5	11	3	1	0	0	0	14	0	0	0	0	0	5	3	0
climaxed	7	.4461	.6812	38.3	1	0	2	0	1	1	2	0	1	1	0	0	0	1	0	0	0	0	0	0	0	1	3	0	0
climaxes	3	.2297	.1496	31.7	0	0	0	1	1	0	1	0	0	0	1	0	0	0	0	0	2	0	0	0	0	0	0	0	0
climb	288	.8693	50.185	57.0	75	68	37	53	31	9	8	7	111	5	6	15	2	25	5	32	4	2	0	0	18	34	9	20	0
climbed	424	.8233	70.640	58.5	111	98	59	55	62	17	17	5	188	15	10	39	4	21	2	12	5	1	0	2	50	53	4	18	0
climber	14	.4754	1.5330	41.9	1	2	5	2	3	1	0	0	7	0	0	1	0	4	0	0	1	0	0	0	0	0	2	0	0
climbers	22	.6278	2.8983	44.6	7	0	3	2	4	5	1	0	6	2	0	2	0	1	0	2	0	0	0	0	0	6	3	0	0
climbing	127	.7692	19.932	53.0	21	20	16	18	28	11	11	2	48	4	0	13	1	5	1	11	0	6	1	0	6	11	9	11	0
climbs	38	.7610	5.8504	47.7	7	7	4	2	13	2	0	3	4	2	0	2	3	5	0	9	0	0	1	0	0	4	1	7	0
climes	2	.2285	.1129	30.5	0	0	0	0	1	1	0	0	0	0	0	0	0	1	0	0	0	0	0	0	0	0	1	0	0

5A cleanness
6R cleanups
7R Clear-Air
5Q clear-minded
9M clearances
4E Clearfield
6A clearin'
8J clearly-written
8D Clears
4N Clearwater's
6D cleat
6R cleaver
8R Cleaver
7A cleaves
9D cleaving
7Q clefts
4H clematis
7R Clements
XR Clendenin
7Q cleric
9F Clericis
3R clerihews
5Q clerked
7Q Clerks
3Q Clermont-Ferrand
7F cleverly-made
9D Cliburn's
6A Cliche
3P Click
4H click-click
3A click-click-click-CLICK
XR clicker
3P clickety
3A clickety-click
7F clientele
7Q clients'
6R cliff's
6A clifflike
9K cliffside
7A Clifton
3H CLIMATE
5Q climatologists
3A Climax
7R climb-out
4A climber's
XB climbing-rope
4P climbing's
9D clime

Word Type	F	D	U	SFI	3 Gr 3	4 Gr 4	5 Gr 5	6 Gr 6	7 Gr 7	8 Gr 8	9 Gr 9	X UnGr	A Read	B Eng & Gr	C Comp	D Lit	E Math	F Soc Stud	G Spell	H Sci	J Music	K Art	L Home Ec	M Shop	N Lib F	P Lib NF	Q Lib Ref	R Mag	S Rel
Clinch	3	.0000	.0434	26.4	0	0	2	0	0	0	1	0	0	0	0	0	0	0	0	0	0	0	0	0	0	3	0	0	0
clinched	3	.2175	.1545	31.9	0	0	0	0	1	2	0	0	0	0	0	2	0	0	0	0	0	0	0	0	0	0	0	1	0
clincher	3	.0000	.0328	25.2	0	0	0	0	0	0	3	0	0	3	0	0	0	0	0	0	0	0	0	0	0	0	0	0	0
cling	36	.7539	5.5283	47.4	3	8	6	5	6	4	2	2	10	2	0	0	0	1	0	6	0	0	2	1	3	3	6	2	0
clinging	42	.7454	6.4252	48.1	2	6	8	6	12	3	3	2	16	0	0	3	0	2	0	3	2	0	0	0	6	3	3	4	0
clings	12	.5193	1.3051	41.2	1	1	1	1	2	3	3	0	0	0	0	1	0	0	0	5	0	0	2	0	0	2	1	1	0
clinic	16	.5146	1.7759	42.5	0	0	0	4	5	3	3	1	2	0	0	0	0	3	0	4	0	0	0	0	0	5	0	2	0
Clinic	4	.2011	.1965	32.9	0	0	1	0	1	1	0	1	0	0	0	0	0	0	0	0	0	0	0	0	1	0	0	3	0
clinical	8	.4738	.8298	39.2	0	0	0	0	3	2	2	1	2	0	0	0	0	0	0	1	0	0	1	0	0	0	1	3	0
clinics	12	.3653	.9876	39.9	3	0	0	1	1	7	0	0	0	0	0	0	0	3	0	5	0	0	0	0	0	0	4	0	0
clink	7	.4086	.6518	38.1	2	0	1	1	2	0	1	0	2	0	0	1	0	0	0	0	0	0	0	0	3	1	0	0	0
clinked	2	.1621	.0746	28.7	0	0	0	0	1	0	1	0	0	0	1	1	0	0	0	0	0	0	0	0	0	0	0	0	0
Clint	6	.1250	.2684	34.3	0	6	0	0	0	0	0	0	2	0	0	0	0	0	0	0	0	0	0	0	4	0	0	0	0
Clinton	37	.4266	3.9268	45.9	0	1	1	0	31	4	0	0	29	0	0	0	0	3	0	0	0	0	0	0	0	0	3	2	0
Clinton's	2	.0000	.0914	29.6	0	0	0	0	2	0	0	0	2	0	0	0	0	0	0	0	0	0	0	0	0	0	0	0	0
clip	41	.3914	3.5350	45.5	5	5	5	3	12	3	6	2	4	0	0	0	2	1	1	13	0	0	13	0	0	3	2	2	0
clipboard	2	.1948	.1250	31.0	1	1	0	0	0	0	0	0	1	0	0	0	0	0	0	0	0	0	0	0	0	1	0	0	0
clipped	17	.5980	2.1684	43.4	0	2	4	6	2	1	1	1	7	2	0	0	0	0	3	0	0	0	1	0	1	3	0	0	0
clipper	28	.5633	3.4476	45.4	9	2	7	4	0	5	1	0	12	0	0	1	0	6	0	0	1	0	0	0	0	7	0	1	0
Clipper	23	.1333	1.4860	41.7	6	4	9	4	0	0	0	0	22	0	0	0	0	0	0	0	0	0	0	0	0	1	0	0	0
clippers	7	.3246	.5299	37.2	2	0	4	1	0	0	0	0	0	0	0	0	0	5	0	0	0	0	0	0	1	1	0	0	0
clippety-clop	2	.0000	.0914	29.6	1	1	0	0	0	0	0	0	2	0	0	0	0	0	0	0	0	0	0	0	0	0	0	0	0
clipping	21	.7284	3.0971	44.9	2	2	7	0	3	0	7	0	4	2	1	4	0	0	4	0	0	0	1	1	3	0	0	1	0
clippings	15	.5317	1.7345	42.4	3	1	4	0	2	2	3	0	4	0	0	0	3	0	0	3	0	0	0	0	0	4	0	1	0
clippity	2	.0000	.0914	29.6	2	0	0	0	0	0	0	0	2	0	0	0	0	0	0	0	0	0	0	0	0	0	0	0	0
clips	30	.4927	3.1845	45.0	13	4	1	1	2	3	5	1	4	0	0	1	0	0	0	14	0	0	1	5	0	3	1	1	0
Clive	2	.2351	.1166	30.7	0	0	0	0	0	0	2	0	0	0	0	0	0	1	0	0	0	0	0	0	0	0	0	1	0
cloaca	2	.0000	.0209	23.2	0	0	0	0	2	0	0	0	0	0	0	0	0	0	0	0	0	0	0	0	0	0	2	0	0
cloak	42	.6962	6.0758	47.8	6	3	5	16	5	4	3	0	17	2	0	9	0	4	0	0	2	0	0	0	3	2	2	1	0
Cloak	2	.1948	.1250	31.0	0	0	1	0	1	0	0	0	1	0	0	0	0	0	0	0	0	0	0	0	0	1	0	0	0
cloakroom	2	.2443	.1130	30.5	1	1	0	0	0	0	0	0	0	0	0	1	0	0	0	0	0	0	0	0	1	0	0	0	0
cloaks	5	.5597	.5840	37.7	0	3	0	1	0	1	0	0	0	0	0	0	0	1	0	1	0	0	0	0	1	1	0	1	0
clobbered	2	.0000	.0243	23.9	0	0	1	0	0	0	0	1	0	0	0	0	0	0	0	0	0	0	0	0	0	0	0	2	0
clock	330	.8339	55.325	57.4	80	63	48	45	37	39	17	1	96	16	10	21	65	14	11	30	13	0	0	0	22	11	2	19	0
Clock	4	.0000	.0323	25.1	4	0	0	0	0	0	0	0	0	0	0	0	0	0	0	0	4	0	0	0	0	0	0	0	0
clock-work	2	.0000	.0162	22.1	0	0	0	0	2	0	0	0	0	0	0	0	0	0	0	0	2	0	0	0	0	0	0	0	0
clocked	4	.2847	.2818	34.5	0	1	0	0	2	0	0	1	1	0	0	0	0	0	0	0	0	0	0	0	0	1	2	0	0
clockface	4	.0000	.0599	27.8	1	0	3	0	0	0	0	0	0	0	0	0	4	0	0	0	0	0	0	0	0	0	0	0	0
clockface-to	2	.0000	.0299	24.8	0	0	2	0	0	0	0	0	0	0	0	0	2	0	0	0	0	0	0	0	0	0	0	0	0
clocks	72	.7925	11.611	50.6	15	17	15	5	7	7	5	1	27	3	1	2	15	9	0	8	0	0	0	1	3	1	1	1	0
clockwise	26	.5403	2.9285	44.7	0	1	2	2	15	2	4	0	1	0	0	1	17	0	0	1	2	0	1	2	0	0	1	0	0
clockwork	8	.4071	.7032	38.5	0	1	1	0	5	0	1	0	0	0	0	0	0	1	0	2	3	0	0	0	2	0	0	0	0
clods	3	.3831	.2447	33.9	0	0	0	1	0	2	0	0	0	0	0	1	0	0	0	0	1	0	0	0	1	0	0	0	0
clog	2	.2446	.1257	31.0	0	1	0	0	1	0	0	0	0	0	0	0	0	1	0	1	0	0	0	0	0	0	0	0	0
clogged	6	.2827	.4028	36.1	0	0	0	3	1	1	1	0	1	0	0	0	0	0	0	0	0	0	0	1	0	0	0	4	0
clogs	7	.2445	.5383	37.3	3	1	0	3	0	0	0	0	5	0	0	0	0	2	0	0	0	0	0	0	0	0	0	0	0
cloister	3	.0000	.0365	25.6	0	0	0	0	0	0	3	0	0	0	0	0	0	0	0	0	0	0	0	0	0	0	0	3	0
cloistered	3	.0000	.0365	25.6	0	0	0	0	0	0	3	0	0	0	0	0	0	0	0	0	0	0	0	0	0	0	0	3	0
clomp	3	.2332	.1690	32.3	0	3	0	0	0	0	0	0	0	0	0	0	0	0	0	0	0	0	0	0	0	2	0	1	0
clong	2	.0000	.0914	29.6	0	0	0	2	0	0	0	0	2	0	0	0	0	0	0	0	0	0	0	0	0	0	0	0	0
clop	5	.3676	.4505	36.5	3	0	0	2	0	0	0	0	2	1	0	0	0	2	0	0	0	0	0	0	0	0	0	0	0
close	1288	.9800	248.66	64.0	201	240	143	172	261	136	111	24	421	45	14	71	31	108	44	122	36	14	33	16	81	145	46	60	1
close-cropped	2	.2440	.1132	30.5	0	0	0	0	2	0	0	0	0	0	0	1	0	0	0	0	0	0	0	0	0	0	0	1	0
close-up	8	.4630	.8219	39.1	1	0	0	3	4	0	0	0	2	0	0	1	0	1	0	2	0	1	0	0	0	0	0	1	0
closed	595	.9058	107.15	60.3	88	104	76	61	101	87	67	11	166	12	5	52	117	24	19	40	13	1	3	8	57	36	15	27	0
Closed	3	.2390	.1719	32.4	2	0	1	0	0	0	0	0	0	0	0	1	2	0	0	0	0	0	0	0	0	0	0	0	0
closed-circuit	4	.2442	.2268	33.6	0	0	1	0	2	0	1	0	0	2	0	0	0	0	0	0	0	0	0	0	0	0	0	2	0
closely	307	.9238	56.161	57.5	34	37	26	32	70	61	42	5	51	34	4	10	6	19	12	65	14	7	12	5	10	18	27	13	0
closely-woven	2	.2137	.1056	30.2	0	0	0	0	1	1	0	0	0	0	0	0	0	1	0	0	1	0	0	0	0	0	0	0	0
closeness	9	.5603	1.0614	40.3	1	0	2	0	3	2	1	0	2	0	0	1	0	0	0	1	0	1	1	0	0	0	2	1	0
closer	354	.9219	64.792	58.1	63	82	45	55	61	24	21	3	108	10	1	15	49	33	5	36	6	2	2	1	22	33	9	22	0
closes	45	.7102	6.5555	48.2	11	3	4	8	9	7	1	2	11	0	0	2	0	5	1	8	7	0	0	3	3	3	3	2	0
closest	82	.8326	13.623	51.3	4	25	6	6	17	12	10	2	3	1	2	0	24	8	2	13	4	0	1	3	5	3	3	10	0
closet	74	.7318	11.112	50.5	19	10	20	3	10	7	4	1	26	0	1	6	0	3	3	6	0	0	7	0	10	6	1	5	0
Closet	3	.0000	.0365	25.6	0	0	0	0	3	0	0	0	0	0	0	0	0	0	0	0	0	0	0	0	0	0	0	3	0
closets	9	.4687	.9286	39.7	2	0	2	0	4	1	0	0	3	0	0	1	0	1	0	0	0	1	2	0	0	0	0	1	0
closing	104	.8675	17.985	52.5	11	26	9	15	26	12	3	2	23	23	2	11	1	2	4	5	4	1	6	1	7	5	2	7	0
closings	8	.3787	.6395	38.1	2	4	0	1	1	0	0	0	0	6	1	0	0	0	0	0	0	0	1	0	0	0	0	0	0
closure	19	.2337	1.0454	40.2	0	0	2	0	6	4	7	0	0	0	0	0	14	0	0	0	0	0	5	0	0	0	0	0	0
clot	6	.3463	.4770	36.8	0	0	3	0	2	0	1	0	0	0	0	0	0	0	0	4	0	0	0	0	1	1	0	0	0
cloth	427	.8307	71.334	58.5	117	92	57	50	41	28	35	7	114	6	3	9	16	103	7	54	1	10	30	16	16	20	13	9	0
cloth-covered	4	.1948	.2500	34.0	1	3	0	0	0	0	0	0	2	0	0	0	0	0	0	0	0	0	0	0	0	2	0	0	0
clothe	14	.6748	1.9639	42.9	1	2	3	2	2	3	1	0	4	1	0	2	0	2	1	2	0	0	0	0	0	2	0	0	0
clothed	17	.3037	1.1807	40.7	3	0	2	1	5	3	3	0	1	1	0	1	0	2	0	1	2	0	0	0	4	1	1	2	0
clothes	678	.7574	104.40	60.2	178	112	56	73	102	72	71	14	180	22	3	42	4	75	17	76	9	4	92	5	49	60	7	33	1
Clothes	2	.0000	.0914	29.6	0	0	0	2	0	0	0	0	2	0	0	0	0	0	0	0	0	0	0	0	0	0	0	0	0
clothesline	15	.6217	1.9105	42.8	3	5	2	1	2	0	0	2	1	3	1	0	0	0	0	2	0	1	0	0	5	1	1	0	0
clotheslines	2	.1733	.1149	30.6	1	0	0	0	1	0	0	0	1	1	0	0	0	0	0	0	0	0	0	0	0	0	0	0	0
clothespin	5	.2000	.2712	34.3	0	1	4	0	0	0	0	0	0	0	0	0	0	0	0	4	0	0	0	0	0	1	0	0	0
clothespins	4	.2405	.2474	33.9	0	2	1	0	1	0	0	0	1	0	1	0	0	0	0	0	0	0	0	0	0	2	0	0	0
clothing	348	.7670	53.867	57.3	68	53	45	38	45	37	56	6	42	13	3	7	8	97	7	40	4	4	48	3	9	22	23	18	0
cloths	16	.5415	1.8797	42.7	3	4	2	1	3	0	3	0	6	0	0	3	0	0	0	2	0	0	2	0	2	0	1	0	0
clots	4	.2335	.2373	33.8	0	0	3	0	0	0	1	0	0	1	0	0	0	0	0	3	0	0	0	0	0	0	0	0	0
clotted	3	.2266	.1614	32.1	0	0	0	0	2	0	0	1	0	0	0	0	0	0	0	0	0	0	0	0	1	0	0	2	0
clotting	3	.2445	.1818	32.6	0	0	1	2	0	0	0	0	0	0	0	0	0	0	0	2	0	0	0	0	0	0	1	0	0
cloud	314	.7570	48.483	56.9	61	44	42	51	56	18	37	5	85	13	11	16	3	5	3	104	7	0	0	2	15	25	9	14	2
Cloud	27	.3458	2.5622	44.1	19	0	0	1	0	5	1	1	23	2	0	0	0	1	0	1	0	0	0	0	0	0	0	0	0
cloud-catching's	2	.0000	.0215	23.3	1	1	0	0	0	0	0	0	0	0	0	2	0	0	0	0	0	0	0	0	0	0	0	0	0
Cloud's	3	.2197	.2090	33.2	1	0	1	0	0	1	0	0	2	0	0	0	0	0	0	0	0	0	0	0	0	0	1	0	0
cloudburst	3	.1650	.1684	32.3	0	0	0	1	0	0	2	0	1	0	0	0	0	0	0	2	0	0	0	0	0	0	0	0	0
clouded	8	.3745	.6471	38.1	0	1	0	2	1	2	2	0	0	0	2	1	0	0	0	2	0	0	0	0	0	1	0	2	0
cloudiness	4	.4055	.3448	35.4	0	1	1	0	1	0	1	0	0	0	0	1	0	1	0	0	0	0	1	0	0	0	1	0	0

4A clinch
7P Cline
7Q clingfish
3P clinking
XH clinoenstatite
XH clinohypersthene
5A clip-clop
8D clip-clopping
4J clipe
5A Clipper's
6A clippity-clop
8D clique
7L cliques
3B clob
7R clobber
7N clobbering
7Q clock-wise
3P clocking
7H clocklike
6R clodbusters
8N clodhopper
8D clodhoppers
9R Cloggers
8F clogging
5Q cloisonne
9R cloisters
9R clomped
3N clomping
6A Clooney
4P clop-clop
9C clopping
4A cloppity-clop
7Q closable
7N close-drawn
4Q close-fitting
5Q close-grained
7C close-growing
5R close-harmony
6A close-lying
7A close-mouthed
6A close-pressing
6F close-set
4F close-to-shore
7B close-trimmed
7A close-wrapped
3R CLOSED
7Q closed-canopy
6R closed-circuit
3A closed-in
7P closed-up
7B Closer
4A CLOSER
XB closer-fitting
6N CLOSES
7R closeted
5P closeup
7L closures
7Q Cloth
4P cloth-wrapped
9B clothers
8N clothes-sack
XR Clotheshorse
4P clothespress
7G clothier
9L Clothing
4F clothing-store
7H cloud-cataloguers
5H cloud-cover
6P cloud-covered
3A cloud-like
7N cloud-rack
8D cloud-shrouded
7D cloud-wreathed
4H cloudbursts
7H cloudcap
6R Cloudcroft
9D clouding

Word Type	F	D	U	SFI	3 Gr 3	4 Gr 4	5 Gr 5	6 Gr 6	7 Gr 7	8 Gr 8	9 Gr 9	X UnGr	A Read	B Eng & Gr	C Comp	D Lit	E Math	F Soc Stud	G Spell	H Sci	J Music	K Art	L Home Ec	M Shop	N Lib F	P Lib NF	Q Lib Ref	R Mag	S Rel
cloudless	15	.5510	1.8125	42.6	2	4	1	3	2	0	2	1	7	0	0	1	0	0	0	0	0	0	0	0	2	2	0	3	0
cloudlike	2	.0000	.0394	26.0	0	1	0	0	0	0	0	1	0	0	0	0	0	0	0	2	0	0	0	0	0	0	0	0	0
clouds	489	.8103	79.955	59.0	133	73	42	82	66	36	47	10	109	29	10	24	0	28	0	181	8	4	0	2	15	52	11	16	0
cloudy	53	.7343	7.9553	49.0	10	9	8	6	6	4	6	4	11	5	0	3	0	2	0	19	1	1	0	0	2	7	2	0	0
clout	3	.0000	.0322	25.1	0	0	0	0	2	0	1	0	0	0	0	3	0	0	0	0	0	0	0	0	0	0	0	0	0
clouts	4	.1919	.1864	32.7	0	0	0	0	1	0	3	0	0	0	0	3	0	0	0	0	0	0	0	0	1	0	0	0	0
clove	3	.3086	.2017	33.0	0	0	1	0	0	0	1	1	0	1	0	0	0	0	0	0	0	0	1	0	0	1	0	0	0
clover	80	.7549	12.382	50.9	24	9	8	21	15	1	1	1	29	2	0	8	1	8	2	16	0	0	0	0	2	3	8	1	0
Clover	7	.2052	.3435	35.4	4	0	0	0	1	0	2	0	0	0	0	5	0	0	0	0	0	0	0	0	2	0	0	0	0
clovers	2	.1948	.1250	31.0	1	0	1	0	0	0	0	0	1	0	0	0	0	0	0	0	0	0	0	0	0	1	0	0	0
cloves	13	.5942	1.5937	42.0	1	2	0	3	3	2	0	2	1	0	0	0	0	2	0	1	2	0	2	0	0	1	2	2	0
Clovis	4	.1873	.1827	32.6	2	0	0	0	1	0	0	1	0	0	0	0	0	0	0	0	0	0	0	0	0	0	3	1	0
clown	62	.6433	8.4097	49.2	37	11	2	3	4	2	1	2	28	0	2	0	0	0	5	0	2	4	0	0	15	3	1	2	0
Clown	7	.2176	.4907	36.9	5	0	0	0	0	0	2	0	5	0	0	0	0	0	0	0	2	0	0	0	0	0	0	0	0
clown's	3	.2747	.1980	33.0	1	1	1	0	0	0	0	0	1	0	1	0	0	0	0	0	0	1	0	0	0	0	0	0	0
clowning	2	.0000	.0290	24.6	0	2	0	0	0	0	0	0	0	0	0	0	0	0	0	0	0	0	0	0	0	2	0	0	0
clowns	33	.5794	3.9432	46.0	17	8	1	3	3	0	1	0	4	4	4	0	0	2	1	0	3	5	0	0	5	3	0	2	0
clowns'	2	.0000	.0914	29.6	0	2	0	0	0	0	0	0	2	0	0	0	0	0	0	0	0	0	0	0	0	0	0	0	0
club	244	.8250	40.483	56.1	62	24	21	22	51	35	18	11	70	41	2	10	13	17	6	3	1	0	13	1	16	16	2	33	0
Club	93	.7422	14.139	51.5	15	11	14	11	14	13	6	9	30	12	0	3	5	11	1	2	0	0	0	0	5	6	1	17	0
club's	2	.0000	.0914	29.6	2	0	0	0	0	0	0	0	2	0	0	0	0	0	0	0	0	0	0	0	0	0	0	0	0
Club's	2	.1814	.1187	30.7	0	0	1	0	0	0	1	0	1	0	0	0	0	0	0	0	0	0	0	0	0	0	0	1	0
clubhouse	25	.4786	2.6603	44.2	8	3	1	5	5	0	0	3	9	0	1	1	1	0	1	0	0	0	0	0	0	0	0	12	0
clublike	3	.2347	.1695	32.3	1	1	0	0	1	0	0	0	0	0	0	0	0	0	0	0	0	0	0	0	1	2	0	0	0
clubs	73	.6998	10.580	50.2	14	8	5	9	16	12	6	3	28	7	0	0	1	5	1	2	0	0	7	1	5	5	0	11	0
Clubs	7	.4613	.6854	38.4	2	2	1	0	0	0	2	0	0	0	0	0	0	2	0	0	2	0	0	0	0	2	1	0	0
cluck	7	.4872	.7831	38.9	4	0	0	0	2	0	0	1	4	0	0	1	0	0	0	0	0	0	0	0	0	1	0	1	0
clucked	3	.2357	.2199	33.4	1	1	0	0	0	1	0	0	2	0	0	0	0	0	0	0	0	0	0	0	0	1	0	0	0
clucking	10	.3201	.8929	39.5	1	3	2	0	1	0	1	2	8	0	0	0	0	1	0	0	0	0	0	0	0	0	0	0	0
clucks	2	.1948	.1250	31.0	1	1	0	0	0	0	0	0	1	0	0	0	0	0	0	0	0	0	1	0	0	1	0	0	0
clue	123	.7282	18.258	52.6	3	36	15	23	17	15	13	1	30	8	3	7	6	5	37	10	4	0	0	1	1	7	2	2	0
clues	125	.7469	19.075	52.8	5	25	14	16	34	18	12	1	41	29	3	6	5	4	14	8	1	0	0	0	0	7	3	4	0
clump	36	.7416	5.4369	47.4	5	12	2	4	9	2	2	0	9	1	1	5	0	1	0	5	1	2	0	0	7	1	2	1	0
clumped	2	.1787	.1174	30.7	0	0	0	2	0	0	0	0	1	0	0	0	0	0	0	0	0	0	0	0	1	0	0	0	0
clumps	17	.5509	2.0274	43.1	4	1	1	2	8	1	0	0	6	1	0	0	0	1	0	0	0	0	0	0	1	4	4	0	0
clumsily	7	.5641	.8565	39.3	1	0	0	3	2	1	0	0	3	0	0	1	0	0	0	0	0	0	0	0	0	1	1	1	0
clumsy	50	.8129	8.2184	49.1	4	11	6	9	9	7	4	0	18	0	0	4	0	3	0	4	4	1	1	0	3	8	2	2	0
clung	54	.6113	7.0411	48.5	2	15	8	9	16	3	1	0	22	1	0	5	0	3	0	1	1	0	0	0	13	7	0	2	0
clunk	3	.2009	.1407	31.5	0	0	0	0	1	2	0	0	0	0	0	0	0	0	0	0	2	0	0	0	1	0	0	0	0
cluster	63	.7102	9.1150	49.6	7	2	9	13	22	3	5	2	7	12	1	0	0	7	0	12	0	0	0	0	2	7	11	4	0
clustered	18	.7053	2.6128	44.2	1	3	0	5	9	0	0	0	5	0	0	2	0	2	0	0	1	0	0	0	2	4	1	1	0
clustering	2	.1814	.1187	30.7	0	0	0	0	1	1	0	0	1	0	0	0	0	0	0	0	0	0	0	0	0	0	0	1	0
clusters	51	.7971	8.1498	49.1	1	5	3	6	20	5	6	5	2	5	0	4	0	8	0	9	1	0	1	0	3	6	3	9	0
clutch	27	.6461	3.6236	45.6	2	4	0	2	16	1	2	0	7	0	0	3	0	0	1	1	0	0	0	1	2	1	1	10	0
clutched	27	.5722	3.3353	45.2	1	5	5	6	8	1	1	0	11	1	0	2	0	0	0	0	0	0	0	0	7	4	0	2	0
clutches	2	.0000	.0914	29.6	0	0	1	1	0	0	0	0	2	0	0	0	0	0	0	0	0	0	0	0	0	0	0	0	0
clutching	23	.6698	3.2148	45.1	4	5	2	4	5	1	2	0	9	1	0	0	0	0	0	0	1	0	1	0	0	2	1	2	0
clutter	5	.4223	.4661	36.7	2	1	0	0	1	1	0	0	1	1	0	2	0	0	0	0	0	0	0	0	6	0	1	0	0
Clutterbuck	3	.0000	.1370	31.4	0	0	0	3	0	0	0	0	3	0	0	0	0	0	0	0	0	0	0	0	0	0	0	0	0
cluttered	6	.4091	.5789	37.6	1	0	2	1	0	2	0	0	3	1	0	0	0	0	0	0	0	0	1	0	0	0	0	1	0
cluttering	2	.2440	.1132	30.5	0	1	0	0	0	0	1	0	0	0	0	1	0	0	0	0	0	0	0	0	0	0	0	1	0
Clyde	46	.5352	5.5535	47.4	5	2	28	0	2	7	2	0	29	0	0	6	1	1	0	1	0	0	0	0	0	0	1	7	0
Clyde's	6	.3621	.5367	37.3	0	0	3	0	1	2	0	0	3	0	0	1	0	0	0	0	0	0	0	0	0	0	0	2	0
Clydesdale	3	.3637	.2412	33.8	1	0	0	0	1	1	0	0	0	0	0	0	0	1	1	0	0	0	0	0	0	1	0	0	0
Clyfton	3	.0000	.0434	26.4	0	3	0	0	0	0	0	0	0	0	0	0	0	0	0	0	0	0	0	0	0	3	0	0	0
Clytemnestra	2	.0000	.0290	24.6	0	0	0	0	2	0	0	0	0	0	0	0	0	0	0	0	0	0	0	0	0	2	0	0	0
cm	33	.1282	1.2666	41.0	0	0	9	2	8	7	5	2	0	0	0	0	30	0	0	2	0	0	0	0	0	0	1	0	0
cm3	7	.0000	.1380	31.4	0	0	0	0	0	0	7	0	0	0	0	0	0	0	0	7	0	0	0	0	0	0	0	0	0
co	2	.0000	.0162	22.1	0	0	1	0	1	0	0	0	0	0	0	0	0	0	2	0	0	0	0	0	0	0	0	0	0
Co	27	.3211	1.9534	42.9	0	3	1	3	8	5	1	6	1	1	0	0	0	0	1	2	0	0	0	0	0	0	2	20	0
CO	4	.2191	.2297	33.6	1	0	0	0	1	2	0	0	0	0	0	0	0	0	0	3	0	0	0	0	0	1	0	0	0
Co-hong	2	.0000	.0290	24.6	0	0	2	0	0	0	0	0	0	0	0	0	0	0	0	0	0	0	0	0	0	2	0	0	0
co-op	7	.2565	.4212	36.2	1	0	0	1	1	1	0	3	0	0	0	0	0	1	0	0	0	0	0	0	1	0	0	5	0
co-operate	8	.4761	.8267	39.2	0	0	0	4	0	3	0	1	1	0	0	0	0	4	1	0	0	0	1	0	0	1	0	0	0
co-operating	2	.2130	.1056	30.2	0	0	0	0	0	1	0	1	0	0	0	0	0	0	1	1	0	0	0	0	0	0	0	0	0
co-operation	18	.4002	1.5991	42.0	3	0	0	10	2	3	0	0	0	0	0	1	0	11	0	2	0	0	0	0	0	0	4	0	0
co-operative	7	.2399	.4129	36.2	0	0	0	3	1	1	2	0	0	0	0	0	0	4	0	0	0	0	0	0	0	0	3	0	0
co-operatively	2	.2285	.1129	30.5	1	0	0	0	0	1	0	0	0	0	0	0	0	1	0	0	0	0	0	0	0	0	1	0	0
co-operatives	6	.2062	.3286	35.2	1	0	0	5	0	0	0	0	0	0	0	0	0	5	0	0	0	0	0	0	0	0	1	0	0
co-ops	10	.0848	.2845	34.5	0	0	0	1	0	0	0	9	0	0	0	0	0	1	0	0	0	0	0	0	0	0	0	9	0
co-ordinate	2	.0000	.0219	23.4	0	0	0	0	0	0	2	0	0	2	0	0	0	0	0	0	0	0	0	0	0	0	0	0	0
co-ordinates	2	.0000	.0209	23.2	0	2	0	0	0	0	0	0	0	0	0	0	0	0	0	0	0	0	0	0	0	0	2	0	0
co-ordinating	2	.0000	.0219	23.4	0	0	0	0	2	0	0	0	0	2	0	0	0	0	0	0	0	0	0	0	0	0	0	0	0
co-ordination	2	.2291	.1135	30.5	0	0	0	0	1	1	0	0	0	0	0	1	0	0	0	1	0	0	0	0	0	0	0	0	0
co-pilot	3	.2279	.2143	33.3	0	1	0	0	1	1	0	0	2	0	0	0	0	0	0	0	0	0	0	0	0	0	0	1	0
co-worker	3	.3406	.2461	33.9	1	0	0	1	1	0	1	0	1	1	0	0	0	0	0	0	0	0	0	0	0	0	0	1	0
COA	3	.0000	.0449	26.5	0	0	2	0	0	0	1	0	0	0	0	0	3	0	0	0	0	0	0	0	0	0	0	0	0
coach	147	.7816	23.431	53.7	21	24	17	24	23	26	12	0	63	8	4	8	4	5	1	1	2	0	1	0	7	18	0	25	0
Coach	27	.4307	2.8558	44.6	2	3	9	4	5	2	2	0	20	1	0	0	0	0	0	0	0	0	0	0	0	2	0	4	0
coach's	3	.3265	.2369	33.7	0	0	0	0	3	0	0	0	1	0	0	0	0	0	1	0	0	0	0	0	0	0	0	1	0
coached	3	.1277	.1363	31.3	0	1	0	2	0	0	0	0	1	0	0	0	0	0	0	0	0	0	0	0	0	0	0	2	0
coaches	29	.6683	3.9761	46.0	2	7	3	5	6	3	3	0	3	0	0	2	3	4	1	1	0	0	0	0	1	6	0	8	0
coaching	8	.2177	.5495	37.4	1	0	2	2	1	2	0	0	5	0	0	0	0	0	0	0	0	0	0	0	0	0	0	3	0
coachman	4	.3755	.3686	35.7	2	1	0	0	1	0	0	0	2	0	0	0	0	0	0	0	0	0	0	0	1	1	0	0	0
Coachman	4	.0000	.0469	26.7	4	0	0	0	0	0	0	0	0	0	0	0	0	0	0	0	0	0	0	0	4	0	0	0	0
coal	419	.6933	59.773	57.8	63	43	51	69	86	78	24	5	52	12	0	10	3	192	4	82	2	0	1	3	2	20	30	6	0
Coal	6	.3797	.5821	37.6	1	0	0	4	0	0	1	0	4	0	0	0	0	1	0	0	0	0	0	0	0	1	0	0	0
coal-black	3	.2138	.1721	32.4	0	0	0	0	3	0	0	0	1	0	1	1	0	0	0	0	0	0	0	0	0	0	0	0	0
coal-tar	3	.2227	.1495	31.7	0	0	0	1	0	1	1	0	0	0	0	0	0	0	0	0	0	0	0	1	0	0	2	0	0
coal's	2	.0000	.0389	25.9	0	0	0	0	0	2	0	0	0	0	0	0	0	2	0	0	0	0	0	0	0	0	0	0	0
coalition	7	.3156	.4893	36.9	1	0	1	1	0	3	1	0	0	0	0	0	0	0	0	0	0	0	0	0	0	1	4	2	0
coals	42	.7060	6.0476	47.8	2	15	6	8	7	1	2	1	6	0	1	4	0	3	0	3	0	0	0	0	10	9	4	2	0

7Q Clouds
4D clouds'
6A clouted
3P cloven
6H clover's
8M cloverleaf
9Q cloverleafs
6N clown-faces
9J Clown's
6A clowned
7R clownish
7P cloy
7R cloying
9P Cloyse
XH club-shaped
9N clubbed
3A clubbing
9D clubfoot
XR clubman's
5G clude
8G Cluett
7N clumb
3A clumping
4N clumpy
7Q clumsiest
6A clumsiness
5Q Cluniac
7Q Clupeiformes
7R clutch-pedal
7P clutch'd
6R Clutter
9M clutters
8A Clymer
9H cm3**
9R Co-Producer
XR co-authors
8R co-chairman
8R co-director
XH co-discoverer
6A co-ed
7R co-founder
4H co-inventor
5R Co-op
7A Co-operative
4Q co-ordinated
7D co-pastors
7R co-producer
8R co-producers
8R co-promoter
4R co-star
5R co-stars
XR Co's**
6A Coachella
9D coachmakers
9J coachmen
9Q coadjutor
6J Coady's
6Q coagulated
4Q coagulation
7F Coahuila-Texas
5P coal-bearing
7F coal-blackened
7F coal-digging
3P coal-making
5Q coal-mine
6F coal-producing
4P coalbin
7R coalesce
9Q coalesced
6F coaling
8R Coalition
7P coalitions
7J coalminer
7J Coalminer's
3K Coals
8H Coalsack
9Q coamings

Word Type	F	D	U	SFI	3 Gr 3	4 Gr 4	5 Gr 5	6 Gr 6	7 Gr 7	8 Gr 8	9 Gr 9	X UnGr	A Read	B Eng & Gr	C Comp	D Lit	E Math	F Soc Stud	G Spell	H Sci	J Music	K Art	L Home Ec	M Shop	N Lib F	P Lib NF	Q Lib Ref	R Mag	S Rel
coarse	63	.7468	9.4919	49.8	4	11	7	13	14	7	7	0	6	1	2	3	0	7	0	15	1	5	3	6	3	6	4	1	0
Coarse	2	.0000	.0050	17.0	0	0	0	0	0	0	2	0	0	0	0	0	0	0	0	0	0	0	0	2	0	0	0	0	0
coarse-grained	3	.1540	.1257	31.0	0	0	0	0	1	0	2	0	0	0	0	0	0	0	0	2	0	1	0	0	0	0	0	0	0
coarsely	3	.2433	.1822	32.6	0	0	0	0	1	0	1	1	0	0	0	0	0	0	0	2	0	0	0	0	1	0	0	0	0
coarseness	3	.1101	.0802	29.0	0	0	0	0	2	1	0	0	0	0	0	0	0	0	0	0	0	0	0	2	0	0	0	1	0
coarser	4	.3743	.3215	35.1	0	1	0	0	0	0	3	0	0	1	0	0	0	0	0	1	0	0	0	1	0	0	1	0	0
coast	594	.7432	89.843	59.5	52	94	120	109	111	64	26	18	78	13	1	8	1	282	5	40	17	2	0	2	12	44	54	35	0
Coast	139	.6718	19.359	52.9	8	23	32	11	32	16	14	3	26	0	0	1	4	53	0	16	4	0	0	0	0	12	10	13	0
coast-to-coast	3	.2321	.1635	32.1	0	0	0	0	2	1	0	0	0	0	0	0	0	0	0	0	0	0	0	0	0	0	1	2	0
coastal	114	.4101	10.450	50.2	2	13	33	14	35	5	4	8	4	0	0	0	0	76	0	11	0	0	0	0	0	5	16	2	0
Coastal	13	.3912	1.1359	40.6	1	0	7	0	2	2	1	0	0	0	0	0	0	9	0	0	0	0	0	0	0	1	1	2	0
coasted	5	.3720	.4658	36.7	1	1	1	2	0	0	0	0	3	0	0	0	0	0	1	0	0	0	0	0	0	1	0	0	0
coaster	9	.4884	.9043	39.6	1	4	2	1	1	0	0	0	0	1	2	0	1	0	0	0	0	1	0	0	0	0	1	3	0
coasting	16	.5279	1.7654	42.5	1	1	1	4	1	0	8	0	1	0	1	0	0	1	0	1	0	0	0	0	1	2	8	1	0
coastline	40	.4608	4.0829	46.1	3	11	6	10	5	1	3	1	5	0	0	0	0	24	0	4	0	0	0	0	0	1	4	2	0
coastlines	9	.4598	.9147	39.6	2	2	0	2	2	1	0	0	1	0	0	1	0	5	0	1	0	0	0	0	0	1	0	0	0
coasts	51	.5512	5.9531	47.7	8	7	7	10	10	4	4	1	4	0	1	0	0	27	0	3	0	0	0	0	0	4	10	2	0
coastwatcher	2	.0000	.0290	24.6	0	0	0	0	2	0	0	0	0	0	0	0	0	0	0	0	0	0	0	0	0	2	0	0	0
coat	391	.8067	63.584	58.0	90	63	38	29	52	72	43	4	118	36	1	27	12	8	10	16	5	1	26	28	40	30	7	26	0
Coat	2	.1674	.0805	29.1	0	0	0	1	0	0	1	0	0	0	0	0	0	0	0	0	0	0	1	0	0	1	0	0	0
coated	31	.7299	4.6125	46.6	3	4	5	1	8	4	5	1	8	1	0	1	0	0	0	6	3	2	2	2	0	1	3	2	0
coating	43	.7896	6.8430	48.4	5	6	6	2	11	2	9	2	9	1	1	1	0	1	1	9	0	1	4	2	0	3	7	3	0
coatings	2	.0000	.0394	26.0	0	0	0	0	0	0	0	2	0	0	0	0	0	0	0	2	0	0	0	0	0	0	0	0	0
coatis	3	.0000	.1370	31.4	0	0	0	0	3	0	0	0	3	0	0	0	0	0	0	0	0	0	0	0	0	0	0	0	0
coats	120	.7683	18.729	52.7	37	21	5	11	17	19	10	0	36	4	2	6	4	12	1	8	0	0	13	6	7	15	2	4	0
coax	5	.2443	.3861	35.9	1	0	0	0	1	2	1	0	4	0	0	0	0	0	0	0	0	0	0	0	0	0	1	0	0
coaxed	17	.5934	2.1238	43.3	6	5	1	2	1	2	0	0	4	1	0	1	1	0	0	0	0	0	0	0	5	4	0	1	0
coaxing	9	.4155	.8589	39.3	0	0	2	1	4	2	0	0	3	0	0	3	0	1	0	0	0	0	0	0	2	0	0	0	0
cob	5	.4505	.5018	37.0	1	0	2	0	0	1	1	0	1	1	0	0	0	2	0	0	0	0	0	0	0	0	0	1	0
COB	2	.0000	.0299	24.8	0	0	1	0	0	0	1	0	0	0	0	0	2	0	0	0	0	0	0	0	0	0	0	0	0
cobalt	16	.3802	1.3922	41.4	0	2	2	0	4	2	1	5	1	0	0	0	0	1	0	11	0	0	0	0	0	1	2	0	0
Cobb	2	.1948	.1250	31.0	1	1	0	0	0	0	0	0	1	0	0	0	0	0	0	0	0	0	0	0	0	1	0	0	0
cobble-stone	2	.2285	.1129	30.5	1	0	0	1	0	0	0	0	0	0	0	0	0	1	0	0	0	0	0	0	0	0	1	0	0
cobbled	11	.5885	1.3736	41.4	3	3	1	4	0	0	0	0	3	0	0	1	0	1	0	0	0	0	0	0	2	3	0	1	0
cobbler	15	.4844	1.6141	42.1	7	3	0	4	0	0	1	0	6	1	0	3	0	0	0	0	4	0	0	0	1	0	0	0	0
cobbler's	4	.3721	.3657	35.6	1	0	0	2	1	0	0	0	2	0	0	1	0	0	0	0	0	0	0	0	0	1	0	0	0
cobbles	4	.3597	.3542	35.5	2	0	0	1	0	1	0	0	2	0	0	0	0	0	0	0	1	0	0	0	0	0	0	1	0
cobblestone	6	.2773	.4266	36.3	1	2	0	2	1	0	0	0	1	0	0	0	0	4	0	0	0	0	0	0	0	1	0	0	0
cobblestones	8	.3625	.6668	38.2	2	1	1	1	0	2	1	0	2	0	2	0	0	1	0	0	0	0	0	0	1	1	1	0	0
Cobh	4	.0000	.0778	28.9	0	0	0	0	4	0	0	0	0	0	0	0	0	4	0	0	0	0	0	0	0	0	0	0	0
cobra	15	.5439	1.7916	42.5	1	3	1	2	7	1	0	0	7	2	0	1	0	0	0	0	0	0	0	0	0	2	3	0	0
Cobra	3	.0000	.0365	25.6	0	0	0	0	3	0	0	0	0	0	0	0	0	0	0	0	0	0	0	0	0	0	0	3	0
cobras	5	.1380	.2415	33.8	0	0	0	1	4	0	0	0	2	0	0	0	0	0	0	0	0	0	0	0	0	0	3	0	0
Cobras	3	.0000	.0328	25.2	0	0	3	0	0	0	0	0	0	3	0	0	0	0	0	0	0	0	0	0	0	0	0	0	0
cobweb	6	.5047	.6504	38.1	0	1	2	1	2	0	0	0	1	0	0	1	0	0	0	1	0	0	0	0	2	0	0	1	0
Cobweb	3	.0000	.0322	25.1	0	0	0	0	0	0	3	0	0	0	0	3	0	0	0	0	0	0	0	0	0	0	0	0	0
COBWEB	4	.0000	.0429	26.3	0	0	0	0	0	0	4	0	0	0	0	4	0	0	0	0	0	0	0	0	0	0	0	0	0
cobwebs	6	.4367	.5967	37.8	3	0	0	2	1	0	0	0	2	0	0	1	0	0	0	1	0	0	0	0	2	0	0	0	0
Coca-Cola	4	.2603	.1916	32.8	0	0	0	0	1	0	3	0	0	0	0	3	0	0	0	0	0	0	0	0	0	0	1	0	0
coca-growing	2	.0000	.0914	29.6	0	0	2	0	0	0	0	0	2	0	0	0	0	0	0	0	0	0	0	0	0	0	0	0	0
cocci	2	.0000	.0394	26.0	0	0	0	1	1	0	0	0	0	0	0	0	0	0	0	2	0	0	0	0	0	0	0	0	0
Cochin	4	.2424	.3036	34.8	3	0	1	0	0	0	0	0	3	0	0	0	0	0	0	0	0	0	0	0	0	0	0	1	0
Cochise	20	.3504	1.6741	42.2	0	0	6	3	11	0	0	0	7	2	0	10	0	0	1	0	0	0	0	0	0	0	0	0	0
Cochise's	6	.1717	.3427	35.3	0	0	3	0	3	0	0	0	3	0	0	3	0	0	0	0	0	0	0	0	0	0	0	0	0
cochlea	8	.3412	.6266	38.0	0	0	0	5	2	1	0	0	0	0	0	0	0	0	0	6	1	0	0	0	0	0	1	0	0
Cochran	5	.2110	.3346	35.2	0	0	3	0	2	0	0	0	3	0	0	0	0	0	0	0	0	0	0	0	0	0	0	2	0
Cochrane	3	.0000	.0434	26.4	1	0	0	2	0	0	0	0	0	0	0	0	0	0	0	0	0	0	0	0	0	3	0	0	0
cock	31	.3553	2.5488	44.1	3	1	0	4	2	1	1	19	7	0	0	1	0	0	0	0	0	0	0	1	20	2	0	0	0
Cock	3	.2009	.1371	31.4	0	0	0	0	0	1	2	0	0	0	0	2	0	0	0	0	0	1	0	0	0	0	0	0	0
cock-a-doodle-doo	7	.1721	.4081	36.1	3	4	0	0	0	0	0	0	4	0	0	0	0	0	0	0	3	0	0	0	0	0	0	0	0
Cock-a-doodle-doo	6	.0000	.0485	26.9	6	0	0	0	0	0	0	0	0	0	0	0	0	0	0	0	6	0	0	0	0	0	0	0	0
cock-eyed	2	.0000	.0914	29.6	0	0	0	2	0	0	0	0	2	0	0	0	0	0	0	0	0	0	0	0	0	0	0	0	0
cock's	2	.2437	.1129	30.5	1	0	0	1	0	0	0	0	0	0	0	0	0	0	0	0	0	0	0	0	0	0	1	1	0
cockatoos	3	.1409	.1472	31.7	2	0	0	1	0	0	0	0	1	0	0	0	0	0	0	0	0	0	0	0	0	2	0	0	0
cocked	24	.6114	3.1098	44.9	4	4	2	4	6	2	1	1	9	0	0	1	0	0	0	0	3	0	0	0	6	3	1	1	0
cocker	3	.2138	.1721	32.4	0	0	1	1	0	0	1	0	1	0	1	1	0	0	0	0	0	0	0	0	0	0	0	0	0
cockfights	2	.2152	.1357	31.3	0	0	0	0	1	1	0	0	1	0	0	0	0	1	0	0	0	0	0	0	0	0	0	0	0
cockpit	24	.5646	2.9445	44.7	4	2	1	7	4	4	1	1	11	1	2	1	0	0	0	0	0	0	0	0	1	4	0	4	0
cockpits	2	.2139	.1057	30.2	0	0	0	0	0	2	0	0	0	0	0	0	0	1	1	0	0	0	0	0	0	0	0	0	0
cockroach	8	.1970	.4003	36.0	0	0	0	2	4	2	0	0	0	0	0	5	0	0	0	3	0	0	0	0	0	0	0	0	0
cockroaches	21	.2446	1.2867	41.1	7	0	0	9	2	1	0	2	0	0	0	0	0	0	0	12	0	0	0	0	0	9	0	0	0
cocks	11	.5170	1.2264	40.9	8	0	1	1	1	0	0	0	3	0	0	0	0	0	0	0	2	0	0	0	1	2	3	0	0
cocksure	2	.1814	.1187	30.7	0	0	0	0	0	0	2	0	1	0	0	0	0	0	0	0	0	0	0	0	0	0	0	1	0
cocksureness	2	.2306	.1140	30.6	0	0	0	0	0	1	1	0	0	1	0	0	0	1	0	0	0	0	0	0	0	0	0	0	0
cocktail	5	.1628	.2128	33.3	0	0	1	0	0	1	2	1	0	0	0	0	0	0	0	0	0	0	0	0	0	1	0	4	0
cocktails	2	.0000	.0394	26.0	0	0	0	0	0	0	2	0	0	0	0	0	0	0	0	2	0	0	0	0	0	0	0	0	0
cocky	2	.2427	.1152	30.6	1	0	0	0	1	0	0	0	0	0	0	0	0	0	0	0	0	0	0	0	1	1	0	0	0
Cocky	4	.0000	.1827	32.6	0	0	0	0	0	4	0	0	4	0	0	0	0	0	0	0	0	0	0	0	0	0	0	0	0
coco	2	.0000	.0914	29.6	0	0	0	2	0	0	0	0	2	0	0	0	0	0	0	0	0	0	0	0	0	0	0	0	0
cocoa	57	.5159	6.1878	47.9	10	9	6	12	3	3	13	1	7	3	0	1	7	3	5	6	0	0	16	0	3	2	3	1	0
cocoanut	2	.0000	.0234	23.7	0	2	0	0	2	0	0	0	0	0	0	0	0	0	0	0	0	0	0	0	2	0	0	0	0
cocoanuts	3	.0000	.0352	25.5	0	1	0	0	2	0	0	0	0	0	0	0	0	0	0	0	0	0	0	0	3	0	0	0	0
coconut	61	.7035	8.9971	49.5	13	7	3	33	3	0	0	2	34	0	0	0	1	7	2	0	5	0	0	0	4	1	4	3	0
coconuts	37	.5764	4.6298	46.7	7	5	0	15	4	4	0	2	16	0	0	0	0	8	1	0	0	0	0	0	0	3	7	2	0
cocoon	34	.5498	3.9820	46.0	22	2	3	2	2	2	1	0	3	0	0	0	0	6	0	17	0	0	1	0	0	5	2	0	0
cocoons	17	.4381	1.6371	42.1	14	2	0	0	0	0	1	0	1	0	0	0	0	4	0	3	0	0	0	0	0	8	1	0	0
cod	28	.5607	3.2965	45.2	3	7	3	6	6	2	1	0	1	0	0	0	0	12	0	2	1	0	0	0	1	7	4	0	0
Cod	16	.6582	2.1653	43.4	0	1	5	2	5	1	0	2	2	0	1	0	0	4	0	1	0	0	0	1	0	2	2	3	0
coda	17	.0000	.1374	31.4	0	1	5	4	3	4	0	0	0	0	0	0	0	0	0	0	17	0	0	0	0	0	0	0	0
coddled	2	.2446	.1125	30.5	0	0	0	0	0	0	2	0	0	1	0	1	0	0	0	0	0	0	0	0	0	0	0	0	0
code	130	.8221	21.510	53.3	9	35	24	11	33	9	7	2	37	11	0	8	12	3	16	12	1	0	0	1	1	8	11	9	0
Code	23	.5016	2.5292	44.0	1	5	6	2	5	4	0	0	7	7	0	4	0	0	0	4	1	0	0	0	0	0	0	0	0
coded	5	.5595	.5799	37.6	0	2	1	1	0	1	0	0	0	1	0	0	1	0	0	1	0	0	0	0	0	0	1	1	0
codes	10	.5697	1.1706	40.7	2	0	1	0	2	1	1	3	0	1	0	1	0	1	1	0	0	0	0	0	0	0	2	4	0

5N coarsest
6A coast-guard
7R coaster-brake
8D coasters
7D coastguardsman
9C coastwise
9D coat-collar
5F coat-of-arms
6N coat-room
8A coat-skirts
3J coat's
7N Coates
7A coati
3A coatimundi
5A coating's
5F coatless
8D coattails
XR coaxes
7Q coaxial
6D cobber
6N cobble
7F cobble-stoned
3Q cobble-stones
4A Cobbler
4P cobblestoned
7Q cobra-injected
5N cobra's
8A Coburg
6R cobwebby
5A coca
5Q cocaine
6B coccospheres
6H coccus
5A Cochran's
4J cock-a-doo-dle-doo
8C cock-a-doodle
3J cock-a-doodle-do
3P cock-crow
8K Cock's
3N cockatoo
9D cockatrice
XR cockbirds
9Q Cockcroft
XR Cocke
4A cockers
3P Cockers
7D cockiness
7A cockleburrs
6R cockles
9A cockney
6H cockroach's
3J cocks'
4Q cockscomb
7B cocoa-colored
7N cocoa-tree
7N cocoanut-tree
6R coconut-husk
6G cocos
6P Cocytus
9B COD
7R code-named
8Q codesigner

Word Type	F	D	U	SFI	3 Gr 3	4 Gr 4	5 Gr 5	6 Gr 6	7 Gr 7	8 Gr 8	9 Gr 9	X UnGr	A Read	B Eng & Gr	C Comp	D Lit	E Math	F Soc Stud	G SpeH	H Sci	J Music	K Art	L Home Ec	M Shop	N Lib F	P Lib NF	Q Lib Ref	R Mag	S Rel
codfish	13	.5064	1.4767	41.7	0	7	2	3	0	1	0	0	5	1	0	0	0	5	0	1	0	0	0	0	0	1	0	0	0
Codner	5	.0000	.2284	33.6	0	0	0	0	5	0	0	0	5	0	0	0	0	0	0	0	0	0	0	0	0	0	0	0	0
Cody	32	.3174	2.4415	43.9	0	4	3	19	0	6	0	0	8	0	0	18	0	2	0	0	0	0	0	0	0	3	0	1	0
coed	5	.0824	.1675	32.2	0	0	0	1	2	1	0	1	1	0	0	0	0	0	0	0	0	0	0	0	0	0	0	4	0
coeducation	2	.0000	.0243	23.9	0	0	0	0	2	0	0	0	0	0	0	0	0	0	0	0	0	0	0	0	0	0	0	2	0
coeducational	9	.2386	.4989	37.0	0	0	3	0	5	1	0	0	0	0	0	0	0	0	0	0	0	0	0	0	0	0	5	4	0
coefficient	13	.1093	.4500	36.5	0	0	0	0	1	0	12	0	0	0	0	0	12	0	0	0	0	0	0	0	0	0	0	1	0
coefficients	6	.1755	.2786	34.5	0	0	0	0	1	0	5	0	0	0	0	0	5	0	0	0	0	0	0	0	0	0	0	1	0
coelacanth	3	.2530	.1734	32.4	0	0	1	0	1	0	1	0	0	0	1	0	0	0	0	1	0	0	0	0	0	0	1	0	0
coelenterates	8	.1824	.4081	36.1	0	0	0	0	7	0	1	0	0	0	0	0	0	0	0	7	0	0	0	0	0	0	1	0	0
coffee	280	.9237	51.258	57.1	28	30	40	55	61	24	37	5	60	14	5	24	10	60	3	11	7	2	9	2	29	14	10	20	0
Coffee	5	.2177	.2519	34.0	0	0	2	3	0	0	0	0	0	0	0	0	0	0	0	0	3	0	0	0	0	0	0	2	0
coffee-growing	2	.0000	.0389	25.9	0	0	0	1	1	0	0	0	0	0	0	0	0	2	0	0	0	0	0	0	0	0	0	0	0
coffee-pot	2	.0000	.0234	23.7	0	0	0	0	2	0	0	0	0	0	0	0	0	0	0	0	0	0	0	0	2	0	0	0	0
coffee-producing	2	.2408	.1204	30.8	0	0	1	0	1	0	0	0	0	0	0	0	0	1	0	0	0	0	0	0	0	1	0	0	0
coffeecake	3	.2435	.2274	33.6	0	1	0	0	2	0	0	0	2	0	0	0	0	1	0	0	0	0	0	0	0	0	0	0	0
coffers	3	.3870	.2492	34.0	1	0	0	1	1	0	0	0	0	0	0	0	0	0	0	0	0	0	0	0	1	0	1	1	0
coffin	22	.6894	3.1565	45.0	0	1	4	6	5	4	2	0	9	0	0	2	0	2	0	0	3	0	0	0	1	1	2	2	0
Coffin	9	.3223	.6369	38.0	0	4	0	0	0	5	0	0	0	0	2	0	0	0	0	0	0	0	0	0	0	4	0	3	0
Coffin's	2	.1948	.1250	31.0	0	0	0	1	1	0	0	0	1	0	0	0	0	0	0	0	0	0	0	0	0	1	0	0	0
coffins	4	.2386	.2998	34.8	0	0	0	1	0	2	1	0	3	0	0	0	0	0	0	0	0	0	0	0	0	0	1	0	0
cog	2	.2427	.1152	30.6	0	0	0	1	1	0	0	0	0	0	0	0	0	0	0	0	0	0	0	0	1	1	0	0	0
Cogia	19	.3344	1.5523	41.9	0	7	8	4	0	0	0	0	7	0	0	4	0	0	0	0	0	0	0	0	8	0	0	0	0
cognac	2	.2442	.1134	30.5	0	0	0	0	1	0	1	0	0	1	0	0	0	0	0	0	0	0	0	0	0	0	0	1	0
cogs	2	.1972	.1262	31.0	0	1	0	0	0	1	0	0	1	0	0	0	1	0	0	0	0	0	0	0	0	0	0	0	0
Cohan	5	.3744	.3962	36.0	0	3	0	0	1	1	0	0	0	0	0	0	0	0	1	0	2	0	0	0	0	0	2	0	0
Cohen	5	.2444	.2887	34.6	2	0	0	0	0	1	2	0	0	0	0	0	0	0	0	0	0	0	0	0	0	3	2	0	0
coherent	4	.0847	.0825	29.2	0	0	0	0	2	0	2	0	0	0	3	1	0	0	0	0	0	0	0	0	0	0	0	0	0
coherently	2	.2407	.1138	30.6	0	0	1	0	1	0	0	0	0	0	0	1	0	0	0	0	0	0	0	0	0	1	0	0	0
cohesion	2	.2408	.1204	30.8	0	0	1	0	0	1	0	0	0	0	0	0	0	1	0	0	0	0	0	0	0	1	0	0	0
cohesive	2	.2278	.1128	30.5	0	0	0	0	2	0	0	0	0	0	0	0	0	0	0	1	0	0	0	0	0	0	1	0	0
coho	7	.0000	.0851	29.3	0	0	0	1	6	0	0	0	0	0	0	0	0	0	0	0	0	0	0	0	0	0	0	7	0
cohort	2	.2444	.1132	30.5	0	1	0	1	0	0	0	0	0	1	0	0	0	0	0	0	0	0	0	0	1	0	0	0	0
cohorts	2	.2412	.1141	30.6	0	0	0	1	0	0	1	0	0	1	0	0	0	0	0	0	0	0	0	0	0	1	0	0	0
cohos	3	.0000	.0365	25.6	0	0	0	0	3	0	0	0	0	0	0	0	0	0	0	0	0	0	0	0	0	0	0	3	0
coil	83	.3691	6.7632	48.3	5	2	2	21	11	30	5	7	6	2	0	4	0	0	0	34	2	1	0	27	1	1	3	2	0
coiled	26	.7478	3.9426	46.0	2	3	4	1	11	2	2	1	4	0	1	2	0	1	0	7	1	0	0	1	5	2	2	0	0
coiling	2	.1717	.1142	30.6	1	0	0	0	0	0	1	0	1	0	0	1	0	0	0	0	0	0	0	0	0	0	0	0	0
coils	32	.4089	2.8405	44.5	0	3	5	9	5	9	0	1	4	1	0	2	1	0	0	5	1	0	0	9	1	0	8	0	0
Coils	2	.0000	.0219	23.4	0	0	2	0	0	0	0	0	0	2	0	0	0	0	0	0	0	0	0	0	0	0	0	0	0
coin	114	.8052	18.465	52.7	21	26	10	11	17	16	9	4	21	4	0	12	29	5	8	8	1	4	0	1	3	14	2	2	0
coinage	8	.3384	.6579	38.2	0	0	2	3	2	0	0	1	3	2	0	0	0	0	0	0	0	0	0	0	0	0	3	0	0
coincide	5	.3898	.4213	36.2	0	0	0	0	2	3	0	0	0	0	0	0	2	0	0	1	0	0	0	1	0	0	1	0	0
coincidence	11	.5104	1.1648	40.7	0	0	0	0	6	1	3	1	0	1	0	4	0	0	0	0	0	0	0	0	0	1	2	3	0
coincident	3	.0000	.0449	26.5	0	0	0	0	3	0	0	0	0	0	0	0	3	0	0	0	0	0	0	0	0	0	0	0	0
coincides	7	.4531	.6739	38.3	0	0	0	0	6	1	0	0	0	0	0	0	3	0	0	0	0	0	0	0	0	1	2	1	0
coined	31	.3891	2.5995	44.1	2	1	19	1	4	2	2	0	2	2	0	2	0	1	18	0	0	0	0	0	0	3	3	0	0
coining	3	.0000	.0243	23.9	0	0	3	0	0	0	0	0	0	0	0	0	0	0	3	0	0	0	0	0	0	0	0	0	0
coins	161	.6265	21.038	53.2	36	38	22	25	16	10	9	5	29	4	0	5	78	13	0	1	0	1	0	1	6	20	2	1	0
coke	24	.4970	2.5471	44.1	3	5	2	1	4	7	2	0	1	2	0	0	0	8	0	7	0	0	0	3	3	0	0	0	0
Coke	6	.2279	.4286	36.3	0	0	1	0	5	0	0	0	4	0	0	0	0	0	0	0	0	0	0	0	0	0	0	2	0
Cokes	6	.3593	.5335	37.3	0	1	0	0	4	0	1	0	3	1	0	0	0	0	0	0	0	0	0	0	2	0	0	0	0
coking	4	.1325	.1944	32.9	1	0	0	2	0	1	0	0	1	0	0	0	0	3	0	0	0	0	0	0	0	0	0	0	0
Col	15	.4457	1.6009	42.0	0	6	0	3	0	6	0	0	10	0	0	0	0	0	0	0	0	0	0	0	0	1	1	3	0
Colbert	3	.0000	.0583	27.7	0	0	3	0	0	0	0	0	0	0	0	0	0	3	0	0	0	0	0	0	0	0	0	0	0
Colby	3	.2277	.1555	31.9	0	0	0	0	3	0	0	0	0	0	0	0	0	0	0	0	0	0	1	0	0	0	0	2	0
Colchester	8	.2179	.4185	36.2	3	0	0	0	5	0	0	0	0	0	0	5	0	0	0	0	0	0	0	0	0	3	0	0	0
Colchians	5	.0000	.2284	33.6	0	0	0	5	0	0	0	0	5	0	0	0	0	0	0	0	0	0	0	0	0	0	0	0	0
Colchis	3	.0000	.1370	31.4	0	0	0	2	0	1	0	0	3	0	0	0	0	0	0	0	0	0	0	0	0	0	0	0	0
cold	1469	.9047	264.37	64.2	361	257	207	168	246	119	91	20	399	58	20	97	2	145	14	304	18	3	40	12	106	135	57	59	0
Cold	9	.5485	1.0300	40.1	0	0	0	2	1	4	2	0	0	0	0	1	0	4	0	0	1	0	0	0	1	0	0	2	0
cold-blooded	23	.4334	2.1891	43.4	7	6	2	4	4	0	0	0	1	0	0	0	0	0	0	10	0	0	0	0	0	9	2	1	0
cold-weather	2	.2278	.1128	30.5	0	0	0	0	2	0	0	0	0	0	0	0	0	0	0	1	0	0	0	0	0	0	1	0	0
coldblooded	2	.2446	.1257	31.0	0	0	0	0	1	0	1	0	0	0	0	0	0	1	0	1	0	0	0	0	0	0	0	0	0
colder	97	.6941	13.940	51.4	19	20	16	13	7	9	12	1	22	2	0	2	2	15	0	40	0	0	1	0	4	4	4	1	0
coldest	31	.6053	3.9281	45.9	7	8	1	1	6	4	3	1	4	0	0	0	4	3	0	12	0	0	3	0	2	1	0	2	0
coldly	21	.5223	2.4135	43.8	0	0	4	3	11	1	2	0	9	0	0	3	0	0	0	0	2	0	0	0	6	0	1	0	0
coldness	7	.4457	.6820	38.3	0	1	0	2	3	1	0	0	1	0	0	3	0	0	0	1	0	0	0	0	0	1	0	1	0
colds	15	.5029	1.6575	42.2	4	2	3	4	1	0	1	0	3	1	0	0	0	3	1	7	0	0	0	0	0	0	0	0	0
Cole	15	.2013	.7552	38.8	0	1	0	1	12	1	0	0	1	0	0	0	0	0	0	0	2	0	0	0	12	0	0	0	0
Cole's	2	.2420	.1154	30.6	0	0	0	0	1	1	0	0	0	0	0	0	1	0	0	0	0	0	0	0	1	0	0	0	0
Coleman	5	.1993	.2508	34.0	0	4	0	0	0	0	1	0	0	0	0	1	0	0	0	0	0	0	0	0	0	4	0	0	0
coleus	2	.0000	.0394	26.0	0	0	0	0	2	0	0	0	0	0	0	0	0	0	0	2	0	0	0	0	0	0	0	0	0
collaborate	3	.3822	.2446	33.9	0	0	0	0	0	1	1	1	0	1	0	0	0	0	0	0	1	0	0	0	0	0	0	1	0
collaborated	2	.2433	.1158	30.6	0	0	1	0	1	0	0	0	0	0	0	0	0	0	0	0	0	0	0	0	0	1	0	1	0
collaborating	2	.0000	.0209	23.2	0	0	0	0	1	0	1	0	0	0	0	0	0	0	0	0	0	0	0	0	0	0	2	0	0
collaboration	7	.4582	.6812	38.3	0	0	1	0	2	1	1	2	0	0	0	0	0	0	0	1	0	0	0	0	0	2	2	2	0
collage	13	.0238	.0942	29.7	4	1	0	2	3	3	0	0	0	0	0	0	0	0	0	0	0	12	0	0	0	0	0	1	0
collages	9	.0368	.0894	29.5	0	1	1	2	5	0	0	0	0	0	0	0	0	0	0	0	0	8	0	0	0	0	1	0	0
collapse	18	.6527	2.4409	43.9	1	0	1	1	4	7	3	1	4	1	0	2	0	3	0	2	0	0	0	0	0	0	3	3	0
collapsed	26	.5507	3.0173	44.8	2	0	3	5	5	8	2	1	4	1	4	1	0	5	0	1	0	0	0	0	1	2	2	5	0
collapses	4	.2287	.2348	33.7	0	3	0	0	1	0	0	0	0	0	0	0	0	0	0	3	0	0	0	0	0	0	0	1	0
collapsing	7	.4417	.6555	38.2	0	0	0	1	1	5	0	0	0	0	1	3	0	1	0	1	0	0	0	0	0	0	0	1	0
collar	126	.5315	14.435	51.6	26	23	18	9	18	7	24	1	42	10	0	5	0	2	2	6	2	0	28	0	15	7	1	6	0
collard	2	.1814	.1187	30.7	0	0	0	1	1	0	0	0	1	0	0	0	0	0	0	0	0	0	0	0	0	0	0	1	0
collards	2	.0000	.0215	23.3	0	0	0	0	0	0	2	0	0	0	0	2	0	0	0	0	0	0	0	0	0	0	0	0	0
collared	3	.1927	.1491	31.7	0	0	0	0	1	0	1	1	0	0	0	0	0	0	0	1	0	0	0	0	0	0	0	2	0
collars	38	.2669	2.2099	43.4	0	2	2	2	6	13	11	2	2	0	0	4	0	0	0	0	1	1	24	0	3	2	1	0	0
colleague	10	.4400	1.0076	40.0	0	0	1	2	5	1	1	0	4	0	0	0	0	0	0	0	0	0	0	0	0	2	3	1	0
colleagues	20	.5462	2.3554	43.7	0	0	0	2	8	4	6	0	6	0	0	0	0	3	0	0	0	0	0	0	1	2	6	2	0
collect	189	.8380	31.686	55.0	30	31	13	23	28	34	21	9	25	8	0	9	6	17	22	58	2	7	2	3	3	9	11	7	0
collected	160	.8263	26.518	54.2	24	21	21	29	31	12	18	4	21	6	0	4	35	24	1	30	3	0	0	3	5	8	11	9	0
collecting	64	.8267	10.618	50.3	8	9	8	8	13	5	5	8	11	5	0	5	0	5	1	17	1	0	1	0	4	3	6	5	0

6F codfishing
8A codger
4H codling
3P codliver
6R Coeur
9Q coexistence
5R COFFEE-OTHERS
4Q coffee-house
7C coffee-room
5P coffeegrowers
5R coffeehouse
8R coffeehouses
6A coffeepot
3N coffeepot's
8F Coffey
9F cogged
7R Coghlan
4A Cogia's
6N cogitations
XR Cognac
7B cognate
8Q Cogniet
6J Coh-dah-ee
8J Cohans
9Q Cohen's
8B coherence
7F cohesiveness
XR cohort's
6Q cohune
5N coiled-up
8Q Coimbra
8E coin-collection
XH coincided
9R coinciding
8A col
8H cola
6A cola-nuts
5K colander
5N Colby's
4P Colbys
8F ColdHarbor
7B cold-bloodedly
7Q cold-bloodedness
8D cold-cream
5Q cold-hearted
9M cold-metal
5H cold-preventing
9A cold-producing
8M cold-rolled
9M cold-type
6R cold-war
4A cold-water
7H cold-wave
7R coleslaw
5Q Colet
5R Colgems
5Q Colin
9R Coliseum
XR collaborations
8F collaborators
5Q Collage
4D collandered
9D collapsible
8R collarbone
6R collard-greens
6N collarless
XQ collated
8Q collateral
5Q Collected
9D collectedly

Word Type	F	D	U	SFI	3 Gr 3	4 Gr 4	5 Gr 5	6 Gr 6	7 Gr 7	8 Gr 8	9 Gr 9	X UnGr	A Read	B Eng & Gr	C Comp	D Lit	E Math	F Soc Stud	G Spell	H Sci	J Music	K Art	L Home Ec	M Shop	N Lib F	P Lib NF	Q Lib Ref	R Mag	S Rel
collection	191	.8924	33.850	55.3	25	38	18	29	40	12	13	16	23	12	3	7	48	7	6	23	5	2	2	0	6	10	14	23	0
collections	52	.6732	7.1135	48.5	6	5	3	2	12	11	1	12	0	1	0	1	13	1	1	11	0	2	0	0	0	3	13	6	0
collective	30	.5982	3.6640	45.6	0	1	11	3	7	6	2	0	0	7	2	1	0	4	0	0	1	0	0	0	1	1	12	1	0
collectively	5	.3304	.3608	35.6	0	0	1	0	2	1	1	0	0	0	0	0	0	0	0	0	1	0	0	0	0	1	3	0	0
collector	33	.6987	4.7358	46.8	4	1	6	2	6	5	1	8	6	4	1	5	0	3	0	11	1	0	0	0	0	0	1	1	0
collector's	3	.3776	.2504	34.0	2	0	0	0	1	0	0	0	0	0	0	1	0	1	0	0	0	0	0	0	0	1	0	0	0
collectors	24	.1665	1.2327	40.9	7	0	4	2	2	0	1	8	6	0	0	0	2	2	0	7	0	0	0	0	0	0	3	2	2
collects	46	.7739	7.1775	48.6	10	10	4	5	9	3	5	0	2	2	1	0	6	10	1	14	0	0	0	0	2	2	3	3	0
college	226	.7857	35.696	55.5	13	25	32	16	68	22	37	13	27	7	1	9	3	27	3	5	5	1	6	1	7	13	27	84	0
College	82	.5878	10.082	50.0	1	9	21	10	12	14	11	4	13	0	0	3	0	13	0	2	4	0	0	0	1	3	28	15	0
college-age	3	.2321	.1635	32.1	1	0	1	0	0	0	1	0	0	0	0	0	0	0	0	0	0	0	0	0	0	0	1	2	0
College-in-the-Woods	2	.0000	.0290	24.6	0	2	0	0	0	0	0	0	0	0	0	0	0	0	0	0	0	0	0	0	0	2	0	0	0
college-trained	2	.2351	.1166	30.7	0	0	0	1	0	1	0	0	0	0	0	0	0	1	0	0	0	0	0	0	0	0	0	1	0
college's	2	.0000	.0243	23.9	0	0	0	0	1	0	0	1	0	0	0	0	0	0	0	0	0	0	0	0	0	0	0	2	0
colleges	43	.6302	5.5885	47.5	2	1	9	2	13	2	13	1	4	1	0	1	1	10	1	0	1	0	0	0	0	2	8	14	0
Colleges	5	.0000	.0523	27.2	0	0	4	0	1	0	0	0	0	0	0	0	0	0	0	0	0	0	0	0	0	0	5	0	0
collegiate	2	.1733	.1149	30.6	0	0	0	0	0	2	0	0	1	1	0	0	0	0	0	0	0	0	0	0	0	0	0	0	0
Collegiate	2	.0000	.0243	23.9	0	1	0	0	1	0	0	0	0	0	0	0	0	0	0	0	0	0	0	0	0	0	0	2	0
collide	14	.4982	1.5033	41.8	0	0	1	4	3	1	4	1	1	0	0	0	0	1	0	8	0	0	0	1	0	1	0	2	0
collided	9	.4045	.8180	39.1	2	1	3	2	0	0	1	0	2	0	2	1	0	1	0	1	0	0	0	0	0	1	0	1	0
colliding	3	.3395	.2468	33.9	1	0	1	1	0	0	0	0	1	0	0	0	0	0	0	0	0	0	0	0	0	1	1	0	0
collie	8	.2445	.6134	37.9	3	0	2	2	0	1	0	0	6	0	0	0	0	0	0	0	0	0	0	0	0	2	0	0	0
Collie	5	.3377	.3703	35.7	1	0	1	0	3	0	0	0	0	0	0	1	0	0	0	0	0	0	0	0	3	0	0	1	0
Collier	8	.0000	.0972	29.9	0	0	0	0	7	0	0	1	0	0	0	0	0	0	0	0	0	0	0	0	0	0	0	8	0
collies	4	.2383	.2466	33.9	0	0	2	1	0	1	0	0	1	0	1	0	2	0	0	0	0	0	0	0	0	0	0	0	0
collinear	6	.0000	.0898	29.5	0	0	0	0	6	0	0	0	0	0	0	0	6	0	0	0	0	0	0	0	0	0	0	0	0
Collins	32	.3875	2.8781	44.6	10	1	0	5	8	8	0	0	10	0	0	6	0	0	0	0	0	0	0	0	0	2	0	14	0
collision	20	.5339	2.2593	43.5	2	0	3	2	4	1	6	2	2	0	2	0	0	0	0	7	0	0	0	0	0	3	3	3	0
collisions	15	.4839	1.5393	41.9	0	2	0	0	3	4	3	3	0	0	0	0	0	0	0	7	0	0	0	1	0	0	4	3	0
collodion	13	.0000	.2563	34.1	0	0	0	0	13	0	0	0	0	0	0	0	0	0	0	13	0	0	0	0	0	0	0	0	0
colloquial	3	.3764	.2475	33.9	0	0	0	0	0	2	0	1	0	1	0	1	0	1	0	0	0	0	0	0	0	0	0	0	0
collotype	2	.0000	.0050	17.0	0	0	0	0	0	0	2	0	0	0	0	0	0	0	0	0	0	0	0	2	0	0	0	0	0
Colo	5	.3278	.4057	36.1	0	0	1	1	2	0	1	0	2	0	0	0	0	0	0	0	0	0	0	0	0	0	2	1	0
cologne	8	.3548	.6259	38.0	0	1	1	0	0	2	0	4	0	1	0	0	0	1	0	0	0	0	0	0	0	1	0	5	0
Colombia	29	.4668	2.9345	44.7	0	0	9	11	8	0	1	0	2	1	0	0	0	12	0	0	0	0	0	0	0	8	6	0	0
Colombia's	10	.2243	.5684	37.5	0	0	6	4	0	0	0	0	0	0	0	0	0	4	0	0	0	0	0	0	0	6	0	0	0
Colombian	4	.3829	.3404	35.3	0	0	2	2	0	0	0	0	0	0	0	0	0	2	0	0	0	0	0	0	0	1	1	0	0
colon	19	.2273	1.0080	40.0	0	1	2	0	8	3	5	0	0	15	0	1	0	0	0	0	0	0	0	0	0	0	3	0	0
Colon	2	.0000	.0914	29.6	0	0	0	0	2	0	0	0	2	0	0	0	0	0	0	0	0	0	0	0	0	0	0	0	0
Colon's	2	.0000	.0914	29.6	0	0	2	0	0	0	0	0	2	0	0	0	0	0	0	0	0	0	0	0	0	0	0	0	0
colonel	41	.6329	5.5534	47.4	1	10	8	5	6	7	1	3	21	0	0	5	0	5	0	1	0	0	0	0	0	2	4	3	0
Colonel	93	.6930	13.381	51.3	2	16	20	14	17	17	6	1	34	2	0	16	0	7	2	1	0	0	0	0	2	19	5	5	0
COLONEL	12	.0000	.1288	31.1	0	0	0	0	12	0	0	0	0	0	0	12	0	0	0	0	0	0	0	0	0	0	0	0	0
colonel's	3	.2212	.2099	33.2	0	0	2	0	1	0	0	0	2	0	0	1	0	0	0	0	0	0	0	0	0	0	0	0	0
Colonel's	4	.3212	.3104	34.9	2	0	0	1	1	0	0	0	1	0	0	1	0	0	0	0	0	0	0	0	0	2	0	0	0
colones	3	.0000	.1370	31.4	0	3	0	0	0	0	0	0	3	0	0	0	0	0	0	0	0	0	0	0	0	0	0	0	0
colonial	102	.6873	14.313	51.6	2	7	19	11	22	34	6	1	3	1	2	2	0	60	0	1	6	0	1	1	1	10	12	2	0
Colonial	21	.4962	2.1505	43.3	0	1	3	0	10	5	0	2	0	1	0	0	0	0	0	0	5	0	0	4	0	6	3	2	0
colonialism	3	.3766	.2497	34.0	0	0	2	0	1	0	0	0	0	0	0	0	0	1	0	0	0	0	0	0	0	1	1	0	0
colonies	265	.5881	32.693	55.1	29	12	69	27	46	70	10	2	21	2	0	1	1	146	1	9	12	0	0	0	3	31	32	6	0
Colonies	15	.3199	1.1271	40.5	0	0	6	0	2	6	0	1	0	0	0	1	0	12	0	0	0	0	0	0	0	1	0	1	0
colonies'	5	.2441	.3058	34.9	2	0	0	0	0	3	0	0	0	0	0	0	0	3	0	0	0	0	0	0	0	2	0	0	0
colonist	7	.4619	.6950	38.4	0	0	1	0	5	1	0	0	0	1	0	0	0	4	0	0	0	0	0	0	1	0	1	0	0
colonists	149	.5758	18.066	52.6	8	7	64	11	19	40	0	0	12	1	0	3	0	97	7	1	10	0	0	1	1	6	10	0	0
colonists'	2	.0000	.0389	25.9	0	0	0	0	0	2	0	0	0	0	0	0	0	2	0	0	0	0	0	0	0	0	0	0	0
colonization	12	.4365	1.1349	40.5	0	0	2	5	3	2	0	0	0	2	0	0	0	8	0	0	1	1	0	0	0	0	0	0	0
colonize	5	.1285	.1797	32.5	3	0	0	0	0	2	0	0	0	0	0	0	0	1	0	0	0	0	0	0	0	0	4	0	0
colonized	4	.4794	.4057	36.1	0	0	1	2	0	1	0	0	0	1	0	0	0	1	0	0	0	0	0	0	0	1	1	0	0
colonizers	2	.2407	.1090	30.4	0	0	0	1	1	0	0	0	0	1	0	0	0	0	0	0	1	0	0	0	0	0	0	0	0
colonizing	3	.1823	.1405	31.5	0	0	2	0	0	1	0	0	0	0	0	0	0	1	0	0	0	0	0	0	0	0	2	0	0
colony	215	.6180	27.614	54.4	23	14	59	27	28	48	15	1	12	2	0	5	2	117	9	17	2	0	0	0	0	15	28	6	0
Colony	11	.4580	1.1045	40.4	0	1	3	0	3	3	1	0	1	1	0	0	0	7	0	0	1	0	0	0	0	0	1	0	0
colony's	4	.0000	.0778	28.9	0	0	0	0	1	2	1	0	0	0	0	0	0	4	0	0	0	0	0	0	0	0	0	0	0
color	1109	.6276	142.93	61.6	188	186	101	138	187	156	115	38	140	50	6	22	54	70	18	169	65	197	97	18	26	56	64	57	0
Color	6	.4404	.5541	37.4	0	0	0	0	3	0	0	3	0	0	0	0	0	0	0	0	1	0	1	0	0	1	0	3	0
Colorado	104	.7458	15.844	52.0	10	7	18	27	23	8	6	5	26	0	3	1	5	25	0	12	2	1	0	0	1	2	3	23	0
ColoradoSprings	3	.2425	.1816	32.6	0	0	0	0	1	1	1	0	0	0	0	0	0	2	0	0	0	0	0	0	0	0	0	1	0
Colorado's	5	.2069	.2483	33.9	0	0	1	2	1	0	0	1	0	0	0	0	0	0	0	0	1	0	0	0	0	0	0	4	0
coloration	10	.3727	.8321	39.2	4	0	1	2	2	1	0	0	0	0	0	0	0	0	0	5	0	0	0	0	0	2	3	0	0
colored	387	.7151	56.322	57.5	96	73	62	49	45	36	20	6	59	5	5	14	62	42	30	48	8	44	4	2	15	22	13	14	0
Colored	2	.2152	.1357	31.3	0	0	0	1	0	1	0	0	1	0	0	0	0	1	0	0	0	0	0	0	0	0	0	0	0
colorfast	2	.0000	.0064	18.1	0	0	0	0	0	1	1	0	0	0	0	0	0	0	0	0	0	0	2	0	0	0	0	0	0
colorful	110	.7801	17.246	52.4	17	17	13	26	14	10	10	3	13	15	4	0	0	17	0	8	15	6	4	0	1	6	8	13	0
colorfully	2	.2446	.1122	30.5	1	0	0	0	0	0	1	0	0	0	0	1	0	0	0	0	0	0	0	0	0	0	1	0	0
coloring	56	.7039	8.1256	49.1	16	13	6	6	7	2	5	1	16	0	0	0	0	3	1	17	0	1	3	4	0	1	6	4	0
coloristic	2	.0000	.0162	22.1	0	0	0	0	0	2	0	0	0	0	0	0	0	0	0	0	2	0	0	0	0	0	0	0	0
colorless	33	.4690	3.3537	45.3	1	3	3	8	5	3	9	1	1	2	0	0	0	0	0	22	1	0	0	0	0	0	4	3	0
colors	648	.4821	66.001	58.2	139	103	58	104	96	83	48	17	79	13	2	11	14	46	5	98	20	179	67	13	7	26	42	26	0
Colors	2	.2109	.0918	29.6	0	0	0	0	1	0	1	0	0	0	0	0	0	0	0	0	1	0	1	0	0	0	0	0	0
colossal	9	.3695	.7540	38.8	0	0	0	1	2	3	2	1	2	1	0	0	0	1	0	0	0	2	0	0	2	0	1	0	0
Colosseum	3	.3849	.2570	34.1	1	1	0	0	1	0	0	0	0	0	0	0	1	1	0	0	0	0	0	0	0	1	0	0	0
colossus	3	.3815	.2447	33.9	0	1	0	1	0	1	0	0	0	0	0	0	0	0	1	0	0	0	0	0	1	0	0	1	0
colour	8	.3998	.7488	38.7	0	1	0	3	3	1	0	0	3	0	0	3	0	1	0	0	0	0	0	0	1	0	0	0	0
coloured	4	.3766	.3696	35.7	1	0	0	2	0	0	0	1	2	0	0	0	0	0	0	0	0	0	0	0	0	1	0	1	0
colours	2	.0000	.0243	23.9	0	0	0	0	0	0	0	2	0	0	0	0	0	0	0	0	0	0	0	0	0	0	0	2	0
colt	125	.5917	15.745	52.0	29	13	18	23	27	8	5	2	45	1	1	36	0	0	0	1	0	1	1	0	29	10	0	0	0
Colt	9	.4951	.9458	39.8	0	0	2	2	4	1	0	0	1	0	0	2	0	0	0	0	0	0	0	0	0	1	2	3	0
colt's	5	.0000	.0537	27.3	0	0	0	0	3	2	0	0	0	0	0	5	0	0	0	0	0	0	0	0	0	0	0	0	0
Colter	24	.0000	1.0964	40.4	0	0	8	0	16	0	0	0	24	0	0	0	0	0	0	0	0	0	0	0	0	0	0	0	0
Colter's	2	.0000	.0914	29.6	0	0	2	0	0	0	0	0	2	0	0	0	0	0	0	0	0	0	0	0	0	0	0	0	0
colts	30	.4943	3.2300	45.1	9	5	1	3	12	0	0	0	8	0	0	1	0	0	0	0	0	1	0	0	14	5	1	0	0
Colts	11	.0000	.1337	31.3	0	0	0	3	3	5	0	0	0	0	0	0	0	0	0	0	0	0	0	0	0	0	0	11	0
Columbia	87	.6420	11.530	50.6	7	4	29	5	25	11	5	1	9	1	0	2	0	31	1	1	7	0	0	0	0	4	10	21	0
Columbia's	4	.2352	.2332	33.7	0	0	0	3	1	0	0	0	0	0	0	0	0	2	0	0	0	0	0	0	0	0	0	2	0
Columbine	5	.2342	.2967	34.7	0	0	0	0	0	0	1	4	0	0	0	0	0	0	0	4	1	0	0	0	0	0	0	0	0

8Q Collection
7A collection-plate
9R Collective
6R collectives
7Q collectivized
8G colleen
6R collegian
4H collides
6A collie's
7R Collier's
9D colliers
8R Colliers
4R colliery
7D Collins'
9M colloid
5Q colloidal
8D colloquialism
8D colloquialisms
9P colloquy
6J colly
9D Colly
6F Cologne
XR colognes
5P Colombians
6F colonial-style
5P colonialism's
5P colonialisms
5P colonialists'
3P COLONIES
8F Colonization
7B colons
8Q Colonus
9Q COLOR
8L color-fast
8R color-field
6R color-glutted
7R color-movie
XR color-over-black
6N color-sergeant
5A color-tagged
9R color-television
7B color-words
3J color's
XR Colorado-Kansas
6F Coloreds
4A colossal-osal
8G Colossus
9Q colourless
5P Coltejer
7D coltish
6R Colton
5F Columbian
6A columbine
7A columbines

Word Type	F	D	U	SFI	3 Gr 3	4 Gr 4	5 Gr 5	6 Gr 6	7 Gr 7	8 Gr 8	9 Gr 9	X UnGr	A Read	B Eng & Gr	C Comp	D Lit	E Math	F Soc Stud	G Spell	H Sci	J Music	K Art	L Home Ec	M Shop	N Lib F	P Lib NF	Q Lib Ref	R Mag	S Rel
Columbus	222	.6140	28.804	54.6	30	24	67	34	40	22	4	1	48	2	2	2	2	125	2	4	2	0	0	0	2	15	10	6	0
Columbus'	19	.4586	1.9662	42.9	1	0	9	1	4	3	1	0	5	0	0	0	0	9	0	1	0	0	0	0	0	1	3	0	0
Columbus's	8	.3351	.6162	37.9	0	2	3	1	2	0	0	0	0	0	0	0	0	6	0	0	0	0	1	0	0	1	0	0	0
column	471	.7758	73.368	58.7	83	56	62	90	68	52	48	12	29	67	6	6	188	6	72	40	17	1	5	4	7	7	3	11	2
Column	26	.3357	2.1098	43.2	0	0	0	10	8	6	2	0	8	0	0	0	12	0	6	0	0	0	0	0	0	0	0	0	0
columnist	2	.1717	.1142	30.6	0	0	0	0	1	0	1	0	1	0	0	1	0	0	0	0	0	0	0	0	0	0	0	0	0
columns	133	.7845	20.942	53.2	19	12	14	18	25	18	25	2	14	18	1	0	44	7	9	2	4	7	2	8	3	5	4	5	0
com	8	.0000	.0649	28.1	0	1	2	1	3	1	0	0	0	0	0	0	0	0	8	0	0	0	0	0	0	0	0	0	0
Com	2	.0000	.0215	23.3	0	0	0	0	2	0	0	0	0	0	0	2	0	0	0	0	0	0	0	0	0	0	0	0	0
com-	2	.0000	.0162	22.1	0	0	0	0	1	1	0	0	0	0	0	0	0	0	2	0	0	0	0	0	0	0	0	0	0
coma	3	.3380	.2498	34.0	0	0	0	0	1	1	1	0	1	1	0	0	0	0	0	1	0	0	0	0	0	0	0	0	0
Comanche	7	.3551	.5757	37.6	0	4	0	2	0	1	0	0	1	0	0	0	0	1	0	0	0	0	0	0	0	4	0	1	0
comb	64	.7860	10.173	50.1	5	8	18	10	14	6	2	1	14	0	0	3	1	0	3	23	1	3	2	1	3	4	4	2	0
combat	34	.6607	4.6606	46.7	1	1	3	6	9	7	5	2	7	0	0	0	0	7	0	3	1	0	0	0	1	5	2	8	0
combatant	2	.0000	.0914	29.6	0	0	0	1	1	0	0	0	2	0	0	0	0	0	0	0	0	0	0	0	0	0	0	0	0
combatants	3	.3773	.2485	34.0	0	0	0	0	1	1	1	0	0	0	0	1	0	1	0	0	0	0	0	0	1	0	0	0	0
combating	6	.3913	.5155	37.1	0	0	0	1	0	2	3	0	0	0	1	0	0	1	1	3	0	0	0	0	0	0	0	0	0
combative	4	.0000	.0789	29.0	0	0	0	4	0	0	0	0	0	0	0	0	0	0	0	4	0	0	0	0	0	0	0	0	0
Combe	3	.0000	.0314	25.0	0	0	0	0	3	0	0	0	0	0	0	0	0	0	0	0	0	0	0	0	0	0	3	0	0
combed	27	.7210	3.9902	46.0	6	2	4	4	6	3	2	0	8	0	0	4	0	1	1	1	0	0	2	0	3	4	1	2	0
combers	3	.3395	.2468	33.9	0	0	0	1	2	0	0	0	1	0	0	0	0	0	0	0	0	0	0	0	0	1	1	0	0
combination	194	.8107	31.364	55.0	6	17	21	17	56	43	30	4	15	13	8	5	3	13	17	16	16	5	23	16	0	9	20	15	0
combinations	140	.7457	20.915	53.2	9	13	23	17	28	32	13	5	5	6	8	1	26	8	14	6	28	5	18	0	0	2	7	6	0
combine	200	.8060	32.181	55.1	14	13	45	21	35	41	24	7	4	26	1	1	9	6	31	56	9	6	17	3	0	5	13	13	0
combined	203	.8809	35.498	55.5	5	22	39	18	46	42	28	3	13	17	1	2	10	17	15	42	25	5	7	2	2	6	26	13	0
combines	69	.7839	10.852	50.4	4	3	16	9	18	14	1	4	3	2	1	1	2	8	6	19	7	0	0	3	0	0	11	6	0
combing	16	.4633	1.6487	42.2	1	6	2	2	0	2	3	0	5	1	0	0	0	0	0	3	0	0	3	0	3	1	0	0	0
combining	66	.7973	10.487	50.2	3	4	12	8	8	21	9	1	1	9	1	1	4	1	17	9	9	2	4	1	1	0	5	1	0
combo	9	.1983	.4189	36.2	0	1	0	6	1	1	0	0	0	0	0	0	0	0	0	0	6	0	0	0	0	0	0	3	0
combos	2	.0000	.0162	22.1	0	0	0	1	1	0	0	0	0	0	0	0	0	0	0	0	2	0	0	0	0	0	0	0	0
combs	14	.5633	1.6504	42.2	3	0	2	7	2	0	0	0	1	0	0	0	0	1	0	3	0	0	0	0	5	1	2	1	0
Combs	2	.1948	.1250	31.0	1	1	0	0	0	0	0	0	1	0	0	0	0	0	0	0	0	0	0	0	0	1	0	0	0
combustion	32	.4381	3.0814	44.9	0	0	2	1	9	12	8	0	2	0	0	0	0	0	0	21	0	0	0	3	0	0	3	3	0
come	4676	.8981	836.75	69.2	1106	890	516	596	784	401	296	87	1588	212	38	415	36	401	118	311	170	15	21	18	565	434	99	220	15
Come	13	.3659	1.0502	40.2	0	2	5	2	3	0	1	0	2	1	0	0	0	0	0	0	8	0	1	0	1	0	0	0	0
comeback	3	.2321	.1635	32.1	0	0	0	0	2	0	1	0	0	0	0	0	0	0	0	0	0	0	0	0	0	0	1	2	0
comedian	3	.2870	.1859	32.7	1	1	0	0	0	1	0	0	0	0	1	1	0	0	0	0	0	0	0	0	0	0	1	0	0
comedians	4	.3778	.3240	35.1	0	0	1	1	0	0	2	0	0	1	0	0	0	0	0	0	1	0	0	0	0	0	0	2	0
comedies	10	.5094	1.0768	40.3	0	2	1	2	2	2	1	0	1	0	0	0	1	1	0	0	1	0	0	0	0	0	4	2	0
comedy	28	.5298	3.0558	44.9	0	0	3	5	4	10	4	2	0	2	0	2	0	2	2	0	12	0	0	0	0	3	0	5	0
Comedy	9	.4938	.9553	39.8	0	0	3	0	2	2	1	1	2	0	0	1	0	0	0	0	2	0	0	0	0	0	3	1	0
comely	2	.2407	.1138	30.6	1	0	0	0	1	0	0	0	0	0	0	1	0	0	0	0	0	0	0	0	0	1	0	0	0
comer	2	.2297	.1135	30.6	0	0	0	0	0	1	1	0	0	0	0	1	0	1	0	0	0	0	0	0	0	0	0	0	0
comers	2	.1432	.0759	28.8	0	0	0	0	0	1	1	0	0	0	0	0	0	0	0	1	0	0	1	0	0	0	0	0	0
comes	1289	.9165	234.30	63.7	263	205	163	200	235	112	91	20	283	109	9	84	23	104	130	190	92	10	17	10	43	81	41	58	5
Comes	8	.0000	.0647	28.1	0	0	3	2	3	0	0	0	0	0	0	0	0	0	0	0	8	0	0	0	0	0	0	0	0
comet	21	.3471	1.7057	42.3	0	9	1	2	2	1	5	1	1	0	0	0	0	2	1	16	0	0	0	0	0	0	1	0	0
Comet	8	.3019	.6154	37.9	0	0	2	0	1	0	0	5	2	0	0	0	0	0	0	5	0	0	0	0	1	0	0	0	0
comets	33	.4777	3.4133	45.3	4	10	2	5	6	2	2	2	1	1	0	0	0	3	0	21	1	0	0	0	0	1	5	0	0
comfort	116	.8131	18.954	52.8	9	8	12	17	31	21	15	3	28	7	1	15	1	10	0	1	3	2	12	1	15	6	7	7	0
comfortable	178	.8599	30.621	54.9	32	22	18	37	26	17	17	9	47	4	2	9	1	18	0	11	2	2	6	0	27	25	7	17	0
comfortably	47	.7429	7.0888	48.5	2	9	4	8	15	5	4	0	11	3	1	1	0	0	1	3	2	0	6	0	5	5	4	5	0
comforted	12	.4759	1.1964	40.8	1	1	3	2	1	2	1	1	0	1	0	2	0	0	0	0	0	0	0	0	6	1	0	2	0
comforters	2	.2337	.1157	30.6	0	0	0	0	0	1	1	0	0	0	0	0	0	1	0	0	0	0	0	0	1	0	0	0	0
comforting	17	.6169	2.2442	43.5	3	2	1	5	2	1	2	1	8	1	0	1	0	0	0	0	0	0	0	0	2	3	0	2	0
comforts	12	.6929	1.7122	42.3	1	1	2	1	1	0	4	2	3	0	0	1	0	1	0	1	1	0	0	0	0	1	2	2	0
comic	39	.7944	6.2045	47.9	4	3	7	6	6	7	6	0	4	8	0	2	0	1	1	1	7	1	1	0	2	6	3	2	0
Comic	3	.0000	.0434	26.4	0	3	0	0	0	0	0	0	0	0	0	0	0	0	0	0	0	0	0	0	0	3	0	0	0
comical	18	.7163	2.6369	44.2	0	7	1	0	5	4	1	0	5	1	0	2	0	0	2	0	1	1	0	0	2	2	0	2	0
comically	2	.2437	.1129	30.5	0	0	0	0	2	0	0	0	0	0	0	0	0	0	0	0	0	0	0	0	0	0	1	1	0
comics	5	.4485	.5011	37.0	0	0	2	0	2	0	1	0	1	0	0	0	0	2	0	0	0	0	0	0	0	1	1	0	0
comin'	7	.4457	.6948	38.4	0	0	1	2	3	1	0	0	2	1	0	2	0	0	0	0	0	0	0	0	2	0	0	0	0
Comin'	4	.0000	.0323	25.1	0	0	0	2	0	2	0	0	0	0	0	0	0	0	0	0	4	0	0	0	0	0	0	0	0
coming	1123	.8528	192.48	62.8	246	229	128	125	214	106	55	20	442	36	12	91	2	82	13	58	32	5	4	0	137	122	19	64	4
Coming	4	.3677	.3659	35.6	1	2	1	0	0	0	0	0	2	0	0	1	0	1	0	0	0	0	0	0	0	0	0	0	0
coming-out	2	.0000	.0290	24.6	0	0	0	0	2	0	0	0	0	0	0	0	0	0	0	0	0	0	0	0	0	2	0	0	0
comings	2	.2441	.1127	30.5	0	0	0	1	1	0	0	0	0	0	0	0	0	0	0	0	0	0	0	0	1	0	1	0	0
comma	90	.3311	6.5473	48.2	13	5	14	4	26	17	11	0	3	71	8	1	5	0	2	0	0	0	0	0	0	0	0	0	0
command	152	.8425	25.661	54.1	11	19	23	22	36	27	12	2	35	6	1	5	0	27	2	2	4	0	1	1	10	14	22	22	0
Command	8	.3486	.6149	37.9	3	0	1	0	3	1	0	0	0	0	0	1	0	0	0	0	0	0	0	0	0	3	0	4	0
commandant	4	.1948	.2500	34.0	0	0	0	2	2	0	0	0	2	0	0	0	0	0	0	0	0	0	0	0	0	2	0	0	0
Commandant	4	.2107	.2095	33.2	1	0	0	0	0	0	3	0	0	0	0	0	0	0	0	0	0	0	0	0	0	3	0	1	0
commanded	63	.5006	6.8547	48.4	9	13	3	11	7	13	7	0	15	0	0	5	0	9	0	0	0	0	0	0	11	10	11	1	1
commander	90	.6998	13.138	51.2	7	27	10	3	10	25	5	3	40	1	0	4	0	15	1	0	0	0	0	0	2	8	8	11	0
Commander	40	.4153	4.1696	46.2	1	24	0	1	7	3	2	2	31	0	0	0	0	0	0	2	0	0	0	0	0	3	0	4	0
Commander-in-Chief	5	.3220	.3933	35.9	0	2	2	0	1	0	0	0	1	0	0	0	0	2	0	0	0	0	0	0	0	2	0	0	0
commander's	2	.1717	.1142	30.6	0	1	0	0	0	0	1	0	1	0	0	1	0	0	0	0	0	0	0	0	0	0	0	0	0
commanders	4	.3359	.2989	34.8	0	0	0	0	1	3	0	0	0	0	0	0	0	1	0	0	0	0	0	0	0	0	2	1	0
commanding	16	.6392	2.1316	43.3	1	2	1	4	2	3	3	0	4	0	0	3	0	2	0	0	0	0	0	0	1	1	2	3	0
commandment	6	.3302	.4267	36.3	0	0	3	0	1	1	1	0	0	0	1	0	0	0	0	0	0	0	0	0	1	0	4	0	0
Commandment	2	.0000	.0234	23.7	0	0	0	0	0	0	2	0	0	0	0	0	0	0	0	0	0	0	0	0	2	0	0	0	0
commandments	10	.2047	.4891	36.9	1	0	7	0	0	1	1	0	0	1	0	0	0	0	0	0	0	0	0	0	0	1	8	0	0
Commandments	6	.3252	.4335	36.4	0	0	3	1	0	0	2	0	0	0	0	0	0	1	0	0	0	0	0	0	2	0	3	0	0
commando	3	.0000	.0365	25.6	0	0	0	1	0	2	0	0	0	0	0	0	0	0	0	0	0	0	0	0	0	0	0	3	0
commands	25	.6637	3.4704	45.4	5	2	4	5	7	0	2	0	9	1	0	1	0	3	0	0	0	0	0	0	4	1	1	5	0
commas	95	.3873	7.9311	49.0	13	10	9	15	22	11	15	0	4	69	7	0	9	0	4	0	1	0	0	0	0	1	0	0	0
commemorate	3	.3756	.2468	33.9	0	0	0	0	1	1	1	0	0	0	0	1	0	1	0	0	0	0	0	0	0	0	1	0	0
commemorated	4	.1737	.1745	32.4	0	2	1	0	0	0	1	0	0	0	0	0	0	0	0	0	0	0	0	0	0	1	3	0	0
commemorates	2	.2303	.1079	30.3	0	0	2	0	0	0	0	0	0	0	0	0	0	0	0	0	1	0	0	0	0	1	0	0	0
commence	5	.4665	.5254	37.2	0	0	0	0	4	0	1	0	2	0	0	0	0	0	1	0	0	0	0	0	1	1	0	0	0
commenced	11	.6220	1.4147	41.5	0	1	0	1	4	4	1	0	1	1	0	1	0	3	0	0	0	0	0	0	3	1	1	0	0
commencement	4	.3647	.3180	35.0	0	0	0	1	2	0	0	1	0	0	0	0	0	0	0	0	0	0	0	0	0	1	1	2	0
Commencement	3	.0000	.0434	26.4	0	3	0	0	0	0	0	0	0	0	0	0	0	0	0	0	0	0	0	0	0	3	0	0	0
commences	2	.2440	.1132	30.5	0	0	0	0	0	0	2	0	0	0	0	1	0	0	0	0	0	0	0	0	0	0	0	1	0
commencing	3	.3772	.2488	34.0	0	1	0	0	0	1	0	1	0	1	0	0	0	0	0	1	0	0	0	0	1	0	0	0	0

XH columbite
8B columbus
7R column-mounted
XH columnar
XP columned
5B columnists
8G com-mand
4G com-pan-ion
4G com-pan-y
3P coma-la
4P Comanche's
9P Comanduras
6H comb-footed
8D combats
7Q combatted
7P comber
6B Combo
9R Combs'
7C combustible
XR Comden
9R Comdr
6A COME
5J Come-All-Ye
5R come-hithery
8F Come-outers
6A comedown
6A comeliness
4H comet's
5N Comet's
6B cometh
7D comets'
8N comf'table
7N comfortable-looking
3B comforter
3A comfortingly
3D comfy
7A comic-book
XR comic-ominous
9B comic-strip
XH Comical
9Q comique
7Q Comique
9A Comiskey
8F commandant-general
7P commandant's
8F commander-in-chief
7R Commander's
7N commandeth
9R commandos'
5Q Commedia

Word Type	F	D	U	SFI	3 Gr 3	4 Gr 4	5 Gr 5	6 Gr 6	7 Gr 7	8 Gr 8	9 Gr 9	X UnGr	A Read	B Eng & Gr	C Comp	D Lit	E Math	F Soc Stud	G Spell	H Sci	J Music	K Art	L Home Ec	M Shop	N Lib F	P Lib NF	Q Lib Ref	R Mag	S Rel
commend	7	.4393	.6448	38.1	0	2	0	0	1	1	3	0	0	0	0	3	0	0	2	0	0	0	0	0	1	0	0	1	0
commendable	4	.3617	.3033	34.8	0	0	0	1	1	1	1	0	0	0	1	0	0	0	0	0	0	0	1	0	0	0	0	2	0
commendation	2	.2443	.1130	30.5	0	0	0	0	1	0	1	0	0	0	0	1	0	0	0	0	0	0	0	0	1	0	0	0	0
commended	4	.4495	.4018	36.0	0	0	0	1	0	2	1	0	1	0	0	1	0	1	0	0	0	0	0	0	0	0	0	1	0
commensalism	4	.0000	.0789	29.0	0	0	0	0	4	0	0	0	0	0	0	0	0	0	0	4	0	0	0	0	0	0	0	0	0
comment	39	.7927	6.2504	48.0	1	2	4	8	11	9	4	0	12	6	1	5	0	0	2	1	0	0	1	0	5	3	1	2	0
commentary	5	.4702	.4939	36.9	0	0	0	0	2	1	0	2	0	1	0	0	0	0	0	0	0	0	0	0	0	1	1	2	0
commentator	2	.2407	.1090	30.4	0	0	0	0	1	1	0	0	0	1	0	0	0	0	0	0	1	0	0	0	0	0	0	0	0
commented	24	.6670	3.3186	45.2	0	2	4	2	10	2	2	2	6	0	0	3	1	2	0	1	0	0	0	0	3	3	0	5	0
comments	23	.6016	2.8538	44.6	1	1	1	1	8	3	8	0	3	3	0	8	0	0	1	1	0	0	3	0	1	0	2	1	0
commerce	88	.4886	9.1165	49.6	10	3	29	6	17	15	7	1	3	0	0	1	0	28	2	1	0	0	1	0	1	5	42	4	0
Commerce	16	.4495	1.5417	41.9	0	1	3	0	2	3	3	4	1	2	0	0	0	2	0	0	0	0	0	0	0	0	4	7	0
commercial	130	.7492	19.597	52.9	10	3	17	11	39	12	30	8	5	1	0	1	5	25	2	8	2	1	4	6	1	5	39	25	0
Commercial	4	.1873	.1827	32.6	0	0	1	1	0	0	2	0	0	0	0	0	0	0	0	0	0	0	0	0	0	0	3	1	0
commercially	7	.4084	.6077	37.8	1	0	0	0	2	1	3	0	0	0	0	0	0	1	0	2	0	0	1	2	0	0	1	0	0
commercials	15	.5742	1.7968	42.5	1	4	0	2	7	1	0	0	2	4	0	1	0	1	1	0	0	0	0	0	0	0	1	5	0
commerical	3	.2679	.1817	32.6	0	0	0	0	0	2	1	0	0	0	0	0	0	1	0	0	0	0	0	1	0	0	1	0	0
commission	73	.7408	10.906	50.4	4	3	10	3	15	7	27	4	3	3	0	3	13	9	0	4	0	1	1	0	0	4	14	18	0
Commission	32	.6084	4.0003	46.0	1	0	6	2	4	6	10	3	0	0	0	0	2	9	0	1	0	0	2	0	0	3	7	8	0
commissioned	16	.6240	2.0347	43.1	2	0	4	1	3	4	2	0	1	2	0	1	0	0	0	0	4	1	0	0	0	1	4	2	0
commissioner	13	.3541	1.1540	40.6	0	2	7	2	0	1	1	0	7	0	0	0	0	0	0	0	0	0	0	0	0	0	4	2	0
Commissioner	6	.2861	.3938	36.0	0	0	1	1	1	1	1	1	0	1	0	0	0	1	0	0	0	0	0	0	0	0	0	4	0
commissioners	9	.3455	.7090	38.5	0	1	1	0	1	0	6	0	0	0	0	0	0	6	0	0	0	0	0	0	0	0	2	1	0
Commissioners	2	.2285	.1129	30.5	0	1	0	0	0	0	1	0	0	0	0	0	0	1	0	0	0	0	0	0	0	0	1	0	0
commissions	9	.4555	.8614	39.4	0	0	2	0	3	2	1	1	0	0	0	0	1	1	0	0	0	1	0	0	0	0	4	2	0
commit	16	.5768	1.9311	42.9	1	0	4	1	5	1	1	3	3	1	0	0	0	0	2	0	0	0	0	0	2	0	4	4	0
commitment	7	.0000	.0851	29.3	0	0	0	0	2	2	2	1	0	0	0	0	0	0	0	0	0	0	0	0	0	0	0	7	0
commits	3	.3873	.2485	34.0	0	0	1	0	0	0	2	0	0	0	0	1	0	0	0	0	0	0	0	0	1	0	1	0	0
committed	35	.4309	3.2870	45.2	2	2	5	0	7	4	14	1	3	2	0	1	0	9	1	0	0	0	0	0	4	3	5	6	1
committee	118	.8096	19.175	52.8	21	22	10	9	29	14	9	4	13	10	1	1	5	23	2	6	0	0	2	0	7	30	4	14	0
Committee	49	.5710	5.8290	47.7	5	5	3	4	6	7	16	3	4	0	2	1	0	10	0	0	0	0	0	0	1	2	9	20	0
committees	30	.7190	4.3491	46.4	4	7	7	0	5	0	5	2	0	1	0	1	4	3	0	2	0	0	2	0	1	5	7	4	0
committing	9	.5927	1.0955	40.4	0	0	0	2	4	1	2	0	0	0	0	0	0	1	0	1	1	0	0	0	2	0	2	2	0
commodities	14	.4296	1.3182	41.2	0	2	5	1	3	1	1	1	2	0	0	0	0	1	0	0	0	0	0	0	0	2	6	3	0
commodity	8	.3679	.6534	38.2	0	2	0	1	2	2	1	0	0	0	0	0	0	3	0	0	0	0	0	0	0	2	3	0	0
Commodore	4	.0000	.0778	28.9	0	0	0	1	1	2	0	0	0	0	0	0	0	4	0	0	0	0	0	0	0	0	0	0	0
common	1174	.8578	200.47	63.0	56	75	123	192	290	223	184	31	68	101	12	21	349	79	66	181	39	3	15	47	12	45	105	31	0
Common	28	.6182	3.6521	45.6	9	1	2	2	3	3	8	0	8	0	0	0	2	6	0	0	0	0	0	0	2	1	2	7	0
common-sense	5	.3833	.4767	36.8	0	0	0	1	4	0	0	0	3	0	0	1	0	0	0	0	0	0	0	0	0	1	0	0	0
commoner	4	.2344	.2377	33.8	0	0	0	1	1	0	0	2	0	0	0	1	0	0	0	3	0	0	0	0	0	0	0	0	0
commoners	3	.3870	.2492	34.0	0	0	0	0	3	0	0	0	0	0	0	0	0	0	0	0	0	0	0	0	1	0	1	1	0
commonest	14	.5969	1.7308	42.4	1	1	0	6	1	1	4	0	1	1	0	0	0	0	0	2	1	0	0	0	1	5	3	0	0
commonly	136	.7090	19.465	52.9	1	4	8	15	40	35	26	7	6	12	0	0	3	11	20	27	10	0	7	16	0	5	15	4	0
commonplace	32	.7040	4.5529	46.6	1	1	2	5	12	3	7	1	3	2	4	1	0	1	1	2	1	2	0	1	0	2	6	6	0
Commons	7	.5294	.7917	39.0	2	0	2	1	0	2	0	0	1	1	0	0	0	2	0	0	0	0	0	0	0	2	1	0	0
commonwealth	3	.0000	.0314	25.0	2	0	0	0	1	0	0	0	0	0	0	0	0	0	0	0	0	0	0	0	0	0	3	0	0
Commonwealth	21	.2903	1.4571	41.6	2	1	9	3	3	3	0	0	0	0	0	0	0	16	0	0	0	0	0	0	0	0	4	1	0
commotion	14	.6162	1.8381	42.6	2	3	0	5	2	1	0	1	6	0	0	0	0	0	0	0	1	0	0	0	1	3	1	2	0
communal	7	.4846	.7051	38.5	0	0	0	0	2	1	3	1	0	0	0	2	0	0	0	0	1	0	0	0	0	0	2	2	0
commune	7	.3077	.4892	36.9	0	0	5	0	0	0	1	1	0	0	0	1	0	0	0	0	0	0	0	0	0	5	0	1	0
communes	5	.3562	.3925	35.9	0	0	3	0	0	1	1	0	0	0	0	0	0	0	0	0	0	0	0	0	0	3	1	1	0
communicable	3	.0000	.0591	27.7	0	0	0	0	0	3	0	0	0	0	0	0	0	0	0	3	0	0	0	0	0	0	0	0	0
communicate	87	.7993	13.951	51.4	7	7	15	9	22	13	12	2	12	28	2	2	1	2	2	7	6	0	1	1	1	5	7	10	0
communicated	10	.5259	1.1212	40.5	0	0	4	0	2	2	1	1	2	4	0	0	1	0	0	0	1	0	0	0	0	1	0	1	0
communicates	8	.1252	.2745	34.4	0	0	1	0	0	6	1	0	0	7	0	0	0	0	0	0	0	0	0	0	0	0	0	1	0
communicating	17	.6718	2.3575	43.7	0	4	1	2	4	0	5	1	5	5	1	0	1	0	0	1	1	1	1	0	0	0	0	1	0
communication	140	.7628	21.468	53.3	12	4	14	11	38	29	29	3	6	38	0	6	3	27	1	9	3	1	0	6	0	13	18	9	0
Communication	2	.2418	.1091	30.4	0	0	1	0	0	1	0	0	0	0	0	0	0	0	1	0	0	0	0	0	0	0	1	0	0
communications	64	.7058	9.1944	49.6	2	3	18	10	7	8	13	3	4	2	0	2	0	10	0	17	1	0	0	1	0	4	14	9	0
communicative	3	.3814	.2446	33.9	0	0	0	0	1	1	0	1	0	0	0	0	0	0	0	0	1	0	0	0	1	0	0	1	0
communion	5	.4119	.4587	36.6	0	0	0	0	3	0	1	1	1	0	0	1	0	0	0	0	0	0	0	0	0	1	2	0	0
communique	2	.2433	.1158	30.6	0	0	0	0	1	0	1	0	0	0	0	0	0	0	0	0	0	0	0	0	0	1	0	1	0
communism	18	.3182	1.3622	41.3	2	0	0	0	0	11	5	0	1	0	0	0	0	14	1	0	0	0	0	0	0	0	2	0	0
Communism	7	.1766	.3250	35.1	0	0	2	0	1	1	3	0	0	0	0	0	0	2	0	0	0	0	0	0	0	0	0	5	0
communist	7	.4652	.6981	38.4	0	0	1	0	3	1	2	0	0	0	0	1	0	4	1	0	0	0	0	0	0	0	0	1	0
Communist	117	.4493	11.373	50.6	2	1	11	25	15	39	24	0	2	0	0	1	0	57	0	0	0	0	0	0	0	6	14	37	0
communistic	3	.0000	.0583	27.7	0	0	0	0	0	3	0	0	0	0	0	0	0	3	0	0	0	0	0	0	0	0	0	0	0
communists	6	.3454	.5132	37.1	0	0	2	1	1	1	1	0	2	0	0	0	0	3	0	0	0	0	0	0	0	0	0	1	0
Communists	76	.4263	7.0747	48.5	3	0	15	29	3	15	10	1	0	0	0	0	0	44	0	0	0	0	0	0	0	4	12	16	0
communities	142	.6372	18.705	52.7	24	11	10	28	26	17	22	4	6	0	2	0	0	52	0	40	3	0	0	0	1	3	20	15	0
community	368	.7979	58.933	57.7	100	28	41	27	74	45	50	3	9	6	3	6	0	145	2	75	16	7	10	0	6	14	28	41	0
Community	9	.3920	.7916	39.0	2	0	2	1	2	0	2	0	0	1	0	0	0	6	0	1	0	0	0	0	0	1	0	0	0
commutative	88	.0000	1.3172	41.2	0	7	12	16	32	15	6	0	0	0	0	0	88	0	0	0	0	0	0	0	0	0	0	0	0
Commutative	5	.0000	.0748	28.7	0	2	0	0	3	0	0	0	0	0	0	0	5	0	0	0	0	0	0	0	0	0	0	0	0
commutator	6	.0659	.0992	30.0	0	0	0	0	1	5	0	0	0	0	0	0	0	0	0	0	0	0	0	5	0	0	1	0	0
commute	2	.1698	.1133	30.5	0	0	1	0	1	0	0	0	1	0	0	0	0	0	0	0	0	0	0	0	0	0	1	0	0
commuter	5	.4143	.4656	36.7	0	0	0	0	0	4	0	1	1	0	0	0	0	1	0	0	0	0	0	0	0	0	1	2	0
commuters	3	.1277	.1363	31.3	0	0	0	0	3	0	0	0	1	0	0	0	0	0	0	0	0	0	0	0	0	0	0	2	0
commutes	2	.2446	.1142	30.6	0	0	0	0	1	0	0	1	0	0	0	0	0	0	0	0	0	0	0	0	1	0	0	1	0
commuting	8	.4118	.7072	38.5	0	0	1	0	2	0	4	1	0	0	0	0	0	1	0	0	0	0	0	0	0	1	3	3	0
comp'ny	6	.3731	.4805	36.8	0	1	0	0	3	0	2	0	0	0	0	2	0	0	0	0	1	0	0	0	3	0	0	0	0
compact	50	.7145	7.2348	48.6	0	9	10	6	9	5	7	4	2	1	0	2	19	1	0	8	0	0	2	1	2	0	8	4	0
Compact	2	.2306	.1140	30.6	0	0	1	0	0	0	1	0	0	1	0	0	0	1	0	0	0	0	0	0	0	0	0	0	0
compactly	3	.3800	.2528	34.0	0	1	0	0	0	1	0	1	0	0	0	0	1	0	0	1	0	0	0	0	1	0	0	0	0
companies	191	.7363	28.489	54.5	13	20	24	8	47	45	28	6	10	2	1	3	1	97	0	5	8	1	1	8	2	8	24	20	0
Companies	6	.1231	.2155	33.3	0	0	0	0	0	1	0	5	0	0	0	0	0	1	0	0	0	0	0	0	0	0	0	5	0
companion	77	.8104	12.577	51.0	5	12	10	13	19	5	11	2	21	4	1	8	0	6	3	2	0	0	0	0	11	8	7	6	0
Companion	3	.0000	.1370	31.4	0	3	0	0	0	0	0	0	3	0	0	0	0	0	0	0	0	0	0	0	0	0	0	0	0
companion's	2	.1948	.1250	31.0	0	1	0	0	0	1	0	0	1	0	0	0	0	0	0	0	0	0	0	0	0	1	0	0	0
companionable	3	.3399	.2456	33.9	0	1	1	1	0	0	0	0	1	0	0	1	0	0	0	0	0	0	0	0	0	0	0	1	0
companions	101	.6924	14.442	51.6	7	12	10	19	21	14	17	1	32	1	5	20	0	2	0	3	0	0	1	0	15	16	2	4	0
companions'	2	.1717	.1142	30.6	0	0	0	0	0	1	1	0	1	0	0	1	0	0	0	0	0	0	0	0	0	0	0	0	0
companionship	16	.5680	1.9088	42.8	0	1	2	4	5	1	3	0	3	0	0	5	0	0	0	0	0	0	1	0	3	3	0	1	0
company	339	.9329	62.602	58.0	24	62	41	44	60	45	49	14	73	19	4	26	8	61	9	5	9	3	4	5	17	30	18	48	0
Company	119	.8374	19.939	53.0	8	10	15	8	39	18	19	2	21	7	1	4	5	14	0	1	10	1	0	0	11	9	14	21	0
company's	13	.5188	1.4298	41.6	0	0	1	6	3	2	1	0	1	0	0	0	5	1	0	1	0	0	0	0	0	0	2	3	0
Company's	6	.4536	.5987	37.8	1	1	0	1	1	1	0	1	1	0	0	0	1	1	0	1	0	0	0	1	0	1	0	0	0

7H commensal
7H commensals
4Q commensurate
6A commentators
6N commenting
XR commercialized
9R Commie
8F commingling
7R commissar
8R commissars
7N commissary-general
7Q Commission's
7R commissionership
7N commitments
8F committeeman
XB commode
6J commodore's
XP Commodus
9F COMMON
4Q commonly-rooted
7P commons
5Q Commune
6R Communications
6R communicator
6A communings
6R communism's
8R Communist-Socialist
8Q Communist-dominated
8F Communist-leaning
8F Communist-led
6R Communist-ruled
9R Communists'
5H community's
6E commutativity
7R commuters'
4B comp
9D compactness
7N Compagnie-Nationale
XR companies'
6P companionway
4N company-front

Word Type	F	D	U	SFI	3 Gr 3	4 Gr 4	5 Gr 5	6 Gr 6	7 Gr 7	8 Gr 8	9 Gr 9	X UnGr	A Read	B Eng & Gr	C Comp	D Lit	E Math	F Soc Stud	G Spell	H Sci	J Music	K Art	L Home Ec	M Shop	N Lib F	P Lib NF	Q Lib Ref	R Mag	S Rel
comparable	30	.6151	3.7718	45.8	0	0	4	0	12	7	2	5	0	1	0	1	0	2	0	3	3	0	0	0	0	3	9	8	0
comparative	42	.5453	4.6666	46.7	0	0	8	0	13	0	20	1	0	12	7	1	0	0	6	0	1	0	0	1	0	0	13	1	0
comparatively	36	.7970	5.7712	47.6	0	0	3	2	17	6	6	2	5	1	0	2	0	8	0	5	3	0	2	1	0	2	4	3	0
compare	467	.8315	77.509	58.9	20	79	67	78	73	98	47	5	20	39	7	15	137	48	33	89	39	14	5	2	1	5	6	7	0
compared	160	.8630	27.548	54.4	16	22	24	15	37	15	28	3	23	13	4	5	11	20	1	31	4	1	0	0	2	12	19	14	0
compares	33	.5546	3.8028	45.8	2	10	3	2	4	8	3	1	0	4	0	0	18	0	2	4	1	0	0	0	0	0	1	3	0
comparing	72	.7965	11.467	50.6	6	7	6	5	12	15	20	1	1	13	0	0	18	8	4	11	3	3	2	3	2	0	3	1	0
comparison	123	.7951	19.539	52.9	2	7	13	3	41	19	35	3	5	29	9	16	9	3	14	16	1	2	2	1	0	2	9	5	0
comparisons	45	.6603	6.0679	47.8	0	1	11	1	14	9	8	1	4	17	2	8	3	2	2	5	0	0	1	0	0	0	0	1	0
compartment	26	.5602	3.0509	44.8	0	2	4	0	12	3	4	1	4	0	0	1	2	1	0	1	0	0	4	0	2	0	2	9	0
compartments	10	.3576	.7880	39.0	0	0	2	2	3	2	1	0	1	0	0	0	0	0	0	1	0	0	0	3	0	1	2	2	0
compass	210	.6500	28.163	54.5	25	27	20	47	33	31	26	1	21	0	0	3	60	12	4	63	0	0	0	15	3	12	15	2	0
compasses	15	.5912	1.8896	42.8	0	4	2	1	4	3	1	0	5	0	0	0	5	1	0	0	0	0	0	1	1	0	1	1	0
compassion	14	.6038	1.7784	42.5	0	0	1	2	5	4	0	2	4	1	0	2	0	0	0	0	0	1	0	0	2	3	0	1	0
compassionate	4	.3605	.3148	35.0	0	0	0	1	1	1	1	0	0	0	0	1	1	0	0	0	0	0	0	0	2	0	0	0	0
compatriots	2	.0000	.0243	23.9	0	0	0	0	0	0	1	1	0	0	0	0	0	0	0	0	0	0	0	0	0	0	0	2	0
compel	8	.3560	.5980	37.8	0	0	0	0	2	4	2	0	0	0	2	0	0	0	4	0	0	0	0	0	0	0	1	1	0
compelled	20	.5515	2.3021	43.6	1	0	0	1	4	13	1	0	2	0	3	4	0	4	0	0	1	0	0	0	2	2	2	0	0
compelling	8	.5850	.9610	39.8	0	0	0	0	2	3	2	1	0	1	0	1	0	1	0	0	0	0	0	0	1	0	1	3	0
compels	3	.1169	.1277	31.1	0	0	1	1	1	0	0	0	1	0	0	0	0	0	0	0	0	0	0	0	0	0	2	0	0
compendium	2	.0000	.0243	23.9	0	0	0	0	0	1	1	0	0	0	0	0	0	0	0	0	0	0	0	0	0	0	0	2	0
compensate	9	.4377	.8333	39.2	0	0	0	1	3	4	1	0	0	0	0	0	0	0	0	1	2	0	0	0	0	0	2	4	0
compensated	2	.2441	.1127	30.5	0	0	0	0	0	0	2	0	0	0	0	0	0	0	0	0	0	0	0	0	1	0	1	0	0
compensates	2	.1948	.1250	31.0	0	0	0	0	0	2	0	0	1	0	0	0	0	0	0	0	0	0	0	0	0	1	0	0	0
compensation	12	.5962	1.4829	41.7	0	0	0	1	3	4	3	1	1	0	1	0	1	3	0	0	2	0	0	0	0	2	0	2	0
compensator	3	.1983	.1396	31.4	0	0	0	0	1	2	0	0	0	0	0	0	0	0	0	0	2	0	0	0	0	0	0	1	0
compete	34	.7172	4.9788	47.0	4	4	2	5	5	6	5	3	6	0	0	3	0	7	0	1	1	0	0	0	3	3	6	4	0
competed	7	.5064	.7602	38.8	0	1	0	1	4	1	0	0	1	0	0	0	0	1	0	0	0	0	0	0	0	2	1	2	0
competence	3	.0000	.0365	25.6	0	0	0	0	2	0	1	0	0	0	0	0	0	0	0	0	0	0	0	0	0	0	0	3	0
competent	11	.5027	1.1890	40.8	0	0	0	1	9	0	1	0	2	0	0	0	0	1	1	0	0	0	0	0	1	1	0	5	0
competing	18	.6153	2.2945	43.6	2	2	1	4	2	1	3	3	2	0	0	0	0	3	0	1	0	0	1	0	0	3	4	4	0
competition	76	.6215	9.8254	49.9	2	4	12	6	28	13	8	3	12	0	0	1	0	14	0	2	2	0	0	0	1	10	12	22	0
Competition	2	.0000	.0215	23.3	0	0	0	0	0	0	2	0	0	0	0	2	0	0	0	0	0	0	0	0	0	0	0	0	0
competitions	4	.2420	.3089	34.9	0	0	0	0	3	1	0	0	3	0	0	0	0	1	0	0	0	0	0	0	0	0	0	0	0
competitive	11	.6086	1.4069	41.5	0	0	1	0	4	3	1	2	3	0	0	1	0	0	0	0	0	0	0	0	1	2	2	2	0
competitor	3	.3380	.2439	33.9	0	0	0	0	1	1	1	0	1	1	0	1	0	0	0	0	0	0	0	0	0	0	0	0	0
competitors	13	.5085	1.3778	41.4	0	3	2	2	1	0	4	1	0	2	1	0	0	0	0	0	0	0	0	0	0	7	1	2	0
compile	4	.3509	.3113	34.9	0	0	0	0	2	1	1	0	0	1	0	0	0	1	0	0	0	0	0	0	0	0	0	2	0
compiled	8	.4674	.7866	39.0	0	0	1	1	2	2	1	1	0	1	0	0	0	0	0	0	0	0	0	0	0	2	2	3	0
complacency	3	.1937	.1495	31.7	0	0	0	0	1	2	0	0	0	0	0	0	0	1	0	0	0	0	0	0	0	0	0	2	0
complacent	5	.4685	.4918	36.9	0	0	1	0	2	1	0	1	0	0	0	1	0	0	0	0	0	0	0	0	2	1	1	0	0
complacently	3	.2212	.2099	33.2	0	0	0	2	0	1	0	0	2	0	0	1	0	0	0	0	0	0	0	0	0	0	0	0	0
complain	31	.7962	5.0010	47.0	5	4	5	6	4	2	4	1	10	2	0	1	0	5	1	0	1	0	0	0	3	3	2	3	0
complained	55	.7330	8.2793	49.2	6	10	4	10	13	8	3	1	19	4	1	1	0	5	0	0	0	0	0	0	8	7	2	8	0
complaining	22	.6015	2.7878	44.5	0	5	4	1	5	2	4	1	6	2	0	2	0	1	0	0	0	0	0	0	6	1	0	4	0
complains	9	.5396	1.0203	40.1	0	0	2	1	3	2	1	0	1	0	0	1	0	1	0	0	0	0	0	0	1	0	3	2	0
complaint	16	.6269	2.0517	43.1	0	1	4	0	0	1	9	1	1	5	0	1	0	0	1	0	0	0	0	0	2	1	1	4	0
complaints	11	.5400	1.2439	40.9	0	0	1	0	3	4	2	1	0	0	0	0	0	2	0	3	0	0	1	0	0	2	0	3	0
complement	83	.4752	8.2203	49.1	0	2	1	2	31	28	11	8	0	53	0	0	14	0	1	1	0	7	2	0	1	0	1	3	0
complementary	14	.3518	1.0438	40.2	0	3	0	0	4	1	6	0	0	0	0	0	6	0	0	0	0	4	3	0	0	0	1	0	0
complements	15	.3154	1.0316	40.1	0	0	0	0	4	6	5	0	0	10	0	0	2	0	0	0	0	0	3	0	0	0	0	0	0
complete	1445	.7558	219.72	63.4	213	254	307	178	213	138	126	16	75	150	45	13	685	34	157	72	44	1	16	34	7	29	35	48	0
Complete	4	.3613	.3132	35.0	0	0	0	0	0	1	2	1	0	2	0	0	0	0	0	0	0	0	0	0	1	0	0	1	0
completed	192	.8099	31.146	54.9	8	27	20	21	45	28	39	4	22	16	1	5	29	25	3	13	4	1	9	19	5	12	16	12	0
completely	337	.9064	60.622	57.8	21	40	46	38	92	36	45	19	63	16	3	16	10	29	8	51	8	3	10	18	14	25	38	25	0
completeness	3	.2630	.1786	32.5	0	0	0	0	2	0	1	0	0	0	0	0	1	0	0	0	0	0	0	1	0	1	0	0	0
completer	2	.0000	.0219	23.4	0	0	0	0	0	0	2	0	0	2	0	0	0	0	0	0	0	0	0	0	0	0	0	0	0
completes	36	.7809	5.6769	47.5	1	4	5	5	15	5	1	0	7	7	1	1	2	2	4	7	0	0	1	0	0	0	2	2	0
completing	31	.6294	3.9844	46.0	1	4	4	5	10	3	4	0	2	4	1	0	3	3	13	1	0	0	0	1	0	1	1	1	0
completion	17	.7212	2.4964	44.0	1	1	4	1	4	1	4	1	3	0	0	1	1	1	0	1	0	0	1	0	1	2	4	2	0
completly	2	.2306	.1140	30.6	0	0	0	0	1	0	1	0	0	1	0	0	0	1	0	0	0	0	0	0	0	0	0	0	0
complex	206	.8043	33.122	55.2	6	18	15	12	63	47	36	9	12	22	10	5	9	5	1	38	26	1	3	3	1	6	52	12	0
Complex	2	.2437	.1129	30.5	0	0	0	0	1	1	0	0	0	0	0	0	0	0	0	0	0	0	0	0	0	0	1	1	0
complexes	3	.3769	.2484	34.0	0	0	0	0	0	2	1	0	0	0	0	0	0	1	0	0	0	0	0	0	0	0	1	1	0
complexion	19	.4943	2.0148	43.0	0	1	0	2	6	2	8	0	4	1	0	5	0	1	0	1	0	0	4	0	2	0	0	1	0
complexions	6	.1300	.1849	32.7	1	0	0	0	0	4	1	0	0	0	0	0	0	0	0	0	0	0	4	0	2	0	0	0	0
complexities	9	.3102	.6258	38.0	0	0	0	0	2	1	4	2	0	0	0	0	0	0	0	1	0	0	0	0	0	0	3	5	0
complexity	20	.4641	1.9943	43.0	0	1	0	0	11	3	4	1	2	0	0	0	1	3	0	1	2	0	0	0	0	0	10	1	0
compliance	3	.3769	.2484	34.0	0	0	1	0	0	1	1	0	0	0	0	0	0	1	0	0	0	0	0	0	0	0	1	1	0
complicated	143	.8183	23.399	53.7	0	11	13	26	27	21	42	3	13	23	7	8	7	13	3	27	3	0	3	9	2	4	17	4	0
complication	2	.2417	.1091	30.4	0	0	0	0	0	2	0	0	0	0	0	0	0	0	0	0	1	0	0	0	0	0	1	0	0
complications	6	.4693	.5858	37.7	0	0	1	0	0	5	0	0	0	0	1	1	1	0	0	0	0	0	0	0	0	0	2	1	0
complied	3	.2609	.1751	32.4	0	0	0	0	1	1	1	0	0	0	1	0	0	0	0	0	0	0	0	0	0	1	0	1	0
compliment	17	.6735	2.3344	43.7	0	2	2	6	1	3	3	0	2	2	0	2	0	1	3	0	1	0	0	0	3	0	0	3	0
complimentary	2	.1693	.0748	28.7	0	0	0	1	0	1	0	0	0	0	0	0	0	0	1	0	0	1	0	0	0	0	0	0	0
complimented	2	.2444	.1132	30.5	0	0	0	0	1	0	1	0	0	1	0	0	0	0	0	0	0	0	0	0	1	0	0	0	0
complimenting	2	.1717	.1142	30.6	0	0	1	0	1	0	0	0	1	0	0	1	0	0	0	0	0	0	0	0	0	0	0	0	0
compliments	8	.5360	.9340	39.7	1	2	0	1	0	3	1	0	3	0	0	2	0	0	0	0	0	0	0	0	1	1	0	1	0
comply	2	.2152	.1357	31.3	0	0	0	1	0	1	0	0	1	0	0	0	0	1	0	0	0	0	0	0	0	0	0	0	0
component	25	.4752	2.5145	44.0	0	0	0	0	2	9	13	1	0	2	0	1	15	0	0	1	0	0	0	0	0	0	4	2	0
components	24	.5661	2.8019	44.5	0	0	0	1	6	1	14	2	0	1	0	0	7	0	0	2	0	0	0	1	0	0	7	6	0
compose	54	.5164	5.7852	47.6	1	20	7	8	7	5	3	3	4	3	3	2	1	0	5	2	30	0	0	0	0	1	1	2	0
composed	223	.6860	30.985	54.9	2	23	22	34	51	46	39	6	14	6	11	4	8	5	1	40	89	1	1	8	4	7	21	3	0
composer	316	.0751	7.1747	48.6	6	60	28	54	67	74	25	2	2	0	0	0	0	1	0	2	296	0	0	0	0	4	10	1	0
composer's	13	.0000	.1051	30.2	0	3	1	3	2	3	1	0	0	0	0	0	0	0	0	0	13	0	0	0	0	0	0	0	0
composers	246	.0935	6.4228	48.1	5	17	26	44	39	103	12	0	1	0	0	0	0	1	0	0	225	0	0	0	0	4	15	0	0
composes	6	.3560	.4727	36.7	1	1	1	0	2	1	0	0	1	0	0	0	0	0	0	0	3	1	0	0	0	0	1	0	0
composing	32	.2737	1.9869	43.0	0	1	5	5	11	5	5	0	2	0	0	2	0	0	0	0	22	0	0	0	0	3	3	0	0
composite	23	.5095	2.4639	43.9	2	3	0	1	8	7	1	1	0	0	0	1	15	0	0	2	0	1	0	0	0	2	1	1	0
composition	378	.5907	45.239	56.6	2	56	45	40	117	63	47	8	4	48	41	12	0	2	5	22	202	17	2	7	1	3	8	4	0
Composition	4	.2224	.1927	32.8	0	0	1	3	0	0	0	0	0	0	2	0	0	0	0	0	1	0	0	0	0	0	1	0	0
compositional	3	.2196	.1435	31.6	0	0	0	0	1	1	1	0	0	0	0	0	0	0	0	0	2	1	0	0	0	0	0	0	0
compositions	130	.4241	11.451	50.6	3	14	23	19	18	37	14	2	0	8	4	1	0	0	0	1	98	6	0	0	3	3	5	1	0
compositor	6	.0000	.0151	21.8	0	0	0	0	0	0	6	0	0	0	0	0	0	0	0	0	0	0	0	6	0	0	0	0	0
compost	2	.2437	.1129	30.5	0	0	0	0	1	0	0	1	0	0	0	0	0	0	0	0	0	0	0	0	0	0	1	1	0
composure	5	.3375	.4157	36.2	0	0	1	1	3	0	0	0	2	0	0	0	0	0	0	0	0	0	0	0	2	0	0	1	0
compound	480	.5969	58.832	57.7	41	74	83	75	73	71	60	3	26	125	16	0	24	12	179	62	0	0	1	3	1	13	13	5	0
compounded	18	.5561	2.0805	43.2	0	0	1	0	4	9	3	1	1	8	0	1	3	0	1	1	0	0	0	0	0	1	0	2	0

7G comparatives
9Q comparativist
XH comparator
7N Compared
7A comparison-contrast
7R compartment's
9R compartmentalized
5Q compartmentizer
5Q Compass
3F compass-rose
7N compassion-inspiring
4R compatriot
9D compellingly
7R compensating
8Q competes
XR Competitive
8F competitiveness
7R competitor's
5P compilation
6B compiler
8F compiling
8A complainingly
7A Complement
XR complexion-consoling
6R complicate
9Q complicates
9Q complicating
7D composedly
8J composers'
6J composit
9M compositors
7Q Compostela
9C compound-complex

Word Type	F	D	U	SFI	3 Gr 3	4 Gr 4	5 Gr 5	6 Gr 6	7 Gr 7	8 Gr 8	9 Gr 9	X UnGr	A Read	B Eng & Gr	C Comp	D Lit	E Math	F Soc Stud	G Spell	H Sci	J Music	K Art	L Home Ec	M Shop	N Lib F	P Lib NF	Q Lib Ref	R Mag	S Rel
compounding	4	.1772	.1782	32.5	0	0	1	1	0	2	0	0	0	3	0	0	0	0	0	0	0	0	0	0	0	1	0	0	0
compounds	243	.4288	22.546	53.5	12	28	47	40	40	42	28	6	5	4	0	0	0	1	88	118	0	0	0	1	0	1	19	6	0
comprehend	13	.4666	1.4358	41.6	0	0	0	1	5	7	0	0	9	0	0	0	0	0	0	0	0	0	0	0	2	0	1	1	0
comprehended	5	.4757	.5327	37.3	0	0	0	0	1	3	1	0	2	1	0	0	0	0	0	0	0	0	0	0	1	0	1	0	0
comprehension	19	.5699	2.4164	43.8	0	0	0	0	5	12	2	0	13	2	0	1	0	0	0	1	0	0	0	0	0	1	1	0	0
comprehensive	7	.2428	.3968	36.0	0	3	1	0	1	0	1	1	0	1	0	0	0	0	0	1	0	0	0	0	0	0	5	0	0
compress	7	.3896	.6516	38.1	0	0	0	1	3	2	1	0	3	0	0	0	0	0	0	2	0	0	0	1	0	0	1	0	0
compressed	45	.7984	7.2574	48.6	3	6	1	6	11	12	6	0	11	4	1	2	0	1	0	13	3	0	0	1	0	2	4	3	0
compresses	5	.2424	.2988	34.8	0	0	1	0	1	0	3	0	0	0	0	0	0	0	0	3	0	0	0	0	0	0	2	0	0
compressibility	10	.0000	.1972	32.9	0	0	0	0	0	0	10	0	0	0	0	0	0	0	0	10	0	0	0	0	0	0	0	0	0
compressible	5	.0000	.0986	29.9	0	0	0	0	0	0	5	0	0	0	0	0	0	0	0	5	0	0	0	0	0	0	0	0	0
compression	20	.6123	2.5284	44.0	0	0	3	1	6	1	4	5	1	0	1	0	0	0	0	8	0	0	0	1	0	1	3	5	0
compressive	5	.3338	.3593	35.6	0	2	0	0	2	1	0	0	0	0	0	0	0	0	0	0	0	1	0	0	0	0	2	2	0
compressor	18	.4386	1.6775	42.2	0	3	0	2	11	0	2	0	0	0	0	0	0	0	0	4	0	0	0	2	0	0	3	9	0
comprise	8	.5289	.8724	39.4	0	3	0	1	2	1	1	0	0	0	1	1	1	1	0	0	1	0	0	0	0	0	3	0	0
comprises	7	.3026	.4582	36.6	1	0	1	0	2	0	1	2	0	0	2	0	0	0	0	0	0	0	0	0	0	0	3	2	0
comprising	6	.4662	.5936	37.7	0	0	1	0	2	3	0	0	0	0	0	0	0	2	0	0	1	0	0	0	0	1	2	0	0
compromise	29	.6342	3.8217	45.8	0	0	2	1	8	10	5	3	4	4	0	1	0	13	0	0	0	0	1	0	0	1	1	4	0
Compromise	23	.2793	1.6409	42.2	0	0	4	0	4	15	0	0	4	0	0	0	0	16	0	0	0	0	0	0	0	0	3	0	0
compromises	7	.1766	.3250	35.1	0	0	0	0	1	2	2	2	0	0	0	0	0	2	0	0	0	0	0	0	0	0	0	5	0
compromising	2	.2440	.1132	30.5	0	0	0	0	1	1	0	0	0	0	0	1	0	0	0	0	0	0	0	0	0	0	0	1	0
Compton's	3	.0000	.0328	25.2	0	0	2	0	0	0	1	0	0	3	0	0	0	0	0	0	0	0	0	0	0	0	0	0	0
Comptroller	2	.0000	.0243	23.9	0	0	0	0	2	0	0	0	0	0	0	0	0	0	0	0	0	0	0	0	0	0	0	2	0
compulsion	5	.1954	.2209	33.4	0	0	1	0	1	3	0	0	0	0	2	0	0	0	0	0	0	0	0	0	0	0	3	0	0
compulsory	12	.4553	1.1557	40.6	1	0	0	0	3	4	4	0	0	0	2	2	0	4	0	0	0	0	0	0	0	0	1	3	0
computation	21	.0000	.3143	35.0	0	0	3	10	2	5	1	0	0	0	0	0	21	0	0	0	0	0	0	0	0	0	0	0	0
computations	25	.2434	1.4695	41.7	0	1	1	2	2	10	9	0	0	0	0	0	21	0	0	0	0	0	0	0	0	1	2	1	0
compute	146	.0462	3.4622	45.4	1	38	48	8	5	23	23	0	2	1	0	0	142	0	0	0	0	0	0	0	0	0	0	1	0
computed	15	.5000	1.5822	42.0	0	1	0	1	0	6	3	4	0	0	0	1	8	0	0	3	0	0	0	1	0	0	0	2	0
computer	78	.5873	9.6320	49.8	7	4	4	13	18	9	20	3	16	2	0	0	12	2	0	7	0	1	0	0	0	0	27	11	0
Computer	2	.2437	.1129	30.5	0	0	0	0	0	0	1	1	0	0	0	0	0	0	0	0	0	0	0	0	0	0	1	1	0
computer-controlled	3	.2321	.1635	32.1	0	0	1	2	0	0	0	0	0	0	0	0	0	0	0	0	0	0	0	0	0	0	1	2	0
computerized	2	.0000	.0243	23.9	0	0	0	0	1	0	0	1	0	0	0	0	0	0	0	0	0	0	0	0	0	0	0	2	0
computers	56	.6760	7.8164	48.9	2	0	6	19	15	10	4	0	12	9	0	0	7	0	0	12	2	0	0	0	0	2	9	3	0
computes	2	.0000	.0394	26.0	0	0	0	1	1	0	0	0	0	0	0	0	0	0	0	2	0	0	0	0	0	0	0	0	0
computing	38	.1075	1.3388	41.3	0	1	3	8	7	14	4	1	1	1	0	0	35	0	0	1	0	0	0	0	0	0	0	0	0
comrade	17	.4567	1.6627	42.2	0	0	0	4	6	3	4	0	2	0	0	7	0	0	0	0	3	0	0	0	4	1	0	0	0
Comrade	2	.0000	.0234	23.7	0	0	0	0	0	0	2	0	0	0	0	0	0	0	0	0	0	0	0	0	2	0	0	0	0
comrades	38	.6497	5.1071	47.1	0	1	0	9	8	9	10	1	9	3	2	6	0	2	0	0	3	0	0	0	11	0	0	2	0
comsumption	2	.0000	.0394	26.0	0	0	0	0	0	0	0	2	0	0	0	0	0	0	0	2	0	0	0	0	0	0	0	0	0
comtemporary	4	.3473	.2974	34.7	0	0	0	0	3	1	0	0	0	0	0	1	0	0	0	0	2	0	0	0	0	0	1	0	0
con	16	.4312	1.4524	41.6	1	0	3	1	5	3	3	0	1	2	0	1	0	0	9	0	0	0	2	0	0	0	0	1	0
con-ver-sa-tion	3	.0000	.0365	25.6	0	0	0	0	3	0	0	0	0	0	0	0	0	0	0	0	0	0	0	0	0	0	0	3	0
Concannon	2	.0000	.0243	23.9	0	0	0	1	1	0	0	0	0	0	0	0	0	0	0	0	0	0	0	0	0	0	0	2	0
concave	10	.3257	.7374	38.7	0	2	0	1	2	1	0	4	0	0	0	0	0	0	0	6	0	0	0	2	0	0	2	0	0
concavity	2	.0000	.0394	26.0	0	0	0	0	0	0	0	2	0	0	0	0	0	0	0	2	0	0	0	0	0	0	0	0	0
conceal	11	.5387	1.2775	41.1	1	0	2	0	4	2	2	0	4	0	0	1	0	0	1	0	0	0	2	0	0	1	1	1	0
concealed	26	.6625	3.5874	45.5	2	0	3	4	11	2	4	0	9	1	2	3	0	1	0	0	0	0	0	0	2	2	2	4	0
concealing	3	.2120	.1548	31.9	0	0	1	0	2	0	0	0	0	0	0	0	0	0	0	0	0	0	0	0	2	1	0	0	0
concealment	7	.2669	.4486	36.5	0	0	0	0	7	0	0	0	1	0	0	0	0	0	0	0	0	0	0	0	2	0	4	0	0
conceals	2	.2417	.1091	30.4	0	1	0	0	1	0	0	0	0	0	0	0	0	0	0	0	1	0	0	0	0	0	1	0	0
concede	5	.4228	.4710	36.7	0	0	0	1	2	1	1	0	1	0	0	0	0	0	0	0	0	0	0	0	1	1	0	2	0
conceded	6	.4764	.6066	37.8	0	1	0	0	0	2	1	2	0	0	0	1	0	2	0	0	0	0	0	0	1	0	0	2	0
concedes	3	.2321	.1635	32.1	0	0	0	0	1	0	1	1	0	0	0	0	0	0	0	0	0	0	0	0	0	0	1	2	0
conceit	3	.2524	.1934	32.9	0	0	1	0	0	0	2	0	1	0	0	1	0	0	0	0	0	0	1	0	0	0	0	0	0
conceited	6	.5570	.7172	38.6	0	1	0	1	3	1	0	0	2	0	0	1	0	0	0	0	0	0	0	0	1	0	1	1	0
conceivably	8	.4500	.7616	38.8	0	0	0	0	4	1	1	2	0	0	0	2	0	0	0	1	0	0	0	0	0	0	2	3	0
conceive	8	.5066	.8391	39.2	0	0	0	0	3	2	3	0	0	1	0	1	0	1	0	0	0	1	0	0	0	0	3	1	0
conceived	29	.7048	4.1359	46.2	0	0	0	2	5	10	11	1	1	0	1	7	1	3	0	4	2	0	0	0	0	1	6	3	0
conceives	2	.2417	.1091	30.4	0	0	0	0	0	2	0	0	0	0	0	0	0	0	0	0	1	0	0	0	0	0	1	0	0
concentrate	37	.7234	5.4107	47.3	2	3	5	2	11	6	6	2	3	7	2	0	0	3	1	3	3	0	0	0	1	1	4	9	0
concentrated	59	.7191	8.6298	49.4	5	1	5	6	18	4	16	4	8	0	0	4	0	8	1	7	2	0	0	2	0	4	16	7	0
concentrates	7	.4480	.6590	38.2	1	0	1	0	0	1	3	1	0	1	0	1	0	0	0	0	0	0	0	0	0	0	3	2	0
concentrating	9	.6409	1.2019	40.8	1	1	1	0	1	0	3	2	2	0	0	2	0	1	0	1	0	0	0	0	1	1	0	1	0
concentration	35	.8395	5.8911	47.7	1	3	2	3	8	10	8	0	9	2	1	1	0	4	2	2	2	0	1	0	0	2	4	5	0
concentrations	7	.4320	.6542	38.2	0	0	0	0	3	1	2	1	0	0	0	0	0	2	0	1	0	0	0	0	0	0	1	3	0
concentric	4	.1901	.1843	32.7	0	1	0	0	2	0	1	0	0	0	0	0	0	0	0	0	0	0	0	0	1	0	3	0	0
concept	89	.7657	13.707	51.4	0	9	4	26	19	15	10	6	3	1	1	2	12	1	0	30	7	1	0	2	0	1	19	9	0
conception	12	.5683	1.4105	41.5	0	0	0	0	1	4	3	4	1	0	1	0	0	1	0	2	1	0	0	2	1	0	3	0	0
conceptions	2	.2417	.1091	30.4	0	0	1	0	0	1	0	0	0	0	0	0	0	0	0	0	1	0	0	0	0	0	1	0	0
concepts	54	.5544	6.3004	48.0	0	9	9	17	8	9	0	2	0	2	0	0	1	6	0	36	2	2	0	0	0	0	4	1	0
Concepts	9	.2204	.5163	37.1	0	7	0	0	0	0	0	2	0	0	0	0	0	0	0	7	0	0	0	0	0	0	0	2	0
conceptual	2	.1378	.0662	28.2	0	0	0	0	0	2	0	0	0	0	0	0	0	0	0	0	0	1	0	0	0	0	0	1	0
concern	96	.8811	16.820	52.3	1	2	12	10	28	25	13	5	15	6	3	4	0	8	5	9	4	1	3	0	4	5	10	19	0
concerned	187	.8597	32.066	55.1	4	13	17	21	59	36	33	4	24	8	4	6	11	36	0	22	6	3	2	0	8	13	21	22	1
concerning	73	.8838	12.801	51.1	1	2	5	13	18	19	11	4	4	6	2	1	5	4	2	13	3	0	3	1	7	3	12	7	0
concerns	38	.5385	4.2149	46.2	0	1	1	2	11	4	19	0	0	1	9	1	0	9	0	3	4	1	1	0	0	0	2	7	0
concert	101	.4481	9.5770	49.8	8	4	11	22	22	18	15	1	6	7	0	0	5	5	2	0	57	0	0	0	3	7	4	5	0
Concert	15	.3042	1.3307	41.2	1	0	0	13	0	0	1	0	13	0	0	0	0	1	0	0	0	0	0	0	0	0	1	0	0
concert-band	2	.0000	.0162	22.1	0	0	0	0	0	2	0	0	0	0	0	0	0	0	0	0	2	0	0	0	0	0	0	0	0
concerted	3	.2321	.1635	32.1	0	1	0	0	0	1	1	0	0	0	0	0	0	0	0	0	0	0	0	0	0	0	1	2	0
concertino	4	.0000	.0323	25.1	0	0	0	0	0	4	0	0	0	0	0	0	0	0	0	0	4	0	0	0	0	0	0	0	0
Concertino	2	.0000	.0162	22.1	0	0	0	2	0	0	0	0	0	0	0	0	0	0	0	0	2	0	0	0	0	0	0	0	0
concerto	27	.2101	1.3946	41.4	0	1	0	4	4	12	6	0	3	1	0	0	0	0	0	1	20	0	0	0	0	1	1	0	0
Concerto	17	.1181	.5238	37.2	1	3	1	2	3	3	4	0	0	0	0	1	0	0	0	0	15	0	0	0	0	1	0	0	0
concertos	8	.3259	.5638	37.5	0	1	0	0	2	2	3	0	0	1	0	0	0	0	0	0	5	0	0	0	0	1	1	0	0
Concertos	2	.2401	.1133	30.5	0	1	0	0	1	0	0	0	0	0	0	0	0	0	0	0	0	0	0	0	0	1	1	0	0
concerts	51	.2051	2.5058	44.0	8	5	12	3	6	13	4	0	2	0	0	0	0	5	0	0	38	0	0	0	0	0	1	5	0
concession	6	.2697	.3782	35.8	0	0	0	0	0	1	2	3	0	0	0	0	0	1	0	0	0	0	0	0	0	1	0	4	0
concessions	14	.4933	1.4851	41.7	0	0	0	0	3	7	3	1	1	0	0	0	0	6	0	0	0	0	0	0	0	3	1	3	0
conch	3	.3395	.2468	33.9	0	1	0	2	0	0	0	0	1	0	0	0	0	0	0	0	0	0	0	0	0	1	1	0	0
conchs	2	.0000	.0209	23.2	0	0	0	0	0	2	0	0	0	0	0	0	0	0	0	0	0	0	0	0	0	0	2	0	0
conciliating	2	.0000	.0215	23.3	0	0	0	0	1	1	0	0	0	0	0	2	0	0	0	0	0	0	0	0	0	0	0	0	0
Conciliation	3	.2043	.1486	31.7	0	0	2	0	0	1	0	0	0	0	0	0	0	0	0	0	0	0	0	0	0	1	2	0	0
concise	3	.2124	.1442	31.6	0	0	0	0	1	0	2	0	0	2	1	0	0	0	0	0	0	0	0	0	0	0	0	0	0
conclude	43	.6988	6.1168	47.9	1	1	1	0	10	15	14	1	1	1	0	1	15	3	2	13	0	0	0	1	1	2	0	3	0
concluded	38	.7619	5.8561	47.7	1	2	1	4	9	15	6	0	4	1	0	3	2	3	1	12	0	0	0	0	1	2	5	4	0

8A comprehending
9C comprehensible
6R compressed-air
9H compressibilities
8D compressing
9N comprised
8F compromised
8Q Compton
5R compulsively
3P computer-automated
3P computer-brained
3P computer-fed
7F computors
7A comradeship
5B comradeships
7Q Comte
8B con-
7A Con-nor
5G con'tent**
8G Conan
8B conant
7H Conant
7Q conceivable
7Q conceiving
7R concentratedly
7F Concepcion
8K CONCEPTUAL
9R concern's
9Q Concerning
9J concert-going
7J concert-master
9B concerti
7J concertmaster
8J concerto-grosso
XH conchoidal
7Q Conchos
7A conciliation
9R conciliatory
7B concisely
7Q conciseness
8F conclave

Word Type	F	D	U	SFI	3 Gr 3	4 Gr 4	5 Gr 5	6 Gr 6	7 Gr 7	8 Gr 8	9 Gr 9	X UnGr	A Read	B Eng & Gr	C Comp	D Lit	E Math	F Soc Stud	G Spell	H Sci	J Music	K Art	L Home Ec	M Shop	N Lib F	P Lib NF	Q Lib Ref	R Mag	S Rel
concludes	10	.5667	1.1776	40.7	0	1	2	0	2	2	3	0	1	3	1	0	1	0	0	1	1	0	0	0	0	0	0	2	0
concluding	6	.5384	.6681	38.2	0	0	2	1	0	2	1	0	0	2	0	1	0	0	0	1	1	0	0	0	1	0	0	0	0
conclusion	126	.7814	19.809	53.0	4	2	15	13	22	31	33	6	14	19	5	5	31	2	1	15	3	0	0	0	4	4	9	14	0
conclusions	62	.6289	8.0623	49.1	1	3	4	6	19	14	13	2	10	7	9	0	7	0	1	14	0	0	2	1	0	1	6	4	0
conclusive	4	.3512	.3114	34.9	0	0	0	0	1	1	2	0	0	0	0	0	0	0	0	1	0	0	0	0	0	0	1	2	0
concocted	5	.2392	.3123	34.9	0	0	1	1	2	1	0	0	1	0	0	0	0	1	0	0	0	0	0	0	0	0	0	3	0
concoction	2	.2346	.1166	30.7	0	0	0	0	1	0	0	1	0	0	0	0	0	0	0	1	0	0	0	0	0	0	0	1	0
Concord	34	.6279	4.6117	46.6	3	1	16	4	2	8	0	0	21	1	0	0	0	1	2	0	0	0	0	0	2	4	3	0	0
concrete	95	.7327	14.067	51.5	11	6	9	13	14	12	20	10	11	1	2	9	3	7	1	4	0	8	0	2	3	7	20	17	0
concurrent	4	.0000	.0599	27.8	0	0	0	0	4	0	0	0	0	0	0	0	4	0	0	0	0	0	0	0	0	0	0	0	0
condemn	5	.4622	.4857	36.9	0	0	0	2	1	1	1	0	0	2	0	1	0	0	0	0	0	0	0	0	1	1	0	0	0
condemnation	6	.5096	.6515	38.1	0	0	0	2	1	1	1	1	1	2	0	1	0	0	0	0	0	0	0	0	0	1	1	0	0
condemned	20	.5910	2.4803	43.9	1	1	2	5	1	6	2	2	4	0	0	0	0	2	0	0	3	0	0	0	3	5	3	0	0
condemning	4	.1325	.1944	32.9	0	0	0	0	1	3	0	0	1	0	0	0	0	3	0	0	0	0	0	0	0	0	0	0	0
condensation	25	.0000	.4929	36.9	2	6	3	1	0	1	12	0	0	0	0	0	0	0	0	25	0	0	0	0	0	0	0	0	0
condense	22	.4712	2.2335	43.5	3	1	0	5	2	3	8	0	0	0	1	0	0	0	1	16	0	0	0	0	3	0	1	0	0
condensed	16	.5889	1.9437	42.9	0	0	0	2	5	4	5	0	0	0	0	1	0	0	1	8	1	0	2	0	1	0	2	0	0
condenser	2	.0000	.0394	26.0	0	0	0	0	0	0	0	2	0	0	0	0	0	0	0	2	0	0	0	0	0	0	0	0	0
condenses	23	.2203	1.3308	41.2	6	6	1	2	4	0	4	0	0	0	0	0	0	0	0	20	0	0	0	0	0	1	2	0	0
condensing	2	.2160	.1362	31.3	0	1	0	0	1	0	0	0	1	0	0	0	0	0	0	1	0	0	0	0	0	0	0	0	0
condescend	4	.3086	.2949	34.7	0	2	0	1	0	1	0	0	1	2	0	0	0	0	0	0	1	0	0	0	0	0	0	0	0
condition	193	.8857	34.013	55.3	9	11	17	24	55	31	36	10	33	8	3	12	2	16	4	39	3	0	8	2	6	16	26	15	0
conditional	3	.3763	.2498	34.0	0	0	0	0	0	2	1	0	0	0	0	0	1	1	0	0	0	0	0	0	0	0	1	0	0
conditioned	10	.6283	1.2787	41.1	1	0	0	1	3	2	2	1	0	1	0	1	0	1	0	0	2	0	0	0	0	1	1	3	0
conditioner	3	.3764	.2483	33.9	0	0	2	0	1	0	0	0	0	0	0	0	0	0	0	1	0	0	0	0	0	0	1	1	0
conditioners	4	.3269	.2809	34.5	1	0	1	0	1	0	1	0	0	0	0	0	0	0	0	0	0	0	0	1	0	0	2	1	0
conditioning	13	.6378	1.7121	42.3	1	0	2	3	2	2	2	1	1	1	0	0	0	2	1	3	0	0	0	0	0	2	0	3	0
Conditioning	2	.2437	.1129	30.5	0	0	1	0	1	0	0	0	0	0	0	0	0	0	0	0	0	0	0	0	0	0	1	1	0
conditions	360	.8256	59.472	57.7	18	20	44	30	98	63	61	26	21	3	3	10	14	55	5	113	3	1	6	4	2	19	66	35	0
condone	2	.2297	.1135	30.6	0	0	1	0	1	0	0	0	0	0	0	1	0	1	0	0	0	0	0	0	0	0	0	0	0
condor	5	.1275	.1790	32.5	0	0	0	0	5	0	0	0	0	0	0	0	0	0	0	1	0	0	0	0	0	0	4	0	0
condors	2	.2437	.1129	30.5	0	1	0	0	1	0	0	0	0	0	0	0	0	0	0	0	0	0	0	0	0	0	1	1	0
conducive	3	.2445	.1818	32.6	0	0	0	0	2	0	0	1	0	0	0	0	0	0	0	2	0	0	0	0	0	0	1	0	0
conduct	76	.7784	11.899	50.8	9	6	9	7	14	10	20	1	8	1	1	3	0	8	1	13	17	0	0	1	5	3	10	5	0
conducted	57	.7895	9.0256	49.6	0	4	3	7	17	15	8	3	4	2	1	1	0	7	2	7	8	0	0	0	3	4	11	7	0
conducting	34	.4078	2.9361	44.7	1	1	9	3	7	5	6	2	1	1	0	0	1	0	0	1	21	0	0	1	0	0	2	6	0
conduction	5	.3749	.4195	36.2	0	0	0	0	2	0	3	0	0	0	0	0	0	0	0	3	0	0	0	0	0	0	1	1	0
conductive	2	.2160	.1362	31.3	1	0	0	0	0	0	1	0	1	0	0	0	0	0	0	1	0	0	0	0	0	0	0	0	0
conductor	115	.5386	13.012	51.1	18	7	20	14	14	36	4	2	19	4	0	1	0	3	1	10	29	0	0	20	0	12	12	4	0
Conductor	3	.2028	.1988	33.0	0	2	0	0	0	1	0	0	2	0	0	0	0	0	0	0	1	0	0	0	0	0	0	0	0
conductor's	3	.2028	.1988	33.0	1	2	0	0	0	0	0	0	2	0	0	0	0	0	0	0	1	0	0	0	0	0	0	0	0
conductors	32	.6130	4.0501	46.1	9	1	4	0	0	13	3	2	1	0	0	1	0	0	0	14	6	0	0	1	0	6	1	2	0
conducts	7	.4610	.6923	38.4	3	0	0	1	1	2	0	0	0	0	0	0	0	1	0	3	0	0	0	1	0	1	0	1	0
conduit	2	.2437	.1129	30.5	0	0	0	0	0	1	0	1	0	0	0	0	0	0	0	0	0	0	0	0	0	0	1	1	0
conduits	4	.1737	.1745	32.4	0	0	1	0	1	0	2	0	0	0	0	0	0	0	0	0	0	0	0	0	0	1	3	0	0
cone	99	.6701	13.797	51.4	18	31	6	12	4	11	16	1	34	0	1	0	13	2	4	11	1	1	0	13	6	4	7	2	0
Cone	2	.1497	.1046	30.2	2	0	0	0	0	0	0	0	1	0	0	0	0	0	1	0	0	0	0	0	0	0	0	0	0
cone-shaped	13	.3665	1.0708	40.3	0	1	3	2	2	4	1	0	1	1	0	0	0	1	0	6	0	0	0	3	0	0	1	0	0
cones	62	.7390	9.3352	49.7	18	10	6	6	13	5	4	0	9	1	0	2	7	3	2	25	0	0	0	1	1	6	5	0	0
Conestoga	4	.3210	.3104	34.9	1	2	0	0	1	0	0	0	1	1	0	0	0	0	0	0	0	0	0	0	0	2	0	0	0
Conestogo	5	.0000	.0537	27.3	0	0	0	0	5	0	0	0	0	0	0	5	0	0	0	0	0	0	0	0	0	0	0	0	0
confectioners'	3	.1148	.0862	29.4	0	1	0	0	1	0	1	0	0	0	0	0	0	0	0	0	0	0	2	0	0	1	0	0	0
confectionery	4	.4866	.4069	36.1	0	1	0	1	1	0	1	0	0	0	0	1	0	0	0	0	0	0	0	0	1	1	1	0	0
confections	2	.2446	.1142	30.6	0	0	0	1	0	0	1	0	0	0	0	0	0	0	0	0	0	0	0	0	1	0	0	1	0
confederacy	3	.0000	.0583	27.7	0	1	0	0	0	2	0	0	0	0	0	0	0	3	0	0	0	0	0	0	0	0	0	0	0
Confederacy	14	.3810	1.2240	40.9	1	0	2	0	2	9	0	0	2	0	0	0	0	7	0	0	0	0	0	0	0	1	4	0	0
Confederate	56	.4318	5.3634	47.3	0	6	17	2	2	27	2	0	6	0	0	1	0	29	0	1	0	0	0	0	1	2	16	0	0
Confederates	16	.4073	1.4411	41.6	1	2	1	0	1	11	0	0	1	0	0	0	0	7	0	0	0	0	0	0	1	1	6	0	0
confederation	5	.2198	.2784	34.4	0	0	0	0	2	2	1	0	0	0	1	0	0	4	0	0	0	0	0	0	0	0	0	0	0
Confederation	22	.2292	1.2863	41.1	0	0	4	0	1	14	3	0	0	0	0	0	0	17	0	0	0	0	0	0	0	0	5	0	0
confer	4	.4806	.4072	36.1	0	1	0	0	2	1	0	0	0	0	0	0	0	1	0	0	0	0	0	0	0	1	1	1	0
conference	39	.6361	5.0862	47.1	0	2	1	4	5	13	14	0	2	2	0	9	0	7	0	1	0	0	0	0	1	2	5	10	0
Conference	13	.6110	1.6414	42.2	0	1	3	2	1	4	2	0	1	0	0	1	0	3	1	0	0	0	0	0	0	1	2	4	0
conferences	10	.5430	1.1453	40.6	0	0	3	1	2	1	2	1	1	1	0	0	0	2	0	1	0	0	0	0	0	0	3	2	0
conferred	8	.5699	.9558	39.8	0	0	2	1	2	0	2	1	1	0	0	0	0	0	0	1	0	0	0	0	1	2	2	1	0
conferring	5	.4297	.4557	36.6	0	0	0	0	1	2	2	0	0	0	1	0	1	1	0	0	0	0	0	0	1	0	1	0	0
confers	3	.0000	.0314	25.0	0	0	0	0	3	0	0	0	0	0	0	0	0	0	0	0	0	0	0	0	0	0	3	0	0
confess	18	.4547	1.7896	42.5	0	1	1	4	7	1	3	1	4	0	0	8	0	0	2	0	0	0	0	0	3	0	0	1	0
confessed	15	.1904	.8722	39.4	3	2	0	2	4	2	2	0	6	1	0	0	0	2	0	0	0	0	0	0	2	0	0	3	1
confessing	3	.3380	.2439	33.9	0	0	0	0	0	2	1	0	1	1	0	1	0	0	0	0	0	0	0	0	0	0	0	0	0
confession	3	.2196	.1554	31.9	0	0	0	0	2	0	1	0	0	0	0	2	0	0	0	0	0	0	0	0	1	0	0	0	0
confessor	2	.2440	.1132	30.5	0	0	0	0	0	0	2	0	0	0	0	1	0	0	0	0	0	0	0	0	0	0	0	1	0
confetti	3	.3431	.2528	34.0	0	1	1	0	0	1	0	0	1	0	0	0	0	1	0	0	0	0	0	0	1	0	0	0	0
confidant	2	.2427	.1152	30.6	1	0	0	0	1	0	0	0	0	0	0	0	0	0	0	0	0	0	0	0	1	1	0	0	0
confide	3	.3267	.2367	33.7	0	0	1	1	0	0	1	0	1	0	0	0	0	0	0	0	1	0	0	0	1	0	0	0	0
confided	6	.4458	.5944	37.7	0	1	0	0	2	1	2	0	2	0	1	1	0	0	1	0	0	0	0	0	1	0	0	0	0
confidence	93	.6877	13.105	51.2	1	3	7	9	31	16	23	3	19	6	0	7	0	4	0	7	0	0	13	1	6	10	5	15	0
confident	37	.8285	6.1588	47.9	2	2	4	5	12	7	4	1	10	1	0	2	1	4	0	0	2	1	1	0	4	3	2	6	0
confidential	10	.4954	1.0372	40.2	0	1	1	1	5	1	1	0	0	0	0	4	0	1	0	0	0	0	0	0	0	2	1	2	0
confidentially	4	.4535	.4003	36.0	0	0	0	1	2	1	0	0	1	0	0	1	0	0	0	0	0	0	0	0	1	0	0	1	0
confidently	13	.7034	1.8845	42.8	0	2	0	2	7	1	1	0	4	1	0	2	0	1	0	0	0	0	0	0	2	1	1	1	0
confiding	2	.1787	.1174	30.7	0	0	0	1	1	0	0	0	1	0	0	0	0	0	0	0	0	0	0	0	1	0	0	0	0
configuration	3	.2159	.1532	31.9	0	1	0	0	2	0	0	0	0	0	0	0	0	0	0	0	0	0	0	0	0	0	2	1	0
configurations	3	.2427	.1822	32.6	0	0	0	0	1	1	0	1	0	0	0	0	0	0	0	2	0	0	0	0	0	0	0	1	0
confine	6	.5089	.6545	38.2	0	0	0	2	3	1	0	0	1	1	0	0	0	1	0	0	0	0	0	0	0	0	1	2	0
confined	34	.7632	5.2212	47.2	2	2	5	2	11	2	10	0	2	1	0	1	0	3	0	3	2	0	0	1	2	8	4	7	0
confinement	5	.4145	.4612	36.6	0	0	1	1	2	1	0	0	1	0	0	2	0	0	0	0	0	0	0	0	0	1	1	0	0
confines	4	.2446	.2243	33.5	0	0	0	0	1	0	3	0	0	0	0	2	0	0	0	0	0	0	0	0	0	0	2	0	0
confining	4	.3354	.3295	35.2	1	2	1	0	0	0	0	0	1	0	0	0	0	2	0	0	0	0	0	0	0	1	0	0	0
confirm	13	.6347	1.6876	42.3	0	0	0	0	7	1	3	2	1	0	0	1	0	0	1	1	2	0	0	0	0	1	4	2	0
confirmation	9	.4489	.8752	39.4	1	0	0	1	3	3	0	1	1	0	0	0	0	1	0	0	0	0	0	0	0	1	3	3	0
Confirmation	3	.2540	.1940	32.9	0	1	0	0	0	0	2	0	1	0	0	0	0	0	0	0	0	0	1	0	0	0	1	0	0
confirmed	28	.5823	3.4022	45.3	0	3	0	3	10	5	5	2	3	0	0	3	0	4	0	3	0	0	0	0	1	0	8	6	0
confirms	3	.2321	.1635	32.1	0	0	0	0	2	0	0	1	0	0	0	0	0	0	0	0	0	0	0	0	0	0	1	2	0
confiscated	6	.4845	.6657	38.2	0	0	0	0	3	3	0	0	3	0	0	0	0	1	0	0	0	0	0	0	0	1	0	1	0
conflict	103	.7961	16.476	52.2	3	0	8	8	24	33	24	3	12	5	0	14	0	25	1	3	2	1	2	0	1	6	17	14	0

8Q Conclusions
7A concoct
7H concoctions
9H concolor
9D concord
9D concourse
XH concretion
5P concubines
7A concurs
6A concussion
8F condemmed
7P condemns
9R condensations
6N condescended
7R condescension
XP condiment
6B Conditional
7D condoled
7B condolence
7D condoling
5Q condominium
7R Condon
7R condones
8Q Conduct
5R CONDUCT
9J Conductors
XH cone-bearing
9H cone-like
7A Coney
7D confabbing
6R confectioner
6N confectioner's
9Q confectioners
7N Confectionery
8F Confederation's
5Q Conferences
5R confesses
8R Confession
9R confessions
8D Confessor
7N Confessor's
7N confirming
8Q confiscation
6N conflagration
XR Conflict

Word Type	F	D	U	SFI	3 Gr 3	4 Gr 4	5 Gr 5	6 Gr 6	7 Gr 7	8 Gr 8	9 Gr 9	X UnGr	A Read	B Eng & Gr	C Comp	D Lit	E Math	F Soc Stud	G Spell	H Sci	J Music	K Art	L Home Ec	M Shop	N Lib F	P Lib NF	Q Lib Ref	R Mag	S Rel
conflicting	7	.4646	.7071	38.5	0	1	0	0	0	4	2	0	1	1	0	0	0	1	0	0	0	0	0	0	0	1	0	3	0
conflicts	26	.5659	3.1309	45.0	2	0	4	0	6	7	5	2	6	0	0	6	0	5	0	2	0	0	0	0	0	0	5	2	0
conform	28	.8043	4.4948	46.5	0	6	0	1	11	3	7	0	0	7	1	1	0	1	1	7	2	0	1	1	0	2	1	3	0
conformal	2	.0000	.0209	23.2	0	2	0	0	0	0	0	0	0	0	0	0	0	0	0	0	0	0	0	0	0	0	2	0	0
conforming	11	.4021	.9822	39.9	0	7	0	1	1	1	1	0	0	1	0	0	0	0	0	8	1	0	0	0	0	0	0	1	0
conformist	4	.0000	.0789	29.0	0	0	0	3	1	0	0	0	0	0	0	0	0	0	0	4	0	0	0	0	0	0	0	0	0
conformity	4	.1772	.1782	32.5	0	0	1	0	0	0	3	0	0	3	0	0	0	0	0	0	0	0	0	0	0	1	0	0	0
conforms	3	.3709	.2499	34.0	0	0	0	1	0	1	1	0	0	0	0	0	0	1	0	1	0	0	0	0	0	0	1	0	0
confound	2	.0000	.0234	23.7	0	0	0	0	2	0	0	0	0	0	0	0	0	0	0	0	0	0	0	0	2	0	0	0	0
confounds	2	.2446	.1122	30.5	0	0	0	0	1	0	1	0	0	0	0	1	0	0	0	0	0	0	0	0	0	0	1	0	0
confront	5	.4616	.4841	36.8	0	0	0	0	2	2	1	0	0	0	0	2	1	0	1	0	0	0	0	0	0	0	0	1	0
confrontation	17	.1561	.6963	38.4	0	0	1	0	4	6	5	1	0	0	0	0	0	0	0	0	0	0	0	0	0	1	1	15	0
confrontations	3	.0000	.0365	25.6	0	0	0	0	0	2	1	0	0	0	0	0	0	0	0	0	0	0	0	0	0	0	0	3	0
confronted	18	.7235	2.6323	44.2	0	1	0	2	6	6	3	0	1	2	0	1	1	1	1	1	0	0	0	0	0	3	3	4	0
confronting	3	.3853	.2436	33.9	0	0	0	0	0	0	2	1	0	0	0	0	0	0	1	0	1	0	0	0	0	0	1	0	0
confronts	5	.3392	.3674	35.7	0	0	0	0	3	0	2	0	0	0	0	0	0	0	0	0	1	0	0	0	0	0	3	1	0
Confucianism	4	.0000	.0778	28.9	0	0	0	0	0	4	0	0	0	0	0	0	0	4	0	0	0	0	0	0	0	0	0	0	0
Confucius	10	.0000	.1945	32.9	0	0	0	8	0	2	0	0	0	0	0	0	0	10	0	0	0	0	0	0	0	0	0	0	0
confuse	27	.7126	3.8882	45.9	0	2	3	0	14	4	4	0	2	6	2	2	1	1	4	2	2	0	0	0	0	3	0	2	0
confused	69	.7445	10.448	50.2	3	6	5	14	23	6	8	4	18	7	5	2	0	3	7	4	4	0	0	0	1	3	6	9	0
confusing	27	.7889	4.2573	46.3	0	2	3	0	11	3	7	1	1	7	2	1	1	1	0	2	1	0	1	1	3	3	1	2	0
confusion	78	.8843	13.715	51.4	5	10	4	7	15	15	20	2	12	3	4	4	3	11	6	7	3	0	1	1	9	6	4	4	0
confusions	2	.2407	.1138	30.6	0	0	0	0	1	0	1	0	0	0	0	1	0	0	0	0	0	0	0	0	0	1	0	0	0
Cong	4	.0000	.0486	26.9	0	0	0	0	0	2	2	0	0	0	0	0	0	0	0	0	0	0	0	0	0	0	0	4	0
conga	2	.2375	.1088	30.4	0	2	0	0	0	0	0	0	0	0	0	0	0	0	0	0	1	0	0	0	0	0	0	1	0
congeners	2	.2444	.1132	30.5	0	0	0	0	2	0	0	0	0	1	0	0	0	0	0	0	0	0	0	0	1	0	0	0	0
congenial	4	.4866	.4070	36.1	0	0	0	1	2	0	1	0	0	0	0	1	0	0	0	0	0	0	0	0	0	1	1	1	0
congenital	7	.3517	.5494	37.4	0	0	0	0	0	3	4	0	0	0	0	1	0	0	0	3	0	0	0	0	0	0	3	0	0
conger	2	.2444	.1132	30.5	0	0	1	1	0	0	0	0	0	1	0	0	0	0	0	0	0	0	0	0	1	0	0	0	0
congested	2	.2427	.1152	30.6	0	1	0	1	0	0	0	0	0	0	0	0	0	0	0	0	0	0	0	0	1	1	0	0	0
congestion	4	.2835	.2871	34.6	0	0	1	0	0	0	3	0	1	0	0	0	0	0	0	1	0	0	0	0	0	0	0	2	0
conglomerate	7	.3738	.5813	37.6	3	0	0	0	0	0	2	2	0	0	0	0	0	0	0	2	0	0	0	0	0	3	0	2	0
conglomeration	3	.3665	.2412	33.8	0	0	0	0	0	2	1	0	0	0	0	0	0	1	0	0	1	0	0	0	0	0	0	1	0
Congo	81	.3911	7.2978	48.6	1	18	11	5	36	2	8	0	11	0	0	0	0	52	0	2	0	0	0	0	0	10	6	0	0
Congo's	2	.0000	.0290	24.6	0	0	2	0	0	0	0	0	0	0	0	0	0	0	0	0	0	0	0	0	0	2	0	0	0
Congolese	7	.1226	.2619	34.2	0	0	6	0	1	0	0	0	0	0	0	0	0	1	0	0	0	0	0	0	0	6	0	0	0
congratulate	8	.4959	.8640	39.4	0	0	0	3	4	0	1	0	2	0	0	0	0	0	0	1	1	0	0	0	1	0	0	3	0
congratulated	9	.4479	.9066	39.6	0	2	0	4	1	0	2	0	3	0	0	0	0	0	0	0	0	0	1	0	2	3	0	0	0
congratulating	2	.1814	.1187	30.7	0	0	0	1	1	0	0	0	1	0	0	0	0	0	0	0	0	0	0	0	0	0	0	1	0
congratulation	2	.2446	.1123	30.5	0	0	0	0	1	0	1	0	0	1	0	0	0	0	0	0	0	0	0	0	0	0	1	0	0
congratulations	18	.6765	2.5344	44.0	1	3	2	5	4	0	3	0	7	3	1	2	0	0	0	0	1	0	0	0	1	2	0	1	0
congregated	3	.1879	.1589	32.0	0	1	0	0	0	1	1	0	1	0	0	0	0	0	0	0	0	1	0	0	1	0	0	0	0
congregation	16	.2622	.9821	39.9	1	2	4	2	4	1	2	0	2	1	0	1	0	0	0	0	8	0	0	0	1	0	0	2	1
congregational	2	.2417	.1091	30.4	0	0	0	0	1	1	0	0	0	0	0	0	0	0	0	0	1	0	0	0	0	0	1	0	0
Congregational	2	.1698	.1133	30.5	0	0	1	0	0	1	0	0	1	0	0	0	0	0	0	0	0	0	0	0	0	0	1	0	0
Congregationalist	2	.2408	.1204	30.8	0	0	1	0	0	1	0	0	0	0	0	0	0	1	0	0	0	0	0	0	0	1	0	0	0
congress	13	.6706	1.7956	42.5	2	0	0	0	2	6	1	2	2	3	0	1	0	3	0	1	0	0	0	0	0	1	1	1	0
Congress	370	.5611	43.906	56.4	66	7	44	17	40	143	44	9	34	1	0	4	1	185	4	4	1	0	0	0	0	70	43	23	0
Congresses	2	.2401	.1133	30.5	1	0	1	0	0	0	0	0	0	0	0	0	0	0	0	0	0	0	0	0	0	1	1	0	0
congressional	4	.3519	.3117	34.9	0	0	1	0	2	1	0	0	0	0	0	0	0	1	0	0	0	0	0	0	0	0	1	2	0
Congressional	9	.5427	1.0124	40.1	0	1	0	1	0	3	4	0	0	0	0	1	0	2	0	0	1	0	0	0	0	0	2	3	0
congressman	11	.5085	1.1959	40.8	0	4	1	0	1	2	1	2	1	0	0	0	0	4	1	0	0	0	0	0	0	2	0	3	0
Congressman	9	.5401	1.0447	40.2	2	0	2	0	2	2	1	0	2	1	0	0	0	2	0	0	0	0	0	0	0	2	0	2	0
congressmen	11	.4352	1.0357	40.2	0	0	1	2	2	4	1	1	0	0	0	0	0	5	0	0	0	0	0	0	1	0	1	4	0
Congressmen	7	.1464	.3624	35.6	1	0	0	0	2	4	0	0	2	0	0	0	0	5	0	0	0	0	0	0	0	0	0	0	0
congruence	7	.0000	.1048	30.2	0	0	0	0	1	6	0	0	0	0	0	0	7	0	0	0	0	0	0	0	0	0	0	0	0
congruences	5	.0000	.0748	28.7	0	0	0	0	4	1	0	0	0	0	0	0	5	0	0	0	0	0	0	0	0	0	0	0	0
congruency	5	.0000	.0748	28.7	0	0	0	0	0	0	5	0	0	0	0	0	5	0	0	0	0	0	0	0	0	0	0	0	0
congruent	205	.0000	3.0685	44.9	0	4	12	41	21	103	24	0	0	0	0	0	205	0	0	0	0	0	0	0	0	0	0	0	0
conic	3	.0000	.0314	25.0	0	3	0	0	0	0	0	0	0	0	0	0	0	0	0	0	0	0	0	0	0	0	3	0	0
conical	8	.4303	.7255	38.6	0	0	2	0	2	1	2	1	0	0	0	1	1	0	0	1	0	0	0	2	2	0	0	1	0
Conie	2	.0000	.0290	24.6	0	2	0	0	0	0	0	0	0	0	0	0	0	0	0	0	0	0	0	0	0	2	0	0	0
conies	4	.1112	.1666	32.2	2	0	1	0	1	0	0	0	1	0	0	0	0	0	0	0	0	0	0	0	0	3	0	0	0
conifer	3	.1813	.1402	31.5	1	0	0	0	1	0	1	0	0	0	0	0	0	0	0	1	0	0	0	0	0	0	2	0	0
coniferous	7	.3415	.5420	37.3	0	2	1	1	1	0	2	0	0	0	0	0	0	2	0	2	0	0	0	0	0	0	3	0	0
conifers	11	.4113	.9875	39.9	5	0	1	0	4	0	0	1	0	0	0	0	0	0	0	5	0	0	0	0	0	1	4	1	0
conj	2	.2408	.1091	30.4	0	0	0	0	0	1	1	0	0	1	0	0	0	0	1	0	0	0	0	0	0	0	0	0	0
conjectural	2	.2278	.1128	30.5	0	0	0	0	1	0	0	1	0	0	0	0	0	0	0	1	0	0	0	0	0	0	1	0	0
conjecture	7	.3591	.5546	37.4	0	0	1	0	3	2	1	0	0	0	0	0	4	0	0	0	0	0	0	0	0	0	1	2	0
conjectured	2	.0000	.0299	24.8	0	0	0	0	2	0	0	0	0	0	0	0	2	0	0	0	0	0	0	0	0	0	0	0	0
conjugate	2	.0000	.0299	24.8	0	0	0	0	0	0	2	0	0	0	0	0	2	0	0	0	0	0	0	0	0	0	0	0	0
conjugation	5	.2432	.3003	34.8	0	0	0	0	3	2	0	0	0	2	0	0	0	0	0	3	0	0	0	0	0	0	0	0	0
conjunction	40	.4155	3.5221	45.5	0	1	3	3	12	12	8	1	1	22	7	0	5	1	1	0	0	0	0	0	0	0	2	1	0
conjunctions	19	.4109	1.6502	42.2	0	0	1	0	7	6	5	0	0	12	2	0	3	0	2	0	0	0	0	0	0	0	0	0	0
conjunctive	9	.0000	.0985	29.9	0	0	0	0	0	9	0	0	0	9	0	0	0	0	0	0	0	0	0	0	0	0	0	0	0
conjure	3	.2159	.1532	31.9	0	0	1	0	2	0	0	0	0	0	0	0	0	0	0	0	0	0	0	0	0	0	2	1	0
conjured	2	.2337	.1157	30.6	0	0	0	0	1	1	0	0	0	0	0	0	0	1	0	0	0	0	0	0	1	0	0	0	0
conjures	3	.2772	.1817	32.6	0	0	2	0	0	1	0	0	0	1	1	0	0	0	0	0	0	0	0	0	0	0	0	1	0
conjuror	2	.2446	.1125	30.5	0	0	0	0	1	0	1	0	0	1	0	1	0	0	0	0	0	0	0	0	0	0	0	0	0
Conn	24	.4014	2.4265	43.8	0	1	5	0	18	0	0	0	18	0	0	0	0	0	0	0	0	0	0	0	0	1	4	1	0
Connally	2	.0000	.0290	24.6	1	0	0	0	1	0	0	0	0	0	0	0	0	0	0	0	0	0	0	0	0	2	0	0	0
connect	92	.6770	12.695	51.0	10	3	11	16	9	18	13	12	3	4	1	2	13	16	3	24	1	0	0	12	1	5	3	4	0
connected	212	.7314	31.470	55.0	11	12	30	32	47	47	25	8	22	6	0	7	11	35	1	51	8	1	0	21	3	17	19	10	0
Connecticut	85	.6515	11.446	50.6	7	7	28	10	10	15	6	2	10	0	0	2	2	31	0	3	1	0	0	0	1	9	9	17	0
connecting	81	.8183	13.279	51.2	4	8	7	12	12	15	17	6	10	9	5	0	16	8	3	9	1	1	0	1	1	6	8	3	0
connection	71	.8055	11.444	50.6	0	3	5	11	21	16	9	6	5	6	0	5	2	5	5	12	6	0	0	4	0	5	9	7	0
connections	25	.5045	2.6257	44.2	1	0	1	2	8	8	4	1	0	0	0	0	0	6	0	1	1	0	0	5	2	2	6	2	0
connective	30	.5322	3.3515	45.3	0	0	0	0	5	12	13	0	2	11	0	0	1	0	0	9	0	0	3	0	0	0	3	1	0
connectives	7	.0000	.0766	28.8	0	0	0	1	0	6	0	0	0	7	0	0	0	0	0	0	0	0	0	0	0	0	0	0	0
connector	14	.1673	.6170	37.9	0	0	0	2	0	2	8	2	0	10	0	0	0	0	0	4	0	0	0	0	0	0	0	0	0
connectors	2	.0000	.0219	23.4	0	0	0	0	0	2	0	0	0	2	0	0	0	0	0	0	0	0	0	0	0	0	0	0	0
connects	36	.5838	4.3796	46.4	0	6	9	7	9	2	1	2	0	1	0	1	1	24	0	1	1	1	0	0	0	0	4	2	0
Connie	12	.5301	1.3550	41.3	5	0	0	4	1	2	0	0	2	2	0	0	3	0	0	0	0	0	0	0	0	2	0	3	0
connoisseur	2	.2446	.1142	30.6	0	0	0	0	1	0	0	1	0	0	0	0	0	0	0	0	0	0	0	0	1	0	0	1	0
Connor	3	.0000	.1370	31.4	0	0	0	0	3	0	0	0	3	0	0	0	0	0	0	0	0	0	0	0	0	0	0	0	0
Connor-Madison	4	.0000	.1827	32.6	0	0	0	0	4	0	0	0	4	0	0	0	0	0	0	0	0	0	0	0	0	0	0	0	0

6P conformation
8F confounded
6A confoundedly
4Q Confraternity
8F Confucian
XH confusedly
7C confuses
5D Confusion
9D confusion's
8B confute
XQ congeal
7Q congenially
8D conglomerations
5P Congolais
5P Congos
8A congregate
7Q congregating
9R Congregation
9R congregations
8F Congress'
7Q Conies
9Q conjectures
6C conjointly
7A conjugating
6B Conjunctive
8B conjuncts
8N conjuration
7N conjurer
6A conjurers
6A conjuring
6A conk
7N conking
8D Conklin
XH conks
7A Conn's
5P Connaught
9M Connections
8E connectivity
6B Connell
9D connesewer
9D connesewers
XR Conni
8R Connie's
6R Conningham
7N connivance
6N connivering
7R Connolly

Word Type	F	D	U	SFI	3 Gr 3	4 Gr 4	5 Gr 5	6 Gr 6	7 Gr 7	8 Gr 8	9 Gr 9	X UnGr	A Read	B Eng & Gr	C Comp	D Lit	E Math	F Soc Stud	G Spell	H Sci	J Music	K Art	L Home Ec	M Shop	N Lib F	P Lib NF	Q Lib Ref	R Mag	S Rel
Connor's	2	.0000	.0914	29.6	0	0	0	0	2	0	0	0	2	0	0	0	0	0	0	0	0	0	0	0	0	0	0	0	0
connotation	4	.2188	.2039	33.1	0	0	0	0	0	0	3	1	0	3	0	0	0	0	0	0	1	0	0	0	0	0	0	0	0
connotative	8	.0836	.1638	32.1	0	0	0	0	0	0	8	0	0	2	6	0	0	0	0	0	0	0	0	0	0	0	0	0	0
Conover	6	.2435	.4680	36.7	0	0	0	0	5	1	0	0	5	0	0	1	0	0	0	0	0	0	0	0	0	0	0	0	0
conquer	49	.7402	7.3392	48.7	3	7	9	8	12	4	3	3	4	3	0	0	1	15	3	2	4	0	0	0	1	3	9	4	0
Conquer	3	.0000	.0328	25.2	0	0	0	0	0	0	3	0	0	3	0	0	0	0	0	0	0	0	0	0	0	0	0	0	0
conquered	86	.7183	12.573	51.0	12	4	15	19	20	14	1	1	9	6	0	2	0	33	5	1	1	1	0	0	2	8	17	1	0
conquering	14	.6382	1.8556	42.7	1	1	1	6	2	2	1	0	3	0	0	0	0	2	2	0	0	0	0	0	1	1	2	3	0
conqueror	12	.6163	1.5294	41.8	0	0	3	1	4	1	1	2	1	1	0	0	0	2	0	0	0	0	0	0	1	4	2	1	0
Conqueror	8	.4879	.8124	39.1	0	0	1	1	3	3	0	0	0	4	0	0	0	0	1	0	0	0	0	0	1	1	1	0	0
conquerors	24	.6663	3.2707	45.1	2	1	3	5	7	4	1	1	1	2	0	0	0	9	2	0	0	0	0	0	1	4	3	2	0
conquest	40	.6736	5.4710	47.4	7	1	5	4	5	9	5	4	1	4	0	0	0	6	1	2	2	2	0	0	0	8	12	2	0
Conquest	3	.2379	.1631	32.1	0	0	0	1	0	2	0	0	0	2	0	0	0	0	1	0	0	0	0	0	0	0	0	0	0
conquests	7	.3613	.5823	37.7	1	0	4	1	0	1	0	0	1	0	0	0	0	1	0	0	0	0	0	0	0	4	1	0	0
conquistador	2	.2285	.1129	30.5	0	0	0	0	1	1	0	0	0	0	0	0	0	1	0	0	0	0	0	0	0	0	1	0	0
conquistadores	2	.2351	.1166	30.7	0	0	0	1	1	0	0	0	0	0	0	0	0	1	0	0	0	0	0	0	0	0	0	1	0
Conquistadores	2	.0000	.0243	23.9	0	1	0	0	0	0	0	1	0	0	0	0	0	0	0	0	0	0	0	0	0	0	0	2	0
conquistadors	5	.0000	.0523	27.2	0	0	0	0	4	0	1	0	0	0	0	0	0	0	0	0	0	0	0	0	0	0	5	0	0
Conrad	12	.4773	1.2549	41.0	2	5	0	0	3	0	2	0	3	1	0	0	0	1	0	0	0	0	0	0	0	0	3	4	0
Conroy	4	.2065	.1985	33.0	0	0	1	3	0	0	0	0	0	0	0	0	0	0	0	0	0	0	0	0	3	0	1	0	0
cons	2	.2433	.1158	30.6	0	0	0	0	1	0	1	0	0	0	0	0	0	0	0	0	0	0	0	0	0	1	0	1	0
conscience	40	.7120	5.8637	47.7	1	0	1	9	10	8	11	0	13	5	0	7	0	3	1	0	0	0	0	0	1	3	2	5	0
Conscience	3	.1639	.1674	32.2	0	0	0	0	1	2	0	0	1	0	0	0	0	2	0	0	0	0	0	0	0	0	0	0	0
consciences	2	.1814	.1187	30.7	0	0	0	0	2	0	0	0	1	0	0	0	0	0	0	0	0	0	0	0	0	0	0	1	0
conscientious	4	.4812	.4019	36.0	0	0	0	0	2	0	2	0	0	1	0	0	0	0	1	0	0	0	0	0	0	1	0	1	0
conscientiously	2	.2446	.1122	30.5	0	0	0	0	0	0	2	0	0	0	0	1	0	0	0	0	0	0	0	0	0	0	1	0	0
conscious	53	.7920	8.3914	49.2	0	3	6	1	13	14	15	1	2	1	4	9	0	1	1	7	2	2	1	0	6	8	3	6	0
consciously	10	.6159	1.2707	41.0	0	0	1	1	4	2	2	0	1	1	0	0	0	1	0	1	0	0	1	0	0	1	3	1	0
consciousness	24	.7360	3.5907	45.6	0	0	5	2	7	5	4	1	4	1	0	0	0	4	1	0	1	0	0	0	2	5	2	4	0
consecrate	3	.3756	.2468	33.9	0	0	0	0	1	2	0	0	0	0	0	1	0	1	0	0	0	0	0	0	0	0	1	0	0
consecrated	6	.3288	.5071	37.1	0	0	0	0	1	5	0	0	3	0	0	2	0	1	0	0	0	0	0	0	0	0	0	0	0
consecutive	27	.5215	2.9763	44.7	0	1	4	2	8	9	3	0	2	1	0	0	16	1	2	1	2	0	0	0	0	0	0	2	0
consecutively	2	.2413	.1212	30.8	0	0	0	0	0	1	1	0	0	0	0	0	1	0	0	1	0	0	0	0	0	0	0	0	0
Conseil	22	.0000	.2579	34.1	0	0	0	0	22	0	0	0	0	0	0	0	0	0	0	0	0	0	0	0	22	0	0	0	0
consensus	2	.2437	.1129	30.5	0	0	0	0	2	0	0	0	0	0	0	0	0	0	0	0	0	0	0	0	0	0	1	1	0
consent	40	.7266	5.9361	47.7	1	7	0	3	15	8	6	0	9	0	0	6	0	6	1	0	1	0	0	0	2	7	5	3	0
consented	18	.6075	2.3127	43.6	2	3	3	5	3	1	1	0	6	0	0	2	0	0	0	0	0	0	0	0	3	3	3	1	0
consequence	26	.6808	3.5941	45.6	0	1	1	4	10	2	5	3	1	2	0	4	0	1	0	2	0	0	0	0	2	4	6	4	0
consequences	33	.6534	4.4357	46.5	1	1	2	5	10	2	10	2	4	3	0	2	0	4	0	2	0	0	0	0	2	2	2	12	0
consequent	5	.3461	.3825	35.8	0	0	0	0	3	0	1	1	0	0	0	0	0	0	0	1	0	0	0	0	0	0	2	2	0
consequently	38	.8310	6.3066	48.0	0	0	4	3	17	4	7	3	4	2	1	1	0	1	1	6	4	0	2	0	3	3	3	7	0
conservation	53	.5650	6.3420	48.0	0	2	8	8	8	2	7	18	4	0	0	0	0	13	1	27	0	0	2	0	0	0	2	4	0
Conservation	7	.2366	.4193	36.2	0	0	0	1	0	0	0	6	0	0	0	0	0	0	0	5	0	0	0	0	0	0	0	2	0
conservationist	2	.2418	.1091	30.4	0	0	0	0	0	1	1	0	0	0	0	0	0	0	1	0	0	0	0	0	0	0	1	0	0
conservationists	5	.4455	.4788	36.8	0	0	0	0	1	2	1	1	0	0	0	0	0	1	0	1	0	0	0	0	0	0	1	2	0
conservatism	4	.3498	.3059	34.9	0	0	1	0	2	1	0	0	0	0	0	0	0	0	0	0	0	0	0	0	0	1	2	1	0
conservative	20	.4523	1.9255	42.8	1	1	3	0	5	5	3	2	1	0	0	0	0	0	0	0	1	0	0	0	0	4	7	7	0
Conservative	2	.0000	.0209	23.2	0	0	1	0	0	0	1	0	0	0	0	0	0	0	0	0	0	0	0	0	0	0	2	0	0
conservatives	2	.2351	.1166	30.7	0	0	0	0	0	1	1	0	0	0	0	0	0	1	0	0	0	0	0	0	0	0	0	1	0
conservatory	3	.0000	.0434	26.4	0	0	0	1	2	0	0	0	0	0	0	0	0	0	0	0	0	0	0	0	0	3	0	0	0
Conservatory	12	.4144	1.0535	40.2	0	0	0	2	5	1	4	0	0	0	0	2	0	0	0	0	5	0	0	0	0	4	1	0	0
conserve	21	.5765	2.5129	44.0	1	2	4	2	6	4	2	0	0	1	0	1	0	9	1	4	0	0	3	0	0	0	1	1	0
conserved	5	.3554	.4063	36.1	0	0	3	0	1	1	0	0	0	0	0	0	0	3	0	1	0	0	0	0	0	0	1	0	0
conserves	3	.2445	.1818	32.6	0	0	0	0	1	0	1	1	0	0	0	0	0	0	0	2	0	0	0	0	0	0	1	0	0
conserving	4	.2336	.2503	34.0	0	1	2	0	1	0	0	0	1	0	0	0	0	2	0	0	0	0	1	0	0	0	0	0	0
consider	346	.8418	58.054	57.6	6	22	30	58	62	82	65	21	25	26	11	14	95	29	12	32	6	7	31	2	4	12	17	23	0
considerable	115	.8583	19.657	52.9	1	1	9	6	45	23	26	4	11	7	2	9	0	17	2	10	7	0	3	0	8	6	20	13	0
considerably	52	.8298	8.6229	49.4	3	2	5	7	15	7	10	3	5	2	0	4	0	6	1	8	3	0	2	1	1	3	11	5	0
considerate	10	.4200	.9408	39.7	0	4	0	3	1	0	2	0	2	0	0	0	0	0	0	4	1	0	2	0	0	1	0	0	0
consideration	59	.7182	8.5434	49.3	0	2	4	4	18	13	11	7	4	5	1	5	0	3	1	8	2	0	11	4	3	4	2	6	0
considerations	11	.6474	1.4526	41.6	0	0	2	0	3	2	4	0	1	0	1	1	0	0	0	1	0	1	1	0	1	3	0	1	0
considered	337	.9251	61.693	57.9	10	22	38	54	64	75	54	20	46	20	3	13	24	36	2	32	30	4	14	6	9	25	41	32	0
considering	56	.8673	9.6637	49.9	2	5	4	7	15	7	13	3	6	3	0	5	4	4	1	7	0	2	3	1	7	4	4	5	0
considers	23	.5375	2.5774	44.1	1	1	3	2	4	3	7	2	1	0	1	1	0	2	0	2	0	0	0	0	0	0	7	9	0
consign	2	.2407	.1090	30.4	0	0	0	0	1	1	0	0	0	1	0	0	0	0	0	0	1	0	0	0	0	0	0	0	0
consist	70	.7615	10.707	50.3	0	1	3	6	29	9	20	2	1	11	0	2	5	3	3	23	4	0	2	5	0	1	8	2	0
consisted	45	.7213	6.5866	48.2	1	1	4	7	11	11	8	2	6	1	0	4	0	6	1	3	8	0	0	1	0	2	11	2	0
consistency	9	.4690	.8866	39.5	0	0	0	0	3	2	2	2	1	0	0	0	0	0	1	1	0	1	3	0	0	0	1	1	0
consistent	27	.5643	3.1596	45.0	5	1	0	2	11	1	5	2	1	2	0	0	1	1	0	2	0	0	0	0	0	4	8	8	0
consistently	18	.6974	2.5391	44.0	2	1	1	1	6	2	3	2	1	2	0	1	0	0	2	1	0	0	1	1	0	4	0	5	0
consisting	62	.8103	10.050	50.0	1	2	4	6	24	12	9	4	3	4	0	1	17	2	3	13	7	0	2	1	0	2	4	3	0
consists	211	.8024	33.900	55.3	2	5	18	36	53	43	44	10	13	17	2	2	22	13	1	57	24	1	5	16	1	2	24	11	0
consolation	3	.3431	.2528	34.0	0	0	0	0	1	1	1	0	1	0	0	0	0	1	0	0	0	0	0	0	1	0	0	0	0
console	7	.4876	.7278	38.6	1	1	0	3	0	2	0	0	1	0	0	1	0	0	0	0	2	0	0	0	0	1	0	2	0
consoled	3	.3385	.2445	33.9	1	0	0	1	1	0	0	0	1	0	0	0	0	0	0	0	0	0	0	0	1	0	1	0	0
consolidate	2	.2433	.1158	30.6	0	0	1	0	0	0	1	0	0	0	0	0	0	0	0	0	0	0	0	0	0	1	0	1	0
consolidated	4	.3874	.3414	35.3	0	0	0	0	1	2	1	0	0	0	0	1	0	2	0	0	0	0	0	0	0	0	1	0	0
Consolidated	3	.0000	.0449	26.5	0	0	0	0	0	0	3	0	0	0	0	0	3	0	0	0	0	0	0	0	0	0	0	0	0
consolidation	2	.2433	.1158	30.6	0	0	1	0	0	0	0	1	0	0	0	0	0	0	0	0	0	0	0	0	0	1	0	1	0
consoling	2	.1787	.1174	30.7	0	0	0	2	0	0	0	0	1	0	0	0	0	0	0	0	0	0	0	0	1	0	0	0	0
consonant	702	.1518	28.448	54.5	161	142	106	106	121	53	13	0	78	71	0	1	1	1	549	0	1	0	0	0	0	0	0	0	0
consonant-shift	2	.0000	.0219	23.4	0	0	0	0	2	0	0	0	0	2	0	0	0	0	0	0	0	0	0	0	0	0	0	0	0
consonant-y	2	.2408	.1091	30.4	0	2	0	0	0	0	0	0	0	1	0	0	0	0	1	0	0	0	0	0	0	0	0	0	0
consonants	248	.2021	12.666	51.0	71	52	30	40	28	17	7	3	40	5	0	0	0	0	189	0	9	1	0	0	0	0	4	0	0
conspicuous	20	.7132	2.8848	44.6	0	0	1	1	12	2	2	2	1	1	1	1	0	0	0	5	0	0	1	0	3	1	5	1	0
conspicuously	2	.2427	.1152	30.6	0	0	1	0	1	0	0	0	0	0	0	0	0	0	0	0	0	0	0	0	1	1	0	0	0
conspiracy	8	.4701	.8507	39.3	0	0	0	0	0	4	4	0	3	0	0	0	0	2	0	0	0	0	0	0	0	0	1	2	0
conspirator	2	.0000	.0914	29.6	0	0	1	1	0	0	0	0	2	0	0	0	0	0	0	0	0	0	0	0	0	0	0	0	0
conspirators	5	.4243	.4716	36.7	0	0	1	0	2	1	1	0	1	0	0	0	0	0	0	0	0	0	0	0	0	1	1	2	0
conspire	2	.2433	.1158	30.6	0	0	2	0	0	0	0	0	0	0	0	0	0	0	0	0	0	0	0	0	0	1	0	1	0
conspiring	5	.3767	.4160	36.2	0	0	0	0	2	2	1	0	0	0	0	0	0	2	0	0	0	0	0	0	0	0	1	2	0
constable	7	.5546	.8372	39.2	0	1	1	2	0	1	1	1	2	0	0	0	0	2	0	0	0	0	0	0	1	1	1	0	0
Constable	6	.1500	.3088	34.9	0	0	0	3	1	0	2	0	3	0	0	0	0	0	0	0	0	2	0	0	0	1	0	0	0
Constable's	3	.0801	.0640	28.1	0	0	0	0	1	0	2	0	0	0	0	0	0	0	0	0	0	2	0	0	0	1	0	0	0
constables	9	.4189	.8447	39.3	0	0	0	1	1	1	6	0	2	0	0	3	0	0	0	0	0	0	0	0	1	3	0	0	0
Constance	23	.2443	1.5923	42.0	12	0	0	10	0	0	1	0	11	0	0	0	0	0	0	0	0	0	0	0	11	1	0	0	0
constancy	2	.0000	.0394	26.0	0	0	0	0	0	0	0	2	0	0	0	0	0	0	0	2	0	0	0	0	0	0	0	0	0
constant	141	.8844	24.790	53.9	3	4	7	21	34	38	27	7	18	4	0	9	5	13	3	29	7	1	7	3	3	6	18	15	0

9B connotations
7R connotes
8Q connoting
7R Conny
9J conquer'd
5P Conqueror's

XR Conrad's
8F consanguinity
5P conscripts
8R consecration
7Q consecrator
7Q Conservancy

XH Conservationist
9Q CONSERVATIVE
5Q conservatively
9R conservatives'
7L Consider
9P considerateness

7N consideringly
7N consigned
7R Consistent
4A consome-trate
8G consomme
9J consonance

7G consonant-vowel
7G consonare
9R consortium
6A Conspiracy
5A conspirator's
6A constable's

6A Constables
3A constance
3A Constance's

Word Type	F	D	U	SFI	3 Gr 3	4 Gr 4	5 Gr 5	6 Gr 6	7 Gr 7	8 Gr 8	9 Gr 9	X UnGr	A Read	B Eng & Gr	C Comp	D Lit	E Math	F Soc Stud	G Spell	H Sci	J Music	K Art	L Home Ec	M Shop	N Lib F	P Lib NF	Q Lib Ref	R Mag	S Rel
Constant	4	.3447	.3156	35.0	0	3	0	0	0	1	0	0	0	0	0	0	0	1	0	1	0	0	0	0	0	2	0	0	0
Constantine	9	.4784	.9127	39.6	2	0	2	0	1	0	2	2	0	0	0	0	0	2	0	0	0	0	0	0	0	3	2	2	0
Constantinople	19	.4303	1.7848	42.5	0	0	6	7	4	1	1	0	0	0	0	1	0	10	0	0	0	0	0	0	0	6	2	0	0
constantly	141	.8325	23.457	53.7	5	16	17	18	45	20	14	6	13	4	1	5	0	13	4	33	1	0	7	5	4	11	21	19	0
constants	5	.0000	.0986	29.9	0	0	0	0	0	0	0	5	0	0	0	0	0	0	0	5	0	0	0	0	0	0	0	0	0
constellarium	2	.0000	.0394	26.0	0	2	0	0	0	0	0	0	0	0	0	0	0	0	0	2	0	0	0	0	0	0	0	0	0
constellation	26	.4336	2.5056	44.0	3	0	1	4	4	5	0	9	2	0	0	0	0	0	1	18	0	0	0	0	1	1	3	0	0
Constellation	2	.2427	.1159	30.6	0	0	0	1	0	1	0	0	0	0	0	0	1	0	0	0	0	0	0	0	0	0	0	1	0
constellations	10	.2198	.5718	37.6	2	1	0	0	0	2	1	4	0	0	0	2	0	0	0	8	0	0	0	0	0	0	0	0	0
constipation	6	.1889	.2743	34.4	0	0	2	0	1	0	3	0	0	0	0	0	0	0	0	2	0	0	3	0	0	1	0	0	0
constituent	10	.2261	.6098	37.9	0	0	1	0	1	0	0	8	1	0	0	0	0	0	0	8	0	0	0	0	0	0	1	0	0
constituents	26	.6004	3.3441	45.2	0	0	0	1	14	2	2	7	10	0	0	0	0	0	0	8	1	0	0	1	0	0	4	2	0
constitute	26	.7449	3.9039	45.9	1	1	1	2	10	4	5	2	1	1	0	1	1	2	2	5	2	0	0	0	0	4	6	1	0
constituted	11	.5864	1.3389	41.3	0	0	1	0	1	2	7	0	1	0	0	1	0	3	0	0	0	0	0	1	1	0	3	1	0
constitutes	6	.4219	.5328	37.3	0	0	1	0	2	1	2	0	0	0	0	0	0	0	0	0	0	0	1	0	0	1	3	1	0
constitution	70	.5339	7.9454	49.0	5	6	9	1	13	24	9	3	7	0	0	0	0	27	1	2	0	0	0	0	0	11	18	4	0
Constitution	162	.4845	16.961	52.3	16	6	24	6	11	67	32	0	5	0	1	0	0	109	0	6	1	0	0	0	1	20	16	3	0
constitutional	18	.4108	1.6545	42.2	1	0	1	1	5	5	5	0	2	0	0	0	0	8	0	1	0	0	0	0	0	0	6	1	0
Constitutional	9	.3112	.7218	38.6	1	0	0	0	3	5	0	0	3	0	0	0	0	5	0	0	0	0	0	0	0	1	0	0	0
constitutionality	2	.0000	.0209	23.2	0	0	1	0	0	0	1	0	0	0	0	0	0	0	0	0	0	0	0	0	0	0	2	0	0
constitutionally	3	.2425	.1816	32.6	0	0	0	1	0	1	1	0	0	0	0	0	0	2	0	0	0	0	0	0	0	0	0	1	0
constitutions	5	.2037	.2562	34.1	0	0	2	0	1	1	1	0	0	0	0	0	0	2	0	0	0	0	0	0	0	0	3	0	0
constrained	2	.2285	.1129	30.5	0	0	0	0	0	1	1	0	0	0	0	0	0	1	0	0	0	0	0	0	0	0	1	0	0
constricted	6	.3693	.4740	36.8	0	0	0	0	2	2	2	0	0	0	0	3	0	0	0	0	1	0	0	0	0	0	2	0	0
constricting	2	.2405	.1205	30.8	1	0	0	0	0	0	1	0	0	0	0	0	0	0	0	1	0	0	0	0	0	1	0	0	0
constriction	3	.2233	.1562	31.9	0	0	0	0	1	1	0	1	0	0	0	1	0	0	0	0	0	0	0	0	0	0	2	0	0
constrictors	2	.2278	.1128	30.5	1	0	0	0	1	0	0	0	0	0	0	0	0	0	0	1	0	0	0	0	0	0	1	0	0
construct	157	.5943	19.259	52.8	1	4	4	16	18	81	31	2	3	8	1	0	113	6	1	5	1	2	2	6	0	2	6	1	0
constructed	82	.8400	13.710	51.4	3	3	7	9	19	14	22	5	2	4	2	3	13	12	3	9	6	1	1	7	0	3	11	5	0
constructing	10	.6325	1.3009	41.1	1	0	0	2	3	3	1	0	1	0	0	0	0	2	0	1	1	0	1	1	0	2	1	0	0
construction	229	.7218	33.105	55.2	9	8	12	14	54	41	70	21	5	5	20	6	13	20	4	10	5	13	28	33	0	12	27	28	0
Construction	9	.4743	.9040	39.6	0	1	0	0	1	1	6	0	1	0	0	2	0	0	0	0	0	0	2	0	1	1	0	2	0
constructional	4	.0000	.0789	29.0	0	0	4	0	0	0	0	0	0	0	0	0	0	0	0	4	0	0	0	0	0	0	0	0	0
constructions	24	.3640	1.8187	42.6	0	1	1	0	4	1	17	0	0	4	11	0	5	0	0	0	0	2	1	0	0	0	1	0	0
constructive	13	.5969	1.6093	42.1	0	1	7	1	1	0	3	0	0	1	0	0	0	4	0	3	0	0	0	0	0	1	1	3	0
constructs	4	.3407	.3120	34.9	0	0	0	1	2	0	1	0	1	1	1	0	0	0	0	0	1	0	0	0	0	0	0	0	0
consul	10	.4844	1.0473	40.2	0	0	0	0	3	7	0	0	1	0	0	0	0	4	0	0	0	0	0	0	0	1	1	3	0
Consul	4	.0974	.1495	31.7	0	0	0	0	4	0	0	0	1	0	0	0	0	0	0	0	0	0	0	0	3	0	0	0	0
Consulate	2	.1787	.1174	30.7	0	0	0	0	2	0	0	0	1	0	0	0	0	0	0	0	0	0	0	0	1	0	0	0	0
consuls	3	.2431	.1816	32.6	0	0	0	1	1	0	1	0	0	0	0	0	0	2	0	0	0	0	0	0	1	0	0	0	0
consult	46	.6780	6.3258	48.0	0	2	6	2	10	14	12	0	3	3	0	1	0	6	9	6	3	0	8	1	1	1	2	2	0
consultant	2	.0000	.0243	23.9	0	0	0	0	0	1	0	1	0	0	0	0	0	0	0	0	0	0	0	0	0	0	0	2	0
consultants	2	.2437	.1129	30.5	0	0	0	0	1	0	1	0	0	0	0	0	0	0	0	0	0	0	0	0	0	0	1	1	0
consultation	4	.3676	.3150	35.0	1	0	0	0	2	1	0	0	0	0	0	0	0	0	0	0	1	0	0	0	0	0	2	1	0
consultations	2	.0000	.0243	23.9	0	0	0	0	0	1	1	0	0	0	0	0	0	0	0	0	0	0	0	0	0	0	0	2	0
consulted	20	.7352	2.9914	44.8	0	2	1	5	6	2	4	0	4	1	0	1	0	2	0	1	0	0	0	1	3	1	2	4	0
consulting	10	.4729	1.0042	40.0	0	0	1	1	1	4	3	0	1	2	0	0	0	0	0	0	0	0	1	0	0	0	1	5	0
consults	2	.0000	.0243	23.9	0	0	0	0	2	0	0	0	0	0	0	0	0	0	0	0	0	0	0	0	0	0	0	2	0
consume	16	.5628	1.8811	42.7	1	1	1	0	7	1	5	0	2	0	0	1	0	2	1	1	0	0	0	2	0	2	5	0	0
consumed	20	.7090	2.9053	44.6	1	3	4	1	6	4	1	0	4	0	0	0	0	3	0	2	0	0	1	0	2	3	2	3	0
consumer	21	.4929	2.1916	43.4	0	0	1	1	3	3	10	3	1	0	0	0	0	4	0	3	0	0	3	0	0	0	2	8	0
consumers	4	.3621	.3145	35.0	1	0	0	0	2	0	1	0	0	0	0	0	0	1	0	0	0	0	0	1	0	1	1	0	0
consumes	5	.5599	.5799	37.6	0	0	0	1	1	0	3	0	0	1	0	0	0	0	0	1	0	0	0	0	0	1	1	1	0
consuming	9	.4652	.8711	39.4	1	0	0	1	4	0	3	0	0	0	0	0	0	1	0	0	1	0	0	2	3	0	1	1	0
consumption	17	.5206	1.8361	42.6	0	0	4	0	2	1	6	4	0	1	0	0	0	0	0	2	0	0	3	0	0	5	2	4	0
contact	121	.7672	18.726	52.7	6	2	9	7	39	21	26	11	14	8	1	4	0	8	2	29	3	0	0	9	2	9	18	14	0
contacted	2	.2433	.1158	30.6	0	0	1	0	0	0	1	0	0	0	0	0	0	0	0	0	0	0	0	0	0	1	0	1	0
contacts	11	.5577	1.2886	41.1	0	0	0	1	5	1	3	1	2	1	0	0	0	0	0	0	0	0	1	0	0	1	3	3	0
contagious	9	.4682	.9326	39.7	0	4	0	1	2	1	1	0	2	0	0	0	0	1	1	1	0	0	0	0	0	4	0	0	0
contain	557	.7151	80.443	59.1	12	72	112	96	127	61	71	6	31	57	8	4	48	19	199	109	10	2	25	3	5	5	19	13	0
contained	148	.8524	25.152	54.0	9	10	23	18	40	31	12	5	11	10	1	2	43	14	1	20	8	0	1	2	6	11	14	4	0
container	93	.6189	11.894	50.8	8	16	10	5	21	18	13	2	6	2	0	0	9	3	0	43	1	0	10	8	0	3	4	4	0
containers	35	.5829	4.2608	46.3	0	4	6	6	6	8	4	1	5	1	0	0	3	2	0	10	0	0	6	3	0	0	3	2	0
containing	253	.7508	38.286	55.8	7	28	26	23	73	45	43	8	17	17	2	5	51	3	59	54	6	0	5	0	1	6	16	11	0
containment	2	.0000	.0389	25.9	0	0	0	0	0	1	1	0	0	0	0	0	0	2	0	0	0	0	0	0	0	0	0	0	0
contains	477	.8460	80.478	59.1	16	50	65	73	117	77	73	6	39	41	16	3	94	25	62	118	16	4	11	10	0	2	27	9	0
contaminated	4	.3303	.3297	35.2	0	0	0	2	0	2	0	0	1	0	0	0	0	1	0	2	0	0	0	0	0	0	0	0	0
contamination	6	.4715	.6028	37.8	0	0	1	0	0	4	1	0	0	0	0	0	0	0	0	2	0	0	0	0	0	1	1	2	0
contemplate	7	.5167	.7610	38.8	0	0	0	0	4	2	0	1	1	0	1	0	0	0	0	1	0	1	0	0	1	0	1	1	0
contemplated	5	.4726	.4945	36.9	0	0	0	0	4	0	1	0	0	1	0	0	0	0	0	0	0	0	0	0	2	0	1	1	0
contemplating	5	.3336	.3687	35.7	0	0	0	1	3	0	1	0	0	0	0	0	0	0	0	0	0	0	0	0	0	1	1	3	0
contemplation	2	.2152	.1357	31.3	0	0	0	0	0	2	0	0	1	0	0	0	0	1	0	0	0	0	0	0	0	0	0	0	0
contemplative	7	.1475	.2751	34.4	0	0	0	0	0	1	6	0	0	0	0	0	0	0	0	0	0	0	0	0	1	0	0	6	0
contemporaneous	2	.2437	.1129	30.5	0	0	0	0	1	1	0	0	0	0	0	0	0	0	0	0	0	0	0	0	0	0	1	1	0
contemporaries	11	.5158	1.1649	40.7	0	0	0	0	5	3	2	1	0	0	0	1	0	0	0	0	3	1	0	0	0	0	4	2	0
contemporary	75	.5648	8.6236	49.4	1	0	4	5	30	23	6	6	1	2	0	0	0	1	0	1	34	7	0	5	0	3	10	11	0
contempt	26	.6638	3.5630	45.5	0	0	5	3	8	6	3	1	6	2	0	3	0	0	0	0	0	0	0	0	3	3	4	5	0
contemptuous	5	.4189	.4641	36.7	0	0	0	0	2	0	1	2	1	1	0	2	0	0	0	0	0	0	0	0	0	0	0	1	0
contemptuously	6	.5060	.6307	38.0	0	0	2	0	2	2	0	0	0	0	1	1	0	1	0	0	0	0	0	0	1	1	1	0	0
contend	8	.4624	.7856	39.0	0	0	0	0	4	2	2	0	0	0	0	0	0	2	0	0	0	0	0	0	2	0	1	3	0
contended	6	.4319	.5772	37.6	0	0	0	0	0	3	2	1	1	0	0	1	0	2	0	0	0	0	0	0	0	0	0	2	0
contender	2	.0000	.0243	23.9	0	0	0	0	1	0	1	0	0	0	0	0	0	0	0	0	0	0	0	0	0	0	0	2	0
contenders	4	.3641	.3177	35.0	0	0	1	0	0	1	1	1	0	0	0	1	0	0	0	0	0	0	0	0	0	1	0	2	0
contending	5	.3684	.4146	36.2	0	0	0	0	1	3	1	0	0	0	0	0	0	3	0	0	0	0	0	0	0	1	1	0	0
contends	5	.1628	.2128	33.3	0	0	1	0	3	1	0	0	0	0	0	0	0	0	0	0	0	0	0	0	0	1	0	4	0
content	114	.8651	19.649	52.9	2	5	9	10	34	24	23	7	18	9	1	7	0	12	4	14	2	1	10	4	3	12	10	7	0
contented	30	.6392	3.9758	46.0	1	5	0	7	9	4	4	0	7	3	0	5	0	0	1	0	0	0	2	0	7	5	0	0	0
contentedly	12	.5320	1.3846	41.4	0	2	1	1	5	1	1	1	4	0	0	2	0	0	0	0	0	0	0	0	3	1	0	2	0
contention	10	.5193	1.0766	40.3	0	0	1	0	3	3	1	2	0	2	0	1	0	0	0	0	0	0	0	0	0	1	2	4	0
contentment	9	.6222	1.1786	40.7	0	1	3	1	1	2	1	0	3	1	0	0	0	0	0	0	1	0	0	0	1	2	1	0	0
contents	67	.8081	10.914	50.4	4	15	6	7	20	7	5	3	17	13	1	1	2	2	1	10	0	0	1	0	5	2	8	4	0
Contents	12	.5428	1.4339	41.6	1	3	1	2	4	1	0	0	5	2	0	0	0	3	1	1	0	0	0	0	0	0	0	0	0
conterminous	3	.0000	.0583	27.7	0	0	3	0	0	0	0	0	0	0	0	0	0	3	0	0	0	0	0	0	0	0	0	0	0
contest	129	.8592	22.184	53.5	29	14	11	22	15	21	11	6	39	15	1	12	3	5	4	1	6	0	1	0	12	16	3	11	0
Contest	2	.1733	.1149	30.6	0	0	1	0	1	0	0	0	1	1	0	0	0	0	0	0	0	0	0	0	0	0	0	0	0
contestants	7	.5210	.7674	38.9	2	2	0	1	1	0	1	0	1	1	0	1	0	0	0	0	0	1	0	0	1	1	1	0	0

7M constant-level
7P Constantin
7F Constantine's
7F Constantinople's
9Q Constantinos
XR constantly-in-view
7A consternation
7A constituency
8Q Constituent
7Q constituting
3P CONSTITUTION
4P constitution's
9F Constitution's
9D constrains
7Q constraints
3H constrictor
6Q constricts
6H CONSTRUCT
9R construction-industry
8P construction-paper
7R constructionist
8E Constructions
8Q constructivists
XB constructor
8F construed
7A consulate
7R Consulich
5Q Consultation
9R consultative
7Q Consumer
7B consummation
4A Contact
8H contact-lens
7P contacting
7P contagion
7A contaminate
7H contaminates
XH contaminating
7R contaminator
9D contemplates
9R contemplatives
8J contempory
9R Contempt
8R contemptible
9B Content
5G content'**
XR contentions
7A contestant

Word Type	F	D	U	SFI	3 Gr 3	4 Gr 4	5 Gr 5	6 Gr 6	7 Gr 7	8 Gr 8	9 Gr 9	X UnGr	A Read	B Eng & Gr	C Comp	D Lit	E Math	F Soc Stud	G Spell	H Sci	J Music	K Art	L Home Ec	M Shop	N Lib F	P Lib NF	Q Lib Ref	R Mag	S Rel
contested	5	.2418	.3070	34.9	0	0	2	1	0	2	0	0	1	0	0	0	0	0	0	0	0	0	0	0	0	1	3	0	0
contests	35	.6722	4.8452	46.9	8	6	0	7	1	4	8	1	7	1	0	9	0	3	0	0	1	0	0	0	3	7	1	3	0
context	61	.5524	7.2686	48.6	1	6	7	6	12	9	19	1	24	18	6	6	0	0	1	0	2	0	0	0	0	1	1	2	0
contexts	6	.3347	.4324	36.4	0	0	0	0	1	2	3	0	0	4	1	1	0	0	0	0	0	0	0	0	0	0	0	0	0
continent	319	.5475	36.954	55.7	20	54	33	64	105	16	23	4	17	1	1	7	5	186	1	14	2	0	0	0	2	15	63	5	0
Continent	14	.4151	1.2964	41.1	0	4	3	2	1	3	1	0	2	0	0	0	0	3	0	0	0	0	0	0	0	5	4	0	0
continent's	4	.3829	.3404	35.3	0	0	1	1	2	0	0	0	0	0	0	0	0	2	0	0	0	0	0	0	0	1	1	0	0
continental	59	.5974	7.3361	48.7	1	6	9	5	13	8	16	1	2	0	0	1	0	12	0	23	0	0	1	0	0	2	13	5	0
Continental	45	.6193	5.7874	47.6	2	6	11	5	10	8	3	0	5	1	0	1	0	17	0	0	3	0	0	0	0	4	10	4	0
continents	179	.4977	19.127	52.8	14	34	38	36	34	4	16	3	4	2	0	0	2	99	1	32	0	0	0	0	3	3	32	1	0
contingent	2	.2446	.1142	30.6	0	1	0	1	0	0	0	0	0	0	0	0	0	0	0	0	0	0	0	0	1	0	0	1	0
continously	2	.2152	.1357	31.3	0	0	0	1	0	0	1	0	1	0	0	0	0	1	0	0	0	0	0	0	0	0	0	0	0
continual	9	.5709	1.0937	40.4	0	0	2	2	2	1	2	0	3	0	0	0	0	0	0	0	1	0	1	0	0	1	2	1	0
continually	59	.8653	10.146	50.1	1	9	3	8	10	17	9	2	4	6	3	9	1	3	1	7	3	1	1	0	3	5	7	5	0
continuance	3	.2233	.1562	31.9	0	0	0	0	0	1	2	0	0	0	0	1	0	0	0	0	0	0	0	0	0	0	2	0	0
continuation	8	.5022	.8649	39.4	1	0	0	2	2	2	1	0	1	0	0	0	0	3	0	0	0	0	0	0	0	1	2	1	0
continue	294	.8719	50.996	57.1	18	34	39	38	63	60	35	7	34	12	1	7	33	32	16	48	22	4	13	20	4	18	17	13	0
continued	413	.8826	72.769	58.6	41	53	63	59	90	60	32	15	129	14	6	20	8	52	2	19	15	1	1	0	29	45	42	30	0
continues	111	.8675	19.182	52.8	6	7	15	15	24	22	19	3	15	3	3	4	6	12	1	20	14	2	0	2	1	3	13	12	0
continuing	55	.8635	9.4514	49.8	3	3	3	5	12	12	12	5	5	1	1	3	2	6	1	7	2	0	2	1	1	3	11	9	0
continuity	7	.3732	.5585	37.5	0	1	0	0	5	1	0	0	0	0	0	0	0	0	0	0	0	0	0	1	0	0	2	4	0
continuous	101	.7668	15.547	51.9	4	6	7	8	20	24	26	6	5	2	3	1	1	11	0	24	2	6	5	7	2	4	24	4	0
continuously	25	.7664	3.8598	45.9	0	1	3	4	7	2	7	1	2	1	0	0	0	3	1	5	1	0	1	0	1	1	5	4	0
contortions	3	.3427	.2477	33.9	0	1	0	1	0	0	1	0	1	0	0	0	0	0	0	0	0	0	0	0	1	0	0	1	0
contour	42	.5185	4.5157	46.5	7	3	7	6	11	3	1	4	0	0	0	0	0	5	0	7	21	1	0	1	0	2	5	0	0
contours	13	.6123	1.6290	42.1	0	0	1	1	4	3	2	2	0	0	1	0	0	0	0	5	0	0	1	1	0	2	3	0	0
contrabassoon	4	.0000	.0323	25.1	0	0	0	0	2	1	1	0	0	0	0	0	0	0	0	0	4	0	0	0	0	0	0	0	0
contraception	4	.2090	.2014	33.0	0	0	0	0	1	1	2	0	0	0	0	0	0	0	0	0	0	0	0	0	0	0	1	3	0
contract	94	.7597	14.346	51.6	4	9	8	5	29	14	17	8	3	13	0	2	0	6	11	16	0	0	0	0	4	5	12	18	0
contracted	18	.7049	2.5648	44.1	0	1	2	3	8	0	3	1	1	3	0	1	0	2	0	0	1	1	4	0	3	1	4	1	0
contractile	2	.0000	.0394	26.0	0	0	0	0	1	0	1	0	0	0	0	0	0	0	0	2	0	0	0	0	0	0	0	0	0
contracting	12	.2736	.8023	39.0	0	0	2	3	0	3	3	1	1	0	0	0	0	0	0	6	0	0	0	0	0	0	5	0	0
contraction	106	.3984	8.9993	49.5	26	19	20	17	11	0	10	3	3	32	1	0	0	0	56	8	1	0	0	0	1	0	4	0	0
contractions	65	.3466	4.8345	46.8	13	25	12	6	4	2	3	0	1	20	2	0	0	0	40	1	0	0	0	0	0	0	1	0	0
contractor	3	.3273	.2365	33.7	0	0	0	0	1	1	1	0	1	1	0	0	0	0	1	0	0	0	0	0	0	0	0	0	0
contractors	3	.1937	.1495	31.7	0	0	0	0	0	1	1	1	0	0	0	0	0	1	0	0	0	0	0	0	0	0	0	2	0
contracts	33	.5330	3.7370	45.7	1	2	7	2	11	4	5	1	1	1	0	1	0	5	0	18	0	0	0	0	0	0	2	5	0
contradance	2	.0000	.0162	22.1	0	0	2	0	0	0	0	0	0	0	0	0	0	0	0	0	2	0	0	0	0	0	0	0	0
contradances	2	.0000	.0162	22.1	0	0	2	0	0	0	0	0	0	0	0	0	0	0	0	0	2	0	0	0	0	0	0	0	0
contradict	4	.3266	.3036	34.8	0	0	0	0	1	1	2	0	1	1	1	1	0	0	0	0	0	0	0	0	0	0	0	0	0
contradicted	4	.4475	.4001	36.0	0	0	0	3	1	0	0	0	1	0	0	0	0	0	0	1	0	0	0	0	1	0	1	0	0
contradicting	3	.3759	.2474	33.9	0	0	0	0	1	1	1	0	0	1	0	1	0	0	0	1	0	0	0	0	0	0	0	0	0
contradiction	9	.5339	1.0024	40.0	0	0	0	2	2	3	2	0	0	0	0	1	3	1	0	0	0	0	0	0	0	2	2	0	0
contradictions	8	.4360	.7474	38.7	0	0	4	0	1	2	1	0	0	0	0	0	0	1	0	0	0	0	0	0	0	3	1	0	0
contradictory	6	.4608	.5847	37.7	0	0	3	0	2	0	1	0	0	1	0	1	0	0	0	0	0	0	0	0	1	3	0	3	0
contradicts	2	.2446	.1122	30.5	0	0	0	0	1	1	0	0	0	0	0	1	0	0	0	0	0	0	0	0	0	0	1	0	0
contralto	5	.0000	.0404	26.1	0	0	0	2	2	1	0	0	0	0	0	0	0	0	0	0	5	0	0	0	0	0	0	0	0
contraption	10	.4176	.9277	39.7	2	0	1	1	2	2	0	2	2	0	1	0	0	0	0	0	0	0	0	0	4	3	0	0	0
contraptions	2	.1362	.0684	28.3	0	0	0	0	1	0	1	0	0	0	1	0	0	0	0	0	0	0	0	0	0	0	0	0	0
contrapuntal	14	.0000	.1132	30.5	0	0	0	0	5	6	3	0	0	0	0	0	1	0	0	0	14	0	0	0	0	0	0	0	0
contrary	59	.8640	10.158	50.1	2	0	6	6	16	13	12	4	9	1	1	6	1	6	0	4	2	0	1	1	3	5	9	10	0
contrast	172	.6534	22.787	53.6	6	7	13	22	57	35	21	11	9	4	2	1	2	14	2	12	40	25	3	5	2	5	27	19	0
contrasted	16	.4812	1.6035	42.1	0	1	0	1	9	4	1	0	0	0	0	1	0	3	8	0	0	1	0	0	0	1	0	2	0
contrasting	50	.4506	4.6465	46.7	4	8	4	4	5	21	4	0	1	1	0	0	0	0	1	0	34	7	2	1	0	1	1	1	0
contrasts	34	.5981	4.1593	46.2	1	2	6	8	4	5	4	4	1	2	0	0	0	8	0	0	12	3	2	0	0	2	2	2	0
contribute	45	.7228	6.5973	48.2	1	3	5	7	14	7	4	4	5	1	1	0	2	10	1	8	5	2	6	0	0	0	2	2	0
contributed	80	.7982	12.827	51.1	2	5	11	11	20	17	13	1	11	4	0	1	3	11	2	7	9	2	0	1	0	7	19	3	0
contributes	17	.5819	2.0544	43.1	1	0	0	2	6	4	3	1	2	0	0	0	0	1	0	4	3	1	3	0	0	1	0	2	0
contributing	13	.5933	1.6164	42.1	0	0	1	1	5	1	3	2	2	0	0	1	0	0	0	3	0	0	0	0	0	2	2	3	0
contribution	52	.7803	8.1557	49.1	2	2	7	5	15	10	10	1	6	2	0	2	4	5	1	5	8	2	0	1	0	1	12	3	0
contributions	59	.7977	9.4485	49.8	2	1	11	3	10	13	17	2	4	4	0	1	10	11	1	8	4	0	0	0	1	2	7	6	0
contributors	2	.2278	.1128	30.5	0	0	0	0	0	1	0	1	0	0	0	0	0	0	0	1	0	0	0	0	0	0	1	0	0
contrivances	4	.1698	.2267	33.6	0	0	1	0	1	1	1	0	2	0	0	0	0	0	0	0	0	0	0	0	0	0	2	0	0
contrive	3	.3805	.2526	34.0	0	1	0	0	1	1	0	0	0	0	0	0	0	1	0	0	0	0	0	0	1	1	0	0	0
contrived	2	.1621	.0746	28.7	0	0	0	0	1	0	1	0	0	0	1	1	0	0	0	0	0	0	0	0	0	0	0	0	0
control	556	.8547	94.840	59.8	36	36	63	92	124	98	83	24	68	6	3	13	4	105	5	97	12	3	18	17	10	30	78	87	0
Control	10	.4293	.9337	39.7	0	0	1	3	2	2	0	2	1	1	0	0	0	1	0	0	0	0	0	0	0	0	2	5	0
controllable	2	.2346	.1166	30.7	0	1	0	1	0	0	0	0	0	0	0	0	0	0	0	1	0	0	0	0	0	0	0	1	0
controlled	120	.7209	17.553	52.4	3	8	21	19	19	27	18	5	7	1	1	1	1	27	0	31	5	0	1	7	0	4	27	7	0
controlling	35	.5373	3.8918	45.9	0	5	1	3	10	7	9	0	1	1	6	0	1	2	0	5	0	0	0	1	1	1	11	6	0
controls	92	.8566	15.730	52.0	6	4	12	25	21	10	13	1	14	0	2	1	1	8	0	19	6	1	2	2	1	9	11	15	0
controversial	15	.3436	1.1314	40.5	0	0	1	0	8	2	4	0	0	0	0	0	0	1	1	0	0	0	0	0	0	0	3	10	0
controversies	4	.1873	.1827	32.6	0	0	1	0	1	1	1	0	0	0	0	0	0	0	0	0	0	0	0	0	0	0	3	1	0
controversy	22	.5692	2.5895	44.1	0	0	0	1	8	7	5	1	0	0	0	1	1	6	0	0	1	0	0	0	0	1	7	5	0
convalescent	2	.1442	.0761	28.8	0	0	0	0	1	0	1	0	0	0	0	0	0	1	0	0	0	0	1	0	0	0	0	0	0
convection	15	.0000	.2957	34.7	0	0	7	2	3	2	1	0	0	0	0	0	0	0	0	15	0	0	0	0	0	0	0	0	0
convene	2	.2139	.1057	30.2	0	0	0	1	0	1	0	0	0	0	0	0	0	1	1	0	0	0	0	0	0	0	0	0	0
convened	2	.0000	.0389	25.9	0	0	0	0	0	1	1	0	0	0	0	0	0	2	0	0	0	0	0	0	0	0	0	0	0
convenience	48	.6442	6.2758	48.0	1	4	3	5	8	8	17	2	2	1	1	1	4	5	3	4	1	0	13	2	2	2	5	2	0
conveniences	2	.0000	.0209	23.2	1	0	0	0	0	0	1	0	0	0	0	0	0	0	0	0	0	0	0	0	0	0	2	0	0
convenient	95	.6278	12.220	50.9	3	6	8	9	18	23	26	2	6	5	0	5	40	5	0	4	0	0	9	10	0	3	4	4	0
conveniently	21	.5116	2.2229	43.5	0	3	1	0	7	5	5	0	1	2	0	1	0	1	0	2	0	0	6	2	0	1	5	0	0
convent	5	.3757	.4097	36.1	0	2	0	0	0	1	2	0	0	0	0	0	0	0	0	0	0	0	0	0	1	2	0	2	0
convention	53	.5652	6.2619	48.0	2	4	4	0	7	28	8	0	2	5	0	0	2	22	0	0	0	0	0	0	2	2	8	12	0
Convention	19	.4035	1.6833	42.3	0	1	1	0	7	8	2	0	0	0	0	0	0	10	0	0	0	0	0	0	0	1	6	2	0
convention's	3	.0000	.0365	25.6	0	0	0	0	0	2	1	0	0	0	0	0	0	0	0	0	0	0	0	0	0	0	0	3	0
conventional	42	.7249	6.1267	47.9	0	2	1	0	21	8	7	3	1	9	0	4	0	1	0	2	1	1	0	1	0	3	7	12	0
conventions	15	.5380	1.6841	42.3	0	0	1	0	2	10	2	0	0	2	0	0	0	6	0	0	1	0	0	0	0	0	4	2	0
convents	2	.0000	.0243	23.9	0	0	0	0	0	0	2	0	0	0	0	0	0	0	0	0	0	0	0	0	0	0	0	2	0
converge	7	.3001	.4730	36.7	0	2	0	1	1	0	1	2	0	0	0	0	0	0	0	1	0	0	0	0	0	0	4	2	0
converged	2	.1170	.0651	28.1	0	0	0	0	0	1	1	0	0	0	1	0	0	1	0	0	0	0	0	0	0	0	0	0	0
converging	3	.0000	.0055	17.4	0	0	0	3	0	0	0	0	0	0	0	0	0	0	0	0	0	3	0	0	0	0	0	0	0
conversation	209	.8086	33.858	55.3	17	22	34	16	42	42	32	4	32	61	8	24	1	7	4	4	10	1	7	0	13	11	9	17	0
conversational	7	.4683	.7057	38.5	0	0	1	0	2	1	3	0	1	3	0	1	0	0	0	0	0	0	0	0	0	1	0	1	0
conversationalist	2	.0000	.0219	23.4	0	0	0	0	1	1	0	0	0	2	0	0	0	0	0	0	0	0	0	0	0	0	0	0	0
conversations	35	.7018	4.9802	47.0	3	5	6	3	4	5	9	0	3	11	2	3	0	3	0	1	1	0	0	0	5	2	2	2	0
converse	24	.4969	2.5234	44.0	0	0	1	1	2	0	20	0	1	1	1	2	17	0	0	1	0	0	1	0	0	0	0	0	0

7Q continent-sized
7P Continental's
8F continentally
7Q continentals
6A Continentals'
7R Contingent
7Q continuations
5F Continuing
6P continuo
9Q continuous-tone
8A contra-dance
9D contraband
7J contrabass
7B contrac'
9R contraceptives
8Q Contract
8Q Contracting
9A contradictoriness
7R Contramaestre
3Q contrariness
5J contras
7N Contrasted
7J Contrasts
XR Contributions
8Q contributor
8F contrite
7D contrition
6A contrivance
7R contriving
7R control-rod
7R controlled-access
XR controllers
7R conundrum
6F conurbation
6F conurbations
3P Convair
9P convalescence
7L convalescing
9R Convent
6A conventionality
7J Conversation
9F conversation's

Word Type	F	D	U	SFI	3 Gr 3	4 Gr 4	5 Gr 5	6 Gr 6	7 Gr 7	8 Gr 8	9 Gr 9	X UnGr	A Read	B Eng & Gr	C Comp	D Lit	E Math	F Soc Stud	G Spell	H Sci	J Music	K Art	L Home Ec	M Shop	N Lib F	P Lib NF	Q Lib Ref	R Mag	S Rel
conversely	8	.5011	.8421	39.3	0	0	0	0	2	1	3	2	0	2	0	0	1	0	0	3	0	0	0	1	0	0	1	0	0
converses	2	.0000	.0299	24.8	0	0	0	0	0	0	2	0	0	0	0	0	2	0	0	0	0	0	0	0	0	0	0	0	0
conversing	2	.1839	.0845	29.3	0	0	0	0	1	1	0	0	0	0	0	0	0	0	0	0	0	0	1	0	1	0	0	0	0
conversion	20	.4852	2.0404	43.1	1	2	0	0	7	4	6	0	0	0	0	0	1	0	0	5	0	0	0	1	0	0	9	4	0
Conversion	3	.3452	.2543	34.1	0	2	0	0	1	0	0	0	1	0	0	0	0	0	0	1	0	0	0	0	0	0	0	1	0
conversions	4	.0000	.0599	27.8	0	0	0	0	0	4	0	0	0	0	0	0	4	0	0	0	0	0	0	0	0	0	0	0	0
convert	42	.6834	5.8238	47.7	2	2	3	3	10	14	6	2	0	2	0	0	14	2	1	5	0	0	0	1	0	3	9	5	0
converted	55	.7106	7.9135	49.0	2	0	7	8	19	10	8	1	1	0	0	2	0	9	2	11	1	0	0	2	2	7	16	2	0
converter	17	.3676	1.3859	41.4	0	7	0	0	9	1	0	0	0	0	0	0	0	0	0	7	0	0	0	1	0	0	0	9	0
converters	2	.0000	.0394	26.0	0	2	0	0	0	0	0	0	0	0	0	0	0	0	0	2	0	0	0	0	0	0	0	0	0
convertible	12	.5718	1.4665	41.7	0	0	0	0	11	1	0	0	4	0	0	0	0	0	0	1	0	0	1	0	3	0	1	2	0
convertibles	4	.2420	.2307	33.6	0	0	2	0	2	0	0	0	0	0	0	0	2	0	0	0	0	0	0	0	2	0	0	0	0
converting	22	.6485	2.9260	44.7	2	2	2	2	6	4	3	1	1	0	0	0	2	1	0	6	0	0	0	1	0	3	5	3	0
converts	11	.4367	1.0469	40.2	0	0	1	0	2	5	1	2	0	0	0	0	0	5	0	2	0	0	0	0	0	1	3	0	0
convex	14	.3565	1.1043	40.4	0	5	0	5	0	0	4	0	0	0	0	0	1	0	0	7	0	0	0	3	0	0	3	0	0
convexity	2	.2405	.1205	30.8	0	0	0	0	1	0	0	1	0	0	0	0	0	0	0	1	0	0	0	0	0	1	0	0	0
convey	41	.6401	5.3116	47.3	0	0	1	1	11	8	20	0	3	5	8	8	0	0	1	0	5	2	0	3	1	1	1	3	0
conveyances	2	.1042	.0600	27.8	0	0	0	0	0	1	1	0	0	0	0	0	0	1	0	0	0	1	0	0	0	0	0	0	0
conveyed	11	.4332	1.0486	40.2	0	0	1	0	3	3	4	0	3	0	3	1	0	1	0	0	0	1	0	0	1	0	1	0	0
conveying	3	.3136	.1997	33.0	0	0	0	1	0	1	1	0	0	1	0	0	0	0	0	0	1	0	0	1	0	0	0	0	0
conveyor	8	.4361	.7508	38.8	0	0	4	0	2	2	0	0	0	0	0	0	0	4	0	0	0	0	0	1	0	1	2	0	0
conveyors	2	.1483	.0728	28.6	0	0	0	0	1	0	1	0	0	0	0	0	0	0	0	0	0	0	0	1	0	1	0	0	0
conveys	6	.4766	.5944	37.7	0	0	1	0	1	1	3	0	0	2	0	2	0	0	0	0	1	0	0	0	0	0	1	0	0
convict	2	.2401	.1133	30.5	0	0	1	0	1	0	0	0	0	0	0	0	0	0	0	0	0	0	0	0	0	1	1	0	0
convicted	17	.6625	2.2926	43.6	0	0	2	1	7	3	4	0	1	1	0	1	0	1	2	0	0	0	0	0	2	1	2	6	0
conviction	25	.5712	3.0316	44.8	1	1	8	1	2	5	7	0	7	2	0	1	0	0	0	0	1	0	0	0	0	1	4	9	0
convictions	5	.3374	.4243	36.3	0	0	1	1	3	0	0	0	2	0	0	0	0	0	0	1	0	0	0	0	0	2	0	0	0
convicts	2	.2297	.1135	30.6	0	0	0	0	0	1	1	0	0	0	0	1	0	1	0	0	0	0	0	0	0	0	0	0	0
convince	47	.8569	8.0243	49.0	0	3	2	3	15	11	10	3	5	4	1	2	4	8	6	1	1	1	0	0	2	4	1	7	0
convinced	85	.7811	13.398	51.3	5	4	17	6	26	7	16	4	15	3	0	5	1	8	2	5	1	0	0	0	7	10	15	13	0
convincing	29	.7614	4.4765	46.5	1	1	3	3	6	8	7	0	7	4	2	2	1	2	0	1	1	0	0	1	0	3	1	4	0
convincingly	4	.2734	.2712	34.3	0	0	0	0	2	1	1	0	1	0	0	0	0	1	0	0	0	1	0	0	0	0	1	0	0
convivial	5	.2384	.2747	34.4	0	0	0	0	0	3	2	0	0	0	0	3	0	0	0	0	0	0	0	0	0	0	2	0	0
convoy	5	.3771	.4747	36.8	0	0	0	4	1	0	0	0	3	0	0	1	0	1	0	0	0	0	0	0	0	0	0	0	0
convoying	3	.2043	.1486	31.7	0	2	0	0	1	0	0	0	0	0	0	0	0	0	0	0	0	0	0	0	0	1	2	0	0
convulsion	2	.1814	.1187	30.7	0	0	0	0	1	0	1	0	1	0	0	0	0	0	0	0	0	0	0	0	0	0	0	1	0
convulsions	3	.3629	.2409	33.8	0	0	0	0	0	1	2	0	0	0	0	0	0	0	0	1	1	0	0	0	0	1	0	0	0
convulsive	4	.3584	.3139	35.0	0	1	0	0	2	0	1	0	0	0	0	0	0	0	0	0	0	0	0	0	2	1	0	1	0
convulsively	3	.2292	.1615	32.1	0	0	0	0	2	0	1	0	0	0	0	1	0	0	0	0	0	0	0	0	2	0	0	0	0
cooed	4	.0000	.0323	25.1	2	0	0	2	0	0	0	0	0	0	0	0	0	0	0	0	4	0	0	0	0	0	0	0	0
cooing	5	.1674	.2532	34.0	0	1	0	1	1	2	0	0	2	0	2	1	0	0	0	0	0	0	0	0	0	0	0	0	0
cook	265	.7035	38.301	55.8	45	60	34	30	32	23	33	8	79	12	3	13	1	16	8	9	8	0	41	1	26	35	2	11	0
Cook	94	.5939	12.054	50.8	30	42	7	2	10	1	2	0	44	1	0	4	0	9	0	0	0	0	0	0	25	4	3	4	0
cook's	5	.1674	.2532	34.0	0	0	0	1	1	2	1	0	2	0	2	1	0	0	0	0	0	0	0	0	0	0	0	0	0
Cook's	6	.3712	.4952	36.9	0	1	3	0	2	0	0	0	0	0	0	2	0	3	0	0	0	0	0	0	1	0	0	0	0
cookbook	11	.2432	.8553	39.3	2	1	8	0	0	0	0	0	9	0	0	0	0	0	0	0	0	0	0	0	0	0	0	2	0
Cookbook	3	.0000	.0097	19.8	0	0	0	0	0	0	3	0	0	0	0	0	0	0	0	0	0	0	3	0	0	0	0	0	0
cookbooks	2	.0857	.0784	28.9	0	0	1	0	0	0	1	0	1	0	0	0	0	0	0	0	0	0	1	0	0	0	0	0	0
Cooke	8	.3475	.6313	38.0	0	0	2	1	1	0	0	4	0	0	0	0	1	0	0	4	0	0	0	0	0	0	0	3	0
cooked	147	.3946	12.949	51.1	23	26	13	16	16	10	41	2	31	2	0	0	0	22	1	4	0	1	51	0	14	14	5	2	0
cooker	6	.4446	.5675	37.5	0	1	0	0	3	0	2	0	0	1	0	0	0	0	0	2	0	0	1	0	0	0	0	2	0
cookers	2	.2351	.1166	30.7	0	0	0	1	0	1	0	0	0	0	0	0	0	1	0	0	0	0	0	0	0	0	0	1	0
cookery	3	.2208	.1563	31.9	0	0	0	0	1	0	1	1	0	2	0	0	0	0	0	0	0	0	0	0	1	0	0	0	0
cookhouse	3	.2261	.2131	33.3	0	0	1	1	1	0	0	0	2	0	0	0	0	0	0	0	0	0	0	0	1	0	0	0	0
cookie	33	.7094	4.8205	46.8	13	7	2	4	2	2	3	0	12	2	1	1	6	0	3	1	0	2	3	0	1	1	0	0	0
Cookie	3	.0000	.0243	23.8	1	2	0	0	0	0	0	0	0	0	0	0	0	0	0	0	3	0	0	0	0	0	0	0	0
cookies	168	.6836	23.738	53.8	78	47	17	3	9	4	7	3	45	7	1	3	72	1	1	1	1	0	7	0	9	12	1	7	0
Cookies	6	.2355	.4634	36.7	5	1	0	0	0	0	0	0	5	0	0	0	0	0	0	0	0	0	0	0	0	1	0	0	0
cookin'	2	.0000	.0234	23.7	0	0	2	0	0	0	0	0	0	0	0	0	0	0	0	0	0	0	0	0	2	0	0	0	0
cooking	212	.5833	25.910	54.1	39	33	23	19	27	23	43	5	44	8	1	11	0	31	4	9	0	0	49	1	16	16	8	14	0
cookout	2	.0000	.0045	16.5	0	0	0	1	0	0	1	0	0	0	2	0	0	0	0	0	0	0	0	0	0	0	0	0	0
cookouts	3	.2443	.1820	32.6	0	2	0	0	0	1	0	0	0	0	0	1	0	0	0	2	0	0	0	0	0	0	0	0	0
cooks	36	.7672	5.6076	47.5	7	6	8	4	5	2	3	1	10	3	0	1	0	1	1	5	3	0	3	0	1	3	1	4	0
cookstove	3	.2212	.2099	33.2	0	2	0	0	0	0	1	0	2	0	0	1	0	0	0	0	0	0	0	0	0	0	0	0	0
cooky	13	.4543	1.2846	41.1	4	7	0	0	1	0	1	0	1	1	0	0	3	2	0	0	0	0	0	0	0	6	0	0	0
Cooky	4	.3318	.2887	34.6	2	2	0	0	0	0	0	0	0	1	0	0	0	0	2	0	0	0	0	0	0	1	0	0	0
cool	500	.8848	88.098	59.4	99	110	74	52	78	39	33	15	93	15	4	15	0	73	3	102	9	14	19	7	32	61	18	35	0
Cool	6	.0706	.1822	32.6	1	0	0	0	1	0	4	0	1	0	0	0	0	0	0	0	0	0	0	0	0	0	0	5	0
cool-down	3	.0000	.0365	25.6	0	0	0	0	0	0	0	3	0	0	0	0	0	0	0	0	0	0	0	0	0	0	0	3	0
coolant	14	.0807	.3806	35.8	0	0	0	0	14	0	0	0	0	0	0	0	0	0	0	0	0	0	0	0	0	1	0	13	0
cooled	133	.6006	16.654	52.2	30	17	21	11	19	11	21	3	5	1	0	3	0	8	1	83	0	0	7	0	4	8	10	3	0
cooler	98	.5824	12.101	50.8	17	27	10	14	15	7	8	0	12	0	0	0	3	30	0	42	0	1	0	0	4	1	5	0	0
coolest	5	.4506	.5019	37.0	0	0	2	0	2	0	0	1	1	0	0	1	0	0	0	2	0	0	0	0	1	0	0	0	0
Coolidge	4	.4516	.4046	36.1	1	0	1	0	0	2	0	0	1	0	0	1	0	1	0	0	0	0	0	0	0	1	0	0	0
cooling	54	.6619	7.2974	48.6	4	7	3	4	13	6	13	4	1	0	0	3	1	2	0	21	1	0	1	4	0	2	4	14	0
coolly	9	.4675	.9391	39.7	0	1	1	2	2	2	1	0	3	0	0	2	0	0	0	0	0	0	0	0	2	2	0	0	0
coolness	11	.5408	1.3108	41.2	1	3	3	1	2	1	0	0	5	0	0	2	0	1	0	0	0	0	0	0	0	2	1	0	0
cools	77	.5196	8.5453	49.3	19	14	13	5	9	5	11	1	3	0	0	1	0	1	0	51	0	0	0	2	0	10	6	3	0
coon	3	.2143	.1568	32.0	1	0	0	0	0	0	0	2	0	0	0	0	0	0	0	0	0	0	0	0	0	1	0	2	0
coonhound	2	.0000	.0243	23.9	0	0	0	0	0	0	0	2	0	0	0	0	0	0	0	0	0	0	0	0	0	0	0	2	0
coons	5	.4826	.5062	37.0	3	0	0	0	1	1	0	0	0	0	0	1	0	0	0	0	0	0	0	0	1	2	1	0	0
coonskin	7	.3571	.5457	37.4	1	4	1	0	0	1	0	0	0	0	0	1	0	0	0	0	2	0	0	0	0	4	0	0	0
coop	24	.3779	2.3878	43.8	20	3	0	0	0	1	0	0	20	0	0	1	0	0	0	1	0	0	0	0	0	2	0	0	0
cooped	7	.2401	.3936	36.0	1	2	1	0	2	0	1	0	0	0	0	0	0	0	0	0	0	0	0	0	4	0	0	3	0
cooper	4	.2393	.3005	34.8	0	0	0	3	1	0	0	0	3	0	0	1	0	0	0	0	0	0	0	0	0	0	0	0	0
Cooper	28	.5910	3.5169	45.5	1	5	8	7	5	2	0	0	9	6	0	1	0	1	0	0	0	0	0	0	0	4	1	6	0
Cooper's	3	.2357	.2199	33.4	0	1	0	2	0	0	0	0	2	0	0	0	0	0	0	0	0	0	0	0	0	1	0	0	0
cooperate	21	.7484	3.2008	45.1	0	1	1	4	6	5	3	1	5	1	1	0	0	2	0	4	0	0	1	0	1	2	3	1	0
cooperated	3	.3847	.2496	34.0	0	1	2	0	0	0	0	0	0	0	0	0	0	0	0	0	0	0	0	0	0	1	1	1	0
cooperates	2	.0000	.0290	24.6	2	0	0	0	0	0	0	0	0	0	0	0	0	0	0	0	0	0	0	0	0	2	0	0	0
cooperating	3	.2581	.1836	32.6	0	0	2	0	1	0	0	0	0	0	0	0	0	1	0	1	0	0	1	0	0	0	0	0	0
cooperation	40	.6887	5.5842	47.5	2	1	8	2	8	6	12	1	0	0	1	0	0	12	0	4	0	0	2	1	1	2	13	4	0
Cooperation	5	.3926	.4468	36.5	0	0	2	0	1	1	1	0	1	0	0	0	0	1	0	0	0	0	0	0	0	1	2	0	0
cooperative	23	.7407	3.4433	45.4	0	0	3	7	5	3	3	2	1	1	1	1	0	9	0	2	0	0	0	1	1	1	3	2	0
Cooperative	2	.0000	.0243	23.9	0	0	0	0	0	1	0	1	0	0	0	0	0	0	0	0	0	0	0	0	0	0	0	2	0
cooperatives	7	.3229	.5280	37.2	0	0	1	4	1	0	0	1	0	0	0	0	0	5	0	0	0	0	0	0	0	1	0	1	0

9N conversed
XR Converter-Dryer
8Q convertibility
5A conveyable
9F conveyance
8B conveyancer
6A conveyer
7R convinces
7Q convoke
7Q convoking
9Q convoluted
7Q convolutions
4N convolvulus-runners
8F convoyed
4Q convoys
7P convulse
4N convulsed
6R convulsing
XR Conway
9D conwey
9P Conyers
3P coo
5Q Cooch's
7B Coogan's
4A cook-brother
8L Cooked
4J Cookie's
6A cooking-stove
7A cooks'
3A Cooks'
3F cookstoves
7R Coolant
3Q coolers
XR Coolidge's
7D coolie
3A Coolie
6A coolies
5R cooly
5P Cooma
5P Cooma's
5J Coon
7N coon's
6A cooper's
7H cooperatively
XR cooperator
XR cooperators
6A Coopers

Word Type	F	D	U	SFI	3 Gr 3	4 Gr 4	5 Gr 5	6 Gr 6	7 Gr 7	8 Gr 8	9 Gr 9	X UnGr	A Read	B Eng & Gr	C Comp	D Lit	E Math	F Soc Stud	G Spell	H Sci	J Music	K Art	L Home Ec	M Shop	N Lib F	P Lib NF	Q Lib Ref	R Mag	S Rel
Cooperstown	3	.1409	.1472	31.7	0	0	0	3	0	0	0	0	1	0	0	0	0	0	0	0	0	0	0	0	0	2	0	0	0
coordinate	49	.3626	3.9426	46.0	4	0	1	0	9	12	23	0	0	0	1	0	40	1	0	2	2	0	0	0	0	0	3	0	0
coordinated	10	.5800	1.1939	40.8	0	0	0	0	2	2	5	1	0	0	1	0	0	2	0	2	0	0	1	0	0	0	2	2	0
coordinates	39	.1961	1.9585	42.9	17	0	0	1	3	8	10	0	0	0	1	0	37	0	0	0	0	0	0	0	0	0	1	0	0
coordinating	6	.3225	.4210	36.2	1	0	0	0	1	0	3	1	0	1	2	0	0	0	0	1	0	0	0	0	0	1	1	0	0
Coordinating	2	.0000	.0243	23.9	0	0	0	0	0	1	0	1	0	0	0	0	0	0	0	0	0	0	0	0	0	0	0	2	0
coordination	9	.4545	.8819	39.5	0	0	1	2	4	1	0	1	0	2	0	0	0	0	0	5	1	0	0	0	0	1	0	0	0
coordinator	10	.1179	.3277	35.2	0	0	1	0	0	9	0	0	0	9	0	0	0	0	0	0	0	0	0	0	0	0	1	0	0
coordinators	2	.0000	.0219	23.4	0	0	0	0	0	2	0	0	0	2	0	0	0	0	0	0	0	0	0	0	0	0	0	0	0
cop	33	.3870	3.3301	45.2	24	0	2	0	5	0	2	0	28	0	0	2	0	0	0	0	0	0	0	0	2	1	0	0	0
cope	20	.4529	1.9273	42.8	0	0	0	3	9	4	4	0	1	0	0	1	0	1	0	4	0	0	0	4	0	0	3	6	0
coped	2	.2446	.1122	30.5	0	0	0	0	1	0	1	0	0	0	0	1	0	0	0	0	0	0	0	0	0	0	1	0	0
Copeland	3	.1910	.1473	31.7	0	1	2	0	0	0	0	0	0	0	0	0	0	1	0	0	0	0	0	0	2	0	0	0	0
Copenhagen	20	.3558	1.6291	42.1	14	0	0	2	2	1	1	0	3	0	0	0	0	3	0	2	1	0	0	0	0	0	11	0	0
copepod	7	.1690	.3428	35.4	1	0	6	0	0	0	0	0	0	0	0	0	0	0	0	6	0	0	0	0	0	1	0	0	0
copepods	5	.2251	.2690	34.3	2	0	0	3	0	0	0	0	0	3	0	0	0	0	0	0	0	0	0	0	0	2	0	0	0
Copernican	3	.0000	.0591	27.7	0	0	0	0	1	0	0	2	0	0	0	0	0	0	0	3	0	0	0	0	0	0	0	0	0
Copernicus	14	.4720	1.4291	41.6	0	0	0	5	1	1	4	3	0	0	0	0	0	2	0	9	1	0	0	0	0	0	1	1	0
copied	24	.6570	3.2511	45.1	4	1	3	7	4	3	2	0	4	6	0	0	0	5	2	0	0	1	0	0	0	4	1	1	0
copies	50	.7181	7.2414	48.6	1	4	10	4	13	9	5	4	3	6	1	2	7	5	2	1	5	0	0	7	1	2	2	6	0
copilot	4	.4502	.4024	36.0	0	0	1	2	1	0	0	0	1	1	0	0	0	1	0	0	0	0	0	0	0	0	0	1	0
coping	7	.2606	.4021	36.0	1	0	0	0	1	4	1	0	0	0	0	1	0	0	0	1	0	0	0	3	0	0	2	0	0
copious	2	.0000	.0209	23.2	0	0	0	0	1	1	0	0	0	0	0	0	0	0	0	0	0	0	0	0	0	0	2	0	0
coplanar	2	.0000	.0299	24.8	0	0	0	0	2	0	0	0	0	0	0	0	2	0	0	0	0	0	0	0	0	0	0	0	0
Copland	9	.0000	.0728	28.6	1	3	0	1	2	2	0	0	0	0	0	0	0	0	0	0	9	0	0	0	0	0	0	0	0
Copland's	2	.2407	.1090	30.4	0	0	0	0	1	0	1	0	0	1	0	0	0	0	0	0	1	0	0	0	0	0	0	0	0
Copley	3	.2432	.1789	32.5	0	0	0	0	1	2	0	0	0	0	0	0	0	2	0	0	1	0	0	0	0	0	0	0	0
copper	326	.6967	46.927	56.7	62	28	41	59	46	52	29	9	89	4	0	6	14	65	2	64	3	2	1	32	4	14	18	8	0
Copper	10	.5407	1.1547	40.6	0	3	0	2	2	0	3	0	2	1	0	0	3	2	0	0	0	0	0	1	0	0	0	1	0
copper-colored	3	.2063	.1600	32.0	1	1	0	1	0	0	0	0	0	0	0	0	0	1	0	0	0	0	0	0	0	2	0	0	0
copperhead	8	.5296	.9270	39.7	1	0	1	0	2	1	1	2	3	1	0	2	0	0	0	1	0	0	0	0	1	0	0	0	0
copperheads	5	.3157	.3891	35.9	3	0	0	0	0	1	0	1	1	0	0	0	0	0	0	3	0	0	0	0	0	0	1	0	0
Coppermine	7	.1912	.3660	35.6	0	6	0	0	1	0	0	0	0	0	0	1	0	6	0	0	0	0	0	0	0	0	0	0	0
coppers	5	.2913	.3570	35.5	3	0	1	0	1	0	0	0	1	0	0	1	0	0	0	0	0	0	0	0	0	3	0	0	0
Coppersmith	7	.0000	.3198	35.0	0	0	0	5	2	0	0	0	7	0	0	0	0	0	0	0	0	0	0	0	0	0	0	0	0
coppery	3	.0000	.1370	31.4	0	0	0	0	3	0	0	0	3	0	0	0	0	0	0	0	0	0	0	0	0	0	0	0	0
Coppino	6	.0000	.0703	28.5	0	0	0	6	0	0	0	0	0	0	0	0	0	0	0	0	0	0	0	0	6	0	0	0	0
Coppinos	2	.0000	.0234	23.7	0	0	0	2	0	0	0	0	0	0	0	0	0	0	0	0	0	0	0	0	2	0	0	0	0
Coppo	5	.0000	.2284	33.6	0	0	0	5	0	0	0	0	5	0	0	0	0	0	0	0	0	0	0	0	0	0	0	0	0
copra	5	.2037	.2562	34.1	3	0	0	1	1	0	0	0	0	0	0	0	0	2	0	0	0	0	0	0	0	0	3	0	0
cops	10	.2300	.5706	37.6	1	0	0	0	3	3	3	0	1	0	0	0	0	0	0	0	0	0	0	0	2	0	0	7	0
copter	13	.2801	.9478	39.8	0	0	4	0	0	0	0	9	3	0	0	0	0	0	1	9	0	0	0	0	0	0	0	0	0
copters	4	.0000	.0789	29.0	0	0	0	0	0	0	0	4	0	0	0	0	0	0	0	4	0	0	0	0	0	0	0	0	0
Coptic	2	.2285	.1129	30.5	0	0	0	0	1	0	0	1	0	0	0	0	0	1	0	0	0	0	0	0	0	0	1	0	0
copy	887	.6396	115.79	60.6	197	143	183	132	109	72	44	7	34	155	58	7	452	10	107	7	2	2	4	13	6	16	5	9	0
copybooks	2	.2427	.1152	30.6	0	1	0	1	0	0	0	0	0	0	0	0	0	0	0	0	0	0	0	0	1	1	0	0	0
copying	25	.6362	3.2739	45.2	1	3	3	3	9	3	2	1	3	5	2	0	3	2	0	0	0	0	0	0	0	5	3	2	0
copyist	2	.0000	.0914	29.6	0	0	0	0	2	0	0	0	2	0	0	0	0	0	0	0	0	0	0	0	0	0	0	0	0
copyists	2	.0000	.0914	29.6	0	0	0	0	2	0	0	0	2	0	0	0	0	0	0	0	0	0	0	0	0	0	0	0	0
copyreaders	2	.1717	.1142	30.6	0	0	0	1	0	0	1	0	1	0	0	1	0	0	0	0	0	0	0	0	0	0	0	0	0
copyright	2	.1814	.1187	30.7	0	0	0	0	0	1	1	0	1	0	0	0	0	0	0	0	0	0	0	0	0	0	0	1	0
Cora	6	.2292	.3230	35.1	2	0	0	0	4	0	0	0	0	0	0	2	0	0	0	0	0	0	0	0	4	0	0	0	0
coracle	3	.0000	.0352	25.5	0	0	0	0	3	0	0	0	0	0	0	0	0	0	0	0	0	0	0	0	3	0	0	0	0
coral	85	.7728	13.414	51.3	14	1	2	19	40	4	3	2	30	3	0	4	0	17	1	9	0	0	0	0	4	6	3	8	0
Coral	4	.1959	.1920	32.8	0	0	0	3	1	0	0	0	0	0	0	0	0	0	0	0	0	0	0	0	3	0	0	1	0
corals	7	.4420	.6750	38.3	0	0	0	2	4	0	1	0	1	0	1	0	0	0	0	2	0	0	0	0	1	0	2	0	0
Corbin	3	.1277	.1363	31.3	2	0	0	0	1	0	0	0	1	0	0	0	0	0	0	0	0	0	0	0	0	0	0	2	0
Corcoran	2	.0000	.0243	23.9	0	0	0	0	1	0	0	1	0	0	0	0	0	0	0	0	0	0	0	0	0	0	0	2	0
cord	115	.7729	18.017	52.6	7	11	30	14	23	10	16	4	24	1	2	9	3	2	1	43	0	0	6	1	3	1	14	5	0
Cord	27	.0000	1.2334	40.9	0	0	0	0	0	27	0	0	27	0	0	0	0	0	0	0	0	0	0	0	0	0	0	0	0
Corday	2	.0000	.0209	23.2	0	0	2	0	0	0	0	0	0	0	0	0	0	0	0	0	0	0	0	0	0	0	2	0	0
corded	2	.0000	.0064	18.1	0	0	0	0	2	0	0	0	0	0	0	0	0	0	0	0	0	0	2	0	0	0	0	0	0
cordial	3	.3815	.2534	34.0	0	0	0	1	1	1	0	0	0	0	0	0	0	1	0	0	0	0	0	0	0	1	0	1	0
cordially	8	.5244	.9015	39.5	1	1	1	1	2	0	1	1	2	0	0	2	0	0	0	0	0	0	0	0	0	1	1	2	0
Cordilleran	2	.0000	.0209	23.2	0	0	0	2	0	0	0	0	0	0	0	0	0	0	0	0	0	0	0	0	0	0	2	0	0
cordless	2	.0000	.0243	23.9	0	0	0	0	0	0	0	2	0	0	0	0	0	0	0	0	0	0	0	0	0	0	0	2	0
Cordoba	2	.2139	.1057	30.2	0	0	0	1	0	1	0	0	0	0	0	0	0	1	1	0	0	0	0	0	0	0	0	0	0
cords	51	.6494	6.8423	48.4	9	2	1	19	5	11	4	0	4	2	0	2	1	2	2	30	5	0	1	0	1	0	1	0	0
Cords	2	.0000	.0914	29.6	0	0	0	0	0	2	0	0	2	0	0	0	0	0	0	0	0	0	0	0	0	0	0	0	0
corduroy	5	.3069	.4062	36.1	0	0	1	1	1	0	2	0	3	0	0	1	0	0	0	0	0	0	1	0	0	0	0	0	0
core	109	.4160	9.9053	50.0	1	7	8	11	28	13	35	6	14	0	2	0	0	2	0	30	0	0	0	29	1	1	20	10	0
coremaker	2	.0000	.0050	17.0	0	0	0	0	0	0	2	0	0	0	0	0	0	0	0	0	0	0	0	2	0	0	0	0	0
cores	14	.5867	1.6996	42.3	0	0	0	0	2	0	12	0	1	0	0	0	0	1	0	3	0	0	1	1	0	0	5	2	0
Corey	13	.1070	.4394	36.4	0	1	0	2	0	0	10	0	0	0	0	0	0	0	0	0	0	0	0	0	0	12	0	1	0
Corey's	5	.0000	.0724	28.6	0	0	0	3	0	0	2	0	0	0	0	0	0	0	0	0	0	0	0	0	0	5	0	0	0
coriander	3	.0000	.0365	25.6	0	0	0	0	0	0	0	3	0	0	0	0	0	0	0	0	0	0	0	0	0	0	0	3	0
coring	2	.0000	.0394	26.0	0	0	0	0	0	1	1	0	0	0	0	0	0	0	0	2	0	0	0	0	0	0	0	0	0
Corinth	6	.3226	.4378	36.4	0	2	0	0	1	3	0	0	0	0	0	0	0	2	0	0	0	0	0	0	0	1	3	0	0
Coriolis	2	.0000	.0209	23.2	0	0	0	0	2	0	0	0	0	0	0	0	0	0	0	0	0	0	0	0	0	0	2	0	0
cork	50	.7598	7.6876	48.9	11	8	12	7	8	2	2	0	6	0	0	0	0	2	3	22	2	2	1	1	2	2	6	1	0
Cork	10	.3384	.7759	38.9	0	1	0	1	7	1	0	0	0	0	0	0	0	6	0	0	0	0	0	0	0	1	0	3	0
Cork's	2	.0000	.0243	23.9	0	0	0	2	0	0	0	0	0	0	0	0	0	0	0	0	0	0	0	0	0	0	0	2	0
Corkonians	2	.0000	.0914	29.6	0	0	0	0	2	0	0	0	2	0	0	0	0	0	0	0	0	0	0	0	0	0	0	0	0
corks	2	.2160	.1362	31.3	1	1	0	0	0	0	0	0	1	0	0	0	0	0	0	1	0	0	0	0	0	0	0	0	0
corkscrew	4	.3603	.3218	35.1	1	0	0	1	0	0	2	0	0	0	0	0	0	0	0	1	0	0	0	0	1	2	0	0	0
Corkscrew	2	.0000	.0914	29.6	0	0	0	2	0	0	0	0	2	0	0	0	0	0	0	0	0	0	0	0	0	0	0	0	0
Corky	4	.0000	.0486	26.9	0	0	0	4	0	0	0	0	0	0	0	0	0	0	0	0	0	0	0	0	0	0	0	4	0
Cormac	2	.0000	.0290	24.6	0	0	2	0	0	0	0	0	0	0	0	0	0	0	0	0	0	0	0	0	0	2	0	0	0
cormorant	3	.2181	.1541	31.9	0	0	0	1	1	0	1	0	0	0	0	0	0	0	0	0	0	0	0	0	1	0	2	0	0
cormorants	6	.3583	.4703	36.7	2	0	0	3	1	0	0	0	0	0	0	0	0	0	0	0	0	0	0	0	3	2	1	0	0
corn	545	.8838	96.264	59.8	189	78	72	60	84	32	17	13	183	12	3	14	12	119	9	56	19	1	14	0	32	41	13	17	0
Corn	26	.5411	2.9463	44.7	2	8	11	0	4	1	0	0	0	2	0	4	0	11	0	0	2	0	0	0	0	7	0	0	0
corn-husk	4	.0000	.1827	32.6	4	0	0	0	0	0	0	0	4	0	0	0	0	0	0	0	0	0	0	0	0	0	0	0	0

5N coops
6R CoosBay
5F Coosa
7Q cooters
3B coots
9D cop's
9D cop'st
4R Copage
7Q copal-burning
3Q Copenhagen's
5H copepod's
3P COPEPODS
XH Copernicus'
3P COPING
8Q Coplas
8N Copp's
8Q Coppelia
5D copper-brown
4R copper-red
5F copper-skinned
6J copper's
9M Copperplate
9D Coppery
7N copse
7R copter's
XH Coptis
9Q Copts
7Q copulation
7Q copulatory
6A copy-reader
XR copyable
6A copybook
7D copywriter
7C coquette
8A coquettes
5A coqui
4N Coquin
3A coral-bell
6A coral-pink
7Q coral-snake
XR Coralburst
8Q Coralli
7Q coralreef
7A corazon
8F Corbett
9K Corbusier
8A Cord's
7A cordage
XH Cordaites
5P cordiality
9F Cordier
XH Cordon
8G Cordovan
7R cordwood
5B Core
8M core-type
7K Coreen
4Q Corelli
8M coretype
4P Corinne
3P Corix
8B cork-heild
7B corker
9Q corkscrews
7H corky
9Q Corliss
5N corn-cakes
7N corn-cob
7N corn-feast
7H corn-grower
5Q corn-husking
4A corn-meal

Word Type	F	D	U	SFI	3 Gr 3	4 Gr 4	5 Gr 5	6 Gr 6	7 Gr 7	8 Gr 8	9 Gr 9	X UnGr	A Read	B Eng & Gr	C Comp	D Lit	E Math	F Soc Stud	G Spell	H Sci	J Music	K Art	L Home Ec	M Shop	N Lib F	P Lib NF	Q Lib Ref	R Mag	S Rel
cornbread	11	.5687	1.3028	41.1	0	3	0	0	5	2	1	0	1	1	0	1	0	0	0	0	0	0	0	0	3	3	0	2	0
corncake	2	.2407	.1138	30.6	0	1	0	0	1	0	0	0	0	0	0	1	0	0	0	0	0	0	0	0	0	1	0	0	0
corncakes	4	.1757	.1766	32.5	0	1	0	0	3	0	0	0	0	0	0	3	0	0	0	0	0	0	0	0	0	1	0	0	0
corncob	6	.4868	.6622	38.2	2	0	0	1	2	1	0	0	3	1	0	0	0	0	0	0	0	0	0	0	1	0	0	1	0
corncobs	5	.3410	.4278	36.3	0	0	1	2	2	0	0	0	2	0	0	0	2	1	0	0	0	0	0	0	0	0	0	0	0
cornea	5	.0000	.0986	29.9	0	0	0	4	0	1	0	0	0	0	0	0	0	0	0	5	0	0	0	0	0	0	0	0	0
corned	9	.3930	.7661	38.8	3	1	0	0	0	0	0	5	0	0	0	0	2	0	0	0	0	0	0	0	1	1	0	5	0
Cornelia	3	.0000	.1370	31.4	0	2	1	0	0	0	0	0	3	0	0	0	0	0	0	0	0	0	0	0	0	0	0	0	0
Cornelius	5	.4789	.5381	37.3	0	1	2	1	0	0	1	0	2	0	0	0	0	0	0	0	0	0	0	0	1	1	0	1	0
Cornell	6	.1453	.2356	33.7	1	0	0	0	2	0	2	1	0	0	0	0	0	0	0	0	0	0	0	0	0	1	0	5	0
corner	579	.9225	105.98	60.3	132	94	78	51	108	48	63	5	179	39	8	48	38	44	2	19	8	9	11	17	57	51	14	35	0
Corner	15	.5548	1.7740	42.5	6	5	0	1	1	0	2	0	4	0	0	0	0	0	1	0	3	0	0	0	1	5	0	1	0
cornered	13	.6017	1.6808	42.3	2	0	2	1	4	3	1	0	6	0	0	1	0	1	0	0	0	0	0	0	2	0	2	1	0
cornering	3	.2300	.1627	32.1	0	0	0	0	3	0	0	0	0	1	0	0	0	0	0	0	0	0	0	0	0	0	0	2	0
corners	152	.8032	24.572	53.9	30	14	22	13	30	12	24	7	36	2	1	14	18	4	1	13	3	3	13	12	6	15	3	8	0
Corners	2	.2446	.1122	30.5	0	1	0	0	0	1	0	0	0	0	0	1	0	0	0	0	0	0	0	0	0	0	1	0	0
cornerstone	5	.4833	.5473	37.4	0	1	1	0	0	3	0	0	2	0	0	0	1	1	0	0	0	0	0	0	0	1	0	0	0
cornet	14	.0000	.1132	30.5	0	4	0	0	0	9	1	0	0	0	0	0	0	0	0	0	14	0	0	0	0	0	0	0	0
cornets	9	.0000	.0728	28.6	0	1	3	1	0	3	1	0	0	0	0	0	0	0	0	0	9	0	0	0	0	0	0	0	0
cornfield	41	.7438	6.2767	48.0	14	6	7	5	6	0	2	1	17	1	0	3	1	1	0	3	0	0	0	0	2	7	2	4	0
cornfields	12	.6913	1.6921	42.3	4	2	0	3	1	1	1	0	1	1	0	0	0	1	0	2	1	0	0	0	2	2	0	2	0
Cornflower	9	.0000	.4111	36.1	9	0	0	0	0	0	0	0	9	0	0	0	0	0	0	0	0	0	0	0	0	0	0	0	0
Cornflower's	2	.0000	.0914	29.6	2	0	0	0	0	0	0	0	2	0	0	0	0	0	0	0	0	0	0	0	0	0	0	0	0
cornhusk	3	.3399	.2456	33.9	0	1	0	0	1	0	0	1	1	0	0	1	0	0	0	0	0	0	0	0	0	0	0	1	0
cornhusks	3	.0978	.0707	28.5	0	0	2	0	1	0	0	0	0	0	0	1	0	0	0	0	0	2	0	0	0	0	0	0	0
cornice	5	.2382	.2754	34.4	0	0	0	0	3	0	2	0	0	3	0	2	0	0	0	0	0	0	0	0	0	0	0	0	0
cornices	2	.1718	.0785	28.9	0	0	0	0	1	0	1	0	0	0	0	1	0	0	0	0	0	0	0	1	0	0	0	0	0
Cornish	5	.3814	.4791	36.8	0	3	0	0	0	1	0	1	3	0	0	0	0	1	0	0	0	0	0	0	0	0	0	1	0
cornmeal	15	.3297	1.3688	41.4	8	2	0	2	3	0	0	0	12	0	0	0	0	0	0	1	0	0	0	0	0	0	0	2	0
Cornplanter	2	.0000	.0914	29.6	0	0	0	0	2	0	0	0	2	0	0	0	0	0	0	0	0	0	0	0	0	0	0	0	0
cornstalk	10	.3438	.9360	39.7	0	2	5	1	2	0	0	0	8	0	0	0	0	0	0	1	0	0	0	0	1	0	0	0	0
cornstalks	12	.4713	1.2795	41.1	4	2	2	2	2	0	0	0	5	0	0	0	2	0	0	0	2	0	0	0	0	3	0	0	0
cornstarch	2	.2331	.1157	30.6	1	0	0	0	1	0	0	0	0	0	0	0	0	0	0	1	0	0	0	0	1	0	0	0	0
cornucopias	4	.1826	.1841	32.7	0	0	1	2	1	0	0	0	0	0	0	0	0	0	0	0	0	0	0	0	3	1	0	0	0
Cornwall	9	.2465	.5350	37.3	0	2	0	1	3	0	0	3	0	0	0	0	0	2	0	1	0	0	0	0	0	0	0	6	0
Cornwallis	10	.2317	.5933	37.7	3	0	1	0	0	6	0	0	0	0	0	0	0	7	0	0	0	0	0	0	0	3	0	0	0
Cornwallis'	2	.2152	.1357	31.3	0	0	1	0	1	0	0	0	1	0	0	0	0	1	0	0	0	0	0	0	0	0	0	0	0
corny	4	.0000	.0486	26.9	0	0	1	0	0	0	3	0	0	0	0	0	0	0	0	0	0	0	0	0	0	0	0	4	0
corolla	7	.0000	.1380	31.4	0	0	0	0	0	0	3	4	0	0	0	0	0	0	0	7	0	0	0	0	0	0	0	0	0
corollaries	2	.0000	.0299	24.8	0	0	0	0	0	0	2	0	0	0	0	0	2	0	0	0	0	0	0	0	0	0	0	0	0
corollary	3	.2233	.1562	31.9	0	0	0	0	0	0	3	0	0	0	0	1	0	0	0	0	0	0	0	0	0	0	2	0	0
corona	5	.2000	.2712	34.3	0	0	0	1	2	0	1	1	0	0	0	0	0	0	0	4	0	0	0	0	0	1	0	0	0
Corona	4	.3831	.3409	35.3	0	0	1	0	2	0	0	1	0	0	0	0	0	0	0	2	0	0	0	0	0	1	1	0	0
Coronado	27	.4614	2.7712	44.4	1	0	11	3	12	0	0	0	6	0	0	0	0	11	0	0	0	0	0	0	0	1	7	2	0
Coronado's	6	.3476	.5208	37.2	0	0	0	1	5	0	0	0	3	0	0	0	0	0	0	0	0	0	0	0	0	0	2	1	0
coronary	4	.2278	.2257	33.5	0	0	2	0	0	2	0	0	0	0	0	0	0	0	0	2	0	0	0	0	0	0	2	0	0
coronation	7	.3199	.5346	37.3	2	0	2	2	0	0	1	0	2	0	0	0	0	0	0	0	2	0	0	0	0	0	3	0	0
Coronation	2	.2443	.1130	30.5	0	0	0	0	2	0	0	0	0	0	0	1	0	0	0	0	0	0	0	0	1	0	0	0	0
coronet	5	.0000	.0608	27.8	0	0	0	5	0	0	0	0	0	0	0	0	0	0	0	0	0	0	0	0	0	0	0	5	0
Coronet	4	.0000	.0486	26.9	0	0	0	0	0	4	0	0	0	0	0	0	0	0	0	0	0	0	0	0	0	0	0	4	0
Corot	4	.1493	.1383	31.4	1	0	1	0	0	1	1	0	0	0	0	0	0	0	0	0	0	2	0	0	0	0	2	0	0
Corp	4	.0000	.0486	26.9	0	0	0	1	1	1	0	1	0	0	0	0	0	0	0	0	0	0	0	0	0	0	0	4	0
corporal	3	.3847	.2448	33.9	0	0	1	0	1	1	0	0	0	0	0	1	0	0	0	0	1	0	0	0	0	0	1	0	0
Corporal	2	.2441	.1127	30.5	0	1	1	0	0	0	0	0	0	0	0	0	0	0	0	0	0	0	0	0	1	0	1	0	0
corporate	7	.2205	.3670	35.6	0	0	0	0	1	4	2	0	0	0	0	0	0	0	0	0	0	0	0	0	0	0	2	5	0
corporation	22	.5714	2.6523	44.2	0	1	4	0	4	5	8	0	2	1	0	0	0	11	0	1	0	0	0	0	0	3	2	2	0
Corporation	17	.5491	1.9234	42.8	0	0	4	0	1	2	5	5	0	1	1	0	0	2	0	0	1	0	0	0	0	0	5	7	0
corporations	20	.5279	2.2178	43.5	0	0	4	2	3	6	5	0	0	0	0	0	1	8	0	1	0	0	0	0	1	0	5	4	0
corps	11	.5348	1.2720	41.0	0	0	3	1	2	4	0	1	3	0	0	0	0	2	0	0	1	0	0	0	0	2	0	3	0
Corps	36	.5779	4.3297	46.4	4	4	3	1	5	15	2	2	2	0	0	0	1	9	0	2	1	0	1	0	0	1	3	16	0
corpse	16	.5484	1.8233	42.6	0	0	1	3	6	2	4	0	1	0	0	2	0	0	0	0	0	0	0	0	4	2	5	2	0
corpses	4	.4538	.4020	36.0	0	1	0	0	1	2	0	0	1	0	0	1	0	0	0	0	0	0	0	0	0	1	0	1	0
corpus	6	.0000	.1183	30.7	0	0	0	0	0	0	6	0	0	0	0	0	0	0	0	6	0	0	0	0	0	0	0	0	0
CorpusChristi	2	.2152	.1357	31.3	0	0	2	0	0	0	0	0	1	0	0	0	0	1	0	0	0	0	0	0	0	0	0	0	0
corpuscles	6	.0000	.1183	30.7	0	0	1	3	0	0	0	2	0	0	0	0	0	0	0	6	0	0	0	0	0	0	0	0	0
corral	57	.6567	7.7463	48.9	22	6	7	7	12	3	0	0	14	3	1	11	0	1	0	0	1	0	0	0	16	3	0	7	0
corrals	6	.5191	.6688	38.3	3	2	0	1	0	0	0	0	1	0	0	0	0	1	0	0	0	0	0	0	1	2	0	1	0
correct	940	.7717	145.51	61.6	84	153	96	162	185	139	107	14	55	148	22	8	321	24	208	42	18	1	11	29	3	14	8	27	1
Correct	6	.1508	.2346	33.7	0	0	3	0	1	1	1	0	0	5	0	0	0	0	0	0	0	0	0	0	0	0	0	1	0
corrected	64	.5290	6.9759	48.4	0	4	10	4	31	2	12	1	3	6	0	2	2	1	37	0	0	0	4	1	3	1	2	2	0
correcting	14	.6415	1.8378	42.6	1	1	1	0	4	3	3	1	1	3	0	0	0	0	3	3	0	0	1	0	1	1	0	1	0
correction	11	.5511	1.2586	41.0	0	0	2	0	0	3	4	2	0	0	0	0	2	0	0	3	0	0	1	0	0	0	2	3	0
corrections	20	.5270	2.1804	43.4	1	1	3	2	5	6	2	0	2	4	0	0	0	0	2	1	0	0	4	4	0	1	1	1	0
corrective	4	.2405	.2410	33.8	1	0	1	0	0	2	0	0	0	0	0	0	0	0	0	2	0	0	0	0	0	2	0	0	0
correctly	485	.5883	58.497	57.7	60	98	73	95	67	33	56	3	36	119	14	0	35	4	225	9	6	0	9	12	1	7	2	6	0
correctness	4	.2501	.2761	34.4	0	0	0	0	0	2	2	0	2	0	0	0	0	0	0	0	0	0	0	1	0	0	0	1	0
corrects	2	.0000	.0243	23.9	1	0	0	0	1	0	0	0	0	0	0	0	0	0	0	0	0	0	0	0	0	0	0	2	0
correlate	7	.3539	.5628	37.5	0	0	0	0	1	0	5	1	0	1	0	0	0	0	0	5	1	0	0	0	0	0	0	0	0
correlated	2	.2300	.1140	30.6	0	0	0	0	1	0	1	0	0	1	0	0	0	0	0	1	0	0	0	0	0	0	0	0	0
correlation	5	.2342	.2967	34.7	0	0	0	0	0	0	4	1	0	0	0	0	0	0	0	4	1	0	0	0	0	0	0	0	0
correspond	29	.6100	3.6266	45.6	0	0	0	2	9	10	7	1	0	3	0	1	14	0	4	3	1	0	0	0	0	0	2	1	0
corresponded	6	.4843	.6601	38.2	0	0	0	1	3	1	0	1	3	0	0	1	0	0	0	0	0	0	0	0	0	1	1	0	0
correspondence	33	.6052	4.1225	46.2	0	1	1	0	15	7	7	2	2	0	1	0	18	2	1	0	0	0	0	1	0	0	5	3	0
correspondent	7	.3862	.5884	37.7	0	0	0	0	2	4	1	0	0	0	0	0	0	1	0	0	0	0	0	0	0	1	1	4	0
correspondents	3	.1277	.1363	31.3	0	0	0	0	1	1	1	0	1	0	0	0	0	0	0	0	0	0	0	0	0	0	0	2	0
corresponding	160	.5487	18.290	52.6	2	20	1	3	28	62	42	2	0	12	0	0	108	16	3	3	2	0	1	4	0	3	6	2	0
correspondingly	3	.3756	.2468	33.9	0	0	0	0	3	0	0	0	0	0	0	1	0	1	0	0	0	0	0	0	0	0	1	0	0
corresponds	36	.4205	3.2996	45.2	0	0	0	3	4	11	17	1	0	0	0	0	22	1	0	8	1	0	0	0	0	1	3	0	0
corridor	28	.6346	3.6421	45.6	3	5	1	4	5	4	6	0	2	1	0	5	0	1	0	0	0	0	0	0	7	5	2	5	0
Corridor	3	.2425	.1816	32.6	0	0	0	3	0	0	0	0	0	0	0	0	0	2	0	0	0	0	0	0	0	0	0	1	0
corridors	11	.5532	1.2683	41.0	0	1	0	1	3	3	2	1	1	0	1	4	0	0	0	1	0	0	0	0	0	2	1	1	0
corrode	3	.3754	.2470	33.9	0	1	0	0	0	1	0	1	0	1	0	0	0	0	0	1	0	0	0	0	0	0	1	0	0
corroded	2	.2437	.1129	30.5	0	0	0	0	1	0	1	0	0	0	0	0	0	0	0	0	0	0	0	0	0	0	1	1	0
corrosion	19	.2818	1.2716	41.0	4	0	1	0	0	10	4	0	4	0	0	0	0	0	0	1	0	0	0	6	0	1	7	0	0
corrosive	3	.1813	.1402	31.5	0	0	0	1	1	0	1	0	0	0	0	0	0	0	0	1	0	0	0	0	0	0	2	0	0
corrugated	11	.3859	.9497	39.8	1	4	1	0	4	0	0	1	1	0	0	0	0	6	0	1	0	2	0	1	0	0	0	0	0
corrupt	9	.4030	.8100	39.1	0	0	2	0	3	2	2	0	2	0	0	0	0	0	0	0	0	1	0	0	0	0	2	4	0

5J corn-picking
7R CORNBREAD
4Q Corneille
9D cornel
6A Cornerstone
9H cornerstones
5R Cornet
4J cornett
9R cornflakes
6A cornhill
5A Corning
5A cornland
6A corns
7R cornstick
7B cornu
7Q cornucopian
5P Coro
7R Corolla
7H coronagraph
XD coroner's
9F corporation's
5Q Corporations
8R corps'
8D corpse-hued
8D corpselike
7P corpsmen
7R corpulency
7P corpulent
8Q corpuscular
7H corralled
XR corralling
5Q Correction
XQ correlates
9L correlating
9B correlative
9R Correspondence
9R Correspondent
8Q Correspondenz
9R Corrington
9D corroborating
7H corrosion-resistant
9M corrosion-resisting

Word Type	F	D	U	SFI	3 Gr 3	4 Gr 4	5 Gr 5	6 Gr 6	7 Gr 7	8 Gr 8	9 Gr 9	X UnGr	A Read	B Eng & Gr	C Comp	D Lit	E Math	F Soc Stud	G Spell	H Sci	J Music	K Art	L Home Ec	M Shop	N Lib F	P Lib NF	Q Lib Ref	R Mag	S Rel
corrupted	2	.2412	.1141	30.6	0	0	0	0	1	0	0	1	0	1	0	0	0	0	0	0	0	0	0	0	0	1	0	0	0
corrupting	2	.1814	.1187	30.7	0	0	0	0	1	0	1	0	1	0	0	0	0	0	0	0	0	0	0	0	0	0	0	1	0
corruption	19	.5925	2.3395	43.7	0	1	0	1	5	6	6	0	2	0	0	1	0	3	0	0	0	0	0	0	2	2	6	3	0
corse	5	.0000	.0537	27.3	0	0	0	0	0	0	5	0	0	0	0	5	0	0	0	0	0	0	0	0	0	0	0	0	0
corselet	2	.1948	.1250	31.0	0	0	0	1	1	0	0	0	1	0	0	0	0	0	0	0	0	0	0	0	0	1	0	0	0
Corsica	4	.2446	.2243	33.5	1	0	0	0	0	2	1	0	0	0	0	2	0	0	0	0	0	0	0	0	0	0	2	0	0
Corsican	2	.0000	.0215	23.3	0	0	0	0	0	2	0	0	0	0	0	2	0	0	0	0	0	0	0	0	0	0	0	0	0
Cortes	24	.3682	2.0079	43.0	1	0	20	0	2	1	0	0	0	0	0	0	0	19	0	0	1	0	0	0	0	2	1	1	0
Cortes'	3	.0000	.0583	27.7	0	0	3	0	0	0	0	0	0	0	0	0	0	3	0	0	0	0	0	0	0	0	0	0	0
cortex	10	.2424	.5976	37.8	0	0	0	0	7	0	3	0	0	0	0	0	0	0	0	6	0	0	0	0	0	0	4	0	0
Cortez	26	.6044	3.2561	45.1	0	12	2	1	9	1	1	0	2	1	0	8	0	8	0	0	1	0	0	0	0	2	3	1	0
Cortina	2	.0000	.0243	23.9	0	0	0	0	1	0	0	1	0	0	0	0	0	0	0	0	0	0	0	0	0	0	0	2	0
Cortinas	2	.0000	.0389	25.9	0	0	0	2	0	0	0	0	0	0	0	0	0	2	0	0	0	0	0	0	0	0	0	0	0
cortisone	2	.2346	.1166	30.7	0	0	0	0	1	0	0	1	0	0	0	0	0	0	0	1	0	0	0	0	0	0	0	1	0
Corvair	9	.0000	.1094	30.4	0	0	0	0	9	0	0	0	0	0	0	0	0	0	0	0	0	0	0	0	0	0	0	9	0
Corvette	10	.0000	.1215	30.8	0	0	0	0	10	0	0	0	0	0	0	0	0	0	0	0	0	0	0	0	0	0	0	10	0
Corvisart	4	.0000	.1827	32.6	0	0	4	0	0	0	0	0	4	0	0	0	0	0	0	0	0	0	0	0	0	0	0	0	0
Cory	2	.0000	.0243	23.9	0	0	2	0	0	0	0	0	0	0	0	0	0	0	0	0	0	0	0	0	0	0	0	2	0
cos	4	.2220	.2176	33.4	0	0	0	0	0	4	0	0	0	0	0	0	3	0	0	0	0	0	0	0	0	0	1	0	0
cosmetic	7	.0869	.2692	34.3	0	0	0	0	7	0	0	0	1	0	0	0	0	0	0	6	0	0	0	0	0	0	0	0	0
Cosmetic	5	.0000	.0986	29.9	0	0	0	0	2	3	0	0	0	0	0	0	0	0	0	5	0	0	0	0	0	0	0	0	0
cosmetics	21	.6960	2.9786	44.7	1	0	6	1	6	1	5	1	3	1	0	1	0	2	0	2	0	1	2	0	0	1	4	4	0
cosmic	17	.3220	1.2301	40.9	0	3	0	2	8	1	1	2	0	0	0	0	1	0	0	4	0	0	0	0	0	2	10	0	0
cosmology	3	.1813	.1402	31.5	0	0	0	0	1	0	2	0	0	0	0	0	0	0	0	1	0	0	0	0	0	0	2	0	0
cosmonaut	2	.2408	.1091	30.4	0	0	0	0	0	1	1	0	0	1	0	0	0	0	1	0	0	0	0	0	0	0	0	0	0
cosmonauts	7	.2202	.3869	35.9	0	4	1	0	2	0	0	0	0	0	0	0	0	0	0	3	0	0	0	0	0	0	0	4	0
cosmopolitan	3	.3847	.2496	34.0	0	0	1	1	1	0	0	0	0	0	0	0	0	0	0	0	0	0	0	0	0	1	1	1	0
cosmos	5	.3014	.3394	35.3	0	1	0	0	3	1	0	0	0	0	0	1	0	0	0	1	0	0	0	0	0	0	3	0	0
Cossack	4	.4448	.3915	35.9	1	0	0	0	1	1	1	0	1	1	0	1	0	0	0	0	1	0	0	0	0	0	0	0	0
Cossacks	2	.0000	.0162	22.1	0	0	0	2	0	0	0	0	0	0	0	0	0	0	0	0	2	0	0	0	0	0	0	0	0
cost	610	.6678	83.630	59.2	118	100	106	72	80	53	56	25	70	5	3	7	334	48	7	9	1	0	25	6	18	17	13	47	0
Costa	6	.3801	.5663	37.5	0	0	2	4	0	0	0	0	3	0	0	0	0	2	0	0	0	0	0	0	0	1	0	0	0
costing	16	.4172	1.4638	41.7	2	1	6	0	1	4	1	1	0	0	0	0	8	3	0	2	0	0	0	0	0	3	0	0	0
costly	53	.6623	7.3184	48.6	6	7	8	3	14	7	7	1	13	0	0	1	0	16	1	7	0	0	0	0	0	5	7	3	0
costs	159	.6562	21.418	53.3	36	22	28	10	22	14	23	4	14	3	1	0	78	17	2	2	0	0	7	0	5	1	11	18	0
costumbres	2	.0000	.0215	23.3	0	0	0	0	2	0	0	0	0	0	0	2	0	0	0	0	0	0	0	0	0	0	0	0	0
costume	77	.8233	12.831	51.1	13	14	12	17	7	5	8	1	36	1	1	5	1	7	0	0	7	1	4	0	3	4	2	5	0
costumes	73	.8264	12.133	50.8	11	23	14	7	9	6	2	1	20	4	0	3	1	13	1	0	7	2	1	0	2	12	3	4	0
Cosway	3	.0000	.0314	25.0	0	0	0	0	0	3	0	0	0	0	0	0	0	0	0	0	0	0	0	0	0	0	3	0	0
cosy	3	.1250	.1342	31.3	0	0	2	1	0	0	0	0	1	0	0	0	0	0	0	0	0	0	0	0	2	0	0	0	0
cot	20	.5525	2.3801	43.8	1	4	3	3	3	0	5	1	7	0	0	6	0	0	0	0	1	0	0	0	3	1	0	2	0
Cotabato	2	.0000	.0209	23.2	0	0	0	0	0	2	0	0	0	0	0	0	0	0	0	0	0	0	0	0	0	0	2	0	0
Cothen	2	.0000	.0290	24.6	0	0	0	0	2	0	0	0	0	0	0	0	0	0	0	0	0	0	0	0	0	2	0	0	0
cotidal	4	.0000	.0789	29.0	0	0	0	0	0	0	0	4	0	0	0	0	0	0	0	4	0	0	0	0	0	0	0	0	0
cotillion	2	.0000	.0389	25.9	0	0	0	0	0	2	0	0	0	0	0	0	0	2	0	0	0	0	0	0	0	0	0	0	0
cotillions	2	.1948	.1250	31.0	0	0	0	0	1	1	0	0	1	0	0	0	0	0	0	0	0	0	0	0	0	1	0	0	0
cottage	85	.7248	12.741	51.1	21	18	5	22	11	3	3	2	40	0	5	5	2	1	1	0	1	0	4	0	6	12	2	6	0
Cottage	3	.0000	.1370	31.4	0	0	0	3	0	0	0	0	3	0	0	0	0	0	0	0	0	0	0	0	0	0	0	0	0
cottages	19	.5379	2.2394	43.5	6	2	6	2	2	1	0	0	6	0	0	0	0	5	0	3	0	0	0	0	1	4	0	0	0
cotton	554	.6879	78.424	58.9	90	64	140	49	99	51	57	4	84	4	2	17	2	277	7	41	4	3	49	1	22	15	17	9	0
Cotton	19	.5712	2.3063	43.6	4	0	8	1	2	3	1	0	4	1	0	4	0	7	0	0	1	0	0	0	0	0	0	2	0
cotton-growing	2	.2152	.1357	31.3	0	0	1	0	1	0	0	0	1	0	0	0	0	1	0	0	0	0	0	0	0	0	0	0	0
cotton-picker	2	.0000	.0234	23.7	2	0	0	0	0	0	0	0	0	0	0	0	0	0	0	0	0	0	0	0	2	0	0	0	0
cotton-picking	2	.0000	.0389	25.9	0	2	0	0	0	0	0	0	0	0	0	0	0	2	0	0	0	0	0	0	0	0	0	0	0
cotton-wool	2	.0000	.0914	29.6	0	2	0	0	0	0	0	0	2	0	0	0	0	0	0	0	0	0	0	0	0	0	0	0	0
cottonmouth	2	.2346	.1166	30.7	1	0	0	1	0	0	0	0	0	0	0	0	0	0	0	1	0	0	0	0	0	0	0	1	0
cottonmouths	4	.0000	.0789	29.0	4	0	0	0	0	0	0	0	0	0	0	0	0	0	0	4	0	0	0	0	0	0	0	0	0
cottons	9	.0672	.1504	31.8	0	1	0	0	0	4	4	0	0	0	0	0	0	0	1	0	0	0	8	0	0	0	0	0	0
cottonseed	9	.4251	.8351	39.2	3	0	2	0	3	1	0	0	0	0	0	0	0	6	0	0	0	0	1	0	0	1	1	0	0
cottonseeds	2	.0000	.0389	25.9	0	2	0	0	0	0	0	0	0	0	0	0	0	2	0	0	0	0	0	0	0	0	0	0	0
cottontail	6	.3751	.4934	36.9	0	0	1	2	2	1	0	0	0	0	0	2	0	0	0	2	0	0	0	0	0	0	2	0	0
cottontail's	2	.0000	.0394	26.0	0	0	0	2	0	0	0	0	0	0	0	0	0	0	0	2	0	0	0	0	0	0	0	0	0
cottontails	6	.1650	.3367	35.3	0	1	0	4	1	0	0	0	2	0	0	0	0	0	0	4	0	0	0	0	0	0	0	0	0
cottonwood	19	.5718	2.3104	43.6	3	1	1	8	2	2	1	1	4	0	0	4	0	0	0	6	0	0	0	0	1	3	1	0	0
cottonwoods	6	.3496	.5232	37.2	0	2	1	2	2	1	0	0	3	0	0	2	0	0	0	0	0	0	0	0	0	0	0	1	0
cottony	2	.2331	.1157	30.6	1	0	0	0	1	0	0	0	0	0	0	0	0	0	0	1	0	0	0	0	1	0	0	0	0
cotylosaurs	5	.0000	.0724	28.6	0	5	0	0	0	0	0	0	0	0	0	0	0	0	0	0	0	0	0	0	0	5	0	0	0
couch	37	.6675	5.1527	47.1	3	8	4	6	11	4	1	0	14	4	1	6	0	0	0	0	0	0	0	0	6	3	0	3	0
couched	3	.3759	.2471	33.9	0	0	0	1	0	1	1	0	0	1	0	0	0	1	0	0	0	0	0	0	0	0	1	0	0
couches	5	.4272	.4803	36.8	1	0	1	3	0	0	0	0	1	0	0	0	0	1	0	0	0	0	0	0	1	2	0	0	0
coudie	4	.2446	.2250	33.5	0	0	0	0	0	2	2	0	0	2	0	2	0	0	0	0	0	0	0	0	0	0	0	0	0
cougar	12	.3341	1.0686	40.3	0	0	7	3	1	0	1	0	8	0	0	0	0	0	0	1	0	0	0	0	0	0	0	3	0
Cougar	8	.0000	.0938	29.7	0	8	0	0	0	0	0	0	0	0	0	0	0	0	0	0	0	0	0	0	8	0	0	0	0
cougar's	3	.0000	.1370	31.4	0	0	3	0	0	0	0	0	3	0	0	0	0	0	0	0	0	0	0	0	0	0	0	0	0
cough	30	.8099	4.8556	46.9	4	9	2	3	6	5	1	0	1	4	1	1	2	1	2	6	1	0	0	0	1	1	3	6	0
coughed	19	.5620	2.3064	43.6	4	5	1	2	7	0	0	0	7	0	0	5	0	0	0	2	0	0	0	0	2	1	0	2	0
coughing	15	.5980	1.9086	42.8	0	1	2	5	5	1	1	0	5	1	0	2	0	0	0	3	0	0	0	0	1	0	3	0	0
coughs	6	.5497	.7166	38.6	1	0	0	2	3	0	0	0	2	1	0	1	0	1	0	1	0	0	0	0	0	0	0	0	0
could	8585	.9459	1607.4	72.1	1631	1625	1112	1096	1566	860	532	163	3107	281	75	631	373	778	102	550	154	47	28	32	883	887	244	407	6
coulda	2	.1787	.1174	30.7	0	0	0	1	1	0	0	0	1	0	0	0	0	0	0	0	0	0	0	0	1	0	0	0	0
couldn't	879	.7213	131.23	61.2	175	229	120	87	157	45	54	12	389	27	10	97	4	10	5	10	2	0	1	0	134	132	1	57	0
couldst	2	.0000	.0215	23.3	0	0	0	0	0	0	2	0	0	0	0	2	0	0	0	0	0	0	0	0	0	0	0	0	0
Coulee	2	.0000	.0299	24.8	0	0	0	2	0	0	0	0	0	0	0	0	2	0	0	0	0	0	0	0	0	0	0	0	0
Coulter	2	.0000	.0914	29.6	0	0	0	2	0	0	0	0	2	0	0	0	0	0	0	0	0	0	0	0	0	0	0	0	0
council	101	.7933	16.134	52.1	6	12	16	9	15	13	28	2	14	3	2	5	0	20	0	9	3	0	0	0	5	18	15	7	0
Council	99	.7646	15.337	51.9	3	7	9	14	33	13	18	2	19	8	2	2	1	25	0	2	0	0	2	0	5	4	21	8	0
CouncilBluffs	2	.0000	.0389	25.9	0	0	2	0	0	0	0	0	0	0	0	0	0	2	0	0	0	0	0	0	0	0	0	0	0
council-manager	4	.1505	.1615	32.1	0	0	3	0	0	0	1	0	0	0	0	0	0	1	0	0	0	0	0	0	0	0	3	0	0
Council's	2	.2446	.1122	30.5	0	0	0	0	2	0	0	0	0	0	0	1	0	0	0	0	0	0	0	0	0	0	1	0	0
councillor	9	.0000	.4111	36.1	0	9	0	0	0	0	0	0	9	0	0	0	0	0	0	0	0	0	0	0	0	0	0	0	0
councilor	6	.2440	.4665	36.7	3	0	0	1	0	2	0	0	5	0	0	0	0	0	1	0	0	0	0	0	0	0	0	0	0
councilors	2	.2152	.1357	31.3	1	0	0	0	0	0	1	0	1	0	0	0	0	1	0	0	0	0	0	0	0	0	0	0	0
councils	8	.3304	.6314	38.0	0	0	3	2	0	0	3	0	2	0	0	0	0	1	0	0	0	0	0	0	0	1	4	0	0
Councils	3	.2043	.1486	31.7	1	0	0	0	1	1	0	0	0	0	0	0	0	0	0	0	0	0	0	0	0	1	2	0	0

7P Corruption
7P corruptions
7P Corsair
9Q corsite
9Q Corsite
9Q cortical
5Q Corumba
9H corundum
9Q Corunna
7R Corvairs
7R Corvettes
5A Corvisart's
8H CORVUS
9D Corwin
5R Cory's
3P Corythosaurus
7A Cosby's
5B Cosgrave
7K Cosimo
XR Cosmetics
8G cosmo
8F cosmography
8C Cosmos
4P Cossine
9R cost-of-living
9R cost-push
8F costlier
6P costliest
7D costumbre
XQ costumed
7B Costumes
4J costureras
8Q COT
8Q Cota
8Q COTA
6B cote
8Q Cote
7A coterie
7D coteries
7Q Cotopaxi
XH cots
8Q cotta
5P cottagers
9L cotton-blend
4N cotton-blond
3P cotton-covered
8L cotton-percale
9F cotton-seed
8L cotton-twill
5Q cottonlike
5F cottonseed-oil
3A Cottontail
9B Cottonwood
6R Couch
8F Coue
4N Cougar's
4F cougars
7Q Coughlin
9D could'a
8Q Coulomb's
7N council-fires
7R council's
4P councillors
3N councilman
9F councilmen

Word Type	F	D	U	SFI	3 Gr 3	4 Gr 4	5 Gr 5	6 Gr 6	7 Gr 7	8 Gr 8	9 Gr 9	X UnGr	A Read	B Eng & Gr	C Comp	D Lit	E Math	F Soc Stud	G Spell	H Sci	J Music	K Art	L Home Ec	M Shop	N Lib F	P Lib NF	Q Lib Ref	R Mag	S Rel
counsel	22	.5132	2.4051	43.8	1	0	4	4	2	4	7	0	4	0	0	8	0	0	0	0	0	0	0	0	2	1	5	2	0
counseled	6	.1814	.3560	35.5	0	0	2	1	1	2	0	0	3	0	0	0	0	0	0	0	0	0	0	0	0	0	0	3	0
counseling	2	.2433	.1158	30.6	1	0	1	0	0	0	0	0	0	0	0	0	0	0	0	0	0	0	0	0	0	1	0	1	0
counselor	8	.5749	.9376	39.7	0	0	0	0	1	2	4	1	0	2	0	0	0	1	1	0	0	0	1	1	0	0	0	2	0
Counselor	2	.0000	.0914	29.6	0	0	2	0	0	0	0	0	2	0	0	0	0	0	0	0	0	0	0	0	0	0	0	0	0
counselors	10	.0460	.2382	33.8	0	1	4	1	1	2	0	1	1	0	0	0	0	0	0	0	0	0	0	0	0	0	0	9	0
Counselors	2	.0000	.0914	29.6	0	0	2	0	0	0	0	0	2	0	0	0	0	0	0	0	0	0	0	0	0	0	0	0	0
count	435	.8253	71.890	58.6	120	64	35	52	56	44	43	21	52	15	3	13	161	10	11	63	44	0	9	1	14	17	5	16	1
Count	21	.5560	2.5470	44.1	0	0	3	1	10	3	3	1	9	0	0	1	0	1	0	3	2	0	0	0	0	0	5	0	0
COUNT	3	.0000	.0449	26.5	3	0	0	0	0	0	0	0	0	0	0	0	3	0	0	0	0	0	0	0	0	0	0	0	0
count-down	2	.1497	.1046	30.2	2	0	0	0	0	0	0	0	1	0	0	0	0	0	1	0	0	0	0	0	0	0	0	0	0
countdown	11	.4525	1.1311	40.5	1	1	2	2	3	2	0	0	4	3	0	0	0	0	0	2	0	0	0	0	0	0	0	2	0
counted	156	.7807	24.668	53.9	33	34	8	20	25	16	18	2	35	10	0	3	38	18	1	5	2	0	0	0	9	20	7	8	0
countenance	12	.4265	1.1196	40.5	0	1	0	0	8	1	1	1	2	0	1	1	0	0	0	0	0	0	0	0	7	0	0	1	0
counter	98	.8260	16.279	52.1	12	12	8	14	13	16	21	2	24	3	1	14	7	4	1	22	2	0	4	0	6	7	0	3	0
counter-attack	2	.0000	.0243	23.9	0	0	0	2	0	0	0	0	0	0	0	0	0	0	0	0	0	0	0	0	0	0	0	2	0
counter-rhythms	2	.0000	.0162	22.1	0	0	0	0	2	0	0	0	0	0	0	0	0	0	0	0	2	0	0	0	0	0	0	0	0
counter-subject	3	.0000	.0243	23.8	0	0	0	0	0	3	0	0	0	0	0	0	0	0	0	0	3	0	0	0	0	0	0	0	0
counteract	4	.4803	.4071	36.1	0	0	1	1	1	0	0	1	0	0	0	0	0	0	0	1	0	0	0	0	0	1	1	1	0
counterattack	3	.3759	.2471	33.9	0	1	0	0	0	1	0	1	0	1	0	0	0	1	0	0	0	0	0	0	0	0	1	0	0
counterbalance	3	.2823	.1882	32.7	0	0	0	1	0	0	2	0	0	0	0	0	0	0	0	1	1	0	0	1	0	0	0	0	0
counterclockwise	8	.5021	.8408	39.2	1	0	4	0	0	0	2	1	0	0	0	0	1	0	0	3	2	0	0	1	0	0	1	0	0
countered	2	.2351	.1166	30.7	0	0	0	0	1	1	0	0	0	0	0	0	0	1	0	0	0	0	0	0	0	0	0	1	0
counterexample	2	.0000	.0299	24.8	0	0	0	0	0	0	2	0	0	0	0	0	2	0	0	0	0	0	0	0	0	0	0	0	0
counterfeit	14	.5616	1.6408	42.2	1	0	0	1	4	3	5	0	1	2	0	2	3	0	0	0	0	0	0	0	0	5	0	1	0
counterfeiter	4	.1948	.2500	34.0	0	0	0	1	3	0	0	0	2	0	0	0	0	0	0	0	0	0	0	0	0	2	0	0	0
counterfeiters	6	.2357	.4397	36.4	1	0	0	4	1	0	0	0	4	0	0	0	0	0	0	0	0	0	0	0	0	2	0	0	0
counterfeiting	2	.0000	.0914	29.6	0	0	0	1	0	0	1	0	2	0	0	0	0	0	0	0	0	0	0	0	0	0	0	0	0
counterman	2	.0000	.0215	23.3	0	0	0	0	0	0	2	0	0	0	0	2	0	0	0	0	0	0	0	0	0	0	0	0	0
countermelody	3	.0000	.0243	23.8	1	0	0	1	1	0	0	0	0	0	0	0	0	0	0	0	3	0	0	0	0	0	0	0	0
counterpart	5	.5552	.5727	37.6	1	0	0	0	2	1	1	0	0	0	0	1	0	0	1	1	0	0	0	0	0	0	1	1	0
counterparts	8	.4118	.7072	38.5	0	0	2	1	3	1	1	0	0	0	0	0	0	1	0	0	0	0	0	0	0	1	3	3	0
counterpoint	22	.0541	.4044	36.1	0	0	6	0	5	8	3	0	0	0	0	0	0	0	0	0	21	0	0	0	0	0	1	0	0
counters	30	.6955	4.2683	46.3	3	2	2	5	6	11	1	0	4	0	1	2	11	3	0	4	0	0	2	0	1	1	1	0	0
countersink	4	.0751	.0794	29.0	0	0	0	0	1	2	1	0	0	0	0	0	0	0	0	0	0	0	0	3	0	1	0	0	0
countersubject	2	.0000	.0162	22.1	0	0	0	0	2	0	0	0	0	0	0	0	0	0	0	0	2	0	0	0	0	0	0	0	0
countersunk	5	.0613	.0833	29.2	0	0	0	0	1	3	1	0	0	0	0	0	0	0	0	0	0	0	0	4	0	1	0	0	0
countess	3	.2074	.1436	31.6	0	0	0	2	1	0	0	0	0	0	0	1	0	0	2	0	0	0	0	0	0	0	0	0	0
Countess	3	.3385	.2445	33.9	0	1	0	0	1	1	0	0	1	0	0	0	0	0	0	0	0	0	0	0	1	0	1	0	0
counties	21	.5381	2.3866	43.8	3	1	0	3	4	2	6	2	2	1	0	0	0	6	0	0	0	0	0	0	0	2	6	4	0
Counties	2	.0000	.0209	23.2	0	0	2	0	0	0	0	0	0	0	0	0	0	0	0	0	0	0	0	0	0	0	2	0	0
counting	254	.5671	30.191	54.8	48	37	34	47	30	42	16	0	22	3	1	4	164	2	1	14	3	0	1	2	19	9	2	7	0
counting-number	9	.0000	.1347	31.3	0	0	9	0	0	0	0	0	0	0	0	0	9	0	0	0	0	0	0	0	0	0	0	0	0
countless	70	.7645	10.773	50.3	5	3	8	3	21	13	14	3	7	3	0	2	0	8	5	8	8	4	0	0	3	5	12	5	0
countries	853	.6917	120.76	60.8	99	137	142	176	146	78	73	2	71	22	1	5	8	444	5	18	64	4	2	2	6	42	126	33	0
Countries	19	.2136	1.0235	40.1	0	4	14	0	1	0	0	0	0	0	0	0	0	3	0	0	0	0	0	0	1	15	0	0	0
countries'	2	.2285	.1129	30.5	0	0	0	0	1	0	1	0	0	0	0	0	0	1	0	0	0	0	0	0	0	0	1	0	0
country	2357	.8638	406.70	66.1	422	350	377	377	397	261	148	25	421	44	19	93	11	862	32	93	135	11	4	9	55	215	202	150	1
Country	47	.6254	6.1770	47.9	5	1	7	9	1	17	2	5	11	1	0	1	0	20	0	0	4	0	0	0	3	2	0	5	0
country-side	2	.0000	.0914	29.6	0	0	0	2	0	0	0	0	2	0	0	0	0	0	0	0	0	0	0	0	0	0	0	0	0
country's	143	.5978	17.851	52.5	26	14	42	13	27	15	3	3	13	2	0	1	0	58	0	1	3	0	0	0	1	30	24	10	0
countryfolk	2	.2297	.1135	30.6	0	0	0	0	1	1	0	0	0	0	0	1	0	1	0	0	0	0	0	0	0	0	0	0	0
countryman	2	.0000	.0243	23.9	0	1	0	0	0	1	0	0	0	0	0	0	0	0	0	0	0	0	0	0	0	0	0	2	0
countrymen	30	.5864	3.7207	45.7	1	2	4	6	6	6	5	0	8	0	0	1	0	3	0	0	3	0	0	0	4	0	1	10	0
countrymen's	2	.2303	.1079	30.3	1	0	0	0	1	0	0	0	0	0	0	0	0	0	0	0	1	0	0	0	0	1	0	0	0
countryside	83	.8354	13.929	51.4	13	11	14	11	19	7	8	0	22	2	1	4	0	14	0	3	3	1	0	0	4	13	10	6	0
counts	43	.5982	5.3577	47.3	6	10	9	6	7	3	2	0	7	1	0	0	7	0	1	4	13	0	0	0	0	3	1	6	0
county	89	.6511	11.900	50.8	15	9	6	5	12	25	13	4	4	8	0	15	2	39	4	0	0	0	0	0	3	5	0	9	0
County	81	.6754	11.154	50.5	4	11	9	5	16	10	10	16	5	1	0	9	0	9	0	6	3	0	0	0	3	9	8	28	0
county's	2	.0000	.0215	23.3	0	0	0	0	0	0	2	0	0	0	0	2	0	0	0	0	0	0	0	0	0	0	0	0	0
coup	4	.3611	.3119	34.9	0	0	0	0	1	2	0	1	0	0	0	1	0	0	0	0	0	0	0	0	0	0	2	1	0
coupe	25	.0000	1.1421	40.6	0	0	0	0	25	0	0	0	25	0	0	0	0	0	0	0	0	0	0	0	0	0	0	0	0
Couperin	4	.0000	.0579	27.6	0	0	0	2	2	0	0	0	0	0	0	0	0	0	0	0	0	0	0	0	0	4	0	0	0
couple	204	.7870	32.400	55.1	13	21	29	19	61	20	31	10	49	6	4	24	1	2	2	4	19	0	2	0	33	15	3	40	0
coupled	8	.4512	.7673	38.8	0	1	1	0	2	1	2	1	0	1	0	0	0	2	0	0	0	0	0	0	0	0	3	2	0
couples	9	.4746	.8947	39.5	0	0	1	0	0	2	4	2	0	0	0	1	0	1	0	0	3	0	0	0	0	1	0	3	0
couplets	2	.2412	.1141	30.6	0	0	0	0	2	0	0	0	0	1	0	0	0	0	0	0	0	0	0	0	0	1	0	0	0
coupling	5	.1306	.1644	32.2	0	1	0	0	0	3	1	0	0	0	0	0	0	1	0	0	0	0	0	3	0	1	0	0	0
coupon	5	.4418	.4883	36.9	1	0	1	0	2	0	1	0	1	1	0	0	2	0	0	0	0	0	0	0	0	0	1	0	0
coupons	5	.4498	.4763	36.8	0	0	2	0	1	1	0	1	0	0	0	0	1	0	0	0	0	0	0	0	0	1	2	1	0
courage	219	.8318	36.827	55.7	9	30	28	46	49	44	12	1	101	7	2	22	0	24	5	3	4	5	0	0	17	16	6	7	0
Courage	8	.3676	.6877	38.4	1	5	0	1	0	1	0	0	1	1	0	0	0	5	0	1	0	0	0	0	0	0	0	0	0
courageous	35	.7076	5.0654	47.0	4	2	3	2	6	7	11	0	7	8	0	3	0	4	0	0	1	0	0	0	1	5	2	4	0
courageously	5	.4627	.4855	36.9	0	1	0	1	1	1	1	0	0	1	0	2	0	0	0	0	0	0	0	0	0	1	1	0	0
Courant	2	.0000	.0914	29.6	0	0	0	0	2	0	0	0	2	0	0	0	0	0	0	0	0	0	0	0	0	0	0	0	0
courier	5	.3833	.4767	36.8	0	1	1	1	1	0	1	0	3	0	0	1	0	0	0	0	0	0	0	0	0	1	0	0	0
Courier	5	.2467	.3124	34.9	0	3	0	0	2	0	0	0	1	3	0	0	0	0	0	0	0	0	0	0	0	1	0	0	0
couriers	3	.2212	.2099	33.2	0	0	0	0	2	1	0	0	2	0	0	1	0	0	0	0	0	0	0	0	0	0	0	0	0
course	1352	.9730	259.30	64.1	144	181	159	196	326	169	141	36	347	88	12	68	45	114	16	161	25	9	30	10	125	102	89	110	1
Course	5	.0804	.1641	32.2	0	0	0	0	2	3	0	0	1	0	0	0	0	0	0	0	0	0	0	0	4	0	0	0	0
coursed	3	.2304	.1619	32.1	2	0	0	0	0	1	0	0	0	0	0	0	0	0	0	0	0	0	0	0	2	0	1	0	0
Courser	7	.0000	.3198	35.0	0	0	0	5	2	0	0	0	7	0	0	0	0	0	0	0	0	0	0	0	0	0	0	0	0
courses	72	.6380	9.4408	49.8	1	5	16	6	17	9	16	2	8	1	0	0	6	6	0	1	0	1	1	1	0	1	25	21	0
court	236	.8898	41.778	56.2	10	17	24	30	58	41	54	2	44	7	2	12	6	57	4	8	16	3	0	1	14	17	28	17	0
Court	140	.5661	16.641	52.2	12	7	15	7	24	33	38	4	6	0	0	2	1	76	0	0	1	0	0	0	9	18	19	8	0
court-room	2	.0000	.0234	23.7	0	2	0	0	0	0	0	0	0	0	0	0	0	0	0	0	0	0	0	0	2	0	0	0	0
court's	2	.2297	.1135	30.6	0	0	0	0	0	1	1	0	0	0	0	1	0	1	0	0	0	0	0	0	0	0	0	0	0
Court's	5	.1990	.2695	34.3	0	0	1	0	0	0	4	0	0	0	0	0	0	4	0	0	0	0	0	0	0	1	0	0	0
courted	2	.0000	.0243	23.9	0	0	0	0	1	0	0	1	0	0	0	0	0	0	0	0	0	0	0	0	0	0	0	2	0
courteous	23	.6971	3.2602	45.1	0	3	2	2	2	3	10	1	3	4	1	6	0	2	1	1	0	0	2	0	0	2	0	1	0
courteously	12	.5650	1.4427	41.6	0	1	1	2	3	3	2	0	3	3	0	2	0	1	0	2	0	0	1	0	0	0	0	0	0
courtesies	4	.4144	.3416	35.3	0	1	0	0	1	1	1	0	0	1	1	1	0	0	0	0	0	0	1	0	0	0	0	0	0
courtesy	33	.8014	5.2983	47.2	1	3	6	3	7	7	5	1	2	1	0	2	0	3	3	6	1	0	2	0	2	6	1	4	0
courthouse	25	.6306	3.3052	45.2	6	3	2	0	0	6	8	0	7	0	1	6	0	5	0	0	0	0	0	0	2	3	1	0	0

9R Counsel
5Q counsel-less
4A count's
7P countenances
5P Counter
7H counter-clockwise
5P counter-cooperative
6R counter-counter-attack
7A Counter-current
8R counter-demonstration
7R counter-revolutionary
6J counter-tenor
XH counteracted
7Q counteracting
7D counterbalanced
7Q counterbalancing
7R counterbore
4R countercurrents
9R counterfeits
XH counterforce
3J countermarching
5P countermeasures
6J countermelodies
XR Counterpoint
7Q counterpoise
9Q counterpull
6A countersign
9D countervail
5E counting-numbers
4B counting-out
7P countinghouse
4J countree
9R country-and-Western
9R country-and-western
7A country-bred
7B country-fresh
5P country-men
XR country-seat
7N country-wards
4N countrybred
6P countrysides
XR countrywide
7F countrywomen
9B coupla
5P couple-color
9R couple's
9F couplers
3P couplings
7D Coupvray
7P courantes
5J Courbet
6A coureur
9Q Cournand
5N coursers
9G court-martial
9R court-ordered
7D court-yard

Word Type	F	D	U	SFI	3 Gr 3	4 Gr 4	5 Gr 5	6 Gr 6	7 Gr 7	8 Gr 8	9 Gr 9	X UnGr	A Read	B Eng & Gr	C Comp	D Lit	E Math	F Soc Stud	G Spell	H Sci	J Music	K Art	L Home Ec	M Shop	N Lib F	P Lib NF	Q Lib Ref	R Mag	S Rel
Courthouse	3	.3390	.2450	33.9	0	0	2	1	0	0	0	0	1	0	0	0	0	0	0	0	0	0	0	0	0	0	1	1	0
courting	6	.1814	.3560	35.5	0	1	0	0	4	0	0	1	3	0	0	0	0	0	0	0	0	0	0	0	0	0	0	3	0
courtly	5	.2355	.2928	34.7	0	0	2	1	0	1	1	0	1	0	0	0	0	0	0	0	3	0	0	0	0	0	1	0	0
courtroom	11	.5805	1.3567	41.3	0	0	0	0	4	3	4	0	3	2	1	1	0	2	0	1	0	0	0	0	0	0	0	1	0
courts	111	.5078	12.029	50.8	6	5	9	5	19	28	39	0	3	0	0	1	0	71	0	1	6	0	0	0	2	7	17	3	0
Courts	18	.0000	.3501	35.4	0	0	0	0	3	0	15	0	0	0	0	0	0	18	0	0	0	0	0	0	0	0	0	0	0
courtship	3	.2197	.2090	33.2	0	0	1	1	1	0	0	0	2	0	0	0	0	0	0	0	0	0	0	0	0	0	1	0	0
courtyard	59	.6700	8.2600	49.2	12	9	8	17	5	5	0	3	23	0	0	4	0	4	0	0	1	3	0	0	6	8	1	9	0
courtyards	7	.4365	.6755	38.3	0	2	1	2	2	0	0	0	1	0	0	0	0	3	0	0	0	0	0	1	0	1	0	1	0
cousin	109	.7369	16.376	52.1	12	23	7	17	18	19	10	3	30	13	5	18	0	4	4	3	0	0	2	1	14	10	1	3	1
Cousin	71	.5651	8.9727	49.5	39	16	1	3	4	7	1	0	48	1	0	4	0	2	0	0	0	0	0	0	5	10	0	1	0
cousin's	5	.3577	.4030	36.1	0	0	0	0	2	1	2	0	1	1	1	2	0	0	0	0	0	0	0	0	0	0	0	0	0
cousins	50	.7441	7.5201	48.8	4	9	4	10	13	5	3	2	5	3	0	11	0	3	0	6	3	0	0	0	2	6	4	7	0
Cousteau	4	.2346	.2332	33.7	0	2	0	1	1	0	0	0	0	0	0	0	0	0	0	2	0	0	0	0	0	0	0	2	0
cove	23	.4481	2.3978	43.8	4	6	0	5	6	2	0	0	11	0	0	0	0	3	0	1	0	0	0	0	7	0	0	1	0
Cove	14	.4980	1.4880	41.7	0	5	2	5	0	2	0	0	1	0	0	0	0	5	0	0	1	0	0	0	3	0	0	4	0
covenant	4	.0379	.0480	26.8	2	1	0	0	0	0	1	0	0	0	0	0	0	0	0	0	1	0	0	0	0	0	1	0	2
Covenant	4	.3287	.2952	34.7	0	0	1	0	0	3	0	0	0	0	0	0	0	1	0	0	0	0	0	0	0	1	2	0	0
Coventry	3	.0000	.0583	27.7	0	0	0	0	2	0	1	0	0	0	0	0	0	3	0	0	0	0	0	0	0	0	0	0	0
cover	604	.9065	108.70	60.4	110	105	81	81	109	51	53	14	111	19	4	12	36	66	31	133	17	13	34	11	13	34	25	45	0
coverage	7	.4224	.6230	37.9	0	1	0	2	0	0	4	0	0	1	0	0	0	0	0	0	0	0	0	1	0	0	1	4	0
coveralls	8	.2995	.6086	37.8	0	0	0	1	3	1	0	3	3	1	0	0	0	0	0	0	0	0	0	0	0	0	0	4	0
covered	844	.9290	155.51	61.9	206	160	120	121	138	44	42	13	251	15	7	28	18	142	5	119	18	13	16	5	55	86	39	25	2
covered-wagon	3	.2060	.1500	31.8	0	1	0	0	0	2	0	0	0	0	0	2	0	0	0	0	0	0	0	0	0	1	0	0	0
covering	165	.8711	28.637	54.6	27	19	23	23	33	20	13	7	21	3	2	3	4	11	4	49	3	0	5	4	8	21	19	8	0
coverings	12	.3712	1.0140	40.1	2	0	2	2	2	0	4	0	2	0	0	0	0	1	0	4	0	0	3	0	0	0	2	0	0
coverlet	4	.3795	.3302	35.2	0	2	0	0	1	0	1	0	0	0	0	1	0	0	0	0	0	0	0	0	1	2	0	0	0
covers	178	.9067	32.062	55.1	32	32	36	20	27	12	17	2	36	5	2	4	12	24	0	36	2	2	7	2	8	15	16	7	0
covert	3	.3870	.2486	34.0	0	0	1	0	2	0	0	0	0	0	0	1	0	0	0	0	0	0	0	0	0	0	1	1	0
coverts	2	.2446	.1142	30.6	0	0	0	0	2	0	0	0	0	0	0	0	0	0	0	0	0	0	0	0	1	0	0	1	0
coves	3	.1865	.1650	32.2	0	1	0	0	1	1	0	0	1	0	0	0	0	1	0	0	0	0	0	1	0	0	0	0	0
covet	4	.3611	.3119	34.9	0	0	1	0	2	0	1	0	0	0	0	1	0	0	0	0	0	0	0	0	0	0	2	1	0
coveted	5	.4794	.4989	37.0	0	0	0	1	3	0	1	0	0	0	0	1	0	0	0	0	1	0	0	0	0	0	1	2	0
Covey	3	.0000	.0583	27.7	0	0	3	0	0	0	0	0	0	0	0	0	0	3	0	0	0	0	0	0	0	0	0	0	0
cow	263	.8835	46.412	56.7	93	36	53	27	26	12	15	1	93	9	5	21	4	16	13	22	9	1	0	0	27	25	12	6	0
Cow	7	.3204	.5411	37.3	0	5	0	2	0	0	0	0	2	3	0	0	0	0	0	0	0	0	0	0	2	0	0	0	0
cow's	14	.5933	1.7531	42.4	3	1	1	3	4	1	1	0	4	0	0	0	0	2	1	0	1	1	0	0	4	0	1	0	0
coward	31	.6794	4.4422	46.5	5	2	12	4	2	2	3	1	17	3	0	3	0	1	1	0	0	0	0	0	3	2	0	1	0
cowardice	2	.1717	.1142	30.6	0	0	0	0	0	0	2	0	1	0	0	1	0	0	0	0	0	0	0	0	0	0	0	0	0
cowardly	15	.5387	1.7454	42.4	4	0	2	1	3	2	3	0	5	1	0	5	0	0	0	0	0	0	0	0	2	1	1	0	0
cowards	13	.4787	1.3670	41.4	0	1	1	1	6	4	0	0	4	0	1	5	0	0	0	0	0	0	0	0	2	1	0	0	0
cowbarn	2	.0000	.0914	29.6	0	0	0	0	2	0	0	0	2	0	0	0	0	0	0	0	0	0	0	0	0	0	0	0	0
cowbells	4	.0759	.1243	30.9	1	1	1	0	0	1	0	0	1	0	0	0	0	0	0	0	3	0	0	0	0	0	0	0	0
cowbird	9	.2437	.6830	38.3	6	0	0	0	0	0	0	3	6	0	0	0	0	0	0	3	0	0	0	0	0	0	0	0	0
cowbirds	3	.0000	.1370	31.4	3	0	0	0	0	0	0	0	3	0	0	0	0	0	0	0	0	0	0	0	0	0	0	0	0
cowboy	214	.7802	34.013	55.3	77	50	27	17	33	8	1	1	89	14	0	21	0	8	7	0	17	4	0	0	32	12	2	8	0
Cowboy	23	.4291	2.1611	43.3	16	6	0	1	0	0	0	0	4	0	0	0	0	0	4	0	1	0	0	0	12	0	0	2	0
cowboy's	24	.6120	3.1358	45.0	3	5	9	0	7	0	0	0	11	1	0	5	0	1	1	0	3	0	0	0	2	0	0	0	0
cowboys	175	.7125	25.877	54.1	60	43	18	16	27	8	1	2	76	5	0	15	0	26	1	1	8	1	0	0	35	3	1	3	0
Cowboys	3	.2309	.1631	32.1	0	0	0	1	1	0	1	0	0	0	0	1	0	0	0	0	0	0	0	0	0	0	0	2	0
Coweeman	2	.0000	.0243	23.9	0	0	0	0	2	0	0	0	0	0	0	0	0	0	0	0	0	0	0	0	0	0	0	2	0
Cowell	5	.0000	.0404	26.1	1	2	0	0	0	2	0	0	0	0	0	0	0	0	0	0	5	0	0	0	0	0	0	0	0
cowered	7	.3930	.6458	38.1	0	1	1	1	4	0	0	0	3	0	1	1	0	0	0	0	0	0	0	0	2	0	0	0	0
cowhand	5	.2446	.3866	35.9	4	0	0	0	0	0	1	0	4	1	0	0	0	0	0	0	0	0	0	0	0	0	0	0	0
cowhands	9	.2378	.6939	38.4	3	1	4	1	0	0	0	0	7	0	0	0	0	2	0	0	0	0	0	0	0	0	0	0	0
cowherd	5	.0000	.2284	33.6	4	1	0	0	0	0	0	0	5	0	0	0	0	0	0	0	0	0	0	0	0	0	0	0	0
cowherders	2	.0000	.0914	29.6	2	0	0	0	0	0	0	0	2	0	0	0	0	0	0	0	0	0	0	0	0	0	0	0	0
cowhide	6	.3704	.5064	37.0	1	2	0	1	2	0	0	0	1	0	0	0	0	1	0	0	0	0	0	0	3	0	1	0	0
cowhides	3	.0000	.0583	27.7	1	0	0	1	1	0	0	0	0	0	0	0	0	3	0	0	0	0	0	0	0	0	0	0	0
cowlick	2	.0000	.0394	26.0	0	0	0	0	2	0	0	0	0	0	0	0	0	0	0	2	0	0	0	0	0	0	0	0	0
cowlike	2	.1948	.1250	31.0	0	1	1	0	0	0	0	0	1	0	0	0	0	0	0	0	0	0	0	0	0	1	0	0	0
cowpoke	2	.2351	.1166	30.7	0	0	0	0	0	1	0	1	0	0	0	0	0	1	0	0	0	0	0	0	0	0	0	1	0
cowpox	2	.0000	.0914	29.6	0	0	0	0	2	0	0	0	2	0	0	0	0	0	0	0	0	0	0	0	0	0	0	0	0
cowpuncher	3	.3674	.2408	33.8	0	1	1	1	0	0	0	0	0	0	0	1	0	1	0	0	1	0	0	0	0	0	0	0	0
cowpunching	3	.3399	.2456	33.9	0	0	0	2	0	0	0	1	1	0	0	1	0	0	0	0	0	0	0	0	0	0	0	1	0
cows	308	.8502	52.554	57.2	118	60	29	37	34	10	12	8	94	8	5	12	14	34	1	27	2	2	0	0	49	33	7	20	0
cows'	6	.2757	.4319	36.4	3	0	0	2	0	0	0	1	2	0	0	0	0	0	0	1	0	0	0	0	0	0	0	3	0
cowshed	2	.2152	.1357	31.3	0	0	1	0	1	0	0	0	1	0	0	0	0	1	0	0	0	0	0	0	0	0	0	0	0
Cox	4	.3869	.3421	35.3	1	1	0	0	0	0	0	2	0	0	0	1	0	0	0	2	0	0	0	0	1	0	0	0	0
coxswain	2	.0000	.0234	23.7	0	0	0	0	2	0	0	0	0	0	0	0	0	0	0	0	0	0	0	0	2	0	0	0	0
Coy	2	.2446	.1142	30.6	0	0	1	0	1	0	0	0	0	0	0	0	0	0	0	0	0	0	0	0	1	0	0	1	0
coyly	3	.2279	.2143	33.3	1	0	0	2	0	0	0	0	2	0	0	0	0	0	0	0	0	0	0	0	0	0	0	1	0
coyote	35	.5431	4.2322	46.3	10	7	2	10	5	0	0	1	19	0	0	7	0	1	2	5	0	0	0	0	0	0	1	0	0
Coyote	34	.2459	2.4520	43.9	18	9	6	0	1	0	0	0	20	0	0	13	0	1	0	0	0	0	0	0	0	0	0	0	0
Coyote's	3	.2212	.2099	33.2	2	1	0	0	0	0	0	0	2	0	0	1	0	0	0	0	0	0	0	0	0	0	0	0	0
coyotes	42	.7407	6.4080	48.1	9	6	4	9	8	4	1	1	17	1	1	6	0	4	0	7	1	0	0	0	0	1	3	1	0
Coyotito	21	.0000	.2254	33.5	0	0	0	0	21	0	0	0	0	0	0	21	0	0	0	0	0	0	0	0	0	0	0	0	0
Coyotito's	3	.0000	.0322	25.1	0	0	0	0	3	0	0	0	0	0	0	3	0	0	0	0	0	0	0	0	0	0	0	0	0
cozy	27	.7553	4.1716	46.2	5	7	3	4	1	1	1	5	10	1	0	2	0	1	0	2	1	1	0	0	1	2	1	5	0
CO2	12	.2085	.6380	38.0	0	1	0	3	2	2	4	0	0	0	0	0	0	0	0	9	0	0	0	3	0	0	0	0	0
cps	4	.0000	.0789	29.0	0	0	0	0	0	1	3	0	0	0	0	0	0	0	0	4	0	0	0	0	0	0	0	0	0
CQ	3	.0000	.1370	31.4	0	0	0	0	3	0	0	0	3	0	0	0	0	0	0	0	0	0	0	0	0	0	0	0	0
cr	9	.0000	.0730	28.6	3	2	3	1	0	0	0	0	0	0	0	0	0	0	9	0	0	0	0	0	0	0	0	0	0
crab	62	.7765	9.8339	49.9	15	13	5	14	10	1	2	2	23	2	1	3	1	1	2	22	0	0	1	0	2	1	1	2	0
Crab	10	.3731	.9748	39.9	8	1	0	0	1	0	0	0	8	0	0	0	0	0	0	0	1	0	0	0	1	0	0	0	0
crab-shells	2	.2411	.1091	30.4	1	0	0	0	1	0	0	0	0	0	0	1	0	0	0	0	1	0	0	0	0	0	0	0	0
crabapple	3	.2279	.2143	33.3	2	0	0	0	0	0	0	1	2	0	0	0	0	0	0	0	0	0	0	0	0	0	0	1	0
Crabapple	6	.0000	.2741	34.4	6	0	0	0	0	0	0	0	6	0	0	0	0	0	0	0	0	0	0	0	0	0	0	0	0
crabapples	3	.2300	.1627	32.1	0	0	0	1	0	0	0	2	0	1	0	0	0	0	0	0	0	0	0	0	0	0	0	2	0
crabbits	7	.0000	.3198	35.0	7	0	0	0	0	0	0	0	7	0	0	0	0	0	0	0	0	0	0	0	0	0	0	0	0
crabs	40	.6729	5.5977	47.5	11	5	3	5	14	1	0	1	11	5	0	3	0	0	0	13	0	0	0	0	1	2	3	2	0
crack	144	.8850	25.452	54.1	38	27	16	18	28	7	7	3	51	8	4	12	0	5	0	22	3	1	1	3	9	12	4	9	0
Crack	2	.2440	.1132	30.5	0	0	0	0	1	0	1	0	0	0	0	1	0	0	0	0	0	0	0	0	0	0	0	1	0

6A courtier
9D courtier's
4N courtiers
9D courtiers'
8R courtside
8B Courvoisier
7B cousine
8C Cousteau's
7R Coutts's
8H covalent
5R cove's
7R Coveleski
8F covenants
7H cover-up
6J cover'd
7A coverall
XR Coveralls
7G Coverdale
4A coverer
6A coverin's
4N covetous
8F covets
7D covey
XR cow-calf
7Q cow-crazy
8N cow-hand
7N cow-horn
7N cow-pea
5A cow-quieting
4Q cow-shaped
4N Coward
6A coward's
3A cowbell
XH cowbird's
4N cowbo-o-oy
4A COWBOYS
5D cowboys'
8R Cowboys'
8R cowering
6A cowhorse
4N cowhorses
4N cowlicks
7R cowling
7R Cowlitz
XH cowmen
7H coworker
XH coworkers
7N cowpeas
3P Cowpens
9R Cowper
5D cowpokes
8Q cowries
4D cowslip
3A coyote's
XR Cozad
XR cozied
6E CR
4A cr-r-rack
6A cr-r-racking
3A crckers
3A cra
3A craes
XR crab-apples
3A crab-eating
4H crab's
3A Crabapple's
5G crabba
3A crabmeat
5A Cracardo
3A crack-brained

Word Type	F	D	U	SFI	3 Gr 3	4 Gr 4	5 Gr 5	6 Gr 6	7 Gr 7	8 Gr 8	9 Gr 9	X UnGr	A Read	B Eng & Gr	C Comp	D Lit	E Math	F Soc Stud	G Spell	H Sci	J Music	K Art	L Home Ec	M Shop	N Lib F	P Lib NF	Q Lib Ref	R Mag	S Rel
crack-up	3	.2051	.1687	32.3	1	0	0	0	0	0	2	0	1	0	1	0	0	0	0	0	0	0	0	0	0	0	0	1	0
cracked	74	.7739	11.693	50.7	17	10	6	11	15	6	8	1	31	1	2	8	2	0	0	6	0	0	2	0	10	5	1	6	0
Crackenberry	2	.0000	.0914	29.6	2	0	0	0	0	0	0	0	2	0	0	0	0	0	0	0	0	0	0	0	0	0	0	0	0
cracker	24	.6577	3.2437	45.1	4	2	11	0	2	3	2	0	3	0	0	4	0	0	1	7	0	0	2	0	1	0	2	4	0
Cracker	2	.0000	.0064	18.1	0	0	0	0	2	0	0	0	0	0	0	0	0	0	0	0	0	0	2	0	0	0	0	0	0
crackers	32	.3267	2.5210	44.0	4	4	5	2	6	3	7	1	12	3	0	0	0	0	0	1	0	0	11	0	1	0	2	2	0
Crackers	2	.2446	.1142	30.6	0	0	1	0	0	1	0	0	0	0	0	0	0	0	0	0	0	0	0	0	1	0	0	1	0
cracking	35	.7847	5.5470	47.4	4	3	5	4	7	6	6	0	9	1	1	6	0	1	0	1	0	1	0	2	5	4	2	2	0
crackle	7	.5517	.8370	39.2	0	0	0	2	4	1	0	0	2	0	0	0	0	1	0	2	0	0	0	0	1	0	0	1	0
crackled	6	.4298	.5688	37.5	1	2	1	0	0	0	2	0	1	0	0	1	0	0	0	0	0	0	0	0	2	2	0	0	0
crackling	23	.5966	2.8796	44.6	1	5	1	3	5	4	3	1	5	2	0	6	0	0	0	2	0	0	0	0	5	2	0	1	0
cracks	81	.7809	12.864	51.1	21	10	8	11	20	5	6	0	25	3	0	5	0	6	0	19	0	0	0	2	5	5	3	8	0
cradle	41	.6489	5.6195	47.5	10	11	3	8	6	3	0	0	17	0	0	1	0	3	0	1	1	0	0	0	2	12	3	1	0
Cradle	4	.3344	.3261	35.1	0	0	1	1	1	1	0	0	1	0	0	0	0	2	0	0	0	0	0	0	0	0	1	0	0
cradleboard	2	.0000	.0290	24.6	0	2	0	0	0	0	0	0	0	0	0	0	0	0	0	0	0	0	0	0	0	2	0	0	0
cradled	8	.4484	.7603	38.8	0	0	0	1	3	2	1	1	0	0	0	2	0	1	0	0	0	0	0	0	3	0	0	2	0
cradlers	2	.0000	.0215	23.3	0	0	0	0	2	0	0	0	0	0	0	2	0	0	0	0	0	0	0	0	0	0	0	0	0
cradles	10	.2127	.5643	37.5	1	6	2	0	1	0	0	0	1	0	0	0	0	2	0	0	0	0	0	0	0	7	0	0	0
craft	87	.8641	15.001	51.8	2	7	6	19	26	13	13	1	18	2	1	4	1	7	1	5	5	1	0	1	7	4	9	21	0
crafted	2	.2408	.1204	30.8	0	0	0	0	1	1	0	0	0	0	0	0	0	1	0	0	0	0	0	0	0	1	0	0	0
crafts	22	.6064	2.7817	44.4	3	2	5	1	7	3	0	1	4	1	0	1	0	2	0	1	0	2	0	0	0	5	3	3	0
craftsman	10	.0702	.2067	33.2	0	0	1	0	8	1	0	0	1	0	0	0	0	0	0	0	1	0	0	8	0	0	0	0	0
craftsmanship	9	.4839	.9239	39.7	0	0	2	0	1	3	1	2	1	0	0	0	0	0	0	0	2	0	0	0	0	1	3	2	0
craftsmen	46	.5521	5.3712	47.3	6	6	1	9	15	2	6	1	8	0	0	1	1	16	0	0	0	2	0	7	0	2	8	1	0
crafty	7	.4346	.6822	38.3	0	0	1	1	3	1	1	0	2	2	0	2	0	0	0	0	0	0	0	0	0	1	0	0	0
crag	10	.5458	1.1668	40.7	2	1	4	1	1	0	1	0	3	2	1	2	0	0	0	0	0	0	0	0	0	1	1	0	0
craggy	5	.1634	.2733	34.4	0	3	0	0	0	0	2	0	2	0	0	0	0	0	0	0	0	0	0	0	0	3	0	0	0
crags	7	.5362	.8078	39.1	1	0	1	3	1	0	1	0	2	0	0	1	0	0	0	0	0	0	0	0	0	1	1	2	0
Craig	18	.4304	1.9154	42.8	0	1	0	6	10	1	0	0	14	1	0	0	1	0	0	0	0	0	0	0	0	0	0	2	0
Craighead	2	.0000	.0914	29.6	0	0	2	0	0	0	0	0	2	0	0	0	0	0	0	0	0	0	0	0	0	0	0	0	0
Craigheads	3	.0000	.1370	31.4	0	0	3	0	0	0	0	0	3	0	0	0	0	0	0	0	0	0	0	0	0	0	0	0	0
Craik	3	.2357	.2199	33.4	0	1	0	2	0	0	0	0	2	0	0	0	0	0	0	0	0	0	0	0	0	1	0	0	0
cram	4	.3647	.3180	35.0	1	0	0	0	2	0	1	0	0	0	0	0	0	0	0	0	0	0	0	0	0	1	1	2	0
crammed	11	.6002	1.4125	41.5	2	0	1	1	4	2	1	0	4	1	0	0	0	2	0	1	0	0	0	0	0	1	2	0	0
cramp	4	.3446	.2950	34.7	1	0	0	0	1	0	2	0	0	0	0	2	0	0	0	0	0	0	1	0	0	0	0	1	0
cramped	14	.6462	1.8854	42.8	0	2	3	3	4	2	0	0	4	2	1	0	0	1	0	1	0	0	0	0	2	0	1	2	0
Crampfurl	7	.0000	.0821	29.1	0	0	7	0	0	0	0	0	0	0	0	0	0	0	0	0	0	0	0	0	7	0	0	0	0
crampons	3	.2236	.1570	32.0	0	0	0	0	1	0	2	0	0	1	0	2	0	0	0	0	0	0	0	0	0	0	0	0	0
cramps	5	.3447	.3792	35.8	0	0	0	0	2	2	1	0	0	0	0	2	0	1	0	0	0	0	0	0	0	0	2	0	0
cranberries	22	.6588	3.0057	44.8	7	4	4	4	1	1	1	0	5	1	1	0	0	5	0	2	0	0	1	0	6	0	1	0	0
cranberry	9	.5566	1.0522	40.2	3	2	0	1	2	0	0	1	1	0	0	0	0	0	0	2	0	0	1	0	2	2	0	1	0
Crandall	3	.2347	.1695	32.3	0	0	0	0	3	0	0	0	0	0	0	0	0	0	0	0	0	0	0	0	1	2	0	0	0
crane	36	.7452	5.5336	47.4	9	8	8	5	2	1	1	2	16	0	0	1	0	4	0	5	1	0	0	1	0	3	3	2	0
Crane	20	.2840	1.4205	41.5	0	0	3	0	16	0	1	0	7	0	4	9	0	0	0	0	0	0	0	0	0	0	0	0	0
craned	3	.2060	.1500	31.8	0	0	0	0	0	0	2	1	0	0	0	2	0	0	0	0	0	0	0	0	0	1	0	0	0
cranes	27	.6446	3.6927	45.7	15	1	2	5	3	0	0	1	12	0	0	0	1	2	0	2	0	0	0	0	0	4	3	3	0
cranial	5	.2424	.2988	34.8	0	0	1	0	0	0	4	0	0	0	0	0	0	0	0	3	0	0	0	0	0	0	2	0	0
craning	4	.3020	.2654	34.2	0	2	0	1	0	1	0	0	0	0	1	0	0	0	0	0	0	0	0	0	2	1	0	0	0
cranium	7	.4474	.6812	38.3	0	0	1	4	1	0	1	0	0	0	0	1	1	0	0	4	0	0	0	0	0	1	0	0	0
crank	36	.5496	4.1970	46.2	5	3	4	4	18	1	1	0	7	0	0	1	1	0	0	3	3	0	0	0	1	2	1	17	0
crankcase	6	.2136	.2941	34.7	0	0	0	0	6	0	0	0	0	0	0	0	0	0	0	0	0	0	0	2	0	0	0	4	0
cranked	9	.3891	.7899	39.0	1	2	1	0	4	1	0	0	2	0	0	0	0	0	0	0	3	0	0	0	0	1	0	3	0
cranking	2	.2437	.1129	30.5	0	0	0	0	1	0	1	0	0	0	0	0	0	0	0	0	0	0	0	0	0	0	1	1	0
cranks	4	.2437	.2257	33.5	0	2	0	0	2	0	0	0	0	0	0	0	0	0	0	0	0	0	0	0	0	0	2	2	0
crankshaft	10	.3089	.6826	38.3	4	0	1	0	5	0	0	0	0	0	0	0	0	0	0	1	0	0	0	3	0	4	0	2	0
cranky	3	.3267	.2367	33.7	0	1	0	0	0	0	1	1	1	0	0	0	0	0	0	0	1	0	0	0	1	0	0	0	0
crannies	6	.4121	.5479	37.4	0	0	0	3	3	0	0	0	1	0	0	0	0	0	0	0	0	0	0	0	0	1	2	2	0
cranny	6	.5577	.7197	38.6	1	2	1	0	1	0	0	1	2	0	0	1	0	0	0	0	0	0	0	0	1	1	0	1	0
crash	106	.8479	18.129	52.6	23	19	11	11	20	10	9	3	53	3	2	4	0	6	1	4	8	1	0	0	4	9	5	6	0
crashed	59	.6896	8.5958	49.3	12	6	3	9	23	4	2	0	36	4	0	5	0	2	0	1	1	0	0	0	4	3	0	3	0
crashes	14	.6859	1.9716	42.9	2	2	2	2	4	2	0	0	3	1	0	2	0	0	0	1	1	0	0	0	0	1	2	3	0
crashing	35	.6786	4.9871	47.0	5	3	3	7	9	1	5	2	17	1	0	5	0	0	0	1	2	0	0	0	3	4	0	2	0
Cratchit	2	.0000	.0215	23.3	0	0	0	0	2	0	0	0	0	0	0	2	0	0	0	0	0	0	0	0	0	0	0	0	0
crate	21	.5819	2.6889	44.3	11	2	2	1	1	3	0	1	13	1	0	2	0	0	0	0	0	0	0	0	3	1	0	1	0
crater	27	.6657	3.7845	45.8	3	7	2	7	6	0	2	0	11	0	0	0	0	3	0	5	0	0	0	0	2	1	2	3	0
Crater	10	.3539	.8127	39.1	0	0	0	2	2	0	6	0	0	0	0	0	0	2	0	6	0	0	0	0	0	0	0	2	0
craters	40	.4045	3.6842	45.7	4	4	3	2	6	1	20	0	4	0	0	0	0	3	0	27	0	0	0	0	0	1	1	4	0
crates	19	.6001	2.4723	43.9	9	1	5	2	2	0	0	0	10	0	0	2	1	3	2	0	0	0	0	0	1	0	0	0	0
cravat	5	.4213	.4686	36.7	0	0	0	0	2	1	1	1	1	0	0	1	0	0	0	0	0	0	0	0	2	1	0	0	0
craved	4	.3071	.2967	34.7	0	0	0	0	3	0	1	0	1	0	0	1	0	0	0	0	0	0	0	0	2	0	0	0	0
craves	2	.2291	.1135	30.5	0	0	0	0	1	0	1	0	0	0	0	1	0	0	0	1	0	0	0	0	0	0	0	0	0
craving	2	.1442	.0761	28.8	0	0	0	0	0	0	2	0	0	0	0	0	0	1	0	0	0	0	1	0	0	0	0	0	0
Crawford	12	.4396	1.1771	40.7	1	0	6	3	0	2	0	0	3	0	0	5	2	1	0	0	0	0	0	0	0	0	1	0	0
Crawfordsville	3	.0000	.0434	26.4	0	3	0	0	0	0	0	0	0	0	0	0	0	0	0	0	0	0	0	0	0	3	0	0	0
crawl	67	.8090	11.010	50.4	20	14	7	7	11	5	2	1	30	2	0	5	1	3	2	6	1	0	0	0	1	8	3	5	0
crawled	112	.6643	15.739	52.0	36	22	12	13	15	7	4	3	58	4	0	9	1	2	1	1	0	0	0	0	18	13	0	5	0
Crawley	3	.0000	.0583	27.7	0	0	0	3	0	0	0	0	0	0	0	0	0	3	0	0	0	0	0	0	0	0	0	0	0
crawling	53	.7263	7.9492	49.0	11	8	4	6	11	6	3	4	20	1	0	4	0	3	0	8	0	0	0	0	4	9	2	2	0
Crawling	8	.0000	.3655	35.6	0	0	0	0	8	0	0	0	8	0	0	0	0	0	0	0	0	0	0	0	0	0	0	0	0
crawls	19	.7683	2.9550	44.7	6	1	1	3	4	2	2	0	4	3	0	0	0	2	1	1	2	0	0	0	1	2	2	1	0
crawly	2	.2446	.1142	30.6	2	0	0	0	0	0	0	0	0	0	0	0	0	0	0	0	0	0	0	0	1	0	0	1	0
Crawshaw	4	.0000	.0419	26.2	0	0	0	0	0	0	4	0	0	0	0	0	0	0	0	0	0	0	0	0	0	0	4	0	0
crayfish	22	.3862	1.9376	42.9	2	2	0	8	9	0	1	0	3	0	0	0	0	0	0	10	0	0	0	0	0	2	7	0	0
Crayne	5	.0804	.1641	32.2	0	0	0	0	4	1	0	0	1	0	0	0	0	0	0	0	0	0	0	0	4	0	0	0	0
crayon	83	.0496	1.3146	41.2	18	29	7	18	7	1	1	2	7	1	0	0	2	0	0	2	0	70	0	1	0	0	0	0	0
crayons	52	.2924	3.4501	45.4	24	15	9	2	1	0	1	0	4	1	0	1	23	1	0	0	1	17	0	1	0	3	0	0	0
craze	2	.1787	.1174	30.7	0	0	0	0	1	1	0	0	1	0	0	0	0	0	0	0	0	0	0	0	1	0	0	0	0
craziest	3	.1187	.1291	31.1	0	1	1	0	0	1	0	0	1	0	0	2	0	0	0	0	0	0	0	0	0	0	0	0	0
crazily	9	.6260	1.2011	40.8	1	1	0	3	3	0	1	0	4	0	0	0	0	1	0	0	0	0	0	0	1	1	1	1	0
crazy	86	.6335	11.472	50.6	6	6	11	12	27	14	8	2	32	1	0	17	0	1	1	0	2	0	0	0	14	5	0	13	0
Crazy	5	.3071	.3634	35.6	0	0	0	2	2	0	1	0	1	2	0	2	0	0	0	0	0	0	0	0	0	0	0	0	0
cre-e-eak	2	.0000	.0914	29.6	0	2	0	0	0	0	0	0	2	0	0	0	0	0	0	0	0	0	0	0	0	0	0	0	0
creak	12	.4966	1.3081	41.2	2	1	1	3	3	1	1	0	4	1	0	4	0	0	0	0	0	0	0	0	2	0	0	1	0
creak-creak	2	.0000	.0914	29.6	0	2	0	0	0	0	0	0	2	0	0	0	0	0	0	0	0	0	0	0	0	0	0	0	0

6A crackbrained
9R crackdown
7F crackdowns
5H crackles
5P crackpot
4R cracky
7A cradle**
6A cradle-rocker
6A Cradles
7Q cradling
8A Craft
6R craft's
8A craftily
6A craftiness
3Q craftmanship
4B Crafts
9K craftsmen's
7A craggy-horned
5Q craig
5Q Craig's
9R cram-packed
7P cramming
5Q cramping
9Q cramplike
7B cramponed
4A Cranberry
7H cranberry-grower
7H cranberry-growers
7N Crandalls
7D Crane's
7M crankpin
5Q Cranmer
7R crap
8F Crapo
4A CRASH-crash-crash
7R Crashley
6A Crat's
7D Cratchits
5A crated
4A crater-shaped
4Q cratered
6A crating
9P crave
9D craven
8R cravenly
8J cravin'
6N Crawfish
9D Crawford's
7P crawl'd
3R crawlers
9Q Crawshaw's
5A Cray's
7H crayfish's
7H crayfishes
9C Crayon
XR crayon-on-cardboard
8N crazed
9D craziness

Word Type	F	D	U	SFI	3 Gr 3	4 Gr 4	5 Gr 5	6 Gr 6	7 Gr 7	8 Gr 8	9 Gr 9	X UnGr	A Read	B Eng & Gr	C Comp	D Lit	E Math	F Soc Stud	G Spell	H Sci	J Music	K Art	L Home Ec	M Shop	N Lib F	P Lib NF	Q Lib Ref	R Mag	S Rel
creaked	14	.5588	1.6836	42.3	0	2	1	4	3	1	2	1	5	2	0	4	0	0	0	0	0	0	0	0	1	1	0	1	0
creaking	20	.6833	2.8266	44.5	3	4	3	0	5	4	1	0	6	1	0	3	0	1	0	0	1	0	0	0	4	2	0	2	0
creaks	5	.3071	.3634	35.6	2	0	0	0	0	2	1	0	1	2	0	2	0	0	0	0	0	0	0	0	0	0	0	0	0
creaky	4	.2417	.3028	34.8	1	1	0	1	0	0	0	1	3	0	0	0	0	0	0	0	0	0	0	0	1	0	0	0	0
cream	300	.6937	42.545	56.3	86	59	34	24	48	15	31	3	62	26	2	9	12	21	19	20	3	2	59	2	21	27	3	12	0
Cream	5	.2097	.2297	33.6	1	0	0	0	2	2	0	0	0	0	0	0	0	0	1	0	0	0	3	0	0	0	0	1	0
cream-colored	6	.5905	.7445	38.7	3	2	0	1	0	0	0	0	1	0	0	0	0	1	1	1	0	0	0	0	0	1	1	0	0
creamed	7	.0741	.1774	32.5	0	0	0	0	2	0	5	0	1	0	0	0	0	0	0	1	0	0	5	0	0	0	0	0	0
creaming	4	.0000	.0129	21.1	0	0	0	0	0	0	4	0	0	0	0	0	0	0	0	0	0	0	4	0	0	0	0	0	0
creams	5	.4827	.5047	37.0	1	0	0	0	1	1	2	0	0	1	0	0	0	0	0	1	0	0	1	0	0	1	1	0	0
creamy	8	.3353	.5939	37.7	0	1	2	0	2	1	1	1	1	1	0	1	0	0	0	0	0	0	3	0	2	0	0	0	0
creamy-white	2	.1717	.1142	30.6	0	0	0	1	0	1	0	0	1	0	0	1	0	0	0	0	0	0	0	0	0	0	0	0	0
crease	22	.2041	.9788	39.9	0	2	1	0	3	12	4	0	0	0	0	0	3	0	0	1	0	0	16	2	0	0	0	0	0
crease-resistant	2	.0000	.0064	18.1	0	0	0	0	0	1	1	0	0	0	0	0	0	0	0	0	0	0	2	0	0	0	0	0	0
creased	6	.4115	.5409	37.3	0	0	0	1	2	1	1	1	1	0	0	2	0	0	0	0	0	0	1	0	0	0	0	2	0
creases	8	.4262	.7216	38.6	0	3	1	1	0	2	1	0	0	0	0	0	3	0	0	0	0	0	2	0	1	1	0	1	0
create	235	.6810	32.309	55.1	12	24	33	32	55	40	35	4	17	10	15	14	3	18	0	4	65	31	8	5	0	9	20	16	0
created	231	.8066	37.279	55.7	4	14	36	36	47	52	32	10	21	4	7	15	3	33	1	12	38	11	1	2	1	22	38	22	0
creates	57	.7847	8.9555	49.5	3	8	8	3	17	8	10	0	5	1	3	4	0	3	1	6	15	3	1	2	0	5	5	3	0
creating	71	.7523	10.719	50.3	3	8	6	4	18	15	8	9	4	4	0	2	0	4	0	3	17	4	3	1	2	7	5	15	0
creation	49	.6513	6.5202	48.1	1	1	4	7	22	5	6	3	4	0	1	1	0	5	0	1	6	0	0	0	3	3	18	7	0
Creation	3	.0995	.1144	30.6	0	1	1	0	0	1	0	0	1	0	0	0	0	0	0	0	2	0	0	0	0	0	0	0	0
creations	5	.3387	.3852	35.9	0	1	1	0	0	0	2	1	1	0	0	1	0	0	0	0	0	1	0	0	0	0	2	0	0
creative	58	.7015	8.2435	49.2	7	4	6	4	13	13	7	4	8	2	0	1	1	0	1	1	6	6	2	2	3	1	14	10	0
Creative	2	.2440	.1132	30.5	0	0	0	0	1	0	0	1	0	0	0	1	0	0	0	0	0	0	0	0	0	0	0	1	0
creatively	2	.1042	.0600	27.8	0	0	2	0	0	0	0	0	0	0	0	0	0	1	0	0	0	1	0	0	0	0	0	0	0
creativity	11	.5846	1.3522	41.3	0	0	1	2	5	2	0	1	2	1	0	0	1	1	0	1	1	0	0	0	0	0	0	4	0
creator	5	.1032	.1409	31.5	1	0	1	0	0	3	0	0	0	0	0	1	0	0	0	0	0	0	0	0	0	0	2	1	1
Creator	8	.3466	.7004	38.5	1	0	0	1	2	3	1	0	4	0	0	0	0	2	0	0	0	1	0	0	0	1	0	0	0
creature	166	.7997	26.940	54.3	19	22	11	35	47	20	9	3	66	10	1	7	1	2	3	8	2	0	0	0	28	13	12	13	0
creatures	225	.8040	36.494	55.6	22	38	20	28	79	15	14	9	60	11	1	14	0	10	2	17	3	4	0	0	9	31	45	17	1
credentials	3	.3321	.2114	33.3	0	0	0	0	2	1	0	0	0	0	0	0	0	0	0	0	1	0	1	0	0	0	0	1	0
credibility	2	.2437	.1129	30.5	0	0	0	0	1	0	1	0	0	0	0	0	0	0	0	0	0	0	0	0	0	0	1	1	0
credit	100	.7338	14.943	51.7	12	3	7	6	23	27	17	5	26	0	2	2	1	8	1	4	5	1	14	2	6	0	4	24	0
Credit	4	.3173	.2747	34.4	0	0	0	2	1	0	1	0	0	0	1	0	0	0	0	0	0	0	0	0	0	0	1	2	0
creditably	2	.2375	.1088	30.4	0	0	0	0	0	0	1	1	0	0	0	0	0	0	0	0	1	0	0	0	0	0	0	1	0
credited	13	.5103	1.4004	41.5	0	0	0	1	6	1	4	1	1	0	0	0	2	0	0	1	0	0	0	0	1	0	4	4	0
creditors	2	.2351	.1166	30.7	0	0	0	0	0	1	1	0	0	0	0	0	0	1	0	0	0	0	0	0	0	0	0	1	0
credits	2	.2437	.1129	30.5	0	0	0	0	2	0	0	0	0	0	0	0	0	0	0	0	0	0	0	0	0	0	1	1	0
creed	8	.3959	.6975	38.4	0	0	2	0	2	3	0	1	1	0	0	1	0	0	0	0	0	0	0	0	0	0	3	3	0
creeds	2	.2401	.1133	30.5	0	0	0	0	0	2	0	0	0	0	0	0	0	0	0	0	0	0	0	0	0	1	1	0	0
creek	102	.7538	15.829	52.0	13	37	15	7	15	10	3	2	47	1	0	3	0	15	2	1	0	1	0	0	13	11	2	6	0
Creek	75	.7351	11.212	50.5	8	7	11	9	7	17	2	14	11	3	1	5	0	14	0	7	0	0	0	0	3	8	3	20	0
creeks	21	.6377	2.8105	44.5	1	3	2	3	2	8	1	1	6	0	0	2	0	6	0	0	1	0	0	0	0	1	1	4	0
Creeks	5	.4391	.4860	36.9	2	1	0	0	2	0	0	0	1	0	0	0	0	0	0	0	0	0	0	0	0	2	1	1	0
creep	36	.7260	5.3256	47.3	11	6	6	2	8	2	1	0	8	3	0	3	0	3	2	2	2	3	0	0	2	4	2	2	0
Creep-Along	2	.0000	.0914	29.6	2	0	0	0	0	0	0	0	2	0	0	0	0	0	0	0	0	0	0	0	0	0	0	0	0
creeper	2	.0000	.0394	26.0	0	0	0	0	2	0	0	0	0	0	0	0	0	0	0	2	0	0	0	0	0	0	0	0	0
Creeper's	5	.0000	.2284	33.6	5	0	0	0	0	0	0	0	5	0	0	0	0	0	0	0	0	0	0	0	0	0	0	0	0
creepers	7	.4023	.6415	38.1	1	1	0	2	3	0	0	0	2	0	0	3	0	0	0	0	0	0	0	0	1	0	0	1	0
creepeth	2	.0000	.0290	24.6	2	0	0	0	0	0	0	0	0	0	0	0	0	0	0	0	0	0	0	0	0	2	0	0	0
creeping	42	.7047	6.1045	47.9	5	4	4	5	16	4	3	1	13	1	0	5	0	1	0	4	1	0	0	0	7	6	4	0	0
creeps	8	.3732	.6806	38.3	2	1	0	2	0	1	1	1	2	0	2	0	0	0	0	1	1	0	0	0	1	1	0	0	0
creepy	3	.3863	.2513	34.0	2	0	0	0	0	1	0	0	0	0	0	0	0	0	0	0	0	0	0	0	1	1	0	1	0
Creesy	4	.0000	.1827	32.6	0	0	0	0	0	4	0	0	4	0	0	0	0	0	0	0	0	0	0	0	0	0	0	0	0
creeturs	2	.0000	.0234	23.7	0	0	0	0	2	0	0	0	0	0	0	0	0	0	0	0	0	0	0	0	2	0	0	0	0
Creighton	13	.2649	.7952	39.0	3	0	0	0	1	9	0	0	0	0	0	0	0	0	0	0	0	0	0	0	9	3	0	1	0
Creighton's	2	.2427	.1152	30.6	1	0	0	0	0	1	0	0	0	0	0	0	0	0	0	0	0	0	0	0	1	1	0	0	0
cremated	2	.0000	.0914	29.6	0	0	0	0	2	0	0	0	2	0	0	0	0	0	0	0	0	0	0	0	0	0	0	0	0
creole	2	.2306	.1140	30.6	0	0	0	1	0	1	0	0	0	1	0	0	0	1	0	0	0	0	0	0	0	0	0	0	0
Creoles	6	.1794	.2611	34.2	5	0	1	0	0	0	0	0	0	0	0	0	0	0	0	0	1	0	0	0	0	0	5	0	0
creosote	5	.2530	.3153	35.0	0	0	0	3	2	0	0	0	1	0	0	0	0	0	0	0	0	0	0	0	0	0	3	1	0
crepe	7	.3236	.5121	37.1	2	0	1	0	1	2	1	0	0	0	0	0	0	3	0	1	0	0	2	0	0	1	0	0	0
crept	89	.7371	13.480	51.3	14	22	10	9	21	9	3	1	35	4	1	13	0	2	2	0	0	0	0	0	13	12	5	2	0
crescendo	6	.0000	.0485	26.9	0	0	0	1	5	0	0	0	0	0	0	0	0	0	0	0	6	0	0	0	0	0	0	0	0
crescent	11	.4860	1.1402	40.6	2	0	1	0	2	0	1	5	0	0	1	0	0	1	0	7	0	0	0	1	0	0	0	1	0
Crescent	13	.0000	.5939	37.7	11	0	0	0	2	0	0	0	13	0	0	0	0	0	0	0	0	0	0	0	0	0	0	0	0
crescent-shaped	2	.2375	.1088	30.4	0	0	0	0	0	1	1	0	0	0	0	0	0	0	0	0	1	0	0	0	0	0	0	1	0
Crespi	4	.0000	.0778	28.9	0	4	0	0	0	0	0	0	0	0	0	0	0	4	0	0	0	0	0	0	0	0	0	0	0
Cress	18	.1446	.6040	37.8	0	0	0	0	10	0	8	0	0	0	10	8	0	0	0	0	0	0	0	0	0	0	0	0	0
crest	41	.7770	6.4070	48.1	4	6	6	4	13	0	7	1	4	2	0	9	0	0	1	8	1	0	0	1	5	3	4	3	0
Crest	2	.0000	.0215	23.3	0	0	0	0	0	2	0	0	0	0	0	2	0	0	0	0	0	0	0	0	0	0	0	0	0
Cresta	2	.0000	.0914	29.6	0	0	0	2	0	0	0	0	2	0	0	0	0	0	0	0	0	0	0	0	0	0	0	0	0
crested	3	.3782	.2435	33.9	2	0	0	1	0	0	0	0	0	0	0	0	0	0	0	0	1	0	0	0	0	1	1	0	0
Creston	3	.0000	.0243	23.8	0	0	0	2	0	1	0	0	0	0	0	0	0	0	0	0	3	0	0	0	0	0	0	0	0
crests	24	.6295	3.1116	44.9	9	0	1	5	4	3	1	1	2	0	1	1	0	0	0	3	0	0	0	0	5	9	2	1	0
Cretaceous	10	.2729	.6279	38.0	0	2	3	0	4	0	0	1	0	0	0	0	0	0	0	1	0	0	0	0	0	3	6	0	0
Crete	13	.3151	.9132	39.6	0	1	0	0	3	4	5	0	1	0	0	2	0	2	0	0	1	4	0	0	0	0	0	3	0
cretinism	3	.0000	.0314	25.0	0	0	0	3	0	0	0	0	0	0	0	0	0	0	0	0	0	0	0	0	0	0	3	0	0
cretins	2	.0000	.0209	23.2	0	0	0	2	0	0	0	0	0	0	0	0	0	0	0	0	0	0	0	0	0	0	2	0	0
crevasses	7	.4832	.7689	38.9	1	1	2	0	0	1	2	0	3	0	0	1	0	0	0	2	0	0	0	0	0	1	0	0	0
crevice	7	.3623	.6333	38.0	0	0	0	4	1	2	0	0	4	0	1	0	0	0	0	0	0	0	0	0	0	1	0	1	0
crevices	2	.2437	.1129	30.5	0	1	0	1	0	0	0	0	0	0	0	0	0	0	0	0	0	0	0	0	0	0	1	1	0
crew	271	.7861	43.668	56.4	12	89	43	33	49	24	19	2	149	1	2	8	0	16	3	7	7	0	0	1	8	31	6	32	0
crew's	8	.5069	.8892	39.5	0	2	0	1	3	0	1	1	3	0	0	1	0	0	0	0	0	0	1	0	1	0	0	2	0
crewman	5	.3861	.4798	36.8	0	2	0	0	3	0	1	0	3	0	0	0	0	0	0	0	0	0	0	0	0	1	0	1	0
crewmen	16	.1414	.7843	38.9	0	0	4	2	4	2	4	0	6	0	0	0	0	0	0	0	0	0	0	0	0	0	0	10	0
crews	39	.7226	5.8172	47.6	5	7	5	6	7	7	1	1	14	0	0	1	0	5	0	3	0	0	0	1	1	8	2	4	0
crib	6	.4391	.5503	37.4	1	1	0	2	1	1	0	0	0	0	1	0	0	0	0	0	1	0	0	0	2	0	0	2	0
cribs	2	.0000	.0394	26.0	1	0	1	0	0	0	0	0	0	0	0	0	0	0	0	2	0	0	0	0	0	0	0	0	0
Crick	2	.0000	.0394	26.0	0	0	0	0	0	0	2	0	0	0	0	0	0	0	0	2	0	0	0	0	0	0	0	0	0
cricked	2	.0000	.0215	23.3	0	0	0	0	2	0	0	0	0	0	0	2	0	0	0	0	0	0	0	0	0	0	0	0	0
cricket	42	.6663	5.9363	47.7	7	22	3	6	1	3	0	0	22	0	0	2	0	2	1	5	0	0	0	0	2	7	0	1	0
Cricket	7	.2366	.5437	37.4	0	5	0	2	0	0	0	0	6	0	0	0	0	0	0	0	0	0	0	0	1	0	0	0	0

7A creakings
3A CREAM
5A Cream-Sponge
9L cream-style
4Q cream-thick
7R creamery
7A Creamery
7A creaminal
4P Creamy
9L creamy/white
4Q creativeness
XR creators
5Q creaturarum
8A creature's
5Q Creatures
3P creatures'
6J creche
9Q credence
8F credible
5Q creditor
XP creditor's
5P credo
5P credos
XR credulity
7A credulous
4R Cree
8F creek-crossings
4P creek's
4B creels
4N creeped
8A Creesy's
XR Creme
3P Cremona
7B Crenshaw's
XH creodonts
3Q Creole
7R creosoted
5A crep'
3A crepe-paper
9L crepes
9D crepey
7J crescendos
7R crescents
8M cresent
4J Crested
7N crestfallen
8B Crestwood
6A Cretheus
6Q cretin
XR cretonnes
5A crevasse
7A Crew
6J crew-ew-ew
9A Crewe
8L crewel
7R cribbing
7N crick
XR crick-cracking
3P CRICKET

Word Type	F	D	U	SFI	3 Gr 3	4 Gr 4	5 Gr 5	6 Gr 6	7 Gr 7	8 Gr 8	9 Gr 9	X UnGr	A Read	B Eng & Gr	C Comp	D Lit	E Math	F Soc Stud	G Spell	H Sci	J Music	K Art	L Home Ec	M Shop	N Lib F	P Lib NF	Q Lib Ref	R Mag	S Rel
cricket's	2	.2407	.1138	30.6	1	0	0	0	0	0	1	0	0	0	0	1	0	0	0	0	0	0	0	0	0	1	0	0	0
crickets	32	.6480	4.3660	46.4	7	3	8	2	4	5	1	2	13	1	3	1	1	0	0	4	1	0	0	0	1	4	2	1	0
cried	1043	.6535	145.74	61.6	355	257	98	170	98	38	14	13	635	20	3	67	0	21	4	4	9	0	0	0	169	85	2	24	0
crier	6	.3801	.5663	37.5	0	1	0	1	2	2	0	0	3	0	0	0	0	2	0	0	0	0	0	0	0	1	0	0	0
cries	89	.7950	14.372	51.6	19	12	11	14	19	8	5	1	37	3	1	7	0	3	5	0	8	0	0	0	10	7	1	7	0
Criger	2	.0000	.0290	24.6	0	0	0	2	0	0	0	0	0	0	0	0	0	0	0	0	0	0	0	0	0	2	0	0	0
crime	52	.6653	7.0628	48.5	2	3	6	4	13	5	16	3	3	2	0	8	0	10	0	0	1	0	0	0	7	4	2	15	0
Crimea	2	.0000	.0209	23.2	0	0	0	0	0	2	0	0	0	0	0	0	0	0	0	0	0	0	0	0	0	0	2	0	0
Crimean	4	.2982	.2887	34.6	0	1	1	0	0	1	1	0	1	0	0	1	0	0	0	0	0	0	0	0	0	0	2	0	0
crimes	29	.5997	3.6029	45.6	1	3	4	3	1	5	11	1	1	0	0	1	0	12	1	0	0	0	0	0	1	3	7	3	0
criminal	25	.7341	3.7177	45.7	0	0	1	2	11	4	7	0	2	2	0	1	0	6	2	1	0	0	0	0	1	4	1	5	0
criminals	17	.6321	2.2231	43.5	0	0	2	1	5	2	6	1	2	1	0	2	0	4	0	0	0	0	0	0	0	4	3	1	0
crimped	3	.3776	.2493	34.0	0	0	0	0	0	1	0	2	0	1	0	0	0	0	0	1	0	0	0	0	0	0	0	1	0
crimping	2	.0000	.0050	17.0	0	0	0	0	1	1	0	0	0	0	0	0	0	0	0	0	0	0	0	2	0	0	0	0	0
crimson	29	.6423	3.9059	45.9	1	3	6	5	6	5	2	1	11	1	1	2	0	0	0	1	7	0	0	0	4	1	0	1	0
crimson-robed	2	.0000	.0234	23.7	2	0	0	0	0	0	0	0	0	0	0	0	0	0	0	0	0	0	0	0	2	0	0	0	0
crimsoned	2	.1787	.1174	30.7	0	0	0	1	1	0	0	0	1	0	0	0	0	0	0	0	0	0	0	0	1	0	0	0	0
cringe	2	.2433	.1158	30.6	0	0	1	0	0	0	0	1	0	0	0	0	0	0	0	0	0	0	0	0	0	1	0	1	0
cringing	3	.3847	.2490	34.0	1	0	0	1	1	0	0	0	0	1	0	1	0	0	0	0	0	0	0	0	0	1	0	0	0
crinkled	5	.3405	.4175	36.2	0	2	1	1	0	0	1	0	2	1	0	0	0	0	0	0	0	0	0	0	2	0	0	0	0
crinkles	3	.3394	.2451	33.9	0	0	0	0	2	1	0	0	1	0	0	1	0	0	0	0	0	0	0	0	1	0	0	0	0
crinoline	2	.2160	.1362	31.3	0	0	0	1	1	0	0	0	1	0	0	0	0	0	0	1	0	0	0	0	0	0	0	0	0
cripple	4	.1787	.2347	33.7	0	0	0	1	2	1	0	0	2	0	0	0	0	0	0	0	0	0	0	0	2	0	0	0	0
crippled	23	.7145	3.4126	45.3	1	1	6	3	6	6	0	0	10	0	0	2	0	1	0	3	1	0	0	0	2	2	0	2	0
crises	11	.4258	1.0017	40.0	0	0	1	0	3	1	6	0	0	0	0	1	0	2	0	0	0	0	0	0	0	0	3	5	0
crisis	29	.4950	3.0699	44.9	0	0	2	0	9	8	10	0	2	1	0	1	0	10	0	0	0	0	0	0	0	2	1	12	0
crisp	62	.3709	5.0047	47.0	5	9	1	6	13	9	17	2	7	4	0	3	0	3	1	1	1	0	26	0	8	3	0	5	0
Crispian	5	.0000	.0547	27.4	0	0	0	0	5	0	0	0	0	5	0	0	0	0	0	0	0	0	0	0	0	0	0	0	0
Crispin	3	.1858	.1432	31.6	0	0	0	0	2	1	0	0	0	2	0	0	0	1	0	0	0	0	0	0	0	0	0	0	0
Crispin's	4	.0000	.0438	26.4	0	0	0	0	4	0	0	0	0	4	0	0	0	0	0	0	0	0	0	0	0	0	0	0	0
crisply	2	.2387	.1089	30.4	1	0	0	0	1	0	0	0	0	0	0	0	0	0	0	0	1	0	0	0	1	0	0	0	0
crispness	2	.0000	.0064	18.1	0	0	0	0	0	0	2	0	0	0	0	0	0	0	0	0	0	0	2	0	0	0	0	0	0
Crispus	2	.0000	.0243	23.9	0	0	0	0	2	0	0	0	0	0	0	0	0	0	0	0	0	0	0	0	0	0	0	2	0
criss-cross	2	.2441	.1127	30.5	1	0	0	1	0	0	0	0	0	0	0	0	0	0	0	0	0	0	0	0	1	0	1	0	0
crisscross	8	.4367	.7755	38.9	1	0	2	2	3	0	0	0	2	0	0	0	0	1	0	0	0	1	0	0	0	0	2	2	0
crisscrossed	8	.6172	1.0420	40.2	1	0	0	1	4	0	1	1	2	0	0	0	0	1	0	2	0	0	0	0	0	1	1	1	0
crisscrossing	2	.1378	.0662	28.2	0	0	0	1	0	0	0	1	0	0	0	0	0	0	0	0	0	1	0	0	0	0	0	1	0
Cristo	2	.1787	.1174	30.7	0	0	1	0	0	1	0	0	1	0	0	0	0	0	0	0	0	0	0	0	1	0	0	0	0
Cristobal	9	.3534	.8522	39.3	0	0	3	1	4	0	0	1	7	0	0	0	0	1	0	0	0	0	0	0	0	0	0	1	0
criteria	11	.5246	1.2199	40.9	0	0	1	0	1	0	7	2	0	0	0	0	0	5	0	1	0	0	0	0	0	2	1	2	0
critic	12	.5898	1.4642	41.7	0	0	2	0	2	4	2	2	1	0	0	1	0	1	0	0	1	0	0	0	0	2	4	2	0
critical	44	.8321	7.3121	48.6	0	1	4	2	18	7	4	8	4	3	1	2	0	3	1	7	2	0	0	1	2	2	5	11	0
critically	13	.5942	1.6273	42.1	0	0	1	4	5	1	2	0	4	2	1	0	0	0	0	1	0	0	2	0	1	1	1	0	0
criticism	25	.7239	3.6922	45.7	0	1	4	1	8	5	6	0	5	0	0	0	0	4	0	2	2	0	1	0	2	1	5	3	0
criticize	12	.6124	1.5317	41.9	0	0	2	1	2	4	3	0	1	0	0	0	0	5	0	1	0	0	0	0	1	2	1	1	0
criticized	15	.5615	1.7941	42.5	0	1	2	2	5	3	2	0	3	0	0	0	0	4	0	1	0	0	0	0	0	1	3	3	0
criticizing	6	.4826	.6161	37.9	0	0	2	1	1	1	1	0	0	0	0	0	0	0	0	2	0	0	0	0	0	2	1	1	0
critics	37	.6300	4.8002	46.8	0	0	3	3	11	9	10	1	3	0	1	1	0	10	0	1	4	0	0	0	0	0	6	11	0
critter	8	.4114	.7418	38.7	2	2	1	1	0	1	0	1	2	0	0	3	0	0	0	0	0	0	0	0	2	1	0	0	0
critters	5	.3547	.4331	36.4	0	2	0	2	1	0	0	0	2	0	0	1	0	0	0	0	0	0	0	0	0	2	0	0	0
Cro-Magnon	6	.2629	.3642	35.6	0	0	0	0	4	1	1	0	0	0	0	0	0	1	0	0	0	0	0	0	0	0	4	1	0
croak	9	.5245	1.0223	40.1	3	2	0	3	0	1	0	0	2	2	0	0	0	0	0	3	0	0	0	0	0	1	0	1	0
croaked	9	.4642	.9527	39.8	5	1	0	1	1	1	0	0	4	0	0	0	0	0	0	0	1	0	0	0	1	3	0	0	0
Croakie	2	.0000	.0162	22.1	0	0	0	0	0	0	2	0	0	0	0	0	0	0	2	0	0	0	0	0	0	0	0	0	0
croaking	11	.5908	1.3627	41.3	2	0	0	4	4	0	1	0	2	1	1	2	0	0	0	3	0	0	0	0	1	0	0	1	0
Croat	2	.0000	.0243	23.9	0	0	0	0	0	0	2	0	0	0	0	0	0	0	0	0	0	0	0	0	0	0	0	2	0
Croatian	3	.3826	.2445	33.9	0	0	1	0	0	1	1	0	0	0	0	0	0	0	0	0	1	0	0	0	0	0	1	1	0
Croatoan	2	.0000	.0290	24.6	0	2	0	0	0	0	0	0	0	0	0	0	0	0	0	0	0	0	0	0	0	2	0	0	0
Croats	2	.0000	.0389	25.9	0	0	0	0	2	0	0	0	0	0	0	0	0	2	0	0	0	0	0	0	0	0	0	0	0
Croce	2	.0000	.0243	23.9	0	0	0	0	2	0	0	0	0	0	0	0	0	0	0	0	0	0	0	0	0	0	0	2	0
crocheted	2	.1812	.0838	29.2	0	0	0	0	0	0	2	0	0	0	0	0	0	0	0	0	0	0	1	0	0	0	0	1	0
crock	3	.2347	.1695	32.3	0	1	1	0	1	0	0	0	0	0	0	0	0	0	0	0	0	0	0	0	1	2	0	0	0
Crocker	2	.2443	.1130	30.5	0	0	0	0	0	0	1	1	0	0	0	1	0	0	0	0	0	0	0	0	1	0	0	0	0
Crockett	25	.4804	2.8218	44.5	3	4	9	2	4	3	0	0	17	0	0	0	0	1	0	0	1	0	0	0	0	5	0	1	0
Crockett's	3	.3454	.2542	34.1	0	0	0	0	1	2	0	0	1	0	0	0	0	1	0	0	0	0	0	0	0	0	0	1	0
crocodile	61	.7309	9.2135	49.6	27	11	3	4	13	3	0	0	27	2	0	6	1	4	0	3	2	0	0	0	2	5	9	0	0
Crocodile	15	.2458	.9529	39.8	0	6	9	0	0	0	0	0	4	0	0	9	0	0	0	0	0	0	0	0	2	0	0	0	0
crocodile's	10	.0000	.4568	36.6	10	0	0	0	0	0	0	0	10	0	0	0	0	0	0	0	0	0	0	0	0	0	0	0	0
crocodiles	71	.5435	8.4521	49.3	35	5	1	6	23	0	0	1	28	0	0	0	0	5	0	9	1	0	0	0	0	12	16	0	0
crocodilians	7	.0000	.0733	28.6	0	0	0	0	7	0	0	0	0	0	0	0	0	0	0	0	0	0	0	0	0	0	7	0	0
crocs	2	.0000	.0914	29.6	0	0	0	2	0	0	0	0	2	0	0	0	0	0	0	0	0	0	0	0	0	0	0	0	0
crocuses	3	.2360	.1709	32.3	0	0	0	3	0	0	0	0	0	0	0	0	2	0	0	0	0	0	0	0	1	0	0	0	0
Cromarty	3	.2304	.1619	32.1	0	0	0	0	2	1	0	0	0	0	0	0	0	0	0	0	0	0	0	0	2	0	1	0	0
Crompton's	2	.1698	.1133	30.5	0	0	0	0	2	0	0	0	1	0	0	0	0	0	0	0	0	0	0	0	0	0	1	0	0
Cromwell	4	.3280	.2948	34.7	0	1	2	0	0	0	1	0	0	0	0	0	0	0	0	1	0	0	0	0	0	1	2	0	0
cronies	5	.3936	.4382	36.4	0	0	0	1	0	1	3	0	1	0	0	1	0	0	2	0	0	0	0	0	0	0	0	1	0
Cronk	3	.0000	.0322	25.1	0	0	0	0	0	0	3	0	0	0	0	3	0	0	0	0	0	0	0	0	0	0	0	0	0
Cronks'	2	.0000	.0215	23.3	0	0	0	0	0	0	2	0	0	0	0	2	0	0	0	0	0	0	0	0	0	0	0	0	0
crook	17	.5601	1.9861	43.0	2	2	0	3	5	3	2	0	2	0	0	6	0	0	0	1	2	0	0	0	4	0	1	1	0
crooked	35	.7067	5.1084	47.1	4	7	5	4	6	5	4	0	12	3	1	7	0	2	0	3	0	0	0	0	4	2	0	1	0
Crooked	2	.0000	.0290	24.6	0	2	0	0	0	0	0	0	0	0	0	0	0	0	0	0	0	0	0	0	0	2	0	0	0
crookedly	3	.3772	.2437	33.9	0	0	1	0	1	0	1	0	0	0	0	0	0	0	0	0	1	0	0	0	1	1	0	0	0
Crookes	2	.0000	.0394	26.0	0	0	0	0	0	2	0	0	0	0	0	0	0	0	0	2	0	0	0	0	0	0	0	0	0
croon	3	.3399	.2456	33.9	0	0	1	0	1	0	1	0	1	0	0	1	0	0	0	0	0	0	0	0	0	0	0	1	0
crooned	2	.2446	.1142	30.6	0	0	0	1	1	0	0	0	0	0	0	0	0	0	0	0	0	0	0	0	1	0	0	1	0
crooning	4	.4525	.3990	36.0	1	0	0	0	2	0	1	0	1	1	0	1	0	0	0	0	0	0	0	0	1	0	0	0	0
crop	215	.6880	30.476	54.8	39	29	31	43	35	13	7	18	29	2	0	7	0	104	2	27	2	0	0	1	5	9	13	14	0
crop-share	2	.0000	.0209	23.2	0	0	2	0	0	0	0	0	0	0	0	0	0	0	0	0	0	0	0	0	0	0	2	0	0
cropland	7	.3298	.5356	37.3	0	0	2	3	0	0	2	0	0	0	0	0	0	5	0	0	0	0	0	0	0	1	1	0	0
cropped	2	.2441	.1127	30.5	0	0	0	0	1	0	1	0	0	0	0	0	0	0	0	0	0	0	0	0	1	0	1	0	0
cropping	8	.5635	.9458	39.8	0	2	2	0	2	0	1	1	1	0	0	2	0	0	0	1	0	0	0	0	1	1	0	2	0
crops	536	.5960	67.161	58.3	88	71	103	125	78	32	28	11	43	3	1	3	0	357	4	46	1	1	0	0	6	27	35	8	1
croquet	7	.2668	.4907	36.9	0	2	0	3	0	0	2	0	3	0	0	0	0	0	0	0	0	0	0	2	0	1	0	1	0

9B crickling
3B Cried
3P crieth
8R crime-prevention
5N crimers
9L crimp
8D crimpy
7R Crimson
6A crimson-crossed
9A cringingly
3P crinoids
7A Crip
9R Crises
XR crisis-filled
7R crisis-intervention
9N crisped
4A crisper
3A crispest
5A Crispi's
4P crispy
9Q criss-crossed
5Q Crisscross
5Q cristobalite
7Q criterion
8J Critic
XR Critical
8D criticising
XB Criticism
7R Critics
8R critiques
5A crittur's
9Q CroMagnon
3A CROAK
3B croak-croak-croak
4P croaks
9R Croatia
9R Croatia's
6B crobble
6A croc
8G crochet
XN Crocker's
7N crockery
9L crocking
4Q crocks
5D crocodile-tears
5D Crocodile's
6A crocodilus
9Q crocus
7P Croesus'
8Q crofter
8F Croix
8D Cronin
8Q Cronje
9D Cronk's
9D Cronks
9D Cronos
8D Cronus
7R cronyism
9R Cronyn
8A Crook
9B crook's
6A crooked-legged
7N crookedy
3P crooks
6N Crookshank
9B Crooner
7R Crop-Growers
XH crop-damaging
5P crop-growing
8F crop-lien
9R croplands
5N croqueted

Word Type	F	D	U	SFI	3 Gr 3	4 Gr 4	5 Gr 5	6 Gr 6	7 Gr 7	8 Gr 8	9 Gr 9	X UnGr	A Read	B Eng & Gr	C Comp	D Lit	E Math	F Soc Stud	G Spell	H Sci	J Music	K Art	L Home Ec	M Shop	N Lib F	P Lib NF	Q Lib Ref	R Mag	S Rel
Crosby	4	.3141	.3005	34.8	0	0	0	2	1	0	0	1	1	0	0	0	0	0	0	0	1	0	0	0	0	0	0	2	0
Crosetti	2	.0000	.0914	29.6	0	0	0	0	2	0	0	0	2	0	0	0	0	0	0	0	0	0	0	0	0	0	0	0	0
cross	498	.9076	89.728	59.5	116	78	71	83	64	35	47	4	104	15	8	12	65	62	64	32	11	3	2	14	34	34	14	24	0
Cross	60	.7501	9.1795	49.6	11	6	21	7	3	8	1	3	14	2	0	1	9	17	1	3	0	0	3	0	0	3	2	5	0
Cross-Florida	2	.0000	.0243	23.9	0	0	0	0	0	0	0	2	0	0	0	0	0	0	0	0	0	0	0	0	0	0	0	2	0
cross-country	5	.0824	.1675	32.2	0	0	0	1	3	1	0	0	1	0	0	0	0	0	0	0	0	0	0	0	0	0	0	4	0
cross-feed	5	.0000	.0126	21.0	0	0	0	0	0	0	5	0	0	0	0	0	0	0	0	0	0	0	0	5	0	0	0	0	0
cross-legged	12	.6580	1.6595	42.2	1	1	1	3	3	1	2	0	5	0	0	0	0	1	0	0	1	0	0	0	1	1	2	1	0
cross-line	3	.0000	.0365	25.6	0	0	0	0	3	0	0	0	0	0	0	0	0	0	0	0	0	0	0	0	0	0	0	3	0
cross-lines	3	.0000	.0365	25.6	0	0	0	0	3	0	0	0	0	0	0	0	0	0	0	0	0	0	0	0	0	0	0	3	0
cross-member	2	.1620	.0760	28.8	0	0	0	0	1	0	1	0	0	0	0	0	0	0	0	0	0	0	0	1	0	0	0	1	0
cross-product	4	.0000	.0599	27.8	0	0	4	0	0	0	0	0	0	0	0	0	4	0	0	0	0	0	0	0	0	0	0	0	0
cross-roads	2	.2427	.1152	30.6	1	0	1	0	0	0	0	0	0	0	0	0	0	0	0	0	0	0	0	0	1	1	0	0	0
cross-section	6	.0412	.0796	29.0	0	0	0	0	0	1	5	0	0	0	0	0	0	0	0	1	0	0	0	5	0	0	0	0	0
cross-sectional	2	.1738	.0790	29.0	0	0	0	0	1	1	0	0	0	0	0	0	0	0	0	0	0	0	0	1	0	0	1	0	0
cross-sections	2	.2440	.0995	30.0	0	0	0	1	0	1	0	0	0	0	1	0	0	0	0	0	0	0	0	1	0	0	0	0	0
cross-stitch	3	.2357	.2199	33.4	1	0	0	2	0	0	0	0	2	0	0	0	0	0	0	0	0	0	0	0	0	1	0	0	0
crossbar	9	.4672	.9963	40.0	0	5	1	0	2	1	0	0	6	0	0	0	1	0	0	1	0	0	0	0	0	0	1	0	0
crossbow	7	.1920	.4372	36.4	0	0	2	2	3	0	0	0	4	0	0	0	0	0	0	0	0	0	0	0	0	0	3	0	0
crosscut	5	.0954	.2223	33.5	0	1	2	0	1	0	1	0	3	0	0	0	0	0	0	0	0	0	0	2	0	0	0	0	0
crosscutting	2	.0000	.0050	17.0	0	0	0	0	2	0	0	0	0	0	0	0	0	0	0	0	0	0	0	2	0	0	0	0	0
crossed	244	.9206	44.616	56.5	38	36	32	40	48	31	16	3	80	8	4	11	10	37	2	16	6	2	2	0	20	21	11	14	0
crosser	3	.3370	.2430	33.9	1	1	0	0	0	1	0	0	1	0	0	1	0	0	0	0	0	0	0	0	0	0	1	0	0
crosses	68	.7949	10.912	50.4	5	12	7	22	6	7	5	4	14	2	2	2	3	13	1	7	0	0	0	0	13	3	3	5	0
crosshatching	4	.0000	.0101	20.0	0	0	0	0	0	0	4	0	0	0	0	0	0	0	0	0	0	0	0	4	0	0	0	0	0
crossing	137	.9142	24.880	54.0	20	14	20	15	30	22	12	4	41	5	4	9	7	17	4	8	4	1	1	0	5	12	12	7	0
Crossing	9	.2348	.6724	38.3	1	0	0	4	4	0	0	0	7	0	0	0	0	0	0	0	2	0	0	0	0	0	0	0	0
crossings	7	.4397	.6986	38.4	0	1	2	0	3	0	1	0	2	0	0	2	1	0	0	2	0	0	0	0	0	0	0	0	0
crosslegged	2	.0000	.0234	23.7	0	0	1	1	0	0	0	0	0	0	0	0	0	0	0	0	0	0	0	0	2	0	0	0	0
crossly	15	.5390	1.7952	42.5	2	5	4	3	0	1	0	0	8	0	1	1	0	1	0	0	0	0	0	0	3	1	0	0	0
crosspieces	2	.0000	.0914	29.6	0	0	0	2	0	0	0	0	2	0	0	0	0	0	0	0	0	0	0	0	0	0	0	0	0
crossroad	4	.3688	.3668	35.6	2	1	1	0	0	0	0	0	2	1	0	0	0	1	0	0	0	0	0	0	0	0	0	0	0
crossroads	18	.6160	2.3491	43.7	7	1	5	1	2	2	0	0	6	0	0	1	0	4	0	0	0	0	0	0	1	1	4	1	0
Crossroads	2	.0000	.0389	25.9	0	0	2	0	0	0	0	0	0	0	0	0	0	2	0	0	0	0	0	0	0	0	0	0	0
Crosstown	2	.0000	.0299	24.8	0	0	0	0	0	2	0	0	0	0	0	0	2	0	0	0	0	0	0	0	0	0	0	0	0
crosswalk	3	.0000	.0591	27.7	0	0	0	0	0	0	3	0	0	0	0	0	0	0	0	3	0	0	0	0	0	0	0	0	0
crosswalks	5	.0000	.0986	29.9	0	0	0	0	3	0	2	0	0	0	0	0	0	0	0	5	0	0	0	0	0	0	0	0	0
crossways	2	.0000	.0045	16.5	0	2	0	0	0	0	0	0	0	0	2	0	0	0	0	0	0	0	0	0	0	0	0	0	0
crosswise	25	.4651	2.4048	43.8	1	1	3	2	6	3	9	0	2	0	0	1	1	0	0	0	0	2	11	3	0	2	3	0	0
crossword	11	.3552	.8808	39.4	0	3	1	2	1	2	1	1	2	0	0	0	1	0	6	0	1	0	0	0	0	0	0	1	0
crotch	11	.1816	.4758	36.8	0	0	0	1	9	1	0	0	1	1	0	0	0	0	0	0	0	0	7	0	0	0	1	1	0
crotches	2	.1698	.1133	30.5	1	0	0	1	0	0	0	0	1	0	0	0	0	0	0	0	0	0	0	0	0	0	1	0	0
crouch	8	.4970	.8626	39.4	3	1	0	2	2	0	0	0	2	0	0	1	0	0	0	1	2	0	0	0	2	0	0	0	0
crouched	44	.5350	5.0888	47.1	1	9	4	8	14	6	2	0	15	0	3	13	0	1	0	0	0	0	0	0	9	1	0	2	0
crouches	3	.3722	.2508	34.0	1	0	0	0	1	1	0	0	0	0	0	1	0	1	0	1	0	0	0	0	0	0	0	0	0
crouching	17	.6083	2.1613	43.3	2	2	3	2	4	0	4	0	4	1	0	5	0	0	0	0	1	0	0	0	2	1	0	3	0
croutons	4	.0000	.0129	21.1	0	0	0	0	2	0	2	0	0	0	0	0	0	0	0	0	0	0	4	0	0	0	0	0	0
crow	49	.7857	7.8572	49.0	14	10	8	3	3	4	2	5	23	2	0	6	0	0	4	5	2	0	0	1	2	2	1	1	0
Crow	29	.3922	2.8551	44.6	9	12	0	2	0	6	0	0	20	1	3	1	0	4	0	0	0	0	0	0	0	0	0	0	0
crow's	6	.4805	.6608	38.2	2	1	2	1	0	0	0	0	3	0	0	0	0	1	0	0	0	0	0	0	0	1	1	0	0
Crow's	2	.0665	.0708	28.5	0	0	0	1	0	1	0	0	1	0	1	0	0	0	0	0	0	0	0	0	0	0	0	0	0
crow's-nest	3	.2347	.1695	32.3	0	0	1	0	0	0	2	0	0	0	0	0	0	0	0	0	0	0	0	0	1	2	0	0	0
crowbar	9	.4564	.8736	39.4	1	1	0	2	3	0	1	1	0	0	0	0	0	0	0	3	0	0	0	1	0	2	3	0	0
crowd	396	.8280	66.213	58.2	59	105	38	56	72	32	28	6	161	16	5	28	0	17	4	12	14	1	1	0	41	58	1	37	0
crowded	223	.8217	36.934	55.7	45	36	36	37	34	11	22	2	61	5	0	18	0	58	0	8	1	1	2	1	16	26	14	12	0
crowding	33	.7140	4.8912	46.9	5	5	3	8	2	7	3	0	15	0	1	3	0	3	0	0	0	0	0	1	3	5	0	2	0
crowds	79	.8341	13.281	51.2	10	16	6	19	13	9	5	1	30	0	1	6	0	9	0	2	3	2	1	0	4	11	3	7	0
Crowe	3	.1937	.1495	31.7	0	0	1	0	0	0	0	2	0	0	0	0	0	1	0	0	0	0	0	0	0	0	0	2	0
crowed	13	.3589	1.1087	40.4	0	3	1	2	1	2	4	0	5	1	3	2	0	1	0	0	0	0	0	0	0	0	0	1	0
crowing	13	.3403	1.1977	40.8	5	3	0	2	2	1	0	0	10	0	0	2	0	1	0	0	0	0	0	0	0	0	0	0	0
Crowley	25	.2725	1.8627	42.7	0	1	1	12	11	0	0	0	13	0	0	11	0	0	0	0	1	0	0	0	0	0	0	0	0
crown	87	.7820	13.765	51.4	11	14	13	11	20	14	1	3	23	0	0	11	0	5	2	3	9	0	1	0	6	8	13	6	0
Crown	30	.6320	3.9362	46.0	2	5	8	3	6	4	1	1	6	0	0	3	0	3	0	1	1	0	0	0	5	1	9	1	0
crowned	26	.6473	3.4923	45.4	1	2	6	3	7	3	4	0	5	1	0	3	0	6	0	1	0	0	0	0	0	2	6	2	0
crowning	3	.2051	.1687	32.3	0	0	2	0	1	0	0	0	1	0	1	0	0	0	0	0	0	0	0	0	0	0	0	1	0
crowns	16	.6604	2.1805	43.4	0	1	3	3	2	1	1	5	3	0	0	1	0	2	1	0	0	0	0	0	1	2	1	5	0
crows	43	.6442	5.9338	47.7	23	10	0	4	1	3	0	2	24	2	0	2	0	0	0	7	0	0	0	0	4	3	1	0	0
Crows	2	.0000	.0914	29.6	1	0	0	0	1	0	0	0	2	0	0	0	0	0	0	0	0	0	0	0	0	0	0	0	0
crucial	23	.5813	2.7559	44.4	2	0	0	3	8	4	4	2	1	0	0	2	0	2	3	0	0	0	0	0	0	2	6	7	0
crucible	5	.0000	.0586	27.7	0	1	0	0	0	4	0	0	0	0	0	0	0	0	0	0	0	0	0	0	5	0	0	0	0
crucified	2	.2408	.1204	30.8	1	0	0	0	1	0	0	0	0	0	0	0	0	1	0	0	0	0	0	0	0	1	0	0	0
Crucis	6	.0000	.1183	30.7	0	0	0	0	0	6	0	0	0	0	0	0	0	0	0	6	0	0	0	0	0	0	0	0	0
crude	67	.7569	10.213	50.1	4	1	12	9	25	8	7	1	5	2	3	1	2	13	0	5	5	0	0	4	0	7	14	6	0
crudely	2	.1703	.0781	28.9	0	0	0	0	0	0	1	1	0	1	0	0	0	0	0	0	0	0	0	1	0	0	0	0	0
crudest	4	.2386	.2998	34.8	0	1	0	2	0	0	1	0	3	0	0	0	0	0	0	0	0	0	0	0	0	0	1	0	0
cruel	95	.7861	15.156	51.8	14	11	19	10	22	10	7	2	32	3	1	15	0	8	1	0	4	0	0	0	5	15	7	4	0
cruelest	5	.3826	.4244	36.3	0	0	1	0	3	1	0	0	0	0	0	1	0	2	0	0	0	0	0	0	0	2	0	0	0
cruelly	8	.2967	.5780	37.6	1	1	1	2	2	1	0	0	1	0	0	0	0	4	0	0	0	0	0	0	3	0	0	0	0
cruelty	20	.7017	2.8813	44.6	2	3	3	3	8	0	1	0	5	2	0	2	0	1	1	0	0	0	0	0	3	4	2	0	0
Cruelty	5	.0000	.2284	33.6	5	0	0	0	0	0	0	0	5	0	0	0	0	0	0	0	0	0	0	0	0	0	0	0	0
Cruickshank	2	.0000	.0394	26.0	0	0	0	0	0	0	0	2	0	0	0	0	0	0	0	2	0	0	0	0	0	0	0	0	0
cruise	21	.4778	2.1922	43.4	0	0	2	4	9	4	1	1	5	0	0	0	1	1	1	0	0	0	0	0	0	0	4	9	0
cruised	5	.5377	.5715	37.6	0	0	0	1	2	0	2	0	1	0	0	1	0	0	0	0	0	0	0	0	0	1	1	1	0
cruiser	14	.3743	1.3190	41.2	0	0	7	3	4	0	0	0	9	0	0	0	0	0	0	0	0	0	0	1	0	0	0	4	0
cruisers	5	.3610	.4506	36.5	0	0	0	1	1	2	0	1	2	0	0	0	0	2	0	1	0	0	0	0	0	0	0	0	0
cruises	3	.2445	.1903	32.8	0	0	1	1	1	0	0	0	1	0	0	0	0	0	0	0	0	0	1	0	0	0	0	1	0
cruising	22	.5666	2.6927	44.3	0	6	1	6	7	1	0	1	8	0	0	1	0	0	0	4	0	0	0	0	1	0	2	6	0
crumb	7	.2616	.4011	36.0	1	0	0	0	2	2	2	0	0	1	0	0	0	0	0	0	0	0	3	0	3	0	0	0	0
crumble	9	.6704	1.2258	40.9	1	1	1	2	2	1	0	1	0	1	0	0	0	1	0	2	0	0	1	0	1	1	1	1	0
crumbled	13	.6533	1.7603	42.5	1	4	0	3	3	2	0	0	3	1	0	2	0	1	0	0	0	0	0	0	0	2	2	2	0
crumbles	5	.2424	.2988	34.8	0	1	1	1	1	1	0	0	0	0	0	0	0	0	0	3	0	0	0	0	0	0	2	0	0

7N croqueting
3P CROSS-CUT
6A CROSS-FADE
4A cross-bred
4Q cross-channel
7R cross-checked
8E cross-cut
9D cross-examination
7D cross-fade
9M cross-grained
7D cross-graining
9M cross-hatching
XH cross-like
3A cross-looking
7M cross-peen
XR cross-pollination
4Q cross-referenced
7N cross-rib
5H cross-stick
6R cross-stitched
8F cross-stitching
9D cross-street
9N cross-trees
XB cross-ways
9B crossbars
6R crossbelts
3P crossbill
7Q crossbills
8E crossbones
4Q crossbreeding
5P crosscurrents
9Q crossfire
7M crossgrain
7R crosshairs
9R crosshatch
8E crosshatched
7R crosshatchings
8J crossin'
8P crossing-the-Delaware
7R crossmember
7R crossmembers
5J crosspoles
6A crosstag
3A crosstown
7R crosswinds
9C crost
7Q Crotalus
7L Crotch
3A crotched
8F crotchety
7A croup
7J Crouse
6D Crow-bait
XR crow-count
8N crowbait
6A crowbars
9D CROWD
7A crowd-pleasing
4A crowd's
XH Crowfoots
3P crowneth
3A crows'
7D Croydon
5A crrrack
9R Crucible
8N crucibles
4A crucifix
7A crucifixion
XH cruciform
7A crucifying
7N crude-looking
9Q crude-oil
7C crudeness
6R cruder
7Q crudities
9R crudity
8R Cruel
XH Cruickshank's
7A Cruiser
7R cruiser's
6A crullers
8D Crumb
7D crumbed
5Q crumblike

Word Type	F	D	U	SFI	3 Gr 3	4 Gr 4	5 Gr 5	6 Gr 6	7 Gr 7	8 Gr 8	9 Gr 9	X UnGr	A Read	B Eng & Gr	C Comp	D Lit	E Math	F Soc Stud	G Spell	H Sci	J Music	K Art	L Home Ec	M Shop	N Lib F	P Lib NF	Q Lib Ref	R Mag	S Rel
crumbling	12	.5213	1.3229	41.2	0	1	2	2	4	2	0	1	1	0	0	1	0	2	0	0	0	0	0	0	0	2	1	5	0
crumbly	7	.3800	.6109	37.9	1	0	0	4	1	0	1	0	1	0	0	0	0	0	0	4	0	0	1	0	0	1	0	0	0
crumbs	38	.4294	3.6860	45.7	5	11	4	3	4	4	6	1	14	2	0	2	0	0	0	0	0	0	10	0	5	3	1	1	0
crumby	2	.1814	.1187	30.7	1	0	0	0	1	0	0	0	1	0	0	0	0	0	0	0	0	0	0	0	0	0	0	1	0
crummy	3	.1250	.1342	31.3	0	0	0	0	1	1	1	0	1	0	0	0	0	0	0	0	0	0	0	0	2	0	0	0	0
Crump	4	.1948	.2500	34.0	2	2	0	0	0	0	0	0	2	0	0	0	0	0	0	0	0	0	0	0	0	2	0	0	0
Crump's	2	.0000	.0290	24.6	0	2	0	0	0	0	0	0	0	0	0	0	0	0	0	0	0	0	0	0	0	2	0	0	0
crumple	6	.4500	.5765	37.6	1	1	1	0	2	0	1	0	1	0	0	0	0	0	0	0	0	1	1	0	1	0	2	0	0
crumpled	24	.6811	3.3562	45.3	2	7	2	2	7	2	1	1	5	0	1	4	0	0	0	1	0	1	0	0	4	5	0	3	0
crumpling	2	.0000	.0914	29.6	0	0	0	0	2	0	0	0	2	0	0	0	0	0	0	0	0	0	0	0	0	0	0	0	0
crunch	7	.4072	.6281	38.0	1	1	1	2	0	0	2	0	1	1	0	2	0	0	0	0	0	0	0	0	0	0	0	3	0
crunched	4	.2995	.2902	34.6	1	0	0	0	1	0	2	0	1	1	0	2	0	0	0	0	0	0	0	0	0	0	0	0	0
Cruncher	9	.0000	.0966	29.8	0	0	0	0	0	0	9	0	0	0	0	9	0	0	0	0	0	0	0	0	0	0	0	0	0
crunching	10	.2940	.7066	38.5	2	0	0	1	1	0	5	1	2	5	0	0	0	0	0	0	0	0	0	0	0	0	0	3	0
crunchy	3	.3772	.2488	34.0	1	0	1	0	0	1	0	0	0	1	0	0	0	0	0	1	0	0	0	0	1	0	0	0	0
crusade	15	.4177	1.3431	41.3	0	0	3	0	2	5	3	2	0	2	0	0	0	2	0	0	0	0	0	0	1	0	1	9	0
Crusade	4	.1505	.1615	32.1	0	2	1	0	0	1	0	0	0	0	0	0	0	1	0	0	0	0	0	0	0	0	3	0	0
crusaded	2	.0000	.0243	23.9	0	0	0	0	0	0	2	0	0	0	0	0	0	0	0	0	0	0	0	0	0	0	0	2	0
Crusader	2	.2441	.1127	30.5	0	1	0	0	1	0	0	0	0	0	0	0	0	0	0	0	0	0	0	0	1	0	1	0	0
crusaders	4	.3287	.2952	34.7	0	0	2	0	1	1	0	0	0	0	0	0	0	1	0	0	0	0	0	0	0	1	2	0	0
Crusaders	38	.5532	4.5255	46.6	0	6	0	3	8	21	0	0	10	1	0	0	0	14	0	0	1	0	0	0	7	0	5	0	0
crusades	2	.2351	.1166	30.7	0	0	0	0	0	1	1	0	0	0	0	0	0	1	0	0	0	0	0	0	0	0	0	1	0
Crusades	16	.4115	1.4447	41.6	0	1	3	2	1	9	0	0	0	0	0	0	0	10	0	0	1	0	0	0	1	0	4	0	0
crusading	3	.2300	.1627	32.1	0	0	1	0	0	0	1	1	0	1	0	0	0	0	0	0	0	0	0	0	0	0	0	2	0
crush	23	.6623	3.1317	45.0	1	3	5	1	5	5	3	0	4	0	0	3	0	1	0	4	0	2	2	0	1	2	2	2	0
crushed	73	.8203	12.063	50.8	7	9	10	13	16	10	3	5	19	2	0	5	0	13	0	10	1	2	0	1	8	3	2	7	0
crushes	2	.1432	.0759	28.8	1	0	0	0	0	0	1	0	0	0	0	0	0	0	0	1	0	0	1	0	0	0	0	0	0
crushing	28	.7468	4.2878	46.3	1	1	7	5	9	3	2	0	11	0	1	3	0	1	0	4	1	0	2	1	0	2	0	2	0
Crusoe	9	.6144	1.1414	40.6	0	0	2	3	1	2	1	0	1	1	0	0	0	1	1	0	0	0	0	0	3	0	1	1	0
crust	160	.6155	20.456	53.1	4	34	32	7	37	6	39	1	14	1	1	3	0	4	3	85	0	0	16	1	1	2	25	4	0
crustacean	2	.0000	.0394	26.0	0	0	0	0	2	0	0	0	0	0	0	0	0	0	0	2	0	0	0	0	0	0	0	0	0
crustaceans	11	.2835	.7604	38.8	0	0	0	0	11	0	0	0	1	0	0	0	0	0	0	6	0	0	0	0	0	0	4	0	0
crustaceous	2	.0000	.0219	23.4	0	0	0	0	0	0	2	0	0	2	0	0	0	0	0	0	0	0	0	0	0	0	0	0	0
crustal	3	.0000	.0591	27.7	0	0	0	0	0	0	3	0	0	0	0	0	0	0	0	3	0	0	0	0	0	0	0	0	0
crusted	4	.2995	.2902	34.6	0	0	1	1	2	0	0	0	1	1	0	2	0	0	0	0	0	0	0	0	0	0	0	0	0
crusts	14	.5104	1.5740	42.0	3	1	1	1	3	0	2	3	5	0	0	0	0	0	0	3	0	0	2	0	1	2	0	1	0
crusty	4	.0857	.1568	32.0	2	0	1	0	1	0	0	0	2	0	0	0	0	0	0	0	0	0	2	0	0	0	0	0	0
crutch	13	.5060	1.3824	41.4	1	1	0	2	6	3	0	0	1	0	0	1	0	0	0	0	2	0	0	0	6	1	0	2	0
crutches	10	.1722	.4625	36.7	0	0	0	7	0	2	1	0	1	0	0	0	0	0	0	0	0	0	0	0	8	0	1	0	0
crux	3	.3667	.2414	33.8	0	0	1	0	1	1	0	0	0	0	0	0	0	1	1	0	0	0	0	0	0	0	0	1	0
CRUX	5	.0000	.0986	29.9	0	0	0	0	0	5	0	0	0	0	0	0	0	0	0	5	0	0	0	0	0	0	0	0	0
Cruz	4	.1325	.1944	32.9	0	0	0	3	1	0	0	0	1	0	0	0	0	3	0	0	0	0	0	0	0	0	0	0	0
cry	327	.7721	51.679	57.1	77	62	30	46	55	30	21	6	154	13	5	40	0	6	8	4	10	0	0	0	42	26	1	18	0
Cry	4	.2442	.2268	33.6	0	0	0	0	2	2	0	0	0	2	0	0	0	0	0	0	0	0	0	0	0	0	0	2	0
crying	164	.7128	24.410	53.9	45	26	14	22	36	10	10	1	91	1	1	16	0	1	2	2	4	0	0	0	27	8	3	8	0
Crying	15	.0000	.6852	38.4	14	0	0	0	1	0	0	0	15	0	0	0	0	0	0	0	0	0	0	0	0	0	0	0	0
cryogenics	4	.0000	.0789	29.0	0	0	0	0	4	0	0	0	0	0	0	0	0	0	0	4	0	0	0	0	0	0	0	0	0
cryolite	2	.1698	.1133	30.5	0	0	2	0	0	0	0	0	1	0	0	0	0	0	0	0	0	0	0	0	0	0	1	0	0
crystal	95	.6653	13.065	51.2	5	10	7	7	9	15	21	21	13	2	0	5	2	1	0	48	0	0	0	2	1	4	11	6	0
Crystal	8	.3720	.7483	38.7	0	0	0	0	1	7	0	0	5	0	0	2	0	0	0	0	0	0	0	0	0	0	1	0	0
crystal-radio	2	.0000	.0394	26.0	0	0	2	0	0	0	0	0	0	0	0	0	0	0	0	2	0	0	0	0	0	0	0	0	0
crystal's	2	.2437	.1129	30.5	0	0	0	0	1	0	1	0	0	0	0	0	0	0	0	0	0	0	0	0	0	0	1	1	0
Crystal's	2	.0000	.0914	29.6	0	0	0	0	0	2	0	0	2	0	0	0	0	0	0	0	0	0	0	0	0	0	0	0	0
crystalline	23	.4026	2.0101	43.0	0	0	5	1	1	10	4	2	1	0	0	0	0	0	0	7	0	0	0	3	0	0	11	1	0
crystallization	4	.2353	.2382	33.8	0	0	0	0	0	3	1	0	0	0	0	0	0	0	0	3	0	0	0	0	0	0	1	0	0
crystallize	5	.4503	.5017	37.0	0	0	0	2	0	1	1	1	1	0	0	0	0	0	0	2	0	0	0	0	0	0	1	1	0
crystallized	2	.2446	.1123	30.5	0	0	0	0	0	0	1	1	0	1	0	0	0	0	0	0	0	0	0	0	0	0	1	0	0
crystallographers	2	.0000	.0914	29.6	0	0	0	2	0	0	0	0	2	0	0	0	0	0	0	0	0	0	0	0	0	0	0	0	0
crystals	152	.4500	15.225	51.8	13	13	18	22	10	8	29	39	18	0	0	0	0	2	0	106	0	0	2	0	1	6	13	4	0
CSA	10	.0000	.1047	30.2	0	0	0	0	10	0	0	0	0	0	0	0	0	0	0	0	0	0	0	0	0	0	10	0	0
CSM	2	.0000	.0243	23.9	0	0	0	0	2	0	0	0	0	0	0	0	0	0	0	0	0	0	0	0	0	0	0	2	0
ctenophores	5	.0000	.0986	29.9	0	0	0	0	5	0	0	0	0	0	0	0	0	0	0	5	0	0	0	0	0	0	0	0	0
cub	53	.5780	6.5748	48.2	5	11	1	5	17	10	4	0	21	1	0	14	0	0	2	0	0	0	0	0	7	0	1	7	0
Cub	21	.5516	2.4206	43.8	7	9	0	4	0	1	0	0	1	2	1	0	11	0	0	1	0	0	0	0	0	3	0	2	0
cub's	11	.3878	.9355	39.7	0	1	0	2	3	5	0	0	1	0	0	5	0	0	0	0	0	0	0	0	3	0	0	2	0
Cuba	77	.4431	7.5489	48.8	2	15	18	9	20	9	1	3	6	0	0	0	0	48	0	1	0	0	0	0	0	12	4	6	0
Cuba's	9	.3336	.6937	38.4	0	0	2	4	3	0	0	0	0	0	0	0	0	6	0	0	0	0	0	0	0	1	0	2	0
Cuban	13	.4810	1.3484	41.3	0	0	1	2	7	2	1	0	1	0	0	0	0	5	0	0	0	0	1	0	0	5	0	1	0
Cubans	7	.2361	.4176	36.2	0	1	2	0	2	2	0	0	0	0	0	0	0	5	0	0	0	0	0	0	0	0	0	2	0
Cubbins	9	.1282	.3180	35.0	8	1	0	0	0	0	0	0	0	1	0	0	0	0	0	0	0	0	0	0	8	0	0	0	0
cube	112	.3646	9.2054	49.6	20	15	14	19	18	14	11	1	4	0	0	0	81	0	0	19	0	1	0	0	1	2	1	3	0
cubed	2	.2446	.1184	30.7	0	1	0	0	0	0	1	0	0	0	0	0	1	0	0	0	0	0	0	0	0	1	0	0	0
cubes	73	.5009	7.8162	48.9	17	20	1	5	11	6	10	3	5	0	0	0	28	0	0	26	0	0	8	0	1	3	1	1	0
cubic	94	.4108	8.4484	49.3	4	11	8	5	11	25	27	3	2	0	0	0	67	0	1	12	0	1	0	0	0	0	8	3	0
cubicle	4	.1948	.2500	34.0	0	0	0	0	2	0	2	0	2	0	0	0	0	0	0	0	0	0	0	0	0	2	0	0	0
cubicles	2	.2433	.1158	30.6	0	0	0	0	1	0	1	0	0	0	0	0	0	0	0	0	0	0	0	0	0	1	0	1	0
Cubism	3	.2027	.1376	31.4	0	0	2	0	0	1	0	0	0	0	0	0	0	0	0	0	0	1	0	0	0	0	2	0	0
Cubists	3	.0000	.0055	17.4	0	0	0	0	0	3	0	0	0	0	0	0	0	0	0	0	0	3	0	0	0	0	0	0	0
Cubists'	2	.0000	.0037	15.7	0	0	0	0	0	2	0	0	0	0	0	0	0	0	0	0	0	2	0	0	0	0	0	0	0
cubit	6	.0000	.0898	29.5	3	0	3	0	0	0	0	0	0	0	0	0	6	0	0	0	0	0	0	0	0	0	0	0	0
cubits	4	.2393	.3005	34.8	0	0	0	0	4	0	0	0	3	0	0	1	0	0	0	0	0	0	0	0	0	0	0	0	0
cubs	32	.6385	4.3849	46.4	5	1	2	9	11	1	3	0	18	1	0	1	0	0	1	4	0	0	0	0	0	3	0	4	0
Cubs	18	.2840	1.1832	40.7	7	1	0	9	1	0	0	0	0	0	0	0	1	0	0	0	0	0	0	0	0	12	0	5	0
cucking	2	.0000	.0219	23.4	0	0	0	0	0	0	0	2	0	2	0	0	0	0	0	0	0	0	0	0	0	0	0	0	0
cuckoo	22	.5589	2.6109	44.2	6	3	1	2	4	4	2	0	6	3	0	7	0	0	0	0	3	0	0	0	0	0	1	2	0
cuckoos	4	.1698	.2267	33.6	0	2	0	0	2	0	0	0	2	0	0	0	0	0	0	0	0	0	0	0	0	0	2	0	0
Cucuface	2	.0000	.0234	23.7	2	0	0	0	0	0	0	0	0	0	0	0	0	0	0	0	0	0	0	0	2	0	0	0	0
cucumber	6	.3902	.5429	37.3	3	0	1	0	2	0	0	0	2	0	0	2	0	0	0	1	0	0	1	0	0	0	0	0	0
cucumbers	15	.6347	1.9770	43.0	3	1	2	1	6	2	0	0	2	1	0	0	0	2	0	4	0	0	0	0	3	1	2	0	0
cud	7	.4542	.7148	38.5	0	2	2	2	0	0	1	0	2	0	0	1	0	0	0	2	0	0	0	0	2	0	0	0	0
cud-chewing	2	.0000	.0394	26.0	0	0	0	0	1	0	1	0	0	0	0	0	0	0	0	2	0	0	0	0	0	0	0	0	0
cuddled	5	.3855	.4777	36.8	0	0	1	3	0	0	0	1	3	0	0	0	0	0	0	0	0	0	0	0	1	0	0	1	0
cudgel	4	.3740	.3661	35.6	0	1	1	1	0	0	1	0	2	0	0	0	0	0	0	0	0	0	0	0	1	0	0	1	0
cue	8	.5379	.8847	39.5	1	0	1	0	2	1	3	0	0	0	0	3	0	0	1	0	1	0	0	0	1	0	0	2	0

5N crumpets
7N crumples
4N crums
3A crunch-crunch-crunched
7F crunches
5A crunchiest
8R crusade's
8F crusader
4R crushers
7D crushing-shed
7L Crust
6Q crustacea
4A crustily
7D crutch/of
7J crwth
8B cryin'
9Q cryogenicist
9Q cryologist
3A cryoton
8Q cryptic
XR crystal-clear
XH crystallizations
9Q crystallizes
9Q crystallizing
6A crystallographer
6A crystallography
6A Crystals
7M Crystolon
7R Cs
6E CS
9H CS2
6G ct
4E CTA
7H Ctenophora
7Q Ctesibius
8E cu
8H CuSO
7R Cuauhtemoc
7B cub-engineer**
7D Cubby
XH cubby-hole
9B cubby-holes
3A cubbyhole
6Q cubical
5Q cubism
7P cubist
8K cubists
6P Cubs'
7N Cuby
4A Cuckoo
7D cuckoo-bird
9D cuckoo's
3A cuddles
3A cuddly
9B cuds
9D cued

Word Type	F	D	U	SFI	3 Gr 3	4 Gr 4	5 Gr 5	6 Gr 6	7 Gr 7	8 Gr 8	9 Gr 9	X UnGr	A Read	B Eng & Gr	C Comp	D Lit	E Math	F Soc Stud	G Spell	H Sci	J Music	K Art	L Home Ec	M Shop	N Lib F	P Lib NF	Q Lib Ref	R Mag	S Rel
cues	13	.3357	.9589	39.8	0	0	0	0	5	1	7	0	0	1	0	8	0	1	0	0	0	0	0	0	0	0	0	3	0
cuff	15	.3095	1.0296	40.1	2	1	0	3	1	4	4	0	2	1	1	0	0	0	0	0	0	0	8	0	0	2	1	0	0
Cuffe	3	.0000	.1370	31.4	0	0	3	0	0	0	0	0	3	0	0	0	0	0	0	0	0	0	0	0	0	0	0	0	0
cuffed	2	.1787	.1174	30.7	0	0	0	1	1	0	0	0	1	0	0	0	0	0	0	0	0	0	0	0	1	0	0	0	0
cuffs	28	.2343	1.5819	42.0	2	5	0	1	1	14	3	2	5	0	0	0	0	1	0	0	1	0	15	0	1	3	1	1	0
Cuhullin	10	.0000	.4568	36.6	0	10	0	0	0	0	0	0	10	0	0	0	0	0	0	0	0	0	0	0	0	0	0	0	0
cuisine	3	.3815	.2534	34.0	0	0	0	0	0	2	0	1	0	0	0	0	0	1	0	0	0	0	0	0	0	1	0	1	0
cul-de-sac	2	.0000	.0914	29.6	0	0	0	0	1	0	1	0	2	0	0	0	0	0	0	0	0	0	0	0	0	0	0	0	0
Cullen	2	.1698	.1133	30.5	0	0	0	0	2	0	0	0	1	0	0	0	0	0	0	0	0	0	0	0	0	0	1	0	0
Cullinan	2	.0000	.0299	24.8	0	0	0	0	0	0	2	0	0	0	0	0	2	0	0	0	0	0	0	0	0	0	0	0	0
culminates	3	.2427	.1822	32.6	0	0	0	0	0	1	0	2	0	0	0	0	0	0	0	2	0	0	0	0	0	0	0	1	0
culminating	5	.4454	.4727	36.7	0	1	1	0	0	0	1	2	0	0	0	0	0	0	0	1	1	0	0	0	0	1	2	0	0
culmination	6	.4634	.5954	37.7	0	0	0	0	1	2	1	2	0	0	0	0	0	1	0	2	1	0	0	0	0	0	0	2	0
culpa	2	.0000	.0914	29.6	0	0	0	2	0	0	0	0	2	0	0	0	0	0	0	0	0	0	0	0	0	0	0	0	0
culprit	9	.4734	.8879	39.5	1	0	0	1	2	0	4	1	0	1	1	0	0	0	0	0	0	0	0	0	1	0	1	5	0
cult	11	.3631	.8691	39.4	0	0	2	0	1	4	2	2	0	0	0	0	0	0	0	0	0	0	0	0	0	3	5	3	0
cultivate	22	.6327	2.8772	44.6	0	2	7	4	5	1	2	1	1	2	0	1	0	12	1	1	0	0	0	0	1	0	1	2	0
cultivated	51	.6754	7.0893	48.5	1	1	13	14	11	4	4	3	6	0	0	1	0	20	0	4	1	0	1	0	1	8	8	1	0
cultivating	13	.5818	1.5827	42.0	1	1	1	4	2	1	3	0	1	0	0	0	0	7	1	0	0	0	1	0	0	1	1	1	0
cultivation	31	.4942	3.2981	45.2	2	2	4	5	8	4	1	5	3	0	0	0	0	11	0	3	0	0	0	0	0	2	10	2	0
cultivator	6	.0000	.2741	34.4	6	0	0	0	0	0	0	0	6	0	0	0	0	0	0	0	0	0	0	0	0	0	0	0	0
cults	3	.1823	.1405	31.5	0	0	0	0	2	0	1	0	0	0	0	0	0	1	0	0	0	0	0	0	0	0	2	0	0
cultural	51	.5465	5.7801	47.6	3	0	10	1	13	7	8	9	0	0	0	0	0	12	0	0	8	0	0	0	0	7	14	10	0
Cultural	3	.1937	.1495	31.7	0	0	0	0	1	1	1	0	0	0	0	0	0	1	0	0	0	0	0	0	0	0	0	2	0
culture	146	.6946	20.550	53.1	18	2	29	10	37	26	20	4	3	1	0	4	0	37	0	8	17	4	1	0	0	13	42	16	0
Culture	6	.3437	.4532	36.6	0	0	3	0	1	2	0	0	0	0	0	0	2	0	0	0	0	0	0	0	1	0	3	0	0
cultured	12	.5845	1.4503	41.6	0	1	6	1	1	0	3	0	0	0	1	2	0	2	0	3	1	0	0	0	0	3	0	0	0
cultures	39	.5716	4.6002	46.6	0	1	10	7	8	2	9	2	0	1	0	0	0	8	0	4	8	0	0	0	0	1	11	6	0
culturist	2	.0000	.0045	16.5	0	0	0	0	0	0	2	0	0	0	2	0	0	0	0	0	0	0	0	0	0	0	0	0	0
culvert	4	.0000	.1827	32.6	0	4	0	0	0	0	0	0	4	0	0	0	0	0	0	0	0	0	0	0	0	0	0	0	0
cum	3	.2187	.1555	31.9	0	0	0	0	0	3	0	0	0	2	0	0	0	0	0	0	0	0	0	0	0	0	0	1	0
Cumberland	19	.5633	2.3210	43.7	1	3	9	4	0	1	0	1	7	0	0	1	0	3	0	0	0	0	0	0	0	6	1	1	0
Cumberlands	4	.1112	.1666	32.2	0	0	4	0	0	0	0	0	1	0	0	0	0	0	0	0	0	0	0	0	0	3	0	0	0
cumbersome	8	.5603	.9251	39.7	0	0	1	0	4	2	1	0	0	0	0	1	1	0	0	1	0	0	0	0	1	0	3	1	0
cumin	2	.2437	.1129	30.5	0	0	0	1	0	0	0	1	0	0	0	0	0	0	0	0	0	0	0	0	0	0	1	1	0
Cummings	2	.2411	.1091	30.4	0	1	0	0	0	1	0	0	0	0	0	1	0	0	0	0	1	0	0	0	0	0	0	0	0
cummingtonite	2	.0000	.0209	23.2	0	0	0	0	0	0	2	0	0	0	0	0	0	0	0	0	0	0	0	0	0	0	2	0	0
cumulative	12	.4525	1.1401	40.6	1	2	1	1	0	4	3	0	0	0	0	0	4	0	1	0	5	0	0	0	0	1	1	0	0
cumulonimbus	4	.0000	.0789	29.0	0	0	0	2	1	0	1	0	0	0	0	0	0	0	0	4	0	0	0	0	0	0	0	0	0
cumulus	22	.1913	1.1610	40.6	8	0	0	4	5	0	5	0	0	0	0	0	0	0	0	18	0	0	0	0	0	4	0	0	0
cuneiform	6	.4017	.5092	37.1	0	0	0	0	2	4	0	0	0	2	0	0	0	1	2	0	0	1	0	0	0	0	0	0	0
cunning	43	.7790	6.7964	48.3	1	1	5	7	18	8	2	1	14	1	0	9	0	1	1	1	0	1	1	0	5	3	4	2	0
Cunningham	2	.0000	.0215	23.3	0	0	0	0	0	0	2	0	0	0	0	2	0	0	0	0	0	0	0	0	0	0	0	0	0
cunningly	4	.2708	.2760	34.4	0	0	0	0	1	2	1	0	1	0	0	2	0	1	0	0	0	0	0	0	0	0	0	0	0
cup	364	.6256	47.278	56.7	68	73	44	19	49	78	27	6	76	7	1	24	29	10	11	53	4	0	75	1	22	17	8	26	0
Cup	6	.2197	.4180	36.2	0	0	0	0	4	0	2	0	4	0	0	0	0	0	0	0	0	0	0	0	0	0	2	0	0
cup-shaped	3	.3160	.2007	33.0	0	0	0	1	1	1	0	0	0	0	0	0	0	0	0	0	1	0	0	1	0	0	1	0	0
cupboard	38	.6418	5.0524	47.0	6	7	8	5	1	5	6	0	9	1	2	8	0	0	0	1	0	0	3	0	7	7	0	0	0
cupboards	14	.4267	1.3401	41.3	4	3	4	0	0	1	2	0	4	0	0	1	0	1	0	0	0	0	2	0	6	0	0	0	0
cupcake	2	.1648	.0800	29.0	0	0	0	0	1	0	0	1	0	0	0	0	1	0	0	0	0	0	1	0	0	0	0	0	0
cupcakes	14	.2831	.9187	39.6	11	0	0	0	0	0	1	2	0	0	0	0	12	0	0	0	0	0	1	0	0	0	0	1	0
cupful	6	.4336	.5836	37.7	3	0	1	0	1	1	0	0	1	0	0	1	0	0	0	3	0	0	0	0	0	0	0	1	0
Cupid	13	.3127	.9087	39.6	0	7	0	5	0	0	1	0	0	7	0	1	0	0	0	0	0	0	0	0	0	5	0	0	0
cupola	8	.3412	.7023	38.5	5	0	2	0	0	1	0	0	5	0	0	0	0	0	0	0	0	0	0	1	0	0	2	0	0
cupped	16	.5066	1.7689	42.5	1	1	1	3	10	0	0	0	5	0	0	4	0	0	0	0	0	0	0	0	4	1	0	2	0
Cuppere	2	.0000	.0389	25.9	0	0	0	2	0	0	0	0	0	0	0	0	0	2	0	0	0	0	0	0	0	0	0	0	0
cupping	3	.3450	.2505	34.0	0	1	1	0	1	0	0	0	1	0	0	0	0	0	0	0	0	0	0	0	1	1	0	0	0
cuprammonium	2	.0000	.0394	26.0	0	0	0	0	0	0	2	0	0	0	0	0	0	0	0	2	0	0	0	0	0	0	0	0	0
cups	128	.6525	17.308	52.4	37	22	13	13	13	18	10	2	31	3	0	3	41	0	0	5	2	0	17	2	6	10	3	5	0
cur	2	.0000	.0914	29.6	0	0	1	0	1	0	0	0	2	0	0	0	0	0	0	0	0	0	0	0	0	0	0	0	0
Curabel	4	.0000	.0579	27.6	4	0	0	0	0	0	0	0	0	0	0	0	0	0	0	0	0	0	0	0	0	4	0	0	0
curator	4	.3512	.3114	34.9	0	0	1	2	0	0	1	0	0	0	0	0	0	0	0	1	0	0	0	0	0	0	1	2	0
curb	33	.7015	4.7672	46.8	3	2	7	5	4	2	10	0	10	4	2	4	0	4	0	0	0	0	0	0	3	1	3	2	0
curbed	2	.0000	.0243	23.9	0	0	0	0	1	0	1	0	0	0	0	0	0	0	0	0	0	0	0	0	0	0	0	2	0
curbing	3	.2143	.1568	32.0	0	0	0	0	2	0	1	0	0	0	0	0	0	0	0	0	0	0	0	0	0	1	0	2	0
curbs	5	.3798	.4228	36.3	1	1	0	1	1	0	1	0	0	0	0	0	0	2	0	0	0	0	0	0	0	2	0	1	0
curbside	3	.2279	.2143	33.3	0	0	0	2	1	0	0	0	2	0	0	0	0	0	0	0	0	0	0	0	0	0	0	1	0
curbstone	2	.0000	.0045	16.5	0	0	0	1	0	1	0	0	0	0	2	0	0	0	0	0	0	0	0	0	0	0	0	0	0
curbstones	2	.2427	.1152	30.6	1	0	0	1	0	0	0	0	0	0	0	0	0	0	0	0	0	0	0	0	1	1	0	0	0
curd	7	.5558	.8373	39.2	1	0	3	1	1	1	0	0	2	1	0	1	0	2	0	0	0	0	0	0	1	0	0	0	0
curdle	3	.1970	.1504	31.8	0	0	0	0	3	0	0	0	0	0	0	0	0	0	0	2	0	0	1	0	0	0	0	0	0
curds	18	.0000	.3549	35.5	0	0	0	0	18	0	0	0	0	0	0	0	0	0	0	18	0	0	0	0	0	0	0	0	0
cure	60	.5944	7.5370	48.8	7	9	8	5	18	4	7	2	17	1	0	5	0	0	2	8	2	0	2	0	5	5	7	5	1
cure-alls	2	.2160	.1362	31.3	0	0	0	0	1	0	1	0	1	0	0	0	0	0	0	1	0	0	0	0	0	0	0	0	0
cured	24	.5302	2.7329	44.4	2	1	6	4	5	0	6	0	7	1	0	2	0	1	0	2	0	0	5	0	2	0	3	1	0
cures	10	.6300	1.3376	41.3	0	0	2	1	2	0	3	2	4	1	0	1	0	0	0	2	0	0	0	0	0	1	1	0	0
curfew	4	.4535	.4003	36.0	0	0	0	1	2	1	0	0	1	0	0	1	0	0	0	0	0	0	0	0	1	0	0	1	0
Curie	24	.5272	2.7316	44.4	1	0	0	11	1	3	1	7	4	1	0	0	0	1	0	10	0	0	0	0	0	6	2	0	0
Curie's	4	.3017	.3031	34.8	0	0	0	1	0	1	0	2	1	0	0	0	0	0	0	1	0	0	0	0	0	2	0	0	0
Curies	9	.3818	.7900	39.0	0	0	0	5	2	1	1	0	1	2	0	0	0	1	0	5	0	0	0	0	0	0	0	0	0
curing	7	.4240	.6968	38.4	0	0	1	1	2	2	0	1	3	0	0	0	0	1	0	1	0	0	0	0	0	0	2	0	0
curiosities	2	.2401	.1133	30.5	0	0	1	0	1	0	0	0	0	0	0	0	0	0	0	0	0	0	0	0	0	1	1	0	0
curiosity	78	.7828	12.374	50.9	5	7	9	15	14	7	12	9	19	0	0	5	2	4	1	19	0	2	0	0	6	6	8	6	0
curious	189	.8509	32.225	55.1	40	17	25	26	42	15	16	8	48	8	2	18	3	13	5	30	2	0	0	0	25	16	7	12	0
curious-looking	2	.0000	.0914	29.6	0	0	0	1	1	0	0	0	2	0	0	0	0	0	0	0	0	0	0	0	0	0	0	0	0
curiously	49	.7238	7.2677	48.6	4	5	4	7	15	4	10	0	15	0	1	9	0	1	2	0	0	0	0	0	6	7	5	3	0
curl	26	.5320	2.9150	44.6	7	3	2	4	1	5	3	1	4	0	0	1	0	0	0	5	0	2	6	0	2	4	0	2	0
curled	73	.7767	11.535	50.6	11	18	8	8	17	5	5	1	27	2	1	10	0	0	0	1	0	1	3	0	7	13	1	7	0
curlers	6	.3436	.4468	36.5	0	0	1	0	3	1	0	1	0	0	0	0	0	0	0	0	0	0	1	0	1	0	0	4	0
curlews	2	.1698	.1133	30.5	0	0	0	0	1	1	0	0	1	0	0	0	0	0	0	0	0	0	0	0	0	0	1	0	0
curlier	2	.2412	.1141	30.6	1	0	0	0	1	0	0	0	0	1	0	0	0	0	0	0	0	0	0	0	0	1	0	0	0
curling	20	.5544	2.3924	43.8	3	5	2	2	4	1	3	0	8	0	0	6	0	0	0	0	0	1	2	0	0	2	0	1	0
curls	42	.5443	4.9007	46.9	3	9	1	9	6	8	5	1	13	1	0	3	0	1	0	2	0	0	8	0	7	4	1	2	0
curly	44	.6538	5.9518	47.7	16	5	6	3	8	5	1	0	10	1	0	5	0	0	0	1	3	0	3	0	5	15	0	1	0
Curly	28	.1303	1.1637	40.7	1	0	0	6	16	0	5	0	6	0	0	21	0	0	0	0	0	0	0	0	0	1	0	0	0

XR Cues
6A cuffing
7Q Cugnot
7Q Cugnot's
4A Cuhullin's
8F cul-de-sacs
7R cul-ti-va-ted
9Q Culdee
8F culinary
7Q culled
5J Culloden
5J Culloden's
6A Cully
7D culminated
7Q Culp's
6R culprits
5P cultivable
9F cultivates
5R cultivators
3P cultive
7R culturally
9H culturing
4B cultus
4N culverins
4N cumbered
8K cumming's
8K cummings
3C Cummins
7N Cunard
9P CunardLine
7Q Cunha
7N cupboard-stairway
6N cupfuls
9L cupids
4A cuplike
3B cupples
3A cuprite
9D cups'n
7R curacas
7N curassavian
3P curassow
7D curative
7A curdled
9L curdling
6N Curdy
8F cure-all
7P cure's
7L curealls
9D cureless
6H Curies'
XR curl-consistency
3P curled-up
9D Curly's
4P Curlytop

Word Type	F	D	U	SFI	3 Gr 3	4 Gr 4	5 Gr 5	6 Gr 6	7 Gr 7	8 Gr 8	9 Gr 9	X UnGr	A Read	B Eng & Gr	C Comp	D Lit	E Math	F Soc Stud	G Spell	H Sci	J Music	K Art	L Home Ec	M Shop	N Lib F	P Lib NF	Q Lib Ref	R Mag	S Rel
currencies	9	.2733	.5589	37.5	0	0	2	1	5	1	0	0	0	0	0	0	0	0	0	0	0	0	0	0	0	2	6	1	0
currency	19	.4389	1.7621	42.5	0	0	1	2	5	6	4	1	0	0	0	0	0	3	0	0	0	0	2	0	0	0	9	5	0
current	473	.6446	62.594	58.0	8	43	55	70	120	134	31	12	50	5	4	10	2	19	5	135	36	1	4	79	14	27	42	40	0
Current	20	.5026	2.2224	43.5	0	4	5	1	6	1	3	0	5	2	0	0	0	3	0	9	0	0	0	0	0	0	1	0	0
current's	3	.2197	.2090	33.2	0	0	0	2	1	0	0	0	2	0	0	0	0	0	0	0	0	0	0	0	0	0	1	0	0
currently	15	.5207	1.6372	42.1	1	0	0	0	8	3	3	0	1	0	0	0	0	1	0	1	1	0	0	1	0	0	2	8	0
currents	171	.6720	23.709	53.7	12	8	26	32	44	25	23	1	23	0	0	2	1	17	0	71	1	0	0	4	2	9	27	14	0
curricula	2	.2437	.1129	30.5	0	0	0	0	0	0	2	0	0	0	0	0	0	0	0	0	0	0	0	0	0	0	1	1	0
curriculum	10	.2977	.6670	38.2	1	0	0	1	0	3	5	0	0	0	0	1	0	0	0	0	0	0	0	0	0	0	2	7	0
curried	6	.3542	.4600	36.6	3	0	0	1	0	2	0	0	0	0	0	1	0	0	0	0	0	0	0	0	2	0	3	0	0
curries	3	.0000	.0365	25.6	0	0	0	1	0	0	0	2	0	0	0	0	0	0	0	0	0	0	0	0	0	0	0	3	0
curry	13	.1256	.4904	36.9	0	1	0	1	0	0	0	11	1	0	0	0	0	0	0	0	0	0	0	0	0	1	0	11	0
currycomb	2	.2427	.1152	30.6	0	1	0	0	0	1	0	0	0	0	0	0	0	0	0	0	0	0	0	0	1	1	0	0	0
currying	3	.2196	.1554	31.9	0	0	0	0	1	1	1	0	0	0	0	2	0	0	0	0	0	0	0	0	1	0	0	0	0
curse	13	.5967	1.6565	42.2	0	1	0	0	6	3	1	2	4	0	0	1	0	1	0	3	0	0	0	0	0	3	0	1	0
cursed	13	.5566	1.5399	41.9	0	0	3	3	6	0	0	1	3	0	0	2	0	0	0	1	0	0	0	0	4	2	0	1	0
curses	8	.3390	.6603	38.2	0	0	1	1	2	2	2	0	3	0	0	3	0	0	0	0	0	0	0	0	2	0	0	0	0
cursing	5	.2251	.2966	34.7	0	0	0	0	2	3	0	0	1	0	0	3	0	1	0	0	0	0	0	0	0	0	0	0	0
cursive	2	.1840	.0808	29.1	0	1	0	0	0	1	0	0	0	0	1	0	0	0	1	0	0	0	0	0	0	0	0	0	0
cursy	2	.0000	.0215	23.3	0	0	0	0	0	0	2	0	0	0	0	2	0	0	0	0	0	0	0	0	0	0	0	0	0
curt	4	.3683	.3188	35.0	0	0	0	1	2	1	0	0	0	0	0	1	0	0	0	0	0	0	0	0	2	0	0	1	0
curtailed	2	.2351	.1166	30.7	0	0	0	0	0	1	1	0	0	0	0	0	0	1	0	0	0	0	0	0	0	0	0	1	0
curtain	80	.8188	13.150	51.2	6	7	11	18	15	8	8	7	15	3	2	11	0	10	2	7	5	0	0	0	14	5	3	3	0
Curtain	3	.2444	.1814	32.6	1	0	0	0	0	1	1	0	0	0	0	0	0	2	0	0	0	0	0	0	0	0	1	0	0
CURTAIN	4	.0000	.0469	26.7	0	0	0	4	0	0	0	0	0	0	0	0	0	0	0	0	0	0	0	0	4	0	0	0	0
curtained	5	.3888	.4322	36.4	0	1	0	1	2	1	0	0	1	0	0	2	0	0	0	0	0	0	1	0	1	0	0	0	0
curtains	49	.7243	7.3751	48.7	11	8	5	6	13	4	2	0	26	0	1	8	2	1	0	0	2	0	0	0	3	3	1	2	0
Curtis	19	.5153	2.0574	43.1	0	9	2	0	1	5	1	1	1	1	0	0	0	0	0	0	1	0	0	0	0	9	3	4	0
curtly	2	.0000	.0215	23.3	0	0	0	0	1	0	1	0	0	0	0	2	0	0	0	0	0	0	0	0	0	0	0	0	0
curtsies	3	.3873	.2495	34.0	0	0	0	0	0	1	1	1	0	0	0	1	0	0	0	0	0	0	0	0	1	0	0	1	0
curtsy	4	.3702	.3170	35.0	0	0	0	0	1	1	2	0	0	0	0	2	0	0	1	0	0	0	0	0	1	0	0	0	0
curvature	4	.2353	.2382	33.8	0	0	1	0	0	0	2	1	0	0	0	0	0	0	0	3	0	0	0	0	0	0	1	0	0
curve	174	.7883	27.545	54.4	29	30	20	15	27	22	24	7	24	8	11	9	44	2	2	17	2	6	4	16	4	7	9	9	0
curved	154	.8134	25.075	54.0	16	20	16	17	38	26	18	3	21	0	3	7	11	9	3	23	7	9	10	13	9	11	6	12	0
curves	68	.5566	7.8629	49.0	9	9	7	8	9	15	10	1	8	0	1	1	15	3	0	8	1	12	2	11	1	3	2	0	0
curving	22	.4777	2.3655	43.7	3	7	3	4	3	1	1	0	9	1	0	1	0	2	0	3	0	3	0	0	1	1	0	1	0
curvy	2	.2433	.1158	30.6	1	0	0	0	0	0	1	0	0	0	0	0	0	0	0	0	0	0	0	0	0	1	0	1	0
cushion	16	.6732	2.1980	43.4	0	2	3	1	4	1	5	0	3	0	1	0	0	0	2	0	0	0	2	1	0	2	3	2	0
cushioned	2	.0000	.0394	26.0	0	0	1	0	0	0	0	1	0	0	0	0	0	0	0	2	0	0	0	0	0	0	0	0	0
cushions	16	.7060	2.3160	43.6	2	4	0	1	6	1	2	0	4	1	1	2	0	2	0	0	0	0	0	0	1	1	2	2	0
Cusi	6	.0000	.2741	34.4	0	0	6	0	0	0	0	0	6	0	0	0	0	0	0	0	0	0	0	0	0	0	0	0	0
Cusi's	2	.0000	.0914	29.6	0	0	2	0	0	0	0	0	2	0	0	0	0	0	0	0	0	0	0	0	0	0	0	0	0
cuspids	4	.0000	.0789	29.0	0	0	4	0	0	0	0	0	0	0	0	0	0	0	0	4	0	0	0	0	0	0	0	0	0
cuss	2	.1497	.1046	30.2	0	0	1	0	0	1	0	0	1	0	0	0	0	0	1	0	0	0	0	0	0	0	0	0	0
cussing	2	.2443	.1130	30.5	0	0	0	0	2	0	0	0	0	0	0	1	0	0	0	0	0	0	0	0	1	0	0	0	0
custard	6	.2133	.3150	35.0	1	1	1	0	1	0	2	0	1	1	0	0	0	0	0	0	0	0	3	0	0	1	0	0	0
Custard	14	.3468	1.2016	40.8	7	0	6	0	0	0	1	0	6	0	0	0	0	0	0	0	0	0	1	0	0	7	0	0	0
custards	2	.0000	.0064	18.1	0	0	0	0	1	1	0	0	0	0	0	0	0	0	0	0	0	0	2	0	0	0	0	0	0
Custer	34	.3287	2.5079	44.0	0	24	0	6	2	2	0	0	0	6	0	3	0	1	0	0	0	0	0	0	0	24	0	0	0
Custer's	3	.2379	.1705	32.3	0	2	0	0	1	0	0	0	0	0	0	1	0	0	0	0	0	0	0	0	0	2	0	0	0
Custis	8	.1117	.2829	34.5	0	7	0	0	0	1	0	0	0	0	0	0	0	1	0	0	0	0	0	0	0	7	0	0	0
custody	4	.3060	.2924	34.7	0	0	2	1	0	0	1	0	1	0	0	0	0	0	1	0	0	0	0	0	0	0	2	0	0
custom	97	.8459	16.410	52.2	7	7	6	9	32	12	15	9	19	9	0	10	2	14	0	1	8	2	1	0	8	11	3	9	0
Custom	3	.2143	.1568	32.0	0	0	0	1	2	0	0	0	0	0	0	0	0	0	0	0	0	0	0	0	0	1	0	2	0
custom-made	2	.2437	.1129	30.5	0	0	0	0	1	0	1	0	0	0	0	0	0	0	0	0	0	0	0	0	0	0	1	1	0
customarily	7	.5452	.7978	39.0	0	0	1	0	2	1	3	0	1	2	0	0	0	0	0	0	0	0	1	0	1	0	1	1	0
customary	26	.6756	3.5408	45.5	0	2	0	0	11	6	5	2	0	2	0	2	4	2	0	1	1	0	5	2	3	1	2	1	0
customer	57	.6528	7.6684	48.8	8	8	5	8	7	8	10	3	12	0	0	13	2	2	1	0	0	0	8	1	3	7	1	7	0
customer's	4	.3766	.3696	35.7	0	1	0	0	2	0	0	1	2	0	0	0	0	0	0	0	0	0	0	0	0	1	0	1	0
customers	71	.8227	11.811	50.7	22	7	7	5	7	18	4	1	28	2	1	6	4	11	0	1	1	0	2	0	1	10	1	3	0
customs	145	.7938	23.131	53.6	10	15	15	51	27	14	11	2	11	6	0	2	0	54	2	10	11	2	2	0	2	8	16	19	0
Customs	3	.0000	.0583	27.7	0	0	0	0	0	0	3	0	0	0	0	0	0	3	0	0	0	0	0	0	0	0	0	0	0
cut	1757	.8201	289.37	64.6	366	242	206	194	316	200	199	34	411	29	15	71	156	145	27	180	33	53	112	156	89	132	42	106	0
cut-and-dried	2	.2303	.1079	30.3	0	0	0	0	1	1	0	0	0	0	0	0	0	0	0	0	1	0	0	0	0	1	0	0	0
cut-and-paste	2	.0000	.0037	15.7	2	0	0	0	0	0	0	0	0	0	0	0	0	0	0	0	0	2	0	0	0	0	0	0	0
cut-and-try	2	.2437	.1129	30.5	0	0	0	0	1	0	1	0	0	0	0	0	0	0	0	0	0	0	0	0	0	0	1	1	0
cut-off	5	.2625	.2852	34.6	0	0	0	0	5	0	0	0	0	0	0	2	0	0	0	0	0	0	0	2	0	0	1	0	0
cut-out	8	.3169	.5628	37.5	2	3	1	0	1	0	0	1	1	0	1	0	0	0	0	0	0	3	0	0	0	2	0	1	0
cut-paper	9	.0000	.0166	22.2	5	3	1	0	0	0	0	0	0	0	0	0	0	0	0	0	0	9	0	0	0	0	0	0	0
cut-up	3	.1980	.1505	31.8	1	1	0	0	0	0	1	0	0	0	0	0	0	2	0	0	0	0	1	0	0	0	0	0	0
cutability	2	.0000	.0243	23.9	0	0	0	0	0	0	0	2	0	0	0	0	0	0	0	0	0	0	0	0	0	0	0	2	0
cutaway	3	.3454	.2542	34.1	0	2	0	0	1	0	0	0	1	0	0	0	0	1	0	0	0	0	0	0	0	0	0	1	0
cutback	3	.2411	.1667	32.2	0	0	0	0	0	1	2	0	0	0	0	0	0	0	0	0	1	0	0	0	0	0	0	2	0
Cutchogue	2	.0000	.0209	23.2	0	0	0	0	0	0	2	0	0	0	0	0	0	0	0	0	0	0	0	0	0	0	2	0	0
cute	27	.6883	3.8556	45.9	3	5	6	3	3	0	6	1	10	4	0	1	0	0	1	0	1	0	0	0	3	2	0	5	0
cutest	6	.3080	.4591	36.6	0	0	3	2	0	1	0	0	2	1	0	0	0	0	0	0	0	0	0	0	0	0	0	3	0
Cuthbert	2	.0000	.0234	23.7	0	0	0	0	2	0	0	0	0	0	0	0	0	0	0	0	0	0	0	0	2	0	0	0	0
cuticle	5	.3691	.4157	36.2	1	3	0	0	1	0	0	0	0	0	0	0	0	0	0	3	0	0	0	0	0	1	1	0	0
Cutie	4	.0000	.1827	32.6	0	4	0	0	0	0	0	0	4	0	0	0	0	0	0	0	0	0	0	0	0	0	0	0	0
cutlass	5	.4661	.5245	37.2	1	0	2	1	1	0	0	0	2	0	0	1	0	0	0	0	1	0	0	0	0	1	0	0	0
Cutler	4	.0000	.0579	27.6	0	4	0	0	0	0	0	0	0	0	0	0	0	0	0	0	0	0	0	0	0	4	0	0	0
cutlery	4	.3154	.3014	34.8	2	0	0	0	1	0	1	0	1	0	0	0	0	1	0	0	0	0	0	1	0	0	1	0	0
cutoff	6	.2184	.3518	35.5	0	2	0	1	1	0	2	0	2	0	0	0	0	0	0	0	0	0	0	2	0	0	0	2	0
cutoffs	2	.0000	.0243	23.9	0	0	0	1	0	0	1	0	0	0	0	0	0	0	0	0	0	0	0	0	0	0	0	2	0
cutout	3	.0000	.0591	27.7	2	1	0	0	0	0	0	0	0	0	0	0	0	0	0	3	0	0	0	0	0	0	0	0	0
cutouts	7	.4786	.6987	38.4	1	4	0	0	0	1	1	0	0	0	0	0	0	0	0	1	0	1	0	1	0	2	0	2	0
cuts	147	.6867	20.477	53.1	19	14	12	14	38	19	25	6	12	4	0	4	12	12	0	13	6	1	18	20	2	19	6	18	0
cutter	38	.2049	1.9131	42.8	1	4	3	2	1	13	13	1	6	0	0	1	0	2	0	1	0	0	1	21	0	4	0	2	0
Cutter	6	.1787	.3521	35.5	0	6	0	0	0	0	0	0	3	0	0	0	0	0	0	0	0	0	0	0	3	0	0	0	0
Cutter's	2	.1787	.1174	30.7	0	2	0	0	0	0	0	0	1	0	0	0	0	0	0	0	0	0	0	0	1	0	0	0	0
cutters	18	.2916	1.1888	40.8	1	2	1	3	8	1	2	0	3	0	0	1	0	0	0	0	0	1	0	9	0	2	2	0	0
cutthroat	5	.0000	.0608	27.8	0	0	0	0	5	0	0	0	0	0	0	0	0	0	0	0	0	0	0	0	0	0	0	5	0
cutthroats	6	.0706	.1822	32.6	0	0	0	0	6	0	0	0	1	0	0	0	0	0	0	0	0	0	0	0	0	0	0	5	0
cuttin'	2	.1717	.1142	30.6	0	0	0	1	1	0	0	0	1	0	0	1	0	0	0	0	0	0	0	0	0	0	0	0	0

7N currant
5N currant-bunny
7A currants
5E currency-breakdown
6H current-carrying
6H current-detector
8B current-events
6A Currey
9Q curriculums
XR currie
5A Currier
9D currish
XR Curry
9D cursed'st
XH cursings
7B cursives
8F curtail
8F curtailing
9R curtails
8L curtaining
4N curtiosity
6N curtsey
8D curtseys
4P curtsied
3E Curve
6H CURVED
7R curved-blade
3A curveting
7R cushiony
4N Cuspid
4N Cuspidor
8A cuspidors
5H cusps
7R cussed
5R cussedness
4P Custers
4K custodian
9B custodians
8N custom's
4R Customer
6C customers'
6F customhouse
7A customize
6F Cut
7D CUT
7N cut-bank
3A cut-cut-a-cut
7L cut-marshmallows
6A cut-out-work
4P cut-outs
XR cut-over
6A cut-steel
9Q cut-stone
4N cutbanks
7N Cuthbert's
5R cuticles
4A cutie
4R cutlasses
7B cutlets
4N cutter-rigged
6A cutter's
4N cutterigsloop

Word Type	F	D	U	SFI	3 Gr 3	4 Gr 4	5 Gr 5	6 Gr 6	7 Gr 7	8 Gr 8	9 Gr 9	X UnGr	A Read	B Eng & Gr	C Comp	D Lit	E Math	F Soc Stud	G Spell	H Sci	J Music	K Art	L Home Ec	M Shop	N Lib F	P Lib NF	Q Lib Ref	R Mag	S Rel
cutting	339	.5634	39.687	56.0	22	17	34	33	94	60	72	7	51	5	2	8	10	25	2	24	9	4	35	92	13	23	11	25	0
cutting-plane	2	.0000	.0050	17.0	0	0	0	0	0	0	2	0	0	0	0	0	0	0	0	0	0	0	0	2	0	0	0	0	0
cuttings	18	.4870	1.8793	42.7	3	2	0	6	5	2	0	0	0	0	0	0	0	2	0	10	0	0	0	0	2	1	3	0	0
cuttlefish	2	.2408	.1204	30.8	1	1	0	0	0	0	0	0	0	0	0	0	0	1	0	0	0	0	0	0	0	1	0	0	0
cutworm	2	.0000	.0914	29.6	0	2	0	0	0	0	0	0	2	0	0	0	0	0	0	0	0	0	0	0	0	0	0	0	0
cutworms	5	.1875	.3065	34.9	0	2	0	2	0	0	0	1	2	0	0	0	0	0	0	3	0	0	0	0	0	0	0	0	0
Cuvier	3	.0000	.0591	27.7	0	0	0	0	3	0	0	0	0	0	0	0	0	0	0	3	0	0	0	0	0	0	0	0	0
Cuyloga	3	.0000	.0322	25.1	0	0	0	0	3	0	0	0	0	0	0	3	0	0	0	0	0	0	0	0	0	0	0	0	0
Cuzco	8	.4028	.7297	38.6	0	3	1	1	3	0	0	0	1	0	0	0	0	5	0	0	1	0	0	0	0	0	1	0	0
cw	3	.2060	.1430	31.6	0	0	2	0	0	0	0	1	0	1	0	0	0	0	2	0	0	0	0	0	0	0	0	0	0
cwen	2	.2408	.1091	30.4	0	0	1	0	0	1	0	0	0	1	0	0	0	0	1	0	0	0	0	0	0	0	0	0	0
cwt	2	.0000	.0243	23.9	0	0	0	0	0	0	0	2	0	0	0	0	0	0	0	0	0	0	0	0	0	0	0	2	0
CX	2	.0000	.0299	24.8	0	0	0	2	0	0	0	0	0	0	0	0	2	0	0	0	0	0	0	0	0	0	0	0	0
cybernetics	2	.0000	.0299	24.8	0	0	0	0	0	0	2	0	0	0	0	0	2	0	0	0	0	0	0	0	0	0	0	0	0
Cyclades	2	.0000	.0209	23.2	0	0	0	0	0	2	0	0	0	0	0	0	0	0	0	0	0	0	0	0	0	0	2	0	0
cyclamate	2	.0000	.0243	23.9	0	0	0	0	0	2	0	0	0	0	0	0	0	0	0	0	0	0	0	0	0	0	0	2	0
cyclamates	4	.2346	.2332	33.7	0	0	0	0	2	2	0	0	0	0	0	0	0	0	0	2	0	0	0	0	0	0	0	2	0
cycle	125	.6410	16.514	52.2	4	28	6	12	34	20	12	9	4	2	0	2	1	6	1	71	3	0	0	5	1	2	19	8	0
cycles	34	.5977	4.1939	46.2	0	2	1	2	14	9	2	4	1	0	0	0	0	1	0	12	8	0	1	0	0	1	4	6	0
cyclic	2	.0000	.0209	23.2	0	0	0	0	2	0	0	0	0	0	0	0	0	0	0	0	0	0	0	0	0	0	2	0	0
cycling	2	.1814	.1187	30.7	0	0	0	0	0	2	0	0	1	0	0	0	0	0	0	0	0	0	0	0	0	0	0	1	0
cyclists	2	.2437	.1129	30.5	0	1	0	0	1	0	0	0	0	0	0	0	0	0	0	0	0	0	0	0	0	0	1	1	0
cyclone	11	.4715	1.1483	40.6	0	1	1	3	2	2	2	0	3	0	0	4	0	0	0	2	0	0	0	0	0	1	1	0	0
Cyclone	11	.3176	.8678	39.4	0	0	0	0	7	4	0	0	4	0	0	0	0	0	0	0	0	0	0	0	5	0	0	2	0
Cyclone's	2	.0000	.0234	23.7	0	0	0	0	2	0	0	0	0	0	0	0	0	0	0	0	0	0	0	0	2	0	0	0	0
cyclones	6	.4298	.5808	37.6	2	1	0	0	0	0	3	0	1	0	0	0	0	0	0	3	0	0	0	0	0	1	1	0	0
cyclonic	3	.1650	.1684	32.3	0	0	0	0	1	2	0	0	1	0	0	0	0	0	0	2	0	0	0	0	0	0	0	0	0
Cyclops	10	.3033	.7698	38.9	0	0	3	0	7	0	0	0	4	0	0	0	0	0	1	0	0	0	0	0	5	0	0	0	0
cyclotron	5	.2028	.2557	34.1	0	0	0	3	0	0	2	0	0	0	0	0	0	0	0	2	0	0	0	0	0	0	3	0	0
Cygnus	2	.0000	.0394	26.0	0	0	0	0	0	1	0	1	0	0	0	0	0	0	0	2	0	0	0	0	0	0	0	0	0
cylinder	116	.6846	16.122	52.1	8	3	11	8	38	19	25	4	3	0	0	0	33	2	0	27	18	1	0	9	4	3	10	6	0
cylinders	35	.6968	4.9458	46.9	7	1	5	3	10	4	5	0	2	0	1	0	4	1	0	6	5	0	0	3	0	7	5	1	0
cylindrical	19	.3978	1.5944	42.0	0	0	1	3	3	3	9	0	1	0	0	0	2	0	0	2	1	2	0	8	1	0	1	1	0
cymbal	7	.0000	.0566	27.5	1	2	0	1	1	1	1	0	0	0	0	0	0	0	0	0	7	0	0	0	0	0	0	0	0
cymbals	19	.3666	1.5141	41.8	4	4	0	5	4	0	2	0	1	0	0	1	0	2	0	0	11	0	0	0	0	0	2	2	0
Cymbeline	2	.0000	.0219	23.4	0	0	0	0	2	0	0	0	0	2	0	0	0	0	0	0	0	0	0	0	0	0	0	0	0
cynical	3	.3769	.2484	34.0	0	0	0	0	0	2	1	0	0	0	0	0	0	1	0	0	0	0	0	0	0	0	1	1	0
cynically	2	.2427	.1152	30.6	0	0	0	0	1	1	0	0	0	0	0	0	0	0	0	0	0	0	0	0	1	1	0	0	0
cynicism	2	.0000	.0243	23.9	0	0	0	0	0	1	1	0	0	0	0	0	0	0	0	0	0	0	0	0	0	0	0	2	0
Cynthia	12	.6291	1.5537	41.9	1	1	1	3	2	0	3	1	2	3	1	1	2	0	1	0	0	1	0	0	0	0	0	1	0
Cynthia's	3	.2665	.1776	32.5	1	0	0	1	0	0	1	0	0	0	1	1	1	0	0	0	0	0	0	0	0	0	0	0	0
cypress	15	.5846	1.8663	42.7	2	0	1	4	2	6	0	0	5	0	0	1	0	1	0	0	1	1	0	0	4	2	0	0	0
cypresses	2	.2437	.1129	30.5	0	0	0	0	2	0	0	0	0	0	0	0	0	0	0	0	0	0	0	0	0	0	1	1	0
Cyprus	6	.1501	.2421	33.8	1	0	2	0	0	0	3	0	1	1	0	0	0	0	0	0	0	3	0	0	0	1	0	0	0
Cyrano	8	.3415	.6117	37.9	0	1	0	0	0	3	0	4	0	0	0	0	0	0	3	4	0	0	0	0	0	0	1	0	0
Cyril	5	.2251	.2567	34.1	0	0	0	0	3	2	0	0	0	0	0	2	0	0	3	0	0	0	0	0	0	0	0	0	0
Cyrillic	3	.0000	.0243	23.9	0	0	0	0	1	2	0	0	0	0	0	0	0	0	3	0	0	0	0	0	0	0	0	0	0
Cyrus	93	.1796	4.6008	46.6	0	82	7	0	1	3	0	0	7	0	0	0	0	10	0	0	1	0	0	0	0	75	0	0	0
Cyrus's	3	.1409	.1472	31.7	0	3	0	0	0	0	0	0	1	0	0	0	0	0	0	0	0	0	0	0	0	2	0	0	0
cystitis	7	.0000	.0733	28.6	0	0	0	0	0	7	0	0	0	0	0	0	0	0	0	0	0	0	0	0	0	0	7	0	0
cytoplasm	15	.2445	.9092	39.6	0	0	3	3	7	0	0	2	0	0	0	0	0	0	0	10	0	0	0	0	0	0	5	0	0
cytosine	2	.0000	.0394	26.0	0	0	0	0	0	0	2	0	0	0	0	0	0	0	0	2	0	0	0	0	0	0	0	0	0
czar	4	.2281	.2337	33.7	0	0	0	3	1	0	0	0	0	0	0	0	0	3	0	0	0	0	0	0	0	0	0	1	0
Czar	21	.1750	.9779	39.9	18	0	1	1	1	0	0	0	0	0	0	0	0	2	0	0	0	0	0	0	0	18	1	0	0
Czar's	6	.1845	.2851	34.5	5	0	1	0	0	0	0	0	0	0	0	0	0	0	0	0	0	0	0	0	0	5	1	0	0
Czarina	3	.0000	.1370	31.4	0	0	3	0	0	0	0	0	3	0	0	0	0	0	0	0	0	0	0	0	0	0	0	0	0
Czech	17	.4700	1.6962	42.3	0	0	1	3	5	2	6	0	0	0	0	0	0	5	0	0	3	0	0	0	0	3	0	6	0
Czechoslovak	7	.0000	.0851	29.3	0	0	0	0	5	2	0	0	0	0	0	0	0	0	0	0	0	0	0	0	0	0	0	7	0
Czechoslovakia	50	.5938	6.1503	47.9	0	1	9	19	11	6	4	0	1	0	0	0	0	24	0	0	9	1	0	0	0	6	3	6	0
Czechs	17	.4194	1.5681	42.0	0	0	0	11	2	1	3	0	0	0	0	0	0	11	0	0	1	0	0	0	0	2	0	3	0
C12H22O11	2	.2405	.1205	30.8	1	0	0	0	1	0	0	0	0	0	0	0	0	0	0	1	0	0	0	0	0	1	0	0	0
C14	10	.0000	.1497	31.8	0	0	0	0	0	10	0	0	0	0	0	0	10	0	0	0	0	0	0	0	0	0	0	0	0
c2	2	.0000	.0299	24.8	0	0	0	0	0	2	0	0	0	0	0	0	2	0	0	0	0	0	0	0	0	0	0	0	0
C2	2	.2278	.1128	30.5	0	0	0	1	0	0	0	1	0	0	0	0	0	0	0	1	0	0	0	0	0	0	1	0	0
C2H4Br2**	2	.0000	.0209	23.2	0	0	0	2	0	0	0	0	0	0	0	0	0	0	0	0	0	0	0	0	0	0	2	0	0
C3H	2	.0000	.0394	26.0	0	0	0	0	0	0	0	2	0	0	0	0	0	0	0	2	0	0	0	0	0	0	0	0	0
C7	3	.0000	.0243	23.8	1	2	0	0	0	0	0	0	0	0	0	0	0	0	0	0	3	0	0	0	0	0	0	0	0
d	407	.6840	56.610	57.5	44	52	42	76	85	65	36	7	38	28	0	5	106	11	120	23	12	0	4	8	2	0	43	7	0
D	476	.7449	71.259	58.5	58	80	62	67	63	81	57	8	13	21	7	2	177	24	11	19	126	2	9	6	4	13	24	18	0
D**	87	.7323	12.992	51.1	20	6	19	11	13	10	6	2	16	3	0	0	8	23	1	3	4	0	0	0	1	3	15	10	0
D-Day	5	.3184	.3581	35.5	0	0	0	0	1	1	3	0	0	0	0	0	0	1	0	0	0	0	0	0	0	0	1	3	0
D-minor	2	.0000	.0162	22.1	0	0	0	2	0	0	0	0	0	0	0	0	0	0	0	0	2	0	0	0	0	0	0	0	0
d'	3	.1187	.1291	31.1	0	1	0	0	0	0	2	0	1	0	0	2	0	0	0	0	0	0	0	0	0	0	0	0	0
d'Argons	2	.0000	.0914	29.6	0	0	0	2	0	0	0	0	2	0	0	0	0	0	0	0	0	0	0	0	0	0	0	0	0
d'Ascoli	2	.0000	.0243	23.9	0	0	0	0	0	0	2	0	0	0	0	0	0	0	0	0	0	0	0	0	0	0	0	2	0
d'Aulaire	2	.1717	.1142	30.6	1	1	0	0	0	0	0	0	1	0	0	1	0	0	0	0	0	0	0	0	0	0	0	0	0
d'Orleans	2	.0000	.0243	23.9	0	0	0	0	2	0	0	0	0	0	0	0	0	0	0	0	0	0	0	0	0	0	0	2	0
d'etat	2	.0000	.0209	23.2	0	0	0	0	1	1	0	0	0	0	0	0	0	0	0	0	0	0	0	0	0	0	2	0	0
D's	4	.3250	.2847	34.5	1	0	1	1	0	1	0	0	0	0	0	0	1	0	0	0	2	0	0	0	0	0	0	1	0
d'ye	2	.1787	.1174	30.7	0	1	1	0	0	0	0	0	1	0	0	0	0	0	0	0	0	0	0	0	1	0	0	0	0
d'you	8	.2301	.6170	37.9	0	0	2	1	2	3	0	0	7	0	0	0	0	0	0	0	0	0	0	0	1	0	0	0	0
da	11	.4524	1.0407	40.2	2	1	1	1	4	1	1	0	0	0	0	0	1	1	0	0	2	2	0	0	0	2	3	0	0
DA	3	.0000	.0449	26.5	0	0	0	0	3	0	0	0	0	0	0	0	3	0	0	0	0	0	0	0	0	0	0	0	0
daGama	4	.2285	.2258	33.5	0	0	2	1	1	0	0	0	0	0	0	0	0	2	0	0	0	0	0	0	0	0	2	0	0
daVinci	11	.3471	.9169	39.6	5	0	0	0	0	0	6	0	5	0	0	0	0	0	1	0	0	3	0	1	0	0	1	0	0
dab	4	.4803	.4052	36.1	0	2	1	0	0	1	0	0	0	1	0	1	0	0	0	1	0	0	0	0	1	0	0	0	0
DAB	2	.0000	.0299	24.8	0	0	0	0	2	0	0	0	0	0	0	0	2	0	0	0	0	0	0	0	0	0	0	0	0
Dab-Dab	12	.1491	.4994	37.0	0	11	1	0	0	0	0	0	1	0	0	1	0	0	0	0	0	0	0	0	10	0	0	0	0
dabbled	3	.3370	.2430	33.9	0	0	0	1	0	1	1	0	1	0	0	1	0	0	0	0	0	0	0	0	0	0	1	0	0
dabbling	3	.2060	.1500	31.8	0	1	1	0	0	0	1	0	0	0	0	2	0	0	0	0	0	0	0	0	0	1	0	0	0
cutters	18	.2916	1.1888	40.8	1	2	1	3	8	1	2	0	3	0	0	1	0	0	0	0	0	1	0	9	0	2	2	0	0
cutthroat	5	.0000	.0608	27.8	0	0	0	0	5	0	0	0	0	0	0	0	0	0	0	0	0	0	0	0	0	0	0	5	0
cutthroats	6	.0706	.1822	32.6	0	0	0	0	6	0	0	0	1	0	0	0	0	0	0	0	0	0	0	0	0	0	0	5	0
cuttin'	2	.1717	.1142	30.6	0	0	0	1	1	0	0	0	1	0	0	1	0	0	0	0	0	0	0	0	0	0	0	0	0

7L Cutting
4D cuttings-up
9R Cuyahoga
3P Cuyler
7D Cuyloga's
6E CW
9D Cwm
6E CY
9Q cyan
9M cyanide
9M cyaniding
7Q cycadeoids
4Q cycads
8R cyclamate-based
9D cyclamen
9D Cyclamen
4H Cycle
8N cycle-path
7R cyclemakers
8Q cyclical
9R cyclists'
9J Cyclopean
8Q cyclopropane
9D Cydonians
7M cylinder-head
8M cylindrically
6R Cymru
9Q cynic
7G cyning
5N cypher
4D Cypress
8Q cypreth
5P Cypriots
8Q cyprome
7R cystadlevaeth
6Q cytoplasm's
8R Czapski
8R Czapski's
7J czardas
7R czars
8F Czechoslovakians
XH COO
XH C1
8Q C2H2**
6Q C2H4Cl2**
5Q C2H5
6Q C2H5OH
5Q C2H6
XH C3
4H C6H12O6
6J C7-chord
9J D-F-A
6N d-d-d
8D d-d-do
4A d-d-don't
8A d-e-e-p
6J D-major
9B d-o-u-g-h
9E d-th
3B D-500

Word Type	F	D	U	SFI	3 Gr 3	4 Gr 4	5 Gr 5	6 Gr 6	7 Gr 7	8 Gr 8	9 Gr 9	X UnGr	A Read	B Eng & Gr	C Comp	D Lit	E Math	F Soc Stud	G Spell	H Sci	J Music	K Art	L Home Ec	M Shop	N Lib F	P Lib NF	Q Lib Ref	R Mag	S Rel
Dachau	2	.0000	.0243	23.9	0	0	0	0	0	0	2	0	0	0	0	0	0	0	0	0	0	0	0	0	0	0	0	2	0
dachshund	2	.2408	.1091	30.4	0	0	0	0	1	1	0	0	0	1	0	0	0	0	1	0	0	0	0	0	0	0	0	0	0
Dacotah	3	.0000	.1370	31.4	0	0	0	0	3	0	0	0	3	0	0	0	0	0	0	0	0	0	0	0	0	0	0	0	0
Dacotahs	2	.0000	.0914	29.6	0	0	0	0	2	0	0	0	2	0	0	0	0	0	0	0	0	0	0	0	0	0	0	0	0
Dacron	7	.0821	.1381	31.4	0	0	0	0	0	3	4	0	0	0	0	0	0	0	1	0	0	0	6	0	0	0	0	0	0
dad	91	.8215	15.100	51.8	30	13	9	3	11	12	13	0	37	5	1	9	7	2	2	0	0	1	1	3	8	0	0	15	0
Dad	330	.7612	51.483	57.1	84	37	17	29	113	31	19	0	149	43	0	40	1	4	10	0	9	0	2	1	14	28	0	29	0
dad's	8	.4845	.8451	39.3	0	1	1	3	3	0	0	0	2	0	0	3	0	0	0	0	0	0	0	0	1	1	0	1	0
Dad's	20	.6482	2.7293	44.4	5	5	3	2	3	1	1	0	8	0	1	2	0	2	0	0	0	0	0	0	2	2	0	3	0
Dadaism	2	.0000	.0209	23.2	0	0	2	0	0	0	0	0	0	0	0	0	0	0	0	0	0	0	0	0	0	0	2	0	0
daddy	14	.4779	1.4850	41.7	4	2	1	1	5	1	0	0	5	0	0	5	0	0	1	1	2	0	0	0	0	0	0	0	0
Daddy	88	.5969	11.138	50.5	39	14	2	9	14	5	4	1	27	0	5	4	0	9	0	0	0	0	0	0	20	20	0	3	0
daddy-o	3	.0000	.0243	23.8	3	0	0	0	0	0	0	0	0	0	0	0	0	0	0	0	3	0	0	0	0	0	0	0	0
daddy's	3	.1735	.1535	31.9	1	1	1	0	0	0	0	0	1	0	0	0	0	0	0	0	0	1	0	0	0	1	0	0	0
Daddy's	4	.3740	.3661	35.6	1	3	0	0	0	0	0	0	2	0	0	0	0	0	0	0	0	0	0	0	1	0	0	1	0
dado	23	.0000	.0581	27.6	0	0	0	0	6	5	12	0	0	0	0	0	0	0	0	0	0	0	0	23	0	0	0	0	0
dado-head	2	.0000	.0050	17.0	0	0	0	0	2	0	0	0	0	0	0	0	0	0	0	0	0	0	0	2	0	0	0	0	0
Daedalus	13	.0000	.5939	37.7	3	9	0	0	0	1	0	0	13	0	0	0	0	0	0	0	0	0	0	0	0	0	0	0	0
daeg	2	.1733	.1149	30.6	0	0	1	1	0	0	0	0	1	1	0	0	0	0	0	0	0	0	0	0	0	0	0	0	0
daffodil	6	.3306	.4637	36.7	1	0	0	0	4	0	1	0	0	0	0	0	0	1	0	4	0	0	0	0	0	0	0	1	0
daffodils	14	.3927	1.1731	40.7	6	2	1	0	2	2	1	0	0	9	1	3	0	0	0	1	0	0	0	0	0	0	0	0	0
daft	3	.2379	.1705	32.3	0	0	0	2	1	0	0	0	0	0	0	1	0	0	0	0	0	0	0	0	0	2	0	0	0
Dag	2	.0000	.0389	25.9	0	0	0	0	0	1	1	0	0	0	0	0	0	2	0	0	0	0	0	0	0	0	0	0	0
dagger	19	.5448	2.2045	43.4	0	2	2	9	3	1	2	0	5	1	0	8	0	0	0	0	0	1	0	0	0	1	2	1	0
daggers	7	.4208	.6853	38.4	1	0	2	1	2	0	1	0	3	0	1	0	0	1	0	0	0	0	0	0	0	1	1	0	0
Dagmar	29	.3356	2.4057	43.8	0	0	0	0	17	12	0	0	12	0	0	5	0	0	0	0	0	0	0	0	12	0	0	0	0
DAGMAR	9	.0000	.0966	29.8	0	0	0	0	9	0	0	0	0	0	0	9	0	0	0	0	0	0	0	0	0	0	0	0	0
Dagmar's	3	.1250	.1342	31.3	0	0	0	0	1	2	0	0	1	0	0	0	0	0	0	0	0	0	0	0	2	0	0	0	0
Dai	2	.2285	.1129	30.5	0	0	0	0	1	1	0	0	0	0	0	0	0	1	0	0	0	0	0	0	0	0	1	0	0
Dailey	2	.0000	.0234	23.7	0	0	0	0	2	0	0	0	0	0	0	0	0	0	0	0	0	0	0	0	2	0	0	0	0
daily	229	.8366	38.328	55.8	15	19	25	27	61	43	32	7	36	11	3	5	10	28	0	41	9	0	21	6	6	8	22	22	1
Daily	22	.5228	2.4292	43.9	1	1	1	4	5	4	3	3	2	1	0	4	0	0	0	7	0	0	3	0	0	0	0	5	0
daintily	11	.5874	1.3794	41.4	3	2	2	2	2	0	0	0	4	0	0	1	0	0	0	0	0	0	0	0	3	1	1	1	0
dainty	22	.6707	3.0424	44.8	4	1	0	2	6	4	4	1	6	1	0	2	0	1	2	0	1	0	3	0	3	1	0	2	0
dairies	7	.2103	.3972	36.0	2	0	1	2	1	1	0	0	0	0	0	0	0	5	0	2	0	0	0	0	0	0	0	0	0
dairy	131	.6518	17.567	52.4	26	11	27	24	16	7	12	8	3	2	0	5	6	78	3	4	0	0	3	0	0	9	8	10	0
Dairy	7	.0000	.1361	31.3	1	0	6	0	0	0	0	0	0	0	0	0	0	7	0	0	0	0	0	0	0	0	0	0	0
dairying	15	.4490	1.4514	41.6	4	0	2	2	1	1	5	0	0	0	0	1	0	7	0	0	0	0	0	0	0	3	4	0	0
Dairymaid	3	.0000	.1370	31.4	3	0	0	0	0	0	0	0	3	0	0	0	0	0	0	0	0	0	0	0	0	0	0	0	0
dairymen	3	.2357	.2199	33.4	0	0	1	0	2	0	0	0	2	0	0	0	0	0	0	0	0	0	0	0	0	1	0	0	0
Dairymen	5	.0000	.0608	27.8	0	0	0	0	0	0	0	5	0	0	0	0	0	0	0	0	0	0	0	0	0	0	0	5	0
dais	2	.0000	.0243	23.9	0	0	0	2	0	0	0	0	0	0	0	0	0	0	0	0	0	0	0	0	0	0	0	2	0
daisies	20	.6274	2.5588	44.1	5	6	5	1	0	1	2	0	0	2	1	0	0	0	0	2	0	0	0	0	5	3	1	6	0
daisy	9	.5367	1.0075	40.0	0	1	2	5	1	0	0	0	0	1	0	0	0	0	2	4	1	0	0	0	1	0	0	0	0
Daisy	8	.5652	.9907	40.0	3	2	0	0	1	0	2	0	4	1	0	0	1	0	0	0	0	0	0	0	1	1	0	0	0
Dakar	2	.2351	.1166	30.7	0	0	0	0	2	0	0	0	0	0	0	0	0	1	0	0	0	0	0	0	0	0	0	1	0
Dakin	2	.0000	.0914	29.6	0	0	0	0	0	2	0	0	2	0	0	0	0	0	0	0	0	0	0	0	0	0	0	0	0
dakota	2	.1733	.1149	30.6	0	0	0	0	1	0	1	0	1	1	0	0	0	0	0	0	0	0	0	0	0	0	0	0	0
Dakota	9	.6077	1.1541	40.6	2	1	0	2	3	0	1	0	2	1	0	0	0	1	0	2	0	0	0	0	0	2	0	1	0
Dakotas	7	.3579	.6270	38.0	0	0	4	0	1	1	1	0	3	0	0	0	0	3	0	0	0	0	0	0	0	1	0	0	0
dale	5	.4202	.4376	36.4	0	0	1	0	4	0	0	0	0	1	1	2	0	0	0	0	1	0	0	0	0	0	0	0	0
Dale	22	.3895	2.0582	43.1	3	3	8	1	6	0	1	0	11	0	0	0	0	0	0	0	0	3	0	0	0	4	1	3	0
Dale's	2	.0580	.0676	28.3	1	0	0	0	0	1	0	0	1	0	0	0	0	0	0	0	0	1	0	0	0	0	0	0	0
Daley	15	.3541	1.1728	40.7	2	8	0	4	1	0	0	0	0	0	0	0	0	0	0	0	0	0	0	0	2	8	0	5	0
Dallapiccola	2	.0000	.0162	22.1	0	0	0	0	0	2	0	0	0	0	0	0	0	0	0	0	2	0	0	0	0	0	0	0	0
Dallas	24	.5605	2.8463	44.5	0	4	5	1	9	2	3	0	3	0	0	0	2	7	0	0	0	0	0	0	0	6	1	5	0
Dalmatia	2	.0000	.0209	23.2	0	0	0	0	0	2	0	0	0	0	0	0	0	0	0	0	0	0	0	0	0	0	2	0	0
Dalmatian	4	.3715	.3214	35.1	2	0	1	0	1	0	0	0	0	0	0	1	0	0	0	0	0	0	0	0	1	0	0	2	0
Dalton	8	.0000	.1577	32.0	0	0	0	0	2	6	0	0	0	0	0	0	0	0	0	8	0	0	0	0	0	0	0	0	0
Dalton's	6	.0000	.1183	30.7	0	0	0	0	4	2	0	0	0	0	0	0	0	0	0	6	0	0	0	0	0	0	0	0	0
Daly	9	.2279	.6936	38.4	0	0	8	0	0	1	0	0	8	0	0	1	0	0	0	0	0	0	0	0	0	0	0	0	0
DALY	2	.0000	.0215	23.3	0	0	0	0	0	2	0	0	0	0	0	2	0	0	0	0	0	0	0	0	0	0	0	0	0
Daly's	5	.0000	.2284	33.6	0	0	5	0	0	0	0	0	5	0	0	0	0	0	0	0	0	0	0	0	0	0	0	0	0
dam	127	.7780	19.967	53.0	33	11	14	27	9	0	7	26	20	1	2	3	0	26	1	14	2	0	0	0	5	16	17	20	0
Dam	24	.6894	3.3840	45.3	4	3	1	4	3	2	3	4	2	0	0	0	3	7	0	1	1	0	0	0	1	3	1	5	0
damage	144	.8024	23.231	53.7	11	18	11	22	36	20	16	10	17	4	1	3	2	15	1	47	2	0	2	7	2	6	14	21	0
damaged	59	.8245	9.7951	49.9	7	9	6	9	11	10	4	3	15	4	1	1	0	12	0	8	0	0	1	1	0	7	5	4	0
damages	11	.4057	1.0102	40.0	1	0	0	0	1	2	6	1	1	0	0	0	0	5	0	4	0	0	0	1	0	0	0	0	0
damaging	13	.6287	1.6671	42.2	0	0	1	0	5	3	3	1	0	0	0	1	0	1	0	3	0	0	1	1	0	0	2	4	0
Damascus	9	.3800	.7396	38.7	0	3	2	1	0	2	1	0	0	0	0	0	0	1	1	0	0	0	0	0	0	2	5	0	0
dame	10	.3100	.7331	38.7	1	0	0	4	1	2	2	0	2	0	0	6	0	0	0	0	0	0	0	0	1	0	0	1	0
Dame	24	.6555	3.2395	45.1	1	1	1	9	4	4	3	1	4	1	0	4	0	2	0	0	0	0	0	0	3	1	3	6	0
Dammam	5	.0000	.0972	29.9	0	0	0	3	2	0	0	0	0	0	0	0	0	5	0	0	0	0	0	0	0	0	0	0	0
dammed	6	.4958	.6395	38.1	0	1	1	0	3	0	0	1	1	0	0	1	0	1	0	0	0	0	0	0	0	0	2	1	0
damn	19	.5716	2.2661	43.6	0	0	0	0	10	4	5	0	2	0	0	3	0	2	0	0	0	0	0	0	3	1	1	7	0
damn'	2	.0000	.0215	23.3	0	0	0	0	2	0	0	0	0	0	0	2	0	0	0	0	0	0	0	0	0	0	0	0	0
damnation	4	.3212	.3104	34.9	0	0	0	0	1	0	3	0	1	0	0	1	0	0	0	0	0	0	0	0	0	2	0	0	0
damned	19	.5627	2.1969	43.4	0	0	1	0	4	5	8	1	0	0	1	8	0	1	0	0	0	0	0	0	1	2	1	5	0
Damon	4	.2306	.2281	33.6	0	0	0	2	0	2	0	0	0	2	0	0	0	2	0	0	0	0	0	0	0	0	0	0	0
damp	111	.8354	18.540	52.7	25	23	9	14	14	12	12	2	14	7	5	8	0	11	3	20	0	4	0	2	12	16	4	5	0
dampen	6	.3836	.5000	37.0	1	1	0	1	2	1	0	0	0	0	0	0	0	0	0	2	0	1	0	0	1	0	0	2	0
dampened	2	.1620	.0760	28.8	0	0	0	1	0	0	1	0	0	0	0	0	0	0	0	0	0	0	0	1	0	0	0	1	0
dampening	3	.2734	.1975	33.0	0	0	1	0	1	0	1	0	1	0	0	0	0	0	0	0	0	1	0	1	0	0	0	0	0
damper	10	.0000	.4568	36.6	0	9	0	1	0	0	0	0	10	0	0	0	0	0	0	0	0	0	0	0	0	0	0	0	0
dampness	7	.3898	.6349	38.0	1	3	1	1	1	0	0	0	2	0	0	0	0	1	0	0	0	0	0	0	0	1	0	3	0
damps	3	.2292	.1615	32.1	0	1	0	0	1	1	0	0	0	0	0	1	0	0	0	0	0	0	0	0	2	0	0	0	0
dams	81	.6487	10.890	50.4	10	5	23	20	9	1	1	12	9	1	0	0	0	31	0	14	0	0	0	1	0	7	10	8	0
damsel	3	.0000	.1370	31.4	0	0	0	3	0	0	0	0	3	0	0	0	0	0	0	0	0	0	0	0	0	0	0	0	0
dan	3	.2074	.1511	31.8	0	0	1	0	0	2	0	0	0	2	0	0	0	0	0	0	0	0	0	0	0	1	0	0	0
Dan	753	.5416	93.375	59.7	143	519	19	28	18	11	15	0	583	8	0	19	16	1	0	0	6	0	0	0	7	78	0	35	0
Dan'l	3	.0000	.1370	31.4	0	0	0	3	0	0	0	0	3	0	0	0	0	0	0	0	0	0	0	0	0	0	0	0	0
Dan's	37	.5839	4.8123	46.8	12	17	2	1	2	2	1	0	27	1	0	1	2	0	1	0	0	0	0	0	1	4	0	0	0
Dana	6	.2255	.3613	35.6	5	0	0	0	1	0	0	0	1	0	0	0	0	0	0	1	0	0	0	0	0	4	0	0	0

4N dace
XR dacha
3R Dachshund
8A dachshunds
9L Dacron-wool
9L Dacrons
7D dad'll
7D Dadda
8D Daddies
7A daddy'll
8M Dado
5D dads
9E DAE
6G daeges
6G daeges-eage
8B daeghwamlican
3R Daffy
6R Daffynishion
7G Dagata
5P dagger-like
8D dagger-pointed
7Q daggerlike
6R Dahl
XN Dahr
9Q Dahshur
4F daikon
9G dailies
6N daintier
4P daintiest
5P daintiness
5F dairy-farm
5F dairy-farmland
4K dairyman
4P dairywoman
5E Daisies
5N daisy-chain
8C daisy's
8P Daisy's
8H Dak
8Q daks
5B dales
4B Dalewood
XR Dall
9R Dallas'
8D dallied
4P dallying
8J Dalry
7R Dalrymple
3N DAM
XR dam-builders
6A dam-building
7R dam's
7P damage-control
4Q Damaged
8G damask
7R Dame's
7A Damien
6A Damisa
7P damnable
9Q Damnable
XR damnably
9P damndest
8D damning
9F Damodar
XR damp-dry
6J dampers
9J Damrosch
7M Dams
7Q damselfly
6A damsels
XR damsite
6P DAN

Word Type	F	D	U	SFI	3 Gr 3	4 Gr 4	5 Gr 5	6 Gr 6	7 Gr 7	8 Gr 8	9 Gr 9	X UnGr	A Read	B Eng & Gr	C Comp	D Lit	E Math	F Soc Stud	G Spell	H Sci	J Music	K Art	L Home Ec	M Shop	N Lib F	P Lib NF	Q Lib Ref	R Mag	S Rel
Danakils	2	.0000	.0389	25.9	0	0	0	0	2	0	0	0	0	0	0	0	0	2	0	0	0	0	0	0	0	0	0	0	0
Danbury	9	.4330	.8324	39.2	2	5	1	0	1	0	0	0	0	1	0	1	0	0	0	0	0	0	0	0	2	5	0	0	0
Danby	5	.0000	.0547	27.4	0	3	0	0	0	1	1	0	0	5	0	0	0	0	0	0	0	0	0	0	0	0	0	0	0
dance	608	.5561	70.982	58.5	140	122	107	77	70	61	23	8	120	13	3	25	0	16	6	9	299	7	2	0	34	37	15	22	0
Dance	47	.5357	5.4363	47.4	6	5	20	6	4	1	3	2	17	2	0	3	0	0	0	0	17	1	0	0	5	0	0	2	0
dance-music	2	.1717	.1142	30.6	0	0	1	0	0	0	1	0	1	0	0	1	0	0	0	0	0	0	0	0	0	0	0	0	0
danced	136	.6083	17.416	52.4	45	26	14	18	13	10	5	5	44	4	1	9	0	2	1	3	46	0	0	0	8	9	2	7	0
dancer	31	.5582	3.6518	45.6	5	6	6	2	2	5	3	2	7	2	0	2	0	1	0	0	11	0	0	0	1	1	1	5	0
dancers	64	.4560	6.3050	48.0	10	9	17	8	8	10	2	0	11	0	0	1	0	7	0	2	34	2	0	0	1	0	2	4	0
dances	139	.5130	14.954	51.7	24	26	35	22	12	18	2	0	14	1	0	6	0	14	0	0	74	3	1	0	3	13	5	5	0
Dances	5	.1563	.1897	32.8	2	0	1	1	0	0	1	0	0	0	0	0	0	0	0	0	4	0	0	0	0	0	1	0	0
dancing	251	.7614	38.701	55.9	75	42	37	32	30	23	10	2	62	9	3	24	0	12	0	1	69	5	1	0	33	14	11	6	1
Dancing	11	.3706	1.0717	40.3	10	0	0	0	0	0	1	0	9	0	0	1	0	0	0	0	1	0	0	0	0	0	0	0	0
dandelion	30	.5959	3.7635	45.8	18	4	0	2	3	0	0	3	4	1	0	1	0	0	0	18	0	1	1	0	0	3	0	1	0
dandelions	9	.2383	.5446	37.4	3	0	0	1	2	0	0	3	0	0	0	0	0	0	0	6	0	0	0	0	0	3	0	0	0
dander	2	.1787	.1174	30.7	1	0	0	0	1	0	0	0	1	0	0	0	0	0	0	0	0	0	0	0	1	0	0	0	0
Dandridge	7	.0000	.1013	30.1	0	7	0	0	0	0	0	0	0	0	0	0	0	0	0	0	0	0	0	0	0	7	0	0	0
Dandridges	3	.0000	.0434	26.4	0	3	0	0	0	0	0	0	0	0	0	0	0	0	0	0	0	0	0	0	0	3	0	0	0
dandy	17	.5234	1.8450	42.7	8	1	1	0	3	0	4	0	1	0	1	4	0	0	0	0	6	0	0	0	0	1	0	4	0
Dandy	7	.1288	.2510	34.0	7	0	0	0	0	0	0	0	0	0	0	0	0	0	0	0	0	0	0	0	6	1	0	0	0
Dane	5	.4886	.5172	37.1	1	0	0	1	1	0	0	2	0	1	0	0	0	0	0	2	0	0	0	0	1	0	1	0	0
Danes	31	.4049	2.6786	44.3	20	0	1	2	6	1	0	1	0	2	0	0	0	4	2	0	2	0	0	0	0	1	20	0	0
Danford	4	.0000	.0599	27.8	0	0	0	0	0	4	0	0	0	0	0	0	4	0	0	0	0	0	0	0	0	0	0	0	0
danger	359	.8892	63.808	58.0	39	72	44	55	78	30	32	9	148	14	3	19	1	36	4	34	2	0	2	3	30	27	16	20	0
Danger	2	.2427	.1152	30.6	0	1	0	0	1	0	0	0	0	0	0	0	0	0	0	0	0	0	0	0	1	1	0	0	0
dangerous	308	.8773	53.929	57.3	45	43	41	31	78	32	33	5	77	15	11	22	0	34	1	53	3	1	4	4	7	33	18	25	0
dangerous-looking	2	.0000	.0914	29.6	1	1	0	0	0	0	0	0	2	0	0	0	0	0	0	0	0	0	0	0	0	0	0	0	0
dangerously	13	.5354	1.5243	41.8	0	2	0	4	3	1	3	0	5	0	0	2	0	0	0	2	0	0	0	0	3	0	0	1	0
dangers	68	.7828	10.821	50.3	5	8	8	4	20	13	8	2	21	5	0	5	0	8	0	12	1	0	0	0	3	3	3	7	0
dangle	6	.5583	.7007	38.5	0	0	1	0	2	1	1	1	0	0	0	1	0	2	0	1	0	0	0	0	0	1	0	1	0
dangled	14	.4270	1.4206	41.5	4	0	3	2	3	1	1	0	8	0	1	0	0	0	0	0	0	0	0	0	4	1	0	0	0
dangles	2	.1432	.0759	28.8	0	0	1	0	0	1	0	0	0	0	0	0	0	0	0	1	0	0	1	0	0	0	0	0	0
dangling	29	.7083	4.2538	46.3	7	2	4	4	4	6	2	0	12	3	0	1	0	0	0	0	1	0	0	0	4	3	3	2	0
Danhasch	4	.0000	.0469	26.7	0	0	4	0	0	0	0	0	0	0	0	0	0	0	0	0	0	0	0	0	4	0	0	0	0
Daniel	158	.7679	24.877	54.0	43	24	34	18	23	9	6	1	73	6	3	2	0	18	0	2	8	0	0	0	21	15	3	7	0
Daniel's	5	.1468	.2522	34.0	3	0	2	0	0	0	0	0	2	0	0	0	0	0	0	0	0	0	0	0	3	0	0	0	0
Daniels	2	.0000	.0219	23.4	0	0	0	0	1	0	1	0	0	2	0	0	0	0	0	0	0	0	0	0	0	0	0	0	0
Danish	81	.5969	10.032	50.0	39	4	7	21	5	0	1	4	8	3	0	1	0	17	0	4	11	0	0	0	1	4	29	3	0
dank	7	.3917	.6024	37.8	0	0	0	0	3	1	1	2	1	0	1	3	0	0	0	0	0	0	0	0	0	0	0	2	0
Danny	253	.4084	24.288	53.9	86	28	14	2	97	3	23	0	112	7	0	34	0	0	0	0	0	0	0	0	97	0	0	3	0
Danny's	17	.1506	.8743	39.4	3	1	2	0	11	0	0	0	7	0	0	0	0	0	0	0	0	0	0	0	10	0	0	0	0
Danse	5	.0000	.0404	26.1	1	4	0	0	0	0	0	0	0	0	0	0	0	0	0	0	5	0	0	0	0	0	0	0	0
Dante	7	.2779	.4364	36.4	1	0	4	0	0	0	1	1	0	0	0	0	0	0	0	0	1	0	0	0	0	1	5	0	0
Dante's	5	.3814	.4107	36.1	0	0	3	1	0	0	0	1	0	0	0	0	0	0	0	0	1	0	0	0	0	2	2	0	0
Danton	3	.1169	.1277	31.1	0	1	1	0	1	0	0	0	1	0	0	0	0	0	0	0	0	0	0	0	0	0	2	0	0
Danube	18	.4918	1.9033	42.8	0	0	1	8	7	0	2	0	1	1	0	0	0	11	0	0	1	0	0	0	0	0	3	1	0
Danubian	4	.0000	.0778	28.9	0	0	0	0	4	0	0	0	0	0	0	0	0	4	0	0	0	0	0	0	0	0	0	0	0
Danzig	2	.0000	.0389	25.9	0	0	0	2	0	0	0	0	0	0	0	0	0	2	0	0	0	0	0	0	0	0	0	0	0
Daphne	16	.4897	1.7915	42.5	6	4	0	4	0	0	0	2	9	4	0	0	0	0	0	0	0	0	0	0	1	1	0	1	0
daphnias	2	.0000	.0394	26.0	0	0	0	0	2	0	0	0	0	0	0	0	0	0	0	2	0	0	0	0	0	0	0	0	0
dappled	9	.4470	.8460	39.3	2	0	2	0	0	3	2	0	0	0	0	3	0	0	0	0	1	1	0	0	0	4	0	0	0
Darby	3	.3826	.2445	33.9	0	1	1	0	1	0	0	0	0	0	0	0	0	0	0	0	1	0	0	0	0	0	1	1	0
Dardanelles	8	.2337	.5029	37.0	0	0	1	1	4	1	1	0	1	0	0	0	0	6	0	0	0	0	0	0	0	1	0	0	0
dare	90	.7333	13.635	51.3	11	18	9	15	18	14	5	0	42	3	2	16	0	2	1	2	1	0	0	0	7	11	1	2	0
Dare	2	.0000	.0914	29.6	0	2	0	0	0	0	0	0	2	0	0	0	0	0	0	0	0	0	0	0	0	0	0	0	0
dared	68	.6296	9.0618	49.6	9	13	8	12	12	2	12	0	28	1	0	15	0	1	0	0	1	0	0	0	11	6	2	3	0
daredevil	4	.4530	.4014	36.0	0	1	0	0	2	0	0	1	1	0	0	0	0	0	0	0	0	0	0	0	0	1	1	1	0
dares	8	.3744	.6766	38.3	1	0	1	1	2	1	2	0	1	0	0	3	0	1	0	0	0	0	0	0	0	3	0	0	0
daresay	3	.2120	.1548	31.9	1	1	0	0	0	0	1	0	0	0	0	0	0	0	0	0	0	0	0	0	2	1	0	0	0
darest	2	.2297	.1135	30.6	0	0	1	0	0	0	1	0	0	0	0	1	0	1	0	0	0	0	0	0	0	0	0	0	0
Dargent	4	.0000	.1827	32.6	0	0	0	0	4	0	0	0	4	0	0	0	0	0	0	0	0	0	0	0	0	0	0	0	0
daring	70	.8128	11.449	50.6	6	12	10	9	14	10	6	3	17	4	3	7	0	12	1	3	4	3	0	0	3	4	5	4	0
daringly	2	.2407	.1138	30.6	0	0	0	1	1	0	0	0	0	0	0	1	0	0	0	0	0	0	0	0	0	1	0	0	0
Darius	10	.3672	.8542	39.3	0	0	3	0	2	5	0	0	3	0	0	0	0	0	0	0	1	0	0	0	0	0	5	1	0
dark	1171	.8339	196.54	62.9	254	230	108	138	252	90	72	27	397	31	12	118	0	63	13	128	15	52	18	6	130	128	18	42	0
Dark	19	.6114	2.4784	43.9	4	1	1	3	4	1	1	4	8	1	0	0	0	3	0	0	1	1	0	0	0	0	1	4	0
dark-blue	4	.3717	.3640	35.6	1	0	0	1	1	1	0	0	2	0	0	1	0	0	0	0	0	0	0	0	0	0	0	1	0
dark-brown	4	.4870	.4078	36.1	0	2	1	0	0	1	0	0	0	0	0	0	0	0	0	0	0	0	0	0	1	1	1	1	0
dark-colored	4	.3307	.3156	35.0	1	1	0	1	0	1	0	0	1	0	0	0	0	0	0	1	0	0	1	0	0	1	0	0	0
dark-eyed	7	.3633	.6318	38.0	1	2	1	0	1	2	0	0	3	0	0	0	0	3	0	0	0	0	0	0	0	0	0	1	0
dark-gray	2	.2278	.1128	30.5	0	0	0	0	1	0	1	0	0	0	0	0	0	0	0	1	0	0	0	0	0	0	1	0	0
dark-green	11	.1801	.5782	37.6	2	0	0	3	0	2	4	0	4	0	0	0	0	1	0	0	0	0	5	0	0	0	0	1	0
dark-haired	10	.5784	1.2154	40.8	1	2	2	1	2	1	1	0	1	0	0	0	0	4	0	0	0	0	0	0	1	2	1	1	0
dark-line	2	.0000	.0394	26.0	0	0	0	0	0	0	2	0	0	0	0	0	0	0	0	2	0	0	0	0	0	0	0	0	0
dark-skinned	12	.4832	1.2367	40.9	2	0	1	1	6	1	0	1	1	0	0	0	0	2	0	1	0	0	1	0	6	0	1	0	0
darken	16	.5567	1.8636	42.7	4	3	0	2	1	1	3	2	1	1	0	0	0	1	0	8	0	2	1	1	0	0	0	1	0
darkened	25	.7264	3.7316	45.7	0	0	3	5	13	3	1	0	8	3	0	2	1	0	0	4	1	0	1	0	4	1	0	1	0
darkening	8	.5965	.9783	39.9	2	0	0	1	1	1	2	1	0	1	0	2	0	0	0	1	0	0	0	0	2	1	1	0	0
darker	61	.6949	8.7577	49.4	12	12	7	7	6	10	4	3	20	1	1	5	0	3	0	8	1	6	2	0	3	6	2	3	0
darkest	16	.7310	2.3638	43.7	2	3	1	3	5	2	0	0	1	1	0	2	1	2	0	1	0	1	0	0	2	3	1	1	0
darkly	9	.4564	.9377	39.7	1	1	0	4	2	1	0	0	4	0	1	0	0	1	0	0	0	0	0	0	2	0	0	1	0
darkness	250	.8205	41.417	56.2	35	36	27	42	52	21	30	7	88	5	4	38	0	12	1	27	5	2	0	0	25	22	3	18	0
Darkness	6	.3504	.4691	36.7	3	0	2	0	0	0	1	0	0	0	0	1	0	2	0	0	0	0	0	0	0	0	0	3	0
darkroom	4	.3644	.3157	35.0	0	0	1	0	0	0	3	0	0	0	0	0	0	0	0	1	0	0	0	1	1	0	0	1	0
darks	3	.1918	.1342	31.3	0	0	0	1	0	0	0	2	0	0	0	0	0	0	0	0	0	1	0	0	0	0	0	2	0
darling	48	.4111	4.5345	46.6	8	5	5	8	18	4	0	0	18	0	0	2	0	0	0	0	17	0	0	0	9	2	0	0	0
Darling	28	.3663	2.6716	44.3	1	1	0	20	2	4	0	0	21	0	0	0	0	0	0	0	4	0	0	0	0	3	0	0	0
Darling's	2	.0000	.0914	29.6	0	0	0	2	0	0	0	0	2	0	0	0	0	0	0	0	0	0	0	0	0	0	0	0	0
darlings	2	.0000	.0914	29.6	0	0	1	1	0	0	0	0	2	0	0	0	0	0	0	0	0	0	0	0	0	0	0	0	0
Darlington	2	.0000	.0243	23.9	0	1	0	0	1	0	0	0	0	0	0	0	0	0	0	0	0	0	0	0	0	0	0	2	0
darn	9	.3283	.7025	38.5	0	0	1	1	2	5	0	0	3	0	0	1	0	0	0	0	0	0	3	0	1	0	0	1	0
Darnay	3	.0000	.0322	25.1	0	0	0	0	0	0	3	0	0	0	0	3	0	0	0	0	0	0	0	0	0	0	0	0	0
darned	6	.3559	.4640	36.7	0	0	3	1	2	0	0	0	0	0	0	2	0	0	0	0	0	0	0	0	3	0	0	1	0
Darnell	7	.0000	.0821	29.1	7	0	0	0	0	0	0	0	0	0	0	0	0	0	0	0	0	0	0	0	7	0	0	0	0
darner	4	.0000	.0129	21.1	0	0	0	0	0	4	0	0	0	0	0	0	0	0	0	0	0	0	4	0	0	0	0	0	0

8N Dana's
XR Danae
9B Danaides
8J Dancairo
9J dance-drama
7J dance-hall
9J danceband
5J dancelike
7B Dancer
6J dancer's
7J dancers'
4N dancin'
4J dancy
3N Dandy's
5Q Danegeld
7D dang
8A dang'rous
8N danged
7A DANGER
6B Dangerous
5A dangerousness
4B dangly
3A DANISH
3Q Danish-Americans
XR Danish-German
5F Danish-owned
XB Danite
XH dankest
7H daphnia
8C Daphnia
6P Daphnis
9B dapper
6A dapple
7A dapple-gray
6A dappling
6A Dar-es-Salaam
6A Daraprim
4R Darby's
5Q Darcy's
7D daren't
5Q Darien
7D Daring
7P dark-coated
4A dark-red
4R dark-rimmed
4P dark's
3J darkens
3K darker-blue
9H darker-colored
4P Darley
8J darlin'
3N Darnells
9D Darney

Word Type	F	D	U	SFI	3 Gr 3	4 Gr 4	5 Gr 5	6 Gr 6	7 Gr 7	8 Gr 8	9 Gr 9	X UnGr	A Read	B Eng & Gr	C Comp	D Lit	E Math	F Soc Stud	G Spell	H Sci	J Music	K Art	L Home Ec	M Shop	N Lib F	P Lib NF	Q Lib Ref	R Mag	S Rel
darning	21	.3224	1.3846	41.4	0	1	1	0	1	17	1	0	0	0	11	0	0	1	0	0	0	1	7	0	1	0	0	0	0
Darrow	2	.1042	.0600	27.8	0	1	0	0	0	1	0	0	0	0	0	0	0	1	0	0	0	1	0	0	0	0	0	0	0
dart	36	.3518	2.8280	44.5	5	3	6	1	13	7	1	0	6	2	0	3	2	1	0	1	0	0	15	0	1	3	1	1	0
Dart	3	.0000	.0314	25.0	0	0	0	0	3	0	0	0	0	0	0	0	0	0	0	0	0	0	0	0	0	0	3	0	0
darted	42	.6423	5.7769	47.6	7	11	6	8	5	2	3	0	24	0	1	2	0	2	0	0	0	0	0	0	5	6	0	2	0
darting	19	.6309	2.5542	44.1	4	3	4	2	4	1	1	0	9	1	0	1	0	1	0	0	0	0	0	0	3	1	0	3	0
Dartmouth	4	.3429	.3033	34.8	0	0	1	0	0	2	1	0	0	0	0	2	0	1	0	0	0	0	0	0	0	0	1	0	0
darts	36	.3141	2.5026	44.0	5	5	0	2	13	7	4	0	3	2	0	1	5	0	0	1	0	0	17	0	1	3	1	2	0
Darwin	27	.3743	2.2258	43.5	0	0	1	19	2	0	3	2	1	0	0	1	0	2	0	2	0	0	0	0	0	0	4	17	0
Darwin's	4	.2090	.2014	33.0	0	0	0	3	1	0	0	0	0	0	0	0	0	0	0	0	0	0	0	0	0	0	1	3	0
Darzee	8	.0000	.3655	35.6	0	3	0	2	3	0	0	0	8	0	0	0	0	0	0	0	0	0	0	0	0	0	0	0	0
Das	2	.0000	.0162	22.1	0	0	0	2	0	0	0	0	0	0	0	0	0	0	0	0	2	0	0	0	0	0	0	0	0
dash	64	.8731	11.161	50.5	4	12	6	5	19	8	7	3	16	2	1	2	6	7	1	8	3	0	0	0	2	7	2	7	0
dashboard	8	.4390	.7994	39.0	1	2	0	1	2	1	1	0	3	0	0	1	0	0	0	0	0	0	0	0	0	0	1	3	0
dashed	107	.7132	15.917	52.0	23	30	12	19	12	8	2	1	56	2	4	5	4	5	0	1	0	0	0	0	11	14	1	4	0
dasher	2	.0000	.0243	23.9	0	0	0	0	0	0	0	2	0	0	0	0	0	0	0	0	0	0	0	0	0	0	0	2	0
dashes	22	.5872	2.7254	44.4	5	2	0	0	6	4	3	2	7	0	0	3	1	0	3	0	1	0	0	3	0	0	2	2	0
dashing	18	.6448	2.4567	43.9	2	3	0	5	3	4	1	0	8	0	0	2	0	1	0	1	2	0	0	0	0	2	0	2	0
dasn't	2	.1787	.1174	30.7	0	0	0	0	2	0	0	0	1	0	0	0	0	0	0	0	0	0	0	0	1	0	0	0	0
dastardly	2	.0000	.0394	26.0	0	0	0	0	0	0	0	2	0	0	0	0	0	0	0	2	0	0	0	0	0	0	0	0	0
dat	5	.2086	.3320	35.2	0	0	0	0	5	0	0	0	3	0	0	0	0	0	0	0	0	0	0	0	2	0	0	0	0
data	157	.6417	20.691	53.2	1	28	18	27	28	27	26	2	3	3	0	1	65	4	0	44	0	1	0	2	0	3	18	13	0
data-processing	3	.2270	.1588	32.0	0	0	0	2	1	0	0	0	0	2	0	0	0	0	0	0	0	0	0	0	0	0	1	0	0
date	201	.8950	35.738	55.5	29	24	21	15	45	20	37	10	35	20	7	9	14	24	1	20	6	2	11	2	3	8	22	17	0
Date	8	.1975	.4358	36.4	0	6	0	0	0	2	0	0	0	0	0	0	0	6	0	2	0	0	0	0	0	0	0	0	0
dated	14	.5215	1.5597	41.9	0	0	3	0	3	4	2	2	3	0	0	0	2	0	0	1	0	0	2	0	0	0	3	3	0
dates	109	.8332	18.210	52.6	17	25	13	11	18	16	7	2	23	15	2	2	7	17	1	5	3	0	4	0	0	6	15	9	0
dating	30	.6506	3.9795	46.0	1	0	4	1	11	9	4	0	1	0	0	0	1	4	0	3	1	0	3	0	1	2	8	6	0
daubed	3	.2435	.2274	33.6	2	0	0	0	1	0	0	0	2	0	0	0	0	1	0	0	0	0	0	0	0	0	0	0	0
Dauberval	2	.0000	.0209	23.2	0	0	0	0	0	2	0	0	0	0	0	0	0	0	0	0	0	0	0	0	0	0	2	0	0
Daubigny	2	.1493	.0692	28.4	0	0	1	0	0	1	0	0	0	0	0	0	0	0	0	0	0	1	0	0	0	0	1	0	0
daubing	2	.2152	.1357	31.3	0	0	1	0	0	1	0	0	1	0	0	0	0	1	0	0	0	0	0	0	0	0	0	0	0
Daugherty	6	.2223	.4212	36.2	0	0	2	4	0	0	0	0	4	2	0	0	0	0	0	0	0	0	0	0	0	0	0	0	0
daughter	288	.8147	47.460	56.8	48	46	32	51	39	32	30	10	115	8	9	38	6	7	4	5	14	0	1	0	16	47	7	10	1
Daughter	7	.4603	.6754	38.3	1	2	0	2	0	1	1	0	0	0	0	0	0	0	0	0	2	0	0	0	2	1	0	2	0
daughter's	12	.3427	1.0355	40.2	2	1	1	1	2	2	3	0	6	0	0	4	0	0	0	0	0	0	0	0	0	2	0	0	0
daughters	52	.3050	3.8506	45.9	7	16	2	4	15	7	1	0	13	0	1	3	2	6	1	0	5	0	0	0	4	7	1	6	3
daunted	2	.1814	.1187	30.7	0	1	0	0	0	1	0	0	1	0	0	0	0	0	0	0	0	0	0	0	0	0	0	1	0
dauntless	3	.3811	.2534	34.0	1	0	0	0	1	0	0	1	0	0	0	0	0	0	0	1	0	0	0	0	0	1	0	1	0
Dauphin	3	.0000	.0314	25.0	0	0	0	0	0	0	3	0	0	0	0	0	0	0	0	0	0	0	0	0	0	0	3	0	0
Dauphine	3	.2222	.1558	31.9	0	0	0	0	1	1	0	1	0	1	0	0	0	0	0	0	0	0	0	0	0	0	2	0	0
Davao	4	.0000	.0419	26.2	3	0	0	0	0	1	0	0	0	0	0	0	0	0	0	0	0	0	0	0	0	0	4	0	0
Dave	122	.5921	15.948	52.0	60	7	10	25	8	8	3	1	83	2	0	3	7	1	0	0	0	0	0	0	4	6	0	16	0
Dave's	6	.2369	.4417	36.5	5	0	0	1	0	0	0	0	4	0	0	0	2	0	0	0	0	0	0	0	0	0	0	0	0
Davey	9	.3737	.8756	39.4	0	0	8	0	0	1	0	0	7	1	0	0	0	0	0	0	0	0	0	0	0	0	0	1	0
Davey's	2	.0000	.0914	29.6	0	0	2	0	0	0	0	0	2	0	0	0	0	0	0	0	0	0	0	0	0	0	0	0	0
David	350	.3155	26.910	54.3	172	47	8	43	30	37	11	2	101	12	0	33	3	24	2	11	2	11	0	0	40	70	11	11	19
David's	32	.4403	3.2176	45.1	14	4	5	2	2	5	0	0	13	1	0	2	3	2	2	1	0	3	0	0	3	1	0	0	1
Davis	72	.6437	9.8227	49.9	13	7	3	13	5	24	7	0	32	0	0	0	0	8	0	0	0	1	0	0	15	9	3	4	0
Davison	2	.0000	.0209	23.2	0	0	2	0	0	0	0	0	0	0	0	0	0	0	0	0	0	0	0	0	0	0	2	0	0
Davy	122	.4664	12.497	51.0	78	6	19	2	4	2	3	8	22	0	0	13	0	2	0	14	1	0	0	0	4	65	1	0	0
Davy's	12	.2407	.6825	38.3	12	0	0	0	0	0	0	0	0	0	0	6	0	0	0	0	0	0	0	0	0	6	0	0	0
Daw	4	.2446	.2243	33.5	0	0	0	0	0	4	0	0	0	0	0	2	0	0	0	0	0	0	0	0	0	0	2	0	0
dawana	2	.0000	.0389	25.9	0	0	0	0	0	2	0	0	0	0	0	0	0	2	0	0	0	0	0	0	0	0	0	0	0
dawdle	3	.3408	.2477	33.9	1	1	0	0	0	0	1	0	1	0	0	1	0	0	0	0	0	0	0	0	0	1	0	0	0
dawdling	2	.1717	.1142	30.6	0	0	1	0	1	0	0	0	1	0	0	1	0	0	0	0	0	0	0	0	0	0	0	0	0
dawn	158	.7689	24.729	53.9	17	21	13	32	32	25	11	7	52	3	3	20	0	12	0	2	3	0	1	0	26	17	1	18	0
Dawn	12	.4404	1.2719	41.0	7	0	0	1	1	1	1	1	8	0	1	0	1	0	0	1	0	0	0	0	0	1	0	0	0
dawned	11	.4776	1.2231	40.9	0	0	1	5	2	0	1	2	7	0	0	1	0	0	0	0	0	0	0	0	0	0	1	2	0
dawning	10	.5644	1.2059	40.8	1	1	0	2	4	1	1	0	3	0	0	3	0	0	0	1	1	0	0	0	0	1	1	0	0
dawns	2	.1733	.1149	30.6	1	0	1	0	0	0	0	0	1	1	0	0	0	0	0	0	0	0	0	0	0	0	0	0	0
Daws	3	.0000	.0322	25.1	0	0	0	0	0	3	0	0	0	0	0	3	0	0	0	0	0	0	0	0	0	0	0	0	0
Dawson	43	.4471	4.5920	46.6	16	1	5	1	13	6	0	1	28	0	0	0	5	0	0	0	0	0	0	0	8	0	0	2	0
Dawson's	4	.2446	.3071	34.9	3	0	1	0	0	0	0	0	3	0	0	0	1	0	0	0	0	0	0	0	0	0	0	0	0
day	5019	.9432	937.06	69.7	1207	955	615	622	770	410	326	114	1601	239	61	342	259	405	99	447	172	16	65	10	398	460	126	306	13
Day	197	.8333	32.990	55.2	44	65	8	22	30	15	6	7	60	9	3	6	8	20	4	0	22	1	0	1	3	17	23	19	1
day-by-day	2	.2331	.1157	30.6	1	0	0	0	1	0	0	0	0	0	0	0	0	0	0	1	0	0	0	0	1	0	0	0	0
day-nursery	3	.0000	.1370	31.4	0	0	0	3	0	0	0	0	3	0	0	0	0	0	0	0	0	0	0	0	0	0	0	0	0
day-old	2	.0857	.0784	28.9	0	1	0	0	0	0	1	0	1	0	0	0	0	0	0	0	0	0	1	0	0	0	0	0	0
day-time	3	.2212	.2099	33.2	0	0	0	0	2	1	0	0	2	0	0	1	0	0	0	0	0	0	0	0	0	0	0	0	0
day-to-day	9	.4675	.8997	39.5	0	0	2	0	3	1	3	0	0	0	0	0	1	1	0	2	0	0	0	0	0	1	0	4	0
day's	95	.7642	14.764	51.7	12	10	13	9	23	19	9	0	29	1	1	9	2	8	1	3	2	0	10	1	7	15	0	6	0
Dayan	3	.1937	.1495	31.7	0	0	0	0	0	2	1	0	0	0	0	0	0	1	0	0	0	0	0	0	0	0	0	2	0
daybreak	28	.5842	3.5143	45.5	0	4	0	11	5	7	1	0	11	0	0	4	0	2	0	0	1	0	0	0	6	4	0	0	0
daydream	22	.4614	2.2240	43.5	1	3	5	1	10	1	1	0	5	10	0	3	0	0	0	1	0	0	0	0	1	0	0	2	0
daydreamer	2	.1787	.1174	30.7	1	0	0	0	0	1	0	0	1	0	0	0	0	0	0	0	0	0	0	0	1	0	0	0	0
daydreaming	13	.6957	1.8523	42.7	4	1	2	0	2	1	1	2	3	1	0	1	0	0	0	0	1	0	1	0	2	2	0	2	0
daydreams	18	.5725	2.1600	43.3	0	2	1	2	10	2	1	0	3	6	0	4	0	0	0	2	1	0	0	0	0	0	1	1	0
daylight	108	.8280	17.997	52.6	19	14	12	13	32	4	11	3	30	4	3	12	0	11	0	16	1	0	2	0	10	10	2	7	0
days	2003	.9604	379.81	65.8	435	351	254	281	307	159	153	63	531	67	17	112	174	235	33	196	59	8	10	3	127	217	78	135	1
Days	9	.5949	1.1243	40.5	0	0	3	0	1	4	1	0	1	0	0	1	0	3	0	2	0	0	0	0	1	0	0	1	0
days'	12	.5886	1.4648	41.7	0	1	1	1	6	0	1	2	1	0	0	3	1	0	0	1	0	0	0	0	3	1	0	2	0
daytime	75	.4953	8.1013	49.1	33	9	3	9	8	7	3	3	12	0	0	5	1	2	0	33	0	0	0	0	5	12	0	4	1
Dayton	15	.6041	1.9620	42.9	0	3	1	5	2	3	1	0	8	1	0	2	2	1	0	0	0	0	0	0	0	0	1	0	0
daze	8	.4552	.8454	39.3	1	1	0	4	2	0	0	0	4	0	0	0	0	0	0	1	0	0	0	0	2	0	0	1	0
dazed	15	.4654	1.5766	42.0	0	1	1	2	6	3	2	0	6	0	0	5	0	1	0	0	0	0	0	0	2	0	0	1	0
dazzle	4	.3778	.3240	35.1	0	1	0	1	0	0	2	0	0	1	0	0	0	0	0	0	1	0	0	0	0	0	0	2	0
dazzled	7	.4061	.6274	38.0	0	0	0	2	3	0	1	1	1	0	0	1	0	0	0	0	0	0	0	0	3	0	0	2	0
Dazzler	5	.0000	.0586	27.7	0	0	0	0	0	5	0	0	0	0	0	0	0	0	0	0	0	0	0	0	5	0	0	0	0
dazzling	30	.6639	4.1181	46.1	2	4	4	7	2	5	4	2	7	0	0	1	0	6	0	0	3	2	0	0	1	2	3	5	0
DB	7	.0000	.1048	30.2	0	0	1	2	0	4	0	0	0	0	0	0	7	0	0	0	0	0	0	0	0	0	0	0	0
DC	13	.0796	.3869	35.9	1	1	2	3	2	2	2	0	0	0	0	0	12	0	0	1	0	0	0	0	0	0	0	0	0

8L darns
9B darr-dit-dit-dit
9B darr-dit-dit-dit-darr
9B Darrel
8E Darrell
3E DART
7Q dart-hurling
7Q Dart's
6R darte
7Q darters
6F dartgun
8D dartles
3J darum
7R Darwinian
6R Daryle
5A Dash
6F Dashan
5Q dashboards
XR dashikis
7A dat's
8H Data
7R data-hunting
9R date-palm
9B datebook
9L dated-looking
7A dateless
9A datelined
5Q Datis
7H datoo
8E datum
7F daub
6H dauber
5B Daugherty's
8A daughter-in-law
8K Daumier's
8D daunting
XB dauphin
8K davenport
7B DAVID
7Q Davidson
5Q Davies
9Q Davis'
4P Davis's
8Q Davisson
9P davits
3D DAVY
8D Daw's
5G Dawes
4D Dawlish
8J dawn's
3B Dawn's
7D dawnlit
8D daws
6A day-break
3A day-dreamed
7B day-dreams
7A day-in
5B day-long
7A day-out
8C Day's
7F Dayak
5A daydreamed
8B daydreamitis
7A Daylight
8A daylights
9J daylong
6N daystar
4A Daytime
3P Daytona
7P dazos
8N Dazzler's
8R dazzles
5E DBY
6R DC-7
7E DCCLIII
4E DCG

Word Type	F	D	U	SFI	3 Gr 3	4 Gr 4	5 Gr 5	6 Gr 6	7 Gr 7	8 Gr 8	9 Gr 9	X UnGr	A Read	B Eng & Gr	C Comp	D Lit	E Math	F Soc Stud	G Spell	H Sci	J Music	K Art	L Home Ec	M Shop	N Lib F	P Lib NF	Q Lib Ref	R Mag	S Rel
DDD	5	.0000	.2284	33.6	0	0	0	0	0	5	0	0	5	0	0	0	0	0	0	0	0	0	0	0	0	0	0	0	0
DDT	9	.3505	.7194	38.6	0	1	0	6	0	0	2	0	0	0	0	0	0	0	0	6	0	0	0	0	0	0	1	2	0
de	127	.7823	19.940	53.0	4	6	16	20	65	12	3	1	14	7	0	3	0	7	12	0	22	1	0	1	22	20	13	5	0
De	17	.4739	1.6944	42.3	6	0	0	0	6	0	5	0	0	2	0	0	0	0	0	0	0	0	0	0	0	6	4	5	0
DE	13	.2240	.7136	38.5	0	4	0	3	1	2	3	0	0	0	0	0	12	0	0	0	0	0	0	1	0	0	0	0	0
deBergerac	3	.3670	.2406	33.8	0	1	0	0	0	1	0	1	0	0	0	0	0	0	1	1	0	0	0	0	0	0	1	0	0
deChamplain	3	.0000	.0583	27.7	0	0	3	0	0	0	0	0	0	0	0	0	0	3	0	0	0	0	0	0	0	0	0	0	0
deCristo	3	.1927	.1491	31.7	0	0	0	0	1	0	1	1	0	0	0	0	0	0	0	1	0	0	0	0	0	0	0	2	0
deDanse	2	.0000	.0209	23.2	0	0	0	0	0	2	0	0	0	0	0	0	0	0	0	0	0	0	0	0	0	0	2	0	0
DeDion	9	.0000	.1303	31.1	0	9	0	0	0	0	0	0	0	0	0	0	0	0	0	0	0	0	0	0	0	9	0	0	0
deFalla	5	.0000	.0404	26.1	0	0	0	2	0	3	0	0	0	0	0	0	0	0	0	0	5	0	0	0	0	0	0	0	0
deForest	2	.0000	.0389	25.9	0	0	2	0	0	0	0	0	0	0	0	0	0	2	0	0	0	0	0	0	0	0	0	0	0
deGaulle	21	.2803	1.3448	41.3	5	0	0	0	0	14	2	0	0	0	0	0	0	2	0	0	0	0	0	0	0	0	5	14	0
DeGaulle	6	.0000	.0729	28.6	0	0	0	0	0	0	6	0	0	0	0	0	0	0	0	0	0	0	0	0	0	0	0	6	0
deGaulle's	2	.0000	.0243	23.9	0	0	0	0	1	0	1	0	0	0	0	0	0	0	0	0	0	0	0	0	0	0	0	2	0
DeGaulle's	4	.0000	.0486	26.9	0	0	0	0	0	0	4	0	0	0	0	0	0	0	0	0	0	0	0	0	0	0	0	4	0
DeGree	19	.0000	.8680	39.4	0	0	0	19	0	0	0	0	19	0	0	0	0	0	0	0	0	0	0	0	0	0	0	0	0
DeGree's	2	.0000	.0914	29.6	0	0	0	2	0	0	0	0	2	0	0	0	0	0	0	0	0	0	0	0	0	0	0	0	0
deJaneiro	9	.3846	.7573	38.8	0	1	2	4	0	2	0	0	0	0	0	0	0	4	0	0	2	0	0	0	0	0	3	0	0
deLeon	15	.3308	1.1447	40.6	0	0	13	1	1	0	0	0	0	0	0	0	0	11	1	0	0	0	0	0	0	0	3	0	0
deMaguaque	2	.0000	.0209	23.2	0	0	0	0	0	2	0	0	0	0	0	0	0	0	0	0	0	0	0	0	0	0	2	0	0
deOjeda	2	.0000	.0389	25.9	0	0	2	0	0	0	0	0	0	0	0	0	0	2	0	0	0	0	0	0	0	0	0	0	0
deParis	2	.1698	.1133	30.5	1	0	0	0	1	0	0	0	1	0	0	0	0	0	0	0	0	0	0	0	0	0	1	0	0
DeParma	7	.0000	.0751	28.8	0	0	0	0	0	7	0	0	0	0	0	7	0	0	0	0	0	0	0	0	0	0	0	0	0
dePasco	2	.0000	.0389	25.9	0	0	0	0	2	0	0	0	0	0	0	0	0	2	0	0	0	0	0	0	0	0	0	0	0
deSolis	3	.0000	.0314	25.0	3	0	0	0	0	0	0	0	0	0	0	0	0	0	0	0	0	0	0	0	0	0	3	0	0
deSoto	6	.1823	.2810	34.5	0	0	2	0	4	0	0	0	0	0	0	0	0	2	0	0	0	0	0	0	0	0	4	0	0
DeSoto	8	.1558	.3721	35.7	1	0	7	0	0	0	0	0	0	0	0	0	0	7	0	0	0	0	0	0	0	1	0	0	0
DeStijl	2	.0000	.0209	23.2	0	0	2	0	0	0	0	0	0	0	0	0	0	0	0	0	0	0	0	0	0	0	2	0	0
deVega	2	.0000	.0209	23.2	0	2	0	0	0	0	0	0	0	0	0	0	0	0	0	0	0	0	0	0	0	0	2	0	0
DeVega's	2	.0000	.0209	23.2	0	2	0	0	0	0	0	0	0	0	0	0	0	0	0	0	0	0	0	0	0	0	2	0	0
deVilliers	2	.0000	.0215	23.3	0	0	0	0	0	2	0	0	0	0	0	2	0	0	0	0	0	0	0	0	0	0	0	0	0
deVincennes	2	.0000	.0914	29.6	2	0	0	0	0	0	0	0	2	0	0	0	0	0	0	0	0	0	0	0	0	0	0	0	0
DeWitt	4	.2152	.2714	34.3	2	0	0	0	1	1	0	0	2	0	0	0	0	2	0	0	0	0	0	0	0	0	0	0	0
de-	2	.2408	.1091	30.4	0	0	0	0	0	2	0	0	0	1	0	0	0	0	1	0	0	0	0	0	0	0	0	0	0
de-mousing	2	.0000	.0234	23.7	0	0	2	0	0	0	0	0	0	0	0	0	0	0	0	0	0	0	0	0	2	0	0	0	0
de'	2	.1247	.0633	28.0	0	0	0	1	0	0	1	0	0	0	0	0	0	0	0	0	0	1	0	0	0	1	0	0	0
dead	590	.8790	103.45	60.1	64	82	59	88	154	68	62	13	155	16	5	93	2	18	3	72	17	3	0	6	84	65	19	31	1
Dead	23	.6044	2.9780	44.7	1	3	6	2	7	4	0	0	9	0	0	3	0	6	0	0	0	0	0	0	0	2	2	1	0
Dead-Come-Back-Man	3	.0000	.1370	31.4	0	0	0	0	3	0	0	0	3	0	0	0	0	0	0	0	0	0	0	0	0	0	0	0	0
deaden	6	.5153	.6594	38.2	0	0	0	2	1	1	2	0	1	0	0	1	0	1	0	1	1	0	1	0	0	0	0	0	0
deadened	2	.0000	.0394	26.0	0	0	0	0	1	0	0	1	0	0	0	0	0	0	0	2	0	0	0	0	0	0	0	0	0
deadening	3	.2427	.1822	32.6	0	0	0	2	0	0	0	1	0	0	0	0	0	0	0	2	0	0	0	0	0	0	0	1	0
deadline	4	.2296	.2103	33.2	0	0	0	0	0	0	4	0	0	0	1	0	0	0	0	0	0	0	0	0	0	0	0	3	0
deadlines	3	.2270	.1588	32.0	0	0	0	0	1	0	2	0	0	2	0	0	0	0	0	0	0	0	0	0	0	0	1	0	0
deadly	56	.8023	9.0862	49.6	0	2	10	14	14	8	4	4	16	2	0	6	0	3	1	9	1	0	0	0	3	8	3	4	0
Deadwood	2	.0000	.0215	23.3	0	0	0	0	2	0	0	0	0	0	0	2	0	0	0	0	0	0	0	0	0	0	0	0	0
deaf	52	.7255	7.7406	48.9	7	5	7	6	9	11	7	0	15	7	0	5	0	3	0	4	0	0	0	0	2	10	2	4	0
Deaf	5	.3441	.4209	36.2	0	0	1	1	0	1	2	0	2	0	0	0	0	0	0	0	0	0	0	0	0	0	1	2	0
deafened	3	.2804	.1831	32.6	0	0	0	0	2	0	1	0	0	0	1	1	0	0	0	0	0	0	0	0	1	0	0	0	0
deafening	9	.4189	.8861	39.5	0	2	0	3	2	0	1	1	4	0	0	0	0	0	0	1	0	0	0	0	3	0	0	1	0
deafeningly	2	.1787	.1174	30.7	0	0	0	1	1	0	0	0	1	0	0	0	0	0	0	0	0	0	0	0	1	0	0	0	0
deafness	3	.2261	.2131	33.3	0	0	2	0	0	1	0	0	2	0	0	0	0	0	0	0	0	0	0	0	1	0	0	0	0
deal	480	.9381	89.047	59.5	49	70	57	76	101	54	59	14	67	23	5	25	9	65	5	109	14	6	12	7	22	49	32	30	0
Deal	9	.0000	.1750	32.4	0	0	0	0	0	9	0	0	0	0	0	0	0	9	0	0	0	0	0	0	0	0	0	0	0
dealer	30	.7234	4.3907	46.4	8	1	0	2	7	4	3	5	2	0	0	2	3	2	1	1	1	0	0	1	0	7	1	9	0
Dealer	3	.2309	.1631	32.1	0	0	0	0	3	0	0	0	0	0	0	1	0	0	0	0	0	0	0	0	0	0	0	2	0
dealer's	2	.0000	.0243	23.9	0	0	0	0	0	0	0	2	0	0	0	0	0	0	0	0	0	0	0	0	0	0	0	2	0
dealers	28	.4594	2.7755	44.4	1	1	4	0	8	4	5	5	3	0	0	3	0	4	0	0	1	0	0	0	0	0	2	15	0
dealers'	2	.2442	.1134	30.5	0	0	0	0	1	1	0	0	0	1	0	0	0	0	0	0	0	0	0	0	0	0	0	1	0
dealership	2	.1814	.1187	30.7	0	0	0	0	1	0	0	1	1	0	0	0	0	0	0	0	0	0	0	0	0	0	0	1	0
dealing	47	.7336	6.9490	48.4	5	3	6	1	14	6	11	1	2	6	2	2	4	5	1	1	1	0	0	0	0	8	13	2	0
dealings	12	.5466	1.3679	41.4	1	0	3	1	3	3	1	0	0	0	0	1	0	5	2	0	0	0	0	0	0	2	2	0	0
deals	37	.8565	6.3072	48.0	1	3	5	5	4	9	9	1	2	2	1	3	5	7	3	3	1	0	1	0	1	1	6	1	0
dealt	21	.6657	2.8562	44.6	2	0	1	1	4	6	6	1	2	0	0	3	0	2	1	1	1	0	0	0	0	1	5	5	0
dean	4	.1873	.1827	32.6	0	0	2	0	0	0	1	1	0	0	0	0	0	0	0	0	0	0	0	0	0	0	3	1	0
Dean	27	.5384	3.2333	45.1	10	0	2	2	9	3	1	0	14	3	0	0	0	2	0	0	0	0	0	0	0	3	0	5	0
Deane	2	.0000	.0914	29.6	0	0	0	2	0	0	0	0	2	0	0	0	0	0	0	0	0	0	0	0	0	0	0	0	0
Deanne	6	.0000	.2741	34.4	0	0	0	6	0	0	0	0	6	0	0	0	0	0	0	0	0	0	0	0	0	0	0	0	0
dear	445	.7303	66.941	58.3	92	84	57	72	68	17	47	8	189	18	5	70	0	5	10	0	49	0	0	0	51	26	0	22	0
Dear	47	.5837	5.7219	47.6	8	14	3	5	9	6	1	1	9	17	4	3	0	2	1	0	6	0	0	0	0	0	0	5	0
Dearborn	5	.3023	.3461	35.4	2	0	0	0	3	0	0	0	0	0	0	0	0	1	0	0	0	0	0	0	0	1	0	3	0
dearer	2	.1717	.1142	30.6	0	0	0	0	0	1	1	0	1	0	0	1	0	0	0	0	0	0	0	0	0	0	0	0	0
dearest	17	.6249	2.2287	43.5	1	0	3	4	3	1	3	2	5	0	0	2	1	1	0	0	3	0	0	0	0	3	0	2	0
dearie	3	.2357	.2199	33.4	0	1	0	1	1	0	0	0	2	0	0	0	0	0	0	0	0	0	0	0	0	1	0	0	0
dearly	18	.7026	2.6036	44.2	2	5	2	0	4	1	3	1	5	1	0	3	0	2	0	0	1	0	0	0	2	3	0	1	0
dears	3	.2261	.2131	33.3	1	1	0	0	0	1	0	0	2	0	0	0	0	0	0	0	0	0	0	0	1	0	0	0	0
dearth	2	.2437	.1129	30.5	0	0	0	0	1	0	1	0	0	0	0	0	0	0	0	0	0	0	0	0	0	0	1	1	0
deary	5	.2446	.3872	35.9	2	0	0	2	1	0	0	0	4	0	0	0	0	0	0	0	0	0	0	0	1	0	0	0	0
death	518	.8754	90.403	59.6	17	42	57	68	148	95	72	19	116	16	4	83	2	43	3	27	22	2	2	0	35	51	67	44	1
Death	56	.7655	8.7250	49.4	0	8	7	8	16	4	11	2	17	4	0	8	2	4	0	1	1	1	0	0	0	12	3	3	0
Death's	3	.3851	.2497	34.0	0	0	0	0	2	0	1	0	0	0	0	1	0	0	0	0	0	0	0	0	1	1	0	0	0
deathbed	2	.2152	.1357	31.3	1	0	0	0	0	1	0	0	1	0	0	0	0	1	0	0	0	0	0	0	0	0	0	0	0
deathbox	3	.0000	.0322	25.1	0	0	0	0	0	3	0	0	0	0	0	3	0	0	0	0	0	0	0	0	0	0	0	0	0
deathless	2	.1814	.1187	30.7	0	0	0	1	0	0	0	1	1	0	0	0	0	0	0	0	0	0	0	0	0	0	0	1	0
deaths	32	.6934	4.5137	46.5	0	0	1	0	13	10	6	2	2	1	1	5	3	4	0	4	0	0	0	0	0	0	3	9	0

7Q deAlvarado
7P deAviles
5Q deBalboa
5Q deBalzac
4Q deBeauregard
8F deBelleau
8Q deBenserade
XH deBlowitz
9F deBrazza
6N deBureford
6R deCardenas
XR DeCarlos
8D deCassagnac
8F deChamplain's
8Q deClavijo
9Q deCorbeil
7Q deCordoba
8Q deCoulomb
XP DeDietrich
4P deDion
9Q DeForest
3P DeFosse
8Q deFrederic
8Q deGasperi
8Q deGasperi's
4A deGrace
3H DeKay
7Q DeKay's
7J DeKoven's
3Q deLaFontaine
5F deLafayette
3P DeLancey
7Q deLaplace
6F deLas
3Q deLegaspi
5R DeLeon
5F deLeon's
5P deLibrari
5Q deLisle
7R DeLorenzo
7A deLorge
7A deLorge's
4N deMalaga
4N deMare
3Q deMendoza
8J deMille
8Q deMindanao
9F deMontcalm
7Q deMonte
7Q deMontejo
8Q deMusique
5Q dePerthes
8F dePortola
5P DePottenzuipers
8Q deRojas
6P deRome
9R DeRosa
7Q deSaint-Exupery
6F deSan
8B deSanMarcos
3Q deSanMartin
7Q DeSaussure
5R DeScherer
6R deSmet
5F deSoto's
7J DeSylva
6N deTodoslosSantos
3A deTriomphe
5Q deUlua
7Q deUrsua
8P deWaal
9D DeWiart
3A DeWitts
9R DeWolfe
5R de-kinkers
8G de-li-cious
9H de-modulation
7R de-press-ing
4F de-salt
9R Deacon
7R Deacon's
8N deacons
7Q deactivated
7N dead-O
5Q dead-air
6P dead-ball
7N dead-beats
6A dead-letter
7P dead-pan
7A dead-right
9M deadcenter
6P deader
XR deadfall
8B deadlie
7A deadlier
9B deadwood
5A deaf-blind
9R deafen
XR Deal's
3A Dean's
6A Deanne's
4A dearskin
9D Deas
7A DeathValley
7A death-bed
9D death-darting
9D death-marked
9J death's
5P deathblow
5F deathlike
8J deathly
3K Deauville
7M debark

Word Type	F	D	U	SFI	3 Gr 3	4 Gr 4	5 Gr 5	6 Gr 6	7 Gr 7	8 Gr 8	9 Gr 9	X UnGr	A Read	B Eng & Gr	C Comp	D Lit	E Math	F Soc Stud	G Spell	H Sci	J Music	K Art	L Home Ec	M Shop	N Lib F	P Lib NF	Q Lib Ref	R Mag	S Rel
debarkation	2	.0000	.0290	24.6	0	0	0	0	2	0	0	0	0	0	0	0	0	0	0	0	0	0	0	0	0	2	0	0	0
debatable	2	.2401	.1133	30.5	0	0	0	0	0	1	0	1	0	0	0	0	0	0	0	0	0	0	0	0	0	1	1	0	0
debate	34	.6274	4.4815	46.5	0	0	0	4	13	14	2	1	9	3	0	2	0	9	0	1	0	0	0	0	0	0	3	7	0
debated	8	.3079	.5787	37.6	0	0	1	2	1	3	1	0	1	1	0	0	0	1	0	0	0	0	0	0	0	0	0	5	0
debates	9	.3198	.6922	38.4	0	1	0	1	3	2	1	1	2	0	0	0	0	1	0	0	0	0	0	0	0	1	0	5	0
debating	5	.3536	.4328	36.4	0	0	1	0	2	1	1	0	2	0	0	0	0	0	0	0	0	0	0	0	1	2	0	0	0
Debbie	9	.4673	.9967	40.0	7	1	1	0	0	0	0	0	6	1	0	0	1	0	0	1	0	0	0	0	0	0	0	0	0
Debby	15	.1409	.7358	38.7	0	10	5	0	0	0	0	0	5	0	0	0	0	0	0	0	0	0	0	0	0	10	0	0	0
Deborah	12	.2445	.7013	38.5	10	1	0	0	0	0	1	0	0	0	0	0	0	0	1	0	0	0	0	0	0	10	0	1	0
Deborah's	5	.0000	.0724	28.6	5	0	0	0	0	0	0	0	0	0	0	0	0	0	0	0	0	0	0	0	0	5	0	0	0
Debre	3	.0000	.0365	25.6	0	0	0	0	0	0	3	0	0	0	0	0	0	0	0	0	0	0	0	0	0	0	0	3	0
debris	20	.5566	2.3021	43.6	2	1	1	5	7	3	1	0	0	0	0	1	0	0	1	4	0	0	0	0	2	0	5	7	0
Debs	4	.2420	.3089	34.9	3	0	0	0	0	1	0	0	3	0	0	0	0	1	0	0	0	0	0	0	0	0	0	0	0
debt	43	.7492	6.5495	48.2	1	2	8	6	6	15	3	2	8	1	0	3	5	11	0	0	1	0	0	0	3	4	6	1	0
debtors'	2	.2152	.1357	31.3	0	0	0	1	0	1	0	0	1	0	0	0	0	1	0	0	0	0	0	0	0	0	0	0	0
debts	36	.5906	4.5106	46.5	0	4	8	2	8	11	3	0	8	1	0	0	0	15	0	0	0	0	0	0	1	3	5	3	0
Debussy	38	.1984	1.7796	42.5	7	2	4	3	5	11	6	0	0	0	0	0	0	1	0	0	28	0	0	0	0	8	1	0	0
Debussy's	7	.3066	.4610	36.6	0	0	0	0	2	3	2	0	0	0	0	0	0	0	0	0	5	1	0	0	0	1	0	0	0
debut	5	.3562	.3925	35.9	0	0	0	1	4	0	0	0	0	0	0	0	0	0	0	0	0	0	0	0	0	3	1	1	0
debutante	2	.2433	.1158	30.6	0	0	0	0	1	0	1	0	0	0	0	0	0	0	0	0	0	0	0	0	0	1	0	1	0
Dec	17	.2212	.8853	39.5	0	0	5	1	5	5	1	0	0	0	0	0	0	0	0	0	0	0	0	0	0	0	11	6	0
DEC	2	.0000	.0299	24.8	0	0	0	0	0	2	0	0	0	0	0	0	2	0	0	0	0	0	0	0	0	0	0	0	0
decade	46	.6177	5.8373	47.7	1	1	1	3	16	12	11	1	1	0	0	1	4	6	0	4	1	0	0	0	0	4	11	14	0
decades	55	.5588	6.3709	48.0	0	1	6	1	19	7	14	7	1	1	0	0	4	3	1	6	0	0	0	0	0	5	21	13	0
decay	67	.5911	8.2958	49.2	5	2	8	8	21	6	15	2	4	1	0	1	0	4	0	41	1	0	3	0	0	5	6	1	0
decayed	18	.5230	1.9972	43.0	2	1	3	1	3	5	2	1	0	0	0	0	0	3	0	10	0	0	1	0	0	2	2	0	0
decaying	19	.4013	1.6969	42.3	4	0	3	3	7	1	1	0	1	0	0	0	0	0	0	10	0	0	0	0	1	1	6	0	0
decays	5	.3426	.3891	35.9	1	0	0	0	3	0	1	0	0	0	0	0	0	1	0	2	0	0	0	0	0	0	2	0	0
deceased	7	.3123	.5115	37.1	0	0	0	0	1	2	4	0	1	0	0	0	0	1	0	0	0	0	0	0	0	0	4	1	0
deceit	4	.4791	.4053	36.1	0	0	0	0	1	1	2	0	0	0	0	1	0	1	0	0	0	0	0	0	0	1	1	0	0
deceitful	3	.2431	.1816	32.6	1	0	0	0	0	2	0	0	0	0	0	0	0	2	0	0	0	0	0	0	1	0	0	0	0
deceive	4	.2399	.3011	34.8	0	0	0	1	2	1	0	0	3	1	0	0	0	0	0	0	0	0	0	0	0	0	0	0	0
deceived	7	.5999	.8614	39.4	0	0	2	1	1	0	3	0	0	1	0	2	0	0	0	1	0	0	0	0	1	1	0	1	0
deceiving	5	.3330	.4105	36.1	0	0	1	0	2	0	2	0	2	2	0	0	0	0	0	0	0	0	0	0	1	0	0	0	0
decem	4	.1511	.1521	31.8	0	0	2	0	1	0	1	0	0	0	0	0	1	0	3	0	0	0	0	0	0	0	0	0	0
December	121	.7911	19.262	52.8	8	37	14	16	17	15	12	2	16	7	3	5	11	19	2	11	6	0	0	1	2	10	14	13	1
decency	2	.1787	.1174	30.7	0	0	0	0	0	1	1	0	1	0	0	0	0	0	0	0	0	0	0	0	1	0	0	0	0
decent	20	.5397	2.3112	43.6	1	1	0	1	11	6	0	0	5	0	0	6	0	1	0	0	0	0	0	0	2	2	0	4	0
decentralize	2	.0000	.0243	23.9	0	0	0	0	0	0	2	0	0	0	0	0	0	0	0	0	0	0	0	0	0	0	0	2	0
deception	2	.2401	.1133	30.5	0	0	0	0	2	0	0	0	0	0	0	0	0	0	0	0	0	0	0	0	0	1	1	0	0
deceptive	6	.5563	.7177	38.6	0	0	1	0	3	0	1	1	2	0	0	1	0	0	0	0	0	0	0	0	0	1	1	1	0
deceptively	2	.2446	.1184	30.7	0	0	1	0	0	0	1	0	0	0	0	0	1	0	0	0	0	0	0	0	0	1	0	0	0
decide	540	.8958	96.193	59.8	68	97	81	66	86	80	51	11	127	74	10	11	52	72	20	37	27	16	27	10	10	21	7	19	0
decided	777	.9204	142.11	61.5	133	147	120	99	130	82	53	13	286	39	6	41	27	121	7	15	11	5	9	3	50	76	20	61	0
decidedly	10	.4948	1.0282	40.1	0	1	0	1	2	2	4	0	0	0	0	1	0	0	0	0	1	0	0	0	5	0	2	1	0
decides	51	.7013	7.3894	48.7	11	3	6	4	10	8	8	1	16	2	4	1	2	13	0	3	0	2	2	0	0	4	0	2	0
deciding	44	.8492	7.4826	48.7	4	6	5	4	8	7	9	1	12	4	2	2	2	5	2	3	1	0	3	1	1	1	1	4	0
deciduous	10	.3457	.7852	38.9	0	0	1	1	5	0	2	1	0	0	0	0	0	0	0	6	0	0	0	0	0	0	3	1	0
decimal	711	.0272	14.137	51.5	1	5	9	302	179	130	84	1	0	4	0	0	704	0	0	1	0	0	0	0	0	1	0	1	0
Decimal	13	.0776	.3331	35.2	0	0	0	2	2	9	0	0	0	12	0	0	1	0	0	0	0	0	0	0	0	0	0	0	0
decimals	94	.0800	2.7616	44.4	0	6	7	15	26	20	20	0	0	0	0	0	93	0	0	0	0	0	0	1	0	0	0	0	0
decimated	4	.3519	.3117	34.9	0	1	0	1	1	1	0	0	0	0	0	0	0	1	0	0	0	0	0	0	0	0	1	2	0
decimeter	4	.0000	.0599	27.8	0	0	0	0	4	0	0	0	0	0	0	0	4	0	0	0	0	0	0	0	0	0	0	0	0
decimeters	7	.0000	.1048	30.2	0	0	3	3	1	0	0	0	0	0	0	0	7	0	0	0	0	0	0	0	0	0	0	0	0
deciphered	2	.2446	.1125	30.5	0	0	0	1	0	0	1	0	0	1	0	1	0	0	0	0	0	0	0	0	0	0	0	0	0
decision	127	.7865	20.104	53.0	4	3	15	12	34	36	20	3	18	7	2	9	1	27	4	2	0	0	10	0	3	14	9	21	0
Decision	3	.2332	.1690	32.3	0	0	0	0	2	0	1	0	0	0	0	0	0	0	0	0	0	0	0	0	0	2	0	1	0
decision-making	3	.1937	.1495	31.7	0	0	0	0	1	1	1	0	0	0	0	0	0	1	0	0	0	0	0	0	0	0	0	2	0
decisions	93	.7284	13.708	51.4	3	11	11	7	18	21	17	5	5	8	0	1	4	18	0	14	0	0	7	0	2	6	14	14	0
decisive	11	.5569	1.2669	41.0	0	1	2	0	2	2	4	0	0	1	0	0	0	2	0	0	0	0	0	0	1	1	4	2	0
decisively	4	.3402	.3011	34.8	0	0	0	0	0	2	2	0	0	0	0	1	0	1	0	0	0	0	0	0	0	0	2	0	0
deck	237	.8086	39.075	55.9	18	91	25	34	36	16	15	2	134	4	2	11	1	7	1	2	8	1	0	0	18	26	6	16	0
Deck	11	.1222	.4016	36.0	0	0	0	0	1	0	10	0	0	0	0	0	0	0	0	0	0	0	0	0	1	10	0	0	0
decked	5	.4293	.4745	36.8	0	0	3	1	1	0	0	0	1	0	0	1	0	0	0	0	0	0	0	0	1	0	0	2	0
Decker	4	.0000	.0486	26.9	0	0	0	0	0	0	0	4	0	0	0	0	0	0	0	0	0	0	0	0	0	0	0	4	0
deckhand	2	.2407	.1090	30.4	0	0	1	0	1	0	0	0	0	1	0	0	0	0	0	0	1	0	0	0	0	0	0	0	0
deckhands	2	.0000	.0389	25.9	0	2	0	0	0	0	0	0	0	0	0	0	0	2	0	0	0	0	0	0	0	0	0	0	0
decking	2	.2297	.1135	30.6	0	0	0	0	0	1	1	0	0	0	0	1	0	1	0	0	0	0	0	0	0	0	0	0	0
decks	24	.6477	3.3064	45.2	3	2	3	7	8	1	0	0	12	1	0	1	0	3	0	0	2	0	0	0	1	4	0	0	0
declaration	12	.4738	1.2782	41.1	0	0	2	3	0	3	4	0	4	0	0	0	0	4	0	0	0	0	0	0	0	0	2	2	0
Declaration	51	.5143	5.6721	47.5	4	4	4	8	5	20	6	0	7	3	0	0	1	31	0	0	3	0	0	0	0	2	4	0	0
declarative	4	.0836	.0819	29.1	1	0	0	0	3	0	0	0	0	1	3	0	0	0	0	0	0	0	0	0	0	0	0	0	0
declare	31	.6909	4.3958	46.4	4	4	3	4	5	9	2	0	5	1	0	2	0	8	0	0	1	0	0	0	6	6	1	1	0
declared	177	.6989	25.514	54.1	11	33	21	23	35	36	16	2	44	2	1	12	0	52	0	0	1	0	0	0	2	29	19	15	0
declares	8	.4752	.8166	39.1	0	1	2	0	2	2	0	1	1	0	0	0	1	0	0	0	0	0	0	0	0	1	2	3	0
declaring	14	.6585	1.8954	42.8	0	0	3	0	4	5	2	0	1	1	0	1	0	6	0	0	0	0	0	0	1	1	1	2	0
declination	3	.0000	.0591	27.7	0	0	0	2	0	0	0	1	0	0	0	0	0	0	0	3	0	0	0	0	0	0	0	0	0
decline	26	.6260	3.3177	45.2	0	1	1	1	12	1	6	4	1	2	1	0	0	3	0	0	0	1	1	0	0	0	12	5	0
declined	23	.5851	2.7789	44.4	1	1	4	1	7	5	1	3	2	0	3	0	0	4	0	0	1	1	0	0	0	1	6	5	0
declines	2	.1641	.0751	28.8	0	0	0	1	1	0	0	0	0	0	1	0	0	0	0	0	0	0	0	0	0	0	1	0	0
declining	11	.5853	1.3269	41.2	0	2	3	1	2	1	2	0	0	1	0	0	0	2	0	0	0	0	0	0	1	3	3	1	0
decode	6	.2280	.3734	35.7	0	2	1	1	1	1	0	0	2	0	0	0	0	0	3	1	0	0	0	0	0	0	0	0	0
decoded	2	.1814	.1187	30.7	0	1	0	0	1	0	0	0	1	0	0	0	0	0	0	0	0	0	0	0	0	0	0	1	0
decompose	8	.0000	.1577	32.0	0	0	0	0	0	4	4	0	0	0	0	0	0	0	0	8	0	0	0	0	0	0	0	0	0
decomposed	5	.0000	.0986	29.9	0	0	0	0	0	2	1	2	0	0	0	0	0	0	0	5	0	0	0	0	0	0	0	0	0
decomposition	6	.3591	.4882	36.9	0	0	0	2	1	0	2	1	0	0	0	0	0	0	0	4	0	0	0	0	1	0	1	0	0
decompression	18	.1532	1.2117	40.8	0	16	0	1	0	0	1	0	17	0	0	0	0	0	0	0	0	0	0	0	0	1	0	0	0
decor	2	.2408	.1204	30.8	0	0	0	1	0	1	0	0	0	0	0	0	0	1	0	0	0	0	0	0	0	1	0	0	0
decorate	29	.6032	3.6078	45.6	4	4	5	8	4	1	2	1	5	2	0	0	1	3	1	0	4	5	1	3	1	0	2	1	0
decorated	63	.7902	10.087	50.0	9	13	10	15	5	4	5	2	21	4	1	2	0	9	0	1	7	3	2	0	0	4	3	6	0
decorating	12	.5892	1.4743	41.7	1	0	1	2	3	2	1	2	3	0	0	1	0	0	0	0	0	1	2	1	1	0	0	3	0
decoration	26	.5307	2.8965	44.6	4	3	0	3	7	3	2	4	6	0	0	1	0	0	1	0	1	6	3	2	1	0	3	2	0
decorations	43	.7326	6.3996	48.1	12	9	1	6	5	7	3	0	10	0	1	0	0	4	3	0	1	4	2	3	1	6	2	6	0
decorative	25	.4890	2.4926	44.0	0	0	3	3	7	4	5	3	0	0	0	0	0	0	1	0	3	4	8	0	0	3	3	3	0

8F debasing
7A debauch
8B debauched
7R debaucher
6J debke
5A debonair
3E Debra
7F debrief
6A debris-filled
7F debris-strewn
7Q debt-free
7A debtors
7Q debunked
7P debutante's
7P debutantes
7P debutantes'
7R debuting
7P debuts
8Q Debye
7E deca
6E deca-
9E decagon
6N decalcomanias
5Q decalogue
8M decals
7N decamp
7R decapitate
4N Decapods
7E decathlon
5Q Decatur
6J Decca
9Q Deccan
9Q deceased's
4N Deceit
9R deceives
7R deceleration
8B december
3J December's
7D decently
9Q decentralization
5P decentralized
5R Deception
7P deceptions
9M decharged
6E deci-
7Q decimate
7Q decimators
8F Decisions
5J Deciso
7N declamatory
6B declarations
6N declivity
5Q Decmocratic-Republican
XD decoction
6R decoding
7H decomposers
4Q decorates
5Q Decoration
7R decoratively

Word Type	F	D	U	SFI	3 Gr 3	4 Gr 4	5 Gr 5	6 Gr 6	7 Gr 7	8 Gr 8	9 Gr 9	X UnGr	A Read	B Eng & Gr	C Comp	D Lit	E Math	F Soc Stud	G Spell	H Sci	J Music	K Art	L Home Ec	M Shop	N Lib F	P Lib NF	Q Lib Ref	R Mag	S Rel
decorator	4	.2932	.2861	34.6	0	2	1	0	0	0	0	1	1	0	0	0	0	0	0	0	0	0	0	0	0	0	2	1	0
decorum	2	.1717	.1142	30.6	0	0	0	0	0	1	1	0	1	0	0	1	0	0	0	0	0	0	0	0	0	0	0	0	0
decoy	5	.2086	.3320	35.2	1	0	0	3	1	0	0	0	3	0	0	0	0	0	0	0	0	0	0	0	2	0	0	0	0
decrease	29	.5523	3.3580	45.3	0	1	2	2	11	4	9	0	0	0	0	0	9	2	0	12	2	0	0	0	0	0	3	1	0
decreased	8	.3510	.6567	38.2	0	0	0	1	1	3	0	3	1	0	1	0	1	0	0	5	0	0	0	0	0	0	0	0	0
decreases	32	.3466	2.4438	43.9	1	1	5	1	3	16	5	0	1	0	0	0	2	0	0	13	2	0	1	11	0	1	1	0	0
decreasing	8	.3943	.6858	38.4	1	0	0	0	4	1	1	1	0	0	0	0	0	1	0	2	1	0	0	0	0	0	4	0	0
decree	12	.4673	1.2334	40.9	0	0	2	0	2	5	3	0	3	0	0	0	0	1	0	0	0	0	0	0	1	0	4	3	0
Decree	2	.0000	.0209	23.2	0	0	0	0	0	2	0	0	0	0	0	0	0	0	0	0	0	0	0	0	0	0	2	0	0
decreed	7	.5546	.8372	39.2	0	1	0	2	2	1	1	0	2	0	0	0	0	2	0	0	0	0	0	0	1	1	1	0	0
decrees	7	.4464	.6758	38.3	0	0	1	1	0	3	2	0	1	0	0	0	0	1	0	0	0	0	1	0	1	0	3	0	0
decrescendo	2	.0000	.0162	22.1	0	0	0	1	1	0	0	0	0	0	0	0	0	0	0	0	2	0	0	0	0	0	0	0	0
dedicate	9	.4575	.8737	39.4	0	0	1	1	0	5	2	0	0	0	0	3	0	3	0	0	2	0	0	0	0	0	0	1	0
dedicated	42	.6706	5.7444	47.6	0	1	5	3	10	14	5	4	3	0	0	5	0	7	0	0	5	0	0	0	1	6	7	8	0
dedication	14	.5624	1.6546	42.2	0	0	3	1	1	5	2	2	2	1	0	0	0	2	0	0	3	0	0	0	0	3	0	3	0
deduce	2	.2446	.1122	30.5	0	0	0	0	0	1	1	0	0	0	0	1	0	0	0	0	0	0	0	0	0	0	1	0	0
deduced	4	.3374	.3006	34.8	0	0	0	0	2	0	0	2	0	0	0	2	0	0	0	1	0	0	0	0	0	0	0	1	0
deduct	3	.1937	.1495	31.7	0	0	0	0	0	1	0	2	0	0	0	0	0	1	0	0	0	0	0	0	0	0	0	2	0
deducted	4	.3328	.2989	34.8	0	0	0	1	0	2	1	0	0	2	0	0	0	1	0	0	0	0	0	0	0	1	0	0	0
deductible	2	.0000	.0243	23.9	0	0	0	0	0	0	0	2	0	0	0	0	0	0	0	0	0	0	0	0	0	0	0	2	0
deduction	3	.3870	.2492	34.0	0	0	1	0	1	0	1	0	0	0	0	0	0	0	0	0	0	0	0	0	1	0	1	1	0
deductions	11	.5958	1.3485	41.3	0	0	0	0	2	1	6	2	0	0	0	1	2	0	0	3	0	0	1	0	0	0	1	3	0
dee	16	.0636	.3246	35.1	4	10	2	0	0	0	0	0	0	0	0	0	0	0	0	0	15	0	0	0	1	0	0	0	0
Deeba	7	.0000	.3198	35.0	0	7	0	0	0	0	0	0	7	0	0	0	0	0	0	0	0	0	0	0	0	0	0	0	0
deed	27	.6538	3.6953	45.7	1	0	9	4	4	4	5	0	9	2	1	5	0	6	0	0	0	0	0	0	2	0	0	2	0
deeds	39	.6116	5.0449	47.0	2	7	5	4	7	7	6	1	14	0	0	11	0	0	0	0	3	0	0	0	2	4	2	3	0
deemed	8	.5541	.9194	39.6	0	0	1	0	3	1	3	0	0	1	0	1	0	2	0	0	0	0	0	0	2	0	0	2	0
deems	2	.2278	.1128	30.5	0	0	0	1	0	1	0	0	0	0	0	0	0	0	0	1	0	0	0	0	0	0	1	0	0
deep	996	.9207	182.05	62.6	178	179	130	150	177	77	73	32	304	21	14	78	10	101	4	125	33	15	11	3	63	102	45	67	0
Deep	10	.4485	.9502	39.8	0	4	0	1	2	0	3	0	0	0	0	5	0	0	0	1	0	0	0	0	0	2	1	1	0
deep-diving	2	.1814	.1187	30.7	0	1	0	0	1	0	0	0	1	0	0	0	0	0	0	0	0	0	0	0	0	0	0	1	0
deep-drifted	2	.2412	.1141	30.6	1	0	0	1	0	0	0	0	0	1	0	0	0	0	0	0	0	0	0	0	0	1	0	0	0
deep-rooted	2	.2303	.1079	30.3	0	0	1	1	0	0	0	0	0	0	0	0	0	0	0	0	1	0	0	0	0	1	0	0	0
deep-sea	25	.5667	3.1625	45.0	0	10	6	3	4	1	1	0	16	1	0	2	0	1	0	4	0	0	0	0	1	0	0	0	0
deep-seated	3	.3811	.2534	34.0	0	0	0	0	0	2	1	0	0	0	0	0	0	0	0	1	0	0	0	0	0	1	0	1	0
deep-set	5	.3967	.4158	36.2	0	0	0	0	1	2	2	0	0	0	0	2	0	0	0	0	1	1	0	0	1	0	0	0	0
deep-throated	4	.1349	.2265	33.6	0	1	0	0	0	2	1	0	3	0	1	0	0	0	0	0	0	0	0	0	0	0	0	0	0
deep-toned	2	.0000	.0914	29.6	0	0	0	0	2	0	0	0	2	0	0	0	0	0	0	0	0	0	0	0	0	0	0	0	0
deep-water	5	.4328	.4654	36.7	0	0	1	1	2	0	1	0	0	0	0	1	0	1	0	1	0	0	0	0	0	0	2	0	0
deep-yellow	2	.0000	.0064	18.1	0	0	0	0	0	0	2	0	0	0	0	0	0	0	0	0	0	0	2	0	0	0	0	0	0
deepen	3	.2437	.2277	33.6	0	0	1	1	0	1	0	0	2	0	0	0	0	0	0	1	0	0	0	0	0	0	0	0	0
deepened	10	.6208	1.2879	41.1	0	2	3	0	2	0	1	2	2	1	1	1	0	1	0	0	0	0	0	0	1	0	2	1	0
deepening	10	.5708	1.1991	40.8	0	0	0	2	5	0	2	1	2	1	0	1	0	0	0	0	0	0	0	0	1	0	3	2	0
deepens	3	.2076	.1697	32.3	0	0	0	0	3	0	0	0	1	0	1	0	0	0	0	0	0	0	0	0	1	0	0	0	0
deeper	137	.8270	22.860	53.6	17	28	16	23	28	13	6	6	49	3	0	8	2	8	0	16	5	0	0	1	6	11	15	13	0
deepest	46	.8448	7.7778	48.9	8	5	8	6	9	7	3	0	8	0	0	2	3	6	0	6	1	1	1	0	2	7	4	5	0
Deepfreeze	2	.1717	.1142	30.6	0	0	0	1	0	1	0	0	1	0	0	1	0	0	0	0	0	0	0	0	0	0	0	0	0
deeply	136	.8746	23.711	53.7	9	12	20	21	32	21	14	7	29	9	1	20	0	14	2	5	5	0	1	1	10	16	7	16	0
deeps	4	.3488	.3091	34.9	0	1	1	0	2	0	0	0	0	0	0	0	0	0	0	1	0	0	0	0	2	0	1	0	0
Deepstar	8	.0000	.1577	32.0	0	8	0	0	0	0	0	0	0	0	0	0	0	0	0	8	0	0	0	0	0	0	0	0	0
deer	316	.8506	54.051	57.3	71	87	43	32	53	21	3	6	124	24	3	24	7	13	9	29	2	0	0	0	27	31	15	8	0
Deer	16	.5584	1.9203	42.8	5	1	1	0	2	6	0	1	5	0	0	1	0	0	0	0	0	0	0	0	1	6	1	2	0
deer-lick	6	.0000	.0703	28.5	0	0	6	0	0	0	0	0	0	0	0	0	0	0	0	0	0	0	0	0	6	0	0	0	0
deer's	5	.3836	.4751	36.8	1	1	0	2	1	0	0	0	3	0	0	0	0	0	0	0	0	0	0	0	1	0	1	0	0
Deere	3	.3350	.2478	33.9	0	0	0	1	1	1	0	0	1	0	0	0	0	1	0	0	0	0	0	0	0	0	1	0	0
Deerfield	7	.3570	.5507	37.4	0	0	0	2	1	0	4	0	0	0	0	0	0	0	0	0	0	0	0	0	0	4	1	2	0
Deering's	2	.2442	.1134	30.5	0	0	0	1	0	1	0	0	0	1	0	0	0	0	0	0	0	0	0	0	0	0	0	1	0
deerskin	20	.3262	1.8320	42.6	9	5	1	1	4	0	0	0	17	0	0	1	0	0	0	0	0	0	0	0	0	2	0	0	0
deerskins	9	.3609	.8077	39.1	1	5	2	1	0	0	0	0	4	0	0	0	0	2	0	0	0	0	0	0	0	3	0	0	0
DEF	20	.0000	.2994	34.8	0	0	0	1	3	13	3	0	0	0	0	0	20	0	0	0	0	0	0	0	0	0	0	0	0
deface	2	.2305	.1080	30.3	0	0	0	0	2	0	0	0	0	0	0	0	0	0	1	0	0	0	0	0	0	1	0	0	0
Defarge	11	.0000	.1180	30.7	0	0	0	0	0	0	11	0	0	0	0	11	0	0	0	0	0	0	0	0	0	0	0	0	0
Defarge's	2	.0000	.0215	23.3	0	0	0	0	0	0	2	0	0	0	0	2	0	0	0	0	0	0	0	0	0	0	0	0	0
Defarges	2	.0000	.0215	23.3	0	0	0	0	0	0	2	0	0	0	0	2	0	0	0	0	0	0	0	0	0	0	0	0	0
defeat	82	.7548	12.591	51.0	3	4	14	11	22	18	6	4	17	4	0	3	0	23	1	1	2	0	0	0	6	15	3	7	0
defeated	96	.7019	13.760	51.4	2	3	11	15	22	21	19	3	12	11	1	2	0	30	0	0	2	0	0	0	1	9	19	9	0
defeating	10	.1686	.4443	36.5	2	0	1	2	2	2	1	0	0	0	0	0	0	4	1	0	0	0	0	0	0	2	2	0	1
defeats	4	.2107	.2095	33.2	2	0	0	1	1	0	0	0	0	0	0	0	0	0	0	0	0	0	0	0	0	3	0	1	0
defect	6	.4293	.5503	37.4	0	0	1	0	2	1	1	1	0	0	0	1	0	0	0	1	0	0	0	0	0	0	1	3	0
defected	2	.2433	.1158	30.6	0	0	1	0	0	1	0	0	0	0	0	0	0	0	0	0	0	0	0	0	0	1	0	1	0
defective	14	.4575	1.3581	41.3	0	0	0	0	3	2	5	4	0	5	0	0	0	0	0	3	0	0	0	0	0	0	2	4	0
defects	27	.5188	2.9640	44.7	2	1	0	0	5	5	11	3	2	0	0	1	0	2	0	10	0	0	5	0	0	2	3	2	0
defence	3	.3131	.2349	33.7	0	0	0	2	0	1	0	0	1	0	0	0	0	1	0	0	1	0	0	0	0	0	0	0	0
defend	69	.7745	10.816	50.3	5	9	15	5	9	17	9	0	13	6	2	6	3	21	1	1	0	0	0	0	1	4	8	3	0
defendant	16	.6169	2.1124	43.2	0	0	1	5	1	1	8	0	7	1	0	1	0	4	1	0	0	0	0	0	2	0	0	0	0
defendants	6	.0000	.0729	28.6	0	0	0	0	0	2	4	0	0	0	0	0	0	0	0	0	0	0	0	0	0	0	0	6	0
defended	16	.6136	2.0933	43.2	2	0	1	2	8	1	2	0	6	0	0	1	0	4	0	0	0	0	0	0	0	2	2	1	0
defender	7	.3897	.5964	37.8	0	1	2	1	1	0	2	0	1	0	0	0	0	0	1	0	3	0	0	0	0	0	2	0	0
defenders	11	.5505	1.3434	41.3	1	1	4	0	2	2	1	0	6	0	0	1	0	1	0	0	1	0	0	0	0	2	0	0	0
defending	20	.7767	3.1352	45.0	0	4	1	1	5	6	2	1	3	1	0	1	0	5	1	0	1	0	0	0	3	2	2	1	0
defense	110	.7581	16.888	52.3	4	5	15	10	31	20	25	0	17	6	2	2	0	18	1	8	0	0	1	0	0	18	15	22	0
Defense	26	.5751	3.1315	45.0	4	1	1	0	1	7	12	0	1	0	0	1	1	13	0	1	0	0	0	0	0	2	2	5	0
defenseless	2	.2401	.1133	30.5	1	0	1	0	0	0	0	0	0	0	0	0	0	0	0	0	0	0	0	0	0	1	.1	0	0
defenses	22	.4910	2.3258	43.7	0	3	0	3	5	8	3	0	1	0	0	0	0	10	0	4	0	0	0	0	0	0	3	4	0
defensive	19	.4854	1.9456	42.9	0	0	2	2	7	6	2	0	1	1	0	0	0	0	2	0	0	0	0	0	0	3	2	10	0
defensively	3	.2159	.1532	31.9	0	0	0	0	2	0	1	0	0	0	0	0	0	0	0	0	0	0	0	0	0	0	2	1	0
deference	2	.2443	.1130	30.5	0	0	0	1	0	0	1	0	0	0	0	1	0	0	0	0	0	0	0	0	1	0	0	0	0
deferent	2	.0000	.0394	26.0	0	0	0	0	0	2	0	0	0	0	0	0	0	0	0	2	0	0	0	0	0	0	0	0	0
deferment	5	.0000	.0523	27.2	0	0	0	0	5	0	0	0	0	0	0	0	0	0	0	0	0	0	0	0	0	0	5	0	0
deferments	2	.0000	.0209	23.2	0	0	0	0	2	0	0	0	0	0	0	0	0	0	0	0	0	0	0	0	0	0	2	0	0
deferred	3	.2143	.1568	32.0	0	0	1	0	0	0	2	0	0	0	0	0	0	0	0	0	0	0	0	0	0	1	0	2	0
Defferre's	2	.0000	.0243	23.9	0	0	0	0	0	2	0	0	0	0	0	0	0	0	0	0	0	0	0	0	0	0	0	2	0
defiance	15	.5323	1.7873	42.5	0	1	1	2	5	4	2	0	8	0	0	0	0	3	0	0	2	0	0	0	0	1	0	1	0
Defiance	2	.1717	.1142	30.6	0	1	0	0	1	0	0	0	1	0	0	1	0	0	0	0	0	0	0	0	0	0	0	0	0

7L decorators
6P decorously
8D decrepit
4N decrepitude
7J decrescendos
XR Decro
9J Dedicated
4F dedicating
6A dedided
6Q deductive
7J Dee-ah-geel-yehf
4A dee-dee-dee
6A Deedee
7N deef
5R deejay
8F deem
6A deeming
7P Deep-River
6A deep-blue
7Q deep-bodied
9N deep-creased
9B deep-dish
6J deep-drenched
7J deep-felt
7P deep-fix'd
9H deep-focus
9A deep-freeze
9Q deep-frozen
9F deep-lying
6H deep-pink
4J deep-pitched
4A deep-running
7A deep-rutted
9H deep-sea-diving
3A deep-shadowed
9B deepfreeze
3H deeply-cut
7Q deepsea
8R deepseated
5F deepwater
7N deer-hound
4A deer-meat
6R Deerfield's
4A Deerford
6R Deering
4F Deerpath
8B Deever
7A defamation
9R defaulted
7R defeatism
7Q defecates
9Q defecation
6G defection
9R defectives
7N defenceless
7J Defender
8R defending-champion
7R defends
7R defense's
7R defenseman's
4Q defensible
8R Defferre
6E DEFG

Word Type	F	D	U	SFI	3 Gr 3	4 Gr 4	5 Gr 5	6 Gr 6	7 Gr 7	8 Gr 8	9 Gr 9	X UnGr	A Read	B Eng & Gr	C Comp	D Lit	E Math	F Soc Stud	G Spell	H Sci	J Music	K Art	L Home Ec	M Shop	N Lib F	P Lib NF	Q Lib Ref	R Mag	S Rel
defiant	6	.6013	.7495	38.7	0	1	2	0	1	0	2	0	1	1	0	1	0	0	0	0	1	0	0	0	1	1	0	0	0
defiantly	8	.3907	.7093	38.5	0	2	0	1	4	1	0	0	2	0	0	0	0	0	0	0	0	0	1	0	4	1	0	0	0
deficiencies	4	.2153	.1980	33.0	0	0	0	0	1	1	0	2	0	0	0	0	0	0	0	1	0	0	2	0	0	0	1	0	0
deficiency	17	.3816	1.4550	41.6	0	3	4	0	2	3	3	2	0	1	0	0	0	0	0	12	0	0	0	0	0	0	3	1	0
deficient	4	.4798	.4048	36.1	0	0	0	0	2	0	2	0	0	0	0	1	0	0	0	1	0	0	0	0	0	0	1	1	0
defied	13	.6783	1.8173	42.6	2	1	3	1	2	3	1	0	3	1	0	1	0	1	0	0	0	0	0	0	1	2	3	1	0
defies	4	.3366	.2993	34.8	0	0	0	0	3	0	1	0	0	0	0	0	0	0	0	1	0	0	0	0	1	0	2	0	0
defile	4	.4530	.4014	36.0	0	0	1	0	3	0	0	0	1	0	0	0	0	0	0	0	0	0	0	0	0	1	1	1	0
defiled	3	.3263	.2368	33.7	0	0	0	0	2	1	0	0	1	0	0	0	0	0	0	0	1	0	0	0	0	0	0	1	0
define	73	.8160	11.993	50.8	0	0	6	4	27	18	18	0	18	12	0	0	14	3	1	11	1	1	2	2	0	2	5	1	0
defined	90	.8106	14.610	51.6	0	1	4	5	31	26	20	3	9	13	0	0	24	5	7	6	3	0	2	1	1	2	10	7	0
defines	9	.5283	.9924	40.0	0	0	0	0	0	6	2	1	1	1	1	0	2	0	1	1	0	0	2	0	0	0	0	0	0
defining	9	.5111	.9567	39.8	0	0	1	1	0	4	3	0	0	1	0	0	2	1	0	0	2	0	0	0	0	0	3	0	0
definite	148	.8536	25.111	54.0	6	10	7	8	32	42	39	4	6	17	6	8	3	6	2	34	15	3	11	7	1	8	14	7	0
definitely	43	.7648	6.6001	48.2	1	1	1	7	18	7	5	3	2	3	0	3	0	3	0	2	1	0	3	1	5	5	2	13	0
definition	182	.7437	27.391	54.4	1	9	18	24	45	40	40	5	28	42	3	1	37	4	29	7	6	0	1	0	0	6	12	6	0
definitional	3	.0000	.0583	27.7	0	0	0	0	0	0	3	0	0	0	0	0	0	3	0	0	0	0	0	0	0	0	0	0	0
definitions	75	.4144	6.7751	48.3	0	1	4	10	42	12	4	2	11	11	0	0	8	1	38	0	1	0	0	0	0	2	3	0	0
definitive	2	.2346	.1166	30.7	0	0	0	0	1	0	0	1	0	0	0	0	0	0	0	1	0	0	0	0	0	0	0	1	0
deflation	2	.0000	.0394	26.0	0	0	0	0	0	0	2	0	0	0	0	0	0	0	0	2	0	0	0	0	0	0	0	0	0
deflect	3	.3781	.2548	34.1	0	1	1	0	0	0	1	0	0	0	0	0	0	1	0	1	0	0	0	0	0	0	0	1	0
deflected	5	.2213	.2870	34.6	0	0	0	2	2	0	1	0	0	0	0	0	0	0	0	4	0	0	0	0	0	0	1	0	0
deflection	3	.0000	.0591	27.7	0	0	0	2	0	1	0	0	0	0	0	0	0	0	0	3	0	0	0	0	0	0	0	0	0
deflector	3	.2915	.1900	32.8	0	0	0	0	2	0	1	0	0	1	0	0	0	0	0	0	0	0	0	1	0	0	0	1	0
Defoe	3	.1823	.1405	31.5	0	0	2	0	1	0	0	0	0	0	0	0	0	1	0	0	0	0	0	0	0	0	2	0	0
Defoe's	2	.0000	.0209	23.2	0	0	2	0	0	0	0	0	0	0	0	0	0	0	0	0	0	0	0	0	0	0	2	0	0
deformation	4	.1249	.1371	31.4	0	0	0	0	0	2	2	0	0	0	0	0	0	0	0	2	0	0	0	2	0	0	0	0	0
deformed	8	.4991	.8391	39.2	0	0	1	0	3	0	3	1	0	0	0	0	0	0	0	3	0	0	0	1	1	1	2	0	0
deforming	2	.0000	.0394	26.0	0	0	0	0	0	0	2	0	0	0	0	0	0	0	0	2	0	0	0	0	0	0	0	0	0
deformity	4	.3359	.2989	34.8	0	0	2	0	0	2	0	0	0	0	0	0	0	1	0	0	0	0	0	0	0	0	2	1	0
defrosting	2	.0000	.0914	29.6	2	0	0	0	0	0	0	0	2	0	0	0	0	0	0	0	0	0	0	0	0	0	0	0	0
deft	5	.3986	.4435	36.5	0	1	0	0	3	1	0	0	1	0	1	0	0	0	0	0	0	0	0	0	1	1	0	1	0
deftly	5	.3507	.3752	35.7	0	0	1	0	4	0	0	0	0	0	1	2	0	0	0	0	0	0	0	0	2	0	0	0	0
defy	6	.5290	.6603	38.2	0	1	0	0	3	0	2	0	0	0	0	1	0	0	0	1	0	0	0	0	1	1	2	0	0
defying	2	.2375	.1088	30.4	0	0	0	1	0	0	1	0	0	0	0	0	0	0	0	0	1	0	0	0	0	0	0	1	0
deg	2	.0000	.0050	17.0	0	0	0	0	0	2	0	0	0	0	0	0	0	0	0	0	0	0	0	2	0	0	0	0	0
degenerate	2	.0000	.0209	23.2	0	0	0	0	1	1	0	0	0	0	0	0	0	0	0	0	0	0	0	0	0	0	2	0	0
degeneration	2	.2278	.1128	30.5	0	0	0	0	0	0	2	0	0	0	0	0	0	0	0	1	0	0	0	0	0	0	1	0	0
degradation	2	.2408	.1204	30.8	0	0	0	0	0	1	1	0	0	0	0	0	0	1	0	0	0	0	0	0	0	1	0	0	0
degrading	4	.3072	.2981	34.7	0	0	0	1	2	0	1	0	1	0	0	0	0	0	0	0	0	0	0	0	1	0	0	2	0
degree	191	.8598	32.624	55.1	2	9	37	12	53	35	33	10	6	12	9	6	35	10	7	18	7	0	5	5	7	8	36	20	0
degree-measure	5	.0000	.0748	28.7	0	0	3	0	1	1	0	0	0	0	0	0	5	0	0	0	0	0	0	0	0	0	0	0	0
degree-measures	3	.0000	.0449	26.5	0	0	2	0	1	0	0	0	0	0	0	0	3	0	0	0	0	0	0	0	0	0	0	0	0
degrees	356	.8416	59.805	57.8	20	46	53	37	91	47	51	11	33	11	3	7	79	38	21	52	7	0	7	22	6	13	25	32	0
dehydrated	7	.1419	.2284	33.6	0	0	0	0	2	2	3	0	0	0	0	0	0	0	0	0	0	0	5	0	0	0	1	1	0
dehydration	2	.2346	.1166	30.7	0	0	0	0	0	0	0	2	0	0	0	0	0	0	0	1	0	0	0	0	0	0	0	1	0
deid	2	.0000	.0219	23.4	0	0	0	0	0	2	0	0	0	2	0	0	0	0	0	0	0	0	0	0	0	0	0	0	0
deir	3	.0000	.0328	25.2	0	0	0	0	0	3	0	0	0	3	0	0	0	0	0	0	0	0	0	0	0	0	0	0	0
deities	5	.3334	.3767	35.8	0	0	0	2	0	1	1	1	0	0	0	1	0	1	0	0	0	0	0	0	0	3	0	0	0
deity	4	.3783	.3298	35.2	0	0	0	1	2	0	0	1	0	1	0	0	0	0	0	0	0	0	0	0	0	2	0	1	0
Deity	3	.3029	.1930	32.9	0	1	0	0	2	0	0	0	0	0	1	0	0	0	0	0	1	0	0	0	0	0	1	0	0
deja	2	.0000	.0243	23.9	0	0	0	0	1	0	0	1	0	0	0	0	0	0	0	0	0	0	0	0	0	0	0	2	0
dejected	4	.3604	.3538	35.5	0	0	0	0	2	2	0	0	2	0	0	1	0	0	0	0	1	0	0	0	0	0	0	0	0
dejectedly	2	.1717	.1142	30.6	0	0	0	0	1	1	0	0	1	0	0	1	0	0	0	0	0	0	0	0	0	0	0	0	0
dekameters	3	.0000	.0449	26.5	0	0	0	0	3	0	0	0	0	0	0	0	3	0	0	0	0	0	0	0	0	0	0	0	0
del	10	.4524	.9737	39.9	3	0	4	0	0	3	0	0	1	0	0	0	0	2	0	0	3	0	0	0	0	1	3	0	0
Del	13	.0335	.2542	34.1	0	0	0	0	13	0	0	0	1	0	0	12	0	0	0	0	0	0	0	0	0	0	0	0	0
delFuego	3	.1823	.1405	31.5	0	0	0	0	3	0	0	0	0	0	0	0	0	1	0	0	0	0	0	0	0	0	2	0	0
delaPlata	3	.0000	.0583	27.7	0	0	0	1	2	0	0	0	0	0	0	0	0	3	0	0	0	0	0	0	0	0	0	0	0
Delacroix	4	.2385	.2074	33.2	0	0	0	0	1	0	1	2	0	0	0	0	0	0	0	0	3	1	0	0	0	0	0	0	0
Delacroix's	2	.1696	.0749	28.7	0	0	0	0	0	1	0	1	0	0	0	0	0	0	0	0	1	1	0	0	0	0	0	0	0
Delafield	2	.0000	.0219	23.4	0	0	0	0	0	0	2	0	0	2	0	0	0	0	0	0	0	0	0	0	0	0	0	0	0
Delahanty	23	.1827	.9580	39.8	0	0	0	0	10	0	13	0	0	0	10	13	0	0	0	0	0	0	0	0	0	0	0	0	0
Delano	4	.3286	.3009	34.8	0	0	1	2	0	0	0	1	0	0	0	0	0	1	0	1	0	0	0	0	0	0	0	2	0
Delaware	73	.6302	9.4719	49.8	14	5	23	7	17	4	1	2	6	1	0	9	0	14	1	0	0	0	0	0	3	14	21	4	0
Delaware's	2	.2285	.1129	30.5	0	0	1	0	0	1	0	0	0	0	0	0	0	1	0	0	0	0	0	0	0	0	1	0	0
Delawareans	2	.0000	.0209	23.2	0	0	2	0	0	0	0	0	0	0	0	0	0	0	0	0	0	0	0	0	0	0	2	0	0
Delawares	5	.3776	.4103	36.1	0	2	0	0	3	0	0	0	0	0	0	1	0	0	0	0	0	0	0	0	2	2	0	0	0
delay	42	.7724	6.5544	48.2	2	3	6	3	11	3	9	5	8	1	3	3	0	4	1	4	0	0	1	0	3	4	5	5	0
delayed	31	.7609	4.7637	46.8	0	1	3	4	11	3	7	2	5	5	1	0	0	2	1	1	1	0	0	0	2	2	5	6	0
delaying	2	.2444	.1132	30.5	0	0	0	1	0	1	0	0	0	1	0	0	0	0	0	0	0	0	0	0	1	0	0	0	0
delays	10	.4969	1.0764	40.3	1	0	1	1	2	0	4	1	2	2	0	0	0	0	0	2	0	0	0	0	0	1	3	0	0
delectable	2	.2444	.1132	30.5	0	1	0	0	0	1	0	0	0	1	0	0	0	0	0	0	0	0	0	0	1	0	0	0	0
delegate	7	.5512	.8434	39.3	0	0	0	1	4	1	1	0	3	0	0	1	0	1	0	0	1	0	0	0	0	1	0	0	0
delegated	2	.2408	.1204	30.8	0	0	0	1	0	1	0	0	0	0	0	0	0	1	0	0	0	0	0	0	0	1	0	0	0
delegates	50	.3972	4.4862	46.5	1	0	8	4	0	34	3	0	4	0	0	1	0	33	0	0	0	0	0	0	0	0	8	4	0
delegates'	2	.2412	.1141	30.6	0	0	1	0	0	0	1	0	0	1	0	0	0	0	0	0	0	0	0	0	0	1	0	0	0
delegation	12	.4221	1.1242	40.5	1	0	2	1	3	4	1	0	1	0	0	0	0	5	0	0	0	0	0	0	0	3	0	3	0
delegations	5	.4085	.4628	36.7	0	0	0	1	2	2	0	0	1	0	0	0	0	1	0	0	0	0	0	0	0	1	0	2	0
delete	3	.0000	.0328	25.2	0	0	0	0	0	2	1	0	0	3	0	0	0	0	0	0	0	0	0	0	0	0	0	0	0
deleted	2	.2442	.1134	30.5	0	0	0	0	1	1	0	0	0	1	0	0	0	0	0	0	0	0	0	0	0	0	0	1	0
deleting	2	.0000	.0219	23.4	0	0	0	0	1	1	0	0	0	2	0	0	0	0	0	0	0	0	0	0	0	0	0	0	0
deletion	2	.0000	.0219	23.4	0	0	0	0	0	2	0	0	0	2	0	0	0	0	0	0	0	0	0	0	0	0	0	0	0
Delft	8	.3803	.6582	38.2	1	0	0	0	1	5	0	1	0	0	0	0	0	1	2	1	0	0	0	0	0	0	4	0	0
Delgado	7	.0000	.0851	29.3	0	0	0	0	5	0	0	2	0	0	0	0	0	0	0	0	0	0	0	0	0	0	0	7	0
Delgados	2	.0000	.0243	23.9	0	0	0	0	2	0	0	0	0	0	0	0	0	0	0	0	0	0	0	0	0	0	0	2	0
Delhi	7	.2644	.4777	36.8	1	4	0	0	0	2	0	0	1	0	0	0	0	5	0	0	0	0	0	0	0	0	0	1	0
deliberate	21	.7544	3.1939	45.0	2	0	2	4	4	2	7	0	3	5	1	1	0	2	1	0	0	1	1	0	4	1	1	0	0
deliberately	38	.8134	6.1915	47.9	2	2	4	6	9	8	5	2	6	3	2	2	0	2	1	1	2	1	0	0	4	2	5	7	0
deliberation	4	.3689	.3351	35.3	0	0	1	0	2	1	0	0	1	0	0	0	0	0	0	0	0	0	1	0	0	0	1	1	0
deliberations	4	.2420	.3089	34.9	0	0	0	0	3	1	0	0	3	0	0	0	0	1	0	0	0	0	0	0	0	0	0	0	0
delicacies	7	.5184	.7879	39.0	1	2	0	0	3	1	0	0	2	1	0	2	0	1	0	0	0	0	0	0	0	0	0	1	0
delicacy	10	.5708	1.1977	40.8	0	0	1	2	1	2	3	1	2	0	0	1	0	0	1	0	2	0	0	0	0	1	0	3	0
delicate	114	.8088	18.483	52.7	8	9	7	17	34	16	18	5	18	2	4	2	0	7	1	11	6	8	5	1	8	11	16	14	0
Delicate	2	.0000	.0243	23.9	0	0	0	0	0	0	2	0	0	0	0	0	0	0	0	0	0	0	0	0	0	0	0	2	0
delicately	20	.7217	2.9191	44.7	0	2	0	0	8	3	6	1	2	0	1	3	0	1	0	2	0	0	2	1	3	4	1	0	0

9R deficit
8B Defining
9F DEFINITIONAL
XR deflate
3P deflated
9R deflator
9D deflowered
8R defoliated
7Q defoliation
7R deforestation
9M deform
7H deforms
8F defraud
4H defroster
3Q defrosters
7R deftness
6R defunct
5R defuzzing
9H degenerates
8Q degenerative
9B degrade
6R degraded
5A deguello
4D dehelm
9P dehook
7B dehul
8M dehumidifiers
5P deified
8B deip
7F deisel
6A dejection
7E deka-
7E dekameter
7R delNorte
7Q del-norte
7D Del's
3A Dela
7R Delco
7R Delcos
5P Deledda
6A delegate's
6R delegently
7B deletes
5H Delia
9D deliberated
7D deliberating
3J Delibes
3N Delicatessa

Word Type	F	D	U	SFI	3 Gr 3	4 Gr 4	5 Gr 5	6 Gr 6	7 Gr 7	8 Gr 8	9 Gr 9	X UnGr	A Read	B Eng & Gr	C Comp	D Lit	E Math	F Soc Stud	G Spell	H Sci	J Music	K Art	L Home Ec	M Shop	N Lib F	P Lib NF	Q Lib Ref	R Mag	S Rel
delicious	83	.7556	12.802	51.1	11	14	16	12	16	1	10	3	30	6	1	2	0	7	5	2	2	0	9	0	7	3	2	7	0
Delicious	2	.0000	.0914	29.6	0	2	0	0	0	0	0	0	2	0	0	0	0	0	0	0	0	0	0	0	0	0	0	0	0
deliciously	2	.1717	.1142	30.6	0	1	0	0	0	1	0	0	1	0	0	1	0	0	0	0	0	0	0	0	0	0	0	0	0
delight	116	.8265	19.331	52.9	12	16	16	30	24	10	4	4	44	2	2	15	1	2	1	1	8	1	0	0	14	12	6	7	0
Delight	3	.0000	.0365	25.6	0	0	0	2	0	0	0	1	0	0	0	0	0	0	0	0	0	0	0	0	0	0	0	3	0
delighted	91	.7893	14.581	51.6	14	23	16	10	13	6	8	1	34	5	3	10	0	2	0	1	2	0	1	0	10	11	2	10	0
delightedly	6	.3501	.5265	37.2	0	2	0	2	2	0	0	0	3	0	0	0	0	0	0	0	0	0	0	0	2	1	0	0	0
delightful	36	.5086	3.9760	46.0	6	5	2	8	4	2	6	3	12	2	7	3	0	1	0	0	1	0	1	0	1	5	0	3	0
delightfully	4	.2819	.2521	34.0	0	0	0	1	2	0	1	0	0	0	0	0	0	0	0	0	0	1	0	0	1	2	0	0	0
delighting	4	.4442	.3918	35.9	0	0	0	1	1	1	1	0	1	0	0	1	0	0	0	0	1	0	0	0	0	0	0	1	0
delights	17	.5389	1.9901	43.0	0	3	2	1	3	1	4	3	6	1	0	3	0	1	0	0	0	0	0	0	0	1	0	5	0
Delilah	2	.0000	.0162	22.1	0	0	0	0	0	2	0	0	0	0	0	0	0	0	0	0	2	0	0	0	0	0	0	0	0
delineated	2	.2437	.1129	30.5	0	0	0	0	2	0	0	0	0	0	0	0	0	0	0	0	0	0	0	0	0	0	1	1	0
delineation	2	.1493	.0692	28.4	0	1	0	0	1	0	0	0	0	0	0	0	0	0	0	0	0	1	0	0	0	0	1	0	0
delinquency	3	.2279	.2143	33.3	0	0	0	0	3	0	0	0	2	0	0	0	0	0	0	0	0	0	0	0	0	0	0	1	0
delirious	6	.4207	.5558	37.4	0	1	0	2	0	1	2	0	1	0	0	2	0	0	0	0	0	0	0	0	1	0	0	2	0
delirium	2	.2160	.1362	31.3	0	0	0	1	0	0	1	0	1	0	0	0	0	0	0	1	0	0	0	0	0	0	0	0	0
Delius	2	.0000	.0162	22.1	0	0	0	0	0	2	0	0	0	0	0	0	0	0	0	0	2	0	0	0	0	0	0	0	0
deliver	81	.6745	11.348	50.5	19	9	9	10	16	12	5	1	25	5	0	6	10	11	4	3	0	0	1	2	7	2	2	2	1
Deliver	2	.2446	.1122	30.5	0	0	1	0	0	0	1	0	0	0	0	1	0	0	0	0	0	0	0	0	0	0	1	0	0
deliverance	10	.0000	.1172	30.7	0	1	0	9	0	0	0	0	0	0	0	0	0	0	0	0	0	0	0	0	10	0	0	0	0
delivered	87	.8662	15.050	51.8	9	7	10	21	21	12	6	1	21	2	3	7	9	8	3	3	0	0	1	1	13	10	3	3	0
deliveries	14	.5747	1.7032	42.3	2	2	0	5	4	0	0	1	3	0	0	0	5	0	0	0	0	0	0	0	2	2	1	1	0
delivering	25	.6713	3.5019	45.4	7	1	0	3	6	3	3	2	9	0	0	2	0	2	0	0	0	0	0	0	2	4	3	3	0
delivers	14	.5737	1.6609	42.2	1	3	0	3	4	1	0	2	0	0	0	0	5	1	0	2	0	0	0	1	0	0	2	3	0
delivery	26	.8529	4.4328	46.5	1	2	2	1	9	5	6	0	5	2	0	1	1	4	1	4	1	0	1	1	1	0	3	1	0
dell	2	.1787	.1174	30.7	0	0	0	0	2	0	0	0	1	0	0	0	0	0	0	0	0	0	0	0	1	0	0	0	0
Dell	10	.2600	.7165	38.6	0	0	0	5	2	3	0	0	5	0	2	0	3	0	0	0	0	0	0	0	0	0	0	0	0
Della	15	.0000	.6852	38.4	0	0	0	7	0	8	0	0	15	0	0	0	0	0	0	0	0	0	0	0	0	0	0	0	0
Dellville	7	.0000	.3198	35.0	0	0	0	0	7	0	0	0	7	0	0	0	0	0	0	0	0	0	0	0	0	0	0	0	0
Delos	8	.0908	.2270	33.6	0	0	0	0	1	7	0	0	0	0	0	0	0	1	0	0	0	0	0	0	0	0	7	0	0
delta	25	.4679	2.5731	44.1	2	4	6	6	5	2	0	0	2	1	0	0	0	14	0	6	0	0	0	0	0	0	1	1	0
Delta	12	.6050	1.5408	41.9	1	2	0	2	1	2	3	1	3	0	0	0	0	2	0	4	0	0	0	0	1	0	1	1	0
deltas	4	.3288	.3285	35.2	0	0	2	1	1	0	0	0	1	0	0	0	0	2	0	1	0	0	0	0	0	0	0	0	0
delude	2	.2388	.1089	30.4	0	0	0	1	1	0	0	0	0	0	0	0	0	0	1	0	0	0	0	0	1	0	0	0	0
deluge	2	.0665	.0708	28.5	0	0	0	0	2	0	0	0	1	0	1	0	0	0	0	0	0	0	0	0	0	0	0	0	0
delusion	2	.2441	.1127	30.5	0	0	0	0	1	0	1	0	0	0	0	0	0	0	0	0	0	0	0	0	1	0	1	0	0
deluxe	2	.0000	.0243	23.9	0	0	0	1	1	0	0	0	0	0	0	0	0	0	0	0	0	0	0	0	0	0	0	2	0
delved	2	.2351	.1166	30.7	0	0	1	0	0	1	0	0	0	0	0	0	0	1	0	0	0	0	0	0	0	0	0	1	0
demagogues	2	.0000	.0914	29.6	0	0	0	0	2	0	0	0	2	0	0	0	0	0	0	0	0	0	0	0	0	0	0	0	0
demand	107	.8033	17.274	52.4	5	2	17	8	17	29	26	3	12	1	0	5	1	37	1	4	7	1	0	1	2	9	12	14	0
demanded	99	.7815	15.700	52.0	13	7	13	13	30	13	9	1	29	2	1	9	0	19	0	1	4	0	0	0	13	3	8	10	0
demanding	25	.5964	3.1046	44.9	2	2	1	2	8	4	5	1	3	0	0	2	0	3	0	0	1	0	0	0	2	6	0	8	0
demands	65	.7154	9.4425	49.8	3	2	3	3	15	19	18	2	5	0	2	1	0	20	0	2	3	0	1	0	1	4	10	16	0
Demarcation	2	.0000	.0209	23.2	0	0	1	0	0	1	0	0	0	0	0	0	0	0	0	0	0	0	0	0	0	0	2	0	0
demeanor	4	.4809	.4076	36.1	0	0	1	0	2	0	0	1	0	0	0	1	0	0	0	1	0	0	0	0	0	1	0	1	0
Demerara	3	.2365	.1616	32.1	0	1	0	0	0	2	0	0	0	0	0	0	0	0	0	0	1	0	0	0	0	0	2	0	0
demerits	2	.0000	.0914	29.6	0	0	2	0	0	0	0	0	2	0	0	0	0	0	0	0	0	0	0	0	0	0	0	0	0
Demeter	7	.0566	.1818	32.6	0	0	1	0	0	6	0	0	1	0	0	6	0	0	0	0	0	0	0	0	0	0	0	0	0
Demetrius	7	.1467	.2657	34.2	0	0	0	0	1	0	6	0	0	0	0	6	0	0	0	0	0	0	0	0	0	0	1	0	0
DEMETRIUS	5	.0000	.0537	27.3	0	0	0	0	0	0	5	0	0	0	0	5	0	0	0	0	0	0	0	0	0	0	0	0	0
demijohn	2	.0000	.0234	23.7	0	0	0	0	2	0	0	0	0	0	0	0	0	0	0	0	0	0	0	0	2	0	0	0	0
Demilitarized	2	.0000	.0243	23.9	0	0	0	1	0	0	1	0	0	0	0	0	0	0	0	0	0	0	0	0	0	0	0	2	0
democracies	3	.2043	.1486	31.7	2	0	1	0	0	0	0	0	0	0	0	0	0	0	0	0	0	0	0	0	0	1	2	0	0
democracy	65	.6404	8.6271	49.4	8	1	9	12	14	16	5	0	7	2	1	0	0	31	0	2	1	0	0	0	0	4	9	8	0
Democracy	3	.0000	.0328	25.2	0	0	0	0	1	0	2	0	0	3	0	0	0	0	0	0	0	0	0	0	0	0	0	0	0
Democrat	5	.3120	.3814	35.8	0	0	0	0	0	4	1	0	1	0	0	0	0	2	0	0	0	0	0	0	0	0	0	2	0
democratic	38	.7420	5.7194	47.6	7	1	4	3	8	11	3	1	5	0	1	1	0	15	0	0	2	1	1	0	1	2	8	1	0
Democratic	34	.5525	4.0031	46.0	0	0	3	0	11	12	6	2	6	1	0	0	0	13	0	0	0	0	0	0	2	0	6	6	0
Democratic-Republican	2	.0000	.0209	23.2	0	0	2	0	0	0	0	0	0	0	0	0	0	0	0	0	0	0	0	0	0	0	2	0	0
Democrats	29	.5317	3.2627	45.1	2	0	3	0	2	15	5	2	1	1	0	0	0	16	0	0	0	0	0	0	1	2	5	3	0
Democritus	5	.2213	.2870	34.6	0	0	0	1	1	1	2	0	0	0	0	0	0	0	0	4	0	0	0	0	0	0	1	0	0
demolish	3	.2437	.2277	33.6	0	1	0	0	1	1	0	0	2	0	0	0	0	0	0	1	0	0	0	0	0	0	0	0	0
demolished	6	.3361	.4370	36.4	1	0	0	0	1	1	2	1	0	0	1	0	0	0	0	0	0	0	0	0	0	0	1	4	0
Demolition	2	.0000	.0914	29.6	0	2	0	0	0	0	0	0	2	0	0	0	0	0	0	0	0	0	0	0	0	0	0	0	0
demon	17	.6093	2.1588	43.3	2	0	4	2	1	0	4	4	3	1	0	0	0	0	0	1	1	0	0	0	4	5	2	0	0
demonic	3	.0000	.0434	26.4	0	0	0	0	0	0	3	0	0	0	0	0	0	0	0	0	0	0	0	0	0	3	0	0	0
demons	15	.5550	1.7175	42.3	0	0	1	2	1	3	8	0	0	3	0	0	0	1	3	0	1	0	0	0	1	6	0	0	0
demonstrate	50	.8249	8.2378	49.2	1	3	4	8	12	8	9	5	4	1	2	0	2	4	6	10	3	1	3	0	0	3	3	8	0
demonstrated	48	.7816	7.5288	48.8	3	1	1	5	13	9	13	3	5	0	0	1	1	3	2	5	3	2	1	3	1	2	13	6	0
demonstrates	18	.7423	2.6862	44.3	0	1	0	2	4	5	5	1	1	1	0	0	0	1	2	4	1	1	2	1	0	0	2	2	0
demonstrating	9	.4042	.7914	39.0	0	0	3	0	0	1	5	0	1	0	0	0	0	1	0	0	1	0	2	0	0	0	0	4	0
demonstration	34	.7123	4.9379	46.9	1	3	4	3	4	12	7	0	5	1	0	1	0	3	0	9	1	0	3	2	0	2	1	6	0
demonstrations	23	.4630	2.2731	43.6	1	0	0	2	5	9	3	3	1	1	0	0	0	5	0	0	0	0	1	0	0	0	2	13	0
demonstrative	4	.0836	.0819	29.1	0	0	0	4	0	0	0	0	0	1	3	0	0	0	0	0	0	0	0	0	0	0	0	0	0
demonstrators	7	.1766	.3250	35.1	0	0	0	0	4	1	1	1	0	0	0	0	0	2	0	0	0	0	0	0	0	0	0	5	0
demoralized	3	.3777	.2489	34.0	0	0	0	0	0	2	1	0	0	1	0	0	0	1	0	0	0	0	0	0	1	0	0	0	0
Dempsey	8	.4506	.8382	39.2	0	0	0	3	4	1	0	0	4	2	0	0	0	1	0	0	0	0	0	0	0	0	0	1	0
demurely	3	.2357	.2199	33.4	0	1	1	0	1	0	0	0	2	0	0	0	0	0	0	0	0	0	0	0	0	1	0	0	0
den	49	.7875	7.8157	48.9	5	13	4	5	11	3	4	4	15	4	0	5	4	0	3	2	4	0	0	0	2	6	0	4	0
Denbooms	7	.0000	.3198	35.0	0	3	0	4	0	0	0	0	7	0	0	0	0	0	0	0	0	0	0	0	0	0	0	0	0
Denbooms'	2	.0000	.0914	29.6	0	0	0	2	0	0	0	0	2	0	0	0	0	0	0	0	0	0	0	0	0	0	0	0	0
dendrites	7	.0000	.1380	31.4	0	0	0	6	0	0	0	1	0	0	0	0	0	0	0	7	0	0	0	0	0	0	0	0	0
Deneb	3	.0000	.0591	27.7	0	0	0	0	0	0	0	3	0	0	0	0	0	0	0	3	0	0	0	0	0	0	0	0	0
denial	3	.1927	.1491	31.7	0	0	0	0	2	1	0	0	0	0	0	0	0	0	0	1	0	0	0	0	0	0	0	2	0
denied	45	.6931	6.4043	48.1	0	1	7	8	12	8	9	0	8	0	0	2	0	12	0	0	0	0	1	0	3	6	4	9	0
denies	3	.0000	.0322	25.1	0	0	0	0	3	0	0	0	0	0	0	3	0	0	0	0	0	0	0	0	0	0	0	0	0
denim	11	.5620	1.2909	41.1	0	2	1	2	3	2	1	0	2	0	0	2	0	0	1	0	0	0	2	0	1	0	1	2	0
Denis	10	.2891	.7472	38.7	0	0	0	9	0	0	1	0	4	0	0	0	0	0	0	0	0	0	0	0	5	0	1	0	0
Denison	3	.1927	.1491	31.7	0	0	0	2	1	0	0	0	0	0	0	0	0	0	0	1	0	0	0	0	0	0	0	2	0
denizens	2	.0000	.0914	29.6	0	0	0	1	0	1	0	0	2	0	0	0	0	0	0	0	0	0	0	0	0	0	0	0	0
Denmark	137	.5255	15.310	51.8	52	2	13	36	19	3	7	5	13	3	0	0	0	55	1	5	6	0	0	0	0	8	45	1	0
Denmark's	17	.1904	.8224	39.2	13	0	3	1	0	0	0	0	1	0	0	0	0	1	0	0	0	0	0	0	0	2	13	0	0
Dennie	2	.0000	.0234	23.7	0	0	0	0	0	2	0	0	0	0	0	0	0	0	0	0	0	0	0	0	2	0	0	0	0

4D delicatessen
6A delicious-tasting
9D deliciousness
8J Delilah's
6R delinquents
7R deliriously
8F Delivered
3A Delivery
9E delivery-truck
XR deliveryman
7C Dell's
6J Deller
8J Dello
7N dells
7Q Delmar
8F Delmonico's
6P Delphi
5P delphinium
8Q deltaic
9Q deltoids
7C deluded
5P delving
7C dem
9R Dem
9H demagnetize
7A demagoguery
3P Dembroski
7D demented
9R Demers
8N demesne
8D Demeter's
7A Demi-Lune
8F demi-gods
7D demigod
4F demilitarized
9H deminsion
8R demise
6A Demo
8A democrat
5Q Democratic-Republican
7P Democratiques
8F democrats
5A Demoiselle
4N demolishing
4A demolition
8F Demon
6A Demonstration
6B Demonstratives
XR demonstrator
8F demoralization
8P Demosthenes
8R demoted
5P demotion
XH demounted
7A Dempsey's
9D demur
4P Den
7Q Dendrobates
9P denials
7A denims
8B Denise
8H denitrifying
3A DENMARK
5P Denmark-Norway
7N denned

Word Type	F	D	U	SFI	3 Gr 3	4 Gr 4	5 Gr 5	6 Gr 6	7 Gr 7	8 Gr 8	9 Gr 9	X UnGr	A Read	B Eng & Gr	C Comp	D Lit	E Math	F Soc Stud	G Spell	H Sci	J Music	K Art	L Home Ec	M Shop	N Lib F	P Lib NF	Q Lib Ref	R Mag	S Rel
Dennis	24	.4520	2.5706	44.1	8	0	9	3	2	1	1	0	15	4	0	0	4	0	0	0	0	0	0	0	0	0	0	1	0
Denny	5	.3343	.4151	36.2	0	0	0	0	3	2	0	0	2	0	0	0	0	0	0	0	0	0	0	0	0	1	0	2	0
denomination	5	.3687	.4014	36.0	0	0	2	1	2	0	0	0	0	0	0	0	0	0	0	0	0	0	0	0	0	2	2	1	0
denominations	4	.2401	.2266	33.6	0	1	2	0	1	0	0	0	0	0	0	0	0	0	0	0	0	0	0	0	0	2	2	0	0
denominator	265	.0264	5.2269	47.2	0	36	21	63	60	33	52	0	0	0	0	0	263	0	0	0	1	0	0	0	0	0	1	0	0
denominators	70	.0000	1.0478	40.2	0	8	6	17	21	6	12	0	0	0	0	0	70	0	0	0	0	0	0	0	0	0	0	0	0
denotation	4	.0000	.0438	26.4	0	0	0	0	0	0	4	0	0	4	0	0	0	0	0	0	0	0	0	0	0	0	0	0	0
denotative	7	.0510	.0933	29.7	0	0	0	0	0	0	7	0	0	1	6	0	0	0	0	0	0	0	0	0	0	0	0	0	0
denote	25	.5002	2.6194	44.2	0	0	0	0	10	8	7	0	0	3	0	0	17	0	0	0	0	0	1	1	0	0	3	0	0
denoted	9	.1502	.3763	35.8	0	1	0	0	5	2	1	0	0	0	0	0	8	0	0	0	0	0	0	0	0	0	1	0	0
denotes	9	.3988	.7796	38.9	0	0	0	1	0	2	6	0	0	1	0	0	6	0	0	1	0	0	1	0	0	0	0	0	0
denoting	3	.3841	.2496	34.0	0	0	0	0	2	0	1	0	0	0	0	0	1	0	0	0	0	0	0	0	0	0	1	1	0
denounce	4	.4802	.4049	36.1	0	0	1	0	0	2	1	0	0	0	0	1	0	1	0	0	0	0	0	0	0	0	1	1	0
denounced	17	.4321	1.7054	42.3	0	0	2	0	4	7	4	0	6	0	0	1	0	8	0	0	0	0	0	0	0	0	2	0	0
denouncing	4	.3677	.3659	35.6	0	0	0	0	2	2	0	0	2	0	0	1	0	1	0	0	0	0	0	0	0	0	0	0	0
dens	8	.4071	.7351	38.7	4	0	2	0	1	0	1	0	2	0	1	0	0	0	0	0	0	0	0	0	2	3	0	0	0
dense	86	.6808	12.034	50.8	1	12	10	13	24	11	13	2	12	0	1	0	5	21	0	16	0	2	0	2	3	3	14	6	1
densely	23	.5330	2.5838	44.1	1	0	4	3	9	2	3	1	0	0	0	0	1	11	0	2	0	0	0	0	0	2	5	2	0
denser	8	.3581	.6472	38.1	0	0	4	1	2	0	0	1	0	0	0	0	0	0	0	5	0	0	0	0	1	0	2	0	0
densities	8	.1542	.3719	35.7	0	0	0	0	0	3	4	1	0	0	0	0	1	0	0	7	0	0	0	0	0	0	0	0	0
density	104	.5672	12.321	50.9	2	1	10	1	6	23	55	6	1	0	9	1	8	7	0	62	0	0	0	5	0	0	8	3	0
dent	20	.1546	1.0177	40.1	3	2	2	3	2	1	7	0	9	0	0	0	0	0	0	2	0	0	0	8	0	1	0	0	0
dental	34	.5250	3.7750	45.8	0	1	6	1	20	2	4	0	1	1	0	0	0	1	0	15	0	0	0	0	0	2	5	9	0
dented	6	.3786	.5475	37.4	3	0	0	0	1	0	2	0	3	1	0	0	0	0	0	0	0	0	0	1	0	0	0	1	0
dentin	7	.0000	.1380	31.4	0	0	2	0	5	0	0	0	0	0	0	0	0	0	0	7	0	0	0	0	0	0	0	0	0
dentist	42	.8031	6.8165	48.3	12	3	4	3	17	2	0	1	11	2	1	2	3	1	2	12	1	0	0	0	1	0	1	5	0
dentist's	10	.3391	.7567	38.8	1	2	2	0	3	1	1	0	1	2	3	1	0	0	0	2	0	0	0	0	0	0	0	1	0
dentistry	6	.3654	.4713	36.7	0	0	4	0	2	0	0	0	0	0	0	0	0	0	1	0	0	0	0	0	0	0	3	2	0
dentists	12	.5222	1.3365	41.3	3	0	0	0	7	1	1	0	1	0	0	0	2	6	0	0	0	0	0	1	0	1	1	0	0
dents	4	.1649	.1534	31.9	0	0	0	1	1	0	2	0	0	0	0	0	0	0	0	0	0	0	0	2	2	0	0	0	0
denunciation	5	.3062	.3620	35.6	0	0	0	0	1	3	1	0	1	0	0	2	0	0	0	0	0	0	0	0	0	0	2	0	0
denunciations	3	.1937	.1495	31.7	0	0	0	0	1	1	1	0	0	0	0	0	0	1	0	0	0	0	0	0	0	0	0	2	0
Denver	32	.6357	4.1948	46.2	1	6	6	4	11	3	0	1	1	2	0	0	8	10	0	3	0	0	0	0	0	2	1	5	0
deny	33	.7361	4.9113	46.9	0	1	4	2	14	3	8	1	4	0	0	6	0	1	2	1	0	0	1	0	5	3	5	5	0
denying	9	.5443	1.0337	40.1	1	0	2	0	1	2	3	0	1	0	0	3	0	0	0	2	0	0	0	0	1	1	0	1	0
deodorant	10	.3061	.6869	38.4	0	0	0	0	4	0	6	0	0	5	0	0	0	0	0	1	0	0	0	0	0	0	0	4	0
deodorized	2	.1787	.1174	30.7	0	2	0	0	0	0	0	0	1	0	0	0	0	0	0	0	0	0	0	0	1	0	0	0	0
deoxyribose	2	.0000	.0394	26.0	0	0	0	0	0	0	2	0	0	0	0	0	0	0	0	2	0	0	0	0	0	0	0	0	0
depart	12	.6557	1.6457	42.2	1	0	1	6	2	1	1	0	4	1	0	0	0	1	0	0	1	0	0	0	1	3	0	1	0
departed	32	.6383	4.2592	46.3	2	1	2	4	9	8	5	1	8	0	0	5	0	1	0	1	0	0	0	0	3	7	1	6	0
departing	15	.6154	1.9618	42.9	1	0	2	0	5	3	4	0	6	0	1	2	0	2	0	0	0	0	0	0	0	1	2	1	0
department	105	.7288	15.624	51.9	15	6	11	11	18	24	19	1	20	8	0	2	1	31	1	7	0	0	6	0	2	4	4	19	0
Department	133	.6907	18.783	52.7	43	5	9	5	13	20	26	12	13	1	0	0	2	23	0	12	0	0	2	1	2	40	9	28	0
department's	4	.2059	.1995	33.0	0	0	1	0	3	0	0	0	0	1	0	0	0	0	0	0	0	0	0	0	0	0	0	3	0
Department's	8	.1854	.3744	35.7	2	0	1	0	3	0	1	1	0	0	0	0	0	0	0	0	0	0	0	0	0	2	0	6	0
departments	34	.7197	4.9592	47.0	2	2	4	2	4	8	11	1	1	1	0	1	0	13	0	2	0	0	1	1	0	4	4	6	0
Departments	5	.4177	.4466	36.5	2	0	1	0	0	0	2	0	0	0	0	0	0	1	0	0	0	0	1	0	0	2	1	0	0
departs	2	.0000	.0162	22.1	0	0	0	0	0	2	0	0	0	0	0	0	0	0	0	0	2	0	0	0	0	0	0	0	0
departure	35	.7033	5.0720	47.1	3	0	1	10	7	3	9	2	11	4	0	5	0	0	0	2	2	0	0	0	1	2	1	7	0
departures	4	.1529	.1647	32.2	0	0	0	0	1	0	3	0	0	3	0	0	0	0	0	1	0	0	0	0	0	0	0	0	0
depend	207	.8329	34.518	55.4	28	13	34	28	44	27	30	3	21	10	0	6	6	56	1	50	1	2	8	8	3	10	13	12	0
dependable	34	.7287	5.0233	47.0	3	1	4	3	10	4	8	1	4	4	0	0	2	2	0	6	0	0	3	1	0	2	4	6	0
depended	57	.7557	8.8052	49.4	6	10	10	10	6	8	5	2	17	2	0	2	0	19	0	4	0	1	0	2	1	2	5	2	0
dependence	14	.5389	1.5742	42.0	0	0	0	1	11	0	1	1	1	0	0	1	0	0	1	1	1	0	0	0	0	0	2	7	0
dependencies	4	.0000	.0778	28.9	0	2	1	0	0	0	1	0	0	0	0	0	0	4	0	0	0	0	0	0	0	0	0	0	0
dependency	2	.2351	.1166	30.7	0	1	0	0	1	0	0	0	0	0	0	0	0	1	0	0	0	0	0	0	0	0	0	1	0
dependent	68	.7800	10.631	50.3	3	2	4	7	19	11	20	2	1	5	0	1	5	7	2	14	5	0	0	3	1	4	16	4	0
dependents	7	.4599	.6914	38.4	1	0	1	0	1	1	3	0	0	0	0	0	3	2	0	0	0	0	0	0	0	1	1	0	0
depending	98	.8304	16.225	52.1	4	6	6	7	31	9	28	7	6	9	1	2	3	6	0	18	5	2	10	5	2	9	11	9	0
depends	235	.8525	39.965	56.0	19	19	16	36	53	45	39	8	27	9	7	6	6	24	3	67	10	2	16	10	2	7	25	14	0
depeopled	2	.1717	.1142	30.6	0	0	0	0	2	0	0	0	1	0	0	1	0	0	0	0	0	0	0	0	0	0	0	0	0
depict	6	.3126	.4195	36.2	0	0	0	1	3	1	1	0	0	0	0	0	0	0	0	2	3	0	0	0	0	0	1	0	0
depicted	4	.3498	.3059	34.9	0	0	0	2	1	0	0	1	0	0	0	0	0	0	0	0	0	0	0	0	0	1	2	1	0
depicting	3	.2365	.1616	32.1	0	0	1	0	0	1	1	0	0	0	0	0	0	0	0	0	1	0	0	0	0	0	2	0	0
depicts	4	.3672	.3092	34.9	0	0	0	1	1	0	1	1	0	0	0	0	0	0	0	0	1	1	0	0	0	0	1	1	0
depleted	4	.1873	.1827	32.6	0	1	0	0	1	1	0	1	0	0	0	0	0	0	0	0	0	0	0	0	0	0	3	1	0
deplorable	6	.4676	.5893	37.7	0	0	1	0	3	1	1	0	0	0	0	0	0	1	0	0	0	0	0	1	0	1	1	2	0
deployed	3	.3847	.2496	34.0	0	0	1	0	2	0	0	0	0	0	0	0	0	0	0	0	0	0	0	0	0	1	1	1	0
deport	2	.2285	.1129	30.5	0	0	0	0	0	2	0	0	0	0	0	0	0	1	0	0	0	0	0	0	0	0	1	0	0
deposed	6	.2521	.3540	35.5	0	0	2	0	2	2	0	0	0	0	0	0	0	1	0	0	0	0	0	0	0	1	4	0	0
deposit	37	.7060	5.3712	47.3	5	1	9	3	4	11	4	0	8	0	0	1	1	5	0	7	0	0	0	0	1	5	6	3	0
deposited	36	.5554	4.2433	46.3	0	0	4	1	6	12	13	0	3	0	0	1	1	1	0	23	0	0	0	1	1	1	4	0	0
depositing	5	.4500	.5006	37.0	0	0	1	0	1	2	0	1	1	0	0	1	0	0	0	2	0	0	0	0	0	0	1	0	0
deposition	11	.2136	.6454	38.1	0	0	0	0	1	4	6	0	1	0	0	0	0	0	0	9	0	0	0	0	0	0	1	0	0
deposits	132	.6263	17.291	52.4	19	5	20	23	20	11	30	4	20	2	0	0	2	48	0	28	0	0	0	1	1	4	23	3	0
depot	19	.6349	2.4962	44.0	3	3	4	3	1	3	2	0	4	2	1	4	0	0	3	0	0	0	0	0	1	4	0	0	0
Depot	2	.0000	.0914	29.6	0	0	0	2	0	0	0	0	2	0	0	0	0	0	0	0	0	0	0	0	0	0	0	0	0
depravity	2	.1948	.1250	31.0	0	0	1	0	1	0	0	0	1	0	0	0	0	0	0	0	0	0	0	0	0	1	0	0	0
deprecated	3	.3374	.2433	33.9	0	0	0	1	1	0	1	0	1	1	0	0	0	0	0	0	0	0	0	0	0	0	1	0	0
depreciate	2	.2437	.1129	30.5	0	0	0	0	1	0	0	1	0	0	0	0	0	0	0	0	0	0	0	0	0	0	1	1	0
depressed	14	.6103	1.7888	42.5	0	0	1	2	3	4	4	0	3	1	1	0	0	0	0	3	0	0	0	0	0	1	2	3	0
depression	29	.7188	4.2348	46.3	0	2	3	1	4	11	6	2	2	0	0	2	0	8	0	3	0	0	0	1	1	4	3	5	0
Depression	6	.5362	.6887	38.4	0	0	1	0	1	4	0	0	1	0	0	1	0	2	0	0	0	0	0	0	0	1	0	1	0
depressions	8	.3774	.6636	38.2	2	0	0	2	0	1	0	3	0	0	0	0	0	1	0	2	0	0	0	0	0	0	4	1	0
deprivation	2	.2152	.1357	31.3	0	0	0	0	0	2	0	0	1	0	0	0	0	1	0	0	0	0	0	0	0	0	0	0	0
deprive	6	.5195	.6418	38.1	0	0	0	0	0	0	5	1	0	1	1	1	0	1	0	0	0	0	1	0	0	1	0	0	0
deprived	18	.7446	2.6990	44.3	0	0	1	2	3	4	5	3	0	1	0	1	0	3	0	3	1	0	0	0	1	2	3	3	0
depriving	2	.0000	.0209	23.2	0	0	0	0	1	1	0	0	0	0	0	0	0	0	0	0	0	0	0	0	0	0	2	0	0
Dept	7	.1564	.2855	34.6	0	0	0	0	7	0	0	0	0	0	0	0	0	0	0	0	0	0	0	0	0	0	1	6	0
depth	167	.6895	23.454	53.7	10	14	15	34	35	16	37	6	18	1	1	6	16	4	0	51	8	15	4	19	3	5	10	6	0
Depth	2	.1442	.0761	28.8	0	0	0	0	1	0	1	0	0	0	0	0	0	1	0	0	0	0	1	0	0	0	0	0	0
depths	83	.7409	12.542	51.0	8	9	9	13	21	8	11	4	16	1	0	4	0	4	0	31	2	1	0	0	3	3	11	7	0
deputies	5	.2222	.2934	34.7	0	0	0	1	3	1	0	0	1	0	0	0	0	1	0	0	0	0	0	0	0	0	3	0	0
Deputies	7	.2399	.4129	36.2	0	0	0	1	5	1	0	0	0	0	0	0	0	4	0	0	0	0	0	0	0	0	3	0	0
deputy	7	.4587	.6816	38.3	0	0	0	2	4	1	0	0	0	0	0	0	0	1	0	0	0	0	0	0	0	2	2	2	0
der	8	.3709	.6282	38.0	0	0	0	0	0	2	6	0	0	0	0	5	0	0	0	0	2	1	0	0	0	0	0	0	0

5A Denny's
5P denominationally
9R denouement
8F denounces
6F densely-populated
7Q densest
7E Density
7R Denson
3A dent
7Q denticles
9B dentifrice
7R Dentistry
5Q dentures
9N dentuso
7Q denudation
7R denuded
7H denudes
9D Denunciation
7H deoxyribonucleic
7H department-store
9Q departmental
8K dependability
XR Dependence-producing
7R Dependent
6R dephyr
7R Depict
7Q depletion
7D deplorably
8R deplore
8J deplored
7A deploring
7R deploying
9R deployment
7Q depopulated
7J deported
7H deportment
4Q depose
9F Deposit
8K Deposition
9R depository
7P Depository
9R depraved
6N deprecatingly
7N deprecatory
7Q depredations
8H depressant
5K depressor
8F Deputy

Word Type	F	D	U	SFI	3 Gr 3	4 Gr 4	5 Gr 5	6 Gr 6	7 Gr 7	8 Gr 8	9 Gr 9	X UnGr	A Read	B Eng & Gr	C Comp	D Lit	E Math	F Soc Stud	G Spell	H Sci	J Music	K Art	L Home Ec	M Shop	N Lib F	P Lib NF	Q Lib Ref	R Mag	S Rel
Der	2	.0000	.0162	22.1	0	0	0	1	0	1	0	0	0	0	0	0	0	0	0	0	2	0	0	0	0	0	0	0	0
derail	3	.0000	.1370	31.4	0	3	0	0	0	0	0	0	3	0	0	0	0	0	0	0	0	0	0	0	0	0	0	0	0
derangement	2	.2437	.1129	30.5	0	0	0	0	0	1	1	0	0	0	0	0	0	0	0	0	0	0	0	0	0	0	1	1	0
derby	3	.1250	.1342	31.3	2	1	0	0	0	0	0	0	1	0	0	0	0	0	0	0	0	0	0	0	2	0	0	0	0
Derby	9	.0000	.1055	30.2	8	0	0	1	0	0	0	0	0	0	0	0	0	0	0	0	0	0	0	0	9	0	0	0	0
derelict	2	.1948	.1250	31.0	1	0	0	0	1	0	0	0	1	0	0	0	0	0	0	0	0	0	0	0	0	1	0	0	0
derision	2	.0000	.0215	23.3	0	0	0	0	0	1	1	0	0	0	0	2	0	0	0	0	0	0	0	0	0	0	0	0	0
derisively	3	.3370	.2430	33.9	0	0	1	0	2	0	0	0	1	0	0	1	0	0	0	0	0	0	0	0	0	0	1	0	0
derivation	6	.2187	.3110	34.9	0	0	0	0	0	0	1	5	0	4	0	0	0	0	0	0	0	0	0	0	0	0	0	2	0
derivations	4	.2129	.2122	33.3	0	0	0	0	0	0	3	1	0	0	0	0	3	0	0	0	0	0	0	0	0	0	0	1	0
derivative	24	.1241	.7664	38.8	0	3	6	8	4	1	2	0	0	2	0	0	0	0	21	0	0	0	0	0	0	1	0	0	0
derivatives	30	.0841	.7234	38.6	0	4	9	9	3	4	1	0	0	1	0	0	0	0	28	0	0	0	0	0	0	0	1	0	0
derive	12	.7066	1.7172	42.3	0	1	0	1	3	3	4	0	0	2	0	1	1	2	0	2	0	0	0	0	0	1	2	1	0
derived	81	.8596	13.830	51.4	0	1	4	19	18	13	13	13	4	10	1	4	3	2	16	10	5	1	1	2	1	3	14	4	0
derives	8	.5415	.9048	39.6	0	0	2	0	4	2	0	0	0	0	0	0	0	1	0	2	1	0	0	0	0	2	2	0	0
deriving	5	.5373	.5765	37.6	0	0	1	0	2	2	0	0	1	0	0	0	1	1	0	0	0	0	0	0	0	1	1	0	0
dermis	11	.0000	.2169	33.4	3	7	0	0	1	0	0	0	0	0	0	0	0	0	0	11	0	0	0	0	0	0	0	0	0
derned	2	.0000	.0215	23.3	0	0	0	0	0	2	0	0	0	0	0	2	0	0	0	0	0	0	0	0	0	0	0	0	0
derogatory	4	.4875	.4085	36.1	0	1	0	0	2	0	1	0	0	1	0	0	0	0	0	0	0	0	0	0	1	1	0	1	0
derrick	6	.3764	.5764	37.6	0	0	0	0	3	3	0	0	4	0	0	0	0	1	0	0	0	0	0	0	0	0	1	0	0
derricks	6	.0000	.1167	30.7	3	0	1	0	2	0	0	0	0	0	0	0	0	6	0	0	0	0	0	0	0	0	0	0	0
Derrill	4	.0000	.1827	32.6	0	0	4	0	0	0	0	0	4	0	0	0	0	0	0	0	0	0	0	0	0	0	0	0	0
derry	8	.0000	.0647	28.1	0	8	0	0	0	0	0	0	0	0	0	0	0	0	0	0	8	0	0	0	0	0	0	0	0
Derry	4	.0000	.1827	32.6	0	0	0	4	0	0	0	0	4	0	0	0	0	0	0	0	0	0	0	0	0	0	0	0	0
Derwin	4	.0000	.0469	26.7	4	0	0	0	0	0	0	0	0	0	0	0	0	0	0	0	0	0	0	0	4	0	0	0	0
des	5	.3630	.3973	36.0	1	0	1	0	1	0	1	1	0	0	0	0	0	0	0	0	1	0	0	0	0	3	0	1	0
Des	3	.2279	.2143	33.3	0	0	2	0	1	0	0	0	2	0	0	0	0	0	0	0	0	0	0	0	0	0	0	1	0
DesMoines	9	.3917	.8067	39.1	0	3	2	0	4	0	0	0	1	0	0	0	2	5	0	0	0	0	0	0	0	1	0	0	0
descant	32	.0000	.2587	34.1	1	10	10	6	1	1	3	0	0	0	0	0	0	0	0	0	32	0	0	0	0	0	0	0	0
descants	3	.0000	.0243	23.8	0	0	0	0	3	0	0	0	0	0	0	0	0	0	0	0	3	0	0	0	0	0	0	0	0
Descartes	9	.3461	.6899	38.4	0	0	0	0	2	1	6	0	0	0	0	0	6	0	0	0	1	0	0	0	0	0	2	0	0
descend	16	.6550	2.1581	43.3	1	5	1	3	4	1	1	0	2	0	0	4	0	1	0	3	0	0	0	0	2	1	1	2	0
descendant	11	.4504	1.0776	40.3	1	0	0	2	1	3	3	1	2	1	0	5	0	0	0	0	0	0	0	0	0	0	2	1	0
descendants	53	.5205	5.9145	47.7	8	3	8	11	13	4	3	3	9	1	0	1	0	15	0	4	3	1	0	0	1	2	14	1	1
descended	53	.5017	5.8270	47.7	5	7	5	8	14	5	8	1	16	0	0	2	4	6	0	0	2	0	0	0	6	5	8	3	1
descendent	3	.2088	.1442	31.6	0	0	0	0	1	2	0	0	0	0	0	0	0	0	0	0	2	0	0	0	0	0	1	0	0
descendents	3	.0000	.0243	23.8	0	0	3	0	0	0	0	0	0	0	0	0	0	0	0	0	3	0	0	0	0	0	0	0	0
descending	30	.6534	4.0017	46.0	3	1	2	3	10	6	5	0	3	0	1	4	4	1	0	0	8	0	0	0	6	1	2	0	0
descends	4	.2558	.2582	34.1	0	1	1	1	0	1	1	0	1	0	0	0	1	0	0	0	2	0	0	0	0	0	0	0	0
descent	33	.7496	5.0139	47.0	3	0	5	3	8	7	3	4	4	0	0	3	1	9	0	3	2	0	0	0	2	1	3	5	0
describe	486	.8411	81.523	59.1	33	58	78	81	89	73	71	3	44	74	37	19	104	29	20	77	30	6	4	13	1	5	17	5	1
described	347	.9126	62.751	58.0	21	18	38	41	87	75	53	14	46	39	8	12	32	31	7	57	14	2	12	13	4	11	34	25	0
describes	113	.8292	18.734	52.7	0	12	16	18	27	25	13	2	17	22	7	11	12	9	3	8	7	4	2	1	0	3	6	1	0
describing	97	.7342	14.377	51.6	4	14	10	10	25	19	15	0	11	28	9	8	6	6	8	5	6	1	1	0	1	4	3	0	0
description	168	.6291	21.684	53.4	7	15	11	15	37	35	43	5	22	37	29	6	11	7	0	14	10	1	0	11	3	5	8	4	0
Description	2	.0000	.0290	24.6	0	0	2	0	0	0	0	0	0	0	0	0	0	0	0	0	0	0	0	0	0	2	0	0	0
descriptions	49	.7692	7.5902	48.8	2	4	9	6	10	13	5	0	7	14	3	1	1	2	2	6	3	0	1	2	0	3	4	0	0
descriptive	62	.5711	7.2232	48.6	5	9	7	7	9	6	17	2	0	28	8	0	0	3	4	3	9	0	1	0	0	1	4	1	0
desecrated	2	.2446	.1142	30.6	0	0	0	0	1	1	0	0	0	0	0	0	0	0	0	0	0	0	0	0	1	0	0	1	0
desecrating	2	.2375	.1088	30.4	1	0	0	0	1	0	0	0	0	0	0	0	0	0	0	0	1	0	0	0	0	0	0	1	0
desegregation	3	.1937	.1495	31.7	0	0	0	0	0	0	3	0	0	0	0	0	0	1	0	0	0	0	0	0	0	0	0	2	0
desert	504	.7686	78.870	59.0	110	119	41	83	88	20	24	19	119	9	1	7	0	146	2	97	4	6	0	0	6	53	20	34	0
Desert	51	.6140	6.5383	48.2	7	9	9	9	10	4	3	0	5	0	1	0	0	27	0	3	0	0	0	0	2	3	4	6	0
DESERT	3	.0000	.0434	26.4	3	0	0	0	0	0	0	0	0	0	0	0	0	0	0	0	0	0	0	0	0	3	0	0	0
desert-like	2	.2346	.1166	30.7	1	0	0	0	0	1	0	0	0	0	0	0	0	0	0	1	0	0	0	0	0	0	0	1	0
desert's	3	.2279	.2143	33.3	0	0	0	1	1	0	0	1	2	0	0	0	0	0	0	0	0	0	0	0	0	0	0	1	0
deserted	52	.6899	7.3760	48.7	4	4	3	6	18	9	7	1	13	4	1	9	0	2	0	0	0	0	0	0	14	3	3	3	0
deserters	4	.3215	.3104	34.9	0	2	1	0	1	0	0	0	1	0	0	0	0	0	0	0	0	0	0	0	0	2	1	0	0
deserting	3	.3553	.2608	34.2	0	0	0	1	1	1	0	0	1	0	0	0	0	1	0	0	0	0	0	0	0	1	0	0	0
desertion	7	.3647	.5642	37.5	0	0	0	0	3	3	0	1	0	0	0	0	0	2	0	0	0	0	0	0	3	0	0	2	0
deserts	157	.6604	21.458	53.3	31	39	16	17	34	8	12	0	15	1	0	3	0	55	0	53	2	2	0	0	0	12	10	4	0
deserve	30	.6201	3.9351	45.9	3	3	5	3	7	2	7	0	11	1	0	8	0	0	0	1	0	0	0	0	2	4	1	2	0
deserved	17	.6610	2.3559	43.7	5	1	1	2	4	2	1	1	7	0	0	3	0	0	0	0	1	0	0	0	1	2	1	2	0
deservedly	2	.2437	.1129	30.5	0	0	0	0	1	0	1	0	0	0	0	0	0	0	0	0	0	0	0	0	0	0	1	1	0
deserves	12	.5333	1.3849	41.4	1	0	0	2	4	2	3	0	4	2	0	3	0	0	0	0	0	0	0	0	1	0	0	2	0
deserving	5	.2242	.2960	34.7	0	0	0	1	2	0	2	0	1	0	0	3	0	0	0	1	0	0	0	0	0	0	0	0	0
Desi	3	.0000	.0365	25.6	0	3	0	0	0	0	0	0	0	0	0	0	0	0	0	0	0	0	0	0	0	0	0	3	0
design	487	.4704	47.222	56.7	40	89	54	84	96	39	63	22	27	10	3	4	13	10	2	15	79	158	17	73	2	9	31	34	0
Design	3	.1169	.1277	31.1	0	0	3	0	0	0	0	0	1	0	0	0	0	0	0	0	0	0	0	0	0	0	2	0	0
designate	15	.4349	1.3892	41.4	0	0	1	0	9	0	4	1	0	0	0	0	9	1	0	0	2	0	0	2	0	1	0	0	0
designated	27	.6408	3.5107	45.5	0	2	0	2	8	6	8	1	0	1	0	1	6	1	0	4	1	0	3	4	0	1	3	2	0
designates	4	.1789	.1692	32.3	0	0	1	0	3	0	0	0	0	0	0	0	0	0	0	0	3	0	0	0	0	0	1	0	0
designating	2	.2391	.1133	30.5	0	0	0	0	1	0	1	0	0	0	0	0	1	0	0	0	0	0	0	0	0	0	1	0	0
designation	6	.4433	.5635	37.5	0	2	0	2	0	1	1	0	0	1	1	0	0	1	0	1	0	0	0	0	0	0	2	0	0
designed	192	.7996	30.711	54.9	2	15	20	19	61	28	34	13	19	8	2	6	3	12	2	15	17	11	8	17	2	12	23	35	0
designer	28	.3237	1.9416	42.9	0	0	2	2	10	0	9	5	2	2	0	0	0	0	0	0	0	3	0	14	0	0	1	6	0
designer's	2	.2437	.1129	30.5	0	0	0	0	2	0	0	0	0	0	0	0	0	0	0	0	0	0	0	0	0	0	1	1	0
designers	18	.4680	1.7598	42.5	4	1	1	2	5	4	1	0	1	0	0	0	0	1	0	1	0	2	0	4	0	1	7	2	0
designing	35	.5524	4.0043	46.0	0	0	2	4	12	8	6	3	3	1	0	0	4	3	0	4	0	5	1	7	0	1	3	3	0
designs	147	.3521	11.227	50.5	24	35	16	30	14	15	6	7	15	1	0	5	5	11	0	5	8	62	5	8	1	8	4	9	0
desirable	59	.5266	6.4128	48.1	0	0	4	2	9	18	22	4	3	0	0	8	5	2	0	5	1	0	18	6	0	2	4	5	0
desire	129	.8625	22.172	53.5	3	2	10	13	34	29	34	4	18	5	1	17	1	23	2	4	7	1	7	0	3	17	12	11	0
desired	131	.5040	13.624	51.3	2	3	4	10	35	30	38	9	6	1	0	5	5	4	0	12	3	0	32	31	4	7	16	5	0
desires	35	.7389	5.2093	47.2	1	2	1	2	10	9	10	0	2	1	1	3	1	6	0	2	2	0	5	0	1	4	4	3	0
desiring	3	.3783	.2436	33.9	1	1	0	0	0	0	0	1	0	0	0	0	0	0	1	0	0	0	0	0	0	1	1	0	0
desist	2	.2442	.1134	30.5	0	0	0	1	0	0	1	0	0	1	0	0	0	0	0	0	0	0	0	0	0	0	0	1	0
desk	324	.8705	56.370	57.5	74	78	32	32	58	20	28	2	97	33	6	16	41	11	17	25	11	0	4	0	38	9	1	15	0
desks	37	.6917	5.2469	47.2	7	12	3	2	7	4	1	1	6	2	0	1	12	2	1	1	1	0	0	0	5	6	0	0	0
desolate	25	.7112	3.6406	45.6	2	1	1	4	7	7	2	1	6	3	1	4	0	3	0	1	0	0	0	0	1	0	4	2	0
desolation	12	.6003	1.4770	41.7	0	2	0	2	8	0	0	0	1	0	1	1	0	0	0	0	2	0	0	0	3	0	3	1	0
despair	52	.6832	7.3277	48.6	4	3	5	12	12	7	7	2	14	1	0	7	0	1	0	1	4	0	0	0	13	5	1	5	0
despairing	8	.5479	.9560	39.8	0	0	0	2	3	1	0	2	3	0	0	0	0	1	0	0	0	0	0	0	1	2	0	1	0
desperados	2	.2412	.1091	30.4	0	0	0	0	2	0	0	0	0	0	0	1	0	0	1	0	0	0	0	0	0	0	0	0	0
desperate	65	.6690	9.0279	49.6	2	6	9	10	17	10	10	1	20	1	4	8	0	6	0	0	0	0	0	0	13	6	2	5	0
desperately	54	.6978	7.8062	48.9	3	6	8	10	12	8	4	3	19	1	1	2	0	4	0	0	0	0	0	0	3	11	2	11	0
desperation	15	.5274	1.6451	42.2	2	1	0	4	4	1	3	0	1	0	2	1	0	0	0	0	0	0	0	0	5	1	2	3	0
despise	12	.4725	1.2345	40.9	0	0	1	1	6	2	2	0	3	0	0	4	0	0	3	0	0	0	0	0	1	0	0	1	0

XH derGrosse
5Q Derain
6R deranged
9D dere
8N derided
5B Derision
7A derisive
6A Derricke
8A derriere
4P dervishes
6R DesBartlett
7A DesMoines'
5F DesPlaines
3Q Descamisados
4P Deschamps
6R Deschutes
7Q desecration
9D desecrator
6R deserter
9Q Deserved
6A desiccated
7Q desiccation
5Q Desiderius
XR design-oriented
9R Desire
9D desisted
4G deske
6J Desmond
7P desolated
7A desolateness
7Q desoxyribonucleic
3P despaired
8A despairers
6A despairingly
7G desperadoes
7A Desperate
7P despicable
7N despisable

Word Type	F	D	U	SFI	3 Gr 3	4 Gr 4	5 Gr 5	6 Gr 6	7 Gr 7	8 Gr 8	9 Gr 9	X UnGr	A Read	B Eng & Gr	C Comp	D Lit	E Math	F Soc Stud	G Spell	H Sci	J Music	K Art	L Home Ec	M Shop	N Lib F	P Lib NF	Q Lib Ref	R Mag	S Rel
despised	17	.6105	2.1781	43.4	1	1	1	2	3	3	5	1	4	1	0	4	0	2	0	1	0	0	0	0	0	2	3	0	0
despite	117	.7579	17.851	52.5	7	2	17	7	29	23	23	9	6	6	2	3	0	20	6	6	2	0	0	0	1	18	23	24	0
despoiled	2	.2440	.1132	30.5	0	0	0	0	0	1	1	0	0	0	0	1	0	0	0	0	0	0	0	0	0	0	0	1	0
despondency	3	.3408	.2477	33.9	0	0	0	2	0	0	1	0	1	0	0	1	0	0	0	0	0	0	0	0	0	1	0	0	0
despondently	2	.2446	.1142	30.6	0	0	1	0	1	0	0	0	0	0	0	0	0	0	0	0	0	0	0	0	1	0	0	1	0
despotism	6	.4091	.5259	37.2	0	0	2	0	1	2	0	1	0	0	0	1	0	1	0	0	0	0	0	0	0	0	3	1	0
dessert	43	.5029	4.5998	46.6	10	4	2	4	12	2	8	1	8	9	0	1	0	2	4	2	0	0	10	0	0	1	0	6	0
Dessert	2	.0000	.0234	23.7	0	2	0	0	0	0	0	0	0	0	0	0	0	0	0	0	0	0	0	0	2	0	0	0	0
desserts	12	.0914	.2908	34.6	1	1	0	0	2	2	6	0	0	0	0	0	0	0	0	2	0	0	9	0	0	1	0	0	0
Dessie	2	.0000	.0389	25.9	0	0	0	0	2	0	0	0	0	0	0	0	0	2	0	0	0	0	0	0	0	0	0	0	0
destination	32	.8075	5.1910	47.2	1	1	4	8	7	3	7	1	5	2	0	2	0	2	1	4	0	0	1	0	2	4	3	6	0
destinations	4	.3286	.3009	34.8	0	0	0	0	2	1	0	1	0	0	0	0	0	1	0	1	0	0	0	0	0	0	0	2	0
destined	19	.7266	2.8195	44.5	0	0	3	4	8	2	2	0	4	1	0	0	0	3	0	1	1	0	0	0	1	2	2	4	0
destinies	2	.0000	.0394	26.0	0	0	0	0	2	0	0	0	0	0	0	0	0	0	0	2	0	0	0	0	0	0	0	0	0
destiny	20	.6359	2.6085	44.2	1	2	1	2	5	2	5	2	1	0	0	2	0	4	0	0	2	0	0	0	3	3	0	5	0
Destiny	3	.3350	.2478	33.9	0	0	1	0	0	1	1	0	1	0	0	0	0	1	0	0	0	0	0	0	0	0	1	0	0
destitute	2	.2285	.1129	30.5	0	0	1	0	0	1	0	0	0	0	0	0	0	1	0	0	0	0	0	0	0	0	1	0	0
destroy	107	.8802	18.808	52.7	5	16	15	15	32	10	11	3	31	4	2	9	7	13	0	16	0	2	1	0	4	6	6	6	0
destroyed	156	.8524	26.588	54.2	11	12	33	24	32	22	16	6	24	3	0	10	3	45	2	18	3	1	2	0	6	10	16	13	0
destroyer	7	.3774	.6121	37.9	0	0	3	1	3	0	0	0	2	0	1	0	0	0	0	0	0	0	0	0	0	3	0	1	0
destroyers	7	.4450	.6646	38.2	0	2	1	1	3	0	0	0	0	0	0	1	0	1	0	0	0	0	0	0	0	3	2	0	0
destroying	34	.8341	5.6725	47.5	1	2	6	5	5	8	5	2	4	2	1	1	0	6	0	6	0	0	1	1	2	2	5	3	0
destroys	19	.7110	2.7591	44.4	1	2	4	1	5	1	3	2	4	0	1	1	0	0	0	4	3	0	0	1	0	1	2	2	0
destruction	55	.6047	6.9060	48.4	3	2	4	5	20	11	9	1	6	0	0	5	0	9	0	4	0	0	0	0	3	5	19	4	0
destructional	5	.0000	.0986	29.9	0	0	5	0	0	0	0	0	0	0	0	0	0	0	0	5	0	0	0	0	0	0	0	0	0
destructive	31	.8058	5.0374	47.0	1	3	4	6	7	5	4	1	8	0	1	1	0	3	1	5	0	0	1	1	1	1	6	2	0
destructiveness	2	.2278	.1128	30.5	0	0	0	0	1	0	1	0	0	0	0	0	0	0	0	1	0	0	0	0	0	0	1	0	0
detach	3	.2580	.1776	32.5	0	0	0	0	2	0	1	0	0	0	0	0	0	0	0	1	0	0	0	1	0	0	0	1	0
detached	21	.6611	2.8250	44.5	0	1	3	1	8	4	3	1	1	0	0	4	0	2	0	1	5	0	0	0	2	2	2	2	0
detachment	3	.2347	.1695	32.3	0	0	0	0	2	0	1	0	0	0	0	0	0	0	0	0	0	0	0	0	1	2	0	0	0
detail	136	.7780	21.249	53.3	1	8	7	13	44	19	39	5	19	15	9	9	0	4	0	12	4	3	4	15	3	10	18	11	0
detailed	54	.7862	8.5062	49.3	0	5	4	8	19	6	9	3	4	5	1	1	2	4	0	7	0	3	4	2	0	3	12	6	0
details	391	.6319	51.530	57.1	16	21	30	37	124	54	105	4	130	77	69	16	0	11	4	7	8	12	11	10	9	10	7	10	0
detained	2	.0000	.0234	23.7	0	0	0	0	2	0	0	0	0	0	0	0	0	0	0	0	0	0	0	0	2	0	0	0	0
detaining	2	.2441	.1127	30.5	0	0	1	0	0	1	0	0	0	0	0	0	0	0	0	0	0	0	0	0	1	0	1	0	0
detect	32	.6046	4.0423	46.1	0	0	3	7	7	6	7	2	4	3	0	0	0	0	0	13	1	0	0	0	0	2	6	3	0
detected	31	.4967	3.3799	45.3	0	0	3	8	5	7	6	2	6	0	0	0	0	0	0	17	0	0	0	0	1	1	3	3	0
detecting	7	.3227	.5109	37.1	0	0	1	1	4	1	0	0	0	1	0	0	0	0	0	2	0	0	0	0	0	0	0	4	0
detection	11	.3494	.8707	39.4	0	0	1	1	4	3	1	1	0	0	0	0	0	0	0	6	0	0	0	0	0	0	1	4	0
detective	67	.7476	10.187	50.1	18	6	7	7	16	8	3	2	17	10	1	1	0	2	3	0	1	0	0	0	14	6	2	10	0
Detective	2	.0000	.0914	29.6	0	0	0	0	2	0	0	0	2	0	0	0	0	0	0	0	0	0	0	0	0	0	0	0	0
detectives	12	.5056	1.3046	41.2	2	1	1	0	1	7	0	0	2	2	1	0	0	1	0	1	0	0	0	0	0	5	0	0	0
detector	17	.4385	1.6442	42.2	1	0	1	6	2	1	2	4	1	0	0	0	0	0	0	12	0	0	0	1	0	0	1	2	0
detectors	4	.2405	.2410	33.8	0	0	3	0	0	0	1	0	0	0	0	0	0	0	0	2	0	0	0	0	0	2	0	0	0
detention	4	.3494	.3094	34.9	0	0	1	0	1	1	1	0	0	0	0	0	0	1	0	0	0	0	0	0	2	0	1	0	0
deter	5	.4662	.5254	37.2	2	0	0	0	1	0	0	2	2	0	0	0	0	0	0	0	1	0	0	0	0	1	0	1	0
detergent	12	.5035	1.3754	41.4	8	0	0	0	0	1	3	0	7	2	0	0	0	0	0	1	0	0	1	0	0	1	0	0	0
detergents	8	.2478	.5030	37.0	1	0	0	0	0	2	5	0	1	0	0	0	0	0	0	5	0	0	2	0	0	0	0	0	0
deteriorate	3	.2321	.1635	32.1	1	0	0	0	1	0	1	0	0	0	0	0	0	0	0	0	0	0	0	0	0	0	1	2	0
deteriorated	2	.2285	.1129	30.5	0	1	0	0	0	1	0	0	0	0	0	0	0	1	0	0	0	0	0	0	0	0	1	0	0
deteriorating	2	.2442	.1134	30.5	0	0	0	0	0	0	1	1	0	1	0	0	0	0	0	0	0	0	0	0	0	0	0	1	0
determination	47	.7808	7.3959	48.7	1	4	5	4	10	10	10	3	5	1	0	2	0	8	0	7	1	0	1	0	3	6	3	10	0
determine	266	.8203	43.593	56.4	0	22	18	26	69	59	62	10	12	13	1	4	77	16	8	60	18	3	20	9	2	4	11	8	0
determined	207	.8623	35.619	55.5	4	17	27	22	62	42	26	7	35	1	0	12	23	27	2	22	17	0	2	7	6	16	21	16	0
determinedly	4	.2107	.2095	33.2	0	2	0	0	1	0	0	1	0	0	0	0	0	0	0	0	0	0	0	0	0	3	0	1	0
determiner	45	.0000	.4924	36.9	16	14	1	2	1	9	2	0	0	45	0	0	0	0	0	0	0	0	0	0	0	0	0	0	0
determiners	21	.0000	.2298	33.6	2	10	1	3	0	5	0	0	0	21	0	0	0	0	0	0	0	0	0	0	0	0	0	0	0
determines	56	.8265	9.2294	49.7	2	5	4	7	10	12	16	0	1	7	1	1	5	8	1	12	4	0	4	2	0	2	7	1	0
determining	54	.8004	8.6374	49.4	0	1	6	1	13	12	20	1	1	3	1	0	9	3	1	11	3	0	3	3	0	1	10	5	0
deterrent	2	.2437	.1129	30.5	0	0	0	0	1	1	0	0	0	0	0	0	0	0	0	0	0	0	0	0	0	0	1	1	0
detestable	2	.0000	.0215	23.3	0	0	0	1	0	0	1	0	0	0	0	2	0	0	0	0	0	0	0	0	0	0	0	0	0
detested	6	.5011	.6483	38.1	0	0	0	1	2	1	1	1	1	0	0	0	0	1	0	0	0	0	0	0	2	1	0	1	0
detonated	2	.2346	.1166	30.7	0	0	0	0	0	1	1	0	0	0	0	0	0	0	0	1	0	0	0	0	0	0	0	1	0
detonation	2	.2446	.1122	30.5	0	0	0	0	0	0	2	0	0	0	0	1	0	0	0	0	0	0	0	0	0	0	1	0	0
detour	11	.5703	1.3168	41.2	3	0	1	1	2	1	2	1	1	2	0	0	0	4	0	0	0	0	0	0	2	1	0	1	0
detours	2	.2297	.1135	30.6	1	0	0	0	0	0	1	0	0	0	0	1	0	1	0	0	0	0	0	0	0	0	0	0	0
detract	4	.4139	.3497	35.4	0	0	0	0	1	2	1	0	0	0	0	1	0	1	1	0	0	0	1	0	0	0	0	0	0
detriment	3	.3870	.2492	34.0	0	0	0	0	2	0	1	0	0	0	0	0	0	0	0	0	0	0	0	0	1	0	1	1	0
detriments	2	.2401	.1133	30.5	0	0	1	0	1	0	0	0	0	0	0	0	0	0	0	0	0	0	0	0	0	1	1	0	0
Detroit	53	.7037	7.6197	48.8	3	15	9	2	7	11	6	0	7	2	0	1	1	13	0	0	2	0	0	0	1	11	6	9	0
Detroit's	2	.0000	.0243	23.9	0	0	0	0	1	1	0	0	0	0	0	0	0	0	0	0	0	0	0	0	0	0	0	2	0
Deuteronomy	3	.2043	.1486	31.7	0	0	2	0	0	1	0	0	0	0	0	0	0	0	0	0	0	0	0	0	0	1	2	0	0
devaluation	8	.0000	.0972	29.9	0	0	0	0	0	0	8	0	0	0	0	0	0	0	0	0	0	0	0	0	0	0	0	8	0
devalued	2	.0000	.0243	23.9	0	0	0	0	1	0	1	0	0	0	0	0	0	0	0	0	0	0	0	0	0	0	0	2	0
devastated	4	.2281	.2337	33.7	0	0	0	0	1	2	1	0	0	0	0	0	0	3	0	0	0	0	0	0	0	0	0	1	0
devastating	6	.3873	.5223	37.2	1	0	1	1	1	0	1	1	1	0	0	0	0	0	0	0	0	0	0	0	0	1	1	3	0
devastation	4	.4767	.4083	36.1	1	0	1	0	0	1	1	0	0	0	0	0	0	1	0	1	0	0	0	0	0	1	1	0	0
develop	378	.8687	65.247	58.1	8	26	58	40	109	58	63	16	15	31	14	2	10	56	22	93	35	5	10	19	1	13	25	27	0
developed	600	.8829	105.18	60.2	26	44	63	84	156	108	89	30	43	26	8	9	18	102	16	85	69	7	7	17	4	44	110	35	0
developers	2	.2351	.1166	30.7	0	0	0	0	0	1	0	1	0	0	0	0	0	1	0	0	0	0	0	0	0	0	0	1	0
developing	131	.8857	23.027	53.6	4	5	13	15	43	26	21	4	10	11	6	4	1	19	4	21	8	3	3	4	1	5	15	16	0
development	348	.8085	56.223	57.5	13	10	41	18	114	75	58	19	12	12	4	1	4	48	4	62	33	2	12	17	0	20	89	28	0
Development	9	.3111	.6213	37.9	1	0	4	0	1	1	0	2	0	0	0	0	0	0	0	0	0	0	0	0	0	1	5	3	0
developmental	9	.4572	.8800	39.4	0	0	0	1	2	2	4	0	0	2	0	0	4	0	0	2	0	0	0	0	0	0	1	0	0
Developmental	3	.0000	.0449	26.5	0	0	0	0	0	0	3	0	0	0	0	0	3	0	0	0	0	0	0	0	0	0	0	0	0
developments	63	.7384	9.3640	49.7	2	2	6	3	13	18	17	2	3	1	0	1	2	7	2	8	6	0	3	6	0	5	14	5	0
develops	50	.6593	6.7373	48.3	1	7	5	9	14	3	9	2	1	2	4	1	0	4	0	22	3	0	1	0	0	0	6	6	0
deviation	8	.4104	.7094	38.5	0	0	0	0	3	2	2	1	0	0	0	0	2	0	0	1	0	0	0	0	0	0	1	4	0
deviations	13	.4506	1.2714	41.0	0	0	0	1	1	5	4	2	1	0	0	0	7	0	0	2	1	0	0	0	0	0	2	0	0
device	146	.7355	21.693	53.4	4	6	10	10	42	40	28	6	13	10	1	9	7	6	3	32	12	0	0	16	2	4	21	10	0
devices	137	.7899	21.673	53.4	1	1	21	17	25	37	32	3	6	16	4	4	5	5	0	37	12	2	0	10	1	3	23	9	0
devil	64	.5562	7.4004	48.7	2	3	3	9	9	15	22	1	4	0	0	22	0	4	0	0	1	0	0	0	18	9	3	3	0
Devil	52	.3321	4.6326	46.7	0	36	1	0	13	0	2	0	37	0	0	13	0	0	0	0	0	0	0	0	0	1	1	0	0
devil's	4	.3566	.3101	34.9	1	0	0	0	1	0	2	0	0	0	0	2	0	0	0	0	0	0	0	0	0	1	1	0	0
Devil's	6	.3688	.5050	37.0	0	2	0	2	1	0	1	0	1	1	0	0	0	1	0	0	0	0	0	0	3	0	0	0	0

5Q despot
8Q despotic
8Q Dessalines
9L Desserts
7R Destresed
XR destructively
8D desultory
9B Det
5Q Detached
9E detaches
XH detaching
9M detailing
XR detains
7R detectably
XR Detective-Inspector
7A detective's
8M detector-mixer
5Q deteriorates
9H deterioration
9Q determinant
9D determinations
6B Determiner
9Q determinism
7Q deterred
8F dethroned
9Q Detlev
5Q detonating
7D detonations
3R DETOUR
7A detracted
9D detractors
8L detracts
8Q Detrick
8B detrimental
5J Dett
9Q Deum
7B deus
5Q Deut
8R deuteride
6H deuterium
9B Deutschland
6R Deva
9R devalue
9R devaluing
8F devastate
XH devastatingly
8J deviates
7R Device
7A device's
XR Devido
7R devil-may-care
7R devil-worshipers

Word Type	F	D	U	SFI	3 Gr 3	4 Gr 4	5 Gr 5	6 Gr 6	7 Gr 7	8 Gr 8	9 Gr 9	X UnGr	A Read	B Eng & Gr	C Comp	D Lit	E Math	F Soc Stud	G Spell	H Sci	J Music	K Art	L Home Ec	M Shop	N Lib F	P Lib NF	Q Lib Ref	R Mag	S Rel
devilfish	4	.3709	.3633	35.6	0	1	0	2	1	0	0	0	2	0	0	0	0	0	0	0	0	0	0	0	0	0	1	1	0
devilish	2	.2160	.1362	31.3	1	0	0	0	0	0	0	1	1	0	0	0	0	0	0	1	0	0	0	0	0	0	0	0	0
devilment	2	.1717	.1142	30.6	0	0	0	0	2	0	0	0	1	0	0	1	0	0	0	0	0	0	0	0	0	0	0	0	0
devils	10	.4006	.9178	39.6	0	1	1	0	5	1	2	0	3	0	0	4	0	0	0	0	0	0	0	0	2	1	0	0	0
devious	5	.3850	.4834	36.8	0	0	1	2	1	1	0	0	3	0	0	0	0	1	0	0	0	0	0	0	0	1	0	0	0
devise	16	.7569	2.4491	43.9	0	2	2	2	2	4	3	1	2	1	0	2	1	0	0	4	0	0	1	0	1	2	1	1	0
devised	61	.7902	9.6902	49.9	2	1	6	7	20	4	19	2	7	3	1	2	3	3	0	12	3	0	0	1	1	4	17	4	0
devising	7	.4962	.7276	38.6	0	1	1	0	2	2	1	0	0	1	0	0	0	0	0	2	0	1	0	0	0	1	1	1	0
devoid	6	.3404	.4555	36.6	0	0	0	0	3	1	2	0	0	0	0	3	0	0	0	2	0	0	0	0	0	0	1	0	0
Devonshire	2	.0000	.0209	23.2	0	0	0	0	0	1	1	0	0	0	0	0	0	0	0	0	0	0	0	0	0	0	2	0	0
Devore's	2	.0000	.0914	29.6	0	0	0	2	0	0	0	0	2	0	0	0	0	0	0	0	0	0	0	0	0	0	0	0	0
devote	15	.6374	1.9697	42.9	1	1	1	3	4	1	4	0	1	2	0	0	0	5	0	0	0	0	0	0	2	2	2	1	0
devoted	73	.7236	10.720	50.3	1	7	15	5	15	16	11	3	8	4	0	3	3	10	1	1	3	0	0	0	1	18	17	4	0
devotees	4	.2437	.2257	33.5	0	0	0	1	2	1	0	0	0	0	0	0	0	0	0	0	0	0	0	0	0	0	2	2	0
devotes	3	.1847	.1428	31.5	0	0	0	0	1	0	2	0	0	2	0	0	0	0	0	1	0	0	0	0	0	0	0	0	0
devoting	4	.4338	.3884	35.9	0	0	0	0	2	1	1	0	1	0	0	0	0	1	0	0	1	0	0	0	0	0	1	0	0
devotion	30	.7287	4.4342	46.5	0	3	4	1	6	9	5	2	4	4	0	4	0	5	0	0	4	0	0	0	1	3	3	2	0
devour	8	.4719	.8307	39.2	0	1	0	1	3	0	3	0	2	0	0	3	0	0	0	1	0	0	0	0	0	1	1	0	0
devoured	13	.5215	1.4520	41.6	0	3	3	1	1	2	3	0	3	0	1	3	0	0	0	0	0	0	0	0	3	3	0	0	0
devouring	7	.4797	.7762	38.9	1	0	0	4	1	1	0	0	4	0	0	1	0	0	0	1	0	0	0	0	0	0	1	0	0
devout	6	.4291	.5437	37.4	0	2	1	0	2	1	0	0	0	0	0	0	0	0	0	0	1	0	0	0	0	1	3	1	0
devoutly	3	.3852	.2500	34.0	0	0	1	0	1	0	1	0	0	0	0	1	0	0	0	0	0	0	0	0	0	1	0	1	0
dew	83	.6066	10.618	50.3	12	14	3	20	7	7	19	1	16	3	0	7	0	0	0	43	5	0	0	0	3	4	1	1	0
dewdrops	4	.3702	.3622	35.6	0	3	0	0	0	1	0	0	2	1	0	1	0	0	0	0	0	0	0	0	0	0	0	0	0
Dewey	35	.4264	3.3316	45.2	0	0	2	2	15	14	1	1	8	18	0	0	1	3	0	0	0	0	0	0	0	1	2	2	0
Dewey's	3	.3418	.2483	33.9	0	0	0	0	1	1	1	0	1	1	0	0	0	0	0	0	0	0	0	0	0	1	0	0	0
dews	2	.2303	.1079	30.3	0	1	1	0	0	0	0	0	0	0	0	0	0	0	0	0	1	0	0	0	0	1	0	0	0
dewy	6	.3690	.4829	36.8	0	0	0	1	2	1	2	0	0	1	0	2	0	0	0	0	0	0	0	0	0	3	0	0	0
Dexter	7	.3493	.5973	37.8	1	1	0	0	3	2	0	0	2	0	0	0	0	0	0	3	0	0	0	0	0	2	0	0	0
dexterity	3	.2279	.2143	33.3	0	0	0	1	0	1	0	1	2	0	0	0	0	0	0	0	0	0	0	0	0	0	0	1	0
dexterous	4	.1973	.1770	32.5	0	0	1	0	2	1	0	0	0	0	2	1	0	0	0	0	0	0	0	0	0	0	0	1	0
dey	10	.2919	.6534	38.2	0	0	0	2	8	0	0	0	0	0	0	0	0	0	0	0	2	0	0	0	7	1	0	0	0
DF	7	.1928	.3442	35.4	0	1	0	2	0	2	2	0	0	0	0	0	6	0	0	0	1	0	0	0	0	0	0	0	0
dge	6	.2379	.3263	35.1	3	0	0	2	0	0	1	0	0	4	0	0	0	0	2	0	0	0	0	0	0	0	0	0	0
DGP	3	.0000	.0449	26.5	0	0	0	0	3	0	0	0	0	0	0	0	3	0	0	0	0	0	0	0	0	0	0	0	0
dhoti	3	.0000	.1370	31.4	0	3	0	0	0	0	0	0	3	0	0	0	0	0	0	0	0	0	0	0	0	0	0	0	0
dhows	3	.2444	.1814	32.6	0	0	1	2	0	0	0	0	0	0	0	0	0	2	0	0	0	0	0	0	0	0	1	0	0
di	9	.2710	.5372	37.3	0	2	3	2	2	0	0	0	0	0	0	0	0	0	6	0	2	0	0	0	0	1	0	0	0
DiMaggio	14	.3654	1.2467	41.0	0	4	0	4	6	0	0	0	6	0	0	0	0	0	0	0	0	0	0	0	0	4	0	4	0
DiMaggio's	2	.0000	.0243	23.9	0	0	0	0	2	0	0	0	0	0	0	0	0	0	0	0	0	0	0	0	0	0	0	2	0
diabase	2	.0000	.0394	26.0	0	0	0	0	0	0	2	0	0	0	0	0	0	0	0	2	0	0	0	0	0	0	0	0	0
diabetes	3	.2233	.1562	31.9	0	0	0	0	0	1	2	0	0	0	0	1	0	0	0	0	0	0	0	0	0	0	2	0	0
diabetics	2	.0000	.0243	23.9	0	0	0	0	0	2	0	0	0	0	0	0	0	0	0	0	0	0	0	0	0	0	0	2	0
Diablo	9	.0000	.4111	36.1	0	0	9	0	0	0	0	0	9	0	0	0	0	0	0	0	0	0	0	0	0	0	0	0	0
diabolical	3	.3465	.2515	34.0	0	0	0	1	1	0	0	1	1	0	0	0	0	0	0	0	0	0	0	0	0	1	0	1	0
diacritical	13	.1901	.6365	38.0	0	4	3	2	4	0	0	0	2	2	0	0	0	0	9	0	0	0	0	0	0	0	0	0	0
diadem	2	.0000	.0209	23.2	0	0	2	0	0	0	0	0	0	0	0	0	0	0	0	0	0	0	0	0	0	0	2	0	0
Diaghilev	6	.0000	.0485	26.9	0	0	0	0	3	0	3	0	0	0	0	0	0	0	0	0	6	0	0	0	0	0	0	0	0
diagnose	7	.5198	.7889	39.0	0	0	1	0	3	2	1	0	2	1	0	2	0	0	0	1	0	0	0	0	0	0	1	0	0
diagnosed	4	.0996	.1523	31.8	0	0	0	0	1	1	1	1	1	0	0	0	0	0	0	0	0	0	0	0	0	0	0	3	0
diagnosis	12	.4648	1.2017	40.8	0	0	1	1	0	6	4	0	1	0	0	0	0	0	0	3	0	0	0	0	0	1	4	3	0
diagnostic	4	.0000	.0419	26.2	0	0	0	0	0	1	3	0	0	0	0	0	0	0	0	0	0	0	0	0	0	0	4	0	0
diagonal	62	.4225	5.6523	47.5	5	2	19	10	9	13	2	2	0	0	0	0	51	0	0	2	0	2	2	0	0	1	1	3	0
diagonally	13	.4905	1.3215	41.2	0	1	0	2	3	3	4	0	1	0	0	1	0	0	0	1	2	0	3	3	0	1	1	0	0
diagonals	15	.2319	.8459	39.3	3	0	8	0	0	3	1	0	0	0	0	0	14	0	0	0	0	1	0	0	0	0	0	0	0
diagram	290	.6836	40.614	56.1	2	33	43	59	72	47	32	2	29	16	6	0	131	8	4	70	10	0	1	6	0	1	7	1	0
Diagram	7	.0847	.1787	32.5	0	0	1	0	6	0	0	0	0	0	0	0	0	1	0	0	6	0	0	0	0	0	0	0	0
diagramed	7	.0000	.0766	28.8	0	0	0	0	0	2	5	0	0	7	0	0	0	0	0	0	0	0	0	0	0	0	0	0	0
diagraming	5	.0000	.0547	27.4	0	0	0	0	3	0	2	0	0	5	0	0	0	0	0	0	0	0	0	0	0	0	0	0	0
diagrams	91	.6791	12.669	51.0	1	7	31	19	16	9	5	3	8	5	0	1	42	4	1	23	1	2	1	1	0	0	1	1	0
dial	43	.7295	6.3444	48.0	6	4	6	3	11	5	8	0	5	4	1	2	5	2	2	5	1	0	0	5	2	0	8	1	0
dialect	16	.5996	1.9665	42.9	2	1	1	1	5	2	4	0	1	3	0	2	0	0	0	0	0	1	0	0	1	1	6	1	0
dialects	13	.5066	1.3608	41.3	1	1	1	1	5	3	1	0	0	6	1	0	0	1	2	0	0	0	0	0	0	0	3	0	0
dialed	8	.4695	.8089	39.1	2	0	0	1	4	0	1	0	1	0	0	0	0	1	0	0	0	0	0	0	3	0	2	1	0
dialing	4	.3719	.3659	35.6	0	0	0	1	0	3	0	0	2	0	0	1	1	0	0	0	0	0	0	0	0	0	0	0	0
dialogue	43	.6027	5.3103	47.3	1	5	0	8	12	6	9	2	4	11	5	2	0	1	1	0	11	0	0	0	1	1	2	4	0
dialogues	3	.2440	.1815	32.6	0	1	0	2	0	0	0	0	0	1	0	0	0	2	0	0	0	0	0	0	0	0	0	0	0
dials	10	.5777	1.2109	40.8	1	1	0	2	4	2	0	0	2	0	0	2	0	0	0	0	2	0	0	0	2	1	0	1	0
diameter	249	.5083	26.570	54.2	3	16	18	43	59	38	59	13	6	1	0	1	106	6	0	47	2	1	1	44	3	3	16	12	0
diameters	22	.3010	1.4940	41.7	1	0	2	4	8	1	6	0	0	0	0	0	10	0	0	5	0	0	0	6	0	0	0	1	0
diametral	3	.0000	.0449	26.5	0	0	0	0	0	3	0	0	0	0	0	0	3	0	0	0	0	0	0	0	0	0	0	0	0
diamond	97	.8836	17.086	52.3	13	13	7	18	25	7	13	1	25	9	2	3	9	12	2	8	3	0	1	5	3	7	4	4	0
Diamond	12	.5398	1.4298	41.6	0	5	1	5	0	1	0	0	6	0	0	0	0	0	0	0	1	0	0	0	1	0	1	3	0
diamond-tipped	2	.1937	.0847	29.3	0	0	0	0	1	0	1	0	0	0	0	0	0	0	0	0	1	0	0	1	0	0	0	0	0
diamondback	4	.3264	.2941	34.7	1	1	0	0	2	0	0	0	0	0	0	0	1	0	0	1	0	0	0	0	0	0	2	0	0
diamonds	57	.7350	8.6925	49.4	6	16	3	4	18	6	2	2	30	1	3	2	2	8	1	2	1	0	0	0	1	1	2	3	0
Diana	6	.4858	.6602	38.2	1	3	0	1	0	0	1	0	3	0	0	1	0	0	0	0	0	0	0	0	1	0	1	0	0
Diana-Kate	3	.0000	.1370	31.4	0	0	0	3	0	0	0	0	3	0	0	0	0	0	0	0	0	0	0	0	0	0	0	0	0
Diane	3	.2031	.1990	33.0	0	1	0	0	2	0	0	0	2	0	0	0	0	0	1	0	0	0	0	0	0	0	0	0	0
diaper	3	.0524	.0803	29.0	1	0	0	0	1	0	1	0	1	0	0	0	0	0	0	0	0	0	2	0	0	0	0	0	0
diapered	2	.2443	.1130	30.5	0	0	0	0	1	1	0	0	0	0	0	1	0	0	0	0	0	0	0	0	1	0	0	0	0
diapers	2	.1717	.1142	30.6	0	0	0	0	0	1	1	0	1	0	0	1	0	0	0	0	0	0	0	0	0	0	0	0	0
diaphragm	35	.4811	3.5482	45.5	1	1	4	3	16	6	4	0	0	0	0	0	0	0	0	15	13	0	0	2	0	0	3	2	0
diarrhea	17	.2163	.8507	39.3	0	0	0	0	0	15	2	0	0	0	0	0	0	0	0	0	0	0	2	0	0	0	15	0	0
diary	57	.6659	8.0675	49.1	2	14	3	9	6	19	4	0	32	0	0	3	0	8	3	0	0	0	0	0	1	7	1	2	0
Diary	2	.0000	.0914	29.6	0	0	0	2	0	0	0	0	2	0	0	0	0	0	0	0	0	0	0	0	0	0	0	0	0
Dias	2	.0000	.0209	23.2	0	0	0	0	0	2	0	0	0	0	0	0	0	0	0	0	0	0	0	0	0	0	2	0	0
Diassigue	6	.0000	.0644	28.1	0	0	0	0	6	0	0	0	0	0	0	6	0	0	0	0	0	0	0	0	0	0	0	0	0
Diassigue-the-Alligator	3	.0000	.0322	25.1	0	0	0	0	3	0	0	0	0	0	0	3	0	0	0	0	0	0	0	0	0	0	0	0	0
diastase	2	.0000	.0394	26.0	0	0	0	1	0	0	0	1	0	0	0	0	0	0	0	2	0	0	0	0	0	0	0	0	0
diastrophism	8	.2353	.4765	36.8	0	0	0	0	2	3	3	0	0	0	0	0	0	0	0	6	0	0	0	0	0	0	2	0	0
diatom	4	.0000	.0789	29.0	0	0	3	0	0	1	0	0	0	0	0	0	0	0	0	4	0	0	0	0	0	0	0	0	0
diatomaceous	2	.0000	.0394	26.0	0	0	0	0	0	2	0	0	0	0	0	0	0	0	0	2	0	0	0	0	0	0	0	0	0

6R Devils
9D devis'd
XR deviser
6A devises
7H devitalizing
6A Devonians
8J devotee
5J devotional
8J devotions
XR devourers
5A devours
8D Dew
3A dew-covered
9D dew-dropping
8D dew-wet
9D dewberries
9D dewberry
7C dexterously
8R DFL
7E DG
7B dh
4Q dharma
6N Dhondaram
7Q diCavour
9D diFrancesco
6P DiMag
7R diMedici
XP diMonza
9Q diTallano
3P diTrevi
9A diabetic
8R Diabetics
5A Diablo's
XH diabolic
8J Diaghilef
8H diagnosing
9Q diagnosticians
9B diagrammed
7B Diagrams
8Q Dial
9D Dialect
9Q dialectics
9Q dialectology
8A Dialing
7B dialog
7Q Dialogues
4F diamond-back
3P diamond-backs
9M diamond-cone
9M diamond-faced
4Q diamond-shaped
7F Diamonds
6A Diana-Kate's
8J diaphragms
XH diapositives
8Q diaries
8Q diarist
8Q diarium
7R diathermy
6Q diatomic

Word Type	F	D	U	SFI	3 Gr 3	4 Gr 4	5 Gr 5	6 Gr 6	7 Gr 7	8 Gr 8	9 Gr 9	X UnGr	A Read	B Eng & Gr	C Comp	D Lit	E Math	F Soc Stud	G Spell	H Sci	J Music	K Art	L Home Ec	M Shop	N Lib F	P Lib NF	Q Lib Ref	R Mag	S Rel
diatoms	14	.3252	1.0392	40.2	1	0	6	6	0	1	0	0	0	6	0	0	0	0	0	7	0	0	0	0	0	0	1	0	0
Diatryma	6	.0000	.1183	30.7	0	0	0	0	0	0	0	6	0	0	0	0	0	0	0	6	0	0	0	0	0	0	0	0	0
Diaz	5	.2956	.3348	35.2	1	0	2	0	1	1	0	0	0	0	0	0	0	1	0	0	0	0	0	0	0	0	3	1	0
Dibbs	14	.0000	.6396	38.1	0	14	0	0	0	0	0	0	14	0	0	0	0	0	0	0	0	0	0	0	0	0	0	0	0
dibromide	2	.0000	.0209	23.2	0	0	0	2	0	0	0	0	0	0	0	0	0	0	0	0	0	0	0	0	0	0	2	0	0
Diccon	7	.0566	.1818	32.6	0	0	1	0	5	1	0	0	1	0	0	6	0	0	0	0	0	0	0	0	0	0	0	0	0
dice	23	.6073	2.9068	44.6	8	1	0	1	3	8	2	0	3	0	0	3	6	1	0	0	0	0	0	0	0	6	1	3	0
Dick	275	.6820	39.496	56.0	127	43	5	26	40	30	4	0	149	29	16	2	19	19	11	0	1	0	0	0	8	8	1	12	0
Dick's	19	.2713	1.3032	41.2	4	8	1	0	1	4	1	0	5	11	0	0	2	1	0	0	0	0	0	0	0	0	0	0	0
Dickens'	2	.2376	.1088	30.4	0	0	0	1	0	1	0	0	0	0	0	0	0	0	1	0	0	0	0	0	0	0	0	1	0
Dickie	10	.1997	.7335	38.7	1	1	0	0	7	1	0	0	9	0	0	0	1	0	0	0	0	0	0	0	0	0	0	0	0
Dickinson	12	.5596	1.4126	41.5	0	0	2	2	3	4	1	0	2	2	0	1	0	1	0	0	0	0	0	0	0	0	3	3	0
Dickson	5	.3317	.4097	36.1	0	2	0	0	0	3	0	0	2	2	0	0	0	0	0	0	0	0	0	0	0	0	0	1	0
Dicksons'	2	.0000	.0914	29.6	0	2	0	0	0	0	0	0	2	0	0	0	0	0	0	0	0	0	0	0	0	0	0	0	0
dictate	10	.6021	1.2291	40.9	0	0	0	1	2	6	1	0	0	2	0	0	0	1	2	0	1	0	0	0	0	2	2	0	0
dictated	12	.6582	1.6025	42.0	0	1	1	0	3	2	3	2	0	1	0	2	0	2	0	0	2	0	0	0	0	1	2	2	0
dictates	16	.6016	1.9645	42.9	1	0	5	2	3	3	2	0	1	1	0	0	0	0	6	0	2	0	1	0	1	0	1	3	0
dictating	6	.4714	.6073	37.8	0	0	0	3	1	0	2	0	0	0	0	0	0	0	0	3	0	0	0	0	1	1	0	1	0
dictation	9	.4146	.7893	39.0	0	3	0	1	2	0	3	0	0	5	0	0	0	0	1	0	0	0	0	0	0	0	2	1	0
dictator	37	.5729	4.4458	46.5	3	0	5	4	11	8	6	0	2	2	0	0	0	20	2	0	0	0	0	0	0	5	4	2	0
Dictator	2	.2437	.1129	30.5	0	1	0	0	0	0	1	0	0	0	0	0	0	0	0	0	0	0	0	0	0	0	1	1	0
dictatorial	3	.2378	.1809	32.6	0	0	1	0	0	1	1	0	0	0	0	0	0	2	0	0	0	0	0	0	0	1	0	0	0
dictators	9	.3932	.8037	39.1	0	0	3	1	1	2	2	0	1	0	0	0	0	5	0	0	0	0	0	0	0	1	2	0	0
dictatorship	9	.4445	.8659	39.4	1	0	1	0	1	1	5	0	0	1	0	0	0	5	0	0	0	0	0	0	0	1	2	0	0
dictatorships	4	.3863	.3414	35.3	0	0	1	0	0	1	2	0	0	0	0	0	0	2	0	0	0	0	0	0	0	0	1	1	0
diction	9	.3159	.6106	37.9	0	0	0	0	2	2	5	0	0	1	0	0	0	0	3	0	5	0	0	0	0	0	0	0	0
dictionaries	57	.3818	4.7193	46.7	0	3	3	6	27	13	5	0	4	30	0	1	1	0	18	0	0	0	0	0	0	0	2	1	0
dictionary	586	.3944	50.252	57.0	31	112	106	82	128	62	56	9	62	218	1	9	10	5	258	7	2	0	0	0	2	6	3	3	0
Dictionary	300	.0341	4.4169	46.5	13	75	72	71	56	9	4	0	1	4	0	0	1	0	293	0	1	0	0	0	0	0	0	0	0
Dictionopolis	2	.0000	.0914	29.6	0	0	2	0	0	0	0	0	2	0	0	0	0	0	0	0	0	0	0	0	0	0	0	0	0
dictum	2	.2443	.1130	30.5	0	0	0	0	2	0	0	0	0	0	0	1	0	0	0	0	0	0	0	0	1	0	0	0	0
did	7169	.9173	1306.6	71.2	1744	1309	888	848	1078	761	435	106	2333	400	38	501	912	734	192	404	147	40	23	4	602	461	119	242	17
Didd	3	.0000	.0352	25.5	3	0	0	0	0	0	0	0	0	0	0	0	0	0	0	0	0	0	0	0	3	0	0	0	0
diddle	16	.1125	.4733	36.8	13	2	1	0	0	0	0	0	0	0	0	2	0	0	0	0	14	0	0	0	0	0	0	0	0
Didelphis	4	.0000	.0419	26.2	0	0	0	0	4	0	0	0	0	0	0	0	0	0	0	0	0	0	0	0	0	0	4	0	0
didn't	2016	.7305	304.35	64.8	426	487	193	202	368	171	140	29	917	64	9	239	5	29	17	21	9	1	3	1	311	261	4	125	0
Didn't	3	.2374	.1625	32.1	0	0	0	0	1	0	2	0	0	0	0	2	0	0	0	0	1	0	0	0	0	0	0	0	0
Didrikson	6	.0000	.0644	28.1	0	0	0	0	0	0	6	0	0	0	0	6	0	0	0	0	0	0	0	0	0	0	0	0	0
didst	5	.4636	.4854	36.9	0	0	0	2	0	0	3	0	0	0	0	2	0	0	0	0	1	0	0	0	1	1	0	0	0
die	360	.8574	61.953	57.9	68	37	31	61	83	31	42	7	133	9	2	40	0	21	2	45	16	0	0	9	28	26	18	10	1
Die	7	.0839	.1779	32.5	0	0	0	5	1	0	1	0	0	0	0	0	0	0	0	1	6	0	0	0	0	0	0	0	0
died	459	.8977	82.041	59.1	52	51	70	60	91	74	38	23	133	8	3	47	11	47	6	33	16	3	0	0	29	49	45	28	1
Diego	12	.3492	1.0944	40.4	0	1	8	2	1	0	0	0	8	0	0	0	0	0	0	0	0	0	0	0	0	1	0	3	0
dielectric	11	.0000	.0278	24.4	0	0	0	0	0	11	0	0	0	0	0	0	0	0	0	0	0	0	0	11	0	0	0	0	0
dielectrics	2	.1738	.0790	29.0	0	0	0	0	0	1	1	0	0	0	0	0	0	0	0	0	0	0	0	1	0	0	1	0	0
Diem	2	.0000	.0209	23.2	0	0	0	0	0	2	0	0	0	0	0	0	0	0	0	0	0	0	0	0	0	0	2	0	0
dies	55	.6380	7.2292	48.6	11	2	3	7	9	10	11	2	8	1	0	4	2	2	0	7	4	0	0	8	1	9	5	4	0
Dies	3	.0000	.0243	23.8	0	0	0	0	3	0	0	0	0	0	0	0	0	0	0	0	3	0	0	0	0	0	0	0	0
diesel	14	.5940	1.7383	42.4	3	1	2	0	6	1	1	0	3	0	1	0	0	2	1	1	0	0	0	2	0	0	2	2	0
Diesel	3	.1727	.1578	32.0	0	0	0	2	0	0	1	0	1	0	1	0	0	0	0	1	0	0	0	0	0	0	0	0	0
diestock	4	.0000	.0101	20.0	0	0	0	0	0	0	4	0	0	0	0	0	0	0	0	0	0	0	0	4	0	0	0	0	0
diet	132	.4933	13.797	51.4	3	1	9	21	40	29	26	3	12	1	0	0	1	8	7	35	1	0	35	0	3	5	11	13	0
dieters	5	.2743	.3370	35.3	0	0	0	0	2	3	0	0	1	1	0	0	0	0	0	0	0	0	0	0	0	0	0	3	0
diethyl	3	.0000	.0314	25.0	0	0	1	2	0	0	0	0	0	0	0	0	0	0	0	0	0	0	0	0	0	0	3	0	0
Dietrich	4	.1724	.1646	32.2	0	0	0	0	0	0	3	1	0	1	2	0	0	0	0	1	0	0	0	0	0	0	0	0	0
diets	17	.3008	1.2115	40.8	0	1	4	1	6	1	4	0	2	1	0	0	0	1	0	8	0	0	5	0	0	0	0	0	0
differ	198	.8580	33.828	55.3	7	24	28	31	43	36	26	3	7	26	0	8	19	22	16	65	3	2	5	3	2	5	11	4	0
differed	16	.6043	2.0094	43.0	1	2	2	3	5	1	1	1	1	0	0	1	0	4	0	3	0	0	0	0	0	2	4	1	0
difference	751	.8713	130.16	61.1	85	104	114	93	136	141	70	8	60	65	5	18	240	33	16	135	50	9	17	19	14	26	20	24	0
difference-sum	5	.0000	.0748	28.7	0	0	0	0	5	0	0	0	0	0	0	0	5	0	0	0	0	0	0	0	0	0	0	0	0
differences	407	.7588	62.228	57.9	29	72	66	64	80	46	45	5	10	22	1	3	176	49	5	66	20	3	1	4	1	9	26	11	0
different	3926	.9339	724.97	68.6	695	649	536	504	694	436	329	83	465	397	34	84	309	453	225	810	354	117	80	69	46	162	190	128	3
Different	3	.1367	.0954	29.8	0	0	0	0	2	1	0	0	0	0	0	1	0	0	0	0	0	0	2	0	0	0	0	0	0
different-looking	2	.2401	.1133	30.5	1	1	0	0	0	0	0	0	0	0	0	0	0	0	0	0	0	0	0	0	0	1	1	0	0
differential	4	.3366	.3291	35.2	0	0	0	0	2	0	1	1	1	0	0	0	0	0	0	2	0	0	0	0	0	0	0	1	0
differentiate	5	.3542	.3897	35.9	0	0	0	0	4	0	1	0	0	2	0	0	0	0	0	2	0	0	1	0	0	0	0	0	0
differentiated	3	.0000	.0314	25.0	0	0	0	0	2	0	1	0	0	0	0	0	0	0	0	0	0	0	0	0	0	0	3	0	0
differently	107	.8017	17.198	52.4	11	17	22	18	19	12	5	3	13	18	1	1	4	14	20	12	3	6	2	1	1	2	4	5	0
differing	7	.3277	.5101	37.1	0	1	1	0	3	2	0	0	0	0	2	0	0	1	0	2	0	0	0	0	0	1	1	0	0
differs	52	.7452	7.8125	48.9	1	4	13	6	16	7	5	0	3	5	0	0	2	7	9	11	6	0	1	1	0	0	7	0	0
difficult	592	.9304	109.01	60.4	28	43	77	76	144	93	113	18	106	41	6	25	19	85	20	68	21	3	26	19	15	53	47	38	0
difficulties	80	.8564	13.655	51.4	6	3	7	8	15	18	20	3	10	6	4	2	5	14	3	8	0	1	6	1	3	5	9	3	0
difficulty	137	.9468	25.621	54.1	3	6	7	19	41	26	29	6	24	13	1	8	7	11	9	10	5	1	6	3	9	10	11	9	0
diffraction	10	.2426	.6051	37.8	0	0	0	2	1	4	0	3	0	0	0	0	0	0	0	7	0	0	0	0	0	0	3	0	0
diffuse	10	.3457	.7852	38.9	2	0	0	0	6	1	1	0	0	0	0	0	0	0	0	6	0	0	0	0	0	0	3	1	0
diffused	5	.5302	.5636	37.5	0	0	1	0	1	0	1	2	1	0	0	0	0	0	0	0	1	0	0	0	0	1	1	1	0
diffuses	6	.2071	.3307	35.2	0	0	0	0	3	0	3	0	0	0	0	0	0	0	0	5	0	0	0	0	0	0	1	0	0
diffusing	2	.0000	.0394	26.0	0	0	0	0	2	0	0	0	0	0	0	0	0	0	0	2	0	0	0	0	0	0	0	0	0
diffusion	11	.3341	.8126	39.1	0	0	2	0	8	1	0	0	0	0	2	0	0	0	0	4	0	0	0	0	0	0	5	0	0
dig	181	.8713	31.554	55.0	74	21	22	20	28	15	1	0	58	6	1	8	1	13	2	28	12	0	0	1	13	20	11	7	0
digest	23	.3979	2.0360	43.1	5	0	3	7	3	2	2	1	0	0	0	0	0	0	0	17	0	0	1	0	0	1	4	0	0
Digest	4	.3622	.3131	35.0	0	0	0	0	2	1	1	0	0	1	0	2	0	0	0	0	0	0	0	0	0	0	0	1	0
digested	37	.4539	3.6772	45.7	6	0	10	5	8	5	2	1	1	1	0	1	0	0	0	29	0	0	1	0	0	1	2	1	0
digester	2	.0000	.0394	26.0	0	0	0	2	0	0	0	0	0	0	0	0	0	0	0	2	0	0	0	0	0	0	0	0	0
digestible	4	.3783	.3305	35.2	0	0	0	0	1	2	1	0	0	1	0	0	0	1	0	1	0	0	1	0	0	0	0	0	0
digesting	4	.2278	.2257	33.5	0	0	1	0	2	1	0	0	0	0	0	0	0	0	0	2	0	0	0	0	0	0	2	0	0
digestion	45	.4327	4.2895	46.3	1	0	10	10	15	2	6	1	2	0	0	2	0	0	0	32	0	0	3	0	0	0	6	0	0
digestive	40	.4300	3.7553	45.7	0	0	8	4	9	3	15	1	1	0	0	0	0	0	1	24	0	0	2	0	0	0	12	0	0
digests	7	.1907	.3670	35.6	1	0	0	1	4	0	0	1	0	1	0	0	0	0	0	6	0	0	0	0	0	0	0	0	0
digger	11	.5815	1.3668	41.4	3	0	0	0	5	0	3	0	4	0	0	1	0	0	2	1	0	0	0	0	0	0	2	1	0
diggerfoot	2	.0000	.0914	29.6	0	0	0	0	2	0	0	0	2	0	0	0	0	0	0	0	0	0	0	0	0	0	0	0	0
diggers	5	.4436	.4942	36.9	1	1	0	0	3	0	0	0	1	0	0	0	0	2	0	0	1	0	0	0	0	0	0	1	0

7J diatonic
7A diatribe
5A Diavolo
5F Diaz's
7N dibs
7D Diccon's
9L diced
6Q dichloride
8Q dichromate
3A Dicked
8D dickens
7B Dickens
9B Dickensian
3A dicker
5N dickey
3P Dickey
7H dicot
7H dicotyledons
8B dict
9Q dicta
7A Did
3B DID
7P didacticism
7Q Didelphidae
8A didn
8D didn'
3A didn'
3B didn'.
5B didnht
9D Dido
3A didos
4Q die-casting
7R die-hard
3P Died
4J diedalum
5A Diego's
9M diemakers
7P DienBienPhu
7R diesel-electric
3P Diesel-electric
7A diesel's
XR diesels
XH diestrous
XH diestrus
5Q Diet
XR diet-proof
8R dieted
7A dieter
9D dietetic
9E dietetics
9E dietician
9E dietician's
7R dieticians
9F dietitian
7R Dietrich's
4G Dieu
4E diez
7G dif-
3E Differences
6H DIFFERENT
4A different-colored
4E different-sized
9P differentiates
7R differentiations
7A Difficult
7N Difficulty
9D diffidence
8F diffident
7C diffidently
6H diffracted
5Q diffusionists
3A DIG
7A Digger
7A Digger's

Word Type	F	D	U	SFI	3 Gr 3	4 Gr 4	5 Gr 5	6 Gr 6	7 Gr 7	8 Gr 8	9 Gr 9	X UnGr	A Read	B Eng & Gr	C Comp	D Lit	E Math	F Soc Stud	G Spell	H Sci	J Music	K Art	L Home Ec	M Shop	N Lib F	P Lib NF	Q Lib Ref	R Mag	S Rel
diggin'	2	.0000	.0914	29.6	0	0	1	1	0	0	0	0	2	0	0	0	0	0	0	0	0	0	0	0	0	0	0	0	0
digging	124	.7575	19.300	52.9	28	24	17	23	24	5	3	0	52	1	0	5	0	16	0	14	2	0	0	0	10	9	3	12	0
diggings	5	.3830	.4247	36.3	1	0	1	0	3	0	0	0	0	0	0	0	0	2	0	0	0	0	0	0	0	2	1	0	0
digit	191	.0293	3.9345	45.9	31	28	18	22	38	30	20	4	2	0	0	0	187	0	0	0	0	0	0	0	0	2	0	0	0
digit's	2	.0000	.0299	24.8	0	1	0	0	0	1	0	0	0	0	0	0	2	0	0	0	0	0	0	0	0	0	0	0	0
digital	3	.3829	.2504	34.0	1	0	0	0	1	1	0	0	0	0	0	0	1	0	0	0	0	0	0	0	0	1	1	0	0
digits	300	.0608	8.0311	49.0	27	48	22	28	51	81	40	3	8	0	0	1	286	0	0	1	0	0	0	0	0	4	0	0	0
dignified	25	.7760	3.9172	45.9	1	1	3	5	6	4	3	2	5	4	0	2	0	2	0	1	2	1	0	0	3	2	2	1	0
dignify	3	.1855	.1344	31.3	0	0	1	0	0	2	0	0	0	0	0	0	0	0	2	0	0	0	0	0	0	1	0	0	0
dignitary	2	.2427	.1152	30.6	0	1	0	0	0	0	0	1	0	0	0	0	0	0	0	0	0	0	0	0	1	1	0	0	0
dignity	49	.7645	7.5780	48.8	4	6	6	5	11	9	6	2	10	1	0	6	0	3	0	0	4	1	0	1	7	6	0	10	0
digraph	63	.0000	.5113	37.1	0	4	17	33	9	0	0	0	0	0	0	0	0	0	63	0	0	0	0	0	0	0	0	0	0
digraphs	20	.0000	.1623	32.1	0	0	8	6	6	0	0	0	0	0	0	0	0	0	20	0	0	0	0	0	0	0	0	0	0
digs	24	.7194	3.5473	45.5	10	5	0	3	5	0	1	0	6	0	0	1	0	1	1	7	1	0	0	0	0	4	2	1	0
dihedral	12	.0000	.1796	32.5	0	0	12	0	0	0	0	0	0	0	0	0	12	0	0	0	0	0	0	0	0	0	0	0	0
dihydrogen	2	.0000	.0394	26.0	0	0	0	0	0	0	0	2	0	0	0	0	0	0	0	2	0	0	0	0	0	0	0	0	0
dike	34	.5364	3.7850	45.8	2	4	17	1	9	1	0	0	0	0	1	9	0	6	0	0	0	0	0	0	14	3	1	0	0
dikes	37	.3740	3.3211	45.2	7	11	0	13	1	1	4	0	10	0	0	0	0	23	0	1	0	0	0	0	0	1	1	1	0
dilapidated	7	.4978	.7393	38.7	0	0	2	3	1	0	1	0	1	0	1	1	0	0	0	0	0	0	0	0	2	1	0	1	0
dilemma	8	.5263	.9100	39.6	0	0	0	0	3	3	2	0	2	0	0	0	0	1	0	0	0	0	0	0	0	2	1	2	0
diligence	2	.2443	.1130	30.5	0	0	0	0	1	0	1	0	0	0	0	1	0	0	0	0	0	0	0	0	1	0	0	0	0
diligent	2	.1948	.1250	31.0	0	1	0	1	0	0	0	0	1	0	0	0	0	0	0	0	0	0	0	0	0	1	0	0	0
diligently	5	.4177	.4477	36.5	0	0	1	0	2	1	1	0	0	1	1	0	0	1	0	1	0	0	0	0	1	0	0	0	0
dill	6	.4933	.6082	37.8	1	1	0	1	2	0	1	0	0	0	1	0	0	0	0	0	0	0	1	0	1	1	2	0	0
Dill	24	.0392	.4408	36.4	0	0	0	0	0	1	23	0	0	0	0	23	0	1	0	0	0	0	0	0	0	0	0	0	0
Dill's	2	.0000	.0215	23.3	0	0	0	0	0	0	2	0	0	0	0	2	0	0	0	0	0	0	0	0	0	0	0	0	0
Dillinger	20	.0000	.9137	39.6	20	0	0	0	0	0	0	0	20	0	0	0	0	0	0	0	0	0	0	0	0	0	0	0	0
Dillinger's	3	.0000	.1370	31.4	3	0	0	0	0	0	0	0	3	0	0	0	0	0	0	0	0	0	0	0	0	0	0	0	0
Dillingham	6	.2419	.4673	36.7	1	0	0	0	0	5	0	0	5	0	0	0	0	0	0	0	0	0	0	0	1	0	0	0	0
Dillworth	12	.0000	.5482	37.4	0	0	12	0	0	0	0	0	12	0	0	0	0	0	0	0	0	0	0	0	0	0	0	0	0
Dillworth's	2	.0000	.0914	29.6	0	0	2	0	0	0	0	0	2	0	0	0	0	0	0	0	0	0	0	0	0	0	0	0	0
dilly	6	.0000	.0485	26.9	0	6	0	0	0	0	0	0	0	0	0	0	0	0	0	0	6	0	0	0	0	0	0	0	0
Dilly	22	.0000	1.0050	40.0	9	0	13	0	0	0	0	0	22	0	0	0	0	0	0	0	0	0	0	0	0	0	0	0	0
dilute	6	.2361	.3556	35.5	0	0	1	0	1	2	2	0	0	0	0	0	0	0	0	5	0	0	0	1	0	0	0	0	0
diluted	4	.2287	.2348	33.7	0	1	0	2	0	0	0	1	0	0	0	0	0	0	0	3	0	0	0	0	0	0	0	1	0
dilutes	2	.2278	.1128	30.5	0	0	0	0	1	1	0	0	0	0	0	0	0	0	0	1	0	0	0	0	0	0	1	0	0
diluting	2	.2278	.1128	30.5	0	0	0	0	1	1	0	0	0	0	0	0	0	0	0	1	0	0	0	0	0	0	1	0	0
Dilworth	2	.0000	.0215	23.3	0	0	0	0	0	0	2	0	0	0	0	2	0	0	0	0	0	0	0	0	0	0	0	0	0
dim	75	.8365	12.602	51.0	5	13	7	13	18	5	9	5	21	1	1	9	0	2	1	11	1	0	1	0	10	7	5	5	0
dime	92	.7761	14.456	51.6	37	16	9	12	11	4	1	2	20	2	0	5	19	1	7	7	0	0	1	0	5	19	1	5	0
dime-store	2	.0000	.0914	29.6	2	0	0	0	0	0	0	0	2	0	0	0	0	0	0	0	0	0	0	0	0	0	0	0	0
dime's	2	.0000	.0914	29.6	0	2	0	0	0	0	0	0	2	0	0	0	0	0	0	0	0	0	0	0	0	0	0	0	0
dimension	44	.2034	2.0128	43.0	0	0	3	1	5	5	27	3	0	1	0	0	4	0	0	3	1	0	0	26	0	4	2	3	0
dimensional	3	.0994	.0714	28.5	0	1	1	0	0	0	1	0	0	0	0	0	0	0	0	0	0	2	0	0	0	0	1	0	0
dimensioning	5	.0000	.0126	21.0	0	0	0	0	0	0	5	0	0	0	0	0	0	0	0	0	0	0	0	5	0	0	0	0	0
dimensions	127	.3425	9.3556	49.7	0	1	2	2	37	18	61	6	1	1	0	1	40	0	0	10	2	1	1	51	1	1	11	6	0
dimes	129	.2137	7.1999	48.6	73	15	16	7	7	1	7	3	11	1	0	1	107	3	0	0	0	0	0	0	1	4	0	1	0
dimes'	3	.0000	.0449	26.5	3	0	0	0	0	0	0	0	0	0	0	0	3	0	0	0	0	0	0	0	0	0	0	0	0
diminish	3	.3267	.2367	33.7	0	0	0	0	2	0	1	0	1	0	0	0	0	0	0	0	1	0	0	0	1	0	0	0	0
diminished	13	.6516	1.7296	42.4	1	1	1	0	2	5	1	2	1	0	1	0	0	0	0	2	2	0	0	0	2	1	2	2	0
diminishing	6	.3873	.4990	37.0	0	0	0	1	2	0	2	1	0	0	0	2	0	0	0	0	0	0	0	0	2	0	0	2	0
diminutive	4	.4861	.4013	36.0	0	0	0	1	2	1	0	0	0	0	0	1	0	0	1	0	1	0	0	0	0	0	1	0	0
dimly	32	.7407	4.8111	46.8	2	4	1	3	7	6	8	1	7	1	2	7	0	0	0	1	1	1	0	0	2	4	2	4	0
dimmed	8	.5223	.9187	39.6	1	0	0	3	2	1	0	1	3	0	0	0	0	0	0	1	0	0	0	0	0	1	2	1	0
dimmer	6	.1808	.2555	34.1	0	0	0	2	1	3	0	0	0	0	0	0	0	0	0	1	0	0	0	3	0	0	0	2	0
dimness	6	.3546	.4886	36.9	0	1	1	0	3	0	1	0	1	0	0	3	0	0	0	1	0	0	0	0	1	0	0	0	0
dimple	2	.1717	.1142	30.6	0	1	0	0	1	0	0	0	1	0	0	1	0	0	0	0	0	0	0	0	0	0	0	0	0
dimpled	5	.4402	.4864	36.9	1	1	1	0	0	1	0	1	1	1	0	1	0	0	0	0	0	0	0	0	0	2	0	0	0
dimples	4	.2417	.3089	34.9	0	1	0	1	0	2	0	0	3	0	0	0	0	0	0	1	0	0	0	0	0	0	0	0	0
dimpling	3	.3772	.2437	33.9	0	2	1	0	0	0	0	0	0	0	0	0	0	0	0	0	1	0	0	0	1	1	0	0	0
din	18	.6587	2.5019	44.0	1	0	3	3	5	4	2	0	9	0	0	2	0	0	1	0	2	0	0	0	1	1	2	0	0
dinars	4	.0000	.0778	28.9	0	4	0	0	0	0	0	0	0	0	0	0	0	4	0	0	0	0	0	0	0	0	0	0	0
Dinarzade	2	.0000	.0234	23.7	0	0	2	0	0	0	0	0	0	0	0	0	0	0	0	0	0	0	0	0	2	0	0	0	0
dine	11	.5540	1.3269	41.2	3	0	1	4	2	0	1	0	5	2	0	1	0	0	1	0	0	0	0	0	0	0	2	0	0
dined	11	.5157	1.2379	40.9	1	1	1	2	2	1	3	0	4	1	0	3	0	0	0	0	2	0	0	0	0	0	0	1	0
diner	8	.4770	.8286	39.2	4	0	1	1	0	2	0	0	2	2	1	1	0	0	0	0	0	0	0	0	0	0	0	2	0
Diner	2	.0000	.0234	23.7	0	0	0	0	2	0	0	0	0	0	0	0	0	0	0	0	0	0	0	0	2	0	0	0	0
diners	3	.3465	.2515	34.0	0	0	1	1	1	0	0	0	1	0	0	0	0	0	0	0	0	0	0	0	0	1	0	1	0
dines	2	.0000	.0243	23.9	0	1	0	1	0	0	0	0	0	0	0	0	0	0	0	0	0	0	0	0	0	0	0	2	0
dinette	3	.0000	.0583	27.7	3	0	0	0	0	0	0	0	0	0	0	0	0	3	0	0	0	0	0	0	0	0	0	0	0
ding	4	.1494	.2089	33.2	4	0	0	0	0	0	0	0	2	0	0	0	0	0	0	0	2	0	0	0	0	0	0	0	0
ding-a-ling-a-ling	2	.2387	.1089	30.4	2	0	0	0	0	0	0	0	0	0	0	0	0	0	0	0	1	0	0	0	1	0	0	0	0
ding-dong-tock	2	.0000	.0914	29.6	0	0	0	0	2	0	0	0	2	0	0	0	0	0	0	0	0	0	0	0	0	0	0	0	0
dingblasted	2	.0000	.0234	23.7	2	0	0	0	0	0	0	0	0	0	0	0	0	0	0	0	0	0	0	0	2	0	0	0	0
dinghy	2	.1497	.1046	30.2	0	0	0	1	1	0	0	0	1	0	0	0	0	0	1	0	0	0	0	0	0	0	0	0	0
Dingo	11	.0000	.5025	37.0	0	11	0	0	0	0	0	0	11	0	0	0	0	0	0	0	0	0	0	0	0	0	0	0	0
dingy	11	.5871	1.3464	41.3	0	0	0	1	6	3	1	0	2	2	1	3	0	1	1	0	0	0	0	0	1	0	0	0	0
Dinh	2	.0000	.0209	23.2	0	0	0	0	0	2	0	0	0	0	0	0	0	0	0	0	0	0	0	0	0	0	2	0	0
dining	96	.7149	13.962	51.4	15	10	13	6	20	12	18	2	19	7	3	10	1	11	1	1	0	1	18	1	5	8	4	6	0
Dining	2	.0000	.0914	29.6	0	0	0	1	1	0	0	0	2	0	0	0	0	0	0	0	0	0	0	0	0	0	0	0	0
dining-room	5	.0804	.1641	32.2	1	2	0	1	0	1	0	0	1	0	0	0	0	0	0	0	0	0	0	0	4	0	0	0	0
dinky	2	.2440	.1132	30.5	0	0	0	1	0	1	0	0	0	0	0	1	0	0	0	0	0	0	0	0	0	0	0	1	0
Dinky	8	.0000	.0938	29.7	0	0	0	0	0	0	0	8	0	0	0	0	0	0	0	0	0	0	0	0	8	0	0	0	0
dinner	430	.8661	74.550	58.7	145	77	41	35	50	28	42	12	147	23	4	42	8	23	17	18	2	1	11	0	63	34	4	33	0
Dinner	6	.4346	.5972	37.8	2	1	1	0	0	0	0	2	2	0	0	0	0	0	0	1	0	0	0	0	0	1	0	2	0
dinners	17	.6208	2.1983	43.4	1	9	4	1	2	0	0	0	3	0	0	2	1	0	0	2	0	0	0	0	4	4	1	0	0
dinnertime	5	.2581	.3344	35.2	1	3	0	0	1	0	0	0	1	0	0	0	0	0	0	1	0	0	0	0	0	3	0	0	0
dinnerware	3	.3132	.2019	33.1	0	0	0	0	1	1	1	0	0	0	0	0	0	1	0	0	0	0	1	1	0	0	0	0	0
Dino	7	.2353	.5425	37.3	0	1	0	6	0	0	0	0	6	0	0	0	0	0	0	0	0	0	0	0	0	0	0	1	0
Dino's	2	.0000	.0914	29.6	0	0	0	2	0	0	0	0	2	0	0	0	0	0	0	0	0	0	0	0	0	0	0	0	0
dinosaur	138	.4940	15.128	51.8	83	15	27	5	4	1	2	1	47	0	1	1	1	0	0	4	0	2	0	0	1	75	2	4	0
dinosaur's	11	.2899	.7699	38.9	10	1	0	0	0	0	0	0	2	0	0	0	0	0	0	1	0	2	0	0	0	6	0	0	0
dinosaurs	189	.3851	16.400	52.1	90	63	10	11	11	2	1	1	21	1	0	0	0	0	0	24	0	1	0	0	0	120	22	0	0
Dinosaurs	4	.1112	.1666	32.2	3	0	0	1	0	0	0	0	1	0	0	0	0	0	0	0	0	0	0	0	0	3	0	0	0
dinosaurs'	2	.0000	.0290	24.6	1	1	0	0	0	0	0	0	0	0	0	0	0	0	0	0	0	0	0	0	0	2	0	0	0
dint	2	.2444	.1132	30.5	0	0	0	1	0	0	0	1	0	1	0	0	0	0	0	0	0	0	0	0	1	0	0	0	0
Dinwiddie	4	.1325	.1944	32.9	0	0	0	0	1	3	0	0	1	0	0	0	0	3	0	0	0	0	0	0	0	0	0	0	0

5P dignifies
7N dignities
6A dik-dik
6R diking
7D dilate
6A dilated
7R dilemmas
9Q dilettantes
8F Diligence
9D Dill'll
7A Dillon's
4A dilly-dallying
4P Dilsey
4P Dilsey's
9M dimensioned
7H dimensionless
3P Dimes
3Q diminishes
7R diminishingly
4J diminuendo
8J diminution
9K dimly-lit
5N dims
5A ding-dong
3N ding-dong-ding-dong
7D dingbat
7D dinged
5R dinghies
8Q Dingwall
4P dinin'-table
9D dining-table
7A Dining's
9D diningroom
6D dinkum
XN Dinky's
3A dinn
XR dinner-party
5N dinner-time
4A dinner's
3A DINOSAURS
6N Dinsmore
8F Dinwiddie's

Word Type	F	D	U	SFI	3 Gr 3	4 Gr 4	5 Gr 5	6 Gr 6	7 Gr 7	8 Gr 8	9 Gr 9	X UnGr	A Read	B Eng & Gr	C Comp	D Lit	E Math	F Soc Stud	G Spell	H Sci	J Music	K Art	L Home Ec	M Shop	N Lib F	P Lib NF	Q Lib Ref	R Mag	S Rel
Diocletian	2	.0000	.0209	23.2	0	0	0	0	1	0	0	1	0	0	0	0	0	0	0	0	0	0	0	0	0	0	2	0	0
diode	3	.0000	.0591	27.7	0	0	0	0	0	2	1	0	0	0	0	0	0	0	0	3	0	0	0	0	0	0	0	0	0
Dionisio	37	.1850	2.6463	44.2	0	34	0	3	0	0	0	0	34	0	0	0	0	0	0	0	0	0	0	0	0	3	0	0	0
diorama	2	.2446	.1257	31.0	0	0	0	1	0	0	1	0	0	0	0	0	0	1	0	1	0	0	0	0	0	0	0	0	0
diorite	2	.2278	.1128	30.5	0	0	0	0	0	0	2	0	0	0	0	0	0	0	0	1	0	0	0	0	0	0	1	0	0
dioxide	198	.3007	14.378	51.6	42	9	35	32	44	15	17	4	4	0	0	0	0	4	0	173	0	0	0	3	0	0	11	3	0
dip	64	.7352	9.5564	49.8	7	12	9	10	13	7	2	4	12	2	0	2	0	0	0	13	3	4	6	1	1	8	3	9	0
Diphda	2	.0000	.0394	26.0	0	0	0	0	0	0	0	2	0	0	0	0	0	0	0	2	0	0	0	0	0	0	0	0	0
diphtheria	16	.3394	1.3149	41.2	2	4	2	1	1	2	1	3	3	0	0	1	0	0	0	11	0	0	0	0	0	0	1	0	0
diphthong	27	.1025	.7482	38.7	0	1	12	11	0	3	0	0	0	3	0	0	0	0	24	0	0	0	0	0	0	0	0	0	0
diphthongs	16	.3724	1.2612	41.0	0	0	3	3	2	3	5	0	0	5	0	0	0	0	7	0	4	0	0	0	0	0	0	0	0
diplodocus	2	.0000	.0290	24.6	0	2	0	0	0	0	0	0	0	0	0	0	0	0	0	0	0	0	0	0	0	2	0	0	0
diploid	2	.2278	.1128	30.5	0	0	0	0	0	0	1	1	0	0	0	0	0	0	0	1	0	0	0	0	0	0	1	0	0
diploma	7	.2927	.4829	36.8	0	0	1	1	1	0	2	2	1	0	0	0	0	0	0	0	0	0	0	0	0	0	3	3	0
diplomacy	15	.4969	1.6141	42.1	3	0	3	0	2	2	5	0	3	0	0	0	0	2	0	0	0	0	0	0	0	2	3	5	0
Diplomacy	2	.0000	.0209	23.2	0	0	2	0	0	0	0	0	0	0	0	0	0	0	0	0	0	0	0	0	0	0	2	0	0
diplomat	7	.5138	.7499	38.7	0	1	1	1	1	2	1	0	0	1	0	0	1	0	0	0	0	0	0	0	1	1	0	3	0
diplomatic	13	.5270	1.4659	41.7	0	0	3	0	8	1	1	0	2	0	0	0	0	3	0	0	0	0	0	0	0	4	2	2	0
diplomats	6	.3704	.5081	37.1	0	1	0	0	1	1	2	1	1	0	0	0	0	1	0	0	0	0	0	0	1	0	0	3	0
dipped	60	.7415	9.1099	49.6	8	10	10	10	13	4	4	1	22	0	1	5	0	1	0	2	1	4	2	0	7	8	3	4	0
dipper	10	.6552	1.3592	41.3	3	2	1	2	1	1	0	0	2	0	0	1	0	1	0	2	1	0	0	0	0	1	0	2	0
Dipper	28	.5290	3.1988	45.0	12	9	0	5	1	0	0	1	4	1	0	2	1	3	1	16	0	0	0	0	0	0	0	0	0
dipping	17	.7485	2.5689	44.1	1	1	0	3	5	3	2	2	2	1	1	1	0	0	1	3	0	0	1	0	0	2	2	3	0
dips	13	.5800	1.5943	42.0	0	2	2	2	5	1	1	0	2	0	0	1	0	2	0	4	0	0	0	0	1	0	0	3	0
dipstick	2	.0000	.0243	23.9	0	0	0	0	2	0	0	0	0	0	0	0	0	0	0	0	0	0	0	0	0	0	0	2	0
dire	8	.5651	.9476	39.8	0	0	1	1	4	0	1	1	1	0	0	2	0	0	0	1	0	0	0	0	0	1	1	2	0
direct	284	.8533	48.232	56.8	13	12	38	19	70	52	65	15	18	68	14	10	4	26	9	44	4	2	5	7	8	12	27	26	0
Direct	2	.1787	.1174	30.7	0	1	0	0	0	1	0	0	1	0	0	0	0	0	0	0	0	0	0	0	1	0	0	0	0
directed	119	.8252	19.646	52.9	3	8	12	13	23	21	36	3	15	6	1	5	27	8	1	7	7	0	9	1	0	10	14	8	0
directing	15	.7476	2.2726	43.6	0	1	2	1	6	2	3	0	3	2	0	0	1	1	0	0	2	0	1	0	2	1	1	1	0
direction	651	.8687	112.76	60.5	97	73	65	82	113	107	94	20	102	18	3	20	62	72	10	151	10	6	17	41	37	34	45	23	0
Direction	3	.2445	.1903	32.8	0	0	0	0	1	1	0	1	1	0	0	0	0	0	0	0	0	0	1	0	0	0	0	1	0
directional	4	.2595	.2168	33.4	0	0	0	0	3	0	1	0	0	0	0	0	0	0	0	0	0	2	1	0	0	0	1	0	0
directionally	6	.0000	.0193	22.9	0	0	0	0	2	0	4	0	0	0	0	0	0	0	0	0	0	0	6	0	0	0	0	0	0
directions	533	.8407	89.750	59.5	87	81	70	68	81	88	50	8	131	90	6	8	31	35	41	59	14	7	48	15	7	20	8	13	0
Directions	37	.2874	3.2401	45.1	35	0	0	1	0	0	1	0	35	0	0	0	0	0	0	0	0	0	1	0	0	0	0	1	0
directly	347	.9063	62.342	57.9	19	29	28	37	92	53	71	18	42	13	10	22	10	24	20	77	8	6	11	16	13	16	41	18	0
directness	4	.3135	.2764	34.4	0	0	0	0	2	1	1	0	0	0	0	0	0	0	0	0	0	0	0	1	0	2	0	1	0
director	79	.6694	10.819	50.3	1	9	8	11	21	13	11	5	11	4	0	4	0	3	1	2	14	0	0	0	0	8	11	21	0
Director	15	.4636	1.4952	41.7	2	0	2	1	5	1	3	1	2	0	0	0	0	0	0	1	3	0	0	0	0	0	3	6	0
director-general	2	.0000	.0389	25.9	0	0	0	0	0	2	0	0	0	0	0	0	0	2	0	0	0	0	0	0	0	0	0	0	0
director's	3	.1277	.1363	31.3	0	0	0	0	1	1	1	0	1	0	0	0	0	0	0	0	0	0	0	0	0	0	0	2	0
directorates	2	.0000	.0209	23.2	0	0	1	0	0	0	1	0	0	0	0	0	0	0	0	0	0	0	0	0	0	0	2	0	0
directors	19	.6274	2.5012	44.0	0	0	3	4	3	4	3	2	5	0	0	0	0	5	0	0	1	0	0	0	1	1	4	2	0
Directors	2	.1698	.1133	30.5	0	0	0	0	1	0	1	0	1	0	0	0	0	0	0	0	0	0	0	0	0	0	1	0	0
directory	5	.3432	.4203	36.2	0	1	1	1	0	0	0	2	2	1	0	0	0	0	0	0	0	0	0	0	0	0	0	2	0
Directory	2	.2437	.1129	30.5	0	1	0	0	0	0	0	1	0	0	0	0	0	0	0	0	0	0	0	0	0	0	1	1	0
directs	14	.6417	1.8623	42.7	1	1	1	2	4	4	1	0	3	2	0	0	0	1	3	1	0	0	0	0	0	1	2	1	0
dirges	2	.2407	.1138	30.6	0	0	0	0	1	0	1	0	0	0	0	1	0	0	0	0	0	0	0	0	0	1	0	0	0
dirigible	2	.2418	.1091	30.4	0	0	0	0	1	1	0	0	0	0	0	0	0	0	1	0	0	0	0	0	0	0	1	0	0
Dirk	50	.2615	3.7542	45.7	20	10	18	0	1	1	0	0	30	1	0	0	0	0	0	0	0	0	0	0	19	0	0	0	0
dirt	185	.8797	32.498	55.1	53	38	14	18	32	13	17	0	55	10	5	14	2	11	4	29	2	0	1	2	12	23	2	13	0
dirtier	2	.2408	.1204	30.8	0	1	0	0	0	0	1	0	0	0	0	0	0	1	0	0	0	0	0	0	0	1	0	0	0
dirtiest	2	.1814	.1187	30.7	0	0	1	0	1	0	0	0	1	0	0	0	0	0	0	0	0	0	0	0	0	0	0	1	0
dirty	143	.8887	25.310	54.0	40	24	16	10	23	11	17	2	36	10	1	17	0	14	6	10	2	0	3	1	16	17	4	6	0
dirty-little	3	.0000	.0352	25.5	0	3	0	0	0	0	0	0	0	0	0	0	0	0	0	0	0	0	0	0	3	0	0	0	0
dis	20	.4015	1.7979	42.5	2	0	0	5	10	2	1	0	5	3	0	2	0	0	9	0	0	0	0	0	1	0	0	0	0
dis-	3	.3843	.2449	33.9	0	0	0	0	1	1	1	0	0	1	0	1	0	0	1	0	0	0	0	0	0	0	0	0	0
disability	4	.3519	.3117	34.9	0	0	0	0	1	0	3	0	0	0	0	0	0	1	0	0	0	0	0	0	0	0	1	2	0
disabled	8	.7121	1.1599	40.6	0	0	0	2	2	3	0	1	1	1	0	1	1	0	0	1	0	0	0	0	1	1	0	1	0
disabling	2	.2446	.1122	30.5	0	0	0	0	0	0	2	0	0	0	0	1	0	0	0	0	0	0	0	0	0	0	1	0	0
disadvantage	16	.7453	2.4215	43.8	0	0	1	2	3	3	4	3	3	1	0	1	1	1	0	3	1	0	1	0	0	0	3	1	0
disadvantages	14	.5524	1.6010	42.0	0	1	3	2	2	1	5	0	0	1	0	0	0	6	0	0	0	1	2	0	0	1	3	0	0
disagree	31	.7055	4.5020	46.5	4	0	3	6	7	2	7	2	7	1	0	0	3	11	1	1	0	1	0	0	0	1	1	4	0
disagreeable	10	.6631	1.3392	41.3	0	0	0	0	3	4	0	3	0	1	1	1	0	0	0	0	1	0	0	0	1	2	1	2	0
disagreed	8	.5401	.9305	39.7	0	1	3	0	3	1	0	0	2	0	0	1	0	2	0	0	0	0	0	0	1	0	0	2	0
disagreeing	3	.3406	.2461	33.9	0	1	1	0	0	1	0	0	1	1	0	0	0	0	0	0	0	0	0	0	0	0	0	1	0
disagreement	13	.5554	1.5094	41.8	0	1	2	0	1	6	3	0	0	3	0	0	0	6	0	1	0	0	0	0	1	0	1	1	0
disagreements	4	.3313	.2956	34.7	1	1	0	0	0	1	1	0	0	0	0	0	0	2	0	0	0	0	1	0	0	0	1	0	0
disagrees	2	.2417	.1211	30.8	0	0	0	0	0	0	2	0	0	0	0	0	1	1	0	0	0	0	0	0	0	0	0	0	0
disappear	79	.7627	12.261	50.9	12	19	7	14	13	8	5	1	18	5	0	6	0	3	3	30	0	0	1	0	3	3	4	3	0
disappearance	14	.4285	1.3064	41.2	1	5	0	2	3	0	3	0	1	0	0	2	0	0	0	4	0	0	0	0	0	1	6	0	0
disappeared	224	.8486	38.238	55.8	35	43	16	33	51	26	17	3	91	10	2	21	0	10	3	11	2	1	1	0	33	20	8	11	0
disappearing	35	.7029	5.0437	47.0	3	9	2	8	6	4	0	3	8	0	0	3	0	0	1	4	0	1	0	0	4	2	2	10	0
disappears	36	.6714	4.9566	47.0	6	6	3	3	7	5	2	4	4	0	0	1	1	1	3	12	5	0	0	0	0	0	5	4	0
disappoint	7	.4859	.7776	38.9	1	1	2	1	1	0	1	0	4	1	0	0	0	0	1	0	0	0	0	0	0	0	1	0	0
disappointed	103	.7545	15.964	52.0	17	40	12	11	9	8	4	2	45	7	2	3	2	5	0	1	2	0	0	0	6	24	1	5	0
disappointedly	3	.1187	.1291	31.1	0	1	0	0	2	0	0	0	1	0	0	2	0	0	0	0	0	0	0	0	0	0	0	0	0
disappointing	7	.4368	.7004	38.5	1	1	0	4	1	0	0	0	3	1	1	0	0	0	0	0	0	0	0	0	0	1	0	1	0
disappointment	50	.6436	6.6794	48.2	8	6	5	6	11	7	6	1	11	0	0	8	0	4	0	0	1	0	0	0	12	6	1	7	0
disappointments	8	.5383	.9067	39.6	2	0	1	0	3	1	1	0	1	0	0	2	0	1	0	0	0	0	1	0	0	2	0	1	0
disapproval	9	.4194	.8249	39.2	0	0	0	0	1	5	3	0	1	2	0	1	0	3	0	0	0	0	2	0	0	0	0	0	0
disapprove	5	.4882	.5167	37.1	0	0	1	1	0	2	1	0	0	1	0	0	0	2	0	0	0	0	0	0	0	0	1	1	0
disapproved	2	.1717	.1142	30.6	0	0	0	0	0	1	1	0	1	0	0	1	0	0	0	0	0	0	0	0	0	0	0	0	0
disapprovingly	3	.3851	.2497	34.0	0	1	1	0	1	0	0	0	0	0	0	1	0	0	0	0	0	0	0	0	1	1	0	0	0
disarmament	2	.0000	.0389	25.9	0	0	0	0	0	1	1	0	0	0	0	0	0	2	0	0	0	0	0	0	0	0	0	0	0
disarmed	2	.0000	.0389	25.9	0	0	0	0	0	1	1	0	0	0	0	0	0	2	0	0	0	0	0	0	0	0	0	0	0
disarming	2	.2407	.1138	30.6	0	0	1	0	1	0	0	0	0	0	0	1	0	0	0	0	0	0	0	0	0	1	0	0	0
disarray	4	.3104	.2995	34.8	0	0	0	0	2	1	1	0	1	0	0	0	0	0	0	0	0	0	0	0	0	0	1	2	0
disassembly	3	.0000	.0076	18.8	0	0	0	0	3	0	0	0	0	0	0	0	0	0	0	0	0	0	0	3	0	0	0	0	0
disaster	43	.6971	6.2025	47.9	4	1	9	8	4	9	4	4	14	2	0	1	0	2	0	3	0	0	0	0	3	5	3	10	0
disasters	8	.5898	.9949	40.0	0	0	0	4	3	1	0	0	2	1	0	1	0	1	0	0	0	0	0	0	1	0	2	0	0
disastrous	13	.7029	1.8717	42.7	0	0	3	2	3	3	1	1	2	0	0	1	0	3	0	1	0	0	0	0	1	2	1	2	0
disavowed	2	.0000	.0243	23.9	0	0	0	1	0	0	1	0	0	0	0	0	0	0	0	0	0	0	0	0	0	0	0	2	0

9R dioceses
9Q diodes
8B Diogenes
6R Diomeders
4A DIONISIO
XR Dior's
7P Dioscuri
7R dip-in-sugar
9H diphosphate
3P Diplocodus
9Q diplomas
9F Diplomatic
6A diplomatically
8D Diplomats
XH dipotassium
7R dippers
8Q Diptera
8B Dirck
8M direct-current
7Q direct-dialing
6J DIRECTIONS
7P directive
7P Directive
9R directorate
XR directories
4N directors'
6A direful
7D direst
9J dirge-like
8A dirigibles
7D dirk
6A Dirks
6R Dirksen's
9L dirndl
6A dirt-and-stick
7D dirt-smeared
4A dirt-stained
3N dirtied
5A dirty-colored
7R dirtying
4A diry
6G dis-cover
5R disabilities
9Q disability-insurance
9C disabuse
8F disaffection
8D disagreeably
9R disallegiance
8J disappearances
6R disappointingly
4A disappoints
9D disarm
8Q disarranged
7M disassembled
7M disassembling
8L disastrously
8F disavow
8F disband
7R disbanded

Word Type	F	D	U	SFI	3 Gr 3	4 Gr 4	5 Gr 5	6 Gr 6	7 Gr 7	8 Gr 8	9 Gr 9	X UnGr	A Read	B Eng & Gr	C Comp	D Lit	E Math	F Soc Stud	G Spell	H Sci	J Music	K Art	L Home Ec	M Shop	N Lib F	P Lib NF	Q Lib Ref	R Mag	S Rel
disbelief	10	.4661	1.0695	40.3	1	0	1	2	4	1	1	0	5	0	0	2	0	0	0	0	0	0	0	0	2	1	0	0	0
Disbeliever	3	.0000	.0322	25.1	0	0	0	0	3	0	0	0	0	0	0	3	0	0	0	0	0	0	0	0	0	0	0	0	0
disc	32	.4660	3.1361	45.0	2	0	5	3	9	4	7	2	0	0	0	0	7	1	0	3	0	0	0	5	0	0	3	13	0
discard	9	.2424	.4814	36.8	0	0	0	0	3	2	3	1	0	1	0	1	0	0	0	1	0	0	5	0	0	0	0	1	0
discarded	28	.7004	3.9936	46.0	3	5	2	7	4	1	4	2	4	1	1	1	0	0	0	6	1	3	1	0	2	4	3	1	0
discarding	2	.1812	.0838	29.2	0	0	0	0	1	1	0	0	0	0	0	0	0	0	0	0	0	0	1	0	0	0	0	1	0
discards	2	.1160	.0650	28.1	0	0	1	0	1	0	0	0	0	0	1	0	0	0	0	1	0	0	0	0	0	0	0	0	0
discern	9	.5063	.9783	39.9	0	0	0	1	3	3	2	0	2	1	1	3	0	1	0	0	0	0	0	0	1	0	0	0	0
discerned	3	.2260	.1580	32.0	0	0	0	0	2	0	1	0	0	0	0	2	0	0	0	0	0	0	0	0	0	0	1	0	0
discernible	2	.1814	.1187	30.7	0	0	0	1	0	0	1	0	1	0	0	0	0	0	0	0	0	0	0	0	0	0	0	1	0
discharge	20	.6636	2.6912	44.3	1	0	2	1	5	6	4	1	0	0	1	1	0	1	1	5	0	0	0	2	0	1	5	3	0
discharged	13	.5046	1.4244	41.5	0	0	0	3	4	3	3	0	3	4	0	2	0	0	0	3	0	0	0	0	1	0	0	0	0
discharges	9	.5098	.9802	39.9	0	0	0	1	3	3	1	1	1	0	1	1	0	0	0	4	0	0	0	0	0	0	1	1	0
discharging	4	.1577	.1755	32.4	0	1	0	0	1	2	0	0	1	0	0	0	0	0	0	0	0	0	0	2	0	0	1	0	0
disciple	5	.3592	.3897	35.9	0	1	2	0	1	0	1	0	0	2	0	0	0	0	0	0	0	0	0	0	0	1	2	0	0
disciples	8	.0742	.1795	32.5	5	0	0	0	2	1	0	0	0	0	1	0	0	2	0	0	0	0	0	0	1	1	0	0	3
Disciples	3	.2043	.1486	31.7	0	0	1	0	2	0	0	0	0	0	0	0	0	0	0	0	0	0	0	0	0	1	2	0	0
disciplinary	2	.0000	.0243	23.9	0	0	0	0	2	0	0	0	0	0	0	0	0	0	0	0	0	0	0	0	0	0	0	2	0
discipline	28	.7699	4.3319	46.4	0	2	3	0	6	9	4	4	2	1	1	4	0	6	0	0	1	0	1	0	1	2	6	3	0
disciplined	13	.6798	1.8009	42.6	1	0	2	0	6	1	2	1	1	0	0	3	0	0	1	2	0	0	0	0	1	2	1	2	0
disciplines	3	.3763	.2498	34.0	0	0	0	0	0	1	2	0	0	0	0	0	1	1	0	0	0	0	0	0	0	0	1	0	0
disclose	6	.3627	.5371	37.3	0	1	0	3	0	1	1	0	3	0	0	0	0	0	0	0	0	0	0	0	0	0	1	2	0
disclosed	8	.5124	.8864	39.5	0	0	0	1	0	4	2	1	2	0	1	1	0	2	0	0	0	0	0	0	0	0	1	1	0
discloses	2	.2417	.1091	30.4	0	1	0	0	0	0	1	0	0	0	0	0	0	0	0	0	1	0	0	0	0	0	1	0	0
disclosing	2	.1717	.1142	30.6	0	1	0	0	0	1	0	0	1	0	0	1	0	0	0	0	0	0	0	0	0	0	0	0	0
disclosure	2	.1523	.0721	28.6	0	0	0	0	1	0	1	0	0	0	1	0	0	0	0	0	0	0	0	0	0	0	0	1	0
discoloration	5	.0000	.0608	27.8	0	0	0	0	4	0	1	0	0	0	0	0	0	0	0	0	0	0	0	0	0	0	0	5	0
discolored	12	.2843	.7365	38.7	1	0	0	4	6	0	1	0	1	0	7	1	0	0	0	0	0	0	1	1	0	1	0	0	0
discomfort	11	.6257	1.4510	41.6	0	0	0	2	6	0	2	1	4	1	0	0	0	0	0	1	0	0	1	0	1	0	1	2	0
discomforts	2	.2160	.1362	31.3	0	0	0	1	0	0	0	1	1	0	0	0	0	0	0	1	0	0	0	0	0	0	0	0	0
disconnect	5	.1389	.1704	32.3	0	0	0	0	4	1	0	0	0	0	0	0	0	0	0	1	0	0	0	3	0	0	0	1	0
disconnected	7	.5512	.8308	39.2	0	0	0	0	3	2	2	0	2	0	0	1	0	0	1	2	0	0	0	0	0	0	0	1	0
disconsolate	3	.1060	.1461	31.6	0	2	0	0	1	0	0	0	2	0	1	0	0	0	0	0	0	0	0	0	0	0	0	0	0
discontent	13	.5558	1.5199	41.8	3	0	2	0	2	3	3	0	1	0	0	2	0	4	0	1	0	0	0	0	0	2	3	0	0
discontented	8	.4711	.8026	39.0	2	1	1	2	1	0	1	0	0	0	0	0	0	2	0	0	0	0	0	0	0	3	1	2	0
discord	5	.4312	.4495	36.5	1	0	1	1	0	0	2	0	0	0	0	0	0	0	0	0	1	0	0	1	0	0	1	2	0
discotheques	2	.0000	.0243	23.9	0	0	0	0	0	0	0	2	0	0	0	0	0	0	0	0	0	0	0	0	0	0	0	2	0
discount	20	.4591	1.9460	42.9	0	0	0	1	5	6	8	0	0	0	0	0	14	0	2	0	0	0	1	0	0	0	2	1	0
discounting	4	.4860	.4069	36.1	0	0	0	0	2	0	2	0	0	0	0	1	1	0	0	0	0	0	0	0	0	0	1	1	0
discounts	2	.0000	.0299	24.8	0	0	0	0	1	1	0	0	0	0	0	0	2	0	0	0	0	0	0	0	0	0	0	0	0
discourage	17	.6098	2.1434	43.3	2	2	1	4	4	2	2	0	1	2	1	0	0	5	0	0	0	0	0	0	0	5	2	1	0
discouraged	58	.7934	9.3777	49.7	4	9	12	5	17	7	3	1	25	4	0	3	1	9	0	2	0	0	0	1	3	6	1	3	0
discouragement	6	.4703	.6479	38.1	0	0	1	1	0	4	0	0	3	0	0	0	0	1	0	0	1	0	0	0	1	0	0	0	0
discourages	5	.4137	.4652	36.7	0	0	1	0	2	0	0	2	1	0	0	0	0	0	0	1	0	0	0	0	0	0	1	2	0
discouraging	7	.5204	.7519	38.8	0	0	2	1	3	1	0	0	0	1	1	0	0	1	0	0	2	0	0	0	1	1	0	0	0
discourse	3	.2196	.1554	31.9	0	0	0	1	0	0	2	0	0	0	0	2	0	0	0	0	0	0	0	0	1	0	0	0	0
discourses	3	.2175	.1545	31.9	0	0	0	0	1	0	2	0	0	0	0	2	0	0	0	0	0	0	0	0	0	0	0	1	0
discover	364	.8029	58.531	57.7	25	49	50	64	61	77	30	8	43	38	4	12	43	25	23	27	85	20	5	2	7	11	7	12	0
discovered	667	.9487	125.09	61.0	79	67	98	103	122	121	57	20	146	29	5	21	51	97	18	113	19	3	5	5	18	54	48	35	0
discoverer	8	.2284	.4794	36.8	2	2	0	1	2	0	1	0	2	0	0	0	0	0	0	0	0	0	0	0	0	0	5	1	0
Discoverer	2	.2427	.1159	30.6	0	0	1	0	1	0	0	0	0	0	0	0	1	0	0	0	0	0	0	0	0	0	0	1	0
discoverers	3	.3380	.2498	34.0	0	0	0	2	1	0	0	0	1	1	0	0	0	0	0	1	0	0	0	0	0	0	0	0	0
discoveries	119	.7112	17.254	52.4	12	14	16	20	19	18	8	12	7	3	0	0	4	15	1	53	3	0	4	0	0	13	12	4	0
discovering	39	.7708	6.0671	47.8	5	4	5	7	6	9	2	1	6	1	3	2	4	8	0	1	2	0	2	0	3	3	1	3	0
discovers	13	.6152	1.6681	42.2	1	1	1	0	3	6	1	0	3	2	0	1	0	0	1	1	3	0	0	0	0	2	0	0	0
discovery	211	.8662	36.499	55.6	19	17	30	33	49	36	16	11	35	5	1	6	9	31	4	60	4	1	1	1	2	17	27	7	0
Discovery	13	.5299	1.4456	41.6	2	1	1	5	1	1	2	0	0	1	0	1	0	6	0	0	0	0	0	0	0	0	2	3	0
discredited	3	.3762	.2496	34.0	0	0	1	0	1	1	0	0	0	0	0	0	0	0	0	1	0	0	0	0	0	1	1	0	0
discreet	6	.3621	.5367	37.3	0	0	1	0	2	2	0	1	3	0	0	1	0	0	0	0	0	0	0	0	0	0	0	2	0
discreetly	2	.2375	.1088	30.4	0	0	0	0	0	1	1	0	0	0	0	0	0	0	0	0	1	0	0	0	0	0	0	1	0
discrepancies	2	.2278	.1128	30.5	0	0	0	0	0	1	0	1	0	0	0	0	0	0	0	1	0	0	0	0	0	0	1	0	0
discrete	2	.0000	.0209	23.2	0	0	0	0	0	2	0	0	0	0	0	0	0	0	0	0	0	0	0	0	0	0	2	0	0
discretion	7	.5721	.8416	39.3	0	0	0	0	1	3	3	0	1	0	0	0	0	1	0	1	1	0	0	0	0	0	1	2	0
discriminate	3	.2222	.1558	31.9	0	0	1	0	0	0	2	0	0	1	0	0	0	0	0	0	0	0	0	0	0	0	2	0	0
discrimination	16	.5186	1.7473	42.4	1	0	4	1	0	1	7	2	0	1	0	0	0	7	0	0	0	0	0	0	0	2	4	2	0
discs	14	.5413	1.5695	42.0	1	0	1	1	8	0	1	2	0	0	0	0	1	0	0	3	0	1	1	0	0	0	1	7	0
discus	4	.4450	.3915	35.9	0	1	0	1	0	1	0	1	1	1	0	0	0	0	1	0	0	0	0	0	0	0	1	0	0
discuss	286	.7820	44.757	56.5	13	69	28	51	39	33	50	3	19	84	9	10	11	18	42	14	35	2	17	0	1	7	6	11	0
discussant	2	.0000	.0389	25.9	0	0	0	0	0	0	2	0	0	0	0	0	0	2	0	0	0	0	0	0	0	0	0	0	0
discussed	109	.8903	19.283	52.9	5	9	10	6	29	24	21	5	18	12	1	3	14	9	0	10	6	3	7	2	4	6	5	9	0
discusses	12	.5678	1.4089	41.5	1	0	1	0	3	3	3	1	1	1	2	0	0	1	1	1	1	0	0	0	0	0	2	2	0
discussing	20	.7483	3.0289	44.8	0	1	4	4	3	1	6	1	3	4	0	1	1	2	0	0	1	0	1	0	0	4	1	2	0
discussion	149	.8112	24.189	53.8	4	10	21	11	38	17	48	0	13	41	5	4	10	24	3	8	8	1	7	0	0	13	2	10	0
discussions	33	.7457	4.9747	47.0	2	2	2	1	4	5	17	0	4	4	0	1	0	5	1	0	2	0	1	0	0	3	3	9	0
disdain	5	.4122	.4599	36.6	1	1	1	0	1	0	1	0	1	0	0	2	0	0	0	0	0	0	0	0	1	1	0	0	0
disdained	4	.2843	.2875	34.6	0	0	0	1	1	2	0	0	1	0	0	0	0	1	0	0	0	0	0	0	0	0	0	2	0
disdainful	2	.2407	.1138	30.6	0	0	0	1	1	0	0	0	0	0	0	1	0	0	0	0	0	0	0	0	0	1	0	0	0
disdainfully	2	.0000	.0914	29.6	1	0	0	1	0	0	0	0	2	0	0	0	0	0	0	0	0	0	0	0	0	0	0	0	0
disease	250	.6693	34.542	55.4	9	22	45	30	43	57	27	17	32	3	0	3	0	23	5	112	0	0	4	0	2	11	40	15	0
disease-causing	2	.0000	.0394	26.0	0	0	2	0	0	0	0	0	0	0	0	0	0	0	0	2	0	0	0	0	0	0	0	0	0
disease-producing	2	.1432	.0759	28.8	0	0	0	0	0	0	1	1	0	0	0	0	0	0	0	1	0	0	1	0	0	0	0	0	0
diseased	12	.5447	1.3973	41.5	0	2	2	1	1	4	1	1	2	0	0	0	0	1	0	4	0	0	0	0	0	1	3	1	0
diseases	161	.6022	20.318	53.1	19	21	19	28	17	23	19	15	14	2	0	2	2	20	3	86	0	0	1	0	0	7	22	2	0
Diseases	2	.2405	.1205	30.8	0	0	0	1	0	0	0	1	0	0	0	0	0	0	0	1	0	0	0	0	0	1	0	0	0
disembarked	3	.2181	.1541	31.9	0	0	0	0	2	1	0	0	0	0	0	0	0	0	0	0	0	0	0	0	1	0	2	0	0
disenchanted	2	.2337	.1157	30.6	0	0	1	0	0	1	0	0	0	0	0	0	0	1	0	0	0	0	0	0	1	0	0	0	0
disfigured	2	.2446	.1142	30.6	0	0	1	0	1	0	0	0	0	0	0	0	0	0	0	0	0	0	0	0	1	0	0	1	0
disfranchised	2	.2351	.1166	30.7	0	0	0	0	1	1	0	0	0	0	0	0	0	1	0	0	0	0	0	0	0	0	0	1	0
disgrace	27	.6264	3.5644	45.5	4	3	2	7	5	3	3	0	10	1	0	7	0	1	3	0	1	0	0	0	3	1	0	0	0
disgraced	3	.3370	.2430	33.9	0	1	1	0	0	0	1	0	1	0	0	1	0	0	0	0	0	0	0	0	0	0	1	0	0
disgraceful	5	.4586	.5209	37.2	0	0	1	2	1	0	1	0	2	0	0	1	0	0	0	1	1	0	0	0	0	0	0	0	0
disgruntled	3	.3781	.2493	34.0	0	0	0	0	0	2	0	1	0	1	0	0	0	1	0	0	0	0	0	0	0	0	0	1	0
disguise	25	.6785	3.4776	45.4	2	1	4	5	3	4	1	5	4	3	0	4	0	1	1	0	0	0	0	0	2	8	1	1	0
disguised	14	.6199	1.8007	42.6	0	3	2	2	2	1	2	2	2	1	0	0	0	2	0	0	0	0	1	0	1	4	0	3	0
disguises	5	.4770	.5360	37.3	0	1	1	0	1	1	1	0	2	0	0	1	0	0	0	0	0	0	0	0	0	1	0	1	0
disgust	20	.6806	2.8411	44.5	0	4	2	4	6	2	1	1	8	1	1	1	0	3	0	0	1	0	0	0	3	2	0	0	0
disgusted	22	.6018	2.8218	44.5	4	4	1	3	3	5	2	0	8	0	0	2	0	3	0	0	0	0	0	0	6	1	1	1	0

5A disbelieved
9L discerning
5P discerns
7R discolorations
7N discoloured
8A discombobulate
6N discomposed
6A disconcerted
7D disconcerting
9Q disconcertingly
5Q disconnects
6B discontinue
9D discontinued
XR discontinuity
7Q Discontinuity
6P Discord
9M discordant
9D discords
5R discos
4R discotheque
9Q discounted
8F discouragements
7F discouragingly
8Q Discourse
7A discoursing
9B discourteous
7Q discrepancy
7Q discriminating
9Q discriminatory
7P disdainfulness
7P disembowel
7N disencumbered
5P disenfranchised
7P disengag(ed)
9D disengage
5A disengaged
7A disfavor
7N disfigure
8F disfranchising
9D disgorged
5Q disguising

Word Type	F	D	U	SFI	3 Gr 3	4 Gr 4	5 Gr 5	6 Gr 6	7 Gr 7	8 Gr 8	9 Gr 9	X UnGr	A Read	B Eng & Gr	C Comp	D Lit	E Math	F Soc Stud	G Spell	H Sci	J Music	K Art	L Home Ec	M Shop	N Lib F	P Lib NF	Q Lib Ref	R Mag	S Rel
disgustedly	3	.0000	.1370	31.4	2	0	0	1	0	0	0	0	3	0	0	0	0	0	0	0	0	0	0	0	0	0	0	0	0
disgusting	2	.1787	.1174	30.7	0	1	1	0	0	0	0	0	1	0	0	0	0	0	0	0	0	0	0	0	1	0	0	0	0
dish	195	.6718	26.927	54.3	51	34	15	15	33	15	23	9	38	12	0	11	0	6	11	40	1	1	34	1	11	14	3	12	0
dish-shaped	3	.3772	.2503	34.0	1	0	0	0	1	1	0	0	0	0	0	1	0	0	0	1	0	0	0	0	0	1	0	0	0
disharmonious	2	.1493	.0692	28.4	0	0	0	0	1	1	0	0	0	0	0	0	0	0	0	0	0	1	0	0	0	0	1	0	0
disheartened	4	.2445	.3067	34.9	1	0	1	1	1	0	0	0	3	0	0	0	0	0	0	0	0	0	0	0	0	1	0	0	0
dishes	266	.8362	44.761	56.5	85	55	16	25	37	18	25	5	101	16	6	16	3	13	8	14	3	2	27	2	23	17	2	12	1
disheveled	5	.2643	.3702	35.7	0	0	1	2	0	0	2	0	3	1	1	0	0	0	0	0	0	0	0	0	0	0	0	0	0
dishonest	7	.4529	.7106	38.5	0	2	0	2	0	1	1	1	2	2	0	0	0	2	1	0	0	0	0	0	0	0	0	0	0
dishonesty	2	.2285	.1129	30.5	0	0	0	0	0	1	1	0	0	0	0	0	0	1	0	0	0	0	0	0	0	0	1	0	0
dishonor	2	.0000	.0914	29.6	0	0	2	0	0	0	0	0	2	0	0	0	0	0	0	0	0	0	0	0	0	0	0	0	0
dishonored	3	.3776	.2504	34.0	1	0	1	0	0	1	0	0	0	0	0	1	0	1	0	0	0	0	0	0	0	1	0	0	0
dishpan	5	.2474	.3588	35.5	4	0	0	0	0	1	0	0	3	0	1	0	0	0	0	0	0	0	0	0	0	1	0	0	0
dishtowel	2	.2446	.1125	30.5	0	0	0	0	0	1	1	0	0	1	0	1	0	0	0	0	0	0	0	0	0	0	0	0	0
dishwasher	6	.2411	.4668	36.7	5	1	0	0	0	0	0	0	5	0	0	0	0	0	0	0	0	0	0	0	0	0	0	1	0
dishwashers	3	.1856	.1648	32.2	0	0	1	0	0	2	0	0	1	0	0	0	0	0	0	1	0	0	0	1	0	0	0	0	0
dishwashing	5	.3841	.4756	36.8	3	1	0	0	0	0	1	0	3	0	0	1	0	0	0	0	0	0	0	0	1	0	0	0	0
dishwater	3	.0000	.1370	31.4	1	1	1	0	0	0	0	0	3	0	0	0	0	0	0	0	0	0	0	0	0	0	0	0	0
disillusioned	3	.2143	.1568	32.0	0	0	0	2	1	0	0	0	0	0	0	0	0	0	0	0	0	0	0	0	0	1	0	2	0
disinclination	2	.0000	.0209	23.2	0	0	2	0	0	0	0	0	0	0	0	0	0	0	0	0	0	0	0	0	0	0	2	0	0
disinfectant	2	.0000	.0290	24.6	0	0	0	1	0	0	1	0	0	0	0	0	0	0	0	0	0	0	0	0	0	2	0	0	0
disintegrate	6	.4454	.5733	37.6	0	0	1	0	2	3	0	0	0	0	0	0	3	0	0	1	0	0	0	0	1	0	1	0	0
disintegrated	3	.2197	.2090	33.2	0	0	0	0	3	0	0	0	2	0	0	0	0	0	0	0	0	0	0	0	0	0	1	0	0
disintegrates	4	.4820	.4132	36.2	0	0	0	0	1	2	1	0	0	0	0	0	1	1	0	1	0	0	0	0	0	0	0	1	0
disintegrating	2	.2278	.1128	30.5	0	0	0	0	2	0	0	0	0	0	0	0	0	0	0	1	0	0	0	0	0	0	1	0	0
disintegration	5	.3816	.4230	36.3	0	0	0	0	1	1	3	0	0	0	0	0	0	0	0	3	1	0	0	0	0	0	1	0	0
disintegrations	2	.2413	.1212	30.8	0	0	0	0	0	1	1	0	0	0	0	0	1	0	0	1	0	0	0	0	0	0	0	0	0
disjoint	4	.0000	.0599	27.8	0	0	1	3	0	0	0	0	0	0	0	0	4	0	0	0	0	0	0	0	0	0	0	0	0
disjointed	2	.1551	.0728	28.6	0	0	0	0	1	0	1	0	0	0	1	0	0	0	0	0	0	0	0	0	1	0	0	0	0
disk	53	.5556	6.2090	47.9	1	0	2	5	18	5	12	10	5	0	2	0	0	2	0	26	13	0	0	0	1	1	1	2	0
disk-shaped	5	.4715	.5340	37.3	0	0	2	0	3	0	0	0	2	0	0	0	0	0	0	1	0	0	0	0	0	0	1	1	0
disks	22	.6161	2.7973	44.5	8	0	2	4	5	2	0	1	1	0	0	0	7	1	0	6	1	0	0	2	1	1	2	0	0
dislike	38	.6456	5.0468	47.0	3	4	4	7	7	4	9	0	8	4	2	4	0	2	2	0	0	0	7	0	5	0	2	2	0
disliked	20	.6950	2.8539	44.6	4	4	4	1	4	1	2	0	4	1	0	2	0	4	0	0	0	0	1	0	3	4	0	1	0
dislikes	9	.4368	.8445	39.3	2	0	0	0	4	1	1	1	1	0	0	0	0	0	0	0	1	0	2	0	0	3	0	2	0
dislodge	2	.2433	.1158	30.6	0	0	0	1	1	0	0	0	0	0	0	0	0	0	0	0	0	0	0	0	0	1	0	1	0
dislodged	7	.4685	.7016	38.5	0	0	0	0	4	1	1	1	0	0	0	0	0	0	0	3	0	0	0	0	2	1	1	0	0
disloyalty	2	.2351	.1166	30.7	0	0	0	0	1	1	0	0	0	0	0	0	0	1	0	0	0	0	0	0	0	0	0	1	0
Dismael	2	.0000	.0914	29.6	0	0	0	2	0	0	0	0	2	0	0	0	0	0	0	0	0	0	0	0	0	0	0	0	0
dismal	22	.6727	3.0994	44.9	0	2	3	2	9	5	1	0	10	1	1	3	0	0	0	0	0	0	0	0	2	1	3	1	0
Dismal	4	.2445	.3067	34.9	0	0	3	0	1	0	0	0	3	0	0	0	0	0	0	0	0	0	0	0	0	1	0	0	0
dismantle	2	.0000	.0219	23.4	0	0	0	0	0	2	0	0	0	2	0	0	0	0	0	0	0	0	0	0	0	0	0	0	0
dismantling	2	.2433	.1158	30.6	0	0	1	0	0	0	1	0	0	0	0	0	0	0	0	0	0	0	0	0	0	1	0	1	0
dismay	32	.6072	4.1822	46.2	2	5	6	5	5	6	3	0	16	2	0	4	0	1	0	0	0	0	0	0	6	2	0	1	0
dismayed	12	.4354	1.1438	40.6	1	0	0	0	4	4	3	0	2	0	0	3	0	0	0	0	0	0	0	0	3	0	0	4	0
dismembered	3	.3870	.2486	34.0	0	0	0	1	1	0	1	0	0	0	0	1	0	0	0	0	0	0	0	0	0	0	1	1	0
dismiss	9	.5993	1.1345	40.5	0	0	0	2	5	1	1	0	2	1	0	0	0	2	0	0	0	0	0	0	1	0	2	1	0
dismissal	4	.3683	.3188	35.0	1	0	1	1	1	0	0	0	0	0	0	1	0	0	0	0	0	0	0	0	2	0	0	1	0
dismissed	21	.6222	2.7435	44.4	0	2	6	2	5	2	4	0	6	0	0	2	0	0	0	1	0	0	0	0	1	5	4	2	0
dismount	5	.2984	.3417	35.3	0	1	0	1	2	1	0	0	0	0	0	0	0	1	0	0	0	0	0	0	3	1	0	0	0
dismounted	16	.5808	2.0035	43.0	0	4	1	3	6	1	0	1	7	0	0	2	0	0	0	0	1	0	0	0	4	1	0	1	0
dismounting	3	.3399	.2456	33.9	0	1	0	0	2	0	0	0	1	0	0	1	0	0	0	0	0	0	0	0	0	0	0	1	0
Disney	21	.3057	1.5256	41.8	0	18	0	0	1	0	1	1	0	0	0	1	0	17	0	0	0	0	0	0	0	1	0	2	0
disobedience	4	.2420	.3089	34.9	0	0	1	1	0	1	1	0	3	0	0	0	0	1	0	0	0	0	0	0	0	0	0	0	0
disobedient	2	.2337	.1157	30.6	0	1	0	1	0	0	0	0	0	0	0	0	0	1	0	0	0	0	0	0	1	0	0	0	0
disobey	11	.4866	1.2118	40.8	0	0	4	0	1	3	3	0	5	0	0	3	0	1	0	1	0	0	0	0	1	0	0	0	0
disobeying	3	.3759	.2471	33.9	0	0	1	0	1	0	1	0	0	1	0	0	0	1	0	0	0	0	0	0	0	0	1	0	0
disobeys	3	.0000	.0097	19.8	0	0	0	0	0	1	2	0	0	0	0	0	0	0	0	0	0	0	3	0	0	0	0	0	0
disorder	15	.5537	1.7709	42.5	1	4	0	5	2	1	1	1	3	0	0	0	0	4	0	2	0	0	0	1	0	0	4	1	0
disordered	5	.3747	.4028	36.1	0	1	0	0	2	1	1	0	0	0	0	2	0	0	0	0	0	0	0	0	2	0	1	0	0
disorderly	5	.4143	.4656	36.7	0	1	0	0	2	0	2	0	1	0	0	0	0	1	0	0	0	0	0	0	0	0	1	2	0
disorders	7	.3001	.4730	36.7	0	0	1	0	0	2	4	0	0	0	0	0	0	0	0	1	0	0	0	0	0	0	4	2	0
disorganized	3	.3766	.2480	33.9	0	0	0	0	0	2	1	0	0	0	0	0	0	1	0	0	0	0	0	0	1	0	1	0	0
disown	2	.1814	.1187	30.7	0	1	0	0	0	0	1	0	1	0	0	0	0	0	0	0	0	0	0	0	0	0	0	1	0
disparagement	2	.2440	.1132	30.5	0	0	0	0	1	0	0	1	0	0	0	1	0	0	0	0	0	0	0	0	0	0	0	1	0
disparate	2	.2446	.1142	30.6	0	0	0	0	1	1	0	0	0	0	0	0	0	0	0	0	0	0	0	0	1	0	0	1	0
disparity	2	.2437	.1129	30.5	0	0	0	0	0	0	2	0	0	0	0	0	0	0	0	0	0	0	0	0	0	0	1	1	0
dispassionate	4	.2988	.2894	34.6	0	0	0	0	1	2	1	0	1	0	1	0	0	1	0	0	0	0	0	0	0	0	1	0	0
dispatch	12	.6481	1.5764	42.0	1	0	1	2	3	2	2	1	0	1	0	1	0	0	1	0	0	0	0	0	3	1	2	3	0
dispatched	7	.3716	.5731	37.6	0	0	0	1	0	3	2	1	0	0	0	1	0	1	0	1	0	0	0	0	0	0	0	4	0
dispatcher	2	.0000	.0389	25.9	0	2	0	0	0	0	0	0	0	0	0	0	0	2	0	0	0	0	0	0	0	0	0	0	0
dispatches	3	.3465	.2515	34.0	0	0	1	0	1	1	0	0	1	0	0	0	0	0	0	0	0	0	0	0	0	1	0	1	0
dispatching	2	.0000	.0209	23.2	0	0	0	0	0	0	2	0	0	0	0	0	0	0	0	0	0	0	0	0	0	0	2	0	0
dispel	3	.1927	.1491	31.7	0	0	0	0	0	1	2	0	0	0	0	0	0	0	0	1	0	0	0	0	0	0	0	2	0
dispelled	4	.4788	.4052	36.1	0	0	1	0	3	0	0	0	0	0	0	1	0	0	0	1	0	0	0	0	0	1	1	0	0
dispensed	5	.4763	.5353	37.3	0	1	0	0	2	1	1	0	2	0	0	0	0	0	0	0	0	0	0	0	0	1	1	1	0
dispersal	5	.3569	.4079	36.1	0	0	0	0	1	1	3	0	0	0	0	0	0	1	0	3	0	0	0	0	0	0	1	0	0
disperse	6	.4857	.6603	38.2	0	0	3	0	0	0	2	1	3	0	0	1	0	0	0	0	0	0	0	0	0	0	1	1	0
dispersed	5	.4385	.4861	36.9	0	0	2	0	1	0	1	1	1	0	0	0	0	0	0	0	0	0	0	0	1	2	0	1	0
disperses	2	.2346	.1166	30.7	0	0	0	0	0	0	1	1	0	0	0	0	0	0	0	1	0	0	0	0	0	0	0	1	0
displaced	12	.6935	1.6929	42.3	0	0	1	1	4	0	6	0	1	1	0	2	0	0	0	2	1	0	0	0	0	2	2	1	0
displacement	12	.5127	1.3058	41.2	0	0	0	0	3	0	5	4	0	0	0	1	3	0	0	6	0	0	0	0	0	1	1	0	0
displacements	3	.0000	.0449	26.5	0	0	0	0	2	1	0	0	0	0	0	0	3	0	0	0	0	0	0	0	0	0	0	0	0
displaces	2	.2433	.1158	30.6	1	0	0	0	1	0	0	0	0	0	0	0	0	0	0	0	0	0	0	0	0	1	0	1	0
display	76	.8795	13.297	51.2	10	5	15	8	14	12	9	3	10	4	1	3	2	9	3	14	4	1	3	0	0	2	8	12	0
displayed	46	.7687	7.1994	48.6	0	17	2	5	6	8	6	2	16	3	3	2	4	7	0	0	1	1	2	0	0	0	3	4	0
displaying	6	.5370	.6882	38.4	0	2	0	0	1	2	1	0	1	0	0	0	0	2	0	0	0	0	0	0	1	0	1	1	0
displays	22	.5699	2.6296	44.2	2	3	4	3	2	6	2	0	4	1	0	0	0	3	0	0	1	3	1	0	0	4	1	4	0
displeased	10	.3079	.7422	38.7	0	1	2	4	1	1	0	1	3	1	3	0	0	1	0	0	0	0	0	0	1	0	0	1	0
displeasure	3	.2197	.2090	33.2	1	1	0	0	0	1	0	0	2	0	0	0	0	0	0	0	0	0	0	0	0	0	1	0	0
disposal	24	.7445	3.6122	45.6	3	0	0	6	4	7	3	1	1	1	0	0	0	4	0	8	0	0	1	1	1	2	2	3	0
dispose	8	.5300	.9222	39.6	1	0	2	2	0	1	2	0	2	0	0	0	0	3	1	1	0	0	0	0	1	0	0	0	0
disposed	17	.5805	2.0656	43.2	0	1	0	1	4	7	4	0	2	3	0	3	0	5	0	0	0	0	0	0	3	0	0	1	0
disposes	2	.1787	.1174	30.7	0	0	0	0	1	1	0	0	1	0	0	0	0	0	0	0	0	0	0	0	1	0	0	0	0
disposition	20	.5064	2.1431	43.3	2	3	2	1	6	3	2	1	4	1	3	1	0	0	0	0	0	0	4	0	0	3	4	0	0
dispositions	2	.0000	.0243	23.9	0	1	0	0	1	0	0	0	0	0	0	0	0	0	0	0	0	0	0	0	0	0	0	2	0

7B dishcloth
8F disheartening
4P dished
7P dishfuls
4G dishonestly
9R disillusionment
7A disillusionments
XR disinclined
6Q disinfectants
8A disinfecting
7P disinterest
5Q disinterested
9D disinterestedly
XR disinterring
9G disirregardless
5P disjunctive
6B Disjunctive
9Q dislocated
8A dislocating
8Q dislodges
6A Dismael-bek
6A Dismael's
7A dismally
8B dismantled
7R dismaying
5A dismays
9Q dismember
7P dismisses
4P dismissing
4F Disneyland
8Q Disobedience
5P disoriented
7D disowned
8R disparages
8R disparaging
7Q disparagingly
7Q dispassionately
9D Dispatch
4J dispels
9R dispensation
7P dispense
7A dispirited
8F displacing
3P displease
9L displeasing
9L disposable
XH disposing
8F dispossessed

Word Type	F	D	U	SFI	3 Gr 3	4 Gr 4	5 Gr 5	6 Gr 6	7 Gr 7	8 Gr 8	9 Gr 9	X UnGr	A Read	B Eng & Gr	C Comp	D Lit	E Math	F Soc Stud	G Spell	H Sci	J Music	K Art	L Home Ec	M Shop	N Lib F	P Lib NF	Q Lib Ref	R Mag	S Rel
disprove	8	.6093	1.0264	40.1	0	0	1	3	1	2	1	0	2	0	0	1	2	0	0	1	0	0	0	0	1	0	0	1	0
disproved	2	.0000	.0389	25.9	0	0	1	0	0	1	0	0	0	0	0	0	0	2	0	0	0	0	0	0	0	0	0	0	0
disputation	2	.2446	.1123	30.5	0	0	0	0	0	1	0	1	0	1	0	0	0	0	0	0	0	0	0	0	0	0	1	0	0
dispute	33	.6417	4.3670	46.4	0	2	2	4	4	10	9	2	4	2	0	4	0	7	0	0	0	0	0	0	2	1	3	10	0
disputed	12	.5320	1.3433	41.3	1	0	2	1	4	1	1	2	0	0	0	0	0	4	0	2	0	0	0	0	0	2	3	1	0
disputes	35	.3724	2.9566	44.7	0	0	7	3	7	6	12	0	3	0	0	0	0	17	0	0	0	0	0	0	0	0	12	3	0
disputing	2	.1717	.1142	30.6	0	0	0	0	0	2	0	0	1	0	0	1	0	0	0	0	0	0	0	0	0	0	0	0	0
disqualified	2	.2351	.1166	30.7	0	0	0	0	1	0	1	0	0	0	0	0	0	1	0	0	0	0	0	0	0	0	0	1	0
disquieting	2	.1170	.0651	28.1	0	0	0	0	1	1	0	0	0	0	1	0	0	1	0	0	0	0	0	0	0	0	0	0	0
Disraeli	2	.0000	.0914	29.6	0	0	0	0	0	2	0	0	2	0	0	0	0	0	0	0	0	0	0	0	0	0	0	0	0
disregard	8	.3548	.6586	38.2	0	0	1	2	0	2	2	1	2	1	2	0	0	1	0	1	0	0	0	0	0	0	1	0	0
disregarded	6	.4232	.5340	37.3	0	0	0	1	3	0	2	0	0	0	0	0	1	0	1	0	0	0	0	1	3	0	0	0	0
disregarding	9	.6018	1.1483	40.6	0	0	0	4	3	1	1	0	3	1	0	2	1	0	0	0	0	0	0	0	0	1	0	1	0
disregards	2	.2413	.1212	30.8	0	0	0	0	0	1	0	1	0	0	0	0	1	0	0	1	0	0	0	0	0	0	0	0	0
disrepair	2	.2285	.1129	30.5	0	0	0	0	1	0	1	0	0	0	0	0	0	1	0	0	0	0	0	0	0	0	1	0	0
disrespect	5	.3833	.4767	36.8	0	0	0	1	4	0	0	0	3	0	0	1	0	0	0	0	0	0	0	0	0	1	0	0	0
disrespectful	2	.1717	.1142	30.6	0	0	0	1	1	0	0	0	1	0	0	1	0	0	0	0	0	0	0	0	0	0	0	0	0
disrupt	3	.2239	.1775	32.5	0	0	0	0	2	0	1	0	0	0	0	0	0	2	0	1	0	0	0	0	0	0	0	0	0
disrupted	5	.4599	.4875	36.9	1	0	0	0	2	2	0	0	0	0	0	0	0	1	0	0	0	0	0	0	1	0	1	2	0
disruption	3	.2425	.1816	32.6	0	0	0	0	1	1	1	0	0	0	0	0	0	2	0	0	0	0	0	0	0	0	0	1	0
disruptions	2	.2437	.1129	30.5	0	0	0	0	1	0	1	0	0	0	0	0	0	0	0	0	0	0	0	0	0	0	1	1	0
dissatisfaction	8	.4859	.8195	39.1	1	0	0	2	0	4	1	0	0	0	1	0	0	3	0	0	0	0	0	0	0	1	2	1	0
dissatisfied	18	.6873	2.5287	44.0	1	0	3	1	6	6	0	1	2	0	0	0	0	5	1	0	1	0	0	0	3	1	2	3	0
dissect	4	.3270	.3198	35.0	0	0	0	1	2	0	1	0	1	0	0	0	0	0	0	2	1	0	0	0	0	0	0	0	0
dissected	5	.2424	.2988	34.8	0	0	0	0	2	1	0	2	0	0	0	0	0	0	0	3	0	0	0	0	0	0	2	0	0
dissection	3	.3781	.2548	34.1	0	0	0	0	1	1	1	0	0	0	0	0	0	1	0	1	0	0	0	0	0	0	0	1	0
dissections	2	.2278	.1128	30.5	0	0	0	0	0	1	1	0	0	0	0	0	0	0	0	1	0	0	0	0	0	0	1	0	0
Dissectograph	2	.0000	.0394	26.0	0	0	0	0	2	0	0	0	0	0	0	0	0	0	0	2	0	0	0	0	0	0	0	0	0
dissension	5	.2857	.3274	35.2	0	0	2	0	2	1	0	0	0	0	0	0	0	1	0	0	0	0	0	0	0	1	3	0	0
dissent	5	.1848	.2301	33.6	0	0	0	0	0	2	3	0	0	1	0	0	0	0	0	0	0	0	0	0	0	0	0	4	0
dissenters	3	.3769	.2484	34.0	0	0	0	0	0	3	0	0	0	0	0	0	0	1	0	0	0	0	0	0	0	0	1	1	0
dissident	2	.2437	.1129	30.5	0	0	0	0	0	1	1	0	0	0	0	0	0	0	0	0	0	0	0	0	0	0	1	1	0
dissidents	2	.2351	.1166	30.7	0	0	0	0	1	0	1	0	0	0	0	0	0	1	0	0	0	0	0	0	0	0	0	1	0
dissimilar	11	.6415	1.4403	41.6	0	0	0	0	6	4	1	0	1	2	0	1	0	1	2	0	0	0	0	1	0	0	2	1	0
dissimulation	2	.0000	.0215	23.3	0	0	0	0	0	1	1	0	0	0	0	2	0	0	0	0	0	0	0	0	0	0	0	0	0
dissipate	2	.2346	.1166	30.7	0	0	0	0	1	0	1	0	0	0	0	0	0	0	0	1	0	0	0	0	0	0	0	1	0
dissipated	2	.0000	.0234	23.7	0	0	0	0	0	2	0	0	0	0	0	0	0	0	0	0	0	0	0	0	2	0	0	0	0
dissociated	2	.2446	.1257	31.0	0	0	0	0	1	1	0	0	0	0	0	0	0	1	0	1	0	0	0	0	0	0	0	0	0
dissolution	3	.1169	.1277	31.1	0	0	0	0	1	1	1	0	1	0	0	0	0	0	0	0	0	0	0	0	0	0	2	0	0
dissolve	69	.6315	9.0172	49.6	13	8	11	8	11	7	10	1	3	2	0	4	0	4	0	42	0	0	3	1	0	2	7	1	0
DISSOLVE	5	.0000	.0537	27.3	0	0	0	0	5	0	0	0	0	0	0	5	0	0	0	0	0	0	0	0	0	0	0	0	0
dissolved	85	.5255	9.5039	49.8	8	9	19	4	19	13	9	4	2	0	0	0	0	2	0	62	0	0	4	1	1	2	7	4	0
dissolves	33	.5709	3.9758	46.0	8	7	6	1	3	2	5	1	3	0	0	1	0	0	0	19	0	0	1	0	0	3	3	3	0
dissolving	6	.4639	.6013	37.8	1	0	0	1	1	2	1	0	0	0	0	0	0	1	0	3	0	0	0	0	0	0	1	1	0
dissonance	2	.0000	.0162	22.1	0	0	1	0	0	0	1	0	0	0	0	0	0	0	0	0	2	0	0	0	0	0	0	0	0
dissonances	3	.2088	.1442	31.6	0	0	0	1	0	1	1	0	0	0	0	0	0	0	0	0	2	0	0	0	0	0	1	0	0
dissonant	9	.2292	.4567	36.6	0	0	0	0	1	6	2	0	0	0	0	0	0	0	0	0	8	1	0	0	0	0	0	0	0
distance	983	.8816	172.60	62.4	66	188	143	157	152	131	124	22	157	8	4	46	247	96	10	188	18	10	8	24	43	49	38	37	0
Distance	2	.1814	.1187	30.7	0	0	0	0	0	1	0	1	1	0	0	0	0	0	0	0	0	0	0	0	0	0	0	1	0
distances	173	.7889	27.505	54.4	18	32	28	25	37	16	17	0	16	2	0	2	12	36	1	56	3	1	0	7	4	9	16	8	0
distant	182	.8847	32.061	55.1	7	24	16	33	61	23	10	8	40	8	6	16	0	17	4	21	6	3	0	1	12	10	22	16	0
Distant	2	.0000	.0914	29.6	0	0	0	2	0	0	0	0	2	0	0	0	0	0	0	0	0	0	0	0	0	0	0	0	0
distantly	2	.0000	.0215	23.3	0	0	0	0	1	1	0	0	0	0	0	2	0	0	0	0	0	0	0	0	0	0	0	0	0
distaste	2	.1787	.1174	30.7	0	0	0	0	2	0	0	0	1	0	0	0	0	0	0	0	0	0	0	0	1	0	0	0	0
distasteful	4	.2386	.2998	34.8	0	2	0	1	1	0	0	0	3	0	0	0	0	0	0	0	0	0	0	0	0	0	1	0	0
distill	3	.2443	.1820	32.6	0	0	1	0	0	0	2	0	0	0	0	1	0	0	0	2	0	0	0	0	0	0	0	0	0
distillate	2	.0000	.0394	26.0	0	0	0	2	0	0	0	0	0	0	0	0	0	0	0	2	0	0	0	0	0	0	0	0	0
distillation	10	.1626	.4769	36.8	0	1	1	2	2	2	2	0	0	0	0	0	0	0	0	9	0	0	0	0	0	0	1	0	0
distilled	13	.4604	1.3047	41.2	0	0	3	2	0	3	5	0	1	0	0	0	1	0	0	7	1	0	0	0	0	0	3	0	0
distilleries	2	.2285	.1129	30.5	1	0	0	0	1	0	0	0	0	0	0	0	0	1	0	0	0	0	0	0	0	0	1	0	0
distilling	3	.0000	.0314	25.0	0	0	1	2	0	0	0	0	0	0	0	0	0	0	0	0	0	0	0	0	0	0	3	0	0
distinct	62	.8924	10.971	50.4	2	2	10	9	21	5	11	2	4	2	0	4	3	3	2	9	4	1	1	1	3	9	12	4	0
distinction	41	.7014	5.8561	47.7	2	0	6	4	10	9	8	2	5	5	0	0	3	6	0	1	2	0	1	0	1	3	13	1	0
distinctions	6	.4083	.5393	37.3	0	0	1	1	2	0	2	0	1	1	0	0	0	0	0	0	0	1	0	0	0	2	1	0	0
distinctive	44	.6818	6.0728	47.8	1	2	4	2	14	8	10	3	2	1	0	0	0	1	0	7	14	2	1	1	0	4	9	2	0
distinctively	7	.1929	.3149	35.0	0	0	0	2	1	3	1	0	0	0	0	0	0	0	0	0	5	0	0	0	0	0	2	0	0
distinctly	36	.7452	5.4075	47.3	4	3	1	5	11	3	8	1	4	4	0	6	0	1	6	1	4	0	0	0	4	2	2	2	0
distinguish	74	.8908	13.078	51.2	0	1	5	10	13	24	19	2	6	16	1	5	3	3	2	16	3	1	3	1	2	3	7	2	0
distinguishable	4	.4712	.3988	36.0	0	0	1	0	2	1	0	0	0	0	0	0	0	1	0	0	1	0	0	0	1	1	0	0	0
distinguished	72	.8058	11.597	50.6	1	3	6	5	20	18	13	6	5	6	3	4	0	4	1	7	9	1	0	0	6	5	17	4	0
Distinguished	10	.4295	.9701	39.9	0	0	1	1	3	5	0	0	2	2	0	0	0	5	0	0	0	0	0	0	0	0	1	0	0
distinguishes	13	.6202	1.6451	42.2	0	0	0	0	3	4	5	1	0	4	1	0	0	2	0	2	0	0	0	1	0	0	2	1	0
distinguishing	16	.5848	1.9419	42.9	1	0	0	0	2	5	5	3	1	1	0	0	1	0	0	7	2	0	1	2	0	1	0	0	0
distort	5	.4871	.5138	37.1	0	0	0	1	1	2	1	0	0	0	0	1	0	0	1	2	0	0	0	0	0	0	1	0	0
distorted	15	.7038	2.1394	43.3	1	2	2	1	4	3	2	0	1	1	0	1	2	3	0	0	0	1	1	0	0	1	3	1	0
distorting	3	.3764	.2483	33.9	0	1	1	0	0	0	0	1	0	0	0	0	0	0	0	1	0	0	0	0	0	0	1	1	0
distortion	6	.3797	.4953	36.9	0	1	1	0	1	2	1	0	0	0	0	0	1	2	0	0	0	1	0	0	0	0	2	0	0
distract	5	.3321	.3618	35.6	0	0	1	0	1	1	2	0	0	1	0	1	0	0	0	0	0	0	0	0	0	0	3	0	0
distracted	11	.6265	1.4451	41.6	1	1	0	1	2	3	3	0	3	1	0	1	1	0	0	1	0	0	0	0	3	1	0	0	0
distracting	4	.3613	.3132	35.0	1	0	0	0	2	1	0	0	0	2	0	0	0	0	0	0	0	0	0	0	1	0	0	1	0
distraction	10	.4882	1.0314	40.1	1	0	4	0	2	0	3	0	1	0	0	1	0	0	0	0	1	0	0	0	1	0	5	1	0
distractions	5	.4003	.4515	36.5	0	1	2	0	0	1	1	0	1	1	0	0	0	1	0	0	0	0	0	0	0	0	2	0	0
distraught	2	.1551	.0728	28.6	0	0	0	0	2	0	0	0	0	0	1	0	0	0	0	0	0	0	0	0	1	0	0	0	0
distress	28	.6740	3.9347	45.9	4	4	2	4	8	3	2	1	11	2	2	3	0	0	0	2	0	0	0	0	2	1	3	2	0
distressed	11	.4043	1.0114	40.0	0	1	1	3	1	1	4	0	3	0	0	4	0	0	0	0	0	0	0	0	0	1	0	3	0
distressing	9	.6087	1.1300	40.5	0	1	2	2	3	0	0	1	1	0	1	1	0	0	0	1	1	0	0	0	2	1	0	1	0
distribute	20	.6432	2.6314	44.2	2	2	4	2	6	1	2	1	0	0	0	1	8	4	0	1	0	0	0	1	0	1	2	2	0
distributed	58	.6928	8.1340	49.1	3	4	10	6	8	7	17	3	2	2	1	1	7	7	0	6	1	0	1	9	2	5	8	6	0
distributes	3	.3390	.2450	33.9	1	0	0	0	0	0	1	1	1	0	0	0	0	0	0	0	0	0	0	0	0	0	1	1	0
distributing	5	.3639	.4034	36.1	1	0	1	2	1	0	0	0	0	0	0	0	0	2	0	0	0	0	0	0	0	0	2	1	0
distribution	54	.6720	7.3581	48.7	1	3	5	7	12	11	12	3	0	1	0	1	2	4	1	11	1	0	1	3	0	2	22	5	0
distributions	2	.2417	.1091	30.4	0	0	0	0	2	0	0	0	0	0	0	0	0	0	0	0	1	0	0	0	0	0	1	0	0
distributive	77	.0000	1.1526	40.6	3	12	12	15	16	6	13	0	0	0	0	0	77	0	0	0	0	0	0	0	0	0	0	0	0
Distributive	2	.0000	.0299	24.8	0	1	1	0	0	0	0	0	0	0	0	0	2	0	0	0	0	0	0	0	0	0	0	0	0
distributor	9	.3838	.7796	38.9	0	0	0	2	6	1	0	0	1	0	0	0	2	0	0	2	0	0	0	0	0	0	0	4	0
distributors	3	.0000	.0365	25.6	0	0	0	0	3	0	0	0	0	0	0	0	0	0	0	0	0	0	0	0	0	0	0	3	0

XH disproportion
9L disproportionately
8E disproves
4J Dispute
7P disqualifications
5H disqualifies
XR disqualify
7C disquietude
XR disquisition
5P disreputable
3Q disrupting
7Q disruptive
6H disrupts
5Q dissatified
9D dissatisfy
9Q dissects
9D dissemblers
9J disseminated
8F dissensions
8R dissents
5R dissertation
9Q dissimilarities
7Q dissipates
5N dissipating
9Q dissociate
9D dissolv'd
6H dissolver
7A dissuading
8A distance-dialing
4P Distances
7N distastefully
7H distend
7H distended
7Q distensible
7B distinctiveness
9R distorter
7M distortions
5F distorts
5B Distraction
6A distressedly
9D distressful
6A distressfully
8F distressingly

Word Type	F	D	U	SFI	3 Gr 3	4 Gr 4	5 Gr 5	6 Gr 6	7 Gr 7	8 Gr 8	9 Gr 9	X UnGr	A Read	B Eng & Gr	C Comp	D Lit	E Math	F Soc Stud	G Spell	H Sci	J Music	K Art	L Home Ec	M Shop	N Lib F	P Lib NF	Q Lib Ref	R Mag	S Rel
district	80	.6889	11.375	50.6	6	1	9	18	22	13	11	0	17	2	0	2	0	26	0	4	0	0	0	0	4	5	9	11	0
District	45	.5594	5.2949	47.2	6	3	5	7	9	2	13	0	2	1	0	1	0	24	0	0	1	0	0	0	0	8	6	2	0
districts	38	.4383	3.6304	45.6	2	0	5	2	9	9	10	1	0	0	0	0	0	23	0	2	0	0	0	0	0	2	8	3	0
distrust	13	.6033	1.6798	42.3	1	0	1	3	3	5	0	0	5	0	0	0	0	2	0	1	0	0	0	0	2	1	0	2	0
distrusts	2	.2407	.1090	30.4	0	0	0	0	0	1	1	0	0	1	0	0	0	0	0	0	1	0	0	0	0	0	0	0	0
disturb	22	.6294	2.8815	44.6	0	3	2	5	3	1	7	1	4	2	0	5	0	0	0	6	2	0	0	0	1	2	0	0	0
disturbance	10	.5159	1.0735	40.3	0	0	1	1	1	4	3	0	0	1	0	0	0	0	0	3	1	0	2	0	0	1	0	2	0
disturbances	28	.5073	2.9894	44.8	0	8	5	0	2	6	7	0	0	0	0	0	0	2	0	12	0	0	4	0	0	1	6	3	0
disturbed	52	.8291	8.6705	49.4	3	5	6	8	13	10	6	1	15	1	0	5	0	4	0	4	1	1	2	0	2	6	5	6	0
disturbing	20	.6384	2.6507	44.2	0	0	2	3	9	2	3	1	4	1	0	3	0	2	0	1	0	0	0	0	2	0	1	6	0
disturbs	6	.3794	.5032	37.0	1	0	1	0	1	2	1	0	0	0	1	0	0	1	0	2	0	0	0	0	0	2	0	0	0
disulfide	2	.2278	.1128	30.5	0	0	1	0	0	0	1	0	0	0	0	0	0	0	0	1	0	0	0	0	0	0	1	0	0
disunion	4	.1325	.1944	32.9	0	0	0	0	1	3	0	0	1	0	0	0	0	3	0	0	0	0	0	0	0	0	0	0	0
disunity	4	.3743	.3712	35.7	0	0	0	0	2	0	1	1	2	0	0	0	0	1	0	0	0	0	0	0	0	0	0	1	0
disuse	2	.1494	.1045	30.2	0	0	0	0	2	0	0	0	1	0	0	0	0	0	0	0	1	0	0	0	0	0	0	0	0
disused	2	.1787	.1174	30.7	0	0	0	0	1	1	0	0	1	0	0	0	0	0	0	0	0	0	0	0	1	0	0	0	0
ditch	63	.7134	9.3304	49.7	15	21	3	12	6	4	2	0	26	1	0	5	0	7	1	6	1	0	0	0	6	10	0	0	0
ditch-digger	3	.0000	.0591	27.7	0	0	0	0	3	0	0	0	0	0	0	0	0	0	0	3	0	0	0	0	0	0	0	0	0
ditches	27	.6795	3.7947	45.8	5	6	5	4	4	3	0	0	5	0	0	1	0	6	0	7	0	0	0	0	3	1	1	3	0
dither	2	.2443	.1130	30.5	0	0	1	0	1	0	0	0	0	0	0	1	0	0	0	0	0	0	0	0	1	0	0	0	0
Ditson	5	.0000	.0547	27.4	0	0	0	0	0	0	5	0	0	5	0	0	0	0	0	0	0	0	0	0	0	0	0	0	0
ditty	2	.2444	.1132	30.5	0	0	0	0	1	0	1	0	0	1	0	0	0	0	0	0	0	0	0	0	1	0	0	0	0
diurnal	4	.2353	.2382	33.8	0	0	0	0	1	0	0	3	0	0	0	0	0	0	0	3	0	0	0	0	0	0	1	0	0
Div	2	.0000	.0243	23.9	0	0	0	0	2	0	0	0	0	0	0	0	0	0	0	0	0	0	0	0	0	0	0	2	0
Divali	5	.0000	.0972	29.9	0	5	0	0	0	0	0	0	0	0	0	0	0	5	0	0	0	0	0	0	0	0	0	0	0
dive	92	.7403	14.076	51.5	17	29	6	13	17	2	3	5	43	5	0	5	0	1	1	12	1	0	0	0	2	16	3	3	0
dived	62	.5587	7.6445	48.8	14	26	6	8	4	3	1	0	33	1	0	2	0	0	0	1	0	0	0	0	6	16	0	3	0
diver	87	.4141	9.0343	49.6	0	36	15	24	7	2	0	3	64	1	0	2	0	0	0	18	0	0	0	0	0	0	0	2	0
diver's	14	.3382	1.2988	41.1	1	5	3	4	0	1	0	0	11	0	0	0	0	0	0	2	0	0	0	0	0	1	0	0	0
diverge	2	.0000	.0209	23.2	0	1	0	0	0	1	0	0	0	0	0	0	0	0	0	0	0	0	0	0	0	0	2	0	0
divergent	2	.0000	.0209	23.2	0	0	0	0	0	1	1	0	0	0	0	0	0	0	0	0	0	0	0	0	0	0	2	0	0
divers	81	.6707	11.625	50.7	1	36	16	12	9	3	3	1	55	0	2	2	0	0	1	13	0	1	0	0	1	0	2	4	0
divers'	3	.2197	.2090	33.2	0	2	0	0	0	1	0	0	2	0	0	0	0	0	0	0	0	0	0	0	0	0	1	0	0
diverse	16	.4503	1.5245	41.8	0	0	0	0	8	2	4	2	0	1	0	0	0	3	0	0	1	0	0	0	0	0	8	3	0
diversification	2	.0000	.0209	23.2	0	0	0	0	1	0	1	0	0	0	0	0	0	0	0	0	0	0	0	0	0	0	2	0	0
diversified	4	.3173	.2747	34.4	0	0	0	0	2	1	0	2	0	0	1	0	0	0	0	0	0	0	0	0	0	0	1	2	0
diversion	10	.4071	.9080	39.6	0	0	1	0	4	1	0	4	2	0	0	1	0	0	0	0	0	0	0	0	0	0	3	4	0
diversions	2	.0000	.0234	23.7	0	1	0	1	0	0	0	0	0	0	0	0	0	0	0	0	0	0	0	0	2	0	0	0	0
diversity	18	.2722	1.1160	40.5	0	0	0	1	14	2	1	0	0	0	0	1	0	0	0	2	0	0	0	0	0	0	13	2	0
divert	4	.4870	.4076	36.1	0	0	0	0	2	1	0	1	0	1	0	1	0	0	0	0	0	0	0	0	0	1	0	1	0
diverted	7	.5686	.8355	39.2	0	0	1	0	0	2	0	4	1	1	0	0	0	1	0	0	0	0	0	0	0	1	2	1	0
diverticula	2	.0000	.0209	23.2	0	0	0	0	0	2	0	0	0	0	0	0	0	0	0	0	0	0	0	0	0	0	2	0	0
dives	15	.5191	1.7498	42.4	4	3	1	1	3	3	0	0	8	0	0	3	0	0	0	1	0	0	0	0	0	2	1	0	0
divide	465	.7176	67.534	58.3	41	57	67	97	87	63	51	2	24	28	2	3	216	27	84	34	9	4	6	4	2	11	9	2	0
Divide	13	.4580	1.2991	41.1	0	5	3	2	2	1	0	0	1	0	1	0	0	8	0	0	0	0	0	0	0	0	1	2	0
divided	520	.8403	87.184	59.4	44	80	67	94	100	67	58	10	29	22	2	7	169	72	55	55	18	1	6	7	7	23	34	13	0
dividend	51	.1027	1.7037	42.3	1	8	6	16	14	4	2	0	0	0	0	0	50	0	0	0	0	0	1	0	0	0	0	0	0
dividends	5	.3973	.4497	36.5	0	0	0	0	1	1	1	2	1	0	0	0	0	0	0	1	0	0	0	0	0	0	2	1	0
divider	7	.3734	.5484	37.4	0	0	0	1	4	2	0	0	0	0	0	0	0	0	0	1	0	0	2	2	0	0	0	2	0
dividers	17	.0622	.2823	34.5	1	0	0	0	11	1	4	0	0	0	0	0	1	0	0	0	0	0	0	14	0	2	0	0	0
divides	57	.7290	8.4380	49.3	9	7	9	6	13	9	2	2	4	0	0	0	9	9	4	17	1	0	1	0	0	1	8	3	0
dividing	159	.6832	22.125	53.4	8	24	20	30	29	21	25	2	6	3	0	0	76	6	20	29	5	1	1	2	1	0	7	1	0
divil	4	.3123	.2986	34.8	0	2	0	1	0	1	0	0	1	0	0	0	0	0	0	0	1	0	0	0	2	0	0	0	0
divine	32	.7349	4.7467	46.8	0	3	1	7	8	1	8	4	3	1	0	5	0	1	1	2	6	0	0	0	2	3	5	3	0
Divine	7	.3235	.5051	37.0	0	1	2	0	1	2	0	1	0	0	0	0	0	2	0	0	1	0	0	0	0	0	4	0	0
divined	2	.0000	.0234	23.7	0	0	0	0	1	1	0	0	0	0	0	0	0	0	0	0	0	0	0	0	2	0	0	0	0
diving	93	.7170	13.950	51.4	5	35	16	16	8	10	2	1	52	4	1	5	0	1	1	21	0	2	0	0	0	1	1	4	0
Diving	11	.1427	.4879	36.9	0	10	0	0	1	0	0	0	0	0	0	0	0	0	0	10	0	0	0	0	0	0	1	1	0
divinities	2	.0290	24.6		0	0	0	1	0	0	0	1	0	0	0	0	0	0	0	0	0	0	0	0	0	2	0	0	0
divinity	4	.4538	.4020	36.0	0	0	0	0	0	1	1	2	1	0	0	1	0	0	0	0	0	0	0	0	0	1	0	1	0
divisibility	15	.0000	.2245	33.5	0	0	0	1	12	0	2	0	0	0	0	0	15	0	0	0	0	0	0	0	0	0	0	0	0
divisible	107	.0149	1.8960	42.8	0	17	14	22	30	2	21	1	0	0	0	0	106	0	0	1	0	0	0	0	0	0	0	0	0
division	454	.4545	44.327	56.5	44	74	46	65	95	69	50	11	10	8	1	7	352	9	5	19	0	0	5	2	1	5	16	14	0
Division	19	.3278	1.4189	41.5	1	2	1	0	5	7	1	1	1	0	0	0	3	2	0	0	0	0	0	0	0	1	0	12	0
divisions	100	.7621	15.307	51.8	3	14	20	8	25	14	11	5	1	9	0	1	39	10	4	7	3	0	1	3	0	2	12	8	0
divisor	64	.0000	.9580	39.8	1	10	4	18	24	3	4	0	0	0	0	0	64	0	0	0	0	0	0	0	0	0	0	0	0
divisors	14	.0000	.2096	33.2	0	0	0	2	2	1	9	0	0	0	0	0	14	0	0	0	0	0	0	0	0	0	0	0	0
divorce	12	.5540	1.3798	41.4	0	0	3	0	4	2	2	1	0	0	0	0	0	3	0	0	0	0	1	0	0	4	2	2	0
divorced	3	.3370	.2430	33.9	0	0	0	0	0	1	1	0	1	0	0	1	0	0	0	0	0	0	0	0	0	0	1	0	0
dix	3	.3758	.2435	33.9	0	1	1	0	0	0	1	0	0	0	0	0	1	0	0	0	1	0	0	0	0	0	0	1	0
Dixie	14	.2233	.7482	38.7	0	0	10	0	2	2	0	0	1	0	0	0	0	1	0	0	10	0	0	0	1	1	0	0	0
Dixieland	12	.0000	.0970	29.9	0	0	0	3	0	9	0	0	0	0	0	0	0	0	0	0	12	0	0	0	0	0	0	0	0
Dixon	2	.2375	.1088	30.4	0	0	1	0	1	0	0	0	0	0	0	0	0	0	0	0	1	0	0	0	0	0	0	1	0
Diz	4	.0000	.1827	32.6	0	0	0	0	4	0	0	0	4	0	0	0	0	0	0	0	0	0	0	0	0	0	0	0	0
dizzy	11	.5852	1.3467	41.3	1	3	2	2	0	1	2	0	2	1	0	1	0	0	0	0	2	0	0	0	0	3	0	2	0
dizzying	3	.2357	.2199	33.4	0	2	0	0	0	1	0	0	2	0	0	0	0	0	0	0	0	0	0	0	0	1	0	0	0
Djakarta	4	.1505	.1615	32.1	0	0	0	0	1	3	0	0	0	0	0	0	0	1	0	0	0	0	0	0	0	0	0	0	0
Djibouti	2	.0000	.0389	25.9	0	0	0	1	1	0	0	0	0	0	0	0	0	2	0	0	0	0	0	0	0	0	3	0	0
Djuanda	2	.0000	.0209	23.2	0	0	0	0	0	2	0	0	0	0	0	0	0	0	0	0	0	0	0	0	0	0	0	0	0
dm	4	.0000	.0599	27.8	0	0	0	0	4	0	0	0	0	0	0	0	4	0	0	0	0	0	0	0	0	0	2	0	0
Dmitri	5	.3816	.4230	36.3	0	0	1	1	1	2	0	0	0	0	0	0	0	0	0	3	1	0	0	0	0	0	1	0	0
DMZ	2	.0000	.0243	23.9	0	0	0	0	0	0	2	0	0	0	0	0	0	0	0	0	0	0	0	0	0	0	0	2	0
DNA	30	.1880	1.5588	41.9	0	0	0	1	15	0	14	0	0	0	0	0	0	0	0	26	0	0	0	0	0	0	4	0	0
Dnepr	6	.1125	.1964	32.9	0	0	0	1	0	5	0	0	0	0	0	0	0	1	0	0	0	0	0	0	0	0	5	0	0
do	12695	.9755	2440.2	73.9	2939	2271	1520	1641	2081	1167	888	188	3140	1118	115	802	971	952	665	1910	400	144	231	75	733	740	209	472	18
Do	15	.4659	1.5127	41.8	7	0	2	2	0	3	1	0	3	1	0	0	0	0	6	1	1	0	0	0	0	0	0	3	0
DO	3	.2918	.1960	32.9	1	0	0	0	1	0	1	0	0	1	0	0	0	0	0	1	0	0	1	0	0	0	0	0	0
do-it-yourself	9	.4987	.9889	40.0	0	0	0	1	0	6	2	0	3	0	0	0	0	1	0	2	0	1	1	0	0	0	0	0	0
do-nothing	2	.0000	.0914	29.6	2	0	0	0	0	0	0	0	2	0	0	0	0	0	0	0	0	0	0	0	0	0	1	0	0
do's	2	.1442	.0761	28.8	0	0	0	0	0	1	1	0	0	0	0	0	0	1	0	0	0	0	1	0	0	0	0	0	0
Doane	8	.0000	.0972	29.9	0	0	0	0	0	8	0	0	0	0	0	0	0	0	0	0	0	0	0	0	0	0	0	8	0
Dobarra	5	.0000	.2284	33.6	0	0	0	5	0	0	0	0	5	0	0	0	0	0	0	0	0	0	0	0	0	0	0	0	0
Dobbin	10	.3817	.8328	39.2	0	7	0	0	1	1	1	0	0	0	1	1	0	1	0	0	0	0	0	0	0	7	0	0	0
Dobby	2	.0000	.0290	24.6	0	2	0	0	0	0	0	0	0	0	0	0	0	0	0	0	0	0	0	0	0	2	0	0	0
Dobie	3	.0000	.1370	31.4	0	2	0	0	1	0	0	0	3	0	0	0	0	0	0	0	0	0	0	0	0	0	0	0	0

5Q districting
5F DistrictofColumbia
8F distrusted
8R distrusting
6A DISTURB
XR disturbingly
7F disunite
5P disunited
9B dit-darr-darr
6A diu
6A dive-bombs
7N dive'
7R diverges
7N diverging
9Q diversify
6B Diversion
8J divertimentos
8R divest
9L divided-collar
9D divideth
4F Dividing
5Q Divina
9D divinest
9Q Divinity
4E divisable
6P divised
6J divisi
9R Division's
8F Divisions
5P divisiveness
9Q divorcement
8G divot
6R diwaniyyah
6A diyu
7A dizzily
6A dizziness
7R Dizzy
8D DKYE
7A dle
5B DLR
8F do-fu
9N do-gooders
3A do-it-your-self
7R do-it-yourselfers
6J do-mi-sol
7A do-re-mi
7A do-re-mi-fa-sol-la
7A do-re-mi-fa-sol-la-l
7J do-si-do
8R do-your-own-thing
5E DOA
8R Doane's
7R Dobbins
XR DobbsFerry

Word Type	F	D	U	SFI	3 Gr 3	4 Gr 4	5 Gr 5	6 Gr 6	7 Gr 7	8 Gr 8	9 Gr 9	X UnGr	A Read	B Eng & Gr	C Comp	D Lit	E Math	F Soc Stud	G Spell	H Sci	J Music	K Art	L Home Ec	M Shop	N Lib F	P Lib NF	Q Lib Ref	R Mag	S Rel
Dobson	5	.0000	.2284	33.6	2	0	3	0	0	0	0	0	5	0	0	0	0	0	0	0	0	0	0	0	0	0	0	0	0
Doc	25	.4580	2.5358	44.0	0	1	1	8	10	5	0	0	7	5	0	1	0	0	0	0	0	0	0	0	10	0	0	2	0
Doc's	4	.0931	.1444	31.6	0	0	0	1	0	3	0	0	1	3	0	0	0	0	0	0	0	0	0	0	0	0	0	0	0
docile	6	.4518	.5771	37.6	1	0	2	0	2	1	0	0	0	0	0	0	0	1	0	0	0	0	0	0	1	2	2	0	0
docility	3	.3465	.2515	34.0	0	0	0	0	2	1	0	0	1	0	0	0	0	0	0	0	0	0	0	0	0	1	0	1	0
dock	86	.7973	13.952	51.4	19	28	6	15	13	1	4	0	37	3	0	9	2	9	2	2	1	0	0	0	6	9	1	5	0
Dock	9	.3279	.6637	38.2	0	0	0	0	0	9	0	0	0	0	0	0	6	0	0	0	0	0	0	0	0	0	1	2	0
docked	15	.6604	2.0524	43.1	2	8	1	2	0	1	1	0	3	0	0	1	0	4	0	0	1	0	0	0	0	3	1	2	0
docking	7	.5295	.7785	38.9	1	3	1	0	2	0	0	0	0	0	0	0	0	1	0	2	0	0	0	0	0	1	2	1	0
docks	45	.7287	6.7270	48.3	11	11	7	6	9	0	1	0	11	3	1	2	0	19	0	1	1	0	0	0	2	2	1	2	0
dockside	2	.1814	.1187	30.7	0	0	0	1	1	0	0	0	1	0	0	0	0	0	0	0	0	0	0	0	0	0	0	1	0
dockworkers	2	.2152	.1357	31.3	1	0	0	0	1	0	0	0	1	0	0	0	0	1	0	0	0	0	0	0	0	0	0	0	0
doctor	406	.8786	71.244	58.5	60	86	54	48	77	32	41	8	120	15	6	34	4	26	6	80	4	0	15	0	37	21	15	22	1
Doctor	180	.4424	17.692	52.5	7	100	24	2	8	11	27	1	44	0	0	33	0	6	1	3	0	0	0	0	82	10	0	1	0
DOCTOR	17	.0000	.1824	32.6	0	0	0	0	17	0	0	0	0	0	0	17	0	0	0	0	0	0	0	0	0	0	0	0	0
doctor's	27	.7098	3.8896	45.9	2	4	5	3	6	2	4	1	4	5	2	3	1	1	0	2	1	0	3	0	3	1	1	0	0
Doctor's	11	.3116	.8292	39.2	0	3	3	0	0	1	4	0	3	0	0	5	0	0	0	0	0	0	0	0	3	0	0	0	0
DOCTOR'S	3	.0000	.0322	25.1	0	0	0	0	3	0	0	0	0	0	0	3	0	0	0	0	0	0	0	0	0	0	0	0	0
doctoral	2	.2437	.1129	30.5	0	0	0	0	0	1	1	0	0	0	0	0	0	0	0	0	0	0	0	0	0	0	1	1	0
doctorate	3	.2159	.1532	31.9	0	0	0	0	1	2	0	0	0	0	0	0	0	0	0	0	0	0	0	0	0	0	2	1	0
doctoring	2	.2297	.1135	30.6	0	0	0	0	1	1	0	0	0	0	0	1	0	1	0	0	0	0	0	0	0	0	0	0	0
doctors	151	.7691	23.708	53.7	24	20	26	10	20	21	13	17	50	0	0	4	0	24	2	26	1	0	1	0	6	6	14	17	0
doctrinaire	2	.2285	.1129	30.5	0	0	0	0	0	1	1	0	0	0	0	0	0	1	0	0	0	0	0	0	0	0	1	0	0
doctrine	16	.4949	1.6538	42.2	0	1	1	0	3	8	2	1	0	2	0	0	0	2	0	0	1	0	0	0	1	2	8	0	0
Doctrine	5	.2205	.2855	34.6	0	1	0	0	0	1	3	0	0	0	0	0	0	4	0	0	0	0	0	0	0	0	1	0	0
doctrines	6	.4473	.5826	37.7	0	0	0	1	1	0	3	1	1	0	0	0	0	1	0	0	1	1	0	0	0	1	1	0	0
document	31	.7009	4.4362	46.5	1	1	5	0	7	11	5	1	3	4	0	2	0	10	0	1	0	0	0	0	2	4	1	4	0
documentary	4	.3104	.2995	34.8	0	0	0	0	1	1	2	0	1	0	0	0	0	0	0	0	0	0	0	0	0	0	1	2	0
documented	3	.2266	.1614	32.1	1	0	0	0	2	0	0	0	0	0	0	0	0	0	0	0	0	0	0	0	1	0	0	2	0
documents	18	.6563	2.4061	43.8	0	2	0	2	4	6	4	0	1	2	0	1	0	2	0	0	3	0	0	0	2	0	2	5	0
dodder	2	.0000	.0394	26.0	0	0	0	2	0	0	0	0	0	0	0	0	0	0	0	2	0	0	0	0	0	0	0	0	0
dodge	11	.5823	1.3627	41.3	2	3	1	1	2	1	1	0	3	0	0	1	0	0	0	2	0	0	0	0	3	1	0	1	0
Dodge	16	.4834	1.6400	42.1	1	2	3	0	8	1	0	1	0	0	0	0	1	3	0	2	1	0	0	0	0	1	0	8	0
DodgeCity	2	.0000	.0389	25.9	0	0	2	0	0	0	0	0	0	0	0	0	0	2	0	0	0	0	0	0	0	0	0	0	0
dodged	14	.5322	1.6352	42.1	0	3	2	1	7	0	1	0	6	0	1	1	0	1	0	0	0	0	0	0	4	0	0	1	0
dodger	2	.0000	.0290	24.6	0	2	0	0	0	0	0	0	0	0	0	0	0	0	0	0	0	0	0	0	0	2	0	0	0
Dodger	9	.2699	.5868	37.7	3	0	0	1	4	0	1	0	1	0	0	0	0	0	0	0	0	0	0	0	0	3	0	5	0
dodgers	6	.1409	.2943	34.7	0	4	0	1	1	0	0	0	2	0	0	0	0	0	0	0	0	0	0	0	0	4	0	0	0
Dodgers	28	.2854	1.9054	42.8	12	0	0	0	6	8	2	0	3	0	0	0	0	0	0	0	0	0	0	0	0	12	0	13	0
dodges	2	.2440	.1132	30.5	0	0	0	0	1	1	0	0	0	0	0	1	0	0	0	0	0	0	0	0	0	0	0	1	0
dodging	11	.5867	1.3472	41.3	1	5	2	2	1	0	0	0	1	0	0	2	0	0	0	3	0	0	0	0	2	2	0	1	0
Dodo	2	.0000	.0914	29.6	2	0	0	0	0	0	0	0	2	0	0	0	0	0	0	0	0	0	0	0	0	0	0	0	0
doe	7	.2839	.4637	36.7	0	3	0	1	0	3	0	0	1	0	0	3	0	0	0	0	3	0	0	0	0	0	0	0	0
doer	9	.3553	.7333	38.7	0	0	6	1	1	0	1	0	2	1	0	0	0	0	1	0	0	0	0	0	0	0	5	0	0
does	4408	.9334	813.78	69.1	957	681	542	579	721	499	368	61	548	532	72	243	704	311	258	951	186	41	59	25	71	157	117	123	10
DOES	3	.0000	.0591	27.7	2	0	0	1	0	0	0	0	0	0	0	0	0	0	0	3	0	0	0	0	0	0	0	0	0
doeskin	3	.2196	.1554	31.9	0	1	0	0	2	0	0	0	0	0	0	2	0	0	0	0	0	0	0	0	1	0	0	0	0
doesn't	590	.8804	103.68	60.2	107	129	56	71	92	67	47	21	180	77	3	37	10	14	10	49	4	3	10	5	44	59	3	82	0
doff	2	.0000	.0215	23.3	0	0	0	0	0	0	2	0	0	0	0	2	0	0	0	0	0	0	0	0	0	0	0	0	0
doffed	2	.0000	.0914	29.6	0	1	0	0	1	0	0	0	2	0	0	0	0	0	0	0	0	0	0	0	0	0	0	0	0
dog	1380	.8291	231.49	63.6	446	266	179	142	211	59	62	15	669	120	35	63	9	22	40	52	6	8	0	6	195	62	23	70	0
Dog	38	.5483	4.4480	46.5	11	17	3	0	3	4	0	0	10	2	0	1	0	0	0	0	2	0	0	0	12	1	0	10	0
DOG	2	.2427	.1152	30.6	1	1	0	0	0	0	0	0	0	0	0	0	0	0	0	0	0	0	0	0	1	1	0	0	0
dog-eared	2	.2446	.1125	30.5	1	0	0	0	1	0	0	0	0	1	0	1	0	0	0	0	0	0	0	0	0	0	0	0	0
dog-headed	2	.2337	.1157	30.6	0	1	0	1	0	0	0	0	0	0	0	0	0	1	0	0	0	0	0	0	1	0	0	0	0
dog-train	2	.0000	.0914	29.6	0	2	0	0	0	0	0	0	2	0	0	0	0	0	0	0	0	0	0	0	0	0	0	0	0
dog's	71	.7711	11.224	50.5	19	15	8	3	15	6	4	1	34	7	1	4	0	0	2	8	1	0	0	0	7	5	0	2	0
Dog's	2	.0000	.0162	22.1	2	0	0	0	0	0	0	0	0	0	0	0	0	0	0	0	2	0	0	0	0	0	0	0	0
dogcarts	2	.1948	.1250	31.0	0	0	1	1	0	0	0	0	1	0	0	0	0	0	0	0	0	0	0	0	0	1	0	0	0
Doge	5	.0000	.2284	33.6	0	0	0	0	5	0	0	0	5	0	0	0	0	0	0	0	0	0	0	0	0	0	0	0	0
dogfish	3	.3871	.2488	34.0	0	1	0	0	1	0	1	0	0	1	0	0	0	0	0	0	0	0	0	0	0	0	1	1	0
Dogfish	3	.0000	.0352	25.5	0	0	0	3	0	0	0	0	0	0	0	0	0	0	0	0	0	0	0	0	3	0	0	0	0
dogged	6	.5051	.6507	38.1	0	1	0	0	3	2	0	0	1	0	0	1	0	1	0	0	0	0	0	0	2	0	0	1	0
doggedly	10	.5800	1.2158	40.8	0	1	0	2	2	2	3	0	2	1	1	2	0	1	0	0	0	0	0	0	2	0	0	1	0
doggie	3	.0995	.1144	30.6	2	0	0	1	0	0	0	0	1	0	0	0	0	0	0	0	2	0	0	0	0	0	0	0	0
Doggie	3	.2227	.1589	32.0	0	0	0	0	3	0	0	0	0	0	0	0	0	0	0	0	0	0	0	0	2	0	0	1	0
doggies	8	.0000	.0647	28.1	8	0	0	0	0	0	0	0	0	0	0	0	0	0	0	0	8	0	0	0	0	0	0	0	0
doggone	2	.2351	.1166	30.7	0	0	0	1	0	1	0	0	0	0	0	0	0	1	0	0	0	0	0	0	0	0	0	1	0
doghouse	20	.5580	2.4134	43.8	1	4	3	8	1	3	0	0	5	0	0	1	0	4	0	8	0	0	0	0	1	0	0	1	0
dogie	4	.3212	.3104	34.9	0	3	0	0	1	0	0	0	1	0	0	1	0	0	0	0	0	0	0	0	0	2	0	0	0
dogies	7	.2409	.3937	36.0	3	3	1	0	0	0	0	0	0	0	0	0	0	0	0	0	3	0	0	0	0	4	0	0	0
dogma	3	.2143	.1568	32.0	0	0	1	1	0	1	0	0	0	0	0	0	0	0	0	0	0	0	0	0	0	1	0	2	0
Dogood	4	.0000	.1827	32.6	0	0	0	0	4	0	0	0	4	0	0	0	0	0	0	0	0	0	0	0	0	0	0	0	0
dogs	651	.8780	114.37	60.6	153	98	91	115	103	37	33	21	258	38	12	41	35	17	10	36	3	6	1	0	76	53	18	47	0
Dogs	14	.2919	1.0880	40.4	6	0	0	7	0	0	0	1	7	0	0	0	0	0	0	0	0	0	0	0	6	0	0	1	0
dogs'	3	.2279	.2143	33.3	2	0	0	0	0	0	0	1	2	0	0	0	0	0	0	0	0	0	0	0	0	0	0	1	0
dogtrot	2	.0000	.0914	29.6	1	0	1	0	0	0	0	0	2	0	0	0	0	0	0	0	0	0	0	0	0	0	0	0	0
dogwood	6	.5318	.6640	38.2	0	1	0	1	1	2	0	1	0	2	0	1	0	0	0	1	0	0	0	0	0	1	0	1	0
Dogwood	2	.1814	.1187	30.7	0	1	1	0	0	0	0	0	1	0	0	0	0	0	0	0	0	0	0	0	0	0	0	1	0
doin'	12	.3510	.9367	39.7	0	0	1	0	5	3	2	1	1	1	0	6	0	0	0	0	0	0	0	0	4	0	0	0	0
doing	927	.9365	171.88	62.4	158	160	117	126	177	93	74	22	257	49	10	69	19	64	82	107	13	8	18	6	70	60	17	78	0
doings	8	.3756	.7544	38.8	2	1	0	1	2	1	1	0	5	0	0	1	0	0	0	0	0	0	0	0	2	0	0	0	0
Dolan	2	.2407	.1138	30.6	0	0	1	0	0	1	0	0	0	0	0	1	0	0	0	0	0	0	0	0	0	1	0	0	0
Dolce	2	.0000	.0209	23.2	0	0	2	0	0	0	0	0	0	0	0	0	0	0	0	0	0	0	0	0	0	0	2	0	0
doldrums	3	.0000	.0591	27.7	0	0	3	0	0	0	0	0	0	0	0	0	0	0	0	3	0	0	0	0	0	0	0	0	0
Dole	6	.2802	.4175	36.2	0	0	0	4	0	2	0	0	1	0	0	0	0	2	0	0	0	0	0	0	0	0	0	3	0
doled	2	.1814	.1187	30.7	0	0	0	1	0	1	0	0	1	0	0	0	0	0	0	0	0	0	0	0	0	0	0	1	0
doleful	2	.2440	.1132	30.5	0	0	0	0	1	0	1	0	0	0	0	1	0	0	0	0	0	0	0	0	0	0	0	1	0
dolefully	2	.0000	.0234	23.7	0	0	1	1	0	0	0	0	0	0	0	0	0	0	0	0	0	0	0	0	2	0	0	0	0
Dolittle	25	.4487	2.5523	44.1	0	18	5	2	0	0	0	0	10	1	0	2	0	0	0	0	0	0	0	0	10	0	0	2	0
doll	144	.8181	23.881	53.8	76	20	21	14	6	2	4	1	66	5	1	1	13	3	6	7	1	0	2	0	24	8	2	5	0
doll-like	2	.1948	.1250	31.0	0	0	1	0	1	0	0	0	1	0	0	0	0	0	0	0	0	0	0	0	0	1	0	0	0
doll's	22	.5433	2.5955	44.1	8	2	8	2	2	0	0	0	8	0	0	1	2	0	1	1	0	0	0	0	8	0	0	1	0
dollar	217	.7796	34.375	55.4	64	29	26	28	21	16	26	7	68	9	4	7	74	6	2	6	2	0	3	0	13	11	3	9	0

4A Dobie's
9D doc
5E DOC
5N Docia
3A docilely
XR doctor-of-divinity
9Q doctor-to-be
3P doctored
4J doctorlum
4R doctors'
6A Doctr
8Q documenting
8R dodderer
8F doddering
XH dodecahedrons
4E dodgeball
9R Dodgem
3P Dodger-killer
9A Dodgers'
7Q Dodoma
6N Dodworth
5Q doers
5E DOF
4N doffing
4N dog-days
7A dog-ear
5A dog-fox
7N dog-musher
5A dog-paddle
9P dog-shopping
XH dog-sized
6F dog-sled
9J dog-vane
5H dog-walkers
4A dog'll
3N dogcatcher's
7A Doge's
6F Dogger
6P Doggett
6P Doggett's
6H doghouses
7H doglike
9R dogmatically
6A dogsled
6A dogsledders
6A Dogtooth
9D dogwood-bloom
3F dogwoods
6A doilies
6H doily
7N doin's
9R Doing
5Q doke
9Q Doktor
5P Dolan's
5P Dolans
8L dole
4D dole-dark
9D Dolios
6R Dolittles

Word Type	F	D	U	SFI	3 Gr 3	4 Gr 4	5 Gr 5	6 Gr 6	7 Gr 7	8 Gr 8	9 Gr 9	X UnGr	A Read	B Eng & Gr	C Comp	D Lit	E Math	F Soc Stud	G Spell	H Sci	J Music	K Art	L Home Ec	M Shop	N Lib F	P Lib NF	Q Lib Ref	R Mag	S Rel
dollar-sized	2	.1787	.1174	30.7	0	2	0	0	0	0	0	0	1	0	0	0	0	0	0	0	0	0	0	0	1	0	0	0	0
dollar's	6	.4312	.5931	37.7	1	0	0	4	0	0	1	0	2	0	0	0	0	0	0	1	0	0	0	0	2	1	0	0	0
dollars	478	.7998	77.493	58.9	125	58	48	48	99	33	57	10	161	17	3	29	113	43	1	9	0	0	4	0	24	26	8	40	0
dollars'	14	.6133	1.8541	42.7	4	2	1	5	2	0	0	0	7	0	0	1	2	1	0	2	0	0	0	0	0	0	0	1	0
dolled	2	.2446	.1142	30.6	0	0	0	0	2	0	0	0	0	0	0	0	0	0	0	0	0	0	0	0	1	0	0	1	0
dollies	5	.2976	.3509	35.5	0	0	0	0	5	0	0	0	1	0	0	2	0	0	0	0	2	0	0	0	0	0	0	0	0
dolls	73	.8146	11.996	50.8	28	19	14	6	5	0	1	0	23	4	0	2	7	7	7	1	7	1	0	0	5	8	1	0	0
Dolls	3	.0000	.1370	31.4	3	0	0	0	0	0	0	0	3	0	0	0	0	0	0	0	0	0	0	0	0	0	0	0	0
Dolls'	3	.0000	.1370	31.4	3	0	0	0	0	0	0	0	3	0	0	0	0	0	0	0	0	0	0	0	0	0	0	0	0
dolly	6	.2407	.3413	35.3	3	0	0	0	1	2	0	0	0	0	0	3	0	0	0	0	0	0	0	0	0	3	0	0	0
Dolly	15	.4356	1.5548	41.9	7	3	1	0	3	0	1	0	9	1	0	1	0	0	0	0	0	0	0	0	4	0	0	0	0
Dolores	2	.2408	.1091	30.4	0	0	1	0	0	1	0	0	0	1	0	0	0	0	1	0	0	0	0	0	0	0	0	0	0
dolphin	29	.5263	3.2853	45.2	6	2	1	2	3	9	5	1	7	9	0	0	0	0	0	3	0	0	0	0	6	3	0	1	0
Dolphin	5	.0926	.1850	32.7	4	0	0	1	0	0	0	0	1	0	0	0	0	0	0	0	0	0	0	0	0	4	0	0	0
dolphin's	2	.1733	.1149	30.6	0	0	0	0	0	2	0	0	1	1	0	0	0	0	0	0	0	0	0	0	0	0	0	0	0
dolphins	29	.6334	3.7893	45.8	7	0	0	5	5	12	0	0	4	7	2	0	0	0	0	3	0	0	0	0	2	5	1	5	0
Dolphins	5	.3756	.4057	36.1	1	0	0	3	1	0	0	0	0	1	0	0	0	0	0	0	0	0	0	0	2	0	0	2	0
dolt	2	.1787	.1174	30.7	0	1	0	1	0	0	0	0	1	0	0	0	0	0	0	0	0	0	0	0	1	0	0	0	0
domain	25	.5575	2.8959	44.6	1	0	1	2	5	5	11	0	0	0	0	0	8	3	0	3	1	0	0	0	0	0	7	3	0
domains	8	.4970	.8594	39.3	0	0	1	0	1	5	1	0	1	0	0	0	1	0	0	3	0	0	0	0	0	1	2	0	0
dome	34	.6164	4.4023	46.4	5	4	4	8	6	4	3	0	7	1	0	3	0	0	0	12	0	0	0	0	1	6	4	0	0
dome-shaped	6	.3493	.5166	37.1	0	1	0	0	2	0	3	0	2	0	0	0	0	0	0	3	0	0	0	0	0	0	1	0	0
domed	5	.3652	.3925	35.9	0	0	0	0	0	2	3	0	0	0	0	1	0	1	0	0	0	0	0	0	0	0	2	0	0
Domenico	2	.0000	.0162	22.1	0	1	0	1	0	0	0	0	0	0	0	0	0	0	0	0	0	1	0	0	0	0	0	0	0
domes	6	.3089	.4599	36.6	2	0	0	1	2	1	0	0	2	0	0	1	0	0	0	0	2	0	0	0	0	0	0	3	0
domestic	56	.6992	7.9765	49.0	2	1	3	3	15	14	12	6	6	3	0	5	0	10	0	3	0	1	0	0	1	2	14	11	0
domesticate	2	.0000	.0209	23.2	0	0	0	0	2	0	0	0	0	0	0	0	0	0	0	0	0	0	0	0	0	0	2	0	0
domesticated	12	.1950	.6111	37.9	0	1	2	1	6	0	2	0	1	0	0	0	0	3	0	0	0	0	0	0	0	0	8	0	0
domestication	2	.0000	.0209	23.2	0	1	0	0	1	0	0	0	0	0	0	0	0	0	0	0	0	0	0	0	0	0	2	0	0
domicile	3	.2266	.1614	32.1	0	1	1	0	0	0	0	1	0	0	0	0	0	0	0	0	0	0	0	0	1	0	0	2	0
DOMIN	22	.0000	.2361	33.7	0	0	0	0	0	0	22	0	0	0	0	22	0	0	0	0	0	0	0	0	0	0	0	0	0
dominance	3	.2043	.1486	31.7	0	0	1	0	2	0	0	0	0	0	0	0	0	0	0	0	0	0	0	0	0	1	2	0	0
dominant	42	.7688	6.4909	48.1	1	2	4	12	11	4	5	3	1	1	1	1	0	3	0	16	3	0	2	1	0	4	8	1	0
dominate	14	.6584	1.8647	42.7	2	0	3	1	4	1	1	2	0	2	0	1	0	1	0	0	2	1	1	0	0	5	1	0	0
dominated	34	.6725	4.6579	46.7	1	2	6	3	11	7	4	0	1	1	0	0	0	7	0	3	3	0	0	0	2	5	9	3	0
dominates	10	.5832	1.2016	40.8	2	0	0	0	3	1	1	3	0	1	0	0	0	2	0	1	1	0	0	0	0	0	3	2	0
dominating	5	.5473	.5687	37.5	0	0	1	0	1	0	2	1	0	0	0	1	0	1	0	1	1	0	0	0	0	0	1	0	0
domination	17	.5028	1.8043	42.6	1	0	4	0	5	5	2	0	1	0	0	0	0	3	0	0	1	0	0	0	0	2	7	3	0
Domingo	7	.3395	.5797	37.6	0	0	3	0	3	0	1	0	2	0	0	0	0	3	0	0	0	0	0	0	0	0	2	0	0
Dominican	11	.2592	.7095	38.5	0	0	6	2	3	0	0	0	0	0	0	0	0	9	0	0	0	0	0	0	1	1	0	0	0
dominie	4	.0000	.0579	27.6	0	4	0	0	0	0	0	0	0	0	0	0	0	0	0	0	0	0	0	0	0	4	0	0	0
dominion	10	.1504	.4633	36.7	1	1	0	3	2	3	0	0	2	0	0	0	0	3	0	0	0	0	0	0	0	1	2	1	1
Dominion	5	.2037	.2562	34.1	0	2	1	1	0	1	0	0	0	0	0	0	0	2	0	0	0	0	0	0	0	0	3	0	0
dominion's	2	.0000	.0209	23.2	0	0	0	0	2	0	0	0	0	0	0	0	0	0	0	0	0	0	0	0	0	0	2	0	0
dominions	5	.4605	.4841	36.8	0	0	2	0	1	0	1	1	0	1	0	2	0	0	0	0	0	0	0	0	1	1	0	0	0
dominoes	2	.1787	.1174	30.7	0	1	0	1	0	0	0	0	1	0	0	0	0	0	0	0	0	0	0	0	1	0	0	0	0
Domitian	4	.0000	.0419	26.2	0	0	0	0	4	0	0	0	0	0	0	0	0	0	0	0	0	0	0	0	0	0	4	0	0
don	11	.5862	1.3419	41.3	0	1	0	0	4	3	3	0	2	3	0	0	0	0	1	0	0	0	1	0	0	0	2	2	0
Don	183	.7824	29.110	54.6	57	39	14	11	32	22	7	1	71	8	0	5	19	1	9	0	23	5	0	0	17	9	2	14	0
Don's	16	.4910	1.6500	42.2	13	2	0	1	0	0	0	0	1	3	0	0	4	0	1	0	0	2	0	0	5	0	0	0	0
don't	2881	.8531	493.93	66.9	582	553	283	346	554	292	217	54	1175	168	26	301	32	59	55	80	46	8	17	11	371	303	3	226	0
Don't	11	.4713	1.1812	40.7	2	3	1	1	2	1	1	0	5	1	0	0	0	0	0	0	0	0	0	0	0	3	0	2	0
DON'T	2	.0000	.0394	26.0	0	0	0	0	0	0	2	0	0	0	0	0	0	0	0	2	0	0	0	0	0	0	0	0	0
don'ts	3	.3454	.2542	34.1	0	0	1	0	0	1	0	1	1	0	0	0	0	1	0	0	0	0	0	0	0	0	0	1	0
Dona	7	.0000	.3198	35.0	0	0	7	0	0	0	0	0	7	0	0	0	0	0	0	0	0	0	0	0	0	0	0	0	0
Donahue	34	.0433	.6462	38.1	0	0	0	0	0	33	0	1	0	33	0	0	0	0	0	0	0	0	0	0	0	0	0	1	0
Donahue's	7	.0000	.0766	28.8	0	0	0	0	0	7	0	0	0	7	0	0	0	0	0	0	0	0	0	0	0	0	0	0	0
Donald	67	.6935	9.7570	49.9	9	6	33	1	14	1	0	3	36	3	0	4	2	1	0	2	0	0	0	0	11	4	1	3	0
Donald's	7	.2362	.5173	37.1	1	3	2	0	1	0	0	0	5	0	0	0	0	0	0	0	0	0	0	0	2	0	0	0	0
donated	11	.5175	1.1922	40.8	0	0	4	2	2	2	0	1	1	1	1	0	1	0	0	0	0	0	0	0	0	0	4	3	0
Donatello	3	.0000	.0314	25.0	0	0	0	0	3	0	0	0	0	0	0	0	0	0	0	0	0	0	0	0	0	0	3	0	0
donation	2	.2417	.1211	30.8	0	0	1	0	0	1	0	0	0	0	0	0	1	1	0	0	0	0	0	0	0	0	0	0	0
donations	4	.3605	.3115	34.9	2	0	0	0	1	1	0	0	0	1	0	0	0	0	0	0	0	0	0	0	0	0	2	1	0
Donatist	2	.0000	.0209	23.2	0	0	0	0	2	0	0	0	0	0	0	0	0	0	0	0	0	0	0	0	0	0	2	0	0
Donatists	5	.0000	.0523	27.2	0	0	0	0	5	0	0	0	0	0	0	0	0	0	0	0	0	0	0	0	0	0	5	0	0
Donatus	2	.0000	.0209	23.2	0	0	0	0	2	0	0	0	0	0	0	0	0	0	0	0	0	0	0	0	0	0	2	0	0
Doncaster	2	.2407	.1138	30.6	0	1	0	1	0	0	0	0	0	0	0	1	0	0	0	0	0	0	0	0	0	1	0	0	0
done	1566	.9290	288.19	64.6	258	282	181	209	262	168	179	27	399	66	58	105	103	145	45	117	34	16	44	65	120	115	45	84	5
Donelson	3	.3766	.2497	34.0	0	1	1	0	0	1	0	0	0	0	0	0	0	1	0	0	0	0	0	0	0	1	1	0	0
doneness	3	.1274	.0913	29.6	0	0	0	0	0	0	2	1	0	0	0	0	0	0	0	0	0	0	2	0	0	0	0	1	0
Donesa	4	.0000	.1827	32.6	0	0	4	0	0	0	0	0	4	0	0	0	0	0	0	0	0	0	0	0	0	0	0	0	0
dong	4	.2278	.2911	34.6	3	0	0	0	1	0	0	0	3	0	0	0	0	0	0	0	1	0	0	0	0	0	0	0	0
Dong	3	.0000	.0314	25.0	0	0	0	0	0	3	0	0	0	0	0	0	0	0	0	0	0	0	0	0	0	0	3	0	0
Donizetti	3	.0000	.0243	23.8	0	0	0	0	1	2	0	0	0	0	0	0	0	0	0	0	3	0	0	0	0	0	0	0	0
donkey	156	.7501	24.192	53.8	61	29	3	25	15	14	2	7	89	8	1	13	0	6	1	1	19	2	0	0	10	3	1	2	0
Donkey	17	.2835	1.0848	40.4	13	3	0	1	0	0	0	0	1	0	0	5	0	0	0	0	10	0	0	0	0	0	0	1	0
donkey's	14	.4646	1.5270	41.8	2	4	0	5	0	0	0	3	9	0	0	0	0	0	0	0	1	0	0	0	3	0	1	0	0
donkeys	39	.6145	5.1823	47.1	3	20	1	7	7	1	0	0	20	0	0	1	0	12	0	0	1	0	0	0	2	1	1	1	0
donkeys'	2	.2337	.1157	30.6	0	1	1	0	0	0	0	0	0	0	0	0	0	1	0	0	0	0	0	0	1	0	0	0	0
Donna	6	.4470	.5637	37.5	1	1	1	3	0	0	0	0	0	1	0	0	1	0	2	0	0	0	0	0	0	0	0	2	0
donned	2	.2444	.1132	30.5	0	0	0	0	2	0	0	0	0	1	0	0	0	0	0	0	0	0	0	0	1	0	0	0	0
Donnelly	5	.0000	.0608	27.8	0	0	0	1	0	0	0	4	0	0	0	0	0	0	0	0	0	0	0	0	0	0	0	5	0
Donnelson	3	.0000	.0591	27.7	0	0	0	0	3	0	0	0	0	0	0	0	0	0	0	3	0	0	0	0	0	0	0	0	0
Donny	2	.0000	.0914	29.6	0	0	2	0	0	0	0	0	2	0	0	0	0	0	0	0	0	0	0	0	0	0	0	0	0
donor	6	.4354	.5847	37.7	0	0	0	0	1	3	0	2	1	1	0	0	0	0	0	3	0	0	0	0	0	0	1	0	0
Donovan	5	.2743	.3370	35.3	0	0	0	0	0	4	1	0	1	1	0	0	0	0	0	0	0	0	0	0	0	0	0	3	0
dons	2	.0000	.0243	23.9	0	0	0	0	0	1	1	0	0	0	0	0	0	0	0	0	0	0	0	0	0	0	0	2	0
Donsoon	4	.0000	.1827	32.6	0	0	4	0	0	0	0	0	4	0	0	0	0	0	0	0	0	0	0	0	0	0	0	0	0
doo-dah	6	.0000	.0485	26.9	0	0	0	6	0	0	0	0	0	0	0	0	0	0	0	0	6	0	0	0	0	0	0	0	0
Doodle	20	.1937	.9361	39.7	1	11	7	1	0	0	0	0	1	0	0	0	0	0	0	0	15	0	0	0	3	1	0	0	0
Doodle-de-do	2	.0000	.0234	23.7	0	0	2	0	0	0	0	0	0	0	0	0	0	0	0	0	0	0	0	0	2	0	0	0	0
Dooley	5	.2226	.2657	34.2	0	0	3	0	2	0	0	0	0	0	0	0	0	0	0	0	0	0	0	0	0	2	3	0	0
doolies	2	.0000	.0243	23.9	2	0	0	0	0	0	0	0	0	0	0	0	0	0	0	0	0	0	0	0	0	0	0	2	0
Doolin	2	.0000	.0389	25.9	0	2	0	0	0	0	0	0	0	0	0	0	0	2	0	0	0	0	0	0	0	0	0	0	0

8F Dollar
7E dollar-days
3A dollhouse
5Q dollmaking
4A dolly's
5Q Dolomites
6R dolphin-ologist
7A Dolphina
9D Dolt
7D dolts
7G dom
7R Dom
5Q Dome
XR dome-like
7Q dome-shelled
5Q Domenichino
9F Domestic
9H domestica
7R domestics
9B Domini
4P Dominic
8Q Dominicans
5Q domino
7Q Domitia
7Q Domitian's
6R Domres
6R Domres'
7Q domus
8A don't-care
3P don't-give-an-inch
9L don't's
7N Donahoe
9Q Donaldson's
8G donare
3A donate
7Q Donatello's
7Q Donatism
4Q Done
9F Donets
4J Doney
8Q Dongola
4A Doni
4A Doni's
3J donkey-engine
9B donna
9Q Donne
8R Donnelley
3F Donnie
7D Donnybrook
XH donor's
XH donors
8B dont
6J doob-kee
4A Dood
4A Doodleberries
5Q Dooley's
7P Dooleys

Word Type	F	D	U	SFI	3 Gr 3	4 Gr 4	5 Gr 5	6 Gr 6	7 Gr 7	8 Gr 8	9 Gr 9	X UnGr	A Read	B Eng & Gr	C Comp	D Lit	E Math	F Soc Stud	G Spell	H Sci	J Music	K Art	L Home Ec	M Shop	N Lib F	P Lib NF	Q Lib Ref	R Mag	S Rel
Doolins	2	.0000	.0389	25.9	0	2	0	0	0	0	0	0	0	0	0	0	0	2	0	0	0	0	0	0	0	0	0	0	0
Doolittle	8	.0496	.1911	32.8	0	0	7	0	1	0	0	0	1	0	0	0	0	0	0	0	0	0	0	0	0	0	7	0	0
doom	11	.5640	1.2873	41.1	0	0	2	3	0	1	4	1	1	0	0	3	0	0	0	0	2	0	0	0	2	1	0	2	0
doomed	13	.6035	1.6263	42.1	0	0	4	3	3	1	0	2	1	0	0	3	0	2	0	1	0	0	0	0	1	2	0	3	0
doomsday	4	.0000	.1827	32.6	0	0	0	0	4	0	0	0	4	0	0	0	0	0	0	0	0	0	0	0	0	0	0	0	0
Doon	3	.0000	.0314	25.0	0	0	3	0	0	0	0	0	0	0	0	0	0	0	0	0	0	0	0	0	0	0	3	0	0
Doone	4	.0000	.0429	26.3	0	0	4	0	0	0	0	0	0	0	0	4	0	0	0	0	0	0	0	0	0	0	0	0	0
Dooner	3	.0000	.0352	25.5	0	0	3	0	0	0	0	0	0	0	0	0	0	0	0	0	0	0	0	0	3	0	0	0	0
door	1748	.8196	290.25	64.6	445	401	187	173	273	140	116	13	811	78	28	199	7	56	16	23	33	0	6	3	240	158	3	83	4
Door	5	.3735	.4140	36.2	0	0	1	2	0	2	0	0	0	0	0	0	0	2	0	0	0	0	0	0	1	0	0	2	0
door's	4	.3212	.3104	34.9	1	0	0	0	1	2	0	0	1	0	0	1	0	0	0	0	0	0	0	0	0	2	0	0	0
doorbell	33	.6494	4.5462	46.6	12	7	3	2	2	4	3	0	16	6	0	1	0	0	0	6	0	0	1	1	2	0	0	0	0
doorbells	3	.0000	.1370	31.4	1	1	0	1	0	0	0	0	3	0	0	0	0	0	0	0	0	0	0	0	0	0	0	0	0
doorjamb	3	.2175	.1545	31.9	0	0	0	0	0	1	2	0	0	0	0	2	0	0	0	0	0	0	0	0	0	0	0	1	0
doorkeeper	2	.1948	.1250	31.0	0	2	0	0	0	0	0	0	1	0	0	0	0	0	0	0	0	0	0	0	0	1	0	0	0
doorknob	10	.4844	1.1238	40.5	5	0	2	1	0	0	0	2	6	0	0	0	0	0	0	2	1	0	0	0	1	0	0	0	0
doorknobs	2	.2331	.1157	30.6	0	1	0	1	0	0	0	0	0	0	0	0	0	0	0	1	0	0	0	0	1	0	0	0	0
doorman	3	.3805	.2526	34.0	1	0	0	1	0	0	1	0	0	0	0	0	0	1	0	0	0	0	0	0	1	1	0	0	0
doorpost	5	.2557	.3182	35.0	1	1	0	0	2	0	1	0	1	0	0	3	0	0	0	0	0	0	0	0	0	0	0	1	0
doors	225	.8715	39.262	55.9	43	36	35	21	46	25	16	3	85	9	4	22	0	20	1	16	9	0	2	7	19	16	4	11	0
doorstep	20	.6615	2.7913	44.5	5	3	2	2	4	2	1	1	10	1	1	3	0	1	0	0	1	0	0	0	1	0	0	2	0
doorsteps	2	.2152	.1357	31.3	1	0	1	0	0	0	0	0	1	0	0	0	0	1	0	0	0	0	0	0	0	0	0	0	0
doorway	117	.7444	17.919	52.5	20	32	15	8	28	6	8	0	52	3	1	16	0	3	1	2	0	3	0	0	19	12	2	3	0
doorways	14	.6478	1.8645	42.7	4	5	2	0	0	0	3	0	2	0	1	1	0	2	1	0	0	0	0	0	2	0	1	4	0
dooryard	3	.2261	.2131	33.3	0	1	1	0	1	0	0	0	2	0	0	0	0	0	0	0	0	0	0	0	1	0	0	0	0
dope	17	.5498	2.0483	43.1	1	3	2	6	2	0	1	2	8	2	0	1	0	0	0	0	0	0	0	0	3	0	0	3	0
Doppler	2	.0000	.0394	26.0	0	0	0	0	2	0	0	0	0	0	0	0	0	0	0	2	0	0	0	0	0	0	0	0	0
Dora	3	.0000	.0434	26.4	0	3	0	0	0	0	0	0	0	0	0	0	0	0	0	0	0	0	0	0	0	3	0	0	0
Dorado	5	.3343	.3773	35.8	3	0	0	0	1	1	0	0	0	0	0	0	0	1	0	0	0	0	0	0	0	3	1	0	0
Dorchester	2	.1814	.1187	30.7	0	0	0	0	0	2	0	0	1	0	0	0	0	0	0	0	0	0	0	0	0	0	0	1	0
Dordogne	3	.3766	.2497	34.0	0	0	0	0	1	1	0	1	0	0	0	0	0	1	0	0	0	0	0	0	0	1	1	0	0
Doria	2	.0000	.0215	23.3	0	0	0	0	0	0	2	0	0	0	0	2	0	0	0	0	0	0	0	0	0	0	0	0	0
Dorian	9	.0000	.0728	28.6	0	1	1	4	3	0	0	0	0	0	0	0	0	0	0	0	9	0	0	0	0	0	0	0	0
Doris	9	.4480	.8545	39.3	0	5	0	2	0	1	1	0	0	1	0	0	3	0	1	0	0	0	0	0	0	0	0	4	0
dorm	2	.1378	.0662	28.2	0	0	0	0	1	1	0	0	0	0	0	0	0	0	0	0	0	1	0	0	0	0	0	1	0
dormant	10	.4298	.9408	39.7	0	0	2	0	6	0	1	1	0	0	0	0	0	0	0	6	0	0	0	0	1	1	0	2	0
dormer	2	.2441	.1127	30.5	0	1	0	0	0	1	0	0	0	0	0	0	0	0	0	0	0	0	0	0	1	0	1	0	0
dormitory	8	.3352	.5990	37.8	0	5	1	0	1	0	1	0	0	0	0	0	0	0	0	0	0	0	0	0	1	5	0	2	0
dormouse	3	.0000	.0328	25.2	0	0	3	0	0	0	0	0	0	3	0	0	0	0	0	0	0	0	0	0	0	0	0	0	0
Dormouse	3	.0000	.1370	31.4	0	0	3	0	0	0	0	0	3	0	0	0	0	0	0	0	0	0	0	0	0	0	0	0	0
Dorothy	16	.6687	2.2167	43.5	5	4	5	0	1	0	1	0	4	2	1	0	0	4	1	1	1	0	0	0	0	0	0	2	0
Dorothy's	2	.1717	.1142	30.6	1	0	0	0	1	0	0	0	1	0	0	1	0	0	0	0	0	0	0	0	0	0	0	0	0
Dorpat	4	.0000	.0419	26.2	0	0	0	0	0	4	0	0	0	0	0	0	0	0	0	0	0	0	0	0	0	0	4	0	0
dorsal	13	.4481	1.2374	40.9	2	1	0	0	5	0	4	1	0	0	0	0	0	0	0	2	0	0	0	0	4	0	2	5	0
Dorset	2	.0000	.0914	29.6	0	0	0	0	2	0	0	0	2	0	0	0	0	0	0	0	0	0	0	0	0	0	0	0	0
Dorsey	4	.0000	.0469	26.7	0	0	4	0	0	0	0	0	0	0	0	0	0	0	0	0	0	0	0	0	4	0	0	0	0
Dort	3	.2222	.1558	31.9	0	0	0	0	0	3	0	0	0	1	0	0	0	0	0	0	0	0	0	0	0	0	2	0	0
dory	12	.3804	1.1748	40.7	1	1	0	9	0	1	0	0	9	0	0	0	0	0	0	0	1	0	0	0	0	2	0	0	0
dose	18	.3601	1.6219	42.1	0	3	2	6	5	0	2	0	8	0	0	0	0	0	0	8	0	0	0	0	0	0	2	0	0
doses	6	.1991	.3231	35.1	0	1	0	0	3	0	1	1	0	0	0	0	0	0	0	5	0	0	0	0	1	0	0	0	0
dosimeter	2	.0000	.0394	26.0	0	0	0	0	0	1	1	0	0	0	0	0	0	0	0	2	0	0	0	0	0	0	0	0	0
dost	23	.5287	2.5613	44.1	0	0	3	5	6	2	7	0	3	1	0	8	0	0	0	0	2	0	0	0	6	3	0	0	0
dot	179	.7299	26.391	54.2	19	29	37	39	24	20	10	1	16	6	3	2	53	10	54	11	9	2	1	4	0	1	1	6	0
Dot	10	.2414	.7744	38.9	7	2	0	0	1	0	0	0	8	0	0	0	2	0	0	0	0	0	0	0	0	0	0	0	0
Dot-and-Go-One	2	.0000	.0234	23.7	0	0	0	0	2	0	0	0	0	0	0	0	0	0	0	0	0	0	0	0	2	0	0	0	0
dote	3	.0000	.0322	25.1	0	0	0	0	0	0	3	0	0	0	0	3	0	0	0	0	0	0	0	0	0	0	0	0	0
doth	33	.4561	3.1902	45.0	3	3	1	3	6	0	17	0	2	4	0	18	0	0	0	0	4	0	0	0	2	3	0	0	0
doting	5	.3909	.4352	36.4	0	0	1	0	1	0	1	2	1	0	0	1	0	0	0	0	0	0	1	0	0	0	0	2	0
dots	254	.5727	30.248	54.8	36	39	17	43	61	47	6	5	9	2	0	7	174	8	19	15	3	2	1	4	0	3	1	6	0
dotted	119	.7898	19.054	52.8	32	16	13	21	20	11	3	3	38	0	1	4	16	9	1	7	20	2	0	0	2	9	1	9	0
Dottie	2	.0000	.0045	16.5	0	0	0	0	0	2	0	0	0	0	2	0	0	0	0	0	0	0	0	0	0	0	0	0	0
dotting	4	.4817	.4082	36.1	0	1	0	0	2	0	0	1	0	1	0	0	0	1	0	0	0	0	0	0	0	1	0	1	0
Dotty	15	.0905	.4260	36.3	14	0	0	0	1	0	0	0	0	1	0	0	0	0	0	0	0	0	0	0	14	0	0	0	0
double	414	.7498	62.315	57.9	62	61	48	56	96	37	42	12	30	18	2	19	27	6	149	26	26	0	14	19	30	14	15	19	0
Double	2	.2417	.1091	30.4	0	1	0	0	0	1	0	0	0	0	0	0	0	0	0	0	1	0	0	0	0	0	1	0	0
double-barreled	2	.2387	.1089	30.4	0	0	0	1	1	0	0	0	0	0	0	0	0	0	0	0	1	0	0	0	1	0	0	0	0
double-base	2	.0000	.0219	23.4	0	0	0	0	0	2	0	0	0	2	0	0	0	0	0	0	0	0	0	0	0	0	0	0	0
double-bit	5	.0000	.2284	33.6	0	0	0	0	5	0	0	0	5	0	0	0	0	0	0	0	0	0	0	0	0	0	0	0	0
double-boiler	4	.0000	.0129	21.1	0	0	0	0	0	0	4	0	0	0	0	0	0	0	0	0	0	0	4	0	0	0	0	0	0
double-knit	2	.0857	.0784	28.9	0	0	0	1	0	0	1	0	1	0	0	0	0	0	0	0	0	0	1	0	0	0	0	0	0
double-quick	3	.2261	.2131	33.3	0	1	2	0	0	0	0	0	2	0	0	0	0	0	0	0	0	0	0	0	1	0	0	0	0
double-reed	4	.0000	.0323	25.1	0	1	2	0	1	0	0	0	0	0	0	0	0	0	0	0	4	0	0	0	0	0	0	0	0
double-space	3	.0000	.0328	25.2	0	0	0	0	1	0	2	0	0	3	0	0	0	0	0	0	0	0	0	0	0	0	0	0	0
double-tracked	2	.0000	.0389	25.9	0	0	0	2	0	0	0	0	0	0	0	0	0	2	0	0	0	0	0	0	0	0	0	0	0
double-vowel	2	.0000	.0162	22.1	0	0	1	1	0	0	0	0	0	0	0	0	0	0	2	0	0	0	0	0	0	0	0	0	0
doublechin	2	.0000	.0219	23.4	2	0	0	0	0	0	0	0	0	2	0	0	0	0	0	0	0	0	0	0	0	0	0	0	0
doubled	93	.6624	12.619	51.0	4	9	14	16	19	19	10	2	12	3	1	1	6	8	33	9	1	0	0	0	3	5	8	3	0
Doubleday	8	.2862	.6031	37.8	0	0	0	8	0	0	0	0	3	0	0	0	0	0	0	1	0	0	0	0	0	4	0	0	0
doubles	24	.5685	2.8313	44.5	6	0	5	1	7	2	2	1	0	1	0	0	14	0	1	4	0	0	1	0	0	1	1	1	0
doublet	2	.2443	.1130	30.5	0	0	0	1	0	0	1	0	0	0	0	1	0	0	0	0	0	0	0	0	1	0	0	0	0
Doubletree	3	.0000	.0352	25.5	0	0	0	0	0	3	0	0	0	0	0	0	0	0	0	0	0	0	0	0	3	0	0	0	0
doublets	3	.2379	.1631	32.1	0	0	0	0	3	0	0	0	0	2	0	0	0	0	1	0	0	0	0	0	0	0	0	0	0
doubling	12	.6934	1.6997	42.3	0	1	2	1	5	0	3	0	2	2	0	1	0	0	2	2	1	0	0	0	0	0	1	1	0
doubloons	3	.2360	.1709	32.3	0	0	0	2	1	0	0	0	0	0	0	0	2	0	0	0	0	0	0	0	1	0	0	0	0
doubly	4	.4458	.3985	36.0	0	1	0	0	1	0	2	0	1	1	0	0	0	0	0	1	0	0	0	0	0	0	1	0	0
doubt	222	.8958	39.541	56.0	12	22	22	24	72	38	27	5	51	16	4	26	4	11	3	15	4	0	7	1	16	25	18	21	0
doubted	18	.6038	2.2833	43.6	1	2	0	4	5	2	4	0	4	0	0	2	0	2	0	0	0	0	0	0	3	4	0	3	0
doubters	3	.3452	.2543	34.1	0	0	0	0	1	1	1	0	1	0	0	0	0	0	0	1	0	0	0	0	0	0	0	1	0
doubtful	32	.7733	5.0171	47.0	1	5	3	2	13	4	3	1	8	4	0	1	0	4	2	0	1	0	0	0	2	6	1	3	0
doubtfully	19	.6089	2.5078	44.0	5	3	3	4	2	2	0	0	11	1	0	2	0	0	0	0	0	0	0	0	2	2	0	1	0
doubting	8	.3282	.6682	38.2	1	1	1	2	1	0	2	0	4	0	0	3	0	0	0	0	0	0	0	0	1	0	0	0	0
doubtless	23	.6161	2.9452	44.7	2	1	1	2	8	2	5	2	3	0	0	4	0	2	0	4	0	0	0	0	6	2	2	0	0
doubts	17	.5770	2.0894	43.2	2	0	2	2	5	1	4	1	5	0	0	4	0	0	0	2	0	0	0	0	2	1	2	3	0
Doug	21	.3837	1.8676	42.7	0	0	0	4	12	2	0	3	6	2	0	0	0	0	0	0	0	0	0	0	0	3	0	10	0

4F Doolins'
5N DOOM
7D doon
4D door-chink
5D doorstone
5P doorstops
7R doped
7H Doppler-shifted
7R dorados
8N Dorcas
9D Doria's
7H dormancy
4N dormice
7R dormitories
4P Dormitory
7R Dorough
7A Dorset's
7R dos
7P Dos
8D dosed
7N dosing
8Q Dositej
7R Dostoevsky
9D dosy-do
5H dot-and-dash
4N dotard
8C doted
3N Dotty's
7G Douai
7G Douay
7Q double-acting
4Q double-bar
7N double-barrelled
7D double-bladed
9B double-check
7R double-checking
9Q double-crested
9R double-cropping
7P double-crossing
XR double-dealing
7R double-deck
5A double-decked
6A double-decker
7R double-ended
9G double-entry
6J double-flute
7M double-ground
9H double-headed
6P double-header
7M double-hung
7G double-letter
8A double-locked
6G double-pointed
6R double-ribbed
9M double-seaming
7M double-strength
7R double-thick
XH double-walled
5N doubled-up
5E Doubling
5D doublings
6E doubloon
8R Doubt
9R doubtlessly
6J douce
6R Doud

Word Type	F	D	U	SFI	3 Gr 3	4 Gr 4	5 Gr 5	6 Gr 6	7 Gr 7	8 Gr 8	9 Gr 9	X UnGr	A Read	B Eng & Gr	C Comp	D Lit	E Math	F Soc Stud	G Spell	H Sci	J Music	K Art	L Home Ec	M Shop	N Lib F	P Lib NF	Q Lib Ref	R Mag	S Rel
dough	55	.6351	7.2134	48.6	4	15	5	8	2	8	13	0	10	5	0	4	0	0	2	5	3	0	9	0	1	13	2	1	0
doughnut	28	.5580	3.2862	45.2	3	9	2	4	0	10	0	0	4	2	0	4	11	0	0	0	0	0	0	0	2	0	5	0	0
doughnut-shaped	2	.2391	.1133	30.5	0	0	0	0	0	1	1	0	0	0	0	0	1	0	0	0	0	0	0	0	0	0	1	0	0
doughnuts	42	.6069	5.4146	47.3	1	7	13	8	6	6	1	0	16	3	0	5	6	0	0	0	0	0	2	0	10	0	0	0	0
doughty	3	.3722	.2508	34.0	0	0	0	0	1	1	0	1	0	0	0	1	0	1	0	1	0	0	0	0	0	0	0	0	0
Douglas	58	.6909	8.2402	49.2	1	4	15	4	9	20	5	0	12	5	4	2	0	18	0	0	1	0	0	0	3	3	6	4	0
Douglass	5	.3770	.4201	36.2	0	0	2	1	0	1	1	0	0	1	0	0	0	3	0	0	0	0	0	0	0	0	1	0	0
dour	2	.1948	.1250	31.0	0	0	1	0	1	0	0	0	1	0	0	0	0	0	0	0	0	0	0	0	0	1	0	0	0
dourness	3	.0000	.0434	26.4	0	0	3	0	0	0	0	0	0	0	0	0	0	0	0	0	0	0	0	0	0	3	0	0	0
doused	3	.2279	.2143	33.3	0	0	0	1	0	2	0	0	2	0	0	0	0	0	0	0	0	0	0	0	0	0	0	1	0
dove	32	.6227	4.1270	46.2	9	7	3	8	4	0	0	1	6	1	0	1	0	0	1	1	10	0	0	0	1	6	2	3	0
Dove	11	.4838	1.1089	40.4	0	0	0	3	1	6	1	0	0	0	0	1	0	0	0	0	0	1	0	0	5	1	0	3	0
Dover	10	.5729	1.2048	40.8	0	0	2	2	2	2	2	0	2	0	0	0	2	0	1	0	0	0	0	0	1	0	3	1	0
doves	23	.6610	3.1773	45.0	3	5	0	7	2	5	0	1	8	3	0	0	0	1	0	2	2	0	0	0	0	1	1	5	0
Dovey	4	.0000	.0469	26.7	0	0	4	0	0	0	0	0	0	0	0	0	0	0	0	0	0	0	0	0	4	0	0	0	0
Dovey's	2	.0000	.0234	23.7	0	0	2	0	0	0	0	0	0	0	0	0	0	0	0	0	0	0	0	0	2	0	0	0	0
Dow	5	.2327	.2720	34.3	0	0	0	0	5	0	0	0	0	0	0	3	0	0	0	0	0	0	0	0	0	0	0	2	0
Dowdey	5	.0000	.0608	27.8	0	5	0	0	0	0	0	0	0	0	0	0	0	0	0	0	0	0	0	0	0	0	0	5	0
dowel	6	.1576	.2595	34.1	0	0	0	0	2	3	0	1	1	0	0	0	0	0	0	1	0	0	0	3	0	1	0	0	0
dowels	11	.1920	.5050	37.0	0	0	0	0	7	4	0	0	0	0	0	0	0	0	0	0	0	0	0	4	0	7	0	0	0
down	7206	.9076	1302.2	71.1	1518	1372	934	880	1276	688	431	107	2758	200	68	609	94	411	58	582	275	28	53	39	840	671	136	384	0
Down	20	.4720	2.0384	43.1	6	2	2	3	4	3	0	0	4	0	0	0	0	0	1	0	8	0	0	0	1	3	0	3	0
down-and-up	2	.0000	.0299	24.8	0	0	2	0	0	0	0	0	0	0	0	0	2	0	0	0	0	0	0	0	0	0	0	0	0
down-right-up	2	.0000	.0162	22.1	2	0	0	0	0	0	0	0	0	0	0	0	0	0	0	0	2	0	0	0	0	0	0	0	0
down-stream	2	.1787	.1174	30.7	0	0	0	1	1	0	0	0	1	0	0	0	0	0	0	0	0	0	0	0	1	0	0	0	0
down-to-earth	4	.3990	.3412	35.3	0	0	0	0	2	1	0	1	0	1	0	0	0	1	0	0	0	0	1	0	0	0	0	1	0
down-up	2	.0000	.0162	22.1	2	0	0	0	0	0	0	0	0	0	0	0	0	0	0	0	2	0	0	0	0	0	0	0	0
downbeat	5	.0000	.0404	26.1	0	3	1	0	1	0	0	0	0	0	0	0	0	0	0	0	5	0	0	0	0	0	0	0	0
downcast	6	.3399	.4913	36.9	1	0	1	1	2	1	0	0	2	0	0	2	0	0	0	0	0	0	0	0	0	0	0	2	0
downed	4	.2424	.3036	34.8	0	2	0	0	2	0	0	0	3	0	0	0	0	0	0	0	0	0	0	0	0	0	0	1	0
Downer	2	.0000	.0299	24.8	0	0	2	0	0	0	0	0	0	0	0	0	2	0	0	0	0	0	0	0	0	0	0	0	0
downfall	6	.4269	.5453	37.4	0	0	2	1	1	1	1	0	0	0	0	1	0	1	0	0	0	1	0	0	0	2	0	1	0
downgrade	6	.2932	.4413	36.4	0	0	1	0	0	0	5	0	1	0	0	1	0	0	0	4	0	0	0	0	0	0	0	0	0
downhill	37	.7799	5.8368	47.7	9	5	4	4	9	2	3	1	7	0	0	3	0	4	1	7	1	0	0	0	3	4	5	2	0
Downing	2	.1733	.1149	30.6	0	0	0	2	0	0	0	0	1	1	0	0	0	0	0	0	0	0	0	0	0	0	0	0	0
downpour	3	.1409	.1472	31.7	0	2	1	0	0	0	0	0	1	0	0	0	0	0	0	0	0	0	0	0	0	2	0	0	0
downrange	2	.0000	.0394	26.0	0	0	0	0	0	0	0	2	0	0	0	0	0	0	0	2	0	0	0	0	0	0	0	0	0
downright	8	.4833	.8100	39.1	0	1	2	1	2	1	0	1	0	0	0	2	0	0	0	0	1	0	0	0	0	3	0	2	0
downriver	3	.3390	.2450	33.9	0	1	0	1	1	0	0	0	1	0	0	0	0	0	0	0	0	0	0	0	0	0	1	1	0
downs	7	.4827	.6952	38.4	0	1	1	0	2	0	2	1	0	1	0	1	0	0	0	1	0	1	2	0	0	0	1	0	0
Downs	13	.3617	1.2418	40.9	0	1	0	11	1	0	0	0	10	0	0	0	0	0	0	0	0	0	0	0	0	2	0	1	0
downstage	10	.2579	.6397	38.1	0	0	0	2	2	6	0	0	2	0	0	6	0	0	0	0	0	0	0	0	2	0	0	0	0
downstairs	90	.7002	13.034	51.2	26	19	12	9	10	9	4	1	32	9	0	9	0	1	2	1	0	0	0	0	16	12	1	7	0
downstream	37	.7495	5.6883	47.5	3	4	4	9	9	6	2	0	13	1	0	1	1	8	2	2	0	0	0	0	0	2	2	5	0
downstroke	3	.2984	.1935	32.9	1	0	0	1	1	0	0	0	0	0	0	0	0	0	1	0	0	0	0	1	0	1	0	0	0
downstrokes	2	.0000	.0162	22.1	0	0	0	2	0	0	0	0	0	0	0	0	0	0	2	0	0	0	0	0	0	0	0	0	0
downtown	60	.8019	9.7494	49.9	11	7	7	11	9	6	9	0	21	3	1	2	2	10	0	0	0	1	0	0	2	4	4	10	0
downward	103	.8079	16.724	52.2	7	23	21	6	25	6	12	3	15	3	5	6	7	5	0	33	8	0	1	2	0	4	10	4	0
downwind	3	.3863	.2513	34.0	1	0	0	0	2	0	0	0	0	0	0	0	0	0	0	0	0	0	0	0	1	1	0	1	0
downy	13	.5405	1.5651	41.9	5	4	1	1	1	0	0	1	7	2	0	1	0	0	0	1	0	0	0	0	0	2	0	0	0
dowry	3	.1187	.1291	31.1	0	0	0	1	0	1	1	0	1	0	0	2	0	0	0	0	0	0	0	0	0	0	0	0	0
Doxiadis	2	.0000	.0209	23.2	0	0	0	0	0	0	2	0	0	0	0	0	0	0	0	0	0	0	0	0	0	0	2	0	0
doze	5	.4686	.4888	36.9	1	1	0	0	0	0	2	1	0	0	0	2	0	0	0	0	1	0	0	0	1	0	0	1	0
Doze	2	.0000	.0219	23.4	0	2	0	0	0	0	0	0	0	2	0	0	0	0	0	0	0	0	0	0	0	0	0	0	0
dozed	16	.4508	1.6582	42.2	1	7	2	2	1	2	1	0	7	1	0	0	0	0	0	0	0	0	0	0	3	5	0	0	0
dozen	253	.7657	39.317	55.9	22	57	36	39	49	16	27	7	58	9	1	13	71	9	1	9	0	0	0	0	20	22	13	27	0
dozenal	3	.0000	.0449	26.5	0	3	0	0	0	0	0	0	0	0	0	0	3	0	0	0	0	0	0	0	0	0	0	0	0
dozens	82	.8309	13.632	51.3	7	12	15	13	21	8	5	1	10	5	3	3	6	15	1	5	0	1	1	0	0	7	9	16	0
dozes	2	.2160	.1362	31.3	1	0	0	1	0	0	0	0	1	0	0	0	0	0	0	1	0	0	0	0	0	0	0	0	0
dozing	17	.5249	1.9342	42.9	2	5	3	1	4	1	1	0	5	0	0	3	0	0	0	0	0	0	0	0	3	5	0	1	0
DPF	4	.0000	.0599	27.8	0	0	0	0	4	0	0	0	0	0	0	0	4	0	0	0	0	0	0	0	0	0	0	0	0
dr	16	.0586	.4125	36.2	5	2	8	1	0	0	0	0	3	0	0	0	0	0	13	0	0	0	0	0	0	0	0	0	0
Dr	409	.7905	65.224	58.1	30	68	70	54	84	43	36	24	82	14	5	33	0	18	6	30	4	0	1	0	30	81	16	89	0
DR	16	.0000	.1717	32.3	0	0	0	0	8	0	8	0	0	0	0	16	0	0	0	0	0	0	0	0	0	0	0	0	0
drab	12	.5523	1.3868	41.4	0	1	0	1	4	1	2	3	1	1	0	2	0	1	0	1	0	0	0	0	0	0	1	5	0
Drachenloch	2	.0000	.0209	23.2	0	0	0	0	2	0	0	0	0	0	0	0	0	0	0	0	0	0	0	0	0	0	2	0	0
Draco	3	.1910	.1473	31.7	0	0	0	0	1	2	0	0	0	0	0	0	0	1	0	0	0	0	0	0	2	0	0	0	0
draft	57	.7250	8.4851	49.3	4	15	11	3	11	4	7	2	19	9	0	2	0	3	0	1	0	0	0	1	3	2	8	9	0
drafted	10	.4015	.9027	39.6	0	0	2	0	0	3	4	1	1	0	0	0	0	5	0	0	0	0	0	0	0	0	1	3	0
drafting	8	.1537	.2817	34.5	0	0	0	0	3	1	4	0	0	0	0	0	0	0	0	0	0	0	0	5	0	0	1	2	0
drafts	13	.7087	1.8969	42.8	0	0	2	4	2	2	1	2	4	1	0	1	0	1	0	0	0	0	0	0	2	1	1	2	0
draftsman	10	.0598	.1646	32.2	0	0	0	0	1	1	8	0	0	0	0	0	2	0	0	0	0	0	0	8	0	0	0	0	0
draftsmen	7	.0998	.1752	32.4	0	0	1	0	2	1	3	0	0	0	0	0	1	0	0	0	0	0	0	5	0	1	0	0	0
drafty	4	.4485	.4009	36.0	0	0	0	0	1	2	0	1	1	0	0	0	0	1	0	0	0	0	0	0	0	0	1	1	0
drag	90	.7904	14.374	51.6	7	17	9	5	35	10	5	2	23	1	2	8	0	3	1	14	0	1	0	6	4	6	5	16	0
dragged	102	.7687	15.997	52.0	14	13	16	15	21	18	5	0	37	2	0	14	0	12	1	2	1	0	0	1	15	6	2	9	0
dragging	37	.6708	5.2216	47.2	5	6	5	6	5	5	2	3	17	1	0	4	0	1	0	3	0	0	0	0	4	2	0	5	0
draggled	2	.1787	.1174	30.7	0	1	0	0	0	1	0	0	1	0	0	0	0	0	0	0	0	0	0	0	1	0	0	0	0
dragon	174	.5047	20.704	53.2	36	4	8	114	6	3	2	1	144	1	0	5	0	0	0	2	4	0	0	0	1	11	0	6	0
Dragon	25	.0000	1.1421	40.6	0	2	2	21	0	0	0	0	25	0	0	0	0	0	0	0	0	0	0	0	0	0	0	0	0
dragon-fly	2	.2407	.1138	30.6	0	0	1	0	1	0	0	0	0	0	0	1	0	0	0	0	0	0	0	0	0	1	0	0	0
dragon's	8	.2089	.5834	37.7	3	0	0	4	0	0	1	0	7	0	0	0	0	0	0	0	0	0	0	1	0	0	0	0	0
Dragon's	2	.1698	.1133	30.5	0	0	0	1	1	0	0	0	1	0	0	0	0	0	0	0	0	0	0	0	0	0	1	0	0
dragonflies	15	.4348	1.5252	41.8	2	2	6	2	0	0	0	3	6	0	0	1	0	0	0	7	1	0	0	0	0	0	0	0	0
dragonfly	21	.5561	2.5046	44.0	12	1	5	0	3	0	0	0	4	0	0	1	1	0	0	11	0	0	0	0	1	1	2	0	0
dragons	26	.6133	3.4636	45.4	8	2	0	8	1	3	2	2	16	0	1	1	0	0	0	1	0	0	0	0	0	3	1	3	0
dragoon	6	.3640	.5364	37.3	0	2	0	0	3	1	0	0	3	0	0	0	0	0	0	0	1	0	0	0	2	0	0	0	0
dragoons	4	.2417	.3028	34.8	0	1	0	0	3	0	0	0	3	0	0	0	0	0	0	0	0	0	0	0	1	0	0	0	0
drags	19	.6790	2.7206	44.3	2	2	3	4	5	1	1	1	10	0	1	1	0	1	0	2	0	0	0	0	1	1	1	1	0
drain	43	.6625	5.8316	47.7	5	4	4	2	16	6	3	3	5	0	2	2	1	5	0	6	0	0	7	0	2	3	3	7	0
drainage	23	.5763	2.7615	44.4	0	1	0	1	6	8	3	4	0	0	0	1	1	8	0	5	0	0	0	0	0	0	4	4	0
drainboard	2	.1787	.1174	30.7	0	1	0	0	1	0	0	0	1	0	0	0	0	0	0	0	0	0	0	0	1	0	0	0	0

7A Doug's
7F dough-mixing
7R doughboy
8D Doughboy
7D doughtier
5Q doughy
5F douglas
8D DOUGLAS
8F Douglas'
7N Doune
7D Dourak
7F Douro
7F douse
9D dove-feathered
9B dove's
7P dovetail-dado
9P dovetailing
XR Dovie
8F Dowager
4R Dowdey's
9D dowdy
8D Dowdy
7N Dowgate
7Q dowitchers
7D Dowitt's
5J Dowland
6A DOWN
3J down-O
3H down-beat
4C down-hearted
5N down-stairs
9R down-to-pavement
9F down-under
7N Downdale
6A downdrafts
5A Downey
6R downgraded
4C downhearted
6A downing
6A downity
7A downthrust
7J downward-moving
8Q downwards
9Q Doxiadis'
7N doxies
4J Doyle
8G Doyle's
4B Doze's
9C Dozen
9R dozer
5B DP
7E DPG
3A drssed
8A drachma
6R Dracula
7R draft-card
7R draftees
9M Drafting
7A drag-line
5D draggin'
7D draggle
5Q dragline
5Q draglines
8B Dragnet
4N Dragon-Seal
6A dragon-cave
6A dragon-end
8F dragon-entwined
7F dragon-ships
9N dragon's-breath
XH dragonfly-like
6A dragonlet
7P dragons'

Word Type	F	D	U	SFI	3 Gr 3	4 Gr 4	5 Gr 5	6 Gr 6	7 Gr 7	8 Gr 8	9 Gr 9	X UnGr	A Read	B Eng & Gr	C Comp	D Lit	E Math	F Soc Stud	G Spell	H Sci	J Music	K Art	L Home Ec	M Shop	N Lib F	P Lib NF	Q Lib Ref	R Mag	S Rel
drained	54	.6331	7.0895	48.5	5	7	8	16	10	2	5	1	3	0	0	2	0	27	0	10	0	0	1	0	2	1	5	3	0
draining	14	.5689	1.6967	42.3	0	0	1	3	4	5	1	0	2	0	0	0	0	4	0	5	0	0	0	0	0	1	1	1	0
drainpipe	4	.2420	.3089	34.9	0	2	0	1	0	1	0	0	3	0	0	0	0	1	0	0	0	0	0	0	0	0	0	0	0
drainpipes	2	.0000	.0394	26.0	0	0	0	2	0	0	0	0	0	0	0	0	0	0	0	2	0	0	0	0	0	0	0	0	0
drains	13	.4666	1.3166	41.2	1	2	1	4	2	2	0	1	1	0	0	0	0	7	1	0	0	0	0	0	0	0	3	1	0
Drake	15	.4997	1.6143	42.1	0	5	1	0	7	2	0	0	2	0	0	0	0	4	0	0	0	0	0	0	2	2	0	5	0
Drakestail	12	.0000	.5482	37.4	12	0	0	0	0	0	0	0	12	0	0	0	0	0	0	0	0	0	0	0	0	0	0	0	0
dram	2	.0000	.0215	23.3	0	0	0	0	1	0	1	0	0	0	0	2	0	0	0	0	0	0	0	0	0	0	0	0	0
drama	84	.6683	11.387	50.6	3	11	2	11	17	15	20	5	4	4	0	10	0	7	0	2	26	2	0	0	0	8	12	9	0
Drama	8	.5585	.9275	39.7	3	0	0	0	1	1	2	1	0	0	0	1	0	3	0	0	1	0	0	0	0	0	1	2	0
dramas	9	.4956	.9694	39.9	0	2	1	0	2	3	0	1	2	0	0	0	0	2	0	0	1	0	0	0	0	1	3	0	0
dramatic	123	.7093	17.533	52.4	2	4	9	8	33	31	31	5	2	6	5	9	0	3	0	3	35	4	0	0	1	11	23	21	0
dramatically	16	.6704	2.1911	43.4	0	0	1	1	6	3	4	1	2	0	1	2	0	1	0	1	1	0	0	0	1	0	4	3	0
dramatics	7	.3716	.6740	38.3	0	1	0	4	0	2	0	0	5	1	0	0	0	0	0	1	0	0	0	0	0	0	0	0	0
dramatist	2	.0000	.0209	23.2	0	2	0	0	0	0	0	0	0	0	0	0	0	0	0	0	0	0	0	0	0	0	2	0	0
dramatists	7	.2626	.4201	36.2	0	5	1	0	0	1	0	0	0	0	0	0	0	1	0	0	1	0	0	0	0	0	5	0	0
Dramatists	2	.0000	.0243	23.9	0	0	0	0	0	0	0	2	0	0	0	0	0	0	0	0	0	0	0	0	0	0	0	2	0
dramatization	7	.3375	.5139	37.1	0	2	2	0	1	1	1	0	0	1	0	0	0	1	0	0	4	0	0	0	0	0	0	1	0
dramatize	9	.1940	.3979	36.0	0	2	3	3	0	0	1	0	0	0	0	0	0	0	0	0	8	0	1	0	0	0	0	0	0
dramatized	7	.3581	.5625	37.5	0	0	0	0	3	1	3	0	1	0	0	4	0	0	0	0	1	0	0	0	0	0	0	1	0
drank	106	.7145	15.591	51.9	28	10	8	16	22	13	8	1	34	5	0	17	7	5	0	2	1	0	0	0	18	10	0	7	0
drape	2	.2152	.1357	31.3	0	0	1	0	0	1	0	0	1	0	0	0	0	1	0	0	0	0	0	0	0	0	0	0	0
draped	15	.5843	1.8790	42.7	2	2	1	3	2	3	2	0	6	0	0	2	0	1	0	0	0	1	0	0	3	1	1	0	0
draperies	5	.4071	.4478	36.5	1	0	0	0	1	1	2	0	1	0	0	0	0	1	0	0	0	1	1	0	0	0	1	0	0
drapery	5	.3750	.4058	36.1	0	0	1	2	1	0	0	1	0	1	0	0	0	2	1	0	0	1	0	0	0	0	0	0	0
drapes	13	.5557	1.6018	42.0	3	4	3	2	0	1	0	0	7	0	0	0	0	3	1	0	0	0	0	0	1	0	0	1	0
drastic	11	.4362	1.0308	40.1	0	0	1	0	3	4	2	1	0	0	1	0	0	5	0	0	0	0	0	0	0	1	4	0	0
drastically	8	.3805	.6483	38.1	1	0	0	2	4	1	0	0	0	0	0	0	0	0	0	0	0	0	0	1	0	0	4	3	0
drat	2	.1787	.1174	30.7	0	1	1	0	0	0	0	0	1	0	0	0	0	0	0	0	0	0	0	0	1	0	0	0	0
Drat	11	.0000	.5025	37.0	0	11	0	0	0	0	0	0	11	0	0	0	0	0	0	0	0	0	0	0	0	0	0	0	0
draught	9	.3672	.8061	39.1	3	0	1	3	0	2	0	0	4	0	0	2	0	0	0	0	0	0	0	0	0	3	0	0	0
draughtsman	2	.0000	.0290	24.6	0	0	0	0	2	0	0	0	0	0	0	0	0	0	0	0	0	0	0	0	0	2	0	0	0
Dravidians	2	.0000	.0389	25.9	0	0	0	0	2	0	0	0	0	0	0	0	0	2	0	0	0	0	0	0	0	0	0	0	0
draw	1623	.7391	242.66	63.9	426	250	206	219	203	160	148	11	230	60	9	16	620	43	324	50	10	98	13	69	14	32	12	20	3
drawback	2	.1717	.1142	30.6	0	0	0	1	0	0	1	0	1	0	0	1	0	0	0	0	0	0	0	0	0	0	0	0	0
drawbridge	10	.5522	1.2130	40.8	2	4	1	2	0	0	1	0	5	1	0	0	0	0	1	0	0	0	0	0	2	1	0	0	0
drawbridges	2	.0000	.0209	23.2	0	0	0	0	1	0	1	0	0	0	0	0	0	0	0	0	0	0	0	0	0	0	2	0	0
drawer	42	.7190	6.1842	47.9	4	10	4	3	9	5	7	0	12	9	0	1	1	1	0	1	0	0	3	1	6	4	0	3	0
drawers	28	.6078	3.4980	45.4	1	4	4	5	8	1	5	0	4	2	1	1	0	0	0	0	0	0	4	3	11	1	1	0	0
drawing	563	.5035	59.221	57.7	29	104	86	58	102	46	131	7	57	11	1	13	83	58	9	30	14	96	5	144	17	11	7	7	0
Drawing	2	.0000	.0299	24.8	2	0	0	0	0	0	0	0	0	0	0	0	2	0	0	0	0	0	0	0	0	0	0	0	0
drawing-room	2	.0000	.0914	29.6	0	0	0	2	0	0	0	0	2	0	0	0	0	0	0	0	0	0	0	0	0	0	0	0	0
drawings	262	.4766	26.239	54.2	19	48	18	20	67	15	69	6	26	4	0	1	24	43	4	13	0	26	1	100	1	3	9	6	1
drawknife	2	.0000	.0050	17.0	0	0	0	0	0	0	2	0	0	0	0	0	0	0	0	0	0	0	0	2	0	0	0	0	0
drawl	7	.4738	.7332	38.7	0	3	1	1	0	1	1	0	2	0	0	0	0	1	0	0	0	0	1	0	1	2	0	0	0
drawled	3	.1250	.1342	31.3	1	0	1	0	1	0	0	0	1	0	0	0	0	0	0	0	0	0	0	0	2	0	0	0	0
Drawling	3	.0000	.0328	25.2	0	0	3	0	0	0	0	0	0	3	0	0	0	0	0	0	0	0	0	0	0	0	0	0	0
Drawling-master	3	.0000	.0328	25.2	0	0	3	0	0	0	0	0	0	3	0	0	0	0	0	0	0	0	0	0	0	0	0	0	0
drawn	344	.7253	50.575	57.0	27	50	34	37	79	44	59	14	49	7	0	11	44	43	6	19	10	23	6	44	12	27	19	24	0
draws	43	.8524	7.3092	48.6	7	4	4	4	9	6	8	1	6	2	0	4	5	1	1	5	6	1	1	0	1	1	4	5	0
drawstring	8	.2187	.6050	37.8	7	1	0	0	0	0	0	0	7	0	0	0	0	0	0	0	0	0	0	0	0	1	0	0	0
Drdla's	2	.0000	.0914	29.6	0	0	0	2	0	0	0	0	2	0	0	0	0	0	0	0	0	0	0	0	0	0	0	0	0
dread	29	.7236	4.3249	46.4	0	4	3	2	11	4	3	2	11	1	0	6	0	2	0	1	2	0	0	0	2	2	1	1	0
dreaded	24	.6674	3.3440	45.2	1	4	0	3	7	6	3	0	8	1	0	4	0	3	0	2	0	0	0	0	4	1	0	1	0
dreadful	53	.7023	7.6590	48.8	2	9	5	16	6	6	8	1	16	0	2	11	0	0	2	2	1	0	0	0	10	6	1	2	0
dreadfully	14	.3036	1.0178	40.1	0	4	5	0	2	0	3	0	3	0	0	4	0	0	0	0	0	0	0	0	7	0	0	0	0
dreads	3	.3465	.2515	34.0	1	0	0	0	1	0	1	0	1	0	0	0	0	0	0	0	0	0	0	0	0	1	0	1	0
dream	232	.8364	39.044	55.9	36	37	19	31	60	20	26	3	77	6	0	35	5	16	1	19	12	0	1	1	20	17	5	17	0
Dream	10	.6993	1.4311	41.6	0	1	1	3	3	1	0	1	2	0	0	2	0	1	0	0	1	0	0	0	1	1	1	1	0
dream-boat	2	.0000	.0914	29.6	0	0	0	0	2	0	0	0	2	0	0	0	0	0	0	0	0	0	0	0	0	0	0	0	0
dreamed	95	.8307	15.950	52.0	19	17	13	14	13	7	6	6	40	2	3	2	2	11	2	8	1	0	1	0	3	12	1	7	0
dreamer	8	.5107	.8838	39.5	0	1	0	2	3	1	1	0	2	0	0	1	0	1	0	1	0	1	0	0	1	0	1	0	0
Dreamer	3	.2378	.1809	32.6	0	3	0	0	0	0	0	0	0	0	0	0	0	2	0	0	0	0	0	0	0	1	0	0	0
dreamers	3	.3394	.2470	33.9	0	1	0	0	0	0	2	0	1	0	0	0	1	0	0	0	0	0	0	0	0	0	1	0	0
dreamily	10	.3841	.9513	39.8	1	3	0	2	3	0	1	0	6	0	0	2	0	0	0	0	0	0	0	0	2	0	0	0	0
dreaming	67	.7740	10.581	50.2	7	15	8	12	19	2	2	2	25	0	1	5	0	3	0	10	2	0	0	0	10	5	2	4	0
dreamland	6	.2217	.3130	35.0	3	0	0	1	1	1	0	0	0	0	0	0	0	1	0	0	4	0	0	0	0	1	0	0	0
dreamless	2	.1787	.1174	30.7	0	0	1	1	0	0	0	0	1	0	0	0	0	0	0	0	0	0	0	0	1	0	0	0	0
dreams	139	.8370	23.409	53.7	18	17	14	16	39	8	22	5	50	6	5	22	3	4	1	9	9	1	1	0	4	17	3	4	0
Dreams	3	.2330	.1860	32.7	0	0	0	0	3	0	0	0	1	0	0	0	0	0	0	0	0	0	1	0	0	1	0	0	0
dreamt	3	.2261	.2131	33.3	0	0	0	2	1	0	0	0	2	0	0	0	0	0	0	0	0	0	0	0	1	0	0	0	0
dreamy	11	.6747	1.5615	41.9	0	1	1	3	4	2	0	0	5	0	0	1	0	1	0	1	0	0	0	0	1	1	0	1	0
drearily	2	.1787	.1174	30.7	0	0	1	0	1	0	0	0	1	0	0	0	0	0	0	0	0	0	0	0	1	0	0	0	0
dreary	19	.6092	2.3920	43.8	1	4	0	1	6	1	5	1	3	2	2	4	0	0	1	0	0	0	0	0	4	1	0	2	0
Dred	10	.1990	.5389	37.3	0	0	1	0	2	7	0	0	0	0	0	0	0	8	0	0	0	0	0	0	0	2	0	0	0
dredge	4	.2932	.2861	34.6	0	0	2	0	2	0	0	0	1	0	0	0	0	0	0	0	0	0	0	0	0	0	2	1	0
dredged	5	.3806	.4395	36.4	1	0	1	1	2	0	0	0	1	0	0	0	0	1	0	1	0	0	0	0	0	0	2	0	0
dredges	4	.3730	.3365	35.3	0	0	2	2	0	0	0	0	0	0	0	0	0	2	0	1	0	0	0	0	0	0	1	0	0
dredging	6	.4494	.5803	37.6	0	0	0	3	0	2	0	1	0	0	0	0	0	2	0	1	0	0	0	0	0	0	2	1	0
Dregg's	2	.0000	.0914	29.6	0	0	0	2	0	0	0	0	2	0	0	0	0	0	0	0	0	0	0	0	0	0	0	0	0
Drem	4	.0000	.1827	32.6	0	0	0	0	4	0	0	0	4	0	0	0	0	0	0	0	0	0	0	0	0	0	0	0	0
drench	2	.2446	.1257	31.0	0	1	0	0	1	0	0	0	0	0	0	0	0	1	0	1	0	0	0	0	0	0	0	0	0
drenched	6	.4808	.6600	38.2	0	0	0	2	1	2	1	0	3	0	0	1	0	1	0	0	0	0	0	0	0	0	0	1	0
drenching	3	.2223	.2106	33.2	0	0	0	2	0	0	1	0	2	1	0	0	0	0	0	0	0	0	0	0	0	0	0	0	0
Dresden	7	.4665	.6914	38.4	0	1	0	3	0	3	0	0	0	0	0	0	0	3	1	0	2	0	0	0	0	0	1	0	0
dress	396	.7886	63.056	58.0	124	41	45	40	73	33	39	1	109	24	7	26	9	36	21	10	18	5	55	1	37	19	7	12	0
dressed	310	.8239	51.675	57.1	87	63	26	34	44	31	22	3	140	11	4	20	0	21	0	3	8	1	16	0	28	31	9	18	0
dressed-up	3	.0000	.1370	31.4	0	1	0	0	2	0	0	0	3	0	0	0	0	0	0	0	0	0	0	0	0	0	0	0	0
dresser	30	.5566	3.5537	45.5	6	7	6	1	0	6	4	0	8	0	0	2	0	0	0	0	0	0	2	0	11	3	0	4	0
Dresser	2	.2433	.1158	30.6	0	1	0	1	0	0	0	0	0	0	0	0	0	0	0	0	0	0	0	0	0	1	0	1	0
dresses	82	.7399	12.337	50.9	25	16	9	6	16	5	5	0	16	2	0	10	12	11	0	2	2	0	7	0	5	9	0	6	0
dressing	72	.2995	5.0586	47.0	3	8	3	4	32	7	11	4	17	0	0	3	0	0	0	3	2	0	32	0	6	3	1	5	0
Dressing	2	.0000	.0064	18.1	0	0	0	0	0	2	0	0	0	0	0	0	0	0	0	0	0	0	2	0	0	0	0	0	0
dressings	19	.0283	.2223	33.5	0	0	1	0	7	1	10	0	1	0	0	0	0	0	0	1	0	0	17	0	0	0	0	0	0
dressmaker	9	.3452	.6956	38.4	3	0	0	2	0	0	4	0	2	0	3	0	1	0	0	0	0	0	2	0	0	0	1	0	0
dressmaker's	2	.0000	.0064	18.1	0	0	0	0	0	0	2	0	0	0	0	0	0	0	0	0	0	0	2	0	0	0	0	0	0

XR drakes
5D drakes'
7A dram-house
6J dramatizations
8J dramatizes
7B dramatizing
XQ Drapers'
9L draping
7A draps
7F Drava
4N Dravidian
6P DRAW
8R drawbacks
4N drawed
7N drawing-pencils
9D drawing-rooms
5Q drawling
3P DRAWN-OUT
7A drawn-out
5H drawn-up
7R drawnout
6A Drdla
8D drea(chipmunk)ming
9Q Dreadful
7A dreading
8J Dreadnaught
8K dream-perfect
7R dreamboat
5A dreamful
9R dreaming-spired
7D dreamlike
4J drear
7A dreariness
5Q Dredges
6A Dreggs'
6A dregs
6A drei
7A Drem's
5R Dreser
6A Dress
3N dress-up
3A dress-ups
9D dressers
7D dressing-gown
3N dressing-room
3A dressmakers
9R dressmaking

Word Type	F	D	U	SFI	3 Gr 3	4 Gr 4	5 Gr 5	6 Gr 6	7 Gr 7	8 Gr 8	9 Gr 9	X UnGr	A Read	B Eng & Gr	C Comp	D Lit	E Math	F Soc Stud	G Spell	H Sci	J Music	K Art	L Home Ec	M Shop	N Lib F	P Lib NF	Q Lib Ref	R Mag	S Rel
dressy	3	.0524	.0803	29.0	1	0	0	0	1	1	0	0	1	0	0	0	0	0	0	0	0	0	2	0	0	0	0	0	0
drew	361	.7045	52.093	57.2	77	54	40	53	79	41	17	0	90	12	4	42	23	23	4	4	7	36	0	2	50	38	15	11	0
Drew	7	.1093	.2329	33.7	0	6	0	0	1	0	0	0	0	0	0	0	0	0	0	1	0	0	0	0	0	0	0	6	0
dreydl	3	.0000	.0243	23.8	0	0	3	0	0	0	0	0	0	0	0	0	0	0	0	0	3	0	0	0	0	0	0	0	0
dribble	12	.4998	1.3059	41.2	1	1	1	0	8	0	1	0	3	1	0	0	0	0	0	0	0	0	0	0	2	5	1	0	0
dribbled	5	.3361	.4093	36.1	0	0	3	0	1	1	0	0	2	1	1	0	0	0	0	0	0	0	0	0	0	1	0	0	0
dribbles	2	.0000	.0290	24.6	0	0	0	0	2	0	0	0	0	0	0	0	0	0	0	0	0	0	0	0	0	2	0	0	0
dribbling	5	.3181	.3528	35.5	0	1	0	0	1	1	2	0	0	3	0	0	0	0	0	0	0	0	0	0	1	1	0	0	0
dried	218	.8522	37.163	55.7	54	34	28	30	29	16	19	8	53	3	1	15	0	29	4	13	5	5	18	3	22	20	18	9	0
dried-out	2	.1814	.1187	30.7	0	0	0	0	2	0	0	0	1	0	0	0	0	0	0	0	0	0	0	0	0	0	0	1	0
dried-up	8	.4677	.8475	39.3	1	2	0	2	3	0	0	0	3	0	0	1	0	0	0	2	0	0	0	0	2	0	0	0	0
drier	23	.5404	2.6382	44.2	1	4	3	1	9	2	3	0	2	0	0	0	0	12	0	1	0	0	0	1	1	1	5	0	0
dries	26	.6210	3.4290	45.4	13	4	0	2	2	0	2	3	8	0	0	0	0	4	0	9	0	0	0	1	1	2	0	1	0
driest	8	.3921	.7161	38.6	1	1	3	1	2	0	0	0	1	0	0	0	0	4	0	1	0	0	0	0	0	0	2	0	0
drift	71	.8079	11.583	50.6	2	14	13	8	15	9	10	0	19	0	1	5	1	7	0	11	1	0	0	0	6	6	7	7	0
Drift	3	.0000	.0583	27.7	0	0	0	3	0	0	0	0	0	0	0	0	0	3	0	0	0	0	0	0	0	0	0	0	0
drifted	78	.7324	11.821	50.7	13	10	6	10	23	9	6	1	38	4	3	10	1	5	0	0	1	0	0	0	4	8	1	3	0
drifting	40	.7229	5.9578	47.8	5	2	5	7	9	7	4	1	16	2	2	7	0	1	0	0	0	1	0	0	1	5	3	2	0
drifts	23	.6074	2.9592	44.7	2	7	2	1	7	3	0	1	7	0	2	1	0	3	0	4	0	0	0	0	0	2	3	1	0
driftwood	16	.4816	1.7243	42.4	1	5	1	4	3	1	1	0	6	0	0	5	0	2	0	0	0	0	0	0	0	1	0	2	0
drill	136	.6333	17.617	52.5	20	7	17	5	47	23	17	0	12	8	1	10	2	8	5	15	12	1	0	27	1	15	2	17	0
Drill	3	.2411	.1667	32.2	0	0	1	0	2	0	0	0	0	0	0	0	0	0	0	0	1	0	0	0	0	0	0	2	0
DRILL	2	.0000	.0290	24.6	2	0	0	0	0	0	0	0	0	0	0	0	0	0	0	0	0	0	0	0	0	2	0	0	0
drilled	45	.5647	5.2860	47.2	3	8	5	3	12	9	4	1	3	0	0	0	0	12	0	2	0	1	0	7	0	5	8	7	0
driller	2	.2128	.1055	30.2	0	1	1	0	0	0	0	0	0	0	0	0	0	0	0	1	1	0	0	0	0	0	0	0	0
drilling	33	.5224	3.5885	45.5	2	8	2	3	6	4	6	2	0	0	0	1	0	8	0	2	1	0	0	6	0	6	3	6	0
drills	27	.6205	3.4272	45.3	2	0	3	3	6	7	5	1	2	2	0	1	0	3	2	1	2	0	0	5	1	2	3	3	0
drink	347	.8842	61.229	57.9	99	52	44	39	56	25	27	5	108	10	5	23	4	17	10	40	5	1	13	0	26	57	10	18	0
Drinker	4	.1750	.1896	32.8	3	0	1	0	0	0	0	0	0	0	0	0	0	0	0	1	0	0	0	0	0	3	0	0	0
drinkers	2	.2405	.1205	30.8	1	0	0	0	0	0	1	0	0	0	0	0	0	0	0	1	0	0	0	0	0	1	0	0	0
drinkin'	2	.0000	.0219	23.4	0	0	0	0	0	2	0	0	0	2	0	0	0	0	0	0	0	0	0	0	0	0	0	0	0
drinking	136	.8172	22.412	53.5	22	19	17	18	23	15	20	2	33	7	1	10	1	14	0	40	2	0	3	0	8	12	1	4	0
drinks	60	.6123	7.5982	48.8	8	8	1	4	9	13	14	3	6	0	1	10	5	7	0	11	0	0	10	0	0	5	0	5	0
drip	29	.7875	4.6215	46.6	3	5	8	2	5	4	1	1	7	1	0	3	0	0	0	9	1	0	1	1	1	2	1	2	0
dripped	13	.5994	1.6480	42.2	2	2	3	0	4	0	2	0	4	2	0	1	0	0	0	0	0	0	0	0	3	2	0	1	0
dripping	48	.8010	7.7572	48.9	7	11	11	4	6	6	2	1	13	3	3	2	0	0	0	10	2	1	1	1	8	0	2	2	0
drippings	7	.0741	.1774	32.5	0	1	0	0	1	3	2	0	1	0	0	0	0	0	0	1	0	0	5	0	0	0	0	0	0
drips	2	.2405	.1205	30.8	1	0	1	0	0	0	0	0	0	0	0	0	0	0	0	1	0	0	0	0	0	1	0	0	0
Driscoll	8	.0000	.3655	35.6	0	0	0	0	2	6	0	0	8	0	0	0	0	0	0	0	0	0	0	0	0	0	0	0	0
Driss	4	.0000	.1827	32.6	0	0	0	4	0	0	0	0	4	0	0	0	0	0	0	0	0	0	0	0	0	0	0	0	0
drive	543	.8994	97.225	59.9	67	75	53	51	173	74	40	10	160	39	2	36	27	69	2	13	9	2	2	4	48	47	17	66	0
Drive	8	.5938	.9908	40.0	3	0	1	1	3	0	0	0	1	1	0	1	0	2	0	0	0	0	0	0	0	0	1	2	0
drive-in	8	.4973	.8627	39.4	1	2	4	0	1	0	0	0	1	0	0	0	1	4	0	0	0	0	0	0	0	0	1	1	0
driven	174	.8551	29.727	54.7	11	25	18	30	49	19	14	8	28	17	0	10	12	31	1	16	1	0	0	3	17	15	12	11	0
driver	305	.8532	52.466	57.2	60	38	11	38	87	30	31	10	151	5	2	17	7	20	3	21	2	0	0	1	20	25	11	20	0
Driver	4	.0000	.0469	26.7	0	0	3	0	1	0	0	0	0	0	0	0	0	0	0	0	0	0	0	0	4	0	0	0	0
driver's	40	.6554	5.5229	47.4	4	5	1	8	13	5	3	1	17	1	0	3	1	1	0	2	0	0	0	0	9	2	0	4	0
Driver's	3	.0000	.0352	25.5	0	0	3	0	0	0	0	0	0	0	0	0	0	0	0	0	0	0	0	0	3	0	0	0	0
drivers	127	.8082	20.866	53.2	12	7	10	18	29	33	16	2	56	4	1	5	3	19	0	7	1	0	0	0	5	14	2	10	0
drivers'	2	.1814	.1187	30.7	0	0	0	1	1	0	0	0	1	0	0	0	0	0	0	0	0	0	0	0	0	0	0	1	0
drives	67	.8879	11.839	50.7	10	12	8	9	16	4	3	5	13	9	0	3	3	10	2	5	1	0	1	1	2	5	4	8	0
driveshaft	5	.0000	.0986	29.9	0	0	1	0	0	4	0	0	0	0	0	0	0	0	0	5	0	0	0	0	0	0	0	0	0
driveway	33	.7101	4.8680	46.9	6	5	1	4	8	5	4	0	15	2	1	2	1	2	0	0	0	0	0	0	5	1	0	4	0
driveways	3	.1910	.1473	31.7	1	0	0	1	0	1	0	0	0	0	0	0	0	1	0	0	0	0	0	0	2	0	0	0	0
driving	248	.8359	41.763	56.2	20	41	17	22	83	47	11	7	95	5	2	19	9	9	2	7	7	0	0	2	25	21	4	41	0
Driving	2	.0000	.0914	29.6	0	2	0	0	0	0	0	0	2	0	0	0	0	0	0	0	0	0	0	0	0	0	0	0	0
drizzle	6	.2657	.3970	36.0	0	3	0	0	1	2	0	0	1	0	0	0	0	0	0	0	0	0	0	0	0	4	1	0	0
drone	11	.4434	1.0543	40.2	1	0	2	2	2	1	1	2	1	1	0	0	0	0	0	3	4	0	0	0	0	0	0	2	0
droned	5	.4252	.4674	36.7	0	0	0	0	3	1	1	0	1	1	0	2	0	0	1	0	0	0	0	0	0	0	0	0	0
drones	12	.3278	.9667	39.9	5	3	0	4	0	0	0	0	3	0	0	0	0	0	0	4	0	0	0	0	0	5	0	0	0
droning	6	.2435	.4680	36.7	1	1	1	1	2	0	0	0	5	0	0	1	0	0	0	0	0	0	0	0	0	0	0	0	0
droop	12	.6258	1.5462	41.9	1	3	2	0	3	2	0	1	1	0	0	1	0	0	0	3	1	1	0	0	2	2	1	0	0
drooped	14	.5492	1.7063	42.3	4	1	2	2	4	1	0	0	8	1	0	2	0	0	0	0	0	0	0	0	2	0	0	1	0
drooping	19	.5978	2.4155	43.8	1	6	5	1	4	2	0	0	7	2	0	3	0	0	0	0	0	0	0	0	4	1	2	0	0
droops	4	.3812	.3773	35.8	2	1	1	0	0	0	0	0	2	0	0	0	0	0	0	1	0	0	0	0	0	1	0	0	0
droopy	3	.3399	.2456	33.9	1	0	0	1	0	1	0	0	1	0	0	1	0	0	0	0	0	0	0	0	0	0	0	1	0
drop	433	.8527	73.860	58.7	71	92	69	58	72	28	31	12	81	9	1	14	9	21	56	139	4	5	5	2	22	24	12	29	0
dropback	3	.0000	.0365	25.6	0	0	0	3	0	0	0	0	0	0	0	0	0	0	0	0	0	0	0	0	0	0	0	3	0
droplet	5	.0000	.0986	29.9	0	3	0	0	0	0	2	0	0	0	0	0	0	0	0	5	0	0	0	0	0	0	0	0	0
droplets	48	.3962	4.3382	46.4	5	16	1	3	9	0	14	0	5	1	0	0	0	0	0	32	0	0	0	0	0	5	5	0	0
dropout	5	.0000	.0608	27.8	0	0	1	0	2	1	1	0	0	0	0	0	0	0	0	0	0	0	0	0	0	0	0	5	0
dropped	427	.8587	73.682	58.7	73	78	59	62	64	57	31	3	184	11	6	18	8	27	36	20	4	1	0	1	45	37	5	24	0
dropper	23	.3272	1.8244	42.6	3	5	6	2	1	4	1	1	3	0	0	0	0	1	0	18	0	1	0	0	0	0	0	0	0
droppers	2	.0000	.0394	26.0	0	1	1	0	0	0	0	0	0	0	0	0	0	0	0	2	0	0	0	0	0	0	0	0	0
dropping	67	.8310	11.224	50.5	10	5	12	11	15	6	7	1	26	5	2	3	0	1	5	5	0	1	0	0	7	5	3	4	0
droppings	6	.4206	.5584	37.5	0	0	1	0	3	1	0	1	1	0	0	0	0	0	0	0	0	0	0	0	0	2	2	1	0
drops	234	.8122	38.346	55.8	80	40	20	32	22	15	20	5	51	3	2	10	3	12	0	104	5	3	6	1	4	17	5	8	0
Drosophila	4	.2278	.2257	33.5	0	0	0	0	1	0	0	3	0	0	0	0	0	0	0	2	0	0	0	0	0	0	2	0	0
Drosselmeyer	2	.0000	.0162	22.1	2	0	0	0	0	0	0	0	0	0	0	0	0	0	0	0	2	0	0	0	0	0	0	0	0
drought	22	.7172	3.2351	45.1	2	1	1	6	5	3	3	1	5	0	1	3	0	5	0	3	1	0	0	0	0	1	2	1	0
droughts	4	.2947	.2869	34.6	1	2	0	0	1	0	0	0	1	0	0	0	0	0	0	0	0	0	0	0	1	0	2	0	0
drouth	3	.2261	.2131	33.3	2	0	0	0	1	0	0	0	2	0	0	0	0	0	0	0	0	0	0	0	1	0	0	0	0
drove	361	.8362	60.811	57.8	61	56	42	34	93	45	25	5	135	12	4	36	18	36	3	1	7	0	0	1	50	24	8	26	0
droves	2	.0000	.0290	24.6	0	0	2	0	0	0	0	0	0	0	0	0	0	0	0	0	0	0	0	0	0	2	0	0	0
drown	29	.6734	4.0992	46.1	4	6	4	6	4	2	2	1	13	0	0	4	0	1	2	2	0	0	0	0	1	2	0	4	0
drowned	64	.7068	9.2849	49.7	12	12	9	15	9	1	3	3	18	1	1	4	0	1	1	0	3	0	0	0	20	3	3	9	0
drowning	11	.3891	1.0186	40.1	3	0	0	3	1	2	0	2	5	0	2	0	0	1	0	0	0	0	0	0	1	1	0	1	0
drowsily	5	.3854	.4790	36.8	2	1	0	2	0	0	0	0	3	0	0	0	0	0	0	0	0	0	0	0	1	1	0	0	0
drowsing	3	.3394	.2451	33.9	1	0	0	1	1	0	0	0	1	0	0	1	0	0	0	0	0	0	0	0	1	0	0	0	0
drowsy	20	.6993	2.9187	44.7	1	6	2	3	3	3	1	1	10	1	1	2	0	1	0	0	1	0	0	0	0	1	2	1	0
drubbing	3	.2060	.1500	31.8	0	0	0	0	1	0	2	0	0	0	0	2	0	0	0	0	0	0	0	0	0	1	0	0	0
drudge	2	.1814	.1187	30.7	0	1	0	1	0	0	0	0	1	0	0	0	0	0	0	0	0	0	0	0	0	0	0	1	0
drudgery	5	.5334	.5711	37.6	0	0	0	0	1	0	4	0	1	0	0	1	0	1	0	0	0	0	0	0	0	1	1	0	0
drug	59	.5514	6.8484	48.4	2	1	5	5	28	3	11	4	4	1	0	0	2	2	0	20	0	0	0	0	3	1	4	22	0
Drug	11	.4581	1.1287	40.5	0	0	0	1	4	4	2	0	2	0	0	0	0	1	0	6	0	0	0	0	1	1	0	0	0
drugged	3	.3406	.2461	33.9	0	0	0	1	1	1	0	0	1	1	0	0	0	0	0	0	0	0	0	0	0	0	0	1	0

4R Drew's
9L dried-fruit
6F dried-mud
7A drier's
8M driers
8R drifter
7D drifters
7D driftin'
7Q Drilling
XR drinkable
8F drinker
9D Drinking
4A drip-drip
7R drippy
6A Driss'
8H driverless
7R driveshafts
9D driveth
4R Drivotrainers
7Q drizzling
8J Dromadaire
7N dronings
7D drool
7R drooled
3N drooling
6P DROOP
7B droopy-headed
6A drop-the-handkerchief
3F dropouts
5H dropsonde
8Q dropsy
4R droshkies
XP droshky
9D dross
6A Drouillard
5J drover
6B drowns
XR Drs
9D drub
8F drubbed
4R drudging
8R drug-company
7R drug-taking

Word Type	F	D	U	SFI	3 Gr 3	4 Gr 4	5 Gr 5	6 Gr 6	7 Gr 7	8 Gr 8	9 Gr 9	X UnGr	A Read	B Eng & Gr	C Comp	D Lit	E Math	F Soc Stud	G Spell	H Sci	J Music	K Art	L Home Ec	M Shop	N Lib F	P Lib NF	Q Lib Ref	R Mag	S Rel
druggist	3	.0000	.0449	26.5	0	0	0	2	0	0	1	0	0	0	0	0	3	0	0	0	0	0	0	0	0	0	0	0	0
druggists	2	.0000	.0389	25.9	0	0	0	0	0	1	1	0	0	0	0	0	0	2	0	0	0	0	0	0	0	0	0	0	0
drugs	96	.5929	11.792	50.7	1	10	9	6	29	18	16	7	1	0	0	1	0	9	2	36	0	0	3	0	0	2	10	32	0
Drugs	2	.2346	.1166	30.7	0	0	0	1	0	0	0	1	0	0	0	0	0	0	0	1	0	0	0	0	0	0	0	1	0
drugstore	50	.7444	7.6538	48.8	14	7	2	7	9	5	6	0	21	3	1	6	0	6	0	3	0	0	3	0	4	1	0	2	0
Drugstore	3	.0000	.0352	25.5	3	0	0	0	0	0	0	0	0	0	0	0	0	0	0	0	0	0	0	0	3	0	0	0	0
drugstores	4	.3741	.3712	35.7	0	0	1	2	1	0	0	0	2	0	0	0	0	0	0	1	0	0	0	0	0	0	0	1	0
Druids	2	.2437	.1129	30.5	0	0	1	0	0	0	0	1	0	0	0	0	0	0	0	0	0	0	0	0	0	0	1	1	0
drum	194	.4997	20.489	53.1	40	36	15	29	37	24	10	3	26	3	0	4	1	0	3	11	98	1	0	0	13	4	8	22	0
Drum	9	.4467	.9284	39.7	2	0	1	4	0	2	0	0	4	0	0	0	0	2	0	0	2	0	0	0	0	0	0	1	0
drumbeat	3	.3668	.2408	33.8	1	0	0	1	0	1	0	0	0	1	0	0	0	0	0	1	1	0	0	0	0	0	0	0	0
drumhead	8	.3356	.6039	37.8	3	0	0	0	4	0	1	0	0	0	0	0	0	0	0	4	3	0	0	0	1	0	0	0	0
drumlin	6	.0000	.1183	30.7	0	0	0	0	0	0	6	0	0	0	0	0	0	0	0	6	0	0	0	0	0	0	0	0	0
drumlins	6	.0000	.1183	30.7	0	0	0	0	0	0	6	0	0	0	0	0	0	0	0	6	0	0	0	0	0	0	0	0	0
drummed	6	.4521	.6070	37.8	2	1	1	1	1	0	0	0	2	0	0	0	0	0	0	0	1	0	0	0	2	0	0	1	0
drummer	24	.3002	1.7798	42.5	6	8	1	3	4	2	0	0	8	0	0	0	0	0	0	1	12	0	0	0	2	1	0	0	0
drummers	6	.3182	.4441	36.5	1	1	0	1	2	0	0	1	1	0	0	0	0	1	0	0	3	0	0	0	1	0	0	0	0
drumming	9	.3965	.8406	39.2	1	0	2	3	2	1	0	0	4	0	0	0	0	0	0	0	3	0	0	0	1	0	0	1	0
Drummond	5	.2446	.3872	35.9	1	0	4	0	0	0	0	0	4	0	0	0	0	0	0	0	0	0	0	0	1	0	0	0	0
drums	128	.5251	14.180	51.5	15	19	16	25	33	13	4	3	20	3	0	18	1	7	0	1	54	0	0	0	6	6	2	10	0
drumsticks	3	.0000	.1370	31.4	1	1	0	1	0	0	0	0	3	0	0	0	0	0	0	0	0	0	0	0	0	0	0	0	0
drunk	29	.6858	4.0640	46.1	1	0	4	3	10	5	6	0	5	2	1	8	2	0	2	0	0	0	0	0	6	2	0	1	0
drunkard	3	.3766	.2497	34.0	0	0	0	0	1	1	1	0	0	0	0	0	0	1	0	0	0	0	0	0	0	1	1	0	0
drunken	7	.4787	.7158	38.5	0	0	0	0	5	1	0	1	1	0	0	3	0	0	0	0	1	0	0	0	1	0	0	1	0
drunkenness	4	.4802	.4049	36.1	0	0	1	0	1	1	1	0	0	0	0	1	0	1	0	0	0	0	0	0	0	0	1	1	0
drupe	3	.0000	.0314	25.0	0	0	0	3	0	0	0	0	0	0	0	0	0	0	0	0	0	0	0	0	0	0	3	0	0
druther	2	.1787	.1174	30.7	0	0	0	0	2	0	0	0	1	0	0	0	0	0	0	0	0	0	0	0	1	0	0	0	0
dry	993	.8927	176.46	62.5	226	186	113	133	149	82	76	28	208	12	8	43	1	183	10	212	17	16	41	19	49	80	49	45	0
Dry	7	.4293	.6438	38.1	0	0	0	0	3	0	4	0	0	0	1	2	0	0	0	3	0	0	0	0	0	0	1	0	0
dry-cell	2	.0000	.0394	26.0	0	0	0	2	0	0	0	0	0	0	0	0	0	0	0	2	0	0	0	0	0	0	0	0	0
dry-cleaning	4	.1995	.2197	33.4	1	0	0	0	0	0	3	0	0	0	0	0	0	1	0	3	0	0	0	0	0	0	0	0	0
dry-goods	3	.2387	.1708	32.3	0	2	0	0	0	0	1	0	0	0	0	0	0	0	0	0	0	0	0	0	0	2	1	0	0
dry-heat	3	.0000	.0097	19.8	0	0	0	0	0	0	3	0	0	0	0	0	0	0	0	0	0	0	3	0	0	0	0	0	0
dry-sand	3	.0000	.0076	18.8	0	0	0	0	0	0	3	0	0	0	0	0	0	0	0	0	0	0	0	3	0	0	0	0	0
drydock	2	.0000	.0209	23.2	1	0	0	0	0	1	0	0	0	0	0	0	0	0	0	0	0	0	0	0	0	0	2	0	0
dryer	8	.5060	.8363	39.2	2	0	0	0	1	0	4	1	0	0	0	0	0	0	0	1	2	0	1	0	0	0	3	1	0
dryers	12	.3418	.8871	39.5	0	0	0	0	1	2	1	8	0	0	0	0	0	0	0	0	0	0	0	2	0	0	2	8	0
drying	57	.6354	7.5681	48.8	14	7	6	6	10	5	5	4	15	0	0	4	0	7	0	10	0	0	1	7	2	2	4	5	0
dryly	8	.6151	1.0308	40.1	0	2	1	1	2	0	2	0	2	1	0	1	0	0	0	0	0	0	0	0	1	2	0	1	0
dryness	7	.4357	.6862	38.4	0	1	2	2	1	1	0	0	1	0	0	0	0	3	0	2	0	0	0	0	0	0	1	0	0
Drysdale	2	.0000	.0243	23.9	0	0	0	0	2	0	0	0	0	0	0	0	0	0	0	0	0	0	0	0	0	0	0	2	0
DTA	4	.0000	.1827	32.6	0	0	0	0	4	0	0	0	4	0	0	0	0	0	0	0	0	0	0	0	0	0	0	0	0
du	10	.5321	1.1021	40.4	0	4	2	1	2	0	1	0	0	0	0	0	0	0	0	0	2	0	0	0	1	4	1	2	0
duMaurier's	2	.0000	.0243	23.9	0	0	0	0	0	0	0	2	0	0	0	0	0	0	0	0	0	0	0	0	0	0	0	2	0
DuPont	3	.2445	.1818	32.6	0	0	0	0	2	1	0	0	0	0	0	0	0	0	0	2	0	0	0	0	0	0	1	0	0
DuPont's	3	.0000	.0365	25.6	0	0	0	0	3	0	0	0	0	0	0	0	0	0	0	0	0	0	0	0	0	0	0	3	0
dual	10	.5609	1.1697	40.7	0	0	0	0	9	1	0	0	1	0	0	0	0	1	0	0	1	0	0	0	3	0	2	2	0
dual-purpose	2	.1812	.0838	29.2	0	0	0	0	2	0	0	0	0	0	0	0	0	0	0	0	0	0	1	0	0	0	0	1	0
dub	3	.3795	.2506	34.0	0	0	0	1	2	0	0	0	0	0	0	0	0	1	0	0	0	0	0	0	1	0	0	1	0
dubbed	3	.0000	.0365	25.6	0	0	0	0	2	1	0	0	0	0	0	0	0	0	0	0	0	0	0	0	0	0	0	3	0
Dublin	18	.4012	1.6447	42.2	2	0	3	0	11	1	1	0	2	1	0	0	0	12	0	0	0	0	0	0	0	2	0	1	0
Dubois	4	.0000	.0419	26.2	0	0	0	0	4	0	0	0	0	0	0	0	0	0	0	0	0	0	0	0	0	0	4	0	0
Dubose	2	.0000	.0215	23.3	0	0	0	0	0	0	2	0	0	0	0	2	0	0	0	0	0	0	0	0	0	0	0	0	0
Dubrovnik	2	.0000	.0209	23.2	0	0	0	0	0	2	0	0	0	0	0	0	0	0	0	0	0	0	0	0	0	0	2	0	0
duc	5	.2042	.2444	33.9	0	1	0	3	0	1	0	0	0	0	0	0	0	0	1	0	0	0	0	0	4	0	0	0	0
Duc	2	.0000	.0243	23.9	0	0	0	0	2	0	0	0	0	0	0	0	0	0	0	0	0	0	0	0	0	0	0	2	0
ducats	4	.2969	.2888	34.6	0	0	0	1	1	0	2	0	1	0	0	2	0	0	0	0	0	0	0	0	1	0	0	0	0
duchess	2	.0000	.0914	29.6	0	0	0	2	0	0	0	0	2	0	0	0	0	0	0	0	0	0	0	0	0	0	0	0	0
Duchess	20	.4581	2.1310	43.3	10	0	1	1	6	0	1	1	11	0	0	1	0	0	0	0	0	0	0	0	6	1	0	1	0
duck	216	.8097	35.793	55.5	120	40	18	15	13	4	2	4	142	1	2	9	1	2	4	23	8	1	1	0	5	8	2	7	0
Duck	25	.5643	3.0524	44.8	19	3	0	1	1	1	0	0	10	0	0	2	0	1	0	0	2	0	0	0	0	3	0	7	0
duck-billed	3	.2053	.1597	32.0	0	2	0	0	0	0	0	1	0	0	0	0	0	0	0	1	0	0	0	0	0	2	0	0	0
duck-chasing	3	.0000	.0322	25.1	0	0	0	0	0	3	0	0	0	0	0	3	0	0	0	0	0	0	0	0	0	0	0	0	0
duck's	11	.4683	1.1665	40.7	6	2	1	0	1	0	0	1	4	0	0	0	0	0	0	2	0	0	0	0	0	3	0	2	0
duckbill	9	.2053	.4792	36.8	6	0	3	0	0	0	0	0	0	0	0	0	0	0	0	3	0	0	0	0	0	6	0	0	0
Duckbill	8	.0000	.1158	30.6	7	0	1	0	0	0	0	0	0	0	0	0	0	0	0	0	0	0	0	0	0	8	0	0	0
duckbills	11	.0881	.3403	35.3	10	0	1	0	0	0	0	0	0	0	0	0	0	0	0	1	0	0	0	0	0	10	0	0	0
ducked	26	.5894	3.3371	45.2	6	9	4	0	4	2	1	0	14	0	0	2	0	1	0	0	0	0	0	0	3	2	0	4	0
ducking	3	.2208	.1563	31.9	0	0	0	0	0	0	1	2	0	2	0	0	0	0	0	0	0	0	0	0	1	0	0	0	0
duckling	42	.5222	4.9815	47.0	26	2	8	1	0	3	0	2	27	0	0	8	0	0	1	2	3	0	0	0	0	1	0	0	0
Duckling	12	.0526	.2872	34.6	10	0	0	2	0	0	0	0	2	0	0	0	0	0	0	0	10	0	0	0	0	0	0	0	0
ducklings	22	.3771	2.1825	43.4	13	3	0	0	0	0	0	6	19	0	1	0	0	0	0	0	2	0	0	0	0	0	0	0	0
ducks	149	.8545	25.553	54.1	62	35	12	11	19	4	1	5	49	6	2	8	1	9	1	21	2	1	0	0	3	24	8	14	0
Ducks	2	.0000	.0162	22.1	2	0	0	0	0	0	0	0	0	0	0	0	0	0	0	0	2	0	0	0	0	0	0	0	0
ducks'	2	.1717	.1142	30.6	0	0	1	0	1	0	0	0	1	0	0	1	0	0	0	0	0	0	0	0	0	0	0	0	0
duckweed	3	.2445	.1818	32.6	0	0	0	2	1	0	0	0	0	0	0	0	0	0	0	2	0	0	0	0	0	0	1	0	0
duckweeds	2	.0000	.0394	26.0	2	0	0	0	0	0	0	0	0	0	0	0	0	0	0	2	0	0	0	0	0	0	0	0	0
duct	3	.0997	.1145	30.6	0	0	2	0	1	0	0	0	1	0	0	0	0	0	2	0	0	0	0	0	0	0	0	0	0
ductile	5	.0488	.0763	28.8	0	0	0	0	2	1	2	0	0	0	0	0	0	0	0	1	0	0	0	4	0	0	0	0	0
ductility	4	.0000	.0101	20.0	0	0	0	0	1	1	2	0	0	0	0	0	0	0	0	0	0	0	0	4	0	0	0	0	0
ductless	2	.0000	.0394	26.0	0	0	0	0	1	0	1	0	0	0	0	0	0	0	0	2	0	0	0	0	0	0	0	0	0
ducts	14	.3988	1.1983	40.8	0	0	1	0	9	0	4	0	0	1	0	0	0	0	0	4	0	0	0	2	0	0	7	0	0
Duddy	3	.0000	.1370	31.4	3	0	0	0	0	0	0	0	3	0	0	0	0	0	0	0	0	0	0	0	0	0	0	0	0
dude	9	.4709	.9774	39.9	0	3	1	1	3	0	0	1	5	2	0	1	0	0	0	0	0	0	0	0	0	0	0	1	0
dudes	2	.1814	.1187	30.7	0	0	1	0	1	0	0	0	1	0	0	0	0	0	0	0	0	0	0	0	0	0	0	1	0
Dudley	14	.0000	.1502	31.8	14	0	0	0	0	0	0	0	0	0	0	14	0	0	0	0	0	0	0	0	0	0	0	0	0
duds	4	.2445	.3067	34.9	1	0	0	0	1	2	0	0	3	0	0	0	0	0	0	0	0	0	0	0	0	1	0	0	0
due	204	.9072	36.687	55.6	10	16	13	15	50	41	34	25	21	5	1	7	8	25	3	28	8	1	5	2	19	13	34	24	0
duel	16	.5372	1.8850	42.8	1	1	6	1	2	3	2	0	7	1	0	3	0	0	0	0	0	0	0	0	0	2	3	0	0
dueling	3	.1187	.1291	31.1	0	0	0	0	0	3	0	0	1	0	0	2	0	0	0	0	0	0	0	0	0	0	0	0	0
duelist	2	.0000	.0215	23.3	0	0	0	0	0	0	2	0	0	0	0	2	0	0	0	0	0	0	0	0	0	0	0	0	0
duelists	2	.0000	.0215	23.3	0	0	0	0	0	2	0	0	0	0	0	2	0	0	0	0	0	0	0	0	0	0	0	0	0
dues	4	.3723	.3645	35.6	2	1	0	0	1	0	0	0	2	1	0	0	0	0	0	0	0	0	0	0	0	0	0	1	0
duet	17	.1672	.6813	38.3	0	4	6	1	1	3	2	0	0	2	0	0	0	0	0	0	14	0	0	0	0	0	0	1	0

5A drum-shaped
4B drum's
4N drumlike
8D Drummer
3N Drummonds
9J drumstick
XH druses
XR dry-docked
5F dry-farming
7A dry-tropical
5F dry-weather
9M dry-writing
8F drygoods
6A Dryopians
8Q Drzic
5B DS
9H DT'S**
XR duMaurier
3A duNation
7Q DuPage
7R duPerron
5Q duPont
6B Dual
7R dual-four
7P dual-hurdling
6R dual-mode
7Q dualism
7Q duality
9R Duane
8R Dubcek
7R dubious
9D Dubose's
8A Dubuque
6N duc's
7N ducal
9D ducat
7G duce
8G ducere
7P Duchess'
XR Duchy
4N duck-language
6R duck-shaped
8B duck-shootin'
3R Duck's
3P duckbill's
3P Duckbills
3J Duckling's
4B dud
9D Dud
6R Dude
7D duded
5A duelists'
6P duels
7P dues-paying
6P Duesseldorf

Word Type	F	D	U	SFI	3 Gr 3	4 Gr 4	5 Gr 5	6 Gr 6	7 Gr 7	8 Gr 8	9 Gr 9	X UnGr	A Read	B Eng & Gr	C Comp	D Lit	E Math	F Soc Stud	G Spell	H Sci	J Music	K Art	L Home Ec	M Shop	N Lib F	P Lib NF	Q Lib Ref	R Mag	S Rel
Duet	2	.0000	.0162	22.1	0	0	0	0	0	2	0	0	0	0	0	0	0	0	0	0	2	0	0	0	0	0	0	0	0
duets	3	.0000	.0243	23.8	0	0	1	0	1	1	0	0	0	0	0	0	0	0	0	0	3	0	0	0	0	0	0	0	0
duff	2	.0000	.0219	23.4	0	0	0	0	0	0	2	0	0	2	0	0	0	0	0	0	0	0	0	0	0	0	0	0	0
Duff	6	.2407	.3413	35.3	0	0	6	0	0	0	0	0	0	0	0	3	0	0	0	0	0	0	0	0	0	3	0	0	0
duffel	3	.2357	.2199	33.4	0	0	0	2	0	0	1	0	2	0	0	0	0	0	0	0	0	0	0	0	0	1	0	0	0
Duffy	16	.0000	.7309	38.6	16	0	0	0	0	0	0	0	16	0	0	0	0	0	0	0	0	0	0	0	0	0	0	0	0
Duffy's	2	.0000	.0914	29.6	2	0	0	0	0	0	0	0	2	0	0	0	0	0	0	0	0	0	0	0	0	0	0	0	0
Dufy	3	.0994	.0714	28.5	2	0	1	0	0	0	0	0	0	0	0	0	0	0	0	0	0	2	0	0	0	0	1	0	0
dug	182	.7373	27.595	54.4	47	33	25	30	27	14	4	2	63	4	1	8	0	39	2	9	1	0	0	0	17	23	5	9	1
dugout	28	.5735	3.4615	45.4	1	2	6	8	8	1	2	0	10	0	0	5	0	5	0	0	0	0	0	0	1	6	1	0	0
dugouts	6	.2952	.4383	36.4	0	2	4	0	0	0	0	0	1	0	0	0	0	2	0	0	0	0	0	0	0	3	0	0	0
Dukas	2	.1696	.0749	28.7	0	0	0	0	1	1	0	0	0	0	0	0	0	0	0	0	1	1	0	0	0	0	0	0	0
duke	20	.4544	1.9624	42.9	0	1	7	3	3	2	3	1	2	0	0	2	0	2	0	1	0	0	0	0	0	4	9	0	0
Duke	85	.7119	12.446	51.0	25	0	14	4	9	8	20	5	26	3	0	16	0	7	1	0	1	0	0	0	7	6	3	15	0
duke's	2	.2401	.1133	30.5	0	0	1	0	1	0	0	0	0	0	0	0	0	0	0	0	0	0	0	0	0	1	1	0	0
Duke's	4	.1112	.1666	32.2	0	0	1	0	3	0	0	0	1	0	0	0	0	0	0	0	0	0	0	0	0	3	0	0	0
dukedom	3	.0000	.0434	26.4	0	0	0	0	3	0	0	0	0	0	0	0	0	0	0	0	0	0	0	0	0	3	0	0	0
dukes	3	.3454	.2542	34.1	0	0	0	0	2	1	0	0	1	0	0	0	0	1	0	0	0	0	0	0	0	0	0	1	0
Dukes	2	.2337	.1157	30.6	1	0	0	0	1	0	0	0	0	0	0	0	0	1	0	0	0	0	0	0	1	0	0	0	0
Dulcey	10	.0000	.1172	30.7	0	0	10	0	0	0	0	0	0	0	0	0	0	0	0	0	0	0	0	0	10	0	0	0	0
dull	147	.8619	25.273	54.0	12	19	7	27	31	27	19	5	34	14	3	15	0	2	4	11	5	6	6	9	11	11	6	10	0
dulled	6	.5236	.6438	38.1	0	1	0	1	0	1	2	1	0	1	0	2	0	0	0	0	1	0	1	0	1	0	0	0	0
duller	2	.2300	.1140	30.6	1	0	0	0	0	0	0	1	0	1	0	0	0	0	0	1	0	0	0	0	0	0	0	0	0
Dulles	5	.3542	.3950	36.0	1	1	0	0	0	1	2	0	0	0	0	0	0	1	0	0	0	0	0	0	0	2	0	2	0
dullness	6	.4007	.5192	37.2	0	1	0	1	3	1	0	0	1	0	0	0	0	0	0	0	0	1	2	0	1	0	0	1	0
dully	8	.3451	.6694	38.3	0	1	1	0	5	1	0	0	3	0	0	2	0	0	0	0	0	0	0	0	3	0	0	0	0
Duluth	4	.2183	.2285	33.6	0	0	2	1	0	0	1	0	0	0	0	0	0	3	0	0	0	0	0	0	0	1	0	0	0
duly	8	.4097	.7024	38.5	0	0	0	0	3	1	4	0	0	3	0	3	0	1	0	0	0	0	0	0	0	1	0	0	0
duma	5	.0000	.0404	26.1	5	0	0	0	0	0	0	0	0	0	0	0	0	0	0	0	5	0	0	0	0	0	0	0	0
Dumas	6	.1698	.3400	35.3	1	2	0	0	3	0	0	0	3	0	0	0	0	0	0	0	0	0	0	0	0	0	3	0	0
dumb	38	.6853	5.4475	47.4	9	5	2	4	7	4	6	1	18	1	0	4	0	0	1	0	0	0	1	0	7	3	0	3	0
dumbfounded	4	.3683	.3188	35.0	0	0	1	1	1	1	0	0	0	0	0	1	0	0	0	0	0	0	0	0	2	0	0	1	0
dumbly	3	.2212	.2099	33.2	0	0	0	1	2	0	0	0	2	0	0	1	0	0	0	0	0	0	0	0	0	0	0	0	0
Dumbo	3	.0000	.0434	26.4	0	0	0	0	0	0	3	0	0	0	0	0	0	0	0	0	0	0	0	0	0	3	0	0	0
Dumfries	8	.0000	.1158	30.6	0	8	0	0	0	0	0	0	0	0	0	0	0	0	0	0	0	0	0	0	0	8	0	0	0
dummies	2	.2331	.1157	30.6	0	1	0	1	0	0	0	0	0	0	0	0	0	0	0	1	0	0	0	0	1	0	0	0	0
dummy	7	.6617	.9526	39.8	0	2	1	1	2	0	1	0	1	1	0	0	0	0	0	1	0	0	0	0	1	1	1	1	0
Dummy	2	.0000	.0162	22.1	2	0	0	0	0	0	0	0	0	0	0	0	0	0	0	0	2	0	0	0	0	0	0	0	0
dump	33	.6895	4.6749	46.7	6	8	4	3	5	4	2	1	6	0	0	3	0	4	1	5	0	0	0	0	6	0	2	6	0
dumped	38	.8233	6.3157	48.0	9	5	5	5	9	4	1	0	14	1	1	1	0	3	0	2	1	0	0	1	2	5	2	5	0
dumping	12	.6375	1.5943	42.0	1	1	2	4	2	0	2	0	2	0	0	1	0	1	0	4	0	0	0	0	1	1	0	2	0
dumpling	4	.0000	.0579	27.6	4	0	0	0	0	0	0	0	0	0	0	0	0	0	0	0	0	0	0	0	0	4	0	0	0
dumplings	4	.4570	.4091	36.1	0	1	0	0	2	1	0	0	1	0	0	0	0	1	0	0	0	0	0	0	0	1	0	1	0
dumps	8	.5332	.9281	39.7	1	3	1	2	1	0	0	0	2	0	0	0	0	1	0	3	0	0	0	0	0	0	1	1	0
Dumpties	2	.0000	.0914	29.6	0	0	0	2	0	0	0	0	2	0	0	0	0	0	0	0	0	0	0	0	0	0	0	0	0
Dumpty	4	.0000	.0486	26.9	4	0	0	0	0	0	0	0	0	0	0	0	0	0	0	0	0	0	0	0	0	0	0	4	0
dumpy	6	.3756	.5424	37.3	2	0	1	0	2	1	0	0	3	0	1	0	0	0	0	0	1	0	0	0	0	0	0	1	0
dun	7	.3828	.6044	37.8	3	2	0	0	2	0	0	0	1	0	0	1	0	0	0	0	0	0	0	0	1	4	0	0	0
Dun	2	.0000	.0162	22.1	0	0	0	0	0	2	0	0	0	0	0	0	0	0	0	0	2	0	0	0	0	0	0	0	0
dun-colored	2	.1814	.1187	30.7	0	1	1	0	0	0	0	0	1	0	0	0	0	0	0	0	0	0	0	0	0	0	0	1	0
Dunbar's	2	.2440	.1132	30.5	0	0	0	0	0	0	2	0	0	0	0	1	0	0	0	0	0	0	0	0	0	0	0	1	0
Duncan	58	.2778	4.9800	47.0	0	52	0	0	3	2	1	0	54	1	0	2	0	0	0	0	0	0	0	0	1	0	0	0	0
Duncan's	6	.0000	.2741	34.4	0	6	0	0	0	0	0	0	6	0	0	0	0	0	0	0	0	0	0	0	0	0	0	0	0
Dundee	5	.1813	.3036	34.8	0	0	2	3	0	0	0	0	3	0	0	0	0	0	0	0	2	0	0	0	0	0	0	0	0
dune	27	.5527	3.1701	45.0	1	1	1	1	11	6	6	0	4	0	0	0	0	0	0	12	0	1	0	0	3	0	6	1	0
dunes	51	.7182	7.4585	48.7	3	7	4	9	7	3	8	10	4	1	1	1	0	12	0	12	0	0	0	0	2	4	3	11	0
Dunes	2	.0000	.0243	23.9	0	0	0	0	0	0	0	2	0	0	0	0	0	0	0	0	0	0	0	0	0	0	0	2	0
dung	4	.2958	.2914	34.6	0	2	0	0	1	1	0	0	1	0	0	0	0	0	0	0	0	0	0	0	2	1	0	0	0
dungarees	5	.5037	.5192	37.2	1	1	0	0	2	0	0	1	0	1	0	1	0	0	0	0	0	0	1	0	1	0	0	1	0
dungeon	5	.5392	.5735	37.6	2	0	1	0	0	1	0	1	1	0	0	1	0	0	0	0	0	0	0	0	1	1	0	1	0
dungeons	2	.2346	.1166	30.7	0	0	0	1	0	0	0	1	0	0	0	0	0	0	0	1	0	0	0	0	0	0	0	1	0
dunk	2	.2446	.1142	30.6	0	0	0	0	1	1	0	0	0	0	0	0	0	0	0	0	0	0	0	0	1	0	0	1	0
Dunkirk	4	.3718	.3639	35.6	0	0	0	1	2	1	0	0	2	1	0	0	0	0	0	0	0	0	0	0	1	0	0	0	0
Dunmore	2	.0000	.0219	23.4	0	0	0	0	0	0	2	0	0	2	0	0	0	0	0	0	0	0	0	0	0	0	0	0	0
Dunn	27	.4043	2.4852	44.0	1	7	7	2	10	0	0	0	7	0	0	0	0	0	0	0	0	0	0	0	4	4	0	12	0
Dunning	5	.0000	.0724	28.6	0	5	0	0	0	0	0	0	0	0	0	0	0	0	0	0	0	0	0	0	0	5	0	0	0
dunno	5	.2387	.2802	34.5	0	0	1	0	4	0	0	0	0	0	0	0	0	0	0	0	0	0	0	0	2	0	0	3	0
Dunnville	4	.0000	.0469	26.7	0	0	0	4	0	0	0	0	0	0	0	0	0	0	0	0	0	0	0	0	4	0	0	0	0
Dunny	2	.0000	.0162	22.1	0	0	0	0	0	2	0	0	0	0	0	0	0	0	0	0	2	0	0	0	0	0	0	0	0
duns	3	.2332	.1690	32.3	2	0	0	0	0	0	0	1	0	0	0	0	0	0	0	0	0	0	0	0	0	2	0	1	0
duodenum	3	.0000	.0314	25.0	0	0	0	0	0	0	3	0	0	0	0	0	0	0	0	0	0	0	0	0	0	0	3	0	0
duple	6	.0000	.0485	26.9	0	0	0	1	4	1	0	0	0	0	0	0	0	0	0	0	6	0	0	0	0	0	0	0	0
duplicate	24	.6395	3.1259	44.9	1	0	2	1	8	2	10	0	0	1	0	0	3	1	0	4	1	0	0	2	0	2	8	2	0
duplicated	10	.7077	1.4377	41.6	0	0	2	0	2	5	0	1	1	0	0	1	0	1	0	1	2	0	0	0	1	1	1	1	0
duplicates	10	.3402	.7178	38.6	0	1	0	0	5	0	4	0	0	0	0	0	0	0	0	0	6	0	0	2	0	0	2	0	0
duplicating	4	.4482	.4009	36.0	0	0	0	1	2	1	0	0	1	0	0	0	0	0	0	1	0	0	0	0	0	0	1	1	0
dupp	7	.0000	.1380	31.4	4	0	0	3	0	0	0	0	0	0	0	0	0	0	0	7	0	0	0	0	0	0	0	0	0
Duquesne	9	.3593	.7292	38.6	0	4	0	0	0	3	2	0	0	0	0	0	0	4	0	0	0	0	0	0	0	4	1	0	0
durability	5	.2827	.3073	34.9	0	0	1	0	2	0	2	0	0	0	0	0	0	0	0	0	0	0	2	0	0	0	1	2	0
durable	25	.4528	2.3965	43.8	1	3	1	1	9	5	5	0	3	0	0	0	0	1	1	2	1	0	5	7	0	4	1	0	0
Durango	5	.3855	.4777	36.8	0	0	0	3	1	0	1	0	3	0	0	0	0	0	0	0	0	0	0	0	1	0	0	1	0
Durant	3	.2431	.1816	32.6	0	0	0	0	0	3	0	0	0	0	0	0	0	2	0	0	0	0	0	0	1	0	0	0	0
duration	21	.5622	2.4380	43.9	1	0	1	4	9	2	3	1	1	1	0	1	0	0	0	2	7	0	0	0	0	2	5	2	0
durations	5	.1101	.1543	31.9	0	0	0	0	4	1	0	0	0	0	0	0	0	1	0	0	4	0	0	0	0	0	0	0	0
Durban	4	.2352	.2332	33.7	0	0	0	4	0	0	0	0	0	0	0	0	0	2	0	0	0	0	0	0	0	0	0	2	0
durbar	4	.0000	.0778	28.9	0	4	0	0	0	0	0	0	0	0	0	0	0	4	0	0	0	0	0	0	0	0	0	0	0
durbars	2	.0000	.0389	25.9	0	2	0	0	0	0	0	0	0	0	0	0	0	2	0	0	0	0	0	0	0	0	0	0	0
Durer	5	.1504	.1970	32.9	0	0	1	0	4	0	0	0	0	0	0	4	1	0	0	0	0	0	0	0	0	0	0	0	0
during	1924	.9505	361.11	65.6	168	210	311	279	384	303	196	73	240	69	24	45	112	372	55	285	125	5	21	19	46	122	219	163	2
Durkee	10	.0000	.4568	36.6	0	0	0	0	10	0	0	0	10	0	0	0	0	0	0	0	0	0	0	0	0	0	0	0	0
Durkee's	6	.0000	.2741	34.4	0	0	0	0	6	0	0	0	6	0	0	0	0	0	0	0	0	0	0	0	0	0	0	0	0
Durrell	7	.2128	.3514	35.5	0	0	0	0	4	3	0	0	0	0	0	5	0	0	0	0	0	0	0	0	0	0	2	0	0
Dusicyon	4	.0000	.0419	26.2	0	0	0	0	4	0	0	0	0	0	0	0	0	0	0	0	0	0	0	0	0	0	4	0	0

8Q Dufay
8D DUFFY
4J Duggan
3P dugong
7D dugway
6A Duivenisse
8Q Dulawan
4G dulband
3A dulce
6J dulcimer
4R dulcimers
3H dull-colored
5P dull-witted
6R dull-yellow
4R dulls
3J dum
5A dumb-waiter
8Q Dumbbell
3R dumbest
9D dumbshow
8B Dumferling
7H dumfounding
8R Dummit
3J Dummy's
7D Dumpground
5A Dumpling
8A dumpy-looking
9R Dunaway
6B dunces
8R Dunderberg
6A dunderheaded
4A Dungannon
7D dungaree
8F Dunkers
9B Dunmores
XR Dunnellen
7R dunning
7D Dunnoo
3P dunny
9Q Dunstaffnage
5G duo
9Q duo-tones
5G duodecem
7E duodecimal
9Q duotones
3H dup
9D dupe
9D duped
3A Dupin
7Q duplication
XQ duplication-deficient
XQ duplications
6J Dupre
9L durable-press
7M durably
8N Durant's
9J Durbach
7N Durham
7A During
7M Durite
8A durn
6F durra
8D Durrell's
9R Durrenmatt
5P Durrow
5A Durston's
4P Duryea

Word Type	F	D	U	SFI	3 Gr 3	4 Gr 4	5 Gr 5	6 Gr 6	7 Gr 7	8 Gr 8	9 Gr 9	X UnGr	A Read	B Eng & Gr	C Comp	D Lit	E Math	F Soc Stud	G Spell	H Sci	J Music	K Art	L Home Ec	M Shop	N Lib F	P Lib NF	Q Lib Ref	R Mag	S Rel
dusk	47	.6809	6.6300	48.2	7	3	4	11	10	7	3	2	15	2	1	12	0	1	0	2	0	0	0	0	8	3	1	2	0
dusky	10	.4282	.9452	39.8	0	2	2	0	4	1	1	0	2	2	0	2	0	0	0	0	0	0	0	0	4	0	0	0	0
Dussel	2	.0000	.0290	24.6	0	0	0	0	0	2	0	0	0	0	0	0	0	0	0	0	0	0	0	0	0	2	0	0	0
dust	340	.8712	59.164	57.7	53	77	36	33	72	32	29	8	81	11	12	34	1	27	2	84	5	2	3	4	20	30	6	18	0
Dust	5	.3844	.4120	36.1	0	2	1	0	2	0	0	0	0	0	0	0	0	0	0	0	1	0	0	0	2	0	0	2	0
dust-free	2	.2440	.1132	30.5	0	0	0	0	1	0	0	1	0	0	0	1	0	0	0	0	0	0	0	0	0	0	0	1	0
dusted	23	.6711	3.2242	45.1	4	9	2	3	4	0	1	0	9	0	0	3	0	1	1	0	1	0	1	0	1	6	0	0	0
duster	3	.2261	.2131	33.3	0	3	0	0	0	0	0	0	2	0	0	0	0	0	0	0	0	0	0	0	1	0	0	0	0
dusters	3	.0000	.1370	31.4	2	1	0	0	0	0	0	0	3	0	0	0	0	0	0	0	0	0	0	0	0	0	0	0	0
dusting	13	.5561	1.5964	42.0	2	4	5	1	0	0	1	0	7	1	0	0	0	0	0	0	0	0	0	0	1	2	0	2	0
dusts	2	.2152	.1357	31.3	1	1	0	0	0	0	0	0	1	0	0	0	0	1	0	0	0	0	0	0	0	0	0	0	0
dusty	79	.7506	12.076	50.8	17	14	11	14	12	3	3	5	21	2	6	11	0	10	0	5	0	1	0	1	4	12	3	3	0
Dusty	23	.3199	2.0904	43.2	20	1	0	0	0	2	0	0	20	0	0	1	0	0	0	0	0	0	0	0	2	0	0	0	0
Dutch	240	.7563	36.858	55.7	17	37	56	39	45	28	15	3	42	4	1	9	1	83	18	2	5	0	0	1	4	45	21	4	0
Dutchie	2	.0000	.0215	23.3	0	0	0	0	0	0	2	0	0	0	0	2	0	0	0	0	0	0	0	0	0	0	0	0	0
Dutchman	12	.7235	1.7936	42.5	0	1	5	2	0	1	2	1	5	1	0	1	0	0	0	1	1	0	0	0	1	1	0	1	0
Dutchmen	6	.3810	.5098	37.1	0	1	4	0	0	0	0	1	0	0	0	0	0	3	0	0	0	0	0	0	0	2	1	0	0
duties	75	.6973	10.700	50.3	5	8	6	12	16	9	18	1	12	4	1	2	0	16	2	4	2	0	1	1	3	9	9	8	1
dutiful	2	.1717	.1142	30.6	0	0	0	1	1	0	0	0	1	0	0	1	0	0	0	0	0	0	0	0	0	0	0	0	0
dutifully	7	.4201	.6650	38.2	1	1	2	2	0	0	0	1	2	0	0	1	0	0	0	0	0	0	0	0	1	0	0	3	0
Duttweiler	4	.0000	.0579	27.6	0	0	4	0	0	0	0	0	0	0	0	0	0	0	0	0	0	0	0	0	0	4	0	0	0
duty	147	.9046	26.406	54.2	9	14	16	18	28	36	24	2	29	7	1	10	3	23	6	3	3	1	2	0	14	24	12	9	0
Duvall	6	.0000	.1167	30.7	0	6	0	0	0	0	0	0	0	0	0	0	0	6	0	0	0	0	0	0	0	0	0	0	0
Duvitch	29	.0779	.9243	39.7	0	0	5	0	7	17	0	0	6	0	0	23	0	0	0	0	0	0	0	0	0	0	0	0	0
Duvitches	8	.1717	.4569	36.6	0	0	2	0	4	2	0	0	4	0	0	4	0	0	0	0	0	0	0	0	0	0	0	0	0
Duvitches'	4	.1717	.2284	33.6	0	0	0	0	0	4	0	0	2	0	0	2	0	0	0	0	0	0	0	0	0	0	0	0	0
dva	2	.1733	.1149	30.6	1	0	0	0	0	0	1	0	1	1	0	0	0	0	0	0	0	0	0	0	0	0	0	0	0
Dvorak	11	.0000	.0889	29.5	1	0	8	0	1	1	0	0	0	0	0	0	0	0	0	0	11	0	0	0	0	0	0	0	0
Dwamish	2	.0000	.0215	23.3	0	0	0	0	2	0	0	0	0	0	0	2	0	0	0	0	0	0	0	0	0	0	0	0	0
dwarf	19	.5092	2.1976	43.4	7	3	4	2	3	0	0	0	11	0	0	0	0	0	0	2	1	0	0	0	1	0	4	0	0
dwarf's	2	.0000	.0914	29.6	1	1	0	0	0	0	0	0	2	0	0	0	0	0	0	0	0	0	0	0	0	0	0	0	0
dwarfed	6	.3644	.4955	37.0	0	0	0	0	4	1	1	0	1	0	0	0	0	0	0	0	0	0	0	0	0	1	3	1	0
dwarfs	13	.6139	1.7324	42.4	0	6	4	1	0	1	1	0	8	0	0	1	0	0	0	0	0	0	0	0	1	1	1	1	0
Dwarfs	2	.2417	.1091	30.4	2	0	0	0	0	0	0	0	0	0	0	0	0	0	0	0	1	0	0	0	0	0	1	0	0
dwell	27	.5502	3.1476	45.0	0	2	2	3	7	8	4	1	6	1	0	11	0	0	0	1	2	0	0	0	1	1	4	0	0
dweller	6	.4279	.5462	37.4	1	2	1	0	0	0	1	1	0	0	0	0	0	1	0	0	0	1	0	0	0	2	1	1	0
dwellers	31	.6450	4.1055	46.1	4	2	1	3	13	4	3	1	2	2	0	2	0	7	0	3	1	0	0	0	0	2	10	2	0
Dwellers	3	.0000	.0314	25.0	0	3	0	0	0	0	0	0	0	0	0	0	0	0	0	0	0	0	0	0	0	0	3	0	0
dwellin'	2	.0000	.0914	29.6	0	0	0	0	2	0	0	0	2	0	0	0	0	0	0	0	0	0	0	0	0	0	0	0	0
dwelling	20	.6246	2.6302	44.2	0	1	6	2	2	6	2	1	7	0	0	0	0	2	0	0	4	0	1	0	0	2	3	1	0
dwelling-place	3	.2379	.1705	32.3	0	0	0	0	1	0	1	1	0	0	0	1	0	0	0	0	0	0	0	0	0	2	0	0	0
dwellings	18	.6509	2.4189	43.8	2	2	2	3	4	2	3	0	3	0	0	0	0	4	0	1	0	1	0	1	0	2	4	2	0
dwells	5	.0887	.1585	32.0	0	1	1	2	1	0	0	0	1	0	0	0	0	0	0	0	1	0	0	0	0	0	0	2	1
dwelt	22	.5545	2.6813	44.3	1	2	3	4	3	5	3	1	11	0	0	5	0	1	0	0	1	0	0	0	0	3	1	0	0
Dwight	22	.4532	2.1197	43.3	0	1	3	7	2	3	5	1	0	1	0	0	0	4	0	0	0	0	0	0	0	2	4	11	0
dwindle	6	.5454	.6762	38.3	0	0	0	1	3	1	1	0	0	0	0	1	0	1	0	0	1	0	0	0	0	0	1	2	0
dwindled	8	.4857	.8305	39.2	0	1	1	1	2	2	1	0	1	0	0	0	0	0	0	0	0	0	0	0	3	1	1	2	0
dwindling	2	.2446	.1142	30.6	0	1	0	1	0	0	0	0	0	0	0	0	0	0	0	0	0	0	0	0	1	0	0	1	0
DX	8	.0000	.1197	30.8	8	0	0	0	0	0	0	0	0	0	0	0	8	0	0	0	0	0	0	0	0	0	0	0	0
dyad	3	.0000	.0314	25.0	0	0	0	3	0	0	0	0	0	0	0	0	0	0	0	0	0	0	0	0	0	0	3	0	0
dyads	2	.0000	.0209	23.2	0	0	0	2	0	0	0	0	0	0	0	0	0	0	0	0	0	0	0	0	0	0	2	0	0
dye	37	.6017	4.6382	46.7	2	11	4	1	6	7	5	1	3	1	0	2	0	1	0	19	1	0	4	0	0	2	1	3	0
dyed	14	.4091	1.2289	40.9	0	6	1	1	1	2	3	0	0	0	0	0	0	4	0	1	0	0	4	0	2	2	0	1	0
dyeing	5	.2846	.3320	35.2	3	0	0	1	0	0	1	0	1	0	0	0	0	0	0	0	3	0	1	0	0	0	0	0	0
Dyer	2	.2440	.1132	30.5	0	0	0	0	1	0	1	0	0	0	0	1	0	0	0	0	0	0	0	0	0	0	0	1	0
dyes	20	.4799	2.0672	43.2	6	4	1	2	2	2	3	0	1	0	0	0	0	7	1	7	0	0	3	0	0	0	1	0	0
Dyhrenfurth	2	.0000	.0914	29.6	0	0	0	0	2	0	0	0	2	0	0	0	0	0	0	0	0	0	0	0	0	0	0	0	0
dyin'	2	.1787	.1174	30.7	0	0	0	0	2	0	0	0	1	0	0	0	0	0	0	0	0	0	0	0	1	0	0	0	0
dying	108	.6216	14.235	51.5	4	8	19	26	19	8	18	6	42	4	0	23	0	5	0	7	2	0	0	0	5	6	5	8	1
dyke	4	.0000	.0579	27.6	1	3	0	0	0	0	0	0	0	0	0	0	0	0	0	0	0	0	0	0	0	4	0	0	0
Dyke	7	.1380	.2554	34.1	0	0	0	1	0	6	0	0	0	0	0	6	0	0	0	0	0	0	0	0	1	0	0	0	0
DYKE	21	.0000	.2254	33.5	0	0	0	0	0	21	0	0	0	0	0	21	0	0	0	0	0	0	0	0	0	0	0	0	0
dykes	2	.0000	.0394	26.0	0	0	0	0	0	0	0	2	0	0	0	0	0	0	0	2	0	0	0	0	0	0	0	0	0
dynamic	28	.3892	2.3178	43.7	2	0	6	1	6	9	3	1	0	0	0	0	0	1	0	1	15	0	0	0	0	2	6	3	0
dynamics	40	.0854	.9838	39.9	9	2	3	3	13	9	1	0	0	0	0	0	0	0	0	1	37	0	0	0	0	0	1	1	0
dynamite	24	.6936	3.4156	45.3	1	4	8	2	5	2	2	0	5	0	0	2	0	2	0	2	2	0	0	0	3	0	3	5	0
dynamometer	5	.2423	.2894	34.6	0	3	0	0	2	0	0	0	0	0	0	0	0	0	0	0	0	0	0	0	0	3	0	2	0
dynasties	4	.3287	.2952	34.7	0	0	1	0	0	1	2	0	0	0	0	0	0	1	0	0	0	0	0	0	0	1	2	0	0
dynasty	16	.5060	1.7051	42.3	0	0	4	1	1	9	1	0	0	0	0	0	0	6	0	0	0	0	0	0	2	1	5	2	0
Dynasty	7	.4716	.7020	38.5	0	0	3	0	3	1	0	0	0	0	0	0	0	2	0	0	0	0	0	0	0	2	2	1	0
Dynel	2	.0000	.0064	18.1	0	0	0	0	0	1	1	0	0	0	0	0	0	0	0	0	0	0	2	0	0	0	0	0	0
dysentery	5	.4858	.5159	37.1	0	0	0	2	0	2	1	0	0	0	0	1	0	0	0	2	0	0	0	0	0	1	1	0	0
Dzea	2	.0000	.0219	23.4	0	0	0	0	0	0	2	0	0	2	0	0	0	0	0	0	0	0	0	0	0	0	0	0	0
D1	2	.0000	.0394	26.0	0	0	0	0	0	0	0	2	0	0	0	0	0	0	0	2	0	0	0	0	0	0	0	0	0
D7	7	.0000	.0566	27.5	1	3	0	3	0	0	0	0	0	0	0	0	0	0	0	0	7	0	0	0	0	0	0	0	0
e	689	.3243	49.389	56.9	149	126	107	126	72	74	25	10	54	53	0	3	28	2	505	6	5	4	1	4	1	6	7	10	0
E	283	.6985	39.972	56.0	36	44	30	36	43	62	25	7	8	10	1	4	101	12	3	16	66	0	0	14	4	9	23	12	0
e/	7	.2301	.3668	35.6	0	0	5	2	0	0	0	0	0	3	0	0	0	0	4	0	0	0	0	0	0	0	0	0	0
E/I	3	.0000	.0076	18.8	0	0	0	0	0	3	0	0	0	0	0	0	0	0	0	0	0	0	0	3	0	0	0	0	0
E/R	3	.0000	.0076	18.8	0	0	0	0	0	3	0	0	0	0	0	0	0	0	0	0	0	0	0	3	0	0	0	0	0
e'en	3	.2071	.1434	31.6	0	0	0	2	0	0	1	0	0	0	0	1	0	0	0	0	2	0	0	0	0	0	0	0	0
e'er	3	.2060	.1500	31.8	0	0	0	0	1	0	2	0	0	0	0	2	0	0	0	0	0	0	0	0	0	1	0	0	0
e's	18	.2211	.9790	39.9	1	4	5	3	4	1	0	0	3	0	1	0	0	0	14	0	0	0	0	0	0	0	0	0	0
ea	45	.1738	1.9214	42.8	10	4	20	6	3	1	1	0	2	9	0	0	0	0	34	0	0	0	0	0	0	0	0	0	0
each	14290	.8513	2426.4	73.8	2796	2669	2045	1946	2113	1382	1173	166	1857	1476	221	198	4210	665	2414	1133	536	97	184	127	177	421	284	284	6
EAD	2	.0000	.0299	24.8	0	0	0	0	2	0	0	0	0	0	0	0	2	0	0	0	0	0	0	0	0	0	0	0	0
Eads	4	.0000	.0486	26.9	0	0	0	0	4	0	0	0	0	0	0	0	0	0	0	0	0	0	0	0	0	0	0	4	0
Eads's	3	.0000	.0365	25.6	0	0	0	0	3	0	0	0	0	0	0	0	0	0	0	0	0	0	0	0	0	0	0	3	0
eager	159	.8163	26.184	54.2	19	36	19	26	28	13	17	1	51	8	6	11	0	15	2	2	2	0	2	0	13	27	5	15	0
eagerly	112	.6603	15.666	51.9	9	44	9	14	22	10	3	1	57	2	0	7	0	4	0	1	1	0	0	0	14	21	1	4	0
eagerness	26	.5680	3.1877	45.0	1	8	3	6	2	6	0	0	10	0	0	4	0	1	0	0	0	0	0	0	5	5	1	0	0
eagle	95	.8223	15.861	52.0	47	7	7	9	18	1	4	2	52	9	1	5	4	1	4	1	2	0	0	0	4	4	5	3	0
Eagle	32	.6004	4.0903	46.1	11	13	1	1	5	1	0	0	11	0	0	0	8	2	1	0	1	0	0	0	7	2	0	0	0
eagle-eyed	3	.2445	.1903	32.8	0	0	0	1	0	1	1	0	1	0	0	0	0	0	0	0	0	0	1	0	0	0	0	1	0

7D Dusk
5N dusk-dark
5A DUST
9R dust-caked
7P dust-collection
9D dust-colored
5P dust-covered
7E dust-speck
4P dustcloth
4A dustcloths
XR dustfree
4A Dusting
3P dustpans
9R dustup
7B dusty-coated
5P Dutch-American
5P Dutti
5F Duty
4F Duvall's
8D Duvitch's
7Q dux
5J Dvorak's
6G dw
9Q dwarfing
4A dwarfs'
8J dwelleth
7R DWI
5A dwindles
XR Dworetsky
6E DY
6F dyewood
4N Dygert
7Q dyings
3P Dykes
9R Dylan
7R dynamism
9F dynamite-laden
8A dynamo
XH dynamos
7R dynanometer
4R Dynastes
5P dynastically
9L Dynel-acetate-viscose
8Q dysuria
7P Dyved
7N E**
3R e-eich
9J e-natural
6A e-nor-mous
8E E's
6D Eadom
6G eage
7Q Eagle-Pass
5N eagle-feathers
3P eagle-like
8F Eagle-scream

Word Type	F	D	U	SFI	3 Gr 3	4 Gr 4	5 Gr 5	6 Gr 6	7 Gr 7	8 Gr 8	9 Gr 9	X UnGr	A Read	B Eng & Gr	C Comp	D Lit	E Math	F Soc Stud	G Spell	H Sci	J Music	K Art	L Home Ec	M Shop	N Lib F	P Lib NF	Q Lib Ref	R Mag	S Rel
eagle's	7	.3817	.6820	38.3	4	0	0	2	1	0	0	0	5	1	0	0	0	0	0	0	0	0	0	0	0	1	0	0	0
Eagle's	2	.0000	.0234	23.7	0	2	0	0	0	0	0	0	0	0	0	0	0	0	0	0	0	0	0	0	2	0	0	0	0
eagles	42	.5952	5.3766	47.3	19	1	5	5	11	0	0	1	18	4	0	0	2	1	0	4	0	0	0	0	0	4	9	0	0
Eagles	5	.2363	.2776	34.4	0	3	0	0	1	0	0	1	0	0	0	0	0	0	0	0	0	0	0	0	3	0	0	2	0
eagles'	5	.2445	.3864	35.9	1	0	1	1	1	1	0	0	4	0	0	1	0	0	0	0	0	0	0	0	0	0	0	0	0
eaglet	3	.0000	.1370	31.4	0	0	0	3	0	0	0	0	3	0	0	0	0	0	0	0	0	0	0	0	0	0	0	0	0
eaglets	7	.0000	.3198	35.0	0	0	0	7	0	0	0	0	7	0	0	0	0	0	0	0	0	0	0	0	0	0	0	0	0
ear	331	.7967	53.336	57.3	60	63	25	52	66	39	23	3	99	9	2	31	1	3	12	57	50	0	4	0	30	16	1	16	0
ear-shattering	2	.1698	.1133	30.5	0	0	1	0	0	0	1	0	1	0	0	0	0	0	0	0	0	0	0	0	0	0	1	0	0
eardrum	17	.1795	.8866	39.5	0	2	0	12	3	0	0	0	1	0	0	0	0	0	0	15	1	0	0	0	0	0	0	0	0
eardrums	10	.4649	1.0195	40.1	0	1	0	7	1	0	1	0	1	1	0	1	0	0	0	6	0	0	0	0	0	0	0	1	0
eared	2	.0000	.0037	15.7	0	0	0	0	0	2	0	0	0	0	0	0	0	0	0	0	0	2	0	0	0	0	0	0	0
earl	6	.4215	.5366	37.3	0	1	1	1	1	0	2	0	0	1	0	0	0	0	0	0	0	0	0	0	1	1	3	0	0
Earl	41	.6836	5.7438	47.6	0	6	7	9	12	4	2	1	7	1	0	0	1	2	3	1	0	0	0	0	9	4	3	10	0
Earle	10	.3259	.7207	38.6	1	0	0	7	0	0	1	1	0	0	0	0	0	0	0	0	0	0	0	0	7	1	1	1	0
earlier	283	.8789	49.514	56.9	20	26	34	32	63	54	46	8	41	15	2	4	16	39	10	40	20	3	0	0	3	29	35	26	0
earliest	139	.7860	21.955	53.4	9	12	25	17	34	20	18	4	13	1	1	3	4	31	2	8	14	3	0	2	1	16	29	10	1
earls	2	.0000	.0389	25.9	0	0	0	0	0	2	0	0	0	0	0	0	0	2	0	0	0	0	0	0	0	0	0	0	0
early	1439	.8722	250.26	64.0	188	199	236	174	290	196	128	28	273	66	13	49	14	278	24	125	105	12	13	12	66	133	163	85	8
Early	15	.5122	1.5958	42.0	0	0	0	0	5	5	4	1	0	2	0	0	0	2	0	0	2	0	0	0	0	0	6	3	0
early-morning	5	.4764	.5339	37.3	2	1	0	0	1	1	0	0	2	0	0	0	0	0	0	0	0	0	0	0	1	0	1	1	0
earmark	3	.0000	.1370	31.4	3	0	0	0	0	0	0	0	3	0	0	0	0	0	0	0	0	0	0	0	0	0	0	0	0
earmarks	12	.3250	1.0958	40.4	10	0	0	0	1	1	0	0	10	0	0	0	0	1	0	0	0	0	0	0	1	0	0	0	0
earmuffs	4	.3141	.3005	34.8	3	1	0	0	0	0	0	0	1	0	0	0	0	0	1	0	0	0	0	0	0	0	0	2	0
earn	166	.8840	29.266	54.7	28	32	24	20	30	17	12	3	42	6	1	12	23	36	2	5	4	0	5	2	3	13	2	10	0
earned	104	.7522	15.905	52.0	18	19	13	14	16	12	11	1	22	3	1	4	38	8	0	1	1	0	2	0	1	10	3	10	0
earners	2	.0000	.0389	25.9	0	0	1	0	0	1	0	0	0	0	0	0	0	2	0	0	0	0	0	0	0	0	0	0	0
earnest	28	.7396	4.2153	46.2	2	3	4	3	9	3	3	1	6	1	0	3	0	2	0	1	1	0	0	0	3	4	1	6	0
earnestly	17	.5477	1.9874	43.0	2	1	1	7	4	1	1	0	4	0	0	3	0	1	0	0	0	0	0	0	5	3	0	1	0
earnestness	5	.4503	.5015	37.0	0	0	0	1	2	2	0	0	1	0	0	1	0	2	0	0	0	0	0	0	0	0	0	1	0
earning	9	.4350	.8740	39.4	0	0	2	1	4	1	1	0	3	0	2	1	0	1	0	0	0	0	1	0	0	0	1	0	0
earnings	27	.6039	3.3611	45.3	0	1	3	5	2	6	10	0	1	1	0	1	11	2	0	0	0	0	1	0	0	1	1	8	0
earns	20	.7053	2.8661	44.6	2	1	3	3	5	1	4	1	1	2	0	0	5	6	1	0	0	0	1	0	0	1	1	2	0
Earnshaw	11	.2434	.8355	39.2	2	3	0	6	0	0	0	0	8	0	0	0	0	0	0	0	0	0	0	0	0	3	0	0	0
earphone	3	.0000	.0591	27.7	0	0	0	0	0	3	0	0	0	0	0	0	0	0	0	3	0	0	0	0	0	0	0	0	0
earphones	12	.6108	1.5733	42.0	2	1	1	6	1	0	1	0	5	0	0	0	0	1	0	3	1	0	0	0	0	1	0	1	0
earring	13	.1806	.9224	39.6	12	1	0	0	0	0	0	0	12	0	0	0	0	0	0	0	0	0	0	0	0	1	0	0	0
earrings	23	.5253	2.7465	44.4	10	8	0	2	2	0	1	0	14	1	0	0	0	5	0	0	0	0	0	0	1	0	0	2	0
ears	505	.8555	86.552	59.4	132	84	61	76	87	38	25	2	152	18	5	47	7	6	6	57	19	9	4	0	98	49	12	16	0
Ears	18	.1983	1.3304	41.2	4	6	0	7	0	1	0	0	17	0	0	0	0	0	0	0	1	0	0	0	0	0	0	0	0
Ears'	5	.0000	.2284	33.6	0	5	0	0	0	0	0	0	5	0	0	0	0	0	0	0	0	0	0	0	0	0	0	0	0
earshot	7	.4626	.7366	38.7	0	1	0	2	3	0	0	1	3	0	0	1	0	0	0	0	0	0	0	0	0	1	0	2	0
earth	2690	.7807	424.82	66.3	615	473	313	319	424	212	246	88	342	24	8	76	79	418	20	1116	37	5	1	20	43	253	182	56	10
Earth	407	.6681	56.025	57.5	95	82	85	33	71	15	19	7	32	44	0	8	13	91	0	162	11	0	0	0	1	1	15	29	0
EARTH	6	.3289	.5019	37.0	3	1	2	0	0	0	0	0	2	0	0	0	0	1	0	3	0	0	0	0	0	0	0	0	0
Earth-born	3	.0000	.1370	31.4	0	0	0	3	0	0	0	0	3	0	0	0	0	0	0	0	0	0	0	0	0	0	0	0	0
earth-covered	2	.2408	.1204	30.8	1	0	0	0	0	1	0	0	0	0	0	0	0	1	0	0	0	0	0	0	0	1	0	0	0
earth-magnet	3	.0000	.0365	25.6	0	0	0	0	3	0	0	0	0	0	0	0	0	0	0	0	0	0	0	0	0	0	0	3	0
earth-moon	2	.2346	.1166	30.7	0	0	0	0	1	1	0	0	0	0	0	0	0	0	0	1	0	0	0	0	0	0	0	1	0
earth's	353	.5779	42.829	56.3	28	46	40	31	76	34	87	11	16	5	1	3	10	42	5	192	0	0	0	0	0	9	62	8	0
Earth's	34	.5563	3.9833	46.0	3	5	13	2	8	0	2	1	0	1	0	3	1	8	1	18	0	0	0	0	0	0	0	2	0
earthbound	2	.2130	.1056	30.2	0	0	0	0	1	1	0	0	0	0	0	0	0	0	1	1	0	0	0	0	0	0	0	0	0
earthen	9	.5563	1.0698	40.3	1	1	1	3	2	0	1	0	3	0	0	0	0	0	0	0	1	0	0	1	2	0	1	1	0
earthenware	10	.6554	1.3289	41.2	2	2	0	0	4	1	1	0	0	0	0	1	0	2	1	0	1	0	1	0	0	2	2	0	0
earthlodge	2	.0000	.0290	24.6	2	0	0	0	0	0	0	0	0	0	0	0	0	0	0	0	0	0	0	0	0	2	0	0	0
earthly	8	.4767	.7927	39.0	0	0	0	1	2	1	3	1	0	0	0	1	0	0	0	0	0	1	0	0	0	1	3	2	0
earthmen	2	.1733	.1149	30.6	0	0	0	1	1	0	0	0	1	1	0	0	0	0	0	0	0	0	0	0	0	0	0	0	0
earthquake	74	.7559	11.366	50.6	5	28	10	8	8	4	10	1	14	1	2	6	0	7	1	19	0	0	0	0	1	5	5	13	0
earthquake-proof	2	.0000	.0243	23.9	0	2	0	0	0	0	0	0	0	0	0	0	0	0	0	0	0	0	0	0	0	0	0	2	0
earthquakes	36	.5301	4.0990	46.1	3	9	5	3	4	1	11	0	4	0	0	3	0	5	0	19	0	0	0	0	0	0	3	2	0
earths	10	.3732	.8497	39.3	2	3	0	1	3	0	0	1	1	0	0	0	0	2	0	3	0	0	0	0	0	0	4	0	0
earthworm	9	.3370	.6985	38.4	5	0	0	1	3	0	0	0	0	2	0	0	0	0	0	6	0	0	0	0	0	1	0	0	0
earthworms	21	.3770	1.8520	42.7	9	1	1	4	5	0	0	1	4	0	0	0	0	0	0	12	0	0	0	0	0	1	4	0	0
earthy	8	.5570	.9259	39.7	0	0	1	1	3	0	1	2	0	1	0	0	0	0	0	2	0	0	0	0	2	2	1	0	0
earwig	2	.0000	.0234	23.7	2	0	0	0	0	0	0	0	0	0	0	0	0	0	0	0	0	0	0	0	2	0	0	0	0
ease	120	.6497	16.003	52.0	6	9	12	15	39	20	19	0	20	6	2	10	1	4	1	6	1	0	24	0	10	11	7	17	0
eased	25	.5678	3.1656	45.0	1	2	1	11	7	1	2	0	17	0	0	2	0	1	0	0	0	0	1	0	3	1	0	0	0
easel	10	.4048	.9965	40.0	1	1	0	2	0	6	0	0	7	0	0	0	0	0	1	0	1	1	0	0	0	0	0	0	0
easels	2	.0000	.0914	29.6	0	0	0	0	1	1	0	0	2	0	0	0	0	0	0	0	0	0	0	0	0	0	0	0	0
eases	3	.3791	.2506	34.0	0	0	2	0	0	0	1	0	0	0	0	0	0	0	0	1	0	0	0	0	1	0	0	1	0
easier	327	.8957	58.182	57.6	54	50	53	45	56	36	29	4	54	22	0	9	42	38	19	36	8	5	19	11	11	26	11	16	0
easiest	50	.8309	8.3216	49.2	8	8	3	11	8	8	3	1	9	5	0	1	10	2	2	4	1	0	2	2	0	4	2	6	0
easily	717	.8735	124.74	61.0	81	96	87	104	146	81	95	27	109	47	14	18	39	59	17	168	19	1	51	25	16	53	45	36	0
easing	9	.6025	1.1228	40.5	3	0	0	0	0	4	1	1	1	0	0	0	0	1	0	0	0	0	1	0	1	2	1	2	0
east	461	.7941	73.740	58.7	75	56	65	77	90	52	29	17	50	6	5	21	14	163	3	54	7	0	1	0	14	34	61	28	0
East	364	.7991	58.526	57.7	36	26	47	59	89	53	45	9	44	5	1	11	7	135	3	9	19	1	0	1	6	22	43	56	1
East-West	3	.1937	.1495	31.7	0	0	0	1	1	0	1	0	0	0	0	0	0	1	0	0	0	0	0	0	0	0	0	2	0
east-central	2	.0000	.0389	25.9	0	0	0	0	2	0	0	0	0	0	0	0	0	2	0	0	0	0	0	0	0	0	0	0	0
east-west	17	.4721	1.7539	42.4	8	1	3	1	3	0	1	0	1	0	0	0	0	8	0	5	0	0	0	0	0	0	1	2	0
East's	2	.2408	.1204	30.8	1	0	0	0	0	0	1	0	0	0	0	0	0	1	0	0	0	0	0	0	0	1	0	0	0
Easter	49	.2951	3.3453	45.2	16	13	1	4	3	2	8	2	6	7	0	0	0	4	1	1	8	4	0	0	2	7	0	5	4
easterly	6	.3327	.4474	36.5	0	1	0	0	3	1	1	0	0	0	0	0	0	0	0	2	0	0	0	0	1	0	3	0	0
eastern	274	.7527	41.694	56.2	29	18	47	50	71	33	21	5	15	4	3	12	2	116	1	23	8	1	0	1	2	20	51	15	0
Eastern	141	.6024	17.810	52.5	4	13	15	37	33	17	16	6	19	0	0	3	1	70	1	3	13	0	0	0	0	2	11	18	0
easternmost	5	.3111	.3857	35.9	0	0	0	1	2	2	0	0	1	0	0	0	0	3	0	0	0	0	0	0	0	0	0	1	0
Eastertide	3	.3380	.2439	33.9	0	0	0	1	1	1	0	0	1	1	0	1	0	0	0	0	0	0	0	0	0	0	0	0	0
Eastman	3	.2223	.2106	33.2	1	1	1	0	0	0	0	0	2	1	0	0	0	0	0	0	0	0	0	0	0	0	0	0	0
Easton	2	.0000	.0243	23.9	0	0	0	0	2	0	0	0	0	0	0	0	0	0	0	0	0	0	0	0	0	0	0	2	0
Eastport	2	.0000	.0914	29.6	0	0	0	0	0	2	0	0	2	0	0	0	0	0	0	0	0	0	0	0	0	0	0	0	0
eastward	72	.7185	10.553	50.2	7	4	12	7	18	13	8	3	6	2	0	4	1	23	0	18	0	0	0	0	4	5	5	4	0
Easty	2	.0000	.0290	24.6	0	0	0	0	0	0	2	0	0	0	0	0	0	0	0	0	0	0	0	0	0	2	0	0	0
easy	894	.9499	167.81	62.2	141	137	100	125	197	87	87	20	206	55	4	52	58	96	27	102	21	8	32	20	65	66	23	59	0
Easy	4	.4889	.4075	36.1	0	0	0	1	2	1	0	0	0	1	0	1	0	0	0	0	0	0	0	0	1	0	0	1	0
easy-going	3	.3263	.2368	33.7	0	0	0	1	2	0	0	0	1	0	0	0	0	0	0	0	1	0	0	0	0	0	0	1	0

4N eaglefeather	6G Earl's	4A earnibbling	6H earth-star	6A earthward	9B easter
6A Eagles'	7N earldom	6A Earnshaw's	9D earth-treading	8R earthworkers	3J Easter-hunt-and-party
3A Ealing	5Q early-American	XH Earoon	7H earth-type	9L eartips	8N Easter's
5G eam	4N early-closing	7J earpiece	4G earth-writing-thing	9D earworms	7B Easterner
3A Ear	7D early-day	9F earplugs	5Q earth-years	7L ease-stitch	7G Easterner's
4G EAR	9D early-risen	7R earth-circling	3H earthlight	7R EASEP	3C Easterners
8R ear-blasting	5A early-roosting	4R Earth-circling	7H earthlike	7J easily-copied	7R Eastland's
5F ear-piercing	8R earlywarning	7R earth-orbiting	9F earthlings	9H easily-evaporated	8F easy-handed
8P ear-splitting	5P earmarked	7M earth-parking	6R Earthly	6J easily-recognized	5A easy-like
3P eared-seal	7R earned-run	5A earth-quivering	7B Earthman's	7R EastGrandForks	XR easy-on-ulcer
4P eargerly	5E Earners	4P earth-shaking	9H Earthquake	3P east-bound	5A easy-shooting

Word Type	F	D	U	SFI	3 Gr 3	4 Gr 4	5 Gr 5	6 Gr 6	7 Gr 7	8 Gr 8	9 Gr 9	X UnGr	A Read	B Eng & Gr	C Comp	D Lit	E Math	F Soc Stud	G Spell	H Sci	J Music	K Art	L Home Ec	M Shop	N Lib F	P Lib NF	Q Lib Ref	R Mag	S Rel
easy-to-eat	2	.0000	.0064	18.1	0	0	0	0	0	1	1	0	0	0	0	0	0	0	0	0	0	0	2	0	0	0	0	0	0
easy-to-follow	2	.0000	.0219	23.4	0	0	0	0	0	0	2	0	0	2	0	0	0	0	0	0	0	0	0	0	0	0	0	0	0
easygoing	9	.5515	1.0892	40.4	2	1	2	0	3	0	1	0	4	0	0	0	0	1	0	0	0	0	0	0	0	2	1	1	0
eat	1616	.8466	274.50	64.4	581	270	167	203	208	82	85	20	441	60	5	56	30	103	35	352	25	1	94	0	125	170	59	55	5
EAT	2	.1812	.0838	29.2	1	0	0	0	1	0	0	0	0	0	0	0	0	0	0	0	0	0	1	0	0	0	0	1	0
eaten	251	.8752	43.859	56.4	67	35	37	37	38	21	14	2	64	28	2	12	12	22	3	40	1	0	10	1	14	21	18	3	0
eater	24	.6108	3.0295	44.8	11	3	0	2	5	0	2	1	2	0	0	2	0	0	1	2	0	0	1	0	0	12	2	2	0
Eater	4	.0000	.0579	27.6	4	0	0	0	0	0	0	0	0	0	0	0	0	0	0	0	0	0	0	0	0	4	0	0	0
eaters	37	.4579	3.6379	45.6	10	7	0	5	12	0	0	3	1	0	0	0	0	0	0	9	0	0	0	0	1	15	10	1	0
eaters-of-men	5	.0000	.0586	27.7	0	0	0	5	0	0	0	0	0	0	0	0	0	0	0	0	0	0	0	0	5	0	0	0	0
eatin'	3	.3399	.2456	33.9	0	0	0	0	3	0	0	0	1	0	0	1	0	0	0	0	0	0	0	0	0	0	0	1	0
eating	419	.7756	66.079	58.2	114	66	34	40	83	31	35	16	137	27	1	22	1	21	2	61	0	2	38	0	29	35	19	22	2
Eaton	10	.1498	.4535	36.6	4	0	0	0	1	5	0	0	0	0	0	0	0	9	0	0	0	0	0	0	0	0	0	1	0
eats	138	.7479	21.100	53.2	49	19	7	28	19	7	4	5	38	7	2	2	2	3	2	43	3	0	2	0	5	15	7	6	1
eau	2	.2433	.1158	30.6	0	1	0	0	0	0	0	1	0	0	0	0	0	0	0	0	0	0	0	0	0	1	0	1	0
EauGalle	2	.0000	.0215	23.3	0	0	0	2	0	0	0	0	0	0	0	2	0	0	0	0	0	0	0	0	0	0	0	0	0
eaves	11	.4994	1.2152	40.8	2	0	0	2	2	4	1	0	4	2	0	3	0	0	0	1	0	0	0	0	0	1	0	0	0
eavesdropper	2	.0000	.0215	23.3	0	0	0	0	0	0	2	0	0	0	0	2	0	0	0	0	0	0	0	0	0	0	0	0	0
eavesdropping	2	.0000	.0914	29.6	0	2	0	0	0	0	0	0	2	0	0	0	0	0	0	0	0	0	0	0	0	0	0	0	0
Eb	7	.2362	.5173	37.1	5	0	0	0	0	2	0	0	5	0	0	0	0	0	0	0	0	0	0	0	2	0	0	0	0
Eb's	2	.1787	.1174	30.7	1	0	0	0	0	1	0	0	1	0	0	0	0	0	0	0	0	0	0	0	1	0	0	0	0
ebb	11	.5537	1.2679	41.0	3	0	1	0	3	2	0	2	0	0	0	0	0	0	0	3	0	0	0	0	2	3	2	1	0
Ebbets	2	.0000	.0290	24.6	2	0	0	0	0	0	0	0	0	0	0	0	0	0	0	0	0	0	0	0	0	2	0	0	0
ebbing	3	.3454	.2542	34.1	0	0	0	1	0	2	0	0	1	0	0	0	0	1	0	0	0	0	0	0	0	0	0	1	0
EBEN	9	.0000	.0966	29.8	0	0	0	0	9	0	0	0	0	0	0	9	0	0	0	0	0	0	0	0	0	0	0	0	0
Ebenezer	8	.2393	.6011	37.8	0	0	1	0	7	0	0	0	6	0	0	2	0	0	0	0	0	0	0	0	0	0	0	0	0
ebony	4	.3863	.3416	35.3	0	1	0	1	0	1	1	0	0	0	0	1	0	2	0	0	0	0	0	0	0	0	0	1	0
Ebony	7	.0000	.0751	28.8	0	0	0	0	7	0	0	0	0	0	0	7	0	0	0	0	0	0	0	0	0	0	0	0	0
ebullience	2	.0000	.0243	23.9	0	0	0	0	0	0	1	1	0	0	0	0	0	0	0	0	0	0	0	0	0	0	0	2	0
eccentric	11	.6069	1.4129	41.5	2	1	0	0	2	1	5	0	4	2	0	0	0	0	0	1	1	0	0	1	1	0	1	0	0
ecclesiastical	9	.3198	.6380	38.0	0	0	3	0	1	3	2	0	0	0	0	1	0	0	0	0	0	0	0	0	0	3	5	0	0
echinoderm	4	.2353	.2382	33.8	0	0	0	0	4	0	0	0	0	0	0	0	0	0	0	3	0	0	0	0	0	0	1	0	0
echinoderms	8	.0000	.1577	32.0	0	0	0	0	8	0	0	0	0	0	0	0	0	0	0	8	0	0	0	0	0	0	0	0	0
echo	78	.7659	12.065	50.8	7	14	8	19	12	10	6	2	12	3	2	5	1	0	4	19	16	0	0	0	3	4	3	6	0
Echo	21	.4467	1.9638	42.9	0	3	12	4	1	1	0	0	0	13	0	0	0	0	0	0	4	0	0	1	1	2	0	0	0
echoed	47	.7304	7.0656	48.5	6	10	8	11	9	2	1	0	19	2	2	3	0	0	0	0	2	0	0	0	6	7	2	4	0
echoes	46	.6718	6.4043	48.1	1	7	8	11	3	5	10	1	14	1	1	10	0	0	0	5	8	0	0	0	3	1	0	3	0
echoic	2	.0000	.0219	23.4	0	0	2	0	0	0	0	0	0	2	0	0	0	0	0	0	0	0	0	0	0	0	0	0	0
echoing	13	.6049	1.6288	42.1	1	1	6	1	3	1	0	0	2	0	1	2	0	0	0	0	1	0	0	0	4	2	0	1	0
echos	2	.2152	.1357	31.3	0	0	1	0	1	0	0	0	1	0	0	0	0	1	0	0	0	0	0	0	0	0	0	0	0
eclectic	2	.0000	.0037	15.7	0	0	0	0	0	2	0	0	0	0	0	0	0	0	0	0	0	2	0	0	0	0	0	0	0
eclipse	31	.3848	2.6517	44.2	1	21	1	3	2	2	0	1	2	2	0	0	0	1	1	1	0	0	0	0	0	22	2	0	0
eclipses	13	.5391	1.4683	41.7	0	3	0	0	6	1	3	0	0	1	0	1	0	1	0	3	0	0	0	0	0	6	1	0	0
eclipsing	5	.2121	.2801	34.5	0	0	0	0	1	0	4	0	0	0	0	0	0	0	0	4	0	0	0	0	0	0	0	1	0
ecological	10	.2363	.5596	37.5	0	0	0	0	10	0	0	0	0	0	0	0	0	0	0	2	0	0	0	0	0	0	7	1	0
ecologically	2	.2437	.1129	30.5	0	0	0	0	1	0	0	1	0	0	0	0	0	0	0	0	0	0	0	0	0	0	1	1	0
ecologist	5	.2213	.2870	34.6	0	0	0	0	5	0	0	0	0	0	0	0	0	0	0	4	0	0	0	0	0	0	1	0	0
ecologist's	2	.0000	.0394	26.0	0	0	0	0	2	0	0	0	0	0	0	0	0	0	0	2	0	0	0	0	0	0	0	0	0
ecologists	2	.2437	.1129	30.5	0	0	0	0	1	1	0	0	0	0	0	0	0	0	0	0	0	0	0	0	0	0	1	1	0
ecology	10	.3429	.7603	38.8	0	0	0	0	8	0	1	1	0	0	0	0	0	0	0	2	0	0	0	0	0	0	3	5	0
economic	170	.5564	19.737	53.0	17	5	28	4	29	33	48	6	3	1	0	1	0	59	0	5	3	0	0	0	0	22	47	29	0
Economic	12	.4659	1.2182	40.9	0	0	1	1	2	3	3	2	1	0	0	0	0	6	0	0	0	0	0	0	0	1	1	3	0
economical	27	.5050	2.8119	44.5	1	0	0	1	4	5	13	3	1	2	0	0	0	2	0	0	1	0	8	2	0	0	7	4	0
economically	25	.4590	2.4434	43.9	3	1	0	3	2	4	8	4	0	0	0	0	0	7	0	3	0	0	1	0	0	0	12	2	0
economics	28	.6219	3.5460	45.5	0	1	6	2	3	4	11	1	0	5	0	0	4	1	0	0	0	0	2	0	0	3	8	5	0
Economics	4	.1873	.1827	32.6	0	0	2	0	0	1	1	0	0	0	0	0	0	0	0	0	0	0	0	0	0	0	3	1	0
economies	7	.4599	.6898	38.4	0	1	1	1	1	1	2	0	0	0	0	0	0	3	0	0	0	0	0	0	0	1	2	1	0
economist	8	.3344	.5897	37.7	0	0	3	0	2	3	0	0	0	0	0	0	0	3	0	0	0	0	2	0	0	0	3	0	0
economists	18	.3776	1.4508	41.6	1	0	0	0	8	2	5	2	0	0	0	0	1	2	0	1	0	0	6	0	0	0	3	5	0
economy	104	.7080	14.929	51.7	2	4	14	6	22	25	26	5	2	4	0	2	1	31	0	6	2	1	0	0	1	14	21	19	0
Economy	4	.0000	.0419	26.2	0	0	2	0	1	1	0	0	0	0	0	0	0	0	0	0	0	0	0	0	0	0	4	0	0
ecosystem	3	.2159	.1532	31.9	0	0	0	0	3	0	0	0	0	0	0	0	0	0	0	0	0	0	0	0	0	0	2	1	0
Ecrette's	2	.0000	.0234	23.7	0	2	0	0	0	0	0	0	0	0	0	0	0	0	0	0	0	0	0	0	2	0	0	0	0
ecstasy	8	.5097	.8594	39.3	0	0	1	1	3	1	1	1	1	0	1	0	0	0	0	0	1	0	0	0	1	1	0	3	0
ecstatic	7	.5057	.7400	38.7	1	0	1	0	2	0	2	1	0	0	0	0	0	0	0	1	1	0	0	0	3	1	0	1	0
ecstatically	3	.0000	.0352	25.5	1	0	1	0	1	0	0	0	0	0	0	0	0	0	0	0	0	0	0	0	3	0	0	0	0
Ector	2	.0000	.0914	29.6	0	0	0	2	0	0	0	0	2	0	0	0	0	0	0	0	0	0	0	0	0	0	0	0	0
Ecuador	25	.2053	1.4019	41.5	5	1	2	9	3	1	4	0	1	1	0	0	0	22	0	0	0	0	0	0	0	0	1	0	0
ed	182	.1690	8.2243	49.2	55	28	31	34	19	3	12	0	29	15	0	0	0	1	135	0	0	0	0	0	0	0	2	0	0
Ed	118	.6114	15.520	51.9	39	19	5	11	21	16	5	2	59	20	0	1	8	0	0	1	0	0	0	0	7	18	0	4	0
ED	5	.0000	.0748	28.7	0	0	0	2	1	2	0	0	0	0	0	0	5	0	0	0	0	0	0	0	0	0	0	0	0
Ed's	12	.5471	1.4216	41.5	4	3	1	2	1	0	1	0	4	2	0	0	3	0	0	0	0	0	0	0	1	2	0	0	0
EDA	2	.0000	.0243	23.9	0	0	0	0	0	0	0	2	0	0	0	0	0	0	0	0	0	0	0	0	0	0	0	2	0
Edam	7	.3455	.6322	38.0	0	0	0	5	1	1	0	0	5	0	0	0	0	0	1	0	0	0	1	0	0	0	0	0	0
Eddie	350	.3265	27.432	54.4	203	111	10	4	14	3	5	0	97	0	0	36	0	0	0	0	0	0	0	0	200	9	0	8	0
Eddie's	44	.4215	4.2977	46.3	23	12	4	1	0	0	4	0	18	0	0	3	0	0	0	0	0	0	0	0	18	1	0	4	0
Eddington	4	.2405	.2410	33.8	0	2	0	0	2	0	0	0	0	0	0	0	0	0	0	2	0	0	0	0	0	2	0	0	0
Eddington's	2	.0000	.0394	26.0	0	0	0	0	2	0	0	0	0	0	0	0	0	0	0	2	0	0	0	0	0	0	0	0	0
eddy	2	.0000	.0219	23.4	2	0	0	0	0	0	0	0	0	2	0	0	0	0	0	0	0	0	0	0	0	0	0	0	0
Eddy	61	.1683	2.6306	44.2	53	1	0	0	5	1	1	0	1	0	1	1	0	0	0	0	0	0	0	0	57	0	1	0	0
eddying	2	.1605	.0742	28.7	2	0	0	0	0	0	0	0	0	1	1	0	0	0	0	0	0	0	0	0	0	0	0	0	0
Ede	2	.0000	.0914	29.6	0	2	0	0	0	0	0	0	2	0	0	0	0	0	0	0	0	0	0	0	0	0	0	0	0
Eden	3	.3811	.2534	34.0	0	0	1	0	0	0	0	2	0	0	0	0	0	0	0	1	0	0	0	0	0	1	0	1	0
Edgar	27	.6254	3.5900	45.6	2	1	6	2	9	5	1	1	12	1	0	6	1	1	0	0	1	0	0	0	0	0	1	4	0
edge	817	.7132	118.56	60.7	125	95	74	94	175	117	125	12	160	5	15	38	51	52	4	83	11	7	113	101	54	60	27	36	0
Edge	2	.0000	.0290	24.6	0	0	0	0	0	0	0	2	0	0	0	0	0	0	0	0	0	0	0	0	0	2	0	0	0
edge-to-edge	2	.0000	.0050	17.0	0	0	0	0	2	0	0	0	0	0	0	0	0	0	0	0	0	0	0	2	0	0	0	0	0
edged	22	.5317	2.4936	44.0	1	2	1	4	7	2	5	0	5	1	2	8	0	1	0	0	0	0	0	0	2	3	0	0	0
edger	3	.1174	.0833	29.2	0	0	0	0	2	0	1	0	0	1	0	0	0	0	0	0	0	0	0	2	0	0	0	0	0
edges	269	.5723	31.736	55.0	31	22	18	24	74	42	53	5	31	0	1	3	30	14	3	21	1	9	72	45	6	15	10	8	0
edging	2	.0000	.0914	29.6	0	0	0	0	2	0	0	0	2	0	0	0	0	0	0	0	0	0	0	0	0	0	0	0	0
edible	16	.7233	2.3569	43.7	0	3	1	2	3	1	4	2	3	1	0	1	0	0	1	3	0	0	1	0	0	1	3	2	0
edict	3	.3871	.2488	34.0	1	0	0	0	1	1	0	0	0	1	0	0	0	0	0	0	0	0	0	0	0	0	1	1	0
Edict	5	.0000	.0523	27.2	1	0	2	0	0	0	2	0	0	0	0	0	0	0	0	0	0	0	0	0	0	0	5	0	0

8N Easy-to-Read
7R easy-to-assemble
8L easy-to-grasp
8L easy-to-handle
7A easy-to-reach
4Q easy-to-use
9D eating-place
8F Eaton's
8A eaves'
7A eavesdrop
4N eavesdroppers
9F Eban
9H ebbed
7F ebony-black
7D Ebony's
7F Ebro
6R Ebsen's
5P ebullient
7F ECAFE
6P eccentrique
7N Ecclesiastical
9R ecclesiasticize
7Q echidna
7A echo-sounders
7K Echoes
3F Eckert
9R Eckstein
7N eclat
3P Eclipse
7P eclipsed
8D Ecole
9R Economists
8L economy-minded
7N ecstasies
9H ectoderm
6A Ector's
5P ecumenical
5P Ecumenical
8G eczema
8G ed/**
5G ed'esen**
6R Eda
8E EDC
8D Eddenburrough
4A eddicated
7D eddied
4Q eddies
4P Eddingtons
5E Eddy's
4A Ede's
6H Edel
8Q Edenton
8L edge-stitch
7P edge-to-surface
9Q Edgerton
8Q Edgeware
3A Edgewood
8N edgy
XH edicts

Word Type	F	D	U	SFI	3 Gr 3	4 Gr 4	5 Gr 5	6 Gr 6	7 Gr 7	8 Gr 8	9 Gr 9	X UnGr	A Read	B Eng & Gr	C Comp	D Lit	E Math	F Soc Stud	G Spell	H Sci	J Music	K Art	L Home Ec	M Shop	N Lib F	P Lib NF	Q Lib Ref	R Mag	S Rel
edification	2	.2387	.1089	30.4	0	0	0	0	1	0	1	0	0	0	0	0	0	0	0	0	1	0	0	0	1	0	0	0	0
edifice	4	.3588	.3039	34.8	0	0	0	0	1	0	2	1	0	1	0	1	0	0	0	0	0	1	0	0	0	0	1	0	0
edifices	2	.2437	.1129	30.5	0	0	0	0	0	0	1	1	0	0	0	0	0	0	0	0	0	0	0	0	0	0	1	1	0
Edinburgh	19	.1707	.9339	39.7	0	0	3	1	3	0	12	0	4	0	0	0	0	2	0	0	0	0	0	0	0	0	13	0	0
Edinburgh's	2	.0000	.0209	23.2	0	0	0	0	0	0	2	0	0	0	0	0	0	0	0	0	0	0	0	0	0	0	2	0	0
Edison	66	.5698	7.9717	49.0	0	9	16	2	24	5	10	0	18	4	0	0	4	7	0	0	21	0	0	1	0	0	10	1	0
Edison's	24	.2603	1.4525	41.6	0	0	2	0	15	2	5	0	2	0	0	0	0	2	0	0	15	0	0	0	0	0	5	0	0
edit	4	.3778	.3240	35.1	0	0	0	0	2	0	1	1	0	1	0	0	0	0	0	0	1	0	0	0	0	0	0	2	0
edited	12	.5502	1.3561	41.3	0	3	1	0	5	0	3	0	0	1	0	1	0	0	0	0	4	0	0	0	0	3	2	1	0
Edith	13	.4537	1.3844	41.4	0	1	8	1	2	0	1	0	8	0	1	2	0	0	0	0	0	0	0	0	2	0	0	0	0
Edith's	3	.2212	.2099	33.2	0	0	2	0	0	0	1	0	2	0	0	1	0	0	0	0	0	0	0	0	0	0	0	0	0
edition	19	.4797	1.9165	42.8	1	2	1	2	4	2	6	1	1	4	0	0	0	0	0	0	2	0	0	0	0	2	9	1	0
Edition	4	.3060	.2924	34.7	0	1	0	0	2	0	1	0	1	0	0	0	0	0	1	0	0	0	0	0	0	0	2	0	0
editions	5	.4150	.4599	36.6	1	1	1	0	1	0	1	0	1	0	0	0	0	0	0	0	1	0	0	0	0	1	2	0	0
editor	69	.7622	10.561	50.2	3	6	6	6	16	17	11	4	3	11	2	9	0	8	2	1	0	0	0	0	5	7	6	15	0
Editor	2	.2446	.1142	30.6	0	0	0	0	0	1	1	0	0	0	0	0	0	0	0	0	0	0	0	0	1	0	0	1	0
Editor-in-Chief	2	.0000	.0290	24.6	0	2	0	0	0	0	0	0	0	0	0	0	0	0	0	0	0	0	0	0	0	2	0	0	0
editor-in-chief	2	.0000	.0243	23.9	0	0	0	0	0	2	0	0	0	0	0	0	0	0	0	0	0	0	0	0	0	0	0	2	0
editor's	5	.1496	.2557	34.1	0	0	1	0	2	1	0	1	2	0	0	0	0	0	0	0	0	0	0	0	0	0	0	3	0
editorial	15	.5070	1.5841	42.0	0	0	1	0	1	9	3	1	1	0	0	1	0	1	4	0	0	2	0	0	0	0	2	4	0
editorials	11	.5222	1.2333	40.9	0	0	1	0	2	2	6	0	2	2	0	1	0	3	0	0	0	0	0	0	0	0	0	3	0
editors	17	.5879	2.1033	43.2	3	4	0	0	5	1	4	0	4	5	0	1	0	1	0	0	0	0	0	0	0	1	3	2	0
Edmond	3	.3670	.2406	33.8	0	1	0	0	0	1	0	1	0	0	0	0	0	0	1	1	0	0	0	0	0	0	1	0	0
Edmonton	5	.2205	.2855	34.6	0	0	4	0	0	1	0	0	0	0	0	0	0	4	0	0	0	0	0	0	0	0	1	0	0
Edmund	31	.6028	3.9013	45.9	0	5	5	9	4	3	3	2	5	1	0	0	0	4	0	1	0	0	0	0	11	3	3	3	0
Edmund's	3	.1250	.1342	31.3	0	0	1	2	0	0	0	0	1	0	0	0	0	0	0	0	0	0	0	0	2	0	0	0	0
Edna	5	.3601	.3927	35.9	0	1	0	0	1	0	2	1	0	0	0	2	1	0	0	0	0	0	0	0	0	0	0	2	0
Eduardo	7	.0000	.3198	35.0	0	0	2	0	5	0	0	0	7	0	0	0	0	0	0	0	0	0	0	0	0	0	0	0	0
educate	11	.6510	1.4628	41.7	1	0	1	2	1	5	1	0	0	2	0	2	1	3	0	1	0	0	0	0	0	0	1	1	0
educated	86	.7389	12.876	51.1	5	3	18	12	16	24	8	0	8	11	0	4	0	25	3	3	2	0	0	0	0	12	11	7	0
educating	4	.3288	.3285	35.2	0	1	0	0	1	1	1	0	1	0	0	0	0	2	0	1	0	0	0	0	0	0	0	0	0
education	294	.8027	47.359	56.8	20	12	35	29	71	37	76	14	30	13	1	13	2	72	6	7	5	1	1	2	6	19	54	62	0
Education	24	.4829	2.4371	43.9	2	1	0	1	1	2	13	4	0	0	0	0	1	3	0	0	1	0	0	0	0	2	5	12	0
educational	40	.6598	5.3900	47.3	2	2	4	4	12	6	7	3	2	3	0	0	0	9	0	3	1	0	0	3	0	3	8	8	0
educations	2	.2306	.1140	30.6	0	0	1	0	0	1	0	0	0	1	0	0	0	1	0	0	0	0	0	0	0	0	0	0	0
educator	3	.3769	.2439	33.9	0	0	1	0	2	0	0	0	0	0	0	0	0	0	1	0	0	0	0	0	0	1	0	1	0
educators	12	.3642	.9789	39.9	1	0	3	0	4	1	3	0	1	0	0	0	0	2	0	0	0	0	0	0	0	0	3	6	0
Edvard	4	.0000	.0323	25.1	0	2	0	2	0	0	0	0	0	0	0	0	0	0	0	0	4	0	0	0	0	0	0	0	0
Edward	252	.5895	30.639	54.9	6	164	33	8	8	16	15	2	12	9	0	2	0	6	0	3	4	4	0	0	113	67	23	9	0
Edward's	16	.2305	.8925	39.5	0	14	2	0	0	0	0	0	0	0	0	0	0	0	0	0	0	0	0	0	5	11	0	0	0
Edwardian	3	.2143	.1568	32.0	0	0	1	0	0	1	0	1	0	0	0	0	0	0	0	0	0	0	0	0	0	1	0	2	0
Edwards	45	.5332	5.0156	47.0	2	1	13	19	2	5	3	0	1	0	0	1	3	12	0	0	0	0	0	4	0	4	1	19	0
Edwin	24	.4916	2.4698	43.9	0	11	2	1	5	2	3	0	0	0	4	1	0	3	0	1	1	0	0	0	0	10	1	3	0
Edwina	7	.0000	.0821	29.1	0	0	0	0	7	0	0	0	0	0	0	0	0	0	0	0	0	0	0	0	7	0	0	0	0
ee	20	.2515	1.1191	40.5	5	3	5	4	0	2	1	0	0	3	0	0	0	0	15	0	1	0	0	0	1	0	0	0	0
ee-ri-gi	3	.0000	.0243	23.8	0	0	0	3	0	0	0	0	0	0	0	0	0	0	0	0	3	0	0	0	0	0	0	0	0
ee-yah	2	.0000	.0162	22.1	0	0	0	2	0	0	0	0	0	0	0	0	0	0	0	0	2	0	0	0	0	0	0	0	0
eel	24	.6275	3.0791	44.9	1	1	8	2	8	2	2	0	0	5	0	2	0	1	1	6	0	0	0	0	4	0	5	0	0
Eel	5	.0000	.2284	33.6	0	5	0	0	0	0	0	0	5	0	0	0	0	0	0	0	0	0	0	0	0	0	0	0	0
Eelka	17	.0000	.1993	33.0	0	0	17	0	0	0	0	0	0	0	0	0	0	0	0	0	0	0	0	0	17	0	0	0	0
eels	23	.5478	2.6772	44.3	2	0	6	10	1	3	1	0	2	1	0	1	0	0	0	13	0	0	0	0	0	2	1	3	0
eerie	21	.6350	2.8224	44.5	1	0	2	7	4	6	0	1	9	2	0	1	0	0	0	0	1	0	0	0	1	2	0	5	0
ef	5	.3854	.4790	36.8	2	1	0	0	1	1	0	0	3	0	0	0	0	0	0	0	0	0	0	0	1	1	0	0	0
EF	24	.0000	.3592	35.6	2	2	1	2	5	11	1	0	0	0	0	0	24	0	0	0	0	0	0	0	0	0	0	0	0
efendi	3	.0000	.0434	26.4	0	0	3	0	0	0	0	0	0	0	0	0	0	0	0	0	0	0	0	0	0	3	0	0	0
effect	399	.8526	67.716	58.3	6	33	41	47	96	81	68	27	27	22	6	17	7	25	4	91	42	21	13	7	9	20	62	26	0
Effect	3	.1169	.1277	31.1	0	1	0	0	0	0	2	0	1	0	0	0	0	0	0	0	0	0	0	0	0	0	2	0	0
effected	8	.4348	.7306	38.6	0	0	1	0	1	3	3	0	0	1	0	0	0	0	0	1	0	0	0	2	0	1	2	1	0
effecting	5	.4296	.4747	36.8	0	0	0	1	1	0	2	1	1	0	0	0	0	0	0	0	0	0	0	0	1	0	1	2	0
effective	136	.8083	21.928	53.4	1	3	18	12	42	27	29	4	4	15	6	4	0	7	1	13	13	5	1	1	1	15	33	17	0
effectively	55	.8373	9.1531	49.6	0	1	7	3	12	16	15	1	1	13	3	2	0	5	2	2	3	1	4	1	1	7	6	4	0
effectiveness	13	.5418	1.4538	41.6	0	0	0	3	3	3	4	0	1	2	2	1	0	0	0	0	3	0	0	0	0	0	2	2	0
effects	158	.8191	25.864	54.1	6	13	17	13	35	29	32	13	7	2	2	5	1	11	1	52	16	6	3	2	2	8	30	10	0
Effendi	3	.0000	.1370	31.4	0	3	0	0	0	0	0	0	3	0	0	0	0	0	0	0	0	0	0	0	0	0	0	0	0
efficiency	40	.7438	5.9823	47.8	0	0	7	5	14	5	9	0	2	2	1	2	0	1	0	4	1	0	1	2	0	3	13	8	0
efficient	94	.7272	13.824	51.4	0	2	8	6	35	11	28	4	8	3	0	0	2	13	1	11	2	0	7	5	2	6	28	6	0
efficiently	27	.6419	3.5619	45.5	0	2	1	0	15	5	3	1	2	2	0	1	0	6	0	4	0	0	2	0	0	0	7	3	0
effigy	3	.2197	.2090	33.2	0	0	0	0	1	1	1	0	2	0	0	0	0	0	0	0	0	0	0	0	0	0	1	0	0
effort	227	.8632	39.060	55.9	12	19	15	38	66	35	34	8	33	7	3	8	0	28	5	28	2	0	10	3	14	18	33	35	0
effortless	6	.5512	.7100	38.5	0	0	0	1	3	1	1	0	2	0	0	0	0	0	0	0	1	0	0	0	1	0	1	1	0
effortlessly	2	.1814	.1187	30.7	0	0	0	1	1	0	0	0	1	0	0	0	0	0	0	0	0	0	0	0	0	0	0	1	0
efforts	117	.8801	20.491	53.1	7	4	14	7	27	23	29	6	19	3	1	4	1	17	1	9	4	2	3	1	4	11	25	12	0
EFG	7	.0000	.1048	30.2	0	0	0	2	2	3	0	0	0	0	0	0	7	0	0	0	0	0	0	0	0	0	0	0	0
EFGH	9	.0000	.1347	31.3	0	2	5	1	0	1	0	0	0	0	0	0	9	0	0	0	0	0	0	0	0	0	0	0	0
EG	2	.0000	.0299	24.8	0	0	0	0	1	1	0	0	0	0	0	0	2	0	0	0	0	0	0	0	0	0	0	0	0
egalite	2	.2285	.1129	30.5	1	0	0	0	1	0	0	0	0	0	0	0	0	1	0	0	0	0	0	0	0	0	1	0	0
Egeria	2	.0000	.0290	24.6	0	0	0	2	0	0	0	0	0	0	0	0	0	0	0	0	0	0	0	0	0	2	0	0	0
EGEUS	2	.0000	.0215	23.3	0	0	0	0	0	0	2	0	0	0	0	2	0	0	0	0	0	0	0	0	0	0	0	0	0
egg	379	.6655	52.026	57.2	114	18	53	37	84	11	46	16	67	7	0	2	6	3	8	122	4	0	40	0	16	33	60	11	0
egg-laying	4	.2672	.2733	34.4	0	1	0	1	2	0	0	0	1	0	0	0	0	0	0	1	0	0	0	0	0	0	2	0	0
egg-shaped	6	.3079	.4501	36.5	1	2	2	0	1	0	0	0	1	0	0	0	0	0	0	3	0	0	0	0	0	0	2	0	0
Eggborn	7	.0000	.1013	30.1	7	0	0	0	0	0	0	0	0	0	0	0	0	0	0	0	0	0	0	0	0	7	0	0	0
eggplant	4	.4756	.4063	36.1	0	1	0	1	0	1	0	1	0	0	0	0	0	1	0	1	0	0	0	0	0	0	1	1	0
eggs	785	.7997	126.89	61.0	299	84	81	103	150	17	36	15	184	27	2	21	42	30	2	232	4	1	19	0	18	104	90	9	0
Eggs	2	.2446	.1257	31.0	1	0	0	1	0	0	0	0	0	0	0	0	0	1	0	1	0	0	0	0	0	0	0	0	0
eggshell	5	.4746	.5331	37.3	0	1	1	1	2	0	0	0	2	0	0	1	0	0	0	0	0	0	0	0	0	1	1	0	0
eggshells	3	.1277	.1363	31.3	0	2	0	0	1	0	0	0	1	0	0	0	0	0	0	0	0	0	0	0	0	0	0	2	0
EGH	2	.0000	.0299	24.8	0	0	1	0	0	1	0	0	0	0	0	0	2	0	0	0	0	0	0	0	0	0	0	0	0
ego	6	.2266	.3513	35.5	0	0	0	0	3	0	1	2	1	0	0	0	0	0	0	0	0	0	0	0	0	1	0	4	0
EGP	2	.0000	.0299	24.8	0	0	0	0	2	0	0	0	0	0	0	0	2	0	0	0	0	0	0	0	0	0	0	0	0
Egypt	164	.6765	22.773	53.6	14	17	18	23	62	11	14	5	14	6	1	2	5	83	0	1	1	6	0	0	1	15	22	7	0
Egypt's	28	.3219	2.0841	43.2	1	0	1	1	14	3	8	0	0	0	0	0	0	16	0	0	0	0	0	0	0	2	0	10	0
Egyptian	131	.5829	15.826	52.0	1	16	22	14	36	22	17	3	10	2	0	1	31	26	7	3	3	18	0	1	0	5	18	6	0

9R Edina
5P Edirne
4Q editing
4Q Editions
6R Editorial
8F editorialized
6G edits
8G editus
7K Edouard
6R Edsel
7R Edson
7A Eduardo's
6B educate-education
9R educationists
5A Educator
7R Edwards'
6R Edwards's
8F Ee-say
8G ee's
9F EEC
4A eee
3A eee-eee-eee-eee-eee
3R EEEEEEEEEEEEEEEK
3R EEEEEEEEEEEEEEK
6A eeeeyiiii-eeeeeee
5H eelgrass
5N Eelka's
4J eels'
7P Eenty
6B eeny
5A eerie-looking
6J eerigi
7Q eerily
5R ees
8D eewoonuck
7A efface
7R effaced
9Q EFFECT
XR Effects
8D effectually
9A effeminacy
7H effervescent
8A Effie
8A Effie's
XP effigies
7P effulgence
8Q effusion
5E EFH
3N Efraim
3N Efraim's
XR Eg
7R Egalite
5Q Egbert
9D Egeus
4P Egg
9L egg-and-milk
5D egg-layer
6F egg-marketing
8L egg-milk
7Q egg-producing
9A eggburgers
8A egged
5N Eggletina's
7A eggplants
8K Eggplants
5Q Egoist
9Q egotists
XR egregious
7Q egret

Word Type	F	D	U	SFI	3 Gr 3	4 Gr 4	5 Gr 5	6 Gr 6	7 Gr 7	8 Gr 8	9 Gr 9	X UnGr	A Read	B Eng & Gr	C Comp	D Lit	E Math	F Soc Stud	G Spell	H Sci	J Music	K Art	L Home Ec	M Shop	N Lib F	P Lib NF	Q Lib Ref	R Mag	S Rel
Egyptians	89	.6752	12.246	50.9	1	3	15	20	21	15	12	2	3	3	0	0	10	32	5	4	1	7	1	0	0	3	14	6	0
eh	37	.4797	4.0315	46.1	6	5	5	2	13	4	1	1	18	0	0	4	0	0	0	0	0	0	0	0	11	1	0	3	0
EH	4	.2129	.2122	33.3	0	0	4	0	0	0	0	0	0	0	0	0	3	0	0	0	0	0	0	0	0	0	0	1	0
Ehmke	5	.0000	.0724	28.6	1	0	0	4	0	0	0	0	0	0	0	0	0	0	0	0	0	0	0	0	0	5	0	0	0
Ehmke's	3	.0000	.0434	26.4	0	0	0	3	0	0	0	0	0	0	0	0	0	0	0	0	0	0	0	0	0	3	0	0	0
Ehre	10	.2353	.7830	38.9	0	0	9	0	0	0	1	0	9	0	0	0	0	0	0	0	1	0	0	0	0	0	0	0	0
Ehrhart	12	.0000	.5482	37.4	0	0	0	0	0	12	0	0	12	0	0	0	0	0	0	0	0	0	0	0	0	0	0	0	0
Ehrich	2	.0000	.0914	29.6	0	2	0	0	0	0	0	0	2	0	0	0	0	0	0	0	0	0	0	0	0	0	0	0	0
Ehrlich	2	.0000	.0394	26.0	0	0	0	0	1	0	1	0	0	0	0	0	0	0	0	2	0	0	0	0	0	0	0	0	0
Ehrlichman	2	.0000	.0243	23.9	0	0	0	0	0	0	2	0	0	0	0	0	0	0	0	0	0	0	0	0	0	0	0	2	0
ei	31	.1745	1.2843	41.1	0	2	1	9	14	3	2	0	0	5	0	1	0	0	25	0	0	0	0	0	0	0	0	0	0
eider	3	.2435	.2274	33.6	0	1	2	0	0	0	0	0	2	0	0	0	0	1	0	0	0	0	0	0	0	0	0	0	0
Eielson	4	.0000	.1827	32.6	0	0	4	0	0	0	0	0	4	0	0	0	0	0	0	0	0	0	0	0	0	0	0	0	0
Eielson's	2	.0000	.0914	29.6	0	0	2	0	0	0	0	0	2	0	0	0	0	0	0	0	0	0	0	0	0	0	0	0	0
eight	651	.9193	118.60	60.7	88	108	73	102	119	82	60	19	118	41	9	20	62	50	55	64	41	1	1	2	30	71	33	53	0
Eight	5	.5243	.5608	37.5	1	1	2	0	0	0	1	0	1	0	0	0	0	1	0	0	1	0	0	0	0	0	1	1	0
eight-foot	5	.4233	.4710	36.7	0	1	0	1	0	0	2	1	1	0	0	0	1	0	0	0	0	0	0	0	0	0	1	2	0
eight-hour	4	.2835	.2871	34.6	0	0	1	1	0	0	0	2	1	0	0	0	0	0	0	1	0	0	0	0	0	0	0	2	0
eight-inch	4	.3766	.3696	35.7	0	0	3	0	1	0	0	0	2	0	0	0	0	0	0	0	0	0	0	0	0	1	0	1	0
eight-measure	2	.0000	.0162	22.1	0	0	0	1	1	0	0	0	0	0	0	0	0	0	0	0	2	0	0	0	0	0	0	0	0
eight-thirty	3	.3553	.2608	34.2	0	2	0	1	0	0	0	0	1	0	0	0	0	1	0	0	0	0	0	0	0	1	0	0	0
eight-year-old	7	.2894	.4890	36.9	0	5	0	0	2	0	0	0	1	0	0	0	0	0	0	0	0	0	0	0	0	4	0	2	0
eighteen	68	.8749	11.895	50.8	10	10	10	9	18	4	5	2	23	4	1	4	4	5	2	2	1	0	2	0	4	12	1	3	0
eighteen-pounders	2	.0000	.0914	29.6	0	0	0	0	2	0	0	0	2	0	0	0	0	0	0	0	0	0	0	0	0	0	0	0	0
eighteen-year-old	4	.2405	.2474	33.9	0	2	0	1	0	0	1	0	1	0	1	0	0	0	0	0	0	0	0	0	0	2	0	0	0
eighteenth	38	.5878	4.5873	46.6	1	1	2	6	14	9	3	2	2	2	0	0	2	3	0	1	16	2	0	0	0	4	3	3	0
Eighteenth	2	.2285	.1129	30.5	0	0	0	0	1	1	0	0	0	0	0	0	0	1	0	0	0	0	0	0	0	0	1	0	0
eighteenth-century	10	.5653	1.1765	40.7	0	0	1	1	4	3	1	0	1	2	0	0	0	0	0	0	2	0	0	0	1	3	0	1	0
eightfold	4	.0000	.0419	26.2	0	0	0	0	1	0	3	0	0	0	0	0	0	0	0	0	0	0	0	0	0	0	4	0	0
eighth	91	.5500	10.384	50.2	18	22	9	11	13	11	7	0	7	9	0	3	11	2	4	4	41	0	0	0	0	3	4	3	0
Eighth	6	.4196	.5543	37.4	0	2	2	0	1	0	0	1	1	0	0	0	0	0	0	0	0	0	0	0	1	0	2	2	0
eighth-grade	2	.2404	.1142	30.6	0	0	0	0	0	2	0	0	0	1	0	0	1	0	0	0	0	0	0	0	0	0	0	0	0
eighths	17	.2348	.9612	39.8	5	4	0	2	4	0	2	0	0	0	0	0	15	0	0	0	0	0	2	0	0	0	0	0	0
eights	30	.2594	1.8981	42.8	0	12	10	2	4	2	0	0	2	0	0	0	24	0	0	0	0	0	0	0	1	1	2	0	0
eighty	41	.8166	6.7801	48.3	5	7	4	6	7	6	2	4	16	0	0	1	2	3	1	5	2	0	0	0	3	4	1	3	0
eighty-eight	6	.3801	.5663	37.5	1	0	2	0	0	3	0	0	3	0	0	0	0	2	0	0	0	0	0	0	0	1	0	0	0
eighty-five	9	.5492	1.0761	40.3	1	1	1	1	1	3	1	0	3	0	0	1	0	3	0	0	0	0	0	0	1	1	0	0	0
eighty-four	3	.3269	.2368	33.7	0	0	1	1	0	0	1	0	1	0	0	0	0	0	1	0	0	0	0	0	1	0	0	0	0
eighty-nine	2	.2417	.1211	30.8	0	0	2	0	0	0	0	0	0	0	0	0	1	1	0	0	0	0	0	0	0	0	0	0	0
eighty-one	2	.0000	.0914	29.6	0	2	0	0	0	0	0	0	2	0	0	0	0	0	0	0	0	0	0	0	0	0	0	0	0
eighty-seven	13	.5929	1.6961	42.3	3	1	0	2	3	3	1	0	8	0	0	0	1	1	0	1	0	0	0	0	1	1	0	0	0
eighty-six	5	.3861	.4798	36.8	0	1	2	1	1	0	0	0	3	0	0	0	0	0	0	0	0	0	0	0	0	1	0	1	0
Eileen	11	.2225	.5662	37.5	0	0	0	1	8	0	2	0	0	0	1	10	0	0	0	0	0	0	0	0	0	0	0	0	0
Eileen's	3	.0397	.0716	28.5	0	0	2	0	0	1	0	0	1	0	2	0	0	0	0	0	0	0	0	0	0	0	0	0	0
ein	2	.1814	.1187	30.7	0	0	0	1	0	1	0	0	1	0	0	0	0	0	0	0	0	0	0	0	0	0	0	1	0
Ein**	2	.0000	.0050	17.0	0	0	0	0	0	2	0	0	0	0	0	0	0	0	0	0	0	0	0	2	0	0	0	0	0
Einstein	63	.6028	7.9031	49.0	0	2	17	11	9	16	8	0	9	1	1	2	9	2	1	10	0	0	0	1	0	0	27	0	0
Einstein's	12	.2304	.6524	38.1	0	0	2	1	3	0	6	0	0	0	0	0	0	0	1	2	0	0	0	0	0	0	9	0	0
Eisenhower	37	.4724	3.6999	45.7	0	2	3	4	6	13	7	2	0	1	0	0	0	11	0	0	0	0	0	2	0	0	4	19	0
Eisenhower's	10	.2634	.6167	37.9	0	0	1	4	2	2	0	1	0	0	0	0	0	2	0	0	0	0	0	0	0	0	1	7	0
Eisteddfod	5	.0000	.0404	26.1	0	0	0	5	0	0	0	0	0	0	0	0	0	0	0	0	5	0	0	0	0	0	0	0	0
either	1033	.9340	190.80	62.8	91	127	98	127	234	160	160	36	163	96	12	54	101	64	58	106	25	6	38	43	51	82	74	60	0
eke	2	.0000	.0162	22.1	0	0	0	0	2	0	0	0	0	0	0	0	0	0	2	0	0	0	0	0	0	0	0	0	0
el	17	.3791	1.4751	41.7	0	2	3	4	4	3	1	0	5	1	0	1	0	0	8	0	0	0	0	0	0	0	2	0	0
El	30	.7150	4.3302	46.4	6	0	2	5	7	8	2	0	2	0	0	2	2	2	0	0	8	1	1	0	0	5	3	4	0
ElPaso	7	.3809	.6033	37.8	0	1	0	0	6	0	0	0	1	0	0	0	0	2	0	0	0	0	0	0	0	0	3	1	0
elaborate	59	.7307	8.7071	49.4	1	4	5	9	14	11	14	1	6	2	0	4	0	7	0	2	2	2	6	0	2	3	15	8	0
elaborated	3	.3833	.2447	33.9	1	0	0	0	0	1	1	0	0	0	0	0	0	0	0	0	1	0	0	0	1	0	1	0	0
elaborately	5	.3682	.4515	36.5	1	0	0	2	1	1	0	0	2	0	0	0	0	2	0	0	0	0	0	0	1	0	0	0	0
Elaine	7	.2607	.4175	36.2	1	0	0	0	5	1	0	0	0	1	0	5	1	0	0	0	0	0	0	0	0	0	0	0	0
Eland	4	.0000	.0469	26.7	0	4	0	0	0	0	0	0	0	0	0	0	0	0	0	0	0	0	0	0	4	0	0	0	0
elapse	4	.4811	.4081	36.1	0	0	0	0	2	2	0	0	0	1	0	0	1	0	0	1	0	0	0	0	0	0	0	1	0
elapsed	7	.5189	.7892	39.0	0	0	0	1	4	1	0	1	2	2	0	0	0	0	0	1	0	0	0	0	1	0	0	1	0
elastic	43	.4839	4.3570	46.4	1	1	4	3	3	9	20	2	1	1	1	0	1	4	1	12	0	0	15	1	1	2	3	0	0
elasticity	15	.4009	1.2928	41.1	0	0	0	0	1	1	10	3	0	0	0	0	0	0	0	8	0	0	3	3	0	0	1	0	0
elated	7	.4804	.7058	38.5	0	0	0	0	1	3	2	1	0	0	1	2	0	2	0	0	0	0	0	0	1	0	0	1	0
elation	3	.2804	.1831	32.6	1	0	0	0	1	1	0	0	0	0	1	1	0	0	0	0	0	0	0	0	1	0	0	0	0
Elba	2	.0000	.0209	23.2	2	0	0	0	0	0	0	0	0	0	0	0	0	0	0	0	0	0	0	0	0	0	2	0	0
Elbe	5	.0000	.0972	29.9	0	0	0	5	0	0	0	0	0	0	0	0	0	5	0	0	0	0	0	0	0	0	0	0	0
Elbert	3	.2037	.1491	31.7	1	0	0	0	0	2	0	0	0	0	0	2	1	0	0	0	0	0	0	0	0	0	0	0	0
elbow	52	.7981	8.3305	49.2	6	4	9	12	12	2	4	3	6	1	1	8	1	0	0	12	3	2	1	0	8	4	0	5	0
elbows	39	.7661	6.0893	47.8	4	9	7	6	7	4	2	0	13	0	1	5	0	1	0	8	1	2	1	0	2	3	1	1	0
Elco	2	.0000	.0290	24.6	0	0	0	0	2	0	0	0	0	0	0	0	0	0	0	0	0	0	0	0	0	2	0	0	0
elder	30	.5938	3.6845	45.7	1	7	7	2	5	4	4	0	4	1	3	4	0	0	0	0	0	0	0	0	4	3	9	2	0
Elder	24	.3978	2.1724	43.4	1	1	2	1	2	17	0	0	2	0	0	1	0	17	0	1	0	0	0	0	0	2	1	0	0
Elder's	2	.2412	.1091	30.4	0	0	0	1	1	0	0	0	0	0	0	1	0	0	1	0	0	0	0	0	0	0	0	0	0
elderberry	2	.0000	.0914	29.6	0	0	2	0	0	0	0	0	2	0	0	0	0	0	0	0	0	0	0	0	0	0	0	0	0
elderly	29	.5651	3.4155	45.3	2	1	4	2	8	4	6	2	4	2	4	2	0	0	0	0	0	0	0	0	3	5	2	7	0
eldern	2	.0000	.0219	23.4	0	0	0	0	0	2	0	0	0	2	0	0	0	0	0	0	0	0	0	0	0	0	0	0	0
elders	24	.7466	3.6530	45.6	1	2	2	8	7	2	2	0	7	0	1	2	0	2	0	0	0	0	1	0	2	3	3	3	0
Elders	5	.0000	.2284	33.6	0	0	0	5	0	0	0	0	5	0	0	0	0	0	0	0	0	0	0	0	0	0	0	0	0
eldest	37	.7468	5.6530	47.5	2	3	6	8	6	4	3	5	13	4	1	2	0	2	0	0	0	0	0	0	3	3	5	4	0
Eldest	7	.0000	.0821	29.1	0	7	0	0	0	0	0	0	0	0	0	0	0	0	0	0	0	0	0	0	7	0	0	0	0
Eldridge	2	.0000	.0162	22.1	0	0	0	0	2	0	0	0	0	0	0	0	0	0	0	0	2	0	0	0	0	0	0	0	0
Eleanor	17	.3330	1.5820	42.0	0	1	0	0	0	16	0	0	15	0	0	1	0	0	1	0	0	0	0	0	0	0	0	0	0
elect	43	.5253	4.7525	46.8	6	9	9	5	3	2	9	0	0	2	0	0	0	23	8	0	0	0	0	0	0	5	4	1	0
elected	151	.6896	21.275	53.3	9	15	25	20	27	32	23	0	10	5	1	4	1	66	2	1	1	0	0	0	4	16	28	12	0
electing	3	.2279	.2143	33.3	0	0	0	1	2	0	0	0	2	0	0	0	0	0	0	0	0	0	0	0	0	0	0	1	0
election	108	.7210	15.858	52.0	8	4	14	11	19	35	17	0	12	5	4	0	4	48	5	0	1	0	0	0	4	5	12	8	0
Election	2	.2437	.1129	30.5	0	0	1	0	1	0	0	0	0	0	0	0	0	0	0	0	0	0	0	0	0	0	1	1	0

4G egz
8E EHFG
6E EHG
5P Eichmann
4F Eiffel
8A eight-and
7A eight-and-eighty-button
6A eight-and-one-half-inch
8J eight-armed
9E eight-cent
XB eight-century
XP eight-cylinder
5J eight-day
8A eight-engined
XR eight-foot-long
XR eight-hour-day
8A eight-hundred-pound
7R eight-lane
3P eight-mule
5A eight-ounce
XB eight-page
8F eight-point
8F eight-room
6R eight-state
6E eight-tenths
4R eight-wheel
4R eight-wheeled
3P eight-wheeler
7P eight-years-olds
8R Eight's
8H eighteen-month
8A eighteen-passenger
8J eighteenth-
5E eighteenths
7J eighth-note
7E eighth-units
7R eighties
5H Eighty
4A eighty-mile
XR Eighty-ninth
XR eighty-one-year-old
6R eighty-some
4A eighty-three
5P eighty-two
8G eighty-year-old
5P Eilat
8E Eilenberg
3A Einar
8J Eine
7P Einsatzgruppen
7H Einsteinian
8B eir
8R Eire's
7D Eisenhowers'
XR Eisner
6J eistedd
6J eisteddfod
8A ejaculated
7N ejaculating
6C ejaculations
9B eject
8H ejecting
9B ejection
XR ejection-seat
6F ejido
7R Ejnar
7G ekenama
5G ekskus'**
5G ekskuz'**
4Q ElAlamein
8A ElDeguello
7Q ElDorado
7R ElSegundo
9B elaboration
7D Elah
XR elan
4R eland
7R elapsed-time
7Q elasmobranchs
8L elasticized
9F Elath
4E Elborus
9Q elbow-rubbing
7B elbowed
5Q elbowroom
7R elbows-inside-the-knees
7F Elburz

Word Type	F	D	U	SFI	3 Gr 3	4 Gr 4	5 Gr 5	6 Gr 6	7 Gr 7	8 Gr 8	9 Gr 9	X UnGr	A Read	B Eng & Gr	C Comp	D Lit	E Math	F Soc Stud	G Spell	H Sci	J Music	K Art	L Home Ec	M Shop	N Lib F	P Lib NF	Q Lib Ref	R Mag	S Rel
elections	38	.6027	4.7319	46.8	3	0	8	3	8	11	4	1	1	0	0	0	0	14	1	0	0	1	0	0	0	6	9	6	0
electoral	14	.4336	1.3092	41.2	1	0	2	0	4	6	1	0	0	0	0	0	0	5	0	0	0	0	0	0	0	3	5	1	0
electorate	7	.4825	.7821	38.9	0	0	1	0	4	0	2	0	4	0	0	0	0	1	0	0	0	0	0	0	0	1	0	1	0
electors	15	.1275	.6225	37.9	0	0	0	0	1	14	0	0	0	0	0	0	0	14	0	0	0	0	0	0	0	0	1	0	0
Electra	7	.0000	.1013	30.1	0	0	0	0	7	0	0	0	0	0	0	0	0	0	0	0	0	0	0	0	0	7	0	0	0
electric	532	.7580	81.479	59.1	63	63	74	83	97	102	36	14	50	9	7	4	6	61	6	183	16	0	10	42	7	25	78	28	0
Electric	13	.2880	.9238	39.7	0	2	0	1	2	2	6	0	3	0	0	0	0	1	0	0	0	0	0	0	0	0	1	8	0
electric-light	2	.0000	.0394	26.0	1	0	0	1	0	0	0	0	0	0	0	0	0	0	0	2	0	0	0	0	0	0	0	0	0
electric-power	3	.2445	.1818	32.6	0	0	1	1	1	0	0	0	0	0	0	0	0	0	0	2	0	0	0	0	0	0	1	0	0
electric-powered	2	.1738	.0790	29.0	0	0	0	0	1	0	1	0	0	0	0	0	0	0	0	0	0	0	0	1	0	0	1	0	0
electrical	191	.4975	20.086	53.0	11	19	19	19	52	56	9	6	19	2	0	0	0	12	2	40	19	0	0	39	3	3	46	6	0
electrically	25	.5898	3.1033	44.9	0	2	5	3	8	1	4	2	5	0	0	0	0	1	0	7	1	0	0	2	0	0	4	5	0
electrically-charged	6	.0000	.1183	30.7	0	2	4	0	0	0	0	0	0	0	0	0	0	0	0	6	0	0	0	0	0	0	0	0	0
electrician	5	.3506	.4194	36.2	0	1	0	0	2	1	1	0	2	1	1	1	0	0	0	0	0	0	0	0	0	0	0	0	0
electricians	4	.2884	.2664	34.3	0	1	0	1	0	1	1	0	0	0	0	0	0	2	0	0	0	0	0	1	0	1	0	0	0
electricity	437	.6634	59.397	57.7	68	55	56	74	67	87	20	10	35	5	19	2	8	64	5	126	8	0	0	55	5	57	34	14	0
Electricity	3	.3830	.2448	33.9	0	1	1	0	0	1	0	0	0	1	0	0	0	0	1	0	0	0	0	0	1	0	0	0	0
electricity's	3	.2153	.1451	31.6	0	0	0	0	2	1	0	0	0	0	1	0	0	0	0	0	0	0	0	0	0	0	2	0	0
electrics	2	.1814	.1187	30.7	0	0	1	1	0	0	0	0	1	0	0	0	0	0	0	0	0	0	0	0	0	0	0	1	0
electrification	2	.2437	.1129	30.5	0	0	0	0	0	1	1	0	0	0	0	0	0	0	0	0	0	0	0	0	0	0	1	1	0
electrified	5	.4090	.4570	36.6	2	0	0	0	1	1	1	0	1	0	0	0	0	0	0	0	0	0	0	0	0	1	2	1	0
Electro-Thinker	17	.0000	.7766	38.9	0	17	0	0	0	0	0	0	17	0	0	0	0	0	0	0	0	0	0	0	0	0	0	0	0
electro-magnetic	2	.0000	.0209	23.2	0	0	0	1	0	0	1	0	0	0	0	0	0	0	0	0	0	0	0	0	0	0	2	0	0
electrochemical	4	.0904	.1412	31.5	1	0	0	0	0	2	1	0	1	0	0	0	0	0	0	0	0	0	0	0	0	0	3	0	0
electrode	8	.2211	.5389	37.3	0	0	0	5	0	2	0	1	5	0	0	0	0	0	0	0	0	0	0	2	0	0	0	1	0
electrodes	10	.1838	.5432	37.3	0	0	0	4	0	4	0	2	4	0	0	0	0	0	0	1	0	0	0	4	0	0	1	0	0
electrolysis	2	.2278	.1128	30.5	0	0	2	0	0	0	0	0	0	0	0	0	0	0	0	1	0	0	0	0	0	0	1	0	0
electrolyte	4	.0000	.1827	32.6	0	0	0	4	0	0	0	0	4	0	0	0	0	0	0	0	0	0	0	0	0	0	0	0	0
electrolytic	2	.1249	.0685	28.4	0	0	0	0	0	1	0	1	0	0	0	0	0	0	0	1	0	0	0	1	0	0	0	0	0
electromagnet	23	.3786	1.9429	42.9	4	0	2	10	6	1	0	0	0	0	0	0	0	0	0	16	0	0	0	2	0	0	5	0	0
electromagnetic	33	.3936	2.8844	44.6	1	1	2	9	5	13	2	0	1	0	0	0	1	0	0	17	0	0	0	0	0	0	11	3	0
electromagnetism	4	.0000	.0419	26.2	0	0	0	0	1	0	3	0	0	0	0	0	0	0	0	0	0	0	0	0	0	0	4	0	0
electromagnets	6	.1785	.2794	34.5	0	0	1	2	1	1	1	0	0	0	0	0	0	0	0	4	0	0	0	2	0	0	0	0	0
electron	67	.5121	7.2405	48.6	1	3	11	4	20	22	3	3	1	0	0	0	0	1	2	35	1	0	0	6	0	0	18	3	0
electronic	109	.7568	16.590	52.2	3	4	8	7	33	34	16	4	5	2	2	2	7	7	0	21	15	0	0	4	0	5	27	12	0
electronically	9	.2088	.4326	36.4	0	0	0	3	0	3	3	0	0	0	0	0	0	0	0	0	6	0	0	0	0	0	3	0	0
electronics	33	.5324	3.6668	45.6	0	0	1	2	6	9	12	3	2	1	0	0	1	4	0	4	1	0	0	5	0	0	11	4	0
electrons	209	.4480	20.413	53.1	0	16	44	28	40	68	5	8	16	0	0	0	0	0	0	118	1	0	0	26	7	0	37	4	0
Electrons	2	.1249	.0685	28.4	0	0	0	0	0	2	0	0	0	0	0	0	0	0	0	1	0	0	0	1	0	0	0	0	0
electroplates	3	.0000	.0314	25.0	0	0	0	0	3	0	0	0	0	0	0	0	0	0	0	0	0	0	0	0	0	0	3	0	0
electroscope	8	.0000	.1577	32.0	0	0	1	0	0	4	3	0	0	0	0	0	0	0	0	8	0	0	0	0	0	0	0	0	0
elects	4	.2330	.2363	33.7	0	0	0	2	2	0	0	0	0	1	0	0	0	3	0	0	0	0	0	0	0	0	0	0	0
elegance	9	.5835	1.0950	40.4	0	0	0	2	2	1	3	1	1	1	0	1	0	2	0	0	0	0	0	0	0	0	2	2	0
elegant	32	.7668	4.9399	46.9	2	3	1	7	4	8	4	3	4	3	1	0	0	3	0	0	3	1	0	0	5	2	3	7	0
elegantly	5	.4720	.4941	36.9	1	0	1	0	2	1	0	0	0	0	0	0	0	0	0	0	1	0	0	0	0	1	1	2	0
elegy	2	.0000	.0215	23.3	0	0	0	0	2	0	0	0	0	0	0	2	0	0	0	0	0	0	0	0	0	0	0	0	0
elektron	6	.2989	.3804	35.8	0	0	0	0	0	6	0	0	0	0	0	0	0	0	3	0	0	0	0	2	0	0	1	0	0
element	258	.7841	40.656	56.1	25	6	22	41	55	67	34	8	8	12	2	2	49	5	3	97	11	0	0	6	3	26	27	7	0
Element	2	.2391	.1133	30.5	0	1	1	0	0	0	0	0	0	0	0	0	1	0	0	0	0	0	0	0	0	0	1	0	0
element's	2	.0000	.0394	26.0	0	0	0	0	1	0	1	0	0	0	0	0	0	0	0	2	0	0	0	0	0	0	0	0	0
elemental	2	.2411	.1091	30.4	0	1	0	0	0	0	1	0	0	0	0	1	0	0	0	0	1	0	0	0	0	0	0	0	0
elementary	38	.6626	5.1428	47.1	2	3	4	5	8	2	8	6	0	3	0	0	5	13	0	4	0	0	0	1	0	0	6	6	0
Elementary	3	.2121	.1560	31.9	1	1	0	1	0	0	0	0	0	0	0	0	1	0	0	0	0	0	0	0	0	0	0	2	0
elements	458	.8013	73.597	58.7	25	23	53	54	80	129	64	30	14	32	4	0	56	9	2	211	34	6	2	13	3	28	33	11	0
Elements	9	.6013	1.1104	40.5	0	1	1	0	2	2	2	1	0	0	0	0	1	1	0	2	1	0	0	1	0	0	2	1	0
elephant	194	.8386	32.899	55.2	40	31	32	52	33	2	3	1	97	3	0	2	15	5	3	18	7	3	0	0	9	13	9	10	0
Elephant	22	.5201	2.6316	44.2	16	5	0	0	1	0	0	0	16	0	0	2	0	0	0	0	0	0	0	0	2	0	1	1	0
ELEPHANT	2	.1948	.1250	31.0	1	0	1	0	0	0	0	0	1	0	0	0	0	0	0	0	0	0	0	0	0	1	0	0	0
elephant's	12	.5306	1.4004	41.5	1	3	1	6	0	1	0	0	5	0	1	0	0	0	0	1	0	0	0	0	1	3	0	1	0
Elephant's	16	.2295	.8585	39.3	0	6	10	0	0	0	0	0	0	0	0	10	0	0	0	0	0	0	0	0	6	0	0	0	0
elephants	157	.7969	25.416	54.1	45	25	16	34	22	4	8	3	60	14	4	0	7	16	0	9	2	0	0	0	5	21	9	10	0
elephants'	3	.1409	.1472	31.7	2	0	1	0	0	0	0	0	1	0	0	0	0	0	0	0	0	0	0	0	0	2	0	0	0
elevated	15	.6093	1.9074	42.8	1	4	2	0	3	1	4	0	3	0	0	0	0	3	0	0	2	1	0	0	1	2	3	0	0
elevating	2	.2401	.1133	30.5	0	0	0	0	2	0	0	0	0	0	0	0	0	0	0	0	0	0	0	0	0	1	1	0	0
elevation	59	.5898	7.2848	48.6	5	4	14	10	15	3	5	3	6	2	0	2	0	29	0	3	0	0	0	5	1	0	6	5	0
elevations	19	.4318	1.7797	42.5	6	1	0	5	3	1	3	0	0	0	0	0	0	9	0	4	0	0	0	3	0	0	2	1	0
elevator	85	.7635	13.191	51.2	29	10	11	16	11	2	4	2	19	8	0	1	9	17	2	5	0	0	0	0	6	7	0	11	0
elevators	25	.6640	3.4261	45.3	7	4	1	5	1	3	4	0	3	0	0	0	0	7	0	6	0	0	0	1	1	2	4	1	0
eleven	146	.8571	25.077	54.0	23	25	15	20	38	16	8	1	46	4	1	20	10	11	10	8	3	0	0	0	10	12	6	5	0
Eleven	5	.3110	.3699	35.7	2	0	0	0	0	1	0	2	1	0	0	0	0	0	0	0	0	0	0	0	2	0	0	2	0
eleven-thirty	2	.2427	.1152	30.6	1	1	0	0	0	0	0	0	0	0	0	0	0	0	0	0	0	0	0	0	1	1	0	0	0
eleven-year-old	4	.3092	.2990	34.8	0	2	1	0	0	1	0	0	1	1	0	0	0	0	0	0	0	0	0	0	0	0	0	2	0
eleventh	21	.6630	2.8671	44.6	3	1	3	2	3	4	4	1	4	2	0	0	1	1	0	1	4	0	0	0	0	3	4	1	0
elf	9	.4541	.9142	39.6	3	4	1	0	0	0	0	1	3	2	0	0	0	0	0	0	1	0	0	0	0	0	0	3	0
Elf	4	.3599	.3543	35.5	1	3	0	0	0	0	0	0	2	0	0	0	0	0	1	0	0	0	0	0	0	0	0	1	0
Elfin	4	.0000	.0486	26.9	0	0	0	0	0	2	0	2	0	0	0	0	0	0	0	0	0	0	0	0	0	0	0	4	0
Elfland	3	.2212	.2099	33.2	0	0	1	1	0	0	1	0	2	0	0	1	0	0	0	0	0	0	0	0	0	0	0	0	0
Elfred	3	.0000	.0352	25.5	0	0	0	3	0	0	0	0	0	0	0	0	0	0	0	0	0	0	0	0	3	0	0	0	0
Elgin	4	.2954	.2881	34.6	0	3	0	0	0	1	0	0	1	0	0	2	0	0	0	0	0	0	0	0	0	0	0	1	0
Eli	20	.4620	2.0829	43.2	2	6	6	0	1	4	1	0	6	0	0	4	0	7	0	0	0	0	0	0	0	3	0	0	0
Elia	5	.1684	.2120	33.3	0	0	0	0	0	0	5	0	0	4	0	0	0	0	0	0	0	0	0	0	0	0	0	1	0
Elias	3	.3766	.2497	34.0	0	0	1	0	1	1	0	0	0	0	0	0	0	1	0	0	0	0	0	0	0	1	1	0	0
eligibility	3	.3871	.2488	34.0	0	0	0	0	0	0	2	1	0	1	0	0	0	0	0	0	0	0	0	0	0	0	1	1	0
eligible	8	.3260	.5937	37.7	0	0	2	0	3	3	0	0	1	0	2	0	0	1	0	0	0	0	0	0	0	1	0	3	0
Elijah	11	.2043	.5576	37.5	1	1	0	1	2	6	0	0	1	0	0	0	0	0	0	0	7	0	0	0	0	3	0	0	0
Eliko	7	.0000	.0766	28.8	0	0	0	0	0	0	7	0	0	7	0	0	0	0	0	0	0	0	0	0	0	0	0	0	0
eliminate	36	.7523	5.4587	47.4	1	1	2	3	13	6	7	3	3	2	1	0	3	3	0	5	0	0	3	1	0	1	5	9	0
eliminated	33	.7620	5.0451	47.0	0	1	2	2	10	6	10	2	1	0	0	1	1	2	1	6	4	0	2	2	0	2	5	6	0
eliminates	7	.4158	.6183	37.9	0	0	0	0	3	1	2	1	0	1	0	0	0	0	0	2	0	0	2	0	0	0	1	1	0
eliminating	13	.6426	1.6898	42.3	0	2	0	2	1	4	4	0	0	2	0	0	1	1	1	0	0	0	1	1	0	0	5	1	0
elimination	11	.5541	1.2696	41.0	0	0	0	1	4	1	2	3	1	0	0	1	0	1	0	1	1	0	2	0	0	1	0	3	0
Elinor	4	.1458	.1365	31.4	0	0	0	0	1	2	1	0	0	2	0	0	0	0	0	0	0	2	0	0	0	0	0	0	0
Eliot	3	.2279	.2143	33.3	0	0	0	0	1	2	0	0	2	0	0	0	0	0	0	0	0	0	0	0	0	0	0	1	0

7D election'd
4A Elective
8J Elector
9Q Electors
7P Electra's
8M electric-arc
6H electric-current
6R electric-drive
9Q electric-driven
9B electric-eye
8M electric-heating
XR electric-motor
8Q electric-shock
9R Electric's
7R electrical-resistance
6A electrically-controlled
4H electrically-driven
5H electrically-neutral
6R Electro-Motive
6R electro-optical
9M electrocharged
4R electrochemistry
7A electrocute
6A electrocuted
9G electrocution
7F electrolytically
9H electrolyzed
9H electrolyzing
4Q Electromagnet
9Q electromotive
6R electromotors
XH electron-shells
8J electronic-age
8J electronically-used
XH electroplating
7Q electroplaxes
7R electroreceptors
8Q electrostatic
8Q electrostatics
9M electrotyping
8G elektor
7H element-hunting
7F elementary-school
6A Elena
5A elephant-legged
7H elephant-like
7D elephant-trunks
4N Elephants
5Q Eleuthere
6A Elevala
6J elevate
7A elevates
3J Elevator
4F Eleven-Cities
7F eleven-hundred
9R eleven-room
3E elevens
7R ELF
7P elf-wife
4A elf's
7Q elfin
8R Elfin's
9D elflocks
7P elfwife
3J Elgar
8Q Elginbrod
7Q Elgon
7D Eliab
8K Elie
3P Elimination

Word Type	F	D	U	SFI	3 Gr 3	4 Gr 4	5 Gr 5	6 Gr 6	7 Gr 7	8 Gr 8	9 Gr 9	X UnGr	A Read	B Eng & Gr	C Comp	D Lit	E Math	F Soc Stud	G Spell	H Sci	J Music	K Art	L Home Ec	M Shop	N Lib F	P Lib NF	Q Lib Ref	R Mag	S Rel
Elis	2	.0000	.0914	29.6	0	0	0	0	0	2	0	0	2	0	0	0	0	0	0	0	0	0	0	0	0	0	0	0	0
Elisabeth	3	.0000	.0322	25.1	0	0	0	0	0	0	3	0	0	0	0	3	0	0	0	0	0	0	0	0	0	0	0	0	0
elite	8	.5070	.8767	39.4	0	0	1	0	3	2	1	1	2	1	0	0	0	0	1	0	0	0	0	0	0	1	0	3	0
Eliza	20	.3234	1.6534	42.2	5	8	6	1	0	0	0	0	9	0	0	0	0	0	0	0	0	0	0	0	2	9	0	0	0
Elizabeth	111	.8222	18.284	52.6	0	43	13	8	31	6	9	1	18	5	2	11	3	4	3	0	2	2	0	0	7	33	10	11	0
ELIZABETH	4	.0000	.0429	26.3	0	0	0	0	0	4	0	0	0	0	0	4	0	0	0	0	0	0	0	0	0	0	0	0	0
Elizabeth's	7	.4543	.7091	38.5	0	1	1	0	3	1	1	0	2	0	0	0	0	0	0	0	0	0	0	0	2	2	1	0	0
Elizabethan	5	.1622	.1793	32.5	0	0	0	1	3	1	0	0	0	0	0	0	0	0	0	0	2	0	0	3	0	0	0	0	0
Elizabethtown	2	.0000	.0914	29.6	0	0	0	2	0	0	0	0	2	0	0	0	0	0	0	0	0	0	0	0	0	0	0	0	0
elk	24	.4989	2.6447	44.2	2	5	10	1	6	0	0	0	8	0	0	1	2	4	0	0	0	0	0	0	0	1	8	0	0
Elk	23	.1885	1.1161	40.5	0	4	0	1	17	1	0	0	2	0	0	18	0	0	0	0	0	0	0	0	0	2	0	1	0
Elka	2	.0000	.0234	23.7	0	0	2	0	0	0	0	0	0	0	0	0	0	0	0	0	0	0	0	0	2	0	0	0	0
Elkhart	2	.0000	.0914	29.6	0	2	0	0	0	0	0	0	2	0	0	0	0	0	0	0	0	0	0	0	0	0	0	0	0
Elkins	6	.0000	.0869	29.4	0	6	0	0	0	0	0	0	0	0	0	0	0	0	0	0	0	0	0	0	0	6	0	0	0
Elkton	3	.0000	.1370	31.4	0	0	0	0	3	0	0	0	3	0	0	0	0	0	0	0	0	0	0	0	0	0	0	0	0
ell	2	.1972	.1262	31.0	2	0	0	0	0	0	0	0	1	0	0	0	1	0	0	0	0	0	0	0	0	0	0	0	0
Ella	49	.2564	4.0320	46.1	3	42	3	0	0	0	1	0	45	0	0	1	0	0	0	0	0	0	0	0	3	0	0	0	0
Ellen	211	.4860	22.586	53.5	103	52	6	6	17	12	2	13	64	5	0	0	6	2	0	4	0	0	1	0	95	10	0	24	0
Ellen's	25	.2857	1.7605	42.5	18	1	0	1	2	2	1	0	6	1	0	0	1	0	0	0	0	0	0	0	16	0	0	1	0
Ellenwood	4	.0000	.0429	26.3	0	0	0	0	4	0	0	0	0	0	0	4	0	0	0	0	0	0	0	0	0	0	0	0	0
Ellesmere	2	.2446	.1122	30.5	0	0	0	0	2	0	0	0	0	0	0	1	0	0	0	0	0	0	0	0	0	0	1	0	0
Elli	7	.0702	.2199	33.4	0	0	0	0	0	7	0	0	1	0	0	0	0	0	0	0	0	0	0	0	0	6	0	0	0
Ellie	3	.2373	.1703	32.3	0	2	0	0	0	0	1	0	0	1	0	0	0	0	0	0	0	0	0	0	0	2	0	0	0
Elliot	6	.4323	.5775	37.6	0	3	1	1	1	0	0	0	1	0	0	0	0	2	0	0	0	0	0	0	0	0	1	2	0
Elliott	10	.4334	1.0011	40.0	0	4	2	0	3	0	0	1	4	0	0	1	0	0	0	0	0	0	0	0	0	4	0	1	0
ellipse	19	.2224	1.0590	40.2	2	0	1	9	1	5	0	1	0	0	0	0	15	0	0	3	0	0	0	0	0	0	1	0	0
ellipses	4	.3163	.2749	34.4	0	2	0	1	0	0	1	0	0	0	0	0	1	0	0	0	0	0	0	1	0	0	2	0	0
elliptical	10	.6055	1.2484	41.0	0	2	2	1	1	2	2	0	0	2	0	0	1	2	0	2	0	0	0	0	0	0	2	1	0
Ellis	16	.5793	2.0431	43.1	8	2	0	1	1	1	2	1	10	1	1	1	0	1	0	0	0	0	0	0	0	1	0	1	0
Ellison	2	.0000	.0290	24.6	0	0	0	0	2	0	0	0	0	0	0	0	0	0	0	0	0	0	0	0	0	2	0	0	0
Ellsworth	2	.1033	.0599	27.8	0	0	0	0	1	1	0	0	0	0	0	0	0	0	0	1	0	1	0	0	0	0	0	0	0
elm	20	.6596	2.7165	44.3	6	2	2	3	2	0	4	1	2	0	0	1	0	2	1	6	0	0	0	0	0	3	4	1	0
Elm	9	.2110	.5002	37.0	1	2	1	0	5	0	0	0	1	0	0	0	7	0	0	0	0	0	0	0	0	0	1	0	0
Elmer	54	.4202	5.5595	47.5	29	23	0	1	0	1	0	0	37	0	0	11	0	0	0	1	0	0	0	0	0	4	0	1	0
Elmer's	3	.2212	.2099	33.2	3	0	0	0	0	0	0	0	2	0	0	1	0	0	0	0	0	0	0	0	0	0	0	0	0
elms	3	.3759	.2474	33.9	0	0	0	0	3	0	0	0	0	1	0	1	0	0	0	1	0	0	0	0	0	0	0	0	0
Elmville	3	.0000	.0583	27.7	3	0	0	0	0	0	0	0	0	0	0	0	0	3	0	0	0	0	0	0	0	0	0	0	0
Elna	8	.0000	.0938	29.7	0	0	0	0	0	8	0	0	0	0	0	0	0	0	0	0	0	0	0	0	8	0	0	0	0
Elna's	2	.0000	.0234	23.7	0	0	0	0	0	2	0	0	0	0	0	0	0	0	0	0	0	0	0	0	2	0	0	0	0
Elochoman	2	.0000	.0243	23.9	0	0	0	0	2	0	0	0	0	0	0	0	0	0	0	0	0	0	0	0	0	0	0	2	0
elocution	2	.0000	.0290	24.6	0	2	0	0	0	0	0	0	0	0	0	0	0	0	0	0	0	0	0	0	0	2	0	0	0
elodea	2	.0000	.0394	26.0	0	2	0	0	0	0	0	0	0	0	0	0	0	0	0	2	0	0	0	0	0	0	0	0	0
elongated	8	.1707	.3929	35.9	0	0	0	0	3	1	1	3	0	0	0	0	0	0	0	7	0	0	0	0	0	0	0	1	0
elongation	4	.3056	.2766	34.4	0	0	0	0	3	1	0	0	0	0	0	0	0	0	0	2	0	0	0	1	0	0	1	0	0
eloquence	6	.4255	.5596	37.5	0	1	0	0	2	3	0	0	1	0	1	0	0	0	0	0	0	0	0	0	1	2	0	1	0
eloquent	9	.5873	1.0953	40.4	1	0	1	0	3	2	2	0	1	1	0	1	0	1	0	0	1	1	0	0	1	2	0	0	0
eloquently	4	.3026	.2923	34.7	0	0	0	0	3	1	0	0	1	2	0	0	0	0	0	0	0	0	0	0	0	0	1	0	0
Elsa	27	.2428	1.7696	42.5	0	0	0	10	17	0	0	0	8	0	0	0	0	0	0	0	0	0	0	0	0	17	0	2	0
Elsa's	3	.2357	.2199	33.4	0	0	0	2	1	0	0	0	2	0	0	0	0	0	0	0	0	0	0	0	0	1	0	0	0
else	859	.9241	157.53	62.0	174	151	110	84	159	83	73	25	284	75	15	69	17	43	7	70	25	3	8	5	69	82	26	61	0
Else	12	.2355	.9268	39.7	0	0	0	10	2	0	0	0	10	0	0	0	0	0	0	0	0	0	0	0	0	2	0	0	0
else's	26	.6675	3.5748	45.5	6	1	3	5	4	4	1	2	4	3	0	1	0	0	1	7	0	0	0	0	4	1	0	5	0
elsewhere	70	.7610	10.761	50.3	5	3	5	14	20	7	8	8	9	2	1	4	0	12	3	3	1	0	0	0	0	9	12	14	0
Elsie	5	.1552	.1773	32.5	1	0	2	1	1	0	0	0	0	1	3	0	0	0	0	0	0	0	0	0	1	0	0	0	0
Elspeth	5	.0000	.2284	33.6	0	0	0	5	0	0	0	0	5	0	0	0	0	0	0	0	0	0	0	0	0	0	0	0	0
eluded	4	.3011	.2909	34.6	0	0	0	0	1	0	3	0	1	0	0	2	0	0	0	0	0	0	0	0	0	0	1	0	0
eludes	2	.2401	.1133	30.5	0	0	1	0	0	0	1	0	0	0	0	0	0	0	0	0	0	0	0	0	0	1	1	0	0
elusive	8	.5649	.9304	39.7	0	0	1	0	4	0	3	0	0	0	0	1	0	0	0	2	1	1	0	0	0	1	1	1	0
Elva	3	.0000	.0434	26.4	0	3	0	0	0	0	0	0	0	0	0	0	0	0	0	0	0	0	0	0	0	3	0	0	0
elves	14	.4992	1.5856	42.0	10	2	1	0	0	0	1	0	8	1	0	1	0	0	0	0	3	0	0	0	0	0	0	1	0
Elvis	6	.1673	.2570	34.1	0	0	0	0	1	5	0	0	0	1	0	0	0	0	0	0	0	0	0	0	0	0	0	5	0
Elwell	2	.0000	.0914	29.6	0	0	0	0	2	0	0	0	2	0	0	0	0	0	0	0	0	0	0	0	0	0	0	0	0
Elysee	2	.0000	.0243	23.9	0	0	0	0	0	1	1	0	0	0	0	0	0	0	0	0	0	0	0	0	0	0	0	2	0
Em	4	.0974	.1495	31.7	2	0	1	0	1	0	0	0	1	0	0	0	0	0	0	0	0	0	0	0	3	0	0	0	0
ema	3	.0000	.1370	31.4	3	0	0	0	0	0	0	0	3	0	0	0	0	0	0	0	0	0	0	0	0	0	0	0	0
emanating	3	.2159	.1532	31.9	0	0	0	0	3	0	0	0	0	0	0	0	0	0	0	0	0	0	0	0	0	0	2	1	0
emancipated	3	.3769	.2484	34.0	0	0	1	0	0	0	2	0	0	0	0	0	0	1	0	0	0	0	0	0	0	0	1	1	0
emancipation	5	.4402	.4864	36.9	0	0	2	0	1	1	1	0	1	1	0	1	0	0	0	0	0	0	0	0	0	2	0	0	0
Emancipation	11	.3310	.8373	39.2	0	0	4	0	1	6	0	0	0	0	0	0	0	7	0	0	0	0	0	0	0	1	3	0	0
Emanuel	2	.2303	.1079	30.3	0	2	0	0	0	0	0	0	0	0	0	0	0	0	0	0	1	0	0	0	0	1	0	0	0
embalmed	2	.2306	.1140	30.6	0	0	0	2	0	0	0	0	0	1	0	0	0	1	0	0	0	0	0	0	0	0	0	0	0
embalming	2	.0000	.0209	23.2	0	0	0	0	0	0	2	0	0	0	0	0	0	0	0	0	0	0	0	0	0	0	2	0	0
embankment	5	.3625	.4611	36.6	0	1	2	0	0	1	1	0	3	0	0	0	0	1	1	0	0	0	0	0	0	0	0	0	0
embankments	4	.3352	.2986	34.8	0	0	0	0	2	0	1	1	0	0	0	0	0	0	0	1	0	0	0	0	0	0	2	1	0
Embargo	4	.1325	.1944	32.9	0	0	0	0	1	3	0	0	1	0	0	0	0	3	0	0	0	0	0	0	0	0	0	0	0
embark	7	.4895	.7317	38.6	0	2	0	0	2	1	2	0	1	0	1	0	0	0	0	1	0	0	0	0	1	0	1	2	0
embarked	7	.5150	.7616	38.8	1	1	0	0	1	1	2	1	1	0	0	1	0	0	0	0	1	0	0	0	0	0	2	2	0
embarrass	7	.3648	.5439	37.4	0	0	0	1	1	3	2	0	0	1	0	1	0	0	4	0	0	0	0	0	0	0	0	1	0
embarrassed	41	.7086	5.9601	47.8	4	4	2	5	15	4	7	0	12	1	1	9	0	2	1	0	0	0	3	0	7	2	0	3	0
embarrasses	2	.1926	.0867	29.4	0	0	0	0	1	1	0	0	0	0	0	0	0	0	0	0	0	0	1	0	0	0	1	0	0
embarrassing	14	.5164	1.5639	41.9	1	1	1	1	3	2	5	0	4	4	0	2	0	0	0	0	0	0	0	0	1	0	0	3	0
embarrassment	19	.6824	2.6708	44.3	0	5	1	0	6	5	2	0	5	2	0	2	0	0	0	0	0	0	1	0	1	2	1	5	0
embassies	2	.2401	.1133	30.5	0	0	2	0	0	0	0	0	0	0	0	0	0	0	0	0	0	0	0	0	0	1	1	0	0
Embassies	2	.1042	.0600	27.8	1	0	0	0	0	1	0	0	0	0	0	0	0	1	0	0	0	1	0	0	0	0	0	0	0
Embassy	6	.3267	.4774	36.8	1	0	0	0	0	4	1	0	2	0	0	0	0	1	0	0	0	1	0	0	0	0	0	2	0
embattled	2	.2285	.1129	30.5	0	1	0	0	0	1	0	0	0	0	0	0	0	1	0	0	0	0	0	0	0	0	1	0	0
embedded	13	.5033	1.3787	41.4	0	0	0	1	6	0	4	2	1	0	0	0	0	0	0	2	0	0	1	0	1	0	6	2	0
embellished	3	.3267	.2367	33.7	0	0	0	1	1	1	0	0	1	0	0	0	0	0	0	0	1	0	0	0	1	0	0	0	0
embellishment	2	.2375	.1088	30.4	0	0	0	0	2	0	0	0	0	0	0	0	0	0	0	0	1	0	0	0	0	0	0	1	0
ember	5	.2025	.3254	35.1	0	0	2	0	1	1	1	0	3	0	0	2	0	0	0	0	0	0	0	0	0	0	0	0	0
embers	14	.5318	1.5665	41.9	1	4	0	3	3	2	1	0	2	1	0	2	0	0	0	0	2	0	0	0	6	0	1	0	0
embittered	4	.3519	.3117	34.9	0	0	0	0	1	2	0	1	0	0	0	0	0	1	0	0	0	0	0	0	0	0	1	2	0
emblem	15	.6323	1.9891	43.0	3	1	0	2	1	4	4	0	5	1	0	4	2	0	1	0	1	0	0	0	0	0	0	1	0
emblems	4	.2851	.2994	34.8	0	0	1	0	1	2	0	0	2	0	0	1	0	0	0	0	0	0	1	0	0	0	0	0	0
embodied	3	.2696	.1807	32.6	0	0	0	0	2	1	0	0	0	0	1	0	0	1	0	0	1	0	0	0	0	0	0	0	0

7P elixir
5N Eliza's
4Q Elizur
7D Elk's
4G ella
4A Ella's
6A Ellicott's
4A Ellinor
6A Elliot's
5A Elliott's
9B ellipsis
8Q ellipsoidal
9Q elliptic
5J Ellsworth's
9E Elmcourt
7R Elmhurst
9A Elmira
8B Elmwood
4H Elodea
XH Elodes
7Q elongate
7P elongating
XH elongations
4P eloping
7D Elouise
6R Eloy
7P Else's
3P Elston
6A elucidate
XR elude
6R Elvar
8B Elvers
4J elves'
8Q Elvey
7A Elvington
7A Elwell's
6P Elysian
6A Elysium
8G em
6J Em'rald
8Q emaciation
9C emanate
3P Emancipator
8Q Emax**
7P embarkation
7R embarking
XR embarrassingly
8Q embassy
7P embellish
9Q embellishments
3A embezzler
7A embittering
XR emblazoned

Word Type	F	D	U	SFI	3 Gr 3	4 Gr 4	5 Gr 5	6 Gr 6	7 Gr 7	8 Gr 8	9 Gr 9	X UnGr	A Read	B Eng & Gr	C Comp	D Lit	E Math	F Soc Stud	G Spell	H Sci	J Music	K Art	L Home Ec	M Shop	N Lib F	P Lib NF	Q Lib Ref	R Mag	S Rel
embodiment	5	.4143	.4656	36.7	0	0	0	0	1	3	1	0	1	0	0	0	0	1	0	0	0	0	0	0	0	0	1	2	0
embody	3	.2799	.1829	32.6	0	0	0	0	1	2	0	0	0	0	1	0	0	0	0	0	0	0	0	0	0	0	1	1	0
embossed	6	.3375	.4366	36.4	0	0	0	0	5	0	1	0	0	0	0	4	0	0	0	0	0	0	1	0	0	0	0	1	0
embossing	9	.2279	.4712	36.7	0	0	0	0	8	1	0	0	0	0	0	8	0	0	0	0	0	0	0	1	0	0	0	0	0
embrace	16	.5285	1.7805	42.5	1	1	0	0	4	5	5	0	2	0	0	6	0	0	0	0	0	0	0	0	2	2	3	1	0
embraced	13	.4649	1.3096	41.2	1	0	2	0	4	2	4	0	2	0	0	6	0	1	0	0	0	0	0	0	1	2	0	1	0
embraces	7	.4787	.7158	38.5	0	0	0	2	0	4	1	0	1	0	0	3	0	0	0	0	1	0	0	0	1	0	0	1	0
embracing	8	.5953	.9770	39.9	0	0	0	0	6	1	1	0	0	0	0	1	0	1	0	0	0	0	0	0	1	1	2	2	0
embroider'd	2	.0000	.0219	23.4	0	0	2	0	0	0	0	0	0	2	0	0	0	0	0	0	0	0	0	0	0	0	0	0	0
embroidered	21	.6364	2.7475	44.4	2	6	3	2	5	1	1	1	2	1	0	2	0	5	0	0	0	2	1	0	3	4	0	1	0
embroidering	2	.2408	.1204	30.8	0	2	0	0	0	0	0	0	0	0	0	0	0	1	0	0	0	0	0	0	0	1	0	0	0
embroidery	12	.6111	1.5153	41.8	0	3	0	2	4	2	1	0	2	0	1	1	0	2	0	0	0	1	2	0	0	2	1	0	0
embryo	40	.3389	3.0746	44.9	0	1	4	3	26	0	2	4	0	0	0	1	0	0	0	21	0	0	0	0	0	2	16	0	0
embryo's	2	.0000	.0209	23.2	0	0	0	0	2	0	0	0	0	0	0	0	0	0	0	0	0	0	0	0	0	0	2	0	0
embryological	2	.0000	.0394	26.0	0	0	0	0	0	0	0	2	0	0	0	0	0	0	0	2	0	0	0	0	0	0	0	0	0
embryology	5	.0000	.0986	29.9	0	0	0	0	5	0	0	0	0	0	0	0	0	0	0	5	0	0	0	0	0	0	0	0	0
embryonic	6	.1339	.2157	33.3	0	0	0	1	4	0	1	0	0	0	0	0	0	0	0	0	0	0	0	0	0	1	5	0	0
embryos	14	.1941	.7415	38.7	0	0	0	2	10	0	0	2	0	0	0	0	0	0	0	12	0	0	0	0	0	0	2	0	0
emerald	12	.5120	1.3646	41.4	0	0	9	0	1	1	1	0	5	2	0	0	0	2	0	1	0	1	0	0	1	0	0	0	0
emerald-green	2	.1733	.1149	30.6	0	0	1	0	0	1	0	0	1	1	0	0	0	0	0	0	0	0	0	0	0	0	0	0	0
emeralds	19	.4121	1.9762	43.0	5	1	9	2	1	0	1	0	15	0	0	0	0	1	0	0	0	0	0	0	0	2	1	0	0
emerge	32	.6077	4.0043	46.0	2	0	2	3	13	5	6	1	2	2	0	1	0	0	0	4	1	0	0	0	1	2	10	9	0
emerged	48	.7549	7.3681	48.7	1	0	3	8	19	14	2	1	14	0	2	2	0	2	0	2	8	1	0	0	6	1	4	6	0
emergence	8	.4200	.7148	38.5	0	0	2	0	2	2	1	1	0	0	0	0	0	0	0	1	3	0	0	0	0	2	2	0	0
emergencies	14	.4912	1.4603	41.6	1	1	1	1	3	3	2	2	2	1	0	0	0	0	0	1	0	0	3	0	0	1	3	3	0
emergency	56	.7553	8.5572	49.3	5	4	4	7	13	11	4	8	8	1	1	1	0	5	1	6	0	0	3	0	3	9	2	16	0
emergent	2	.2446	.1123	30.5	0	0	0	0	1	0	1	0	0	1	0	0	0	0	0	0	0	0	0	0	0	0	1	0	0
emerges	10	.4844	1.0166	40.1	0	0	1	1	3	1	3	1	0	0	0	1	0	1	0	2	3	0	0	0	0	0	3	0	0
emerging	13	.6299	1.6676	42.2	1	0	0	1	3	6	1	1	0	1	0	1	0	3	0	0	2	0	0	1	0	0	1	4	0
Emerson	22	.5626	2.6092	44.2	0	3	4	0	5	10	0	0	4	1	0	0	0	2	0	0	1	0	0	0	0	3	8	3	0
Emerson's	5	.3602	.3954	36.0	0	0	3	0	1	1	0	0	0	1	0	0	0	0	0	0	0	0	0	0	0	3	1	0	0
emery	15	.4488	1.4534	41.6	2	0	0	0	9	0	3	1	2	0	0	0	0	1	0	2	0	0	2	3	0	5	0	0	0
emigrant	9	.4839	.9325	39.7	1	0	0	2	4	0	1	1	1	2	0	1	0	0	0	0	0	0	0	0	0	4	0	1	0
emigrants	6	.3323	.4455	36.5	2	1	0	0	2	1	0	0	0	0	0	1	0	0	0	0	0	0	0	0	1	4	0	0	0
emigrate	5	.5615	.5818	37.6	0	0	2	1	0	1	1	0	0	1	0	0	0	1	0	0	0	0	0	0	1	1	0	1	0
emigrated	7	.5067	.7726	38.9	0	0	2	1	0	1	2	1	1	0	0	0	1	3	0	1	0	0	0	0	0	1	0	0	0
emigratin'	2	.0000	.0914	29.6	0	0	2	0	0	0	0	0	2	0	0	0	0	0	0	0	0	0	0	0	0	0	0	0	0
emigration	4	.2408	.2408	33.8	0	0	2	0	1	1	0	0	0	0	0	0	0	2	0	0	0	0	0	0	0	2	0	0	0
Emil	11	.3529	.8797	39.4	0	0	0	2	6	2	0	1	2	0	0	7	0	0	0	0	0	1	0	0	0	0	0	1	0
Emile	9	.5441	1.0212	40.1	0	0	1	1	2	3	1	1	1	0	0	1	0	1	0	0	2	1	0	0	0	1	2	0	0
Emilia	6	.0000	.0657	28.2	0	0	0	0	0	0	6	0	0	6	0	0	0	0	0	0	0	0	0	0	0	0	0	0	0
Emilio	3	.1019	.0750	28.7	0	0	0	0	0	0	2	1	0	0	2	0	0	0	0	0	0	0	0	0	0	0	0	1	0
Emily	68	.6762	9.6971	49.9	30	15	3	7	2	8	3	0	36	7	0	2	1	0	0	0	1	0	0	0	6	11	1	3	0
Emily's	4	.2958	.2914	34.6	1	1	0	2	0	0	0	0	1	0	0	0	0	0	0	0	0	0	0	0	2	1	0	0	0
eminence	8	.2828	.5178	37.1	0	0	0	0	3	2	3	0	0	1	0	0	0	2	0	0	0	0	0	0	0	0	5	0	0
eminent	9	.4870	.9143	39.6	0	0	1	1	3	2	2	0	0	1	0	0	0	0	0	0	0	0	0	0	1	1	4	2	0
eminently	7	.4651	.7077	38.5	0	0	1	1	2	0	1	2	1	0	0	0	0	0	0	1	0	0	0	0	0	1	1	3	0
emissary	2	.2440	.1132	30.5	0	0	0	0	0	0	1	1	0	0	0	1	0	0	0	0	0	0	0	0	0	0	0	1	0
emission	4	.0000	.0419	26.2	0	0	2	0	0	2	0	0	0	0	0	0	0	0	0	0	0	0	0	0	0	0	4	0	0
emit	10	.4165	.9237	39.7	0	0	1	1	3	4	0	1	1	0	0	0	0	0	0	4	0	0	0	0	0	0	3	2	0
emits	3	.3764	.2483	33.9	0	0	0	2	1	0	0	0	0	0	0	0	0	0	0	1	0	0	0	0	0	0	1	1	0
emitted	15	.4693	1.5218	41.8	0	0	1	1	1	5	4	3	1	1	0	0	0	0	0	7	0	0	0	0	0	0	4	2	0
emitter	5	.0000	.0986	29.9	0	0	0	0	0	5	0	0	0	0	0	0	0	0	0	5	0	0	0	0	0	0	0	0	0
emitting	5	.2444	.3032	34.8	0	0	0	2	0	0	2	1	0	0	0	0	0	0	0	3	0	0	0	0	0	0	0	2	0
Emma	32	.6088	4.1662	46.2	2	10	18	0	1	0	1	0	14	2	0	7	3	0	0	0	0	0	0	0	1	4	0	1	0
Emma's	2	.0000	.0914	29.6	0	0	2	0	0	0	0	0	2	0	0	0	0	0	0	0	0	0	0	0	0	0	0	0	0
Emmanuel	11	.3608	.8781	39.4	3	0	0	3	5	0	0	0	1	0	0	0	0	0	0	0	2	0	0	0	0	2	6	0	0
Emmett	7	.2299	.3665	35.6	0	0	4	0	0	3	0	0	0	3	0	0	0	0	0	0	4	0	0	0	0	0	0	0	0
Emmons	3	.0000	.0365	25.6	0	0	0	0	0	0	3	0	0	0	0	0	0	0	0	0	0	0	0	0	0	0	0	3	0
Emory	2	.0000	.0219	23.4	0	0	0	0	0	0	2	0	0	2	0	0	0	0	0	0	0	0	0	0	0	0	0	0	0
emotion	42	.6546	5.6230	47.5	0	0	3	7	15	7	8	2	6	6	0	9	0	0	1	1	5	4	0	0	1	4	3	2	0
emotional	97	.7292	14.208	51.5	1	0	10	2	26	25	27	6	2	10	4	2	0	2	0	18	20	2	11	0	0	3	5	18	0
emotionalism	3	.0000	.0243	23.8	0	0	0	0	0	3	0	0	0	0	0	0	0	0	0	0	3	0	0	0	0	0	0	0	0
emotionally	15	.6464	1.9890	43.0	0	1	3	0	5	2	3	1	1	0	0	0	0	1	0	6	0	1	1	1	0	0	2	2	0
emotions	55	.7884	8.6985	49.4	0	0	7	3	18	15	9	3	7	1	2	1	0	1	0	9	8	3	5	1	1	5	7	4	0
emperor	37	.4411	3.6381	45.6	2	4	7	4	11	6	3	0	8	0	0	0	0	11	0	0	2	0	0	0	0	2	14	0	0
Emperor	76	.6434	10.431	50.2	5	20	7	15	19	6	2	2	39	0	0	1	0	13	0	0	4	0	0	0	1	6	10	2	0
emperor's	5	.3926	.4468	36.5	0	0	2	1	1	0	1	0	1	0	0	0	0	1	0	0	0	0	0	0	0	1	2	0	0
Emperor's	12	.3059	1.0053	40.0	0	4	3	4	1	0	0	0	8	0	0	0	0	1	0	0	3	0	0	0	0	0	0	0	0
emperors	21	.5088	2.2857	43.6	0	0	6	6	3	3	2	1	2	0	0	0	0	9	1	0	0	0	0	0	0	2	6	1	0
emphasis	66	.8167	10.751	50.3	2	2	4	3	21	14	17	3	4	12	5	3	0	8	1	2	7	2	1	1	1	3	8	8	0
emphasize	34	.7781	5.2757	47.2	1	0	1	2	11	9	9	1	0	6	2	1	2	1	1	2	7	1	3	0	0	4	3	1	0
emphasized	24	.7043	3.3941	45.3	1	2	0	2	8	5	6	0	0	3	0	0	1	4	0	0	3	1	4	1	1	0	4	2	0
emphasizes	18	.5981	2.1725	43.4	0	0	0	0	7	7	4	0	0	2	2	2	1	0	0	1	4	3	2	0	0	1	0	0	0
emphasizing	9	.5840	1.0702	40.3	0	0	1	1	4	1	2	0	0	1	0	0	0	0	0	1	1	1	1	0	0	1	3	0	0
emphatic	4	.3415	.3124	34.9	0	0	0	1	1	1	1	0	1	0	1	1	0	0	1	0	0	0	0	0	0	0	0	0	0
emphatically	7	.2594	.4649	36.7	0	0	0	1	2	2	2	0	2	0	0	4	0	0	0	0	0	0	0	0	1	0	0	0	0
empire	91	.5861	11.148	50.5	7	2	15	22	23	13	8	1	5	0	0	1	0	48	3	0	1	0	0	0	1	12	12	8	0
Empire	118	.7219	17.325	52.4	10	4	22	20	19	23	12	8	12	5	0	0	7	42	3	2	4	1	0	0	1	8	27	6	0
empire-building	2	.0000	.0290	24.6	0	0	2	0	0	0	0	0	0	0	0	0	0	0	0	0	0	0	0	0	0	2	0	0	0
empire's	2	.2408	.1204	30.8	0	0	1	0	0	1	0	0	0	0	0	0	0	1	0	0	0	0	0	0	0	1	0	0	0
empires	14	.3567	1.1353	40.6	1	0	2	1	7	1	0	2	0	0	0	0	0	9	0	0	0	0	0	0	0	3	2	0	0
Empires	2	.2278	.1128	30.5	0	0	0	0	0	0	0	2	0	0	0	0	0	0	0	1	0	0	0	0	0	0	1	0	0
empirical	4	.0000	.0419	26.2	0	0	0	0	0	1	3	0	0	0	0	0	0	0	0	0	0	0	0	0	0	0	4	0	0
emplaced	3	.3465	.2515	34.0	0	0	0	0	2	0	1	0	1	0	0	0	0	0	0	0	0	0	0	0	0	1	0	1	0
employ	34	.6866	4.7593	46.8	1	0	5	3	12	4	8	1	3	0	3	3	2	3	0	6	2	0	0	0	0	5	5	2	0
employed	87	.7835	13.686	51.4	4	1	12	11	16	25	14	4	5	2	0	5	3	22	1	7	6	1	0	3	1	6	23	2	0
employee	17	.6763	2.3464	43.7	2	1	0	0	9	2	3	0	2	2	2	1	2	2	1	0	0	0	0	0	1	2	1	1	0
employees	33	.4943	3.4524	45.4	0	0	5	2	13	8	5	0	1	1	0	0	3	9	0	0	0	0	0	0	0	2	14	3	0
employer	15	.6563	2.0410	43.1	1	1	0	2	7	0	3	1	4	1	1	0	2	0	1	1	0	0	0	0	0	0	3	2	0
employer's	3	.2063	.1600	32.0	0	0	1	0	2	0	0	0	0	0	0	0	0	1	0	0	0	0	0	0	0	2	0	0	0
employers	28	.5476	3.1902	45.0	3	0	2	1	6	6	10	0	1	2	0	1	0	4	0	0	0	0	0	0	0	3	9	8	0
employing	13	.5471	1.5285	41.8	1	2	2	1	4	2	1	0	3	0	0	0	0	4	0	0	0	0	0	0	0	2	2	2	0
employment	21	.6357	2.7481	44.4	2	0	1	1	2	6	9	0	1	2	0	1	0	9	0	1	0	0	1	0	0	0	4	2	0
Employment	4	.2408	.2408	33.8	2	0	0	0	0	2	0	0	0	0	0	0	0	2	0	0	0	0	0	0	0	2	0	0	0
employs	25	.6018	3.1107	44.9	2	0	6	2	7	3	5	0	2	0	0	0	1	6	0	1	4	0	0	3	0	4	1	3	0

8Q embodying
6A embonpoint
8A embosomed
7J embouchure
7A embowered
8D embrasure
7A embroiled
7H Embryology
6Q Embryophyta
7J embued
6R EMD
9F Emerald
7M Emeri
6R Emeritus
5P Emersonian
7R Emery
5P emigrators
9Q emigres
9B Emilia's
7R Emiliano
4R Emilie
7Q eminences
9A eminency
4F emir
5P emirates
5P emirs
8R emissaries
7H Emission
9H emissions
3P Emmanuel's
5P Emmanuele
7L Emmenthaler
8R Emmerich
4P Emmitsburg
9R Emmons'
9B Emmy
7J Emotions
XR empathize
9D empathy
7N emperor-holocanthus
7R EMPI
7R EMPI'S
8F Empire's
7P emplacements
9E employee's
5R employees'

Word Type	F	D	U	SFI	3 Gr 3	4 Gr 4	5 Gr 5	6 Gr 6	7 Gr 7	8 Gr 8	9 Gr 9	X UnGr	A Read	B Eng & Gr	C Comp	D Lit	E Math	F Soc Stud	G Spell	H Sci	J Music	K Art	L Home Ec	M Shop	N Lib F	P Lib NF	Q Lib Ref	R Mag	S Rel
empowered	2	.0000	.0209	23.2	0	0	0	0	0	2	0	0	0	0	0	0	0	0	0	0	0	0	0	0	0	0	2	0	0
empresarios	2	.0000	.0389	25.9	0	0	0	0	2	0	0	0	0	0	0	0	0	2	0	0	0	0	0	0	0	0	0	0	0
empress	4	.3755	.3689	35.7	1	0	1	0	0	2	0	0	2	0	0	0	1	0	0	0	0	0	0	0	1	0	0	0	0
Empress	16	.6132	2.1151	43.3	0	7	5	1	1	2	0	0	8	0	0	1	0	3	0	0	0	0	0	0	0	1	1	2	0
emptied	22	.6832	3.1204	44.9	6	5	2	4	1	2	2	0	7	0	0	2	0	2	0	1	1	0	0	0	3	5	1	0	0
empties	6	.4622	.5953	37.7	1	0	2	1	2	0	0	0	0	0	0	0	0	1	0	2	0	0	0	0	0	0	1	2	0
emptiness	7	.6188	.9117	39.6	0	1	2	0	4	0	0	0	2	0	0	1	0	1	0	0	0	0	0	0	0	1	1	1	0
empty	384	.8874	67.988	58.3	84	63	67	38	70	23	30	9	117	13	7	34	43	25	6	48	6	0	3	0	32	27	11	12	0
empty-handed	4	.2958	.2914	34.6	1	1	2	0	0	0	0	0	1	0	0	0	0	0	0	0	0	0	0	0	2	1	0	0	0
emptying	12	.7123	1.7542	42.4	1	0	3	1	3	0	4	0	3	1	0	1	0	2	0	1	0	0	1	0	1	1	0	1	0
emu	3	.3709	.2499	34.0	1	1	0	0	1	0	0	0	0	0	0	0	0	1	0	1	0	0	0	0	0	0	1	0	0
emu's	2	.2408	.1204	30.8	1	1	0	0	0	0	0	0	0	0	0	0	0	1	0	0	0	0	0	0	0	1	0	0	0
en	42	.5153	4.5962	46.6	2	3	6	2	25	3	1	0	7	5	0	0	0	0	6	1	1	0	0	0	20	0	1	1	0
Ena	2	.0000	.0914	29.6	0	0	0	2	0	0	0	0	2	0	0	0	0	0	0	0	0	0	0	0	0	0	0	0	0
enable	77	.8031	12.421	50.9	4	8	7	12	13	13	17	3	8	4	4	2	6	4	0	28	2	0	1	3	1	4	5	5	0
enabled	45	.7863	7.0894	48.5	3	3	8	2	11	5	12	1	0	1	1	2	1	9	0	7	1	0	1	0	3	6	11	2	0
enables	60	.7458	9.0005	49.5	0	2	2	8	20	7	17	4	1	0	1	1	4	2	0	20	1	2	3	4	0	1	16	4	0
enabling	15	.5716	1.7844	42.5	0	0	0	0	7	3	5	0	1	1	0	0	0	3	0	1	1	0	0	0	0	1	6	1	0
enact	4	.2281	.2337	33.7	0	0	1	0	0	1	2	0	0	0	0	0	0	3	0	0	0	0	0	0	0	0	0	1	0
enacted	10	.5066	1.0736	40.3	1	0	1	0	2	2	3	1	1	0	0	0	0	2	0	0	0	1	0	0	0	1	2	3	0
enamel	55	.3540	4.2657	46.3	0	1	6	4	19	12	10	3	2	0	0	0	0	0	0	19	0	1	1	20	0	8	3	1	0
enamels	5	.1044	.1632	32.1	0	0	0	1	2	2	0	0	1	0	0	0	0	0	0	0	0	0	0	3	0	1	0	0	0
enamored	2	.1948	.1250	31.0	0	0	0	2	0	0	0	0	1	0	0	0	0	0	0	0	0	0	0	0	0	1	0	0	0
encamped	4	.4802	.4047	36.1	0	0	1	0	1	1	1	0	0	0	0	1	0	1	0	0	0	0	0	0	1	0	1	0	0
encampment	7	.3807	.5803	37.6	0	0	1	0	3	3	0	0	0	0	0	1	0	1	0	0	0	0	0	0	4	1	0	0	0
encase	2	.1033	.0599	27.8	0	0	0	0	1	0	1	0	0	0	0	0	0	0	0	1	0	1	0	0	0	0	0	0	0
encased	7	.5219	.7532	38.8	0	0	1	0	1	0	4	1	0	1	0	0	0	0	0	0	0	0	1	0	0	1	2	2	0
ence	16	.0670	.3346	35.2	0	0	0	1	11	3	1	0	0	1	0	0	0	0	15	0	0	0	0	0	0	0	0	0	0
enchanted	16	.6570	2.1747	43.4	1	4	0	2	5	0	3	1	4	1	0	2	0	0	0	0	1	1	0	0	0	4	1	2	0
Enchanted	2	.1494	.1045	30.2	1	0	0	0	1	0	0	0	1	0	0	0	0	0	0	0	1	0	0	0	0	0	0	0	0
enchanting	7	.3813	.6089	37.8	0	1	1	2	2	0	1	0	2	0	0	0	0	0	0	0	1	1	0	0	3	0	0	0	0
Enchanting	4	.0000	.0323	25.1	0	0	0	0	0	0	4	0	0	0	0	0	0	0	0	0	4	0	0	0	0	0	0	0	0
enchantment	7	.4769	.7542	38.8	1	0	0	1	2	1	2	0	3	1	0	1	0	0	0	0	0	0	0	0	0	2	0	0	0
enchantress	5	.0804	.1641	32.2	0	0	4	1	0	0	0	0	1	0	0	0	0	0	0	0	0	0	0	0	4	0	0	0	0
encircle	5	.3947	.4409	36.4	0	0	0	1	2	0	2	0	1	0	1	0	1	0	0	0	0	0	0	0	0	1	1	0	0
encircled	6	.4245	.5347	37.3	0	0	0	1	3	1	1	0	0	1	0	1	0	0	0	0	0	0	0	1	3	0	0	0	0
encircles	2	.2303	.1079	30.3	1	0	0	0	1	0	0	0	0	0	0	0	0	0	0	0	1	0	0	0	0	1	0	0	0
encircling	5	.3414	.4194	36.2	0	1	0	2	1	1	0	0	2	0	0	0	0	0	0	0	0	0	0	0	1	0	0	2	0
enclaves	2	.2433	.1158	30.6	0	0	1	0	0	0	1	0	0	0	0	0	0	0	0	0	0	0	0	0	0	1	0	1	0
enclose	21	.5629	2.4222	43.8	0	1	2	2	5	8	3	0	0	11	0	1	3	0	2	0	0	1	0	0	0	0	2	1	0
enclosed	39	.6911	5.4905	47.4	2	1	4	2	16	6	7	1	5	4	3	1	9	3	0	2	0	0	0	3	1	0	6	2	0
encloses	10	.4649	1.0062	40.0	0	0	0	1	6	0	3	0	0	0	0	0	1	3	0	4	0	0	0	0	0	0	2	0	0
enclosing	10	.5073	1.0858	40.4	0	2	1	2	1	3	0	1	2	3	0	0	0	1	0	0	0	1	0	0	0	0	1	2	0
enclosure	5	.4115	.4585	36.6	0	2	1	1	1	0	0	0	1	1	0	0	0	0	0	0	0	0	0	0	0	1	2	0	0
encomienda	2	.0000	.0209	23.2	2	0	0	0	0	0	0	0	0	0	0	0	0	0	0	0	0	0	0	0	0	0	2	0	0
encompass	7	.4391	.6513	38.1	1	0	1	1	4	0	0	0	0	0	0	0	0	0	0	0	0	0	0	0	1	2	3	1	0
encompasses	3	.3782	.2435	33.9	0	0	1	0	2	0	0	0	0	0	0	0	0	0	0	0	1	0	0	0	0	1	1	0	0
encompassing	5	.4564	.4807	36.8	0	0	1	1	1	0	2	0	0	0	0	0	0	0	0	0	0	0	0	0	1	1	2	1	0
encore	2	.2411	.1091	30.4	0	0	0	0	0	1	1	0	0	0	0	1	0	0	0	0	1	0	0	0	0	0	0	0	0
encounter	38	.6658	5.2079	47.2	1	4	3	4	12	7	6	1	7	0	0	2	0	3	0	3	0	0	2	0	3	3	12	3	0
encountered	39	.8405	6.5615	48.2	0	1	6	3	16	5	5	3	7	1	1	1	1	3	1	5	1	0	0	0	5	5	5	3	0
encountering	2	.0000	.0299	24.8	0	0	0	0	0	1	1	0	0	0	0	0	2	0	0	0	0	0	0	0	0	0	0	0	0
encounters	7	.5788	.8478	39.3	0	0	0	1	2	3	1	0	1	0	0	0	0	1	1	0	0	0	0	0	0	1	1	2	0
encourage	43	.8144	7.0161	48.5	0	3	7	7	9	5	9	3	4	2	1	2	0	13	3	3	5	0	1	0	0	3	1	5	0
encouraged	79	.8592	13.518	51.3	6	3	13	14	15	13	13	2	8	6	3	5	0	14	0	3	4	1	2	0	4	13	9	7	0
encouragement	23	.7898	3.6672	45.6	0	0	6	3	5	5	4	0	5	0	0	2	1	2	1	2	1	0	0	0	1	1	4	3	0
encourages	10	.2253	.5376	37.3	0	2	1	1	2	1	2	1	0	0	0	0	0	2	0	2	1	0	1	0	1	0	2	0	1
encouraging	26	.7621	4.0008	46.0	0	1	4	3	8	6	3	1	3	2	1	1	0	8	1	2	1	0	2	0	2	0	0	3	0
encouragingly	3	.1250	.1342	31.3	0	1	0	1	1	0	0	0	1	0	0	0	0	0	0	0	0	0	0	0	2	0	0	0	0
encroach	3	.3709	.2499	34.0	0	0	0	0	1	1	0	1	0	0	0	0	0	1	0	1	0	0	0	0	0	0	1	0	0
encroachments	2	.2407	.1138	30.6	0	0	1	0	0	1	0	0	0	0	0	1	0	0	0	0	0	0	0	0	0	1	0	0	0
encrusted	2	.2446	.1122	30.5	0	0	0	0	1	0	0	1	0	0	0	1	0	0	0	0	0	0	0	0	0	0	1	0	0
encyclical	2	.2437	.1129	30.5	0	0	0	0	1	1	0	0	0	0	0	0	0	0	0	0	0	0	0	0	0	0	1	1	0
encyclopedia	69	.6956	9.8685	49.9	3	27	22	4	10	1	2	0	17	14	0	1	3	3	1	9	1	2	0	0	0	1	16	1	0
Encyclopedia	18	.3320	1.5841	42.0	0	0	14	0	0	1	3	0	12	5	0	0	0	0	0	0	0	0	0	0	0	0	1	0	0
encyclopedias	30	.6050	3.7869	45.8	0	6	7	5	6	2	3	1	5	10	0	0	1	2	0	5	0	0	0	1	0	0	5	1	0
end	2961	.9352	547.78	67.4	591	418	386	375	533	338	250	70	597	292	27	118	135	201	402	292	101	20	49	105	136	207	111	167	1
End	12	.4360	1.1064	40.4	2	0	0	2	7	1	0	0	0	0	1	0	0	0	0	0	1	0	0	0	0	3	0	7	0
end-to-end	4	.2009	.2054	33.1	0	0	0	0	2	1	0	1	0	0	0	0	3	0	0	0	0	0	0	0	0	1	0	0	0
endanger	3	.3756	.2468	33.9	0	0	0	0	1	1	1	0	0	0	0	1	0	1	0	0	0	0	0	0	0	0	1	0	0
endangered	10	.5141	1.0966	40.4	0	0	1	1	5	1	1	1	1	0	0	0	0	2	0	1	0	0	0	0	0	1	1	4	0
endangering	4	.1597	.1815	32.6	0	1	1	0	2	0	0	0	1	0	0	0	0	0	0	0	0	0	2	0	0	1	0	0	0
endeared	2	.1948	.1250	31.0	0	0	1	0	1	0	0	0	1	0	0	0	0	0	0	0	0	0	0	0	0	1	0	0	0
endearing	4	.1854	.1872	32.7	0	0	0	2	1	0	0	1	0	0	0	0	0	0	0	0	0	0	0	0	0	1	0	3	0
endeavor	12	.6254	1.5523	41.9	0	0	0	1	3	4	3	1	1	0	0	2	0	1	0	4	1	0	0	0	0	0	2	1	0
Endeavor	3	.2387	.1708	32.3	0	2	0	0	0	0	1	0	0	0	0	0	0	0	0	0	0	0	0	0	0	2	1	0	0
endeavored	3	.2197	.2090	33.2	0	0	0	0	1	2	0	0	2	0	0	0	0	0	0	0	0	0	0	0	0	0	1	0	0
endeavoring	3	.3465	.2515	34.0	0	0	0	1	1	0	1	0	1	0	0	0	0	0	0	0	0	0	0	0	0	1	0	1	0
endeavors	3	.3805	.2526	34.0	0	0	0	1	1	0	1	0	0	0	0	0	0	1	0	0	0	0	0	0	1	1	0	0	0
endeavour	2	.2297	.1135	30.6	0	0	0	0	1	1	0	0	0	0	0	1	0	1	0	0	0	0	0	0	0	0	0	0	0
endeavoured	4	.3394	.3015	34.8	0	0	0	1	0	1	2	0	0	0	0	2	0	1	0	0	0	0	0	0	1	0	0	0	0
ended	240	.7967	38.718	55.9	30	48	31	33	43	35	16	4	72	7	0	8	2	40	5	3	16	0	0	0	13	42	14	18	0
endemic	3	.1169	.1277	31.1	0	0	0	0	2	1	0	0	1	0	0	0	0	0	0	0	0	0	0	0	0	0	2	0	0
Enders	2	.0000	.0234	23.7	0	0	2	0	0	0	0	0	0	0	0	0	0	0	0	0	0	0	0	0	2	0	0	0	0
endgate	2	.0000	.0215	23.3	0	0	0	0	0	2	0	0	0	0	0	2	0	0	0	0	0	0	0	0	0	0	0	0	0
Endicott	2	.0000	.0234	23.7	0	0	0	0	0	0	2	0	0	0	0	0	0	0	0	0	0	0	0	0	2	0	0	0	0
ending	482	.5437	54.557	57.4	83	65	51	70	82	77	53	1	62	89	17	11	6	10	230	8	35	0	2	0	4	1	3	4	0
endings	133	.3874	11.165	50.5	20	18	21	32	18	20	4	0	9	26	1	0	0	1	74	17	4	0	0	0	0	0	1	0	0
endive	2	.0000	.0064	18.1	0	0	0	0	2	0	0	0	0	0	0	0	0	0	0	0	0	0	2	0	0	0	0	0	0
endless	81	.7101	11.786	50.7	8	10	9	9	19	14	10	2	18	4	2	1	4	11	2	7	1	0	2	0	6	8	7	7	1
endlessly	15	.7482	2.2690	43.6	0	1	2	0	6	2	2	2	2	2	0	1	0	1	1	1	0	0	0	0	2	1	3	1	0
endocrine	10	.2426	.6051	37.8	0	0	0	0	1	5	4	0	0	0	0	0	0	0	0	7	0	0	0	0	0	0	3	0	0
endocrines	3	.0000	.0314	25.0	0	0	0	0	0	0	3	0	0	0	0	0	0	0	0	0	0	0	0	0	0	0	3	0	0
endorsed	2	.2152	.1357	31.3	0	0	0	0	1	1	0	0	1	0	0	0	0	1	0	0	0	0	0	0	0	0	0	0	0

8Q empowers
4A Empress'
5A emprise
9B emptor
8Q empyema
6P emulate
7N emulating
9H emulsifying
7L emulsion
4F emus
3J En
7G en-
3P en-jine
6B en-1
6B en-2
7N en'
8M enameled
3Q enameling
XQ enamelists
XR enamelled
9D enamor'd
3A enargite
9Q encamp
XB encases
6H encephalitis
3Q enchant
7A enchante
8R enchanter
5N enchantments
7D Encinal
4F Encino
8A encirclement
XH Encke
XH Encke's
5P enclave
4A encode
4N encompassed
7P encrease
8A encroaching
XQ encroachment
8D encumbered
8G ency
9H encysted
XH end-member
9E end-of-the-month
8E end-points
XH end-products
7P end-to-edge
7P end-to-face
6A endear
8F Endeavour
7D endeth
9Q endocrinology
9H endoderm
9Q endorse

Word Type	F	D	U	SFI	3 Gr 3	4 Gr 4	5 Gr 5	6 Gr 6	7 Gr 7	8 Gr 8	9 Gr 9	X UnGr	A Read	B Eng & Gr	C Comp	D Lit	E Math	F Soc Stud	G Spell	H Sci	J Music	K Art	L Home Ec	M Shop	N Lib F	P Lib NF	Q Lib Ref	R Mag	S Rel
endorsement	4	.0000	.0486	26.9	0	0	0	0	1	1	2	0	0	0	0	0	0	0	0	0	0	0	0	0	0	0	0	4	0
endorsing	2	.2351	.1166	30.7	0	0	0	0	1	0	1	0	0	0	0	0	0	1	0	0	0	0	0	0	0	0	0	1	0
endoskeleton	2	.0000	.0394	26.0	0	0	0	1	0	0	1	0	0	0	0	0	0	0	0	2	0	0	0	0	0	0	0	0	0
endoskeletons	2	.0000	.0394	26.0	0	0	0	2	0	0	0	0	0	0	0	0	0	0	0	2	0	0	0	0	0	0	0	0	0
endosperm	2	.0000	.0064	18.1	0	0	0	0	0	0	2	0	0	0	0	0	0	0	0	0	0	0	2	0	0	0	0	0	0
endow	4	.2847	.2818	34.5	0	0	0	0	2	1	1	0	1	0	0	0	0	0	0	0	0	0	0	0	0	1	2	0	0
endowed	11	.5801	1.3220	41.2	0	0	0	0	6	1	3	1	1	0	0	1	0	1	0	0	1	0	0	0	1	0	4	2	0
endowment	3	.3771	.2489	34.0	0	0	0	0	2	1	0	0	0	0	0	1	0	0	0	1	0	0	0	0	0	0	0	1	0
endpoint	36	.0000	.5389	37.3	10	1	3	4	13	4	1	0	0	0	0	0	36	0	0	0	0	0	0	0	0	0	0	0	0
endpoints	18	.0000	.2694	34.3	7	0	1	1	4	5	0	0	0	0	0	0	18	0	0	0	0	0	0	0	0	0	0	0	0
ends	600	.8294	99.402	60.0	136	71	77	63	115	73	51	14	88	51	5	18	36	16	138	62	29	7	31	38	21	19	18	23	0
endurance	26	.6697	3.6465	45.6	3	1	5	3	8	5	0	1	10	0	0	1	0	1	0	3	0	0	0	1	0	5	1	4	0
Endurance	2	.0000	.0914	29.6	0	0	0	2	0	0	0	0	2	0	0	0	0	0	0	0	0	0	0	0	0	0	0	0	0
endure	39	.6762	5.4539	47.4	0	2	4	2	12	10	8	1	10	0	0	4	0	6	0	1	4	0	0	0	0	5	7	2	0
endured	18	.6438	2.4163	43.8	1	0	1	4	7	3	2	0	5	1	0	3	0	1	0	0	0	0	0	0	3	3	2	0	0
enduring	17	.5962	2.0775	43.2	0	2	1	1	5	3	5	0	1	1	0	1	0	1	0	1	7	1	0	0	0	1	2	1	0
enema	3	.0000	.0434	26.4	0	0	0	0	3	0	0	0	0	0	0	0	0	0	0	0	0	0	0	0	0	3	0	0	0
enemies	226	.6742	31.547	55.0	54	31	22	36	40	22	18	3	48	7	0	11	0	32	2	46	2	0	0	1	7	41	17	10	2
Enemies	2	.2337	.1157	30.6	0	1	0	0	0	1	0	0	0	0	0	0	0	1	0	0	0	0	0	0	1	0	0	0	0
enemy	301	.7977	48.675	56.9	38	40	43	54	65	34	21	6	96	10	1	26	0	38	5	29	0	0	0	0	16	51	15	14	0
Enemy	7	.3431	.5241	37.2	0	4	1	0	1	1	0	0	0	1	0	2	0	0	0	0	0	0	0	0	4	0	0	0	0
enemy's	15	.5080	1.6353	42.1	1	4	2	0	2	1	5	0	3	1	0	3	0	0	0	0	0	0	0	0	0	4	4	0	0
energetic	27	.7462	4.0729	46.1	0	0	3	4	6	6	5	3	2	4	0	0	0	5	0	5	2	0	1	0	2	3	3	0	0
energetically	2	.2440	.1132	30.5	0	0	0	0	1	0	1	0	0	0	0	1	0	0	0	0	0	0	0	0	0	0	0	1	0
energies	14	.6010	1.7264	42.4	1	0	0	2	5	3	2	1	0	2	0	0	0	2	0	2	0	1	0	0	0	1	4	2	0
energized	4	.0000	.0419	26.2	0	0	0	0	0	4	0	0	0	0	0	0	0	0	0	0	0	0	0	0	0	0	4	0	0
energizers	2	.0000	.0394	26.0	0	0	0	0	0	2	0	0	0	0	0	0	0	0	0	2	0	0	0	0	0	0	0	0	0
energy	1190	.5973	148.77	61.7	194	131	181	180	240	141	99	24	72	2	2	6	10	30	8	804	14	0	24	12	6	40	141	19	0
Energy	5	.4303	.4639	36.7	0	0	1	0	1	2	1	0	0	0	0	0	0	1	0	1	0	0	0	0	0	0	2	1	0
energy-producing	2	.0000	.0394	26.0	0	0	0	1	0	1	0	0	0	0	0	0	0	0	0	2	0	0	0	0	0	0	0	0	0
enfolded	2	.1787	.1174	30.7	0	0	0	0	1	1	0	0	1	0	0	0	0	0	0	0	0	0	0	0	1	0	0	0	0
enforce	24	.6649	3.2752	45.2	0	0	4	4	5	9	2	0	1	1	0	1	0	11	1	3	0	0	0	0	1	0	3	2	0
enforced	10	.5451	1.1503	40.6	1	0	1	1	5	2	0	0	1	0	0	0	0	3	0	0	0	0	0	0	1	1	3	1	0
enforcement	2	.2278	.1128	30.5	0	0	1	0	0	1	0	0	0	0	0	0	0	0	0	1	0	0	0	0	0	0	1	0	0
enforces	6	.4590	.5969	37.8	1	1	0	0	2	0	2	0	0	0	0	0	0	3	0	1	0	0	0	0	0	1	1	0	0
enforcing	5	.3116	.3461	35.4	0	1	0	0	3	1	0	0	0	0	0	0	0	0	0	0	0	0	0	0	0	1	3	1	0
Eng	3	.0000	.0314	25.0	0	0	0	0	0	2	1	0	0	0	0	0	0	0	0	0	0	0	0	0	0	0	3	0	0
engage	29	.7308	4.2969	46.3	1	0	2	5	12	3	6	0	3	0	0	0	1	7	4	1	0	0	0	1	1	4	4	3	0
engaged	77	.8804	13.464	51.3	5	5	8	8	9	23	15	4	7	6	1	6	0	16	0	2	4	1	3	2	3	6	13	7	0
engagement	18	.7260	2.6464	44.2	2	2	1	4	6	2	1	0	2	3	0	1	0	1	0	0	1	0	0	0	3	3	2	2	0
engagements	4	.3402	.3011	34.8	1	0	0	0	1	2	0	0	0	0	0	1	0	1	0	0	0	0	0	0	0	0	2	0	0
engages	4	.3394	.2961	34.7	0	0	0	1	1	0	2	0	0	0	1	0	0	2	0	0	0	0	1	0	0	0	0	0	0
engaging	8	.5108	.8725	39.4	0	0	0	2	3	1	2	0	1	0	0	0	0	1	0	2	0	0	0	1	0	0	1	2	0
Engelbert	2	.0000	.0162	22.1	0	0	0	2	0	0	0	0	0	0	0	0	0	0	0	0	2	0	0	0	0	0	0	0	0
engendered	2	.2440	.1132	30.5	0	0	0	0	1	0	1	0	0	0	0	1	0	0	0	0	0	0	0	0	0	0	0	1	0
engine	582	.8110	95.737	59.8	91	95	67	55	136	85	36	17	235	16	6	6	6	23	6	100	4	0	0	10	3	73	23	71	0
engine's	10	.4527	1.0064	40.0	1	1	1	0	6	0	1	0	2	0	0	0	0	1	0	2	0	0	0	0	0	1	0	4	0
engineer	167	.7824	26.446	54.2	28	26	18	19	17	13	44	2	44	9	1	1	4	13	2	11	2	1	0	8	0	14	37	20	0
Engineer	6	.3790	.5800	37.6	1	2	0	1	1	0	1	0	4	0	0	0	0	1	0	0	0	0	0	0	0	0	0	1	0
engineer's	14	.4713	1.3925	41.4	2	1	0	1	1	0	9	0	1	0	0	0	0	0	1	0	0	0	0	1	0	2	8	1	0
engineered	6	.2437	.3386	35.3	0	0	0	0	3	1	1	1	0	0	0	0	0	0	0	0	0	0	0	0	0	0	3	3	0
engineering	89	.4194	8.0580	49.1	0	7	2	8	12	6	52	2	7	0	0	0	2	3	0	3	0	3	0	0	0	3	58	10	0
engineers	155	.6651	21.006	53.2	2	16	9	19	26	18	63	2	10	3	1	2	3	16	2	19	7	0	0	12	0	2	55	23	0
Engineers	6	.5540	.7194	38.6	0	0	2	1	1	1	0	1	2	0	0	0	1	1	0	0	0	0	0	0	0	0	1	1	0
engines	246	.7751	38.646	55.9	29	48	30	16	61	38	21	3	54	5	6	6	2	31	2	55	0	0	0	14	4	16	21	30	0
England	859	.8130	140.28	61.5	65	101	204	119	139	130	75	26	124	61	3	26	5	271	23	29	64	1	1	1	22	86	114	28	0
England's	35	.6661	4.8063	46.8	1	3	7	1	7	8	7	1	4	1	0	0	1	16	0	1	4	0	0	0	2	3	1	2	0
Englanders	6	.0000	.1167	30.7	0	0	3	0	0	2	1	0	0	0	0	0	0	6	0	0	0	0	0	0	0	0	0	0	0
Englewood	2	.0000	.0914	29.6	0	0	0	0	0	2	0	0	2	0	0	0	0	0	0	0	0	0	0	0	0	0	0	0	0
english	2	.0000	.0219	23.4	0	0	0	0	0	1	1	0	0	2	0	0	0	0	0	0	0	0	0	0	0	0	0	0	0
English	1564	.7221	228.35	63.6	72	138	213	245	365	313	175	43	145	565	16	57	27	164	236	29	81	1	4	1	21	75	105	37	0
English-speaking	22	.5171	2.3738	43.8	0	0	7	3	6	4	2	0	1	10	2	0	0	2	3	1	0	0	0	0	0	3	0	0	0
Englishes	3	.0000	.0434	26.4	0	0	0	0	0	0	3	0	0	0	0	0	0	0	0	0	0	0	0	0	0	3	0	0	0
Englishman	44	.8543	7.5055	48.8	3	7	2	6	9	7	10	0	7	4	1	3	3	5	3	3	0	0	0	0	2	6	4	3	0
Englishman's	2	.0000	.0219	23.4	0	0	0	0	1	0	0	1	0	2	0	0	0	0	0	0	0	0	0	0	0	0	0	0	0
Englishmen	26	.6056	3.2950	45.2	2	2	5	3	5	8	0	1	3	1	0	0	0	13	2	1	0	0	0	0	0	2	3	1	0
engraved	3	.2946	.1913	32.8	0	0	0	1	0	1	1	0	0	0	0	1	0	0	0	0	0	0	0	1	1	0	0	0	0
engraving	3	.2184	.1759	32.5	0	0	0	0	1	0	1	1	1	0	0	0	0	0	0	0	0	0	0	1	0	0	0	1	0
engravings	3	.2286	.1800	32.6	0	0	2	0	0	0	1	0	1	0	0	0	0	0	0	0	0	0	0	1	0	0	1	0	0
engrossed	3	.3408	.2477	33.9	0	0	1	0	1	1	0	0	1	0	0	1	0	0	0	0	0	0	0	0	0	1	0	0	0
engrossing	3	.2304	.1619	32.1	0	0	0	0	2	1	0	0	0	0	0	0	0	0	0	0	0	0	0	0	2	0	1	0	0
Engstrom	2	.0000	.0243	23.9	0	0	0	0	0	2	0	0	0	0	0	0	0	0	0	0	0	0	0	0	0	0	0	2	0
engulf	8	.5261	.8737	39.4	3	0	1	0	1	0	3	0	0	2	0	2	0	0	0	1	0	0	0	0	0	1	2	0	0
engulfed	7	.4090	.6743	38.3	0	0	0	0	6	0	1	0	3	0	1	0	0	1	0	1	0	0	0	0	0	0	1	0	0
engulfing	3	.2159	.1532	31.9	0	0	0	1	2	0	0	0	0	0	0	0	0	0	0	0	0	0	0	0	0	0	2	1	0
enhance	7	.4791	.6958	38.4	0	0	0	0	4	0	2	1	0	2	0	0	0	0	0	0	1	1	0	0	0	1	0	2	0
enhanced	6	.4725	.5911	37.7	0	0	0	0	0	3	1	2	0	0	1	0	0	1	0	0	1	0	0	0	0	0	1	2	0
enhances	2	.0000	.0162	22.1	0	0	0	1	0	0	1	0	0	0	0	0	0	0	0	0	2	0	0	0	0	0	0	0	0
Enich	10	.0000	.1073	30.3	0	0	0	0	5	5	0	0	0	0	0	10	0	0	0	0	0	0	0	0	0	0	0	0	0
Enid	2	.0000	.0299	24.8	0	2	0	0	0	0	0	0	0	0	0	0	2	0	0	0	0	0	0	0	0	0	0	0	0
Enif	2	.0000	.0394	26.0	0	0	0	0	0	0	0	2	0	0	0	0	0	0	0	2	0	0	0	0	0	0	0	0	0
enigma	2	.2401	.1133	30.5	0	0	1	0	1	0	0	0	0	0	0	0	0	0	0	0	0	0	0	0	0	1	1	0	0
enigmatic	4	.3582	.3103	34.9	0	0	0	0	4	0	0	0	0	0	0	0	0	0	0	0	0	0	0	0	1	0	2	1	0
enjoined	4	.3011	.2909	34.6	0	0	1	0	1	0	2	0	1	0	0	2	0	0	0	0	0	0	0	0	0	0	1	0	0
enjoins	2	.2351	.1166	30.7	0	0	0	0	0	1	0	1	0	0	0	0	0	1	0	0	0	0	0	0	0	0	0	1	0
enjoy	422	.8374	70.658	58.5	64	86	58	49	75	50	36	4	75	45	20	21	2	69	9	26	55	13	22	0	9	20	18	18	0
enjoyable	32	.6945	4.4929	46.5	1	9	1	5	8	2	5	1	2	6	1	3	3	1	1	4	0	1	6	0	2	0	0	2	0
enjoyed	212	.8490	36.079	55.6	25	49	26	25	29	36	17	5	62	26	5	10	3	29	4	5	23	1	2	0	4	18	8	11	1
enjoying	61	.8385	10.285	50.1	6	11	12	10	8	9	5	0	22	4	2	7	0	4	0	2	2	1	3	0	3	4	1	6	0
enjoyment	51	.7832	8.0428	49.1	3	8	8	4	9	10	7	2	9	5	0	2	0	5	2	3	12	0	1	1	1	3	6	1	0
enjoys	35	.6568	4.7390	46.8	3	6	8	4	8	3	3	0	7	6	4	4	0	6	0	1	2	0	1	0	1	2	0	1	0
enlarge	12	.7162	1.7300	42.4	0	0	2	2	3	3	2	0	0	2	0	1	0	2	1	1	1	0	0	1	0	0	1	2	0
enlarged	37	.7543	5.6177	47.5	1	3	6	5	7	7	8	0	1	1	0	2	0	6	1	10	3	0	1	3	0	2	5	2	0
enlargement	3	.3668	.2408	33.8	0	0	0	1	1	1	0	0	0	1	0	0	0	0	0	1	1	0	0	0	0	0	0	0	0
enlarges	5	.3468	.3884	35.9	0	0	0	1	1	2	0	1	0	0	0	0	0	0	0	3	0	0	1	0	0	0	1	0	0

8Q endowing
6A endurable
7Q endures
9D endureth
9Q endwise
8Q enemas
7P enemy-defended
4N Energetic
8H energy-converting
XR energy-filled
7Q energy-laden
9H energy-yielding
6P Enfant
6A Enfields
7R enfold
8F Enforcement
8R enforcer
8F enfranchised
8B engag'd
8F Engels
5A Engine
3A engine-driven
7R engine-mounting
7D engine-power
9M Engineering
5Q enginemen
8B Enginer
4R enginewright
7G Engla
8B england
3P Englander
7C Engle
7G Englisc
6B English-French
XR English-made
9Q English-style
8R English-trained
XR English-type
7D Englishwoman
4J engraven
9M engraver
3P Engraving
6B engrosses
8J Engulfed
9Q Engynes
9Q enhancement
8J enharmonic
8D Enich's
7B Enjoy
7R Enjoyable
8Q enlargements

Word Type	F	D	U	SFI	3 Gr 3	4 Gr 4	5 Gr 5	6 Gr 6	7 Gr 7	8 Gr 8	9 Gr 9	X UnGr	A Read	B Eng & Gr	C Comp	D Lit	E Math	F Soc Stud	G Spell	H Sci	J Music	K Art	L Home Ec	M Shop	N Lib F	P Lib NF	Q Lib Ref	R Mag	S Rel
enlarging	6	.4267	.5450	37.4	0	0	0	0	2	3	1	0	0	0	0	1	0	2	0	0	0	0	0	1	0	0	2	0	0
enlightened	12	.3754	.9818	39.9	2	0	1	2	2	0	3	2	0	0	0	0	0	1	0	0	0	0	0	0	0	2	2	7	0
enlist	5	.4657	.4823	36.8	0	0	0	0	4	1	0	0	0	1	1	0	0	1	0	0	0	0	1	0	0	0	1	0	0
enlisted	11	.4602	1.0916	40.4	0	1	1	0	4	4	0	1	2	0	2	2	0	0	0	0	0	0	0	0	0	2	2	1	0
enlisting	3	.2435	.2274	33.6	0	0	1	1	0	1	0	0	2	0	0	0	0	1	0	0	0	0	0	0	0	0	0	0	0
enlistment	2	.0000	.0389	25.9	0	0	0	0	0	2	0	0	0	0	0	0	0	2	0	0	0	0	0	0	0	0	0	0	0
enlistments	2	.0000	.0209	23.2	0	0	0	0	2	0	0	0	0	0	0	0	0	0	0	0	0	0	0	0	0	0	2	0	0
enliven	2	.1698	.1133	30.5	0	0	1	0	0	1	0	0	1	0	0	0	0	0	0	0	0	0	0	0	0	0	1	0	0
enlivened	2	.2401	.1133	30.5	0	0	0	1	0	0	1	0	0	0	0	0	0	0	0	0	0	0	0	0	0	1	1	0	0
enmities	2	.2152	.1357	31.3	0	0	0	0	1	1	0	0	1	0	0	0	0	1	0	0	0	0	0	0	0	0	0	0	0
enmity	6	.5118	.6534	38.2	0	0	0	1	1	1	1	2	1	2	0	1	0	0	0	0	0	0	0	0	1	0	0	1	0
Enoch	13	.0000	.0290	24.6	0	0	0	0	0	13	0	0	0	0	13	0	0	0	0	0	0	0	0	0	0	0	0	0	0
enormity	2	.2408	.1204	30.8	0	0	1	0	0	1	0	0	0	0	0	0	0	1	0	0	0	0	0	0	0	1	0	0	0
enormous	169	.8421	28.561	54.6	24	14	19	22	47	23	15	5	47	8	3	8	0	14	1	16	2	0	0	1	19	12	23	15	0
enormously	17	.5581	1.9875	43.0	3	2	0	1	9	1	1	0	2	0	0	1	0	1	0	1	1	0	0	0	0	3	7	1	0
enough	2363	.9520	444.76	66.5	433	382	291	289	458	218	215	77	723	87	18	132	44	270	14	304	24	20	61	25	183	220	69	168	1
enow	2	.2446	.1125	30.5	0	0	0	0	1	0	1	0	0	1	0	1	0	0	0	0	0	0	0	0	0	0	0	0	0
enquired	2	.1551	.0728	28.6	0	0	1	0	0	1	0	0	0	0	1	0	0	0	0	0	0	0	0	0	1	0	0	0	0
enquiries	2	.2446	.1142	30.6	0	0	0	0	1	0	0	1	0	0	0	0	0	0	0	0	0	0	0	0	1	0	0	1	0
enraged	13	.5177	1.4683	41.7	0	0	2	1	4	4	1	1	4	0	0	3	0	1	0	0	0	0	0	0	0	3	0	2	0
enrich	11	.6049	1.3893	41.4	0	0	1	0	4	2	3	1	2	1	0	1	0	4	0	0	0	0	1	1	0	0	1	0	0
enriched	30	.6104	3.7425	45.7	2	1	6	4	6	6	4	1	1	0	0	0	1	1	1	7	4	0	6	1	0	1	6	1	0
enriches	3	.3369	.2489	34.0	0	0	1	0	1	0	1	0	1	0	0	1	0	1	0	0	0	0	0	0	0	0	0	0	0
enriching	7	.4287	.6425	38.1	1	0	3	0	1	1	1	0	0	1	1	0	0	3	0	0	0	0	0	0	0	0	2	0	0
enrichment	3	.2859	.1854	32.7	0	0	0	0	1	1	1	0	0	1	1	0	0	0	0	0	0	0	0	0	0	0	1	0	0
Enrico	9	.4910	.9561	39.8	1	0	0	1	6	0	0	1	1	0	0	0	0	4	0	1	1	0	0	0	0	0	2	0	0
Enrique	6	.1881	.2759	34.4	0	5	0	1	0	0	0	0	0	0	0	0	0	0	0	0	1	0	0	0	5	0	0	0	0
enroll	4	.3192	.3100	34.9	0	0	0	0	3	0	1	0	1	0	0	0	0	0	0	0	0	0	0	0	0	2	0	1	0
enrolled	23	.5374	2.6384	44.2	3	1	2	2	9	4	2	0	3	0	0	0	10	5	0	1	0	0	0	0	0	1	1	2	0
enrolling	3	.3848	.2500	34.0	0	0	0	1	0	1	1	0	0	1	0	0	1	0	0	0	0	0	0	0	1	0	0	0	0
enrollment	17	.4422	1.6007	42.0	0	0	4	0	5	1	7	0	0	1	0	0	8	0	0	0	0	0	0	0	0	0	4	4	0
ensemble	12	.0683	.2574	34.1	0	0	1	1	8	2	0	0	0	0	0	0	0	0	0	0	11	0	0	0	0	1	0	0	0
ensembles	14	.2250	.7048	38.5	0	0	0	3	6	3	2	0	0	0	0	0	0	0	0	0	12	0	1	0	0	0	1	0	0
ensign	4	.4415	.3910	35.9	0	0	0	0	2	0	2	0	1	0	0	0	0	0	0	0	1	0	0	0	0	1	1	0	0
Ensign	2	.0000	.0290	24.6	0	0	0	0	2	0	0	0	0	0	0	0	0	0	0	0	0	0	0	0	0	2	0	0	0
ensilage	2	.1621	.0746	28.7	0	0	0	0	1	1	0	0	0	0	1	1	0	0	0	0	0	0	0	0	0	0	0	0	0
enslaved	3	.2444	.1814	32.6	0	0	1	0	0	2	0	0	0	0	0	0	0	2	0	0	0	0	0	0	0	0	1	0	0
enstatite	3	.0000	.0591	27.7	0	0	0	0	0	0	0	3	0	0	0	0	0	0	0	3	0	0	0	0	0	0	0	0	0
ensued	6	.4382	.5577	37.5	0	0	1	0	3	2	0	0	0	0	0	0	0	0	0	0	0	0	0	0	1	1	1	3	0
ensuing	7	.5549	.8380	39.2	0	0	0	1	5	1	0	0	2	0	0	0	0	0	0	2	0	0	0	0	0	1	1	1	0
ensure	20	.5493	2.2589	43.5	1	0	3	0	7	2	6	1	0	0	0	0	0	1	0	3	0	0	4	1	0	2	6	3	0
ent	23	.0858	.5636	37.5	0	0	1	1	15	4	2	0	0	2	0	0	0	0	21	0	0	0	0	0	0	0	0	0	0
entail	3	.3709	.2499	34.0	0	0	0	0	0	1	1	1	0	0	0	0	0	1	0	1	0	0	0	0	0	0	1	0	0
entangled	11	.3896	1.0262	40.1	2	0	0	2	3	4	0	0	5	0	0	4	0	0	0	1	0	0	0	0	0	0	1	0	0
entanglement	2	.1814	.1187	30.7	0	0	1	1	0	0	0	0	1	0	0	0	0	0	0	0	0	0	0	0	0	0	0	1	0
entanglements	4	.2856	.2574	34.1	0	0	0	0	1	1	1	1	0	0	1	0	0	1	0	0	0	0	0	0	0	0	0	2	0
enter	249	.9029	44.653	56.5	46	32	33	36	43	29	29	1	41	12	1	21	2	25	6	61	12	0	3	2	19	15	15	14	0
entered	257	.8266	42.759	56.3	17	40	36	41	72	30	15	6	73	10	1	23	2	37	1	11	6	0	0	0	29	25	21	18	0
entering	71	.8618	12.244	50.9	2	6	9	8	20	15	11	0	21	2	1	9	0	8	1	5	5	0	2	0	2	4	6	5	0
enterprise	35	.6679	4.7847	46.8	1	1	2	5	6	9	9	2	3	0	1	2	0	10	0	0	0	0	0	0	4	2	8	5	0
enterprises	20	.5606	2.3499	43.7	0	1	5	0	1	4	9	0	1	0	0	2	0	8	0	1	0	0	0	0	0	1	5	2	0
enterprising	7	.4067	.6337	38.0	0	0	2	0	1	1	3	0	1	0	0	0	0	2	0	0	0	1	0	0	0	1	0	2	0
enters	126	.7772	19.793	53.0	13	10	14	28	26	13	16	6	18	1	1	11	0	8	0	50	7	0	0	4	9	4	8	5	0
entertain	33	.6895	4.7491	46.8	1	3	7	7	6	3	6	0	14	2	0	0	0	2	1	2	3	0	0	0	0	6	0	3	0
entertained	23	.7443	3.4730	45.4	0	5	4	1	6	4	3	0	5	4	1	3	0	1	0	1	3	0	1	0	0	2	0	2	0
entertainer	5	.4459	.5028	37.0	1	1	0	0	0	0	2	1	1	0	0	0	0	1	0	2	0	0	0	0	0	0	0	1	0
entertainers	8	.4390	.7789	38.9	0	1	1	2	3	0	1	0	2	1	0	0	0	1	0	0	3	0	0	0	0	0	0	1	0
entertaining	20	.5448	2.2774	43.6	1	5	1	1	4	4	2	2	2	3	3	1	0	1	0	1	0	0	0	0	1	4	0	4	0
entertainment	64	.6642	8.6682	49.4	3	5	7	12	14	11	9	3	8	1	0	3	0	3	1	2	26	1	2	0	2	3	5	7	0
entertainments	4	.3546	.3122	34.9	0	1	1	0	1	0	0	1	0	0	0	0	0	1	0	0	1	0	0	0	0	0	0	2	0
entertains	2	.2285	.1129	30.5	1	0	1	0	0	0	0	0	0	0	0	0	0	1	0	0	0	0	0	0	0	0	1	0	0
enthralled	2	.2411	.1091	30.4	0	0	0	0	1	0	1	0	0	0	0	1	0	0	0	0	1	0	0	0	0	0	0	0	0
enthusiasm	59	.8416	9.9015	50.0	5	6	6	4	16	12	6	4	6	1	1	3	0	7	1	3	3	1	5	0	7	8	6	7	0
enthusiast	5	.3204	.4069	36.1	0	0	0	0	2	1	0	2	2	0	0	0	0	0	0	1	0	0	0	0	0	0	0	2	0
enthusiastic	30	.7077	4.3123	46.3	0	2	4	6	5	9	3	1	5	2	3	2	0	2	0	0	5	0	1	0	3	1	2	4	0
enthusiastically	20	.6726	2.7663	44.4	1	4	2	3	4	1	3	2	4	2	1	4	0	0	0	1	0	0	0	0	2	4	0	2	0
entire	377	.8849	66.284	58.2	19	26	41	44	104	48	77	18	47	12	10	16	14	49	1	44	58	7	5	6	8	20	52	28	0
entirely	204	.8764	35.558	55.5	11	9	27	36	62	19	31	9	27	5	1	7	4	26	2	19	13	6	2	7	15	13	39	18	0
entirety	7	.3998	.6032	37.8	0	0	2	0	2	0	1	2	0	0	0	0	0	0	0	2	3	0	0	0	0	1	1	0	0
entities	4	.4737	.3981	36.0	0	1	0	0	2	0	1	0	0	0	0	1	0	0	0	1	1	0	0	0	0	0	1	0	0
entitle	2	.2152	.1357	31.3	0	0	0	0	1	1	0	0	1	0	0	0	0	1	0	0	0	0	0	0	0	0	0	0	0
entitled	40	.8135	6.5186	48.1	1	4	6	1	7	8	11	2	3	5	1	0	2	10	0	3	1	1	0	0	1	5	3	5	0
entitles	2	.2446	.1123	30.5	0	0	1	0	0	0	1	0	0	1	0	0	0	0	0	0	0	0	0	0	0	0	1	0	0
entity	6	.2868	.3877	35.9	0	1	0	0	3	2	0	0	0	0	0	0	0	1	0	0	1	0	0	0	0	0	4	0	0
entomologist	3	.3764	.2483	33.9	0	0	0	0	0	1	0	2	0	0	0	0	0	0	0	1	0	0	0	0	0	0	1	1	0
entomologists	2	.0000	.0209	23.2	0	0	0	0	2	0	0	0	0	0	0	0	0	0	0	0	0	0	0	0	0	0	2	0	0
entourage	2	.2433	.1158	30.6	0	0	0	0	2	0	0	0	0	0	0	0	0	0	0	0	0	0	0	0	0	1	0	1	0
entrails	4	.4522	.3988	36.0	0	0	0	1	2	1	0	0	1	1	0	0	0	0	0	0	0	0	0	0	0	0	1	1	0
entrance	106	.8468	17.938	52.5	16	16	12	16	24	7	14	1	20	4	1	10	1	4	3	4	7	0	1	0	20	16	9	6	0
Entrance	3	.0000	.0243	23.8	0	0	0	2	0	0	1	0	0	0	0	0	0	0	0	0	3	0	0	0	0	0	0	0	0
entranced	2	.1787	.1174	30.7	0	1	0	0	1	0	0	0	1	0	0	0	0	0	0	0	0	0	0	0	1	0	0	0	0
entrances	11	.6718	1.5347	41.9	0	0	2	7	2	0	0	0	3	0	0	1	0	3	0	0	1	0	0	0	0	1	1	1	0
entrancing	2	.1814	.1187	30.7	0	0	0	1	0	1	0	0	1	0	0	0	0	0	0	0	0	0	0	0	0	0	0	1	0
entrants	2	.0000	.0290	24.6	0	2	0	0	0	0	0	0	0	0	0	0	0	0	0	0	0	0	0	0	0	2	0	0	0
entrapped	2	.2346	.1166	30.7	0	0	0	0	1	0	1	0	0	0	0	0	0	0	0	1	0	0	0	0	0	0	0	1	0
entreat	5	.0000	.0537	27.3	0	0	0	0	0	0	5	0	0	0	0	5	0	0	0	0	0	0	0	0	0	0	0	0	0
entreated	2	.0000	.0215	23.3	0	0	0	0	0	1	1	0	0	0	0	2	0	0	0	0	0	0	0	0	0	0	0	0	0
entreaties	2	.1787	.1174	30.7	0	0	0	1	1	0	0	0	1	0	0	0	0	0	0	0	0	0	0	0	1	0	0	0	0
entreating	3	.2060	.1500	31.8	0	0	0	0	1	0	2	0	0	0	0	2	0	0	0	0	0	0	0	0	0	1	0	0	0
entreaty	2	.1787	.1174	30.7	0	1	0	0	0	1	0	0	1	0	0	0	0	0	0	0	0	0	0	0	1	0	0	0	0
entrenched	5	.3568	.3984	36.0	0	0	1	0	1	2	1	0	0	0	0	0	0	2	0	0	0	0	0	0	0	1	2	0	0
entrepreneurs	2	.2408	.1204	30.8	0	0	1	0	0	1	0	0	0	0	0	0	0	1	0	0	0	0	0	0	0	1	0	0	0
entries	41	.5683	4.8809	46.9	0	6	13	6	8	3	5	0	6	11	0	1	14	0	5	0	0	0	0	0	2	0	2	0	0
entrust	3	.3660	.2695	34.3	0	0	1	0	0	0	2	0	1	0	0	0	0	1	0	1	0	0	0	0	0	0	0	0	0
entrusted	7	.4924	.7393	38.7	0	1	0	1	1	3	1	0	1	0	0	0	0	1	0	0	0	0	0	0	1	0	2	2	0

7C enlighten
7Q enlightening
8D enlightenment
8Q Enlightenment
XR enmeshed
8D ennoble
5Q enormities
4R Enos
6A Enough
7R enplaned
XR enquiry
7D enraptured
6A Enrico's
7R Enriques
9D enrobe
9F enroute
8G ens
5P enshrine
7Q enshrined
6J enshrining
7B enslave
5Q enslavement
7D enslaving
6R ensues
6R ensured
XR ensures
7A Ensuring
8A entablatures
7P entails
8A Entangled
7Q enterpriser
7R Enterprises
9R enterprize
5B Entertainment
7H enthralling
6J enthrone
9R enthusiasms
9Q enthusiasts
7R enticements
8J enticing
7P entitling
7P Entombment
5R entomological
7N Entomological
XH entrapment
7Q entraps
7A entreatings
8R entrepreneur
7R entrusting

Word Type	F	D	U	SFI	3 Gr 3	4 Gr 4	5 Gr 5	6 Gr 6	7 Gr 7	8 Gr 8	9 Gr 9	X UnGr	A Read	B Eng & Gr	C Comp	D Lit	E Math	F Soc Stud	G Spell	H Sci	J Music	K Art	L Home Ec	M Shop	N Lib F	P Lib NF	Q Lib Ref	R Mag	S Rel
entry	162	.4582	16.020	52.0	20	43	31	21	24	10	11	2	29	32	0	1	3	4	75	1	2	0	0	0	3	6	2	4	0
enumerated	2	.1948	.1250	31.0	0	0	0	1	1	0	0	0	1	0	0	0	0	0	0	0	0	0	0	0	0	1	0	0	0
enunciate	3	.2380	.1632	32.1	0	0	0	0	2	1	0	0	0	2	0	0	0	0	0	0	1	0	0	0	0	0	0	0	0
enunciation	3	.0000	.0314	25.0	0	0	3	0	0	0	0	0	0	0	0	0	0	0	0	0	0	0	0	0	0	0	3	0	0
envelop	4	.4756	.4063	36.1	0	0	1	0	2	0	1	0	0	0	0	0	0	1	0	1	0	0	0	0	0	0	1	1	0
envelope	70	.6614	9.6387	49.8	13	4	8	13	23	5	3	1	23	22	1	6	0	1	2	4	0	0	0	0	4	1	6	0	0
enveloped	8	.5002	.8675	39.4	1	0	0	2	3	1	1	0	2	0	0	1	0	0	0	0	0	0	0	0	3	1	1	0	0
envelopes	10	.4824	1.0437	40.2	2	1	1	1	2	3	0	0	2	4	0	0	2	0	1	0	0	0	0	0	1	0	0	0	0
envelops	2	.2278	.1128	30.5	0	0	0	0	0	1	1	0	0	0	0	0	0	0	0	1	0	0	0	0	0	0	1	0	0
enviable	5	.4705	.4940	36.9	0	0	0	0	1	0	2	2	0	0	0	1	0	0	0	0	0	0	0	0	0	1	1	2	0
envied	8	.4114	.7585	38.8	0	4	0	0	0	2	1	1	3	0	1	2	0	0	0	0	0	0	0	0	0	2	0	0	0
envious	9	.3674	.7091	38.5	0	0	0	0	2	0	7	0	0	1	0	6	0	0	0	0	1	0	0	0	0	0	1	0	0
enviously	2	.0665	.0708	28.5	1	0	0	0	1	0	0	0	1	0	1	0	0	0	0	0	0	0	0	0	0	0	0	0	0
environment	271	.6174	34.687	55.4	14	55	31	19	89	24	26	13	7	0	0	2	0	18	3	161	1	1	6	1	0	4	39	28	0
environmental	18	.5102	1.9209	42.8	4	0	0	0	10	1	2	1	0	0	0	0	0	1	0	4	3	0	0	0	0	0	4	6	0
environments	32	.3813	2.7205	44.3	4	8	2	0	14	1	3	0	0	0	0	0	0	1	0	20	0	0	1	0	0	0	10	0	0
envisage	2	.2418	.1091	30.4	0	0	0	0	1	0	1	0	0	0	0	0	0	0	1	0	0	0	0	0	0	0	1	0	0
envision	3	.3390	.2450	33.9	0	0	0	1	1	1	0	0	1	0	0	0	0	0	0	0	0	0	0	0	0	0	1	1	0
envisioned	2	.1733	.1149	30.6	0	0	0	0	1	0	1	0	1	1	0	0	0	0	0	0	0	0	0	0	0	0	0	0	0
envoy	3	.3769	.2484	34.0	0	0	0	0	1	1	1	0	0	0	0	0	0	1	0	0	0	0	0	0	0	0	1	1	0
envy	24	.7729	3.7529	45.7	5	2	3	2	4	5	3	0	6	3	0	3	0	1	0	0	2	0	1	0	1	2	3	2	0
enzyme	8	.0000	.1577	32.0	0	0	0	2	4	0	1	1	0	0	0	0	0	0	0	8	0	0	0	0	0	0	0	0	0
enzymes	16	.2353	.9529	39.8	0	0	0	4	3	0	4	5	0	0	0	0	0	0	0	12	0	0	0	0	0	0	4	0	0
Eocene	8	.2353	.4765	36.8	0	0	0	0	4	0	0	4	0	0	0	0	0	0	0	6	0	0	0	0	0	0	2	0	0
EOD	3	.0000	.0449	26.5	0	0	3	0	0	0	0	0	0	0	0	0	3	0	0	0	0	0	0	0	0	0	0	0	0
Eohippus	6	.0000	.1183	30.7	0	0	0	0	5	0	0	1	0	0	0	0	0	0	0	6	0	0	0	0	0	0	0	0	0
eons	6	.2655	.3986	36.0	0	0	0	0	4	1	1	0	1	0	0	0	0	0	0	2	0	0	0	0	0	0	3	0	0
eous	2	.0000	.0162	22.1	0	0	0	0	1	1	0	0	0	0	0	0	0	0	2	0	0	0	0	0	0	0	0	0	0
Eout**	2	.0000	.0050	17.0	0	0	0	0	0	2	0	0	0	0	0	0	0	0	0	0	0	0	0	2	0	0	0	0	0
EP	5	.0000	.0748	28.7	0	0	5	0	0	0	0	0	0	0	0	0	5	0	0	0	0	0	0	0	0	0	0	0	0
Epaminondas	2	.0000	.0290	24.6	0	2	0	0	0	0	0	0	0	0	0	0	0	0	0	0	0	0	0	0	0	2	0	0	0
EPF	4	.0000	.0599	27.8	0	0	0	0	4	0	0	0	0	0	0	0	4	0	0	0	0	0	0	0	0	0	0	0	0
Ephialtes	3	.0000	.1370	31.4	0	0	0	0	3	0	0	0	3	0	0	0	0	0	0	0	0	0	0	0	0	0	0	0	0
Ephraim	2	.2285	.1129	30.5	0	0	0	0	1	0	1	0	0	0	0	0	0	1	0	0	0	0	0	0	0	0	1	0	0
epic	13	.5035	1.3861	41.4	0	0	0	0	5	5	1	2	1	1	0	1	0	2	0	1	0	0	0	0	0	0	6	1	0
epics	3	.3815	.2534	34.0	0	0	1	0	1	0	1	0	0	0	0	0	0	1	0	0	0	0	0	0	0	1	0	1	0
epicycle	2	.0000	.0394	26.0	0	0	0	0	0	2	0	0	0	0	0	0	0	0	0	2	0	0	0	0	0	0	0	0	0
epidemic	15	.6250	1.9483	42.9	0	3	1	0	5	4	2	0	2	0	0	1	0	2	0	3	0	0	0	0	0	1	3	3	0
epidemics	8	.3123	.5704	37.6	0	2	0	1	0	3	2	0	0	0	0	0	0	0	0	3	0	0	0	0	0	1	4	0	0
epidermis	9	.1719	.4433	36.5	0	3	2	1	3	0	0	0	0	0	0	0	0	0	0	8	0	0	0	0	0	0	1	0	0
epiglottis	3	.2443	.1820	32.6	0	0	0	0	1	0	2	0	0	0	0	1	0	0	0	2	0	0	0	0	0	0	0	0	0
Epimetheus	26	.0000	1.1877	40.7	0	0	9	13	0	4	0	0	26	0	0	0	0	0	0	0	0	0	0	0	0	0	0	0	0
epiphytes	2	.0000	.0394	26.0	0	0	0	0	2	0	0	0	0	0	0	0	0	0	0	2	0	0	0	0	0	0	0	0	0
epiphytic	2	.0000	.0209	23.2	0	0	0	0	2	0	0	0	0	0	0	0	0	0	0	0	0	0	0	0	0	0	2	0	0
Epirus	2	.0000	.0389	25.9	0	0	0	0	2	0	0	0	0	0	0	0	0	2	0	0	0	0	0	0	0	0	0	0	0
Episcopal	9	.2798	.5941	37.7	0	1	3	1	0	4	0	0	1	0	0	0	0	0	0	0	0	0	0	0	0	0	3	5	0
episode	22	.6065	2.7731	44.4	0	3	1	1	6	5	6	0	3	2	0	6	0	5	0	0	3	0	0	0	0	1	0	2	0
episodes	13	.4221	1.1991	40.8	0	0	2	0	6	4	1	0	2	0	0	0	0	0	0	1	6	0	0	0	0	1	1	2	0
Epistle	2	.0299	.0221	23.4	1	0	0	0	0	1	0	0	0	0	0	0	0	0	0	0	0	0	0	0	0	0	1	0	1
epitaph	3	.3831	.2447	33.9	1	0	0	1	0	0	1	0	0	0	0	1	0	0	0	0	1	0	0	0	1	0	0	0	0
epithelial	6	.0000	.1183	30.7	0	0	0	0	1	0	5	0	0	0	0	0	0	0	0	6	0	0	0	0	0	0	0	0	0
epithets	6	.4228	.5577	37.5	0	1	0	0	2	2	1	0	1	1	0	2	0	0	0	0	0	0	0	0	0	0	0	2	0
epitome	2	.1814	.1187	30.7	0	0	0	0	1	0	0	1	1	0	0	0	0	0	0	0	0	0	0	0	0	0	0	1	0
epitomized	2	.0000	.0389	25.9	0	0	0	0	0	2	0	0	0	0	0	0	0	2	0	0	0	0	0	0	0	0	0	0	0
epoch	10	.4707	.9893	40.0	0	0	0	0	1	1	7	1	0	0	0	4	0	1	0	1	1	0	0	0	0	0	3	0	0
epoch-making	4	.3372	.2996	34.8	0	1	2	0	0	1	0	0	0	0	0	0	0	1	0	0	0	0	0	0	1	0	2	0	0
epochs	3	.0000	.0314	25.0	0	0	0	0	3	0	0	0	0	0	0	0	0	0	0	0	0	0	0	0	0	0	3	0	0
Epsom	5	.2144	.2818	34.5	0	0	1	0	1	3	0	0	0	0	0	0	0	0	0	4	0	0	0	0	1	0	0	0	0
equable	4	.2401	.2266	33.6	0	0	1	1	2	0	0	0	0	0	0	0	0	0	0	0	0	0	0	0	0	2	2	0	0
equal	565	.6948	79.943	59.0	28	47	53	63	94	112	146	22	38	2	5	11	303	32	7	57	12	0	8	28	4	18	23	17	0
equal-area	4	.0000	.0419	26.2	0	4	0	0	0	0	0	0	0	0	0	0	0	0	0	0	0	0	0	0	0	0	4	0	0
equal-sized	2	.0000	.0394	26.0	0	0	1	0	0	1	0	0	0	0	0	0	0	0	0	2	0	0	0	0	0	0	0	0	0
equaled	7	.5457	.8192	39.1	2	0	1	2	1	0	1	0	2	0	0	0	0	0	0	0	1	0	0	0	0	2	1	1	0
equaling	6	.4196	.5417	37.3	1	0	1	0	1	1	1	1	0	0	0	0	0	1	0	0	0	0	0	0	0	1	1	3	0
equality	41	.6130	5.1658	47.1	0	1	5	1	10	5	19	0	0	1	0	1	23	4	0	0	1	0	0	1	1	6	2	1	0
Equality	2	.1493	.0692	28.4	1	0	0	0	0	0	1	0	0	0	0	0	0	0	0	0	0	1	0	0	0	0	1	0	0
equalize	4	.3352	.2986	34.8	0	1	0	0	3	0	0	0	0	0	0	0	0	0	0	1	0	0	0	0	0	0	2	1	0
equalized	2	.0000	.0394	26.0	0	1	0	0	0	1	0	0	0	0	0	0	0	0	0	2	0	0	0	0	0	0	0	0	0
equally	144	.8695	24.904	54.0	12	8	13	15	31	28	24	13	13	8	2	1	26	14	0	11	3	5	6	1	7	12	14	21	0
equals	98	.4837	10.056	50.0	9	15	7	18	11	15	23	0	3	1	0	0	60	4	0	10	0	0	2	12	0	3	2	1	0
equated	3	.2260	.1580	32.0	0	0	0	0	0	2	1	0	0	0	0	2	0	0	0	0	0	0	0	0	0	0	1	0	0
equation	673	.0767	19.401	52.9	86	177	89	91	69	90	71	0	0	0	0	0	657	1	0	4	0	0	0	2	0	0	9	0	0
equations	654	.0334	13.792	51.4	107	138	118	112	58	71	50	0	1	0	0	0	644	0	0	4	0	0	0	0	0	2	3	0	0
equator	236	.4835	24.707	53.9	22	60	39	28	49	21	17	0	5	1	0	0	18	120	0	65	0	0	0	0	0	4	23	0	0
Equator	11	.1717	.5720	37.6	1	1	0	6	0	0	3	0	1	0	0	0	0	1	0	9	0	0	0	0	0	0	0	0	0
equatorial	21	.5531	2.4232	43.8	0	1	1	5	8	3	0	3	0	0	0	0	0	5	0	6	0	0	0	1	1	0	7	1	0
Equatorial	7	.3793	.6388	38.1	1	0	0	1	4	0	1	0	3	0	0	0	0	0	0	1	0	1	0	0	0	0	1	0	0
equestrian	4	.2975	.2883	34.6	0	1	0	0	1	0	1	1	1	1	0	0	0	1	0	0	0	0	0	0	0	0	2	0	0
equidistant	2	.2446	.1257	31.0	0	0	1	0	0	0	1	0	0	0	0	0	0	1	0	1	0	0	0	0	0	0	0	0	0
equilateral	20	.0717	.5594	37.5	0	0	0	6	4	4	6	0	0	0	0	0	19	0	0	0	0	0	0	0	0	1	0	0	0
equilibrium	5	.4858	.5164	37.1	0	0	0	1	2	1	0	1	0	0	0	0	0	0	0	2	0	0	0	0	1	1	1	0	0
equinox	7	.4099	.6515	38.1	0	0	0	1	1	0	0	5	1	0	0	0	0	0	0	4	0	0	0	0	1	0	0	1	0
equip	2	.0000	.0209	23.2	1	0	0	0	1	0	0	0	0	0	0	0	0	0	0	0	0	0	0	0	0	0	2	0	0
equipment	302	.7654	46.507	56.7	22	14	35	41	67	62	48	13	35	10	6	10	3	34	4	35	7	1	36	27	6	14	36	38	0
equipments	2	.1551	.0728	28.6	0	0	0	0	1	0	1	0	0	0	1	0	0	0	0	0	0	0	0	0	1	0	0	0	0
equipped	73	.7244	10.641	50.3	1	6	4	8	29	9	16	0	2	2	1	2	1	6	0	8	4	0	3	9	1	8	16	10	0
equipping	4	.3344	.3261	35.1	0	0	1	0	0	2	1	0	1	0	0	0	0	2	0	0	0	0	0	0	0	0	1	0	0
equity	2	.2446	.1142	30.6	0	0	0	1	0	0	0	1	0	0	0	0	0	0	0	0	0	0	0	0	1	0	0	1	0
equivalence	5	.2207	.2647	34.2	0	0	2	0	3	0	0	0	0	0	0	0	2	0	0	0	0	0	0	0	0	0	3	0	0
equivalent	339	.2782	22.090	53.4	9	63	50	75	62	44	30	6	0	2	0	0	302	1	3	3	5	0	1	1	1	2	11	7	0
equivalents	7	.3252	.5115	37.1	1	0	0	0	3	2	1	0	0	0	0	0	5	0	0	0	1	0	0	0	0	0	0	1	0
Equus	2	.0000	.0394	26.0	0	0	0	0	2	0	0	0	0	0	0	0	0	0	0	2	0	0	0	0	0	0	0	0	0
er	157	.3213	11.388	50.6	30	25	31	50	12	7	2	0	22	20	2	0	0	0	104	0	2	0	0	0	5	1	0	1	0
era	65	.7061	9.3215	49.7	2	1	4	14	10	17	14	3	3	0	0	1	1	13	0	10	4	0	0	1	0	8	15	9	0

6A entryway
8D entwined
4N entymologist
8R Enugu
7A Enumclaw
XD enumerate
5R enunciating
6N enveloping
6R Environmental
7R environs
9Q envisaged
4Q envisions
7A envoys
7P Envoys
9E Enyart
5E EOC
5E EOF
5E EOG
7D eon
8M Eout
8D ep
8R epaulets
7E EPG
9Q Ephraem
9K epic-loving
9H epicenter
XR epicurean
XH epicycles
7H epidermal
6B epigrams
9Q epilepsy
6A Epimetheus'
5A Epiphany
8H epiphysis
8R Episcopalians
8R Episcopalians'
8Q Episcopius
9F episode's
7R episodic
8Q epithalamium
9H epithelium
9D epithet
7Q epitomize
9R epitomizes
7H Epoch
6R epochal
4N Epps'
7D equably
7J Equador
8J equalization
5H equalizes
XR equalled
4Q equally-spaced
9Q equate
9B equating
4F Equidistant
6H Equinox
XH equinoxes
9H equisetums
7Q equitable

Word Type	F	D	U	SFI	3 Gr 3	4 Gr 4	5 Gr 5	6 Gr 6	7 Gr 7	8 Gr 8	9 Gr 9	X UnGr	A Read	B Eng & Gr	C Comp	D Lit	E Math	F Soc Stud	G Spell	H Sci	J Music	K Art	L Home Ec	M Shop	N Lib F	P Lib NF	Q Lib Ref	R Mag	S Rel
Era	9	.3679	.7503	38.8	0	0	1	2	0	3	2	1	1	1	0	0	0	0	0	3	0	0	0	0	0	0	4	0	0
eras	7	.4512	.6651	38.2	0	0	1	0	1	1	2	2	0	0	0	0	0	1	0	0	0	1	0	0	0	1	2	2	0
erase	14	.6003	1.7498	42.4	4	0	0	1	6	0	3	0	2	2	0	1	6	0	1	0	0	0	0	0	1	0	0	1	0
ERASE	2	.0000	.0299	24.8	0	0	2	0	0	0	0	0	0	0	0	0	2	0	0	0	0	0	0	0	0	0	0	0	0
erased	12	.6393	1.5877	42.0	3	2	0	0	6	0	1	0	2	1	0	0	4	0	1	0	0	0	0	0	0	2	1	1	0
eraser	27	.6453	3.5540	45.5	12	3	4	4	2	0	2	0	0	4	0	0	9	0	0	5	0	1	0	1	6	1	0	0	0
erasers	15	.5183	1.6313	42.1	5	2	3	4	1	0	0	0	0	0	0	0	5	0	0	4	0	1	0	0	4	0	0	1	0
erasing	5	.3100	.4022	36.0	2	1	0	1	1	0	0	0	3	0	0	0	0	0	0	0	0	1	0	1	0	0	0	0	0
Erasmus	3	.1813	.1402	31.5	0	0	2	0	0	0	0	1	0	0	0	0	0	0	0	1	0	0	0	0	0	0	2	0	0
Eratosthenes	15	.2408	.8851	39.5	0	2	0	1	8	0	4	0	0	0	0	0	12	1	0	1	0	0	0	0	0	0	0	1	0
Erde	2	.0000	.0162	22.1	0	0	2	0	0	0	0	0	0	0	0	0	0	0	0	0	2	0	0	0	0	0	0	0	0
ere	24	.2966	1.6339	42.1	0	1	1	2	7	2	11	0	2	0	0	17	0	0	0	0	1	0	0	0	2	2	0	0	0
erebh	2	.0000	.0389	25.9	0	0	0	2	0	0	0	0	0	0	0	0	0	2	0	0	0	0	0	0	0	0	0	0	0
erect	36	.8118	5.8719	47.7	1	5	6	4	14	3	3	0	6	1	1	5	1	3	0	6	1	0	0	0	4	3	4	1	0
erected	25	.7224	3.6603	45.6	1	0	6	4	4	1	7	2	2	3	1	0	0	7	0	0	0	0	0	1	1	4	4	2	0
erection	4	.3395	.3008	34.8	0	0	0	0	3	0	1	0	0	0	0	1	0	0	0	1	0	0	0	0	0	0	2	0	0
erectus	6	.1116	.1956	32.9	0	0	0	0	6	0	0	0	0	0	0	0	0	0	0	1	0	0	0	0	0	0	5	0	0
Eric	56	.4789	6.3533	48.0	7	21	16	10	1	1	0	0	42	4	0	0	0	0	0	0	0	0	0	0	7	0	1	2	0
Eric's	8	.2399	.6021	37.8	0	3	1	4	0	0	0	0	6	2	0	0	0	0	0	0	0	0	0	0	0	0	0	0	0
Ericson	7	.3665	.6345	38.0	1	0	0	0	3	3	0	0	3	0	0	0	0	3	0	0	0	0	0	0	0	0	1	0	0
Ericsson	2	.0000	.0389	25.9	0	1	0	0	0	1	0	0	0	0	0	0	0	2	0	0	0	0	0	0	0	0	0	0	0
Erie	72	.6376	9.4663	49.8	5	7	18	7	14	17	4	0	5	12	0	0	4	30	0	0	8	0	0	0	0	4	4	5	0
Erik	8	.2889	.5320	37.3	0	0	2	0	3	2	1	0	0	0	0	0	0	0	0	0	0	0	0	0	0	6	1	1	0
Erikson	6	.0000	.0729	28.6	0	0	0	0	0	6	0	0	0	0	0	0	0	0	0	0	0	0	0	0	0	0	0	6	0
Erikson's	2	.0000	.0243	23.9	0	0	0	0	0	2	0	0	0	0	0	0	0	0	0	0	0	0	0	0	0	0	0	2	0
Erin	2	.2446	.1184	30.7	1	0	0	0	0	1	0	0	0	0	0	0	1	0	0	0	0	0	0	0	0	1	0	0	0
Eris	3	.0000	.1370	31.4	0	0	0	0	0	3	0	0	3	0	0	0	0	0	0	0	0	0	0	0	0	0	0	0	0
Eritrea	3	.0000	.0583	27.7	0	0	0	3	0	0	0	0	0	0	0	0	0	3	0	0	0	0	0	0	0	0	0	0	0
Erl-King	10	.0000	.0808	29.1	0	0	0	0	10	0	0	0	0	0	0	0	0	0	0	0	10	0	0	0	0	0	0	0	0
Erlking	9	.0000	.0728	28.6	0	0	0	0	9	0	0	0	0	0	0	0	0	0	0	0	9	0	0	0	0	0	0	0	0
Erlking's	2	.0000	.0162	22.1	0	0	0	0	2	0	0	0	0	0	0	0	0	0	0	0	2	0	0	0	0	0	0	0	0
ermine	2	.0000	.0215	23.3	0	0	0	1	1	0	0	0	0	0	0	2	0	0	0	0	0	0	0	0	0	0	0	0	0
Ernest	28	.6091	3.6797	45.7	0	14	2	2	3	4	3	0	15	1	1	0	1	1	0	1	0	0	0	0	0	0	6	2	0
Ernestine	28	.2075	2.0812	43.2	0	0	25	0	3	0	0	0	25	0	0	0	0	0	0	0	0	0	0	0	0	3	0	0	0
Ernestine's	2	.0000	.0914	29.6	0	0	2	0	0	0	0	0	2	0	0	0	0	0	0	0	0	0	0	0	0	0	0	0	0
Ernie	23	.5614	2.7765	44.4	0	2	0	8	5	0	8	0	8	2	0	1	0	0	0	0	0	0	0	0	7	2	0	3	0
Ernst	8	.4272	.8028	39.0	0	4	1	1	1	1	0	0	4	0	0	0	0	0	0	1	2	0	0	0	0	0	1	0	0
erode	4	.0000	.0789	29.0	0	0	0	0	1	3	0	0	0	0	0	0	0	0	0	4	0	0	0	0	0	0	0	0	0
eroded	20	.5099	2.1624	43.3	5	0	1	2	5	4	3	0	0	0	0	0	0	2	0	8	0	0	0	0	0	5	4	1	0
erodes	2	.2278	.1128	30.5	0	0	0	0	1	1	0	0	0	0	0	0	0	0	0	1	0	0	0	0	0	0	1	0	0
eroding	4	.3739	.3373	35.3	0	1	0	1	0	0	1	1	0	0	0	0	0	1	0	2	0	0	0	0	0	0	1	0	0
Eroica	3	.0000	.0243	23.8	0	0	0	0	1	1	1	0	0	0	0	0	0	0	0	0	3	0	0	0	0	0	0	0	0
Eros	4	.0000	.0789	29.0	0	0	0	0	0	4	0	0	0	0	0	0	0	0	0	4	0	0	0	0	0	0	0	0	0
erosion	67	.4494	6.5857	48.2	5	5	5	1	14	9	23	5	2	1	0	0	0	6	0	41	0	0	0	0	0	1	13	3	0
Erosion	2	.0000	.0394	26.0	0	0	0	0	0	0	0	2	0	0	0	0	0	0	0	2	0	0	0	0	0	0	0	0	0
erosional	2	.0000	.0394	26.0	0	0	0	0	0	0	2	0	0	0	0	0	0	0	0	2	0	0	0	0	0	0	0	0	0
erosive	2	.2437	.1129	30.5	0	1	0	0	1	0	0	0	0	0	0	0	0	0	0	0	0	0	0	0	0	0	1	1	0
erotic	4	.0000	.0486	26.9	0	0	0	0	0	1	1	2	0	0	0	0	0	0	0	0	0	0	0	0	0	0	0	4	0
err	3	.2410	.1667	32.2	0	0	0	0	1	0	0	2	0	0	0	0	0	0	1	0	0	0	0	0	0	0	0	2	0
errand	14	.6146	1.8177	42.6	1	5	0	1	2	2	2	1	5	0	1	2	1	0	0	0	0	0	0	0	2	1	0	2	0
errands	17	.6958	2.4457	43.9	0	4	4	3	4	1	1	0	5	1	1	1	2	3	0	1	0	0	0	0	0	1	0	2	0
erratic	10	.3475	.7581	38.8	0	0	1	1	6	0	1	1	0	0	0	2	0	0	0	0	0	0	0	0	0	0	2	6	0
erratics	4	.2287	.2348	33.7	1	0	0	0	0	0	3	0	0	0	0	0	0	0	0	3	0	0	0	0	0	0	0	1	0
erred	2	.2391	.1133	30.5	0	0	0	0	1	1	0	0	0	0	0	0	1	0	0	0	0	0	0	0	0	0	1	0	0
erroneous	3	.2222	.1558	31.9	0	0	0	0	2	0	0	1	0	1	0	0	0	0	0	0	0	0	0	0	0	0	2	0	0
error	86	.7816	13.502	51.3	2	3	3	13	24	14	22	5	6	20	1	1	23	2	3	11	1	0	0	1	2	3	8	4	0
errors	122	.5838	14.539	51.6	1	12	23	18	31	13	18	6	1	42	1	1	8	1	48	6	1	0	1	2	0	2	3	5	0
ers	2	.1717	.1142	30.6	1	0	0	0	0	0	1	0	1	0	0	1	0	0	0	0	0	0	0	0	0	0	0	0	0
erudite	2	.2376	.1088	30.4	0	0	0	0	0	0	1	1	0	0	0	0	0	0	1	0	0	0	0	0	0	0	0	1	0
erupt	11	.2577	.7757	38.9	0	2	2	1	4	1	0	1	3	0	0	0	0	1	0	7	0	0	0	0	0	0	0	0	0
erupted	16	.5017	1.7829	42.5	0	0	2	7	2	2	3	0	5	1	0	0	0	6	0	1	0	0	0	0	0	0	0	3	0
erupting	2	.2440	.1132	30.5	0	0	0	0	1	0	1	0	0	0	0	1	0	0	0	0	0	0	0	0	0	0	0	1	0
eruption	23	.4553	2.4552	43.9	0	3	0	10	6	0	4	0	12	0	0	0	0	0	0	7	0	0	0	0	1	0	3	0	0
eruptions	15	.5268	1.6610	42.2	3	0	2	0	4	2	4	0	0	0	0	0	0	1	0	7	0	0	1	0	0	0	3	3	0
erupts	5	.3689	.4527	36.6	0	1	1	1	0	0	2	0	2	0	0	0	0	0	0	2	0	0	0	0	0	0	0	1	0
ery	3	.0000	.0243	23.9	0	0	0	0	0	3	0	0	0	0	0	0	0	0	3	0	0	0	0	0	0	0	0	0	0
Erymanthus	2	.0000	.0914	29.6	0	0	0	0	0	2	0	0	2	0	0	0	0	0	0	0	0	0	0	0	0	0	0	0	0
es	144	.1981	6.9970	48.4	42	36	20	22	7	4	10	3	13	20	0	0	3	0	107	0	1	0	0	0	0	0	0	0	0
Esau	2	.2437	.1129	30.5	0	0	0	0	1	0	0	1	0	0	0	0	0	0	0	0	0	0	0	0	0	0	1	1	0
Esbjerg	2	.0000	.0209	23.2	2	0	0	0	0	0	0	0	0	0	0	0	0	0	0	0	0	0	0	0	0	0	2	0	0
escalation	3	.0000	.0365	25.6	0	0	0	0	0	3	0	0	0	0	0	0	0	0	0	0	0	0	0	0	0	0	0	3	0
escalator	3	.3273	.2365	33.7	0	0	0	2	1	0	0	0	1	1	0	0	0	0	1	0	0	0	0	0	0	0	0	0	0
escalators	4	.2968	.2661	34.2	0	0	0	1	0	1	2	0	0	0	0	0	0	0	0	1	0	0	0	1	0	0	0	2	0
Escamillo	10	.0000	.0808	29.1	0	0	0	0	6	4	0	0	0	0	0	0	0	0	0	0	10	0	0	0	0	0	0	0	0
escapade	2	.2443	.1130	30.5	0	0	0	1	0	0	1	0	0	0	0	1	0	0	0	0	0	0	0	0	1	0	0	0	0
escape	257	.8613	44.338	56.5	19	43	33	37	72	18	28	7	79	5	3	23	1	10	4	46	8	0	2	0	22	16	25	13	0
escaped	97	.7793	15.385	51.9	7	17	14	19	25	5	9	1	35	2	1	11	0	7	0	2	1	0	0	0	7	15	8	8	0
escapees	2	.0000	.0215	23.3	0	0	0	0	2	0	0	0	0	0	0	2	0	0	0	0	0	0	0	0	0	0	0	0	0
escapes	26	.6870	3.6980	45.7	4	3	2	6	6	2	3	0	8	3	0	2	0	0	0	4	1	0	0	0	1	2	5	0	0
escaping	28	.5923	3.5336	45.5	1	8	1	4	6	2	4	2	7	0	0	2	0	1	0	12	0	0	0	0	0	3	2	1	0
escarole	2	.1812	.0838	29.2	0	0	0	0	1	0	0	1	0	0	0	0	0	0	0	0	0	0	1	0	0	0	0	1	0
escarpment	5	.4688	.4985	37.0	0	0	3	1	1	0	0	0	0	0	0	1	0	1	0	0	0	0	0	0	0	2	0	1	0
escort	13	.5481	1.5214	41.8	0	1	3	2	4	3	0	0	3	0	0	0	0	2	0	0	0	0	0	0	1	1	4	2	0
escorted	11	.6395	1.4432	41.6	1	2	1	2	1	2	2	0	1	1	0	1	0	0	0	0	0	0	0	0	2	3	1	2	0
escorting	2	.2427	.1152	30.6	2	0	0	0	0	0	0	0	0	0	0	0	0	0	0	0	0	0	0	0	1	1	0	0	0
escorts	5	.1901	.2435	33.9	0	0	0	0	5	0	0	0	0	0	0	0	0	0	0	0	0	0	0	0	0	4	0	1	0
Eskimo	42	.6638	5.7479	47.6	12	10	5	4	7	0	4	0	10	4	0	1	0	6	4	0	11	2	0	0	0	1	2	1	0
Eskimos	92	.6931	13.287	51.2	19	37	19	4	9	1	3	0	35	2	0	3	0	28	1	0	7	0	0	0	0	7	4	5	0
Eskimos'	2	.1948	.1250	31.0	1	1	0	0	0	0	0	0	1	0	0	0	0	0	0	0	0	0	0	0	0	1	0	0	0
Esmat's	3	.0000	.0583	27.7	0	3	0	0	0	0	0	0	0	0	0	0	0	3	0	0	0	0	0	0	0	0	0	0	0
Esmeralda	4	.0000	.1827	32.6	4	0	0	0	0	0	0	0	4	0	0	0	0	0	0	0	0	0	0	0	0	0	0	0	0
esophagus	10	.2213	.5740	37.6	0	0	0	0	4	1	4	1	0	0	0	0	0	0	0	8	0	0	0	0	0	0	2	0	0
esoteric	3	.2159	.1532	31.9	0	0	0	0	1	0	1	1	0	0	0	0	0	0	0	0	0	0	0	0	0	0	2	1	0
Espana	2	.1698	.1133	30.5	1	1	0	0	0	0	0	0	1	0	0	0	0	0	0	0	0	0	0	0	0	0	1	0	0

7R ERA
7Q eradicate
5R Eradicate
7P eradicated
7B erasures
7Q Ercilla
6J Erda
XQ Erectheum
7P erecting
6R erectly
7Q erectness
4N erector
8A erects
6F erg
XH ergotine
8E ergs
7J erh-hu
8F Erich
6R Erickson
6P Erisichthon
8Q Erivan
7J Erl
7J Erl-King's
7J Erlkonig
6R ermine-trimmed
7D ermine's
5G ern
5G ern**
9B Erna's
4F Ernesto
9N Ernie's
4A Ernst's
7R Erofei
XR erogenous
XR erosion-control
9N erosions
XR erotica
7P errest
9Q erring
8H erroneously
9D errs
XR Ersabas
9R ersatz
6N erstwhile
5G erth
9P eruptive
9Q Erwin
3P Eryops
6E ES
XR escalating
4A Escalator
8J Escamillo's
6K Escher
7R eschew
8D escrime
8D Escrime
XR escrow
7M escutcheon
XR ESEA
7A Esk
9H esker
4F Esmat
6P espagnole
6P Espagnole
5F Espanola

Word Type	F	D	U	SFI	3 Gr 3	4 Gr 4	5 Gr 5	6 Gr 6	7 Gr 7	8 Gr 8	9 Gr 9	X UnGr	A Read	B Eng & Gr	C Comp	D Lit	E Math	F Soc Stud	G Spell	H Sci	J Music	K Art	L Home Ec	M Shop	N Lib F	P Lib NF	Q Lib Ref	R Mag	S Rel
especial	4	.3289	.3049	34.8	0	0	0	1	0	1	2	0	1	0	1	1	0	0	0	0	0	0	0	0	0	0	1	0	0
especially	611	.9531	114.95	60.6	61	70	78	70	128	99	87	18	94	40	9	25	5	98	12	63	33	5	28	14	31	53	60	40	1
Esperanto	2	.0000	.0243	23.9	0	0	0	2	0	0	0	0	0	0	0	0	0	0	0	0	0	0	0	0	0	0	0	2	0
espionage	2	.2351	.1166	30.7	0	0	0	0	1	1	0	0	0	0	0	0	0	1	0	0	0	0	0	0	0	0	0	1	0
esplanade	2	.2437	.1129	30.5	0	0	1	0	0	1	0	0	0	0	0	0	0	0	0	0	0	0	0	0	0	0	1	1	0
espoused	2	.2433	.1158	30.6	0	0	0	1	0	0	0	1	0	0	0	0	0	0	0	0	0	0	0	0	0	1	0	1	0
espresso	2	.0000	.0243	23.9	0	0	0	0	1	0	1	0	0	0	0	0	0	0	0	0	0	0	0	0	0	0	0	2	0
esprit	2	.2152	.1357	31.3	0	0	0	0	0	2	0	0	1	0	0	0	0	1	0	0	0	0	0	0	0	0	0	0	0
Esputa	20	.0000	.2895	34.6	0	20	0	0	0	0	0	0	0	0	0	0	0	0	0	0	0	0	0	0	0	20	0	0	0
Esquimo	3	.0000	.0322	25.1	0	0	0	0	0	0	3	0	0	0	0	3	0	0	0	0	0	0	0	0	0	0	0	0	0
Esquimos	2	.2443	.1130	30.5	0	0	0	1	0	0	1	0	0	0	0	1	0	0	0	0	0	0	0	0	1	0	0	0	0
Esquire	4	.3717	.3640	35.6	0	2	0	0	1	1	0	0	2	0	0	1	0	0	0	0	0	0	0	0	0	0	0	1	0
Essa	2	.0000	.0394	26.0	0	0	0	0	2	0	0	0	0	0	0	0	0	0	0	2	0	0	0	0	0	0	0	0	0
essay	44	.4970	4.5664	46.6	1	0	3	1	4	10	25	0	3	8	9	10	0	0	0	2	0	0	0	0	4	2	3	3	0
Essay	2	.0000	.0219	23.4	0	0	1	0	0	0	0	1	0	2	0	0	0	0	0	0	0	0	0	0	0	0	0	0	0
essayed	3	.2261	.2131	33.3	0	0	0	0	2	1	0	0	2	0	0	0	0	0	0	0	0	0	0	0	1	0	0	0	0
essayist	4	.3444	.3047	34.8	0	0	0	0	2	2	0	0	0	2	0	0	0	1	0	0	0	0	0	0	0	0	1	0	0
essays	9	.3745	.7392	38.7	0	0	0	0	0	5	4	0	1	2	2	0	0	1	0	0	0	0	0	0	0	0	3	0	0
Essays	3	.1250	.1342	31.3	0	0	1	0	0	2	0	0	1	0	0	0	0	0	0	0	0	0	0	0	2	0	0	0	0
essed	2	.0000	.0914	29.6	2	0	0	0	0	0	0	0	2	0	0	0	0	0	0	0	0	0	0	0	0	0	0	0	0
essence	10	.4940	1.0725	40.3	1	0	1	0	4	2	0	2	2	0	0	0	0	1	0	0	0	0	0	0	0	3	1	3	0
essences	2	.0000	.0209	23.2	0	0	0	0	0	0	2	0	0	0	0	0	0	0	0	0	0	0	0	0	0	0	2	0	0
essential	155	.7540	23.458	53.7	1	4	10	14	39	32	45	10	5	15	1	1	4	5	3	38	5	3	24	6	1	11	25	8	0
essentially	37	.7068	5.2699	47.2	0	2	3	0	13	4	10	5	0	1	0	0	0	4	0	3	3	1	0	2	1	2	10	10	0
essentials	6	.5066	.6278	38.0	0	1	0	0	2	3	0	0	0	1	0	0	0	0	0	0	0	0	1	0	0	1	2	1	0
Essex	9	.2292	.6951	38.4	0	0	1	0	2	6	0	0	8	0	0	0	0	0	0	0	0	0	0	0	0	0	1	0	0
Essie	9	.0000	.1055	30.2	1	0	8	0	0	0	0	0	0	0	0	0	0	0	0	0	0	0	0	0	9	0	0	0	0
est	55	.2402	3.1870	45.0	19	8	7	19	2	0	0	0	9	1	2	0	0	0	42	0	0	0	0	0	0	0	1	0	0
establish	87	.8188	14.237	51.5	2	4	14	8	22	21	12	4	3	2	2	5	3	33	2	3	5	0	1	5	1	8	9	5	0
established	267	.7237	39.183	55.9	13	9	49	32	63	59	32	10	21	7	0	3	2	65	0	18	15	0	1	3	3	28	73	28	0
establishes	6	.4058	.5053	37.0	0	0	0	0	3	2	1	0	0	0	2	0	0	0	0	1	1	0	0	1	0	0	1	0	0
establishing	23	.6222	2.9269	44.7	0	0	4	2	5	5	3	4	0	2	0	1	0	4	0	1	1	0	0	0	0	4	8	2	0
establishment	42	.5991	5.1839	47.1	4	0	3	4	9	6	15	1	2	0	0	1	0	5	0	2	1	1	0	0	0	5	17	8	0
Establishment	4	.0996	.1523	31.8	0	0	0	0	2	0	1	1	1	0	0	0	0	0	0	0	0	0	0	0	0	0	0	3	0
establishments	4	.2285	.2258	33.5	0	1	0	0	1	1	1	0	0	0	0	0	0	2	0	0	0	0	0	0	0	0	2	0	0
estancia	5	.3016	.3700	35.7	2	1	1	1	0	0	0	0	1	0	0	0	0	2	0	0	0	0	0	0	0	0	2	0	0
Estancia	6	.0000	.1167	30.7	0	6	0	0	0	0	0	0	0	0	0	0	0	6	0	0	0	0	0	0	0	0	0	0	0
estancias	3	.0000	.0583	27.7	0	1	0	1	0	0	1	0	0	0	0	0	0	3	0	0	0	0	0	0	0	0	0	0	0
estate	46	.8773	8.0129	49.0	0	3	1	4	15	9	10	4	2	3	0	2	5	10	3	1	2	1	1	0	6	2	3	5	0
Estate	3	.0000	.0583	27.7	0	0	0	0	3	0	0	0	0	0	0	0	0	3	0	0	0	0	0	0	0	0	0	0	0
estates	23	.4912	2.4011	43.8	2	0	6	7	4	4	0	0	0	0	0	0	0	11	0	0	0	0	0	0	2	3	6	1	0
Estates-General	2	.0000	.0389	25.9	0	0	0	0	0	0	2	0	0	0	0	0	0	2	0	0	0	0	0	0	0	0	0	0	0
esteem	7	.5094	.7565	38.8	0	2	0	1	3	1	0	0	1	2	0	0	0	0	0	0	0	0	0	0	2	0	1	1	0
esteemed	4	.4870	.4078	36.1	0	1	0	1	0	0	1	1	0	0	0	0	0	0	0	0	0	0	0	0	1	1	1	1	0
Esther	22	.3585	2.1064	43.2	7	0	9	0	0	6	0	0	18	0	0	0	0	0	0	0	2	0	0	0	0	2	0	0	0
esthetic	4	.2978	.2586	34.1	0	0	0	0	0	1	3	0	0	0	0	0	0	0	0	0	0	1	0	0	0	0	2	1	0
estimate	220	.4724	22.221	53.5	11	23	29	36	26	46	45	4	8	0	1	0	171	2	1	10	0	0	4	5	2	2	6	8	0
estimated	107	.7437	16.086	52.1	8	7	4	17	20	15	28	8	9	0	1	1	19	11	0	14	0	0	4	1	1	2	21	23	0
estimates	29	.5662	3.4513	45.4	0	7	2	4	2	8	6	0	3	0	0	0	11	1	0	6	0	0	1	0	0	0	6	1	0
estimating	15	.4105	1.3870	41.4	1	2	1	3	1	5	2	0	2	0	0	0	8	1	0	3	0	0	0	0	0	0	1	0	0
estimation	7	.2446	.4060	36.1	0	0	1	3	1	0	2	0	0	0	0	3	4	0	0	0	0	0	0	0	0	0	0	0	0
Estonia	2	.2437	.1129	30.5	0	0	0	1	0	1	0	0	0	0	0	0	0	0	0	0	0	0	0	0	0	0	1	1	0
estranged	2	.2433	.1158	30.6	0	0	0	0	0	1	1	0	0	0	0	0	0	0	0	0	0	0	0	0	0	1	0	1	0
estrogen	2	.0000	.0394	26.0	0	0	0	0	0	0	2	0	0	0	0	0	0	0	0	2	0	0	0	0	0	0	0	0	0
estrus	3	.0000	.0591	27.7	0	0	0	0	0	0	0	3	0	0	0	0	0	0	0	3	0	0	0	0	0	0	0	0	0
estuaries	3	.3660	.2695	34.3	0	0	0	1	0	1	1	0	1	0	0	0	0	1	0	1	0	0	0	0	0	0	0	0	0
estuary	12	.4925	1.2347	40.9	2	0	1	1	6	1	1	0	0	0	0	3	0	1	0	0	0	0	0	0	0	1	4	3	0
et	14	.5854	1.6887	42.3	0	1	1	2	4	4	2	0	1	0	0	1	0	0	4	0	0	0	0	0	2	2	1	3	0
etait	2	.0000	.0162	22.1	0	0	2	0	0	0	0	0	0	0	0	0	0	0	0	0	2	0	0	0	0	0	0	0	0
etatism	2	.0000	.0290	24.6	0	0	2	0	0	0	0	0	0	0	0	0	0	0	0	0	0	0	0	0	0	2	0	0	0
etc	175	.8662	30.059	54.8	12	11	26	18	42	22	32	12	4	18	2	9	23	1	18	11	24	6	1	10	14	14	11	9	0
etch	2	.2160	.1362	31.3	1	0	0	0	0	0	0	1	1	0	0	0	0	0	0	1	0	0	0	0	0	0	0	0	0
etched	14	.2130	.7462	38.7	2	2	0	0	4	1	5	0	3	0	0	1	0	0	0	1	1	0	0	7	0	0	1	0	0
Etches	2	.0000	.0290	24.6	0	0	0	0	0	0	2	0	0	0	0	0	0	0	0	0	0	0	0	0	0	2	0	0	0
etching	9	.3226	.6024	37.8	0	0	1	0	5	1	2	0	0	0	0	0	0	0	0	0	1	4	0	2	0	1	0	1	0
etchings	2	.0000	.0050	17.0	0	0	0	0	0	0	2	0	0	0	0	0	0	0	0	0	0	0	0	2	0	0	0	0	0
etci	5	.0000	.0586	27.7	0	0	0	5	0	0	0	0	0	0	0	0	0	0	0	0	0	0	0	0	5	0	0	0	0
eternal	26	.5737	3.0664	44.9	0	2	4	0	10	5	5	0	0	0	0	6	0	1	0	0	1	0	0	0	2	8	7	1	0
Eternal	4	.2201	.2150	33.3	3	0	1	0	0	0	0	0	0	0	0	0	0	0	0	0	0	0	0	0	0	3	1	0	0
eternally	7	.5134	.7434	38.7	0	1	1	0	2	1	2	0	0	0	0	1	0	0	0	0	1	0	0	0	1	1	3	0	0
eternity	6	.4109	.5504	37.4	1	0	3	0	2	0	0	0	1	1	0	0	0	0	0	0	0	0	0	0	1	3	0	0	0
Eternity	2	.2337	.1157	30.6	0	1	0	0	0	1	0	0	0	0	0	0	0	1	0	0	0	0	0	0	1	0	0	0	0
eth	3	.2379	.1631	32.1	0	1	0	0	2	0	0	0	0	2	0	0	0	0	1	0	0	0	0	0	0	0	0	0	0
Ethan	7	.4847	.7684	38.9	0	0	1	1	3	2	0	0	3	1	0	0	0	2	0	0	0	0	0	0	0	0	1	0	0
ethane	6	.0000	.0628	28.0	0	0	4	2	0	0	0	0	0	0	0	0	0	0	0	0	0	0	0	0	0	0	6	0	0
Ethel	4	.2989	.2660	34.2	2	0	0	1	0	0	0	1	0	0	1	0	2	0	0	0	0	0	0	0	0	0	0	1	0
ether	27	.2235	1.4163	41.5	0	0	10	9	1	5	0	2	0	0	0	1	0	0	2	2	0	0	0	0	0	0	22	0	0
ethereal	2	.2417	.1091	30.4	0	0	0	0	0	1	1	0	0	0	0	0	0	0	0	0	1	0	0	0	0	0	1	0	0
ethic	3	.3465	.2515	34.0	1	0	2	0	0	0	0	0	1	0	0	0	0	0	0	0	0	0	0	0	0	1	0	1	0
ethical	7	.3643	.5564	37.5	0	1	0	0	4	0	2	0	0	1	0	0	0	0	0	1	0	0	0	0	0	1	4	0	0
ethics	4	.3605	.3115	34.9	0	0	0	0	0	0	3	1	0	1	0	0	0	0	0	0	0	0	0	0	0	0	2	1	0
Ethiopia	69	.1702	3.3829	45.3	0	0	4	27	35	0	3	0	0	0	0	0	0	63	0	0	0	0	0	0	0	2	4	0	0
Ethiopia's	2	.0000	.0389	25.9	0	0	0	0	2	0	0	0	0	0	0	0	0	2	0	0	0	0	0	0	0	0	0	0	0
Ethiopian	24	.3492	1.9166	42.8	0	5	1	3	15	0	0	0	0	0	0	0	0	17	0	0	0	0	0	0	5	1	1	0	0
Ethiopians	11	.4243	1.0181	40.1	0	0	1	4	3	0	3	0	0	0	0	3	0	6	0	0	0	0	0	0	1	1	0	0	0
ethnic	13	.4128	1.1702	40.7	0	0	6	0	5	0	2	0	0	0	0	0	0	2	0	1	0	0	0	0	0	8	1	1	0
ethnocentric	2	.0000	.0389	25.9	0	0	0	0	2	0	0	0	0	0	0	0	0	2	0	0	0	0	0	0	0	0	0	0	0
ethnological	3	.2043	.1486	31.7	0	0	1	0	0	1	0	1	0	0	0	0	0	0	0	0	0	0	0	0	0	1	2	0	0
ethyl	17	.0000	.1779	32.5	0	0	1	11	0	5	0	0	0	0	0	0	0	0	0	0	0	0	0	0	0	0	17	0	0
ethylene	19	.0000	.1989	33.0	0	0	1	8	0	10	0	0	0	0	0	0	0	0	0	0	0	0	0	0	0	0	19	0	0
Etienne	2	.0000	.0389	25.9	0	0	0	2	0	0	0	0	0	0	0	0	0	2	0	0	0	0	0	0	0	0	0	0	0
etiquette	9	.4645	.8886	39.5	0	2	0	1	5	1	0	0	0	0	0	0	0	1	0	1	0	0	1	0	0	5	1	0	0
Etiquette	3	.1858	.1432	31.6	0	1	0	0	2	0	0	0	0	2	0	0	0	1	0	0	0	0	0	0	0	0	0	0	0
Etna	9	.3558	.8547	39.3	7	0	0	0	1	0	1	0	7	0	0	0	0	0	0	1	0	0	0	0	0	0	1	0	0

4R Esposito
4P Esputa's
7P espy
8A Espy
7N Esq
6R esquamulose
6B ess
7R ESSA
8F essayist-poet
6P essayists
4Q Essence
8L ESSENTIAL
5P Essequibo
6R EST
8B establish'd
5F Estados
6A estanica
7F Estates
9F EstatesGeneral
8F Este
3P esteemeth
7P esteeming
9D Estella
9D Estella's
6Q ester
5J Esterhazy
3A Esther's
8R esthetically
7L Estimate
9F Estonians
7P Estrada
XQ estrangement
3A Estrellita
3A Estrellita's
XH estrous
XH Eta
XH Etamin
7Q etat
7N etcetera
8Q etcher
5Q etches
8Q Eteocles
3P Eterna
5Q Ethelred
5P Ethelreda
5Q Ethelwulf
9J ethereally
6Q ethers
8Q ethnographic
5Q Ethnological
8Q ethnologist
8Q ethnology
5Q Ethnology
7J ethnomusicologists
XR ethologists
5Q Ethylene
7H etiolated
4J Eto
7R ETO

Word Type	F	D	U	SFI	3 Gr 3	4 Gr 4	5 Gr 5	6 Gr 6	7 Gr 7	8 Gr 8	9 Gr 9	X UnGr	A Read	B Eng & Gr	C Comp	D Lit	E Math	F Soc Stud	G Spell	H Sci	J Music	K Art	L Home Ec	M Shop	N Lib F	P Lib NF	Q Lib Ref	R Mag	S Rel
Eton	3	.0000	.0328	25.2	0	0	0	3	0	0	0	0	0	3	0	0	0	0	0	0	0	0	0	0	0	0	0	0	0
Etruscan	2	.0000	.0209	23.2	0	0	0	0	0	0	2	0	0	0	0	0	0	0	0	0	0	0	0	0	0	0	2	0	0
Etruscans	17	.4125	1.4903	41.7	8	0	0	1	4	0	4	0	0	2	0	0	0	1	2	0	0	0	0	0	0	2	10	0	0
Etty	6	.0000	.0869	29.4	0	6	0	0	0	0	0	0	0	0	0	0	0	0	0	0	0	0	0	0	0	6	0	0	0
Etude	3	.0000	.0243	23.8	1	0	0	0	2	0	0	0	0	0	0	0	0	0	0	0	3	0	0	0	0	0	0	0	0
Etudes	2	.2303	.1079	30.3	0	0	0	0	1	1	0	0	0	0	0	0	0	0	0	0	1	0	0	0	0	1	0	0	0
etymologies	2	.2408	.1091	30.4	0	0	0	0	2	0	0	0	0	1	0	0	0	0	1	0	0	0	0	0	0	0	0	0	0
etymology	15	.1531	.5615	37.5	0	0	1	1	9	4	0	0	0	3	0	0	0	0	12	0	0	0	0	0	0	0	0	0	0
Euboea	4	.3874	.3414	35.3	0	0	1	0	2	1	0	0	0	0	0	1	0	2	0	0	0	0	0	0	0	0	1	0	0
eucalyptus	15	.3283	1.1336	40.5	0	2	0	9	3	0	1	0	0	0	0	1	0	10	0	0	0	0	0	0	0	0	4	0	0
euchh	4	.0000	.1827	32.6	0	0	0	4	0	0	0	0	4	0	0	0	0	0	0	0	0	0	0	0	0	0	0	0	0
Euclid	10	.5698	1.1957	40.8	0	1	1	2	1	3	2	0	1	0	0	0	3	2	0	0	0	0	0	0	1	1	2	0	0
Euclidean	3	.0000	.0449	26.5	0	0	0	0	1	2	0	0	0	0	0	0	3	0	0	0	0	0	0	0	0	0	0	0	0
Eugene	18	.5832	2.1552	43.3	0	2	1	0	6	4	5	0	1	1	1	0	0	2	0	0	1	2	0	0	0	0	6	4	0
euglena	5	.2442	.3066	34.9	2	0	1	0	0	0	2	0	0	0	0	0	0	0	0	3	0	0	0	0	0	2	0	0	0
Eulalie	2	.0000	.0234	23.7	0	1	0	0	1	0	0	0	0	0	0	0	0	0	0	0	0	0	0	0	2	0	0	0	0
Eulenspiegel's	2	.0000	.0162	22.1	0	0	0	1	0	1	0	0	0	0	0	0	0	0	0	0	2	0	0	0	0	0	0	0	0
Euler	9	.0000	.1347	31.3	0	0	1	0	0	8	0	0	0	0	0	0	9	0	0	0	0	0	0	0	0	0	0	0	0
eulogy	2	.1948	.1250	31.0	0	-0	0	0	1	0	0	1	1	0	0	0	0	0	0	0	0	0	0	0	0	1	0	0	0
Eunice	4	.0000	.0429	26.3	0	0	0	0	4	0	0	0	0	0	0	4	0	0	0	0	0	0	0	0	0	0	0	0	0
euphemisms	2	.2433	.1158	30.6	0	0	0	0	0	1	1	0	0	0	0	0	0	0	0	0	0	0	0	0	0	1	0	1	0
euphonium	2	.0000	.0162	22.1	0	0	0	0	0	2	0	0	0	0	0	0	0	0	0	0	2	0	0	0	0	0	0	0	0
Euphrates	10	.5095	1.0748	40.3	0	1	0	4	2	1	1	1	0	1	0	0	1	5	0	0	0	1	0	0	0	1	1	0	0
Eur-Af-Asia	3	.0000	.0583	27.7	0	0	0	3	0	0	0	0	0	0	0	0	0	3	0	0	0	0	0	0	0	0	0	0	0
Eurasia	41	.1031	1.5384	41.9	0	1	0	21	12	0	7	0	0	0	0	0	0	39	0	1	0	0	0	0	0	0	1	0	0
Eurasian	2	.0000	.0389	25.9	0	0	1	0	0	0	1	0	0	0	0	0	0	2	0	0	0	0	0	0	0	0	0	0	0
Eureka	9	.4642	.9711	39.9	0	4	1	0	0	2	0	2	5	0	0	0	0	1	0	0	1	0	0	0	0	0	0	2	0
Euridice	2	.0000	.0290	24.6	0	0	0	2	0	0	0	0	0	0	0	0	0	0	0	0	0	0	0	0	0	2	0	0	0
Europe	760	.7231	111.67	60.5	44	69	130	158	158	117	73	11	40	18	3	6	17	397	7	18	38	7	0	1	6	61	100	41	0
Europe's	20	.4947	2.1290	43.3	1	0	6	2	6	3	2	0	1	0	0	0	1	11	0	0	0	0	0	0	0	4	2	1	0
European	323	.6967	45.751	56.6	22	5	62	35	91	68	32	8	10	2	1	2	4	124	4	9	29	0	0	2	2	38	69	27	0
Europeans	123	.5166	13.539	51.3	3	9	27	20	32	21	9	2	2	1	0	1	0	88	1	0	2	1	0	0	0	8	12	7	0
Eurus	2	.2408	.1204	30.8	0	0	0	2	0	0	0	0	0	0	0	0	0	1	0	0	0	0	0	0	0	1	0	0	0
Eurydice	7	.2445	.5495	37.4	0	0	6	0	0	1	0	0	6	0	0	0	0	0	0	0	1	0	0	0	0	0	0	0	0
Eurylochos	4	.0000	.0429	26.3	0	0	0	0	0	0	4	0	0	0	0	4	0	0	0	0	0	0	0	0	0	0	0	0	0
Eurymachus	3	.0000	.1370	31.4	0	0	0	0	3	0	0	0	3	0	0	0	0	0	0	0	0	0	0	0	0	0	0	0	0
Eurystheus	2	.0000	.0914	29.6	0	0	0	0	0	2	0	0	2	0	0	0	0	0	0	0	0	0	0	0	0	0	0	0	0
eustachian	3	.0000	.0591	27.7	0	0	0	3	0	0	0	0	0	0	0	0	0	0	0	3	0	0	0	0	0	0	0	0	0
Eustachian	3	.0000	.0591	27.7	0	0	0	1	2	0	0	0	0	0	0	0	0	0	0	3	0	0	0	0	0	0	0	0	0
eutectic	3	.0000	.1370	31.4	3	0	0	0	0	0	0	0	3	0	0	0	0	0	0	0	0	0	0	0	0	0	0	0	0
Ev	6	.0000	.0644	28.1	0	0	0	0	0	0	6	0	0	0	0	6	0	0	0	0	0	0	0	0	0	0	0	0	0
ev'ry	11	.1564	.4789	36.8	3	0	2	5	1	0	0	0	2	1	0	0	0	0	0	0	8	0	0	0	0	0	0	0	0
ev'rybody	3	.2058	.1429	31.5	2	0	0	1	0	0	0	0	0	1	0	0	0	0	0	0	2	0	0	0	0	0	0	0	0
Eva	16	.6378	2.0837	43.2	5	1	1	6	0	2	1	0	1	1	0	2	1	0	0	0	2	0	0	0	0	1	3	5	0
EVA	3	.2121	.1560	31.9	0	0	0	0	2	0	1	0	0	0	0	0	1	0	0	0	0	0	0	0	0	0	0	2	0
evacuate	2	.2351	.1166	30.7	0	0	0	0	1	1	0	0	0	0	0	0	0	1	0	0	0	0	0	0	0	0	0	1	0
evacuated	8	.5461	.9231	39.7	0	0	1	1	2	3	0	1	1	2	0	0	0	1	0	1	0	0	0	0	0	1	2	0	0
evade	4	.4443	.3917	35.9	0	0	0	0	3	1	0	0	1	0	0	0	0	0	1	0	0	0	0	0	0	0	1	1	0
evading	3	.3408	.2477	33.9	0	0	0	0	2	0	1	0	1	0	0	1	0	0	0	0	0	0	0	0	0	1	0	0	0
evaluate	34	.5582	3.9089	45.9	0	0	5	3	4	10	12	0	0	4	0	0	7	6	3	2	0	0	7	0	0	0	4	1	0
evaluated	5	.3274	.3649	35.6	0	0	0	0	3	1	1	0	0	0	0	0	0	0	1	1	0	0	0	0	0	0	0	3	0
evaluation	8	.5539	.9463	39.8	0	0	3	0	2	0	1	2	2	0	0	0	0	1	0	1	2	0	0	0	0	0	1	1	0
evaluations	2	.2442	.1134	30.5	0	0	0	1	0	0	0	1	0	1	0	0	0	0	0	0	0	0	0	0	0	0	0	1	0
Evan	18	.1871	.8939	39.5	0	13	0	0	5	0	0	0	0	0	0	0	0	5	0	0	0	0	0	0	0	13	0	0	0
Evan's	5	.1990	.2695	34.3	0	1	0	0	4	0	0	0	0	0	0	0	0	4	0	0	0	0	0	0	0	1	0	0	0
evanescent	2	.0000	.0162	22.1	0	0	0	0	0	0	2	0	0	0	0	0	0	0	0	0	2	0	0	0	0	0	0	0	0
evangel	2	.2442	.1134	30.5	0	0	0	0	1	0	1	0	0	1	0	0	0	0	0	0	0	0	0	0	0	0	0	1	0
evangelical	5	.2316	.2703	34.3	0	0	0	0	1	3	1	0	0	0	0	0	0	0	0	0	0	0	0	0	0	0	3	2	0
Evangelical	2	.0000	.0209	23.2	0	0	0	0	2	0	0	0	0	0	0	0	0	0	0	0	0	0	0	0	0	0	2	0	0
Evangeline	4	.3480	.3055	34.8	0	0	1	1	0	2	0	0	0	0	0	2	0	1	0	0	1	0	0	0	0	0	0	0	0
evangelist	4	.1854	.1872	32.7	0	1	0	0	0	0	3	0	0	0	0	0	0	0	0	0	0	0	0	0	0	1	0	3	0
evangelization	2	.0000	.0209	23.2	0	0	0	0	0	2	0	0	0	0	0	0	0	0	0	0	0	0	0	0	0	0	2	0	0
Evans	19	.4791	1.9848	43.0	2	7	0	0	0	1	9	0	5	1	3	0	2	0	0	0	0	0	0	0	0	2	1	5	0
Evans's	2	.0000	.0045	16.5	0	0	0	0	0	0	2	0	0	0	2	0	0	0	0	0	0	0	0	0	0	0	0	0	0
Evansville	2	.0000	.0914	29.6	0	0	0	0	0	2	0	0	2	0	0	0	0	0	0	0	0	0	0	0	0	0	0	0	0
evaporate	27	.3238	2.0920	43.2	3	4	4	1	3	10	1	1	2	0	0	0	0	1	2	21	0	0	0	0	0	0	0	1	0
evaporated	24	.3062	1.6891	42.3	6	5	0	0	4	1	8	0	1	0	0	0	0	4	0	9	0	0	8	0	0	1	0	1	0
evaporates	37	.4413	3.5813	45.5	10	9	4	5	6	2	1	0	0	0	0	0	0	2	0	28	0	0	1	0	0	2	3	1	0
evaporating	6	.2427	.3643	35.6	0	1	0	3	1	1	0	0	0	0	0	0	0	0	0	4	0	0	0	0	0	0	0	2	0
evaporation	35	.3786	3.0490	44.8	5	5	7	6	3	4	2	3	3	0	0	0	0	0	0	25	0	0	0	0	0	2	2	3	0
evasion	4	.3740	.3226	35.1	0	0	0	0	1	1	2	0	0	1	0	0	0	0	0	0	0	0	0	0	0	0	1	2	0
evasive	2	.2351	.1166	30.7	0	0	0	1	0	1	0	0	0	0	0	0	0	1	0	0	0	0	0	0	0	0	0	1	0
eve	15	.6376	1.9893	43.0	2	2	2	2	1	4	2	0	3	0	0	1	0	4	0	0	2	0	0	0	0	1	1	3	0
Eve	59	.6241	7.7747	48.9	14	8	7	14	6	6	4	0	23	4	0	6	1	2	1	0	15	0	0	0	1	4	2	0	0
Evelyn	5	.2742	.3281	35.2	0	1	1	2	0	1	0	0	1	3	1	0	0	0	0	0	0	0	0	0	0	0	0	0	0
even	4225	.9684	806.95	69.1	641	622	462	563	899	460	412	166	1072	166	46	267	233	427	45	417	86	29	71	23	286	380	291	385	1
Even	2	.2137	.1056	30.2	0	1	0	0	1	0	0	0	0	0	0	0	0	1	0	0	1	0	0	0	0	0	0	0	0
even-numbered	3	.0000	.0591	27.7	0	0	3	0	0	0	0	0	0	0	0	0	0	0	0	3	0	0	0	0	0	0	0	0	0
even-tempered	2	.2405	.1205	30.8	0	0	1	0	0	1	0	0	0	0	0	0	0	0	0	1	0	0	0	0	0	1	0	0	0
evening	543	.8674	94.341	59.7	109	109	58	71	99	54	33	10	201	24	5	65	6	26	7	21	21	1	10	0	50	68	4	34	0
Evening	10	.5708	1.2161	40.8	1	4	1	0	2	1	1	0	3	1	0	2	0	0	0	1	2	0	0	0	0	1	0	0	0
evening's	4	.3408	.2936	34.7	0	1	0	0	2	1	0	0	0	0	0	1	0	0	0	0	2	0	0	0	0	0	0	1	0
evenings	34	.7443	5.1474	47.1	5	6	7	5	6	3	2	0	8	2	0	1	0	2	0	0	1	0	1	0	8	4	2	5	0
evenly	67	.7658	10.285	50.1	3	16	12	6	9	7	12	2	3	3	5	0	11	2	1	13	2	1	8	5	1	4	5	3	0
evenly-spaced	2	.0000	.0209	23.2	0	2	0	0	0	0	0	0	0	0	0	0	0	0	0	0	0	0	0	0	0	0	2	0	0
event	179	.7986	28.805	54.6	7	26	17	34	45	24	18	8	38	20	12	6	2	14	6	24	5	1	0	0	3	16	13	19	0
eventful	2	.2405	.1205	30.8	0	0	1	0	0	0	0	1	0	0	0	0	0	0	0	1	0	0	0	0	0	1	0	0	0
events	305	.8868	53.859	57.3	16	35	47	48	62	52	42	3	73	36	14	13	5	47	7	21	16	2	5	3	3	10	24	26	0
eventual	8	.3824	.6837	38.3	0	0	0	2	1	2	3	0	1	0	0	0	0	0	0	0	0	0	0	0	0	2	1	4	0
eventually	178	.8056	28.763	54.6	2	7	17	25	72	23	22	10	17	12	0	7	4	20	2	31	11	0	0	2	2	11	33	26	0
ever	2036	.9377	378.11	65.8	397	356	219	282	383	193	168	38	630	99	18	178	28	128	40	191	67	23	19	6	175	206	89	139	0
Ever	2	.0000	.0215	23.3	0	0	0	0	2	0	0	0	0	0	0	2	0	0	0	0	0	0	0	0	0	0	0	0	0
ever-changing	6	.5960	.7458	38.7	2	0	1	0	0	2	1	0	1	1	0	0	0	0	0	1	1	0	0	0	1	0	1	0	0

3P Etowah
8Q Etruscan-Roman
4P Etty's
7J etude
7D Etukishook
6B etymological
XQ euchromatin
5P Eucumbene
7R Eufemio
6P Eugenie
7H Euglena
3P EUGLENA
6H euglenas
7J Eulenspiegel
8E Euler's
9D Eumaeos
7A Eumaeus
8Q Eumenides
7D Eunice's
7Q Eunotosaurus
5N eunuchs
XR euphemism
7Q euphorbias
8R euphorically
5P EUR
XH eureka
7F Euripides
6F Europa
6F European-owned
7F European-style
3F Europoort
9D Euryalos
9D Eurycleia
9D Eurymachos
6H Eustachean
XR Eustis
3A eutectics
7Q euthytonon
6P Euxine
3J Ev'ry
3J ev'ryone
3J ev'rything
3J ev'rywhere
7D evacuation
8Q evacuations
7A Evageline
7A evaluating
8D Evangeline's
8R evangelism
6R evangelistic
5P evangelize
7R Evans'
8B Evanston
7R evaporator
7N evasions
3E EVEN
7P even-pace
7H even-toed
9C eveners
4Q evenly-placed
5J evenness
6A Events
8P ever-broadening
9Q ever-broader
4Q ever-cloudless
9H ever-expanding

Word Type	F	D	U	SFI	3 Gr 3	4 Gr 4	5 Gr 5	6 Gr 6	7 Gr 7	8 Gr 8	9 Gr 9	X UnGr	A Read	B Eng & Gr	C Comp	D Lit	E Math	F Soc Stud	G Spell	H Sci	J Music	K Art	L Home Ec	M Shop	N Lib F	P Lib NF	Q Lib Ref	R Mag	S Rel
ever-increasing	3	.1277	.1363	31.3	0	1	0	1	0	1	0	0	1	0	0	0	0	0	0	0	0	0	0	0	0	0	0	2	0
ever-present	7	.3511	.5318	37.3	0	0	0	1	2	2	1	1	0	0	0	0	0	0	0	0	2	0	0	0	0	0	1	4	0
ever'	2	.1717	.1142	30.6	1	0	0	0	0	0	1	0	1	0	0	1	0	0	0	0	0	0	0	0	0	0	0	0	0
Everest	33	.6427	4.4454	46.5	3	8	3	6	7	3	3	0	8	2	0	1	8	6	0	5	0	0	0	0	0	3	0	0	0
Everett	10	.4615	.9543	39.8	0	1	2	0	0	6	0	1	0	0	0	0	0	0	0	0	0	1	3	0	0	3	2	1	0
Everett's	3	.0000	.0097	19.8	0	0	0	0	0	3	0	0	0	0	0	0	0	0	0	0	0	0	3	0	0	0	0	0	0
everglades	2	.0000	.0209	23.2	0	2	0	0	0	0	0	0	0	0	0	0	0	0	0	0	0	0	0	0	0	0	2	0	0
Everglades	2	.0000	.0290	24.6	2	0	0	0	0	0	0	0	0	0	0	0	0	0	0	0	0	0	0	0	0	2	0	0	0
evergreen	27	.4846	2.8789	44.6	3	4	3	4	5	5	1	2	7	1	0	0	0	2	0	5	0	0	0	0	0	0	10	2	0
evergreens	11	.6090	1.3667	41.4	1	1	2	3	2	1	0	1	0	1	1	0	0	1	0	1	1	0	0	0	1	1	4	0	0
Evering	3	.0000	.0322	25.1	0	0	0	0	3	0	0	0	0	0	0	3	0	0	0	0	0	0	0	0	0	0	0	0	0
everlasting	9	.3175	.6358	38.0	2	0	0	1	2	1	3	0	0	0	0	5	0	0	0	0	0	0	0	0	1	3	0	0	0
evermore	6	.1143	.1995	33.0	0	0	0	0	0	1	5	0	0	0	0	5	0	1	0	0	0	0	0	0	0	0	0	0	0
every	3398	.9772	654.20	68.2	627	578	398	410	605	372	325	83	835	179	27	178	224	366	69	390	130	30	33	24	231	292	189	194	7
Every	3	.3394	.2145	33.3	0	0	0	1	1	1	0	0	0	0	0	0	0	0	0	0	1	0	1	0	0	0	1	0	0
everybody	390	.7418	59.341	57.7	82	100	39	29	68	37	30	5	144	35	2	38	0	12	4	7	7	0	0	0	67	54	0	20	0
Everybody	3	.2279	.2143	33.3	3	0	0	0	0	0	0	0	2	0	0	0	0	0	0	0	0	0	0	0	0	0	0	1	0
everybody's	14	.5900	1.7271	42.4	2	2	1	1	3	4	1	0	2	0	0	1	0	1	0	1	0	0	0	0	4	2	0	3	0
everyday	117	.8493	19.829	53.0	10	14	12	14	26	22	18	1	18	10	0	6	5	16	3	8	7	5	4	7	1	9	12	6	0
everyone	953	.9572	180.18	62.6	234	212	112	113	113	95	64	10	277	75	12	51	14	110	35	75	51	5	31	9	51	87	16	52	2
Everyone	2	.0857	.0784	28.9	0	0	0	1	1	0	0	0	1	0	0	0	0	0	0	0	0	0	1	0	0	0	0	0	0
everyone's	24	.7076	3.4805	45.4	4	3	4	1	7	4	1	0	5	3	0	2	1	5	0	1	0	0	1	0	1	0	0	5	0
everything	1005	.8960	179.55	62.5	227	179	131	106	177	73	87	25	362	39	11	100	2	80	10	70	14	3	14	4	102	100	18	76	0
everything's	15	.4375	1.4442	41.6	2	1	1	3	2	2	3	1	3	0	0	6	0	0	0	0	0	0	0	0	4	1	0	1	0
everytime	4	.2963	.2703	34.3	1	0	0	0	1	1	0	1	0	0	0	0	0	1	0	1	0	1	0	0	0	0	0	1	0
everywhere	308	.9195	56.236	57.5	68	63	39	50	44	20	14	10	90	9	4	15	2	52	2	37	12	4	1	2	14	32	15	17	0
evidence	221	.7281	32.659	55.1	9	10	17	16	62	35	62	10	13	4	4	4	1	19	1	93	5	0	2	0	4	4	40	27	0
evidenced	5	.3493	.3767	35.8	0	0	1	0	0	1	2	1	0	0	0	0	0	0	0	0	2	0	0	0	0	1	2	0	0
evidences	13	.5470	1.4876	41.7	1	2	1	0	1	1	7	0	0	2	1	0	0	0	0	7	0	0	0	0	0	1	1	1	0
evident	47	.7491	7.0921	48.5	3	2	3	4	7	14	11	3	4	0	0	2	1	3	0	4	2	2	0	2	4	2	12	9	0
evidently	48	.8015	7.7389	48.9	2	2	3	9	16	7	6	3	10	1	1	9	0	1	0	2	2	0	1	0	7	4	4	6	0
evil	132	.3534	10.880	50.4	13	15	6	19	46	15	15	3	35	7	2	35	0	6	4	2	7	0	0	0	11	7	2	8	6
Evil	9	.5198	.9674	39.9	0	3	2	1	1	1	1	0	0	0	1	2	0	0	0	0	0	0	0	0	0	3	2	1	0
evil-smelling	3	.2261	.2131	33.3	0	1	0	1	0	1	0	0	2	0	0	0	0	0	0	0	0	0	0	0	1	0	0	0	0
evilly	2	.0000	.0914	29.6	0	0	0	1	0	0	1	0	2	0	0	0	0	0	0	0	0	0	0	0	0	0	0	0	0
evils	8	.4529	.7684	38.9	0	1	0	0	1	5	1	0	0	0	1	2	0	3	0	0	0	0	0	0	0	0	2	0	0
evoke	4	.4737	.3981	36.0	0	0	0	0	0	0	3	1	0	0	0	1	0	0	0	1	1	0	0	0	0	0	1	0	0
evoked	2	.1948	.1250	31.0	0	0	1	1	0	0	0	0	1	0	0	0	0	0	0	0	0	0	0	0	0	1	0	0	0
evolution	44	.3813	3.6098	45.6	1	0	5	2	27	1	7	1	0	0	0	0	1	1	0	4	2	0	0	1	0	1	32	2	0
evolutionary	23	.1099	.7354	38.7	0	0	0	0	21	0	2	0	0	0	0	0	0	1	0	2	0	0	0	0	0	0	20	0	0
evolutionists	2	.0000	.0209	23.2	0	0	2	0	0	0	0	0	0	0	0	0	0	0	0	0	0	0	0	0	0	0	2	0	0
evolve	11	.5746	1.3045	41.2	0	1	0	1	6	0	1	2	0	0	0	0	0	1	0	2	1	0	0	0	1	0	3	3	0
evolved	45	.4617	4.4055	46.4	0	1	4	2	24	4	10	0	1	0	0	0	0	3	0	7	6	0	0	0	0	3	23	2	0
evolving	3	.1813	.1402	31.5	0	0	0	0	2	0	0	1	0	0	0	0	0	0	0	1	0	0	0	0	0	0	2	0	0
ew	4	.0000	.0325	25.1	2	1	0	0	1	0	0	0	0	0	0	0	0	0	4	0	0	0	0	0	0	0	0	0	0
ewe	4	.3688	.3668	35.6	1	0	1	2	0	0	0	0	2	1	0	0	0	1	0	0	0	0	0	0	0	0	0	0	0
Ewell	5	.1786	.2193	33.4	0	0	0	0	1	0	4	0	0	0	0	4	0	0	0	0	0	0	0	0	0	0	1	0	0
Ewells	3	.0000	.0322	25.1	0	0	0	0	0	0	3	0	0	0	0	3	0	0	0	0	0	0	0	0	0	0	0	0	0
ewes	2	.0000	.0389	25.9	2	0	0	0	0	0	0	0	0	0	0	0	0	2	0	0	0	0	0	0	0	0	0	0	0
Ewing	2	.1948	.1250	31.0	0	1	1	0	0	0	0	0	1	0	0	0	0	0	0	0	0	0	0	0	0	1	0	0	0
ex	12	.1511	.4564	36.6	3	1	2	1	4	1	0	0	0	0	0	0	3	0	9	0	0	0	0	0	0	0	0	0	0
Ex	2	.2391	.1133	30.5	1	0	1	0	0	0	0	0	0	0	0	0	1	0	0	0	0	0	0	0	0	0	1	0	0
ex-	2	.0000	.0162	22.1	0	0	0	0	2	0	0	0	0	0	0	0	0	0	2	0	0	0	0	0	0	0	0	0	0
ex-slave	2	.1948	.1250	31.0	0	0	0	0	2	0	0	0	1	0	0	0	0	0	0	0	0	0	0	0	0	1	0	0	0
ex-slaves	5	.0000	.0724	28.6	0	0	0	0	5	0	0	0	0	0	0	0	0	0	0	0	0	0	0	0	0	5	0	0	0
exact	236	.8527	40.034	56.0	21	37	31	24	57	26	38	2	16	55	10	9	45	10	7	18	9	3	2	12	8	10	13	9	0
exacted	2	.1717	.1142	30.6	0	0	0	1	0	1	0	0	1	0	0	1	0	0	0	0	0	0	0	0	0	0	0	0	0
exacting	4	.2045	.1813	32.6	0	0	0	0	0	2	2	0	0	1	2	0	0	0	0	0	0	0	0	0	0	0	1	0	0
exactly	641	.9494	120.25	60.8	73	95	82	88	119	93	65	26	144	52	8	44	72	49	13	75	41	3	20	9	31	37	13	30	0
exactness	3	.3134	.1996	33.0	0	0	0	0	0	1	2	0	0	1	0	0	0	0	1	0	0	0	0	1	0	0	0	0	0
exaggerate	8	.2971	.5919	37.7	0	1	1	1	0	4	0	1	3	0	0	1	0	0	0	0	0	2	0	0	1	1	0	0	0
exaggerated	21	.5986	2.6437	44.2	2	3	2	0	2	9	1	2	5	0	0	0	0	4	0	1	1	2	0	0	1	1	3	3	0
exaggerates	3	.3454	.2542	34.1	0	0	1	0	2	0	0	0	1	0	0	0	0	1	0	0	0	0	0	0	0	0	0	1	0
exaggerating	7	.4398	.6830	38.3	0	0	0	0	4	2	1	0	2	0	1	0	0	1	0	0	0	1	0	0	0	0	0	2	0
exaggeration	19	.7194	2.8098	44.5	4	2	1	1	5	3	3	0	6	1	1	1	0	3	0	0	1	0	0	0	1	3	2	0	0
exaggerations	9	.3139	.7833	38.9	1	1	3	2	1	0	1	0	7	0	1	0	0	0	0	0	0	0	0	0	0	0	1	0	0
exalted	8	.5517	.9256	39.7	0	0	0	2	4	2	0	0	1	1	0	1	0	1	0	0	1	0	0	0	3	0	0	0	0
exam	6	.3511	.5250	37.2	0	1	2	0	1	0	2	0	3	2	0	0	0	0	0	0	0	0	0	0	0	0	0	1	0
examination	65	.8323	10.824	50.3	2	3	5	7	14	9	24	1	8	12	1	1	3	4	2	13	0	0	1	0	2	6	7	5	0
examinations	24	.5310	2.7476	44.4	4	3	9	1	0	3	3	1	5	0	0	0	0	1	0	7	0	0	0	0	0	4	6	1	0
examine	190	.8500	32.192	55.1	4	19	29	20	55	39	21	3	10	22	6	2	16	13	14	68	5	3	7	0	5	7	4	8	0
examined	115	.9003	20.573	53.1	12	12	12	21	23	11	19	5	24	7	4	9	4	5	0	20	2	2	2	2	11	13	8	2	0
examiner	4	.1873	.1827	32.6	1	1	2	0	0	0	0	0	0	0	0	0	0	0	0	0	0	0	0	0	0	0	3	1	0
Examiner	6	.2760	.3823	35.8	1	0	0	0	0	4	1	0	0	0	0	0	0	1	0	0	0	0	0	0	4	0	0	1	0
examiners	3	.2159	.1532	31.9	0	2	0	0	0	0	0	1	0	0	0	0	0	0	0	0	0	0	0	0	0	0	2	1	0
examines	8	.3905	.6710	38.3	1	1	0	2	2	1	1	0	0	0	2	0	0	1	0	1	0	0	0	0	2	1	0	1	0
examining	44	.7408	6.6284	48.2	2	8	3	8	8	6	7	2	7	4	0	1	1	3	0	14	0	2	2	0	4	3	0	3	0
example	1939	.8801	338.75	65.3	90	157	247	270	485	341	314	35	82	218	41	20	533	136	138	329	98	20	46	46	7	37	121	67	0
Example	61	.1506	2.6268	44.2	6	0	7	5	5	22	16	0	2	0	0	0	57	1	0	0	0	0	0	1	0	0	0	0	0
examples	674	.8021	108.11	60.3	42	61	83	104	127	132	119	6	31	105	21	17	283	18	55	48	25	12	14	8	1	8	22	6	0
Examples	6	.0000	.0898	29.5	0	0	0	0	0	2	4	0	0	0	0	0	6	0	0	0	0	0	0	0	0	0	0	0	0
exams	6	.3421	.4505	36.5	0	1	0	1	2	0	2	0	0	3	0	0	0	0	0	0	0	0	0	0	0	1	0	2	0
exasperated	4	.4538	.4019	36.0	1	0	0	0	2	0	0	1	1	1	0	0	0	0	0	0	0	0	0	0	1	1	0	0	0
exasperating	6	.5244	.6574	38.2	0	0	0	0	4	1	1	0	0	1	0	2	0	1	0	1	0	0	0	0	0	0	1	0	0
exasperation	4	.3717	.3640	35.6	0	1	0	0	1	1	1	0	2	0	0	1	0	0	0	0	0	0	0	0	0	0	0	1	0
excavate	5	.2390	.2757	34.4	0	0	2	0	2	1	0	0	0	3	0	0	0	0	0	0	0	0	0	0	0	0	2	0	0
excavated	8	.1737	.3490	35.4	2	0	1	0	4	0	1	0	0	0	0	0	0	0	0	0	0	0	0	0	0	2	6	0	0
excavating	5	.5297	.5634	37.5	1	1	0	0	2	1	0	0	1	0	0	0	1	0	0	0	1	0	0	0	0	0	1	1	0
excavation	4	.3665	.3130	35.0	0	0	0	0	1	2	1	0	0	0	1	0	1	0	0	0	0	0	0	0	1	0	1	0	0
excavations	4	.3104	.2995	34.8	0	0	0	1	2	1	0	0	1	0	0	0	0	0	0	0	0	0	0	0	0	0	1	2	0
exceed	17	.7442	2.5673	44.1	0	0	1	1	7	3	4	1	2	0	0	1	1	2	1	4	0	0	0	0	0	2	2	2	0
exceeded	14	.6364	1.8310	42.6	1	0	2	1	3	3	4	0	1	0	0	1	0	1	0	1	0	0	0	0	1	3	2	4	0
exceeding	10	.5916	1.2389	40.9	1	1	2	0	4	0	2	0	2	0	0	2	0	0	0	1	0	0	0	1	0	2	1	1	0

9H ever-flowing
9Q ever-greater
8F ever-improving
6P ever-new
8F ever-optimistic
9R ever-rising
8F ever-widening
3A ever'wheres
7J everchanging
8P Everetts
3P EVERGREENS
6N everlastingly
5Q everlengthening
7A evermounting
5A Everson
7Q everted
8J everwidening
8R Everybody's
7H everyman's
8B everyones
7A everythin's
9R Everything
7D EVERYTHING
7N everywheres
3A Evian
7G evict
8D evicted
XB Evidence
9P evil-doing
6A evil-natured
5A evil-tasting
9A evildoers
8F evinces
9Q evisceration
XR evocation
7Q evocative
7R evokes
6Q evolutional
XH evolutionarily
5Q evolutionist
9J evolves
9D Evremonde
5P ewe's
9J Ewigen
8R ex-Communists
8F ex-Populist
8R ex-Presidents
5R ex-actress
8D Ex-as-per-at-ing
4D ex-ballplayer
9R ex-convict
8R ex-cop
9D ex-florist
7R ex-managers
8F ex-officers
7R ex-production
XR ex-publisher's
7R ex-reformer
8F ex-servicemen
8D ex-soldier
7Q exactitude
4A exaggeratedly
4Q examiner's
8E ExampleC
8R exbanker
8D exc
6A Excalibur
5Q excavator
3P excavators

Word Type	F	D	U	SFI	3 Gr 3	4 Gr 4	5 Gr 5	6 Gr 6	7 Gr 7	8 Gr 8	9 Gr 9	X UnGr	A Read	B Eng & Gr	C Comp	D Lit	E Math	F Soc Stud	G Spell	H Sci	J Music	K Art	L Home Ec	M Shop	N Lib F	P Lib NF	Q Lib Ref	R Mag	S Rel
exceedingly	20	.7051	2.8856	44.6	1	2	2	4	5	1	4	1	4	0	1	2	0	1	0	4	0	0	1	0	2	1	4	0	0
exceeds	14	.5814	1.6726	42.2	1	0	0	1	5	1	6	0	0	1	0	0	2	2	0	1	0	0	0	2	0	1	3	2	0
excel	2	.2407	.1138	30.6	0	0	2	0	0	0	0	0	0	0	0	1	0	0	0	0	0	0	0	0	0	1	0	0	0
excelled	4	.2969	.2888	34.6	0	0	1	0	1	0	2	0	1	0	0	2	0	0	0	0	0	0	0	0	1	0	0	0	0
excellence	11	.5744	1.3171	41.2	1	0	0	1	4	1	1	3	1	1	0	0	0	1	0	1	0	0	0	0	1	0	2	4	0
Excellency	7	.5157	.7866	39.0	1	2	0	1	0	1	2	0	2	2	0	0	0	1	0	0	0	0	0	0	0	1	0	1	0
excellent	175	.9119	31.626	55.0	8	7	17	30	49	21	29	14	22	4	3	11	0	26	2	22	6	3	6	4	10	12	19	25	0
excelsis	2	.0000	.0162	22.1	0	0	2	0	0	0	0	0	0	0	0	0	0	0	0	0	2	0	0	0	0	0	0	0	0
except	716	.9546	134.95	61.3	91	95	81	88	162	83	99	17	150	44	9	44	32	89	21	49	28	6	9	23	54	65	55	38	0
excepted	4	.1952	.1875	32.7	0	0	0	0	2	0	2	0	0	1	0	0	0	0	0	0	0	0	0	0	0	0	3	0	0
excepting	5	.4376	.4695	36.7	1	0	0	0	0	2	2	0	0	0	0	2	1	1	0	0	0	0	0	0	0	1	0	0	0
exception	73	.8918	12.910	51.1	2	5	3	10	20	11	21	1	8	11	1	4	1	3	5	4	3	1	5	1	3	6	11	6	0
exceptional	12	.5652	1.4437	41.6	0	0	4	1	5	1	1	0	3	0	0	0	0	2	0	0	0	0	0	1	0	3	2	1	0
exceptionally	17	.6723	2.3362	43.7	0	1	5	0	5	2	3	1	2	3	0	0	0	3	1	0	0	0	0	1	0	1	3	3	0
exceptions	52	.6549	6.9376	48.4	2	1	4	5	19	6	12	3	3	9	0	1	0	4	15	7	0	0	0	3	0	3	5	2	0
excerpt	21	.5145	2.2514	43.5	0	1	0	3	7	8	2	0	1	6	0	3	1	2	0	0	7	0	0	0	0	0	1	0	0
excerpts	22	.5313	2.4271	43.9	0	0	4	1	9	5	3	0	2	2	2	0	0	0	0	0	8	0	0	0	1	0	1	6	0
excess	48	.6575	6.4179	48.1	0	3	2	5	13	9	9	7	1	0	0	1	1	1	1	12	0	0	5	3	0	2	8	13	0
excesses	8	.5894	.9933	40.0	0	0	0	0	1	5	2	0	2	0	0	1	0	1	0	0	1	0	0	0	0	0	2	1	0
excessive	23	.7284	3.3802	45.3	0	0	2	1	6	5	4	5	1	3	1	0	0	1	0	4	0	0	1	0	1	2	5	4	0
excessively	3	.3870	.2486	34.0	0	0	0	0	2	0	1	0	0	0	0	1	0	0	0	0	0	0	0	0	0	0	1	1	0
exchange	140	.8334	23.358	53.7	16	15	19	8	30	23	25	4	22	10	0	6	2	21	13	15	1	0	5	0	7	14	19	5	0
Exchange	11	.6165	1.3993	41.5	2	0	0	0	5	0	4	0	1	0	0	1	0	1	0	0	0	0	0	0	1	2	2	3	0
exchanged	34	.7055	4.9290	46.9	4	5	5	2	7	10	1	0	8	0	0	4	1	8	0	1	1	0	0	0	5	0	4	2	0
exchanges	11	.4809	1.2201	40.9	0	0	1	1	1	5	2	1	6	0	0	0	0	2	0	0	0	0	0	0	0	0	1	2	0
exchanging	10	.4511	1.0483	40.2	0	1	1	2	4	1	1	0	5	0	0	0	0	2	0	0	0	0	1	0	0	0	0	2	0
Exchequer	6	.3983	.5052	37.0	0	0	0	1	1	3	0	1	0	1	0	0	0	0	0	0	3	0	0	0	1	0	0	1	0
excise	9	.3393	.6950	38.4	0	0	2	0	0	0	7	0	0	0	0	0	1	5	0	0	0	0	0	0	0	0	3	0	0
excitable	6	.5536	.7186	38.6	1	1	0	1	1	1	1	0	2	0	0	0	0	1	0	0	0	0	0	0	1	1	1	0	0
excite	8	.4816	.8771	39.4	3	1	1	2	1	0	0	0	4	0	0	0	0	0	1	0	0	0	0	0	1	2	0	0	0
excited	270	.7917	43.559	56.4	53	69	45	42	31	20	6	4	120	11	4	9	2	17	1	4	4	0	2	0	34	50	3	9	0
excitedly	74	.6775	10.566	50.2	11	23	9	15	6	4	5	1	39	0	2	7	0	1	0	1	1	0	0	0	6	12	0	5	0
excitement	259	.8195	42.718	56.3	39	49	29	38	50	28	20	6	77	14	9	23	0	14	1	3	27	6	0	0	27	29	7	22	0
excites	6	.5962	.7461	38.7	0	1	0	1	2	1	1	0	1	1	0	0	0	1	0	0	1	0	0	0	0	0	1	1	0
exciting	357	.8212	58.937	57.7	61	96	28	61	52	34	14	11	93	51	14	6	1	37	2	16	28	14	4	0	16	43	8	24	0
exclaim	15	.5873	1.8373	42.6	1	2	1	4	3	2	2	0	3	2	2	2	0	0	0	0	1	0	0	0	2	2	0	1	0
exclaimed	225	.7384	34.486	55.4	62	68	30	26	24	11	3	1	127	3	5	11	2	10	1	0	0	0	0	2	27	28	1	8	0
exclaiming	7	.4649	.7094	38.5	1	1	3	0	0	1	1	0	2	0	0	1	0	0	0	0	0	1	1	0	2	0	0	0	0
exclaims	5	.3852	.4252	36.3	0	0	2	0	1	1	0	1	0	0	0	0	0	2	0	0	1	0	0	0	0	2	0	0	0
exclamation	34	.4261	3.0462	44.8	5	4	6	2	7	2	7	1	1	17	7	4	0	0	1	0	1	0	0	0	1	2	0	0	0
exclamations	2	.1494	.1045	30.2	1	0	0	1	0	0	0	0	1	0	0	0	0	0	0	0	1	0	0	0	0	0	0	0	0
exclamatory	4	.1605	.1483	31.7	1	1	0	0	1	0	1	0	0	2	2	0	0	0	0	0	0	0	0	0	0	0	0	0	0
exclude	7	.6009	.8841	39.5	0	0	0	0	3	1	3	0	1	0	0	0	1	2	0	1	0	0	0	0	0	1	1	0	0
excluded	14	.6970	1.9893	43.0	0	1	0	0	4	4	5	0	1	0	0	0	3	4	0	1	1	0	1	0	0	1	1	1	0
excludes	2	.0000	.0209	23.2	0	0	0	0	1	0	1	0	0	0	0	0	0	0	0	0	0	0	0	0	0	0	2	0	0
excluding	2	.0000	.0389	25.9	0	0	0	0	0	1	1	0	0	0	0	0	0	2	0	0	0	0	0	0	0	0	0	0	0
exclusion	3	.3815	.2534	34.0	0	0	1	0	1	1	0	0	0	0	0	0	0	1	0	0	0	0	0	0	0	1	0	1	0
exclusive	18	.6821	2.5041	44.0	0	1	2	0	5	5	4	1	1	0	0	1	0	5	0	1	1	0	0	0	1	1	3	4	0
exclusively	18	.6753	2.4671	43.9	0	0	1	0	7	2	6	2	1	1	1	0	1	0	0	1	1	0	0	0	1	2	6	3	0
excrement	2	.2401	.1133	30.5	0	0	0	0	1	0	1	0	0	0	0	0	0	0	0	0	0	0	0	0	0	1	1	0	0
excreta	2	.2446	.1142	30.6	0	0	0	0	1	0	0	1	0	0	0	0	0	0	0	0	0	0	0	0	1	0	0	1	0
excrete	3	.2445	.1818	32.6	0	0	0	0	2	0	1	0	0	0	0	0	0	0	0	2	0	0	0	0	0	0	1	0	0
excretes	2	.2278	.1128	30.5	0	0	0	0	1	1	0	0	0	0	0	0	0	0	0	1	0	0	0	0	0	0	1	0	0
excretion	3	.2445	.1818	32.6	0	0	0	2	0	0	1	0	0	0	0	0	0	0	0	2	0	0	0	0	0	0	1	0	0
excretory	6	.2445	.3637	35.6	0	0	0	0	4	0	2	0	0	0	0	0	0	0	0	4	0	0	0	0	0	0	2	0	0
excruciating	2	.2446	.1122	30.5	0	0	0	0	2	0	0	0	0	0	0	1	0	0	0	0	0	0	0	0	0	0	1	0	0
excursion	9	.3953	.7963	39.0	1	0	1	1	1	2	2	1	1	0	0	0	0	3	1	0	0	0	0	0	0	0	0	4	0
excursions	4	.0996	.1523	31.8	0	0	0	1	1	1	0	1	1	0	0	0	0	0	0	0	0	0	0	0	0	0	0	3	0
excuse	75	.8051	12.216	50.9	12	16	7	7	17	5	9	2	27	6	1	8	0	2	4	3	0	0	2	0	6	5	0	11	0
excused	16	.6326	2.1367	43.3	0	3	3	2	4	1	2	1	6	2	0	3	1	0	0	1	0	0	0	0	0	1	0	2	0
excuses	12	.6805	1.6986	42.3	0	1	2	3	1	1	3	1	4	0	0	1	0	0	1	2	0	0	0	0	1	2	0	1	0
execute	13	.6397	1.7054	42.3	0	0	2	0	2	7	2	0	1	0	0	3	0	3	1	0	1	0	0	0	0	0	2	2	0
executed	25	.6699	3.4028	45.3	0	0	4	2	7	5	7	0	0	2	0	0	1	8	0	0	0	1	0	1	0	3	7	2	0
executing	3	.3847	.2496	34.0	0	0	0	0	3	0	0	0	0	0	0	0	0	0	0	0	0	0	0	0	0	1	1	1	0
execution	23	.6715	3.1616	45.0	5	0	3	0	7	4	3	1	3	0	0	3	0	2	0	0	1	0	0	0	5	2	2	5	0
executioner	6	.3814	.4892	36.9	2	0	0	0	0	2	2	0	0	0	0	0	0	0	0	0	2	0	0	0	2	0	0	2	0
Executioner	3	.0000	.0243	23.8	0	0	0	0	0	3	0	0	0	0	0	0	0	0	0	0	3	0	0	0	0	0	0	0	0
executioners	2	.0000	.0389	25.9	0	0	0	0	0	2	0	0	0	0	0	0	0	2	0	0	0	0	0	0	0	0	0	0	0
executions	2	.2297	.1135	30.6	0	0	0	0	0	2	0	0	0	0	0	1	0	1	0	0	0	0	0	0	0	0	0	0	0
executive	50	.5903	6.1144	47.9	5	0	6	0	10	13	16	0	2	2	1	0	0	15	0	0	0	0	0	0	0	5	10	15	0
Executive	7	.4587	.6816	38.3	2	0	2	1	1	1	0	0	0	0	0	0	0	1	0	0	0	0	0	0	0	2	2	2	0
executives	6	.4121	.5479	37.4	0	0	0	1	1	0	4	0	1	0	0	0	0	0	0	0	0	0	0	0	0	1	2	2	0
Executors	2	.0000	.0234	23.7	0	0	0	0	2	0	0	0	0	0	0	0	0	0	0	0	0	0	0	0	2	0	0	0	0
exemplified	4	.3435	.2952	34.7	0	0	0	1	0	1	1	1	0	0	0	0	0	0	0	0	2	0	0	0	1	0	1	0	0
exempt	5	.5389	.5772	37.6	0	0	1	1	2	0	1	0	1	0	0	0	0	1	0	0	0	0	0	0	1	1	0	1	0
exemption	4	.3628	.3241	35.1	0	0	0	0	1	1	2	0	0	0	0	0	2	1	0	0	0	0	0	0	1	0	0	0	0
exemptions	3	.0000	.0449	26.5	0	0	0	0	0	0	3	0	0	0	0	0	3	0	0	0	0	0	0	0	0	0	0	0	0
exercise	580	.6477	77.077	58.9	65	100	94	71	98	92	58	2	31	45	3	6	313	12	52	74	2	0	9	1	4	9	6	13	0
Exercise	134	.3521	10.482	50.2	8	8	13	18	47	23	16	1	2	30	0	0	89	0	12	1	0	0	0	0	0	0	0	0	0
exercised	10	.6181	1.2758	41.1	0	1	2	2	3	2	0	0	1	1	0	0	0	1	0	1	0	0	0	1	0	2	2	1	0
exercises	343	.4901	35.596	55.5	29	51	46	60	83	46	26	2	17	17	1	2	209	1	73	7	5	0	0	1	2	1	3	4	0
Exercises	92	.0768	2.7064	44.3	4	2	2	6	15	29	34	0	2	1	0	0	88	0	1	0	0	0	0	0	0	0	0	0	0
exercising	11	.5748	1.3146	41.2	0	1	0	1	2	5	2	0	1	0	1	0	0	0	0	2	0	0	0	0	1	1	3	2	0
exert	18	.5794	2.1840	43.4	0	0	0	1	3	7	5	2	2	0	0	0	0	1	0	6	0	0	2	0	0	2	3	2	0
exerted	15	.7167	2.1949	43.4	0	0	2	1	1	6	5	0	2	0	0	1	1	1	0	5	1	0	0	0	0	1	2	1	0
exertion	6	.5514	.7101	38.5	0	1	1	0	2	2	0	0	2	0	0	0	0	0	1	0	0	0	0	0	1	0	1	1	0
exertions	2	.2441	.1127	30.5	0	0	0	0	0	1	1	0	0	0	0	0	0	0	0	0	0	0	0	0	1	0	1	0	0
exerts	6	.3613	.4864	36.9	0	0	1	2	1	1	1	0	0	0	0	0	0	0	0	3	0	0	0	0	0	1	2	0	0
Exeter	11	.5585	1.3668	41.4	0	1	0	0	9	0	0	1	7	1	0	0	0	0	1	0	0	0	0	0	0	0	1	1	0
exeunt	2	.0000	.0215	23.3	0	0	0	0	0	0	2	0	0	0	0	2	0	0	0	0	0	0	0	0	0	0	0	0	0
exhale	6	.4603	.5902	37.7	1	0	1	0	4	0	0	0	0	0	0	2	1	0	0	2	0	0	0	0	0	0	0	1	0
exhaled	9	.4785	.9308	39.7	0	0	1	0	5	1	2	0	1	0	0	3	0	0	0	3	0	0	0	0	0	1	1	0	0
exhales	4	.3865	.3420	35.3	0	0	0	1	2	0	1	0	0	0	0	1	0	0	0	2	0	0	0	0	0	0	0	1	0
exhaling	3	.1650	.1684	32.3	0	1	0	0	2	0	0	0	1	0	0	0	0	0	0	2	0	0	0	0	0	0	0	0	0
exhaust	33	.7089	4.7736	46.8	8	2	3	3	10	2	5	0	3	0	1	0	1	1	0	14	0	0	0	1	1	5	2	4	0
exhausted	49	.8001	7.9381	49.0	1	9	7	7	13	9	3	0	16	2	1	1	0	5	0	2	2	0	0	0	7	6	2	5	0
exhausting	3	.2357	.2199	33.4	1	0	0	1	1	0	0	0	2	0	0	0	0	0	0	0	0	0	0	0	0	1	0	0	0
exhaustion	17	.6371	2.2661	43.6	1	2	2	2	5	3	2	0	5	0	0	2	0	1	0	0	1	0	0	0	0	3	1	4	0

9C Excellent
7N excellently
4R excels
6R ExcelsiorSprings
7R excerpted
5Q exchangeable
XH exchangers
8F excises
8Q excitation
8D excitements
8F Exclusion
5Q excommunicated
7Q excrescence
7Q excrescences
9H excreted
7Q excreting
7Q excretions
9H excurrent
9E Excursion
5Q excusable
5A EXCUSE
7Q Exec
9B execute/execution
9R Executives
4N executor
7C exemplify
8F exempting
8F Exemptions
6E Exercize
8E exerting
4D exhalant
XR exhalations
XP Exhaust

Word Type	F	D	U	SFI	3 Gr 3	4 Gr 4	5 Gr 5	6 Gr 6	7 Gr 7	8 Gr 8	9 Gr 9	X UnGr	A Read	B Eng & Gr	C Comp	D Lit	E Math	F Soc Stud	G Spell	H Sci	J Music	K Art	L Home Ec	M Shop	N Lib F	P Lib NF	Q Lib Ref	R Mag	S Rel
exhaustive	5	.2129	.2689	34.3	0	0	0	0	2	2	0	1	0	0	0	0	0	0	0	2	0	0	0	0	0	0	0	3	0
exhausts	3	.3762	.2496	34.0	0	0	0	0	2	0	1	0	0	0	0	0	0	0	0	1	0	0	0	0	0	1	1	0	0
exhibit	46	.7665	7.0882	48.5	7	15	3	5	7	6	3	0	1	6	0	2	3	10	0	3	1	0	0	0	2	5	7	6	0
Exhibit	3	.2321	.1635	32.1	0	0	0	0	1	0	2	0	0	0	0	0	0	0	0	0	0	0	0	0	0	0	1	2	0
exhibited	15	.6491	2.0007	43.0	0	2	3	0	2	5	2	1	2	1	0	0	0	1	0	0	1	0	0	0	1	2	4	3	0
exhibiting	7	.6800	.9656	39.8	0	0	0	1	3	1	1	1	0	0	0	1	1	0	0	1	0	0	0	0	1	1	1	1	0
exhibition	18	.5937	2.2257	43.5	2	1	2	3	2	4	2	2	3	1	0	3	1	0	0	0	0	0	0	0	1	0	4	5	0
Exhibition	5	.3562	.3925	35.9	1	2	0	0	0	0	2	0	0	0	0	0	0	0	0	0	0	0	0	0	0	3	1	1	0
exhibitions	6	.5614	.6929	38.4	1	0	0	1	1	2	1	0	0	0	0	1	0	0	1	0	0	0	0	0	0	2	1	1	0
exhibits	17	.4700	1.6890	42.3	4	2	1	1	0	6	3	0	0	1	0	0	0	1	0	3	0	0	0	0	0	1	8	3	0
exhilarated	2	.2440	.1132	30.5	0	0	0	0	0	2	0	0	0	0	0	1	0	0	0	0	0	0	0	0	0	0	0	1	0
exhilarating	3	.3847	.2490	34.0	0	0	0	0	1	2	0	0	0	1	0	1	0	0	0	0	0	0	0	0	0	1	0	0	0
exhilaration	2	.1812	.0838	29.2	0	0	0	0	0	1	0	1	0	0	0	0	0	0	0	0	0	0	1	0	0	0	0	1	0
exhort	4	.2440	.2264	33.5	0	0	0	1	1	0	2	0	0	0	0	2	0	0	0	0	0	0	0	0	0	0	0	2	0
exile	17	.5961	2.0964	43.2	0	0	6	1	6	3	0	1	1	0	0	1	0	2	0	0	1	0	0	0	0	6	2	4	0
exiled	5	.3753	.4112	36.1	0	0	2	0	1	2	0	0	0	0	0	0	0	2	0	0	1	0	0	0	0	0	2	0	0
exiles	4	.3604	.3538	35.5	0	0	2	0	2	0	0	0	2	0	0	1	0	0	0	0	1	0	0	0	0	0	0	0	0
exist	135	.8698	23.353	53.7	7	5	17	16	29	23	31	7	7	6	3	2	5	17	3	35	6	0	2	3	2	8	21	15	0
existed	71	.7382	10.587	50.2	6	4	8	5	19	15	8	6	2	2	0	2	1	17	0	12	4	0	0	1	3	7	18	2	0
existence	89	.8010	14.280	51.5	0	6	6	5	25	17	17	13	6	2	1	6	3	5	0	18	9	0	0	2	1	6	19	11	0
existing	45	.7040	6.4030	48.1	1	0	8	2	13	7	9	5	1	0	0	0	0	6	4	5	1	2	0	1	0	3	12	10	0
exists	66	.8520	11.215	50.5	3	2	8	7	23	14	6	3	5	1	1	2	6	10	1	14	4	0	0	1	1	3	10	7	0
exit	26	.7248	3.7917	45.8	0	1	3	5	4	4	8	1	1	0	1	7	1	0	1	0	2	0	0	0	5	3	2	3	0
exits	14	.4858	1.4616	41.6	0	1	2	6	0	2	1	2	2	0	0	1	0	0	0	1	0	0	0	0	6	1	0	3	0
Exodus	3	.2159	.1532	31.9	0	0	2	0	0	0	0	1	0	0	0	0	0	0	0	0	0	0	0	0	0	0	2	1	0
exorbitant	3	.2672	.1778	32.5	0	0	1	0	1	0	1	0	0	1	1	0	0	0	0	0	0	0	0	0	0	1	0	0	0
exoskeleton	14	.1341	.5998	37.8	0	0	0	7	5	0	2	0	0	0	0	0	0	0	0	13	0	0	0	0	0	0	1	0	0
exoskeletons	5	.0000	.0986	29.9	0	0	0	5	0	0	0	0	0	0	0	0	0	0	0	5	0	0	0	0	0	0	0	0	0
exotic	25	.6345	3.2227	45.1	3	0	3	1	8	6	1	3	0	0	1	0	0	4	0	0	3	2	0	0	0	3	5	7	0
expand	87	.8319	14.461	51.6	6	6	11	20	22	7	15	0	6	16	2	1	6	5	1	28	5	0	1	2	1	1	6	6	0
expanded	153	.6343	19.885	53.0	17	32	18	15	30	28	12	1	4	8	4	1	95	6	0	4	10	2	0	0	0	7	6	6	0
expanding	37	.6335	4.8402	46.8	4	1	4	3	13	7	4	1	2	0	1	0	0	4	0	17	0	0	0	2	0	2	7	2	0
expands	52	.5727	6.2861	48.0	8	4	9	11	7	6	5	2	5	1	0	0	0	0	0	33	0	0	1	2	0	1	4	5	0
expanse	26	.7341	3.8723	45.9	2	0	6	7	8	2	1	0	3	1	0	2	0	7	0	1	0	1	0	0	2	2	4	3	0
expanses	6	.6230	.7678	38.9	0	3	1	1	1	0	0	0	0	0	0	1	0	1	0	1	0	0	0	0	1	1	0	1	0
expansion	70	.7347	10.393	50.2	7	1	4	6	16	15	20	1	2	6	2	0	3	14	0	16	0	0	0	2	1	1	16	7	0
Expansion	2	.2337	.1157	30.6	0	1	1	0	0	0	0	0	0	0	0	0	0	1	0	0	0	0	0	0	1	0	0	0	0
expansionist	3	.2425	.1816	32.6	0	0	0	0	1	2	0	0	0	0	0	0	0	2	0	0	0	0	0	0	0	0	0	1	0
expansions	3	.2222	.1558	31.9	0	0	0	1	0	1	1	0	0	1	0	0	0	0	0	0	0	0	0	0	0	0	2	0	0
expansive	7	.5178	.7387	38.7	1	0	0	0	3	2	1	0	0	0	0	2	0	0	0	0	1	1	0	1	0	0	2	0	0
expecially	7	.4219	.6364	38.0	0	2	3	0	0	0	2	0	0	0	0	0	0	2	0	1	0	0	1	0	3	0	0	0	0
expect	360	.8980	64.264	58.1	32	46	68	62	57	32	51	12	71	27	2	22	7	37	27	59	11	1	4	0	27	22	3	40	0
expectancy	5	.4860	.5175	37.1	1	0	0	0	0	3	0	1	0	0	0	0	0	0	0	2	0	0	0	0	1	1	0	1	0
expectant	7	.3967	.6326	38.0	0	1	1	1	3	1	0	0	2	0	1	2	0	0	0	0	0	0	0	0	0	2	0	0	0
expectantly	11	.6352	1.4423	41.6	1	3	0	0	1	5	1	0	2	1	0	2	0	0	0	0	2	0	0	0	2	1	0	1	0
expectation	16	.6450	2.1344	43.3	0	1	1	2	4	2	5	1	3	1	0	4	0	1	0	1	0	0	0	0	3	0	1	2	0
expectations	11	.5690	1.2868	41.1	0	1	0	0	3	2	4	1	0	0	1	0	0	2	0	0	1	0	0	0	2	0	1	4	0
expected	292	.9113	52.811	57.2	17	25	30	46	78	48	40	8	64	12	5	32	7	28	4	26	7	2	10	0	25	21	16	33	0
expecting	43	.3994	4.0422	46.1	5	12	5	4	12	3	2	0	18	3	0	4	0	0	0	0	0	0	0	0	8	4	0	5	1
expects	29	.7964	4.6803	46.7	6	3	6	5	2	3	4	0	9	1	1	3	1	4	1	3	0	0	0	0	1	3	0	2	0
expedient	5	.2553	.3169	35.0	0	0	1	0	4	0	0	0	1	0	0	0	0	0	0	0	0	0	0	0	1	0	3	0	0
expedite	2	.0665	.0708	28.5	0	0	0	1	0	1	0	0	1	0	1	0	0	0	0	0	0	0	0	0	0	0	0	0	0
expedition	107	.6705	14.819	51.7	9	6	19	26	21	18	7	1	22	2	0	6	1	20	0	3	0	0	0	0	2	14	25	12	0
Expedition	2	.1948	.1250	31.0	1	0	0	0	1	0	0	0	1	0	0	0	0	0	0	0	0	0	0	0	0	1	0	0	0
expedition's	2	.1948	.1250	31.0	1	0	0	1	0	0	0	0	1	0	0	0	0	0	0	0	0	0	0	0	0	1	0	0	0
Expeditionary	5	.0000	.0972	29.9	0	0	0	0	0	5	0	0	0	0	0	0	0	5	0	0	0	0	0	0	0	0	0	0	0
expeditions	38	.6779	5.2819	47.2	8	5	6	5	5	6	0	3	5	0	0	4	0	4	0	2	0	0	0	0	4	10	5	4	0
expel	3	.3670	.2406	33.8	0	0	0	0	1	1	1	0	0	0	0	0	0	0	1	1	0	0	0	0	0	0	1	0	0
expelled	14	.5431	1.5848	42.0	1	1	2	0	2	8	0	0	0	0	0	1	0	1	1	4	0	0	0	0	0	2	5	0	0
expelling	3	.3709	.2499	34.0	0	1	0	0	0	1	0	1	0	0	0	0	0	1	0	1	0	0	0	0	0	0	1	0	0
expels	2	.2418	.1091	30.4	0	0	0	0	0	1	1	0	0	0	0	0	0	0	1	0	0	0	0	0	0	0	1	0	0
expend	2	.2437	.1129	30.5	0	0	0	0	1	0	0	1	0	0	0	0	0	0	0	0	0	0	0	0	0	0	1	1	0
expended	6	.4059	.5230	37.2	0	0	0	0	3	0	3	0	0	0	0	0	0	1	0	0	0	0	0	0	1	0	3	1	0
expenditure	5	.4638	.4999	37.0	0	0	1	0	0	1	2	1	1	0	0	1	0	0	0	0	0	0	1	0	0	0	1	1	0
expenditures	14	.1131	.3754	35.7	0	0	1	0	2	1	10	0	0	0	0	0	0	0	0	0	0	0	11	0	0	1	1	1	0
expense	38	.6913	5.3652	47.3	3	3	5	2	9	6	7	3	5	2	0	1	2	5	0	4	0	0	3	0	1	0	8	7	0
expenses	51	.6082	6.4407	48.1	4	5	3	5	9	9	16	0	8	3	0	2	17	5	1	0	1	0	8	0	3	0	2	1	0
expensive	129	.8187	21.181	53.3	9	25	16	8	29	17	20	5	22	5	0	3	5	22	1	14	3	2	12	7	5	8	11	9	0
expensively	3	.3454	.2542	34.1	0	0	1	0	1	0	1	0	1	0	0	0	0	1	0	0	0	0	0	0	0	0	0	1	0
experience	361	.8452	60.932	57.8	9	24	28	27	112	70	74	17	61	37	26	36	2	33	4	31	11	3	11	6	4	23	32	41	0
experienced	76	.8545	12.963	51.1	6	8	4	8	28	9	10	3	14	8	1	5	1	2	1	7	1	0	1	3	3	5	11	13	0
experiences	157	.7819	24.670	53.9	6	8	32	9	51	25	19	7	21	22	16	17	0	11	0	19	6	2	6	2	3	7	10	15	0
experiencing	9	.3956	.8144	39.1	0	0	2	2	4	0	1	0	2	0	0	0	0	0	0	2	0	0	0	0	0	0	1	4	0
experiment	497	.7318	74.018	58.7	114	106	34	94	54	30	41	24	50	4	1	7	27	15	4	266	30	20	5	2	3	23	22	18	0
Experiment	3	.0737	.0659	28.2	0	0	0	0	0	0	3	0	0	0	2	0	0	0	0	1	0	0	0	0	0	0	0	0	0
experimental	42	.6617	5.6746	47.5	0	2	4	7	9	6	9	5	1	1	0	0	2	2	0	12	1	0	0	1	0	2	8	12	0
experimentally	7	.0995	.2112	33.2	0	1	0	0	3	1	1	1	0	0	0	0	0	0	0	1	0	0	0	0	0	0	6	0	0
experimentation	30	.6314	3.8997	45.9	0	5	1	5	8	3	6	2	2	0	0	0	1	0	0	13	3	0	2	1	0	0	7	1	0
experimented	21	.5703	2.4781	43.9	0	4	2	3	3	5	4	0	1	0	0	1	0	3	0	5	3	3	1	0	0	0	3	1	0
experimenter	6	.3593	.4929	36.9	0	0	0	0	2	0	3	1	1	0	0	3	0	0	0	1	0	0	0	0	0	0	1	0	0
experimenters	6	.3256	.5038	37.0	0	0	0	0	2	2	2	0	3	0	0	0	0	0	0	1	0	0	0	0	0	0	2	0	0
experimenting	45	.6916	6.3828	48.1	4	11	5	6	8	6	1	4	7	0	0	2	2	2	0	17	8	2	1	0	0	1	1	2	0
experiments	247	.7676	38.402	55.8	23	33	30	37	48	18	39	19	32	2	0	8	11	10	0	121	3	4	4	3	4	4	27	14	0
Experiments	4	.2090	.2014	33.0	0	0	0	0	3	0	1	0	0	0	0	0	0	0	0	0	0	0	0	0	0	0	1	3	0
expert	89	.8960	15.866	52.0	9	6	14	9	24	4	14	9	23	5	1	7	1	9	3	2	1	0	2	2	4	13	4	12	0
expert's	2	.1948	.1250	31.0	2	0	0	0	0	0	0	0	1	0	0	0	0	0	0	0	0	0	0	0	0	1	0	0	0
expertise	2	.0000	.0243	23.9	0	0	0	0	0	1	0	1	0	0	0	0	0	0	0	0	0	0	0	0	0	0	0	2	0
expertly	8	.5942	1.0039	40.0	0	1	0	0	3	3	1	0	2	1	0	0	0	1	0	0	0	0	0	0	2	1	0	1	0
experts	85	.6710	11.772	50.7	5	7	8	15	24	10	9	7	16	4	0	1	0	13	1	6	0	0	0	0	0	14	10	20	0
expiration	2	.0000	.0219	23.4	0	0	0	1	0	1	0	0	0	2	0	0	0	0	0	0	0	0	0	0	0	0	0	0	0
expire	5	.4140	.4655	36.7	0	0	0	0	2	0	2	1	1	0	0	1	0	1	0	0	0	0	0	0	0	0	0	2	0
expired	5	.4613	.4882	36.9	0	0	0	0	1	1	3	0	0	0	0	1	0	1	0	0	0	0	0	0	0	0	1	2	0
expiring	2	.0000	.0234	23.7	0	0	1	0	1	0	0	0	0	0	0	0	0	0	0	0	0	0	0	0	2	0	0	0	0
explain	891	.8321	148.27	61.7	87	161	129	102	160	125	119	8	74	85	15	45	316	64	19	168	12	3	2	12	18	28	10	17	3
explained	314	.9041	56.501	57.5	47	57	39	37	55	47	27	5	100	19	2	14	12	17	6	27	3	1	0	5	27	36	9	36	0
explaining	59	.6981	8.4463	49.3	4	9	6	8	6	12	13	1	13	18	2	4	2	8	1	0	2	0	0	0	0	4	0	5	0
explains	86	.7214	12.623	51.0	6	10	14	7	24	14	7	4	13	5	7	3	3	14	5	13	3	0	1	1	0	4	4	9	1

9Q exhibitionist
4P Exhibits
9R exhortation
9D exhorting
XJ exigencies
7F exiling
9R existential
7R existentialist
9J Exit
8D exit-hole
7R exiting
7H exo
9Q exocrine
9Q exocrines
5P exodus
9R exonerate
7B exorciser
5H exosphere
8F exotic-looking
7J exotic-sounding
3E expanded-numeral
7R expanding-point
XH expansible
8F expansively
5P expatriates
4Q expectancies
7K Expectancy
9B expectedness
5N expectin'
7N expectoration
8F expediency
8F expedients
XR expeditionary
7Q expeditious
XR expense-paid
9R Experience
7H Experimental
7H experimentations
8J Experimenting
7B Explaining

Word Type	F	D	U	SFI	3 Gr 3	4 Gr 4	5 Gr 5	6 Gr 6	7 Gr 7	8 Gr 8	9 Gr 9	X UnGr	A Read	B Eng & Gr	C Comp	D Lit	E Math	F Soc Stud	G Spell	H Sci	J Music	K Art	L Home Ec	M Shop	N Lib F	P Lib NF	Q Lib Ref	R Mag	S Rel
explanation	140	.8198	23.044	53.6	1	12	8	23	38	19	35	4	26	26	6	3	7	8	1	30	5	0	1	1	4	1	10	11	0
explanations	45	.6423	5.9289	47.7	0	2	4	4	18	8	9	0	4	19	1	3	0	0	0	7	1	0	0	0	2	4	3	1	0
explanatory	9	.3876	.7565	38.8	0	1	0	4	0	2	2	0	0	5	1	0	0	1	0	2	0	0	0	0	0	0	0	0	0
expletives	2	.0000	.0219	23.4	0	0	0	0	0	0	2	0	0	2	0	0	0	0	0	0	0	0	0	0	0	0	0	2	0
explicit	9	.5950	1.0976	40.4	0	0	2	1	2	1	3	0	0	2	0	1	0	1	0	0	0	0	0	0	0	1	2	2	0
explode	15	.6542	2.0181	43.0	3	1	2	2	2	1	4	0	1	1	0	0	0	2	0	5	0	1	0	0	1	2	1	1	0
exploded	34	.7262	5.0584	47.0	4	1	2	6	9	6	6	0	10	2	1	3	0	2	0	2	0	0	0	0	3	0	4	7	0
explodes	13	.3475	1.0431	40.2	6	0	1	1	1	2	2	0	1	0	0	0	0	0	0	4	0	0	0	0	0	7	0	1	0
exploding	10	.5310	1.1378	40.6	0	2	4	0	3	1	0	0	2	0	1	0	0	0	0	3	0	0	0	0	2	1	1	0	0
exploit	12	.5358	1.3517	41.3	1	0	1	0	3	4	2	1	1	1	0	0	0	2	0	1	1	0	0	0	0	1	5	0	0
exploitation	14	.4246	1.2977	41.1	0	0	0	0	7	3	4	0	1	0	0	0	0	4	0	0	0	0	0	0	0	1	6	2	0
exploited	10	.3380	.7444	38.7	0	0	0	0	7	1	1	1	0	0	0	0	0	1	0	0	0	0	0	0	0	1	6	2	0
exploiters	2	.1698	.1133	30.5	0	0	0	0	1	1	0	0	1	0	0	0	0	0	0	0	0	0	0	0	0	0	1	0	0
exploiting	8	.2999	.5410	37.3	0	0	0	0	5	3	0	0	0	0	0	0	0	2	0	0	1	0	0	0	0	0	5	0	0
exploits	12	.5328	1.3370	41.3	0	1	2	0	4	3	0	2	1	1	0	0	0	0	0	1	2	0	0	0	0	0	3	4	0
exploration	68	.8803	11.910	50.8	7	4	11	11	14	10	8	3	8	1	1	2	5	11	1	13	5	0	1	1	0	4	6	9	0
explorations	19	.6610	2.5917	44.1	0	1	5	5	1	4	3	0	3	1	0	2	0	6	0	2	3	0	0	1	0	0	0	1	0
explore	180	.8101	29.373	54.7	15	41	45	34	21	12	8	4	37	5	2	4	6	34	1	37	31	2	0	1	1	3	6	10	0
explored	91	.8561	15.563	51.9	8	11	31	10	14	11	4	2	12	3	0	4	1	31	4	12	5	1	0	1	2	6	5	4	0
explorer	60	.6974	8.6067	49.3	7	13	17	10	6	3	4	0	11	3	0	1	0	25	3	2	2	0	0	0	0	4	7	2	0
Explorer	20	.4573	2.0104	43.0	1	5	3	6	4	0	0	1	3	0	0	0	0	1	0	4	0	0	0	0	0	5	0	7	0
explorers	144	.7193	21.218	53.3	19	21	35	32	25	7	3	2	25	3	0	1	1	59	4	12	4	0	0	0	2	12	14	7	0
Explorers	12	.5735	1.4537	41.6	2	1	1	3	3	1	0	1	2	2	0	0	1	3	0	0	0	0	0	0	0	1	0	3	0
explorers'	2	.2152	.1357	31.3	0	0	1	0	0	1	0	0	1	0	0	0	0	1	0	0	0	0	0	0	0	0	0	0	0
Explorers'	2	.2306	.1140	30.6	0	1	0	0	1	0	0	0	0	1	0	0	0	1	0	0	0	0	0	0	0	0	0	0	0
explores	11	.4843	1.1684	40.7	3	0	1	0	4	0	1	2	2	0	0	0	0	0	0	6	1	0	1	0	0	1	0	0	0
exploring	85	.8491	14.475	51.6	5	13	24	20	12	6	3	2	22	3	3	2	0	21	1	11	2	1	2	0	1	5	3	8	0
Exploring	2	.1494	.1045	30.2	0	1	0	0	1	0	0	0	1	0	0	0	0	0	0	0	1	0	0	0	0	0	0	0	0
explosion	73	.7953	11.725	50.7	2	11	3	6	17	22	8	4	16	4	2	4	1	2	0	21	0	1	0	0	6	1	8	7	0
explosions	22	.5709	2.7218	44.3	4	3	2	6	2	3	0	2	9	0	0	0	0	0	0	2	0	0	0	0	1	4	1	5	0
explosive	29	.6902	4.1498	46.2	0	7	3	2	10	3	4	0	10	0	2	1	0	1	0	4	1	0	0	0	1	2	3	4	0
explosively	4	.2672	.2733	34.4	0	0	0	0	2	1	1	0	1	0	0	0	0	0	0	1	0	0	0	0	0	0	2	0	0
explosives	29	.6361	3.9626	46.0	1	15	4	1	2	4	2	0	17	1	0	0	0	1	1	1	0	0	0	0	0	1	4	3	0
exponent	55	.1334	2.1765	43.4	0	2	0	4	9	21	17	2	1	0	0	0	50	0	0	0	0	0	0	0	0	2	0	2	0
exponential	52	.0394	1.1478	40.6	0	0	0	0	1	50	0	1	0	0	0	0	51	0	0	0	0	0	0	0	0	0	0	1	0
exponents	50	.0000	.7484	38.7	0	0	5	3	6	27	9	0	0	0	0	0	50	0	0	0	0	0	0	0	0	0	0	0	0
export	51	.3913	4.4660	46.5	5	1	6	18	14	2	5	0	1	0	0	0	0	34	0	1	0	0	0	0	0	1	10	4	0
exported	37	.3247	2.7764	44.4	8	1	5	11	11	1	0	0	0	0	0	0	0	24	0	0	0	0	0	0	0	3	10	0	0
exporter	5	.0000	.0972	29.9	0	0	0	1	3	1	0	0	0	0	0	0	0	5	0	0	0	0	0	0	0	0	0	0	0
exporters	2	.2408	.1204	30.8	0	0	2	0	0	0	0	0	0	0	0	0	0	1	0	0	0	0	0	0	0	1	0	0	0
exporting	5	.3742	.4184	36.2	0	0	1	1	2	1	0	0	0	0	0	0	0	3	0	0	0	0	0	0	0	0	1	1	0
exports	59	.4783	5.9926	47.8	6	4	15	11	12	3	8	0	0	0	0	0	0	22	0	0	1	0	0	0	0	7	20	9	0
expose	11	.6844	1.5373	41.9	1	2	0	0	2	1	3	2	1	0	0	2	0	1	0	2	1	0	0	0	0	1	1	2	0
exposed	73	.7996	11.721	50.7	0	4	10	8	14	7	23	7	8	2	1	3	0	3	1	23	1	0	2	5	4	3	8	9	0
exposing	11	.5390	1.2784	41.1	0	0	1	2	5	0	3	0	3	0	1	0	0	0	0	3	0	0	0	0	0	1	2	1	0
exposition	29	.4977	2.9791	44.7	0	0	0	1	12	10	6	0	1	4	4	5	0	0	0	0	12	0	0	0	0	0	1	2	0
Exposition	6	.4330	.5823	37.7	0	0	2	1	0	3	0	0	1	0	0	0	0	3	0	0	0	0	0	0	0	0	1	1	0
expository	3	.1088	.0779	28.9	0	0	0	0	0	0	3	0	0	1	2	0	0	0	0	0	0	0	0	0	0	0	0	0	0
exposure	31	.5597	3.5979	45.6	0	0	1	0	7	5	14	4	1	1	2	0	0	0	0	11	0	0	0	4	0	0	4	8	0
expounded	2	.2412	.1141	30.6	0	0	0	0	2	0	0	0	0	1	0	0	0	0	0	0	0	0	0	0	0	1	0	0	0
express	437	.7173	63.407	58.0	13	47	45	75	103	83	67	4	42	48	15	16	160	12	19	4	60	31	0	2	3	7	15	3	0
Express	36	.5713	4.4763	46.5	16	5	5	0	2	8	0	0	16	3	1	1	0	4	0	0	0	0	0	0	0	11	0	0	0
expressed	190	.8265	31.365	55.0	5	13	10	21	54	43	37	7	18	11	9	13	57	11	1	7	21	4	0	2	5	4	14	13	0
expresses	83	.5973	10.206	50.1	2	15	11	8	25	12	8	2	13	11	17	8	3	0	5	8	10	4	0	0	1	2	6	3	0
expressing	75	.7158	10.808	50.3	1	8	4	7	27	16	10	2	4	11	3	5	19	0	5	1	8	8	0	1	0	3	4	3	0
expression	287	.8058	46.269	56.7	4	25	20	28	54	82	65	9	30	35	7	14	75	4	7	4	54	11	5	0	13	11	10	7	0
Expression	2	.0000	.0243	23.9	0	0	0	0	0	0	0	2	0	0	0	0	0	0	0	0	0	0	0	0	0	0	0	2	0
expressionism	2	.2437	.1129	30.5	0	0	0	0	0	2	0	0	0	0	0	0	0	0	0	0	0	0	0	0	0	0	1	1	0
Expressionism	5	.1812	.2068	33.2	0	0	2	0	1	2	0	0	0	0	0	0	0	0	0	0	0	2	0	0	0	0	3	0	0
expressions	142	.5734	16.832	52.3	2	1	19	14	32	33	39	2	13	47	20	5	38	0	6	0	5	1	1	0	0	4	1	1	0
expressive	23	.5595	2.6285	44.2	0	2	0	3	5	9	3	1	1	3	1	1	0	0	0	0	9	3	0	0	3	0	2	0	0
expressively	3	.0995	.1144	30.6	0	1	2	0	0	0	0	0	1	0	0	0	0	0	0	0	2	0	0	0	0	0	0	0	0
expressiveness	2	.2431	.0986	29.9	0	0	0	0	0	2	0	0	0	0	1	0	0	0	0	0	0	1	0	0	0	0	0	0	0
expressly	6	.3612	.4858	36.9	0	1	2	0	0	2	1	0	0	0	0	0	0	3	0	0	0	0	0	0	0	1	2	0	0
expressway	4	.3519	.3117	34.9	1	0	1	0	1	0	1	0	0	0	0	0	0	1	0	0	0	0	0	0	0	0	1	2	0
expressways	7	.4531	.6861	38.4	1	0	3	1	2	0	0	0	0	0	0	0	0	4	0	0	0	0	0	0	0	1	1	1	0
expulsion	4	.3831	.3409	35.3	0	0	0	0	1	0	3	0	0	0	0	0	0	0	0	2	0	0	0	0	0	1	1	0	0
exquisite	15	.7016	2.1538	43.3	1	0	3	2	3	2	2	2	3	0	0	1	0	1	0	0	1	0	0	0	2	3	2	2	0
exquisitely	2	.1698	.1133	30.5	0	0	0	1	0	1	0	0	1	0	0	0	0	0	0	0	0	0	0	0	0	0	1	0	0
extant	2	.2441	.1127	30.5	0	0	0	0	1	0	1	0	0	0	0	0	0	0	0	0	0	0	0	0	1	0	1	0	0
extend	137	.8037	22.067	53.4	3	4	15	23	42	22	22	6	8	1	0	4	12	43	5	17	5	1	10	5	1	3	19	3	0
extended	114	.8971	20.291	53.1	2	9	12	10	38	19	18	6	14	2	2	5	13	7	0	13	9	1	2	4	7	5	19	11	0
extending	56	.8036	9.0088	49.5	2	2	2	8	12	17	10	3	2	0	0	2	2	12	1	12	2	1	4	2	0	2	9	5	0
extends	101	.7448	15.218	51.8	3	13	15	18	27	11	13	1	3	2	1	1	5	46	0	15	3	0	3	1	0	2	16	3	0
extens-	2	.0000	.0162	22.1	0	0	0	0	0	2	0	0	0	0	0	0	0	0	2	0	0	0	0	0	1	0	0	0	0
extension	38	.5797	4.5434	46.6	1	2	1	0	9	13	11	1	3	0	0	0	4	5	2	2	3	0	1	8	0	0	5	4	0
Extension	3	.1277	.1363	31.3	0	1	0	0	0	0	0	2	1	0	0	0	0	0	0	0	0	0	0	0	0	0	0	2	0
extensions	8	.4009	.7146	38.5	1	0	0	1	3	2	1	1	1	0	0	0	0	0	0	2	0	0	0	0	0	0	3	2	0
extensive	60	.6479	7.9294	49.0	2	1	4	4	16	14	15	4	2	1	0	0	0	9	1	6	1	1	1	1	0	2	29	6	0
extensively	24	.5934	2.8891	44.6	0	0	0	3	8	4	8	1	0	0	0	1	0	2	0	3	5	2	1	5	0	0	4	1	0
extent	88	.8440	14.789	51.7	3	1	6	8	29	24	17	0	4	3	2	3	1	8	4	17	2	1	6	1	2	6	23	5	0
exterior	26	.5883	3.1468	45.0	1	0	1	1	11	2	8	2	1	0	0	2	12	0	0	0	0	0	1	3	0	2	3	2	0
exteriors	2	.2446	.1122	30.5	0	0	0	0	0	1	1	0	0	0	0	1	0	0	0	0	0	0	0	0	0	0	1	0	0
exterminate	5	.4305	.4752	36.8	0	1	0	0	4	0	0	0	1	1	0	1	0	0	0	0	0	0	0	0	0	3	0	2	0
exterminated	10	.4352	.9960	40.0	0	0	0	4	5	1	0	0	4	0	1	0	0	0	0	0	0	0	0	0	0	1	2	0	0
external	34	.5071	3.6067	45.6	0	2	3	2	6	5	15	1	2	0	0	1	1	1	2	6	0	0	0	7	1	0	10	2	0
External	2	.2437	.1129	30.5	0	0	0	0	0	2	0	0	0	0	0	0	0	0	0	0	0	0	0	0	0	0	1	1	0
externally	5	.3732	.4026	36.0	0	0	2	0	1	1	0	1	0	0	1	0	0	0	0	1	0	0	0	0	0	1	2	0	0
extinct	31	.6168	3.9634	46.0	1	5	4	8	8	2	3	0	3	0	0	1	0	3	0	6	0	0	0	0	1	4	9	4	0
extinction	13	.5011	1.3635	41.3	0	0	0	1	7	1	2	2	0	0	0	1	0	1	0	1	0	0	0	0	0	1	4	5	0
extinguished	5	.3416	.4181	36.2	1	0	0	1	2	1	0	0	2	0	0	0	0	0	0	0	0	0	0	0	2	0	1	0	0
extinguisher	4	.2059	.1995	33.0	0	0	0	0	3	0	1	0	0	1	0	0	0	0	0	0	0	0	0	0	0	0	0	3	0
extinguishing	3	.0000	.0365	25.6	0	0	0	0	3	0	0	0	0	0	0	0	0	0	0	0	0	0	0	0	0	0	1	1	0
extirpation	2	.2437	.1129	30.5	0	0	0	1	1	0	0	0	0	0	0	0	0	0	0	0	0	0	0	0	0	0	0	0	0
extol	4	.0000	.0323	25.1	0	1	1	1	1	0	0	0	0	0	0	0	0	0	0	0	4	0	0	0	0	0	0	0	0
extra	284	.8816	49.882	57.0	38	52	26	37	56	31	35	9	67	23	1	13	19	13	9	28	10	0	14	11	9	31	6	30	0
extract	25	.6715	3.4555	45.4	3	0	2	5	8	2	4	1	4	0	0	0	1	4	4	4	0	0	0	0	2	0	4	2	0

8R explayer
9B expletive
7R Exploration
3N explorin
4Q Explosive
7R explosiveness
8F exportation
4R Expos
8R exposes
8J expositions
6N expostulated
8F expostulations
9B exposures
6G expound
7A expounders
9D expounding
7K Expressionist
5Q expressionists
8K Expressionists
4A expressionless
8Q expropriation
7J Exquise
8Q exstrophy
9B extemporaneous
9L extenders
8G extention
7R exterminating
9D extermination
8H external-combustion
5P externalized
7C extinguish
6H extinguishers
6R extirpated
4A extolling
9A extort
4A Extra
7R extra-fresh
XP extra-good
8A extra-powerful
7N extra-special
6A extra-tall
7H extracellular

Word Type	F	D	U	SFI	3 Gr 3	4 Gr 4	5 Gr 5	6 Gr 6	7 Gr 7	8 Gr 8	9 Gr 9	X UnGr	A Read	B Eng & Gr	C Comp	D Lit	E Math	F Soc Stud	G Spell	H Sci	J Music	K Art	L Home Ec	M Shop	N Lib F	P Lib NF	Q Lib Ref	R Mag	S Rel
extracted	20	.7375	2.9936	44.8	0	0	1	6	7	1	4	1	3	0	0	1	0	4	0	2	1	0	1	1	1	0	1	5	0
extracting	2	.2420	.1154	30.6	0	0	0	1	0	0	1	0	0	0	0	0	1	0	0	0	0	0	0	0	1	0	0	0	0
extracts	5	.3480	.3989	36.0	0	0	0	1	1	0	2	1	1	0	1	0	0	0	0	0	0	0	0	0	0	2	1	0	0
extramusical	3	.0000	.0243	23.8	0	0	0	0	2	1	0	0	0	0	0	0	0	0	0	0	3	0	0	0	0	0	0	0	0
extraordinarily	11	.3579	.8813	39.5	0	0	3	1	2	2	3	0	1	0	0	0	0	0	0	0	0	0	0	0	1	4	5	0	0
extraordinary	63	.7575	9.6556	49.8	3	5	4	8	20	13	7	3	11	5	0	3	0	7	2	2	0	2	0	0	5	3	14	9	0
extras	6	.4418	.5550	37.4	0	1	1	0	3	0	0	1	0	1	0	0	0	0	0	0	0	0	1	0	0	0	1	3	0
extravagant	8	.3744	.6537	38.2	2	0	0	0	0	1	5	0	1	1	0	1	0	0	0	0	0	2	0	0	0	0	2	1	0
extravagantly	3	.2435	.1694	32.3	0	0	0	0	3	0	0	0	0	0	1	0	0	0	0	1	0	0	0	0	0	0	0	1	0
extreme	88	.8624	15.117	51.8	8	4	8	5	22	14	21	6	11	3	1	4	2	8	0	10	0	2	3	3	3	12	16	10	0
extremely	135	.8157	22.089	53.4	4	8	6	22	49	19	21	6	24	6	4	5	0	10	0	15	7	0	2	9	6	15	23	9	0
extremes	24	.7681	3.7138	45.7	1	1	1	2	9	6	4	0	2	2	0	1	3	4	0	2	1	1	0	0	0	3	4	1	0
extremists	3	.2159	.1532	31.9	0	0	2	1	0	0	0	0	0	0	0	0	0	0	0	0	0	0	0	0	0	0	2	1	0
extremities	2	.2278	.1128	30.5	0	0	0	1	1	0	0	0	0	0	0	0	0	0	0	1	0	0	0	0	0	0	1	0	0
extremity	6	.4222	.5373	37.3	0	0	1	0	1	3	1	0	0	0	0	1	0	0	0	0	0	0	0	0	1	1	3	0	0
extruded	4	.3864	.3418	35.3	0	0	0	0	1	0	3	0	0	0	0	0	0	0	0	2	0	0	0	0	0	0	1	1	0
extrusion	3	.2197	.2090	33.2	2	0	1	0	0	0	0	0	2	0	0	0	0	0	0	0	0	0	0	0	0	0	1	0	0
extrusive	3	.0000	.0591	27.7	0	0	0	0	0	0	3	0	0	0	0	0	0	0	0	3	0	0	0	0	0	0	0	0	0
exuberance	3	.3465	.2515	34.0	0	0	0	0	0	1	2	0	1	0	0	0	0	0	0	0	0	0	0	0	0	1	0	1	0
exuberant	10	.4143	.8987	39.5	0	0	1	2	2	4	0	1	1	0	0	0	0	1	0	0	4	0	0	0	0	0	1	3	0
exudate	2	.0000	.0209	23.2	0	0	0	0	0	2	0	0	0	0	0	0	0	0	0	0	0	0	0	0	0	0	2	0	0
exultant	3	.3851	.2497	34.0	0	0	1	0	1	0	1	0	0	0	0	1	0	0	0	0	0	0	0	0	1	1	0	0	0
exultantly	3	.2435	.2274	33.6	0	0	0	2	0	1	0	0	2	0	0	0	0	1	0	0	0	0	0	0	0	0	0	0	0
exultation	8	.3545	.6378	38.0	1	3	0	0	1	2	1	0	1	0	0	0	0	1	0	0	3	0	0	0	3	0	0	0	0
exulted	2	.2297	.1135	30.6	0	0	0	0	1	1	0	0	0	0	0	1	0	1	0	0	0	0	0	0	0	0	0	0	0
exulting	2	.2411	.1091	30.4	0	0	0	0	0	1	1	0	0	0	0	1	0	0	0	0	1	0	0	0	0	0	0	0	0
ey	3	.0000	.0243	23.9	0	0	1	0	0	2	0	0	0	0	0	0	0	0	3	0	0	0	0	0	0	0	0	0	0
eye	707	.8926	125.64	61.0	101	86	60	111	164	96	67	22	194	43	6	79	6	12	12	109	11	21	26	14	64	53	18	39	0
Eye	17	.6583	2.3741	43.8	4	0	1	5	4	1	2	0	9	0	0	2	0	0	0	1	1	0	0	0	1	2	1	0	0
eye-care	2	.0000	.0394	26.0	0	0	2	0	0	0	0	0	0	0	0	0	0	0	0	2	0	0	0	0	0	0	0	0	0
eye-catching	3	.2486	.1687	32.3	0	0	0	0	1	2	0	0	0	0	0	0	0	1	0	0	1	1	0	0	0	0	0	0	0
eyeball	3	.1650	.1684	32.3	0	0	0	3	0	0	0	0	1	0	0	0	0	0	0	2	0	0	0	0	0	0	0	0	0
eyeballs	10	.5983	1.2605	41.0	3	0	0	0	2	4	1	0	2	0	0	0	0	0	0	3	0	0	0	0	2	1	1	1	0
eyebars	2	.0000	.0209	23.2	0	0	0	0	0	0	2	0	0	0	0	0	0	0	0	0	0	0	0	0	0	0	2	0	0
eyebrow	9	.6236	1.1819	40.7	0	2	2	0	2	1	2	0	3	1	0	1	0	0	0	0	0	0	0	0	1	2	1	0	0
eyebrows	25	.6077	3.2068	45.1	1	7	3	3	5	4	2	0	8	0	0	5	0	0	0	1	0	1	0	0	6	2	0	2	0
eyed	28	.5479	3.4577	45.4	8	2	4	1	8	5	0	0	19	0	0	3	0	1	0	0	0	0	0	0	3	1	1	0	0
eyedropper	3	.0000	.1370	31.4	0	0	0	3	0	0	0	0	3	0	0	0	0	0	0	0	0	0	0	0	0	0	0	0	0
eyeglasses	12	.5725	1.4692	41.7	3	2	2	2	1	0	2	0	4	1	0	3	0	0	0	1	0	0	0	0	0	0	2	1	0
eyeing	9	.5088	1.0173	40.1	1	0	2	0	5	0	0	1	4	0	1	1	0	1	0	0	0	0	0	0	1	0	0	1	0
eyelashes	10	.5582	1.1969	40.8	1	3	1	1	4	0	0	0	3	1	0	3	0	0	0	1	0	0	0	0	1	1	0	0	0
eyelets	3	.2359	.1459	31.6	0	0	0	0	2	1	0	0	0	0	0	0	0	0	0	0	0	0	2	1	0	0	0	0	0
eyelid	6	.4743	.6417	38.1	0	0	0	3	1	2	0	0	2	0	0	0	0	0	0	2	0	0	0	0	1	1	0	0	0
eyelids	25	.7174	3.6797	45.7	3	5	0	3	8	3	2	1	6	2	1	2	0	0	0	8	0	0	0	0	2	1	1	2	0
eyepiece	18	.1444	.9256	39.7	0	0	2	3	9	0	1	3	5	0	0	0	0	0	0	13	0	0	0	0	0	0	0	0	0
eyes	2303	.8397	389.32	65.9	398	414	230	330	520	218	164	29	885	62	32	341	8	38	28	162	28	26	16	3	344	199	29	102	0
Eyes	29	.1877	2.0908	43.2	18	0	1	1	8	1	0	0	27	0	0	0	0	0	0	0	0	0	0	0	2	0	0	0	0
eyeshade	2	.0000	.0914	29.6	0	0	0	2	0	0	0	0	2	0	0	0	0	0	0	0	0	0	0	0	0	0	0	0	0
eyesight	13	.6843	1.8279	42.6	1	4	1	0	4	2	1	0	3	2	1	1	0	0	0	2	0	0	1	0	1	1	0	1	0
eyesore	4	.2399	.3011	34.8	0	0	0	1	3	0	0	0	3	1	0	0	0	0	0	0	0	0	0	0	0	0	0	0	0
eyestrain	2	.2160	.1362	31.3	0	0	0	0	1	0	1	0	1	0	0	0	0	0	0	1	0	0	0	0	0	0	0	0	0
eyewitness	4	.2399	.3011	34.8	0	0	0	2	0	2	0	0	3	1	0	0	0	0	0	0	0	0	0	0	0	0	0	0	0
eying	5	.3313	.4088	36.1	0	0	0	0	3	1	1	0	2	0	0	2	0	0	0	0	0	0	0	0	1	0	0	0	0
eyrie	2	.0000	.0243	23.9	0	0	0	2	0	0	0	0	0	0	0	0	0	0	0	0	0	0	0	0	0	0	0	2	0
Ezekiel	3	.3780	.2436	33.9	0	0	1	0	1	0	1	0	0	0	0	1	0	0	0	0	1	0	0	0	0	1	0	0	0
Ezra	3	.0000	.0365	25.6	0	0	0	0	0	0	0	3	0	0	0	0	0	0	0	0	0	0	0	0	0	0	0	3	0
f	249	.4637	24.367	53.9	26	47	47	61	36	21	10	1	12	18	1	0	74	2	122	5	5	0	1	1	0	1	0	7	0
F	544	.6475	71.604	58.5	61	126	97	64	65	55	72	4	15	14	5	2	100	4	3	82	211	0	26	4	0	11	47	20	0
F**	2	.0000	.0290	24.6	0	0	0	0	2	0	0	0	0	0	0	0	0	0	0	0	0	0	0	0	0	2	0	0	0
F-major	3	.0000	.0243	23.8	0	0	2	1	0	0	0	0	0	0	0	0	0	0	0	0	3	0	0	0	0	0	0	0	0
f-p	2	.2446	.1084	30.3	0	0	0	1	1	0	0	0	0	0	0	0	0	0	1	0	1	0	0	0	0	0	0	0	0
F-1	3	.0000	.0076	18.8	0	0	0	0	3	0	0	0	0	0	0	0	0	0	0	0	0	0	0	3	0	0	0	0	0
F-104A	2	.0000	.0299	24.8	0	0	0	2	0	0	0	0	0	0	0	0	2	0	0	0	0	0	0	0	0	0	0	0	0
F-106	2	.0000	.0290	24.6	2	0	0	0	0	0	0	0	0	0	0	0	0	0	0	0	0	0	0	0	0	2	0	0	0
F's	3	.1200	.1302	31.1	0	0	0	1	0	0	2	0	1	2	0	0	0	0	0	0	0	0	0	0	0	0	0	0	0
fa	23	.0164	.2941	34.7	3	9	2	4	3	2	0	0	1	0	0	0	0	0	0	0	22	0	0	0	0	0	0	0	0
FAA	3	.0000	.0365	25.6	0	0	0	0	0	0	0	3	0	0	0	0	0	0	0	0	0	0	0	0	0	0	0	3	0
Faber's	2	.2443	.1130	30.5	0	0	0	0	1	0	1	0	0	0	0	1	0	0	0	0	0	0	0	0	1	0	0	0	0
fable	37	.4111	3.4743	45.4	6	7	0	6	3	12	2	1	12	10	0	13	0	0	0	0	0	0	0	0	0	1	0	1	0
fabled	6	.4196	.5417	37.3	1	1	1	1	1	0	0	1	0	0	0	0	0	1	0	0	0	0	0	0	0	1	1	3	0
fables	27	.5009	2.9834	44.7	3	0	0	1	5	17	1	0	10	4	0	9	0	1	0	0	0	0	0	0	1	0	0	2	0
Fables	2	.1698	.1133	30.5	1	0	0	0	0	1	0	0	1	0	0	0	0	0	0	0	0	0	0	0	0	0	1	0	0
Fabre	6	.3577	.4870	36.9	0	0	0	4	2	0	0	0	0	0	0	0	0	0	0	4	0	0	0	0	0	0	1	1	0
fabric	212	.1400	6.5750	48.2	0	1	3	6	26	69	104	3	0	3	0	1	3	2	1	0	2	6	185	0	1	1	3	4	0
fabric-to-fabric	2	.0000	.0064	18.1	0	0	0	0	0	0	2	0	0	0	0	0	0	0	0	0	0	0	2	0	0	0	0	0	0
fabricate	3	.0437	.0743	28.7	1	0	0	0	0	0	2	0	1	0	0	0	0	0	0	0	0	0	0	2	0	0	0	0	0
fabricated	7	.4868	.7337	38.7	0	0	1	0	4	1	1	0	1	0	0	0	0	1	0	0	0	0	0	0	0	1	2	2	0
fabrication	3	.3390	.2450	33.9	1	0	0	0	1	0	0	1	1	0	0	0	0	0	0	0	0	0	0	0	0	0	1	1	0
fabrics	117	.0807	2.5373	44.0	2	0	6	2	6	31	67	3	3	0	0	0	3	9	0	1	0	0	96	0	0	0	3	2	0
Fabritius	4	.2003	.1916	32.8	0	0	0	0	3	1	0	0	0	0	0	3	0	0	0	0	0	0	0	0	0	0	1	0	0
Fabry	3	.0000	.0322	25.1	0	0	0	0	0	0	3	0	0	0	0	3	0	0	0	0	0	0	0	0	0	0	0	0	0
FABRY	13	.0000	.1395	31.4	0	0	0	0	0	0	13	0	0	0	0	13	0	0	0	0	0	0	0	0	0	0	0	0	0
fabulous	19	.6132	2.4201	43.8	1	0	1	8	3	2	1	3	2	0	1	1	0	6	0	0	0	0	0	0	0	4	1	4	0
fabulously	2	.2285	.1129	30.5	0	0	0	0	2	0	0	0	0	0	0	0	0	1	0	0	0	0	0	0	0	0	1	0	0
facade	3	.3756	.2468	33.9	0	0	0	1	0	0	2	0	0	0	0	1	0	1	0	0	0	0	0	0	0	0	1	0	0
facades	3	.1735	.1580	32.0	0	0	0	1	1	1	0	0	1	0	1	0	0	1	0	0	0	0	0	0	0	0	0	0	0
face	1629	.8962	290.91	64.6	261	274	168	178	392	153	168	35	581	54	20	197	38	46	18	46	20	11	41	29	243	133	51	101	0
Face	35	.3778	3.0824	44.9	24	0	2	0	0	6	1	2	11	0	1	0	0	0	0	0	0	0	0	0	20	1	0	2	0
faced	130	.8325	21.760	53.4	13	16	22	18	29	21	10	1	36	2	1	4	1	28	0	5	2	0	7	1	13	12	9	9	0
faceless	3	.2239	.1775	32.5	0	0	0	0	1	2	0	0	0	0	0	0	0	2	0	1	0	0	0	0	0	0	0	0	0
faceplate	8	.1237	.3341	35.2	0	3	0	0	5	0	0	0	3	0	0	0	0	0	0	0	0	0	0	4	0	0	0	1	0
faces	351	.9115	63.529	58.0	50	40	63	48	80	27	25	18	83	10	2	34	51	20	4	32	7	4	1	2	43	29	10	19	0

7G extraction
3A extractive
9F extracurricular
XH Extraordinary
8G extraordinary**
9R extrapolate
8C extrapolating
7H extrapolation
7H extrapolations
9Q extrasensory
3Q extravagance
7R extravehicular
XP Extreme
8Q extremist
6A extricated
8R extricating
7Q extrudes
8M extrusion-type
9J exuberantly
7Q exudations
7N exult
7D exultingly
7D Exundas
5H eye-blinking
9Q eye-filling
7N eye-lashes
XR eye-opening
5A eye-piece
7N eye-reach
3P eye-section
3F eye-sore
6K eye-spacing
7H eye-twisting
8B eye-witnesses
7R Eyebrow
6H eyecup
7R eyefilling
5N eyelash
8D eyelike
9D eyes'
7A Eyes'
8D eyeshine
8R eyetalian
5A eyewitnesses
9D eyne
6R eyries
XR Ezra's
6E E2
6E E6
7J F-A
5A f-a-m-i-s-h-e-d
7E f-h
3D F-o-r-
XR F-104
9E f/N
XH f/7
3A fzz
6R f'r
3B f's
3A fa-tee-gay
6R FA'S
6R fab
9R Fabbio
9B Fabian's
8R Fabians
8R Fabians'
9Q Fabius
6H Fabre's
5P Fabricants
5P Fabricato
6E FAC
3P FACE
9M face-planing
6R facedown
5B facere
3P Faces

Word Type	F	D	U	SFI	3 Gr 3	4 Gr 4	5 Gr 5	6 Gr 6	7 Gr 7	8 Gr 8	9 Gr 9	X UnGr	A Read	B Eng & Gr	C Comp	D Lit	E Math	F Soc Stud	G Spell	H Sci	J Music	K Art	L Home Ec	M Shop	N Lib F	P Lib NF	Q Lib Ref	R Mag	S Rel
facet	3	.1927	.1491	31.7	0	0	0	2	0	0	1	0	0	0	0	0	0	0	0	1	0	0	0	0	0	0	0	2	0
facetiously	2	.2442	.1134	30.5	0	0	0	0	0	2	0	0	0	1	0	0	0	0	0	0	0	0	0	0	0	0	0	1	0
facets	7	.3664	.5656	37.5	0	0	0	4	1	0	1	1	0	0	1	0	0	0	0	4	2	0	0	0	0	0	0	0	0
facial	22	.6436	2.8724	44.6	1	1	2	1	4	7	5	1	2	6	3	0	0	0	1	1	2	2	2	0	0	0	1	2	0
facilitate	5	.4862	.5004	37.0	0	0	0	0	1	1	2	1	0	1	0	0	0	0	0	0	1	0	0	1	0	0	1	1	0
facilitated	2	.2401	.1133	30.5	0	0	1	0	0	1	0	0	0	0	0	0	0	0	0	0	0	0	0	0	0	1	1	0	0
facilities	49	.6854	6.8036	48.3	5	0	5	2	13	7	14	3	1	0	0	0	0	7	0	3	1	0	4	2	1	8	8	14	0
facility	9	.4066	.7726	38.9	0	0	0	2	2	0	4	1	0	0	0	1	0	0	0	0	4	0	0	0	0	0	1	3	0
facing	178	.6057	22.307	53.5	26	18	18	14	41	14	44	3	27	3	1	9	2	12	1	25	14	0	45	3	7	11	9	9	0
Facing	3	.2359	.1459	31.6	0	0	0	0	0	1	2	0	0	0	0	0	0	0	0	0	0	0	2	1	0	0	0	0	0
facings	21	.0500	.2883	34.6	0	0	0	0	3	3	15	0	0	0	0	1	0	0	0	0	0	0	19	0	0	1	0	0	0
facsimile	2	.2351	.1166	30.7	0	0	0	0	1	1	0	0	0	0	0	0	0	1	0	0	0	0	0	0	0	0	0	1	0
fact	925	.9498	173.52	62.4	57	82	101	135	238	136	134	42	152	65	15	37	85	117	14	117	19	9	10	6	39	67	79	94	0
fact-finding	4	.2090	.2014	33.0	0	1	0	1	0	0	1	1	0	0	0	0	0	0	0	0	0	0	0	0	0	0	1	3	0
faction	4	.3359	.2989	34.8	0	0	2	0	0	1	1	0	0	0	0	0	0	1	0	0	0	0	0	0	0	0	2	1	0
factions	5	.0824	.1675	32.2	0	0	0	0	2	2	1	0	1	0	0	0	0	0	0	0	0	0	0	0	0	0	0	4	0
facto	2	.0000	.0389	25.9	0	2	0	0	0	0	0	0	0	0	0	0	0	2	0	0	0	0	0	0	0	0	0	0	0
factor	460	.3434	35.546	55.5	38	49	51	69	97	87	65	4	4	2	0	1	390	6	4	12	3	0	5	1	1	6	16	9	0
factor-product	2	.0000	.0299	24.8	0	0	0	0	0	2	0	0	0	0	0	0	2	0	0	0	0	0	0	0	0	0	0	0	0
factored	15	.0000	.2245	33.5	0	0	0	0	3	9	3	0	0	0	0	0	15	0	0	0	0	0	0	0	0	0	0	0	0
factories	413	.5041	44.826	56.5	67	48	100	90	58	33	17	0	17	3	1	3	2	298	0	24	2	0	0	4	0	23	31	5	0
factoring	10	.0000	.1497	31.8	0	0	0	0	3	2	5	0	0	0	0	0	10	0	0	0	0	0	0	0	0	0	0	0	0
factorization	53	.0000	.7933	39.0	0	0	6	22	19	4	2	0	0	0	0	0	53	0	0	0	0	0	0	0	0	0	0	0	0
factorizations	30	.0000	.4491	36.5	0	0	1	10	17	2	0	0	0	0	0	0	30	0	0	0	0	0	0	0	0	0	0	0	0
factors	545	.3790	45.656	56.6	41	64	66	102	123	77	60	12	4	1	0	1	443	8	0	35	10	0	6	4	0	4	24	5	0
factory	237	.8415	39.917	56.0	51	25	33	35	43	24	15	11	31	6	5	9	3	96	6	8	1	1	1	2	9	20	16	23	0
factory's	2	.2408	.1204	30.8	0	1	0	0	0	1	0	0	0	0	0	0	0	1	0	0	0	0	0	0	0	1	0	0	0
facts	519	.8430	87.627	59.4	65	88	65	48	102	60	69	22	104	79	10	12	139	48	7	48	0	2	5	7	7	11	21	19	0
Facts	6	.4316	.5770	37.6	0	1	1	1	0	0	1	2	1	1	0	0	0	2	0	0	0	0	0	0	0	0	0	2	0
factual	19	.5047	2.0623	43.1	1	0	3	2	4	1	8	0	5	2	4	1	0	2	0	0	0	0	1	0	1	1	2	0	0
faculties	7	.5064	.7424	38.7	0	0	0	0	4	2	1	0	0	0	0	1	0	1	0	0	0	0	0	0	1	1	0	3	0
faculty	22	.5154	2.3757	43.8	0	0	0	6	4	4	8	0	1	0	0	0	2	0	2	1	0	0	0	0	1	1	2	12	0
Faculty	6	.3716	.4872	36.9	1	0	2	1	0	0	0	2	0	0	0	0	0	0	0	0	0	0	0	0	0	3	1	2	0
fad	4	.2657	.2272	33.6	0	0	0	0	1	1	2	0	0	0	0	0	0	0	0	0	1	0	2	0	0	0	1	0	0
fade	42	.7435	6.3901	48.1	2	4	4	5	15	9	1	2	14	1	0	4	0	4	0	4	3	0	3	0	2	0	2	5	0
faded	63	.6966	9.1008	49.6	10	12	2	11	16	7	4	1	24	2	0	13	0	2	0	1	0	1	0	0	9	7	1	3	0
fades	9	.6457	1.1901	40.8	0	0	3	1	2	2	1	0	1	0	0	0	0	0	0	1	1	0	1	0	1	1	2	1	0
fading	40	.6050	5.0322	47.0	1	0	3	4	19	8	5	0	7	0	0	17	0	3	1	0	0	0	2	0	3	3	1	3	0
fads	10	.2239	.5960	37.8	0	0	1	0	3	2	4	0	3	0	0	0	0	2	0	0	0	0	4	0	0	0	0	1	0
Faggett	5	.0000	.2284	33.6	0	0	0	0	5	0	0	0	5	0	0	0	0	0	0	0	0	0	0	0	0	0	0	0	0
faggots	12	.2845	.7698	38.9	0	0	8	2	2	0	0	0	0	0	0	8	0	0	0	0	0	0	0	0	2	2	0	0	0
fagot	2	.0000	.0290	24.6	2	0	0	0	0	0	0	0	0	0	0	0	0	0	0	0	0	0	0	0	0	2	0	0	0
Fahrenheit	61	.6912	8.6818	49.4	2	12	9	11	11	13	3	0	11	0	0	0	12	3	0	21	0	0	1	2	3	0	7	1	0
fail	83	.8596	14.266	51.5	5	10	7	6	25	13	17	0	20	7	0	8	1	9	2	7	2	0	1	0	3	6	7	10	0
failed	194	.8169	31.903	55.0	12	13	36	31	46	29	23	4	45	9	1	11	0	40	2	7	4	0	0	0	15	20	23	17	0
failing	14	.6666	1.9293	42.9	1	0	2	0	5	3	2	1	3	1	0	1	1	2	0	0	0	0	0	0	0	1	1	4	0
failings	5	.1668	.2098	33.2	0	0	0	0	4	1	0	0	0	0	0	4	0	0	0	0	0	0	0	0	0	0	0	1	0
fails	24	.7979	3.8391	45.8	1	0	2	1	10	4	4	2	2	1	0	2	1	2	0	2	1	0	1	0	1	4	5	2	0
failure	71	.8495	12.026	50.8	2	5	8	7	24	12	12	1	8	7	3	5	0	8	0	5	2	1	1	0	3	10	9	9	0
failures	12	.6438	1.5837	42.0	0	1	3	2	5	0	0	1	1	0	0	0	0	1	1	1	1	0	0	0	2	0	1	4	0
fain	11	.2642	.7056	38.5	0	0	0	2	3	1	5	0	2	0	0	7	0	0	0	0	2	0	0	0	0	0	0	0	0
faint	117	.8477	19.937	53.0	13	13	14	13	41	10	6	7	44	3	1	11	0	2	1	13	7	0	1	0	12	8	5	9	0
fainted	17	.5398	2.0092	43.0	1	5	3	5	1	0	1	1	7	0	0	1	0	1	0	0	0	0	0	0	5	1	0	2	0
fainter	20	.5991	2.5635	44.1	0	3	2	7	7	0	0	1	7	0	0	2	0	0	0	7	1	0	0	0	2	0	1	0	0
faintest	7	.5731	.8382	39.2	0	0	0	0	4	3	0	0	1	1	0	0	0	1	0	0	1	0	0	0	1	0	2	0	0
fainthearted	3	.2279	.2143	33.3	1	1	0	0	0	0	0	1	2	0	0	0	0	0	0	0	0	0	0	0	0	0	0	1	0
fainting	6	.3315	.5003	37.0	0	1	1	2	1	1	0	0	3	0	0	0	0	0	0	0	0	0	1	0	2	0	0	0	0
Fainting	2	.0000	.0219	23.4	0	0	2	0	0	0	0	0	0	2	0	0	0	0	0	0	0	0	0	0	0	0	0	0	0
faintly	28	.6103	3.6415	45.6	0	5	6	4	6	4	2	1	12	0	1	6	0	0	0	1	0	0	0	0	5	0	1	2	0
faints	3	.3759	.2474	33.9	0	0	0	0	0	1	2	0	0	1	0	1	0	0	0	1	0	0	0	0	0	0	0	0	0
fair	402	.8585	69.056	58.4	90	54	43	47	68	41	48	11	112	27	1	54	10	34	15	16	29	0	4	0	38	31	3	28	0
Fair	50	.7687	7.8443	48.9	12	8	13	3	6	6	2	0	18	2	0	0	10	4	0	0	1	0	0	1	4	6	2	2	0
FAIR	2	.0000	.0914	29.6	0	2	0	0	0	0	0	0	2	0	0	0	0	0	0	0	0	0	0	0	0	0	0	0	0
fair-lined	2	.0000	.0219	23.4	0	0	2	0	0	0	0	0	0	2	0	0	0	0	0	0	0	0	0	0	0	0	0	0	0
Fairbanks	8	.5625	.9795	39.9	1	0	3	3	0	0	1	0	3	0	0	0	1	2	0	0	0	0	0	0	0	1	0	1	0
Fairchild	2	.0000	.0914	29.6	0	0	2	0	0	0	0	0	2	0	0	0	0	0	0	0	0	0	0	0	0	0	0	0	0
faire	3	.0000	.0322	25.1	0	0	0	0	0	3	0	0	0	0	0	3	0	0	0	0	0	0	0	0	0	0	0	0	0
fairer	6	.3998	.5542	37.4	2	0	1	1	2	0	0	0	2	0	0	1	0	0	0	1	2	0	0	0	0	0	0	0	0
fairest	9	.3529	.7625	38.8	0	0	0	2	2	1	4	0	3	0	0	4	0	1	0	0	0	0	0	0	0	1	0	0	0
Fairfax	5	.4446	.4943	36.9	1	0	3	0	0	1	0	0	1	0	0	1	0	2	0	0	1	0	0	0	0	0	0	0	0
Fairfax's	2	.2297	.1135	30.6	0	0	1	0	0	1	0	0	0	0	0	1	0	1	0	0	0	0	0	0	0	0	0	0	0
Fairfield	9	.2732	.6229	37.9	5	2	1	0	0	1	0	0	1	0	0	0	2	6	0	0	0	0	0	0	0	0	0	0	0
fairgrounds	2	.0665	.0708	28.5	0	0	1	0	0	1	0	0	1	0	1	0	0	0	0	0	0	0	0	0	0	0	0	0	0
fairies	39	.6610	5.3963	47.3	11	16	7	4	0	0	1	0	15	1	1	6	0	0	0	2	4	0	0	0	0	9	1	0	0
Fairlane	2	.0000	.0243	23.9	0	0	0	0	2	0	0	0	0	0	0	0	0	0	0	0	0	0	0	0	0	0	0	2	0
fairly	167	.8911	29.611	54.7	13	18	23	24	40	22	20	7	33	8	1	13	3	20	2	28	10	0	4	0	9	8	13	15	0
fairness	7	.4874	.7834	38.9	0	1	0	3	2	1	0	0	4	1	0	0	0	0	0	0	0	0	0	0	0	1	0	1	0
fairs	14	.6398	1.8572	42.7	4	2	3	0	2	2	1	0	2	0	0	0	0	3	0	1	0	0	0	0	2	3	2	1	0
Fairview	11	.1259	.4553	36.6	10	0	1	0	0	0	0	0	0	0	0	0	1	10	0	0	0	0	0	0	0	0	0	0	0
Fairweather	3	.2444	.1728	32.4	0	2	1	0	0	0	0	0	0	0	0	0	2	0	0	0	1	0	0	0	0	0	0	0	0
fairy	71	.8301	11.884	50.7	24	16	10	9	5	6	1	0	29	5	3	6	0	2	2	2	5	1	0	0	3	3	6	4	0
Fairy	32	.3294	2.5243	44.0	11	1	11	7	1	0	1	0	10	0	0	0	0	1	0	0	13	0	0	0	8	0	0	0	0
fairy-tale	4	.2333	.2229	33.5	0	0	3	1	0	0	0	0	0	0	0	0	0	0	0	0	1	0	0	0	0	3	0	0	0
Fairy's	2	.0000	.0234	23.7	0	0	0	2	0	0	0	0	0	0	0	0	0	0	0	0	0	0	0	0	2	0	0	0	0
fairyland	6	.3876	.5822	37.7	3	1	0	0	2	0	0	0	4	1	0	1	0	0	0	0	0	0	0	0	0	0	0	0	0
faith	124	.2582	7.8725	49.0	10	11	7	9	21	30	30	6	21	3	0	16	0	12	1	2	4	0	1	0	10	9	21	15	9
Faith	5	.1848	.2301	33.6	1	0	0	0	0	4	0	0	0	1	0	0	0	0	0	0	0	0	0	0	0	0	0	4	0
faithful	50	.3030	3.6829	45.7	3	4	2	10	10	13	8	0	12	3	0	3	0	7	1	3	4	0	0	1	4	3	2	4	3
Faithful	2	.2130	.1056	30.2	0	0	0	1	0	0	1	0	0	0	0	0	0	0	1	1	0	0	0	0	0	0	0	0	0
faithfully	20	.7895	3.1650	45.0	0	4	4	2	6	2	1	1	1	1	0	2	0	4	0	1	2	0	1	0	2	2	1	3	0
faithfulness	2	.2387	.1089	30.4	0	0	0	2	0	0	0	0	0	0	0	0	0	0	0	0	1	0	0	0	1	0	0	0	0
faithless	2	.2412	.1091	30.4	0	0	0	0	1	0	1	0	0	0	0	1	0	0	1	0	0	0	0	0	0	0	0	0	0
faiths	8	.4919	.8376	39.2	0	1	4	1	0	2	0	0	1	0	0	0	0	1	0	0	3	0	0	0	0	1	1	1	0
fake	5	.4509	.5024	37.0	0	0	0	0	2	1	1	1	1	1	0	0	0	0	0	2	0	0	0	0	0	0	0	1	0
faked	3	.1250	.1342	31.3	0	0	0	0	2	1	0	0	1	0	0	0	0	0	0	0	0	0	0	0	2	0	0	0	0
fakes	2	.1698	.1133	30.5	0	0	0	0	1	1	0	0	1	0	0	0	0	0	0	0	0	0	0	0	0	0	1	0	0

7P facetious	7G faeger	3B fahg	3Q fair-haired	9D fairies'	8R Faith's
6E Factor	XB Faerie	8M Fahnestock	3Q fair-sized	3A fairy-land	7P faithlessness
4R factory-built	5P Faeroe	8A faience	XR fair-skinned	4D fairy-lanterns	7F Faiyum
6J factotum	8Q Faesulae	7N faileth	7A fair-to-middlers	3A fairy-story	7R Fajen
6P FAD	6R Fagaras	7N failin'	7Q fair-to-middling	6A fairy-tales	7D Fake
8A faddist	6R Fagin	3P fainteth	8R fair's	6A fairy's	
7D FADE	8A fagots	7H faintness	9M faired	5P fairytale	
8B fadom	6J fah-yah	9D fair-flowing	6A fairhaired	5A faith's	

Word Type	F	D	U	SFI	3 Gr 3	4 Gr 4	5 Gr 5	6 Gr 6	7 Gr 7	8 Gr 8	9 Gr 9	X UnGr	A Read	B Eng & Gr	C Comp	D Lit	E Math	F Soc Stud	G Spell	H Sci	J Music	K Art	L Home Ec	M Shop	N Lib F	P Lib NF	Q Lib Ref	R Mag	S Rel
faking	2	.2433	.1158	30.6	0	0	0	0	1	0	0	1	0	0	0	0	0	0	0	0	0	0	0	0	0	1	0	1	0
fakirs	2	.2411	.1091	30.4	0	1	0	0	1	0	0	0	0	0	0	1	0	0	0	0	1	0	0	0	0	0	0	0	0
Falal	5	.0000	.2284	33.6	0	0	0	0	5	0	0	0	5	0	0	0	0	0	0	0	0	0	0	0	0	0	0	0	0
falcon	14	.1906	1.0145	40.1	0	0	0	13	1	0	0	0	13	0	0	0	0	0	0	0	0	0	0	0	1	0	0	0	0
Falcon	11	.3869	1.0650	40.3	2	0	5	2	2	0	0	0	7	0	0	0	0	0	0	0	0	0	0	0	0	2	0	2	0
falcon's	4	.2386	.2998	34.8	0	0	0	3	1	0	0	0	3	0	0	0	0	0	0	0	0	0	0	0	0	0	1	0	0
falconry	2	.2160	.1362	31.3	0	0	0	2	0	0	0	0	1	0	0	0	0	0	0	1	0	0	0	0	0	0	0	0	0
falcons	7	.3816	.6817	38.3	1	0	0	5	1	0	0	0	5	0	0	0	0	0	0	0	0	0	0	0	0	1	1	0	0
Falcons	2	.0000	.0243	23.9	0	0	0	0	0	2	0	0	0	0	0	0	0	0	0	0	0	0	0	0	0	0	0	2	0
Faline	2	.0000	.0914	29.6	0	0	0	2	0	0	0	0	2	0	0	0	0	0	0	0	0	0	0	0	0	0	0	0	0
Falkland	3	.0000	.0314	25.0	2	0	0	0	1	0	0	0	0	0	0	0	0	0	0	0	0	0	0	0	0	0	3	0	0
fall	824	.9341	152.49	61.8	179	141	113	100	144	73	48	26	224	23	10	67	15	77	20	146	35	2	5	5	39	63	37	56	0
Fall	7	.4284	.6439	38.1	1	0	4	0	1	1	0	0	0	0	0	1	0	2	0	0	0	0	0	0	0	1	3	0	0
fallacy	14	.1868	.6374	38.0	0	0	0	0	3	0	11	0	0	11	0	0	0	0	0	0	0	0	0	0	0	0	3	0	0
Fallbrook	2	.0000	.0299	24.8	0	0	0	0	0	2	0	0	0	0	0	0	2	0	0	0	0	0	0	0	0	0	0	0	0
fallen	176	.8791	30.941	54.9	27	33	20	21	39	19	9	8	63	9	1	17	2	15	0	16	4	1	0	1	13	17	3	14	0
Fallen	2	.0000	.0914	29.6	0	2	0	0	0	0	0	0	2	0	0	0	0	0	0	0	0	0	0	0	0	0	0	0	0
faller	4	.0000	.0778	28.9	0	0	4	0	0	0	0	0	0	0	0	0	0	4	0	0	0	0	0	0	0	0	0	0	0
falling	239	.8993	42.807	56.3	38	28	31	41	47	33	16	5	73	9	4	24	1	18	5	41	6	1	2	0	19	14	13	9	0
Fallopian	3	.0000	.0591	27.7	0	0	0	0	0	0	3	0	0	0	0	0	0	0	0	3	0	0	0	0	0	0	0	0	0
fallout	7	.1941	.3707	35.7	0	0	0	0	1	1	0	5	0	0	0	0	0	0	0	6	0	0	0	0	0	0	1	0	0
fallow	8	.5616	.9414	39.7	2	0	2	0	3	1	0	0	1	2	0	2	0	1	0	0	0	0	0	0	0	1	1	0	0
Fallows	4	.0000	.0486	26.9	0	0	0	0	4	0	0	0	0	0	0	0	0	0	0	0	0	0	0	0	0	0	0	4	0
falls	329	.8614	56.627	57.5	60	52	73	48	43	25	21	7	52	10	6	10	4	64	3	100	20	2	2	2	1	18	26	9	0
Falls	49	.4508	4.7496	46.8	14	3	17	6	5	1	0	3	4	0	0	0	0	4	0	2	0	0	0	0	2	1	18	18	0
Falorie	2	.0000	.0162	22.1	0	2	0	0	0	0	0	0	0	0	0	0	0	0	0	0	2	0	0	0	0	0	0	0	0
false	225	.6052	28.293	54.5	13	38	27	26	41	46	31	3	21	11	0	5	137	7	1	10	5	1	1	0	5	5	9	7	0
false-hearted	2	.0000	.0162	22.1	0	0	1	1	0	0	0	0	0	0	0	0	0	0	0	0	2	0	0	0	0	0	0	0	0
falsehood	5	.3796	.4256	36.3	1	0	0	0	3	0	1	0	1	0	0	2	0	0	0	0	0	0	1	0	0	1	0	0	0
falsehoods	2	.2346	.1166	30.7	0	0	0	1	1	0	0	0	0	0	0	0	0	0	0	1	0	0	0	0	0	0	0	1	0
falsetto	2	.0000	.0162	22.1	0	0	0	0	1	1	0	0	0	0	0	0	0	0	0	0	2	0	0	0	0	0	0	0	0
falsified	2	.1948	.1250	31.0	0	0	0	0	1	1	0	0	1	0	0	0	0	0	0	0	0	0	0	0	0	1	0	0	0
Falstaff	3	.3244	.2330	33.7	0	0	0	0	1	2	0	0	1	0	0	0	0	0	1	0	1	0	0	0	0	0	0	0	0
falter	2	.1698	.1133	30.5	0	0	0	0	1	0	1	0	1	0	0	0	0	0	0	0	0	0	0	0	0	0	1	0	0
faltered	11	.5665	1.3286	41.2	0	1	1	3	2	4	0	0	3	0	0	2	0	1	0	0	0	0	0	0	3	1	0	1	0
faltering	4	.3310	.2973	34.7	0	0	0	0	2	1	1	0	0	0	0	2	0	1	0	0	0	0	0	0	0	1	0	0	0
fame	85	.7670	13.210	51.2	5	6	10	16	18	15	12	3	22	5	0	7	0	3	1	0	13	1	0	0	3	10	13	7	0
Fame	4	.4502	.4024	36.0	0	0	0	1	0	1	2	0	1	1	0	0	0	1	0	0	0	0	0	0	0	0	0	1	0
famed	23	.6718	3.1367	45.0	0	1	6	6	5	1	4	0	1	1	1	1	0	2	0	0	2	0	0	0	0	3	5	7	0
familar	2	.1362	.0684	28.3	0	0	0	1	0	0	1	0	0	0	1	0	1	0	0	0	0	0	0	0	0	0	0	0	0
familiar	406	.8711	70.333	58.5	33	33	47	58	113	61	50	11	55	41	25	24	18	18	9	49	58	8	5	10	15	14	36	21	0
familiarity	13	.6268	1.6678	42.2	0	1	1	0	5	2	4	0	1	4	0	0	0	0	0	1	1	0	1	0	0	1	3	1	0
familiarize	3	.2074	.1511	31.8	0	0	0	0	3	0	0	0	0	2	0	0	0	0	0	0	0	0	0	0	0	1	0	0	0
families	394	.8418	66.364	58.2	76	48	49	42	77	57	39	6	54	14	2	7	4	148	4	19	23	1	18	0	9	28	30	32	1
Families	2	.1926	.0867	29.4	0	0	0	0	1	0	1	0	0	0	0	0	0	0	0	0	0	0	1	0	0	0	1	0	0
family	1768	.8239	292.91	64.7	309	352	206	183	303	202	167	46	476	86	24	103	64	217	16	100	55	9	136	4	70	176	102	118	12
Family	28	.6657	3.8091	45.8	1	4	2	2	7	8	3	1	4	1	0	5	0	2	2	1	1	3	1	0	0	1	1	6	0
family's	40	.5205	4.5012	46.5	5	7	4	4	8	9	1	2	13	0	0	1	1	6	0	0	1	2	10	0	0	2	2	2	0
famine	5	.5387	.5729	37.6	0	1	0	3	1	0	0	0	1	0	0	0	0	0	0	0	0	0	0	0	1	1	1	1	0
famines	5	.4845	.5126	37.1	0	0	0	4	1	0	0	0	0	0	0	0	0	2	1	0	0	0	0	0	1	0	0	1	0
famished	8	.3811	.6909	38.4	0	0	1	2	1	4	0	0	2	0	1	4	0	0	0	0	0	0	0	0	1	0	0	0	0
famous	717	.8713	124.65	61.0	91	118	120	118	132	83	40	15	161	47	7	25	15	134	14	34	93	16	2	2	11	62	68	26	0
Famous	2	.1733	.1149	30.6	1	0	0	0	0	0	1	0	1	1	0	0	0	0	0	0	0	0	0	0	0	0	0	0	0
fan	72	.7416	10.957	50.4	18	8	13	11	10	6	5	1	24	1	0	3	2	0	0	17	2	0	0	0	3	4	6	10	0
Fan	3	.0000	.0591	27.7	0	0	0	0	0	3	0	0	0	0	0	0	0	0	0	3	0	0	0	0	0	0	0	0	0
Fan-Tan	4	.0000	.1827	32.6	0	0	4	0	0	0	0	0	4	0	0	0	0	0	0	0	0	0	0	0	0	0	0	0	0
fan-shaped	2	.1948	.1250	31.0	0	0	0	0	2	0	0	0	1	0	0	0	0	0	0	0	0	0	0	0	0	1	0	0	0
fanatic	2	.0000	.0389	25.9	0	0	0	0	0	1	1	0	0	0	0	0	0	2	0	0	0	0	0	0	0	0	0	0	0
fanatical	2	.0000	.0914	29.6	0	0	0	1	1	0	0	0	2	0	0	0	0	0	0	0	0	0	0	0	0	0	0	0	0
fanatics	3	.0000	.0365	25.6	0	0	0	0	3	0	0	0	0	0	0	0	0	0	0	0	0	0	0	0	0	0	0	3	0
fanbearers	2	.0000	.0914	29.6	0	0	0	0	2	0	0	0	2	0	0	0	0	0	0	0	0	0	0	0	0	0	0	0	0
fancied	11	.4372	1.0501	40.2	0	0	4	1	2	3	0	1	2	0	1	1	0	0	0	0	0	0	0	0	6	0	0	1	0
fancier	5	.4178	.4625	36.7	1	0	0	0	3	0	1	0	1	1	0	0	0	0	0	0	0	0	0	0	1	0	2	0	0
fancies	2	.1717	.1142	30.6	0	1	0	0	0	0	1	0	1	0	0	1	0	0	0	0	0	0	0	0	0	0	0	0	0
fanciest	2	.2440	.1132	30.5	0	0	0	0	1	0	1	0	0	0	0	1	0	0	0	0	0	0	0	0	0	0	0	1	0
fanciful	16	.5687	1.9245	42.8	0	5	2	1	4	2	0	2	4	4	0	0	0	0	0	1	0	1	0	0	0	1	4	1	0
fancy	103	.8002	16.694	52.2	15	13	10	17	30	6	9	3	37	3	1	16	0	3	3	3	1	0	0	1	15	9	1	10	0
fancy-dress	2	.0000	.0290	24.6	0	0	2	0	0	0	0	0	0	0	0	0	0	0	0	0	0	0	0	0	0	2	0	0	0
fandango	3	.2365	.1616	32.1	0	0	0	0	0	3	0	0	0	0	0	0	0	0	0	0	1	0	0	0	0	0	2	0	0
Faneuil	8	.0496	.1911	32.8	0	0	0	0	1	7	0	0	1	0	0	0	0	0	0	0	0	0	0	0	0	0	7	0	0
Fanfani	3	.0000	.0314	25.0	0	0	0	0	0	3	0	0	0	0	0	0	0	0	0	0	0	0	0	0	0	0	3	0	0
fanfares	2	.0000	.0162	22.1	0	0	1	0	1	0	0	0	0	0	0	0	0	0	0	0	2	0	0	0	0	0	0	0	0
Fang	32	.0000	.3752	35.7	0	0	0	0	32	0	0	0	0	0	0	0	0	0	0	0	0	0	0	0	32	0	0	0	0
Fang's	4	.0000	.0469	26.7	0	0	0	0	4	0	0	0	0	0	0	0	0	0	0	0	0	0	0	0	4	0	0	0	0
fangs	23	.4132	2.1238	43.3	6	0	0	3	11	1	2	0	1	1	0	1	0	0	0	17	0	0	0	0	2	0	1	0	0
fanned	18	.6192	2.3542	43.7	4	2	2	3	6	1	0	0	6	0	0	4	0	1	0	1	0	0	0	0	0	2	2	2	0
Fannin	5	.0000	.0724	28.6	0	5	0	0	0	0	0	0	0	0	0	0	0	0	0	0	0	0	0	0	0	5	0	0	0
Fannin's	4	.2183	.2285	33.6	0	1	0	0	3	0	0	0	0	0	0	0	0	3	0	0	0	0	0	0	0	1	0	0	0
fanning	7	.4642	.7436	38.7	2	2	0	1	1	0	0	1	3	0	0	0	0	0	0	1	0	0	0	0	0	2	1	0	0
Fanny	19	.3871	1.6551	42.2	2	11	0	0	3	0	3	0	3	0	0	2	0	0	0	0	3	0	0	0	0	11	0	0	0
fans	79	.7188	11.652	50.7	12	12	5	20	18	7	5	0	22	3	1	0	1	2	2	5	0	0	0	1	1	17	2	22	0
Fantasia	6	.0000	.0485	26.9	0	0	0	5	0	0	1	0	0	0	0	0	0	0	0	0	6	0	0	0	0	0	0	0	0
fantasies	6	.4389	.5960	37.8	2	0	1	1	1	0	0	1	2	2	0	0	0	0	0	0	0	0	0	0	0	1	0	1	0
fantastic	58	.8082	9.4001	49.7	3	2	5	9	17	5	14	3	9	5	1	6	0	4	1	2	2	3	0	0	4	5	8	8	0
fantastically	4	.4809	.4076	36.1	0	0	0	0	2	1	0	1	0	0	0	1	0	0	0	1	0	0	0	0	0	1	0	1	0
fantasy	18	.6656	2.4791	43.9	1	0	1	5	3	3	3	2	5	2	0	3	1	0	0	0	1	1	0	0	0	2	0	3	0
far	2250	.9516	423.22	66.3	362	418	271	321	400	229	184	65	618	59	19	144	157	273	31	227	61	25	11	13	139	193	123	157	0
Far	82	.6533	11.094	50.5	6	12	7	14	21	15	7	0	9	0	0	0	1	45	0	4	3	1	0	0	6	5	5	3	0
FAR	2	.1972	.1262	31.0	1	1	0	0	0	0	0	0	1	0	0	0	1	0	0	0	0	0	0	0	0	0	0	0	0
far-away	26	.5659	3.1047	44.9	15	3	1	4	1	2	0	0	4	0	0	2	0	7	0	0	1	2	0	0	2	8	0	0	0
far-flung	6	.3567	.4852	36.9	0	0	0	0	2	2	1	1	0	0	0	0	0	4	0	0	0	0	0	0	0	0	1	1	0
far-off	47	.7708	7.3775	48.7	7	9	6	7	7	6	5	0	16	2	2	6	0	6	0	1	2	0	0	0	3	4	1	4	0
far-out	2	.0000	.0243	23.9	0	0	0	1	1	0	0	0	0	0	0	0	0	0	0	0	0	0	0	0	0	0	0	2	0

7D fakir
5P Falasha
8D falce
5A Falcon's
9D Falconbridge
8D Falcone's
6A falconer
8Q Falconer
7Q falconets
6J Falke
7A Fall-of-the-
7A Fall-of-the-leaf
7R fall-spawning
9H fall-winter
7Q fallacies
7R fallacious
6J Falling
6A falls'
7Q Falmouth
7D false-fronted
9D falsely
7D falseness
9F falsity
7R Falstaffian
3Q Falster
7D falters
5P Faluja
7R Famers
8A familiar-looking
7H familiaris
8A familiarly
7R family-life
5Q family-operated
XR family-owned
9F family-size
8K family-style
9E Family's
9B familys
6R Famine
7A famous-brand
6A famously
3K fan-like
3N fan-tail
8F fanatically
7D fanaticism
8J Fancy
7A fancy-play
6A fancying
7A Fand
7A Fand's
7D Fanelli
7R fanfare
6R fang
5N fangled
9H fanjet
4A Fanny's
9H fanshaped
5G fant
6J fantasia
9D fantasticoes
9J Fantasy
3P fanwise
6F Fao
4N Far-Off
7Q Far-Traveler
7H far-distant
5J far-fallen
9D far-famed
7P far-fetched
9H far-inks

Word Type	F	D	U	SFI	3 Gr 3	4 Gr 4	5 Gr 5	6 Gr 6	7 Gr 7	8 Gr 8	9 Gr 9	X UnGr	A Read	B Eng & Gr	C Comp	D Lit	E Math	F Soc Stud	G Spell	H Sci	J Music	K Art	L Home Ec	M Shop	N Lib F	P Lib NF	Q Lib Ref	R Mag	S Rel
far-ranging	3	.3125	.2347	33.7	0	0	0	1	1	1	0	0	1	0	0	0	0	0	0	1	1	0	0	0	0	0	0	0	0
far-reaching	17	.4919	1.8148	42.6	2	2	0	2	3	2	5	1	3	0	0	0	0	2	0	3	0	0	0	0	0	0	4	5	0
far-sighted	3	.1650	.1684	32.3	0	1	0	0	0	2	0	0	1	0	0	0	0	0	0	2	0	0	0	0	0	0	0	0	0
farad	4	.0000	.0101	20.0	0	0	0	0	0	4	0	0	0	0	0	0	0	0	0	0	0	0	0	4	0	0	0	0	0
Faraday	13	.2257	.7884	39.0	0	8	0	2	1	2	0	0	3	0	0	0	0	0	0	2	0	0	0	0	0	0	0	8	0
Faraday's	4	.2346	.2332	33.7	0	2	0	2	0	0	0	0	0	0	0	0	0	0	0	2	0	0	0	0	0	0	0	2	0
faraway	69	.8154	11.379	50.6	27	19	2	5	11	2	2	1	23	2	0	4	1	15	0	8	1	2	0	1	1	6	2	3	0
farce	4	.2248	.2112	33.2	0	0	0	1	1	0	2	0	0	0	0	0	0	0	0	0	1	0	0	0	0	0	0	3	0
Fardowners	4	.0000	.1827	32.6	0	0	0	0	4	0	0	0	4	0	0	0	0	0	0	0	0	0	0	0	0	0	0	0	0
fare	54	.6775	7.5014	48.8	5	12	9	10	6	3	8	1	10	2	0	14	5	2	0	0	9	0	0	0	1	4	2	5	0
fared	3	.3852	.2500	34.0	0	1	0	0	0	0	2	0	0	0	0	1	0	0	0	0	0	0	0	0	0	1	0	1	0
fares	3	.3569	.2619	34.2	0	0	1	0	0	2	0	0	1	0	0	0	1	1	0	0	0	0	0	0	0	0	0	0	0
farewell	48	.7361	7.1892	48.6	3	4	2	14	7	5	13	0	12	1	1	12	0	2	4	0	6	0	0	0	5	2	2	1	0
Farewell	3	.1983	.1396	31.4	0	0	1	1	0	0	1	0	0	0	0	0	0	0	0	0	2	0	0	0	0	0	0	1	0
farfetched	4	.2418	.2183	33.4	1	0	0	0	2	1	0	0	0	0	0	0	0	0	2	0	0	0	0	0	0	0	2	0	0
Farley	4	.0000	.1827	32.6	0	1	0	3	0	0	0	0	4	0	0	0	0	0	0	0	0	0	0	0	0	0	0	0	0
Farley's	2	.0000	.0914	29.6	0	0	0	2	0	0	0	0	2	0	0	0	0	0	0	0	0	0	0	0	0	0	0	0	0
farm	900	.8055	146.54	61.7	189	159	168	135	109	56	62	22	223	25	8	25	8	361	19	18	6	4	1	1	43	75	41	42	0
Farm	18	.5399	2.1442	43.3	4	1	3	2	0	3	3	2	8	0	0	0	0	3	0	0	0	0	0	0	3	1	0	3	0
farmed	31	.3331	2.5180	44.0	4	5	6	4	7	3	2	0	6	0	0	0	0	20	0	0	0	0	0	0	0	4	0	1	0
farmer	414	.8676	71.956	58.6	125	50	40	69	45	37	35	13	129	9	2	15	14	116	16	32	10	1	1	0	14	23	10	22	0
Farmer	46	.6097	5.8990	47.7	17	4	0	10	6	3	3	3	11	1	0	3	1	0	1	9	0	0	0	0	2	2	0	16	0
farmer's	71	.7522	10.962	50.4	31	11	7	7	4	5	3	3	27	1	0	3	0	9	6	10	3	0	0	0	0	9	2	1	0
Farmer's	2	.1717	.1142	30.6	0	0	0	0	1	0	1	0	1	0	0	1	0	0	0	0	0	0	0	0	0	0	0	0	0
farmers	750	.6455	100.86	60.0	124	122	136	174	82	65	20	27	104	2	2	7	2	465	7	32	7	2	0	0	5	43	44	27	1
Farmers	6	.3697	.4939	36.9	0	0	0	0	0	1	5	0	0	0	0	2	0	3	0	0	0	0	0	0	0	0	0	1	0
farmers'	14	.5290	1.6628	42.2	3	5	2	2	1	1	0	0	7	0	0	1	0	4	0	1	0	0	0	0	0	0	0	1	0
Farmers'	5	.0619	.1340	31.3	4	0	0	0	1	0	0	0	1	0	0	0	0	0	0	0	4	0	0	0	0	0	0	0	0
farmhouse	55	.6519	7.5820	48.8	13	9	4	6	13	2	7	1	26	1	1	11	0	3	0	0	0	0	0	0	7	3	0	3	0
Farmhouse	2	.2440	.1132	30.5	0	0	1	0	0	0	0	1	0	0	0	1	0	0	0	0	0	0	0	0	0	0	0	1	0
farmhouses	11	.4001	1.0329	40.1	2	4	1	3	0	1	0	0	3	0	0	0	0	6	0	0	0	0	0	0	1	1	0	0	0
farming	284	.3780	24.726	53.9	28	20	65	65	54	25	24	3	26	0	0	1	0	209	3	2	0	0	0	0	0	14	25	4	0
Farmington	24	.0000	.4668	36.7	24	0	0	0	0	0	0	0	0	0	0	0	0	24	0	0	0	0	0	0	0	0	0	0	0
farmland	36	.5452	4.1352	46.2	0	3	13	3	8	5	2	2	2	0	3	0	0	19	0	1	1	0	0	0	0	1	4	5	0
farmlands	21	.4198	1.9414	42.9	1	1	4	4	6	2	1	2	0	0	0	0	0	13	0	2	0	0	0	0	0	0	3	3	0
farms	481	.5016	52.235	57.2	105	73	99	91	54	33	21	5	41	0	1	4	0	335	1	7	2	2	0	0	2	32	37	17	0
Farms	3	.0000	.0365	25.6	0	3	0	0	0	0	0	0	0	0	0	0	0	0	0	0	0	0	0	0	0	0	0	3	0
farmstead	2	.2408	.1204	30.8	0	0	1	1	0	0	0	0	0	0	0	0	0	1	0	0	0	0	0	0	0	1	0	0	0
Farmville	5	.0000	.0724	28.6	0	5	0	0	0	0	0	0	0	0	0	0	0	0	0	0	0	0	0	0	0	5	0	0	0
farmyard	14	.6219	1.8532	42.7	5	3	1	1	2	2	0	0	6	0	0	2	0	2	0	0	1	0	0	0	2	0	1	0	0
Farnsworth	12	.2003	.8839	39.5	0	1	11	0	0	0	0	0	11	0	0	0	0	0	0	0	0	0	0	0	0	0	0	1	0
Farnsworth's	2	.0000	.0914	29.6	0	0	2	0	0	0	0	0	2	0	0	0	0	0	0	0	0	0	0	0	0	0	0	0	0
Farnum	5	.0000	.2284	33.6	5	0	0	0	0	0	0	0	5	0	0	0	0	0	0	0	0	0	0	0	0	0	0	0	0
faroff	2	.2442	.1134	30.5	0	2	0	0	0	0	0	0	0	1	0	0	0	0	0	0	0	0	0	0	0	0	0	1	0
Farragut	5	.2007	.3235	35.1	0	0	0	0	1	4	0	0	3	0	0	0	0	0	0	0	0	0	0	0	0	0	2	0	0
Farrar	2	.0000	.0243	23.9	0	0	0	0	0	0	0	2	0	0	0	0	0	0	0	0	0	0	0	0	0	0	0	2	0
Farrington	5	.0000	.2284	33.6	5	0	0	0	0	0	0	0	5	0	0	0	0	0	0	0	0	0	0	0	0	0	0	0	0
farseeing	2	.2391	.1133	30.5	0	0	1	0	0	0	1	0	0	0	0	0	1	0	0	0	0	0	0	0	0	0	1	0	0
farsighted	4	.4514	.3975	36.0	1	0	0	0	1	2	0	0	1	1	0	1	0	0	0	0	0	0	0	0	0	0	1	0	0
farther	443	.8922	78.755	59.0	86	86	50	74	85	40	18	4	106	12	1	17	36	84	1	67	7	6	2	1	16	48	25	14	0
farthest	53	.8847	9.3303	49.7	7	15	5	6	13	1	4	2	7	1	1	4	5	9	1	11	1	0	0	1	2	4	4	2	0
Farthest-Thrower	5	.0000	.2284	33.6	5	0	0	0	0	0	0	0	5	0	0	0	0	0	0	0	0	0	0	0	0	0	0	0	0
Farwell	2	.0000	.0234	23.7	2	0	0	0	0	0	0	0	0	0	0	0	0	0	0	0	0	0	0	0	2	0	0	0	0
fascinated	47	.7798	7.4272	48.7	1	4	6	7	14	10	5	0	14	3	0	5	0	1	1	1	4	0	0	0	7	3	4	4	0
fascinates	2	.2442	.1134	30.5	0	0	0	1	0	1	0	0	0	1	0	0	0	0	0	0	0	0	0	0	0	0	0	1	0
fascinating	70	.8641	12.033	50.8	6	8	4	10	26	8	5	3	8	5	2	3	1	2	0	7	4	3	1	3	4	8	8	11	0
fascination	12	.6151	1.5393	41.9	0	0	1	0	8	2	1	0	3	0	1	1	0	1	0	0	0	1	0	0	0	1	2	2	0
fascism	5	.4505	.5037	37.0	0	0	1	0	0	1	3	0	1	0	0	0	0	2	0	0	0	0	0	0	0	1	0	1	0
Fascism	3	.2043	.1486	31.7	1	0	1	0	0	0	1	0	0	0	0	0	0	0	0	0	0	0	0	0	0	1	2	0	0
Fascist	4	.3829	.3404	35.3	1	0	1	0	1	1	0	0	0	0	0	0	0	2	0	0	0	0	0	0	0	1	1	0	0
fashion	118	.8865	20.786	53.2	9	7	5	13	35	25	19	5	19	9	0	14	2	8	2	7	5	2	7	1	9	10	11	12	0
fashion-right	2	.0000	.0064	18.1	0	0	0	0	0	0	2	0	0	0	0	0	0	0	0	0	0	0	2	0	0	0	0	0	0
fashionable	18	.6982	2.5714	44.1	0	0	1	3	6	6	2	0	4	1	1	1	1	1	0	0	0	1	0	0	0	1	3	4	0
fashioned	17	.6658	2.3583	43.7	1	3	0	3	3	5	1	1	6	0	0	0	0	1	0	1	0	1	0	1	1	1	2	3	0
fashioning	3	.3766	.2497	34.0	0	0	0	0	1	1	1	0	0	0	0	0	0	1	0	0	0	0	0	0	0	1	1	0	0
fashions	13	.6382	1.6677	42.2	2	0	1	0	4	2	3	1	0	1	1	0	0	0	0	0	1	0	3	1	1	1	3	1	0
fast	1173	.9058	211.75	63.3	354	214	143	125	198	78	45	16	478	39	7	41	46	52	23	115	47	6	0	6	105	142	26	40	0
Fast	25	.1971	1.8313	42.6	0	0	0	0	23	0	0	2	23	0	0	0	0	0	0	0	0	0	0	0	0	0	0	2	0
fast-beating	2	.0000	.0234	23.7	0	0	1	1	0	0	0	0	0	0	0	0	0	0	0	0	0	0	0	0	2	0	0	0	0
fast-flowing	3	.3263	.2368	33.7	0	1	0	1	1	0	0	0	1	0	0	0	0	0	0	0	1	0	0	0	0	0	0	1	0
fast-flying	2	.2291	.1135	30.5	0	0	0	1	0	1	0	0	0	0	0	1	0	0	0	1	0	0	0	0	0	0	0	0	0
fast-growing	5	.3016	.3700	35.7	0	1	0	1	2	1	0	0	1	0	0	0	0	2	0	0	0	0	0	0	0	0	2	0	0
fast-moving	14	.6741	1.9235	42.8	0	3	0	3	5	1	2	0	1	0	0	1	0	1	0	3	0	0	1	1	1	0	1	4	0
fast-talking	2	.2137	.1056	30.2	0	0	0	0	0	2	0	0	0	0	0	0	0	1	0	0	1	0	0	0	0	0	0	0	0
Fast's	3	.0000	.1370	31.4	0	0	0	0	3	0	0	0	3	0	0	0	0	0	0	0	0	0	0	0	0	0	0	0	0
fasted	4	.2707	.2665	34.3	0	1	1	2	0	0	0	0	1	0	0	0	0	0	2	0	0	0	0	0	1	0	0	0	0
fasten	109	.6415	14.329	51.6	14	11	21	21	17	6	14	5	13	2	1	2	2	1	1	30	3	7	5	22	7	5	4	4	0
fastened	187	.8286	31.234	54.9	29	37	35	37	23	10	12	4	68	4	2	11	0	10	2	26	5	7	2	11	15	15	4	5	0
fastener	6	.2601	.4044	36.1	0	0	0	1	4	0	0	1	2	0	0	0	0	0	0	1	0	0	2	0	0	1	0	0	0
fasteners	15	.2813	.8788	39.4	0	2	0	0	4	2	7	0	0	0	0	0	0	0	0	1	0	0	9	4	0	0	1	0	0
fastening	15	.5523	1.7269	42.4	1	2	3	1	3	1	3	1	2	0	1	1	0	1	0	2	0	0	2	3	0	3	0	0	0
fastens	14	.5797	1.7533	42.4	0	2	2	2	3	2	1	2	6	1	0	0	0	1	0	2	0	1	0	1	0	2	0	0	0
faster	536	.9164	97.601	59.9	146	91	69	60	81	55	32	2	167	14	2	15	15	24	6	107	31	2	5	4	39	55	17	33	0
faster-moving	2	.0000	.0394	26.0	0	0	0	2	0	0	0	0	0	0	0	0	0	0	0	2	0	0	0	0	0	0	0	0	0
fastest	69	.9038	12.393	50.9	11	14	11	10	11	7	2	3	14	3	1	2	9	9	2	8	1	0	1	0	4	8	2	5	0
fastest-growing	4	.2348	.2372	33.8	0	0	3	0	1	0	0	0	0	0	0	0	0	3	0	0	0	0	0	0	0	0	1	0	0
fastidious	2	.1523	.0721	28.6	0	0	0	0	1	1	0	0	0	0	1	0	0	0	0	0	0	0	0	0	0	0	0	1	0
fasting	2	.0000	.0389	25.9	0	0	0	0	1	1	0	0	0	0	0	0	0	2	0	0	0	0	0	0	0	0	0	0	0
fastness	2	.1698	.1133	30.5	0	0	0	0	2	0	0	0	1	0	0	0	0	0	0	0	0	0	0	0	0	0	1	0	0
fastnesses	2	.0000	.0914	29.6	0	0	0	2	0	0	0	0	2	0	0	0	0	0	0	0	0	0	0	0	0	0	0	0	0
fat	386	.6436	51.702	57.1	95	53	46	27	49	21	79	16	112	13	4	15	2	12	7	50	6	3	78	0	26	21	9	28	0
Fat	9	.4066	.8502	39.3	6	0	1	1	0	1	0	0	4	0	1	0	0	0	0	0	3	0	0	0	1	0	0	0	0
fatal	37	.7554	5.6813	47.5	1	0	5	9	6	6	7	3	9	1	0	7	0	2	0	4	0	0	1	0	4	2	4	3	0

3Q far-seeing
3P Far-shooter
8B far-surrounding
7A fare's
7P Farenholt
6A farewells
8J Fargo
6A faring
4D Farjeon
4E FARM
9R farm-equipment
4J farm-er
8F farm-holiday
8D farm-mates
7R farm-to-market
XP Farman
7D farmboy
XR farmer-gas
7Q farmer-mechanics
XR farmer-turned-realtor
7E farmhand
8A farmhands
5F farming-regions
3F Farmington's
9D farmwork
6A farmyards
7A Farns
XH Faroes
8A Farraguts
7Q farre
9D Farrel
7Q Farrell
7Q Farrell's
9D Farrels
7F Farther
7A farther**
9D farthing
5N farthings
7P Fartlek
3N Farwell's
7N fas'
9Q fasciculations
7Q fascinate
4A Fascinating
8F fascist
3Q Fascists
3Q fashionably
9D fashionmongers
3A FAST
8N fast-a
3P fast-balling
8A fast-break
7H fast-burning
8H fast-changing
6A fast-falling
XR fast-flashing
6R fast-paced
6A fast-rising
6A fast-rolling
3P fast-running
3N fastenings
7Q faster-growing
9H faster-than-sound
XH fastest-moving
3A fastidiously
8R fasts
XH fat-filled
6R fat-tailed

Word Type	F	D	U	SFI	3 Gr 3	4 Gr 4	5 Gr 5	6 Gr 6	7 Gr 7	8 Gr 8	9 Gr 9	X UnGr	A Read	B Eng & Gr	C Comp	D Lit	E Math	F Soc Stud	G Spell	H Sci	J Music	K Art	L Home Ec	M Shop	N Lib F	P Lib NF	Q Lib Ref	R Mag	S Rel
fatalist	2	.0000	.0290	24.6	0	0	0	0	0	0	0	2	0	0	0	0	0	0	0	0	0	0	0	0	0	2	0	0	0
fatalities	4	.3864	.3418	35.3	0	0	0	0	2	0	2	0	0	0	0	0	0	0	0	2	0	0	0	0	0	0	1	1	0
fatally	2	.1698	.1133	30.5	0	0	0	1	1	0	0	0	1	0	0	0	0	0	0	0	0	0	0	0	0	0	1	0	0
fate	61	.7396	9.2502	49.7	2	5	7	8	18	9	9	3	20	0	1	9	0	8	0	3	0	0	0	0	7	5	2	6	0
Fate	3	.2374	.1625	32.1	0	0	0	0	1	0	2	0	0	0	0	2	0	0	0	0	1	0	0	0	0	0	0	0	0
fated	2	.2303	.1079	30.3	0	0	1	0	0	0	1	0	0	0	0	0	0	0	0	0	1	0	0	0	0	1	0	0	0
fateful	5	.4085	.4628	36.7	1	0	1	1	0	1	0	1	1	0	0	0	0	1	0	0	0	0	0	0	0	1	0	2	0
father	2245	.9059	405.23	66.1	538	493	281	252	377	146	117	41	940	79	26	240	58	134	17	49	46	9	15	3	260	228	50	89	2
Father	785	.4002	72.972	58.6	205	280	104	80	58	37	17	4	262	16	10	64	1	102	11	4	27	1	0	0	82	152	2	26	25
FATHER	47	.0000	.5044	37.0	0	0	0	0	28	11	8	0	0	0	0	47	0	0	0	0	0	0	0	0	0	0	0	0	0
Father-Abbot	4	.0000	.1827	32.6	0	4	0	0	0	0	0	0	4	0	0	0	0	0	0	0	0	0	0	0	0	0	0	0	0
father-and-son	2	.0000	.0243	23.9	0	0	0	0	2	0	0	0	0	0	0	0	0	0	0	0	0	0	0	0	0	0	0	2	0
father-in-law	2	.0000	.0243	23.9	0	0	0	1	0	0	1	0	0	0	0	0	0	0	0	0	0	0	0	0	0	0	0	2	0
father-son	2	.2446	.1122	30.5	0	0	0	0	0	0	2	0	0	0	0	1	0	0	0	0	0	0	0	0	0	0	1	0	0
father'll	3	.0000	.1370	31.4	0	0	0	3	0	0	0	0	3	0	0	0	0	0	0	0	0	0	0	0	0	0	0	0	0
father's	246	.7929	39.670	56.0	39	68	30	28	46	19	14	2	105	6	8	26	2	9	5	1	5	0	1	0	24	38	5	10	1
Father's	48	.4403	4.6513	46.7	10	22	6	6	1	3	0	0	8	0	0	1	3	4	0	0	4	0	0	0	12	15	0	0	1
fatherhood	2	.2437	.1129	30.5	0	0	0	0	1	0	0	1	0	0	0	0	0	0	0	0	0	0	0	0	0	0	1	1	0
fatherland	4	.2003	.1916	32.8	0	0	0	0	0	1	3	0	0	0	0	3	0	0	0	0	0	0	0	0	0	0	1	0	0
Fatherland	2	.2417	.1091	30.4	0	0	1	0	0	1	0	0	0	0	0	0	0	0	0	0	1	0	0	0	0	0	1	0	0
fatherly	2	.1717	.1142	30.6	0	0	0	0	2	0	0	0	1	0	0	1	0	0	0	0	0	0	0	0	0	0	0	0	0
fathers	80	.7653	12.448	51.0	25	13	8	6	18	4	5	1	20	2	0	5	2	18	0	0	4	0	0	0	6	13	3	7	0
Fathers	8	.5332	.9338	39.7	3	1	1	0	1	2	0	0	3	0	0	0	0	1	0	0	0	0	0	0	2	1	1	0	0
fathers'	7	.1602	.3048	34.8	1	4	0	2	0	0	0	0	1	0	0	0	0	0	0	0	5	0	0	0	0	1	0	0	0
fathom	5	.4538	.4728	36.7	0	1	0	0	1	0	3	0	0	1	1	1	1	0	0	0	0	0	0	0	0	0	1	0	0
fathometer	3	.2437	.2277	33.6	0	0	2	0	0	0	1	0	2	0	0	0	0	0	0	1	0	0	0	0	0	0	0	0	0
fathoms	18	.4961	1.9884	43.0	1	7	1	0	3	1	5	0	7	0	0	1	4	0	0	0	0	0	0	0	5	1	0	0	0
fatigue	32	.7440	4.8048	46.8	0	2	3	4	6	5	12	0	5	1	0	4	0	0	2	1	1	0	4	1	3	1	4	5	0
fatigued	2	.1787	.1174	30.7	0	0	0	1	1	0	0	0	1	0	0	0	0	0	0	0	0	0	0	0	1	0	0	0	0
fatigues	2	.0000	.0243	23.9	0	0	0	0	0	1	1	0	0	0	0	0	0	0	0	0	0	0	0	0	0	0	0	2	0
fats	63	.2902	4.3464	46.4	1	3	19	4	19	11	5	1	5	0	0	0	0	0	1	38	0	0	17	0	0	0	2	0	0
Fats	35	.2427	2.6695	44.3	0	27	0	0	0	8	0	0	27	8	0	0	0	0	0	0	0	0	0	0	0	0	0	0	0
Fats'	3	.0000	.1370	31.4	0	3	0	0	0	0	0	0	3	0	0	0	0	0	0	0	0	0	0	0	0	0	0	0	0
fatten	9	.3932	.8037	39.1	1	1	1	1	2	3	0	0	1	0	0	0	0	5	0	0	0	0	0	0	0	1	2	0	0
fattened	9	.3065	.6520	38.1	0	0	3	2	3	1	0	0	0	0	0	0	0	7	0	0	0	0	0	0	1	0	1	0	0
fattening	11	.5441	1.2574	41.0	0	5	2	1	2	0	0	1	0	0	0	1	0	1	0	6	0	0	1	0	0	1	0	1	0
fattens	2	.0000	.0209	23.2	1	0	0	0	1	0	0	0	0	0	0	0	0	0	0	0	0	0	0	0	0	0	2	0	0
fatter	14	.6098	1.7867	42.5	9	2	0	0	0	2	1	0	3	0	0	4	0	2	0	0	0	0	0	0	2	1	1	1	0
fattest	5	.3833	.4767	36.8	3	0	0	1	0	0	1	0	3	0	0	1	0	0	0	0	0	0	0	0	0	1	0	0	0
fatty	13	.2715	.8752	39.4	0	0	1	4	4	3	0	1	1	0	0	0	0	0	0	10	0	0	2	0	0	0	0	0	0
Fatty	4	.3740	.3661	35.6	2	0	1	0	1	0	0	0	2	0	0	0	0	0	0	0	0	0	0	0	1	0	0	1	0
faucet	21	.2735	1.4748	41.7	2	8	8	1	2	0	0	0	3	0	0	0	0	0	0	16	0	0	0	0	1	0	0	1	0
faucets	6	.3940	.5367	37.3	1	2	1	1	1	0	0	0	1	0	1	0	0	1	0	2	0	0	0	0	0	0	0	1	0
Faulkner	5	.3716	.4099	36.1	0	0	2	0	1	0	2	0	0	2	0	0	0	2	0	0	0	0	0	0	0	0	1	0	0
fault	120	.6848	17.028	52.3	20	18	10	17	22	13	19	1	38	6	0	20	0	3	1	11	1	0	0	1	17	12	3	6	1
fault-block	4	.0000	.0789	29.0	0	0	0	0	0	0	4	0	0	0	0	0	0	0	0	4	0	0	0	0	0	0	0	0	0
faulted	4	.2287	.2348	33.7	0	0	0	0	1	0	3	0	0	0	0	0	0	0	0	3	0	0	0	0	0	0	0	1	0
faulting	4	.0000	.0789	29.0	0	0	1	0	0	0	3	0	0	0	0	0	0	0	0	4	0	0	0	0	0	0	0	0	0
faultless	2	.1948	.1250	31.0	0	0	0	1	1	0	0	0	1	0	0	0	0	0	0	0	0	0	0	0	0	1	0	0	0
faultlessly	2	.1551	.0728	28.6	0	0	0	0	1	0	1	0	0	0	1	0	0	0	0	0	0	0	0	0	1	0	0	0	0
faults	26	.7585	3.9825	46.0	1	0	2	2	5	8	7	1	4	1	0	4	0	0	1	4	1	0	2	0	1	1	3	4	0
faulty	10	.4418	.9703	39.9	0	0	2	0	6	1	1	0	2	2	0	0	0	2	0	0	0	0	2	0	0	0	0	2	0
Faun	2	.2417	.1091	30.4	0	0	0	0	2	0	0	0	0	0	0	0	0	0	0	0	1	0	0	0	0	0	1	0	0
fauna	19	.0789	.4949	36.9	0	0	0	0	17	0	0	2	0	0	0	0	0	0	0	2	0	0	0	0	0	0	17	0	0
faunal	2	.0000	.0209	23.2	0	0	0	0	2	0	0	0	0	0	0	0	0	0	0	0	0	0	0	0	0	0	2	0	0
Faure	2	.2401	.1133	30.5	0	0	0	1	1	0	0	0	0	0	0	0	0	0	0	0	0	0	0	0	0	1	1	0	0
Faust	15	.1963	.6991	38.4	0	0	0	0	3	0	12	0	0	0	0	0	0	0	0	0	3	0	0	0	0	0	12	0	0
Faustino	5	.0000	.2284	33.6	0	0	0	0	0	0	5	0	5	0	0	0	0	0	0	0	0	0	0	0	0	0	0	0	0
Faustus	5	.0000	.0523	27.2	0	0	0	0	0	0	5	0	0	0	0	0	0	0	0	0	0	0	0	0	0	0	5	0	0
Favonius	2	.0000	.0290	24.6	0	0	0	2	0	0	0	0	0	0	0	0	0	0	0	0	0	0	0	0	0	2	0	0	0
favor	107	.8966	19.064	52.8	6	9	11	14	24	26	14	3	21	10	1	8	0	14	7	4	2	0	1	1	8	9	12	9	0
favorable	51	.8069	8.2563	49.2	5	0	7	10	13	2	8	6	3	3	1	1	0	16	1	8	0	0	1	0	2	5	3	7	0
favorably	12	.5257	1.3294	41.2	5	0	1	0	4	1	1	0	1	0	1	0	0	2	0	0	0	0	1	0	0	6	0	1	0
favored	55	.5804	6.6619	48.2	5	3	11	7	11	12	4	2	4	0	0	1	0	17	0	1	1	0	0	0	0	9	14	8	0
favoring	6	.4608	.5821	37.7	0	0	0	1	5	0	0	0	0	0	0	2	0	0	0	0	0	0	0	0	1	1	0	2	0
favorite	291	.9166	52.889	57.2	43	51	37	50	55	27	21	7	70	25	6	10	5	22	15	8	35	6	8	3	11	27	9	31	0
favorites	27	.6682	3.6806	45.7	3	2	3	6	8	1	3	1	4	2	0	0	0	1	0	0	9	1	1	0	1	1	3	4	0
Favorites	2	.2387	.1089	30.4	0	1	0	1	0	0	0	0	0	0	0	0	0	0	0	0	1	0	0	0	1	0	0	0	0
favors	19	.7011	2.7122	44.3	2	0	0	0	7	5	5	0	3	1	0	1	0	2	0	0	0	1	2	0	1	2	2	4	0
favour	4	.3030	.2949	34.7	0	0	1	0	1	0	1	1	1	0	0	0	0	0	0	0	0	0	0	0	2	0	0	1	0
favourable	4	.2847	.2818	34.5	0	0	0	0	1	1	2	0	1	0	0	0	0	0	0	0	0	0	0	0	0	1	2	0	0
favoured	3	.1187	.1291	31.1	0	0	0	0	0	1	2	0	1	0	0	2	0	0	0	0	0	0	0	0	0	0	0	0	0
favourite	3	.2261	.2131	33.3	0	0	0	2	1	0	0	0	2	0	0	0	0	0	0	0	0	0	0	0	1	0	0	0	0
Fawcett	2	.2391	.1133	30.5	0	0	0	0	1	1	0	0	0	0	0	0	1	0	0	0	0	0	0	0	0	0	1	0	0
fawn	23	.5970	2.9642	44.7	5	2	4	1	5	3	3	0	12	0	1	3	0	0	2	0	0	0	0	0	4	1	0	0	0
fawns	6	.3364	.5162	37.1	0	2	2	2	0	0	0	0	3	0	0	0	0	0	0	1	0	0	0	0	2	0	0	0	0
fay	2	.2287	.1077	30.3	1	1	0	0	0	0	0	0	0	0	0	0	1	0	0	0	1	0	0	0	0	0	0	0	0
Fay	3	.1434	.1493	31.7	3	0	0	0	0	0	0	0	1	0	0	0	2	0	0	0	0	0	0	0	0	0	0	0	0
Fay's	3	.1434	.1493	31.7	0	0	2	0	0	1	0	0	1	0	0	0	2	0	0	0	0	0	0	0	0	0	0	0	0
Faysal	3	.0000	.0434	26.4	0	0	0	0	3	0	0	0	0	0	0	0	0	0	0	0	0	0	0	0	0	3	0	0	0
FBI	18	.3576	1.6137	42.1	0	0	7	1	0	1	9	0	8	2	0	0	0	8	0	0	0	0	0	0	0	0	0	0	0
FDA	6	.0000	.1183	30.7	0	0	0	0	0	6	0	0	0	0	0	0	0	0	0	6	0	0	0	0	0	0	0	0	0
Fdr	13	.0000	.5939	37.7	0	0	0	0	0	13	0	0	13	0	0	0	0	0	0	0	0	0	0	0	0	0	0	0	0
fe	16	.0670	.3346	35.2	0	4	4	5	0	2	1	0	0	1	0	0	0	0	15	0	0	0	0	0	0	0	0	0	0
Fe	11	.5057	1.2169	40.9	1	0	4	2	0	3	1	0	2	0	0	0	0	5	0	2	1	0	0	0	0	1	0	0	0
FE	2	.0000	.0299	24.8	0	2	0	0	0	0	0	0	0	0	0	0	2	0	0	0	0	0	0	0	0	0	0	0	0
FeO	2	.0000	.0394	26.0	0	0	0	0	0	0	0	2	0	0	0	0	0	0	0	2	0	0	0	0	0	0	0	0	0
fear	439	.8891	77.895	58.9	24	55	61	71	125	42	56	5	158	19	3	64	0	25	6	29	7	5	7	1	41	34	14	26	0
Fear	3	.2107	.1527	31.8	0	0	1	1	0	1	0	0	0	0	0	0	0	0	0	1	0	1	0	0	0	1	0	0	0
feared	113	.7601	17.566	52.4	6	12	21	21	18	19	13	3	39	3	0	8	0	24	0	3	2	0	0	0	12	10	6	6	0
fearful	72	.8198	11.887	50.8	3	5	11	8	24	11	9	1	19	2	1	10	0	7	3	10	1	0	0	0	10	4	2	3	0
fearfully	9	.4858	.9734	39.9	0	2	0	2	3	1	1	0	3	0	0	1	0	1	0	1	0	0	0	0	3	0	0	0	0
fearing	7	.6230	.9141	39.6	0	0	0	1	3	2	1	0	2	1	0	1	0	0	0	0	0	0	0	0	1	1	0	1	0
Fearing	2	.0000	.0037	15.7	1	0	0	0	1	0	0	0	0	0	0	0	0	0	0	0	0	2	0	0	0	0	0	0	0

7R fatality
3J Fath'r
7A Father-Sun
7N Father'll
9Q fathering
7A fatherless
5P fathers-forth
7Q fatigue-ridden
3A fatiguee
7N fatiguing
9Q Fatimid
5N Fatso
8P Fatu
8N fatuous
7D fatuously
7H Fauchard
7D fault-finding
9H fault-scarp
7H faunas
9Q Faust-book
9Q Faust's
9Q Fausten
8K Fauves
8J faux-bourdon
8J fauxbourdon
5R fave
7R Favell
9Q Faversham
7R favor-doing
8R Favorite
7P favoritism
7Q Favre
7Q Fawcett's
3B fawg
5Q fawn-
9D fawn-froth
4G fawn's
9R Faye
XR Fayerweather
5Q Fayette
7D Fayetteville
8R Faygo
4N faze
4E FB
7E FBD
4G FBS
6E FC
6E FCA
7A FCC
6E FCT
4E FD
9F FDIC
8F FDR'S**
6R fealty
3B Fear-not
3Q fear-provoking
3P fearest
XR fearfuls

					3	4	5	6	7	8	9	X	A	B	C	D	E	F	G	H	J	K	L	M	N	P	Q	R	S
Word Type	F	D	U	SFI	Gr 3	Gr 4	Gr 5	Gr 6	Gr 7	Gr 8	Gr 9	UnGr	Read	Eng & Gr	Comp	Lit	Math	Soc Stud	Spell	Sci	Music	Art	Home Ec	Shop	Lib F	Lib NF	Lib Ref	Mag	Rel
fearless	18	.5801	2.2128	43.4	2	2	4	2	2	3	3	0	5	4	0	0	0	0	1	0	0	0	0	0	4	3	0	1	0
fearlessly	6	.3599	.5352	37.3	1	0	2	0	1	1	1	0	3	0	0	0	0	0	0	0	0	0	0	0	1	0	0	2	0
fears	37	.7522	5.6755	47.5	0	2	4	6	11	7	7	0	10	0	0	3	0	5	0	5	2	1	0	0	3	0	2	6	0
fearsome	5	.2422	.3874	35.9	1	1	0	2	1	0	0	0	4	0	0	0	0	0	0	0	0	0	0	0	0	1	0	0	0
feasibility	3	.2321	.1635	32.1	0	0	0	0	1	0	1	1	0	0	0	0	0	0	0	0	0	0	0	0	0	0	1	2	0
feasible	6	.4409	.5646	37.5	0	0	0	1	2	0	1	2	0	0	0	0	1	0	0	1	0	0	0	0	0	0	2	2	0
feast	103	.8045	16.799	52.3	20	25	15	12	16	4	8	3	41	3	0	9	0	4	3	6	8	3	0	0	4	13	2	7	0
Feast	8	.2486	.4790	36.8	0	1	3	2	2	0	0	0	1	0	0	0	0	1	0	0	5	0	0	0	1	0	0	0	0
feasted	8	.4499	.8368	39.2	0	0	0	3	4	1	0	0	4	0	0	2	0	1	0	0	0	0	0	0	1	0	0	0	0
feasting	15	.5220	1.7307	42.4	2	1	2	7	1	2	0	0	7	0	0	0	0	1	1	0	4	0	0	0	1	0	1	0	0
feasts	8	.5697	.9522	39.8	2	2	1	0	1	1	1	0	1	1	0	2	0	1	0	0	0	0	0	0	2	0	1	0	0
feat	19	.6025	2.3878	43.8	2	0	4	1	8	2	2	0	4	0	0	2	0	0	1	0	1	0	0	0	0	1	5	5	0
feather	106	.7992	17.185	52.4	38	18	13	6	19	12	0	0	41	2	3	9	0	0	1	10	4	0	0	0	8	11	9	8	0
Feather	5	.2360	.3663	35.6	0	3	2	0	0	0	0	0	3	0	0	0	0	2	0	0	0	0	0	0	0	0	0	0	0
feather-planting	3	.0000	.1370	31.4	3	0	0	0	0	0	0	0	3	0	0	0	0	0	0	0	0	0	0	0	0	0	0	0	0
feathered	11	.5523	1.3137	41.2	2	3	2	1	2	0	0	1	4	0	0	1	0	0	0	0	0	0	0	0	0	2	2	2	0
feathers	304	.8233	50.559	57.0	133	77	21	28	22	12	7	4	111	8	2	13	2	6	2	53	8	8	0	0	14	49	16	12	0
Feathers	9	.2261	.6392	38.1	3	6	0	0	0	0	0	0	6	0	0	0	0	0	0	0	0	0	0	0	3	0	0	0	0
Feathertop	10	.0000	.1073	30.3	0	0	0	0	1	9	0	0	0	0	0	10	0	0	0	0	0	0	0	0	0	0	0	0	0
FEATHERTOP	12	.0000	.1288	31.1	0	0	0	0	0	12	0	0	0	0	0	12	0	0	0	0	0	0	0	0	0	0	0	0	0
Feathertop's	2	.0000	.0215	23.3	0	0	0	0	1	1	0	0	0	0	0	2	0	0	0	0	0	0	0	0	0	0	0	0	0
feathery	18	.5412	2.1180	43.3	2	4	2	2	5	2	1	0	7	0	0	6	0	0	0	1	0	1	0	0	1	1	0	1	0
feats	16	.6106	2.0410	43.1	2	1	1	2	4	2	4	0	4	2	0	2	0	0	0	0	0	1	0	0	0	2	4	1	0
feature	70	.8613	11.990	50.8	4	2	13	8	15	8	17	3	4	6	0	1	0	11	1	8	4	2	2	2	3	7	12	7	0
featured	14	.6413	1.8481	42.7	1	0	0	0	10	3	0	0	2	0	0	1	0	2	0	1	2	0	1	0	1	0	4	0	0
featureless	2	.2446	.1122	30.5	0	0	0	0	2	0	0	0	0	0	0	1	0	0	0	0	0	0	0	0	0	0	1	0	0
features	194	.7994	31.054	54.9	11	17	16	14	43	46	39	8	12	6	0	12	1	31	0	32	8	12	12	4	11	8	23	22	0
featuring	6	.1277	.1964	32.9	0	0	0	1	1	3	0	1	0	0	0	0	0	0	0	0	5	0	0	0	0	0	0	1	0
Feb	9	.3797	.7301	38.6	0	0	4	0	1	1	2	1	0	0	0	0	0	0	2	0	0	0	0	0	0	0	4	3	0
February	119	.7831	18.825	52.7	14	19	10	20	14	16	23	3	22	4	0	3	20	15	4	4	2	0	0	0	1	14	8	22	0
fed	182	.8851	32.143	55.1	44	29	28	23	31	14	12	1	55	5	1	8	3	23	6	15	7	0	0	5	9	23	15	7	0
Fed	2	.0000	.0209	23.2	0	0	0	0	2	0	0	0	0	0	0	0	0	0	0	0	0	0	0	0	0	0	2	0	0
fedayeen	12	.1231	.4309	36.3	0	0	0	0	0	0	12	0	0	0	0	0	0	2	0	0	0	0	0	0	0	0	0	10	0
federal	165	.5157	18.132	52.6	1	17	14	2	24	42	63	2	5	0	0	1	2	106	2	3	0	0	2	0	0	2	23	19	0
Federal	107	.6443	14.141	51.5	2	3	7	5	31	32	21	6	5	3	0	0	4	27	0	7	0	0	3	0	0	8	29	21	0
Federalist	12	.3030	.9190	39.6	0	0	6	0	4	2	0	0	4	0	0	0	0	3	0	0	0	0	0	0	0	0	5	0	0
Federalists	12	.4392	1.1685	40.7	0	0	3	0	5	4	0	0	2	0	0	0	0	4	0	0	0	0	0	0	0	0	3	3	0
federally	3	.3847	.2496	34.0	0	0	1	0	1	0	1	0	0	0	0	0	0	0	0	0	0	0	0	0	0	1	1	1	0
Federals	7	.3401	.5466	37.4	0	0	0	0	0	7	0	0	0	0	0	0	0	5	0	0	0	0	0	0	1	0	1	0	0
federated	2	.2351	.1166	30.7	0	0	0	1	0	0	0	1	0	0	0	0	0	1	0	0	0	0	0	0	0	0	0	1	0
federation	10	.3779	.8376	39.2	0	0	4	1	1	1	1	2	0	0	0	0	0	3	0	0	0	0	0	0	0	4	0	3	0
Federation	13	.4439	1.2496	41.0	0	0	0	4	4	2	0	3	0	0	0	0	0	7	0	0	0	0	1	0	0	1	2	3	0
fee	20	.7776	3.1371	45.0	1	2	1	5	2	6	0	3	3	2	0	1	2	4	0	0	1	1	0	0	0	2	1	3	0
Fee-ona	2	.0000	.0215	23.3	0	0	0	0	2	0	0	0	0	0	0	2	0	0	0	0	0	0	0	0	0	0	0	0	0
feeble	19	.6870	2.6889	44.3	1	1	3	3	7	3	1	0	5	1	1	0	0	1	1	1	0	0	0	0	4	2	3	0	0
feebly	4	.4491	.4015	36.0	0	0	0	0	1	2	0	1	1	1	0	0	0	0	0	1	0	0	0	0	1	0	0	0	0
feed	372	.8847	65.633	58.2	88	61	50	41	64	30	30	8	93	6	1	15	6	62	8	60	2	3	2	14	33	26	21	20	0
feedback	2	.1843	.0808	29.1	0	0	0	1	0	1	0	0	0	0	1	0	0	0	0	0	1	0	0	0	0	0	0	0	0
feeder	32	.4601	3.2467	45.1	2	8	1	7	3	6	1	4	10	1	0	2	0	0	0	0	0	0	0	6	0	1	6	6	0
feeders	9	.4217	.8397	39.2	0	1	0	2	1	0	2	3	1	0	0	0	0	0	0	3	0	0	0	0	0	0	2	3	0
feeding	126	.8252	20.862	53.2	17	16	10	13	48	8	10	4	26	3	1	4	0	6	1	13	0	1	1	3	9	18	30	10	0
feedle	4	.0000	.0323	25.1	4	0	0	0	0	0	0	0	0	0	0	0	0	0	0	0	4	0	0	0	0	0	0	0	0
feeds	46	.8544	7.8569	49.0	8	6	4	5	15	3	3	2	8	3	1	1	0	7	1	10	0	1	0	1	1	5	5	2	0
feel	1275	.8934	226.78	63.6	269	222	157	124	243	134	99	27	338	77	17	131	4	43	11	228	49	30	40	3	92	85	25	102	0
feeler	3	.1650	.1684	32.3	0	0	0	3	0	0	0	0	1	0	0	0	0	0	0	2	0	0	0	0	0	0	0	0	0
feelers	33	.6130	4.2861	46.3	16	2	3	7	4	1	0	0	9	2	0	0	0	0	0	14	0	1	0	0	2	4	1	0	0
feelin'	3	.1250	.1342	31.3	0	1	0	1	1	0	0	0	1	0	0	0	0	0	0	0	0	0	0	0	2	0	0	0	0
feeling	540	.8085	87.815	59.4	61	85	69	51	124	70	66	14	135	36	5	55	1	24	3	24	62	30	20	0	65	25	15	40	0
feelings	229	.8072	37.075	55.7	17	28	18	26	71	42	22	5	38	18	2	34	0	10	4	27	40	11	6	0	8	6	10	15	0
feels	182	.8339	30.437	54.8	40	17	34	17	43	16	10	5	45	20	7	18	0	5	2	29	9	8	5	0	6	10	6	12	0
fees	12	.5958	1.4978	41.8	1	0	2	3	3	1	2	0	2	0	0	1	0	2	0	0	0	0	0	0	0	3	2	2	0
feet	2545	.9169	463.34	66.7	380	413	340	434	502	220	211	45	682	53	18	153	410	186	21	273	55	13	5	11	165	217	154	129	0
Feigen	2	.0000	.0243	23.9	0	0	0	0	0	2	0	0	0	0	0	0	0	0	0	0	0	0	0	0	0	0	0	2	0
feigned	3	.3842	.2485	34.0	0	0	0	0	1	1	1	0	0	0	0	1	0	0	0	0	0	0	0	0	0	1	1	0	0
feir	3	.0000	.0328	25.2	0	0	0	0	0	3	0	0	0	3	0	0	0	0	0	0	0	0	0	0	0	0	0	0	0
feist	2	.0000	.0234	23.7	0	0	0	0	2	0	0	0	0	0	0	0	0	0	0	0	0	0	0	0	2	0	0	0	0
feldspar	12	.3672	.9930	40.0	0	2	1	0	1	5	3	0	0	0	0	0	0	0	0	9	0	0	0	1	0	0	2	0	0
felicitations	3	.0000	.0328	25.2	0	0	0	0	0	0	3	0	0	3	0	0	0	0	0	0	0	0	0	0	0	0	0	0	0
feline	2	.2446	.1142	30.6	1	0	0	0	1	0	0	0	0	0	0	0	0	0	0	0	0	0	0	0	1	0	0	1	0
Felis	7	.0000	.1380	31.4	0	0	0	0	3	0	4	0	0	0	0	0	0	0	0	7	0	0	0	0	0	0	0	0	0
Felix	14	.4635	1.4507	41.6	0	3	1	5	3	1	1	0	5	0	0	0	0	1	0	0	4	0	0	0	0	0	1	3	0
fell	790	.8474	134.73	61.3	167	145	74	124	143	73	53	11	331	42	17	83	7	43	4	31	18	1	0	0	81	66	18	46	2
fella	5	.3496	.3978	36.0	0	0	1	0	4	0	0	0	1	0	1	0	0	0	0	0	0	0	0	0	2	0	0	1	0
fellahin	4	.0000	.0778	28.9	0	0	0	0	4	0	0	0	0	0	0	0	0	4	0	0	0	0	0	0	0	0	0	0	0
fellahs	2	.0000	.0234	23.7	0	0	0	0	2	0	0	0	0	0	0	0	0	0	0	0	0	0	0	0	2	0	0	0	0
felled	13	.6268	1.7052	42.3	1	1	3	3	4	0	1	0	4	0	0	1	0	0	0	0	1	0	0	1	3	2	1	0	0
feller	20	.5164	2.2412	43.5	3	2	4	1	5	5	0	0	6	0	0	5	0	0	0	0	1	0	0	0	5	3	0	0	0
Feller	7	.2353	.5425	37.3	0	0	0	0	1	6	0	0	6	0	0	0	0	0	0	0	0	0	0	0	0	0	0	1	0
fellers	7	.2444	.4065	36.1	4	0	0	0	3	0	0	0	0	0	0	0	0	0	0	0	0	0	0	0	3	4	0	0	0
fellow	291	.8317	48.776	56.9	40	43	17	43	68	36	38	6	110	18	1	46	0	12	1	6	12	1	1	1	21	31	5	25	0
Fellow	18	.2959	1.5806	42.0	0	0	17	0	0	1	0	0	16	0	0	0	0	1	0	0	1	0	0	0	0	0	0	0	0
fellow's	5	.2664	.3459	35.4	1	0	0	0	2	1	1	0	2	0	0	2	0	0	0	0	0	1	0	0	0	0	0	0	0
Fellow's	2	.0000	.0914	29.6	0	0	2	0	0	0	0	0	2	0	0	0	0	0	0	0	0	0	0	0	0	0	0	0	0
fellows	81	.7466	12.434	50.9	7	13	4	15	21	12	9	0	35	3	0	13	0	4	0	1	1	0	0	1	8	10	3	2	0
fellowship	9	.5001	.9285	39.7	1	1	0	1	3	3	0	0	0	0	1	2	0	0	0	0	1	0	0	0	0	1	4	0	0
felony	4	.1622	.1743	32.4	0	0	0	0	2	2	0	0	0	0	0	0	0	1	0	0	0	0	0	0	0	0	0	3	0
felt	1231	.8540	211.37	63.3	191	254	154	174	208	134	97	19	529	41	10	144	1	69	8	25	12	14	12	3	171	99	26	67	0
felts	3	.2540	.1940	32.9	0	0	1	0	1	0	1	0	1	0	0	0	0	0	0	0	0	0	1	0	0	0	1	0	0
female	147	.7324	21.870	53.4	21	9	16	24	59	6	9	3	17	3	2	3	0	4	1	49	3	1	0	0	3	14	37	10	0
female's	5	.3636	.4034	36.1	0	0	0	2	3	0	0	0	0	0	0	0	0	0	0	2	0	0	0	0	0	0	2	1	0
females	27	.4472	2.6458	44.2	8	1	2	0	4	5	5	2	5	0	5	4	0	1	0	5	0	0	0	0	0	5	2	0	0
feminine	12	.4910	1.2715	41.0	0	0	3	2	3	0	2	2	3	0	1	0	0	0	0	0	0	0	2	0	0	2	0	4	0
femininity	2	.2412	.1141	30.6	0	0	0	0	2	0	0	0	0	1	0	0	0	0	0	0	0	0	0	0	0	1	0	0	0
fence	346	.8182	57.176	57.6	88	60	41	39	69	25	20	4	134	22	7	36	33	5	7	2	1	4	0	15	52	18	1	9	0

9R Fearsome
6R fearsomely
6R feast-or-famine
6N feather-light
3A feather-shaped
3R feather's
4A Feather's
4R featherbed
4A featherless
9B federal-aid
9Q federal-state
5Q federations
7P federative
4P feeble-minded
6G feeblest
6J Feed
7N feedin'
7N feedn'
6H feeler-legs
6R Feelin'
9B Feeling
7A feeling-out
9D feelingly
7A feex
6N fei
XR Feiffer
8D feign
7Q feigning
3K Feininger
6A feint
6A feinting
7P feints
8B feit
XR Feldman
9Q Feldspar
9H feldspars
7A Felician
4D felicity
XP Felicity
5A Felippe
9D fell-frowning
8J Fella
8R fellas
7N feller'll
3Q felling
6N fellow-Christians
8F fellow-citizens
9J fellow-composer
7N fellow-rascal
9G fellow-scientists
3P fellow-vendors
9Q fellowmen
8A fellows'
7R Fellowship
8D fellowships
9F felonies
7N felonious
XR Felse
7J felt-covered
XN felt-lined
6R femininely
7E femur

Word Type	F	D	U	SFI	3 Gr 3	4 Gr 4	5 Gr 5	6 Gr 6	7 Gr 7	8 Gr 8	9 Gr 9	X UnGr	A Read	B Eng & Gr	C Comp	D Lit	E Math	F Soc Stud	G Spell	H Sci	J Music	K Art	L Home Ec	M Shop	N Lib F	P Lib NF	Q Lib Ref	R Mag	S Rel
Fence	2	.2440	.1132	30.5	0	0	0	0	1	0	0	1	0	0	0	1	0	0	0	0	0	0	0	0	0	0	0	1	0
fenced	12	.4918	1.3145	41.2	3	1	1	4	2	0	1	0	4	0	1	0	2	4	0	0	0	0	0	0	1	0	0	0	0
fenced-in	7	.4825	.7821	38.9	2	4	1	0	0	0	0	0	4	0	0	0	0	1	0	0	0	0	0	0	0	1	0	1	0
fences	59	.7796	9.3123	49.7	13	5	7	11	10	9	1	3	13	2	2	10	2	12	0	6	0	2	0	0	2	4	1	3	0
fencin'	2	.0000	.0234	23.7	0	0	2	0	0	0	0	0	0	0	0	0	0	0	0	0	0	0	0	0	2	0	0	0	0
fencing	11	.5521	1.3291	41.2	2	1	1	3	0	3	0	1	5	1	0	2	2	0	0	0	0	0	0	0	0	0	0	1	0
fend	2	.1698	.1133	30.5	1	0	0	0	1	0	0	0	1	0	0	0	0	0	0	0	0	0	0	0	0	0	1	0	0
fender	18	.5374	2.1895	43.4	4	1	2	3	4	3	1	0	12	0	0	1	0	0	0	0	0	0	0	0	1	2	0	2	0
fenders	22	.6074	2.9074	44.6	6	3	1	1	5	3	3	0	14	1	0	1	0	0	0	0	0	1	0	1	0	1	0	3	0
fending	3	.2143	.1568	32.0	0	0	0	0	2	0	1	0	0	0	0	0	0	0	0	0	0	0	0	0	0	1	0	2	0
Fenimore	2	.2306	.1140	30.6	0	0	0	0	1	1	0	0	0	1	0	0	0	1	0	0	0	0	0	0	0	0	0	0	0
fennel	3	.3370	.2430	33.9	0	0	0	2	0	0	1	0	1	0	0	1	0	0	0	0	0	0	0	0	0	0	1	0	0
Fenwick	2	.1814	.1187	30.7	0	0	0	0	1	0	0	1	1	0	0	0	0	0	0	0	0	0	0	0	0	0	0	1	0
Feodorovna	3	.0000	.0328	25.2	0	0	0	0	0	0	3	0	0	3	0	0	0	0	0	0	0	0	0	0	0	0	0	0	0
Feodorovna's	2	.0000	.0219	23.4	0	0	0	0	0	0	2	0	0	2	0	0	0	0	0	0	0	0	0	0	0	0	0	0	0
fer	20	.2812	1.2945	41.1	1	0	4	1	2	12	0	0	1	0	0	4	0	0	0	0	0	0	0	0	14	0	1	0	0
Ferde	2	.1696	.0749	28.7	0	1	0	0	0	1	0	0	0	0	0	0	0	0	0	0	1	1	0	0	0	0	0	0	0
Ferdinand	18	.4147	1.6728	42.2	3	2	6	1	2	3	0	1	2	0	0	0	0	9	0	0	0	0	0	0	0	3	4	0	0
fergit	2	.0000	.0234	23.7	0	0	0	0	1	1	0	0	0	0	0	0	0	0	0	0	0	0	0	0	2	0	0	0	0
Ferguson	4	.3766	.3696	35.7	0	0	0	2	1	1	0	0	2	0	0	0	0	0	0	0	0	0	0	0	0	1	0	1	0
Ferhat	2	.0000	.0290	24.6	0	0	0	0	2	0	0	0	0	0	0	0	0	0	0	0	0	0	0	0	0	2	0	0	0
feria	2	.0000	.0162	22.1	0	0	0	0	2	0	0	0	0	0	0	0	0	0	2	0	0	0	0	0	0	0	0	0	0
fermata	9	.0000	.0728	28.6	2	0	4	3	0	0	0	0	0	0	0	0	0	0	0	0	9	0	0	0	0	0	0	0	0
fermatas	4	.0000	.0323	25.1	3	0	0	1	0	0	0	0	0	0	0	0	0	0	0	0	4	0	0	0	0	0	0	0	0
ferment	6	.3530	.4827	36.8	0	0	1	1	0	3	0	1	0	0	0	0	0	1	0	3	0	0	0	0	0	0	0	2	0
fermentation	9	.0000	.1774	32.5	0	0	0	0	0	1	7	1	0	0	0	0	0	0	0	9	0	0	0	0	0	0	0	0	0
fermented	3	.2345	.1568	32.0	0	0	0	2	0	0	1	0	0	0	0	0	0	0	0	0	0	0	1	0	0	0	2	0	0
fermenting	3	.2514	.1727	32.4	0	0	0	0	1	1	0	1	0	0	1	1	0	0	0	1	0	0	0	0	0	0	0	0	0
Fermi	14	.2949	.9655	39.8	0	0	0	0	13	0	0	1	0	0	0	0	0	7	0	1	0	0	0	0	0	0	6	0	0
Fermi's	2	.2285	.1129	30.5	0	0	0	0	2	0	0	0	0	0	0	0	0	1	0	0	0	0	0	0	0	0	1	0	0
fern	25	.4756	2.5935	44.1	3	0	1	2	6	1	10	2	2	0	0	2	0	0	0	16	0	0	0	0	0	2	2	1	0
Fern	36	.1520	1.4459	41.6	0	33	0	0	0	3	0	0	0	0	0	0	3	0	0	0	0	0	0	0	31	2	0	0	0
Fern's	4	.0000	.0469	26.7	0	4	0	0	0	0	0	0	0	0	0	0	0	0	0	0	0	0	0	0	4	0	0	0	0
Fernand	6	.1600	.3820	35.8	5	0	0	0	0	1	0	0	5	0	0	0	0	0	0	0	0	1	0	0	0	0	0	0	0
Fernanda	6	.0000	.2741	34.4	6	0	0	0	0	0	0	0	6	0	0	0	0	0	0	0	0	0	0	0	0	0	0	0	0
ferns	38	.6140	4.8433	46.9	7	3	4	4	14	2	3	1	2	2	0	1	0	2	0	17	0	0	0	0	3	5	6	0	0
ferny	6	.2435	.4680	36.7	4	0	1	0	1	0	0	0	5	0	0	1	0	0	0	0	0	0	0	0	0	0	0	0	0
ferocious	15	.5577	1.8398	42.6	3	1	2	2	1	5	0	1	8	2	1	2	0	0	0	1	0	0	0	0	0	0	0	1	0
ferociously	4	.3030	.2949	34.7	0	1	0	1	1	0	1	0	1	0	0	0	0	0	0	0	0	0	0	0	2	0	0	1	0
ferocity	6	.4644	.5827	37.7	0	0	0	1	4	0	1	0	0	1	0	2	0	0	0	0	0	0	0	0	0	0	2	1	0
ferret	2	.0000	.0234	23.7	0	0	2	0	0	0	0	0	0	0	0	0	0	0	0	0	0	0	0	0	2	0	0	0	0
ferric	2	.0000	.0215	23.3	0	0	0	0	0	0	2	0	0	0	0	2	0	0	0	0	0	0	0	0	0	0	0	0	0
ferried	4	.3470	.3506	35.4	0	0	1	0	0	1	0	2	2	0	0	0	0	0	0	1	1	0	0	0	0	0	0	0	0
ferries	10	.4804	1.0343	40.1	1	0	5	1	1	2	0	0	0	0	0	0	0	6	0	1	0	0	0	0	0	1	1	1	0
Ferris	19	.1707	1.3284	41.2	17	1	0	0	1	0	0	0	18	1	0	0	0	0	0	0	0	0	0	0	0	0	0	0	0
ferry	41	.6352	5.4961	47.4	0	15	10	8	2	6	0	0	13	0	0	2	0	13	0	0	0	0	0	0	3	6	1	3	0
Ferry	42	.3011	3.6733	45.7	0	0	3	34	0	2	3	0	34	1	0	0	0	7	0	0	0	0	0	0	0	0	0	0	0
Ferry's	5	.0000	.2284	33.6	0	0	0	5	0	0	0	0	5	0	0	0	0	0	0	0	0	0	0	0	0	0	0	0	0
ferryboat	13	.4513	1.3302	41.2	0	1	3	1	5	3	0	0	5	0	1	0	0	1	0	0	0	0	0	0	5	1	0	0	0
ferryboats	6	.4278	.5790	37.6	0	0	2	2	1	1	0	0	1	0	0	0	0	3	0	0	0	0	0	0	1	1	0	0	0
ferrying	2	.2433	.1158	30.6	0	0	0	0	1	0	0	1	0	0	0	0	0	0	0	0	0	0	0	0	0	1	0	1	0
ferryman	5	.2218	.3471	35.4	0	0	0	5	0	0	0	0	3	0	0	0	0	0	0	0	0	0	0	0	0	2	0	0	0
fertile	124	.4970	13.215	51.2	12	2	27	27	34	8	9	5	4	1	0	0	0	75	1	7	1	0	0	0	1	4	25	5	0
fertility	29	.4468	2.7846	44.4	1	0	3	1	19	2	1	2	1	0	0	0	0	4	0	2	0	0	0	0	0	3	4	15	0
fertilization	17	.3606	1.3800	41.4	1	1	1	0	9	0	4	1	0	0	0	0	0	1	0	9	0	0	0	0	0	1	6	0	0
fertilize	4	.3134	.2876	34.6	0	0	1	0	3	0	0	0	0	0	0	0	0	1	0	1	0	0	0	0	0	0	2	0	0
fertilized	22	.3438	1.7417	42.4	1	0	9	0	7	1	2	2	0	0	0	1	0	0	0	17	0	0	0	0	1	0	3	0	0
fertilizer	53	.5707	6.4620	48.1	16	3	10	7	3	4	6	4	10	0	0	0	0	21	0	8	0	0	0	0	0	7	2	5	0
Fertilizer	3	.0000	.1370	31.4	0	0	0	0	3	0	0	0	3	0	0	0	0	0	0	0	0	0	0	0	0	0	0	0	0
fertilizers	24	.4687	2.4534	43.9	7	1	3	6	3	3	1	0	1	0	0	0	0	11	1	8	0	0	0	0	0	0	3	0	0
fertilizes	2	.2278	.1128	30.5	0	0	0	0	1	0	1	0	0	0	0	0	0	0	0	1	0	0	0	0	0	0	1	0	0
fertilizing	3	.3764	.2483	33.9	0	0	1	0	1	0	0	1	0	0	0	0	0	0	0	1	0	0	0	0	0	0	1	1	0
fervent	6	.5142	.6573	38.2	0	0	1	0	1	4	0	0	1	1	0	0	0	0	0	0	0	0	0	0	2	1	1	0	0
fervently	6	.4441	.5992	37.8	0	0	1	0	2	1	2	0	2	1	0	2	0	0	0	0	0	0	0	0	0	0	0	1	0
fervor	8	.4761	.7993	39.0	0	0	1	3	2	0	2	0	0	0	0	0	0	0	0	0	1	0	0	0	2	2	0	3	0
festering	4	.3786	.3298	35.2	0	0	1	0	1	1	0	1	0	0	0	1	0	0	0	0	0	0	0	0	0	2	0	1	0
festival	61	.7330	9.0869	49.6	13	6	5	8	6	15	5	3	10	0	0	3	1	16	0	0	10	1	2	0	0	3	4	11	0
Festival	38	.6336	5.0860	47.1	9	10	2	6	2	2	5	2	13	1	0	1	1	12	0	0	4	0	0	0	0	0	1	5	0
festivals	44	.5508	5.0766	47.1	10	8	5	9	8	2	1	1	1	0	0	0	0	21	1	0	7	0	0	0	0	8	5	1	0
festive	9	.4042	.7939	39.0	1	0	1	2	1	2	0	2	1	0	0	0	0	0	0	1	4	0	0	0	0	0	1	2	0
festivities	11	.5483	1.2844	41.1	1	1	0	3	2	3	0	1	3	0	0	1	0	0	0	0	3	0	0	0	0	1	2	1	0
festivity	2	.2437	.1129	30.5	0	1	0	1	0	0	0	0	0	0	0	0	0	0	0	0	0	0	0	0	0	0	1	1	0
festooned	3	.2227	.1589	32.0	0	0	1	0	1	0	1	0	0	0	0	0	0	0	0	0	0	0	0	0	2	0	0	1	0
festoons	3	.3390	.2450	33.9	0	0	0	1	1	0	0	1	1	0	0	0	0	0	0	0	0	0	0	0	0	0	1	1	0
fetal	2	.0000	.0394	26.0	0	0	0	0	0	0	0	2	0	0	0	0	0	0	0	2	0	0	0	0	0	0	0	0	0
fetch	65	.5891	8.3018	49.2	10	5	9	18	11	7	2	3	34	3	2	7	0	0	0	0	0	0	0	0	16	1	0	2	0
fetched	13	.4897	1.3775	41.4	1	3	0	2	4	1	2	0	3	0	0	2	0	0	0	0	2	0	0	0	5	1	0	0	0
fetches	2	.0000	.0215	23.3	0	0	0	0	1	0	1	0	0	0	0	2	0	0	0	0	0	0	0	0	0	0	0	0	0
fetching	5	.3833	.4767	36.8	0	0	0	1	3	1	0	0	3	0	0	1	0	0	0	0	0	0	0	0	0	1	0	0	0
fetters	2	.1814	.1187	30.7	0	0	1	1	0	0	0	0	1	0	0	0	0	0	0	0	0	0	0	0	0	0	0	1	0
fetus	4	.2191	.2297	33.6	0	0	0	0	0	0	1	3	0	0	0	0	0	0	0	3	0	0	0	0	0	1	0	0	0
feud	8	.5664	.9603	39.8	0	0	0	0	1	2	4	1	2	1	0	1	0	0	0	1	2	0	0	0	0	0	0	1	0
Feud	3	.0000	.0243	23.8	0	0	0	0	0	0	3	0	0	0	0	0	0	0	0	0	3	0	0	0	0	0	0	0	0
feudal	20	.5434	2.2752	43.6	3	0	4	1	6	4	2	0	0	0	0	0	0	10	0	1	1	1	0	0	0	2	5	0	0
feudalism	6	.2663	.3991	36.0	2	0	0	0	2	2	0	0	1	0	0	0	0	2	0	0	0	0	0	0	0	0	3	0	0
feuds	3	.2279	.2143	33.3	0	0	0	0	1	1	0	1	2	0	0	0	0	0	0	0	0	0	0	0	0	0	0	1	0
fever	150	.7114	22.021	53.4	6	26	18	32	23	22	9	14	42	0	0	6	0	9	2	45	0	0	0	0	10	19	11	6	0
fevered	3	.1900	.1470	31.7	0	0	0	0	2	0	0	1	0	0	0	0	0	0	0	1	0	0	0	0	2	0	0	0	0
feverish	8	.4745	.8154	39.1	0	0	1	1	3	2	1	0	1	0	0	2	0	1	0	0	0	0	0	0	3	0	1	0	0
feverishly	2	.1717	.1142	30.6	0	0	1	0	1	0	0	0	1	0	0	1	0	0	0	0	0	0	0	0	0	0	0	0	0
fevers	3	.2757	.1896	32.8	0	1	0	0	0	0	1	1	0	0	0	0	0	0	0	1	0	0	1	0	0	1	0	0	0
few	2685	.9625	510.04	67.1	390	401	332	390	528	289	262	93	640	135	37	130	21	467	47	299	60	26	34	23	125	245	172	223	1
fewer	155	.8791	27.118	54.3	31	11	11	26	24	22	22	8	15	4	4	2	34	24	2	36	2	1	3	2	2	7	7	10	0
fewest	18	.1857	.9028	39.6	8	6	1	0	0	2	1	0	1	0	0	0	15	1	0	0	0	0	0	0	0	0	0	1	0

8A fence-post
8N fencerow
3A fend
8A fended
6J Feng
XH Fenner
3P Fenton
XR fenugreek
7R Feodor
3P fer-de-lance
8R Ferber
8N ferine
6H ferments
7F Fermis
7Q fern-choked
8P fern-clad
7N fern-table
7Q Fernandez
8Q Fernando
5P ferned
XR ferociousness
8B ferre
6R ferreting
3A ferris
3A ferroalloy
4Q ferromagnetic
9M ferrous
9M ferrous-metal
9Q Ferruccio
3P ferrum
7N ferry-boat
4F ferry's
7N fervency
7A Fessenden
8A Fessler
6A festal
8N festerin'
8J Festivals
5J fests
7L feta
7D fetchin'
8K Fetes
7Q fetish
8K fetishes
3P fetlocks
6A fettered
9Q Fettes
6N fettle
XR fetuses
5Q Feudalism
6R feuding
4N fever-trees
8A feverishness
4F Few
7Q fewness

Word Type	F	D	U	SFI	3 Gr 3	4 Gr 4	5 Gr 5	6 Gr 6	7 Gr 7	8 Gr 8	9 Gr 9	X UnGr	A Read	B Eng & Gr	C Comp	D Lit	E Math	F Soc Stud	G Spell	H Sci	J Music	K Art	L Home Ec	M Shop	N Lib F	P Lib NF	Q Lib Ref	R Mag	S Rel
fez	6	.3477	.5147	37.1	0	2	2	0	1	0	1	0	2	1	0	0	0	3	0	0	0	0	0	0	0	0	0	0	0
Fez	24	.1089	1.4674	41.7	10	0	0	13	1	0	0	0	23	0	0	0	0	1	0	0	0	0	0	0	0	0	0	0	0
fezzes	2	.2401	.1133	30.5	1	0	0	1	0	0	0	0	0	0	0	0	0	0	0	0	0	0	0	0	0	1	1	0	0
ff	7	.3400	.5150	37.1	2	3	0	1	0	0	1	0	0	4	0	0	0	0	2	0	0	0	0	0	1	0	0	0	0
FG	4	.0000	.0599	27.8	1	1	0	1	0	1	0	0	0	0	0	0	4	0	0	0	0	0	0	0	0	0	0	0	0
FH	2	.0000	.0299	24.8	0	0	0	0	0	2	0	0	0	0	0	0	2	0	0	0	0	0	0	0	0	0	0	0	0
FHA	9	.0000	.0942	29.7	0	0	9	0	0	0	0	0	0	0	0	0	0	0	0	0	0	0	0	0	0	0	9	0	0
fiance	2	.2433	.1158	30.6	0	0	1	0	1	0	0	0	0	0	0	0	0	0	0	0	0	0	0	0	0	1	0	1	0
Fianna	2	.0000	.0290	24.6	0	0	2	0	0	0	0	0	0	0	0	0	0	0	0	0	0	0	0	0	0	2	0	0	0
fiasco	2	.2285	.1129	30.5	0	0	0	0	1	1	0	0	0	0	0	0	0	1	0	0	0	0	0	0	0	0	1	0	0
Fiat	21	.0000	.9593	39.8	0	0	0	0	0	21	0	0	21	0	0	0	0	0	0	0	0	0	0	0	0	0	0	0	0
fiber	57	.4508	5.4142	47.3	0	1	4	5	10	16	19	2	3	0	0	0	0	8	0	8	1	0	21	5	3	1	5	2	0
fibers	137	.3576	10.738	50.3	3	1	27	14	13	36	38	5	5	0	1	0	0	21	5	36	1	0	54	0	1	2	9	2	0
fibre	3	.2266	.1614	32.1	0	0	0	0	1	0	0	2	0	0	0	0	0	0	0	0	0	0	0	0	1	0	0	2	0
fibril	2	.0000	.0394	26.0	0	0	0	0	0	0	0	2	0	0	0	0	0	0	0	2	0	0	0	0	0	0	0	0	0
fibrillation	2	.0000	.0209	23.2	0	0	0	0	0	2	0	0	0	0	0	0	0	0	0	0	0	0	0	0	0	0	2	0	0
fibrils	5	.0000	.0986	29.9	0	0	0	0	0	0	0	5	0	0	0	0	0	0	0	5	0	0	0	0	0	0	0	0	0
fibrous	13	.4988	1.3903	41.4	1	0	0	2	2	2	4	2	1	0	0	0	0	0	0	7	0	0	1	0	2	0	2	0	0
fibs	2	.2427	.1152	30.6	0	2	0	0	0	0	0	0	0	0	0	0	0	0	0	0	0	0	0	0	1	1	0	0	0
fickle	6	.2845	.3849	35.9	0	1	1	0	1	0	3	0	0	0	0	4	0	0	0	0	0	0	0	0	1	1	0	0	0
fiction	68	.6533	9.2032	49.6	2	3	15	12	9	10	14	3	17	20	2	3	0	2	0	1	0	0	0	0	0	5	9	9	0
Fiction	2	.1733	.1149	30.6	0	0	1	0	1	0	0	0	1	1	0	0	0	0	0	0	0	0	0	0	0	0	0	0	0
fictional	9	.5335	1.0258	40.1	0	0	1	1	2	2	2	1	2	1	0	0	0	0	0	0	0	0	0	0	0	2	2	2	0
fictions	2	.2412	.1141	30.6	0	0	0	1	1	0	0	0	0	1	0	0	0	0	0	0	0	0	0	0	0	1	0	0	0
fictitious	4	.2454	.2714	34.3	0	0	0	3	0	1	0	0	2	0	1	0	0	0	0	0	0	0	0	0	0	0	1	0	0
FID	7	.0000	.0851	29.3	0	0	0	0	7	0	0	0	0	0	0	0	0	0	0	0	0	0	0	0	0	0	0	7	0
fiddle	65	.5909	8.2532	49.2	4	9	22	7	21	0	1	1	29	1	0	5	0	0	0	1	13	0	0	0	7	8	0	1	0
fiddled	2	.1717	.1142	30.6	0	0	0	1	1	0	0	0	1	0	0	1	0	0	0	0	0	0	0	0	0	0	0	0	0
fiddler	21	.5143	2.3294	43.7	3	3	5	5	2	2	1	0	5	0	0	4	0	0	0	4	5	0	0	0	3	0	0	0	0
Fiddler	11	.3640	1.0363	40.2	0	0	8	0	2	1	0	0	8	0	0	0	0	0	0	0	2	0	0	0	0	0	1	0	0
FIDDLER	3	.0000	.0322	25.1	0	0	0	0	0	0	3	0	0	0	0	3	0	0	0	0	0	0	0	0	0	0	0	0	0
fiddler's	3	.3267	.2367	33.7	1	0	0	1	0	1	0	0	1	0	0	0	0	0	0	0	1	0	0	0	1	0	0	0	0
fiddlers	5	.3541	.4309	36.3	0	3	0	0	2	0	0	0	2	0	0	0	0	0	0	0	1	0	0	0	0	2	0	0	0
fiddles	5	.3626	.4123	36.2	1	1	0	0	1	0	0	2	0	0	0	0	0	1	0	2	0	0	0	0	0	2	0	0	0
fiddling	5	.4433	.4638	36.7	0	3	0	0	1	1	0	0	0	0	0	1	0	0	0	0	2	0	0	0	1	0	0	1	0
Fidel	4	.2352	.2332	33.7	0	0	1	0	2	1	0	0	0	0	0	0	0	2	0	0	0	0	0	0	0	0	0	2	0
Fidele	2	.0000	.0219	23.4	0	0	0	0	2	0	0	0	0	2	0	0	0	0	0	0	0	0	0	0	0	0	0	0	0
fidelity	8	.0000	.1577	32.0	0	0	0	0	0	8	0	0	0	0	0	0	0	0	0	8	0	0	0	0	0	0	0	0	0
Fidelity	3	.0000	.0243	23.8	0	0	0	0	0	3	0	0	0	0	0	0	0	0	0	0	3	0	0	0	0	0	0	0	0
fidgeted	4	.3231	.3016	34.8	0	0	0	1	2	0	1	0	1	0	1	1	0	0	0	0	0	0	0	0	1	0	0	0	0
fidgeting	3	.2223	.2106	33.2	0	1	0	2	0	0	0	0	2	1	0	0	0	0	0	0	0	0	0	0	0	0	0	0	0
fidgets	2	.0000	.0914	29.6	1	0	0	0	1	0	0	0	2	0	0	0	0	0	0	0	0	0	0	0	0	0	0	0	0
fie	6	.2827	.4100	36.1	1	2	0	0	0	0	3	0	1	0	0	3	0	0	0	0	0	0	0	0	0	2	0	0	0
field	919	.8931	163.40	62.1	164	152	82	134	157	112	89	29	230	18	8	48	32	85	16	120	14	6	1	41	68	76	79	77	0
Field	37	.7320	5.5285	47.4	6	2	7	6	5	6	2	3	7	1	0	0	0	8	1	4	2	0	0	0	3	7	4	0	0
Field's	2	.2285	.1129	30.5	0	0	0	0	1	1	0	0	0	0	0	0	0	1	0	0	0	0	0	0	0	0	1	0	0
fielded	6	.3860	.5837	37.7	0	4	1	0	1	0	0	0	4	0	0	0	0	0	0	0	0	0	0	0	0	1	0	1	0
fielder	20	.5683	2.3966	43.8	2	8	7	2	0	1	0	0	3	1	1	0	0	0	0	7	0	0	0	0	0	1	6	1	0
fielder's	2	.1787	.1174	30.7	1	0	1	0	0	0	0	0	1	0	0	0	0	0	0	0	0	0	0	0	1	0	0	0	0
fielders	2	.1948	.1250	31.0	1	0	1	0	0	0	0	0	1	0	0	0	0	0	0	0	0	0	0	0	0	1	0	0	0
fielding	9	.2269	.5374	37.3	2	0	1	3	2	1	0	0	2	0	0	0	0	0	0	0	0	0	0	0	1	0	0	6	0
Fielding	3	.2159	.1532	31.9	0	0	3	0	0	0	0	0	0	0	0	0	0	0	0	0	0	0	0	0	0	0	2	1	0
fields	604	.8616	104.03	60.2	110	86	71	103	117	63	40	14	118	8	6	42	12	203	5	43	10	9	0	4	35	34	47	28	0
Fields	9	.2844	.6262	38.0	5	0	1	0	1	1	0	1	1	0	0	0	0	4	0	0	0	0	0	0	0	0	0	4	0
fiend	10	.2450	.5958	37.8	0	0	1	1	0	0	7	1	1	1	0	7	0	0	0	1	0	0	0	0	0	0	0	0	0
fiendish	2	.1948	.1250	31.0	0	0	1	0	0	1	0	0	1	0	0	0	0	0	0	0	0	0	0	0	0	1	0	0	0
fierce	146	.8339	24.540	53.9	31	28	21	16	30	11	6	3	55	5	2	11	0	16	3	3	0	1	0	0	19	15	7	9	0
Fierce	2	.0000	.0290	24.6	0	2	0	0	0	0	0	0	0	0	0	0	0	0	0	0	0	0	0	0	0	2	0	0	0
fierce-eyed	2	.0000	.0914	29.6	0	1	0	1	0	0	0	0	2	0	0	0	0	0	0	0	0	0	0	0	0	0	0	0	0
fierce-looking	3	.3553	.2609	34.2	1	1	0	0	0	0	1	0	1	0	0	0	0	0	0	1	0	0	0	0	0	1	0	0	0
fiercely	64	.7471	9.8026	49.9	8	13	6	10	17	4	5	1	24	3	2	7	0	7	0	0	0	0	0	0	8	6	3	4	0
fierceness	6	.3859	.5833	37.7	1	2	1	0	2	0	0	0	4	0	0	0	0	0	0	0	0	0	0	0	1	1	0	0	0
fiercer	6	.5066	.6515	38.1	0	0	0	1	5	0	0	0	1	0	0	1	0	1	0	0	0	0	0	0	2	0	1	0	0
fiercest	7	.4962	.7518	38.8	1	0	0	2	3	1	0	0	1	0	0	0	0	2	0	1	0	0	0	0	0	0	2	1	0
fiery	49	.8838	8.6299	49.4	4	8	5	11	11	6	3	1	13	4	1	4	0	2	2	4	2	1	0	0	3	5	4	4	0
fiesta	17	.4637	1.7973	42.5	10	3	2	1	1	1	0	0	7	0	0	0	0	4	0	0	0	0	0	0	2	0	4	0	0
fiestas	6	.0971	.2435	33.9	0	4	0	1	0	1	0	0	1	0	0	0	0	5	0	0	0	0	0	0	0	0	0	0	0
fife	9	.2276	.5480	37.4	1	2	2	1	2	1	0	0	3	0	0	1	0	0	0	0	5	0	0	0	0	0	0	0	0
fifes	4	.4417	.3913	35.9	0	1	1	1	0	0	1	0	1	0	0	1	0	0	0	0	1	0	0	0	0	1	0	0	0
fifteen	233	.8908	41.324	56.2	28	35	32	40	51	23	17	7	55	16	3	17	8	26	11	16	2	1	1	0	22	38	2	15	0
fifteen-minute	4	.4818	.4128	36.2	0	1	0	0	1	1	1	0	0	0	0	0	0	1	0	1	0	0	0	0	0	1	0	1	0
fifteen-year-old	7	.3517	.5514	37.4	0	0	2	1	2	0	2	0	1	0	2	1	0	1	0	0	0	0	0	0	1	0	0	1	0
fifteenth	25	.6888	3.4870	45.4	2	4	1	3	7	2	3	3	2	5	0	0	1	3	1	0	4	1	0	3	0	1	1	3	0
Fifteenth	2	.0000	.0389	25.9	0	0	0	0	0	1	1	0	0	0	0	0	0	2	0	0	0	0	0	0	0	0	0	0	0
fifteenth-century	2	.2412	.1091	30.4	0	0	0	0	1	0	1	0	0	0	0	1	0	0	1	0	0	0	0	0	0	0	0	0	0
fifth	185	.7662	28.503	54.5	33	41	25	30	25	19	11	1	18	10	1	3	19	13	15	11	53	3	0	0	3	18	8	10	0
Fifth	30	.6971	4.2811	46.3	6	1	0	3	5	2	12	1	6	2	0	0	2	2	0	0	5	0	0	0	6	3	1	3	0
fifth-grade	3	.1900	.1470	31.7	0	2	1	0	0	0	0	0	0	0	0	0	0	0	0	1	0	0	0	0	2	0	0	0	0
fifths	34	.4457	3.2405	45.1	0	3	14	6	5	4	2	0	1	2	0	0	14	5	0	0	11	0	0	0	0	0	1	0	0
fifties	5	.4407	.4881	36.9	1	0	1	0	0	3	0	0	1	0	0	1	2	0	0	0	0	0	0	0	0	0	0	1	0
fiftieth	7	.5655	.8325	39.2	1	3	0	0	1	2	0	0	1	2	0	1	0	1	1	1	0	0	0	0	0	0	0	0	0
fifty	306	.8911	54.387	57.4	51	49	34	43	64	36	17	12	96	18	1	22	10	44	7	26	8	0	4	0	25	30	7	8	0
Fifty	10	.2397	.5579	37.5	0	2	4	3	0	0	1	0	0	4	0	0	0	0	0	0	0	0	0	0	6	0	0	0	0
Fifty-Mile	2	.0000	.0914	29.6	0	0	2	0	0	0	0	0	2	0	0	0	0	0	0	0	0	0	0	0	0	0	0	0	0
fifty-cent	7	.4775	.7559	38.8	2	0	2	1	1	0	0	1	3	1	0	0	2	0	0	0	0	0	0	0	1	0	0	0	0
fifty-eight	2	.2152	.1357	31.3	0	0	1	0	0	0	1	0	1	0	0	0	0	1	0	0	0	0	0	0	0	0	0	0	0
fifty-five	5	.4743	.5375	37.3	2	0	1	0	0	1	1	0	2	0	0	1	0	1	0	0	0	0	0	0	0	1	0	0	0
fifty-four	3	.3467	.2520	34.0	1	0	1	0	1	0	0	0	1	0	0	0	1	0	0	0	0	0	0	0	0	0	0	0	0
fifty-nine	2	.2152	.1357	31.3	0	0	0	1	0	1	0	0	1	0	0	0	0	1	0	0	0	0	0	0	0	0	0	1	0
fifty-nines	2	.0000	.0299	24.8	0	0	0	2	0	0	0	0	0	0	0	0	2	0	0	0	0	0	0	0	0	0	0	0	0
fifty-one	2	.2152	.1357	31.3	1	0	0	0	0	1	0	0	1	0	0	0	0	1	0	0	0	0	0	0	0	0	0	0	0
fifty-pound	2	.1787	.1174	30.7	0	0	0	0	0	2	0	0	1	0	0	0	0	0	0	0	0	0	0	0	1	0	0	0	0
fifty-seven	2	.2408	.1204	30.8	1	0	1	0	0	0	0	0	0	0	0	0	0	1	0	0	0	0	0	0	0	1	0	0	0
fifty-six	6	.4530	.6191	37.9	2	1	1	0	1	1	0	0	2	0	0	0	2	1	0	0	0	0	0	0	0	1	0	0	0

4B ffe
7R Ffrancis
4E FGC
8E FGH
6E FHG
3A fi
9D fia
XN fib
9H fiber-glass
7H fiberboard
4H fiberglass
9Q fibres
7Q fibrillae
XH fibro-vascular
4R fibroblasts
8H fibroplasia
6A Fichtenhorst
7D fiction-writing
7D fictionalizes
7N ficuses
7M fid
7R fiddleback
7A Fiddlers'
8J fiddlin'
8J Fidelio
7N fidgetin'
7N fidgety
7Q field-glass
7P field-slave
7R field-test
7R Fielder
6A fieldglasses
5Q Fielding's
3N Fieldmouse's
5P fieldpiece
7A fiendishly
6A fierce-burning
8D fierce-hued
7D fieriest
7Q Fiers
5H fiery-hot
8F fiery-tempered
8Q Fiesole
6J Fiesta
3P Fifteen
5H fifteen-hour
7R fifteen-mile
7R fifteenth-anniversary
7D fifteenth-early
4B fifth-
6R fifth-best
6B fifth-hand
8R fifth-place
7R fifth-round
8B fiftie
3A Fifty-Fifty
6F fifty-fifth
3A fifty-fifty
5A Fifty-first
4H fifty-foot

Word Type	F	D	U	SFI	3 Gr 3	4 Gr 4	5 Gr 5	6 Gr 6	7 Gr 7	8 Gr 8	9 Gr 9	X UnGr	A Read	B Eng & Gr	C Comp	D Lit	E Math	F Soc Stud	G Spell	H Sci	J Music	K Art	L Home Ec	M Shop	N Lib F	P Lib NF	Q Lib Ref	R Mag	S Rel
fifty-three	2	.2303	.1079	30.3	0	1	0	0	0	0	1	0	0	0	0	0	0	0	0	0	1	0	0	0	0	1	0	0	0
fifty-two	8	.4652	.8482	39.3	0	2	0	5	1	0	0	0	3	0	0	0	1	3	0	0	1	0	0	0	0	0	0	0	0
fig	55	.4586	5.4454	47.4	6	1	1	4	9	7	19	8	7	1	0	1	1	0	0	15	0	0	0	12	2	7	8	1	0
Fig	501	.0864	11.752	50.7	0	1	0	0	133	152	206	9	0	0	0	0	25	0	0	113	0	0	0	358	0	0	5	0	0
Figaro	8	.1042	.2253	33.5	0	1	0	3	0	3	1	0	0	0	0	0	0	0	0	0	7	0	0	0	0	0	0	1	0
figger	2	.0000	.0234	23.7	0	0	0	0	2	0	0	0	0	0	0	0	0	0	0	0	0	0	0	0	2	0	0	0	0
figgering	2	.2443	.1130	30.5	0	1	0	0	0	1	0	0	0	0	0	1	0	0	0	0	0	0	0	0	1	0	0	0	0
figgy	2	.0000	.0162	22.1	0	2	0	0	0	0	0	0	0	0	0	0	0	0	0	0	2	0	0	0	0	0	0	0	0
fight	529	.8425	89.612	59.5	90	90	48	81	98	76	38	8	178	19	9	49	1	64	5	23	13	0	1	0	51	65	13	38	0
fighter	48	.6202	6.3743	48.0	6	9	7	14	8	3	1	0	23	3	0	6	0	2	0	0	0	0	0	0	1	11	1	1	0
Fighter	6	.3545	.5377	37.3	0	1	0	3	1	1	0	0	3	0	0	0	0	1	0	0	0	0	0	0	0	2	0	0	0
fighters	35	.6210	4.5514	46.6	2	5	3	3	9	8	3	2	6	0	0	1	0	12	0	2	1	0	0	0	0	9	3	1	0
fightin'	2	.1717	.1142	30.6	0	0	0	1	0	1	0	0	1	0	0	1	0	0	0	0	0	0	0	0	0	0	0	0	0
fighting	321	.7685	50.152	57.0	23	57	40	40	65	61	27	8	79	2	0	21	0	93	1	6	5	2	0	0	27	36	19	30	0
Fighting	2	.2285	.1129	30.5	0	0	0	0	0	2	0	0	0	0	0	0	0	1	0	0	0	0	0	0	0	0	1	0	0
fights	39	.7206	5.8275	47.7	1	8	4	10	8	5	3	0	18	2	0	5	0	4	0	0	2	1	0	0	1	5	0	1	0
figs	13	.6613	1.7712	42.5	4	0	3	1	2	1	2	0	2	0	0	1	0	4	0	0	1	0	0	1	1	2	1	0	0
Figs	42	.0358	.4974	37.0	0	0	0	0	14	2	26	0	0	0	0	0	0	0	0	6	0	0	0	36	0	0	0	0	0
figurative	15	.2875	.9170	39.6	0	0	0	0	1	7	7	0	0	3	6	1	0	0	5	0	0	0	0	0	0	0	0	0	0
figuratively	4	.4820	.4018	36.0	0	0	1	0	0	1	1	1	0	1	0	1	0	0	1	0	0	0	0	0	0	1	0	0	0
figure	863	.7763	134.86	61.3	67	112	96	84	217	156	110	21	97	21	5	44	385	16	10	47	15	42	24	12	27	60	22	36	0
Figure	171	.5748	20.485	53.1	4	8	10	0	8	47	87	7	7	0	0	0	91	11	0	37	11	9	3	1	0	0	1	0	0
figured	93	.8525	15.907	52.0	9	15	4	12	29	13	10	1	34	1	2	13	5	0	0	3	5	0	2	1	6	7	4	10	0
figurehead	4	.4866	.4070	36.1	1	0	0	1	1	0	1	0	0	0	0	1	0	0	0	0	0	0	0	0	0	1	1	1	0
figures	447	.6786	61.927	57.9	42	72	55	45	82	92	41	18	51	12	4	14	147	38	2	17	18	50	1	7	9	26	28	23	0
Figures	6	.2906	.4002	36.0	0	1	0	0	1	1	3	0	0	0	0	0	4	1	0	0	0	1	0	0	0	0	0	0	0
figurines	3	.2321	.1635	32.1	1	0	0	1	1	0	0	0	0	0	0	0	0	0	0	0	0	0	0	0	0	0	1	2	0
figuring	20	.6313	2.6805	44.3	2	6	3	2	2	2	0	3	8	0	1	0	0	2	0	3	0	0	0	0	2	1	0	3	0
Fiji	3	.0000	.0583	27.7	0	2	0	0	1	0	0	0	0	0	0	0	0	3	0	0	0	0	0	0	0	0	0	0	0
filament	30	.5365	3.4442	45.4	3	0	3	4	1	7	11	1	4	0	0	0	0	0	0	18	0	0	1	1	1	0	5	0	0
filaments	10	.2621	.5914	37.7	0	0	0	1	0	4	4	1	0	0	0	0	0	0	0	3	0	0	4	0	0	0	3	0	0
Filcher	3	.0000	.0352	25.5	0	0	0	0	3	0	0	0	0	0	0	0	0	0	0	0	0	0	0	0	3	0	0	0	0
file	97	.6022	11.995	50.8	5	13	7	9	21	13	25	4	11	6	3	3	0	3	19	11	1	0	3	22	2	4	2	7	0
File	6	.0000	.0487	26.9	0	0	0	0	6	0	0	0	0	0	0	0	0	0	6	0	0	0	0	0	0	0	0	0	0
filed	23	.6367	2.9871	44.8	0	2	0	4	10	3	4	0	2	4	0	2	1	0	0	0	0	0	1	3	4	0	1	5	0
files	17	.4226	1.5395	41.9	1	3	0	1	3	5	4	0	2	2	0	0	0	0	0	1	1	0	0	5	1	0	3	2	0
filibuster	2	.0000	.0914	29.6	0	0	0	0	2	0	0	0	2	0	0	0	0	0	0	0	0	0	0	0	0	0	0	0	0
filigree	2	.1814	.1187	30.7	0	1	0	0	0	0	0	1	1	0	0	0	0	0	0	0	0	0	0	0	0	0	0	1	0
filing	10	.4087	.8538	39.3	0	2	2	2	1	1	2	0	0	0	0	0	0	0	1	0	0	0	0	3	1	1	3	1	0
filings	16	.3744	1.3550	41.3	3	2	0	6	2	2	1	0	1	0	0	0	0	0	0	10	0	0	0	2	0	0	0	3	0
Filipinos	22	.2848	1.4313	41.6	14	0	0	5	0	3	0	0	0	0	0	0	0	6	0	0	2	0	0	0	0	0	14	0	0
fill	487	.9238	89.149	59.5	143	84	52	51	67	39	39	12	105	16	12	11	99	15	53	68	10	7	14	6	14	29	14	13	1
filled	656	.9347	121.51	60.8	152	124	86	78	97	57	45	17	212	22	11	44	17	45	9	83	15	10	6	5	61	57	22	35	2
filled-in	3	.1986	.1398	31.5	0	0	0	0	1	2	0	0	0	0	0	0	0	0	2	0	0	0	0	0	0	0	0	1	0
fillet	2	.2427	.1152	30.6	1	0	0	1	0	0	0	0	0	0	0	0	0	0	0	0	0	0	0	0	1	1	0	0	0
fillets	4	.3232	.2801	34.5	0	0	0	0	2	0	1	1	0	0	0	0	0	0	0	0	0	0	0	1	1	0	0	2	0
filling	126	.6531	16.886	52.3	14	10	8	19	29	15	26	5	24	2	4	11	9	4	3	5	4	1	30	0	12	5	5	7	0
fillings	7	.1160	.2019	33.1	0	0	0	0	3	0	4	0	0	0	0	0	0	0	0	1	0	0	5	0	0	0	0	1	0
Fillmore	2	.1814	.1187	30.7	0	0	0	0	1	0	1	0	1	0	0	0	0	0	0	0	0	0	0	0	0	0	0	1	0
fills	49	.8532	8.3658	49.2	12	9	4	4	4	6	9	1	12	2	1	3	4	3	0	8	3	2	0	2	1	2	3	3	0
filly	9	.4679	.9732	39.9	0	0	2	4	0	3	0	0	5	0	0	2	0	0	0	0	0	0	0	0	1	0	0	1	0
filly's	3	.2212	.2099	33.2	0	0	1	1	0	1	0	0	2	0	0	1	0	0	0	0	0	0	0	0	0	0	0	0	0
film	164	.7329	24.272	53.9	5	9	7	20	43	16	46	18	9	4	0	5	8	2	3	31	9	1	0	5	2	6	13	66	0
Film	4	.1854	.1872	32.7	0	1	0	0	1	0	1	1	0	0	0	0	0	0	0	0	0	0	0	0	0	1	0	3	0
film-making	2	.0000	.0243	23.9	0	0	0	0	2	0	0	0	0	0	0	0	0	0	0	0	0	0	0	0	0	0	0	2	0
filmed	9	.3609	.7315	38.6	0	1	0	2	3	2	0	1	1	0	0	3	0	1	0	0	0	0	0	0	0	0	0	4	0
filming	3	.3769	.2439	33.9	0	1	0	1	1	0	0	0	0	0	0	0	0	0	1	0	0	0	0	0	0	1	0	1	0
filmmaker	2	.0000	.0243	23.9	0	0	0	0	0	0	0	2	0	0	0	0	0	0	0	0	0	0	0	0	0	0	0	2	0
films	31	.6151	3.8989	45.9	0	4	2	4	5	6	6	4	0	1	0	0	2	3	0	4	2	2	0	0	0	0	6	11	0
filmstrip	2	.0000	.0394	26.0	0	1	0	1	0	0	0	0	0	0	0	0	0	0	0	2	0	0	0	0	0	0	0	0	0
filmstrips	2	.2351	.1166	30.7	0	0	0	0	1	0	0	1	0	0	0	0	0	1	0	0	0	0	0	0	0	0	0	1	0
filmy	3	.2443	.1820	32.6	0	1	0	0	1	1	0	0	0	0	0	1	0	0	0	2	0	0	0	0	0	0	0	0	0
filoplumes	2	.2401	.1133	30.5	1	0	0	0	1	0	0	0	0	0	0	0	0	0	0	0	0	0	0	0	0	1	1	0	0
filter	39	.4447	3.7715	45.8	3	0	7	3	20	1	3	2	0	0	0	5	0	0	0	26	0	0	0	0	1	0	5	2	0
filtered	13	.5750	1.5799	42.0	1	1	2	1	2	1	4	1	2	0	0	0	0	2	0	4	1	0	0	0	0	0	3	1	0
filtering	4	.3396	.2945	34.7	0	0	0	0	0	2	2	0	0	0	0	0	0	0	0	1	1	1	0	0	0	0	0	1	0
filters	9	.3315	.6752	38.3	0	1	0	1	1	2	4	0	0	0	0	0	0	0	0	4	0	0	0	0	0	0	4	1	0
filth	8	.4690	.7982	39.0	2	0	0	0	2	3	1	0	0	0	0	2	0	0	0	2	0	0	0	0	0	3	1	0	0
filthiest	2	.2442	.1134	30.5	0	0	0	0	1	0	1	0	0	1	0	0	0	0	0	0	0	0	0	0	0	0	0	1	0
filthy	12	.5460	1.4000	41.5	1	0	0	1	4	4	1	1	2	0	0	3	0	4	0	1	0	0	0	0	0	1	0	1	0
filtration	8	.3474	.6430	38.1	0	0	3	1	1	2	1	0	0	1	0	0	0	2	0	5	0	0	0	0	0	0	0	0	0
fin	34	.5545	4.0070	46.0	5	7	2	2	14	1	2	1	8	2	0	0	0	0	0	2	0	0	0	0	6	0	8	8	0
Fin	3	.2184	.1759	32.5	0	1	0	0	0	0	1	1	1	0	0	0	0	0	0	0	0	0	0	1	0	0	0	1	0
fin'lly	2	.0000	.0162	22.1	0	0	0	0	2	0	0	0	0	0	0	0	0	0	0	0	2	0	0	0	0	0	0	0	0
final	460	.7485	69.380	58.4	42	43	52	76	105	63	63	16	61	48	12	14	14	16	169	19	16	2	3	12	9	18	9	38	0
Final	37	.0000	.3003	34.8	19	8	3	4	1	2	0	0	0	0	0	0	0	0	37	0	0	0	0	0	0	0	0	0	0
finale	5	.1446	.1801	32.6	0	1	0	1	0	1	2	0	0	0	0	0	0	0	0	0	4	0	0	0	0	0	0	1	0
finality	3	.3873	.2495	34.0	0	0	0	0	1	1	1	0	0	0	0	1	0	0	0	0	0	0	0	0	1	0	0	1	0
finally	1032	.9080	186.39	62.7	117	152	142	143	219	118	105	36	324	54	15	68	18	149	6	67	30	2	2	4	49	88	67	89	0
finals	3	.2187	.1555	31.9	0	0	0	0	0	1	1	1	0	2	0	0	0	0	0	0	0	0	0	0	0	0	0	1	0
finance	19	.5664	2.2480	43.5	3	0	3	2	6	1	3	1	2	0	0	1	0	3	1	0	0	0	0	0	0	2	7	3	0
Finance	7	.4256	.6379	38.0	0	0	2	0	0	2	3	0	0	0	0	0	0	1	0	0	0	0	0	0	0	1	2	3	0
financed	7	.4366	.6546	38.2	0	0	2	0	1	1	1	2	0	0	0	1	0	0	0	1	0	0	0	0	0	2	0	3	0
financial	58	.6694	7.9395	49.0	2	0	6	2	14	15	18	1	6	2	0	1	2	11	1	0	0	0	5	0	0	6	10	14	0
financially	3	.2159	.1532	31.9	0	0	1	0	0	1	1	0	0	0	0	0	0	0	0	0	0	0	0	0	0	0	2	1	0
financier	3	.3390	.2450	33.9	0	0	1	0	0	1	0	1	1	0	0	0	0	0	0	0	0	0	0	0	0	0	1	1	0
financing	7	.2210	.3873	35.9	0	0	0	0	1	3	3	0	0	0	0	0	0	3	0	0	0	0	0	0	0	0	0	4	0
finch	6	.3015	.4021	36.0	4	0	0	0	1	0	1	0	0	4	0	1	0	0	0	0	0	0	0	0	0	0	0	1	0
Finch	8	.2185	.4186	36.2	0	0	0	0	0	0	8	0	0	0	0	6	0	1	0	0	0	0	0	0	0	0	0	1	0
Finch's	2	.2297	.1135	30.6	0	0	0	0	0	0	2	0	0	0	0	1	0	1	0	0	0	0	0	0	0	0	0	0	0
finches	4	.2847	.2818	34.5	1	0	0	1	1	1	0	0	1	0	0	0	0	0	0	0	0	0	0	0	0	1	2	0	0
find	6916	.8936	1228.5	70.9	1363	1269	953	909	1139	721	462	100	1138	405	60	162	2183	494	546	773	321	85	66	30	144	227	89	188	5
Find	5	.4459	.5028	37.0	1	0	1	2	0	1	0	0	1	0	0	0	0	1	0	2	0	0	0	0	0	0	0	1	0
finder	5	.2279	.3264	35.1	1	0	4	0	0	0	0	0	2	0	0	0	0	0	0	2	0	1	0	0	0	0	0	0	0
finders	4	.1335	.1958	32.9	2	0	1	1	0	0	0	0	1	0	0	0	0	0	0	3	0	0	0	0	0	0	0	0	0
finding	392	.8718	68.136	58.3	48	58	42	65	76	53	43	7	68	21	6	15	132	19	9	44	4	3	3	3	16	15	11	23	0

9B fifty-story
XH fifty-thousandth
8A fifty-yard
7A fifty's
7D fiftyseven
3A fig-eater
7D figgered
4A FIGHT
3B Fight-the-good-fight-of**
7N fight'n
8D fight's
XR figment
9R figura
7J figure-eight
8E figure-wheels
8B figurin'
4P figurine
9P filamental
3R Filbert
7R file-drawers
XR filet
7D filial
7N Filial
7A filibustering
6J Filipino
7K Filippino
XR Fillet
9Q Filling
9F filling-station
XR fillip
9M fillister
8R Fillmores
9M Film-o-type
XR filmic
6R filmmakers
XR Films
6A fin-out
8B finalists
XR Finalizer
9D finances
8F financiers
9D Finches
5P finches'
8A Finder

Word Type	F	D	U	SFI	3 Gr 3	4 Gr 4	5 Gr 5	6 Gr 6	7 Gr 7	8 Gr 8	9 Gr 9	X UnGr	A Read	B Eng & Gr	C Comp	D Lit	E Math	F Soc Stud	G Spell	H Sci	J Music	K Art	L Home Ec	M Shop	N Lib F	P Lib NF	Q Lib Ref	R Mag	S Rel
findings	52	.6547	6.9958	48.4	1	4	6	7	17	10	6	1	3	3	0	0	4	2	0	22	0	0	3	0	0	1	6	8	0
Findlay	2	.2433	.1158	30.6	0	0	0	0	0	1	1	0	0	0	0	0	0	0	0	0	0	0	0	0	0	1	0	1	0
Findley	2	.0000	.0219	23.4	2	0	0	0	0	0	0	0	0	2	0	0	0	0	0	0	0	0	0	0	0	0	0	0	0
finds	137	.8798	24.034	53.8	31	17	15	24	29	10	6	5	30	4	1	4	4	9	3	27	5	0	0	2	5	15	17	11	0
fine	1079	.9273	198.46	63.0	235	208	111	135	186	109	71	24	353	29	18	88	3	135	13	62	44	18	17	18	102	94	33	52	0
Fine	12	.3477	.9152	39.6	1	4	3	2	0	0	1	1	1	0	0	1	0	0	0	0	7	0	0	0	0	0	2	1	0
fine-grained	4	.3280	.2948	34.7	0	0	1	1	0	1	1	0	0	0	0	0	0	0	0	1	0	0	0	0	0	1	2	0	0
fine-looking	5	.2422	.3874	35.9	4	1	0	0	0	0	0	0	4	0	0	0	0	0	0	0	0	0	0	0	0	1	0	0	0
fine-tooth	2	.1249	.0685	28.4	0	0	0	0	1	0	0	1	0	0	0	0	0	0	0	1	0	0	0	1	0	0	0	0	0
fined	3	.0000	.0365	25.6	0	0	0	1	0	0	1	1	0	0	0	0	0	0	0	0	0	0	0	0	0	0	0	3	0
finely	14	.6721	1.9090	42.8	0	1	0	0	8	1	1	3	0	0	0	1	0	1	0	2	0	0	1	0	1	2	2	4	0
finer	35	.7686	5.4250	47.3	8	8	1	1	2	5	8	2	6	0	1	4	0	4	0	3	5	0	2	3	2	2	1	2	0
finer-grained	2	.2433	.1158	30.6	0	0	0	1	0	1	0	0	0	0	0	0	0	0	0	0	0	0	0	0	0	1	0	1	0
finery	2	.1717	.1142	30.6	0	0	0	1	1	0	0	0	1	0	0	1	0	0	0	0	0	0	0	0	0	0	0	0	0
fines	3	.2239	.1775	32.5	0	0	0	0	0	0	3	0	0	0	0	0	0	2	0	1	0	0	0	0	0	0	0	0	0
finest	134	.8238	22.224	53.5	32	18	7	27	25	9	10	6	40	3	0	6	0	16	0	2	11	0	3	1	7	17	16	12	0
fing	2	.0000	.0219	23.4	0	0	0	2	0	0	0	0	0	2	0	0	0	0	0	0	0	0	0	0	0	0	0	0	0
finger	370	.8735	64.363	58.1	89	81	43	46	46	23	35	7	66	9	5	20	26	13	4	51	62	3	5	17	29	38	7	15	0
Finger	2	.2408	.1204	30.8	1	0	1	0	0	0	0	0	0	0	0	0	0	1	0	0	0	0	0	0	0	1	0	0	0
fingered	11	.4806	1.2270	40.9	0	2	1	3	1	3	1	0	7	0	0	1	0	0	0	0	1	0	0	0	2	0	0	0	0
fingering	7	.4356	.6528	38.1	0	2	0	1	3	0	1	0	1	0	1	1	0	0	0	0	3	0	0	0	0	0	0	1	0
fingerlike	3	.2053	.1597	32.0	0	1	0	0	1	1	0	0	0	0	0	0	0	0	0	1	0	0	0	0	0	2	0	0	0
fingerlings	3	.0000	.0365	25.6	0	0	0	0	3	0	0	0	0	0	0	0	0	0	0	0	0	0	0	0	0	0	0	3	0
fingernail	12	.4887	1.2491	41.0	1	1	0	6	0	1	2	1	0	2	1	0	1	0	0	7	0	0	0	0	1	0	0	0	0
fingernails	21	.6347	2.7600	44.4	3	4	1	1	7	1	4	0	4	1	0	3	0	0	0	4	1	0	3	0	2	1	0	2	0
fingerprint	3	.3465	.2515	34.0	1	0	0	1	0	1	0	0	1	0	0	0	0	0	0	0	0	0	0	0	0	1	0	1	0
fingerprinting	3	.3824	.2447	33.9	0	0	0	0	2	0	1	0	0	1	0	0	0	0	1	0	0	0	0	0	0	0	0	1	0
fingerprints	30	.6518	4.1411	46.2	11	1	0	13	3	1	1	0	13	1	0	0	0	0	0	10	0	1	0	1	0	2	1	1	0
fingers	489	.9118	88.509	59.5	93	109	42	78	79	39	34	15	124	7	9	40	28	15	4	50	55	7	13	9	44	57	8	19	0
fingertip	9	.5361	1.0442	40.2	0	1	2	2	4	0	0	0	2	0	0	0	2	0	0	3	0	0	0	0	0	1	0	1	0
fingertips	15	.5446	1.7152	42.3	0	2	5	4	3	0	1	0	2	0	0	0	1	0	0	0	3	0	0	0	0	2	2	5	0
finish	395	.7589	60.744	57.8	98	68	42	28	59	41	55	4	108	17	9	14	26	15	55	6	6	3	32	43	14	32	0	15	0
finished	594	.8999	106.41	60.3	120	106	55	87	96	59	56	15	198	39	6	38	7	51	10	18	9	13	20	23	46	67	13	36	0
finishes	36	.4125	3.1476	45.0	0	3	4	1	7	6	11	4	3	1	1	1	0	1	0	0	0	0	16	1	0	5	1	6	0
finishing	73	.4210	6.6282	48.2	5	6	2	7	28	13	12	0	13	2	0	4	1	1	0	3	1	1	7	28	3	7	0	2	0
finite	21	.0931	.6780	38.3	0	5	6	0	4	2	4	0	0	0	0	0	19	0	0	2	0	0	0	0	0	0	0	0	0
Fink	21	.1186	1.3120	41.2	0	0	0	20	0	1	0	0	20	0	0	0	0	1	0	0	0	0	0	0	0	0	0	0	0
Finland	47	.4957	4.9775	47.0	0	1	4	28	0	4	6	4	1	0	0	0	2	27	0	1	8	0	0	0	0	4	0	4	0
Finland's	3	.2411	.1667	32.2	0	0	0	1	0	0	0	2	0	0	0	0	0	0	0	0	1	0	0	0	0	0	0	2	0
Finlandia	6	.0000	.0485	26.9	0	0	0	4	0	2	0	0	0	0	0	0	0	0	0	0	6	0	0	0	0	0	0	0	0
Finlay	2	.0000	.0914	29.6	0	0	0	0	0	2	0	0	2	0	0	0	0	0	0	0	0	0	0	0	0	0	0	0	0
Finley	45	.0886	1.4080	41.5	0	41	3	0	0	0	0	1	1	0	0	0	0	1	0	0	0	0	0	0	0	42	0	1	0
Finley's	6	.0797	.2027	33.1	0	5	1	0	0	0	0	0	1	0	0	0	0	0	0	0	0	0	0	0	0	5	0	0	0
Finn	26	.4154	2.7339	44.4	0	16	2	1	1	5	1	0	22	0	1	0	0	0	0	0	0	0	0	0	0	1	0	2	0
Finn's	4	.3723	.3645	35.6	0	2	0	0	1	0	1	0	2	1	0	0	0	0	0	0	0	0	0	0	0	0	0	1	0
Finney	2	.2412	.1141	30.6	1	0	1	0	0	0	0	0	0	1	0	0	0	0	0	0	0	0	0	0	0	1	0	0	0
Finnish	10	.5264	1.0995	40.4	0	0	2	3	1	1	0	3	0	0	0	0	0	3	0	0	2	0	0	0	1	1	0	3	0
Finns	12	.1344	.5126	37.1	0	0	0	10	0	0	1	1	0	0	0	0	0	11	0	0	0	0	0	0	0	0	0	1	0
Finny	39	.0000	.5646	37.5	0	39	0	0	0	0	0	0	0	0	0	0	0	0	0	0	0	0	0	0	0	39	0	0	0
fins	45	.6492	6.1220	47.9	17	7	3	1	13	2	2	0	14	0	0	1	0	0	0	10	0	0	0	0	6	3	5	6	0
Fiona	9	.0000	.0966	29.8	0	0	0	0	9	0	0	0	0	0	0	9	0	0	0	0	0	0	0	0	0	0	0	0	0
fiord	7	.0861	.2668	34.3	0	5	0	2	0	0	0	0	1	0	0	0	0	6	0	0	0	0	0	0	0	0	0	0	0
Fiord	7	.3665	.6345	38.0	2	1	0	2	2	0	0	0	3	0	0	0	0	3	0	0	0	0	0	0	0	0	1	0	0
fiords	20	.2194	1.2409	40.9	5	3	1	11	0	0	0	0	4	0	0	0	0	15	0	0	0	0	0	0	0	0	1	0	0
fir	35	.8299	5.8333	47.7	7	4	12	5	4	1	2	0	9	2	1	0	0	5	3	1	1	0	0	1	1	4	4	3	0
fire	1227	.9291	226.28	63.5	281	284	152	175	151	109	65	10	485	29	20	88	5	86	27	98	13	6	3	11	125	130	39	61	1
Fire	19	.6712	2.6175	44.2	2	3	6	2	3	1	2	0	3	1	0	3	0	3	0	0	1	0	0	0	0	1	4	3	0
Fire-Boy	2	.0000	.0914	29.6	0	0	2	0	0	0	0	0	2	0	0	0	0	0	0	0	0	0	0	0	0	0	0	0	0
fire-breathing	4	.3743	.3712	35.7	0	1	1	0	1	1	0	0	2	0	0	0	0	1	0	0	0	0	0	0	0	0	0	0	0
fire-crackers	2	.0000	.0914	29.6	0	2	0	0	0	0	0	0	2	0	0	0	0	0	0	0	0	0	0	0	0	0	0	1	0
fire-drill	2	.0000	.0914	29.6	2	0	0	0	0	0	0	0	2	0	0	0	0	0	0	0	0	0	0	0	0	0	0	0	0
fire-eater	2	.0000	.0290	24.6	0	2	0	0	0	0	0	0	0	0	0	0	0	0	0	0	0	0	0	0	0	2	0	0	0
Fire-eater	3	.0000	.0352	25.5	0	0	0	3	0	0	0	0	0	0	0	0	0	0	0	0	0	0	0	0	0	0	0	0	0
fire-god	3	.0000	.1370	31.4	0	3	0	0	0	0	0	0	3	0	0	0	0	0	0	0	0	0	0	0	3	0	0	0	0
fire-irons	2	.0000	.0234	23.7	0	0	2	0	0	0	0	0	0	0	0	0	0	0	0	0	0	0	0	0	2	0	0	0	0
fire's	2	.0000	.0290	24.6	0	2	0	0	0	0	0	0	0	0	0	0	0	0	0	0	0	0	0	0	0	2	0	0	0
firearms	10	.2906	.7516	38.8	2	0	1	0	6	1	0	0	4	1	0	0	0	0	0	0	0	0	0	0	0	0	0	5	0
fireball	7	.3748	.6666	38.2	0	0	0	0	4	1	2	0	4	0	0	0	0	1	0	2	0	0	0	0	0	0	0	0	0
fireballs	4	.0000	.1827	32.6	0	0	0	0	4	0	0	0	4	0	0	0	0	0	0	0	0	0	0	0	0	0	0	0	0
Firebird	2	.0000	.0162	22.1	1	0	0	0	1	0	0	0	0	0	0	0	0	0	0	0	2	0	0	0	0	0	0	0	0
fireboat	3	.0000	.0322	25.1	3	0	0	0	0	0	0	0	0	0	0	3	0	0	0	0	0	0	0	0	0	0	0	0	0
firebox	11	.3140	.8806	39.4	2	2	7	0	0	0	0	0	3	0	0	0	0	2	0	6	0	0	0	0	0	0	0	0	0
firebrats	3	.0000	.0434	26.4	3	0	0	0	0	0	0	0	0	0	0	0	0	0	0	0	0	0	0	0	0	3	0	0	0
firecracker	6	.3586	.4696	36.7	3	0	0	0	0	2	1	0	1	0	1	1	0	0	0	0	0	2	0	0	0	0	1	0	0
firecrackers	13	.4947	1.4209	41.5	2	1	2	4	2	2	0	0	5	1	0	0	0	0	0	0	1	1	0	0	0	0	2	4	0
fired	131	.8624	22.645	53.5	9	25	27	7	31	21	9	2	47	4	1	7	2	8	2	7	2	4	0	1	6	23	6	11	0
firefighters	2	.1717	.1142	30.6	0	0	1	1	1	0	0	0	1	0	0	1	0	0	0	0	0	0	0	0	0	0	0	0	0
fireflies	9	.5140	.9928	40.0	2	3	1	1	1	0	1	0	1	0	0	1	0	0	0	4	1	0	0	0	0	2	0	0	0
firefly	12	.4590	1.2845	41.1	0	8	1	1	1	0	1	0	6	0	0	0	0	1	0	3	0	0	0	0	0	0	2	0	0
firehouse	5	.1118	.2195	33.4	3	1	0	0	1	0	0	0	1	0	0	0	0	4	0	0	0	0	0	0	0	0	0	0	0
firelight	13	.3715	1.0854	40.4	0	1	2	4	5	0	0	1	2	0	0	4	0	0	0	0	0	0	0	0	6	0	0	1	0
firelock	3	.2196	.1554	31.9	0	0	0	1	1	1	0	0	0	0	0	2	0	0	0	0	0	0	0	0	1	0	0	0	0
fireman	39	.6761	5.5917	47.5	24	0	6	2	2	1	4	0	24	1	1	1	0	0	0	0	2	0	1	0	0	7	0	2	0
firemen	49	.7548	7.5955	48.8	31	8	4	1	2	2	1	0	21	1	0	1	0	8	1	1	2	2	0	0	3	3	1	5	0
Firenze	2	.2446	.1123	30.5	0	0	0	0	0	1	1	0	0	1	0	0	0	0	0	0	0	0	0	0	0	0	1	0	0
fireplace	134	.8280	22.385	53.5	34	35	19	13	16	12	5	0	53	0	1	12	0	3	5	5	1	2	5	0	16	21	4	6	0
fireplaces	13	.5389	1.5586	41.9	2	6	2	1	1	1	0	0	7	0	0	2	0	1	0	0	0	0	0	0	2	0	1	0	0
fireproof	2	.2285	.1129	30.5	0	0	1	0	0	1	0	0	0	0	0	0	0	1	0	0	0	0	0	0	0	0	0	0	0
fires	154	.7799	24.403	53.9	18	43	18	31	27	13	1	3	43	1	0	3	1	29	0	18	1	0	0	3	16	13	6	20	0
fireside	11	.6820	1.5237	41.8	3	2	0	1	0	4	0	1	1	2	0	1	0	0	1	0	2	0	0	0	1	2	0	1	0
firewater	2	.2412	.1141	30.6	1	0	0	0	1	0	0	0	0	1	0	0	0	0	0	0	0	0	0	0	0	1	0	0	0
firewood	35	.7244	5.1929	47.2	8	9	8	4	2	3	0	1	10	1	1	2	0	2	0	0	3	0	0	0	4	6	6	3	0
fireworks	35	.8134	5.7587	47.6	9	10	3	6	1	2	4	0	13	1	0	4	1	4	2	2	3	0	0	0	1	1	1	2	0

6R fine-featured
7M fine-mesh
3A fine-tasting
4F fine-tipped
7A finegrained
7M fineness
7R finesse
5N finest-blooded
4A finger-marks
9Q finger-stop
5N finger's
4J fingerboard

XP fingerbreadth
XP fingerbreadths
7J fingerings
7R fingerlings'
9Q fingernail-sized
7P fingerprinted
6B fings
7B finish'd
8F finishers
4E Finite
7R Finkbine
6R Finladn

5A Finlay's
7R Finletter
7Q finlike
XR Finnair
5B Finney's
8B fio
8E Fiore
4Q Fiorello
5F FIRE
7Q fire-belching
9Q fire-control
8G fire-cracker

7R fire-detection
4A fire-eaten
3A fire-eating
7R fire-extinguishing
8M fire-fighting
7F fire-insurance
8D fire-lock
XP fire-making
7B fire-reel
8M fire-resistant
8Q fire-safe
7D fire-wand

5A firearm
7R Firearms
5J Fireball
5A fireboats
8F firedrill
7R firefighting
XR fireflies'
4P Firefly
8A fireguard
3P fireman's
9B firemen's
8F firepit

8F firepits
3P fireplug
5A firepot
5P firepower
5Q fireproofed
6F Fires
7D firesticks
5Q firewoods
7D firewrought

Word Type	F	D	U	SFI	3 Gr 3	4 Gr 4	5 Gr 5	6 Gr 6	7 Gr 7	8 Gr 8	9 Gr 9	X UnGr	A Read	B Eng & Gr	C Comp	D Lit	E Math	F Soc Stud	G Spell	H Sci	J Music	K Art	L Home Ec	M Shop	N Lib F	P Lib NF	Q Lib Ref	R Mag	S Rel
firing	43	.6912	6.1360	47.9	1	5	9	4	13	7	4	0	12	0	0	2	0	5	0	5	0	2	0	3	3	5	0	6	0
firm	159	.7753	24.935	54.0	27	14	20	13	28	23	25	9	36	9	0	13	0	15	5	16	2	0	17	1	10	12	7	16	0
firmament	3	.2325	.1651	32.2	1	0	0	0	1	0	0	1	0	0	1	0	0	0	0	1	0	0	0	0	0	1	0	0	0
firmer	5	.3225	.3493	35.4	0	0	1	0	0	1	3	0	0	0	0	0	0	2	0	0	0	0	2	1	0	0	0	0	0
firmly	172	.7709	26.793	54.3	13	29	18	16	39	24	26	7	39	5	0	10	0	6	1	15	3	5	15	15	9	22	13	14	0
firmness	7	.3007	.4636	36.7	0	0	1	0	1	3	2	0	0	0	0	0	0	1	0	1	0	0	3	0	0	0	1	1	0
firms	28	.5248	3.0681	44.9	0	0	3	1	8	3	12	1	0	0	0	0	0	8	0	0	0	0	0	2	0	3	4	11	0
firs	2	.0000	.0914	29.6	0	1	0	0	0	1	0	0	2	0	0	0	0	0	0	0	0	0	0	0	0	0	0	0	0
first	7655	.9805	1477.9	71.7	1278	1107	1066	1053	1367	931	676	177	1749	598	150	355	577	685	446	579	562	50	88	83	293	539	423	474	4
First	119	.7476	18.205	52.6	24	11	17	9	25	17	12	4	38	3	0	5	1	21	0	1	2	0	0	0	19	9	10	10	0
FIRST	2	.0000	.0215	23.3	0	0	0	0	0	0	2	0	0	0	0	2	0	0	0	0	0	0	0	0	0	0	0	0	0
first-aid	4	.2942	.2513	34.0	0	0	1	0	0	2	1	0	0	0	1	0	0	0	0	1	0	0	2	0	0	0	0	0	0
first-born	5	.4755	.5327	37.3	1	0	1	2	1	0	0	0	2	0	0	1	0	0	0	0	0	0	0	0	0	0	1	1	0
first-cabin	2	.2446	.1125	30.5	0	0	0	0	0	1	1	0	0	1	0	1	0	0	0	0	0	0	0	0	0	0	0	0	0
first-class	15	.5638	1.7799	42.5	2	0	0	0	6	1	2	4	2	0	0	2	3	1	0	0	0	0	0	0	0	5	2	0	0
first-floor	4	.2381	.2674	34.3	2	0	1	0	0	1	0	0	2	0	1	0	0	0	0	0	0	0	0	0	1	0	0	0	0
first-generation	2	.2351	.1166	30.7	0	0	0	0	1	1	0	0	0	0	0	0	0	1	0	0	0	0	0	0	0	0	0	1	0
first-hand	2	.2306	.1140	30.6	0	0	0	1	1	0	0	0	0	1	0	0	0	1	0	0	0	0	0	0	0	0	0	0	0
first-magnitude	3	.0000	.0591	27.7	0	0	0	0	0	0	3	0	0	0	0	0	0	0	0	3	0	0	0	0	0	0	0	0	0
first-order	2	.2278	.1128	30.5	0	1	0	0	1	0	0	0	0	0	0	0	0	0	0	1	0	0	0	0	0	0	1	0	0
first-place	2	.2427	.1159	30.6	0	0	1	1	0	0	0	0	0	0	0	0	1	0	0	0	0	0	0	0	0	0	0	1	0
first-rate	5	.4524	.4818	36.8	1	0	0	0	2	1	1	0	0	0	0	1	0	1	0	0	0	0	0	0	2	1	0	0	0
first-syllable	2	.0000	.0162	22.1	0	1	1	0	0	0	0	0	0	0	0	0	0	0	2	0	0	0	0	0	0	0	0	0	0
firsthand	15	.6576	2.0143	43.0	0	1	2	5	3	1	3	0	1	3	1	0	0	0	0	4	0	0	0	1	0	1	2	2	0
firsts	3	.0524	.0803	29.0	0	0	0	0	3	0	0	0	1	0	0	0	0	0	0	0	0	0	2	0	0	0	0	0	0
firth	4	.0000	.0579	27.6	0	4	0	0	0	0	0	0	0	0	0	0	0	0	0	0	0	0	0	0	0	4	0	0	0
Firth	2	.2401	.1133	30.5	0	1	1	0	0	0	0	0	0	0	0	0	0	0	0	0	0	0	0	0	0	1	1	0	0
fiscal	2	.0000	.0243	23.9	0	0	0	0	1	0	1	0	0	0	0	0	0	0	0	0	0	0	0	0	0	0	0	2	0
fish	1513	.9410	281.81	64.5	409	291	192	172	249	90	91	19	406	36	22	64	48	198	20	231	14	22	24	0	113	112	92	110	1
Fish	78	.7461	11.952	50.8	25	24	9	3	10	2	2	3	32	2	0	6	0	2	0	3	0	1	0	0	13	5	5	9	0
fish-eating	2	.2446	.1257	31.0	2	0	0	0	0	0	0	0	0	0	0	0	0	1	0	1	0	0	0	0	0	0	0	0	0
fish-liver	2	.1432	.0759	28.8	0	0	0	0	1	1	0	0	0	0	0	0	0	0	0	1	0	0	1	0	0	0	0	0	0
fish-market	2	.1787	.1174	30.7	1	0	0	0	1	0	0	0	1	0	0	0	0	0	0	0	0	0	0	0	1	0	0	0	0
fish-shaped	2	.1698	.1133	30.5	0	0	1	0	1	0	0	0	1	0	0	0	0	0	0	0	0	0	0	0	0	0	1	0	0
fish-tale	2	.0000	.0215	23.3	0	0	0	0	0	2	0	0	0	0	0	2	0	0	0	0	0	0	0	0	0	0	0	0	0
fish's	16	.7168	2.3462	43.7	6	2	0	2	4	1	1	0	4	1	0	1	0	0	0	1	1	0	0	0	1	1	3	3	0
Fish's	2	.0000	.0914	29.6	0	2	0	0	0	0	0	0	2	0	0	0	0	0	0	0	0	0	0	0	0	0	0	0	0
fishbone	5	.2446	.3872	35.9	0	1	3	1	0	0	0	0	4	0	0	0	0	0	0	0	0	0	0	0	1	0	0	0	0
fished	35	.7641	5.4211	47.3	4	7	4	3	8	2	2	5	8	2	0	5	0	4	1	0	2	0	0	0	4	2	1	6	0
fisher	8	.3730	.6846	38.4	0	2	0	0	4	0	2	0	2	0	0	4	0	0	0	0	0	0	0	0	1	0	1	0	0
Fisher	16	.4165	1.5272	41.8	3	9	0	3	0	1	0	0	5	3	0	0	0	0	0	0	0	0	0	0	0	7	1	0	0
Fisher's	3	.1169	.1277	31.1	1	0	0	0	0	2	0	0	1	0	0	0	0	0	0	0	0	0	0	0	0	0	2	0	0
fisheries	11	.2580	.6587	38.2	3	0	3	0	3	2	0	0	0	0	0	0	0	1	0	0	0	0	0	0	0	3	7	0	0
Fisheries	8	.2390	.4458	36.5	0	0	1	1	5	0	0	1	0	0	0	0	0	0	0	0	0	0	0	0	0	0	3	5	0
fisherman	77	.6457	10.541	50.2	31	20	8	9	5	1	1	2	37	2	6	9	0	8	0	3	1	0	0	0	3	1	2	5	0
fisherman's	9	.3891	.8558	39.3	1	5	0	0	0	1	1	1	5	0	1	0	0	1	0	0	0	0	0	0	0	0	0	2	0
Fisherman's	3	.1060	.1461	31.6	0	0	1	1	0	1	0	0	2	0	1	0	0	0	0	0	0	0	0	0	0	0	0	0	0
fishermen	137	.7852	21.837	53.4	25	26	28	23	22	6	6	1	37	0	1	6	0	50	1	4	5	1	0	0	8	7	8	9	0
Fishermen	2	.0000	.0234	23.7	0	0	0	2	0	0	0	0	0	0	0	0	0	0	0	0	0	0	0	0	2	0	0	0	0
fishermen's	4	.3354	.3295	35.2	1	0	1	2	0	0	0	0	1	0	0	0	0	2	0	0	0	0	0	0	0	1	0	0	0
fishers	2	.1814	.1187	30.7	0	1	0	0	1	0	0	0	1	0	0	0	0	0	0	0	0	0	0	0	0	0	0	1	0
Fishers	3	.0000	.0243	23.8	0	0	0	0	0	3	0	0	0	0	0	0	0	0	0	0	3	0	0	0	0	0	0	0	0
fisherwoman	2	.0000	.0914	29.6	0	0	2	0	0	0	0	0	2	0	0	0	0	0	0	0	0	0	0	0	0	0	0	0	0
fishery	3	.0000	.0314	25.0	0	0	0	0	3	0	0	0	0	0	0	0	0	0	0	0	0	0	0	0	0	0	3	0	0
Fishery	2	.1814	.1187	30.7	0	0	0	0	1	0	1	0	1	0	0	0	0	0	0	0	0	0	0	0	0	0	0	1	0
fishes	133	.4137	11.971	50.8	23	4	2	5	89	4	5	1	9	1	0	7	0	0	0	26	2	0	0	0	4	5	77	2	0
Fishes	2	.2446	.1142	30.6	0	0	0	1	0	1	0	0	0	0	0	0	0	0	0	0	0	0	0	0	1	0	0	1	0
fishes'	3	.0000	.0314	25.0	0	0	0	0	3	0	0	0	0	0	0	0	0	0	0	0	0	0	0	0	0	0	3	0	0
fishhead	3	.2261	.2131	33.3	0	0	2	0	1	0	0	0	2	0	0	0	0	0	0	0	0	0	0	0	1	0	0	0	0
fishhook	3	.2357	.2199	33.4	0	2	1	0	0	0	0	0	2	0	0	0	0	0	0	0	0	0	0	0	0	1	0	0	0
fishhooks	2	.2152	.1357	31.3	0	0	1	1	0	0	0	0	1	0	0	0	0	1	0	0	0	0	0	0	0	0	0	0	0
fishin'	3	.2196	.1554	31.9	0	1	0	0	2	0	0	0	0	0	0	2	0	0	0	0	0	0	0	0	1	0	0	0	0
fishing	376	.8391	63.425	58.0	85	80	50	52	58	25	16	10	109	9	11	14	5	110	7	6	10	1	0	2	11	24	19	38	0
fishlike	6	.4603	.5986	37.8	0	1	2	0	1	1	1	0	0	0	0	0	0	1	0	3	0	0	0	0	0	1	1	0	0
fishline	3	.2120	.1548	31.9	0	1	0	2	0	0	0	0	0	0	0	0	0	0	0	0	0	0	0	0	2	1	0	0	0
Fishmonger	2	.0000	.0234	23.7	0	0	2	0	0	0	0	0	0	0	0	0	0	0	0	0	0	0	0	0	2	0	0	0	0
fishy	4	.2440	.2264	33.5	1	1	0	0	0	1	0	1	0	0	0	2	0	0	0	0	0	0	0	0	0	0	0	2	0
Fishye	2	.0000	.0215	23.3	0	2	0	0	0	0	0	0	0	0	0	2	0	0	0	0	0	0	0	0	0	0	0	0	0
fisk	2	.0000	.0219	23.4	0	0	0	0	0	0	0	2	0	2	0	0	0	0	0	0	0	0	0	0	0	0	0	0	0
Fisk	4	.3141	.3005	34.8	1	0	0	1	0	2	0	0	1	0	0	0	0	0	0	0	1	0	0	0	0	0	0	2	0
Fiske	3	.2444	.1649	32.2	0	1	1	0	0	0	1	0	0	0	0	1	1	0	0	0	0	1	0	0	0	0	0	0	0
fission	24	.3731	2.0503	43.1	0	0	2	11	3	5	3	0	2	0	0	0	0	0	0	15	0	0	0	0	0	0	5	2	0
fissionable	2	.0000	.0394	26.0	0	0	0	1	0	0	1	0	0	0	0	0	0	0	0	2	0	0	0	0	0	0	0	0	0
fissure	4	.3647	.3180	35.0	0	0	0	1	0	0	3	0	0	0	0	0	0	0	0	0	0	0	0	0	0	1	1	2	0
fissures	4	.3512	.3114	34.9	1	0	0	0	1	0	2	0	0	0	0	0	0	0	0	1	0	0	0	0	0	0	1	2	0
fist	74	.7253	11.075	50.4	11	9	6	9	21	8	8	2	29	2	0	13	0	1	0	9	1	1	0	0	8	7	0	3	0
fists	35	.6979	5.0695	47.0	3	4	6	4	9	3	5	1	14	0	1	7	0	2	0	1	2	0	0	0	4	3	1	0	0
fistula	2	.0000	.0209	23.2	0	0	0	0	0	0	2	0	0	0	0	0	0	0	0	0	0	0	0	0	0	0	2	0	0
fit	461	.8728	80.050	59.0	58	55	60	64	91	70	49	14	77	26	6	32	34	20	45	49	15	15	43	15	26	11	15	32	0
fitful	4	.3619	.3155	35.0	0	0	0	2	1	0	1	0	0	0	0	1	0	0	0	0	0	0	0	0	2	1	0	0	0
fitfully	4	.4445	.3917	35.9	0	1	0	1	1	0	1	0	1	0	0	1	0	0	0	0	1	0	0	0	1	0	0	0	0
FITH	2	.0000	.0243	23.9	0	0	0	0	2	0	0	0	0	0	0	0	0	0	0	0	0	0	0	0	0	0	0	2	0
fitness	10	.5516	1.1552	40.6	0	0	0	5	1	3	1	0	0	1	0	0	0	1	0	5	0	0	1	0	0	1	1	1	0
fits	180	.8560	30.874	54.9	31	37	30	18	25	18	16	5	61	10	0	5	12	2	24	17	6	3	8	6	5	12	1	8	0
fitted	99	.7935	15.855	52.0	12	16	10	11	22	15	9	4	26	1	0	4	2	3	1	8	3	0	8	4	6	10	14	9	0
fitten	3	.0000	.0352	25.5	0	0	1	0	2	0	0	0	0	0	0	0	0	0	0	0	0	0	0	0	3	0	0	0	0
fitting	57	.6428	7.4983	48.7	3	2	4	6	15	12	10	5	7	1	0	5	3	3	0	4	1	0	12	4	5	5	2	5	0
fittingly	2	.2278	.1128	30.5	1	0	0	0	1	0	0	0	0	0	0	0	0	0	0	1	0	0	0	0	0	0	1	0	0
fittings	8	.4890	.8203	39.1	0	1	0	0	3	3	1	0	1	0	0	1	0	0	0	0	0	0	2	1	0	1	2	0	0
Fitz	2	.0000	.0243	23.9	0	0	0	2	0	0	0	0	0	0	0	0	0	0	0	0	0	0	0	0	0	0	0	2	0
five	1725	.9006	308.51	64.9	245	261	251	246	329	177	138	78	325	164	45	63	259	133	188	109	62	3	11	5	70	97	62	129	0
Five	34	.7435	5.1690	47.1	14	7	4	1	5	3	0	0	10	3	0	0	3	2	0	2	2	0	0	0	2	5	0	5	0
five-cent	3	.2369	.2208	33.4	0	0	0	0	2	0	1	0	2	0	0	0	1	0	0	0	0	0	0	0	0	0	0	0	0

8D firings
XR firm's
8R firmed
5A firmest
XR Firming
7A Firpo
4A First-Aiders
9Q first-amendment
3P first-base
8H first-come-first-served
8R first-down
3E first-grade
3Q first-graders
8R first-half
8J first-movement
XR first-name
7B first-person
9H first-quarter
3R first-sign-of-spring
6J first-space
4P first-term
7R first-year
3P firstborn
8R Fischbach
8R Fischer
3D fish-bait
4A fish-like
8B fish-line
7Q fish-lizards
7B fish'hook**
3E fishbowl
3E fishbowls
6A fisherfolk
9R Fisherman
4A Fishers'
5A fisherwoman's
6N Fishhook
9D fishified
3J Fishing
4N fishing-boat
3A fishing-pole's
4N fishing-sloop
8D fishknife
9N fishless
5A fishmonger's
5N Fishmonger's
8D fishpond
6A fishtailed
4A fishwheel
4A fishwheels
8D fishwives
9H fission-fusion-fission
9H fissions
4P fist-flying
7F Fists
9J fists-full
8A fit'n
3P Fitch
7R fitly
6A fitments
9L Fitted
9D fittest
7R Fitzgerald
9D Fitzgerald's
4P Fitzpatrick
4F FIVE
8A five-and-dime
7N five-and-thirty
9D five-and-twentieth
9H five-carbon

Word Type	F	D	U	SFI	3 Gr 3	4 Gr 4	5 Gr 5	6 Gr 6	7 Gr 7	8 Gr 8	9 Gr 9	X UnGr	A Read	B Eng & Gr	C Comp	D Lit	E Math	F Soc Stud	G Spell	H Sci	J Music	K Art	L Home Ec	M Shop	N Lib F	P Lib NF	Q Lib Ref	R Mag	S Rel
Five-clawed	4	.0000	.1827	32.6	0	0	0	4	0	0	0	0	4	0	0	0	0	0	0	0	0	0	0	0	0	0	0	0	0
five-clock	4	.0000	.0599	27.8	0	0	0	4	0	0	0	0	0	0	0	0	4	0	0	0	0	0	0	0	0	0	0	0	0
five-day	3	.3569	.2621	34.2	0	0	1	1	0	0	0	1	1	0	0	0	1	0	0	1	0	0	0	0	0	0	0	0	0
five-dollar	7	.2326	.5117	37.1	3	0	0	2	1	1	0	0	5	0	0	2	0	0	0	0	0	0	0	0	0	0	0	0	0
five-eighths	2	.1648	.0800	29.0	0	0	0	1	0	1	0	0	0	0	0	0	1	0	0	0	0	0	1	0	0	0	0	0	0
five-fifteen	2	.1814	.1187	30.7	0	0	0	0	0	1	0	1	1	0	0	0	0	0	0	0	0	0	0	0	0	0	0	1	0
five-figure	4	.2107	.2095	33.2	3	0	0	0	0	0	0	1	0	0	0	0	0	0	0	0	0	0	0	0	0	3	0	1	0
five-foot	4	.4546	.4042	36.1	0	0	1	0	1	0	2	0	1	0	0	1	1	0	0	0	0	0	0	0	0	1	0	0	0
five-gallon	3	.2357	.2199	33.4	0	0	0	1	1	0	1	0	2	0	0	0	0	0	0	0	0	0	0	0	0	1	0	0	0
five-hundred	3	.3854	.2500	34.0	0	2	0	0	0	0	1	0	0	1	0	0	0	0	0	0	0	0	0	0	1	1	0	0	0
five-man	2	.2437	.1129	30.5	0	0	1	0	0	1	0	0	0	0	0	0	0	0	0	0	0	0	0	0	0	0	1	1	0
five-minute	6	.1755	.2786	34.5	0	0	0	0	5	0	1	0	0	0	0	0	5	0	0	0	0	0	0	0	0	0	0	1	0
five-note	2	.0000	.0162	22.1	0	0	1	0	1	0	0	0	0	0	0	0	0	0	0	0	2	0	0	0	0	0	0	0	0
five-pound	4	.1948	.2500	34.0	1	0	0	1	2	0	0	0	2	0	0	0	0	0	0	0	0	0	0	0	0	2	0	0	0
five-sided	3	.3759	.2471	33.9	1	0	1	1	0	0	0	0	0	1	0	0	0	1	0	0	0	0	0	0	0	0	1	0	0
five-syllable	4	.0000	.0325	25.1	0	0	2	1	0	1	0	0	0	0	0	0	0	0	4	0	0	0	0	0	0	0	0	0	0
five-thirty	3	.3406	.2461	33.9	1	0	0	0	0	0	1	1	1	1	0	0	0	0	0	0	0	0	0	0	0	0	0	1	0
five-ton	5	.2581	.3344	35.2	0	0	2	3	0	0	0	0	1	0	0	0	0	0	0	1	0	0	0	0	0	3	0	0	0
five-tone	6	.0000	.0485	26.9	0	1	1	3	0	1	0	0	0	0	0	0	0	0	0	0	6	0	0	0	0	0	0	0	0
five-year	9	.4596	.8832	39.5	0	1	0	3	2	3	0	0	0	0	0	0	0	3	0	0	0	0	0	0	0	1	2	3	0
five-year-old	7	.1683	.3126	35.0	0	5	1	0	0	1	0	0	0	0	0	1	0	0	0	0	0	0	0	0	0	6	0	0	0
fives	31	.0000	.4640	36.7	3	8	17	1	0	1	0	1	0	0	0	0	31	0	0	0	0	0	0	0	0	0	0	0	0
fives'	2	.0000	.0299	24.8	0	0	2	0	0	0	0	0	0	0	0	0	2	0	0	0	0	0	0	0	0	0	0	0	0
fix	156	.8367	26.386	54.2	67	11	10	19	25	12	6	6	75	3	5	8	19	3	0	16	2	1	0	2	6	3	3	10	0
Fix	24	.0642	.5656	37.5	0	0	0	0	23	0	1	0	0	1	0	0	0	0	0	0	0	0	0	0	23	0	0	0	0
fix'em	2	.0000	.0234	23.7	2	0	0	0	0	0	0	0	0	0	0	0	0	0	0	0	0	0	0	0	2	0	0	0	0
fixatives	2	.2437	.1129	30.5	0	0	0	1	0	0	0	1	0	0	0	0	0	0	0	0	0	0	0	0	0	0	1	1	0
fixed	196	.8875	34.700	55.4	41	16	30	13	42	25	23	6	62	2	2	9	9	9	7	22	0	2	0	6	22	18	10	16	0
fixedly	4	.3065	.2965	34.7	0	0	1	0	3	0	0	0	1	1	0	0	0	0	0	0	0	0	0	0	2	0	0	0	0
fixes	9	.4831	1.0069	40.0	6	1	0	1	0	0	1	0	5	0	0	0	1	0	0	2	0	0	0	0	0	0	0	1	0
fixin'	5	.0804	.1641	32.2	0	0	4	0	1	0	0	0	1	0	0	0	0	0	0	0	0	0	0	0	4	0	0	0	0
fixing	36	.6466	5.0177	47.0	19	5	2	2	3	3	2	0	24	1	0	1	2	0	0	1	1	0	0	0	3	3	0	0	0
fixture	4	.3799	.3292	35.2	1	1	0	2	0	0	0	0	0	0	0	0	0	0	1	0	0	0	0	0	0	2	0	1	0
fixtures	8	.4709	.8053	39.1	2	0	0	0	4	0	2	0	0	0	0	1	2	2	0	0	0	0	0	0	0	3	0	0	0
fizz	3	.3234	.2368	33.7	0	0	0	2	0	1	0	0	1	0	0	0	0	0	1	0	0	0	0	0	0	1	0	0	0
fizzled	2	.1814	.1187	30.7	0	0	0	1	0	1	0	0	1	0	0	0	0	0	0	0	0	0	0	0	0	0	0	1	0
fjord	2	.2387	.1089	30.4	0	1	0	0	0	1	0	0	0	0	0	0	0	0	0	0	1	0	0	0	1	0	0	0	0
fjords	2	.0000	.0290	24.6	0	0	2	0	0	0	0	0	0	0	0	0	0	0	0	0	0	0	0	0	0	2	0	0	0
fl	8	.0409	.1627	32.1	2	3	0	2	1	0	0	0	1	0	0	0	0	0	7	0	0	0	0	0	0	0	0	0	0
Fla	4	.3512	.3114	34.9	0	0	1	1	1	0	0	1	0	0	0	0	0	0	0	1	0	0	0	0	0	0	1	2	0
flabbergasted	2	.1698	.1133	30.5	0	0	0	1	0	0	1	0	1	0	0	0	0	0	0	0	0	0	0	0	0	0	1	0	0
flabby	3	.2880	.1944	32.9	0	0	2	0	0	0	1	0	0	0	0	0	0	0	0	1	0	0	1	0	1	0	0	0	0
flaccid	2	.2446	.1122	30.5	0	0	0	0	1	0	1	0	0	0	0	1	0	0	0	0	0	0	0	0	0	0	1	0	0
flag	248	.8464	42.256	56.3	55	72	20	24	28	31	16	2	99	6	2	14	8	29	5	9	19	0	0	0	13	31	5	8	0
Flag	14	.4760	1.4211	41.5	0	2	0	7	3	2	0	0	2	0	0	0	0	0	4	0	0	0	0	0	3	0	4	1	0
flagella	3	.0000	.0591	27.7	0	0	0	1	1	0	1	0	0	0	0	0	0	0	0	3	0	0	0	0	0	0	0	0	0
flagellated	2	.0000	.0394	26.0	0	0	0	0	2	0	0	0	0	0	0	0	0	0	0	2	0	0	0	0	0	0	0	0	0
flagellates	4	.0000	.0789	29.0	0	0	0	3	0	0	1	0	0	0	0	0	0	0	0	4	0	0	0	0	0	0	0	0	0
flagged	4	.2446	.2283	33.6	0	0	0	0	2	0	0	2	0	0	0	0	0	0	0	0	0	0	0	0	2	0	0	2	0
flagon	7	.2461	.4508	36.5	1	0	1	0	2	3	0	0	2	0	0	4	0	0	0	0	0	0	0	0	0	1	0	0	0
flagpole	15	.5492	1.7842	42.5	3	1	3	6	1	0	0	1	5	1	1	1	5	0	0	2	0	0	0	0	0	0	0	0	0
flagrant	3	.2851	.1858	32.7	0	0	0	1	1	0	0	1	0	0	1	0	0	0	0	0	1	0	0	0	0	1	0	0	0
flagrantly	2	.2437	.1129	30.5	0	0	0	0	2	0	0	0	0	0	0	0	0	0	0	0	0	0	0	0	0	0	1	1	0
flags	66	.7946	10.653	50.3	10	24	9	9	4	6	3	1	25	0	1	1	2	10	0	2	2	2	0	0	2	7	8	4	0
flagship	3	.2063	.1600	32.0	0	0	0	1	2	0	0	0	0	0	0	0	0	1	0	0	0	0	0	0	0	2	0	0	0
flagstaff	6	.3465	.5030	37.0	0	2	0	3	1	0	0	0	2	0	0	0	0	0	0	0	0	0	0	0	0	2	0	2	0
flagstaffs	2	.2152	.1357	31.3	0	1	0	0	1	0	0	0	1	0	0	0	0	1	0	0	0	0	0	0	0	0	0	0	0
flail	5	.3707	.4004	36.0	0	0	0	0	1	3	1	0	0	0	0	2	0	0	0	0	0	0	0	0	1	0	0	2	0
flailed	3	.2261	.2131	33.3	0	0	2	0	1	0	0	0	2	0	0	0	0	0	0	0	0	0	0	0	1	0	0	0	0
flailing	3	.3870	.2486	34.0	1	0	0	1	0	0	1	0	0	0	0	1	0	0	0	0	0	0	0	0	0	0	1	1	0
flair	3	.2159	.1532	31.9	1	0	1	1	0	0	0	0	0	0	0	0	0	0	0	0	0	0	0	0	0	0	2	1	0
flake	8	.5608	.9854	39.9	0	3	3	0	1	0	1	0	4	1	0	1	0	0	0	1	0	0	0	0	0	0	0	1	0
flakes	24	.7210	3.5514	45.5	2	6	0	4	5	1	6	0	7	1	0	4	0	0	0	5	0	0	1	1	1	1	0	3	0
flaking	2	.2351	.1166	30.7	0	0	0	0	0	1	0	1	0	0	0	0	0	1	0	0	0	0	0	0	0	0	0	1	0
flaky	7	.3606	.5708	37.6	0	1	0	0	2	1	3	0	1	1	0	0	0	0	0	2	0	0	2	0	0	1	0	0	0
flamboyant	4	.3104	.2995	34.8	0	0	0	0	1	1	1	1	1	0	0	0	0	0	0	0	0	0	0	0	0	0	1	2	0
flamboyantly	2	.2437	.1129	30.5	0	0	0	0	1	1	0	0	0	0	0	0	0	0	0	0	0	0	0	0	0	0	1	1	0
flame	151	.8648	26.069	54.2	17	14	22	23	32	24	15	4	26	4	2	14	0	5	1	52	3	2	1	4	15	10	6	6	0
flamed	5	.4122	.4599	36.6	0	0	0	0	4	0	1	0	1	0	0	2	0	0	0	0	0	0	0	0	1	1	0	0	0
flamenco	10	.0000	.0808	29.1	0	0	0	3	7	0	0	0	0	0	0	0	0	0	0	0	10	0	0	0	0	0	0	0	0
flameout	2	.0000	.0290	24.6	2	0	0	0	0	0	0	0	0	0	0	0	0	0	0	0	0	0	0	0	0	2	0	0	0
flames	81	.7076	11.979	50.8	15	23	6	15	10	10	2	0	41	0	0	9	0	5	0	8	1	0	0	0	4	7	1	5	0
flaming	31	.7894	4.9498	46.9	3	4	4	5	8	3	2	2	9	1	1	5	0	1	0	2	1	1	0	0	5	2	1	2	0
Flaming	6	.2063	.3201	35.1	2	2	2	0	0	0	0	0	0	0	0	0	0	2	0	0	0	0	0	0	0	4	0	0	0
flamingo	7	.4262	.6760	38.3	2	0	4	0	0	0	0	1	2	2	0	0	0	0	0	1	0	0	0	0	2	0	0	0	0
flamingos	4	.2975	.2883	34.6	1	0	1	0	2	0	0	0	1	1	0	0	0	0	0	0	0	0	0	0	0	0	2	0	0
flammable	2	.1738	.0790	29.0	0	0	1	0	1	0	0	0	0	0	0	0	0	0	0	0	0	0	0	1	0	0	1	0	0
Flan	9	.0000	.4111	36.1	0	0	9	0	0	0	0	0	9	0	0	0	0	0	0	0	0	0	0	0	0	0	0	0	0
Flanders	12	.5781	1.4712	41.7	0	1	2	5	1	2	0	1	3	0	0	1	0	2	0	0	0	0	0	0	2	1	3	0	0
Flandin	6	.0000	.2741	34.4	6	0	0	0	0	0	0	0	6	0	0	0	0	0	0	0	0	0	0	0	0	0	0	0	0
Flandins	6	.0000	.2741	34.4	6	0	0	0	0	0	0	0	6	0	0	0	0	0	0	0	0	0	0	0	0	0	0	0	0
flanges	2	.0000	.0243	23.9	0	0	0	0	2	0	0	0	0	0	0	0	0	0	0	0	0	0	0	0	0	0	0	2	0
flank	16	.6302	2.1145	43.3	0	0	0	5	3	3	5	0	5	0	1	3	0	2	0	0	0	0	0	0	2	0	1	2	0
flanked	4	.2090	.2014	33.0	0	0	2	0	2	0	0	0	0	0	0	0	0	0	0	0	0	0	0	0	0	0	1	3	0
flanking	2	.2337	.1157	30.6	0	1	0	0	0	1	0	0	0	0	0	0	0	1	0	0	0	0	0	0	1	0	0	0	0
flanks	5	.3547	.4331	36.4	2	1	1	0	1	0	0	0	2	0	0	1	0	0	0	0	0	0	0	0	0	2	0	0	0
flannel	22	.5692	2.6261	44.2	1	4	9	3	1	2	1	1	4	0	0	3	0	0	0	1	0	0	2	0	9	1	1	1	0
flannels	2	.1814	.1187	30.7	0	1	0	0	1	0	0	0	1	0	0	0	0	0	0	0	0	0	0	0	0	0	0	1	0
Flannigans	2	.1717	.1142	30.6	1	0	0	0	0	0	1	0	1	0	0	1	0	0	0	0	0	0	0	0	0	0	0	0	0
flap	36	.7211	5.3212	47.3	13	4	0	0	8	0	9	2	10	2	0	2	0	0	0	4	0	0	0	2	4	7	3	2	0
flapjacks	3	.0000	.1370	31.4	0	0	3	0	0	0	0	0	3	0	0	0	0	0	0	0	0	0	0	0	0	0	0	0	0
flapped	17	.4440	1.8421	42.7	4	5	2	4	2	0	0	0	13	0	0	1	0	0	0	0	0	0	0	0	1	2	0	0	0
flapping	42	.6471	5.7304	47.6	14	8	0	8	6	3	3	0	18	1	2	3	0	0	0	1	0	0	0	0	8	5	0	4	0

9Q five-color
7E five-cubed
5E five-fives
8B five-haired
4P five-hundred-mile
6P five-hundred-pound
9H five-inch
XB five-letter
7J five-line
XH five-lobed
6F five-mile
5E five-month
6E five-ninths
6A five-part
XH five-parted
4H five-penny
8D five-point-nine
4P five-pointed
5Q five-quarter
9E five-room
6J five-seven
4B five-seven-five
6E five-sevenths
4R five-shooter
7E five-squared
4E five-step
9E five-tenths
7E five-thirds
8A five-word
9R five-year-olds
8B fix'd
6K fixative
XR fixed-wing
5N fixin
6A fixings
4N fizzed
3A fizzing
5P Fjord
3B flabbed
5Q flach
6D Flack
8N fladbrod
4Q flag-raising
4P flageolet
9D flagman
6F flagship's
4R Flagstaff
XP Flaherty's
8A Flail
5D flailsome
9R flak
8L flaked
6A Flamborough
XH Flame
XR flame-blue
7N flame-jets
7Q flamethrowers
6R Flamm
9H flammability
6J flams
5A Flan's
7M flange
9M flanged
5A flankers
3A Flannigan
9L Flap
6A flap-hopping
6P Flapdoodle
5A flapjack
5A Flapjack
5B flappers
5N flappy

Word Type	F	D	U	SFI	3 Gr 3	4 Gr 4	5 Gr 5	6 Gr 6	7 Gr 7	8 Gr 8	9 Gr 9	X UnGr	A Read	B Eng & Gr	C Comp	D Lit	E Math	F Soc Stud	G Spell	H Sci	J Music	K Art	L Home Ec	M Shop	N Lib F	P Lib NF	Q Lib Ref	R Mag	S Rel
flaps	31	.8084	5.0418	47.0	10	8	4	4	4	1	0	0	7	3	0	3	1	0	0	4	3	1	1	0	2	4	2	0	0
flare	14	.6026	1.7894	42.5	1	1	4	2	1	2	3	0	5	0	1	3	0	2	0	0	0	0	0	1	0	1	0	1	0
flare-out	2	.0000	.0290	24.6	2	0	0	0	0	0	0	0	0	0	0	0	0	0	0	0	0	0	0	0	0	2	0	0	0
flared	10	.5234	1.0823	40.3	1	0	1	1	3	1	3	0	1	0	1	2	0	0	0	1	0	0	3	1	1	0	0	0	0
flares	19	.4832	2.1351	43.3	2	1	6	1	4	4	1	0	12	0	0	0	0	1	0	2	0	0	2	0	0	1	0	1	0
flaring	9	.5839	1.0939	40.4	0	0	1	2	3	1	2	0	2	1	1	0	0	0	0	0	2	0	0	1	1	0	0	1	0
flash	114	.7740	18.037	52.6	15	17	9	23	22	17	6	5	47	2	0	9	0	2	1	17	2	0	0	0	10	8	5	11	0
Flash	2	.0000	.0914	29.6	0	0	2	0	0	0	0	0	2	0	0	0	0	0	0	0	0	0	0	0	0	0	0	0	0
flashed	74	.6585	10.283	50.1	15	9	14	10	20	5	1	0	35	1	0	10	2	1	0	0	1	0	0	0	14	6	1	3	0
flashes	30	.7014	4.3189	46.4	3	2	3	9	4	6	0	3	5	1	0	1	0	1	0	11	1	0	0	0	3	1	1	5	0
flashing	57	.7764	9.0813	49.6	4	10	7	10	14	7	4	1	31	1	0	4	1	0	0	2	4	1	0	0	4	3	2	4	0
flashlight	94	.6500	12.837	51.1	24	9	11	14	28	7	0	1	28	1	1	6	0	0	1	43	0	0	0	1	2	1	0	10	0
flashlights	5	.2144	.2818	34.5	1	0	0	2	2	0	0	0	0	0	0	0	0	0	0	4	0	0	0	0	1	0	0	0	0
flashy	6	.3396	.5199	37.2	0	0	4	1	1	0	0	0	3	0	0	0	0	0	0	1	0	0	0	0	0	0	0	2	0
flask	59	.3499	4.7567	46.8	1	4	21	2	6	5	11	9	0	0	0	1	0	0	0	52	1	0	0	3	0	1	1	0	0
flasks	12	.3290	.9170	39.6	0	0	0	0	5	0	2	5	0	0	0	1	0	0	0	10	0	0	0	1	0	0	0	0	0
flat	662	.8579	113.32	60.5	128	101	70	61	140	75	70	17	125	10	18	31	30	79	9	75	42	25	26	50	29	55	29	29	0
Flat	7	.4730	.6846	38.4	1	1	0	1	1	0	3	0	0	1	0	0	0	0	0	0	3	0	0	1	0	1	0	1	0
flat-bottomed	2	.1948	.1250	31.0	0	2	0	0	0	0	0	0	1	0	0	0	0	0	0	0	0	0	0	0	0	1	0	0	0
flat-topped	12	.3501	1.1137	40.5	4	3	0	4	1	0	0	0	8	0	0	0	0	3	0	1	0	0	0	0	0	0	0	0	0
flatboat	11	.5082	1.1962	40.8	3	0	6	0	1	1	0	0	1	0	0	1	0	4	0	0	0	0	0	0	0	3	2	0	0
flatboats	14	.5331	1.5873	42.0	4	1	7	0	2	0	0	0	1	0	0	1	0	7	0	0	0	0	0	0	0	3	1	1	0
flatcar	3	.1434	.1493	31.7	0	2	0	0	1	0	0	0	1	0	0	0	2	0	0	0	0	0	0	0	0	0	0	0	0
flatcars	5	.4347	.4733	36.8	0	1	2	1	0	0	1	0	1	0	0	0	1	0	0	0	1	0	0	1	0	0	1	0	0
flatiron	2	.1717	.1142	30.6	0	0	1	0	0	0	1	0	1	0	0	1	0	0	0	0	0	0	0	0	0	0	0	0	0
flatlands	2	.2346	.1166	30.7	0	1	0	1	0	0	0	0	0	0	0	0	0	0	0	1	0	0	0	0	0	0	0	1	0
flatly	9	.3265	.6240	38.0	0	0	0	0	5	1	2	1	0	1	0	2	0	0	0	0	0	0	4	0	1	0	0	1	0
flatness	4	.1847	.1655	32.2	0	0	1	1	0	2	0	0	0	0	0	1	0	0	0	0	0	2	0	0	0	0	1	0	0
flats	37	.4048	3.2380	45.1	8	6	1	2	11	4	1	4	3	0	0	1	0	1	0	3	21	0	0	0	2	2	1	3	0
Flats	5	.3077	.3486	35.4	0	1	0	0	0	1	2	1	0	0	0	0	0	1	0	0	0	0	0	0	3	0	0	1	0
flatt'ring	2	.0000	.0162	22.1	0	0	0	0	2	0	0	0	0	0	0	0	0	0	0	0	2	0	0	0	0	0	0	0	0
flatten	13	.5999	1.6000	42.0	2	1	4	1	2	1	2	0	0	0	0	1	0	2	0	4	1	0	1	2	1	0	0	1	0
flattened	42	.8179	6.8820	48.4	4	6	7	2	11	6	5	1	4	2	1	2	2	4	0	10	0	0	0	2	5	3	3	4	0
flattening	5	.2664	.3459	35.4	0	2	0	0	2	1	0	0	2	0	0	2	0	0	0	0	0	1	0	0	0	0	0	0	0
flattens	5	.3640	.3990	36.0	1	0	1	0	0	2	1	0	0	0	0	0	0	0	0	3	0	0	1	1	0	0	0	0	0
flatter	11	.5668	1.3265	41.2	0	0	4	0	3	1	3	0	3	0	0	3	0	2	1	0	0	0	1	0	0	1	0	0	0
flattered	5	.4699	.4937	36.9	1	0	1	1	1	0	1	0	0	1	0	1	0	0	0	0	0	0	0	0	0	1	0	0	0
flattering	5	.4761	.5332	37.3	0	1	0	0	4	0	0	0	2	1	0	1	0	0	0	0	0	0	0	0	1	0	0	2	0
flattery	5	.3875	.4309	36.3	0	1	0	0	2	2	0	0	1	0	0	0	0	0	1	0	0	1	0	0	1	1	0	0	0
flatting	3	.0000	.0243	23.8	0	0	0	1	0	0	2	0	0	0	0	0	0	0	0	0	3	0	0	0	0	0	0	0	0
flatworm	3	.0000	.0591	27.7	0	0	0	0	3	0	0	0	0	0	0	0	0	0	0	3	0	0	0	0	0	0	0	0	0
flatworms	7	.0000	.1380	31.4	0	0	0	0	6	0	1	0	0	0	0	0	0	0	0	7	0	0	0	0	0	0	0	0	0
Flaubert	3	.0000	.0314	25.0	0	0	3	0	0	0	0	0	0	0	0	0	0	0	0	0	0	0	0	0	0	0	3	0	0
flavor	81	.4066	7.0447	48.5	3	4	9	6	13	7	34	5	9	5	1	1	1	5	2	4	4	1	38	0	0	2	3	5	0
flavored	10	.2435	.5720	37.6	0	0	0	2	3	0	4	1	1	0	0	0	0	1	0	1	0	0	5	0	0	0	1	1	0
flavorful	5	.0000	.0161	22.1	0	0	0	0	0	0	5	0	0	0	0	0	0	0	0	0	0	0	5	0	0	0	0	0	0
flavoring	7	.2441	.3817	35.8	0	0	2	1	0	1	3	0	0	0	0	0	0	0	0	1	0	0	3	0	0	0	3	0	0
flavorings	4	.3134	.2876	34.6	0	0	0	2	2	0	0	0	0	0	0	0	0	1	0	1	0	0	0	0	0	0	2	0	0
flavors	12	.3546	.9685	39.9	1	0	0	0	5	0	5	1	3	1	0	0	0	1	0	1	0	1	5	0	0	0	0	0	0
flaw	8	.5558	.9768	39.9	1	0	2	0	3	1	1	0	4	1	0	1	0	1	0	0	1	0	0	0	0	0	0	0	0
flawed	2	.2297	.1135	30.6	0	0	0	0	0	1	1	0	0	0	0	1	0	1	0	0	0	0	0	0	0	0	0	0	0
flawless	2	.0000	.0243	23.9	0	0	0	0	1	0	0	1	0	0	0	0	0	0	0	0	0	0	0	0	0	0	0	2	0
flaws	6	.3882	.5354	37.3	1	0	1	0	1	1	2	0	2	0	0	0	0	0	0	0	0	0	0	1	0	0	2	1	0
flax	19	.6853	2.6573	44.2	4	1	0	4	6	2	1	1	2	2	0	0	0	5	2	2	1	0	2	0	1	0	2	0	0
flaxen	3	.3851	.2497	34.0	0	0	0	2	1	0	0	0	0	0	0	1	0	0	0	0	0	0	0	0	1	1	0	0	0
flayed	2	.2440	.1132	30.5	0	0	0	0	0	0	2	0	0	0	0	1	0	0	0	0	0	0	0	0	0	0	0	1	0
flea	25	.6723	3.4679	45.4	9	3	5	2	1	4	1	0	6	3	2	0	2	1	1	1	2	0	0	0	1	6	0	0	0
Flea	5	.0000	.2284	33.6	5	0	0	0	0	0	0	0	5	0	0	0	0	0	0	0	0	0	0	0	0	0	0	0	0
flea-bitten	3	.2357	.2199	33.4	2	0	0	1	0	0	0	0	2	0	0	0	0	0	0	0	0	0	0	0	0	1	0	0	0
flea's	3	.2053	.1597	32.0	2	0	0	0	0	1	0	0	0	0	0	0	0	0	0	1	0	0	0	0	0	2	0	0	0
fleas	13	.4926	1.4178	41.5	4	0	1	3	3	2	0	0	3	0	0	0	0	1	0	6	0	0	0	0	0	2	1	0	0
Fleas	2	.0000	.0243	23.9	0	0	0	0	2	0	0	0	0	0	0	0	0	0	0	0	0	0	0	0	0	0	0	2	0
fleck	2	.2375	.1088	30.4	0	0	0	1	0	1	0	0	0	0	0	0	0	0	0	0	1	0	0	0	0	0	0	1	0
flecked	2	.0000	.0914	29.6	1	0	1	0	0	0	0	0	2	0	0	0	0	0	0	0	0	0	0	0	0	0	0	0	0
flecks	5	.4213	.4686	36.7	1	0	0	2	1	0	1	0	1	0	0	1	0	0	0	0	0	0	0	0	2	1	0	0	0
fled	79	.8614	13.606	51.3	4	9	9	18	19	13	6	1	21	3	2	8	0	10	3	1	3	0	0	1	10	8	3	6	0
Fledermaus	3	.0000	.0243	23.8	0	0	0	3	0	0	0	0	0	0	0	0	0	0	0	0	3	0	0	0	0	0	0	0	0
fledge	2	.2440	.1132	30.5	0	0	0	0	1	0	1	0	0	0	0	1	0	0	0	0	0	0	0	0	0	0	0	1	0
fledgling	2	.2437	.1129	30.5	0	0	0	0	1	0	1	0	0	0	0	0	0	0	0	0	0	0	0	0	0	0	1	1	0
fledglings	2	.1717	.1142	30.6	0	0	0	0	1	1	0	0	1	0	0	1	0	0	0	0	0	0	0	0	0	0	0	0	0
flee	26	.7533	3.9873	46.0	2	5	3	3	6	5	2	0	7	2	0	3	0	4	1	0	3	0	0	0	2	2	0	2	0
fleece	13	.6271	1.7063	42.3	5	1	1	0	1	3	2	0	3	1	0	1	0	5	0	0	1	0	1	0	0	0	0	1	0
Fleece	10	.2025	.6507	38.1	0	0	0	6	4	0	0	0	6	0	0	4	0	0	0	0	0	0	0	0	0	0	0	0	0
fleeces	2	.2412	.1141	30.6	0	1	1	0	0	0	0	0	0	1	0	0	0	0	0	0	0	0	0	0	0	1	0	0	0
fleecy	6	.2432	.4679	36.7	0	0	0	1	4	0	1	0	5	1	0	0	0	0	0	0	0	0	0	0	0	0	0	0	0
fleeing	18	.6688	2.4914	44.0	1	2	3	4	2	4	2	0	4	0	1	2	0	4	0	1	0	0	0	0	1	3	2	0	0
fleet	95	.7291	14.154	51.5	5	11	13	13	24	24	4	1	19	4	0	4	2	28	0	2	0	0	0	0	5	10	12	9	0
Fleet	21	.4838	2.2135	43.5	0	0	0	3	1	3	14	0	4	0	0	3	0	2	0	0	0	0	0	0	0	9	0	3	0
fleet-footed	2	.1698	.1133	30.5	0	0	0	1	1	0	0	0	1	0	0	0	0	0	0	0	0	0	0	0	0	0	1	0	0
fleeting	5	.3451	.4196	36.2	0	0	0	1	3	1	0	0	2	0	0	0	0	0	0	0	1	0	0	0	2	0	0	0	0
fleets	20	.4035	1.8109	42.6	0	7	5	1	3	3	1	0	1	0	0	1	0	13	0	0	0	0	0	0	0	4	1	0	0
Fleming	16	.5196	1.7768	42.5	0	2	0	3	4	3	4	0	1	0	0	1	0	0	0	9	0	0	0	0	0	2	1	2	0
Fleming's	2	.0000	.0394	26.0	0	0	0	0	0	0	2	0	0	0	0	0	0	0	0	2	0	0	0	0	0	0	0	0	0
Flemings	2	.0000	.0914	29.6	0	0	0	2	0	0	0	0	2	0	0	0	0	0	0	0	0	0	0	0	0	0	0	0	0
Flemish	11	.3244	.8184	39.1	1	2	2	2	1	1	2	0	2	0	0	0	1	0	0	0	0	3	0	0	1	2	2	0	0
flensing	4	.0000	.1827	32.6	0	0	4	0	0	0	0	0	4	0	0	0	0	0	0	0	0	0	0	0	0	0	0	0	0
flesh	95	.7457	14.325	51.6	9	12	6	9	36	6	14	3	13	4	0	28	0	0	3	10	0	0	1	2	11	12	8	3	0
flesh-eating	3	.3350	.2478	33.9	0	0	0	1	2	0	0	0	1	0	0	0	0	1	0	0	0	0	0	0	0	0	1	0	0
fleshed	2	.1839	.0845	29.3	0	0	0	1	0	0	1	0	0	0	0	0	0	0	0	0	0	0	1	0	1	0	0	0	0
fleshy	15	.5464	1.7457	42.4	3	0	0	1	9	1	0	1	2	0	0	1	0	0	0	7	0	0	0	0	3	0	1	1	0
Fletcher	7	.1020	.2156	33.3	6	0	1	0	0	0	0	0	0	0	0	6	0	1	0	0	0	0	0	0	0	0	0	0	0
Fletcher's	2	.0000	.0215	23.3	2	0	0	0	0	0	0	0	0	0	0	2	0	0	0	0	0	0	0	0	0	0	0	0	0
Fleury	2	.0000	.0234	23.7	0	0	0	2	0	0	0	0	0	0	0	0	0	0	0	0	0	0	0	0	2	0	0	0	0
flew	403	.7806	64.464	58.1	131	85	45	68	35	19	16	4	211	15	0	32	16	5	9	10	8	0	0	0	38	32	3	24	0
flexed	3	.2357	.2199	33.4	1	0	0	0	1	1	0	0	2	0	0	0	0	0	0	0	0	0	0	0	0	1	0	0	0
flexibility	16	.6326	2.0471	43.1	0	0	0	1	6	3	2	4	0	1	0	0	0	0	0	1	0	1	1	2	0	1	4	5	0
flexible	41	.7309	6.0439	47.8	0	2	3	4	15	6	5	6	4	2	0	0	0	0	2	8	2	1	4	5	3	2	4	4	0

4H flash-evaporation
4H flash-evaporator
3P flashback
7R flasher
5H flat-bodied
8N flat-brimmed
8L flat-edged
8M flat-head
7R flat-rate
7H flat-sided
8F flat-soled
9M flat-surface
8F Flatbush
5Q flatfish
5Q Flatfish
8D flatfooted
7M flathead
6R Flatheads
4N flatirons
3H flattened-out
8J flatters
7Q flattish
8F flattops
9L flatware
5N flatwoods
7F flaxseed
3P FLEA
5H flea-like
7R flecking
5R fledged
6A Fleet's
8D fleeter
9N fleetingly
6N fleetness
7R Flemming
5J Flemmons
7J Flentrop
5P flesh-eater
8J fleugel
8G flex
5H Flex
4N Flexible

					3	4	5	6	7	8	9	X	A	B	C	D	E	F	G	H	J	K	L	M	N	P	Q	R	S
Word Type	F	D	U	SFI	Gr 3	Gr 4	Gr 5	Gr 6	Gr 7	Gr 8	Gr 9	UnGr	Read	Eng & Gr	Comp	Lit	Math	Soc Stud	Spell	Sci	Music	Art	Home Ec	Shop	Lib F	Lib NF	Lib Ref	Mag	Rel
flick	14	.5610	1.6950	42.3	2	3	1	6	2	0	0	0	5	0	0	0	0	0	0	1	0	0	0	0	2	1	1	4	0
Flicka	6	.1717	.3427	35.3	0	0	3	0	0	3	0	0	3	0	0	3	0	0	0	0	0	0	0	0	0	0	0	0	0
flicked	25	.4849	2.8136	44.5	11	5	1	0	3	2	3	0	16	0	0	5	0	0	0	0	0	0	0	0	1	2	0	1	0
flicker	10	.4834	1.0580	40.2	1	2	0	1	5	0	1	0	3	0	1	3	0	0	0	0	0	0	0	0	2	1	0	0	0
Flicker	2	.1814	.1187	30.7	0	1	0	0	0	0	0	1	1	0	0	0	0	0	0	0	0	0	0	0	0	0	0	1	0
flickered	7	.4770	.7542	38.8	1	5	0	0	1	0	0	0	3	1	0	0	0	0	0	0	0	0	0	0	0	2	1	0	0
flickering	25	.5410	2.8843	44.6	2	3	5	8	5	1	1	0	6	0	4	1	0	1	0	3	1	0	0	0	4	3	1	1	0
flickers	4	.3215	.3104	34.9	0	0	0	2	0	0	0	2	1	0	0	0	0	0	0	0	0	0	0	0	0	2	1	0	0
flicking	6	.3599	.5352	37.3	1	2	0	1	1	0	1	0	3	0	0	0	0	0	0	0	0	0	0	0	1	0	0	2	0
flicks	4	.4242	.3545	35.5	0	1	0	0	1	1	1	0	0	0	0	1	0	0	0	0	0	0	1	0	0	0	1	1	0
flier	8	.6080	1.0233	40.1	2	0	2	2	0	2	0	0	2	1	0	1	0	0	0	1	0	0	0	0	0	2	1	0	0
flier's	2	.1814	.1187	30.7	0	0	0	1	1	0	0	0	1	0	0	0	0	0	0	0	0	0	0	0	0	0	0	1	0
fliers	22	.5349	2.6643	44.3	5	1	0	8	5	0	2	1	14	0	0	0	0	2	0	0	0	0	0	0	0	3	1	2	0
flies	220	.8839	38.732	55.9	56	29	27	35	41	13	10	9	42	4	3	14	18	18	3	40	9	0	0	1	6	24	23	15	0
flight	328	.8498	55.895	57.5	27	52	30	40	96	35	34	14	97	17	3	24	7	11	1	38	4	4	0	0	10	28	44	40	0
Flight	12	.4503	1.2060	40.8	3	0	3	1	0	5	0	0	3	0	0	0	5	1	0	0	0	1	0	0	0	2	0	0	0
flightless	3	.1823	.1405	31.5	0	0	0	0	2	0	1	0	0	0	0	0	0	1	0	0	0	0	0	0	0	0	2	0	0
flights	73	.7567	11.258	50.5	8	11	8	10	18	8	6	4	18	2	0	3	7	8	1	12	0	0	0	0	0	6	3	13	0
flighty	4	.1717	.2284	33.6	0	0	1	1	1	0	1	0	2	0	0	2	0	0	0	0	0	0	0	0	0	0	0	0	0
flimsy	7	.5250	.7984	39.0	0	1	2	1	1	0	1	1	2	0	0	0	0	0	0	1	0	0	0	0	0	1	1	2	0
flinch	4	.2969	.2888	34.6	0	0	2	0	2	0	0	0	1	0	0	2	0	0	0	0	0	0	0	0	1	0	0	0	0
flinching	3	.3400	.2455	33.9	0	1	0	1	0	1	0	0	1	1	0	0	0	0	0	0	0	0	0	0	1	0	0	0	0
fling	17	.6071	2.2171	43.5	2	1	3	2	6	1	1	1	8	0	0	2	0	2	0	0	2	0	0	0	0	1	0	2	0
flinging	12	.5171	1.3887	41.4	0	0	3	5	1	1	2	0	6	1	0	1	0	1	0	0	0	0	0	0	3	0	0	0	0
flint	32	.5303	3.5293	45.5	0	4	6	1	12	7	2	0	1	5	0	4	0	1	0	6	0	0	0	6	3	5	1	0	0
Flint	4	.2348	.2372	33.8	0	0	0	1	0	3	0	0	0	0	0	0	0	3	0	0	0	0	0	0	0	0	1	0	0
flintlock	2	.0000	.0290	24.6	0	1	0	0	0	0	1	0	0	0	0	0	0	0	0	0	0	0	0	0	0	2	0	0	0
flints	2	.2441	.1127	30.5	0	0	0	0	1	0	1	0	0	0	0	0	0	0	0	0	0	0	0	0	1	0	1	0	0
flinty	3	.2260	.1580	32.0	0	0	0	0	3	0	0	0	0	0	0	2	0	0	0	0	0	0	0	0	0	0	1	0	0
flip	18	.6483	2.4274	43.9	5	2	1	2	3	2	0	3	4	1	0	1	0	0	0	5	0	1	0	0	1	2	0	3	0
Flip	18	.3760	1.6916	42.3	4	11	0	2	1	0	0	0	11	0	0	0	0	0	2	0	0	0	0	0	0	0	0	5	0
FLIP	3	.0000	.0591	27.7	0	0	0	0	3	0	0	0	0	0	0	0	0	0	0	3	0	0	0	0	0	0	0	0	0
flip-flops	2	.2433	.1158	30.6	0	1	0	0	0	0	0	1	0	0	0	0	0	0	0	0	0	0	0	0	0	1	0	1	0
Flip's	2	.2376	.1088	30.4	0	0	0	1	1	0	0	0	0	0	0	0	0	0	1	0	0	0	0	0	0	0	0	1	0
flipped	13	.5514	1.5673	42.0	2	1	1	2	6	1	0	0	6	0	1	2	0	0	0	1	0	0	0	0	1	0	0	2	0
flipper	4	.4452	.3980	36.0	0	1	1	1	0	1	0	0	1	0	0	1	0	0	0	1	0	0	0	0	0	0	1	0	0
flippers	28	.4750	3.1563	45.0	4	16	2	2	3	1	0	0	21	1	2	0	0	0	1	2	0	0	0	0	1	0	0	0	0
flipping	6	.3121	.4562	36.6	0	1	0	1	1	1	0	2	1	0	0	0	0	0	0	3	0	0	0	0	2	0	0	0	0
flips	9	.3791	.7876	39.0	7	1	0	0	1	0	0	0	2	0	0	0	0	0	0	1	0	0	0	0	0	2	0	4	0
flirt	3	.1101	.0785	28.9	0	0	0	0	0	2	1	0	0	0	2	1	0	0	0	0	0	0	0	0	0	0	0	0	0
flirting	5	.3819	.4299	36.3	1	0	1	0	1	2	0	0	1	0	0	0	0	0	0	0	2	0	0	0	0	1	0	1	0
flirts	4	.2389	.2497	34.0	0	0	0	0	2	2	0	0	1	0	0	0	0	1	0	0	2	0	0	0	0	0	0	0	0
flit	5	.5304	.5639	37.5	1	1	0	1	1	1	0	0	1	0	0	1	0	0	0	0	1	0	0	0	0	1	0	1	0
flitted	8	.3810	.6935	38.4	2	0	0	1	3	0	1	1	2	0	1	0	0	0	0	0	0	0	0	0	4	0	0	1	0
flitting	2	.1814	.1187	30.7	0	1	0	1	0	0	0	0	1	0	0	0	0	0	0	0	0	0	0	0	0	0	0	1	0
Flo	2	.2443	.1130	30.5	0	0	0	0	1	0	1	0	0	0	0	1	0	0	0	0	0	0	0	0	1	0	0	0	0
float	125	.8358	21.032	53.2	27	18	20	21	20	11	5	3	40	3	1	1	0	2	3	34	5	3	1	0	3	12	7	10	0
floated	84	.8351	14.155	51.5	22	13	17	14	8	3	5	2	34	2	1	7	0	11	0	5	3	0	0	1	8	8	1	3	0
floating	134	.8819	23.647	53.7	24	27	19	24	22	6	10	2	54	4	1	9	2	9	0	20	3	1	1	0	7	7	12	4	0
Floating	2	.2446	.1257	31.0	0	0	0	1	1	0	0	0	0	0	0	0	0	1	0	1	0	0	0	0	0	0	0	0	0
floats	34	.7175	5.0009	47.0	6	7	1	3	11	4	1	1	8	2	0	2	0	3	0	7	5	0	0	0	0	2	1	4	0
flock	69	.7875	11.054	50.4	18	12	1	12	17	4	3	2	27	3	1	6	1	6	0	0	0	2	0	0	5	11	2	5	0
flocked	13	.5992	1.6345	42.1	1	2	2	2	1	4	1	0	2	1	0	0	0	6	0	0	0	0	1	0	1	1	1	0	0
flocking	2	.2408	.1204	30.8	0	0	0	1	1	0	0	0	0	0	0	0	0	1	0	0	0	0	0	0	0	1	0	0	0
flocks	62	.5865	7.6987	48.9	11	8	8	13	12	5	4	1	14	2	1	6	0	14	1	7	2	0	0	0	1	6	5	2	1
floes	5	.4715	.5340	37.3	0	2	0	0	2	1	0	0	2	0	0	0	0	0	0	1	0	0	0	0	0	0	1	1	0
flogging	3	.2279	.2143	33.3	0	0	0	2	1	0	0	0	2	0	0	0	0	0	0	0	0	0	0	0	0	0	0	1	0
flood	127	.8032	20.548	53.1	11	16	14	20	40	11	7	8	21	1	4	5	4	23	2	23	1	0	0	0	7	10	5	21	0
Flood	4	.3141	.3005	34.8	0	0	0	1	1	0	0	2	1	0	0	0	0	0	0	0	1	0	0	0	0	0	0	2	0
flood-circled	2	.0000	.0215	23.3	0	0	0	0	0	0	2	0	0	0	0	2	0	0	0	0	0	0	0	0	0	0	0	0	0
flooded	47	.7631	7.2764	48.6	11	5	8	7	6	6	4	0	10	5	1	0	0	10	2	0	0	0	0	0	4	7	4	4	0
flooding	21	.6867	2.9690	44.7	4	1	6	0	5	2	2	1	3	0	0	1	0	6	0	5	1	0	0	0	0	1	2	2	0
floodlights	2	.2160	.1362	31.3	0	0	0	1	0	1	0	0	1	0	0	0	0	0	0	1	0	0	0	0	0	0	0	0	0
floods	73	.5294	8.2744	49.2	5	8	20	11	14	3	3	9	6	0	0	0	0	29	0	19	0	0	0	0	0	3	3	13	0
floodwaters	6	.5049	.6522	38.1	1	1	0	0	2	0	1	1	1	1	0	0	0	1	0	0	0	0	0	0	0	1	0	2	0
Floogle	6	.0000	.0644	28.1	6	0	0	0	0	0	0	0	0	0	0	6	0	0	0	0	0	0	0	0	0	0	0	0	0
Floogles	5	.0000	.0537	27.3	5	0	0	0	0	0	0	0	0	0	0	5	0	0	0	0	0	0	0	0	0	0	0	0	0
floor	935	.9419	174.34	62.4	186	162	109	118	177	91	76	16	302	47	8	43	52	51	8	92	24	5	6	19	91	79	35	73	0
floor's	2	.0000	.0914	29.6	1	0	0	0	1	0	0	0	2	0	0	0	0	0	0	0	0	0	0	0	0	0	0	0	0
floorboard	2	.2443	.1130	30.5	0	0	0	0	1	0	1	0	0	0	0	1	0	0	0	0	0	0	0	0	1	0	0	0	0
floorboards	6	.3521	.4792	36.8	0	1	2	0	3	0	0	0	1	0	1	0	0	0	0	0	0	0	0	0	0	1	0	3	0
flooring	7	.4536	.7032	38.5	0	1	4	0	2	0	0	0	2	0	0	1	0	1	0	0	0	0	0	1	0	0	2	0	0
floors	80	.8426	13.501	51.3	13	9	15	15	11	8	9	0	15	4	1	2	13	7	0	13	0	0	1	2	1	8	11	2	0
flop	8	.5004	.8640	39.4	0	4	1	0	1	1	0	1	2	1	0	3	0	0	0	0	1	0	0	0	0	0	0	1	0
flopped	15	.5680	1.8297	42.6	2	3	2	2	3	1	1	1	5	0	0	3	0	1	0	1	0	0	0	0	2	0	0	3	0
flopping	8	.5608	.9866	39.9	3	1	1	1	1	0	1	0	4	0	0	1	0	1	0	0	0	0	0	0	1	1	0	0	0
floppy	6	.3657	.5386	37.3	1	2	1	1	0	0	0	1	3	0	0	0	0	0	0	0	1	0	0	0	0	0	0	2	0
Floppy	2	.0000	.0914	29.6	2	0	0	0	0	0	0	0	2	0	0	0	0	0	0	0	0	0	0	0	0	0	0	0	0
flops	3	.2437	.2277	33.6	1	0	1	0	1	0	0	0	2	0	0	0	0	0	0	1	0	0	0	0	0	0	0	0	0
flora	6	.3327	.4474	36.5	0	1	0	0	3	0	0	2	0	0	0	0	0	0	0	2	0	0	0	0	1	0	3	0	0
Flora	13	.6018	1.6128	42.1	2	1	2	2	6	0	0	0	1	0	0	2	0	1	0	0	2	0	0	0	4	2	1	0	0
Florabel	2	.0000	.0243	23.9	2	0	0	0	0	0	0	0	0	0	0	0	0	0	0	0	0	0	0	0	0	0	0	2	0
floral	3	.3346	.2478	33.9	0	1	0	0	0	1	1	0	1	0	0	0	0	0	0	1	0	0	0	0	0	0	1	0	0
Floral	2	.0000	.0209	23.2	0	0	0	0	0	2	0	0	0	0	0	0	0	0	0	0	0	0	0	0	0	0	2	0	0
Florence	49	.6759	6.8705	48.4	5	2	15	5	4	11	5	2	16	2	0	4	0	3	0	0	1	1	0	0	0	4	14	4	0
Florentine	3	.0801	.0640	28.1	0	0	1	0	1	0	1	0	0	0	0	0	0	0	0	0	0	2	0	0	0	1	0	0	0
Flores	5	.0000	.0547	27.4	0	0	0	0	0	0	5	0	0	5	0	0	0	0	0	0	0	0	0	0	0	0	0	0	0
Florey	3	.0000	.0591	27.7	0	0	0	1	0	1	1	0	0	0	0	0	0	0	0	3	0	0	0	0	0	0	0	0	0
Florian's	4	.0000	.0323	25.1	0	0	0	0	0	0	4	0	0	0	0	0	0	0	0	0	4	0	0	0	0	0	0	0	0
florid	2	.2417	.1091	30.4	0	0	1	0	0	1	0	0	0	0	0	0	0	0	0	0	1	0	0	0	0	0	1	0	0
Florida	174	.7788	27.418	54.4	42	24	43	18	27	9	6	5	29	1	1	1	4	52	3	13	0	1	0	0	6	25	18	20	0
Florida's	7	.3896	.6186	37.9	1	0	3	0	0	0	0	3	1	0	0	0	0	2	0	0	0	0	0	0	0	1	0	3	0
florins	2	.1717	.1142	30.6	0	0	0	0	2	0	0	0	1	0	0	1	0	0	0	0	0	0	0	0	0	0	0	0	0
Florizel	11	.0000	.5025	37.0	0	0	11	0	0	0	0	0	11	0	0	0	0	0	0	0	0	0	0	0	0	0	0	0	0
Flossie	6	.0000	.0729	28.6	0	0	0	0	0	0	0	6	0	0	0	0	0	0	0	0	0	0	0	0	0	0	0	6	0

8D Flicka's
7N flicker's
9D flied
6A Flier
3P FLIES
7A Flight-Lieutenant
7R Flights
3J flinched
7N flinders
4A Flinders
6R flings
7A flint-headed
6R flintlocks
3A flip-flop
4D flipflops
6C flippant
3J Flipper-Flopper
9J flirtatious
7N flirted
8R Flit
5A flitter
3B flitter-twitters
9Q flivvers
4J floatin'
6J Flock
8G floe
6A flogged
7H flood-control
3P floodings
8D floodlike
4Q floodlit
XR floodplains
3B floofle
3D Floogle's
3D Floogles'
XH floored
5G floorwalker
7A Flor
7H floras
8Q florentia
8Q Florentia
7R Florentines
5C florid-faced
9H florist
XH florists
6A florists'
XR Flossie's
3A flot
3A flot's

Word Type	F	D	U	SFI	3 Gr 3	4 Gr 4	5 Gr 5	6 Gr 6	7 Gr 7	8 Gr 8	9 Gr 9	X UnGr	A Read	B Eng & Gr	C Comp	D Lit	E Math	F Soc Stud	G Spell	H Sci	J Music	K Art	L Home Ec	M Shop	N Lib F	P Lib NF	Q Lib Ref	R Mag	S Rel
flotation	2	.2160	.1362	31.3	1	0	0	0	0	0	1	0	1	0	0	0	0	0	0	1	0	0	0	0	0	0	0	0	0
flotsam	5	.2435	.2726	34.4	0	0	0	0	5	0	0	0	0	0	1	0	0	0	0	0	0	0	0	0	0	0	4	0	0
flounder	10	.4935	1.0385	40.2	3	0	5	0	1	0	0	1	0	0	0	0	0	0	0	3	1	0	0	0	0	1	4	1	0
floundered	6	.3765	.5074	37.1	1	0	1	1	2	1	0	0	1	0	0	3	0	0	0	0	0	0	0	0	1	0	0	1	0
floundering	7	.4287	.6565	38.2	0	2	0	1	2	2	0	0	1	0	0	2	0	0	0	0	0	0	0	0	0	2	2	0	0
flour	224	.4331	21.083	53.2	31	32	29	17	27	37	50	1	38	8	1	2	2	39	4	9	2	1	81	0	5	7	16	9	0
floured	9	.3145	.6282	38.0	0	6	0	1	0	0	2	0	0	0	0	0	0	0	0	0	0	0	2	0	1	6	0	0	0
flourish	28	.6736	3.8690	45.9	2	5	2	2	8	5	4	0	4	0	0	1	0	5	0	1	1	0	1	0	3	4	8	0	0
flourished	43	.6959	6.0969	47.9	1	2	2	3	17	9	5	4	3	1	1	1	0	13	0	3	2	0	0	0	0	5	11	3	0
flourishes	10	.5126	1.0635	40.3	0	2	0	2	3	1	1	1	0	0	0	0	0	1	0	0	2	0	0	0	1	0	3	3	0
flourishing	3	.2444	.1814	32.6	0	0	0	0	1	1	1	0	0	0	0	0	0	2	0	0	0	0	0	0	0	0	1	0	0
flow	352	.7729	54.861	57.4	35	48	65	35	54	56	48	11	31	8	2	6	10	66	4	108	13	6	1	30	3	13	36	15	0
Flow	2	.0000	.0162	22.1	0	0	0	2	0	0	0	0	0	0	0	0	0	0	0	0	2	0	0	0	0	0	0	0	0
flowed	68	.7596	10.493	50.2	10	15	9	7	13	6	4	4	13	2	0	8	0	13	1	11	0	0	0	1	0	11	6	2	0
flower	283	.9085	51.062	57.1	64	43	33	52	43	17	19	12	54	15	3	10	10	17	14	90	4	4	2	1	10	16	17	16	0
Flower	25	.1749	1.1898	40.8	1	21	0	0	0	2	1	0	1	0	0	0	0	2	0	0	0	0	0	0	0	21	0	1	0
Flower's	2	.0000	.0290	24.6	0	2	0	0	0	0	0	0	0	0	0	0	0	0	0	0	0	0	0	0	0	2	0	0	0
flowered	6	.4696	.6398	38.1	2	1	0	0	0	0	0	3	2	0	0	0	0	1	0	2	0	0	0	0	0	0	0	1	0
flowering	48	.5423	5.5292	47.4	4	4	6	10	11	7	0	6	5	1	0	0	0	3	0	21	2	0	0	0	0	2	13	1	0
flowerpot	5	.4490	.5022	37.0	1	0	2	0	1	1	0	0	1	0	0	1	1	0	0	2	0	0	0	0	0	0	0	0	0
flowerpots	4	.2805	.2842	34.5	1	0	0	0	3	0	0	0	1	0	0	0	0	1	0	0	0	0	0	0	2	0	0	0	0
flowers	695	.8885	123.22	60.9	184	155	59	137	59	30	31	40	220	20	8	42	5	49	13	150	17	16	4	1	15	53	51	31	0
Flowers	5	.5336	.5703	37.6	0	0	2	1	0	2	0	0	1	1	0	0	0	1	0	0	0	0	0	0	0	0	1	1	0
flowery	3	.3870	.2486	34.0	0	0	0	0	0	1	1	1	0	0	0	1	0	0	0	0	0	0	0	0	0	0	1	1	0
flowing	130	.8264	21.517	53.3	12	13	18	25	20	26	13	3	18	5	2	5	0	11	1	36	15	5	0	6	5	7	7	7	0
Flowing	3	.2425	.1816	32.6	0	0	2	0	0	0	0	1	0	0	0	0	0	2	0	0	0	0	0	0	0	0	0	1	0
flown	55	.8089	9.0272	49.6	6	15	5	12	10	3	3	1	23	3	0	4	2	4	0	3	1	0	0	0	3	4	2	6	0
flows	218	.6827	30.499	54.8	23	48	39	41	25	20	17	5	7	3	2	1	1	67	2	95	5	0	0	9	0	6	13	7	0
Floyd	4	.0847	.0825	29.2	0	0	0	0	3	1	0	0	0	0	3	1	0	0	0	0	0	0	0	0	0	0	0	0	0
flu	7	.5201	.7858	39.0	1	2	2	1	0	0	1	0	1	0	0	0	2	1	0	2	0	0	0	0	0	0	0	1	0
fluctuating	3	.3709	.2499	34.0	0	0	0	0	1	1	0	1	0	0	0	0	0	1	0	1	0	0	0	0	0	0	1	0	0
fluctuation	2	.2278	.1128	30.5	0	0	0	0	1	0	0	1	0	0	0	0	0	0	0	1	0	0	0	0	0	0	1	0	0
fluctuations	7	.3452	.5533	37.4	0	0	0	0	1	0	1	5	0	0	0	1	0	0	0	5	0	0	0	0	0	0	1	0	0
flue	6	.5081	.6494	38.1	1	0	2	0	1	1	0	1	1	2	0	0	0	0	1	0	0	0	0	0	0	1	0	1	0
fluff	11	.3489	.9155	39.6	1	3	1	1	2	1	1	1	4	0	0	0	0	0	0	1	0	0	3	0	2	0	0	1	0
Fluff	3	.2283	.1611	32.1	1	0	0	0	2	0	0	0	0	1	0	0	0	0	0	0	0	0	0	0	2	0	0	0	0
fluffed	2	.1787	.1174	30.7	0	1	0	0	1	0	0	0	1	0	0	0	0	0	0	0	0	0	0	0	1	0	0	0	0
fluffy	45	.6227	5.8180	47.6	12	7	3	4	5	4	9	1	8	3	1	3	0	1	0	11	1	0	8	0	1	6	0	2	0
fluid	55	.5774	6.6032	48.2	1	2	4	6	9	19	9	5	2	0	0	0	2	0	0	25	0	0	4	1	1	1	17	2	0
fluidity	2	.1247	.0633	28.0	0	0	1	0	0	0	1	0	0	0	0	0	0	0	0	0	0	1	0	0	0	1	0	0	0
fluids	13	.4325	1.2475	41.0	0	0	2	0	4	3	2	2	1	0	0	0	0	0	0	9	0	0	1	0	0	1	1	0	0
fluke	8	.1494	.3218	35.1	0	0	6	0	2	0	0	0	0	0	0	0	0	0	0	2	0	0	0	0	0	0	6	0	0
flukes	11	.3095	.8091	39.1	2	0	5	2	2	0	0	0	2	0	0	0	0	0	0	1	0	0	0	0	0	2	6	0	0
flung	70	.5548	8.3845	49.2	9	11	5	11	20	8	6	0	25	1	0	8	0	0	0	1	0	0	0	0	23	8	1	3	0
fluoresce	3	.0000	.0591	27.7	0	0	0	0	0	1	1	1	0	0	0	0	0	0	0	3	0	0	0	0	0	0	0	0	0
fluorescence	8	.1494	.3218	35.1	0	0	6	0	0	2	0	0	0	0	0	0	0	0	0	2	0	0	0	0	0	0	6	0	0
Fluorescence	2	.0000	.0209	23.2	0	0	2	0	0	0	0	0	0	0	0	0	0	0	0	0	0	0	0	0	0	0	2	0	0
fluorescent	18	.3932	1.5619	41.9	0	1	6	1	2	2	1	5	1	0	0	0	0	0	0	8	0	0	0	2	0	0	7	0	0
fluoresces	2	.0000	.0209	23.2	0	0	2	0	0	0	0	0	0	0	0	0	0	0	0	0	0	0	0	0	0	0	2	0	0
fluoridated	2	.2346	.1166	30.7	0	0	0	0	1	1	0	0	0	0	0	0	0	0	0	1	0	0	0	0	0	0	0	1	0
fluoridation	4	.2287	.2348	33.7	0	0	0	0	1	3	0	0	0	0	0	0	0	0	0	3	0	0	0	0	0	0	0	1	0
fluoride	12	.3237	.8654	39.4	0	0	6	0	4	0	1	1	0	0	0	0	0	0	0	2	0	0	0	0	0	0	6	4	0
fluorides	3	.2321	.1635	32.1	0	0	1	0	2	0	0	0	0	0	0	0	0	0	0	0	0	0	0	0	0	0	1	2	0
fluorine	22	.3815	1.8457	42.7	0	0	9	0	6	6	1	0	0	0	0	0	0	0	0	11	0	0	2	0	0	0	9	0	0
fluorspar	3	.0000	.0314	25.0	0	0	3	0	0	0	0	0	0	0	0	0	0	0	0	0	0	0	0	0	0	0	3	0	0
Flupp	6	.0000	.0703	28.5	6	0	0	0	0	0	0	0	0	0	0	0	0	0	0	0	0	0	0	0	6	0	0	0	0
flurry	4	.3713	.3634	35.6	2	1	1	0	0	0	0	0	2	0	0	1	0	0	0	0	0	0	0	0	1	0	0	0	0
flush	13	.5970	1.6123	42.1	1	0	1	1	4	5	1	0	2	2	1	1	0	1	0	2	0	0	0	2	1	1	0	0	0
flushed	37	.5630	4.4632	46.5	3	4	2	6	16	5	1	0	12	0	0	7	0	0	0	1	0	0	0	0	11	2	2	2	0
flushing	3	.3465	.2515	34.0	0	1	0	0	1	0	1	0	1	0	0	0	0	0	0	0	0	0	0	0	0	1	0	1	0
Flushing	2	.1698	.1133	30.5	0	0	0	0	1	0	1	0	1	0	0	0	0	0	0	0	0	0	0	0	0	0	1	0	0
flustered	2	.1787	.1174	30.7	0	1	0	1	0	0	0	0	1	0	0	0	0	0	0	0	0	0	0	0	1	0	0	0	0
flute	80	.1765	3.5939	45.6	11	18	16	10	17	4	4	0	8	1	0	2	0	1	0	0	63	0	0	0	0	3	0	2	0
Flute	4	.0000	.0323	25.1	0	0	1	1	0	1	1	0	0	0	0	0	0	0	0	0	4	0	0	0	0	0	0	0	0
fluted	4	.2358	.2662	34.3	0	1	0	2	0	0	1	0	2	0	1	0	0	0	0	0	0	0	0	0	0	0	0	1	0
flutes	34	.4695	3.3808	45.3	4	5	6	4	8	3	4	0	3	0	0	3	0	1	0	0	16	0	0	0	4	5	1	1	0
flutter	21	.6848	2.9649	44.7	4	4	3	2	4	2	2	0	6	1	1	5	0	1	0	0	0	1	0	0	0	3	1	2	0
fluttered	33	.6752	4.6575	46.7	6	7	4	5	5	6	0	0	14	1	1	4	0	0	0	0	1	0	0	0	6	5	0	1	0
fluttering	26	.6714	3.6453	45.6	2	6	4	5	4	3	1	1	11	2	1	3	0	1	0	0	0	2	0	0	2	1	1	2	0
flutters	3	.2155	.1729	32.4	0	0	1	0	2	0	0	0	1	0	1	0	0	0	0	0	0	0	0	0	0	0	1	0	0
fluttery	2	.0000	.0914	29.6	1	0	0	1	0	0	0	0	2	0	0	0	0	0	0	0	0	0	0	0	0	0	0	0	0
flux	28	.1068	.7671	38.8	1	0	2	0	2	10	13	0	1	0	0	0	0	0	0	3	0	0	0	20	0	1	3	0	0
fly	785	.9105	142.25	61.5	266	125	85	116	111	41	13	28	289	27	15	25	47	54	16	96	31	4	0	1	27	78	27	48	0
Fly	2	.0000	.0162	22.1	1	0	0	0	1	0	0	0	0	0	0	0	0	0	0	0	2	0	0	0	0	0	0	0	0
fly-away	2	.0000	.0234	23.7	2	0	0	0	0	0	0	0	0	0	0	0	0	0	0	0	0	0	0	0	2	0	0	0	0
fly's	2	.0000	.0209	23.2	0	0	2	0	0	0	0	0	0	0	0	0	0	0	0	0	0	0	0	0	0	0	2	0	0
Flyaway	11	.0000	.5025	37.0	11	0	0	0	0	0	0	0	11	0	0	0	0	0	0	0	0	0	0	0	0	0	0	0	0
Flyaway's	2	.0000	.0914	29.6	2	0	0	0	0	0	0	0	2	0	0	0	0	0	0	0	0	0	0	0	0	0	0	0	0
flycatchers	2	.0000	.0394	26.0	1	0	0	1	0	0	0	0	0	0	0	0	0	0	0	2	0	0	0	0	0	0	0	0	0
flyer	5	.2754	.3628	35.6	3	1	0	0	1	0	0	0	2	0	0	0	0	0	0	1	2	0	0	0	0	0	0	0	0
Flyer	9	.3804	.8678	39.4	0	4	0	0	5	0	0	0	6	0	0	0	0	0	0	0	0	0	0	0	1	2	0	0	0
flyers	4	.2191	.2297	33.6	1	0	0	2	0	1	0	0	0	0	0	0	0	0	0	3	0	0	0	0	0	1	0	0	0
flyin'	3	.2028	.1988	33.0	0	1	1	0	1	0	0	0	2	0	0	0	0	0	0	0	1	0	0	0	0	0	0	0	0
flying	508	.8955	90.749	59.6	116	78	48	81	93	39	30	23	184	8	5	30	15	32	6	57	11	8	0	2	21	74	17	38	0
Flying	22	.4030	2.1250	43.3	0	0	0	4	9	8	0	1	11	0	0	7	0	2	0	0	0	0	0	0	0	0	0	2	0
flypaper	3	.1169	.1277	31.1	0	0	0	0	3	0	0	0	1	0	0	0	0	0	0	0	0	0	0	0	0	0	2	0	0
flyway	11	.3618	1.0054	40.0	3	0	0	5	3	0	0	0	6	0	0	0	0	0	0	2	0	0	0	0	0	0	0	3	0
Flyway	10	.3617	.9146	39.6	0	1	0	8	1	0	0	0	5	0	0	0	0	0	0	4	0	0	0	0	0	0	0	1	0
flyways	10	.2574	.7013	38.5	0	2	0	3	4	0	0	1	4	0	0	0	0	0	0	1	0	0	0	0	0	0	0	5	0
flywheel	11	.2590	.6274	38.0	0	0	0	0	11	0	0	0	0	0	0	0	0	0	0	0	1	0	0	4	0	0	0	6	0
flywheels	2	.2346	.1166	30.7	0	0	1	0	1	0	0	0	0	0	0	0	0	0	0	1	0	0	0	0	0	0	0	1	0
FM	15	.2522	.8915	39.5	0	0	0	1	0	8	6	0	0	0	0	0	1	0	0	6	8	0	0	0	0	0	0	0	0
FMCS	8	.0000	.0837	29.2	0	0	8	0	0	0	0	0	0	0	0	0	0	0	0	0	0	0	0	0	0	0	8	0	0

9P flotilla
3A flots
5Q Flounder
5Q flour-milling
8L flours
7A flouted
9Q flow-meter
9Q flow-rate
9D flow'ring
3N flower-bed
3N flower-beds
6F flower-decked
6A flower-peckers
9L flower-shaped
6A flower-strewn
6A flower-women
7A flower's
5E flowerbeds
9L flowerets
5Q Flowering
7Q flowerlike
8D flowers'
XA Flowery
9A Flt
7Q fluctuate
7Q fluctuated
7Q fluctuates
6J Fludde
9J fluent
7R fluently
3P fluffed-up
6B fluffiest
9L fluffy-to-moist
9L Fluflon
XQ flumes
XR flummadiddle
7D flunk
5A flunked
8J flunky
5Q Fluorescent
7L fluorescents
5Q fluorescing
5Q fluoridating
8Q fluorine-containing
9H fluorite
7R fluorocarbon
5Q fluorocarbons
9Q fluoroscope
5Q Fluoroscope
5Q fluoroscopes
XH fluorospar
5Q fluosilicate
7D flurried
3A flurries
7B flushes
9D FLUTE
7J flute-like
8J flute's
5A flutist
7D flutter-butterfly
6A flutter-kicking
7M fluxes
3P fly-boy
4N fly-whisk
8E flyby
9A flying-doctor
3P flying-instruction
3P flying-officer
7P flying-trapeze
7Q flyingfish
4F flyleaf
4P flyweight

Word Type	F	D	U	SFI	3 Gr 3	4 Gr 4	5 Gr 5	6 Gr 6	7 Gr 7	8 Gr 8	9 Gr 9	X UnGr	A Read	B Eng & Gr	C Comp	D Lit	E Math	F Soc Stud	G Spell	H Sci	J Music	K Art	L Home Ec	M Shop	N Lib F	P Lib NF	Q Lib Ref	R Mag	S Rel
fo'	9	.0000	.4111	36.1	0	0	0	0	9	0	0	0	9	0	0	0	0	0	0	0	0	0	0	0	0	0	0	0	0
fo'c's'tle	2	.0000	.0914	29.6	0	0	0	0	0	2	0	0	2	0	0	0	0	0	0	0	0	0	0	0	0	0	0	0	0
foal	19	.6075	2.4368	43.9	0	10	2	3	3	1	0	0	6	0	0	3	0	0	0	0	1	0	0	0	4	3	0	2	0
foal's	3	.2060	.1500	31.8	0	1	0	0	2	0	0	0	0	0	0	2	0	0	0	0	0	0	0	0	0	1	0	0	0
foaled	2	.0000	.0234	23.7	0	1	0	1	0	0	0	0	0	0	0	0	0	0	0	0	0	0	0	0	2	0	0	0	0
foals	4	.3192	.3100	34.9	0	2	0	2	0	0	0	0	1	0	0	0	0	0	0	0	0	0	0	0	0	2	0	1	0
foam	36	.7760	5.6462	47.5	5	1	4	9	7	6	4	0	9	2	0	9	0	1	0	2	2	2	1	1	2	2	2	1	0
foamed	2	.1717	.1142	30.6	0	0	1	0	0	0	1	0	1	0	0	1	0	0	0	0	0	0	0	0	0	0	0	0	0
foaming	13	.6572	1.7881	42.5	2	3	2	1	3	2	0	0	5	0	0	1	0	0	0	0	2	0	0	0	1	2	1	1	0
foamy	5	.3722	.4330	36.4	0	0	0	1	1	2	1	0	2	0	0	1	0	0	0	0	0	1	1	0	0	0	0	0	0
focal	11	.5858	1.3215	41.2	0	3	0	4	2	1	1	0	0	0	0	0	0	0	0	2	1	0	1	0	0	1	3	3	0
Foch	4	.0000	.0778	28.9	0	0	0	0	0	4	0	0	0	0	0	0	0	4	0	0	0	0	0	0	0	0	0	0	0
foci	6	.1870	.2899	34.6	0	0	0	5	0	1	0	0	0	0	0	0	5	0	0	0	0	0	0	0	0	0	1	0	0
focus	56	.7947	8.9241	49.5	0	4	2	9	20	7	8	6	2	5	0	3	0	5	0	17	1	1	0	1	2	2	7	10	0
focused	27	.7836	4.2496	46.3	2	2	1	4	9	6	1	2	2	3	0	1	1	4	0	4	3	0	0	1	1	0	3	4	0
focuses	9	.5166	.9659	39.8	0	0	0	1	4	0	4	0	0	2	1	0	0	0	0	2	1	0	0	0	0	0	0	3	0
focusing	20	.5418	2.2942	43.6	0	1	2	1	14	0	2	0	1	1	1	0	0	0	0	14	0	0	0	1	0	0	1	1	0
fodder	7	.4757	.6989	38.4	0	1	1	2	2	1	0	0	0	0	1	1	0	1	0	0	0	0	0	0	2	2	0	0	0
foe	26	.7332	3.8701	45.9	0	1	2	3	11	6	3	0	4	2	0	4	0	6	2	0	1	1	0	0	0	3	3	0	0
foe's	2	.1494	.1045	30.2	0	1	0	1	0	0	0	0	1	0	0	0	0	0	0	0	1	0	0	0	0	0	0	0	0
Foerstner	2	.0000	.0050	17.0	0	0	0	0	0	2	0	0	0	0	0	0	0	0	0	0	0	0	0	2	0	0	0	0	0
foes	15	.6554	2.0659	43.2	3	1	2	0	5	2	2	0	6	0	0	1	0	1	0	0	1	0	0	0	0	3	2	1	0
fog	212	.7749	33.553	55.3	41	36	17	35	38	17	24	4	80	9	4	14	0	12	0	44	2	0	0	0	19	20	1	7	0
Fog	7	.3738	.5840	37.7	0	4	0	1	2	0	0	0	1	0	0	1	0	0	0	0	1	0	0	0	4	0	0	0	0
fogbound	2	.1948	.1250	31.0	0	0	1	0	1	0	0	0	1	0	0	0	0	0	0	0	0	0	0	0	0	1	0	0	0
Fogg	53	.0349	.9620	39.8	0	0	0	1	52	0	0	0	0	1	0	0	0	0	0	0	0	0	0	0	52	0	0	0	0
fogging	2	.2440	.1132	30.5	0	0	0	0	2	0	0	0	0	0	0	1	0	0	0	0	0	0	0	0	0	0	0	1	0
foggy	37	.7359	5.6150	47.5	10	6	7	6	7	0	1	0	15	0	1	0	0	8	2	3	3	1	0	0	0	3	0	1	0
foghorn	18	.5427	2.1961	43.4	11	2	0	2	0	0	2	1	11	2	0	0	0	2	0	0	0	0	0	0	0	2	0	1	0
foghorns	4	.0000	.1827	32.6	3	0	1	0	0	0	0	0	4	0	0	0	0	0	0	0	0	0	0	0	0	0	0	0	0
fogs	11	.2922	.8340	39.2	2	0	0	1	1	1	6	0	3	0	0	1	0	0	0	7	0	0	0	0	0	0	0	0	0
fohn	2	.0000	.0394	26.0	0	0	0	0	2	0	0	0	0	0	0	0	0	0	0	2	0	0	0	0	0	0	0	0	0
foil	53	.5781	6.3210	48.0	3	12	4	4	21	2	4	3	7	0	0	1	0	0	0	6	6	4	4	12	0	3	1	9	0
fol	2	.0000	.0162	22.1	0	0	0	0	2	0	0	0	0	0	0	0	0	0	0	0	2	0	0	0	0	0	0	0	0
fold	168	.5357	18.808	52.7	32	20	14	15	21	25	38	3	23	8	0	8	31	1	1	15	1	5	54	4	0	4	4	9	0
folded	141	.7430	21.238	53.3	27	18	17	13	21	21	23	1	29	0	0	15	14	2	0	15	4	8	17	6	13	9	3	6	0
folder	12	.3560	.9309	39.7	5	0	1	0	1	1	4	0	1	0	0	0	5	0	1	0	0	0	1	4	0	0	0	0	0
folders	10	.4314	.9105	39.6	2	2	1	3	0	0	2	0	0	4	0	0	2	0	3	0	0	0	0	0	0	0	0	1	0
folding	49	.7134	7.0390	48.5	5	4	3	9	6	3	16	3	4	0	1	2	7	0	1	1	0	3	7	6	5	4	2	6	0
folds	51	.7837	8.0414	49.1	5	8	6	3	12	4	6	7	7	2	0	4	4	1	0	10	0	3	3	1	3	3	8	2	0
Foley	2	.2303	.1079	30.3	0	0	0	1	0	0	1	0	0	0	0	0	0	0	0	0	1	0	0	0	0	1	0	0	0
Folger	7	.2979	.4980	37.0	0	3	0	1	3	0	0	0	1	0	0	0	0	0	0	0	0	0	0	0	0	3	0	3	0
Folger's	3	.1409	.1472	31.7	0	2	0	1	0	0	0	0	1	0	0	0	0	0	0	0	0	0	0	0	0	2	0	0	0
Folgil	5	.0000	.2284	33.6	0	0	0	0	0	5	0	0	5	0	0	0	0	0	0	0	0	0	0	0	0	0	0	0	0
foliage	18	.6446	2.3792	43.8	0	0	1	2	6	4	1	4	2	0	0	0	0	0	0	1	1	1	0	0	2	3	4	4	0
folk	280	.3185	19.858	53.0	11	36	54	59	61	45	14	0	24	1	0	15	3	3	2	1	196	0	1	0	8	13	5	8	0
Folk	11	.4245	1.0015	40.0	2	3	0	0	2	0	0	4	0	0	0	0	0	0	0	4	4	0	0	0	0	0	1	2	0
folk-music	3	.0000	.0243	23.8	0	0	0	0	0	0	3	0	0	0	0	0	0	0	0	0	3	0	0	0	0	0	0	0	0
folk-rock	2	.0000	.0243	23.9	0	0	1	0	0	1	0	0	0	0	0	0	0	0	0	0	0	0	0	0	0	0	0	2	0
folklike	2	.2417	.1091	30.4	0	0	0	0	0	1	1	0	0	0	0	0	0	0	0	0	1	0	0	0	0	0	1	0	0
folklore	7	.4029	.6192	37.9	0	0	1	3	2	1	0	0	1	0	0	0	0	0	0	0	2	0	0	0	0	0	1	3	0
folks	153	.7427	23.215	53.7	25	29	21	11	37	17	9	4	48	4	1	24	0	3	2	0	7	1	0	0	28	27	0	8	0
Folks	11	.3193	.7699	38.9	7	3	0	0	0	0	1	0	0	0	0	1	0	0	0	0	3	0	0	0	7	0	0	0	0
Folksong	2	.0000	.0290	24.6	0	0	0	0	2	0	0	0	0	0	0	0	0	0	0	0	0	0	0	0	0	2	0	0	0
Foll	2	.0000	.0290	24.6	0	0	0	0	2	0	0	0	0	0	0	0	0	0	0	0	0	0	0	0	0	2	0	0	0
follicle	10	.2235	.5679	37.5	6	0	0	0	0	0	4	0	0	0	0	0	0	0	0	4	0	0	0	0	0	6	0	0	0
follicles	9	.0000	.1303	31.1	9	0	0	0	0	0	0	0	0	0	0	0	0	0	0	0	0	0	0	0	0	9	0	0	0
follow	1022	.8883	180.44	62.6	155	161	166	138	174	104	111	13	199	149	13	39	48	60	138	70	100	4	43	26	38	39	24	32	0
Follow	4	.0759	.1243	30.9	2	1	1	0	0	0	0	0	1	0	0	0	0	0	0	0	3	0	0	0	0	0	0	0	0
follow-my-leader	2	.0000	.0290	24.6	0	2	0	0	0	0	0	0	0	0	0	0	0	0	0	0	0	0	0	0	0	2	0	0	0
follow-up	2	.2346	.1166	30.7	0	0	0	0	0	1	1	0	0	0	0	0	0	0	0	1	0	0	0	0	0	0	0	1	0
followed	880	.9190	160.47	62.1	92	174	132	109	184	117	57	15	252	50	18	65	7	93	54	17	47	1	8	7	82	79	54	46	0
follower	4	.4777	.4012	36.0	1	0	0	1	1	0	1	0	0	0	0	0	1	0	0	0	1	0	0	0	1	1	0	0	0
followers	50	.6643	6.8117	48.3	5	0	10	7	16	8	3	1	4	2	0	2	0	17	2	0	0	0	0	0	1	6	11	5	0
following	2680	.7361	398.14	66.0	166	289	336	371	640	455	391	32	258	654	173	44	762	68	329	90	96	4	40	18	21	44	33	46	0
follows	346	.8578	59.043	57.7	25	44	48	38	73	57	58	3	27	79	11	8	59	18	33	35	20	1	11	8	2	8	18	8	0
folly	7	.5335	.8006	39.0	0	0	0	1	3	0	3	0	2	0	0	2	0	0	1	0	0	0	0	0	1	0	1	0	0
Folly	4	.0000	.1827	32.6	0	3	1	0	0	0	0	0	4	0	0	0	0	0	0	0	0	0	0	0	0	0	0	0	0
fomites	3	.0000	.1370	31.4	0	0	0	0	0	3	0	0	3	0	0	0	0	0	0	0	0	0	0	0	0	0	0	0	0
fond	82	.8326	13.710	51.4	12	14	7	12	18	12	4	3	24	5	2	10	1	1	2	1	4	0	1	0	14	9	2	6	0
fonder	4	.0000	.1827	32.6	3	1	0	0	0	0	0	0	4	0	0	0	0	0	0	0	0	0	0	0	0	0	0	0	0
fondling	2	.2443	.1130	30.5	0	0	1	0	1	0	0	0	0	0	0	1	0	0	0	0	0	0	0	0	1	0	0	0	0
fondly	11	.5060	1.1941	40.8	2	4	0	2	3	0	0	0	2	0	0	1	0	0	1	0	0	0	0	0	3	4	0	0	0
fondness	5	.4755	.5327	37.3	0	0	3	1	0	0	1	0	2	0	0	1	0	0	0	0	0	0	0	0	0	0	1	1	0
Fong	11	.1717	.7657	38.8	0	10	0	0	0	1	0	0	10	0	0	0	0	1	0	0	0	0	0	0	0	0	0	0	0
font	2	.2440	.1132	30.5	0	0	0	0	0	0	1	1	0	0	0	1	0	0	0	0	0	0	0	0	0	0	0	1	0
Fontainebleau	2	.1493	.0692	28.4	0	0	1	0	0	0	1	0	0	0	0	0	0	0	0	0	0	1	0	0	0	0	1	0	0
Fontana	2	.0000	.0290	24.6	2	0	0	0	0	0	0	0	0	0	0	0	0	0	0	0	0	0	0	0	0	2	0	0	0
fooba	6	.0000	.0729	28.6	6	0	0	0	0	0	0	0	0	0	0	0	0	0	0	0	0	0	0	0	0	0	0	6	0
food	2801	.8306	467.35	66.7	714	338	398	396	481	210	219	45	544	54	9	59	22	390	34	887	7	7	174	9	90	249	179	84	3
Food	27	.4676	2.7531	44.4	5	1	1	5	3	8	3	1	3	0	0	0	0	3	0	13	0	0	4	0	0	0	1	3	0
FOOD	3	.2123	.1792	32.5	0	0	0	2	0	1	0	0	1	0	0	0	0	0	0	1	0	0	1	0	0	0	0	0	0
food-chain	4	.2353	.2382	33.8	0	0	0	0	1	3	0	0	0	0	0	0	0	0	0	3	0	0	0	0	0	0	1	0	0
food-gatherer	2	.2446	.1257	31.0	0	0	0	2	0	0	0	0	0	0	0	0	0	1	0	1	0	0	0	0	0	0	0	0	0
food-gatherers	2	.2401	.1133	30.5	1	0	0	0	1	0	0	0	0	0	0	0	0	0	0	0	0	0	0	0	0	1	1	0	0
food-getting	3	.1813	.1402	31.5	0	0	0	0	3	0	0	0	0	0	0	0	0	0	0	1	0	0	0	0	0	0	2	0	0
food-making	4	.0000	.0789	29.0	0	1	0	3	0	0	0	0	0	0	0	0	0	0	0	4	0	0	0	0	0	0	0	0	0
food-processing	6	.1822	.3062	34.9	0	0	3	0	3	0	0	0	0	0	0	0	0	5	0	0	0	0	0	0	0	1	0	0	0
food-producing	2	.2285	.1129	30.5	0	0	1	0	1	0	0	0	0	0	0	0	0	1	0	0	0	0	0	0	0	0	1	0	0
foodmaking	2	.0000	.0394	26.0	0	0	0	0	2	0	0	0	0	0	0	0	0	0	0	2	0	0	0	0	0	0	0	0	0
foods	518	.4647	52.082	57.2	91	62	83	42	91	59	78	12	48	7	2	7	2	62	6	222	0	0	117	0	0	13	24	8	0
Foods	2	.1432	.0759	28.8	1	0	0	0	0	0	1	0	0	0	0	0	0	0	0	1	0	0	1	0	0	0	0	0	0

8E FMH
8E FN
7N fo'c's'le
6P fo'c'sle
9Q Foa
9Q Foa's
6R foaling
6R foam-flecked
6A foam-laced
7R foam-padded
4N foamite
8P fob
5E FOB
5P fobs
8R Foccart
8F Foch's
7N Fodder-wing
5P Fodio
6J foeman's
5E FOG
7A fog-bound
XH fog-horn
3A fog's
7N Fogg's
7R fogged
9B foglights
7H foibles
7Q foiled
7K foils
3J fol-de-rol
7R fold-back
3F foldaway
3P Folded
8A Folgil's
6P folia
9R folk-hero
XH folk-inventiveness
XH folk-shrewdness
5J folk-sing
6J folk-singing
5J folk-song
9J folk-songs
8Q folksong
3Q folksongs
6A folktale
6R folktales
7R folkways
6J foller
9H follicle-stimulating
3P FOLLICLES
7A follies
5G follis
9D follow'd
6A followin'
XH Fomalhaut
7A fondest
7D fondled
9D Fong's
7R food-bearing
9L food-budget
9L food-buying
8H food-chains
4P food-laden
5H food-makers
8L food-preparation
6H food-producer
8H food-product
7Q food-rich
8H food-web
7L food's
5A foodless
4H foodmaker

Word Type	F	D	U	SFI	3 Gr 3	4 Gr 4	5 Gr 5	6 Gr 6	7 Gr 7	8 Gr 8	9 Gr 9	X UnGr	A Read	B Eng & Gr	C Comp	D Lit	E Math	F Soc Stud	G Spell	H Sci	J Music	K Art	L Home Ec	M Shop	N Lib F	P Lib NF	Q Lib Ref	R Mag	S Rel
foodstuffs	7	.4788	.7158	38.5	0	0	3	2	1	1	0	0	0	0	0	0	0	3	0	0	0	0	0	0	1	2	1	0	0
fool	117	.7179	17.418	52.4	20	16	13	11	34	17	6	0	55	2	2	22	0	3	4	1	1	0	0	0	13	7	0	7	0
Fool	56	.1604	2.5406	44.0	55	0	0	0	1	0	0	0	4	0	0	0	0	0	0	0	0	0	0	0	0	47	0	5	0
fool's	9	.4793	.9847	39.9	3	1	0	0	0	4	1	0	4	1	0	0	0	0	0	3	0	0	0	0	0	0	1	0	0
Fool's	2	.0000	.0290	24.6	2	0	0	0	0	0	0	0	0	0	0	0	0	0	0	0	0	0	0	0	0	2	0	0	0
Foolanian	2	.0000	.0299	24.8	0	0	0	0	2	0	0	0	0	0	0	0	2	0	0	0	0	0	0	0	0	0	0	0	0
fooled	32	.6403	4.4012	46.4	14	4	4	2	5	3	0	0	19	1	0	1	0	1	1	1	0	0	0	0	4	4	0	0	0
foolers	4	.1675	.1620	32.1	0	2	0	1	1	0	0	0	0	0	0	0	0	0	3	0	0	0	0	0	0	0	0	1	0
foolhardy	6	.6035	.7598	38.8	1	1	0	0	3	1	0	0	1	0	0	1	0	1	0	1	0	0	0	0	1	1	0	0	0
fooling	17	.6604	2.3654	43.7	6	0	1	0	5	1	4	0	8	2	1	1	0	0	1	1	0	0	0	0	1	2	0	0	0
foolish	126	.8674	21.948	53.4	23	29	17	17	19	13	7	1	60	3	1	14	1	5	4	5	1	1	0	2	13	8	2	6	0
foolishly	15	.6278	2.0019	43.0	1	3	1	0	5	3	1	1	7	2	1	0	0	0	0	2	1	0	1	0	1	0	0	0	0
foolishness	11	.2853	.8268	39.2	1	1	2	2	0	1	4	0	5	0	0	5	0	0	0	0	0	0	0	0	1	0	0	0	0
foolproof	2	.1698	.1133	30.5	0	1	0	0	0	1	0	0	1	0	0	0	0	0	0	0	0	0	0	0	0	0	1	0	0
fools	17	.5088	1.8308	42.6	0	3	2	1	5	2	4	0	2	0	0	5	0	0	0	0	0	0	0	0	6	2	1	1	0
Fools	2	.0000	.0243	23.9	1	0	0	0	0	0	0	1	0	0	0	0	0	0	0	0	0	0	0	0	0	0	0	2	0
foolscap	2	.0000	.0234	23.7	0	0	0	0	0	2	0	0	0	0	0	0	0	0	0	0	0	0	0	0	2	0	0	0	0
foot	849	.9424	158.32	62.0	127	131	118	127	184	77	69	16	249	26	5	58	98	38	29	55	51	3	24	7	70	66	23	47	0
Foot	4	.3609	.3221	35.1	1	0	0	0	1	2	0	0	0	0	0	0	0	1	0	0	0	0	0	0	1	2	0	0	0
foot-and-mouth	2	.0000	.0394	26.0	0	0	2	0	0	0	0	0	0	0	0	0	0	0	0	2	0	0	0	0	0	0	0	0	0
football	216	.8984	38.575	55.9	15	26	18	37	45	38	34	3	52	25	2	8	23	11	7	5	10	1	3	4	14	5	3	43	0
Football	6	.0000	.0729	28.6	0	0	0	1	2	1	2	0	0	0	0	0	0	0	0	0	0	0	0	0	0	0	0	6	0
footballs	4	.3708	.3650	35.6	3	0	1	0	0	0	0	0	2	0	0	0	1	0	0	0	0	0	0	0	0	0	1	0	0
footbridge	3	.1200	.1302	31.1	0	0	0	0	0	3	0	0	1	2	0	0	0	0	0	0	0	0	0	0	0	0	0	0	0
footfall	2	.1948	.1250	31.0	1	0	0	1	0	0	0	0	1	0	0	0	0	0	0	0	0	0	0	0	0	1	0	0	0
foothill	2	.2441	.1127	30.5	0	0	0	0	0	2	0	0	0	0	0	0	0	0	0	0	0	0	0	0	1	0	1	0	0
foothills	21	.6400	2.8374	44.5	2	5	3	2	5	1	1	2	7	0	0	1	0	6	0	1	0	0	0	0	0	3	1	2	0
foothold	10	.6047	1.2856	41.1	0	3	3	2	3	2	0	0	3	0	0	0	0	2	0	1	0	0	0	0	1	1	0	2	0
footing	18	.4549	1.8918	42.8	1	7	1	6	2	1	0	0	9	0	0	1	0	0	0	0	0	0	0	0	6	1	0	1	0
footings	3	.0000	.0076	18.8	0	0	0	0	0	0	3	0	0	0	0	0	0	0	0	0	0	0	0	3	0	0	0	0	0
footless	2	.0000	.0215	23.3	0	0	0	0	0	0	2	0	0	0	0	2	0	0	0	0	0	0	0	0	0	0	0	0	0
footlights	2	.2443	.1130	30.5	0	0	0	1	0	0	1	0	0	0	0	1	0	0	0	0	0	0	0	0	1	0	0	0	0
footman	5	.2422	.3874	35.9	4	1	0	0	0	0	0	0	4	0	0	0	0	0	0	0	0	0	0	0	0	1	0	0	0
Footman	3	.0000	.1370	31.4	2	0	1	0	0	0	0	0	3	0	0	0	0	0	0	0	0	0	0	0	0	0	0	0	0
footmen	3	.2435	.2274	33.6	0	0	1	1	1	0	0	0	2	0	0	0	0	1	0	0	0	0	0	0	0	0	0	0	0
footnotes	3	.0000	.0434	26.4	0	0	3	0	0	0	0	0	0	0	0	0	0	0	0	0	0	0	0	0	0	3	0	0	0
footpath	3	.2197	.2090	33.2	2	0	0	0	0	0	1	0	2	0	0	0	0	0	0	0	0	0	0	0	0	0	1	0	0
footprint	7	.5404	.7843	38.9	1	2	1	1	0	1	1	0	0	1	0	2	0	0	0	1	1	0	0	0	0	2	0	0	0
footprints	45	.5832	5.7473	47.6	16	9	4	9	6	1	0	0	25	2	0	5	0	3	0	0	0	0	0	0	2	8	0	0	0
footrest	2	.0000	.0064	18.1	0	0	0	0	0	1	1	0	0	0	0	0	0	0	0	0	0	0	2	0	0	0	0	0	0
footsore	4	.2708	.2760	34.4	0	1	2	0	0	0	1	0	1	0	0	2	0	1	0	0	0	0	0	0	0	0	0	0	0
footstep	2	.0000	.0290	24.6	0	0	1	1	0	0	0	0	0	0	0	0	0	0	0	0	0	0	0	0	0	2	0	0	0
footsteps	92	.7357	13.949	51.4	19	8	11	15	22	8	9	0	41	2	3	18	0	2	0	2	4	1	0	0	9	8	0	2	0
footstool	3	.3418	.2483	33.9	0	1	0	0	2	0	0	0	1	1	0	0	0	0	0	0	0	0	0	0	0	1	0	0	0
footwear	5	.4740	.5375	37.3	0	0	2	1	1	0	0	1	2	0	0	1	0	0	0	1	0	0	0	0	0	1	0	0	0
footwork	5	.4724	.5348	37.3	0	0	1	0	2	2	0	0	2	0	0	1	0	0	0	1	0	0	0	0	0	0	0	1	0
for	39322	.9942	7687.0	78.9	6107	5796	4760	5184	7526	4819	4162	968	8804	2150	387	1945	4215	3960	1584	3102	1611	313	018	599	2144	2800	2024	2628	38
For	11	.4601	1.0483	40.2	2	1	1	0	3	2	2	0	0	0	0	0	0	0	0	0	4	0	0	2	2	1	0	2	0
forage	7	.4696	.7000	38.5	0	0	0	2	5	0	0	0	0	0	0	1	0	3	0	0	0	0	0	0	1	0	2	0	0
forager	2	.0000	.0209	23.2	0	0	0	0	2	0	0	0	0	0	0	0	0	0	0	0	0	0	0	0	0	0	2	0	0
foraging	9	.3692	.7640	38.8	0	0	0	3	6	0	0	0	2	0	0	0	0	1	0	0	0	0	0	0	2	0	4	0	0
foraminifers	2	.0000	.0394	26.0	0	0	0	0	0	0	2	0	0	0	0	0	0	0	0	2	0	0	0	0	0	0	0	0	0
Foran	7	.0000	.0821	29.1	0	0	7	0	0	0	0	0	0	0	0	0	0	0	0	0	0	0	0	0	7	0	0	0	0
foray	4	.2440	.2264	33.5	0	0	0	0	1	2	0	1	0	0	0	2	0	0	0	0	0	0	0	0	0	0	0	2	0
forays	3	.2321	.1635	32.1	0	0	0	0	1	1	1	0	0	0	0	0	0	0	0	0	0	0	0	0	0	0	1	2	0
forbade	14	.6303	1.8117	42.6	0	0	1	3	6	3	1	0	1	0	0	1	0	2	1	0	0	0	0	0	5	1	2	1	0
forbear	3	.3874	.2487	34.0	0	0	0	0	3	0	0	0	0	1	0	0	0	0	0	0	0	0	0	0	1	0	1	0	0
Forbes	2	.1387	.0689	28.4	0	1	0	0	0	1	0	0	0	0	1	0	0	0	0	0	0	0	0	0	0	1	0	0	0
forbid	16	.5058	1.7410	42.4	0	0	1	2	4	8	1	0	3	0	0	7	0	2	0	1	0	0	0	0	1	0	1	1	0
forbidden	43	.7233	6.3598	48.0	1	3	8	6	10	11	3	1	10	2	0	3	0	8	0	0	0	0	2	0	3	7	7	1	0
Forbidden	2	.1814	.1187	30.7	0	0	0	0	1	0	0	1	1	0	0	0	0	0	0	0	0	0	0	0	0	0	0	1	0
forbidding	24	.5801	2.9655	44.7	2	3	3	4	5	5	2	0	5	1	0	3	0	11	0	2	0	0	0	0	1	0	1	0	0
forbids	4	.3287	.2952	34.7	0	0	2	0	1	0	1	0	0	0	0	0	0	1	0	0	0	0	0	0	0	1	2	0	0
force	651	.8499	110.60	60.4	64	75	65	98	120	119	89	21	80	13	6	18	18	60	13	251	11	2	4	22	8	47	51	47	0
Force	97	.6390	13.005	51.1	20	7	8	9	21	16	6	10	28	0	0	3	0	15	0	6	1	0	0	0	0	14	6	24	0
forced	238	.8651	41.151	56.1	27	19	31	38	58	32	30	3	57	4	2	18	0	39	1	22	5	0	3	2	10	25	34	16	0
forceful	17	.5472	1.9943	43.0	0	1	1	1	6	5	3	0	5	2	0	0	0	2	0	0	1	2	0	0	0	3	1	1	0
forcefully	10	.5191	1.0883	40.4	0	0	1	0	4	4	0	1	1	2	0	0	0	0	0	1	2	1	0	0	0	0	0	3	0
forces	344	.7530	52.394	57.2	13	45	38	19	85	81	55	8	29	2	1	8	3	63	2	85	7	0	1	11	0	25	72	35	0
Forces	13	.5268	1.4676	41.7	0	0	1	2	6	4	0	0	3	0	1	0	0	1	0	1	0	0	0	0	0	1	5	1	0
forcibly	3	.3847	.2494	34.0	0	0	0	1	2	0	0	0	0	0	0	0	0	0	0	0	0	0	0	0	1	1	1	0	0
forcing	22	.7702	3.4446	45.4	0	2	2	4	5	2	5	2	6	1	0	2	0	3	0	3	0	0	0	1	1	2	2	1	0
ford	5	.3622	.4609	36.6	2	0	1	1	0	1	0	0	3	0	0	0	0	1	0	0	1	0	0	0	0	0	0	0	0
Ford	100	.6149	12.948	51.1	7	4	12	4	31	33	7	2	25	3	0	3	1	26	0	0	0	0	0	0	2	7	4	29	0
Ford's	9	.3161	.6546	38.2	1	0	0	1	5	0	2	0	1	0	0	1	0	0	0	0	0	0	0	0	0	0	1	6	0
forded	4	.2843	.2875	34.6	0	0	0	2	2	0	0	0	1	0	0	0	0	1	0	0	0	0	0	0	0	0	0	2	0
Fords	4	.0996	.1523	31.8	0	0	1	1	1	0	1	0	1	0	0	0	0	0	0	0	0	0	0	0	0	0	0	3	0
fore	21	.6856	2.9404	44.7	4	0	4	2	1	6	3	1	4	1	0	0	0	0	3	1	2	0	0	2	4	1	2	1	0
fore-and-aft	4	.3647	.3180	35.0	0	0	1	0	3	0	0	0	0	0	0	0	0	0	0	0	0	0	0	0	0	1	1	2	0
forearm	8	.5007	.8539	39.3	0	1	2	4	1	0	0	0	1	0	0	1	0	0	1	3	1	1	0	0	0	0	0	0	0
forebears	7	.4552	.6710	38.3	0	2	1	0	1	0	2	1	0	1	0	0	0	1	0	0	0	1	0	0	0	2	2	0	0
foreboding	6	.6046	.7580	38.8	0	0	3	1	0	0	1	1	1	0	0	0	0	1	0	0	0	0	0	0	1	1	1	1	0
forecast	32	.6701	4.4293	46.5	0	2	7	9	5	5	4	0	5	0	0	1	0	1	2	13	1	0	0	0	0	3	1	5	0
Forecast	2	.2346	.1166	30.7	0	0	0	1	0	0	1	0	0	0	0	0	0	0	0	1	0	0	0	0	0	0	0	1	0
forecaster	3	.1650	.1684	32.3	0	0	1	1	1	0	0	0	1	0	0	0	0	0	0	2	0	0	0	0	0	0	0	0	0
forecasters	4	.1335	.1958	32.9	0	0	2	1	1	0	0	0	1	0	0	0	0	0	0	3	0	0	0	0	0	0	0	0	0
forecasting	12	.2007	.6761	38.3	0	1	3	0	4	4	0	0	1	0	0	1	0	0	0	10	0	0	0	0	0	0	0	0	0
forecastle	4	.2445	.3067	34.9	0	0	0	1	0	2	1	0	3	0	0	0	0	0	0	0	0	0	0	0	0	1	0	0	0
forecasts	25	.3612	2.0791	43.2	5	2	5	5	7	1	0	0	1	1	0	0	0	0	0	19	0	0	0	0	0	0	2	2	0
forefathers	21	.5689	2.5709	44.1	1	4	2	1	8	1	4	0	6	0	0	0	0	8	1	0	0	0	0	0	1	4	1	0	0
forefeet	7	.4190	.6478	38.1	2	1	1	2	0	1	0	0	1	0	0	0	0	0	0	0	0	0	0	0	2	3	1	0	0
forefinger	24	.5946	2.9396	44.7	1	2	3	2	6	3	7	0	3	1	0	4	1	0	1	1	0	0	5	1	6	0	1	0	0
forefingers	2	.2421	.0995	30.0	0	0	0	0	0	0	2	0	0	0	0	0	0	0	0	0	0	0	1	1	0	0	0	0	0

7L FOODS
7E Foolania
3A Fooled
3R foolery
7A foolin'
7H foot-deep
6R foot-locker
4F foot-powered
8A foot-race
9R foot-slogging
6P foot-stamping
4A foot-trail

5J foot-weary
9R footage
7Q football-sized
7R football's
7R footboard
7A footed
6N footfalls
7P footmaiden
8F footmarks
5A Footmen
6G footnote
7D footpaths

4A footraces
3R Footsore
5A footwalk
9H for-uh-min-i-ferz
5G for'hed**
5G for'id
XQ fora
7D foraged
7Q foragers
7Q forages
7Q foramen
7N forasmuch

8R forbearance
7D force-break
3P Force's
7R forced-labor
9M forcefulness
8D forceless
XH forceps
7N forcible
7R FORD
7R Ford-O-Matic
6A fordin'
5Q fording

9F Fordlandia
7R Fords's
9D fore-legs
9D fore-paws
7N fore-quarter
7N fore-quarters
3P fore-runner
5N fore-topsail
6A forearms
5R forebear
8Q Forebearance
XR foreboded

8A forebodings
7Q forebrain
8A forecaster's
7A forecastles
8B foreclaws
7A forecloser
8F foreclosure
9D forecourt
6F foredeck
8D foreflipper

Word Type	F	D	U	SFI	3 Gr 3	4 Gr 4	5 Gr 5	6 Gr 6	7 Gr 7	8 Gr 8	9 Gr 9	X UnGr	A Read	B Eng & Gr	C Comp	D Lit	E Math	F Soc Stud	G Spell	H Sci	J Music	K Art	L Home Ec	M Shop	N Lib F	P Lib NF	Q Lib Ref	R Mag	S Rel
forefoot	10	.4340	.9538	39.8	0	0	1	0	8	0	1	0	2	0	0	3	0	0	0	0	0	0	0	0	2	0	3	0	0
forefront	4	.2741	.2683	34.3	0	0	0	1	1	2	0	0	1	1	0	0	0	0	0	0	2	0	0	0	0	0	0	0	0
foregoing	3	.3845	.2448	33.9	0	0	0	1	1	0	1	0	0	1	0	0	0	0	0	0	1	0	0	0	0	0	1	0	0
foregone	3	.2159	.1532	31.9	0	0	1	0	1	0	1	0	0	0	0	0	0	0	0	0	0	0	0	0	0	0	2	1	0
foreground	16	.5300	1.7621	42.5	0	4	0	1	7	1	2	1	0	0	0	0	1	5	0	0	0	2	0	1	0	3	4	0	0
forehead	100	.7590	15.466	51.9	10	22	13	13	25	11	5	1	32	2	1	15	0	1	3	3	0	0	1	0	19	15	2	6	0
foreheads	7	.4821	.7814	38.9	0	1	2	1	1	0	2	0	4	0	0	0	0	1	0	0	0	0	0	0	1	1	0	0	0
foreign	263	.7138	38.203	55.8	20	15	41	31	59	46	41	10	23	26	0	6	1	86	5	10	3	0	0	0	3	28	47	25	0
Foreign	15	.5073	1.6105	42.1	0	0	3	1	3	3	4	1	1	1	0	0	0	3	0	0	0	0	0	0	0	1	3	6	0
foreign-born	2	.2306	.1140	30.6	0	0	2	0	0	0	0	0	0	1	0	0	0	1	0	0	0	0	0	0	0	0	0	0	0
foreign-owned	2	.2351	.1166	30.7	0	0	0	1	1	0	0	0	0	0	0	0	0	1	0	0	0	0	0	0	0	0	0	1	0
foreign-policy	2	.0000	.0243	23.9	0	0	0	0	0	1	1	0	0	0	0	0	0	0	0	0	0	0	0	0	0	0	0	2	0
foreigner	16	.5344	1.8326	42.6	1	1	1	2	7	0	4	0	4	2	0	5	0	1	0	0	0	0	0	0	3	1	0	0	0
foreigners	29	.6161	3.7127	45.7	3	0	4	2	8	7	4	1	3	2	0	2	0	9	0	0	0	0	0	0	0	6	1	6	0
forelands	3	.0000	.0328	25.2	3	0	0	0	0	0	0	0	0	3	0	0	0	0	0	0	0	0	0	0	0	0	0	0	0
foreleg	7	.3266	.5724	37.6	0	1	2	2	1	0	1	0	3	0	0	1	0	0	0	0	0	0	0	0	3	0	0	0	0
forelegs	11	.5185	1.2365	40.9	2	2	2	0	2	1	0	2	3	1	0	1	0	0	0	0	0	0	0	0	2	4	0	0	0
forelimbs	5	.0000	.0523	27.2	0	0	0	0	5	0	0	0	0	0	0	0	0	0	0	0	0	0	0	0	0	0	5	0	0
forelock	4	.3648	.3145	35.0	1	0	1	0	1	0	1	0	0	0	0	2	0	0	0	0	0	0	0	0	1	0	1	0	0
foreman	24	.6232	3.2213	45.1	7	2	4	4	1	3	3	0	14	2	0	2	0	1	1	0	3	0	0	0	0	1	0	0	0
foremast	3	.2357	.2199	33.4	0	0	0	3	0	0	0	0	2	0	0	0	0	0	0	0	0	0	0	0	0	1	0	0	0
foremost	21	.6870	2.9432	44.7	1	0	4	2	5	7	2	0	4	2	2	2	0	1	2	0	3	0	0	0	1	0	3	1	0
forenoon	6	.3859	.5833	37.7	2	0	1	2	1	0	0	0	4	0	0	0	0	0	0	0	0	0	0	0	1	1	0	0	0
forepaw	4	.0000	.0469	26.7	2	0	0	1	1	0	0	0	0	0	0	0	0	0	0	0	0	0	0	0	4	0	0	0	0
forepaws	3	.2304	.1619	32.1	0	0	1	2	0	0	0	0	0	0	0	0	0	0	0	0	0	0	0	0	2	0	1	0	0
forequarters	2	.2427	.1152	30.6	0	0	0	0	1	0	0	1	0	0	0	0	0	0	0	0	0	0	0	0	1	1	0	0	0
forerunner	11	.4929	1.1623	40.7	0	1	2	1	3	1	3	0	2	0	0	0	0	2	0	0	2	0	0	1	0	0	4	0	0
forerunners	7	.2829	.4415	36.4	0	0	2	0	3	1	0	1	0	0	0	0	0	0	0	1	4	0	0	0	0	0	2	0	0
foresail	4	.1462	.1667	32.2	0	0	0	1	2	0	1	0	1	0	2	0	0	0	0	0	0	0	0	0	0	0	1	0	0
foresaw	5	.5329	.5694	37.6	0	0	0	1	1	1	2	0	1	0	0	1	0	1	0	0	0	0	0	0	1	0	1	0	0
foresee	11	.6105	1.3948	41.4	0	1	1	2	0	3	3	1	2	1	0	1	0	0	0	1	0	1	0	0	2	0	1	2	0
foreseeable	4	.1737	.1745	32.4	0	2	1	0	0	0	1	0	0	0	0	0	0	0	0	0	0	0	0	0	0	1	3	0	0
foreseeing	2	.0000	.0914	29.6	0	0	0	0	1	1	0	0	2	0	0	0	0	0	0	0	0	0	0	0	0	0	0	0	0
foreseen	8	.4284	.7870	39.0	0	1	0	1	2	0	2	2	3	0	0	1	0	0	0	0	0	0	0	0	0	1	0	3	0
foreshadow	3	.3406	.2461	33.9	0	0	0	0	0	1	2	0	1	1	0	0	0	0	0	0	0	0	0	0	0	0	0	1	0
foreshadowed	3	.2365	.1616	32.1	0	0	0	0	1	1	0	1	0	0	0	0	0	0	0	0	1	0	0	0	0	0	2	0	0
foreshortened	2	.1483	.0728	28.6	0	0	0	0	1	0	1	0	0	0	0	0	0	0	0	0	0	0	0	1	0	1	0	0	0
foreshortening	2	.0000	.0290	24.6	0	0	0	0	2	0	0	0	0	0	0	0	0	0	0	0	0	0	0	0	0	2	0	0	0
foresight	13	.5421	1.4800	41.7	2	1	1	0	3	4	2	0	2	0	2	2	0	1	0	0	0	0	0	0	2	1	2	1	0
forest	684	.8384	115.29	60.6	105	149	80	101	161	46	32	10	197	15	7	52	0	164	7	36	5	1	0	7	23	46	85	39	0
Forest	60	.6851	8.5875	49.3	5	19	9	10	12	3	0	2	24	0	0	3	0	11	0	0	0	0	0	1	1	10	2	8	0
forest-clad	2	.1948	.1250	31.0	1	0	1	0	0	0	0	0	1	0	0	0	0	0	0	0	0	0	0	0	0	1	0	0	0
forest-covered	4	.0000	.0778	28.9	0	0	1	2	0	0	1	0	0	0	0	0	0	4	0	0	0	0	0	0	0	0	0	0	0
forestall	2	.2446	.1142	30.6	0	0	0	0	0	1	0	1	0	0	0	0	0	0	0	0	0	0	0	0	1	0	0	1	0
forested	27	.4298	2.5810	44.1	0	1	8	8	8	2	0	0	2	0	0	2	0	19	0	0	0	0	0	0	1	0	2	1	0
forester	6	.2611	.4137	36.2	0	1	0	1	0	0	4	0	2	0	0	3	0	0	0	1	0	0	0	0	0	0	0	0	0
foresters	10	.3237	.7530	38.8	3	4	0	1	0	1	0	1	0	0	0	0	0	6	0	1	0	0	0	0	0	0	0	3	0
Forestier	4	.0000	.1827	32.6	0	0	0	4	0	0	0	0	4	0	0	0	0	0	0	0	0	0	0	0	0	0	0	0	0
forestry	10	.4276	.9181	39.6	0	1	5	1	0	1	2	0	0	0	0	0	0	2	0	0	0	0	0	0	1	3	4	0	0
forests	380	.7415	57.299	57.6	66	65	71	63	68	20	17	10	38	2	3	5	0	190	2	40	5	1	0	3	2	32	46	10	1
Forests	2	.2152	.1357	31.3	1	0	0	0	1	0	0	0	1	0	0	0	0	1	0	0	0	0	0	0	0	0	0	0	0
foretell	7	.5019	.7452	38.7	0	1	1	1	3	1	0	0	1	1	0	0	0	0	2	0	1	0	0	0	0	2	0	0	0
foretells	3	.3380	.2439	33.9	1	0	0	1	1	0	0	0	1	1	0	1	0	0	0	0	0	0	0	0	0	0	0	0	0
forethought	4	.3711	.3648	35.6	0	0	0	2	1	0	1	0	2	0	0	0	0	0	0	0	0	0	0	0	0	1	1	0	0
foretold	2	.2160	.1362	31.3	0	0	0	1	1	0	0	0	1	0	0	0	0	0	0	1	0	0	0	0	0	0	0	0	0
foretop	4	.1787	.2347	33.7	0	0	2	0	2	0	0	0	2	0	0	0	0	0	0	0	0	0	0	0	2	0	0	0	0
forever	162	.4819	17.180	52.4	20	15	20	32	29	26	15	5	49	3	2	37	0	8	2	9	14	0	0	0	13	6	6	9	4
Forever	6	.0526	.1436	31.6	1	0	3	0	0	1	1	0	1	0	0	0	0	0	0	0	5	0	0	0	0	0	0	0	0
forewings	3	.2043	.1486	31.7	1	0	0	0	1	0	1	0	0	0	0	0	0	0	0	0	0	0	0	0	0	1	2	0	0
foreword	4	.0996	.1523	31.8	0	0	0	0	3	0	1	0	1	0	0	0	0	0	0	0	0	0	0	0	0	0	0	3	0
forfeit	7	.5155	.7414	38.7	0	1	0	1	0	1	4	0	0	1	0	3	0	0	0	0	1	0	1	0	0	0	0	1	0
forfeiture	2	.2446	.1122	30.5	0	0	0	0	0	0	2	0	0	0	0	1	0	0	0	0	0	0	0	0	0	0	1	0	0
forgave	4	.0562	.1157	30.6	1	1	1	0	0	1	0	0	1	0	0	0	0	1	0	0	0	0	0	0	0	0	1	0	1
forge	21	.2567	1.3582	41.3	0	5	6	1	2	4	3	0	5	0	0	0	0	6	0	0	0	0	0	7	0	2	1	0	0
Forge	9	.4409	.8922	39.5	0	2	1	0	2	4	0	0	2	0	0	2	0	4	0	0	0	0	0	0	0	0	1	0	0
forged	12	.5841	1.4309	41.6	0	1	3	2	4	0	2	0	0	1	1	0	0	0	0	0	0	1	0	0	0	4	3	2	0
forges	2	.2417	.1091	30.4	0	0	0	1	0	0	1	0	0	0	0	0	0	0	0	0	1	0	0	0	0	0	1	0	0
forget	314	.8910	55.704	57.5	51	68	35	45	50	28	29	8	83	18	1	33	20	15	19	10	7	1	7	1	36	33	0	30	0
forget-me-nots	3	.2236	.1570	32.0	2	0	0	0	0	1	0	0	0	1	0	2	0	0	0	0	0	0	0	0	0	0	0	0	0
forgetful	9	.5480	1.0793	40.3	3	0	0	2	2	1	0	1	4	0	0	1	0	0	0	0	0	0	0	0	2	1	0	1	0
forgetfulness	3	.3450	.2505	34.0	1	0	0	0	1	0	1	0	1	0	0	0	0	0	0	0	0	0	0	0	1	1	0	0	0
forgets	18	.5910	2.2894	43.6	5	7	2	3	0	1	0	0	8	0	1	0	0	1	0	1	3	0	0	0	0	3	0	1	0
forgettable	2	.0000	.0243	23.9	0	0	0	1	0	1	0	0	0	0	0	0	0	0	0	0	0	0	0	0	0	0	0	2	0
forgetting	21	.6580	2.8896	44.6	3	4	5	5	2	0	2	0	8	2	0	3	0	0	1	0	0	0	0	0	4	0	1	2	0
forging	16	.1560	.5569	37.5	0	0	0	1	2	6	6	1	0	0	0	0	0	0	0	0	2	0	0	11	0	0	1	2	0
forgive	26	.1527	1.2294	40.9	6	7	0	5	1	4	3	0	8	0	0	4	0	1	4	0	0	0	0	0	5	0	1	0	3
forgiven	5	.4023	.4462	36.5	0	1	0	0	2	0	2	0	1	0	1	1	0	0	0	0	0	0	0	0	0	1	0	1	0
forgiveness	7	.0925	.2844	34.5	4	0	1	0	1	0	1	0	3	0	0	2	0	0	0	0	0	0	0	0	0	1	0	0	1
forgot	225	.7521	34.809	55.4	64	55	21	26	28	16	8	7	103	9	1	14	0	12	2	2	3	0	1	0	38	32	1	7	0
forgotten	200	.8576	34.424	55.4	31	32	17	42	36	20	15	7	78	7	7	18	5	9	2	6	2	1	2	1	30	19	3	10	0
fork	122	.6156	15.531	51.9	18	15	5	17	33	20	11	3	17	1	0	4	2	0	5	31	9	1	25	0	7	9	1	10	0
Fork	9	.4067	.8256	39.2	0	0	1	0	2	5	1	0	1	0	0	1	0	0	0	5	0	0	0	0	0	0	0	2	0
fork's	2	.0000	.0290	24.6	2	0	0	0	0	0	0	0	0	0	0	0	0	0	0	0	0	0	0	0	0	2	0	0	0
forked	17	.6764	2.4076	43.8	3	4	2	2	3	1	1	1	7	1	0	0	0	0	0	2	0	0	0	0	2	2	1	2	0
forkful	2	.1787	.1174	30.7	0	0	0	1	1	0	0	0	1	0	0	0	0	0	0	0	0	0	0	0	1	0	0	0	0
forking	2	.1948	.1250	31.0	0	1	1	0	0	0	0	0	1	0	0	0	0	0	0	0	0	0	0	0	0	1	0	0	0
forklift	8	.0000	.3655	35.6	8	0	0	0	0	0	0	0	8	0	0	0	0	0	0	0	0	0	0	0	0	0	0	0	0
forks	20	.6854	2.8165	44.5	6	2	1	0	4	3	2	2	4	1	0	4	0	1	0	1	0	0	0	0	1	3	1	4	0
Forks	3	.1187	.1291	31.1	0	1	0	0	2	0	0	0	1	0	0	2	0	0	0	0	0	0	0	0	0	0	0	0	0
forlorn	8	.4420	.7836	38.9	0	1	0	1	4	2	0	0	2	0	1	1	0	1	0	0	0	0	0	0	3	0	0	0	0
form	2720	.8711	470.54	66.7	308	410	378	321	505	396	335	67	144	466	46	25	443	124	381	411	189	43	40	83	24	76	167	58	0
form-class	3	.0000	.0328	25.2	0	0	0	0	2	0	1	0	0	3	0	0	0	0	0	0	0	0	0	0	0	0	0	0	0
formal	85	.8994	15.173	51.8	1	1	12	8	20	26	16	1	16	9	1	2	2	7	5	1	12	1	3	1	3	4	10	8	0
formaldehyde	4	.2090	.2014	33.0	0	0	0	1	3	0	0	0	0	0	0	0	0	0	0	0	0	0	0	0	0	0	1	3	0
formalin	3	.1409	.1472	31.7	0	0	0	0	1	0	2	0	1	0	0	0	0	0	0	0	0	0	0	0	0	2	0	0	0
formalities	2	.0000	.0290	24.6	0	0	0	0	2	0	0	0	0	0	0	0	0	0	0	0	0	0	0	0	0	2	0	0	0
formality	8	.6274	1.0110	40.0	0	0	1	0	3	1	3	0	0	1	0	1	0	0	1	0	1	1	0	1	1	0	0	1	0

9Q foregoes
XR foreign-accent
9R foreign-exchange
9F foreign-made
6R foreigner's
8Q foreknowledge
3B foreland
XH Foreland
9Q foremen
7Q forepart
9Q foresails
6A Foreseer
9D foreshadowing
9D foreshadows
7Q forest-loving
6R forest-ringed
7D forest-roof
5A forest's
9P forestalled
7C forestaysail
6A forester's
9D Forestville
3B foresty
4D Forever-Mountain
7R Forgedtrue
7Q forgings
8D forgit
3P forgiveth
6B forgo
6B forgott
6A Forgotten
9P forgottne
XR fork-tongued
XR Forked
8N forkfuls
6N forlornly
9B Form
8J formalism

Word Type	F	D	U	SFI	3 Gr 3	4 Gr 4	5 Gr 5	6 Gr 6	7 Gr 7	8 Gr 8	9 Gr 9	X UnGr	A Read	B Eng & Gr	C Comp	D Lit	E Math	F Soc Stud	G Spell	H Sci	J Music	K Art	L Home Ec	M Shop	N Lib F	P Lib NF	Q Lib Ref	R Mag	S Rel
formalized	3	.3847	.2496	34.0	0	0	2	0	1	0	0	0	0	0	0	0	0	0	0	0	0	0	0	0	0	1	1	1	0
formally	18	.6320	2.3592	43.7	0	0	2	3	6	5	2	0	4	0	1	2	0	2	3	0	0	0	0	0	0	0	4	2	0
formation	72	.7165	10.499	50.2	0	3	8	3	15	14	26	3	4	4	3	2	1	13	0	30	5	0	0	0	3	3	4	0	0
formations	17	.6259	2.1676	43.4	0	1	2	0	4	5	4	1	0	0	2	1	0	1	0	5	3	1	0	0	0	0	2	2	0
formed	673	.8802	117.80	60.7	46	101	117	93	106	90	107	13	58	48	4	12	67	84	40	190	14	2	4	27	17	33	51	22	0
former	157	.8224	25.849	54.1	10	7	12	21	36	34	26	11	17	5	0	10	0	32	1	5	4	1	1	1	10	16	21	33	0
formerly	59	.8512	10.003	50.0	3	3	4	13	16	4	15	1	3	4	1	3	0	15	1	6	1	0	1	3	4	5	8	4	0
formidable	26	.6671	3.5211	45.5	0	0	2	1	13	4	6	0	0	0	1	1	0	6	0	0	1	0	0	0	5	1	4	7	0
formidably	2	.2285	.1129	30.5	0	0	0	0	1	1	0	0	0	0	0	0	0	1	0	0	0	0	0	0	0	0	1	0	0
forming	143	.6648	19.362	52.9	10	7	8	20	28	28	33	9	8	12	2	3	4	12	7	36	1	0	3	25	5	8	13	4	0
formless	3	.2443	.1820	32.6	0	0	0	0	2	0	0	1	0	0	0	1	0	0	0	2	0	0	0	0	0	0	0	0	0
Formosa	6	.2444	.3628	35.6	0	0	2	2	1	0	1	0	0	0	0	0	0	4	0	0	0	0	0	0	0	0	2	0	0
forms	992	.7715	153.20	61.9	84	132	151	106	179	157	142	41	31	162	9	7	74	37	228	172	50	61	7	33	5	16	84	16	0
Forms	2	.2446	.1142	30.6	0	0	0	0	1	0	0	1	0	0	0	0	0	0	0	0	0	0	0	0	1	0	0	1	0
formula	167	.6215	21.399	53.3	6	3	10	13	35	62	31	7	5	3	0	2	85	4	0	35	0	0	2	7	0	12	8	4	0
formulas	16	.5890	1.9607	42.9	0	0	3	1	2	6	3	1	1	0	0	0	5	1	0	4	0	0	0	1	0	0	3	1	0
formulate	3	.2442	.1815	32.6	0	0	0	0	0	2	1	0	0	0	0	1	0	2	0	0	0	0	0	0	0	0	0	0	0
formulated	8	.4897	.8239	39.2	0	0	0	0	2	2	2	2	0	1	0	0	0	1	0	1	0	0	0	0	0	0	3	2	0
formulating	2	.2446	.1123	30.5	0	0	0	0	0	0	2	0	0	1	0	0	0	0	0	0	0	0	0	0	0	0	1	0	0
formulation	2	.2437	.1129	30.5	0	0	0	0	0	0	2	0	0	0	0	0	0	0	0	0	0	0	0	0	0	0	1	1	0
forrard	2	.0000	.0243	23.9	0	0	0	2	0	0	0	0	0	0	0	0	0	0	0	0	0	0	0	0	0	0	0	2	0
Forrester	9	.0000	.1055	30.2	0	0	0	0	9	0	0	0	0	0	0	0	0	0	0	0	0	0	0	0	9	0	0	0	0
Forresters	6	.0000	.0703	28.5	0	0	0	0	6	0	0	0	0	0	0	0	0	0	0	0	0	0	0	0	6	0	0	0	0
forsaken	8	.4259	.7184	38.6	0	0	1	4	1	1	0	1	0	1	0	1	0	1	0	0	4	0	0	0	1	0	0	0	0
forsook	3	.2181	.1541	31.9	1	0	0	0	1	1	0	0	0	0	0	0	0	0	0	0	0	0	0	0	1	0	2	0	0
Forssmann	4	.0000	.0419	26.2	0	0	0	0	0	0	4	0	0	0	0	0	0	0	0	0	0	0	0	0	0	0	4	0	0
Forster	2	.2442	.1134	30.5	0	0	1	0	0	0	1	0	0	1	0	0	0	0	0	0	0	0	0	0	0	0	0	1	0
forsworn	2	.2446	.1125	30.5	0	0	0	0	1	0	1	0	0	1	0	1	0	0	0	0	0	0	0	0	0	0	0	0	0
fort	150	.7988	24.274	53.9	25	36	44	15	11	12	7	0	47	5	3	9	4	29	3	1	0	1	0	0	2	34	7	5	0
Fort	115	.7023	16.520	52.2	4	17	31	6	28	18	8	3	16	1	0	14	1	36	0	1	1	0	0	1	1	17	18	8	0
FortLaramie	2	.0000	.0389	25.9	0	0	2	0	0	0	0	0	0	0	0	0	0	2	0	0	0	0	0	0	0	0	0	0	0
FortWorth	6	.0971	.2435	33.9	0	0	5	0	1	0	0	0	1	0	0	0	0	5	0	0	0	0	0	0	0	0	0	0	0
fort's	2	.2278	.1128	30.5	0	1	0	0	0	0	0	1	0	0	0	0	0	0	0	1	0	0	0	0	0	0	1	0	0
Fort's	2	.0000	.0914	29.6	0	0	0	0	2	0	0	0	2	0	0	0	0	0	0	0	0	0	0	0	0	0	0	0	0
Fortas	2	.2351	.1166	30.7	0	0	0	0	2	0	0	0	0	0	0	0	0	1	0	0	0	0	0	0	0	0	0	1	0
forte	2	.2446	.1084	30.3	0	0	2	0	0	0	0	0	0	0	0	0	0	0	1	0	1	0	0	0	0	0	0	0	0
Forte	4	.1494	.2089	33.2	2	0	0	0	2	0	0	0	2	0	0	0	0	0	0	0	2	0	0	0	0	0	0	0	0
forth	412	.9170	75.000	58.8	77	61	45	56	53	67	44	9	121	15	4	30	6	13	6	42	29	3	7	15	31	52	12	26	0
forthcoming	2	.2351	.1166	30.7	0	0	0	0	1	1	0	0	0	0	0	0	0	1	0	0	0	0	0	0	0	0	0	1	0
forthright	2	.2433	.1158	30.6	0	0	1	0	0	1	0	0	0	0	0	0	0	0	0	0	0	0	0	0	0	1	0	1	0
forties	8	.2650	.5048	37.0	1	0	5	0	0	2	0	0	0	0	0	1	6	1	0	0	0	0	0	0	0	0	0	0	0
fortieth	2	.0000	.0215	23.3	0	0	0	0	0	2	0	0	0	0	0	2	0	0	0	0	0	0	0	0	0	0	0	0	0
fortification	2	.2437	.1129	30.5	0	0	0	0	2	0	0	0	0	0	0	0	0	0	0	0	0	0	0	0	0	0	1	1	0
fortifications	7	.3643	.5717	37.6	0	0	0	0	0	5	2	0	0	0	0	0	0	4	0	0	0	0	0	0	0	0	2	1	0
fortified	15	.4674	1.4872	41.7	0	1	1	1	6	3	3	0	1	0	0	0	0	2	0	0	0	0	2	0	0	2	7	1	0
fortify	3	.2223	.2106	33.2	1	0	0	1	0	1	0	0	2	1	0	0	0	0	0	0	0	0	0	0	0	0	0	0	0
fortitude	6	.4491	.6073	37.8	1	0	1	0	1	2	1	0	2	1	0	0	0	0	0	0	0	0	0	0	0	1	0	2	0
fortnight	9	.5449	1.0623	40.3	0	2	0	0	2	4	1	0	3	1	0	0	2	0	0	0	0	0	0	0	0	1	0	2	0
fortress	22	.6946	3.1488	45.0	0	1	3	6	2	5	4	1	6	1	0	0	0	2	0	0	1	0	0	0	2	3	4	3	0
fortresses	5	.4699	.4987	37.0	1	1	1	1	1	0	0	0	0	1	0	0	0	1	0	0	0	0	0	0	0	2	1	0	0
forts	32	.5478	3.6979	45.7	0	4	12	2	6	5	2	1	1	0	0	0	0	20	0	0	0	0	0	1	1	3	3	3	0
Fortunata	2	.0000	.0914	29.6	0	0	0	2	0	0	0	0	2	0	0	0	0	0	0	0	0	0	0	0	0	0	0	0	0
fortunate	52	.7134	7.6233	48.8	3	6	8	9	10	8	8	0	12	0	0	4	0	18	0	5	2	0	3	0	1	3	3	1	0
fortunately	78	.8387	13.125	51.2	1	12	9	13	20	12	10	1	19	2	1	3	1	12	0	10	1	3	4	0	5	6	4	7	0
fortune	98	.7776	15.533	51.9	12	5	14	16	19	14	15	3	38	5	0	12	1	8	1	0	4	0	0	0	7	14	3	5	0
Fortune	22	.5143	2.4000	43.8	0	3	10	0	2	3	4	0	3	0	0	4	0	1	0	0	1	0	0	0	10	1	0	2	0
fortune-teller	2	.1787	.1174	30.7	2	0	0	0	0	0	0	0	1	0	0	0	0	0	0	0	0	0	0	0	1	0	0	0	0
fortune-telling	2	.2443	.1130	30.5	0	0	0	0	1	1	0	0	0	0	0	1	0	0	0	0	0	0	0	0	1	0	0	0	0
fortunes	31	.5625	3.7747	45.8	2	6	5	3	7	5	3	0	11	0	0	4	0	6	0	0	0	0	0	0	4	6	0	0	0
Fortunes	2	.2152	.1357	31.3	0	0	0	0	1	1	0	0	1	0	0	0	0	1	0	0	0	0	0	0	0	0	0	0	0
fortuneteller	4	.0000	.1827	32.6	0	2	0	1	1	0	0	0	4	0	0	0	0	0	0	0	0	0	0	0	0	0	0	0	0
forty	153	.8498	26.090	54.2	23	22	12	22	36	14	17	7	47	17	1	11	3	21	3	7	6	0	1	0	13	18	0	5	0
Forty	4	.3571	.3132	35.0	0	3	0	0	0	0	1	0	0	0	0	0	1	0	0	0	0	0	0	0	2	0	0	1	0
Forty-Niners	3	.1621	.1254	31.0	0	1	2	0	0	0	0	0	0	0	0	0	0	1	0	0	2	0	0	0	0	0	0	0	0
forty-eight	11	.4444	1.1085	40.4	1	3	3	1	3	0	0	0	3	0	0	2	0	5	0	0	0	0	0	0	0	0	1	0	0
forty-eighth	2	.0000	.0914	29.6	2	0	0	0	0	0	0	0	2	0	0	0	0	0	0	0	0	0	0	0	0	0	0	0	0
Forty-first	3	.0000	.0365	25.6	0	0	0	0	0	0	0	3	0	0	0	0	0	0	0	0	0	0	0	0	0	0	0	3	0
forty-five	19	.6313	2.5280	44.0	2	0	3	3	7	1	3	0	7	0	1	3	2	0	0	1	0	0	0	0	3	0	0	2	0
forty-foot	2	.2398	.1138	30.6	0	0	0	0	1	0	1	0	0	0	0	1	1	0	0	0	0	0	0	0	0	0	0	0	0
forty-four	5	.2804	.3481	35.4	0	2	0	0	1	2	0	0	1	0	0	0	0	2	2	0	0	0	0	0	0	0	0	0	0
forty-nine	8	.5863	.9821	39.9	0	0	1	3	2	2	0	0	1	0	0	1	1	2	0	0	0	0	0	0	2	0	0	1	0
Forty-nine	2	.1698	.1133	30.5	0	0	1	0	1	0	0	0	1	0	0	0	0	0	0	0	0	0	0	0	0	0	1	0	0
forty-niners	5	.0000	.0972	29.9	0	0	4	0	0	1	0	0	0	0	0	0	0	5	0	0	0	0	0	0	0	0	0	0	0
forty-ninth	5	.3601	.4423	36.5	2	1	1	0	0	1	0	0	2	0	0	0	0	2	0	0	1	0	0	0	0	0	0	0	0
forty-one	3	.3795	.2506	34.0	1	1	0	0	0	1	0	0	0	0	0	0	0	1	0	0	0	0	0	0	1	0	0	1	0
Forty-second	2	.1733	.1149	30.6	0	0	0	1	0	0	1	0	1	1	0	0	0	0	0	0	0	0	0	0	0	0	0	0	0
forty-seven	8	.5443	.9451	39.8	2	0	0	3	2	1	0	0	3	0	0	0	1	0	1	0	0	0	0	0	1	0	0	2	0
forty-six	8	.4559	.8086	39.1	2	1	2	0	2	0	1	0	2	0	0	0	2	0	0	0	0	0	0	0	2	0	0	2	0
forty-three	3	.2357	.2199	33.4	0	0	0	0	1	1	0	1	2	0	0	0	0	0	0	0	0	0	0	0	0	1	0	0	0
forty-two	12	.6728	1.6616	42.2	2	2	3	1	0	4	0	0	2	1	0	1	4	1	0	0	0	0	0	0	0	1	1	1	0
forum	4	.0996	.1523	31.8	0	0	0	0	1	0	3	0	1	0	0	0	0	0	0	0	0	0	0	0	0	0	0	3	0
Forum	5	.3474	.3866	35.9	0	2	1	0	1	0	0	1	0	0	0	0	0	1	0	0	0	0	0	0	0	2	2	0	0
forward	591	.9162	107.51	60.3	64	90	66	80	151	65	59	16	172	23	10	52	6	28	5	61	17	2	4	8	75	61	31	36	0
Forward	4	.3192	.3100	34.9	0	1	2	0	0	0	0	1	1	0	0	0	0	0	0	0	0	0	0	0	0	2	0	1	0
forwards	10	.3980	.9217	39.6	0	0	0	8	1	0	1	0	2	0	0	0	0	0	0	6	0	0	0	0	1	0	1	0	0
Foss	3	.2441	.1719	32.4	0	0	0	0	2	1	0	0	0	0	0	0	0	0	0	0	1	0	0	0	0	2	0	0	0
fossil	72	.4140	6.4874	48.1	11	9	7	4	29	1	7	4	0	0	0	0	0	1	0	24	0	0	0	0	0	22	24	1	0
fossil-hunting	2	.0000	.0394	26.0	0	0	2	0	0	0	0	0	0	0	0	0	0	0	0	2	0	0	0	0	0	0	0	0	0
fossilized	6	.3613	.4864	36.9	0	1	1	0	1	2	0	1	0	0	0	0	0	0	0	3	0	0	0	0	0	1	2	0	0
fossils	117	.5472	13.487	51.3	37	9	11	7	22	17	10	4	5	0	0	0	0	1	0	48	5	0	0	1	0	41	14	2	0
foster	9	.4415	.8640	39.4	0	0	1	1	5	1	1	0	1	0	0	1	0	2	0	0	0	0	0	0	1	0	4	0	0
Foster	60	.6003	7.5330	48.8	2	14	11	12	14	5	1	1	13	2	0	14	1	0	0	1	11	0	0	0	0	14	1	3	0
foster-father	2	.1787	.1174	30.7	0	0	1	0	0	1	0	0	1	0	0	0	0	0	0	0	0	0	0	0	1	0	0	0	0
Foster's	2	.2303	.1079	30.3	0	1	1	0	0	0	0	0	0	0	0	0	0	0	0	0	1	0	0	0	0	1	0	0	0
fostered	5	.4485	.5011	37.0	0	0	1	1	0	0	3	0	1	0	0	0	0	2	0	0	0	0	0	0	0	1	1	0	0
fostering	2	.1926	.0867	29.4	0	0	0	0	0	1	1	0	0	0	0	0	0	0	0	0	0	0	1	0	0	0	1	0	0

4A Forman
9P format
9M Format
8F formative
5Q Former
8G Formica
7B formidable-looking
8D formin'
9M forming-press
7R Formula
8A Formulae
6A forsake
9D forswear
XR FortMyers
XH FortSill
XR FortWorth-Dallas
4A Fortain
9Q Forteviot
8F fortful
5N Forth
XR fortifier
9L fortifying
8J fortissimo
XH fortnightly
5N Fortnightly
7A Fortress
7R Fortresses
6A fortresslike
4P Forts
7H fortuitous
7R Fortunato
5D fortune's
8A Forty-eighters
8N forty-fifth
3P forty-five-degree
4J forty-niner
5J Forty-niners
7D forty-odd
4G forty-sixth
4F forty-story
7F forward-looking
8P forward-reaching
9P forwarded
5Q forwarders
9B Fosdick
9H fossil-containing
5P fosters
4P Fosters

Word Type	F	D	U	SFI	3 Gr 3	4 Gr 4	5 Gr 5	6 Gr 6	7 Gr 7	8 Gr 8	9 Gr 9	X UnGr	A Read	B Eng & Gr	C Comp	D Lit	E Math	F Soc Stud	G Spell	H Sci	J Music	K Art	L Home Ec	M Shop	N Lib F	P Lib NF	Q Lib Ref	R Mag	S Rel
fought	278	.8067	45.299	56.6	25	44	54	40	47	48	14	6	76	15	2	19	0	66	3	2	6	0	0	0	16	37	22	14	0
foul	35	.6938	4.9536	46.9	5	4	1	4	10	3	6	2	4	3	0	8	0	1	0	4	0	0	0	0	3	7	2	3	0
foul-smelling	3	.3418	.2483	33.9	0	0	0	0	2	0	1	0	1	1	0	0	0	0	0	0	0	0	0	0	0	1	0	0	0
fouled	4	.4495	.4018	36.0	0	0	0	0	1	3	0	0	1	0	0	1	0	1	0	0	0	0	0	0	0	0	0	1	0
Foulis	3	.0000	.1370	31.4	0	0	3	0	0	0	0	0	3	0	0	0	0	0	0	0	0	0	0	0	0	0	0	0	0
fouls	3	.3811	.2534	34.0	0	0	0	0	1	0	1	1	0	0	0	0	0	0	0	1	0	0	0	0	0	1	0	1	0
found	3362	.9784	648.07	68.1	582	548	478	461	600	363	248	82	940	134	17	144	213	349	74	493	90	28	17	27	180	268	214	172	2
Found	3	.2357	.2199	33.4	3	0	0	0	0	0	0	0	2	0	0	0	0	0	0	0	0	0	0	0	0	1	0	0	0
foundation	56	.7433	8.3450	49.2	2	3	7	14	8	8	7	7	1	1	6	2	0	6	0	4	1	3	2	2	1	6	14	7	0
Foundation	11	.5496	1.2436	40.9	1	1	0	1	1	2	5	0	0	0	1	1	0	0	0	1	0	0	0	0	1	1	5	1	0
foundations	31	.5384	3.5020	45.4	1	3	2	3	4	1	12	5	3	1	0	0	0	3	0	1	1	0	0	0	1	1	13	7	0
founded	112	.6360	14.647	51.7	7	4	25	12	24	23	15	2	4	2	0	3	1	45	2	1	3	0	0	0	1	12	29	9	0
founder	21	.5785	2.5378	44.0	0	1	4	2	4	7	2	1	2	0	0	0	0	5	0	1	1	0	0	0	0	2	6	4	0
founders	7	.5091	.7742	38.9	1	0	0	1	0	3	1	1	1	0	0	0	0	3	0	1	0	0	0	0	0	1	0	1	0
founding	25	.5943	3.0702	44.9	5	1	5	3	6	2	3	0	1	0	0	0	0	6	1	0	2	0	0	0	0	6	7	2	0
Founding	2	.1948	.1250	31.0	1	0	0	0	0	1	0	0	1	0	0	0	0	0	0	0	0	0	0	0	0	1	0	0	0
foundries	5	.3128	.3441	35.4	0	0	0	0	0	3	2	0	0	0	0	0	0	1	0	0	0	0	0	1	0	0	3	0	0
foundry	9	.1325	.3516	35.5	1	1	0	0	0	2	5	0	2	0	0	0	0	1	0	0	0	0	0	5	1	0	0	0	0
fount	2	.2441	.1127	30.5	0	0	1	0	1	0	0	0	0	0	0	0	0	0	0	0	0	0	0	0	1	0	1	0	0
fountain	62	.8221	10.228	50.1	8	6	7	11	20	5	5	0	14	2	1	10	1	5	3	5	2	4	1	2	6	5	1	0	0
Fountain	5	.3668	.4060	36.1	0	0	2	0	3	0	0	0	0	0	0	2	0	2	0	0	0	0	0	0	1	0	0	0	0
fountains	19	.6778	2.6469	44.2	2	2	0	0	7	2	5	1	4	4	0	0	1	0	0	0	1	0	0	0	2	3	3	1	0
four	2357	.9459	440.50	66.4	394	348	304	317	425	294	212	63	420	141	27	77	306	190	216	199	153	9	25	28	80	186	108	192	0
Four	54	.7421	8.1884	49.1	10	3	10	2	14	7	6	2	18	13	0	0	0	2	0	0	5	0	2	1	3	4	2	4	0
four-	2	.2418	.1091	30.4	0	0	1	0	0	0	1	0	0	0	0	0	0	0	1	0	0	0	0	0	0	0	1	0	0
Four-Eyes	2	.2407	.1138	30.6	0	1	0	0	0	1	0	0	0	0	0	1	0	0	0	0	0	0	0	0	0	1	0	0	0
four-and-twenty	2	.0000	.0914	29.6	2	0	0	0	0	0	0	0	2	0	0	0	0	0	0	0	0	0	0	0	0	0	0	0	0
four-barrel	3	.0000	.0365	25.6	0	0	0	0	3	0	0	0	0	0	0	0	0	0	0	0	0	0	0	0	0	0	0	3	0
four-cent	2	.0000	.0290	24.6	0	0	0	2	0	0	0	0	0	0	0	0	0	0	0	0	0	0	0	0	0	2	0	0	0
four-clawed	2	.2446	.1125	30.5	0	1	0	0	1	0	0	0	0	1	0	1	0	0	0	0	0	0	0	0	0	0	0	0	0
four-cylinder	2	.0000	.0290	24.6	0	0	0	0	0	0	0	2	0	0	0	0	0	0	0	0	0	0	0	0	0	2	0	0	0
four-day	4	.2843	.2875	34.6	0	0	1	0	0	1	2	0	1	0	0	0	0	1	0	0	0	0	0	0	0	0	0	2	0
four-digit	3	.1434	.1493	31.7	0	0	0	0	1	0	2	0	1	0	0	0	2	0	0	0	0	0	0	0	0	0	0	0	0
four-fifths	8	.5635	.9430	39.7	0	1	2	1	3	0	1	0	0	0	0	0	2	2	0	2	0	0	0	0	0	0	1	1	0
four-foot	3	.3452	.2543	34.1	0	0	0	1	1	0	0	1	1	0	0	0	0	0	0	1	0	0	0	0	0	0	0	1	0
four-footed	3	.3390	.2450	33.9	0	1	0	0	1	0	0	1	1	0	0	0	0	0	0	0	0	0	0	0	0	0	1	1	0
four-footers	3	.0000	.0583	27.7	0	0	0	0	0	3	0	0	0	0	0	0	0	3	0	0	0	0	0	0	0	0	0	0	0
four-hour	4	.3810	.3743	35.7	0	0	1	0	1	1	1	0	2	0	0	0	1	0	0	0	0	0	0	0	0	1	0	0	0
four-inch	2	.1698	.1133	30.5	1	0	0	0	1	0	0	0	1	0	0	0	0	0	0	0	0	0	0	0	0	0	1	0	0
four-inch-long	2	.2437	.1129	30.5	0	0	0	0	1	0	1	0	0	0	0	0	0	0	0	0	0	0	0	0	0	0	1	1	0
four-lane	4	.2352	.2332	33.7	0	1	0	2	0	0	1	0	0	0	0	0	0	2	0	0	0	0	0	0	0	0	0	2	0
four-leaf	2	.1733	.1149	30.6	1	1	0	0	0	0	0	0	1	1	0	0	0	0	0	0	0	0	0	0	0	0	0	0	0
four-legged	13	.6215	1.6598	42.2	1	6	1	0	4	0	1	0	1	2	1	0	1	0	0	1	0	0	1	0	0	5	1	0	0
four-letter	11	.5166	1.2429	40.9	5	0	0	1	1	1	2	1	4	1	0	0	0	0	2	0	0	0	0	0	0	1	0	3	0
four-line	2	.0000	.0162	22.1	0	0	0	0	2	0	0	0	0	0	0	0	0	0	0	0	2	0	0	0	0	0	0	0	0
four-man	3	.2279	.2143	33.3	0	0	0	2	1	0	0	0	2	0	0	0	0	0	0	0	0	0	0	0	0	0	0	1	0
four-measure	3	.0000	.0243	23.8	0	0	1	1	1	0	0	0	0	0	0	0	0	0	0	0	3	0	0	0	0	0	0	0	0
four-o'clock	13	.0000	.2563	34.1	0	0	0	13	0	0	0	0	0	0	0	0	0	0	0	13	0	0	0	0	0	0	0	0	0
four-part	7	.0000	.0566	27.5	0	1	3	2	0	1	0	0	0	0	0	0	0	0	0	0	7	0	0	0	0	0	0	0	0
four-poster	2	.1948	.1250	31.0	1	1	0	0	0	0	0	0	1	0	0	0	0	0	0	0	0	0	0	0	0	1	0	0	0
four-room	3	.2425	.1816	32.6	0	1	1	0	1	0	0	0	0	0	0	0	0	2	0	0	0	0	0	0	0	0	0	1	0
four-sided	12	.5295	1.3199	41.2	1	1	7	0	0	1	2	0	0	0	0	0	7	0	0	1	1	1	0	1	0	1	0	0	0
four-speed	2	.0000	.0243	23.9	0	0	0	0	2	0	0	0	0	0	0	0	0	0	0	0	0	0	0	0	0	0	0	2	0
four-story	2	.2408	.1204	30.8	1	0	0	1	0	0	0	0	0	0	0	0	0	1	0	0	0	0	0	0	0	1	0	0	0
four-stroke	3	.1785	.1397	31.5	0	0	2	0	1	0	0	0	0	0	0	0	0	0	0	2	0	0	0	1	0	0	0	0	0
four-syllable	11	.0000	.0893	29.5	0	3	1	3	3	1	0	0	0	0	0	0	0	0	11	0	0	0	0	0	0	0	0	0	0
four-tenths	2	.2152	.1357	31.3	0	0	0	0	2	0	0	0	1	0	0	0	0	1	0	0	0	0	0	0	0	0	0	0	0
four-thirty	2	.0000	.0914	29.6	0	0	0	2	0	0	0	0	2	0	0	0	0	0	0	0	0	0	0	0	0	0	0	0	0
four-week	2	.0000	.0243	23.9	0	0	0	0	0	2	0	0	0	0	0	0	0	0	0	0	0	0	0	0	0	0	0	2	0
four-wheel	5	.4755	.4973	37.0	1	1	0	1	1	0	1	0	0	0	0	1	0	0	0	0	0	0	0	0	1	0	1	2	0
four-wheeled	2	.2427	.1152	30.6	0	0	1	0	1	0	0	0	0	0	0	0	0	0	0	0	0	0	0	0	1	1	0	0	0
four-year	10	.4240	.8883	39.5	0	0	2	2	1	2	3	0	0	0	2	1	0	0	0	0	0	0	0	0	0	1	4	2	0
four-year-old	8	.3578	.6525	38.1	1	6	0	0	0	1	0	0	1	0	0	0	0	0	0	0	0	0	0	0	1	5	1	0	0
fours	47	.4130	4.3646	46.4	6	5	7	14	10	2	1	2	8	0	0	1	30	1	0	1	0	0	0	0	2	2	2	0	0
fourscore	3	.3274	.2364	33.7	0	1	1	0	0	1	0	0	1	0	0	1	0	0	1	0	0	0	0	0	0	0	0	0	0
foursome	2	.2346	.1166	30.7	0	0	0	0	0	1	1	0	0	0	0	0	0	0	0	1	0	0	0	0	0	0	0	1	0
foursquare	2	.1948	.1250	31.0	0	0	1	1	0	0	0	0	1	0	0	0	0	0	0	0	0	0	0	0	0	1	0	0	0
fourteen	93	.8912	16.540	52.2	11	9	12	13	29	12	7	0	34	2	1	4	6	7	7	6	5	0	1	0	6	10	2	2	0
Fourteen	2	.0000	.0389	25.9	0	0	0	0	0	1	1	0	0	0	0	0	0	2	0	0	0	0	0	0	0	0	0	0	0
fourteen-year-old	3	.3863	.2513	34.0	0	1	1	0	0	1	0	0	0	0	0	0	0	0	0	0	0	0	0	0	1	1	0	1	0
fourteenth	9	.7478	1.3582	41.3	1	0	1	1	4	1	0	1	1	1	0	1	0	1	1	0	1	0	0	0	1	1	0	1	0
Fourteenth	4	.0000	.0778	28.9	0	1	0	0	0	1	2	0	0	0	0	0	0	4	0	0	0	0	0	0	0	0	0	0	0
fourth	311	.9095	56.067	57.5	44	54	48	39	48	44	27	7	45	24	4	8	44	24	19	21	51	3	4	4	6	21	12	21	0
Fourth	55	.8327	9.1727	49.6	15	11	8	5	4	4	8	0	11	3	1	4	2	4	1	0	5	0	0	0	9	6	5	4	0
fourth-floor	2	.2160	.1362	31.3	1	0	1	0	0	0	0	0	1	0	0	0	0	0	0	1	0	0	0	0	0	0	0	0	0
fourth-grade	5	.1310	.2243	33.5	0	5	0	0	0	0	0	0	2	0	0	0	1	0	0	0	0	2	0	0	0	0	0	0	0
fourths	61	.4448	5.8256	47.7	19	12	13	5	9	0	3	0	0	1	0	0	44	7	0	1	4	0	2	0	0	1	1	0	0
Fouser	6	.0000	.0729	28.6	0	0	0	0	6	0	0	0	0	0	0	0	0	0	0	0	0	0	0	0	0	0	0	6	0
fowl	24	.6402	3.1764	45.0	9	0	0	2	6	4	1	2	5	0	0	1	0	0	1	0	1	0	2	0	0	6	6	2	0
fowling	2	.1814	.1187	30.7	0	0	0	0	1	0	0	1	1	0	0	0	0	0	0	0	0	0	0	0	0	0	0	1	0
fowling-piece	2	.1621	.0746	28.7	0	0	0	0	1	1	0	0	0	0	1	1	0	0	0	0	0	0	0	0	0	0	0	0	0
fowls	10	.5031	1.0848	40.4	4	2	0	2	1	1	0	0	2	1	0	2	0	0	0	0	0	0	0	0	1	4	0	0	0
fox	163	.7922	26.322	54.2	43	34	29	15	22	11	4	5	76	9	0	7	0	1	10	10	8	0	0	0	8	20	5	9	0
Fox	83	.6641	11.630	50.7	28	8	14	9	4	15	5	0	41	1	2	14	0	3	0	0	0	0	0	0	7	8	0	7	0
fox's	5	.2038	.3268	35.1	1	0	0	3	1	0	0	0	3	2	0	0	0	0	0	0	0	0	0	0	0	0	0	0	0
foxes	57	.7747	9.0374	49.6	7	11	14	12	6	6	1	0	25	1	0	3	0	2	1	7	1	0	0	0	2	9	4	2	0
Foxes	2	.0000	.0234	23.7	0	2	0	0	0	0	0	0	0	0	0	0	0	0	0	0	0	0	0	0	2	0	0	0	0
foxhole	2	.0000	.0219	23.4	0	0	0	0	0	2	0	0	0	2	0	0	0	0	0	0	0	0	0	0	0	0	0	0	0
foxhounds	4	.2445	.3067	34.9	0	3	0	0	0	0	1	0	3	0	0	0	0	0	0	0	0	0	0	0	0	1	0	0	0
Foxie	2	.0000	.0162	22.1	0	0	0	0	0	0	2	0	0	0	0	0	0	0	2	0	0	0	0	0	0	0	0	0	0
Foxx	6	.2379	.3410	35.3	2	2	0	2	0	0	0	0	0	0	0	2	0	0	0	0	0	0	0	0	0	4	0	0	0
Foxy	21	.0000	.9593	39.8	15	0	0	0	6	0	0	0	21	0	0	0	0	0	0	0	0	0	0	0	0	0	0	0	0

9M Fotosetter
9B foul-shooting
9B foulard
XH fouler
5P Foulke
7N foun'
8R Foundation-funded
XR Foundations
5P Founder
5F foundered
9R Founders
9M foundrymen
8A Four-Ring
4P four-acre
3P four-and-a-half
XR four-and-five-letter
7R four-banger
4J four-beat
9R four-bedroom
5E four-clock
5P four-dimensional
6E four-eighths
8R four-engine
8F four-footer
8D four-forty
3P four-horse
6F four-hundred-year-old
5J Four-in-Line
9D four-layered
7E four-mile
7J four-minute
7E four-month
6H four-o'clocks
9J four-octave
5H four-passenger
XR four-piece
5E four-place
9C four-ply
9R four-power
6E four-sevenths
5A four-stage
7G four-step
6H four-strand
7R four-stroker
7R four-throat
8J four-voice
7R four-wheel-drive
4A four-winged
3Q four-year-olds
7Q Fourneyron
9R Foursome
7L fourteen-day
4A fourteen-day-old
4B fourth-
6A Fourth-Class
9H Fourth-of-July
6A fourth-place
8R fourth-story
8D Fourtou
5B fourty
7H fovea
8D fowerscore
7Q fowl's
7Q fowle
7R Fowler
9Q Fox-Davies
6A fox-and-geese
5A fox-bats
7N fox-hearted
8F fox-trot
8D Fox's
9D Foxfire
5P foxgloves
6R foxhound
8A foxtrot
8A foxy

Word Type	F	D	U	SFI	3 Gr 3	4 Gr 4	5 Gr 5	6 Gr 6	7 Gr 7	8 Gr 8	9 Gr 9	X UnGr	A Read	B Eng & Gr	C Comp	D Lit	E Math	F Soc Stud	G Spell	H Sci	J Music	K Art	L Home Ec	M Shop	N Lib F	P Lib NF	Q Lib Ref	R Mag	S Rel
Foxy's	4	.0000	.1827	32.6	3	0	0	0	1	0	0	0	4	0	0	0	0	0	0	0	0	0	0	0	0	0	0	0	0
Foyega	2	.0000	.0243	23.9	0	0	0	0	2	0	0	0	0	0	0	0	0	0	0	0	0	0	0	0	0	0	0	2	0
foyer	3	.3390	.2450	33.9	0	0	0	0	0	1	1	1	1	0	0	0	0	0	0	0	0	0	0	0	0	0	1	1	0
fps	5	.0000	.0126	21.0	0	0	0	0	5	0	0	0	0	0	0	0	0	0	0	0	0	0	0	5	0	0	0	0	0
fr	4	.0761	.1245	31.0	1	2	1	0	0	0	0	0	1	0	0	0	0	0	3	0	0	0	0	0	0	0	0	0	0
fraction	480	.1637	21.558	53.3	25	53	54	96	122	67	63	0	5	1	0	2	445	2	2	9	0	0	0	1	0	3	7	3	0
fractional	292	.0459	6.8016	48.3	27	57	53	85	47	11	12	0	0	0	0	0	289	0	0	2	0	0	0	1	0	0	0	0	0
fractions	421	.1346	16.545	52.2	7	50	76	69	96	50	73	0	0	1	0	2	406	0	0	5	1	0	0	4	0	1	1	0	0
fracture	19	.4688	1.9178	42.8	0	2	1	1	2	5	4	4	1	1	0	0	0	0	0	8	0	0	0	0	0	0	5	4	0
fractured	6	.3780	.5036	37.0	0	1	1	0	2	2	0	0	0	0	0	0	0	0	0	3	0	0	0	0	2	0	1	0	0
fractures	7	.4520	.6838	38.3	0	3	0	0	0	1	3	0	1	0	0	0	0	0	0	1	0	0	0	1	0	0	2	2	0
fracturing	3	.2940	.1911	32.8	0	1	0	0	0	1	1	0	0	0	0	0	0	0	0	0	0	0	0	1	0	0	1	1	0
frae	2	.0000	.0162	22.1	0	0	0	2	0	0	0	0	0	0	0	0	0	0	0	0	2	0	0	0	0	0	0	0	0
fragile	21	.7400	3.1409	45.0	0	2	0	3	6	4	6	0	3	0	1	1	0	0	0	1	0	1	1	0	3	3	2	5	0
fragment	26	.4307	2.3680	43.7	1	0	3	0	6	9	6	1	0	15	0	1	0	0	0	2	5	0	0	0	0	2	1	0	0
fragmentation	8	.2303	.4315	36.3	0	0	3	0	5	0	0	0	0	0	0	0	0	0	0	0	4	0	0	0	0	4	0	0	0
fragmented	3	.3815	.2534	34.0	0	0	1	0	0	1	1	0	0	0	0	0	0	1	0	0	0	0	0	0	0	1	0	1	0
fragments	52	.7342	7.7305	48.9	0	0	5	6	15	15	10	1	7	15	0	2	0	0	0	8	4	1	0	1	1	1	9	3	0
Fragonard	2	.1493	.0692	28.4	0	0	1	0	0	1	0	0	0	0	0	0	0	0	0	0	0	1	0	0	0	0	1	0	0
fragrance	26	.7123	3.7957	45.8	3	4	3	2	5	2	2	5	6	2	1	1	0	2	0	3	0	0	0	0	3	2	0	6	0
fragrances	2	.0000	.0243	23.9	0	0	1	0	0	0	0	1	0	0	0	0	0	0	0	0	0	0	0	0	0	0	0	2	0
fragrant	22	.7737	3.4608	45.4	1	2	4	7	4	1	2	1	7	2	0	2	0	1	0	2	1	0	0	0	2	1	3	1	0
frail	30	.7680	4.7052	46.7	2	3	5	5	7	4	2	2	12	1	1	0	1	1	1	1	0	1	0	0	5	4	1	1	0
frail-looking	2	.2440	.1132	30.5	0	0	0	1	0	0	1	0	0	0	0	1	0	0	0	0	0	0	0	0	0	0	0	1	0
frailties	2	.1698	.1133	30.5	0	0	0	0	0	1	1	0	1	0	0	0	0	0	0	0	0	0	0	0	0	0	1	0	0
Fram	4	.0000	.0778	28.9	0	4	0	0	0	0	0	0	0	0	0	0	0	4	0	0	0	0	0	0	0	0	0	0	0
frame	249	.8183	40.733	56.1	35	32	15	36	59	50	20	2	29	18	2	10	61	14	22	8	8	10	4	22	7	11	6	17	0
framed	16	.6554	2.1470	43.3	1	0	0	4	2	4	3	2	2	1	1	1	0	3	0	0	0	0	2	0	1	0	1	4	0
frames	151	.5496	17.279	52.4	42	30	3	29	7	30	3	7	4	8	1	0	98	4	21	2	0	0	0	3	0	3	4	3	0
Frames	2	.0000	.0243	23.9	0	0	0	0	0	0	0	2	0	0	0	0	0	0	0	0	0	0	0	0	0	0	0	2	0
framework	51	.8562	8.7042	49.4	5	4	6	7	13	3	10	3	6	8	2	3	0	6	1	9	2	0	1	2	1	2	4	4	0
framing	2	.0725	.0732	28.6	0	1	0	0	0	1	0	0	1	0	0	0	0	0	0	0	0	0	0	1	0	0	0	0	0
Framton	2	.0000	.0215	23.3	0	0	0	0	0	0	2	0	0	0	0	2	0	0	0	0	0	0	0	0	0	0	0	0	0
Fran	10	.3635	.8117	39.1	2	0	0	3	1	4	0	0	1	4	0	0	1	0	0	0	0	0	0	0	0	0	0	4	0
franc	5	.1496	.2557	34.1	2	0	0	0	0	0	3	0	2	0	0	0	0	0	0	0	0	0	0	0	0	0	0	3	0
France	633	.7458	95.471	59.8	108	37	94	95	97	91	90	21	48	23	1	14	3	245	13	10	37	9	3	0	8	37	150	32	0
France's	32	.4890	3.2920	45.2	11	0	2	3	4	4	7	1	0	0	0	0	0	9	0	0	0	1	0	0	0	1	13	8	0
Frances	23	.6100	2.9477	44.7	1	7	7	0	3	0	3	2	6	3	0	1	1	0	2	0	0	0	0	0	0	8	0	2	0
Francie	16	.0000	.7309	38.6	0	0	0	0	16	0	0	0	16	0	0	0	0	0	0	0	0	0	0	0	0	0	0	0	0
Francis	68	.8223	11.264	50.5	0	23	12	4	9	6	12	2	23	3	1	10	2	1	2	1	6	0	0	0	3	4	7	5	0
Franciscan	4	.3519	.3117	34.9	0	0	0	2	0	2	0	0	0	0	0	0	0	1	0	0	0	0	0	0	0	0	1	2	0
Franciscans	4	.3709	.3633	35.6	0	0	0	3	0	1	0	0	2	0	0	0	0	0	0	0	0	0	0	0	0	0	1	1	0
Francisco	22	.6105	2.7762	44.4	2	2	5	4	7	1	1	0	1	0	0	2	0	9	0	0	0	1	0	0	0	2	4	3	0
Francke	3	.0000	.0322	25.1	0	0	0	0	3	0	0	0	0	0	0	3	0	0	0	0	0	0	0	0	0	0	0	0	0
Franco	6	.1361	.2398	33.8	0	0	5	0	0	0	1	0	0	0	0	0	0	1	0	0	0	0	0	0	0	5	0	0	0
Franco-Prussian	3	.0000	.0434	26.4	1	0	0	1	1	0	0	0	0	0	0	0	0	0	0	0	0	0	0	0	0	3	0	0	0
Francois	28	.5287	3.1848	45.0	0	10	0	0	11	4	2	1	8	0	0	0	0	0	0	1	1	2	0	0	12	1	2	1	0
Francoise	2	.0000	.0914	29.6	2	0	0	0	0	0	0	0	2	0	0	0	0	0	0	0	0	0	0	0	0	0	0	0	0
francs	13	.3660	1.2316	40.9	9	1	0	3	0	0	0	0	9	0	0	0	3	0	0	0	0	0	0	0	1	0	0	0	0
frank	10	.4084	.9541	39.8	0	1	1	1	4	2	1	0	4	0	0	0	0	0	0	0	0	0	0	0	0	1	1	4	0
Frank	295	.7686	46.734	56.7	135	44	31	12	32	27	9	5	173	13	2	6	6	4	1	0	7	1	0	0	14	35	2	31	0
Frank's	16	.4223	1.6923	42.3	13	1	0	0	0	1	1	0	13	1	0	0	0	0	0	0	0	0	0	0	1	1	0	0	0
Frankel	8	.1363	.2895	34.6	0	0	7	0	0	0	1	0	0	7	0	0	0	0	0	0	0	0	0	0	0	0	1	0	0
Frankel's	3	.0000	.0328	25.2	0	0	3	0	0	0	0	0	0	3	0	0	0	0	0	0	0	0	0	0	0	0	0	0	0
Frankenstein	2	.2412	.1091	30.4	0	0	0	0	0	2	0	0	0	0	0	1	0	0	1	0	0	0	0	0	0	0	0	0	0
Frankfort	5	.0926	.1850	32.7	0	4	0	1	0	0	0	0	1	0	0	0	0	0	0	0	0	0	0	0	0	4	0	0	0
Frankfurt	3	.3845	.2449	33.9	0	1	1	0	0	1	0	0	0	1	0	0	0	0	1	0	0	0	0	0	0	0	1	0	0
frankfurter	7	.1323	.2181	33.4	0	1	1	0	0	0	5	0	0	1	0	0	0	0	0	0	0	0	5	0	0	1	0	0	0
frankfurters	10	.2019	.4763	36.8	1	1	0	0	0	2	6	0	1	0	0	0	0	0	1	0	0	0	6	0	0	1	0	1	0
Frankie	49	.3096	3.4633	45.4	0	45	1	0	1	0	0	2	2	0	0	0	0	0	0	0	0	0	0	0	25	20	0	2	0
Frankie's	8	.3507	.6196	37.9	0	7	0	0	0	0	0	1	0	0	0	0	0	0	0	0	0	0	0	0	3	4	0	1	0
frankincense	3	.3263	.2368	33.7	0	1	0	1	0	0	0	1	1	0	0	0	0	0	0	0	1	0	0	0	0	0	0	1	0
Frankish	4	.0000	.0419	26.2	2	0	0	0	1	0	1	0	0	0	0	0	0	0	0	0	0	0	0	0	0	0	4	0	0
Franklin	130	.7969	20.993	53.2	6	26	29	5	11	37	14	2	37	5	0	6	2	39	1	8	2	0	1	0	3	5	13	8	0
Franklin's	15	.5040	1.6474	42.2	2	4	1	0	4	3	1	0	4	0	0	1	0	4	0	0	0	0	0	2	0	2	2	0	0
frankly	16	.6166	2.0572	43.1	0	1	0	3	2	5	3	2	3	2	0	3	0	2	0	1	0	0	0	0	0	0	1	4	0
frankness	4	.1854	.1872	32.7	0	0	0	0	1	0	3	0	0	0	0	0	0	0	0	0	0	0	0	0	0	1	0	3	0
Franks	16	.2477	.9418	39.7	1	0	0	0	8	4	1	2	1	0	0	0	0	1	0	0	0	0	0	0	0	0	11	3	0
Franny	9	.0000	.1094	30.4	0	0	0	9	0	0	0	0	0	0	0	0	0	0	0	0	0	0	0	0	0	0	0	9	0
frantic	27	.6337	3.5717	45.5	0	3	3	3	9	7	2	0	8	0	1	5	0	0	0	0	1	0	0	0	5	0	1	6	0
frantically	33	.7466	4.9852	47.0	3	1	6	5	12	2	2	2	5	2	1	4	0	1	1	2	0	0	0	0	6	1	2	8	0
Franz	37	.4479	3.4865	45.4	1	5	8	5	7	7	2	2	2	2	2	0	0	0	0	1	22	0	0	0	0	4	3	1	0
Frasquita	3	.0000	.0243	23.8	0	0	0	0	0	3	0	0	0	0	0	0	0	0	0	0	3	0	0	0	0	0	0	0	0
fraternal	3	.1813	.1402	31.5	0	0	1	0	0	0	1	1	0	0	0	0	0	0	0	1	0	0	0	0	0	0	2	0	0
fraternite	2	.2285	.1129	30.5	1	0	0	0	1	0	0	0	0	0	0	0	0	1	0	0	0	0	0	0	0	0	1	0	0
fraternity	9	.4843	.9040	39.6	0	0	0	0	2	1	5	1	0	0	1	0	0	0	0	1	2	0	0	0	0	0	4	1	0
Fratianno	11	.0000	.1337	31.3	0	0	0	0	0	0	11	0	0	0	0	0	0	0	0	0	0	0	0	0	0	0	0	11	0
fraud	7	.4579	.7233	38.6	0	0	0	1	2	3	1	0	2	1	0	0	0	3	0	0	0	0	0	0	1	0	0	0	0
fraudulent	4	.2386	.2998	34.8	0	0	1	0	1	2	0	0	3	0	0	0	0	0	0	0	0	0	0	0	0	0	1	0	0
fraught	3	.3815	.2534	34.0	0	0	0	0	2	1	0	0	0	0	0	0	0	1	0	0	0	0	0	0	0	1	0	1	0
fray	7	.3611	.5916	37.7	1	3	0	2	0	0	0	1	2	0	1	0	0	0	0	1	0	0	0	0	3	0	0	0	0
frayed	11	.6141	1.3940	41.4	1	1	1	1	2	3	2	0	1	3	0	1	0	1	0	0	0	0	0	0	0	2	1	2	0
frays	2	.0000	.0215	23.3	0	0	0	0	0	0	2	0	0	0	0	2	0	0	0	0	0	0	0	0	0	0	0	0	0
freak	3	.1927	.1491	31.7	0	0	0	0	1	1	1	0	0	0	0	0	0	0	0	1	0	0	0	0	0	0	0	2	0
freckle	2	.2412	.1091	30.4	0	1	0	1	0	0	0	0	0	0	0	1	0	0	1	0	0	0	0	0	0	0	0	0	0
freckled	7	.4044	.6281	38.0	1	1	2	0	2	0	0	1	1	0	0	1	0	0	0	0	0	0	0	0	3	2	0	0	0
freckles	13	.6032	1.6891	42.3	3	5	1	1	1	2	0	0	6	0	0	0	1	0	0	1	0	0	0	0	2	2	0	1	0
Fred	223	.5467	25.853	54.1	137	20	15	7	25	7	12	0	43	18	0	5	24	2	4	2	0	0	0	0	103	10	0	12	0
Fred's	18	.5109	2.0007	43.0	7	4	3	0	1	0	3	0	5	1	0	0	7	0	2	0	0	0	0	0	3	0	0	0	0
Freddie	7	.0000	.3198	35.0	0	6	0	1	0	0	0	0	7	0	0	0	0	0	0	0	0	0	0	0	0	0	0	0	0
Freddy	197	.0572	4.8066	46.8	164	13	13	0	0	0	1	6	13	0	0	0	0	0	1	0	0	0	0	0	182	1	0	0	0
Freddy's	5	.0804	.1641	32.2	1	1	2	0	0	0	0	1	1	0	0	0	0	0	0	0	0	0	0	0	4	0	0	0	0

7R Foyt
7R Foyt's
5Q FPC
7Q FPO
5A Fra
5K frabjous
5G frac
3A fracas
7H Fracastoro
6J Frackenpohl
5Q Fragment
7B fragmentary
8K Fragonard's
6J Fragrant
3A fraidy-cat
7Q frailer
7D frailest
7A Fraley
7A Fraley's
XR framboise
8A Frame
8F framers
XR Framing
8Q Franc
6R franca
7R Francaise
9R France-Soir
6P Francesca
9R Francesco
7R franchise
8F Franchise
7A Francie's
8Q Franciscus
4Q francium
8Q Franck
7J Franck's
9R Franco-American
5P Franco-Belge
5P Franco-Belgian
7F Franco-Ethiopian
9R Francois-Marie
7A Francois's
9Q Franconia
8Q Frane
5B frangere
6R frangipani
9Q Frankfurt-on-Oder
9F Frankfurter
7J Frankincense
4N FRANKLIN
4F Franklins
8J Franko
6R Franny's
XQ Frans
8H Frasch
7R Fraser
9K Fraternity
8R fratricidal
7R fratricide
7P Frau
7D Fraud
7D frauds
8F Fraunces
9H Fraunhofer
5A Fray
8B Fre
3A fre
7R freaked
8R freakiest
3A freakish
6H freaks
6N freckle-faced
8D freckle-nosed
8N freckled-faced
7B FRED

Word Type	F	D	U	SFI	3 Gr 3	4 Gr 4	5 Gr 5	6 Gr 6	7 Gr 7	8 Gr 8	9 Gr 9	X UnGr	A Read	B Eng & Gr	C Comp	D Lit	E Math	F Soc Stud	G Spell	H Sci	J Music	K Art	L Home Ec	M Shop	N Lib F	P Lib NF	Q Lib Ref	R Mag	S Rel
Frederic	4	.3060	.2924	34.7	0	1	2	0	1	0	0	0	1	0	0	0	0	0	0	0	1	0	0	0	0	0	2	0	0
Frederick	57	.6713	7.7998	48.9	0	1	12	2	9	13	18	2	1	2	1	1	0	23	0	2	6	0	0	0	1	2	14	4	0
Frederick's	2	.2285	.1129	30.5	0	0	0	0	0	1	1	0	0	0	0	0	0	1	0	0	0	0	0	0	0	0	1	0	0
Fredericksburg	11	.5317	1.2483	41.0	2	2	0	0	0	7	0	0	1	0	0	0	0	6	0	0	0	0	0	0	1	1	1	1	0
free	805	.8351	134.83	61.3	105	93	98	112	166	134	75	22	174	26	5	52	21	152	9	57	48	4	12	9	52	75	53	50	6
Free	19	.5655	2.2437	43.5	1	1	2	0	3	7	2	3	1	0	0	0	0	6	0	0	1	0	0	0	0	3	4	4	0
free-dom	2	.0000	.0215	23.3	0	0	0	0	0	0	2	0	0	0	0	2	0	0	0	0	0	0	0	0	0	0	0	0	0
free-enterprise	2	.0000	.0209	23.2	0	0	2	0	0	0	0	0	0	0	0	0	0	0	0	0	0	0	0	0	0	0	2	0	0
free-flowing	2	.2375	.1088	30.4	0	0	0	1	0	1	0	0	0	0	0	0	0	0	0	0	1	0	0	0	0	0	0	1	0
free-for-all	3	.3872	.2490	34.0	0	0	0	0	0	1	2	0	0	1	0	1	0	0	0	0	0	0	0	0	0	0	0	1	0
free-form	3	.1927	.1491	31.7	0	0	0	0	1	1	1	0	0	0	0	0	0	0	0	1	0	0	0	0	0	0	0	2	0
free-soil	2	.0000	.0389	25.9	0	0	0	0	0	2	0	0	0	0	0	0	0	2	0	0	0	0	0	0	0	0	0	0	0
free-style	2	.0000	.0914	29.6	0	0	0	0	0	2	0	0	2	0	0	0	0	0	0	0	0	0	0	0	0	0	0	0	0
free-throw	2	.0000	.0290	24.6	0	0	0	0	2	0	0	0	0	0	0	0	0	0	0	0	0	0	0	0	0	2	0	0	0
Freebody	6	.2196	.3108	34.9	2	0	4	0	0	0	0	0	0	0	0	4	0	0	0	0	0	0	0	0	2	0	0	0	0
Freebody's	2	.2443	.1130	30.5	1	0	1	0	0	0	0	0	0	0	0	1	0	0	0	0	0	0	0	0	1	0	0	0	0
Freebus	3	.0000	.0328	25.2	0	0	0	0	0	3	0	0	0	3	0	0	0	0	0	0	0	0	0	0	0	0	0	0	0
freed	57	.3363	4.5548	46.6	6	7	12	9	12	10	0	1	12	0	0	1	0	12	0	4	0	0	0	0	2	9	12	3	2
Freedman	2	.0000	.0219	23.4	0	0	0	0	0	0	2	0	0	2	0	0	0	0	0	0	0	0	0	0	0	0	0	0	0
Freedmen's	2	.0000	.0389	25.9	0	0	0	0	0	2	0	0	0	0	0	0	0	2	0	0	0	0	0	0	0	0	0	0	0
freedom	386	.6080	49.189	56.9	27	36	44	65	49	103	58	4	73	1	1	23	1	129	4	12	31	6	1	0	20	25	32	21	6
Freedom	11	.6154	1.3941	41.4	0	1	2	0	3	2	0	3	0	0	0	0	0	2	0	3	1	0	0	0	0	1	2	2	0
freedom-loving	2	.2285	.1129	30.5	1	0	0	1	0	0	0	0	0	0	0	0	0	1	0	0	0	0	0	0	0	0	1	0	0
freedom's	8	.2093	.3873	35.9	1	4	1	1	0	0	1	0	0	0	0	1	0	0	0	0	6	0	0	0	0	1	0	0	0
Freedom's	2	.0000	.0162	22.1	1	1	0	0	0	0	0	0	0	0	0	0	0	0	0	0	2	0	0	0	0	0	0	0	0
freedoms	16	.4370	1.5611	41.9	1	0	0	2	3	8	2	0	2	0	0	0	0	10	0	0	0	0	0	0	1	0	1	2	0
Freedoms	4	.2152	.2714	34.3	0	0	0	0	0	2	2	0	2	0	0	0	0	2	0	0	0	0	0	0	0	0	0	0	0
freehand	5	.0000	.0126	21.0	0	0	0	0	0	0	5	0	0	0	0	0	0	0	0	0	0	0	0	5	0	0	0	0	0
freeing	9	.5957	1.1399	40.6	0	0	4	2	1	1	1	0	3	1	0	1	0	1	0	0	0	0	0	0	0	1	2	0	0
freely	89	.8150	14.537	51.6	11	11	2	18	19	14	12	2	10	1	0	5	2	9	0	20	5	5	2	2	2	11	7	8	0
freeman	2	.2152	.1357	31.3	0	0	0	1	0	1	0	0	1	0	0	0	0	1	0	0	0	0	0	0	0	0	0	0	0
freemen	7	.4201	.6603	38.2	0	1	0	2	2	1	1	0	1	0	0	0	0	4	0	0	1	0	0	0	0	0	1	0	0
freer	4	.2090	.2014	33.0	0	0	1	0	2	0	1	0	0	0	0	0	0	0	0	0	0	0	0	0	0	0	1	3	0
frees	3	.0050	.0487	26.9	1	2	0	0	0	0	0	0	1	0	0	0	0	0	0	0	0	0	0	0	0	0	0	0	2
freeway	8	.5426	.8973	39.5	0	0	0	0	3	1	3	1	0	0	0	2	0	1	1	0	0	0	0	0	2	0	0	2	0
Freeway	2	.0000	.0299	24.8	0	2	0	0	0	0	0	0	0	0	0	0	2	0	0	0	0	0	0	0	0	0	0	0	0
freeways	6	.3350	.4461	36.5	2	1	0	0	1	0	2	0	0	0	0	0	0	1	0	0	0	0	0	0	0	0	2	3	0
freeze	61	.7656	9.5457	49.8	14	12	6	9	10	1	9	0	22	2	0	6	0	4	2	12	0	0	2	0	1	7	3	0	0
freezer	10	.2889	.6847	38.4	4	2	0	0	0	0	4	0	1	0	0	0	0	0	0	5	0	0	3	0	0	0	1	0	0
freezers	3	.3676	.2407	33.8	1	0	1	0	0	1	0	0	0	0	0	0	0	1	1	0	0	0	0	0	0	0	1	0	0
freezes	42	.7067	6.1658	47.9	18	6	9	2	4	1	2	0	15	0	0	2	3	5	0	11	0	0	0	0	1	1	3	1	0
freezing	98	.7298	14.673	51.7	18	11	22	11	14	9	11	2	27	2	0	7	2	8	0	26	0	0	4	0	3	3	15	1	0
freight	101	.6901	14.453	51.6	24	16	19	13	11	12	3	3	27	3	0	1	3	42	2	1	0	0	0	0	4	5	6	7	0
freighter	12	.5927	1.4966	41.8	2	2	1	4	1	0	2	0	2	1	0	2	0	4	0	0	0	0	0	0	0	2	0	1	0
freighters	21	.5591	2.4944	44.0	10	0	3	2	0	3	3	0	3	0	1	0	2	10	0	0	0	0	0	0	0	2	3	0	0
Fremont	4	.3358	.3279	35.2	0	0	0	1	0	3	0	0	1	0	0	0	0	2	0	0	0	0	0	0	1	0	0	0	0
French	886	.8438	149.08	61.7	72	86	142	124	139	169	121	33	69	75	0	32	6	233	64	9	80	8	10	1	34	77	128	60	0
French-Canadian	3	.3390	.2450	33.9	0	0	0	1	0	0	2	0	1	0	0	0	0	0	0	0	0	0	0	0	0	0	1	1	0
French-English	2	.2440	.1132	30.5	0	0	0	1	0	1	0	0	0	0	0	1	0	0	0	0	0	0	0	0	0	0	0	1	0
French-speaking	2	.2139	.1057	30.2	0	0	1	0	1	0	0	0	0	0	0	0	0	1	1	0	0	0	0	0	0	0	0	0	0
Frenchman	43	.7369	6.4088	48.1	3	8	10	5	10	1	5	1	4	1	0	5	0	7	2	2	0	2	0	0	2	8	8	2	0
Frenchmen	44	.6340	5.7286	47.6	4	5	15	4	7	1	8	0	0	2	0	0	0	19	1	1	2	0	0	0	0	8	7	4	0
Frenchy	5	.0000	.0537	27.3	0	0	0	0	0	0	5	0	0	0	0	5	0	0	0	0	0	0	0	0	0	0	0	0	0
Frenchy's	2	.0000	.0215	23.3	0	0	0	0	0	0	2	0	0	0	0	2	0	0	0	0	0	0	0	0	0	0	0	0	0
frenetic	4	.0000	.0486	26.9	0	0	0	0	0	1	3	0	0	0	0	0	0	0	0	0	0	0	0	0	0	0	0	4	0
frenzied	3	.2236	.1570	32.0	0	0	1	0	0	1	1	0	0	1	0	2	0	0	0	0	0	0	0	0	0	0	0	0	0
frenziedly	2	.2440	.1132	30.5	0	0	0	0	1	1	0	0	0	0	0	1	0	0	0	0	0	0	0	0	0	0	0	1	0
frenzy	20	.6326	2.6422	44.2	0	0	2	2	9	3	4	0	6	0	1	2	0	0	0	0	1	0	0	0	4	0	1	5	0
Freon	6	.1708	.2605	34.2	0	0	1	0	5	0	0	0	0	0	0	0	0	0	0	0	0	0	0	0	0	0	1	5	0
frequencies	30	.4611	2.9070	44.6	2	0	3	7	2	15	0	1	0	0	0	0	0	0	0	10	11	0	0	4	0	0	4	1	0
frequency	113	.5135	12.142	50.8	7	0	3	14	19	53	12	5	1	2	1	0	8	1	0	50	17	0	0	20	0	0	11	2	0
frequent	47	.8781	8.2012	49.1	1	1	4	4	15	10	12	0	5	2	1	2	0	7	0	3	2	1	1	1	4	2	8	8	0
frequented	3	.3399	.2456	33.9	0	0	0	0	1	2	0	0	1	0	0	1	0	0	0	0	0	0	0	0	0	0	0	1	0
frequently	241	.8745	41.866	56.2	5	7	16	21	76	53	53	10	24	33	7	11	16	13	15	24	20	0	16	5	1	13	25	18	0
Frere	5	.0000	.0404	26.1	1	0	2	1	1	0	0	0	0	0	0	0	0	0	0	0	5	0	0	0	0	0	0	0	0
Fresca	2	.0000	.0243	23.9	0	0	0	0	0	2	0	0	0	0	0	0	0	0	0	0	0	0	0	0	0	0	0	2	0
frescoes	2	.1698	.1133	30.5	0	0	0	0	0	1	0	1	1	0	0	0	0	0	0	0	0	0	0	0	0	0	1	0	0
fresh	573	.8522	97.778	59.9	133	82	61	68	101	54	56	18	138	16	7	34	1	76	11	91	8	3	40	0	42	52	21	33	0
fresh-baked	2	.1948	.1250	31.0	0	1	0	0	0	0	0	1	1	0	0	0	0	0	0	0	0	0	0	0	0	1	0	0	0
fresh-cut	3	.2076	.1697	32.3	0	1	0	0	0	1	1	0	1	0	1	0	0	0	0	0	0	0	0	0	1	0	0	0	0
fresh-water	16	.5433	1.8204	42.6	2	2	2	2	7	1	0	0	0	0	0	0	1	2	0	5	0	0	0	0	1	2	5	0	0
freshened	7	.3999	.6007	37.8	0	0	1	3	2	1	0	0	0	1	0	0	0	0	0	0	0	0	0	0	4	1	0	1	0
fresher	9	.5427	.9996	40.0	0	0	3	0	2	1	3	0	0	1	0	0	0	1	0	0	0	1	2	0	2	1	1	0	0
freshest	3	.3662	.2412	33.8	0	0	0	1	1	0	1	0	0	0	0	0	0	0	1	1	0	0	0	0	0	0	0	1	0
freshly	24	.7500	3.6798	45.7	2	3	3	4	2	4	3	3	8	3	1	1	0	1	0	4	0	0	1	0	3	0	1	1	0
freshman	31	.5617	3.7269	45.7	1	1	1	2	7	9	10	0	10	2	0	1	0	0	1	0	0	0	0	0	0	1	6	10	0
freshmen	6	.3779	.5077	37.1	0	0	0	1	1	0	4	0	1	1	0	0	0	0	0	0	0	0	0	0	1	0	3	0	0
freshness	10	.5530	1.1548	40.6	0	0	1	1	2	5	1	0	2	1	0	2	0	0	0	0	1	1	2	0	0	0	0	1	0
freshwater	9	.5001	.9409	39.7	3	0	0	1	4	1	0	0	0	1	1	0	0	0	0	2	0	0	0	0	0	2	3	0	0
Fresno	6	.3369	.4978	37.0	0	2	0	0	3	1	0	0	2	0	0	2	0	2	0	0	0	0	0	0	0	0	0	0	0
fret	16	.4543	1.5334	41.9	4	5	1	3	2	0	0	1	1	4	0	0	0	0	0	0	7	0	0	0	1	0	1	2	0
fretful	3	.2295	.1558	31.9	0	0	2	0	1	0	0	0	0	0	0	0	0	0	0	0	0	0	1	0	2	0	0	0	0
fretfully	3	.2279	.2143	33.3	2	0	1	0	0	0	0	0	2	0	0	0	0	0	0	0	0	0	0	0	0	0	0	1	0
frets	3	.3842	.2448	33.9	1	1	1	0	0	0	0	0	0	1	0	1	0	0	0	0	1	0	0	0	0	0	0	0	0
fretted	6	.3598	.5339	37.3	2	0	1	0	2	1	0	0	3	0	0	1	0	0	0	0	0	0	0	0	2	0	0	0	0
fretting	2	.1814	.1187	30.7	0	0	0	0	0	1	1	0	1	0	0	0	0	0	0	0	0	0	0	0	0	0	0	1	0
Freud	3	.3452	.2543	34.1	0	0	0	1	0	0	2	0	1	0	0	0	0	0	0	1	0	0	0	0	0	0	0	1	0
Freudian	3	.2159	.1532	31.9	0	0	0	0	0	2	1	0	0	0	0	0	0	0	0	0	0	0	0	0	0	0	2	1	0
Frey	3	.3465	.2515	34.0	2	0	1	0	0	0	0	0	1	0	0	0	0	0	0	0	0	0	0	0	0	1	0	1	0
Freylinck	2	.0000	.0914	29.6	0	0	0	0	0	2	0	0	2	0	0	0	0	0	0	0	0	0	0	0	0	0	0	0	0
Fri	2	.2427	.1159	30.6	1	0	0	1	0	0	0	0	0	0	0	0	1	0	0	0	0	0	0	0	0	0	0	1	0
friar	3	.3773	.2485	34.0	0	0	0	1	1	0	1	0	0	0	0	1	0	1	0	0	0	0	0	0	1	0	0	0	0
Friar	15	.2833	.9457	39.8	0	1	0	0	0	0	14	0	0	0	0	10	0	0	0	0	4	0	0	0	0	1	0	0	0

7J Frederica
4A Fredrick
9D Free-Soilers
7Q free-born
9R free-floating
7R free-flying
3Q free-lance
7H free-living
3A free-milling
9H free-piston
7D free-roaming
9R free-spoken
7Q free-swimming
9D free-verse
9R free-wheeling
3N Freebody'll
7R freebooter
XR Freeborn
8F freedmen
8J freeflowing
8F freeholder
8F freeholders
7P freeholds
5R freelance
8F Freeman
8F Freeman's
9D Freemason
5Q Freemasons
5F Freeport
XR Freestone
7A freewheeled
8R freewheeling
8Q FreigatPullada
9B Freiberg
5Q freight-train
5A freight-yard
6R freighted
3P FREIGHTERS
3P freighting
8F freights
8J Freischuetz
8F Fremont's
5N french
6A French-Cajun
5P French-Dutch
5P French-colonial
7A French-fried
7R French-made
7N Frenchers
6P Frenchies
5F Frenchmen's
6A Freneau's
8Q Freons
8J Frequency
7G fresche
8K fresco
7R Fresco
3N Fresh
5A fresh-fallen
5P fresh-firecoal
5A fresh-killed
4H fresh-looking
4A fresh-picked
7N fresh-turned
7H freshen
7D freshet
7D freshets
9B fretwork
6A Freuchen
4K Freund
9F fria
XR Fria

Word Type	F	D	U	SFI	3 Gr 3	4 Gr 4	5 Gr 5	6 Gr 6	7 Gr 7	8 Gr 8	9 Gr 9	X UnGr	A Read	B Eng & Gr	C Comp	D Lit	E Math	F Soc Stud	G Spell	H Sci	J Music	K Art	L Home Ec	M Shop	N Lib F	P Lib NF	Q Lib Ref	R Mag	S Rel
friars	9	.4181	.8282	39.2	1	0	1	1	3	3	0	0	0	0	0	1	0	6	0	0	0	0	0	0	0	1	1	0	0
friction	91	.5036	9.7242	49.9	5	24	7	16	14	15	6	4	3	1	0	3	0	1	0	51	0	0	1	13	0	3	11	4	0
frictional	3	.3762	.2496	34.0	1	0	0	1	1	0	0	0	0	0	0	0	0	0	0	1	0	0	0	0	0	1	1	0	0
Friday	139	.7883	22.219	53.5	32	25	9	18	22	19	12	2	47	13	5	6	16	7	4	0	6	0	0	0	20	4	0	11	0
Fridays	3	.3431	.2528	34.0	0	1	0	0	1	1	0	0	1	0	0	0	0	1	0	0	0	0	0	0	1	0	0	0	0
Frideric	2	.0000	.0162	22.1	0	0	0	0	1	1	0	0	0	0	0	0	0	0	0	0	2	0	0	0	0	0	0	0	0
fried	61	.7145	8.8957	49.5	9	7	6	5	12	5	15	2	12	8	0	7	1	2	0	1	0	0	1	0	8	9	0	12	0
Fried	2	.0000	.0243	23.9	0	0	0	0	0	0	2	0	0	0	0	0	0	0	0	0	0	0	0	0	0	0	0	2	0
Friedrich	14	.5778	1.6937	42.3	1	1	3	1	4	2	2	0	2	0	0	0	1	0	1	3	1	0	0	0	0	0	5	1	0
friend	923	.8158	152.34	61.8	209	172	100	130	154	81	64	13	377	111	22	63	9	30	29	34	22	2	4	1	77	75	8	54	5
Friend	21	.6006	2.6991	44.3	3	6	5	2	0	4	1	0	9	4	0	0	0	0	0	0	1	0	0	0	3	3	1	0	0
friend's	29	.3885	2.6380	44.2	6	3	5	6	4	3	2	0	9	3	1	1	1	2	1	6	0	0	0	0	0	3	0	1	1
friendless	2	.1674	.0805	29.1	0	0	0	0	0	1	1	0	0	0	0	0	0	0	0	0	0	0	1	0	0	1	0	0	0
friendliest	3	.2261	.2131	33.3	1	1	0	0	0	1	0	0	2	0	0	0	0	0	0	0	0	0	0	0	1	0	0	0	0
friendliness	12	.6781	1.6763	42.2	2	2	3	1	1	1	2	0	3	0	0	1	0	1	1	0	0	0	1	0	1	2	2	0	0
friendly	317	.8680	55.004	57.4	62	75	40	31	61	33	10	5	92	51	8	16	0	37	10	14	3	1	6	0	24	32	5	17	1
Friendly	5	.3489	.3894	35.9	2	0	0	1	1	1	0	0	0	2	0	0	2	0	0	1	0	0	0	0	0	0	0	0	0
friends	1061	.9010	190.35	62.8	282	193	104	91	165	114	81	31	354	84	18	72	21	91	12	66	28	6	42	2	36	103	14	112	0
Friends	9	.6085	1.1535	40.6	1	3	3	1	0	1	0	0	2	1	0	0	0	3	0	0	0	0	0	0	1	1	1	0	0
friends'	9	.5378	1.0466	40.2	3	0	3	1	1	0	1	0	3	1	0	0	0	1	0	1	2	0	1	0	0	0	0	0	0
friendship	58	.5943	7.2137	48.6	7	10	5	3	13	13	4	3	9	5	0	5	1	16	1	1	2	0	2	0	2	4	2	7	1
Friendship	5	.2599	.3221	35.1	0	0	0	0	1	4	0	0	1	3	0	0	0	0	0	0	0	0	0	0	1	0	0	0	0
friendships	13	.2881	.7999	39.0	0	0	1	2	4	6	0	0	0	2	0	1	0	0	0	0	1	0	7	0	0	1	0	1	0
fries	2	.1892	.0858	29.3	0	0	0	1	0	0	1	0	0	1	0	0	0	0	0	0	0	0	1	0	0	0	0	0	0
Friesland	2	.2337	.1157	30.6	0	1	1	0	0	0	0	0	0	0	0	0	0	1	0	0	0	0	0	0	1	0	0	0	0
frigate	6	.3793	.5091	37.1	1	0	1	0	2	2	0	0	1	0	0	0	0	0	0	0	1	0	0	0	0	1	3	0	0
Frigga	4	.2158	.2006	33.0	0	1	3	0	0	0	0	0	0	0	0	0	0	0	1	0	0	0	0	0	0	0	3	0	0
fright	62	.7750	9.8026	49.9	13	14	7	16	6	3	2	1	26	2	1	6	0	1	2	0	2	0	0	0	9	4	1	8	0
frighten	56	.7709	8.8494	49.5	9	20	11	7	4	1	2	2	27	1	0	2	0	1	2	4	2	0	1	0	9	3	0	4	0
frightened	262	.7630	41.162	56.1	52	69	31	33	40	27	8	2	143	13	7	21	0	5	1	4	7	0	0	0	23	22	3	13	0
frightening	66	.7778	10.460	50.2	11	11	9	6	14	8	6	1	26	3	1	10	0	3	0	3	0	0	3	0	4	6	1	6	0
frightens	6	.4730	.6108	37.9	0	2	1	1	0	1	0	1	1	1	1	1	0	1	0	0	0	0	0	0	1	0	0	0	0
frightful	20	.4943	2.3054	43.6	3	6	4	4	1	2	0	0	14	0	0	0	0	1	0	0	0	0	0	0	3	0	1	1	0
frightfully	6	.3548	.5245	37.2	0	0	1	3	1	1	0	0	3	0	1	1	0	0	0	0	0	0	0	0	0	1	0	0	0
frigid	7	.5353	.8073	39.1	1	0	1	1	2	0	2	0	2	1	0	0	0	0	0	0	0	0	0	0	1	1	0	2	0
frill	2	.2407	.1138	30.6	1	1	0	0	1	0	0	0	0	1	0	1	0	0	0	0	0	0	0	0	0	1	0	0	0
frilled	2	.2407	.1138	30.6	0	0	0	0	1	0	0	1	0	0	0	1	0	0	0	0	0	0	0	0	0	1	0	0	0
frills	2	.1717	.1142	30.6	1	0	0	0	1	0	0	0	1	0	0	1	0	0	0	0	0	0	0	0	0	0	0	0	0
frilly	3	.2028	.1988	33.0	3	0	0	0	0	0	0	0	2	0	0	0	0	0	0	0	1	0	0	0	0	0	0	0	0
Friml	2	.0000	.0162	22.1	0	0	0	0	2	0	0	0	0	0	0	0	0	0	0	0	2	0	0	0	0	0	0	0	0
fringe	19	.5098	2.0906	43.2	4	2	1	2	5	0	3	2	4	1	0	2	0	0	0	3	0	0	0	0	0	0	1	8	0
fringed	22	.6425	2.8975	44.6	6	3	5	2	3	2	1	0	2	2	0	1	0	2	0	1	2	2	0	0	3	6	1	0	0
fringes	15	.6507	2.0108	43.0	2	1	0	2	3	2	1	4	1	0	0	1	0	1	0	6	0	0	0	0	1	1	2	2	0
Frisch	2	.0000	.0394	26.0	0	0	0	0	2	0	0	0	0	0	0	0	0	0	0	2	0	0	0	0	0	0	0	0	0
Frisco	8	.3406	.6067	37.8	0	0	0	0	0	3	5	0	0	0	0	0	1	0	0	0	0	0	0	0	3	4	0	0	0
Frisette	2	.0000	.0914	29.6	2	0	0	0	0	0	0	0	2	0	0	0	0	0	0	0	0	0	0	0	0	0	0	0	0
frisked	3	.2261	.2131	33.3	1	1	0	1	0	0	0	0	2	0	0	0	0	0	0	0	0	0	0	0	1	0	0	0	0
Friskies	3	.0000	.0449	26.5	0	0	3	0	0	0	0	0	0	0	0	0	3	0	0	0	0	0	0	0	0	0	0	0	0
frisking	5	.2718	.3338	35.2	0	2	1	0	1	1	0	0	1	0	0	1	0	0	0	0	0	0	0	0	3	0	0	0	0
frisky	13	.4918	1.4226	41.5	7	3	1	1	0	1	0	0	6	1	2	0	0	0	0	1	2	1	0	0	0	0	0	0	0
Fritz	13	.3784	1.2687	41.0	1	7	1	1	3	0	0	0	10	0	0	0	0	0	0	0	1	0	0	0	0	0	2	0	0
Fritzl	6	.0000	.2741	34.4	5	1	0	0	0	0	0	0	6	0	0	0	0	0	0	0	0	0	0	0	0	0	0	0	0
frivolity	2	.1814	.1187	30.7	0	0	0	1	1	0	0	0	1	0	0	0	0	0	0	0	0	0	0	0	0	0	0	1	0
frivolous	9	.5285	.9791	39.9	0	0	1	0	3	4	1	0	0	3	0	0	0	1	0	0	2	1	0	0	1	0	0	1	0
fro	29	.7693	4.5357	46.6	2	3	0	11	5	3	5	0	9	2	1	4	1	0	0	3	2	0	0	0	3	3	1	0	0
frock	2	.1717	.1142	30.6	0	0	0	0	1	0	1	0	1	0	0	1	0	0	0	0	0	0	0	0	0	0	0	0	0
frocks	3	.3863	.2513	34.0	1	0	0	0	0	1	0	1	0	0	0	0	0	0	0	0	0	0	0	0	1	1	0	1	0
frog	171	.7484	26.143	54.2	58	36	5	32	25	6	9	0	41	8	1	7	10	0	1	75	0	0	2	6	3	11	5	1	0
Frog	5	.4252	.4674	36.7	1	1	1	0	0	2	0	0	1	1	0	2	0	0	0	0	1	0	0	0	0	0	0	0	0
frog's	5	.2187	.2850	34.5	0	2	1	0	0	0	1	1	0	1	0	0	0	0	0	4	0	0	0	0	0	0	0	0	0
Froggie	2	.0000	.0914	29.6	0	0	0	0	2	0	0	0	2	0	0	0	0	0	0	0	0	0	0	0	0	0	0	0	0
frogman	19	.0000	.8680	39.4	0	19	0	0	0	0	0	0	19	0	0	0	0	0	0	0	0	0	0	0	0	0	0	0	0
frogman's	3	.0000	.1370	31.4	0	3	0	0	0	0	0	0	3	0	0	0	0	0	0	0	0	0	0	0	0	0	0	0	0
frogmen	43	.0000	1.9644	42.9	0	42	0	0	1	0	0	0	43	0	0	0	0	0	0	0	0	0	0	0	0	0	0	0	0
frogs	140	.6911	20.004	53.0	45	11	8	52	21	1	2	0	31	1	1	5	2	0	0	66	2	0	2	0	1	13	13	3	0
frogs'	4	.3362	.3304	35.2	0	0	0	3	1	0	0	0	1	0	0	0	0	0	0	2	0	0	0	0	0	1	0	0	0
Frogtown	2	.0000	.0914	29.6	0	2	0	0	0	0	0	0	2	0	0	0	0	0	0	0	0	0	0	0	0	0	0	0	0
Frokowski	4	.0000	.0486	26.9	0	0	0	0	4	0	0	0	0	0	0	0	0	0	0	0	0	0	0	0	0	0	0	4	0
frolic	7	.4152	.6549	38.2	0	0	1	0	1	4	1	0	2	0	0	3	0	0	0	0	1	0	0	0	1	0	0	0	0
frolicked	4	.3771	.3293	35.2	1	1	0	1	1	0	0	0	0	0	0	0	0	0	0	0	0	0	0	0	1	2	0	1	0
frolicking	3	.2197	.2090	33.2	0	0	1	1	0	1	0	0	2	0	0	0	0	0	0	0	0	0	0	0	0	0	1	0	0
frolics	5	.4086	.4291	36.3	0	0	0	1	1	3	0	0	0	2	1	0	0	0	0	0	1	0	0	0	0	1	0	0	0
from	22799	.9940	4456.2	76.5	3394	3440	3127	3198	4332	2615	2076	617	4721	1027	230	1027	1239	3142	1026	3030	947	204	356	266	1012	1573	1497	1482	20
From	9	.3979	.7864	39.0	1	1	3	3	1	0	0	0	1	0	0	0	0	0	0	1	4	0	0	0	0	2	1	0	0
FROM	2	.0000	.0215	23.3	1	0	0	0	0	1	0	0	0	0	0	2	0	0	0	0	0	0	0	0	0	0	0	0	0
fronds	4	.3384	.3042	34.8	1	0	0	2	0	0	1	0	0	0	0	0	0	0	0	1	0	0	0	0	2	1	0	0	0
front	1438	.9040	258.87	64.1	302	304	144	147	253	135	132	21	546	42	15	109	14	48	31	121	22	11	39	54	133	131	35	87	0
Front	8	.5370	.8810	39.4	0	2	1	0	1	2	2	0	0	1	0	0	0	0	1	0	0	0	1	0	0	0	2	3	0
front-page	3	.2309	.1631	32.1	2	0	0	0	0	0	1	0	0	0	0	1	0	0	0	0	0	0	0	0	0	0	0	2	0
front-room	2	.0000	.0914	29.6	0	2	0	0	0	0	0	0	2	0	0	0	0	0	0	0	0	0	0	0	0	0	0	0	0
front-wheel	2	.0000	.0243	23.9	0	0	0	0	2	0	0	0	0	0	0	0	0	0	0	0	0	0	0	0	0	0	0	2	0
frontal	6	.3123	.4169	36.2	0	0	0	0	2	1	3	0	0	0	0	0	0	1	0	1	0	0	0	2	0	1	0	1	0
frontier	117	.7117	17.018	52.3	1	12	36	14	26	15	10	3	19	3	0	6	0	31	0	3	6	0	0	0	1	14	20	14	0
Frontier	5	.4586	.5229	37.2	0	1	2	0	2	0	0	0	2	0	0	0	0	1	0	0	1	0	0	0	0	1	0	0	0
frontiers	21	.6999	2.9864	44.8	2	0	5	1	5	6	1	1	1	0	1	1	0	7	0	0	0	0	1	0	2	5	2	1	0
frontiersman	2	.0000	.0219	23.4	0	0	1	0	1	0	0	0	0	2	0	0	0	0	0	0	0	0	0	0	0	0	0	0	0
frontiersmen	9	.3554	.7277	38.6	0	3	4	0	0	2	0	0	0	0	0	0	0	6	1	0	0	0	0	0	0	2	0	0	0
fronting	3	.3776	.2489	34.0	0	0	0	0	2	1	0	0	0	0	0	1	0	1	0	0	0	0	0	0	0	0	0	1	0
fronts	17	.6358	2.2630	43.5	1	1	0	4	2	6	3	0	4	0	0	3	0	4	0	3	0	0	1	0	0	1	0	1	0
frontways	2	.0000	.0219	23.4	0	1	0	0	0	0	1	0	0	2	0	0	0	0	0	0	0	0	0	0	0	0	0	0	0
frost	83	.8148	13.601	51.3	10	8	9	16	18	10	6	6	14	2	1	8	0	5	0	27	2	0	1	0	6	6	3	8	0
Frost	59	.4531	6.0234	47.8	1	23	16	14	2	1	2	0	21	2	0	2	2	0	0	0	0	0	0	0	27	0	1	4	0
frost-free	5	.2205	.2855	34.6	0	0	1	0	1	2	1	0	0	0	0	0	0	4	0	0	0	0	0	0	0	0	1	0	0
frostbitten	6	.4033	.5583	37.5	0	0	1	0	3	2	0	0	2	1	1	0	0	0	0	1	0	0	0	0	0	1	0	0	0

9J Friar's
XQ fricatives
8Q Frick
7R frictionless
3B Friday's
5P Fridtjof
7R FRIED
4A Friedman
4A Friedricks
7G friend-like
5A Friend's
3A friendlier
8A friendlylike
7K Frienze
8Q Frietchie
8Q Frietchie's
7K frieze
7F friezes
6N frigate's
7R Frigatebirds
9D frighted
6B frighteningly
8B frigidaire
8F frijoles
XH fringe-shift
6A fringing
8F Frisbie
3A Frisette's
5P Frisian
7A frisk
7J Friska
7D frisks
7N Frisky
8J frittering
9K frivolities
5G frivolously
XR frizz
3P frizzle
7G Frobel
6B frobish
9D frock-coat
7N frockcoat
4P Frogeye
3J froggie
7Q froglets
7J frolicsome
9H frond
8L front-bodice
7H front-line
9D front-parlor
8A front-porch
4P front-row
XR front-runner
7R front-spring
3P front-view
3R front-yard
8F frontier-style
7D frontline
6A frontward
7R frontwheel
7A froon
8A frost-biters
5P frost-stunted
7B Frost's

Word Type	F	D	U	SFI	3 Gr 3	4 Gr 4	5 Gr 5	6 Gr 6	7 Gr 7	8 Gr 8	9 Gr 9	X UnGr	A Read	B Eng & Gr	C Comp	D Lit	E Math	F Soc Stud	G Spell	H Sci	J Music	K Art	L Home Ec	M Shop	N Lib F	P Lib NF	Q Lib Ref	R Mag	S Rel
frosted	15	.5589	1.7841	42.5	1	1	0	4	3	1	3	2	4	3	0	0	0	0	0	3	0	0	1	2	0	1	0	1	0
frosting	11	.6736	1.5256	41.8	1	3	1	2	1	0	2	1	3	1	1	1	0	0	0	0	0	0	1	0	1	1	1	1	0
Frostproof	8	.0000	.1556	31.9	8	0	0	0	0	0	0	0	0	0	0	0	0	8	0	0	0	0	0	0	0	0	0	0	0
frosts	7	.3655	.5841	37.7	0	0	1	2	3	0	1	0	0	0	0	0	0	2	0	4	0	0	0	0	0	0	1	0	0
Frosts	2	.0000	.0234	23.7	0	1	1	0	0	0	0	0	0	0	0	0	0	0	0	0	0	0	0	0	2	0	0	0	0
frosty	38	.7608	5.8909	47.7	9	10	3	5	4	3	4	0	13	5	1	5	0	1	0	0	2	0	0	0	4	2	1	4	0
froth	4	.3071	.2967	34.7	0	1	0	1	1	1	0	0	1	0	0	1	0	0	0	0	0	0	0	0	2	0	0	0	0
frothy	4	.3723	.3645	35.6	0	0	0	1	2	0	1	0	2	1	0	0	0	0	0	0	0	0	0	0	0	0	0	1	0
frown	41	.6878	5.8167	47.6	8	7	6	2	8	2	8	0	12	7	0	6	0	0	0	0	1	0	0	0	6	3	2	4	0
frowned	45	.7349	6.8125	48.3	8	17	3	3	11	3	0	0	18	1	1	2	0	3	0	1	0	0	0	0	5	9	1	4	0
frowning	21	.5885	2.7009	44.3	2	6	0	3	8	0	2	0	12	0	0	2	0	0	0	0	0	0	0	0	1	4	1	1	0
frowns	2	.2407	.1138	30.6	1	0	0	0	0	0	1	0	0	0	0	1	0	0	0	0	0	0	0	0	0	1	0	0	0
froze	23	.5765	2.7956	44.5	2	8	3	4	3	2	1	0	5	0	0	0	0	0	0	0	2	0	0	0	6	6	1	3	0
frozen	209	.8106	34.210	55.3	44	35	27	23	32	25	21	2	64	10	4	11	0	38	7	14	2	0	16	0	12	16	6	9	0
Frozen	5	.3826	.4759	36.8	1	3	0	0	0	1	0	0	3	0	0	0	0	0	0	0	0	0	0	0	0	1	1	0	0
frozen-food	2	.0000	.0389	25.9	2	0	0	0	0	0	0	0	0	0	0	0	0	2	0	0	0	0	0	0	0	0	0	0	0
fructose	3	.0000	.0591	27.7	0	0	0	0	3	0	0	0	0	0	0	0	0	0	0	3	0	0	0	0	0	0	0	0	0
frugal	4	.1497	.2092	33.2	0	0	0	2	1	1	0	0	2	0	0	0	0	0	2	0	0	0	0	0	0	0	0	0	0
frugality	3	.0000	.0314	25.0	0	0	0	0	0	0	3	0	0	0	0	0	0	0	0	0	0	0	0	0	0	0	3	0	0
fruit	456	.7109	66.232	58.2	98	59	43	73	79	20	72	12	84	9	4	10	18	74	9	72	5	1	72	1	14	34	26	23	0
Fruit	3	.2936	.1967	32.9	0	0	0	0	3	0	0	0	0	0	0	1	0	1	0	0	0	0	1	0	0	0	0	0	0
fruit-flavored	3	.0000	.0097	19.8	0	0	0	0	1	0	2	0	0	0	0	0	0	0	0	0	0	0	3	0	0	0	0	0	0
fruit-growing	2	.2408	.1204	30.8	1	0	0	0	0	1	0	0	0	0	0	0	0	1	0	0	0	0	0	0	0	1	0	0	0
fruitades	3	.0000	.0097	19.8	0	0	0	0	0	0	3	0	0	0	0	0	0	0	0	0	0	0	3	0	0	0	0	0	0
fruited	2	.2433	.1158	30.6	0	0	1	0	0	0	0	1	0	0	0	0	0	0	0	0	0	0	0	0	0	1	0	1	0
fruitful	13	.5744	1.5567	41.9	1	0	1	3	4	1	1	2	1	1	0	0	0	2	0	1	0	0	0	0	0	1	3	4	0
fruiting	5	.3177	.3576	35.5	0	0	0	0	1	0	0	4	0	0	0	0	0	0	0	1	0	0	0	0	0	0	1	3	0
Fruitlands	3	.0000	.0434	26.4	0	0	0	3	0	0	0	0	0	0	0	0	0	0	0	0	0	0	0	0	0	3	0	0	0
fruitless	7	.4378	.6875	38.4	0	1	0	2	2	0	2	0	2	0	0	2	0	0	0	0	0	0	0	0	0	1	0	2	0
fruits	240	.6672	32.821	55.2	49	13	18	48	58	22	21	11	13	3	0	0	0	66	5	75	3	0	30	0	3	8	22	11	1
Fruits	2	.2278	.1128	30.5	2	0	0	0	0	0	0	0	0	0	0	0	0	0	0	1	0	0	0	0	0	0	1	0	0
frumiously	2	.0000	.0219	23.4	0	0	0	2	0	0	0	0	0	2	0	0	0	0	0	0	0	0	0	0	0	0	0	0	0
Frumkin	3	.0000	.0365	25.6	0	0	0	0	0	3	0	0	0	0	0	0	0	0	0	0	0	0	0	0	0	0	0	3	0
frustrate	2	.2106	.0917	29.6	0	0	0	0	0	2	0	0	0	0	0	0	0	0	1	0	0	0	1	0	0	0	0	0	0
frustrated	15	.5717	1.7757	42.5	1	0	2	0	8	2	2	0	1	0	1	0	0	0	0	1	0	0	0	0	1	3	5	3	0
frustrating	2	.0000	.0243	23.9	0	0	0	0	1	0	1	0	0	0	0	0	0	0	0	0	0	0	0	0	0	0	0	2	0
frustration	10	.4665	1.0069	40.0	0	0	1	1	4	2	0	2	1	0	0	2	0	2	0	0	0	0	0	0	0	1	0	4	0
frustrations	2	.2446	.1142	30.6	0	0	0	0	1	0	0	1	0	0	0	0	0	0	0	0	0	0	0	0	1	0	0	1	0
fry	38	.7147	5.6180	47.5	15	6	6	2	6	2	0	1	16	1	0	0	0	0	5	1	0	0	1	0	3	6	2	3	0
frying	37	.6565	5.0532	47.0	8	5	1	4	7	4	8	0	13	2	1	3	0	1	2	2	4	0	6	0	2	1	0	0	0
ft	140	.3106	9.9094	50.0	3	31	15	3	20	38	27	3	0	0	0	0	116	0	1	0	0	0	0	2	0	0	16	5	0
FTA	2	.0000	.0299	24.8	0	0	0	2	0	0	0	0	0	0	0	0	2	0	0	0	0	0	0	0	0	0	0	0	0
FTC	5	.2364	.2883	34.6	3	0	0	2	0	0	0	0	0	0	0	0	2	0	0	0	0	0	0	0	0	3	0	0	0
Fu	3	.1937	.1495	31.7	0	0	0	1	0	0	2	0	0	0	0	0	0	1	0	0	0	0	0	0	0	0	0	2	0
Fuchs	6	.2355	.4634	36.7	0	6	0	0	0	0	0	0	5	0	0	0	0	0	0	0	0	0	0	0	0	1	0	0	0
Fuddy	3	.0000	.1370	31.4	3	0	0	0	0	0	0	0	3	0	0	0	0	0	0	0	0	0	0	0	0	0	0	0	0
fudge	22	.4498	2.3387	43.7	3	5	1	12	1	0	0	0	13	3	0	0	5	0	0	0	0	0	0	0	0	1	0	0	0
Fuego	4	.1505	.1615	32.1	3	0	0	0	0	1	0	0	0	0	0	0	0	1	0	0	0	0	0	0	0	0	3	0	0
Fuehrer	6	.1361	.2398	33.8	0	0	0	0	5	0	1	0	0	0	0	0	0	1	0	0	0	0	0	0	0	5	0	0	0
fuel	262	.7134	38.144	55.8	26	36	46	34	56	33	23	8	31	1	0	3	5	35	5	93	1	0	3	19	3	13	30	20	0
fuel-and-water	3	.0000	.0365	25.6	0	0	0	3	0	0	0	0	0	0	0	0	0	0	0	0	0	0	0	0	0	0	0	3	0
fuels	41	.5998	5.1372	47.1	7	4	7	8	4	8	3	0	2	0	0	0	0	8	0	19	1	0	0	1	0	6	4	0	0
fugitive	8	.5097	.8831	39.5	0	0	0	1	4	2	1	0	2	0	1	0	0	2	0	0	0	0	0	0	1	0	1	1	0
Fugitive	6	.2920	.4393	36.4	0	0	0	0	2	4	0	0	1	0	0	1	0	4	0	0	0	0	0	0	0	0	0	0	0
fugitives	6	.3756	.4936	36.9	0	0	0	0	4	2	0	0	0	0	0	2	0	2	0	0	0	0	0	0	0	0	2	0	0
fugue	18	.0000	.1455	31.6	0	0	5	2	6	5	0	0	0	0	0	0	0	0	0	0	18	0	0	0	0	0	0	0	0
Fugue	7	.0000	.0566	27.5	0	0	1	3	2	1	0	0	0	0	0	0	0	0	0	0	7	0	0	0	0	0	0	0	0
fugues	2	.2303	.1079	30.3	0	0	0	0	1	1	0	0	0	0	0	0	0	0	0	0	1	0	0	0	0	1	0	0	0
Fugues	2	.0000	.0162	22.1	0	0	0	0	0	2	0	0	0	0	0	0	0	0	0	0	2	0	0	0	0	0	0	0	0
Fuji	2	.2440	.1132	30.5	0	0	0	0	2	0	0	0	0	0	0	1	0	0	0	0	0	0	0	0	0	0	0	1	0
Fujiyama	2	.2285	.1129	30.5	0	0	0	1	1	0	0	0	0	0	0	0	0	1	0	0	0	0	0	0	0	0	1	0	0
ful	27	.1232	.8937	39.5	0	4	7	9	7	0	0	0	1	2	0	0	0	0	23	1	0	0	0	0	0	0	0	0	0
Fulani	5	.2242	.2842	34.5	0	2	3	0	0	0	0	0	0	0	0	0	0	2	0	0	0	0	0	0	0	3	0	0	0
fulcrum	38	.4366	3.6273	45.6	2	1	0	17	7	5	0	6	0	0	0	0	10	0	0	20	0	0	0	0	0	6	2	0	0
fulfill	20	.7345	2.9566	44.7	1	1	2	1	7	5	3	0	1	2	0	1	0	1	2	1	1	1	0	0	0	3	5	2	0
fulfilled	12	.6202	1.5483	41.9	1	0	2	4	3	0	1	1	2	0	0	1	0	0	0	1	0	0	0	0	2	4	1	1	0
fulfilling	4	.3444	.3221	35.1	0	0	1	0	1	1	1	0	1	0	0	0	1	0	0	0	0	0	1	0	0	1	0	0	0
fulfillment	6	.3638	.4717	36.7	0	0	1	1	1	2	1	0	0	0	0	0	0	1	0	0	0	1	0	0	0	1	3	0	0
fulfills	3	.3109	.2027	33.1	0	0	0	0	1	1	1	0	0	0	0	0	0	0	0	0	0	0	1	0	0	1	1	0	0
Fulke	5	.0000	.2284	33.6	0	0	0	5	0	0	0	0	5	0	0	0	0	0	0	0	0	0	1	0	0	1	0	0	0
full	1144	.9762	220.07	63.4	192	199	142	136	210	118	103	44	335	32	19	103	36	66	23	112	40	13	16	16	95	109	46	82	1
full-blooded	8	.4619	.7838	38.9	0	0	1	2	4	1	0	0	0	0	0	2	0	2	0	0	0	0	0	0	0	0	1	3	0
full-blown	3	.3781	.2493	34.0	0	0	0	1	0	2	0	0	0	1	0	0	0	1	0	0	0	0	0	0	0	0	0	1	0
full-employment	2	.0000	.0243	23.9	0	0	0	0	0	0	2	0	0	0	0	0	0	0	0	0	0	0	0	0	0	0	0	2	0
full-fledged	3	.1169	.1277	31.1	0	0	0	1	1	0	1	0	1	0	0	0	0	0	0	0	0	0	0	0	0	0	2	0	0
full-grown	50	.6833	7.1039	48.5	12	8	10	11	4	2	1	2	14	1	0	1	7	0	0	17	1	0	0	0	1	6	1	1	0
full-length	9	.6012	1.1264	40.5	1	0	0	0	5	1	2	0	2	1	0	2	0	0	0	0	1	0	0	1	1	0	0	1	0
full-pressure	2	.0000	.0290	24.6	2	0	0	0	0	0	0	0	0	0	0	0	0	0	0	0	0	0	0	0	0	2	0	0	0
full-rigged	2	.2303	.1079	30.3	1	0	1	0	0	0	0	0	0	0	0	0	0	0	0	0	1	0	0	0	0	1	0	0	0
full-scale	7	.1289	.2539	34.0	0	1	0	1	4	1	0	0	0	0	0	0	1	0	0	0	0	0	0	0	0	0	0	6	0
full-size	8	.0847	.1692	32.3	0	0	0	0	4	0	4	0	0	0	0	0	0	0	0	0	0	0	0	6	0	0	0	2	0
full-sized	7	.3717	.6748	38.3	3	0	0	2	2	0	0	0	5	0	0	0	0	0	0	1	0	0	0	0	0	0	0	1	0
full-time	13	.5327	1.4521	41.6	0	0	2	1	4	2	3	1	1	1	0	1	0	1	0	1	0	0	0	0	0	0	5	3	0
fullback	4	.3717	.3640	35.6	0	0	0	1	1	0	2	0	2	0	0	1	0	0	0	0	0	0	0	0	0	0	0	1	0
fuller	6	.4781	.5998	37.8	0	1	0	2	1	1	1	0	0	0	0	1	0	1	0	1	2	0	1	0	0	0	0	0	0
Fuller	7	.2022	.3746	35.7	0	0	1	0	5	1	0	0	1	0	0	0	0	0	0	0	0	0	0	0	0	1	0	5	0
Fullerton	2	.2442	.1134	30.5	1	0	0	0	0	0	0	1	0	1	0	0	0	0	0	0	0	0	0	0	0	0	0	1	0
fullest	8	.5138	.8407	39.2	1	0	0	0	4	3	0	0	0	0	0	2	0	1	0	0	1	1	2	0	0	0	1	0	0
fullness	10	.1973	.4676	36.7	0	0	1	1	0	6	2	0	1	0	0	1	0	0	0	0	0	0	6	0	1	0	0	1	0
fulltime	3	.3465	.2515	34.0	0	0	0	0	1	1	0	1	1	0	0	0	0	0	0	0	0	0	0	0	0	1	0	1	0
fully	141	.8798	24.683	53.9	3	6	15	20	48	17	26	6	21	5	2	11	3	6	1	25	5	0	3	2	3	13	21	20	0
Fulton	14	.4278	1.4149	41.5	1	6	5	1	1	0	0	0	6	0	0	1	0	6	0	0	0	0	0	0	0	1	0	0	0

9N frosted-glass
4P Frosting
7R frosty-cold
9B frothing
3A frow
7A Frow
4P frowningly
7N frozen-hearted
7R frozen-rubber
5E FRS
3P FRUIT
7Q fruit-eating
7H fruit-grower
7H fruit-growers
5A fruit-picking
7F fruit-raising
9L fruitade
5A fruitcake
5Q fruitflies
7Q fruitfull
8C fruitfulness
8D fruitlessly
6A fruity
5K frumious
3B frums
9M frustum
7R fryed
5A fryer
7R fryers
7N frying-pan
8L frypan
6E FS
9H FSH
3R Ft
7E ft-lb
4E ft-long**
8E ft/sec
3A fu
6R fuchsia
7N fuchsias
3P fuddled
4P fudgy
7F fuel-driven
7Q fuel-eating
7R fueled
3A fueling
7A Fuerteventura
5A Fuff
9E fugit
6J fuguing
5P Fukienese
5F Fulfillment
7R Fulgencio
6A Fulke's
7B Full
7R full-blade
6R full-bloods
9L full-bodied
9Q full-color
4P full-colored
7R full-course
8A full-flavored
9H full-moon
XR full-page
6R full-powered
7N full-stretch
9M full-thread
9A full-throttle
5Q fully-developed
9P fully-grown
XR fully-independent
4P Fulsom
7D fulsome

Word Type	F	D	U	SFI	3 Gr 3	4 Gr 4	5 Gr 5	6 Gr 6	7 Gr 7	8 Gr 8	9 Gr 9	X UnGr	A Read	B Eng & Gr	C Comp	D Lit	E Math	F Soc Stud	G Spell	H Sci	J Music	K Art	L Home Ec	M Shop	N Lib F	P Lib NF	Q Lib Ref	R Mag	S Rel
Fulton's	5	.2326	.3837	35.8	0	4	0	1	0	0	0	0	4	0	0	0	0	1	0	0	0	0	0	0	0	0	0	0	0
fumble	4	.2399	.3011	34.8	2	0	1	0	0	0	1	0	3	1	0	0	0	0	0	0	0	0	0	0	0	0	0	0	0
fumbled	12	.4244	1.2216	40.9	1	1	2	2	3	1	1	1	7	0	0	3	0	0	0	1	0	0	0	0	1	0	0	0	0
fumbles	3	.2309	.1631	32.1	0	0	0	0	1	2	0	0	0	0	0	1	0	0	0	0	0	0	0	0	0	0	0	2	0
fumbling	8	.4526	.8195	39.1	0	1	1	1	4	0	0	1	3	0	0	2	0	0	0	0	0	0	0	0	0	1	0	2	0
fumed	4	.2424	.3036	34.8	3	0	1	0	0	0	0	0	3	0	0	0	0	0	0	0	0	0	0	0	0	0	0	1	0
fumes	26	.6838	3.6477	45.6	6	0	5	1	4	5	5	0	3	0	1	1	0	8	0	4	0	0	0	0	2	1	5	1	0
Fumiko	7	.0000	.3198	35.0	7	0	0	0	0	0	0	0	7	0	0	0	0	0	0	0	0	0	0	0	0	0	0	0	0
Fumiko's	2	.0000	.0914	29.6	2	0	0	0	0	0	0	0	2	0	0	0	0	0	0	0	0	0	0	0	0	0	0	0	0
fuming	3	.3346	.2478	33.9	0	0	0	2	0	0	1	0	1	0	0	0	0	0	0	1	0	0	0	0	0	0	1	0	0
fun	695	.8749	121.47	60.8	216	169	81	71	78	48	20	12	223	48	6	30	11	41	30	33	26	23	16	0	83	77	4	44	0
Fun	13	.4726	1.3199	41.2	5	4	1	0	0	1	1	1	2	2	0	0	1	0	3	0	0	0	0	0	0	0	0	5	0
fun-loving	2	.0857	.0784	28.9	0	0	1	0	1	0	0	0	1	0	0	0	0	0	0	0	0	0	1	0	0	0	0	0	0
function	298	.6777	41.089	56.1	5	18	65	48	53	50	50	9	5	42	1	1	152	1	1	43	6	4	1	2	1	5	25	8	0
functional	17	.5780	2.0067	43.0	0	0	2	1	3	6	4	1	0	0	0	0	0	3	0	0	0	2	1	1	0	1	7	2	0
functioning	18	.5816	2.1569	43.3	1	0	0	0	2	7	7	1	2	3	0	0	0	0	2	0	1	0	3	0	0	0	3	4	0
functions	111	.7479	16.699	52.2	0	4	10	7	25	28	33	4	2	36	1	2	13	4	0	22	2	1	3	0	1	5	17	2	0
fund	21	.8173	3.4380	45.4	0	2	3	3	3	4	5	1	2	2	0	2	2	4	1	1	0	0	0	0	2	2	1	2	0
Fund	18	.4460	1.7176	42.3	0	1	2	1	12	1	1	0	1	1	0	0	0	2	1	1	0	0	0	0	0	0	10	2	0
fund-raising	2	.2440	.1132	30.5	0	0	0	1	0	1	0	0	0	0	0	1	0	0	0	0	0	0	0	0	0	0	0	1	0
fundamental	48	.6519	6.3594	48.0	2	0	6	2	16	9	9	4	2	2	0	0	1	1	0	6	11	0	2	1	0	1	17	4	0
fundamentally	6	.3869	.5158	37.1	0	0	0	1	3	0	1	1	1	0	0	0	0	0	0	0	1	0	0	0	0	0	3	1	0
fundamentals	5	.4401	.4616	36.6	0	0	0	0	2	1	2	0	0	1	0	0	0	0	0	0	2	0	0	0	0	1	1	0	0
FUNDAMENTALS	2	.0000	.0162	22.1	0	0	0	0	0	0	2	0	0	0	0	0	0	0	0	0	2	0	0	0	0	0	0	0	0
funds	52	.7073	7.4493	48.7	1	0	6	2	15	8	15	5	3	2	0	1	0	7	0	2	1	0	1	1	1	4	14	15	0
Fundy	3	.0000	.0591	27.7	0	0	0	0	0	0	3	0	0	0	0	0	0	0	0	3	0	0	0	0	0	0	0	0	0
funeral	38	.5834	4.5782	46.6	3	5	2	4	8	3	11	2	3	1	0	11	0	1	0	0	5	0	0	0	7	1	0	9	0
funerals	3	.3399	.2456	33.9	0	0	0	0	1	0	2	0	1	0	0	1	0	0	0	0	0	0	0	0	0	0	0	1	0
fungi	91	.1784	4.6012	46.6	7	0	16	22	13	1	2	30	0	0	0	0	0	0	1	83	0	0	0	0	0	0	7	0	0
fungus	41	.3574	3.3721	45.3	4	0	3	13	5	3	0	13	1	2	0	0	0	0	3	33	0	0	0	0	1	0	0	1	0
Funjo	3	.0000	.0322	25.1	0	0	3	0	0	0	0	0	0	0	0	3	0	0	0	0	0	0	0	0	0	0	0	0	0
funnel	73	.4567	7.3739	48.7	16	9	21	10	9	4	2	2	7	0	0	2	0	0	0	53	0	0	0	1	0	4	3	3	0
funnel-shaped	3	.2445	.1818	32.6	0	0	0	0	1	0	0	2	0	0	0	0	0	0	0	2	0	0	0	0	0	0	1	0	0
funnels	2	.2405	.1205	30.8	0	0	1	0	0	0	1	0	0	0	0	0	0	0	0	1	0	0	0	0	0	1	0	0	0
funnier	2	.2446	.1125	30.5	0	1	0	1	0	0	0	0	0	1	0	1	0	0	0	0	0	0	0	0	0	0	0	0	0
funniest	12	.5986	1.5179	41.8	4	2	1	0	3	0	2	0	4	2	0	3	0	0	1	0	1	0	0	0	1	0	0	0	0
funny	312	.7961	50.344	57.0	100	65	30	30	45	26	12	4	120	35	9	24	0	6	20	1	5	9	0	0	44	19	2	18	0
Funny	70	.0783	3.9918	46.0	69	0	0	0	0	0	1	0	69	0	0	1	0	0	0	0	0	0	0	0	0	0	0	0	0
funny-looking	7	.3397	.6064	37.8	5	1	1	0	0	0	0	0	4	0	0	0	0	0	0	0	2	0	0	0	1	0	0	0	0
Funny's	7	.0000	.3198	35.0	7	0	0	0	0	0	0	0	7	0	0	0	0	0	0	0	0	0	0	0	0	0	0	0	0
fur	259	.8752	45.221	56.6	64	34	43	27	42	40	7	2	54	7	5	16	0	48	4	35	5	3	0	1	27	28	13	12	1
fur-bearing	10	.5235	1.1507	40.6	0	0	5	1	4	0	0	0	3	0	0	1	0	4	0	1	0	0	0	0	0	0	1	0	0
fur-clad	2	.1948	.1250	31.0	0	0	2	0	0	0	0	0	1	0	0	0	0	0	0	0	0	0	0	0	0	1	0	0	0
fur-lined	4	.3513	.3115	34.9	2	0	0	0	2	0	0	0	0	0	0	1	0	1	0	0	0	0	0	0	0	0	0	2	0
fur-trading	8	.1813	.4050	36.1	0	0	7	0	0	1	0	0	0	0	0	0	0	7	0	0	0	0	0	0	0	0	1	0	0
Furies	3	.2379	.1705	32.3	0	0	0	2	0	0	1	0	0	0	0	1	0	0	0	0	0	0	0	0	0	2	0	0	0
Furillo	2	.0000	.0290	24.6	2	0	0	0	0	0	0	0	0	0	0	0	0	0	0	0	0	0	0	0	0	2	0	0	0
furious	44	.6203	5.7696	47.6	4	2	4	9	14	7	3	1	16	5	0	8	0	2	0	0	0	0	0	0	8	2	0	3	0
furiously	34	.6907	4.8534	46.9	3	6	6	8	5	2	4	0	11	1	1	1	0	1	0	0	1	0	0	0	9	2	1	6	0
furl	2	.0000	.0234	23.7	0	0	2	0	0	0	0	0	0	0	0	0	0	0	0	0	0	0	0	0	2	0	0	0	0
furled	5	.3827	.4088	36.1	0	1	0	0	1	1	2	0	0	0	0	2	0	0	0	0	1	0	0	0	2	0	0	0	0
furlongs	2	.0000	.0299	24.8	0	2	0	0	0	0	0	0	0	0	0	0	2	0	0	0	0	0	0	0	0	0	0	0	0
Furloy	4	.0000	.1827	32.6	0	0	0	4	0	0	0	0	4	0	0	0	0	0	0	0	0	0	0	0	0	0	0	0	0
furnace	93	.7157	13.789	51.4	21	22	12	4	10	19	3	2	36	2	0	3	0	22	1	8	0	0	0	5	8	2	3	3	0
furnaces	31	.5930	3.8563	45.9	7	0	5	4	7	5	3	0	5	3	0	0	0	6	0	6	0	0	0	3	0	3	5	0	0
furnish	53	.8013	8.5188	49.3	6	2	4	13	10	7	8	3	4	1	0	2	0	10	1	14	2	1	3	4	3	4	2	2	0
furnished	43	.8101	7.0076	48.5	2	1	7	4	11	9	6	3	8	0	0	6	0	9	0	7	1	1	1	2	2	1	3	2	0
furnishes	14	.5407	1.5965	42.0	1	1	2	4	2	2	2	0	0	0	0	1	0	3	0	6	0	0	0	0	0	2	2	0	0
furnishing	3	.3840	.2493	34.0	0	0	0	1	1	1	0	0	0	0	0	0	1	0	0	0	0	0	0	0	1	0	1	0	0
furnishings	17	.6529	2.2564	43.5	0	0	3	2	4	4	2	2	1	0	0	1	0	4	0	0	0	1	3	1	2	0	2	2	0
furniture	231	.7668	35.670	55.5	21	37	18	18	68	34	32	3	31	14	0	12	3	38	3	11	5	6	23	23	18	26	7	11	0
furred	2	.0000	.0215	23.3	0	0	0	0	2	0	0	0	0	0	0	2	0	0	0	0	0	0	0	0	0	0	0	0	0
furring	10	.0000	.1448	31.6	0	0	0	0	10	0	0	0	0	0	0	0	0	0	0	0	0	0	0	0	0	10	0	0	0
furrow	8	.5158	.8894	39.5	1	0	1	0	2	3	1	0	2	0	0	1	0	1	0	0	0	0	0	1	2	1	0	0	0
furrowed	2	.1698	.1133	30.5	0	0	0	0	0	1	1	0	1	0	0	0	0	0	0	0	0	0	0	0	0	0	1	0	0
furrows	6	.5372	.6886	38.4	1	2	1	1	1	0	0	0	1	0	0	1	0	2	0	0	0	0	0	0	1	0	0	1	0
furry	31	.7003	4.4987	46.5	10	6	2	5	6	2	0	0	11	1	0	1	0	1	0	3	0	0	0	0	5	3	1	5	0
furs	92	.5928	11.572	50.6	6	33	20	7	6	18	2	0	20	0	0	5	0	41	0	0	3	0	0	0	6	15	1	1	0
further	324	.9127	58.639	57.7	12	24	31	26	94	67	53	17	48	21	1	11	7	36	3	68	10	2	7	8	14	21	41	26	0
furtherance	2	.2446	.1125	30.5	0	0	0	0	1	0	1	0	0	1	0	1	0	0	0	0	0	0	0	0	0	0	0	0	0
furthering	3	.3350	.2478	33.9	0	0	0	0	1	2	0	0	1	0	0	0	0	1	0	0	0	0	0	0	0	0	1	0	0
furthermore	69	.8135	11.267	50.5	1	5	7	4	20	16	14	2	10	5	0	6	5	13	0	7	5	0	1	0	3	1	11	2	0
furthest	6	.3047	.4368	36.4	4	2	0	0	0	0	0	0	1	0	0	0	3	0	0	0	0	0	0	0	0	0	2	0	0
furtively	2	.2446	.1142	30.6	0	0	0	0	1	0	1	0	0	0	0	0	0	0	0	0	0	0	0	0	1	0	0	1	0
fury	35	.6028	4.4239	46.5	1	6	5	5	11	3	3	1	9	0	2	3	0	0	0	0	0	0	0	0	11	2	2	6	0
Fuschi	2	.0000	.0215	23.3	0	0	0	0	0	0	2	0	0	0	0	2	0	0	0	0	0	0	0	0	0	0	0	0	0
fuse	22	.4573	2.1954	43.4	1	10	0	3	2	4	1	1	3	0	1	0	0	0	1	12	1	0	0	4	0	0	0	0	0
fused	9	.3793	.7417	38.7	0	0	0	0	7	2	0	0	0	0	0	0	0	0	0	3	0	0	0	2	0	2	2	0	0
fuselage	13	.4449	1.3751	41.4	0	0	1	6	3	1	1	1	8	0	0	0	0	0	1	1	0	0	0	0	0	0	0	3	0
fuses	10	.5901	1.2288	40.9	0	3	1	0	1	1	2	2	1	1	0	0	0	0	0	4	1	0	0	1	0	0	1	1	0
fusibility	2	.0000	.0050	17.0	0	0	0	0	0	0	2	0	0	0	0	0	0	0	0	0	0	0	0	2	0	0	0	0	0
fusible	2	.1249	.0685	28.4	0	0	0	0	1	0	0	1	0	0	0	0	0	0	0	1	0	0	0	1	0	0	0	0	0
fusion	17	.5223	1.8626	42.7	0	2	1	5	0	2	5	2	0	0	0	0	0	0	0	8	0	0	0	2	1	1	2	3	0
fuss	25	.6672	3.5237	45.5	3	6	0	7	3	2	3	1	13	0	0	2	1	0	0	1	0	0	1	0	4	1	0	2	0
fussed	8	.3958	.7063	38.5	0	5	1	0	1	1	0	0	1	0	0	0	0	0	0	0	0	0	0	0	2	4	0	1	0
fussing	9	.3732	.8542	39.3	0	1	0	1	5	1	0	1	6	0	0	0	0	0	0	0	0	0	0	0	2	0	0	1	0
fussy	10	.5380	1.1501	40.6	2	0	1	1	3	1	0	2	3	0	0	1	0	0	0	0	0	1	1	0	1	0	0	3	0
Fust	4	.2446	.2246	33.5	0	0	2	2	0	0	0	0	0	2	0	0	0	0	0	0	0	0	0	0	0	0	2	0	0
futhermore	3	.3855	.2503	34.0	0	0	1	0	1	1	0	0	0	1	0	0	0	0	0	0	0	0	0	0	0	1	0	1	0
futile	9	.6056	1.1068	40.4	0	1	0	1	3	0	3	1	0	0	1	2	0	0	2	1	1	0	0	0	0	0	1	1	0
futility	4	.3584	.3139	35.0	0	0	0	0	3	0	1	0	0	0	0	0	0	0	0	0	0	0	0	0	2	1	0	1	0
future	354	.8610	60.841	57.8	10	27	49	48	85	57	64	14	58	21	1	10	4	67	8	37	7	0	9	2	8	20	45	57	0
Future	8	.3193	.5747	37.6	0	0	0	0	2	1	5	0	1	0	0	2	0	1	0	0	0	0	3	0	0	0	1	0	0
futures	2	.2285	.1129	30.5	0	0	0	0	2	0	0	0	0	0	0	0	0	1	0	0	0	0	0	0	0	0	1	0	0

7H fulva
5G fumare
6P Fumblefinger
5G fume
4R Fumio
9F fun-food
7A fun-making
8F Func
5Q functionalism
5P functionary
8F Functionary
7F functioned
8F Fundamental
7Q fundamentalist
8D Fundamentalist
9J Fundamentals
8J Funeral
6G fung
7G fungo
8Q fungous
7Q fungus-blighted
7Q funiculars
9R funky
5J funmaking
XR funnel's
9H funneling
6A funnily
3G funny**
3J funny-man
4P Fur
4A fur-animals
3D fur-hooded
7K fur-like
7D fur's
7D furbish
5F furfural
7N Furina
6N furlong
6A Furlong
9B furlough
5Q Furman
5Q Furnace
7R furnace-brazed
4A furnace-tending
3A furnace's
7A furnacelike
6H Furnaces
8J Furnberg
8D Furness
9E Furniture
8J furor
7J furthered
5A furtive
7R Fury
XH fused-quartz
8F Fusiliers
8R fusillade
8F fusing
3N fusses
8A fust
6B Fust's
6R fustiness
6A fusty
5Q futa

Word Type	F	D	U	SFI	3 Gr 3	4 Gr 4	5 Gr 5	6 Gr 6	7 Gr 7	8 Gr 8	9 Gr 9	X UnGr	A Read	B Eng & Gr	C Comp	D Lit	E Math	F Soc Stud	G Spell	H Sci	J Music	K Art	L Home Ec	M Shop	N Lib F	P Lib NF	Q Lib Ref	R Mag	S Rel
futuristic	2	.2437	.1129	30.5	0	0	0	0	0	0	2	0	0	0	0	0	0	0	0	0	0	0	0	0	0	0	1	1	0
fuzz	7	.4635	.7298	38.6	3	1	0	3	0	0	0	0	2	0	0	0	0	0	0	2	0	0	0	0	0	2	0	1	0
fuzziness	3	.1540	.1257	31.0	0	0	1	1	1	0	0	0	0	0	0	0	0	0	0	2	0	1	0	0	0	0	0	0	0
fuzzy	17	.5139	1.9225	42.8	5	4	1	3	2	1	1	0	7	0	0	0	0	0	0	3	1	2	2	0	1	1	0	0	0
Fuzzy-top	2	.0000	.0914	29.6	0	0	0	2	0	0	0	0	2	0	0	0	0	0	0	0	0	0	0	0	0	0	0	0	0
Fyn	2	.1698	.1133	30.5	2	0	0	0	0	0	0	0	1	0	0	0	0	0	0	0	0	0	0	0	0	0	1	0	0
g	227	.3944	19.594	52.9	30	24	31	51	54	26	9	2	30	16	1	0	29	0	133	7	5	0	1	0	1	0	1	3	0
G	242	.4461	22.709	53.6	44	60	44	31	23	19	15	6	6	4	2	2	36	3	1	11	148	0	1	1	0	8	11	8	0
G**	12	.4547	1.1705	40.7	0	1	0	0	6	3	1	1	0	0	0	0	5	3	0	0	0	0	0	0	0	0	1	3	0
Gls	3	.0000	.0434	26.4	0	0	3	0	0	0	0	0	0	0	0	0	0	0	0	0	0	0	0	0	0	3	0	0	0
G-Man	2	.0000	.0914	29.6	0	0	0	2	0	0	0	0	2	0	0	0	0	0	0	0	0	0	0	0	0	0	0	0	0
g-h-o-t-i	3	.0000	.0243	23.9	0	0	0	0	3	0	0	0	0	0	0	0	0	0	3	0	0	0	0	0	0	0	0	0	0
G-major	6	.0000	.0485	26.9	0	2	2	2	0	0	0	0	0	0	0	0	0	0	0	0	6	0	0	0	0	0	0	0	0
G-2	3	.0000	.0365	25.6	0	0	0	0	3	0	0	0	0	0	0	0	0	0	0	0	0	0	0	0	0	0	0	3	0
g/cm3	3	.0000	.0591	27.7	0	0	0	0	0	0	3	0	0	0	0	0	0	0	0	3	0	0	0	0	0	0	0	0	0
g's	4	.3272	.3199	35.1	0	2	0	0	0	0	0	2	1	0	0	0	0	0	1	2	0	0	0	0	0	0	0	0	0
G's	5	.2183	.2661	34.3	5	0	0	0	0	0	0	0	0	0	0	0	0	0	0	0	1	0	0	0	0	4	0	0	0
ga	5	.0000	.0126	21.0	0	0	0	0	0	5	0	0	0	0	0	0	0	0	0	0	0	0	0	5	0	0	0	0	0
ga-lumping	3	.0000	.1370	31.4	0	3	0	0	0	0	0	0	3	0	0	0	0	0	0	0	0	0	0	0	0	0	0	0	0
ga'nzas	3	.0000	.0434	26.4	0	0	0	0	3	0	0	0	0	0	0	0	0	0	0	0	0	0	0	0	0	3	0	0	0
gabardine	2	.0000	.0064	18.1	0	0	0	0	0	1	1	0	0	0	0	0	0	0	0	0	0	0	2	0	0	0	0	0	0
gabble	2	.2407	.1138	30.6	0	0	1	0	0	0	1	0	0	0	0	1	0	0	0	0	0	0	0	0	0	1	0	0	0
gabbling	2	.0000	.0914	29.6	2	0	0	0	0	0	0	0	2	0	0	0	0	0	0	0	0	0	0	0	0	0	0	0	0
gabbro	3	.1813	.1402	31.5	0	0	0	0	0	0	3	0	0	0	0	0	0	0	0	1	0	0	0	0	0	0	2	0	0
Gabby	64	.2438	5.1545	47.1	2	0	61	1	0	0	0	0	59	0	0	0	0	0	0	0	0	0	0	0	2	3	0	0	0
Gabby's	7	.3858	.6848	38.4	0	0	6	1	0	0	0	0	5	0	0	1	0	0	0	0	0	0	0	0	1	0	0	0	0
Gabe	2	.0000	.0914	29.6	0	0	2	0	0	0	0	0	2	0	0	0	0	0	0	0	0	0	0	0	0	0	0	0	0
Gabee	11	.0000	.5025	37.0	0	0	0	11	0	0	0	0	11	0	0	0	0	0	0	0	0	0	0	0	0	0	0	0	0
Gabilan	9	.2439	.5081	37.1	0	0	0	0	4	5	0	0	0	0	0	4	0	0	0	0	0	0	0	0	5	0	0	0	0
Gabilan's	2	.0000	.0234	23.7	0	0	0	0	0	2	0	0	0	0	0	0	0	0	0	0	0	0	0	0	2	0	0	0	0
gable	5	.3081	.3654	35.6	0	2	0	0	2	0	1	0	1	0	0	2	0	0	0	0	0	0	0	0	2	0	0	0	0
Gable	2	.0000	.0243	23.9	0	0	0	0	2	0	0	0	0	0	0	0	0	0	0	0	0	0	0	0	0	0	0	2	0
gabled	2	.2446	.1125	30.5	0	0	0	0	0	1	1	0	0	1	0	1	0	0	0	0	0	0	0	0	0	0	0	0	0
gables	4	.1934	.1880	32.7	0	0	0	0	0	3	0	1	0	3	0	0	0	0	0	0	0	0	0	0	1	0	0	0	0
Gabriel	38	.5392	4.5200	46.6	2	0	18	3	5	0	10	0	18	0	0	0	0	0	0	1	1	0	0	0	0	4	4	10	0
Gabriel's	3	.3263	.2368	33.7	0	1	1	0	0	0	1	0	1	0	0	0	0	0	0	0	1	0	0	0	0	0	0	1	0
Gacrux	2	.0000	.0394	26.0	0	0	0	0	0	2	0	0	0	0	0	0	0	0	0	2	0	0	0	0	0	0	0	0	0
gad	2	.0000	.0234	23.7	0	0	0	0	0	2	0	0	0	0	0	0	0	0	0	0	0	0	0	0	2	0	0	0	0
gadfly	5	.2443	.3861	35.9	0	0	4	0	1	0	0	0	4	0	0	0	0	0	0	0	0	0	0	0	0	0	1	0	0
gadget	10	.6009	1.2624	41.0	0	3	0	3	0	1	2	1	3	1	0	0	1	0	0	0	0	0	1	1	2	0	0	1	0
gadgets	11	.5407	1.2691	41.0	0	1	2	3	1	3	1	0	3	0	0	0	1	0	0	0	1	0	2	0	0	2	1	1	0
Gadja	3	.0000	.1370	31.4	0	0	0	0	3	0	0	0	3	0	0	0	0	0	0	0	0	0	0	0	0	0	0	0	0
Gaelic	3	.2379	.1705	32.3	0	0	2	0	1	0	0	0	0	0	0	1	0	0	0	0	0	0	0	0	0	2	0	0	0
Gaetano	2	.2401	.1133	30.5	0	0	1	1	0	1	0	0	0	0	0	0	0	0	0	0	0	0	0	0	0	1	1	0	0
gaff	6	.3334	.4466	36.5	0	4	0	0	0	0	2	0	0	0	0	0	0	0	0	0	0	0	0	0	1	4	1	0	0
gaff-topsail	2	.0000	.0209	23.2	0	0	0	0	2	0	0	0	0	0	0	0	0	0	0	0	0	0	0	0	0	0	2	0	0
GAFFER	2	.0000	.0215	23.3	0	0	0	0	0	0	2	0	0	0	0	2	0	0	0	0	0	0	0	0	0	0	0	0	0
gag	2	.1787	.1174	30.7	0	0	0	0	0	1	0	1	1	0	0	0	0	0	0	0	0	0	0	0	1	0	0	0	0
gage	28	.0815	.5734	37.6	0	0	0	0	18	7	3	0	0	0	0	0	0	0	1	0	0	0	0	22	0	5	0	0	0
Gage	3	.2261	.2131	33.3	0	0	0	0	2	1	0	0	2	0	0	0	0	0	0	0	0	0	0	0	1	0	0	0	0
gages	2	.0000	.0050	17.0	0	0	0	0	2	0	0	0	0	0	0	0	0	0	0	0	0	0	0	2	0	0	0	0	0
gagged	5	.1530	.1990	33.0	0	1	0	0	3	0	1	0	0	0	0	4	0	0	0	0	0	0	0	0	0	1	0	0	0
Gagnon	4	.0000	.0469	26.7	0	4	0	0	0	0	0	0	0	0	0	0	0	0	0	0	0	0	0	0	4	0	0	0	0
gags	2	.2442	.1134	30.5	0	0	0	0	0	1	1	0	0	1	0	0	0	0	0	0	0	0	0	0	0	0	0	1	0
gaiety	12	.4742	1.2169	40.9	2	1	1	2	2	3	1	0	2	0	0	3	0	1	0	0	1	2	0	0	1	0	2	0	0
Gail	4	.3723	.3645	35.6	0	0	0	0	3	1	0	0	2	1	0	0	0	0	0	0	0	0	0	0	0	0	0	1	0
gaily	33	.7657	5.1664	47.1	4	8	4	7	5	3	2	0	14	2	0	2	0	1	0	1	4	1	0	0	2	3	1	2	0
gaily-colored	2	.2128	.1055	30.2	0	0	0	1	0	1	0	0	0	0	0	0	0	0	0	1	1	0	0	0	0	0	0	0	0
gain	173	.9162	31.402	55.0	10	15	17	31	45	22	30	3	19	11	2	7	20	25	6	30	4	0	7	2	6	6	12	16	0
gained	148	.8805	25.913	54.1	9	7	37	19	30	27	15	4	13	2	1	5	9	33	3	24	14	1	0	1	9	6	18	9	0
gaining	39	.8024	6.2920	48.0	0	7	8	4	9	7	2	2	5	0	1	2	0	7	1	7	0	0	1	0	4	2	2	7	0
gains	41	.7462	6.1961	47.9	1	2	6	4	7	3	15	3	3	0	0	3	2	13	1	6	0	0	1	0	1	1	2	8	0
gait	18	.6126	2.3816	43.8	4	2	2	4	5	1	0	0	10	2	0	1	0	0	0	0	0	0	0	0	2	2	0	1	0
gaiters	2	.0000	.0234	23.7	0	0	2	0	0	0	0	0	0	0	0	0	0	0	0	0	0	0	0	0	2	0	0	0	0
gal	7	.5388	.7766	38.9	0	2	2	3	0	0	0	0	0	1	0	0	2	0	1	0	2	0	0	0	1	0	0	0	0
Gal	3	.0000	.0243	23.8	0	1	2	0	0	0	0	0	0	0	0	0	0	0	0	0	3	0	0	0	0	0	0	0	0
gala	4	.3778	.3240	35.1	1	0	1	1	0	1	0	0	0	1	0	0	0	0	0	0	1	0	0	0	0	0	0	2	0
galactic	2	.2437	.1129	30.5	0	0	0	0	2	0	0	0	0	0	0	0	0	0	0	0	0	0	0	0	0	0	1	1	0
Galapagos	2	.0000	.0243	23.9	0	0	0	2	0	0	0	0	0	0	0	0	0	0	0	0	0	0	0	0	0	0	0	2	0
galaxies	47	.2797	3.2246	45.1	8	2	6	0	24	2	2	3	1	0	0	1	0	0	0	39	0	0	0	0	0	0	5	1	0
galaxy	52	.3649	4.3457	46.4	5	2	9	9	6	10	5	6	1	0	0	3	2	0	0	41	0	0	0	0	0	0	3	2	0
Galaxy	9	.1601	.4259	36.3	5	1	0	2	1	0	0	0	0	0	0	0	0	0	0	8	0	0	0	0	0	0	0	1	0
gale	27	.7229	4.0218	46.0	0	3	6	10	7	0	1	0	10	1	1	0	0	3	0	0	1	0	0	0	4	2	1	4	0
Gale	7	.3780	.6760	38.3	5	0	1	0	1	0	0	0	5	0	0	0	0	0	0	0	1	0	0	0	0	1	0	0	0
Galen	11	.3591	.8854	39.5	0	2	0	0	0	5	4	0	0	0	0	0	2	0	0	5	0	0	0	0	0	0	4	0	0
Galen's	3	.0000	.0314	25.0	0	0	0	0	0	0	3	0	0	0	0	0	0	0	0	0	0	0	0	0	0	0	3	0	0
galena	2	.0000	.0394	26.0	0	0	0	0	0	0	2	0	0	0	0	0	0	0	0	2	0	0	0	0	0	0	0	0	0
gales	7	.3665	.6345	38.0	0	2	1	1	1	2	0	0	3	0	0	0	0	3	0	0	0	0	0	0	0	0	1	0	0
Galilee	15	.1817	.7996	39.0	2	0	1	2	10	0	0	0	3	2	0	0	0	8	0	0	1	0	0	0	0	0	0	0	1
Galilei	5	.4026	.4530	36.6	0	0	0	1	3	0	1	0	1	0	0	0	1	0	0	0	0	0	0	0	0	1	2	0	0
Galileo	41	.5850	5.1655	47.1	3	5	1	13	15	3	0	1	14	0	0	0	2	3	0	14	1	0	0	0	0	1	6	0	0
Galileo's	11	.4047	1.0208	40.1	1	0	0	5	4	0	1	0	2	0	0	0	0	0	0	6	0	0	0	0	0	1	2	0	0
gall	6	.5284	.6599	38.2	0	0	0	0	5	0	1	0	0	0	0	1	0	0	0	1	0	0	0	0	0	1	2	1	0
Gall	3	.0000	.0322	25.1	0	0	0	0	0	0	3	0	0	0	0	3	0	0	0	0	0	0	0	0	0	0	0	0	0
GALL	8	.0000	.0859	29.3	0	0	0	0	0	0	8	0	0	0	0	8	0	0	0	0	0	0	0	0	0	0	0	0	0
gallant	17	.4879	1.8523	42.7	0	3	2	4	5	1	2	0	7	1	0	5	0	0	0	0	0	0	0	0	3	1	0	0	0
gallantly	9	.4416	.8795	39.4	1	0	0	2	1	5	0	0	2	0	0	4	0	1	0	0	1	0	0	0	0	1	0	0	0
gallantry	5	.4694	.5313	37.3	0	0	1	1	2	1	0	0	2	0	0	1	0	1	0	0	0	0	0	0	0	0	1	0	0
Gallas	3	.0000	.0583	27.7	0	0	0	0	3	0	0	0	0	0	0	0	0	3	0	0	0	0	0	0	0	0	0	0	0
galleon	15	.3462	1.3569	41.3	0	4	6	3	0	2	0	0	10	1	0	0	0	0	0	0	0	0	0	0	4	0	0	0	0
galleons	2	.2285	.1129	30.5	1	0	0	0	1	0	0	0	0	0	0	0	0	1	0	0	0	0	0	0	0	0	1	0	0
galleries	16	.5444	1.8452	42.7	6	3	0	0	6	0	1	0	2	0	0	0	0	2	0	3	1	0	0	0	0	3	5	0	0
gallery	16	.5919	1.9927	43.0	2	4	0	0	3	4	1	2	4	0	0	0	0	2	0	0	2	1	0	0	1	0	1	5	0
Gallery	10	.1046	.3008	34.8	0	0	3	0	1	3	2	1	0	0	0	0	0	0	0	0	0	0	0	0	0	0	9	1	0

4P Futurity
4R fuzzlike
3R G-One
4A g-g-got
4A g-gave
7D G-men
9D G-o-d
4P G-r-o-u-n-d
4N G-type
9H g/10
3A gfts
3A grl's
3A gve
5A g'morning
7D g'nite
7A g'wan
4N ga-loups
8D Gaa-kl
8R gab
5A Gabe's
9D Gabelle
8N Gabilans
8R Gabon
5R Gabor
4Q Gabriele
7J Gabrielli
XR Gabrielson
9Q gadgetry
8F Gadsden
5P Gaels
6P Gagarin
8Q gagging
5N gaggle
7A gagman
8F Gahma
8B Gail's
6F Gaillard
6A gainsay
7Q Gaite
7D gaited
7A gal-bride
7F galabias
7D Galagos
7D Galagos'
6B Galahad
7F Galata
4H galaxy's
7H gale-force
7A Galena
7N galeolaria
7P Gales'
3N Galilean
3N Galileans
7Q gall-making
6F Galla
4R Gallant
8F Gallatin
7N gallberry
6R galleass
7C Gallegher
5P Galleria
9Q gallery-going
8R gallery-theaters
8R Gallery's

Word Type	F	D	U	SFI	3 Gr 3	4 Gr 4	5 Gr 5	6 Gr 6	7 Gr 7	8 Gr 8	9 Gr 9	X UnGr	A Read	B Eng & Gr	C Comp	D Lit	E Math	F Soc Stud	G Spell	H Sci	J Music	K Art	L Home Ec	M Shop	N Lib F	P Lib NF	Q Lib Ref	R Mag	S Rel
galley	15	.5888	1.8899	42.8	1	2	4	2	5	0	1	0	6	0	0	2	0	0	0	0	0	0	0	1	1	2	0	3	0
gallon	90	.4028	7.9907	49.0	29	21	10	5	14	4	5	2	2	2	0	0	64	1	0	15	0	1	0	0	1	1	0	3	0
gallons	118	.5695	14.056	51.5	10	15	26	15	26	11	14	1	7	0	0	4	66	2	0	19	0	0	0	3	1	3	5	8	0
gallop	35	.6740	4.9066	46.9	5	9	4	4	7	5	1	0	13	0	0	3	0	0	1	0	6	1	0	0	4	6	0	1	0
galloped	42	.6531	5.7479	47.6	4	17	3	2	7	5	4	0	16	3	1	8	0	0	0	0	0	0	0	0	7	5	0	2	0
galloping	33	.6559	4.5405	46.6	5	8	1	3	12	2	1	1	13	3	0	5	0	1	0	1	2	0	0	0	6	2	0	0	0
gallops	4	.3075	.2938	34.7	0	0	0	1	1	0	2	0	1	0	0	2	0	0	0	0	1	0	0	0	0	0	0	0	0
gallows	7	.3134	.5554	37.4	0	0	0	2	2	1	2	0	3	0	0	3	0	0	0	0	0	0	0	0	1	0	0	0	0
galls	10	.1692	.4425	36.5	0	0	0	0	10	0	0	0	0	0	0	0	0	0	0	3	0	0	0	0	0	0	7	0	0
Gallup	4	.0996	.1523	31.8	0	1	0	1	1	0	1	0	1	0	0	0	0	0	0	0	0	0	0	0	0	0	0	3	0
galore	3	.2346	.1705	32.3	1	0	0	0	1	0	0	1	0	0	0	0	2	0	0	0	0	0	0	0	0	0	0	1	0
galoshes	2	.2446	.1142	30.6	0	1	1	0	0	0	0	0	0	0	0	0	0	0	0	0	0	0	0	0	1	0	0	1	0
gals	4	.2375	.2175	33.4	0	0	1	2	1	0	0	0	0	0	0	0	0	0	0	0	2	0	0	0	0	0	0	2	0
Gals	2	.1717	.1142	30.6	0	0	0	1	1	0	0	0	1	0	0	1	0	0	0	0	0	0	0	0	0	0	0	0	0
Galt'd	2	.0000	.0914	29.6	0	0	0	0	2	0	0	0	2	0	0	0	0	0	0	0	0	0	0	0	0	0	0	0	0
Galts	2	.0000	.0914	29.6	0	0	0	0	2	0	0	0	2	0	0	0	0	0	0	0	0	0	0	0	0	0	0	0	0
Galvani	2	.2278	.1128	30.5	0	0	0	0	1	0	0	1	0	0	0	0	0	0	0	1	0	0	0	0	0	0	1	0	0
galvanized	9	.3758	.7581	38.8	1	0	2	0	4	0	0	2	1	0	0	0	0	0	0	4	1	0	0	2	0	0	0	1	0
galvanizing	2	.0000	.0914	29.6	1	0	0	0	1	0	0	0	2	0	0	0	0	0	0	0	0	0	0	0	0	0	0	0	0
galvanometer	9	.0000	.1774	32.5	0	0	3	4	0	2	0	0	0	0	0	0	0	0	0	9	0	0	0	0	0	0	0	0	0
Galveston	5	.2055	.2584	34.1	0	0	0	0	5	0	0	0	0	0	0	3	0	2	0	0	0	0	0	0	0	0	0	0	0
gam	5	.0000	.2284	33.6	0	5	0	0	0	0	0	0	5	0	0	0	0	0	0	0	0	0	0	0	0	0	0	0	0
Gama	2	.2285	.1129	30.5	0	0	1	0	0	1	0	0	0	0	0	0	0	1	0	0	0	0	0	0	0	0	1	0	0
Gamal	5	.1990	.2695	34.3	0	0	1	1	1	1	1	0	0	0	0	0	0	4	0	0	0	0	0	0	0	1	0	0	0
Gamanio	7	.0000	.3198	35.0	0	0	7	0	0	0	0	0	7	0	0	0	0	0	0	0	0	0	0	0	0	0	0	0	0
gamba	3	.3768	.2437	33.9	0	1	0	1	0	0	0	1	0	0	0	0	0	0	0	0	1	0	0	0	0	1	0	1	0
Gambetta	2	.0000	.0215	23.3	0	0	0	0	0	2	0	0	0	0	0	2	0	0	0	0	0	0	0	0	0	0	0	0	0
Gambia	4	.0000	.0419	26.2	0	4	0	0	0	0	0	0	0	0	0	0	0	0	0	0	0	0	0	0	0	0	4	0	0
gamble	7	.5257	.7663	38.8	0	2	1	0	2	1	1	0	0	0	0	0	0	1	0	0	0	0	0	0	1	1	2	2	0
Gamble	3	.0000	.0434	26.4	3	0	0	0	0	0	0	0	0	0	0	0	0	0	0	0	0	0	0	0	0	3	0	0	0
gambler	3	.2379	.1705	32.3	0	0	0	0	2	0	1	0	0	0	0	1	0	0	0	0	0	0	0	0	0	2	0	0	0
gamblers	8	.7027	1.1471	40.6	0	0	0	1	3	3	1	0	1	0	0	1	1	1	0	1	1	0	0	0	1	0	0	1	0
gambling	6	.2673	.3696	35.7	0	1	0	0	4	0	1	0	0	0	0	4	0	0	0	1	0	0	0	0	1	0	0	0	0
gambol	2	.0000	.0215	23.3	0	0	0	0	0	1	1	0	0	0	0	2	0	0	0	0	0	0	0	0	0	0	0	0	0
gamboling	3	.3395	.2468	33.9	0	0	1	1	1	0	0	0	1	0	0	0	0	0	0	0	0	0	0	0	0	1	1	0	0
game	974	.9284	179.22	62.5	205	194	101	103	174	110	65	22	273	78	17	46	102	30	38	53	22	8	7	2	57	114	24	103	0
Game	17	.5224	1.8631	42.7	0	0	1	1	6	6	2	1	1	1	0	0	4	0	0	0	2	0	0	0	0	2	0	7	0
game's	4	.2424	.3036	34.8	0	0	0	2	0	1	1	0	3	0	0	0	0	0	0	0	0	0	0	0	0	0	0	1	0
gamefish	3	.0000	.0365	25.6	0	0	0	0	3	0	0	0	0	0	0	0	0	0	0	0	0	0	0	0	0	0	0	3	0
gamekeeper	2	.0000	.0162	22.1	0	0	0	2	0	0	0	0	0	0	0	0	0	0	0	0	2	0	0	0	0	0	0	0	0
gamelan	2	.0000	.0162	22.1	0	0	0	0	2	0	0	0	0	0	0	0	0	0	0	0	2	0	0	0	0	0	0	0	0
gamely	3	.1277	.1363	31.3	0	0	1	1	0	0	1	0	1	0	0	0	0	0	0	0	0	0	0	0	0	0	0	2	0
games	349	.8885	61.697	57.9	66	71	34	45	52	61	20	0	73	36	4	17	28	27	3	12	13	1	10	0	8	44	17	56	0
Games	24	.6487	3.2869	45.2	5	3	4	3	3	5	1	0	10	0	0	0	2	3	0	0	1	0	0	0	0	1	3	4	0
gametes	6	.1813	.2803	34.5	0	0	0	0	2	0	0	4	0	0	0	0	0	0	0	2	0	0	0	0	0	0	4	0	0
gametophyte	3	.0000	.0591	27.7	0	0	0	0	0	0	3	0	0	0	0	0	0	0	0	3	0	0	0	0	0	0	0	0	0
gamma	13	.3111	.9187	39.6	0	0	0	3	4	6	0	0	0	0	0	0	0	0	1	5	0	0	0	0	0	0	7	0	0
gamut	3	.3782	.2435	33.9	0	0	0	0	1	2	0	0	0	0	0	0	0	0	0	0	1	0	0	0	0	1	1	0	0
gander	10	.3854	.9580	39.8	0	9	0	1	0	0	0	0	6	0	0	0	0	0	0	0	0	0	0	0	2	2	0	0	0
ganders	2	.0000	.0215	23.3	0	0	2	0	0	0	0	0	0	0	0	2	0	0	0	0	0	0	0	0	0	0	0	0	0
Gandhi	17	.3376	1.5078	41.8	0	0	0	1	0	16	0	0	11	0	0	0	0	0	0	0	0	0	0	0	0	0	1	5	0
Gandhi's	9	.0502	.2245	33.5	0	0	0	0	0	9	0	0	1	0	0	0	0	0	0	0	0	0	0	0	0	0	0	8	0
gang	74	.6723	10.321	50.1	4	11	9	8	24	13	5	0	25	9	4	8	0	0	0	0	2	0	0	0	17	3	1	5	0
Gang	7	.2934	.4844	36.9	0	0	1	1	1	4	0	0	1	0	0	3	0	0	0	0	0	0	0	0	0	0	0	3	0
Ganges	6	.3703	.4939	36.9	0	2	2	1	1	0	0	0	0	0	0	0	0	3	0	0	0	0	0	0	1	0	2	0	0
ganglia	3	.1813	.1402	31.5	0	0	0	0	0	0	3	0	0	0	0	0	0	0	0	1	0	0	0	0	0	0	2	0	0
gangplank	13	.6121	1.6972	42.3	1	3	2	2	2	2	1	0	5	1	0	1	0	2	0	0	0	0	0	0	1	3	0	0	0
gangplanks	2	.0000	.0299	24.8	0	0	0	0	0	2	0	0	0	0	0	0	2	0	0	0	0	0	0	0	0	0	0	0	0
gangs	6	.4962	.6398	38.1	0	2	1	0	0	1	2	0	1	1	0	0	0	1	0	0	0	0	0	0	1	0	2	0	0
gangster	8	.4758	.8913	39.5	5	0	0	0	0	0	3	0	5	1	0	0	0	1	0	0	0	0	0	0	0	1	0	0	0
gangsters	4	.2393	.3005	34.8	1	0	0	2	1	0	0	0	3	0	0	1	0	0	0	0	0	0	0	0	0	0	0	0	0
gangway	4	.3721	.3657	35.6	0	1	0	2	0	0	1	0	2	0	0	1	0	0	0	0	0	0	0	0	0	1	0	0	0
gannets	2	.2401	.1133	30.5	1	0	0	0	1	0	0	0	0	0	0	0	0	0	0	0	0	0	0	0	0	1	1	0	0
Gant	7	.2353	.5425	37.3	6	0	1	0	0	0	0	0	6	0	0	0	0	0	0	0	0	0	0	0	0	0	0	1	0
gantry	2	.0000	.0299	24.8	0	0	0	2	0	0	0	0	0	0	0	0	2	0	0	0	0	0	0	0	0	0	0	0	0
gaol	2	.0000	.0215	23.3	0	0	0	0	2	0	0	0	0	0	0	2	0	0	0	0	0	0	0	0	0	0	0	0	0
gap	46	.7813	7.2017	48.6	5	2	3	11	6	8	8	3	1	7	0	3	0	2	0	10	0	0	2	2	3	5	4	7	0
Gap	14	.3729	1.3354	41.3	1	7	4	2	0	0	0	0	9	0	0	0	0	2	0	0	0	0	0	0	0	3	0	0	0
gape	9	.3948	.8149	39.1	0	1	0	2	6	0	0	0	3	0	1	0	0	0	0	0	0	0	0	0	1	0	4	0	0
gaped	8	.4943	.8761	39.4	1	1	2	1	0	1	2	0	3	0	1	1	0	1	0	0	0	0	0	0	1	1	0	0	0
gaping	18	.6255	2.3529	43.7	2	1	2	3	5	3	2	0	5	0	1	4	0	0	0	0	0	0	0	0	3	3	1	1	0
gaps	19	.7294	2.8121	44.5	1	0	1	3	5	5	4	0	2	3	0	0	0	4	0	2	0	0	1	0	2	1	2	2	0
Gar	2	.1787	.1174	30.7	0	0	0	0	1	1	0	0	1	0	0	0	0	0	0	0	0	0	0	0	1	0	0	0	0
garage	157	.7333	24.089	53.8	31	14	8	21	31	44	8	0	106	9	1	1	8	3	2	6	0	1	1	0	17	0	0	2	0
garages	8	.4848	.8488	39.3	2	1	2	0	2	1	0	0	1	0	0	0	0	4	0	1	0	0	0	0	0	1	1	0	0
Garagiola	2	.0000	.0243	23.9	0	0	0	0	2	0	0	0	0	0	0	0	0	0	0	0	0	0	0	0	0	0	0	2	0
garb	5	.3706	.4110	36.1	0	1	0	0	1	0	3	0	0	0	0	0	0	2	0	0	0	0	0	0	2	0	0	1	0
garbage	60	.8418	10.134	50.1	14	3	5	16	12	7	3	0	15	3	0	3	0	6	1	11	0	0	1	2	4	4	3	7	0
garbage-disposal	2	.1703	.0781	28.9	0	0	0	0	0	1	1	0	0	1	0	0	0	0	0	0	0	0	0	1	0	0	0	0	0
Garcilaso	2	.0000	.0243	23.9	0	0	0	0	2	0	0	0	0	0	0	0	0	0	0	0	0	0	0	0	0	0	0	2	0
gard	2	.0000	.0162	22.1	0	0	2	0	0	0	0	0	0	0	0	0	0	0	2	0	0	0	0	0	0	0	0	0	0
garde	3	.2410	.1667	32.2	0	0	0	0	1	0	0	2	0	0	0	0	0	0	1	0	0	0	0	0	0	0	0	2	0
Gardel	2	.0000	.0209	23.2	0	0	0	0	0	2	0	0	0	0	0	0	0	0	0	0	0	0	0	0	0	0	2	0	0
garden	600	.8775	105.63	60.2	238	106	63	78	52	33	16	14	294	23	7	26	19	44	7	55	2	4	2	0	55	34	11	17	0
Garden	40	.5971	5.0791	47.1	6	4	10	4	2	4	7	3	13	1	0	0	2	4	0	1	1	0	0	0	0	1	3	14	0
gardener	20	.6905	2.8525	44.6	6	3	0	5	3	2	1	0	5	3	0	1	1	0	0	5	0	0	0	0	2	1	0	2	0
Gardener	3	.0000	.1370	31.4	0	0	0	3	0	0	0	0	3	0	0	0	0	0	0	0	0	0	0	0	0	0	0	0	0
gardener's	2	.1948	.1250	31.0	1	1	0	0	0	0	0	0	1	0	0	0	0	0	0	0	0	0	0	0	0	1	0	0	0
Gardener's	2	.0000	.0914	29.6	0	0	0	2	0	0	0	0	2	0	0	0	0	0	0	0	0	0	0	0	0	0	0	0	0
gardeners	11	.3102	.8554	39.3	2	0	0	2	2	2	1	2	2	0	0	0	0	3	0	6	0	0	0	0	0	0	0	0	0
Gardenia	2	.0000	.0914	29.6	0	2	0	0	0	0	0	0	2	0	0	0	0	0	0	0	0	0	0	0	0	0	0	0	0
gardening	7	.6006	.8782	39.4	2	0	0	1	1	1	1	1	1	1	0	0	0	2	1	0	0	0	0	0	0	1	0	1	0
gardens	134	.8111	21.968	53.4	41	20	17	30	13	6	1	6	38	2	0	3	0	34	0	13	3	2	0	1	5	18	10	5	0
Gardens	13	.6156	1.6566	42.2	1	6	0	1	2	2	0	1	2	0	0	3	0	1	0	0	1	0	0	0	1	0	3	2	0

5Q galleys
6A gallied
XR galling
5P Gallipolli
7D gallipot
7N gallopin'
6R Galloping
5N gallumph
5K galumphing
XH Galvani's

XH galvanism
7Q galvanize
6F Galvao
5P Galway
8D Gambetta's
4Q Gambia's
7R gambit
9N gambits
3P Gamble's
9R gambles

9D Gambling
7J gambols
3P game-fixing
7Q game-rich
7A game-tracks
8D gamecocks
6R gamekeepers
6R Gamelan
7J gamelans
8H Gamma

7A Gamper
7N Gamut
7D Ganawese
6F Gander
9N gang's
7P Gangbusters
5A gangling
9P gangrenous
6A gangsters'
7Q gap-jawed

XR Garaci
8A Garage
7A garbage-can
6P garbed
7R garble
9P garbled
6R Garcia
3A gard
3P Garda
6H GardenCity

9D garden-chair
4A garden-path
6A garden's
XR gardened
7D GARDENER
3A gardenias
8H Gardiner
6P Gardiner's
7R Gardner
7D Gardner's

Word Type	F	D	U	SFI	3 Gr 3	4 Gr 4	5 Gr 5	6 Gr 6	7 Gr 7	8 Gr 8	9 Gr 9	X UnGr	A Read	B Eng & Gr	C Comp	D Lit	E Math	F Soc Stud	G Spell	H Sci	J Music	K Art	L Home Ec	M Shop	N Lib F	P Lib NF	Q Lib Ref	R Mag	S Rel
Gareth	5	.0000	.2284	33.6	0	0	5	0	0	0	0	0	5	0	0	0	0	0	0	0	0	0	0	0	0	0	0	0	0
Garfield	3	.3674	.2408	33.8	0	0	1	0	0	1	1	0	0	0	0	1	0	1	0	0	1	0	0	0	0	0	0	0	0
gargoyle	3	.2208	.1563	31.9	0	0	0	0	1	0	0	2	0	2	0	0	0	0	0	0	0	0	0	0	1	0	0	0	0
Garibaldi	5	.2226	.2657	34.2	3	0	0	0	2	0	0	0	0	0	0	0	0	0	0	0	0	0	0	0	0	2	3	0	0
garish	2	.2433	.1158	30.6	0	0	1	0	0	0	1	0	0	0	0	0	0	0	0	0	0	0	0	0	0	1	0	1	0
garland	4	.4857	.4029	36.1	0	0	2	0	2	0	0	0	0	0	0	1	0	0	0	0	1	0	0	0	1	0	1	0	0
garlands	4	.3713	.3634	35.6	0	0	0	2	2	0	0	0	2	0	0	1	0	0	0	0	0	0	0	0	1	0	0	0	0
garlic	13	.4346	1.1783	40.7	2	1	0	1	2	0	5	2	0	1	0	1	0	0	0	0	1	0	4	0	0	2	0	4	0
garment	117	.0915	2.7581	44.4	1	6	0	6	22	40	42	0	4	2	0	2	0	3	4	4	0	0	97	0	1	0	0	0	0
garments	64	.1522	2.4697	43.9	0	2	1	8	8	26	19	0	6	0	0	5	0	5	0	3	0	0	42	0	3	0	0	0	0
garnered	3	.3390	.2450	33.9	0	0	0	0	0	1	1	1	1	0	0	0	0	0	0	0	0	0	0	0	0	0	1	1	0
Garnerin	3	.0000	.1370	31.4	0	0	3	0	0	0	0	0	3	0	0	0	0	0	0	0	0	0	0	0	0	0	0	0	0
garnet	11	.1769	.5201	37.2	0	0	0	3	7	0	0	1	2	0	0	0	0	0	0	1	0	0	0	5	0	3	0	0	0
Garnet	28	.2048	1.3823	41.4	21	0	7	0	0	0	0	0	0	0	0	7	0	0	0	0	0	0	0	0	21	0	0	0	0
Garnet's	2	.2443	.1130	30.5	1	0	1	0	0	0	0	0	0	0	0	1	0	0	0	0	0	0	0	0	1	0	0	0	0
garnish	6	.0929	.1315	31.2	0	0	0	0	4	0	2	0	0	0	0	0	0	0	0	0	1	0	5	0	0	0	0	0	0
garnished	3	.3096	.2022	33.1	1	0	0	0	0	0	2	0	0	0	0	1	0	0	0	0	0	0	1	0	0	1	0	0	0
garnishes	3	.0000	.0097	19.8	0	0	0	0	2	0	1	0	0	0	0	0	0	0	0	0	0	0	3	0	0	0	0	0	0
garret	4	.4873	.4082	36.1	1	1	0	0	1	0	1	0	0	0	0	1	0	0	0	0	0	0	0	0	1	1	0	1	0
Garrett	6	.4221	.5602	37.5	2	0	0	2	2	0	0	0	1	0	0	2	0	0	0	0	0	0	0	0	0	2	0	1	0
garrison	9	.3725	.7876	39.0	0	3	2	1	1	1	1	0	3	0	0	0	0	0	0	0	0	0	0	0	1	1	4	0	0
garrisoned	2	.0000	.0243	23.9	0	0	0	0	1	0	0	1	0	0	0	0	0	0	0	0	0	0	0	0	0	0	0	2	0
garrisons	3	.1823	.1405	31.5	0	0	2	0	0	1	0	0	0	0	0	0	0	1	0	0	0	0	0	0	0	0	2	0	0
Garry	2	.0000	.0299	24.8	2	0	0	0	0	0	0	0	0	0	0	0	2	0	0	0	0	0	0	0	0	0	0	0	0
garter	14	.3426	1.1244	40.5	9	2	1	0	2	0	0	0	1	0	0	0	0	0	0	10	0	0	0	0	2	0	1	0	0
garters	3	.1367	.0954	29.8	0	0	0	1	0	0	2	0	0	0	0	1	0	0	0	0	0	0	2	0	0	0	0	0	0
Garver	15	.0000	.6852	38.4	0	0	0	0	0	15	0	0	15	0	0	0	0	0	0	0	0	0	0	0	0	0	0	0	0
Garver's	2	.0000	.0914	29.6	0	0	0	0	0	2	0	0	2	0	0	0	0	0	0	0	0	0	0	0	0	0	0	0	0
Garvey	2	.0000	.0389	25.9	0	0	0	0	0	2	0	0	0	0	0	0	0	2	0	0	0	0	0	0	0	0	0	0	0
Garwick	9	.0000	.4111	36.1	0	0	0	9	0	0	0	0	9	0	0	0	0	0	0	0	0	0	0	0	0	0	0	0	0
Gary	44	.5948	5.6863	47.5	1	1	22	6	6	4	4	0	24	1	0	1	6	0	1	0	2	0	0	0	0	0	0	9	0
gas	583	.7202	86.136	59.4	76	92	74	69	103	71	90	8	106	7	1	7	14	54	7	274	0	0	1	9	5	26	49	23	0
Gas	8	.2995	.6086	37.8	0	1	1	0	6	0	0	0	3	1	0	0	0	0	0	0	0	0	0	0	0	0	0	4	0
gas-pipe	4	.0000	.0469	26.7	0	0	4	0	0	0	0	0	0	0	0	0	0	0	0	0	0	0	0	0	4	0	0	0	0
GASCOIGNE	12	.0000	.1288	31.1	0	0	0	0	12	0	0	0	0	0	0	12	0	0	0	0	0	0	0	0	0	0	0	0	0
gaseous	22	.3481	1.7524	42.4	0	2	1	4	3	5	7	0	0	0	0	0	0	1	0	15	0	0	0	0	0	0	5	1	0
gases	276	.2904	19.441	52.9	49	31	25	16	50	36	58	11	3	0	0	0	0	5	0	229	0	0	0	0	0	8	25	6	0
gash	3	.3431	.2528	34.0	0	0	2	1	0	0	0	0	1	0	0	0	0	1	0	0	0	0	0	0	1	0	0	0	0
gashes	6	.4715	.6261	38.0	0	0	2	0	3	0	1	0	2	0	0	0	0	0	0	0	0	0	1	0	1	1	0	1	0
gasket	10	.1968	.4446	36.5	0	0	0	3	6	1	0	0	0	0	0	1	0	0	0	0	0	0	0	5	0	0	0	4	0
gasoline	189	.7835	29.911	54.8	32	29	39	28	23	27	10	1	26	3	6	0	34	27	3	44	1	0	0	1	1	25	9	9	0
gasoline-powered	3	.2440	.1815	32.6	0	0	2	0	0	1	0	0	0	1	0	0	0	2	0	0	0	0	0	0	0	0	0	0	0
gasolines	4	.0000	.0419	26.2	0	0	0	3	0	0	1	0	0	0	0	0	0	0	0	0	0	0	0	0	0	0	4	0	0
gasp	19	.6289	2.4934	44.0	2	2	2	4	7	0	1	1	5	2	0	2	0	0	0	0	0	0	0	0	5	1	1	3	0
Gaspard	3	.0000	.0434	26.4	0	0	0	2	1	0	0	0	0	0	0	0	0	0	0	0	0	0	0	0	0	3	0	0	0
Gasparilla	5	.0000	.2284	33.6	0	0	5	0	0	0	0	0	5	0	0	0	0	0	0	0	0	0	0	0	0	0	0	0	0
gasped	69	.5484	8.2863	49.2	6	21	13	12	13	1	1	2	31	0	0	5	0	0	0	1	0	0	0	0	20	6	1	5	0
Gasper	2	.1494	.1045	30.2	0	0	2	0	0	0	0	0	1	0	0	0	0	0	0	0	1	0	0	0	0	0	0	0	0
gasping	19	.5752	2.3277	43.7	1	1	1	7	4	3	2	0	6	2	0	5	0	0	0	0	0	0	0	0	2	1	0	3	0
gasps	8	.5496	.9497	39.8	0	0	1	2	3	0	2	0	3	1	0	1	0	0	0	0	1	0	0	0	2	0	0	0	0
gasses	2	.0000	.0394	26.0	2	0	0	0	0	0	0	0	0	0	0	0	0	0	0	2	0	0	0	0	0	0	0	0	0
gastric	6	.3623	.4910	36.9	0	0	0	0	3	0	1	2	0	0	0	1	0	0	0	4	0	0	0	0	0	0	1	0	0
gastropods	2	.2278	.1128	30.5	0	0	0	0	1	1	0	0	0	0	0	0	0	0	0	1	0	0	0	0	0	0	1	0	0
gastrovascular	2	.0000	.0394	26.0	0	0	0	0	2	0	0	0	0	0	0	0	0	0	0	2	0	0	0	0	0	0	0	0	0
Gata	12	.0000	.5482	37.4	12	0	0	0	0	0	0	0	12	0	0	0	0	0	0	0	0	0	0	0	0	0	0	0	0
gate	267	.7808	42.571	56.3	72	70	26	22	45	19	12	1	124	8	2	30	2	5	7	1	6	0	0	7	40	30	2	3	0
Gate	25	.5853	3.1051	44.9	6	0	5	7	5	2	0	0	6	0	0	1	1	7	0	0	0	0	0	0	1	0	2	7	0
gatekeeper	6	.2261	.4261	36.3	4	0	0	0	2	0	0	0	4	0	0	0	0	0	0	0	0	0	0	0	2	0	0	0	0
gateposts	2	.0000	.0290	24.6	0	2	0	0	0	0	0	0	0	0	0	0	0	0	0	0	0	0	0	0	0	2	0	0	0
gates	67	.8112	11.008	50.4	9	12	8	11	7	9	6	5	27	4	1	7	0	6	1	2	2	0	0	1	11	3	0	2	0
Gates	25	.3756	2.4048	43.8	11	7	1	0	4	2	0	0	17	0	0	0	0	4	0	0	0	0	0	0	0	0	4	0	0
Gates's	3	.0000	.1370	31.4	0	3	0	0	0	0	0	0	3	0	0	0	0	0	0	0	0	0	0	0	0	0	0	0	0
gateway	25	.4118	2.2507	43.5	4	3	8	4	4	1	1	0	3	0	0	0	1	3	0	0	0	5	0	0	1	7	4	1	0
Gateway	8	.3209	.5990	37.8	4	1	2	0	0	1	0	0	0	0	0	0	0	6	0	0	0	0	0	0	0	0	1	1	0
gateways	5	.2426	.2985	34.7	0	0	1	1	0	0	3	0	0	0	0	0	0	3	0	0	0	0	0	0	0	0	2	0	0
Gath	2	.0000	.0215	23.3	0	0	0	0	1	1	0	0	0	0	0	2	0	0	0	0	0	0	0	0	0	0	0	0	0
gather	208	.8767	36.376	55.6	35	47	19	40	41	12	9	5	50	5	6	11	3	17	4	33	19	2	3	0	13	21	9	11	1
gathered	297	.8956	53.086	57.2	38	66	35	58	40	31	23	6	120	6	2	17	2	30	2	16	11	4	5	0	31	26	12	13	0
gatherers	2	.2285	.1129	30.5	0	1	0	1	0	0	0	0	0	0	0	0	0	1	0	0	0	0	0	0	0	0	1	0	0
gathering	91	.8521	15.558	51.9	11	7	24	13	15	8	10	3	30	1	3	8	0	9	2	10	4	0	2	0	9	5	5	3	0
gatherings	11	.6139	1.3786	41.4	0	1	1	2	1	4	1	1	0	0	0	0	2	2	0	0	3	0	1	0	0	1	1	1	0
gathers	30	.7038	4.3000	46.3	6	3	3	6	2	3	5	2	3	1	1	0	0	3	0	7	2	0	3	0	1	7	0	2	0
Gato	6	.0000	.0485	26.9	6	0	0	0	0	0	0	0	0	0	0	0	0	0	0	0	6	0	0	0	0	0	0	0	0
Gatun	7	.0000	.1361	31.3	0	0	5	2	0	0	0	0	0	0	0	0	0	7	0	0	0	0	0	0	0	0	0	0	0
Gatundu	2	.0000	.0243	23.9	0	0	0	2	0	0	0	0	0	0	0	0	0	0	0	0	0	0	0	0	0	0	0	2	0
gaucho	6	.3657	.5386	37.3	0	0	0	6	0	0	0	0	3	0	0	0	0	0	0	0	1	0	0	0	0	0	0	2	0
Gaucho	3	.3272	.2361	33.7	1	0	1	1	0	0	0	0	1	0	0	0	0	0	0	0	1	0	0	0	0	0	1	0	0
gauchos	4	.3743	.3712	35.7	0	0	0	3	1	0	0	0	2	0	0	0	0	1	0	0	0	0	0	0	0	0	0	1	0
Gauchos	3	.0000	.0314	25.0	3	0	0	0	0	0	0	0	0	0	0	0	0	0	0	0	0	0	0	0	0	0	3	0	0
gaudy	8	.5815	.9551	39.8	1	1	1	1	2	2	0	0	0	0	0	0	0	2	0	0	1	0	1	0	0	1	2	1	0
gauge	53	.6989	7.5653	48.8	3	12	2	8	17	7	2	2	8	0	1	2	4	1	0	15	0	0	7	2	0	3	3	7	0
gauged	2	.2291	.1135	30.5	0	0	0	0	2	0	0	0	0	0	0	1	0	0	0	1	0	0	0	0	0	0	0	0	0
gauges	8	.4585	.7877	39.0	0	0	0	0	6	1	1	0	1	0	1	0	0	2	0	1	0	0	2	0	0	0	1	0	0
Gauguin	2	.2303	.1079	30.3	0	1	0	0	1	0	0	0	0	0	0	0	0	0	0	0	1	0	0	0	0	1	0	0	0
Gaul	2	.0000	.0209	23.2	1	0	0	0	1	0	0	0	0	0	0	0	0	0	0	0	0	0	0	0	0	0	2	0	0
Gaulle	7	.2771	.4435	36.5	0	0	1	0	0	2	4	0	0	1	0	0	0	0	0	0	0	0	0	0	0	1	0	5	0
Gaullist	3	.0000	.0365	25.6	0	0	0	0	0	3	0	0	0	0	0	0	0	0	0	0	0	0	0	0	0	0	0	3	0
Gauls	2	.2446	.1123	30.5	0	0	0	0	2	0	0	0	0	1	0	0	0	0	0	0	0	0	0	0	0	0	1	0	0
gaunt	20	.6901	2.8376	44.5	0	0	2	2	5	7	4	0	5	1	0	5	0	1	0	0	1	0	0	0	3	1	1	2	0
Gaunt	2	.0000	.0209	23.2	0	0	2	0	0	0	0	0	0	0	0	0	0	0	0	0	0	0	0	0	0	0	2	0	0
gauntlet	3	.2309	.1631	32.1	0	0	0	0	3	0	0	0	0	0	0	1	0	0	0	0	0	0	0	0	0	0	0	2	0
Gauss	4	.0000	.0599	27.8	0	0	0	0	0	4	0	0	0	0	0	0	4	0	0	0	0	0	0	0	0	0	0	0	0
Gautama	5	.0000	.0972	29.9	0	0	0	5	0	0	0	0	0	0	0	0	0	5	0	0	0	0	0	0	0	0	0	0	0

4N garfish
4A Gargantua
XB gargled
XB gargouille
3P Garibaldi's
7Q garishly
9R garlic-reeking
7R Garlits
3P garment's
8A Garmisch
7R Garner
7Q garnering
6P garnets
8D Garoghlanian
9F Garonne
3P Garrett's
7G garten
3B Garth
6A Garwick's
5A Gary's
4R gas-burning
9R gas-escape
8H gas-filled
7B gas-light
7R gas-power
7R gas-powered
8A gas-scorching
9D gas-station
6R gas-turbine
4H gas-water
9M gas-welding
7D Gascoigne
7A Gascon
4D gashed
9P gashing
4A gasholder
7R gasket-sealed
7M gaskets
7A Gaskets
4A gaslight
7R gasoline-driven
8F gasometers
8F Gaspar
XR Gasperi
5N gaspipe
7A gassed
9N Gassers
3R Gaston
XH gastric-juice
XH gastrocnemius
5P gastronomic
XN gastroscope
3P GASTROTRICH
7D gat
7F Gat
7A gate-leg
3A gatekeeper's
9Q gatherer
6K Gathering
XR gatherum
9R Gator
7Q Gattamelata
6A Gatwick
9D gaud
9A gaudiest
6E gauge-reading
XH gauging
8K Gauguin's
9R Gaulle's
8D gauntleted
5P gauntly
6F Gautama's

Word Type	F	D	U	SFI	3 Gr 3	4 Gr 4	5 Gr 5	6 Gr 6	7 Gr 7	8 Gr 8	9 Gr 9	X UnGr	A Read	B Eng & Gr	C Comp	D Lit	E Math	F Soc Stud	G Spell	H Sci	J Music	K Art	L Home Ec	M Shop	N Lib F	P Lib NF	Q Lib Ref	R Mag	S Rel
gauze	12	.6458	1.5677	42.0	0	1	0	0	4	5	1	1	0	0	1	4	0	0	1	1	0	0	0	1	1	2	1	0	0
gave	1534	.8857	271.42	64.3	341	268	164	195	263	179	106	18	574	71	9	108	95	127	33	32	49	7	0	1	132	149	59	83	5
gavel	5	.3330	.4105	36.1	2	0	0	0	3	0	0	0	2	2	0	0	0	0	0	0	0	0	0	0	1	0	0	0	0
gavotte	7	.0000	.0566	27.5	0	5	1	0	0	1	0	0	0	0	0	0	0	0	0	0	7	0	0	0	0	0	0	0	0
Gavotte	2	.0000	.0162	22.1	0	2	0	0	0	0	0	0	0	0	0	0	0	0	0	0	2	0	0	0	0	0	0	0	0
gaw	2	.1787	.1174	30.7	1	1	0	0	0	0	0	0	1	0	0	0	0	0	0	0	0	0	0	0	1	0	0	0	0
Gawain	7	.0000	.3198	35.0	0	0	0	2	5	0	0	0	7	0	0	0	0	0	0	0	0	0	0	0	0	0	0	0	0
gawk	3	.3370	.2430	33.9	0	0	0	0	1	2	0	0	1	0	0	1	0	0	0	0	0	0	0	0	0	0	1	0	0
gawking	2	.0000	.0243	23.9	0	0	0	1	1	0	0	0	0	0	0	0	0	0	0	0	0	0	0	0	0	0	0	2	0
gawky	2	.0000	.0219	23.4	0	0	0	0	0	0	2	0	0	2	0	0	0	0	0	0	0	0	0	0	0	0	0	0	0
gay	131	.7710	20.405	53.1	23	28	15	17	21	9	12	6	30	7	3	13	0	10	3	2	36	0	4	1	6	6	1	9	0
Gay	5	.2040	.2436	33.9	1	1	0	0	2	1	0	0	0	0	0	0	2	0	0	0	3	0	0	0	0	0	0	0	0
Gay's	2	.1733	.1149	30.6	1	0	0	0	0	1	0	0	1	1	0	0	0	0	0	0	0	0	0	0	0	0	0	0	0
gayer	4	.4448	.3915	35.9	1	0	1	0	1	0	0	1	1	1	0	1	0	0	0	0	1	0	0	0	0	0	0	0	0
gayest	4	.4516	.4046	36.1	0	2	0	1	0	1	0	0	1	0	0	1	0	1	0	0	0	0	0	0	0	1	0	0	0
Gaylord	5	.1738	.2196	33.4	0	0	3	0	1	1	0	0	0	0	0	0	0	0	0	0	0	0	0	0	4	0	0	1	0
Gaylord's	2	.0000	.0234	23.7	0	0	2	0	0	0	0	0	0	0	0	0	0	0	0	0	0	0	0	0	2	0	0	0	0
gayly	5	.3082	.3848	35.9	1	1	0	2	1	0	0	0	2	1	0	0	0	0	2	0	0	0	0	0	0	0	0	0	0
gaz'd	2	.0000	.0290	24.6	0	0	0	0	2	0	0	0	0	0	0	0	0	0	0	0	0	0	0	0	0	2	0	0	0
Gaza	14	.5152	1.5191	41.8	0	2	2	0	4	1	1	4	0	4	0	0	0	6	1	0	0	0	0	0	0	2	0	1	0
gaze	39	.6400	5.1712	47.1	1	5	3	6	15	4	5	0	7	1	0	9	0	3	0	5	0	1	0	0	10	0	0	3	0
gazed	68	.6716	9.6550	49.8	9	11	14	14	12	4	3	1	38	1	3	6	0	0	0	2	1	0	0	0	10	3	1	3	0
gazelle	8	.4614	.7855	39.0	0	2	0	4	2	0	0	0	1	0	0	0	0	0	0	0	1	1	0	0	3	0	2	0	0
gazelles	7	.4766	.7174	38.6	0	0	0	5	2	0	0	0	1	0	0	0	0	0	0	0	0	0	0	0	3	1	1	1	0
gazes	7	.3715	.5904	37.7	1	0	2	0	4	0	0	0	1	0	0	3	0	1	0	0	0	0	0	0	0	2	0	0	0
Gazette	3	.1200	.1302	31.1	0	0	0	1	0	0	2	0	1	2	0	0	0	0	0	0	0	0	0	0	0	0	0	0	0
Gazetteer-Index	4	.0000	.0419	26.2	0	4	0	0	0	0	0	0	0	0	0	0	0	0	0	0	0	0	0	0	0	0	4	0	0
gazing	23	.5327	2.6377	44.2	0	1	1	3	10	2	4	2	7	0	2	7	0	0	0	1	0	0	0	0	4	1	0	1	0
GCF	27	.0000	.4041	36.1	0	0	2	11	7	7	0	0	0	0	0	0	27	0	0	0	0	0	0	0	0	0	0	0	0
ge	9	.1636	.3552	35.5	2	0	0	5	0	2	0	0	0	2	0	0	0	0	7	0	0	0	0	0	0	0	0	0	0
GE	7	.0620	.1965	32.9	0	0	0	0	2	0	5	0	1	0	0	0	0	0	0	0	0	0	0	0	0	0	0	6	0
GE'S	2	.0000	.0243	23.9	0	0	0	0	0	0	2	0	0	0	0	0	0	0	0	0	0	0	0	0	0	0	0	2	0
gear	80	.7263	12.062	50.8	14	19	3	6	22	9	6	1	41	1	1	2	1	0	0	1	0	1	0	0	2	13	4	13	0
gearbox	3	.2321	.1635	32.1	0	1	0	0	1	0	0	1	0	0	0	0	0	0	0	0	0	0	0	0	0	0	1	2	0
geared	12	.6165	1.5100	41.8	0	0	0	0	6	4	2	0	0	0	0	2	1	1	0	1	0	0	0	1	0	1	4	1	0
gears	20	.6167	2.5407	44.0	3	1	1	1	2	10	2	0	2	0	0	1	1	1	0	4	0	2	0	2	0	1	4	2	0
gebeta	4	.0000	.1827	32.6	0	4	0	0	0	0	0	0	4	0	0	0	0	0	0	0	0	0	0	0	0	0	0	0	0
gecko	3	.2357	.2199	33.4	1	2	0	0	0	0	0	0	2	0	0	0	0	0	0	0	0	0	0	0	0	1	0	0	0
geckos	4	.1335	.1958	32.9	0	1	0	0	0	0	3	0	1	0	0	0	0	0	0	3	0	0	0	0	0	0	0	0	0
Gedney	2	.0000	.0234	23.7	0	0	0	2	0	0	0	0	0	0	0	0	0	0	0	0	0	0	0	0	2	0	0	0	0
gee	42	.6503	5.8135	47.6	9	10	3	8	6	3	2	1	23	1	0	6	1	0	0	0	1	0	0	0	5	3	0	2	0
gee-haw	3	.0000	.0243	23.8	0	0	0	3	0	0	0	0	0	0	0	0	0	0	0	0	3	0	0	0	0	0	0	0	0
geese	74	.8360	12.437	50.9	22	15	7	14	13	0	3	0	23	4	1	6	1	4	0	5	5	0	0	0	5	10	7	3	0
Geese	8	.0000	.3655	35.6	0	0	0	8	0	0	0	0	8	0	0	0	0	0	0	0	0	0	0	0	0	0	0	0	0
Gehrig	11	.1945	.8000	39.0	1	2	0	0	8	0	0	0	10	0	0	0	0	0	0	0	0	0	0	0	0	1	0	0	0
Geiger	22	.2454	1.4989	41.8	0	0	3	6	0	10	3	0	6	0	0	0	0	0	0	15	0	0	0	0	0	0	1	0	0
gel	6	.1314	.2134	33.3	0	0	5	0	0	0	1	0	0	0	0	0	1	0	0	0	0	0	0	0	0	0	5	0	0
gelatin	17	.0550	.2580	34.1	0	1	0	1	2	5	8	0	0	0	0	0	0	0	0	1	0	0	15	0	0	0	1	0	0
gelatine	4	.2517	.2137	33.3	0	1	1	0	0	0	2	0	0	0	0	0	0	0	1	0	1	0	0	2	0	0	0	0	0
gelatinous	2	.0000	.0209	23.2	0	0	0	1	1	0	0	0	0	0	0	0	0	0	0	0	0	0	0	0	0	0	2	0	0
gelding	5	.1738	.2196	33.4	0	3	0	0	0	1	1	0	0	0	0	0	0	0	0	0	0	0	0	0	4	0	0	1	0
Gell-Mann	4	.0000	.0419	26.2	0	0	0	0	0	0	4	0	0	0	0	0	0	0	0	0	0	0	0	0	0	0	4	0	0
gem	19	.6250	2.5372	44.0	0	0	2	3	5	2	4	3	9	0	0	1	0	1	3	3	1	0	0	0	0	0	1	0	0
GEM	3	.0000	.1370	31.4	0	3	0	0	0	0	0	0	3	0	0	0	0	0	0	0	0	0	0	0	0	0	0	0	0
Gemini	12	.4803	1.2702	41.0	0	4	2	1	2	2	0	1	3	0	0	0	0	0	0	4	0	1	0	0	0	0	1	3	0
gemmed	3	.0000	.0591	27.7	0	0	0	3	0	0	0	0	0	0	0	0	0	0	0	3	0	0	0	0	0	0	0	0	0
Gempylus	4	.0000	.1827	32.6	0	0	0	0	4	0	0	0	4	0	0	0	0	0	0	0	0	0	0	0	0	0	0	0	0
gems	18	.5811	2.3170	43.6	1	0	1	0	12	1	2	1	12	0	0	0	0	1	0	1	0	0	0	1	1	0	1	1	0
gen	3	.3670	.2406	33.8	0	0	0	0	2	1	0	0	0	0	0	0	0	0	1	1	0	0	0	0	0	0	1	0	0
Gen	40	.1220	1.3339	41.3	0	0	1	3	19	16	1	0	0	0	0	0	0	0	0	0	0	0	0	0	0	0	35	5	0
gendarmes	3	.0000	.0352	25.5	1	0	0	2	0	0	0	0	0	0	0	0	0	0	0	0	0	0	0	0	3	0	0	0	0
gene	21	.3128	1.5461	41.9	0	0	0	7	8	0	2	4	0	0	0	0	0	0	0	16	0	0	0	0	0	0	3	2	0
Gene	5	.1848	.2301	33.6	0	0	0	1	3	1	0	0	0	1	0	0	0	0	0	0	0	0	0	0	0	0	0	4	0
genera	5	.0000	.0523	27.2	0	0	0	0	5	0	0	0	0	0	0	0	0	0	0	0	0	0	0	0	0	0	5	0	0
general	619	.8862	108.84	60.4	18	32	66	54	150	152	124	23	58	74	15	30	33	62	10	43	24	4	31	28	15	34	113	45	0
General	254	.7019	36.544	55.6	11	39	23	24	39	82	32	4	37	2	1	9	5	97	0	1	2	0	0	0	9	37	22	32	0
general's	7	.3423	.5256	37.2	0	1	0	0	0	4	2	0	0	0	0	3	0	0	0	0	0	0	0	0	0	1	0	3	0
General's	2	.2152	.1357	31.3	0	0	0	0	2	0	0	0	1	0	0	0	0	1	0	0	0	0	0	0	0	0	0	0	0
generalization	13	.3671	1.0530	40.2	0	0	0	1	3	5	4	0	1	8	0	0	0	0	1	1	0	0	0	0	0	0	2	0	0
generalizations	14	.6618	1.8868	42.8	0	0	3	1	4	4	2	0	1	2	1	0	0	1	3	1	0	0	0	0	0	2	2	1	0
generalize	4	.3444	.3047	34.8	0	0	0	2	0	1	1	0	0	2	0	0	0	1	0	0	0	0	0	0	0	0	1	0	0
generalized	5	.4561	.4818	36.8	0	0	0	1	1	2	1	0	0	2	0	0	1	0	0	0	0	0	0	0	0	1	1	0	0
generally	314	.8537	53.373	57.3	9	11	34	31	76	63	74	16	27	26	5	6	8	40	5	37	12	1	18	19	10	17	55	28	0
generals	24	.5744	2.9015	44.6	1	0	5	0	5	8	4	1	3	0	0	0	0	8	0	0	0	0	0	0	1	4	4	4	0
generate	18	.5995	2.2316	43.5	1	3	1	0	10	2	0	1	0	1	0	0	0	3	0	5	0	0	0	0	0	3	4	2	0
generated	28	.4902	2.8597	44.6	0	2	2	1	10	7	5	1	0	0	0	0	2	5	0	2	3	0	0	6	0	0	5	5	0
generates	7	.4922	.7245	38.6	0	1	1	0	2	2	1	0	0	0	0	0	0	0	0	2	0	0	0	1	0	2	1	1	0
generating	11	.5240	1.2065	40.8	1	0	1	0	5	1	3	0	0	0	0	0	0	1	0	3	2	0	0	0	0	2	3	0	0
generation	107	.8255	17.616	52.5	3	3	11	10	27	25	18	10	6	5	1	3	1	8	4	13	12	5	2	1	0	5	19	22	0
Generation	6	.0000	.0729	28.6	0	0	0	4	0	0	2	0	0	0	0	0	0	0	0	0	0	0	0	0	0	0	0	6	0
generations	80	.8836	14.041	51.5	0	2	6	11	27	8	15	11	7	2	1	6	1	11	3	12	4	2	1	0	2	5	10	13	0
generator	37	.5389	4.1954	46.2	3	12	0	10	5	4	3	0	1	0	0	0	0	2	0	20	3	0	0	4	0	3	3	1	0
generators	32	.5081	3.4223	45.3	3	6	2	7	4	4	5	1	0	1	0	0	0	3	0	13	0	0	0	5	0	3	3	4	0
generic	6	.1290	.1795	32.5	0	2	1	0	3	0	0	0	0	0	4	0	0	0	0	0	0	0	0	0	0	0	1	1	0
generosity	8	.5643	.9785	39.9	0	0	1	0	2	2	2	1	3	1	0	1	0	2	0	0	0	0	0	0	0	0	0	1	0
generous	54	.8195	8.8646	49.5	2	6	7	10	17	4	5	3	8	3	0	2	0	7	6	2	3	1	1	0	11	4	0	6	0
generously	12	.5391	1.3434	41.3	0	2	1	2	4	2	0	1	1	0	2	0	0	1	0	0	0	1	0	0	1	1	1	4	0
genes	37	.3075	2.6958	44.3	0	0	0	16	9	1	3	8	0	0	0	0	0	0	1	30	0	0	0	0	0	0	5	1	0
Genesis	3	.1169	.1277	31.1	0	0	0	0	2	1	0	0	1	0	0	0	0	0	0	0	0	0	0	0	0	0	2	0	0
genetic	16	.4666	1.5979	42.0	0	0	2	0	5	0	4	5	0	0	0	0	0	0	0	7	0	0	0	0	0	2	4	3	0
genetically	2	.2346	.1166	30.7	0	0	0	0	1	0	0	1	0	0	0	0	0	0	0	1	0	0	0	0	0	0	0	1	0
geneticists	2	.0000	.0394	26.0	0	0	0	2	0	0	0	0	0	0	0	0	0	0	0	2	0	0	0	0	0	0	0	0	0
genetics	2	.2346	.1166	30.7	0	0	1	0	0	0	0	1	0	0	0	0	0	0	0	1	0	0	0	0	0	0	0	1	0
Geneva	32	.5562	3.7534	45.7	5	2	2	10	3	3	6	1	3	0	0	1	1	12	0	0	0	0	0	0	0	5	8	2	0

7D Gauthier
5Q Gautier
4D gauzy
7R gavels
3P gavest
7P gavottes
7A Gawain's
8D Gawd
4A gay-colored
6A gay-coloured
6J Gayane
6A Gazelle
4Q gazetteer
8Q GazzetedesBeaux-Arts
6J GBD
7B GC
6F Gdynia
8F gear-cutting
7R gearing
8C Geary
7A geave
6P Gedalge
4A Gedovius
8N gee-pole
3A geez
8E GEF
9D geh
6A gehts
8E Geis
5Q geisha
9H gek-ohz
5G gelata
8L Gelatin
6H gelatin-like
5G gelatina
9L gelatinize
5G gelee
8R Gellis
5R gels
XR Geminis
6N Gemma
XR gemmologist
9R Gemutlichkeit
7R gen-er-a-tion
7P gendarme
XH gene-loci
8B Gene's
7P genealogical
7R genealogies
XR general-in-chief
9M general-purpose
9Q general-studies
8D generaled
5P Generalissimo
8Q generalogy
7R generalship
9D generation's
XP generative
8R Genesco
7R Genesee
7Q genet
XH genetical
9Q geneticist
7H Genetics

Word Type	F	D	U	SFI	3 Gr 3	4 Gr 4	5 Gr 5	6 Gr 6	7 Gr 7	8 Gr 8	9 Gr 9	X UnGr	A Read	B Eng & Gr	C Comp	D Lit	E Math	F Soc Stud	G Spell	H Sci	J Music	K Art	L Home Ec	M Shop	N Lib F	P Lib NF	Q Lib Ref	R Mag	S Rel
Genevieve	7	.0000	.0821	29.1	7	0	0	0	0	0	0	0	0	0	0	0	0	0	0	0	0	0	0	0	7	0	0	0	0
Genghis	22	.4666	2.2224	43.5	7	0	0	4	2	6	3	0	2	0	0	0	0	6	0	0	0	0	0	0	0	7	6	1	0
genial	3	.3874	.2487	34.0	1	0	0	0	1	1	0	0	0	1	0	0	0	0	0	0	0	0	0	0	1	0	1	0	0
genially	2	.1787	.1174	30.7	0	0	0	0	2	0	0	0	1	0	0	0	0	0	0	0	0	0	0	0	1	0	0	0	0
genie	16	.5058	1.7929	42.5	0	1	10	0	3	1	1	0	6	0	0	0	0	3	1	0	0	0	0	0	5	0	1	0	0
genii	3	.3431	.2528	34.0	0	1	2	0	0	0	0	0	1	0	0	0	0	1	0	0	0	0	0	0	1	0	0	0	0
genital	3	.3764	.2483	33.9	0	0	0	0	1	0	1	1	0	0	0	0	0	0	0	1	0	0	0	0	0	0	1	1	0
genius	68	.7656	10.561	50.2	3	6	15	7	12	7	14	4	19	2	1	0	0	1	0	1	4	1	0	1	5	8	19	6	0
geniuses	2	.1787	.1174	30.7	0	0	0	0	0	1	0	1	1	0	0	0	0	0	0	0	0	0	0	0	1	0	0	0	0
Genoa	15	.5487	1.7548	42.4	3	0	3	3	3	1	2	0	2	0	0	1	0	7	0	0	0	0	0	0	0	3	1	1	0
Genoese	2	.2306	.1140	30.6	0	0	0	1	0	0	0	1	0	1	0	0	0	1	0	0	0	0	0	0	0	0	0	0	0
genre	7	.4108	.6076	37.8	0	0	0	0	1	2	4	0	0	0	0	0	0	0	0	0	0	1	0	0	0	1	3	2	0
genteel	2	.2442	.1134	30.5	0	0	0	0	0	1	1	0	0	1	0	0	0	0	0	0	0	0	0	0	0	0	0	1	0
gentle	200	.8830	35.235	55.5	35	27	24	19	47	18	23	7	62	12	1	25	0	10	3	10	10	1	1	1	28	19	8	9	0
gentled	3	.2212	.2099	33.2	0	1	0	1	1	0	0	0	2	0	0	1	0	0	0	0	0	0	0	0	0	0	0	0	0
gentlefolk	2	.2440	.1132	30.5	0	0	0	0	1	0	1	0	0	0	0	1	0	0	0	0	0	0	0	0	0	0	0	1	0
gentleman	121	.8028	19.592	52.9	8	14	9	25	31	3	30	1	35	3	1	25	1	1	4	0	3	1	1	0	23	7	7	9	0
Gentleman	6	.2687	.4022	36.0	0	0	3	0	1	2	0	0	1	0	0	3	0	2	0	0	0	0	0	0	0	0	0	0	0
GENTLEMAN	9	.0000	.0966	29.8	0	0	0	0	9	0	0	0	0	0	0	9	0	0	0	0	0	0	0	0	0	0	0	0	0
gentleman's	4	.3713	.3634	35.6	1	0	0	2	0	1	0	0	2	0	0	1	0	0	0	0	0	0	0	0	1	0	0	0	0
Gentleman's	2	.0000	.0914	29.6	0	0	0	0	2	0	0	0	2	0	0	0	0	0	0	0	0	0	0	0	0	0	0	0	0
gentlemanly	7	.5355	.7945	39.0	0	1	1	1	1	3	0	0	1	0	0	1	0	2	0	0	0	0	1	0	1	1	0	0	0
gentlemen	94	.7293	14.039	51.5	8	19	6	15	25	7	12	2	29	2	0	18	0	4	1	0	8	0	1	0	13	14	2	2	0
Gentlemen	8	.3393	.6122	37.9	0	1	1	0	2	1	3	0	1	5	0	1	0	0	0	0	1	0	0	0	0	0	0	0	0
gentlemen's	3	.3863	.2513	34.0	0	1	0	0	2	0	0	0	0	0	0	0	0	0	0	0	0	0	0	0	1	1	0	1	0
gentleness	9	.5941	1.1229	40.5	1	0	1	2	3	1	1	0	2	1	0	0	0	0	0	0	1	0	0	0	1	3	0	1	0
gentler	3	.2365	.1616	32.1	0	1	0	1	0	1	0	0	0	0	0	0	0	0	0	0	1	0	0	0	0	0	2	0	0
gently	245	.8598	42.130	56.2	35	54	23	26	53	25	16	13	63	3	2	30	1	14	1	27	14	1	9	0	22	32	5	21	0
gentry	7	.4533	.6887	38.4	0	0	1	1	0	4	1	0	1	0	0	0	0	1	0	0	1	0	0	0	0	1	3	0	0
Gentry	4	.2386	.2998	34.8	0	0	1	3	0	0	0	0	3	0	0	0	0	0	0	0	0	0	0	0	0	0	1	0	0
Gentry's	2	.0000	.0209	23.2	0	0	2	0	0	0	0	0	0	0	0	0	0	0	0	0	0	0	0	0	0	0	2	0	0
gents	3	.0000	.0243	23.8	0	0	3	0	0	0	0	0	0	0	0	0	0	0	0	0	3	0	0	0	0	0	0	0	0
genuine	26	.7465	3.9253	45.9	2	1	1	5	4	6	4	3	4	0	1	3	2	1	0	1	1	0	2	0	3	2	0	6	0
genuinely	5	.2766	.3388	35.3	1	0	1	1	3	0	0	0	1	0	0	0	0	0	0	0	0	0	0	0	0	0	1	3	0
genus	31	.3850	2.6075	44.2	0	6	3	0	15	0	5	2	0	0	0	1	0	0	1	11	0	0	0	0	2	0	16	0	0
geo	4	.2999	.2714	34.3	0	2	0	1	0	0	1	0	0	0	0	0	1	0	2	1	0	0	0	0	0	0	0	0	0
Geo	3	.0000	.0314	25.0	0	0	0	0	3	0	0	0	0	0	0	0	0	0	0	0	0	0	0	0	0	0	3	0	0
geodesic	2	.0000	.0243	23.9	0	0	0	0	1	1	0	0	0	0	0	0	0	0	0	0	0	0	0	0	0	0	0	2	0
Geoffrey	5	.3454	.3692	35.7	0	0	0	3	1	0	1	0	0	0	1	0	0	0	1	0	0	0	0	0	3	0	0	0	0
geographer	3	.3769	.2484	34.0	0	1	1	0	0	0	0	1	0	0	0	0	0	1	0	0	0	0	0	0	0	0	1	1	0
geographers	15	.2345	.8665	39.4	2	1	8	2	1	0	1	0	0	0	0	0	0	8	0	0	0	0	0	0	0	0	7	0	0
geographic	28	.5212	3.0856	44.9	0	4	4	1	9	2	8	0	0	0	0	0	0	13	0	6	1	0	0	1	0	0	7	0	0
Geographic	6	.3738	.5111	37.1	0	1	0	4	1	0	0	0	1	0	0	0	0	0	0	1	0	0	0	0	0	0	1	3	0
geographical	28	.4678	2.8324	44.5	1	5	2	3	6	4	7	0	3	1	0	0	0	7	0	3	2	0	0	0	0	0	12	0	0
geographically	5	.3562	.3925	35.9	1	1	2	1	0	0	0	0	0	0	0	0	0	0	0	0	0	0	0	0	0	3	1	1	0
geographies	3	.2031	.1990	33.0	1	0	1	1	1	0	0	0	2	0	0	0	0	0	1	0	0	0	0	0	0	0	0	0	0
geography	104	.6512	14.035	51.5	10	14	26	9	33	3	9	0	15	2	0	2	2	53	7	0	2	0	0	1	1	2	16	1	0
Geography	4	.4810	.4060	36.1	1	0	2	0	1	0	0	0	0	0	0	0	0	1	0	0	0	0	0	0	1	0	1	1	0
geologic	32	.3460	2.5154	44.0	0	1	0	2	15	7	6	1	1	0	0	0	0	2	0	14	0	0	0	0	0	0	14	1	0
geological	17	.5023	1.8396	42.6	0	0	1	3	3	2	8	0	1	0	0	0	0	2	0	9	0	0	0	0	1	1	0	3	0
Geological	8	.4526	.7808	38.9	1	0	0	1	1	4	1	0	0	0	0	0	0	0	0	4	0	0	0	0	0	1	2	1	0
geologically	4	.2437	.2257	33.5	0	1	0	2	1	0	0	0	0	0	0	0	0	0	0	0	0	0	0	0	0	0	2	2	0
geologist	18	.4306	1.6998	42.3	2	1	1	3	7	0	3	1	0	0	0	1	0	1	0	12	0	0	0	0	0	0	3	1	0
geologist's	2	.0000	.0394	26.0	0	0	1	1	0	0	0	0	0	0	0	0	0	0	0	2	0	0	0	0	0	0	0	0	0
geologists	45	.4468	4.4145	46.4	4	6	4	5	6	12	8	0	2	0	0	0	0	3	0	28	0	0	0	0	0	1	7	4	0
geology	32	.4786	3.2819	45.2	0	0	2	4	12	6	6	2	0	2	0	1	0	0	0	19	0	0	0	0	0	0	4	6	0
geometric	73	.4814	7.3999	48.7	7	0	4	5	7	30	18	2	0	0	0	0	49	1	0	5	0	8	2	1	0	1	6	0	0
geometrical	8	.4243	.7014	38.5	0	0	1	0	1	1	5	0	0	1	0	0	0	0	0	0	0	1	0	2	0	0	4	0	0
geometrically	7	.3955	.6024	37.8	0	0	0	0	0	2	3	2	0	0	0	0	3	0	0	2	0	1	0	0	0	0	1	0	0
geometries	2	.0000	.0299	24.8	0	0	0	0	0	2	0	0	0	0	0	0	2	0	0	0	0	0	0	0	0	0	0	0	0
geometry	106	.4184	9.6313	49.8	2	1	2	20	22	26	32	1	2	0	0	0	74	4	0	2	0	1	0	0	0	3	17	3	0
Geophysical	11	.5915	1.3893	41.4	0	0	2	4	1	3	1	0	3	0	0	1	0	1	0	4	0	0	0	0	0	1	1	0	0
geophysicist	2	.2278	.1128	30.5	0	0	0	0	1	0	1	0	0	0	0	0	0	0	0	1	0	0	0	0	0	0	1	0	0
geophysicists	3	.3346	.2478	33.9	0	0	1	1	1	0	0	0	1	0	0	0	0	0	0	1	0	0	0	0	0	0	1	0	0
Georg	6	.5329	.5697	37.6	1	0	0	1	0	2	1	0	1	0	0	1	0	0	0	1	0	0	0	0	0	0	1	1	0
George	828	.7843	131.38	61.2	140	323	79	48	121	78	31	8	191	27	3	47	17	91	3	3	27	7	0	1	29	281	36	65	0
GEORGE	8	.0000	.0859	29.3	0	0	0	0	8	0	0	0	0	0	0	8	0	0	0	0	0	0	0	0	0	0	0	0	0
George's	30	.6230	3.8666	45.9	3	13	2	0	4	2	6	0	4	3	0	3	0	0	1	0	0	0	0	0	3	13	1	2	0
Georges	17	.5387	1.8799	42.7	1	0	2	1	4	7	2	0	0	0	0	0	0	0	0	1	4	2	0	0	1	1	3	5	0
Georgetown	10	.3525	.7994	39.0	3	1	1	0	1	4	0	0	1	0	0	0	0	1	0	0	0	0	0	0	0	4	4	0	0
Georgia	93	.5973	11.658	50.7	12	3	33	6	19	13	6	1	11	2	0	3	2	44	0	0	0	0	0	0	0	15	7	9	0
Georgia's	4	.3743	.3712	35.7	0	0	1	0	0	0	2	1	2	0	0	0	0	1	0	0	0	0	0	0	0	0	0	1	0
Georgian	4	.3444	.3047	34.8	0	0	0	0	0	1	3	0	0	2	0	0	0	1	0	0	0	0	0	0	0	0	1	0	0
Georgie	66	.3723	5.3949	47.3	6	55	5	0	0	0	0	0	1	0	0	5	0	0	0	0	8	0	0	0	5	47	0	0	0
Georgie's	3	.2347	.1695	32.3	1	2	0	0	0	0	0	0	0	0	0	0	0	0	0	0	0	0	0	0	1	2	0	0	0
geosynclinal	3	.0000	.0591	27.7	0	0	0	0	0	0	3	0	0	0	0	0	0	0	0	3	0	0	0	0	0	0	0	0	0
geosyncline	4	.0000	.0789	29.0	0	0	0	0	0	0	4	0	0	0	0	0	0	0	0	4	0	0	0	0	0	0	0	0	0
geosynclines	6	.0000	.1183	30.7	0	0	0	0	0	0	6	0	0	0	0	0	0	0	0	6	0	0	0	0	0	0	0	0	0
geotropism	4	.0000	.0789	29.0	0	0	0	0	4	0	0	0	0	0	0	0	0	0	0	4	0	0	0	0	0	0	0	0	0
Gerald	9	.4399	.8302	39.2	1	0	0	0	3	1	0	4	0	0	0	3	0	0	0	0	0	1	0	0	0	0	1	4	0
Geraldine	3	.2279	.2143	33.3	2	0	0	0	1	0	0	0	2	0	0	0	0	0	0	0	0	0	0	0	0	0	0	1	0
geranium	10	.3666	.8450	39.3	2	3	0	0	3	1	1	0	1	0	1	1	0	0	0	7	0	0	0	0	0	0	0	0	0
geraniums	10	.3631	.9167	39.6	3	1	3	3	0	0	0	0	5	0	0	0	0	0	0	4	0	0	0	0	1	0	0	0	0
Gerard	3	.3845	.2449	33.9	0	1	0	0	1	0	1	0	0	1	0	0	0	0	1	0	0	0	0	0	0	0	1	0	0
Gerbert	2	.0000	.0219	23.4	0	0	0	0	0	0	2	0	0	2	0	0	0	0	0	0	0	0	0	0	0	0	0	0	0
Gerbertovna	4	.0000	.0438	26.4	0	0	0	0	0	0	4	0	0	4	0	0	0	0	0	0	0	0	0	0	0	0	0	0	0
Gerd	2	.0000	.0914	29.6	0	0	0	0	2	0	0	0	2	0	0	0	0	0	0	0	0	0	0	0	0	0	0	0	0
germ	32	.4223	2.9192	44.7	2	1	2	3	4	5	2	13	0	0	0	0	0	0	0	17	0	0	6	0	0	1	6	2	0
germ-fighting	3	.0000	.0591	27.7	0	0	0	3	0	0	0	0	0	0	0	0	0	0	0	3	0	0	0	0	0	0	0	0	0
Germain-en-Laye	3	.0000	.1370	31.4	3	0	0	0	0	0	0	0	3	0	0	0	0	0	0	0	0	0	0	0	0	0	0	0	0
German	343	.8045	55.347	57.4	24	37	33	56	53	71	56	13	35	13	0	6	8	74	15	24	53	5	0	1	0	31	43	35	0
Germanic	41	.4503	3.8647	45.9	0	4	7	3	15	6	4	2	0	17	0	1	0	2	14	0	0	0	0	0	0	2	5	0	0
germanium	10	.4609	1.0589	40.2	3	1	0	1	1	4	0	0	4	0	0	0	0	0	0	4	0	0	0	0	0	0	1	1	0
Germans	89	.6543	11.965	50.8	3	13	10	22	11	17	12	1	6	3	0	2	0	37	3	0	3	0	0	0	0	8	17	10	0

5N genie's
8D genies
7A genista
XH genitalia
7R genitals
7N genlman's
3P Gennesaret
5P genocide
7Q Gens
6B Gensfleisch
8J gent
9C Gent
3R gent-ly
3B gentian
6B Gentile
7G gentiles
8P gentle-hearted
9R gentle-voiced
5A gentlefolks
6A gentlest
6N gentlewoman
9R genuflection
4G geo-graph-y
7Q geochemist
7Q geoduck's
6R GEOGRAPHIC
6R Geographic's
8F Geographical
7H Geologist
9B Geologists
9P Geology
7Q geomagnetic
9E geometer
8E Geometric
9Q geometrizing
9Q Geometry
6R geophagy
8Q Georgetown's
9A Georgians
9Q Georgius
8G geous
6N Geppetto
6N Geppetto's
8Q Ger
6J Gerakina
XR gerbils
8P Gerbrandy
7P gerenuk
XR Gerhart
9K Gericault
XH Germ
8H germ-free
4H germ-killing
8B germ-laden
8F Germain
8F German-American
9D German-English
6A German-born
6J German-speaking
3Q German's
7D germane

Word Type	F	D	U	SFI	3 Gr 3	4 Gr 4	5 Gr 5	6 Gr 6	7 Gr 7	8 Gr 8	9 Gr 9	X UnGr	A Read	B Eng & Gr	C Comp	D Lit	E Math	F Soc Stud	G Spell	H Sci	J Music	K Art	L Home Ec	M Shop	N Lib F	P Lib NF	Q Lib Ref	R Mag	S Rel
Germantown	7	.3715	.5815	37.6	1	0	1	2	0	3	0	0	0	0	0	0	0	3	0	0	0	0	0	0	0	3	1	0	0
Germany	336	.7631	51.754	57.1	23	17	42	78	78	53	40	5	30	8	0	5	13	120	3	6	40	1	1	3	0	25	49	32	0
Germany's	12	.4847	1.2591	41.0	0	1	0	2	2	5	2	0	1	0	0	0	2	6	0	0	0	0	0	0	0	0	2	1	0
germinate	14	.3414	1.0813	40.3	8	2	0	0	4	0	0	0	0	0	0	0	0	0	0	4	0	0	0	0	0	8	2	0	0
germinated	2	.2405	.1205	30.8	1	0	0	0	0	0	1	0	0	0	0	0	0	0	0	1	0	0	0	0	0	1	0	0	0
germinates	2	.2405	.1205	30.8	1	0	0	0	0	0	1	0	0	0	0	0	0	0	0	1	0	0	0	0	0	1	0	0	0
germinating	3	.2427	.1822	32.6	0	1	0	1	0	0	0	1	0	0	0	0	0	0	0	2	0	0	0	0	0	0	0	1	0
germination	4	.0000	.0789	29.0	0	2	0	0	2	0	0	0	0	0	0	0	0	0	0	4	0	0	0	0	0	0	0	0	0
germs	152	.2515	9.8145	49.9	33	23	9	57	0	18	0	12	6	0	0	0	0	3	0	134	0	0	1	0	1	2	1	4	0
Geronimo	3	.3399	.2456	33.9	0	0	1	0	2	0	0	0	1	0	0	1	0	0	0	0	0	0	0	0	0	0	0	1	0
Gerry	6	.2456	.3324	35.2	0	3	0	0	0	1	2	0	0	3	2	0	0	1	0	0	0	0	0	0	0	0	0	0	0
Gershwin	13	.0000	.1051	30.2	0	0	4	0	4	3	2	0	0	0	0	0	0	0	0	0	13	0	0	0	0	0	0	0	0
Gerson	2	.0000	.0290	24.6	0	0	0	0	0	0	2	0	0	0	0	0	0	0	0	0	0	0	0	0	0	2	0	0	0
Gertie	33	.0000	1.5075	41.8	0	33	0	0	0	0	0	0	33	0	0	0	0	0	0	0	0	0	0	0	0	0	0	0	0
Gertrud	2	.0000	.0215	23.3	0	0	0	0	0	0	2	0	0	0	0	2	0	0	0	0	0	0	0	0	0	0	0	0	0
Gertrude	22	.4334	2.0100	43.0	0	15	2	0	1	0	3	1	0	0	2	1	0	0	0	0	0	0	0	0	15	1	1	2	0
Gertrudis	4	.0000	.0778	28.9	0	0	1	0	0	3	0	0	0	0	0	0	0	4	0	0	0	0	0	0	0	0	0	0	0
gerund	4	.2408	.2182	33.4	0	0	0	0	0	2	2	0	0	2	0	0	0	0	2	0	0	0	0	0	0	0	0	0	0
Gesler	9	.0000	.0728	28.6	0	9	0	0	0	0	0	0	0	0	0	0	0	0	0	0	9	0	0	0	0	0	0	0	0
Gessler	22	.0000	1.0050	40.0	12	0	5	5	0	0	0	0	22	0	0	0	0	0	0	0	0	0	0	0	0	0	0	0	0
Gessler's	4	.0000	.1827	32.6	2	0	2	0	0	0	0	0	4	0	0	0	0	0	0	0	0	0	0	0	0	0	0	0	0
Gestapo	3	.3380	.2439	33.9	0	0	0	0	0	2	1	0	1	1	0	1	0	0	0	0	0	0	0	0	0	0	0	0	0
gestation	2	.2405	.1205	30.8	0	0	0	2	0	0	0	0	0	0	0	0	0	0	0	1	0	0	0	0	0	1	0	0	0
gesticulating	2	.2443	.1130	30.5	0	0	0	0	0	2	0	0	0	0	0	1	0	0	0	0	0	0	0	0	0	0	0	0	0
gesture	31	.7222	4.5738	46.6	3	3	1	6	10	5	3	0	8	3	1	7	0	1	0	0	1	0	0	0	5	3	1	1	0
gestured	6	.2212	.4198	36.2	0	0	0	0	2	1	3	0	4	0	0	2	0	0	0	0	0	0	0	0	0	0	0	0	0
gestures	43	.6668	5.8732	47.7	4	5	3	11	8	7	5	0	8	15	0	2	0	1	1	0	2	3	2	0	6	2	1	0	0
gesturing	4	.3730	.3206	35.1	0	1	0	2	0	1	0	0	0	0	0	0	0	0	1	0	0	0	0	0	2	0	0	1	0
get	5700	.9485	1069.7	70.3	1477	1201	579	640	865	531	315	92	1958	180	30	329	303	367	76	717	63	36	63	25	552	537	71	390	3
Get	9	.5256	1.0243	40.1	2	1	2	0	1	2	1	0	3	0	0	0	0	0	0	0	2	0	0	0	1	0	1	2	0
get-together	2	.2375	.1088	30.4	0	0	0	1	0	0	0	1	0	0	0	0	0	0	0	0	1	0	0	0	0	0	0	1	0
geta	12	.2332	.8697	39.4	0	5	0	7	0	0	0	0	7	0	0	0	0	5	0	0	0	0	0	0	0	0	0	0	0
getaway	4	.2280	.2913	34.6	0	1	0	0	2	1	0	0	3	0	0	0	0	0	1	0	0	0	0	0	0	0	0	0	0
gets	541	.8957	96.440	59.8	154	83	59	60	88	53	32	12	113	16	5	25	18	39	15	153	24	3	4	0	13	53	14	46	0
gettin	2	.2297	.1135	30.6	0	1	0	0	1	0	0	0	0	0	0	1	0	1	0	0	0	0	0	0	0	0	0	0	0
gettin'	11	.3817	.9440	39.7	0	1	0	1	7	1	1	0	2	1	0	5	0	0	0	0	0	0	0	0	0	0	0	3	0
getting	913	.9277	168.09	62.3	195	180	101	120	140	99	67	11	319	28	3	65	13	66	8	116	8	7	15	3	93	70	16	82	1
Gettysburg	19	.5603	2.3094	43.6	1	6	3	3	5	1	0	0	8	2	0	3	0	0	0	0	0	0	0	0	0	3	3	0	0
Gewandhaus	2	.0000	.0290	24.6	0	0	0	1	1	0	0	0	0	0	0	0	0	0	0	0	0	0	0	0	0	2	0	0	0
geyser	12	.4717	1.2197	40.9	0	0	1	1	2	0	8	0	0	1	0	0	0	0	0	8	0	0	0	0	1	0	1	1	0
geysers	11	.2761	.7911	39.0	0	1	1	1	2	0	6	0	2	0	0	0	0	2	0	7	0	0	0	0	0	0	0	0	0
gh	53	.1353	1.9261	42.8	6	18	9	8	4	7	0	1	4	6	0	0	0	0	43	0	0	0	0	0	0	0	0	0	0
GH	12	.0000	.1796	32.5	0	0	2	1	1	6	2	0	0	0	0	0	12	0	0	0	0	0	0	0	0	0	0	0	0
Ghalas-at	3	.0000	.0352	25.5	0	0	0	3	0	0	0	0	0	0	0	0	0	0	0	0	0	0	0	0	3	0	0	0	0
Ghana	7	.1953	.4416	36.4	3	0	0	2	2	0	0	0	3	0	0	0	0	4	0	0	0	0	0	0	0	0	0	0	0
ghastly	10	.4374	.9628	39.8	0	0	1	1	2	1	5	0	2	0	0	3	0	0	0	0	0	0	0	0	2	0	0	3	0
ghetto	10	.1628	.4256	36.3	0	0	1	0	6	0	3	0	0	0	0	0	0	0	0	0	0	0	0	0	0	2	0	8	0
ghettos	10	.2880	.7023	38.5	0	0	0	0	1	8	1	0	1	0	0	0	0	5	0	0	0	0	0	0	0	0	0	4	0
GHI	3	.0000	.0449	26.5	0	0	0	0	2	0	1	0	0	0	0	0	3	0	0	0	0	0	0	0	0	0	0	0	0
ghost	138	.7701	21.774	53.4	13	62	13	10	14	17	6	3	66	11	1	20	0	2	5	3	4	0	0	0	2	15	2	7	0
Ghost	33	.4869	3.6182	45.6	0	3	2	1	14	13	0	0	15	1	0	11	0	2	0	0	1	0	0	0	0	0	0	3	0
ghost-writing	2	.0000	.0243	23.9	0	0	0	0	0	0	0	2	0	0	0	0	0	0	0	0	0	0	0	0	0	0	0	2	0
ghostly	21	.6506	2.8877	44.6	0	2	1	6	6	4	2	0	10	2	0	3	0	0	0	1	2	0	0	0	2	0	1	0	0
ghosts	48	.6504	6.6270	48.2	6	16	4	4	6	10	1	1	24	0	1	0	0	2	1	0	0	0	0	0	2	9	1	8	0
ghoul	2	.2411	.1091	30.4	1	0	0	0	0	0	1	0	0	0	0	1	0	0	0	0	1	0	0	0	0	0	0	0	0
ghouls	2	.1497	.1046	30.2	0	0	0	0	1	1	0	0	1	0	0	0	0	0	1	0	0	0	0	0	0	0	0	0	0
gi	2	.0000	.0162	22.1	0	0	0	2	0	0	0	0	0	0	0	0	0	0	2	0	0	0	0	0	0	0	0	0	0
GI	7	.5485	.8001	39.0	0	0	2	0	1	1	3	0	0	0	0	0	2	1	0	0	0	0	0	0	0	2	1	1	0
GI'S	2	.2376	.1088	30.4	0	0	0	0	0	1	1	0	0	0	0	0	0	0	1	0	0	0	0	0	0	0	0	1	0
Giacomo	4	.3603	.3110	34.9	0	0	2	0	0	1	1	0	0	0	0	0	0	0	0	0	1	0	0	0	0	1	2	0	0
Gian	4	.0000	.0323	25.1	0	0	0	3	0	1	0	0	0	0	0	0	0	0	0	0	4	0	0	0	0	0	0	0	0
Gian-Carlo	3	.0000	.1370	31.4	0	0	0	3	0	0	0	0	3	0	0	0	0	0	0	0	0	0	0	0	0	0	0	0	0
Gian-Carlo's	2	.0000	.0914	29.6	0	0	0	2	0	0	0	0	2	0	0	0	0	0	0	0	0	0	0	0	0	0	0	0	0
giant	316	.8761	55.274	57.4	55	56	43	48	69	23	18	4	79	12	7	7	6	42	5	43	4	2	0	1	6	43	33	26	0
Giant	31	.5316	3.6691	45.6	6	12	0	8	2	2	1	0	16	1	0	0	0	3	6	0	0	0	0	0	0	4	0	1	0
giant-sized	3	.1148	.0862	29.4	1	0	0	0	2	0	0	0	0	0	0	0	0	0	0	0	0	0	2	0	0	1	0	0	0
giant's	9	.1557	.4758	36.8	5	0	0	3	1	0	0	0	4	5	0	0	0	0	0	0	0	0	0	0	0	0	0	0	0
Giant's	3	.2279	.2143	33.3	0	0	0	2	1	0	0	0	2	0	0	0	0	0	0	0	0	0	0	0	0	0	0	1	0
giants	61	.7317	9.2818	49.7	7	23	3	4	13	6	2	3	34	1	0	0	0	1	1	4	2	0	0	0	3	4	5	6	0
Giants	36	.3769	2.9389	44.7	9	6	0	7	1	13	0	0	0	0	0	0	0	0	7	0	0	0	0	0	0	12	0	17	0
gib	2	.2303	.1079	30.3	1	0	0	0	1	0	0	0	0	0	0	0	0	0	0	0	1	0	0	0	0	1	0	0	0
Gibbons	3	.2365	.1616	32.1	0	0	2	0	0	1	0	0	0	0	0	0	0	0	0	0	1	0	0	0	0	0	2	0	0
Gibbs	3	.2181	.1541	31.9	0	0	0	0	1	0	2	0	0	0	0	0	0	0	0	0	0	0	0	0	1	0	2	0	0
Gibraltar	14	.6147	1.7812	42.5	0	0	2	5	3	3	1	0	0	1	0	1	0	7	0	2	0	0	0	0	1	1	1	0	0
gibs	2	.0000	.0290	24.6	0	0	0	0	2	0	0	0	0	0	0	0	0	0	0	0	0	0	0	0	0	2	0	0	0
Gibson	4	.3710	.3211	35.1	0	0	1	1	0	0	2	0	0	1	0	0	0	0	0	0	0	0	0	0	1	0	0	2	0
gid	2	.0000	.0162	22.1	0	1	1	0	0	0	0	0	0	0	0	0	0	0	2	0	0	0	0	0	0	0	0	0	0
giddap	7	.3784	.6594	38.2	1	5	1	0	0	0	0	0	4	0	0	0	0	0	0	0	0	0	0	0	1	2	0	0	0
giddy	7	.3503	.5335	37.3	0	1	1	1	2	1	1	0	0	0	0	3	0	0	0	0	0	0	0	0	3	0	0	1	0
giddyap	2	.0000	.0914	29.6	0	2	0	0	0	0	0	0	2	0	0	0	0	0	0	0	0	0	0	0	0	0	0	0	0
Gideon	6	.2427	.3457	35.4	2	0	1	3	0	0	0	0	0	0	0	0	0	0	0	0	0	0	0	0	3	3	0	0	0
gif	2	.0000	.0234	23.7	0	0	0	0	0	2	0	0	0	0	0	0	0	0	0	0	0	0	0	0	2	0	0	0	0
gift	177	.7498	27.233	54.4	34	31	14	33	24	17	19	5	78	17	4	11	4	9	7	0	9	4	2	2	4	11	6	7	2
Gift	11	.4808	1.2309	40.9	1	3	0	1	1	5	0	0	7	0	0	0	0	0	0	0	1	0	0	0	0	2	0	1	0
gift-giving	4	.0000	.0323	25.1	0	0	2	1	0	1	0	0	0	0	0	0	0	0	0	0	4	0	0	0	0	0	0	0	0
gift-wrapping	2	.1812	.0838	29.2	0	0	0	0	1	0	1	0	0	0	0	0	0	0	0	0	0	0	1	0	0	0	0	1	0
gifted	16	.6669	2.1912	43.4	1	1	1	3	3	4	2	1	3	0	0	1	1	0	0	1	2	1	0	0	0	1	3	3	0
gifts	115	.8601	19.796	53.0	15	26	23	19	13	5	10	4	34	1	3	7	4	21	1	0	11	3	3	0	5	10	5	7	0
gigantic	43	.6338	5.6640	47.5	7	1	4	4	8	10	5	4	9	1	5	1	0	6	0	3	2	0	0	0	2	8	4	2	0
gigas	3	.0000	.0314	25.0	0	0	1	0	1	1	0	0	0	0	0	0	0	0	0	0	0	0	0	0	0	0	3	0	0
giggle	11	.5572	1.3662	41.4	5	2	1	2	0	0	1	0	7	1	0	1	0	0	0	0	0	0	0	0	1	0	0	1	0
giggled	26	.5427	3.0871	44.9	6	6	5	4	1	3	1	0	11	0	0	3	0	0	0	0	0	0	0	0	6	4	0	2	0
giggles	9	.5019	1.0217	40.1	1	1	1	2	2	1	1	0	5	0	0	1	0	0	0	0	0	0	1	0	0	1	0	1	0
giggling	10	.5597	1.2419	40.9	2	3	2	0	3	0	0	0	6	1	0	1	0	0	0	0	0	0	0	0	0	1	0	1	0

8G Germanys
8Q Germer
XH germicides
9Q Gernsback
9Q Gernsback's
8J Gershwin's
9P Gerson's
8G gerunds
3A Gerzah
XR Gesell
7Q Gesner

5G gess
8G gesse
3P Gestalt
7D geste
6R Geste
4Q gestes
7N gesticulation
XR get-away
5N get-up
6H get-up-and-stretch
7N getchu

7A Gethsemane
7B getter
7P getters
6R getup
7G gewgaw
9H geyserite
8B geyserlike
3B gg
6A ghastlier
8F Ghent
6P Gherman

XQ Ghetto
7R Ghias
7Q Ghiberti
6Q Ghiorso
9D ghost-footfall
7A ghost-like
8F ghost-quiet
8B ghost-writer
6R ghosting
7P ghostlike
4A ghurush

9D gi'
8K Giacometti
8K Giacometti's
5N Giafar
5J Giannini
9D giant-like
9C giants'
5P Giants'
6A gibberish
8F gibes
7R Gibsons

5P Gide
6J gie's
7A Giedzinski
9Q Giessen
4P gif's
7R Gifford
7A gift-wraps
6P gig
4A gigantic-antic
7Q gigantism
8R Gigi

Word Type	F	D	U	SFI	3 Gr 3	4 Gr 4	5 Gr 5	6 Gr 6	7 Gr 7	8 Gr 8	9 Gr 9	X UnGr	A Read	B Eng & Gr	C Comp	D Lit	E Math	F Soc Stud	G Spell	H Sci	J Music	K Art	L Home Ec	M Shop	N Lib F	P Lib NF	Q Lib Ref	R Mag	S Rel
gigs	2	.1814	.1187	30.7	0	0	0	0	1	0	1	0	1	0	0	0	0	0	0	0	0	0	0	0	0	0	0	1	0
Gil	10	.3318	.7443	38.7	0	1	0	6	1	1	0	1	0	0	0	0	5	0	0	0	0	0	0	0	0	1	0	4	0
Gila	2	.1698	.1133	30.5	0	0	0	0	2	0	0	0	1	0	0	0	0	0	0	0	0	0	0	0	0	0	1	0	0
Gilbert	26	.7193	3.7843	45.8	2	4	0	2	11	5	2	0	2	3	0	0	0	2	1	4	3	0	0	1	0	1	7	2	0
Gilbert's	2	.0000	.0209	23.2	0	0	0	0	2	0	0	0	0	0	0	0	0	0	0	0	0	0	0	0	0	0	2	0	0
Gilbreth	6	.1409	.2943	34.7	0	0	0	0	6	0	0	0	2	0	0	0	0	0	0	0	0	0	0	0	0	4	0	0	0
gilded	8	.5265	.9237	39.7	1	0	1	2	0	3	1	0	3	0	0	2	0	1	0	0	0	0	0	0	0	1	1	0	0
gilding	2	.1814	.1187	30.7	0	0	0	1	1	0	0	0	1	0	0	0	0	0	0	0	0	0	0	0	0	0	0	1	0
Giles	15	.2230	1.1414	40.6	13	0	0	0	0	0	2	0	13	0	0	0	0	0	0	0	0	0	0	0	0	2	0	0	0
gill	8	.2440	.4818	36.8	2	0	0	0	6	0	0	0	0	0	0	0	0	0	0	5	0	0	0	0	0	0	3	0	0
gills	58	.4333	5.5583	47.4	19	10	1	8	13	2	5	0	2	2	0	2	0	0	0	42	0	0	0	0	1	6	3	0	0
Gilman	2	.0000	.0290	24.6	0	0	0	0	0	2	0	0	0	0	0	0	0	0	0	0	0	0	0	0	0	2	0	0	0
Gilmore	3	.1621	.1254	31.0	0	0	0	1	0	2	0	0	0	0	0	0	0	1	0	0	2	0	0	0	0	0	0	0	0
Gilson	11	.1926	.6850	38.4	0	0	0	0	5	6	0	0	6	0	0	0	0	0	0	0	0	0	0	0	5	0	0	0	0
gilt	2	.2446	.1142	30.6	0	0	0	0	1	0	0	1	0	0	0	0	0	0	0	0	0	0	0	0	1	0	0	1	0
Gilvaethwy	2	.0000	.0290	24.6	0	0	0	0	2	0	0	0	0	0	0	0	0	0	0	0	0	0	0	0	0	2	0	0	0
gimble	4	.2254	.2040	33.1	0	0	1	3	0	0	0	0	0	3	0	0	0	0	0	0	0	1	0	0	0	0	0	0	0
gimmicks	2	.2442	.1134	30.5	0	0	0	0	1	1	0	0	0	1	0	0	0	0	0	0	0	0	0	0	0	0	0	1	0
gin	40	.3676	3.4899	45.4	8	6	13	0	8	2	3	0	8	2	0	0	0	27	1	0	0	0	0	0	0	2	0	0	0
Ginastera	2	.0000	.0162	22.1	0	0	0	2	0	0	0	0	0	0	0	0	0	0	0	0	2	0	0	0	0	0	0	0	0
ginger	35	.7093	5.0993	47.1	10	7	1	5	4	4	2	2	11	1	1	0	4	1	2	0	0	0	4	0	1	2	2	6	0
Ginger	19	.3660	1.6310	42.1	6	0	0	0	11	2	0	0	6	0	0	0	0	0	0	0	0	1	0	0	11	0	0	1	0
Ginger's	2	.1787	.1174	30.7	1	0	0	0	1	0	0	0	1	0	0	0	0	0	0	0	0	0	0	0	1	0	0	0	0
gingerale	2	.0000	.0234	23.7	1	1	0	0	0	0	0	0	0	0	0	0	0	0	0	0	0	0	0	0	2	0	0	0	0
gingerbread	30	.7136	4.4054	46.4	21	2	1	0	1	3	0	2	10	2	0	1	2	0	0	0	0	0	1	0	1	5	6	2	0
Gingerbread	2	.0000	.0914	29.6	2	0	0	0	0	0	0	0	2	0	0	0	0	0	0	0	0	0	0	0	0	0	0	0	0
gingerly	12	.6019	1.5450	41.9	2	1	1	4	0	0	3	1	5	0	0	2	0	0	0	1	0	0	0	0	2	0	1	1	0
gingham	11	.0000	.5025	37.0	5	5	0	0	1	0	0	0	11	0	0	0	0	0	0	0	0	0	0	0	0	0	0	0	0
ginning	3	.0953	.0796	29.0	1	0	0	0	0	1	1	0	0	0	0	0	0	1	0	0	0	0	2	0	0	0	0	0	0
Ginny	5	.2414	.3872	35.9	0	1	0	4	0	0	0	0	4	0	0	0	1	0	0	0	0	0	0	0	0	0	0	0	0
Gino	5	.0000	.2284	33.6	0	0	0	5	0	0	0	0	5	0	0	0	0	0	0	0	0	0	0	0	0	0	0	0	0
gins	2	.0000	.0389	25.9	0	0	2	0	0	0	0	0	0	0	0	0	0	2	0	0	0	0	0	0	0	0	0	0	0
Ginza	3	.3769	.2484	34.0	0	0	1	1	0	0	0	1	0	0	0	0	0	1	0	0	0	0	0	0	0	0	1	1	0
Gioacchino	3	.0000	.0243	23.8	0	1	0	2	0	0	0	0	0	0	0	0	0	0	0	0	3	0	0	0	0	0	0	0	0
Gioconda	2	.1247	.0633	28.0	0	0	1	0	0	0	1	0	0	0	0	0	0	0	0	0	0	1	0	0	0	1	0	0	0
Gionfriddo	2	.0000	.0290	24.6	2	0	0	0	0	0	0	0	0	0	0	0	0	0	0	0	0	0	0	0	0	2	0	0	0
Giotto	2	.1693	.0748	28.7	0	0	1	0	0	1	0	0	0	0	0	0	0	0	1	0	0	1	0	0	0	0	0	0	0
Giovanni	12	.4164	1.1142	40.5	1	0	3	4	2	2	0	0	3	0	0	0	0	0	0	0	5	0	0	0	0	1	1	2	0
giraffe	40	.5730	4.9830	47.0	16	5	1	4	10	0	2	2	19	0	0	1	3	3	1	2	0	4	0	0	1	2	3	1	0
Giraffe	10	.3065	.6779	38.3	2	7	1	0	0	0	0	0	0	0	0	1	0	0	0	0	2	0	0	0	7	0	0	0	0
giraffe's	3	.2063	.1600	32.0	2	1	0	0	0	0	0	0	0	0	0	0	0	1	0	0	0	0	0	0	0	2	0	0	0
giraffes	24	.5259	2.6645	44.3	13	2	0	5	3	0	0	1	2	1	0	0	0	4	0	0	0	2	0	0	0	11	2	2	0
gird	3	.2236	.1570	32.0	0	0	0	0	1	0	1	1	0	1	0	2	0	0	0	0	0	0	0	0	0	0	0	0	0
girded	3	.3795	.2506	34.0	0	0	0	0	1	2	0	0	0	0	0	0	0	1	0	0	0	0	0	0	1	0	0	1	0
girders	11	.3754	.9142	39.6	0	2	0	0	2	2	5	0	2	0	0	0	0	2	0	0	0	1	0	4	1	0	1	0	0
girdle	8	.5042	.8715	39.4	0	1	2	0	5	0	0	0	1	0	0	0	0	0	0	4	0	0	0	0	1	0	1	1	0
girl	1084	.9032	194.91	62.9	285	212	151	101	161	112	55	7	392	89	16	79	39	24	25	36	35	14	26	0	110	92	12	95	0
Girl	60	.8395	10.057	50.0	8	20	16	1	6	7	2	0	8	6	1	1	9	1	0	1	7	1	1	0	2	12	2	8	0
GIRL	9	.1143	.2890	34.6	0	0	1	0	0	8	0	0	0	0	0	8	0	0	0	0	0	0	0	0	0	0	0	1	0
GIRL-FRIEND	3	.0000	.0322	25.1	0	0	0	0	0	3	0	0	0	0	0	3	0	0	0	0	0	0	0	0	0	0	0	0	0
girl-daughter	3	.0000	.0352	25.5	0	3	0	0	0	0	0	0	0	0	0	0	0	0	0	0	0	0	0	0	3	0	0	0	0
girl's	48	.8072	7.8032	48.9	13	8	4	8	3	9	1	2	13	4	2	4	1	1	0	2	4	0	3	0	2	7	2	3	0
girls	1107	.8901	196.09	62.9	288	252	156	103	138	88	67	15	254	85	18	39	146	68	8	57	44	11	52	0	118	123	9	75	0
Girls	23	.4418	2.3045	43.6	8	3	5	5	0	2	0	0	9	1	0	0	0	0	0	0	7	0	0	0	1	0	0	5	0
girls'	24	.7420	3.6304	45.6	3	3	5	2	5	6	0	0	7	1	1	0	3	0	0	0	3	0	1	0	3	3	0	2	0
Girls'	2	.2427	.1159	30.6	0	0	0	2	0	0	0	0	0	0	0	0	1	0	0	0	0	0	0	0	0	0	0	1	0
Giron	2	.0000	.0290	24.6	0	2	0	0	0	0	0	0	0	0	0	0	0	0	0	0	0	0	0	0	0	2	0	0	0
girth	8	.6662	1.0770	40.3	0	1	0	2	3	1	1	0	0	1	0	1	0	0	1	0	0	0	0	0	1	1	2	1	0
Girty	4	.1112	.1666	32.2	0	0	4	0	0	0	0	0	1	0	0	0	0	0	0	0	0	0	0	0	0	3	0	0	0
GIS	2	.2408	.1204	30.8	0	0	1	0	0	1	0	0	0	0	0	0	0	1	0	0	0	0	0	0	0	1	0	0	0
Giselle	2	.0000	.0209	23.2	0	0	0	0	1	1	0	0	0	0	0	0	0	0	0	0	0	0	0	0	0	0	2	0	0
Gist	2	.0000	.0389	25.9	0	0	0	0	0	2	0	0	0	0	0	0	0	2	0	0	0	0	0	0	0	0	0	0	0
git	39	.3762	3.3373	45.2	6	2	10	1	11	8	1	0	8	1	0	4	0	0	0	0	0	0	0	0	23	2	1	0	0
Gitler	18	.0000	.2110	33.2	18	0	0	0	0	0	0	0	0	0	0	0	0	0	0	0	0	0	0	0	18	0	0	0	0
gits	5	.2542	.3208	35.1	3	1	1	0	0	0	0	0	1	0	0	0	0	0	0	0	0	0	0	0	3	1	0	0	0
gittin'	3	.2292	.1615	32.1	1	0	1	0	1	0	0	0	0	0	0	1	0	0	0	0	0	0	0	0	2	0	0	0	0
Giuseppe	11	.4753	1.1425	40.6	0	0	1	4	4	2	0	0	3	0	0	0	0	0	0	0	3	0	0	0	0	1	3	1	0
give	3366	.9090	607.43	67.8	511	549	402	459	578	418	382	67	720	286	41	176	876	158	84	256	90	26	69	32	158	201	63	118	12
Give	3	.3826	.2445	33.9	0	0	0	0	1	2	0	0	0	0	0	0	0	0	0	0	1	0	0	0	0	0	1	1	0
give-and-take	3	.3668	.2405	33.8	0	0	0	0	1	0	2	0	0	0	0	0	0	0	0	1	1	0	0	0	0	0	1	0	0
given	1661	.9118	300.37	64.8	163	184	179	187	385	279	244	40	285	136	11	40	444	103	77	144	60	1	49	33	45	77	83	69	4
Given	2	.0000	.0234	23.7	0	0	0	0	0	0	2	0	0	0	0	0	0	0	0	0	0	0	0	0	2	0	0	0	0
giver	5	.3956	.4593	36.6	0	1	0	1	3	0	0	0	2	0	0	0	0	0	0	0	0	0	1	0	1	0	1	0	0
gives	650	.9380	120.52	60.8	87	87	64	90	136	84	83	19	97	51	8	22	63	28	18	124	51	15	28	15	13	38	41	36	2
giveth	2	.2401	.1133	30.5	1	0	1	0	0	0	0	0	0	0	0	0	0	0	0	0	0	0	0	0	0	1	1	0	0
giving	379	.9595	71.762	58.6	40	63	30	48	95	53	40	10	81	43	9	21	20	30	12	29	11	4	8	3	38	21	26	22	1
Giza	5	.3036	.3812	35.8	1	0	0	3	0	0	1	0	1	0	0	0	1	3	0	0	0	0	0	0	0	0	0	0	0
Gizeh	3	.2398	.1721	32.4	0	0	0	1	0	0	2	0	0	0	0	0	2	0	0	0	0	0	0	0	0	0	1	0	0
gizzard	2	.2291	.1135	30.5	0	0	0	0	2	0	0	0	0	0	0	1	0	0	0	1	0	0	0	0	0	0	0	0	0
gl	5	.0621	.1343	31.3	1	1	2	1	0	0	0	0	1	0	0	0	0	0	4	0	0	0	0	0	0	0	0	0	0
glacial	19	.4725	1.9218	42.8	2	0	1	0	3	3	10	0	0	0	0	1	0	0	0	10	0	0	0	0	0	1	5	2	0
glaciated	2	.2278	.1128	30.5	0	0	0	0	0	1	1	0	0	0	0	0	0	0	0	1	0	0	0	0	0	0	1	0	0
glaciation	3	.2445	.1818	32.6	0	0	0	0	0	1	2	0	0	0	0	0	0	0	0	2	0	0	0	0	0	0	1	0	0
glacier	41	.4342	4.1058	46.1	4	11	15	1	2	0	7	1	12	0	0	0	0	0	0	22	0	0	0	0	1	3	0	3	0
Glacier	4	.4501	.4035	36.1	1	0	3	0	0	0	0	0	1	0	0	0	0	0	0	1	0	0	0	0	0	1	1	0	0
glacier's	2	.0000	.0394	26.0	0	0	0	0	0	0	2	0	0	0	0	0	0	0	0	2	0	0	0	0	0	0	0	0	0
glaciers	94	.6001	11.943	50.8	14	14	35	7	15	2	5	2	19	2	0	0	0	18	0	33	0	0	0	0	0	4	13	5	0
glad	523	.8270	87.321	59.4	160	150	43	49	62	26	30	3	208	17	3	30	0	35	14	5	18	1	6	0	102	69	0	14	1
gladdened	2	.1733	.1149	30.6	0	0	0	0	1	1	0	0	1	1	0	0	0	0	0	0	0	0	0	0	0	0	0	0	0
gladdest	2	.0000	.0914	29.6	1	1	0	0	0	0	0	0	2	0	0	0	0	0	0	0	0	0	0	0	0	0	0	0	0
glade	6	.5558	.6856	38.4	0	2	0	0	2	0	0	2	0	1	0	1	0	0	0	0	0	0	0	0	1	0	1	2	0
glades	2	.2401	.1133	30.5	1	0	0	0	1	0	0	0	0	0	0	0	0	0	0	0	0	0	0	0	0	1	1	0	0
gladiators	2	.2408	.1204	30.8	0	2	0	0	0	0	0	0	0	0	0	0	0	1	0	0	0	0	0	0	0	1	0	0	0
gladly	20	.5840	2.4671	43.9	3	2	1	2	5	3	3	1	6	0	1	5	0	0	0	0	3	0	0	0	4	0	0	1	0

8J gigue
7P gigues
8D gila
6F Gilberts
7D Gilbreths
3P Gilead
9D Giles'
4F Gilham
7Q gill-breathing
7Q gill-like
7R gill-rattling

9Q Gilles
3P Gilliam
8Q Gillmore
8P Gilman's
6J Gilmore's
6N Giltspur
9Q gimcrack
7N gimlet
6A Gimlet
7A gimme
4P gingerbread-boy

4P Gingham
7Q ginkgoes
4F ginned
7A ginner
6A Ginny's
6A Gino's
8Q Ginsburg
7N ginseng
8Q Gintings
XH Giordano
8A Gipson's

9D gipsy's
XP Girardot
9L girdles
5F girdling
XR girl-boy
4N girl-daughter's
7A girlfriend
3N girlie
7N girlish
6R Girona
6R Girona's

5Q Girondists
7A girt
8D girted
6A girths
9R Giscard
7R Gish
9D gist
8N Gitano
8N Gitano's
6A Giuseppe's
7P giveaway

7N givin'
7L gjetost
3A gla
5P glacier-scored
7Q glaciers'
7Q glaciologists
5Q Glackens
XR glad-hearted
7R Gladewater
4P Gladiators

Word Type	F	D	U	SFI	3 Gr 3	4 Gr 4	5 Gr 5	6 Gr 6	7 Gr 7	8 Gr 8	9 Gr 9	X UnGr	A Read	B Eng & Gr	C Comp	D Lit	E Math	F Soc Stud	G Spell	H Sci	J Music	K Art	L Home Ec	M Shop	N Lib F	P Lib NF	Q Lib Ref	R Mag	S Rel
gladness	13	.4859	1.3662	41.4	1	2	1	1	0	4	2	2	3	0	0	5	0	0	0	0	2	0	0	0	1	0	0	2	0
glamor	4	.3676	.3150	35.0	0	0	0	0	2	1	0	1	0	0	0	0	0	0	0	0	1	0	0	0	0	0	2	1	0
glamorized	2	.2440	.1132	30.5	0	0	0	0	2	0	0	0	0	0	0	1	0	0	0	0	0	0	0	0	0	0	0	1	0
glamorous	5	.3760	.4077	36.1	0	0	0	0	2	0	3	0	0	2	0	0	0	0	0	0	0	0	0	0	0	2	1	0	0
glamour	5	.4319	.4750	36.8	0	0	0	2	1	0	1	1	1	1	0	0	0	0	0	0	1	0	0	0	0	0	0	2	0
Glamour	2	.1814	.1187	30.7	0	0	1	0	1	0	0	0	1	0	0	0	0	0	0	0	0	0	0	0	0	0	0	1	0
glance	130	.8279	21.692	53.4	4	22	26	16	30	16	11	5	44	9	2	13	7	10	0	8	1	0	0	1	21	8	1	5	0
glanced	114	.6502	15.610	51.9	9	27	12	15	29	13	8	1	48	1	3	15	1	1	0	0	0	0	0	0	21	18	0	6	0
glances	25	.4904	2.7235	44.4	0	1	2	2	10	6	4	0	9	0	0	8	0	2	0	1	0	0	0	0	4	1	0	0	0
glancing	31	.5859	3.8799	45.9	2	5	4	6	7	3	3	1	12	0	0	3	0	0	0	0	0	1	0	1	11	0	0	3	0
gland	29	.4647	2.8636	44.6	0	2	0	11	2	5	8	1	0	0	0	0	0	0	0	12	0	0	3	0	0	2	11	1	0
glands	82	.4899	8.6087	49.3	4	14	3	5	28	14	13	1	0	1	0	0	0	1	0	58	0	0	3	0	1	3	12	3	0
glandular	10	.4328	.9182	39.6	0	0	0	2	2	2	4	0	0	0	0	0	0	1	0	2	0	0	2	0	0	0	4	1	0
glare	36	.6890	5.0749	47.1	2	3	6	4	7	3	9	2	7	2	4	4	0	2	1	2	0	0	1	0	2	3	1	7	0
glared	20	.5349	2.3556	43.7	1	6	1	2	7	1	2	0	9	0	0	4	0	0	0	0	0	0	0	0	3	3	0	1	0
glaring	25	.6563	3.4278	45.4	1	7	2	3	9	2	0	1	9	2	1	5	0	0	0	0	0	0	0	0	3	3	0	2	0
Glarus	2	.0000	.0290	24.6	0	0	2	0	0	0	0	0	0	0	0	0	0	0	0	0	0	0	0	0	0	2	0	0	0
Glasgow	9	.3932	.7967	39.0	0	0	2	2	3	0	2	0	1	0	0	0	0	4	0	0	0	0	0	0	0	0	3	1	0
glass	913	.8601	157.04	62.0	248	175	120	82	151	51	57	29	180	22	9	30	11	42	6	356	8	16	17	21	27	73	64	31	0
Glass	12	.4730	1.3085	41.2	0	1	1	6	3	0	1	0	7	1	0	2	0	0	0	0	0	1	0	0	0	0	0	1	0
glass-bottomed	3	.2257	.1583	32.0	2	0	0	0	1	0	0	0	0	2	0	1	0	0	0	0	0	0	0	0	0	0	0	0	0
glass-walled	2	.2351	.1166	30.7	0	1	0	0	1	0	0	0	0	0	0	0	0	1	0	0	0	0	0	0	0	0	0	1	0
glassed-in	3	.2197	.2090	33.2	0	0	1	2	0	0	0	0	2	0	0	0	0	0	0	0	0	0	0	0	0	0	1	0	0
glasses	150	.7920	24.070	53.8	45	26	9	21	21	12	14	2	46	8	0	12	18	0	3	19	0	0	8	1	5	21	0	9	0
glassful	5	.1294	.1816	32.6	1	0	0	0	0	0	4	0	0	0	0	4	0	0	0	1	0	0	0	0	0	0	0	0	0
glasslike	3	.0000	.0591	27.7	0	1	2	0	0	0	0	0	0	0	0	0	0	0	0	3	0	0	0	0	0	0	0	0	0
glassmaking	2	.2285	.1129	30.5	0	0	0	0	2	0	0	0	0	0	0	0	0	1	0	0	0	0	0	0	0	0	1	0	0
glassware	5	.2373	.2950	34.7	0	0	1	0	2	1	1	0	0	0	0	0	0	4	0	0	0	0	1	0	0	0	0	0	0
glassy	20	.5200	2.2250	43.5	3	1	1	1	6	0	5	3	2	1	0	4	0	0	0	10	0	0	0	0	0	1	2	0	0
glassy-smooth	2	.2437	.1129	30.5	0	0	0	0	0	1	1	0	0	0	0	0	0	0	0	0	0	0	0	0	0	0	1	1	0
glaze	3	.2027	.1376	31.4	0	2	0	1	0	0	0	0	0	0	0	0	0	0	0	0	0	1	0	0	0	0	2	0	0
glazed	13	.4395	1.2124	40.8	0	1	1	2	5	2	2	0	1	0	0	0	0	0	0	2	0	3	2	0	2	2	1	0	0
gleam	28	.7092	4.0714	46.1	0	3	3	7	8	4	1	2	8	1	1	5	0	1	0	0	3	0	0	0	4	0	1	4	0
gleamed	27	.5785	3.4069	45.3	7	5	4	4	3	3	1	0	14	2	0	3	0	1	0	0	0	0	0	0	5	2	0	0	0
gleaming	41	.7094	5.9382	47.7	6	7	5	5	9	6	2	1	8	1	0	9	0	3	0	1	5	1	0	0	4	8	1	0	0
gleams	3	.2236	.1570	32.0	0	0	0	0	1	1	1	0	0	1	0	2	0	0	0	0	0	0	0	0	0	0	0	0	0
gleaned	2	.2437	.1129	30.5	0	0	0	0	1	1	0	0	0	0	0	0	0	0	0	0	0	0	0	0	0	0	1	1	0
glee	16	.5018	1.7687	42.5	6	4	1	1	2	1	1	0	6	0	0	2	0	0	0	0	4	0	0	0	0	3	0	1	0
gleefully	10	.6134	1.2916	41.1	2	2	0	3	1	1	0	1	3	1	0	1	0	0	0	0	0	0	0	0	2	2	0	1	0
glen	5	.2620	.3230	35.1	0	0	1	0	0	3	1	0	1	1	0	3	0	0	0	0	0	0	0	0	0	0	0	0	0
Glen	31	.4916	3.5967	45.6	0	3	23	0	3	0	2	0	24	2	0	0	2	0	0	0	0	0	0	0	1	0	0	2	0
Glendale	2	.2408	.1204	30.8	0	0	1	0	0	0	0	1	0	0	0	0	0	1	0	0	0	0	0	0	0	1	0	0	0
Glendy	3	.0000	.0243	23.8	0	0	1	2	0	0	0	0	0	0	0	0	0	0	0	0	3	0	0	0	0	0	0	0	0
Glenn	34	.4698	3.7564	45.7	1	15	0	7	8	3	0	0	21	0	0	0	0	1	0	5	0	0	0	0	0	1	0	6	0
Glennie	7	.0000	.3198	35.0	0	0	0	0	7	0	0	0	7	0	0	0	0	0	0	0	0	0	0	0	0	0	0	0	0
glens	3	.2212	.2099	33.2	0	0	1	1	0	0	1	0	2	0	0	1	0	0	0	0	0	0	0	0	0	0	0	0	0
Glick	4	.0000	.0429	26.3	0	0	0	0	0	0	4	0	0	0	0	4	0	0	0	0	0	0	0	0	0	0	0	0	0
glide	28	.6786	3.9593	46.0	7	3	4	5	5	3	0	1	10	0	0	0	0	1	1	5	3	0	0	0	0	1	3	4	0
glided	19	.5975	2.4631	43.9	4	1	2	3	4	3	1	1	10	0	0	2	0	1	0	0	0	0	0	0	2	3	0	1	0
glider	38	.6549	5.2341	47.2	6	6	7	9	10	0	0	0	15	6	0	3	0	1	1	5	0	0	0	0	0	1	0	6	0
glider's	2	.0000	.0914	29.6	0	0	0	2	0	0	0	0	2	0	0	0	0	0	0	0	0	0	0	0	0	0	0	0	0
gliders	9	.4605	.9900	40.0	3	1	2	2	1	0	0	0	6	0	0	0	0	1	0	1	0	0	0	0	0	0	0	1	0
glides	9	.5580	1.0514	40.2	2	0	0	3	1	2	1	0	1	1	0	0	0	0	0	1	2	0	0	0	0	2	0	2	0
gliding	18	.6634	2.4681	43.9	4	2	1	1	5	3	1	1	5	0	1	0	0	0	1	2	4	0	1	0	3	0	0	1	0
glimmer	5	.3827	.4088	36.1	0	0	0	0	3	2	0	0	0	0	0	2	0	0	0	0	1	0	0	0	2	0	0	0	0
glimmered	2	.1948	.1250	31.0	2	0	0	0	0	0	0	0	1	0	0	0	0	0	0	0	0	0	0	0	0	1	0	0	0
glimmering	4	.3055	.2919	34.7	0	1	0	2	0	0	1	0	1	0	1	0	0	0	0	0	0	0	0	0	0	1	0	1	0
glimpse	51	.8315	8.5266	49.3	7	7	7	13	8	4	4	1	15	1	0	5	0	4	0	2	1	1	0	1	5	8	4	4	0
glimpsed	10	.5583	1.1830	40.7	1	3	0	1	4	0	1	0	2	0	0	0	0	0	0	1	0	0	0	0	1	1	2	3	0
glimpses	11	.5349	1.2585	41.0	0	1	0	1	4	2	0	3	3	0	0	1	0	0	0	0	0	1	0	0	2	0	1	3	0
Glinka's	2	.0000	.0162	22.1	0	0	0	0	0	0	2	0	0	0	0	0	0	0	0	0	2	0	0	0	0	0	0	0	0
glint	4	.3709	.3633	35.6	0	1	0	0	2	0	0	1	2	0	0	0	0	0	0	0	0	0	0	0	0	0	1	1	0
glinted	5	.4770	.5360	37.3	1	0	0	1	3	0	0	0	2	0	0	1	0	0	0	0	0	0	0	0	0	1	0	1	0
glinting	4	.3387	.3012	34.8	0	0	0	0	2	0	2	0	0	0	0	2	0	0	0	1	0	0	0	0	1	0	0	0	0
glisten	4	.0974	.1495	31.7	0	1	1	0	2	0	0	0	1	0	0	0	0	0	0	0	0	0	0	0	3	0	0	0	0
glistened	11	.4782	1.1538	40.6	1	3	2	1	3	0	1	0	3	0	0	4	0	0	0	0	0	0	0	0	2	1	0	1	0
glistening	24	.7407	3.6689	45.6	2	4	2	4	4	3	4	1	11	1	0	2	0	1	0	2	0	0	0	0	2	1	2	2	0
glistens	2	.1814	.1187	30.7	0	0	0	0	1	0	0	1	1	0	0	0	0	0	0	0	0	0	0	0	0	0	0	1	0
glitter	11	.5346	1.2110	40.8	1	0	0	3	4	3	0	0	0	0	0	5	0	1	2	0	0	0	1	0	0	1	0	1	0
glittered	15	.5543	1.8132	42.6	4	1	6	1	0	3	0	0	7	1	1	0	0	0	0	0	1	0	0	0	4	1	0	0	0
glittering	44	.7824	6.9850	48.4	7	6	4	11	6	7	2	1	13	0	1	3	0	5	0	2	2	0	0	0	2	7	3	6	0
glitters	2	.2440	.1132	30.5	0	0	0	1	0	1	0	0	0	0	0	1	0	0	0	0	0	0	0	0	0	0	0	1	0
gloat	2	.0857	.0784	28.9	0	1	0	0	0	1	0	0	1	0	0	0	0	0	0	0	0	0	1	0	0	0	0	0	0
gloating	2	.1717	.1142	30.6	0	0	0	0	1	0	1	0	1	0	0	1	0	0	0	0	0	0	0	0	0	0	0	0	0
gloatingly	2	.0000	.0914	29.6	0	0	0	1	1	0	0	0	2	0	0	0	0	0	0	0	0	0	0	0	0	0	0	0	0
glob	2	.2433	.1158	30.6	0	0	0	0	0	0	2	0	0	0	0	0	0	0	0	0	0	0	0	0	0	1	0	1	0
global	14	.5669	1.6551	42.2	0	0	7	0	3	2	1	1	0	0	0	0	0	6	0	2	0	0	0	1	0	1	1	3	0
globe	278	.5733	33.730	55.3	57	107	24	22	36	12	13	7	23	2	0	0	1	148	4	62	2	0	1	0	2	8	21	4	0
Globe	3	.2425	.1816	32.6	0	1	0	0	0	1	0	1	0	0	0	0	0	2	0	0	0	0	0	0	0	0	0	1	0
globe-map	4	.0000	.0778	28.9	0	4	0	0	0	0	0	0	0	0	0	0	0	4	0	0	0	0	0	0	0	0	0	0	0
globe's	4	.2680	.2737	34.4	0	1	0	1	2	0	0	0	1	0	0	0	0	1	0	0	0	0	0	0	0	0	2	0	0
globes	24	.1862	1.3370	41.3	6	11	4	1	1	0	0	1	4	0	0	0	0	19	0	0	0	0	0	0	1	0	0	0	0
globular	10	.3714	.8086	39.1	0	0	0	0	9	0	0	1	0	0	0	0	0	0	0	1	0	0	0	0	1	0	2	6	0
globule	4	.2417	.3089	34.9	0	0	0	0	3	0	0	1	3	0	0	0	0	0	0	1	0	0	0	0	0	0	0	0	0
globules	3	.0803	.0701	28.5	0	0	0	0	0	0	2	1	0	0	0	0	0	0	0	1	0	0	0	2	0	0	0	0	0
glockenspiel	6	.2088	.2884	34.6	0	2	0	0	3	0	1	0	0	0	0	0	0	0	0	0	4	0	0	0	0	0	2	0	0
glomeruli	3	.0000	.0314	25.0	0	0	0	0	0	0	3	0	0	0	0	0	0	0	0	0	0	0	0	0	0	0	3	0	0
Glomstulen	3	.0000	.0243	23.8	0	0	0	3	0	0	0	0	0	0	0	0	0	0	0	0	3	0	0	0	0	0	0	0	0
gloom	28	.6689	3.8792	45.9	1	4	4	3	9	5	2	0	8	2	0	8	0	1	0	0	1	0	0	0	3	2	1	2	0
gloomily	12	.5408	1.4497	41.6	2	5	2	0	2	0	1	0	7	0	0	2	0	0	0	0	0	0	0	0	1	1	0	1	0
gloomy	29	.6990	4.1328	46.2	4	3	3	3	10	2	4	0	5	1	2	7	0	0	3	2	1	0	0	0	2	4	0	2	0
gloria	2	.0000	.0162	22.1	0	0	2	0	0	0	0	0	0	0	0	0	0	0	0	0	2	0	0	0	0	0	0	0	0
Gloria	108	.4439	11.964	50.8	1	16	1	84	3	2	1	0	98	1	0	3	0	0	0	0	2	0	1	0	2	0	1	0	0
Gloria's	3	.0000	.1370	31.4	0	0	0	3	0	0	0	0	3	0	0	0	0	0	0	0	0	0	0	0	0	0	0	0	0
Glorianna	8	.0000	.3655	35.6	0	5	3	0	0	0	0	0	8	0	0	0	0	0	0	0	0	0	0	0	0	0	0	0	0

4J Gladness
4N gladsome
9Q Gladsome
3A Gladys
4H glares
6A glaringly
6A glass-stoppered
7Q glassblowing
7R glassed
8C glassily
7R glassing
7Q glassmaker
7Q glassmakers
7Q glassworkers
9C glassy-eyed
5R Glatthorn
7A glazing
7A gle
7R glean
8B Glee
9D gleek
7Q gleemen
4E Glen's
9D Glenfield
7D glent
9Q glia
7L glibly
5Q Glidden
5P glider-borne
8J Gliere
8J Gliere's
4A glimmerings
9J Glinka
9P glio
9D glisters
8B gloatin'
8R Globetrotters
7N globicephali
7Q globus
5Q Glockner
XR Gloeilampenfabrieken
7Q Glomar
3B gloobed
8P Gloom
7R gloomey
7G gloomier
7G gloomiest
XR Gloriana
7F gloried

Word Type	F	D	U	SFI	3 Gr 3	4 Gr 4	5 Gr 5	6 Gr 6	7 Gr 7	8 Gr 8	9 Gr 9	X UnGr	A Read	B Eng & Gr	C Comp	D Lit	E Math	F Soc Stud	G Spell	H Sci	J Music	K Art	L Home Ec	M Shop	N Lib F	P Lib NF	Q Lib Ref	R Mag	S Rel
glories	7	.4824	.7296	38.6	3	0	0	0	2	2	0	0	1	0	0	0	0	0	0	2	2	0	0	0	1	1	0	0	0
glorified	7	.5194	.7824	38.9	0	0	1	1	3	1	1	0	2	0	0	1	0	0	0	0	0	0	0	1	1	1	1	0	0
glorifies	2	.0000	.0243	23.9	0	0	0	0	0	1	0	1	0	0	0	0	0	0	0	0	0	0	0	0	0	0	0	2	0
glorify	5	.5244	.5606	37.5	0	1	1	1	1	1	0	0	1	0	0	0	0	1	0	0	1	0	0	0	1	0	1	0	0
glorious	54	.6465	7.1398	48.5	5	4	4	8	9	4	15	5	7	1	5	9	0	3	1	1	8	2	0	0	1	5	5	5	1
Glorious	4	.3270	.3194	35.0	0	0	1	2	0	1	0	0	1	0	0	0	0	2	0	0	1	0	0	0	0	0	0	0	0
gloriously	2	.2433	.1158	30.6	0	0	0	0	1	0	0	1	0	0	0	0	0	0	0	0	0	0	0	0	0	1	0	1	0
glory	93	.3687	7.8981	49.0	9	12	8	20	24	8	8	4	22	4	1	3	0	7	2	2	13	0	0	0	7	18	4	6	4
Glory	3	.1187	.0817	29.1	1	1	1	0	0	0	0	0	0	1	1	0	0	0	0	0	0	0	0	0	0	0	0	0	1
glorying	2	.0665	.0708	28.5	0	0	0	1	0	0	1	0	1	0	1	0	0	0	0	0	0	0	0	0	0	0	0	0	0
gloss	8	.2715	.4853	36.9	1	0	1	0	1	2	1	2	0	0	0	0	0	1	0	0	0	0	0	3	0	2	0	2	0
glossary	30	.2697	2.2168	43.5	11	2	2	0	13	1	1	0	16	0	0	0	0	0	12	1	0	0	0	0	0	0	1	0	0
Glossary	8	.3787	.7502	38.8	0	4	0	2	1	1	0	0	4	0	0	0	0	3	0	0	1	0	0	0	0	0	0	0	0
glossy	17	.6650	2.3394	43.7	2	2	3	2	5	2	0	1	4	0	0	1	0	3	0	2	0	0	2	1	1	2	1	0	0
glottal	6	.0000	.0628	28.0	0	0	0	0	0	0	0	6	0	0	0	0	0	0	0	0	0	0	0	0	0	0	6	0	0
glottis	2	.0000	.0209	23.2	0	0	0	0	0	0	0	2	0	0	0	0	0	0	0	0	0	0	0	0	0	0	2	0	0
Gloucester	8	.5626	.9771	39.9	0	0	3	0	3	2	0	0	3	1	0	0	0	2	0	0	0	0	0	0	0	1	1	0	0
glove	42	.7241	6.2899	48.0	11	10	4	3	10	2	2	0	18	1	0	0	2	0	4	6	3	0	0	0	4	1	0	3	0
gloved	2	.0000	.0215	23.3	0	0	0	0	1	0	1	0	0	0	0	2	0	0	0	0	0	0	0	0	0	0	0	0	0
gloves	55	.7556	8.4010	49.2	9	9	5	6	12	6	8	0	10	2	1	5	0	2	3	3	0	1	7	0	3	13	4	1	0
glow	102	.7407	15.469	51.9	16	21	11	17	15	9	9	4	33	3	1	9	0	1	1	15	3	2	1	0	7	13	5	7	1
glowed	35	.6463	4.7609	46.8	5	7	6	5	9	1	2	0	14	1	3	4	0	1	0	3	0	0	0	0	3	3	1	2	0
glowered	5	.2086	.3320	35.2	2	0	1	0	2	0	0	0	3	0	0	0	0	0	0	0	0	0	0	0	2	0	0	0	0
glowering	2	.2440	.1132	30.5	0	0	0	0	0	0	2	0	0	0	0	1	0	0	0	0	0	0	0	0	0	0	0	1	0
glowing	74	.6914	10.627	50.3	6	7	7	11	21	8	11	3	24	0	0	3	0	3	0	25	4	3	0	0	3	1	5	3	0
glows	12	.5857	1.4435	41.6	2	0	2	3	3	2	0	0	0	0	0	0	0	0	2	4	1	1	0	0	0	0	2	2	0
glowworm	4	.3284	.2866	34.6	1	0	1	0	0	2	0	0	0	0	0	0	0	0	0	0	2	0	0	0	1	1	0	0	0
glub	2	.2444	.1132	30.5	1	1	0	0	0	0	0	0	0	1	0	0	0	0	0	0	0	0	0	0	1	0	0	0	0
glucose	23	.0974	.8413	39.2	0	2	0	5	11	0	5	0	0	0	0	0	0	0	0	22	0	0	0	0	0	0	1	0	0
glue	123	.5484	14.579	51.6	54	6	11	11	15	18	6	2	48	0	2	0	0	3	0	15	1	6	0	24	1	9	7	7	0
Glueck	3	.0000	.0434	26.4	0	0	3	0	0	0	0	0	0	0	0	0	0	0	0	0	0	0	0	0	0	3	0	0	0
glued	17	.5693	2.0295	43.1	3	2	0	3	4	2	3	0	4	0	0	2	0	0	0	0	0	1	0	3	3	1	2	1	0
glues	4	.1371	.1640	32.1	1	0	0	0	1	2	0	0	1	0	0	0	0	0	0	0	0	0	0	2	0	1	0	0	0
gluey	2	.1698	.1133	30.5	0	0	0	0	2	0	0	0	1	0	0	0	0	0	0	0	0	0	0	0	0	0	1	0	0
gluggle-gluggle-gluggle	2	.0000	.0914	29.6	0	0	0	2	0	0	0	0	2	0	0	0	0	0	0	0	0	0	0	0	0	0	0	0	0
gluing	8	.5407	.9019	39.6	1	1	2	1	0	0	3	0	1	0	0	0	0	2	0	0	0	1	1	1	0	0	2	0	0
glum	2	.1814	.1187	30.7	1	1	0	0	0	0	0	0	1	0	0	0	0	0	0	0	0	0	0	0	0	0	0	1	0
glumly	4	.2417	.3028	34.8	0	0	1	2	1	0	0	0	3	0	0	0	0	0	0	0	0	0	0	0	1	0	0	0	0
glycerin	2	.2346	.1166	30.7	0	0	0	0	0	1	1	0	0	0	0	0	0	0	0	1	0	0	0	0	0	0	0	1	0
glycol	2	.0000	.0209	23.2	0	0	0	1	0	1	0	0	0	0	0	0	0	0	0	0	0	0	0	0	0	0	2	0	0
Glynn	2	.0000	.0243	23.9	0	0	0	2	0	0	0	0	0	0	0	0	0	0	0	0	0	0	0	0	0	0	0	2	0
glyph	8	.0000	.3655	35.6	0	0	0	0	8	0	0	0	8	0	0	0	0	0	0	0	0	0	0	0	0	0	0	0	0
glyphs	3	.0000	.1370	31.4	0	0	0	0	3	0	0	0	3	0	0	0	0	0	0	0	0	0	0	0	0	0	0	0	0
gm	3	.0000	.0449	26.5	0	0	0	0	0	3	0	0	0	0	0	0	3	0	0	0	0	0	0	0	0	0	0	0	0
GM	8	.0000	.0972	29.9	0	0	0	0	7	0	1	0	0	0	0	0	0	0	0	0	0	0	0	0	0	0	0	8	0
GM'S	2	.0000	.0243	23.9	0	0	0	0	2	0	0	0	0	0	0	0	0	0	0	0	0	0	0	0	0	0	0	2	0
GMC	5	.0000	.0608	27.8	0	0	0	0	5	0	0	0	0	0	0	0	0	0	0	0	0	0	0	0	0	0	0	5	0
gnarled	12	.6278	1.5737	42.0	2	3	1	1	3	2	0	0	3	0	0	2	0	1	0	0	0	0	0	0	3	1	1	1	0
gnashings	2	.0000	.0219	23.4	0	0	0	0	0	2	0	0	0	2	0	0	0	0	0	0	0	0	0	0	0	0	0	0	0
gnat	4	.4866	.4069	36.1	1	0	1	0	1	0	1	0	0	0	0	1	0	0	0	0	0	0	0	0	1	1	1	0	0
gnats	9	.5299	1.0003	40.0	1	1	0	2	4	0	1	0	0	0	0	2	0	1	0	2	0	0	0	0	0	3	1	0	0
gnaw	14	.5273	1.5542	41.9	4	0	0	1	5	2	2	0	2	1	1	6	0	0	0	0	0	0	0	0	0	2	2	0	0
gnawed	17	.3674	1.3726	41.4	1	2	0	2	8	3	1	0	1	0	0	10	0	0	0	0	0	0	0	0	3	2	0	1	0
gnawing	22	.5532	2.5903	44.1	1	2	2	9	5	3	0	0	5	0	0	4	0	1	0	2	0	0	0	0	1	2	7	0	0
gnaws	3	.2212	.2099	33.2	0	0	0	1	1	0	1	0	2	0	0	1	0	0	0	0	0	0	0	0	0	0	0	0	0
gneiss	3	.2043	.1486	31.7	0	0	0	2	1	0	0	0	0	0	0	0	0	0	0	0	0	0	0	0	0	1	2	0	0
go	5388	.9453	1008.1	70.0	1485	1131	543	615	807	443	296	68	1883	178	65	410	155	448	88	374	174	32	49	14	520	604	67	325	2
Go	14	.4552	1.3224	41.2	2	0	3	2	6	0	1	0	0	0	0	1	0	0	0	0	8	0	1	0	2	1	0	1	0
GO	7	.4055	.6674	38.2	1	3	0	1	2	0	0	0	3	0	0	0	0	0	0	1	0	0	1	0	0	0	0	2	0
go-between	4	.0000	.0579	27.6	3	0	0	0	1	0	0	0	0	0	0	0	0	0	0	0	0	0	0	0	0	4	0	0	0
go-getter	2	.0000	.0243	23.9	0	0	0	0	0	0	0	2	0	0	0	0	0	0	0	0	0	0	0	0	0	0	0	2	0
go-to-meeting	2	.2427	.1152	30.6	0	1	0	0	0	1	0	0	0	0	0	0	0	0	0	0	0	0	0	0	1	1	0	0	0
goaded	4	.2991	.2943	34.7	0	0	1	2	0	0	1	0	1	0	0	0	0	0	0	0	0	0	0	0	0	1	0	2	0
goading	2	.2440	.1132	30.5	0	0	0	0	2	0	0	0	0	0	0	1	0	0	0	0	0	0	0	0	0	0	0	1	0
goal	128	.8756	22.345	53.5	9	13	12	22	30	19	21	2	24	7	0	3	3	12	4	23	3	2	3	0	2	21	7	14	0
goal-insight	3	.0000	.0591	27.7	0	0	0	3	0	0	0	0	0	0	0	0	0	0	0	3	0	0	0	0	0	0	0	0	0
goalies	5	.0000	.0608	27.8	0	0	0	0	5	0	0	0	0	0	0	0	0	0	0	0	0	0	0	0	0	0	0	5	0
goals	54	.6602	7.2980	48.6	0	4	8	6	8	15	11	2	3	1	0	0	0	15	0	2	1	0	3	0	1	8	4	16	0
goat	130	.7517	20.278	53.1	66	16	8	11	22	5	1	1	82	7	0	3	0	4	12	6	1	1	0	0	2	3	5	4	0
Goat	9	.4242	.8560	39.3	3	0	0	6	0	0	0	0	2	0	0	2	0	0	0	2	0	0	0	0	0	0	3	0	0
goat's	7	.2366	.5437	37.4	1	3	0	2	1	0	0	0	6	0	0	0	0	0	0	0	0	0	0	0	1	0	0	0	0
goatee	4	.4421	.3922	35.9	0	2	0	0	2	0	0	0	1	0	0	0	0	0	1	0	0	0	0	0	1	1	0	0	0
goatherd	10	.2215	.7638	38.8	9	0	0	0	0	0	1	0	9	0	0	1	0	0	0	0	0	0	0	0	0	0	0	0	0
goats	99	.5527	11.975	50.8	29	11	16	15	20	2	5	1	38	1	0	2	1	37	1	2	0	0	1	0	0	5	7	3	1
goats'	5	.0000	.2284	33.6	4	1	0	0	0	0	0	0	5	0	0	0	0	0	0	0	0	0	0	0	0	0	0	0	0
goatskin	9	.3840	.8785	39.4	4	1	1	0	2	1	0	0	6	0	0	1	0	2	0	0	0	0	0	0	0	0	0	0	0
goatskins	4	.3271	.3195	35.0	1	0	0	1	1	1	0	0	1	0	0	0	0	2	1	0	0	0	0	0	0	0	0	0	0
gob	2	.1698	.1133	30.5	0	1	0	0	1	0	0	0	1	0	0	0	0	0	0	0	0	0	0	0	0	0	1	0	0
gobble	10	.4292	.9674	39.9	6	1	2	0	0	0	0	1	3	3	0	0	0	0	0	0	0	0	0	0	3	0	0	1	0
gobbled	14	.4721	1.5327	41.9	3	6	2	1	1	0	1	0	8	2	0	0	0	0	0	0	0	0	0	0	0	3	0	1	0
gobbler	4	.0000	.0486	26.9	0	0	0	0	4	0	0	0	0	0	0	0	0	0	0	0	0	0	0	0	0	0	0	4	0
gobblers	5	.2766	.3388	35.3	0	0	1	0	4	0	0	0	1	0	0	0	0	0	0	0	0	0	0	0	0	0	1	3	0
gobbles	2	.2291	.1135	30.5	0	1	0	1	0	0	0	0	0	0	0	1	0	0	0	1	0	0	0	0	0	0	0	0	0
gobbling	6	.2279	.4286	36.3	1	1	0	1	2	0	1	0	4	0	0	0	0	0	0	0	0	0	0	0	0	0	0	2	0
Gobbo	6	.0000	.0644	28.1	0	0	0	0	0	0	6	0	0	0	0	6	0	0	0	0	0	0	0	0	0	0	0	0	0
Gobi	12	.2898	.8154	39.1	7	3	0	1	1	0	0	0	0	0	0	1	0	0	0	3	0	0	0	0	0	8	0	0	0
goblet	2	.1814	.1187	30.7	0	0	0	1	0	0	0	1	1	0	0	0	0	0	0	0	0	0	0	0	0	0	0	1	0
goblets	5	.2353	.2584	34.1	0	0	0	0	5	0	0	0	0	0	0	0	0	0	0	0	4	0	1	0	0	0	0	0	0
goblin	9	.3706	.8710	39.4	5	0	1	2	1	0	0	0	7	0	0	0	0	0	0	0	1	0	0	0	0	1	0	0	0
Goblin	6	.3906	.5236	37.2	1	0	0	0	0	5	0	0	1	0	0	0	0	0	0	0	0	0	0	0	3	0	1	1	0
goblins	14	.4689	1.5420	41.9	1	9	0	2	0	2	0	0	9	0	0	0	0	0	1	0	0	0	0	0	1	3	0	0	0
Gobo	2	.0000	.0914	29.6	0	0	0	2	0	0	0	0	2	0	0	0	0	0	0	0	0	0	0	0	0	0	0	0	0
god	125	.8383	20.955	53.2	10	15	25	20	21	9	20	5	22	8	2	21	0	16	12	3	9	3	0	0	4	15	8	2	0

8J glorification
5Q glory-hole
7R glory-seeking
5A glory-singing
XH glossitis
8P Gloster's
7A Gloucestershire
6R Glove
8B Glover's
6R Gloves
9D glow-worm's
7C glow'd
4P Gloworm
5H Glowworm
8A glub-glub
XH gluconic
6A Glue
3A Glue-All
8A glued-on
8H gluelike
3P glug
3P Glug
9Q gluteal
7N glutinous
5P glutted
9B glutteral
6N glutton
5G gluvz
7Q glyptodons
8E GMJ
6N gnapan
9D gnashed
XR Gnats
6N gnawin'
9H gneisses
3P gnitten
3J gnome
6A gnomelike
4P gnomes
3J Gnomes
3A gnu
6A gnu-tail
6D go-ahead
9D go-den
8R go-go
7R go-kart
5A go-o-o
4N go-o-o-ne
XR go-round
7D goa
6P Goal
7R goalie
7R goaltenders
6F goat-raising
6N goatsack
5E GOB
3A Gobble-uns
4P gobble-uns'll
3A Gobble-uns'll
7R gobbler-chasing
9R Gobel
7Q gobies
8N Goblin's
7N goby
5E GOC
4F Gochiso-sama

Word Type	F	D	U	SFI	3 Gr 3	4 Gr 4	5 Gr 5	6 Gr 6	7 Gr 7	8 Gr 8	9 Gr 9	X UnGr	A Read	B Eng & Gr	C Comp	D Lit	E Math	F Soc Stud	G Spell	H Sci	J Music	K Art	L Home Ec	M Shop	N Lib F	P Lib NF	Q Lib Ref	R Mag	S Rel
God	473	.1492	19.583	52.9	96	82	39	77	72	41	44	22	55	16	3	45	2	50	9	1	63	2	0	0	45	56	19	31	76
god-forsaken	2	.0000	.0219	23.4	0	0	0	0	0	2	0	0	0	2	0	0	0	0	0	0	0	0	0	0	0	0	0	0	0
god-spirits	2	.0000	.0914	29.6	0	0	0	2	0	0	0	0	2	0	0	0	0	0	0	0	0	0	0	0	0	0	0	0	0
god's	2	.0000	.0234	23.7	0	0	0	0	2	0	0	0	0	0	0	0	0	0	0	0	0	0	0	0	2	0	0	0	0
God's	59	.1061	1.9684	42.9	9	10	2	7	10	4	13	4	8	4	0	6	0	2	0	0	3	0	0	0	9	2	3	10	12
Goddard	13	.3677	1.2583	41.0	0	0	4	0	1	7	1	0	10	0	0	0	0	0	1	2	0	0	0	0	0	0	0	0	0
Goddard's	2	.0000	.0914	29.6	0	0	0	0	0	2	0	0	2	0	0	0	0	0	0	0	0	0	0	0	0	0	0	0	0
goddess	53	.6272	6.9626	48.4	4	4	9	10	1	10	12	3	18	5	0	11	0	2	1	0	3	5	1	0	1	0	6	0	0
Goddess	10	.4858	1.1265	40.5	4	3	0	0	0	3	0	0	6	0	0	1	0	2	0	0	0	0	0	0	0	0	1	0	0
goddesses	27	.5758	3.4679	45.4	0	5	4	6	0	12	0	0	19	2	0	0	0	1	1	2	0	1	0	0	0	1	0	0	0
godlike	4	.2694	.2494	34.0	0	0	0	0	0	2	2	0	0	0	0	1	0	2	0	0	0	1	0	0	0	0	0	0	0
godly	8	.2431	.4404	36.4	0	0	0	0	0	0	8	0	0	0	0	7	0	0	0	0	0	1	0	0	0	0	0	0	0
godmother	7	.0000	.3198	35.0	7	0	0	0	0	0	0	0	7	0	0	0	0	0	0	0	0	0	0	0	0	0	0	0	0
Godmother	3	.0000	.0243	23.8	3	0	0	0	0	0	0	0	0	0	0	0	0	0	0	0	3	0	0	0	0	0	0	0	0
Godolphin	2	.0000	.0234	23.7	0	0	0	2	0	0	0	0	0	0	0	0	0	0	0	0	0	0	0	0	2	0	0	0	0
Godounov	3	.0000	.0243	23.8	0	0	0	3	0	0	0	0	0	0	0	0	0	0	0	0	3	0	0	0	0	0	0	0	0
gods	180	.7923	28.841	54.6	10	23	21	48	34	22	18	4	46	13	0	29	0	35	4	7	9	2	0	0	2	20	12	1	0
Gods	10	.4106	.9280	39.7	0	0	0	3	2	4	1	0	3	0	0	3	0	0	0	0	3	0	0	0	0	0	0	1	0
godson	2	.0000	.0290	24.6	0	0	0	0	2	0	0	0	0	0	0	0	0	0	0	0	0	0	0	0	0	2	0	0	0
Godspeed	2	.2152	.1357	31.3	0	1	0	0	1	0	0	0	1	0	0	0	0	1	0	0	0	0	0	0	0	0	0	0	0
Godwin	4	.2160	.2724	34.4	0	0	4	0	0	0	0	0	2	0	0	0	0	0	0	2	0	0	0	0	0	0	0	0	0
Goering	2	.0000	.0914	29.6	0	0	0	0	0	0	2	0	2	0	0	0	0	0	0	0	0	0	0	0	0	0	0	0	0
Goering's	2	.1948	.1250	31.0	0	0	0	0	1	0	1	0	1	0	0	0	0	0	0	0	0	0	0	0	0	1	0	0	0
goes	930	.9402	172.94	62.4	240	143	116	114	155	70	66	26	180	49	12	70	62	58	35	169	55	5	5	2	34	83	37	74	0
Goes	5	.2063	.2450	33.9	2	0	1	1	1	0	0	0	0	0	0	0	0	0	0	0	3	0	0	0	0	2	0	0	0
goest	2	.2407	.1138	30.6	1	0	0	0	0	0	1	0	0	0	0	1	0	0	0	0	0	0	0	0	0	1	0	0	0
goeth	4	.2186	.2141	33.3	2	0	1	0	0	0	1	0	0	0	0	1	0	0	0	0	0	0	0	0	0	3	0	0	0
Goethe	7	.4178	.6189	37.9	0	0	0	0	2	3	2	0	0	0	0	0	0	0	0	0	3	0	0	0	0	2	1	1	0
Goethe's	4	.2160	.2008	33.0	0	0	0	0	1	0	3	0	0	0	0	0	0	0	0	0	1	0	0	0	0	0	3	0	0
Goewin	2	.0000	.0290	24.6	0	0	0	0	2	0	0	0	0	0	0	0	0	0	0	0	0	0	0	0	0	2	0	0	0
GOF	2	.0000	.0299	24.8	0	0	2	0	0	0	0	0	0	0	0	0	2	0	0	0	0	0	0	0	0	0	0	0	0
Gog	3	.0000	.0352	25.5	0	0	0	2	1	0	0	0	0	0	0	0	0	0	0	0	0	0	0	0	3	0	0	0	0
goggle-eyed	2	.2446	.1142	30.6	0	0	0	1	0	0	0	1	0	0	0	0	0	0	0	0	0	0	0	0	1	0	0	1	0
goggled	2	.0000	.0234	23.7	1	1	0	0	0	0	0	0	0	0	0	0	0	0	0	0	0	0	0	0	2	0	0	0	0
goggles	18	.4875	1.9710	42.9	6	3	1	2	1	3	0	2	9	0	3	2	0	0	0	1	1	0	0	1	1	0	0	0	0
goggling	5	.4385	.4861	36.9	2	0	0	0	2	0	1	0	1	0	0	0	0	0	0	0	0	0	0	0	1	2	0	1	0
Gogh	2	.1247	.0633	28.0	0	0	0	0	1	1	0	0	0	0	0	0	0	0	0	0	0	1	0	0	0	1	0	0	0
Gogh's	2	.0000	.0037	15.7	0	1	0	0	0	1	0	0	0	0	0	0	0	0	0	0	0	2	0	0	0	0	0	0	0
goin'	60	.6038	7.5626	48.8	5	8	0	12	16	15	4	0	13	4	0	11	0	0	0	0	9	0	0	0	15	7	0	1	0
going	2832	.8583	487.80	66.9	622	655	297	293	489	250	173	53	1064	127	31	230	50	163	31	109	24	11	9	3	373	373	25	209	0
Going	4	.3259	.2859	34.6	1	1	0	0	0	1	0	1	0	0	0	1	0	1	0	0	0	1	0	0	0	0	0	1	0
going-away	2	.0000	.0243	23.9	0	0	2	0	0	0	0	0	0	0	0	0	0	0	0	0	0	0	0	0	0	0	0	2	0
goings	3	.2304	.1619	32.1	1	0	0	1	1	0	0	0	0	0	0	0	0	0	0	0	0	0	0	0	2	0	1	0	0
goiter	2	.0000	.0064	18.1	0	0	0	0	0	2	0	0	0	0	0	0	0	0	0	0	0	0	2	0	0	0	0	0	0
GOK	3	.0000	.0322	25.1	0	0	0	0	3	0	0	0	0	0	0	3	0	0	0	0	0	0	0	0	0	0	0	0	0
gold	895	.8776	157.28	62.0	240	152	118	118	131	85	39	12	359	12	6	48	10	141	2	54	45	5	0	2	54	59	49	49	0
Gold	34	.6602	4.6373	46.7	0	15	7	6	2	2	2	0	9	7	0	1	1	1	0	0	7	2	0	0	1	1	1	3	0
gold-bearing	2	.1814	.1187	30.7	1	0	0	1	0	0	0	0	1	0	0	0	0	0	0	0	0	0	0	0	0	0	0	1	0
gold-crowned	2	.0000	.0914	29.6	0	0	1	1	0	0	0	0	2	0	0	0	0	0	0	0	0	0	0	0	0	0	0	0	0
gold-leafed	2	.0000	.0045	16.5	0	0	0	0	0	0	2	0	0	0	2	0	0	0	0	0	0	0	0	0	0	0	0	0	0
gold-rush	2	.1523	.0721	28.6	0	0	0	1	0	1	0	0	0	0	1	0	0	0	0	0	0	0	0	0	0	0	0	1	0
Golda	3	.2425	.1816	32.6	0	0	0	0	0	1	2	0	0	0	0	0	0	2	0	0	0	0	0	0	0	0	0	1	0
Goldberg	2	.2446	.1142	30.6	0	0	0	0	0	0	0	2	0	0	0	0	0	0	0	0	0	0	0	0	1	0	0	1	0
Goldberger	3	.0000	.0365	25.6	0	0	0	0	0	0	3	0	0	0	0	0	0	0	0	0	0	0	0	0	0	0	0	3	0
golden	298	.8966	53.273	57.3	75	29	22	47	41	41	23	20	114	26	4	23	4	13	4	16	18	1	9	0	21	19	7	19	0
Golden	75	.7518	11.542	50.6	14	3	8	22	19	6	1	2	25	1	0	5	1	18	0	1	7	0	0	0	3	5	3	6	0
golden-brown	7	.3842	.5922	37.7	1	2	0	0	2	0	2	0	1	0	0	1	0	0	0	0	0	0	2	0	1	2	0	0	0
goldenrod	3	.3390	.2450	33.9	1	0	0	0	1	0	1	0	1	0	0	0	0	0	0	0	0	0	0	0	0	0	1	1	0
goldfish	45	.7131	6.5438	48.2	23	11	4	1	0	1	4	1	7	4	0	3	5	0	0	5	1	0	0	0	11	6	0	3	0
Goldie	2	.0000	.0914	29.6	2	0	0	0	0	0	0	0	2	0	0	0	0	0	0	0	0	0	0	0	0	0	0	0	0
Goldilocks	3	.1187	.1291	31.1	0	1	2	0	0	0	0	0	1	0	0	2	0	0	0	0	0	0	0	0	0	0	0	0	0
Goldman	3	.0000	.0243	23.8	0	0	0	0	0	3	0	0	0	0	0	0	0	0	0	0	3	0	0	0	0	0	0	0	0
Goldoni	2	.2401	.1133	30.5	0	1	1	0	0	0	0	0	0	0	0	0	0	0	0	0	0	0	0	0	0	1	1	0	0
goldsmith	3	.2223	.2106	33.2	1	0	0	1	1	0	0	0	2	1	0	0	0	0	0	0	0	0	0	0	0	0	0	0	0
goldsmiths	2	.2440	.1132	30.5	0	0	0	0	1	1	0	0	0	0	0	1	0	0	0	0	0	0	0	0	0	0	0	1	0
Goldsmiths'	2	.0000	.0914	29.6	2	0	0	0	0	0	0	0	2	0	0	0	0	0	0	0	0	0	0	0	0	0	0	0	0
golf	52	.7495	7.9082	49.0	4	8	3	9	6	7	13	2	9	1	1	2	2	5	1	6	0	0	0	1	1	2	2	19	0
Golf	2	.0000	.0243	23.9	0	0	0	0	0	0	2	0	0	0	0	0	0	0	0	0	0	0	0	0	0	0	0	2	0
golfer	5	.3432	.4203	36.2	0	0	0	3	0	1	1	0	2	1	0	0	0	0	0	0	0	0	0	0	0	0	0	2	0
golfers	2	.2427	.1159	30.6	0	1	0	0	0	0	1	0	0	0	0	0	1	0	0	0	0	0	0	0	0	0	0	1	0
golfing	3	.1060	.1461	31.6	0	0	0	2	0	0	1	0	2	0	1	0	0	0	0	0	0	0	0	0	0	0	0	0	0
Golgi	2	.0000	.0394	26.0	0	0	0	0	2	0	0	0	0	0	0	0	0	0	0	2	0	0	0	0	0	0	0	0	0
Goliad	4	.2183	.2285	33.6	0	1	0	0	3	0	0	0	0	0	0	0	0	3	0	0	0	0	0	0	0	1	0	0	0
goliath	3	.2398	.1721	32.4	0	0	0	0	1	0	2	0	0	0	0	0	2	0	0	0	0	0	0	0	0	0	1	0	0
Goliath	11	.2382	.6351	38.0	0	1	1	0	5	4	0	0	1	0	0	8	0	0	0	0	0	0	0	0	1	1	0	0	0
Goliath's	3	.0000	.0322	25.1	0	0	0	0	0	3	0	0	0	0	0	3	0	0	0	0	0	0	0	0	0	0	0	0	0
Golliwog's	2	.2303	.1079	30.3	1	0	0	0	1	0	0	0	0	0	0	0	0	0	0	0	1	0	0	0	0	1	0	0	0
golly	14	.6340	1.8437	42.7	1	4	2	4	1	1	0	1	3	1	0	1	0	0	0	0	1	0	0	0	3	4	0	1	0
Gomez	12	.3815	1.1171	40.5	1	1	2	4	0	0	4	0	6	0	0	4	1	1	0	0	0	0	0	0	0	0	0	0	0
Gompton	6	.0000	.2741	34.4	0	0	0	6	0	0	0	0	6	0	0	0	0	0	0	0	0	0	0	0	0	0	0	0	0
gon'	2	.0000	.0215	23.3	0	0	0	0	2	0	0	0	0	0	0	2	0	0	0	0	0	0	0	0	0	0	0	0	0
Gona	3	.0000	.0314	25.0	0	0	0	0	0	3	0	0	0	0	0	0	0	0	0	0	0	0	0	0	0	0	3	0	0
gonads	3	.2445	.1818	32.6	0	0	0	0	1	0	0	2	0	0	0	0	0	0	0	2	0	0	0	0	0	0	1	0	0
Gonaives	5	.0000	.0523	27.2	0	0	0	0	0	5	0	0	0	0	0	0	0	0	0	0	0	0	0	0	0	0	5	0	0
Goncalves	2	.0000	.0209	23.2	0	0	0	0	0	2	0	0	0	0	0	0	0	0	0	0	0	0	0	0	0	0	2	0	0
gondola	5	.4533	.4780	36.8	0	0	4	0	0	1	0	0	0	1	0	0	0	0	1	1	0	0	0	0	0	0	2	0	0
gone	1077	.8689	187.53	62.7	227	199	99	132	221	102	77	20	427	32	14	129	17	51	10	29	20	2	1	1	146	106	22	69	1
Gone	9	.2831	.5729	37.6	1	0	0	0	7	0	1	0	0	2	0	6	0	0	0	0	0	0	0	0	0	1	0	0	0
Gone-the-Child	2	.0000	.0215	23.3	0	0	0	0	2	0	0	0	0	0	0	2	0	0	0	0	0	0	0	0	0	0	0	0	0
gong	22	.6139	2.8035	44.5	2	1	1	7	6	3	0	2	3	0	0	3	0	3	0	3	5	0	0	0	3	0	0	2	0
gongs	4	.0759	.1243	30.9	0	0	1	0	3	0	0	0	1	0	0	0	0	0	0	0	3	0	0	0	0	0	0	0	0
gonna	57	.6309	7.5262	48.8	0	4	3	5	24	3	17	1	18	11	0	11	0	0	0	0	5	0	0	0	5	0	1	6	0

7A God-blesses
9D god-den
9F God-fearing
5P God-given
7N Godamighty
9R Godard
9R goddam
7R goddamned
7N goddaughter
6A goddess'
8F Godey's
3J godfather
9D godfathers
9P Godfrey
3A godmother's
3Q godparents
9D gods'
8A godsend
6B goed
6F Goethals
8J Goethe-Lieder
9B Gogio
7D Gogo
6N going-to-bed
8A goings-on
6A GOLD
5A Gold-Digging
4P gold-colored
6F gold-covered
8K gold-enameled
3A gold-eye
4N gold-fish
5A gold-flecked
6F gold-handled
4R gold-laced
6F gold-mining
7R gold-plated
7F gold-producing
5A gold-roofed
XR gold-tiled
3P gold-town
7D gold-white
XQ gold-work
7A gold-worked
6E Gold's
9R Golddiggers
5A golden-eyed
7D golden-haired
7N golden-tailed
9D golden-throated
7Q goldenrods
3A Goldens
7R Goldfarb
8N goldfields
6A goldfinch
7D Goldfinch
4P goldmining
3H golds
5Q Goldsmith
6J Goldsworthy
XH Goldthread
8R Goldwater
7R golf-bag
9R golfers'
4A gollee
8Q Golosov
8Q Gomarus
5A Gomera
8F Gompers
8F Gompers'
6A Gompton's
8Q Goncharov
5Q gondola-style
7B gonnagetit
XR Gonzaga

Word Type	F	D	U	SFI	3 Gr 3	4 Gr 4	5 Gr 5	6 Gr 6	7 Gr 7	8 Gr 8	9 Gr 9	X UnGr	A Read	B Eng & Gr	C Comp	D Lit	E Math	F Soc Stud	G Spell	H Sci	J Music	K Art	L Home Ec	M Shop	N Lib F	P Lib NF	Q Lib Ref	R Mag	S Rel
Gonzales	9	.4207	.8209	39.1	0	5	0	0	3	1	0	0	0	0	0	1	0	2	0	0	0	0	0	0	0	5	1	0	0
Gonzalez	4	.2059	.1995	33.0	0	0	0	0	0	1	0	3	0	1	0	0	0	0	0	0	0	0	0	0	0	0	0	3	0
goober	2	.1494	.1045	30.2	0	0	1	0	1	0	0	0	1	0	0	0	0	0	0	0	1	0	0	0	0	0	0	0	0
Goober	5	.0000	.2284	33.6	5	0	0	0	0	0	0	0	5	0	0	0	0	0	0	0	0	0	0	0	0	0	0	0	0
good	5343	.9542	1007.3	70.0	1210	969	539	685	840	525	468	107	1555	406	46	359	41	476	124	428	146	61	172	68	546	484	91	330	10
Good	50	.7282	7.3809	48.7	4	5	9	8	11	7	6	0	8	7	1	7	0	3	0	0	9	0	0	0	4	1	2	8	0
good-	2	.1787	.1174	30.7	1	0	1	0	0	0	0	0	1	0	0	0	0	0	0	0	0	0	0	0	1	0	0	0	0
good-by	145	.7398	22.123	53.4	33	46	14	15	27	6	3	1	66	4	1	7	0	12	8	0	6	0	0	0	24	16	0	1	0
Good-by	2	.2412	.1141	30.6	1	1	0	0	0	0	0	0	0	1	0	0	0	0	0	0	0	0	0	0	0	1	0	0	0
good-bye	33	.5656	3.9320	45.9	9	4	0	7	6	4	2	1	6	1	0	10	0	4	0	0	1	0	0	0	8	0	0	3	0
good-bys	3	.1639	.1674	32.2	0	1	1	0	0	1	0	0	1	0	0	0	0	2	0	0	0	0	0	0	0	0	0	0	0
good-day	2	.2303	.1079	30.3	1	1	0	0	0	0	0	0	0	0	0	0	0	0	0	0	1	0	0	0	0	1	0	0	0
good-for-nothing	2	.1717	.1142	30.6	0	0	1	0	1	0	0	0	1	0	0	1	0	0	0	0	0	0	0	0	0	0	0	0	0
good-humored	4	.3711	.3648	35.6	0	0	1	1	1	1	0	0	2	0	0	0	0	0	0	0	0	0	0	0	0	1	1	0	0
good-looking	7	.4543	.7043	38.5	0	1	2	1	0	1	2	0	2	0	1	0	0	0	0	1	0	0	1	0	0	2	0	0	0
good-luck	3	.2437	.2277	33.6	0	0	0	1	1	0	0	1	2	0	0	0	0	0	0	1	0	0	0	0	0	0	0	0	0
good-morning	2	.1787	.1174	30.7	0	0	2	0	0	0	0	0	1	0	0	0	0	0	0	0	0	0	0	0	1	0	0	0	0
good-natured	29	.6908	4.2177	46.3	2	7	2	2	6	10	0	0	17	1	1	3	0	0	0	1	0	1	0	0	2	2	0	1	0
good-naturedly	6	.1409	.2943	34.7	0	4	0	1	1	0	0	0	2	0	0	0	0	0	0	0	0	0	0	0	0	4	0	0	0
good-night	7	.4701	.7421	38.7	3	0	2	1	0	1	0	0	3	0	0	1	0	0	0	0	1	0	0	0	0	0	0	2	0
good-sized	6	.4801	.6592	38.2	2	2	0	0	2	0	0	0	3	0	0	1	0	0	0	1	0	0	0	0	1	0	0	0	0
good-spell	2	.0000	.0219	23.4	0	0	0	0	2	0	0	0	0	2	0	0	0	0	0	0	0	0	0	0	0	0	0	0	0
good-tasting	2	.0000	.0389	25.9	1	1	0	0	0	0	0	0	0	0	0	0	0	2	0	0	0	0	0	0	0	0	0	0	0
good-tempered	5	.3444	.3754	35.7	1	1	0	0	3	0	0	0	0	0	0	1	0	0	0	0	0	0	0	0	3	0	1	0	0
goodby	8	.2426	.6298	38.0	5	1	0	1	0	1	0	0	7	0	0	0	0	0	0	0	1	0	0	0	0	0	0	0	0
goodbye	15	.3801	1.2730	41.0	10	1	0	2	0	0	1	1	2	0	0	0	0	0	0	0	1	0	0	0	9	2	0	1	0
Goode	10	.0000	.1448	31.6	0	0	0	0	0	0	10	0	0	0	0	0	0	0	0	0	0	0	0	0	0	10	0	0	0
goodies	6	.3596	.4727	36.7	1	2	1	0	2	0	0	0	0	0	0	1	0	0	0	0	0	0	0	0	0	2	0	3	0
goodly	12	.6722	1.6558	42.2	1	2	0	2	3	1	1	2	2	1	0	2	0	0	0	1	0	0	0	0	3	1	1	1	0
Goodman	7	.4701	.7421	38.7	1	0	1	1	3	1	0	0	3	0	0	1	0	0	0	0	1	0	0	0	0	0	0	2	0
goodness	89	.7051	13.023	51.1	14	16	16	16	16	5	4	2	38	1	1	9	0	3	1	0	3	0	0	0	20	7	0	6	0
goodness'	5	.2446	.3866	35.9	0	1	0	3	0	0	1	0	4	1	0	0	0	0	0	0	0	0	0	0	0	0	0	0	0
goodnight	3	.2212	.2099	33.2	0	0	0	2	0	0	1	0	2	0	0	1	0	0	0	0	0	0	0	0	0	0	0	0	0
goods	420	.6223	54.419	57.4	62	67	77	57	63	50	43	1	35	4	0	7	2	264	6	4	1	0	2	6	12	23	44	10	0
Goods	2	.2391	.1133	30.5	0	1	0	1	0	0	0	0	0	0	0	0	1	0	0	0	0	0	0	0	0	0	1	0	0
Goodsell	2	.0000	.0215	23.3	0	0	0	0	2	0	0	0	0	0	0	2	0	0	0	0	0	0	0	0	0	0	0	0	0
Goodwill	7	.1205	.2337	33.7	0	0	6	1	0	0	0	0	0	0	0	0	0	0	0	0	0	0	0	0	0	1	6	0	0
Goodwin	5	.2342	.2967	34.7	1	0	0	0	0	0	0	4	0	0	0	0	0	0	0	4	1	0	0	0	0	0	0	0	0
goody	7	.4744	.7505	38.8	3	3	0	0	0	0	1	0	3	0	0	0	0	0	1	0	0	0	0	0	0	2	0	1	0
Goody	15	.3534	1.2050	40.8	0	0	7	2	0	0	6	0	2	7	0	0	0	0	0	0	0	0	0	0	0	5	0	1	0
Goody's	2	.1733	.1149	30.6	0	0	1	1	0	0	0	0	1	1	0	0	0	0	0	0	0	0	0	0	0	0	0	0	0
Goodyear	12	.0000	.1256	31.0	0	0	12	0	0	0	0	0	0	0	0	0	0	0	0	0	0	0	0	0	0	0	12	0	0
Goodyear's	2	.2285	.1129	30.5	0	0	1	0	0	1	0	0	0	0	0	0	0	1	0	0	0	0	0	0	0	0	1	0	0
gooey	3	.3874	.2497	34.0	1	0	1	0	0	0	1	0	0	1	0	0	0	0	0	0	0	0	0	0	1	0	0	1	0
goof	3	.2266	.1614	32.1	0	0	1	0	0	0	2	0	0	0	0	0	0	0	0	0	0	0	0	0	1	0	0	2	0
Goofus	2	.0000	.0243	23.9	0	2	0	0	0	0	0	0	0	0	0	0	0	0	0	0	0	0	0	0	0	0	0	2	0
goofy	8	.2862	.5310	37.3	1	0	7	0	0	0	0	0	0	0	0	0	6	0	0	0	0	0	0	0	1	0	0	1	0
googol	2	.0000	.0209	23.2	0	0	2	0	0	0	0	0	0	0	0	0	0	0	0	0	0	0	0	0	0	0	2	0	0
gook	4	.2417	.3028	34.8	1	3	0	0	0	0	0	0	3	0	0	0	0	0	0	0	0	0	0	0	1	0	0	0	0
Gookin	6	.0000	.0644	28.1	0	0	0	0	2	4	0	0	0	0	0	6	0	0	0	0	0	0	0	0	0	0	0	0	0
gooney	2	.2433	.1158	30.6	1	0	0	0	1	0	0	0	0	0	0	0	0	0	0	0	0	0	0	0	0	1	0	1	0
goose	184	.6335	25.423	54.1	138	26	8	4	4	0	2	2	139	4	0	2	0	0	8	2	6	0	0	0	9	11	1	2	0
Goose	21	.6095	2.7709	44.4	11	4	1	3	1	1	0	0	12	2	0	1	0	0	0	0	1	0	0	0	0	2	0	3	0
goose-house	2	.0000	.0914	29.6	0	2	0	0	0	0	0	0	2	0	0	0	0	0	0	0	0	0	0	0	0	0	0	0	0
goose's	4	.1112	.1666	32.2	1	3	0	0	0	0	0	0	1	0	0	0	0	0	0	0	0	0	0	0	0	3	0	0	0
gooseberries	3	.0000	.0591	27.7	0	0	0	0	3	0	0	0	0	0	0	0	0	0	0	3	0	0	0	0	0	0	0	0	0
gooseberry	2	.2444	.1132	30.5	1	0	0	0	1	0	0	0	0	1	0	0	0	0	0	0	0	0	0	0	1	0	0	0	0
Goosie	9	.0000	.4111	36.1	9	0	0	0	0	0	0	0	9	0	0	0	0	0	0	0	0	0	0	0	0	0	0	0	0
Goover	2	.0000	.0219	23.4	0	0	0	0	0	0	2	0	0	2	0	0	0	0	0	0	0	0	0	0	0	0	0	0	0
gopher	11	.3667	.8697	39.4	0	1	0	0	3	7	0	0	0	0	0	5	0	0	0	0	0	0	0	0	4	0	2	0	0
gophers	3	.3385	.2445	33.9	0	1	0	0	1	1	0	0	1	0	0	0	0	0	0	0	0	0	0	0	1	0	1	0	0
Gordie	6	.1493	.2320	33.7	0	0	0	0	6	0	0	0	0	0	0	5	0	0	0	0	0	0	0	0	0	0	0	1	0
Gordon	23	.6831	3.2401	45.1	6	1	0	0	10	1	1	4	6	2	0	1	0	1	0	0	1	0	0	0	2	2	1	7	0
Gordy	9	.0000	.4111	36.1	0	0	0	9	0	0	0	0	9	0	0	0	0	0	0	0	0	0	0	0	0	0	0	0	0
Gordy's	2	.0000	.0914	29.6	0	0	0	2	0	0	0	0	2	0	0	0	0	0	0	0	0	0	0	0	0	0	0	0	0
gore	3	.1320	.1599	32.0	0	0	0	0	2	1	0	0	2	0	0	0	0	0	0	0	0	0	1	0	0	0	0	0	0
gored	3	.3427	.2477	33.9	0	0	0	0	1	0	2	0	1	0	0	0	0	0	0	0	0	0	0	0	1	0	0	1	0
gorge	10	.4921	1.0378	40.2	1	2	0	3	2	1	1	0	1	0	1	0	0	0	0	0	0	0	0	0	2	0	3	3	0
Gorge	7	.4598	.6930	38.4	0	2	1	3	0	0	1	0	0	0	0	0	1	3	0	0	0	0	0	0	0	1	0	2	0
gorgeous	17	.5579	2.0264	43.1	0	1	3	4	5	1	3	0	5	0	2	2	0	1	0	1	0	0	0	0	3	1	0	2	0
gorgeously	3	.3665	.2412	33.8	0	0	1	1	0	0	1	0	0	0	0	0	0	1	0	0	1	0	0	0	0	0	0	1	0
gorges	9	.5745	1.0888	40.4	0	1	2	1	4	0	1	0	1	0	0	1	0	4	0	0	0	0	0	0	1	1	1	0	0
gorging	3	.3452	.2543	34.1	0	1	0	1	1	0	0	0	1	0	0	0	0	0	0	1	0	0	0	0	0	0	0	1	0
Gorgonzola	2	.1442	.0761	28.8	0	0	0	1	1	0	0	0	0	0	0	0	0	1	0	0	0	0	1	0	0	0	0	0	0
gorilla	9	.3471	.8192	39.1	0	1	0	0	8	0	0	0	6	0	0	0	0	1	0	0	0	0	0	0	0	0	2	0	0
gorillas	12	.4493	1.2505	41.0	0	2	0	2	6	0	2	0	5	0	0	0	0	4	0	1	0	0	0	0	0	0	2	0	0
gork	3	.2261	.2131	33.3	0	3	0	0	0	0	0	0	2	0	0	0	0	0	0	0	0	0	0	0	1	0	0	0	0
Gorman	2	.0000	.0219	23.4	0	0	0	0	0	2	0	0	0	2	0	0	0	0	0	0	0	0	0	0	0	0	0	0	0
gorse	2	.2443	.1130	30.5	0	0	0	0	2	0	0	0	0	0	0	1	0	0	0	0	0	0	0	0	1	0	0	0	0
gosh	16	.4196	1.5649	41.9	0	3	2	3	7	1	0	0	7	0	0	5	0	0	0	0	0	0	0	0	3	1	0	0	0
goslings	2	.0000	.0290	24.6	2	0	0	0	0	0	0	0	0	0	0	0	0	0	0	0	0	0	0	0	0	2	0	0	0
Gosnold	3	.0000	.0434	26.4	0	3	0	0	0	0	0	0	0	0	0	0	0	0	0	0	0	0	0	0	0	3	0	0	0
gospel	6	.4389	.5960	37.8	0	1	2	0	2	0	1	0	2	2	0	0	0	0	0	0	0	0	0	0	0	1	0	1	0
Gospel	5	.1068	.1501	31.8	1	0	0	1	1	0	1	1	0	0	0	0	0	0	0	1	1	0	0	0	0	0	1	1	1
gossamer	5	.4716	.4938	36.9	0	1	0	0	1	0	2	1	0	0	0	1	0	0	0	0	1	0	0	0	0	1	0	2	0
gossip	13	.7327	1.9275	42.8	0	1	1	2	6	2	1	0	2	2	0	1	0	0	1	0	1	0	1	0	1	2	0	2	0
gossiped	3	.3408	.2477	33.9	0	0	1	1	0	1	0	0	1	0	0	1	0	0	0	0	0	0	0	0	0	1	0	0	0
gossiping	5	.3544	.4006	36.0	0	1	0	0	1	2	1	0	1	0	1	2	0	0	0	0	0	0	0	0	1	0	0	0	0
gossips	2	.2152	.1357	31.3	0	0	0	0	0	2	0	0	1	0	0	0	0	1	0	0	0	0	0	0	0	0	0	0	0
got	2626	.8037	428.73	66.3	557	452	267	308	553	276	169	44	1159	80	14	294	35	101	17	55	40	5	1	0	439	188	11	186	1
Gota	2	.0000	.0389	25.9	0	0	0	0	2	0	0	0	0	0	0	0	0	2	0	0	0	0	0	0	0	0	0	0	0
Gothic	18	.3313	1.3393	41.3	0	0	4	1	1	3	6	3	3	0	0	1	0	0	0	0	2	5	0	0	0	1	6	0	0
Gothics	3	.0000	.0076	18.8	0	0	0	0	0	0	3	0	0	0	0	0	0	0	0	0	0	0	0	3	0	0	0	0	0
Goto	2	.0000	.0914	29.6	0	0	2	0	0	0	0	0	2	0	0	0	0	0	0	0	0	0	0	0	0	0	0	0	0

4F Good-bye
7A good-government
8D good-morrow
6A good-nights
8N good-payin'
7R good-performing
8L good-quality
XR good-size
9R good-will
7R good-working
7N good's
5A Goodall
6J Goodbye
9P Goode's
XR Goodell
5A goodhearted
8P Goodhue
XR Goodlad
3G Goodman's
7P goodwill
XH Goodwin's
4R goody-goody
6A goofed
5Q googolplex
8D Gookin's
7A goon
7R gooneys
5R goopy
5Q goose-flesh
3N Gooseberry
3H gooseneck
8P Goosens
8D gopher's
6B gorbed
XP Gordius
7N Gordons
XR Gore
9D gore-blood
8D gorged
9D Gorgon
8A Gorgons
8D Gorgons'
8B Gorham
8F Goro
9D Gortyn
4P Goshen
XQ Gospels
9Q Gospertie
6P Goss
9D gossamers
9R Gosse
7D gossipings
4N Gossips
9A gossipy
8J Got
4A GOT
8D got'm
8D gota
7H Goteborg
5Q Goth
6J Goths
9D Gott

Word Type	F	D	U	SFI	3 Gr 3	4 Gr 4	5 Gr 5	6 Gr 6	7 Gr 7	8 Gr 8	9 Gr 9	X UnGr	A Read	B Eng & Gr	C Comp	D Lit	E Math	F Soc Stud	G Spell	H Sci	J Music	K Art	L Home Ec	M Shop	N Lib F	P Lib NF	Q Lib Ref	R Mag	S Rel
gotta	15	.4167	1.4279	41.5	2	4	0	2	5	1	1	0	5	0	0	4	0	0	0	0	0	0	0	0	5	0	0	1	0
gotten	50	.7089	7.3854	48.7	9	11	6	6	12	2	2	2	24	0	0	2	0	4	0	2	0	1	0	0	9	3	2	3	0
Gottfried	2	.0000	.0299	24.8	0	0	0	0	0	2	0	0	0	0	0	0	2	0	0	0	0	0	0	0	0	0	0	0	0
Gottschalk	8	.0000	.0647	28.1	0	0	7	0	0	1	0	0	0	0	0	0	0	0	0	0	8	0	0	0	0	0	0	0	0
gouache	3	.0000	.0055	17.4	0	2	0	0	1	0	0	0	0	0	0	0	0	0	0	0	0	3	0	0	0	0	0	0	0
gouge	13	.2769	.7569	38.8	0	0	0	1	9	0	3	0	0	0	0	0	0	0	0	1	0	2	0	8	0	1	1	0	0
gouged	5	.3926	.4468	36.5	0	0	1	1	2	1	0	0	1	0	0	0	0	1	0	0	0	0	0	0	0	1	2	0	0
gouges	5	.2002	.2062	33.1	0	0	0	0	3	0	2	0	0	0	0	0	0	0	0	0	0	1	0	4	0	0	0	0	0
Gould	5	.1101	.1543	31.9	0	0	1	1	1	2	0	0	0	0	0	0	0	1	0	0	4	0	0	0	0	0	0	0	0
Gounod	7	.1929	.3149	35.0	0	0	0	0	4	1	2	0	0	0	0	0	0	0	0	0	5	0	0	0	0	0	2	0	0
Gounod's	2	.2417	.1091	30.4	0	0	0	0	1	0	1	0	0	0	0	0	0	0	0	0	1	0	0	0	0	0	1	0	0
Gouraud	2	.0000	.0389	25.9	0	0	0	2	0	0	0	0	0	0	0	0	0	2	0	0	0	0	0	0	0	0	0	0	0
gourd	17	.3426	1.3942	41.4	2	2	5	3	4	1	0	0	6	0	0	1	0	2	0	0	1	4	0	0	1	2	0	0	0
gourds	19	.2564	1.1072	40.4	3	2	9	3	2	0	0	0	2	0	0	1	0	1	0	0	4	8	0	0	0	0	2	1	0
gourmet	2	.0000	.0243	23.9	0	0	0	0	0	0	0	2	0	0	0	0	0	0	0	0	0	0	0	0	0	0	0	2	0
Goury	3	.0000	.0365	25.6	0	3	0	0	0	0	0	0	0	0	0	0	0	0	0	0	0	0	0	0	0	0	0	3	0
gout	2	.2446	.1142	30.6	0	0	0	1	0	0	0	1	0	0	0	0	0	0	0	0	0	0	0	0	1	0	0	1	0
Gouverneur	3	.1937	.1495	31.7	0	0	0	0	2	1	0	0	0	0	0	0	0	1	0	0	0	0	0	0	0	0	0	2	0
Gouyave	2	.0000	.0243	23.9	0	0	2	0	0	0	0	0	0	0	0	0	0	0	0	0	0	0	0	0	0	0	0	2	0
Gov	4	.2437	.2257	33.5	0	0	0	0	3	1	0	0	0	0	0	0	0	0	0	0	0	0	0	0	0	0	2	2	0
govern	35	.6819	4.8712	46.9	3	2	4	8	8	5	5	0	2	1	0	0	1	13	2	0	1	0	0	0	2	3	8	2	0
governed	42	.5631	4.9815	47.0	2	1	6	9	7	11	6	0	4	0	0	2	0	21	1	0	0	1	0	0	0	1	11	1	0
governess	7	.3296	.5964	37.8	0	1	4	0	0	0	2	0	4	0	0	0	0	0	0	0	2	0	0	0	0	1	0	0	0
governing	24	.5949	2.9573	44.7	2	0	2	5	6	4	4	1	1	1	0	0	0	8	1	1	0	0	0	0	1	1	8	2	0
government	1095	.5846	133.99	61.3	101	55	170	147	160	286	164	12	49	8	4	18	6	670	4	24	9	0	2	1	4	60	161	75	0
Government	89	.6025	11.111	50.5	8	6	8	7	8	12	36	4	6	1	0	1	5	15	1	2	1	0	0	0	1	17	3	36	0
government-owned	2	.1698	.1133	30.5	0	0	1	0	0	1	0	0	1	0	0	0	0	0	0	0	0	0	0	0	0	0	1	0	0
government's	12	.4825	1.2527	41.0	1	0	3	2	1	4	0	1	1	0	0	0	0	6	0	0	0	0	0	0	0	1	2	2	0
Government's	5	.3608	.3926	35.9	0	0	1	0	0	0	4	0	0	0	0	0	0	0	0	0	0	0	0	0	0	1	2	2	0
governmental	16	.5117	1.7220	42.4	1	0	3	0	4	4	3	1	0	0	0	1	0	5	0	1	0	0	0	0	0	2	6	1	0
governments	121	.4954	12.852	51.1	4	1	22	17	19	36	21	1	4	1	0	0	0	75	1	1	1	0	0	0	1	6	22	9	0
Governments	2	.1698	.1133	30.5	0	0	1	0	1	0	0	0	1	0	0	0	0	0	0	0	0	0	0	0	0	0	1	0	0
governor	106	.7007	15.253	51.8	4	9	28	11	19	27	4	4	19	3	0	3	0	44	2	1	3	0	0	1	1	5	19	5	0
Governor	74	.6543	10.233	50.1	7	16	20	4	10	9	6	2	32	0	0	3	0	12	0	0	0	0	0	0	5	14	3	5	0
governor's	6	.5161	.6632	38.2	0	2	1	1	0	1	1	0	1	0	0	1	0	1	1	0	0	0	0	0	0	2	0	0	0
Governor's	8	.4803	.8919	39.5	0	1	4	0	1	1	1	0	5	0	0	0	0	0	0	0	1	0	0	0	0	1	0	1	0
governors	21	.3406	1.6482	42.2	0	1	1	1	4	14	0	0	0	1	0	0	0	16	0	0	0	0	0	0	0	1	3	0	0
Governors	6	.0000	.0628	28.0	0	0	0	0	6	0	0	0	0	0	0	0	0	0	0	0	0	0	0	0	0	0	6	0	0
governorship	2	.0000	.0914	29.6	0	0	1	0	0	0	1	0	2	0	0	0	0	0	0	0	0	0	0	0	0	0	0	0	0
governs	11	.6587	1.4848	41.7	0	0	0	3	3	1	3	1	1	0	0	0	0	3	1	1	1	0	1	0	0	1	2	0	0
Gowdy	4	.0000	.1827	32.6	0	4	0	0	0	0	0	0	4	0	0	0	0	0	0	0	0	0	0	0	0	0	0	0	0
Gowdy's	2	.0000	.0914	29.6	0	2	0	0	0	0	0	0	2	0	0	0	0	0	0	0	0	0	0	0	0	0	0	0	0
gown	25	.7297	3.7657	45.8	9	2	3	3	4	2	2	0	12	3	1	3	0	0	2	0	1	0	1	0	1	1	0	0	0
gowns	9	.6257	1.1720	40.7	4	0	2	0	3	0	0	0	2	0	0	1	0	1	0	0	2	0	0	0	0	1	1	1	0
Gowrie	2	.0000	.0209	23.2	0	0	0	0	0	0	2	0	0	0	0	0	0	0	0	0	0	0	0	0	0	0	2	0	0
Goya's	2	.1378	.0662	28.2	0	0	0	0	0	1	0	1	0	0	0	0	0	0	0	0	0	1	0	0	0	0	0	1	0
Gozaimasu	2	.0000	.0914	29.6	2	0	0	0	0	0	0	0	2	0	0	0	0	0	0	0	0	0	0	0	0	0	0	0	0
GP	2	.0000	.0243	23.9	0	0	0	2	0	0	0	0	0	0	0	0	0	0	0	0	0	0	0	0	0	0	0	2	0
gr	10	.0337	.1810	32.6	2	4	2	2	0	0	0	0	1	0	0	0	0	0	9	0	0	0	0	0	0	0	0	0	0
grab	73	.7366	11.060	50.4	16	13	13	9	11	8	3	0	30	2	2	9	0	1	5	3	0	0	0	0	11	4	0	6	0
grab-bag	2	.1698	.1133	30.5	0	0	0	1	0	1	0	0	1	0	0	0	0	0	0	0	0	0	0	0	0	0	1	0	0
grabbed	161	.7064	23.720	53.8	26	58	15	16	29	11	6	0	80	1	1	11	0	3	2	1	2	0	0	0	18	21	0	21	0
grabbing	13	.3810	1.1816	40.7	2	3	2	0	3	2	1	0	6	0	2	2	0	0	0	0	0	0	0	0	0	0	0	3	0
Graben	2	.0000	.0209	23.2	0	0	0	0	0	0	2	0	0	0	0	0	0	0	0	0	0	0	0	0	0	0	2	0	0
Grabow	5	.0000	.0537	27.3	0	0	0	0	0	0	5	0	0	0	0	5	0	0	0	0	0	0	0	0	0	0	0	0	0
grabs	13	.4374	1.3980	41.5	6	1	2	1	1	1	0	1	10	0	0	0	0	1	0	0	0	0	0	0	0	0	1	1	0
grace	55	.6088	6.9663	48.4	4	7	4	9	13	7	10	1	11	2	0	5	0	3	1	1	5	4	0	0	7	6	2	7	1
Grace	37	.6636	5.0228	47.0	9	3	9	0	7	2	6	1	3	2	0	12	5	8	0	0	0	1	0	0	3	0	2	1	0
graced	2	.2285	.1129	30.5	0	0	0	0	2	0	0	0	0	0	0	0	0	1	0	0	0	0	0	0	0	0	1	0	0
graceful	59	.5881	7.2390	48.6	9	12	7	8	14	6	3	0	10	4	0	2	0	6	0	4	7	8	0	0	2	8	3	5	0
gracefully	18	.6695	2.4632	43.9	2	2	5	2	4	2	1	0	2	2	0	2	0	0	0	3	3	1	0	0	0	3	0	2	0
gracefulness	4	.3727	.3183	35.0	0	0	0	0	2	0	2	0	0	1	0	2	0	0	0	0	1	0	0	0	0	0	0	0	0
graces	5	.4604	.4840	36.8	0	0	1	2	0	0	2	0	0	0	0	2	0	0	0	0	0	0	0	0	0	1	1	1	0
gracias	8	.2284	.6152	37.9	7	0	0	1	0	0	0	0	7	0	0	0	0	0	0	0	0	0	0	0	0	0	0	1	0
Gracie	4	.1112	.1666	32.2	0	0	0	0	1	0	3	0	1	0	0	0	0	0	0	0	0	0	0	0	0	3	0	0	0
gracious	27	.6846	3.8084	45.8	4	6	3	4	2	4	3	1	7	1	0	5	0	1	0	0	1	0	0	0	6	2	1	3	0
Gracious	3	.1250	.1342	31.3	0	2	0	0	1	0	0	0	1	0	0	0	0	0	0	0	0	0	0	0	2	0	0	0	0
graciously	13	.7217	1.9063	42.8	0	1	1	2	2	1	5	1	2	1	0	2	0	0	0	2	1	0	1	0	1	1	0	2	0
grackles	3	.3782	.2437	33.9	1	0	0	0	1	1	0	0	0	0	0	1	0	0	1	0	0	0	0	0	0	1	0	0	0
grad	2	.0000	.0243	23.9	0	0	1	0	1	0	0	0	0	0	0	0	0	0	0	0	0	0	0	0	0	0	0	2	0
gradations	5	.2111	.2294	33.6	0	0	0	0	1	0	4	0	0	0	0	0	0	0	0	1	0	3	0	1	0	0	0	0	0
grade	175	.7950	27.912	54.5	38	30	8	20	31	19	24	5	21	16	2	9	29	19	10	6	1	14	8	1	9	10	1	19	0
Grade	16	.3564	1.2581	41.0	1	0	0	0	6	1	7	1	1	0	0	0	9	0	1	0	0	0	4	0	0	0	0	1	0
grade-school	3	.3454	.2542	34.1	1	0	0	0	1	1	0	0	1	0	0	0	0	1	0	0	0	0	0	0	0	0	0	1	0
graded	10	.5250	1.0797	40.3	0	1	2	1	2	1	2	1	0	0	0	0	1	0	0	1	0	0	1	2	0	1	3	1	0
grader	3	.2266	.1614	32.1	0	1	0	1	0	0	1	0	0	0	0	0	0	0	0	0	0	0	0	0	1	0	0	2	0
graders	13	.4522	1.2465	41.0	1	3	0	5	4	0	0	0	0	4	0	0	5	0	0	0	0	0	0	0	1	0	0	3	0
grades	62	.7173	9.0088	49.5	1	8	8	4	18	11	8	4	7	0	1	0	12	4	3	5	0	0	8	4	1	2	4	11	0
Grades	3	.0000	.0449	26.5	0	0	0	0	1	0	2	0	0	0	0	0	3	0	0	0	0	0	0	0	0	0	0	0	0
gradient	3	.0000	.0314	25.0	0	0	0	0	0	1	2	0	0	0	0	0	0	0	0	0	0	0	0	0	0	0	3	0	0
gradients	2	.2437	.1129	30.5	0	0	0	0	2	0	0	0	0	0	0	0	0	0	0	0	0	0	0	0	0	0	1	1	0
grading	5	.4932	.5024	37.0	0	0	0	1	1	1	2	0	0	0	1	0	1	0	0	0	0	0	1	1	0	0	0	1	0
gradual	26	.7738	4.0374	46.1	1	1	1	2	7	3	9	2	1	0	0	1	0	4	0	4	3	1	1	0	2	1	4	4	0
gradually	239	.8787	41.755	56.2	14	20	27	27	62	45	34	10	28	2	1	11	1	30	8	39	28	3	9	3	7	16	40	12	1
graduate	44	.6151	5.5707	47.5	7	0	12	2	11	7	5	0	3	0	0	2	0	7	0	1	2	0	1	0	0	2	14	12	0
graduated	48	.6346	6.2922	48.0	2	0	10	2	20	8	6	0	7	0	0	2	4	6	0	0	1	0	1	0	0	1	12	14	0
graduates	14	.4955	1.4737	41.7	5	0	1	0	4	3	1	0	0	0	1	0	0	8	0	0	0	0	0	0	0	1	1	3	0
graduating	4	.1698	.2267	33.6	1	1	0	1	0	1	0	0	2	0	0	0	0	0	0	0	0	0	0	0	0	0	2	0	0
graduation	28	.7200	4.1606	46.2	1	3	2	4	8	5	4	1	11	5	0	2	0	2	1	0	0	0	0	0	2	1	1	3	0
Grady	2	.0000	.0389	25.9	0	0	0	0	0	2	0	0	0	0	0	0	0	2	0	0	0	0	0	0	0	0	0	0	0
Graff	3	.0000	.1370	31.4	0	0	0	0	0	3	0	0	3	0	0	0	0	0	0	0	0	0	0	0	0	0	0	0	0
graft	5	.3053	.3433	35.4	0	0	0	0	3	0	1	1	0	0	0	3	0	0	0	1	0	0	0	0	0	0	1	0	0
grafted	2	.0000	.0394	26.0	0	0	0	0	1	0	0	1	0	0	0	0	0	0	0	2	0	0	0	0	0	0	0	0	0
graham	4	.3641	.3324	35.2	2	1	0	0	1	0	0	0	1	0	0	0	0	0	0	0	0	0	1	0	1	0	0	1	0
Graham	48	.6732	6.6294	48.2	10	1	2	1	11	5	18	0	6	2	0	0	7	9	0	1	1	0	2	0	0	2	2	16	0
Graham's	4	.2427	.2319	33.7	0	0	0	0	0	2	2	0	0	0	0	0	2	0	0	0	0	0	0	0	0	0	0	2	0

6J Gotterdammerung
6F Gotthard
9Q Gotthold
5P Gottlieb
5J Gottschalk's
7L Gouda
9Q gouged-out
5A gougers
8F gouging
3A gourdful
4P governess'
6F government-built
8F government-business
5P government-controlled
8F government-led
5F government-operated
6R government-run
7Q government-sponsored
5Q governor-general
6R GOW-choz
6A gowned
8K Goya
8M Graaff
7R Grabber
9H grabens
5Q Grabner
9D Grace's
XR Graceful
8R Graceland
3J Gracieuse
8A gracious'
6R graciousness
5P gradated
9M gradation
9L gradings
6A gradual-like
5P gradualism
8A Graduation
8M graduations
7A Gradys
9R graffiti
7F grafting
5Q Grafton
7R grafts
6J grah-nah-dohs
8R Graham-style

Word Type	F	D	U	SFI	3 Gr 3	4 Gr 4	5 Gr 5	6 Gr 6	7 Gr 7	8 Gr 8	9 Gr 9	X UnGr	A Read	B Eng & Gr	C Comp	D Lit	E Math	F Soc Stud	G Spell	H Sci	J Music	K Art	L Home Ec	M Shop	N Lib F	P Lib NF	Q Lib Ref	R Mag	S Rel
Grahame	2	.0000	.0219	23.4	0	0	2	0	0	0	0	0	0	2	0	0	0	0	0	0	0	0	0	0	0	0	0	0	0
grain	340	.7642	52.532	57.2	50	48	54	57	38	46	39	8	53	1	2	8	2	97	10	33	2	7	36	20	7	35	24	3	0
grained	3	.2427	.1822	32.6	0	0	0	0	1	1	0	1	0	0	0	0	0	0	0	2	0	0	0	0	0	0	0	1	0
grainline	2	.0000	.0064	18.1	0	0	0	0	1	0	1	0	0	0	0	0	0	0	0	0	0	0	2	0	0	0	0	0	0
grains	142	.7813	22.452	53.5	27	22	17	23	20	8	14	11	26	1	1	1	0	20	2	44	1	0	6	2	2	14	20	2	0
grainy	3	.2383	.1815	32.6	0	0	1	1	0	0	1	0	0	0	0	0	0	0	0	2	0	0	0	0	0	1	0	0	0
gram	13	.3310	.9793	39.9	0	0	0	4	1	7	1	0	0	0	0	0	8	0	0	3	0	0	0	0	0	0	2	0	0
grama	2	.2446	.1122	30.5	0	0	0	0	0	0	2	0	0	0	0	1	0	0	0	0	0	0	0	0	0	0	1	0	0
grammar	61	.5165	6.6784	48.2	0	2	6	1	21	10	19	2	10	34	1	3	0	0	5	1	0	0	0	0	0	2	3	2	0
Grammar	3	.2153	.1451	31.6	0	0	1	1	0	0	1	0	0	0	1	0	0	0	0	0	0	0	0	0	0	0	2	0	0
grammarian	2	.2408	.1091	30.4	0	0	2	0	0	0	0	0	0	1	0	0	0	0	1	0	0	0	0	0	0	0	0	0	0
grammarians	2	.0000	.0219	23.4	0	0	0	0	1	1	0	0	0	2	0	0	0	0	0	0	0	0	0	0	0	0	0	0	0
grammars	2	.0000	.0219	23.4	0	0	1	0	0	1	0	0	0	2	0	0	0	0	0	0	0	0	0	0	0	0	0	0	0
grammatical	19	.3034	1.2526	41.0	0	0	2	1	9	1	6	0	0	13	4	0	0	0	0	0	0	0	0	0	0	0	2	0	0
grammatically	4	.1853	.1704	32.3	0	0	0	0	4	0	0	0	0	1	2	0	1	0	0	0	0	0	0	0	0	0	0	0	0
gramophone	2	.0000	.0209	23.2	0	0	0	0	0	2	0	0	0	0	0	0	0	0	0	0	0	0	0	0	0	0	2	0	0
Gramp	11	.2152	.8321	39.2	10	0	0	0	1	0	0	0	10	0	0	1	0	0	0	0	0	0	0	0	0	0	0	0	0
grampa	5	.1751	.2165	33.4	0	0	0	0	4	0	1	0	0	1	0	4	0	0	0	0	0	0	0	0	0	0	0	0	0
Gramps	3	.2435	.2274	33.6	1	0	1	0	0	1	0	0	2	0	0	0	0	1	0	0	0	0	0	0	0	0	0	0	0
grams	29	.4107	2.6057	44.2	1	0	0	2	11	0	15	0	0	0	0	0	17	0	0	7	0	0	0	0	1	1	3	0	0
Gran	3	.2435	.2274	33.6	2	0	0	0	1	0	0	0	2	0	0	0	0	1	0	0	0	0	0	0	0	0	0	0	0
Gran'maw	2	.0000	.0914	29.6	0	0	2	0	0	0	0	0	2	0	0	0	0	0	0	0	0	0	0	0	0	0	0	0	0
Granada	3	.3431	.2528	34.0	0	0	0	1	1	1	0	0	1	0	0	0	0	1	0	0	0	0	0	0	1	0	0	0	0
grand	109	.8213	17.964	52.5	10	11	12	14	28	21	9	4	23	5	3	10	0	12	0	3	12	2	0	0	8	6	5	20	0
Grand	101	.7647	15.652	51.9	11	28	10	21	7	7	8	9	17	1	0	2	4	24	0	9	6	0	0	0	12	5	5	16	0
grand-vizir	6	.0000	.0703	28.5	0	0	6	0	0	0	0	0	0	0	0	0	0	0	0	0	0	0	0	0	6	0	0	0	0
grandchild	2	.1787	.1174	30.7	0	1	0	0	0	1	0	0	1	0	0	0	0	0	0	0	0	0	0	0	1	0	0	0	0
grandchildren	16	.6341	2.1118	43.2	5	3	1	3	2	1	1	0	3	0	0	1	0	2	0	2	0	0	0	0	4	2	2	0	0
grandcolts	2	.0000	.0290	24.6	1	1	0	0	0	0	0	0	0	0	0	0	0	0	0	0	0	0	0	0	0	2	0	0	0
granddad	2	.0000	.0914	29.6	0	0	0	2	0	0	0	0	2	0	0	0	0	0	0	0	0	0	0	0	0	0	0	0	0
Granddad	12	.1975	.7654	38.8	0	0	0	2	10	0	0	0	7	0	0	5	0	0	0	0	0	0	0	0	0	0	0	0	0
granddaddy	2	.0000	.0914	29.6	2	0	0	0	0	0	0	0	2	0	0	0	0	0	0	0	0	0	0	0	0	0	0	0	0
granddaughter	6	.4859	.6625	38.2	0	1	0	2	1	1	0	1	3	1	0	0	0	0	0	0	0	0	0	0	1	1	0	0	0
Grande	45	.5204	4.9934	47.0	1	15	2	4	17	4	0	2	4	0	0	1	0	22	0	1	3	0	0	0	0	0	11	3	0
grandeur	14	.4841	1.4513	41.6	0	0	0	2	4	4	3	1	2	0	0	3	0	2	0	0	4	0	0	0	0	0	0	3	0
grandfather	186	.7928	30.095	54.8	67	50	24	16	15	8	3	3	91	4	2	16	1	16	5	1	3	0	1	0	18	24	0	4	0
Grandfather	283	.5965	37.221	55.7	138	105	5	5	11	17	2	0	189	3	0	12	0	28	1	0	1	0	2	0	3	43	0	1	0
GRANDFATHER	11	.0000	.1180	30.7	0	0	0	0	0	11	0	0	0	0	0	11	0	0	0	0	0	0	0	0	0	0	0	0	0
grandfather's	23	.7300	3.4395	45.4	3	6	0	5	3	3	2	1	8	2	0	3	0	0	1	0	0	1	1	1	1	5	0	0	0
Grandfather's	21	.5695	2.5869	44.1	12	8	0	0	0	1	0	0	8	1	0	0	0	2	0	0	0	0	0	0	1	6	0	3	0
grandfathers	11	.5493	1.2706	41.0	4	3	1	2	0	0	0	1	1	0	0	0	0	2	0	1	2	0	0	0	3	2	0	0	0
grandiose	4	.1307	.1407	31.5	0	0	1	0	0	3	0	0	0	0	0	0	0	1	0	0	3	0	0	0	0	0	0	0	0
grandly	8	.4871	.9006	39.5	1	2	0	3	0	2	0	0	5	0	0	1	0	0	0	0	0	0	0	0	1	0	0	1	0
grandma	5	.4281	.4726	36.7	0	1	1	0	2	0	1	0	1	1	0	1	0	0	0	0	0	0	0	0	2	0	0	0	0
Grandma	97	.4883	10.314	50.1	22	25	21	5	17	2	5	0	24	1	1	5	0	3	1	0	0	0	0	0	51	3	0	8	0
Grandma's	15	.3912	1.2657	41.0	8	2	1	0	2	0	2	0	0	0	0	2	0	1	0	0	0	0	0	0	4	0	0	8	0
Grandmarina	4	.0000	.1827	32.6	0	0	4	0	0	0	0	0	4	0	0	0	0	0	0	0	0	0	0	0	0	0	0	0	0
grandmother	140	.8121	23.135	53.6	52	30	10	13	6	13	12	4	76	5	1	15	3	7	3	1	2	0	4	0	14	3	2	4	0
Grandmother	89	.6703	12.492	51.0	22	43	2	0	7	9	6	0	33	14	0	5	0	24	1	0	0	0	2	0	4	6	0	0	0
GRANDMOTHER	2	.0000	.0215	23.3	0	0	0	0	0	0	2	0	0	0	0	2	0	0	0	0	0	0	0	0	0	0	0	0	0
grandmother's	15	.5222	1.7310	42.4	5	2	3	2	2	1	0	0	7	0	2	1	1	1	0	0	1	0	0	0	1	0	0	1	0
Grandmother's	17	.6457	2.2946	43.6	3	6	2	0	1	2	3	0	5	1	0	3	1	3	1	0	0	0	0	0	3	0	0	0	0
grandmothers	5	.3541	.3828	35.8	1	0	1	0	1	0	1	1	0	0	0	1	0	0	0	0	1	0	0	0	3	0	0	0	0
grandpa	7	.4187	.6621	38.2	1	0	2	0	3	1	0	0	2	1	0	1	0	0	0	0	0	0	0	0	3	0	0	0	0
Grandpa	71	.4897	7.8721	49.0	20	10	21	9	3	2	0	6	35	0	1	0	0	2	2	0	0	0	0	0	25	6	0	0	0
grandpa's	2	.1787	.1174	30.7	0	0	0	0	2	0	0	0	1	0	0	0	0	0	0	0	0	0	0	0	1	0	0	0	0
Grandpa's	8	.2155	.5456	37.4	3	0	3	0	2	0	0	0	5	0	0	0	0	0	0	0	0	0	0	0	3	0	0	0	0
grandparent	2	.2160	.1362	31.3	0	0	1	0	0	0	0	1	1	0	0	0	0	0	0	1	0	0	0	0	0	0	0	0	0
grandparents	46	.5158	5.1717	47.1	7	5	5	7	8	8	4	2	13	7	1	1	1	9	0	6	0	0	3	0	0	2	2	0	1
grandparents'	5	.3274	.3627	35.6	0	3	1	0	1	0	0	0	0	0	0	1	1	0	0	0	0	0	0	0	3	0	0	0	0
grandson	12	.1826	.6336	38.0	1	1	3	1	2	2	2	0	3	0	0	1	0	2	0	0	0	0	0	0	0	1	1	3	1
grandsons	4	.2417	.3028	34.8	2	0	0	0	1	1	0	0	3	0	0	0	0	0	0	0	0	0	0	0	1	0	0	0	0
grandstand	23	.5749	2.8748	44.6	5	8	2	5	2	0	1	0	11	0	1	2	0	1	0	1	0	0	0	0	6	1	0	0	0
grandstands	3	.1277	.1363	31.3	0	1	0	1	0	0	0	1	1	0	0	0	0	0	0	0	0	0	0	0	0	0	0	2	0
Grange	3	.0000	.0583	27.7	0	0	0	0	0	0	3	0	0	0	0	0	0	3	0	0	0	0	0	0	0	0	0	0	0
Granger	13	.2480	.7732	38.9	2	1	7	0	3	0	0	0	0	0	0	2	0	1	0	0	0	0	0	0	0	10	0	0	0
Granger's	2	.2407	.1138	30.6	0	0	1	0	1	0	0	0	0	0	0	1	0	0	0	0	0	0	0	0	0	1	0	0	0
granite	62	.6954	8.8028	49.4	6	5	10	12	10	7	11	1	6	1	0	4	0	2	0	19	0	2	0	0	1	8	12	7	0
Granite	4	.3717	.3640	35.6	0	0	2	1	1	0	0	0	2	0	0	1	0	0	0	0	0	0	0	0	0	0	0	1	0
granitic	2	.0000	.0209	23.2	0	0	0	0	2	0	0	0	0	0	0	0	0	0	0	0	0	0	0	0	0	0	2	0	0
grannies	4	.0000	.0429	26.3	0	0	0	0	4	0	0	0	0	0	0	4	0	0	0	0	0	0	0	0	0	0	0	0	0
granny	2	.0000	.0215	23.3	0	0	0	0	2	0	0	0	0	0	0	2	0	0	0	0	0	0	0	0	0	0	0	0	0
Granny	27	.2839	2.3191	43.7	24	0	0	2	1	0	0	0	24	0	0	0	0	0	0	0	0	0	0	0	0	1	0	2	0
Granny's	6	.1277	.2726	34.4	6	0	0	0	0	0	0	0	2	0	0	0	0	0	0	0	0	0	0	0	0	0	0	4	0
grant	31	.6278	4.0767	46.1	3	5	2	1	9	5	6	0	9	0	0	6	0	2	1	0	0	0	0	0	1	4	7	1	0
Grant	94	.6596	12.895	51.1	8	11	12	2	11	43	6	1	20	1	1	0	1	38	0	0	1	0	0	0	9	13	9	1	0
Grant's	19	.4033	1.6958	42.3	2	3	3	0	1	3	7	0	2	0	0	0	0	4	0	0	0	0	0	0	1	3	9	0	0
granted	117	.8936	20.767	53.2	8	9	15	10	20	24	28	3	14	8	1	4	6	24	0	14	2	1	2	1	4	6	20	10	0
granting	5	.4035	.4527	36.6	0	0	1	1	2	1	0	0	1	0	0	0	0	1	1	0	0	0	0	0	0	0	2	0	0
grants	13	.4264	1.2313	40.9	0	0	0	1	2	6	2	2	2	0	0	0	0	4	0	0	0	0	0	0	0	0	4	3	0
Grantville	3	.0000	.1370	31.4	3	0	0	0	0	0	0	0	3	0	0	0	0	0	0	0	0	0	0	0	0	0	0	0	0
granular	3	.2445	.1818	32.6	0	0	0	1	0	0	1	1	0	0	0	0	0	0	0	2	0	0	0	0	0	0	1	0	0
granulated	3	.0000	.0097	19.8	0	0	0	0	3	0	0	0	0	0	0	0	0	0	0	0	0	0	3	0	0	0	0	0	0
grape	18	.6245	2.3509	43.7	4	1	3	1	4	4	1	0	5	0	0	5	1	2	2	0	0	1	0	0	1	0	0	1	0
grapefruit	18	.6597	2.4290	43.9	5	4	0	2	7	0	0	0	0	1	0	0	4	7	0	1	0	0	1	0	1	1	0	2	0
grapes	80	.8007	12.907	51.1	11	19	4	18	22	4	2	0	14	8	0	4	0	27	3	3	0	1	1	0	2	2	8	7	0
grapeshot	2	.0000	.0914	29.6	0	0	0	0	2	0	0	0	2	0	0	0	0	0	0	0	0	0	0	0	0	0	0	0	0
grapevine	7	.3154	.5582	37.5	0	5	0	0	2	0	0	0	3	3	0	0	0	0	0	0	0	0	0	0	1	0	0	0	0
grapevines	3	.1639	.1674	32.2	0	1	0	1	1	0	0	0	1	0	0	0	0	2	0	0	0	0	0	0	0	0	0	0	0
graph	379	.3961	32.908	55.2	18	57	57	48	30	72	95	2	0	4	0	1	299	18	6	32	1	0	1	14	0	2	0	1	0
graphed	4	.0000	.0599	27.8	0	0	1	0	0	2	1	0	0	0	0	0	4	0	0	0	0	0	0	0	0	0	0	0	0
graphein	2	.2408	.1091	30.4	0	2	0	0	0	0	0	0	0	1	0	0	0	0	1	0	0	0	0	0	0	0	0	0	0
grapheme	5	.0000	.0547	27.4	0	0	0	1	1	3	0	0	0	5	0	0	0	0	0	0	0	0	0	0	0	0	0	0	0
graphemes	25	.0000	.2736	34.4	0	0	0	1	8	11	5	0	0	25	0	0	0	0	0	0	0	0	0	0	0	0	0	0	0
graphic	14	.1526	.4916	36.9	0	1	0	0	3	2	7	1	0	1	0	0	0	0	0	1	0	0	0	9	0	0	3	0	0
graphic-relief	2	.0000	.0389	25.9	0	0	0	2	0	0	0	0	0	0	0	0	0	2	0	0	0	0	0	0	0	0	0	0	0
graphically	4	.3639	.3251	35.1	0	0	0	0	1	2	1	0	1	1	1	0	0	0	0	0	0	0	0	1	0	0	0	0	0

7N Grahamsville
8R Grail
5R grain-devouring
XH grain-infesting
4A grainfields
5N graining
7L grainlines
6G gram-mar
9B grammaticality
7J Gramophone
3A Gramp's
7N Gran'
6J Granados
6R granaries
4A Grancher
8K GrandCanyonSuite
5F GrandIsland
4A grand-slam
4P Granddaddy
6A Granddad's
3S Granddaughter
7A granddaughters
XR grandee
7N grandees
3A Grandes
7Q Grandeur
5P grandiosely
9L grandma's
9R grandmas
6A grandpas
6A Grandpere
7A Grandpop
9D grandsir
4N grandsire
5A Grandy
8F grantee
7R grape-like
9L grapefruits
9R grapeless
5G graper
6A grapeskin
7R Graphic

Word Type	F	D	U	SFI	3 Gr 3	4 Gr 4	5 Gr 5	6 Gr 6	7 Gr 7	8 Gr 8	9 Gr 9	X UnGr	A Read	B Eng & Gr	C Comp	D Lit	E Math	F Soc Stud	G Spell	H Sci	J Music	K Art	L Home Ec	M Shop	N Lib F	P Lib NF	Q Lib Ref	R Mag	S Rel
graphing	5	.0000	.0748	28.7	0	0	0	0	1	1	3	0	0	0	0	0	5	0	0	0	0	0	0	0	0	0	0	0	0
graphite	13	.4132	1.1895	40.8	0	0	2	5	4	1	1	0	1	0	0	0	0	0	0	7	0	0	0	1	0	0	4	0	0
Graphophone	8	.0000	.0647	28.1	0	0	0	0	8	0	0	0	0	0	0	0	0	0	0	0	8	0	0	0	0	0	0	0	0
graphs	68	.3944	5.9689	47.8	0	18	3	4	8	15	20	0	3	0	0	0	44	14	0	4	0	0	0	3	0	0	0	0	0
grapple	3	.3385	.2445	33.9	0	0	0	0	3	0	0	0	1	0	0	0	0	0	0	0	0	0	0	0	1	0	1	0	0
grappled	3	.0000	.1370	31.4	0	0	0	0	2	1	0	0	3	0	0	0	0	0	0	0	0	0	0	0	0	0	0	0	0
grappling	2	.2446	.1122	30.5	0	0	0	0	2	0	0	0	0	0	0	1	0	0	0	0	0	0	0	0	0	0	1	0	0
Gras	3	.3635	.2410	33.8	0	1	1	0	1	0	0	0	0	0	0	0	0	1	0	0	1	0	0	0	0	1	0	0	0
grasp	69	.7990	11.135	50.5	2	9	7	13	18	9	9	2	21	4	0	1	0	2	0	8	6	1	3	5	2	4	5	7	0
grasped	31	.6622	4.2348	46.3	3	8	4	3	9	1	3	0	6	1	0	5	0	1	0	1	0	0	0	0	7	6	1	3	0
grasping	17	.6112	2.1803	43.4	1	5	1	1	6	1	2	0	4	0	0	0	0	0	2	3	0	0	0	0	2	3	3	0	0
grasps	2	.2137	.1056	30.2	0	0	1	0	1	0	0	0	0	0	0	0	0	1	0	0	1	0	0	0	0	0	0	0	0
grass	761	.8705	132.49	61.2	232	153	80	120	92	37	36	11	215	21	12	60	10	124	9	99	7	4	0	1	83	72	18	26	0
Grass	4	.3702	.3622	35.6	0	0	0	0	3	1	0	0	2	1	0	1	0	0	0	0	0	0	0	0	0	0	0	0	0
grass-eating	2	.2446	.1257	31.0	0	0	0	0	1	0	0	1	0	0	0	0	0	1	0	1	0	0	0	0	0	0	0	0	0
grass-lands	3	.0000	.0591	27.7	0	0	0	3	0	0	0	0	0	0	0	0	0	0	0	3	0	0	0	0	0	0	0	0	0
grass-like	2	.2331	.1157	30.6	0	0	0	0	1	0	0	1	0	0	0	0	0	0	0	1	0	0	0	0	1	0	0	0	0
grasses	87	.7737	13.640	51.3	14	14	11	18	15	5	9	1	17	0	2	6	0	20	0	15	0	0	3	0	5	6	11	2	0
grasshopper	46	.6548	6.2975	48.0	8	13	7	12	3	2	1	0	11	0	0	1	2	1	0	21	1	1	0	0	0	6	1	1	0
grasshopper's	2	.0000	.0394	26.0	0	0	0	2	0	0	0	0	0	0	0	0	0	0	0	2	0	0	0	0	0	0	0	0	0
grasshoppers	48	.6667	6.7073	48.3	12	5	9	7	4	7	2	2	16	2	0	2	1	1	0	16	0	0	0	0	3	6	1	0	0
grasshoppers'	2	.2443	.1130	30.5	0	0	1	0	0	1	0	0	0	0	0	1	0	0	0	0	0	0	0	0	1	0	0	0	0
grassland	22	.5390	2.5559	44.1	2	4	5	5	3	1	2	0	5	0	0	0	0	6	1	3	0	0	0	0	0	1	6	0	0
grasslands	83	.4499	8.3356	49.2	12	18	12	13	21	3	4	0	12	0	0	1	0	47	0	10	0	0	0	0	0	2	11	0	0
grassy	47	.8009	7.6044	48.8	8	11	4	9	8	1	4	2	12	5	0	2	0	8	1	3	1	0	0	0	1	5	4	5	0
grate	5	.3830	.4740	36.8	0	2	0	1	2	0	0	0	3	0	0	1	0	0	0	0	0	0	0	0	0	0	1	0	0
grated	9	.1432	.3287	35.2	0	1	1	0	2	2	2	1	1	1	0	0	0	0	0	0	0	0	6	0	0	0	0	1	0
grateful	61	.7666	9.5323	49.8	4	6	10	12	17	6	6	0	22	3	3	4	0	7	1	0	4	0	0	0	8	2	2	5	0
gratefully	13	.5025	1.4538	41.6	2	2	0	1	6	1	1	0	6	0	1	1	0	0	0	0	1	0	0	0	4	0	0	0	0
grater	2	.0000	.0037	15.7	0	0	2	0	0	0	0	0	0	0	0	0	0	0	0	0	0	2	0	0	0	0	0	0	0
Gratiano	18	.0000	.1932	32.9	0	0	0	0	0	0	18	0	0	0	0	18	0	0	0	0	0	0	0	0	0	0	0	0	0
gratification	2	.1787	.1174	30.7	0	0	0	0	1	0	1	0	1	0	0	0	0	0	0	0	0	0	0	0	1	0	0	0	0
gratified	2	.2446	.1142	30.6	0	0	0	0	0	1	1	0	0	0	0	0	0	0	0	0	0	0	0	0	1	0	0	1	0
gratify	2	.2291	.1135	30.5	0	0	0	1	0	0	1	0	0	0	0	1	0	0	0	1	0	0	0	0	0	0	0	0	0
gratifying	6	.3810	.4867	36.9	0	1	0	0	3	2	0	0	0	0	0	0	0	0	0	0	0	0	1	0	0	0	2	3	0
grating	24	.5224	2.6971	44.3	1	1	0	4	4	8	0	6	3	0	0	0	0	0	0	13	0	0	0	0	2	1	2	3	0
gratitude	22	.4616	2.3364	43.7	1	0	3	6	4	4	4	0	11	0	0	4	0	0	0	0	0	0	0	0	5	2	0	0	0
grave	78	.7597	11.946	50.8	7	2	11	7	22	12	15	2	9	4	0	20	0	7	1	2	4	0	1	0	10	9	9	2	0
gravel	82	.8168	13.480	51.3	12	14	16	13	18	3	6	0	17	2	2	5	0	9	0	18	4	0	0	0	6	9	3	7	0
graveled	4	.3619	.3167	35.0	0	2	0	0	2	0	0	0	0	0	0	0	0	0	0	0	0	0	0	0	1	1	0	2	0
gravelly	2	.1717	.1142	30.6	0	0	0	0	2	0	0	0	1	0	0	1	0	0	0	0	0	0	0	0	0	0	0	0	0
gravels	2	.2446	.1257	31.0	0	0	0	0	1	0	1	0	0	0	0	0	0	1	0	1	0	0	0	0	0	0	0	0	0
gravely	29	.5143	3.1969	45.0	1	11	4	3	3	3	3	1	5	0	0	3	0	2	0	0	0	0	0	0	9	9	0	1	0
graven	2	.2446	.1122	30.5	0	0	1	0	0	0	1	0	0	0	0	1	0	0	0	0	0	0	0	0	0	0	1	0	0
graves	11	.4603	1.0886	40.4	0	2	3	2	2	1	0	1	0	2	0	0	0	6	0	0	0	0	0	0	0	0	1	2	0
Graves	3	.2357	.2199	33.4	0	0	0	3	0	0	0	0	2	0	0	0	0	0	0	0	0	0	0	0	0	1	0	0	0
gravestone	2	.1787	.1174	30.7	0	0	1	1	0	0	0	0	1	0	0	0	0	0	0	0	0	0	0	0	1	0	0	0	0
gravestones	3	.2425	.1816	32.6	0	0	2	0	0	0	0	1	0	0	0	0	0	2	0	0	0	0	0	0	0	0	0	1	0
graveyard	19	.6460	2.6249	44.2	2	1	3	2	11	0	0	0	11	1	0	2	0	1	0	0	1	0	0	0	0	1	0	2	0
gravitation	19	.3263	1.4602	41.6	1	1	1	4	1	8	3	0	1	0	0	0	1	0	0	13	0	0	0	0	0	0	4	0	0
Gravitation	4	.0000	.0789	29.0	0	4	0	0	0	0	0	0	0	0	0	0	0	0	0	4	0	0	0	0	0	0	0	0	0
gravitational	39	.4156	3.6527	45.6	0	5	7	4	8	8	5	2	4	0	0	0	2	1	0	25	0	0	0	0	0	0	6	1	0
gravity	257	.4234	24.564	53.9	33	28	63	36	32	33	20	12	29	1	0	0	7	1	1	183	0	0	0	1	0	20	13	1	0
gravity's	2	.2278	.1128	30.5	0	0	0	0	1	0	1	0	0	0	0	0	0	0	0	1	0	0	0	0	0	0	1	0	0
gravure	3	.2227	.1495	31.7	0	0	0	0	0	0	3	0	0	0	0	0	0	0	0	0	0	0	0	1	0	0	2	0	0
gravy	19	.6896	2.6843	44.3	1	2	5	1	4	2	3	1	3	0	1	2	0	4	0	2	0	0	1	0	3	0	0	3	0
gray	457	.9066	82.388	59.2	96	71	51	56	93	37	45	8	139	16	10	46	41	16	1	31	8	10	6	2	41	49	15	26	0
Gray	74	.6612	10.190	50.1	18	19	1	8	21	7	0	0	21	1	0	2	1	14	0	0	1	0	0	0	19	4	2	9	0
GRAY	6	.0000	.0644	28.1	0	0	0	0	6	0	0	0	0	0	0	6	0	0	0	0	0	0	0	0	0	0	0	0	0
gray-blue	2	.1787	.1174	30.7	0	0	0	0	2	0	0	0	1	0	0	0	0	0	0	0	0	0	0	0	1	0	0	0	0
gray-brown	3	.2387	.1708	32.3	0	2	0	0	1	0	0	0	0	0	0	0	0	0	0	0	0	0	0	0	0	2	1	0	0
gray-green	6	.3163	.4639	36.7	3	2	0	1	0	0	0	0	1	0	0	0	0	3	0	0	0	0	0	0	0	2	0	0	0
gray-haired	4	.4588	.4078	36.1	0	1	0	2	0	1	0	0	1	0	0	0	1	0	0	0	0	0	0	0	0	1	0	1	0
gray-headed	2	.2427	.1152	30.6	0	0	0	0	2	0	0	0	0	0	0	0	0	0	0	0	0	0	0	0	1	1	0	0	0
gray-white	2	.2405	.1205	30.8	0	0	1	0	1	0	0	0	0	0	0	0	0	0	0	1	0	0	0	0	0	1	0	0	0
Gray's	8	.5356	.9307	39.7	0	4	1	1	1	1	0	0	2	0	0	0	1	3	0	0	0	0	0	0	1	1	0	0	0
Grayback	2	.0000	.0215	23.3	0	0	0	0	2	0	0	0	0	0	0	2	0	0	0	0	0	0	0	0	0	0	0	0	0
grayed	4	.3533	.3175	35.0	0	1	0	0	2	0	1	0	1	0	0	1	0	0	0	0	0	1	1	0	0	0	0	0	0
graying	2	.2433	.1158	30.6	1	0	0	0	0	0	1	0	0	0	0	0	0	0	0	0	0	0	0	0	0	1	0	1	0
grayish	10	.5516	1.1500	40.6	0	1	1	1	3	0	2	2	0	0	0	1	0	1	0	4	0	0	0	1	0	1	2	0	0
grayish-brown	3	.2437	.2277	33.6	0	1	0	2	0	0	0	0	2	0	0	0	0	0	0	1	0	0	0	0	0	0	0	0	0
Graylegs	11	.0000	.5025	37.0	11	0	0	0	0	0	0	0	11	0	0	0	0	0	0	0	0	0	0	0	0	0	0	0	0
grayling	10	.0000	.1215	30.8	0	0	0	0	0	0	0	10	0	0	0	0	0	0	0	0	0	0	0	0	0	0	0	10	0
grays	4	.2031	.2455	33.9	1	0	0	1	0	2	0	0	2	0	0	0	0	0	0	0	0	1	0	0	0	1	0	0	0
Grayson	2	.0000	.0914	29.6	1	0	0	1	0	0	0	0	2	0	0	0	0	0	0	0	0	0	0	0	0	0	0	0	0
Grayson's	5	.0000	.2284	33.6	4	0	0	1	0	0	0	0	5	0	0	0	0	0	0	0	0	0	0	0	0	0	0	0	0
Grayville	2	.0000	.0299	24.8	0	0	0	0	0	2	0	0	0	0	0	0	2	0	0	0	0	0	0	0	0	0	0	0	0
graze	46	.7534	7.0273	48.5	5	7	13	8	7	1	5	0	5	1	0	1	3	19	1	2	2	0	0	0	1	5	4	2	0
grazed	21	.5773	2.5849	44.1	2	7	4	3	3	0	2	0	5	0	1	0	0	9	0	0	0	0	0	0	2	2	2	0	0
grazie	2	.0000	.0234	23.7	0	0	0	2	0	0	0	0	0	0	0	0	0	0	0	0	0	0	0	0	2	0	0	0	0
grazing	102	.6897	14.552	51.6	3	21	25	24	16	6	2	5	23	1	0	6	0	40	0	7	1	0	0	0	4	9	8	3	0
grease	55	.8418	9.2598	49.7	7	14	11	4	14	1	4	0	10	4	0	2	1	3	1	3	2	1	3	1	2	17	1	4	0
greased	19	.2793	1.2085	40.8	3	2	2	1	4	3	4	0	2	0	0	1	0	1	0	0	0	0	9	0	1	3	0	2	0
Greased	6	.0000	.2741	34.4	6	0	0	0	0	0	0	0	6	0	0	0	0	0	0	0	0	0	0	0	0	0	0	0	0
greasewood	3	.0000	.1370	31.4	0	0	0	0	3	0	0	0	3	0	0	0	0	0	0	0	0	0	0	0	0	0	0	0	0
greasy	28	.6576	3.8044	45.8	2	2	2	6	4	2	7	3	5	6	0	1	0	1	0	7	0	0	0	2	2	2	0	2	0
great	3855	.8946	686.78	68.4	544	575	513	652	713	444	325	89	996	101	26	239	52	644	42	405	172	34	31	23	225	391	260	197	17
Great	411	.7929	65.925	58.2	29	38	147	43	55	51	33	15	90	5	3	16	21	146	2	16	9	1	0	0	8	20	48	26	0
GREAT	3	.0000	.1370	31.4	3	0	0	0	0	0	0	0	3	0	0	0	0	0	0	0	0	0	0	0	0	0	0	0	0
GreatBritain	106	.4934	11.298	50.5	3	10	17	12	29	22	12	1	6	3	0	0	0	73	1	2	1	0	0	0	1	4	11	4	0
GreatBritain's	6	.2444	.3628	35.6	0	0	2	0	2	1	1	0	0	0	0	0	0	4	0	0	0	0	0	0	0	0	2	0	0
great-	2	.2412	.1141	30.6	0	0	2	0	0	0	0	0	0	1	0	0	0	0	0	0	0	0	0	0	0	1	0	0	0
Great-Aunt	2	.0000	.0914	29.6	2	0	0	0	0	0	0	0	2	0	0	0	0	0	0	0	0	0	0	0	0	0	0	0	0
Great-Uncle	4	.0000	.1827	32.6	0	4	0	0	0	0	0	0	4	0	0	0	0	0	0	0	0	0	0	0	0	0	0	0	0

XR Graphics
4F gras
5F grass-covered
3A grass-eater
9C grass-grown
5H grass-lined
7N grass-patches
7D grass-thatched
7Q grass-tree
3P Grasshoppers
5F Grasslands
8F Grassmere
8N gratefulness
XR gratia
7P Gratiana
9D Gratiano's
XR gratifyingly
6Q gratings
9D gratis
9R gratuitous
9Q grave-stones
9D graved
8N gravelled
5Q graveside
7A gravest
7A graveyards
8L gravies
8J gravitated
8H Gravitational
8H gravities
4N gray-and
4N gray-and-white
6A gray-bearded
XR gray-black
8F gray-clad
9D gray-coated
3A gray-colored
4P gray-shingled
3P gray-silk
3A gray-tin
7N gray-trunked
7D Grayback's
3P graybeards
5A Graycheek
5A Graycheek's
7A grayed-green
5A grayish-red
3P grayish-white
7Q graylag
7R Grayling
7N grayness
4Q Grays
3R Graysquirrel
7F Graz
7F grazes
5P Grazia
4J grazioso
9H grease-spot
7R greasepaint
7B greasiest
9D greasiness
9P greasy-spoon
5F GREATBRITAIN
5Q GreatBritian
4A GreatUncle
4N Great-Grandfather

Word Type	F	D	U	SFI	3 Gr 3	4 Gr 4	5 Gr 5	6 Gr 6	7 Gr 7	8 Gr 8	9 Gr 9	X UnGr	A Read	B Eng & Gr	C Comp	D Lit	E Math	F Soc Stud	G Spell	H Sci	J Music	K Art	L Home Ec	M Shop	N Lib F	P Lib NF	Q Lib Ref	R Mag	S Rel
Great-aunt	2	.2427	.1152	30.6	0	0	0	0	1	1	0	0	0	0	0	0	0	0	0	0	0	0	0	0	1	1	0	0	0
great-grandchildren	2	.0000	.0389	25.9	0	1	0	1	0	0	0	0	0	0	0	0	0	2	0	0	0	0	0	0	0	0	0	0	0
great-grandfather	8	.5631	.9783	39.9	3	3	1	1	0	0	0	0	3	1	0	0	0	2	0	0	0	0	0	0	1	1	0	0	0
great-grandmother	4	.2420	.3089	34.9	4	0	0	0	0	0	0	0	3	0	0	0	0	1	0	0	0	0	0	0	0	0	0	0	0
great-grandparents	2	.1432	.0759	28.8	0	0	0	1	0	1	0	0	0	0	0	0	0	0	0	1	0	0	1	0	0	0	0	0	0
great-grandson	2	.0000	.0290	24.6	0	0	1	0	1	0	0	0	0	0	0	0	0	0	0	0	0	0	0	0	0	2	0	0	0
great-grandsons	2	.1814	.1187	30.7	1	0	0	1	0	0	0	0	1	0	0	0	0	0	0	0	0	0	0	0	0	0	0	1	0
great-great-grand father	3	.2435	.2274	33.6	0	1	1	0	1	0	0	0	2	0	0	0	0	1	0	0	0	0	0	0	0	0	0	0	0
great-great-great -great**	2	.0000	.0394	26.0	0	0	0	2	0	0	0	0	0	0	0	0	0	0	0	2	0	0	0	0	0	0	0	0	0
great-hearted	2	.0000	.0215	23.3	0	0	0	0	0	0	2	0	0	0	0	2	0	0	0	0	0	0	0	0	0	0	0	0	0
great-uncle	3	.0000	.1370	31.4	0	3	0	0	0	0	0	0	3	0	0	0	0	0	0	0	0	0	0	0	0	0	0	0	0
greatcoat	4	.3795	.3302	35.2	0	1	0	1	0	0	2	0	0	0	0	1	0	0	0	0	0	0	0	0	1	2	0	0	0
greater	646	.8029	104.05	60.2	68	82	82	100	127	92	83	12	44	21	3	13	278	58	4	91	18	5	8	7	8	17	44	27	0
Greater	12	.4571	1.2046	40.8	7	1	0	2	1	0	1	0	1	0	0	0	0	7	0	0	0	0	0	0	0	2	1	1	0
greatest	486	.9023	87.065	59.4	46	65	68	68	90	82	53	14	73	17	2	16	114	62	3	36	20	2	8	4	19	35	51	24	0
Greatest	2	.2427	.1159	30.6	0	1	0	1	0	0	0	0	0	0	0	0	1	0	0	0	0	0	0	0	0	0	0	1	0
greatly	216	.8744	37.657	55.8	13	15	37	27	62	31	27	4	38	15	1	7	1	50	2	31	15	3	4	0	7	11	25	6	0
greatness	30	.7802	4.7347	46.8	2	4	8	1	6	4	5	0	8	1	1	2	0	1	1	0	1	1	0	0	1	7	5	1	0
grebes	2	.2401	.1133	30.5	1	0	0	0	1	0	0	0	0	0	0	0	0	0	0	0	0	0	0	0	0	1	1	0	0
Grech	2	.0000	.0243	23.9	0	0	0	0	0	2	0	0	0	0	0	0	0	0	0	0	0	0	0	0	0	0	0	2	0
Grechko	14	.0000	.1701	32.3	0	0	0	0	3	11	0	0	0	0	0	0	0	0	0	0	0	0	0	0	0	0	0	14	0
Grechko's	2	.0000	.0243	23.9	0	0	0	0	0	2	0	0	0	0	0	0	0	0	0	0	0	0	0	0	0	0	0	2	0
Grecian	6	.5128	.6304	38.0	0	1	0	0	5	0	0	0	0	0	0	1	0	0	1	0	1	0	0	1	2	0	0	0	0
Grecians	2	.0000	.0162	22.1	0	0	0	0	2	0	0	0	0	0	0	0	0	0	2	0	0	0	0	0	0	0	0	0	0
Greece	186	.7025	26.781	54.3	8	31	17	32	68	19	8	3	21	7	1	5	1	115	2	0	4	3	1	1	1	11	11	2	0
greed	12	.5407	1.3927	41.4	0	0	1	1	7	1	2	0	3	0	0	4	0	2	0	0	0	0	0	0	0	1	1	1	0
greedily	11	.5283	1.2824	41.1	1	1	3	1	3	0	1	1	5	1	0	1	0	0	0	0	0	0	0	0	3	0	0	1	0
greedy	28	.5046	3.3271	45.2	12	8	0	3	2	1	1	1	23	1	0	1	0	1	1	0	0	0	0	0	1	0	0	0	0
greek	3	.1829	.1333	31.2	0	0	2	0	0	0	1	0	0	0	0	0	1	0	2	0	0	0	0	0	0	0	0	0	0
Greek	412	.7868	65.257	58.1	12	43	29	79	110	89	34	16	61	42	0	7	18	73	76	28	5	10	0	3	1	20	56	12	0
Greeks	184	.8414	30.994	54.9	3	12	13	45	55	25	19	12	30	18	1	2	5	57	10	14	7	4	0	3	0	9	21	3	0
Greeley	4	.2947	.2869	34.6	0	0	0	0	1	1	2	0	1	0	0	0	0	0	0	0	0	0	0	0	1	0	2	0	0
green	1216	.9209	222.21	63.5	344	187	168	164	188	77	68	20	311	34	4	73	60	112	11	253	36	23	30	5	81	87	38	58	0
Green	128	.7850	20.542	53.1	25	19	24	22	21	11	3	3	62	2	0	7	3	14	0	1	0	1	0	1	9	2	10	16	0
green-sand	2	.0000	.0050	17.0	0	0	0	0	0	0	2	0	0	0	0	0	0	0	0	0	0	0	0	2	0	0	0	0	0
green-speckled	2	.2443	.1130	30.5	0	0	0	0	1	1	0	0	0	0	0	1	0	0	0	0	0	0	0	0	1	0	0	0	0
green-turtle	2	.0000	.0209	23.2	0	0	0	0	2	0	0	0	0	0	0	0	0	0	0	0	0	0	0	0	0	0	2	0	0
Green's	8	.4191	.7365	38.7	1	0	0	1	4	2	0	0	1	0	0	2	2	0	0	0	0	0	0	0	0	0	0	3	0
Greenback	2	.0000	.0209	23.2	0	0	0	0	2	0	0	0	0	0	0	0	0	0	0	0	0	0	0	0	0	0	2	0	0
greenbacks	2	.2446	.1122	30.5	0	0	0	0	1	0	1	0	0	0	0	1	0	0	0	0	0	0	0	0	0	0	1	0	0
Greenbaum	11	.0000	.1290	31.1	0	11	0	0	0	0	0	0	0	0	0	0	0	0	0	0	0	0	0	0	11	0	0	0	0
Greene	9	.3350	.7433	38.7	0	2	3	0	1	3	0	0	3	0	0	0	0	3	0	0	0	0	0	0	0	0	3	0	0
greener	6	.4743	.6396	38.1	2	1	1	0	1	0	1	0	2	1	0	0	0	2	0	0	0	0	0	0	1	0	0	0	0
greenery	5	.4764	.5339	37.3	1	0	0	1	3	0	0	0	2	0	0	0	0	0	0	0	0	0	0	0	1	0	1	1	0
greenest	2	.2446	.1125	30.5	1	0	0	1	0	0	0	0	0	1	0	1	0	0	0	0	0	0	0	0	0	0	0	0	0
Greenfield	7	.4530	.7194	38.6	5	1	0	0	1	0	0	0	2	0	0	0	0	3	0	0	0	0	0	0	1	1	0	0	0
greenhorn	7	.4507	.6984	38.4	0	0	2	0	0	3	2	0	2	2	0	2	0	0	0	0	1	0	0	0	0	0	0	0	0
greenhouse	6	.4675	.6370	38.0	0	3	1	1	0	0	1	0	2	0	0	1	0	1	0	2	0	0	0	0	0	0	0	0	0
greenhouses	7	.4203	.6609	38.2	1	3	1	2	0	0	0	0	1	0	0	0	0	3	0	0	0	0	0	0	0	1	0	2	0
Greenie	2	.0000	.0290	24.6	0	2	0	0	0	0	0	0	0	0	0	0	0	0	0	0	0	0	0	0	0	2	0	0	0
greenish	20	.5572	2.3493	43.7	2	0	1	2	8	0	1	6	1	0	0	2	0	1	0	11	0	0	0	0	2	0	2	1	0
greenish-blue	4	.3696	.3616	35.6	1	0	0	0	3	0	0	0	2	1	0	0	0	0	0	0	0	0	0	0	0	0	1	0	0
greenish-yellow	2	.2446	.1122	30.5	1	0	1	0	0	0	0	0	0	0	0	1	0	0	0	0	0	0	0	0	0	0	1	0	0
Greenland	39	.5578	4.7350	46.8	4	5	8	6	12	0	3	1	12	2	0	0	0	13	0	9	0	0	0	0	0	2	1	0	0
Greenlanders	2	.0000	.0914	29.6	0	0	2	0	0	0	0	0	2	0	0	0	0	0	0	0	0	0	0	0	0	0	0	0	0
Greenleaf	8	.2351	.6222	37.9	0	0	2	4	0	2	0	0	7	0	0	0	0	0	0	0	0	0	0	0	0	0	1	0	0
greens	47	.4583	4.6598	46.7	3	4	3	7	22	4	4	0	11	0	0	1	0	4	1	2	2	3	17	0	0	2	3	1	0
Greens	4	.1972	.2524	34.0	2	0	0	0	0	2	0	0	2	0	0	0	2	0	0	0	0	0	0	0	0	0	0	0	0
Greensboro	5	.0000	.0523	27.2	0	0	5	0	0	0	0	0	0	0	0	0	0	0	0	0	0	0	0	0	0	0	5	0	0
Greensleeves	11	.0000	.0889	29.5	0	0	0	10	0	0	1	0	0	0	0	0	0	0	0	0	11	0	0	0	0	0	0	0	0
greenstick	2	.0000	.0243	23.9	0	2	0	0	0	0	0	0	0	0	0	0	0	0	0	0	0	0	0	0	0	0	0	2	0
Greentown	2	.0000	.0219	23.4	0	0	0	0	0	2	0	0	0	2	0	0	0	0	0	0	0	0	0	0	0	0	0	0	0
Greenville	24	.5367	2.7156	44.3	4	2	13	0	1	1	3	0	2	1	0	1	6	5	0	0	0	0	0	0	0	1	8	0	0
Greenway	2	.0000	.0209	23.2	0	0	2	0	0	0	0	0	0	0	0	0	0	0	0	0	0	0	0	0	0	0	2	0	0
Greenwich	22	.5047	2.3575	43.7	2	7	3	0	0	7	1	2	1	0	0	1	12	1	1	3	0	0	0	0	0	0	3	0	0
greenwood	4	.3075	.2938	34.7	1	0	0	3	0	0	0	0	1	0	0	2	0	0	0	0	1	0	0	0	0	0	0	0	0
Greenwood	8	.0000	.3655	35.6	8	0	0	0	0	0	0	0	8	0	0	0	0	0	0	0	0	0	0	0	0	0	0	0	0
greet	42	.7390	6.3646	48.0	9	11	1	6	4	6	3	2	15	5	0	0	0	4	1	0	2	0	1	0	6	2	0	6	0
greeted	70	.7649	10.888	50.4	3	23	8	9	15	4	7	1	20	1	0	4	0	7	1	0	3	0	2	0	11	16	2	3	0
greeting	74	.7533	11.299	50.5	18	19	7	6	18	5	0	1	17	22	3	8	0	3	4	0	2	0	1	0	5	5	2	2	0
greetings	19	.4782	2.0044	43.0	1	7	2	3	3	1	1	1	6	7	0	2	0	0	0	0	0	0	0	0	3	0	0	1	0
greets	8	.5409	.9081	39.6	2	0	1	1	0	2	2	0	1	0	0	2	0	1	0	0	0	0	1	0	1	0	0	2	0
Greg	7	.3766	.5679	37.5	0	0	0	2	2	0	3	0	0	0	0	3	0	0	0	0	0	0	0	0	2	0	0	2	0
Gregor	6	.0979	.2456	33.9	1	0	0	3	0	1	1	0	1	0	0	0	0	0	0	5	0	0	0	0	0	0	0	0	0
Gregorian	4	.2380	.2493	34.0	0	1	1	0	0	1	1	0	1	0	0	0	0	0	0	1	2	0	0	0	0	0	0	0	0
Gregorio	6	.0000	.0644	28.1	0	0	0	0	6	0	0	0	0	0	0	6	0	0	0	0	0	0	0	0	0	0	0	0	0
Gregory	40	.5126	4.4200	46.5	1	8	2	4	10	0	15	0	9	0	0	16	0	2	1	1	0	0	0	0	1	8	0	2	0
Gregory's	3	.2357	.2199	33.4	0	1	0	0	2	0	0	0	2	0	0	0	0	0	0	0	0	0	0	0	0	1	0	0	0
Greig	2	.0000	.0162	22.1	0	0	0	0	0	1	1	0	0	0	0	0	0	0	0	0	2	0	0	0	0	0	0	0	0
Grenada	2	.0000	.0243	23.9	0	0	2	0	0	0	0	0	0	0	0	0	0	0	0	0	0	0	0	0	0	0	0	2	0
grenade	5	.0000	.0724	28.6	0	0	5	0	0	0	0	0	0	0	0	0	0	0	0	0	0	0	0	0	0	5	0	0	0
grenades	9	.4181	.8260	39.2	0	1	5	1	1	1	0	0	1	0	0	0	0	0	0	0	0	0	0	0	0	4	2	2	0
grenadiers	2	.0000	.0162	22.1	0	0	0	0	2	0	0	0	0	0	0	0	0	0	0	0	2	0	0	0	0	0	0	0	0
Grenal	3	.0000	.0314	25.0	0	0	0	0	3	0	0	0	0	0	0	0	0	0	0	0	0	0	0	0	0	0	3	0	0
Grenelle	2	.0000	.0914	29.6	2	0	0	0	0	0	0	0	2	0	0	0	0	0	0	0	0	0	0	0	0	0	0	0	0
Grenfell	8	.1990	.5845	37.7	0	0	0	7	0	0	1	0	7	0	0	0	0	1	0	0	0	0	0	0	0	0	0	0	0
Grenoble	3	.1169	.1277	31.1	0	0	0	0	2	1	0	0	1	0	0	0	0	0	0	0	0	0	0	0	0	0	2	0	0
Grenville	2	.0000	.0389	25.9	0	0	2	0	0	0	0	0	0	0	0	0	0	2	0	0	0	0	0	0	0	0	0	0	0
Greshkin	2	.0000	.0219	23.4	0	0	0	0	0	0	2	0	0	2	0	0	0	0	0	0	0	0	0	0	0	0	0	0	0
Greta	4	.0000	.0469	26.7	0	4	0	0	0	0	0	0	0	0	0	0	0	0	0	0	0	0	0	0	4	0	0	0	0

6Q great-berried
4Q great-circle
6A great-coats
4N Great-grandfather's
3A great-grandfathers
3A Great-grandmother
3N great-grandmother's
6A great-granduncle
XB great-great
3A great-great-grandfathers
7C great-great-grandmother
5A great-great-grandparent
6A great-great-granduncle
5P great-nephew
7P great-niece
6R greatgrandson
7R greats
7D greaves
9Q grebe
3P Grecia
7P Greco
8K Greco's
9R Gredy
6N greedier
XH Greek-derived
5P Greek-speaking
6A Greeks'
5Q Greely
6Q GreenBay
6R green-and-gold
7A green-and-white
XR green-and-yellow
XH green-black
9Q green-blue
6A green-eyed
3A green-feathered
7D green-figured
6A green-filtered
6Q green-gray
3A green-leaf
7D green-plush
5E green-tinted
8Q green-tipped
7D green-white
7Q greenback
4N Greenbaum's
7R Greenberg
7R Greenbriar
4N greenbug
7Q Greeneville
3F Greenfield's
7P greenish-brown
7Q greenish-gray
XH greenish-white
5A Greenland's
6A Greenleaf'll
3P greenness
4D greensilver
6A greenstone
7A greensward
3A Greer
3B grees
8A Greetings
3B greez
4E Greg's
6R gregaria
8C gregarious
6R Gregg
8J greggers
6F gregory
9H gremlin
9B Gremlin
9H gremlins
8E Gren-ich
5R Grenadian
7J Grenadiers
6A Grenfells
7N Grennan

Word Type	F	D	U	SFI	3 Gr 3	4 Gr 4	5 Gr 5	6 Gr 6	7 Gr 7	8 Gr 8	9 Gr 9	X UnGr	A Read	B Eng & Gr	C Comp	D Lit	E Math	F Soc Stud	G Spell	H Sci	J Music	K Art	L Home Ec	M Shop	N Lib F	P Lib NF	Q Lib Ref	R Mag	S Rel
Gretel	51	.4415	5.1290	47.1	32	0	0	17	1	0	1	0	21	0	1	23	0	0	0	0	4	0	0	0	0	0	2	0	0
Gretel's	2	.0000	.0215	23.3	0	0	0	2	0	0	0	0	0	0	0	2	0	0	0	0	0	0	0	0	0	0	0	0	0
grew	847	.8879	150.21	61.8	177	165	118	122	133	85	34	13	298	17	2	58	6	142	10	63	35	1	2	0	57	87	42	26	1
grey	32	.5832	3.8980	45.9	1	11	1	3	10	2	4	0	5	0	0	6	0	3	0	1	0	3	0	0	7	5	1	1	0
Grey	22	.0685	.5359	37.3	19	1	0	0	1	0	1	0	0	1	0	0	0	0	0	0	0	0	0	0	21	0	0	0	0
grey-	2	.0000	.0219	23.4	0	0	2	0	0	0	0	0	0	2	0	0	0	0	0	0	0	0	0	0	0	0	0	0	0
grey-green	3	.2292	.1615	32.1	0	2	0	0	0	1	0	0	0	0	0	1	0	0	0	0	0	0	0	0	2	0	0	0	0
Grey's	4	.0000	.0469	26.7	4	0	0	0	0	0	0	0	0	0	0	0	0	0	0	0	0	0	0	0	4	0	0	0	0
greyhound	9	.4645	.9272	39.7	1	1	4	0	2	0	1	0	3	3	1	1	0	0	0	0	0	0	0	0	0	1	0	0	0
greys	3	.0000	.0097	19.8	0	0	0	0	3	0	0	0	0	0	0	0	0	0	0	0	0	0	3	0	0	0	0	0	0
grid	21	.6473	2.7876	44.5	5	2	3	2	5	3	1	0	0	0	0	0	5	7	0	3	0	0	0	1	1	0	2	2	0
griddle	16	.1814	.8231	39.2	0	4	5	0	0	4	3	0	5	0	0	0	0	0	0	0	0	0	7	0	0	4	0	0	0
gridiron	3	.3274	.2364	33.7	0	0	0	0	1	1	1	0	1	0	0	1	0	0	1	0	0	0	0	0	0	0	0	0	0
grids	5	.3186	.3628	35.6	2	0	1	0	1	1	0	0	0	0	0	0	0	3	0	0	0	0	0	1	0	0	0	1	0
grief	48	.6231	6.3132	48.0	2	5	8	10	7	6	9	1	18	1	0	11	0	0	0	0	5	0	0	0	5	4	0	4	0
grief-stricken	3	.3395	.2468	33.9	0	0	1	1	0	1	0	0	1	0	0	0	0	0	0	0	0	0	0	0	0	1	1	0	0
griefs	4	.3530	.3083	34.9	0	0	0	1	1	0	2	0	0	0	0	2	0	0	0	0	0	0	0	0	1	1	0	0	0
Grieg	17	.2145	.8359	39.2	7	2	0	3	3	1	1	0	0	0	0	0	0	0	0	0	11	0	0	0	0	0	6	0	0
Grieg's	3	.2088	.1442	31.6	1	0	0	1	1	0	0	0	0	0	0	0	0	0	0	0	2	0	0	0	0	0	1	0	0
grievances	9	.5185	1.0163	40.1	0	0	1	2	1	4	1	0	2	1	0	0	0	4	0	0	0	0	0	0	1	1	0	0	0
grieve	8	.5120	.8963	39.5	0	3	1	2	1	0	1	0	3	1	1	1	0	0	0	0	0	0	0	0	1	1	0	0	0
grieved	12	.4312	1.1240	40.5	0	0	1	4	1	3	3	0	2	0	1	7	0	0	0	0	1	0	0	0	1	0	0	0	0
Grieves	2	.0000	.0215	23.3	0	0	0	0	2	0	0	0	0	0	0	2	0	0	0	0	0	0	0	0	0	0	0	0	0
grieving	6	.1717	.3427	35.3	0	0	0	1	1	1	3	0	3	0	0	3	0	0	0	0	0	0	0	0	0	0	0	0	0
grievous	4	.3168	.2732	34.4	0	1	0	0	1	1	1	0	0	0	1	2	0	0	0	0	0	0	0	0	1	0	0	0	0
griffin	2	.2412	.1141	30.6	0	0	1	0	1	0	0	0	0	1	0	0	0	0	0	0	0	0	0	0	0	1	0	0	0
Griffin	9	.3859	.7718	38.9	0	0	4	0	2	0	3	0	0	0	0	0	0	4	0	0	0	0	0	0	0	3	0	2	0
Griffith	3	.2143	.1568	32.0	1	0	0	0	1	0	1	0	0	0	0	0	0	0	0	0	0	0	0	0	0	1	0	2	0
Griggs	2	.0000	.0215	23.3	0	0	0	0	2	0	0	0	0	0	0	2	0	0	0	0	0	0	0	0	0	0	0	0	0
grill	8	.4894	.8429	39.3	1	3	0	1	2	0	1	0	1	0	0	1	0	0	0	1	0	0	0	0	0	3	0	2	0
grilled	2	.1948	.1250	31.0	0	0	0	0	1	0	1	0	1	0	0	0	0	0	0	0	0	0	0	0	0	1	0	0	0
grillwork	2	.1948	.1250	31.0	0	1	1	0	0	0	0	0	1	0	0	0	0	0	0	0	0	0	0	0	0	1	0	0	0
grim	46	.7750	7.1983	48.6	2	1	7	9	11	9	6	1	9	2	2	6	0	3	0	1	3	0	0	0	6	6	2	6	0
grimace	4	.3693	.3613	35.6	0	2	0	0	2	0	0	0	2	0	0	1	0	0	0	0	0	0	0	0	0	0	1	0	0
grimaced	2	.0000	.0215	23.3	0	0	0	0	1	0	1	0	0	0	0	2	0	0	0	0	0	0	0	0	0	0	0	0	0
Grimalkin	6	.0000	.0703	28.5	0	0	0	6	0	0	0	0	0	0	0	0	0	0	0	0	0	0	0	0	6	0	0	0	0
grime	5	.4431	.4730	36.7	1	0	0	0	3	0	1	0	0	0	0	2	0	1	0	0	0	0	0	0	0	1	0	1	0
Grimes	18	.2416	1.1940	40.8	0	2	8	0	7	1	0	0	7	0	0	0	0	0	0	0	0	0	0	0	10	0	1	0	0
grimly	26	.5456	3.0146	44.8	1	1	2	3	13	1	5	0	6	2	0	10	0	0	0	0	0	0	0	0	4	1	1	2	0
Grimm	8	.4764	.8926	39.5	2	5	0	0	1	0	0	0	5	0	0	0	0	1	0	0	0	0	0	0	0	1	0	1	0
Grimm's	2	.2137	.1056	30.2	0	1	0	1	0	0	0	0	0	0	0	0	0	1	0	0	1	0	0	0	0	0	0	0	0
grimness	3	.3394	.2451	33.9	0	0	0	0	2	1	0	0	1	0	0	1	0	0	0	0	0	0	0	0	1	0	0	0	0
Grimsby	4	.0000	.0778	28.9	0	0	0	4	0	0	0	0	0	0	0	0	0	4	0	0	0	0	0	0	0	0	0	0	0
Grimsey's	2	.0000	.0243	23.9	0	0	0	2	0	0	0	0	0	0	0	0	0	0	0	0	0	0	0	0	0	0	0	2	0
grimy	3	.3399	.2456	33.9	0	0	0	2	1	0	0	0	1	0	0	1	0	0	0	0	0	0	0	0	0	0	0	1	0
grin	75	.6366	10.159	50.1	13	9	14	9	20	6	3	1	37	2	1	6	0	0	0	1	0	0	0	0	16	3	0	9	0
grind	38	.8446	6.4458	48.1	2	10	4	4	7	6	3	2	11	1	0	3	0	4	1	8	1	0	1	1	0	3	2	2	0
grinder	19	.7056	2.7003	44.3	1	7	0	1	6	0	4	0	1	1	1	3	0	0	0	0	2	0	1	2	2	2	1	4	0
grinders	8	.1612	.2983	34.7	0	0	1	0	1	1	5	0	0	0	0	1	0	0	0	1	0	0	0	5	0	0	1	0	0
grinding	63	.7062	9.0020	49.5	9	8	5	8	13	6	13	1	5	0	1	3	0	4	1	4	6	0	0	8	6	9	7	9	0
grindstone	6	.3859	.5833	37.7	0	2	0	3	1	0	0	0	4	0	0	0	0	0	0	0	0	0	0	0	1	1	0	0	0
grinned	120	.5087	13.741	51.4	24	42	8	9	24	11	2	0	61	0	0	7	0	0	0	0	1	0	0	0	20	30	0	1	0
grinning	54	.5425	6.4679	48.1	9	9	2	6	16	7	4	1	27	0	0	8	0	0	0	0	0	0	0	0	9	3	0	7	0
grins	24	.5357	2.9443	44.7	19	0	0	0	3	1	1	0	18	0	0	2	0	1	0	0	0	0	0	0	0	1	1	1	0
grip	46	.7054	6.7239	48.3	4	5	4	4	15	6	6	2	19	1	0	2	0	4	2	1	1	0	0	4	2	2	2	6	0
gripes	2	.1814	.1187	30.7	0	0	0	0	1	1	0	0	1	0	0	0	0	0	0	0	0	0	0	0	0	0	0	1	0
gripped	37	.6216	4.8440	46.9	5	2	0	9	11	3	5	2	12	1	0	11	0	1	0	1	0	0	0	0	2	5	2	2	0
gripping	11	.5676	1.3323	41.2	0	0	2	3	1	2	3	0	4	0	1	2	0	0	0	0	0	0	0	1	0	0	1	2	0
grips	5	.3732	.4026	36.0	0	0	0	0	4	0	1	0	0	0	1	0	0	0	0	1	0	0	0	0	0	1	2	0	0
Griscom	5	.0000	.0724	28.6	0	5	0	0	0	0	0	0	0	0	0	0	0	0	0	0	0	0	0	0	0	5	0	0	0
Grisdale	4	.0000	.0778	28.9	4	0	0	0	0	0	0	0	0	0	0	0	0	4	0	0	0	0	0	0	0	0	0	0	0
grisly	5	.4135	.4652	36.7	0	0	0	0	1	1	2	1	1	0	0	1	0	0	0	1	0	0	0	0	0	0	0	2	0
Grissom	2	.2405	.1205	30.8	0	0	0	1	1	0	0	0	0	0	0	0	0	0	0	1	0	0	0	0	0	1	0	0	0
gristle	2	.0000	.0064	18.1	0	0	0	0	1	0	1	0	0	0	0	0	0	0	0	0	0	0	2	0	0	0	0	0	0
gristmill	3	.3777	.2489	34.0	1	0	1	0	0	1	0	0	0	1	0	0	0	1	0	0	0	0	0	0	1	0	0	0	0
grit	9	.1515	.3756	35.7	1	1	0	0	6	0	0	1	2	0	0	1	0	0	0	0	0	0	0	5	0	0	0	1	0
grits	5	.4854	.5066	37.0	0	0	2	0	0	2	1	0	0	1	0	0	0	1	0	0	0	0	1	0	1	0	0	1	0
gritted	4	.3740	.3661	35.6	1	0	0	0	1	2	0	0	2	0	0	0	0	0	0	0	0	0	0	0	1	0	0	1	0
gritty	3	.3764	.2483	33.9	0	1	0	0	1	0	1	0	0	0	0	0	0	0	0	1	0	0	0	0	0	0	1	1	0
Grizzle	4	.1907	.1863	32.7	0	3	0	0	1	0	0	0	0	3	0	0	0	0	0	0	0	0	0	0	0	0	0	1	0
grizzled	4	.3071	.2967	34.7	0	0	0	1	2	0	1	0	1	0	0	1	0	0	0	0	0	0	0	0	2	0	0	0	0
grizzlies	6	.2757	.4319	36.4	0	0	1	1	3	0	1	0	2	0	0	0	0	0	0	1	0	0	0	0	0	0	0	3	0
grizzly	33	.6526	4.5353	46.6	5	3	5	6	5	4	2	3	14	0	1	6	0	0	0	3	1	0	0	0	1	1	0	6	0
Grizzly	5	.3540	.3848	35.9	0	2	0	3	0	0	0	0	0	0	0	0	0	0	0	0	2	0	0	0	0	2	0	1	0
groan	26	.5687	3.2242	45.1	0	11	3	4	7	1	0	0	13	1	0	3	0	0	2	0	0	0	0	0	6	1	0	0	0
groaned	47	.6415	6.3816	48.0	8	14	4	6	8	7	0	0	21	0	0	5	0	1	1	0	1	0	0	0	10	5	0	3	0
groaning	15	.5380	1.7915	42.5	2	1	2	2	6	1	1	0	8	1	0	2	0	0	0	0	0	0	0	0	3	0	0	1	0
groans	14	.5380	1.6681	42.2	1	6	2	1	1	0	3	0	7	0	0	1	0	0	0	0	0	0	0	0	3	2	0	1	0
grocer	14	.5992	1.7784	42.5	3	4	1	1	2	2	1	0	4	0	1	0	3	2	0	1	0	0	0	0	2	0	0	1	0
groceries	23	.7090	3.3348	45.2	8	3	3	1	3	2	3	0	4	6	0	1	2	1	0	4	0	0	0	0	2	1	1	1	0
grocers	4	.3519	.3117	34.9	0	0	0	0	0	2	2	0	0	0	0	0	0	1	0	0	0	0	0	0	0	0	1	2	0
grocery	48	.7735	7.5548	48.8	10	7	8	4	12	4	2	1	16	2	3	2	6	4	4	4	1	0	0	0	2	1	1	2	0
Grocery	3	.2279	.2143	33.3	0	1	0	0	1	0	0	1	2	0	0	0	0	0	0	0	0	0	0	0	0	0	0	1	0
Grofe	4	.2385	.2074	33.2	1	1	0	0	0	2	0	0	0	0	0	0	0	0	0	0	3	1	0	0	0	0	0	0	0
grog	2	.1948	.1250	31.0	1	0	1	0	0	0	0	0	1	0	0	0	0	0	0	0	0	0	0	0	0	1	0	0	0
Grogan	7	.0000	.3198	35.0	0	0	0	0	0	7	0	0	7	0	0	0	0	0	0	0	0	0	0	0	0	0	0	0	0
groggy	2	.2446	.1142	30.6	0	1	0	0	1	0	0	0	0	0	0	0	0	0	0	0	0	0	0	0	1	0	0	1	0
Gromyko	4	.0000	.0778	28.9	0	0	0	0	4	0	0	0	0	0	0	0	0	4	0	0	0	0	0	0	0	0	0	0	0
groom	20	.4638	2.0009	43.0	3	0	0	8	6	2	1	0	3	2	0	4	0	0	0	0	0	0	0	0	9	0	0	2	0
groom's	2	.2443	.1130	30.5	0	0	0	1	1	0	0	0	0	0	0	1	0	0	0	0	0	0	0	0	1	0	0	0	0
groomed	15	.2310	.8268	39.2	3	1	1	0	3	5	2	0	2	0	0	0	0	0	0	0	0	0	7	0	4	2	0	0	0
grooming	15	.1235	.4372	36.4	0	0	3	1	0	0	11	0	0	0	0	0	0	0	0	0	0	0	11	0	1	0	0	3	0
grooms	3	.1250	.1342	31.3	0	0	0	1	1	1	0	0	1	0	0	0	0	0	0	0	0	0	0	0	2	0	0	0	0
groove	54	.4490	5.1652	47.1	3	3	1	2	29	7	8	1	5	0	0	0	0	2	0	5	11	0	0	13	0	11	3	4	0
grooved	10	.1857	.4662	36.7	0	1	0	1	2	2	3	1	1	0	0	0	0	0	0	2	0	0	0	5	0	1	0	1	0

9Q Gretchen
9N Greyhound
7N greyhounds
4N greyish-brownish
4N greyish-yellowish
4N greyish-yellowish-reddish
3Q greystone
7G Grg
3B gribble
5A Griddle
9L griddlecakes
5B Grief
XR grief's
6P Griefs
9R Grier
6R Griese
8F grievance
7R grieves
3P grievously
8J Griffes
8R Grill
7A grille
8C grilles
7P Grimari
5P Grimbert
XD Grimesby
5N Grimeses'
XR Grimme
8N grimmer
7B grimmest
6R Grimsey
3J grinder's
6N grinds
7G gringo
7A Gringo
7R gringos
7R gripe
6R griping
4P Griscoms
9H Griseus
5P Grisons
8D grist
9H gristlelike
5F gristmills
7P grito
6J griz-ze-ly
8A gro-o-o
8F Groaners
7P groanings
3R GROAR
5A groceryman
7N grog-shop
9R groin
7N grooms'

Word Type	F	D	U	SFI	3 Gr 3	4 Gr 4	5 Gr 5	6 Gr 6	7 Gr 7	8 Gr 8	9 Gr 9	X UnGr	A Read	B Eng & Gr	C Comp	D Lit	E Math	F Soc Stud	G Spell	H Sci	J Music	K Art	L Home Ec	M Shop	N Lib F	P Lib NF	Q Lib Ref	R Mag	S Rel
groover	7	.0000	.0177	22.5	0	0	0	0	0	5	2	0	0	0	0	0	0	0	0	0	0	0	0	7	0	0	0	0	0
grooves	43	.4509	4.0315	46.1	2	1	1	4	24	5	6	0	0	0	0	0	0	2	0	5	14	1	0	12	1	5	0	3	0
grooving	4	.0847	.0846	29.3	0	0	0	0	2	0	2	0	0	0	0	0	0	0	0	0	0	0	0	3	0	0	0	1	0
groovy	3	.0000	.0365	25.6	0	0	1	1	0	1	0	0	0	0	0	0	0	0	0	0	0	0	0	0	0	0	0	3	0
grope	5	.5560	.5787	37.6	1	0	0	1	1	1	1	0	0	1	0	1	0	1	0	1	0	0	0	0	0	0	0	1	0
groped	13	.5754	1.5776	42.0	0	2	2	1	6	0	1	1	3	1	1	4	0	0	0	1	0	0	0	0	1	2	0	0	0
gropes	2	.2446	.1125	30.5	0	1	0	0	1	0	0	0	0	1	0	1	0	0	0	0	0	0	0	0	0	0	0	0	0
groping	12	.3849	1.0320	40.1	0	1	2	1	5	1	2	0	2	0	0	5	0	0	0	0	0	0	0	0	4	0	1	0	0
grosbeaks	2	.0000	.0209	23.2	0	0	0	0	2	0	0	0	0	0	0	0	0	0	0	0	0	0	0	0	0	0	2	0	0
grosgrain	2	.0000	.0064	18.1	0	0	0	0	0	1	1	0	0	0	0	0	0	0	0	0	0	0	2	0	0	0	0	0	0
gross	32	.4549	3.1538	45.0	1	11	6	0	4	0	8	2	3	0	0	3	19	0	0	0	0	0	0	0	0	1	2	4	0
grossly	4	.4866	.4070	36.1	0	0	1	0	0	0	3	0	0	0	0	1	0	0	0	0	0	0	0	0	0	1	1	1	0
grosso	5	.1563	.1897	32.8	0	1	0	0	0	4	0	0	0	0	0	0	0	0	0	0	4	0	0	0	0	0	1	0	0
Grote	2	.0000	.0394	26.0	0	0	0	0	0	2	0	0	0	0	0	0	0	0	0	2	0	0	0	0	0	0	0	0	0
grotesque	11	.6372	1.4460	41.6	0	0	1	1	5	2	1	1	2	1	0	1	0	0	0	0	2	0	0	0	0	1	2	2	0
grotesquely	2	.2443	.1130	30.5	0	0	0	0	2	0	0	0	0	0	0	1	0	0	0	0	0	0	0	0	1	0	0	0	0
grotto	2	.2433	.1158	30.6	0	0	0	1	0	0	1	0	0	0	0	0	0	0	0	0	0	0	0	0	0	1	0	1	0
Grouch	20	.0000	.9137	39.6	15	0	0	5	0	0	0	0	20	0	0	0	0	0	0	0	0	0	0	0	0	0	0	0	0
grouchy	2	.2375	.1088	30.4	0	1	0	0	1	0	0	0	0	0	0	0	0	0	0	0	1	0	0	0	0	0	0	1	0
ground	1511	.8845	266.87	64.3	372	258	175	214	261	110	80	41	466	32	13	71	17	155	15	269	35	6	8	12	102	167	62	75	6
Ground	2	.1948	.1250	31.0	0	1	1	0	0	0	0	0	1	0	0	0	0	0	0	0	0	0	0	0	0	1	0	0	0
ground-up	3	.3765	.2537	34.0	0	0	1	2	0	0	0	0	0	0	0	0	0	1	0	1	0	0	0	0	1	0	0	0	0
grounded	15	.5116	1.6418	42.2	1	1	0	4	6	2	0	1	3	0	0	0	0	1	0	1	0	0	0	2	0	1	4	3	0
grounder	4	.1948	.2500	34.0	1	1	0	1	1	0	0	0	2	0	0	0	0	0	0	0	0	0	0	0	0	2	0	0	0
grounding	2	.2401	.1133	30.5	0	0	1	0	0	1	0	0	0	0	0	0	0	0	0	0	0	0	0	0	0	1	1	0	0
groundless	2	.2337	.1157	30.6	0	1	0	0	0	1	0	0	0	0	0	0	0	1	0	0	0	0	0	0	1	0	0	0	0
grounds	95	.8307	15.839	52.0	10	20	10	7	25	12	8	3	19	1	1	5	4	21	1	3	0	1	0	0	5	13	12	9	0
groundwork	5	.3592	.3915	35.9	0	0	1	1	1	0	2	0	0	0	0	0	1	0	0	0	0	0	0	0	0	0	2	2	0
group	1570	.9204	286.05	64.6	189	238	203	176	337	208	184	35	181	198	11	36	94	174	100	196	152	21	33	4	24	110	115	121	0
Group	43	.6256	5.6359	47.5	2	5	0	9	19	7	1	0	15	3	0	0	0	2	2	2	9	2	6	0	0	1	1	0	0
group's	5	.4143	.4656	36.7	0	1	1	1	0	1	0	1	1	0	0	0	0	1	0	0	0	0	0	0	0	0	1	2	0
grouped	82	.7666	12.638	51.0	5	13	15	12	20	7	8	2	2	6	1	1	29	8	2	16	9	2	1	0	0	0	5	0	0
grouping	108	.5592	12.583	51.0	12	11	17	13	31	11	12	1	3	3	1	0	78	1	3	7	3	0	2	1	0	1	4	1	0
groupings	22	.5329	2.4799	43.9	2	5	3	1	9	0	2	0	3	1	0	0	4	0	0	4	6	0	0	0	0	0	4	0	0
groups	795	.9067	142.77	61.5	115	88	108	97	185	117	78	7	56	123	20	8	62	120	30	97	89	6	27	4	2	38	76	35	2
grouse	16	.5872	1.9421	42.9	2	1	1	0	8	0	1	3	1	1	0	1	0	0	0	2	0	0	0	0	1	1	6	3	0
grove	37	.7734	5.8122	47.6	7	6	5	5	8	5	1	0	11	1	1	3	0	4	0	1	0	1	0	0	7	5	2	1	0
Grove	20	.6217	2.5806	44.1	1	4	0	5	6	3	1	0	3	0	0	3	4	0	0	0	0	0	0	0	2	6	1	1	0
Grover	4	.4338	.3884	35.9	0	1	2	0	0	1	0	0	1	0	0	0	0	1	0	0	1	0	0	0	0	0	1	0	0
Grover's	4	.0000	.1827	32.6	0	2	0	0	2	0	0	0	4	0	0	0	0	0	0	0	0	0	0	0	0	0	0	0	0
groves	30	.6779	4.1594	46.2	3	0	7	7	8	3	1	1	1	2	0	1	0	15	0	1	1	0	0	0	2	2	3	2	0
grow	1418	.8596	243.77	63.9	494	211	186	195	201	61	47	23	235	38	1	37	5	285	18	459	18	11	16	3	21	140	76	53	2
Grow	3	.3507	.2194	33.4	1	0	1	0	1	0	0	0	0	0	0	0	0	0	1	0	1	0	1	0	0	0	0	0	0
GROW	2	.1432	.0759	28.8	1	0	0	0	1	0	0	0	0	0	0	0	0	0	0	1	0	0	1	0	0	0	0	0	0
growed	4	.2228	.2087	33.2	0	1	0	0	1	2	0	0	0	0	0	0	0	0	0	0	1	0	0	0	3	0	0	0	0
grower	6	.3345	.4658	36.7	1	1	0	0	1	3	0	0	0	0	0	0	1	4	0	0	0	0	0	0	0	1	0	0	0
growers	27	.5997	3.4276	45.3	7	4	4	3	4	3	2	0	5	0	0	1	0	11	0	5	0	0	0	0	2	1	0	2	0
growin'	2	.0000	.0914	29.6	0	0	0	1	1	0	0	0	2	0	0	0	0	0	0	0	0	0	0	0	0	0	0	0	0
growing	734	.8199	121.09	60.8	167	94	138	104	117	53	45	16	136	8	0	23	5	165	10	179	16	5	12	0	17	53	63	39	3
Growing	2	.2160	.1362	31.3	0	1	0	0	1	0	0	0	1	0	0	0	0	0	0	1	0	0	0	0	0	0	0	0	0
growl	25	.6655	3.4364	45.4	4	5	2	5	5	2	2	0	7	2	2	4	0	0	1	0	2	0	0	0	5	1	0	1	0
growled	55	.6767	7.7983	48.9	9	13	11	8	8	4	2	0	25	6	1	5	0	0	0	0	0	0	0	0	7	8	0	3	0
growling	18	.5862	2.2254	43.5	4	2	3	4	4	0	1	0	5	0	2	3	0	0	0	1	1	0	0	0	3	1	0	2	0
growls	11	.6324	1.4394	41.6	2	0	2	0	4	1	2	0	2	1	0	1	0	0	0	1	2	0	0	0	2	0	0	2	0
grown	501	.8331	83.844	59.2	82	89	78	77	99	36	28	12	95	5	2	16	2	192	5	52	7	2	5	3	24	49	30	12	0
grown-up	71	.7625	10.980	50.4	24	23	6	8	7	1	1	1	13	2	1	3	0	1	0	19	1	0	2	0	10	16	1	2	0
grown-up's	2	.0000	.0219	23.4	2	0	0	0	0	0	0	0	0	2	0	0	0	0	0	0	0	0	0	0	0	0	0	0	0
grown-ups	30	.6394	4.0604	46.1	17	3	3	4	2	0	0	1	13	4	0	0	1	2	0	0	0	0	1	0	1	1	0	7	0
grownup	9	.3536	.7369	38.7	6	1	1	0	0	0	0	1	2	0	0	0	0	0	0	0	0	0	0	0	5	0	1	1	0
grownups	21	.6210	2.7780	44.4	4	9	2	2	2	2	0	0	9	0	0	1	0	1	1	0	1	0	0	0	2	6	0	0	0
grows	331	.8289	55.039	57.4	94	48	45	56	49	13	15	11	38	10	1	7	5	46	6	135	8	1	2	1	8	26	24	13	0
growth	322	.7344	47.954	56.8	13	26	48	34	96	46	47	12	18	7	0	2	2	57	3	117	1	1	12	1	5	11	61	24	0
Growth	5	.1174	.1473	31.7	0	0	0	0	3	1	0	1	0	1	0	0	0	0	0	1	0	3	0	0	0	0	0	0	0
growths	6	.3688	.4931	36.9	1	0	0	0	1	2	1	1	0	0	0	0	0	0	0	3	0	0	0	0	0	0	2	1	0
Grrrr	2	.0000	.0243	23.9	2	0	0	0	0	0	0	0	0	0	0	0	0	0	0	0	0	0	0	0	0	0	0	2	0
grub	13	.4749	1.4501	41.6	0	0	6	1	5	0	1	0	9	0	0	2	0	0	0	0	1	0	0	0	0	0	1	0	0
grub-box	2	.0000	.0234	23.7	0	0	0	0	0	2	0	0	0	0	0	0	0	0	0	0	0	0	0	0	2	0	0	0	0
grub's	3	.2060	.1500	31.8	1	0	0	0	0	2	0	0	0	0	0	2	0	0	0	0	0	0	0	0	0	1	0	0	0
grubby	3	.3408	.2477	33.9	2	0	0	0	1	0	0	0	1	0	0	1	0	0	0	0	0	0	0	0	0	1	0	0	0
Gruber	3	.0000	.0243	23.8	0	0	0	3	0	0	0	0	0	0	0	0	0	0	0	0	3	0	0	0	0	0	0	0	0
grubs	15	.4847	1.5707	42.0	7	1	1	0	5	0	0	1	2	0	0	1	0	0	0	3	0	0	0	0	0	5	4	0	0
grudge	7	.4307	.6605	38.2	0	0	0	4	1	0	2	0	1	0	0	2	0	0	0	0	0	0	0	0	2	2	0	0	0
grudgingly	4	.4525	.3990	36.0	0	0	0	2	2	0	0	0	1	1	0	1	0	0	0	0	0	0	0	0	1	0	0	0	0
gruel	5	.3121	.3863	35.9	0	3	0	0	1	1	0	0	1	0	0	0	0	3	0	0	0	0	0	0	1	0	0	0	0
grueling	8	.4161	.7502	38.8	0	1	0	0	3	1	3	0	2	0	0	3	0	0	0	0	0	0	0	0	0	2	0	1	0
gruesome	4	.2107	.2095	33.2	0	0	0	0	2	2	0	0	0	0	0	0	0	0	0	0	0	0	0	0	0	3	0	1	0
gruff	8	.3016	.6378	38.0	1	1	0	2	2	2	0	0	4	0	0	3	0	1	0	0	0	0	0	0	0	0	0	0	0
Gruff	3	.0000	.1370	31.4	3	0	0	0	0	0	0	0	3	0	0	0	0	0	0	0	0	0	0	0	0	0	0	0	0
gruffly	4	.3755	.3686	35.7	0	4	0	0	0	0	0	0	2	0	0	0	0	0	0	0	0	0	0	0	1	1	0	0	0
Grumbie	5	.0000	.2284	33.6	0	0	5	0	0	0	0	0	5	0	0	0	0	0	0	0	0	0	0	0	0	0	0	0	0
grumble	8	.3406	.6862	38.4	2	2	0	2	1	1	0	0	4	0	0	1	0	0	0	0	0	0	0	0	3	0	0	0	0
grumbled	25	.5783	3.1002	44.9	5	6	4	3	4	3	0	0	10	0	2	4	0	0	0	0	0	0	0	0	5	2	1	1	0
grumbling	18	.6032	2.3241	43.7	2	3	3	3	3	3	1	0	8	0	1	2	0	0	0	0	0	0	0	0	2	3	0	2	0
Grummick	2	.0000	.0215	23.3	0	0	0	0	0	0	2	0	0	0	0	2	0	0	0	0	0	0	0	0	0	0	0	0	0
grumple	2	.0000	.0219	23.4	0	0	0	0	2	0	0	0	0	2	0	0	0	0	0	0	0	0	0	0	0	0	0	0	0
grumpy	9	.4713	.9806	39.9	4	0	3	0	1	1	0	0	5	1	0	0	0	0	0	0	0	0	0	0	0	1	0	2	0
Grundy	2	.1948	.1250	31.0	2	0	0	0	0	0	0	0	1	0	0	0	0	0	0	0	0	0	0	0	0	1	0	0	0
grunt	9	.5608	1.0999	40.4	1	3	2	1	2	0	0	0	4	0	0	0	0	0	0	0	0	0	0	0	1	2	1	1	0
grunted	36	.6251	4.7711	46.8	5	10	6	1	8	4	1	1	15	0	1	5	0	0	0	0	0	0	0	0	6	4	0	5	0
grunting	12	.6725	1.6867	42.3	2	3	1	2	2	2	0	0	5	1	0	1	0	0	0	0	1	0	0	0	2	1	0	1	0
grunts	13	.6446	1.7344	42.4	3	1	0	3	3	1	2	0	3	2	1	1	0	0	0	1	1	0	0	0	3	0	0	1	0
GrussGott	2	.0000	.0914	29.6	0	0	0	0	0	2	0	0	2	0	0	0	0	0	0	0	0	0	0	0	0	0	0	0	0
Gryphon	11	.0000	.1204	30.8	0	0	11	0	0	0	0	0	0	11	0	0	0	0	0	0	0	0	0	0	0	0	0	0	0
GT	5	.0000	.0608	27.8	0	0	0	0	5	0	0	0	0	0	0	0	0	0	0	0	0	0	0	0	0	0	0	5	0

XR groovier
6R Groovy
6B grop
7D grosbeak
4A Grosbeaks
9R Grospiron
5Q Gross
8R grosser
8A grosses
8Q Grosseteste
7N grossing
9D grossness
5P grot
8Q Grotius
5F Groton
7R Grotto
3A grouching
5J Ground-Gopher's
9F ground-breaking
7Q ground-clinging
6R ground-floor
6A ground-gainers
4F ground-hitched
3P ground-nesting
3P ground-roll
4A grounders
4F groundnuts
6P Grounds
7F groundskeeper
7R groundskeepers
5F groundwater
7P group-contact
8D groveled
6P grovelling
5R grower's
XR Growers
4N Growers'
8H growing-up
9R growingly
9R Grown-up
5N Grows
9R growth-minded
7H growth-stimulating
3R GRRRRRRRR
8P Grub
9D grubbiness
8D grubbing
3A grubbly
7R grudges
7A grudging
XN gruesome-looking
3P Grumpy
8A Grune
6A grunter
6A gruntingly
6A gruntings
7L Gruyere
5B gryphon
5B Gryphon's
5B gryphons
3R GSNARRRRRRRL
7R GT-18
4K Guadalajara

Word Type	F	D	U	SFI	3 Gr 3	4 Gr 4	5 Gr 5	6 Gr 6	7 Gr 7	8 Gr 8	9 Gr 9	X UnGr	A Read	B Eng & Gr	C Comp	D Lit	E Math	F Soc Stud	G Spell	H Sci	J Music	K Art	L Home Ec	M Shop	N Lib F	P Lib NF	Q Lib Ref	R Mag	S Rel
Guadalcanal	4	.3354	.3295	35.2	0	0	2	0	2	0	0	0	1	0	0	0	0	2	0	0	0	0	0	0	0	1	0	0	0
Guaira	3	.2444	.1814	32.6	0	0	1	2	0	0	0	0	0	0	0	0	0	2	0	0	0	0	0	0	0	0	1	0	0
Guam	15	.2458	.9395	39.7	0	0	1	3	1	8	2	0	0	0	0	0	0	12	0	2	0	0	0	0	0	0	0	1	0
guanacos	4	.2835	.2871	34.6	2	0	0	0	2	0	0	0	1	0	0	0	0	0	0	1	0	0	0	0	0	0	0	2	0
guanine	2	.0000	.0394	26.0	0	0	0	0	0	0	2	0	0	0	0	0	0	0	0	2	0	0	0	0	0	0	0	0	0
Guarani	2	.0000	.0389	25.9	0	0	0	2	0	0	0	0	0	0	0	0	0	2	0	0	0	0	0	0	0	0	0	0	0
guarantee	30	.6530	3.9878	46.0	0	0	3	2	9	9	6	1	1	2	0	2	0	5	0	2	1	0	5	0	1	3	3	5	0
guaranteed	25	.7120	3.6009	45.6	1	0	2	2	7	6	7	2	0	0	1	1	0	11	1	1	0	1	1	0	0	1	1	6	0
guaranteeing	4	.4820	.4018	36.0	0	0	1	0	0	2	1	0	0	1	0	1	0	0	1	0	0	0	0	0	0	1	0	0	0
guarantees	9	.5775	1.0934	40.4	0	1	1	3	0	0	4	0	2	1	1	0	0	2	0	0	0	0	1	0	1	0	0	1	0
guard	158	.8211	26.181	54.2	20	23	23	23	39	12	15	3	57	4	2	19	0	10	6	8	3	1	0	2	15	9	8	13	1
Guard	47	.6421	6.4431	48.1	3	21	3	2	11	2	5	0	25	0	0	0	0	3	0	0	1	0	0	0	3	5	3	7	0
Guard's	3	.0000	.1370	31.4	0	3	0	0	0	0	0	0	3	0	0	0	0	0	0	0	0	0	0	0	0	0	0	0	0
guarded	29	.7138	4.2408	46.3	0	6	1	4	8	3	6	1	7	2	0	4	0	1	0	2	0	0	0	0	5	3	1	4	0
guardhouse	2	.2427	.1152	30.6	0	0	0	0	1	1	0	0	0	0	0	0	0	0	0	0	0	0	0	0	1	1	0	0	0
guardian	12	.5547	1.4178	41.5	1	0	1	2	4	3	1	0	3	0	0	2	0	2	0	0	3	0	0	0	0	1	1	0	0
Guardian	2	.2152	.1357	31.3	0	0	0	0	0	2	0	0	1	0	0	0	0	1	0	0	0	0	0	0	0	0	0	0	0
guardians	3	.3450	.2505	34.0	0	0	1	0	1	1	0	0	1	0	0	0	0	0	0	0	0	0	0	0	1	1	0	0	0
guardianship	2	.1814	.1187	30.7	0	0	0	1	1	0	0	0	1	0	0	0	0	0	0	0	0	0	0	0	0	0	0	1	0
guarding	26	.6677	3.6547	45.6	5	3	5	2	5	6	0	0	12	0	0	3	0	3	0	1	1	0	0	0	1	0	4	1	0
guards	65	.7929	10.478	50.2	8	5	14	12	9	13	4	0	27	2	0	10	0	3	0	3	1	1	2	0	2	2	3	9	0
Guards	15	.4072	1.3407	41.3	5	4	0	0	0	5	1	0	0	0	0	1	0	8	0	0	0	0	0	0	5	0	0	1	0
Guatemala	10	.4536	1.0262	40.1	0	3	3	3	0	0	1	0	3	1	0	0	0	4	0	0	0	0	0	0	0	0	2	0	0
Guayaquil	4	.3270	.3194	35.0	1	1	0	0	1	1	0	0	1	0	0	0	0	2	0	0	1	0	0	0	0	0	0	0	0
guayule	2	.0000	.0209	23.2	0	0	0	0	2	0	0	0	0	0	0	0	0	0	0	0	0	0	0	0	0	0	2	0	0
Gub-Gub	5	.0000	.0586	27.7	0	5	0	0	0	0	0	0	0	0	0	0	0	0	0	0	0	0	0	0	5	0	0	0	0
Guelou	4	.0000	.1827	32.6	0	0	0	4	0	0	0	0	4	0	0	0	0	0	0	0	0	0	0	0	0	0	0	0	0
Guericke	2	.0000	.0209	23.2	0	0	0	0	0	0	2	0	0	0	0	0	0	0	0	0	0	0	0	0	0	0	2	0	0
Guernsey	3	.1624	.1256	31.0	0	0	0	0	0	2	1	0	0	0	0	0	0	1	2	0	0	0	0	0	0	0	0	0	0
guerrilla	11	.3207	.7871	39.0	0	0	1	2	2	1	5	0	0	0	1	0	0	2	0	0	0	0	0	0	0	0	0	8	0
guerrillas	12	.3228	.8702	39.4	0	0	0	3	2	1	6	0	0	0	0	0	0	2	0	0	0	0	0	0	0	1	1	8	0
guess	637	.8413	107.75	60.3	156	121	83	76	90	57	41	13	212	38	2	48	46	26	13	52	6	2	0	0	99	59	4	30	0
guessed	55	.7669	8.6621	49.4	15	7	10	5	7	6	4	1	26	3	0	4	1	3	0	5	0	0	0	0	3	6	2	2	0
guesser	5	.2112	.2785	34.4	0	2	0	0	0	0	0	3	0	0	0	0	0	4	0	0	0	0	0	0	0	0	0	1	0
guesses	21	.7800	3.3182	45.2	2	2	2	2	7	4	2	0	4	1	0	1	3	3	1	5	0	0	0	0	0	1	1	1	0
guessing	19	.6094	2.4184	43.8	2	7	0	3	2	2	3	0	3	2	0	0	8	1	0	1	1	0	0	0	1	2	0	0	0
guesswork	5	.3167	.3807	35.8	0	0	2	0	0	1	1	1	1	0	1	0	0	0	0	2	0	0	0	0	0	1	0	0	0
guest	94	.6839	13.285	51.2	7	12	6	9	27	19	11	3	30	5	0	14	0	1	1	2	3	0	10	0	8	12	0	8	0
guests	162	.7705	25.209	54.0	7	12	23	33	25	28	33	1	32	7	3	17	0	11	1	7	10	0	17	0	12	28	3	14	0
guffawed	2	.1948	.1250	31.0	0	1	0	0	1	0	0	0	1	0	0	0	0	0	0	0	0	0	0	0	0	1	0	0	0
Guggenheim	4	.2218	.2339	33.7	0	0	0	0	0	2	2	0	1	0	0	0	0	0	0	0	0	1	0	0	0	2	0	0	0
Guglielmo	3	.2445	.1818	32.6	0	0	1	0	0	1	1	0	0	0	0	0	0	0	0	2	0	0	0	0	0	0	1	0	0
Guiana	18	.4204	1.6464	42.2	0	1	2	0	11	3	1	0	0	0	0	0	0	9	0	0	1	0	0	0	0	2	6	0	0
Guianas	5	.0000	.0972	29.9	0	0	0	0	5	0	0	0	0	0	0	0	0	5	0	0	0	0	0	0	0	0	0	0	0
guid	4	.0000	.0438	26.4	0	0	0	0	0	4	0	0	0	4	0	0	0	0	0	0	0	0	0	0	0	0	0	0	0
guidance	30	.6953	4.2202	46.3	0	1	3	1	7	8	9	1	2	0	1	1	0	3	0	2	1	0	4	1	0	2	9	4	0
guide	347	.8456	58.546	57.7	31	65	72	42	65	39	31	2	56	39	4	12	7	41	71	16	11	1	29	12	3	15	10	19	1
Guide	31	.5579	3.5734	45.5	0	1	1	5	8	2	2	12	1	3	0	1	0	0	0	5	5	0	3	0	0	0	0	13	0
GUIDE	12	.0000	.1288	31.1	0	0	0	0	12	0	0	0	0	0	0	12	0	0	0	0	0	0	0	0	0	0	0	0	0
guide-sheet	2	.0000	.0064	18.1	0	0	0	0	0	2	0	0	0	0	0	0	0	0	0	0	0	0	2	0	0	0	0	0	0
guided	46	.5989	5.7814	47.6	0	5	9	8	7	9	6	2	11	3	1	2	0	4	2	3	0	0	1	1	4	2	6	5	1
guided-missile	2	.2285	.1129	30.5	0	0	1	0	0	0	1	0	0	0	0	0	0	1	0	0	0	0	0	0	0	0	1	0	0
guideline	5	.3343	.4151	36.2	0	0	2	0	3	0	0	0	2	0	0	0	0	0	0	0	0	0	0	0	0	1	0	2	0
guidelines	7	.2829	.4468	36.5	0	0	1	0	3	0	2	1	0	0	0	0	0	2	0	0	0	0	0	2	0	0	0	3	0
guides	71	.6158	9.0230	49.6	6	14	11	2	14	7	16	1	8	27	0	1	0	8	0	6	0	0	8	1	0	4	5	3	0
Guides	27	.0885	.7476	38.7	1	7	4	11	4	0	0	0	0	25	0	0	0	1	0	0	0	0	0	0	0	0	0	1	0
guideway	2	.0000	.0243	23.9	0	0	0	2	0	0	0	0	0	0	0	0	0	0	0	0	0	0	0	0	0	0	0	2	0
guiding	22	.3436	1.7555	42.4	1	2	1	4	7	2	4	1	4	1	0	0	0	3	0	2	1	0	1	0	0	1	2	6	1
Guido	4	.2160	.2008	33.0	0	0	3	0	1	0	0	0	0	0	0	0	0	0	0	0	1	0	0	0	0	0	3	0	0
guidon	2	.0000	.0290	24.6	0	2	0	0	0	0	0	0	0	0	0	0	0	0	0	0	0	0	0	0	0	2	0	0	0
guild	6	.1698	.3400	35.3	0	0	0	2	2	2	0	0	3	0	0	0	0	0	0	0	0	0	0	0	0	0	3	0	0
Guild	11	.3058	.7503	38.8	2	0	1	1	1	0	4	2	1	1	0	0	0	1	0	0	1	4	0	0	0	1	1	1	0
guilders	2	.2152	.1357	31.3	0	0	0	0	1	1	0	0	1	0	0	0	0	1	0	0	0	0	0	0	0	0	0	0	0
guilds	5	.2379	.3486	35.4	0	0	0	2	2	0	1	0	3	0	0	0	0	0	0	0	0	1	0	0	1	0	0	0	0
guile	5	.1668	.2098	33.2	0	0	0	3	2	0	0	0	0	0	0	4	0	0	0	0	0	0	0	0	0	0	0	1	0
Guilford	3	.0000	.0314	25.0	0	0	3	0	0	0	0	0	0	0	0	0	0	0	0	0	0	0	0	0	0	0	3	0	0
Guillaume	4	.2065	.1985	33.0	0	3	0	0	1	0	0	0	0	0	0	0	0	0	0	0	0	0	0	0	3	0	1	0	0
guillotine	5	.4280	.4411	36.4	0	0	1	1	0	1	2	0	0	0	0	1	0	0	0	0	0	1	0	1	0	0	2	0	0
guillotined	3	.2159	.1532	31.9	0	0	1	0	1	0	1	0	0	0	0	0	0	0	0	0	0	0	0	0	0	0	2	1	0
guilt	12	.5335	1.3651	41.4	0	0	1	0	3	3	1	4	2	0	0	0	0	2	2	1	0	0	0	0	0	1	0	4	0
guiltily	6	.4328	.5514	37.4	0	2	2	0	1	1	0	0	0	0	0	1	0	0	0	0	0	0	0	0	3	1	0	1	0
guiltless	2	.2401	.1133	30.5	0	0	1	0	1	0	0	0	0	0	0	0	0	0	0	0	0	0	0	0	0	1	1	0	0
guilty	44	.7201	6.4636	48.1	2	2	6	5	16	5	7	1	9	1	0	10	0	3	2	2	0	0	0	0	2	4	6	5	0
guinea	16	.5914	1.9634	42.9	1	1	1	4	6	2	0	1	1	1	0	0	0	2	0	2	0	0	0	0	0	2	4	4	0
Guinea	25	.3751	2.2010	43.4	0	0	4	11	3	5	2	0	5	1	0	0	0	15	0	0	0	0	0	0	0	0	4	0	0
guineas	2	.1787	.1174	30.7	0	0	1	0	1	0	0	0	1	0	0	0	0	0	0	0	0	0	0	0	1	0	0	0	0
Guinevere	3	.0000	.1370	31.4	0	0	0	3	0	0	0	0	3	0	0	0	0	0	0	0	0	0	0	0	0	0	0	0	0
guiros	2	.0000	.0162	22.1	0	0	1	0	1	0	0	0	0	0	0	0	0	0	0	0	2	0	0	0	0	0	0	0	0
guise	2	.2128	.1055	30.2	0	1	0	0	0	0	0	1	0	0	0	0	0	0	0	1	1	0	0	0	0	0	0	0	0
guises	2	.0000	.0209	23.2	0	0	0	0	1	0	1	0	0	0	0	0	0	0	0	0	0	0	0	0	0	0	2	0	0
guitar	101	.5081	10.702	50.3	9	14	7	17	39	11	4	0	9	5	1	5	0	1	4	3	60	2	0	0	1	1	1	8	0
guitarist	4	.2375	.2175	33.4	0	1	0	0	2	1	0	0	0	0	0	0	0	0	0	0	2	0	0	0	0	0	0	2	0
guitarists	2	.2375	.1088	30.4	0	0	0	0	1	0	1	0	0	0	0	0	0	0	0	0	1	0	0	0	0	0	0	1	0
guitars	14	.6975	1.9818	43.0	0	3	3	0	4	2	2	0	1	0	0	1	0	3	1	0	3	0	0	0	1	1	1	2	0
Gulch	3	.2223	.2106	33.2	0	2	0	0	0	0	1	0	0	1	0	0	0	0	0	0	0	0	0	0	0	0	0	0	0
gulf	15	.5908	1.8673	42.7	1	5	0	2	2	1	3	1	2	0	0	1	0	7	0	1	0	0	0	0	0	1	1	2	0
Gulf	181	.7069	26.230	54.2	9	25	47	30	36	8	21	5	23	1	1	9	0	70	0	36	0	1	0	0	2	5	16	17	0
gulfs	5	.3775	.4204	36.2	0	3	0	0	2	0	0	0	0	0	0	1	0	3	0	0	0	0	0	0	0	0	1	0	0
gull	25	.5688	3.1341	45.0	9	4	3	6	1	1	1	0	15	2	0	0	0	0	0	0	1	1	0	0	5	0	0	1	0
Gull	10	.1904	.5138	37.1	0	8	1	0	0	0	1	0	1	1	0	0	0	0	0	0	0	0	0	0	0	8	0	0	0
gullet	5	.3780	.4214	36.2	0	0	1	0	2	0	2	0	0	0	0	1	0	0	0	3	0	0	0	0	0	0	1	0	0
gulley	2	.0000	.0394	26.0	2	0	0	0	0	0	0	0	0	0	0	0	0	0	0	2	0	0	0	0	0	0	0	0	0
gullies	9	.5070	.9622	39.8	0	5	1	1	1	1	0	0	0	0	0	1	0	1	0	4	0	1	0	0	1	0	1	0	0
Gulliver	2	.0000	.0219	23.4	0	0	0	0	0	2	0	0	0	2	0	0	0	0	0	0	0	0	0	0	0	0	0	0	0
Gulliver's	2	.1733	.1149	30.6	0	0	0	1	0	1	0	0	1	1	0	0	0	0	0	0	0	0	0	0	0	0	0	0	0

7F Guadalquivir
7R guamil
3A guanaco
7R Guanajay
7Q guanay
7P Guantanamo
6F Guaranis
7D Guaranteed
4A GUARD
7N guardedly
3P Guardian's
9Q guardrail
6B Gubser
9M Gudea
9C gudgeon
6A Guelou's
7F guenon
XR Guernica
8F Guerre
6R Guerrilla
7R guerrillero
7R guesstimate
6R guesthouse
7L Guests
9L guests'
7D guff
8C Guggenheim's
5P Guiana's
5Q Guibert
6R guidebooks
7Q guideposts
4N Guilderland
7N Guildhall
5Q guilding
8A guileful
4N Guilty
XH guinea-pigs
5Q Guinicelli
4J guiro
9D Guiseppe
8R Guitar
9R guitar-plucking
9R Guitarist-Composer
8R Gujarati
6R gulches
4A gulf's
5A gull's
7A gullibility
6J gullible
6J Gulliby

Word Type	F	D	U	SFI	3 Gr 3	4 Gr 4	5 Gr 5	6 Gr 6	7 Gr 7	8 Gr 8	9 Gr 9	X UnGr	A Read	B Eng & Gr	C Comp	D Lit	E Math	F Soc Stud	G Spell	H Sci	J Music	K Art	L Home Ec	M Shop	N Lib F	P Lib NF	Q Lib Ref	R Mag	S Rel
Gullport	2	.0000	.0389	25.9	0	2	0	0	0	0	0	0	0	0	0	0	0	2	0	0	0	0	0	0	0	0	0	0	0
gulls	61	.6530	8.5039	49.3	12	15	14	12	7	1	0	0	36	3	0	0	0	1	0	2	0	1	0	0	11	2	4	1	0
gulls'	3	.2261	.2131	33.3	1	1	0	1	0	0	0	0	2	0	0	0	0	0	0	0	0	0	0	0	1	0	0	0	0
gully	12	.2957	.9363	39.7	2	0	0	1	6	3	0	0	6	0	0	5	0	0	0	0	0	0	0	0	1	0	0	0	0
gulp	12	.6035	1.5349	41.9	3	4	2	1	1	0	1	0	4	0	0	2	0	0	0	0	0	0	0	0	1	3	1	1	0
gulped	18	.5851	2.2615	43.5	3	3	2	4	4	2	0	0	7	0	0	3	0	1	0	0	0	0	0	0	3	3	0	1	0
gulping	7	.3421	.5971	37.8	2	0	1	2	1	0	1	0	3	0	0	0	0	0	0	0	0	0	0	0	1	3	0	0	0
gulps	6	.3793	.5819	37.6	1	0	1	1	1	0	1	1	4	0	0	0	0	0	0	1	0	0	0	0	0	1	0	0	0
gum	68	.9013	12.179	50.9	14	7	4	17	15	3	7	1	15	10	1	2	12	6	3	4	1	1	0	1	3	2	4	3	0
gum-chewing	2	.0000	.0219	23.4	0	0	0	0	0	0	2	0	0	2	0	0	0	0	0	0	0	0	0	0	0	0	0	0	0
Gumdrop	5	.0000	.0608	27.8	5	0	0	0	0	0	0	0	0	0	0	0	0	0	0	0	0	0	0	0	0	0	0	5	0
gumdrops	5	.3090	.3462	35.4	1	2	0	1	1	0	0	0	0	0	1	0	3	0	0	0	0	0	0	0	0	1	0	0	0
gummed	2	.1458	.0682	28.3	0	1	0	0	0	0	1	0	0	1	0	0	0	0	0	0	0	1	0	0	0	0	0	0	0
gummite	2	.0000	.0394	26.0	0	0	0	0	0	0	0	2	0	0	0	0	0	0	0	2	0	0	0	0	0	0	0	0	0
gummy	3	.3847	.2494	34.0	1	0	1	0	0	1	0	0	0	0	0	0	0	0	0	0	0	0	0	0	1	1	1	0	0
gums	13	.5467	1.4891	41.7	0	1	8	0	2	0	2	0	0	1	0	0	0	1	0	7	0	0	0	1	0	0	2	1	0
gun	422	.7731	66.501	58.2	39	147	67	16	90	40	20	3	160	4	3	49	1	8	6	18	4	0	0	16	55	75	8	15	0
Gun	8	.4745	.7992	39.0	0	4	1	0	1	1	0	1	0	0	0	0	0	0	0	1	1	0	0	0	4	1	0	1	0
Gunboat	2	.0000	.0290	24.6	0	0	0	0	2	0	0	0	0	0	0	0	0	0	0	0	0	0	0	0	0	2	0	0	0
gunboats	2	.2285	.1129	30.5	0	0	1	0	1	0	0	0	0	0	0	0	0	1	0	0	0	0	0	0	0	0	1	0	0
Gunde	8	.0000	.3655	35.6	0	8	0	0	0	0	0	0	8	0	0	0	0	0	0	0	0	0	0	0	0	0	0	0	0
Gundulic	2	.0000	.0209	23.2	0	0	0	0	0	2	0	0	0	0	0	0	0	0	0	0	0	0	0	0	0	0	2	0	0
gunfire	3	.1409	.1472	31.7	0	0	1	1	1	0	0	0	1	0	0	0	0	0	0	0	0	0	0	0	0	2	0	0	0
gunman	3	.0000	.1370	31.4	0	0	3	0	0	0	0	0	3	0	0	0	0	0	0	0	0	0	0	0	0	0	0	0	0
Gunn	58	.2671	4.8629	46.9	0	0	0	0	2	53	0	3	53	0	0	0	0	0	0	0	0	0	0	0	2	0	0	3	0
Gunn's	4	.0000	.1827	32.6	0	0	0	0	0	4	0	0	4	0	0	0	0	0	0	0	0	0	0	0	0	0	0	0	0
gunned	4	.0000	.1827	32.6	0	2	0	0	1	1	0	0	4	0	0	0	0	0	0	0	0	0	0	0	0	0	0	0	0
gunner	7	.2147	.4730	36.7	0	0	2	1	4	0	0	0	4	0	0	0	0	0	0	0	0	0	0	0	0	3	0	0	0
Gunner	8	.2187	.6050	37.8	0	0	7	0	1	0	0	0	7	0	0	0	0	0	0	0	0	0	0	0	0	1	0	0	0
gunners	9	.5597	1.0571	40.2	0	1	0	0	5	3	0	0	1	0	0	2	0	1	0	0	0	0	0	0	0	3	1	1	0
gunnery	5	.3009	.3636	35.6	0	0	0	1	4	0	0	0	1	0	0	0	0	0	0	0	1	0	0	0	0	3	0	0	0
gunny	2	.2337	.1157	30.6	0	0	0	1	0	1	0	0	0	0	0	0	0	1	0	0	0	0	0	0	1	0	0	0	0
gunpowder	20	.6195	2.5622	44.1	2	4	2	1	6	4	1	0	3	0	0	0	0	2	0	1	0	2	1	0	3	3	4	1	0
Gunpowder	3	.3370	.2430	33.9	0	0	1	0	0	2	0	0	1	0	0	1	0	0	0	0	0	0	0	0	0	0	1	0	0
guns	175	.7832	27.820	54.4	17	41	20	21	44	23	5	4	53	4	1	19	0	20	1	3	2	0	0	1	7	44	9	11	0
gunsmith	2	.0000	.0234	23.7	0	0	0	0	0	2	0	0	0	0	0	0	0	0	0	0	0	0	0	0	2	0	0	0	0
Guntar	3	.0000	.0434	26.4	0	0	0	0	0	0	3	0	0	0	0	0	0	0	0	0	0	0	0	0	0	3	0	0	0
gunwales	2	.1717	.1142	30.6	1	0	0	0	0	0	1	0	1	0	0	1	0	0	0	0	0	0	0	0	0	0	0	0	0
guppies	36	.5487	4.3324	46.4	1	18	3	11	1	2	0	0	14	2	0	0	0	0	0	13	0	0	0	0	5	0	1	1	0
guppy	11	.2937	.8365	39.2	0	3	0	7	1	0	0	0	3	0	0	0	0	0	0	7	0	0	0	0	0	0	1	0	0
gurgle	7	.3722	.6487	38.1	1	1	2	3	0	0	0	0	4	0	0	1	0	0	0	0	0	0	0	0	0	0	0	2	0
gurgled	3	.2260	.1580	32.0	0	0	0	0	3	0	0	0	0	0	0	2	0	0	0	0	0	0	0	0	0	0	1	0	0
gurgling	6	.3506	.5208	37.2	0	2	1	0	2	1	0	0	3	0	1	0	0	0	0	0	0	0	0	0	1	1	0	0	0
Gurt	3	.0000	.1370	31.4	3	0	0	0	0	0	0	0	3	0	0	0	0	0	0	0	0	0	0	0	0	0	0	0	0
guru	2	.0000	.0243	23.9	0	0	0	0	0	1	1	0	0	0	0	0	0	0	0	0	0	0	0	0	0	0	0	2	0
Gus	16	.4654	1.6174	42.1	0	2	6	0	1	2	5	0	3	1	0	6	0	0	0	0	0	0	0	0	4	2	0	0	0
gush	9	.3430	.7219	38.6	0	1	1	0	5	0	1	1	2	1	0	0	0	0	0	0	0	0	0	0	5	1	0	0	0
gushed	7	.2664	.4726	36.7	0	1	1	0	5	0	0	0	2	0	0	4	0	0	0	0	0	0	0	0	0	0	1	0	0
gusher	2	.2442	.1134	30.5	0	0	0	0	0	1	1	0	0	1	0	0	0	0	0	0	0	0	0	0	0	0	0	1	0
gushes	4	.4492	.4017	36.0	0	0	1	1	1	0	0	1	1	0	0	1	0	0	0	1	0	0	0	0	0	0	0	1	0
gushing	3	.3452	.2543	34.1	0	0	1	1	0	0	1	0	1	0	0	0	0	0	0	1	0	0	0	0	0	0	0	1	0
gusset	2	.2421	.0995	30.0	0	0	0	0	1	0	1	0	0	0	0	0	0	0	0	0	0	0	1	1	0	0	0	0	0
gust	16	.5251	1.8566	42.7	2	4	1	6	2	1	0	0	7	1	0	3	0	0	0	0	0	0	0	0	0	4	0	1	0
Gustaf's	2	.0000	.0162	22.1	0	2	0	0	0	0	0	0	0	0	0	0	0	0	0	0	2	0	0	0	0	0	0	0	0
Gustav	9	.4103	.7799	38.9	0	2	1	0	1	4	1	0	0	0	0	0	0	0	0	0	4	0	0	0	0	1	2	2	0
Gustave	2	.2285	.1129	30.5	0	0	1	0	0	1	0	0	0	0	0	0	0	1	0	0	0	0	0	0	0	0	1	0	0
Gustavus	7	.1205	.2337	33.7	0	0	1	0	0	0	6	0	0	0	0	0	0	0	0	0	0	0	0	0	0	1	6	0	0
gusting	2	.1814	.1187	30.7	0	0	0	1	1	0	0	0	1	0	0	0	0	0	0	0	0	0	0	0	0	0	0	1	0
gusto	2	.1787	.1174	30.7	0	0	0	2	0	0	0	0	1	0	0	0	0	0	0	0	0	0	0	0	1	0	0	0	0
gusts	16	.6576	2.1672	43.4	0	3	1	2	8	1	1	0	3	1	1	3	0	0	0	1	0	0	0	0	3	2	0	2	0
gusty	4	.3710	.3211	35.1	0	0	0	1	2	0	0	1	0	1	0	0	0	0	0	0	0	0	0	0	1	0	0	2	0
gut	4	.3097	.2992	34.8	0	0	0	1	1	0	2	0	1	0	0	1	0	0	0	0	0	0	0	0	0	0	0	2	0
Gutenberg	22	.4290	1.9986	43.0	0	0	4	9	2	2	5	0	1	8	0	0	0	3	2	0	0	0	0	5	0	0	3	0	0
Gutenberg's	3	.3781	.2493	34.0	0	0	0	2	1	0	0	0	0	1	0	0	0	1	0	0	0	0	0	0	0	0	0	1	0
guts	10	.4532	1.0285	40.1	0	1	0	0	5	2	2	0	4	0	0	2	0	0	0	0	0	0	0	0	1	0	0	3	0
gutta	2	.0000	.0209	23.2	0	0	2	0	0	0	0	0	0	0	0	0	0	0	0	0	0	0	0	0	0	0	2	0	0
gutta-percha	10	.0000	.1047	30.2	0	0	10	0	0	0	0	0	0	0	0	0	0	0	0	0	0	0	0	0	0	0	10	0	0
gutted	2	.2351	.1166	30.7	0	0	0	1	0	1	0	0	0	0	0	0	0	1	0	0	0	0	0	0	0	0	0	1	0
gutter	12	.5986	1.5035	41.8	2	0	0	5	2	3	0	0	3	1	1	0	0	0	2	0	0	0	0	0	1	1	0	3	0
gutters	4	.3348	.3266	35.1	2	1	0	0	0	0	1	0	1	0	0	1	0	2	0	0	0	0	0	0	0	0	0	0	0
guttural	7	.4852	.7253	38.6	0	2	2	0	0	2	1	0	1	0	0	0	0	0	0	0	2	0	0	0	1	1	0	2	0
guv'nor	5	.0000	.0537	27.3	0	0	0	0	5	0	0	0	0	0	0	5	0	0	0	0	0	0	0	0	0	0	0	0	0
guy	68	.5548	8.1783	49.1	0	2	3	1	26	18	15	3	27	3	0	5	1	0	0	0	0	0	0	0	17	1	0	14	0
Guy	9	.4725	.8915	39.5	1	2	1	1	1	2	1	0	0	0	0	1	0	0	0	0	1	0	0	0	1	1	0	5	0
guys	76	.4380	7.5645	48.8	1	7	2	8	25	19	13	1	27	1	0	2	0	1	0	0	0	0	0	0	25	0	0	20	0
Gwai-lin-di	2	.0000	.0215	23.3	0	0	2	0	0	0	0	0	0	0	0	2	0	0	0	0	0	0	0	0	0	0	0	0	0
Gwendolyn	8	.2341	.6211	37.9	0	7	0	0	0	0	1	0	7	0	0	1	0	0	0	0	0	0	0	0	0	0	0	0	0
Gwendolyn's	2	.0000	.0914	29.6	0	2	0	0	0	0	0	0	2	0	0	0	0	0	0	0	0	0	0	0	0	0	0	0	0
Gwydion	2	.0000	.0290	24.6	0	0	0	0	2	0	0	0	0	0	0	0	0	0	0	0	0	0	0	0	0	2	0	0	0
gwyne	3	.0000	.0352	25.5	0	0	0	0	3	0	0	0	0	0	0	0	0	0	0	0	0	0	0	0	3	0	0	0	0
Gyko	4	.0000	.1827	32.6	0	0	0	0	4	0	0	0	4	0	0	0	0	0	0	0	0	0	0	0	0	0	0	0	0
gym	36	.6474	4.8688	46.9	1	5	5	4	5	7	8	1	11	10	0	0	3	1	1	1	0	0	0	0	2	3	0	4	0
gymnasium	21	.7891	3.3545	45.3	4	2	2	0	6	4	3	0	6	2	0	1	0	0	1	3	1	0	0	0	1	1	2	3	0
gymnasiums	3	.3454	.2542	34.1	1	0	0	0	2	0	0	0	1	0	0	0	0	1	0	0	0	0	0	0	0	0	0	1	0
gymnastics	2	.0000	.0243	23.9	0	1	0	0	0	1	0	0	0	0	0	0	0	0	0	0	0	0	0	0	0	0	0	2	0
Gynt	7	.1929	.3149	35.0	2	2	0	1	2	0	0	0	0	0	0	0	0	0	0	0	5	0	0	0	0	0	2	0	0
gypsies	8	.6047	.9903	40.0	4	0	0	0	2	1	1	0	0	1	0	0	0	1	0	0	1	0	0	0	0	2	2	1	0
Gypsies	10	.1835	.4760	36.8	1	0	8	1	0	0	0	0	1	8	0	0	0	0	0	0	1	0	0	0	0	0	0	0	0
gypsum	5	.2213	.2870	34.6	0	0	0	0	0	1	4	0	0	0	0	0	0	0	0	4	0	0	0	0	0	0	1	0	0
gypsy	46	.5333	5.3798	47.3	5	19	3	2	5	9	3	0	20	1	1	1	0	5	1	1	15	0	0	0	0	1	0	0	0
Gypsy	10	.3647	.8929	39.5	4	1	3	1	0	1	0	0	5	3	0	0	0	0	0	0	2	0	0	0	0	0	0	0	0
gyrating	2	.2346	.1166	30.7	0	0	0	0	1	1	0	0	0	0	0	0	0	0	0	1	0	0	0	0	0	0	0	1	0
gyre	4	.2254	.2040	33.1	0	0	1	3	0	0	0	0	0	3	0	0	0	0	0	0	0	1	0	0	0	0	0	0	0

8B Gulls	4A gun-shot	9D gunning	4J Gustaf	8A guvs	7P gymnast
7Q gullying	4P gun's	4N gunny-sack	7R Gustavo	8D guy's	4R gymnasts
7G gulyas	8F gunboat	7N gunshop	7L Gustavson	7A guzzle	7Q gymnocercus
6F GUM	7H guncotton	3C gunshot	9Q Gustavus's	7A gwine	3P gyms
4A gumbo	7D gunfight	7D gunshots	3P gustily	7P Gwydion's	7J Gynt's
3R Gump	5A gunfights	5F gunsmiths	8J Gut	9Q gybing	9H Gypsum
6F gumwood	8R gung-ho	6J Gunther	3R guten	7P Gyffe's	7J gypsy-like
9D gun-club	5A Gungner	7F Gupta	8D Guthrie	7P Gyffes	3P gyrate
7R gun-control	7D Gunlock	3B gurgle-gurgle	8D Guthrie's	5A gym's	7H gyrates
5A gun-deck	8B gunnels	7R gurgles	5Q Gutta-Percha	7N gymkhana	
7R gun-fetishist	6N gunner's	4A Gurley	7Q guttation	7N Gymkhana's	
9H gun-firing	7R gunners'	3N Gussie	4A guttinke	XP Gymnasium	

Word Type	F	D	U	SFI	3 Gr 3	4 Gr 4	5 Gr 5	6 Gr 6	7 Gr 7	8 Gr 8	9 Gr 9	X UnGr	A Read	B Eng & Gr	C Comp	D Lit	E Math	F Soc Stud	G Spell	H Sci	J Music	K Art	L Home Ec	M Shop	N Lib F	P Lib NF	Q Lib Ref	R Mag	S Rel
gyrfalcon	5	.0000	.2284	33.6	0	0	0	5	0	0	0	0	5	0	0	0	0	0	0	0	0	0	0	0	0	0	0	0	0
gyrfalcon's	2	.0000	.0914	29.6	0	0	0	2	0	0	0	0	2	0	0	0	0	0	0	0	0	0	0	0	0	0	0	0	0
h	174	.4645	17.003	52.3	18	21	14	28	32	27	11	23	2	4	0	0	56	0	74	2	1	0	1	0	0	25	2	7	0
H	120	.7226	17.574	52.4	10	16	16	15	18	28	11	6	7	3	4	0	41	7	1	19	0	0	0	2	0	9	20	7	0
H**	6	.2480	.3712	35.7	1	0	1	3	0	0	0	1	1	0	0	0	0	0	0	0	0	0	0	0	0	0	1	4	0
H-bomb	6	.3577	.4870	36.9	0	0	0	0	1	1	4	0	0	0	0	0	0	0	0	4	0	0	0	0	0	0	1	1	0
H/A	2	.0000	.0243	23.9	0	0	0	0	2	0	0	0	0	0	0	0	0	0	0	0	0	0	0	0	0	0	0	2	0
h'm	4	.3721	.3657	35.6	0	1	0	1	1	0	1	0	2	0	0	1	0	0	0	0	0	0	0	0	0	1	0	0	0
ha	53	.6075	6.8180	48.3	10	24	1	3	2	3	2	8	18	0	0	7	0	0	0	0	4	0	0	0	3	13	0	8	0
Ha	2	.0000	.0290	24.6	0	0	2	0	0	0	0	0	0	0	0	0	0	0	0	0	0	0	0	0	0	2	0	0	0
Ha-ha	2	.0000	.0914	29.6	0	2	0	0	0	0	0	0	2	0	0	0	0	0	0	0	0	0	0	0	0	0	0	0	0
Ha-ho	2	.0000	.0914	29.6	0	2	0	0	0	0	0	0	2	0	0	0	0	0	0	0	0	0	0	0	0	0	0	0	0
ha-ja-ha	2	.0000	.0162	22.1	0	0	0	2	0	0	0	0	0	0	0	0	0	0	0	0	2	0	0	0	0	0	0	0	0
Ha'penny	5	.0000	.2284	33.6	0	0	0	0	5	0	0	0	5	0	0	0	0	0	0	0	0	0	0	0	0	0	0	0	0
Haaga	2	.0000	.0290	24.6	0	2	0	0	0	0	0	0	0	0	0	0	0	0	0	0	0	0	0	0	0	2	0	0	0
Haakon	5	.1901	.2435	33.9	0	0	4	0	0	1	0	0	0	0	0	0	0	0	0	0	0	0	0	0	0	4	0	1	0
Haarlem	4	.1737	.1745	32.4	0	0	1	0	0	3	0	0	0	0	0	0	0	0	0	0	0	0	0	0	0	1	3	0	0
Hab	8	.1581	.3426	35.3	0	0	0	7	0	1	0	0	0	0	0	0	0	0	0	0	0	0	0	0	0	7	1	0	0
Hab's	2	.0000	.0290	24.6	0	0	0	2	0	0	0	0	0	0	0	0	0	0	0	0	0	0	0	0	0	2	0	0	0
habanera	4	.0000	.0323	25.1	0	0	2	0	0	2	0	0	0	0	0	0	0	0	0	0	4	0	0	0	0	0	0	0	0
Haber	2	.2278	.1128	30.5	0	0	0	1	0	1	0	0	0	0	0	0	0	0	0	1	0	0	0	0	0	0	1	0	0
habit	130	.8581	22.303	53.5	11	5	22	27	29	15	12	9	27	8	0	8	0	4	5	35	2	1	2	0	11	6	11	10	0
habit-forming	3	.3202	.2063	33.1	0	0	1	0	1	1	0	0	0	0	0	0	0	0	0	0	0	0	1	0	0	0	1	1	0
habitable	2	.2278	.1128	30.5	0	0	0	0	2	0	0	0	0	0	0	0	0	0	0	1	0	0	0	0	0	0	1	0	0
habitat	34	.3763	2.8251	44.5	12	2	0	1	12	1	2	4	0	0	0	0	0	0	0	14	0	0	0	0	0	0	12	8	0
habitation	12	.5921	1.4704	41.7	2	0	0	1	5	3	1	0	1	0	0	3	0	0	0	1	0	0	0	0	1	2	3	1	0
habitats	12	.3543	.9487	39.8	2	1	0	0	8	0	0	1	0	0	0	0	0	0	0	5	0	0	0	0	0	0	5	2	0
habits	162	.7267	23.832	53.8	12	14	9	28	57	15	24	3	12	20	1	1	0	5	3	52	0	0	18	3	3	13	20	11	0
habitual	7	.5120	.7593	38.8	0	0	0	0	4	1	1	1	1	1	0	2	0	0	0	0	0	0	0	0	0	0	1	2	0
habitually	4	.4738	.4043	36.1	0	0	1	0	1	1	1	0	0	1	0	0	0	1	0	1	0	0	0	0	0	0	1	0	0
Hacha	2	.0000	.0290	24.6	0	0	0	0	2	0	0	0	0	0	0	0	0	0	0	0	0	0	0	0	0	2	0	0	0
haciendas	5	.0000	.0972	29.9	0	2	0	2	0	0	1	0	0	0	0	0	0	5	0	0	0	0	0	0	0	0	0	0	0
hack	7	.1985	.3733	35.7	0	1	1	2	3	0	0	0	2	0	0	0	0	0	0	0	0	0	0	3	1	1	0	0	0
Hack	3	.2347	.1695	32.3	2	0	0	1	0	0	0	0	0	0	0	0	0	0	0	0	0	0	0	0	1	2	0	0	0
hacked	4	.3726	.3697	35.7	0	0	2	1	1	0	0	0	2	0	0	0	0	1	0	0	0	0	0	0	1	0	0	0	0
Hackett	2	.0000	.0914	29.6	0	0	0	2	0	0	0	0	2	0	0	0	0	0	0	0	0	0	0	0	0	0	0	0	0
hacking	7	.5607	.8553	39.3	0	0	0	1	4	2	0	0	3	0	0	1	0	1	0	0	0	0	0	0	1	0	0	1	0
hackles	2	.2412	.1091	30.4	0	0	0	0	1	1	0	0	0	0	0	1	0	0	1	0	0	0	0	0	0	0	0	0	0
hacksaw	8	.1581	.3191	35.0	0	1	1	0	1	2	3	0	0	0	0	0	0	0	0	3	0	0	0	4	0	1	0	0	0
had	20511	.8865	3633.8	75.6	3482	3651	2473	2854	3913	2447	1320	371	8013	569	131	1779	503	1994	149	536	308	55	44	6	2434	2255	562	1162	11
Had	7	.2689	.4530	36.6	0	1	0	0	0	6	0	0	1	4	0	0	0	0	0	0	0	0	0	0	0	0	0	2	0
haddock	4	.3730	.3365	35.3	0	0	0	2	2	0	0	0	0	0	0	0	0	2	0	1	0	0	0	0	0	0	1	0	0
Haddock	2	.0000	.0243	23.9	0	0	0	0	0	0	0	2	0	0	0	0	0	0	0	0	0	0	0	0	0	0	0	2	0
Hades	6	.2435	.4680	36.7	0	0	5	0	0	1	0	0	5	0	0	1	0	0	0	0	0	0	0	0	0	0	0	0	0
hadn't	284	.7001	41.315	56.2	35	63	34	34	58	21	36	3	121	10	4	39	0	2	1	3	1	0	0	0	51	30	1	21	0
hadst	4	.1757	.1766	32.5	0	0	0	0	1	0	3	0	0	0	0	3	0	0	0	0	0	0	0	0	0	1	0	0	0
haff	2	.0000	.0215	23.3	0	0	0	0	0	0	2	0	0	0	0	2	0	0	0	0	0	0	0	0	0	0	0	0	0
hag	3	.2212	.2099	33.2	0	0	0	0	2	0	1	0	2	0	0	1	0	0	0	0	0	0	0	0	0	0	0	0	0
hagfishes	2	.0000	.0209	23.2	0	0	0	0	2	0	0	0	0	0	0	0	0	0	0	0	0	0	0	0	0	0	2	0	0
haggard	4	.4533	.4015	36.0	0	1	1	0	1	0	1	0	1	0	0	1	0	0	0	0	0	0	0	0	1	1	0	0	0
Haggerty	2	.0000	.0243	23.9	0	0	0	0	0	0	2	0	0	0	0	0	0	0	0	0	0	0	0	0	0	0	0	2	0
Haggin	20	.1140	.8364	39.2	0	0	0	0	20	0	0	0	6	0	0	0	0	0	0	0	0	0	0	0	14	0	0	0	0
Haggin's	5	.0000	.0586	27.7	0	0	0	0	5	0	0	0	0	0	0	0	0	0	0	0	0	0	0	0	5	0	0	0	0
haggled	3	.3873	.2495	34.0	0	0	0	1	1	1	0	0	0	0	0	1	0	0	0	0	0	0	0	0	1	0	0	1	0
haggling	2	.2351	.1166	30.7	0	0	0	0	1	0	1	0	0	0	0	0	0	1	0	0	0	0	0	0	0	0	0	1	0
Hague	18	.3315	1.3295	41.2	1	0	2	0	11	3	1	0	0	0	0	0	0	2	0	0	0	0	0	0	0	2	2	12	0
Hagy	2	.0000	.0243	23.9	0	0	0	0	0	0	0	2	0	0	0	0	0	0	0	0	0	0	0	0	0	0	0	2	0
hah	4	.3065	.2965	34.7	1	0	2	0	0	1	0	0	1	1	0	0	0	0	0	0	0	0	0	0	2	0	0	0	0
Hahalaba	2	.0000	.0215	23.3	0	0	0	0	0	2	0	0	0	0	0	2	0	0	0	0	0	0	0	0	0	0	0	0	0
Hahn	6	.3493	.5166	37.1	0	0	0	0	4	2	0	0	2	0	0	0	0	0	0	3	0	0	0	0	0	0	1	0	0
hai	2	.0000	.0914	29.6	2	0	0	0	0	0	0	0	2	0	0	0	0	0	0	0	0	0	0	0	0	0	0	0	0
Haifa	2	.2408	.1204	30.8	0	0	1	0	1	0	0	0	0	0	0	0	0	1	0	0	0	0	0	0	0	1	0	0	0
haiku	37	.3823	3.0706	44.9	3	19	1	4	10	0	0	0	2	22	0	8	0	0	2	0	0	0	0	0	0	0	0	3	0
hail	45	.7493	6.8509	48.4	8	3	5	10	4	4	10	1	9	1	0	9	0	1	2	10	4	0	0	0	3	3	1	2	0
Hail	4	.3075	.2938	34.7	0	0	2	1	1	0	0	0	1	0	0	2	0	0	0	0	1	0	0	0	0	0	0	0	0
Haile	5	.0000	.0972	29.9	0	0	0	2	3	0	0	0	0	0	0	0	0	5	0	0	0	0	0	0	0	0	0	0	0
hailed	22	.6164	2.8519	44.6	0	2	1	8	6	5	0	0	6	0	0	1	0	4	0	0	2	0	0	0	6	1	0	2	0
hailing	2	.2408	.1204	30.8	0	0	1	0	0	1	0	0	0	0	0	0	0	1	0	0	0	0	0	0	0	1	0	0	0
hails	2	.0000	.0394	26.0	1	1	0	0	0	0	0	0	0	0	0	0	0	0	0	2	0	0	0	0	0	0	0	0	0
hailstone	5	.0000	.0986	29.9	5	0	0	0	0	0	0	0	0	0	0	0	0	0	0	5	0	0	0	0	0	0	0	0	0
hailstones	5	.3624	.4519	36.5	3	0	0	2	0	0	0	0	2	0	0	0	0	1	0	2	0	0	0	0	0	0	0	0	0
hailstorms	2	.2160	.1362	31.3	0	0	0	0	1	1	0	0	1	0	0	0	0	0	0	1	0	0	0	0	0	0	0	0	0
hain't	3	.3394	.2451	33.9	0	0	0	1	0	1	1	0	1	0	0	1	0	0	0	0	0	0	0	0	1	0	0	0	0
Haines	3	.1783	.1304	31.2	0	0	0	2	0	0	1	0	0	0	0	0	0	0	0	0	0	1	0	0	0	2	0	0	0
Haiphong	5	.0000	.0724	28.6	0	0	0	0	5	0	0	0	0	0	0	0	0	0	0	0	0	0	0	0	0	5	0	0	0
hair	867	.8268	144.02	61.6	173	146	90	97	176	89	77	19	227	21	5	95	11	29	9	61	9	6	56	4	140	135	7	52	0
Hair	6	.4226	.5320	37.3	0	0	1	1	0	1	2	1	0	0	1	0	0	0	0	0	1	0	0	0	1	0	0	3	0
hair-like	3	.2357	.2199	33.4	1	2	0	0	0	0	0	0	2	0	0	0	0	0	0	0	0	0	0	0	0	1	0	0	0
hair-raising	4	.3011	.2909	34.6	0	0	1	0	0	0	3	0	1	0	0	2	0	0	0	0	0	0	0	0	0	0	1	0	0
hairbreadth	2	.2446	.1123	30.5	0	0	0	1	1	0	0	0	0	1	0	0	0	0	0	0	0	0	0	0	0	0	1	0	0
hairbrush	2	.1787	.1174	30.7	1	0	0	1	0	0	0	0	1	0	0	0	0	0	0	0	0	0	0	0	1	0	0	0	0
haircut	13	.5893	1.6012	42.0	2	0	1	3	1	3	2	1	2	4	0	1	0	0	0	1	0	0	0	0	1	3	0	1	0
Haircut	2	.2446	.1125	30.5	0	0	0	0	0	2	0	0	0	1	0	1	0	0	0	0	0	0	0	0	0	0	0	0	0
haircuts	4	.4829	.4095	36.1	1	0	1	0	1	0	0	1	0	0	0	0	0	1	0	0	0	0	0	0	1	1	0	1	0
hairless	2	.2446	.1142	30.6	0	1	0	0	0	1	0	0	0	0	0	0	0	0	0	0	0	0	0	0	1	0	0	1	0
hairlike	10	.4110	.9125	39.6	1	2	0	1	5	1	0	0	1	0	0	0	0	0	0	5	0	0	0	1	0	0	3	0	0
hairline	4	.1648	.1599	32.0	0	0	0	0	0	2	2	0	0	0	0	0	2	0	0	0	0	0	2	0	0	0	0	0	0
hairpin	4	.3709	.3633	35.6	1	2	1	0	0	0	0	0	2	0	0	0	0	0	0	0	0	0	0	0	0	0	1	1	0
hairpins	6	.2261	.4261	36.3	2	1	1	0	2	0	0	0	4	0	0	0	0	0	0	0	0	0	0	0	2	0	0	0	0
hairs	70	.5628	8.3225	49.2	30	7	6	7	17	0	3	0	7	0	0	3	3	0	0	26	0	0	0	0	1	23	6	1	0
hairy	29	.6341	3.8797	45.9	10	8	3	2	3	1	2	0	11	0	0	3	0	0	0	1	0	0	0	0	4	5	4	1	0
Hairy	3	.0000	.1370	31.4	3	0	0	0	0	0	0	0	3	0	0	0	0	0	0	0	0	0	0	0	0	0	0	0	0
Haiti	18	.3475	1.4354	41.6	0	0	9	2	1	2	3	1	0	0	0	1	0	14	0	0	0	0	0	0	0	0	2	1	0

XR Gyrocopter
XH gyroscopic
5G gz
3J G7
XR H&G
9H H-bombs
3N h-h-h-h-h
7A h-h-headless
8Q h/mc
8Q h/mv
3A hnd
3J H'
9N h'mm
9B h'ugh
5E HA
4P ha-yu
8N ha'
7A ha'nted
6A ha'pence
7A Ha'penny's
6R haaa-raaam-bayyy
3F Haarlem's
4A haawwnk
4A haawwnnkk
8J Habanera
3P habergeon
8A habitants
5Q Habitat
5P habituated
7P Hacha's
3F hachures
9Q hackberry
XR Hackettstown
5Q hackneyed
5P Haddonfield
6H Hader
8Q Hadfield
6A Hadji
6R Hadl
6R Hadley
7N hadn'
5P Hadrosaurus
9D hafta
7N Haggin'll
7R Hague's
3D Hah-nee's
6B hahf
7H Hahn's
7P Haiduong
7D haiku-like
9D hail'd
3B Hailstones
6F hailstorm
5P Hainan
6P Haineses
7P Haiphong's
9Q hair-coloring
7D hair-dye
6R hair-oil
7D hair-pulling
4P hair-ribbon
4N hair-stiffening
9D hair-tip
4N hair's
5A hairbrushes
XR hairdos
3A hairdresser
7Q hairiness
5R hairstyling
XH hairy-skinned

Word Type	F	D	U	SFI	3 Gr 3	4 Gr 4	5 Gr 5	6 Gr 6	7 Gr 7	8 Gr 8	9 Gr 9	X UnGr	A Read	B Eng & Gr	C Comp	D Lit	E Math	F Soc Stud	G Spell	H Sci	J Music	K Art	L Home Ec	M Shop	N Lib F	P Lib NF	Q Lib Ref	R Mag	S Rel
Haji	22	.0000	1.0050	40.0	0	0	0	22	0	0	0	0	22	0	0	0	0	0	0	0	0	0	0	0	0	0	0	0	0
Haji's	2	.0000	.0914	29.6	0	0	0	2	0	0	0	0	2	0	0	0	0	0	0	0	0	0	0	0	0	0	0	0	0
Hak-Tak	17	.0000	.7766	38.9	0	17	0	0	0	0	0	0	17	0	0	0	0	0	0	0	0	0	0	0	0	0	0	0	0
Hak-Taks	4	.0000	.1827	32.6	0	4	0	0	0	0	0	0	4	0	0	0	0	0	0	0	0	0	0	0	0	0	0	0	0
Hal	30	.4388	3.1027	44.9	2	0	5	0	2	13	8	0	17	2	0	8	0	0	0	0	0	0	0	0	3	0	0	0	0
Hal's	2	.1733	.1149	30.6	1	0	1	0	0	0	0	0	1	1	0	0	0	0	0	0	0	0	0	0	0	0	0	0	0
hala	2	.0000	.0914	29.6	2	0	0	0	0	0	0	0	2	0	0	0	0	0	0	0	0	0	0	0	0	0	0	0	0
Haldeman	3	.0000	.0365	25.6	0	0	0	0	0	0	3	0	0	0	0	0	0	0	0	0	0	0	0	0	0	0	0	3	0
hale	3	.2060	.1430	31.6	0	0	0	2	0	1	0	0	0	1	0	0	0	0	2	0	0	0	0	0	0	0	0	0	0
Hale	31	.2254	1.8944	42.8	7	2	0	1	1	20	0	0	9	19	0	0	0	0	0	2	0	0	0	0	0	1	0	0	0
Hale's	3	.0000	.0328	25.2	0	0	0	0	0	3	0	0	0	3	0	0	0	0	0	0	0	0	0	0	0	0	0	0	0
Haley	3	.0000	.0322	25.1	0	0	0	0	3	0	0	0	0	0	0	3	0	0	0	0	0	0	0	0	0	0	0	0	0
half	1514	.9528	284.86	64.5	258	194	182	204	311	174	164	27	292	51	11	107	114	173	23	143	125	6	27	19	118	119	83	103	0
Half	34	.1647	1.5011	41.8	0	1	1	1	28	3	0	0	3	0	0	28	0	1	0	0	0	0	0	0	0	0	1	1	0
Half-Chick	10	.0000	.4568	36.6	10	0	0	0	0	0	0	0	10	0	0	0	0	0	0	0	0	0	0	0	0	0	0	0	0
half-acre	2	.1787	.1174	30.7	0	0	0	1	0	1	0	0	1	0	0	0	0	0	0	0	0	0	0	0	1	0	0	0	0
half-afraid	2	.1717	.1142	30.6	0	0	0	1	1	0	0	0	1	0	0	1	0	0	0	0	0	0	0	0	0	0	0	0	0
half-asleep	2	.2427	.1152	30.6	0	0	0	1	0	0	1	0	0	0	0	0	0	0	0	0	0	0	0	0	1	1	0	0	0
half-ball	2	.0000	.0394	26.0	0	0	2	0	0	0	0	0	0	0	0	0	0	0	0	2	0	0	0	0	0	0	0	0	0
half-breed	3	.3873	.2495	34.0	0	0	1	0	2	0	0	0	0	0	0	1	0	0	0	0	0	0	0	0	1	0	0	1	0
half-buried	3	.2599	.1710	32.3	0	0	0	1	1	0	1	0	0	0	0	0	0	0	0	0	0	1	0	0	1	0	1	0	0
half-chick	2	.0000	.0914	29.6	2	0	0	0	0	0	0	0	2	0	0	0	0	0	0	0	0	0	0	0	0	0	0	0	0
half-circle	3	.2120	.1548	31.9	0	0	0	2	1	0	0	0	0	0	0	0	0	0	0	0	0	0	0	0	2	1	0	0	0
half-closed	2	.1787	.1174	30.7	0	0	0	1	1	0	0	0	1	0	0	0	0	0	0	0	0	0	0	0	1	0	0	0	0
half-dollar	2	.2446	.1142	30.6	1	0	0	0	0	0	0	1	0	0	0	0	0	0	0	0	0	0	0	0	1	0	0	1	0
half-dollars	4	.0000	.0599	27.8	1	1	1	0	1	0	0	0	0	0	0	0	4	0	0	0	0	0	0	0	0	0	0	0	0
half-dozen	10	.5396	1.1622	40.7	0	3	2	0	3	0	2	0	3	0	1	1	2	0	0	0	0	0	0	0	0	2	0	1	0
half-drowned	2	.2152	.1357	31.3	1	0	0	0	1	0	0	0	1	0	0	0	0	1	0	0	0	0	0	0	0	0	0	0	0
half-eaten	2	.2440	.1132	30.5	0	0	0	0	2	0	0	0	0	0	0	1	0	0	0	0	0	0	0	0	0	0	0	1	0
half-filled	3	.2437	.2277	33.6	1	0	1	0	1	0	0	0	2	0	0	0	0	0	0	1	0	0	0	0	0	0	0	0	0
half-finished	4	.3394	.3015	34.8	0	0	1	0	1	1	1	0	0	0	0	2	0	1	0	0	0	0	0	0	1	0	0	0	0
half-forgotten	2	.1814	.1187	30.7	0	0	0	1	1	0	0	0	1	0	0	0	0	0	0	0	0	0	0	0	0	0	0	1	0
half-formed	2	.1698	.1133	30.5	0	0	0	0	1	1	0	0	1	0	0	0	0	0	0	0	0	0	0	0	0	0	1	0	0
half-gallon	8	.1131	.2882	34.6	2	4	0	0	1	0	1	0	0	0	0	0	7	0	0	1	0	0	0	0	0	0	0	0	0
half-gallons	2	.0000	.0299	24.8	0	2	0	0	0	0	0	0	0	0	0	0	2	0	0	0	0	0	0	0	0	0	0	0	0
half-globes	2	.0000	.0389	25.9	0	0	0	2	0	0	0	0	0	0	0	0	0	2	0	0	0	0	0	0	0	0	0	0	0
half-grown	6	.5567	.7164	38.6	0	0	0	1	4	1	0	0	2	1	0	1	0	0	0	0	0	0	0	0	1	0	1	0	0
half-heartedly	3	.3450	.2505	34.0	1	1	0	0	1	0	0	0	1	0	0	0	0	0	0	0	0	0	0	0	1	1	0	0	0
half-hidden	2	.2152	.1357	31.3	1	0	1	0	0	0	0	0	1	0	0	0	0	1	0	0	0	0	0	0	0	0	0	0	0
half-hitch	2	.2427	.1152	30.6	0	0	0	0	0	1	0	1	0	0	0	0	0	0	0	0	0	0	0	0	1	1	0	0	0
half-hour	10	.3410	.8356	39.2	0	2	0	2	3	1	2	0	4	0	0	2	0	0	0	0	0	0	0	0	4	0	0	0	0
half-inch	3	.3849	.2503	34.0	0	0	0	0	1	0	1	1	0	1	0	0	1	0	0	0	0	0	0	0	0	0	0	1	0
half-life	4	.1494	.1609	32.1	0	0	0	1	2	1	0	0	0	0	0	0	0	0	0	1	0	0	0	0	0	0	3	0	0
half-light	3	.3394	.2451	33.9	0	0	0	1	1	0	1	0	1	0	0	1	0	0	0	0	0	0	0	0	1	0	0	0	0
half-line	7	.0000	.1048	30.2	0	0	0	0	6	0	1	0	0	0	0	0	7	0	0	0	0	0	0	0	0	0	0	0	0
half-lines	16	.0000	.2395	33.8	0	0	0	0	13	0	3	0	0	0	0	0	16	0	0	0	0	0	0	0	0	0	0	0	0
half-lives	2	.0000	.0209	23.2	0	0	0	0	2	0	0	0	0	0	0	0	0	0	0	0	0	0	0	0	0	0	2	0	0
half-mast	2	.2444	.1132	30.5	0	0	0	0	1	0	1	0	0	1	0	0	0	0	0	0	0	0	0	0	1	0	0	0	0
half-mile	10	.5487	1.2297	40.9	0	1	1	0	4	2	1	1	6	0	0	0	1	0	0	1	0	0	0	0	0	1	0	1	0
half-miler	2	.1948	.1250	31.0	0	0	0	0	1	1	0	0	1	0	0	0	0	0	0	0	0	0	0	0	0	1	0	0	0
half-moon	2	.2412	.1141	30.6	0	1	1	0	0	0	0	0	0	1	0	0	0	0	0	0	0	0	0	0	0	1	0	0	0
half-naked	3	.2060	.1500	31.8	0	0	1	0	0	1	1	0	0	0	0	2	0	0	0	0	0	0	0	0	0	1	0	0	0
half-note	3	.0000	.0243	23.8	0	2	1	0	0	0	0	0	0	0	0	0	0	0	0	0	3	0	0	0	0	0	0	0	0
half-ounce	2	.0000	.0219	23.4	0	0	0	0	0	2	0	0	0	2	0	0	0	0	0	0	0	0	0	0	0	0	0	0	0
half-past	16	.5450	1.9404	42.9	3	4	0	2	3	2	1	1	9	1	0	2	0	0	0	0	0	0	0	0	1	3	0	0	0
half-pint	3	.3800	.2528	34.0	1	0	1	0	0	1	0	0	0	0	0	0	1	0	0	1	0	0	0	0	1	0	0	0	0
half-plane	5	.0000	.0748	28.7	0	0	0	0	5	0	0	0	0	0	0	0	5	0	0	0	0	0	0	0	0	0	0	0	0
half-planes	5	.0000	.0748	28.7	0	0	0	0	5	0	0	0	0	0	0	0	5	0	0	0	0	0	0	0	0	0	0	0	0
half-round	2	.0000	.0050	17.0	0	0	0	0	0	1	1	0	0	0	0	0	0	0	0	0	0	0	0	2	0	0	0	0	0
half-shaved	2	.0000	.0234	23.7	0	0	0	0	0	2	0	0	0	0	0	0	0	0	0	0	0	0	0	0	2	0	0	0	0
half-squat	2	.0000	.0394	26.0	0	0	0	2	0	0	0	0	0	0	0	0	0	0	0	2	0	0	0	0	0	0	0	0	0
half-starved	4	.3721	.3657	35.6	0	0	1	0	2	1	0	0	2	0	0	1	0	0	0	0	0	0	0	0	0	1	0	0	0
half-step	2	.0000	.0162	22.1	0	0	0	1	1	0	0	0	0	0	0	0	0	0	0	0	2	0	0	0	0	0	0	0	0
half-submerged	2	.0000	.0914	29.6	0	0	0	1	0	1	0	0	2	0	0	0	0	0	0	0	0	0	0	0	0	0	0	0	0
half-timbered	2	.1738	.0790	29.0	1	0	0	0	1	0	0	0	0	0	0	0	0	0	0	0	0	0	0	1	0	0	1	0	0
half-time	6	.0526	.1436	31.6	0	0	0	0	0	6	0	0	1	0	0	0	0	0	0	0	5	0	0	0	0	0	0	0	0
half-way	7	.5636	.8615	39.4	3	0	0	3	1	0	0	0	3	0	0	0	1	1	0	0	0	0	0	0	1	1	0	0	0
half-wild	3	.1409	.1472	31.7	0	3	0	0	0	0	0	0	1	0	0	0	0	0	0	0	0	0	0	0	0	2	0	0	0
half's	2	.2446	.1142	30.6	0	0	0	1	1	0	0	0	0	0	0	0	0	0	0	0	0	0	0	0	1	0	0	1	0
halfback	3	.2212	.2099	33.2	0	0	0	1	1	1	0	0	2	0	0	1	0	0	0	0	0	0	0	0	0	0	0	0	0
halfbacks	3	.0000	.0591	27.7	0	0	0	3	0	0	0	0	0	0	0	0	0	0	0	3	0	0	0	0	0	0	0	0	0
halfbreed	2	.0000	.0234	23.7	0	2	0	0	0	0	0	0	0	0	0	0	0	0	0	0	0	0	0	0	2	0	0	0	0
halfheartedly	2	.2441	.1127	30.5	1	0	0	0	1	0	0	0	0	0	0	0	0	0	0	0	0	0	0	0	1	0	1	0	0
halftime	2	.0000	.0243	23.9	0	0	0	0	2	0	0	0	0	0	0	0	0	0	0	0	0	0	0	0	0	0	0	2	0
halftone	4	.1738	.1581	32.0	0	0	0	0	0	0	4	0	0	0	0	0	0	0	0	0	0	0	0	2	0	0	2	0	0
halfway	149	.9140	27.029	54.3	13	37	22	20	26	18	13	0	35	2	4	8	30	17	6	9	7	2	1	1	6	4	5	12	0
halibut	4	.1975	.2179	33.4	0	0	3	0	0	0	1	0	0	0	0	0	0	3	0	1	0	0	0	0	0	0	0	0	0
Halibut	2	.2444	.1132	30.5	1	0	1	0	0	0	0	0	0	1	0	0	0	0	0	0	0	0	0	0	1	0	0	0	0
Halifax	2	.2408	.1204	30.8	0	0	0	1	0	0	1	0	0	0	0	0	0	1	0	0	0	0	0	0	0	1	0	0	0
halite	6	.0000	.1183	30.7	0	0	0	0	0	4	2	0	0	0	0	0	0	0	0	6	0	0	0	0	0	0	0	0	0
hall	279	.8437	47.373	56.8	59	45	45	28	45	32	20	5	115	12	0	28	2	13	5	2	15	6	3	0	33	20	15	10	0
Hall	108	.8065	17.560	52.4	17	10	11	15	35	11	8	1	30	2	2	6	1	10	0	0	12	1	0	0	9	5	12	18	0
hallelujah	2	.2411	.1091	30.4	0	0	0	0	0	0	2	0	0	0	0	1	0	0	0	0	1	0	0	0	0	0	0	0	0
Hallelujah	7	.2250	.3611	35.6	2	1	0	0	4	0	0	0	0	0	0	0	0	0	0	0	5	0	0	0	1	1	0	0	0
HALLEMEIER	7	.0000	.0751	28.8	0	0	0	0	0	0	7	0	0	0	0	7	0	0	0	0	0	0	0	0	0	0	0	0	0
Halley	2	.1698	.1133	30.5	0	1	0	0	0	1	0	0	1	0	0	0	0	0	0	0	0	0	0	0	0	0	1	0	0
Halley's	10	.2213	.5740	37.6	0	4	0	0	1	0	0	5	0	0	0	0	0	0	0	8	0	0	0	0	0	0	2	0	0
Halliburton	2	.0000	.0219	23.4	0	0	0	0	0	0	2	0	0	2	0	0	0	0	0	0	0	0	0	0	0	0	0	0	0

5A hal-loo
6A Haleakala
3A Half-Chick's
7D half-Indian
6A half-admiring
6A half-an-hour
6N half-awake
9R half-back-option
7D half-bald
9L half-bang
6F half-barbarian
8A half-black
9D half-block
7N half-blown
4G half-boot
7B half-boots
7P half-brother
9Q half-built
8A half-burned
9Q half-century
7A half-choked
9D half-column
7A half-cropping
9D half-crying
3A half-darkness
7F half-day
3A half-dead
9D half-decks
7D half-degree
7N half-devoured
8A half-dissolved
9P half-dozed
7N half-drunken
5H half-empty
XB half-familiar
6A half-foot
5A half-full
4A half-gay
9D half-grin
6R half-hearted
7F half-island
9D half-laughing
5N half-looking
7E half-million
7D half-moons
5N half-not-looking
7N half-open
5N half-opened
6N half-piece
9L half-pound
8N half-reluctantly
8A half-reveal
7N half-rotten
7E half-ruined
6N half-savage
7A half-scream
4A half-serious
3A half-shut
7P half-sister
4P half-slouched
7A half-smiled
8N half-sob
7F half-sphere
8E half-spheres
8N half-started
6J half-steps
6R half-stood
3N half-suspended
7N half-tamed
7R half-told
6J half-tones
7L half-truths
9N half-turned
7E half-unit
3E half-units
7D half-white
5A half-witted
3P half-won
7D half-world
4A halfhearted
6R halfmile
5N halfpenny
9M halfround
5A Halfway
4N halfways
5P Halket
3A Hall-Heroult
7N hall-oo
9D hall's
3A Hall's
7R Hallam
7Q Halleck
7N Hallek
5A hallelujah
5J Hallelujahs
9D HALLENMEIER
9B Halliburton's

Word Type	F	D	U	SFI	3 Gr 3	4 Gr 4	5 Gr 5	6 Gr 6	7 Gr 7	8 Gr 8	9 Gr 9	X UnGr	A Read	B Eng & Gr	C Comp	D Lit	E Math	F Soc Stud	G Spell	H Sci	J Music	K Art	L Home Ec	M Shop	N Lib F	P Lib NF	Q Lib Ref	R Mag	S Rel
Halliday	3	.0000	.1370	31.4	0	0	0	0	3	0	0	0	3	0	0	0	0	0	0	0	0	0	0	0	0	0	0	0	0
Hallidie	2	.0000	.0914	29.6	0	0	0	2	0	0	0	0	2	0	0	0	0	0	0	0	0	0	0	0	0	0	0	0	0
Hallie	2	.1494	.1045	30.2	0	1	0	1	0	0	0	0	1	0	0	0	0	0	0	0	1	0	0	0	0	0	0	0	0
hallo	3	.0000	.1370	31.4	1	0	0	2	0	0	0	0	3	0	0	0	0	0	0	0	0	0	0	0	0	0	0	0	0
halloo	2	.0000	.0914	29.6	0	0	2	0	0	0	0	0	2	0	0	0	0	0	0	0	0	0	0	0	0	0	0	0	0
hallow	2	.2297	.1135	30.6	0	0	0	0	0	2	0	0	0	0	0	1	0	1	0	0	0	0	0	0	0	0	0	0	0
Hallowe'en	7	.4102	.6130	37.9	2	3	0	2	0	0	0	0	1	0	2	0	0	0	0	0	2	1	0	0	0	1	0	0	0
hallowed	5	.0996	.1423	31.5	1	0	2	2	0	0	0	0	0	0	0	0	0	0	0	0	1	0	0	0	0	2	0	1	1
Halloween	53	.7411	8.0750	49.1	32	8	6	2	2	2	1	0	23	4	0	2	5	0	6	0	2	2	0	0	1	4	0	4	0
Halloweening	3	.0000	.1370	31.4	0	3	0	0	0	0	0	0	3	0	0	0	0	0	0	0	0	0	0	0	0	0	0	0	0
halls	47	.6399	6.1968	47.9	2	6	3	4	10	10	10	2	7	3	0	6	0	2	0	6	14	0	0	0	4	2	2	1	0
hallucinations	4	.2278	.2257	33.5	0	0	0	0	0	0	4	0	0	0	0	0	0	0	0	2	0	0	0	0	0	0	2	0	0
hallway	20	.5385	2.3799	43.8	4	5	2	0	4	1	3	1	10	1	0	3	0	0	0	0	0	0	0	0	4	0	0	2	0
hallways	2	.1787	.1174	30.7	0	0	0	2	0	0	0	0	1	0	0	0	0	0	0	0	0	0	0	0	1	0	0	0	0
Halmoni	3	.0000	.1370	31.4	0	3	0	0	0	0	0	0	3	0	0	0	0	0	0	0	0	0	0	0	0	0	0	0	0
halo	12	.5774	1.4573	41.6	1	1	1	2	5	0	1	1	2	1	0	0	0	0	0	4	1	1	0	0	0	1	2	0	0
halos	3	.2445	.1818	32.6	1	0	0	0	0	0	0	2	0	0	0	0	0	0	0	2	0	0	0	0	0	0	1	0	0
Halpern	2	.0000	.0243	23.9	0	0	0	0	0	0	2	0	0	0	0	0	0	0	0	0	0	0	0	0	0	0	0	2	0
Hals	2	.0000	.0209	23.2	0	0	0	0	0	0	0	2	0	0	0	0	0	0	0	0	0	0	0	0	0	0	2	0	0
Halstead	5	.0000	.2284	33.6	0	0	0	0	0	5	0	0	5	0	0	0	0	0	0	0	0	0	0	0	0	0	0	0	0
halt	44	.7167	6.4732	48.1	1	5	3	5	15	7	8	0	12	2	0	5	0	5	0	1	0	0	0	0	3	4	3	9	0
Halt	2	.2446	.1123	30.5	0	0	0	1	0	1	0	0	0	1	0	0	0	0	0	0	0	0	0	0	0	0	1	0	0
halted	23	.6228	3.0102	44.8	1	4	2	7	5	1	3	0	7	0	0	2	0	1	0	0	0	0	0	0	6	2	2	3	0
halter	16	.4995	1.7302	42.4	1	2	1	5	3	2	2	0	4	0	0	4	0	0	0	0	0	0	0	0	5	0	1	2	0
halteres	2	.0000	.0209	23.2	0	0	2	0	0	0	0	0	0	0	0	0	0	0	0	0	0	0	0	0	0	0	2	0	0
halters	3	.2357	.2199	33.4	0	1	2	0	0	0	0	0	2	0	0	0	0	0	0	0	0	0	0	0	0	1	0	0	0
halting	5	.4281	.4726	36.7	0	0	1	0	3	1	0	0	1	1	0	1	0	0	0	0	0	0	0	0	2	0	0	0	0
halts	9	.5580	1.0544	40.2	1	0	1	1	2	2	1	1	1	0	0	1	0	0	0	1	0	0	0	0	0	3	2	1	0
halve	3	.2346	.1705	32.3	0	0	1	0	1	1	0	0	0	0	0	0	2	0	0	0	0	0	0	0	0	0	0	1	0
halved	2	.2413	.1212	30.8	0	0	0	0	1	1	0	0	0	0	0	0	1	0	0	1	0	0	0	0	0	0	0	0	0
halves	69	.7384	10.308	50.1	21	9	5	5	17	6	3	3	5	1	0	3	26	1	1	13	5	0	3	0	3	5	2	1	0
halyards	2	.1843	.0808	29.1	0	1	0	0	1	0	0	0	0	0	1	0	0	0	0	0	1	0	0	0	0	0	0	0	0
ham	69	.6620	9.5139	49.8	21	11	4	3	5	3	19	3	25	5	0	7	5	3	2	0	1	0	10	0	3	1	3	4	0
Ham	12	.2424	.9107	39.6	3	0	0	4	2	0	3	0	9	0	0	0	0	0	0	0	0	0	0	0	0	0	0	3	0
Haman	4	.1494	.2089	33.2	0	2	0	0	0	2	0	0	2	0	0	0	0	0	0	0	2	0	0	0	0	0	0	0	0
Hambletonian	3	.0000	.0434	26.4	0	3	0	0	0	0	0	0	0	0	0	0	0	0	0	0	0	0	0	0	0	3	0	0	0
Hambletonian's	2	.0000	.0290	24.6	0	2	0	0	0	0	0	0	0	0	0	0	0	0	0	0	0	0	0	0	0	2	0	0	0
hamburg	2	.0000	.0234	23.7	0	2	0	0	0	0	0	0	0	0	0	0	0	0	0	0	0	0	0	0	2	0	0	0	0
Hamburg	6	.4789	.6071	37.8	0	0	1	2	2	1	0	0	0	1	0	0	0	2	1	0	0	0	0	0	2	0	0	0	0
hamburger	28	.6639	3.9034	45.9	11	6	2	2	2	1	4	0	12	4	0	2	4	0	2	0	0	0	0	0	1	3	0	0	0
hamburgers	22	.7170	3.2156	45.1	5	4	3	1	2	3	4	0	4	4	0	1	5	2	1	0	0	0	1	0	3	0	0	1	0
Hamelin	11	.3308	.9525	39.8	3	0	0	0	8	0	0	0	7	0	0	1	0	0	0	0	3	0	0	0	0	0	0	0	0
hames	2	.2411	.1091	30.4	0	0	1	0	1	0	0	0	0	0	0	1	0	0	0	0	1	0	0	0	0	0	0	0	0
Hamilton	60	.5446	7.1333	48.5	3	8	25	6	7	9	2	0	20	0	0	1	0	24	1	0	0	0	0	0	0	4	9	1	0
Hamilton's	13	.5309	1.5155	41.8	0	0	7	1	2	2	1	0	5	0	0	1	2	2	0	0	0	0	0	0	0	0	3	0	0
Hamitic	2	.0000	.0389	25.9	0	0	0	0	2	0	0	0	0	0	0	0	0	2	0	0	0	0	0	0	0	0	0	0	0
hamlet	6	.1787	.3521	35.5	0	1	0	1	3	1	0	0	3	0	0	0	0	0	0	0	0	0	0	0	3	0	0	0	0
Hamlet	29	.1838	1.6076	42.1	6	0	23	0	0	0	0	0	5	0	0	0	0	23	0	0	0	0	0	0	0	0	1	0	0
Hamlet's	2	.1787	.1174	30.7	1	1	0	0	0	0	0	0	1	0	0	0	0	0	0	0	0	0	0	0	1	0	0	0	0
Hamlin	2	.0000	.0219	23.4	0	0	0	0	0	2	0	0	0	2	0	0	0	0	0	0	0	0	0	0	0	0	0	0	0
Hammarskjold	3	.0000	.0583	27.7	0	0	0	0	0	1	2	0	0	0	0	0	0	3	0	0	0	0	0	0	0	0	0	0	0
Hamme	2	.0000	.0243	23.9	0	0	2	0	0	0	0	0	0	0	0	0	0	0	0	0	0	0	0	0	0	0	0	2	0
hammer	155	.6392	20.519	53.1	24	16	14	17	47	25	9	3	36	0	3	21	0	1	0	17	10	1	0	25	7	18	4	12	0
Hammer	3	.2321	.1635	32.1	0	0	0	0	1	0	0	2	0	0	0	0	0	0	0	0	0	0	0	0	0	0	1	2	0
HAMMER	2	.0000	.0290	24.6	2	0	0	0	0	0	0	0	0	0	0	0	0	0	0	0	0	0	0	0	0	2	0	0	0
hammer'll	2	.0000	.0914	29.6	0	0	0	0	2	0	0	0	2	0	0	0	0	0	0	0	0	0	0	0	0	0	0	0	0
hammered	32	.6606	4.3957	46.4	4	5	3	3	7	5	3	2	10	0	1	2	0	1	0	5	4	0	0	3	1	0	0	5	0
Hammerfest	3	.0000	.0583	27.7	0	3	0	0	0	0	0	0	0	0	0	0	0	3	0	0	0	0	0	0	0	0	0	0	0
hammerhead	13	.3188	.9890	40.0	0	2	0	5	6	0	0	0	3	0	0	0	0	0	0	0	0	0	0	0	5	0	0	5	0
hammering	41	.5547	4.6973	46.7	1	5	1	1	9	13	4	7	2	0	0	11	0	0	0	1	1	0	0	5	5	4	0	12	0
hammers	22	.6990	3.0826	44.9	5	3	2	1	10	0	1	0	0	0	1	1	0	0	0	1	6	1	0	2	3	0	4	3	0
Hammerstein	5	.1101	.1543	31.9	0	0	0	1	1	3	0	0	0	0	0	0	0	1	0	0	4	0	0	0	0	0	0	0	0
hammock	14	.5810	1.6755	42.2	3	2	0	1	5	0	2	1	1	3	2	1	0	0	0	1	1	0	0	0	1	1	0	3	0
hammocks	9	.4260	.8797	39.4	1	1	0	2	4	0	0	1	3	0	0	3	0	2	0	0	0	0	0	0	1	0	0	0	0
Hammond	3	.0000	.0314	25.0	0	3	0	0	0	0	0	0	0	0	0	0	0	0	0	0	0	0	0	0	0	0	3	0	0
hamper	4	.4456	.3981	36.0	0	0	1	0	2	0	1	0	1	0	0	1	0	1	0	0	0	0	0	0	0	0	1	0	0
hampered	9	.4926	.9493	39.8	2	0	2	2	2	0	1	0	1	0	0	0	0	1	0	0	0	0	0	0	0	3	2	2	0
hampers	2	.0000	.0290	24.6	1	1	0	0	0	0	0	0	0	0	0	0	0	0	0	0	0	0	0	0	0	2	0	0	0
Hampshire	2	.1494	.1045	30.2	0	0	0	0	2	0	0	0	1	0	0	0	0	0	0	0	1	0	0	0	0	0	0	0	0
Hampstead	2	.1493	.0692	28.4	0	0	0	0	0	0	2	0	0	0	0	0	0	0	0	0	0	1	0	0	0	0	1	0	0
Hampton	14	.5552	1.6600	42.2	1	5	1	0	3	2	1	1	4	0	0	1	0	0	0	0	1	0	0	0	0	1	2	5	0
hams	16	.5247	1.8104	42.6	4	5	3	1	2	0	1	0	4	0	0	1	0	2	0	0	0	0	0	0	6	1	2	0	0
hamster	5	.3775	.4753	36.8	1	0	0	0	3	1	0	0	3	1	0	0	0	0	0	1	0	0	0	0	0	0	0	0	0
hamsters	14	.5023	1.4800	41.7	9	0	0	0	2	1	2	0	0	3	0	0	4	0	0	1	0	0	0	0	0	5	0	1	0
Hamwi	4	.0000	.1827	32.6	0	4	0	0	0	0	0	0	4	0	0	0	0	0	0	0	0	0	0	0	0	0	0	0	0
han	2	.0000	.0162	22.1	0	0	0	2	0	0	0	0	0	0	0	0	0	0	0	0	2	0	0	0	0	0	0	0	0
Hanae	3	.0000	.0365	25.6	0	0	0	0	0	0	0	3	0	0	0	0	0	0	0	0	0	0	0	0	0	0	0	3	0
Hancock	15	.5302	1.7909	42.5	0	0	2	9	2	2	0	0	9	2	0	0	0	1	0	0	0	0	0	0	0	0	2	1	0
hand	2316	.9185	422.15	66.3	345	375	214	325	537	263	235	22	682	59	23	214	97	109	25	184	163	17	64	112	235	181	64	86	1
Hand	8	.5600	.9869	39.9	0	0	1	0	1	4	1	1	4	0	0	0	1	1	0	0	0	0	0	0	0	1	1	0	0
hand-clapping	5	.2063	.2450	33.9	0	1	1	3	0	0	0	0	0	0	0	0	0	0	0	0	3	0	0	0	0	2	0	0	0
hand-picked	2	.2427	.1152	30.6	1	0	0	0	0	0	1	0	0	0	0	0	0	0	0	0	0	0	0	0	1	1	0	0	0
hand-to-hand	5	.3761	.4737	36.8	0	0	1	0	2	1	1	0	3	0	0	0	0	1	0	0	0	0	0	0	0	0	1	0	0
hand's	5	.4746	.5335	37.3	0	0	0	1	2	1	1	0	2	1	0	0	1	0	0	0	0	0	0	0	0	0	1	0	0
Hand's	3	.0000	.1370	31.4	0	0	0	0	0	3	0	0	3	0	0	0	0	0	0	0	0	0	0	0	0	0	0	0	0
handbags	2	.0000	.0389	25.9	1	1	0	0	0	0	0	0	0	0	0	0	0	2	0	0	0	0	0	0	0	0	0	0	0
handball	3	.2279	.2143	33.3	1	0	0	0	1	1	0	0	2	0	0	0	0	0	0	0	0	0	0	0	0	0	0	1	0
handbill	2	.0000	.0914	29.6	0	0	2	0	0	0	0	0	2	0	0	0	0	0	0	0	0	0	0	0	0	0	0	0	0
handbills	6	.4044	.5466	37.4	0	0	1	0	4	1	0	0	1	0	0	0	3	0	0	0	0	0	0	0	0	1	0	1	0
handbook	5	.4587	.4755	36.8	0	1	0	0	3	0	1	0	0	1	1	0	0	0	0	1	0	0	0	1	0	0	1	0	0
Handbook	17	.0649	.3940	36.0	1	2	3	0	8	2	0	1	0	16	0	0	0	0	0	0	0	0	0	0	0	1	0	0	0
handbooks	5	.3399	.3636	35.6	0	0	0	0	0	1	4	0	0	1	0	0	0	0	0	0	0	0	0	1	0	0	3	0	0

XB hallmark
6R Hallmark
3A hallmarked
9Q hallmarks
4A Halloweens
XR hallucinogenic
5Q halogens
7R Halon
4J Halowe'en
7D haltered
6A haltingly
8Q Halton
4F halv
4F halvoy**
4A halyard
8A hamadryad
XH Hamal
8Q Hamatreya
9R hambone
3A Hamburger
5Q Hamiltonians
4A Hamiltons'
6J Hamishah
5P Hamite
5P Hamite-Negro
7F Hamites
8D hamlets
XR Hammacher-Schlemmer
5P Hammer-Handle
7R hammer-thrower
7R hammerhead's
7R hammerheads
5J hammerin'
8R Hammerin'
XR hammermill
6F Hammurabi
6A Hampden
7R hampering
4A Hampton's
4A Hamwi's
8F Han
7A han'
8A Han's
6A Hana
7C Hance's
8F Hancock's
3P HAND
7N hand-barrow
3Q hand-blown
6A hand-clappings
3P hand-crafted
9C hand-crank
6R hand-cutting
6A hand-drawn
9N hand-forged
9M hand-hammering
7H hand-held
9D hand-hold
4A hand-knitted
3A hand-lettered
4F hand-made
5D hand-me-down
5N hand-painted
3N hand-pick
8L hand-printed
7M hand-screw
7L hand-sew
6J hand-sewn
7H hand-sized
7L hand-stitching
7Q hand-stuffed
3Q hand-sucking
8F hand-talk
7M hand-tool
9P hand-washing
7F hand-woven
7P hand-writing
8B handbag

Word Type	F	D	U	SFI	3 Gr 3	4 Gr 4	5 Gr 5	6 Gr 6	7 Gr 7	8 Gr 8	9 Gr 9	X UnGr	A Read	B Eng & Gr	C Comp	D Lit	E Math	F Soc Stud	G Spell	H Sci	J Music	K Art	L Home Ec	M Shop	N Lib F	P Lib NF	Q Lib Ref	R Mag	S Rel
handcarts	2	.2375	.1088	30.4	0	0	1	0	0	0	0	1	0	0	0	0	0	0	0	0	1	0	0	0	0	0	0	0	0
handcrafts	2	.0000	.0389	25.9	0	0	2	0	0	0	0	0	0	0	0	0	2	0	0	0	0	0	0	0	0	0	0	0	0
handcuffs	6	.1814	.3560	35.5	0	2	2	1	1	0	0	0	3	0	0	0	0	0	0	0	0	0	0	0	0	0	0	3	0
handed	196	.8223	32.598	55.1	33	44	16	27	40	20	13	3	83	12	1	16	5	8	0	1	3	1	1	0	27	23	2	13	0
Handel	25	.2011	.1655	40.7	2	3	8	3	3	5	1	0	0	0	0	0	0	0	0	0	20	0	0	0	0	1	0	0	0
Handel's	4	.1534	.1534	31.9	0	0	2	2	0	0	0	0	0	0	0	0	0	0	0	0	3	0	0	0	0	0	0	0	0
handful	66	.8330	11.079	50.4	14	9	6	9	16	9	3	0	24	0	1	0	6	1	5	2	4	1	0	0	6	8	4	4	0
handfuls	8	.5643	.9459	39.8	0	3	1	1	2	1	0	0	1	0	0	0	1	0	1	0	0	0	0	0	2	1	1	0	0
handgun	3	.0000	.0365	25.6	0	0	0	0	3	0	0	0	0	0	0	0	0	0	0	0	0	0	0	0	0	0	0	3	0
handguns	2	.0000	.0243	23.9	0	0	0	0	2	0	0	0	0	0	0	0	0	0	0	0	0	0	0	0	0	0	0	2	0
handholds	2	.2446	.1142	30.6	1	0	0	1	0	0	0	0	1	0	0	0	0	0	0	0	0	0	0	0	1	0	0	1	0
handicap	8	.4210	.7739	38.9	0	3	1	2	1	1	0	0	2	0	0	0	1	0	2	0	0	0	0	0	3	0	0	0	0
handicapped	24	.5582	2.7896	44.5	0	1	16	1	1	2	3	0	2	0	0	1	0	0	3	1	0	1	0	0	0	0	7	9	0
handicaps	11	.5177	1.1890	40.8	3	0	2	3	2	0	1	0	0	0	0	0	4	0	1	0	0	1	0	0	0	0	4	0	0
handicraft	7	.5288	.7914	39.0	3	1	1	0	0	0	2	0	1	0	0	0	2	0	0	0	0	0	0	0	1	2	1	0	0
handicrafts	12	.5995	1.4811	41.7	3	0	0	0	5	0	3	1	0	0	0	0	4	0	0	0	1	0	0	0	3	2	1	0	0
handing	26	.7228	3.8737	45.9	3	9	1	3	3	2	3	2	10	1	0	3	0	2	1	0	0	1	0	0	3	3	0	2	0
handiwork	12	.6713	1.6580	42.2	2	2	1	0	3	1	2	1	2	0	0	1	0	2	0	0	0	1	0	0	0	2	1	2	0
handkerchief	68	.7612	10.563	50.2	15	21	9	4	9	5	3	2	22	3	2	2	0	3	4	10	2	0	0	0	7	13	0	1	0
handkerchiefs	22	.5558	2.6528	44.2	1	2	4	8	1	4	1	1	9	1	0	0	0	5	0	0	0	0	0	2	0	0	1	0	0
handle	301	.8405	50.729	57.1	51	44	25	35	75	38	28	5	84	9	10	16	1	26	5	22	7	1	15	21	26	26	8	24	0
handle-bar	2	.0000	.0290	24.6	2	0	0	0	0	0	0	0	2	0	0	0	0	0	0	0	0	0	0	0	0	0	0	0	0
handlebar	3	.2754	.1835	32.6	0	0	0	1	0	1	1	0	0	0	0	0	0	0	0	0	0	1	0	0	1	0	0	1	0
handled	59	.8097	9.5996	49.8	3	6	5	8	19	6	10	2	11	2	0	3	0	9	1	6	3	0	3	4	2	5	4	6	0
handler	4	.2805	.2842	34.5	0	0	0	0	2	2	0	0	1	0	0	0	0	0	0	0	0	0	0	0	2	0	0	0	0
handlers	4	.3658	.3646	35.6	0	0	0	0	2	2	0	0	2	0	0	0	0	1	0	0	0	0	0	0	1	0	0	0	0
handles	59	.7331	8.7590	49.4	10	7	8	8	19	4	2	1	7	2	0	0	0	7	0	4	3	0	0	5	6	8	7	8	0
handling	92	.7953	14.676	51.7	6	6	3	7	26	11	30	3	11	3	1	4	0	6	0	12	1	1	10	5	4	10	8	16	0
handloads	2	.0000	.0243	23.9	0	0	0	0	2	0	0	0	0	0	0	0	0	0	0	0	0	0	0	0	0	0	0	2	0
handmade	11	.5316	1.2434	40.9	1	1	0	3	2	1	0	3	2	0	0	0	0	3	0	0	0	0	2	0	1	0	1	1	0
handmaidens	4	.3604	.3536	35.5	0	0	1	1	1	0	0	1	2	0	0	0	0	0	0	0	1	0	0	0	0	0	1	0	0
handrails	2	.0000	.0394	26.0	0	0	1	0	1	0	0	0	0	0	0	0	0	0	0	2	0	0	0	0	0	0	0	0	0
hands	1357	.8929	241.40	63.8	222	216	179	199	264	139	123	15	421	25	12	187	23	69	9	82	74	14	17	7	183	136	26	72	0
Hands	3	.3431	.2528	34.0	1	0	0	0	1	1	0	0	1	0	0	0	0	1	0	0	0	0	0	0	1	0	0	0	0
hands-off	2	.1814	.1187	30.7	0	0	0	0	1	0	0	1	1	0	0	0	0	0	0	0	0	0	0	0	0	1	0	0	0
handset	4	.0000	.0419	26.2	0	0	0	0	0	0	0	4	0	0	0	0	0	0	0	0	0	0	0	0	0	0	0	4	0
handshake	4	.4522	.3988	36.0	0	1	0	1	0	0	2	0	0	0	0	0	0	0	0	0	0	0	0	0	1	1	0	0	0
handshakes	3	.0000	.0365	25.6	0	0	0	0	2	0	0	0	0	0	0	0	0	0	0	0	0	0	0	0	0	0	0	3	0
handsome	155	.8683	26.887	54.3	14	20	19	32	36	17	15	2	45	12	2	20	0	12	3	1	10	3	2	0	17	11	2	15	0
Handsome	2	.2446	.1125	30.5	0	0	0	1	1	0	0	0	0	1	0	1	0	0	0	0	0	0	0	0	0	0	0	0	0
handsomely	7	.4654	.6836	38.3	0	2	2	0	0	1	0	0	2	0	0	0	0	0	0	0	2	0	0	0	1	2	0	2	0
handsomer	4	.3726	.3697	35.7	0	0	1	2	0	1	0	0	2	0	0	0	0	0	0	0	0	0	0	0	1	0	0	0	0
handsomest	9	.3679	.8453	39.3	1	1	0	1	0	5	0	0	6	0	1	0	0	1	0	0	0	0	0	0	0	0	0	1	0
handstand	2	.2440	.1132	30.5	0	0	1	1	0	0	0	0	0	0	0	0	0	0	0	0	0	0	0	0	0	0	0	1	0
handwheel	5	.0613	.0833	29.2	0	0	0	0	1	0	0	4	0	0	0	0	0	0	0	0	0	0	0	0	0	1	0	0	0
handwriting	60	.6266	7.7366	48.9	8	17	3	11	9	10	2	0	10	21	5	1	0	1	13	0	1	0	0	0	2	3	0	2	0
Handwriting	49	.0000	.3977	36.0	4	8	18	19	0	0	0	0	0	0	0	0	0	0	49	0	0	0	0	0	0	0	0	0	0
handwritten	5	.0000	.0547	27.4	0	0	0	0	4	0	0	1	0	5	0	0	0	0	0	0	0	0	0	0	0	0	0	0	0
handy	47	.7665	7.2804	48.6	7	9	2	3	11	6	5	4	11	3	1	3	0	0	0	0	1	1	1	4	9	2	1	10	0
handyman	2	.2441	.1127	30.5	0	1	0	0	0	1	0	0	0	0	0	0	0	0	0	0	0	0	0	0	0	0	0	0	0
Haneda	2	.2285	.1129	30.5	0	1	1	0	0	0	0	0	0	0	0	0	0	1	0	0	0	0	0	0	0	0	1	0	0
hang	159	.9278	29.244	54.7	38	33	19	20	26	13	6	4	44	6	1	11	1	7	4	21	8	1	2	1	19	19	7	7	0
hangar	2	.0000	.0914	29.6	0	0	0	2	0	0	0	0	2	0	0	0	0	0	0	0	0	0	0	0	0	0	0	0	0
hangars	2	.0000	.0914	29.6	0	0	0	1	1	0	0	0	2	0	0	0	0	0	0	0	0	0	0	0	0	0	0	0	0
hanged	17	.5123	1.9240	42.8	1	3	4	4	2	2	3	0	6	1	0	4	0	5	0	0	0	0	0	0	1	1	0	0	0
hanger	6	.4696	.6014	37.8	0	1	1	1	2	0	0	0	0	0	0	0	0	0	0	2	0	0	0	0	1	1	0	0	0
hangers	4	.2171	.2287	33.6	2	1	0	0	0	0	0	1	0	0	0	0	1	0	0	3	0	0	0	0	0	0	0	0	0
hangin'	2	.2443	.1130	30.5	1	0	0	0	1	0	0	0	0	0	0	1	0	0	0	0	0	0	0	0	1	0	0	0	0
hanging	205	.8595	35.373	55.5	39	39	23	26	41	15	18	4	84	6	2	22	0	7	2	12	5	3	1	0	27	17	8	9	0
Hanging	2	.0000	.0209	23.2	0	2	0	0	0	0	0	0	0	0	0	0	0	0	0	0	0	0	0	0	0	0	2	0	0
hangman	2	.1717	.1142	30.6	0	0	0	0	1	0	0	1	1	0	0	1	0	0	0	0	0	0	0	0	0	0	0	0	0
hangnails	2	.1432	.0759	28.8	0	1	0	0	0	1	0	0	0	0	0	0	0	0	0	1	0	0	1	0	0	0	0	0	0
hangs	60	.7937	9.6005	49.8	10	6	12	9	17	3	3	0	12	3	2	6	0	8	1	8	0	3	3	0	2	7	0	5	0
Hank	118	.4102	11.695	50.7	24	7	2	7	40	38	0	0	68	0	0	0	5	0	1	0	0	0	0	0	39	0	0	0	0
Hank's	11	.2384	.8205	39.1	1	2	0	2	3	3	0	0	8	0	0	0	0	0	0	0	0	0	0	0	3	0	0	0	0
hankering	2	.0000	.0234	23.7	0	2	0	0	0	0	0	0	0	0	0	0	0	0	0	0	0	0	0	0	2	0	0	0	0
Hanks	9	.1010	.3518	35.5	0	6	0	1	1	0	0	1	2	0	0	0	0	0	0	0	0	0	0	0	7	0	0	0	0
hanky	2	.2375	.1088	30.4	0	1	0	0	0	0	1	0	0	0	0	0	0	0	0	1	0	0	0	0	0	0	0	1	0
Hannah	17	.3914	1.4841	41.7	1	8	2	1	4	0	1	0	2	0	0	2	0	0	0	0	0	0	0	0	4	9	0	0	0
Hannibal	11	.0976	.4103	36.1	0	0	1	0	3	0	7	0	3	0	0	0	0	0	0	0	0	0	0	0	0	0	8	0	0
Hanno	4	.0000	.0778	28.9	0	0	0	4	0	0	0	0	0	0	0	0	0	4	0	0	0	0	0	0	0	0	0	0	0
Hanoi	8	.1001	.2513	34.0	0	0	0	1	1	0	6	0	0	0	0	0	0	0	0	0	0	0	0	0	0	0	1	7	0
Hanover	3	.3833	.2447	33.9	0	0	0	0	1	2	0	0	0	0	0	0	0	1	0	1	0	0	0	0	0	1	0	0	0
Hanratty	11	.0000	.1337	31.3	0	0	0	10	1	0	0	0	0	0	0	0	0	0	0	0	0	0	0	0	0	0	0	11	0
Hans	85	.7226	12.727	51.0	5	14	9	31	11	4	8	3	42	7	1	17	0	1	1	2	4	3	0	0	0	3	3	1	0
Hans'	3	.0000	.0322	25.1	0	0	0	0	0	0	3	0	0	0	0	0	0	0	0	0	0	0	0	0	0	0	2	0	0
Hansel	40	.4375	4.1265	46.2	29	0	0	10	0	0	1	0	23	0	0	11	0	0	0	0	4	0	0	0	0	0	2	0	0
Hansen	13	.3377	.9748	39.9	0	8	0	1	3	0	1	0	0	0	0	0	0	3	0	0	1	0	0	0	1	0	0	0	0
Hanson	2	.2387	.1089	30.4	0	1	0	0	0	0	0	1	0	0	0	0	0	0	0	0	0	0	0	0	1	0	0	0	0
Hansonville	4	.0000	.1827	32.6	0	0	0	4	0	0	0	0	4	0	0	0	0	0	0	0	0	0	0	0	0	0	0	0	0
Hanukkah	5	.0000	.0404	26.1	0	0	0	0	1	4	0	0	0	0	0	0	0	0	0	0	0	5	0	0	0	0	0	0	0
Hap	3	.1187	.1291	31.1	0	0	0	0	1	0	2	0	1	0	0	2	0	0	0	0	0	0	0	0	0	0	0	0	0
haphazard	5	.3004	.3386	35.3	1	1	0	1	1	0	0	1	0	1	0	0	0	0	0	0	0	0	0	0	0	0	3	0	0
haphazardly	2	.2351	.1166	30.7	0	0	0	0	1	0	1	0	0	0	0	1	0	0	0	0	0	0	0	0	0	0	2	0	0
hapless	3	.1169	.1277	31.1	0	0	0	0	2	0	0	1	1	0	0	0	0	0	0	0	0	0	0	0	0	0	2	0	0
happen	468	.9050	84.270	59.3	76	115	78	50	78	45	19	7	131	28	7	30	12	26	9	107	8	1	4	1	36	36	7	25	0
happened	910	.8692	158.76	62.0	228	161	112	113	128	98	61	9	419	79	12	82	6	49	24	57	11	6	5	0	66	59	3	32	0
happening	179	.7454	27.166	54.3	36	36	27	33	24	13	10	0	43	14	16	13	5	22	5	19	4	1	1	0	12	12	0	13	0
happenings	42	.6064	5.3238	47.3	7	6	5	9	6	4	5	0	11	2	7	4	0	2	1	2	2	0	1	0	3	3	4	0	0
happens	520	.8356	87.046	59.4	128	105	68	49	79	50	30	11	59	21	2	22	20	27	27	256	18	4	7	4	7	13	13	20	0
happier	51	.8007	8.2490	49.2	6	10	4	8	10	7	3	3	15	2	2	6	0	4	2	4	2	0	2	0	3	1	7	3	0
happiest	27	.7615	4.1961	46.2	4	4	8	4	3	2	2	0	10	0	1	2	0	2	2	0	1	0	0	4	1	1	3	0	0
happily	143	.8168	23.701	53.7	49	27	12	18	21	10	4	2	71	1	1	12	0	5	2	5	1	1	3	0	18	11	1	13	0
happiness	79	.8185	13.005	51.1	10	11	9	9	13	12	13	2	21	2	0	12	0	0	7	2	0	1	1	3	10	6	4	10	0

4P handcar	3P Handicraft	3A handprints	8R hang-ups
5J handcart	6P handie	7R handsaw	6A hangar-top
9H handclap	6G handier	7N handspike	6F Hangchow
9D handclasps	6P handies	3N handspring	8D hange'd
7D handfulla	7R handlebars	3A handsprings	7R hangers-on
7R handgun-carrying	7D Handley	4R handstands	8L hangings
7R handheld	7D Handley-Page	3H handwoven	9D hangman's
5N handhold	3H handloom	8J Handy	8Q Hanibal
4P Handicap	8F handmarks	5A handy-boy	6N Hankinsons
5R Handicapped	3K handprint	6N hang-dog	5Q Hankow

8D Hanlon	5R HAPPENED
9Q Hannibal's	9D happenin's
XR Hansbrough-Newlands	4F Happens
5P Hanseatic	7A Happily
3A Hansel's	7A Happiness
4N Hansen's	
XR Hanslin	
3A hap'	
4R Hapgood	
8D Happened	

Word Type	F	D	U	SFI	3 Gr 3	4 Gr 4	5 Gr 5	6 Gr 6	7 Gr 7	8 Gr 8	9 Gr 9	X UnGr	A Read	B Eng & Gr	C Comp	D Lit	E Math	F Soc Stud	G Spell	H Sci	J Music	K Art	L Home Ec	M Shop	N Lib F	P Lib NF	Q Lib Ref	R Mag	S Rel
happy	774	.9062	139.55	61.4	229	147	84	96	75	76	52	15	282	62	15	58	2	26	25	13	55	8	27	0	70	71	5	54	1
Happy	21	.7343	3.1529	45.0	5	0	2	2	6	1	5	0	6	2	0	3	2	1	0	0	2	0	0	0	1	3	0	1	0
happy-go-lucky	3	.2279	.2143	33.3	0	0	0	1	1	1	0	0	2	0	0	0	0	0	0	0	0	0	0	0	0	0	0	1	0
Hapsburg	2	.0000	.0389	25.9	0	0	0	0	0	0	2	0	0	0	0	0	0	2	0	0	0	0	0	0	0	0	0	0	0
Hapsburgs	2	.0000	.0290	24.6	0	0	2	0	0	0	0	0	0	0	0	0	0	0	0	0	0	0	0	0	0	2	0	0	0
Harald	2	.0000	.0389	25.9	0	2	0	0	0	0	0	0	0	0	0	0	0	2	0	0	0	0	0	0	0	0	0	0	0
harambee	2	.0000	.0243	23.9	0	0	0	2	0	0	0	0	0	0	0	0	0	0	0	0	0	0	0	0	0	0	0	2	0
harangued	3	.3399	.2456	33.9	0	0	0	1	1	1	0	0	1	0	0	1	0	0	0	0	0	0	0	0	0	0	0	1	0
Harar	2	.0000	.0389	25.9	0	0	0	0	2	0	0	0	0	0	0	0	0	2	0	0	0	0	0	0	0	0	0	0	0
harass	3	.3766	.2480	33.9	1	0	0	0	1	1	0	0	0	0	0	0	0	1	0	0	0	0	0	0	1	0	1	0	0
harassed	8	.4544	.7700	38.9	0	0	1	2	4	1	0	0	0	0	0	0	0	0	0	0	0	0	0	0	1	3	1	3	0
harassment	5	.2138	.2693	34.3	0	0	0	0	0	2	3	0	0	0	0	0	0	2	0	0	0	0	0	0	0	0	0	3	0
harbor	184	.7058	26.666	54.3	33	39	25	34	25	15	10	3	34	6	3	5	0	73	0	4	0	0	0	0	4	17	20	18	0
Harbor	47	.7551	7.2366	48.6	5	6	9	8	4	12	3	0	12	0	0	2	3	14	0	0	1	1	0	0	1	5	4	4	0
harbored	2	.2437	.1129	30.5	0	0	1	0	1	0	0	0	0	0	0	0	0	0	0	0	0	0	0	0	0	0	1	1	0
harboring	2	.0000	.0914	29.6	0	0	0	0	2	0	0	0	2	0	0	0	0	0	0	0	0	0	0	0	0	0	0	0	0
harbors	51	.4890	5.4316	47.3	7	10	8	9	4	7	5	1	5	0	0	0	0	32	0	3	1	0	0	0	0	3	5	2	0
Harcourt	3	.1927	.1491	31.7	0	0	0	1	0	1	0	1	0	0	0	0	0	0	0	1	0	0	0	0	0	0	0	2	0
hard	1980	.9495	371.85	65.7	460	380	232	230	334	187	117	40	645	78	6	117	11	184	78	201	34	22	12	41	175	212	48	114	2
Hard	11	.5612	1.3366	41.3	1	9	0	0	0	0	1	0	5	0	0	0	0	0	2	0	1	0	0	1	1	1	0	0	0
hard-baked	2	.2285	.1129	30.5	0	0	0	1	1	0	0	0	0	0	0	0	0	1	0	0	0	0	0	0	0	0	1	0	0
hard-bitten	3	.2143	.1568	32.0	1	0	1	0	0	0	0	1	0	0	0	0	0	0	0	0	0	0	0	0	0	1	0	2	0
hard-boiled	11	.5058	1.2441	40.9	4	1	2	1	1	0	1	1	5	0	0	0	0	0	0	1	0	0	1	0	0	3	1	0	0
hard-cooked	2	.1674	.0805	29.1	0	1	0	0	0	0	1	0	0	0	0	0	0	0	0	0	0	0	1	0	0	1	0	0	0
hard-core	2	.2433	.1158	30.6	0	0	1	0	1	0	0	0	0	0	0	0	0	0	0	0	0	0	0	0	0	1	0	1	0
hard-earned	2	.0000	.0914	29.6	1	0	0	0	1	0	0	0	2	0	0	0	0	0	0	0	0	0	0	0	0	0	0	0	0
hard-hitting	2	.2433	.1158	30.6	0	0	1	0	0	0	1	0	0	0	0	0	0	0	0	0	0	0	0	0	0	1	0	1	0
hard-line	3	.0000	.0365	25.6	0	0	0	0	1	0	2	0	0	0	0	0	0	0	0	0	0	0	0	0	0	0	0	3	0
Hard-nuts	3	.0000	.0322	25.1	0	0	0	0	0	0	3	0	0	0	0	3	0	0	0	0	0	0	0	0	0	0	0	0	0
hard-packed	7	.5384	.7902	39.0	0	1	3	1	1	1	0	0	0	0	0	1	0	2	0	1	0	0	0	0	2	1	0	0	0
hard-pressed	2	.0000	.0290	24.6	0	1	1	0	0	0	0	0	0	0	0	0	0	0	0	0	0	0	0	0	0	2	0	0	0
hard-to-spell	2	.0000	.0162	22.1	0	0	0	0	1	1	0	0	0	0	0	0	0	0	2	0	0	0	0	0	0	0	0	0	0
hard-won	2	.0000	.0914	29.6	0	0	0	1	1	0	0	0	2	0	0	0	0	0	0	0	0	0	0	0	0	0	0	0	0
hard-working	20	.7149	2.9133	44.6	8	1	1	2	4	3	0	1	3	1	0	0	0	4	1	1	3	0	0	0	0	2	3	2	0
harden	19	.3475	1.4942	41.7	3	0	2	1	2	4	5	2	3	1	0	0	0	0	0	4	0	0	0	5	0	2	2	1	1
Harden	3	.2181	.1541	31.9	0	0	1	0	2	0	0	0	0	0	0	0	0	0	0	0	0	0	0	0	1	0	2	0	0
hardenability	4	.0000	.0101	20.0	0	0	0	0	0	0	4	0	0	0	0	0	0	0	0	0	0	0	0	4	0	0	0	0	0
hardened	42	.3655	3.3403	45.2	1	4	1	2	8	9	17	0	4	1	0	3	0	4	2	3	0	0	1	17	3	2	2	0	0
hardening	4	.1199	.1563	31.9	0	0	1	1	0	0	2	0	1	0	0	0	0	0	0	1	0	0	0	2	0	0	0	0	0
hardens	18	.5481	2.0765	43.2	3	4	5	1	1	2	2	0	0	0	0	0	0	2	0	10	0	0	0	1	0	3	1	1	0
harder	217	.9022	38.944	55.9	45	52	24	25	36	17	17	1	58	5	2	11	3	13	6	36	2	1	2	7	15	24	5	27	0
hardest	99	.3461	7.6642	48.8	4	22	23	16	26	4	3	1	12	1	0	3	1	6	62	4	0	0	0	0	4	1	2	3	0
hardhead	2	.0000	.0234	23.7	0	0	0	0	2	0	0	0	0	0	0	0	0	0	0	0	0	0	0	0	2	0	0	0	0
hardheaded	5	.3141	.3764	35.8	0	1	3	0	0	0	0	1	1	0	0	0	0	0	0	0	0	0	0	0	0	2	0	2	0
hardier	2	.0000	.0389	25.9	0	0	0	1	0	0	1	0	0	0	0	0	0	2	0	0	0	0	0	0	0	0	0	0	0
hardiest	3	.2043	.1486	31.7	1	0	0	0	2	0	0	0	0	0	0	0	0	0	0	0	0	0	0	0	0	1	2	0	0
hardihood	2	.2433	.1158	30.6	1	0	0	1	0	0	0	0	0	0	0	0	0	0	0	0	0	0	0	0	0	1	0	1	0
Harding	4	.3662	.3647	35.6	0	0	0	0	0	3	1	0	2	0	0	0	0	1	0	0	0	0	0	0	0	0	1	0	0
hardly	409	.8569	70.316	58.5	93	82	48	41	71	26	31	17	147	29	8	34	0	22	5	24	6	0	1	1	39	46	13	34	0
hardness	63	.1902	2.8960	44.6	0	1	3	2	4	6	42	5	2	1	0	1	2	1	0	19	0	0	0	33	2	1	1	0	0
Hardness	5	.0000	.0126	21.0	0	0	0	0	0	0	5	0	0	0	0	0	0	0	0	0	0	0	0	5	0	0	0	0	0
hardship	32	.6548	4.3620	46.4	3	2	13	2	7	4	1	0	8	1	0	4	0	9	0	0	3	0	0	0	0	4	3	0	0
hardships	34	.6899	4.8565	46.9	3	2	7	4	7	10	1	0	9	0	0	1	1	12	0	1	4	0	0	0	2	2	1	1	0
hardtack	2	.2128	.1055	30.2	0	1	1	0	0	0	0	0	0	0	0	0	0	0	0	1	1	0	0	0	0	0	0	0	0
hardware	33	.6180	4.3539	46.4	10	5	2	1	11	0	3	1	15	1	0	2	1	4	0	0	0	0	0	3	0	2	1	4	0
Hardware	2	.1717	.1142	30.6	1	0	0	0	0	0	1	0	1	0	0	1	0	0	0	0	0	0	0	0	0	0	0	0	0
hardwood	15	.5702	1.7848	42.5	2	1	2	1	5	0	4	0	2	0	0	1	0	3	0	0	1	0	0	2	0	1	4	1	0
hardwoods	10	.5008	1.0521	40.2	1	0	1	1	6	0	1	0	0	0	0	0	0	2	0	1	0	0	0	1	0	3	3	0	0
hardworking	7	.3715	.5815	37.6	1	1	0	0	4	1	0	0	0	0	0	0	0	3	0	0	0	0	0	0	0	3	1	0	0
hardy	24	.7028	3.4275	45.3	5	0	2	2	8	2	2	3	2	0	0	1	0	4	1	0	0	0	0	1	1	6	4	4	0
Hardy	11	.2713	.7007	38.5	9	0	0	0	2	0	0	0	0	0	0	2	0	1	0	0	0	0	0	0	0	8	0	0	0
hare	16	.5462	1.8087	42.6	5	0	3	5	1	0	1	1	1	4	0	0	0	0	0	0	4	0	0	0	1	0	3	3	0
Hare	12	.2003	.8839	39.5	0	2	7	2	0	0	1	0	11	0	0	0	0	0	0	0	0	0	0	0	0	0	0	1	0
harelip	2	.2437	.1129	30.5	0	0	2	0	0	0	0	0	0	0	0	0	0	0	0	0	0	0	0	0	0	0	1	1	0
harems	2	.2285	.1129	30.5	0	0	0	0	1	1	0	0	0	0	0	0	0	1	0	0	0	0	0	0	0	0	1	0	0
hares	11	.3962	.9711	39.9	3	0	6	2	0	0	0	0	2	2	0	0	0	0	0	0	0	0	0	0	0	0	5	2	0
Hargreaves'	2	.1698	.1133	30.5	0	0	0	0	2	0	0	0	1	0	0	0	0	0	0	0	0	0	0	0	0	0	1	0	0
hark	15	.6878	2.1113	43.2	2	0	2	4	4	0	1	2	3	1	0	3	0	0	0	0	2	0	0	0	2	1	1	2	0
Harkness	6	.1250	.2684	34.3	0	0	0	2	0	0	0	4	2	0	0	0	0	0	0	0	0	0	0	0	4	0	0	0	0
Harlem	14	.4238	1.3636	41.3	1	4	0	0	5	1	3	0	4	0	0	0	0	5	0	0	0	0	0	0	0	1	0	4	0
Harlequin	4	.2228	.2087	33.2	0	0	0	3	0	0	1	0	0	0	0	0	0	0	0	0	1	0	0	0	3	0	0	0	0
Harley	2	.2442	.1134	30.5	0	0	0	0	0	0	2	0	0	1	0	0	0	0	0	0	0	0	0	0	0	0	0	1	0
Harlow	12	.3119	.8427	39.3	0	0	0	4	6	0	2	0	0	1	0	0	4	0	0	0	0	0	0	0	0	0	0	7	0
harm	148	.6087	19.032	52.8	29	24	13	26	27	19	5	5	42	2	1	22	0	3	3	34	1	0	3	0	15	14	2	4	2
harm's	3	.2208	.1563	31.9	0	1	0	0	0	0	2	0	0	2	0	0	0	0	0	0	0	0	0	0	1	0	0	0	0
harmed	8	.4681	.8478	39.3	0	2	1	2	3	0	0	0	3	0	0	0	0	0	0	2	0	0	0	0	2	0	1	0	0
harmful	94	.6343	12.452	51.0	17	16	16	15	12	7	9	2	13	1	0	1	0	10	0	50	1	0	1	0	1	5	7	4	0
harming	6	.4293	.5878	37.7	0	1	2	1	2	0	0	0	2	0	0	2	0	0	0	1	0	0	0	0	0	0	1	0	0
harmless	32	.6397	4.3192	46.4	6	3	2	7	11	1	2	0	10	0	0	2	0	1	0	12	0	0	0	0	1	3	2	1	0
Harmon	7	.2104	.3814	35.8	0	0	0	1	1	0	0	5	1	0	0	0	0	0	0	0	0	0	0	0	5	0	0	1	0
harmonic	26	.1907	1.2121	40.8	0	1	2	3	2	11	1	6	0	0	0	0	0	0	0	7	18	0	0	0	0	0	1	0	0
harmonica	19	.5342	2.1909	43.4	3	6	4	4	0	0	2	0	6	0	0	0	0	0	0	0	4	0	0	0	3	3	0	3	0
Harmonica	2	.2387	.1089	30.4	1	0	0	0	1	0	0	0	0	0	0	0	0	0	0	0	1	0	0	0	1	0	0	0	0
harmonically	3	.0995	.1144	30.6	0	0	0	0	1	1	1	0	1	0	0	0	0	0	0	0	2	0	0	0	0	0	0	0	0
harmonics	7	.0839	.1779	32.5	0	0	0	0	0	7	0	0	0	0	0	0	0	0	0	1	6	0	0	0	0	0	0	0	0
harmonies	19	.3504	1.4010	41.5	0	0	2	4	2	8	3	0	0	0	0	0	0	0	0	0	15	2	1	0	0	1	0	0	0
harmonious	9	.5789	1.0509	40.2	0	1	1	0	3	2	2	0	0	0	0	0	0	0	1	0	1	1	1	2	2	1	0	0	0
harmoniously	2	.2407	.1090	30.4	0	0	0	0	2	0	0	0	0	1	0	0	0	0	0	0	1	0	0	0	0	0	0	0	0
harmonization	5	.0000	.0404	26.1	0	0	1	0	3	1	0	0	0	0	0	0	0	0	0	0	5	0	0	0	0	0	0	0	0
harmonize	17	.2505	.9461	39.8	0	1	4	3	4	4	1	0	1	0	0	0	0	0	0	0	10	0	6	0	0	0	0	0	0
harmonized	5	.0000	.0404	26.1	0	1	1	1	1	1	0	0	0	0	0	0	0	0	0	0	5	0	0	0	0	0	0	0	0
harmonizes	2	.2109	.0918	29.6	0	0	0	0	1	1	0	0	0	0	0	0	0	0	0	0	1	0	1	0	0	0	0	0	0
harmonizing	14	.1563	.5213	37.2	0	1	8	2	1	1	1	0	0	0	0	0	0	0	0	0	13	0	1	0	0	0	0	0	0
harmony	194	.4354	17.508	52.4	23	21	29	25	36	36	21	3	2	0	0	1	0	5	0	0	150	10	5	9	1	3	5	3	0

6E Happyborough
8Q Hara
7R hara-kiri
8D harangue
7F Hararge
7Q harassing
9Q harassments
7J Harbach
4P Harbin
8F Harbord
7N harbour
6E Harbour
XR hard-bodied
7Q hard-coated
7L hard-crusted
4A hard-driven
5R hard-driving
9D hard-fated
7A hard-frozen
7Q hard-hat
7N hard-headed
4A hard-hit
7D hard-looking
9N hard-nosed
4P hard-riding
9R hard-rock
7D hard-rutted
4H hard-shell
6G hard-shelled
9M hard-soldered
6B hard-surface
6F hard-surfaced
7D hard-tipped
8A hard-to-comprehend
9B hard-to-get
8M hard-to-get-to
3P hard-to-remember
8J hard-wood
XR hardcover
7M hardened-steel
5N Hardens
7Q Harder
8C hardest-earned
8C hardest-to-beat
9H hardpan
7R harem
7Q Hares
9D Hargest
9D harkened
5P Harlan
9D harlots
5Q Harlowe
5A harm-doing
4F harmattan
8B harme
8K Harmens
8K Harmenszoon
9R harmfulness
8Q harmlessness
7F Harmonious

Column codes: 3=Gr 3, 4=Gr 4, 5=Gr 5, 6=Gr 6, 7=Gr 7, 8=Gr 8, 9=Gr 9, X=UnGr, A=Read, B=Eng & Gr, C=Comp, D=Lit, E=Math, F=Soc Stud, G=Spell, H=Sci, J=Music, K=Art, L=Home Ec, M=Shop, N=Lib F, P=Lib NF, Q=Lib Ref, R=Mag, S=Rel

Word Type	F	D	U	SFI	Gr3	Gr4	Gr5	Gr6	Gr7	Gr8	Gr9	UnGr	Read	Eng&Gr	Comp	Lit	Math	SocStud	Spell	Sci	Music	Art	HomeEc	Shop	LibF	LibNF	LibRef	Mag	Rel
handcarts	2	.2375	.1088	30.4	0	0	1	0	0	0	0	1	0	0	0	0	0	0	0	0	1	0	0	0	0	0	0	1	0
handcrafts	2	.0000	.0389	25.9	0	0	2	0	0	0	0	0	0	0	0	0	0	2	0	0	0	0	0	0	0	0	0	0	0
handcuffs	6	.1814	.3560	35.5	0	2	2	1	1	0	0	0	3	0	0	0	0	0	0	0	0	0	0	0	0	0	0	3	0
handed	196	.8223	32.598	55.1	33	44	16	27	40	20	13	3	83	12	1	16	5	8	0	1	3	1	1	0	27	23	2	13	0
Handel	25	.2011	1.1655	40.7	2	3	8	3	3	5	1	0	0	0	0	0	1	0	0	0	20	0	0	0	0	2	0	0	0
Handel's	4	.1534	.1534	31.9	0	0	2	2	0	0	0	0	0	0	0	0	0	0	0	0	3	0	0	0	0	0	0	0	0
handful	66	.8330	11.079	50.4	14	9	6	9	16	9	3	0	24	0	1	6	1	5	2	4	1	0	0	0	6	8	4	4	0
handfuls	8	.5643	.9459	39.8	0	3	1	1	2	1	0	0	1	0	0	2	0	1	0	0	0	0	0	0	2	1	1	1	0
handgun	3	.0000	.0365	25.6	0	0	0	0	3	0	0	0	0	0	0	0	0	0	0	0	0	0	0	0	0	0	0	3	0
handguns	2	.0000	.0243	23.9	0	0	0	0	2	0	0	0	0	0	0	0	0	0	0	0	0	0	0	0	0	0	0	2	0
handholds	2	.2446	.1142	30.6	1	0	0	1	0	0	0	0	0	0	0	0	0	0	0	0	0	0	0	0	1	0	0	1	0
handicap	8	.4210	.7739	38.9	0	3	1	2	1	1	0	0	2	0	0	0	1	0	2	0	0	0	1	0	0	3	0	0	0
handicapped	24	.5582	2.7896	44.5	0	1	16	1	1	2	3	0	2	0	1	0	0	4	0	3	1	0	1	0	0	0	7	9	0
handicaps	11	.5177	1.1890	40.8	3	0	2	3	2	0	1	0	0	0	0	0	0	4	0	1	0	0	1	1	0	0	4	0	0
handicraft	7	.5288	.7914	39.0	3	1	1	0	0	0	2	0	1	0	0	0	0	2	0	0	0	0	0	0	1	2	1	0	0
handicrafts	12	.5995	1.4811	41.7	3	0	0	0	5	0	3	1	0	0	0	1	0	4	0	0	0	0	1	0	0	3	2	1	0
handing	26	.7228	3.8737	45.9	3	9	1	3	3	2	3	2	10	1	0	3	0	2	1	0	1	0	0	0	3	3	0	2	0
handiwork	12	.6713	1.6580	42.2	2	2	1	0	3	1	2	1	2	0	0	1	0	1	0	2	0	0	1	0	0	2	1	2	0
handkerchief	68	.7612	10.563	50.2	15	21	9	4	9	5	3	2	22	3	2	2	0	3	4	10	2	0	0	0	7	13	0	0	0
handkerchiefs	22	.5558	2.6528	44.2	1	2	4	8	1	4	1	1	9	1	0	2	0	5	0	0	0	0	2	0	0	4	0	0	0
handle	301	.8405	50.729	57.1	51	44	25	35	75	38	28	5	84	9	10	16	1	26	5	22	7	1	15	21	26	26	8	24	0
handle-bar	2	.0000	.0290	24.6	2	0	0	0	0	0	0	0	2	0	0	0	0	0	0	0	0	0	0	0	0	2	0	0	0
handlebar	3	.2754	.1835	32.6	0	0	0	0	1	0	1	0	0	0	0	0	0	0	0	0	0	0	1	0	1	0	1	0	0
handled	59	.8097	9.5996	49.8	3	6	5	8	19	6	10	2	11	2	0	3	0	9	1	6	3	0	3	4	2	5	4	6	0
handler	4	.2805	.2842	34.5	0	0	0	0	2	2	0	0	1	0	0	0	0	1	0	0	0	0	0	0	2	0	0	0	0
handlers	4	.3658	.3646	35.6	0	0	0	0	2	2	0	0	2	0	0	0	0	1	0	0	0	0	0	0	0	0	0	0	0
handles	59	.7331	8.7590	49.4	10	7	8	8	19	4	2	1	7	2	0	2	0	7	0	4	3	0	0	5	6	8	7	8	0
handling	92	.7953	14.676	51.7	6	6	3	7	26	11	30	3	11	3	1	4	0	6	0	12	1	1	10	5	4	10	8	16	0
handloads	2	.0000	.0243	23.9	0	0	0	0	2	0	0	0	0	0	0	0	0	0	0	0	0	0	0	0	0	0	0	2	0
handmade	11	.5316	1.2434	40.9	1	1	0	3	2	1	0	3	2	0	0	0	0	3	0	0	0	0	2	0	1	0	1	1	0
handmaidens	4	.3604	.3536	35.5	0	0	0	1	1	0	1	0	2	0	0	0	0	0	0	2	0	0	0	0	0	0	0	1	0
handrails	2	.0000	.0394	26.0	0	0	1	0	1	0	0	0	0	0	0	0	0	0	0	2	0	0	0	0	0	0	0	0	0
hands	1357	.8929	241.40	63.8	222	216	179	199	264	139	123	15	421	25	12	187	23	69	9	82	74	14	17	7	183	136	26	72	0
Hands	3	.3431	.2528	34.0	1	0	0	0	1	1	0	0	1	0	0	0	0	0	0	0	0	0	0	0	1	0	0	0	0
hands-off	2	.1814	.1187	30.7	0	0	0	0	1	0	0	1	1	0	0	0	0	0	0	0	0	0	0	0	0	0	0	1	0
handset	4	.0000	.0419	26.2	0	0	0	0	0	0	0	4	0	0	0	0	0	0	0	0	0	0	0	0	0	0	0	4	0
handshake	4	.4522	.3988	36.0	0	1	0	1	0	0	0	0	1	1	0	0	0	0	0	0	0	0	0	0	0	1	1	0	0
handshakes	3	.0000	.0365	25.6	0	0	0	1	2	0	0	0	0	0	0	0	0	0	0	0	0	0	0	0	0	0	0	3	0
handsome	155	.8683	26.887	54.3	14	20	19	32	36	17	15	2	45	12	2	20	0	12	3	1	10	3	2	0	17	11	2	15	0
Handsome	2	.2446	.1125	30.5	0	0	0	1	1	0	0	0	0	1	0	1	0	0	0	0	0	0	0	0	0	0	0	0	0
handsomely	7	.4654	.6836	38.3	0	2	2	0	1	0	1	2	0	0	0	0	0	0	0	0	2	0	0	0	1	2	0	2	0
handsomer	4	.3726	.3697	35.7	0	1	0	2	0	1	0	0	2	0	0	0	0	1	0	0	0	0	0	0	1	0	0	0	0
handsomest	9	.3679	.8453	39.3	1	1	1	0	1	5	0	0	6	0	1	0	0	1	0	0	0	0	0	0	1	0	0	1	0
handstand	2	.2440	.1132	30.5	0	0	1	1	0	0	0	0	0	0	0	0	0	0	0	0	0	0	0	4	0	1	0	0	0
handwheel	5	.0613	.0833	29.2	0	0	0	0	1	0	0	4	0	0	0	0	0	0	0	0	0	0	0	0	0	1	0	0	0
handwriting	60	.6266	7.7366	48.9	8	17	3	11	9	10	2	0	10	21	5	1	0	1	13	0	1	0	0	0	2	3	0	2	0
Handwriting	49	.0000	.3977	36.0	4	8	18	19	0	0	0	0	0	0	0	0	0	0	49	0	0	0	0	0	0	0	0	0	0
handwritten	5	.0000	.0547	27.4	0	0	0	0	4	0	1	0	0	5	0	0	0	0	0	0	0	0	0	0	0	0	0	0	0
handy	47	.7665	7.2804	48.6	7	9	2	3	11	6	5	4	11	3	1	3	0	0	0	0	1	1	1	4	9	2	1	10	0
handyman	2	.2441	.1127	30.5	0	1	0	0	0	1	0	0	0	0	0	0	0	0	0	0	0	0	0	0	1	0	1	0	0
Haneda	2	.2285	.1129	30.5	0	1	1	0	0	0	0	0	0	0	0	0	0	1	0	0	0	0	0	0	0	1	0	0	0
hang	159	.9278	29.244	54.7	38	33	19	20	26	13	6	4	44	6	1	11	1	7	4	21	8	1	2	1	19	19	7	7	0
hangar	2	.0000	.0914	29.6	0	0	0	2	0	0	0	0	2	0	0	0	0	0	0	0	0	0	0	0	0	0	0	0	0
hangars	2	.0000	.0914	29.6	0	0	0	1	1	0	0	0	2	0	0	0	0	0	0	0	0	0	0	0	0	0	0	0	0
hanged	17	.5123	1.9240	42.8	1	3	4	0	4	2	3	0	6	1	0	4	0	5	0	0	0	0	0	0	0	1	0	0	0
hanger	6	.4696	.6014	37.8	0	0	1	1	2	0	0	2	0	0	0	0	0	0	0	2	0	0	0	0	1	1	0	2	0
hangers	4	.2171	.2287	33.6	2	1	0	0	0	0	0	1	0	0	0	0	0	1	0	0	3	0	0	0	0	0	0	0	0
hangin'	2	.2443	.1130	30.5	1	0	0	0	1	0	0	0	0	0	0	0	0	1	0	0	0	0	0	0	1	0	0	0	0
hanging	205	.8595	35.373	55.5	39	39	23	26	41	15	18	4	84	6	2	22	0	7	2	12	5	3	1	0	27	17	8	9	0
Hanging	2	.0000	.0209	23.2	0	2	0	0	0	0	0	0	0	0	0	0	0	0	0	0	0	0	0	0	0	0	0	0	0
hangman	2	.1717	.1142	30.6	0	0	0	0	1	0	0	1	1	0	0	1	0	0	0	0	0	0	0	0	1	0	0	0	0
hangnails	2	.1432	.0759	28.8	0	1	0	0	0	1	0	0	0	0	0	0	0	0	0	1	0	0	1	0	0	0	0	0	0
hangs	60	.7937	9.6005	49.8	10	6	12	9	17	3	3	0	12	3	2	6	0	8	1	8	0	3	3	0	2	7	0	5	0
Hank	118	.4102	11.695	50.7	24	7	2	7	40	38	0	0	68	0	0	5	0	0	0	1	2	4	0	0	39	0	0	0	0
Hank's	11	.2384	.8205	39.1	1	2	0	2	3	3	0	0	8	0	0	0	0	0	0	0	0	0	0	0	3	0	0	0	0
hankering	2	.0000	.0234	23.7	0	2	0	0	0	0	0	0	2	0	0	0	0	0	0	0	0	0	0	0	2	0	0	0	0
Hanks	9	.1010	.3518	35.5	0	6	0	1	1	0	0	1	2	0	0	0	0	0	0	1	0	0	0	0	7	0	0	0	0
hanky	2	.2375	.1088	30.4	0	1	0	0	0	0	1	0	0	0	0	0	0	0	0	0	1	0	0	0	0	0	0	1	0
Hannah	17	.3914	1.4841	41.7	1	8	2	1	4	0	1	0	2	0	0	2	0	0	0	0	0	0	0	0	4	9	0	0	0
Hannibal	11	.0976	.4103	36.1	0	0	1	0	3	0	0	7	3	0	0	0	0	0	0	0	0	0	0	0	0	0	8	0	0
Hanno	4	.0000	.0778	28.9	0	0	0	4	0	0	0	0	0	0	0	0	0	4	0	0	0	0	0	0	0	0	0	0	0
Hanoi	8	.1001	.2513	34.0	0	0	0	1	0	1	6	0	0	0	0	0	0	1	0	0	0	0	0	0	0	7	0	0	0
Hanover	3	.3833	.2447	33.9	0	0	0	0	1	2	0	0	0	0	0	0	0	1	0	0	0	0	0	0	1	0	0	0	0
Hanratty	11	.0000	.1337	31.3	0	0	0	10	1	0	0	0	0	0	0	0	0	0	0	0	0	0	0	0	0	0	0	11	0
Hans	85	.7226	12.727	51.0	5	14	9	31	11	4	8	3	42	7	1	17	0	1	1	2	4	3	0	0	3	3	1	0	0
Hans'	3	.0000	.0322	25.1	0	0	0	0	3	0	0	0	3	0	0	0	0	0	0	0	0	0	0	0	0	0	0	0	0
Hansel	40	.4375	4.1265	46.2	29	0	0	10	0	0	0	1	23	0	0	11	0	0	0	0	4	0	0	0	0	0	0	0	0
Hansen	13	.3377	.9748	39.9	0	4	0	0	1	3	0	0	0	0	0	1	0	3	0	0	1	0	0	0	8	0	0	0	0
Hanson	2	.2387	.1089	30.4	0	0	0	0	0	1	0	0	0	0	0	0	0	0	0	0	0	0	0	0	0	4	0	0	0
Hansonville	4	.0000	.1827	32.6	0	0	0	4	0	0	0	0	4	0	0	0	0	0	0	0	0	0	0	0	0	0	0	0	0
Hanukkah	5	.0000	.0404	26.1	0	0	0	1	4	0	0	0	0	0	0	0	0	0	0	0	0	0	0	0	5	0	0	0	0
Hap	3	.1187	.1291	31.1	0	1	0	0	0	0	2	0	1	0	0	2	0	0	0	0	0	0	0	0	0	0	0	0	0
haphazard	5	.3004	.3386	35.3	1	0	0	1	1	0	1	0	0	1	0	0	0	0	1	0	0	0	0	0	0	0	0	3	0
haphazardly	2	.2351	.1166	30.7	0	0	0	0	2	0	0	0	0	0	0	0	0	0	0	0	0	0	0	0	0	0	1	1	0
hapless	3	.1169	.1277	31.1	0	0	0	1	2	0	0	0	0	0	0	0	0	0	0	0	0	0	0	0	0	0	0	3	0
happen	468	.9050	84.270	59.3	76	115	78	50	78	45	19	7	131	28	7	30	12	26	9	107	8	1	4	1	36	36	7	25	0
happened	910	.8692	158.76	62.0	228	161	112	113	128	98	61	9	419	79	12	82	6	49	24	57	11	6	5	0	66	59	3	32	0
happening	179	.7454	27.166	54.3	36	36	27	33	24	13	10	0	43	14	16	13	5	22	5	19	4	1	0	0	12	12	0	13	0
happenings	42	.6064	5.3238	47.3	7	6	5	9	6	4	5	0	11	2	7	4	0	2	1	2	2	0	0	0	5	3	3	4	0
happens	520	.8356	87.046	59.4	128	105	68	49	79	50	30	11	59	21	2	22	20	27	27	256	18	4	7	4	7	13	13	20	0
happier	51	.8007	8.2490	49.2	6	10	4	8	10	7	3	3	15	2	2	6	0	4	2	2	4	2	0	3	0	1	7	3	0
happiest	27	.7615	4.1961	46.2	4	4	8	4	3	2	2	0	10	0	1	2	0	2	2	0	1	0	0	0	4	1	1	3	0
happily	143	.8168	23.701	53.7	49	27	12	18	21	10	4	2	71	1	1	12	0	5	2	0	1	3	0	18	11	1	13	0	0
happiness	79	.8185	13.005	51.1	10	11	9	9	13	12	13	2	21	2	0	12	0	7	2	0	1	1	3	0	10	6	4	10	0

4P handcar	3P Handicraft	3A handprints	8R hang-ups	8D Hanlon	5R HAPPENED
5J handcart	6P handie	7R handsaw	6A hangar-top	9Q Hannibal's	9D happenin'
9H handclap	6G handier	7N handspike	6F Hangchow	XR Hansbrough-Newlands	4F Happens
9D handclasps	6P handies	3N handspring	8D hange'd	5P Hanseatic	7A Happily
7D handfulla	7R handlebars	3A handsprings	7R hangers-on	3A Hansel's	7A Happiness
7R handgun-carrying	7D Handley-Page	4R handstands	8L hangings	4N Hansen's	
7R handheld	3H handloom	3H handwoven	9D hangman's	XR Hanslin	
5N handhold	8F handmarks	8J Handy	8Q Hanibal	3A hap'	
4P Handicap	3K handprint	5A handy-boy	6N Hankinsons	4R Hapgood	
5R Handicapped		6N hang-dog	5Q Hankow	8D Happened	

Word Type	F	D	U	SFI	Gr 3	Gr 4	Gr 5	Gr 6	Gr 7	Gr 8	Gr 9	UnGr	A Read	B Eng & Gr	C Comp	D Lit	E Math	F Soc Stud	G Spell	H Sci	J Music	K Art	L Home Ec	M Shop	N Lib F	P Lib NF	Q Lib Ref	R Mag	S Rel
happy	774	.9062	139.55	61.4	229	147	84	96	75	76	52	15	282	62	15	58	2	26	25	13	55	8	27	0	70	71	5	54	1
Happy	21	.7343	3.1529	45.0	5	0	2	2	6	1	5	0	6	2	0	3	2	1	0	0	2	0	0	0	1	3	0	1	0
happy-go-lucky	3	.2279	.2143	33.3	0	0	0	1	1	1	0	0	2	0	0	0	0	0	0	0	0	0	0	0	0	0	0	1	0
Hapsburg	2	.0000	.0389	25.9	0	0	0	0	0	0	0	2	0	0	0	0	0	0	0	0	0	0	0	0	0	0	0	0	0
Hapsburgs	2	.0000	.0290	24.6	0	0	2	0	0	0	0	0	0	0	0	0	0	0	0	0	0	0	0	0	0	0	0	0	0
Harald	2	.0000	.0389	25.9	0	2	0	0	0	0	0	0	0	0	0	0	0	2	0	0	0	0	0	0	0	0	0	0	0
harambee	2	.0000	.0243	23.9	0	0	0	2	0	0	0	0	0	0	0	0	0	0	0	0	0	0	0	0	0	0	0	2	0
harangued	3	.3399	.2456	33.9	0	0	0	1	1	1	0	0	1	0	0	1	0	0	0	0	0	0	0	0	0	0	0	1	0
Harar	2	.0000	.0389	25.9	0	0	0	0	2	0	0	0	0	0	0	0	0	2	0	0	0	0	0	0	0	0	0	0	0
harass	3	.3766	.2480	33.9	1	0	0	0	1	1	0	0	0	0	0	0	0	1	0	0	0	0	0	0	0	1	1	0	0
harassed	8	.4544	.7700	38.9	0	0	1	2	4	1	0	0	0	0	0	0	0	0	0	0	0	0	0	0	1	3	1	3	0
harassment	5	.2138	.2693	34.3	0	0	0	0	0	2	0	3	0	0	0	0	0	2	0	0	0	0	0	0	0	0	0	3	0
harbor	184	.7058	26.666	54.3	33	39	25	34	25	15	10	3	34	6	3	5	0	73	0	4	0	0	0	0	4	17	20	18	0
Harbor	47	.7551	7.2366	48.6	5	6	9	8	4	12	3	0	12	0	0	0	3	14	0	0	1	1	0	0	1	5	4	4	0
harbored	2	.2437	.1129	30.5	0	0	1	0	1	0	0	0	0	0	0	0	0	0	0	0	0	0	0	0	1	0	1	0	0
harboring	2	.0000	.0914	29.6	0	0	0	0	2	0	0	0	2	0	0	0	0	0	0	0	0	0	0	0	0	0	0	0	0
harbors	51	.4890	5.4316	47.3	7	10	8	9	4	7	5	1	5	0	0	0	0	32	0	3	0	0	0	0	3	5	2	0	0
Harcourt	3	.1927	.1491	31.7	0	0	0	0	0	1	1	1	0	0	0	0	0	0	0	1	0	0	0	0	0	0	2	0	0
hard	1980	.9495	371.85	65.7	460	380	232	230	334	187	117	40	645	78	6	117	11	184	78	201	34	22	12	41	175	212	48	114	2
Hard	11	.5612	1.3366	41.3	1	9	0	0	0	0	1	0	5	0	0	0	0	0	2	0	1	0	0	0	1	1	1	0	0
hard-baked	2	.2285	.1129	30.5	0	0	0	1	1	0	0	0	0	0	0	0	0	1	0	0	0	0	0	0	0	1	0	0	0
hard-bitten	3	.2143	.1568	32.0	1	0	1	0	0	0	0	1	0	0	0	0	0	0	0	0	0	0	0	0	0	1	0	2	0
hard-boiled	11	.5058	1.2441	40.9	4	1	2	1	1	0	1	1	5	0	0	0	0	0	0	1	0	0	1	0	0	3	1	0	0
hard-cooked	2	.1674	.0805	29.1	0	1	0	0	1	0	0	0	0	0	0	0	0	0	0	1	0	0	0	0	0	1	0	0	0
hard-core	2	.2433	.1158	30.6	0	0	0	1	0	1	0	0	0	0	0	0	0	0	0	0	0	0	0	0	0	1	0	0	1
hard-earned	2	.0000	.0914	29.6	1	0	0	0	1	0	0	0	2	0	0	0	0	0	0	0	0	0	0	0	0	0	0	0	0
hard-hitting	2	.2433	.1158	30.6	0	0	1	0	0	0	1	0	0	0	0	0	0	0	0	0	0	0	0	0	0	1	0	1	0
hard-line	3	.0000	.0365	25.6	0	0	0	0	1	0	2	0	0	0	0	0	0	0	0	0	0	0	0	0	0	0	0	3	0
Hard-nuts	3	.0000	.0322	25.1	0	0	0	0	0	0	3	0	0	0	0	0	0	0	0	3	0	0	0	0	0	0	0	0	0
hard-packed	7	.5384	.7902	39.0	0	1	3	1	1	1	0	0	0	0	0	0	0	1	0	2	0	0	1	0	0	2	0	1	0
hard-pressed	2	.0000	.0290	24.6	0	1	1	0	0	0	0	0	0	0	0	0	0	0	0	0	0	0	0	0	0	2	0	0	0
hard-to-spell	2	.0000	.0162	22.1	0	0	0	0	1	1	0	0	0	0	0	0	0	0	0	0	0	0	0	0	0	0	0	0	0
hard-won	2	.0000	.0914	29.6	0	0	0	1	1	0	0	0	2	0	0	0	0	0	0	0	0	0	0	0	0	0	0	0	0
hard-working	20	.7149	2.9133	44.6	8	1	1	2	4	3	0	1	3	1	0	0	0	1	1	1	3	0	0	0	2	3	2	0	1
harden	19	.3475	1.4942	41.7	3	0	2	1	2	4	5	2	3	1	0	0	0	0	0	4	0	0	0	0	5	0	2	1	1
Harden	3	.2181	.1541	31.9	0	0	1	0	2	0	0	0	0	0	0	0	0	0	0	0	0	0	0	0	1	0	2	0	0
hardenability	4	.0000	.0101	20.0	0	0	0	0	0	0	4	0	0	0	0	0	0	0	0	0	0	0	0	0	4	0	0	0	0
hardened	42	.3655	3.3403	45.2	1	4	1	2	8	9	17	0	4	1	0	3	0	4	2	3	0	0	1	0	17	3	2	2	0
hardening	4	.1199	.1563	31.9	0	0	1	1	0	1	0	0	1	0	0	0	0	0	0	1	0	0	0	0	2	0	0	0	0
hardens	18	.5481	2.0765	43.2	3	4	5	1	1	2	2	0	1	0	0	0	0	0	0	10	0	0	0	0	1	0	3	1	1
Hardness	5	.0000	.0126	21.0	0	0	0	0	0	0	5	0	0	0	0	0	0	0	0	5	0	0	0	0	0	0	0	0	0
hardship	32	.6548	4.3620	46.4	3	2	13	2	7	4	1	0	8	1	0	4	0	9	0	0	3	0	0	0	5	0	0	0	0
hardships	34	.6899	4.8565	46.9	3	2	7	4	7	10	1	0	9	0	0	1	1	12	0	1	4	0	0	0	2	2	1	1	0
hardtack	2	.2128	.1055	30.2	0	1	1	0	0	0	0	0	0	0	0	0	0	0	0	1	1	0	0	0	0	0	0	0	0
hardware	33	.6180	4.3539	46.4	10	5	2	1	11	0	3	1	15	1	0	2	1	4	0	0	0	0	0	3	0	2	1	4	0
Hardware	2	.1717	.1142	30.6	1	0	0	0	0	0	1	0	1	0	0	0	0	0	0	0	0	0	0	0	1	0	0	0	0
hardwood	15	.5702	1.7848	42.5	2	1	2	1	5	0	4	0	2	0	0	1	0	2	0	1	0	0	0	0	3	1	4	1	0
hardwoods	10	.5008	1.0521	40.2	1	0	1	1	6	0	1	0	2	0	0	0	0	2	0	1	0	0	0	0	1	0	3	1	0
hardworking	7	.3715	.5815	37.6	1	1	0	0	4	1	0	0	0	0	0	0	0	3	0	0	0	0	0	0	0	3	1	0	0
hardy	24	.7028	3.4275	45.3	5	0	2	2	8	2	2	3	2	0	0	1	0	4	1	0	0	0	0	0	1	1	6	4	4
Hardy	11	.2713	.7007	38.5	9	0	0	0	2	0	0	0	1	0	0	2	0	1	0	0	4	0	0	0	1	0	0	2	0
hare	16	.5462	1.8087	42.6	5	0	3	5	1	0	1	1	1	4	0	0	0	1	0	0	4	0	0	0	1	0	3	2	0
Hare	12	.2003	.8839	39.5	0	2	7	2	0	0	1	0	11	0	0	0	0	0	0	0	0	0	0	0	1	0	0	0	0
harelip	2	.2437	.1129	30.5	0	0	0	0	1	1	0	0	0	0	0	0	0	0	0	1	0	0	0	0	0	1	0	0	0
harems	2	.2285	.1129	30.5	0	0	0	0	1	1	0	0	0	0	0	0	0	0	0	0	0	0	0	0	0	0	0	2	0
hares	11	.3962	.9711	39.9	3	0	6	0	2	0	0	0	2	2	0	0	0	0	0	0	0	0	0	0	0	0	5	2	0
Hargreaves'	2	.1698	.1133	30.5	0	0	0	0	2	0	0	0	1	0	0	0	0	0	0	0	0	0	0	0	1	0	0	0	0
hark	15	.6878	2.1113	43.2	2	0	2	4	4	0	1	2	3	1	0	3	0	0	0	0	2	0	0	0	2	1	1	2	0
Harkness	6	.1250	.2684	34.3	0	0	0	2	0	0	0	4	2	0	0	0	0	0	0	0	0	0	0	0	4	0	0	0	0
Harlem	14	.4238	1.3636	41.3	1	4	0	0	5	1	0	3	4	0	0	0	0	5	0	0	0	0	0	0	1	0	0	4	0
Harlequin	4	.2228	.2087	33.2	0	0	0	3	0	0	0	1	0	0	0	0	0	0	0	0	1	0	0	0	3	0	0	0	0
Harley	2	.2442	.1134	30.5	0	0	0	0	0	0	0	2	0	1	0	0	0	0	0	0	0	0	0	0	0	0	1	0	0
Harlow	12	.3119	.8427	39.3	0	0	0	4	6	0	2	0	0	2	0	0	4	0	0	0	0	0	0	0	0	0	0	7	0
harm	148	.6087	19.032	52.8	29	24	13	26	27	19	5	5	42	2	1	22	0	3	3	34	1	0	3	0	15	14	2	4	2
harm's	3	.2208	.1563	31.9	0	1	0	0	0	2	0	0	0	1	0	0	0	0	0	0	0	0	0	0	1	0	1	0	0
harmed	8	.4681	.8478	39.3	0	2	1	2	3	0	0	0	3	0	0	0	0	0	0	2	0	0	0	0	1	0	1	1	0
harmful	94	.6343	12.452	51.0	17	16	16	15	12	7	9	2	13	1	0	4	0	10	0	50	1	0	1	0	1	5	7	4	0
harming	6	.4293	.5878	37.7	0	1	2	1	2	0	0	0	2	0	0	0	0	0	0	1	0	0	0	0	0	0	0	3	0
harmless	32	.6397	4.3192	46.4	6	3	2	7	11	1	2	0	10	0	0	2	0	1	0	12	0	0	0	0	0	1	3	2	1
Harmon	7	.2104	.3814	35.8	0	0	0	1	1	0	0	5	1	0	0	0	0	0	0	0	0	0	0	0	0	0	5	0	1
harmonic	26	.1907	1.2121	40.8	0	1	2	3	2	11	1	6	0	0	0	0	0	0	0	7	18	0	0	0	0	0	0	1	0
harmonica	19	.5342	2.1909	43.4	3	6	4	4	0	2	0	0	6	0	0	0	0	0	0	0	4	0	0	0	0	3	0	3	0
Harmonica	2	.2387	.1089	30.4	1	0	0	0	1	0	0	0	1	0	0	0	0	0	0	0	1	0	0	0	0	0	0	0	0
harmonically	3	.0995	.1144	30.6	0	0	0	0	1	1	1	0	1	0	0	0	0	0	0	0	2	0	0	0	0	0	0	0	0
harmonics	7	.0839	.1779	32.5	0	0	0	0	0	7	0	0	0	0	0	0	0	0	0	1	6	0	0	0	0	0	0	0	0
harmonies	19	.3504	1.4010	41.5	0	0	2	4	2	8	3	0	0	0	0	0	0	0	0	0	15	2	1	0	0	0	1	0	0
harmonious	9	.5789	1.0509	40.2	0	1	1	0	3	2	2	0	0	0	0	1	0	0	0	0	1	1	1	0	2	2	1	0	0
harmoniously	2	.2407	.1090	30.4	0	0	0	0	2	0	0	0	0	0	0	0	0	0	0	1	1	0	0	0	0	0	0	0	0
harmonization	5	.0000	.0404	26.1	0	0	0	1	3	1	0	0	0	0	0	0	0	0	0	0	5	0	0	0	0	0	0	0	0
harmonize	17	.2505	.9461	39.8	0	1	4	3	4	4	1	0	1	0	0	0	0	0	0	0	10	0	6	0	0	0	0	0	0
harmonized	5	.0000	.0404	26.1	0	1	1	1	1	0	1	0	0	0	0	0	0	0	0	0	5	0	0	0	0	0	0	0	0
harmonizes	2	.2109	.0918	29.6	0	0	0	0	1	1	0	0	0	0	0	0	0	0	0	0	1	0	1	0	0	0	0	0	0
harmonizing	14	.1563	.5213	37.2	0	0	0	2	8	2	1	1	0	0	0	0	0	0	0	0	13	0	1	0	0	0	0	0	0
harmony	194	.4354	17.508	52.4	23	21	29	25	36	36	21	3	2	0	0	1	0	5	0	0	150	10	5	0	9	1	3	5	3

6E Happyborough	7N harbour	7N hard-headed	6B hard-surface	5N Hardens	9D harlots
8Q Hara	6E Harbour	4A hard-hit	6F hard-surfaced	7Q Harder	5Q Harlowe
7R hara-kiri	XR hard-bodied	7D hard-looking	7D hard-tipped	8C hardest-earned	5A harm-doing
8D harangue	7Q hard-coated	9N hard-nosed	8A hard-to-comprehend	8C hardest-to-beat	4F harmattan
7F Hararge	7L hard-crusted	4P hard-riding	9B hard-to-get	9H hardpan	8B harme
7Q harassing	4A hard-driven	9R hard-rock	8M hard-to-get-to	7R harem	8K Harmens
9Q harassments	5R hard-driving	7D hard-rutted	3P hard-to-remember	7Q Hares	8K Harmenszoon
7J Harbach	9D hard-fated	4H hard-shell	8J hard-wood	9D Hargest	9R harmfulness
4P Harbin	7A hard-frozen	6G hard-shelled	XR hardcover	9D harkened	8Q harmlessness
8F Harbord	7Q hard-hat	9M hard-soldered	7M hardened-steel	5P Harlan	7F Harmonious

Word Type	F	D	U	SFI	3 Gr 3	4 Gr 4	5 Gr 5	6 Gr 6	7 Gr 7	8 Gr 8	9 Gr 9	X UnGr	A Read	B Eng & Gr	C Comp	D Lit	E Math	F Soc Stud	G Spell	H Sci	J Music	K Art	L Home Ec	M Shop	N Lib F	P Lib NF	Q Lib Ref	R Mag	S Rel
Harmony	3	.3635	.2410	33.8	0	1	0	0	1	1	0	0	0	0	0	0	0	1	0	0	1	0	0	0	0	1	0	0	0
harms	3	.3751	.2467	33.9	0	0	0	1	0	0	1	1	0	0	0	1	0	0	0	1	0	0	0	0	0	0	1	0	0
harness	82	.7272	12.388	50.9	14	24	9	10	15	6	3	1	42	1	1	9	0	5	0	3	0	0	0	0	7	10	1	3	0
harness-maker	3	.1639	.1674	32.2	1	0	0	2	0	0	0	0	1	0	0	0	0	2	0	0	0	0	0	0	0	0	0	0	0
harness-room	2	.0000	.0234	23.7	0	0	0	0	0	0	2	0	0	0	0	0	0	0	0	0	0	0	0	0	2	0	0	0	0
harnessed	20	.6711	2.8006	44.5	6	2	1	2	2	4	3	0	7	0	0	4	0	1	0	2	0	0	0	0	1	2	2	1	0
harnesses	8	.4850	.8378	39.2	1	2	2	2	1	0	0	0	1	0	0	1	0	2	0	0	0	0	0	0	0	1	0	3	0
harnessing	8	.3962	.7436	38.7	1	1	1	0	3	1	1	0	3	0	0	0	0	0	0	1	0	0	0	0	1	0	3	0	0
Harnett	2	.0000	.0215	23.3	0	0	0	0	2	0	0	0	0	0	0	2	0	0	0	0	0	0	0	0	0	0	0	0	0
Harold	54	.7477	8.2426	49.2	12	1	4	4	12	11	7	3	18	2	1	8	1	0	0	1	7	0	0	0	1	4	3	8	0
Harold's	2	.2446	.1125	30.5	0	1	0	0	1	0	0	0	0	1	0	1	0	0	0	0	0	0	0	0	0	0	0	0	0
Haroun-al-Raschid	2	.0000	.0234	23.7	0	0	2	0	0	0	0	0	0	0	0	0	0	0	0	0	0	0	0	0	2	0	0	0	0
harp	37	.2574	2.2614	43.5	3	0	3	15	6	4	4	2	5	2	0	0	0	0	0	1	25	0	0	0	2	2	0	0	0
harp-strings	3	.0000	.1370	31.4	0	0	0	3	0	0	0	0	3	0	0	0	0	0	0	0	0	0	0	0	0	0	0	0	0
Harper	11	.5885	1.3817	41.4	1	3	2	2	2	0	1	0	3	0	0	0	1	1	0	2	0	0	0	0	1	3	0	0	0
Harper's	5	.3830	.4247	36.3	0	2	1	0	1	1	0	0	0	0	0	0	0	2	0	0	0	0	0	0	0	2	1	0	0
Harpers	6	.3819	.5658	37.5	0	0	1	2	0	0	3	0	3	1	0	0	0	2	0	0	0	0	0	0	0	0	0	0	0
harpoon	42	.6273	5.7414	47.6	3	26	3	3	4	0	3	0	30	0	0	2	0	1	1	0	1	0	0	0	4	2	1	0	0
harpooned	2	.0000	.0914	29.6	0	1	0	0	1	0	0	0	2	0	0	0	0	0	0	0	0	0	0	0	0	0	0	0	0
harpooner	2	.1787	.1174	30.7	0	0	0	1	1	0	0	0	1	0	0	0	0	0	0	0	0	0	0	0	1	0	0	0	0
harpoons	3	.3380	.2498	34.0	0	1	0	0	1	0	1	0	1	1	0	0	0	0	0	1	0	0	0	0	0	0	0	0	0
harps	3	.3674	.2408	33.8	0	0	0	0	2	1	0	0	0	0	0	1	0	1	0	0	1	0	0	0	0	0	0	0	0
harpsichord	37	.1167	1.2349	40.9	2	4	9	3	12	6	1	0	3	0	0	0	0	0	0	0	30	0	0	0	0	4	0	0	0
harpsichords	3	.2088	.1442	31.6	0	1	1	0	1	0	0	0	0	0	0	0	0	0	0	0	2	0	0	0	0	0	1	0	0
harpy	2	.2417	.1091	30.4	0	0	0	1	1	0	0	0	0	0	0	0	0	0	0	0	1	0	0	0	0	0	1	0	0
Harriet	62	.2460	3.7760	45.8	50	0	3	1	5	1	2	0	4	0	0	1	1	4	0	0	0	0	0	0	1	50	1	0	0
Harriet's	3	.2373	.1703	32.3	2	0	0	0	0	1	0	0	0	1	0	0	0	0	0	0	0	0	0	0	0	2	0	0	0
Harriett	9	.0000	.0966	29.8	0	0	0	0	0	0	9	0	0	0	0	9	0	0	0	0	0	0	0	0	0	0	0	0	0
Harris	36	.6811	5.0306	47.0	6	2	15	1	2	6	2	2	4	2	0	1	3	1	0	12	5	0	0	0	0	5	0	3	0
Harrisburg	23	.4757	2.5987	44.1	0	17	0	0	1	4	1	0	16	0	0	0	1	4	0	1	0	0	0	0	0	0	0	1	0
Harrison	8	.5545	.9176	39.6	0	0	1	2	2	1	2	0	0	1	0	0	0	2	0	0	1	0	0	0	0	0	2	2	0
Harrodsburg	7	.3613	.6446	38.1	0	5	1	0	1	0	0	0	4	0	0	0	0	1	0	0	0	0	0	0	0	2	0	0	0
harrow	5	.3850	.4834	36.8	3	0	1	0	1	0	0	0	3	0	0	0	0	1	0	0	0	0	0	0	0	1	0	0	0
Harrow	4	.0000	.0438	26.4	0	0	0	4	0	0	0	0	0	4	0	0	0	0	0	0	0	0	0	0	0	0	0	0	0
harry	5	.4234	.4662	36.7	0	0	0	2	1	0	2	0	1	0	0	2	0	0	1	0	0	0	0	0	1	0	0	0	0
Harry	153	.7648	23.739	53.8	39	31	5	15	36	14	11	2	38	11	2	28	23	5	1	0	1	0	1	0	3	13	1	26	0
Harry's	6	.3156	.4753	36.8	1	4	0	0	0	1	0	0	2	0	0	0	3	0	0	0	0	0	0	0	0	1	0	0	0
harsh	61	.8227	10.044	50.0	4	5	6	5	14	15	12	0	9	2	4	10	0	12	2	1	4	1	2	0	4	2	3	5	0
harsher	2	.2152	.1357	31.3	0	0	1	0	1	0	0	0	1	0	0	0	0	1	0	0	0	0	0	0	0	0	0	0	0
harshest	2	.2337	.1157	30.6	0	0	0	0	1	1	0	0	0	0	0	0	0	1	0	0	0	0	0	0	1	0	0	0	0
harshly	12	.4182	1.1728	40.7	0	2	1	2	6	0	1	0	5	0	0	4	0	2	0	0	0	0	0	0	0	0	1	0	0
harshness	2	.2401	.1133	30.5	0	0	0	0	1	0	1	0	0	0	0	0	0	0	0	0	0	0	0	0	0	1	1	0	0
hart	2	.0000	.0290	24.6	2	0	0	0	0	0	0	0	0	0	0	0	0	0	0	0	0	0	0	0	0	2	0	0	0
Hart	8	.3471	.7133	38.5	2	0	0	0	5	1	0	0	5	0	0	0	0	0	0	0	2	0	0	0	0	0	0	1	0
hartebeest	9	.1871	.5507	37.4	0	0	4	0	0	0	5	0	5	0	0	0	0	0	0	0	0	0	0	0	0	0	4	0	0
hartebeests	5	.0000	.0523	27.2	0	0	3	0	2	0	0	0	0	0	0	0	0	0	0	0	0	0	0	0	0	0	5	0	0
Hartford	13	.3302	.9736	39.9	0	1	10	0	0	0	2	0	1	0	0	0	0	2	0	0	0	0	0	0	0	0	7	3	0
Harvard	35	.6803	4.8855	46.9	0	1	5	2	9	6	9	3	6	3	0	2	1	4	0	1	4	0	0	0	0	2	1	11	0
Harve	9	.0457	.2064	33.1	0	0	0	0	1	0	8	0	1	0	0	8	0	0	0	0	0	0	0	0	0	0	0	0	0
harvest	112	.7219	16.462	52.2	27	25	18	11	11	7	5	8	15	5	0	6	0	29	5	8	10	0	1	0	6	16	4	6	1
Harvest	7	.0000	.1013	30.1	0	7	0	0	0	0	0	0	0	0	0	0	0	0	0	0	0	0	0	0	0	7	0	0	0
harvested	45	.5286	5.1137	47.1	1	13	11	5	7	4	1	3	6	0	0	1	0	27	0	2	0	0	2	0	0	0	5	2	0
harvester	3	.2254	.1785	32.5	2	1	0	0	0	0	0	0	0	0	0	0	0	1	0	2	0	0	0	0	0	0	0	0	0
harvesters	3	.3350	.2478	33.9	0	0	1	0	1	1	0	0	1	0	0	0	0	1	0	0	0	0	0	0	0	0	1	0	0
harvesting	26	.5742	3.1571	45.0	4	4	5	4	2	3	2	2	3	0	0	1	0	12	0	2	0	0	0	0	1	3	0	4	0
harvests	14	.5399	1.5782	42.0	3	2	3	2	0	1	2	1	0	0	0	0	0	5	0	1	0	1	0	0	0	2	4	1	0
Harvey	46	.4432	4.4126	46.4	9	3	1	0	6	6	3	18	2	0	0	0	6	0	1	12	0	0	0	0	0	1	1	23	0
Harvey's	6	.3399	.5100	37.1	1	1	0	2	0	1	1	0	2	0	0	0	1	0	0	3	0	0	0	0	0	0	0	0	0
Hary	2	.0000	.0162	22.1	0	2	0	0	0	0	0	0	0	0	0	0	0	0	0	0	2	0	0	0	0	0	0	0	0
has	10369	.9812	2002.9	73.0	1760	1331	1198	1419	2007	1203	1134	317	1690	727	121	300	976	1331	590	1297	473	118	141	143	169	603	831	849	10
Has	2	.1494	.1045	30.2	0	0	1	1	0	0	0	0	1	0	0	0	0	0	0	0	1	0	0	0	0	0	0	0	0
Has-ka	12	.0000	.5482	37.4	0	12	0	0	0	0	0	0	12	0	0	0	0	0	0	0	0	0	0	0	0	0	0	0	0
Has-ka's	3	.0000	.1370	31.4	0	3	0	0	0	0	0	0	3	0	0	0	0	0	0	0	0	0	0	0	0	0	0	0	0
hash	21	.5814	2.6978	44.3	15	0	1	0	2	2	1	0	14	1	0	0	0	0	0	0	1	0	1	0	0	1	0	3	0
Haskell	10	.3764	.9244	39.7	0	7	0	1	0	0	2	0	5	0	0	0	0	0	0	0	0	0	0	0	0	3	0	2	0
hasn't	98	.7447	14.954	51.7	18	21	9	21	10	6	13	0	37	7	4	11	0	2	3	2	0	0	0	0	14	10	1	7	0
Hassan	5	.2382	.2754	34.4	0	0	0	0	0	2	3	0	0	3	0	2	0	0	0	0	0	0	0	0	0	0	0	0	0
hast	40	.6111	5.0278	47.0	7	0	4	6	6	3	14	0	3	5	0	15	0	2	0	0	1	1	0	0	5	8	0	0	0
haste	36	.5747	4.5057	46.5	3	3	4	9	7	5	5	0	18	0	0	7	0	1	0	0	3	0	0	0	3	4	0	0	0
hasten	10	.4484	1.0162	40.1	0	1	7	0	2	0	0	0	4	0	0	1	0	0	0	0	2	0	0	0	3	0	0	0	0
hastened	20	.6042	2.5156	44.0	1	6	2	3	2	2	3	1	4	0	1	3	0	0	0	0	0	0	0	0	6	1	4	1	0
hastening	3	.0000	.0322	25.1	0	1	0	1	1	0	0	0	0	0	0	3	0	0	0	0	0	0	0	0	0	0	0	0	0
hastens	3	.3660	.2411	33.8	0	0	0	1	0	0	0	2	0	0	0	0	0	0	0	1	1	0	0	0	0	0	0	1	0
hastily	53	.7118	7.8164	48.9	8	11	7	8	12	5	2	0	22	2	1	4	0	4	0	0	0	0	0	0	11	5	1	3	0
Hastings	59	.4276	6.1289	47.9	0	41	14	0	2	2	0	0	40	0	0	0	0	1	0	0	0	1	0	0	16	0	1	0	0
hasty	10	.6645	1.3769	41.4	2	0	0	2	4	0	1	1	3	0	0	2	0	0	1	0	1	0	0	0	0	1	1	1	0
hat	511	.8052	83.116	59.2	200	88	43	37	80	39	21	3	174	23	24	40	4	12	20	2	16	3	9	0	108	25	4	47	0
Hat	9	.4940	.9588	39.8	1	4	0	3	0	1	0	0	2	0	0	0	1	0	0	0	2	0	0	0	3	0	1	0	0
hatband	3	.2292	.1615	32.1	0	0	1	0	0	2	0	0	0	0	0	1	0	0	0	0	0	0	0	0	2	0	0	0	0
hatch	114	.5372	13.253	51.2	56	10	14	13	17	1	2	1	24	0	0	1	0	2	0	53	0	0	0	0	0	19	8	7	0
hatched	56	.5908	7.0663	48.5	14	6	4	19	11	1	0	1	16	2	0	0	0	0	0	19	0	0	0	0	1	12	4	2	0
hatcheries	4	.3134	.2876	34.6	0	0	1	0	2	0	0	1	0	0	0	0	0	1	0	1	0	0	0	0	0	0	2	0	0
hatchery	4	.1611	.1738	32.4	0	0	2	0	2	0	0	0	0	0	0	0	0	0	0	1	0	0	0	0	0	0	0	3	0
hatches	16	.4024	1.4618	41.6	5	0	1	3	7	0	0	0	2	0	0	0	0	0	0	9	0	0	0	0	0	2	3	0	0
hatchet	12	.5542	1.3999	41.5	3	2	2	2	2	0	1	0	2	1	0	1	0	0	0	0	0	0	0	1	3	4	0	0	0
Hatchet	4	.0000	.0579	27.6	4	0	0	0	0	0	0	0	0	0	0	0	0	0	0	0	0	0	0	0	0	4	0	0	0
hatchets	2	.2152	.1357	31.3	0	0	1	1	0	0	0	0	1	0	0	0	0	1	0	0	0	0	0	0	0	0	0	0	0
hatching	15	.4387	1.4575	41.6	2	1	0	1	6	0	3	2	3	0	2	1	0	0	0	5	0	0	0	0	0	0	4	0	0
hatchway	2	.0000	.0914	29.6	0	0	0	2	0	0	0	0	2	0	0	0	0	0	0	0	0	0	0	0	0	0	0	0	0
hate	107	.7964	17.277	52.4	12	20	7	17	26	10	15	0	41	6	2	19	0	1	1	1	3	2	0	0	13	9	2	7	0
hated	96	.7167	14.227	51.5	13	17	9	12	26	12	4	3	39	2	0	10	0	5	0	1	2	0	0	0	18	7	6	6	0
hateful	14	.2663	.9225	39.6	0	3	1	0	1	2	7	0	3	0	0	9	0	0	0	0	0	0	0	0	0	1	1	0	0
hates	16	.6673	2.2382	43.5	4	3	1	1	2	2	3	0	7	2	0	2	0	0	0	0	1	0	0	0	2	1	0	1	0
hath	71	.5213	7.7169	48.9	10	3	6	7	12	2	31	0	3	4	0	30	0	1	0	0	7	0	0	0	10	16	0	0	0

5A Harmony's
XR Harmsworth
4P harness-racing
7D Harnett's
5Q Haro
7A Haroun
6J harp-like
4J harp's
6P Harpies
4A Harpoon
6A harpoon's
7P harpsichordists
7A harpstrings
8F harried
5A Harrington
5H Harris'
9N Harrisville
5F Harrod
XP Harroun
3N harrowed
7H harrowing
8K harsh-sounding
6P Harsimus
5Q Harte
5Q Harte's
4N Hartebeest
6P Hartnett
5B Hartshorne
3J harum
XR harum-scarum
4E Harun
8B harvard
8F Harvard-Yale
7R Harvard's
7R Harvester
7H harvestings
7F Harvre
7R Hasanlu
9Q Hasdrubal
4F hashi
4A Haskell's
5A Haskins
7R Hasler
3A hasn'
6A Hasn't
8N hasp
8M hasps
5N hassock
3A HASTA
XH hastiness
4A Hastings'
7R Haswell
7C hat-securer
8G hat's
3N hatboxes
9H hatchet-footed
9H hatchet-shaped
7Q hatchlings
3B Hate-evil
7R hate-mongers
9D hateth
5B Hathaway's
XR Hathorn

Word Type	F	D	U	SFI	3 Gr 3	4 Gr 4	5 Gr 5	6 Gr 6	7 Gr 7	8 Gr 8	9 Gr 9	X UnGr	A Read	B Eng & Gr	C Comp	D Lit	E Math	F Soc Stud	G Spell	H Sci	J Music	K Art	L Home Ec	M Shop	N Lib F	P Lib NF	Q Lib Ref	R Mag	S Rel
Hathorne	5	.0000	.0724	28.6	0	0	0	0	0	0	5	0	0	0	0	0	0	0	0	0	0	0	0	0	0	5	0	0	0
hating	10	.4231	.9700	39.9	1	0	1	3	2	2	1	0	4	0	0	2	0	0	3	0	0	0	0	0	1	0	0	0	0
hatred	30	.6270	3.8925	45.9	2	0	3	0	9	7	6	3	4	0	0	7	0	4	0	0	1	0	0	0	4	6	0	4	0
hatreds	3	.2378	.1809	32.6	1	0	0	0	1	1	0	0	0	0	0	0	0	2	0	0	0	0	0	0	0	1	0	0	0
hats	139	.8561	23.834	53.8	38	32	26	20	12	4	6	1	42	11	2	8	20	7	2	1	4	0	3	0	22	10	4	3	0
hatter	2	.2303	.1079	30.3	0	1	1	0	0	0	0	0	0	0	0	0	0	0	0	0	1	0	0	0	0	1	0	0	0
Hatter	6	.0000	.2741	34.4	0	0	6	0	0	0	0	0	6	0	0	0	0	0	0	0	0	0	0	0	0	0	0	0	0
Hatteras	10	.3332	.7548	38.8	0	1	3	5	1	0	0	0	0	0	0	0	0	0	0	4	0	0	0	0	0	0	1	5	0
Hattie	17	.2301	1.3132	41.2	15	0	0	0	0	0	2	0	15	2	0	0	0	0	0	0	0	0	0	0	0	0	0	0	0
Hattie's	3	.0000	.1370	31.4	3	0	0	0	0	0	0	0	3	0	0	0	0	0	0	0	0	0	0	0	0	0	0	0	0
haughtily	8	.4712	.8620	39.4	0	1	2	4	0	0	1	0	4	1	0	0	0	0	0	0	0	0	0	0	2	0	0	1	0
haughty	7	.4633	.7109	38.5	0	2	1	1	2	0	1	0	2	0	1	0	0	0	0	0	1	0	0	0	2	0	0	1	0
haul	53	.8732	9.2488	49.7	8	12	10	4	11	7	1	0	17	1	1	4	1	5	3	2	6	0	0	1	2	5	2	3	0
haulaway	2	.1494	.1045	30.2	0	1	0	0	1	0	0	0	1	0	0	0	0	0	0	0	1	0	0	0	0	0	0	0	0
hauled	59	.7694	9.2887	49.7	11	4	11	11	13	4	5	0	23	3	0	2	3	12	0	2	0	0	0	0	3	5	4	2	0
hauling	22	.7270	3.2885	45.2	1	3	8	6	2	0	1	1	7	1	0	1	0	5	0	1	2	0	0	0	1	0	1	3	0
hauls	5	.3978	.4500	36.5	0	0	1	0	3	1	0	0	1	0	0	0	0	1	0	0	0	0	0	0	0	0	2	1	0
haunches	13	.4321	1.3244	41.2	0	2	2	3	3	2	1	0	7	1	0	1	0	0	0	0	0	0	0	0	4	0	0	0	0
haunt	5	.4746	.5331	37.3	0	0	0	1	3	1	0	0	2	0	0	1	0	0	0	0	0	0	0	0	0	1	1	0	0
haunted	43	.7375	6.5023	48.1	11	4	7	3	9	7	2	0	16	2	2	7	0	1	2	0	0	0	0	0	3	4	2	4	0
haunting	16	.6189	2.0632	43.1	1	0	4	1	3	5	1	1	4	2	0	2	0	0	0	0	3	1	0	0	0	3	0	1	0
haunts	12	.5509	1.4069	41.5	2	0	0	2	7	0	0	1	3	1	0	4	0	0	0	0	0	0	0	0	0	1	1	2	0
Hausa	4	.3829	.3404	35.3	0	2	1	0	0	0	1	0	0	0	0	0	0	2	0	0	0	0	0	0	0	1	1	0	0
Hauser	6	.2292	.3230	35.1	4	0	2	0	0	0	0	0	0	0	0	2	0	0	0	0	0	0	0	0	4	0	0	0	0
Hausers'	3	.0000	.0352	25.5	3	0	0	0	0	0	0	0	0	0	0	0	0	0	0	0	0	0	0	0	3	0	0	0	0
Havana	24	.5034	2.6429	44.2	0	0	2	4	9	6	2	1	5	0	0	0	0	10	0	0	0	0	0	0	1	4	0	4	0
have	22337	.9889	4345.8	76.4	4060	3455	2688	3185	4061	2321	2068	499	4800	1607	230	1028	1501	2330	1370	3114	603	252	430	168	1072	1536	1013	1255	28
Have	11	.5817	1.3568	41.3	3	2	0	2	2	2	0	0	3	0	0	1	0	0	0	0	1	0	0	0	1	4	0	1	0
haven	7	.3116	.5109	37.1	3	2	0	0	1	0	0	1	1	0	0	0	0	0	0	1	0	0	0	0	0	0	4	1	0
Haven	2	.2433	.1158	30.6	0	1	0	0	1	0	0	0	0	0	0	0	0	0	0	0	0	0	0	0	0	1	0	1	0
haven't	237	.7874	37.908	55.8	54	53	27	20	48	17	15	3	88	12	4	20	0	4	9	6	0	0	2	0	42	30	2	18	0
haversack	4	.1717	.2284	33.6	0	2	0	0	0	2	0	0	2	0	0	2	0	0	0	0	0	0	0	0	0	0	0	0	0
havin'	2	.0000	.0234	23.7	0	0	1	0	1	0	0	0	0	0	0	0	0	0	0	0	0	0	0	0	2	0	0	0	0
having	881	.9766	169.49	62.3	104	88	90	126	214	132	100	27	192	55	15	49	68	62	41	86	16	9	30	4	79	75	43	56	1
Havisham	5	.0000	.0537	27.3	0	0	0	0	0	0	5	0	0	0	0	5	0	0	0	0	0	0	0	0	0	0	0	0	0
Havisham's	2	.0000	.0215	23.3	0	0	0	0	0	0	2	0	0	0	0	2	0	0	0	0	0	0	0	0	0	0	0	0	0
havoc	6	.4250	.5837	37.7	0	0	0	0	4	1	1	0	2	0	0	0	0	0	0	1	0	0	0	0	1	0	2	0	0
Havre	2	.1717	.1142	30.6	0	1	0	0	0	0	1	0	1	0	0	1	0	0	0	0	0	0	0	0	0	0	0	0	0
haw	11	.4221	1.0628	40.3	1	4	2	1	1	2	0	0	4	0	0	0	0	0	0	0	2	0	0	0	4	1	0	0	0
Haw	7	.0000	.0851	29.3	0	0	0	0	0	0	7	0	0	0	0	0	0	0	0	0	0	0	0	0	0	0	0	7	0
Hawaii	155	.4276	14.939	51.7	13	41	68	10	4	16	3	0	18	0	1	0	2	111	0	9	1	0	0	0	0	0	5	8	0
Hawaii's	14	.3778	1.2227	40.9	0	2	9	2	0	1	0	0	2	0	0	0	0	9	0	0	2	0	0	0	0	0	0	1	0
Hawaiian	45	.5996	5.6903	47.6	1	4	20	6	5	7	2	0	7	0	0	0	1	21	1	7	4	0	0	0	0	0	1	3	0
Hawaiians	17	.2606	1.0983	40.4	1	0	14	0	0	2	0	0	0	0	0	0	0	14	0	1	2	0	0	0	0	0	0	0	0
hawk	48	.6275	6.4987	48.1	17	3	7	9	9	1	0	2	28	0	0	2	0	0	0	6	0	0	0	0	4	1	5	2	0
Hawk	39	.6794	5.5579	47.4	3	18	3	3	10	1	1	0	18	3	0	2	0	1	0	1	0	0	0	0	6	6	1	1	0
hawk's	3	.2212	.2099	33.2	2	0	0	0	1	0	0	0	2	0	0	1	0	0	0	0	0	0	0	0	0	0	0	0	0
Hawk's	3	.2357	.2199	33.4	0	1	0	0	2	0	0	0	2	0	0	0	0	0	0	0	0	0	0	0	0	1	0	0	0
Hawke's	2	.0000	.0914	29.6	0	0	2	0	0	0	0	0	2	0	0	0	0	0	0	0	0	0	0	0	0	0	0	0	0
Hawkeye	9	.2616	.5383	37.3	0	0	0	0	7	0	1	1	0	0	0	0	0	0	1	0	0	0	0	0	7	0	0	1	0
Hawkins	11	.2200	.5786	37.6	0	0	0	1	1	8	1	0	0	1	0	0	0	0	0	0	0	0	0	0	1	0	0	9	0
hawks	54	.5470	6.4581	48.1	11	1	15	12	7	5	0	3	19	1	0	0	0	0	0	20	0	0	0	0	0	5	7	2	0
Hawks	4	.2424	.3036	34.8	3	0	0	0	1	0	0	0	3	0	0	0	0	0	0	0	0	0	0	0	0	0	0	1	0
hawksbill	6	.0000	.0628	28.0	0	0	0	0	6	0	0	0	0	0	0	0	0	0	0	0	0	0	0	0	0	0	6	0	0
Hawktown	2	.0000	.0389	25.9	0	2	0	0	0	0	0	0	0	0	0	0	0	2	0	0	0	0	0	0	0	0	0	0	0
hawnk	2	.0000	.0914	29.6	0	2	0	0	0	0	0	0	2	0	0	0	0	0	0	0	0	0	0	0	0	0	0	0	0
hawthorn	3	.3385	.2445	33.9	0	0	0	1	1	0	1	0	1	0	0	0	0	0	0	0	0	0	0	0	1	0	1	0	0
Hawthorne	8	.4553	.7734	38.9	0	0	3	0	0	5	0	0	0	2	0	0	0	1	0	0	0	0	0	0	0	3	2	0	0
Hawthorne's	3	.0000	.0434	26.4	0	0	3	0	0	0	0	0	0	0	0	0	0	0	0	0	0	0	0	0	0	3	0	0	0
haxa	3	.0000	.0583	27.7	0	0	0	0	0	3	0	0	0	0	0	0	0	3	0	0	0	0	0	0	0	0	0	0	0
hay	171	.7733	26.775	54.3	53	15	28	33	17	15	8	2	38	5	3	9	0	32	8	6	16	0	0	0	39	9	1	5	0
Hay	3	.2442	.1815	32.6	0	0	0	0	1	2	0	0	0	0	0	1	0	2	0	0	0	0	0	0	0	0	0	0	0
Hayakawa	5	.3733	.4179	36.2	0	0	0	0	0	4	1	0	0	1	0	0	0	3	0	0	0	0	0	0	0	0	0	1	0
haybales	4	.0000	.0429	26.3	0	0	0	0	0	0	4	0	0	0	0	4	0	0	0	0	0	0	0	0	0	0	0	0	0
Hayden	3	.3452	.2543	34.1	0	1	0	1	0	1	0	0	1	0	0	0	0	0	0	1	0	0	0	0	0	0	0	1	0
Haydn	68	.0529	1.2340	40.9	6	7	24	7	6	16	2	0	0	0	0	0	0	0	0	0	65	0	0	0	0	0	3	0	0
Haydn's	14	.0000	.1132	30.5	1	1	6	0	3	3	0	0	0	0	0	0	0	0	0	0	14	0	0	0	0	0	0	0	0
Hayes	22	.6006	2.7849	44.4	0	0	2	4	10	6	0	0	5	0	0	0	1	6	0	0	1	0	0	0	6	0	2	1	0
hayfield	2	.1717	.1142	30.6	0	1	1	0	0	0	0	0	1	0	0	1	0	0	0	0	0	0	0	0	0	0	0	0	0
haying	3	.3873	.2495	34.0	0	0	0	1	0	1	0	1	0	0	0	1	0	0	0	0	0	0	0	0	1	0	0	1	0
hayloft	6	.2894	.4192	36.2	1	2	2	0	1	0	0	0	1	0	0	0	0	0	0	0	0	0	0	0	3	2	0	0	0
haymow	10	.4436	1.0130	40.1	0	3	3	1	3	0	0	0	4	0	0	2	0	0	0	0	0	0	0	0	3	1	0	0	0
Hayne	2	.0000	.0914	29.6	0	0	0	0	2	0	0	0	2	0	0	0	0	0	0	0	0	0	0	0	0	0	0	0	0
hays	2	.0000	.0389	25.9	0	0	0	0	2	0	0	0	0	0	0	0	0	2	0	0	0	0	0	0	0	0	0	0	0
haystack	11	.5636	1.2978	41.1	1	0	2	1	1	6	0	0	2	1	0	1	0	0	0	0	1	1	0	0	4	0	0	1	0
haystacks	3	.0000	.1370	31.4	2	1	0	0	0	0	0	0	3	0	0	0	0	0	0	0	0	0	0	0	0	0	0	0	0
hazard	25	.6931	3.5174	45.5	0	1	0	3	4	5	10	2	2	1	0	5	0	1	0	4	0	0	1	2	0	1	5	3	0
hazardous	19	.6634	2.5928	44.1	0	1	3	1	3	5	4	2	3	1	1	0	0	1	0	3	0	0	0	0	1	1	5	3	0
hazards	16	.5963	1.9509	42.9	0	0	1	2	7	2	3	1	0	0	1	1	0	0	1	2	0	0	0	0	0	1	5	5	0
haze	28	.6610	3.8269	45.8	3	3	1	3	6	6	3	3	6	1	0	8	0	2	0	2	1	0	0	0	0	3	1	4	0
hazel	12	.6110	1.5759	42.0	1	2	1	4	2	1	1	0	6	1	0	1	0	0	0	1	1	0	0	0	2	0	0	0	0
Hazel	3	.2257	.1583	32.0	0	0	0	0	1	2	0	0	0	2	0	1	0	0	0	0	0	0	0	0	0	0	0	0	0
hazelnut	2	.2297	.1135	30.6	0	0	0	0	1	0	1	0	0	0	0	1	0	1	0	0	0	0	0	0	0	0	0	0	0
hazelnuts	4	.3832	.3414	35.3	0	0	1	1	2	0	0	0	0	0	0	0	0	2	0	0	0	0	0	0	1	1	0	0	0
Hazleton	9	.0000	.1750	32.4	9	0	0	0	0	0	0	0	0	0	0	0	0	9	0	0	0	0	0	0	0	0	0	0	0
hazy	7	.6607	.9509	39.8	0	0	2	1	2	0	2	0	1	1	0	1	0	0	0	1	0	0	0	0	1	1	1	0	0
Hd	2	.0000	.0050	17.0	0	0	0	0	0	0	2	0	0	0	0	0	0	0	0	0	0	0	0	2	0	0	0	0	0
he	46249	.8928	8244.5	79.2	9206	9518	5248	5809	8355	4418	3040	655	19114	1409	427	4724	1081	2606	351	1281	939	192	133	38	5479	4781	1071	2549	74
He	69	.0946	2.1692	43.4	13	12	4	14	13	6	7	0	12	10	1	4	0	2	1	2	14	0	0	0	5	1	0	0	17
HE	6	.0000	.0485	26.9	6	0	0	0	0	0	0	0	0	0	0	0	0	0	0	0	6	0	0	0	0	0	0	0	0
he'	3	.0000	.1370	31.4	3	0	0	0	0	0	0	0	3	0	0	0	0	0	0	0	0	0	0	0	0	0	0	0	0
he'd	358	.6297	47.572	56.8	34	64	46	54	100	29	28	3	137	6	0	67	0	1	0	0	11	0	1	0	73	28	0	34	0
He'd	4	.1787	.2347	33.7	0	0	0	0	2	0	2	0	2	0	0	0	0	0	0	0	0	0	0	0	2	0	0	0	0
he'll	198	.7107	29.083	54.6	29	49	28	21	49	14	8	0	76	6	1	23	0	2	1	0	7	0	0	0	29	32	0	21	0

8J Hatikvah
8D hatless
6A hatmaker
4A hatmakers
3A hatrack
3A Hats
9K Hatshepsut
5A Hatten
9P Hattiesburg
8J haud
5Q haulage
6A haulin'
7N haunch
7B Haunted
7F hauntingly
5P Hausas
5J Hauschka
7J hautboy
7R hav-a-leena
3R Havasupai
8F haversacks
8C Having
9R Haw's
7R hawk-bill
5A hawk-watching
7A hawked
8D hawking
5A hawks'
7N hawksbills
5N haws
9J hawse
7D Hawthorn
4R HAY
6N haycock
8F Hayes's
6H hayfever
8F Haym
5J Haymaker's
8F Haymarket
7F Haynsworth
6B hayrack
8F hayrake
9D hayseed
4A haywire
4Q Hazard
9D hazarded
6A hazel-tree
3F Hazleton's
9M HB
4A He-Who-Cries-When-**
7D He-Who-Knows-the-Marks
3J he-bear
4N He-e-enry
9Q he-man
7D he-men

					3	4	5	6	7	8	9	X	A	B	C	D	E	F	G	H	J	K	L	M	N	P	Q	R	S
Word Type	F	D	U	SFI	Gr 3	Gr 4	Gr 5	Gr 6	Gr 7	Gr 8	Gr 9	UnGr	Read	Eng & Gr	Comp	Lit	Math	Soc Stud	Spell	Sci	Music	Art	Home Ec	Shop	Lib F	Lib NF	Lib Ref	Mag	Rel
He'll	4	.0000	.0579	27.6	1	3	0	0	0	0	0	0	0	0	0	0	0	0	0	0	0	0	0	0	0	4	0	0	0
he's	767	.7144	113.43	60.5	117	163	84	109	148	72	65	9	329	24	2	113	0	7	3	0	23	0	5	0	122	67	0	72	0
He's	7	.1146	.2114	33.3	1	4	1	0	0	0	1	0	0	0	0	0	0	0	0	0	6	0	0	0	0	0	0	1	0
head	2487	.8832	439.00	66.4	497	424	264	322	534	245	168	33	975	62	14	263	27	61	16	130	63	24	14	34	360	244	64	136	0
Head	22	.4101	1.9835	43.0	3	5	1	2	3	4	4	0	4	1	0	2	2	0	0	0	1	5	0	0	0	4	0	3	0
Head-Tilt	2	.0000	.0394	26.0	0	0	0	0	0	2	0	0	0	0	0	0	0	0	0	2	0	0	0	0	0	0	0	0	0
head-on	3	.2212	.2099	33.2	0	0	1	0	1	0	1	0	2	0	0	1	0	0	0	0	0	0	0	0	0	0	0	0	0
head-shy	2	.0000	.0290	24.6	0	2	0	0	0	0	0	0	0	0	0	0	0	0	0	0	0	0	0	0	0	2	0	0	0
headache	16	.5397	1.9165	42.8	0	5	0	0	7	2	2	0	8	3	0	0	0	0	0	2	0	0	0	0	0	2	1	0	0
headaches	7	.5165	.7701	38.9	0	0	0	2	1	1	3	0	1	1	0	0	0	1	0	1	0	0	1	0	0	0	0	2	0
headband	8	.3766	.7392	38.7	4	1	0	0	1	1	0	1	4	0	0	0	0	0	0	0	0	0	0	0	0	2	0	2	0
headbands	6	.4845	.6657	38.2	4	2	0	0	0	0	0	0	3	0	0	0	0	1	0	0	0	0	0	0	0	1	0	1	0
headboard	4	.3641	.3324	35.2	0	0	0	1	2	0	1	0	1	0	0	0	0	0	0	0	0	0	1	0	1	0	0	1	0
headdress	10	.6262	1.3266	41.2	0	6	2	1	0	0	0	1	4	1	0	0	0	0	0	0	0	0	0	0	1	2	1	1	0
headdresses	6	.6046	.7580	38.8	1	2	1	1	0	0	0	1	1	0	0	0	0	1	0	0	0	0	0	0	1	1	1	1	0
headed	173	.8050	28.243	54.5	16	36	21	15	43	24	14	4	68	3	0	9	8	19	0	0	6	0	0	1	19	11	10	19	0
headers	3	.2321	.1635	32.1	0	0	0	0	2	0	1	0	0	0	0	0	0	0	0	0	0	0	0	0	0	0	1	2	0
headfirst	4	.3726	.3697	35.7	1	0	2	0	0	1	0	0	2	0	0	0	0	1	0	0	0	0	0	0	1	0	0	0	0
headgear	2	.0000	.0394	26.0	0	0	2	0	0	0	0	0	0	0	0	0	0	0	0	2	0	0	0	0	0	0	0	0	0
headin'	3	.1250	.1342	31.3	1	0	1	1	0	0	0	0	1	0	0	0	0	0	0	0	0	0	0	0	2	0	0	0	0
heading	152	.7275	22.589	53.5	16	37	25	14	46	10	4	0	42	54	5	3	4	2	7	4	1	0	1	1	11	6	1	10	0
headings	98	.4723	10.176	50.1	4	20	21	11	31	6	4	1	31	31	17	0	7	1	2	4	1	0	2	0	0	0	1	1	0
headland	9	.1083	.2882	34.6	0	0	0	8	0	1	0	0	0	0	0	0	0	0	0	0	0	0	0	0	8	1	0	0	0
headlands	3	.3390	.2450	33.9	1	0	0	1	1	0	0	0	1	0	0	0	0	0	0	0	0	0	0	0	0	0	1	1	0
Headless	2	.1523	.0721	28.6	0	0	0	1	0	0	1	0	0	0	1	0	0	0	0	0	0	0	0	0	0	0	0	1	0
headlight	7	.2626	.4497	36.5	0	1	0	3	1	0	2	0	1	0	2	1	0	0	0	3	0	0	0	0	0	0	0	0	0
headlights	13	.6595	1.8109	42.6	1	3	2	1	3	0	3	0	6	0	0	1	0	1	0	1	0	0	0	0	1	0	1	2	0
headline	26	.4615	2.5073	44.0	11	0	2	2	1	3	5	2	0	15	3	1	0	1	1	1	0	0	0	0	0	0	0	4	0
headlines	29	.7483	4.4025	46.4	6	2	6	4	2	7	2	0	6	5	2	0	1	4	2	3	0	1	0	1	0	0	2	3	0
headlong	20	.7076	2.9447	44.7	2	3	2	2	1	7	2	1	9	1	0	2	0	2	0	0	0	0	0	0	1	3	1	1	0
headman	6	.3089	.4509	36.5	0	3	2	1	0	0	0	0	1	0	0	2	0	3	0	0	0	0	0	0	0	0	0	0	0
Headman	5	.2190	.2843	34.5	0	0	0	0	0	4	1	0	0	0	0	1	0	4	0	0	0	0	0	0	0	0	0	0	0
HEADMAN	2	.0000	.0215	23.3	0	0	0	0	0	0	2	0	0	0	0	2	0	0	0	0	0	0	0	0	0	0	0	0	0
headmaster	5	.4614	.4852	36.9	0	1	0	3	0	1	0	0	0	2	0	1	0	0	0	0	0	0	0	0	0	1	0	1	0
headphone	4	.1995	.2197	33.4	0	0	1	3	0	0	0	0	0	0	0	0	0	1	0	3	0	0	0	0	0	0	0	0	0
headphones	3	.0000	.0583	27.7	0	0	3	0	0	0	0	0	0	0	0	0	0	3	0	0	0	0	0	0	0	0	0	0	0
headquartered	2	.0000	.0243	23.9	0	0	1	0	0	0	1	0	0	0	0	0	0	0	0	0	0	0	0	0	0	0	0	2	0
headquarters	65	.6008	8.1817	49.1	4	3	17	9	12	8	11	1	10	0	0	1	0	20	1	1	0	0	0	0	0	9	13	10	0
Headquarters	4	.2991	.2943	34.7	1	0	1	1	0	0	1	0	1	0	0	0	0	0	0	0	0	0	0	0	0	1	0	2	0
heads	358	.8765	62.651	58.0	76	60	39	45	59	35	39	5	108	8	2	40	13	27	1	13	7	11	2	10	40	35	14	27	0
Heads	2	.2437	.1129	30.5	0	0	1	0	0	0	0	1	0	0	0	0	0	0	0	0	0	0	0	0	0	0	1	1	0
headsaw	3	.0000	.0076	18.8	0	0	0	0	0	0	3	0	0	0	0	0	0	0	0	0	0	0	0	3	0	0	0	0	0
headstall	2	.2443	.1130	30.5	0	0	0	0	1	1	0	0	0	0	0	1	0	0	0	0	0	0	0	0	0	1	0	0	0
headstock	8	.2351	.4292	36.3	0	0	0	0	6	0	2	0	0	0	0	0	0	0	0	0	0	0	0	2	0	0	0	6	0
headstones	2	.2444	.1132	30.5	1	0	1	0	0	0	0	0	0	1	0	0	0	0	0	0	0	0	0	0	1	0	0	0	0
headstrong	4	.2445	.3067	34.9	0	1	1	1	1	0	0	0	3	0	0	0	0	0	0	0	0	0	0	0	0	1	0	0	0
headwaters	13	.4523	1.3255	41.2	0	1	6	0	4	1	1	0	4	0	0	0	0	3	0	0	0	0	0	0	0	0	2	4	0
headway	7	.4781	.7292	38.6	1	0	1	2	2	0	1	0	2	0	1	0	0	1	0	0	0	1	0	0	1	0	1	0	0
headwind	3	.2279	.2143	33.3	0	0	0	3	0	0	0	0	2	0	0	0	0	0	0	0	0	0	0	0	0	0	0	1	0
headword	18	.0000	.1970	32.9	0	0	10	2	6	0	0	0	0	18	0	0	0	0	0	0	0	0	0	0	0	0	0	0	0
heady	3	.3870	.2492	34.0	0	0	0	0	0	0	2	1	0	0	0	0	0	0	0	0	0	0	0	0	1	0	1	1	0
heah	4	.1787	.2347	33.7	0	0	0	0	2	2	0	0	2	0	0	0	0	0	0	0	0	0	0	0	2	0	0	0	0
heal	20	.2569	1.3721	41.4	2	4	4	2	4	2	2	0	7	0	0	4	0	2	0	2	0	0	0	0	1	0	1	2	1
healed	19	.1026	.7900	39.0	2	3	3	4	4	0	3	0	8	0	0	2	0	0	1	0	0	0	0	0	0	1	3	1	3
healer	2	.2291	.1135	30.5	0	0	0	0	1	0	0	1	0	0	0	1	0	0	0	1	0	0	0	0	0	0	0	0	0
healing	17	.6906	2.4164	43.8	0	4	1	4	3	4	1	0	4	2	0	0	0	2	0	1	1	0	0	0	3	0	1	3	0
heals	3	.1832	.1417	31.5	0	0	0	0	2	1	0	0	0	0	0	2	0	0	0	1	0	0	0	0	0	0	0	0	0
health	331	.6678	45.362	56.6	26	19	32	47	68	84	48	7	24	7	0	8	0	46	5	134	5	0	34	0	3	15	28	22	0
Health	19	.6066	2.3858	43.8	2	0	1	0	5	3	5	3	1	0	0	2	0	3	0	3	0	0	0	0	0	2	2	6	0
healthful	20	.5838	2.4408	43.9	1	0	2	5	6	6	0	0	2	0	0	0	0	8	3	2	0	0	2	0	0	0	1	2	0
healthier	9	.5533	1.0625	40.3	1	1	1	1	0	1	3	1	2	0	0	0	0	2	0	1	0	0	1	0	0	0	1	2	0
healthiest	2	.2152	.1357	31.3	0	0	0	0	1	1	0	0	1	0	0	0	0	1	0	0	0	0	0	0	0	0	0	0	0
healthily	2	.2440	.1132	30.5	0	0	0	0	0	0	1	1	0	0	0	1	0	0	0	0	0	0	0	0	0	0	0	1	0
healthy	140	.6760	19.572	52.9	18	25	21	17	18	20	12	9	30	0	0	4	0	17	6	42	1	0	13	0	2	12	2	10	1
Healthy	2	.0000	.0914	29.6	0	0	0	0	2	0	0	0	2	0	0	0	0	0	0	0	0	0	0	0	0	0	0	0	0
heap	52	.7064	7.5760	48.8	5	9	9	9	9	3	7	1	18	0	0	14	0	1	2	1	1	0	1	0	3	5	1	5	0
heaped	21	.7056	3.0597	44.9	4	0	5	2	6	2	1	1	7	0	0	4	0	1	0	2	1	0	0	0	3	1	1	1	0
heaping	4	.4798	.4045	36.1	1	0	1	0	1	0	1	0	0	0	0	1	0	0	0	1	0	0	0	0	1	0	1	0	0
heaps	20	.5519	2.3697	43.7	3	6	4	2	2	1	1	1	6	0	0	6	0	0	0	2	0	0	0	0	3	0	1	2	0
hear	2154	.7829	339.90	65.3	597	418	302	280	298	143	99	17	467	102	40	139	2	65	548	133	325	5	2	4	101	137	17	63	4
Hear	5	.3846	.4764	36.8	2	0	1	1	0	0	1	0	3	1	0	0	0	0	0	0	0	0	0	0	0	0	0	1	0
heard	1988	.8464	338.68	65.3	371	387	260	285	329	190	132	34	837	94	19	182	7	96	50	62	143	3	2	2	223	164	13	91	0
Heard	2	.2411	.1091	30.4	0	0	0	1	0	1	0	0	0	0	0	1	0	0	0	0	1	0	0	0	0	0	0	0	0
hearing	199	.7938	31.918	55.0	17	23	25	34	52	34	14	0	55	17	4	23	0	3	7	26	31	0	0	0	6	12	6	9	0
hearings	12	.4943	1.2525	41.0	1	0	0	0	3	5	2	1	0	0	0	0	0	4	0	0	1	0	0	0	0	1	1	5	0
hearken	2	.2291	.1135	30.5	0	0	0	0	0	0	1	1	0	0	0	1	0	0	0	1	0	0	0	0	0	0	0	0	0
hears	67	.7439	10.121	50.1	15	11	8	6	10	8	7	2	14	6	5	5	1	3	2	6	6	0	0	0	0	12	3	4	0
hearsay	3	.3842	.2485	34.0	1	0	0	0	1	1	0	0	0	0	0	1	0	0	0	0	0	0	0	0	0	1	1	0	0
hearse	2	.1733	.1149	30.6	0	0	0	1	1	0	0	0	1	1	0	0	0	0	0	0	0	0	0	0	0	0	0	0	0
heart	1032	.8151	169.64	62.3	132	141	151	160	149	119	134	46	282	22	6	99	6	40	2	231	37	1	6	1	88	58	69	79	5
Heart	19	.6032	2.3571	43.7	0	4	3	3	4	3	2	0	1	0	0	8	0	2	1	1	1	0	0	0	3	0	1	1	0
heart-breaking	2	.0000	.0290	24.6	1	0	1	0	0	0	0	0	0	0	0	0	0	0	0	0	0	0	0	0	0	2	0	0	0
heart-broken	2	.2411	.1091	30.4	0	0	0	0	0	1	1	0	0	0	0	1	0	0	0	0	1	0	0	0	0	0	0	0	0
heart-lung	3	.2445	.1818	32.6	0	0	0	0	0	1	2	0	0	0	0	0	0	0	0	2	0	0	0	0	0	0	1	0	0
heart-rending	3	.3369	.2489	34.0	0	0	1	0	1	1	0	0	1	0	0	1	0	1	0	0	0	0	0	0	0	0	0	0	0
heart-shaped	6	.3143	.4867	36.9	4	0	0	0	0	0	2	0	3	0	0	1	0	0	0	1	0	1	0	0	0	0	0	0	0
heart's	10	.6622	1.3772	41.4	2	1	1	2	1	0	1	2	3	0	0	1	0	0	0	1	1	0	0	0	0	1	1	2	0
Heart's	2	.0000	.0215	23.3	0	0	1	0	0	0	1	0	0	0	0	2	0	0	0	0	0	0	0	0	0	0	0	0	0
heartaches	3	.3756	.2468	33.9	1	0	0	0	1	0	1	0	0	0	0	1	0	1	0	0	0	0	0	0	0	0	1	0	0
heartbeat	18	.4459	1.7999	42.6	2	0	6	5	2	1	1	1	3	0	0	1	0	0	0	11	1	0	0	0	0	2	0	0	0
heartbeats	6	.4819	.6140	37.9	1	0	1	0	3	1	0	0	0	0	0	1	0	0	0	3	1	0	0	0	0	0	1	0	0
heartbreak	3	.3824	.2446	33.9	0	0	1	0	0	1	1	0	0	0	0	1	0	0	0	0	1	0	0	0	0	0	0	1	0
Heartbreak	2	.0000	.0243	23.9	0	0	0	0	0	2	0	0	0	0	0	0	0	0	0	0	0	0	0	0	0	0	0	2	0
heartbreaking	4	.2958	.2914	34.6	0	0	0	2	2	0	0	0	1	0	0	0	0	0	0	0	0	0	0	0	2	1	0	0	0
heartbroken	4	.2445	.3067	34.9	0	1	1	2	0	0	0	0	3	0	0	0	0	0	0	0	0	0	0	0	0	1	0	0	0
heartened	2	.0000	.0914	29.6	0	0	0	1	0	1	0	0	2	0	0	0	0	0	0	0	0	0	0	0	0	0	0	0	0

7N he'p
7N he'ped
4N head-down
7D head-dress
3A head-end
7D head-high
7Q head-hunters
4B Head-in-Air
4A head-over-heels
8R head-shop
8D head's
7R header
7F headhunter
9Q headlamp
6R Headlamp
6F headless
9A headline-diplomacy
7R headliner
7A Headmaster's
XR headmasters
5A headpiece
9M headrig
6D headsails
XH headset
6R headsets
4A headshake
9N Headshrinkers
6N headstalls
6B headwords
5J heal-all
3P healeth
8D healthgiving
9D healths
4H healthy-looking
3P heardest
8B hearer
XH hearers
9D hearest
5A hearkening
XR Hearl
9D heart-in-throat
5P heart-stirring
7Q heart-stopper
6A heart'll
9D heart's-ease
9Q heartburn
7N hearten
7D heartening

Word Type	F	D	U	SFI	3 Gr 3	4 Gr 4	5 Gr 5	6 Gr 6	7 Gr 7	8 Gr 8	9 Gr 9	X UnGr	A Read	B Eng & Gr	C Comp	D Lit	E Math	F Soc Stud	G Spell	H Sci	J Music	K Art	L Home Ec	M Shop	N Lib F	P Lib NF	Q Lib Ref	R Mag	S Rel
heartfelt	3	.3408	.2477	33.9	0	0	0	1	0	2	0	0	1	0	0	1	0	0	0	0	0	0	0	0	0	1	0	0	0
hearth	33	.5342	3.7829	45.8	4	11	4	6	3	0	4	1	8	0	0	4	0	0	0	0	1	0	0	0	7	12	0	1	0
hearthstone	3	.2260	.1580	32.0	0	0	0	0	3	0	0	0	0	0	0	2	0	0	0	0	0	0	0	0	0	0	1	0	0
heartily	15	.4808	1.5467	41.9	1	3	1	4	2	1	3	0	2	1	0	4	0	1	0	0	0	0	0	0	6	1	0	0	0
heartiness	2	.1717	.1142	30.6	0	0	0	1	1	0	0	0	1	0	0	1	0	0	0	0	0	0	0	0	0	0	0	0	0
heartland	5	.3639	.4034	36.1	1	0	0	0	2	1	1	0	0	0	0	0	0	2	0	0	0	0	0	0	0	0	2	1	0
Heartland	2	.0000	.0243	23.9	0	0	0	0	0	0	0	2	0	0	0	0	0	0	0	0	0	0	0	0	0	0	0	2	0
heartless	7	.2517	.4817	36.8	0	0	3	2	0	0	1	1	3	0	0	0	0	0	0	1	3	0	0	0	0	0	0	0	0
hearts	103	.2419	6.5636	48.2	19	15	6	15	18	8	13	9	32	4	1	12	0	0	0	8	15	0	1	0	4	7	2	9	8
Hearts	2	.0000	.0162	22.1	0	0	0	0	0	2	0	0	0	0	0	0	0	0	0	0	2	0	0	0	0	0	0	0	0
heartsick	3	.3369	.2489	34.0	0	0	0	0	1	2	0	0	1	0	0	1	0	1	0	0	0	0	0	0	0	0	0	0	0
hearty	41	.6720	5.7215	47.6	6	3	4	3	10	9	6	0	14	0	1	7	0	3	1	1	1	0	5	0	0	6	1	1	0
heat	1003	.7374	150.32	61.8	166	133	140	122	176	141	109	16	122	12	4	17	6	38	9	470	4	1	53	54	22	68	82	41	0
Heat	4	.2278	.2257	33.5	0	0	2	2	0	0	0	0	0	0	0	0	0	0	0	2	0	0	0	0	0	0	2	0	0
heat-producing	2	.2278	.1128	30.5	0	0	0	1	1	0	0	0	0	0	0	0	0	0	0	1	0	0	0	0	0	0	1	0	0
heat-treating	3	.0000	.0076	18.8	0	0	0	0	0	0	3	0	0	0	0	0	0	0	0	0	0	0	0	3	0	0	0	0	0
heat-treatment	2	.0000	.0050	17.0	0	0	0	0	0	0	2	0	0	0	0	0	0	0	0	0	0	0	0	2	0	0	0	0	0
heated	170	.6584	23.086	53.6	38	18	20	25	18	18	31	2	13	2	0	5	0	21	1	93	2	0	4	11	2	5	8	3	0
heatedly	2	.1814	.1187	30.7	0	1	0	0	1	0	0	0	1	0	0	0	0	0	0	0	0	0	0	0	0	0	0	1	0
heater	13	.4961	1.4385	41.6	2	1	5	4	0	0	0	1	4	0	0	0	0	0	0	6	0	0	0	0	1	1	0	1	0
heaters	8	.4935	.8282	39.2	1	1	2	0	0	4	0	0	1	0	1	2	0	0	0	0	0	0	0	1	0	0	3	0	0
heath	3	.2197	.2090	33.2	0	0	0	0	3	0	0	0	2	0	0	0	0	0	0	0	0	0	0	0	0	0	1	0	0
Heath	5	.2868	.3232	35.1	0	0	0	0	3	0	1	1	0	0	0	0	0	0	0	1	0	1	0	0	0	0	0	3	0
heathen	11	.5703	1.3029	41.1	0	1	4	2	3	0	1	0	1	0	0	3	0	0	0	0	0	0	0	0	2	2	2	1	0
heathens	3	.2260	.1580	32.0	1	0	0	0	0	0	2	0	0	0	0	2	0	0	0	0	0	0	0	0	0	0	1	0	0
heather	7	.4889	.7832	38.9	0	1	3	0	3	0	0	0	4	1	0	1	0	0	0	0	0	0	0	0	0	0	0	1	0
Heather	2	.0000	.0299	24.8	0	2	0	0	0	0	0	0	0	0	0	0	2	0	0	0	0	0	0	0	0	0	0	0	0
Heathkit	3	.0000	.0365	25.6	0	0	0	0	3	0	0	0	0	0	0	0	0	0	0	0	0	0	0	0	0	0	0	3	0
heating	105	.4499	10.096	50.0	7	7	17	13	9	34	16	2	6	1	0	0	0	7	1	38	0	0	6	26	0	0	16	4	0
heats	35	.6098	4.4445	46.5	9	5	8	3	5	4	0	1	2	0	0	0	0	1	1	21	0	0	0	1	2	1	3	3	0
heav'n	3	.0000	.0243	23.8	1	2	0	0	0	0	0	0	0	0	0	0	0	0	0	0	3	0	0	0	0	0	0	0	0
Heav'n	2	.0000	.0162	22.1	1	1	0	0	0	0	0	0	0	0	0	0	0	0	0	0	2	0	0	0	0	0	0	0	0
heave	20	.4431	1.9388	42.9	11	1	1	3	2	2	0	0	4	0	0	1	0	0	0	1	7	0	0	0	6	1	0	0	0
Heave	2	.0000	.0162	22.1	0	0	0	0	0	0	2	0	0	0	0	0	0	0	0	0	2	0	0	0	0	0	0	0	0
heaved	20	.6317	2.6242	44.2	1	1	4	3	5	2	4	0	4	2	0	5	0	0	0	2	1	0	0	0	3	3	0	0	0
heaven	103	.2083	5.5706	47.5	14	12	13	9	19	3	30	3	18	3	0	34	0	3	0	1	10	0	0	0	7	13	1	4	9
Heaven	30	.6124	3.8133	45.8	3	1	5	5	9	2	5	0	5	0	0	9	0	2	0	0	3	0	0	0	4	4	3	0	0
heaven-rescued	2	.0000	.0162	22.1	0	1	0	1	0	0	0	0	0	0	0	0	0	0	0	0	2	0	0	0	0	0	0	0	0
heaven's	11	.4309	1.0615	40.3	0	0	0	5	1	3	2	0	3	1	0	5	0	0	0	0	0	0	0	0	0	1	0	1	0
Heaven's	2	.2440	.1132	30.5	0	0	0	0	0	0	1	1	0	0	0	1	0	0	0	0	0	0	0	0	0	0	0	1	0
heavenly	33	.4103	2.9834	44.7	4	5	1	9	2	3	5	4	4	1	0	1	0	1	0	7	6	0	0	0	0	2	8	2	1
Heavenly	4	.0000	.1827	32.6	3	0	0	1	0	0	0	0	4	0	0	0	0	0	0	0	0	0	0	0	0	0	0	0	0
heavens	69	.8360	11.618	50.7	4	8	7	15	12	8	10	5	25	1	1	7	0	4	0	10	6	1	0	0	4	3	4	3	0
Heavens	5	.3355	.4048	36.1	1	0	0	1	0	1	2	0	2	0	0	0	0	0	0	0	1	1	0	0	1	0	0	0	0
heaves	4	.1514	.1630	32.1	0	0	1	0	3	0	0	0	0	0	0	3	0	0	0	1	0	0	0	0	0	0	0	0	0
heavier	133	.7924	21.200	53.3	17	14	27	13	31	19	11	1	14	5	0	5	5	9	3	50	0	2	6	9	2	9	8	6	0
heaviest	35	.7842	5.5292	47.4	3	7	5	3	8	5	4	0	3	1	0	2	6	8	1	5	0	0	0	0	2	2	4	1	0
heavily	106	.8474	17.911	52.5	5	11	12	13	31	17	17	0	13	3	2	14	0	13	6	2	0	2	3	0	18	5	13	12	0
heaviness	3	.3399	.2456	33.9	0	1	0	0	0	0	1	1	1	0	0	1	0	0	0	0	0	0	0	0	0	0	0	1	0
heaving	10	.4436	1.0130	40.1	0	1	1	2	1	5	0	0	4	0	0	2	0	0	0	0	0	0	0	0	3	1	0	0	0
heavy	984	.9275	180.93	62.6	177	195	128	113	151	106	92	22	273	37	21	55	11	120	25	113	16	22	32	18	55	110	33	43	0
heavy-duty	8	.2918	.5583	37.5	0	1	0	1	5	1	0	0	1	0	0	0	0	0	0	1	0	0	0	0	0	1	0	5	0
heavy-footed	2	.1948	.1250	31.0	0	1	0	0	1	0	0	0	1	0	0	0	0	0	0	0	0	0	0	0	0	1	0	0	0
heavy-hearted	3	.2261	.2131	33.3	0	0	0	0	1	2	0	0	2	0	0	0	0	0	0	0	0	0	0	0	1	0	0	0	0
heavy-in	2	.0000	.0050	17.0	0	0	0	0	0	0	2	0	0	0	0	0	0	0	0	0	0	0	0	2	0	0	0	0	0
heavy-set	2	.1948	.1250	31.0	0	1	0	0	0	0	1	0	1	0	0	0	0	0	0	0	0	0	0	0	0	1	0	0	0
heavyweight	7	.2794	.5122	37.1	0	1	0	0	4	2	0	0	3	0	0	0	0	1	0	0	0	0	2	0	0	1	0	0	0
Heber	2	.2437	.1129	30.5	0	0	0	0	1	1	0	0	0	0	0	0	0	0	0	0	0	0	0	0	0	0	1	1	0
Hebrew	27	.5446	3.1596	45.0	6	2	5	5	3	1	4	1	8	2	0	0	0	4	0	0	7	0	0	0	0	2	4	0	0
Hebrews	8	.1778	.4005	36.0	0	0	0	6	1	0	1	0	0	1	0	0	0	7	0	0	0	0	0	0	0	0	0	0	0
Hebrides	2	.2297	.1135	30.6	0	0	0	0	2	0	0	0	0	0	0	1	0	1	0	0	0	0	0	0	0	0	0	0	0
heck	9	.3270	.7191	38.6	0	1	1	0	6	0	0	1	3	0	0	0	0	0	0	0	0	0	0	0	2	0	0	4	0
Heck	4	.2073	.2003	33.0	0	0	0	0	0	3	1	0	0	0	0	1	0	0	0	0	0	0	0	0	0	0	0	3	0
hectic	3	.2266	.1614	32.1	0	0	0	0	1	0	1	1	0	0	0	0	0	0	0	0	0	0	0	0	1	0	0	2	0
hecto-	2	.0000	.0299	24.8	0	0	0	1	1	0	0	0	0	0	0	0	2	0	0	0	0	0	0	0	0	0	0	0	0
hectometer	2	.0000	.0299	24.8	0	0	0	0	2	0	0	0	0	0	0	0	2	0	0	0	0	0	0	0	0	0	0	0	0
Hector	50	.4447	5.4788	47.4	42	0	0	0	2	3	3	0	42	1	0	1	0	0	0	0	2	0	0	0	0	0	4	0	0
Hector's	2	.0000	.0914	29.6	2	0	0	0	0	0	0	0	2	0	0	0	0	0	0	0	0	0	0	0	0	0	0	0	0
hedge	27	.5615	3.2282	45.1	1	9	1	8	5	0	3	0	8	0	3	1	1	0	0	0	1	0	0	0	7	3	0	3	0
hedged	3	.2292	.1615	32.1	0	0	0	0	1	1	1	0	0	0	0	1	0	0	0	0	0	0	0	0	2	0	0	0	0
hedgehog	11	.4028	.9765	39.9	0	2	4	3	0	1	0	1	1	1	0	1	0	0	0	2	0	0	0	0	6	0	0	0	0
hedgehogs	2	.0000	.0234	23.7	0	1	1	0	0	0	0	0	0	0	0	0	0	0	0	0	0	0	0	0	2	0	0	0	0
hedgerow	4	.4560	.4041	36.1	0	1	1	1	0	0	0	1	1	0	0	0	0	0	0	0	0	0	0	0	1	1	0	1	0
hedgerows	10	.5339	1.1505	40.6	0	0	2	2	2	1	0	3	3	1	1	0	0	1	0	0	0	0	0	0	2	0	0	2	0
hedges	20	.7070	2.8975	44.6	3	2	6	5	2	0	2	0	5	1	1	1	0	2	0	0	1	0	0	0	3	2	4	0	0
Hedges	2	.1814	.1187	30.7	0	0	1	0	0	0	0	1	1	0	0	0	0	0	0	0	0	0	0	0	0	0	0	1	0
Hedingham	2	.0000	.0209	23.2	0	0	0	0	0	2	0	0	0	0	0	0	0	0	0	0	0	0	0	0	0	0	2	0	0
hee	4	.3604	.3538	35.5	1	2	0	0	0	1	0	0	2	0	0	1	0	0	0	0	1	0	0	0	0	0	0	0	0
Hee	9	.0000	.1094	30.4	0	0	0	1	0	0	8	0	0	0	0	0	0	0	0	0	0	0	0	0	0	0	0	9	0
heed	22	.6359	2.9369	44.7	1	1	4	4	9	0	3	0	8	0	1	4	0	0	0	0	3	0	0	0	1	4	1	0	0
heeded	7	.4701	.7421	38.7	0	1	2	0	1	0	3	0	3	0	0	1	0	0	0	0	1	0	0	0	0	0	0	2	0
heeding	2	.0000	.0914	29.6	0	0	0	1	0	1	0	0	2	0	0	0	0	0	0	0	0	0	0	0	0	0	0	0	0
heedless	9	.5970	1.1143	40.5	1	0	0	1	4	1	2	0	1	0	0	3	0	1	1	1	1	0	0	0	1	0	0	0	0
heehaw	2	.0000	.0914	29.6	0	0	1	1	0	0	0	0	2	0	0	0	0	0	0	0	0	0	0	0	0	0	0	0	0
heel	38	.6445	5.0173	47.0	3	4	5	10	6	3	6	1	6	0	0	2	0	1	0	1	8	0	5	3	6	4	0	2	0
heel-toe	4	.0000	.0323	25.1	0	3	0	1	0	0	0	0	0	0	0	0	0	0	0	0	4	0	0	0	0	0	0	0	0
heeled	2	.1843	.0808	29.1	0	0	0	1	1	0	0	0	0	0	1	0	0	0	0	0	1	0	0	0	0	0	0	0	0
heels	109	.7808	17.363	52.4	22	22	14	12	19	10	9	1	49	0	2	9	0	5	1	1	7	0	4	0	18	7	2	4	0
heem	5	.2086	.3320	35.2	0	0	0	0	3	2	0	0	3	0	0	0	0	0	0	0	0	0	0	0	2	0	0	0	0
heerd	3	.2212	.2099	33.2	2	0	0	0	1	0	0	0	2	0	0	1	0	0	0	0	0	0	0	0	0	0	0	0	0
heered	2	.0000	.0234	23.7	0	0	0	0	1	1	0	0	0	0	0	0	0	0	0	0	0	0	0	0	2	0	0	0	0
hefty	5	.0824	.1675	32.2	0	0	1	0	4	0	0	0	1	0	0	0	0	0	0	0	0	0	0	0	0	0	0	4	0
Hegel	2	.0000	.0209	23.2	0	0	0	0	0	2	0	0	0	0	0	0	0	0	0	0	0	0	0	0	0	0	2	0	0

9B heartful
7N hearth-brush
4A hearth-fire
7Q hearthside
7A heartier
6A hearties
5A heartiest
4A heartwarming
7Q heartwood
5A Hearty
5A Hearty's
7A hease
8H heat-absorbing
8A heat-measuring
8L heat-sensitive
9M heat-treat
9M heat-treated
4H heated-up
6H HEATER
6A heathenish
9D heathpacks
7A heaths
5Q Heating
4H heatproof
4N heatpump
3J heav'nly
3J Heav'nly
7J heav'ns
XR heaven-sent
4J heaven-thoughts
4A heavenward
4P heavier-built
7Q heavier-featured
9Q heavier-than-air
8D heavies
4A heavily-built
4Q heavily-fortified
3K Heaving
7Q Heavy
8B heavy-bodied
XR heavy-handed
7Q heavy-industry
7N heavy-jowled
7R heavy-thighed
7R heavyset
6P Hecate
8F hecklers
7E hecto
3A Hedge
6A Hedgehog
5A Hedges'
7D Hedin
8R Hedley
3J hee-haw
8D hee'd
6R heedlessly
3P heehaws
3P heehawses
6J heel-tapping
4J heel-toe-step-step-step
6E heelbones
6D heeling
8A heelless
8E HEF
6R hefted
9R heftier

Word Type	F	D	U	SFI	3 Gr 3	4 Gr 4	5 Gr 5	6 Gr 6	7 Gr 7	8 Gr 8	9 Gr 9	X UnGr	A Read	B Eng & Gr	C Comp	D Lit	E Math	F Soc Stud	G Spell	H Sci	J Music	K Art	L Home Ec	M Shop	N Lib F	P Lib NF	Q Lib Ref	R Mag	S Rel
heh	5	.2718	.3338	35.2	0	1	0	0	3	1	0	0	1	0	0	1	0	0	0	0	0	0	0	0	3	0	0	0	0
Heidegger	6	.0000	.0644	28.1	0	0	0	0	6	0	0	0	0	0	0	6	0	0	0	0	0	0	0	0	0	0	0	0	0
HEIDEGGER	8	.0000	.0859	29.3	0	0	0	0	8	0	0	0	0	0	0	8	0	0	0	0	0	0	0	0	0	0	0	0	0
Heidelberg	2	.1698	.1133	30.5	0	0	1	0	0	1	0	0	1	0	0	0	0	0	0	0	0	0	0	0	0	0	1	0	0
Heidi	9	.0829	.2993	34.8	0	2	7	0	0	0	0	0	2	0	0	7	0	0	0	0	0	0	0	0	0	0	0	0	0
heifer	5	.4130	.4651	36.7	0	0	3	0	0	0	0	2	1	0	0	0	0	1	0	0	0	0	0	0	1	0	0	2	0
heigh-ho	2	.2443	.1130	30.5	1	1	0	0	0	0	0	0	0	0	0	1	0	0	0	0	0	0	0	0	1	0	0	0	0
height	346	.7989	55.436	57.4	17	56	39	34	82	51	62	5	29	6	10	13	118	19	2	53	2	3	8	25	9	14	24	11	0
heighten	2	.2407	.1090	30.4	0	0	0	0	0	2	0	0	0	1	0	0	0	0	0	0	1	0	0	0	0	0	0	0	0
heightened	12	.5021	1.2669	41.0	0	0	0	1	3	4	4	0	1	0	0	1	0	0	0	0	3	0	0	0	0	1	1	5	0
heightens	2	.0000	.0037	15.7	0	0	0	0	1	0	1	0	0	0	0	0	0	0	0	0	0	2	0	0	0	0	0	0	0
heights	85	.7439	12.763	51.1	6	15	11	4	18	11	14	6	6	0	1	2	24	2	0	12	4	0	0	5	1	6	14	8	0
Heights	8	.6030	.9858	39.9	0	0	1	1	3	2	1	0	0	0	0	1	0	1	0	0	1	0	0	0	1	0	2	2	0
Heine	3	.2197	.2090	33.2	0	0	0	2	0	0	1	0	2	0	0	0	0	0	0	0	0	0	0	0	0	0	1	0	0
Heinold	3	.0000	.0365	25.6	0	0	0	3	0	0	0	0	0	0	0	0	0	0	0	0	0	0	0	0	0	0	0	3	0
Heinold's	2	.0000	.0243	23.9	0	0	0	2	0	0	0	0	0	0	0	0	0	0	0	0	0	0	0	0	0	0	0	2	0
heinous	2	.2443	.1130	30.5	0	0	0	1	0	0	1	0	0	0	0	1	0	0	0	0	0	0	0	0	1	0	0	0	0
Heinrich	10	.3801	.8913	39.5	0	0	3	0	1	2	3	1	3	0	0	0	0	0	0	2	0	0	0	0	0	1	4	0	0
Heinz	2	.2446	.1257	31.0	0	0	0	0	0	1	1	0	0	0	0	0	0	1	0	1	0	0	0	0	0	0	0	0	0
heir	18	.7334	2.6885	44.3	0	2	2	0	5	6	2	1	4	1	0	2	0	1	1	0	0	0	0	0	1	3	3	2	0
heirs	13	.5530	1.5277	41.8	0	1	1	0	2	7	2	0	2	1	0	0	0	5	0	0	0	0	0	0	1	1	3	0	0
Heiskell	2	.0000	.0243	23.9	0	0	0	0	0	2	0	0	0	0	0	0	0	0	0	0	0	0	0	0	0	0	0	2	0
Heisman	5	.0824	.1675	32.2	0	0	0	1	4	0	0	0	1	0	0	0	0	0	0	0	0	0	0	0	0	0	0	4	0
Hela	4	.0000	.0579	27.6	0	0	0	0	0	0	0	4	0	0	0	0	0	0	0	0	0	0	0	0	0	4	0	0	0
held	1049	.9136	190.46	62.8	168	182	119	129	204	126	102	19	338	25	8	72	16	114	8	60	31	5	9	34	95	106	68	60	0
Helen	155	.6665	21.674	53.4	4	55	54	12	3	6	19	2	63	11	0	11	13	3	1	0	0	1	1	0	0	48	0	3	0
Helen's	33	.4945	3.6765	45.7	0	13	13	1	0	1	4	1	15	1	0	3	1	0	0	0	0	0	0	0	0	12	0	1	0
Helena	23	.5375	2.5436	44.1	0	0	1	2	1	3	16	0	0	8	2	8	0	1	0	0	0	0	0	0	0	1	1	2	0
HELENA	35	.0000	.3756	35.7	0	0	0	0	0	0	35	0	0	0	0	35	0	0	0	0	0	0	0	0	0	0	0	0	0
Helene	2	.1814	.1187	30.7	1	0	0	0	0	0	0	1	1	0	0	0	0	0	0	0	0	0	0	0	0	0	0	1	0
helicopter	74	.7029	10.942	50.4	24	5	5	13	11	5	0	11	42	3	1	0	7	3	1	12	0	0	0	0	0	2	0	3	0
helicopters	46	.5954	5.9961	47.8	18	2	3	11	2	2	0	8	26	0	0	0	0	3	0	8	0	0	0	0	0	3	2	4	0
helium	51	.3634	4.2948	46.3	1	1	4	8	9	12	13	3	3	0	0	0	0	0	0	42	0	0	0	1	1	0	2	2	0
hell	58	.6264	7.5005	48.8	1	0	1	1	18	6	25	6	8	1	0	16	0	1	0	0	2	0	0	0	10	10	1	9	0
Hell	11	.6346	1.4472	41.6	1	0	0	0	3	2	0	5	2	0	0	0	0	1	0	0	1	0	0	0	1	2	1	3	0
hell-devil	2	.0000	.0215	23.3	0	0	0	0	0	0	2	0	0	0	0	2	0	0	0	0	0	0	0	0	0	0	0	0	0
Hellas	2	.1948	.1250	31.0	0	0	0	1	1	0	0	0	1	0	0	0	0	0	0	0	0	0	0	0	0	1	0	0	0
Hellenistic	10	.1615	.4730	36.7	0	0	0	0	1	0	9	0	0	0	0	0	0	9	0	0	0	0	0	0	0	0	1	0	0
Heller	2	.0000	.0243	23.9	0	0	0	0	0	0	2	0	0	0	0	0	0	0	0	0	0	0	0	0	0	0	0	2	0
Hellespont	4	.3354	.3295	35.2	1	0	0	0	2	1	0	0	1	0	0	0	0	2	0	0	0	0	0	0	0	1	0	0	0
hello	162	.7693	25.531	54.1	66	25	6	16	22	21	6	0	75	7	1	20	0	8	3	4	5	0	0	0	21	11	0	7	0
Hello	3	.3465	.2515	34.0	1	0	0	0	1	1	0	0	1	0	0	0	0	0	0	0	0	0	0	0	0	1	0	1	0
helm	5	.3456	.4158	36.2	0	0	1	1	3	0	0	0	2	0	1	1	0	0	0	0	0	0	0	0	0	0	0	1	0
helmet	80	.7254	12.137	50.8	14	23	11	12	6	9	2	3	49	1	1	3	0	6	0	2	0	0	0	0	5	6	1	6	0
helmets	28	.6461	3.7489	45.7	7	2	4	1	2	6	5	1	6	2	3	4	0	4	0	2	1	0	0	0	0	3	2	1	0
help	3875	.9671	739.09	68.7	858	752	584	492	510	352	280	47	877	333	43	121	344	503	229	545	107	38	93	24	159	207	78	173	1
Help	5	.5244	.5612	37.5	0	0	1	2	2	0	0	0	1	1	0	0	0	0	0	1	1	0	0	0	0	0	0	1	0
HELP	2	.1717	.1142	30.6	1	0	0	0	1	0	0	0	1	0	0	1	0	0	0	0	0	0	0	0	0	0	0	0	0
helped	696	.8671	120.71	60.8	178	117	133	81	72	69	36	10	186	28	4	36	7	165	9	44	19	6	4	1	47	71	37	29	3
helper	41	.7022	6.0046	47.8	14	11	4	3	4	1	4	0	20	5	0	1	0	2	2	1	0	0	2	0	4	4	0	0	0
Helper	10	.0000	.4568	36.6	10	0	0	0	0	0	0	0	10	0	0	0	0	0	0	0	0	0	0	0	0	0	0	0	0
helpers	44	.6641	6.1713	47.9	10	11	9	3	1	3	7	0	23	6	0	0	0	2	0	0	4	2	0	0	2	2	1	2	0
Helpers	7	.0000	.3198	35.0	7	0	0	0	0	0	0	0	7	0	0	0	0	0	0	0	0	0	0	0	0	0	0	0	0
helpful	209	.8355	34.933	55.4	24	25	27	31	47	31	20	4	30	23	2	5	28	15	15	46	0	3	18	4	4	10	4	2	0
helping	294	.8404	49.561	57.0	73	54	31	43	39	26	22	6	73	58	3	14	2	39	10	28	1	0	8	0	14	16	10	18	0
Helping	2	.0000	.0914	29.6	2	0	0	0	0	0	0	0	2	0	0	0	0	0	0	0	0	0	0	0	0	0	0	0	0
helpings	3	.2757	.1896	32.8	1	0	0	0	1	1	0	0	0	0	0	0	0	0	0	1	0	0	1	0	0	1	0	0	0
helpless	55	.8156	9.0951	49.6	9	8	12	8	9	6	3	0	24	2	1	4	0	5	0	4	2	0	0	0	5	4	1	3	0
helplessly	30	.6324	4.0420	46.1	3	2	5	3	10	3	3	1	14	0	0	4	0	1	0	2	0	0	0	0	4	2	0	3	0
helplessness	4	.2851	.2994	34.8	0	1	0	0	2	0	1	0	2	0	0	1	0	0	0	0	0	0	1	0	0	0	0	0	0
helps	554	.9195	100.91	60.0	146	103	83	67	69	49	27	10	66	45	6	5	45	71	33	141	14	14	25	5	6	41	14	22	1
Helps	34	.0640	.6913	38.4	0	14	4	5	11	0	0	0	0	2	0	0	0	0	32	0	0	0	0	0	0	0	0	0	0
Helsinki	7	.1103	.2338	33.7	0	0	0	1	0	0	0	6	0	0	0	0	0	1	0	0	0	0	0	0	0	0	0	6	0
helter-skelter	4	.3766	.3696	35.7	1	1	0	0	1	0	0	1	2	0	0	0	0	0	0	0	0	0	0	0	0	1	0	1	0
Helvi	4	.0000	.0469	26.7	0	0	0	0	4	0	0	0	0	0	0	0	0	0	0	0	0	0	0	0	4	0	0	0	0
hem	65	.0367	.8689	39.4	4	0	0	0	10	19	32	0	4	0	0	0	0	1	0	0	0	0	58	0	1	1	0	0	0
hematite	17	.2831	1.1769	40.7	2	5	0	0	0	3	7	0	2	0	0	0	0	0	0	8	0	0	0	0	0	0	7	0	0
hemi	5	.2446	.2802	34.5	0	2	0	0	3	0	0	0	0	0	0	0	0	0	2	0	0	0	0	0	0	0	0	3	0
Hemingford	2	.0000	.0389	25.9	0	2	0	0	0	0	0	0	0	0	0	0	0	2	0	0	0	0	0	0	0	0	0	0	0
hemipenes	2	.0000	.0209	23.2	0	0	0	0	2	0	0	0	0	0	0	0	0	0	0	0	0	0	0	0	0	0	2	0	0
hemisphere	40	.5517	4.6638	46.7	5	3	3	8	9	2	7	3	1	1	0	0	0	23	1	8	2	0	0	0	0	0	3	1	0
Hemisphere	107	.4263	10.111	50.0	12	6	6	31	33	14	4	1	3	0	0	0	4	75	0	9	2	0	0	0	0	0	12	2	0
hemispheres	20	.5504	2.3167	43.6	3	3	4	1	4	2	3	0	0	0	0	0	2	11	0	2	1	0	0	0	0	2	2	0	0
Hemispheres	4	.3829	.3404	35.3	0	0	1	1	1	0	1	0	0	0	0	0	0	2	0	0	0	0	0	0	0	1	1	0	0
hemline	2	.2316	.0949	29.8	0	0	0	0	0	2	0	0	0	0	0	0	0	0	0	0	0	1	1	0	0	0	0	0	0
hemlock	9	.6517	1.2106	40.8	2	0	3	0	3	1	0	0	1	0	0	1	0	2	0	1	0	0	0	0	0	2	1	1	0
hemlocks	6	.1187	.2583	34.1	0	0	0	1	1	4	0	0	2	0	0	4	0	0	0	0	0	0	0	0	0	0	0	0	0
hemmed	6	.3185	.4451	36.5	1	0	0	0	1	1	3	0	1	0	0	1	0	1	0	1	0	0	2	0	0	0	0	0	0
hemming	12	.0136	.1121	30.5	0	0	0	1	0	0	11	0	1	0	0	0	0	0	0	0	0	0	11	0	0	0	0	0	0
hemoglobin	5	.2368	.2953	34.7	0	0	1	0	3	1	0	0	0	0	0	0	0	0	0	4	0	0	1	0	0	0	0	0	0
hemp	18	.6149	2.3150	43.6	2	2	5	3	5	1	0	0	3	0	0	0	0	3	0	4	0	0	1	0	0	1	1	5	0
hems	10	.1324	.2875	34.6	0	0	0	0	2	4	4	0	0	0	0	0	0	0	0	0	0	0	9	1	0	0	0	0	0
hen	77	.7914	12.410	50.9	34	9	10	3	8	1	0	12	34	3	0	4	1	0	3	8	8	0	0	0	5	4	3	4	0
Hen	5	.3765	.4671	36.7	4	1	0	0	0	0	0	0	3	0	0	1	0	0	0	0	1	0	0	0	0	0	0	0	0
hen's	7	.3672	.6359	38.0	0	1	2	1	1	0	0	2	3	0	0	0	0	0	0	3	0	0	0	0	0	0	1	0	0
hence	61	.7739	9.4712	49.8	4	1	2	3	19	6	22	4	3	3	5	6	8	5	0	8	2	0	0	2	3	3	10	3	0
henceforth	10	.5346	1.1709	40.7	0	0	0	3	1	2	4	0	4	0	0	2	0	1	0	0	0	0	0	0	0	0	1	2	0
Henderson	15	.3724	1.2682	41.0	0	8	0	1	2	4	0	0	3	3	0	0	0	0	0	0	1	0	0	0	8	0	0	0	0
Henderson's	4	.4577	.4069	36.1	0	1	1	1	1	0	0	0	1	0	0	0	1	0	0	0	0	0	0	0	1	1	0	0	0
Hendon	10	.0000	.1172	30.7	0	0	0	0	10	0	0	0	0	0	0	0	0	0	0	0	0	0	0	0	10	0	0	0	0
Hendon's	2	.0000	.0234	23.7	0	0	0	0	2	0	0	0	0	0	0	0	0	0	0	0	0	0	0	0	2	0	0	0	0

5P hegemony
7D Heidegger's
5D Heidi's
7N heifers
7R heightening
4P Heiman
8R Hein
8A heiress
9L heirloom
9Q Heisenberg
8R Heiskell's
6J Heitor
6F Hekla
9L Helanca
4P Helder
4N Helderbergs
9D HELENA'S
9H Helens
9D Helens's
8A Helfer
5G heli
7R heliarc
9H helical
XR Helicom
7Q heliconiids
7Q Heliconius
9Q helicopter-landing
8R helicoptered
6F Helidon
6A Helios
3A heliport
XH heliports
8H Helium
8H helium-filled
9H helix
7R HELL
8F hell-fire
7R hell-for-leather
7R hell-raising
8D hell-roosters
9N hell's
9R Hell's
8A Helle
XH Hellebore
XH Helleborus
XR Hellenes
XR Hellenic
6R hellgrammite
3D HELLO
4A helloes
3P helloworm
6B Helluland
7Q helmet-like
6R helmeted
9Q Helmont
5Q Helms
6R helmsman
7R helmsman's
5A Helped
6H Helpful
6A helpfully
9A helpfulness
3Q Helsingor
6F Helsinki's
7N Helvetia
4N Helvetius
7N Helvi's
XQ hemilaryngectomized
7A Hemingway
3P Hemingway's
7Q hemipenis
7R hemis
7Q hemisphere's
5H Hemisphere's
7D Hemlock
9L Hemmed
9Q hemorrhage
7D hemorrhaged
7R hemorrhaging
7P hemp-wine
XR Hempstead
9D Hemstreet
6A hen-roost
8F henceforward

Word Type	F	D	U	SFI	3 Gr 3	4 Gr 4	5 Gr 5	6 Gr 6	7 Gr 7	8 Gr 8	9 Gr 9	X UnGr	A Read	B Eng & Gr	C Comp	D Lit	E Math	F Soc Stud	G Spell	H Sci	J Music	K Art	L Home Ec	M Shop	N Lib F	P Lib NF	Q Lib Ref	R Mag	S Rel
Hendrik	2	.0000	.0290	24.6	0	0	2	0	0	0	0	0	0	0	0	0	0	0	0	0	0	0	0	0	0	2	0	0	0
henhouse	6	.3860	.5837	37.7	1	1	0	3	0	1	0	0	4	0	0	0	0	0	0	0	0	0	0	0	0	1	0	1	0
Henke	5	.0000	.0608	27.8	0	0	0	0	5	0	0	0	0	0	0	0	0	0	0	0	0	0	0	0	0	0	0	5	0
Henke's	2	.0000	.0243	23.9	0	0	0	0	2	0	0	0	0	0	0	0	0	0	0	0	0	0	0	0	0	0	0	2	0
Henley	3	.2074	.1511	31.8	1	0	1	1	0	0	0	0	0	2	0	0	0	0	0	0	0	0	0	0	0	1	0	0	0
Hennessey	23	.0000	1.0507	40.2	23	0	0	0	0	0	0	0	23	0	0	0	0	0	0	0	0	0	0	0	0	0	0	0	0
Henny	35	.0000	1.5989	42.0	0	35	0	0	0	0	0	0	35	0	0	0	0	0	0	0	0	0	0	0	0	0	0	0	0
Henny's	2	.0000	.0914	29.6	0	2	0	0	0	0	0	0	2	0	0	0	0	0	0	0	0	0	0	0	0	0	0	0	0
Henri	32	.3639	2.9008	44.6	16	4	3	1	2	3	2	1	18	0	0	0	0	1	0	2	0	5	0	0	0	2	3	1	0
Henrich	2	.0000	.0290	24.6	1	0	0	1	0	0	0	0	0	0	0	0	0	0	0	0	0	0	0	0	0	2	0	0	0
Henrik	3	.3674	.2406	33.8	1	1	0	1	0	0	0	0	0	0	0	0	0	1	0	0	1	0	0	0	0	0	1	0	0
Henry	636	.7642	98.894	60.0	122	188	97	37	108	34	24	26	197	12	8	37	13	41	3	1	21	3	0	0	187	45	46	22	0
Henry's	36	.6181	4.7334	46.8	15	4	6	0	9	0	1	1	15	0	0	4	4	1	0	0	0	0	0	0	6	1	5	0	0
Henrys	7	.3291	.5359	37.3	0	1	0	0	0	5	1	0	0	1	0	0	0	0	0	5	0	0	0	0	0	1	0	0	0
hens	50	.7350	7.6028	48.8	12	9	10	4	10	4	1	0	24	3	0	5	4	2	0	1	3	0	0	0	1	6	0	1	0
Hepburn	2	.2437	.1129	30.5	0	0	1	0	0	1	0	0	0	0	0	0	0	0	0	0	0	0	0	0	0	0	1	1	0
Hephaestion	4	.0000	.1827	32.6	0	4	0	0	0	0	0	0	4	0	0	0	0	0	0	0	0	0	0	0	0	0	0	0	0
Hephaestus	5	.0756	.1562	31.9	0	0	0	0	0	5	0	0	1	0	0	4	0	0	0	0	0	0	0	0	0	0	0	0	0
Hepzibah	2	.0000	.0243	23.9	0	0	0	2	0	0	0	0	0	0	0	0	0	0	0	0	0	0	0	0	0	0	0	2	0
her	11375	.8147	1876.6	72.7	2583	2135	1399	1493	1867	961	807	130	4836	359	156	1247	236	284	81	119	192	24	84	0	1860	1232	111	554	0
Her	7	.4896	.7306	38.6	1	1	3	0	1	0	1	0	1	0	0	1	0	0	0	0	1	0	0	0	3	0	0	1	0
Hera	8	.3413	.6626	38.2	0	0	3	0	0	5	0	0	3	3	0	2	0	0	0	0	0	0	0	0	0	0	0	0	0
Heracles	17	.0000	.7766	38.9	0	0	0	17	0	0	0	0	17	0	0	0	0	0	0	0	0	0	0	0	0	0	0	0	0
herald	7	.4093	.6282	38.0	0	0	0	1	1	2	1	2	1	0	0	3	0	0	1	0	0	0	0	0	0	0	0	2	0
Herald	8	.5302	.9167	39.6	0	0	0	0	2	3	2	1	2	2	0	0	0	2	0	0	0	0	0	0	0	1	1	0	0
heralded	4	.3648	.3145	35.0	0	0	0	0	0	1	3	0	0	0	0	2	0	0	0	0	0	0	0	0	1	0	1	0	0
heraldic	3	.2292	.1615	32.1	0	0	0	0	2	1	0	0	0	0	0	1	0	0	0	0	0	0	0	0	2	0	0	0	0
heralding	3	.3824	.2446	33.9	0	0	0	1	0	0	2	0	0	0	0	1	0	0	0	0	1	0	0	0	0	0	0	1	0
heralds	2	.2443	.1130	30.5	0	0	0	0	1	0	1	0	0	0	0	1	0	0	0	0	0	0	0	0	1	0	0	0	0
herb	11	.6312	1.4096	41.5	0	0	0	3	3	2	2	1	0	1	0	2	0	1	0	0	0	0	1	0	1	0	3	2	0
Herb	10	.5144	1.1369	40.6	1	1	0	5	1	1	0	1	4	1	0	0	1	0	0	0	0	0	0	0	0	1	0	3	0
herbaceous	10	.2424	.5976	37.8	0	0	0	2	7	0	1	0	0	0	0	0	0	0	0	6	0	0	0	0	0	0	4	0	0
herbage	3	.3854	.2500	34.0	0	1	1	0	0	1	0	0	0	1	0	0	0	0	0	0	0	0	0	0	1	1	0	0	0
herbarium	3	.0000	.0314	25.0	0	0	0	2	0	1	0	0	0	0	0	0	0	0	0	0	0	0	0	0	0	0	3	0	0
Herbert	44	.6728	6.1863	47.9	0	4	17	3	6	5	5	4	18	2	0	2	0	3	0	0	6	0	0	0	0	2	4	7	0
Herbert's	4	.0000	.1827	32.6	0	0	4	0	0	0	0	0	4	0	0	0	0	0	0	0	0	0	0	0	0	0	0	0	0
Herbie	9	.0000	.0966	29.8	0	0	0	0	9	0	0	0	0	0	0	9	0	0	0	0	0	0	0	0	0	0	0	0	0
herbivore	3	.1813	.1402	31.5	0	0	0	0	2	1	0	0	0	0	0	0	0	0	0	1	0	0	0	0	0	0	2	0	0
herbivores	13	.1981	.6524	38.1	0	0	0	5	3	5	0	0	0	0	0	0	0	0	0	5	0	0	0	0	0	0	8	0	0
herbivorous	3	.0000	.0314	25.0	0	0	0	0	3	0	0	0	0	0	0	0	0	0	0	0	0	0	0	0	0	0	3	0	0
herbs	27	.6146	3.4299	45.4	0	2	2	14	4	2	1	2	4	1	0	3	0	1	0	0	0	0	1	0	2	1	11	3	0
Herculaneum	2	.0000	.0914	29.6	0	0	0	2	0	0	0	0	2	0	0	0	0	0	0	0	0	0	0	0	0	0	0	0	0
Hercules	22	.6069	2.8863	44.6	0	3	1	0	5	9	2	2	12	0	0	1	0	0	1	2	0	1	0	0	0	0	1	4	0
herd	168	.8039	27.438	54.4	28	49	24	15	35	8	8	1	73	1	5	15	7	19	2	2	7	0	0	0	14	15	4	4	0
herded	2	.2407	.1138	30.6	0	1	0	0	0	0	1	0	0	0	0	1	0	0	0	0	0	0	0	0	0	1	0	0	0
herder	13	.5326	1.4951	41.7	2	0	0	6	2	0	3	0	3	0	0	1	3	3	0	0	0	0	0	0	0	0	0	3	0
herders	11	.4225	1.0544	40.2	0	6	0	4	1	0	0	0	2	0	0	0	0	5	0	0	0	0	0	0	0	3	0	1	0
herding	19	.4840	2.0389	43.1	4	5	2	5	2	0	1	0	5	0	0	1	0	9	0	0	3	0	0	0	0	0	1	0	0
herds	126	.7484	19.164	52.8	17	28	27	23	22	6	2	1	19	4	0	5	0	42	0	9	2	1	0	0	2	15	18	9	0
herdsman	7	.5937	.8726	39.4	0	0	1	3	2	0	1	0	1	0	0	1	0	2	0	1	1	0	0	0	0	1	0	0	0
Herdsman	11	.0000	.5025	37.0	11	0	0	0	0	0	0	0	11	0	0	0	0	0	0	0	0	0	0	0	0	0	0	0	0
herdsmen	15	.4832	1.5719	42.0	1	0	2	4	3	1	4	0	2	0	0	2	0	6	0	0	0	0	0	0	0	1	4	0	0
here	4184	.9614	794.18	69.0	830	783	477	523	757	446	289	79	1267	303	49	325	189	445	127	214	182	34	31	16	358	363	80	200	1
Here	8	.3577	.7145	38.5	5	0	0	2	0	0	1	0	4	0	0	1	0	0	0	0	0	0	0	0	0	3	0	0	0
here's	118	.8049	19.256	52.8	32	33	8	7	21	4	10	3	46	7	2	10	5	3	0	6	4	0	0	0	10	17	0	8	0
hereafter	5	.4186	.4468	36.5	0	0	0	1	1	0	3	0	0	0	0	0	1	1	2	0	0	0	0	0	0	0	1	0	0
hereby	9	.3442	.7051	38.5	1	1	0	0	2	5	0	0	0	0	0	0	0	5	0	0	0	0	0	0	3	1	0	0	0
hereditary	13	.5170	1.4401	41.6	0	0	0	2	4	3	1	3	1	0	0	1	0	1	0	7	0	0	0	0	0	0	2	1	0
heredity	24	.4379	2.2800	43.6	0	0	7	4	1	5	4	3	0	0	0	1	0	0	0	16	0	0	3	0	0	1	3	0	0
Hereford	2	.2139	.1057	30.2	0	0	1	0	0	1	0	0	0	0	0	0	0	1	1	0	0	0	0	0	0	0	0	0	0
heresy	5	.4303	.4639	36.7	0	0	1	0	0	3	1	0	0	0	0	0	0	1	0	1	0	0	0	0	0	0	2	1	0
heretical	2	.0000	.0209	23.2	0	0	0	0	1	1	0	0	0	0	0	0	0	0	0	0	0	0	0	0	0	0	2	0	0
heretofore	10	.5744	1.1883	40.7	0	0	0	0	4	4	0	2	0	0	0	3	0	2	0	1	0	0	0	0	0	1	1	2	0
heritable	3	.2445	.1818	32.6	0	0	0	0	3	0	0	0	0	0	0	0	0	0	0	2	0	0	0	0	0	0	1	0	0
heritage	46	.6297	5.8800	47.7	2	0	2	5	15	11	7	4	0	1	1	0	0	8	0	0	18	2	0	0	2	2	5	7	0
Heritage	2	.2351	.1166	30.7	0	0	0	0	1	0	1	0	0	0	0	0	0	1	0	0	0	0	0	0	0	0	0	1	0
heritages	3	.2088	.1442	31.6	0	0	0	0	1	2	0	0	0	0	0	0	0	0	0	0	2	0	0	0	0	0	1	0	0
Herkimer	2	.0000	.0219	23.4	0	0	2	0	0	0	0	0	0	2	0	0	0	0	0	0	0	0	0	0	0	0	0	0	0
Herman	53	.5574	6.3482	48.0	18	5	2	0	4	20	4	0	17	15	0	4	0	1	0	1	0	0	0	0	0	9	0	6	0
Hermann	3	.1813	.1402	31.5	0	0	1	1	0	1	0	0	0	0	0	0	0	0	0	1	0	0	0	0	0	0	2	0	0
Hermes	8	.2512	.5444	37.4	0	0	0	0	0	4	4	0	3	0	0	4	0	0	0	1	0	0	0	0	0	0	0	0	0
hermetically	4	.3192	.3100	34.9	0	0	0	0	2	2	0	0	1	0	0	0	0	0	0	0	0	0	0	0	0	2	0	1	0
Hermia	5	.0000	.0537	27.3	0	0	0	0	0	0	5	0	0	0	0	5	0	0	0	0	0	0	0	0	0	0	0	0	0
HERMIA	10	.0000	.1073	30.3	0	0	0	0	0	0	10	0	0	0	0	10	0	0	0	0	0	0	0	0	0	0	0	0	0
Hermia's	3	.0000	.0322	25.1	0	0	0	0	0	0	3	0	0	0	0	3	0	0	0	0	0	0	0	0	0	0	0	0	0
hermit	18	.5463	2.1504	43.3	6	5	0	0	6	1	0	0	7	1	0	0	0	0	2	5	0	0	0	0	3	0	0	0	0
Hermit	4	.2387	.2178	33.4	0	2	2	0	0	0	0	0	0	0	0	0	0	0	0	0	2	0	0	0	2	0	0	0	0
Hernandez	13	.1573	.8803	39.4	12	0	0	1	0	0	0	0	12	0	0	0	0	1	0	0	0	0	0	0	0	0	0	0	0
Hernandez's	2	.0000	.0914	29.6	2	0	0	0	0	0	0	0	2	0	0	0	0	0	0	0	0	0	0	0	0	0	0	0	0
Hernando	5	.3568	.3984	36.0	1	0	3	0	1	0	0	0	0	0	0	0	0	2	0	0	0	0	0	0	0	1	2	0	0
Herne	2	.0000	.0914	29.6	0	0	0	0	2	0	0	0	2	0	0	0	0	0	0	0	0	0	0	0	0	0	0	0	0
hero	129	.8316	21.596	53.3	6	22	14	21	28	27	10	1	46	9	0	12	1	8	9	0	11	0	2	0	7	12	4	8	0
Hero	5	.4354	.4679	36.7	0	0	0	2	0	1	2	0	0	0	0	2	0	1	0	1	0	0	0	0	0	0	1	0	0
hero's	3	.2357	.2199	33.4	0	1	0	1	1	0	0	0	2	0	0	0	0	0	0	0	0	0	0	0	0	1	0	0	0
Hero's	4	.0000	.0789	29.0	0	0	0	4	0	0	0	0	0	0	0	0	0	0	0	4	0	0	0	0	0	0	0	0	0
Herodotus	14	.3386	1.1113	40.5	1	1	1	8	2	0	1	0	1	0	0	0	0	9	0	1	0	0	0	0	0	0	3	0	0
heroes	74	.7435	11.367	50.6	2	8	10	22	9	16	7	0	36	3	0	6	0	11	1	0	3	0	0	0	1	5	1	7	0
heroes'	2	.1814	.1187	30.7	0	0	0	0	1	0	1	0	1	0	0	0	0	0	0	0	0	0	0	0	0	0	0	1	0
heroic	29	.7477	4.3951	46.4	3	1	0	4	8	6	4	3	5	1	0	2	0	3	0	2	4	0	0	0	2	2	5	3	0
heroically	3	.3852	.2500	34.0	0	0	0	0	1	0	2	0	0	0	0	1	0	0	0	0	0	0	0	0	0	1	0	1	0
heroin	4	.2346	.2332	33.7	0	0	0	0	3	0	1	0	0	0	0	0	0	0	0	2	0	0	0	0	0	0	0	2	0
heroine	12	.6408	1.5970	42.0	1	1	2	2	3	1	2	0	3	2	0	1	0	1	0	0	2	0	0	0	2	0	1	0	0
heroines	2	.2285	.1129	30.5	0	0	0	0	0	1	1	0	0	0	0	0	0	1	0	0	0	0	0	0	0	0	1	0	0
heroism	6	.5520	.7154	38.5	0	0	1	1	1	1	2	0	2	0	0	1	0	1	0	0	0	0	0	0	0	0	1	1	0

5N Hendreary
8F Hendrickson
3A Hennessey's
8G Hennig
7D henpecked
3A Henri's
7R Henrietta
3A Henriette
3J Hens
3A Henson
6A hepaticas
5P hepatitis
6R hephyr
6R Hepzibah's
3A HER
8H Heraclides
6A Heraclius
9D HERALD
7B heraldry
9Q Heralds'
8Q Herault
6A Herb's
7Q Herbart
7Q Herbart's
9R herculean
4R hercules
5A herdboy
7D herdboys
6F herders'
7G herdsman's
4R Here's
4P hereabouts
7H Heredity
9D Herefords
9D herein
8B heres
XH heretic
8F hereunto
4A herewith
8G Herfordshire
9Q Heriot-Watt
XB herisson
6B Herjolfsson
9D Herman's
8Q Hermanns
6R Hermannstadt
8Q Hermansen
7N hermit's
8Q hermits
7F Hermon
7F Hernad
8Q Hernan
8A Herndon
8Q hernia
3B herns
8N hero-commander
XB hero-tales
6R hero-turned-traitor
9R hero-worship
8N hero-worshiping
4R hero-worshipped
8N Herod
8B Heroes
8J Heroic
7J heroine's
8F Heroism

Word Type	F	D	U	SFI	3 Gr 3	4 Gr 4	5 Gr 5	6 Gr 6	7 Gr 7	8 Gr 8	9 Gr 9	X UnGr	A Read	B Eng & Gr	C Comp	D Lit	E Math	F Soc Stud	G Spell	H Sci	J Music	K Art	L Home Ec	M Shop	N Lib F	P Lib NF	Q Lib Ref	R Mag	S Rel
heron	9	.5862	1.0812	40.3	3	0	4	0	1	0	1	0	0	2	0	0	0	0	0	1	1	0	0	0	3	0	1	1	0
Heron	3	.2309	.1631	32.1	0	0	0	0	1	2	0	0	0	0	0	1	0	0	0	0	0	0	0	0	0	0	0	2	0
herons	11	.4444	1.0980	40.4	3	3	1	0	4	0	0	0	3	0	0	0	0	1	0	1	0	0	0	0	0	2	4	0	0
Heroult	3	.0000	.1370	31.4	3	0	0	0	0	0	0	0	3	0	0	0	0	0	0	0	0	0	0	0	0	0	0	0	0
Herr	18	.2896	1.5624	41.9	16	0	1	1	0	0	0	0	16	0	0	0	0	0	0	0	0	0	0	0	0	1	0	1	0
Herrick	5	.1634	.2733	34.4	0	3	0	2	0	0	0	0	2	0	0	0	0	0	0	0	0	0	0	0	0	3	0	0	0
herring	25	.6851	3.4968	45.4	1	5	4	6	4	1	4	0	1	5	0	2	0	8	0	4	1	0	0	0	0	2	1	1	0
herrings	4	.4475	.4001	36.0	0	1	0	0	3	0	0	0	1	0	0	0	0	0	0	1	0	0	0	0	1	0	1	0	0
hers	61	.6553	8.4190	49.3	10	12	7	8	13	2	9	0	27	9	0	6	0	0	2	0	0	0	0	0	6	9	2	0	0
Herschel	4	.2353	.2382	33.8	0	0	1	0	0	1	0	2	0	0	0	0	0	0	0	3	0	0	0	0	0	0	1	0	0
herself	432	.7822	68.852	58.4	89	83	60	52	76	32	33	7	179	9	4	44	2	9	0	5	0	3	6	0	76	54	7	34	0
Hertford	10	.0000	.1172	30.7	0	0	0	0	10	0	0	0	0	0	0	0	0	0	0	0	0	0	0	0	10	0	0	0	0
Hertford's	2	.0000	.0234	23.7	0	0	0	0	2	0	0	0	0	0	0	0	0	0	0	0	0	0	0	0	2	0	0	0	0
hertz	3	.0000	.0076	18.8	0	0	0	0	0	3	0	0	0	0	0	0	0	0	0	0	0	0	0	3	0	0	0	0	0
Hertz	5	.2028	.2557	34.1	0	0	0	0	0	3	1	1	0	0	0	0	0	0	0	2	0	0	0	0	0	0	3	0	0
Herzen	5	.0000	.0523	27.2	0	0	0	0	0	5	0	0	0	0	0	0	0	0	0	0	0	0	0	0	0	0	5	0	0
Herzl	2	.0000	.0389	25.9	0	0	0	0	2	0	0	0	0	0	0	0	0	2	0	0	0	0	0	0	0	0	0	0	0
Hesburgh	7	.1766	.3250	35.1	0	0	0	0	0	0	7	0	0	0	0	0	0	2	0	0	0	0	0	0	0	0	0	5	0
hesitant	5	.3814	.4791	36.8	0	0	2	0	0	3	0	0	3	0	0	0	0	1	0	0	0	0	0	0	0	0	0	1	0
hesitantly	7	.4673	.7408	38.7	0	0	0	0	5	1	0	1	3	0	0	1	0	0	0	0	0	0	0	0	1	0	0	2	0
hesitate	29	.8244	4.8039	46.8	1	2	5	0	11	5	5	0	7	2	0	1	1	1	0	3	1	0	1	0	3	2	2	5	0
hesitated	60	.6401	8.1038	49.1	3	14	5	6	17	6	6	3	24	3	0	9	0	1	0	1	0	0	0	0	10	8	0	4	0
hesitates	2	.1814	.1187	30.7	0	0	0	0	0	2	0	0	1	0	0	0	0	0	0	0	0	0	0	0	0	0	0	1	0
hesitating	7	.3934	.6131	37.9	0	0	0	0	4	0	3	0	1	0	0	3	0	0	0	0	0	0	0	0	1	2	0	0	0
hesitatingly	4	.0974	.1495	31.7	0	0	1	1	2	0	0	0	1	0	0	0	0	0	0	0	0	0	0	0	3	0	0	0	0
hesitation	19	.6800	2.6297	44.2	1	3	1	0	8	4	2	0	2	4	1	3	0	0	1	0	0	0	0	0	2	4	0	2	0
Hesperides	3	.2223	.2106	33.2	0	0	0	0	2	1	0	0	2	1	0	0	0	0	0	0	0	0	0	0	0	0	0	0	0
Hessians	6	.2212	.4538	36.6	0	2	0	3	0	1	0	0	5	0	0	0	0	1	0	0	0	0	0	0	0	0	0	0	0
het	2	.2305	.1080	30.3	0	0	1	0	0	0	1	0	0	0	0	0	0	0	1	0	0	0	0	0	0	1	0	0	0
Hetch	2	.0000	.0209	23.2	0	0	2	0	0	0	0	0	0	0	0	0	0	0	0	0	0	0	0	0	0	0	2	0	0
Hetchy	2	.0000	.0209	23.2	0	0	2	0	0	0	0	0	0	0	0	0	0	0	0	0	0	0	0	0	0	0	2	0	0
heterochromatic	2	.0000	.0209	23.2	0	0	0	0	0	0	0	2	0	0	0	0	0	0	0	0	0	0	0	0	0	0	2	0	0
heterodyne	2	.0000	.0215	23.3	0	0	0	0	2	0	0	0	0	0	0	2	0	0	0	0	0	0	0	0	0	0	0	0	0
heterozygote	2	.0000	.0209	23.2	0	0	0	0	0	0	0	2	0	0	0	0	0	0	0	0	0	0	0	0	0	0	2	0	0
heterozygotes	5	.2028	.2557	34.1	0	0	0	0	0	0	0	5	0	0	0	0	0	0	0	2	0	0	0	0	0	0	3	0	0
Hetrick	5	.0000	.0608	27.8	0	0	0	0	5	0	0	0	0	0	0	0	0	0	0	0	0	0	0	0	0	0	0	5	0
Hetty	28	.3023	2.1923	43.4	11	0	0	4	13	0	0	0	13	0	0	12	0	0	0	0	0	0	0	0	3	0	0	0	0
Hetty's	3	.2292	.1615	32.1	0	0	0	2	1	0	0	0	0	0	0	1	0	0	0	0	0	0	0	0	2	0	0	0	0
hev	4	.0000	.0469	26.7	0	0	0	0	0	4	0	0	0	0	0	0	0	0	0	0	0	0	0	0	4	0	0	0	0
hew	3	.3399	.2456	33.9	0	0	0	1	0	2	0	0	1	0	0	1	0	0	0	0	0	0	0	0	0	0	0	1	0
hewed	4	.3078	.2971	34.7	0	0	1	2	1	0	0	0	1	0	0	0	0	0	0	0	0	0	0	0	2	0	1	0	0
hewing	2	.2443	.1130	30.5	0	0	0	1	1	0	0	0	0	0	0	1	0	0	0	0	0	0	0	0	1	0	0	0	0
hexachlorophene	2	.0000	.0243	23.9	0	0	1	0	1	0	0	0	0	0	0	0	0	0	0	0	0	0	0	0	0	0	0	2	0
hexagon	27	.3106	1.9113	42.8	0	0	4	6	2	3	12	0	0	0	0	0	23	0	0	0	0	0	0	1	0	1	2	0	0
hexagonal	4	.2016	.1828	32.6	0	0	0	0	1	2	1	0	0	0	0	0	1	0	0	0	0	0	0	2	0	0	1	0	0
hey	159	.5862	20.009	53.0	47	38	14	20	19	12	6	3	68	1	0	10	0	1	0	0	35	0	0	0	13	16	0	15	0
Hey	6	.2343	.3251	35.1	4	0	0	0	0	2	0	0	0	0	0	0	0	0	0	1	4	0	0	0	1	0	0	0	0
heyday	5	.4098	.4297	36.3	0	1	0	0	2	1	1	0	0	0	1	0	0	0	0	0	1	0	0	0	0	1	2	0	0
Heyerdahl	3	.1650	.1684	32.3	0	2	0	1	0	0	0	0	1	0	0	0	0	0	0	2	0	0	0	0	0	0	0	0	0
Heyward	7	.0000	.0821	29.1	0	0	0	0	7	0	0	0	0	0	0	0	0	0	0	0	0	0	0	0	7	0	0	0	0
hi	85	.6449	11.440	50.6	26	17	13	4	12	4	8	1	27	8	0	5	0	1	0	0	5	0	2	0	28	1	0	8	0
Hi	5	.2901	.3447	35.4	0	0	0	1	1	0	3	0	1	0	0	0	0	0	0	0	0	0	1	0	3	0	0	0	0
HI	6	.2398	.3414	35.3	3	1	0	0	0	0	2	0	0	0	0	3	3	0	0	0	0	0	0	0	0	0	0	0	0
Hi-Wah	3	.0000	.0322	25.1	0	0	0	0	3	0	0	0	0	0	0	3	0	0	0	0	0	0	0	0	0	0	0	0	0
Hi-dee-roon	3	.0000	.0243	23.8	3	0	0	0	0	0	0	0	0	0	0	0	0	0	0	0	3	0	0	0	0	0	0	0	0
hi-ee	2	.0000	.0914	29.6	2	0	0	0	0	0	0	0	2	0	0	0	0	0	0	0	0	0	0	0	0	0	0	0	0
hi-fi	9	.4876	1.0092	40.0	1	0	0	5	0	3	0	0	5	0	0	0	0	0	0	2	1	0	0	0	0	0	1	0	0
Hi-no-yo-o-jin	2	.0000	.0914	29.6	0	0	0	2	0	0	0	0	2	0	0	0	0	0	0	0	0	0	0	0	0	0	0	0	0
hi's	2	.2446	.1142	30.6	1	0	1	0	0	0	0	0	0	0	0	0	0	0	0	0	0	0	0	0	1	0	0	1	0
Hiawatha	7	.4812	.7787	38.9	0	0	4	1	1	1	0	0	4	0	0	1	0	1	0	0	0	0	0	0	0	0	0	1	0
hibernate	23	.2722	1.5841	42.0	6	0	1	0	14	1	1	0	2	1	0	0	0	0	0	18	0	0	0	0	0	2	0	0	0
hibernated	3	.2427	.1822	32.6	0	0	0	0	2	0	0	1	0	0	0	0	0	0	0	2	0	0	0	0	0	0	0	1	0
hibernating	13	.5804	1.5848	42.0	1	0	1	1	8	0	1	1	1	1	0	0	0	0	0	7	0	0	0	0	1	1	1	1	0
hibernation	21	.4676	2.2148	43.5	2	0	2	0	11	0	4	2	6	0	0	1	0	0	0	11	0	0	0	0	2	0	1	0	0
hibiscus	3	.1187	.1291	31.1	0	0	0	1	2	0	0	0	1	0	0	2	0	0	0	0	0	0	0	0	0	0	0	0	0
hiccups	2	.1733	.1149	30.6	0	1	0	0	0	0	1	0	1	1	0	0	0	0	0	0	0	0	0	0	0	0	0	0	0
Hickel	2	.0000	.0243	23.9	0	0	0	0	0	0	2	0	0	0	0	0	0	0	0	0	0	0	0	0	0	0	0	2	0
Hickok	3	.3553	.2608	34.2	0	1	1	1	0	0	0	0	1	0	0	0	0	1	0	0	0	0	0	0	0	1	0	0	0
hickory	15	.6394	1.9952	43.0	2	3	4	2	3	1	0	0	3	0	0	0	0	1	1	2	0	0	0	0	2	4	2	0	0
Hickory	10	.4013	.8935	39.5	0	7	0	1	0	0	1	1	1	1	0	0	0	1	0	0	0	0	0	0	0	6	0	1	0
hid	127	.6524	17.385	52.4	20	30	20	22	22	8	5	0	47	8	0	17	0	8	3	0	0	0	0	0	21	22	0	1	0
Hidalgo	6	.3509	.4797	36.8	0	0	0	0	3	3	0	0	0	0	0	0	0	3	0	1	0	0	0	0	2	0	0	0	0
hidden	210	.9067	37.896	55.8	23	35	30	39	41	24	15	3	76	5	1	15	2	12	7	15	3	2	1	7	16	18	18	12	0
Hidden	3	.3427	.2477	33.9	1	0	1	1	0	0	0	0	1	0	0	0	0	0	0	0	0	0	0	0	1	0	0	1	0
hide	241	.8695	41.918	56.2	57	48	23	49	45	15	4	0	78	8	2	22	0	10	7	22	6	4	0	1	35	31	6	9	0
hide-and-seek	8	.4871	.9006	39.5	2	2	0	1	2	1	0	0	5	0	0	1	0	0	0	0	0	0	0	0	1	0	0	1	0
hide-out	4	.0000	.1827	32.6	0	1	0	1	2	0	0	0	4	0	0	0	0	0	0	0	0	0	0	0	0	0	0	0	0
hideaway	2	.2440	.1132	30.5	1	0	0	0	1	0	0	0	0	0	0	1	0	0	0	0	0	0	0	0	0	0	0	1	0
hideous	7	.4547	.6723	38.3	1	0	2	0	1	0	3	0	0	1	0	1	0	0	0	0	0	0	0	0	3	2	0	0	0
hideout	4	.2891	.2856	34.6	0	0	0	0	4	0	0	0	1	2	0	0	0	0	0	0	0	0	0	0	0	1	0	0	0
hiders	3	.0000	.0322	25.1	0	0	0	0	0	0	3	0	0	0	0	3	0	0	0	0	0	0	0	0	0	0	0	0	0
hides	91	.7427	13.790	51.4	30	11	13	19	11	4	1	2	18	4	0	3	0	31	0	8	3	0	0	0	6	8	8	2	0
hiding	134	.7834	21.502	53.3	25	37	11	14	26	17	2	2	71	4	0	14	1	2	0	4	3	1	0	0	7	14	6	7	0
hiding-place	3	.3429	.2528	34.0	0	0	1	2	0	0	0	0	1	0	0	0	0	0	0	1	0	0	0	0	1	0	0	0	0
hierarchy	2	.1387	.0689	28.4	0	0	1	0	0	1	0	0	0	0	1	0	0	0	0	0	0	0	0	0	0	1	0	0	0
hieroglyphic	5	.0000	.0406	26.1	0	2	0	0	2	1	0	0	0	0	0	0	0	0	5	0	0	0	0	0	0	0	0	0	0
hieroglyphics	18	.3405	1.3242	41.2	0	4	5	0	7	1	0	1	1	5	0	0	0	1	5	0	0	5	0	0	0	0	0	1	0
hierogylph	2	.0000	.0037	15.7	0	0	2	0	0	0	0	0	0	0	0	0	0	0	0	0	0	2	0	0	0	0	0	0	0
Higgins	6	.2818	.4318	36.4	0	0	0	1	1	1	3	0	2	3	0	0	0	0	0	0	0	0	0	0	0	1	0	0	0
Higginson	3	.0000	.0352	25.5	0	0	0	0	3	0	0	0	0	0	0	0	0	0	0	0	0	0	0	0	3	0	0	0	0
high	2237	.9522	420.88	66.2	398	371	268	280	413	219	212	76	524	66	22	117	67	315	32	293	99	10	23	27	131	169	140	202	0

7D HERREN
9E Herrick's
6R Herring
7Q herringbone
7P Hershey
7Q Herstal
5P Hertfordshire
7A Hertwig
7R Hertzsprung
5P Herut
8Q Herzen's
9B hes
9R Hesburgh's
9R Hesikiah
7A hesitancy
6A Hesper
XH Hesperornis
7C Hesperus
8F Hesse
9Q Hesse-Cassel
6R Hessian
8M heterodyning
XH heterozygosis
XH heterozygous
7F hevea
9F HEW
6R Hewitt
8M hex
9M Hex
9M hexagonal-shaped
9M hexagons
XB hexameter
XB hexameters
4P Hey-yo
9R Heyman
8A hez
3N Hezron
5Q HF
XR hgl
5Q hhd
8J Hi-Fi
6A hi-fi's
8C hi-ho
3P hi-o
5N hi-yi
7H hibernates
5R hibernations
5Q hibernicus
7N hibisci
5Q Hibiya
6R hiccough
4A hiccup
3R hiccuped
8N hiccuping
9C hick'ry
7P Hickerson
XR Hicketheier
XR Hickethier
XR Hickethier's
4P Hicks
7N hid'n
3N HIDDEN
6B Hide-and-Go-Seek
8R hide-outs
7N hide's
7Q hideousness
4R hideouts
3N hidin'
4P Hiding
9D hie
6J hieland
5P hierarchically
8R hierarchies
8F hiered
7A hieroglyph
9Q Hieron
9N hifi
9R Higby
8D higgled

Word Type	F	D	U	SFI	3 Gr 3	4 Gr 4	5 Gr 5	6 Gr 6	7 Gr 7	8 Gr 8	9 Gr 9	X UnGr	A Read	B Eng & Gr	C Comp	D Lit	E Math	F Soc Stud	G Spell	H Sci	J Music	K Art	L Home Ec	M Shop	N Lib F	P Lib NF	Q Lib Ref	R Mag	S Rel
High	131	.7924	20.958	53.2	3	19	12	10	36	32	16	3	34	12	0	8	8	3	1	2	12	0	2	0	16	5	2	26	0
high-	2	.2375	.1088	30.4	0	0	0	0	0	1	1	0	0	0	0	0	0	0	0	0	1	0	0	0	0	0	0	1	0
high-altitude	5	.3467	.3861	35.9	0	0	1	1	1	1	1	0	0	0	0	0	0	0	0	1	0	0	0	0	0	2	2	0	0
high-arched	2	.0000	.0162	22.1	0	0	0	0	0	0	2	0	0	0	0	0	0	0	0	0	2	0	0	0	0	0	0	0	0
high-brow	2	.2303	.1079	30.3	0	0	0	1	0	0	1	0	0	0	0	0	0	0	0	0	1	0	0	0	0	1	0	0	0
high-calorie	2	.0000	.0394	26.0	0	0	0	0	2	0	0	0	0	0	0	0	0	0	0	2	0	0	0	0	0	0	0	0	0
high-carbon	4	.0000	.0101	20.0	0	0	0	0	0	2	2	0	0	0	0	0	0	0	0	0	0	0	0	4	0	0	0	0	0
high-class	2	.1814	.1187	30.7	0	0	0	0	0	1	0	1	1	0	0	0	0	0	0	0	0	0	0	0	0	0	0	1	0
high-compression	3	.2940	.1911	32.8	0	0	0	0	1	0	2	0	0	0	0	0	0	0	0	0	0	0	0	1	0	0	1	1	0
high-councillor	3	.0000	.1370	31.4	0	3	0	0	0	0	0	0	3	0	0	0	0	0	0	0	0	0	0	0	0	0	0	0	0
high-energy	8	.2278	.4514	36.5	0	0	0	3	2	1	2	0	0	0	0	0	0	0	0	4	0	0	0	0	0	0	4	0	0
high-fashion	2	.1814	.1187	30.7	1	0	0	0	0	0	0	1	1	0	0	0	0	0	0	0	0	0	0	0	0	0	0	1	0
high-flying	3	.3452	.2543	34.1	0	0	0	0	2	1	0	0	1	0	0	0	0	0	0	1	0	0	0	0	0	0	0	1	0
high-frequency	3	.0000	.0591	27.7	0	0	0	0	1	0	2	0	0	0	0	0	0	0	0	3	0	0	0	0	0	0	0	0	0
high-grade	10	.4112	.9121	39.6	1	0	0	3	2	0	4	0	1	0	0	0	0	5	0	0	0	0	0	1	0	0	3	0	0
high-heeled	3	.3756	.2468	33.9	0	1	0	0	2	0	0	0	0	0	0	1	0	1	0	0	0	0	0	0	0	0	1	0	0
high-level	2	.1814	.1187	30.7	0	0	0	2	0	0	0	0	1	0	0	0	0	0	0	0	0	0	0	0	0	0	0	1	0
high-performance	2	.0000	.0243	23.9	0	0	0	0	2	0	0	0	0	0	0	0	0	0	0	0	0	0	0	0	0	0	0	2	0
high-pitched	22	.7408	3.3246	45.2	0	1	1	9	6	2	3	0	5	1	0	2	0	0	0	6	2	0	0	0	2	2	1	1	0
high-power	10	.1626	.4769	36.8	0	1	1	1	7	0	0	0	0	0	0	0	0	0	0	9	0	0	0	0	0	0	1	0	0
high-powered	5	.4730	.5355	37.3	0	1	0	1	3	0	0	0	2	1	0	0	0	0	0	1	0	0	0	0	0	0	0	1	0
high-pressure	6	.3131	.4579	36.6	0	0	0	1	1	3	1	0	1	0	0	0	0	0	0	3	0	0	0	0	0	0	0	2	0
high-quality	12	.5935	1.4667	41.7	1	0	2	1	4	1	3	0	0	0	0	0	0	5	0	0	0	0	1	1	0	2	2	1	0
high-ranking	2	.1948	.1250	31.0	0	0	0	1	1	0	0	0	1	0	0	0	0	0	0	0	0	0	0	0	0	1	0	0	0
high-rise	3	.1918	.1342	31.3	0	0	0	1	1	1	0	0	0	0	0	0	0	0	0	0	0	1	0	0	0	0	0	2	0
high-school	29	.6223	3.7218	45.7	6	0	6	4	5	4	3	1	2	0	0	1	0	7	0	1	2	0	0	0	1	1	4	10	0
high-scoring	2	.0000	.0243	23.9	0	0	0	1	0	1	0	0	0	0	0	0	0	0	0	0	0	0	0	0	0	0	0	2	0
high-speed	30	.6318	3.8842	45.9	2	1	0	2	18	3	3	1	1	1	0	1	0	3	0	4	0	0	0	2	0	4	3	11	0
high-spirited	3	.1250	.1342	31.3	0	3	0	0	0	0	0	0	1	0	0	0	0	0	0	0	0	0	0	0	2	0	0	0	0
high-strength	3	.0803	.0701	28.5	0	0	0	0	1	0	2	0	0	0	0	0	0	0	0	1	0	0	0	2	0	0	0	0	0
high-strung	2	.0000	.0045	16.5	0	0	0	0	0	2	0	0	0	0	2	0	0	0	0	0	0	0	0	0	0	0	0	0	0
high-temperature	2	.2433	.1158	30.6	0	0	0	0	2	0	0	0	0	0	0	0	0	0	0	0	0	0	0	0	0	1	0	1	0
high-tension	2	.2437	.1129	30.5	0	0	0	0	2	0	0	0	0	0	0	0	0	0	0	0	0	0	0	0	0	0	1	1	0
high-tide	5	.1127	.2213	33.4	1	3	0	0	0	0	1	0	1	0	0	0	0	0	0	4	0	0	0	0	0	0	0	0	0
high-water	2	.2437	.1129	30.5	0	0	1	0	0	0	0	1	0	0	0	0	0	0	0	0	0	0	0	0	0	0	1	1	0
higher	544	.8577	93.231	59.7	93	79	83	72	107	53	47	10	86	3	0	12	41	93	2	115	46	3	3	6	9	29	56	40	0
Higher	2	.0000	.0914	29.6	0	0	0	0	2	0	0	0	2	0	0	0	0	0	0	0	0	0	0	0	0	0	0	0	0
highest	283	.8363	47.343	56.8	50	54	34	33	48	35	22	7	36	4	0	7	29	58	0	24	30	1	3	1	5	14	39	31	1
highest-pitched	3	.1610	.1250	31.0	0	0	0	1	2	0	0	0	0	0	0	0	0	0	0	1	2	0	0	0	0	0	0	0	0
Highflyer	4	.0000	.1827	32.6	0	0	0	0	4	0	0	0	4	0	0	0	0	0	0	0	0	0	0	0	0	0	0	0	0
highland	28	.3863	2.4469	43.9	2	0	6	14	4	2	0	0	1	0	0	0	0	20	0	0	0	0	0	0	0	3	2	2	0
Highland	16	.6269	2.0772	43.2	3	0	1	5	3	3	1	0	2	0	0	3	0	5	0	0	2	0	0	0	0	1	2	1	0
Highlanders	6	.3072	.4231	36.3	1	0	0	3	1	1	0	0	0	0	0	0	0	1	0	0	0	0	0	0	0	4	1	0	0
highlands	73	.2680	4.8699	46.9	6	3	11	38	4	4	6	1	2	0	0	0	0	61	0	0	0	0	0	0	0	4	5	1	0
Highlands	36	.4008	3.1986	45.0	0	0	21	2	5	3	5	0	0	0	0	3	0	26	0	0	2	0	0	0	0	0	5	0	0
highlight	6	.4077	.5099	37.1	0	0	0	0	1	3	1	1	0	0	1	1	0	0	0	0	3	0	0	0	0	0	0	1	0
highlights	9	.5380	1.0094	40.0	0	0	0	3	1	1	4	0	1	2	1	1	0	0	0	0	1	0	0	0	0	0	0	3	0
HIGHLIGHTS	4	.0000	.0486	26.9	0	4	0	0	0	0	0	0	0	0	0	0	0	0	0	0	0	0	0	0	0	0	0	4	0
highly	202	.8612	34.619	55.4	12	12	20	21	63	26	36	12	19	11	3	7	0	12	2	35	10	3	4	10	6	15	45	20	0
highness	4	.3155	.2801	34.5	0	1	0	0	2	1	0	0	0	1	0	0	0	0	0	1	2	0	0	0	0	0	0	0	0
Highness	6	.3171	.4658	36.7	3	0	0	0	3	0	0	0	2	0	0	0	0	0	0	0	1	0	0	0	3	0	0	0	0
highroad	5	.3126	.3746	35.7	1	0	1	3	0	0	0	0	1	0	0	0	0	0	0	0	0	0	0	0	2	2	0	0	0
highs	7	.2293	.3949	36.0	0	1	0	0	2	3	1	0	0	0	0	0	0	0	0	4	3	0	0	0	0	0	0	0	0
Hightower	2	.0000	.0243	23.9	0	0	0	0	2	0	0	0	0	0	0	0	0	0	0	0	0	0	0	0	0	0	0	2	0
highway	190	.8319	31.715	55.0	33	30	19	25	36	22	20	5	40	9	4	9	4	45	3	5	1	0	0	5	9	8	13	35	0
Highway	38	.5459	4.4435	46.5	2	17	6	3	2	5	0	3	6	2	0	0	3	19	0	0	0	0	0	0	0	1	1	6	0
highwayman	8	.4596	.8256	39.2	0	0	1	2	0	3	2	0	3	2	0	2	0	0	0	0	0	0	0	0	0	0	1	0	0
highwaymen	2	.1948	.1250	31.0	0	0	0	0	1	0	1	0	1	0	0	0	0	0	0	0	0	0	0	0	0	1	0	0	0
highways	119	.7086	17.235	52.4	23	10	27	18	22	9	9	1	15	4	2	1	1	57	2	2	1	0	0	5	0	5	17	7	0
Highways	6	.1814	.3560	35.5	0	0	0	1	2	0	0	3	3	0	0	0	0	0	0	0	0	0	0	0	0	0	0	3	0
hijacked	2	.0000	.0389	25.9	0	1	0	0	0	0	1	0	0	0	0	0	0	2	0	0	0	0	0	0	0	0	0	0	0
hijacker	2	.0000	.0389	25.9	0	2	0	0	0	0	0	0	0	0	0	0	0	2	0	0	0	0	0	0	0	0	0	0	0
hijackings	2	.0000	.0389	25.9	0	2	0	0	0	0	0	0	0	0	0	0	0	2	0	0	0	0	0	0	0	0	0	0	0
hike	37	.7571	5.6475	47.5	4	4	3	5	10	5	1	5	3	6	1	0	6	3	0	1	1	0	0	0	2	6	1	7	0
hiked	11	.2348	.6527	38.1	0	0	2	4	5	0	0	0	1	0	0	0	8	0	0	0	0	0	0	0	0	0	0	2	0
hikers	6	.3511	.5250	37.2	0	3	0	0	0	1	1	1	3	2	0	0	0	0	0	0	0	0	0	0	0	0	0	1	0
hikes	4	.3624	.3169	35.0	1	0	1	1	0	0	0	1	0	1	0	0	1	0	0	0	0	0	0	0	0	0	0	2	0
hiking	28	.7471	4.2340	46.3	4	3	3	4	1	7	0	6	4	5	0	0	2	2	0	2	3	1	1	0	0	6	0	2	0
Hikueru	11	.0000	.1290	31.1	0	0	0	11	0	0	0	0	0	0	0	0	0	0	0	0	0	0	0	0	11	0	0	0	0
hilarious	3	.2212	.2099	33.2	0	0	0	0	2	1	0	0	2	0	0	1	0	0	0	0	0	0	0	0	0	0	0	0	0
Hilda	7	.3858	.6824	38.3	5	0	1	1	0	0	0	0	5	0	0	0	0	0	0	0	1	0	0	0	0	0	1	0	0
hill	430	.8357	72.611	58.6	106	77	48	60	75	37	18	9	197	21	4	31	2	28	9	32	7	0	0	0	46	26	7	20	0
Hill	139	.7973	22.645	53.5	28	14	21	11	30	21	8	6	77	2	2	16	1	7	2	3	4	0	0	0	9	4	6	6	0
Hillary	5	.1294	.1816	32.6	0	0	0	0	1	0	4	0	0	0	0	4	0	0	0	1	0	0	0	0	0	0	0	0	0
hillbilly	8	.3824	.7622	38.8	0	0	1	0	5	0	2	0	5	0	0	0	0	0	0	0	1	0	0	0	0	0	0	2	0
Hiller	9	.0000	.1055	30.2	0	0	0	0	0	0	9	0	0	0	0	0	0	0	0	0	0	0	0	0	9	0	0	0	0
hillfolk	2	.0000	.0215	23.3	0	0	0	0	0	2	0	0	0	0	0	2	0	0	0	0	0	0	0	0	0	0	0	0	0
hillock	5	.4122	.4599	36.6	0	1	0	1	1	2	0	0	1	0	0	2	0	0	0	0	0	0	0	0	1	1	0	0	0
hills	410	.8866	72.540	58.6	95	77	57	55	68	35	16	7	120	16	3	21	2	100	4	24	15	2	0	2	22	38	16	25	0
Hills	35	.7349	5.2304	47.2	4	1	9	4	8	0	8	1	4	1	0	2	2	13	0	3	2	0	0	0	1	1	5	1	0
hillside	45	.7142	6.6243	48.2	7	11	5	6	10	1	3	2	14	2	0	8	0	2	0	7	0	0	0	0	3	5	1	3	0
hillsides	36	.5516	4.2470	46.3	5	1	6	7	7	7	2	1	5	0	0	1	0	22	0	1	1	0	0	0	1	2	2	1	0
hilltop	17	.5128	1.9511	42.9	4	5	1	2	2	1	2	0	8	0	0	4	0	2	0	0	0	0	0	0	0	2	0	1	0
Hilltop	3	.0000	.1370	31.4	0	0	3	0	0	0	0	0	3	0	0	0	0	0	0	0	0	0	0	0	0	0	0	0	0
hilltops	7	.4646	.7443	38.7	1	2	1	1	0	1	1	0	3	1	0	0	0	1	0	0	0	0	0	0	0	2	0	0	0
Hilltown	7	.0719	.2247	33.5	1	0	3	0	0	0	3	0	1	0	0	0	6	0	0	0	0	0	0	0	0	0	0	0	0
hilly	55	.3376	4.4095	46.4	6	6	15	12	9	6	1	0	5	0	0	0	0	44	1	0	1	0	0	0	0	1	2	1	0
Hilo	9	.3086	.7158	38.5	3	4	2	0	0	0	0	0	4	0	0	0	0	2	0	0	3	0	0	0	0	0	0	0	0
hilt	4	.4641	.3966	36.0	0	1	0	0	2	0	0	1	0	0	0	0	0	1	0	1	1	0	0	0	0	0	0	1	0

5Q HighPoint
8J High-School
8F high-back
6R high-beam
3P high-bibbed
3F high-button
7B high-buttoned
9D high-caste
8N high-ceilinged
8N high-collared
7R high-compressions
6N high-crested
7N high-crowned
6R high-desert
8B high-diving
7Q high-efficiency
6A high-explosive
6R high-fire
5N high-flyin'
8M high-gloss
3P high-handed
7D high-headed
6N high-held
6E high-jump
7R high-living
7Q high-mountain
6R high-octane
4P high-placed
7R high-pressured
5P high-priced
9Q high-resistance
5P high-stepping
9P high-strutting
6A high-styled
9Q high-technology
9Q high-test
9H high-tides
8D high-toned
5A high-top
7P high-voltage
7F high-walled
7R high-wheeler
9L high-yoked
8D High's
3P highball
8D highborn
8Q Highbury
XH highbush
9H higher-grade
7B Highest
7R highest-grade
7R highest-level
7R highest-powered
7R highest-ranking
6Q HighlandPark
6P Highlanders'
6F Highlands-Coastal
7R highline
5N Highness's
5F Highnesses
6R highpoint
7F highpriced
8K highrise
3P highroads
3P Highsaddle
7A highscorer's
4N hightail
8N hightailed
XB highty-tighty
5A highwater
9D Highwayman
7R highwing
4F hijackers
4F hijacking
5D hijjus
7R hiker
8B Hilaire
5D hilarity
9D hildings
7D hildy
8Q hill-city
6P hill-tops
9D Hillary's
9N Hiller's
8D hillfolks
8D hillfolks'
9F hillier
8F hilliness
3A hillman
9K Hillmer
9C Hillock
8P hillocks
6P Hillside

Word Type	F	D	U	SFI	3 Gr 3	4 Gr 4	5 Gr 5	6 Gr 6	7 Gr 7	8 Gr 8	9 Gr 9	X UnGr	A Read	B Eng & Gr	C Comp	D Lit	E Math	F Soc Stud	G Spell	H Sci	J Music	K Art	L Home Ec	M Shop	N Lib F	P Lib NF	Q Lib Ref	R Mag	S Rel
him	10703	.8129	1762.3	72.5	1874	2023	1125	1400	2300	991	844	146	4470	290	74	1425	72	383	55	173	170	14	37	2	1645	1066	210	588	29
Him	46	.0515	.7555	38.8	9	14	3	11	7	0	2	0	1	1	0	4	0	0	0	0	15	0	0	0	2	4	0	0	19
Himalaya	8	.4458	.7777	38.9	1	3	1	0	0	0	1	2	0	0	0	0	0	4	0	1	0	0	0	0	0	2	0	1	0
Himalayan	4	.4518	.3982	36.0	0	1	0	1	1	1	0	0	1	0	0	1	0	0	0	0	0	0	0	0	1	0	1	0	0
Himalayas	15	.6072	1.8861	42.8	0	2	1	2	7	2	1	0	1	0	0	1	0	3	0	2	0	0	0	0	1	1	5	1	0
himation	4	.0000	.1827	32.6	0	0	0	4	0	0	0	0	4	0	0	0	0	0	0	0	0	0	0	0	0	0	0	0	0
Himmel	3	.0000	.0243	23.8	0	0	2	0	0	0	1	0	0	0	0	0	0	0	0	0	3	0	0	0	0	0	0	0	0
himself	1789	.8568	307.83	64.9	268	292	206	250	392	200	147	34	723	54	10	216	6	84	5	40	31	6	12	2	253	151	64	128	4
Himself	4	.0366	.0447	26.5	1	1	0	2	0	0	0	0	0	0	0	0	0	0	0	0	2	0	0	0	0	0	0	0	2
Hinch	3	.0000	.0322	25.1	0	0	0	0	0	0	3	0	0	0	0	3	0	0	0	0	0	0	0	0	0	0	0	0	0
hind	102	.6501	13.830	51.4	23	17	12	13	31	2	2	2	29	0	0	10	0	0	0	8	1	0	0	0	10	27	14	3	0
Hindemith	4	.0000	.0323	25.1	0	1	0	0	0	3	0	0	0	0	0	0	0	0	0	0	4	0	0	0	0	0	0	0	0
hinder	10	.4831	1.0430	40.2	1	1	1	1	0	3	3	0	2	2	0	1	0	2	0	0	0	0	2	0	1	0	0	0	0
hindered	9	.5903	1.1234	40.5	2	0	1	0	4	2	0	0	2	0	0	1	0	1	0	2	0	0	0	0	1	0	2	0	0
hindering	3	.2051	.1687	32.3	0	0	0	0	3	0	0	0	1	0	1	0	0	0	0	0	0	0	0	0	0	0	0	1	0
Hindi	2	.2306	.1140	30.6	0	1	0	0	1	0	0	0	0	1	0	0	0	1	0	0	0	0	0	0	0	0	0	0	0
hindquarters	4	.2441	.2254	33.5	0	0	1	0	2	0	1	0	0	0	0	0	0	0	0	0	0	0	0	0	2	0	2	0	0
hindrance	6	.4794	.6585	38.2	0	2	0	2	0	0	1	1	3	0	0	0	0	0	0	1	0	0	0	0	1	0	1	0	0
Hindu	26	.6634	3.5491	45.5	0	5	1	7	8	2	0	3	2	0	0	0	1	9	0	3	1	0	0	0	0	4	3	3	0
Hindu-Arabic	27	.0000	.4041	36.1	0	2	0	3	15	5	2	0	0	0	0	0	27	0	0	0	0	0	0	0	0	0	0	0	0
Hinduism	9	.3046	.6491	38.1	0	1	0	1	7	0	0	0	0	0	0	0	0	7	0	0	0	0	0	0	0	0	1	1	0
Hinduist	2	.0000	.0389	25.9	0	0	0	0	2	0	0	0	0	0	0	0	0	2	0	0	0	0	0	0	0	0	0	0	0
Hindus	19	.4914	1.9909	43.0	0	4	0	1	13	0	1	0	0	0	0	0	2	10	0	0	0	0	0	0	1	2	4	0	0
Hindustani	2	.0000	.0219	23.4	0	0	0	0	2	0	0	0	0	2	0	0	0	0	0	0	0	0	0	0	0	0	0	0	0
Hines	2	.2375	.1088	30.4	0	0	0	0	0	1	1	0	0	0	0	0	0	0	0	0	1	0	0	0	0	0	0	1	0
hinge	19	.4007	1.6896	42.3	0	0	7	4	2	3	3	0	1	0	0	1	0	0	0	12	0	0	0	3	0	0	1	1	0
hinged	9	.4758	.9366	39.7	0	2	0	0	6	0	1	0	2	0	0	0	0	0	0	1	0	0	0	0	0	1	3	2	0
hinges	13	.5865	1.6370	42.1	1	2	0	2	4	2	2	0	5	1	0	3	0	2	0	0	0	0	0	0	0	1	1	0	0
Hinsdale	2	.0000	.0243	23.9	0	0	0	0	0	0	2	0	0	0	0	0	0	0	0	0	0	0	0	0	0	0	0	2	0
hint	57	.7964	9.1370	49.6	4	3	7	5	14	14	8	2	10	8	1	4	17	2	3	3	3	0	0	0	2	1	1	2	0
hinted	6	.4540	.6108	37.9	0	1	2	1	0	2	0	0	2	0	0	1	0	0	0	0	0	0	0	0	1	0	0	2	0
hinterland	2	.2401	.1133	30.5	0	0	1	0	1	0	0	0	0	0	0	0	0	0	0	0	0	0	0	0	0	1	1	0	0
hinterlands	2	.2351	.1166	30.7	0	0	0	0	0	2	0	0	0	0	0	0	0	1	0	0	0	0	0	0	0	0	0	1	0
hinting	2	.2440	.1132	30.5	0	0	0	0	0	0	1	1	0	0	0	1	0	0	0	0	0	0	0	0	0	0	0	1	0
hints	27	.6108	3.4568	45.4	0	4	4	2	9	5	3	0	8	0	0	3	5	0	1	0	2	0	4	0	0	0	2	2	0
Hints	45	.0000	.3652	35.6	0	8	18	19	0	0	0	0	0	0	0	0	0	0	45	0	0	0	0	0	0	0	0	0	0
hip	33	.5772	4.0243	46.0	3	8	9	0	9	2	1	1	9	0	0	3	0	0	0	2	0	3	4	0	1	8	0	3	0
Hip	20	.0000	.9137	39.6	0	0	13	7	0	0	0	0	20	0	0	0	0	0	0	0	0	0	0	0	0	0	0	0	0
Hipparchus	2	.2446	.1257	31.0	0	0	0	0	0	0	1	1	0	0	0	0	0	1	0	1	0	0	0	0	0	0	0	0	0
hippie	3	.2266	.1614	32.1	0	0	0	0	2	0	1	0	0	0	0	0	0	0	0	0	0	0	0	0	1	0	0	2	0
hippies	9	.2173	.4754	36.8	0	0	1	0	2	2	4	0	0	0	0	0	0	1	0	0	0	0	0	0	1	0	0	7	0
hippity	3	.0995	.1144	30.6	3	0	0	0	0	0	0	0	1	0	0	0	0	0	0	0	2	0	0	0	0	0	0	0	0
hippo	20	.3138	1.6648	42.2	9	9	0	0	2	0	0	0	11	0	0	0	0	0	0	0	0	0	0	0	0	8	1	0	0
Hippo	12	.0000	.5482	37.4	12	0	0	0	0	0	0	0	12	0	0	0	0	0	0	0	0	0	0	0	0	0	0	0	0
Hippocrates	5	.2213	.2928	34.7	0	0	0	0	2	0	3	0	1	0	0	0	0	0	0	1	0	0	0	0	0	0	3	0	0
Hippocratic	2	.1698	.1133	30.5	0	0	0	0	1	0	1	0	1	0	0	0	0	0	0	0	0	0	0	0	0	0	1	0	0
Hippolyta	2	.0000	.0215	23.3	0	0	0	0	0	0	2	0	0	0	0	2	0	0	0	0	0	0	0	0	0	0	0	0	0
hippopotamus	42	.7913	6.7094	48.3	12	8	0	8	11	1	2	0	9	5	0	1	0	3	1	6	1	1	0	0	0	4	5	6	0
Hippopotamus	4	.3071	.2967	34.7	1	2	1	0	0	0	0	0	1	0	0	1	0	0	0	0	0	0	0	0	2	0	0	0	0
hippopotamuses	5	.1865	.3050	34.8	0	0	1	2	2	0	0	0	2	0	0	0	0	3	0	0	0	0	0	0	0	0	0	0	0
hippos	11	.3875	.9533	39.8	6	0	0	2	3	0	0	0	1	0	0	0	0	0	0	2	0	0	0	0	0	5	3	0	0
hippos'	2	.0000	.0290	24.6	2	0	0	0	0	0	0	0	0	0	0	0	0	0	0	0	0	0	0	0	0	2	0	0	0
hips	36	.7073	5.2108	47.2	2	10	7	1	12	3	1	0	8	1	0	2	0	1	0	7	2	2	3	0	7	2	1	0	0
Hipshank	2	.0000	.0219	23.4	0	0	0	0	0	2	0	0	0	2	0	0	0	0	0	0	0	0	0	0	0	0	0	0	0
Hiram	25	.3040	2.2182	43.5	0	1	7	16	1	0	0	0	22	0	0	0	0	0	0	0	0	0	0	0	1	0	0	2	0
Hiram's	8	.0000	.3655	35.6	0	0	0	8	0	0	0	0	8	0	0	0	0	0	0	0	0	0	0	0	0	0	0	0	0
hire	37	.7322	5.5538	47.4	10	5	4	2	5	4	4	3	11	3	0	2	1	4	1	0	1	0	0	0	3	10	0	1	0
hired	69	.8228	11.435	50.6	11	8	8	8	14	9	5	6	19	2	1	4	1	12	0	2	2	0	0	0	4	11	4	7	0
hires	3	.3766	.2497	34.0	0	1	1	0	1	0	0	0	0	0	0	0	0	1	0	0	0	0	0	0	0	1	1	0	0
hiring	10	.6641	1.3745	41.4	1	0	3	0	2	3	1	0	2	0	0	1	0	3	0	0	1	0	0	0	1	1	0	1	0
Hiro	4	.0000	.0486	26.9	4	0	0	0	0	0	0	0	0	0	0	0	0	0	0	0	0	0	0	0	0	0	0	4	0
Hiromu	2	.0000	.0389	25.9	0	2	0	0	0	0	0	0	0	0	0	0	0	2	0	0	0	0	0	0	0	0	0	0	0
Hiroshima	8	.5417	.9345	39.7	0	0	2	2	0	3	1	0	2	0	0	1	0	3	1	0	0	0	0	0	0	0	0	1	0
Hirsch	2	.2446	.1122	30.5	0	0	0	0	0	0	2	0	0	0	0	1	0	0	0	0	0	0	0	0	0	0	1	0	0
Hirsch's	2	.2446	.1122	30.5	0	0	0	0	0	0	2	0	0	0	0	1	0	0	0	0	0	0	0	0	0	0	1	0	0
his	29268	.9134	5316.2	77.3	4750	5279	3269	3846	6122	3188	2310	504	10901	967	349	3205	497	1728	274	738	932	219	93	38	3514	2876	1041	1861	35
His	119	.0823	3.1361	45.0	17	36	7	23	17	8	9	2	13	6	0	8	0	4	1	0	38	0	1	0	6	3	2	3	34
Hispaniola	13	.3491	1.0346	40.1	0	0	7	2	4	0	0	0	0	0	0	0	0	9	0	0	0	0	0	0	2	0	2	0	0
hiss	15	.6320	1.9383	42.9	0	3	1	1	4	4	1	1	2	1	2	1	0	0	2	1	3	0	1	0	2	0	0	0	0
hissed	13	.4831	1.3819	41.4	2	0	4	1	4	0	0	2	4	1	0	2	0	0	0	0	0	0	0	0	5	0	0	1	0
hisself	3	.3380	.2439	33.9	0	0	0	0	1	1	1	0	1	1	0	1	0	0	0	0	0	0	0	0	0	0	0	0	0
hisses	2	.2405	.1205	30.8	2	0	0	0	0	0	0	0	0	0	0	0	0	0	0	1	0	0	0	0	0	1	0	0	0
hissing	20	.5758	2.4571	43.9	5	2	1	6	6	0	0	0	6	0	0	0	0	0	0	1	1	0	0	0	4	5	0	3	0
hist	3	.0000	.1370	31.4	0	0	0	1	1	1	0	0	3	0	0	0	0	0	0	0	0	0	0	0	0	0	0	0	0
Histadrut	6	.0000	.1167	30.7	0	0	0	0	6	0	0	0	0	0	0	0	0	6	0	0	0	0	0	0	0	0	0	0	0
histogram	7	.1240	.2665	34.3	0	6	0	0	1	0	0	0	0	0	0	0	6	0	0	1	0	0	0	0	0	0	0	0	0
historian	22	.5286	2.4336	43.9	0	1	4	0	7	4	4	2	1	2	0	1	0	3	0	1	0	0	0	0	0	0	7	7	0
historians	31	.5920	3.8086	45.8	0	4	3	6	9	5	4	0	3	1	0	0	0	6	0	0	3	0	0	0	2	0	7	9	0
Historians	2	.2306	.1140	30.6	0	0	0	0	0	1	1	0	0	1	0	0	0	1	0	0	0	0	0	0	0	0	0	0	0
historic	65	.7140	9.4564	49.8	5	5	8	7	23	8	7	2	8	2	1	1	0	18	1	2	1	0	0	0	0	8	14	9	0
Historic	3	.2387	.1708	32.3	0	0	0	0	1	0	0	2	0	0	0	0	0	0	0	0	0	0	0	0	0	2	1	0	0
historical	86	.8229	14.192	51.5	1	8	11	9	14	28	9	6	16	6	1	4	1	11	2	4	4	2	0	0	0	7	18	10	0
Historical	6	.3512	.5237	37.2	0	0	4	0	1	0	1	0	3	1	0	0	0	0	0	0	0	0	0	0	0	0	2	0	0
historically	10	.4734	.9882	39.9	0	0	0	0	6	1	3	0	0	0	0	1	0	0	0	0	1	0	0	0	0	1	5	2	0
histories	15	.6880	2.1084	43.2	0	0	4	1	2	5	3	0	2	2	1	0	0	3	2	1	0	0	0	0	0	1	2	1	0
history	726	.8979	129.48	61.1	58	48	119	84	183	126	77	31	111	33	2	24	15	162	11	50	54	7	2	3	11	58	111	71	1
History	39	.6684	5.3073	47.2	4	5	3	2	9	7	6	3	2	2	2	0	1	4	0	1	0	0	0	0	2	6	8	11	0
history-making	3	.2279	.2143	33.3	0	0	1	1	1	0	0	0	2	0	0	0	0	0	0	0	0	0	0	0	0	0	0	1	0
hit	595	.8639	103.17	60.1	117	115	54	74	123	63	41	8	249	32	2	32	2	10	9	50	14	2	1	2	57	63	9	61	0
hit-and-run	3	.2373	.1703	32.3	0	0	1	1	1	0	0	0	0	1	0	0	0	0	0	0	0	0	0	0	0	2	0	0	0
hit-or-miss	5	.4767	.5121	37.1	0	0	0	0	2	3	0	0	0	0	0	0	0	2	0	1	0	0	0	0	0	1	1	0	0
hit's	5	.0000	.0586	27.7	0	0	1	0	4	0	0	0	0	0	0	0	0	0	0	0	0	0	0	0	5	0	0	0	0
hitch	14	.4958	1.5546	41.9	4	2	0	1	0	1	1	5	6	0	1	0	0	1	0	0	0	0	0	0	0	4	0	2	0
Hitchcock	3	.2440	.1815	32.6	0	0	0	0	0	3	0	0	0	1	0	0	0	2	0	0	0	0	0	0	0	0	0	0	0

3A HIM
6R hin
4N Hin
3J hinched
9C Hinckley
7Q hind-gut
4N hind-leg
XP hind-quarters
9D hind'red
4A Hindbad
7J Hindemith's
7Q Hindenburg
5F hinders
4N hindlegs
6A Hindoo
4A hindquarter
9R Hinds
9R hindsight
4E Hindu-
4Q Hindu's
6R Hinduism's
8R Hine's
7R Hingham
7P hinging
3Q hinny
6A hinoyojin
6R hins
8L hip-length
9R hippie-esque
8R hippie-haired
3D hippity-hop
4A hippo's
4R hippocampus
3P Hippodrome
7P Hippolito
9D HIPPOLYTA
5Q Hippolyte
4A hippotomuscle
4A hippopotomusses
4A hippopotomust
4A hippopotomustard
6R hippy
8B hir
7R Hiroshi
7H Hiroshima-type
7R Hirshberg's
9R hirsute
8A his'n
7R Hispanic
8R Hispanic-studies
6P Histoires
XR histologist
9Q Historia
7F Historian
XR historiographer
7Q history's
7N Hit
5R hit-run

Word Type	F	D	U	SFI	3 Gr 3	4 Gr 4	5 Gr 5	6 Gr 6	7 Gr 7	8 Gr 8	9 Gr 9	X UnGr	A Read	B Eng & Gr	C Comp	D Lit	E Math	F Soc Stud	G Spell	H Sci	J Music	K Art	L Home Ec	M Shop	N Lib F	P Lib NF	Q Lib Ref	R Mag	S Rel
Hitchcock's	2	.2337	.1157	30.6	0	0	0	1	0	1	0	0	0	0	0	0	0	1	0	0	0	0	0	0	1	0	0	0	0
hitched	32	.7228	4.7845	46.8	5	8	3	7	6	1	2	0	14	0	1	5	0	3	1	0	1	0	0	0	0	4	1	2	0
hitches	4	.3024	.3033	34.8	0	0	1	1	0	0	0	2	1	0	0	0	0	1	0	0	0	0	0	0	0	2	0	0	0
hitchhiked	2	.2437	.1129	30.5	0	0	0	0	1	1	0	0	0	0	0	0	0	0	0	0	0	0	0	0	0	0	1	1	0
hitchhiker	3	.0000	.0365	25.6	0	0	0	0	0	3	0	0	0	0	0	0	0	0	0	0	0	0	0	0	0	0	0	3	0
hitchhikers	2	.0000	.0243	23.9	0	0	0	0	0	2	0	0	0	0	0	0	0	0	0	0	0	0	0	0	0	0	0	2	0
hitchhiking	7	.1117	.2888	34.6	0	0	1	1	1	4	0	0	2	0	0	0	0	0	0	0	0	0	0	0	0	0	0	5	0
hitching	14	.5301	1.6250	42.1	2	4	4	1	2	0	1	0	5	0	0	3	0	2	0	0	0	0	0	0	1	3	0	0	0
hither	18	.3272	1.3877	41.4	0	1	3	4	3	2	5	0	4	0	0	10	0	0	0	0	0	0	0	0	2	2	0	0	0
hitherto	21	.7002	2.9949	44.8	0	1	2	2	7	3	4	2	2	0	0	1	0	1	0	4	1	0	0	0	5	2	3	2	0
Hitler	55	.4658	5.5841	47.5	1	2	1	8	27	6	10	0	6	0	0	0	0	15	0	0	0	0	0	0	0	24	3	7	0
Hitler's	13	.2696	.8307	39.2	0	1	1	0	11	0	0	0	0	0	0	0	0	1	0	1	0	0	0	0	0	10	1	0	0
hits	76	.7425	11.524	50.6	17	12	11	5	19	4	5	3	17	1	0	1	5	1	1	24	2	0	0	0	2	7	3	12	0
hitter	11	.4453	1.0608	40.3	5	2	2	1	0	1	0	0	1	1	0	2	0	0	0	0	0	0	0	0	0	6	0	1	0
hitters	11	.3445	.8641	39.4	6	1	1	3	0	0	0	0	1	1	0	0	0	0	0	0	0	0	0	0	0	7	0	2	0
hitting	64	.8297	10.706	50.3	7	13	3	12	17	7	5	0	22	4	0	5	1	1	1	12	1	0	0	1	4	4	1	7	0
Hitty	2	.0000	.0219	23.4	0	2	0	0	0	0	0	0	0	2	0	0	0	0	0	0	0	0	0	0	0	0	0	0	0
hive	61	.5119	6.6047	48.2	37	4	2	7	10	1	0	0	4	0	1	1	0	0	4	4	0	0	0	0	0	39	5	3	0
hives	10	.5424	1.1499	40.6	3	2	0	2	0	3	0	0	1	0	0	1	0	2	0	1	0	0	0	0	0	4	1	0	0
hiya	3	.1409	.1472	31.7	0	2	0	0	0	1	0	0	1	0	0	0	0	0	0	0	0	0	0	0	0	2	0	0	0
hm	4	.2708	.2760	34.4	1	0	0	1	1	1	0	0	1	0	0	2	0	1	0	0	0	0	0	0	0	0	0	0	0
hm-m	2	.1787	.1174	30.7	0	1	0	0	1	0	0	0	1	0	0	0	0	0	0	0	0	0	0	0	1	0	0	0	0
hmm	4	.2958	.2914	34.6	0	3	0	1	0	0	0	0	1	0	0	0	0	0	0	0	0	0	0	0	2	1	0	0	0
hmmmm	6	.3394	.4902	36.9	0	3	1	0	0	2	0	0	2	0	0	2	0	0	0	0	0	0	0	0	2	0	0	0	0
ho	77	.5931	9.5913	49.8	33	16	4	6	5	9	4	0	20	6	0	12	0	2	0	0	21	0	0	0	9	4	0	3	0
Ho	6	.4776	.6111	37.9	0	0	0	0	2	2	2	0	0	1	0	0	0	3	0	0	0	0	0	0	0	0	1	1	0
HO	2	.0000	.0219	23.4	0	0	0	0	2	0	0	0	0	2	0	0	0	0	0	0	0	0	0	0	0	0	0	0	0
ho-ho-ho	3	.2212	.2099	33.2	2	1	0	0	0	0	0	0	2	0	0	1	0	0	0	0	0	0	0	0	0	0	0	0	0
ho-hum	3	.3427	.2477	33.9	0	0	0	2	0	0	1	0	1	0	0	0	0	0	0	0	0	0	0	0	1	0	0	1	0
hoard	4	.3072	.2981	34.7	0	0	0	2	1	0	0	1	1	0	0	0	0	0	0	0	0	0	0	0	1	0	0	2	0
hoarded	2	.0000	.0209	23.2	0	0	0	0	2	0	0	0	0	0	0	0	0	0	0	0	0	0	0	0	0	0	2	0	0
hoarding	3	.3390	.2450	33.9	0	0	0	0	3	0	0	0	1	0	0	0	0	0	0	0	0	0	0	0	0	0	1	1	0
hoards	4	.0000	.0323	25.1	4	0	0	0	0	0	0	0	0	0	0	0	0	0	0	0	4	0	0	0	0	0	0	0	0
hoarse	28	.5646	3.4187	45.3	3	1	3	5	9	5	1	1	12	1	1	5	0	0	0	0	1	0	0	0	8	0	0	0	0
hoarsely	10	.6003	1.2524	41.0	0	2	2	2	2	1	1	0	2	2	0	1	0	0	0	0	0	0	0	0	2	0	1	2	0
hoary	5	.4216	.4687	36.7	1	2	1	0	1	0	0	0	1	0	0	0	0	0	0	0	0	0	0	0	2	1	1	0	0
hoax	5	.4274	.4693	36.7	0	0	0	0	0	5	0	0	1	2	0	0	0	0	0	0	1	0	0	0	0	0	1	0	0
Hobbie	2	.0000	.0914	29.6	0	0	2	0	0	0	0	0	2	0	0	0	0	0	0	0	0	0	0	0	0	0	0	0	0
hobbies	21	.6866	2.9372	44.7	0	3	1	4	3	3	2	5	1	2	1	1	0	3	0	6	0	0	2	0	0	3	0	2	0
hobble	5	.2445	.3864	35.9	4	0	0	0	1	0	0	0	4	0	0	1	0	0	0	0	0	0	0	0	0	0	0	0	0
hobbled	12	.5242	1.3544	41.3	2	2	2	1	1	2	2	0	3	0	0	3	0	0	0	0	0	0	0	0	1	3	0	2	0
hobbles	4	.2393	.3005	34.8	0	0	1	1	1	1	0	0	3	0	0	1	0	0	0	0	0	0	0	0	0	0	0	0	0
hobbling	3	.1187	.1291	31.1	1	0	0	0	0	1	1	0	1	0	0	2	0	0	0	0	0	0	0	0	0	0	0	0	0
hobby	74	.7538	11.270	50.5	10	9	6	17	10	4	6	12	9	8	5	0	1	4	3	20	1	0	2	4	2	2	0	13	0
hobo	2	.0665	.0708	28.5	1	0	0	0	1	0	0	0	1	0	1	0	0	0	0	0	0	0	0	0	0	0	0	0	0
hockey	13	.5880	1.6094	42.1	1	1	1	0	6	3	1	0	3	1	1	1	0	2	0	0	0	0	0	0	1	0	0	4	0
Hockley	5	.0000	.0724	28.6	0	5	0	0	0	0	0	0	0	0	0	0	0	0	0	0	0	0	0	0	0	5	0	0	0
hocks	3	.3852	.2500	34.0	0	1	0	0	1	1	0	0	0	0	0	1	0	0	0	0	0	0	0	0	0	1	0	1	0
Hod	7	.0000	.0766	28.8	0	0	0	0	0	7	0	0	0	7	0	0	0	0	0	0	0	0	0	0	0	0	0	0	0
Hoda	5	.0000	.2284	33.6	5	0	0	0	0	0	0	0	5	0	0	0	0	0	0	0	0	0	0	0	0	0	0	0	0
Hodges	12	.3766	1.1088	40.4	6	2	0	3	0	0	1	0	6	0	0	0	0	0	0	0	0	0	0	0	0	3	0	3	0
Hodja	15	.0000	.6852	38.4	0	15	0	0	0	0	0	0	15	0	0	0	0	0	0	0	0	0	0	0	0	0	0	0	0
Hodja's	2	.0000	.0914	29.6	0	2	0	0	0	0	0	0	2	0	0	0	0	0	0	0	0	0	0	0	0	0	0	0	0
hoe	33	.5913	4.2678	46.3	20	3	0	3	4	2	1	0	19	0	0	4	0	3	0	0	0	0	0	0	3	3	0	1	0
hoecakes	2	.0000	.0290	24.6	0	2	0	0	0	0	0	0	0	0	0	0	0	0	0	0	0	0	0	0	0	2	0	0	0
hoed	5	.0000	.2284	33.6	2	1	1	1	0	0	0	0	5	0	0	0	0	0	0	0	0	0	0	0	0	0	0	0	0
hoedown	2	.0000	.0162	22.1	0	2	0	0	0	0	0	0	0	0	0	0	0	0	0	0	2	0	0	0	0	0	0	0	0
hoeing	9	.3747	.8768	39.4	6	0	0	1	1	0	1	0	7	1	0	0	0	0	0	0	0	0	0	0	1	0	0	0	0
hoes	4	.1325	.1944	32.9	1	1	0	1	1	0	0	0	1	0	0	0	0	3	0	0	0	0	0	0	0	0	0	0	0
Hoevenberg	2	.0000	.0914	29.6	0	0	0	2	0	0	0	0	2	0	0	0	0	0	0	0	0	0	0	0	0	0	0	0	0
Hoff	7	.0000	.1361	31.3	7	0	0	0	0	0	0	0	0	0	0	0	0	7	0	0	0	0	0	0	0	0	0	0	0
Hoffer	4	.0000	.0429	26.3	0	0	0	0	0	0	4	0	0	0	0	4	0	0	0	0	0	0	0	0	0	0	0	0	0
Hoffman	6	.2432	.4679	36.7	0	0	0	0	5	0	1	0	5	1	0	0	0	0	0	0	0	0	0	0	0	0	0	0	0
Hofmann	6	.2414	.3321	35.2	1	0	0	5	0	0	0	0	0	0	0	0	0	0	0	0	0	1	0	0	0	0	0	5	0
Hofus	8	.0000	.3655	35.6	8	0	0	0	0	0	0	0	8	0	0	0	0	0	0	0	0	0	0	0	0	0	0	0	0
hog	33	.7430	5.0096	47.0	6	1	7	3	6	5	3	2	11	6	0	4	0	1	1	0	1	1	0	0	4	2	2	0	0
hogan	8	.3414	.6862	38.4	6	1	0	0	1	0	0	0	3	0	0	0	0	4	0	0	0	0	0	0	0	0	0	1	0
Hogan	2	.0000	.0914	29.6	2	0	0	0	0	0	0	0	2	0	0	0	0	0	0	0	0	0	0	0	0	0	0	0	0
hogans	4	.2281	.2337	33.7	3	1	0	0	0	0	0	0	0	0	0	0	0	3	0	0	0	0	0	0	0	0	0	1	0
hognose	3	.0000	.0591	27.7	3	0	0	0	0	0	0	0	0	0	0	0	0	0	0	3	0	0	0	0	0	0	0	0	0
hogs	65	.6128	8.2431	49.2	16	6	11	3	21	3	4	1	2	0	2	1	3	27	0	2	0	0	0	0	16	10	0	2	0
hoist	9	.6729	1.2575	41.0	0	0	3	3	2	1	0	0	3	0	0	1	0	1	1	0	1	0	0	0	0	0	1	1	0
hoisted	21	.6920	2.9701	44.7	0	3	2	3	5	6	1	1	4	0	2	3	0	1	1	1	1	0	0	0	3	1	1	3	0
hoisting	4	.4538	.4007	36.0	0	1	0	0	0	1	1	1	1	1	0	0	0	0	0	0	0	0	0	0	1	0	0	1	0
Hokkaido	9	.0000	.1750	32.4	0	3	0	0	0	6	0	0	0	0	0	0	0	9	0	0	0	0	0	0	0	0	0	0	0
Holcomb	5	.1820	.2261	33.5	0	0	0	0	4	0	1	0	0	1	0	0	0	0	0	0	0	0	0	0	4	0	0	0	0
hold	1192	.9162	216.70	63.4	264	223	128	149	179	120	108	21	280	39	15	63	49	82	10	220	37	16	41	48	79	128	32	53	0
holder	28	.5156	3.0677	44.9	2	1	2	5	2	2	6	8	4	1	0	0	11	0	0	2	1	0	0	4	1	0	0	4	0
holders	8	.5381	.9027	39.6	1	1	0	0	2	1	0	3	0	0	0	0	3	0	0	2	0	0	0	0	1	1	0	1	0
holdin'	2	.0000	.0234	23.7	0	0	0	0	2	0	0	0	0	0	0	0	0	0	0	0	0	0	0	0	2	0	0	0	0
holding	362	.8769	63.414	58.0	63	71	44	44	68	35	27	10	123	8	7	31	3	9	3	27	11	3	8	18	44	38	10	19	0
holdings	17	.5339	1.9117	42.8	4	0	4	3	3	0	2	1	1	0	0	1	0	5	0	1	0	0	0	0	0	1	6	2	0
holds	228	.9115	41.250	56.2	48	34	32	20	46	24	18	6	46	5	2	9	45	9	2	43	10	3	3	6	4	18	9	14	0
hole	602	.7296	90.312	59.6	211	75	56	57	67	83	42	11	229	11	2	32	18	10	8	84	35	1	13	67	24	35	14	19	0
Hole	13	.6277	1.6638	42.2	0	5	1	1	4	2	0	0	0	1	0	0	0	0	0	1	1	0	0	0	3	2	1	4	0
holes	278	.8021	45.033	56.5	81	39	35	23	50	27	20	3	84	1	1	8	6	15	3	36	17	4	7	26	12	22	22	14	0
holiday	109	.8037	17.643	52.5	21	24	16	13	12	10	12	1	29	18	4	3	0	7	7	0	9	5	1	0	1	13	6	6	0
Holiday	6	.4493	.6059	37.8	0	0	0	2	0	2	2	0	2	0	0	0	0	0	0	0	1	0	0	0	0	1	0	2	0
holidays	56	.7585	8.5878	49.3	14	12	10	4	3	6	6	1	9	4	4	3	3	10	6	1	4	0	0	0	2	6	0	4	0
Holland	73	.8068	11.902	50.8	9	14	10	13	11	9	4	3	21	0	2	2	1	20	1	2	1	2	1	0	2	9	8	1	0

9D hitchpost
5D hitchrail
4Q Hittin
8P Hiva
4A hive's
6A hiyup
8E HJ
8B hlaf
4B hlafdige
4B hlafweard
3A hmmm
6A hmmmmm
4R hmmmmph
6N hmph
4A ho-ho
3A ho-ho-hoing
6A ho-ka-he
6P ho-o-o-o-o-o
8R Ho-shu
7L hoagy
6R hoar
7H hoarfrost
6N hoarhound
7R hob
9A hobbes
5A Hobbie's
5B Hobbies
7N Hobbs
3B Hobby
4A hobgoblins
6P Hoboken
7R Hockey
4R hockey's
4P Hockley's
9A hocus-pocus
3A Hodag
7R Hodaka
5Q Hoder
XR Hodge
8F hodgepodge
8R Hodson
6A hoein'
4R hoelike
9Q Hof
9R Hoffert
6R Hoffmann-LaRoche
3K Hofmann's
5P Hofmeyr
7F Hofuf
3R hog-calling
9B hog-nosed
6F hog-slaughtering
3N Hogarth
7N hogged
4B hogger
4B hogger's
4N hoghouse
3D Hognose
5Q hogshead
4P hogsheads
7R hogwash
5Q Hohe
9Q Hoher
7H hoists
XB hoiting
XB hoity
XB hoity-toity
3A hoksila
4R Holbrook
8A Hold
6R Holden
8D Holderness
7Q holdfast
6A Holdfast
9Q Holdheim
7B holdless
7R holdout
5R holdover
6A hole-in-the-wall
9M hole-machining
8R holed
3P HOLIDAY
5P holidaymakers
6A Holidays
6J holiness

Word Type	F	D	U	SFI	3 Gr 3	4 Gr 4	5 Gr 5	6 Gr 6	7 Gr 7	8 Gr 8	9 Gr 9	X UnGr	A Read	B Eng & Gr	C Comp	D Lit	E Math	F Soc Stud	G Spell	H Sci	J Music	K Art	L Home Ec	M Shop	N Lib F	P Lib NF	Q Lib Ref	R Mag	S Rel
Holland's	3	.2279	.2143	33.3	0	2	0	0	0	0	0	1	2	0	0	0	0	0	0	0	0	0	0	0	0	0	0	1	0
Hollander	10	.0000	.1945	32.9	10	0	0	0	0	0	0	0	0	0	0	0	0	10	0	0	0	0	0	0	0	0	0	0	0
holler	11	.6431	1.4684	41.7	0	1	0	1	5	4	0	0	3	1	1	1	0	0	0	0	1	0	0	0	1	1	0	2	0
hollered	8	.3470	.6043	37.8	1	0	0	2	4	0	1	0	0	1	0	3	0	0	0	0	0	0	0	0	4	0	0	0	0
hollerin'	2	.2446	.1125	30.5	0	0	0	0	0	2	0	0	0	1	0	1	0	0	0	0	0	0	0	0	0	0	0	0	0
hollering	5	.4712	.4906	36.9	1	0	0	1	1	1	1	0	0	1	0	2	0	0	0	0	1	0	0	0	1	0	0	0	0
hollers	2	.1787	.1174	30.7	0	0	2	0	0	0	0	0	1	0	0	0	0	0	0	0	0	0	0	0	1	0	0	0	0
Hollerville	5	.0000	.0972	29.9	5	0	0	0	0	0	0	0	0	0	0	0	0	5	0	0	0	0	0	0	0	0	0	0	0
Holley	2	.0000	.0243	23.9	0	0	0	0	2	0	0	0	0	0	0	0	0	0	0	0	0	0	0	0	0	0	0	2	0
Holleys	2	.0000	.0243	23.9	0	0	0	0	2	0	0	0	0	0	0	0	0	0	0	0	0	0	0	0	0	0	0	2	0
Hollis	33	.0000	1.5075	41.8	33	0	0	0	0	0	0	0	33	0	0	0	0	0	0	0	0	0	0	0	0	0	0	0	0
Hollis's	2	.0000	.0914	29.6	2	0	0	0	0	0	0	0	2	0	0	0	0	0	0	0	0	0	0	0	0	0	0	0	0
hollow	164	.9016	29.393	54.7	27	17	23	23	36	12	24	2	40	4	2	16	2	4	3	29	11	1	1	6	6	17	12	10	0
Hollow	10	.4381	.9710	39.9	1	1	0	2	3	1	2	0	3	0	2	1	0	0	1	0	0	0	0	0	2	0	0	1	0
Holloways	2	.2420	.1154	30.6	1	0	0	0	0	1	0	0	0	0	0	0	1	0	0	0	0	0	0	0	1	0	0	0	0
hollowed	13	.5975	1.6346	42.1	2	2	0	2	4	1	2	0	3	0	0	3	0	2	0	0	1	0	0	0	2	2	0	0	0
hollowed-out	2	.2137	.1056	30.2	0	0	1	0	1	0	0	0	0	0	0	0	0	1	0	0	1	0	0	0	0	0	0	0	0
hollowing	3	.3773	.2485	34.0	0	0	0	1	0	0	1	1	0	0	0	1	0	1	0	0	0	0	0	0	1	0	0	0	0
hollowness	2	.1473	.0686	28.4	0	0	0	0	0	1	1	0	0	0	0	1	0	0	0	0	0	1	0	0	0	0	0	0	0
hollows	22	.6053	2.8239	44.5	2	6	6	0	7	0	1	0	7	0	0	1	0	5	0	1	0	0	0	2	1	2	3	0	0
holly	24	.5724	2.9226	44.7	7	4	1	7	4	0	1	0	7	1	0	1	0	1	0	2	7	0	0	0	3	2	0	0	0
Holly	9	.2348	.6724	38.3	1	3	0	5	0	0	0	0	7	0	0	0	0	0	0	0	2	0	0	0	0	0	0	0	0
hollyhocks	3	.3779	.2508	34.0	0	0	1	0	1	0	1	0	0	1	0	0	0	0	0	1	0	0	0	0	0	1	0	0	0
Hollywood	24	.5099	2.5976	44.1	0	4	2	2	4	8	3	1	2	2	0	1	0	4	0	1	0	0	0	0	1	1	0	12	0
Hollywood's	2	.2351	.1166	30.7	0	0	0	0	0	1	1	0	0	0	0	0	0	1	0	0	0	0	0	0	0	0	0	1	0
Holmes	49	.5385	5.7238	47.6	12	6	1	1	3	8	15	3	18	1	3	18	1	1	1	1	0	0	0	0	0	5	0	0	0
Holmes's	2	.2407	.1138	30.6	0	1	0	0	0	0	1	0	0	0	0	1	0	0	0	0	0	0	0	0	0	1	0	0	0
holograms	2	.0000	.0243	23.9	0	0	0	0	2	0	0	0	0	0	0	0	0	0	0	0	0	0	0	0	0	0	0	2	0
holosteans	2	.0000	.0209	23.2	0	0	0	0	2	0	0	0	0	0	0	0	0	0	0	0	0	0	0	0	0	0	2	0	0
Holst	4	.0000	.0323	25.1	1	1	0	0	1	1	0	0	0	0	0	0	0	0	0	0	4	0	0	0	0	0	0	0	0
Holstein	2	.2337	.1157	30.6	0	0	0	1	1	0	0	0	0	0	0	0	0	1	0	0	0	0	0	0	1	0	0	0	0
holster	5	.3343	.4151	36.2	0	0	1	2	1	1	0	0	2	0	0	0	0	0	0	0	0	0	0	0	0	1	0	2	0
Holston	2	.0000	.0290	24.6	0	0	2	0	0	0	0	0	0	0	0	0	0	0	0	0	0	0	0	0	0	2	0	0	0
holy	74	.3804	6.3647	48.0	11	7	7	10	23	4	9	3	15	4	0	10	0	7	4	0	12	0	0	0	3	8	4	4	3
Holy	60	.2933	4.2349	46.3	2	7	10	10	9	17	4	1	9	0	0	3	0	19	0	0	6	0	0	0	1	5	10	4	3
holyday	3	.0000	.0243	23.9	0	0	3	0	0	0	0	0	0	0	0	0	0	0	3	0	0	0	0	0	0	0	0	0	0
homage	3	.3814	.2446	33.9	0	0	0	3	0	0	0	0	0	0	0	0	0	0	0	0	1	0	0	0	1	0	0	1	0
home	3308	.9335	612.07	67.9	786	717	364	366	512	285	222	56	1141	164	31	213	57	276	29	165	158	23	123	43	263	290	110	222	0
Home	62	.6883	8.6995	49.4	6	15	3	17	12	4	5	0	10	1	2	2	0	3	1	0	19	0	3	0	1	12	1	7	0
Home-coming	2	.0000	.0914	29.6	0	2	0	0	0	0	0	0	2	0	0	0	0	0	0	0	0	0	0	0	0	0	0	0	0
home-made	5	.3839	.4167	36.2	0	0	0	3	2	0	0	0	0	0	1	1	0	0	0	2	0	0	0	0	1	0	0	0	0
home-making	2	.2297	.1135	30.6	0	0	1	0	0	0	1	0	0	0	0	1	0	1	0	0	0	0	0	0	0	0	0	0	0
home-run	5	.2422	.3874	35.9	3	1	0	0	1	0	0	0	4	0	0	0	0	0	0	0	0	0	0	0	0	1	0	0	0
homecoming	6	.4467	.6041	37.8	0	1	1	2	1	0	1	0	2	0	0	1	0	0	0	0	0	0	0	0	2	1	0	0	0
homeland	40	.5717	4.8517	46.9	2	5	8	9	8	3	5	0	7	1	0	2	0	20	0	0	6	0	0	0	2	0	1	1	0
homelands	10	.3730	.8242	39.2	0	0	8	1	0	0	1	0	0	0	0	0	0	4	0	0	3	0	0	0	0	3	0	0	0
homeless	10	.6565	1.3590	41.3	0	2	1	1	2	4	0	0	2	0	0	2	0	2	0	0	0	0	0	0	1	1	1	1	0
homelike	3	.0524	.0803	29.0	0	0	0	0	1	2	0	0	1	0	0	0	0	0	0	0	0	0	2	0	0	0	0	0	0
homely	11	.4572	1.1712	40.7	0	3	0	1	1	4	2	0	6	2	0	2	0	1	0	0	0	0	0	0	0	0	0	0	0
homemade	30	.6740	4.2326	46.3	2	4	2	5	5	7	5	0	13	0	1	5	0	3	0	1	0	0	0	2	2	1	0	2	0
homemaker	9	.1008	.2225	33.5	0	1	1	0	1	1	5	0	0	0	0	0	0	0	0	0	0	0	7	0	0	1	0	1	0
homemakers	9	.1905	.3917	35.9	0	0	0	1	2	0	4	2	0	0	0	0	1	0	0	0	0	0	5	0	0	0	0	3	0
Homemakers	3	.0000	.0097	19.8	0	0	0	0	1	1	1	0	0	0	0	0	0	0	0	0	0	0	3	0	0	0	0	0	0
homemaking	15	.0000	.0483	26.8	0	0	0	0	6	5	4	0	0	0	0	0	0	0	0	0	0	0	15	0	0	0	0	0	0
homeowners	3	.0000	.0583	27.7	3	0	0	0	0	0	0	0	0	0	0	0	0	3	0	0	0	0	0	0	0	0	0	0	0
homer	3	.2187	.1555	31.9	0	0	1	1	0	1	0	0	0	2	0	0	0	0	0	0	0	0	0	0	0	0	0	1	0
Homer	145	.4725	15.146	51.8	0	12	48	41	2	9	32	1	45	2	0	44	0	2	0	0	0	1	0	0	48	1	2	0	0
Homer's	18	.4249	1.7580	42.5	0	2	8	5	0	1	2	0	7	0	0	4	0	0	0	0	0	0	0	0	6	0	1	0	0
homers	3	.1409	.1472	31.7	1	0	0	1	1	0	0	0	1	0	0	0	0	0	0	0	0	0	0	0	0	2	0	0	0
homes	581	.8474	98.522	59.9	133	94	96	96	80	51	25	6	87	5	1	9	3	217	4	69	28	12	13	12	4	49	34	32	2
homesick	17	.5927	2.1758	43.4	1	4	7	2	2	0	1	0	8	0	0	1	0	2	0	0	2	0	0	0	3	1	0	0	0
homesickness	4	.2995	.2902	34.6	0	1	0	0	3	0	0	0	1	1	0	2	0	0	0	0	0	0	0	0	0	0	0	0	0
homesite	2	.0000	.0243	23.9	0	2	0	0	0	0	0	0	0	0	0	0	0	0	0	0	0	0	0	0	0	0	0	2	0
homespun	9	.4788	.9331	39.7	0	5	0	0	1	2	1	0	1	0	0	1	0	2	0	0	0	0	0	0	0	4	0	1	0
homestead	9	.5660	1.0771	40.3	1	0	4	2	1	0	1	0	2	0	1	1	0	1	0	0	0	0	0	0	0	2	1	1	0
Homestead	8	.4753	.8904	39.5	1	1	5	0	0	1	0	0	5	0	0	0	0	1	0	0	0	0	0	0	0	1	1	0	0
homesteaded	2	.2437	.1129	30.5	0	0	1	0	1	0	0	0	0	0	0	0	0	0	0	0	0	0	0	0	0	0	1	1	0
homesteaders	6	.2152	.4071	36.1	0	0	4	0	2	0	0	0	3	0	0	0	0	3	0	0	0	0	0	0	0	0	0	0	0
homesteads	4	.3212	.3104	34.9	1	0	1	1	1	0	0	0	1	0	0	1	0	0	0	0	0	0	0	0	0	2	0	0	0
hometown	12	.4451	1.1731	40.7	0	1	1	2	6	2	0	0	2	0	0	5	0	2	0	0	0	0	0	0	0	1	0	2	0
homeward	24	.6481	3.2941	45.2	5	2	4	2	8	3	0	0	12	0	1	3	0	1	0	0	2	0	0	0	3	0	2	0	0
homeward-bound	2	.0000	.0243	23.9	0	0	0	1	0	1	0	0	0	0	0	0	0	0	0	0	0	0	0	0	0	0	0	2	0
homewards	2	.0000	.0914	29.6	0	0	0	1	0	1	0	0	2	0	0	0	0	0	0	0	0	0	0	0	0	0	0	0	0
homework	67	.6900	9.6154	49.8	9	13	7	2	15	13	8	0	28	14	3	2	7	2	0	0	0	0	3	0	0	1	1	6	0
homey	2	.1812	.0838	29.2	0	0	0	0	0	0	1	1	0	0	0	0	0	0	0	0	0	0	1	0	0	0	0	1	0
Homily	42	.0000	.4924	36.9	0	0	42	0	0	0	0	0	0	0	0	0	0	0	0	0	0	0	0	0	42	0	0	0	0
Homily's	3	.0000	.0352	25.5	0	0	3	0	0	0	0	0	0	0	0	0	0	0	0	0	0	0	0	0	3	0	0	0	0
homing	11	.3538	.9873	39.9	5	0	0	2	3	1	0	0	6	0	0	0	4	0	0	0	0	0	0	0	0	0	1	0	0
hominid	2	.0000	.0209	23.2	0	0	0	0	2	0	0	0	0	0	0	0	0	0	0	0	0	0	0	0	0	0	2	0	0
hominy	7	.3934	.6054	37.8	0	0	1	1	2	1	0	2	1	0	0	3	0	0	2	0	0	0	0	0	1	0	0	0	0
homo	2	.2417	.1091	30.4	0	1	0	1	0	0	0	0	0	0	0	0	0	0	0	0	1	0	0	0	0	0	1	0	0
Homo	10	.2553	.6070	37.8	0	0	0	0	9	1	0	0	0	0	0	0	0	1	0	3	0	0	0	0	0	0	6	0	0
homogeneous	3	.0000	.0314	25.0	0	0	0	0	1	1	1	0	0	0	0	0	0	0	0	0	0	0	0	0	0	0	3	0	0
homogenized	2	.2130	.1056	30.2	0	0	0	0	0	2	0	0	0	0	0	0	0	0	1	1	0	0	0	0	0	0	0	0	0
homograph	9	.1636	.3552	35.5	0	0	2	0	5	2	0	0	0	2	0	0	0	0	7	0	0	0	0	0	0	0	0	0	0
homographs	10	.2379	.5644	37.5	0	0	3	1	2	2	2	0	1	3	0	0	0	0	6	0	0	0	0	0	0	0	0	0	0
homologous	4	.2278	.2257	33.5	0	0	0	2	0	0	0	2	0	0	0	0	0	0	0	2	0	0	0	0	0	0	2	0	0
homonym	45	.1222	1.4795	41.7	11	8	10	11	3	1	0	1	2	5	0	0	0	0	38	0	0	0	0	0	0	0	0	0	0
homonyms	92	.1642	3.7870	45.8	18	17	18	22	8	5	2	2	5	16	0	0	0	0	71	0	0	0	0	0	0	0	0	0	0
homophone	9	.2444	.4981	37.0	0	4	1	2	2	0	0	0	0	5	0	0	0	0	4	0	0	0	0	0	0	0	0	0	0
homophones	11	.2253	.5736	37.6	0	5	1	2	3	0	0	0	0	8	0	0	0	0	3	0	0	0	0	0	0	0	0	0	0
homophonic	9	.0851	.2230	33.5	0	0	0	4	0	5	0	0	0	0	0	0	0	0	0	0	8	0	0	0	0	1	0	0	0
homos	3	.0000	.0243	23.9	0	2	0	1	0	0	0	0	0	0	0	0	0	0	3	0	0	0	0	0	0	0	0	0	0
homotransplantation	2	.0000	.0394	26.0	0	0	0	0	0	0	0	2	0	0	0	0	0	0	0	2	0	0	0	0	0	0	0	0	0
homozygous	3	.2427	.1822	32.6	0	0	0	0	1	0	0	2	0	0	0	0	0	0	0	2	0	0	0	0	0	0	0	1	0

3F Hollander's
4G Hollanders
3A hollar
5Q hollow-horned
7J hollow-log
8E Holloway
7D hollowly
5Q Holman
4A Holmes'
8Q Holnicote
7R hologram
5F holokus
7Q holostean
9D holp
4P Holsopple
9F Holstein-Friesian
6A holsters
6R Holtzman
3P HOLYDAY
4G hom
7P Homage
8D hombre
5A hombres
5P hombria
3A Home-Run
9R home-building
7J home-built
5Q home-disposal
5J home-feeling
8N home-hearths
6A home-sick
3P home-town
9R home-turf
4A home's
8A homebound
8F homebuilder
7R homebuilts
7H homecomings
5Q homelier
5C homered
7B homeroom
4A homeseekers
8F homesteader
7B Homework
XR homicidal
XR homicide
7A Homme
6G homo-
9L homogenization
XH homograft
XH homografts
8R homosexuals
XH homozygotes

Word Type	F	D	U	SFI	3 Gr 3	4 Gr 4	5 Gr 5	6 Gr 6	7 Gr 7	8 Gr 8	9 Gr 9	X UnGr	A Read	B Eng & Gr	C Comp	D Lit	E Math	F Soc Stud	G Spell	H Sci	J Music	K Art	L Home Ec	M Shop	N Lib F	P Lib NF	Q Lib Ref	R Mag	S Rel
hon	2	.0000	.0914	29.6	0	0	0	1	1	0	0	0	2	0	0	0	0	0	0	0	0	0	0	0	0	0	0	0	0
Honda	2	.0000	.0243	23.9	0	0	0	0	2	0	0	0	0	0	0	0	0	0	0	0	0	0	0	0	0	0	0	2	0
Honduras	3	.0000	.0583	27.7	0	0	0	2	0	1	0	0	0	0	0	0	0	3	0	0	0	0	0	0	0	0	0	0	0
honest	84	.7853	13.378	51.3	4	10	4	11	25	12	18	0	27	7	1	18	0	7	1	0	1	0	0	1	6	10	2	3	0
honest-to-goodness	2	.2433	.1158	30.6	1	0	0	0	1	0	0	0	0	0	0	0	0	0	0	0	0	0	0	0	0	1	0	1	0
honestly	20	.7119	2.9188	44.7	2	0	1	6	3	5	2	1	4	3	0	2	0	3	0	3	0	0	0	0	1	2	0	2	0
honesty	19	.7075	2.7309	44.4	1	3	2	3	5	3	2	0	2	3	0	2	0	3	0	0	0	1	0	0	2	2	1	3	0
honey	113	.7811	17.899	52.5	32	12	14	12	23	6	10	4	33	2	0	6	0	4	7	6	1	0	3	0	6	29	12	4	0
Honey	7	.0000	.3198	35.0	5	0	2	0	0	0	0	0	7	0	0	0	0	0	0	0	0	0	0	0	0	0	0	0	0
honey-bees	3	.2383	.1815	32.6	0	0	1	2	0	0	0	0	0	0	0	0	0	0	0	2	0	0	0	0	0	1	0	0	0
honeybee	5	.4730	.5364	37.3	1	3	0	0	1	0	0	0	2	0	0	0	0	0	0	1	0	0	0	0	0	1	1	0	0
honeybees	13	.4605	1.3072	41.2	2	6	1	0	4	0	0	0	2	0	0	1	0	0	0	3	0	0	0	0	0	2	5	0	0
honeycomb	7	.5092	.7591	38.8	2	0	1	1	1	0	2	0	1	0	0	0	0	0	0	0	0	0	0	0	1	2	2	1	0
honeycombed	4	.4456	.3981	36.0	0	0	0	2	1	0	1	0	1	0	0	1	0	1	0	0	0	0	0	0	0	0	1	0	0
honeycombs	2	.2401	.1133	30.5	1	0	0	0	1	0	0	0	0	0	0	0	0	0	0	0	0	0	0	0	0	1	1	0	0
Honeycreeper	2	.0000	.0243	23.9	0	0	0	0	2	0	0	0	0	0	0	0	0	0	0	0	0	0	0	0	0	0	0	2	0
Honeycutt	4	.0000	.1827	32.6	0	0	0	4	0	0	0	0	4	0	0	0	0	0	0	0	0	0	0	0	0	0	0	0	0
honeydew	18	.5440	2.1739	43.4	6	3	0	2	6	0	1	0	9	0	0	0	0	0	0	5	0	0	1	0	0	0	1	2	0
honeymoon	3	.2143	.1568	32.0	0	1	0	1	0	1	0	0	0	0	0	0	0	0	0	0	0	0	0	0	0	1	0	2	0
honeypot	5	.0000	.0523	27.2	0	0	0	0	5	0	0	0	0	0	0	0	0	0	0	0	0	0	0	0	0	0	5	0	0
honeysuckle	7	.4194	.6838	38.3	0	0	2	1	1	1	1	1	3	0	1	1	0	0	0	1	0	0	0	0	0	1	0	0	0
Honeywell	2	.0000	.0209	23.2	0	0	1	0	1	0	0	0	0	0	0	0	0	0	0	0	0	0	0	0	0	0	2	0	0
Hong	6	.1639	.3347	35.2	0	3	1	1	1	0	0	0	2	0	0	0	0	4	0	0	0	0	0	0	0	0	0	0	0
HongKong	7	.1787	.3475	35.4	0	0	0	1	5	1	0	0	1	0	0	0	0	1	0	0	0	0	0	0	5	0	0	0	0
honing	3	.0437	.0743	28.7	0	0	0	1	0	0	2	0	1	0	0	0	0	0	0	0	0	0	0	2	0	0	0	0	0
honk	6	.2435	.4548	36.6	4	0	0	0	0	1	1	0	4	0	0	0	0	2	0	0	0	0	0	0	0	0	0	0	0
Honkebeest	8	.0000	.3655	35.6	0	8	0	0	0	0	0	0	8	0	0	0	0	0	0	0	0	0	0	0	0	0	0	0	0
honked	13	.3439	1.2232	40.9	7	1	0	2	2	0	1	0	11	1	0	0	0	0	0	0	0	0	0	0	1	0	0	0	0
Honkey	9	.0000	.1094	30.4	9	0	0	0	0	0	0	0	0	0	0	0	0	0	0	0	0	0	0	0	0	0	0	9	0
honking	9	.2837	.6857	38.4	5	1	0	1	0	1	0	1	5	0	2	0	0	0	0	0	0	0	0	0	1	0	0	1	0
Honolulu	20	.4323	1.9282	42.9	0	1	10	4	1	3	1	0	2	0	0	0	2	11	0	1	0	0	0	0	0	0	0	4	0
honor	204	.8973	36.487	55.6	21	40	30	30	32	28	20	3	73	6	1	14	0	27	3	0	7	2	3	1	13	22	17	15	0
Honor	15	.5098	1.6121	42.1	5	1	1	0	1	5	1	1	1	0	0	4	0	1	0	1	0	0	0	0	6	1	1	0	0
honorable	22	.6672	3.0259	44.8	2	0	0	3	5	2	9	1	5	5	0	5	0	1	1	0	0	0	0	0	2	1	1	1	0
Honorable	17	.4231	1.6909	42.3	3	4	0	2	1	3	0	4	8	0	0	0	0	1	0	0	0	0	0	0	3	0	0	5	0
honorably	2	.1717	.1142	30.6	0	0	0	1	0	1	0	0	1	0	0	1	0	0	0	0	0	0	0	0	0	0	0	0	0
honoraries	2	.0000	.0243	23.9	0	0	0	0	0	0	0	2	0	0	0	0	0	0	0	0	0	0	0	0	0	0	0	2	0
honorary	14	.1103	.4677	36.7	0	0	1	1	1	2	0	9	0	0	0	0	0	2	0	0	0	0	0	0	0	0	0	12	0
Honore	3	.0994	.0714	28.5	0	0	1	0	0	2	0	0	0	0	0	0	0	0	0	0	0	2	0	0	0	0	1	0	0
honored	45	.7773	7.0896	48.5	2	9	5	7	3	7	6	6	12	4	0	6	0	7	1	1	3	1	0	0	2	1	0	7	0
honoring	8	.5512	.9314	39.7	1	2	2	0	1	1	1	0	2	0	0	1	0	0	0	0	0	1	1	0	0	1	1	1	0
honors	34	.8040	5.5195	47.4	4	10	1	8	7	0	3	1	9	2	0	2	1	5	0	1	2	0	0	0	1	4	3	4	0
honour	14	.5249	1.6172	42.1	0	0	0	2	3	4	5	0	6	1	0	3	0	0	0	0	0	0	0	0	3	0	0	1	0
honourable	6	.5143	.6574	38.2	0	0	0	1	2	0	2	1	1	0	0	1	0	0	0	0	0	0	0	0	2	1	1	0	0
honoured	2	.1948	.1250	31.0	0	0	0	1	0	0	0	1	1	0	0	0	0	0	0	0	0	0	0	0	0	1	0	0	0
honours	2	.0000	.0162	22.1	0	0	0	0	0	2	0	0	0	0	0	0	0	0	0	0	2	0	0	0	0	0	0	0	0
Honshu	5	.1118	.2195	33.4	1	2	0	0	0	2	0	0	1	0	0	0	0	4	0	0	0	0	0	0	0	0	0	0	0
hoo	6	.1717	.3427	35.3	1	4	0	0	0	1	0	0	3	0	0	3	0	0	0	0	0	0	0	0	0	0	0	0	0
hoo-oo	3	.0000	.0434	26.4	0	3	0	0	0	0	0	0	0	0	0	0	0	0	0	0	0	0	0	0	0	3	0	0	0
hood	28	.6768	3.9712	46.0	2	4	2	7	12	1	0	0	13	1	0	4	0	0	1	0	0	0	0	0	3	1	1	4	0
Hood	36	.7186	5.4107	47.3	1	3	6	13	7	4	2	0	21	0	0	3	0	2	1	2	1	0	0	0	0	3	2	1	0
Hood's	2	.1717	.1142	30.6	0	0	1	0	1	0	0	0	1	0	0	1	0	0	0	0	0	0	0	0	0	0	0	0	0
hooded	5	.5382	.5720	37.6	0	1	1	2	1	0	0	0	1	1	0	1	0	0	0	0	0	0	0	0	1	1	0	0	0
hoodlum	2	.0000	.0243	23.9	0	0	0	0	2	0	0	0	0	0	0	0	0	0	0	0	0	0	0	0	0	0	0	2	0
hoods	11	.5771	1.3292	41.2	0	2	1	3	4	0	1	0	2	0	0	2	0	0	0	0	0	0	1	0	1	2	0	3	0
hoof	16	.5106	1.7119	42.3	7	1	2	0	3	1	2	0	0	0	0	1	0	1	0	2	1	0	0	0	7	4	0	0	0
hoofbeats	6	.3153	.4866	36.9	3	1	0	1	1	0	0	0	3	0	0	0	0	0	0	0	2	0	0	0	0	1	0	0	0
hoofed	9	.2744	.6060	37.8	0	0	0	2	5	0	0	2	1	0	0	0	0	0	0	4	0	0	0	0	0	0	4	0	0
hoofprints	4	.2445	.3067	34.9	1	0	0	3	0	0	0	0	3	0	0	0	0	0	0	0	0	0	0	0	0	1	0	0	0
hoofs	66	.6899	9.4820	49.8	6	20	8	14	13	1	4	0	25	0	2	9	0	5	0	8	1	0	0	0	6	10	0	0	0
hook	112	.8083	18.208	52.6	20	27	5	19	22	9	10	0	27	5	7	2	5	6	3	8	4	0	10	2	15	9	4	5	0
Hook	33	.0000	1.5075	41.8	0	0	0	33	0	0	0	0	33	0	0	0	0	0	0	0	0	0	0	0	0	0	0	0	0
Hook's	3	.0000	.1370	31.4	0	0	0	3	0	0	0	0	3	0	0	0	0	0	0	0	0	0	0	0	0	0	0	0	0
Hooke	9	.2285	.5268	37.2	0	0	5	0	3	0	1	0	0	0	0	0	0	0	0	7	0	0	0	0	0	0	2	0	0
hooked	50	.8072	8.1655	49.1	14	8	6	5	10	2	3	2	18	1	1	3	0	1	1	2	1	0	0	0	6	7	5	4	0
Hooker	15	.2444	.9069	39.6	0	0	3	0	5	7	0	0	0	0	0	0	0	10	0	0	0	0	0	0	0	0	5	0	0
Hooker's	2	.2337	.1157	30.6	0	0	0	0	1	1	0	0	0	0	0	0	0	1	0	0	0	0	0	0	1	0	0	0	0
hookers	2	.1948	.1250	31.0	0	0	1	1	0	0	0	0	1	0	0	0	0	0	0	0	0	0	0	0	0	1	0	0	0
hooking	10	.4746	1.0274	40.1	1	5	0	0	3	0	1	0	2	0	1	0	0	0	0	3	0	0	0	2	0	0	1	1	0
hooks	49	.7299	7.2971	48.6	14	3	5	3	10	11	3	0	11	1	0	3	0	5	0	8	0	0	5	2	1	5	5	3	0
hookup	2	.2433	.1158	30.6	1	0	0	0	1	0	0	0	0	0	0	0	0	0	0	0	0	0	0	0	0	1	0	1	0
hookworm	3	.2445	.1818	32.6	0	0	0	0	2	1	0	0	0	0	0	0	0	0	0	2	0	0	0	0	0	0	1	0	0
hooky	4	.0000	.1827	32.6	0	0	0	0	2	2	0	0	4	0	0	0	0	0	0	0	0	0	0	0	0	0	0	0	0
hoop	41	.7502	6.3438	48.0	11	4	0	9	9	5	1	2	20	0	0	2	1	1	3	5	0	1	0	0	2	3	0	3	0
hoops	8	.3811	.7656	38.8	2	3	1	1	1	0	0	0	5	0	0	0	0	0	0	0	0	0	0	0	1	2	0	0	0
hooray	11	.4749	1.2163	40.9	2	1	1	5	2	0	0	0	7	0	0	2	0	0	0	0	1	0	0	0	0	0	0	1	0
hoosband	2	.0000	.0290	24.6	2	0	0	0	0	0	0	0	0	0	0	0	0	0	0	0	0	0	0	0	0	2	0	0	0
hoot	10	.5268	1.1624	40.7	3	1	0	0	5	0	1	0	4	0	0	1	0	0	0	1	0	0	0	0	0	3	0	1	0
hooted	9	.5460	1.0377	40.2	2	2	0	3	0	0	2	0	2	0	1	2	0	0	0	0	1	0	0	0	2	0	0	1	0
hooting	6	.3548	.5245	37.2	2	1	0	1	1	1	0	0	3	0	1	1	0	0	0	0	0	0	0	0	0	1	0	0	0
hoots	2	.1621	.0746	28.7	0	1	0	0	1	0	0	0	0	0	1	1	0	0	0	0	0	0	0	0	0	0	0	0	0
hooved	2	.1674	.0805	29.1	0	0	0	0	0	0	1	1	0	0	0	0	0	0	0	0	0	0	1	0	0	1	0	0	0
Hoover	22	.6375	2.9043	44.6	3	0	0	2	6	3	6	2	4	1	0	1	0	1	0	1	0	0	0	0	2	1	4	7	0
Hoover's	3	.3781	.2493	34.0	0	0	0	0	1	1	1	0	0	1	0	0	0	1	0	0	0	0	0	0	0	0	0	1	0
Hoovers	6	.2279	.4286	36.3	0	0	0	0	6	0	0	0	4	0	0	0	0	0	0	0	0	0	0	0	0	0	0	2	0
hooves	21	.4866	2.1687	43.4	0	1	3	3	11	1	1	1	2	0	1	3	0	1	0	0	0	0	0	0	12	1	0	1	0
hop	75	.7160	11.038	50.4	36	12	12	8	3	1	2	1	24	9	0	2	0	1	4	6	12	0	0	0	2	10	0	5	0
Hop	3	.0000	.1370	31.4	0	0	0	3	0	0	0	0	3	0	0	0	0	0	0	0	0	0	0	0	0	0	0	0	0
hop-scotch	2	.1812	.0838	29.2	0	1	0	0	0	0	1	0	0	0	0	0	0	0	0	0	0	0	1	0	0	0	0	1	0
hopak	2	.0000	.0162	22.1	0	0	0	0	0	2	0	0	0	0	0	0	0	0	0	0	2	0	0	0	0	0	0	0	0
Hopalong	3	.2060	.1500	31.8	0	0	1	0	2	0	0	0	0	0	0	2	0	0	0	0	0	0	0	0	0	1	0	0	0
hope	544	.8839	95.992	59.8	89	93	55	60	101	69	66	11	184	33	4	64	1	36	15	13	10	0	2	2	63	51	16	49	1
Hope	33	.6377	4.4518	46.5	15	2	3	1	5	3	4	0	13	4	0	0	2	5	0	0	0	0	0	0	0	1	2	6	0
Hope's	5	.4138	.4638	36.7	3	0	0	0	1	0	1	0	1	0	0	0	0	1	1	0	0	0	0	0	0	0	0	2	0
hoped	201	.8153	33.146	55.2	33	47	26	26	28	22	15	4	70	5	1	8	1	40	3	4	1	0	1	0	19	24	5	19	0

9R Hondas
6A Honest
4H honey-bee
7Q honey-clear
7D honey-coloured
5H Honey-comb
6A honey-suckle
4A honeyed
4N honeyjar
5H honeylike
7Q honeypots
XH Honeysuckle
4A honker
6R Honker
4A honks
3A Honks
6R Honolulu's
7B honor's
XR honorary-degree
7D Honored
7N Honourable
4A hoo-hoo
7R hoodlum-haunted
8F hoodlums
8N hoof-beats
5A hoohooed
5A hoohooing
9L hook-and-eye
8L hook-and-ladder
3N hook-and-ladders
8F hook-shaped
5N hookah
5H Hooke's
8A Hookerville
5A hookey
7Q hooklets
4P hoop-skirts
7D hooraw
3J hooraying
9D hooroar
9D hooroaring
9D hooroars
XR Hoosiers
8F Hooverville
3P hop-and-skip
7A hop-skip-and-jump
3J hop-skip-jumping
7R hop-up
XR Hopa
7D Hopalong's

Word Type	F	D	U	SFI	3 Gr 3	4 Gr 4	5 Gr 5	6 Gr 6	7 Gr 7	8 Gr 8	9 Gr 9	X UnGr	A Read	B Eng & Gr	C Comp	D Lit	E Math	F Soc Stud	G Spell	H Sci	J Music	K Art	L Home Ec	M Shop	N Lib F	P Lib NF	Q Lib Ref	R Mag	S Rel
hoped-for	7	.5525	.8044	39.1	1	1	0	0	1	1	3	0	0	1	0	1	0	2	0	0	0	0	0	0	0	1	0	2	0
hopeful	23	.6491	3.1032	44.9	1	4	2	1	6	3	6	0	5	1	0	2	0	5	0	0	0	0	0	0	4	2	0	4	0
hopefully	30	.7030	4.2962	46.3	3	8	3	3	5	4	3	1	4	2	0	2	0	3	0	0	1	0	0	0	8	3	2	5	0
hopeless	30	.7359	4.5403	46.6	3	2	4	0	9	6	6	0	12	0	0	3	0	3	0	0	3	0	1	0	4	2	1	1	0
hopelessly	14	.5839	1.7229	42.4	0	2	0	3	6	2	1	0	3	0	0	3	0	1	0	0	0	0	0	0	2	3	0	2	0
hopelessness	5	.4770	.5360	37.3	0	0	1	0	2	1	1	0	2	0	0	1	0	0	0	0	0	0	0	0	0	1	0	1	0
hopes	112	.8514	19.100	52.8	7	16	9	18	22	19	19	2	29	4	4	3	0	21	4	4	5	1	0	0	9	10	5	13	0
Hopeville	2	.0000	.0299	24.8	0	0	2	0	0	0	0	0	0	0	0	0	2	0	0	0	0	0	0	0	0	0	0	0	0
Hopi	8	.3753	.6681	38.2	3	2	0	2	0	0	0	1	1	0	0	0	0	0	0	0	2	0	0	0	0	1	0	4	0
hoping	94	.8008	15.288	51.8	9	16	22	14	20	4	7	2	40	7	1	4	0	4	0	1	3	0	1	0	13	9	1	10	0
Hopkins	19	.6973	2.7659	44.4	8	0	2	0	4	2	2	1	9	2	0	1	0	1	1	1	0	0	0	0	0	0	2	2	0
Hopkinson	5	.0619	.1340	31.3	0	0	0	0	4	1	0	0	1	0	0	0	0	0	0	0	4	0	0	0	0	0	0	0	0
hopped	68	.6867	9.8854	49.9	21	24	3	11	5	3	1	0	43	4	0	5	0	1	3	1	2	0	0	0	3	6	0	0	0
hopper	15	.4970	1.6125	42.1	2	8	3	0	0	2	0	0	3	1	0	0	1	0	0	0	0	0	0	1	1	8	0	0	0
Hopper	11	.3569	.9024	39.6	3	4	0	0	0	4	0	0	3	0	3	0	0	0	0	0	0	1	0	0	0	4	0	0	0
hoppers	6	.3295	.5083	37.1	0	0	4	0	0	1	1	0	3	0	0	0	0	1	0	1	0	0	0	1	0	0	0	0	0
hopping	27	.6658	3.7628	45.8	9	4	4	3	5	0	1	1	10	2	0	2	0	1	0	2	2	0	0	0	1	7	0	0	0
hoppity	2	.1717	.1142	30.6	2	0	0	0	0	0	0	0	1	0	0	1	0	0	0	0	0	0	0	0	0	0	0	0	0
hoppity-hop	4	.0000	.0429	26.3	0	4	0	0	0	0	0	0	0	0	0	4	0	0	0	0	0	0	0	0	0	0	0	0	0
hops	23	.6964	3.3332	45.2	9	7	2	3	1	1	0	0	10	1	0	0	2	0	0	1	2	1	0	0	3	2	0	1	0
hopscotch	5	.3861	.4329	36.4	4	0	0	1	0	0	0	0	1	1	0	0	0	0	2	0	0	0	0	0	0	1	0	0	0
Hor	9	.0000	.4111	36.1	0	0	0	0	9	0	0	0	9	0	0	0	0	0	0	0	0	0	0	0	0	0	0	0	0
Horace	29	.5710	3.6840	45.7	10	7	4	1	3	2	2	0	19	0	0	0	0	1	0	1	0	0	0	0	1	2	4	1	0
Horace's	3	.0000	.1370	31.4	3	0	0	0	0	0	0	0	3	0	0	0	0	0	0	0	0	0	0	0	0	0	0	0	0
Horatio	7	.5686	.8340	39.2	1	0	1	0	0	3	2	0	1	0	0	0	0	1	0	0	1	0	0	0	1	1	2	0	0
horde	11	.3694	.9449	39.8	1	1	5	0	3	1	0	0	3	5	0	0	0	1	0	0	0	0	0	0	0	0	2	0	0
hordes	10	.3971	.8760	39.4	0	0	2	1	5	2	0	0	1	0	0	0	0	1	0	0	0	0	0	0	0	2	5	1	0
Horican	3	.0000	.0352	25.5	0	0	0	0	3	0	0	0	0	0	0	0	0	0	0	0	0	0	0	0	3	0	0	0	0
horizon	89	.7175	13.038	51.2	2	11	14	7	25	9	18	3	17	2	2	14	0	8	1	18	1	7	0	0	4	8	3	4	0
horizons	15	.5429	1.7152	42.3	0	0	0	0	4	2	9	0	0	2	0	2	0	4	0	6	0	0	0	0	0	0	0	1	0
Horizons	4	.0000	.1827	32.6	0	3	0	1	0	0	0	0	4	0	0	0	0	0	0	0	0	0	0	0	0	0	0	0	0
horizontal	123	.5621	14.170	51.5	3	15	11	13	25	15	37	4	4	3	1	0	32	1	0	8	3	12	1	30	2	7	13	6	0
horizontally	22	.6158	2.7688	44.4	0	0	2	2	8	3	7	0	1	0	0	0	3	2	0	2	2	0	2	4	1	2	1	2	0
hormone	17	.2497	1.0844	40.4	0	0	0	2	7	0	8	0	1	0	0	0	0	0	0	13	0	0	0	0	0	0	3	0	0
hormone-producing	2	.0000	.0394	26.0	0	0	0	0	2	0	0	0	0	0	0	0	0	0	0	2	0	0	0	0	0	0	0	0	0
hormones	10	.1626	.4769	36.8	0	0	0	0	8	0	2	0	0	0	0	0	0	0	0	9	0	0	0	0	0	0	1	0	0
horn	185	.6830	25.903	54.1	31	40	12	21	48	20	13	0	40	2	3	11	2	3	3	7	62	0	1	1	16	28	4	2	0
Horn	22	.5927	2.7962	44.5	1	5	6	1	5	4	0	0	8	0	0	1	0	5	0	0	2	0	0	0	1	5	0	0	0
hornblende	10	.3372	.7715	38.9	0	0	2	1	0	0	4	3	0	0	0	0	0	0	0	6	0	0	0	0	0	1	3	0	0
Horne	2	.0000	.0914	29.6	1	1	0	0	0	0	0	0	2	0	0	0	0	0	0	0	0	0	0	0	0	0	0	0	0
horned	17	.6144	2.1753	43.4	6	3	0	3	3	1	1	0	2	0	0	2	0	0	0	5	0	0	0	0	1	5	1	0	0
Horner	12	.2028	.8883	39.5	1	0	0	11	0	0	0	0	11	0	0	0	0	0	0	0	0	0	0	0	1	0	0	1	0
hornet	2	.0000	.0914	29.6	0	1	0	0	1	0	0	0	2	0	0	0	0	0	0	0	0	0	0	0	0	0	0	0	0
hornet's	3	.2435	.2274	33.6	2	0	0	0	0	0	1	0	2	0	0	0	0	1	0	0	0	0	0	0	0	0	0	0	0
hornets	3	.3450	.2505	34.0	2	0	1	0	0	0	0	0	1	0	0	0	0	0	0	0	0	0	0	0	1	1	0	0	0
hornets'	2	.2337	.1157	30.6	0	1	0	0	0	0	1	0	0	0	0	0	0	1	0	0	0	0	0	0	1	0	0	0	0
horns	158	.7639	24.596	53.9	51	31	18	14	23	11	10	0	55	2	3	7	0	10	0	5	27	5	0	0	5	25	7	7	0
Hornsby	3	.2332	.1690	32.3	1	0	0	2	0	0	0	0	0	0	0	0	0	0	0	0	0	0	0	0	0	2	0	1	0
horny	20	.6802	2.8094	44.5	5	1	2	1	9	0	2	0	4	1	1	1	0	0	0	6	0	0	0	0	1	4	2	1	0
horrible	39	.6626	5.4127	47.3	6	4	6	5	9	2	4	3	16	0	1	8	0	1	1	0	0	0	0	0	6	3	3	0	0
horribly	8	.4176	.7511	38.8	2	0	2	1	2	0	1	0	2	0	0	2	0	0	0	0	0	0	0	0	3	1	0	0	0
horrid	21	.6228	2.7441	44.4	0	7	2	4	5	1	1	1	6	0	0	3	0	0	0	1	0	0	0	0	5	3	2	1	0
horrified	13	.7207	1.9252	42.8	1	3	1	3	2	3	0	0	4	0	0	1	0	2	0	0	1	0	0	0	2	1	1	1	0
horrify	4	.4444	.3919	35.9	0	0	1	0	1	1	1	0	1	0	0	1	0	0	1	0	0	0	0	0	0	0	0	1	0
horrifying	5	.4595	.4872	36.9	0	0	1	0	1	2	1	0	0	0	0	0	0	0	0	1	0	0	0	0	1	0	1	2	0
horror	41	.6921	5.8297	47.7	0	4	6	5	14	4	7	1	11	4	3	8	0	0	0	1	2	0	0	0	4	3	1	4	0
horror-stricken	2	.1494	.1045	30.2	0	0	0	0	2	0	0	0	1	0	0	0	0	0	0	0	1	0	0	0	0	0	0	0	0
horrors	7	.5712	.8387	39.2	0	0	0	0	1	4	1	1	1	0	0	2	0	1	0	0	0	0	0	0	1	1	1	0	0
Horrors	2	.1717	.1142	30.6	0	0	0	0	0	0	2	0	1	0	0	1	0	0	0	0	0	0	0	0	0	0	0	0	0
horse	1263	.8148	208.34	63.2	303	253	122	201	204	120	49	11	527	46	22	126	5	41	17	33	22	12	0	0	212	140	20	40	0
Horse	32	.6224	4.2156	46.2	9	2	4	7	8	0	0	2	12	1	0	5	0	1	0	0	0	0	0	0	3	4	0	6	0
horse-and-buggy	3	.2442	.1815	32.6	0	0	2	0	0	1	0	0	0	0	0	0	0	2	0	0	0	0	0	0	0	0	0	0	0
horse-drawn	9	.4447	.8617	39.4	0	2	1	2	0	4	0	0	0	0	0	1	0	6	1	0	1	0	0	1	0	0	0	0	0
horse-hoofs	2	.1717	.1142	30.6	0	0	0	0	0	1	1	0	1	0	0	1	0	0	0	0	0	0	0	0	0	0	0	0	0
horse-radish	4	.0000	.0129	21.1	0	0	0	0	0	0	4	0	0	0	0	0	0	0	0	0	0	0	4	0	0	0	0	0	0
horse's	67	.7055	9.8450	49.9	15	12	5	12	16	3	3	1	31	1	1	3	0	1	0	4	1	0	0	0	12	10	0	3	0
horseback	94	.7602	14.624	51.7	18	25	11	9	20	7	3	1	33	2	2	3	1	21	0	2	2	0	0	0	2	18	2	6	0
horseboy	3	.0000	.0352	25.5	0	0	0	3	0	0	0	0	0	0	0	0	0	0	0	0	0	0	0	0	3	0	0	0	0
horseboys	6	.0000	.0703	28.5	0	0	0	6	0	0	0	0	0	0	0	0	0	0	0	0	0	0	0	0	6	0	0	0	0
horseflesh	3	.2120	.1548	31.9	1	1	0	1	0	0	0	0	0	0	0	0	0	0	0	0	0	0	0	0	2	1	0	0	0
horsefly	3	.0000	.1370	31.4	0	3	0	0	0	0	0	0	3	0	0	0	0	0	0	0	0	0	0	0	0	0	0	0	0
horsehair	11	.4904	1.2044	40.8	1	2	0	5	0	0	3	0	4	0	0	3	0	1	0	1	0	0	0	0	0	2	0	0	0
horsehide	4	.3702	.3622	35.6	0	0	1	1	1	0	1	0	2	1	0	1	0	0	0	0	0	0	0	0	0	0	0	0	0
horseless	6	.2152	.4071	36.1	1	1	2	2	0	0	0	0	3	0	0	0	0	3	0	0	0	0	0	0	0	0	0	0	0
horseman	18	.6287	2.3812	43.8	1	2	1	6	6	0	2	0	6	0	0	4	0	1	0	0	1	0	0	0	1	3	0	2	0
Horseman	2	.1523	.0721	28.6	0	0	0	1	0	0	1	0	0	0	1	0	0	0	0	0	0	0	0	0	0	0	0	1	0
horsemanship	5	.4405	.4864	36.9	2	0	1	0	0	2	0	0	1	0	0	1	0	0	0	0	0	0	0	0	0	2	1	0	0
horsemen	27	.6753	3.7707	45.8	3	8	3	6	3	2	1	1	6	1	0	0	0	7	0	0	1	1	0	0	2	6	0	3	0
Horsemen	2	.1948	.1250	31.0	1	0	0	1	0	0	0	0	1	0	0	0	0	0	0	0	0	0	0	0	0	1	0	0	0
Horsepepper	2	.0000	.0234	23.7	0	0	2	0	0	0	0	0	0	0	0	0	0	0	0	0	0	0	0	0	2	0	0	0	0
horsepower	9	.4339	.8440	39.3	0	1	0	0	5	2	1	0	1	0	0	0	0	1	2	0	0	0	0	0	0	0	4	1	0
horses	776	.8557	133.30	61.2	173	190	73	122	126	63	21	8	280	20	9	59	11	96	9	12	8	9	0	2	91	118	14	38	0
Horses	4	.2417	.3028	34.8	3	0	1	0	0	0	0	0	3	0	0	0	0	0	0	0	0	0	0	0	1	0	0	0	0
horses'	19	.6036	2.4892	44.0	3	7	2	2	3	2	0	0	11	0	0	1	0	0	0	0	2	1	0	0	2	2	0	1	0
horseshoe	23	.7213	3.4265	45.3	10	2	3	3	3	1	1	0	8	0	0	1	0	5	0	4	0	0	0	1	1	0	1	1	0
Horseshoe	3	.1277	.1363	31.3	2	0	0	1	0	0	0	0	1	0	0	0	0	0	0	0	0	0	0	0	0	0	0	2	0
horseshoe-shaped	2	.2291	.1135	30.5	0	0	0	0	0	0	2	0	0	0	0	1	0	0	0	1	0	0	0	0	0	0	0	0	0
horseshoes	8	.5566	.9835	39.9	6	0	1	0	0	1	0	0	4	1	0	0	0	1	0	1	0	0	0	0	1	0	0	0	0
horsetail	2	.2446	.1257	31.0	0	0	0	0	1	0	1	0	0	0	0	0	0	1	0	1	0	0	0	0	0	0	0	0	0
horsie	4	.0000	.1827	32.6	0	0	0	4	0	0	0	0	4	0	0	0	0	0	0	0	0	0	0	0	0	0	0	0	0
Hortense	5	.0000	.2284	33.6	0	0	0	5	0	0	0	0	5	0	0	0	0	0	0	0	0	0	0	0	0	0	0	0	0
hose	64	.8437	10.910	50.4	7	25	7	14	8	0	3	0	33	2	1	6	0	2	1	8	1	1	1	0	3	3	0	2	0
hoses	10	.3814	.9581	39.8	4	2	0	2	2	0	0	0	6	0	0	0	0	2	0	0	0	0	0	0	0	0	0	2	0
Hoshour	3	.0000	.0434	26.4	0	3	0	0	0	0	0	0	0	0	0	0	0	0	0	0	0	0	0	0	0	3	0	0	0

5R hopefuls
8J Hopes
4R Hopewell
6A Hopis
7G hopital
7J Hopkinson's
5F hoppers'
3N Hopping
7L hopsacking
5G hor
7D Hor-rid
8J hora
5J Hora
8Q Horde
7C horehound
4A Horiuchi-san
9Q hormon
9Q hormonal
8B Horn-Webler
3R horn-blowing
3P Horn-faced
3P horn-like
7N Hornback
6A hornbills
4A Horned
6A Horner's
5Q Hornet
7Q hornified
3P hornlike
4F hornos
5J Hornpipe
4N hornpipes
5G hornswoggle
XH horoscopes
8R Horowitz
7D horray
7Q Horror
7Q horror-struck
9C horrorstricken
6N horse-breaker
6N horse-colt
4A horse-hair
6R horse-loving
7N horse-noises
4P horse-pulling
4N horse-skin
3Q horsedrawn
7N horsefeathers
4J horsehairs
3P HORSELESS
7H horseman's
6N horseplay
6Q horseradish
6R HORSES
3P horsetails
8N horsewhipping
3P horsewrangler
6R horsey
9N horsing
9D horticultural
7H Horwitz's
5Q Hosea

Word Type	F	D	U	SFI	3 Gr 3	4 Gr 4	5 Gr 5	6 Gr 6	7 Gr 7	8 Gr 8	9 Gr 9	X UnGr	A Read	B Eng & Gr	C Comp	D Lit	E Math	F Soc Stud	G Spell	H Sci	J Music	K Art	L Home Ec	M Shop	N Lib F	P Lib NF	Q Lib Ref	R Mag	S Rel
hosiery	8	.1440	.2972	34.7	1	0	0	0	1	2	4	0	1	0	0	0	0	0	0	0	0	0	5	0	0	0	2	0	0
hospitable	12	.5704	1.4437	41.6	0	0	1	2	4	3	2	0	2	0	0	3	0	3	0	0	0	0	0	0	0	1	2	1	0
hospitably	2	.0000	.0914	29.6	0	0	0	1	1	0	0	0	2	0	0	0	0	0	0	0	0	0	0	0	0	0	0	0	0
hospital	154	.8090	25.221	54.0	24	30	12	21	25	17	23	2	55	3	4	7	1	24	4	5	0	0	1	0	8	13	4	25	0
Hospital	14	.5880	1.7540	42.4	1	2	1	0	3	4	3	0	5	3	0	1	0	0	0	0	0	0	0	0	1	0	1	3	0
hospital's	2	.0000	.0243	23.9	0	0	0	1	1	0	0	0	0	0	0	0	0	0	0	0	0	0	0	0	0	0	0	2	0
hospitality	17	.6161	2.1940	43.4	3	1	0	2	4	5	2	0	5	3	0	2	0	0	2	0	0	0	0	0	2	0	3	0	0
hospitalization	4	.3485	.3103	34.9	0	0	0	0	2	2	0	0	0	0	0	0	0	0	0	1	0	0	0	0	1	0	0	2	0
hospitalized	3	.2530	.1734	32.4	0	0	0	0	1	1	1	0	0	0	1	0	0	0	0	1	0	0	0	0	0	0	1	0	0
hospitals	52	.6216	6.7404	48.3	5	4	12	3	13	13	2	0	6	0	0	0	0	18	0	10	0	0	1	0	0	2	6	9	0
hoss	4	.3480	.3055	34.8	0	0	0	0	2	2	0	0	0	0	0	2	0	1	0	0	1	0	0	0	0	0	0	0	0
host	84	.7881	13.294	51.2	3	8	6	8	25	15	12	7	7	10	1	8	0	2	1	24	3	0	6	0	1	4	9	8	0
hostages	3	.2212	.2099	33.2	0	0	0	2	1	0	0	0	2	0	0	1	0	0	0	0	0	0	0	0	0	0	0	0	0
hostess	27	.2003	1.3282	41.2	0	1	0	4	8	5	8	1	4	5	0	0	0	1	0	0	0	0	15	0	0	1	0	1	0
hostile	35	.7517	5.3625	47.3	1	4	1	5	10	10	3	1	9	2	0	3	0	8	1	0	0	0	0	0	2	3	4	3	0
hostilities	6	.2352	.3498	35.4	0	0	0	0	3	1	1	1	0	0	0	0	0	3	0	0	0	0	0	0	0	0	0	3	0
hostility	9	.5094	.9832	39.9	0	1	1	0	1	4	0	2	1	0	0	0	0	3	0	0	1	0	0	0	0	3	0	1	0
Hostilius	2	.0000	.0290	24.6	0	2	0	0	0	0	0	0	0	0	0	0	0	0	0	0	0	0	0	0	0	2	0	0	0
hostler	3	.1250	.1342	31.3	0	0	1	0	2	0	0	0	1	0	0	0	0	0	0	0	0	0	0	0	2	0	0	0	0
hosts	10	.6395	1.3029	41.1	2	1	0	0	6	0	1	0	0	0	0	1	0	0	0	2	1	0	0	0	1	1	3	1	0
hot	1233	.8851	217.70	63.4	276	222	152	116	206	106	115	40	333	37	13	49	5	139	14	253	12	5	60	6	67	115	55	70	0
Hot	11	.4991	1.2138	40.8	2	0	1	0	2	4	2	0	4	0	0	0	0	1	0	0	2	0	0	0	0	1	0	3	0
hot-	2	.0000	.0243	23.9	0	1	0	1	0	0	0	0	0	0	0	0	0	0	0	0	0	0	0	0	0	0	0	2	0
hot-air	3	.3764	.2483	33.9	1	0	2	0	0	0	0	0	0	0	0	0	0	0	0	1	0	0	0	0	0	0	1	1	0
hot-rod	5	.0000	.2284	33.6	0	0	0	0	5	0	0	0	5	0	0	0	0	0	0	0	0	0	0	0	0	0	0	0	0
hot-water	12	.4793	1.2550	41.0	7	1	3	0	1	0	0	0	3	0	0	0	0	0	0	1	0	0	1	0	5	0	2	0	0
hotel	106	.7676	16.583	52.2	28	15	7	18	22	8	6	2	35	4	1	9	3	16	3	1	0	0	0	0	15	4	0	15	0
Hotel	35	.5117	4.0098	46.0	10	3	2	4	6	8	2	0	17	0	0	0	1	1	0	0	0	0	0	0	3	1	1	11	0
hotels	44	.5348	5.0080	47.0	7	9	3	5	5	7	4	4	5	0	0	0	0	16	0	0	0	0	0	0	2	5	3	13	0
hotheaded	2	.2152	.1357	31.3	0	0	0	0	1	1	0	0	1	0	0	0	0	1	0	0	0	0	0	0	0	0	0	0	0
hotheads	3	.1639	.1674	32.2	0	0	0	0	1	2	0	0	1	0	0	0	0	2	0	0	0	0	0	0	0	0	0	0	0
hothouses	2	.0000	.0389	25.9	0	0	0	0	2	0	0	0	0	0	0	0	0	2	0	0	0	0	0	0	0	0	0	0	0
hotly	10	.6089	1.2834	41.1	1	2	0	1	5	0	1	0	3	0	0	2	0	0	0	0	0	0	0	0	1	2	1	1	0
Hottentot	3	.2270	.1588	32.0	0	2	0	0	0	0	1	0	0	2	0	0	0	0	0	0	0	0	0	0	0	0	1	0	0
Hottentots	5	.0000	.0972	29.9	0	0	0	1	4	0	0	0	0	0	0	0	0	5	0	0	0	0	0	0	0	0	0	0	0
hotter	46	.7343	6.9142	48.4	14	11	3	7	8	0	2	1	10	0	0	2	3	6	0	12	0	0	0	0	1	5	4	3	0
hottest	26	.7076	3.8015	45.8	5	3	4	4	5	2	2	1	7	0	0	0	2	4	0	6	0	0	0	0	1	3	1	2	0
Houdini	7	.2215	.3961	36.0	0	5	1	0	1	0	0	0	1	1	0	0	0	0	0	0	0	0	0	0	0	0	0	5	0
Houdini's	2	.0000	.0243	23.9	0	2	0	0	0	0	0	0	0	0	0	0	0	0	0	0	0	0	0	0	0	0	0	2	0
Houei	3	.0000	.0434	26.4	0	0	0	0	0	0	3	0	0	0	0	0	0	0	0	0	0	0	0	0	0	3	0	0	0
Houghton	13	.4775	1.4402	41.6	0	0	1	11	0	0	1	0	8	1	0	0	0	0	0	0	0	0	0	0	0	0	2	2	0
Houghton's	2	.0000	.0914	29.6	0	0	0	2	0	0	0	0	2	0	0	0	0	0	0	0	0	0	0	0	0	0	0	0	0
houn'	3	.0000	.1370	31.4	2	0	0	0	1	0	0	0	3	0	0	0	0	0	0	0	0	0	0	0	0	0	0	0	0
hound	44	.6328	5.9623	47.8	11	9	5	8	8	2	0	1	24	4	1	0	0	0	0	0	0	0	0	0	6	7	1	1	0
Hound	3	.2563	.1695	32.3	0	0	1	0	0	2	0	0	0	0	0	1	0	0	0	0	0	1	0	0	0	0	0	1	0
hound's	3	.0000	.0352	25.5	0	0	0	1	2	0	0	0	0	0	0	0	0	0	0	0	0	0	0	0	3	0	0	0	0
hounds	40	.5591	4.7804	46.8	1	7	1	18	7	4	1	1	12	0	0	5	0	0	0	0	2	0	0	0	6	2	0	13	0
hour	908	.8799	159.37	62.0	96	133	110	151	185	108	107	18	224	31	9	62	223	39	8	82	9	1	14	3	59	62	21	61	0
Hour	6	.2887	.4130	36.2	0	0	0	1	3	1	1	0	1	0	0	3	0	0	0	0	0	0	0	0	0	0	0	2	0
hour-glass	3	.3762	.2496	34.0	1	0	1	0	0	1	0	0	0	0	0	0	0	0	0	1	0	0	0	0	0	1	1	0	0
hour's	6	.4868	.6622	38.2	1	1	0	1	1	1	1	0	3	1	0	0	0	0	0	0	0	0	0	0	1	0	0	1	0
hourglass	14	.5463	1.7122	42.3	0	0	3	10	0	0	1	0	8	1	0	1	1	0	0	3	0	0	0	0	0	0	0	0	0
hourly	9	.5438	1.0280	40.1	0	1	1	1	2	2	2	0	1	0	0	2	3	1	0	0	0	0	1	0	0	0	1	0	0
hours	990	.8924	175.88	62.5	117	164	114	103	207	126	123	36	222	34	14	46	215	84	6	112	10	0	20	6	43	64	39	75	0
Hours	5	.2190	.2843	34.5	0	0	0	0	1	4	0	0	0	0	0	1	0	4	0	0	0	0	0	0	0	0	0	0	0
hours'	7	.5892	.8587	39.3	2	0	1	1	1	0	1	1	1	0	0	1	0	0	0	0	0	0	0	0	1	1	1	2	0
house	2705	.9249	496.81	67.0	785	479	341	282	383	220	160	55	1068	138	30	233	42	172	47	43	49	23	31	23	340	248	50	162	6
House	257	.6809	36.156	55.6	44	37	29	13	28	53	33	20	58	9	0	3	0	62	0	0	0	2	0	0	7	41	18	57	0
HOUSE	3	.2212	.2099	33.2	1	0	1	0	1	0	0	0	2	0	0	1	0	0	0	0	0	0	0	0	0	0	0	0	0
house-dwellers	3	.0000	.0434	26.4	3	0	0	0	0	0	0	0	0	0	0	0	0	0	0	0	0	0	0	0	0	3	0	0	0
house-raising	2	.0000	.0914	29.6	0	2	0	0	0	0	0	0	2	0	0	0	0	0	0	0	0	0	0	0	0	0	0	0	0
house's	2	.2443	.1130	30.5	0	0	0	0	1	0	1	0	0	0	0	1	0	0	0	0	0	0	0	0	1	0	0	0	0
houseboat	8	.2399	.6021	37.8	0	6	1	1	0	0	0	0	6	2	0	0	0	0	0	0	0	0	0	0	0	0	0	0	0
housecleaning	4	.3030	.2949	34.7	2	1	0	0	1	0	0	0	1	0	0	0	0	0	0	0	0	0	0	0	2	0	0	1	0
housed	10	.6121	1.2679	41.0	1	0	2	0	2	3	0	2	1	0	0	0	1	1	0	0	0	0	0	0	1	2	1	3	0
houseflies	4	.1737	.1745	32.4	1	0	3	0	0	0	0	0	0	0	0	0	0	0	0	0	0	0	0	0	0	1	3	0	0
household	89	.8514	15.073	51.8	11	9	14	10	20	16	8	1	5	3	1	4	0	14	3	6	3	1	4	6	8	9	18	4	0
householders	3	.3399	.2456	33.9	0	0	0	0	0	1	2	0	1	0	0	1	0	0	0	0	0	0	0	0	0	0	0	1	0
households	11	.5495	1.2638	41.0	1	0	1	1	3	0	4	1	1	0	0	1	0	0	0	2	0	0	1	0	0	0	2	4	0
housekeeper	10	.4698	1.0943	40.4	5	1	1	0	1	0	2	0	6	0	0	1	0	0	0	0	0	0	0	0	2	1	0	0	0
Housekeeper	10	.0000	.4568	36.6	4	0	0	6	0	0	0	0	10	0	0	0	0	0	0	0	0	0	0	0	0	0	0	0	0
housekeeping	7	.4888	.7394	38.7	2	1	1	1	1	0	1	0	1	0	0	0	0	1	0	0	0	0	0	0	0	3	1	1	0
housemaid	4	.1814	.2373	33.8	1	0	0	1	0	0	2	0	2	0	0	0	0	0	0	0	0	0	0	0	0	0	0	2	0
housemaids	3	.3431	.2528	34.0	0	0	0	1	0	2	0	0	1	0	0	0	0	1	0	0	0	0	0	0	1	0	0	0	0
Houseman's	2	.0000	.0234	23.7	0	0	0	0	0	0	2	0	0	0	0	0	0	0	0	0	0	0	0	0	2	0	0	0	0
houses	702	.8937	124.85	61.0	163	103	111	109	89	57	47	23	145	14	10	51	15	222	7	29	15	16	2	2	21	49	53	50	1
Houses	2	.0000	.0914	29.6	0	0	0	1	0	0	1	0	2	0	0	0	0	0	0	0	0	0	0	0	0	0	0	0	0
housewares	2	.2404	.1142	30.6	0	0	0	0	0	0	2	0	0	1	0	0	1	0	0	0	0	0	0	0	0	0	0	0	0
housewife	29	.7202	4.2719	46.3	3	6	0	7	6	2	5	0	6	3	0	2	2	6	0	1	0	0	0	0	2	2	5	0	0
housewives	16	.7069	2.2960	43.6	1	2	1	3	5	2	2	0	1	0	0	2	0	4	0	1	1	0	1	0	3	1	0	2	0
housework	14	.4259	1.3632	41.3	3	1	0	2	3	1	4	0	5	0	0	1	0	3	0	0	0	0	3	0	1	1	0	0	0
housewreckers	4	.0000	.1827	32.6	4	0	0	0	0	0	0	0	4	0	0	0	0	0	0	0	0	0	0	0	0	0	0	0	0
housing	63	.6827	8.7651	49.4	8	1	16	3	13	8	13	1	5	1	1	0	2	17	0	1	2	0	6	0	0	3	11	14	0
Housing	3	.2043	.1486	31.7	1	0	2	0	0	0	0	0	0	0	0	0	0	0	0	0	0	0	0	0	0	1	2	0	0
housings	2	.2446	.1142	30.6	0	0	0	1	1	0	0	0	0	0	0	0	0	0	0	0	0	0	0	0	1	0	0	1	0
Houssain	4	.0000	.0429	26.3	0	0	0	4	0	0	0	0	0	0	0	4	0	0	0	0	0	0	0	0	0	0	0	0	0
Houston	77	.4576	7.8677	49.0	9	19	16	3	26	1	3	0	15	0	0	0	0	38	0	0	0	0	0	0	0	11	1	12	0
Houston's	9	.2279	.6395	38.1	0	3	1	0	4	1	0	0	5	0	0	0	0	4	0	0	0	0	0	0	0	0	0	0	0
hove	4	.1901	.1843	32.7	0	1	0	0	0	0	3	0	0	0	0	0	0	0	0	0	0	0	0	0	1	0	3	0	0
hovel	2	.2411	.1091	30.4	0	0	1	0	1	0	0	0	0	0	0	1	0	0	0	0	1	0	0	0	0	0	0	0	0
hovels	3	.3768	.2437	33.9	0	0	1	1	1	0	0	0	0	0	0	0	0	0	0	0	1	0	0	0	0	1	0	1	0
hover	9	.5592	1.1054	40.4	1	0	0	4	2	1	0	1	4	0	0	0	0	2	0	1	0	0	0	0	0	0	1	1	0
Hovercraft	2	.0000	.0243	23.9	0	0	0	2	0	0	0	0	0	0	0	0	0	0	0	0	0	0	0	0	0	0	0	2	0

6R Hosmer
8F Hospitality
4B hospitalium
9J Hospodi
9Q Hoss
5N hosses
7Q hostage
5P Hostages
6F hostel
7R Hostetler
9R Hosts
3A Hot-Potato
4A hot-chick-pea
9D hot-cool-headed
6J hot-cross
8A hot-dog
8R hot-dogs
5P hot-heads
5N hot-pot
7A hot-rods
6R hot-spot
4F hot-weather
5Q hotbox
9E Hotchkins
3R hotplate
7R hotspots
7R Hotz
9R Hough
3P Houk
3P Houk's
7N hound'll
8F hounded
6A hounds'
9R Hour-Radio
8D hour-long
5A hourglasses
7R house-bound
6A house-building
8N house-dog
6A house-flannel
7A house-moving
3C house-painter
7A house-place
9F house-to-house
3N house-trailer
8M house-wiring
6A house-work
4A houseboats
7F houseboy
9D housebreaker
4A housebreaking
8F housebroken
7H housecat
4R housecats
9L housecoats
7D housefly
8M household-use
4Q householder
9J households'
7L housekeeper's
3A housekeepers
7N houseless
8J houselights
3A housetop
6A housetops
7D housewife's
5F housewifes
7B Housman
8P Houtman
9D hov'ring

Word Type	F	D	U	SFI	3 Gr 3	4 Gr 4	5 Gr 5	6 Gr 6	7 Gr 7	8 Gr 8	9 Gr 9	X UnGr	A Read	B Eng & Gr	C Comp	D Lit	E Math	F Soc Stud	G Spell	H Sci	J Music	K Art	L Home Ec	M Shop	N Lib F	P Lib NF	Q Lib Ref	R Mag	S Rel
hovered	15	.5419	1.7508	42.4	1	0	1	5	5	1	2	0	5	0	0	3	0	0	0	0	0	0	1	0	4	0	0	2	0
hovering	14	.6847	1.9804	43.0	2	1	2	1	6	1	0	1	4	1	0	2	0	1	0	0	0	0	0	0	3	1	1	1	0
hovers	7	.5608	.8567	39.3	0	2	0	1	2	0	1	1	3	0	0	1	0	0	0	1	0	0	0	0	0	1	0	1	0
how	13303	.9154	2414.2	73.8	3043	2560	1701	1691	1936	1347	853	172	2105	1014	120	528	4081	952	636	1517	504	182	124	114	440	502	139	331	14
How	37	.6696	5.0876	47.1	4	5	2	5	16	1	1	3	7	13	0	2	1	1	5	2	0	0	1	0	0	1	1	3	0
HOW	9	.1464	.4059	36.1	5	0	0	4	0	0	0	0	0	0	0	0	0	0	0	8	0	0	0	0	0	1	0	0	0
how-to-do-it	2	.1814	.1187	30.7	0	1	0	0	1	0	0	0	1	0	0	0	0	0	0	0	0	0	0	0	0	0	0	1	0
how-wow-wow-in-is h-a-shin	2	.0000	.0914	29.6	2	0	0	0	0	0	0	0	2	0	0	0	0	0	0	0	0	0	0	0	0	0	0	0	0
how'd	10	.4789	1.0558	40.2	1	0	1	1	5	1	1	0	3	1	0	1	0	0	0	0	0	0	0	0	4	1	0	0	0
how'm	2	.1814	.1187	30.7	1	0	0	1	0	0	0	0	1	0	0	0	0	0	0	0	0	0	0	0	0	0	0	1	0
how're	2	.0000	.0215	23.3	0	0	0	0	2	0	0	0	0	0	0	2	0	0	0	0	0	0	0	0	0	0	0	0	0
how's	26	.5182	2.8758	44.6	3	0	0	5	10	4	4	0	5	1	0	10	0	0	0	0	0	0	0	0	4	3	0	3	0
Howard	66	.6930	9.4501	49.8	23	2	4	18	8	7	4	0	20	4	0	5	5	0	0	3	1	0	0	0	0	7	4	17	0
Howard's	6	.4878	.6666	38.2	3	1	0	2	0	0	0	0	3	0	0	0	1	0	0	0	0	0	0	0	0	1	0	1	0
howdah	3	.3274	.2364	33.7	0	0	1	0	2	0	0	0	1	0	0	1	0	0	1	0	0	0	0	0	0	0	0	0	0
howdy	15	.4542	1.5202	41.8	5	0	2	1	6	0	1	0	5	0	0	5	0	0	0	0	0	0	1	0	4	0	0	0	0
Howe	25	.5269	2.8996	44.6	0	0	1	0	6	18	0	0	9	0	0	0	0	9	3	0	0	0	0	0	0	0	1	3	0
Howe's	4	.0000	.0778	28.9	0	0	0	0	0	4	0	0	0	0	0	0	0	4	0	0	0	0	0	0	0	0	0	0	0
Howell	8	.2292	.5710	37.6	5	3	0	0	0	0	0	0	5	0	0	0	3	0	0	0	0	0	0	0	0	0	0	0	0
Howells	3	.1409	.1472	31.7	0	0	1	0	0	2	0	0	1	0	0	0	0	0	0	0	0	0	0	0	0	2	0	0	0
however	1914	.9527	359.99	65.6	96	191	247	247	472	300	303	58	265	136	24	52	40	362	43	322	89	11	43	44	55	109	199	119	1
Howie	27	.1250	1.2078	40.8	18	0	9	0	0	0	0	0	9	0	0	0	0	0	0	0	0	0	0	0	18	0	0	0	0
Howie's	3	.0000	.0352	25.5	3	0	0	0	0	0	0	0	0	0	0	0	0	0	0	0	0	0	0	0	3	0	0	0	0
howitzer	2	.1948	.1250	31.0	0	0	1	0	1	0	0	0	1	0	0	0	0	0	0	0	0	0	0	0	0	1	0	0	0
howitzers	3	.2212	.2099	33.2	0	0	0	0	2	1	0	0	2	0	0	1	0	0	0	0	0	0	0	0	0	0	0	0	0
howl	32	.6279	4.3386	46.4	8	3	6	5	7	2	0	1	20	0	1	4	0	0	0	0	0	0	0	0	2	3	1	1	0
Howland	5	.0000	.0608	27.8	0	0	0	2	3	0	0	0	0	0	0	0	0	0	0	0	0	0	0	0	0	0	0	5	0
howled	38	.5597	4.6268	46.7	6	10	8	4	7	3	0	0	17	1	1	3	0	0	0	0	0	0	0	0	13	2	0	1	0
howling	42	.6703	5.9248	47.7	8	14	5	3	7	4	1	0	20	0	1	5	0	2	0	0	0	0	0	0	5	7	1	1	0
howls	10	.3885	.8998	39.5	1	1	0	1	3	3	1	0	3	0	0	4	0	1	0	0	0	0	0	0	2	0	0	0	0
hows	2	.1892	.0858	29.3	0	0	0	0	1	1	0	0	0	1	0	0	0	0	0	0	0	0	1	0	0	0	0	0	0
Hoyt	7	.0000	.1013	30.1	0	5	0	0	0	0	2	0	0	0	0	0	0	0	0	0	0	0	0	0	0	7	0	0	0
hp	2	.0000	.0243	23.9	0	0	0	0	2	0	0	0	0	0	0	0	0	0	0	0	0	0	0	0	0	0	0	2	0
hr	15	.0000	.2245	33.5	1	2	4	0	2	2	4	0	0	0	0	0	15	0	0	0	0	0	0	0	0	0	0	0	0
HR	6	.1453	.2356	33.7	1	0	0	0	5	0	0	0	0	0	0	0	0	0	0	0	0	0	0	0	0	1	0	5	0
Hroudland	2	.0000	.0209	23.2	0	0	0	0	2	0	0	0	0	0	0	0	0	0	0	0	0	0	0	0	0	0	2	0	0
Hsi	2	.0000	.0914	29.6	0	2	0	0	0	0	0	0	2	0	0	0	0	0	0	0	0	0	0	0	0	0	0	0	0
Hualachi	13	.0000	.5939	37.7	0	0	13	0	0	0	0	0	13	0	0	0	0	0	0	0	0	0	0	0	0	0	0	0	0
Hualachi's	3	.0000	.1370	31.4	0	0	3	0	0	0	0	0	3	0	0	0	0	0	0	0	0	0	0	0	0	0	0	0	0
Huang	2	.0000	.0389	25.9	0	0	0	2	0	0	0	0	0	0	0	0	0	2	0	0	0	0	0	0	0	0	0	0	0
hub	21	.6133	2.7103	44.3	3	2	4	6	5	0	1	0	5	0	0	1	0	6	0	0	0	0	0	0	1	1	2	5	0
Hub	2	.2285	.1129	30.5	0	0	0	0	1	1	0	0	0	0	0	0	0	1	0	0	0	0	0	0	0	0	1	0	0
Hub-bub	4	.0000	.0429	26.3	4	0	0	0	0	0	0	0	0	0	0	4	0	0	0	0	0	0	0	0	0	0	0	0	0
Hubbard	7	.5136	.7722	38.9	2	0	2	2	1	0	0	0	1	0	0	1	2	0	0	1	0	0	0	0	0	2	0	0	0
Hubble	6	.0000	.1183	30.7	0	0	4	0	2	0	0	0	0	0	0	0	0	0	0	6	0	0	0	0	0	0	0	0	0
hubbub	6	.5179	.6589	38.2	1	0	2	0	2	1	0	0	1	0	0	1	0	0	0	0	1	0	0	0	2	0	0	1	0
Huber	7	.0000	.3198	35.0	7	0	0	0	0	0	0	0	7	0	0	0	0	0	0	0	0	0	0	0	0	0	0	0	0
Huber's	4	.0000	.1827	32.6	4	0	0	0	0	0	0	0	4	0	0	0	0	0	0	0	0	0	0	0	0	0	0	0	0
Hubert	18	.2999	1.4484	41.6	0	0	0	3	2	12	0	1	10	0	0	0	0	0	0	0	0	0	0	0	1	0	0	7	0
hubs	8	.2163	.4745	36.8	0	0	0	1	6	1	0	0	2	0	0	0	0	1	0	0	0	0	0	0	0	0	0	5	0
Huck	36	.3989	3.4739	45.4	0	0	6	7	14	2	7	0	21	5	5	0	0	0	0	0	0	0	0	0	4	0	0	1	0
Huck's	6	.0192	.0784	28.9	0	0	0	0	1	0	5	0	1	0	5	0	0	0	0	0	0	0	0	0	0	0	0	0	0
Huckabuck	13	.1104	.5306	37.2	0	13	0	0	0	0	0	0	4	0	0	9	0	0	0	0	0	0	0	0	0	0	0	0	0
huckleberry	3	.3450	.2505	34.0	0	2	1	0	0	0	0	0	1	0	0	0	0	0	0	0	0	0	0	0	1	1	0	0	0
Huckleberry	12	.3351	1.0810	40.3	0	3	1	6	1	1	0	0	9	0	0	0	0	0	0	0	0	1	0	0	0	0	0	2	0
huddle	12	.4885	1.2778	41.1	2	0	1	3	2	1	3	0	3	1	0	0	0	0	0	0	0	0	0	0	4	1	0	3	0
huddled	41	.7288	6.1342	47.9	1	7	7	9	12	2	3	0	14	3	0	3	0	1	0	0	1	0	0	0	7	5	3	4	0
Hudson	97	.7630	15.017	51.8	13	9	16	11	22	18	5	3	19	1	3	8	1	24	0	4	0	0	0	0	6	14	7	10	0
Hudson's	5	.2392	.3123	34.9	0	0	0	0	4	1	0	0	1	0	0	0	0	1	0	0	0	0	0	0	0	0	0	3	0
hue	20	.4100	1.7129	42.3	1	0	0	1	9	3	4	2	1	0	1	4	0	0	0	1	0	7	3	0	0	1	0	2	0
hues	9	.5769	1.0621	40.3	1	0	0	0	3	2	2	1	0	0	0	2	0	0	0	1	1	1	0	0	0	1	2	1	0
huff	5	.3771	.4747	36.8	1	1	0	1	2	0	0	0	3	0	0	1	0	1	0	0	0	0	0	0	0	0	0	0	0
Huffman	11	.2432	.8553	39.3	9	0	0	0	2	0	0	0	9	0	0	0	0	0	0	0	0	0	0	0	0	0	0	2	0
hug	18	.6438	2.4295	43.9	7	4	0	3	2	0	2	0	6	1	0	2	0	1	1	0	0	0	0	0	3	4	0	0	0
huge	607	.8861	107.34	60.3	101	97	106	92	97	51	45	18	176	17	6	19	1	127	8	58	6	9	1	2	29	58	43	47	0
hugely	3	.2279	.2143	33.3	0	0	0	1	1	0	1	0	2	0	0	0	0	0	0	0	0	0	0	0	0	0	0	1	0
hugged	42	.4845	4.6139	46.6	10	13	6	4	5	2	1	1	20	0	0	1	0	1	0	0	0	0	0	0	13	5	0	2	0
hugging	15	.4749	1.5983	42.0	1	5	1	2	4	1	1	0	6	0	0	5	0	0	0	0	0	0	0	0	2	1	0	1	0
Huggins	17	.2432	1.2974	41.1	6	7	2	0	2	0	0	0	13	0	0	0	0	0	0	0	0	0	0	0	4	0	0	0	0
Hugh	34	.6503	4.5564	46.6	6	2	7	2	12	0	1	4	5	0	0	4	1	1	0	3	0	0	0	0	11	3	3	3	0
Hughes	5	.5332	.5699	37.6	0	2	0	1	0	2	0	0	1	0	0	1	0	1	0	0	0	0	0	0	0	0	1	1	0
Hughes'	2	.2297	.1135	30.6	0	0	0	0	1	1	0	0	0	0	0	1	0	1	0	0	0	0	0	0	0	0	0	0	0
Hugo	17	.5049	1.8566	42.7	1	1	1	5	4	1	2	2	5	1	0	0	0	1	0	0	2	2	0	0	0	0	5	1	0
hugs	4	.4344	.3899	35.9	1	1	0	0	0	1	0	1	1	0	0	0	0	0	0	1	1	0	0	0	0	0	0	1	0
Huguenots	11	.3847	.9374	39.7	2	0	7	0	2	0	0	0	0	0	0	0	0	5	0	0	0	0	0	0	0	3	3	0	0
huh	23	.4293	2.2887	43.6	3	3	4	1	7	3	2	0	10	0	0	2	0	0	0	0	0	0	0	0	9	1	0	1	0
Huilliche	2	.0000	.0209	23.2	0	0	0	0	2	0	0	0	0	0	0	0	0	0	0	0	0	0	0	0	0	0	2	0	0
hula	8	.3270	.6388	38.1	1	0	5	1	1	0	0	0	2	0	0	0	0	4	0	0	2	0	0	0	0	0	0	0	0
Hulda	13	.0746	.4226	36.3	0	11	0	2	0	0	0	0	2	0	0	0	0	0	0	0	0	0	0	0	0	11	0	0	0
Huldah	8	.0000	.1158	30.6	0	8	0	0	0	0	0	0	0	0	0	0	0	0	0	0	0	0	0	0	0	8	0	0	0
Huleh	2	.0000	.0389	25.9	0	0	0	0	2	0	0	0	0	0	0	0	0	2	0	0	0	0	0	0	0	0	0	0	0
hulk	5	.4763	.5353	37.3	0	1	0	1	2	0	1	0	2	0	0	0	0	0	0	0	0	0	0	0	0	1	1	1	0
hulking	2	.0000	.0234	23.7	0	0	1	1	0	0	0	0	0	0	0	0	0	0	0	0	0	0	0	0	2	0	0	0	0
hull	35	.6555	4.7861	46.8	3	3	5	5	14	1	3	1	10	0	0	2	2	0	0	6	0	0	0	0	2	1	3	9	0
Hull	14	.2175	.8361	39.2	0	3	1	1	7	2	0	0	4	0	0	0	0	0	0	0	0	0	0	0	1	0	0	9	0
Hull's	5	.0000	.0608	27.8	0	0	0	0	5	0	0	0	0	0	0	0	0	0	0	0	0	0	0	0	0	0	0	5	0
hulled	2	.2351	.1166	30.7	1	1	0	0	0	0	0	0	0	0	0	0	0	1	0	0	0	0	0	0	0	0	0	1	0
hulling	3	.2444	.1814	32.6	1	2	0	0	0	0	0	0	0	0	0	0	0	2	0	0	0	0	0	0	0	0	1	0	0
hullo	4	.0000	.1827	32.6	0	0	0	4	0	0	0	0	4	0	0	0	0	0	0	0	0	0	0	0	0	0	0	0	0
Hullocks	4	.0000	.0469	26.7	0	0	0	0	4	0	0	0	0	0	0	0	0	0	0	0	0	0	0	0	4	0	0	0	0
hulls	7	.1920	.4372	36.4	4	0	0	2	1	0	0	0	4	0	0	0	0	0	0	0	0	0	0	0	0	0	3	0	0
hum	65	.6751	9.0391	49.6	17	7	8	8	17	2	3	3	15	6	0	8	0	2	0	6	14	0	0	0	2	2	1	9	0

6J Hovhaness
7A how-d'you-do's
5N how-do
8D how-do-you-do
4N how-does-it-make
3N how'll
8A howdydo
3A Howell's
6R Howes
7D However
6R Howland's
3A howler
3A Howler
4P Howlett
4A HOY
XB hoyden
4A hoyee
4P Hoyt's
3A Hozak
7E HRL
7R HRM
3P HR511
3P Hsieh
3P Hsin-hung
XH HSS
8F Hsueh-liang
9R ht
6A hu-hu
7F hubble-bubble
6R hubcaps
8R Hubert's
9F Hubertusburg
3C huddles
5F Hudson-Mohawk
4R hudsonius
XR hued
5J huehuetls
8F Huerta
7Q Huey
7G Huey's
8E Huff
3R huffed
3A huffing
4A huffle
9R huffs
XR huffy
8D Hug
8D huge-appearing
6R hugeness
7R Hugger
3N Huggins'
6N Hugh's
5Q Hugo's
8Q Huguenot
3A hui
5F hukilau
7H Hula-Hoop
8Q Hulagu
5F hulas
6R Hulick
3A hulla
3D Hulla-Baloo's
4R hullabaloo
4N hulloa
7R Hulme
9M hultgren
9M Hultgren
5A Hulton
7D hum-clack

Word Type	F	D	U	SFI	3 Gr 3	4 Gr 4	5 Gr 5	6 Gr 6	7 Gr 7	8 Gr 8	9 Gr 9	X UnGr	A Read	B Eng & Gr	C Comp	D Lit	E Math	F Soc Stud	G Spell	H Sci	J Music	K Art	L Home Ec	M Shop	N Lib F	P Lib NF	Q Lib Ref	R Mag	S Rel
hum-m-m-m	2	.0000	.0914	29.6	2	0	0	0	0	0	0	0	2	0	0	0	0	0	0	0	0	0	0	0	0	0	0	0	0
Humabom	2	.0000	.0209	23.2	2	0	0	0	0	0	0	0	0	0	0	0	0	0	0	0	0	0	0	0	0	0	2	0	0
human	710	.8956	126.25	61.0	33	30	54	79	214	104	142	54	100	52	5	53	18	45	10	112	25	18	11	2	25	50	122	62	0
Human	11	.5789	1.3491	41.3	0	0	3	0	4	4	0	0	3	0	0	1	0	0	0	0	0	0	0	0	1	2	3	1	0
human-factors	4	.0000	.0419	26.2	0	0	0	0	0	0	4	0	0	0	0	0	0	0	0	0	0	0	0	0	0	0	4	0	0
human-interest	2	.1814	.1187	30.7	0	0	1	0	0	0	1	0	1	0	0	0	0	0	0	0	0	0	0	0	0	0	0	1	0
humane	6	.4336	.5711	37.6	0	0	0	0	3	2	1	0	1	0	1	1	0	2	1	0	0	0	0	0	0	0	0	0	0
humanism	2	.0000	.0162	22.1	0	0	0	0	0	0	0	2	0	0	0	0	0	0	0	0	2	0	0	0	0	0	0	0	0
humanist	2	.0000	.0209	23.2	0	0	0	0	0	1	1	0	0	0	0	0	0	0	0	0	0	0	0	0	0	0	2	0	0
humanitarian	6	.4343	.5625	37.5	0	0	2	1	1	0	2	0	0	0	0	0	0	1	0	1	0	0	0	0	0	2	2	0	0
humanities	5	.2437	.2754	34.4	0	0	0	0	0	0	3	2	0	0	0	0	0	0	0	0	2	0	0	0	0	0	3	0	0
humanity	22	.6699	3.0187	44.8	0	1	0	0	4	9	7	1	3	0	0	1	0	3	1	0	3	0	0	0	0	3	5	3	0
humans	49	.7465	7.4505	48.7	2	4	7	10	18	6	1	1	12	1	1	1	0	4	0	6	0	1	0	0	2	4	13	4	0
Humason	2	.0000	.0394	26.0	0	0	0	0	2	0	0	0	0	0	0	0	0	0	0	2	0	0	0	0	0	0	0	0	0
Humbert	2	.0000	.0209	23.2	0	0	0	0	2	0	0	0	0	0	0	0	0	0	0	0	0	0	0	0	0	0	2	0	0
humble	42	.7220	6.2192	47.9	5	3	4	5	14	7	3	1	12	2	0	7	0	6	0	0	1	0	0	0	6	2	4	2	0
humbled	2	.2405	.1205	30.8	0	0	0	1	0	0	0	1	0	0	0	0	0	0	0	1	0	0	0	0	0	1	0	0	0
humbling	2	.2346	.1166	30.7	0	0	0	0	1	0	1	0	0	0	0	0	0	0	0	1	0	0	0	0	0	0	0	1	0
humbly	8	.4070	.7195	38.6	1	0	0	1	2	2	2	0	1	0	0	4	0	1	0	0	0	0	0	0	1	1	0	0	0
Humboldt	4	.2991	.2943	34.7	0	0	1	0	2	0	0	1	1	0	0	0	0	0	0	0	0	0	0	0	0	1	0	2	0
humbug	4	.3702	.3622	35.6	0	0	0	0	1	2	0	1	2	1	0	1	0	0	0	0	0	0	0	0	0	0	0	0	0
humdrum	2	.1698	.1133	30.5	0	0	0	0	2	0	0	0	1	0	0	0	0	0	0	0	0	0	0	0	0	0	1	0	0
Hume	3	.3764	.2483	33.9	0	0	0	0	1	0	2	0	0	0	0	0	0	0	0	1	0	0	0	0	0	0	1	1	0
humerus	5	.2439	.3070	34.9	0	0	0	1	2	0	0	2	0	0	0	0	2	0	0	3	0	0	0	0	0	0	0	0	0
humid	38	.7167	5.5433	47.4	0	7	3	3	7	6	8	4	3	0	2	0	0	17	2	5	0	1	1	0	0	1	2	4	0
humid-continental	3	.0000	.0583	27.7	0	0	0	0	0	0	3	0	0	0	0	0	0	3	0	0	0	0	0	0	0	0	0	0	0
humid-subtropical	4	.0000	.0778	28.9	0	0	0	0	0	0	4	0	0	0	0	0	0	4	0	0	0	0	0	0	0	0	0	0	0
humidity	25	.5225	2.7993	44.5	0	3	7	2	8	1	4	0	2	0	0	0	1	4	0	12	0	0	0	0	0	0	4	2	0
humiliated	5	.3375	.4157	36.2	1	0	0	2	0	2	0	0	2	0	0	0	0	0	0	0	0	0	0	0	2	0	0	1	0
humiliating	7	.4543	.7146	38.5	1	0	0	1	1	3	1	0	2	0	0	1	0	2	0	0	0	0	0	0	2	0	0	0	0
humiliation	7	.4312	.6618	38.2	0	0	0	1	1	3	1	1	1	0	1	0	0	1	0	0	0	0	0	0	0	2	0	2	0
humility	4	.3622	.3131	35.0	0	0	0	1	0	1	2	0	0	1	0	2	0	0	0	0	0	0	0	0	0	0	0	1	0
hummed	16	.6327	2.1265	43.3	0	2	3	1	3	3	0	2	5	0	0	3	0	1	0	2	2	0	0	0	2	1	0	0	0
humming	42	.7434	6.3827	48.1	12	9	4	7	4	1	3	2	14	1	2	2	0	3	0	2	6	0	0	0	5	1	3	3	0
Humming-bird	2	.0000	.0290	24.6	2	0	0	0	0	0	0	0	0	0	0	0	0	0	0	0	0	0	0	0	0	2	0	0	0
hummingbird	21	.5288	2.5112	44.0	5	2	0	4	5	2	0	3	12	0	0	0	3	0	0	4	0	0	0	0	1	1	0	0	0
hummingbird's	3	.1409	.1472	31.7	2	0	0	0	1	0	0	0	1	0	0	0	0	0	0	0	0	0	0	0	0	2	0	0	0
hummingbirds	12	.5420	1.4587	41.6	1	0	1	1	8	1	0	0	7	0	0	0	2	1	0	0	0	0	0	0	0	1	1	0	0
hummock	3	.2304	.1619	32.1	0	0	0	2	0	0	1	0	0	0	0	0	0	0	0	0	0	0	0	0	2	0	1	0	0
humor	72	.7982	11.539	50.6	2	8	9	7	16	16	11	3	13	5	3	13	0	1	2	1	9	0	3	0	2	10	3	7	0
humorist	4	.3479	.3510	35.5	0	2	0	0	0	2	0	0	2	0	0	0	0	1	1	0	0	0	0	0	0	0	0	0	0
humorous	49	.6958	6.9063	48.4	0	3	7	9	10	14	6	0	6	8	2	11	0	0	2	0	13	1	0	0	1	2	3	0	0
humors	2	.1698	.1133	30.5	0	0	0	1	0	0	1	0	1	0	0	0	0	0	0	0	0	0	0	0	0	0	1	0	0
humour	2	.0000	.0914	29.6	0	0	0	2	0	0	0	0	2	0	0	0	0	0	0	0	0	0	0	0	0	0	0	0	0
hump	27	.4672	2.7396	44.4	4	6	5	8	2	2	0	0	6	1	0	0	0	0	11	1	1	0	0	0	5	2	0	0	0
Hump	3	.0000	.1370	31.4	0	1	0	2	0	0	0	0	3	0	0	0	0	0	0	0	0	0	0	0	0	0	0	0	0
hump-backed	2	.1787	.1174	30.7	0	0	0	0	1	1	0	0	1	0	0	0	0	0	0	0	0	0	0	0	1	0	0	0	0
humpback	4	.2107	.2095	33.2	2	0	1	0	1	0	0	0	0	0	0	0	0	0	0	0	0	0	0	0	0	3	0	1	0
humpbacked	4	.2298	.2346	33.7	0	0	2	1	1	0	0	0	0	0	0	0	0	3	0	0	0	0	0	0	1	0	0	0	0
humped	4	.3755	.3686	35.7	1	1	0	1	1	0	0	0	2	0	0	0	0	0	0	0	0	0	0	0	1	1	0	0	0
Humperdinck	4	.0000	.0323	25.1	1	0	0	3	0	0	0	0	0	0	0	0	0	0	0	0	4	0	0	0	0	0	0	0	0
humph	11	.5208	1.2395	40.9	4	2	3	1	0	1	0	0	3	1	0	1	0	0	0	0	0	0	0	0	3	3	0	0	0
Humphrey	11	.1073	.4412	36.4	0	2	3	0	4	0	1	1	3	0	0	0	0	0	0	0	0	0	0	0	0	0	0	8	0
Humphreys	2	.2401	.1133	30.5	0	1	1	0	0	0	0	0	0	0	0	0	0	0	0	0	0	0	0	0	0	1	1	0	0
Humphry	4	.0000	.0789	29.0	0	0	1	1	0	0	1	1	0	0	0	0	0	0	0	4	0	0	0	0	0	0	0	0	0
humps	13	.5317	1.4544	41.6	2	4	2	3	1	0	0	1	2	1	1	0	0	0	5	1	0	0	0	0	1	2	0	0	0
Humpty	2	.0000	.0914	29.6	0	0	0	2	0	0	0	0	2	0	0	0	0	0	0	0	0	0	0	0	0	0	0	0	0
hums	5	.5325	.5641	37.5	1	0	0	1	2	1	0	0	1	1	0	1	0	0	0	0	1	0	0	0	0	0	0	1	0
humus	20	.2727	1.3760	41.4	9	0	4	3	0	1	3	0	1	0	0	0	0	8	0	11	0	0	0	0	0	0	0	0	0
hun	2	.0000	.0162	22.1	0	0	0	2	0	0	0	0	0	0	0	0	0	0	0	0	2	0	0	0	0	0	0	0	0
Hunan	2	.2408	.1204	30.8	0	0	1	0	0	1	0	0	0	0	0	0	0	1	0	0	0	0	0	0	0	1	0	0	0
hunch	6	.4557	.6118	37.9	0	2	1	0	1	0	2	0	2	0	0	1	0	0	0	0	0	0	0	0	0	0	1	2	0
Hunchback	2	.0000	.0209	23.2	1	0	1	0	0	0	0	0	0	0	0	0	0	0	0	0	0	0	0	0	0	0	2	0	0
hunched	14	.5942	1.7847	42.5	6	1	0	0	3	1	3	0	6	0	0	3	0	0	0	0	0	0	0	0	1	2	1	1	0
hunches	4	.2424	.3036	34.8	0	3	0	0	0	1	0	0	3	0	0	0	0	0	0	0	0	0	0	0	0	0	0	1	0
Hundley	2	.0000	.0914	29.6	0	0	0	0	2	0	0	0	2	0	0	0	0	0	0	0	0	0	0	0	0	0	0	0	0
hundred	1187	.9132	215.32	63.3	183	178	196	177	232	103	75	43	312	40	8	75	146	175	29	84	45	3	0	3	84	103	36	44	0
Hundred	7	.3800	.5835	37.7	0	0	3	1	0	3	0	0	0	0	0	0	0	3	0	0	2	0	0	0	2	0	0	0	0
hundred-pound	3	.1409	.1472	31.7	1	0	2	0	0	0	0	0	1	0	0	0	0	0	0	0	0	0	0	0	0	2	0	0	0
hundred-yard	4	.4538	.4020	36.0	0	1	0	0	2	0	1	0	1	0	0	1	0	0	0	0	0	0	0	0	0	1	0	1	0
hundred-year-old	2	.0000	.0215	23.3	0	0	0	0	0	0	2	0	0	0	0	2	0	0	0	0	0	0	0	0	0	0	0	0	0
hundredfold	2	.0000	.0209	23.2	0	0	0	0	0	0	2	0	0	0	0	0	0	0	0	0	0	0	0	0	0	0	2	0	0
hundreds	568	.8500	96.587	59.8	130	110	73	87	71	41	42	14	90	8	4	10	129	104	9	64	14	1	1	1	7	50	39	37	0
hundreds'	15	.0000	.2245	33.5	1	1	8	4	1	0	0	0	0	0	0	0	15	0	0	0	0	0	0	0	0	0	0	0	0
hundredth	30	.4276	2.8327	44.5	0	2	2	9	4	8	4	1	3	0	0	0	19	0	0	4	1	0	0	0	1	1	1	0	0
Hundredth	2	.0000	.0162	22.1	0	0	2	0	0	0	0	0	0	0	0	0	0	0	0	0	2	0	0	0	0	0	0	0	0
hundredths	59	.0994	1.9456	42.9	0	0	4	34	12	5	3	1	0	0	0	0	56	0	0	1	0	0	0	0	0	0	1	1	0
hundredths'	2	.0000	.0299	24.8	0	0	0	1	1	0	0	0	0	0	0	0	2	0	0	0	0	0	0	0	0	0	0	0	0
hung	321	.8225	53.356	57.3	57	63	43	53	58	33	8	6	129	9	6	31	1	22	0	9	5	2	2	0	57	26	7	15	0
Hungarian	43	.5031	4.5518	46.6	0	4	7	10	12	6	4	0	4	0	0	4	1	5	1	0	20	0	0	0	0	2	3	3	0
Hungarians	12	.5203	1.3118	41.2	0	0	2	3	3	1	3	0	0	0	0	2	0	5	0	0	0	0	0	0	0	1	3	1	0
Hungary	29	.6730	4.0076	46.0	1	4	3	6	5	5	4	1	3	0	0	2	0	12	1	1	4	0	0	0	0	2	2	2	0
Hungary's	3	.0000	.0583	27.7	0	0	0	3	0	0	0	0	0	0	0	0	0	3	0	0	0	0	0	0	0	0	0	0	0
hunger	95	.6973	13.661	51.4	8	7	16	15	17	14	15	3	31	3	2	5	0	7	0	1	0	0	11	0	16	8	4	7	0
Hunger	2	.0000	.0290	24.6	0	0	0	1	1	0	0	0	0	0	0	0	0	0	0	0	0	0	0	0	0	2	0	0	0
hungered	3	.3805	.2526	34.0	1	0	0	0	1	1	0	0	0	0	0	0	0	1	0	0	0	0	0	0	1	1	0	0	0
hungrier	8	.2386	.5997	37.8	2	4	1	1	0	0	0	0	6	0	0	0	0	0	0	0	0	0	0	0	0	0	2	0	0
hungrily	14	.5204	1.6667	42.2	5	2	2	3	0	2	0	0	9	0	0	1	0	1	0	1	0	0	0	0	0	2	0	0	0
hungry	399	.8516	68.420	58.4	109	107	61	33	51	17	19	2	185	27	9	25	1	16	5	23	1	1	10	0	36	36	9	15	0
hunk	4	.2417	.3028	34.8	0	1	0	3	0	0	0	0	3	0	0	0	0	0	0	0	0	0	0	0	1	0	0	0	0
Huns	4	.3134	.2876	34.6	0	0	0	0	1	0	2	1	0	0	0	0	0	1	0	1	0	0	0	0	0	0	2	0	0
Hunsaker	5	.0000	.2284	33.6	0	0	0	0	5	0	0	0	5	0	0	0	0	0	0	0	0	0	0	0	0	0	0	0	0
hunt	263	.8180	43.467	56.4	65	68	28	39	45	14	3	1	89	12	0	15	0	23	7	24	5	1	0	0	15	50	3	19	0
Hunt	16	.5046	1.8227	42.6	9	0	2	0	0	3	2	0	9	0	2	0	1	1	0	0	0	1	0	0	0	1	1	0	0

8H human-directed
8R Humanae
4A Humane
XJ humanistic
9Q humanists
7Q humanization
9A humanized
8Q humanly
9D humanness
8D humanoids
9D humble-bees
9D humbleness
9N humbler
4P Humbolt
5A Humbug
4N humbugged
5D humdinger
6R Humenick
7G humidor
7Q humiliatingly
5P humiliations
5N hummin'
3A Hummingbird
4A hummingbirds'
5B hummmmm
7A hummocks
7D humored
9D Humoresque
5P humorless
4A hump-back
5A humpf
5A Humphrey's
8R Humphries
7J Humpty-Dumpty
4B humpy
5Q Hun
9D hunchbacked
5N hunching
7R hundred-act
5E hundred-millions'
3E hundred-thousands
XH hundred-thousandth
6H hundred-thousandths
7E hundred's
8E hundreds-tens-ones
6R Hunedoara
6J Hung
7A hung-g-g
7R hung-over
8N hunger-madness
7R hungering
9Q hungers
7Q hungriest
6R hunker
7R hunkered
7D hunks
4N hunkydory
3A Hunt's
9D hunt's-up

Word Type	F	D	U	SFI	3 Gr 3	4 Gr 4	5 Gr 5	6 Gr 6	7 Gr 7	8 Gr 8	9 Gr 9	X UnGr	A Read	B Eng & Gr	C Comp	D Lit	E Math	F Soc Stud	G Spell	H Sci	J Music	K Art	L Home Ec	M Shop	N Lib F	P Lib NF	Q Lib Ref	R Mag	S Rel
hunted	124	.7972	20.112	53.0	31	22	14	17	19	9	7	5	53	3	0	11	0	17	3	2	4	0	0	0	5	10	9	7	0
hunter	151	.7548	23.356	53.7	30	32	27	17	26	10	3	6	62	4	8	6	2	9	1	3	4	0	0	0	5	21	16	10	0
Hunter	16	.4699	1.7110	42.3	0	4	2	5	3	2	0	0	7	0	1	0	0	1	0	0	0	0	0	0	0	6	0	1	0
hunter's	10	.5854	1.2540	41.0	0	3	1	2	4	0	0	0	4	1	0	0	0	0	2	1	1	0	0	0	0	0	0	1	0
hunters	225	.8090	36.795	55.7	29	69	39	28	27	19	2	12	69	4	8	10	0	33	4	25	4	0	0	0	9	29	19	11	0
Hunters	6	.3321	.4442	36.5	0	3	0	0	2	1	0	0	0	0	0	0	0	1	0	0	0	0	0	0	3	0	0	2	0
huntin'	7	.2168	.3610	35.6	0	0	0	0	7	0	0	0	0	0	0	2	0	0	0	0	0	0	0	0	5	0	0	0	0
hunting	346	.8302	57.856	57.6	57	72	47	41	61	35	15	18	114	9	15	22	6	39	3	16	10	0	1	1	17	54	11	28	0
Huntington	6	.3452	.5086	37.1	2	0	0	0	2	0	0	2	2	0	0	0	0	0	0	2	0	0	0	0	0	0	0	2	0
HuntingtonBeach	2	.0000	.0243	23.9	0	0	0	2	0	0	0	0	0	0	0	0	0	0	0	0	0	0	0	0	0	0	0	2	0
hunts	25	.7534	3.8432	45.8	8	9	1	1	5	1	0	0	8	1	0	1	0	2	1	0	0	1	0	0	2	4	2	3	0
huntsman	7	.0000	.3198	35.0	0	0	0	7	0	0	0	0	7	0	0	0	0	0	0	0	0	0	0	0	0	0	0	0	0
huntsmen	2	.0000	.0215	23.3	0	0	1	0	0	0	1	0	0	0	0	2	0	0	0	0	0	0	0	0	0	0	0	0	0
Huntsville	3	.3766	.2497	34.0	0	1	2	0	0	0	0	0	0	0	0	0	0	1	0	0	0	0	0	0	0	1	1	0	0
hurdle	20	.3415	1.5487	41.9	0	1	2	0	17	0	0	0	1	0	0	0	2	0	0	0	0	0	0	0	2	14	0	1	0
Hurdle	6	.0000	.0487	26.9	0	0	3	3	0	0	0	0	0	0	0	0	0	0	6	0	0	0	0	0	0	0	0	0	0
hurdler	15	.2023	.7712	38.9	0	0	4	0	11	0	0	0	0	0	0	0	4	0	0	0	0	0	0	0	0	11	0	0	0
hurdlers	5	.0000	.0724	28.6	0	0	0	0	5	0	0	0	0	0	0	0	0	0	0	0	0	0	0	0	0	5	0	0	0
hurdles	30	.1959	1.5485	41.9	0	1	0	3	25	0	1	0	2	0	0	0	0	0	0	0	0	0	0	0	1	25	0	2	0
Hurdles	2	.0000	.0162	22.1	0	0	1	1	0	0	0	0	0	0	0	0	0	0	2	0	0	0	0	0	0	0	0	0	0
hurdling	8	.0629	.2367	33.7	0	0	0	1	7	0	0	0	1	0	0	0	0	0	0	0	0	0	0	0	0	7	0	0	0
hurl	4	.4336	.3884	35.9	0	0	1	0	1	0	2	0	1	0	0	0	0	0	1	1	0	0	0	0	0	0	1	0	0
hurled	31	.7263	4.6492	46.7	5	2	2	5	9	5	3	0	13	0	0	2	0	1	2	1	1	0	0	0	3	4	0	4	0
hurlers	2	.1948	.1250	31.0	1	0	0	0	0	1	0	0	1	0	0	0	0	0	0	0	0	0	0	0	0	1	0	0	0
hurling	6	.4856	.6621	38.2	0	2	0	3	0	0	1	0	3	0	0	1	0	0	0	0	0	0	0	0	1	1	0	0	0
Hurlock	7	.0000	.1013	30.1	0	7	0	0	0	0	0	0	0	0	0	0	0	0	0	0	0	0	0	0	0	7	0	0	0
Huron	20	.6785	2.7955	44.5	1	3	5	3	4	4	0	0	4	0	0	1	3	4	0	0	3	0	0	0	3	1	1	0	0
Hurons	6	.2655	.3724	35.7	1	0	1	0	4	0	0	0	0	0	0	0	0	1	0	0	0	0	0	0	4	1	0	0	0
hurrah	23	.5316	2.6634	44.3	7	4	2	6	1	3	0	0	9	0	0	4	0	0	1	0	3	0	0	0	6	0	0	0	0
hurray	15	.4940	1.6246	42.1	7	1	0	2	4	0	1	0	5	1	0	3	0	0	0	0	4	0	0	0	0	2	0	0	0
hurricane	74	.6931	10.633	50.3	11	2	8	30	17	4	1	1	19	1	2	0	4	7	0	31	0	0	1	0	2	2	0	5	0
Hurricane	3	.3722	.2508	34.0	1	1	0	1	0	0	0	0	0	0	0	1	0	1	0	1	0	0	0	0	0	0	0	0	0
hurricane-proof	2	.0000	.0215	23.3	0	0	0	0	2	0	0	0	0	0	0	2	0	0	0	0	0	0	0	0	0	0	0	0	0
hurricanes	25	.4425	2.5401	44.0	5	1	6	8	4	1	0	0	7	0	0	0	0	3	0	13	0	0	0	0	0	0	1	1	0
hurried	279	.7152	41.507	56.2	77	73	34	27	30	21	12	5	136	8	3	20	0	7	0	5	3	0	0	0	33	49	0	15	0
hurriedly	33	.6477	4.4551	46.5	2	4	7	7	5	2	6	0	10	5	2	3	0	3	0	0	0	0	0	0	7	1	2	0	0
hurries	14	.5597	1.6729	42.2	5	1	2	3	2	1	0	0	4	1	2	1	0	2	0	1	1	0	0	0	0	1	0	1	0
hurry	314	.8104	51.610	57.1	87	77	35	38	35	20	17	5	138	10	6	28	1	10	7	3	3	0	2	1	38	51	2	14	0
hurrying	69	.6912	10.032	50.0	21	14	6	4	9	9	5	1	39	0	3	8	0	5	0	0	1	0	1	0	4	5	0	3	0
hurt	457	.7994	74.255	58.7	120	94	50	43	85	46	13	6	196	16	2	48	0	13	7	31	1	0	5	1	73	29	3	32	0
hurtful	2	.2407	.1138	30.6	0	0	0	0	1	1	0	0	0	0	0	1	0	0	0	0	0	0	0	0	0	1	0	0	0
hurting	16	.5795	2.0373	43.1	3	3	2	1	2	3	1	1	9	0	0	0	0	0	0	3	0	0	1	0	1	1	0	1	0
hurtled	5	.3300	.4080	36.1	0	0	0	0	3	2	0	0	2	0	0	2	0	0	0	0	0	0	0	0	0	0	0	1	0
hurtling	8	.4432	.8118	39.1	1	1	0	0	5	1	0	0	3	0	0	0	0	0	0	1	0	0	0	0	0	2	2	0	0
hurts	23	.7305	3.4781	45.4	11	5	1	3	1	1	1	0	10	1	0	1	0	1	1	5	0	0	0	0	2	1	0	1	0
Husak	2	.0000	.0243	23.9	0	0	0	0	0	2	0	0	0	0	0	0	0	0	0	0	0	0	0	0	0	0	0	2	0
husband	233	.7159	34.408	55.4	43	45	23	26	42	21	24	9	84	5	0	44	2	11	2	2	5	0	0	0	15	42	4	17	0
Husband	3	.2223	.2106	33.2	0	1	0	1	1	0	0	0	2	1	0	0	0	0	0	0	0	0	0	0	0	0	0	0	0
husband's	20	.5958	2.5297	44.0	3	0	5	1	8	2	1	0	6	2	0	4	0	3	0	0	0	0	0	0	0	4	1	0	0
husbands	23	.5625	2.8945	44.6	0	1	14	1	2	0	5	0	16	0	1	2	0	0	0	0	0	0	0	0	1	1	0	2	0
hush	58	.6481	7.9186	49.0	3	10	6	7	23	5	4	0	24	1	0	12	0	5	0	0	5	0	0	0	6	3	0	2	0
hushed	17	.5200	1.9458	42.9	3	3	0	3	4	1	3	0	7	0	0	2	0	0	0	0	0	0	0	0	5	0	1	2	0
husk	4	.0000	.1827	32.6	2	0	1	1	0	0	0	0	4	0	0	0	0	0	0	0	0	0	0	0	0	0	0	0	0
husked	2	.0000	.0914	29.6	0	1	1	0	0	0	0	0	2	0	0	0	0	0	0	0	0	0	0	0	0	0	0	0	0
huskies	13	.2395	1.0118	40.1	0	6	1	1	3	2	0	0	11	0	0	0	0	0	0	0	0	0	0	0	2	0	0	0	0
huskily	6	.3427	.5178	37.1	0	1	0	3	1	1	0	0	3	0	0	2	0	0	0	0	0	0	0	0	0	1	0	0	0
husking	3	.1060	.1461	31.6	0	2	0	0	1	0	0	0	2	0	1	0	0	0	0	0	0	0	0	0	0	0	0	0	0
husks	13	.2339	.9452	39.8	8	0	4	0	0	1	0	0	9	0	0	0	0	2	0	0	0	2	0	0	0	0	0	0	0
husky	26	.6069	3.3581	45.3	1	6	8	1	6	1	3	0	10	1	0	4	0	0	0	0	0	0	0	0	3	5	0	3	0
hustle	3	.3321	.2114	33.3	0	1	0	0	1	0	1	0	0	0	0	0	0	0	0	0	1	0	1	0	0	0	0	1	0
hustled	5	.3375	.4157	36.2	1	2	0	1	1	0	0	0	2	0	0	0	0	0	0	0	0	0	0	0	2	0	0	1	0
hustling	7	.4031	.6377	38.0	0	0	0	0	6	1	0	0	2	0	1	2	0	0	0	0	0	0	0	0	0	0	0	2	0
hut	86	.7553	13.309	51.2	14	26	9	10	17	5	5	0	35	1	1	15	0	4	0	0	1	1	0	0	7	14	2	5	0
hutch	4	.3199	.3102	34.9	3	0	0	1	0	0	0	0	1	0	0	0	0	0	0	0	0	0	0	0	1	2	0	0	0
huts	62	.6526	8.4361	49.3	8	9	7	12	16	6	4	0	14	0	0	2	0	22	1	0	2	0	0	0	4	14	1	2	0
Hutschnecker	3	.0000	.0365	25.6	0	0	0	0	0	0	3	0	0	0	0	0	0	0	0	0	0	0	0	0	0	0	0	3	0
Hutterite	9	.0000	.1094	30.4	0	0	0	0	9	0	0	0	0	0	0	0	0	0	0	0	0	0	0	0	0	0	0	9	0
Hutterites	13	.0000	.1580	32.0	0	0	0	0	13	0	0	0	0	0	0	0	0	0	0	0	0	0	0	0	0	0	0	13	0
Hutto	5	.0000	.0586	27.7	0	0	0	0	5	0	0	0	0	0	0	0	0	0	0	0	0	0	0	0	5	0	0	0	0
Hutton	6	.3079	.4501	36.5	0	0	2	0	3	0	1	0	1	0	0	0	0	0	0	3	0	0	0	0	0	0	2	0	0
Huxley	2	.0000	.0209	23.2	0	0	0	0	2	0	0	0	0	0	0	0	0	0	0	0	0	0	0	0	0	0	2	0	0
Huygens	3	.2445	.1818	32.6	0	0	0	2	0	0	1	0	0	0	0	0	0	0	0	2	0	0	0	0	0	0	1	0	0
hv	6	.1555	.2368	33.7	0	0	0	0	1	5	0	0	0	1	0	0	0	0	0	0	0	0	0	0	0	0	5	0	0
hw	9	.0000	.0730	28.6	1	3	0	2	3	0	0	0	0	0	0	0	0	0	9	0	0	0	0	0	0	0	0	0	0
Hwang	2	.2306	.1140	30.6	0	0	0	0	1	1	0	0	0	1	0	0	0	1	0	0	0	0	0	0	0	0	0	0	0
Hyacinth	5	.0000	.2284	33.6	5	0	0	0	0	0	0	0	5	0	0	0	0	0	0	0	0	0	0	0	0	0	0	0	0
Hyatt	3	.0000	.0314	25.0	0	0	3	0	0	0	0	0	0	0	0	0	0	0	0	0	0	0	0	0	0	0	3	0	0
hybrid	17	.3687	1.4291	41.6	0	0	0	13	0	1	1	2	0	0	0	0	0	1	0	13	0	0	0	0	0	1	1	1	0
hybrids	4	.0000	.0789	29.0	0	0	0	2	0	0	0	2	0	0	0	0	0	0	0	4	0	0	0	0	0	0	0	0	0
Hydarnes	2	.0000	.0914	29.6	0	0	0	0	2	0	0	0	2	0	0	0	0	0	0	0	0	0	0	0	0	0	0	0	0
Hyde	16	.4283	1.5642	41.9	0	0	1	1	12	2	0	0	6	1	0	7	0	0	1	0	0	0	0	0	0	0	0	1	0
hydra	4	.3617	.3220	35.1	2	0	0	0	2	0	0	0	0	0	0	0	0	0	0	1	0	0	0	0	0	2	1	0	0
Hydra	2	.0000	.0394	26.0	0	0	0	0	2	0	0	0	0	0	0	0	0	0	0	2	0	0	0	0	0	0	0	0	0
hydra's	3	.0000	.0434	26.4	3	0	0	0	0	0	0	0	0	0	0	0	0	0	0	0	0	0	0	0	0	3	0	0	0
hydrant	5	.2320	.3834	35.8	3	1	1	0	0	0	0	0	4	0	0	0	0	0	0	1	0	0	0	0	0	0	0	0	0
hydrants	2	.0000	.0914	29.6	0	2	0	0	0	0	0	0	2	0	0	0	0	0	0	0	0	0	0	0	0	0	0	0	0
hydras	2	.0000	.0394	26.0	0	0	0	0	2	0	0	0	0	0	0	0	0	0	0	2	0	0	0	0	0	0	0	0	0
hydrate	2	.0000	.0394	26.0	0	0	1	0	0	1	0	0	0	0	0	0	0	0	0	2	0	0	0	0	0	0	0	0	0
hydrated	2	.2278	.1128	30.5	0	0	0	0	0	1	1	0	0	0	0	0	0	0	0	1	0	0	0	0	0	0	1	0	0
hydraulic	8	.3141	.5649	37.5	1	0	2	0	2	1	1	1	0	0	0	0	0	1	0	1	0	0	0	0	0	0	5	1	0
hydrazine	2	.2278	.1128	30.5	0	1	0	0	0	0	1	0	0	0	0	0	0	0	0	1	0	0	0	0	0	0	1	0	0
hydride	2	.0000	.0394	26.0	0	0	0	0	0	0	2	0	0	0	0	0	0	0	0	2	0	0	0	0	0	0	0	0	0
Hydrion	2	.0000	.0394	26.0	0	0	0	0	0	2	0	0	0	0	0	0	0	0	0	2	0	0	0	0	0	0	0	0	0
hydrocarbon	4	.2353	.2382	33.8	0	0	3	0	0	1	0	0	0	0	0	0	0	0	0	3	0	0	0	0	0	0	1	0	0

7N hunter-build
4P Hunter's
XR Hunterdon
7Q hunters'
6A hunting-dogs
6A hunting-grounds
5N hunting-knife
7N hunting-shirt
8Q Huntly
6A huntress
7P Hunts
8J huntsman's
6A huntsmanship
8R Huong
8R Huong's
6A hurdy-gurdy
3P hurler
8F Hurley
7A hurricane's
3B Hurry
XB hurry-scurry
7R Hurst/Airheart
5F Hurston
7N hurted
7N hurtfulness
5D hurtig
7R hurtle
7H hurtles
7G hus
XH HUS
9D husband-friend
6N husbanded
7F husbands'
3B hushes
4G huskie
5J Husky
6P Hussar
8Q Hussayn
8Q Hussein
7Q hustles
7A hutches
8N Hutchinson's
9R Hutschnecker's
5H Hutton's
7N Huttos
7Q Huxley's
8F huzzahs
8Q hv/c
8Q Hvar
4N Hwang-tao
4G hwit
4G hwiz
XR hyacinth-dotted
3A Hyacinth's
4F hyacinths
6H hybird
8Q Hyderabad
3P HYDRA
6P Hydras
8H hydrates
8H hydration
5P hydraulically
5Q hydraulicking
7R hydrides
XR hydro-generators
5Q Hydrocarbon

Word Type	F	D	U	SFI	3 Gr 3	4 Gr 4	5 Gr 5	6 Gr 6	7 Gr 7	8 Gr 8	9 Gr 9	X UnGr	A Read	B Eng & Gr	C Comp	D Lit	E Math	F Soc Stud	G Spell	H Sci	J Music	K Art	L Home Ec	M Shop	N Lib F	P Lib NF	Q Lib Ref	R Mag	S Rel
hydrocarbons	6	.3764	.4966	37.0	0	0	2	0	1	1	2	0	0	0	0	0	0	0	0	2	0	0	0	0	0	0	2	2	0
hydrochloric	8	.0000	.1577	32.0	0	0	1	0	1	0	2	4	0	0	0	0	0	0	0	8	0	0	0	0	0	0	0	0	0
hydroelectirc	2	.0000	.0389	25.9	0	0	0	0	2	0	0	0	0	0	0	0	0	2	0	0	0	0	0	0	0	0	0	0	0
hydroelectric	32	.3462	2.5450	44.1	2	1	14	6	7	1	1	0	0	0	0	0	0	23	0	1	0	0	0	0	0	3	5	0	0
hydroelectricity	3	.0000	.0583	27.7	0	0	2	0	1	0	0	0	0	0	0	0	0	3	0	0	0	0	0	0	0	0	0	0	0
hydrofluoric	4	.1494	.1609	32.1	0	0	3	0	0	0	1	0	0	0	0	0	0	0	0	1	0	0	0	0	0	0	3	0	0
hydrogen	197	.5102	21.422	53.3	10	3	41	27	51	33	32	0	1	0	0	0	6	1	1	140	1	0	0	7	0	8	24	8	0
hydrogen-1	2	.0000	.0394	26.0	0	0	0	2	0	0	0	0	0	0	0	0	0	0	0	2	0	0	0	0	0	0	0	0	0
hydrogen-3	2	.0000	.0394	26.0	0	0	0	2	0	0	0	0	0	0	0	0	0	0	0	2	0	0	0	0	0	0	0	0	0
hydrographic	3	.3769	.2484	34.0	0	0	0	1	1	1	0	0	0	0	0	0	0	1	0	0	0	0	0	0	0	0	1	1	0
hydrology	2	.0000	.0243	23.9	0	0	0	0	2	0	0	0	0	0	0	0	0	0	0	0	0	0	0	0	0	0	0	2	0
hydrolysis	2	.0000	.0394	26.0	0	0	0	0	2	0	0	0	0	0	0	0	0	0	0	2	0	0	0	0	0	0	0	0	0
hydrometer	2	.0000	.0394	26.0	0	0	0	0	0	2	0	0	0	0	0	0	0	0	0	2	0	0	0	0	0	0	0	0	0
hydrophones	2	.0000	.0243	23.9	0	0	0	0	2	0	0	0	0	0	0	0	0	0	0	0	0	0	0	0	0	0	0	2	0
hydroponics	2	.2446	.1257	31.0	0	1	0	0	0	1	0	0	0	0	0	0	0	1	0	1	0	0	0	0	0	0	0	0	0
hydrosphere	4	.0000	.0789	29.0	0	0	0	1	2	1	0	0	0	0	0	0	0	0	0	4	0	0	0	0	0	0	0	0	0
hydrous	4	.2353	.2382	33.8	0	0	0	0	0	1	0	3	0	0	0	0	0	0	0	3	0	0	0	0	0	0	1	0	0
hydroxide	10	.0000	.1972	32.9	0	0	3	0	2	0	5	0	0	0	0	0	0	0	0	10	0	0	0	0	0	0	0	0	0
hyena	8	.3590	.7035	38.5	0	2	0	0	2	4	0	0	3	0	0	0	0	0	0	3	0	0	0	0	0	0	2	0	0
hyenas	4	.2437	.2257	33.5	1	1	0	1	1	0	0	0	0	0	0	0	0	0	0	0	0	0	0	0	0	0	2	2	0
Hyer	2	.0000	.0290	24.6	0	0	0	2	0	0	0	0	0	0	0	0	0	0	0	0	0	0	0	0	0	2	0	0	0
hygiene	5	.4163	.4416	36.5	0	0	1	0	2	2	0	0	0	0	0	0	0	1	0	0	0	0	1	0	0	0	2	1	0
hygrometer	3	.0000	.0591	27.7	0	0	0	0	2	1	0	0	0	0	0	0	0	0	0	3	0	0	0	0	0	0	0	0	0
hygroscope	2	.0000	.0914	29.6	0	0	0	0	2	0	0	0	2	0	0	0	0	0	0	0	0	0	0	0	0	0	0	0	0
hygroscopic	2	.0000	.0394	26.0	0	0	0	0	0	0	2	0	0	0	0	0	0	0	0	2	0	0	0	0	0	0	0	0	0
Hyksos	3	.2444	.1814	32.6	0	0	0	0	3	0	0	0	0	0	0	0	0	2	0	0	0	0	0	0	0	0	1	0	0
Hylas	8	.0000	.3655	35.6	0	0	0	8	0	0	0	0	8	0	0	0	0	0	0	0	0	0	0	0	0	0	0	0	0
Hyman	6	.3496	.5232	37.2	0	3	0	2	1	0	0	0	3	0	0	2	0	0	0	0	0	0	0	0	0	0	0	1	0
Hymenoptera	2	.2278	.1128	30.5	0	0	0	0	1	0	1	0	0	0	0	0	0	0	0	1	0	0	0	0	0	0	1	0	0
hymenopterans	2	.0000	.0209	23.2	0	0	0	0	0	0	2	0	0	0	0	0	0	0	0	0	0	0	0	0	0	0	2	0	0
hymn	54	.2919	3.4889	45.4	2	8	19	6	6	4	9	0	2	1	0	0	0	0	2	0	39	0	0	0	2	3	5	0	0
Hymn	8	.2204	.4024	36.0	0	0	3	0	1	2	2	0	0	0	0	0	0	0	0	0	5	0	0	0	0	0	3	0	0
hymnbook	3	.0000	.0352	25.5	0	0	0	0	3	0	0	0	0	0	0	0	0	0	0	0	0	0	0	0	3	0	0	0	0
hymns	24	.2634	1.4517	41.6	0	0	10	1	2	2	9	0	2	0	0	2	0	0	0	0	16	0	0	0	0	0	4	0	0
Hyperboreans	2	.0000	.0290	24.6	0	0	0	2	0	0	0	0	0	0	0	0	0	0	0	0	0	0	0	0	0	2	0	0	0
Hyperion	3	.0000	.0322	25.1	0	0	0	0	0	0	3	0	0	0	0	3	0	0	0	0	0	0	0	0	0	0	0	0	0
hypersthene	4	.0000	.0789	29.0	0	0	0	0	0	0	0	4	0	0	0	0	0	0	0	4	0	0	0	0	0	0	0	0	0
hyphen	26	.2290	1.3568	41.3	4	3	6	4	0	3	6	0	0	11	0	0	0	0	15	0	0	0	0	0	0	0	0	0	0
hyphenated	19	.2844	1.3167	41.2	4	1	0	4	5	2	3	0	5	5	0	0	0	0	9	0	0	0	0	0	0	0	0	0	0
hyphens	11	.2417	.6051	37.8	0	3	3	2	0	3	0	0	0	7	0	0	0	0	4	0	0	0	0	0	0	0	0	0	0
hypnotized	2	.1717	.1142	30.6	0	0	0	0	1	1	0	0	1	0	0	1	0	0	0	0	0	0	0	0	0	0	0	0	0
hypo	5	.0000	.0986	29.9	0	0	5	0	0	0	0	0	0	0	0	0	0	0	0	5	0	0	0	0	0	0	0	0	0
hypocrisies	2	.2433	.1158	30.6	0	0	0	0	1	0	0	1	0	0	0	0	0	0	0	0	0	0	0	0	0	1	0	1	0
hypocrites	3	.0000	.0365	25.6	0	0	0	0	0	0	3	0	0	0	0	0	0	0	0	0	0	0	0	0	0	0	0	3	0
hypotenuse	24	.0626	.6316	38.0	4	0	0	1	1	7	11	0	0	0	0	0	23	0	0	0	0	0	0	0	0	1	0	0	0
hypothalamus	2	.0000	.0394	26.0	0	0	0	0	2	0	0	0	0	0	0	0	0	0	0	2	0	0	0	0	0	0	0	0	0
hypotheses	25	.3383	1.9974	43.0	0	1	10	3	3	6	2	0	1	0	0	0	0	9	0	14	0	0	0	0	0	0	1	0	0
hypothesis	58	.3616	4.9128	46.9	0	3	17	9	9	4	12	4	6	0	0	0	7	1	0	41	0	0	0	0	0	0	2	1	0
hyrax	2	.0000	.0290	24.6	0	0	0	0	2	0	0	0	0	0	0	0	0	0	0	0	0	0	0	0	0	2	0	0	0
hysteria	2	.2437	.1129	30.5	0	0	1	0	0	0	1	0	0	0	0	0	0	0	0	0	0	0	0	0	0	0	1	1	0
hysterical	11	.5122	1.1828	40.7	1	0	1	1	2	1	4	1	1	0	1	2	0	0	0	0	0	0	0	0	0	1	1	5	0
hysterically	11	.4548	1.0656	40.3	0	1	0	1	8	1	0	0	1	0	1	5	0	0	0	0	0	0	0	0	3	1	0	0	0
hysterics	2	.2446	.1125	30.5	0	0	0	0	2	0	0	0	0	1	0	1	0	0	0	0	0	0	0	0	0	0	0	0	0
Hz	4	.0000	.0486	26.9	0	0	0	0	4	0	0	0	0	0	0	0	0	0	0	0	0	0	0	0	0	0	0	4	0
H2	3	.0000	.0591	27.7	0	0	0	0	1	0	2	0	0	0	0	0	0	0	0	3	0	0	0	0	0	0	0	0	0
H2O	7	.4130	.6305	38.0	1	1	0	2	0	2	1	0	0	0	0	0	0	0	0	4	0	0	0	1	0	1	1	0	0
i	523	.5031	55.038	57.4	99	108	72	74	71	51	36	12	47	61	5	13	19	3	297	12	5	0	1	3	16	19	17	5	0
I	25932	.8440	4405.2	76.4	5080	4130	2516	3648	5007	2610	2503	438	10718	1502	300	3362	250	587	453	148	607	45	43	22	3656	2008	169	2017	45
I**	6	.3041	.4355	36.4	0	2	0	1	1	2	0	0	1	0	0	2	0	0	0	0	0	0	0	0	0	3	0	0	0
I-am-blowing	3	.0000	.0434	26.4	3	0	0	0	0	0	0	0	0	0	0	0	0	0	0	0	0	0	0	0	0	3	0	0	0
i%	2	.0000	.0394	26.0	0	0	0	0	0	0	0	2	0	0	0	0	0	0	0	2	0	0	0	0	0	0	0	0	0
i'	3	.1187	.1291	31.1	0	0	0	0	1	1	1	0	1	0	0	2	0	0	0	0	0	0	0	0	0	0	0	0	0
I'	4	.0000	.1827	32.6	4	0	0	0	0	0	0	0	4	0	0	0	0	0	0	0	0	0	0	0	0	0	0	0	0
I'd	534	.7365	80.846	59.1	85	138	57	63	110	32	44	5	211	9	3	69	1	5	7	3	10	0	3	0	84	73	0	56	0
I'll	1604	.7590	250.01	64.0	473	379	114	176	240	126	83	13	752	31	16	174	21	23	6	8	73	0	3	1	197	226	0	73	0
I'm	1848	.7854	296.06	64.7	412	400	166	242	321	176	110	21	844	63	18	189	36	18	23	6	50	0	5	1	243	205	1	146	0
i's	17	.3393	1.2704	41.0	1	6	3	4	1	1	1	0	2	2	2	0	0	0	11	0	0	0	0	0	0	0	0	0	0
I's	2	.1717	.1142	30.6	0	0	0	0	1	0	1	0	1	0	0	1	0	0	0	0	0	0	0	0	0	0	0	0	0
I've	730	.7453	111.75	60.5	133	140	84	92	143	73	48	17	305	28	9	84	6	9	3	1	25	0	0	0	104	83	0	73	0
ia	3	.0000	.0243	23.9	0	0	0	0	0	3	0	0	0	0	0	0	0	0	3	0	0	0	0	0	0	0	0	0	0
IA	2	.2418	.1091	30.4	0	1	0	0	0	0	1	0	0	0	0	0	0	0	1	0	0	0	0	0	0	0	1	0	0
iar	2	.0000	.0162	22.1	0	0	0	0	2	0	0	0	0	0	0	0	0	0	2	0	0	0	0	0	0	0	0	0	0
Iberian	8	.0000	.1556	31.9	0	0	1	7	0	0	0	0	0	0	0	0	0	8	0	0	0	0	0	0	0	0	0	0	0
Iberians	2	.0000	.0389	25.9	0	0	0	2	0	0	0	0	0	0	0	0	0	2	0	0	0	0	0	0	0	0	0	0	0
ible	6	.0000	.0487	26.9	0	0	0	0	6	0	0	0	0	0	0	0	0	0	6	0	0	0	0	0	0	0	0	0	0
Ibn	4	.2201	.2150	33.3	0	0	0	0	3	1	0	0	0	0	0	0	0	0	0	0	0	0	0	0	0	3	1	0	0
Ibsen	2	.2417	.1091	30.4	1	1	0	0	0	0	0	0	0	0	0	0	0	0	0	0	1	0	0	0	0	0	1	0	0
ic	10	.0000	.0812	29.1	0	0	1	3	5	0	1	0	0	0	0	0	0	0	10	0	0	0	0	0	0	0	0	0	0
Icarus	21	.3431	1.9312	42.9	7	7	0	0	3	3	1	0	16	0	0	4	0	0	0	0	0	0	0	0	0	0	1	0	0
ice	995	.8736	173.96	62.4	248	225	151	105	118	63	83	2	318	35	15	31	22	77	26	268	5	0	15	2	29	64	45	43	0
Ice	23	.6264	2.9784	44.7	4	0	2	3	4	4	5	1	1	0	1	0	0	7	1	7	0	0	1	0	0	0	0	5	0
ice-age	2	.0000	.0209	23.2	0	0	0	0	2	0	0	0	0	0	0	0	0	0	0	0	0	0	0	0	0	0	2	0	0
ice-bound	3	.2239	.1775	32.5	0	0	0	0	3	0	0	0	0	0	0	0	0	2	0	1	0	0	0	0	0	0	0	0	0
ice-breaking	2	.2446	.1257	31.0	0	0	0	0	2	0	0	0	0	0	0	0	0	1	0	1	0	0	0	0	0	0	0	0	0
ice-choked	2	.0000	.0394	26.0	0	1	0	0	1	0	0	0	0	0	0	0	0	0	0	2	0	0	0	0	0	0	0	0	0
ice-cold	4	.2576	.2681	34.3	2	0	0	1	0	0	1	0	1	0	0	0	0	0	0	2	0	0	1	0	0	0	0	0	0
ice-covered	6	.3816	.5652	37.5	1	1	1	0	1	1	1	0	3	0	0	0	0	2	0	0	0	0	0	0	0	0	1	0	0
ice-cream	33	.6725	4.7417	46.8	7	19	2	1	1	2	1	0	23	2	1	1	1	0	1	2	0	1	0	0	1	0	0	0	0
ice-cube	2	.1839	.0845	29.3	0	1	0	0	0	0	1	0	0	0	0	0	0	0	0	0	0	0	1	0	1	0	0	0	0
ice-locked	2	.0000	.0914	29.6	0	2	0	0	0	0	0	0	2	0	0	0	0	0	0	0	0	0	0	0	0	0	0	0	0
ice-skate	2	.1733	.1149	30.6	1	0	0	1	0	0	0	0	1	1	0	0	0	0	0	0	0	0	0	0	0	0	0	0	0

4H hydrofoil
7Q hydrogen-filled
6H hydrogen-2
4H Hydrologic
6R hydrologists
9H hydrolyzes
7Q hydrophytes
8A hydroplane
6Q hydroxyl
3R Hyena
8G hygienic
6H Hyla
4A Hyman's
5Q Hymen
7H hymeno
9Q HYMETTUS
9Q HYMN
5J hymn-like
7R hypalon
7R hyped-up
9Q hyperacidity
6P Hyperborean
9H hypertension
8Q hypertrophy
9B hypnotism
3H hypnotize
6A hypnotizes
7H hypnum
9Q hypochondriac
XR hypochondriacal
3N hypocritical
7Q hypodermic
9E hypothesis/conclusion
7R hypothesized
XH hypothetical
9D Hyrcanian
5Q Hysteria
7D Hyyenaes
9H H2SO4
7J H2O
6Q H5
7A I-I
7Q I-S
8M i-f
4G i-n-g
3B I-1
7R I-270
7R i-5
7R i-95
7R I-95
3A i
7D I'da
4J I'se
9R Ia
5A Iagoo
9Q iambic
5G ian
6R Ian
9D Iardanos
9G IB
7P Iberia
6F Ibernian
3J Ibert
XH Ibex
4F Ibibio
7Q ibises
9R IBM
7P ibn
4F Ibo
4J Ibsen's
7G ical
9D Icarios'
9D ice-axe
9D ice-axes
3P ice-blocks
7F ice-clogged
8A ice-coated
7N ice-edged
3R ice-filled
6F ice-lined
6R ice-packed

Word Type	F	D	U	SFI	3 Gr 3	4 Gr 4	5 Gr 5	6 Gr 6	7 Gr 7	8 Gr 8	9 Gr 9	X UnGr	A Read	B Eng & Gr	C Comp	D Lit	E Math	F Soc Stud	G Spell	H Sci	J Music	K Art	L Home Ec	M Shop	N Lib F	P Lib NF	Q Lib Ref	R Mag	S Rel
ice-skating	6	.3838	.4828	36.8	1	0	1	0	1	3	0	0	0	4	1	0	0	0	0	0	0	0	1	0	0	0	0	0	0
iceberg	34	.7423	5.2014	47.2	0	14	4	3	10	0	3	0	14	1	0	1	1	1	0	7	0	0	1	0	0	4	3	1	0
icebergs	28	.6057	3.6482	45.6	4	15	3	1	3	0	2	0	12	0	0	1	0	0	0	7	0	0	0	0	0	4	2	2	0
iceboats	3	.0000	.0243	23.9	3	0	0	0	0	0	0	0	0	0	0	0	0	0	3	0	0	0	0	0	0	0	0	0	0
icebox	24	.4034	2.3322	43.7	7	9	0	3	2	1	2	0	13	2	0	1	0	0	0	0	0	0	0	0	8	0	0	0	0
Icebox	2	.0000	.0389	25.9	0	0	2	0	0	0	0	0	0	0	0	0	0	2	0	0	0	0	0	0	0	0	0	0	0
icebreaker	5	.2444	.3032	34.8	1	4	0	0	0	0	0	0	0	0	0	0	0	0	0	3	0	0	0	0	0	0	0	2	0
icebreakers	2	.2446	.1257	31.0	0	1	0	1	0	0	0	0	0	0	0	0	0	1	0	1	0	0	0	0	0	0	0	0	0
icecap	3	.0000	.0583	27.7	0	0	2	1	0	0	0	0	0	0	0	0	0	3	0	0	0	0	0	0	0	0	0	0	0
icecaps	4	.3348	.3267	35.1	0	0	0	1	1	1	0	1	1	0	0	0	0	0	0	2	0	0	0	0	0	0	1	0	0
iced	3	.2468	.1912	32.8	0	1	0	1	1	0	0	0	1	0	0	0	0	0	0	0	0	0	1	0	1	0	0	0	0
icehouse	7	.3040	.5671	37.5	4	2	0	1	0	0	0	0	4	0	1	0	0	0	0	0	0	0	0	0	0	2	0	0	0
Icehouse	2	.0000	.0914	29.6	2	0	0	0	0	0	0	0	2	0	0	0	0	0	0	0	0	0	0	0	0	0	0	0	0
Iceland	43	.5780	5.2393	47.2	1	0	7	23	4	0	6	2	4	2	0	0	0	23	0	3	1	0	0	0	0	4	5	1	0
Iceland's	4	.2152	.2714	34.3	0	0	0	4	0	0	0	0	2	0	0	0	0	2	0	0	0	0	0	0	0	0	0	0	0
Icelandic	3	.3553	.2608	34.2	2	0	0	1	0	0	0	0	1	0	0	0	0	1	0	0	0	0	0	0	0	1	0	0	0
iceman	2	.2440	.0995	30.0	0	0	0	0	0	1	1	0	0	0	1	0	0	0	0	0	0	0	0	1	0	0	0	0	0
ices	2	.0857	.0784	28.9	0	0	0	0	1	1	0	0	1	0	0	0	0	0	0	0	0	0	1	0	0	0	0	0	0
Ichabod	30	.3679	2.9047	44.6	0	0	3	0	15	12	0	0	24	0	0	3	0	0	0	0	0	0	0	0	3	0	0	0	0
ichthyosaurs	4	.0000	.0419	26.2	0	0	0	0	4	0	0	0	0	0	0	0	0	0	0	0	0	0	0	0	0	0	4	0	0
icicle	3	.3759	.2474	33.9	1	0	0	1	0	0	1	0	0	1	0	1	0	0	0	1	0	0	0	0	0	0	0	0	0
icicles	16	.4513	1.5825	42.0	0	3	3	3	1	1	5	0	3	7	0	2	0	0	0	2	0	0	0	0	2	0	0	0	0
icing	10	.5211	1.1279	40.5	5	0	2	0	1	2	0	0	3	2	0	0	0	0	0	0	0	0	0	0	3	0	1	1	0
ick	5	.2042	.2444	33.9	0	4	1	0	0	0	0	0	0	0	0	0	0	0	1	0	0	0	0	0	4	0	0	0	0
Ickes	2	.0000	.0243	23.9	0	0	0	0	0	0	0	2	0	0	0	0	0	0	0	0	0	0	0	0	0	0	0	2	0
icy	89	.7846	14.123	51.5	11	16	10	10	24	8	10	0	22	12	4	12	0	8	1	9	1	0	0	0	5	4	6	5	0
Ida	5	.2557	.3182	35.0	3	0	0	0	0	1	0	1	1	0	0	3	0	0	0	0	0	0	0	0	0	0	0	1	0
Idaho	43	.4552	4.3464	46.4	0	2	19	9	6	4	2	1	6	0	0	1	0	24	0	3	0	0	0	0	0	0	1	8	0
idea	1397	.8896	247.56	63.9	171	242	168	157	312	185	145	17	400	163	56	67	85	86	10	118	59	46	17	13	77	97	40	63	0
Idea	2	.1733	.1149	30.6	0	1	0	1	0	0	0	0	1	1	0	0	0	0	0	0	0	0	0	0	0	0	0	0	0
ideal	59	.7893	9.3552	49.7	2	1	8	8	14	12	8	6	8	3	0	3	0	7	1	3	4	4	1	2	1	5	4	13	0
idealism	2	.1814	.1187	30.7	0	0	0	0	1	1	0	0	1	0	0	0	0	0	0	0	0	0	0	0	0	0	0	1	0
idealistic	5	.2956	.3348	35.2	0	0	0	0	1	3	1	0	0	0	0	0	0	1	0	0	0	0	0	0	0	0	3	1	0
idealists	2	.1698	.1133	30.5	0	0	0	0	1	1	0	0	1	0	0	0	0	0	0	0	0	0	0	0	0	0	1	0	0
idealized	4	.1493	.1383	31.4	0	0	0	0	3	0	1	0	0	0	0	0	0	0	0	0	0	2	0	0	0	0	2	0	0
ideally	11	.6213	1.4044	41.5	0	1	1	1	6	2	0	0	1	0	0	0	0	1	0	1	2	0	1	0	0	1	3	1	0
ideals	27	.5470	3.1207	44.9	1	0	0	2	2	13	8	1	3	0	0	1	0	13	0	0	4	2	0	0	0	1	3	0	0
ideas	978	.7618	150.56	61.8	102	157	158	114	186	139	110	12	189	175	76	15	67	100	10	59	82	63	15	4	5	41	38	39	0
idee	2	.1717	.1142	30.6	0	0	0	0	0	1	1	0	1	0	0	1	0	0	0	0	0	0	0	0	0	0	0	0	0
Idell	6	.0000	.0703	28.5	0	0	0	0	0	0	6	0	0	0	0	0	0	0	0	0	0	0	0	0	6	0	0	0	0
identical	46	.7834	7.2433	48.6	2	0	2	1	14	11	9	7	5	2	2	1	5	1	0	11	2	0	4	1	0	1	7	4	0
identifiable	5	.4470	.4760	36.8	0	0	1	0	1	1	2	0	0	2	0	0	0	0	0	1	0	0	0	0	0	1	1	0	0
identification	30	.6364	3.9252	45.9	0	2	3	4	11	1	5	4	3	4	0	1	0	0	0	7	0	0	0	3	1	2	6	3	0
identified	83	.8036	13.331	51.2	0	1	6	7	38	14	16	1	3	6	1	4	3	4	1	19	4	0	4	6	0	6	16	6	0
identifies	19	.5068	2.0350	43.1	0	1	2	2	6	3	5	0	3	7	3	0	0	0	2	1	1	0	0	0	0	1	1	0	0
identify	242	.7947	38.430	55.8	11	9	20	23	100	46	31	2	10	35	17	5	22	5	40	45	32	1	3	7	1	5	7	7	0
identifying	19	.7257	2.7756	44.4	0	0	1	3	4	5	5	1	0	3	0	1	2	0	0	5	1	1	0	1	0	0	3	2	0
identities	6	.2398	.3441	35.4	0	0	0	0	4	0	2	0	0	0	0	0	4	0	0	0	0	0	0	0	0	0	2	0	0
identity	79	.5017	8.4056	49.2	0	0	6	2	37	26	7	1	4	1	1	1	60	0	0	1	0	0	1	2	0	4	1	3	0
ideograms	2	.0000	.0162	22.1	0	0	0	0	1	1	0	0	0	0	0	0	0	0	2	0	0	0	0	0	0	0	0	0	0
ideographs	2	.2300	.1140	30.6	0	0	0	0	2	0	0	0	0	1	0	0	0	0	0	1	0	0	0	0	0	0	0	0	0
ideologies	3	.0000	.0583	27.7	0	0	0	0	0	2	1	0	0	0	0	0	0	3	0	0	0	0	0	0	0	0	0	0	0
ideology	3	.3395	.2468	33.9	0	0	1	0	0	0	2	0	1	0	0	0	0	0	0	0	0	0	0	0	0	1	1	0	0
idiocy	3	.0000	.1370	31.4	0	0	0	0	1	2	0	0	3	0	0	0	0	0	0	0	0	0	0	0	0	0	0	0	0
idiom	11	.2925	.7605	38.8	0	1	0	5	1	1	3	0	2	6	0	0	0	0	0	0	3	0	0	0	0	0	0	0	0
idioms	10	.1964	.4824	36.8	0	0	1	6	1	2	0	0	0	7	0	0	0	0	0	0	0	0	0	0	0	3	0	0	0
idiophones	3	.0000	.0243	23.8	0	0	0	0	3	0	0	0	0	0	0	0	0	0	0	0	3	0	0	0	0	0	0	0	0
idiot	10	.5619	1.1861	40.7	0	1	0	0	1	5	2	1	2	0	0	3	0	0	0	1	1	0	0	0	2	0	0	1	0
idiotic	3	.2143	.1568	32.0	0	0	0	1	0	1	1	0	0	0	0	0	0	0	0	0	0	0	0	0	0	1	0	2	0
idiots	2	.1717	.1142	30.6	0	0	0	0	0	2	0	0	1	0	0	1	0	0	0	0	0	0	0	0	0	0	0	0	0
idle	32	.6801	4.4822	46.5	1	4	3	5	8	5	5	1	8	1	2	7	0	3	1	0	0	0	0	0	6	1	1	2	0
Idle	2	.1948	.1250	31.0	1	0	0	1	0	0	0	0	1	0	0	0	0	0	0	0	0	0	0	0	0	1	0	0	0
idleness	2	.2407	.1138	30.6	0	1	0	0	1	0	0	0	0	0	0	1	0	0	0	0	0	0	0	0	0	1	0	0	0
idling	2	.0000	.0290	24.6	0	0	0	0	1	0	0	1	0	0	0	0	0	0	0	0	0	0	0	0	0	2	0	0	0
idly	9	.6048	1.1559	40.6	0	1	2	1	1	1	1	2	3	1	0	0	0	0	0	1	0	0	0	0	1	1	0	2	0
idol	10	.5763	1.2234	40.9	0	1	1	1	4	2	1	0	3	0	0	3	0	0	0	0	1	0	0	0	0	1	1	1	0
idolized	2	.0000	.0234	23.7	0	0	0	0	1	1	0	0	0	0	0	0	0	0	0	0	0	0	0	0	2	0	0	0	0
idols	7	.3986	.6015	37.8	1	0	0	2	1	3	0	0	0	1	0	0	0	2	0	0	3	0	0	0	0	1	0	0	0
idols'	2	.0000	.0215	23.3	0	0	0	0	2	0	0	0	0	0	0	2	0	0	0	0	0	0	0	0	0	0	0	0	0
idyllic	5	.4395	.4863	36.9	0	1	2	1	0	0	1	0	1	0	0	1	0	0	0	0	0	0	0	0	1	2	0	0	0
ie	34	.1874	1.4977	41.8	2	2	2	7	14	5	2	0	0	7	0	0	0	0	26	0	0	0	0	0	0	1	0	0	0
ie-ei	2	.0000	.0162	22.1	0	0	0	0	2	0	0	0	0	0	0	0	0	0	2	0	0	0	0	0	0	0	0	0	0
if	12907	.9667	2460.7	73.9	1981	1913	1523	1717	2436	1651	1421	265	2961	966	130	722	1961	662	428	1501	251	115	411	195	739	885	288	687	5
If	3	.1983	.1396	31.4	0	0	1	0	0	2	0	0	0	0	0	0	0	0	0	0	2	0	0	0	0	0	0	1	0
IF	2	.0000	.0394	26.0	0	2	0	0	0	0	0	0	0	0	0	0	0	0	0	2	0	0	0	0	0	0	0	0	0
if-then	3	.0000	.0449	26.5	0	0	2	1	0	0	0	0	0	0	0	0	3	0	0	0	0	0	0	0	0	0	0	0	0
iffen	2	.0000	.0234	23.7	0	0	2	0	0	0	0	0	0	0	0	0	0	0	0	0	0	0	0	0	2	0	0	0	0
ifs	3	.0000	.0322	25.1	0	0	0	0	0	3	0	0	0	0	0	3	0	0	0	0	0	0	0	0	0	0	0	0	0
Iggy	2	.0000	.0290	24.6	0	2	0	0	0	0	0	0	0	0	0	0	0	0	0	0	0	0	0	0	0	2	0	0	0
igloo	7	.2310	.4012	36.0	1	1	1	0	0	0	4	0	1	5	0	0	0	0	1	0	0	0	0	0	0	0	0	0	0
igloos	5	.2038	.3268	35.1	2	1	0	0	0	0	2	0	3	2	0	0	0	0	0	0	0	0	0	0	0	0	0	0	0
Ignazio	2	.0000	.0290	24.6	0	0	1	0	1	0	0	0	0	0	0	0	0	0	0	0	0	0	0	0	0	2	0	0	0
igneous	40	.1975	2.1612	43.3	1	9	1	6	1	3	16	3	0	0	0	0	0	0	0	35	0	0	0	0	0	4	1	0	0
ignite	9	.5829	1.1074	40.4	1	0	4	0	3	1	0	0	2	0	0	0	0	1	1	2	0	0	0	1	0	0	1	1	0
ignited	5	.3253	.4059	36.1	1	0	1	0	1	1	1	0	2	0	0	0	0	1	0	0	0	0	0	1	0	1	0	0	0
igniting	2	.0665	.0708	28.5	0	0	0	0	2	0	0	0	1	0	1	0	0	0	0	0	0	0	0	0	0	0	0	0	0
ignition	25	.4365	2.3759	43.8	0	0	1	2	15	2	4	1	3	2	0	1	0	0	0	2	0	0	0	0	0	0	3	14	0
ignominiously	2	.1717	.1142	30.6	0	0	0	1	1	0	0	0	1	0	0	1	0	0	0	0	0	0	0	0	0	0	0	0	0
ignorance	22	.7347	3.2998	45.2	0	0	2	3	7	5	4	1	5	1	0	3	0	3	0	2	0	0	1	0	2	4	0	1	0
ignorant	30	.8086	4.8968	46.9	1	0	2	8	8	6	3	2	9	1	0	2	0	3	2	2	0	0	0	1	3	1	3	3	0
ignore	28	.7328	4.1686	46.2	1	1	1	1	12	4	7	1	5	0	1	2	2	4	0	1	0	0	3	0	1	2	3	4	0
ignored	41	.7932	6.5724	48.2	1	5	4	2	13	5	10	1	10	2	0	3	1	7	0	1	0	1	0	0	4	4	5	3	0
ignores	4	.2889	.2536	34.0	1	0	0	0	1	1	1	0	0	0	0	0	0	0	0	0	0	1	0	0	0	1	2	0	0
ignoring	14	.6528	1.9023	42.8	0	0	1	1	6	1	4	1	4	1	0	0	0	1	0	1	0	0	1	0	0	1	3	2	0

7A ice-storms
8Q icebound
3F iceboxes
4A icefall
8R Ich
7Q ichthyological
7Q ichthyologist
7N ichthyologists
4N ichthyophthirius
6A Icicle
7D icily
7Q iciness
9B icon
8Q iconoclast
6F Ictinus
6A icy-cold
5G id
8Q ida-maia
9B idaho
5F Idaho's
8K IDEA
7K idealization
3B idear
8K IDEAS
9N Idell's
7J identically
7R Identification
7R identification-card
7H identifications
5E Identity
6J ideo-o-o
5P ideological
7R ideologues
7P Ides
9D Idiots
8F idler
8A idlers
9D idles
8F idlest
9R idolaters
8Q idolatrous
7P idolatry
9J idolize
4J Idue
XR idyllically
7Q Ieper
4A ies
9E IG
XB Igel
7R IGFA**
4A igg-puh
8G igh
XR Ignatius
8R ignoble
9K ignominious
4J ignoramus

Word Type	F	D	U	SFI	3 Gr 3	4 Gr 4	5 Gr 5	6 Gr 6	7 Gr 7	8 Gr 8	9 Gr 9	X UnGr	A Read	B Eng & Gr	C Comp	D Lit	E Math	F Soc Stud	G Spell	H Sci	J Music	K Art	L Home Ec	M Shop	N Lib F	P Lib NF	Q Lib Ref	R Mag	S Rel
Igor	18	.2268	.9886	39.9	0	8	0	0	3	1	6	0	2	0	0	0	0	0	0	0	11	0	0	0	0	0	0	5	0
Iguacu	2	.0000	.0209	23.2	0	0	2	0	0	0	0	0	0	0	0	0	0	0	0	0	0	0	0	0	0	0	2	0	0
iguana	8	.2360	.5112	37.1	2	1	0	0	2	2	1	0	2	0	0	0	0	0	0	1	0	0	0	0	0	5	0	0	0
iguanas	4	.1335	.1958	32.9	0	0	0	0	1	0	3	0	1	0	0	0	0	0	0	3	0	0	0	0	0	0	0	0	0
iguanodon	2	.0000	.0290	24.6	0	2	0	0	0	0	0	0	0	0	0	0	0	0	0	0	0	0	0	0	0	2	0	0	0
Iguanodon	4	.0000	.0579	27.6	1	0	3	0	0	0	0	0	0	0	0	0	0	0	0	0	0	0	0	0	0	4	0	0	0
Iguassu	2	.2285	.1129	30.5	0	0	1	0	1	0	0	0	0	0	0	0	0	1	0	0	0	0	0	0	0	0	1	0	0
IGY	11	.3409	.9104	39.6	0	0	6	3	0	1	1	0	2	0	0	0	0	1	0	7	0	0	0	0	0	1	0	0	0
ih	3	.0000	.0352	25.5	0	0	0	3	0	0	0	0	0	0	0	0	0	0	0	0	0	0	0	0	3	0	0	0	0
ii	3	.2444	.1728	32.4	0	1	0	0	1	0	1	0	0	0	0	0	2	0	1	0	0	0	0	0	0	0	0	0	0
II	307	.7628	47.222	56.7	18	25	59	53	51	49	46	6	28	7	0	2	16	73	7	16	29	0	0	8	0	26	66	29	0
iii	2	.2404	.1142	30.6	0	1	0	0	1	0	0	0	0	1	0	0	1	0	0	0	0	0	0	0	0	0	0	0	0
III	69	.7924	10.955	50.4	4	2	18	6	16	4	13	6	7	4	0	1	6	2	8	1	4	0	1	3	0	8	15	9	0
ij	2	.0000	.0162	22.1	0	0	1	1	0	0	0	0	0	0	0	0	0	0	2	0	0	0	0	0	0	0	0	0	0
IJ	5	.0000	.0748	28.7	0	1	0	1	0	3	0	0	0	0	0	0	5	0	0	0	0	0	0	0	0	0	0	0	0
IJKL	2	.0000	.0299	24.8	0	0	1	1	0	0	0	0	0	0	0	0	2	0	0	0	0	0	0	0	0	0	0	0	0
Ike	28	.4052	2.4661	43.9	1	0	0	8	5	9	5	0	0	1	0	5	0	9	0	0	0	0	0	0	0	0	0	13	0
Ike's	5	.0000	.0608	27.8	0	0	0	5	0	0	0	0	0	0	0	0	0	0	0	0	0	0	0	0	0	0	0	5	0
Ikhnaton	2	.0000	.0389	25.9	0	0	0	0	2	0	0	0	0	0	0	0	0	2	0	0	0	0	0	0	0	0	0	0	0
Iki	4	.1787	.2347	33.7	0	2	0	2	0	0	0	0	2	0	0	0	0	0	0	0	0	0	0	0	2	0	0	0	0
il	5	.0000	.0406	26.1	0	1	0	4	0	0	0	0	0	0	0	0	0	0	5	0	0	0	0	0	0	0	0	0	0
Il	4	.0000	.0323	25.1	0	0	2	0	1	1	0	0	0	0	0	0	0	0	0	0	4	0	0	0	0	0	0	0	0
ile	2	.2408	.1091	30.4	0	0	0	1	0	0	0	1	0	1	0	0	0	0	1	0	0	0	0	0	0	0	0	0	0
Iliad	6	.4332	.5826	37.7	0	0	1	1	3	1	0	0	1	1	0	0	0	3	0	0	0	0	0	0	1	0	0	0	0
ill	148	.8703	25.734	54.1	5	26	15	26	28	28	17	3	41	11	2	15	0	13	6	15	1	0	5	0	15	10	8	6	0
Ill	7	.1564	.2855	34.6	0	0	1	0	0	2	1	3	0	0	0	0	0	0	0	0	0	0	0	0	0	0	1	6	0
ill-fated	7	.3829	.6211	37.9	0	2	1	0	0	1	3	0	2	0	0	1	0	1	0	0	0	0	0	0	0	0	3	0	0
ill-feeling	2	.0000	.0209	23.2	0	0	0	0	0	2	0	0	0	0	0	0	0	0	0	0	0	0	0	0	0	0	2	0	0
ill-smelling	2	.2408	.1204	30.8	0	0	1	0	0	1	0	0	0	0	0	0	0	1	0	0	0	0	0	0	0	1	0	0	0
ill-tempered	4	.3713	.3634	35.6	0	0	0	2	2	0	0	0	2	0	0	1	0	0	0	0	0	0	0	0	1	0	0	0	0
Illarion	2	.0000	.0219	23.4	0	0	0	0	0	0	2	0	0	2	0	0	0	0	0	0	0	0	0	0	0	0	0	0	0
illegal	12	.6145	1.5187	41.8	0	1	3	2	4	1	1	0	1	1	0	1	0	1	1	0	0	0	0	0	0	1	1	5	0
illegally	4	.2090	.2014	33.0	0	0	1	2	0	0	1	0	0	0	0	0	0	0	0	0	0	0	0	0	0	0	1	3	0
Illinois	145	.7947	23.203	53.7	5	24	28	12	21	37	10	8	16	8	1	5	6	56	1	6	2	1	0	0	2	9	9	23	0
Illinois's	2	.2408	.1204	30.8	0	1	1	0	0	0	0	0	0	0	0	0	0	1	0	0	0	0	0	0	0	1	0	0	0
illiteracy	6	.4782	.6116	37.9	1	0	1	0	2	1	0	1	0	1	0	0	0	3	0	0	0	0	0	0	1	0	1	0	0
illiterate	15	.7150	2.2037	43.4	0	0	1	0	1	9	3	1	4	0	0	1	2	3	1	0	0	0	0	0	0	1	2	1	0
illness	78	.6706	10.750	50.3	3	3	5	10	18	21	18	0	14	3	1	3	0	2	1	16	0	0	12	0	5	7	3	11	0
illnesses	17	.4505	1.6717	42.2	1	1	5	3	0	4	3	0	3	0	0	0	0	1	0	4	0	0	4	0	1	0	3	1	0
illogical	4	.3141	.2718	34.3	0	0	0	1	0	0	2	1	0	2	1	0	0	0	0	0	0	0	0	0	0	0	0	1	0
ills	11	.5016	1.1583	40.6	0	0	0	0	2	3	6	0	1	0	0	2	0	0	0	0	0	0	1	0	0	0	4	3	0
illuminate	5	.3933	.4170	36.2	0	0	1	0	3	0	0	1	0	2	1	0	0	0	0	0	0	0	0	0	1	1	0	0	0
illuminated	20	.5588	2.3128	43.6	0	0	2	5	6	0	1	6	0	0	2	0	0	0	0	7	3	0	0	0	4	1	0	3	0
illuminating	5	.3157	.3891	35.9	0	0	0	0	0	4	1	0	1	0	0	0	0	0	0	3	0	0	0	0	0	0	1	0	0
illumination	4	.3231	.2911	34.6	0	0	0	0	2	0	0	2	0	0	0	0	0	0	0	2	0	0	1	0	0	0	0	1	0
illumined	2	.1717	.1142	30.6	0	0	0	1	1	0	0	0	1	0	0	1	0	0	0	0	0	0	0	0	0	0	0	0	0
illusion	17	.5095	1.7972	42.5	0	0	1	5	3	4	2	2	0	0	0	1	0	0	0	3	0	3	1	0	3	3	0	3	0
illusions	7	.4970	.7479	38.7	0	0	1	0	4	2	0	0	1	0	0	2	0	1	0	0	0	0	0	0	0	2	0	1	0
illustrate	119	.7546	18.070	52.6	1	4	10	11	40	28	23	2	6	11	9	6	39	8	10	17	3	3	0	1	0	0	4	2	0
illustrated	115	.7570	17.539	52.4	5	5	7	13	35	24	23	3	10	8	0	2	39	5	2	13	8	2	2	10	0	1	9	4	0
Illustrated	2	.0000	.0243	23.9	0	0	0	1	0	1	0	0	0	0	0	0	0	0	0	0	0	0	0	0	0	0	0	2	0
illustrates	63	.6424	8.3248	49.2	0	3	1	12	19	12	13	3	4	2	1	0	32	4	1	8	4	0	0	0	0	0	4	3	0
illustrating	12	.5916	1.5009	41.8	0	1	1	4	2	3	1	0	3	1	0	1	3	0	2	2	0	0	0	0	0	0	0	0	0
illustration	93	.7615	14.176	51.5	3	5	9	8	22	35	8	3	2	10	1	1	9	1	17	20	5	2	12	6	0	4	2	1	0
Illustration	16	.0000	.0296	24.7	0	0	0	0	0	0	16	0	0	0	0	0	0	0	0	0	0	16	0	0	0	0	0	0	0
illustrations	56	.6589	7.4815	48.7	4	6	8	8	8	11	9	2	3	10	0	0	8	4	0	4	3	2	12	3	0	0	4	3	0
illustrative	8	.3101	.5448	37.4	0	0	0	0	2	4	2	0	0	6	0	0	1	0	0	0	0	0	0	1	0	0	0	0	0
illustrator	7	.2446	.3875	35.9	4	0	0	0	2	1	0	0	0	6	0	0	0	0	0	0	0	1	0	0	0	0	0	0	0
illustrious	10	.5195	1.0985	40.4	0	0	0	0	3	3	4	0	1	0	0	4	0	2	0	0	1	0	0	0	1	1	0	0	0
ilmenite	2	.0000	.0914	29.6	2	0	0	0	0	0	0	0	2	0	0	0	0	0	0	0	0	0	0	0	0	0	0	0	0
Ilse	7	.0000	.3198	35.0	0	7	0	0	0	0	0	0	7	0	0	0	0	0	0	0	0	0	0	0	0	0	0	0	0
Ilyitch	4	.0000	.0323	25.1	1	1	0	0	0	1	1	0	0	0	0	0	0	0	0	0	4	0	0	0	0	0	0	0	0
im	9	.2934	.6542	38.2	2	0	2	2	1	2	0	0	3	2	0	0	0	0	4	0	0	0	0	0	0	0	0	0	0
image	148	.7840	23.327	53.7	1	12	10	27	32	23	27	16	13	1	4	18	0	5	1	45	1	1	0	7	3	9	24	16	0
imagery	5	.5324	.5639	37.5	0	0	0	1	0	1	2	1	1	0	0	1	0	0	0	0	1	0	0	0	0	0	1	1	0
images	60	.7512	9.0936	49.6	2	3	6	16	9	3	14	7	5	3	0	5	0	6	0	7	4	0	0	1	0	8	14	7	0
imaginable	3	.3800	.2528	34.0	0	0	0	1	1	1	0	0	0	0	0	0	1	0	0	1	0	0	0	0	1	0	0	0	0
imaginary	93	.6393	12.162	50.9	10	28	13	7	9	8	12	6	6	4	14	6	6	20	6	14	0	8	0	1	2	1	4	1	0
imagination	150	.7243	21.988	53.4	2	26	6	21	46	25	18	6	23	21	8	15	5	5	0	8	11	18	4	1	8	8	4	11	0
imaginations	4	.1733	.2298	33.6	0	0	0	0	3	1	0	0	2	2	0	0	0	0	0	0	0	0	0	0	0	0	0	0	0
imaginative	32	.7247	4.6964	46.7	0	4	3	5	5	7	6	2	4	6	1	0	0	3	1	3	3	2	0	0	0	0	5	4	0
imaginatively	2	.2306	.1140	30.6	0	0	1	1	0	0	0	0	0	1	0	0	0	1	0	0	0	0	0	0	0	0	0	0	0
imagine	381	.9295	70.135	58.5	61	73	43	51	70	50	26	7	80	41	12	23	43	27	10	58	18	5	2	3	13	29	4	12	1
imagined	68	.7598	10.483	50.2	4	9	5	6	18	16	9	1	19	2	1	15	0	0	2	0	4	3	0	0	7	6	7	2	0
imagines	4	.2708	.2760	34.4	1	0	0	0	2	0	1	0	1	0	0	2	0	1	0	0	0	0	0	0	0	0	0	0	0
imagining	16	.7570	2.4408	43.9	2	4	0	1	3	5	0	1	2	3	0	2	1	0	1	0	1	0	0	0	3	1	1	1	0
imaginings	3	.2196	.1554	31.9	0	0	0	1	2	0	0	0	0	0	0	2	0	0	0	0	0	0	0	0	1	0	0	0	0
imagist	2	.0000	.0209	23.2	0	0	2	0	0	0	0	0	0	0	0	0	0	0	0	0	0	0	0	0	0	0	2	0	0
imams	2	.0000	.0209	23.2	0	0	0	0	0	0	2	0	0	0	0	0	0	0	0	0	0	0	0	0	0	0	2	0	0
imbedded	4	.3366	.2993	34.8	0	0	0	0	3	0	1	0	0	0	0	0	0	0	0	1	0	0	0	0	1	0	2	0	0
imitate	51	.6521	6.7699	48.3	6	6	7	9	10	4	9	0	6	4	5	5	0	2	1	0	16	0	4	0	1	4	3	0	0
imitated	17	.5432	1.9571	42.9	1	2	1	6	2	4	1	0	3	1	0	0	0	3	0	1	6	0	0	0	0	1	1	1	0
imitates	11	.2503	.6222	37.9	0	3	1	1	2	4	0	0	0	0	0	3	0	1	0	0	7	0	0	0	0	0	0	0	0
imitating	13	.5872	1.5798	42.0	0	1	5	4	3	0	0	0	2	1	2	1	0	0	0	0	2	0	0	0	1	1	2	1	0
imitation	38	.5406	4.2059	46.2	0	11	3	8	6	6	3	1	2	0	10	3	0	1	4	0	9	1	1	0	1	4	1	1	0
imitations	11	.1543	.3844	35.8	0	1	5	2	2	0	1	0	0	1	7	2	0	0	0	0	0	0	0	0	0	0	0	1	0
imitators	3	.2772	.2004	33.0	1	0	1	0	1	0	0	0	1	0	1	0	0	0	0	0	0	0	1	0	0	0	0	0	0
immaculate	2	.1717	.1142	30.6	0	0	0	0	2	0	0	0	1	0	0	1	0	0	0	0	0	0	0	0	0	0	0	0	0
immature	10	.2620	.6202	37.9	0	0	0	1	9	0	0	0	1	0	0	0	0	0	0	0	0	0	0	0	1	0	7	1	0
immeasurable	6	.4082	.5269	37.2	0	0	4	0	2	0	0	0	0	3	0	0	0	1	0	0	0	0	0	0	0	1	1	0	0
immeasurably	2	.1698	.1133	30.5	0	0	1	0	0	0	1	0	1	0	0	0	0	0	0	0	0	0	0	0	0	0	1	0	0
immediate	62	.7966	9.9162	50.0	1	3	9	4	16	16	9	4	7	2	0	3	0	7	2	9	3	0	4	0	2	4	9	10	0
immediately	295	.9083	53.151	57.3	23	28	33	40	61	54	43	13	55	28	6	16	8	11	4	28	16	0	9	3	25	18	28	40	0
immemorial	2	.2278	.1128	30.5	0	0	0	0	0	0	1	1	0	0	0	0	0	0	0	1	0	0	0	0	0	0	1	0	0

4R Igor's
4J Igorot
3Q Igorots
5P Iguanodons
XH Il-16
7Q Ill-A
5E IJK
5E IJL
9R Ikarus
4F ikebana
6R Ileana
5G ilekt'**
5Q Ilion
9R ilk
8F ill-advised
7A ill-concealed
9J ill-favored
7Q ill-fitted
6P ill-fitting
5A ill-gotten
5P ill-health
6A ill-humored
4N ill-informed
7N ill-looking
4N ill-paved
7N ill-temper
8R ill-trained
9Q ill-treated
8Q Illana
6A Illegal
9F illegality
8B illegible
5Q Illilouette
7N illimitable
9R Illinois'
XR illogic
5R illuminates
8D illuminations
8D illumine
XR illusive
5P illusory
4Q illustrators
7F Illyushin
4D Ilsebill
7G im-
7Q imaginal
5Q imagists
7R imbalance
4Q imbalances
7H imbat
9Q imbued
9R imitative
XR immaculately
XJ immanent
7Q Immanuel

Word Type	F	D	U	SFI	3 Gr 3	4 Gr 4	5 Gr 5	6 Gr 6	7 Gr 7	8 Gr 8	9 Gr 9	X UnGr	A Read	B Eng & Gr	C Comp	D Lit	E Math	F Soc Stud	G Spell	H Sci	J Music	K Art	L Home Ec	M Shop	N Lib F	P Lib NF	Q Lib Ref	R Mag	S Rel
immense	46	.6801	6.3613	48.0	1	0	9	2	18	5	10	1	3	1	0	3	0	7	0	1	1	2	0	0	4	4	16	4	0
immensely	14	.4430	1.3920	41.4	0	1	2	1	4	4	1	1	4	0	0	0	0	1	0	1	0	0	0	0	1	1	6	0	0
immersed	2	.0000	.0243	23.9	0	0	0	0	2	0	0	0	0	0	0	0	0	0	0	0	0	0	0	0	0	0	0	2	0
immigrant	11	.4982	1.1728	40.7	1	0	3	0	3	4	0	0	1	1	0	0	0	5	0	0	2	0	0	0	0	0	2	0	0
immigrants	60	.6301	7.8075	48.9	2	2	13	8	14	19	2	0	2	3	0	0	3	33	1	0	4	0	0	0	0	4	5	5	0
immigrated	3	.1169	.1277	31.1	0	0	1	1	0	0	1	0	1	0	0	0	0	0	0	0	0	0	0	0	0	0	2	0	0
immigration	16	.4152	1.4602	41.6	3	0	1	1	1	8	1	1	0	0	0	0	0	10	0	0	0	0	0	0	0	1	3	2	0
immobility	3	.2159	.1532	31.9	0	0	1	0	2	0	0	0	0	0	0	0	0	0	0	0	0	0	0	0	0	0	2	1	0
immobilized	2	.0000	.0243	23.9	0	0	0	2	0	0	0	0	0	0	0	0	0	0	0	0	0	0	0	0	0	0	0	2	0
immoral	6	.3745	.5116	37.1	0	0	0	2	0	3	1	0	1	0	0	0	0	1	0	0	0	0	0	0	0	0	1	3	0
immortal	11	.5805	1.3497	41.3	0	0	0	3	1	3	3	1	3	3	0	2	0	0	0	0	1	0	0	0	0	1	0	1	0
immortality	8	.4281	.7499	38.7	1	0	0	3	3	1	0	0	1	0	0	0	0	0	0	0	0	0	0	0	0	3	2	2	0
immortalized	2	.2278	.1128	30.5	0	0	0	0	0	1	0	1	0	0	0	0	0	0	0	1	0	0	0	0	0	0	1	0	0
immortals	6	.2129	.3322	35.2	0	0	0	0	1	0	4	1	1	0	0	4	0	0	0	0	0	0	0	0	0	1	0	0	0
Immortals	3	.0000	.1370	31.4	0	0	0	0	2	1	0	0	3	0	0	0	0	0	0	0	0	0	0	0	0	0	0	0	0
immovable	5	.3683	.4536	36.6	0	0	0	3	1	0	1	0	2	0	0	0	0	0	0	2	0	0	0	0	0	1	0	0	0
immune	18	.6254	2.3109	43.6	0	2	1	1	7	1	5	1	0	0	0	1	0	2	0	6	0	0	0	1	0	1	4	3	0
immunities	2	.2285	.1129	30.5	0	0	0	0	0	1	1	0	0	0	0	0	0	1	0	0	0	0	0	0	0	0	1	0	0
immunity	8	.2353	.4765	36.8	0	0	0	0	4	3	1	0	0	0	0	0	0	0	0	6	0	0	0	0	0	0	2	0	0
immunization	4	.2446	.2515	34.0	0	0	0	1	0	1	2	0	0	0	0	0	0	2	0	2	0	0	0	0	0	0	0	0	0
immunological	4	.0000	.0789	29.0	0	0	0	0	0	0	0	4	0	0	0	0	0	0	0	4	0	0	0	0	0	0	0	0	0
immured	2	.1717	.1142	30.6	0	0	0	1	0	0	1	0	1	0	0	1	0	0	0	0	0	0	0	0	0	0	0	0	0
imp	3	.1250	.1342	31.3	1	0	0	0	1	1	0	0	1	0	0	0	0	0	0	0	0	0	0	0	2	0	0	0	0
impact	77	.7218	11.260	50.5	2	0	5	6	15	13	32	4	5	4	0	3	0	5	0	16	4	0	0	1	1	4	11	23	0
impacted	2	.0000	.0394	26.0	0	0	0	0	2	0	0	0	0	0	0	0	0	0	0	2	0	0	0	0	0	0	0	0	0
impair	3	.2153	.1451	31.6	0	0	1	0	1	1	0	0	0	0	1	0	0	0	0	0	0	0	0	0	0	0	2	0	0
impaired	5	.4707	.5371	37.3	0	0	0	1	1	2	1	0	2	0	0	0	0	1	0	1	0	0	0	0	0	0	1	0	0
impalas	2	.0000	.0209	23.2	0	0	0	0	2	0	0	0	0	0	0	0	0	0	0	0	0	0	0	0	0	0	2	0	0
impart	3	.3768	.2437	33.9	0	0	0	0	1	0	1	1	0	0	0	0	0	0	0	0	1	0	0	0	0	1	0	1	0
imparted	7	.4187	.6103	37.9	0	0	1	0	2	1	3	0	0	0	2	1	0	0	0	0	0	0	1	0	1	2	0	0	0
impartial	4	.4818	.4128	36.2	0	0	0	0	0	2	1	1	0	0	0	0	0	1	0	1	0	0	0	0	0	1	0	1	0
impartially	2	.1787	.1174	30.7	0	0	0	0	1	0	1	0	1	0	0	0	0	0	0	0	0	0	0	0	1	0	0	0	0
impassable	10	.6153	1.2554	41.0	1	0	2	1	3	1	2	0	0	1	1	2	0	2	1	0	0	0	0	0	0	1	0	2	0
impassible	2	.2433	.1158	30.6	0	2	0	0	0	0	0	0	0	0	0	0	0	0	0	0	0	0	0	0	0	1	0	1	0
impassioned	5	.2177	.2519	34.0	0	0	0	0	2	0	3	0	0	0	0	0	0	0	0	0	3	0	0	0	0	0	0	2	0
impassive	4	.1919	.1864	32.7	0	0	0	0	3	0	1	0	0	0	0	3	0	0	0	0	0	0	0	0	1	0	0	0	0
impatience	14	.6006	1.7578	42.4	1	3	3	2	2	0	2	1	3	0	0	1	0	0	0	0	1	0	0	0	5	1	1	2	0
impatient	35	.7833	5.5495	47.4	4	5	3	7	9	4	2	1	10	5	1	3	2	1	1	0	1	0	0	0	3	2	0	6	0
impatiently	37	.6370	5.0417	47.0	9	9	2	7	3	4	2	1	20	0	1	2	0	1	0	0	0	0	0	0	3	7	0	3	0
impeached	7	.0000	.0733	28.6	0	0	7	0	0	0	0	0	0	0	0	0	0	0	0	0	0	0	0	0	0	0	7	0	0
impeachment	11	.2613	.7338	38.7	2	0	4	0	5	0	0	0	3	0	0	0	0	0	0	0	0	0	0	0	0	2	6	0	0
impeccable	2	.2442	.1134	30.5	0	0	0	0	0	1	1	0	0	1	0	0	0	0	0	0	0	0	0	0	0	0	0	1	0
impeccably	2	.2437	.1129	30.5	0	1	0	0	0	0	1	0	0	0	0	0	0	0	0	0	0	0	0	0	0	0	1	1	0
impede	2	.2437	.1129	30.5	0	0	0	0	0	1	1	0	0	0	0	0	0	0	0	0	0	0	0	0	0	0	1	1	0
impeded	3	.3370	.2430	33.9	0	0	0	1	0	2	0	0	1	0	0	1	0	0	0	0	0	0	0	0	0	0	1	0	0
impel	2	.2152	.1357	31.3	0	0	0	0	1	1	0	0	1	0	0	0	0	1	0	0	0	0	0	0	0	0	0	0	0
impelled	3	.3764	.2483	33.9	0	0	0	0	1	1	0	1	0	0	0	0	0	0	0	1	0	0	0	0	0	0	1	1	0
impending	9	.5236	.9730	39.9	0	2	0	2	1	2	2	0	0	1	0	3	0	0	0	0	1	0	0	0	3	0	0	1	0
impenetrable	7	.4685	.6938	38.4	0	0	0	1	2	2	1	1	0	0	1	2	0	2	0	1	0	0	0	0	0	0	1	0	0
imperative	13	.4288	1.1660	40.7	1	0	1	2	6	2	1	0	0	4	3	0	0	0	0	0	0	0	0	0	1	1	1	3	0
imperceptible	4	.4866	.4070	36.1	1	0	0	0	2	0	1	0	0	0	0	1	0	0	0	0	0	0	0	0	0	1	1	1	0
imperceptibly	3	.2027	.1376	31.4	0	1	0	0	1	0	1	0	0	0	0	0	0	0	0	0	0	1	0	0	0	0	2	0	0
imperfect	8	.5907	.9858	39.9	0	0	2	0	3	1	0	2	1	1	0	0	0	0	1	2	0	0	0	0	2	0	0	1	0
imperfections	5	.3661	.4112	36.1	0	0	0	1	2	1	1	0	1	0	0	0	0	0	0	0	0	0	0	1	0	0	2	1	0
imperfectly	2	.2437	.1129	30.5	0	0	0	0	1	0	1	0	0	0	0	0	0	0	0	0	0	0	0	0	0	0	1	1	0
imperial	10	.4942	1.0687	40.3	0	0	1	2	1	5	1	0	1	0	0	1	0	5	0	0	0	0	0	0	0	2	1	0	0
Imperial	18	.5783	2.1966	43.4	1	0	4	3	1	6	1	2	3	1	0	0	0	5	0	1	0	0	0	0	0	2	5	1	0
imperialism	3	.2425	.1816	32.6	0	0	0	0	0	3	0	0	0	0	0	0	0	2	0	0	0	0	0	0	0	0	0	1	0
imperious	4	.3437	.3043	34.8	0	0	0	0	0	2	2	0	0	2	0	1	0	1	0	0	0	0	0	0	0	0	0	0	0
imperiously	3	.1250	.1342	31.3	0	0	0	1	1	1	0	0	1	0	0	0	0	0	0	0	0	0	0	0	2	0	0	0	0
impersonal	7	.5337	.7658	38.8	0	0	0	0	1	3	2	1	0	1	1	0	0	0	0	0	2	0	0	0	1	1	0	1	0
impersonality	3	.1277	.1363	31.3	0	0	1	0	0	2	0	0	1	0	0	0	0	0	0	0	0	0	0	0	0	0	0	2	0
impersonally	2	.1160	.0650	28.1	0	0	0	0	1	0	1	0	0	0	1	0	0	0	0	1	0	0	0	0	0	0	0	0	0
impersonating	2	.2387	.1089	30.4	0	0	0	0	0	2	0	0	0	0	0	0	0	0	0	0	1	0	0	0	1	0	0	0	0
impervious	4	.1901	.1843	32.7	0	0	0	0	2	0	0	2	0	0	0	0	0	0	0	0	0	0	0	0	1	0	3	0	0
impetuous	3	.3385	.2445	33.9	0	0	2	1	0	0	0	0	1	0	0	0	0	0	0	0	0	0	0	0	1	0	1	0	0
impetus	8	.2938	.5278	37.2	0	0	2	0	4	0	2	0	0	0	0	0	0	0	0	0	0	0	0	0	0	2	5	1	0
impish	2	.2443	.1130	30.5	0	0	0	1	0	1	0	0	0	0	0	1	0	0	0	0	0	0	0	0	1	0	0	0	0
implacable	7	.5866	.8555	39.3	0	0	0	2	1	3	1	0	1	1	0	1	0	0	0	0	0	0	0	0	2	1	0	1	0
implanted	4	.1873	.1827	32.6	0	0	0	0	1	1	1	1	0	0	0	0	0	0	0	0	0	0	0	0	0	0	3	1	0
implement	9	.5518	1.0352	40.2	0	0	1	2	2	2	1	1	1	0	0	0	0	0	1	1	0	1	0	0	1	0	2	2	0
implements	9	.3791	.7406	38.7	0	3	0	0	2	2	1	1	0	1	0	1	0	2	0	0	0	0	0	0	0	0	5	0	0
implicated	3	.2321	.1635	32.1	0	0	1	0	1	1	0	0	0	0	0	0	0	0	0	0	0	0	0	0	0	0	1	2	0
implication	2	.2437	.1129	30.5	0	0	0	0	1	0	1	0	0	0	0	0	0	0	0	0	0	0	0	0	0	0	1	1	0
implications	10	.6208	1.2685	41.0	0	0	1	0	6	1	2	0	0	0	0	1	0	1	0	1	1	0	0	0	0	1	3	2	0
implicit	5	.5336	.5703	37.6	0	0	0	0	0	3	2	0	1	1	0	0	0	1	0	0	0	0	0	0	0	0	1	1	0
implied	13	.5360	1.4654	41.7	0	0	1	4	1	4	3	0	2	3	2	2	1	1	0	0	1	0	0	0	0	1	0	0	0
implies	15	.6022	1.8442	42.7	0	0	0	1	3	4	4	3	1	1	0	0	0	0	0	3	3	2	2	1	0	0	2	0	0
implored	2	.2337	.1157	30.6	0	1	0	0	0	1	0	0	0	0	0	0	0	1	0	0	0	0	0	0	1	0	0	0	0
imploring	3	.2261	.2131	33.3	0	0	1	1	0	1	0	0	2	0	0	0	0	0	0	0	0	0	0	0	1	0	0	0	0
imploringly	5	.2086	.3320	35.2	0	0	0	4	0	1	0	0	3	0	0	0	0	0	0	0	0	0	0	0	2	0	0	0	0
imply	11	.5795	1.3254	41.2	0	0	2	1	2	1	3	2	1	1	1	0	2	0	0	1	0	0	0	0	0	3	2	0	0
impolite	8	.4198	.7560	38.8	0	1	0	3	0	3	1	0	2	3	1	0	0	1	0	1	0	0	0	0	0	0	0	0	0
import	38	.5270	4.2570	46.3	3	0	9	7	7	7	5	0	2	1	0	0	0	22	0	1	2	0	0	0	0	2	7	1	0
importance	232	.8579	39.628	56.0	12	11	25	23	59	46	41	15	20	15	5	3	3	27	3	43	19	2	14	4	4	12	49	9	0
important	2588	.9326	477.62	66.8	278	370	396	374	481	352	283	54	397	195	34	55	81	638	37	393	113	43	95	54	41	132	185	94	1
Important	2	.0857	.0784	28.9	0	0	0	0	2	0	0	0	1	0	0	0	0	0	0	0	0	0	1	0	0	0	0	0	0
importantly	9	.6250	1.1937	40.8	1	1	0	3	3	1	0	0	4	0	0	0	0	0	1	0	1	0	0	0	1	1	1	0	0
importation	2	.2408	.1204	30.8	0	0	0	1	0	1	0	0	0	0	0	0	0	1	0	0	0	0	0	0	0	1	0	0	0
imported	56	.5391	6.3587	48.0	9	3	4	19	9	6	3	3	1	3	0	0	0	33	0	1	1	0	0	1	0	1	13	2	0
importers	3	.2425	.1816	32.6	0	0	0	0	1	0	1	1	0	0	0	0	0	2	0	0	0	0	0	0	0	0	0	1	0
importing	5	.3767	.4160	36.2	0	0	0	3	1	0	1	0	0	0	0	0	0	2	0	0	0	0	0	0	0	0	1	2	0
imports	35	.4899	3.6508	45.6	3	4	7	4	10	1	6	0	1	0	0	0	0	13	0	0	0	0	0	0	0	5	8	8	0
impose	8	.4643	.7918	39.0	0	0	1	1	5	1	0	0	0	0	0	0	0	2	0	0	0	0	0	0	0	3	2	1	0
imposed	24	.6431	3.1663	45.0	2	0	2	4	7	3	4	2	2	1	0	1	0	3	0	1	1	0	0	0	1	3	9	2	0
imposes	3	.3668	.2405	33.8	0	0	0	0	1	0	0	2	0	0	0	0	0	0	0	1	1	0	0	0	0	0	1	0	0

9H immerse
8C immersing
9Q immersion
6A immigrate
9Q imminence
7R imminent
7R immobile
XB immodest
9R immorality
XP Immortal
8A immunes
9H immunized
7H immunology
7Q immutable
7B Imogen
7B imoto
9P impairment
3Q impala
9J impalpable
7P imparting
9L imparts
7A impassively
XQ impasto
9D impediment
XR impediments
9Q imperfection
9Q imperialist
9D imperil
9C imperishable
8J impersonation
9Q impersonator
8N imperturbability
8F imperturbable
7R impetuosity
7Q impinge
XR implacably
XH implants
9F implemented
6A implicitly
9D implore
9Q imponderable
5P import-export
4A important-looking
8A importanter'n
7R importations
7R importuning
9D importunity

Word Type	F	D	U	SFI	3 Gr 3	4 Gr 4	5 Gr 5	6 Gr 6	7 Gr 7	8 Gr 8	9 Gr 9	X UnGr	A Read	B Eng & Gr	C Comp	D Lit	E Math	F Soc Stud	G Spell	H Sci	J Music	K Art	L Home Ec	M Shop	N Lib F	P Lib NF	Q Lib Ref	R Mag	S Rel
imposing	13	.7730	2.0274	43.1	0	0	0	1	4	4	2	2	2	1	0	1	0	1	0	1	1	0	0	0	1	1	2	2	0
imposition	2	.0000	.0215	23.3	0	0	0	0	1	0	1	0	0	0	0	2	0	0	0	0	0	0	0	0	0	0	0	0	0
impossibility	7	.5023	.7466	38.7	0	0	0	1	2	1	3	0	1	0	0	2	0	0	0	0	0	0	0	0	1	0	2	1	0
impossible	231	.8931	41.070	56.1	9	25	22	32	58	47	29	9	57	9	5	20	11	24	5	22	6	0	0	1	9	18	17	27	0
impossibly	2	.0000	.0243	23.9	0	0	0	0	1	0	1	0	0	0	0	0	0	0	0	0	0	0	0	0	0	0	0	2	0
impost	4	.0000	.0778	28.9	0	0	0	0	0	4	0	0	0	0	0	0	0	4	0	0	0	0	0	0	0	0	0	0	0
impotence	3	.3454	.2542	34.1	0	0	0	0	1	2	0	0	1	0	0	0	0	1	0	0	0	0	0	0	0	0	0	1	0
impoverished	2	.1814	.1187	30.7	0	0	0	0	1	0	1	0	1	0	0	0	0	0	0	0	0	0	0	0	0	0	0	1	0
impractical	8	.6058	1.0042	40.0	0	0	2	1	1	2	2	0	1	0	0	1	1	1	1	1	0	0	0	1	0	0	1	0	0
imprecise	3	.1823	.1405	31.5	0	0	0	0	2	1	0	0	0	0	0	0	0	1	0	0	0	0	0	0	0	0	2	0	0
impregnated	5	.4543	.4843	36.9	0	0	0	0	3	0	0	2	0	1	0	0	0	0	0	1	0	0	0	0	0	1	0	2	0
impress	18	.6652	2.4433	43.9	0	3	1	1	7	1	3	2	1	0	0	3	1	1	0	1	0	0	0	0	2	3	1	5	0
impressed	58	.8438	9.7717	49.9	4	1	7	8	16	13	8	1	9	2	0	6	0	6	2	2	4	3	1	1	4	8	7	3	0
impresses	2	.2376	.1088	30.4	0	0	0	1	0	1	0	0	0	0	0	0	0	0	1	0	0	0	0	0	0	0	0	1	0
impressing	2	.1170	.0651	28.1	0	0	0	0	1	1	0	0	0	0	1	0	0	1	0	0	0	0	0	0	0	0	0	0	0
impression	109	.7981	17.352	52.4	1	4	15	5	23	13	46	2	6	11	9	17	0	4	0	3	13	1	8	6	8	9	4	10	0
Impression	2	.0000	.0162	22.1	0	0	2	0	0	0	0	0	0	0	0	0	0	0	0	0	2	0	0	0	0	0	0	0	0
impressionable	3	.3450	.2505	34.0	0	0	1	0	0	1	0	1	1	0	0	0	0	0	0	0	0	0	0	0	1	1	0	0	0
impressionism	6	.1389	.2076	33.2	0	0	3	0	0	0	3	0	0	0	0	0	0	0	0	0	5	0	0	0	0	0	1	0	0
Impressionism	11	.3108	.7246	38.6	0	0	0	0	1	9	0	1	0	0	0	0	0	0	0	0	6	3	0	0	0	0	1	1	0
impressionist	5	.2915	.3213	35.1	0	0	0	1	0	2	2	0	0	0	0	0	0	0	0	0	3	0	0	0	0	1	1	0	0
Impressionist	2	.1696	.0749	28.7	0	0	0	0	0	1	1	0	0	0	0	0	0	0	0	0	1	1	0	0	0	0	0	0	0
impressionistic	4	.1534	.1534	31.9	0	0	1	0	1	2	0	0	0	0	0	0	0	0	0	0	3	0	0	0	0	1	0	0	0
Impressionistic	2	.0000	.0162	22.1	0	0	0	0	0	2	0	0	0	0	0	0	0	0	0	0	2	0	0	0	0	0	0	0	0
impressions	55	.6979	7.7479	48.9	1	0	6	2	14	6	26	0	5	2	8	7	0	2	0	2	4	1	1	6	2	5	8	2	0
impressive	48	.7779	7.4906	48.7	4	0	2	3	15	10	6	8	1	1	0	2	0	8	0	5	1	1	1	0	2	7	7	12	0
impressively	6	.3509	.5242	37.2	0	0	0	2	3	1	0	0	3	0	0	2	0	0	0	0	0	0	0	0	1	0	0	0	0
impressiveness	3	.3369	.2489	34.0	0	0	0	0	2	1	0	0	1	0	0	1	0	1	0	0	0	0	0	0	0	0	0	0	0
imprint	13	.6211	1.6581	42.2	0	1	0	4	1	4	3	0	2	0	0	1	0	0	0	0	1	0	1	2	1	1	3	1	0
imprinted	7	.5844	.8506	39.3	0	0	0	2	3	0	2	0	1	1	0	2	0	0	0	0	0	0	0	0	1	0	1	1	0
imprinting	3	.0000	.0314	25.0	0	0	0	0	3	0	0	0	0	0	0	0	0	0	0	0	0	0	0	0	0	0	3	0	0
imprints	3	.2028	.1988	33.0	1	0	0	2	0	0	0	0	2	0	0	0	0	0	0	0	1	0	0	0	0	0	0	0	0
imprison	6	.3772	.5070	37.1	0	0	2	1	2	1	0	0	1	0	0	1	0	0	0	0	0	0	0	0	0	0	3	1	0
imprisoned	27	.7167	3.9449	46.0	0	0	7	5	9	2	3	1	5	3	0	2	0	3	0	2	5	0	0	0	1	1	4	1	0
imprisonment	12	.5065	1.2616	41.0	0	0	5	0	4	1	2	0	0	0	0	3	0	0	0	0	0	0	0	0	3	1	4	1	0
improbable	2	.2278	.1128	30.5	0	0	0	0	2	0	0	0	0	0	0	0	0	0	0	1	0	0	0	0	0	0	1	0	0
impromptu	3	.2233	.1562	31.9	0	0	0	0	0	0	3	0	0	0	0	1	0	0	0	0	0	0	0	0	0	0	2	0	0
improper	43	.1589	1.8724	42.7	0	3	12	14	10	2	2	0	0	0	0	0	40	0	1	0	1	0	0	0	0	1	0	0	0
improperly	2	.2346	.1166	30.7	0	0	1	0	1	0	0	0	0	0	0	0	0	0	0	1	0	0	0	0	0	0	0	1	0
improve	201	.8161	32.879	55.2	18	14	26	31	45	26	37	4	24	34	2	5	0	49	2	28	10	1	16	4	1	3	10	12	0
improved	116	.8616	19.928	53.0	9	12	21	12	27	17	15	3	14	7	1	5	2	33	1	10	7	0	5	1	2	6	15	7	0
improvement	46	.8125	7.4840	48.7	0	3	2	2	17	9	10	3	4	4	0	4	1	7	0	5	0	0	2	1	2	2	5	9	0
Improvement	2	.2306	.1140	30.6	0	1	0	0	0	1	0	0	0	1	0	0	0	1	0	0	0	0	0	0	0	0	0	0	0
improvements	53	.6721	7.2814	48.6	5	4	5	7	17	10	5	0	4	3	0	2	0	17	0	2	10	0	0	0	2	1	8	4	0
improves	9	.5848	1.0906	40.4	0	1	1	1	3	1	0	2	1	1	0	0	0	1	0	1	0	1	1	0	0	0	1	2	0
improving	53	.7664	8.2108	49.1	5	1	9	6	7	12	12	1	8	8	0	2	0	13	2	5	0	0	4	1	0	2	4	4	0
improvisation	7	.0000	.0566	27.5	0	1	0	1	0	5	0	0	0	0	0	0	0	0	0	0	7	0	0	0	0	0	0	0	0
Improvisation	2	.0000	.0162	22.1	0	0	0	0	0	2	0	0	0	0	0	0	0	0	0	0	2	0	0	0	0	0	0	0	0
improvise	27	.1420	.9844	39.9	3	5	4	4	4	4	3	0	1	0	0	1	0	0	0	0	23	0	0	0	0	1	0	1	0
improvised	16	.3836	1.2937	41.1	1	0	2	5	4	2	1	1	0	0	0	1	0	0	0	0	10	1	0	0	0	0	0	4	0
improvises	4	.0000	.0323	25.1	0	0	1	1	0	2	0	0	0	0	0	0	0	0	0	0	4	0	0	0	0	0	0	0	0
improvising	4	.0000	.0323	25.1	1	0	0	1	0	1	1	0	0	0	0	0	0	0	0	0	4	0	0	0	0	0	0	0	0
imps	3	.3408	.2477	33.9	0	1	0	0	0	2	0	0	1	0	0	1	0	0	0	0	0	0	0	0	0	1	0	0	0
impudence	3	.2227	.1589	32.0	2	0	0	0	0	0	1	0	0	0	0	0	0	0	0	0	0	0	0	0	2	0	0	1	0
impudent	5	.3628	.3885	35.9	1	1	0	0	0	1	2	0	0	0	0	1	0	0	0	0	2	0	0	0	2	0	0	0	0
impulse	43	.7671	6.6786	48.2	0	2	6	6	8	13	6	2	7	4	1	2	0	0	0	15	0	1	0	0	5	3	2	3	0
impulses	44	.4145	4.1127	46.1	1	0	13	17	7	2	4	0	4	1	0	0	0	0	0	33	0	0	0	1	0	1	4	0	0
impulsive	2	.2401	.1133	30.5	0	0	1	0	0	0	1	0	0	0	0	0	0	0	0	0	0	0	0	0	0	1	1	0	0
impulsively	2	.2408	.1204	30.8	0	1	0	0	0	0	1	0	0	0	0	0	0	1	0	0	0	0	0	0	0	1	0	0	0
impunity	3	.2309	.1631	32.1	0	0	0	0	0	2	1	0	0	0	0	1	0	0	0	0	0	0	0	0	0	0	0	2	0
Impunity	3	.0000	.0328	25.2	0	3	0	0	0	0	0	0	0	3	0	0	0	0	0	0	0	0	0	0	0	0	0	0	0
impure	9	.4611	.9057	39.6	0	3	2	0	1	3	0	0	1	0	0	0	0	3	0	1	0	0	0	0	0	0	3	1	0
impurities	11	.5199	1.2077	40.8	0	0	3	1	1	4	2	0	0	0	0	0	0	4	0	3	0	0	0	1	0	1	2	0	0
impurity	6	.2942	.4422	36.5	1	0	0	0	0	3	2	0	1	0	0	0	0	0	0	4	0	0	0	0	0	0	1	0	0
imputation	2	.0000	.0914	29.6	0	0	0	0	1	1	0	0	2	0	0	0	0	0	0	0	0	0	0	0	0	0	0	0	0
in	99108	.9938	19366	82.9	14636	13995	12971	13202	18926	12579	10302	2497	18511	6346	1116	4451	8068	12274	5923	10752	4631	906	1612	1364	4081	6344	6768	5892	69
In	40	.4278	3.6634	45.6	5	3	5	8	12	5	1	1	4	1	0	1	0	2	0	0	24	1	0	0	1	1	0	5	0
IN	9	.3813	.7691	38.9	6	0	0	2	1	0	0	0	1	0	0	1	0	0	0	0	0	0	0	0	0	5	0	2	0
in-	5	.1531	.1872	32.7	0	0	0	0	3	1	1	0	0	1	0	0	0	0	4	0	0	0	0	0	0	0	0	0	0
in-between	9	.5542	1.0514	40.2	1	4	1	0	1	1	1	0	1	2	0	1	0	2	0	2	0	0	1	0	0	0	0	0	0
in-depth	2	.0000	.0243	23.9	0	0	0	0	1	0	1	0	0	0	0	0	0	0	0	0	0	0	0	0	0	0	0	2	0
in-doors	2	.2412	.1091	30.4	0	0	0	1	0	1	0	0	0	0	0	1	0	0	1	0	0	0	0	0	0	0	0	0	0
in-feed	5	.0000	.0126	21.0	0	0	0	0	0	0	5	0	0	0	0	0	0	0	0	0	0	0	0	5	0	0	0	0	0
in-laws	2	.2401	.1133	30.5	1	0	0	0	1	0	0	0	0	0	0	0	0	0	0	0	0	0	0	0	0	1	1	0	0
inability	6	.6199	.7598	38.8	0	0	1	0	2	2	1	0	0	1	0	0	0	0	1	1	0	0	0	0	0	1	1	1	0
inaccessible	7	.4927	.7488	38.7	0	0	0	1	3	0	1	2	1	0	0	0	0	1	0	2	0	0	0	0	0	1	2	0	0
inaccuracy	3	.3160	.2007	33.0	0	0	0	1	2	0	0	0	0	0	0	0	0	0	0	0	1	0	0	1	0	0	1	0	0
inaccurate	5	.4606	.4878	36.9	0	0	0	1	2	0	2	0	0	1	0	0	0	0	0	1	0	0	0	0	0	0	1	2	0
inaccurately	2	.1698	.1133	30.5	0	0	0	1	1	0	0	0	1	0	0	0	0	0	0	0	0	0	0	0	0	0	1	0	0
inactive	5	.3581	.3971	36.0	0	0	1	0	1	2	0	1	0	0	0	0	0	0	1	3	0	0	1	0	0	0	0	0	0
inactivity	2	.0000	.0064	18.1	0	0	0	0	1	0	1	0	0	0	0	0	0	0	0	0	0	0	2	0	0	0	0	0	0
inadequate	14	.6732	1.9412	42.9	0	0	1	0	7	3	3	0	2	0	0	0	0	4	0	2	0	0	1	0	1	1	1	2	0
inadvertently	5	.3270	.3578	35.5	0	0	0	0	4	0	1	0	0	0	0	1	0	0	0	0	0	0	0	0	0	0	3	1	0
inalienable	2	.2401	.1133	30.5	0	0	1	0	1	0	0	0	0	0	0	0	0	0	0	0	0	0	0	0	0	1	1	0	0
inanimate	7	.3050	.4773	36.8	0	0	0	0	6	0	1	0	0	2	0	0	0	1	0	0	0	0	0	0	0	0	4	0	0
inappropriate	8	.5074	.8694	39.4	0	0	0	0	3	3	2	0	2	0	0	0	0	0	2	0	0	0	1	0	0	0	1	2	0
inappropriately	2	.2442	.1134	30.5	0	0	0	0	0	1	1	0	0	1	0	0	0	0	0	0	0	0	0	0	0	0	0	1	0
inarticulate	4	.3816	.3310	35.2	0	0	2	0	0	1	1	0	0	0	0	1	0	0	0	0	0	0	0	0	0	2	1	0	0
inasmuch	8	.3856	.6676	38.2	0	0	0	0	6	0	2	0	1	0	1	0	0	0	0	0	0	0	0	2	4	0	0	0	0
inaudible	4	.3366	.3291	35.2	0	0	0	2	0	0	0	2	1	0	0	0	0	0	0	2	0	0	0	0	0	0	0	1	0
inaugural	13	.4354	1.2320	40.9	0	0	0	0	6	4	2	1	1	1	0	0	0	2	0	0	0	0	0	0	0	3	0	6	0
Inaugural	3	.2440	.1815	32.6	0	0	1	1	0	1	0	0	0	1	0	0	0	2	0	0	0	0	0	0	0	0	0	0	0
inaugurated	4	.3287	.2952	34.7	0	1	1	1	0	1	0	0	0	0	0	0	0	1	0	0	0	0	0	0	0	1	2	0	0
inaugurating	3	.2143	.1568	32.0	0	0	0	1	1	0	0	1	0	0	0	0	0	0	0	0	0	0	0	0	0	1	0	2	0
inauguration	9	.3793	.7841	38.9	0	0	1	0	1	6	1	0	1	0	0	0	0	6	0	0	1	0	0	0	0	0	0	1	0
Inauguration	5	.2304	.2767	34.4	0	0	1	0	1	0	3	0	0	0	0	0	0	0	0	0	0	0	0	0	0	2	0	3	0
inboard	2	.2441	.1127	30.5	0	0	0	0	0	1	1	0	0	0	0	0	0	0	0	0	0	0	0	0	1	0	1	0	0
inborn	19	.0683	.6525	38.1	0	4	1	10	3	0	1	0	2	0	0	0	0	0	0	17	0	0	0	0	0	0	0	0	0

8E impossibilities
5A Impossible
9A impostors
8F imposts
7A impotency
7N impotent
9R impounded
7R impoundments
9Q impracticable
9Q impregnable
8J Impressionists
8K Impressionists'
8R improvisational
8J improvision
9P impudently
8D impute
7D in-and-out
9R in-person
7R in-school
3P in-space
7D in-under
5G in'crease**
4C Ina
7H inactivation
9R inadequacy
9J inadequately
7G inadvisable
8Q inapplicable
9J inartistic
7G inattention
6A inattentiveness
8D inaudibly
7R inaugurals
XR inaugurate
8D inaugurates
9Q inauspicious

Word Type	F	D	U	SFI	3 Gr 3	4 Gr 4	5 Gr 5	6 Gr 6	7 Gr 7	8 Gr 8	9 Gr 9	X UnGr	A Read	B Eng & Gr	C Comp	D Lit	E Math	F Soc Stud	G Spell	H Sci	J Music	K Art	L Home Ec	M Shop	N Lib F	P Lib NF	Q Lib Ref	R Mag	S Rel
inbred	8	.0000	.1577	32.0	0	0	0	0	0	0	0	8	0	0	0	0	0	0	0	8	0	0	0	0	0	0	0	0	0
inbreeding	5	.0000	.0608	27.8	0	0	0	0	5	0	0	0	0	0	0	0	0	0	0	0	0	0	0	0	0	0	0	5	0
Inc	29	.3132	2.0481	43.1	0	1	2	0	4	10	5	7	1	2	0	0	0	1	0	0	1	0	0	0	0	0	2	22	0
Inc's**	3	.0000	.0365	25.6	0	0	0	0	0	3	0	0	0	0	0	0	0	0	0	0	0	0	0	0	0	0	0	3	0
Inca	48	.5509	5.7396	47.6	0	4	24	9	9	0	1	1	16	0	0	0	0	16	0	0	5	0	0	0	0	0	4	7	0
incalculable	4	.4708	.3982	36.0	0	0	1	0	2	0	1	0	0	1	0	0	0	0	0	1	1	0	0	0	0	1	0	0	0
incandescence	3	.2260	.1580	32.0	0	0	1	0	2	0	0	0	0	0	0	2	0	0	0	0	0	0	0	0	0	0	1	0	0
incandescent	7	.2395	.4133	36.2	0	0	1	2	1	1	2	0	0	0	0	0	0	0	0	4	0	0	0	0	0	0	3	0	0
incapable	8	.5843	.9641	39.8	0	2	1	0	1	2	0	2	0	0	0	1	0	1	0	1	0	0	0	0	0	1	2	2	0
Incas	19	.5864	2.3711	43.7	0	1	8	2	7	0	1	0	5	1	0	0	0	7	0	0	1	0	0	0	0	0	3	2	0
incendiary	5	.1634	.2733	34.4	0	0	3	0	2	0	0	0	2	0	0	0	0	0	0	0	0	0	0	0	0	3	0	0	0
incense	8	.4869	.8155	39.1	1	0	0	2	3	1	1	0	0	0	0	0	0	2	0	0	3	0	0	0	1	0	1	1	0
incentive	4	.4846	.4028	36.1	0	1	1	0	0	1	1	0	0	0	0	0	0	0	1	0	0	0	0	0	1	0	1	1	0
incentives	3	.2321	.1635	32.1	0	0	0	0	0	0	2	1	0	0	0	0	0	0	0	0	0	0	0	0	0	0	1	2	0
inception	3	.3766	.2480	33.9	0	0	0	0	1	2	0	0	0	0	0	0	0	1	0	0	0	0	0	0	1	0	1	0	0
incessant	9	.3889	.7568	38.8	3	2	0	1	1	1	1	0	0	0	0	0	0	1	0	0	0	0	0	0	5	0	1	2	0
incessantly	4	.2969	.2888	34.6	0	0	1	1	1	1	0	0	1	0	0	2	0	0	0	0	0	0	0	0	1	0	0	0	0
inch	590	.6582	79.481	59.0	62	54	89	33	137	66	129	20	57	16	1	8	195	14	5	104	0	2	81	45	7	14	17	24	0
inch-long	5	.4274	.4648	36.7	0	2	0	0	1	2	0	0	1	0	1	0	0	0	1	0	0	0	0	0	1	0	1	0	0
Inchcape	9	.0000	.1303	31.1	0	0	9	0	0	0	0	0	0	0	0	0	0	0	0	0	0	0	0	0	0	9	0	0	0
inched	11	.5435	1.3469	41.3	1	3	2	1	3	1	0	0	7	1	0	0	0	1	0	0	0	0	0	0	0	1	0	1	0
inches	846	.7714	131.53	61.2	127	103	113	104	154	129	85	31	71	15	4	8	351	56	3	118	1	3	17	33	14	50	50	52	0
incidence	4	.3512	.3114	34.9	0	0	0	0	2	1	0	1	0	0	0	0	0	0	0	1	0	0	0	0	0	0	1	2	0
incident	70	.5979	8.7319	49.4	3	1	5	10	21	22	8	0	17	9	12	8	0	3	0	0	2	2	0	0	4	2	8	3	0
incidental	4	.3192	.2719	34.3	0	0	1	1	2	0	0	0	0	0	0	0	0	0	0	0	1	1	0	0	0	0	2	0	0
incidentally	12	.4988	1.2410	40.9	1	0	1	0	4	4	0	2	0	0	1	0	0	0	1	0	0	0	0	0	0	1	3	6	0
incidents	34	.6756	4.6972	46.7	0	1	1	2	15	7	8	0	6	2	4	2	0	2	0	0	1	1	0	0	5	1	3	7	0
incinerators	2	.0000	.0394	26.0	0	0	0	2	0	0	0	0	0	0	0	0	0	0	0	2	0	0	0	0	0	0	0	0	0
incision	4	.4809	.4076	36.1	0	0	0	1	0	0	2	1	0	0	0	1	0	0	0	1	0	0	0	0	0	1	0	1	0
incisive	3	.3350	.2478	33.9	0	0	0	0	0	1	2	0	1	0	0	0	0	1	0	0	0	0	0	0	0	0	1	0	0
incisor	5	.2444	.3032	34.8	0	0	2	0	3	0	0	0	0	0	0	0	0	0	0	3	0	0	0	0	0	0	0	2	0
incisors	8	.2278	.4514	36.5	0	0	4	1	3	0	0	0	0	0	0	0	0	0	0	4	0	0	0	0	0	0	4	0	0
inclination	17	.6545	2.3045	43.6	0	0	2	4	2	8	1	0	3	0	0	0	0	3	0	3	0	0	0	1	4	1	1	1	0
inclinations	2	.2427	.1152	30.6	0	0	1	1	0	0	0	0	0	0	0	0	0	0	0	0	0	0	0	0	1	1	0	0	0
incline	9	.5061	.9783	39.9	1	0	1	3	0	2	2	0	2	1	0	3	0	0	0	0	0	0	0	0	2	0	1	0	0
inclined	69	.5024	7.3071	48.6	4	10	5	14	6	7	22	1	5	3	0	0	0	3	1	20	1	1	0	17	3	3	3	9	0
inclosed	3	.3408	.2477	33.9	1	0	0	0	0	2	0	0	1	0	0	1	0	0	0	0	0	0	0	0	0	1	0	0	0
include	483	.8497	81.573	59.1	20	37	88	54	99	72	99	14	17	65	19	6	13	65	22	54	43	7	42	14	2	16	75	23	0
included	218	.8857	38.314	55.8	6	25	27	25	43	43	46	3	21	24	6	4	18	30	4	7	17	4	12	9	2	13	33	14	0
includes	271	.8445	45.581	56.6	5	20	49	37	68	37	48	7	8	20	11	2	5	71	11	40	21	1	7	12	0	7	35	20	0
including	278	.8754	48.329	56.8	10	15	48	38	66	37	51	13	14	11	1	12	16	54	5	14	16	2	6	8	2	22	53	42	0
inclusion	7	.5680	.8161	39.1	0	0	1	0	0	2	2	2	0	0	0	0	1	1	0	0	1	0	1	0	0	0	1	2	0
inclusive	3	.0000	.0449	26.5	0	0	0	0	0	0	3	0	0	0	0	0	3	0	0	0	0	0	0	0	0	0	0	0	0
income	209	.6642	28.313	54.5	22	0	14	11	22	25	101	14	6	6	0	3	48	53	0	1	1	0	15	0	0	7	36	33	0
income-tax	2	.2433	.1158	30.6	1	0	0	0	0	0	1	0	0	0	0	0	0	0	0	0	0	0	0	0	0	1	0	1	0
incomes	27	.5474	3.1127	44.9	5	0	3	0	4	4	11	0	1	0	0	0	1	14	0	1	0	0	1	0	0	0	3	6	0
incoming	16	.6027	1.9920	43.0	2	0	0	1	5	3	3	2	0	1	0	0	0	0	0	8	0	0	0	1	1	1	1	3	0
incomparable	2	.2401	.1133	30.5	0	0	1	0	1	0	0	0	0	0	0	0	0	0	0	0	0	0	0	0	0	1	1	0	0
incompatible	2	.2401	.1133	30.5	0	0	1	0	0	1	0	0	0	0	0	0	0	0	0	0	0	0	0	0	0	1	1	0	0
incompetence	2	.2437	.1129	30.5	0	0	0	0	1	1	0	0	0	0	0	0	0	0	0	0	0	0	0	0	0	0	1	1	0
incomplete	47	.7504	7.1872	48.6	4	4	8	7	18	5	1	0	14	10	0	0	3	0	4	6	5	0	1	1	0	1	2	0	0
incompletely	2	.0000	.0394	26.0	0	0	1	1	0	0	0	0	0	0	0	0	0	0	0	2	0	0	0	0	0	0	0	0	0
incomprehensible	6	.4244	.5403	37.3	0	0	0	1	2	1	2	0	0	0	0	3	0	0	0	0	0	0	0	0	0	1	1	1	0
incompressible	3	.2445	.1818	32.6	0	0	0	0	1	0	2	0	0	0	0	0	0	0	0	2	0	0	0	0	0	0	1	0	0
inconceivable	2	.2407	.1090	30.4	0	0	0	0	0	1	1	0	0	1	0	0	0	0	0	0	1	0	0	0	0	0	0	0	0
incongruity	2	.1717	.1142	30.6	0	0	0	0	0	1	1	0	1	0	0	1	0	0	0	0	0	0	0	0	0	0	0	0	0
incongruous	8	.3388	.5929	37.7	0	0	0	1	1	4	1	1	0	0	0	4	0	0	0	0	0	0	0	0	1	0	0	3	0
inconsequential	2	.0000	.0243	23.9	0	0	0	0	2	0	0	0	0	0	0	0	0	0	0	0	0	0	0	0	0	0	0	2	0
inconsiderate	5	.1848	.2301	33.6	0	0	0	0	0	1	0	4	0	1	0	0	0	0	0	0	0	0	0	0	0	0	0	4	0
inconsistent	8	.2740	.5153	37.1	0	0	1	1	0	0	6	0	0	0	0	0	6	0	0	0	0	0	0	0	0	1	0	1	0
inconspicuous	7	.4536	.6761	38.3	0	0	1	0	3	0	2	1	0	0	0	0	0	0	0	3	0	0	1	0	0	0	2	1	0
inconstant	2	.2446	.1122	30.5	0	0	0	0	0	1	1	0	0	0	0	1	0	0	0	0	0	0	0	0	0	0	1	0	0
inconvenience	4	.3686	.3350	35.2	0	0	0	2	0	0	2	0	1	1	0	0	0	0	0	0	0	0	1	0	1	0	0	0	0
inconvenient	6	.4719	.6387	38.1	0	2	1	0	0	3	0	0	2	0	0	0	1	2	0	0	0	0	0	0	0	0	1	0	0
incorporate	6	.4315	.5418	37.3	0	0	0	0	5	0	1	0	0	0	1	1	0	0	0	0	0	0	0	0	0	0	2	2	0
incorporated	19	.5006	1.9843	43.0	0	0	3	0	1	12	2	1	0	1	0	0	0	3	0	0	2	0	0	0	0	1	9	3	0
incorporates	2	.2437	.1129	30.5	0	0	1	0	1	0	0	0	0	0	0	0	0	0	0	0	0	0	0	0	0	0	1	1	0
incorporating	2	.1696	.0749	28.7	0	0	0	0	0	2	0	0	0	0	0	0	0	0	0	0	1	1	0	0	0	0	0	0	0
incorrect	37	.5843	4.4501	46.5	0	1	3	5	12	5	11	0	2	17	1	0	9	1	5	0	1	0	0	1	0	0	0	0	0
incorrectly	17	.4569	1.6279	42.1	0	3	0	6	3	3	2	0	0	7	0	0	3	0	5	0	0	0	0	0	0	1	1	0	0
increase	244	.8962	43.379	56.4	6	28	16	26	64	43	50	11	13	12	5	4	19	43	3	56	8	1	4	6	5	7	28	30	0
increased	223	.9052	40.046	56.0	9	9	30	23	62	36	50	4	29	6	2	9	12	44	1	24	10	1	3	7	8	16	33	18	0
increases	102	.7039	14.567	51.6	2	8	7	17	24	20	21	3	5	5	1	0	3	4	0	35	5	0	2	10	1	1	10	20	0
increasing	132	.8879	23.277	53.7	5	6	18	12	33	27	23	8	12	4	1	6	4	21	0	21	10	1	3	2	1	10	20	16	0
increasingly	80	.7592	12.233	50.9	1	0	4	5	19	21	23	7	5	2	2	0	1	15	0	7	6	0	2	0	0	9	14	17	0
incredible	37	.7270	5.4380	47.4	1	3	5	3	12	7	4	2	4	1	1	4	0	1	2	0	1	0	0	0	1	4	8	10	0
incredibly	19	.6353	2.4856	44.0	1	0	3	1	6	6	1	1	2	0	0	3	0	1	0	2	0	0	0	0	1	2	5	3	0
incredulity	4	.2700	.2756	34.4	0	0	0	1	0	0	2	1	1	0	0	2	0	0	0	1	0	0	0	0	0	0	0	0	0
incredulously	4	.2954	.2881	34.6	0	0	0	0	1	2	0	1	1	0	0	2	0	0	0	0	0	0	0	0	0	0	0	1	0
incrusted	2	.2443	.1130	30.5	0	0	0	0	1	1	0	0	0	0	0	1	0	0	0	0	0	0	0	0	1	0	0	0	0
incubate	2	.0000	.0209	23.2	0	0	0	0	2	0	0	0	0	0	0	0	0	0	0	0	0	0	0	0	0	0	2	0	0
incubation	8	.2786	.5075	37.1	0	0	0	0	6	0	0	2	0	0	0	0	0	0	0	1	0	0	0	0	0	0	5	2	0
incubator	3	.1813	.1402	31.5	0	0	0	0	2	0	0	1	0	0	0	0	0	0	0	1	0	0	0	0	0	0	2	0	0
incumbent	6	.5406	.6739	38.3	0	0	1	0	2	2	1	0	0	0	0	1	0	1	0	1	0	0	0	0	0	1	1	2	0
incurred	4	.4802	.4047	36.1	0	0	0	0	1	1	2	0	0	0	0	1	0	1	0	0	0	0	0	0	1	0	1	0	0
Ind	3	.2321	.1635	32.1	0	0	0	0	2	0	0	1	0	0	0	0	0	0	0	0	0	0	0	0	0	0	1	2	0
indebted	5	.5594	.5787	37.6	0	0	0	0	2	1	2	0	0	1	0	1	0	1	0	0	0	0	0	0	0	1	1	0	0
indecent	2	.1814	.1187	30.7	0	0	1	0	0	1	0	0	1	0	0	0	0	0	0	0	0	0	0	0	0	0	0	1	0
indecision	5	.3375	.4157	36.2	0	0	0	1	3	1	0	0	2	0	0	0	0	0	0	0	0	0	0	0	2	0	0	1	0
indecisive	3	.3674	.2406	33.8	0	0	0	0	0	3	0	0	0	0	0	0	0	1	0	0	1	0	0	0	0	0	1	0	0
indeed	423	.8385	71.222	58.5	48	55	48	63	84	48	49	28	119	9	1	43	4	21	2	35	12	0	1	1	42	40	43	50	0
indefinite	38	.5105	4.0175	46.0	11	3	3	5	3	8	5	0	0	23	0	0	0	2	1	2	5	0	0	2	0	1	2	0	0
indefinitely	22	.6651	2.9724	44.7	1	1	0	0	7	8	4	1	0	0	0	0	10	0	0	3	1	0	1	1	1	0	3	2	0

5F Inca's
9Q Incan
4A incantations
7R incapacitated
8F incarceration
7N incarnation
4S Incarnation
6A incautiously
9P incense-permeated
7A incensed
8Q incertain
9D Incestuous
7R Inch
7N inch-by-inch
8N inch-square
7R inching
6R inchoate
6H incinerator
9M incised
9Q incisions
5Q incited
8N incitement
9Q inclemencies
9D inclemency
4N inclement
5Q inclined-type
8D inclines
5P inclosure
8D incoherent
8Q incombustible
8F Income
7N incommunicable
7Q incommunicado
7H incomparably
7A incompetent
7R incompetently
5P incomprehension
7Q incompressibility
7H inconceivably
XB inconclusive
6P incongruously
6Q inconsistencies
7Q inconspicuously
8A incontinently
XH inconveniences
8F inconveniencing
8F Increase
5G increase'**
3P increaseth
4H incrustation
7Q incrustations
7Q incubating
7Q incubations
9D incur
9R incurable
6A incurably
9Q incurious
9H incurrent
7A incurring
7J Ind'ans
7A indebtedness
7D indecencies
7R indecipherable
3A Indeed
9Q indefatigably
6B indefinites

Word Type	F	D	U	SFI	3 Gr 3	4 Gr 4	5 Gr 5	6 Gr 6	7 Gr 7	8 Gr 8	9 Gr 9	X UnGr	A Read	B Eng & Gr	C Comp	D Lit	E Math	F Soc Stud	G Spell	H Sci	J Music	K Art	L Home Ec	M Shop	N Lib F	P Lib NF	Q Lib Ref	R Mag	S Rel
indelible	2	.2441	.1127	30.5	1	0	0	0	0	0	1	0	0	0	0	0	0	0	0	0	0	0	0	0	1	0	1	0	0
indelicate	2	.1814	.1187	30.7	0	0	0	0	1	0	1	0	1	0	0	0	0	0	0	0	0	0	0	0	0	0	0	1	0
indent	12	.1825	.5331	37.3	6	2	0	0	2	0	2	0	0	10	0	0	0	0	2	0	0	0	0	0	0	0	0	0	0
indented	23	.3208	1.6397	42.1	8	3	1	3	7	0	1	0	0	16	0	1	0	3	0	0	0	0	0	0	0	1	2	0	0
indenting	6	.2434	.3298	35.2	2	2	0	0	1	0	1	0	0	5	0	0	0	0	0	0	0	1	0	0	0	0	0	0	0
indenture	3	.2120	.1548	31.9	0	0	2	1	0	0	0	0	0	0	0	0	0	0	0	0	0	0	0	0	2	1	0	0	0
indentured	10	.4969	1.0598	40.3	0	1	1	1	7	0	0	0	0	0	0	0	0	6	0	0	0	0	0	0	1	1	1	1	0
independence	161	.6114	20.419	53.1	17	7	27	31	36	24	18	1	6	3	0	0	0	87	1	0	6	1	0	0	1	23	22	11	0
Independence	71	.6653	9.7438	49.9	7	10	15	9	6	17	5	2	8	4	0	1	1	37	1	0	4	0	0	0	1	4	4	6	0
independent	161	.7558	24.522	53.9	5	6	22	26	41	33	24	4	8	11	5	2	0	53	1	7	14	0	1	0	2	11	32	14	0
Independent	5	.3742	.4184	36.2	0	0	1	0	0	3	0	1	0	0	0	0	0	3	0	0	0	0	0	0	0	0	1	1	0
independently	18	.5805	2.1491	43.3	0	1	1	4	6	1	4	1	0	1	0	0	1	1	0	3	3	0	0	0	0	0	6	3	0
independents	3	.3390	.2450	33.9	0	0	0	0	1	1	0	1	1	0	0	0	0	0	0	0	0	0	0	0	0	0	1	1	0
indescribable	3	.1250	.1342	31.3	0	0	0	0	3	0	0	0	1	0	0	0	0	0	0	0	0	0	0	0	2	0	0	0	0
indescribably	2	.1494	.1045	30.2	0	0	0	0	1	1	0	0	1	0	0	0	0	0	0	0	1	0	0	0	0	0	0	0	0
indestructible	3	.2181	.1541	31.9	0	0	0	0	3	0	0	0	0	0	0	0	0	0	0	0	0	0	0	0	1	0	2	0	0
indeterminate	2	.2433	.1158	30.6	0	0	1	0	0	0	1	0	0	0	0	0	0	0	0	0	0	0	0	0	0	1	0	1	0
index	91	.7330	13.463	51.3	2	44	9	6	5	12	12	1	7	21	0	0	10	8	1	3	12	0	2	0	1	2	16	8	0
Index	9	.2255	.5212	37.2	0	4	3	2	0	0	0	0	0	2	0	0	0	7	0	0	0	0	0	0	0	0	0	0	0
indexed	2	.0000	.0389	25.9	0	2	0	0	0	0	0	0	0	0	0	0	0	2	0	0	0	0	0	0	0	0	0	0	0
indexes	9	.2568	.5583	37.5	1	6	0	0	1	0	1	0	1	0	0	0	0	1	0	0	0	0	0	0	0	0	6	1	0
India	304	.6675	41.746	56.2	14	67	23	60	76	37	23	4	23	9	0	3	3	175	3	6	3	11	1	0	11	15	29	12	0
India-Pakistan	2	.0000	.0389	25.9	0	0	0	2	0	0	0	0	0	0	0	0	0	2	0	0	0	0	0	0	0	0	0	0	0
India's	7	.1931	.3682	35.7	0	0	0	1	3	1	2	0	0	0	0	0	0	6	0	0	0	0	0	0	0	0	1	0	0
Indian	1044	.8729	182.15	62.6	237	258	156	105	174	65	24	25	325	33	11	113	6	160	51	12	33	16	0	0	69	116	46	53	0
Indian's	12	.5344	1.4407	41.6	3	4	3	1	1	0	0	0	7	0	0	1	0	1	0	0	0	0	0	0	2	1	0	0	0
Indiana	53	.6433	7.0299	48.5	4	13	8	9	9	6	3	1	6	1	0	1	2	10	0	0	1	0	0	0	0	11	11	10	0
Indianapolis	17	.5928	2.0979	43.2	0	3	0	0	4	1	2	7	2	0	0	1	2	0	0	0	1	0	0	0	0	7	1	3	0
indians	2	.0000	.0219	23.4	0	0	1	0	0	0	1	0	0	2	0	0	0	0	0	0	0	0	0	0	0	0	0	0	0
Indians	1283	.7991	207.77	63.2	331	334	242	128	135	90	14	9	389	26	3	48	4	402	19	8	32	17	0	0	62	166	60	47	0
Indians'	23	.5258	2.7214	44.3	7	5	3	3	4	1	0	0	12	0	0	0	0	5	0	0	0	0	0	0	1	4	0	1	0
indicate	275	.8661	47.277	56.7	6	12	17	27	81	66	63	3	10	53	12	4	55	8	20	26	18	2	11	9	3	9	17	18	0
indicated	247	.7911	39.067	55.9	2	9	23	31	57	48	72	5	8	16	5	3	94	6	43	9	13	0	6	10	4	7	11	12	0
indicates	161	.8270	26.521	54.2	1	23	10	9	43	29	46	0	4	17	10	1	23	19	7	20	28	1	6	4	0	2	12	7	0
indicating	44	.8116	7.1260	48.5	1	1	6	6	12	4	12	2	2	5	0	2	2	0	1	5	2	0	2	3	3	5	7	5	0
indication	30	.7491	4.5297	46.6	0	1	3	0	12	6	6	2	3	1	2	1	0	0	0	4	3	0	0	1	1	4	5	5	0
indications	12	.5865	1.4608	41.6	0	0	0	1	3	3	4	1	1	0	0	1	0	1	0	2	1	1	0	0	0	1	0	4	0
indicative	3	.2159	.1532	31.9	0	0	0	1	0	1	1	0	0	0	0	0	0	0	0	0	0	0	0	0	0	0	2	1	0
indicator	7	.3368	.5462	37.4	0	0	1	0	5	0	1	0	1	1	0	0	0	0	0	1	0	0	0	0	0	0	0	4	0
indicators	13	.4764	1.3194	41.2	0	0	3	7	0	0	3	0	1	6	0	0	2	0	0	1	0	0	0	0	0	0	1	2	0
indictment	2	.2446	.1123	30.5	0	0	0	0	1	0	1	0	0	1	0	0	0	0	0	0	0	0	0	0	0	0	1	0	0
Indies	80	.5744	9.6488	49.8	7	5	23	17	15	9	4	0	4	1	0	0	0	49	0	3	6	0	1	0	0	6	8	2	0
indifference	10	.6153	1.3070	41.2	0	0	1	2	5	0	2	0	4	1	0	0	0	0	0	0	0	0	0	0	2	1	1	1	0
indifferent	24	.6634	3.2943	45.2	1	0	2	3	8	3	6	1	7	0	2	4	0	1	0	0	1	0	2	0	2	3	0	2	0
indifferently	4	.3030	.2949	34.7	1	0	0	1	2	0	0	0	1	0	0	0	0	0	0	0	0	0	0	0	2	0	0	1	0
indigenous	7	.4616	.6819	38.3	0	0	3	0	2	0	1	1	0	0	0	1	0	0	0	0	0	0	0	0	0	3	2	1	0
indigestible	4	.3957	.3394	35.3	0	0	1	1	1	0	1	0	0	0	0	0	0	0	0	1	0	0	1	0	1	0	0	1	0
indigestion	2	.0000	.0064	18.1	0	0	0	0	1	0	1	0	0	0	0	0	0	0	0	0	0	0	2	0	0	0	0	0	0
indignant	13	.6220	1.7124	42.3	1	3	1	1	6	0	0	1	5	0	0	1	0	0	0	0	0	0	0	0	2	2	1	2	0
indignantly	11	.5844	1.3841	41.4	1	1	3	1	2	0	2	1	5	1	1	1	0	0	0	0	0	0	0	0	1	1	0	1	0
indignation	13	.6485	1.7241	42.4	0	2	1	1	4	0	4	1	1	3	0	2	0	1	0	0	0	0	0	0	3	1	1	1	0
indigo	11	.4677	1.1076	40.4	1	1	0	4	1	1	1	2	0	0	0	0	0	2	0	6	0	1	0	0	0	0	1	1	0
indios	2	.0000	.0215	23.3	0	0	0	0	2	0	0	0	0	0	0	2	0	0	0	0	0	0	0	0	0	0	0	0	0
indirect	40	.7288	5.8675	47.7	0	2	0	3	12	12	11	0	1	17	1	2	2	0	2	7	0	0	1	1	1	0	3	2	0
indirectly	24	.7129	3.4972	45.4	0	2	3	3	3	6	5	2	4	3	0	2	0	3	2	5	0	0	0	0	0	2	3	0	0
indiscriminate	3	.0000	.0365	25.6	0	0	0	0	2	1	0	0	0	0	0	0	0	0	0	0	0	0	0	0	0	0	0	3	0
indiscriminately	2	.2405	.1205	30.8	0	0	0	0	2	0	0	0	0	0	0	0	0	0	0	1	0	0	0	0	0	1	0	0	0
indispensable	10	.5878	1.2128	40.8	0	0	1	2	3	1	1	2	0	0	1	0	0	1	0	3	0	0	0	0	1	1	2	1	0
indisputable	2	.0000	.0243	23.9	0	0	0	0	1	0	0	1	0	0	0	0	0	0	0	0	0	0	0	0	0	0	0	2	0
indistinct	3	.3394	.2451	33.9	0	0	0	0	1	1	1	0	1	0	0	1	0	0	0	0	0	0	0	0	1	0	0	0	0
individual	278	.8711	48.086	56.8	5	17	26	13	88	54	49	26	11	15	4	9	3	27	11	47	27	4	12	1	4	13	57	33	0
individual's	8	.4837	.8126	39.1	1	0	2	0	3	0	2	0	0	0	0	0	0	1	1	0	0	0	0	0	0	1	1	4	0
individualism	5	.5389	.5772	37.6	0	0	1	0	2	1	0	1	1	0	0	0	0	1	0	0	0	0	0	0	1	1	0	1	0
individualistic	2	.2401	.1133	30.5	0	0	1	0	0	1	0	0	0	0	0	0	0	0	0	0	0	0	0	0	0	1	1	0	0
individuality	13	.4422	1.2024	40.8	0	0	1	1	2	3	4	2	0	0	0	0	0	0	0	2	4	0	2	0	0	0	5	0	0
individually	16	.6492	2.1114	43.2	1	1	1	0	3	4	4	2	0	0	0	0	0	3	1	1	1	0	0	1	0	1	5	3	0
individuals	85	.7736	13.198	51.2	2	2	5	6	34	8	23	5	3	6	0	2	1	13	0	10	1	0	3	2	3	6	23	12	0
indivisible	10	.5538	1.1678	40.7	1	1	1	3	0	1	3	0	1	1	0	0	0	0	0	4	2	0	0	0	0	1	0	1	0
Indo-European	19	.1851	.8589	39.3	0	0	0	0	11	4	4	0	0	15	0	0	0	0	0	0	0	0	0	0	0	0	4	0	0
Indo-Pacific	3	.1927	.1491	31.7	0	0	0	2	0	0	1	0	0	0	0	0	0	0	0	1	0	0	0	0	0	0	0	2	0
Indochina	6	.2062	.3286	35.2	1	0	0	4	1	0	0	0	0	0	0	0	0	5	0	0	0	0	0	0	0	0	1	0	0
Indochinese	2	.2437	.1129	30.5	0	0	0	0	1	1	0	0	0	0	0	0	0	0	0	0	0	0	0	0	0	0	1	1	0
indomitable	5	.2800	.3594	35.6	0	0	0	0	4	1	0	0	2	0	1	0	0	0	0	0	0	0	0	0	2	0	0	0	0
Indonesia	35	.4583	3.4880	45.4	2	0	4	10	13	2	3	1	1	0	0	0	0	23	0	1	2	0	0	0	0	0	4	4	0
Indonesian	6	.3626	.4817	36.8	0	0	1	2	2	1	0	0	0	0	0	0	0	3	0	0	2	0	0	0	0	0	1	0	0
Indonesians	2	.2285	.1129	30.5	1	0	0	0	1	0	0	0	0	0	0	0	0	1	0	0	0	0	0	0	0	0	1	0	0
indoor	10	.5648	1.1785	40.7	1	0	1	3	2	1	2	0	1	1	0	1	0	0	1	0	0	0	0	0	0	4	0	2	0
indoors	57	.8150	9.3708	49.7	14	9	8	10	8	5	3	0	17	1	1	3	0	4	1	12	1	2	1	2	10	0	0	2	0
induce	12	.4851	1.2364	40.9	0	0	0	0	4	4	3	1	1	0	0	0	0	0	2	2	0	0	0	0	0	0	4	3	0
induced	28	.6739	3.8367	45.8	0	1	0	4	11	4	6	2	1	1	0	2	0	1	0	6	0	0	0	2	2	1	6	6	0
inducement	2	.1717	.1142	30.6	0	0	0	1	0	0	1	0	1	0	0	1	0	0	0	0	0	0	0	0	0	0	0	0	0
inducements	2	.0000	.0243	23.9	0	0	0	0	0	0	2	0	0	0	0	0	0	0	0	0	0	0	0	0	0	0	0	2	0
induces	2	.1249	.0685	28.4	0	0	0	0	0	1	0	1	0	0	0	0	0	0	0	1	0	0	0	1	0	0	0	0	0
inductance	2	.0000	.0050	17.0	0	0	0	0	0	2	0	0	0	0	0	0	0	0	0	0	0	0	0	2	0	0	0	0	0
induction	13	.3401	.9914	40.0	0	0	0	4	7	2	0	0	0	0	0	0	0	0	0	5	0	0	0	0	0	0	6	2	0
inductive	3	.0000	.0449	26.5	0	0	0	0	0	3	0	0	0	0	0	0	3	0	0	0	0	0	0	0	0	0	0	0	0
indulge	5	.3923	.4350	36.4	0	0	0	0	0	1	4	0	1	2	0	1	0	0	0	0	0	0	1	0	0	0	0	0	0
indulged	4	.4870	.4074	36.1	0	1	0	1	0	0	1	1	0	1	0	1	0	0	0	0	0	0	0	0	1	1	0	0	0
indulgence	2	.0000	.0234	23.7	1	1	0	0	0	0	0	0	0	0	0	0	0	0	0	0	0	0	0	0	2	0	0	0	0
indulges	2	.0000	.0243	23.9	0	0	0	0	1	0	0	1	0	0	0	0	0	0	0	0	0	0	0	0	0	0	0	2	0
Indus	7	.2924	.4696	36.7	0	0	2	1	2	2	0	0	0	0	0	0	0	2	0	0	0	0	0	0	0	1	4	0	0
industrial	243	.5641	28.545	54.6	24	6	45	32	61	41	33	1	6	1	0	2	1	104	1	10	2	0	0	24	0	19	59	14	0
Industrial	33	.5166	3.6113	45.6	1	1	4	5	9	8	5	0	1	0	0	0	0	17	0	0	0	1	0	0	0	3	9	2	0
industrialist	2	.1814	.1187	30.7	0	0	0	1	0	0	0	1	1	0	0	0	0	0	0	0	0	0	0	0	0	0	0	1	0
industrialists	3	.2431	.1816	32.6	0	0	0	0	1	1	1	0	0	0	0	0	0	2	0	0	0	0	0	0	1	0	0	0	0
industrialization	18	.3172	1.3266	41.2	1	0	6	1	7	1	2	0	1	0	0	0	0	8	0	0	0	0	0	0	0	1	8	0	0
industrialized	9	.3729	.7461	38.7	0	2	3	0	1	1	2	0	0	0	0	0	0	4	0	0	0	0	0	0	0	2	3	0	0

6B Indefinites
7R indelicacy
7A indemnification
8R indemnity
6B indention
6P Independents
5A Indepentia
4Q indexers
4Q indexing
4P Indian-fashion
8F Indian-fighter
7E Indian-head
7D Indian-sacred
6R Indianapolis-Attucks
9R Indianhead
4B indicare
8B indict
8R indicted
8R indicts
8F indignities
9Q indignity
7A Indio
6R Indira
7R indiscernible
8Q indiscriminatingly
9Q indisposition
8F indissolubly
9A indistinguishable
6P indite
5Q Individual
5P IndoEuropean
7B Indo-Iranian
8Q Indo-Pakistan
8Q indolence
7Q inducing
8E inductively
8M inductor
7A indulgently
XR indulging
8Q indus
8F industrialize
3Q industrializing

Word Type	F	D	U	SFI	3 Gr 3	4 Gr 4	5 Gr 5	6 Gr 6	7 Gr 7	8 Gr 8	9 Gr 9	X UnGr	A Read	B Eng & Gr	C Comp	D Lit	E Math	F Soc Stud	G Spell	H Sci	J Music	K Art	L Home Ec	M Shop	N Lib F	P Lib NF	Q Lib Ref	R Mag	S Rel
industrially	2	.0000	.0389	25.9	0	0	1	1	0	0	0	0	0	0	0	0	0	2	0	0	0	0	0	0	0	0	0	0	0
industries	219	.5954	27.117	54.3	24	5	57	36	39	19	37	2	9	1	1	0	1	117	2	2	0	0	0	8	0	13	46	19	0
Industries	7	.1334	.2484	34.0	0	0	6	0	0	0	0	1	0	0	0	0	0	0	0	0	0	0	0	0	0	0	6	1	0
industrious	8	.5162	.9121	39.6	0	0	0	3	2	2	1	0	3	0	0	1	0	1	0	1	0	0	0	0	0	0	2	0	0
industriousness	2	.2285	.1129	30.5	1	0	0	1	0	0	0	0	0	0	0	0	0	1	0	0	0	0	0	0	0	0	1	0	0
industry	429	.6509	57.313	57.6	30	14	78	66	94	65	73	9	22	5	0	2	5	192	6	18	5	1	2	37	1	25	76	32	0
Industry	5	.5554	.5729	37.6	1	0	1	0	0	2	1	0	0	1	0	0	0	1	0	0	1	0	0	0	0	0	1	1	0
inedible	4	.3689	.3171	35.0	0	0	0	0	1	1	1	1	0	2	0	1	0	0	0	0	0	0	0	0	0	0	1	0	0
ineffective	5	.4680	.4836	36.8	0	0	0	1	2	0	2	0	0	0	1	0	0	0	1	0	0	0	0	0	1	0	1	1	0
ineffectual	4	.2433	.2315	33.6	0	0	1	0	2	0	1	0	0	0	0	0	0	0	0	0	0	0	0	0	0	2	0	2	0
inefficiency	3	.3766	.2497	34.0	0	0	1	0	1	1	0	0	0	0	0	0	0	1	0	0	0	0	0	0	0	1	1	0	0
inefficient	8	.4657	.8013	39.0	0	0	2	0	3	2	1	0	0	0	0	1	0	4	0	0	0	0	0	0	0	2	0	1	0
ineligible	2	.2351	.1166	30.7	0	0	0	0	1	0	1	0	0	0	0	0	0	1	0	0	0	0	0	0	0	0	0	1	0
inept	4	.4817	.4082	36.1	1	0	0	0	0	1	1	1	0	1	0	0	0	1	0	0	0	0	0	0	0	1	0	1	0
inequalities	28	.1004	.9654	39.8	0	3	1	1	3	7	13	0	1	0	0	0	25	2	0	0	0	0	0	0	0	0	0	0	0
inequality	46	.0911	1.4428	41.6	0	3	1	12	2	9	19	0	0	0	0	0	44	0	0	0	0	0	0	0	0	0	1	1	0
inert	16	.3266	1.1744	40.7	0	0	2	2	8	3	1	0	0	0	0	0	0	0	0	5	0	0	0	0	1	1	9	0	0
inertia	9	.4646	.8985	39.5	3	0	0	0	1	4	1	0	0	0	0	1	0	0	0	4	0	0	0	0	0	3	1	0	0
inescapable	4	.4514	.4045	36.1	0	0	1	0	1	1	1	0	1	0	0	1	0	0	0	1	0	0	0	0	0	1	0	0	0
inescapably	3	.3764	.2483	33.9	0	0	0	0	3	0	0	0	0	0	0	0	0	0	0	1	0	0	0	0	0	0	1	1	0
inestimable	2	.2401	.1133	30.5	0	0	0	0	1	0	1	0	0	0	0	0	0	0	0	0	0	0	0	0	0	1	1	0	0
inevitable	31	.7353	4.6139	46.6	0	1	6	4	9	6	5	0	4	1	0	4	0	1	1	0	1	0	0	0	3	6	5	5	0
inevitably	21	.6661	2.8576	44.6	0	0	2	3	4	6	4	2	1	0	0	2	0	3	0	3	0	0	0	0	2	2	5	3	0
inexorably	2	.2401	.1133	30.5	0	0	0	0	0	0	2	0	0	0	0	0	0	0	0	0	0	0	0	0	0	1	1	0	0
inexpensive	26	.6443	3.4069	45.3	1	2	0	1	4	7	8	3	2	1	0	1	0	1	0	2	0	1	5	3	0	4	3	3	0
inexperience	4	.4802	.4049	36.1	0	0	0	0	1	1	2	0	0	0	0	1	0	1	0	0	0	0	0	0	0	0	1	1	0
inexperienced	8	.4858	.8626	39.4	0	0	0	1	3	3	1	0	3	0	0	1	0	2	0	0	0	0	1	1	0	0	0	0	0
inexpert	2	.2375	.1088	30.4	0	0	0	0	1	0	1	0	0	0	0	0	0	0	0	0	1	0	0	0	0	0	0	1	0
inexplicable	4	.3078	.2971	34.7	0	0	0	0	3	1	0	0	1	0	0	0	0	0	0	0	0	0	0	0	2	0	1	0	0
infallibility	2	.2441	.1127	30.5	0	0	0	0	2	0	0	0	0	0	0	0	0	0	0	0	0	0	0	0	1	0	1	0	0
infamous	5	.3750	.4036	36.1	0	0	0	1	2	0	2	0	0	0	0	2	0	0	0	0	0	0	0	0	0	0	1	2	0
infancy	6	.4347	.5844	37.7	0	0	0	1	3	2	0	0	2	1	1	0	0	0	0	0	0	0	0	0	0	0	1	1	0
infant	31	.6220	3.9929	46.0	1	3	4	7	8	4	3	1	6	3	3	2	0	1	0	0	0	0	0	0	2	2	8	4	0
Infant	4	.0000	.0323	25.1	1	1	1	1	0	0	0	0	0	0	0	0	0	0	0	0	4	0	0	0	0	0	0	0	0
infant's	2	.1717	.1142	30.6	0	0	0	1	0	1	0	0	1	0	0	1	0	0	0	0	0	0	0	0	0	0	0	0	0
Infanta	2	.0000	.0290	24.6	0	0	0	1	1	0	0	0	0	0	0	0	0	0	0	0	0	0	0	0	0	2	0	0	0
infantile	3	.2443	.1820	32.6	0	0	0	1	1	1	0	0	0	0	0	1	0	0	0	2	0	0	0	0	0	0	0	0	0
infantry	15	.5796	1.8235	42.6	0	0	1	1	0	10	1	2	2	0	0	3	0	4	0	0	0	0	0	0	0	1	2	3	0
Infantry	5	.2392	.3123	34.9	0	0	0	0	1	1	0	3	1	0	0	0	0	1	0	0	0	0	0	0	0	0	0	3	0
infantryman	4	.1772	.1782	32.5	0	0	1	3	0	0	0	0	0	3	0	0	0	0	0	0	0	0	0	0	0	1	0	0	0
infantrymen	4	.4808	.4056	36.1	0	0	0	1	0	2	1	0	0	1	0	1	0	1	0	0	0	0	0	0	0	0	0	1	0
infants	6	.3717	.4649	36.7	0	0	0	1	1	4	0	0	0	0	2	0	0	0	0	0	0	0	1	0	0	0	1	2	0
infect	2	.1698	.1133	30.5	0	0	0	0	1	1	0	0	1	0	0	0	0	0	0	0	0	0	0	0	0	0	1	0	0
infected	21	.6252	2.7279	44.4	0	1	5	2	6	5	1	1	2	1	0	0	0	1	0	10	0	0	1	0	0	2	3	1	0
infection	37	.5419	4.2214	46.3	0	0	6	6	11	8	6	0	0	0	1	1	0	0	0	24	0	0	0	0	1	1	5	4	0
infections	21	.3696	1.7352	42.4	0	2	2	3	0	5	8	1	0	0	0	0	0	0	0	13	0	0	1	0	0	0	7	0	0
infectious	15	.3291	1.1685	40.7	0	3	7	0	2	1	2	0	1	0	0	0	0	0	0	11	0	0	0	0	0	0	2	1	0
infeed	5	.0000	.0724	28.6	0	0	0	0	5	0	0	0	0	0	0	0	0	0	0	0	0	0	0	0	0	5	0	0	0
infer	12	.3022	.8276	39.2	0	1	0	0	2	1	8	0	1	8	0	1	0	0	0	0	0	0	0	0	0	0	2	0	0
inference	4	.4526	.3993	36.0	0	0	0	0	1	0	2	1	1	1	0	1	0	0	0	0	0	0	0	0	0	0	0	1	0
inferences	14	.3105	1.0256	40.1	0	0	0	1	2	3	8	0	2	8	0	0	0	0	0	3	0	0	0	0	0	0	1	0	0
inferior	18	.6169	2.3404	43.7	2	0	0	1	6	7	2	0	5	0	0	1	0	5	0	0	1	0	0	0	0	1	4	1	0
inferiority	6	.3585	.4833	36.8	0	0	0	0	4	2	0	0	0	0	0	0	0	2	0	0	0	0	0	0	0	3	0	1	0
inferiors	2	.1814	.1187	30.7	0	0	0	0	1	1	0	0	1	0	0	0	0	0	0	0	0	0	0	0	0	0	0	1	0
infernal	6	.2988	.4153	36.2	0	0	0	3	0	1	1	1	0	0	0	0	0	0	0	1	0	0	0	0	0	4	0	1	0
inferno	5	.1669	.3184	35.0	0	3	0	1	1	0	0	0	4	0	0	0	0	0	0	0	0	0	0	1	0	0	0	0	0
inferred	3	.2159	.1532	31.9	0	0	0	0	1	1	1	0	0	0	0	0	0	0	0	0	0	0	0	0	0	0	2	1	0
infertile	2	.2285	.1129	30.5	0	0	0	0	2	0	0	0	0	0	0	0	0	1	0	0	0	0	0	0	0	0	1	0	0
infest	4	.2160	.2008	33.0	0	0	0	0	4	0	0	0	0	0	0	0	0	0	0	0	1	0	0	0	0	0	3	0	0
infested	2	.2446	.1123	30.5	0	0	0	0	0	2	0	0	0	1	0	0	0	0	0	0	0	0	0	0	0	0	1	0	0
infidel	3	.2233	.1562	31.9	0	0	0	0	2	0	1	0	0	0	0	1	0	0	0	0	0	0	0	0	0	0	2	0	0
infidelity	2	.2401	.1133	30.5	0	0	2	0	0	0	0	0	0	0	0	0	0	0	0	0	0	0	0	0	0	1	1	0	0
infield	11	.5431	1.3110	41.2	0	2	5	3	1	0	0	0	5	0	0	0	0	0	0	0	0	0	0	0	1	1	2	2	0
infielder	2	.2433	.1158	30.6	0	0	0	1	1	0	0	0	0	0	0	0	0	0	0	0	0	0	0	0	0	1	0	1	0
infielders	3	.0000	.1370	31.4	0	1	0	0	2	0	0	0	3	0	0	0	0	0	0	0	0	0	0	0	0	0	0	0	0
infiltrated	2	.2437	.1129	30.5	0	0	0	1	0	0	0	1	0	0	0	0	0	0	0	0	0	0	0	0	0	0	1	1	0
infiltration	2	.2351	.1166	30.7	0	0	0	0	1	0	1	0	0	0	0	0	0	1	0	0	0	0	0	0	0	0	0	1	0
infinite	38	.6147	4.7681	46.8	0	7	3	8	11	4	5	0	0	0	2	3	21	0	0	0	1	0	0	3	3	2	3	0	0
infinite-resource -and-s**	3	.0000	.0352	25.5	0	3	0	0	0	0	0	0	0	0	0	0	0	0	0	0	0	0	0	0	3	0	0	0	0
infinitely	18	.6799	2.4827	43.9	0	1	1	2	8	1	4	1	0	0	0	2	3	1	0	2	0	0	0	0	4	1	3	2	0
infinitesimal	3	.2159	.1532	31.9	0	0	0	0	2	0	0	1	0	0	0	0	0	0	0	0	0	0	0	0	0	0	2	1	0
infinitive	17	.0964	.4876	36.9	0	0	0	0	2	1	14	0	0	16	0	0	0	0	1	0	0	0	0	0	0	0	0	0	0
infinitives	5	.0000	.0547	27.4	0	0	0	0	0	0	5	0	0	5	0	0	0	0	0	0	0	0	0	0	0	0	0	0	0
infinity	9	.5502	1.0333	40.1	0	0	0	1	3	1	2	2	1	0	1	0	1	0	0	1	1	0	0	0	1	0	3	0	0
infirm	2	.2139	.1057	30.2	0	0	0	0	0	2	0	0	0	0	0	0	0	1	1	0	0	0	0	0	0	0	0	0	0
infirmities	3	.0000	.1370	31.4	0	0	0	2	0	0	1	0	3	0	0	0	0	0	0	0	0	0	0	0	0	0	0	0	0
infirmity	3	.0000	.0352	25.5	0	1	0	0	2	0	0	0	0	0	0	0	0	0	0	0	0	0	0	0	3	0	0	0	0
inflamed	6	.5273	.6591	38.2	0	0	0	0	4	1	0	1	0	0	0	0	0	0	0	1	0	0	0	0	1	1	2	1	0
inflammable	3	.3844	.2487	34.0	0	0	2	0	0	0	1	0	0	1	0	0	0	0	0	0	0	0	0	0	0	1	1	0	0
inflammation	8	.2440	.4818	36.8	0	0	3	0	0	3	0	2	0	0	0	0	0	0	0	5	0	0	0	0	0	0	3	0	0
inflammatory	7	.3479	.5279	37.2	0	0	0	0	2	3	2	0	0	0	0	3	0	0	0	0	0	0	0	0	0	0	3	1	0
inflatable	4	.2835	.2871	34.6	0	0	1	1	2	0	0	0	1	0	0	0	0	0	0	1	0	0	0	0	0	0	0	2	0
inflated	6	.5185	.6677	38.2	1	1	1	0	3	0	0	0	1	0	0	0	0	0	0	1	0	0	0	0	0	2	1	1	0
inflation	31	.0544	.6862	38.4	0	0	0	3	1	0	26	1	0	1	0	0	0	0	0	0	0	0	0	0	0	0	0	30	0
inflationary	3	.1277	.1363	31.3	0	0	0	0	1	0	2	0	1	0	0	0	0	0	0	0	0	0	0	0	0	0	0	2	0
inflected	6	.1825	.2666	34.3	0	0	0	0	1	1	4	0	0	5	0	0	0	0	1	0	0	0	0	0	0	0	0	0	0
inflection	6	.2729	.3611	35.6	0	0	0	0	1	2	3	0	0	1	0	1	0	0	0	0	4	0	0	0	0	0	0	0	0
inflectional	4	.0000	.0438	26.4	0	0	0	0	4	0	0	0	0	4	0	0	0	0	0	0	0	0	0	0	0	0	0	0	0
inflections	5	.2238	.2558	34.1	0	0	0	0	4	1	0	0	0	2	0	0	0	0	0	0	3	0	0	0	0	0	0	0	0
inflict	3	.3801	.2525	34.0	1	0	1	1	0	0	0	0	0	0	0	0	0	0	0	1	0	0	0	0	1	1	0	0	0
inflicted	6	.5650	.7041	38.5	0	0	0	1	1	3	0	1	0	1	0	1	0	2	0	0	0	0	0	0	0	1	0	1	0
inflicting	2	.2285	.1129	30.5	0	0	0	0	1	1	0	0	0	0	0	0	0	1	0	0	0	0	0	0	0	0	1	0	0
influence	200	.8396	33.486	55.2	9	6	24	19	51	54	25	12	17	9	1	4	0	27	6	23	32	2	7	2	4	7	43	16	0
influenced	97	.7268	14.258	51.5	3	2	8	19	27	27	8	3	9	8	0	1	0	16	1	8	24	4	2	0	0	8	13	3	0
influences	42	.6538	5.5923	47.5	1	0	4	8	9	12	5	3	2	5	0	0	0	3	1	8	9	0	5	0	0	3	5	1	0
influencing	3	.3756	.2468	33.9	0	0	0	0	1	1	1	0	0	0	0	1	0	1	0	0	0	0	0	0	0	0	1	0	0

8A industriously
9R industry's
7R ineffectively
8F ineffectiveness
7P ineffectuality
5Q inelastic
XB inelegant
7R ineluctably
7Q ineradicable
7A inertial
3J Ines
9D inexecrable
7Q inexhaustible
5A inexpensively
6N inexpressible
7Q inextricable
7A infamy
6B infans
7A infatuated
9R infatuation
9Q infection-free
6P Inferno
8Q infestation
9H infestations
5Q infests
5Q Infielders
5P infiltrating
5P infiltrations
4E Infinite
6B infinitesimally
7D infirmary
7A Infirmary
7R inflatable-type
6K inflate
9R INFLATION
7R inflator
7N inflexibility
9R inflexible
XR inflight
9H inflow
7L Influence

Word Type	F	D	U	SFI	3 Gr 3	4 Gr 4	5 Gr 5	6 Gr 6	7 Gr 7	8 Gr 8	9 Gr 9	X UnGr	A Read	B Eng & Gr	C Comp	D Lit	E Math	F Soc Stud	G Spell	H Sci	J Music	K Art	L Home Ec	M Shop	N Lib F	P Lib NF	Q Lib Ref	R Mag	S Rel
influential	22	.5680	2.5953	44.1	1	1	4	0	4	9	3	0	2	0	0	1	0	1	0	0	3	0	0	0	0	3	7	5	0
influenza	10	.4197	.9106	39.6	0	1	1	4	4	0	0	0	0	0	0	0	0	0	3	5	0	0	0	0	0	1	1	0	0
influx	7	.3579	.5672	37.5	0	0	1	1	0	4	1	0	0	0	0	0	0	4	0	0	0	0	0	0	0	1	0	2	0
inform	21	.6515	2.7999	44.5	1	0	2	1	5	2	10	0	2	5	1	3	0	1	0	0	0	0	0	0	0	5	1	3	0
informal	31	.7836	4.8901	46.9	0	0	1	0	11	13	6	0	7	6	1	1	0	1	2	0	3	0	3	1	3	0	2	1	0
informality	3	.3319	.2114	33.3	0	0	0	0	1	0	1	1	0	0	0	0	0	0	1	0	0	0	1	0	0	0	0	1	0
informally	4	.4443	.3917	35.9	0	0	0	0	3	1	0	0	1	0	0	0	0	0	1	0	0	0	0	0	0	0	1	1	0
information	817	.8232	135.03	61.3	40	119	139	83	160	126	131	19	173	143	40	6	49	89	12	125	5	1	23	30	6	21	61	33	0
Information	6	.3421	.4505	36.5	1	1	0	0	2	0	2	0	0	3	0	0	0	0	0	0	0	0	0	0	0	1	0	2	0
informative	5	.4052	.4260	36.3	0	0	0	0	3	0	2	0	0	2	1	0	0	0	0	0	0	0	0	0	0	0	1	1	0
informed	48	.7332	7.1921	48.6	1	3	6	9	10	12	4	3	12	1	0	3	1	6	0	3	0	0	0	2	4	3	1	12	0
informer	3	.3399	.2456	33.9	0	0	0	0	2	0	1	0	1	0	0	1	0	0	0	0	0	0	0	0	0	0	0	1	0
informs	7	.1707	.3344	35.2	0	1	0	0	1	2	3	0	1	5	0	0	0	0	0	1	0	0	0	0	0	0	0	0	0
infrared	19	.3264	1.4337	41.6	0	0	0	6	7	3	0	3	1	0	0	0	0	0	0	9	0	0	0	0	0	0	8	1	0
infrequent	8	.4654	.7901	39.0	0	1	0	0	5	1	1	0	0	1	0	0	0	1	0	1	0	0	0	0	0	0	1	4	0
infringe	3	.3769	.2484	34.0	0	1	0	0	1	1	0	0	0	0	0	0	0	1	0	0	0	0	0	0	0	0	1	1	0
infuriated	3	.3454	.2542	34.1	0	0	0	0	0	2	1	0	1	0	0	0	0	1	0	0	0	0	0	0	0	0	0	1	0
infused	3	.3870	.2486	34.0	0	0	0	0	0	1	2	0	0	0	0	1	0	0	0	0	0	0	0	0	0	0	1	1	0
infusible	2	.0000	.0394	26.0	0	0	0	0	0	0	0	2	0	0	0	0	0	0	0	2	0	0	0	0	0	0	0	0	0
ing	298	.1562	11.899	50.8	94	44	71	53	14	12	10	0	20	34	1	0	0	0	243	0	0	0	0	0	0	0	0	0	0
Ingalls	6	.4307	.5897	37.7	2	0	0	3	0	1	0	0	2	2	0	1	0	0	0	1	0	0	0	0	0	0	0	0	0
Ingenhousz	2	.0000	.0394	26.0	0	0	0	0	2	0	0	0	0	0	0	0	0	0	0	2	0	0	0	0	0	0	0	0	0
ingenious	15	.5262	1.6310	42.1	1	1	1	3	9	0	0	0	1	0	1	0	0	0	0	0	1	2	0	0	2	0	7	1	0
ingenuity	18	.6673	2.4616	43.9	2	0	0	1	4	3	6	2	3	2	0	1	0	0	0	2	1	0	2	0	0	1	4	2	0
ingots	2	.2446	.1142	30.6	0	0	0	0	0	1	1	0	0	0	0	0	0	0	0	0	0	0	0	0	1	0	0	1	0
ingrained	4	.2073	.2003	33.0	0	0	0	0	1	1	1	1	0	0	0	1	0	0	0	0	0	0	0	0	0	0	0	3	0
ingredient	13	.6852	1.7965	42.5	1	1	1	3	2	0	3	2	0	1	1	0	1	1	0	1	1	0	1	0	0	0	3	3	0
ingredients	65	.4045	5.5149	47.4	2	3	2	5	18	14	18	3	0	4	0	0	4	1	0	9	1	0	29	3	0	4	3	7	0
Ingri	2	.1717	.1142	30.6	1	1	0	0	0	0	0	0	1	0	0	1	0	0	0	0	0	0	0	0	0	0	0	0	0
Ingrid	4	.0931	.1444	31.6	0	0	1	0	3	0	0	0	1	3	0	0	0	0	0	0	0	0	0	0	0	0	0	0	0
inhabit	10	.5817	1.1994	40.8	0	1	0	0	6	0	2	1	0	0	0	0	0	1	0	2	1	0	0	0	1	0	3	2	0
inhabitant	7	.4423	.7016	38.5	2	1	0	0	1	0	2	1	2	2	0	0	0	0	0	2	0	0	0	0	0	1	0	0	0
inhabitants	78	.7688	12.096	50.8	6	2	6	10	26	14	12	2	7	4	1	4	2	25	1	4	0	1	0	0	1	7	18	3	0
inhabited	32	.5684	3.8251	45.8	4	3	2	4	9	4	4	2	4	1	0	0	0	8	0	2	0	0	0	0	1	2	11	3	0
inhabiting	4	.3540	.3081	34.9	0	0	1	0	2	0	1	0	0	0	0	1	0	0	0	0	0	0	0	0	0	1	2	0	0
inhale	10	.5767	1.2084	40.8	3	0	1	0	5	1	0	0	1	0	0	2	1	0	1	4	1	0	0	0	0	0	0	0	0
inhaled	10	.5662	1.1927	40.8	0	1	3	0	3	0	3	0	1	0	0	2	0	0	0	4	0	0	0	0	1	1	0	1	0
inhales	2	.2346	.1166	30.7	0	1	0	1	0	0	0	0	0	0	0	0	0	0	0	1	0	0	0	0	0	0	0	1	0
inhaling	4	.3812	.3773	35.8	1	1	0	0	2	0	0	0	2	0	0	0	0	0	0	1	0	0	0	0	0	1	0	0	0
inherent	12	.6418	1.5817	42.0	1	0	1	0	4	4	2	0	1	0	0	0	0	1	0	2	2	0	0	0	1	1	3	1	0
inherently	3	.2159	.1532	31.9	0	0	0	0	0	1	2	0	0	0	0	0	0	0	0	0	0	0	0	0	0	0	2	1	0
inherit	19	.5990	2.3451	43.7	1	0	2	2	1	9	1	3	1	0	0	1	0	4	1	3	1	0	4	0	1	1	1	1	0
inheritance	14	.6293	1.8102	42.6	0	3	3	1	1	3	2	1	1	0	0	1	0	1	0	3	0	0	2	0	2	1	2	1	0
inherited	37	.6530	4.9685	47.0	0	2	4	3	8	10	8	2	5	0	0	3	0	2	0	9	3	0	5	0	1	1	3	5	0
inherits	3	.3771	.2489	34.0	0	1	0	0	1	0	1	0	0	0	0	1	0	0	0	1	0	0	0	0	0	0	0	1	0
inhibit	4	.4803	.4071	36.1	0	0	1	0	2	0	1	0	0	0	0	0	0	0	0	1	0	0	0	0	0	1	1	1	0
inhibition	3	.2043	.1486	31.7	0	0	1	0	0	2	0	0	0	0	0	0	0	0	0	0	0	0	0	0	0	1	2	0	0
inhospitable	9	.6144	1.1342	40.5	0	1	2	1	3	1	1	0	0	0	0	1	0	2	0	0	0	0	0	0	1	2	2	1	0
inhuman	5	.5392	.5735	37.6	0	0	1	1	1	1	1	0	1	0	0	1	0	0	0	0	0	0	0	0	1	1	0	1	0
iniquity	2	.2441	.1127	30.5	0	0	1	1	0	0	0	0	0	0	0	0	0	0	0	0	0	0	0	0	1	0	1	0	0
initial	65	.5591	7.4769	48.7	1	5	8	3	22	7	17	2	2	8	13	9	5	1	4	6	1	0	0	0	0	6	3	7	0
initially	2	.1814	.1187	30.7	0	0	0	0	1	1	0	0	1	0	0	0	0	0	0	0	0	0	0	0	0	0	0	1	0
initials	21	.5734	2.5012	44.0	0	2	1	3	4	0	2	9	3	10	1	1	0	0	0	0	0	0	0	2	0	2	1	1	0
initiate	4	.3352	.2986	34.8	0	0	0	0	2	1	1	0	0	0	0	0	0	0	0	1	0	0	0	0	0	0	2	1	0
initiated	9	.5925	1.1251	40.5	0	0	1	1	3	2	1	1	2	0	0	0	1	1	0	0	0	0	0	0	0	2	1	2	0
initiation	2	.1814	.1187	30.7	0	0	0	1	1	0	0	0	1	0	0	0	0	0	0	0	0	0	0	0	0	0	0	1	0
initiative	13	.5596	1.5281	41.8	0	0	3	0	2	7	1	0	1	0	0	0	0	5	0	0	1	0	0	0	0	2	3	1	0
inject	6	.4189	.5626	37.5	0	0	1	2	2	0	1	0	1	0	0	0	0	0	0	2	0	0	0	0	0	0	2	1	0
injected	11	.4122	1.0282	40.1	0	0	2	2	5	1	0	1	2	0	0	0	0	0	0	5	0	0	0	0	0	0	3	1	0
injection	11	.3980	1.0244	40.1	0	2	2	1	3	0	1	2	3	0	0	0	0	0	0	6	0	0	0	1	0	1	0	0	0
injections	2	.2401	.1133	30.5	0	0	0	0	1	1	0	0	0	0	0	0	0	0	0	0	0	0	0	0	0	1	1	0	0
injects	3	.3764	.2483	33.9	1	0	0	0	1	0	0	1	0	0	0	0	0	0	0	1	0	0	0	0	0	0	1	1	0
Injun	12	.3619	.9466	39.8	0	2	1	0	8	0	1	0	0	0	0	3	0	0	0	0	0	0	0	0	6	3	0	0	0
injunction	2	.2437	.1129	30.5	0	0	0	0	2	0	0	0	0	0	0	0	0	0	0	0	0	0	0	0	0	0	1	1	0
injunctions	4	.0000	.0419	26.2	0	0	0	0	4	0	0	0	0	0	0	0	0	0	0	0	0	0	0	0	0	0	4	0	0
Injuns	18	.3114	1.3014	41.1	2	1	0	1	3	2	9	0	1	0	0	3	0	2	0	0	0	0	0	0	0	12	0	0	0
injure	17	.6274	2.2247	43.5	1	1	3	3	6	0	3	0	4	0	2	1	0	1	1	3	0	0	0	0	2	1	1	1	0
injured	64	.8211	10.602	50.3	6	7	5	11	23	7	4	1	21	3	2	4	0	6	1	7	0	0	1	0	2	5	2	10	0
injures	2	.2405	.1205	30.8	0	0	0	1	1	0	0	0	0	0	0	0	0	0	0	1	0	0	0	0	0	1	0	0	0
injuries	35	.7187	5.0975	47.1	1	2	8	3	9	4	7	1	2	1	2	2	2	1	1	9	0	0	0	0	0	4	3	8	0
injuring	3	.3131	.2349	33.7	0	0	0	0	1	1	1	0	1	0	0	0	0	1	0	0	1	0	0	0	0	0	0	0	0
injurious	6	.2040	.3278	35.2	0	0	0	0	0	3	0	3	0	1	0	0	0	0	0	5	0	0	0	0	0	0	0	0	0
injury	51	.7094	7.4247	48.7	2	2	6	5	18	12	6	0	12	0	0	0	0	2	1	9	0	0	0	2	4	5	5	11	0
injustice	9	.5420	1.0365	40.2	1	1	0	1	1	4	1	0	2	1	0	0	0	1	0	0	0	1	0	0	1	0	1	2	0
injustices	3	.3852	.2500	34.0	0	0	0	0	2	1	0	0	0	0	0	1	0	0	0	0	0	0	0	0	0	1	0	1	0
ink	136	.5322	15.181	51.8	24	21	11	24	26	12	16	2	23	8	2	5	4	7	5	8	1	32	0	12	14	9	4	2	0
Ink	15	.1847	.8995	39.5	8	0	6	0	1	0	0	0	7	0	0	0	0	0	0	0	0	0	0	0	0	8	0	0	0
inked	9	.1843	.3735	35.7	0	0	2	3	2	1	1	0	0	0	0	1	0	0	1	1	0	5	0	0	0	0	1	0	0
inking	4	.2404	.1956	32.9	0	0	2	0	0	0	2	0	0	0	0	0	0	0	0	0	0	2	0	2	0	0	0	0	0
inkling	4	.3693	.3613	35.6	1	0	0	1	1	0	1	0	2	0	0	1	0	0	0	0	0	0	0	0	0	0	1	0	0
inkpot	2	.0000	.0234	23.7	1	0	1	0	0	0	0	0	0	0	0	0	0	0	0	0	0	0	0	0	2	0	0	0	0
inks	10	.3081	.6672	38.2	0	0	0	1	0	0	9	0	0	1	0	0	0	0	0	0	0	0	0	2	0	0	7	0	0
Inkslinger	4	.0000	.0429	26.3	0	0	0	0	4	0	0	0	0	0	0	4	0	0	0	0	0	0	0	0	0	0	0	0	0
inkstand	2	.1787	.1174	30.7	0	0	1	1	0	0	0	0	1	0	0	0	0	0	0	0	0	0	0	0	1	0	0	0	0
inkwell	3	.1187	.1291	31.1	0	1	0	0	2	0	0	0	1	0	0	2	0	0	0	0	0	0	0	0	0	0	0	0	0
inky	7	.4807	.7781	38.9	0	1	2	1	3	0	0	0	4	0	0	1	0	0	0	1	0	0	0	0	1	0	0	0	0
Inky	2	.0000	.0037	15.7	2	0	0	0	0	0	0	0	0	0	0	0	0	0	0	0	0	2	0	0	0	0	0	0	0
inlaid	7	.3302	.5979	37.8	1	0	0	1	3	2	0	0	4	0	0	0	0	1	0	0	0	1	0	0	0	0	1	0	0
inland	108	.6272	14.123	51.5	10	11	17	25	25	9	9	2	12	1	0	1	0	58	0	9	2	0	1	0	1	5	12	6	0
Inland	4	.3360	.3283	35.2	0	1	1	0	0	1	0	1	1	0	0	0	0	2	0	0	0	0	0	0	0	0	0	1	0
inlet	12	.4661	1.2803	41.1	0	1	1	6	3	1	0	0	5	0	0	0	0	4	0	0	0	0	0	0	0	0	2	1	0
Inlet	3	.2357	.2199	33.4	2	1	0	0	0	0	0	0	2	0	0	0	0	0	0	0	0	0	0	0	0	1	0	0	0
Inman	2	.0000	.0234	23.7	0	0	0	0	2	0	0	0	0	0	0	0	0	0	0	0	0	0	0	0	2	0	0	0	0
inmates	2	.1787	.1174	30.7	0	0	0	1	0	0	1	0	1	0	0	0	0	0	0	0	0	0	0	0	1	0	0	0	0

9D infold
7R informants
8A information-please
XH infra-red
8D infractions
7R infrared-sensing
7Q infrastructure
7B infrequently
5Q infringement
7R infringing
9D infuse
8A infusing
7H infusion
9Q ingeniators
6N ingenio
7Q ingeniously
7M ingenius
4R Ingenue
7N ingenuous
8B ingersoll
9C Ingersoll
9Q ingested
XR Inglis
4F ingot
6A ingrates
7N ingratiating
3P ingratitude
9K Ingres
XH inhabits
XH inhalation
9A inhibitions
8Q inhibitors
9A inhibits
5Q inhumane
5P inhumanity
9Q inhumation
3P iniquities
XR Initial
8D initial-letter
9E initialization
5Q Initiative
9Q initiator
4N injun
3P INK
8E ink-blot
3P ink-slab
4N inkbottle
4G inkiness
8D inkstands
6R inland-waterway
7R inlay
7P inlays
5F inlets
5Q inmate
6A Inmate

Word Type	F	D	U	SFI	3 Gr 3	4 Gr 4	5 Gr 5	6 Gr 6	7 Gr 7	8 Gr 8	9 Gr 9	X UnGr	A Read	B Eng & Gr	C Comp	D Lit	E Math	F Soc Stud	G Spell	H Sci	J Music	K Art	L Home Ec	M Shop	N Lib F	P Lib NF	Q Lib Ref	R Mag	S Rel
inmost	2	.2337	.1157	30.6	0	0	1	0	1	0	0	0	0	0	0	0	0	1	0	0	0	0	0	0	1	0	0	0	0
inn	79	.6543	10.964	50.4	16	21	4	17	15	5	1	0	40	1	0	2	0	2	0	0	3	0	0	0	10	16	1	4	0
Inn	14	.3504	1.3150	41.2	1	2	0	0	11	0	0	0	11	0	0	0	0	0	0	0	0	0	0	0	2	1	0	0	0
inn-door	2	.1717	.1142	30.6	0	0	0	0	0	1	1	0	1	0	0	1	0	0	0	0	0	0	0	0	0	0	0	0	0
innards	5	.3750	.4036	36.1	0	0	0	0	2	1	1	1	0	0	0	2	0	0	0	0	0	0	0	0	0	0	1	2	0
innate	7	.5177	.7543	38.8	0	0	2	0	0	1	2	2	0	0	0	0	0	0	0	1	2	0	0	0	0	2	1	1	0
inner	128	.8275	21.201	53.3	2	18	15	15	33	28	11	6	14	8	0	3	6	6	0	37	4	2	5	0	7	4	18	14	0
innermost	8	.5189	.9033	39.6	0	0	1	2	2	1	1	1	2	0	0	1	0	1	0	2	0	0	0	0	0	0	2	0	0
inning	43	.6118	5.5756	47.5	16	9	3	3	5	2	4	1	15	0	0	3	0	0	2	1	0	0	0	0	7	12	0	3	0
innings	8	.5163	.8953	39.5	3	2	0	0	0	1	1	1	2	1	0	0	1	0	0	0	0	0	0	0	0	3	0	1	0
innkeeper	17	.4637	1.8429	42.7	6	4	2	3	2	0	0	0	10	0	0	2	0	0	0	0	0	0	0	0	1	4	0	0	0
innocence	13	.5633	1.5405	41.9	0	0	3	1	4	0	5	0	2	1	0	2	0	0	0	0	0	0	0	0	1	5	0	2	0
innocent	45	.7097	6.5471	48.2	1	3	8	8	10	4	10	1	11	1	0	7	0	3	0	1	1	0	0	0	5	4	2	10	0
innocent-looking	4	.3641	.3177	35.0	0	0	0	0	2	1	1	0	0	0	0	1	0	0	0	0	0	0	0	0	0	1	0	2	0
innocently	8	.3263	.6695	38.3	1	1	0	1	4	0	1	0	4	0	0	0	0	0	0	0	0	0	0	0	3	1	0	0	0
innocuous	3	.3769	.2484	34.0	0	0	0	0	1	1	0	1	0	0	0	0	0	1	0	0	0	0	0	0	0	0	1	1	0
innovation	8	.2454	.4781	36.8	0	0	1	0	3	0	4	0	1	0	0	0	0	0	0	0	0	0	0	0	0	0	5	2	0
innovations	14	.5654	1.6337	42.1	0	0	1	1	5	4	2	1	1	0	0	0	0	0	0	0	3	0	0	1	0	2	4	3	0
innovative	4	.2090	.2014	33.0	0	0	0	0	1	1	1	1	0	0	0	0	0	0	0	0	0	0	0	0	0	0	1	3	0
innovator	3	.2321	.1635	32.1	0	1	0	1	0	0	0	1	0	0	0	0	0	0	0	0	0	0	0	0	0	0	1	2	0
inns	8	.5321	.9331	39.7	0	0	2	1	3	2	0	0	3	0	0	0	0	1	0	0	0	0	0	0	2	1	0	1	0
Inns	2	.0000	.0243	23.9	0	0	0	0	0	0	2	0	0	0	0	0	0	0	0	0	0	0	0	0	0	0	0	2	0
Innsbruck	2	.2417	.1091	30.4	0	0	1	0	1	0	0	0	0	0	0	0	0	0	0	0	1	0	0	0	0	0	1	0	0
innumerable	20	.7145	2.9021	44.6	1	2	3	2	6	4	2	0	3	1	2	3	0	1	1	1	1	0	0	0	1	3	2	1	0
inoculated	4	.2160	.2724	34.4	0	0	0	0	2	0	1	1	2	0	0	0	0	0	0	2	0	0	0	0	0	0	0	0	0
inoculation	3	.2437	.2277	33.6	0	0	0	0	2	1	0	0	2	0	0	0	0	0	0	1	0	0	0	0	0	0	0	0	0
inoculations	6	.3488	.4627	36.7	2	0	0	0	0	2	1	1	0	0	0	0	0	0	1	2	0	0	0	0	0	0	3	0	0
inoperative	2	.2437	.1129	30.5	0	0	0	0	1	1	0	0	0	0	0	0	0	0	0	0	0	0	0	0	0	0	1	1	0
inordinately	2	.2405	.1205	30.8	0	0	0	0	1	0	1	0	0	0	0	0	0	0	0	1	0	0	0	0	0	1	0	0	0
inorganic	12	.3691	1.0152	40.1	1	0	1	0	6	0	3	1	1	0	0	0	0	0	0	7	0	0	0	0	0	1	3	0	0
input	35	.2855	2.3532	43.7	0	0	12	10	8	5	0	0	0	0	0	0	27	0	0	7	0	0	0	1	0	0	0	0	0
input-output	5	.2035	.2560	34.1	0	0	4	0	0	0	1	0	0	0	0	0	4	0	0	0	0	0	0	0	0	0	1	0	0
inquire	6	.5515	.7099	38.5	1	0	0	0	2	2	1	0	2	1	0	0	0	0	1	0	0	0	0	0	0	0	1	1	0
inquired	33	.6441	4.4915	46.5	4	3	5	5	9	3	3	1	15	4	1	2	0	0	0	0	0	0	0	0	8	1	1	1	0
inquires	3	.1832	.1417	31.5	0	0	0	0	1	1	1	0	0	0	0	2	0	0	0	1	0	0	0	0	0	0	0	0	0
inquiries	6	.4798	.6590	38.2	0	0	0	1	3	0	2	0	3	0	0	0	0	0	0	1	0	0	0	0	0	0	1	1	0
inquiring	10	.5748	1.2094	40.8	1	0	1	2	1	2	2	1	2	0	1	2	0	0	0	1	0	0	0	0	1	2	0	1	0
inquiringly	6	.3394	.4902	36.9	0	0	1	1	3	1	0	0	2	0	0	2	0	0	0	0	0	0	0	0	2	0	0	0	0
inquiry	17	.4476	1.6383	42.1	0	1	0	1	4	1	9	1	1	0	0	2	0	0	0	3	0	0	0	0	3	0	0	8	0
Inquiry	4	.0000	.0486	26.9	0	0	0	0	0	0	0	4	0	0	0	0	0	0	0	0	0	0	0	0	0	0	0	4	0
Inquisition	2	.0000	.0209	23.2	0	0	0	0	0	2	0	0	0	0	0	0	0	0	0	0	0	0	0	0	0	0	2	0	0
inquisitive	16	.6409	2.1408	43.3	2	1	0	2	7	2	2	0	5	0	1	4	0	0	1	1	0	0	0	0	2	1	1	0	0
inroads	5	.4465	.4743	36.8	0	0	0	1	2	1	1	0	0	0	0	0	0	1	0	0	0	0	0	0	1	0	2	1	0
insane	14	.6603	1.8930	42.8	0	0	1	1	5	2	3	2	2	0	0	2	0	0	3	1	1	0	0	0	0	1	2	2	0
insanely	5	.2553	.2944	34.7	0	0	0	0	3	0	1	1	0	0	0	0	0	0	3	1	0	0	0	0	0	1	0	0	0
insatiable	4	.4535	.4003	36.0	0	0	0	1	2	0	1	0	1	0	0	1	0	0	0	0	0	0	0	0	1	0	0	1	0
inscribed	10	.4974	1.0786	40.3	0	2	0	2	4	0	2	0	2	0	0	0	4	0	0	0	0	0	0	0	2	1	0	1	0
inscription	9	.5741	1.0857	40.4	3	1	1	1	1	2	0	0	1	0	0	0	1	2	0	0	0	0	0	0	1	3	1	0	0
inscriptions	3	.3842	.2485	34.0	0	0	2	0	0	0	1	0	0	0	0	1	0	0	0	0	0	0	0	0	0	1	1	0	0
insect	202	.6473	27.049	54.3	31	19	23	36	79	5	4	5	25	1	0	2	2	3	8	80	1	1	0	0	2	20	49	8	0
insect-eaters	2	.2278	.1128	30.5	0	1	0	0	1	0	0	0	0	0	0	0	0	0	0	1	0	0	0	0	0	0	1	0	0
insect-eating	2	.2401	.1133	30.5	0	0	0	0	2	0	0	0	0	0	0	0	0	0	0	0	0	0	0	0	0	1	1	0	0
insect's	9	.4218	.8160	39.1	2	0	1	2	4	0	0	0	0	0	0	1	0	0	0	2	0	0	0	0	0	2	4	0	0
insecticide	3	.3374	.2433	33.9	0	0	1	0	0	0	2	0	1	1	0	0	0	0	0	0	0	0	0	0	0	0	1	0	0
insecticides	5	.4793	.5136	37.1	0	0	0	2	2	0	0	1	0	1	0	0	0	1	0	2	0	0	0	0	0	0	0	1	0
insectivorous	3	.0000	.0314	25.0	0	0	0	0	3	0	0	0	0	0	0	0	0	0	0	0	0	0	0	0	0	0	3	0	0
insects	561	.6430	74.762	58.7	147	92	32	120	126	21	9	14	57	4	1	3	3	15	4	280	1	5	1	1	3	75	98	10	0
insects'	3	.3395	.2468	33.9	1	0	0	0	1	0	1	0	1	0	0	0	0	0	0	0	0	0	0	0	0	1	1	0	0
insecure	4	.3443	.3228	35.1	0	0	1	0	1	1	1	0	1	1	0	0	0	0	0	1	0	0	1	0	0	0	0	0	0
insecurity	4	.3364	.2938	34.7	0	0	3	0	0	1	0	0	0	0	0	0	0	0	0	0	0	0	1	0	0	2	0	1	0
insensitive	3	.1169	.1277	31.1	0	0	0	0	2	0	1	0	1	0	0	0	0	0	0	0	0	0	0	0	0	0	2	0	0
inseparable	6	.5299	.6600	38.2	0	0	1	2	3	0	0	0	0	0	0	0	0	0	0	1	1	0	0	0	1	1	2	0	0
insert	70	.5571	7.9940	49.0	7	5	11	6	10	13	18	0	6	9	16	0	7	0	1	6	0	1	7	13	0	1	1	2	0
Insert	15	.0000	.1641	32.2	0	0	0	0	0	15	0	0	0	15	0	0	0	0	0	0	0	0	0	0	0	0	0	0	0
inserted	30	.6047	3.7196	45.7	0	3	2	3	9	6	6	1	3	1	0	1	1	1	0	1	0	0	5	4	1	3	7	2	0
inserting	18	.3782	1.4282	41.5	0	3	2	1	4	4	4	0	0	5	7	0	2	0	0	2	0	0	1	1	0	0	0	0	0
insertion	3	.1970	.1504	31.8	0	0	0	0	0	0	1	2	0	0	0	0	0	0	0	2	0	0	1	0	0	0	0	0	0
inserts	3	.3847	.2496	34.0	0	0	0	0	3	0	0	0	0	0	0	0	0	0	0	0	0	0	0	0	0	1	1	1	0
inset	4	.3219	.2826	34.5	0	3	0	0	1	0	0	0	0	0	0	0	0	1	0	0	0	0	1	0	0	0	2	0	0
inshore	5	.2110	.3346	35.2	3	0	0	0	1	0	1	0	3	0	0	0	0	0	0	0	0	0	0	0	0	0	0	2	0
inside	1398	.9249	256.66	64.1	361	229	164	172	224	109	102	37	457	53	6	68	86	52	13	264	25	11	19	37	99	103	38	67	0
Inside	5	.2190	.2843	34.5	0	0	3	0	2	0	0	0	0	0	0	1	0	4	0	0	0	0	0	0	0	0	0	0	0
insiders	5	.3428	.3756	35.7	0	0	1	0	1	2	0	1	0	0	0	0	0	0	1	0	0	0	0	0	0	1	0	3	0
insides	12	.5938	1.4942	41.7	1	0	5	0	3	0	2	1	2	0	0	0	0	0	0	2	0	0	0	0	1	3	2	2	0
insidious	5	.1275	.1790	32.5	0	0	0	0	2	1	1	1	0	0	0	0	0	0	0	1	0	0	0	0	0	0	4	0	0
insight	25	.7321	3.7393	45.7	1	0	1	2	4	11	5	1	7	1	0	1	2	0	0	2	2	0	1	0	0	1	6	2	0
insights	7	.2844	.4888	36.9	0	0	0	0	6	1	0	0	1	0	0	0	0	0	0	3	0	0	0	0	0	0	3	0	0
insignia	3	.3263	.2368	33.7	0	0	0	2	0	1	0	0	1	0	0	0	0	0	0	0	1	0	0	0	0	0	0	1	0
insignificant	13	.6619	1.7462	42.4	0	0	1	2	3	5	2	0	1	0	1	2	0	1	0	1	1	1	1	0	0	0	4	0	0
insincerity	2	.2446	.1142	30.6	0	1	0	0	1	0	0	0	0	0	0	0	0	0	0	0	0	0	0	0	1	0	0	1	0
insist	32	.8373	5.3524	47.3	3	4	4	3	6	3	8	1	4	2	1	1	0	3	2	2	1	0	1	0	2	5	1	7	0
insisted	115	.7409	17.423	52.4	10	20	19	17	20	12	13	4	34	4	0	13	0	11	0	2	1	0	0	0	13	14	6	17	0
insistence	8	.4118	.7072	38.5	0	0	1	0	1	2	3	1	0	0	0	0	0	1	0	0	0	0	0	0	0	1	3	3	0
insistent	6	.3674	.4993	37.0	0	0	0	0	2	1	2	1	1	0	0	3	0	0	0	0	0	0	0	0	0	1	0	1	0
insistently	4	.2991	.2943	34.7	0	0	1	0	0	1	1	1	1	0	0	0	0	0	0	0	0	0	0	0	0	1	0	2	0
insisting	4	.3092	.2990	34.8	0	0	1	0	1	1	1	0	1	1	0	0	0	0	0	0	0	0	0	0	0	0	0	2	0
insists	15	.5440	1.7083	42.3	1	0	0	2	4	1	7	0	2	0	0	1	0	0	0	0	0	0	2	0	2	1	1	6	0
insofar	6	.5522	.6833	38.3	1	0	0	0	2	1	1	1	0	0	0	0	0	0	0	1	0	0	1	0	1	1	1	1	0
insolent	5	.4305	.4752	36.8	0	0	0	1	1	1	1	1	1	1	0	1	0	0	0	0	0	0	0	0	0	0	0	2	0
insoluble	4	.1249	.1371	31.4	0	0	0	0	2	0	2	0	0	0	0	0	0	0	0	2	0	0	0	2	0	0	0	0	0
inspect	12	.6490	1.6287	42.1	0	2	2	2	2	4	0	0	3	0	0	1	0	4	1	1	0	0	0	0	0	1	0	1	0
inspected	18	.7669	2.7995	44.5	1	2	3	5	2	3	2	0	4	1	0	1	1	4	0	1	0	0	1	1	0	1	1	2	0
inspecting	7	.5624	.8590	39.3	1	2	0	3	1	0	0	0	3	0	0	0	0	0	0	1	0	0	0	0	1	1	0	1	0
inspection	34	.6782	4.6758	46.7	2	2	2	0	8	5	13	2	1	3	0	2	2	2	0	5	0	0	5	0	4	2	5	3	0
inspections	2	.2427	.1159	30.6	0	0	0	2	0	0	0	0	0	0	0	0	1	0	0	0	0	0	0	0	0	0	0	1	0
inspector	17	.7315	2.5103	44.0	2	0	0	0	5	5	5	0	1	1	0	1	1	3	0	0	1	0	0	1	4	2	2	0	0

8A inn-yard
4D innately
5Q Inner
7R inner-wall
5P Innerschweiz
3P Inness
7P Inness'
4F innkeepers
6A Innocence
4J Innocent
6R Innovations
XR innovators
XH inoculate
8F Inouye
XR inpatients
7R inputs
9D inquisitively
6G ins
8D insanity
7E inscribe
8Q Inscribed
9D inscrolled
5P inscrutable
9D insculped
6G insecare
6H insect-pollinated
7Q insect-ridden
8A insect-size
7H insect-type
7H Insecta
7H insensibility
5N insensible
7R insensitivity
4Q insets
3D inside-out
4P insidiously
8P insignificance
9B insipid
7N insolence
8B insolently
6F insoles
5Q insolvency
9L insomnia
7Q insomniacs
9D insomuch
5P insouciance
8H Inspection

Word Type	F	D	U	SFI	3 Gr 3	4 Gr 4	5 Gr 5	6 Gr 6	7 Gr 7	8 Gr 8	9 Gr 9	X UnGr	A Read	B Eng & Gr	C Comp	D Lit	E Math	F Soc Stud	G Spell	H Sci	J Music	K Art	L Home Ec	M Shop	N Lib F	P Lib NF	Q Lib Ref	R Mag	S Rel
Inspector	2	.2443	.1130	30.5	0	0	0	0	1	1	0	0	0	0	0	1	0	0	0	0	0	0	0	0	1	0	0	0	0
inspectors	10	.4635	1.0065	40.0	0	0	0	2	0	6	2	0	0	1	0	1	0	4	0	4	0	0	0	0	0	0	0	0	0
inspects	4	.4764	.4070	36.1	0	1	0	2	0	1	0	0	0	0	0	1	0	1	0	1	0	0	0	0	0	0	0	1	0
inspiration	35	.6536	4.6754	46.7	0	1	3	3	13	10	3	2	5	2	0	1	0	0	0	0	13	1	0	1	1	3	2	6	0
inspirational	2	.2437	.1129	30.5	0	0	1	0	0	1	0	0	0	0	0	0	0	0	0	0	0	0	0	0	0	0	1	1	0
inspirations	2	.2433	.1158	30.6	0	0	1	0	0	1	0	0	0	0	0	0	0	0	0	0	0	0	0	0	0	1	0	1	0
inspire	10	.4661	.9752	39.9	0	0	0	5	1	0	4	0	0	0	0	2	0	0	0	0	0	0	0	0	0	2	0	3	0
inspired	60	.6146	7.5933	48.8	3	3	9	5	16	15	7	2	7	1	0	0	1	6	3	1	17	3	0	0	1	4	16	3	0
inspires	4	.1854	.1872	32.7	0	0	1	0	1	0	0	2	0	0	0	0	0	0	0	0	0	0	0	0	0	1	0	3	0
inspiring	7	.4081	.6120	37.9	0	0	2	0	2	3	0	0	0	0	0	1	0	2	0	0	3	0	0	0	1	0	0	0	0
install	25	.3701	2.0216	43.1	0	0	1	1	16	4	2	1	2	0	0	0	0	0	0	2	0	0	0	7	0	4	3	7	0
installation	19	.5958	2.3287	43.7	0	0	0	2	6	6	5	0	1	0	0	0	0	0	0	2	0	0	1	1	0	2	5	7	0
installations	8	.4561	.7783	38.9	0	0	3	0	0	3	1	1	0	0	0	0	0	1	0	1	0	0	0	0	0	1	1	4	0
installed	50	.7512	7.5810	48.8	1	2	2	3	21	10	7	4	4	3	0	3	0	6	0	4	0	0	1	1	1	9	3	15	0
installing	9	.4288	.8235	39.2	0	1	0	0	8	0	0	0	0	0	0	0	0	1	0	0	0	0	0	1	0	3	0	4	0
installment	15	.2810	.9193	39.6	0	1	0	0	3	7	1	3	0	1	0	0	2	0	0	0	0	0	7	0	0	1	0	4	0
installments	3	.3849	.2570	34.1	0	0	0	1	1	1	0	0	0	0	0	0	1	1	0	0	0	0	0	0	0	1	0	0	0
installs	2	.0000	.0290	24.6	0	0	0	0	2	0	0	0	0	0	0	0	0	0	0	0	0	0	0	0	0	2	0	0	0
instance	292	.9015	52.222	57.2	17	21	37	36	88	43	42	8	35	27	3	25	19	13	6	64	8	0	11	5	9	15	35	17	0
instances	39	.7847	6.1558	47.9	2	2	5	6	8	6	8	2	3	1	0	2	1	7	0	8	1	0	1	1	0	5	8	1	0
instant	135	.8448	22.834	53.6	16	17	15	16	33	11	24	3	32	7	1	12	2	5	0	6	2	0	4	1	24	11	7	21	0
Instant	2	.0000	.0243	23.9	0	0	1	0	0	0	0	1	0	0	0	0	0	0	0	0	0	0	0	0	0	0	0	2	0
instantaneous	4	.3352	.2986	34.8	0	0	0	0	3	0	0	1	0	0	0	0	0	0	0	1	0	0	0	0	0	0	2	1	0
instantaneously	5	.4655	.4866	36.9	0	0	0	0	4	0	1	0	0	1	0	1	0	0	0	0	0	0	0	0	0	0	2	1	0
instantly	76	.7356	11.486	50.6	5	7	8	10	23	13	5	5	29	3	2	9	0	0	0	3	0	0	0	0	11	9	4	6	0
instead	998	.9699	190.82	62.8	148	152	125	137	172	125	106	33	219	68	7	36	56	112	32	123	35	11	19	16	62	93	43	66	0
instep	2	.1717	.1142	30.6	0	0	1	0	1	0	0	0	1	0	0	1	0	0	0	0	0	0	0	0	0	0	0	0	0
instigated	2	.2351	.1166	30.7	0	0	0	0	1	1	0	0	0	0	0	0	0	1	0	0	0	0	0	0	0	0	0	1	0
instill	2	.2401	.1133	30.5	0	0	0	1	0	0	1	0	0	0	0	0	0	0	0	0	0	0	0	0	0	1	1	0	0
instinct	46	.8087	7.5135	48.8	2	3	3	11	12	4	10	1	14	0	0	5	0	2	1	6	0	1	1	0	6	5	3	2	0
instinctive	9	.6195	1.1323	40.5	1	0	0	0	4	1	3	0	0	0	0	1	0	0	1	1	1	1	0	0	0	1	2	1	0
instinctively	22	.7344	3.3120	45.2	0	2	3	2	10	1	3	1	8	1	0	4	0	0	1	0	0	0	1	0	2	2	2	1	0
instincts	6	.3780	.5308	37.2	0	1	0	1	2	0	2	0	2	0	0	0	0	0	0	1	0	1	0	0	1	0	0	1	0
institute	10	.3626	.7913	39.0	0	0	3	0	3	1	3	0	0	0	0	3	0	1	0	1	0	0	0	0	0	0	5	0	0
Institute	50	.7031	7.1300	48.5	3	1	16	4	10	6	8	2	5	0	2	3	1	3	0	2	2	2	0	0	0	3	13	14	0
instituted	6	.5191	.6688	38.3	0	0	2	0	2	2	0	0	1	0	0	0	0	1	0	0	0	0	0	0	1	2	0	1	0
institutes	3	.2043	.1486	31.7	1	0	0	0	0	0	2	0	0	0	0	0	0	0	0	0	0	0	0	0	0	1	2	0	0
Institutes	2	.2437	.1129	30.5	0	0	0	0	0	0	2	0	0	0	0	0	0	0	0	0	0	0	0	0	0	0	1	1	0
institution	28	.6526	3.6993	45.7	0	1	3	1	8	8	5	2	0	1	0	1	0	1	0	0	3	0	1	0	2	2	9	8	0
Institution	13	.4772	1.3414	41.3	1	1	2	0	2	2	0	5	1	0	0	0	0	0	0	6	0	0	0	0	0	1	3	2	0
institutions	37	.6477	4.8864	46.9	2	0	11	0	10	8	6	0	2	1	0	1	0	3	2	0	1	1	0	0	0	6	15	5	0
instruct	4	.4417	.3913	35.9	1	0	0	1	0	0	2	0	1	0	0	1	0	0	0	0	1	0	0	0	0	1	0	0	0
instructed	24	.5542	2.8214	44.5	0	0	1	7	9	5	2	0	6	3	1	0	0	4	0	0	0	0	5	0	2	1	0	2	0
instructing	2	.2441	.1127	30.5	0	0	0	0	2	0	0	0	0	0	0	0	0	0	0	0	0	0	0	0	1	0	1	0	0
instruction	51	.7853	8.0529	49.1	1	0	7	4	20	7	10	2	7	2	2	3	0	5	0	2	2	0	2	0	1	7	11	7	0
instructional	2	.0000	.0243	23.9	0	0	0	0	0	0	0	2	0	0	0	0	0	0	0	0	0	0	0	0	0	0	0	2	0
instructions	91	.7330	13.603	51.3	11	4	4	16	26	14	14	2	27	9	0	6	2	4	4	1	5	0	4	10	5	0	4	10	0
instructive	3	.3847	.2496	34.0	0	0	0	0	1	1	1	0	0	0	0	0	0	0	0	0	0	0	0	0	0	1	1	1	0
instructor	29	.2932	1.8949	42.8	3	1	0	1	5	5	11	3	2	1	0	0	2	1	0	0	0	0	0	12	0	2	2	7	0
instructor's	3	.0000	.0434	26.4	0	3	0	0	0	0	0	0	0	0	0	0	0	0	0	0	0	0	0	0	0	3	0	0	0
instructors	2	.2351	.1166	30.7	0	0	0	0	0	0	1	1	0	0	0	0	0	1	0	0	0	0	0	0	0	0	0	1	0
instrument	386	.5042	40.567	56.1	36	82	30	51	102	62	19	4	19	6	3	1	3	7	5	49	230	4	0	4	3	16	22	14	0
Instrument	3	.2580	.1776	32.5	0	0	0	0	2	0	1	0	0	0	0	0	0	0	0	1	0	0	0	1	0	0	0	1	0
instrumental	53	.2012	2.4799	43.9	2	3	9	11	11	13	4	0	0	0	0	0	2	1	0	0	43	0	0	0	0	2	3	2	0
Instrumental	4	.0000	.0323	25.1	0	0	0	0	3	1	0	0	0	0	0	0	0	0	0	0	4	0	0	0	0	0	0	0	0
instrumentalists	2	.0000	.0162	22.1	0	0	1	0	0	1	0	0	0	0	0	0	0	0	0	0	2	0	0	0	0	0	0	0	0
instrumentation	19	.1093	.5528	37.4	1	0	2	0	1	13	2	0	0	0	0	0	0	0	0	0	17	0	0	0	0	1	1	0	0
instrumented	3	.2321	.1635	32.1	0	0	0	0	1	1	1	0	0	0	0	0	0	0	0	0	0	0	0	0	0	0	1	2	0
instruments	656	.4568	63.301	58.0	79	128	85	70	141	120	28	5	32	2	0	2	9	25	1	94	401	5	3	11	6	21	31	13	0
Instruments	3	.0000	.0243	23.8	0	1	0	0	2	0	0	0	0	0	0	0	0	0	0	0	3	0	0	0	0	0	0	0	0
insubstantial	2	.2446	.1122	30.5	0	0	0	0	2	0	0	0	0	0	0	1	0	0	0	0	0	0	0	0	0	0	1	0	0
insufferable	2	.2446	.1142	30.6	0	0	0	0	0	1	0	1	0	0	0	0	0	0	0	0	0	0	0	0	1	0	0	1	0
insufficient	4	.3779	.3297	35.2	0	0	1	0	0	0	2	1	0	0	0	0	1	0	0	1	0	0	1	0	0	1	0	0	0
insulated	12	.5076	1.2634	41.0	1	0	1	2	2	4	0	2	0	1	0	0	0	0	0	2	0	0	0	2	1	0	3	3	0
insulates	2	.1698	.1133	30.5	0	0	1	1	0	0	0	0	1	0	0	0	0	0	0	0	0	0	0	0	0	0	1	0	0
insulating	10	.4264	.9111	39.6	0	1	2	2	2	3	0	0	1	0	0	0	0	0	0	2	0	1	0	3	0	0	2	1	0
insulation	39	.5718	4.5994	46.6	3	4	12	1	7	8	0	4	0	0	0	0	0	0	0	12	0	0	1	4	1	5	13	3	0
insulator	10	.3560	.7936	39.0	0	2	1	0	2	3	2	0	0	0	0	0	0	0	0	6	0	0	0	2	0	0	1	1	0
insulators	11	.3093	.8089	39.1	0	0	1	0	2	8	0	0	1	0	0	0	0	0	0	7	0	0	0	2	0	1	0	0	0
insulin	3	.0000	.0591	27.7	0	0	0	0	3	0	0	0	0	0	0	0	0	0	0	3	0	0	0	0	0	0	0	0	0
Insull	5	.0000	.0972	29.9	0	0	0	0	0	5	0	0	0	0	0	0	0	5	0	0	0	0	0	0	0	0	0	0	0
Insull's	2	.0000	.0389	25.9	0	0	0	0	0	2	0	0	0	0	0	0	0	2	0	0	0	0	0	0	0	0	0	0	0
insult	17	.5720	2.0882	43.2	0	0	2	1	9	3	2	0	6	1	0	3	0	1	0	0	0	0	0	0	0	2	0	4	0
insulted	9	.5731	1.0971	40.4	0	0	0	0	4	1	3	1	2	1	0	1	0	1	0	1	0	0	0	0	0	3	0	0	0
insulting	11	.5028	1.1952	40.8	0	0	0	0	5	3	2	1	2	0	0	3	0	2	0	0	0	0	0	0	0	3	0	1	0
insults	7	.3402	.6156	37.9	1	0	0	0	4	1	1	0	4	0	0	2	0	1	0	0	0	0	0	0	0	0	0	0	0
insurance	71	.5587	8.3569	49.2	11	22	7	0	11	4	15	1	11	2	0	0	9	9	0	1	0	0	1	0	1	3	31	3	0
Insurance	7	.4714	.6917	38.4	0	1	1	0	0	2	2	1	0	0	1	0	1	1	0	0	0	0	0	0	0	0	2	2	0
insure	29	.6989	4.1389	46.2	0	2	2	4	9	7	4	1	4	0	2	1	0	6	1	5	0	0	2	0	0	1	5	2	0
insured	11	.6405	1.4493	41.6	0	0	1	3	3	0	4	0	1	1	0	2	2	2	0	0	0	0	0	0	0	0	2	1	0
insures	3	.2345	.1568	32.0	0	0	2	0	0	0	1	0	0	0	0	0	0	0	0	0	0	0	1	0	0	0	2	0	0
insurgent	2	.2446	.1123	30.5	0	0	0	1	0	0	1	0	0	1	0	0	0	0	0	0	0	0	0	0	0	0	1	0	0
insuring	4	.3863	.3414	35.3	0	1	0	1	1	0	1	0	0	0	0	0	0	2	0	0	0	0	0	0	0	0	1	1	0
insurrection	2	.1948	.1250	31.0	0	0	0	1	1	0	0	0	1	0	0	0	0	0	0	0	0	0	0	0	0	1	0	0	0
int	2	.2408	.1091	30.4	0	0	0	0	0	1	1	0	0	1	0	0	0	0	1	0	0	0	0	0	0	0	0	0	0
intact	8	.4867	.8537	39.3	1	1	1	0	0	4	1	0	2	0	0	0	0	0	0	1	0	0	0	0	0	1	1	3	0
intake	31	.6181	3.9489	46.0	0	0	3	2	14	4	6	2	3	0	0	3	0	1	0	8	0	0	3	3	0	0	3	7	0
intakes	2	.1814	.1187	30.7	0	0	0	1	1	0	0	0	1	0	0	0	0	0	0	0	0	0	0	0	0	0	0	1	0
intangible	2	.2437	.1129	30.5	0	0	0	0	1	0	0	1	0	0	0	0	0	0	0	0	0	0	0	0	0	0	1	1	0
integer	98	.0268	1.9392	42.9	0	0	25	2	14	35	22	0	0	0	0	0	97	0	0	0	0	0	0	0	0	0	1	0	0
integers	118	.0000	1.7663	42.5	0	0	10	1	17	46	44	0	0	0	0	0	118	0	0	0	0	0	0	0	0	0	0	0	0
integral	16	.4974	1.6670	42.2	0	1	1	0	4	1	9	0	0	0	2	0	7	1	0	0	0	0	0	0	1	3	2	0	0
integrated	12	.5051	1.2670	41.0	0	0	1	0	1	4	5	1	0	0	0	0	0	2	0	1	2	0	0	0	0	0	4	3	0
integration	14	.4094	1.2617	41.0	0	0	1	0	3	2	8	0	0	0	0	0	0	8	0	0	0	0	0	0	0	1	1	4	0
integrity	11	.5205	1.2397	40.9	0	0	0	1	4	4	2	0	3	0	0	0	0	2	0	0	2	0	0	0	0	0	1	3	0
intellect	11	.5326	1.2414	40.9	0	1	0	0	4	3	3	0	2	1	0	2	1	0	0	0	0	0	0	0	0	0	4	1	0
intellectual	32	.6873	4.4478	46.5	2	0	3	0	11	5	7	4	0	2	0	1	0	5	0	1	0	1	2	0	0	4	5	11	0

8F Inspirationists
9Q instability
XR instant-fit
8A instant's
7N instants
3R INSTEAD
8A instigates
5Q instigating
8R instigation
7R instilled
7R instilling
9R Institut
9R institutional
5P institutionalize
6F Institutions
9F instructs
6R instrument-lined
9Q instrument-maker
9Q instrument-makers
7A instrumentalist
XR insufficiency
7R insular
5P insularity
5Q Insulation
7C insuperable
6P insupportable
6B insurgents
9N insurmountable
8F insurrectionary
7A insurrectionists
8F insurrections
9M intaglio
9Q intangibles
9F integrate
4D integument
9H integumentary
7N intellects
9Q Intellectual

Word Type	F	D	U	SFI	3 Gr 3	4 Gr 4	5 Gr 5	6 Gr 6	7 Gr 7	8 Gr 8	9 Gr 9	X UnGr	A Read	B Eng & Gr	C Comp	D Lit	E Math	F Soc Stud	G Spell	H Sci	J Music	K Art	L Home Ec	M Shop	N Lib F	P Lib NF	Q Lib Ref	R Mag	S Rel
intellectually	3	.0000	.0314	25.0	0	1	0	0	0	1	1	0	0	0	0	0	0	0	0	0	0	0	0	0	0	0	3	0	0
intellectuals	6	.4716	.6026	37.8	0	0	0	0	2	3	1	0	0	0	0	0	0	2	0	0	0	0	0	0	0	1	1	2	0
intelligence	73	.7549	11.173	50.5	4	1	5	14	21	10	16	2	14	1	1	7	0	6	0	7	0	1	1	0	0	4	10	21	0
intelligent	70	.8270	11.601	50.6	1	2	10	10	20	9	12	6	13	6	1	4	0	4	0	7	2	0	3	0	5	4	7	14	0
intelligently	12	.6439	1.5720	42.0	1	0	1	0	2	3	5	0	1	1	1	0	2	0	0	1	0	0	2	1	0	0	2	1	0
intelligible	4	.3833	.3412	35.3	0	0	0	0	1	1	1	1	0	0	0	1	0	0	0	2	0	0	0	0	0	1	0	0	0
intend	34	.6299	4.4775	46.5	2	2	3	3	10	7	6	1	11	1	4	3	0	2	1	0	0	0	3	0	4	3	0	2	0
intendant	5	.0000	.0586	27.7	0	0	5	0	0	0	0	0	0	0	0	0	0	0	0	0	0	0	0	0	5	0	0	0	0
intended	113	.8346	18.859	52.8	2	7	11	11	24	17	34	7	21	16	6	9	2	9	2	4	9	5	0	2	4	5	5	14	0
intendere	2	.0000	.0162	22.1	0	0	0	0	1	1	0	0	0	0	0	0	0	0	2	0	0	0	0	0	0	0	0	0	0
intending	10	.4710	1.1150	40.5	0	2	1	2	4	0	1	0	7	0	0	0	0	0	0	0	0	0	0	0	1	1	0	1	0
intends	9	.5383	1.0128	40.1	0	0	0	0	1	4	4	0	1	0	1	1	1	1	0	0	0	1	0	0	0	0	0	3	0
intense	58	.7136	8.4047	49.2	0	1	5	10	16	14	6	6	7	3	1	3	0	4	0	9	1	6	1	0	3	6	6	8	0
intensely	18	.6286	2.3476	43.7	1	0	4	4	3	1	2	3	3	0	0	2	0	0	0	2	0	0	0	0	1	4	4	2	0
intensified	15	.6373	1.9756	43.0	1	0	2	1	3	6	2	0	2	0	0	2	0	3	0	0	1	0	0	0	0	2	1	4	0
intensifiers	5	.0000	.0547	27.4	0	0	0	0	4	1	0	0	0	5	0	0	0	0	0	0	0	0	0	0	0	0	0	0	0
intensify	4	.3408	.2936	34.7	0	0	0	0	1	1	2	0	0	0	0	1	0	0	0	0	2	0	0	0	0	0	0	1	0
intensifying	3	.1823	.1405	31.5	0	0	0	0	1	1	1	0	0	0	0	0	0	1	0	0	0	0	0	0	0	0	2	0	0
intensities	4	.0758	.0744	28.7	0	0	0	0	0	4	0	0	0	0	0	0	0	0	0	0	0	3	0	0	0	0	1	0	0
intensity	68	.6282	8.6825	49.4	0	0	1	2	21	30	11	3	2	0	0	1	0	5	0	10	22	8	4	2	0	3	6	5	0
intensive	13	.4827	1.3309	41.2	0	0	1	0	3	1	8	0	0	0	0	0	0	3	0	2	0	0	0	0	0	1	5	2	0
intensively	5	.2948	.3343	35.2	0	0	2	0	1	2	0	0	0	0	0	0	0	0	0	1	0	0	0	0	0	0	3	1	0
intent	31	.7127	4.5041	46.5	1	2	1	3	9	6	9	0	5	2	0	8	0	4	0	1	1	0	0	0	4	2	1	3	0
intention	25	.6830	3.5109	45.5	1	0	2	5	7	3	6	1	6	0	1	3	0	3	1	0	0	2	0	0	1	2	1	5	0
intentionally	3	.3380	.2498	34.0	0	0	0	0	1	0	1	1	1	1	0	0	0	0	0	1	0	0	0	0	0	0	0	0	0
intentions	15	.6388	2.0128	43.0	1	1	1	2	5	2	3	0	5	0	0	2	0	1	0	0	1	0	0	0	1	4	0	1	0
intently	24	.5312	2.7539	44.4	3	8	1	3	5	3	1	0	7	1	0	2	0	0	0	0	0	0	0	0	8	5	0	1	0
inter	3	.2432	.1790	32.5	0	0	1	0	2	0	0	0	0	0	0	0	0	2	1	0	0	0	0	0	0	0	0	0	0
inter-American	2	.0000	.0209	23.2	0	0	2	0	0	0	0	0	0	0	0	0	0	0	0	0	0	0	0	0	0	0	2	0	0
interact	8	.3864	.6837	38.3	4	0	0	0	1	1	0	2	0	0	0	0	0	0	0	4	0	0	0	0	0	0	2	2	0
interacting	5	.3749	.4195	36.2	1	0	0	0	1	2	0	1	0	0	0	0	0	0	0	3	0	0	0	0	0	0	1	1	0
interaction	13	.4769	1.3158	41.2	3	1	2	0	4	2	1	0	0	0	0	0	0	0	0	5	0	0	0	1	0	3	4	0	0
interactions	2	.0000	.0394	26.0	0	0	0	0	2	0	0	0	0	0	0	0	0	0	0	2	0	0	0	0	0	0	0	0	0
interbreed	2	.0000	.0209	23.2	0	0	0	0	2	0	0	0	0	0	0	0	0	0	0	0	0	0	0	0	0	0	2	0	0
intercept	7	.5587	.8535	39.3	1	0	0	1	4	1	0	0	3	0	0	1	0	0	0	1	0	0	0	0	0	1	1	0	0
intercepted	4	.4870	.4078	36.1	0	0	0	1	2	0	1	0	0	0	0	0	0	0	0	0	0	0	0	0	1	1	1	1	0
interceptions	2	.0000	.0243	23.9	0	0	0	1	0	1	0	0	0	0	0	0	0	0	0	0	0	0	0	0	0	0	0	2	0
interchange	6	.3804	.4943	36.9	0	0	1	0	3	1	1	0	0	0	0	0	3	0	0	0	1	0	0	0	0	0	2	0	0
interchangeable	8	.5673	.9412	39.7	0	0	0	0	4	2	1	1	1	0	0	0	0	0	0	1	2	0	1	1	0	1	0	1	0
interchangeably	7	.5155	.7579	38.8	1	0	0	0	2	2	2	0	1	1	0	0	1	0	0	0	2	0	0	1	0	0	1	0	0
interchanged	3	.2398	.1721	32.4	0	0	0	0	1	0	2	0	0	0	0	0	2	0	0	0	0	0	0	0	0	0	1	0	0
interchanges	2	.2418	.1091	30.4	0	0	1	0	0	0	1	0	0	0	0	0	0	0	1	0	0	0	0	0	0	0	1	0	0
interchanging	2	.2446	.1123	30.5	0	0	0	0	1	0	1	0	0	1	0	0	0	0	0	0	0	0	0	0	0	0	1	0	0
intercom	3	.0000	.0365	25.6	0	0	1	1	1	0	0	0	0	0	0	0	0	0	0	0	0	0	0	0	0	0	0	3	0
interconnected	2	.2437	.1129	30.5	0	0	0	0	1	0	1	0	0	0	0	0	0	0	0	0	0	0	0	0	0	0	1	1	0
intercourse	8	.5423	.9030	39.6	0	0	2	0	2	4	0	0	0	0	0	0	0	2	0	0	0	0	0	0	1	1	2	2	0
interdependence	3	.0000	.0591	27.7	0	0	0	0	3	0	0	0	0	0	0	0	0	0	0	3	0	0	0	0	0	0	0	0	0
interdependent	7	.4496	.6824	38.3	0	0	2	0	4	0	1	0	0	0	0	0	0	4	0	1	1	0	0	0	0	0	1	0	0
interdisciplinary	2	.0000	.0209	23.2	0	0	0	0	0	0	2	0	0	0	0	0	0	0	0	0	0	0	0	0	0	0	2	0	0
interest	560	.8973	99.688	60.0	35	34	71	65	151	88	100	16	80	43	11	19	79	36	1	24	41	18	31	11	26	36	65	39	0
interested	438	.9408	81.543	59.1	38	63	72	65	78	56	56	10	118	43	2	19	10	52	5	36	30	3	7	7	15	30	27	34	0
interesting	712	.8302	118.19	60.7	82	116	104	95	137	88	70	20	114	132	15	27	40	72	24	51	68	50	19	12	10	28	30	20	0
interestingly	9	.5651	1.0679	40.3	0	0	0	2	2	2	3	0	2	0	0	2	0	0	1	0	1	1	0	0	0	1	0	1	0
interests	132	.8410	22.129	53.4	4	6	20	15	22	35	25	5	12	12	6	3	1	24	2	11	14	1	9	3	0	5	20	9	0
interface	4	.1432	.1519	31.8	0	0	0	0	1	1	2	0	0	0	0	0	0	0	0	2	0	0	2	0	0	0	0	0	0
interfaced	3	.0000	.0097	19.8	0	0	0	0	0	3	0	0	0	0	0	0	0	0	0	0	0	0	3	0	0	0	0	0	0
interfaces	2	.0000	.0394	26.0	0	0	0	0	2	0	0	0	0	0	0	0	0	0	0	2	0	0	0	0	0	0	0	0	0
interfacing	11	.0000	.0354	25.5	0	0	0	0	1	10	0	0	0	0	0	0	0	0	0	0	0	0	11	0	0	0	0	0	0
interfacings	3	.0000	.0097	19.8	0	0	0	0	0	1	2	0	0	0	0	0	0	0	0	0	0	0	3	0	0	0	0	0	0
interfere	37	.6673	5.0712	47.1	1	1	3	7	8	9	7	1	4	0	0	3	0	6	1	9	0	0	4	0	0	5	3	2	0
interfered	9	.6114	1.1393	40.6	0	0	1	0	4	2	1	1	1	1	0	0	0	1	0	0	0	0	0	0	1	1	1	3	0
interference	15	.6373	1.9513	42.9	0	0	1	0	5	5	1	3	0	1	0	1	0	0	1	4	0	0	0	0	1	0	3	4	0
interferes	6	.2781	.3828	35.8	0	0	3	0	2	1	0	0	0	0	0	0	0	0	0	3	0	0	2	0	0	0	1	0	0
interfering	11	.6064	1.3726	41.4	0	0	3	2	1	3	2	0	0	0	0	0	0	4	0	0	1	0	0	0	2	1	2	1	0
interferometer	3	.0000	.0591	27.7	0	0	0	0	0	0	0	3	0	0	0	0	0	0	0	3	0	0	0	0	0	0	0	0	0
intergranular	2	.0000	.0209	23.2	0	0	0	0	0	2	0	0	0	0	0	0	0	0	0	0	0	0	0	0	0	0	2	0	0
interim	4	.2090	.2014	33.0	0	0	1	0	0	1	1	1	0	0	0	0	0	0	0	0	0	0	0	0	0	0	1	3	0
interior	166	.7592	25.408	54.0	4	15	25	21	45	11	40	5	6	1	0	6	30	41	0	29	0	7	0	4	8	4	21	9	0
Interior	25	.6159	3.1704	45.0	2	1	8	0	1	4	3	6	0	0	0	1	0	8	0	3	0	0	1	0	0	2	2	8	0
interiors	12	.4920	1.2671	41.0	1	0	0	1	6	1	2	1	1	0	0	0	1	1	0	3	0	0	0	0	0	0	1	5	0
interjected	2	.2446	.1123	30.5	0	0	0	0	1	1	0	0	0	1	0	0	0	0	0	0	0	0	0	0	0	0	1	0	0
interjection	10	.0987	.2376	33.8	0	0	4	0	3	0	3	0	0	3	7	0	0	0	0	0	0	0	0	0	0	0	0	0	0
interjections	3	.2793	.1826	32.6	0	0	1	0	1	0	1	0	0	1	1	0	0	0	0	0	0	0	0	0	1	0	0	0	0
interlaced	2	.1674	.0805	29.1	0	1	0	0	0	1	0	0	0	0	0	0	0	0	0	0	0	0	1	0	0	1	0	0	0
interlining	2	.0000	.0064	18.1	0	0	0	0	0	2	0	0	0	0	0	0	0	0	0	0	0	0	2	0	0	0	0	0	0
interlock	3	.2942	.1970	32.9	0	0	0	0	1	1	1	0	0	0	0	0	0	0	0	1	0	0	1	0	0	0	1	0	0
interlocked	6	.5063	.6328	38.0	0	1	0	1	2	0	2	0	0	0	0	0	0	0	0	1	2	0	0	0	1	1	1	0	0
interlocking	4	.4336	.3884	35.9	0	0	0	1	1	1	1	0	1	0	0	0	0	0	1	1	0	0	0	0	0	0	1	0	0
interlude	7	.2304	.3675	35.7	0	0	0	0	4	0	3	0	0	0	0	1	0	0	0	0	5	0	0	0	0	1	0	0	0
interludes	4	.1789	.1692	32.3	0	0	2	1	1	0	0	0	0	0	0	0	0	0	0	0	3	0	0	0	0	0	1	0	0
intermarried	2	.0000	.0389	25.9	0	0	0	1	0	1	0	0	0	0	0	0	0	2	0	0	0	0	0	0	0	0	0	0	0
intermarrying	2	.2408	.1204	30.8	0	0	1	0	0	1	0	0	0	0	0	0	0	1	0	0	0	0	0	0	0	1	0	0	0
intermediate	26	.5886	3.1247	44.9	0	1	4	1	9	5	5	1	0	0	1	0	4	0	0	2	1	0	0	5	1	5	4	3	0
Intermediate	2	.0000	.0389	25.9	0	0	0	0	2	0	0	0	0	0	0	0	0	2	0	0	0	0	0	0	0	0	0	0	0
Intermezzo	2	.0000	.0162	22.1	0	0	0	0	0	2	0	0	0	0	0	0	0	0	0	0	2	0	0	0	0	0	0	0	0
interminable	7	.3634	.5435	37.4	0	0	0	0	2	2	3	0	0	0	1	4	0	0	0	0	0	0	0	0	2	0	0	0	0
interminably	2	.2446	.1142	30.6	0	0	0	0	1	0	0	1	0	0	0	0	0	0	0	0	0	0	0	0	1	0	0	1	0
intermingle	2	.2278	.1128	30.5	0	0	0	1	1	0	0	0	0	0	0	0	0	0	0	1	0	0	0	0	0	0	1	0	0
intermingled	2	.2375	.1088	30.4	1	0	0	0	0	1	0	0	0	0	0	0	0	0	0	0	1	0	0	0	0	0	0	1	0
intermission	8	.5530	.9053	39.6	0	0	2	0	2	1	2	1	0	1	1	1	0	0	0	0	1	0	0	0	1	0	0	3	0
intermittent	6	.5280	.6740	38.3	0	0	1	2	1	1	0	1	1	0	0	0	0	0	0	0	0	0	0	0	1	2	1	1	0
intermittently	6	.2870	.4107	36.1	0	0	0	2	2	0	2	0	1	0	0	0	0	0	0	0	0	0	0	0	0	0	3	2	0
intern	2	.2152	.1357	31.3	0	0	0	0	1	0	1	0	1	0	0	0	0	1	0	0	0	0	0	0	0	0	0	0	0
internal	85	.6874	11.844	50.7	0	2	8	3	24	20	25	3	2	2	1	2	0	5	2	21	0	0	1	8	1	8	26	6	0
Internal	6	.3304	.4470	36.5	0	0	0	0	2	1	3	0	0	0	0	0	2	1	0	0	0	0	0	0	0	0	0	3	0
internal-combustion	8	.0782	.2923	34.7	0	0	4	0	1	3	0	0	1	0	0	0	0	0	0	7	0	0	0	0	0	0	0	0	0

9R intelligentsia
8A intelligibly
7B intensifier
8B intensifies
7R intensive-training
8A intentional
7Q Inter-American
7Q inter-church
XR inter-relationship
3H interacted
9J interactive
7R interacts
9R intercede
7Q intercellular
3A interceptor
7D intercession
7P interchangeability
XR intercity
6P interclass
7Q Intercollegian
8F intercolonial
7Q intercommunication
7Q interconnecting
8R intercontinental
8F Intercourse
5F Interdependence
5Q Interest
XR interest-bearing
4P interestedly
5Q Interesting
XH interferometric
7Q interfold
7Q interglacial
9Q intergrowths
7R Interior's
8G interj
8N interlacing
7R interlarded
9L interlinings
9D interlopers
5F intermarriage
9H intermediate-
8M intermediate-frequency
7F intermediate-school
7R intermediate-size
7Q intermeshing
8Q intermingling
4Q intermolecular

Word Type	F	D	U	SFI	3 Gr 3	4 Gr 4	5 Gr 5	6 Gr 6	7 Gr 7	8 Gr 8	9 Gr 9	X UnGr	A Read	B Eng & Gr	C Comp	D Lit	E Math	F Soc Stud	G Spell	H Sci	J Music	K Art	L Home Ec	M Shop	N Lib F	P Lib NF	Q Lib Ref	R Mag	S Rel
internally	6	.3613	.4864	36.9	0	0	2	0	2	1	0	1	0	0	0	0	0	0	0	3	0	0	0	0	0	1	2	0	0
international	121	.5968	14.964	51.8	4	10	22	13	23	17	26	6	7	3	2	0	0	36	0	4	2	0	0	0	0	10	43	14	0
International	69	.7149	10.091	50.0	1	10	12	12	13	10	11	0	12	1	0	2	0	17	4	9	1	0	0	0	0	3	13	7	0
INTERNATIONAL	2	.2446	.1122	30.5	0	1	0	0	1	0	0	0	0	0	0	1	0	0	0	0	0	0	0	0	0	0	1	0	0
internationally	4	.3790	.3299	35.2	0	0	2	0	0	0	1	1	0	0	0	0	0	0	0	0	0	0	0	0	0	2	1	1	0
interned	2	.2285	.1129	30.5	0	0	0	0	0	2	0	0	0	0	0	0	0	1	0	0	0	0	0	0	0	0	1	0	0
interpersonal	2	.0000	.0243	23.9	0	0	0	0	0	0	0	2	0	0	0	0	0	0	0	0	0	0	0	0	0	0	0	2	0
interplanetary	14	.3177	1.0734	40.3	0	1	0	0	4	3	6	0	1	0	0	0	0	2	0	10	0	0	0	0	0	0	1	0	0
interplay	3	.3668	.2405	33.8	0	0	0	0	1	1	1	0	0	0	0	0	0	0	0	1	1	0	0	0	0	0	1	0	0
interposed	2	.2443	.1130	30.5	0	0	0	0	1	1	0	0	0	0	0	1	0	0	0	0	0	0	0	0	1	0	0	0	0
interpret	48	.8529	8.1773	49.1	0	4	5	4	14	9	9	3	7	1	1	2	2	4	3	15	3	1	0	1	0	0	5	3	0
interpretation	53	.7324	7.9255	49.0	4	0	7	3	3	21	11	4	14	3	0	2	1	5	0	3	10	1	0	0	0	3	9	2	0
interpretations	15	.5616	1.7535	42.4	0	0	2	0	3	5	3	2	1	0	0	0	0	2	0	1	2	0	0	0	0	1	5	3	0
interpreted	35	.6895	4.9218	46.9	0	1	2	3	10	10	7	2	3	3	0	2	4	5	0	6	1	3	0	0	0	2	3	3	0
interpreter	11	.4604	1.1216	40.5	0	1	1	0	2	6	1	0	3	0	0	2	0	1	0	0	0	0	0	0	0	1	4	0	0
interpreting	10	.5615	1.1839	40.7	0	1	0	2	1	4	1	1	2	0	0	0	1	2	1	0	2	1	0	0	0	0	0	1	0
interprets	4	.3739	.3373	35.3	0	2	1	0	1	0	0	0	0	0	0	0	0	1	0	2	0	0	0	0	0	0	1	0	0
interrelated	6	.1339	.2157	33.3	0	1	2	0	1	0	2	0	0	0	0	0	0	0	0	0	0	0	0	0	0	1	5	0	0
interrelationship	3	.0000	.0314	25.0	0	1	0	0	1	0	1	0	0	0	0	0	0	0	0	0	0	0	0	0	0	0	3	0	0
interrelationships	5	.3569	.4079	36.1	0	0	1	0	4	0	0	0	0	0	0	0	0	1	0	3	0	0	0	0	0	0	1	0	0
interrogative	8	.1605	.2966	34.7	1	0	0	0	3	0	4	0	0	4	4	0	0	0	0	0	0	0	0	0	0	0	0	0	0
interrupt	18	.6716	2.5202	44.0	1	4	3	1	3	3	3	0	7	4	0	0	0	1	1	0	1	0	1	0	2	1	0	0	0
interrupted	81	.8116	13.222	51.2	4	21	10	10	16	9	7	4	18	4	1	10	1	6	0	3	4	1	0	0	19	9	2	3	0
Interrupted	2	.0000	.0162	22.1	0	0	0	0	0	2	0	0	0	0	0	0	0	0	0	0	2	0	0	0	0	0	0	0	0
interrupting	6	.6052	.7586	38.8	0	1	0	2	1	1	1	0	1	0	0	1	0	1	0	0	0	0	0	0	1	1	0	1	0
interruption	9	.5364	1.0257	40.1	0	0	1	0	4	3	0	1	2	0	0	2	0	0	1	0	0	0	0	0	0	0	2	2	0
interruptions	4	.4525	.3990	36.0	0	0	0	0	1	2	1	0	1	1	0	1	0	0	0	0	0	0	0	0	1	0	0	0	0
interrupts	4	.1717	.2284	33.6	1	0	1	0	1	1	0	0	2	0	0	2	0	0	0	0	0	0	0	0	0	0	0	0	0
interschool	2	.0000	.0394	26.0	0	0	0	0	0	0	2	0	0	0	0	0	0	0	0	2	0	0	0	0	0	0	0	0	0
intersect	79	.1937	3.9383	46.0	1	16	13	17	21	8	3	0	0	2	0	0	74	0	0	0	0	0	0	1	0	0	1	1	0
intersected	4	.3785	.3310	35.2	0	0	0	2	1	0	1	0	0	0	0	0	2	0	0	0	0	0	0	0	1	0	0	1	0
intersecting	33	.2330	1.8612	42.7	0	6	7	1	8	8	3	0	0	0	0	0	30	0	0	0	0	0	0	3	0	0	0	0	0
intersection	118	.4290	10.935	50.4	5	10	25	13	27	17	19	2	1	1	1	1	95	3	0	5	0	0	0	5	1	0	2	3	0
intersectional	2	.0000	.0914	29.6	0	0	0	0	2	0	0	0	2	0	0	0	0	0	0	0	0	0	0	0	0	0	0	0	0
intersections	17	.3299	1.2947	41.1	1	3	3	4	2	2	2	0	1	0	0	0	12	0	0	2	0	0	0	0	0	0	1	1	0
intersects	18	.0623	.4776	36.8	0	2	3	0	5	5	2	1	0	0	0	0	17	0	0	1	0	0	0	0	0	0	0	0	0
interspersed	6	.4426	.5660	37.5	1	1	0	0	1	0	2	1	0	0	0	0	0	1	0	0	0	0	0	0	0	1	2	2	0
interstate	26	.5141	2.7964	44.5	0	2	14	0	3	5	2	0	1	1	0	0	0	3	1	2	0	0	1	0	0	0	14	3	0
Interstate	11	.1178	.3711	35.7	0	0	1	0	7	0	0	3	0	0	0	0	0	0	0	0	0	0	0	0	0	0	1	10	0
Interstates	3	.0000	.0365	25.6	0	0	0	0	3	0	0	0	0	0	0	0	0	0	0	0	0	0	0	0	0	0	0	3	0
interstellar	5	.4137	.4652	36.7	0	0	1	1	2	0	0	1	1	0	0	0	0	0	0	1	0	0	0	0	0	0	1	2	0
interstitial	2	.2437	.1129	30.5	0	0	0	0	1	0	0	1	0	0	0	0	0	0	0	0	0	0	0	0	0	0	1	1	0
intertwined	3	.3390	.2450	33.9	0	0	0	0	1	0	2	0	1	0	0	0	0	0	0	0	0	0	0	0	0	0	1	1	0
interval	57	.3502	4.3882	46.4	0	2	19	16	8	2	9	1	4	0	0	1	4	0	0	4	35	0	0	0	2	1	6	0	0
intervals	86	.6161	10.834	50.3	0	3	19	18	26	8	9	3	6	0	0	2	2	1	0	9	38	0	3	3	3	2	11	6	0
intervene	4	.1854	.1872	32.7	0	0	0	0	2	0	2	0	0	0	0	0	0	0	0	0	0	0	0	0	0	1	0	3	0
intervened	4	.4803	.4067	36.1	0	0	1	1	1	1	0	0	0	0	0	0	0	1	0	0	0	0	0	0	1	1	1	0	0
intervenes	2	.0000	.0209	23.2	0	0	2	0	0	0	0	0	0	0	0	0	0	0	0	0	0	0	0	0	0	0	2	0	0
intervening	3	.2442	.1820	32.6	0	0	0	0	1	0	1	1	0	1	0	0	0	0	0	2	0	0	0	0	0	0	0	0	0
intervention	8	.5150	.8606	39.3	0	0	0	0	3	3	2	0	0	0	0	1	0	2	0	0	0	0	0	0	1	0	3	1	0
interview	25	.5634	3.0523	44.8	0	4	1	7	5	5	3	0	10	1	0	0	0	2	2	0	0	0	0	0	0	3	0	7	0
interviewed	7	.4730	.7156	38.5	0	1	2	0	3	0	1	0	1	1	0	0	0	0	0	1	0	0	0	0	0	0	1	3	0
interviewing	2	.0000	.0243	23.9	0	0	0	0	1	0	0	1	0	0	0	0	0	0	0	0	0	0	0	0	0	0	0	2	0
interviews	9	.3501	.7343	38.7	0	0	1	2	2	1	1	2	2	0	0	0	0	0	0	0	0	0	0	0	0	1	1	5	0
interweaving	3	.0646	.0600	27.8	0	0	0	2	1	0	0	0	0	0	0	0	0	0	0	1	0	2	0	0	0	0	0	0	0
interwoven	5	.5605	.5787	37.6	1	0	0	1	2	1	0	0	0	1	0	1	0	1	0	0	0	0	0	0	0	0	1	1	0
intestinal	11	.3616	.8675	39.4	0	0	0	0	2	3	5	1	0	0	0	0	0	0	0	4	0	0	3	0	0	1	3	0	0
intestine	55	.1926	2.9285	44.7	2	0	29	0	5	15	3	1	0	0	0	0	0	0	0	52	0	0	1	0	0	0	2	0	0
intestines	24	.2439	1.4705	41.7	2	0	5	2	7	1	5	2	0	0	0	0	0	0	0	21	0	0	3	0	0	0	0	0	0
intimacy	5	.4639	.4856	36.9	0	0	0	1	2	0	1	1	0	0	0	1	0	0	0	0	0	0	0	0	1	0	2	1	0
intimate	21	.6799	2.9026	44.6	0	0	0	0	11	5	4	1	2	1	1	2	0	0	0	0	3	0	0	0	0	5	3	4	0
intimated	2	.2441	.1127	30.5	0	0	0	0	0	0	2	0	0	0	0	0	0	0	0	0	0	0	0	0	1	0	1	0	0
intimately	5	.4856	.5165	37.1	0	0	0	0	4	0	0	1	0	0	0	0	0	0	0	2	0	0	0	0	0	1	1	1	0
intimations	2	.0000	.0209	23.2	0	0	0	0	0	0	1	1	0	0	0	0	0	0	0	0	0	0	0	0	0	0	2	0	0
intimidated	3	.2321	.1635	32.1	0	0	0	0	1	0	1	1	0	0	0	0	0	0	0	0	0	0	0	0	0	0	1	2	0
into	10620	.9865	2061.9	73.1	1909	1605	1330	1383	2056	1167	907	263	2879	406	111	575	347	1002	266	1539	223	92	180	111	724	844	614	697	10
intolerable	13	.6729	1.7818	42.5	0	0	2	0	4	4	2	1	1	0	0	2	0	0	0	1	1	0	0	0	3	2	2	1	0
intolerance	4	.1622	.1743	32.4	0	0	0	0	0	4	0	0	0	0	0	0	0	1	0	0	0	0	0	0	0	0	0	3	0
intolerant	2	.1814	.1187	30.7	0	0	0	0	2	0	0	0	1	0	0	0	0	0	0	0	0	0	0	0	0	0	0	1	0
intonation	22	.3260	1.5716	42.0	0	0	0	2	14	5	1	0	0	17	0	0	0	0	1	0	1	0	0	0	1	1	0	1	0
intonations	2	.2412	.1141	30.6	0	0	0	0	2	0	0	0	0	1	0	0	0	0	0	0	0	0	0	0	0	1	0	0	0
intoned	3	.3768	.2437	33.9	0	0	0	1	0	1	1	0	0	0	0	0	0	0	0	0	1	0	0	0	0	1	0	1	0
intoxicated	2	.2446	.1142	30.6	0	1	0	0	1	0	0	0	0	0	0	0	0	0	0	0	0	0	0	0	1	0	0	1	0
intoxicating	2	.2306	.1140	30.6	0	0	0	0	0	1	1	0	0	1	0	0	0	1	0	0	0	0	0	0	0	0	0	0	0
Intracoastal	2	.2408	.1204	30.8	1	0	1	0	0	0	0	0	0	0	0	0	0	1	0	0	0	0	0	0	0	1	0	0	0
intractable	5	.2435	.2726	34.4	0	0	0	0	3	2	0	0	0	0	1	0	0	0	0	0	0	0	0	0	0	0	4	0	0
intransitive	30	.0533	.6246	38.0	0	0	1	0	9	7	13	0	0	29	0	0	0	0	0	0	0	0	0	0	0	0	1	0	0
intransitively	5	.0000	.0547	27.4	0	0	0	0	3	0	2	0	0	5	0	0	0	0	0	0	0	0	0	0	0	0	0	0	0
intrastate	2	.2446	.1123	30.5	0	0	1	0	0	0	1	0	0	1	0	0	0	0	0	0	0	0	0	0	0	0	1	0	0
intrepid	3	.3400	.2455	33.9	0	1	0	1	1	0	0	0	1	1	0	0	0	0	0	0	0	0	0	0	1	0	0	0	0
intricacies	3	.2222	.1558	31.9	0	0	1	0	1	0	1	0	0	1	0	0	0	0	0	0	0	0	0	0	0	0	2	0	0
intricacy	2	.2278	.1128	30.5	0	0	1	0	1	0	0	0	0	0	0	0	0	0	0	1	0	0	0	0	0	0	1	0	0
intricate	31	.6749	4.2679	46.3	0	2	0	2	10	8	8	1	4	1	0	3	0	1	0	2	8	0	0	1	0	1	4	6	0
intricately	7	.3855	.5767	37.6	0	0	0	0	4	1	2	0	0	0	1	0	0	0	0	1	0	0	0	0	1	0	4	0	0
intrigue	7	.3375	.5469	37.4	0	0	0	0	3	2	1	1	1	1	0	0	0	1	0	0	0	0	0	0	0	0	0	4	0
intrigued	10	.5929	1.2132	40.8	0	0	2	1	3	2	2	0	0	0	0	0	2	0	0	1	1	1	0	0	2	0	1	2	0
intriguing	5	.4507	.4762	36.8	0	1	0	0	2	0	2	0	0	0	0	0	0	0	0	1	1	0	0	0	0	0	2	1	0
intrinsic	3	.2445	.1818	32.6	0	0	0	0	1	0	1	1	0	0	0	0	0	0	0	2	0	0	0	0	0	0	1	0	0
introduce	69	.7217	10.035	50.0	15	6	4	8	16	5	12	3	5	18	7	0	4	1	4	5	4	0	4	0	6	2	5	4	0
introduced	152	.8973	27.052	54.3	12	11	14	19	42	22	25	7	17	18	2	6	7	13	3	9	12	1	3	0	8	11	25	17	0
introduces	27	.4526	2.5591	44.1	2	6	1	0	8	5	4	1	2	3	8	0	1	1	2	1	6	0	1	0	0	0	0	2	0
introducing	14	.6755	1.9145	42.8	0	1	0	2	5	4	2	0	0	2	0	1	1	0	0	2	1	0	0	0	1	0	4	2	0
introduction	97	.5833	11.658	50.7	12	3	13	14	17	17	20	1	9	18	3	4	0	6	1	3	44	0	0	1	0	2	5	1	0
Introduction	2	.2407	.1090	30.4	0	0	1	0	1	0	0	0	0	1	0	0	0	0	0	0	1	0	0	0	0	0	0	0	0
introductions	14	.5283	1.5333	41.9	4	1	1	2	2	1	2	1	0	7	0	1	0	0	0	3	1	0	1	0	1	0	0	0	0
introductory	10	.3715	.8235	39.2	0	0	0	0	1	1	8	0	1	6	0	1	0	0	0	0	0	0	0	0	0	1	0	1	0
introspective	3	.3870	.2486	34.0	0	0	0	0	0	2	0	1	0	0	0	1	0	0	0	0	0	0	0	0	0	0	1	1	0
intrude	4	.3606	.3539	35.5	0	0	0	1	2	1	0	0	2	0	0	1	0	0	1	0	0	0	0	0	0	0	0	0	0

8D Internationale
9Q interneurons
9B internship
7D interoffice
7J interpolated
8E interpolation
8F interpositions
8J interpretative
8A interpreters
4A interracial
8F Interracial
8A interred
9R interregnum
9Q interrelation
9B interrogated
8A interrogation
8Q intertwining
7R interviewer
5R INTERVIEWS
7P interwar
8F intimates
6A intimation
7R intimidation
9R intones
XR intoxicates
6A intoxication
5F intra
9H intramural
XR intranauts
7B Intransitive
8Q intravenous
9D intrigues
XR intriguingly
7B Introductions
7Q intruded

Word Type	F	D	U	SFI	3 Gr 3	4 Gr 4	5 Gr 5	6 Gr 6	7 Gr 7	8 Gr 8	9 Gr 9	X UnGr	A Read	B Eng & Gr	C Comp	D Lit	E Math	F Soc Stud	G Spell	H Sci	J Music	K Art	L Home Ec	M Shop	N Lib F	P Lib NF	Q Lib Ref	R Mag	S Rel
intruder	5	.0000	.2284	33.6	0	0	3	1	0	1	0	0	5	0	0	0	0	0	0	0	0	0	0	0	0	0	0	0	0
intruders	7	.3941	.6163	37.9	0	1	2	2	1	1	0	0	1	0	0	0	0	1	0	0	0	1	0	0	0	3	0	1	0
intruding	2	.2306	.1140	30.6	0	0	1	0	1	0	0	0	0	1	0	0	0	1	0	0	0	0	0	0	0	0	0	0	0
intrusion	4	.3463	.2960	34.7	0	0	0	1	2	0	1	0	0	0	0	2	0	0	0	0	0	0	1	0	1	0	0	0	0
intrusions	3	.3764	.2483	33.9	0	0	0	0	1	0	1	1	0	0	0	0	0	0	0	1	0	0	0	0	0	0	1	1	0
intrusive	8	.0000	.1577	32.0	0	0	0	0	0	0	8	0	0	0	0	0	0	0	0	8	0	0	0	0	0	0	0	0	0
intuition	6	.2437	.3386	35.3	0	1	0	0	1	0	3	1	0	0	0	0	0	0	0	0	0	0	0	0	0	0	3	3	0
intuitions	2	.2446	.1122	30.5	0	0	0	0	0	0	2	0	0	0	0	1	0	0	0	0	0	0	0	0	0	0	1	0	0
intuitive	2	.1814	.1187	30.7	0	0	0	2	0	0	0	0	1	0	0	0	0	0	0	0	0	0	0	0	0	0	0	1	0
inundated	3	.0000	.0365	25.6	0	0	0	1	1	0	1	0	0	0	0	0	0	0	0	0	0	0	0	0	0	0	0	3	0
inundation	6	.3147	.4198	36.2	0	0	0	0	5	0	1	0	0	0	0	1	0	0	0	0	0	0	0	0	1	0	0	4	0
invade	20	.5547	2.3721	43.8	0	1	1	3	8	3	1	3	4	0	0	0	0	6	1	3	0	0	0	0	0	0	5	1	0
invaded	69	.7280	10.168	50.1	4	2	12	23	16	5	3	4	5	11	0	1	0	19	2	0	1	2	0	0	1	8	13	6	0
invader	6	.4794	.6585	38.2	0	0	3	0	3	0	0	0	3	0	0	0	0	0	0	1	0	0	0	0	1	0	1	0	0
invaders	40	.7303	5.9193	47.7	4	2	3	5	19	4	2	1	4	2	0	1	0	10	4	0	2	0	0	0	1	5	8	3	0
invades	2	.2346	.1166	30.7	0	0	0	1	1	0	0	0	0	0	0	0	0	0	0	1	0	0	0	0	0	0	0	1	0
invading	21	.6602	2.8414	44.5	2	1	3	2	5	5	1	2	2	0	1	1	0	5	0	0	1	0	0	0	0	4	5	2	0
invalid	8	.5261	.9235	39.7	0	0	1	1	2	3	0	1	3	1	0	2	0	1	0	0	0	0	0	0	0	1	0	0	0
invaluable	4	.3395	.3008	34.8	0	1	0	0	2	0	0	1	0	0	0	1	0	0	0	1	0	0	0	0	0	0	2	0	0
invariably	25	.7406	3.7161	45.7	0	0	3	0	10	4	6	2	0	1	2	3	0	1	0	3	1	1	0	0	1	5	4	3	0
invariant	3	.0000	.0449	26.5	0	0	0	0	0	3	0	0	0	0	0	0	3	0	0	0	0	0	0	0	0	0	0	0	0
invariants	3	.0000	.0314	25.0	0	3	0	0	0	0	0	0	0	0	0	0	0	0	0	0	0	0	0	0	0	0	3	0	0
invasion	53	.6382	6.9343	48.4	3	4	4	8	19	8	6	1	2	5	0	1	0	12	1	2	0	0	0	0	0	7	14	9	0
Invasion	3	.2279	.2143	33.3	0	0	2	0	0	0	1	0	2	0	0	0	0	0	0	0	0	0	0	0	0	0	0	1	0
invasions	13	.4025	1.1387	40.6	3	0	2	1	3	4	0	0	1	1	0	0	0	2	2	0	0	0	0	0	0	0	7	0	0
invective	3	.3427	.2477	33.9	0	0	0	0	2	1	0	0	1	0	0	0	0	0	0	0	0	0	0	0	1	0	0	1	0
invent	73	.7974	11.711	50.7	2	11	15	22	9	7	3	4	13	2	2	3	5	5	11	14	4	4	0	0	2	2	4	2	0
invented	241	.8921	42.808	56.3	30	32	40	39	50	32	13	5	57	14	0	8	28	27	15	37	18	2	1	3	0	11	16	4	0
inventing	20	.7255	2.9649	44.7	2	3	4	4	5	0	2	0	5	1	0	3	0	1	2	3	0	0	0	1	2	0	2	0	0
invention	151	.8533	25.829	54.1	13	22	31	24	26	20	13	2	45	9	2	4	5	21	7	19	10	1	0	4	1	1	22	0	0
inventions	80	.7436	12.168	50.9	9	15	14	10	12	12	7	1	21	5	0	1	3	25	5	7	6	0	0	0	0	1	5	1	0
inventive	12	.2869	.7543	38.8	0	0	0	3	3	2	3	1	0	0	0	0	0	1	0	0	0	4	0	0	0	1	3	3	0
inventiveness	4	.4499	.4023	36.0	0	0	1	1	1	0	0	1	1	1	0	0	0	0	0	1	0	0	0	0	0	0	0	1	0
inventor	49	.7753	7.7280	48.9	6	7	10	4	7	9	3	3	18	4	1	1	0	2	3	2	5	0	0	0	1	0	7	5	0
inventors	17	.6378	2.2509	43.5	1	3	4	1	5	1	2	0	3	1	0	0	0	5	1	1	0	0	0	1	0	1	4	0	0
inventory	7	.5861	.8540	39.3	0	1	1	1	2	1	0	1	1	0	0	0	1	0	1	1	0	0	1	0	1	0	0	1	0
invents	2	.0000	.0394	26.0	0	0	0	1	0	0	1	0	0	0	0	0	0	0	0	2	0	0	0	0	0	0	0	0	0
inverse	57	.1238	2.1503	43.3	0	0	0	3	19	25	10	0	1	0	0	0	55	0	0	0	0	0	0	1	0	0	0	0	0
inversely	4	.3352	.2986	34.8	0	0	0	0	1	2	1	0	0	0	0	0	0	0	0	1	0	0	0	0	0	0	2	1	0
inverses	7	.0000	.1048	30.2	0	0	0	0	5	2	0	0	0	0	0	0	7	0	0	0	0	0	0	0	0	0	0	0	0
inversion	11	.2570	.6424	38.1	0	0	0	0	1	6	2	2	0	0	0	0	0	0	0	2	7	0	0	0	0	0	2	0	0
inversions	4	.3855	.3387	35.3	0	0	0	0	1	0	2	1	0	0	0	0	0	0	0	2	1	0	0	0	0	0	1	0	0
invert	6	.3095	.4309	36.3	1	0	1	0	4	0	0	0	0	0	1	0	0	0	0	4	0	0	0	0	0	1	0	0	0
invertebrate	5	.2213	.2870	34.6	0	0	1	0	3	0	1	0	0	0	0	0	0	0	0	4	0	0	0	0	0	0	1	0	0
invertebrates	13	.2308	.7655	38.8	4	0	2	0	6	1	0	0	0	0	0	0	0	0	0	10	0	0	0	0	0	0	3	0	0
inverted	21	.4854	2.0991	43.2	1	1	0	3	9	1	5	1	0	4	6	0	0	0	1	3	1	0	2	0	0	1	2	1	0
invest	8	.4305	.7650	38.8	1	0	1	1	1	1	3	0	1	0	0	0	2	3	0	0	0	0	0	0	0	0	2	0	0
invested	24	.5006	2.5569	44.1	0	0	0	3	4	2	14	1	1	1	0	2	13	5	0	0	0	0	0	0	0	0	1	1	0
investigate	73	.8047	11.817	50.7	3	7	11	8	20	8	11	5	8	5	0	1	5	4	1	32	1	1	1	0	2	2	4	6	0
investigated	14	.6534	1.9194	42.8	0	0	2	0	4	3	2	3	5	1	0	1	1	0	0	2	0	0	0	0	0	0	1	3	0
investigates	9	.4413	.8541	39.3	0	2	2	0	0	1	4	0	0	2	0	0	0	1	0	3	0	0	0	0	0	0	3	0	0
investigating	22	.4945	2.3621	43.7	1	1	1	3	3	6	5	2	2	0	1	1	0	2	0	14	0	0	0	0	0	0	0	2	0
investigation	127	.4963	13.614	51.3	0	28	12	17	31	18	19	2	5	2	0	2	1	3	1	98	0	1	1	0	0	0	6	7	0
Investigation	9	.2777	.6128	37.9	0	0	0	0	3	1	5	0	0	1	0	0	0	1	0	7	0	0	0	0	0	0	0	0	0
investigations	38	.3975	3.3711	45.3	0	4	4	3	7	10	8	2	1	0	0	2	0	0	0	25	0	0	0	0	0	0	8	2	0
investigative	3	.2321	.1635	32.1	0	0	0	0	0	1	1	1	0	0	0	0	0	0	0	0	0	0	0	0	0	0	1	2	0
investigator	3	.2435	.1694	32.3	0	0	0	0	1	1	0	1	0	0	1	0	0	0	0	1	0	0	0	0	0	0	0	1	0
investigators	16	.4687	1.6136	42.1	0	0	0	0	9	2	5	0	1	0	0	1	0	0	0	6	0	0	0	0	0	0	5	3	0
investing	3	.3814	.2537	34.0	0	0	0	0	1	0	1	1	0	0	0	0	1	1	0	0	0	0	0	0	0	0	0	1	0
investiture	4	.0000	.0486	26.9	0	0	0	3	1	0	0	0	0	0	0	0	0	0	0	0	0	0	0	0	0	0	0	4	0
investment	20	.6083	2.4979	44.0	0	1	4	1	3	0	8	3	0	1	0	1	3	4	0	0	0	0	0	0	0	1	4	6	0
investments	19	.5964	2.3248	43.7	0	0	2	0	3	5	9	0	0	2	0	1	2	5	0	0	0	0	3	0	0	1	1	4	0
investors	11	.3678	.9056	39.6	0	0	1	2	2	1	5	0	0	0	0	0	0	5	0	0	0	0	0	0	0	2	0	4	0
inveterate	5	.4289	.4730	36.7	0	0	0	0	3	1	1	0	1	0	0	1	0	0	0	0	0	0	0	0	2	0	1	0	0
inviable	2	.0000	.0209	23.2	0	0	0	0	0	0	0	2	0	0	0	0	0	0	0	0	0	0	0	0	0	0	2	0	0
invigorating	2	.1641	.0751	28.8	0	1	0	1	0	0	0	0	0	0	1	0	0	0	0	0	0	0	0	0	0	0	1	0	0
invincible	4	.2761	.2537	34.0	0	0	0	1	0	1	2	0	0	0	1	0	0	1	0	0	0	0	0	0	0	2	0	0	0
inviolable	2	.2408	.1204	30.8	0	0	1	0	0	1	0	0	0	0	0	0	0	1	0	0	0	0	0	0	0	1	0	0	0
invisibility	4	.0000	.1827	32.6	0	0	3	0	0	1	0	0	4	0	0	0	0	0	0	0	0	0	0	0	0	0	0	0	0
invisible	117	.7787	18.441	52.7	12	7	17	18	16	16	22	9	22	3	0	4	0	2	2	49	0	1	5	5	5	8	4	7	0
invisibly	3	.0945	.0794	29.0	0	0	0	0	0	0	3	0	0	0	0	0	0	0	0	1	0	0	2	0	0	0	0	0	0
invitation	67	.5896	8.1669	49.1	1	17	0	19	9	6	14	1	8	28	7	3	0	2	2	0	0	0	2	0	0	10	1	4	0
invitations	19	.6499	2.5688	44.1	1	5	0	3	2	6	1	1	5	4	0	0	0	1	1	0	0	0	0	0	1	5	1	1	0
invite	93	.7624	14.363	51.6	12	23	7	10	11	16	6	8	24	14	3	6	0	3	8	1	3	1	4	0	8	5	2	10	1
invited	150	.8363	25.204	54.0	24	26	17	28	28	17	8	2	47	18	4	10	4	14	1	1	3	1	3	1	14	12	4	12	1
invites	10	.2230	.5940	37.7	2	3	1	2	0	2	0	0	3	1	1	0	0	1	0	0	2	0	0	0	0	1	0	0	1
inviting	23	.6482	3.0462	44.8	2	1	2	4	3	2	7	2	2	2	2	1	0	3	0	0	0	0	2	0	2	2	0	7	0
invoked	3	.3766	.2497	34.0	0	0	1	0	0	2	0	0	0	0	0	0	0	1	0	0	0	0	0	0	0	1	1	0	0
invokes	2	.2306	.1140	30.6	0	0	0	1	0	1	0	0	0	1	0	0	0	1	0	0	0	0	0	0	0	0	0	0	0
involuntarily	2	.2443	.1130	30.5	0	0	0	0	2	0	0	0	0	0	0	1	0	0	0	0	0	0	0	0	1	0	0	0	0
involuntary	24	.4831	2.5083	44.0	0	0	0	4	2	9	8	1	2	0	0	6	0	1	0	12	0	0	0	0	1	0	2	0	0
involve	36	.7934	5.7327	47.6	1	1	2	1	4	8	17	2	3	3	1	0	6	4	0	5	0	0	1	1	0	1	7	4	0
involved	203	.8754	35.302	55.5	6	6	12	19	60	31	56	13	15	15	4	12	19	14	1	18	7	1	4	2	1	13	36	41	0
involvement	14	.2525	.8566	39.3	0	0	0	1	3	5	4	1	1	0	0	0	0	2	0	0	0	0	0	0	0	0	1	10	0
involves	65	.7774	10.139	50.1	0	3	8	9	12	11	17	5	3	6	2	0	8	2	0	16	3	0	1	5	1	3	11	4	0
involving	52	.8066	8.3956	49.2	0	0	3	3	17	10	17	2	2	4	2	1	16	10	0	3	1	0	1	1	0	3	3	5	0
invulnerable	2	.2401	.1133	30.5	0	0	1	0	1	0	0	0	0	0	0	0	0	0	0	0	0	0	0	0	0	1	1	0	0
inward	24	.6396	3.1494	45.0	5	0	2	2	4	4	7	0	2	0	1	6	0	0	0	4	0	0	0	1	0	6	4	0	0
inwardly	6	.3408	.4953	36.9	0	1	0	1	2	2	0	0	2	0	0	2	0	0	0	0	0	0	0	0	0	2	0	0	0
iodide	2	.2160	.1362	31.3	0	0	0	1	0	0	1	0	1	0	0	0	0	0	0	1	0	0	0	0	0	0	0	0	0
iodine	43	.3869	3.7424	45.7	9	4	5	8	5	6	6	0	2	0	0	0	0	1	0	30	0	0	6	0	0	2	2	0	0
Iolanda	3	.0000	.0365	25.6	0	0	0	0	0	0	3	0	0	0	0	0	0	0	0	0	0	0	0	0	0	0	0	3	0
Iolcus	10	.2294	.7220	38.6	0	0	0	7	3	0	0	0	7	0	0	3	0	0	0	0	0	0	0	0	0	0	0	0	0
ion	25	.2709	1.5141	41.8	0	0	0	8	3	3	9	2	0	9	0	0	0	0	14	2	0	0	0	0	0	0	0	0	0
Ionian	9	.3448	.6787	38.3	0	0	0	2	3	4	0	0	0	0	0	0	0	2	0	0	3	0	0	0	0	0	4	0	0
Ionians	3	.0000	.0314	25.0	0	0	2	0	0	1	0	0	0	0	0	0	0	0	0	0	0	0	0	0	0	0	3	0	0
Ionisation	4	.0000	.0323	25.1	0	4	0	0	0	0	0	0	0	0	0	0	0	0	0	0	4	0	0	0	0	0	0	0	0
ionization	3	.2088	.1442	31.6	0	1	1	0	1	0	0	0	0	0	0	0	0	0	0	0	2	0	0	0	0	0	1	0	0

9Q intuitionism
7Q Invaded
7L invalid's
6R invariable
7J Invention
9Q Inventions
3A Inventor
4A inventors'
9D Inversnaid
6A inverts
8Q Investiture
8A inveteracy
6B invidious
7H invigorated
7R invincibility
7P Invisible
XR invitational
6B Invitations
6J invocation
6J Invocation
7Q invoices
9E involution
XR Involvement
9N inwards
5F Inyo
9B IO
4J io-la
4J io-li
8L iodized
8Q Iofan
5Q Ionia
3Q Ionian-Greek
8Q ionic

Word Type	F	D	U	SFI	3 Gr 3	4 Gr 4	5 Gr 5	6 Gr 6	7 Gr 7	8 Gr 8	9 Gr 9	X UnGr	A Read	B Eng & Gr	C Comp	D Lit	E Math	F Soc Stud	G Spell	H Sci	J Music	K Art	L Home Ec	M Shop	N Lib F	P Lib NF	Q Lib Ref	R Mag	S Rel
ionize	2	.0000	.0394	26.0	0	0	0	0	0	0	2	0	0	0	0	0	0	0	0	2	0	0	0	0	0	0	0	0	0
ionized	6	.2278	.3385	35.3	0	0	1	0	0	3	2	0	0	0	0	0	0	0	0	3	0	0	0	0	0	0	3	0	0
ionizing	5	.1275	.1790	32.5	0	0	1	0	0	3	1	0	0	0	0	0	0	0	0	1	0	0	0	0	0	0	4	0	0
ionosphere	6	.2160	.4085	36.1	0	0	1	0	4	0	1	0	3	0	0	0	0	0	0	3	0	0	0	0	0	0	0	0	0
ions	34	.3863	2.9232	44.7	0	16	0	2	2	3	2	9	0	0	0	0	0	0	0	16	0	0	0	0	0	10	0	8	0
ious	3	.0000	.0243	23.9	0	0	0	0	1	2	0	0	0	0	0	0	0	0	3	0	0	0	0	0	0	0	0	0	0
Iowa	47	.7422	7.1029	48.5	3	7	9	3	8	8	3	6	10	1	0	2	2	7	1	3	6	0	0	0	0	4	1	10	0
IowaCity	3	.0000	.0449	26.5	0	0	0	3	0	0	0	0	0	0	0	0	3	0	0	0	0	0	0	0	0	0	0	0	0
IP'S	2	.0000	.0290	24.6	2	0	0	0	0	0	0	0	0	0	0	0	0	0	0	0	0	0	0	0	0	2	0	0	0
ipecac	2	.0000	.0215	23.3	0	0	0	0	0	0	0	2	0	0	0	2	0	0	0	0	0	0	0	0	0	0	0	0	0
Iphias	3	.0000	.1370	31.4	0	0	0	3	0	0	0	0	3	0	0	0	0	0	0	0	0	0	0	0	0	0	0	0	0
Ipswich	2	.2401	.1133	30.5	0	0	0	1	0	1	0	0	0	0	0	0	0	0	0	0	0	0	0	0	0	1	1	0	0
IQ	5	.0824	.1675	32.2	0	0	0	1	3	1	0	0	1	0	0	0	0	0	0	0	0	0	0	0	0	0	0	4	0
ir	2	.0000	.0162	22.1	0	1	0	0	1	0	0	0	0	0	0	0	0	0	2	0	0	0	0	0	0	0	0	0	0
Ira	2	.2417	.1091	30.4	0	0	0	0	1	1	0	0	0	0	0	0	0	0	0	0	1	0	0	0	0	0	1	0	0
Irae	3	.0000	.0243	23.8	0	0	0	0	3	0	0	0	0	0	0	0	0	0	0	0	3	0	0	0	0	0	0	0	0
Iran	28	.4829	2.9108	44.6	1	1	1	4	12	2	7	0	1	2	0	0	0	17	0	0	0	0	0	0	0	1	4	3	0
Iranian	4	.2352	.2332	33.7	0	0	0	0	3	0	1	0	0	0	0	0	0	2	0	0	0	0	0	0	0	0	0	2	0
Iraq	38	.3956	3.3919	45.3	2	2	2	24	3	1	4	0	2	0	0	0	0	29	0	0	0	1	0	0	0	1	5	0	0
Iraq's	3	.0000	.0583	27.7	0	0	0	3	0	0	0	0	0	0	0	0	0	3	0	0	0	0	0	0	0	0	0	0	0
irascible	2	.2437	.1129	30.5	0	0	0	0	2	0	0	0	0	0	0	0	0	0	0	0	0	0	0	0	0	0	1	1	0
Irby	8	.0000	.3655	35.6	0	0	8	0	0	0	0	0	8	0	0	0	0	0	0	0	0	0	0	0	0	0	0	0	0
Irby's	3	.0000	.1370	31.4	0	0	3	0	0	0	0	0	3	0	0	0	0	0	0	0	0	0	0	0	0	0	0	0	0
ire	2	.1497	.1046	30.2	2	0	0	0	0	0	0	0	1	0	0	0	0	0	1	0	0	0	0	0	0	0	0	0	0
Ireland	111	.7205	16.329	52.1	11	10	34	22	22	7	3	2	20	3	0	0	0	27	0	0	12	1	1	0	1	28	7	11	0
Ireland's	7	.4375	.6942	38.4	0	0	3	0	2	2	0	0	2	0	0	0	0	1	0	0	0	0	0	0	0	2	0	2	0
Irene	20	.5284	2.2786	43.6	6	9	0	1	3	0	1	0	6	1	1	3	1	0	0	0	0	0	0	0	8	0	0	0	0
Irian	2	.2285	.1129	30.5	0	0	0	0	1	1	0	0	0	0	0	0	0	1	0	0	0	0	0	0	0	0	1	0	0
iridescent	2	.2446	.1257	31.0	0	0	0	1	1	0	0	0	0	0	0	0	0	1	0	1	0	0	0	0	0	0	0	0	0
iridium	2	.0000	.0209	23.2	0	2	0	0	0	0	0	0	0	0	0	0	0	0	0	0	0	0	0	0	0	0	2	0	0
iris	15	.2729	1.0296	40.1	1	1	1	9	1	1	0	1	1	0	0	0	0	1	0	12	1	0	0	0	0	0	0	0	0
irises	3	.3874	.2497	34.0	0	0	0	0	0	2	1	0	0	1	0	0	0	0	0	0	0	0	0	0	1	0	0	1	0
Irish	129	.7238	18.990	52.8	0	15	36	25	26	13	5	9	21	3	1	4	0	14	2	1	22	0	1	0	1	33	3	23	0
Irishman	11	.5485	1.2643	41.0	0	3	1	2	1	0	2	2	1	1	0	0	1	0	0	0	1	0	0	0	0	4	0	3	0
Irishmen	2	.2412	.1141	30.6	0	0	0	0	0	1	1	0	0	1	0	0	0	0	0	0	0	0	0	0	0	1	0	0	0
iron	817	.7403	122.91	60.9	130	104	126	116	142	118	71	10	116	16	6	29	5	176	5	201	8	0	19	76	25	68	54	13	0
Iron	21	.4193	1.9950	43.0	4	1	5	1	4	1	4	1	5	0	0	0	0	6	0	0	0	0	0	0	0	1	8	1	0
iron-and-steel	8	.0000	.1556	31.9	0	0	2	1	5	0	0	0	0	0	0	0	0	8	0	0	0	0	0	0	0	0	0	0	0
iron-bearing	4	.0904	.1412	31.5	1	0	0	0	0	0	3	0	1	0	0	0	0	0	0	0	0	0	0	0	0	0	3	0	0
iron-ore	6	.0971	.2435	33.9	0	0	0	4	1	1	0	0	1	0	0	0	0	5	0	0	0	0	0	0	0	0	0	0	0
ironclad	5	.4552	.4847	36.9	0	0	0	1	1	2	1	0	0	0	0	0	0	1	0	0	0	0	0	0	0	1	1	2	0
ironed	8	.4122	.7518	38.8	1	1	2	0	1	2	1	0	3	0	0	0	0	1	0	0	0	1	2	0	1	0	0	0	0
ironic	7	.3917	.6024	37.8	0	0	0	0	3	0	3	1	1	0	1	3	0	0	0	0	0	0	0	0	0	0	0	2	0
ironically	16	.5901	1.9592	42.9	0	0	1	2	6	4	3	0	1	1	0	0	0	2	0	1	0	0	0	0	0	4	3	4	0
ironies	2	.2351	.1166	30.7	0	0	0	0	0	1	1	0	0	0	0	0	0	1	0	0	0	0	0	0	0	0	0	1	0
ironing	19	.2435	1.0881	40.4	1	2	1	1	4	7	3	0	3	2	0	2	0	0	0	0	0	0	10	0	1	0	0	1	0
irons	15	.5762	1.8304	42.6	3	5	1	0	2	4	0	0	4	0	1	0	0	1	0	2	0	0	0	2	1	1	0	3	0
ironwork	2	.1259	.0687	28.4	0	1	0	0	0	0	1	0	0	0	0	0	0	1	0	0	0	0	0	1	0	0	0	0	0
irony	9	.3566	.7009	38.5	0	1	0	1	0	0	3	4	0	1	0	1	0	0	0	0	0	0	0	0	0	1	0	6	0
Iroquoian	2	.0000	.0209	23.2	0	0	0	0	2	0	0	0	0	0	0	0	0	0	0	0	0	0	0	0	0	0	2	0	0
Iroquoians	3	.0000	.0434	26.4	3	0	0	0	0	0	0	0	0	0	0	0	0	0	0	0	0	0	0	0	0	3	0	0	0
Iroquois	28	.4254	2.7403	44.4	3	0	5	0	8	12	0	0	7	0	0	1	0	16	0	0	0	0	0	0	0	3	1	0	0
irradiated	2	.0000	.0394	26.0	0	0	0	0	0	1	0	1	0	0	0	0	0	0	0	2	0	0	0	0	0	0	0	0	0
irrational	25	.2157	1.3432	41.3	0	0	0	0	3	13	9	0	0	0	0	0	21	0	0	0	0	0	0	0	0	0	1	3	0
irregular	72	.7030	10.183	50.1	1	2	4	16	22	8	18	1	2	16	0	6	0	3	9	4	7	1	0	9	0	3	9	3	0
irregularities	6	.5259	.6457	38.1	0	0	0	0	3	2	1	0	0	1	0	1	0	0	1	0	0	0	1	0	0	0	2	0	0
irregularity	2	.2300	.1140	30.6	0	0	0	0	1	0	1	0	0	1	0	0	0	0	0	1	0	0	0	0	0	0	0	0	0
irregularly	8	.4583	.7886	39.0	1	0	0	0	1	0	5	1	0	2	0	0	0	0	0	4	0	0	0	0	0	1	1	0	0
irrelevant	3	.3847	.2496	34.0	0	0	1	0	1	0	0	1	0	0	0	0	0	0	0	0	0	0	0	0	0	1	1	1	0
irreparable	3	.2051	.1687	32.3	1	0	0	0	2	0	0	0	1	0	1	0	0	0	0	0	0	0	0	0	0	0	0	1	0
irreplaceable	2	.2437	.1129	30.5	0	1	0	0	0	0	1	0	0	0	0	0	0	0	0	0	0	0	0	0	0	0	1	1	0
irresistible	15	.6292	1.9513	42.9	1	1	0	0	6	5	1	1	2	0	0	2	0	2	0	0	0	0	0	0	4	2	2	1	0
irresistibly	4	.3720	.3216	35.1	0	0	0	1	3	0	0	0	0	0	0	0	0	0	0	0	0	0	0	0	1	0	1	2	0
irresolute	2	.2443	.1130	30.5	0	0	0	0	1	0	1	0	0	0	0	1	0	0	0	0	0	0	0	0	1	0	0	0	0
irrespective	2	.1814	.1187	30.7	0	0	0	1	1	0	0	0	1	0	0	0	0	0	0	0	0	0	0	0	0	0	0	1	0
irresponsibility	3	.2196	.1554	31.9	0	0	0	0	0	2	1	0	0	0	0	2	0	0	0	0	0	0	0	0	1	0	0	0	0
irresponsible	3	.3427	.2477	33.9	1	0	0	0	2	0	0	0	1	0	0	0	0	0	0	0	0	0	0	0	1	0	0	1	0
irreverent	2	.2442	.1134	30.5	0	0	0	1	0	0	1	0	0	1	0	0	0	0	0	0	0	0	0	0	0	0	0	1	0
irrevocably	2	.2278	.1128	30.5	0	0	0	0	2	0	0	0	0	0	0	0	0	0	0	1	0	0	0	0	0	0	1	0	0
irrigate	20	.3365	1.5660	41.9	5	4	6	1	4	0	0	0	0	1	0	0	0	16	0	1	0	0	0	0	0	1	1	0	0
irrigated	47	.2231	2.7434	44.4	3	5	12	17	6	3	1	0	0	0	0	0	0	40	0	3	0	0	0	0	0	0	4	0	0
irrigates	2	.0000	.0219	23.4	0	0	0	0	1	0	1	0	0	2	0	0	0	0	0	0	0	0	0	0	0	0	0	0	0
irrigating	4	.0000	.0778	28.9	0	2	0	2	0	0	0	0	0	0	0	0	0	4	0	0	0	0	0	0	0	0	0	0	0
irrigation	92	.4610	9.2231	49.6	1	8	17	27	22	6	7	4	1	0	0	2	1	61	0	9	0	0	0	0	0	2	12	4	0
irritability	2	.1432	.0759	28.8	0	0	0	0	0	0	2	0	0	0	0	0	0	0	0	1	0	0	1	0	0	0	0	0	0
irritable	10	.4547	.9411	39.7	0	2	0	0	5	1	2	0	0	0	1	3	0	0	0	1	0	0	3	0	2	0	0	0	0
irritably	5	.2422	.3874	35.9	1	0	1	1	1	0	1	0	4	0	0	0	0	0	0	0	0	0	0	0	0	1	0	0	0
irritated	13	.5010	1.3906	41.4	0	0	2	1	3	4	3	0	2	0	0	5	1	0	0	0	0	0	0	0	3	1	0	1	0
irritates	4	.3863	.3414	35.3	0	2	1	0	0	0	1	0	0	0	0	0	0	2	0	0	0	0	0	0	0	0	1	1	0
irritating	8	.3836	.7075	38.5	0	0	3	0	2	2	1	0	1	0	0	1	0	0	0	5	0	0	0	0	0	1	0	0	0
irritation	5	.4326	.4543	36.6	0	0	2	0	0	0	3	0	0	0	0	0	0	0	0	0	0	0	1	0	2	1	1	0	0
irritations	2	.2306	.1140	30.6	0	0	0	0	0	1	0	1	0	1	0	0	0	1	0	0	0	0	0	0	0	0	0	0	0
Irvin	2	.2437	.1129	30.5	0	1	0	0	0	0	0	1	0	0	0	0	0	0	0	0	0	0	0	0	0	0	1	1	0
Irving	36	.2766	2.3879	43.8	7	1	0	1	4	9	14	0	9	1	14	0	2	2	0	0	5	0	0	0	0	0	2	1	0
Irving's	2	.0000	.0045	16.5	0	0	0	0	0	0	2	0	0	0	2	0	0	0	0	0	0	0	0	0	0	0	0	0	0
is	60852	.9710	11643	80.7	10121	8304	7716	8078	10782	7276	7026	1549	8611	4501	738	1791	9158	6528	2706	9361	3219	504	1214	1530	1173	3078	3576	3086	78
Is	17	.6709	2.3254	43.7	1	2	0	1	7	2	4	0	2	3	0	4	0	1	0	0	1	0	1	0	0	0	2	3	0
IS	10	.3414	.8452	39.3	5	1	1	3	0	0	0	0	3	0	0	0	0	0	0	5	0	0	0	0	0	2	0	0	0
is't	3	.0000	.0322	25.1	0	0	0	0	0	0	3	0	0	0	0	3	0	0	0	0	0	0	0	0	0	0	0	0	0
Isaac	40	.1311	1.7147	42.3	9	5	4	9	4	8	1	0	8	0	0	1	3	1	0	11	1	0	0	0	0	4	6	0	5
Isabel	26	.5381	2.9254	44.7	12	1	0	7	0	1	1	4	2	7	2	0	2	0	0	0	0	0	0	0	0	9	0	4	0
Isabella	18	.3713	1.6428	42.2	1	0	5	8	0	4	0	0	8	0	0	0	0	6	0	0	0	0	0	0	0	0	4	0	0
Isabelle	2	.2408	.1204	30.8	0	2	0	0	0	0	0	0	0	0	0	0	0	1	0	0	0	0	0	0	0	1	0	0	0
Isaiah	5	.3022	.3399	35.3	0	0	2	1	1	1	0	0	0	0	0	1	0	1	0	0	0	0	0	0	0	0	3	0	0

8H ionizes
6G ior
7E iota
6F Iowan
3P IP
7P Iphigenia
7Q ipse
5J ipu
XR IQS
7F Iquique
7F Iquitos
8M IR
9G ir-
7F Iranians
4A irate
5F IRELAND
5Q Irenee
5P Irgun
8Q iridescence
8J Irish-American
8Q Irish-Italian
4N Irishman's
9Q irked
8L irks
7C irksome
4P Irkutsk
8G irl
9H iron-filing
6R iron-fisted
8N iron-gray
7N iron-like
9H iron-magnesium
6F iron-mining
9Q iron-poor
7A iron-studded
7Q iron-tipped
8C ironbarred
7N ironbound
5A ironhearted
6B ironical
7R ironmasters
9Q ironmonger
6A Irons
7R Ironworkers
3P Iroquois'
8Q irradiation
8F irreconcilables
7A irrecoverably
7M irregular-grained
7N irreproachable
7R irresistibility
6N irresolutely
9F irreversible
7Q irrevocable
4F Irrigate
8L irritate
7Q irruptive
7P Irus'
8B Irvings's
8A Irwin
4A Isaac's
6B Isabel's

Word Type	F	D	U	SFI	3 Gr 3	4 Gr 4	5 Gr 5	6 Gr 6	7 Gr 7	8 Gr 8	9 Gr 9	X UnGr	A Read	B Eng & Gr	C Comp	D Lit	E Math	F Soc Stud	G Spell	H Sci	J Music	K Art	L Home Ec	M Shop	N Lib F	P Lib NF	Q Lib Ref	R Mag	S Rel
Isannah	3	.0000	.0352	25.5	0	0	0	0	0	3	0	0	0	0	0	0	0	0	0	0	0	0	0	0	3	0	0	0	0
ish	2	.0000	.0162	22.1	0	0	0	0	1	1	0	0	0	0	0	0	0	0	2	0	0	0	0	0	0	0	0	0	0
Ishan	2	.0000	.0914	29.6	2	0	0	0	0	0	0	0	2	0	0	0	0	0	0	0	0	0	0	0	0	0	0	0	0
Ishi	35	.0000	.6807	38.3	0	0	0	0	0	35	0	0	0	0	0	0	0	35	0	0	0	0	0	0	0	0	0	0	0
Ishi's	4	.0000	.0778	28.9	0	0	0	0	0	4	0	0	0	0	0	0	0	4	0	0	0	0	0	0	0	0	0	0	0
Isiolo	6	.0000	.0869	29.4	0	0	0	0	6	0	0	0	0	0	0	0	0	0	0	0	0	0	0	0	0	6	0	0	0
Iskenderun	2	.0000	.0389	25.9	0	0	0	0	2	0	0	0	0	0	0	0	0	2	0	0	0	0	0	0	0	0	0	0	0
Islam	26	.4516	2.5689	44.1	0	1	5	2	9	4	5	0	2	0	0	0	0	13	0	0	0	0	0	0	0	4	6	1	0
Islamic	6	.4746	.6076	37.8	0	0	1	2	2	0	0	1	0	0	0	0	0	3	1	0	0	0	0	0	0	1	1	0	0
island	619	.8146	101.74	60.1	106	106	103	118	89	56	30	11	168	22	1	25	1	169	7	15	5	6	0	0	65	56	42	37	0
Island	201	.7601	31.164	54.9	35	24	31	44	32	15	15	5	62	7	0	4	1	28	1	8	3	0	0	0	10	21	27	29	0
island's	4	.0996	.1523	31.8	0	0	0	2	2	0	0	0	1	0	0	0	0	0	0	0	0	0	0	0	0	0	0	3	0
islanders	10	.5315	1.1173	40.5	2	0	1	2	4	0	1	0	1	0	0	0	0	1	0	0	1	0	0	0	0	1	3	3	0
Islanders	4	.2183	.2285	33.6	0	1	3	0	0	0	0	0	0	0	0	0	0	3	0	0	0	0	0	0	0	1	0	0	0
islands	460	.5901	57.043	57.6	66	63	85	93	99	41	11	2	46	7	0	4	2	260	3	17	5	1	0	0	3	21	71	20	0
Islands	120	.6802	16.863	52.3	9	13	31	20	19	19	5	4	21	1	1	0	0	54	1	10	3	0	0	1	0	3	18	7	0
islands'	3	.0000	.0365	25.6	1	0	0	0	2	0	0	0	0	0	0	0	0	0	0	0	0	0	0	0	0	0	0	3	0
isle	8	.4306	.7495	38.7	0	2	1	1	2	0	2	0	1	1	0	4	0	0	1	1	0	0	0	0	0	0	0	0	0
Isle	16	.5736	1.9617	42.9	3	0	1	1	5	5	1	0	4	0	0	2	0	7	0	0	1	0	0	0	0	0	1	1	0
isles	6	.5514	.6869	38.4	2	0	0	0	1	1	2	0	0	0	0	1	0	0	0	1	0	0	0	0	0	2	1	1	0
Isles	59	.6327	7.6938	48.9	1	5	8	22	16	4	3	0	3	3	0	5	0	25	0	4	11	0	0	0	0	2	2	4	0
islets	4	.3540	.3081	34.9	0	0	0	1	1	1	1	0	0	0	0	1	0	0	0	0	0	0	0	0	0	1	2	0	0
Ismay	3	.0000	.0434	26.4	0	0	0	0	0	0	3	0	0	0	0	0	0	0	0	0	0	0	0	0	0	3	0	0	0
isn't	645	.8341	108.49	60.4	157	142	71	73	104	45	33	20	260	41	4	49	5	19	4	33	2	0	11	5	94	64	2	52	0
isobar	2	.0000	.0394	26.0	0	0	0	0	0	2	0	0	0	0	0	0	0	0	0	2	0	0	0	0	0	0	0	0	0
isobars	4	.0000	.0789	29.0	0	0	0	0	0	4	0	0	0	0	0	0	0	0	0	4	0	0	0	0	0	0	0	0	0
isolate	2	.2346	.1166	30.7	0	0	0	0	1	0	0	1	0	0	0	0	0	0	0	1	0	0	0	0	0	0	0	1	0
isolated	55	.6479	7.3035	48.6	2	0	10	9	14	6	10	4	2	1	0	2	0	14	0	4	2	0	0	0	0	10	14	6	0
isolating	2	.2408	.1204	30.8	0	0	1	0	1	0	0	0	0	0	0	0	0	1	0	0	0	0	0	0	0	1	0	0	0
isolation	34	.7471	5.1397	47.1	0	1	4	3	13	7	6	0	4	0	1	3	0	8	1	2	0	0	0	2	0	4	5	4	0
isolationism	3	.3454	.2542	34.1	0	0	0	0	1	0	1	1	1	0	0	0	0	1	0	0	0	0	0	0	0	0	0	1	0
isometric	11	.2770	.7068	38.5	0	0	1	4	3	0	3	0	0	0	0	0	0	0	0	5	0	0	0	3	0	3	0	0	0
isoprene	3	.0000	.0591	27.7	0	0	0	0	3	0	0	0	0	0	0	0	0	0	0	3	0	0	0	0	0	0	0	0	0
isosceles	35	.0549	.8699	39.4	3	0	0	2	4	12	14	0	0	0	0	0	34	0	0	0	0	0	0	0	1	0	0	0	0
isotope	19	.2955	1.3278	41.2	0	0	0	13	5	1	0	0	0	0	0	0	0	1	0	12	0	0	0	0	0	0	6	0	0
isotopes	30	.1285	1.2570	41.0	0	0	2	23	1	1	3	0	0	0	0	0	0	0	0	28	0	0	0	0	0	0	2	0	0
Israel	197	.4157	17.985	52.5	15	49	29	23	54	11	13	3	9	3	0	6	0	66	0	1	6	1	0	0	1	73	6	20	5
Israel's	10	.3651	.8254	39.2	0	1	1	3	3	1	1	0	0	0	0	0	0	6	0	0	0	0	0	0	0	2	0	2	0
Israeli	40	.4330	3.7607	45.8	2	2	7	5	3	12	9	0	2	0	0	0	0	9	0	0	1	0	0	0	0	7	1	20	0
Israeli-held	2	.0000	.0243	23.9	0	0	0	0	0	0	2	0	0	0	0	0	0	0	0	0	0	0	0	0	0	0	0	2	0
Israelis	17	.3465	1.3257	41.2	0	0	3	0	2	6	6	0	0	0	0	0	0	6	0	0	0	0	0	0	0	3	0	8	0
Israelite	2	.2446	.1122	30.5	0	0	1	0	0	1	0	0	0	0	0	1	0	0	0	0	0	0	0	0	0	0	1	0	0
Israelites	27	.3892	2.2438	43.5	0	0	14	2	7	4	0	0	0	0	0	6	0	2	0	0	4	0	0	0	0	0	15	0	0
iss	2	.2440	.1132	30.5	0	0	1	0	0	1	0	0	0	0	0	1	0	0	0	0	0	0	0	0	0	0	0	1	0
Issa	2	.0000	.0389	25.9	0	0	0	0	2	0	0	0	0	0	0	0	0	2	0	0	0	0	0	0	0	0	0	0	0
Issas	2	.0000	.0389	25.9	0	0	0	2	0	0	0	0	0	0	0	0	0	2	0	0	0	0	0	0	0	0	0	0	0
issuance	3	.2321	.1635	32.1	0	0	0	0	2	1	0	0	0	0	0	0	0	0	0	0	0	0	0	0	0	0	1	2	0
issue	97	.6598	13.207	51.2	2	5	9	8	21	16	28	8	13	4	0	2	1	30	1	4	0	0	0	0	1	6	9	26	0
issued	57	.6875	7.9893	49.0	1	0	15	3	15	13	8	2	5	1	1	2	0	11	0	2	1	0	0	0	1	6	16	11	0
issues	59	.4973	6.3438	48.0	2	0	0	2	14	10	25	6	8	0	0	0	1	21	1	2	0	0	0	0	0	1	3	22	0
issuing	9	.6002	1.1347	40.5	0	0	2	0	2	2	3	0	2	0	0	0	0	2	0	0	1	0	0	0	1	0	2	1	0
ist	3	.3849	.2435	33.9	1	0	1	0	0	0	1	0	0	0	0	1	0	0	1	0	1	0	0	0	0	0	0	0	0
Istanbul	18	.4522	1.7629	42.5	0	0	4	2	10	2	0	0	0	0	0	0	0	11	0	0	0	1	0	0	0	4	0	2	0
isthmus	14	.3497	1.1143	40.5	0	1	4	6	3	0	0	0	0	0	0	0	0	10	2	0	0	0	0	0	2	0	0	0	0
Isthmus	10	.3803	.8699	39.4	0	2	3	5	0	0	0	0	1	0	0	0	0	6	0	0	0	0	0	0	0	1	2	0	0
it	47284	.9863	9179.4	79.6	9135	7453	5682	6315	8506	5109	4027	1057	13361	2301	456	3056	1810	3825	1110	5877	1566	396	717	662	3618	3936	1968	2606	19
It	55	.6458	7.3823	48.7	5	23	11	9	1	3	0	3	10	6	0	2	0	0	0	18	1	0	0	0	0	10	7	1	0
IT	18	.1795	.8878	39.5	0	15	0	3	0	0	0	0	3	13	0	0	0	0	0	0	0	0	0	0	0	2	0	0	0
it'd	11	.3752	1.0176	40.1	0	3	1	1	2	3	1	0	6	0	0	2	0	0	0	0	0	0	0	0	3	0	0	0	0
it'll	65	.6039	8.2681	49.2	4	7	5	15	18	10	4	2	18	1	0	11	1	1	0	0	0	0	0	0	14	8	0	11	0
It'll	2	.1787	.1174	30.7	1	0	0	0	0	1	0	0	1	0	0	0	0	0	0	0	0	0	0	0	1	0	0	0	0
it's	2178	.8045	355.61	65.5	487	428	250	270	386	182	111	64	929	68	6	191	10	52	18	27	51	4	11	10	306	210	3	282	0
It's	3	.3822	.2446	33.9	0	0	1	0	0	1	1	0	0	1	0	0	0	0	0	0	1	0	0	0	0	0	0	1	0
IT'S	2	.0000	.0914	29.6	2	0	0	0	0	0	0	0	2	0	0	0	0	0	0	0	0	0	0	0	0	0	0	0	0
Italian	248	.7770	38.663	55.9	54	19	49	28	40	34	13	11	17	13	1	1	3	26	13	11	33	1	2	2	1	41	72	11	0
Italian's	3	.0000	.0434	26.4	0	0	2	1	0	0	0	0	0	0	0	0	0	0	0	0	0	0	0	0	0	3	0	0	0
Italians	54	.5964	6.7290	48.3	12	8	13	4	11	1	3	2	7	1	0	0	0	14	2	0	1	0	0	0	0	14	13	2	0
italic	11	.3253	.9544	39.8	0	0	0	7	2	0	1	0	7	3	0	0	0	0	0	1	0	0	0	0	0	0	0	0	0
italicized	99	.4691	10.111	50.0	0	6	10	10	22	26	25	0	24	44	1	5	1	1	22	0	0	0	0	0	0	0	1	0	0
italics	42	.3800	3.5083	45.5	1	2	9	11	11	3	5	0	5	27	0	0	0	0	8	0	1	0	0	1	0	0	0	0	0
Italy	348	.7375	51.916	57.2	95	19	46	69	41	37	33	8	25	16	1	5	4	107	5	2	18	3	1	1	2	47	98	13	0
Italy's	30	.4093	2.6685	44.3	15	0	5	7	2	0	1	0	0	0	0	0	0	9	0	0	0	0	0	0	0	9	11	1	0
itch	8	.4284	.7870	39.0	1	1	2	2	1	0	1	0	3	0	0	1	0	0	0	0	0	0	0	0	0	1	0	3	0
itched	6	.3859	.5833	37.7	0	2	0	0	3	1	0	0	4	0	0	0	0	0	0	0	0	0	0	0	1	1	0	0	0
itches	3	.3429	.2528	34.0	0	0	1	2	0	0	0	0	1	0	0	0	0	0	0	1	0	0	0	0	1	0	0	0	0
itching	7	.4879	.7843	38.9	0	3	1	0	2	0	0	1	4	0	0	0	0	0	0	0	0	0	0	0	1	1	0	1	0
itchy	4	.0000	.1827	32.6	1	0	3	0	0	0	0	0	4	0	0	0	0	0	0	0	0	0	0	0	0	0	0	0	0
ite	3	.0000	.0243	23.9	0	0	1	1	0	1	0	0	0	0	0	0	0	0	3	0	0	0	0	0	0	0	0	0	0
item	124	.7584	18.932	52.8	8	10	7	13	45	20	19	2	9	12	2	4	56	2	4	4	0	0	8	2	3	4	4	10	0
itemize	2	.1812	.0838	29.2	0	0	0	0	1	0	1	0	0	0	0	0	0	0	0	0	0	0	1	0	0	0	0	1	0
items	196	.7401	29.217	54.7	9	7	18	21	49	47	41	4	14	46	10	2	58	13	1	4	0	1	17	7	0	3	12	8	0
iteration	2	.0000	.0299	24.8	0	0	0	0	0	0	2	0	0	0	0	0	2	0	0	0	0	0	0	0	0	0	0	0	0
Ithaca	17	.5691	2.0862	43.2	0	0	1	0	5	6	5	0	7	0	1	4	0	1	0	0	0	0	0	0	0	0	2	2	0
its	7512	.9512	1411.3	71.5	1079	765	889	1016	1671	975	855	262	1326	288	83	241	353	929	260	1296	265	83	44	63	238	599	918	525	1
itself	872	.9460	162.97	62.1	92	66	72	103	237	124	137	41	121	38	10	39	61	99	15	147	31	6	7	17	40	76	104	61	0
ity	12	.1757	.5017	37.0	0	0	0	1	3	5	3	0	0	3	0	0	0	0	9	0	0	0	0	0	0	0	0	0	0
iv	3	.2249	.1514	31.8	0	0	0	0	0	2	1	0	0	0	0	0	0	0	2	0	1	0	0	0	0	0	0	0	0
IV	50	.5232	5.4590	47.4	1	5	7	14	7	10	6	0	3	2	0	0	9	5	0	0	22	0	0	1	0	3	5	0	0
Iva	3	.0000	.1370	31.4	3	0	0	0	0	0	0	0	3	0	0	0	0	0	0	0	0	0	0	0	0	0	0	0	0
Ivald	3	.0000	.1370	31.4	0	0	3	0	0	0	0	0	3	0	0	0	0	0	0	0	0	0	0	0	0	0	0	0	0
Ivan	42	.4976	4.8166	46.8	16	7	4	0	5	5	5	0	26	0	0	0	0	4	0	1	0	0	0	0	0	0	4	7	0
Ivan's	3	.0000	.1370	31.4	2	0	1	0	0	0	0	0	3	0	0	0	0	0	0	0	0	0	0	0	0	0	0	0	0
Ivar	9	.2212	.6853	38.4	0	8	0	0	0	0	1	0	8	0	0	0	0	0	0	0	0	0	0	0	0	0	0	1	0
ive	4	.0000	.0325	25.1	0	0	0	2	0	2	0	0	0	0	0	0	0	0	4	0	0	0	0	0	0	0	0	0	0

7R Iselin
5P Isengrim
8F Ishikari
8B isinglass
9Q Isis
7R Iskenderian
7R Isky
9Q Islamabad
4F island-country
7Q island-hopping
6F island-studded
9Q Island's
5F ISLES
9R islet
8G ism
6N Ismael
9Q Ismailis
7A Ismarus
8Q Ismene
8H iso
7Q isogonic
7A isolationist
5P isolationists
XR Isolda
XR Isolda's
7H isoprene's
8Q isopropyl
5P Israelis'
7D Issa's
8F Issei
3A Issippi
5Q issuer
7R Issues
9F ISSUES
8Q istoriya
3A it'
4F itadakimasu
5P Italian-Americans
7Q Italian-born
9R Italian-style
5P Italys
8L itemized
9L itemizes
7A itemizing
9D Ithakos
7Q ithomiids
8R itinerary
7F Its
7B its-it's
7Q Itza
6F Itzcoatl
5Q IUD
7Q IV-A
7G IV-1
9B Ivanitch
3A Ivanova
4A Ivar's
8B Ive

Word Type	F	D	U	SFI	3 Gr 3	4 Gr 4	5 Gr 5	6 Gr 6	7 Gr 7	8 Gr 8	9 Gr 9	X UnGr	A Read	B Eng & Gr	C Comp	D Lit	E Math	F Soc Stud	G Spell	H Sci	J Music	K Art	L Home Ec	M Shop	N Lib F	P Lib NF	Q Lib Ref	R Mag	S Rel
Iverson	5	.0000	.2284	33.6	5	0	0	0	0	0	0	0	5	0	0	0	0	0	0	0	0	0	0	0	0	0	0	0	0
Iverson's	2	.0000	.0914	29.6	2	0	0	0	0	0	0	0	2	0	0	0	0	0	0	0	0	0	0	0	0	0	0	0	0
Ives	10	.2646	.6215	37.9	0	0	4	0	0	4	2	0	1	0	0	0	0	1	0	0	6	0	0	0	0	0	0	2	0
Ivik	57	.0000	2.6039	44.2	0	0	57	0	0	0	0	0	57	0	0	0	0	0	0	0	0	0	0	0	0	0	0	0	0
Ivik's	14	.0000	.6396	38.1	0	0	14	0	0	0	0	0	14	0	0	0	0	0	0	0	0	0	0	0	0	0	0	0	0
Ivorsens	2	.0000	.0914	29.6	0	0	0	2	0	0	0	0	2	0	0	0	0	0	0	0	0	0	0	0	0	0	0	0	0
ivory	29	.7007	4.1401	46.2	2	5	5	5	7	2	3	0	4	3	1	3	0	6	0	0	0	1	0	0	0	1	8	2	0
ivy	11	.5279	1.2195	40.9	0	3	2	2	3	0	1	0	1	1	1	0	0	0	0	2	3	0	0	0	0	3	0	0	0
Ivy	5	.2447	.2801	34.5	0	0	0	4	0	0	0	1	0	0	0	0	0	0	0	0	2	0	0	0	0	0	0	3	0
ivy-covered	2	.2446	.1142	30.6	0	0	1	1	0	0	0	0	0	0	0	0	0	0	0	0	0	0	0	0	1	0	0	1	0
Iwanovski	2	.0000	.0394	26.0	0	0	2	0	0	0	0	0	0	0	0	0	0	0	0	2	0	0	0	0	0	0	0	0	0
IX	6	.3240	.4397	36.4	2	1	0	0	2	0	0	1	0	1	0	0	4	0	0	0	0	0	0	0	0	1	0	0	0
Ixtlapan	6	.0000	.0644	28.1	0	0	0	0	6	0	0	0	0	0	0	6	0	0	0	0	0	0	0	0	0	0	0	0	0
Izak	3	.0000	.1370	31.4	3	0	0	0	0	0	0	0	3	0	0	0	0	0	0	0	0	0	0	0	0	0	0	0	0
Izbushka	2	.0000	.0243	23.9	2	0	0	0	0	0	0	0	0	0	0	0	0	0	0	0	0	0	0	0	0	0	0	2	0
ize	6	.0000	.0487	26.9	0	1	0	0	3	2	0	0	0	0	0	0	0	0	6	0	0	0	0	0	0	0	0	0	0
Izmir	4	.0000	.0778	28.9	0	0	0	0	4	0	0	0	0	0	0	0	0	4	0	0	0	0	0	0	0	0	0	0	0
j	87	.4246	7.8707	49.0	7	12	15	26	17	6	3	1	8	4	5	1	8	0	56	0	0	0	1	0	0	2	0	2	0
J	101	.8208	16.602	52.2	3	12	7	10	27	22	11	9	14	5	2	1	20	5	7	5	3	0	0	1	0	6	14	18	0
J**	4	.0919	.1430	31.6	0	0	0	1	3	0	0	0	1	0	0	3	0	0	0	0	0	0	0	0	0	0	0	0	0
J-2	2	.0000	.0050	17.0	0	0	0	0	2	0	0	0	0	0	0	0	0	0	0	0	0	0	0	2	0	0	0	0	0
j's	2	.0000	.0045	16.5	0	2	0	0	0	0	0	0	0	0	2	0	0	0	0	0	0	0	0	0	0	0	0	0	0
ja	5	.3228	.4034	36.1	1	1	1	0	0	0	2	0	2	0	0	2	0	0	0	0	0	0	0	0	0	1	0	0	0
JA	3	.0000	.0449	26.5	0	2	0	0	1	0	0	0	0	0	0	0	3	0	0	0	0	0	0	0	0	0	0	0	0
jab	2	.0000	.0914	29.6	1	0	0	0	1	0	0	0	2	0	0	0	0	0	0	0	0	0	0	0	0	0	0	0	0
jabbed	8	.4736	.8644	39.4	1	1	3	0	1	1	1	0	4	1	0	1	0	0	0	0	0	0	0	0	2	0	0	0	0
jabbered	2	.2440	.1132	30.5	0	1	0	0	0	1	0	0	0	0	0	1	0	0	0	0	0	0	0	0	0	0	0	1	0
Jabberwock	3	.0000	.0055	17.4	0	0	3	0	0	0	0	0	0	0	0	0	0	0	0	0	0	3	0	0	0	0	0	0	0
Jabez	9	.0829	.2993	34.8	0	0	0	0	0	2	7	0	2	0	0	7	0	0	0	0	0	0	0	0	0	0	0	0	0
JABEZ	5	.0000	.0537	27.3	0	0	0	0	0	0	5	0	0	0	0	5	0	0	0	0	0	0	0	0	0	0	0	0	0
Jabizri	3	.0000	.0352	25.5	0	3	0	0	0	0	0	0	0	0	0	0	0	0	0	0	0	0	0	0	3	0	0	0	0
jabs	2	.0000	.0914	29.6	0	0	0	0	2	0	0	0	2	0	0	0	0	0	0	0	0	0	0	0	0	0	0	0	0
Jacalevna	5	.0000	.0547	27.4	0	0	0	0	0	0	5	0	0	5	0	0	0	0	0	0	0	0	0	0	0	0	0	0	0
Jacaranda	3	.0000	.1370	31.4	0	0	0	3	0	0	0	0	3	0	0	0	0	0	0	0	0	0	0	0	0	0	0	0	0
Jacinto	4	.2982	.2887	34.6	0	2	0	0	0	2	0	0	1	0	0	1	0	0	0	0	0	0	0	0	0	0	2	0	0
jack	35	.5709	4.3188	46.4	10	3	6	6	2	5	1	2	14	3	0	0	0	4	2	5	0	0	0	4	0	2	1	0	0
Jack	532	.8570	91.810	59.6	232	78	59	49	50	34	27	3	266	42	6	18	48	23	28	13	1	0	2	1	23	19	9	33	0
JACK	2	.0000	.0215	23.3	0	0	0	0	2	0	0	0	0	0	0	2	0	0	0	0	0	0	0	0	0	0	0	0	0
jack-in-the-box	2	.2420	.1154	30.6	1	1	0	0	0	0	0	0	0	0	0	0	1	0	0	0	0	0	0	0	1	0	0	0	0
jack-knife	4	.2048	.1975	33.0	0	3	0	0	1	0	0	0	0	0	0	1	0	0	0	0	0	0	0	0	3	0	0	0	0
jack-o'-lantern	4	.4820	.4018	36.0	1	0	0	1	0	1	1	0	0	1	0	1	0	0	1	0	0	0	0	0	0	1	0	0	0
jack-o'-lanterns	2	.0000	.0243	23.9	2	0	0	0	0	0	0	0	0	0	0	0	0	0	0	0	0	0	0	0	0	0	0	2	0
Jack's	29	.6893	4.2061	46.2	16	4	1	1	2	2	1	2	16	1	1	0	3	2	3	1	0	0	0	0	1	0	1	0	0
jackal	3	.1169	.1277	31.1	0	0	0	1	2	0	0	0	1	0	0	0	0	0	0	0	0	0	0	0	0	0	2	0	0
jackals	12	.3358	.9537	39.8	0	1	0	4	6	0	1	0	3	0	0	0	0	1	0	0	0	0	0	0	0	0	6	2	0
jackass	2	.2285	.1129	30.5	1	0	0	1	0	0	0	0	0	0	0	0	0	1	0	0	0	0	0	0	0	0	1	0	0
jackdaws	3	.3842	.2485	34.0	1	0	0	0	1	1	0	0	0	0	0	1	0	0	0	0	0	0	0	0	0	1	1	0	0
jacket	143	.7151	21.250	53.3	46	24	12	15	17	16	12	1	75	3	3	11	1	1	3	4	2	3	17	0	5	8	0	7	0
Jacket	2	.1674	.0805	29.1	1	0	0	0	0	0	1	0	0	0	0	0	0	0	0	0	0	0	1	0	0	1	0	0	0
jackets	35	.6298	4.6065	46.6	3	3	3	8	9	1	8	0	10	1	0	2	1	3	0	0	0	0	5	0	3	4	1	5	0
jackhammer	3	.2332	.1804	32.6	1	0	0	0	1	1	0	0	1	0	1	0	0	0	0	0	1	0	0	0	0	0	0	0	0
Jackie	19	.4470	2.0618	43.1	1	2	0	0	14	0	2	0	14	0	0	0	2	0	0	0	0	0	0	0	0	2	0	1	0
jackknife	9	.3961	.8108	39.1	0	5	0	4	0	0	0	0	2	0	0	1	0	0	1	0	0	0	0	0	0	5	0	0	0
jackrabbit	5	.4418	.4883	36.9	0	0	0	0	3	2	0	0	1	1	0	0	2	0	0	0	0	0	0	0	0	0	1	0	0
jacks	4	.4543	.4025	36.0	0	1	0	1	2	0	0	0	1	1	0	0	0	0	0	0	0	0	0	0	0	1	0	1	0
Jackson	104	.8121	17.038	52.3	26	20	12	7	9	21	5	4	27	7	1	7	1	25	0	2	3	0	0	0	10	11	3	7	0
Jackson's	18	.5168	2.0993	43.2	3	1	1	4	1	7	1	0	9	1	0	1	0	6	0	0	0	0	0	0	1	0	0	0	0
Jacksons	2	.0000	.0243	23.9	0	0	0	0	0	0	0	2	0	0	0	0	0	0	0	0	0	0	0	0	0	0	0	2	0
Jacksons'	2	.2337	.1157	30.6	1	1	0	0	0	0	0	0	0	0	0	0	0	1	0	0	0	0	0	0	1	0	0	0	0
Jacksonville	11	.4743	1.1253	40.5	2	0	3	2	1	0	1	2	1	0	0	0	4	1	0	0	0	0	0	0	0	2	0	3	0
Jacob	99	.5702	12.663	51.0	10	21	17	33	9	8	1	0	72	0	0	5	0	3	0	1	3	0	0	0	2	12	1	0	0
Jacob's	11	.5619	1.3607	41.3	1	1	5	2	1	1	0	0	6	0	0	1	0	0	0	0	1	0	0	0	1	2	0	0	0
Jacobson	2	.1814	.1187	30.7	0	1	1	0	0	0	0	0	1	0	0	0	0	0	0	0	0	0	0	0	0	0	0	1	0
Jacobus	2	.1698	.1133	30.5	0	0	0	1	0	1	0	0	1	0	0	0	0	0	0	0	0	0	0	0	0	0	1	0	0
Jacot	7	.0000	.3198	35.0	7	0	0	0	0	0	0	0	7	0	0	0	0	0	0	0	0	0	0	0	0	0	0	0	0
Jacqueline	4	.2814	.2738	34.4	1	0	0	0	1	0	0	2	1	0	0	0	0	0	0	0	0	0	1	0	0	0	0	2	0
Jacques	31	.6596	4.2149	46.2	1	3	7	6	4	3	5	2	6	0	0	3	0	3	0	4	6	2	0	0	0	1	3	3	0
jade	21	.3202	1.9210	42.8	0	0	2	0	17	1	0	1	19	0	0	0	0	0	0	0	0	1	0	0	0	0	0	1	0
Jaffrey	4	.0000	.0469	26.7	0	0	4	0	0	0	0	0	0	0	0	0	0	0	0	0	0	0	0	0	4	0	0	0	0
Jagatai	2	.0000	.0209	23.2	0	0	0	0	0	2	0	0	0	0	0	0	0	0	0	0	0	0	0	0	0	0	2	0	0
jagged	39	.8144	6.3958	48.1	8	4	7	5	7	2	4	2	10	1	0	2	0	1	1	5	1	1	1	0	5	5	0	6	0
jaguar	9	.4770	.9033	39.6	2	1	0	0	1	0	1	4	0	0	0	4	0	0	0	1	0	0	0	0	0	2	1	1	0
Jaguar	10	.0000	.4568	36.6	0	0	0	0	0	10	0	0	10	0	0	0	0	0	0	0	0	0	0	0	0	0	0	0	0
jaguars	2	.2285	.1129	30.5	0	0	0	1	1	0	0	0	0	0	0	0	0	1	0	0	0	0	0	0	0	0	1	0	0
Jahn	2	.0000	.0209	23.2	0	0	2	0	0	0	0	0	0	0	0	0	0	0	0	0	0	0	0	0	0	0	2	0	0
jai-alai	4	.0000	.1827	32.6	0	0	0	0	4	0	0	0	4	0	0	0	0	0	0	0	0	0	0	0	0	0	0	0	0
jail	51	.7495	7.8489	48.9	11	3	2	10	10	3	12	0	21	0	2	5	3	5	1	0	0	0	0	0	3	5	1	5	0
jailed	4	.4889	.4075	36.1	0	0	0	0	3	0	1	0	0	1	0	1	0	0	0	0	0	0	0	0	1	0	0	1	0
jailhouse	2	.2440	.1132	30.5	0	0	0	0	0	0	1	1	0	0	0	1	0	0	0	0	0	0	0	0	0	0	0	1	0
jails	4	.1505	.1615	32.1	0	0	3	0	1	0	0	0	0	0	0	0	0	1	0	0	0	0	0	0	0	0	3	0	0
Jake	53	.2967	4.6013	46.6	40	0	0	3	8	2	0	0	45	0	0	1	0	0	0	0	0	0	0	0	7	0	0	0	0
Jake's	5	.2446	.3872	35.9	1	0	0	1	3	0	0	0	4	0	0	0	0	0	0	0	0	0	0	0	1	0	0	0	0
jalopy	6	.3876	.5828	37.7	1	0	2	0	3	0	0	0	4	1	0	0	0	0	0	0	0	0	0	0	1	0	0	0	0
Jalpa	2	.0000	.0215	23.3	0	0	0	0	2	0	0	0	0	0	0	2	0	0	0	0	0	0	0	0	0	0	0	0	0
jam	46	.7250	6.8380	48.3	15	6	1	7	5	9	3	0	13	3	2	0	0	6	0	2	1	0	0	0	9	6	1	3	0
Jam	6	.1948	.3750	35.7	3	0	3	0	0	0	0	0	3	0	0	0	0	0	0	0	0	0	0	0	0	3	0	0	0
Jamaica	20	.3274	1.5625	41.9	0	1	1	4	13	1	0	0	2	0	0	0	1	14	0	0	0	0	0	0	0	0	3	0	0
jamb	2	.0000	.0234	23.7	0	0	2	0	0	0	0	0	0	0	0	0	0	0	0	0	0	0	0	0	2	0	0	0	0
jamcloset	2	.1717	.1142	30.6	0	0	1	0	1	0	0	0	1	0	0	1	0	0	0	0	0	0	0	0	0	0	0	0	0
James	300	.8568	51.539	57.1	59	55	26	31	59	42	23	5	100	5	3	13	12	26	8	13	9	0	0	0	25	19	36	31	0
James'	2	.0000	.0914	29.6	0	1	0	1	0	0	0	0	2	0	0	0	0	0	0	0	0	0	0	0	0	0	0	0	0
James's	6	.4369	.5566	37.5	0	3	1	0	1	1	0	0	0	0	0	0	1	0	0	0	0	0	0	0	1	0	1	3	0

4D ivied
6A Ivorsen
7F Ivory
6H ivory-billed
8H ivorylike
4P ivver
8F IWW
5P Ixelles
6D IXL
6F Ixtaccihuatl
4B J-La
3J J-i-n-g-o
6N j-j-jumps
7A j-j-just
7D J-79
3A jzz
5A Ja-Nez
4A Ja's
3A jabbers
6B Jabberwocky
4N jabbing
9D Jabez's
7Q jabiru
4N Jabizri's
9B Jacalevna's
7Q jacanas
8A Jack-and-the-beanstalk
4H jack-in-the-pulpit
4A jack-o-lantern
3G jack-o-lanterns
3B Jack-o'-Lantern
7A jackal's
7Q jackals'
9R jackboots
8D jackdaw
3P jackdawses
7R jacketed
7R jacking
7Q jackknife-and-baling-wire
8A jackknife's
5J Jackman's
8E jackrabbit's
7A jackrabbits
9D Jacks
8N Jackson-fork
6A jackstones
4D jackstraws
8F JACL'S
9D Jacobin
6A Jacobins
4B Jacobs
5Q Jacopone
7Q Jacquard
6A Jacques's
XR jaded
7P jaded-looking
XR jag
8Q Jagello
8Q Jagiello
5Q Jagiellonian
8A Jaguars
9B jail-breaker
8D jail-house
9N jailbird
6A jailer
8R Jailhouse
8D jailing
4K Jalisco
7A jalopies
5R Jaloux
4P jam-jams
8B jam-packed
4A Jam's
6E Jamaican
5Q jambiya
5N jamboree
8B james
9Q JAMES

Word Type	F	D	U	SFI	3 Gr 3	4 Gr 4	5 Gr 5	6 Gr 6	7 Gr 7	8 Gr 8	9 Gr 9	X UnGr	A Read	B Eng & Gr	C Comp	D Lit	E Math	F Soc Stud	G Spell	H Sci	J Music	K Art	L Home Ec	M Shop	N Lib F	P Lib NF	Q Lib Ref	R Mag	S Rel
Jamestown	59	.5301	6.7030	48.3	13	8	8	5	19	3	3	0	9	0	0	0	2	23	2	0	0	0	0	0	0	10	13	0	0
Jamie	15	.4462	1.5878	42.0	0	13	0	0	1	0	1	0	9	1	0	0	0	0	0	0	0	0	0	0	0	4	0	1	0
Jamison	6	.1493	.2320	33.7	0	1	0	0	0	5	0	0	0	0	0	5	0	0	0	0	0	0	0	0	0	0	0	1	0
jammed	41	.7004	5.9165	47.7	8	7	6	4	5	4	7	0	12	3	1	3	0	4	1	0	0	0	0	0	0	3	2	12	0
jamming	3	.1983	.1396	31.4	0	0	0	1	0	2	0	0	0	0	0	0	0	0	0	0	2	0	0	0	0	0	0	1	0
jams	12	.5758	1.4957	41.7	2	3	1	2	3	0	0	1	5	0	0	0	0	2	0	1	0	0	1	0	0	0	1	2	0
Jan	85	.7921	13.613	51.3	10	13	16	6	15	11	14	0	23	1	1	1	15	4	2	2	3	0	0	0	13	1	10	9	0
Jan's	6	.5210	.6707	38.3	0	2	1	1	1	1	0	0	1	1	0	0	2	1	0	0	0	0	0	0	1	0	0	0	0
Jancsi	5	.0000	.2284	33.6	0	0	0	5	0	0	0	0	5	0	0	0	0	0	0	0	0	0	0	0	0	0	0	0	0
Jane	444	.7530	67.821	58.3	100	98	72	24	98	5	44	3	88	28	1	32	88	22	22	5	2	0	3	0	115	24	2	12	0
Jane's	50	.5413	5.8489	47.7	8	17	8	8	5	2	2	0	15	1	0	1	22	1	5	0	0	0	0	0	4	0	0	1	0
Janeiro	5	.3975	.4517	36.5	0	0	1	2	1	1	0	0	1	2	0	0	0	1	0	0	0	0	0	0	0	1	0	0	0
Janet	35	.6180	4.6655	46.7	23	4	0	2	3	2	1	0	19	3	0	0	4	1	1	0	0	0	0	0	1	6	0	0	0
Janet's	3	.1434	.1493	31.7	1	2	0	0	0	0	0	0	1	0	0	0	2	0	0	0	0	0	0	0	0	0	0	0	0
Janey	103	.1468	6.8980	48.4	0	3	4	20	76	0	0	0	100	0	0	2	0	0	0	0	0	0	0	0	1	0	0	0	0
Janey's	7	.2389	.5456	37.4	1	0	0	0	6	0	0	0	6	1	0	0	0	0	0	0	0	0	0	0	0	0	0	0	0
jangled	2	.1551	.0728	28.6	0	0	1	0	0	0	1	0	0	0	1	0	0	0	0	0	0	0	0	0	1	0	0	0	0
jangling	7	.4658	.7063	38.5	4	1	1	0	0	1	0	0	1	0	0	0	0	1	0	0	1	0	0	0	3	1	0	0	0
Janice	13	.4220	1.1705	40.7	2	1	0	0	0	4	6	0	0	2	0	0	3	0	1	0	0	0	0	0	0	0	0	7	0
Janie	45	.3331	3.9358	46.0	18	10	0	11	6	0	0	0	28	0	0	0	0	0	0	0	0	0	0	0	3	0	0	14	0
Janie's	4	.1814	.2373	33.8	2	1	0	1	0	0	0	0	2	0	0	0	0	0	0	0	0	0	0	0	0	0	0	2	0
Janis	3	.2321	.1635	32.1	0	0	1	0	0	0	2	0	0	0	0	0	0	0	0	0	0	0	0	0	0	0	1	2	0
Janissaries	2	.0000	.0290	24.6	0	0	2	0	0	0	0	0	0	0	0	0	0	0	0	0	0	0	0	0	0	2	0	0	0
janitor	3	.3269	.2368	33.7	1	1	0	1	0	0	0	0	1	0	0	0	0	0	1	0	0	0	0	0	1	0	0	0	0
janitors	2	.1948	.1250	31.0	0	0	0	1	0	1	0	0	1	0	0	0	0	0	0	0	0	0	0	0	0	1	0	0	0
Janos	2	.2287	.1077	30.3	0	1	0	0	1	0	0	0	0	0	0	0	1	0	0	0	1	0	0	0	0	0	0	0	0
Jansky	2	.0000	.0394	26.0	0	0	0	0	0	2	0	0	0	0	0	0	0	0	0	2	0	0	0	0	0	0	0	0	0
Janssen	3	.2076	.1618	32.1	0	1	1	0	0	1	0	0	0	0	0	0	2	0	0	1	0	0	0	0	0	0	0	0	0
January	156	.7651	24.212	53.8	10	48	22	18	18	16	23	1	31	2	2	1	9	39	5	8	5	0	0	0	5	12	15	21	1
Janus	22	.4269	2.0026	43.0	2	3	8	0	0	0	1	8	0	0	0	1	0	0	3	0	0	0	0	0	8	10	0	0	0
Japan	337	.5165	37.673	55.8	33	87	35	61	28	84	6	3	43	7	0	4	4	231	0	2	9	1	0	0	1	6	14	15	0
Japan's	32	.4087	2.9085	44.6	0	7	4	9	2	9	1	0	1	0	0	0	0	22	0	0	1	0	0	0	0	0	4	4	0
Japanese	354	.6419	47.264	56.7	22	85	24	44	64	104	8	3	46	4	2	28	0	213	5	2	9	1	0	0	3	12	13	16	0
Japeth	2	.0000	.0914	29.6	0	0	0	0	2	0	0	0	2	0	0	0	0	0	0	0	0	0	0	0	0	0	0	0	0
jar	299	.6862	42.554	56.3	74	103	53	8	32	17	8	4	70	0	7	10	10	6	1	158	1	2	5	0	13	15	0	1	0
Jar	6	.1600	.3820	35.8	5	0	0	0	0	1	0	0	5	0	0	0	0	0	0	0	0	1	0	0	0	0	0	0	0
jargon	2	.2437	.1129	30.5	0	0	0	0	0	1	1	0	0	0	0	0	0	0	0	0	0	0	0	0	0	0	1	1	0
Jarman	2	.0000	.0243	23.9	0	0	0	0	0	2	0	0	0	0	0	0	0	0	0	0	0	0	0	0	0	0	0	2	0
jarred	4	.0000	.1827	32.6	0	1	0	2	1	0	0	0	4	0	0	0	0	0	0	0	0	0	0	0	0	0	0	0	0
jarring	8	.4652	.8026	39.0	0	0	0	1	4	2	1	0	1	0	0	3	0	1	0	0	0	0	0	0	1	0	0	2	0
jars	80	.7794	12.644	51.0	17	35	5	6	6	7	2	2	19	0	0	1	16	2	0	23	0	2	3	2	3	4	3	2	0
Jase	7	.0000	.0751	28.8	0	0	0	0	7	0	0	0	0	0	0	7	0	0	0	0	0	0	0	0	0	0	0	0	0
Jase's	2	.0000	.0215	23.3	0	0	0	0	2	0	0	0	0	0	0	2	0	0	0	0	0	0	0	0	0	0	0	0	0
Jasim	6	.0000	.1167	30.7	0	6	0	0	0	0	0	0	0	0	0	0	0	6	0	0	0	0	0	0	0	0	0	0	0
Jasim's	2	.0000	.0389	25.9	0	2	0	0	0	0	0	0	0	0	0	0	0	2	0	0	0	0	0	0	0	0	0	0	0
jasmine	5	.4638	.4999	37.0	0	0	0	2	0	0	2	1	1	0	0	1	0	0	0	0	0	0	1	0	0	0	1	1	0
Jason	52	.2990	4.5250	46.6	0	0	13	30	7	1	1	0	44	1	0	7	0	0	0	0	0	0	0	0	0	0	0	0	0
Jason's	8	.2393	.6011	37.8	0	0	0	4	4	0	0	0	6	0	0	2	0	0	0	0	0	0	0	0	0	0	0	0	0
Jasper	8	.5791	.9674	39.9	1	4	0	0	2	0	1	0	1	0	0	2	2	0	0	0	0	0	0	0	1	1	0	1	0
jauntily	5	.3181	.3528	35.5	4	0	1	0	0	0	0	0	0	3	0	0	0	0	0	0	0	0	0	0	1	1	0	0	0
jaunty	3	.2175	.1545	31.9	0	0	1	0	1	1	0	0	0	0	0	2	0	0	0	0	0	0	0	0	0	0	0	1	0
Java	23	.4888	2.5203	44.0	0	0	3	8	8	4	0	0	9	0	0	0	0	4	0	1	0	0	0	0	0	1	7	1	0
Javanese	5	.3684	.4146	36.2	0	0	1	0	4	0	0	0	0	0	0	0	0	3	0	0	0	0	0	0	0	1	1	0	0
javelin	3	.3873	.2495	34.0	0	0	1	0	2	0	0	0	0	0	0	1	0	0	0	0	0	0	0	0	1	0	0	1	0
javelina	3	.2266	.1614	32.1	0	0	0	0	3	0	0	0	0	0	0	0	0	0	0	0	0	0	0	0	1	0	0	2	0
javelinas	4	.2446	.2283	33.6	0	0	0	0	4	0	0	0	0	0	0	0	0	0	0	0	0	0	0	0	2	0	0	2	0
jaw	42	.7681	6.5016	48.1	12	2	3	2	10	7	6	0	6	4	0	6	0	1	1	4	2	0	0	3	4	6	4	1	0
jaw-breaking	2	.2437	.1129	30.5	0	0	0	1	0	0	1	0	0	0	0	0	0	0	0	0	0	0	0	0	0	0	1	1	0
jawbone	3	.3811	.2534	34.0	1	0	0	0	1	0	1	0	0	0	0	0	0	0	0	1	0	0	0	0	0	1	0	1	0
jaws	126	.7459	19.065	52.8	36	10	9	12	38	12	9	0	22	1	0	8	0	1	1	23	0	2	0	7	8	21	25	7	0
jay	16	.4509	1.7282	42.4	7	0	0	2	5	2	0	0	11	2	0	2	0	0	0	1	0	0	0	0	0	0	0	0	0
Jay	53	.6143	6.8192	48.3	20	9	12	1	4	2	5	0	13	0	0	1	1	5	0	0	1	0	0	0	14	1	11	6	0
Jayme	2	.0000	.0389	25.9	0	2	0	0	0	0	0	0	0	0	0	0	0	2	0	0	0	0	0	0	0	0	0	0	0
jays	8	.3962	.7436	38.7	4	0	1	0	3	0	0	0	3	0	0	0	0	0	0	1	0	0	0	0	1	0	3	0	0
Jayvees	5	.0000	.2284	33.6	0	0	0	0	0	5	0	0	5	0	0	0	0	0	0	0	0	0	0	0	0	0	0	0	0
jaywalking	2	.0000	.0394	26.0	0	0	0	0	2	0	0	0	0	0	0	0	0	0	0	2	0	0	0	0	0	0	0	0	0
Jazbo	7	.0000	.3198	35.0	7	0	0	0	0	0	0	0	7	0	0	0	0	0	0	0	0	0	0	0	0	0	0	0	0
jazz	108	.1524	4.0915	46.1	1	0	5	37	6	43	16	0	3	1	0	0	0	0	0	0	97	1	0	0	1	2	0	3	0
Jazz	8	.0762	.1901	32.8	0	0	0	2	0	4	2	0	0	0	0	0	0	1	0	0	7	0	0	0	0	0	0	0	0
jealous	28	.3813	2.4057	43.8	0	3	3	3	4	10	5	0	4	1	0	4	1	5	0	0	2	0	0	0	3	5	0	2	1
jealousies	4	.2912	.2656	34.2	0	0	0	0	0	3	1	0	0	0	1	1	0	2	0	0	0	0	0	0	0	0	0	0	0
jealously	4	.3006	.2666	34.3	0	2	0	0	0	1	0	1	0	0	1	0	0	0	0	0	0	0	0	0	0	2	0	1	0
jealousy	14	.5937	1.7525	42.4	0	2	1	2	4	2	3	0	4	0	0	2	0	0	0	0	1	0	1	0	0	2	0	4	0
Jean	164	.6132	21.146	53.3	39	26	14	27	15	31	12	0	52	14	2	15	8	3	1	16	2	22	1	0	10	3	13	2	0
Jean's	13	.3989	1.1262	40.5	8	4	0	0	1	0	0	0	2	1	1	0	1	0	1	1	0	4	0	0	2	0	0	0	0
Jeanette	15	.0000	.6852	38.4	0	0	0	0	15	0	0	0	15	0	0	0	0	0	0	0	0	0	0	0	0	0	0	0	0
Jeanette's	3	.0000	.1370	31.4	0	0	0	0	3	0	0	0	3	0	0	0	0	0	0	0	0	0	0	0	0	0	0	0	0
Jeanie	14	.4585	1.5119	41.8	9	0	1	0	3	0	1	0	9	1	0	3	0	0	0	0	1	0	0	0	0	0	0	0	0
Jeanie's	2	.0000	.0914	29.6	2	0	0	0	0	0	0	0	2	0	0	0	0	0	0	0	0	0	0	0	0	0	0	0	0
Jeanne	4	.2399	.3011	34.8	3	0	0	0	0	0	1	0	3	1	0	0	0	0	0	0	0	0	0	0	0	0	0	0	0
Jeannie	2	.1814	.1187	30.7	1	0	0	0	0	0	1	0	1	0	0	0	0	0	0	0	0	0	0	0	0	0	0	1	0
jeans	24	.6415	3.2330	45.1	0	7	3	4	3	7	0	0	9	0	0	1	0	2	0	0	0	0	2	1	6	1	0	2	0
Jeans	2	.0000	.0394	26.0	0	0	0	0	0	0	2	0	0	0	0	0	0	0	0	2	0	0	0	0	0	0	0	0	0
Jeb	22	.4174	2.2924	43.6	0	7	4	10	1	0	0	0	17	1	0	0	0	0	0	0	0	0	0	0	3	1	0	0	0
Jeb's	2	.0000	.0914	29.6	0	2	0	0	0	0	0	0	2	0	0	0	0	0	0	0	0	0	0	0	0	0	0	0	0
Jed	65	.1122	2.4010	43.8	0	63	0	0	1	0	1	0	5	1	0	0	0	0	0	0	0	0	0	0	1	58	0	0	0
Jed's	14	.0000	.2027	33.1	0	14	0	0	0	0	0	0	0	0	0	0	0	0	0	0	0	0	0	0	0	14	0	0	0
jedges	3	.0000	.1370	31.4	0	0	0	0	3	0	0	0	3	0	0	0	0	0	0	0	0	0	0	0	0	0	0	0	0
Jee-rusalem	2	.0000	.0914	29.6	0	0	0	0	2	0	0	0	2	0	0	0	0	0	0	0	0	0	0	0	0	0	0	0	0
jeep	43	.5419	5.1498	47.1	9	1	2	2	28	0	1	0	21	2	0	0	0	1	0	0	0	0	0	0	9	8	0	2	0
Jeep	11	.2223	.5918	37.7	0	0	4	0	1	0	6	0	0	0	0	0	0	0	0	0	0	0	0	0	0	4	0	7	0
Jeep's	2	.0000	.0243	23.9	0	0	0	0	0	0	2	0	0	0	0	0	0	0	0	0	0	0	0	0	0	0	0	2	0
jeepers	6	.3598	.5339	37.3	1	2	2	0	0	0	1	0	3	0	0	1	0	0	0	0	0	0	0	0	2	0	0	0	0
jeepney	2	.0000	.0914	29.6	2	0	0	0	0	0	0	0	2	0	0	0	0	0	0	0	0	0	0	0	0	0	0	0	0

9B Jameses
4P Jameson
4P Jamie's
3N Jamin
7D Jamshedpur
8J Janacek
7D JANE
5E Janes's
3A jangle
5P Janissary
8N Jannough's
6A Jansci
8H Jansky's
XP Januarius
5N Janus'
7R Jap
8F Japanese-Americans
5F Japanese-held
8F Japanized
6R jarad
XP Jarrott
6A jas
7Q Jas
9Q Jasomirgott
5Q jasper
8A Jataka
9R jaundiced
8R jaunt
7P jauntiness
6R Java's
9B jaw-wagging
8R Jawaharlal
7N jawin'
3P jawses
3J jay-bird
7N jay-birds
7E Jay's
7B jaybirds
7R Jaycees
8A Jayvee
9J jazzmen
7E JB
8E JD
9D jealious
9K Jean-Baptiste
7A Jean-Claude
9K Jean-Francois
9R Jean-Luc
9R Jean-Paul
4Q Jean-Philippe
9R Jean-Pierre
8F Jeannette
5N jedgin'
4P Jedidiah
4R jeep's

Word Type	F	D	U	SFI	3 Gr 3	4 Gr 4	5 Gr 5	6 Gr 6	7 Gr 7	8 Gr 8	9 Gr 9	X UnGr	A Read	B Eng & Gr	C Comp	D Lit	E Math	F Soc Stud	G Spell	H Sci	J Music	K Art	L Home Ec	M Shop	N Lib F	P Lib NF	Q Lib Ref	R Mag	S Rel
jeeps	8	.2395	.5946	37.7	0	0	0	1	7	0	0	0	5	0	0	0	0	3	0	0	0	0	0	0	0	0	0	0	0
Jeeps	2	.0000	.0290	24.6	0	0	2	0	0	0	0	0	0	0	0	0	0	0	0	0	0	0	0	0	0	2	0	0	0
jeer	2	.2331	.1157	30.6	0	0	0	1	0	0	1	0	0	0	0	0	0	0	0	1	0	0	0	0	1	0	0	0	0
jeered	5	.4733	.5356	37.3	0	1	0	1	1	1	1	0	2	1	0	0	0	1	0	0	0	0	0	0	0	0	0	1	0
jeering	5	.3854	.4790	36.8	1	0	0	2	2	0	0	0	3	0	0	0	0	0	0	0	0	0	0	0	1	1	0	0	0
jeers	3	.3854	.2500	34.0	1	0	1	0	0	0	0	1	0	1	0	0	0	0	0	0	0	0	0	0	1	1	0	0	0
Jeff	213	.4879	24.847	54.0	15	16	6	15	152	1	1	7	181	6	1	3	1	1	0	0	0	0	0	0	5	0	0	15	0
Jeff's	11	.3581	.9439	39.7	1	6	0	0	4	0	0	0	4	5	0	0	1	0	0	0	0	0	0	0	0	0	0	1	0
Jefferson	115	.7183	16.933	52.3	5	12	39	9	19	26	5	0	23	7	0	5	2	46	1	1	2	0	0	0	1	8	11	8	0
Jefferson's	18	.5563	2.1992	43.4	1	2	2	1	5	7	0	0	8	0	0	1	0	4	0	0	0	0	0	0	0	3	0	2	0
Jeffersonians	2	.1698	.1133	30.5	0	0	1	0	1	0	0	0	1	0	0	0	0	0	0	0	0	0	0	0	0	0	1	0	0
Jeffrey	11	.2234	.8394	39.2	0	8	1	2	0	0	0	0	10	0	1	0	0	0	0	0	0	0	0	0	0	0	0	0	0
Jeffries	3	.2427	.1822	32.6	0	0	0	1	0	0	2	0	0	0	0	0	0	0	0	2	0	0	0	0	0	0	0	1	0
Jehovah	3	.2071	.1434	31.6	0	0	0	0	0	3	0	0	0	0	0	1	0	0	0	0	2	0	0	0	0	0	0	0	0
Jekyll	6	.3834	.5765	37.6	0	0	0	1	4	1	0	0	4	1	0	0	0	0	1	0	0	0	0	0	0	0	0	0	0
Jelena	2	.0000	.0162	22.1	0	0	2	0	0	0	0	0	0	0	0	0	0	0	0	0	2	0	0	0	0	0	0	0	0
Jella	7	.0000	.0821	29.1	0	0	7	0	0	0	0	0	0	0	0	0	0	0	0	0	0	0	0	0	7	0	0	0	0
jellies	6	.1991	.3231	35.1	0	0	0	0	6	0	0	0	0	0	0	0	0	0	0	5	0	0	0	0	1	0	0	0	0
jello	2	.1787	.1174	30.7	1	0	0	1	0	0	0	0	1	0	0	0	0	0	0	0	0	0	0	0	1	0	0	0	0
jelly	87	.7675	13.620	51.3	37	22	5	12	6	2	1	2	29	1	0	0	2	2	3	13	0	0	2	0	4	16	4	11	0
jelly-like	3	.2212	.2099	33.2	1	1	0	0	1	0	0	0	2	0	0	1	0	0	0	0	0	0	0	0	0	0	0	0	0
jellyfish	28	.4641	2.8637	44.6	4	2	4	1	15	0	2	0	5	0	0	1	0	0	0	14	0	3	0	0	0	1	3	1	0
jellyfishes	2	.2443	.1130	30.5	1	0	0	1	0	0	0	0	0	0	0	1	0	0	0	0	0	0	0	0	1	0	0	0	0
Jem	54	.0000	.5795	37.6	0	0	0	0	0	0	54	0	0	0	0	54	0	0	0	0	0	0	0	0	0	0	0	0	0
Jem's	5	.0000	.0537	27.3	0	0	0	0	0	0	5	0	0	0	0	5	0	0	0	0	0	0	0	0	0	0	0	0	0
Jemima	12	.2261	.9283	39.7	0	1	11	0	0	0	0	0	11	0	0	0	0	0	0	0	1	0	0	0	0	0	0	0	0
Jemmy	6	.0000	.0485	26.9	0	6	0	0	0	0	0	0	0	0	0	0	0	0	0	0	6	0	0	0	0	0	0	0	0
Jen	9	.0000	.1303	31.1	9	0	0	0	0	0	0	0	0	0	0	0	0	0	0	0	0	0	0	0	0	9	0	0	0
Jen's	2	.0000	.0290	24.6	2	0	0	0	0	0	0	0	0	0	0	0	0	0	0	0	0	0	0	0	0	2	0	0	0
Jencks	3	.0000	.0434	26.4	0	3	0	0	0	0	0	0	0	0	0	0	0	0	0	0	0	0	0	0	0	3	0	0	0
Jeni	5	.0000	.0972	29.9	0	5	0	0	0	0	0	0	0	0	0	0	0	5	0	0	0	0	0	0	0	0	0	0	0
Jenkins	105	.2735	8.9595	49.5	2	92	5	0	5	1	0	0	98	0	0	3	0	1	0	0	0	0	0	0	1	0	0	2	0
Jenkins'	3	.1277	.1363	31.3	0	1	0	0	2	0	0	0	1	0	0	0	0	0	0	0	0	0	0	0	0	0	0	2	0
Jenks	10	.0000	.4568	36.6	0	0	0	8	1	1	0	0	10	0	0	0	0	0	0	0	0	0	0	0	0	0	0	0	0
Jenner	7	.2444	.5386	37.3	0	1	0	0	5	0	1	0	5	0	0	0	0	0	0	2	0	0	0	0	0	0	0	0	0
jennet	2	.2441	.1127	30.5	1	0	0	1	0	0	0	0	0	0	0	0	0	0	0	0	0	0	0	0	1	0	1	0	0
Jennie	6	.3560	.4730	36.7	0	4	0	2	0	0	0	0	0	0	0	0	1	0	0	0	0	0	0	0	0	3	0	2	0
Jennifer	24	.4612	2.6922	44.3	17	3	3	1	0	0	0	0	20	1	0	0	1	0	1	0	0	0	0	0	0	0	0	1	0
Jennifer's	2	.1972	.1262	31.0	0	1	0	0	1	0	0	0	1	0	0	0	1	0	0	0	0	0	0	0	0	0	0	0	0
Jennings	5	.4751	.5383	37.3	0	2	0	0	1	2	0	0	2	1	0	0	0	1	0	0	0	0	0	0	0	1	0	0	0
jenny	4	.3662	.3647	35.6	1	0	0	0	2	0	1	0	2	0	0	0	0	1	0	0	0	0	0	0	0	0	1	0	0
Jenny	43	.5879	5.2356	47.2	8	13	2	0	9	11	0	0	5	12	0	3	1	0	0	0	5	0	0	0	11	0	0	6	0
JENNY	9	.0000	.0966	29.8	0	0	0	0	9	0	0	0	0	0	0	9	0	0	0	0	0	0	0	0	0	0	0	0	0
Jenny-O	4	.0000	.0323	25.1	4	0	0	0	0	0	0	0	0	0	0	0	0	0	0	0	4	0	0	0	0	0	0	0	0
Jenny's	3	.2227	.1589	32.0	0	1	0	0	0	2	0	0	0	0	0	0	0	0	0	0	0	0	0	0	2	0	0	1	0
Jensen	23	.4055	2.2869	43.6	5	0	0	16	2	0	0	0	14	0	0	0	0	0	0	0	0	0	0	0	0	7	1	1	0
Jere	3	.0000	.0365	25.6	0	0	0	0	3	0	0	0	0	0	0	0	0	0	0	0	0	0	0	0	0	0	0	3	0
Jeremiah	4	.4741	.3983	36.0	0	0	0	1	0	2	1	0	0	0	0	1	0	1	0	0	1	0	0	0	0	0	1	0	0
Jeremy	17	.3459	1.5955	42.0	0	11	2	3	0	0	0	1	14	0	0	0	0	0	0	0	0	0	0	0	0	0	2	1	0
Jericho	6	.2956	.3997	36.0	1	2	0	0	1	2	0	0	0	0	0	0	0	1	0	0	3	0	0	0	0	2	0	0	0
jerk	24	.6364	3.2286	45.1	3	2	3	2	9	3	2	0	11	1	1	4	0	0	0	0	0	0	2	0	2	0	0	3	0
jerked	63	.6029	8.1513	49.1	8	17	10	7	12	6	3	0	29	0	1	11	0	0	0	1	0	0	0	0	12	7	0	2	0
jerkily	3	.2236	.1570	32.0	0	0	0	0	3	0	0	0	0	1	0	2	0	0	0	0	0	0	0	0	0	0	0	0	0
jerkin	4	.4889	.4075	36.1	0	0	1	2	1	0	0	0	0	1	0	1	0	0	0	0	0	0	0	0	1	0	0	1	0
jerking	11	.3189	.8445	39.3	1	2	0	0	5	1	2	0	3	0	0	6	0	0	0	0	0	0	0	0	1	1	0	0	0
jerks	8	.4197	.7149	38.5	1	1	0	0	2	3	1	0	0	0	0	2	0	0	0	0	0	0	0	0	4	1	0	1	0
jerky	13	.5181	1.4669	41.7	0	3	1	0	5	3	1	0	3	0	0	1	0	0	0	6	1	0	0	0	2	0	0	0	0
Jernegan	15	.2434	1.1572	40.6	0	0	0	11	0	0	0	4	11	0	0	0	0	0	0	4	0	0	0	0	0	0	0	0	0
Jernegan's	3	.0000	.1370	31.4	0	0	0	3	0	0	0	0	3	0	0	0	0	0	0	0	0	0	0	0	0	0	0	0	0
Jerome	38	.4172	3.8386	45.8	18	0	9	5	2	3	1	0	24	0	0	9	1	0	0	0	4	0	0	0	0	0	0	0	0
Jerry	131	.6610	18.067	52.6	31	18	23	14	27	8	10	0	47	27	5	21	15	0	1	1	0	0	0	0	8	0	0	6	0
Jerry's	17	.4671	1.7612	42.5	5	2	7	0	3	0	0	0	5	6	0	1	4	0	0	0	0	0	0	0	0	0	0	1	0
jersey	4	.3686	.3350	35.2	1	0	0	0	1	1	1	0	1	1	0	0	0	0	0	0	0	0	1	0	1	0	0	0	0
Jersey	12	.5598	1.4152	41.5	0	4	2	0	3	2	1	0	2	1	0	2	0	2	3	0	0	0	0	0	0	2	0	0	0
JerseyCity	6	.4697	.6013	37.8	1	0	2	0	3	0	0	0	0	0	0	0	0	2	0	0	0	0	0	0	1	1	0	2	0
Jerseys	2	.0000	.0389	25.9	0	0	0	0	0	2	0	0	0	0	0	0	0	2	0	0	0	0	0	0	0	0	0	0	0
Jerusalem	64	.2910	4.4178	46.5	5	4	8	17	20	5	3	2	3	3	0	1	0	32	0	1	4	0	0	0	1	8	7	1	3
jes'	3	.0000	.0322	25.1	0	0	0	0	3	0	0	0	0	0	0	3	0	0	0	0	0	0	0	0	0	0	0	0	0
Jespersen	2	.0000	.0219	23.4	0	0	0	0	2	0	0	0	0	2	0	0	0	0	0	0	0	0	0	0	0	0	0	0	0
Jess	14	.3210	1.0126	40.1	9	0	0	0	0	4	0	1	1	0	0	8	0	0	0	0	0	0	0	0	4	0	0	1	0
jessamine	2	.2427	.1152	30.6	0	1	0	0	1	0	0	0	0	0	0	0	0	0	0	0	0	0	0	0	1	1	0	0	0
Jesse	28	.4418	2.8440	44.5	2	0	2	0	5	6	2	11	12	2	0	2	0	0	0	0	0	0	0	0	0	1	0	11	0
Jesse's	4	.0000	.0486	26.9	0	0	0	0	0	0	0	4	0	0	0	0	0	0	0	0	0	0	0	0	0	0	0	4	0
Jessica	9	.1143	.2890	34.6	0	0	0	0	0	1	8	0	0	0	0	8	0	0	0	0	0	0	0	0	0	0	0	1	0
Jessie	44	.0917	1.3293	41.2	35	0	1	1	4	0	3	0	2	0	0	1	0	1	0	0	0	0	0	0	40	0	0	0	0
jest	29	.3457	2.2312	43.5	5	2	3	0	7	5	6	1	2	3	0	7	0	0	0	0	0	0	0	0	17	0	0	0	0
Jest	2	.0000	.0215	23.3	0	0	0	0	0	2	0	0	0	0	0	2	0	0	0	0	0	0	0	0	0	0	0	0	0
jestbooks	2	.0000	.0209	23.2	0	2	0	0	0	0	0	0	0	0	0	0	0	0	0	0	0	0	0	0	0	0	2	0	0
jester	3	.2197	.2090	33.2	0	1	0	2	0	0	0	0	2	0	0	0	0	0	0	0	0	0	0	0	0	0	1	0	0
jesters	9	.2246	.4753	36.8	0	8	0	1	0	0	0	0	0	0	0	0	0	1	0	0	1	0	0	0	0	0	7	0	0
jests	2	.0000	.0215	23.3	0	0	0	0	0	0	2	0	0	0	0	2	0	0	0	0	0	0	0	0	0	0	0	0	0
Jests	2	.0000	.0209	23.2	0	2	0	0	0	0	0	0	0	0	0	0	0	0	0	0	0	0	0	0	0	0	2	0	0
Jesuit	10	.5192	1.0863	40.4	0	0	1	4	1	1	3	0	0	0	0	0	0	3	0	0	1	0	0	0	1	0	1	4	0
Jesuits	7	.4435	.6659	38.2	0	0	1	3	0	1	2	0	0	0	0	0	0	2	0	0	0	0	0	0	0	1	1	3	0
Jesus	136	.0217	1.3135	41.2	62	46	4	9	5	5	4	1	3	0	0	2	0	5	0	0	10	0	0	0	8	16	0	6	86
JESUS	2	.0000	.0004	5.5	2	0	0	0	0	0	0	0	0	0	0	0	0	0	0	0	0	0	0	0	0	0	0	0	2
Jesus'	7	.0465	.1049	30.2	5	0	0	2	0	0	0	0	0	0	0	0	0	0	0	0	2	0	0	0	1	1	0	0	3
jet	221	.8473	37.449	55.7	62	32	10	24	51	18	19	5	32	10	2	7	40	12	2	60	3	2	0	9	1	14	11	16	0
Jet	7	.4888	.7829	38.9	3	0	1	0	2	0	1	0	4	1	0	0	0	0	0	0	0	0	0	0	0	0	1	1	0
jet-age	2	.0000	.0243	23.9	0	0	0	1	0	0	0	1	0	0	0	0	0	0	0	0	0	0	0	0	0	0	0	2	0
jet-propelled	3	.2223	.2106	33.2	0	0	2	0	0	0	1	0	2	1	0	0	0	0	0	0	0	0	0	0	0	0	0	0	0
Jeth	7	.0000	.0821	29.1	0	0	0	0	0	7	0	0	0	0	0	0	0	0	0	0	0	0	0	0	7	0	0	0	0
Jethro	32	.0852	.9399	39.7	0	0	1	0	2	29	0	0	2	0	0	0	0	0	0	0	0	0	0	0	29	0	1	0	0
Jethro's	3	.2304	.1619	32.1	0	0	1	0	0	2	0	0	0	0	0	0	0	0	0	0	0	0	0	0	2	0	1	0	0
jets	34	.5923	4.2576	46.3	12	5	0	8	5	1	2	1	8	2	0	0	2	0	0	5	0	0	0	0	1	6	0	10	0
Jets	10	.2574	.7013	38.5	0	0	3	2	3	2	0	0	4	0	0	0	0	0	0	1	0	0	0	0	0	0	0	5	0

XN Jeff'll
4A Jeffrey's
7N Jehoshaphat
9A Jehovah's
9R Jekyll-to-Hyde
7L jellied
9E jelling
3R JELLY
6G jellybean
3A Jellyfish
5Q jelutong
4J Jemmy's
4P Jenckses
6R Jennie's
6A Jensen's
7G jeopardize
8F jeopardized
7R jeopardy
7Q jerboas
6A Jeremy's
8A jerkers
6N jerkins
9P Jerky
6A Jerome's
8D Jerries
7R JerseyCity's
3D JESS
6J jesting
5P jestingly
9D Jesu
7R Jesup
8D jet-black
9B jet-blast
3P jet-control
5H jet-hours
8B jet-piercer
8E jet-plane
4F jet-powered
5R jet-setters
7H jet-stream
3R jet's
9G jetliner
6R jetliners
5E JETS

Word Type	F	D	U	SFI	3 Gr 3	4 Gr 4	5 Gr 5	6 Gr 6	7 Gr 7	8 Gr 8	9 Gr 9	X UnGr	A Read	B Eng & Gr	C Comp	D Lit	E Math	F Soc Stud	G Spell	H Sci	J Music	K Art	L Home Ec	M Shop	N Lib F	P Lib NF	Q Lib Ref	R Mag	S Rel
jetted	2	.1717	.1142	30.6	0	0	0	1	0	1	0	0	1	0	0	1	0	0	0	0	0	0	0	0	0	0	0	0	0
jettisoned	2	.1620	.0760	28.8	0	0	0	0	2	0	0	0	0	0	0	0	0	0	0	0	0	0	0	1	0	0	0	1	0
jetty	4	.0996	.1523	31.8	0	0	0	4	0	0	0	0	1	0	0	0	0	0	0	0	0	0	0	0	0	0	0	3	0
Jew	23	.2387	1.2954	41.1	0	0	1	0	1	1	20	0	1	0	0	17	0	0	0	0	0	0	0	0	0	1	4	0	0
Jew's	2	.2411	.1091	30.4	0	0	1	0	0	0	1	0	0	0	0	1	0	0	0	0	1	0	0	0	0	0	0	0	0
Jewan	2	.0000	.0914	29.6	0	0	0	0	0	2	0	0	2	0	0	0	0	0	0	0	0	0	0	0	0	0	0	0	0
jewel	20	.7062	2.9365	44.7	1	0	3	6	5	1	4	0	9	0	0	2	0	3	0	0	1	0	1	0	2	0	1	1	0
jewel-like	2	.1698	.1133	30.5	1	0	0	0	0	0	1	0	1	0	0	0	0	0	0	0	0	0	0	0	0	0	1	0	0
jeweled	7	.4128	.6365	38.0	0	2	1	1	2	0	0	1	1	0	0	0	0	1	0	0	0	1	0	0	0	2	2	0	0
jeweler	5	.2218	.3471	35.4	0	0	0	5	0	0	0	0	3	0	0	0	0	0	0	0	0	0	0	0	0	2	0	0	0
jeweler's	3	.3795	.2506	34.0	0	1	1	0	1	0	0	0	0	0	0	0	0	1	0	0	0	0	0	0	1	0	0	1	0
jewelers	3	.1169	.1277	31.1	0	0	1	0	1	1	0	0	1	0	0	0	0	0	0	0	0	0	0	0	0	0	2	0	0
jewelled	2	.2387	.1089	30.4	1	0	0	0	1	0	0	0	0	0	0	0	0	0	0	0	1	0	0	0	1	0	0	0	0
jewelry	67	.7882	10.745	50.3	14	4	12	10	17	2	8	0	26	1	1	1	1	15	0	2	0	3	2	2	1	2	2	8	0
jewels	71	.7557	11.068	50.4	8	10	12	7	25	5	3	1	38	3	3	6	0	9	0	0	2	1	0	0	3	3	1	2	0
Jewish	72	.5399	8.1988	49.1	4	11	9	10	18	7	11	2	7	1	0	1	0	22	0	1	11	0	0	0	0	10	15	3	1
Jewry	2	.2427	.1152	30.6	0	0	1	0	1	0	0	0	0	0	0	0	0	0	0	0	0	0	0	0	1	1	0	0	0
Jews	74	.4915	7.8102	48.9	4	2	9	20	23	12	2	2	5	1	0	0	0	34	0	0	5	0	0	0	0	17	10	1	1
Jezreel	5	.0000	.0972	29.9	0	0	0	0	5	0	0	0	0	0	0	0	0	5	0	0	0	0	0	0	0	0	0	0	0
jib	9	.3772	.7620	38.8	0	0	0	3	3	2	1	0	2	0	2	1	0	0	0	0	0	0	0	0	3	0	1	0	0
jibes	2	.1733	.1149	30.6	0	0	0	0	1	1	0	0	1	1	0	0	0	0	0	0	0	0	0	0	0	0	0	0	0
jibs	2	.1698	.1133	30.5	0	0	0	1	0	0	1	0	1	0	0	0	0	0	0	0	0	0	0	0	0	0	1	0	0
jiffy	6	.4050	.5403	37.3	1	1	0	2	1	0	0	1	1	0	1	0	0	0	0	1	0	0	0	0	2	1	0	0	0
jig	18	.3128	1.2713	41.0	9	1	2	0	5	0	1	0	3	0	0	0	0	0	0	0	10	0	0	4	1	0	0	0	0
Jig	2	.0000	.0162	22.1	0	0	1	1	0	0	0	0	0	0	0	0	0	0	0	0	2	0	0	0	0	0	0	0	0
jiggin'	2	.0000	.0162	22.1	0	2	0	0	0	0	0	0	0	0	0	0	0	0	0	0	2	0	0	0	0	0	0	0	0
jiggle	2	.1733	.1149	30.6	1	1	0	0	0	0	0	0	1	1	0	0	0	0	0	0	0	0	0	0	0	0	0	0	0
jiggling	3	.3452	.2543	34.1	0	0	0	2	1	0	0	0	1	0	0	0	0	0	0	1	0	0	0	0	0	0	0	1	0
Jigori	4	.0000	.1827	32.6	0	0	0	4	0	0	0	0	4	0	0	0	0	0	0	0	0	0	0	0	0	0	0	0	0
jigsaw	8	.5876	.9834	39.9	1	1	0	1	2	0	2	1	1	0	0	1	1	0	0	2	0	0	0	0	2	0	1	0	0
Jill	66	.5427	7.8320	48.9	33	6	11	2	10	4	0	0	28	9	1	15	13	0	0	0	0	0	0	0	0	0	0	0	0
Jill's	4	.2446	.3071	34.9	1	1	0	0	0	2	0	0	3	0	0	0	1	0	0	0	0	0	0	0	0	0	0	0	0
Jillson	2	.0000	.0243	23.9	0	0	0	0	0	2	0	0	0	0	0	0	0	0	0	0	0	0	0	0	0	0	0	2	0
Jim	779	.7469	120.22	60.8	293	165	52	64	114	68	13	10	399	65	2	14	109	30	21	8	1	0	0	0	69	24	0	37	0
Jim's	83	.5824	10.712	50.3	50	18	5	2	5	3	0	0	56	6	0	0	12	0	2	0	0	0	0	0	2	1	0	4	0
Jimma	5	.0000	.0972	29.9	0	0	0	0	5	0	0	0	0	0	0	0	0	5	0	0	0	0	0	0	0	0	0	0	0
Jimmie	2	.2407	.1138	30.6	0	0	0	0	1	0	1	0	0	0	0	1	0	0	0	0	0	0	0	0	0	1	0	0	0
Jimmy	233	.7214	34.676	55.4	32	92	16	29	46	13	3	2	87	5	3	31	4	9	1	4	0	0	0	0	12	61	4	12	0
Jimmy's	22	.5327	2.5285	44.0	3	8	4	0	5	0	2	0	6	2	0	5	0	0	0	1	0	0	0	0	0	7	0	1	0
jingle	13	.5569	1.5128	41.8	4	2	1	3	1	2	0	0	2	0	0	0	0	0	3	0	3	0	0	0	0	2	1	2	0
Jingle	2	.0000	.0219	23.4	0	0	2	0	0	0	0	0	0	2	0	0	0	0	0	0	0	0	0	0	0	0	0	0	0
Jinglebob	7	.0000	.0751	28.8	0	0	7	0	0	0	0	0	0	0	0	7	0	0	0	0	0	0	0	0	0	0	0	0	0
jingled	5	.3536	.4328	36.4	3	2	0	0	0	0	0	0	2	0	0	0	0	0	0	0	0	0	0	0	1	2	0	0	0
jingles	2	.2306	.1140	30.6	0	1	0	0	1	0	0	0	0	1	0	0	0	1	0	0	0	0	0	0	0	0	0	0	0
jingling	9	.3695	.8474	39.3	3	1	2	3	0	0	0	0	6	0	1	0	0	1	0	0	0	0	0	0	1	0	0	0	0
jingo	3	.2071	.1434	31.6	2	0	0	0	0	0	1	0	0	0	0	1	0	0	0	0	2	0	0	0	0	0	0	0	0
jings	2	.1787	.1174	30.7	0	0	0	1	1	0	0	0	1	0	0	0	0	0	0	0	0	0	0	0	1	0	0	0	0
jinni	2	.0000	.0914	29.6	0	0	0	0	2	0	0	0	2	0	0	0	0	0	0	0	0	0	0	0	0	0	0	0	0
Jinny	4	.0000	.1827	32.6	4	0	0	0	0	0	0	0	4	0	0	0	0	0	0	0	0	0	0	0	0	0	0	0	0
Jinny's	3	.0000	.1370	31.4	3	0	0	0	0	0	0	0	3	0	0	0	0	0	0	0	0	0	0	0	0	0	0	0	0
jinx	9	.0000	.4111	36.1	0	0	0	0	9	0	0	0	9	0	0	0	0	0	0	0	0	0	0	0	0	0	0	0	0
jinxed	7	.0000	.3198	35.0	0	0	0	0	7	0	0	0	7	0	0	0	0	0	0	0	0	0	0	0	0	0	0	0	0
Jip	10	.2111	.5602	37.5	0	9	1	0	0	0	0	0	2	0	0	1	0	0	0	0	0	0	0	0	7	0	0	0	0
jittery	2	.2407	.1138	30.6	0	0	0	1	1	0	0	0	0	0	0	1	0	0	0	0	0	0	0	0	0	1	0	0	0
Jiya	46	.0449	1.0442	40.2	0	0	12	0	34	0	0	0	5	0	0	41	0	0	0	0	0	0	0	0	0	0	0	0	0
JIYA	17	.0000	.1824	32.6	0	0	0	0	17	0	0	0	0	0	0	17	0	0	0	0	0	0	0	0	0	0	0	0	0
Jiya's	2	.0000	.0215	23.3	0	0	1	0	1	0	0	0	0	0	0	2	0	0	0	0	0	0	0	0	0	0	0	0	0
JK	5	.0000	.0748	28.7	0	1	0	0	4	0	0	0	0	0	0	0	5	0	0	0	0	0	0	0	0	0	0	0	0
JKLM	3	.0000	.0449	26.5	0	1	1	0	0	1	0	0	0	0	0	0	3	0	0	0	0	0	0	0	0	0	0	0	0
JKPO	2	.0000	.0299	24.8	0	0	2	0	0	0	0	0	0	0	0	0	2	0	0	0	0	0	0	0	0	0	0	0	0
Jo	76	.4532	7.2970	48.6	0	20	1	3	43	0	9	0	1	0	0	7	0	1	1	0	0	0	1	0	43	19	0	3	0
JoAnn	5	.0000	.0986	29.9	0	0	0	0	5	0	0	0	0	0	0	0	0	0	0	5	0	0	0	0	0	0	0	0	0
JoAnn's	2	.0000	.0394	26.0	0	0	0	0	2	0	0	0	0	0	0	0	0	0	0	2	0	0	0	0	0	0	0	0	0
Jo's	5	.2414	.2745	34.4	1	0	0	0	4	0	0	0	0	0	1	0	0	0	0	0	0	0	0	0	4	0	0	0	0
Joaby	8	.0000	.3655	35.6	0	0	8	0	0	0	0	0	8	0	0	0	0	0	0	0	0	0	0	0	0	0	0	0	0
Joan	64	.5800	7.7171	48.9	15	6	14	11	8	2	5	3	5	13	0	0	30	2	0	1	1	0	4	0	0	4	0	4	0
Joan's	6	.1851	.2880	34.6	0	1	2	0	1	0	2	0	0	0	0	1	5	0	0	0	0	0	0	0	0	0	0	0	0
Joanie	2	.0000	.0243	23.9	0	0	0	0	0	0	0	2	0	0	0	0	0	0	0	0	0	0	0	0	0	0	0	2	0
Joanne	9	.2031	.4885	36.9	3	3	0	3	0	0	0	0	1	0	0	0	7	0	0	0	0	0	0	0	1	0	0	0	0
Joanne's	4	.0000	.0599	27.8	0	1	0	3	0	0	0	0	0	0	0	0	4	0	0	0	0	0	0	0	0	0	0	0	0
Joaquin	8	.6211	1.0558	40.2	0	1	1	0	4	1	1	0	3	0	0	1	0	1	0	1	0	0	0	0	0	0	1	1	0
job	855	.8883	151.64	61.8	173	128	88	65	173	104	108	16	315	47	6	49	12	84	9	47	16	1	10	32	40	72	20	95	0
Job	3	.3385	.2445	33.9	0	1	0	0	2	0	0	0	1	0	0	0	0	0	0	0	0	0	0	0	1	0	1	0	0
Jobe	11	.1645	.4641	36.7	9	0	0	0	0	2	0	0	0	0	0	0	0	0	0	0	0	0	0	0	9	0	0	2	0
jobless	2	.0000	.0243	23.9	0	0	0	0	0	1	1	0	0	0	0	0	0	0	0	0	0	0	0	0	0	0	0	2	0
jobs	258	.7918	41.163	56.1	34	24	49	26	49	32	34	10	36	16	2	8	3	95	0	16	1	1	7	17	6	18	10	22	0
Jocasta	4	.0000	.0419	26.2	0	0	0	0	0	4	0	0	0	0	0	0	0	0	0	0	0	0	0	0	0	0	4	0	0
jockey	7	.3465	.5216	37.2	0	0	0	3	2	2	0	0	0	0	1	0	0	0	0	0	1	0	0	0	5	0	0	0	0
jockeying	3	.3553	.2609	34.2	1	0	0	0	1	0	0	1	1	0	0	0	0	0	0	1	0	0	0	0	0	1	0	0	0
jockeys	3	.2332	.1690	32.3	0	1	0	2	0	0	0	0	0	0	0	0	0	0	0	0	0	0	0	0	0	2	0	1	0
Jocko	6	.2187	.3110	34.9	2	4	0	0	0	0	0	0	0	4	0	0	0	0	0	0	0	0	0	0	0	0	0	2	0
jocund	5	.3431	.3712	35.7	0	0	0	1	0	2	2	0	0	0	0	3	0	0	0	0	1	0	0	0	1	0	0	0	0
Jody	145	.2830	9.8867	50.0	36	0	0	1	54	54	0	0	25	0	0	9	0	0	1	0	0	0	0	0	99	0	0	11	0
JODY	6	.0000	.0644	28.1	0	0	0	0	0	6	0	0	0	0	0	6	0	0	0	0	0	0	0	0	0	0	0	0	0
Jody's	13	.2615	.9052	39.6	5	0	0	0	4	4	0	0	5	0	0	1	0	0	0	0	0	0	0	0	7	0	0	0	0
joe	4	.1497	.2092	33.2	1	1	0	1	1	0	0	0	2	0	0	0	0	0	2	0	0	0	0	0	0	0	0	0	0
Joe	680	.8509	116.47	60.7	174	167	73	69	101	50	38	8	310	24	5	43	51	22	13	0	18	9	4	0	102	37	3	39	0
Joe's	61	.7794	9.6493	49.8	17	15	2	6	13	4	4	0	18	5	0	4	8	7	2	0	0	1	0	0	7	1	0	8	0
Joel	28	.2613	1.7099	42.3	26	0	1	0	1	0	0	0	1	0	0	0	0	0	0	0	0	0	0	0	13	0	0	14	0
Joes	3	.2143	.1568	32.0	0	0	2	0	1	0	0	0	0	0	0	0	0	0	0	0	0	0	0	0	0	1	0	2	0
joey	9	.1890	.6465	38.1	0	1	0	8	0	0	0	0	8	0	0	0	0	1	0	0	0	0	0	0	0	0	0	0	0
Joey	72	.5427	8.4958	49.3	28	14	7	0	14	9	0	0	28	3	0	11	0	0	1	0	0	0	0	0	8	0	0	21	0
Joey's	3	.3845	.2500	34.0	1	0	0	0	2	0	0	0	0	0	0	1	1	0	0	0	0	0	0	0	0	0	0	1	0

6A jetties
XR jetting
6R jettisons
7P Jeux
8J Jevan
8Q Jevric
7P Jew-free
7D jew's
8R Jewel
6N jewel-bag
6A jewel-bright
8D jewellers
7N jewellery
4H jewelweed
8E JH
7N jib-boom
6D jibe
9P jibed
5R jibing
9M jig-boring
9H jig-saw
5N jigged
5N jigging
5H jiggled
6H jiggles
7P jigs
5P jihad
7N jillion
8R Jillson's
8D jiminey
7N jimpson
7R jims
4P jimson
7B jinan
XB jine
6A jing
3J jingle-jangle
3B jingle-jingle
9B jingle-jingling
5D Jinglebob'd
5D jinglebobbed
9D jingly
5N Jinks
8D jinn
3A Jiquipilco
9Q Jiro
7N jis'
5Q jist
7F jitney
8G jiujitsu
7E JKL
6R JLIT
5E JO
8D Joab
5A Joaby's
XH Joachimstal
3P Joany
5A Joao
9D job-stealer
7J job's
5J jobber's
7R jobbers
3N Jobe's
6N jockey's
3R Jocko's
6A Jod
6R JOD
6A Jod's
5F Jodhpur
8D JODY'S
7D JOE
7D Joe'd

Word Type	F	D	U	SFI	3 Gr 3	4 Gr 4	5 Gr 5	6 Gr 6	7 Gr 7	8 Gr 8	9 Gr 9	X UnGr	A Read	B Eng & Gr	C Comp	D Lit	E Math	F Soc Stud	G Spell	H Sci	J Music	K Art	L Home Ec	M Shop	N Lib F	P Lib NF	Q Lib Ref	R Mag	S Rel
jog	3	.3427	.2477	33.9	0	0	1	0	2	0	0	0	1	0	0	0	0	0	0	0	0	0	0	0	1	0	0	1	0
jogged	9	.4434	.9021	39.6	0	2	2	0	3	2	0	0	3	0	0	1	0	0	0	0	0	0	0	0	3	2	0	0	0
jogging	5	.3833	.4767	36.8	1	1	1	1	1	0	0	0	3	0	0	1	0	0	0	0	0	0	0	0	0	1	0	0	0
joggled	2	.1787	.1174	30.7	0	0	2	0	0	0	0	0	1	0	0	0	0	0	0	0	0	0	0	0	1	0	0	0	0
Jogues	2	.0000	.0914	29.6	0	2	0	0	0	0	0	0	2	0	0	0	0	0	0	0	0	0	0	0	0	0	0	0	0
Johann	80	.5589	9.7303	49.9	19	22	4	14	8	5	5	3	37	4	0	0	0	2	0	4	23	0	0	2	0	3	5	0	0
Johann's	6	.0000	.2741	34.4	0	6	0	0	0	0	0	0	6	0	0	0	0	0	0	0	0	0	0	0	0	0	0	0	0
Johanna	9	.2261	.6392	38.1	5	1	0	3	0	0	0	0	6	0	0	0	0	0	0	0	0	0	0	0	3	0	0	0	0
Johannes	16	.2364	.8616	39.4	1	5	1	1	3	4	1	0	0	1	0	0	1	0	0	1	12	0	0	0	0	0	0	1	0
Johannesburg	7	.1679	.3402	35.3	0	0	1	1	5	0	0	0	0	0	0	0	0	6	0	0	0	0	0	0	0	1	0	0	0
John	1347	.8982	240.80	63.8	236	252	153	245	239	116	91	15	383	119	12	66	123	79	35	28	45	8	1	0	124	192	49	83	0
JOHN	8	.4521	.8390	39.2	0	0	0	0	5	1	2	0	4	0	0	2	0	1	0	0	0	0	0	0	0	0	1	0	0
John-go-in-the-Wynd	7	.0000	.0821	29.1	0	0	0	7	0	0	0	0	0	0	0	0	0	0	0	0	0	0	0	0	7	0	0	0	0
John-the-Fletcher	2	.0000	.0234	23.7	0	0	0	2	0	0	0	0	0	0	0	0	0	0	0	0	0	0	0	0	2	0	0	0	0
John's	81	.7780	12.740	51.1	14	12	10	17	12	8	7	1	18	6	1	3	23	2	5	1	1	3	0	0	11	4	0	3	0
Johnie	11	.0000	.1180	30.7	0	0	0	0	0	11	0	0	0	0	0	11	0	0	0	0	0	0	0	0	0	0	0	0	0
Johnie's	2	.0000	.0215	23.3	0	0	0	0	0	2	0	0	0	0	0	2	0	0	0	0	0	0	0	0	0	0	0	0	0
Johnnie	10	.2407	.7487	38.7	0	3	7	0	0	0	0	0	7	0	0	0	0	0	0	0	0	0	0	0	0	3	0	0	0
Johnny	617	.6504	84.543	59.3	107	304	8	38	47	73	40	0	254	19	0	27	2	2	6	0	18	0	0	0	71	172	0	46	0
JOHNNY	5	.0000	.0537	27.3	0	0	0	0	0	0	5	0	0	0	0	5	0	0	0	0	0	0	0	0	0	0	0	0	0
Johnny's	56	.5631	6.8761	48.4	10	28	0	5	2	7	4	0	26	1	0	0	0	0	0	0	5	0	0	0	10	12	0	2	0
JOHNNY'S	7	.0000	.0751	28.8	0	0	0	0	0	0	7	0	0	0	0	7	0	0	0	0	0	0	0	0	0	0	0	0	0
johnnycake	2	.0000	.0914	29.6	1	0	1	0	0	0	0	0	2	0	0	0	0	0	0	0	0	0	0	0	0	0	0	0	0
Johns	13	.6599	1.8029	42.6	0	0	6	0	3	4	0	0	5	1	0	1	0	2	0	1	0	0	0	0	0	1	2	0	0
Johnson	179	.7578	27.495	54.4	35	24	13	7	49	32	15	4	31	10	0	15	3	38	2	0	5	0	0	0	4	22	14	35	0
Johnson's	17	.6326	2.2349	43.5	5	1	0	0	5	3	3	0	3	0	0	1	0	3	0	0	1	0	0	0	0	4	1	4	0
Johnsons	11	.4176	1.0096	40.0	5	1	0	0	3	0	2	0	0	1	0	2	1	7	0	0	0	0	0	0	0	0	0	0	0
Johnsons'	2	.0000	.0914	29.6	2	0	0	0	0	0	0	0	2	0	0	0	0	0	0	0	0	0	0	0	0	0	0	0	0
Johnston	5	.4485	.5011	37.0	0	1	0	1	1	2	0	0	1	0	0	0	0	2	0	0	0	0	0	0	0	1	1	0	0
Johnston's	2	.0000	.0290	24.6	0	2	0	0	0	0	0	0	0	0	0	0	0	0	0	0	0	0	0	0	0	2	0	0	0
Johnstown	12	.0831	.3175	35.0	1	0	0	0	0	11	0	0	0	0	0	11	0	0	0	0	0	0	0	0	0	1	0	0	0
Johnty	12	.0000	.1737	32.4	0	12	0	0	0	0	0	0	0	0	0	0	0	0	0	0	0	0	0	0	0	12	0	0	0
Johnty's	2	.0000	.0290	24.6	0	2	0	0	0	0	0	0	0	0	0	0	0	0	0	0	0	0	0	0	0	2	0	0	0
join	363	.9522	68.268	58.3	59	80	55	49	46	36	29	9	79	24	3	8	35	41	19	19	29	6	11	4	9	32	12	31	1
joined	385	.9422	71.701	58.6	52	57	52	47	65	60	49	3	70	32	4	23	16	53	12	28	13	1	10	11	17	31	39	25	0
joining	65	.8009	10.407	50.2	4	10	8	3	14	17	7	2	5	7	4	1	13	4	5	3	1	0	4	5	4	3	2	4	0
joins	50	.8195	8.2162	49.1	11	4	10	5	9	7	3	1	7	2	0	0	1	8	2	12	4	1	2	3	0	2	4	2	0
joint	142	.4083	12.369	50.9	1	4	29	13	33	25	37	0	5	1	0	2	2	2	1	31	1	3	0	50	2	20	11	11	0
Joint	4	.1889	.1768	32.5	0	0	0	0	0	2	2	0	0	0	0	0	0	1	0	0	0	0	0	2	0	0	1	0	0
jointed	18	.4377	1.7110	42.3	5	2	0	2	6	3	0	0	0	0	0	0	0	0	0	12	0	0	0	2	0	1	2	1	0
jointer	12	.0520	.1740	32.4	0	0	0	0	2	1	9	0	0	0	0	0	0	0	0	0	0	0	0	10	0	2	0	0	0
jointing	4	.0935	.0899	29.5	0	0	0	0	1	0	2	1	0	0	0	0	0	0	0	0	0	0	0	3	0	0	1	0	0
jointly	6	.3779	.5077	37.1	0	0	0	0	3	0	3	0	1	1	0	0	0	0	0	0	0	0	0	0	1	0	3	0	0
joints	77	.4250	7.0065	48.5	1	3	10	18	21	13	10	1	4	0	0	2	0	0	0	28	0	6	0	23	1	7	6	0	0
Jojep	6	.0000	.1167	30.7	0	6	0	0	0	0	0	0	0	0	0	0	0	6	0	0	0	0	0	0	0	0	0	0	0
Joji	7	.0000	.3198	35.0	7	0	0	0	0	0	0	0	7	0	0	0	0	0	0	0	0	0	0	0	0	0	0	0	0
joke	109	.7981	17.601	52.5	24	19	7	12	19	15	8	5	37	10	0	14	0	2	2	2	2	4	1	0	6	10	5	14	0
Joke	2	.2375	.1088	30.4	0	0	0	0	0	0	2	0	0	0	0	0	0	0	0	0	1	0	0	0	0	0	0	1	0
joke's	2	.1814	.1187	30.7	2	0	0	0	0	0	0	0	1	0	0	0	0	0	0	0	0	0	0	0	0	0	0	1	0
joked	8	.4081	.7432	38.7	1	2	2	0	0	0	3	0	2	0	0	1	0	0	0	0	0	0	0	0	1	4	0	0	0
joker	2	.1814	.1187	30.7	0	1	1	0	0	0	0	0	1	0	0	0	0	0	0	0	0	0	0	0	0	0	0	1	0
jokes	77	.7731	12.067	50.8	12	18	6	3	8	20	6	4	20	12	0	5	0	5	0	2	1	2	0	0	3	12	8	7	0
joking	25	.6042	3.2863	45.2	7	9	2	2	3	0	0	2	15	1	0	0	0	0	0	0	1	0	0	0	3	3	2	0	0
jokingly	7	.0000	.3198	35.0	1	1	5	0	0	0	0	0	7	0	0	0	0	0	0	0	0	0	0	0	0	0	0	0	0
Jolliginki	2	.0000	.0234	23.7	0	2	0	0	0	0	0	0	0	0	0	0	0	0	0	0	0	0	0	0	2	0	0	0	0
jollily	2	.0000	.0234	23.7	0	2	0	0	0	0	0	0	0	0	0	0	0	0	0	0	0	0	0	0	2	0	0	0	0
jolly	41	.6987	5.9436	47.7	7	13	4	11	3	2	0	1	18	2	1	5	0	0	0	0	8	0	1	0	3	1	0	2	0
Jolly	14	.2165	1.0672	40.3	4	0	1	1	0	8	0	0	13	0	0	0	0	0	0	0	1	0	0	0	0	0	0	0	0
Jolly's	2	.0000	.0914	29.6	1	0	0	0	0	1	0	0	2	0	0	0	0	0	0	0	0	0	0	0	0	0	0	0	0
jolt	8	.5203	.8962	39.5	0	2	0	1	2	0	3	0	2	0	0	2	0	0	0	0	0	0	0	0	2	1	0	1	0
jolted	6	.3629	.5312	37.3	0	1	0	0	3	2	0	0	3	0	1	1	0	0	0	0	0	0	0	0	0	0	0	1	0
jolting	4	.4538	.4020	36.0	1	0	0	2	0	0	1	0	1	0	0	1	0	0	0	0	0	0	0	0	0	1	0	1	0
jolts	2	.1814	.1187	30.7	0	0	0	0	2	0	0	0	1	0	0	0	0	0	0	0	0	0	0	0	0	0	0	1	0
Jomo	3	.0000	.0365	25.6	0	0	0	1	0	1	1	0	0	0	0	0	0	0	0	0	0	0	0	0	0	0	0	3	0
Jon	33	.3928	3.1981	45.0	15	11	6	0	0	1	0	0	17	0	0	0	2	13	0	0	0	0	0	0	0	0	0	1	0
Jon's	2	.0000	.0914	29.6	0	2	0	0	0	0	0	0	2	0	0	0	0	0	0	0	0	0	0	0	0	0	0	0	0
Jonah	7	.2808	.4602	36.6	5	0	0	0	0	1	1	0	0	1	0	0	0	1	0	0	0	0	0	0	0	5	0	0	0
Jonah's	2	.0000	.0914	29.6	2	0	0	0	0	0	0	0	2	0	0	0	0	0	0	0	0	0	0	0	0	0	0	0	0
Jonas	37	.5223	4.1147	46.1	0	33	1	1	0	2	0	0	3	0	0	10	2	11	0	3	0	0	0	0	0	8	0	0	0
Jonathan	59	.5628	7.3470	48.7	7	39	2	4	1	6	0	0	33	1	0	1	0	4	2	0	0	0	0	0	1	16	0	1	0
Jonathan's	3	.2223	.2106	33.2	2	0	1	0	0	0	0	0	2	1	0	0	0	0	0	0	0	0	0	0	0	0	0	0	0
Jones	180	.7802	28.432	54.5	41	25	13	39	21	13	27	1	45	11	2	5	23	9	4	0	0	0	0	0	36	22	5	18	0
Jones'	7	.4775	.7559	38.8	1	0	0	3	0	1	2	0	3	1	0	0	2	0	0	0	0	0	0	0	1	0	0	0	0
Jones's	5	.4597	.5223	37.2	0	2	1	0	1	1	0	0	2	0	0	0	0	1	1	0	0	0	0	0	1	0	0	0	0
Joneses	5	.1979	.2497	34.0	4	0	0	0	0	0	1	0	0	1	0	0	0	0	0	0	0	0	0	0	0	4	0	0	0
jongleurs	2	.0000	.0162	22.1	0	2	0	0	0	0	0	0	0	0	0	0	0	0	0	0	2	0	0	0	0	0	0	0	0
Joplin	4	.3267	.2856	34.6	0	0	0	2	0	1	1	0	0	0	0	0	0	0	0	0	2	0	0	0	0	1	0	1	0
Jordan	38	.6740	5.2549	47.2	7	2	6	7	9	1	6	0	3	0	1	0	2	16	0	0	2	0	0	0	1	7	1	5	0
Jordan's	10	.4688	1.0987	40.4	6	1	0	1	1	0	1	0	6	0	0	0	2	1	0	0	0	0	0	0	0	0	1	0	0
Jordanian	2	.0000	.0243	23.9	0	0	0	0	0	1	1	0	0	0	0	0	0	0	0	0	0	0	0	0	0	0	0	2	0
Jorge	29	.0000	1.3248	41.2	27	0	2	0	0	0	0	0	29	0	0	0	0	0	0	0	0	0	0	0	0	0	0	0	0
Jorgensen	2	.0000	.0290	24.6	2	0	0	0	0	0	0	0	0	0	0	0	0	0	0	0	0	0	0	0	0	2	0	0	0
Jorinda	3	.0000	.1370	31.4	0	0	0	3	0	0	0	0	3	0	0	0	0	0	0	0	0	0	0	0	0	0	0	0	0
Joringel	7	.0000	.3198	35.0	0	0	0	7	0	0	0	0	7	0	0	0	0	0	0	0	0	0	0	0	0	0	0	0	0
Jos	2	.0000	.0209	23.2	0	0	0	0	2	0	0	0	0	0	0	0	0	0	0	0	0	0	0	0	0	0	2	0	0
Jose	29	.3980	2.6620	44.3	5	0	1	2	12	7	0	2	10	0	0	0	0	2	0	0	12	0	0	0	0	1	1	3	0
Jose's	2	.1494	.1045	30.2	1	0	0	0	0	1	0	0	1	0	0	0	0	0	0	0	1	0	0	0	0	0	0	0	0
Josef	7	.3894	.6045	37.8	1	0	0	2	2	1	1	0	1	0	0	0	0	0	0	0	2	0	0	0	0	1	0	3	0
Josefina	2	.0000	.0914	29.6	2	0	0	0	0	0	0	0	2	0	0	0	0	0	0	0	0	0	0	0	0	0	0	0	0
Joseph	126	.6581	17.387	52.4	26	26	18	14	12	9	18	3	50	1	0	7	2	1	0	6	17	1	0	0	0	23	13	4	1
Joseph's	11	.5381	1.2845	41.1	4	2	2	1	0	1	0	1	4	0	0	0	0	0	0	0	0	0	1	0	2	2	0	2	0
Josephine	8	.0000	.3655	35.6	0	8	0	0	0	0	0	0	8	0	0	0	0	0	0	0	0	0	0	0	0	0	0	0	0
Josephson	2	.0000	.0243	23.9	0	0	0	0	0	0	2	0	0	0	0	0	0	0	0	0	0	0	0	0	0	0	0	2	0
Josh	29	.1840	1.7418	42.4	3	25	1	0	0	0	0	0	15	0	0	0	0	0	0	0	0	0	0	0	14	0	0	0	0
joshing	2	.0000	.0215	23.3	0	0	0	0	1	1	0	0	0	0	0	2	0	0	0	0	0	0	0	0	0	0	0	0	0
Joshua	10	.5099	1.0957	40.4	3	0	3	1	2	0	1	0	2	0	0	1	0	0	0	0	0	0	0	0	3	3	1	0	0
Josiah	13	.3208	1.1812	40.7	0	0	0	0	11	1	1	0	11	0	0	0	0	1	0	0	0	0	0	0	0	0	1	0	0
Joss	8	.0000	.3655	35.6	0	0	0	8	0	0	0	0	8	0	0	0	0	0	0	0	0	0	0	0	0	0	0	0	0

4F joeys
8D joggle
7N joggling
XR jogs
4R Johnny's
7R johnboats
4A Johnny-on-the-spot
9D johnson
9D join-stools
9D joiner
7M Joining
7A jointless
8J Joio
7A joists
4F Jojep's
4Q joke-telling
7B jokebox
3A jokers
7P jokesters
8A Jolanna
5F Joliet
XH Joly
5B Jonesville
4N Jong
7H Jons
8P Jopie
6A Joppers
9Q Jord
9R Jordanians
3A Jorge's
8B Joris
9Q JOSEPH
XH Josephus
3A Josh's
7A Josiah's
7R Josip

Word Type	F	D	U	SFI	3 Gr 3	4 Gr 4	5 Gr 5	6 Gr 6	7 Gr 7	8 Gr 8	9 Gr 9	X UnGr	A Read	B Eng & Gr	C Comp	D Lit	E Math	F Soc Stud	G Spell	H Sci	J Music	K Art	L Home Ec	M Shop	N Lib F	P Lib NF	Q Lib Ref	R Mag	S Rel
jostle	3	.3131	.2349	33.7	0	1	0	0	0	1	1	0	1	0	0	0	0	1	0	0	1	0	0	0	0	0	0	0	0
jostled	5	.2446	.3872	35.9	1	1	1	2	0	0	0	0	4	0	0	0	0	0	0	0	0	0	0	0	1	0	0	0	0
jot	14	.4329	1.3549	41.3	1	1	1	3	1	2	5	0	4	7	0	0	0	0	0	0	0	0	1	0	0	1	0	1	0
jotted	6	.6073	.7575	38.8	0	1	0	0	2	3	0	0	1	1	0	0	0	0	0	0	0	0	0	0	1	1	1	1	0
jounced	2	.2442	.1134	30.5	0	0	1	1	0	0	0	0	0	1	0	0	0	0	0	0	0	0	0	0	0	0	0	1	0
journal	21	.5953	2.5904	44.1	0	1	2	2	7	3	6	0	2	2	0	1	0	1	1	2	0	0	0	0	0	0	4	8	0
Journal	17	.5018	1.7910	42.5	0	3	0	0	2	2	2	8	0	0	0	1	0	0	0	3	0	0	0	0	0	3	3	7	0
journalism	8	.3438	.5995	37.8	0	0	2	0	3	1	2	0	0	0	0	0	0	0	1	0	0	0	0	0	0	0	2	5	0
journalist	7	.4704	.6852	38.4	0	0	1	0	2	2	1	1	0	0	0	1	0	0	0	0	2	0	0	0	0	0	2	2	0
journalistic	3	.2143	.1568	32.0	0	1	1	0	0	0	1	0	0	0	0	0	0	0	0	0	0	0	0	0	0	1	0	2	0
journalists	3	.0000	.0365	25.6	0	0	0	1	1	1	0	0	0	0	0	0	0	0	0	0	0	0	0	0	0	0	0	3	0
journals	12	.6533	1.6238	42.1	1	0	0	1	2	5	1	2	2	0	0	1	0	2	0	2	0	0	0	0	0	1	2	2	0
journey	257	.7544	39.568	56.0	19	41	50	57	40	32	10	8	69	2	2	20	2	59	4	28	9	1	0	1	7	23	10	18	2
Journey	8	.3306	.5862	37.7	5	1	0	0	0	2	0	0	0	0	0	0	0	2	0	0	0	1	0	0	5	0	0	0	0
journey's	3	.1983	.1396	31.4	1	0	0	1	0	1	0	0	0	0	0	0	0	0	0	0	2	0	0	0	0	0	0	1	0
journeyed	16	.6609	2.1853	43.4	2	2	2	4	2	2	1	1	3	0	0	2	0	4	0	0	2	0	0	0	0	2	1	2	0
journeying	4	.4340	.3885	35.9	0	2	1	0	1	0	0	0	1	0	0	0	0	1	1	0	0	0	0	0	0	0	1	0	0
journeyman	2	.2137	.1056	30.2	0	1	0	0	0	1	0	0	0	0	0	0	0	1	0	0	1	0	0	0	0	0	0	0	0
journeymen	4	.3071	.2967	34.7	0	0	0	2	2	0	0	0	1	0	0	1	0	0	0	0	0	0	0	0	2	0	0	0	0
journeys	17	.6472	2.2754	43.6	3	0	0	4	5	3	2	0	2	1	0	3	0	4	0	3	0	0	0	0	0	2	2	0	0
Journeys	2	.0000	.0389	25.9	0	2	0	0	0	0	0	0	0	0	0	0	0	2	0	0	0	0	0	0	0	0	0	0	0
jousting	2	.1523	.0721	28.6	0	0	0	0	0	0	1	1	0	0	1	0	0	0	0	0	0	0	0	0	0	0	0	1	0
Jove	3	.3272	.2363	33.7	0	0	0	0	0	1	2	0	1	0	0	1	0	0	0	0	1	0	0	0	0	0	0	0	0
jovial	4	.4448	.3915	35.9	0	0	0	0	1	2	1	0	1	1	0	1	0	0	0	0	1	0	0	0	0	0	0	0	0
jowls	2	.2407	.1138	30.6	0	0	0	0	2	0	0	0	0	0	0	1	0	0	0	0	0	0	0	0	0	1	0	0	0
joy	236	.8001	38.222	55.8	43	40	40	30	43	16	15	9	88	6	2	33	0	1	6	1	35	3	1	0	19	21	3	16	1
Joy	22	.5045	2.5713	44.1	13	0	0	1	1	6	1	0	16	0	0	0	0	0	0	0	2	1	0	0	0	1	0	2	0
Joybells	5	.0000	.2284	33.6	0	0	0	5	0	0	0	0	5	0	0	0	0	0	0	0	0	0	0	0	0	0	0	0	0
Joyce	26	.4868	2.7106	44.3	17	1	4	1	1	1	1	0	4	1	0	0	2	0	1	0	0	0	1	0	15	0	0	2	0
Joyce's	2	.1839	.0845	29.3	1	0	0	0	0	1	0	0	0	0	0	0	0	0	0	0	0	0	1	0	1	0	0	0	0
joyful	23	.7078	3.3210	45.2	2	3	4	3	3	2	5	1	5	3	1	6	0	0	1	0	2	0	0	0	1	2	0	2	0
joyfully	20	.5380	2.4078	43.8	4	5	3	4	4	0	0	0	12	0	0	3	0	0	0	0	2	0	0	0	2	1	0	0	0
joyous	20	.6825	2.8108	44.5	3	2	2	2	7	1	2	1	5	0	0	2	0	1	0	0	3	0	0	0	3	2	1	3	0
joyously	9	.5006	.9745	39.9	0	0	1	4	2	2	0	0	2	0	0	1	0	2	0	0	0	1	0	0	2	0	0	1	0
joys	23	.5632	2.6863	44.3	1	2	2	2	5	5	3	3	2	1	0	3	0	0	0	0	6	0	0	0	0	3	1	7	0
Jozef	2	.0000	.0389	25.9	0	0	0	0	2	0	0	0	0	0	0	0	0	2	0	0	0	0	0	0	0	0	0	0	0
JQ	2	.0000	.0299	24.8	0	0	2	0	0	0	0	0	0	0	0	0	2	0	0	0	0	0	0	0	0	0	0	0	0
Jr	40	.6148	5.1124	47.1	0	4	4	11	5	5	7	4	7	1	0	0	0	2	0	1	3	0	0	0	2	3	6	15	0
Juan	87	.5679	10.560	50.2	15	2	23	13	28	2	4	0	27	0	0	26	0	12	0	0	8	0	0	0	0	0	7	7	0
Juan's	10	.3805	.9604	39.8	4	0	2	3	1	0	0	0	6	0	0	1	0	3	0	0	0	0	0	0	0	0	0	0	0
Juana	64	.0086	.8243	39.2	0	0	0	0	64	0	0	0	1	0	0	63	0	0	0	0	0	0	0	0	0	0	0	0	0
Juana's	8	.0000	.0859	29.3	0	0	0	0	8	0	0	0	0	0	0	8	0	0	0	0	0	0	0	0	0	0	0	0	0
Juanito	15	.0000	.6852	38.4	15	0	0	0	0	0	0	0	15	0	0	0	0	0	0	0	0	0	0	0	0	0	0	0	0
Juarez	4	.3709	.3633	35.6	0	2	0	0	2	0	0	0	2	0	0	0	0	0	0	0	0	0	0	0	0	0	1	1	0
juba	2	.0000	.0162	22.1	0	0	2	0	0	0	0	0	0	0	0	0	0	0	0	0	2	0	0	0	0	0	0	0	0
Juba	2	.0000	.0162	22.1	0	0	2	0	0	0	0	0	0	0	0	0	0	0	0	0	2	0	0	0	0	0	0	0	0
Jubal	2	.0000	.0209	23.2	0	0	0	0	1	1	0	0	0	0	0	0	0	0	0	0	0	0	0	0	0	0	2	0	0
jubilant	5	.4222	.4492	36.5	0	0	0	0	3	1	1	0	0	0	0	0	0	1	0	0	2	0	0	0	1	0	0	1	0
jubilantly	2	.1814	.1187	30.7	0	0	0	2	0	0	0	0	1	0	0	0	0	0	0	0	0	0	0	0	0	0	0	1	0
jubilation	5	.4311	.4734	36.8	0	0	1	2	1	0	1	0	1	0	0	0	0	0	0	0	1	0	0	0	2	0	1	0	0
jubilee	3	.1983	.1396	31.4	1	0	0	1	1	0	0	0	0	0	0	0	0	0	0	0	2	0	0	0	0	0	0	1	0
Judah	5	.1882	.2328	33.7	0	0	0	0	0	1	0	4	0	0	0	0	0	0	0	0	0	0	0	0	0	0	1	4	0
Judaism	16	.2819	1.0265	40.1	0	0	3	0	2	1	10	0	0	0	0	0	0	2	0	0	0	0	0	0	0	2	11	1	0
JUDAISM	3	.0000	.0314	25.0	0	0	0	0	0	0	3	0	0	0	0	0	0	0	0	0	0	0	0	0	0	0	3	0	0
Judas	4	.2303	.2158	33.3	0	0	0	0	2	2	0	0	0	0	0	0	0	0	0	0	2	0	0	0	0	2	0	0	0
Judea	3	.2432	.1790	32.5	0	0	1	0	2	0	0	0	0	0	0	0	0	2	1	0	0	0	0	0	0	0	0	0	0
Judean	3	.3769	.2484	34.0	0	0	0	0	1	1	0	1	0	0	0	0	0	1	0	0	0	0	0	0	0	0	1	1	0
judge	173	.8675	29.953	54.8	23	21	17	26	36	22	26	2	42	12	2	8	2	17	5	5	6	0	6	3	41	5	11	8	0
Judge	95	.7040	13.854	51.4	7	3	19	7	22	24	13	0	36	2	0	8	10	1	0	0	1	0	0	0	15	15	1	6	0
judge's	4	.3602	.3543	35.5	2	0	1	1	0	0	0	0	2	0	0	0	0	0	1	0	0	0	0	0	1	0	0	0	0
Judge's	8	.3113	.6217	37.9	0	2	0	1	1	4	0	0	3	0	0	0	0	0	0	0	1	0	0	0	4	0	0	0	0
judged	31	.7124	4.5076	46.5	4	3	2	6	7	3	5	1	7	1	2	2	0	1	1	0	1	0	1	0	9	5	1	0	0
judgement	5	.4755	.5327	37.3	0	0	1	1	1	0	2	0	2	0	0	1	0	0	0	0	0	0	0	0	0	0	1	1	0
judges	81	.7983	13.058	51.2	15	10	16	9	5	10	16	0	19	1	1	3	8	17	1	0	1	0	0	0	7	8	12	3	0
judges'	6	.2991	.4499	36.5	0	4	0	2	0	0	0	0	2	0	0	0	0	0	0	0	0	0	0	0	3	0	0	1	0
judging	34	.8026	5.4710	47.4	5	2	4	2	11	7	2	1	5	3	1	3	0	3	1	1	0	0	3	1	5	1	1	6	0
judgment	55	.9142	9.9692	50.0	0	3	5	8	10	14	12	3	10	4	1	3	1	9	4	4	3	1	0	1	3	1	3	7	0
judgments	14	.5640	1.6882	42.3	0	0	4	5	1	1	2	1	3	0	0	0	0	5	1	1	0	0	0	0	0	1	0	3	0
judicial	22	.3864	1.9139	42.8	1	0	1	1	9	8	2	0	1	0	0	0	0	14	0	0	0	0	0	0	1	1	5	0	0
judiciary	3	.2378	.1809	32.6	1	0	0	0	0	2	0	0	0	0	0	0	0	2	0	0	0	0	0	0	0	1	0	0	0
Judiciary	4	.2183	.2285	33.6	1	0	0	0	0	1	2	0	0	0	0	0	0	3	0	0	0	0	0	0	0	1	0	0	0
judicious	4	.3301	.2948	34.7	0	0	0	0	1	2	1	0	0	0	0	1	0	2	0	0	0	0	1	0	0	0	0	0	0
Judith	5	.3152	.3888	35.9	0	0	1	0	3	0	1	0	1	0	0	1	0	0	0	3	0	0	0	0	0	0	0	0	0
judo	2	.2401	.1133	30.5	0	0	1	0	1	0	0	0	0	0	0	0	0	0	0	0	0	0	0	0	0	1	1	0	0
Judson	4	.0000	.0486	26.9	0	0	3	0	0	0	1	0	0	0	0	0	0	0	0	0	0	0	0	0	0	0	0	4	0
Judy	107	.6169	13.929	51.4	64	8	3	8	12	10	2	0	40	3	0	0	5	8	4	0	3	11	7	0	18	0	0	8	0
Judy's	12	.5216	1.3135	41.2	9	1	0	0	1	1	0	0	1	1	0	0	7	0	1	0	0	1	1	0	0	0	0	0	0
jug	48	.6145	6.2729	48.0	2	19	5	10	8	3	1	0	19	0	3	8	6	4	0	0	0	0	0	0	3	5	0	0	0
Jug	9	.0000	.1303	31.1	9	0	0	0	0	0	0	0	0	0	0	0	0	0	0	0	0	0	0	0	0	9	0	0	0
jug-o-rum	4	.0000	.0789	29.0	0	0	0	4	0	0	0	0	0	0	0	0	0	0	0	4	0	0	0	0	0	0	0	0	0
juggle	3	.3465	.2515	34.0	0	1	1	0	1	0	0	0	1	0	0	0	0	0	0	0	0	0	0	0	0	1	0	1	0
juggled	2	.2408	.1204	30.8	0	0	0	0	0	1	1	0	0	0	0	0	0	1	0	0	0	0	0	0	0	1	0	0	0
juggler	5	.2446	.3872	35.9	0	4	0	1	0	0	0	0	4	0	0	0	0	0	0	0	0	0	0	0	1	0	0	0	0
jugglers	10	.5517	1.2167	40.9	0	7	0	0	2	0	1	0	5	0	0	1	0	1	0	0	1	0	0	0	0	2	0	0	0
juggling	6	.2526	.4448	36.5	2	0	0	0	4	0	0	0	4	0	0	0	0	0	0	0	0	1	0	0	0	0	0	1	0
jugs	4	.2991	.2840	34.5	0	1	0	1	1	0	1	0	1	0	0	0	0	0	0	0	0	1	0	0	1	0	1	0	0
juice	170	.6193	21.722	53.4	46	21	17	18	23	20	18	7	14	4	0	4	25	15	2	41	1	0	32	1	9	7	2	13	0
juices	51	.3822	4.3478	46.4	4	5	8	5	12	5	12	0	5	0	0	0	0	1	0	22	0	0	13	0	1	2	7	0	0
juicier	3	.2685	.2000	33.0	0	1	0	0	1	0	1	0	1	0	0	0	0	0	1	0	0	0	1	0	0	0	0	0	0
juicy	40	.7785	6.3612	48.0	18	7	6	4	0	1	3	1	17	4	1	0	0	4	0	3	0	0	1	0	2	5	2	1	0
juju	2	.0000	.0389	25.9	0	2	0	0	0	0	0	0	0	0	0	0	0	2	0	0	0	0	0	0	0	0	0	0	0
juke	3	.3780	.2436	33.9	0	0	0	0	1	0	2	0	0	0	0	1	0	0	0	0	1	0	0	0	0	1	0	0	0
Jules	15	.5793	1.8256	42.6	0	1	1	5	3	0	3	2	3	4	0	0	1	0	0	2	0	1	0	0	0	0	3	1	0
Julia	24	.5306	2.8266	44.5	12	3	0	0	7	2	0	0	12	0	1	0	0	1	0	0	0	0	0	0	7	1	0	2	0
Julian	6	.4334	.5835	37.7	0	0	0	0	3	0	3	0	1	1	0	0	0	0	0	3	0	0	0	0	0	0	0	1	0

6A Joss's
5P Jostedalsbreen
6J jota
8A Jotham
7A jotting
7P jottings
5P Joueurs
7Q Joule
7D jouncing
9A jour
8K Jour
6A Journal's
3N Journey's
6A journeyings
4J Journeyman's
8G jousted
7A joviality
7R Joxer
7N joy-flames
5P joyance
3J Joyeuse
5P Joyeux
6J joyful'st
8B joyless
5J Joyous
6R JS
6R JSH
7D ju
3A Juanito's
6J Jubilee
5K Jubjub
8Q Juchi
3P Judaea
6B Judd
6F Judeans
7Q Judges
7R judgeship
3N judgings
7Q Judgment
7H Judith's
4A juggler's
7B juggles
3P juggly
6R juice-making
5A juiciest
7D Juicy
9B jujitsu
7A jukebox
7D jukella
6A Jukes
4B Julia's

Word Type	F	D	U	SFI	3 Gr 3	4 Gr 4	5 Gr 5	6 Gr 6	7 Gr 7	8 Gr 8	9 Gr 9	X UnGr	A Read	B Eng & Gr	C Comp	D Lit	E Math	F Soc Stud	G Spell	H Sci	J Music	K Art	L Home Ec	M Shop	N Lib F	P Lib NF	Q Lib Ref	R Mag	S Rel
Juliana	16	.1630	1.0982	40.4	15	0	0	0	1	0	0	0	15	0	0	0	0	0	0	0	0	0	0	0	0	1	0	0	0
Julie	63	.5139	6.8395	48.4	13	0	16	1	23	5	5	0	7	11	0	3	3	0	0	0	0	0	0	0	21	0	0	18	0
Julie's	11	.3349	.8105	39.1	0	0	5	0	5	0	1	0	0	0	0	1	0	0	0	0	0	0	0	0	5	0	0	5	0
Juliet	73	.2193	3.8737	45.9	0	0	0	1	1	7	64	0	5	0	0	57	0	0	0	0	10	0	0	0	1	0	0	0	0
Juliska	8	.0000	.3655	35.6	0	8	0	0	0	0	0	0	8	0	0	0	0	0	0	0	0	0	0	0	0	0	0	0	0
Julius	18	.6612	2.4737	43.9	2	1	0	0	5	7	3	0	5	2	1	0	0	1	0	2	0	0	0	0	0	3	3	1	0
July	199	.8368	33.318	55.2	20	45	25	21	32	22	26	8	28	7	4	6	13	34	4	12	4	0	0	0	9	18	28	32	0
jumble	11	.6204	1.4491	41.6	2	0	2	2	3	2	0	0	4	0	0	1	0	3	0	0	1	0	0	0	0	1	1	0	0
jumbled	6	.3570	.4916	36.9	0	0	1	4	0	0	1	0	1	3	0	0	0	0	0	1	0	0	0	0	1	0	0	0	0
jumbling	2	.2441	.1127	30.5	0	0	1	1	0	0	0	0	0	0	0	0	0	0	0	0	0	0	0	0	1	0	1	0	0
jumbo	3	.0000	.1370	31.4	2	0	0	0	0	1	0	0	3	0	0	0	0	0	0	0	0	0	0	0	0	0	0	0	0
Jumbo	12	.0956	.3429	35.4	0	0	0	1	0	11	0	0	0	0	0	11	0	0	0	0	0	0	0	0	1	0	0	0	0
Jumbo's	3	.2292	.1615	32.1	0	0	0	2	0	1	0	0	0	0	0	1	0	0	0	0	0	0	0	0	2	0	0	0	0
jump	356	.9151	64.792	58.1	118	78	32	47	45	15	17	4	131	9	1	11	35	10	12	48	12	2	2	1	22	39	5	16	0
jumped	476	.7551	74.199	58.7	150	118	44	44	71	32	13	4	261	19	3	25	11	6	4	2	13	0	0	0	64	51	2	15	0
jumper	16	.5214	1.8159	42.6	4	3	5	0	1	0	3	0	5	0	0	1	4	0	0	1	0	0	2	0	0	3	0	0	0
Jumper	16	.2308	1.1573	40.6	0	0	0	11	5	0	0	0	11	0	0	0	0	0	0	0	0	0	0	0	5	0	0	0	0
jumpers	3	.2765	.1899	32.8	1	1	0	0	1	0	0	0	0	0	0	0	0	1	0	0	0	0	1	0	0	1	0	0	0
Jumpin'	2	.2443	.1130	30.5	0	0	0	0	2	0	0	0	0	0	0	1	0	0	0	0	0	0	0	0	1	0	0	0	0
jumping	119	.8217	19.736	53.0	24	38	13	14	21	5	4	0	42	2	0	9	1	3	3	13	3	4	1	0	12	16	2	8	0
jumping-off	4	.2904	.2847	34.5	0	1	1	0	0	0	1	1	1	0	1	0	0	1	0	0	0	0	0	0	0	0	0	1	0
jumps	82	.7210	12.114	50.8	33	13	9	11	7	8	1	0	19	2	0	5	30	2	1	8	2	0	0	1	2	9	1	0	0
jumpy	6	.4467	.6041	37.8	2	1	0	0	1	1	0	1	2	0	0	1	0	0	0	0	0	0	0	0	2	1	0	0	0
juncos	3	.2437	.2277	33.6	0	0	0	2	0	1	0	0	2	0	0	0	0	0	0	1	0	0	0	0	0	0	0	0	0
junction	8	.5919	.9938	40.0	1	2	1	0	0	1	1	2	1	1	0	0	0	1	0	2	0	0	0	0	0	2	1	0	0
Junction	3	.0000	.1370	31.4	0	0	0	3	0	0	0	0	3	0	0	0	0	0	0	0	0	0	0	0	0	0	0	0	0
junctions	5	.3691	.4157	36.2	0	1	1	0	0	0	0	3	0	0	0	0	0	0	0	3	0	0	0	0	0	1	1	0	0
juncture	13	.0000	.1423	31.5	0	0	0	0	2	10	1	0	0	13	0	0	0	0	0	0	0	0	0	0	0	0	0	0	0
junctures	2	.2388	.1089	30.4	0	0	0	0	2	0	0	0	0	0	0	0	0	0	1	0	0	0	0	0	1	0	0	0	0
June	205	.8115	33.400	55.2	40	38	23	16	29	29	15	15	29	12	2	5	12	31	3	11	3	0	0	0	4	28	25	40	0
Juneau	6	.2366	.3612	35.6	0	0	4	0	0	2	0	0	0	0	0	0	2	4	0	0	0	0	0	0	0	0	0	0	0
jungle	178	.6893	25.373	54.0	60	33	9	31	26	11	8	0	54	0	2	13	1	14	1	3	0	10	0	0	7	53	9	11	0
Jungle	3	.0939	.1398	31.5	1	1	1	0	0	0	0	0	2	0	0	0	0	0	0	0	0	1	0	0	0	0	0	0	0
jungles	71	.6353	9.3641	49.7	32	6	8	11	10	1	2	1	11	0	0	3	0	12	0	8	1	4	0	0	2	23	7	0	0
jungly	3	.2699	.1789	32.5	1	0	0	0	1	1	0	0	0	0	1	0	0	0	0	0	0	0	0	0	0	1	1	0	0
junior	44	.7931	7.0373	48.5	2	1	6	3	18	13	1	0	11	7	0	1	1	1	1	1	0	1	2	1	2	1	2	12	0
Junior	111	.5321	12.639	51.0	59	5	5	9	14	9	9	1	25	13	0	4	4	4	2	0	0	0	0	0	0	5	2	52	0
Junior's	2	.1814	.1187	30.7	2	0	0	0	0	0	0	0	1	0	0	0	0	0	0	0	0	0	0	0	0	0	0	1	0
juniors	3	.2121	.1560	31.9	0	0	0	1	1	0	1	0	0	0	0	0	1	0	0	0	0	0	0	0	0	0	0	2	0
juniper	4	.4811	.4016	36.0	1	0	1	1	0	0	1	0	0	0	0	0	0	0	0	0	1	0	0	0	0	1	1	1	0
Junipero	2	.2351	.1166	30.7	0	0	0	1	0	1	0	0	0	0	0	0	0	1	0	0	0	0	0	0	0	0	0	1	0
junipers	3	.1277	.1363	31.3	0	0	0	1	1	0	0	1	1	0	0	0	0	0	0	0	0	0	0	0	0	0	0	2	0
junk	43	.6770	6.0904	47.8	17	14	2	2	3	2	2	1	19	1	0	5	0	2	1	0	0	1	0	0	10	0	1	3	0
junked	3	.0000	.0365	25.6	0	2	0	0	1	0	0	0	0	0	0	0	0	0	0	0	0	0	0	0	0	0	0	3	0
junks	5	.3441	.4209	36.2	1	2	0	2	0	0	0	0	2	0	0	0	0	0	0	0	0	0	0	0	0	0	1	2	0
junkyard	3	.3427	.2477	33.9	1	1	1	0	0	0	0	0	1	0	0	0	0	0	0	0	0	0	0	0	1	0	0	1	0
junkyards	4	.1611	.1738	32.4	0	3	0	1	0	0	0	0	0	0	0	0	0	0	0	1	0	0	0	0	0	0	0	3	0
Juno	2	.0000	.0290	24.6	0	0	0	0	0	0	0	2	0	0	0	0	0	0	0	0	0	0	0	0	0	2	0	0	0
junta	8	.3481	.6134	37.9	2	0	4	0	0	1	1	0	0	0	0	0	0	0	0	0	0	0	0	0	0	4	3	1	0
Jupiter	101	.6875	14.410	51.6	10	25	9	17	10	21	5	4	29	4	0	11	6	0	2	34	0	0	0	0	1	7	7	0	0
Jupiter's	8	.2160	.5447	37.4	0	1	1	1	0	2	2	1	4	0	0	0	0	0	0	4	0	0	0	0	0	0	0	0	0
Jura	4	.3617	.3220	35.1	1	0	2	0	0	0	0	1	0	0	0	0	0	0	0	1	0	0	0	0	0	2	1	0	0
Jurassic	3	.0000	.0314	25.0	0	0	0	0	3	0	0	0	0	0	0	0	0	0	0	0	0	0	0	0	0	0	3	0	0
Jurgensen	2	.0000	.0243	23.9	0	0	0	2	0	0	0	0	0	0	0	0	0	0	0	0	0	0	0	0	0	0	0	2	0
juries	3	.2440	.1815	32.6	0	0	0	1	0	1	1	0	0	1	0	0	0	2	0	0	0	0	0	0	0	0	0	0	0
jurisdiction	24	.3042	1.7358	42.4	0	0	0	0	6	6	11	1	0	0	0	0	0	20	1	0	0	0	0	0	0	1	2	0	0
jurisdictions	2	.0000	.0243	23.9	0	0	0	0	2	0	0	0	0	0	0	0	0	0	0	0	0	0	0	0	0	0	0	2	0
Jurisprudence	2	.0000	.0162	22.1	0	0	0	0	0	0	2	0	0	0	0	0	0	0	0	0	2	0	0	0	0	0	0	0	0
Jurjis	7	.0000	.3198	35.0	7	0	0	0	0	0	0	0	7	0	0	0	0	0	0	0	0	0	0	0	0	0	0	0	0
Jurjis's	2	.0000	.0914	29.6	2	0	0	0	0	0	0	0	2	0	0	0	0	0	0	0	0	0	0	0	0	0	0	0	0
juror	2	.2376	.1088	30.4	0	0	0	0	1	1	0	0	0	0	0	0	0	0	1	0	0	0	0	0	0	0	0	1	0
jurors	3	.1937	.1495	31.7	0	0	0	0	1	2	0	0	0	0	0	0	0	1	0	0	0	0	0	0	0	0	0	2	0
jury	43	.6885	6.0151	47.8	1	2	6	3	8	5	18	0	1	2	0	5	0	16	7	1	1	0	0	0	5	0	2	3	0
jurymen	2	.0000	.0234	23.7	0	2	0	0	0	0	0	0	0	0	0	0	0	0	0	0	0	0	0	0	2	0	0	0	0
jus'	4	.0000	.0469	26.7	1	0	0	0	3	0	0	0	0	0	0	0	0	0	0	0	0	0	0	0	4	0	0	0	0
just	5858	.9536	1104.6	70.4	1314	1093	625	696	1038	573	393	126	2262	263	50	396	132	302	160	414	132	49	91	33	547	461	111	454	1
Just	7	.4442	.6699	38.3	0	1	0	0	3	1	2	0	1	0	0	2	0	0	0	0	1	1	0	0	0	2	0	0	0
justice	80	.8136	13.089	51.2	3	6	15	9	15	19	13	0	17	2	1	9	2	16	2	0	3	0	0	0	5	5	13	5	0
Justice	41	.5493	4.7530	46.8	5	1	2	1	7	10	14	1	2	0	0	0	0	22	0	0	2	0	0	0	1	5	2	7	0
justices	11	.1878	.5724	37.6	0	0	0	0	0	6	5	0	0	0	0	0	2	9	0	0	0	0	0	0	0	0	0	0	0
Justices	6	.4273	.5787	37.6	1	0	0	1	3	0	1	0	1	0	0	0	0	3	0	0	0	0	0	0	0	1	0	1	0
justifiable	2	.2433	.1158	30.6	0	0	0	0	1	0	0	1	0	0	0	0	0	0	0	0	0	0	0	0	0	1	0	1	0
justifiably	2	.2408	.1204	30.8	0	1	0	0	0	1	0	0	0	0	0	0	0	1	0	0	0	0	0	0	0	1	0	0	0
justification	3	.1927	.1388	31.4	0	0	2	1	0	0	0	0	0	0	1	0	0	0	0	0	0	0	0	0	0	2	0	0	0
justified	15	.7009	2.1395	43.3	0	0	1	2	7	2	3	0	1	0	0	1	2	3	0	2	0	0	1	0	0	1	3	1	0
justifies	5	.1926	.2474	33.9	0	0	1	0	0	1	3	0	0	0	0	0	4	0	0	0	0	0	0	0	0	0	0	1	0
justify	15	.5780	1.7903	42.5	0	0	2	2	5	1	5	0	1	0	2	4	0	1	1	1	0	0	0	0	1	2	0	2	0
justifying	2	.2401	.1133	30.5	0	0	1	0	1	0	0	0	0	0	0	0	0	0	0	0	0	0	0	0	0	1	1	0	0
Justin	12	.4136	1.1016	40.4	3	0	5	0	2	0	0	2	1	0	0	0	0	4	0	0	0	0	0	0	0	3	0	4	0
justly	11	.5385	1.2286	40.9	0	0	0	3	1	2	5	0	0	3	0	2	0	2	0	0	0	0	0	0	0	0	1	3	0
jute	7	.2446	.4271	36.3	0	2	0	2	1	1	1	0	0	0	0	0	0	6	0	0	0	0	1	0	0	0	0	0	0
Jutes	4	.2408	.2182	33.4	0	0	0	2	2	0	0	0	0	2	0	0	0	0	2	0	0	0	0	0	0	0	0	0	0
Jutland	12	.0000	.1256	31.0	12	0	0	0	0	0	0	0	0	0	0	0	0	0	0	0	0	0	0	0	0	0	12	0	0
Jutta	2	.0000	.0914	29.6	0	0	0	2	0	0	0	0	2	0	0	0	0	0	0	0	0	0	0	0	0	0	0	0	0
jutted	3	.3385	.2445	33.9	1	0	0	1	0	1	0	0	1	0	0	0	0	0	0	0	0	0	0	0	1	0	1	0	0
jutting	8	.4633	.8181	39.1	1	0	0	1	5	1	0	0	2	0	0	0	0	1	0	1	0	1	0	0	0	0	1	2	0
juvenile	19	.3610	1.5313	41.9	0	0	0	6	9	3	0	1	2	0	1	0	0	0	0	0	0	0	0	0	3	0	0	13	0
juveniles	3	.1019	.0750	28.7	0	0	0	0	1	2	0	0	0	0	2	0	0	0	0	0	0	0	0	0	0	0	0	1	0
juxtaposition	3	.2321	.1635	32.1	0	0	0	0	0	0	2	1	0	0	0	0	0	0	0	0	0	0	0	0	0	0	1	2	0
k	263	.3478	20.358	53.1	79	33	26	43	46	18	12	6	32	23	0	5	22	1	162	0	1	0	0	0	8	4	0	5	0
K	57	.5705	6.8373	48.3	1	6	14	4	18	9	2	3	5	0	0	1	26	1	0	13	1	0	0	0	0	4	2	4	0
K**	3	.3399	.2456	33.9	1	0	0	0	0	0	2	0	1	0	0	1	0	0	0	0	0	0	0	0	0	0	0	1	0
k's	2	.0000	.0162	22.1	0	1	0	0	0	1	0	0	0	0	0	0	0	0	2	0	0	0	0	0	0	0	0	0	0
Kaang	6	.0000	.2741	34.4	0	0	0	6	0	0	0	0	6	0	0	0	0	0	0	0	0	0	0	0	0	0	0	0	0
Kaaren	2	.0000	.0234	23.7	0	0	0	0	0	2	0	0	0	0	0	0	0	0	0	0	0	0	0	0	2	0	0	0	0

9J Juliet's
9D Juliets
XR Julio
4A Juliska's
8B july
7A July's
4P jumbies
3D jumbly
5Q Jumhuriyah
6H Jump
5N Jumpin
4H Jumping
4N jumpsome
4J June-bug
XR jungle-gym
4N jungle-paths
3P jungle's
8A jungleland
7N junior-class
7K junior-high-school
7N Juniper
7R Junius
3A Junk
4R junk-car
5R junky
5P junta's
8B Junto
5A Jupiter-C
8F Jupka
7H Jurg
9F juridical
9F Jurisdiction
8F jurists
9D Jury
9D jury's
7G jus
7R just-plain-fun
8F justiciaries
9A justifications
7D justling
9Q Justus
5A jut
7R jut-jawed
4N Jute
3Q juts
9F Juvenile
7K juxtapose
XR juxtaposed
8F jyow-dzuh
9B k'hinkali
XP K'un-lun
3D KA-chow

Word Type	F	D	U	SFI	3 Gr 3	4 Gr 4	5 Gr 5	6 Gr 6	7 Gr 7	8 Gr 8	9 Gr 9	X UnGr	A Read	B Eng & Gr	C Comp	D Lit	E Math	F Soc Stud	G Spell	H Sci	J Music	K Art	L Home Ec	M Shop	N Lib F	P Lib NF	Q Lib Ref	R Mag	S Rel
Kaata	2	.0000	.0290	24.6	0	0	0	0	0	2	0	0	0	0	0	0	0	0	0	0	0	0	0	0	0	2	0	0	0
Kaatskill	2	.2446	.1125	30.5	0	0	0	0	1	1	0	0	0	1	0	1	0	0	0	0	0	0	0	0	0	0	0	0	0
kabuki	2	.0000	.0209	23.2	0	0	2	0	0	0	0	0	0	0	0	0	0	0	0	0	0	0	0	0	0	0	2	0	0
Kabuki	8	.1001	.2513	34.0	0	7	0	0	0	1	0	0	0	0	0	0	0	1	0	0	0	0	0	0	0	0	0	7	0
kabunkit	6	.0000	.2741	34.4	0	0	6	0	0	0	0	0	6	0	0	0	0	0	0	0	0	0	0	0	0	0	0	0	0
kachinas	3	.0000	.0243	23.8	3	0	0	0	0	0	0	0	0	0	0	0	0	0	0	0	3	0	0	0	0	0	0	0	0
Kafa	2	.0000	.0389	25.9	0	0	0	0	2	0	0	0	0	0	0	0	0	2	0	0	0	0	0	0	0	0	0	0	0
Kaffirs	2	.2401	.1133	30.5	1	0	1	0	0	0	0	0	0	0	0	0	0	0	0	0	0	0	0	0	0	1	1	0	0
Kahan	3	.1119	.0792	29.0	0	0	0	0	0	3	0	0	0	0	2	0	0	0	0	0	0	0	0	0	0	0	1	0	0
Kahn	3	.2437	.2277	33.6	2	0	0	1	0	0	0	0	2	0	0	0	0	0	0	1	0	0	0	0	0	0	0	0	0
Kai-shek	6	.2285	.3387	35.3	0	0	3	2	0	1	0	0	0	0	0	0	0	3	0	0	0	0	0	0	0	0	3	0	0
Kaibab	2	.0000	.0243	23.9	0	0	0	2	0	0	0	0	0	0	0	0	0	0	0	0	0	0	0	0	0	0	0	2	0
Kaihsienkung	2	.0000	.0389	25.9	0	0	0	2	0	0	0	0	0	0	0	0	0	2	0	0	0	0	0	0	0	0	0	0	0
kain't	2	.0000	.0215	23.3	0	0	0	0	2	0	0	0	0	0	0	2	0	0	0	0	0	0	0	0	0	0	0	0	0
Kaiser	11	.3288	.8141	39.1	0	0	0	0	2	0	4	5	0	0	0	0	0	2	0	1	0	0	0	0	0	0	1	7	0
Kaiser's	5	.1398	.1959	32.9	0	0	0	0	0	0	3	2	0	0	0	0	0	1	0	0	0	0	0	0	0	0	0	4	0
Kakapateyuo	2	.0000	.0914	29.6	0	1	0	1	0	0	0	0	2	0	0	0	0	0	0	0	0	0	0	0	0	0	0	0	0
Kalahari	10	.3449	.8450	39.3	0	0	0	3	6	0	1	0	3	0	0	0	0	5	0	0	0	0	0	0	0	0	2	0	0
kale	3	.1970	.1504	31.8	0	0	0	0	2	0	1	0	0	0	0	0	0	0	0	2	0	0	1	0	0	0	0	0	0
kaleidoscope	4	.1611	.1738	32.4	0	0	0	0	0	1	1	2	0	0	0	0	0	0	0	1	0	0	0	0	0	0	0	3	0
Kalgoorlie	2	.0000	.0389	25.9	0	2	0	0	0	0	0	0	0	0	0	0	0	2	0	0	0	0	0	0	0	0	0	0	0
Kalmar	3	.0000	.0434	26.4	0	0	3	0	0	0	0	0	0	0	0	0	0	0	0	0	0	0	0	0	0	3	0	0	0
Kaltsuna	2	.0000	.0389	25.9	0	0	0	0	0	2	0	0	0	0	0	0	0	2	0	0	0	0	0	0	0	0	0	0	0
Kamehameha	6	.0000	.1167	30.7	0	0	6	0	0	0	0	0	0	0	0	0	0	6	0	0	0	0	0	0	0	0	0	0	0
Kampala	3	.0000	.0365	25.6	0	3	0	0	0	0	0	0	0	0	0	0	0	0	0	0	0	0	0	0	0	0	0	3	0
Kana	4	.0000	.0469	26.7	0	0	0	4	0	0	0	0	0	0	0	0	0	0	0	0	0	0	0	0	4	0	0	0	0
Kanana	3	.0000	.1370	31.4	0	0	0	3	0	0	0	0	3	0	0	0	0	0	0	0	0	0	0	0	0	0	0	0	0
Kandahar	2	.0000	.0209	23.2	0	0	0	0	0	2	0	0	0	0	0	0	0	0	0	0	0	0	0	0	0	0	2	0	0
Kane	3	.3394	.2470	33.9	0	0	0	1	1	1	0	0	1	0	0	0	1	0	0	0	0	0	0	0	0	0	1	0	0
Kanele	6	.0000	.2741	34.4	0	0	0	0	0	6	0	0	6	0	0	0	0	0	0	0	0	0	0	0	0	0	0	0	0
kangaroo	43	.7584	6.6414	48.2	7	11	4	8	1	6	0	6	11	1	0	1	8	2	2	6	2	0	0	0	0	4	0	6	0
Kangaroo	16	.2071	1.2010	40.8	1	11	4	0	0	0	0	0	15	0	0	0	0	0	0	0	1	0	0	0	0	0	0	0	0
kangaroo's	2	.2408	.1204	30.8	1	1	0	0	0	0	0	0	0	0	0	0	0	1	0	0	0	0	0	0	0	1	0	0	0
kangaroos	15	.5039	1.6651	42.2	2	7	1	3	2	0	0	0	4	0	0	0	0	7	0	0	1	0	0	0	0	1	2	0	0
Kannon	3	.1823	.1405	31.5	0	1	2	0	0	0	0	0	0	0	0	0	0	1	0	0	0	0	0	0	0	0	2	0	0
Kano	12	.0000	.2334	33.7	0	1	0	11	0	0	0	0	0	0	0	0	0	12	0	0	0	0	0	0	0	0	0	0	0
Kansas	102	.7235	15.037	51.8	5	9	34	10	12	17	13	2	11	2	1	6	1	43	0	5	0	0	0	0	5	7	10	11	0
KansasCity	14	.5766	1.7128	42.3	0	1	4	3	1	0	5	0	2	0	0	0	1	4	0	4	0	0	0	0	0	1	2	0	0
Kansas-Nebraska	7	.2727	.4867	36.9	0	0	1	0	1	4	1	0	1	0	0	0	0	5	0	0	0	0	0	0	0	0	1	0	0
Kantchil	13	.0000	.5939	37.7	0	0	0	0	13	0	0	0	13	0	0	0	0	0	0	0	0	0	0	0	0	0	0	0	0
kaoliang	4	.0000	.0778	28.9	0	4	0	0	0	0	0	0	0	0	0	0	0	4	0	0	0	0	0	0	0	0	0	0	0
kaolin	7	.2407	.4351	36.4	0	3	4	0	0	0	0	0	0	0	0	0	0	4	0	3	0	0	0	0	0	0	0	0	0
kapok	4	.3313	.2956	34.7	0	2	1	0	0	1	0	0	0	0	0	0	0	2	0	0	0	0	1	0	0	0	1	0	0
kapusta	2	.0000	.0290	24.6	2	0	0	0	0	0	0	0	0	0	0	0	0	0	0	0	0	0	0	0	0	2	0	0	0
Kara	21	.1027	.7821	38.9	0	20	0	0	0	1	0	0	0	0	0	0	0	20	0	0	0	0	0	0	0	0	1	0	0
Karachi	2	.0000	.0209	23.2	0	0	0	0	0	2	0	0	0	0	0	0	0	0	0	0	0	0	0	0	0	0	2	0	0
karakul	8	.2446	.4501	36.5	0	0	0	0	0	4	4	0	0	4	0	4	0	0	0	0	0	0	0	0	0	0	0	0	0
Karana	2	.0000	.0219	23.4	0	0	0	0	2	0	0	0	0	2	0	0	0	0	0	0	0	0	0	0	0	0	0	0	0
Karasik	4	.0000	.0429	26.3	0	0	0	0	4	0	0	0	0	0	0	4	0	0	0	0	0	0	0	0	0	0	0	0	0
karat	2	.1698	.1133	30.5	1	0	0	1	0	0	0	0	1	0	0	0	0	0	0	0	0	0	0	0	0	0	1	0	0
Karboe	3	.0000	.0352	25.5	0	0	0	0	0	3	0	0	0	0	0	0	0	0	0	0	0	0	0	0	3	0	0	0	0
Karen	29	.5025	3.1663	45.0	2	16	0	7	4	0	0	0	4	3	0	0	5	15	0	0	0	0	0	0	0	1	0	1	0
Karen's	5	.1660	.2768	34.4	0	0	0	5	0	0	0	0	2	0	0	0	3	0	0	0	0	0	0	0	0	0	0	0	0
Karin	3	.1434	.1493	31.7	0	0	0	2	1	0	0	0	1	0	0	0	2	0	0	0	0	0	0	0	0	0	0	0	0
Karl	51	.6570	7.0925	48.5	13	9	1	13	10	4	1	0	25	2	0	0	4	2	0	1	0	0	0	0	6	0	3	8	0
Karl's	2	.1698	.1133	30.5	1	1	0	0	0	0	0	0	1	0	0	0	0	0	0	0	0	0	0	0	0	0	1	0	0
Karlstead	6	.1250	.2684	34.3	0	0	0	0	4	2	0	0	2	0	0	0	0	0	0	0	0	0	0	0	4	0	0	0	0
Karn	2	.0000	.0219	23.4	0	0	0	0	2	0	0	0	0	2	0	0	0	0	0	0	0	0	0	0	0	0	0	0	0
Karnak	2	.0000	.0037	15.7	0	0	2	0	0	0	0	0	0	0	0	0	0	0	0	0	0	2	0	0	0	0	0	0	0
Karpur	2	.0000	.0389	25.9	0	2	0	0	0	0	0	0	0	0	0	0	0	2	0	0	0	0	0	0	0	0	0	0	0
Karroo	5	.0000	.0972	29.9	0	0	0	5	0	0	0	0	0	0	0	0	0	5	0	0	0	0	0	0	0	0	0	0	0
Kasai	3	.0000	.0583	27.7	0	0	0	0	3	0	0	0	0	0	0	0	0	3	0	0	0	0	0	0	0	0	0	0	0
Kasavubu	4	.0000	.0579	27.6	0	0	4	0	0	0	0	0	0	0	0	0	0	0	0	0	0	0	0	0	0	4	0	0	0
Kaseek	5	.0000	.0537	27.3	0	0	0	0	5	0	0	0	0	0	0	5	0	0	0	0	0	0	0	0	0	0	0	0	0
Kasim	3	.0000	.1370	31.4	0	0	0	2	1	0	0	0	3	0	0	0	0	0	0	0	0	0	0	0	0	0	0	0	0
Kaskaskia	8	.2443	.4819	36.8	0	0	5	0	0	0	3	0	0	0	0	3	0	5	0	0	0	0	0	0	0	0	0	0	0
Kass	2	.0000	.0215	23.3	0	0	0	0	2	0	0	0	0	0	0	2	0	0	0	0	0	0	0	0	0	0	0	0	0
Kasson	7	.0000	.3198	35.0	0	7	0	0	0	0	0	0	7	0	0	0	0	0	0	0	0	0	0	0	0	0	0	0	0
Katalin	7	.0000	.3198	35.0	7	0	0	0	0	0	0	0	7	0	0	0	0	0	0	0	0	0	0	0	0	0	0	0	0
Kate	77	.5985	10.060	50.0	12	7	26	15	7	1	8	1	48	0	2	14	1	0	0	0	1	0	0	0	7	1	0	3	0
Kate's	4	.3030	.2949	34.7	0	0	1	0	3	0	0	0	1	0	0	0	0	0	0	0	0	0	0	0	2	0	0	1	0
Katherine	7	.3296	.5114	37.1	0	0	1	4	2	0	0	0	0	0	0	0	0	0	0	0	0	0	0	0	2	1	0	4	0
Kathleen	3	.3849	.2503	34.0	0	0	1	0	1	0	1	0	0	1	0	0	1	0	0	0	0	0	0	0	0	0	0	1	0
Kathryn	3	.2078	.1429	31.5	0	0	0	0	0	3	0	0	0	0	1	0	0	0	0	0	0	0	0	0	2	0	0	0	0
Kathy	64	.6025	8.1571	49.1	46	12	0	2	4	0	0	0	14	0	1	3	9	30	5	0	0	0	0	0	0	0	0	2	0
Kathy's	8	.5313	.8784	39.4	1	4	0	1	2	0	0	0	0	1	0	2	1	0	1	0	0	0	0	0	0	0	0	3	0
Katie	110	.2371	8.7742	49.4	88	6	11	4	0	0	1	0	103	0	0	4	0	0	0	0	0	0	0	0	3	0	0	0	0
Katie's	2	.0000	.0914	29.6	2	0	0	0	0	0	0	0	2	0	0	0	0	0	0	0	0	0	0	0	0	0	0	0	0
Kato	5	.0000	.0972	29.9	0	5	0	0	0	0	0	0	0	0	0	0	0	5	0	0	0	0	0	0	0	0	0	0	0
Katrin	11	.2197	.6005	37.8	1	0	0	0	2	8	0	0	1	0	0	2	0	0	0	0	0	0	0	0	8	0	0	0	0
KATRIN	6	.0000	.0644	28.1	0	0	0	0	6	0	0	0	0	0	0	6	0	0	0	0	0	0	0	0	0	0	0	0	0
Katrina	17	.2420	1.3642	41.3	0	0	0	0	17	0	0	0	16	0	1	0	0	0	0	0	0	0	0	0	0	0	0	0	0
Kattegat	5	.2037	.2562	34.1	3	0	0	1	1	0	0	0	0	0	0	0	0	2	0	0	0	0	0	0	0	0	3	0	0
Katy	15	.6003	1.9059	42.8	5	7	0	1	0	0	2	0	4	0	0	2	0	0	1	3	0	0	0	0	0	4	0	1	0
katydid	6	.1833	.3085	34.9	1	5	0	0	0	0	0	0	0	0	0	0	0	0	0	5	0	0	0	0	0	1	0	0	0
katydids	7	.4548	.7213	38.6	3	1	0	1	2	0	0	0	2	0	0	0	0	0	0	3	0	0	0	0	0	1	1	0	0
Katz	2	.0000	.0299	24.8	0	0	0	0	0	2	0	0	0	0	0	0	2	0	0	0	0	0	0	0	0	0	0	0	0
Kauai	9	.1212	.4142	36.2	0	3	6	0	0	0	0	0	2	0	0	0	0	7	0	0	0	0	0	0	0	0	0	0	0
Kaug	2	.0000	.0243	23.9	0	0	0	2	0	0	0	0	0	0	0	0	0	0	0	0	0	0	0	0	0	0	0	2	0

5Q Kabukiza
8Q Kabul
3J kachina
8R Kadar
5A kaffakalas
5A kaffet
4A kaffir
7Q Kaffir
6R Kahuku
5F Kain-tuck
3Q kaingin
8F Kaintuck
6A Kaiva's
8D kaka
7P Kal
7P Kal's
7R Kalama
7R Kalamazoo
5F Kalapana
9R Kalashnikov
8J Kaleidoscope
9R kaleidoscopes
6R kaleidoscopic
5Q Kalgan
8Q Kalimantan
8E Kaliningrad
7R Kalitta
7H kalium
5A Kaller
XH Kalm
XH Kalmia
6R Kalstrom
4F Kamakura
7Q Kamchatka
5F Kamehameha's
9H kames
8G kamikaze
7J Kammermusik
8F Kan
7D Kanahawas
6A Kanana's
8K Kandinsky
5R Kandy
9D Kangshung
8R Kans
8F Kansans
9B kansas
5P Kansu
7Q Kant
7A Kantchil's
9Q Kantrowitz
4F Kanuri
5F kapa
4A Kapaa
7H kapalilua
9J Kapellmeister
5F Kapiolani
9Q Kaplan
6R Kapp
9Q Kappa
9Q Kappas
6R kaput
5G kar'ver**
7D Karait
3A karats
9R Karel
7D Karendouah
XR kari
9F Kariba
8Q Karo
7R Karwat
5G kas**
7F Kaschau
8Q Kashgar
7D Kasimar
7F Kassa
4F kassalalia
4A Kasson's
7R kat
7Q Katahdin
5J Katharine
4C Kathie
5E Kathleen's
8B kathy
3A KATIE'D
7Q Katmai
4F Kato's
4P Katrin's
6D Katrinka
4P Katydid
4P Katydid's
8R Katzenberg
8A Katzenellenbogen
5F Kauai's
5K Kauffer
6R Kaug's

Word Type	F	D	U	SFI	3 Gr 3	4 Gr 4	5 Gr 5	6 Gr 6	7 Gr 7	8 Gr 8	9 Gr 9	X UnGr	A Read	B Eng & Gr	C Comp	D Lit	E Math	F Soc Stud	G Spell	H Sci	J Music	K Art	L Home Ec	M Shop	N Lib F	P Lib NF	Q Lib Ref	R Mag	S Rel
kauri	2	.0000	.0209	23.2	0	0	0	0	2	0	0	0	0	0	0	0	0	0	0	0	0	0	0	0	0	0	2	0	0
Kaweki	5	.0000	.0972	29.9	0	5	0	0	0	0	0	0	0	0	0	0	0	5	0	0	0	0	0	0	0	0	0	0	0
Kay	30	.4550	3.1701	45.0	0	0	2	10	16	0	2	0	15	2	0	0	11	0	0	0	0	0	0	0	0	0	1	1	0
Kay's	3	.1908	.1634	32.1	0	0	0	1	1	0	1	0	1	0	1	0	1	0	0	0	0	0	0	0	0	0	0	0	0
kayak	20	.2651	1.6686	42.2	0	9	9	1	0	0	1	0	18	1	0	0	0	0	0	1	0	0	0	0	0	0	0	0	0
kayaks	3	.2028	.1988	33.0	2	1	0	0	0	0	0	0	2	0	0	0	0	0	0	0	1	0	0	0	0	0	0	0	0
Kayapo	3	.0000	.0365	25.6	0	0	0	0	3	0	0	0	0	0	0	0	0	0	0	0	0	0	0	0	0	0	0	3	0
Kazan	3	.0000	.0365	25.6	0	0	0	0	0	0	3	0	0	0	0	0	0	0	0	0	0	0	0	0	0	0	0	3	0
Kazan's	2	.0000	.0243	23.9	0	0	0	0	0	0	2	0	0	0	0	0	0	0	0	0	0	0	0	0	0	0	0	2	0
KDKA	3	.1621	.1254	31.0	0	0	0	0	2	1	0	0	0	0	0	0	0	1	0	0	2	0	0	0	0	0	0	0	0
ke	3	.0000	.0243	23.9	0	0	0	2	1	0	0	0	0	0	0	0	0	0	3	0	0	0	0	0	0	0	0	0	0
ke-mo	2	.0000	.0914	29.6	0	2	0	0	0	0	0	0	2	0	0	0	0	0	0	0	0	0	0	0	0	0	0	0	0
Ke-ya	6	.0000	.2741	34.4	0	6	0	0	0	0	0	0	6	0	0	0	0	0	0	0	0	0	0	0	0	0	0	0	0
Kea	2	.0000	.0389	25.9	0	0	2	0	0	0	0	0	0	0	0	0	0	2	0	0	0	0	0	0	0	0	0	0	0
Kearns	3	.0000	.1370	31.4	0	0	0	0	3	0	0	0	3	0	0	0	0	0	0	0	0	0	0	0	0	0	0	0	0
Keas	2	.0000	.0243	23.9	0	0	2	0	0	0	0	0	0	0	0	0	0	0	0	0	0	0	0	0	0	0	0	2	0
keastentroom	3	.0000	.1370	31.4	0	0	0	3	0	0	0	0	3	0	0	0	0	0	0	0	0	0	0	0	0	0	0	0	0
Keats	3	.0000	.0328	25.2	0	0	0	0	0	3	0	0	0	3	0	0	0	0	0	0	0	0	0	0	0	0	0	0	0
kedgeree	2	.0000	.0234	23.7	0	0	0	0	2	0	0	0	0	0	0	0	0	0	0	0	0	0	0	0	2	0	0	0	0
keel	18	.6583	2.4757	43.9	1	2	2	6	4	2	1	0	6	4	0	0	0	1	0	1	0	0	0	0	1	2	2	1	0
Keel	3	.0000	.0243	23.8	0	0	0	3	0	0	0	0	0	0	0	0	0	0	0	0	3	0	0	0	0	0	0	0	0
keelboat	2	.1170	.0651	28.1	0	0	0	0	0	2	0	0	0	0	1	0	0	1	0	0	0	0	0	0	0	0	0	0	0
keelboats	2	.2408	.1204	30.8	1	0	1	0	0	0	0	0	0	0	0	0	0	1	0	0	0	0	0	0	0	1	0	0	0
keen	58	.8191	9.5559	49.8	7	3	6	12	12	7	7	4	15	3	2	8	0	1	1	6	0	1	0	0	5	5	4	7	0
keen-eyed	2	.2401	.1133	30.5	0	1	1	0	0	0	0	0	0	0	0	0	0	0	0	0	0	0	0	0	0	1	1	0	0
keener	3	.0000	.0322	25.1	0	0	0	0	0	0	3	0	0	0	0	3	0	0	0	0	0	0	0	0	0	0	0	0	0
keenly	6	.3206	.4255	36.3	0	0	0	0	1	3	2	0	0	0	0	1	0	0	0	0	0	0	0	0	0	0	1	4	0
keep	2509	.9388	466.41	66.7	570	482	285	319	407	229	176	41	735	99	24	111	44	198	81	404	60	20	88	35	163	230	86	123	8
Keep	22	.3487	1.6620	42.2	1	0	0	2	6	11	0	2	1	1	0	0	0	0	15	1	0	0	0	1	0	0	0	3	0
Keep-Off-the-Grass	2	.0000	.0045	16.5	0	0	0	0	2	0	0	0	0	0	2	0	0	0	0	0	0	0	0	0	0	0	0	0	0
keeper	44	.7416	6.7576	48.3	18	12	4	3	3	2	1	1	23	2	0	3	0	1	1	6	3	0	0	0	1	1	0	3	0
Keeper	4	.2958	.2914	34.6	2	1	0	0	0	1	0	0	1	0	0	0	0	0	0	0	0	0	0	0	2	1	0	0	0
keeper's	5	.4091	.4615	36.6	2	2	0	0	0	1	0	0	1	0	0	0	0	1	0	0	0	0	0	0	2	0	0	1	0
keepers	7	.3813	.6823	38.3	6	0	1	0	0	0	0	0	5	0	0	0	0	0	0	0	0	0	0	0	0	1	0	1	0
keepin'	2	.1494	.1045	30.2	0	0	0	1	0	1	0	0	1	0	0	0	0	0	0	0	1	0	0	0	0	0	0	0	0
keeping	323	.9107	58.464	57.7	45	43	41	46	68	38	36	6	96	6	4	19	5	22	4	47	12	1	15	2	25	28	14	23	0
keeps	288	.8807	50.625	57.0	68	60	31	39	55	17	15	3	70	2	3	15	4	18	4	89	7	1	2	3	6	33	12	19	0
keepsake	3	.3399	.2456	33.9	1	0	0	1	1	0	0	0	1	0	0	1	0	0	0	0	0	0	0	0	0	0	0	1	0
keer	2	.0000	.0215	23.3	0	0	0	0	0	2	0	0	0	0	0	2	0	0	0	0	0	0	0	0	0	0	0	0	0
Kees	37	.0000	1.6903	42.3	0	0	0	37	0	0	0	0	37	0	0	0	0	0	0	0	0	0	0	0	0	0	0	0	0
keg	13	.4980	1.4350	41.6	1	2	1	5	3	1	0	0	6	1	1	1	0	0	0	0	1	2	0	0	0	1	0	0	0
kegs	9	.2442	.6954	38.4	1	0	2	3	3	0	0	0	7	0	0	0	0	0	0	0	0	0	0	0	0	2	0	0	0
Keith	14	.4553	1.5286	41.8	0	11	0	1	1	0	1	0	10	0	0	0	1	0	0	0	0	0	0	0	0	0	1	2	0
Keith's	2	.0000	.0914	29.6	0	2	0	0	0	0	0	0	2	0	0	0	0	0	0	0	0	0	0	0	0	0	0	0	0
Keller	31	.5300	3.5510	45.5	1	9	9	0	0	3	8	1	9	1	1	7	0	0	0	0	0	0	0	0	0	12	0	1	0
Keller's	2	.2407	.1138	30.6	0	0	0	0	0	1	1	0	0	0	0	1	0	0	0	0	0	0	0	0	0	1	0	0	0
Kellers	5	.2218	.3471	35.4	0	2	3	0	0	0	0	0	3	0	0	0	0	0	0	0	0	0	0	0	0	2	0	0	0
Kelley	2	.0000	.0215	23.3	0	0	0	0	0	2	0	0	0	0	0	2	0	0	0	0	0	0	0	0	0	0	0	0	0
Kellogg	3	.0000	.0314	25.0	0	0	3	0	0	0	0	0	0	0	0	0	0	0	0	0	0	0	0	0	0	0	3	0	0
Kellogg-Briand	2	.2285	.1129	30.5	0	0	1	0	0	1	0	0	0	0	0	0	0	1	0	0	0	0	0	0	0	0	1	0	0
Kells	2	.2401	.1133	30.5	0	0	2	0	0	0	0	0	0	0	0	0	0	0	0	0	0	0	0	0	0	1	1	0	0
Kelly	56	.6600	7.7329	48.9	3	8	11	8	4	17	4	1	22	0	0	1	0	2	2	0	0	3	0	0	6	4	10	6	0
Kellys	2	.2376	.1088	30.4	0	0	1	0	0	0	1	0	0	0	0	0	0	0	1	0	0	0	0	0	0	0	0	1	0
kelp	15	.5846	1.8592	42.7	1	0	1	9	1	3	0	0	4	0	0	3	0	1	0	1	0	0	0	0	4	1	0	1	0
kelps	2	.2446	.1122	30.5	0	0	0	1	1	0	0	0	0	0	0	1	0	0	0	0	0	0	0	0	0	0	1	0	0
Kelsey	3	.2187	.1555	31.9	0	0	0	0	0	2	0	1	0	2	0	0	0	0	0	0	0	0	0	0	0	0	0	1	0
Kelton	2	.1948	.1250	31.0	0	1	0	0	0	1	0	0	1	0	0	0	0	0	0	0	0	0	0	0	0	1	0	0	0
Kelvin	11	.3782	.9389	39.7	0	0	4	0	1	5	1	0	0	0	0	0	1	0	0	8	0	0	0	0	0	0	1	1	0
Kemal	5	.2112	.2785	34.4	0	0	0	0	4	0	0	1	0	0	0	0	0	4	0	0	0	0	0	0	0	0	0	1	0
Kemp	11	.1604	.4474	36.5	2	0	0	0	9	0	0	0	0	0	0	9	0	0	0	0	0	0	0	0	2	0	0	0	0
Kemper	2	.0000	.0290	24.6	0	2	0	0	0	0	0	0	0	0	0	0	0	0	0	0	0	0	0	0	0	2	0	0	0
ken	3	.1813	.1402	31.5	0	0	0	0	2	0	1	0	0	0	0	0	0	0	0	1	0	0	0	0	0	0	2	0	0
Ken	20	.5693	2.4183	43.8	4	1	1	5	2	6	1	0	5	1	0	2	6	0	1	0	0	0	0	0	0	0	0	5	0
Ken's	6	.1972	.3786	35.8	4	1	0	0	1	0	0	0	3	0	0	0	3	0	0	0	0	0	0	0	0	0	0	0	0
Kendall	3	.1200	.1302	31.1	0	0	0	0	1	2	0	0	1	2	0	0	0	0	0	0	0	0	0	0	0	0	0	0	0
Kenji	4	.0000	.1827	32.6	0	0	4	0	0	0	0	0	4	0	0	0	0	0	0	0	0	0	0	0	0	0	0	0	0
Kennedy	75	.6339	9.9244	50.0	1	4	8	6	31	12	9	4	18	1	0	1	2	6	0	2	1	0	0	0	0	13	9	22	0
Kennedy's	10	.4646	1.0006	40.0	0	0	2	0	3	2	3	0	1	0	0	0	0	1	0	0	0	0	0	0	0	2	2	4	0
Kennedys	2	.1948	.1250	31.0	0	0	0	0	1	1	0	0	1	0	0	0	0	0	0	0	0	0	0	0	0	1	0	0	0
kennel	15	.5516	1.8440	42.7	5	0	3	3	3	0	1	0	9	1	0	1	2	0	0	0	0	0	0	0	2	0	0	0	0
Kennel	4	.2445	.3067	34.9	0	0	0	2	2	0	0	0	3	0	0	0	0	0	0	0	0	0	0	0	0	1	0	0	0
kennels	5	.4761	.5332	37.3	0	0	0	0	2	2	1	0	2	1	0	1	0	0	0	0	0	0	0	0	1	0	0	0	0
Kenneth	10	.4959	1.0169	40.1	1	1	2	0	0	2	2	2	0	3	1	1	0	0	0	0	0	2	0	0	0	0	1	2	0
Kennie	13	.1596	.7011	38.5	0	0	6	0	0	7	0	0	6	0	0	7	0	0	0	0	0	0	0	0	0	0	0	0	0
Kennie's	2	.1717	.1142	30.6	0	0	1	0	0	1	0	0	1	0	0	1	0	0	0	0	0	0	0	0	0	0	0	0	0
Kenny	30	.4090	2.8992	44.6	21	0	3	2	4	0	0	0	14	3	0	0	0	0	0	0	0	0	0	0	11	0	0	2	0
Kent	9	.7247	1.3107	41.2	0	2	2	1	3	1	0	0	0	1	0	0	1	0	1	0	1	0	0	0	1	2	1	1	0
Kenton	10	.0952	.3227	35.1	0	9	1	0	0	0	0	0	0	0	0	0	0	1	0	0	0	0	0	0	0	9	0	0	0
Kentons	2	.0000	.0290	24.6	0	2	0	0	0	0	0	0	0	0	0	0	0	0	0	0	0	0	0	0	0	2	0	0	0
Kentuck	3	.0000	.1370	31.4	0	0	0	3	0	0	0	0	3	0	0	0	0	0	0	0	0	0	0	0	0	0	0	0	0
Kentucky	98	.7160	14.339	51.6	7	26	32	10	7	5	8	3	15	1	0	4	3	24	1	3	1	0	0	0	2	28	6	10	0
Kenya	36	.5268	4.0162	46.0	0	3	0	17	13	3	0	0	2	2	0	0	0	16	0	0	0	0	0	0	0	2	7	7	0
Kenya's	3	.0000	.0365	25.6	0	0	0	2	0	1	0	0	0	0	0	0	0	0	0	0	0	0	0	0	0	0	0	3	0
Kenyans	2	.0000	.0243	23.9	0	0	0	1	0	0	1	0	0	0	0	0	0	0	0	0	0	0	0	0	0	0	0	2	0
Kenyatta	5	.0000	.0608	27.8	0	0	0	3	0	1	1	0	0	0	0	0	0	0	0	0	0	0	0	0	0	0	0	5	0
Keokuk	2	.1733	.1149	30.6	0	1	0	0	0	0	1	0	1	1	0	0	0	0	0	0	0	0	0	0	0	0	0	0	0
Kepler	9	.3245	.6669	38.2	0	2	0	0	1	6	0	0	0	4	0	0	1	0	0	4	0	0	0	0	0	0	0	0	0
Kepler's	4	.0000	.0438	26.4	0	0	0	0	0	4	0	0	0	4	0	0	0	0	0	0	0	0	0	0	0	0	0	0	0
kept	1131	.9421	211.04	63.2	208	207	146	154	213	101	83	19	420	25	4	90	15	116	21	51	16	9	21	8	117	125	39	53	1
ker-choo	2	.0000	.0290	24.6	0	2	0	0	0	0	0	0	0	0	0	0	0	0	0	0	0	0	0	0	0	2	0	0	0
Kerezan	5	.0000	.2284	33.6	0	0	0	5	0	0	0	0	5	0	0	0	0	0	0	0	0	0	0	0	0	0	0	0	0
kerf	5	.0000	.0126	21.0	0	0	0	0	2	0	3	0	0	0	0	0	0	0	0	0	0	0	0	5	0	0	0	0	0
Kerlan	10	.0000	.1215	30.8	0	0	0	0	0	10	0	0	0	0	0	0	0	0	0	0	0	0	0	0	0	0	0	10	0
Kern	5	.2731	.3081	34.9	0	0	0	0	2	1	2	0	0	0	0	1	0	0	0	1	3	0	0	0	0	0	0	0	0

4F Kawata
4F Kawata's
4F Kaweki's
8R Kay-O
8D Kaye
7R Kazakh
7R Kazakhs
7Q Kazinga
7R Keach
7A keads
XB keck

4P Keefer
4P Keefer's
8C keelboatman's
8C keelboatmen
6A keeled
3K Keelmen
7R keels
5R Keen
5R Keen's
5N Keene
6A keenest

7A keenin'
9D keenness
6D keepest
7A Keeping
8D keerful
7D Keerist
6A Kees'
6R Kel
9R Kellogg's
6A Kelly's
6R kelpfish

9R Kelvinator
8B kembs
4G ken-tah-ten
4F Kenai
4P Kendallville
7Q Kendeigh
9B Kendrick
6N Kenilworth
5A Kenji's
7J Kennan
8F Kennebec

7R Kennecott
8N kennel-dog
8B Kenneth's
4P Kent's
4P Kentuckians
8B kentucky
6A Kentucky-born
4P Kentucky's
9R Kenyan
XR Keokee
7N kep'

XR Kepes
3A ker-chunking
7L kerchief
4R kerchiefs
9M kerfs
4A Kermit

Word Type	F	D	U	SFI	3 Gr 3	4 Gr 4	5 Gr 5	6 Gr 6	7 Gr 7	8 Gr 8	9 Gr 9	X UnGr	A Read	B Eng & Gr	C Comp	D Lit	E Math	F Soc Stud	G Spell	H Sci	J Music	K Art	L Home Ec	M Shop	N Lib F	P Lib NF	Q Lib Ref	R Mag	S Rel
Kern's	2	.2446	.1084	30.3	0	0	0	0	2	0	0	0	0	0	0	0	0	0	1	0	1	0	0	0	0	0	0	0	0
kernel	77	.3137	5.4124	47.3	1	0	5	0	27	32	12	0	3	60	0	0	0	0	0	6	0	0	4	0	2	0	1	1	0
kernels	29	.3820	2.4449	43.9	1	2	0	1	7	18	0	0	3	19	0	0	1	2	0	0	0	0	1	0	0	0	3	0	0
kernite	2	.0000	.0394	26.0	0	0	0	0	0	0	2	0	0	0	0	0	0	0	0	2	0	0	0	0	0	0	0	0	0
kerosene	23	.7519	3.4802	45.4	2	2	3	1	4	7	3	1	1	1	0	6	0	2	1	3	0	0	0	1	3	2	1	2	0
kerosine	2	.2351	.1166	30.7	0	1	1	0	0	0	0	0	0	0	0	0	0	1	0	0	0	0	0	0	0	0	0	1	0
Kerr	2	.0000	.0243	23.9	0	0	0	0	0	1	1	0	0	0	0	0	0	0	0	0	0	0	0	0	0	0	0	2	0
Kerry	22	.1654	.9410	39.7	0	0	2	17	0	3	0	0	0	1	0	0	0	0	0	0	0	0	0	0	0	2	0	19	0
Ket	8	.0000	.3655	35.6	0	0	0	8	0	0	0	0	8	0	0	0	0	0	0	0	0	0	0	0	0	0	0	0	0
ketch	7	.2762	.4876	36.9	0	0	0	1	4	1	1	0	2	0	0	0	0	0	0	0	0	0	0	0	4	0	1	0	0
ketches	2	.0000	.0914	29.6	0	0	0	2	0	0	0	0	2	0	0	0	0	0	0	0	0	0	0	0	0	0	0	0	0
Ketchikan	8	.0775	.2896	34.6	0	0	8	0	0	0	0	0	1	0	0	0	0	7	0	0	0	0	0	0	0	0	0	0	0
ketchup	2	.1972	.1262	31.0	0	0	1	0	1	0	0	0	1	0	0	0	1	0	0	0	0	0	0	0	0	0	0	0	0
kettle	88	.7902	14.175	51.5	18	17	18	14	12	7	1	1	40	1	1	4	0	4	1	8	4	0	4	0	13	4	0	4	0
kettledrum	3	.3231	.2367	33.7	0	0	0	1	1	1	0	0	1	0	0	0	0	0	0	0	1	0	0	0	0	1	0	0	0
kettledrums	2	.0000	.0162	22.1	0	0	0	1	1	0	0	0	0	0	0	0	0	0	0	0	2	0	0	0	0	0	0	0	0
kettles	20	.6807	2.8307	44.5	3	8	1	3	0	1	2	2	6	0	1	0	0	4	0	3	1	0	0	0	1	3	1	0	0
Keukenhof	3	.0000	.1370	31.4	3	0	0	0	0	0	0	0	3	0	0	0	0	0	0	0	0	0	0	0	0	0	0	0	0
Kevin	33	.3546	2.6240	44.2	10	3	1	0	6	0	13	0	3	1	0	0	0	0	0	1	0	0	0	0	13	0	0	15	0
key	652	.5823	78.946	59.0	91	106	107	79	122	49	92	6	115	34	3	15	6	24	48	17	317	0	6	8	6	13	13	27	0
Key	28	.4488	2.7079	44.3	13	7	1	3	2	1	1	0	5	1	0	0	0	0	5	0	13	0	0	0	0	1	2	1	0
KeyWest	2	.2446	.1257	31.0	0	1	1	0	0	0	0	0	0	0	0	0	0	1	0	1	0	0	0	0	0	0	0	0	0
keyboard	67	.1636	2.6888	44.3	12	14	13	9	12	5	1	1	2	1	0	3	0	0	0	0	57	0	0	0	0	0	3	1	0
keyboards	10	.0976	.2668	34.3	0	0	2	5	3	0	0	0	0	0	0	0	0	0	0	0	9	0	0	0	0	0	1	0	0
keyed	4	.3256	.2923	34.7	0	1	0	0	0	1	2	0	0	0	0	0	0	2	0	0	0	0	1	0	1	0	0	0	0
Keyes	7	.0000	.0851	29.3	0	0	0	0	7	0	0	0	0	0	0	0	0	0	0	0	0	0	0	0	0	0	0	7	0
keyhole	4	.2287	.1993	33.0	1	0	0	1	0	2	0	0	0	0	0	0	0	0	0	0	1	0	0	2	0	0	0	1	0
keying	2	.0000	.0064	18.1	0	0	0	0	0	0	2	0	0	0	0	0	0	0	0	0	0	0	2	0	0	0	0	0	0
keynote	8	.1112	.2348	33.7	0	0	0	1	4	3	0	0	0	1	0	0	0	0	0	0	7	0	0	0	0	0	0	0	0
keys	156	.4437	14.656	51.7	24	41	28	22	20	15	6	0	12	1	3	8	2	5	1	3	101	0	0	1	8	3	3	5	0
keystone	3	.3668	.2407	33.8	0	0	0	1	0	1	1	0	0	0	0	1	0	0	0	1	1	0	0	0	0	0	0	0	0
kg	3	.0000	.0449	26.5	0	0	0	0	0	0	3	0	0	0	0	0	3	0	0	0	0	0	0	0	0	0	0	0	0
Kha	2	.0000	.0290	24.6	0	0	0	0	0	0	2	0	0	0	0	0	0	0	0	0	0	0	0	0	0	2	0	0	0
Khachaturian	2	.0000	.0162	22.1	0	0	0	0	0	2	0	0	0	0	0	0	0	0	0	0	2	0	0	0	0	0	0	0	0
khaghan	2	.0000	.0209	23.2	0	0	0	0	0	2	0	0	0	0	0	0	0	0	0	0	0	0	0	0	0	0	2	0	0
khaki	6	.5563	.7177	38.6	1	2	1	0	1	0	1	0	2	0	0	1	0	0	0	0	0	0	0	0	0	1	1	1	0
Khaled	3	.0000	.1370	31.4	0	0	0	3	0	0	0	0	3	0	0	0	0	0	0	0	0	0	0	0	0	0	0	0	0
Khalil	2	.0000	.0243	23.9	0	0	0	2	0	0	0	0	0	0	0	0	0	0	0	0	0	0	0	0	0	0	0	2	0
Khan	32	.5176	3.5502	45.5	9	0	7	4	3	5	4	0	4	0	0	1	0	10	0	0	0	0	0	0	0	11	5	1	0
Khan's	4	.2408	.2408	33.8	0	0	2	1	0	1	0	0	0	0	0	0	0	2	0	0	0	0	0	0	0	2	0	0	0
Khazars	7	.0000	.0733	28.6	0	0	0	0	0	7	0	0	0	0	0	0	0	0	0	0	0	0	0	0	0	0	7	0	0
Kherson	4	.0000	.0419	26.2	0	0	0	0	0	4	0	0	0	0	0	0	0	0	0	0	0	0	0	0	0	0	4	0	0
Kho	2	.0000	.0290	24.6	0	0	0	0	0	0	2	0	0	0	0	0	0	0	0	0	0	0	0	0	0	2	0	0	0
Khosrove	3	.0000	.0322	25.1	0	0	0	0	0	3	0	0	0	0	0	3	0	0	0	0	0	0	0	0	0	0	0	0	0
Khotan	2	.0000	.0914	29.6	0	0	0	2	0	0	0	0	2	0	0	0	0	0	0	0	0	0	0	0	0	0	0	0	0
Khrushchev	5	.1398	.1959	32.9	0	0	0	1	1	1	2	0	0	0	0	0	0	1	0	0	0	0	0	0	0	0	0	4	0
Khufu	2	.0000	.0209	23.2	0	1	0	0	0	0	1	0	0	0	0	0	0	0	0	0	0	0	0	0	0	0	2	0	0
Khufu-onekh	2	.0000	.0209	23.2	0	0	0	0	0	0	2	0	0	0	0	0	0	0	0	0	0	0	0	0	0	0	2	0	0
ki	2	.0000	.0162	22.1	0	0	0	2	0	0	0	0	0	0	0	0	0	0	2	0	0	0	0	0	0	0	0	0	0
Ki	3	.1409	.1472	31.7	0	1	0	0	0	2	0	0	1	0	0	0	0	0	0	0	0	0	0	0	0	2	0	0	0
ki-me-oh	10	.0000	.4568	36.6	0	10	0	0	0	0	0	0	10	0	0	0	0	0	0	0	0	0	0	0	0	0	0	0	0
ki-mo	2	.0000	.0914	29.6	0	2	0	0	0	0	0	0	2	0	0	0	0	0	0	0	0	0	0	0	0	0	0	0	0
ki-yi	4	.0000	.0579	27.6	4	0	0	0	0	0	0	0	0	0	0	0	0	0	0	0	0	0	0	0	0	4	0	0	0
ki-yi'd	2	.0000	.0234	23.7	0	0	0	0	2	0	0	0	0	0	0	0	0	0	0	0	0	0	0	0	2	0	0	0	0
Kiche	3	.0000	.0352	25.5	0	0	0	0	3	0	0	0	0	0	0	0	0	0	0	0	0	0	0	0	3	0	0	0	0
kick	89	.8468	15.121	51.8	21	13	8	12	20	4	8	3	27	5	0	8	0	5	4	6	2	0	0	1	11	10	3	7	0
Kickapoo	7	.4104	.6410	38.1	1	4	0	2	0	0	0	0	1	0	0	0	0	2	0	0	2	0	0	0	0	2	0	0	0
Kickapoos	8	.0000	.1556	31.9	0	8	0	0	0	0	0	0	0	0	0	0	0	8	0	0	0	0	0	0	0	0	0	0	0
kickball	2	.2404	.1142	30.6	2	0	0	0	0	0	0	0	0	1	0	0	1	0	0	0	0	0	0	0	0	0	0	0	0
kicked	85	.6720	11.930	50.8	18	21	9	10	14	9	4	0	33	0	0	10	0	2	3	2	1	0	0	0	17	8	0	9	0
kicker	10	.2121	.5602	37.5	0	8	0	0	0	1	1	0	0	0	0	0	0	0	0	8	0	0	0	0	0	0	0	2	0
kicking	43	.7635	6.7387	48.3	9	9	4	6	5	4	5	1	21	1	0	3	0	0	1	1	2	0	1	0	4	4	0	5	0
kickoff	2	.1814	.1187	30.7	0	0	1	1	0	0	0	0	1	0	0	0	0	0	0	0	0	0	0	0	0	0	0	1	0
kicks	23	.7130	3.3610	45.3	3	6	3	2	4	4	1	0	5	0	0	0	0	2	1	5	0	1	1	0	4	3	0	1	0
kickshaw	2	.0000	.0219	23.4	0	0	0	0	0	0	0	2	0	2	0	0	0	0	0	0	0	0	0	0	0	0	0	0	0
kid	92	.6087	12.029	50.8	13	4	2	8	38	14	12	1	46	2	1	21	0	0	0	0	0	0	0	0	11	2	1	8	0
Kid	27	.4575	2.6571	44.2	1	4	1	1	16	4	0	0	4	0	0	12	0	0	0	0	5	0	0	0	4	0	0	2	0
kid's	2	.2446	.1142	30.6	0	0	0	0	2	0	0	0	0	0	0	0	0	0	0	0	0	0	0	0	1	0	0	1	0
Kidd	4	.2278	.2911	34.6	0	1	0	0	3	0	0	0	3	0	0	0	0	0	0	0	1	0	0	0	0	0	0	0	0
kidding	14	.6947	2.0099	43.0	7	1	0	2	1	0	3	0	4	1	0	1	0	1	0	1	0	0	0	0	1	3	0	2	0
kidnap	2	.1814	.1187	30.7	0	0	0	1	0	0	0	1	1	0	0	0	0	0	0	0	0	0	0	0	0	0	0	1	0
kidnaped	5	.3838	.4772	36.8	1	0	0	2	1	1	0	0	3	1	0	0	0	0	0	0	0	0	0	0	0	1	0	0	0
kidnaping	3	.2279	.2143	33.3	0	0	0	0	2	0	0	1	2	0	0	0	0	0	0	0	0	0	0	0	0	0	0	1	0
kidney	10	.3407	.7535	38.8	0	1	0	0	0	1	6	2	0	0	0	1	0	0	0	2	0	0	0	0	0	1	6	0	0
kidneys	35	.3802	2.9777	44.7	1	3	7	0	5	8	10	1	0	0	0	0	0	0	0	24	0	0	1	0	0	1	9	0	0
kids	168	.6745	23.738	53.8	34	21	11	12	38	18	31	3	74	3	2	16	0	5	0	0	1	0	0	0	20	9	1	37	0
kids'	2	.1814	.1187	30.7	0	0	0	1	0	0	0	1	1	0	0	0	0	0	0	0	0	0	0	0	0	0	0	1	0
Kidwell	6	.0000	.2741	34.4	0	6	0	0	0	0	0	0	6	0	0	0	0	0	0	0	0	0	0	0	0	0	0	0	0
Kiehl	4	.0000	.1827	32.6	0	0	0	0	4	0	0	0	4	0	0	0	0	0	0	0	0	0	0	0	0	0	0	0	0
Kiesinger	3	.0000	.0365	25.6	0	0	0	0	0	3	0	0	0	0	0	0	0	0	0	0	0	0	0	0	0	0	0	3	0
Kiev	11	.3590	.8886	39.5	0	1	0	4	0	3	3	0	0	0	0	0	0	7	0	0	1	0	0	0	0	0	3	0	0
Kilauea	5	.0000	.2284	33.6	0	5	0	0	0	0	0	0	5	0	0	0	0	0	0	0	0	0	0	0	0	0	0	0	0
Kilimanjaro	12	.4196	1.0868	40.4	0	5	0	1	5	0	1	0	0	0	0	0	3	3	0	0	0	0	0	0	0	0	5	1	0
kill	326	.7194	48.413	56.8	57	52	35	59	66	35	16	6	116	8	0	33	0	21	4	49	3	0	0	0	36	22	13	19	2
Kill	3	.1250	.1342	31.3	0	2	0	0	1	0	0	0	1	0	0	0	0	0	0	0	0	0	0	0	2	0	0	0	0
killdeer	3	.3553	.2609	34.2	3	0	0	0	0	0	0	0	1	0	0	0	0	0	0	1	0	0	0	0	0	1	0	0	0
killed	443	.7848	70.484	58.5	42	87	48	62	126	37	31	10	121	8	0	52	4	55	2	41	6	0	1	0	31	52	34	34	2
killer	30	.6974	4.3200	46.4	4	10	0	5	9	0	2	0	9	0	0	5	0	0	0	4	2	0	0	0	2	5	2	1	0
Killer	12	.0000	.5482	37.4	11	0	0	0	1	0	0	0	12	0	0	0	0	0	0	0	0	0	0	0	0	0	0	0	0
killers	18	.5948	2.2363	43.5	3	3	2	0	8	1	0	1	3	0	0	1	0	1	0	1	0	0	0	0	1	2	6	3	0
KILLIGREW	2	.0000	.0215	23.3	0	0	0	0	2	0	0	0	0	0	0	2	0	0	0	0	0	0	0	0	0	0	0	0	0

3N Kernstawk
XR kerplunk
6R Kerry's
7A kersplack
5N Kessie
7N ketched
7N kettle-holder
8A kettleful
9N Kevin's
9D Kewpie
7R KeyBiscayne
4A key's
9R Keynes
9C Keys
7R Keystone
7R keyways
8E kgm
5G kh
7R Khabarov
7R Khabarov's
7F Khafre
8Q Khaghan
6J Khah-tchah-too-ree-ahn
8Q Khairpar
8Q Khairpur
6A Khaled's
7P Khalid
8Q Khalifa
6R Khalil's
5P khamsin
8Q khan
6R Khan-style
9F khan's
6R Khartoum
6J Khatchaturian
8Q Khazar
9B KHCAL
8Q Khersonskaya
8Q KHITAN
7D Khoda
6A Khoda-verdikol
7P khomp
9Q Khrushchev's
7Q Khyber
XR KH3
7N ki-yi's
5A Kia-wa-wa
7N kick'm
5R kickboards
5A kicked-up
7D kickety
7D kickin'
7P Kicva
7D Kid's
XR kidded
4J kiddies
8D kiddo
XR kidnaper's
7A kidnapers
9F kidnapped
7B Kidnapped
9F kidnappers
9F kidnapping
9Q Kidney
8F kidney-shaped
4A Kidwells
7A Kiehl's
8K Kienholz
8K Kienholz's
9F Kievan
9R kike
3P Kiki
6R Kikuyu
XH Kilborne
9D Kilbourne
3A Kildare
3P Kilkenny
XR Killan
8R Killarney
XR Killdeer
7R Killebrew
3P killer's

Word Type	F	D	U	SFI	3 Gr 3	4 Gr 4	5 Gr 5	6 Gr 6	7 Gr 7	8 Gr 8	9 Gr 9	X UnGr	A Read	B Eng & Gr	C Comp	D Lit	E Math	F Soc Stud	G Spell	H Sci	J Music	K Art	L Home Ec	M Shop	N Lib F	P Lib NF	Q Lib Ref	R Mag	S Rel
killin'	2	.1787	.1174	30.7	0	0	0	1	1	0	0	0	1	0	0	0	0	0	0	0	0	0	0	0	1	0	0	0	0
killing	90	.7718	14.032	51.5	6	8	10	19	27	9	8	3	12	0	1	10	1	6	0	21	1	0	0	0	7	9	12	10	0
kills	37	.7689	5.7497	47.6	6	2	1	7	13	4	3	1	5	2	1	4	0	2	0	11	2	0	0	0	0	3	4	3	0
kiln	7	.3098	.4543	36.6	2	0	1	0	2	0	2	0	0	0	0	0	0	0	0	0	0	3	0	1	1	0	2	0	0
kilns	2	.1259	.0687	28.4	1	0	0	0	1	0	0	0	0	0	0	0	0	1	0	0	0	0	0	1	0	0	0	0	0
kilo	2	.0000	.0299	24.8	0	0	0	0	1	1	0	0	0	0	0	0	2	0	0	0	0	0	0	0	0	0	0	0	0
kilogram	3	.0000	.0449	26.5	0	0	0	1	0	2	0	0	0	0	0	0	3	0	0	0	0	0	0	0	0	0	0	0	0
kilograms	7	.0000	.1048	30.2	0	0	3	0	2	0	2	0	0	0	0	0	7	0	0	0	0	0	0	0	0	0	0	0	0
kilohertz	3	.0000	.0076	18.8	0	0	0	0	0	3	0	0	0	0	0	0	0	0	0	0	0	0	0	3	0	0	0	0	0
kilometer	9	.3779	.7558	38.8	0	0	1	0	5	1	2	0	0	0	0	2	4	0	0	3	0	0	0	0	0	0	0	0	0
kilometers	22	.3060	1.5826	42.0	0	0	0	1	8	0	13	0	0	0	0	0	11	0	0	10	0	0	0	0	0	0	0	1	0
kilowatt	2	.2413	.1212	30.8	0	0	0	0	1	1	0	0	0	0	0	0	1	0	0	1	0	0	0	0	0	0	0	0	0
kilowatts	2	.2405	.1205	30.8	0	0	1	0	0	1	0	0	0	0	0	0	0	0	0	1	0	0	0	0	0	1	0	0	0
Kilpatrick	44	.1570	2.3367	43.7	37	7	0	0	0	0	0	0	19	0	0	0	0	0	0	0	0	0	0	0	25	0	0	0	0
Kilpatrick's	5	.0000	.0586	27.7	5	0	0	0	0	0	0	0	0	0	0	0	0	0	0	0	0	0	0	0	5	0	0	0	0
kilt	8	.2351	.6222	37.9	0	0	7	0	1	0	0	0	7	0	0	0	0	0	0	0	0	0	0	0	0	0	1	0	0
Kiltie	2	.0000	.0914	29.6	0	2	0	0	0	0	0	0	2	0	0	0	0	0	0	0	0	0	0	0	0	0	0	0	0
Kim	33	.3973	3.2640	45.1	15	2	9	7	0	0	0	0	22	0	0	0	1	0	0	0	0	0	0	0	2	0	0	8	0
Kimberley	5	.2205	.2855	34.6	0	0	0	1	3	1	0	0	0	0	0	0	0	4	0	0	0	0	0	0	0	0	1	0	0
Kimo	4	.0000	.1827	32.6	0	4	0	0	0	0	0	0	4	0	0	0	0	0	0	0	0	0	0	0	0	0	0	0	0
kimono	4	.2393	.3005	34.8	2	0	0	1	1	0	0	0	3	0	0	1	0	0	0	0	0	0	0	0	0	0	0	0	0
kimonos	5	.1118	.2195	33.4	0	1	1	3	0	0	0	0	1	0	0	0	0	4	0	0	0	0	0	0	0	0	0	0	0
kin	18	.5315	1.9974	43.0	0	4	1	0	7	3	3	0	1	0	0	2	0	0	0	0	1	0	0	0	7	5	2	0	0
kind	2262	.9736	433.99	66.4	430	392	239	256	406	264	228	47	454	218	20	139	73	235	58	398	81	26	46	47	93	160	115	98	1
Kind	2	.0000	.0914	29.6	1	0	0	1	0	0	0	0	2	0	0	0	0	0	0	0	0	0	0	0	0	0	0	0	0
kind-hearted	6	.3370	.5167	37.1	1	2	2	0	1	0	0	0	3	0	0	0	0	1	0	0	0	0	0	0	2	0	0	0	0
kinda	8	.3374	.5902	37.7	0	2	0	0	5	1	0	0	0	0	0	4	0	0	0	0	0	0	0	0	3	0	0	1	0
kinder	6	.2513	.3687	35.7	0	0	1	0	2	2	1	0	1	0	0	4	0	0	1	0	0	0	0	0	0	0	0	0	0
kindergarten	25	.7122	3.5793	45.5	11	3	0	0	4	2	4	1	0	3	1	0	1	1	2	0	0	1	0	0	7	1	1	7	0
Kinderhook	2	.0000	.0219	23.4	0	0	0	0	0	0	0	2	0	2	0	0	0	0	0	0	0	0	0	0	0	0	0	0	0
kindest	7	.3621	.6358	38.0	0	2	0	0	2	3	0	0	4	0	0	2	0	0	0	0	0	0	0	0	1	0	0	0	0
kindhearted	2	.1948	.1250	31.0	0	2	0	0	0	0	0	0	1	0	0	0	0	0	0	0	0	0	0	0	0	1	0	0	0
kindle	3	.1983	.1396	31.4	0	0	0	0	1	2	0	0	0	0	0	0	0	0	0	0	2	0	0	0	0	0	0	1	0
kindled	4	.3693	.3613	35.6	1	0	0	0	1	1	1	0	2	0	0	1	0	0	0	0	0	0	0	0	0	0	1	0	0
kindling	9	.4854	.9614	39.8	0	1	2	2	4	0	0	0	3	0	1	1	0	0	0	0	0	0	0	0	0	2	2	0	0
kindly	83	.7802	13.210	51.2	7	16	10	20	12	8	10	0	36	5	1	9	1	2	1	0	2	0	0	0	11	11	2	2	0
kindness	66	.7299	9.9100	50.0	9	16	11	10	10	2	8	0	25	5	0	14	0	6	3	0	1	0	1	0	5	5	0	1	0
kindred	4	.3402	.3011	34.8	0	0	0	0	1	1	2	0	0	0	0	1	0	1	0	0	0	0	0	0	0	0	2	0	0
kinds	1545	.8845	271.86	64.3	396	245	166	223	232	141	107	35	194	104	24	25	27	219	29	464	53	44	28	37	12	148	98	39	0
Kinds	2	.2306	.1140	30.6	0	2	0	0	0	0	0	0	0	1	0	0	0	1	0	0	0	0	0	0	0	0	0	0	0
kinescope	2	.1249	.0685	28.4	0	0	0	0	1	1	0	0	0	0	0	0	0	0	0	1	0	0	0	1	0	0	0	0	0
kinetic	23	.2891	1.6100	42.1	0	0	0	18	1	1	3	0	0	0	0	0	0	0	0	21	0	1	0	0	0	0	1	0	0
Kinetic	2	.0000	.0394	26.0	0	0	0	2	0	0	0	0	0	0	0	0	0	0	0	2	0	0	0	0	0	0	0	0	0
king	688	.6628	96.339	59.8	188	80	118	119	91	62	21	9	327	28	1	38	3	123	12	5	17	2	0	0	29	38	47	12	6
King	790	.7349	119.81	60.8	210	115	119	111	137	53	28	17	355	18	1	51	1	62	9	6	61	2	0	0	86	59	37	37	5
king-size	3	.2121	.1560	31.9	1	0	0	0	0	0	1	1	0	0	0	0	1	0	0	0	0	0	0	0	0	0	0	2	0
king's	68	.6348	9.2226	49.6	12	13	13	15	10	4	0	1	34	3	0	8	0	13	0	0	3	0	0	0	0	1	6	0	0
King's	85	.5946	10.682	50.3	19	17	5	14	21	3	4	2	25	2	0	10	0	3	0	0	4	0	0	0	32	3	2	4	0
kingdom	117	.2427	7.6488	48.8	16	12	13	20	32	15	5	4	34	2	0	5	0	19	0	19	6	0	0	0	4	10	9	2	7
Kingdom	49	.5741	5.8899	47.7	8	2	9	6	16	2	5	1	2	0	0	0	0	27	0	0	4	0	0	0	3	5	3	5	0
kingdoms	25	.5341	2.8406	44.5	1	0	8	5	7	2	2	0	1	0	0	0	0	11	0	6	0	0	0	0	0	3	3	1	0
kingfisher	5	.4392	.4839	36.8	4	0	0	0	1	0	0	0	1	0	0	1	0	0	0	0	1	0	0	0	0	2	0	0	0
Kingfisher	3	.1187	.1291	31.1	0	1	0	0	0	2	0	0	1	0	0	2	0	0	0	0	0	0	0	0	0	0	0	0	0
kingly	9	.5778	1.0908	40.4	0	3	0	0	6	0	0	0	2	0	0	2	0	0	1	0	2	0	0	0	1	1	0	0	0
kings	131	.7499	19.926	53.0	26	13	25	32	18	8	6	3	23	11	0	0	0	35	2	1	10	3	0	1	5	7	30	3	0
Kings	17	.5033	1.7867	42.5	6	1	3	1	0	5	1	0	0	1	0	0	0	4	0	1	7	0	0	0	1	1	2	0	0
kings'	2	.1948	.1250	31.0	1	0	0	0	1	0	0	0	1	0	0	0	0	0	0	0	0	0	0	0	0	1	0	0	0
Kingsland	2	.0000	.0914	29.6	0	0	0	2	0	0	0	0	2	0	0	0	0	0	0	0	0	0	0	0	0	0	0	0	0
kingsnake	2	.0000	.0394	26.0	2	0	0	0	0	0	0	0	0	0	0	0	0	0	0	2	0	0	0	0	0	0	0	0	0
kingsnakes	2	.0000	.0394	26.0	2	0	0	0	0	0	0	0	0	0	0	0	0	0	0	2	0	0	0	0	0	0	0	0	0
Kingston	15	.1616	.7127	38.5	12	2	0	0	1	0	0	0	0	0	0	0	0	13	0	0	0	0	0	0	0	2	0	0	0
kinks	5	.2446	.3872	35.9	0	0	0	4	0	1	0	0	4	0	0	0	0	0	0	0	0	0	0	0	1	0	0	0	0
kinky	2	.0000	.0389	25.9	0	0	0	0	2	0	0	0	0	0	0	0	0	2	0	0	0	0	0	0	0	0	0	0	0
Kino	161	.0232	2.6935	44.3	0	0	8	0	153	0	0	0	8	0	0	153	0	0	0	0	0	0	0	0	0	0	0	0	0
KINO	15	.0000	.1610	32.1	0	0	0	0	15	0	0	0	0	0	0	15	0	0	0	0	0	0	0	0	0	0	0	0	0
Kino's	39	.0238	.6591	38.2	0	0	2	0	37	0	0	0	2	0	0	37	0	0	0	0	0	0	0	0	0	0	0	0	0
Kinsale	3	.3406	.2461	33.9	0	0	0	1	1	0	1	0	1	1	0	0	0	0	0	0	0	0	0	0	0	0	0	1	0
Kinshasa	9	.0000	.1750	32.4	0	1	0	0	8	0	0	0	0	0	0	0	0	9	0	0	0	0	0	0	0	0	0	0	0
kinship	6	.1794	.2611	34.2	1	0	0	0	4	0	1	0	0	0	0	0	0	0	0	0	1	0	0	0	0	0	5	0	0
kinsman	5	.2445	.3100	34.9	0	1	0	0	0	1	3	0	1	0	0	3	0	0	0	0	0	0	0	0	0	1	0	0	0
Kioto	5	.0000	.2284	33.6	0	0	0	5	0	0	0	0	5	0	0	0	0	0	0	0	0	0	0	0	0	0	0	0	0
Kipling	8	.1892	.3956	36.0	0	0	0	1	7	0	0	0	1	1	0	6	0	0	0	0	0	0	0	0	0	0	0	0	0
Kipp	2	.0000	.0914	29.6	2	0	0	0	0	0	0	0	2	0	0	0	0	0	0	0	0	0	0	0	0	0	0	0	0
Kippur	4	.0000	.1827	32.6	0	4	0	0	0	0	0	0	4	0	0	0	0	0	0	0	0	0	0	0	0	0	0	0	0
Kirby	89	.0672	4.9348	46.9	0	0	0	88	1	0	0	0	88	0	0	0	0	0	0	0	0	0	0	0	0	0	1	0	0
Kirby's	14	.0000	.6396	38.1	0	0	0	14	0	0	0	0	14	0	0	0	0	0	0	0	0	0	0	0	0	0	0	0	0
Kiril	2	.0000	.0243	23.9	0	0	0	0	0	0	2	0	0	0	0	0	0	0	0	0	0	0	0	0	0	0	0	2	0
kirk	3	.2074	.1511	31.8	2	1	0	0	0	0	0	0	0	2	0	0	0	0	0	0	0	0	0	0	0	1	0	0	0
Kirk	11	.2591	.7566	38.8	0	10	0	0	0	0	1	0	4	0	0	0	0	0	0	0	0	0	0	0	6	0	0	1	0
Kirkland	2	.0000	.0914	29.6	0	0	2	0	0	0	0	0	2	0	0	0	0	0	0	0	0	0	0	0	0	0	0	0	0
Kirsten	24	.1752	1.6998	42.3	16	7	0	0	0	0	1	0	23	0	0	0	0	0	0	0	1	0	0	0	0	0	0	0	0
Kirsten's	2	.0000	.0914	29.6	1	1	0	0	0	0	0	0	2	0	0	0	0	0	0	0	0	0	0	0	0	0	0	0	0
Kirthar	2	.0000	.0209	23.2	0	0	0	0	0	2	0	0	0	0	0	0	0	0	0	0	0	0	0	0	0	0	2	0	0
kirtle	2	.2442	.1134	30.5	1	0	1	0	0	0	0	0	0	1	0	0	0	0	0	0	0	0	0	0	0	0	0	1	0
Kisangani	5	.0000	.0972	29.9	0	1	0	0	4	0	0	0	0	0	0	0	0	5	0	0	0	0	0	0	0	0	0	0	0
kiss	43	.7255	6.3861	48.1	6	7	3	4	8	3	11	1	12	1	1	9	0	5	3	0	0	0	0	0	4	3	0	5	0
Kiss	2	.2411	.1091	30.4	0	0	0	1	0	1	0	0	0	0	0	1	0	0	0	0	1	0	0	0	0	0	0	0	0
kissed	65	.6212	8.4464	49.3	8	15	6	6	16	2	12	0	17	3	1	22	0	4	1	0	0	0	0	0	10	6	0	1	0
kisses	13	.5955	1.6129	42.1	0	0	1	3	2	1	5	1	2	0	0	2	0	0	0	0	1	0	0	0	2	4	0	2	0
Kissimmee	5	.1628	.2128	33.3	1	0	0	0	0	0	0	4	0	0	0	0	0	0	0	0	0	0	0	0	0	1	0	4	0
kissing	15	.5626	1.7907	42.5	4	2	0	4	0	1	3	1	3	0	0	3	0	3	0	0	0	0	0	0	1	1	0	4	0
Kissinger	3	.0000	.0365	25.6	0	0	0	0	0	0	3	0	0	0	0	0	0	0	0	0	0	0	0	0	0	0	0	3	0
kit	43	.6771	6.0047	47.8	7	3	4	1	18	6	1	3	11	2	0	2	2	2	2	2	0	0	1	3	0	1	0	15	0
Kit	36	.4163	3.4432	45.4	1	21	12	1	1	0	0	0	12	0	0	0	0	1	7	0	0	0	0	0	0	15	0	1	0

7A Killy
4E Kilmanjaro
XR Kilmarth
6R Kilmer
7P kiln-drying
6E kilo-
9H kilometerstones
8F kilowatt-hours
8F kilts
3A Kim's
4J Kimio
6A Kimmel
6A Kimmel's
7N kin-folks
7L KIND
8A kind-faced
9R kindergarteners
8C kindheartedness
XR kindlier
7R kindliest
7A kindnesses
9Q kindreds
5A kinfolks
7D KING
5Q king-maker
3P king-sized
3A kingbirds
6R kingcraft
9R Kingdom's
8D Kingfisher's
7Q kingfishers
7A kingpin
3F Kings'
4N Kingsbridge
6A kingship
3F Kingston's
4Q Kingstown
5Q Kingsville
7N Kingsworthy
7A kink
7N kinked
3P Kinnan
3A Kinndli
7D KINO'S
9L kinsfolk
9D kinsmen
7A Kinzua
6B kiosk
7N Kiouni
5A Kipling's
7R Kirgiz
4E Kirk's
6F Kirkuk
8Q Kirov
5B kirtel
7Q Kirtland's
6F Kiruna
7F Kiryat
8A Kish
9J Kismet
7P kiss'd
XH Kissenger
3F kisser
9R Kissinger's
5F Kit's
8Q Kitai

Word Type	F	D	U	SFI	3 Gr 3	4 Gr 4	5 Gr 5	6 Gr 6	7 Gr 7	8 Gr 8	9 Gr 9	X UnGr	A Read	B Eng & Gr	C Comp	D Lit	E Math	F Soc Stud	G Spell	H Sci	J Music	K Art	L Home Ec	M Shop	N Lib F	P Lib NF	Q Lib Ref	R Mag	S Rel
kitch	2	.0000	.0914	29.6	2	0	0	0	0	0	0	0	2	0	0	0	0	0	0	0	0	0	0	0	0	0	0	0	0
kitchen	497	.8549	85.435	59.3	123	112	44	60	60	54	38	6	220	26	8	34	1	21	2	15	3	4	13	2	78	46	7	17	0
Kitchen	8	.1990	.5845	37.7	7	1	0	0	0	0	0	0	7	0	0	0	0	1	0	0	0	0	0	0	0	0	0	0	0
kitchen-floor	2	.0000	.0234	23.7	0	2	0	0	0	0	0	0	0	0	0	0	0	0	0	0	0	0	0	0	2	0	0	0	0
kitchen-girl	3	.0000	.1370	31.4	3	0	0	0	0	0	0	0	3	0	0	0	0	0	0	0	0	0	0	0	0	0	0	0	0
Kitchener	2	.0000	.0209	23.2	0	0	0	0	0	2	0	0	0	0	0	0	0	0	0	0	0	0	0	0	0	0	2	0	0
kitchens	18	.4558	1.7083	42.3	1	2	2	0	4	4	4	1	0	0	0	0	1	2	2	0	0	0	6	0	2	2	1	2	0
kitchenware	2	.2160	.1362	31.3	0	1	0	1	0	0	0	0	1	0	0	0	0	0	0	1	0	0	0	0	0	0	0	0	0
kite	84	.7370	12.567	51.0	26	39	6	6	4	3	0	0	18	9	1	6	6	7	13	0	1	7	0	1	7	2	0	6	0
kites	19	.4017	1.6620	42.2	4	7	2	1	3	1	1	0	3	1	0	2	1	0	3	1	0	5	0	0	0	0	2	1	0
kits	19	.6468	2.5171	44.0	2	1	0	0	10	2	1	3	2	2	0	2	1	0	0	0	0	1	0	0	0	3	2	6	0
kitten	105	.6864	14.919	51.7	54	24	6	4	6	8	3	0	34	22	0	5	0	5	11	3	0	0	0	0	1	7	2	15	0
kittens	42	.6921	5.9887	47.8	22	9	2	3	3	3	0	0	11	11	1	2	6	2	3	2	0	0	0	0	0	4	0	0	0
kittens'	2	.0000	.0394	26.0	0	0	0	2	0	0	0	0	0	0	0	0	0	0	0	2	0	0	0	0	0	0	0	0	0
Kittery	2	.0000	.0914	29.6	0	0	0	0	2	0	0	0	2	0	0	0	0	0	0	0	0	0	0	0	0	0	0	0	0
kitty	22	.3265	2.0365	43.1	0	12	1	2	6	0	0	1	20	0	1	0	0	0	0	0	0	0	0	0	0	0	0	1	0
Kitty	32	.6911	4.6231	46.6	7	9	2	7	2	4	1	0	15	3	0	5	0	1	1	1	1	0	0	0	0	4	0	1	0
Kitty-Cat	12	.0000	.1288	31.1	0	0	0	0	12	0	0	0	0	0	0	12	0	0	0	0	0	0	0	0	0	0	0	0	0
kivas	2	.0000	.0209	23.2	0	2	0	0	0	0	0	0	0	0	0	0	0	0	0	0	0	0	0	0	0	0	2	0	0
Kivi	3	.0000	.0352	25.5	0	0	0	3	0	0	0	0	0	0	0	0	0	0	0	0	0	0	0	0	3	0	0	0	0
kiwi	2	.0000	.0209	23.2	0	0	0	0	2	0	0	0	0	0	0	0	0	0	0	0	0	0	0	0	0	0	2	0	0
Kiyago	2	.0000	.0290	24.6	0	2	0	0	0	0	0	0	0	0	0	0	0	0	0	0	0	0	0	0	0	2	0	0	0
Kiyoko	2	.0000	.0914	29.6	2	0	0	0	0	0	0	0	2	0	0	0	0	0	0	0	0	0	0	0	0	0	0	0	0
KL	4	.0000	.0599	27.8	1	0	0	1	1	1	0	0	0	0	0	0	4	0	0	0	0	0	0	0	0	0	0	0	0
Klamath	4	.0000	.0789	29.0	0	0	0	0	0	0	4	0	0	0	0	0	0	0	0	4	0	0	0	0	0	0	0	0	0
Klee's	2	.0000	.0037	15.7	1	0	0	0	0	1	0	0	0	0	0	0	0	0	0	0	0	2	0	0	0	0	0	0	0
Kleine	2	.0000	.0162	22.1	0	0	0	0	1	1	0	0	0	0	0	0	0	0	0	0	2	0	0	0	0	0	0	0	0
Klickitat	3	.1250	.1342	31.3	0	3	0	0	0	0	0	0	1	0	0	0	0	0	0	0	0	0	0	0	2	0	0	0	0
klong	2	.0000	.0914	29.6	0	0	0	0	2	0	0	0	2	0	0	0	0	0	0	0	0	0	0	0	0	0	0	0	0
Kloo-Teekl	2	.0000	.0215	23.3	0	0	0	0	0	2	0	0	0	0	0	2	0	0	0	0	0	0	0	0	0	0	0	0	0
KM	2	.0000	.0299	24.8	0	1	0	1	0	0	0	0	0	0	0	0	2	0	0	0	0	0	0	0	0	0	0	0	0
KMN	2	.0000	.0299	24.8	0	0	0	0	0	2	0	0	0	0	0	0	2	0	0	0	0	0	0	0	0	0	0	0	0
knack	8	.5317	.9072	39.6	0	2	0	1	1	2	2	0	2	2	0	0	0	0	0	0	0	0	0	1	1	1	1	0	0
knapsack	3	.2196	.1554	31.9	0	1	1	0	1	0	0	0	0	0	0	2	0	0	0	0	0	0	0	0	1	0	0	0	0
knapsacks	2	.2412	.1141	30.6	1	0	0	0	0	0	1	0	0	1	0	0	0	0	0	0	0	0	0	0	0	1	0	0	0
knave	2	.2443	.1130	30.5	0	0	0	0	1	0	1	0	0	0	0	1	0	0	0	0	0	0	0	0	1	0	0	0	0
Knave	3	.2227	.1589	32.0	0	0	2	0	0	0	0	1	0	0	0	0	0	0	0	0	0	0	0	0	2	0	0	1	0
knead	3	.3482	.2141	33.3	0	0	0	0	2	0	1	0	0	0	1	0	0	0	1	0	0	0	1	0	0	0	0	0	0
kneaded	5	.3752	.4067	36.1	1	1	1	0	2	0	0	0	0	0	0	2	0	0	0	0	0	0	0	0	0	2	1	0	0
knee	93	.7735	14.549	51.6	12	9	16	21	17	5	12	1	23	2	2	10	1	0	1	9	11	1	2	3	10	5	1	11	1
knee-deep	7	.3784	.6594	38.2	1	1	2	1	0	1	0	1	4	0	0	0	0	0	0	0	0	0	0	0	1	2	0	0	0
knee-high	2	.0000	.0914	29.6	0	0	0	1	1	0	0	0	2	0	0	0	0	0	0	0	0	0	0	0	0	0	0	0	0
kneecap	4	.2346	.2332	33.7	0	0	0	2	0	1	0	1	0	0	0	0	0	0	0	2	0	0	0	0	0	0	0	2	0
kneel	9	.5539	1.0432	40.2	1	4	1	1	0	0	2	0	1	0	0	1	0	1	0	1	3	0	0	0	0	0	1	1	0
kneeled	4	.2969	.2888	34.6	1	0	1	1	0	0	1	0	1	0	0	2	0	0	0	0	0	0	0	0	1	0	0	0	0
kneeling	14	.6019	1.8183	42.6	2	2	2	1	5	1	1	0	7	0	0	2	0	1	0	0	1	0	0	0	0	1	0	2	0
kneels	5	.4858	.5170	37.1	0	0	1	1	3	0	0	0	0	0	0	0	0	2	0	0	0	0	0	0	1	1	0	1	0
knees	213	.7455	32.516	55.1	22	50	28	30	49	15	18	1	75	2	1	30	0	3	0	17	10	6	0	0	30	31	0	8	0
knelt	59	.6951	8.5397	49.3	6	15	9	10	15	2	2	0	25	2	0	3	0	3	0	0	2	0	0	0	11	9	1	3	0
Knesset	4	.0000	.0579	27.6	0	0	4	0	0	0	0	0	0	0	0	0	0	0	0	0	0	0	0	0	0	4	0	0	0
knew	2044	.8667	355.65	65.5	379	428	266	285	350	193	126	17	914	52	17	214	16	143	18	62	24	6	4	3	258	200	22	89	2
knicht	3	.0000	.0328	25.2	0	0	0	0	0	3	0	0	0	3	0	0	0	0	0	0	0	0	0	0	0	0	0	0	0
Knickerbocker	5	.1994	.2383	33.8	0	0	0	2	0	1	2	0	0	0	2	0	0	1	0	0	0	0	0	0	0	2	0	0	0
knickers	2	.0000	.0215	23.3	0	0	0	0	1	0	1	0	0	0	0	2	0	0	0	0	0	0	0	0	0	0	0	0	0
knife	318	.8699	55.169	57.4	24	92	28	36	69	35	24	10	75	7	5	38	9	6	15	11	5	1	19	7	36	55	5	24	0
knife-edge	4	.0718	.0837	29.2	0	0	0	0	1	3	0	0	0	0	0	0	0	0	0	1	0	0	3	0	0	0	0	0	0
knight	67	.7897	10.757	50.3	7	18	4	20	14	3	1	0	24	3	0	2	1	13	2	0	2	0	0	0	3	10	2	5	0
Knight	20	.2892	1.3971	41.5	0	0	11	4	1	0	4	0	4	5	0	0	0	0	0	0	0	0	0	0	11	0	0	0	0
knight's	2	.2408	.1204	30.8	1	0	0	1	0	0	0	0	0	0	0	0	0	1	0	0	0	0	0	0	0	1	0	0	0
knighthood	5	.4138	.4637	36.7	0	1	0	2	0	1	0	1	1	0	0	0	0	1	0	0	1	0	0	0	0	0	0	2	0
knights	70	.6040	9.2282	49.7	11	15	2	28	10	4	0	0	41	0	0	0	3	10	0	0	1	0	0	0	1	9	0	5	0
Knights	11	.5247	1.2587	41.0	1	0	3	3	0	4	0	0	3	0	0	0	0	4	0	0	0	0	0	0	1	1	2	0	0
knit	29	.6403	3.7775	45.8	6	3	8	1	1	6	4	0	1	0	0	3	1	2	0	1	2	0	5	0	6	4	2	2	0
knits	6	.1349	.1977	33.0	0	0	0	0	0	0	5	1	0	0	0	0	0	0	0	1	0	0	4	0	0	0	0	1	0
knitted	21	.4182	1.9111	42.8	1	1	1	4	3	2	8	1	3	0	0	2	0	1	1	3	0	0	7	0	1	1	0	2	0
knitting	26	.6668	3.5912	45.6	9	5	3	2	4	1	2	0	6	1	0	4	0	4	0	3	0	0	1	0	6	1	0	0	0
knives	65	.7702	10.151	50.1	6	11	10	9	12	7	6	4	15	0	0	7	0	11	1	3	0	0	1	3	5	11	1	7	0
Knives	2	.0000	.0290	24.6	0	2	0	0	0	0	0	0	0	0	0	0	0	0	0	0	0	0	0	0	0	2	0	0	0
knob	47	.7495	7.1455	48.5	6	2	6	7	19	6	1	0	8	2	0	4	1	2	1	11	1	0	0	4	5	4	2	2	0
knobbed	2	.2446	.1123	30.5	1	0	0	0	1	0	0	0	0	1	0	0	0	0	0	0	0	0	0	0	0	0	1	0	0
knobbly	3	.0000	.1370	31.4	3	0	0	0	0	0	0	0	3	0	0	0	0	0	0	0	0	0	0	0	0	0	0	0	0
knobby	7	.5607	.8553	39.3	0	1	1	2	2	0	1	0	3	0	0	1	0	1	0	0	0	0	0	0	1	0	0	1	0
knobs	24	.6619	3.2558	45.1	1	2	3	4	8	2	3	1	3	0	0	0	0	2	0	5	3	0	1	2	1	1	6	0	0
knock	85	.7794	13.461	51.3	21	6	11	11	17	12	6	1	30	9	5	8	2	2	1	5	4	0	0	0	5	5	3	6	0
knockdown	2	.1814	.1187	30.7	0	0	0	1	1	0	0	0	1	0	0	0	0	0	0	0	0	0	0	0	0	0	0	1	0
knocked	139	.6699	19.591	52.9	27	30	17	16	24	22	1	2	65	1	4	15	0	8	0	6	1	0	0	0	16	14	0	8	1
knocker	5	.1835	.2274	33.6	3	0	0	1	0	0	1	0	0	0	0	1	0	0	0	0	0	0	0	0	4	0	0	0	0
knocking	48	.4298	4.7459	46.8	7	14	8	6	2	3	8	0	19	3	0	8	0	2	0	0	0	0	0	0	8	4	0	3	1
Knockmany	3	.0000	.1370	31.4	0	3	0	0	0	0	0	0	3	0	0	0	0	0	0	0	0	0	0	0	0	0	0	0	0
knocks	12	.6539	1.6278	42.1	4	1	1	1	1	4	0	0	2	0	0	1	0	2	0	2	0	0	0	0	1	3	0	1	0
knoll	11	.5901	1.3693	41.4	1	2	0	3	1	3	1	0	3	2	0	1	0	0	0	0	1	0	0	0	0	1	0	3	0
knolls	2	.2351	.1166	30.7	0	0	0	0	1	1	0	0	0	0	0	0	0	1	0	0	0	0	0	0	0	0	0	1	0
Knoop	2	.0000	.0243	23.9	0	0	0	0	0	0	0	2	0	0	0	0	0	0	0	0	0	0	0	0	0	0	0	2	0
knot	82	.7507	12.709	51.0	32	5	6	7	15	11	3	3	43	7	0	2	4	2	1	7	2	0	5	0	3	4	0	2	0
knothole	7	.0000	.3198	35.0	7	0	0	0	0	0	0	0	7	0	0	0	0	0	0	0	0	0	0	0	0	0	0	0	0
knotholes	3	.0939	.1398	31.5	0	1	0	0	0	2	0	0	2	0	0	0	0	0	0	0	0	1	0	0	0	0	0	0	0
knots	60	.8037	9.6820	49.9	9	2	6	8	13	13	8	1	10	4	0	3	8	0	3	1	4	0	0	3	3	13	5	3	0
knotted	20	.5781	2.4510	43.9	1	3	3	3	4	3	2	1	6	1	0	6	0	0	0	0	0	0	1	0	3	0	0	3	0
knotting	3	.2283	.1611	32.1	1	0	0	0	1	1	0	0	0	1	0	0	0	0	0	0	0	0	0	0	2	0	0	0	0
knotty	3	.3298	.2055	33.1	0	0	1	0	2	0	0	0	0	0	1	0	0	0	0	0	0	0	0	1	1	0	0	0	0
know	5655	.9601	1072.0	70.3	1112	1035	713	723	923	609	412	128	1675	429	51	377	494	309	163	638	181	48	57	20	480	390	71	261	11

6A kitchen-maid
7A kitchenette-furnished
7Q Kitchens
4N kite-flying
7N kited
4K Kites
7Q Kitimat
8P Kits
6A Kitt
7D Kittaniny
4F Kitten
4A kitten's
3A Kitten's
7Q Kitts
4F Kitts-Nevis-Anguilla
3A Kitty's
4Q kiva
3A kivvers
8R Kiwanis
7Q kiwis
8F Kiyo
7H Klaproth
6A klaxons
3K Klee
8B kleenex
3A Kleenex
8E Klein
7H Kleitman
XR klepto
8H Klien
8E Kline
9E Kline's
6R Klinger
7R Kloman
6A klompen
5Q Klondike
8D Kloo-teekl
5G kloun
4H klunk
9Q klystron
5G kn
8E KN
4P Knapp
6N knaves
8B kne
4B kneader
4B kneads
5H knee-jerk
3F knee-length
6N knee'd
9B Kneeaz
5H kneecaps
3A kneed
7A kneepads
5P knell
7P knicker
6P knickerbocker
7P knickers'
8E knife-axe
7R knife-sharp
9D knifed
8A knifes
9N knifing
8D knight-errant
9Q knighted
7F knighting
6F knightly
6N Knightrider
6A knights'
6B Knit
5N knitter
8Q Knjizevnost
5Q knob-kneed
9H knoblike
7R knock-back
9R knock-kneed
5H knock-knees
9R knockabout
7A knockouts
XR Knopf
8E Knot
5A knot-tying
3A Knots
6A knottings

Word Type	F	D	U	SFI	3 Gr 3	4 Gr 4	5 Gr 5	6 Gr 6	7 Gr 7	8 Gr 8	9 Gr 9	X UnGr	A Read	B Eng & Gr	C Comp	D Lit	E Math	F Soc Stud	G Spell	H Sci	J Music	K Art	L Home Ec	M Shop	N Lib F	P Lib NF	Q Lib Ref	R Mag	S Rel
Know	22	.0171	.2864	34.6	0	2	8	4	8	0	0	0	1	0	0	0	0	0	21	0	0	0	0	0	0	0	0	0	0
Know-Nothing	2	.0000	.0243	23.9	0	0	0	0	0	0	0	2	0	0	0	0	0	0	0	0	0	0	0	0	0	0	0	2	0
know-how	9	.3452	.7145	38.5	0	0	0	0	5	4	0	0	1	0	0	0	0	4	0	0	0	0	2	0	0	2	0	0	0
knowed	22	.4061	1.9472	42.9	0	4	1	1	8	7	1	0	2	3	0	4	0	0	0	0	0	0	0	0	12	1	0	0	0
knoweth	2	.0000	.0290	24.6	1	0	1	0	0	0	0	0	0	0	0	0	0	0	0	0	0	0	0	0	0	2	0	0	0
knowin'	4	.3065	.2965	34.7	0	0	1	0	2	1	0	0	1	1	0	0	0	0	0	0	0	0	0	0	2	0	0	0	0
knowing	249	.9063	44.889	56.5	15	32	45	31	56	33	28	9	82	28	3	21	6	12	12	18	3	2	10	1	21	16	2	12	0
knowingly	7	.3814	.6017	37.8	1	0	2	0	4	0	0	0	1	0	0	0	0	1	0	0	0	0	0	0	3	0	0	2	0
knowledge	424	.8889	74.876	58.7	8	21	36	54	104	85	105	11	55	28	6	14	16	49	6	70	10	12	12	18	7	27	72	22	0
known	1401	.9313	258.18	64.1	86	134	169	202	362	239	153	56	203	36	7	58	38	197	12	264	88	11	17	34	49	94	211	81	1
knows	505	.9488	94.771	59.8	104	86	49	72	100	41	43	10	166	26	8	37	11	37	9	45	17	4	6	3	29	56	15	36	0
Knows	2	.2411	.1091	30.4	0	0	1	0	1	0	0	0	0	0	0	1	0	0	0	0	1	0	0	0	0	0	0	0	0
Knox	9	.4677	.9498	39.8	1	1	1	1	3	1	1	0	3	0	0	0	0	3	0	0	0	0	0	0	0	0	1	2	0
knuckle	5	.4611	.4785	36.8	1	2	0	0	1	1	0	0	0	0	1	1	0	0	1	0	0	0	0	0	1	1	0	0	0
knuckles	15	.3311	1.2271	40.9	1	1	0	0	10	2	1	0	6	0	0	7	0	0	0	0	0	0	0	0	1	1	0	0	0
knurled	3	.0000	.0076	18.8	0	0	0	0	0	2	1	0	0	0	0	0	0	0	0	0	0	0	0	3	0	0	0	0	0
knurling	3	.0000	.0076	18.8	0	0	0	0	0	3	0	0	0	0	0	0	0	0	0	0	0	0	0	3	0	0	0	0	0
Knut	12	.3850	1.1636	40.7	0	0	0	0	2	8	2	0	8	0	0	2	0	0	0	0	0	0	0	0	0	2	0	0	0
Knute	2	.1733	.1149	30.6	0	0	0	2	0	0	0	0	1	1	0	0	0	0	0	0	0	0	0	0	0	0	0	0	0
Ko-Ko	13	.0000	.1051	30.2	0	0	0	0	0	13	0	0	0	0	0	0	0	0	0	0	13	0	0	0	0	0	0	0	0
Ko-Ngai	4	.0000	.0469	26.7	0	4	0	0	0	0	0	0	0	0	0	0	0	0	0	0	0	0	0	0	4	0	0	0	0
koala	3	.2239	.1775	32.5	0	2	1	0	0	0	0	0	0	0	0	0	0	2	0	1	0	0	0	0	0	0	0	0	0
Kobi	31	.0000	1.4162	41.5	20	11	0	0	0	0	0	0	31	0	0	0	0	0	0	0	0	0	0	0	0	0	0	0	0
Kobi's	4	.0000	.1827	32.6	3	1	0	0	0	0	0	0	4	0	0	0	0	0	0	0	0	0	0	0	0	0	0	0	0
Kobo	20	.0000	.9137	39.6	20	0	0	0	0	0	0	0	20	0	0	0	0	0	0	0	0	0	0	0	0	0	0	0	0
Kobuk	2	.0000	.0243	23.9	0	0	0	2	0	0	0	0	0	0	0	0	0	0	0	0	0	0	0	0	0	0	0	2	0
Koch	9	.1719	.4433	36.5	0	0	4	0	0	0	1	4	0	0	0	0	0	0	0	8	0	0	0	0	0	0	1	0	0
Koch's	5	.0000	.0986	29.9	0	0	3	0	0	0	0	2	0	0	0	0	0	0	0	5	0	0	0	0	0	0	0	0	0
Kodaly	5	.0000	.0404	26.1	1	2	0	1	0	1	0	0	0	0	0	0	0	0	0	0	5	0	0	0	0	0	0	0	0
Kodiak	3	.3350	.2478	33.9	0	1	1	0	1	0	0	0	1	0	0	0	0	1	0	0	0	0	0	0	0	0	1	0	0
Koelle	2	.0000	.0209	23.2	0	0	0	0	0	0	2	0	0	0	0	0	0	0	0	0	0	0	0	0	0	0	2	0	0
Koenigsberg	6	.0000	.0898	29.5	0	0	0	0	0	6	0	0	0	0	0	0	6	0	0	0	0	0	0	0	0	0	0	0	0
Kogler	2	.0000	.0209	23.2	0	0	0	0	2	0	0	0	0	0	0	0	0	0	0	0	0	0	0	0	0	0	2	0	0
Kogler's	2	.0000	.0209	23.2	0	0	0	0	2	0	0	0	0	0	0	0	0	0	0	0	0	0	0	0	0	0	2	0	0
Kohara	2	.0000	.0209	23.2	0	0	0	0	0	0	2	0	0	0	0	0	0	0	0	0	0	0	0	0	0	0	2	0	0
Kokichi	3	.0000	.0583	27.7	0	3	0	0	0	0	0	0	0	0	0	0	0	3	0	0	0	0	0	0	0	0	0	0	0
kolo	2	.2417	.1091	30.4	0	0	0	1	0	1	0	0	0	0	0	0	0	0	0	0	1	0	0	0	0	0	1	0	0
Kon	3	.0000	.0591	27.7	0	3	0	0	0	0	0	0	0	0	0	0	0	0	0	3	0	0	0	0	0	0	0	0	0
Kon-Tiki	17	.3455	1.4739	41.7	0	0	0	4	4	7	2	0	8	0	0	2	0	0	0	0	0	0	0	0	0	7	0	0	0
Kon-Tiki's	2	.1948	.1250	31.0	0	0	0	0	1	1	0	0	1	0	0	0	0	0	0	0	0	0	0	0	0	1	0	0	0
Kong	6	.1639	.3347	35.2	0	3	1	1	1	0	0	0	2	0	0	0	0	4	0	0	0	0	0	0	0	0	0	0	0
Koni	4	.0000	.0486	26.9	0	0	0	0	4	0	0	0	0	0	0	0	0	0	0	0	0	0	0	0	0	0	0	4	0
Konigsberg	2	.0000	.0394	26.0	0	0	0	0	2	0	0	0	0	0	0	0	0	0	0	2	0	0	0	0	0	0	0	0	0
Konrad	5	.3834	.4164	36.2	0	0	0	1	1	2	0	1	0	0	1	0	0	0	0	2	0	0	0	0	0	0	1	1	0
konsepsi	2	.0000	.0209	23.2	0	0	0	0	0	2	0	0	0	0	0	0	0	0	0	0	0	0	0	0	0	0	2	0	0
Koodoo	4	.0000	.0469	26.7	0	4	0	0	0	0	0	0	0	0	0	0	0	0	0	0	0	0	0	0	4	0	0	0	0
Kook	2	.0000	.0243	23.9	0	0	0	0	0	0	0	2	0	0	0	0	0	0	0	0	0	0	0	0	0	0	0	2	0
kookaburra	4	.3270	.3194	35.0	1	0	0	3	0	0	0	0	1	0	0	0	0	2	0	0	1	0	0	0	0	0	0	0	0
Kookie	2	.0000	.0914	29.6	0	0	0	2	0	0	0	0	2	0	0	0	0	0	0	0	0	0	0	0	0	0	0	0	0
kooky	2	.0000	.0243	23.9	0	1	1	0	0	0	0	0	0	0	0	0	0	0	0	0	0	0	0	0	0	0	0	2	0
Koom	15	.0000	.6852	38.4	0	0	0	15	0	0	0	0	15	0	0	0	0	0	0	0	0	0	0	0	0	0	0	0	0
Koons	2	.0000	.0394	26.0	0	0	0	0	0	0	0	2	0	0	0	0	0	0	0	2	0	0	0	0	0	0	0	0	0
Koophuis	6	.3408	.4953	36.9	0	0	0	0	0	4	2	0	2	0	0	2	0	0	0	0	0	0	0	0	0	2	0	0	0
Koopman	4	.0000	.0486	26.9	0	0	0	4	0	0	0	0	0	0	0	0	0	0	0	0	0	0	0	0	0	0	0	4	0
Koran	4	.2152	.2714	34.3	0	0	2	0	2	0	0	0	2	0	0	0	0	2	0	0	0	0	0	0	0	0	0	0	0
Korea	39	.4620	3.8862	45.9	0	6	4	16	6	1	6	0	2	1	0	0	0	15	0	0	2	0	0	0	0	1	1	17	0
Korea's	2	.0000	.0243	23.9	0	0	0	2	0	0	0	0	0	0	0	0	0	0	0	0	0	0	0	0	0	0	0	2	0
Korean	13	.3385	.9676	39.9	0	4	0	3	1	2	3	0	0	0	0	0	0	1	0	0	2	0	0	0	0	0	1	9	0
Korth	2	.0000	.0914	29.6	0	2	0	0	0	0	0	0	2	0	0	0	0	0	0	0	0	0	0	0	0	0	0	0	0
Kosciusko	4	.3805	.3414	35.3	0	1	1	2	0	0	0	0	0	0	0	0	1	2	0	0	0	0	0	0	0	1	0	0	0
koto	4	.0000	.0323	25.1	0	2	0	0	2	0	0	0	0	0	0	0	0	0	0	0	4	0	0	0	0	0	0	0	0
Kouan-Yu	3	.0000	.0352	25.5	0	3	0	0	0	0	0	0	0	0	0	0	0	0	0	0	0	0	0	0	3	0	0	0	0
Koufax	9	.3465	.6911	38.4	5	0	0	1	2	0	1	0	0	1	0	0	0	0	0	0	0	0	0	0	0	5	0	3	0
kraal	3	.0000	.1370	31.4	0	0	0	3	0	0	0	0	3	0	0	0	0	0	0	0	0	0	0	0	0	0	0	0	0
Krakow	4	.3465	.3040	34.8	0	0	3	1	0	0	0	0	0	0	0	0	0	1	0	0	1	0	0	0	0	0	2	0	0
Kraler	5	.1634	.2733	34.4	0	0	0	0	0	5	0	0	2	0	0	0	0	0	0	0	0	0	0	0	0	3	0	0	0
Kranz	8	.0000	.0972	29.9	8	0	0	0	0	0	0	0	0	0	0	0	0	0	0	0	0	0	0	0	0	0	0	8	0
Kremlin	7	.2210	.3873	35.9	0	0	0	3	2	2	0	0	0	0	0	0	0	3	0	0	0	0	0	0	0	0	0	4	0
krill	7	.2412	.4224	36.3	0	0	0	5	2	0	0	0	0	0	0	0	0	0	0	5	0	0	0	0	0	0	2	0	0
Kris	2	.0000	.0299	24.8	0	0	0	0	2	0	0	0	0	0	0	0	2	0	0	0	0	0	0	0	0	0	0	0	0
Krishna	19	.1742	1.3382	41.3	1	17	0	0	0	1	0	0	18	0	0	0	0	0	0	0	0	0	0	0	0	0	1	0	0
Krishna's	3	.0000	.1370	31.4	0	3	0	0	0	0	0	0	3	0	0	0	0	0	0	0	0	0	0	0	0	0	0	0	0
Krispy-Krackles	3	.0000	.1370	31.4	0	0	0	3	0	0	0	0	3	0	0	0	0	0	0	0	0	0	0	0	0	0	0	0	0
Kristy	5	.0000	.0748	28.7	0	5	0	0	0	0	0	0	0	0	0	0	5	0	0	0	0	0	0	0	0	0	0	0	0
Kriternerk	10	.0000	.4568	36.6	0	0	10	0	0	0	0	0	10	0	0	0	0	0	0	0	0	0	0	0	0	0	0	0	0
Kroger	2	.0000	.0389	25.9	0	2	0	0	0	0	0	0	0	0	0	0	0	2	0	0	0	0	0	0	0	0	0	0	0
Krogers	4	.0000	.0778	28.9	0	4	0	0	0	0	0	0	0	0	0	0	0	4	0	0	0	0	0	0	0	0	0	0	0
Krolugta	8	.0000	.3655	35.6	0	0	8	0	0	0	0	0	8	0	0	0	0	0	0	0	0	0	0	0	0	0	0	0	0
Kronborg	2	.0000	.0209	23.2	2	0	0	0	0	0	0	0	0	0	0	0	0	0	0	0	0	0	0	0	0	0	2	0	0
Kruesi	8	.0000	.3655	35.6	0	0	8	0	0	0	0	0	8	0	0	0	0	0	0	0	0	0	0	0	0	0	0	0	0
Kruger	3	.0000	.0314	25.0	0	0	0	0	3	0	0	0	0	0	0	0	0	0	0	0	0	0	0	0	0	0	3	0	0
Krumm	3	.0000	.1370	31.4	3	0	0	0	0	0	0	0	3	0	0	0	0	0	0	0	0	0	0	0	0	0	0	0	0
Kruper	2	.0000	.0215	23.3	0	0	0	0	2	0	0	0	0	0	0	2	0	0	0	0	0	0	0	0	0	0	0	0	0
Kruper's	2	.1717	.1142	30.6	0	0	0	0	2	0	0	0	1	0	0	1	0	0	0	0	0	0	0	0	0	0	0	0	0
kryos	2	.2278	.1128	30.5	0	0	0	0	1	0	1	0	0	0	0	0	0	0	0	1	0	0	0	0	0	0	1	0	0
krypton	4	.2353	.2382	33.8	0	0	1	0	2	1	0	0	0	0	0	0	0	0	0	3	0	0	0	0	0	0	1	0	0
ks	7	.0000	.0568	27.5	2	1	2	1	0	1	0	0	0	0	0	0	0	0	7	0	0	0	0	0	0	0	0	0	0

XR Know-Nothings
8P know-alls
8A know's
5P knowledgeable
9B Knowles
3P knowns
3P knowworm
5F Knoxville
6Q KNO3
8R Knuckler
6A knucklers
5A knuckling
7M knurl
4N Ko-Nagi
4F koala's
4F koalas
4P Kobas
3A Kobo's
9A Kochendorfer
4P Kochersperger
4D kochokochokocho
4J Kodaly's
7R Kodiak-bear-class
7Q Koehler
4P Koeppen
7R Kogaku
7H Kogan
9H koh-per-ni-kus
9Q Kohara's
8Q Kohistan
XR Kohl's
4Q Koldewey
4N Kolokolo
9B komatics
3A komiks
4R kongoni
7R Koni-Stahl
8Q Koodoesberg
7R kooks
8D Kool-Aid
6R Koolau
8Q Koornheert
9F Kopechne
5A Koponen
7D Koppelberg
3J Kopylow
7D Koquaeunquas
6D Korbes
9R Koreans
8R Korianinen
6A Korn
5R Korner
6R Kororareka
4Q Korps
XB Korrect
7P Korson
5F kortez'**
9D Kortschagins
7F Kosice
5N Kossie
8Q Kotah
4F Kotoku
8Q Kotri
6R Kotzebue
3P Koufax's
7P kouloungoulou
5P Kourou
8J Koussevitsky
5Q Koussevitzky
7R Koy
7D Koyo
8E KPM
5E KPQL
8Q Kqq'/r2**
6G kr
7P Krachi
7B Kraft
8E Kraitchik
7Q Krakatoa
8P Kraler's
3R Kranz's
6A Krasnin
8H Krause
5Q Krefeld
7J Kreisler
8R Kremlin's
8J Krenek
8R kreplach
6N Kreutznaer
7E KRG
7D Krieger
9R Krishnas
6A Krisps
5A Kristen
5G kro
4F Krogers'
5G krol
7A kroner
8Q Krsinic
6A Kruger's
7D Kruif
8Q Krym
7D Kschippihelleu
4Q Kshatriyas

Word Type	F	D	U	SFI	3 Gr 3	4 Gr 4	5 Gr 5	6 Gr 6	7 Gr 7	8 Gr 8	9 Gr 9	X UnGr	A Read	B Eng & Gr	C Comp	D Lit	E Math	F Soc Stud	G Spell	H Sci	J Music	K Art	L Home Ec	M Shop	N Lib F	P Lib NF	Q Lib Ref	R Mag	S Rel
Ku	5	.0000	.0724	28.6	5	0	0	0	0	0	0	0	0	0	0	0	0	0	0	0	0	0	0	0	0	5	0	0	0
Kuassi	2	.0000	.0243	23.9	2	0	0	0	0	0	0	0	0	0	0	0	0	0	0	0	0	0	0	0	0	0	0	2	0
Kublai	5	.3734	.4048	36.1	0	0	4	0	1	0	0	0	0	0	0	1	0	0	0	0	0	0	0	0	0	2	2	0	0
Kuiper	2	.0000	.0209	23.2	0	0	0	0	2	0	0	0	0	0	0	0	0	0	0	0	0	0	0	0	0	0	2	0	0
Kul	6	.0000	.2741	34.4	6	0	0	0	0	0	0	0	6	0	0	0	0	0	0	0	0	0	0	0	0	0	0	0	0
Kul's	2	.0000	.0914	29.6	2	0	0	0	0	0	0	0	2	0	0	0	0	0	0	0	0	0	0	0	0	0	0	0	0
Kula	2	.0000	.0290	24.6	2	0	0	0	0	0	0	0	0	0	0	0	0	0	0	0	0	0	0	0	0	2	0	0	0
Kullak	2	.0000	.0162	22.1	2	0	0	0	0	0	0	0	0	0	0	0	0	0	0	0	2	0	0	0	0	0	0	0	0
Kum	4	.0000	.0323	25.1	4	0	0	0	0	0	0	0	0	0	0	0	0	0	0	0	4	0	0	0	0	0	0	0	0
Kuma	5	.0000	.2284	33.6	5	0	0	0	0	0	0	0	5	0	0	0	0	0	0	0	0	0	0	0	0	0	0	0	0
kun	4	.0000	.0469	26.7	0	4	0	0	0	0	0	0	0	0	0	0	0	0	0	0	0	0	0	0	4	0	0	0	0
Kurdish	2	.2446	.1123	30.5	0	1	0	0	1	0	0	0	0	1	0	0	0	0	0	0	0	0	0	0	0	0	1	0	0
Kurds	2	.0000	.0389	25.9	0	0	0	2	0	0	0	0	0	0	0	0	0	2	0	0	0	0	0	0	0	0	0	0	0
Kurt	5	.4132	.4634	36.7	0	0	0	1	1	3	0	0	1	0	0	0	0	0	0	1	1	0	0	0	0	0	0	2	0
Kurtis	2	.0000	.0290	24.6	0	0	0	0	0	0	0	2	0	0	0	0	0	0	0	0	0	0	0	0	0	2	0	0	0
kuwa	2	.0000	.0389	25.9	0	2	0	0	0	0	0	0	0	0	0	0	0	2	0	0	0	0	0	0	0	0	0	0	0
Kuwait	8	.1622	.3487	35.4	0	0	0	5	1	0	2	0	0	0	0	0	0	2	0	0	0	0	0	0	0	0	0	6	0
Kuwi	8	.0000	.1556	31.9	0	0	0	0	0	8	0	0	0	0	0	0	0	8	0	0	0	0	0	0	0	0	0	0	0
Kvidal	2	.0000	.0290	24.6	0	0	0	0	2	0	0	0	0	0	0	0	0	0	0	0	0	0	0	0	0	2	0	0	0
kw	22	.0171	.2864	34.6	0	6	8	4	2	2	0	0	1	0	0	0	0	0	21	0	0	0	0	0	0	0	0	0	0
Kwaku	7	.0000	.3198	35.0	7	0	0	0	0	0	0	0	7	0	0	0	0	0	0	0	0	0	0	0	0	0	0	0	0
kwashiorkor	3	.0000	.0591	27.7	0	0	0	0	3	0	0	0	0	0	0	0	0	0	0	3	0	0	0	0	0	0	0	0	0
Ky	4	.3647	.3180	35.0	0	0	0	2	2	0	0	0	0	0	0	0	0	0	0	0	0	0	0	0	0	1	1	2	0
Kya	5	.0000	.2284	33.6	0	0	0	5	0	0	0	0	5	0	0	0	0	0	0	0	0	0	0	0	0	0	0	0	0
Kyklops	3	.0000	.0322	25.1	0	0	0	0	0	0	3	0	0	0	0	3	0	0	0	0	0	0	0	0	0	0	0	0	0
kyklos	2	.1497	.1046	30.2	0	0	0	1	1	0	0	0	1	0	0	0	0	0	1	0	0	0	0	0	0	0	0	0	0
Kyoto	5	.3081	.3943	36.0	0	1	2	0	0	2	0	0	2	0	0	2	0	1	0	0	0	0	0	0	0	0	0	0	0
Kyrios	5	.0000	.2284	33.6	0	5	0	0	0	0	0	0	5	0	0	0	0	0	0	0	0	0	0	0	0	0	0	0	0
Kyushu	3	.0000	.0583	27.7	0	3	0	0	0	0	0	0	0	0	0	0	0	3	0	0	0	0	0	0	0	0	0	0	0
K3	3	.0000	.0322	25.1	0	0	0	0	0	3	0	0	0	0	0	3	0	0	0	0	0	0	0	0	0	0	0	0	0
l	226	.3929	19.262	52.8	22	23	39	24	70	29	18	1	14	7	0	2	84	0	108	0	3	1	0	0	0	0	0	7	0
L	99	.7776	15.480	51.9	2	15	24	12	21	14	5	6	8	6	2	1	39	6	0	5	1	2	2	0	0	5	11	11	0
L**	11	.0000	.1647	32.2	0	0	0	0	6	2	3	0	0	0	0	0	11	0	0	0	0	0	0	0	0	0	0	0	0
l-l-lad	3	.0000	.0352	25.5	0	0	0	3	0	0	0	0	0	0	0	0	0	0	0	0	0	0	0	0	3	0	0	0	0
L'Enfant	3	.1937	.1495	31.7	0	0	1	0	2	0	0	0	0	0	0	0	0	1	0	0	0	0	0	0	0	0	0	2	0
L'Heure	2	.2303	.1079	30.3	0	0	0	1	1	0	0	0	0	0	0	0	0	0	0	0	1	0	0	0	0	1	0	0	0
l's	4	.2744	.2686	34.3	0	2	1	0	1	0	0	0	1	1	0	0	0	0	2	0	0	0	0	0	0	0	0	0	0
la	91	.1610	3.6238	45.6	8	14	3	37	12	10	6	1	3	2	0	0	0	0	0	0	77	0	0	0	0	2	5	2	0
La	44	.5681	5.1827	47.1	3	1	7	15	6	7	2	3	3	0	0	1	0	9	0	0	16	2	0	0	0	8	3	2	0
LaBrea	2	.0000	.0914	29.6	0	0	2	0	0	0	0	0	2	0	0	0	0	0	0	0	0	0	0	0	0	0	0	0	0
LaCenter	2	.0000	.0243	23.9	0	0	0	0	2	0	0	0	0	0	0	0	0	0	0	0	0	0	0	0	0	0	0	2	0
LaFollette	2	.2152	.1357	31.3	0	0	0	0	1	1	0	0	1	0	0	0	0	1	0	0	0	0	0	0	0	0	0	0	0
LaFontaine	2	.1698	.1133	30.5	0	0	1	0	0	1	0	0	1	0	0	0	0	0	0	0	0	0	0	0	0	0	1	0	0
LaGuardia	2	.2437	.1129	30.5	0	1	0	0	1	0	0	0	0	0	0	0	0	0	0	0	0	0	0	0	0	0	1	1	0
LaPorte	6	.0000	.0729	28.6	0	0	0	0	0	0	6	0	0	0	0	0	0	0	0	0	0	0	0	0	0	0	0	6	0
LaRabida	6	.0000	.2741	34.4	0	0	6	0	0	0	0	0	6	0	0	0	0	0	0	0	0	0	0	0	0	0	0	0	0
LaSalle	16	.2753	1.0728	40.3	0	0	12	0	3	1	0	0	0	0	0	0	0	13	0	0	0	0	0	0	0	0	2	1	0
LaVerne	14	.0337	.2842	34.5	0	0	0	0	13	1	0	0	1	0	0	0	0	0	0	0	0	0	0	0	13	0	0	0	0
la-la-de-da	2	.0000	.0234	23.7	0	2	0	0	0	0	0	0	0	0	0	0	0	0	0	0	0	0	0	0	2	0	0	0	0
lab	16	.5325	1.8195	42.6	0	2	1	4	2	0	6	1	4	0	1	0	0	0	0	0	0	0	0	0	3	0	4	4	0
Lab	2	.0000	.0243	23.9	2	0	0	0	0	0	0	0	0	0	0	0	0	0	0	0	0	0	0	0	0	0	0	2	0
Labadie	7	.1560	.3699	35.7	0	4	0	3	0	0	0	0	3	0	0	0	0	0	0	0	0	0	0	0	4	0	0	0	0
label	184	.6476	24.486	53.9	15	30	18	17	31	41	26	6	12	13	0	1	97	16	5	19	1	0	9	1	1	1	4	4	0
labeled	98	.6761	13.517	51.3	4	12	10	5	14	25	25	3	4	4	0	0	40	16	3	10	2	0	8	0	1	2	3	5	0
labeling	11	.4957	1.1564	40.6	0	0	0	0	3	2	6	0	0	0	0	0	5	3	0	1	0	0	1	0	0	0	0	1	0
labelled	3	.1983	.1396	31.4	0	0	0	0	3	0	0	0	0	0	0	0	0	0	0	0	2	0	0	0	0	0	0	1	0
labelling	2	.0000	.0162	22.1	0	0	0	0	2	0	0	0	0	0	0	0	0	0	0	0	2	0	0	0	0	0	0	0	0
labels	46	.5754	5.4699	47.4	1	3	4	1	13	14	9	1	4	13	1	0	2	2	0	8	1	1	11	0	0	0	2	1	0
labor	164	.7435	24.659	53.9	9	5	18	10	50	37	33	2	11	1	2	8	1	64	3	1	4	0	2	1	0	11	35	20	0
Labor	26	.4439	2.4635	43.9	6	0	7	0	6	2	3	2	0	0	0	0	0	3	0	0	0	0	0	0	0	11	7	5	0
Labor-Management	2	.0000	.0209	23.2	0	0	1	0	1	0	0	0	0	0	0	0	0	0	0	0	0	0	0	0	0	0	2	0	0
labor-saving	7	.2867	.4915	36.9	0	1	3	3	0	0	0	0	1	0	0	3	0	3	0	0	0	0	0	0	0	0	0	0	0
laboratories	45	.6104	5.7311	47.6	2	0	8	13	6	4	8	4	5	2	0	0	1	0	0	21	0	0	1	0	0	2	8	5	0
Laboratories	2	.1698	.1133	30.5	0	0	1	0	0	1	0	0	1	0	0	0	0	0	0	0	0	0	0	0	0	0	1	0	0
laboratory	138	.7325	20.623	53.1	8	14	10	23	21	19	28	15	23	6	0	2	2	10	0	54	1	0	2	3	2	2	25	6	0
Laboratory	16	.4445	1.5347	41.9	0	0	1	3	7	1	4	0	2	0	0	0	0	0	0	1	0	0	0	1	0	1	9	2	0
labored	11	.4819	1.1695	40.7	0	0	0	4	4	2	1	0	4	0	2	0	0	1	0	0	0	1	0	0	1	1	0	1	0
laborer	8	.5066	.8706	39.4	0	0	1	0	3	2	2	0	1	0	0	2	0	3	0	0	0	0	0	0	0	1	1	0	0
laborers	21	.6986	2.9984	44.8	2	3	3	3	3	4	3	0	3	1	1	0	1	6	1	0	1	0	0	0	0	3	4	0	0
laboring	7	.4418	.7128	38.5	1	0	1	0	3	2	0	0	3	0	0	1	0	1	0	0	0	0	0	0	0	0	2	0	0
laborious	4	.2278	.2257	33.5	0	0	0	0	3	0	0	1	0	0	0	0	0	0	0	2	0	0	0	0	0	0	2	0	0
laboriously	7	.4357	.6841	38.4	0	1	1	0	4	1	0	0	2	0	0	0	0	0	0	0	0	0	0	0	2	1	2	0	0
labors	7	.5590	.8537	39.3	0	0	1	0	2	3	1	0	3	0	0	1	0	1	0	0	0	0	0	0	0	1	1	0	0
laborsaving	2	.2285	.1129	30.5	0	0	0	0	1	0	1	0	0	0	0	0	0	1	0	0	0	0	0	0	0	0	1	0	0
labour	14	.4741	1.4042	41.5	1	0	0	7	1	0	4	1	1	0	1	2	0	0	0	0	0	0	0	0	8	1	0	1	0
Labrador	32	.6270	4.2623	46.3	0	3	8	9	8	1	2	1	12	1	0	0	0	2	0	8	0	0	0	0	4	0	4	1	0
Labs	2	.0000	.0243	23.9	0	0	0	0	2	0	0	0	0	0	0	0	0	0	0	0	0	0	0	0	0	0	0	2	0
labyrinths	2	.1473	.0686	28.4	0	0	0	0	0	0	2	0	0	0	0	1	0	0	0	0	0	1	0	0	0	0	0	0	0
lac	2	.0000	.0209	23.2	0	0	2	0	0	0	0	0	0	0	0	0	0	0	0	0	0	0	0	0	0	0	2	0	0
Lac	2	.2401	.1133	30.5	1	0	1	0	0	0	0	0	0	0	0	0	0	0	0	0	0	0	0	0	0	1	1	0	0
lace	62	.6395	8.1434	49.1	16	5	5	8	14	3	10	1	12	0	0	1	2	4	3	2	9	1	7	11	7	1	1	1	0
laced	15	.5192	1.6387	42.1	1	4	1	3	4	1	1	0	2	0	0	1	0	0	0	0	0	0	0	2	6	1	2	1	0
Lacedemon	2	.0000	.0215	23.3	0	0	0	0	0	0	2	0	0	0	0	2	0	0	0	0	0	0	0	0	0	0	0	0	0
laces	11	.5084	1.1775	40.7	4	1	0	2	0	1	3	0	2	0	0	1	0	0	0	0	1	1	3	0	2	1	0	0	0
Lachine	2	.0000	.0389	25.9	0	0	2	0	0	0	0	0	0	0	0	0	0	2	0	0	0	0	0	0	0	0	0	0	0
Lachish	3	.0000	.0583	27.7	0	0	0	0	3	0	0	0	0	0	0	0	0	3	0	0	0	0	0	0	0	0	0	0	0
lacing	9	.2118	.4577	36.6	1	1	0	0	5	1	1	0	1	0	0	0	0	0	0	0	0	0	0	4	3	1	0	0	0
lack	193	.8262	31.983	55.0	7	7	22	19	53	32	45	8	31	6	3	11	1	36	0	33	4	0	10	0	5	13	21	19	0

3P Ku's
3P Kubek
5B Kubie
XR Kuchel
7C Kuching
XR kudo
XP Kuei
6A Kukupi
5G kul
6R Kullyspell
7G kum
8D Kumba
4F Kunari
9R Kundera
9R Kundera's
6F Kung
6A Kunming
8Q Kunsthistorisches
XR Kupperman
7R Kurdistan
4F Kure
7Q Kuriles
8Q Kurland
7Q Kush
8Q Kutch
6R Kutenais
6R Kuwait's
6R Kuwaitis
9F Kuznetsk
8D kvas
7P Kvidal's
8F Kwai
5R Kwame
3P ky-yi
9D Kyklops'
XR Kylmerth
3A Kypros
7J Kyrie
4A Kyrios's
5A l-a-u-g-h
7R L-e-r-o-y
4P l-l-let's
4A l-lady
5H L-shape
6N L-shaped
3B L-50
7R L-88
5Q l'Abbe
8Q L'Academie
5Q L'Ami
5P l'Avenir
4K L'Avion
5P l'Ecole
5B L'Engle
5P l'Espoir
5P l'Harmonie
7A l'Orient
7A l'Orient's
5F L'Ouverture
XB l'anglaise
3R l'ile
3A LA
4A LaBahia
5F LaChine
8Q LaFilleMalCardee
8A LaFontaine's
6A LaJolla
7N LaLongue
5A LaMesa
6F LaPlata
9R LaPorte's
6R LaRoche's
9J la-ah
6A la-dee-da
8C la-di-da
9Q lab's
7B labboard
5Q labella
5K labo
8F labor-degrading
5Q labor-management
9R labor-relations
8F labor's
6A laboratory's
5P Laborites
7Q Labourer
5N labours
5A Labrador's
6A Labradors
7N labre
7N labres
7R labs
5P labyrinth
7Q Lacandon
XR lace-and-carnation
9D lace-curtain-Irish
8K lace-like
3Q lacemaking
7N lacerations
7Q Lacerta
7Q lacertas
7A lackadaisical

Word Type	F	D	U	SFI	3 Gr 3	4 Gr 4	5 Gr 5	6 Gr 6	7 Gr 7	8 Gr 8	9 Gr 9	X UnGr	A Read	B Eng & Gr	C Comp	D Lit	E Math	F Soc Stud	G Spell	H Sci	J Music	K Art	L Home Ec	M Shop	N Lib F	P Lib NF	Q Lib Ref	R Mag	S Rel
lacked	43	.8180	7.0336	48.5	0	2	6	6	15	8	4	2	3	1	0	2	0	10	0	2	1	1	1	1	2	3	8	8	0
lacking	32	.7055	4.6215	46.6	0	2	5	6	10	1	7	1	6	0	0	2	0	5	1	4	0	0	1	0	1	1	9	2	0
lacks	24	.6866	3.3646	45.3	2	1	3	3	10	2	2	1	2	1	0	0	0	7	0	1	1	0	1	0	0	2	3	6	0
laconic	5	.4662	.5247	37.2	0	0	1	1	1	1	1	0	2	0	0	1	0	0	1	0	0	0	0	0	0	1	0	0	0
lacquer	35	.2759	2.0379	43.1	0	0	4	1	21	2	1	6	0	0	0	1	0	0	0	0	0	3	0	21	0	2	1	7	0
lacquered	4	.2094	.2127	33.3	0	2	0	1	0	1	0	0	0	0	0	0	0	3	0	0	0	0	0	1	0	0	0	0	0
lacrosse	8	.2110	.5379	37.3	0	0	1	4	3	0	0	0	5	3	0	0	0	0	0	0	0	0	0	0	0	0	0	0	0
Lacrosse	3	.0000	.0328	25.2	0	0	0	0	3	0	0	0	0	3	0	0	0	0	0	0	0	0	0	0	0	0	0	0	0
lactation	2	.0000	.0394	26.0	0	0	0	0	0	0	0	2	0	0	0	0	0	0	0	2	0	0	0	0	0	0	0	0	0
lactic	3	.0000	.0591	27.7	0	1	0	0	0	0	2	0	0	0	0	0	0	0	0	3	0	0	0	0	0	0	0	0	0
lactose	4	.0000	.0789	29.0	0	0	0	0	4	0	0	0	0	0	0	0	0	0	0	4	0	0	0	0	0	0	0	0	0
lacy	6	.3702	.5104	37.1	0	1	1	2	1	1	0	0	1	1	0	0	0	1	0	2	0	1	0	0	0	0	0	0	0
lad	126	.7179	18.886	52.8	24	38	12	31	11	5	2	3	72	3	2	8	1	0	0	0	3	0	0	0	10	19	1	7	0
Lad	2	.2440	.1132	30.5	0	0	0	0	1	1	0	0	0	0	0	1	0	0	0	0	0	0	0	0	0	0	0	1	0
lad's	4	.2417	.3028	34.8	2	1	0	0	0	1	0	0	3	0	0	0	0	0	0	0	0	0	0	0	1	0	0	0	0
ladder	127	.8694	22.149	53.5	33	21	15	13	24	11	7	3	55	2	4	7	7	8	3	11	3	2	0	0	8	7	3	7	0
Ladder	6	.2634	.3859	35.9	1	0	0	1	0	0	0	4	1	0	0	0	0	0	0	0	1	0	0	0	0	0	0	4	0
ladders	24	.7441	3.6662	45.6	3	9	1	1	4	5	1	0	9	1	0	2	0	3	0	2	0	0	0	1	2	0	2	2	0
laddie	2	.1948	.1250	31.0	1	0	0	1	0	0	0	0	1	0	0	0	0	0	0	0	0	0	0	0	0	1	0	0	0
laden	20	.6973	2.8866	44.6	2	0	0	6	8	3	0	1	6	0	0	1	0	6	0	0	1	0	0	0	2	1	1	2	0
ladies	127	.7815	20.124	53.0	23	26	9	22	17	16	13	1	41	9	1	8	0	6	2	0	19	2	0	0	22	11	1	5	0
Ladies	3	.3267	.2367	33.7	0	1	2	0	0	0	0	0	1	0	0	0	0	0	0	0	1	0	0	0	1	0	0	0	0
ladies'	13	.5282	1.5033	41.8	1	5	2	1	0	2	2	0	5	0	0	3	0	0	0	0	0	0	0	0	1	3	1	0	0
Ladies'	6	.4087	.5221	37.2	0	3	1	1	1	0	0	0	0	0	1	1	0	0	0	0	0	0	0	0	1	3	0	0	0
ladle	9	.3781	.8495	39.3	4	0	3	0	0	2	0	0	5	0	0	0	0	2	0	0	0	0	0	0	2	0	0	0	0
ladled	6	.2895	.4416	36.4	1	2	1	0	2	0	0	0	2	0	0	0	0	0	0	0	0	0	0	0	3	1	0	0	0
ladles	4	.2165	.2524	34.0	1	0	1	1	1	0	0	0	2	0	0	0	0	0	0	0	0	1	0	0	1	0	0	0	0
lads	18	.6165	2.3274	43.7	2	2	0	4	6	2	0	2	5	2	0	0	0	0	0	1	3	0	0	0	4	2	0	1	0
lady	539	.7954	87.444	59.4	176	106	55	62	53	30	49	8	277	30	4	76	0	6	9	1	13	3	1	0	55	31	8	25	0
Lady	103	.6402	13.860	51.4	16	7	10	26	14	12	15	3	40	1	5	21	0	1	0	0	3	0	0	0	18	4	0	10	0
lady-friend	2	.0000	.0234	23.7	0	0	0	0	2	0	0	0	0	0	0	0	0	0	0	0	0	0	0	0	2	0	0	0	0
lady-in-waiting	9	.2232	.6878	38.4	3	5	0	1	0	0	0	0	8	0	0	0	0	0	0	0	0	0	0	0	1	0	0	0	0
lady's	23	.5909	2.9766	44.7	7	3	1	0	9	0	3	0	14	1	0	3	0	0	0	0	0	0	0	0	2	2	0	1	0
Lady's	3	.2465	.1705	32.3	1	0	0	0	0	2	0	0	0	0	1	0	0	1	0	0	0	0	0	0	1	0	0	0	0
ladybird	2	.1948	.1250	31.0	0	0	1	0	0	0	0	1	1	0	0	0	0	0	0	0	0	0	0	0	0	1	0	0	0
ladybug	14	.4265	1.3766	41.4	7	2	3	1	0	1	0	0	5	0	0	0	0	0	1	3	0	0	0	0	5	0	0	0	0
Ladye	2	.0000	.0162	22.1	0	0	0	2	0	0	0	0	0	0	0	0	0	0	0	0	2	0	0	0	0	0	0	0	0
ladyfingers	3	.0000	.1370	31.4	0	0	0	3	0	0	0	0	3	0	0	0	0	0	0	0	0	0	0	0	0	0	0	0	0
ladylike	3	.2212	.2099	33.2	1	0	1	0	0	0	1	0	2	0	0	1	0	0	0	0	0	0	0	0	0	0	0	0	0
ladyslipper	2	.2278	.1128	30.5	0	0	0	1	1	0	0	0	0	0	0	0	0	0	0	1	0	0	0	0	0	0	1	0	0
Laennec	6	.0000	.2741	34.4	0	0	6	0	0	0	0	0	6	0	0	0	0	0	0	0	0	0	0	0	0	0	0	0	0
Laertes	2	.2446	.1122	30.5	0	0	0	0	0	1	1	0	0	0	0	1	0	0	0	0	0	0	0	0	0	0	1	0	0
Lafayette	14	.3585	1.2011	40.8	0	0	0	2	5	6	1	0	3	0	0	1	0	9	0	0	0	0	0	0	0	0	0	1	0
Lafleur	3	.0000	.0322	25.1	0	0	0	0	0	3	0	0	0	0	0	3	0	0	0	0	0	0	0	0	0	0	0	0	0
lag	7	.3908	.6286	38.0	0	0	2	1	3	0	1	0	2	0	0	0	0	0	0	0	0	0	0	0	0	1	3	1	0
lagged	3	.3394	.2451	33.9	0	0	0	0	1	1	1	0	1	0	0	1	0	0	0	0	0	0	0	0	1	0	0	0	0
lagoon	23	.6289	3.1380	45.0	0	10	0	7	4	0	1	1	15	1	0	1	0	2	0	0	0	0	0	0	2	1	0	1	0
lagoons	7	.5294	.7917	39.0	1	0	2	2	1	1	0	0	1	1	0	0	0	2	0	0	0	0	0	0	0	2	1	0	0
Lagos	3	.0000	.0583	27.7	0	3	0	0	0	0	0	0	0	0	0	0	0	3	0	0	0	0	0	0	0	0	0	0	0
laid	369	.9201	67.307	58.3	49	53	45	44	82	37	50	9	82	15	4	38	9	26	6	24	8	2	2	9	48	36	35	25	0
Laika	8	.0000	.3655	35.6	8	0	0	0	0	0	0	0	8	0	0	0	0	0	0	0	0	0	0	0	0	0	0	0	0
lain	18	.5466	2.0713	43.2	0	3	2	1	6	4	1	1	3	4	1	7	0	0	0	1	0	0	0	0	1	1	0	0	0
lair	6	.3876	.5836	37.7	0	0	4	2	0	0	0	0	4	0	0	0	0	0	0	0	0	0	0	0	1	0	0	1	0
Laird	2	.0000	.0243	23.9	0	0	0	0	0	0	2	0	0	0	0	0	0	0	0	0	0	0	0	0	0	0	0	2	0
Laius	4	.0000	.0419	26.2	0	0	0	0	0	4	0	0	0	0	0	0	0	0	0	0	0	0	0	0	0	0	4	0	0
Lajoi	4	.0000	.1827	32.6	0	0	0	4	0	0	0	0	4	0	0	0	0	0	0	0	0	0	0	0	0	0	0	0	0
lake	319	.8916	56.643	57.5	62	61	44	61	43	18	14	16	67	19	3	8	10	79	6	41	1	1	1	1	19	20	14	29	0
Lake	286	.7457	43.347	56.4	29	34	64	43	49	36	22	9	40	10	1	5	18	106	2	13	7	0	0	0	2	11	25	46	0
lake's	3	.3847	.2494	34.0	0	0	1	1	1	0	0	0	0	0	0	0	0	0	0	0	0	0	0	0	1	1	1	0	0
lakes	261	.7590	40.088	56.0	56	20	52	41	46	15	15	16	19	5	1	1	5	86	2	52	1	1	0	1	1	30	29	27	0
Lakes	85	.5835	10.397	50.2	6	9	31	8	10	13	3	5	6	0	0	0	5	44	0	2	3	0	0	0	0	5	12	8	0
lakeside	2	.1698	.1133	30.5	0	0	0	1	1	0	0	0	1	0	0	0	0	0	0	0	0	0	0	0	0	0	1	0	0
Lakeside	4	.0000	.1827	32.6	4	0	0	0	0	0	0	0	4	0	0	0	0	0	0	0	0	0	0	0	0	0	0	0	0
Lamar	8	.3669	.7460	38.7	0	1	0	0	6	0	1	0	5	0	0	0	0	0	0	0	0	0	0	0	0	1	0	2	0
lamb	94	.6652	12.947	51.1	14	26	10	8	17	2	16	1	28	2	0	12	5	4	3	2	6	0	14	0	6	9	3	0	0
Lamb	5	.0063	.0975	29.9	3	0	2	0	0	0	0	0	2	0	0	0	0	0	0	0	0	0	0	0	0	0	0	0	3
lamb's	3	.2357	.2199	33.4	0	1	1	1	0	0	0	0	2	0	0	0	0	0	0	0	0	0	0	0	0	1	0	0	0
Lambert	2	.1698	.1133	30.5	0	2	0	0	0	0	0	0	1	0	0	0	0	0	0	0	0	0	0	0	0	0	1	0	0
lambs	46	.6278	6.0949	47.8	8	16	12	1	7	0	1	1	14	8	0	1	0	14	0	0	0	0	0	0	1	5	2	1	0
Lambs	2	.0000	.0219	23.4	0	0	2	0	0	0	0	0	0	2	0	0	0	0	0	0	0	0	0	0	0	0	0	0	0
Lambu	3	.0000	.0434	26.4	0	0	0	0	3	0	0	0	0	0	0	0	0	0	0	0	0	0	0	0	0	3	0	0	0
lame	28	.7508	4.2612	46.3	3	6	1	7	5	3	3	0	6	1	0	3	0	1	3	0	2	0	0	0	6	2	2	2	0
Lame	5	.3915	.4394	36.4	0	0	0	0	1	3	1	0	1	0	1	0	0	1	0	0	0	0	0	0	0	0	1	1	0
lamed	3	.3394	.2451	33.9	0	1	0	0	1	1	0	0	1	0	0	1	0	0	0	0	0	0	0	0	1	0	0	0	0
lamely	3	.3394	.2451	33.9	0	1	0	0	1	0	1	0	1	0	0	1	0	0	0	0	0	0	0	0	1	0	0	0	0
lament	7	.5273	.7948	39.0	1	0	0	2	1	1	2	0	2	0	0	2	0	0	0	0	1	0	0	0	1	1	0	0	0
Lament	2	.2417	.1091	30.4	0	0	0	0	1	0	1	0	0	0	0	0	0	0	0	0	1	0	0	0	0	0	1	0	0
lamentable	3	.2260	.1580	32.0	0	0	0	0	0	1	2	0	0	0	0	2	0	0	0	0	0	0	0	0	0	0	1	0	0
lamentation	3	.2060	.1500	31.8	0	0	0	1	0	1	1	0	0	0	0	2	0	0	0	0	0	0	0	0	0	1	0	0	0
lamentations	7	.4153	.6359	38.0	0	0	1	3	0	0	3	0	1	0	0	2	0	0	0	0	1	0	0	0	3	0	0	0	0
lamented	6	.3704	.5081	37.1	0	1	0	1	2	1	1	0	1	0	0	0	0	1	0	0	0	0	0	0	1	0	0	3	0
lamenting	5	.3544	.4006	36.0	0	0	1	2	0	0	2	0	1	0	1	2	0	0	0	0	0	0	0	0	1	0	0	0	0
laments	2	.2411	.1091	30.4	0	0	0	0	0	0	2	0	0	0	0	1	0	0	0	0	1	0	0	0	0	0	0	0	0
laminae	2	.0000	.0394	26.0	0	0	0	0	0	0	0	2	0	0	0	0	0	0	0	2	0	0	0	0	0	0	0	0	0
laminated	5	.2429	.2560	34.1	0	0	0	1	1	2	1	0	0	0	0	0	0	0	0	0	0	0	1	3	0	0	0	1	0
laminating	2	.0000	.0209	23.2	0	0	2	0	0	0	0	0	0	0	0	0	0	0	0	0	0	0	0	0	0	0	2	0	0
lamp	179	.8532	30.638	54.9	50	41	27	10	19	14	14	4	56	4	2	20	4	7	3	36	1	0	1	4	23	10	3	5	0
Lamp	2	.1698	.1133	30.5	0	1	1	0	0	0	0	0	1	0	0	0	0	0	0	0	0	0	0	0	0	0	1	0	0
lampblack	3	.2383	.1458	31.6	0	0	1	0	0	1	1	0	0	0	0	0	0	0	0	0	0	1	0	2	0	0	0	0	0
lamplight	3	.3427	.2477	33.9	0	1	1	0	0	0	0	1	1	0	0	0	0	0	0	0	0	0	0	0	1	0	0	1	0
Lamplighter	3	.2441	.1719	32.4	3	0	0	0	0	0	0	0	0	0	0	0	0	0	0	0	1	0	0	0	0	2	0	0	0
lamppost	2	.0000	.0914	29.6	1	0	1	0	0	0	0	0	2	0	0	0	0	0	0	0	0	0	0	0	0	0	0	0	0
lampposts	2	.2408	.1204	30.8	0	1	0	0	0	1	0	0	0	0	0	0	0	1	0	0	0	0	0	0	0	1	0	0	0

4P Lackawanna
XR Lackland
8G Laconia
8F laconically
3A Lacour
6F Lacq
XR lacquer's
XR lacquerers
XR lacquering
5Q lacquerware
4P ladder-backed
5A ladder-rack
6A ladder's
3F Laddie
4A ladies-in-waiting
6P Ladislas
7A ladling
7B Ladner
6F Ladoga
4A Ladrones
6A Lady-day
4A lady-in-wating
3A lady-size
4N Lady-who-asks-a-very-man*
5A ladybugs
9D ladyship
8P Lafayette's
4F Lafitte
6N laggard
6Q Lagrange
3B lags
8N Laguna
6R LagunaBeach
9F Laicos
5F laipala
7Q Lair
7Q lairs
4A laise
8B laith
6Q LAKE
3A LakeCity
5P lake-shore
XR lake-side
3A Lake's
7Q Lakehurst
6A Lakemanu
5F lakeshore
4E Lakeville
5C Lalley
6A lama
8P Lamb's
6B Lambarene
7D lambaste
6R Lambeau
7D lambing
XH Lambkill
7D lameness
7P lamentest
9L laminates
9L lamination
6R Lamonica
8H Lamont
7Q Lamont-Doherty
3B Lamorisse
XH lamp's
4Q Lampedusa
4Q Lampedusa's
7A lamplit
9H lamprey

Word Type	F	D	U	SFI	3 Gr 3	4 Gr 4	5 Gr 5	6 Gr 6	7 Gr 7	8 Gr 8	9 Gr 9	X UnGr	A Read	B Eng & Gr	C Comp	D Lit	E Math	F Soc Stud	G Spell	H Sci	J Music	K Art	L Home Ec	M Shop	N Lib F	P Lib NF	Q Lib Ref	R Mag	S Rel
lampreys	2	.2441	.1127	30.5	0	0	0	0	2	0	0	0	0	0	0	0	0	0	0	0	0	0	0	0	1	0	1	0	0
lamps	60	.8949	10.687	50.3	11	6	9	8	8	11	5	2	16	1	2	5	0	6	0	6	2	1	1	1	3	7	3	6	0
lampshade	3	.2369	.2208	33.4	0	0	2	0	0	1	0	0	2	0	0	0	1	0	0	0	0	0	0	0	0	0	0	0	0
Lamson	2	.0000	.0290	24.6	0	0	0	0	0	2	0	0	0	0	0	0	0	0	0	0	0	0	0	0	0	2	0	0	0
Lancaster	9	.5395	1.0395	40.2	0	0	1	2	3	1	0	2	2	0	0	3	0	1	0	1	0	0	0	0	0	0	1	1	0
Lancastrian	2	.0000	.0209	23.2	0	0	2	0	0	0	0	0	0	0	0	0	0	0	0	0	0	0	0	0	0	0	2	0	0
lance	18	.5661	2.2150	43.5	0	2	3	5	8	0	0	0	7	0	1	0	0	6	0	0	0	0	0	0	1	2	1	0	0
Lance	11	.1147	.3652	35.6	10	0	0	0	0	0	1	0	0	1	0	0	0	0	0	0	0	0	0	0	0	0	0	10	0
lances	6	.5363	.6888	38.4	0	1	0	3	2	0	0	0	1	1	0	0	0	2	0	0	0	0	0	0	1	1	0	0	0
Lancet	2	.0000	.0243	23.9	0	0	0	0	0	0	2	0	0	0	0	0	0	0	0	0	0	0	0	0	0	0	0	2	0
Lanciotti	5	.0000	.0608	27.8	0	0	0	0	0	0	5	0	0	0	0	0	0	0	0	0	0	0	0	0	0	0	0	5	0
land	2953	.7707	461.77	66.6	525	442	569	558	441	219	132	67	475	30	7	53	29	1333	21	297	76	4	0	3	49	233	211	130	2
Land	104	.7641	16.085	52.1	11	13	19	9	27	19	1	5	16	1	0	3	12	24	1	2	8	0	0	0	18	7	2	10	0
Land-Rover	3	.0000	.0365	25.6	0	0	0	3	0	0	0	0	0	0	0	0	0	0	0	0	0	0	0	0	0	0	0	3	0
land-crabs	2	.0000	.0219	23.4	2	0	0	0	0	0	0	0	0	2	0	0	0	0	0	0	0	0	0	0	0	0	0	0	0
land-dwelling	2	.0000	.0209	23.2	0	0	0	0	2	0	0	0	0	0	0	0	0	0	0	0	0	0	0	0	0	0	2	0	0
land-hungry	3	.0000	.0583	27.7	0	0	0	0	0	3	0	0	0	0	0	0	0	3	0	0	0	0	0	0	0	0	0	0	0
land's	4	.4519	.3985	36.0	0	0	0	2	2	0	0	0	1	0	0	1	0	0	0	0	0	0	0	0	0	0	1	1	0
Land's	3	.2054	.1422	31.5	0	0	0	0	2	1	0	0	0	0	1	0	0	0	0	0	0	0	0	0	0	0	0	2	0
landed	178	.8665	30.911	54.9	45	24	26	20	31	24	6	2	65	5	1	9	1	23	3	7	4	0	0	1	19	13	12	15	0
landfall	2	.2351	.1166	30.7	0	0	0	0	1	1	0	0	0	0	0	0	0	1	0	0	0	0	0	0	0	0	0	1	0
landform	4	.0000	.0778	28.9	0	0	2	1	0	0	1	0	0	0	0	0	0	4	0	0	0	0	0	0	0	0	0	0	0
landforms	9	.2239	.5325	37.3	0	1	1	1	0	0	6	0	0	0	0	0	0	6	0	3	0	0	0	0	0	0	0	0	0
landholders	2	.2285	.1129	30.5	0	0	0	0	0	2	0	0	0	0	0	0	0	1	0	0	0	0	0	0	0	0	1	0	0
landholding	2	.2408	.1204	30.8	0	0	1	0	0	1	0	0	0	0	0	0	0	1	0	0	0	0	0	0	0	1	0	0	0
landholdings	2	.2285	.1129	30.5	1	0	0	0	0	1	0	0	0	0	0	0	0	1	0	0	0	0	0	0	0	0	1	0	0
landing	171	.8813	30.104	54.8	32	27	26	24	31	13	16	2	55	7	1	11	6	23	0	10	2	1	0	1	18	8	8	20	0
Landing	8	.3831	.7676	38.9	0	3	4	0	0	0	1	0	5	0	0	1	0	0	0	0	0	0	0	0	0	2	0	0	0
landings	12	.5817	1.4692	41.7	3	0	2	1	3	1	1	1	2	2	0	0	0	3	0	0	0	0	0	0	0	1	1	3	0
landlady	16	.3413	1.4884	41.7	11	2	0	1	0	0	2	0	13	2	0	0	0	0	0	0	0	0	0	0	0	1	0	0	0
landlocked	9	.1212	.4142	36.2	0	0	0	4	4	1	0	0	2	0	0	0	0	7	0	0	0	0	0	0	0	0	0	0	0
landlord	22	.4871	2.4191	43.8	11	4	1	1	0	4	1	0	10	0	0	2	0	4	0	0	5	0	0	0	0	1	0	0	0
landlord's	7	.3402	.6156	37.9	0	0	0	0	0	5	2	0	4	0	0	2	0	1	0	0	0	0	0	0	0	0	0	0	0
landlords	6	.2930	.4402	36.4	1	0	0	0	2	1	2	0	1	0	0	0	0	4	0	0	0	0	0	0	0	0	1	0	0
landmark	12	.5164	1.3324	41.2	2	4	0	2	1	2	1	0	2	2	0	0	0	5	0	0	2	0	0	0	0	0	1	0	0
landmarks	24	.6298	3.1458	45.0	6	4	1	3	5	3	1	1	4	3	0	0	1	8	1	0	0	0	0	0	0	0	3	4	0
landmass	3	.0000	.0583	27.7	0	0	2	0	0	0	1	0	0	0	0	0	0	3	0	0	0	0	0	0	0	0	0	0	0
landmasses	4	.0000	.0778	28.9	0	0	1	0	0	0	3	0	0	0	0	0	0	4	0	0	0	0	0	0	0	0	0	0	0
landowner	7	.4745	.7173	38.6	1	1	1	0	1	1	0	2	0	0	0	0	0	3	0	2	0	0	0	0	0	1	1	0	0
landowners	29	.6126	3.7116	45.7	5	0	2	9	3	3	1	6	4	0	0	1	0	9	0	3	0	0	0	0	0	2	5	5	0
Landry	5	.0000	.0608	27.8	0	0	0	0	5	0	0	0	0	0	0	0	0	0	0	0	0	0	0	0	0	0	0	5	0
lands	602	.6114	77.099	58.9	57	91	125	152	81	49	37	10	62	8	2	7	3	380	2	32	14	2	0	0	5	28	41	16	0
Lands	9	.0706	.3119	34.9	0	1	1	6	1	0	0	0	1	0	0	0	0	8	0	0	0	0	0	0	0	0	0	0	0
landscape	93	.6221	11.883	50.7	7	7	10	10	33	10	12	4	8	1	0	19	0	13	0	3	0	10	0	1	4	7	16	11	0
landscaped	3	.2143	.1568	32.0	0	1	1	0	0	0	0	1	0	0	0	0	0	0	0	0	0	0	0	0	0	1	0	2	0
landscapes	17	.2231	.8639	39.4	0	1	1	0	7	5	3	0	0	0	0	0	0	2	0	1	0	7	0	0	0	2	5	0	0
landscaping	5	.1882	.2328	33.7	2	0	1	0	0	0	0	2	0	0	0	0	0	0	0	0	0	0	0	0	0	0	1	4	0
Landshort	2	.0000	.0914	29.6	0	0	0	0	0	2	0	0	2	0	0	0	0	0	0	0	0	0	0	0	0	0	0	0	0
landslide	4	.4350	.3902	35.9	0	1	0	1	0	1	1	0	1	0	0	0	0	1	1	0	0	0	0	0	0	0	0	1	0
landslides	6	.3781	.5096	37.1	1	2	0	2	0	0	1	0	0	0	0	0	0	2	0	2	0	0	0	0	0	0	0	2	0
landward	2	.1387	.0689	28.4	0	0	0	0	1	0	1	0	0	0	1	0	0	0	0	0	0	0	0	0	0	1	0	0	0
lane	61	.6960	8.7656	49.4	5	22	7	7	15	4	1	0	18	1	0	5	0	3	1	1	2	0	0	0	8	17	0	5	0
Lane	38	.7595	5.8620	47.7	2	7	7	8	2	7	4	1	9	1	1	2	3	6	0	0	3	0	0	0	8	3	0	2	0
Lane's	3	.3553	.2608	34.2	0	0	0	1	0	2	0	0	1	0	0	0	0	1	0	0	0	0	0	0	0	1	0	0	0
lanes	27	.6152	3.4784	45.4	5	4	1	6	6	4	1	0	7	1	3	0	2	4	0	0	1	0	0	0	2	0	3	4	0
Lanes	5	.0000	.2284	33.6	5	0	0	0	0	0	0	0	5	0	0	0	0	0	0	0	0	0	0	0	0	0	0	0	0
lang	5	.0000	.0547	27.4	0	0	0	0	0	5	0	0	0	5	0	0	0	0	0	0	0	0	0	0	0	0	0	0	0
Lang	2	.2375	.1088	30.4	0	0	0	0	1	1	0	0	0	0	0	0	0	0	0	0	1	0	0	0	0	0	0	1	0
Langanes	2	.0000	.0243	23.9	0	0	0	2	0	0	0	0	0	0	0	0	0	0	0	0	0	0	0	0	0	0	0	2	0
Langelinie	2	.0000	.0209	23.2	2	0	0	0	0	0	0	0	0	0	0	0	0	0	0	0	0	0	0	0	0	0	2	0	0
Langewiesche	3	.0000	.0067	18.3	0	0	0	0	0	0	3	0	0	0	3	0	0	0	0	0	0	0	0	0	0	0	0	0	0
Langley	7	.3829	.6802	38.3	0	5	0	1	0	1	0	0	5	0	0	0	0	0	0	0	1	0	0	0	0	0	0	1	0
Langmier	2	.0000	.0914	29.6	0	0	0	0	2	0	0	0	2	0	0	0	0	0	0	0	0	0	0	0	0	0	0	0	0
Langston	3	.1843	.1420	31.5	0	0	0	0	1	2	0	0	0	0	0	2	0	1	0	0	0	0	0	0	0	0	0	0	0
language	1041	.7199	151.81	61.8	115	86	125	162	271	149	117	16	131	446	26	26	17	86	115	2	30	5	1	7	14	50	55	30	0
Language	47	.3994	4.0113	46.0	1	14	8	7	6	7	4	0	1	24	0	0	0	3	14	0	0	0	0	0	0	1	4	0	0
languages	249	.6112	31.266	55.0	16	35	43	29	58	26	36	6	20	88	0	2	2	25	45	1	4	2	0	0	0	6	49	5	0
languid	5	.3679	.4143	36.2	0	0	0	0	1	2	2	0	0	0	0	1	0	3	0	0	0	0	0	0	0	1	0	0	0
languor	2	.2446	.1122	30.5	0	0	0	0	0	1	1	0	0	0	0	1	0	0	0	0	0	0	0	0	0	0	1	0	0
Lank	3	.0000	.0352	25.5	0	0	3	0	0	0	0	0	0	0	0	0	0	0	0	0	0	0	0	0	3	0	0	0	0
lanky	21	.3462	1.7284	42.4	2	14	0	2	1	2	0	0	7	0	0	0	0	1	0	0	10	0	0	0	1	1	0	1	0
Lansing	6	.3643	.4733	36.8	0	2	0	1	1	2	0	0	0	2	0	0	0	0	0	0	0	0	0	0	0	0	1	3	0
lantern	72	.7561	11.134	50.5	2	27	10	9	6	11	4	3	27	2	0	8	1	3	2	2	0	0	1	0	16	5	2	3	0
Lantern	2	.0000	.0914	29.6	0	2	0	0	0	0	0	0	2	0	0	0	0	0	0	0	0	0	0	0	0	0	0	0	0
lanterns	12	.5417	1.4506	41.6	3	2	1	3	3	0	0	0	7	1	0	0	0	0	0	0	0	0	0	0	1	1	2	0	0
Lanterns	2	.0000	.0914	29.6	2	0	0	0	0	0	0	0	2	0	0	0	0	0	0	0	0	0	0	0	0	0	0	0	0
lanx	3	.2379	.1631	32.1	0	0	0	0	1	0	0	2	0	2	0	0	0	0	1	0	0	0	0	0	0	0	0	0	0
lanyard	3	.2120	.1548	31.9	1	0	0	0	2	0	0	0	0	0	0	0	0	0	0	0	0	0	0	0	2	1	0	0	0
Lao	11	.2266	.6037	37.8	0	0	0	0	3	3	5	0	0	0	0	0	0	0	0	0	0	0	0	0	0	8	3	0	0
Laos	22	.4440	2.1067	43.2	0	0	3	2	8	0	9	0	0	0	0	0	0	7	0	0	0	0	0	0	0	10	3	2	0
lap	104	.8148	17.066	52.3	15	22	13	9	22	10	4	9	29	3	0	8	3	0	0	9	0	3	3	3	16	17	2	8	0
lapels	2	.1839	.0845	29.3	0	0	0	0	0	1	0	1	0	0	0	0	0	0	0	0	0	0	1	0	1	0	0	0	0
Lapham	11	.0000	.1290	31.1	0	0	0	0	0	11	0	0	0	0	0	0	0	0	0	0	0	0	0	0	11	0	0	0	0
Lapland	8	.3803	.7820	38.9	0	4	0	2	0	1	0	1	6	1	0	0	0	0	0	0	0	0	0	0	0	0	0	1	0
Laporte	2	.0000	.0243	23.9	0	0	0	0	0	0	2	0	0	0	0	0	0	0	0	0	0	0	0	0	0	0	0	2	0
Lapp	2	.0000	.0914	29.6	0	2	0	0	0	0	0	0	2	0	0	0	0	0	0	0	0	0	0	0	0	0	0	0	0
lapped	10	.1841	.5073	37.1	1	1	0	1	7	0	0	0	3	0	0	1	0	0	0	0	0	0	5	0	0	1	0	0	0
lapping	9	.3464	.7069	38.5	1	2	0	2	0	1	3	0	2	0	0	0	0	0	0	0	0	1	0	3	0	3	0	0	0
Lapps	17	.1579	1.1553	40.6	4	11	2	0	0	0	0	0	16	0	0	0	0	0	0	0	0	0	0	0	0	1	0	0	0
laps	13	.6578	1.7645	42.5	1	1	2	1	4	1	2	1	3	0	0	1	1	0	0	0	0	0	1	1	1	2	0	3	0
lapse	4	.4560	.4041	36.1	0	0	1	1	2	0	0	0	1	0	0	0	0	0	0	0	0	0	0	0	1	1	0	1	0
Laramie	5	.5627	.5847	37.7	1	2	0	0	1	1	0	0	0	0	0	0	1	1	0	0	0	0	0	0	1	1	0	1	0
lard	5	.3145	.3397	35.3	0	1	0	0	2	1	1	0	0	0	0	0	0	0	0	0	0	0	2	0	1	1	0	1	0

7P Lamu
7N lan'
6A Lana
8Q Lanao
5Q lance-shaped
6A lanced
9R Lanciotti's
XH land-
5Q land-based
5F land-form
6F land-forms
9R land-grant
7F land-holding
XH land-life
7R land-locked
XR land-management
5P land-poor
9F land-reform
3P land-roaming
7F land-sea
7D land-spies
4H land-world
3A land
7R landing-gear
6J Landler
6F landless
XR landloving
7Q landlubber
7D landlubbers
7A Landrum
7R Landry's
7R Landsburg
7D Landscape
7P landscapist
6J lang's
8B Lang's
7Q Langenaltheim
XR Langer
6Q Langerhans
5A Langford
XB Langland
9A Langmuir
7R Langrenus
7B Langro
XR Langsley
7B Languages
7Q languidly
9D languish
7A languished
4D languors
4Q Lanham
8N lank
7D lankly
9D Lansdale
7Q lanthanide
9R Laocoon
9D Laodamas
7F Laotian
4D lap-elephant
8N Laphams
7A Lapice
8D lapis
8A lapis-lazuli
6Q Laplace
7F lappa
7B lapsed
6R lapses
6R Lapwai
7G laqueus
6A larboard
7R larcenous
4F larch

Word Type	F	D	U	SFI	3 Gr 3	4 Gr 4	5 Gr 5	6 Gr 6	7 Gr 7	8 Gr 8	9 Gr 9	X UnGr	A Read	B Eng & Gr	C Comp	D Lit	E Math	F Soc Stud	G Spell	H Sci	J Music	K Art	L Home Ec	M Shop	N Lib F	P Lib NF	Q Lib Ref	R Mag	S Rel
larder	5	.4660	.4877	36.9	0	0	1	0	2	0	1	1	0	0	0	2	0	0	0	0	0	0	0	0	1	0	1	1	0
Laredo	12	.4717	1.2122	40.8	0	0	0	4	5	3	0	0	2	0	0	3	0	0	0	0	4	0	0	0	0	0	2	1	0
large	2777	.9050	499.21	67.0	418	423	394	407	484	277	279	95	464	80	13	72	116	737	30	444	67	54	35	62	69	203	206	125	0
Large	3	.0000	.0322	25.1	0	3	0	0	0	0	0	0	0	0	0	3	0	0	0	0	0	0	0	0	0	0	0	0	0
large-scale	21	.5537	2.4259	43.8	0	1	4	1	3	2	6	4	0	0	0	0	0	9	0	1	0	0	0	1	0	1	3	6	0
largely	144	.7259	21.194	53.3	4	1	24	14	33	27	36	5	11	0	0	3	0	34	1	20	5	0	3	4	0	12	40	11	0
largemouth	2	.0000	.0243	23.9	0	0	0	0	1	0	0	1	0	0	0	0	0	0	0	0	0	0	0	0	0	0	0	2	0
larger	736	.8859	129.69	61.1	91	116	64	102	156	100	83	24	86	19	9	18	99	142	1	155	15	5	10	28	16	40	62	31	0
largest	667	.7942	106.58	60.3	77	84	112	96	144	76	62	16	56	16	0	9	140	211	5	55	10	1	3	9	3	42	72	35	0
Largo	4	.1982	.1818	32.6	0	0	2	2	0	0	0	0	0	0	0	0	0	0	1	0	3	0	0	0	0	0	0	0	0
largus	2	.0000	.0162	22.1	0	0	0	2	0	0	0	0	0	0	0	0	0	0	2	0	0	0	0	0	0	0	0	0	0
lariat	15	.4873	1.6466	42.2	4	2	3	1	2	3	0	0	7	0	0	3	0	1	0	0	3	0	0	0	0	1	0	0	0
lark	27	.4445	2.6987	44.3	7	0	0	7	3	0	9	1	9	2	0	12	0	0	2	1	0	0	0	0	0	1	0	0	0
Lark	13	.0000	.1524	31.8	0	0	13	0	0	0	0	0	0	0	0	0	0	0	0	0	0	0	0	0	13	0	0	0	0
Lark's	3	.0000	.0352	25.5	0	0	3	0	0	0	0	0	0	0	0	0	0	0	0	0	0	0	0	0	3	0	0	0	0
Larkin	18	.3200	1.6324	42.1	2	0	0	1	13	2	0	0	15	0	0	0	0	2	0	0	0	0	0	0	1	0	0	0	0
Larkin's	4	.0000	.0469	26.7	4	0	0	0	0	0	0	0	0	0	0	0	0	0	0	0	0	0	0	0	4	0	0	0	0
Larkins	4	.0000	.1827	32.6	0	0	0	1	3	0	0	0	4	0	0	0	0	0	0	0	0	0	0	0	0	0	0	0	0
larks	5	.3766	.4670	36.7	1	0	0	3	1	0	0	0	3	0	0	0	0	0	0	0	1	0	0	0	0	0	1	0	0
larkspur	3	.1847	.1428	31.5	1	0	0	1	1	0	0	0	0	2	0	0	0	0	0	1	0	0	0	0	0	0	0	0	0
Larry	57	.5450	6.7344	48.3	9	10	6	17	8	0	5	2	20	4	0	0	12	0	4	1	0	0	0	0	0	0	0	16	0
Larry's	3	.2279	.2143	33.3	1	2	0	0	0	0	0	0	2	0	0	0	0	0	0	0	0	0	0	0	0	0	0	1	0
Lars	14	.1972	1.0279	40.1	7	5	0	0	2	0	0	0	13	0	0	1	0	0	0	0	0	0	0	0	0	0	0	0	0
Larsen	10	.4557	1.0399	40.2	7	0	0	0	2	0	0	1	4	0	0	0	1	0	0	0	0	0	0	0	0	3	0	2	0
Larsen's	3	.2332	.1690	32.3	2	0	0	0	0	0	0	1	0	0	0	0	0	0	0	0	0	0	0	0	0	2	0	1	0
larva	26	.3034	1.8226	42.6	4	0	1	0	20	0	1	0	0	0	0	0	0	0	0	12	0	0	0	0	0	2	12	0	0
larvae	53	.3831	4.6057	46.6	30	3	5	10	5	0	0	0	3	0	0	0	0	0	0	30	0	0	0	0	0	15	5	0	0
larval	6	.3754	.4940	36.9	0	0	0	2	4	0	0	0	0	2	0	0	0	0	0	2	0	0	0	0	0	0	2	0	0
laryngeal	2	.0000	.0209	23.2	0	0	0	0	0	0	0	2	0	0	0	0	0	0	0	0	0	0	0	0	0	0	2	0	0
larynx	12	.4470	1.1404	40.6	3	0	0	1	0	3	2	3	0	1	0	0	0	0	3	4	0	0	0	0	0	0	4	0	0
las	2	.0000	.0162	22.1	0	2	0	0	0	0	0	0	0	0	0	0	0	0	0	0	2	0	0	0	0	0	0	0	0
Las	7	.1437	.3145	35.0	0	0	0	6	0	0	0	1	0	0	0	0	0	6	0	1	0	0	0	0	0	0	0	0	0
LasLomas	2	.0000	.0389	25.9	2	0	0	0	0	0	0	0	0	0	0	0	0	2	0	0	0	0	0	0	0	0	0	0	0
LasVegas	3	.0000	.0365	25.6	0	0	0	0	0	3	0	0	0	0	0	0	0	0	0	0	0	0	0	0	0	0	0	3	0
laser	13	.4383	1.2411	40.9	0	0	0	1	9	2	1	0	0	0	0	0	0	2	0	6	0	0	0	0	0	0	1	4	0
lasers	2	.2413	.1212	30.8	0	1	0	0	0	0	1	0	0	0	0	0	1	0	0	1	0	0	0	0	0	0	0	0	0
lash	13	.5214	1.4244	41.5	0	1	1	1	5	2	2	1	1	0	0	2	0	1	0	0	0	0	0	0	3	0	1	5	0
lashed	32	.6449	4.2715	46.3	3	3	4	9	4	6	3	0	7	1	2	2	0	0	0	0	1	0	0	0	7	7	0	5	0
lashes	5	.3841	.4756	36.8	0	0	0	1	1	1	2	0	3	0	0	1	0	0	0	0	0	0	0	0	1	0	0	0	0
lashing	9	.5918	1.1177	40.5	0	2	1	2	2	1	1	0	2	2	0	1	0	0	0	0	0	0	0	0	2	1	0	1	0
lashings	5	.3854	.4790	36.8	0	0	0	2	1	2	0	0	3	0	0	0	0	0	0	0	0	0	0	0	1	1	0	0	0
Lasky	3	.0000	.1370	31.4	0	0	0	0	0	3	0	0	3	0	0	0	0	0	0	0	0	0	0	0	0	0	0	0	0
lass	14	.4388	1.4643	41.7	4	0	5	3	2	0	0	0	9	3	1	0	0	0	0	0	0	0	0	0	1	0	0	0	0
Lass	3	.0000	.0322	25.1	0	0	0	0	3	0	0	0	0	0	0	3	0	0	0	0	0	0	0	0	0	0	0	0	0
Lassen	6	.3503	.4804	36.8	0	0	3	1	1	0	1	0	0	0	0	0	0	0	0	4	0	0	0	0	0	1	1	0	0
lasses	2	.0000	.0162	22.1	0	0	0	1	0	1	0	0	0	0	0	0	0	0	0	0	2	0	0	0	0	0	0	0	0
lassie	3	.0000	.1370	31.4	0	0	3	0	0	0	0	0	3	0	0	0	0	0	0	0	0	0	0	0	0	0	0	0	0
Lassie	3	.0000	.0328	25.2	0	0	0	2	1	0	0	0	0	3	0	0	0	0	0	0	0	0	0	0	0	0	0	0	0
lasso	17	.6189	2.2099	43.4	6	3	4	2	1	1	0	0	5	0	0	2	0	1	1	0	1	0	0	0	5	2	0	0	0
lassos	3	.3134	.2351	33.7	0	0	1	0	1	1	0	0	1	0	0	0	0	1	1	0	0	0	0	0	0	0	0	0	0
last	3030	.9346	560.99	67.5	610	566	332	375	516	308	258	65	955	228	36	207	109	175	190	110	125	2	16	6	258	216	79	314	4
Last	13	.6617	1.7655	42.5	1	0	2	3	6	0	0	1	2	0	0	2	0	1	1	0	1	0	0	0	0	1	1	4	0
last-minute	8	.5348	.8982	39.5	1	2	0	0	1	2	2	0	1	0	0	1	0	1	0	0	1	0	1	0	0	0	0	3	0
lasted	89	.7727	14.005	51.5	11	16	13	8	22	12	7	0	28	2	0	9	3	17	0	1	3	0	0	0	4	14	3	5	0
lasting	33	.7144	4.8036	46.8	1	0	7	1	12	3	6	3	5	1	0	1	0	8	0	1	1	0	1	2	0	1	3	9	0
lastly	6	.4658	.6220	37.9	1	0	0	1	3	1	0	0	2	0	0	0	0	1	0	0	0	0	1	0	1	0	1	0	0
lasts	40	.8107	6.5366	48.2	12	4	4	6	5	2	5	2	9	2	0	1	1	8	0	5	2	0	1	0	0	3	4	4	0
Lasuen	2	.0000	.0389	25.9	0	2	0	0	0	0	0	0	0	0	0	0	0	2	0	0	0	0	0	0	0	0	0	0	0
lat	2	.2441	.1127	30.5	0	0	0	0	1	1	0	0	0	0	0	0	0	0	0	0	0	0	0	0	1	0	1	0	0
latch	12	.3740	1.1174	40.5	5	0	0	2	1	1	3	0	7	0	0	3	0	0	0	0	0	0	0	0	0	0	0	2	0
latched	2	.0000	.0914	29.6	2	0	0	0	0	0	0	0	2	0	0	0	0	0	0	0	0	0	0	0	0	0	0	0	0
late	689	.9033	123.90	60.9	110	104	76	74	149	84	70	22	233	38	9	60	8	62	14	29	17	1	7	0	56	51	42	62	0
Late	2	.2418	.1091	30.4	0	0	1	0	1	0	0	0	0	0	0	0	0	0	1	0	0	0	0	0	0	0	1	0	0
late-afternoon	2	.1787	.1174	30.7	0	0	0	0	0	2	0	0	1	0	0	0	0	0	0	0	0	0	0	0	1	0	0	0	0
late-blooming	2	.2437	.1129	30.5	0	0	0	0	1	0	0	1	0	0	0	0	0	0	0	0	0	0	0	0	0	0	1	1	0
late-model	5	.1398	.1959	32.9	0	0	0	0	4	0	0	1	0	0	0	0	0	1	0	0	0	0	0	0	0	0	0	4	0
lateen	3	.1823	.1405	31.5	0	0	0	0	0	1	2	0	0	0	0	0	0	1	0	0	0	0	0	0	0	0	2	0	0
lately	44	.6795	6.2293	47.9	4	4	7	8	8	4	5	4	16	3	0	5	0	1	0	4	0	0	0	0	4	3	0	8	0
latency	2	.0000	.0243	23.9	0	0	0	0	2	0	0	0	0	0	0	0	0	0	0	0	0	0	0	0	0	0	0	2	0
latent	6	.3969	.5149	37.1	0	0	1	0	2	0	2	1	0	0	0	0	0	0	0	1	0	0	0	0	0	1	3	1	0
later	1599	.9201	291.86	64.7	193	222	213	211	324	237	143	56	377	53	14	76	53	244	21	147	65	1	16	8	66	149	177	132	0
Later	2	.0000	.0389	25.9	0	0	2	0	0	0	0	0	0	0	0	0	0	2	0	0	0	0	0	0	0	0	0	0	0
lateral	31	.4341	2.8220	44.5	0	0	0	1	21	2	7	0	0	0	1	0	15	0	0	0	4	0	0	8	0	0	1	2	0
latest	93	.7925	14.782	51.7	5	11	12	17	17	12	12	7	8	10	1	5	0	8	0	7	5	0	0	1	8	4	9	27	0
latex	10	.3016	.7400	38.7	0	2	5	0	2	0	1	0	2	0	0	0	0	4	0	0	0	0	0	0	0	0	4	0	0
Lath	8	.0000	.0938	29.7	0	0	0	8	0	0	0	0	0	0	0	0	0	0	0	0	0	0	0	0	8	0	0	0	0
Latham	2	.2446	.1123	30.5	0	0	2	0	0	0	0	0	0	1	0	0	0	0	0	0	0	0	0	0	0	0	1	0	0
lathe	37	.1542	1.3108	41.2	0	0	0	1	19	8	9	0	0	2	0	0	0	0	0	0	0	0	0	23	0	0	1	11	0
lather	6	.3427	.4955	37.0	1	0	2	0	1	1	0	1	2	0	0	0	0	0	0	0	0	0	0	0	2	0	0	2	0
latigo	2	.2443	.1130	30.5	0	1	0	0	1	0	0	0	0	0	0	1	0	0	0	0	0	0	0	0	1	0	0	0	0
Latin	447	.5571	51.583	57.1	8	35	65	117	106	78	29	9	10	61	0	3	4	126	169	14	10	1	0	0	3	16	27	3	0
LatinAmerica	8	.3037	.5773	37.6	0	0	1	0	2	5	0	0	0	0	0	0	0	6	0	0	0	0	0	0	0	1	0	1	0
LatinAmerican	2	.0000	.0389	25.9	0	0	0	0	0	2	0	0	0	0	0	0	0	2	0	0	0	0	0	0	0	0	0	0	0
LatinAmericans	2	.0000	.0389	25.9	0	0	0	0	0	2	0	0	0	0	0	0	0	2	0	0	0	0	0	0	0	0	0	0	0
Latin-American	26	.4103	2.3541	43.7	0	0	7	2	13	4	0	0	1	0	0	1	0	16	0	0	6	0	0	0	0	0	2	0	0
Latin-speaking	2	.2305	.1080	30.3	0	0	2	0	0	0	0	0	0	0	0	0	0	0	1	0	0	0	0	0	0	1	0	0	0
Latins	5	.2226	.2657	34.2	4	0	0	0	0	0	0	1	0	0	0	0	0	0	0	0	0	0	0	0	0	2	3	0	0
latitude	98	.5710	11.755	50.7	2	18	12	19	14	20	12	1	2	0	0	0	15	47	1	19	0	0	0	0	4	0	8	2	0
Latitude	2	.0000	.0389	25.9	0	0	2	0	0	0	0	0	0	0	0	0	0	2	0	0	0	0	0	0	0	0	0	0	0
latitudes	48	.5277	5.4664	47.4	0	6	5	12	12	7	6	0	7	0	1	0	1	24	0	8	0	0	0	0	0	0	7	0	0
latitudinal	2	.0000	.0389	25.9	0	0	0	0	0	0	2	0	0	0	0	0	0	2	0	0	0	0	0	0	0	0	0	0	0
latter	91	.8018	14.630	51.7	1	7	1	5	28	22	18	9	11	2	1	11	4	5	0	5	7	0	1	0	4	6	21	13	0
latter-day	3	.2159	.1532	31.9	0	0	0	0	2	0	1	0	0	0	0	0	0	0	0	0	0	0	0	0	0	0	2	1	0
Latter-day	2	.2351	.1166	30.7	0	0	0	1	0	1	0	0	0	0	0	0	0	1	0	0	0	0	0	0	0	0	0	1	0
latter's	3	.3274	.2362	33.7	0	0	0	0	1	1	1	0	1	0	0	0	0	0	1	0	0	0	0	0	0	0	1	0	0

XR larder's
7Q larders
9L larding
8B Lardner
XH large-diameter
9D large-eyed
7R large-headed
5H large-intestine
5D large-pattern
4A large-size
7A large-wheeled
7R largemouths
8F larger-than-life
9R largesse
5J larghetto
6G largo
6A Larraby
9D larrup
6A Lars'
4A Lars's
3A Larsens'
6Q Larsh
7H larvas
7N las'
6A lascar
9R Lascaux
7P lascivious
7D Lasher
7J Lassan
7A lassoed
3A last-forever
9Q last-mentioned
5E last-place
8Q Lat
9R late-November
3P late-comers
7R late-summer
9B lateness
9K later-day
7R laterally
9H laterites
6N lath
7Q lathes
9N laths
5P latifundios
6Q Latimer
5F Latin-America
6J Latin-Americans
8G Latin-French
8Q Latinized
XP Latium
8N Latour
7H latrans
5N Latrelle

Word Type	F	D	U	SFI	3 Gr 3	4 Gr 4	5 Gr 5	6 Gr 6	7 Gr 7	8 Gr 8	9 Gr 9	X UnGr	A Read	B Eng & Gr	C Comp	D Lit	E Math	F Soc Stud	G Spell	H Sci	J Music	K Art	L Home Ec	M Shop	N Lib F	P Lib NF	Q Lib Ref	R Mag	S Rel
lattice	5	.4107	.4579	36.6	1	0	0	1	0	2	1	0	1	0	0	1	1	0	0	0	0	0	0	0	0	0	2	0	0
lattices	2	.0000	.0299	24.8	2	0	0	0	0	0	0	0	0	0	0	0	2	0	0	0	0	0	0	0	0	0	0	0	0
Lattimore	2	.0000	.0389	25.9	0	0	0	0	0	2	0	0	0	0	0	0	0	2	0	0	0	0	0	0	0	0	0	0	0
Latvia	15	.0781	.3766	35.8	0	0	14	1	0	0	0	0	0	0	0	0	0	0	0	0	0	0	0	0	0	0	14	1	0
Latvian	6	.1555	.2368	33.7	0	0	5	0	1	0	0	0	0	1	0	0	0	0	0	0	0	0	0	0	0	0	5	0	0
Latvians	7	.0000	.0733	28.6	0	0	7	0	0	0	0	0	0	0	0	0	0	0	0	0	0	0	0	0	0	0	7	0	0
laud	2	.2407	.1090	30.4	0	0	0	1	0	0	0	1	0	1	0	0	0	0	0	0	1	0	0	0	0	0	0	0	0
laudable	2	.2440	.1132	30.5	0	0	0	0	1	0	1	0	0	0	0	1	0	0	0	0	0	0	0	0	0	0	0	1	0
laugh	287	.8379	48.431	56.9	59	74	21	29	45	36	20	3	117	19	5	41	0	4	8	1	12	2	1	0	27	31	7	12	0
Laugh-In	3	.0000	.0365	25.6	0	0	0	0	0	0	3	0	0	0	0	0	0	0	0	0	0	0	0	0	0	0	0	3	0
laughable	6	.4801	.6592	38.2	1	0	0	1	1	1	2	0	3	0	0	1	0	0	0	1	0	0	0	0	1	0	0	0	0
laughed	639	.6507	88.023	59.4	217	158	40	55	89	50	23	7	304	10	0	47	0	10	5	3	6	0	0	1	131	99	3	20	0
laughin'	3	.1200	.1302	31.1	0	0	0	0	1	2	0	0	1	2	0	0	0	0	0	0	0	0	0	0	0	0	0	0	0
laughing	265	.7378	40.414	56.1	64	61	41	32	36	12	10	9	131	5	3	21	0	4	1	1	8	0	0	0	43	30	4	14	0
Laughing	11	.3636	1.0612	40.3	0	0	1	0	9	1	0	0	9	1	0	0	0	0	0	0	0	0	0	0	0	0	1	0	0
laughingstock	2	.0000	.0914	29.6	0	1	1	0	0	0	0	0	2	0	0	0	0	0	0	0	0	0	0	0	0	0	0	0	0
laughs	37	.7393	5.5534	47.4	6	9	7	3	9	0	2	1	7	4	1	7	0	2	0	1	3	0	0	0	1	6	0	5	0
laughter	135	.7640	21.134	53.2	13	17	14	21	32	8	25	5	62	6	3	10	0	2	1	2	3	2	0	0	28	9	0	7	0
laughter-silvered	3	.0000	.0322	25.1	0	0	0	0	0	0	3	0	0	0	0	3	0	0	0	0	0	0	0	0	0	0	0	0	0
Launcelot	20	.0000	.2146	33.3	0	0	0	0	0	0	20	0	0	0	0	20	0	0	0	0	0	0	0	0	0	0	0	0	0
launch	40	.6891	5.6074	47.5	0	3	3	5	21	1	5	2	5	1	1	1	1	1	1	4	3	0	0	5	1	1	3	12	0
Launch	3	.2143	.1568	32.0	1	0	0	2	0	0	0	0	0	0	0	0	0	0	0	0	0	0	0	0	0	1	0	2	0
launched	68	.6503	9.1443	49.6	1	4	7	9	15	19	11	2	8	0	0	3	2	15	0	14	0	0	0	0	0	3	12	11	0
launcher	5	.0000	.0724	28.6	0	0	5	0	0	0	0	0	0	0	0	0	0	0	0	0	0	0	0	0	0	5	0	0	0
launches	3	.3665	.2412	33.8	0	0	0	2	1	0	0	0	0	0	0	0	0	1	0	0	1	0	0	0	0	0	0	1	0
launching	30	.7243	4.4246	46.5	0	2	3	9	4	3	8	1	3	3	0	1	3	1	0	10	0	0	0	0	1	5	1	2	0
launchings	3	.3776	.2493	34.0	0	0	0	1	1	1	0	0	0	1	0	0	0	0	0	1	0	0	0	0	0	0	0	1	0
launder	5	.1768	.2036	33.1	0	0	1	0	0	2	1	1	0	0	0	0	0	0	0	0	0	0	3	0	0	1	0	1	0
laundered	2	.0000	.0064	18.1	0	0	0	0	0	2	0	0	0	0	0	0	0	0	0	0	0	0	2	0	0	0	0	0	0
laundering	6	.0000	.0193	22.9	0	0	0	0	0	4	2	0	0	0	0	0	0	0	0	0	0	0	6	0	0	0	0	0	0
laundry	39	.6990	5.5918	47.5	10	2	0	10	3	3	6	5	8	1	0	1	2	6	1	4	0	0	4	0	6	1	0	5	0
Laura	147	.3898	13.086	51.2	3	12	97	20	8	2	5	0	37	12	0	7	1	1	0	0	0	0	0	0	82	6	0	1	0
Laura's	7	.2736	.4847	36.9	1	0	5	0	1	0	0	0	2	1	0	0	0	0	0	0	0	0	0	0	4	0	0	0	0
laureate	2	.0000	.0209	23.2	0	0	0	0	0	0	2	0	0	0	0	0	0	0	0	0	0	0	0	0	0	0	2	0	0
laureates	3	.0000	.0314	25.0	0	0	0	0	0	0	3	0	0	0	0	0	0	0	0	0	0	0	0	0	0	0	3	0	0
laurel	12	.5673	1.4166	41.5	0	1	0	2	7	1	0	1	1	1	0	0	0	1	0	0	1	0	0	0	5	2	1	0	0
Laurel	7	.1475	.3648	35.6	0	0	0	0	0	2	0	5	2	0	0	0	0	0	0	5	0	0	0	0	0	0	0	0	0
laurels	2	.2306	.1140	30.6	0	1	0	0	0	1	0	0	0	1	0	0	0	1	0	0	0	0	0	0	0	0	0	0	0
Laurence	6	.4893	.6254	38.0	0	0	2	0	1	0	3	0	1	0	0	1	0	0	0	0	2	0	0	0	1	0	1	0	0
Laurie	35	.4565	3.7552	45.7	12	2	0	9	6	0	0	6	21	0	0	0	2	0	0	0	0	0	0	0	6	0	0	6	0
Laurie's	3	.2279	.2143	33.3	0	0	0	2	0	0	0	1	2	0	0	0	0	0	0	0	0	0	0	0	0	0	0	1	0
Laurinchen	2	.0000	.0914	29.6	0	0	0	2	0	0	0	0	2	0	0	0	0	0	0	0	0	0	0	0	0	0	0	0	0
Lauritz	5	.0000	.2284	33.6	0	0	0	0	5	0	0	0	5	0	0	0	0	0	0	0	0	0	0	0	0	0	0	0	0
Lauterbach	4	.0000	.0323	25.1	0	0	0	4	0	0	0	0	0	0	0	0	0	0	0	0	4	0	0	0	0	0	0	0	0
lava	88	.6564	12.133	50.8	2	21	19	20	8	11	6	1	28	2	0	0	0	3	2	33	0	0	0	0	5	8	6	1	0
Lava	2	.0000	.0243	23.9	0	0	0	2	0	0	0	0	0	0	0	0	0	0	0	0	0	0	0	0	0	0	0	2	0
Lavardens	2	.0000	.0290	24.6	0	0	0	0	2	0	0	0	0	0	0	0	0	0	0	0	0	0	0	0	0	2	0	0	0
lavas	3	.3762	.2496	34.0	0	0	0	1	0	1	1	0	0	0	0	0	0	0	0	1	0	0	0	0	0	1	1	0	0
Lavendar	22	.0000	1.0050	40.0	0	0	22	0	0	0	0	0	22	0	0	0	0	0	0	0	0	0	0	0	0	0	0	0	0
Lavendar's	2	.0000	.0914	29.6	0	0	2	0	0	0	0	0	2	0	0	0	0	0	0	0	0	0	0	0	0	0	0	0	0
lavender	10	.4952	1.0415	40.2	1	0	1	4	4	0	0	0	1	0	0	2	0	0	0	0	0	0	1	0	2	0	4	0	0
Lavinia	4	.0000	.0469	26.7	0	0	0	0	0	4	0	0	0	0	0	0	0	0	0	0	0	0	0	0	4	0	0	0	0
lavish	10	.6145	1.2498	41.0	0	1	0	1	0	3	4	1	0	0	0	2	0	2	0	0	1	1	1	0	1	0	0	2	0
Lavoisier	8	.1951	.3965	36.0	0	0	0	5	3	0	0	0	0	0	0	0	0	0	0	3	0	0	0	0	0	0	5	0	0
Lavoisier's	4	.2278	.2257	33.5	0	0	0	1	0	0	3	0	0	0	0	0	0	0	0	2	0	0	0	0	0	0	2	0	0
law	445	.7774	69.683	58.4	46	33	56	36	79	100	79	16	44	26	0	20	17	95	6	35	6	0	6	2	16	45	84	40	3
Law	36	.6557	4.8418	46.9	3	7	5	2	4	10	5	0	3	0	0	1	0	5	0	10	1	0	2	4	1	4	5	0	0
law-abiding	3	.3781	.2493	34.0	0	0	0	1	0	2	0	0	0	1	0	0	0	1	0	0	0	0	0	0	0	0	0	1	0
law-making	2	.0000	.0389	25.9	0	0	1	0	1	0	0	0	0	0	0	0	0	2	0	0	0	0	0	0	0	0	0	0	0
lawbreaker	4	.3422	.3073	34.9	0	1	0	2	0	1	0	0	0	0	0	0	0	1	0	0	0	0	0	0	0	1	0	2	0
lawbreakers	3	.1277	.1363	31.3	0	0	0	3	0	0	0	0	1	0	0	0	0	0	0	0	0	0	0	0	0	0	0	2	0
lawful	7	.4594	.7243	38.6	1	0	2	0	0	3	1	0	2	0	0	1	0	3	0	0	0	0	0	0	0	0	1	0	0
lawfully	3	.0000	.0583	27.7	0	0	1	0	0	2	0	0	0	0	0	0	0	3	0	0	0	0	0	0	0	0	0	0	0
lawgiver	2	.2408	.1091	30.4	0	0	0	0	1	1	0	0	0	1	0	0	0	0	1	0	0	0	0	0	0	0	0	0	0
lawless	4	.3358	.3279	35.2	0	0	2	0	0	2	0	0	1	0	0	0	0	2	0	0	0	0	0	0	1	0	0	0	0
Lawless	2	.0000	.0209	23.2	0	0	2	0	0	0	0	0	0	0	0	0	0	0	0	0	0	0	0	0	0	0	2	0	0
lawlessness	3	.3781	.2493	34.0	0	0	0	0	2	0	1	0	0	1	0	0	0	1	0	0	0	0	0	0	0	0	0	1	0
lawmakers	10	.3009	.7772	38.9	1	0	2	1	1	2	3	0	3	0	0	0	0	6	0	0	0	0	0	0	0	0	0	1	0
lawmaking	4	.2183	.2285	33.6	1	0	1	0	1	0	1	0	0	0	0	0	0	3	0	0	0	0	0	0	0	1	0	0	0
lawn	121	.8424	20.385	53.1	19	21	20	9	23	11	11	7	20	10	3	2	30	4	5	11	0	1	0	2	19	6	1	7	0
lawnmower	5	.4699	.5002	37.0	0	0	1	2	1	1	0	0	0	1	0	0	2	0	0	1	0	0	0	0	0	0	0	1	0
lawns	37	.7098	5.3695	47.3	5	7	4	6	7	4	2	2	6	2	1	0	12	2	0	5	0	0	0	0	3	0	3	3	0
Lawrence	70	.6631	9.5587	49.8	1	3	22	9	15	11	7	2	7	3	1	9	0	32	0	1	0	0	0	0	0	4	7	6	0
Lawrence's	2	.2401	.1133	30.5	0	1	0	0	0	0	1	0	0	0	0	0	0	0	0	0	0	0	0	0	0	1	1	0	0
Lawrenceville	3	.0000	.0434	26.4	0	3	0	0	0	0	0	0	0	0	0	0	0	0	0	0	0	0	0	0	0	3	0	0	0
lawrencium	4	.1494	.1609	32.1	0	0	0	3	0	1	0	0	0	0	0	0	0	0	0	1	0	0	0	0	0	0	3	0	0
Lawrrrrence	3	.0000	.0322	25.1	0	0	0	0	3	0	0	0	0	0	0	3	0	0	0	0	0	0	0	0	0	0	0	0	0
laws	371	.7353	55.451	57.4	25	37	57	50	58	84	54	6	28	4	1	7	4	176	5	48	2	1	1	2	5	21	50	16	0
Laws	3	.3553	.2608	34.2	0	0	1	0	2	0	0	0	1	0	0	0	0	1	0	0	0	0	0	0	0	1	0	0	0
Lawson	2	.2401	.1133	30.5	0	0	1	0	1	0	0	0	0	0	0	0	0	0	0	0	0	0	0	0	0	1	1	0	0
lawsuit	5	.4686	.4962	37.0	0	0	0	1	1	0	3	0	0	1	0	0	0	1	1	0	0	0	0	0	0	2	0	0	0
lawsuits	3	.2254	.1785	32.5	0	0	0	0	2	0	1	0	0	0	0	0	0	1	0	2	0	0	0	0	0	0	0	0	0
Lawton	4	.2353	.2382	33.8	0	0	0	0	0	4	0	0	0	0	0	0	0	0	0	3	0	0	0	0	0	0	1	0	0
lawyer	43	.7883	6.8810	48.4	0	4	11	4	7	11	4	2	14	5	0	2	1	8	1	0	1	0	0	0	1	3	2	5	0
lawyer's	5	.1273	.1779	32.5	0	0	0	0	3	1	1	0	1	0	3	0	0	0	1	0	0	0	0	0	0	0	0	0	0
lawyers	43	.6375	5.7077	47.6	2	4	6	1	16	7	7	0	6	1	1	1	0	25	1	0	0	0	0	1	0	4	3	0	0
lax	4	.3141	.3005	34.8	0	0	1	0	1	2	0	0	1	0	0	0	0	0	1	0	0	0	0	0	0	0	0	2	0
lay	951	.8795	167.03	62.2	178	114	111	124	215	110	85	14	303	53	10	101	11	58	4	79	12	0	13	29	109	94	35	40	0
lay-away	3	.0000	.0097	19.8	0	0	0	0	0	3	0	0	0	0	0	0	0	0	0	0	0	0	3	0	0	0	0	0	0
layer	259	.6510	34.770	55.4	26	39	45	25	57	21	36	10	22	2	2	4	4	8	1	144	1	20	8	2	0	9	23	9	0
layer-cake	4	.1907	.1725	32.4	0	0	0	0	0	0	4	0	0	0	0	2	0	0	0	0	0	0	2	0	0	0	0	0	0
layered	2	.2418	.1091	30.4	0	0	0	0	1	1	0	0	0	0	0	0	0	0	1	0	0	0	0	0	0	0	1	0	0
layers	225	.7881	35.709	55.5	28	33	28	14	33	33	51	5	16	2	4	0	3	14	2	114	0	4	6	4	5	20	20	11	0
laying	54	.7253	7.9430	49.0	4	8	5	6	20	4	6	1	8	3	0	7	0	4	0	5	0	2	0	5	8	1	6	5	0
layman	6	.1794	.2611	34.2	0	0	0	0	0	0	5	1	0	0	0	0	0	0	0	0	1	0	0	0	0	0	5	0	0

7D latticed
8F Lattimore's
9Q laudamus
XJ laudas
8R laude
7Q lauded
5Q Laudes
5Q Laudi
XR laugh-filled
3P laugheth
7D laughing-stock
7R launchers
9L launders
9D Laureate
XH Laurels
9J Laurence's
7Q Laurier
7Q lava-built
5H lava-cinder
9F Laval
4J lavanderas
7A lavatories
8P lavatory
5A Lavendars
7D lavender's
9B Laverne
7Q laves
9R Lavin
6P Lavine
9Q lavished
7Q lavishing
8A lavishly
4Q LAW
XP Law-Courts
5F law-maker
7D lawbooks
5A Lawk
3N lawn-mower
7N laws-a-me
9R Lawson's
9D lawyers'
8A laxative
8Q laxatives
7R laxity
7P Lay
8A lay-ups
9D layest
3P layeth
9Q layman's

Word Type	F	D	U	SFI	3 Gr 3	4 Gr 4	5 Gr 5	6 Gr 6	7 Gr 7	8 Gr 8	9 Gr 9	X UnGr	A Read	B Eng & Gr	C Comp	D Lit	E Math	F Soc Stud	G Spell	H Sci	J Music	K Art	L Home Ec	M Shop	N Lib F	P Lib NF	Q Lib Ref	R Mag	S Rel
laymen	6	.4416	.5686	37.5	0	0	3	0	0	0	2	1	0	0	0	0	0	0	0	1	0	0	0	0	0	3	1	1	0
layout	18	.1133	.4609	36.6	0	0	0	0	3	2	12	1	0	0	0	0	0	0	0	0	0	0	1	15	0	1	0	1	0
layouts	7	.0000	.0177	22.5	0	0	0	0	1	0	6	0	0	0	0	0	0	0	0	0	0	0	0	7	0	0	0	0	0
lays	71	.7332	10.606	50.3	25	12	7	6	15	0	5	1	11	2	2	2	2	3	0	21	0	0	0	0	1	15	8	4	0
Laysan	7	.0000	.0851	29.3	0	0	0	0	7	0	0	0	0	0	0	0	0	0	0	0	0	0	0	0	0	0	0	7	0
Lazare	2	.0000	.0234	23.7	0	2	0	0	0	0	0	0	0	0	0	0	0	0	0	0	0	0	0	0	2	0	0	0	0
Lazarus	2	.0000	.0290	24.6	0	0	0	0	2	0	0	0	0	0	0	0	0	0	0	0	0	0	0	0	0	2	0	0	0
Lazear	9	.2442	.6954	38.4	0	2	4	0	0	3	0	0	7	0	0	0	0	0	0	0	0	0	0	0	0	2	0	0	0
lazier	4	.2446	.3071	34.9	3	0	1	0	0	0	0	0	3	0	0	0	1	0	0	0	0	0	0	0	0	0	0	0	0
lazily	18	.6561	2.4663	43.9	2	5	4	1	2	3	0	1	6	3	0	2	0	1	1	0	0	0	0	0	2	3	0	0	0
laziness	4	.3584	.3139	35.0	0	0	1	0	1	2	0	0	0	0	0	0	0	0	0	0	0	0	0	0	2	1	0	1	0
lazy	102	.7854	16.360	52.1	30	14	13	18	12	7	6	2	51	7	3	7	1	1	6	1	6	0	0	0	10	6	2	1	0
lb	45	.2392	2.6045	44.2	1	2	3	5	11	6	15	2	0	0	0	0	39	0	3	0	0	0	0	0	0	0	1	2	0
LBJ	3	.0000	.0365	25.6	0	0	0	0	0	3	0	0	0	0	0	0	0	0	0	0	0	0	0	0	0	0	0	3	0
lbs	12	.4739	1.1933	40.8	0	0	2	3	5	0	2	0	0	0	0	0	4	0	0	0	0	0	0	1	0	0	2	5	0
LCD	4	.0000	.0599	27.8	0	0	0	0	1	3	0	0	0	0	0	0	4	0	0	0	0	0	0	0	0	0	0	0	0
LCM	24	.0000	.3592	35.6	0	0	0	14	8	2	0	0	0	0	0	0	24	0	0	0	0	0	0	0	0	0	0	0	0
le	58	.3035	4.1138	46.1	16	4	8	20	5	4	1	0	11	2	0	0	0	2	36	0	0	0	0	0	4	1	1	1	0
Le	8	.3411	.6091	37.8	1	0	0	1	2	2	2	0	1	0	0	0	0	0	0	0	1	2	0	0	0	2	0	2	0
LeClerc	2	.0000	.0914	29.6	2	0	0	0	0	0	0	0	2	0	0	0	0	0	0	0	0	0	0	0	0	0	0	0	0
LeClerc's	2	.0000	.0914	29.6	2	0	0	0	0	0	0	0	2	0	0	0	0	0	0	0	0	0	0	0	0	0	0	0	0
LeHavre	4	.2441	.2254	33.5	2	0	0	0	2	0	0	0	0	0	0	0	0	0	0	0	0	0	0	0	2	0	2	0	0
LeMans	2	.0000	.0243	23.9	0	0	0	0	2	0	0	0	0	0	0	0	0	0	0	0	0	0	0	0	0	0	0	2	0
LeMatin	3	.0000	.0434	26.4	0	3	0	0	0	0	0	0	0	0	0	0	0	0	0	0	0	0	0	0	0	3	0	0	0
lePelican	7	.0000	.3198	35.0	0	0	7	0	0	0	0	0	7	0	0	0	0	0	0	0	0	0	0	0	0	0	0	0	0
lea	2	.0000	.0290	24.6	1	0	1	0	0	0	0	0	0	0	0	0	0	0	0	0	0	0	0	0	0	2	0	0	0
leached	5	.3636	.4034	36.1	0	0	1	0	2	0	2	0	0	0	0	0	0	0	0	2	0	0	0	0	0	0	2	1	0
leaching	3	.2239	.1775	32.5	0	0	0	0	1	0	2	0	0	0	0	0	0	2	0	1	0	0	0	0	0	0	0	0	0
lead	520	.9436	97.007	59.9	43	60	70	66	113	74	75	19	109	22	8	34	7	60	13	70	19	3	6	21	17	38	53	39	1
lead-off	2	.1814	.1187	30.7	0	0	0	1	1	0	0	0	1	0	0	0	0	0	0	0	0	0	0	0	0	0	0	1	0
leaded	2	.1814	.1187	30.7	0	0	0	1	1	0	0	0	1	0	0	0	0	0	0	0	0	0	0	0	0	0	0	1	0
leaden	5	.4026	.4248	36.3	0	0	1	0	2	1	1	0	0	0	1	1	0	0	0	0	0	0	0	0	1	0	0	2	0
leader	310	.8646	53.597	57.3	43	53	49	50	47	40	25	3	82	9	3	15	1	67	4	2	30	1	1	1	14	33	20	27	0
Leader	10	.5305	1.0964	40.4	1	0	1	2	2	1	0	3	0	1	0	3	0	0	0	0	2	0	0	0	0	3	0	1	0
leader's	9	.3836	.8041	39.1	0	1	0	1	3	4	0	0	3	0	0	4	0	0	0	0	0	0	0	0	1	0	0	1	0
leaders	238	.6171	30.478	54.8	26	13	52	19	29	58	37	4	14	3	0	1	0	125	0	1	6	2	0	1	2	26	18	37	2
leadership	81	.6104	10.263	50.1	5	0	5	10	15	17	26	3	6	1	0	1	0	30	0	1	3	0	0	0	1	8	7	23	0
leadeth	4	.3075	.2938	34.7	1	0	0	0	1	2	0	0	1	0	0	2	0	0	1	0	0	0	0	0	0	0	0	0	0
leadin'	2	.2444	.1132	30.5	0	1	0	0	0	1	0	0	0	1	0	0	0	0	0	0	0	0	0	0	1	0	0	0	0
leading	315	.7966	50.568	57.0	26	41	49	59	68	41	30	1	52	6	4	14	3	92	1	19	16	2	2	0	12	21	40	29	2
Leading	2	.0000	.0234	23.7	2	0	0	0	0	0	0	0	0	0	0	0	0	0	0	0	0	0	0	0	2	0	0	0	0
leads	120	.8099	19.500	52.9	8	7	19	13	31	16	16	10	14	1	1	9	7	19	1	21	10	1	1	2	2	6	14	10	1
leadsmen	2	.1948	.1250	31.0	0	0	0	1	0	1	0	0	1	0	0	0	0	0	0	0	0	0	0	0	0	1	0	0	0
leaf	214	.8403	36.066	55.6	60	27	30	27	52	8	5	5	45	3	3	5	0	5	7	75	4	4	4	0	15	19	20	5	0
Leaf	5	.2590	.3349	35.2	1	2	0	0	1	1	0	0	1	0	0	0	0	1	0	0	0	0	0	0	0	3	0	0	0
leaf-nosed	2	.0000	.0290	24.6	0	0	0	0	2	0	0	0	0	0	0	0	0	0	0	0	0	0	0	0	0	2	0	0	0
leafless	5	.5363	.5745	37.6	1	0	1	1	1	0	0	1	1	1	0	0	0	0	0	1	0	0	0	0	1	1	0	0	0
leaflets	8	.3554	.6368	38.0	1	0	1	1	2	0	0	3	0	1	0	0	0	0	0	4	0	0	0	0	0	0	3	0	0
leaflike	3	.2445	.1818	32.6	0	0	1	1	0	0	1	0	0	0	0	0	0	0	0	2	0	0	0	0	0	0	1	0	0
leafy	30	.6544	4.1056	46.1	12	2	5	1	6	2	1	1	11	0	1	0	0	4	0	1	1	0	4	0	1	1	3	3	0
league	53	.7280	7.8211	48.9	3	3	5	13	13	10	5	1	7	10	1	1	1	3	3	0	1	0	0	0	2	7	1	16	0
League	106	.6390	14.063	51.5	13	7	15	16	20	23	8	4	17	3	0	1	1	27	0	0	0	0	0	0	4	21	8	24	0
league's	3	.0000	.0365	25.6	0	0	0	0	0	2	0	1	0	0	0	0	0	0	0	0	0	0	0	0	0	0	0	3	0
leagues	16	.5777	1.9742	43.0	0	1	1	3	6	4	1	0	5	0	0	0	0	1	0	0	0	0	0	0	2	3	1	4	0
Leagues	2	.2446	.1123	30.5	0	0	0	1	0	0	1	0	0	1	0	0	0	0	0	0	0	0	0	0	0	0	1	0	0
Leah	7	.0000	.0821	29.1	7	0	0	0	0	0	0	0	0	0	0	0	0	0	0	0	0	0	0	0	7	0	0	0	0
leak	29	.6959	4.1636	46.2	4	4	4	5	8	1	2	1	8	1	1	0	2	3	3	3	0	0	0	0	0	1	0	7	0
leakage	2	.0000	.0243	23.9	0	0	0	0	1	0	1	0	0	0	0	0	0	0	0	0	0	0	0	0	0	0	0	2	0
leaked	10	.6052	1.2860	41.1	0	0	1	3	1	2	2	1	3	0	0	1	0	2	0	1	0	0	0	0	0	1	0	2	0
leaking	12	.5161	1.3384	41.3	2	3	1	1	4	1	0	0	3	1	0	0	0	0	0	1	0	0	0	0	1	0	1	5	0
leaks	14	.5899	1.7460	42.4	3	1	0	4	3	2	1	0	3	1	0	0	0	3	0	0	0	0	0	0	1	4	0	2	0
leaky	10	.5943	1.2436	40.9	1	0	0	2	4	3	0	0	2	0	1	1	0	0	1	2	0	0	0	0	0	0	1	2	0
lean	99	.8266	16.439	52.2	10	11	14	8	29	21	4	2	26	5	0	16	0	5	4	6	3	2	4	0	12	10	0	6	0
lean-to	8	.5447	.9444	39.8	1	0	4	2	0	0	1	0	3	0	0	0	0	0	0	0	1	0	0	0	2	1	1	0	0
Leander	2	.0000	.0389	25.9	0	0	2	0	0	0	0	0	0	0	0	0	0	2	0	0	0	0	0	0	0	0	0	0	0
leaned	138	.6101	17.849	52.5	24	38	7	20	24	12	13	0	51	1	5	22	0	3	0	0	0	0	0	0	36	15	0	5	0
leaner	6	.5520	.7154	38.5	0	0	0	0	4	1	0	1	2	0	0	1	0	1	0	0	0	0	0	0	0	0	1	1	0
leaning	75	.7474	11.490	50.6	12	11	13	9	20	2	7	1	30	2	3	6	1	2	0	0	2	1	0	0	15	6	0	7	0
Leaning	2	.2408	.1204	30.8	1	0	0	1	0	0	0	0	0	0	0	0	0	1	0	0	0	0	0	0	0	1	0	0	0
leans	18	.6495	2.4336	43.9	4	2	2	3	2	1	3	1	5	1	0	2	0	2	0	0	0	1	0	0	2	1	0	4	0
leant	5	.0804	.1641	32.2	0	0	2	1	2	0	0	0	1	0	0	0	0	0	0	0	0	0	0	0	4	0	0	0	0
leap	99	.8289	16.490	52.2	17	20	11	11	23	6	11	0	25	2	0	10	3	2	3	15	1	2	0	0	15	8	5	8	0
Leap	2	.0000	.0290	24.6	0	0	2	0	0	0	0	0	0	0	0	0	0	0	0	0	0	0	0	0	0	2	0	0	0
leaped	118	.6810	16.788	52.3	19	19	12	12	35	18	3	0	51	6	2	11	0	3	1	0	0	0	0	0	30	9	2	3	0
leaping	41	.6340	5.4633	47.4	3	3	4	15	9	6	1	0	15	1	0	5	0	0	0	1	0	3	0	0	6	4	3	3	0
leaps	36	.7336	5.3587	47.3	5	5	5	7	4	5	5	0	6	1	3	3	1	2	0	6	6	1	0	0	0	3	2	2	0
leapt	10	.4818	1.1154	40.5	2	0	0	5	2	1	0	0	6	0	0	1	0	0	0	0	0	0	0	0	1	2	0	0	0
Lear	4	.3809	.3307	35.2	0	1	0	0	1	1	1	0	0	1	0	1	0	0	0	0	0	0	0	0	0	2	0	0	0
learn	1674	.9458	312.98	65.0	335	326	224	184	293	149	138	25	380	138	17	48	65	223	152	203	74	40	44	46	46	95	25	77	1
Learn	3	.2425	.1816	32.6	0	0	3	0	0	0	0	0	0	0	0	0	0	2	0	0	0	0	0	0	0	0	0	1	0
learn'd	2	.0000	.0914	29.6	0	0	0	0	2	0	0	0	2	0	0	0	0	0	0	0	0	0	0	0	0	0	0	0	0
learned	1345	.9360	249.17	64.0	251	226	185	181	211	155	104	32	293	129	21	42	80	218	69	165	54	19	15	13	49	89	32	52	5
learnin'	4	.2393	.3005	34.8	0	3	0	0	1	0	0	0	3	0	0	1	0	0	0	0	0	0	0	0	0	0	0	0	0
learning	377	.9192	68.699	58.4	58	49	53	62	57	44	40	14	73	36	5	8	2	52	20	62	20	9	9	2	9	17	26	27	0
Learning	2	.2442	.1134	30.5	0	0	0	1	0	1	0	0	0	1	0	0	0	0	0	0	0	0	0	0	0	0	0	1	0
learnings	13	.1589	.6091	37.8	0	0	12	0	1	0	0	0	0	0	0	0	0	12	1	0	0	0	0	0	0	0	0	0	0
learns	56	.7829	8.8932	49.5	9	14	6	3	9	8	6	1	18	1	4	1	1	7	2	6	3	0	4	1	1	2	1	4	0
learnt	4	.1787	.2347	33.7	1	1	0	1	1	0	0	0	2	0	0	0	0	0	0	0	0	0	0	0	2	0	0	0	0
lease	11	.1641	.4931	36.9	1	0	1	0	1	0	1	7	1	0	0	0	0	0	0	0	0	0	0	0	0	0	1	9	0
leased	7	.2210	.3873	35.9	0	0	1	0	1	3	1	1	0	0	0	0	0	3	0	0	0	0	0	0	0	0	0	4	0
leases	2	.2437	.1129	30.5	0	0	1	0	0	0	0	1	0	0	0	0	0	0	0	0	0	0	0	0	0	0	1	1	0
leash	16	.6225	2.0826	43.2	4	3	1	0	6	2	0	0	4	2	1	0	0	0	0	2	0	0	0	0	3	1	0	3	0
leashes	4	.2417	.3028	34.8	0	0	0	3	1	0	0	0	3	0	0	0	0	0	0	0	0	0	0	0	1	0	0	0	0
leasing	3	.1937	.1495	31.7	0	0	0	0	0	0	1	2	0	0	0	0	0	1	0	0	0	0	0	0	0	0	0	2	0

3J Layo
7R layoff
7M layover
7J Lazaroni
5N lazing
8D lazuli
3A Lazy
9D lazy-pacing
6A lazybones
9P lazyness
3P Lazzeri

8F LeBourget
5A LeGrand
8A LeMonde
7N LeRenard
8A LeRoy
7N LeSubtil
8D Le-jardin
8D le's
7R Lea
5F Lead
8M lead-alloy-coated

8Q lead-bismuth
XH lead-blue
8M lead-coated
7A lead-dog
7R lead-in
8N lead-pencil
9H lead-206
9D leadcolour
4A LEADER
7D Leader's
8F leaderless

9R Leaders
7D Leadership
3P leadoff
8A leadsman's
XH Leadville
4A leady
5A leaf-fringed
7Q leaf's
8F leafed
7Q leafhoppers
7A leafing

5R leaflet
3P LEAFLETS
9H leafy-shoot
3P League's
5A Leaguers
9F Leakey
8B leakproof
XR Lean
8N lean-bellied
6A lean-bodied
XP lean-tos

5N leanness
4A leapfrog
3P Leaping
5R learn-to-sail
3B Learn-wisdom
3F Learned
7B learning-knight
8F Leary

Word Type	F	D	U	SFI	3 Gr 3	4 Gr 4	5 Gr 5	6 Gr 6	7 Gr 7	8 Gr 8	9 Gr 9	X UnGr	A Read	B Eng & Gr	C Comp	D Lit	E Math	F Soc Stud	G Spell	H Sci	J Music	K Art	L Home Ec	M Shop	N Lib F	P Lib NF	Q Lib Ref	R Mag	S Rel
least	878	.9247	160.77	62.1	68	98	92	112	195	130	136	47	142	72	12	28	168	53	23	69	9	3	21	6	42	80	55	95	0
leastways	2	.1717	.1142	30.6	1	0	0	0	1	0	0	0	1	0	0	1	0	0	0	0	0	0	0	0	0	0	0	0	0
leather	226	.7781	35.663	55.5	48	45	29	29	56	10	7	2	62	4	5	10	0	55	5	6	6	1	0	18	23	17	8	6	0
leather-and-rope	2	.0000	.0914	29.6	0	0	2	0	0	0	0	0	2	0	0	0	0	0	0	0	0	0	0	0	0	0	0	0	0
leather-bound	2	.2306	.1140	30.6	0	1	1	0	0	0	0	0	0	1	0	0	0	1	0	0	0	0	0	0	0	0	0	0	0
leathered	2	.0000	.0243	23.9	0	0	0	1	1	0	0	0	0	0	0	0	0	0	0	0	0	0	0	0	0	0	0	2	0
leathery	13	.6441	1.7353	42.4	3	0	1	2	4	2	0	1	2	0	0	2	0	0	0	4	0	0	0	0	2	1	1	1	0
leave	964	.9418	179.67	62.5	175	167	102	126	184	100	90	20	283	83	13	63	24	74	14	92	24	6	24	1	93	88	22	58	2
leavened	2	.1698	.1133	30.5	0	1	0	0	1	0	0	0	1	0	0	0	0	0	0	0	0	0	0	0	0	0	1	0	0
leavening	2	.0000	.0209	23.2	0	0	2	0	0	0	0	0	0	0	0	0	0	0	0	0	0	0	0	0	0	0	2	0	0
leaves	939	.8963	167.40	62.2	286	127	105	140	169	38	43	31	181	30	15	58	17	68	12	261	29	21	11	2	34	105	64	31	0
Leaves	8	.3347	.6581	38.2	0	4	1	0	3	0	0	0	3	0	0	0	0	0	0	0	0	0	1	0	0	4	0	0	0
leavin'	2	.0000	.0234	23.7	0	0	0	0	1	1	0	0	0	0	0	0	0	0	0	0	0	0	0	0	2	0	0	0	0
leaving	301	.9327	55.614	57.5	42	47	30	33	71	39	30	9	86	18	4	24	8	24	3	18	6	4	13	4	23	33	13	20	0
Lebanese	15	.3474	1.3652	41.4	9	0	1	4	0	0	1	0	9	0	0	0	0	5	0	0	0	0	0	0	0	1	0	0	0
Lebanon	40	.5142	4.5626	46.6	15	0	2	11	3	2	7	0	15	0	0	0	0	10	0	0	0	0	0	0	0	5	1	9	0
Lebanons	7	.0000	.3198	35.0	0	0	0	0	0	7	0	0	7	0	0	0	0	0	0	0	0	0	0	0	0	0	0	0	0
Lebarge	2	.0000	.0914	29.6	0	0	0	0	2	0	0	0	2	0	0	0	0	0	0	0	0	0	0	0	0	0	0	0	0
Leblanc	6	.1787	.3521	35.5	0	6	0	0	0	0	0	0	3	0	0	0	0	0	0	0	0	0	0	0	3	0	0	0	0
lectern	4	.2073	.2003	33.0	0	0	0	0	1	0	3	0	0	0	0	1	0	0	0	0	0	0	0	0	0	0	0	3	0
lecture	22	.6671	3.0218	44.8	1	1	3	0	4	8	1	4	4	5	0	0	0	2	1	0	0	0	0	0	1	5	2	2	0
lectured	2	.1717	.1142	30.6	0	0	0	1	0	1	0	0	1	0	0	1	0	0	0	0	0	0	0	0	0	0	0	0	0
lecturer	8	.5665	.9451	39.8	0	0	1	1	2	3	1	0	1	1	0	1	2	0	0	0	2	0	0	0	0	0	0	1	0
lectures	12	.6012	1.4941	41.7	1	3	0	0	1	2	4	1	1	2	0	1	0	0	0	2	0	0	0	0	0	1	1	4	0
lecturing	5	.5474	.5694	37.6	0	0	1	1	0	2	1	0	0	0	0	0	0	1	0	1	1	0	0	0	0	0	1	1	0
led	598	.8861	105.63	60.2	82	80	97	99	120	71	36	13	158	9	2	38	8	92	8	23	24	4	0	0	44	68	68	51	1
Lederer	2	.0000	.0243	23.9	0	0	0	0	0	0	0	2	0	0	0	0	0	0	0	0	0	0	0	0	0	0	0	2	0
ledge	61	.7113	9.0546	49.6	3	7	14	16	15	5	1	0	33	3	1	6	0	1	0	0	1	0	0	0	10	3	1	2	0
ledger	4	.1700	.1635	32.1	0	0	0	0	3	1	0	0	0	0	0	0	0	0	0	0	3	0	0	0	1	0	0	0	0
ledgers	2	.1787	.1174	30.7	0	0	0	0	0	2	0	0	1	0	0	0	0	0	0	0	0	0	0	0	1	0	0	0	0
ledges	10	.5616	1.2237	40.9	0	1	1	3	1	1	0	3	4	0	0	1	0	0	0	2	0	0	0	0	0	2	0	1	0
lee	21	.4507	2.0895	43.2	6	2	2	1	6	0	4	0	6	0	0	1	0	0	0	0	8	0	0	0	0	1	4	1	0
Lee	146	.7925	23.388	53.7	23	10	32	7	18	41	11	4	31	2	2	3	7	45	3	1	2	0	0	0	5	16	10	19	0
Lee's	17	.6002	2.2060	43.4	4	2	2	0	2	6	1	0	8	0	0	0	0	4	0	0	0	0	0	0	1	1	2	1	0
leeboard	2	.0000	.0209	23.2	0	0	0	0	0	0	2	0	0	0	0	0	0	0	0	0	0	0	0	0	0	0	2	0	0
leeboards	2	.0000	.0209	23.2	0	0	0	0	0	0	2	0	0	0	0	0	0	0	0	0	0	0	0	0	0	0	2	0	0
leech	4	.4526	.3993	36.0	0	0	1	1	2	0	0	0	1	1	0	1	0	0	0	0	0	0	0	0	0	0	0	1	0
Leeds	2	.0000	.0389	25.9	0	0	0	0	2	0	0	0	0	0	0	0	0	2	0	0	0	0	0	0	0	0	0	0	0
Leeds'	2	.0000	.0234	23.7	2	0	0	0	0	0	0	0	0	0	0	0	0	0	0	0	0	0	0	0	2	0	0	0	0
leetle	3	.1250	.1342	31.3	0	0	0	0	2	1	0	0	1	0	0	0	0	0	0	0	0	0	0	0	2	0	0	0	0
Leeuwenhoek	9	.1719	.4433	36.5	0	1	0	1	1	0	0	6	0	0	0	0	0	0	0	8	0	0	0	0	0	0	1	0	0
Leeuwenhoek's	2	.2160	.1362	31.3	1	0	0	0	0	0	0	1	1	0	0	0	0	0	0	1	0	0	0	0	0	0	0	0	0
leeward	6	.2942	.4422	36.5	1	0	0	0	4	0	1	0	1	0	0	0	0	0	0	4	0	0	0	0	0	0	1	0	0
Leeward	2	.0000	.0243	23.9	0	0	0	0	2	0	0	0	0	0	0	0	0	0	0	0	0	0	0	0	0	0	0	2	0
leeway	5	.4691	.4932	36.9	0	0	1	1	2	0	1	0	0	0	0	0	0	0	0	0	0	0	0	0	1	1	1	2	0
Lefevre	2	.0000	.0243	23.9	0	0	0	0	0	0	2	0	0	0	0	0	0	0	0	0	0	0	0	0	0	0	0	2	0
left	2885	.9762	554.95	67.4	602	486	337	330	543	327	229	31	827	132	23	175	438	182	67	147	138	19	56	47	217	177	94	144	2
Left	38	.2314	2.1323	43.3	3	0	0	29	6	0	0	0	2	0	0	0	0	1	0	0	0	0	0	0	29	1	0	5	0
Left-Distributive	5	.0000	.0748	28.7	0	0	0	0	0	0	5	0	0	0	0	0	5	0	0	0	0	0	0	0	0	0	0	0	0
left-footed	2	.2433	.1158	30.6	0	0	0	0	1	1	0	0	0	0	0	0	0	0	0	0	0	0	0	0	0	1	0	1	0
left-hand	44	.7366	6.5788	48.2	2	8	7	6	6	3	12	0	7	5	0	2	8	2	6	8	0	1	0	3	1	1	0	0	0
left-handed	17	.4825	1.7054	42.3	4	6	1	1	0	1	4	0	0	0	2	0	0	0	0	1	1	0	0	3	0	9	1	0	0
left-hander	2	.0000	.0914	29.6	1	0	0	1	0	0	0	0	2	0	0	0	0	0	0	0	0	0	0	0	0	0	0	0	0
left-over	4	.3314	.3159	35.0	1	1	1	0	0	0	1	0	1	0	0	0	0	1	0	0	0	0	1	0	0	1	0	0	0
left-overs	3	.0000	.0434	26.4	3	0	0	0	0	0	0	0	0	0	0	0	0	0	0	0	0	0	0	0	0	3	0	0	0
left-wing	2	.0000	.0243	23.9	0	0	0	1	0	0	0	1	0	0	0	0	0	0	0	0	0	0	0	0	0	0	0	2	0
lefthanded	2	.2346	.1166	30.7	0	0	1	0	1	0	0	0	0	0	0	0	0	0	0	1	0	0	0	0	0	0	0	1	0
leftist	2	.2437	.1129	30.5	0	0	0	0	0	2	0	0	0	0	0	0	0	0	0	0	0	0	0	0	0	0	1	1	0
leftover	13	.5469	1.5380	41.9	3	5	2	0	2	1	0	0	5	1	1	0	0	1	0	1	0	0	2	0	2	0	0	0	0
leftovers	5	.4356	.4810	36.8	1	0	0	0	1	1	1	1	1	0	0	1	0	0	0	1	0	0	1	0	0	1	0	0	0
Lefty	9	.3196	.7113	38.5	4	0	3	1	1	0	0	0	3	0	0	0	0	0	0	0	0	0	0	0	0	2	0	4	0
leg	313	.9251	57.498	57.6	73	45	31	51	53	23	32	5	123	9	3	11	11	2	11	32	3	2	6	6	30	27	11	26	0
legacies	3	.2332	.1690	32.3	0	0	2	1	0	0	0	0	0	0	0	0	0	0	0	0	0	0	0	0	0	2	0	1	0
legacy	6	.5515	.6813	38.3	0	0	2	0	3	0	1	0	0	0	0	0	0	0	0	0	1	0	0	0	1	1	1	2	0
legal	66	.6513	8.7822	49.4	1	0	8	4	21	16	16	0	2	1	0	0	2	15	2	0	1	0	1	0	0	9	13	20	0
legality	5	.3468	.3830	35.8	0	0	0	0	1	2	2	0	0	0	0	0	0	1	0	0	0	0	0	0	0	0	2	2	0
legally	4	.3831	.3415	35.3	0	0	1	1	1	1	0	0	0	0	0	0	0	2	0	0	0	0	0	0	0	1	0	1	0
legato	12	.0000	.0970	29.9	3	1	1	0	2	0	5	0	0	0	0	0	0	0	0	0	12	0	0	0	0	0	0	0	0
legend	116	.7155	16.992	52.3	13	15	17	24	19	20	4	4	26	3	0	5	0	27	0	1	15	0	0	0	6	5	17	11	0
Legend	2	.2407	.1090	30.4	1	0	0	1	0	0	0	0	0	1	0	0	0	0	0	0	1	0	0	0	0	0	0	0	0
legendary	20	.7684	3.1333	45.0	1	0	4	2	2	7	3	1	7	1	0	3	0	2	0	1	1	0	0	0	1	1	2	1	0
legends	68	.7575	10.497	50.2	2	7	13	15	9	14	4	4	22	5	1	3	0	9	0	2	11	3	0	0	2	3	6	1	0
legged	4	.0971	.1385	31.4	0	0	0	0	2	2	0	0	1	0	0	0	0	1	0	0	0	2	0	0	0	0	0	0	0
leggings	6	.4934	.6389	38.1	0	1	3	0	2	0	0	0	1	0	0	2	0	1	0	0	0	0	0	0	1	1	0	0	0
leggy	2	.0000	.0243	23.9	0	0	0	0	1	0	0	1	0	0	0	0	0	0	0	0	0	0	0	0	0	0	0	2	0
legible	10	.4362	.9107	39.6	0	0	0	5	2	1	2	0	0	6	0	0	0	0	2	0	0	0	0	1	0	0	1	0	0
legibly	4	.0931	.1444	31.6	0	0	0	0	3	0	1	0	1	3	0	0	0	0	0	0	0	0	0	0	0	0	0	0	0
legion	5	.4660	.4877	36.9	0	0	0	0	1	2	1	1	0	0	0	2	0	0	0	0	0	0	0	0	1	0	1	1	0
Legion	16	.5767	1.9226	42.8	0	0	6	1	1	7	0	1	1	1	0	3	0	2	0	1	0	0	0	0	0	6	0	2	0
legionaries	2	.2401	.1133	30.5	0	0	1	0	1	0	0	0	0	0	0	0	0	0	0	0	0	0	0	0	0	1	1	0	0
legions	5	.2444	.2887	34.6	0	0	1	1	1	0	2	0	0	0	0	0	0	0	0	0	0	0	0	0	0	3	2	0	0
legislate	2	.0000	.0162	22.1	0	0	0	0	1	1	0	0	0	0	0	0	0	0	2	0	0	0	0	0	0	0	0	0	0
legislation	27	.5208	2.9339	44.7	0	0	4	0	7	8	8	0	0	1	0	0	0	6	1	0	0	0	0	0	0	2	9	8	0
legislative	44	.5142	4.8185	46.8	9	1	10	0	13	6	3	2	5	0	0	0	0	10	1	0	0	0	0	0	0	9	15	4	0
legislator	4	.4350	.3902	35.9	0	0	0	0	1	1	2	0	1	0	0	0	0	1	1	0	0	0	0	0	0	0	0	1	0
legislators	10	.4267	.9292	39.7	0	0	4	1	1	1	1	2	1	0	0	0	0	0	0	1	0	0	0	0	0	1	4	3	0
legislature	50	.5368	5.6813	47.5	1	2	14	0	5	24	3	1	4	0	0	1	0	23	3	0	0	0	0	0	0	1	12	6	0
Legislature	7	.4646	.7440	38.7	1	0	1	0	4	1	0	0	3	0	0	0	0	1	0	0	0	0	0	0	0	2	1	0	0
legislature's	2	.2437	.1129	30.5	0	0	1	0	0	0	1	0	0	0	0	0	0	0	0	0	0	0	0	0	0	0	1	1	0
legislatures	26	.5468	3.0210	44.8	1	0	7	2	7	7	2	0	4	0	0	0	1	7	0	0	0	0	0	0	0	4	7	3	0
legitimate	18	.5081	1.9015	42.8	0	1	4	0	3	4	6	0	0	1	0	0	0	2	0	0	0	0	2	0	0	1	3	9	0

6E Least
7N least-religious
7D leastwise
6G leath-er
5A leather-cheeked
7A leather-covered
6A leather-lined
8D leathern
3Q leathernecks
5N leathers
8F Leatherstocking
6A leatherworking
6R leathery-leafed
7A leatle
3A Leave
3N leave-
6A leave-taking
3P Leavenworth
6N leavings
7R Leavitt
7P lecher
XB lecherous
9Q Lechfeld
8A lecons
5Q Leconte
7Q Lectureship
8D leead-er
7H leeches
9R leek
7N leer
7Q leering
9N Leeroy's
7D leers
8Q Leesburg
7R Leewards
7R Leewards'
9E Left-
4A Left-Over
5R left-arm
5A left-behind
6R left-field
9M left-handers
7L left-off
3J left-right
4B left-to-right
6B leftenant
8R leftists
7R Leftists
8R Leftover
7A lefts
7N leftward
7P leg-and-rail
8D leg-iron
7N leg's
5N legal-like
9R legal-size
8F legalistic
6P legalize
8Q legalized
6R legally-elected
4J legalum
3Q Legaspi
4N legatee
8Q legation
8F legations
5Q legend-like
8P Legends
8K Leger
7D legerdemain
3H legger
8G Leghorn
9M legibility
5P Legion's
6N Legions
6P legislated
5Q legislates
5Q Legislative
7A Legislature's
5P legitimacy
XR legitimately

Word Type	F	D	U	SFI	3 Gr 3	4 Gr 4	5 Gr 5	6 Gr 6	7 Gr 7	8 Gr 8	9 Gr 9	X UnGr	A Read	B Eng & Gr	C Comp	D Lit	E Math	F Soc Stud	G Spell	H Sci	J Music	K Art	L Home Ec	M Shop	N Lib F	P Lib NF	Q Lib Ref	R Mag	S Rel
legless	3	.3754	.2470	33.9	0	0	0	1	2	0	0	0	0	1	0	0	0	0	0	1	0	0	0	0	0	0	1	0	0
legs	836	.8362	140.57	61.5	233	142	90	96	154	55	55	11	261	23	6	56	33	14	3	123	1	34	4	8	78	120	38	34	0
Legs	3	.0000	.1370	31.4	3	0	0	0	0	0	0	0	3	0	0	0	0	0	0	0	0	0	0	0	0	0	0	0	0
legumes	7	.3567	.5642	37.5	0	0	1	0	3	1	2	0	0	0	0	0	0	0	0	4	0	0	0	0	0	1	2	0	0
leguminous	3	.3762	.2479	33.9	0	0	0	0	3	0	0	0	0	0	0	0	0	0	0	1	0	0	0	0	1	0	1	0	0
Lehar	2	.0000	.0162	22.1	0	0	0	0	2	0	0	0	0	0	0	0	0	0	0	0	2	0	0	0	0	0	0	0	0
lei	6	.2440	.4665	36.7	5	0	0	0	0	1	0	0	5	0	0	0	0	0	1	0	0	0	0	0	0	0	0	0	0
Lei	5	.0000	.2284	33.6	5	0	0	0	0	0	0	0	5	0	0	0	0	0	0	0	0	0	0	0	0	0	0	0	0
Leibniz	9	.0000	.1347	31.3	0	0	0	0	0	9	0	0	0	0	0	0	9	0	0	0	0	0	0	0	0	0	0	0	0
Leiden	12	.3704	1.0207	40.1	2	0	2	0	2	6	0	0	2	0	0	0	0	4	0	0	0	0	0	0	0	0	5	1	0
Leidesdorff	2	.0000	.0389	25.9	0	0	0	0	0	2	0	0	0	0	0	0	0	2	0	0	0	0	0	0	0	0	0	0	0
Leif	24	.3036	1.7833	42.5	1	0	0	13	6	4	0	0	6	13	0	0	0	4	0	0	0	0	0	0	0	0	1	0	0
Leif's	2	.1733	.1149	30.6	0	0	0	1	1	0	0	0	1	1	0	0	0	0	0	0	0	0	0	0	0	0	0	0	0
Leighton	2	.2446	.1142	30.6	0	0	1	0	0	0	0	1	0	0	0	0	0	0	0	0	0	0	0	0	1	0	0	1	0
Leinster	4	.3212	.3104	34.9	0	0	2	1	1	0	0	0	1	0	0	1	0	0	0	0	0	0	0	0	0	2	0	0	0
Leipsic	3	.0000	.0434	26.4	0	0	0	3	0	0	0	0	0	0	0	0	0	0	0	0	0	0	0	0	0	3	0	0	0
Leipzig	9	.5196	1.0187	40.1	0	3	0	0	3	1	1	1	3	0	0	0	1	0	0	0	2	0	0	0	0	2	1	0	0
leis	4	.2399	.3011	34.8	3	0	0	1	0	0	0	0	3	1	0	0	0	0	0	0	0	0	0	0	0	0	0	0	0
leisure	47	.6603	6.3722	48.0	3	1	0	2	10	10	20	1	8	6	6	3	0	10	2	1	2	0	2	0	0	0	5	2	0
leisure-time	5	.1990	.2695	34.3	0	0	0	0	0	1	3	1	0	0	0	0	0	4	0	0	0	0	0	0	0	1	0	0	0
leisurely	17	.5484	1.9530	42.9	2	1	1	0	6	2	3	2	2	0	0	4	0	1	0	0	0	0	0	0	2	0	4	4	0
LEM	2	.0000	.0299	24.8	0	0	0	0	0	0	2	0	0	0	0	0	2	0	0	0	0	0	0	0	0	0	0	0	0
Lemke	2	.0000	.0209	23.2	0	0	0	0	2	0	0	0	0	0	0	0	0	0	0	0	0	0	0	0	0	0	2	0	0
lemme	9	.3975	.8826	39.5	0	5	1	0	2	0	1	0	6	1	1	1	0	0	0	0	0	0	0	0	0	0	0	0	0
lemmings	4	.0000	.0789	29.0	0	0	0	3	0	1	0	0	0	0	0	0	0	0	0	4	0	0	0	0	0	0	0	0	0
Lemmons	2	.0000	.0914	29.6	0	0	0	0	2	0	0	0	2	0	0	0	0	0	0	0	0	0	0	0	0	0	0	0	0
lemon	44	.5814	5.3058	47.2	9	6	3	6	9	2	7	2	5	1	0	2	0	3	2	8	3	0	10	0	3	0	2	5	0
lemon-yellow	2	.0000	.0234	23.7	2	0	0	0	0	0	0	0	0	0	0	0	0	0	0	0	0	0	0	0	2	0	0	0	0
lemonade	40	.7667	6.2322	47.9	16	6	4	6	6	1	1	0	11	2	0	1	9	1	5	3	0	0	1	0	3	2	0	2	0
lemons	19	.6743	2.6102	44.2	4	2	2	2	8	1	0	0	0	1	0	4	0	6	0	2	0	0	0	0	1	2	2	1	0
lemur	2	.0000	.0209	23.2	0	0	0	0	2	0	0	0	0	0	0	0	0	0	0	0	0	0	0	0	0	0	2	0	0
lemurs	8	.1494	.3218	35.1	0	0	0	0	7	0	0	1	0	0	0	0	0	0	0	2	0	0	0	0	0	0	6	0	0
Len	2	.0000	.0914	29.6	0	0	0	2	0	0	0	0	2	0	0	0	0	0	0	0	0	0	0	0	0	0	0	0	0
Lena	5	.0000	.0972	29.9	0	3	0	0	0	0	2	0	0	0	0	0	0	5	0	0	0	0	0	0	0	0	0	0	0
Lenape	7	.1380	.2554	34.1	0	0	0	0	7	0	0	0	0	0	0	6	0	0	0	0	0	0	0	0	1	0	0	0	0
Lenard	2	.0000	.0209	23.2	0	0	0	0	0	2	0	0	0	0	0	0	0	0	0	0	0	0	0	0	0	0	2	0	0
lend	61	.5534	7.1351	48.5	14	19	4	8	3	5	5	3	12	1	0	3	0	7	2	0	14	0	0	0	6	6	1	8	1
lender	4	.4802	.4049	36.1	0	0	1	1	0	1	0	1	0	0	0	1	0	1	0	0	0	0	0	0	0	0	1	1	0
lenders	2	.0000	.0243	23.9	0	0	0	0	0	0	2	0	0	0	0	0	0	0	0	0	0	0	0	0	0	0	0	2	0
lending	12	.6081	1.5691	42.0	4	1	2	0	3	1	0	1	6	1	0	0	1	0	0	0	0	0	0	0	1	0	2	1	0
lends	14	.5647	1.6508	42.2	1	0	2	2	4	2	0	3	2	0	0	0	0	1	0	1	2	0	0	2	0	1	2	3	0
length	962	.6998	136.78	61.4	87	91	116	86	209	190	153	30	66	14	5	16	504	35	2	67	23	2	28	67	31	30	49	23	0
lengthen	8	.3415	.5707	37.6	0	1	0	0	2	5	0	0	0	0	0	0	0	0	0	1	2	0	4	1	0	0	0	0	0
lengthened	10	.5496	1.1575	40.6	0	1	1	1	7	0	0	0	2	0	0	0	0	0	0	0	1	0	1	0	4	0	1	1	0
lengthening	8	.3878	.6600	38.2	0	0	1	0	3	2	2	0	0	0	0	0	0	0	0	2	3	0	2	0	0	0	0	1	0
lengthens	2	.0000	.0394	26.0	0	1	0	0	0	0	1	0	0	0	0	0	0	0	0	2	0	0	0	0	0	0	0	0	0
lengths	171	.6776	23.507	53.7	10	15	21	11	35	33	43	3	7	4	2	3	80	3	0	10	15	1	4	20	1	3	13	5	0
lengthwise	40	.4324	3.6586	45.6	1	1	2	0	7	11	16	2	2	1	0	0	1	1	0	10	0	1	17	2	0	2	2	1	0
lengthy	18	.6886	2.5655	44.1	0	1	2	0	5	2	8	0	5	3	0	0	1	3	0	1	0	0	0	0	0	2	2	1	0
lenient	5	.4515	.4782	36.8	0	1	0	0	2	1	1	0	0	0	0	2	0	1	0	0	0	0	0	0	1	0	1	0	0
Lenin	2	.0000	.0389	25.9	0	0	0	2	0	0	0	0	0	0	0	0	0	2	0	0	0	0	0	0	0	0	0	0	0
Leningrad	6	.4134	.5321	37.3	0	1	1	1	1	1	1	0	0	0	0	0	0	1	0	1	2	0	0	0	0	0	2	0	0
Lenni	4	.0000	.0429	26.3	0	0	0	0	4	0	0	0	0	0	0	4	0	0	0	0	0	0	0	0	0	0	0	0	0
Lennie	17	.1908	.7782	38.9	0	0	0	0	9	0	8	0	0	0	1	16	0	0	0	0	0	0	0	0	0	0	0	0	0
Lennon	2	.0000	.0243	23.9	0	0	0	0	0	0	1	1	0	0	0	0	0	0	0	0	0	0	0	0	0	0	0	2	0
Lenore	5	.0756	.1562	31.9	0	1	0	0	0	0	4	0	1	0	0	4	0	0	0	0	0	0	0	0	0	0	0	0	0
lens	123	.5737	14.837	51.7	16	25	12	30	22	8	5	5	7	0	1	0	0	1	0	81	1	0	0	4	3	4	16	5	0
lenses	40	.5491	4.6436	46.7	4	7	2	8	11	3	1	4	3	1	0	1	0	0	0	19	0	0	0	0	0	5	8	3	0
lent	14	.6359	1.8531	42.7	1	2	2	2	2	3	1	1	3	1	0	1	0	2	0	0	0	0	0	0	0	3	3	1	0
Lent	4	.2376	.2177	33.4	0	0	0	2	0	2	0	0	0	0	0	0	0	0	2	0	0	0	0	0	0	0	0	2	0
lentils	4	.3801	.3316	35.2	0	0	0	1	2	0	1	0	0	0	0	0	0	1	0	1	0	0	1	0	0	0	1	0	0
leo	3	.2445	.1818	32.6	0	0	0	0	2	0	1	0	0	0	0	0	0	0	0	2	0	0	0	0	0	0	1	0	0
Leo	17	.4805	1.7928	42.5	8	0	0	4	4	0	1	0	5	0	0	0	0	0	0	0	1	0	0	0	6	0	4	1	0
Leodegrance	4	.0000	.1827	32.6	0	0	0	4	0	0	0	0	4	0	0	0	0	0	0	0	0	0	0	0	0	0	0	0	0
leoht	2	.0000	.0162	22.1	0	0	0	0	0	2	0	0	0	0	0	0	0	0	2	0	0	0	0	0	0	0	0	0	0
Leon	10	.2087	.5110	37.1	6	0	1	0	1	1	0	1	0	0	0	0	0	0	0	1	0	0	0	0	0	0	1	8	0
Leona	8	.0000	.3655	35.6	0	8	0	0	0	0	0	0	8	0	0	0	0	0	0	0	0	0	0	0	0	0	0	0	0
Leona's	4	.0000	.1827	32.6	0	4	0	0	0	0	0	0	4	0	0	0	0	0	0	0	0	0	0	0	0	0	0	0	0
Leonard	24	.4825	2.5459	44.1	2	5	3	1	1	9	2	1	8	4	0	0	1	0	0	0	8	0	0	0	0	0	2	1	0
Leonardo	18	.3531	1.4081	41.5	3	0	0	0	5	0	9	1	3	0	0	0	0	0	1	0	0	6	0	1	0	3	3	1	0
Leonardo's	2	.0000	.0037	15.7	0	0	0	0	0	0	2	0	0	0	0	0	0	0	0	0	0	2	0	0	0	0	0	0	0
Leonidas	8	.2351	.6222	37.9	0	7	0	0	1	0	0	0	7	0	0	0	0	0	0	0	0	0	0	0	0	0	1	0	0
leopard	34	.6366	4.5148	46.5	7	7	0	7	9	4	0	0	9	3	0	6	0	1	1	1	0	0	0	0	0	7	6	0	0
Leopard	10	.2111	.5602	37.5	0	8	0	1	1	0	0	0	2	0	0	1	0	0	0	0	0	0	0	0	7	0	0	0	0
leopard's	2	.2444	.1132	30.5	0	0	0	1	0	1	0	0	0	1	0	0	0	0	0	0	0	0	0	0	1	0	0	0	0
Leopardi	3	.2387	.1708	32.3	0	0	2	0	0	0	1	0	0	0	0	0	0	0	0	0	0	0	0	0	0	2	1	0	0
leopards	12	.5939	1.5157	41.8	2	3	0	1	4	2	0	0	4	2	0	0	0	1	0	0	0	0	0	0	0	1	2	2	0
Leopold	11	.4725	1.1927	40.8	0	0	5	0	3	0	3	0	5	0	0	0	0	4	0	0	1	0	0	0	0	0	1	0	0
Leopoldville	3	.2063	.1600	32.0	0	1	2	0	0	0	0	0	0	0	0	0	0	1	0	0	0	0	0	0	0	2	0	0	0
Lepidoptera	3	.0000	.0591	27.7	0	0	0	1	2	0	0	0	0	0	0	0	0	0	0	3	0	0	0	0	0	0	0	0	0
leprechaun	6	.3941	.5282	37.2	0	1	3	1	0	0	1	0	1	1	0	0	0	0	0	0	0	0	0	0	1	0	0	3	0
leprechauns	2	.2442	.1134	30.5	0	0	2	0	0	0	0	0	0	1	0	0	0	0	0	0	0	0	0	0	0	0	0	1	0
Lerner	2	.1494	.1045	30.2	0	0	0	0	0	2	0	0	1	0	0	0	0	0	0	0	1	0	0	0	0	0	0	0	0
Leroy	15	.4214	1.3762	41.4	0	0	2	6	6	0	1	0	2	0	0	0	0	0	1	0	1	0	0	1	0	0	0	10	0
les	2	.1948	.1250	31.0	0	0	0	1	0	1	0	0	1	0	0	0	0	0	0	0	0	0	0	0	0	1	0	0	0
Les	7	.4504	.6639	38.2	0	0	2	1	1	2	1	0	0	0	0	0	0	0	0	0	1	0	0	0	0	2	3	1	0
Lescaut	2	.2417	.1091	30.4	0	0	1	0	0	1	0	0	0	0	0	0	0	0	0	0	1	0	0	0	0	0	1	0	0
Leslie	4	.1828	.1857	32.7	0	1	0	2	0	0	1	0	0	0	0	0	1	0	0	0	0	0	0	0	0	0	0	3	0
less	1366	.8877	240.98	63.8	158	154	163	176	290	205	172	48	150	44	8	35	376	131	18	183	28	3	33	24	47	64	117	105	0
less-tender	2	.0000	.0064	18.1	0	0	0	0	0	0	2	0	0	0	0	0	0	0	0	0	0	0	2	0	0	0	0	0	0
lessen	10	.6482	1.3375	41.3	1	1	3	0	2	1	2	0	2	1	1	0	0	1	0	1	0	0	1	0	1	0	1	1	0

8F Legree
4Q Lehman
9K Lehmbruck
3A lei-making
8E Leibniz's
5P Leidy
9A Leigh
XR Leighton's
7B Leiningen
9Q Leitha
7R leitmotiv
4A Leland
4A Leland's
5Q Lelia
7N Lem
4A lemarkable
6R Lemhi
7Q lemming
6B Lemmon
8D Lemnos
8F Lemon
4A lemon-meringue
5J Lemuel
7Q lemur-and
7Q Lemuria
7Q lemurlike
8Q Lenard's
8F lender's
XR Lending
8Q leng
7L lengthening-shortening
7C lengthier
8E Lengths
7D Lennie's
3F Lenny
XR Lenor
XH Lenouvel
4P Lenox
7Q lens-shaped
6A Lenten
7A lentil
3R Lentil
5Q lento
7R Lentz
8R Lenya
8M Lenz's
7A Leominster
3R Leon's
8E Leonhard
9F Leoni
8R Leonid
7Q Leonide
7H leonine
7J Leonore
5F Leontyne
6A leopard-panther
8R leopard-skin
7A Leopard's
5Q Leopardi's
8R leopardskins
5R leotard-like
XB Lepanto
9P leper
7A lepers
7H lepido
XH Lepidodendron
7Q lepidopterist
3N Lepine
4N lepped
5R Leprechaun
9P leprosy
5J Leron
5Q LesFauves
3B Lesley
7Q less-charged
7P less-expensive
5Q less-than-carload
9R less-well-known
9D less'ned

Word Type	F	D	U	SFI	3 Gr 3	4 Gr 4	5 Gr 5	6 Gr 6	7 Gr 7	8 Gr 8	9 Gr 9	X UnGr	A Read	B Eng & Gr	C Comp	D Lit	E Math	F Soc Stud	G Spell	H Sci	J Music	K Art	L Home Ec	M Shop	N Lib F	P Lib NF	Q Lib Ref	R Mag	S Rel
lessened	8	.6260	1.0611	40.3	1	0	1	4	1	0	1	0	3	0	0	1	0	1	0	0	0	0	0	0	1	1	0	1	0
lessening	3	.3762	.2496	34.0	0	0	1	0	0	0	2	0	0	0	0	0	0	0	0	1	0	0	0	0	0	1	1	0	0
lessens	5	.2548	.3115	34.9	1	1	0	0	0	0	3	0	1	0	0	0	0	1	0	0	0	0	2	0	0	0	1	0	0
lesser	29	.6582	3.8995	45.9	2	6	2	5	8	3	2	1	1	0	0	2	9	2	0	4	0	0	1	0	0	1	7	2	0
lesson	256	.7446	38.720	55.9	49	47	33	44	32	28	19	4	61	25	4	13	29	11	71	1	2	0	0	1	12	13	0	12	1
Lesson	29	.3549	2.2438	43.5	1	2	2	0	3	17	4	0	2	8	0	1	1	0	16	0	1	0	0	0	0	0	0	0	0
lesson's	2	.0000	.0162	22.1	0	0	0	0	0	1	1	0	0	0	0	0	0	0	2	0	0	0	0	0	0	0	0	0	0
lessons	141	.8542	24.106	53.8	27	35	21	11	17	11	15	4	39	20	0	7	4	8	7	0	3	3	1	1	12	22	1	13	0
Lessons	2	.2376	.1088	30.4	0	0	0	0	1	1	0	0	0	0	0	0	0	0	1	0	0	0	0	0	0	0	0	1	0
lest	35	.6095	4.4629	46.5	4	0	3	2	12	5	7	2	9	0	1	12	0	0	0	0	3	0	0	0	5	3	0	2	0
Lester	9	.4155	.7873	39.0	1	0	0	2	2	3	1	0	0	2	0	0	1	0	0	0	0	2	0	0	0	1	1	2	0
Lestrade	4	.0000	.0429	26.3	0	0	0	0	0	0	4	0	0	0	0	4	0	0	0	0	0	0	0	0	0	0	0	0	0
let	2176	.9358	403.53	66.1	465	418	233	287	386	202	160	25	747	88	25	224	119	91	18	178	90	19	19	5	232	204	22	94	1
Let	4	.0000	.0579	27.6	4	0	0	0	0	0	0	0	0	0	0	0	0	0	0	0	0	0	0	0	0	4	0	0	0
let's	892	.9066	160.92	62.1	224	188	92	90	124	128	31	15	287	37	14	38	109	38	22	106	31	0	6	6	81	72	3	42	0
lethal	4	.2672	.2733	34.4	0	0	0	0	3	0	0	1	1	0	0	0	0	0	0	1	0	0	0	0	0	0	2	0	0
lethargy	3	.1409	.1472	31.7	0	0	1	1	0	0	1	0	1	0	0	0	0	0	0	0	0	0	0	0	0	2	0	0	0
Leto	5	.2443	.3861	35.9	0	0	0	4	0	1	0	0	4	0	0	0	0	0	0	0	0	0	0	0	0	0	1	0	0
lets	70	.8436	11.845	50.7	18	11	6	9	15	5	4	2	17	8	1	3	2	6	1	12	1	0	0	0	2	6	2	9	0
letter	1738	.6711	238.16	63.8	411	448	213	204	214	121	113	14	269	555	55	26	76	38	503	18	35	11	1	12	28	61	13	37	0
Letter	8	.3984	.7135	38.5	0	0	1	0	2	4	1	0	1	0	0	0	0	2	0	0	0	0	0	0	0	2	3	0	0
lettered	20	.5293	2.2210	43.5	0	0	2	2	6	2	8	0	3	0	0	1	5	0	2	0	0	1	0	4	0	0	0	4	0
lettering	27	.1854	1.0738	40.3	0	1	4	5	0	11	6	0	1	0	0	0	1	0	0	0	0	19	0	6	0	0	0	0	0
letterpress	5	.1420	.1640	32.1	0	0	0	0	0	0	5	0	0	0	0	0	0	0	0	0	0	0	0	3	0	0	2	0	0
letters	1798	.6396	235.23	63.7	425	474	244	255	182	112	92	14	242	347	92	21	81	43	767	20	36	25	1	24	9	46	15	29	0
Letters	8	.4867	.8109	39.1	0	2	1	3	1	1	0	0	0	4	0	0	0	0	1	0	0	0	0	0	0	1	1	1	0
letterwriting	2	.1605	.0742	28.7	0	1	0	0	1	0	0	0	0	1	1	0	0	0	0	0	0	0	0	0	0	0	0	0	0
letting	74	.7442	11.257	50.5	10	11	8	7	12	13	11	2	25	3	4	8	5	5	1	3	1	4	0	0	9	1	0	5	0
lettuce	56	.4932	5.9410	47.7	14	7	5	7	20	1	2	0	10	3	0	3	1	5	0	11	0	0	14	0	1	5	2	1	0
lettuces	2	.2444	.1132	30.5	1	0	0	0	0	0	1	0	0	1	0	0	0	0	0	0	0	0	0	0	1	0	0	0	0
letup	2	.0000	.0914	29.6	1	0	0	0	1	0	0	0	2	0	0	0	0	0	0	0	0	0	0	0	0	0	0	0	0
leucocytes	10	.0000	.1972	32.9	0	0	0	10	0	0	0	0	0	0	0	0	0	0	0	10	0	0	0	0	0	0	0	0	0
levee	2	.2160	.1362	31.3	0	0	1	0	0	1	0	0	1	0	0	0	0	0	0	1	0	0	0	0	0	0	0	0	0
levees	12	.5254	1.3394	41.3	0	1	8	0	1	1	0	1	0	0	0	0	1	4	0	5	1	0	0	0	0	0	0	1	0
level	531	.8554	90.704	59.6	31	68	86	75	103	89	55	24	61	4	1	15	22	168	8	83	6	3	15	13	7	21	51	53	0
leveled	14	.6666	1.9229	42.8	2	0	3	2	2	0	3	2	2	0	0	1	1	1	0	2	0	0	0	0	0	4	2	1	0
leveling	7	.5764	.8447	39.3	0	0	2	1	0	3	1	0	1	0	0	0	0	1	0	1	0	0	1	0	1	0	1	1	0
levelled	2	.0000	.0243	23.9	0	0	0	0	2	0	0	0	0	0	0	0	0	0	0	0	0	0	0	0	0	0	0	2	0
levels	86	.8154	14.024	51.5	1	6	6	7	24	19	18	5	5	6	1	1	3	8	4	20	5	0	0	2	1	1	18	11	0
lever	128	.5371	14.492	51.6	6	18	7	30	21	16	11	19	12	1	0	1	6	1	0	46	1	0	3	22	0	19	3	13	0
leverage	2	.0000	.0243	23.9	0	0	0	0	0	0	2	0	0	0	0	0	0	0	0	0	0	0	0	0	0	0	0	2	0
levers	40	.6609	5.4426	47.4	5	8	0	5	7	5	3	7	4	0	0	0	3	4	0	13	2	0	0	3	0	7	3	1	0
Levi	11	.0000	.1592	32.0	0	11	0	0	0	0	0	0	0	0	0	0	0	0	0	0	0	0	0	0	0	11	0	0	0
leviathan	2	.2446	.1257	31.0	0	0	0	0	1	1	0	0	0	0	0	0	0	1	0	1	0	0	0	0	0	0	0	0	0
levied	6	.3350	.4955	37.0	0	0	0	2	1	2	1	0	2	0	0	0	0	2	0	0	0	0	0	0	0	0	2	0	0
Levin	2	.0000	.0299	24.8	0	0	0	0	0	2	0	0	0	0	0	0	2	0	0	0	0	0	0	0	0	0	0	0	0
levy	8	.2891	.5766	37.6	2	0	0	1	0	4	1	0	1	0	0	0	0	5	0	0	0	0	0	0	0	2	0	0	0
Lew	7	.3387	.5241	37.2	0	3	0	1	0	3	0	0	0	0	0	0	0	0	0	0	0	0	0	0	0	2	1	4	0
Lewis	128	.6320	16.832	52.3	2	58	21	10	13	18	4	2	23	4	0	8	2	17	1	0	0	0	0	0	1	50	6	16	0
lexicon	4	.3444	.3047	34.8	0	0	0	2	0	1	1	0	0	2	0	0	0	1	0	0	0	0	0	0	0	0	1	0	0
Lexington	36	.6098	4.7028	46.7	2	12	7	5	3	7	0	0	16	1	0	0	0	1	0	0	0	0	0	0	4	9	2	3	0
Leyden	3	.0803	.0701	28.5	0	0	0	0	0	2	0	1	0	0	0	0	0	0	0	1	0	0	0	2	0	0	0	0	0
Lg	2	.0000	.0050	17.0	0	0	0	0	0	0	2	0	0	0	0	0	0	0	0	0	0	0	0	2	0	0	0	0	0
LH	3	.0803	.0701	28.5	0	0	0	0	0	0	3	0	0	0	0	0	0	0	0	1	0	0	0	2	0	0	0	0	0
Lhevinne	3	.0000	.0322	25.1	0	0	0	0	0	0	3	0	0	0	0	3	0	0	0	0	0	0	0	0	0	0	0	0	0
li	3	.2249	.1514	31.8	0	2	1	0	0	0	0	0	0	0	0	0	0	0	2	0	1	0	0	0	0	0	0	0	0
Li	16	.4416	1.5534	41.9	10	0	4	0	0	2	0	0	2	0	0	0	0	1	0	1	0	0	0	0	0	9	1	2	0
Li'l	2	.0000	.0290	24.6	2	0	0	0	0	0	0	0	0	0	0	0	0	0	0	0	0	0	0	0	0	2	0	0	0
Li's	2	.1698	.1133	30.5	1	0	1	0	0	0	0	0	1	0	0	0	0	0	0	0	0	0	0	0	0	0	1	0	0
liability	2	.2437	.1129	30.5	0	0	0	0	1	1	0	0	0	0	0	0	0	0	0	0	0	0	0	0	0	0	1	1	0
liable	12	.4125	1.0739	40.3	0	0	2	0	3	3	4	0	1	0	0	5	0	1	0	0	0	0	0	0	1	0	4	0	0
Liam	4	.0000	.0486	26.9	0	0	0	4	0	0	0	0	0	0	0	0	0	0	0	0	0	0	0	0	0	0	0	4	0
lianas	2	.2285	.1129	30.5	0	0	0	1	1	0	0	0	0	0	0	0	0	1	0	0	0	0	0	0	0	0	1	0	0
Liao	5	.2418	.2811	34.5	0	0	0	0	0	5	0	0	0	0	0	0	0	0	0	0	0	0	0	0	0	0	2	3	0
liar	10	.4169	.9897	40.0	0	1	0	2	2	4	1	0	5	0	0	3	0	1	0	0	0	0	0	0	0	0	0	1	0
lib	2	.0000	.0234	23.7	0	0	0	2	0	0	0	0	0	0	0	0	0	0	0	0	0	0	0	0	2	0	0	0	0
liberal	30	.6074	3.7081	45.7	1	0	6	1	3	3	15	1	0	5	0	1	0	0	1	0	1	0	0	1	0	1	10	10	0
liberalism	3	.1277	.1363	31.3	0	0	0	0	1	0	2	0	1	0	0	0	0	0	0	0	0	0	0	0	0	0	0	2	0
liberalization	2	.0000	.0243	23.9	0	0	0	0	0	0	2	0	0	0	0	0	0	0	0	0	0	0	0	0	0	0	0	2	0
liberally	2	.2433	.1158	30.6	0	1	0	0	1	0	0	0	0	0	0	0	0	0	0	0	0	0	0	0	0	1	0	1	0
liberals	4	.1622	.1743	32.4	0	0	0	0	1	3	0	0	0	0	0	0	0	1	0	0	0	0	0	0	0	0	0	3	0
liberate	5	.2530	.3153	35.0	0	0	0	0	1	4	0	0	1	0	0	0	0	0	0	0	0	0	0	0	0	0	3	1	0
liberated	11	.5095	1.1681	40.7	1	0	2	1	3	2	1	1	0	0	0	0	0	2	0	0	0	0	0	1	0	1	3	4	0
liberating	5	.3207	.3659	35.6	0	0	0	2	0	2	1	0	0	0	0	0	0	2	0	1	2	0	0	0	0	0	0	0	0
liberation	7	.5388	.8163	39.1	0	0	0	1	2	2	2	0	2	1	0	0	0	1	0	0	0	0	0	0	0	2	0	1	0
Liberation	2	.2437	.1129	30.5	0	0	1	0	0	0	1	0	0	0	0	0	0	0	0	0	0	0	0	0	0	0	1	1	0
Liberia	4	.0000	.0778	28.9	0	0	0	0	4	0	0	0	0	0	0	0	0	4	0	0	0	0	0	0	0	0	0	0	0
Liberian	3	.1937	.1495	31.7	0	0	0	0	2	1	0	0	0	0	0	0	0	1	0	0	0	0	0	0	0	0	0	2	0
libertarian	2	.0000	.0209	23.2	0	0	0	0	0	0	2	0	0	0	0	0	0	0	0	0	0	0	0	0	0	0	2	0	0
liberte	2	.2285	.1129	30.5	1	0	0	0	1	0	0	0	0	0	0	0	0	1	0	0	0	0	0	0	0	0	1	0	0
liberties	8	.4050	.7312	38.6	0	0	2	0	1	4	1	0	1	0	0	0	0	4	0	0	0	0	0	0	0	1	2	0	0
liberty	82	.7323	12.186	50.9	9	5	8	9	11	30	10	0	12	3	0	7	0	18	2	0	13	0	0	0	4	5	13	5	0
Liberty	85	.7143	12.579	51.0	13	15	18	12	13	11	3	0	35	0	0	13	4	14	0	0	4	1	0	0	1	4	9	0	0
Liberty's	2	.0000	.0914	29.6	1	0	0	1	0	0	0	0	2	0	0	0	0	0	0	0	0	0	0	0	0	0	0	0	0
libra	4	.1792	.1694	32.3	0	3	1	0	0	0	0	0	0	0	0	0	0	0	3	0	0	0	0	0	0	0	1	0	0
librarian	23	.4968	2.4640	43.9	4	3	1	1	5	4	1	4	5	9	0	1	0	0	0	1	2	0	0	0	0	0	0	5	0
librarians	10	.3184	.7162	38.6	0	2	0	0	0	1	1	6	0	0	0	0	0	2	0	0	0	0	0	0	0	0	2	6	0
libraries	51	.7588	7.8371	48.9	8	3	9	5	11	7	5	3	8	10	0	0	0	12	0	4	2	1	1	0	0	2	5	6	0
library	276	.9037	49.596	57.0	64	64	22	26	47	30	14	9	76	50	4	10	30	22	9	17	8	2	2	4	6	6	4	26	0
Library	33	.6191	4.2574	46.3	4	3	11	4	2	5	2	2	6	2	0	0	0	6	0	0	0	0	0	0	2	3	8	6	0
library's	4	.3381	.3009	34.8	1	1	0	0	2	0	0	0	0	0	0	2	0	1	0	0	0	0	0	0	0	0	0	1	0
libretto	8	.3126	.5452	37.4	0	0	1	0	3	2	2	0	0	0	0	0	0	0	0	0	4	0	0	0	0	1	3	0	0

7N Lesseps
6F Lesser
9F lesser-known
9Q Lessing
9D Lestrade's
7A let's-go-easies
6N Letham
7Q letter-carrier
4Q letter-number
3P letter-perfect
9B letter-wide
7D letter-writing
7D letter'll
9D letter's
9M Lettering
6R letterman
6H Leucippus
6A leukemia
8A Levant
XP Levassor
4F Level
XR level-compensating
4A level-headed
5Q leveling-off
7R lever-action
7D lever-wise
7B levered
9Q Leverkuhn
6H Levers
3S Levi's
9P Levitan
3P Levite
5A Levittown
XR Levy
9D lewd
XR Lewellen
5Q Lewes
7A Lex
6B lexicographer
3Q Leyte
8E LF
6E LG
9E lh
7M LH2
7P li'nghas
7R liaison
9R Liaison
6N Lianas
5J Liang
7A liar's
8F liars
6N Lib
9D libation
6N libbing
8Q Libby
5Q libel
5P libera
9Q Liberal
8R liberal-arts
7Q liberalist
7R liberalize
9Q liberalizing
8R Liberals
9F liberator
6J Liberians
7R libertad
7P Libertes
9A Liberties
7R Libertyville
7P Libra
5Q librarianship
8Q librettists

Word Type	F	D	U	SFI	3 Gr 3	4 Gr 4	5 Gr 5	6 Gr 6	7 Gr 7	8 Gr 8	9 Gr 9	X UnGr	A Read	B Eng & Gr	C Comp	D Lit	E Math	F Soc Stud	G Spell	H Sci	J Music	K Art	L Home Ec	M Shop	N Lib F	P Lib NF	Q Lib Ref	R Mag	S Rel
Libya	12	.3584	1.0182	40.1	0	1	0	6	3	0	2	0	2	0	0	0	0	8	0	0	0	0	0	0	0	0	1	1	0
Libyans	2	.0000	.0389	25.9	0	0	0	2	0	0	0	0	0	0	0	0	0	2	0	0	0	0	0	0	0	0	0	0	0
lice	18	.4808	1.9572	42.9	2	7	0	2	1	1	3	2	7	0	0	3	0	0	0	5	0	0	0	0	0	3	0	0	0
license	36	.6251	4.6946	46.7	3	1	7	7	11	2	3	2	7	0	0	2	1	7	0	0	0	0	0	0	4	3	1	11	0
licensed	9	.5441	1.0185	40.1	0	2	1	2	1	0	1	2	0	0	0	0	0	0	0	2	1	0	0	0	0	2	1	3	0
licenses	5	.3414	.4194	36.2	2	0	1	1	1	0	0	0	2	0	0	0	0	0	0	0	0	0	0	0	1	0	0	2	0
licensing	4	.2090	.2014	33.0	0	1	0	0	2	0	0	1	0	0	0	0	0	0	0	0	0	0	0	0	0	0	1	3	0
lichen	4	.4734	.4039	36.1	0	0	0	0	3	1	0	0	0	0	0	1	0	1	0	1	0	0	0	0	0	0	1	0	0
lichens	16	.3181	1.1848	40.7	0	1	0	4	8	1	0	2	0	0	0	0	0	0	0	11	0	0	0	0	0	0	4	1	0
Lichtenstein	2	.0000	.0243	23.9	0	0	0	0	0	0	0	2	0	0	0	0	0	0	0	0	0	0	0	0	0	0	0	2	0
lick	34	.6487	4.5876	46.6	11	5	5	3	7	1	1	1	9	1	1	0	0	0	0	2	0	0	1	0	10	8	2	0	0
Lick	12	.5054	1.3369	41.3	0	2	7	0	1	2	0	0	4	0	0	0	0	1	0	0	0	0	0	0	0	4	2	1	0
licked	65	.5943	8.3460	49.2	8	23	7	11	9	5	1	1	32	0	0	10	0	0	1	1	0	0	0	0	11	6	0	4	0
licker	2	.1948	.1250	31.0	0	0	0	0	2	0	0	0	1	0	0	0	0	0	0	0	0	0	0	0	0	1	0	0	0
licking	21	.6060	2.7317	44.4	4	5	0	4	6	1	1	0	10	2	0	2	0	0	0	0	0	0	0	0	4	2	1	0	0
licks	9	.3679	.8689	39.4	2	3	1	0	3	0	0	0	7	1	0	0	0	0	0	0	0	0	0	0	0	1	0	0	0
Licks	19	.2359	1.0457	40.2	0	0	0	0	19	0	0	0	0	0	0	7	0	0	0	0	0	0	0	0	12	0	0	0	0
licorice	7	.4606	.6896	38.4	0	1	2	0	3	0	1	0	1	1	1	2	0	0	0	0	0	0	0	0	2	0	0	0	0
lid	94	.8101	15.421	51.9	26	19	7	18	9	6	4	5	35	1	2	2	0	4	0	16	1	0	3	2	10	7	0	11	0
Lida	5	.0000	.2284	33.6	0	0	5	0	0	0	0	0	5	0	0	0	0	0	0	0	0	0	0	0	0	0	0	0	0
Liddell	4	.0000	.0469	26.7	0	0	0	0	4	0	0	0	0	0	0	0	0	0	0	0	0	0	0	0	4	0	0	0	0
Liddy	11	.0000	.1290	31.1	0	0	11	0	0	0	0	0	0	0	0	0	0	0	0	0	0	0	0	0	11	0	0	0	0
lids	23	.5265	2.6268	44.2	3	5	2	1	3	6	3	0	9	0	0	2	0	0	1	0	0	1	0	4	5	0	1	0	0
Lidya	3	.0000	.1370	31.4	3	0	0	0	0	0	0	0	3	0	0	0	0	0	0	0	0	0	0	0	0	0	0	0	0
lie	379	.9248	69.461	58.4	45	35	50	53	96	40	54	6	79	24	5	43	40	62	3	27	6	3	8	1	9	24	27	18	0
Lie	3	.2366	.1806	32.6	0	0	0	0	0	2	1	0	0	0	0	0	1	2	0	0	0	0	0	0	0	0	0	0	0
lied	13	.6075	1.6627	42.2	0	0	2	2	5	4	0	0	4	0	0	2	0	0	0	0	1	0	0	0	3	0	1	2	0
liege	3	.3874	.2497	34.0	0	0	1	1	1	0	0	0	0	1	0	0	0	0	0	0	0	0	0	0	1	0	0	1	0
lies	312	.8179	51.242	57.1	32	17	55	47	86	26	36	13	43	15	1	21	18	96	1	24	4	1	1	0	5	15	46	21	0
Lies	3	.0000	.0434	26.4	0	0	0	0	0	3	0	0	0	0	0	0	0	0	0	0	0	0	0	0	0	3	0	0	0
Liesi	6	.0000	.2741	34.4	6	0	0	0	0	0	0	0	6	0	0	0	0	0	0	0	0	0	0	0	0	0	0	0	0
lieu	4	.3011	.2909	34.6	0	1	0	0	0	0	3	0	1	0	0	2	0	0	0	0	0	0	0	0	0	0	1	0	0
lieutenant	31	.6551	4.1904	46.2	1	0	3	9	4	4	9	1	7	1	0	7	0	0	4	0	0	0	0	0	2	1	4	5	0
Lieutenant	37	.6921	5.3688	47.3	3	4	9	4	8	5	1	3	18	0	0	3	0	3	1	2	0	0	0	0	0	6	2	2	0
lieutenants	3	.2143	.1568	32.0	1	0	1	0	1	0	0	0	0	0	0	0	0	0	0	0	0	0	0	0	0	1	0	2	0
Lieve	16	.0000	.2316	33.6	0	16	0	0	0	0	0	0	0	0	0	0	0	0	0	0	0	0	0	0	0	16	0	0	0
life	2612	.8615	449.34	66.5	198	319	375	335	650	350	309	76	523	105	27	220	20	328	36	327	125	38	35	14	125	190	295	187	17
Life	44	.7088	6.3715	48.0	2	2	5	7	8	14	4	2	10	1	0	4	0	0	0	1	3	2	0	0	3	3	6	11	0
LIFE	3	.0000	.0365	25.6	0	0	0	1	2	0	0	0	0	0	0	0	0	0	0	0	0	0	0	0	0	0	0	3	0
life-giving	7	.4770	.7242	38.6	0	0	0	2	2	0	1	2	1	0	0	0	0	1	0	1	0	0	0	0	0	0	2	2	0
life-long	4	.3277	.2829	34.5	0	1	0	0	1	2	0	0	0	0	0	1	0	0	0	0	0	0	0	1	0	0	0	2	0
life-saving	5	.2213	.2870	34.6	0	0	0	1	0	0	1	3	0	0	0	0	0	0	0	4	0	0	0	0	0	0	0	0	0
life-sized	2	.0000	.0914	29.6	0	1	0	0	0	0	0	1	2	0	0	0	0	0	0	0	0	0	0	0	0	0	1	0	0
life-style	2	.2351	.1166	30.7	0	0	1	0	0	0	1	0	0	0	0	0	0	1	0	0	0	0	0	0	0	0	0	1	0
life-support	2	.0000	.0243	23.9	0	0	0	0	1	0	1	0	0	0	0	0	0	0	0	0	0	0	0	0	0	0	0	2	0
life's	15	.7054	2.1837	43.4	0	0	2	1	5	4	2	1	5	2	0	0	0	1	1	2	1	0	0	1	0	1	0	1	0
lifebelt	2	.2427	.1152	30.6	1	0	0	0	0	0	1	0	0	0	0	0	0	0	0	0	0	0	0	0	1	1	0	0	0
lifebelts	2	.0000	.0290	24.6	0	0	0	0	0	0	2	0	0	0	0	0	0	0	0	0	0	0	0	0	0	2	0	0	0
lifeblood	2	.2446	.1257	31.0	0	0	0	0	0	0	2	0	0	0	0	0	0	1	0	1	0	0	0	0	0	0	0	0	0
lifeboat	10	.3757	.9699	39.9	0	7	0	1	2	0	0	0	7	0	0	0	0	2	0	0	0	0	0	0	0	0	0	1	0
lifeboats	4	.3813	.3772	35.8	0	1	0	0	1	0	2	0	2	0	0	0	0	1	0	0	0	0	0	0	0	1	0	0	0
lifeguard	6	.3486	.5162	37.1	3	0	2	0	0	0	1	0	2	1	0	0	0	0	0	3	0	0	0	0	0	0	0	0	0
lifeguards	2	.0000	.0914	29.6	0	0	0	0	2	0	0	0	2	0	0	0	0	0	0	0	0	0	0	0	0	0	0	0	0
lifeless	17	.7290	2.4988	44.0	0	0	3	4	5	1	4	0	0	1	0	2	0	5	0	1	1	1	0	0	2	2	1	1	0
lifelike	7	.3838	.6520	38.1	2	3	0	0	0	0	2	0	4	0	1	0	0	0	0	0	0	1	0	0	0	1	0	0	0
lifeline	2	.2152	.1357	31.3	0	0	1	0	1	0	0	0	1	0	0	0	0	1	0	0	0	0	0	0	0	0	0	0	0
lifelong	4	.3192	.3100	34.9	0	0	2	0	0	0	1	1	1	0	0	0	0	0	0	0	0	0	0	0	0	2	0	1	0
lifesaver	2	.1814	.1187	30.7	0	0	0	1	0	1	0	0	1	0	0	0	0	0	0	0	0	0	0	0	0	0	0	1	0
lifesaving	7	.2395	.5461	37.4	3	1	0	1	1	1	0	0	6	0	0	1	0	0	0	0	0	0	0	0	0	0	0	0	0
lifetime	78	.8675	13.488	51.3	4	6	9	9	20	16	11	3	13	5	1	6	2	6	1	12	7	0	1	0	3	2	11	8	0
lifetimes	8	.4663	.8001	39.0	0	1	1	0	2	1	1	2	0	0	0	1	0	0	0	4	0	0	0	0	1	0	0	2	0
lifework	4	.3696	.3616	35.6	0	0	0	1	1	0	2	0	2	1	0	0	0	0	0	0	0	0	0	0	0	0	1	0	0
lift	267	.8700	46.462	56.7	57	58	29	45	30	33	11	4	71	12	2	10	8	6	3	92	5	1	4	6	8	22	2	15	0
lift-off	4	.2059	.1995	33.0	0	1	0	2	0	1	0	0	0	1	0	0	0	0	0	0	0	0	0	0	0	0	0	3	0
lifted	298	.8550	51.253	57.1	52	64	36	50	58	19	17	2	131	11	3	24	1	7	1	28	3	1	1	4	43	24	4	12	0
liftin'	2	.1717	.1142	30.6	0	0	0	1	1	0	0	0	1	0	0	1	0	0	0	0	0	0	0	0	0	0	0	0	0
lifting	70	.8504	11.899	50.8	5	12	10	6	12	14	11	0	14	2	0	7	4	1	1	15	3	1	5	2	8	3	2	2	0
lifts	42	.7018	6.0931	47.8	4	11	9	7	4	2	3	2	12	0	0	3	2	1	0	12	0	0	0	0	4	1	2	5	0
ligaments	2	.2278	.1128	30.5	0	0	0	0	0	0	2	0	0	0	0	0	0	0	0	1	0	0	0	0	0	0	1	0	0
light	2376	.8715	413.06	66.2	347	337	239	423	422	230	236	142	436	52	24	158	36	83	35	818	49	65	49	52	125	138	150	95	11
Light	39	.1491	2.0264	43.1	4	5	3	3	20	2	2	0	18	1	0	1	0	0	0	3	2	0	0	0	2	2	4	2	4
light-and-dark	2	.1033	.0599	27.8	0	0	0	0	0	2	2	0	0	0	0	0	0	0	0	1	0	1	0	0	0	0	0	0	0
light-blue	2	.2152	.1357	31.3	1	0	0	0	0	1	0	0	1	0	0	0	0	1	0	0	0	0	0	0	0	0	0	0	0
light-brown	2	.0000	.0914	29.6	1	0	0	1	0	0	0	0	2	0	0	0	0	0	0	0	0	0	0	0	0	0	0	0	0
light-colored	12	.5258	1.3464	41.3	3	0	2	0	1	2	3	1	2	0	0	0	0	1	0	4	0	1	2	0	0	1	0	1	0
light-hearted	6	.2034	.3105	34.9	0	0	3	2	1	0	0	0	1	0	0	1	0	0	0	0	4	0	0	0	0	0	0	0	0
light-sensitive	2	.0000	.0394	26.0	0	0	0	0	2	0	0	0	0	0	0	0	0	0	0	2	0	0	0	0	0	0	0	0	0
light-weight	3	.2540	.1940	32.9	1	0	0	0	0	1	1	0	1	0	0	0	0	0	0	0	0	0	1	0	0	0	1	0	0
light-year	12	.3924	1.0678	40.3	0	0	0	4	2	6	0	0	1	0	0	0	4	0	0	6	0	0	0	0	0	0	1	0	0
light-years	22	.2993	1.5491	41.9	0	3	0	6	11	2	0	0	0	0	0	0	1	0	0	14	0	0	0	0	0	0	7	0	0
lighted	145	.8456	24.676	53.9	30	38	12	22	18	9	14	2	54	6	2	15	0	12	2	24	7	1	0	0	10	9	2	1	0
lighten	7	.2526	.3803	35.8	1	2	0	0	1	3	0	0	0	0	0	0	0	0	0	0	2	3	0	0	1	0	1	0	0
lightened	2	.2443	.1130	30.5	0	0	0	0	2	0	0	0	0	0	0	1	0	0	0	0	0	0	0	0	1	0	0	0	0
lightening	8	.4793	.8259	39.2	1	0	1	1	4	0	1	0	1	0	0	3	0	2	0	0	0	0	0	0	1	0	1	0	0
lightens	2	.1948	.1250	31.0	1	0	0	1	0	0	0	0	1	0	0	0	0	0	0	0	0	0	0	0	0	1	0	0	0
lighter	95	.8043	15.321	51.9	17	7	12	16	16	10	11	6	11	1	1	4	2	7	3	23	4	4	4	9	1	12	5	4	0
lighter-than-air	2	.2160	.1362	31.3	0	0	1	0	0	1	0	0	1	0	0	0	0	0	0	1	0	0	0	0	0	0	0	0	0
lighters	3	.3848	.2449	33.9	0	0	0	0	1	1	1	0	0	0	0	1	0	0	1	0	0	0	0	0	0	0	1	0	0
lightest	15	.5819	1.8219	42.6	2	5	4	1	1	2	0	0	1	0	0	2	6	1	0	2	0	0	0	0	0	2	1	0	0
lighthearted	7	.5850	.8501	39.3	1	1	1	1	0	2	0	1	1	0	0	2	0	0	0	0	1	0	0	0	1	0	1	1	0
lightheartedness	3	.1735	.1535	31.9	0	0	0	2	0	0	1	0	1	0	0	0	0	0	0	0	0	1	0	0	0	1	0	0	0
lighthouse	51	.5230	5.9153	47.7	36	5	0	2	3	4	0	1	23	0	1	0	2	4	0	0	0	0	0	0	18	2	0	1	0

8J librettos
6N libs
7R license-holders
XR Licensed
8F licentious
9D Lichas
8C lichee
XR Lichtenstein's
3P lickety
4A lickety-split
5P Licking
7D lickings
7D Licksians

7N Liddell's
5G lide
6J lieber
9Q Liebig's
5Q Liechtenstein
7R Lief
5Q Lienz
4A Liesi's
7Q lieut
9R Lieut
6N lieutenant-colonel
7R life-and-death
7H life-bearing

3A life-boats
7F life-groupings
9Q life-or-death
7D life-sapping
6A life-size
7R life-span
8H life-sustaining
9D lifeboat's
5N Lifebuoy
5R lifejacketed
7A lifelines
3A Liffey
8L lifter

5R liftoff
4A liger
6H LIGHT
8F Light-Horse
7Q light-activated
6H light-and
8M light-dark
7P light-edged
9M light-faced
XP light-filled
5A light-foot
6A light-footed
XH light-gathering

7H light-giving
6A light-headed
8A light-heeled
6Q light-pink
7A light-purple
7Q light-reacting
7Q light-requiring
9M light-sensitized
7R light-skinned
XQ light-splashed
6A light-stand
4R light-tan
8Q light's

7A Light's
5R lightbulb
3P lightcolored
8G lighte
8D lighter-hued
8A lighter-than-aircraft
5H lighter-than-water
4P Lightfoot
8A lightheartedly

Word Type	F	D	U	SFI	3 Gr 3	4 Gr 4	5 Gr 5	6 Gr 6	7 Gr 7	8 Gr 8	9 Gr 9	X UnGr	A Read	B Eng & Gr	C Comp	D Lit	E Math	F Soc Stud	G Spell	H Sci	J Music	K Art	L Home Ec	M Shop	N Lib F	P Lib NF	Q Lib Ref	R Mag	S Rel
Lighthouse	5	.4776	.5409	37.3	3	1	0	0	0	1	0	0	2	0	0	0	0	1	0	0	0	0	0	0	1	1	0	0	0
lighthouses	8	.4574	.8552	39.3	4	0	1	1	0	1	1	0	4	0	0	0	0	1	0	1	0	0	0	0	0	2	0	0	0
lighting	33	.5382	3.7359	45.7	1	4	2	9	4	7	2	4	5	0	1	0	0	2	1	2	1	0	1	2	2	2	7	6	1
lightkeeper	2	.0000	.0914	29.6	2	0	0	0	0	0	0	0	2	0	0	0	0	0	0	0	0	0	0	0	0	0	0	0	0
lightly	152	.7091	21.913	53.4	18	32	6	16	37	25	16	2	30	3	5	11	0	3	1	10	17	0	25	11	7	20	2	7	0
lightness	14	.5788	1.6814	42.3	0	1	1	0	8	2	1	1	2	0	0	1	0	1	0	1	1	2	0	1	0	0	3	2	0
lightning	166	.5857	20.730	53.2	35	24	20	39	27	13	4	4	52	2	3	7	0	4	1	36	7	0	0	6	12	17	4	12	3
Lightning	28	.4476	2.9772	44.7	25	1	2	0	0	0	0	0	18	1	0	7	0	0	0	0	1	0	0	0	0	1	0	0	0
lightning-fast	2	.2433	.1158	30.6	1	0	0	1	0	0	0	0	0	0	0	0	0	0	0	0	0	0	0	0	0	1	0	1	0
lightning's	2	.1494	.1045	30.2	0	0	2	0	0	0	0	0	1	0	0	0	0	0	0	0	1	0	0	0	0	0	0	0	0
lightnings	3	.3831	.2447	33.9	0	1	0	1	0	1	0	0	0	0	0	1	0	0	0	0	1	0	0	0	1	0	0	0	0
Lightnings	5	.0000	.2284	33.6	0	4	0	1	0	0	0	0	5	0	0	0	0	0	0	0	0	0	0	0	0	0	0	0	0
Lightoller	12	.0000	.1737	32.4	0	0	0	0	0	0	12	0	0	0	0	0	0	0	0	0	0	0	0	0	0	12	0	0	0
lights	376	.8685	65.344	58.2	67	42	28	42	88	68	33	8	127	15	13	28	20	28	2	35	3	8	1	17	16	18	13	32	0
Lights	10	.3615	.8327	39.2	0	3	3	0	3	0	1	0	2	0	0	0	0	2	0	0	4	0	0	0	0	2	0	0	0
lightship	7	.2658	.4804	36.8	0	0	1	1	0	0	0	5	1	0	0	0	0	0	0	5	0	0	0	0	0	0	0	1	0
lightships	2	.2351	.1166	30.7	0	0	0	1	0	0	1	0	0	0	0	0	0	1	0	0	0	0	0	0	0	0	0	1	0
lightweight	37	.5542	4.2579	46.3	1	5	1	3	7	11	8	1	5	0	0	0	0	0	2	4	0	1	11	2	0	4	5	3	0
lignite	7	.3415	.5420	37.3	1	0	0	0	2	2	2	0	0	0	0	0	0	2	0	2	0	0	0	0	0	0	3	0	0
likable	3	.2309	.1631	32.1	0	0	0	1	1	0	1	0	0	0	0	1	0	0	0	0	0	0	0	0	0	0	0	2	0
like	9696	.9781	1868.2	72.7	2110	1725	1069	1226	1727	955	716	168	2641	740	158	726	301	799	297	918	344	133	108	55	781	828	291	566	10
Like	10	.5374	1.1380	40.6	0	1	0	1	2	5	0	1	2	1	0	0	0	0	0	0	3	0	0	0	1	1	0	2	0
liked	610	.8637	105.73	60.2	172	148	75	61	77	41	30	6	251	24	5	38	2	58	6	15	18	10	5	1	75	76	1	25	0
likelihood	5	.3011	.3700	35.7	0	0	2	1	1	0	1	0	1	0	0	0	0	0	0	2	0	0	0	0	0	0	2	0	0
likely	334	.8594	57.237	57.6	20	27	40	30	79	64	57	17	46	19	1	33	7	27	8	55	2	1	22	1	16	27	28	41	0
likeness	16	.5455	1.8391	42.6	1	0	3	1	5	2	4	0	4	1	1	2	0	0	0	1	0	3	0	2	0	1	1	0	0
likenesses	7	.4492	.6732	38.3	1	1	0	1	1	2	1	0	0	0	0	0	0	0	0	3	2	0	0	0	0	1	1	0	0
likes	229	.8571	39.323	55.9	76	39	23	26	27	16	18	4	77	40	1	7	2	7	14	12	8	5	7	0	12	12	3	22	0
likewise	40	.8022	6.4292	48.1	1	3	2	8	11	6	7	2	5	4	1	5	7	1	0	1	3	0	3	0	5	1	3	1	0
Likimani	5	.0000	.0608	27.8	0	5	0	0	0	0	0	0	0	0	0	0	0	0	0	0	0	0	0	0	0	0	0	5	0
liking	30	.7293	4.4621	46.5	1	5	7	9	4	2	1	1	7	0	0	2	0	0	0	4	5	0	1	0	3	3	1	4	0
Lila	2	.0000	.0215	23.3	0	0	0	0	0	0	2	0	0	0	0	2	0	0	0	0	0	0	0	0	0	0	0	0	0
lilac	10	.5813	1.2439	40.9	3	2	0	1	1	1	0	2	3	1	0	0	0	1	0	1	0	0	0	0	0	3	0	1	0
lilacs	2	.0000	.0290	24.6	0	2	0	0	0	0	0	0	0	0	0	0	0	0	0	0	0	0	0	0	0	2	0	0	0
lilies	22	.7501	3.3770	45.3	8	2	1	2	7	0	2	0	7	1	0	1	1	0	0	5	1	0	0	0	2	2	2	0	0
Liliuokalani	4	.2425	.2409	33.8	0	0	1	1	0	2	0	0	0	0	0	0	0	3	0	0	1	0	0	0	0	0	0	0	0
Lill	5	.0000	.0724	28.6	0	0	0	0	5	0	0	0	0	0	0	0	0	0	0	0	0	0	0	0	0	5	0	0	0
Lille	2	.2139	.1057	30.2	0	0	0	1	0	1	0	0	0	0	0	0	0	1	1	0	0	0	0	0	0	0	0	0	0
Lillian	10	.3004	.6512	38.1	0	0	0	3	6	1	0	0	0	0	3	5	0	0	0	0	0	0	0	0	0	1	0	1	0
Lillian's	2	.1387	.0689	28.4	0	0	0	0	2	0	0	0	0	0	1	0	0	0	0	0	0	0	0	0	0	1	0	0	0
Lilliput	3	.3273	.2365	33.7	0	0	0	0	1	2	0	0	1	1	0	0	0	0	1	0	0	0	0	0	0	0	0	0	0
Lilliputians	2	.1497	.1046	30.2	0	0	0	0	1	1	0	0	1	0	0	0	0	0	0	0	0	0	0	0	0	0	0	0	0
Lilly	4	.0996	.1523	31.8	0	0	0	3	1	0	0	0	1	0	0	0	0	0	0	0	0	0	0	0	0	0	0	3	0
Lillybell	10	.0000	.1172	30.7	8	2	0	0	0	0	0	0	0	0	0	0	0	0	0	0	0	0	0	0	10	0	0	0	0
Lillybell's	3	.0000	.0352	25.5	3	0	0	0	0	0	0	0	0	0	0	0	0	0	0	0	0	0	0	0	3	0	0	0	0
lilt	2	.1787	.1174	30.7	0	1	0	1	0	0	0	0	1	0	0	0	0	0	0	0	0	0	0	0	1	0	0	0	0
lilting	4	.1672	.1617	32.1	1	0	0	1	1	0	1	0	0	0	0	0	0	0	0	0	3	0	0	0	0	0	0	1	0
lily	37	.5730	4.5075	46.5	18	2	6	3	6	1	1	0	6	0	0	0	0	1	1	19	0	0	0	0	1	4	4	1	0
Lily	16	.2238	.9271	39.7	8	0	3	3	0	2	0	0	3	2	0	0	0	0	0	0	0	0	0	0	11	0	0	0	0
Lily's	3	.1250	.1342	31.3	1	0	1	1	0	0	0	0	1	0	0	0	0	0	0	0	0	0	0	0	2	0	0	0	0
lima	8	.5405	.9355	39.7	0	1	1	0	3	0	1	2	2	1	0	1	0	0	0	3	0	0	0	0	0	1	0	0	0
Lima	25	.2394	1.5383	41.9	0	7	0	8	9	0	1	0	1	0	0	0	0	19	0	0	0	0	0	0	0	0	0	5	0
limb	32	.7020	4.6346	46.7	2	5	3	5	11	4	1	1	11	0	0	3	0	0	3	1	0	0	0	2	3	5	1	3	0
limber	7	.4748	.6972	38.4	1	3	1	0	1	1	0	0	0	2	0	2	0	0	0	0	0	0	0	0	1	2	0	0	0
limbs	69	.7448	10.477	50.2	2	14	3	8	28	7	6	1	20	0	1	7	0	3	1	4	2	4	0	0	5	8	12	2	0
Limburger	2	.2106	.0917	29.6	0	0	0	0	1	1	0	0	0	0	0	0	0	0	1	0	0	0	1	0	0	0	0	0	0
lime	49	.6913	6.9571	48.4	6	2	0	5	13	12	9	2	7	1	0	2	0	2	0	20	0	1	0	0	4	3	8	1	0
limelight	4	.4889	.4075	36.1	0	0	0	0	2	1	1	0	0	1	0	1	0	0	0	0	0	0	0	1	1	0	0	1	0
limerick	5	.3071	.3634	35.6	0	0	1	1	3	0	0	0	1	2	0	2	0	0	0	0	0	0	0	0	0	0	0	0	0
Limerick	2	.2297	.1135	30.6	0	0	0	0	2	0	0	0	0	0	0	1	0	1	0	0	0	0	0	0	0	0	0	0	0
limericks	3	.2223	.2106	33.2	0	0	0	0	3	0	0	0	2	1	0	0	0	0	0	0	0	0	0	0	0	0	0	0	0
limes	8	.3608	.6591	38.2	0	0	1	0	7	0	0	0	1	0	0	0	0	2	0	0	0	0	0	0	4	0	0	1	0
limestone	64	.6267	8.3147	49.2	18	8	6	10	5	4	11	2	4	0	0	0	0	17	0	22	0	4	0	1	0	7	5	4	0
limestones	2	.0000	.0394	26.0	0	0	0	0	0	0	2	0	0	0	0	0	0	0	0	2	0	0	0	0	0	0	0	0	0
limewater	13	.0000	.2563	34.1	0	7	2	0	0	0	4	0	0	0	0	0	0	0	0	13	0	0	0	0	0	0	0	0	0
limit	92	.8820	16.121	52.1	0	5	13	2	27	16	26	3	9	10	1	1	9	11	3	9	1	1	2	3	0	4	15	13	0
limitation	4	.1873	.1827	32.6	0	0	0	0	1	1	2	0	0	0	0	0	0	0	0	0	0	0	0	0	0	0	3	1	0
limitations	22	.6395	2.8652	44.6	1	0	3	1	7	4	6	0	0	1	0	0	0	4	0	1	0	0	2	0	2	2	6	4	0
limited	151	.8591	25.799	54.1	6	11	4	10	51	30	31	8	5	10	2	3	3	17	2	34	10	1	5	4	0	9	33	13	0
limiting	12	.5220	1.3505	41.3	1	0	1	0	3	2	4	1	3	2	0	0	1	0	0	1	0	0	0	0	0	1	4	0	0
limitless	4	.3624	.3126	34.9	0	1	0	1	1	1	0	0	0	0	0	1	0	0	0	0	0	0	0	0	1	0	2	0	0
limits	71	.8502	12.037	50.8	5	6	5	7	19	10	13	6	7	6	3	2	2	13	0	7	2	0	1	2	2	5	10	9	0
limonite	2	.0000	.0394	26.0	0	0	0	0	0	2	0	0	0	0	0	0	0	0	0	2	0	0	0	0	0	0	0	0	0
limousine	2	.2351	.1166	30.7	0	0	0	0	1	1	0	0	0	0	0	0	0	1	0	0	0	0	0	0	0	0	0	1	0
limousines	2	.2285	.1129	30.5	0	0	0	0	0	1	1	0	0	0	0	0	0	1	0	0	0	0	0	0	0	0	1	0	0
limp	31	.7455	4.6904	46.7	4	3	2	4	10	3	5	0	7	2	1	5	0	0	0	1	0	0	2	0	5	3	1	4	0
limped	12	.4345	1.1527	40.6	2	2	1	0	3	3	1	0	3	1	2	4	0	1	0	0	0	0	0	0	1	0	0	0	0
limpid	3	.2292	.1615	32.1	0	0	1	0	2	0	0	0	0	0	0	1	0	0	0	0	0	0	0	0	2	0	0	0	0
limping	8	.3614	.6702	38.3	1	2	0	0	3	1	1	0	2	1	0	4	0	0	0	0	0	0	0	0	0	1	0	0	0
limply	5	.3767	.4746	36.8	0	0	0	3	1	0	0	1	3	0	0	1	0	0	0	1	0	0	0	0	0	0	0	0	0
Limpopo	3	.0000	.0352	25.5	0	3	0	0	0	0	0	0	0	0	0	0	0	0	0	0	0	0	0	0	3	0	0	0	0
Lin	5	.2326	.3837	35.8	3	0	1	0	0	1	0	0	4	0	0	0	0	1	0	0	0	0	0	0	0	0	0	0	0
Lina	19	.0000	.2228	33.5	0	0	19	0	0	0	0	0	0	0	0	0	0	0	0	0	0	0	0	0	19	0	0	0	0
Lincoln	261	.8131	42.989	56.3	79	22	57	14	33	47	9	0	103	8	4	22	3	50	3	1	9	0	0	0	4	21	21	12	0
Lincoln's	40	.7150	5.8749	47.7	8	3	4	2	7	11	5	0	11	1	0	8	0	6	1	1	2	0	0	0	1	6	3	1	0
Lincolns	3	.2378	.1809	32.6	1	0	2	0	0	0	0	0	0	0	0	0	0	2	0	0	0	0	0	0	0	1	0	0	0
Lincolnshire	3	.3782	.2435	33.9	0	1	1	1	0	0	0	0	0	0	0	0	0	0	0	0	1	0	0	0	0	1	1	0	0
Linda	85	.7183	12.546	51.0	39	5	15	1	2	14	9	0	28	15	1	3	10	2	2	0	0	0	2	0	19	0	0	3	0
LINDA	9	.0000	.0966	29.8	0	0	0	0	0	9	0	0	0	0	0	9	0	0	0	0	0	0	0	0	0	0	0	0	0
Linda's	4	.4535	.4020	36.0	3	0	0	0	0	1	0	0	1	1	0	0	1	0	0	0	0	0	0	0	1	0	0	0	0
Lindbergh	7	.3650	.5730	37.6	0	0	0	2	1	4	0	0	0	2	0	0	0	4	0	0	0	0	0	0	0	0	0	1	0
Linden	4	.1826	.1841	32.7	4	0	0	0	0	0	0	0	0	0	0	0	0	0	0	0	0	0	0	0	3	1	0	0	0
Lindsay	14	.3343	1.0267	40.1	0	0	1	11	2	0	0	0	0	1	0	0	0	0	0	0	1	0	0	0	10	0	0	2	0
Lindy	66	.0534	3.5218	45.5	11	0	0	0	54	1	0	0	65	0	0	0	0	1	0	0	0	0	0	0	0	0	0	0	0
Lindy's	4	.0000	.1827	32.6	1	0	0	0	3	0	0	0	4	0	0	0	0	0	0	0	0	0	0	0	0	0	0	0	0
line	3293	.8923	583.88	67.7	635	528	374	361	557	450	344	44	556	178	76	80	1097	177	261	169	165	46	78	78	55	117	63	96	1

6F Lighting
3A lightkeepers
5J lightnin'
7B lightning-flash
4N lightning-rods
6R Lightship
XH lightship's
7N lightsome
4Q lightweights
5N lightwood
8Q Liguasan
3Q Ligurian
5F Lihue
6A Lijembe's
5P likeable
7N likeliest
7F likely-looking
8J likened
5J Liking
7A likings
3A Lilac
7D lilac-bush
8Q Liliaceae
7R Lilienfield
8N lille
XH Lilliputian
6A lily-white
8Q Liman
4P limbering
9D Limberlock
XR limbic-lobe
7D limbo
4D lime-filled
7R lime-green
8H limelike
7A Limited
7Q limiters
4R Limoges
7H limy
7R Lincoln-Mercury
7R Lincoln-Roosevelt
8J Lind's
9Q Lindberg
6A linden
7K Lindner
7A Lindsay's

Word Type	F	D	U	SFI	3 Gr 3	4 Gr 4	5 Gr 5	6 Gr 6	7 Gr 7	8 Gr 8	9 Gr 9	X UnGr	A Read	B Eng & Gr	C Comp	D Lit	E Math	F Soc Stud	G Spell	H Sci	J Music	K Art	L Home Ec	M Shop	N Lib F	P Lib NF	Q Lib Ref	R Mag	S Rel
Line	31	.7009	4.4168	46.5	4	7	6	2	6	4	1	1	1	0	0	0	2	10	0	2	3	0	0	0	5	3	3	2	0
line-of-sight	7	.2416	.4240	36.3	0	0	5	0	0	1	1	0	0	0	0	0	0	0	0	6	0	0	0	1	0	0	0	0	0
line-up	3	.2357	.2199	33.4	1	1	1	0	0	0	0	0	2	0	0	0	0	0	0	0	0	0	0	0	0	1	0	0	0
linear	22	.4566	2.1065	43.2	0	1	0	3	6	2	9	1	0	0	0	0	8	0	0	2	0	4	0	1	0	0	6	1	0
linearly	2	.2278	.1128	30.5	0	0	0	0	0	0	0	2	0	0	0	0	0	0	0	1	0	0	0	0	0	0	1	0	0
lined	126	.8826	22.190	53.5	18	21	14	19	20	19	14	1	38	6	2	6	8	5	1	10	0	0	4	3	5	21	10	7	0
lineman	2	.2442	.1134	30.5	0	1	0	0	1	0	0	0	0	1	0	0	0	0	0	0	0	0	0	0	0	0	0	1	0
linemen	3	.2031	.1990	33.0	0	1	1	1	0	0	0	0	2	0	0	0	0	0	1	0	0	0	0	0	0	0	0	0	0
linen	58	.5060	6.3815	48.0	7	8	5	9	10	12	6	1	17	1	0	6	0	7	0	3	0	0	12	0	5	6	0	1	0
Linen	5	.0000	.0608	27.8	0	0	0	0	0	5	0	0	0	0	0	0	0	0	0	0	0	0	0	0	0	0	0	5	0
Linen's	2	.0000	.0243	23.9	0	0	0	0	0	2	0	0	0	0	0	0	0	0	0	0	0	0	0	0	0	0	0	2	0
linens	12	.3150	.8322	39.2	2	1	3	1	0	1	4	0	1	0	0	0	0	0	0	0	0	0	5	0	2	0	2	2	0
liner	19	.7128	2.7843	44.4	5	1	2	2	7	0	1	1	5	2	0	0	0	2	0	2	0	0	0	0	3	2	1	2	0
liners	17	.6953	2.4255	43.8	9	1	3	1	0	0	2	1	3	2	0	0	2	3	0	1	2	0	0	0	0	3	1	0	0
lines	1715	.7772	266.85	64.3	187	267	206	220	358	182	269	26	110	115	31	62	335	102	259	120	68	116	26	175	15	46	84	51	0
Lines	4	.1814	.2373	33.8	0	2	0	0	0	2	0	0	2	0	0	0	0	0	0	0	0	0	0	0	0	0	0	2	0
linesmen	3	.2143	.1568	32.0	1	0	0	0	2	0	0	0	0	0	0	0	0	0	0	0	0	0	0	0	0	1	0	2	0
lineup	5	.2580	.3252	35.1	0	2	0	1	1	0	0	1	1	0	0	0	0	0	0	0	0	0	0	0	0	1	0	3	0
ling-tum	2	.0000	.0914	29.6	0	2	0	0	0	0	0	0	2	0	0	0	0	0	0	0	0	0	0	0	0	0	0	0	0
linger	13	.7021	1.8713	42.7	2	1	2	4	2	1	0	1	3	2	0	2	0	0	1	1	0	0	0	0	1	2	0	1	0
lingered	22	.6327	2.9510	44.7	2	1	3	1	7	4	4	0	10	0	1	3	0	0	0	0	0	0	0	0	4	1	1	2	0
lingerie	4	.1092	.1038	30.2	0	0	1	0	0	3	0	0	0	0	0	0	0	0	0	0	0	0	3	0	0	0	1	0	0
lingering	11	.5785	1.3336	41.3	2	1	2	0	3	0	2	1	2	0	0	1	0	0	0	0	0	0	0	0	3	1	2	2	0
lingers	6	.4394	.5885	37.7	0	0	0	1	1	2	1	1	2	1	1	1	0	0	0	0	0	0	0	0	0	0	1	0	0
lingo	4	.3641	.3147	35.0	1	0	2	0	1	0	0	0	0	2	0	1	0	0	0	0	0	0	0	0	0	0	0	1	0
lingua	3	.3824	.2447	33.9	0	0	0	2	1	0	0	0	0	1	0	0	0	0	1	0	0	0	0	0	0	0	0	1	0
linguist	6	.2270	.3177	35.0	0	0	0	3	1	0	2	0	0	4	0	0	0	0	0	0	0	0	0	0	0	0	2	0	0
linguistic	17	.4781	1.6880	42.3	0	0	2	0	3	3	8	1	0	2	1	0	0	0	2	0	0	0	0	0	0	2	10	0	0
Linguistic	12	.0000	.0974	29.9	0	3	3	3	3	0	0	0	0	0	0	0	0	0	12	0	0	0	0	0	0	0	0	0	0
linguistics	6	.1555	.2368	33.7	0	0	0	0	1	0	5	0	0	1	0	0	0	0	0	0	0	0	0	0	0	0	5	0	0
linguists	10	.3257	.7078	38.5	0	0	1	0	3	5	1	0	0	6	0	0	0	0	3	0	0	0	0	0	0	0	1	0	0
lining	101	.4993	10.567	50.2	5	13	11	5	37	8	22	0	7	2	2	1	0	1	0	29	2	0	34	3	5	1	8	6	0
Lining	2	.1937	.0847	29.3	0	0	0	0	1	0	1	0	0	0	0	0	0	0	0	0	1	0	0	1	0	0	0	0	0
linings	13	.4436	1.2434	40.9	1	3	1	0	3	2	3	0	1	0	0	0	0	0	0	4	0	0	3	0	0	2	1	2	0
link	71	.8351	11.801	50.7	5	6	8	12	17	8	12	3	1	11	1	0	2	5	0	10	3	2	2	2	1	4	13	14	0
Link	23	.1564	1.5639	41.9	0	0	0	0	22	0	1	0	22	0	0	1	0	0	0	0	0	0	0	0	0	0	0	0	0
Link's	6	.0000	.2741	34.4	0	0	0	0	6	0	0	0	6	0	0	0	0	0	0	0	0	0	0	0	0	0	0	0	0
linkage	2	.0000	.0209	23.2	0	0	0	0	0	0	1	1	0	0	0	0	0	0	0	0	0	0	0	0	0	0	2	0	0
linked	52	.7510	7.8455	48.9	1	4	3	9	9	6	15	5	1	11	0	1	1	7	1	3	2	0	1	0	3	2	13	6	0
linking	62	.4593	5.9686	47.8	0	1	6	14	20	10	11	0	0	43	4	0	0	3	3	3	1	0	0	0	0	1	2	2	0
links	47	.8350	7.8281	48.9	3	1	9	11	8	7	5	3	3	3	2	0	2	5	4	8	1	0	1	2	1	6	8	1	0
Linn	23	.2210	1.1788	40.7	6	0	0	0	17	0	0	0	0	0	0	17	0	0	0	0	6	0	0	0	0	0	0	0	0
Linnaean	2	.0000	.0394	26.0	0	0	0	0	0	0	2	0	0	0	0	0	0	0	0	2	0	0	0	0	0	0	0	0	0
Linnaeus	4	.0000	.0789	29.0	0	1	0	0	0	0	2	1	0	0	0	0	0	0	0	4	0	0	0	0	0	0	0	0	0
linoleum	17	.3964	1.4358	41.6	1	1	0	3	5	0	6	1	2	1	0	2	1	0	0	0	0	5	0	4	0	1	0	1	0
linotype	5	.0000	.0537	27.3	0	0	0	0	5	0	0	0	0	0	0	5	0	0	0	0	0	0	0	0	0	0	0	0	0
linseed	4	.0609	.0733	28.6	0	0	0	1	0	1	2	0	0	0	0	0	0	1	0	0	0	0	0	3	0	0	0	0	0
lint	4	.1409	.1725	32.4	0	0	1	0	1	1	1	0	1	0	0	0	0	0	0	1	0	0	2	0	0	0	0	0	0
Linton	2	.2346	.1166	30.7	0	0	1	0	0	0	0	1	0	0	0	0	0	0	0	1	0	0	0	0	0	0	0	1	0
lion	264	.8213	44.017	56.4	87	42	29	23	52	20	8	3	138	8	5	21	0	6	3	16	3	4	0	0	3	28	13	16	0
Lion	31	.5176	3.5576	45.5	9	6	1	12	1	1	1	0	15	0	0	1	0	1	0	0	6	2	0	0	6	0	0	0	0
lion's	20	.6329	2.6975	44.3	7	1	3	2	4	2	1	0	10	1	0	3	0	0	0	1	0	1	0	0	2	1	0	1	0
Lion's	4	.3600	.3541	35.5	1	0	0	2	1	0	0	0	2	0	0	0	0	0	0	0	1	0	0	0	1	0	0	0	0
Lionel	15	.2925	1.1063	40.4	0	1	0	5	0	9	0	0	6	0	4	0	0	0	0	0	0	0	0	0	3	1	0	1	0
lioness	15	.3504	1.3681	41.4	0	1	1	10	1	0	2	0	10	0	0	0	0	0	0	0	0	0	0	0	0	0	1	4	0
Lioness	4	.0000	.0579	27.6	0	4	0	0	0	0	0	0	0	0	0	0	0	0	0	0	0	0	0	0	0	4	0	0	0
lionesses	5	.3826	.4759	36.8	0	2	0	0	2	0	1	0	3	0	0	0	0	0	0	0	0	0	0	0	0	1	1	0	0
lions	128	.6621	17.851	52.5	58	16	13	14	18	6	2	1	57	7	0	1	3	3	1	7	0	0	1	0	3	20	10	14	1
Lions	10	.4988	1.0716	40.3	3	0	0	0	2	4	1	0	2	1	0	0	0	0	0	0	1	0	0	0	2	0	0	4	0
lions'	7	.5311	.8041	39.1	1	3	0	1	1	1	0	0	2	0	0	0	1	0	0	0	0	0	0	0	1	1	0	2	0
lip	47	.6853	6.6586	48.2	5	7	8	5	10	7	4	1	14	4	0	6	0	0	0	3	0	0	0	0	10	3	4	3	0
lip-stretching	2	.0000	.0914	29.6	0	0	0	0	0	2	0	0	2	0	0	0	0	0	0	0	0	0	0	0	0	0	0	0	0
Lippmann	3	.3454	.2542	34.1	0	0	0	0	2	1	0	0	1	0	0	0	0	1	0	0	0	0	0	0	0	0	0	1	0
lips	248	.7994	40.038	56.0	16	44	18	28	81	39	17	5	73	5	5	44	0	8	5	6	11	0	3	0	45	25	5	13	0
lipstick	10	.4374	.9564	39.8	2	0	1	1	4	2	0	0	2	0	0	0	0	0	0	0	0	0	2	0	2	1	0	3	0
lipsticks	3	.3769	.2484	34.0	1	0	0	0	1	0	1	0	0	0	0	0	0	1	0	0	0	0	0	0	0	0	1	1	0
liquefied	5	.3724	.4180	36.2	0	1	0	0	2	0	2	0	0	0	0	0	0	0	0	3	0	0	0	0	1	0	0	1	0
liquefy	3	.1785	.1397	31.5	0	0	0	0	1	0	2	0	0	0	0	0	0	0	0	2	0	0	0	1	0	0	0	0	0
liqueurs	2	.2278	.1128	30.5	0	0	0	0	1	0	1	0	0	0	0	0	0	0	0	1	0	0	0	0	0	0	1	0	0
liquid	442	.6835	61.925	57.9	41	84	63	43	76	61	68	6	34	1	2	5	18	8	5	259	3	1	34	10	4	18	34	6	0
liquid-fuel	2	.0000	.0299	24.8	0	1	0	0	0	1	0	0	0	0	0	0	2	0	0	0	0	0	0	0	0	0	0	0	0
liquids	89	.5336	10.121	50.1	9	18	10	12	4	14	21	1	5	0	0	0	5	1	0	63	0	0	4	1	1	1	7	1	0
liquor	6	.4692	.5895	37.7	0	0	0	0	3	2	1	0	0	1	0	2	0	0	0	0	0	0	0	0	1	0	0	2	0
liquors	2	.2285	.1129	30.5	0	0	1	0	0	1	0	0	0	0	0	0	0	1	0	0	0	0	0	0	0	0	1	0	0
lira	5	.1446	.1801	32.6	4	0	0	1	0	0	0	0	0	0	0	0	0	0	0	0	4	0	0	0	0	0	0	1	0
Lisa	18	.4534	1.8649	42.7	9	1	1	3	1	0	3	0	8	1	0	0	5	0	0	0	0	2	0	0	0	0	1	1	0
Lisbeth	6	.2120	.3097	34.9	0	2	0	0	4	0	0	0	0	0	0	0	0	0	0	0	0	0	0	0	4	2	0	0	0
Lisbon	4	.2065	.1985	33.0	0	0	0	3	1	0	0	0	0	0	0	0	0	0	0	0	0	0	0	0	3	0	1	0	0
lisping	2	.2440	.1132	30.5	0	1	0	0	0	0	1	0	0	0	0	1	0	0	0	0	0	0	0	0	0	0	0	1	0
Lissa	3	.0000	.0365	25.6	0	3	0	0	0	0	0	0	0	0	0	0	0	0	0	0	0	0	0	0	0	0	0	3	0
list	1781	.5893	216.13	63.3	159	350	341	303	326	173	111	18	149	212	32	14	273	65	845	83	9	2	30	14	6	19	12	16	0
List	19	.1284	.6360	38.0	12	1	4	2	0	0	0	0	0	1	0	0	0	2	16	0	0	0	0	0	0	0	0	0	0
listed	307	.7775	47.993	56.8	25	61	39	34	64	50	32	2	35	58	4	2	55	22	58	21	25	1	3	0	1	3	13	6	0
listen	1148	.6358	150.17	61.8	230	269	200	180	146	85	29	9	206	134	2	39	2	20	155	40	455	4	6	0	30	22	4	28	1
Listen	4	.3740	.3661	35.6	1	1	1	0	0	1	0	0	2	0	0	0	0	0	0	0	0	0	0	0	1	0	0	1	0
listened	260	.7701	40.919	56.1	65	50	36	32	30	26	17	4	108	17	1	29	0	20	0	0	12	0	1	0	32	27	2	11	0
listener	79	.3925	6.7695	48.3	3	5	10	13	13	21	14	0	8	43	0	3	0	2	0	1	20	0	0	0	0	1	1	0	0
Listener	6	.0000	.0869	29.4	6	0	0	0	0	0	0	0	0	0	0	0	0	0	0	0	0	0	0	0	0	6	0	0	0
listeners	57	.6244	7.3287	48.7	6	3	5	8	17	5	12	1	8	21	2	3	0	1	0	1	11	0	0	0	0	5	1	4	0
listening	256	.7145	37.482	55.7	34	59	31	32	53	33	13	1	75	55	2	20	1	5	4	4	45	0	0	0	23	9	3	10	0
Listening	6	.2407	.3271	35.1	3	1	0	2	0	0	0	0	0	3	0	0	0	0	0	0	3	0	0	0	0	0	0	0	0
listens	38	.6572	5.1850	47.1	8	7	4	5	5	4	5	0	10	8	0	3	0	3	0	4	6	0	0	0	2	0	0	2	0
Lister	4	.2335	.2373	33.8	0	1	0	0	0	3	0	0	0	1	0	0	0	0	0	3	0	0	0	0	0	0	0	0	0

5A line-drive
8E line-segment
4P lineage
7N lineaments
XR Linear
7R linebacker
7Q lined-up
9R Linemen
9P Liner
3P LINERS
9Q Lingala
6R Lingo
5A lingonberry
8B linguistically
9Q Linguistics
7N lingy
5A Linian
XR liniment
5Q liniments
5J linin'
7A link's
7B Linking
9B linking-verb
4D linkmen
7D Linn's
9H Linnaeus'
7R Linnea
6A linnet
7R linseed-oil
4A linsey
8C linsey-woolsey
4B Linsky
6J Linstead
8A lintel
9H linters
7R Linville
7F Linz
XB Lion-Hearted
8A lion-hearted
4Q Lion-hearted
7F lion-like
8A Lionel's
6P LIP
7D lip-like
7H lipids
3P Lipizzans
6N lipped
7K Lippi
7R Liquefied
6Q liquefying
7H liqueur
7H liquid-drop
8J liquid-filled
7H liquid-in-liquid
7R liquid-level
9M liquid-salt
7Q liquidation
5H liquidlike
7H liquified
9E lire
7B LISA
7H Lise
8G lisle
7N Lisle
7N lisped
7A Liss
7B listener's
6B listeners'
3A Listening-to-Me-Humming

Word Type	F	D	U	SFI	3 Gr 3	4 Gr 4	5 Gr 5	6 Gr 6	7 Gr 7	8 Gr 8	9 Gr 9	X UnGr	A Read	B Eng & Gr	C Comp	D Lit	E Math	F Soc Stud	G Spell	H Sci	J Music	K Art	L Home Ec	M Shop	N Lib F	P Lib NF	Q Lib Ref	R Mag	S Rel
listing	35	.6544	4.6920	46.7	1	4	3	2	15	2	7	1	3	6	1	0	16	2	1	0	0	0	1	0	0	0	1	4	0
listings	2	.1497	.1046	30.2	0	0	0	1	1	0	0	0	1	0	0	0	0	0	1	0	0	0	0	0	0	0	0	0	0
listless	6	.4522	.5949	37.7	0	0	1	0	2	1	2	0	1	0	0	0	0	1	0	1	2	0	0	0	1	0	0	0	0
listlessly	4	.4857	.4029	36.1	0	0	0	1	3	0	0	0	0	0	0	1	0	0	0	0	1	0	0	0	1	0	1	0	0
listlessness	2	.2278	.1128	30.5	0	0	0	1	1	0	0	0	0	0	0	0	0	0	0	1	0	0	0	0	0	0	1	0	0
lists	98	.7225	14.278	51.5	5	22	15	13	19	12	11	1	5	33	1	2	9	7	22	7	1	0	2	1	1	1	4	2	0
Liszt	19	.0606	.3727	35.7	0	0	0	2	11	5	1	0	0	0	0	0	0	0	0	0	18	0	0	0	0	0	1	0	0
Liszt's	3	.0000	.0243	23.8	0	0	0	0	1	2	0	0	0	0	0	0	0	0	0	0	3	0	0	0	0	0	0	0	0
lit	92	.7586	14.276	51.5	21	13	8	12	22	12	3	1	35	2	1	17	0	2	0	8	1	1	0	0	11	6	0	8	0
lit-up	4	.0000	.0789	29.0	4	0	0	0	0	0	0	0	0	0	0	0	0	0	0	4	0	0	0	0	0	0	0	0	0
litany	3	.3815	.2447	33.9	0	1	0	1	1	0	0	0	0	0	0	0	0	0	1	0	0	0	0	0	1	0	0	1	0
lite	2	.0000	.0914	29.6	0	0	0	0	0	2	0	0	2	0	0	0	0	0	0	0	0	0	0	0	0	0	0	0	0
liter	6	.2076	.3235	35.1	0	1	0	0	2	3	0	0	0	0	0	0	4	0	0	2	0	0	0	0	0	0	0	0	0
literacy	9	.3113	.6590	38.2	1	0	1	5	1	0	1	0	0	0	0	1	0	7	0	0	0	0	0	0	0	0	1	0	0
literal	12	.3222	.8295	39.2	0	0	0	0	1	8	2	1	0	1	0	1	0	0	8	0	2	0	0	0	0	0	0	0	0
literally	55	.6933	7.7388	48.9	1	3	3	2	19	10	8	9	3	6	0	2	0	2	0	8	5	0	0	0	1	4	13	11	0
literary	39	.6488	5.1670	47.1	1	2	9	0	11	9	3	4	2	4	0	5	0	3	0	0	2	0	0	0	0	11	9	3	0
Literary	6	.3014	.4177	36.2	0	4	0	0	1	1	0	0	0	0	0	0	0	1	0	0	0	0	0	0	1	4	0	0	0
literate	4	.1622	.1743	32.4	0	0	0	1	1	2	0	0	0	0	0	0	0	1	0	0	0	0	0	0	0	0	0	3	0
literature	127	.7018	18.110	52.6	4	6	25	13	22	32	19	6	14	12	1	12	0	11	1	2	11	0	0	0	0	20	38	5	0
Literature	5	.4236	.4668	36.7	0	0	0	0	2	0	1	2	1	2	0	0	0	0	0	0	1	0	0	0	0	0	0	1	0
liters	7	.4495	.6753	38.3	0	0	2	0	0	1	0	4	0	0	0	0	2	0	0	1	0	0	0	0	0	3	1	0	0
lithe	6	.4649	.5827	37.7	0	1	0	0	4	1	0	0	0	1	1	2	0	1	0	0	0	0	0	0	0	0	1	0	0
lithium	19	.4225	1.7766	42.5	0	1	5	1	1	6	3	2	0	0	0	0	1	2	0	13	0	0	0	0	0	0	1	2	0
lithograph	5	.2522	.2759	34.4	0	0	0	0	2	0	2	1	0	1	0	1	0	0	0	0	0	2	0	0	0	0	0	1	0
lithographic	2	.0000	.0209	23.2	0	0	0	0	0	0	2	0	0	0	0	0	0	0	0	0	0	0	0	0	0	0	2	0	0
lithography	6	.1205	.1694	32.3	0	0	0	0	0	0	6	0	0	0	0	0	0	0	0	0	0	0	0	4	0	0	2	0	0
lithosphere	6	.0000	.1183	30.7	0	0	0	0	3	2	1	0	0	0	0	0	0	0	0	6	0	0	0	0	0	0	0	0	0
lithotomy	2	.0000	.0209	23.2	0	0	0	0	0	2	0	0	0	0	0	0	0	0	0	0	0	0	0	0	0	0	2	0	0
Lithuania	2	.2437	.1129	30.5	0	0	1	1	0	0	0	0	0	0	0	0	0	0	0	0	0	0	0	0	0	0	1	1	0
litigation	2	.0000	.0243	23.9	0	0	0	0	2	0	0	0	0	0	0	0	0	0	0	0	0	0	0	0	0	0	0	2	0
litmus	19	.0000	.3746	35.7	0	0	16	0	0	3	0	0	0	0	0	0	0	0	0	19	0	0	0	0	0	0	0	0	0
litter	26	.6686	3.6390	45.6	4	5	2	6	6	0	1	2	10	0	0	1	0	1	0	1	0	0	0	0	2	5	2	4	0
littered	9	.4668	.9377	39.7	2	1	1	1	3	0	1	0	3	0	0	0	0	0	0	0	0	0	0	0	2	2	2	0	0
litters	2	.1698	.1133	30.5	0	0	2	0	0	0	0	0	1	0	0	0	0	0	0	0	0	0	0	0	0	1	0	0	0
little	6204	.9347	1149.9	70.6	1773	1123	631	780	962	469	335	131	2398	211	46	517	45	455	52	452	238	41	57	27	643	579	155	286	2
Little	364	.7187	54.623	57.4	147	77	39	22	52	20	5	2	209	5	4	38	0	19	0	2	13	0	0	0	46	11	3	14	0
little-known	4	.4485	.4009	36.0	0	1	0	0	1	1	1	0	1	0	0	0	0	1	0	0	0	0	0	0	0	0	1	1	0
Little's	3	.1060	.1461	31.6	0	0	1	0	2	0	0	0	2	0	1	0	0	0	0	0	0	0	0	0	0	0	0	0	0
littlest	11	.5199	1.2689	41.0	1	3	1	4	1	0	0	1	5	0	0	1	0	0	0	1	1	0	0	0	3	0	0	0	0
live	2431	.8919	431.78	66.4	689	436	316	343	365	143	104	35	461	53	15	94	29	656	16	485	66	20	18	2	72	205	121	113	5
Live	7	.3626	.6400	38.1	0	1	2	1	1	0	1	1	4	0	0	0	0	0	0	0	0	0	0	0	0	1	0	2	0
live-bearing	5	.2028	.2557	34.1	0	0	0	0	5	0	0	0	0	0	0	0	0	0	0	2	0	0	0	0	0	0	3	0	0
lived	1372	.9039	247.03	63.9	313	291	198	200	186	111	53	20	476	38	13	80	21	259	10	58	65	8	0	0	90	132	67	54	1
livelier	2	.1787	.1174	30.7	0	0	0	1	1	0	0	0	1	0	0	0	0	0	0	0	0	0	0	0	1	0	0	0	0
liveliest	5	.4113	.4594	36.6	0	2	1	1	1	0	0	0	1	0	0	2	0	0	0	0	0	0	0	0	0	1	0	1	0
livelihood	8	.5245	.8882	39.5	1	0	2	1	2	1	1	0	1	0	0	1	0	2	0	0	0	1	0	0	1	1	1	0	0
liveliness	4	.3723	.3645	35.6	0	0	1	0	2	0	0	1	2	1	0	0	0	0	0	0	0	0	0	0	0	0	0	1	0
livelong	2	.1733	.1149	30.6	2	0	0	0	0	0	0	0	1	1	0	0	0	0	0	0	0	0	0	0	0	0	0	0	0
lively	128	.8475	21.712	53.4	13	25	19	15	32	12	9	3	33	17	5	6	0	5	2	7	12	4	1	0	7	14	7	8	0
liven	2	.0000	.0215	23.3	0	0	1	0	1	0	0	0	0	0	0	2	0	0	0	0	0	0	0	0	0	0	0	0	0
liver	51	.7041	7.3677	48.7	4	1	11	3	12	5	11	4	10	0	0	2	0	0	0	20	1	0	4	1	3	3	5	2	0
Liverpool	16	.6557	2.1820	43.4	1	1	2	5	6	0	1	0	4	0	0	0	0	4	0	0	2	0	0	0	2	1	1	2	0
liverworts	3	.0000	.0591	27.7	0	0	0	0	3	0	0	0	0	0	0	0	0	0	0	3	0	0	0	0	0	0	0	0	0
liverwurst	2	.0000	.0914	29.6	0	2	0	0	0	0	0	0	2	0	0	0	0	0	0	0	0	0	0	0	0	0	0	0	0
livery	8	.4694	.8277	39.2	0	2	1	1	1	0	3	0	2	0	0	3	0	1	0	0	0	0	0	0	1	1	0	0	0
lives	742	.9083	133.81	61.3	135	98	77	111	154	73	73	21	141	41	7	47	28	123	9	107	26	4	10	2	18	72	52	52	3
Lives	2	.2152	.1357	31.3	0	0	0	0	1	1	0	0	1	0	0	0	0	1	0	0	0	0	0	0	0	0	0	0	0
Livesey	2	.0000	.0234	23.7	0	0	0	0	2	0	0	0	0	0	0	0	0	0	0	0	0	0	0	0	2	0	0	0	0
livestock	57	.5137	6.2922	48.0	2	3	16	12	15	3	4	2	5	0	0	1	0	34	1	0	0	0	0	0	0	6	6	4	0
Livestock	7	.2361	.4176	36.2	0	4	1	0	0	0	1	1	0	0	0	0	0	5	0	0	0	0	0	0	0	0	0	2	0
livid	8	.4800	.8216	39.1	1	0	1	2	1	3	0	0	1	0	0	2	0	0	0	0	0	0	0	0	3	1	0	1	0
livin'	6	.3416	.4646	36.7	0	3	1	0	0	1	1	0	1	0	0	0	0	0	0	0	3	0	0	0	1	0	0	1	0
living	1645	.8427	277.61	64.4	304	219	223	221	362	151	117	48	215	39	3	55	13	312	6	589	27	7	34	17	40	93	118	77	0
Living	9	.3557	.7740	38.9	0	0	2	0	1	1	4	1	3	0	0	0	0	1	0	1	0	0	0	0	0	0	0	4	0
living-area	2	.0000	.0064	18.1	0	0	0	0	0	2	0	0	0	0	0	0	0	0	0	0	0	0	2	0	0	0	0	0	0
living-room	10	.4756	1.0507	40.2	2	0	0	1	4	2	1	0	3	0	0	1	0	0	0	0	0	0	0	0	4	1	0	1	0
livingroom	4	.0000	.0429	26.3	0	0	0	0	1	0	3	0	0	0	0	4	0	0	0	0	0	0	0	0	0	0	0	0	0
Livingston	18	.3738	1.5413	41.9	0	0	11	0	0	2	5	0	2	0	0	5	0	10	0	0	0	0	0	0	0	0	1	0	0
Livingstone	9	.2278	.5242	37.2	0	0	0	1	3	0	5	0	0	0	0	0	0	7	0	0	0	0	0	0	0	0	2	0	0
Livonia	2	.0000	.0209	23.2	0	0	1	0	0	1	0	0	0	0	0	0	0	0	0	0	0	0	0	0	0	0	2	0	0
Liza	16	.1655	.7330	38.7	0	13	0	3	0	0	0	0	3	0	0	0	0	0	0	0	11	0	0	0	0	2	0	0	0
lizard	54	.5919	6.8113	48.3	28	7	1	7	6	1	4	0	16	0	0	1	1	0	0	9	0	0	0	0	2	19	4	2	0
Lizard	12	.1155	.4235	36.3	11	0	1	0	0	0	0	0	0	0	0	0	0	0	0	0	0	0	0	0	1	11	0	0	0
lizard-like	2	.2405	.1205	30.8	1	0	0	0	1	0	0	0	0	0	0	0	0	0	0	1	0	0	0	0	0	1	0	0	0
lizardlike	2	.2401	.1133	30.5	0	1	0	0	1	0	0	0	0	0	0	0	0	0	0	0	0	0	0	0	0	1	1	0	0
lizards	69	.6284	9.0890	49.6	27	8	2	3	16	1	11	1	15	2	0	1	0	1	0	22	0	0	0	0	1	15	9	3	0
Lizards	7	.1613	.3045	34.8	6	1	0	0	0	0	0	0	0	0	0	0	0	0	0	0	0	0	0	0	1	6	0	0	0
Lizzie	5	.3803	.4779	36.8	1	2	1	0	0	1	0	0	3	0	0	0	0	1	0	0	0	0	0	0	1	0	0	0	0
Lizzie's	2	.0000	.0243	23.9	0	0	2	0	0	0	0	0	0	0	0	0	0	0	0	0	0	0	0	0	0	0	0	2	0
Lizzy	4	.0000	.1827	32.6	0	0	4	0	0	0	0	0	4	0	0	0	0	0	0	0	0	0	0	0	0	0	0	0	0
Ljubljana	3	.2321	.1635	32.1	0	0	0	0	0	1	2	0	0	0	0	0	0	0	0	0	0	0	0	0	0	0	1	2	0
lk	3	.2060	.1430	31.6	1	0	1	0	1	0	0	0	0	1	0	0	0	0	2	0	0	0	0	0	0	0	0	0	0
ll	7	.0000	.0568	27.5	2	1	1	2	0	1	0	0	0	0	0	0	0	0	7	0	0	0	0	0	0	0	0	0	0
llama	18	.4491	1.8492	42.7	1	9	5	1	1	1	0	0	7	0	0	0	0	7	0	0	0	2	1	0	0	0	1	0	0
llama's	3	.0652	.0601	27.8	0	3	0	0	0	0	0	0	0	0	0	0	0	1	0	0	0	2	0	0	0	0	0	0	0
llamas	20	.4727	2.1465	43.3	1	9	8	0	2	0	0	0	7	0	0	0	0	9	0	1	0	0	0	0	0	0	2	1	0
llamo	2	.0000	.0914	29.6	2	0	0	0	0	0	0	0	2	0	0	0	0	0	0	0	0	0	0	0	0	0	0	0	0
Llangollen	2	.0000	.0162	22.1	0	0	0	2	0	0	0	0	0	0	0	0	0	0	0	0	2	0	0	0	0	0	0	0	0
llanos	3	.2444	.1814	32.6	0	0	0	2	1	0	0	0	0	0	0	0	0	2	0	0	0	0	0	0	0	0	1	0	0
Llanos	2	.0000	.0389	25.9	0	0	0	0	0	0	2	0	0	0	0	0	0	2	0	0	0	0	0	0	0	0	0	0	0
Llaw	2	.0000	.0290	24.6	0	0	0	0	2	0	0	0	0	0	0	0	0	0	0	0	0	0	0	0	0	2	0	0	0
Llew	2	.0000	.0290	24.6	0	0	0	0	2	0	0	0	0	0	0	0	0	0	0	0	0	0	0	0	0	2	0	0	0
Llewelyn	2	.1814	.1187	30.7	0	0	0	1	1	0	0	0	1	0	0	0	0	0	0	0	0	0	0	0	0	0	0	1	0

7A lit'l
7H Litchfield
8F litchi
8F litchis
5A Litefoot
XR litera-graphic
8A lites
5A lithographs
9M lithoink
9F Lithuanians
9B litigant
5J Lititz
8R Litman
8G littera
6G litterbug
7B litterbugs
3A LITTLE
7F LittleRock
7F little-developed
7N little-girlish
7Q little-seen
9B little-used
7R Littlefield
3A littler
5A Littles
5A Littleton
7G liturgies
7G liturgy
8F Liu
7P livable
7F live-and-let-live
7Q live-born
7H live-virus
8D live'd
XR liveable
7D livelihoods
7N liveried
9Q Livermore
7N livers
7N livery-man
7N livery-stable-man
6A lives'
3P liveth
3H LIVING
8L living-dining
7J living's
9D livings
XR Liz
6A Liza's
6A Lizabeth
6N lizard's
6P Lizza
8E LK
7B lkd
5G lks
6A lllama

Word Type	F	D	U	SFI	3 Gr 3	4 Gr 4	5 Gr 5	6 Gr 6	7 Gr 7	8 Gr 8	9 Gr 9	X UnGr	A Read	B Eng & Gr	C Comp	D Lit	E Math	F Soc Stud	G Spell	H Sci	J Music	K Art	L Home Ec	M Shop	N Lib F	P Lib NF	Q Lib Ref	R Mag	S Rel
Lloyd	8	.3558	.7066	38.5	0	0	1	0	0	5	2	0	4	0	0	0	0	0	0	1	0	1	0	0	0	0	0	2	0
Lloyd's	2	.0000	.0209	23.2	0	2	0	0	0	0	0	0	0	0	0	0	0	0	0	0	0	0	0	0	0	0	2	0	0
LM	11	.2712	.6951	38.4	1	0	1	2	6	1	0	0	0	0	0	0	3	1	0	0	0	0	0	0	0	0	0	7	0
LNG	2	.0000	.0243	23.9	0	0	0	0	2	0	0	0	0	0	0	0	0	0	0	0	0	0	0	0	0	0	0	2	0
lo	17	.5512	1.9998	43.0	3	1	3	4	4	1	1	0	5	0	0	4	0	0	1	0	4	0	0	0	0	2	0	1	0
Lo	19	.2438	1.1216	40.5	19	0	0	0	0	0	0	0	0	0	0	0	9	0	0	0	0	0	0	0	0	10	0	0	0
Lo's	3	.2228	.1655	32.2	3	0	0	0	0	0	0	0	0	0	0	0	1	0	0	0	0	0	0	0	0	2	0	0	0
Loa	8	.2160	.5447	37.4	0	6	2	0	0	0	0	0	4	0	0	0	0	0	0	4	0	0	0	0	0	0	0	0	0
load	214	.8558	36.646	55.6	23	51	25	46	26	20	22	1	43	4	1	7	5	24	1	58	4	1	0	8	16	17	11	14	0
loaded	170	.8301	28.499	54.5	39	37	26	26	21	9	7	5	67	4	1	9	1	32	1	2	2	0	0	4	10	19	6	12	0
loaders	3	.2411	.1667	32.2	0	0	0	0	3	0	0	0	0	0	0	0	0	0	0	0	1	0	0	0	0	0	0	2	0
loading	40	.7156	5.8744	47.7	4	5	4	6	14	0	6	1	11	0	0	1	1	6	0	1	2	0	0	3	2	5	2	6	0
loads	80	.6506	10.852	50.4	21	18	5	14	11	2	8	1	21	0	0	3	0	14	0	7	2	0	0	7	1	17	2	6	0
loadstone	3	.0000	.1370	31.4	0	0	0	3	0	0	0	0	3	0	0	0	0	0	0	0	0	0	0	0	0	0	0	0	0
loaf	68	.6980	9.6798	49.9	9	18	4	7	14	4	9	3	9	3	0	7	19	3	4	3	1	0	6	0	1	12	0	0	0
Loaf	2	.1733	.1149	30.6	0	0	0	1	0	1	0	0	1	1	0	0	0	0	0	0	0	0	0	0	0	0	0	0	0
loafers	6	.2443	.3659	35.6	0	0	0	1	4	0	1	0	1	0	0	0	0	0	0	0	0	0	0	0	4	0	1	0	0
loafing	4	.4494	.4016	36.0	0	0	0	0	1	2	1	0	1	1	0	0	0	1	0	0	0	0	0	0	1	0	0	0	0
loam	9	.3683	.8454	39.3	0	0	1	2	5	0	0	1	6	0	0	0	0	0	0	0	0	0	0	0	0	0	2	1	0
loan	32	.6505	4.2607	46.3	0	0	1	6	12	2	10	1	3	2	0	3	7	1	5	0	0	0	0	0	1	0	1	9	0
loaned	22	.5885	2.7342	44.4	3	3	1	4	5	2	3	1	4	0	0	0	1	8	0	0	0	0	0	0	1	1	2	5	0
loans	26	.4120	2.3067	43.6	2	0	5	1	6	2	10	0	0	0	0	0	2	5	0	0	0	0	0	0	0	0	9	10	0
loanwords	5	.0000	.0547	27.4	0	0	0	0	5	0	0	0	0	5	0	0	0	0	0	0	0	0	0	0	0	0	0	0	0
loath	5	.2042	.2444	33.9	0	0	0	2	1	1	1	0	0	0	0	0	0	0	1	0	0	0	0	0	4	0	0	0	0
loathe	5	.4749	.4969	37.0	0	0	1	0	1	2	1	0	0	1	0	1	0	0	0	0	0	0	0	0	1	0	0	2	0
loaves	31	.6565	4.1919	46.2	9	4	3	6	3	0	4	2	5	0	0	4	8	1	1	0	0	1	0	0	7	4	0	0	0
lob	4	.3192	.3100	34.9	1	0	0	0	2	1	0	0	1	0	0	0	0	0	0	0	0	0	0	0	0	2	0	1	0
Lobachevsky	2	.0000	.0299	24.8	0	0	0	0	2	0	0	0	0	0	0	0	2	0	0	0	0	0	0	0	0	0	0	0	0
lobby	13	.5848	1.6251	42.1	2	3	1	2	1	0	3	1	5	2	0	1	1	0	0	0	0	0	1	0	0	0	0	3	0
lobbyists	2	.0000	.0389	25.9	0	0	0	0	0	1	1	0	0	0	0	0	0	2	0	0	0	0	0	0	0	0	0	0	0
lobe	2	.2278	.1128	30.5	0	0	0	0	0	0	2	0	0	0	0	0	0	0	0	1	0	0	0	0	0	0	1	0	0
lobed	3	.2383	.1815	32.6	1	0	0	0	0	0	0	2	0	0	0	0	0	0	0	2	0	0	0	0	0	1	0	0	0
lobes	2	.1814	.1187	30.7	0	0	0	0	2	0	0	0	1	0	0	0	0	0	0	0	0	0	0	0	0	0	0	1	0
Loble	2	.0000	.0243	23.9	0	0	0	2	0	0	0	0	0	0	0	0	0	0	0	0	0	0	0	0	0	0	0	2	0
lobo	2	.0000	.0914	29.6	2	0	0	0	0	0	0	0	2	0	0	0	0	0	0	0	0	0	0	0	0	0	0	0	0
lobster	29	.6076	3.7389	45.7	5	5	2	9	8	0	0	0	7	0	1	1	0	7	0	11	1	0	0	0	0	0	1	0	0
Lobster	9	.2232	.6878	38.4	8	0	1	0	0	0	0	0	8	0	0	0	0	0	0	0	0	0	0	0	1	0	0	0	0
lobster's	3	.0000	.0591	27.7	0	0	0	0	3	0	0	0	0	0	0	0	0	0	0	3	0	0	0	0	0	0	0	0	0
lobsterman	2	.0000	.0914	29.6	0	0	0	0	2	0	0	0	2	0	0	0	0	0	0	0	0	0	0	0	0	0	0	0	0
lobstermen	3	.0000	.0583	27.7	0	3	0	0	0	0	0	0	0	0	0	0	0	3	0	0	0	0	0	0	0	0	0	0	0
lobsters	36	.5904	4.5546	46.6	5	13	5	4	8	1	0	0	10	1	1	0	0	14	1	8	0	0	0	0	0	1	0	0	0
loc	2	.0000	.0162	22.1	0	0	0	0	2	0	0	0	0	0	0	0	0	0	2	0	0	0	0	0	0	0	0	0	0
local	286	.7726	44.569	56.5	45	12	37	16	76	64	26	10	27	8	3	6	0	97	1	15	4	1	1	2	3	19	55	44	0
Local	4	.3739	.3373	35.3	1	1	0	0	2	0	0	0	0	0	0	0	0	1	0	2	0	0	0	0	0	0	1	0	0
localities	12	.4913	1.2489	41.0	0	1	2	0	2	1	2	4	0	0	0	0	0	1	0	5	0	0	1	0	0	1	4	0	0
locality	10	.4373	.9221	39.6	0	0	1	1	2	2	1	3	0	0	1	0	0	1	0	3	0	0	3	0	0	0	2	0	0
localized	2	.1717	.1142	30.6	0	0	0	0	1	0	1	0	1	0	0	1	0	0	0	0	0	0	0	0	0	0	0	0	0
locally	13	.3991	1.1083	40.4	1	0	2	3	3	2	2	0	0	1	0	0	0	3	0	1	0	0	4	0	0	1	3	0	0
locals	4	.3733	.3369	35.3	0	0	0	0	1	3	0	0	0	0	0	1	0	2	0	1	0	0	0	0	0	0	0	0	0
locate	188	.8082	30.490	54.8	7	16	35	25	38	28	34	5	19	6	1	2	45	40	8	27	9	1	3	13	2	3	3	6	0
located	350	.7827	55.325	57.4	25	41	75	64	64	31	41	9	40	7	3	4	19	147	1	44	2	0	6	5	0	9	35	28	0
locates	12	.5081	1.3136	41.2	4	0	0	2	3	2	1	0	2	1	0	0	6	0	0	1	1	0	0	0	0	1	0	0	0
locating	27	.7283	3.9973	46.0	2	0	3	3	8	4	6	1	3	4	0	0	5	5	0	3	0	0	0	1	0	2	1	3	0
location	175	.7062	25.104	54.0	11	11	27	32	30	18	40	6	10	8	1	1	17	55	1	24	2	0	6	19	2	2	21	6	0
locations	44	.6860	6.1918	47.9	2	1	5	7	7	7	9	6	4	1	0	0	4	11	0	15	0	0	2	2	0	0	4	1	0
Loch	5	.2365	.3671	35.6	0	0	0	0	5	0	0	0	3	0	0	0	0	0	0	2	0	0	0	0	0	0	0	0	0
loci	3	.2019	.1477	31.7	0	0	0	0	0	0	1	2	0	0	0	0	1	0	0	0	0	0	0	0	0	0	2	0	0
lock	123	.7904	19.751	53.0	16	28	23	15	19	11	7	4	48	7	0	11	0	12	4	4	4	0	1	8	11	5	3	5	0
Lock	3	.0000	.0365	25.6	0	0	0	1	0	0	0	2	0	0	0	0	0	0	0	0	0	0	0	0	0	0	0	3	0
Locke	29	.3658	2.6789	44.3	0	0	0	18	0	9	2	0	18	0	0	0	0	0	0	0	1	0	0	0	0	0	9	1	0
Locke's	5	.1677	.2094	33.2	0	0	0	0	0	2	3	0	0	0	0	0	0	0	0	0	0	0	0	0	1	0	4	0	0
locked	116	.7415	17.684	52.5	35	19	9	9	16	12	15	1	47	9	1	7	0	5	1	7	1	0	1	2	7	15	3	9	1
locker	18	.5564	2.1476	43.3	1	0	2	2	5	6	1	1	6	3	1	1	0	0	0	0	0	0	0	0	1	0	0	6	0
lockers	4	.1349	.2265	33.6	0	0	0	2	1	1	0	0	3	0	1	0	0	0	0	0	0	0	0	0	0	0	0	0	0
locket	2	.1733	.1149	30.6	1	0	0	0	1	0	0	0	1	1	0	0	0	0	0	0	0	0	0	0	0	0	0	0	0
locking	8	.3542	.6370	38.0	0	1	0	1	3	1	2	0	2	1	1	0	0	0	0	0	0	0	0	3	0	0	0	1	0
lockings	2	.0000	.0243	23.9	0	0	0	2	0	0	0	0	0	0	0	0	0	0	0	0	0	0	0	0	0	0	0	2	0
locks	37	.8166	6.0974	47.9	6	2	7	5	4	7	4	2	12	1	0	6	0	6	0	1	1	0	1	1	2	2	2	2	0
locksmith	2	.0000	.0914	29.6	0	0	2	0	0	0	0	0	2	0	0	0	0	0	0	0	0	0	0	0	0	0	0	0	0
loco	2	.2442	.1134	30.5	0	0	0	0	0	1	1	0	0	1	0	0	0	0	0	0	0	0	0	0	0	0	0	1	0
Locomobile	2	.0000	.0290	24.6	0	2	0	0	0	0	0	0	0	0	0	0	0	0	0	0	0	0	0	0	0	2	0	0	0
locomotion	14	.4646	1.3984	41.5	0	0	2	1	7	1	1	2	1	0	0	0	0	0	2	5	0	0	0	0	1	0	5	0	0
locomotive	55	.7466	8.3712	49.2	17	8	22	1	6	1	0	0	12	3	1	0	1	1	1	15	3	0	0	0	0	13	3	2	0
Locomotive	8	.1757	.3532	35.5	2	0	0	0	6	0	0	0	0	0	0	6	0	0	0	0	0	0	0	0	0	2	0	0	0
locomotives	21	.6898	2.9673	44.7	1	2	6	4	4	0	3	1	2	1	1	0	0	7	0	5	0	0	0	1	0	1	2	1	0
locos	2	.0000	.0243	23.9	0	0	0	2	0	0	0	0	0	0	0	0	0	0	0	0	0	0	0	0	0	0	0	2	0
locus	6	.2057	.3084	34.9	0	0	1	0	0	0	5	0	0	0	0	0	5	0	1	0	0	0	0	0	0	0	0	0	0
locust	19	.4787	1.9254	42.8	2	6	0	8	1	0	1	1	0	0	0	0	0	1	0	3	0	0	0	0	0	4	3	8	0
locusts	16	.5551	1.8882	42.8	1	6	1	4	3	0	0	1	2	0	0	0	0	0	1	8	0	0	0	0	0	2	1	2	0
lodestone	9	.3552	.7017	38.5	3	0	0	0	6	0	0	0	0	0	0	0	0	0	0	3	0	0	0	1	0	0	5	0	0
lodge	40	.6539	5.4391	47.4	6	4	2	5	12	0	9	2	11	2	0	12	0	0	1	4	0	0	0	0	3	2	1	4	0
Lodge	13	.5022	1.3784	41.4	6	0	0	0	3	2	2	0	0	0	0	1	0	3	0	0	0	0	0	0	1	6	0	2	0
Lodge's	2	.0000	.0389	25.9	0	0	0	0	0	2	0	0	0	0	0	0	0	2	0	0	0	0	0	0	0	0	0	0	0
lodged	13	.5054	1.4262	41.5	0	0	1	3	5	1	3	0	3	0	0	4	0	0	0	3	0	0	0	0	2	0	1	0	0
lodger	2	.2443	.1130	30.5	0	0	0	1	0	0	1	0	0	0	0	1	0	0	0	0	0	0	0	0	1	0	0	0	0
lodges	8	.4925	.8547	39.3	0	3	0	1	4	0	0	0	2	1	0	3	0	0	0	0	0	0	0	0	1	0	0	1	0
lodging	18	.5916	2.1934	43.4	2	4	1	1	1	2	7	0	1	1	0	7	0	1	0	0	2	0	0	0	2	3	0	1	0
lodgings	2	.1494	.1045	30.2	0	0	0	1	0	1	0	0	1	0	0	0	0	0	0	0	1	0	0	0	0	0	0	0	0
Lodi	2	.0000	.0209	23.2	0	0	0	0	0	2	0	0	0	0	0	0	0	0	0	0	0	0	0	0	0	0	2	0	0
Lodz	2	.0000	.0389	25.9	0	0	0	2	0	0	0	0	0	0	0	0	0	2	0	0	0	0	0	0	0	0	0	0	0
loess	8	.1340	.3470	35.4	0	0	0	1	0	0	7	0	0	0	0	0	0	1	0	7	0	0	0	0	0	0	0	0	0
Loesser	8	.0000	.0647	28.1	0	0	0	0	0	8	0	0	0	0	0	0	0	0	0	0	8	0	0	0	0	0	0	0	0
Loesser's	2	.0000	.0162	22.1	0	0	0	0	0	2	0	0	0	0	0	0	0	0	0	0	2	0	0	0	0	0	0	0	0
Loffler	2	.0000	.0394	26.0	0	0	2	0	0	0	0	0	0	0	0	0	0	0	0	2	0	0	0	0	0	0	0	0	0
Lofoten	2	.0000	.0389	25.9	0	2	0	0	0	0	0	0	0	0	0	0	0	2	0	0	0	0	0	0	0	0	0	0	0
loft	31	.6118	4.0339	46.1	0	9	3	6	1	5	4	3	12	1	0	0	0	4	0	0	0	0	0	2	4	2	0	6	0

7P Llyr
6R Llywelyn
5G lm
7R LM'S
8E LMN
5E LNO
7A loa
7R load-pulling
9D loafed
9D loafer
9B loamy
9R loanable
7B loanword
9D loathed
7D loathing
9D loathsome
7A lobbing
7R lobsterback
XR locale
4G Locality
9Q Lockean
6N Lockhart
7R Lockheed
7R Lockheed-Georgia
7R Lockheed-Georgia's
7R lockjaw
3B Locklin
8N lockouts
4R Lockridge
9M lockup
7R Lockwood
6R Loco
7Q locomotive's
5P Locust
8A Lode
9Q lodes
7M lodestones
8D lodgefire
7R lodgepole
8J Loeffler
4F Loess
8Q Loew
8J Loewe
8R Lofchie

Word Type	F	D	U	SFI	3 Gr 3	4 Gr 4	5 Gr 5	6 Gr 6	7 Gr 7	8 Gr 8	9 Gr 9	X UnGr	A Read	B Eng & Gr	C Comp	D Lit	E Math	F Soc Stud	G Spell	H Sci	J Music	K Art	L Home Ec	M Shop	N Lib F	P Lib NF	Q Lib Ref	R Mag	S Rel
loftier	3	.3831	.2447	33.9	0	1	0	1	0	0	1	0	0	0	0	1	0	0	0	0	1	0	0	0	1	0	0	0	0
loftiest	3	.2043	.1486	31.7	1	1	1	0	0	0	0	0	0	0	0	0	0	0	0	0	0	0	0	0	0	1	2	0	0
lofting	3	.0000	.0076	18.8	0	0	0	0	0	0	3	0	0	0	0	0	0	0	0	0	0	0	0	3	0	0	0	0	0
Lofting	9	.0000	.4111	36.1	0	9	0	0	0	0	0	0	9	0	0	0	0	0	0	0	0	0	0	0	0	0	0	0	0
lofty	32	.7788	5.0485	47.0	0	1	3	5	10	5	7	1	9	0	1	5	0	4	0	0	2	1	0	0	2	2	3	3	0
log	243	.8795	42.701	56.3	56	40	35	35	41	22	13	1	81	6	6	13	9	32	3	13	5	3	0	9	27	24	5	7	0
Log	4	.1733	.2298	33.6	0	2	0	0	1	0	1	0	2	2	0	0	0	0	0	0	0	0	0	0	0	0	0	0	0
Logan	6	.2991	.4180	36.2	0	0	2	1	1	0	2	0	1	0	0	0	0	0	0	0	0	0	2	0	0	2	0	1	0
logarithm	5	.0000	.0748	28.7	0	0	0	0	0	5	0	0	0	0	0	0	5	0	0	0	0	0	0	0	0	0	0	0	0
logarithms	9	.0000	.1347	31.3	0	0	0	0	0	9	0	0	0	0	0	0	9	0	0	0	0	0	0	0	0	0	0	0	0
logbook	4	.1948	.2500	34.0	0	0	0	3	0	1	0	0	2	0	0	0	0	0	0	0	0	0	0	0	0	2	0	0	0
logged	8	.4039	.7537	38.8	0	0	2	0	4	0	2	0	3	0	0	3	0	1	0	0	0	0	0	0	0	0	1	0	0
logger	4	.3677	.3659	35.6	0	1	2	0	1	0	0	0	2	0	0	1	0	1	0	0	0	0	0	0	0	0	0	0	0
loggerhead	3	.0000	.0314	25.0	0	0	0	0	3	0	0	0	0	0	0	0	0	0	0	0	0	0	0	0	0	0	3	0	0
loggers	15	.5252	1.7545	42.4	1	5	5	1	2	1	0	0	7	0	0	1	0	3	0	0	0	0	0	1	0	3	0	0	0
logging	32	.6158	4.1440	46.2	3	4	8	5	7	1	1	3	9	0	0	4	0	8	0	0	2	0	0	3	0	1	1	4	0
logic	21	.5760	2.5091	44.0	0	0	1	1	8	4	6	1	1	1	0	0	4	1	0	2	0	0	0	0	0	1	7	4	0
logical	58	.8120	9.4113	49.7	2	3	2	5	19	11	13	3	4	12	3	2	7	2	3	6	2	1	0	0	1	1	8	6	0
logically	5	.5554	.5729	37.6	0	0	0	1	2	1	1	0	0	1	0	0	0	1	0	0	1	0	0	0	0	0	1	1	0
logs	216	.7603	33.389	55.2	53	33	35	40	29	17	7	2	48	4	1	8	0	62	0	15	5	0	0	13	15	24	10	11	0
logy	2	.2405	.1205	30.8	0	0	0	1	0	0	0	1	0	0	0	0	0	0	0	1	0	0	0	0	0	1	0	0	0
loin	4	.1812	.1676	32.2	0	0	0	0	0	0	2	2	0	0	0	0	0	0	0	0	0	0	2	0	0	0	0	2	0
loincloths	2	.2433	.1158	30.6	0	0	1	0	0	0	0	1	0	0	0	0	0	0	0	0	0	0	0	0	0	1	0	1	0
loins	4	.3734	.3223	35.1	0	0	0	0	0	0	2	2	0	1	0	1	0	0	0	0	0	0	0	0	0	0	0	2	0
Loire	3	.1823	.1405	31.5	1	0	1	1	0	0	0	0	0	0	0	0	0	1	0	0	0	0	0	0	0	0	2	0	0
Lois	15	.3347	1.1093	40.5	2	8	3	1	0	1	0	0	0	9	0	0	4	0	0	0	0	0	0	0	1	1	0	0	0
Loisel	2	.0000	.0914	29.6	0	0	0	2	0	0	0	0	2	0	0	0	0	0	0	0	0	0	0	0	0	0	0	0	0
loiter	2	.0000	.0914	29.6	0	0	0	1	1	0	0	0	2	0	0	0	0	0	0	0	0	0	0	0	0	0	0	0	0
Lokanon	15	.0000	.2171	33.4	0	15	0	0	0	0	0	0	0	0	0	0	0	0	0	0	0	0	0	0	0	15	0	0	0
Loki	28	.3365	2.6053	44.2	10	7	11	0	0	0	0	0	24	0	0	0	0	0	1	0	0	0	0	0	0	0	3	0	0
Loki's	5	.0000	.2284	33.6	0	2	3	0	0	0	0	0	5	0	0	0	0	0	0	0	0	0	0	0	0	0	0	0	0
Lola	9	.3488	.6946	38.4	7	0	1	0	0	1	0	0	0	1	0	0	4	0	0	0	0	0	0	0	0	0	0	4	0
Lolita	5	.0000	.0586	27.7	5	0	0	0	0	0	0	0	0	0	0	0	0	0	0	0	0	0	0	0	5	0	0	0	0
lolling	5	.3855	.4777	36.8	2	0	1	0	2	0	0	0	3	0	0	0	0	0	0	0	0	0	0	0	1	0	0	1	0
lollipop	9	.4386	.9059	39.6	4	2	1	0	2	0	0	0	4	0	0	1	0	0	0	0	0	0	1	0	3	0	0	0	0
lollipops	2	.2417	.1211	30.8	2	0	0	0	0	0	0	0	0	0	0	0	1	1	0	0	0	0	0	0	0	0	0	0	0
Lollo	3	.0000	.0322	25.1	0	0	0	0	3	0	0	0	0	0	0	3	0	0	0	0	0	0	0	0	0	0	0	0	0
lolly	8	.0000	.0647	28.1	0	0	0	0	8	0	0	0	0	0	0	0	0	0	0	0	8	0	0	0	0	0	0	0	0
LOM	3	.0000	.0449	26.5	0	0	0	0	3	0	0	0	0	0	0	0	3	0	0	0	0	0	0	0	0	0	0	0	0
Lombard	3	.0000	.0314	25.0	0	0	2	0	0	1	0	0	0	0	0	0	0	0	0	0	0	0	0	0	0	0	3	0	0
Lombardi	2	.0000	.0243	23.9	0	0	0	0	0	2	0	0	0	0	0	0	0	0	0	0	0	0	0	0	0	0	0	2	0
Lombardy	4	.1737	.1745	32.4	0	0	3	0	1	0	0	0	0	0	0	0	0	0	0	0	0	0	0	0	0	1	3	0	0
Lon	9	.2430	.6880	38.4	7	0	0	0	0	0	2	0	7	0	0	2	0	0	0	0	0	0	0	0	0	0	0	0	0
London	254	.8348	42.497	56.3	16	47	32	56	39	34	25	5	50	5	1	14	8	36	4	10	16	0	0	0	16	30	34	30	0
London's	7	.4246	.6715	38.3	0	0	2	2	1	0	2	0	2	0	1	0	0	1	0	0	0	0	0	0	0	1	0	2	0
Londonderry	2	.2303	.1079	30.3	0	1	0	1	0	0	0	0	0	0	0	0	0	0	0	0	1	0	0	0	0	1	0	0	0
lone	47	.7641	7.2504	48.6	10	2	6	3	19	3	3	1	8	5	1	13	0	2	1	1	1	1	0	0	6	6	0	2	0
Lone	3	.3272	.2363	33.7	0	1	2	0	0	0	0	0	1	0	0	1	0	0	0	0	1	0	0	0	0	0	0	0	0
lonelier	4	.0996	.1523	31.8	0	0	0	0	3	1	0	0	1	0	0	0	0	0	0	0	0	0	0	0	0	0	0	3	0
loneliness	29	.7267	4.2741	46.3	0	2	6	6	8	5	2	0	4	3	0	4	0	4	0	0	3	1	0	0	6	2	0	2	0
lonely	207	.8099	33.971	55.3	38	37	24	34	31	22	17	4	88	13	8	21	0	11	1	1	6	2	0	0	21	14	8	13	0
loner	2	.1814	.1187	30.7	0	0	0	1	0	1	0	0	1	0	0	0	0	0	0	0	0	0	0	0	0	0	0	1	0
lonesome	49	.7051	7.1416	48.5	6	9	6	3	11	7	5	2	20	2	2	8	0	0	0	0	7	0	1	0	5	1	0	3	0
Lonesome	2	.1787	.1174	30.7	0	0	0	0	2	0	0	0	1	0	0	0	0	0	0	0	0	0	0	0	1	0	0	0	0
lonesome-looking	2	.0000	.0219	23.4	0	0	0	0	0	2	0	0	0	2	0	0	0	0	0	0	0	0	0	0	0	0	0	0	0
long	6220	.9570	1175.6	70.7	1400	1128	798	830	938	574	425	127	1654	161	68	336	414	649	514	555	193	40	58	50	424	543	257	304	0
Long	94	.7891	15.019	51.8	17	13	9	9	18	16	9	3	27	0	0	4	7	4	2	3	3	0	0	0	10	14	12	8	0
LongBeach	3	.1639	.1674	32.2	0	0	2	0	1	0	0	0	1	0	0	0	0	2	0	0	0	0	0	0	0	0	0	0	0
LongIsland	7	.4621	.6936	38.4	0	1	1	1	4	0	0	0	0	2	0	0	0	0	0	3	0	0	0	0	0	1	0	1	0
long-ago	4	.4556	.4079	36.1	1	1	0	1	0	1	0	0	1	0	0	0	0	1	0	0	0	0	0	0	1	1	0	0	0
long-day	5	.0000	.0986	29.9	0	0	0	0	5	0	0	0	0	0	0	0	0	0	0	5	0	0	0	0	0	0	0	0	0
long-dead	3	.2325	.1651	32.2	0	0	1	0	0	0	1	1	0	0	1	0	0	0	0	1	0	0	0	0	0	1	0	0	0
long-distance	14	.5679	1.6627	42.2	2	3	1	3	2	1	2	0	2	1	0	0	0	0	0	0	0	0	0	1	0	4	2	4	0
long-drawn	3	.3465	.2515	34.0	0	0	0	1	2	0	0	0	1	0	0	0	0	0	0	0	0	0	0	0	0	1	0	1	0
long-eared	4	.3215	.3104	34.9	1	0	1	1	1	0	0	0	1	0	0	0	0	0	0	0	0	0	0	0	0	2	1	0	0
long-established	2	.2351	.1166	30.7	0	0	0	0	0	2	0	0	0	0	0	0	0	1	0	0	0	0	0	0	0	0	0	1	0
long-existing	2	.2137	.1056	30.2	0	0	0	0	0	2	0	0	0	0	0	0	0	1	0	0	1	0	0	0	0	0	0	0	0
long-forgotten	2	.2407	.1138	30.6	0	1	0	0	1	0	0	0	0	0	0	1	0	0	0	0	0	0	0	0	0	1	0	0	0
long-haired	3	.0000	.0365	25.6	0	0	1	1	0	1	0	0	0	0	0	0	0	0	0	0	0	0	0	0	0	0	0	3	0
long-handled	3	.3395	.2468	33.9	1	1	1	0	0	0	0	0	1	0	0	0	0	0	0	0	0	0	0	0	0	1	1	0	0
long-horned	3	.3553	.2609	34.2	1	2	0	0	0	0	0	0	1	0	0	0	0	0	0	1	0	0	0	0	0	1	0	0	0
long-lasting	6	.4826	.6161	37.9	1	2	1	1	1	0	0	0	0	0	0	0	0	0	0	2	0	0	0	0	0	2	1	1	0
long-legged	10	.4642	1.0869	40.4	3	2	1	3	1	0	0	0	6	0	0	0	0	0	0	1	1	0	0	0	0	0	0	2	0
long-lived	3	.1169	.1277	31.1	0	0	0	0	2	0	1	0	1	0	0	0	0	0	0	0	0	0	0	0	0	0	2	0	0
long-lost	3	.2435	.2274	33.6	0	0	0	1	2	0	0	0	2	0	0	0	0	1	0	0	0	0	0	0	0	1	3	0	0
long-necked	4	.1737	.1745	32.4	1	0	0	0	3	0	0	0	0	0	0	0	0	0	0	0	0	0	0	0	0	0	0	0	0
long-nosed	4	.0000	.1827	32.6	3	0	0	0	1	0	0	0	4	0	0	0	0	0	0	0	0	0	0	0	0	0	0	0	0
long-playing	2	.2404	.1142	30.6	0	0	0	0	0	2	0	0	0	1	0	0	1	0	0	0	0	0	0	0	0	0	0	0	0
long-range	13	.5219	1.4133	41.5	0	1	3	0	5	2	1	1	0	0	0	0	0	0	0	3	0	0	1	0	0	1	4	4	0
long-reach	2	.0000	.0243	23.9	0	0	0	0	2	0	0	0	0	0	0	0	0	0	0	0	0	0	0	0	0	0	0	2	0
long-standing	5	.5414	.5831	37.7	1	0	1	1	0	0	1	1	1	0	0	0	0	1	0	1	0	0	0	0	0	1	0	1	0
long-staple	2	.0000	.0064	18.1	0	0	0	0	0	2	0	0	0	0	0	0	0	0	0	0	0	0	2	0	0	0	0	0	0
long-suffering	5	.4113	.4594	36.6	0	0	0	0	3	0	1	1	1	0	0	2	0	0	0	0	0	0	0	0	0	1	0	1	0
long-term	9	.5321	1.0083	40.0	0	0	0	0	1	0	5	3	0	0	0	1	0	1	0	4	0	0	0	0	0	0	1	2	0
long-time	8	.4660	.7932	39.0	0	0	1	2	2	1	2	0	0	0	0	1	0	3	0	0	1	0	0	0	0	0	0	3	0
long-vowel	7	.0000	.0568	27.5	0	2	0	5	0	0	0	0	0	0	0	0	0	0	7	0	0	0	0	0	0	0	0	0	0
long-wave	9	.0000	.1774	32.5	0	0	0	0	1	0	2	6	0	0	0	0	0	0	0	9	0	0	0	0	0	0	0	0	0
long-winded	2	.2442	.1134	30.5	0	0	0	0	2	0	0	0	0	1	0	0	0	0	0	0	0	0	0	0	0	0	0	1	0
longed	45	.6754	6.3522	48.0	6	6	7	6	9	6	4	1	19	3	0	10	0	2	0	0	1	0	1	0	6	2	0	1	0
longed-for	2	.2444	.1132	30.5	0	0	1	0	1	0	0	0	0	1	0	0	0	0	0	0	0	0	0	0	1	0	0	0	0

8D loftily
6J loftiness
7N log-books
5A log-cabin
6G log-roller
6D log-rolling
7A log's
9L Logan's
9L Logans
8E logarithmic
7P logbooks
8D logged-out
4A logger's
XR Logging
5Q Logic
9Q Logick
7Q logistics
7B logographs
9H logos
7R logotype
7A logrolling
8J Lohengrin
8A loike
XR Loin
7F loincloth
4B Lois's
3N Lolita's
8D loll
3Q Lolland
7A lollapaloozing
6A lolled
7D lollipop-hard
7A Loma
8F lombard
5F lomilomi
8R Lompoc
5G lon
7N Londoner
4D loneliest
XR Loneliness
7P lonelinesses
8R Lonely
9Q loners
7A lonesome-born
5N lonesome-like
7N lonesomest
7F LongBeach's
5R LongBranch
XH long-
8J Long-Playing
8C long-anticipated
3P long-awaited
6A long-boats
7A long-cherished
7A long-continued
7A long-controlled
4N long-departed
6A long-drawn-out
3A long-expected
9D long-experienced
7H long-exposure
4A long-faced
4D long-forgotton
8A long-gone
9Q long-haul
8L long-leg
7D long-leggedness
3D long-neck
9C long-projected
9L long-pronged
7Q long-run
5Q long-running
XH long-shafted
7R long-shot
9R long-simmering
4P long-skirted
XR long-sought-after
XH long-spurred
9B long-stemmed
9F long-suspected
4R long-tailed
9R long-unchallenged
8A long-unused
4P Long's
6N longbladed
6N longbows
5P longdead
3A longdistance
7A longdraft
8A longdrawn

Word Type	F	D	U	SFI	3 Gr 3	4 Gr 4	5 Gr 5	6 Gr 6	7 Gr 7	8 Gr 8	9 Gr 9	X UnGr	A Read	B Eng & Gr	C Comp	D Lit	E Math	F Soc Stud	G Spell	H Sci	J Music	K Art	L Home Ec	M Shop	N Lib F	P Lib NF	Q Lib Ref	R Mag	S Rel
longer	955	.9721	183.00	62.6	163	138	133	122	168	107	100	24	242	42	10	64	59	93	26	113	34	6	13	8	56	78	54	57	0
longest	111	.7991	17.864	52.5	11	18	16	21	24	10	11	0	16	9	1	4	30	20	0	11	4	0	0	0	4	4	5	3	0
Longest	2	.2433	.1158	30.6	1	0	0	0	0	0	1	0	0	0	0	0	0	0	0	0	0	0	0	0	0	1	0	1	0
Longfellow	7	.5103	.7649	38.8	0	1	1	1	3	1	0	0	1	0	0	2	0	2	0	0	1	0	0	0	0	1	0	0	0
Longfellow's	2	.2440	.1132	30.5	0	0	0	1	1	0	0	0	0	0	0	1	0	0	0	0	0	0	0	0	0	0	0	1	0
longhorn	2	.1042	.0600	27.8	0	0	0	2	0	0	0	0	0	0	0	0	0	1	0	0	0	1	0	0	0	0	0	0	0
longhorns	6	.3718	.5494	37.4	2	0	1	0	3	0	0	0	3	0	0	1	0	0	0	0	0	0	0	0	0	2	0	0	0
longhouses	2	.0000	.0914	29.6	0	1	0	0	1	0	0	0	2	0	0	0	0	0	0	0	0	0	0	0	0	0	0	0	0
longing	26	.6771	3.6169	45.6	3	2	5	5	7	1	2	1	5	1	0	4	0	2	0	0	2	0	0	0	6	3	0	3	0
longingly	5	.4698	.4988	37.0	0	3	0	0	1	1	0	0	0	1	0	1	0	1	0	0	0	0	0	0	0	2	0	0	0
longings	6	.4039	.5374	37.3	0	1	1	2	1	1	0	0	1	0	0	0	0	0	0	0	2	0	0	0	1	2	0	0	0
longish	2	.2446	.1123	30.5	0	0	0	0	1	0	0	1	0	1	0	0	0	0	0	0	0	0	0	0	0	0	1	0	0
longitude	52	.5701	6.2089	47.9	2	15	8	5	3	15	4	0	0	0	0	0	13	18	2	14	0	0	0	0	2	0	3	0	0
Longitude	6	.0000	.1167	30.7	0	0	0	0	6	0	0	0	0	0	0	0	0	6	0	0	0	0	0	0	0	0	0	0	0
longitudinal	11	.2302	.6052	37.8	0	0	0	0	2	2	6	1	1	0	0	0	0	1	0	2	0	0	0	5	0	0	1	1	0
longitudinally	3	.3764	.2483	33.9	0	0	0	0	2	0	1	0	0	0	0	0	0	0	0	1	0	0	0	0	0	0	1	1	0
longleaf	2	.2441	.1127	30.5	0	0	2	0	0	0	0	0	0	0	0	0	0	0	0	0	0	0	0	0	1	0	1	0	0
Longridge	5	.0000	.0586	27.7	0	0	0	0	5	0	0	0	0	0	0	0	0	0	0	0	0	0	0	0	5	0	0	0	0
Longstocking	5	.0804	.1641	32.2	5	0	0	0	0	0	0	0	1	0	0	0	0	0	0	0	0	0	0	0	4	0	0	0	0
Longstreet	3	.3766	.2480	33.9	0	0	0	0	1	2	0	0	0	0	0	0	0	1	0	0	0	0	0	0	1	0	1	0	0
longtime	3	.3454	.2542	34.1	0	1	0	0	0	2	0	0	1	0	0	0	0	1	0	0	0	0	0	0	0	0	0	1	0
Longview	4	.0000	.0486	26.9	0	0	0	0	4	0	0	0	0	0	0	0	0	0	0	0	0	0	0	0	0	0	0	4	0
longways	2	.0000	.0162	22.1	0	0	2	0	0	0	0	0	0	0	0	0	0	0	0	0	2	0	0	0	0	0	0	0	0
Lonnie	13	.1776	.5705	37.6	1	0	0	1	6	0	5	0	0	0	0	11	0	0	0	0	0	0	0	0	1	0	0	1	0
Lonnie's	4	.0000	.0429	26.3	0	0	0	0	3	0	1	0	0	0	0	4	0	0	0	0	0	0	0	0	0	0	0	0	0
Lono	2	.0000	.0389	25.9	0	0	2	0	0	0	0	0	0	0	0	0	0	2	0	0	0	0	0	0	0	0	0	0	0
Lonz	3	.0000	.1370	31.4	3	0	0	0	0	0	0	0	3	0	0	0	0	0	0	0	0	0	0	0	0	0	0	0	0
loo	11	.0000	.0889	29.5	1	2	4	2	2	0	0	0	0	0	0	0	0	0	0	0	11	0	0	0	0	0	0	0	0
look	4933	.9124	894.00	69.5	1334	1016	553	549	784	367	254	76	1384	358	32	295	229	368	309	638	168	183	55	26	365	290	51	181	1
Look	15	.5397	1.6868	42.3	1	1	0	0	4	0	9	0	1	3	0	1	0	0	0	0	1	0	0	0	1	1	0	7	0
LOOK	2	.1497	.1046	30.2	1	0	0	0	0	1	0	0	1	0	0	0	0	0	1	0	0	0	0	0	0	0	0	0	0
looked	3197	.7725	506.25	67.0	858	730	324	367	498	237	158	25	1558	91	17	299	26	139	16	57	27	16	0	1	508	324	15	103	0
lookin'	5	.4687	.5254	37.2	0	0	1	2	0	2	0	0	2	1	0	0	0	0	0	0	1	0	0	0	1	0	0	0	0
looking	1331	.9302	245.72	63.9	270	275	149	145	273	118	75	26	539	47	8	129	48	72	33	69	24	14	10	3	142	90	13	88	2
Looking	5	.4762	.5335	37.3	0	1	1	1	2	0	0	0	2	1	0	1	0	0	0	0	0	0	0	0	0	0	0	1	0
lookout	45	.7282	6.7860	48.3	9	6	6	10	4	6	4	0	22	2	0	2	1	1	0	0	0	0	0	2	5	4	2	4	0
Lookout	6	.4596	.5865	37.7	0	0	1	0	3	0	2	0	0	0	0	0	0	0	0	1	0	0	0	0	2	2	1	0	0
lookout's	2	.2412	.1141	30.6	0	0	0	2	0	0	0	0	0	1	0	0	0	0	0	0	0	0	0	0	0	1	0	0	0
lookouts	6	.1948	.3750	35.7	2	0	0	2	0	0	2	0	3	0	0	0	0	0	0	0	0	0	0	0	0	3	0	0	0
looks	756	.9073	136.38	61.3	201	138	100	87	113	65	43	9	220	54	8	46	11	55	8	111	8	24	10	8	49	72	29	43	0
lookyhere	2	.0000	.0914	29.6	0	0	0	0	2	0	0	0	2	0	0	0	0	0	0	0	0	0	0	0	0	0	0	0	0
loom	41	.6506	5.5663	47.5	9	4	4	8	8	4	4	0	12	0	0	3	0	2	0	8	0	3	1	0	7	2	3	0	0
loomed	12	.5345	1.4390	41.6	2	1	1	5	2	0	0	1	7	0	0	2	0	0	0	1	0	0	0	0	0	0	1	1	0
looming	12	.4297	1.1973	40.8	2	0	1	3	2	0	3	1	6	1	2	1	0	0	0	0	0	0	0	0	0	0	1	1	0
looms	17	.6899	2.4098	43.8	6	0	0	2	3	3	2	1	2	0	0	0	0	5	0	4	1	0	0	0	1	2	1	1	0
loon	7	.3854	.6844	38.4	0	0	0	0	6	0	1	0	5	0	0	0	0	0	0	0	0	0	0	0	0	0	1	1	0
loons	2	.2331	.1157	30.6	0	0	0	2	0	0	0	0	0	0	0	0	0	0	0	1	0	0	0	0	1	0	0	0	0
loop	138	.5673	16.402	52.1	22	47	14	15	18	13	8	1	32	9	29	3	11	0	18	9	0	0	11	3	0	4	1	8	0
looped	10	.5145	1.1006	40.4	2	1	1	3	0	2	1	0	3	0	0	1	0	0	2	0	0	1	2	0	0	0	0	1	0
loopholes	4	.2073	.2003	33.0	0	0	0	0	1	0	3	0	0	0	0	1	0	0	0	0	0	0	0	0	0	0	0	3	0
looping	2	.0000	.0215	23.3	0	0	0	0	1	0	1	0	0	0	0	2	0	0	0	0	0	0	0	0	0	0	0	0	0
loops	37	.6708	5.0610	47.0	0	9	3	6	8	3	6	2	6	6	2	3	3	0	7	1	0	0	5	0	0	0	3	1	0
loose	227	.8844	40.059	56.0	28	44	34	17	49	23	28	4	75	9	4	17	0	8	3	24	3	1	9	8	29	17	8	12	0
loose-fitting	4	.3743	.3712	35.7	2	1	0	1	0	0	0	0	2	0	0	0	0	1	0	0	0	0	0	0	0	0	0	1	0
loosed	8	.5326	.9140	39.6	2	0	0	0	4	1	1	0	2	0	0	2	0	0	0	0	0	0	0	0	1	2	1	0	0
loosely	39	.6262	5.0340	47.0	2	7	2	2	8	14	3	1	5	0	0	1	1	2	1	7	0	0	8	1	4	4	3	2	0
loosen	31	.5838	3.8076	45.8	3	4	4	5	8	2	5	0	7	0	0	1	0	2	0	7	1	0	2	5	4	0	1	1	0
loosened	26	.7555	4.0207	46.0	2	4	1	4	8	2	5	0	10	1	0	3	0	1	0	2	0	0	0	1	3	1	2	2	0
loosening	4	.1937	.1693	32.3	0	1	0	0	3	0	0	0	0	0	0	0	0	0	0	0	2	0	0	2	0	0	0	0	0
loosens	5	.2926	.3754	35.7	0	0	1	1	0	2	1	0	1	0	0	0	0	1	0	3	0	0	0	0	0	0	0	0	0
loot	7	.5328	.8000	39.0	0	1	2	0	2	1	1	0	2	0	0	2	0	0	1	0	0	0	0	0	0	0	1	1	0
looted	4	.4820	.4016	36.0	1	0	0	0	3	0	0	0	0	0	0	1	0	0	0	0	1	0	0	0	0	1	1	0	0
lop-eared	7	.0000	.3198	35.0	5	0	0	0	2	0	0	0	7	0	0	0	0	0	0	0	0	0	0	0	0	0	0	0	0
lope	3	.3267	.2367	33.7	0	2	1	0	0	0	0	0	1	0	0	0	0	0	0	0	1	0	0	0	1	0	0	0	0
Lope	2	.0000	.0209	23.2	0	2	0	0	0	0	0	0	0	0	0	0	0	0	0	0	0	0	0	0	0	0	2	0	0
loped	4	.2393	.3005	34.8	2	1	0	0	0	0	1	0	3	0	0	1	0	0	0	0	0	0	0	0	0	0	0	0	0
Lopez	4	.0996	.1523	31.8	0	0	1	2	1	0	0	0	1	0	0	0	0	0	0	0	0	0	0	0	0	0	0	3	0
loping	3	.3267	.2367	33.7	0	0	1	0	2	0	0	0	1	0	0	0	0	0	0	0	1	0	0	0	1	0	0	0	0
lopsided	4	.3030	.2949	34.7	2	0	1	0	0	1	0	0	1	0	0	0	0	0	0	0	0	0	0	0	2	0	0	1	0
loqu	2	.0000	.0162	22.1	0	0	0	0	2	0	0	0	0	0	0	0	0	0	2	0	0	0	0	0	0	0	0	0	0
loquacious	2	.1605	.0742	28.7	0	0	1	1	0	0	0	0	0	1	1	0	0	0	0	0	0	0	0	0	0	0	0	0	0
lord	78	.5372	8.8219	49.5	2	7	3	17	10	10	28	1	7	4	0	34	0	20	0	0	1	0	0	0	3	3	4	2	0
Lord	296	.1523	13.200	51.2	72	33	33	27	72	30	25	4	61	5	0	40	1	8	0	3	36	0	0	0	33	47	15	8	39
LORD	2	.0000	.0004	5.5	2	0	0	0	0	0	0	0	0	0	0	0	0	0	0	0	0	0	0	0	0	0	0	0	2
lord's	9	.4459	.8695	39.4	0	0	1	6	0	1	1	0	0	0	0	1	0	5	0	0	0	0	0	0	2	1	0	0	0
Lord's	7	.5376	.7711	38.9	0	1	0	1	3	2	0	0	0	0	1	1	0	1	2	0	1	0	0	0	1	0	0	0	0
lordly	3	.3394	.2451	33.9	0	0	1	1	0	0	1	0	1	0	0	1	0	0	0	0	0	0	0	0	1	0	0	0	0
lords	44	.7126	6.4356	48.1	3	0	3	16	10	7	4	1	10	4	0	4	0	13	0	1	3	0	0	0	5	3	1	0	0
Lords	3	.1250	.1342	31.3	2	0	1	0	0	0	0	0	1	0	0	0	0	0	0	0	0	0	0	0	2	0	0	0	0
lordship	3	.2292	.1615	32.1	0	0	0	1	1	0	1	0	0	0	0	1	0	0	0	0	0	0	0	0	2	0	0	0	0
lore	8	.2277	.4276	36.3	0	1	0	0	1	0	4	2	0	0	0	5	0	0	0	0	0	0	0	0	0	0	0	3	0
Lorenz	5	.1769	.1946	32.9	0	0	0	0	1	4	0	0	0	0	3	0	0	0	0	0	1	0	0	0	0	0	1	0	0
Lorenzo	22	.4108	1.9327	42.9	0	0	0	2	3	0	17	0	1	0	0	14	0	1	0	0	0	2	0	0	0	0	1	3	0
Loreto	2	.2297	.1135	30.6	0	0	1	0	1	0	0	0	0	0	0	1	0	1	0	0	0	0	0	0	0	0	0	0	0
Loretta	5	.2442	.3018	34.8	2	0	0	0	0	0	3	0	0	0	0	0	0	3	0	0	0	0	0	0	2	0	0	0	0
lorikeet	3	.0000	.1370	31.4	0	0	0	3	0	0	0	0	3	0	0	0	0	0	0	0	0	0	0	0	0	0	0	0	0
Lorne	13	.2948	.9304	39.7	0	0	0	0	0	13	0	0	3	0	0	3	0	0	0	0	0	0	0	0	7	0	0	0	0
Lorraine	6	.1822	.3062	34.9	0	0	0	4	0	0	2	0	0	0	0	0	0	5	0	0	0	0	0	0	0	1	0	0	0
Lorry	17	.0000	.1824	32.6	0	0	0	0	0	0	17	0	0	0	0	17	0	0	0	0	0	0	0	0	0	0	0	0	0
los	3	.2425	.1816	32.6	0	0	0	0	3	0	0	0	0	0	0	0	0	2	0	0	0	0	0	0	0	0	0	1	0
Los	3	.2425	.1816	32.6	0	1	0	1	1	0	0	0	0	0	0	0	0	2	0	0	0	0	0	0	0	0	0	1	0
LosAlamos	4	.3513	.3115	34.9	0	0	1	0	0	3	0	0	0	0	0	1	0	1	0	0	0	0	0	0	0	0	0	2	0
LosAngeles	112	.5188	12.323	50.9	12	17	17	8	15	31	11	1	2	1	0	1	18	53	0	2	0	0	0	0	0	3	3	29	0
los'	2	.0000	.0234	23.7	0	0	0	0	2	0	0	0	0	0	0	0	0	0	0	0	0	0	0	0	2	0	0	0	0

3P longer-horned
7A longer-legged
7R longer-reach
7R longest-surviving
5F Longhorns
4A longhouse
7N Longings
4E longitudes
5Q longjeray
4P Longnecker
6R longs
3E Longs
5R longshoreman
7R longshoremen
7Q longstanding
7P Longueval
7Q Lonigan
8B Lonny
7A looekd
4F Look-It-Up
7H look-alike
9D look-arounds
8R Look-in
4A look-out
9D look'd
9N looka
5A looker
6P lookers
8K LOOKING
5A looking-glass
4J looking'
9N lookit
4A looky
5R loop-the-loop
XR loopwind
5R loose-jointed
7N loose-kneed
7R loose-tongued
7M looseness
8J looser
4R loosing
9C looters
9F looting
7B Looy
9D lop
6P Lopat
5J lopes
6A lopped
7A loquacity
9R Lorain
7R loran
7D lorded
7D lording
4A Lordliness
7F lords'
6N Lordship
7Q Lorentz
3G Loretta's
5Q Lorient
5R Lorna
8D Lorne's
8N Lornes'
XQ Lorrain
9D Lorry's
6H Lorus

Word Type	F	D	U	SFI	3 Gr 3	4 Gr 4	5 Gr 5	6 Gr 6	7 Gr 7	8 Gr 8	9 Gr 9	X UnGr	A Read	B Eng & Gr	C Comp	D Lit	E Math	F Soc Stud	G Spell	H Sci	J Music	K Art	L Home Ec	M Shop	N Lib F	P Lib NF	Q Lib Ref	R Mag	S Rel
lose	268	.9034	48.104	56.8	44	36	23	28	65	27	34	11	55	17	2	17	5	23	8	44	3	0	10	1	26	23	14	20	0
loser	9	.5383	1.0299	40.1	3	1	1	0	2	1	1	0	1	0	0	0	0	1	0	3	0	0	1	0	0	2	0	1	0
losers	8	.5358	.8816	39.5	0	2	1	0	2	0	3	0	0	0	1	3	0	1	1	0	0	0	0	0	0	0	1	1	0
loses	70	.8304	11.647	50.7	16	5	4	12	10	10	11	2	9	4	1	3	0	2	2	26	1	0	1	1	0	9	5	6	0
losing	92	.8398	15.509	51.9	14	11	9	11	14	17	16	0	24	6	1	6	0	10	1	9	0	0	1	0	7	8	4	15	0
loss	162	.9081	29.173	54.6	8	5	22	13	52	24	30	8	19	3	1	9	21	16	3	28	5	0	6	2	6	14	16	13	0
losses	39	.7910	6.1711	47.9	3	1	0	1	6	14	6	8	0	1	1	1	5	9	1	2	0	0	1	2	1	1	3	11	0
lost	820	.9043	147.55	61.7	146	130	74	111	172	106	62	19	255	35	16	64	20	89	17	50	24	0	5	1	63	76	37	68	0
Lost	16	.6240	2.0865	43.2	3	0	2	2	3	5	1	0	4	4	0	0	0	1	0	0	0	0	0	0	2	2	2	1	0
lost-and-found	3	.2223	.2106	33.2	0	0	0	0	2	0	1	0	2	1	0	0	0	0	0	0	0	0	0	0	0	0	0	0	0
lot	679	.8816	119.60	60.8	147	107	66	59	150	80	58	12	238	30	2	55	25	42	2	24	7	3	7	6	60	86	6	86	0
Lot	7	.0383	.3165	35.0	2	0	1	0	0	4	0	0	6	0	0	0	0	0	0	0	0	0	0	0	0	0	0	0	1
lotion	10	.5540	1.1859	40.7	1	1	0	3	1	2	0	2	3	1	0	1	0	0	0	1	0	0	1	0	0	0	0	3	0
Lotion	6	.2411	.4668	36.7	0	0	0	5	0	0	0	1	5	0	0	0	0	0	0	0	0	0	0	0	0	0	0	1	0
lotions	5	.3177	.3576	35.5	0	0	2	1	1	0	0	1	0	0	0	0	0	0	0	1	0	0	0	0	0	0	1	3	0
lots	233	.8405	39.453	56.0	80	40	27	21	28	19	14	4	93	7	1	16	4	7	2	12	4	1	1	0	21	30	2	32	0
Lott	3	.0000	.0365	25.6	0	0	0	0	0	0	0	3	0	0	0	0	0	0	0	0	0	0	0	0	0	0	0	3	0
lotta	2	.2442	.1134	30.5	0	0	0	0	1	0	1	0	0	1	0	0	0	0	0	0	0	0	0	0	0	0	0	1	0
lotus	3	.0939	.1398	31.5	0	1	0	0	1	1	0	0	2	0	0	0	0	0	0	0	0	1	0	0	0	0	0	0	0
Lou	44	.5300	4.9792	47.0	4	11	12	2	12	0	3	0	11	3	0	7	1	0	0	0	15	0	0	0	1	5	0	1	0
loud	410	.8366	69.110	58.4	118	78	58	43	49	45	18	1	165	15	10	33	2	8	8	28	48	1	1	1	41	34	4	11	0
loud-speaker	2	.0000	.0389	25.9	1	1	0	0	0	0	0	0	0	0	0	0	0	2	0	0	0	0	0	0	0	0	0	0	0
louder	126	.7141	18.496	52.7	29	35	14	17	11	10	8	2	41	7	0	8	0	2	7	7	24	0	0	0	14	10	0	6	0
loudest	13	.5511	1.5107	41.8	7	2	0	1	1	1	0	1	2	0	0	4	0	0	1	2	1	0	0	0	3	0	0	1	0
loudly	142	.7358	21.538	53.3	27	41	14	15	27	14	3	1	63	12	0	11	0	4	3	2	13	0	0	0	18	13	1	2	0
loudmouth	5	.2445	.3875	35.9	4	0	0	0	0	0	0	1	4	0	0	0	0	0	0	0	0	0	0	0	0	0	0	1	0
loudness	17	.4620	1.6358	42.1	1	1	4	0	3	7	1	0	0	5	0	1	0	0	0	2	8	1	0	0	0	0	0	0	0
loudspeaker	11	.6105	1.3797	41.4	0	2	0	1	4	2	2	0	1	2	0	3	0	1	1	0	2	0	0	0	0	0	1	0	0
Louella	16	.0000	.7309	38.6	16	0	0	0	0	0	0	0	16	0	0	0	0	0	0	0	0	0	0	0	0	0	0	0	0
Louie	5	.3844	.4760	36.8	1	0	0	0	0	3	1	0	3	1	0	0	0	0	0	0	0	0	0	0	1	0	0	0	0
Louis	212	.8417	35.861	55.5	33	18	34	40	51	17	16	3	67	10	0	18	7	36	1	9	8	3	0	0	12	5	24	12	0
LOUIS	2	.0000	.0209	23.2	0	0	0	0	0	0	2	0	0	0	0	0	0	0	0	0	0	0	0	0	0	0	2	0	0
Louis'	6	.1717	.3427	35.3	0	0	0	3	3	0	0	0	3	0	0	3	0	0	0	0	0	0	0	0	0	0	0	0	0
Louisa	31	.4629	3.2863	45.2	0	18	1	11	0	1	0	0	14	0	0	0	0	0	0	0	1	0	0	0	0	12	1	3	0
Louisa's	2	.2433	.1158	30.6	0	1	0	1	0	0	0	0	0	0	0	0	0	0	0	0	0	0	0	0	0	1	0	1	0
Louise	36	.5121	4.2189	46.3	22	6	5	0	0	0	3	0	23	4	0	1	2	0	0	0	0	0	0	0	0	6	0	0	0
Louise's	3	.0000	.1370	31.4	3	0	0	0	0	0	0	0	3	0	0	0	0	0	0	0	0	0	0	0	0	0	0	0	0
Louisiana	90	.4697	9.1699	49.6	1	11	38	2	11	24	2	1	3	1	0	1	0	66	0	2	10	1	0	0	0	0	6	0	0
Louisiana's	9	.1591	.4224	36.3	0	0	7	0	0	1	1	0	0	0	0	0	0	8	0	0	0	0	0	0	0	0	0	1	0
Louisville	11	.5173	1.2102	40.8	1	2	2	5	0	0	1	0	1	1	0	0	2	1	0	0	0	0	0	0	0	5	0	1	0
lounge	5	.3143	.3491	35.4	0	0	2	0	0	0	3	0	0	0	0	3	0	0	0	0	0	0	0	0	0	1	0	1	0
lounged	2	.1717	.1142	30.6	0	0	0	0	2	0	0	0	1	0	0	1	0	0	0	0	0	0	0	0	0	0	0	0	0
lounging	9	.4225	.8569	39.3	0	2	0	1	3	1	1	1	3	0	0	1	0	0	0	0	0	0	2	0	2	0	0	1	0
loup-garou	2	.1787	.1174	30.7	0	1	0	1	0	0	0	0	1	0	0	0	0	0	0	0	0	0	0	0	1	0	0	0	0
Lourenco	2	.0000	.0389	25.9	0	0	0	2	0	0	0	0	0	0	0	0	0	2	0	0	0	0	0	0	0	0	0	0	0
louse	2	.2401	.1133	30.5	0	0	0	0	2	0	0	0	0	0	0	0	0	0	0	0	0	0	0	0	0	1	1	0	0
lousy	8	.3864	.6864	38.4	0	1	0	0	6	0	1	0	1	0	0	1	0	0	0	0	0	0	0	0	2	0	0	4	0
Louvre	2	.1493	.0692	28.4	0	0	0	0	0	1	1	0	0	0	0	0	0	0	0	0	0	1	0	0	0	0	1	0	0
Lovaas	2	.0000	.0243	23.9	0	0	0	0	0	0	2	0	0	0	0	0	0	0	0	0	0	0	0	0	0	0	0	2	0
lovable	9	.4976	.9861	39.9	1	2	0	2	0	4	0	0	3	1	0	0	0	2	0	0	1	1	0	0	0	1	0	0	0
Lovanium	2	.0000	.0389	25.9	0	0	0	0	2	0	0	0	0	0	0	0	0	2	0	0	0	0	0	0	0	0	0	0	0
love	735	.5673	88.175	59.5	113	95	68	90	123	110	112	24	185	32	1	127	1	22	9	6	113	9	6	0	46	76	20	67	15
Love	29	.5262	3.2847	45.2	2	0	2	9	3	4	8	1	9	1	0	2	0	0	0	0	10	0	0	0	1	0	3	3	0
love's	5	.3765	.4671	36.7	0	0	1	1	1	1	1	0	3	0	0	1	0	0	0	0	1	0	0	0	0	0	0	0	0
Love's	2	.2446	.1122	30.5	0	0	0	0	0	1	1	0	0	0	0	1	0	0	0	0	0	0	0	0	0	0	1	0	0
loved	347	.6783	49.250	56.9	75	65	57	46	51	22	23	8	152	7	0	32	1	20	0	1	26	1	4	0	33	44	5	18	3
lovelessness	2	.0000	.0914	29.6	0	0	2	0	0	0	0	0	2	0	0	0	0	0	0	0	0	0	0	0	0	0	0	0	0
loveliest	22	.6598	3.0308	44.8	2	0	3	6	7	2	2	0	8	3	0	1	0	0	1	0	2	0	0	0	4	3	0	0	0
loveliness	7	.5253	.7602	38.8	1	2	2	0	1	0	1	0	0	1	0	1	0	0	0	0	1	0	0	0	3	1	0	0	0
Lovell	5	.1398	.1959	32.9	0	0	1	2	1	1	0	0	0	0	0	0	0	1	0	0	0	0	0	0	0	0	0	4	0
lovely	263	.8273	43.865	56.4	58	58	31	38	36	22	15	5	97	12	1	23	0	22	2	1	28	1	3	0	34	17	4	18	0
Lovely	2	.0000	.0162	22.1	0	1	0	1	0	0	0	0	0	0	0	0	0	0	0	0	2	0	0	0	0	0	0	0	0
lover	41	.6404	5.4666	47.4	1	4	6	10	8	7	2	3	11	2	0	3	0	2	2	0	9	0	0	0	1	10	0	1	0
LOVER	4	.0000	.0429	26.3	0	0	0	0	0	4	0	0	0	0	0	4	0	0	0	0	0	0	0	0	0	0	0	0	0
lover's	2	.1948	.1250	31.0	0	0	0	1	1	0	0	0	1	0	0	0	0	0	0	0	0	0	0	0	0	1	0	0	0
lovers	37	.6573	5.0305	47.0	0	3	3	4	9	6	9	3	10	4	0	4	0	0	0	0	9	1	0	0	0	3	1	5	0
LOVERS	2	.0000	.0215	23.3	0	0	0	0	0	2	0	0	0	0	0	2	0	0	0	0	0	0	0	0	0	0	0	0	0
lovers'	4	.2176	.2025	33.1	0	0	0	0	0	0	4	0	0	0	0	3	0	0	0	0	1	0	0	0	0	0	0	0	0
loves	75	.4590	7.6529	48.8	21	11	7	12	8	8	6	2	24	4	0	6	0	1	0	0	10	0	2	0	4	7	1	14	2
loveth	3	.0000	.0067	18.3	0	0	3	0	0	0	0	0	0	0	3	0	0	0	0	0	0	0	0	0	0	0	0	0	0
loving	57	.3335	4.4464	46.5	4	11	4	6	9	8	11	4	13	2	0	11	0	2	0	0	5	1	0	0	7	6	2	5	3
lovingly	8	.4511	.8411	39.2	0	1	1	3	1	1	0	1	4	0	0	0	0	0	0	1	0	0	0	0	2	1	0	0	0
low	857	.9285	157.64	62.0	115	123	84	143	190	101	81	20	194	27	11	47	7	136	9	96	79	5	22	9	61	48	34	72	0
Low	32	.5279	3.5526	45.5	2	6	16	3	2	2	1	0	2	0	0	1	0	4	0	0	6	0	0	0	2	15	0	2	0
low-bid	2	.2407	.1138	30.6	0	0	0	0	2	0	0	0	0	0	0	1	0	0	0	0	0	0	0	0	0	1	0	0	0
low-branching	2	.0000	.0243	23.9	0	0	0	0	0	0	0	2	0	0	0	0	0	0	0	0	0	0	0	0	0	0	0	2	0
low-calorie	3	.1927	.1491	31.7	0	0	0	0	1	1	0	1	0	0	0	0	0	0	0	1	0	0	0	0	0	0	0	2	0
low-carbon	4	.0000	.0101	20.0	0	0	0	0	0	2	2	0	0	0	0	0	0	0	0	0	0	0	0	4	0	0	0	0	0
low-cost	2	.1442	.0761	28.8	0	0	0	0	1	0	1	0	0	0	0	0	0	1	0	0	0	0	1	0	0	0	0	0	0
low-energy	2	.0000	.0394	26.0	0	0	0	2	0	0	0	0	0	0	0	0	0	0	0	2	0	0	0	0	0	0	0	0	0
low-flying	3	.3131	.2349	33.7	0	0	2	0	0	1	0	0	1	0	0	0	0	1	0	0	1	0	0	0	0	0	0	0	0
low-frequency	2	.0000	.0394	26.0	0	0	0	0	0	1	1	0	0	0	0	0	0	0	0	2	0	0	0	0	0	0	0	0	0
low-grade	5	.2037	.2562	34.1	0	0	2	0	0	0	3	0	0	0	0	0	0	2	0	0	0	0	0	0	0	0	3	0	0
low-growing	2	.2446	.1142	30.6	0	0	0	1	1	0	0	0	0	0	0	0	0	0	0	0	0	0	0	0	1	0	0	1	0
low-hanging	3	.2261	.2131	33.3	0	2	0	1	0	0	0	0	2	0	0	0	0	0	0	0	0	0	0	0	1	0	0	0	0
low-income	3	.2321	.1635	32.1	0	0	0	0	1	0	2	0	0	0	0	0	0	0	0	0	0	0	0	0	0	0	1	2	0
low-lying	8	.4181	.7484	38.7	0	0	0	4	3	0	0	1	1	0	0	2	0	0	0	4	0	0	0	0	0	0	1	0	0
low-pitched	8	.3033	.5478	37.4	0	1	1	3	1	2	0	0	0	0	0	0	0	0	0	3	4	0	0	0	0	0	1	0	0
low-power	7	.0000	.1380	31.4	0	1	1	0	4	1	0	0	0	0	0	0	0	0	0	7	0	0	0	0	0	0	0	0	0
low-pressure	4	.4348	.3900	35.9	0	0	0	1	1	1	0	1	1	0	0	0	0	1	0	0	1	0	0	0	0	0	0	1	0
low-tide	3	.0000	.0591	27.7	0	2	0	0	0	0	1	0	0	0	0	0	0	0	0	3	0	0	0	0	0	0	0	0	0
low-voltage	2	.2401	.1133	30.5	0	0	0	0	1	1	0	0	0	0	0	0	0	0	0	0	0	0	0	0	0	1	1	0	0

6A Loss
7Q Losses
8A lost-plane
7R lost-time
5A losted
7Q Lothair
7F Lothaire
9D lott'ry
8R Lotte
9R lottery
XR Lotts
XR Lotus
7J Loud
5R loud-and-soft
8C loudest-talking
XR loudmouthed
9P Loudoun
7A Loudspeakers
6A Loues
8A Louie's
6N louis
6F LouisXVI
7R Louis-Philippe
7A Louis's
3A Louisey
8B louisiana
6A Lounge
5A louring
3N louts
8B lov'd
8R Lovat
4J Love-Song
9D love-devouring
8R love-in
8A love-knot
9D love-lord
7N love-lornity
9D love-news
7R loveable
8B lovebirds
9R Loved
8F lovelier
5N Lover
7J lovesick
5P lovesome
7A lovin'
7N loving-cup
5A loving-kindness
3Q low-altitude
7D low-beamed
6A low-bent
9H low-boiling-point
9R low-budget
XR low-cholesterol
4G low-heeled
7F low-interest
5P low-level
8K low-life
3A low-melting
3Q low-paid
8F low-paying
7R low-pitch
6A low-powered
6F low-quality
9Q low-resistance
6N low-skimming
XR low-sodium
5A low-spread
8M low-temperature
9H low-tides
7Q low-veld
9Q low-yield

Word Type	F	D	U	SFI	3 Gr 3	4 Gr 4	5 Gr 5	6 Gr 6	7 Gr 7	8 Gr 8	9 Gr 9	X UnGr	A Read	B Eng & Gr	C Comp	D Lit	E Math	F Soc Stud	G Spell	H Sci	J Music	K Art	L Home Ec	M Shop	N Lib F	P Lib NF	Q Lib Ref	R Mag	S Rel
Low's	2	.0000	.0914	29.6	1	1	0	0	0	0	0	0	2	0	0	0	0	0	0	0	0	0	0	0	0	0	0	0	0
Lowdermilk	6	.0000	.0644	28.1	0	0	0	6	0	0	0	0	0	0	0	6	0	0	0	0	0	0	0	0	0	0	0	0	0
Lowe	12	.0000	.1737	32.4	0	0	0	0	0	0	12	0	0	0	0	0	0	0	0	0	0	0	0	0	0	12	0	0	0
Lowell	9	.4181	.8629	39.4	0	4	1	0	3	1	0	0	2	0	0	0	0	0	0	5	0	0	0	0	1	0	1	0	0
lower	659	.8651	113.57	60.6	74	92	65	64	133	106	100	25	86	12	6	17	26	80	7	136	78	5	44	24	15	24	52	47	0
Lower	25	.4377	2.3807	43.8	0	3	12	5	1	1	2	1	1	0	0	0	1	11	0	0	0	0	0	0	0	2	9	1	0
lower-case	2	.2404	.0978	29.9	0	0	1	0	0	0	1	0	0	0	0	0	0	0	0	0	0	1	0	1	0	0	0	0	0
lowered	95	.8348	15.927	52.0	13	13	10	24	18	10	7	0	26	5	0	4	1	4	0	11	7	0	2	1	18	7	2	7	0
lowering	24	.6978	3.4625	45.4	0	3	2	5	6	3	2	3	7	0	0	0	0	2	0	5	3	0	0	0	1	2	2	2	0
lowermost	2	.2346	.1166	30.7	0	0	0	1	0	0	1	0	0	0	0	0	0	0	0	1	0	0	0	0	0	0	0	1	0
lowers	17	.5965	2.0825	43.2	1	7	1	1	5	1	1	0	0	0	0	0	0	2	0	4	5	0	0	1	0	1	1	3	0
lowest	195	.5891	23.902	53.8	20	23	27	27	46	25	25	2	14	2	0	5	103	13	0	17	25	0	1	0	2	4	6	3	0
lowest-pitched	3	.0000	.0591	27.7	0	0	0	3	0	0	0	0	0	0	0	0	0	0	0	3	0	0	0	0	0	0	0	0	0
lowest-terms	37	.0000	.5538	37.4	0	1	3	9	12	12	0	0	0	0	0	0	37	0	0	0	0	0	0	0	0	0	0	0	0
lowing	4	.4442	.3918	35.9	1	0	0	2	0	0	1	0	1	0	0	1	0	0	0	0	1	0	0	0	0	0	0	1	0
lowland	71	.3850	6.5435	48.2	1	3	6	22	34	3	2	0	23	0	0	0	0	38	0	1	0	0	0	0	0	0	8	1	0
Lowland	20	.2446	1.2037	40.8	0	0	5	12	2	1	0	0	0	0	0	0	0	14	0	0	6	0	0	0	0	0	0	0	0
lowlands	96	.3971	8.5875	49.3	9	17	16	33	13	2	4	2	4	0	0	1	0	72	0	1	1	0	0	0	0	3	10	4	0
Lowlands	8	.2007	.4308	36.3	0	0	4	3	1	0	0	0	0	0	0	0	0	7	0	0	1	0	0	0	0	0	0	0	0
lowly	18	.5953	2.2938	43.6	4	1	0	2	8	1	2	0	8	0	0	1	0	1	0	0	3	1	0	0	1	0	3	0	0
lowness	4	.3155	.2801	34.5	0	1	0	0	2	1	0	0	0	1	0	0	0	0	0	1	2	0	0	0	0	0	0	0	0
Lowry	2	.1814	.1187	30.7	1	0	0	0	1	0	0	0	1	0	0	0	0	0	0	0	0	0	0	0	0	0	0	1	0
lows	6	.2429	.3584	35.5	0	1	0	0	2	2	1	0	0	0	0	0	0	0	0	4	2	0	0	0	0	0	0	0	0
Lowy	2	.0000	.0215	23.3	0	0	0	0	2	0	0	0	0	0	0	2	0	0	0	0	0	0	0	0	0	0	0	0	0
lox	3	.0000	.0591	27.7	0	2	0	0	0	0	1	0	0	0	0	0	0	0	0	3	0	0	0	0	0	0	0	0	0
loyal	38	.7366	5.7140	47.6	1	0	8	4	11	11	3	0	9	1	0	5	0	9	0	0	3	0	0	0	4	3	2	2	0
Loyalists	3	.2378	.1809	32.6	0	0	1	0	0	1	1	0	0	0	0	0	0	2	0	0	0	0	0	0	0	1	0	0	0
loyally	4	.3693	.3613	35.6	0	0	0	3	0	1	0	0	2	0	0	1	0	0	0	0	0	0	0	0	0	0	1	0	0
loyalties	4	.4802	.4049	36.1	0	0	1	0	2	0	0	1	0	0	0	1	0	1	0	0	0	0	0	0	0	0	1	1	0
loyalty	30	.6551	4.0275	46.1	1	0	3	0	8	13	5	0	2	0	2	5	0	12	0	0	1	0	2	0	1	4	0	1	0
Loyola	2	.0000	.0394	26.0	0	0	0	0	2	0	0	0	0	0	0	0	0	0	0	2	0	0	0	0	0	0	0	0	0
LP	12	.0772	.2753	34.4	0	0	0	0	2	9	0	1	0	0	0	0	0	0	0	0	11	0	0	0	0	0	0	1	0
LP'S	2	.0000	.0162	22.1	0	0	0	0	1	1	0	0	0	0	0	0	0	0	0	0	2	0	0	0	0	0	0	0	0
LSD	8	.2011	.3931	35.9	0	0	0	2	1	2	3	0	0	0	0	0	0	0	0	0	0	0	0	0	2	0	0	6	0
Lt	18	.4550	1.9283	42.9	0	1	0	9	5	2	1	0	11	0	0	0	0	0	0	0	0	0	0	0	0	1	3	3	0
Ltd	3	.1277	.1363	31.3	0	0	0	0	2	0	1	0	1	0	0	0	0	0	0	0	0	0	0	0	0	0	0	2	0
lu	6	.0000	.2741	34.4	0	0	0	0	6	0	0	0	6	0	0	0	0	0	0	0	0	0	0	0	0	0	0	0	0
Lu	2	.2433	.1158	30.6	0	1	0	0	0	0	0	1	0	0	0	0	0	0	0	0	0	0	0	0	0	1	0	1	0
Luath	4	.0000	.0469	26.7	0	0	0	0	4	0	0	0	0	0	0	0	0	0	0	0	0	0	0	0	4	0	0	0	0
luau	5	.0000	.0986	29.9	0	0	5	0	0	0	0	0	0	0	0	0	0	0	0	5	0	0	0	0	0	0	0	0	0
Luba	3	.0000	.0328	25.2	0	0	0	0	0	0	3	0	0	3	0	0	0	0	0	0	0	0	0	0	0	0	0	0	0
lubb	7	.0000	.1380	31.4	4	0	0	3	0	0	0	0	0	0	0	0	0	0	0	7	0	0	0	0	0	0	0	0	0
lubbers	2	.0000	.0162	22.1	0	2	0	0	0	0	0	0	0	0	0	0	0	0	0	0	2	0	0	0	0	0	0	0	0
Lubis	2	.0000	.0209	23.2	0	0	0	0	0	2	0	0	0	0	0	0	0	0	0	0	0	0	0	0	0	0	2	0	0
lubricant	2	.1738	.0790	29.0	0	0	0	0	0	1	1	0	0	0	0	0	0	0	0	0	0	0	0	1	0	0	1	0	0
lubricants	2	.0000	.0209	23.2	1	0	0	0	0	0	1	0	0	0	0	0	0	0	0	0	0	0	0	0	0	0	2	0	0
lubricate	3	.2442	.1820	32.6	0	1	0	1	1	0	0	0	0	1	0	0	0	0	0	2	0	0	0	0	0	0	0	0	0
lubricated	3	.2345	.1568	32.0	0	0	0	0	0	1	2	0	0	0	0	0	0	0	0	0	0	0	1	0	0	0	2	0	0
lubricating	6	.5399	.6765	38.3	0	0	2	0	2	2	0	0	0	0	0	0	0	1	1	1	0	0	0	0	0	2	1	0	0
lubrication	7	.4585	.7244	38.6	0	3	1	0	3	0	0	0	2	0	0	0	0	0	0	3	0	0	0	0	0	0	1	1	0
Lubumbashi	3	.0000	.0583	27.7	0	0	0	0	3	0	0	0	0	0	0	0	0	3	0	0	0	0	0	0	0	0	0	0	0
Lucas	3	.2028	.1988	33.0	0	0	0	0	1	2	0	0	2	0	0	0	0	0	0	0	1	0	0	0	0	0	0	0	0
Luce	3	.2300	.1627	32.1	0	0	0	0	0	2	1	0	0	1	0	0	0	0	0	0	0	0	0	0	0	0	0	2	0
Luce's	2	.0000	.0243	23.9	0	0	0	0	0	2	0	0	0	0	0	0	0	0	0	0	0	0	0	0	0	0	0	2	0
Lucia	14	.3607	1.1580	40.6	0	4	1	8	0	0	1	0	2	0	0	0	0	6	0	0	5	0	0	0	0	0	1	0	0
lucid	4	.3745	.3228	35.1	0	0	0	0	0	2	1	1	0	0	0	1	0	0	0	0	0	0	0	0	0	0	1	2	0
Lucie	7	.1352	.2522	34.0	0	0	0	0	0	0	6	1	0	0	0	6	0	0	0	0	0	0	0	0	0	0	0	1	0
Lucifer	2	.0000	.0914	29.6	0	0	0	0	2	0	0	0	2	0	0	0	0	0	0	0	0	0	0	0	0	0	0	0	0
Lucille	13	.2070	.8611	39.4	0	8	0	0	5	0	0	0	8	0	0	5	0	0	0	0	0	0	0	0	0	0	0	0	0
Lucinda	81	.0348	1.6667	42.2	0	0	0	76	0	5	0	0	6	0	0	0	0	0	0	0	0	0	0	0	75	0	0	0	0
Lucinda's	5	.0000	.0586	27.7	0	0	0	5	0	0	0	0	0	0	0	0	0	0	0	0	0	0	0	0	5	0	0	0	0
Lucio	8	.0000	.3655	35.6	0	0	8	0	0	0	0	0	8	0	0	0	0	0	0	0	0	0	0	0	0	0	0	0	0
luck	193	.7976	31.283	55.0	46	48	15	25	32	19	6	2	81	9	3	20	0	12	1	2	2	1	0	0	28	21	2	11	0
Luck	6	.2355	.4634	36.7	0	5	1	0	0	0	0	0	5	0	0	0	0	0	0	0	0	0	0	0	0	1	0	0	0
luckier	2	.2440	.1132	30.5	0	0	0	0	2	0	0	0	0	0	0	1	0	0	0	0	0	0	0	0	0	0	0	1	0
luckily	40	.7194	5.9495	47.7	8	10	4	3	8	3	3	1	15	2	0	6	0	6	0	3	0	0	0	0	2	4	1	1	0
lucky	166	.8364	28.014	54.5	58	34	15	20	15	13	8	3	70	5	0	16	3	11	4	6	4	0	1	0	11	19	3	13	0
Lucky	21	.3385	1.9476	42.9	15	1	3	1	1	0	0	0	17	1	0	0	3	0	0	0	0	0	0	0	0	0	0	0	0
lucrative	4	.3498	.3059	34.9	0	0	1	0	1	1	1	0	0	0	0	0	0	0	0	0	0	0	0	0	0	1	2	1	0
Lucretia	31	.0000	.4488	36.5	0	31	0	0	0	0	0	0	0	0	0	0	0	0	0	0	0	0	0	0	0	31	0	0	0
Lucretia's	2	.0000	.0290	24.6	0	2	0	0	0	0	0	0	0	0	0	0	0	0	0	0	0	0	0	0	0	2	0	0	0
Lucy	82	.6726	11.703	50.7	39	25	4	5	3	1	5	0	47	3	0	2	4	7	0	0	4	0	0	0	1	13	0	1	0
Lucy's	3	.2212	.2099	33.2	1	1	0	0	1	0	0	0	2	0	0	1	0	0	0	0	0	0	0	0	0	0	0	0	0
ludicrous	2	.1698	.1133	30.5	0	0	0	0	0	0	2	0	1	0	0	0	0	0	0	0	0	0	0	0	0	0	1	0	0
Ludlow	4	.0000	.0429	26.3	0	0	0	0	4	0	0	0	0	0	0	4	0	0	0	0	0	0	0	0	0	0	0	0	0
LUDLOW	2	.0000	.0215	23.3	0	0	0	0	2	0	0	0	0	0	0	2	0	0	0	0	0	0	0	0	0	0	0	0	0
Ludwig	11	.4171	.9870	39.9	0	3	1	2	2	1	1	1	1	0	0	0	0	0	0	0	4	0	0	0	0	1	4	1	0
lug	6	.5978	.7446	38.7	1	0	1	0	2	1	1	0	1	0	0	1	0	0	1	0	1	0	0	0	1	1	0	0	0
Luga	2	.0000	.0914	29.6	0	0	0	0	2	0	0	0	2	0	0	0	0	0	0	0	0	0	0	0	0	0	0	0	0
luggage	17	.5480	1.9978	43.0	0	3	2	2	3	1	2	4	5	1	2	0	1	1	0	1	0	0	0	0	3	0	0	3	0
lugged	5	.3854	.4790	36.8	2	2	0	0	1	0	0	0	3	0	0	0	0	0	0	0	0	0	0	0	1	1	0	0	0
lugging	3	.3399	.2456	33.9	0	0	0	1	2	0	0	0	1	0	0	1	0	0	0	0	0	0	0	0	0	0	0	1	0
lugs	5	.2431	.2776	34.4	0	0	0	0	4	1	0	0	0	0	0	0	0	0	0	0	0	0	0	1	0	0	0	4	0
Luigi	10	.4791	1.0495	40.2	0	1	3	3	1	2	0	0	3	0	0	0	0	0	0	0	1	1	0	0	0	2	3	0	0
Luigia	5	.0000	.2284	33.6	0	0	0	5	0	0	0	0	5	0	0	0	0	0	0	0	0	0	0	0	0	0	0	0	0
Luis	28	.2258	2.1311	43.3	13	13	0	1	1	0	0	0	23	0	0	0	0	5	0	0	0	0	0	0	0	0	0	0	0
LUKA	5	.0000	.0537	27.3	0	0	0	0	0	0	5	0	0	0	0	5	0	0	0	0	0	0	0	0	0	0	0	0	0
Luke	77	.2006	3.8076	45.8	5	12	1	57	1	0	0	1	1	0	0	0	1	0	0	0	0	0	0	0	63	10	1	1	0
lukewarm	4	.3250	.2921	34.7	0	0	1	0	2	1	0	0	0	0	0	0	0	0	0	2	0	0	1	0	1	0	0	0	0
lull	6	.3477	.4702	36.7	0	1	1	1	2	0	1	0	1	0	0	1	0	0	0	0	3	0	0	0	1	0	0	0	0
lullabies	4	.1770	.1679	32.3	1	2	0	1	0	0	0	0	0	0	0	1	0	0	0	0	3	0	0	0	0	0	0	0	0
lullaby	17	.3269	1.2355	40.9	3	5	1	3	4	1	0	0	2	0	1	1	0	0	0	0	12	0	0	0	1	0	0	0	0
Lullaby	5	.3026	.3808	35.8	0	2	2	0	0	0	0	1	2	0	0	0	0	0	0	0	2	0	0	0	0	0	0	1	0
Lullah	31	.0000	.3634	35.6	31	0	0	0	0	0	0	0	0	0	0	0	0	0	0	0	0	0	0	0	31	0	0	0	0

9D low'r
5J Lowd
8N lowed
4H Lowell's
5P lower-class
XH lower-cost
9Q lower-grade
8J lower-pitched
9L lower-priced
4J lowest-sounding
7Q Lowestoft
3P Lowlanders
7M LOX
5N Loy
3Q loyalists
8R loyality
7L LOYALTY
6G lphbt
3E LS
7R LSU
6E Lu-Ann
3H lub
8Q Lubarda
7N lubber
7D lucent
4F Lucerne
4J Lucia's
8Q Lucic
XR Lucie-FortMyers
5J Lucien
7D Lucille's
7A Lucius
8P luck's
4A Luck's
7Q luckananee
6R Luckey
4R luckiest
3P luckless
3N LUCKY
7A lucre
7Q Lucretius
8F Ludendorff
6N Ludgate
7D ludicrously
XR Ludington
7D Ludlow's
8R Ludvik
7A Luella
6J Luening
6D luff
8D Lug
7A Luga's
6A Luigia's
4P Luke's
9R lukewarmly
5Q Luks

Word Type	F	D	U	SFI	3 Gr 3	4 Gr 4	5 Gr 5	6 Gr 6	7 Gr 7	8 Gr 8	9 Gr 9	X UnGr	A Read	B Eng & Gr	C Comp	D Lit	E Math	F Soc Stud	G Spell	H Sci	J Music	K Art	L Home Ec	M Shop	N Lib F	P Lib NF	Q Lib Ref	R Mag	S Rel
Lullah's	2	.0000	.0234	23.7	2	0	0	0	0	0	0	0	0	0	0	0	0	0	0	0	0	0	0	0	2	0	0	0	0
lulled	3	.3873	.2495	34.0	0	1	0	0	2	0	0	0	0	0	0	1	0	0	0	0	0	0	0	0	1	0	0	1	0
lulls	2	.2337	.1157	30.6	0	0	0	0	1	0	1	0	0	0	0	0	0	1	0	0	0	0	0	0	1	0	0	0	0
Lully	3	.2365	.1616	32.1	0	0	0	0	0	3	0	0	0	0	0	0	0	0	0	0	1	0	0	0	0	0	2	0	0
lumber	154	.6777	21.302	53.3	21	20	44	21	22	12	10	4	13	3	2	3	3	53	7	4	3	0	0	17	3	7	31	5	0
lumbered	11	.5997	1.3761	41.4	1	1	2	1	5	0	1	0	2	2	0	2	0	0	0	0	0	0	0	0	2	2	0	1	0
lumbering	23	.4665	2.3549	43.7	1	2	5	3	4	2	5	1	6	0	0	1	0	5	0	0	1	0	0	5	1	1	2	1	0
lumberjack	8	.2187	.6050	37.8	0	4	2	0	0	2	0	0	7	0	0	0	0	0	0	0	0	0	0	0	0	1	0	0	0
lumberjacks	9	.3683	.8693	39.4	0	2	2	1	1	3	0	0	7	0	0	1	0	0	0	0	0	0	0	0	0	1	0	0	0
lumberman	2	.1840	.0808	29.1	0	0	0	0	0	2	0	0	0	0	1	0	0	0	1	0	0	0	0	0	0	0	0	0	0
lumbermen	9	.3855	.7930	39.0	5	1	2	0	1	0	0	0	1	0	0	0	0	6	0	0	1	0	0	0	0	0	1	0	0
lumbers	2	.1494	.1045	30.2	2	0	0	0	0	0	0	0	1	0	0	0	0	0	0	0	1	0	0	0	0	0	0	0	0
lumberyard	2	.0000	.0914	29.6	0	0	1	0	0	1	0	0	2	0	0	0	0	0	0	0	0	0	0	0	0	0	0	0	0
lumberyards	3	.3270	.2028	33.1	1	0	1	0	1	0	0	0	0	0	0	0	0	0	0	0	0	1	0	1	0	0	1	0	0
luminescence	2	.0000	.0209	23.2	0	0	2	0	0	0	0	0	0	0	0	0	0	0	0	0	0	0	0	0	0	0	2	0	0
luminescent	2	.1738	.0790	29.0	0	0	0	0	2	0	0	0	0	0	0	0	0	0	0	0	0	0	0	1	0	0	1	0	0
luminosity	2	.2278	.1128	30.5	0	0	0	0	0	1	1	0	0	0	0	0	0	0	0	1	0	0	0	0	0	0	1	0	0
luminous	32	.3918	2.8328	44.5	2	0	0	15	3	4	3	5	1	0	0	1	0	0	0	24	0	0	0	0	2	2	0	2	0
Lummox	2	.0000	.0290	24.6	0	2	0	0	0	0	0	0	0	0	0	0	0	0	0	0	0	0	0	0	0	2	0	0	0
lump	80	.7834	12.746	51.1	12	17	4	19	18	9	1	0	26	0	1	4	0	2	0	23	0	0	2	2	9	6	1	4	0
Lump	4	.0000	.0486	26.9	0	0	0	0	4	0	0	0	0	0	0	0	0	0	0	0	0	0	0	0	0	0	0	4	0
lump-nosed	2	.0000	.0290	24.6	0	0	0	0	2	0	0	0	0	0	0	0	0	0	0	0	0	0	0	0	0	2	0	0	0
lumped	2	.0000	.0209	23.2	0	0	0	0	2	0	0	0	0	0	0	0	0	0	0	0	0	0	0	0	0	0	2	0	0
lumping	3	.1148	.0862	29.4	1	0	0	0	0	0	2	0	0	0	0	0	0	0	0	0	0	0	2	0	0	1	0	0	0
lumps	43	.6861	6.1638	47.9	8	8	8	12	6	1	0	0	17	0	0	0	0	1	0	14	1	0	2	2	2	2	1	1	0
lumpy	6	.4977	.6125	37.9	0	1	0	1	1	2	1	0	0	2	1	0	0	0	0	0	0	0	1	0	1	0	0	1	0
Lumumba	2	.0000	.0290	24.6	0	0	2	0	0	0	0	0	0	0	0	0	0	0	0	0	0	0	0	0	0	2	0	0	0
Luna	3	.1409	.1472	31.7	2	0	1	0	0	0	0	0	1	0	0	0	0	0	0	0	0	0	0	0	0	2	0	0	0
lunar	55	.5893	6.7858	48.3	2	5	2	10	15	0	16	5	7	0	0	0	5	1	0	13	0	0	0	1	0	3	4	21	0
Lunar	8	.1177	.2734	34.4	0	0	0	0	7	0	1	0	0	0	0	0	1	0	0	0	0	0	0	0	0	0	0	7	0
lunars	2	.0000	.0290	24.6	0	0	0	2	0	0	0	0	0	0	0	0	0	0	0	0	0	0	0	0	0	2	0	0	0
lunatic	5	.2418	.2811	34.5	0	1	0	0	0	0	4	0	0	0	0	0	0	0	0	0	0	0	0	0	0	0	2	3	0
lunatics	2	.1698	.1133	30.5	0	0	0	0	0	0	2	0	1	0	0	0	0	0	0	0	0	0	0	0	0	0	1	0	0
lunch	357	.7303	53.454	57.3	113	51	27	31	47	41	40	7	124	26	4	21	37	13	12	10	1	0	43	0	27	8	3	28	0
Lunch	2	.2413	.1212	30.8	1	0	1	0	0	0	0	0	0	0	0	0	1	0	0	1	0	0	0	0	0	0	0	0	0
lunch-box	2	.0000	.0064	18.1	0	0	0	0	2	0	0	0	0	0	0	0	0	0	0	0	0	0	2	0	0	0	0	0	0
lunchbox	2	.0000	.0914	29.6	0	0	1	0	0	1	0	0	2	0	0	0	0	0	0	0	0	0	0	0	0	0	0	0	0
luncheon	31	.4155	2.8622	44.6	0	4	3	4	4	2	11	3	8	1	0	1	0	0	2	1	0	0	9	0	0	2	0	7	0
lunches	21	.3836	1.8539	42.7	5	2	1	2	4	2	5	0	7	1	0	0	3	0	1	0	0	0	6	0	0	0	0	3	0
lunchman	2	.0000	.0219	23.4	0	0	0	0	0	0	2	0	0	2	0	0	0	0	0	0	0	0	0	0	0	0	0	0	0
lunchroom	7	.2361	.4786	36.8	1	1	0	2	1	0	2	0	4	0	0	0	0	0	0	0	0	0	2	0	0	0	0	1	0
lunchtime	7	.3059	.5242	37.2	2	1	0	0	3	0	1	0	2	0	0	0	0	0	0	2	0	0	2	0	1	0	0	0	0
Lundquist	6	.0000	.1167	30.7	0	0	0	6	0	0	0	0	0	0	0	0	0	6	0	0	0	0	0	0	0	0	0	0	0
Luneburg	2	.0000	.0243	23.9	0	0	0	0	0	0	2	0	0	0	0	0	0	0	0	0	0	0	0	0	0	0	0	2	0
Lunenberg	2	.0000	.0234	23.7	0	0	2	0	0	0	0	0	0	0	0	0	0	0	0	0	0	0	0	0	2	0	0	0	0
lung	34	.5000	3.5908	45.6	1	1	9	2	4	9	7	1	0	0	0	1	0	0	1	14	0	0	0	0	0	3	12	3	0
lunge	7	.4094	.6526	38.1	1	2	0	2	1	1	0	0	2	0	0	0	0	0	0	0	0	0	0	0	3	1	1	0	0
lunged	9	.5239	1.0214	40.1	0	0	3	2	3	0	1	0	3	0	1	2	0	0	0	0	0	0	0	0	1	1	0	1	0
lungfishes	2	.0000	.0209	23.2	0	0	0	0	2	0	0	0	0	0	0	0	0	0	0	0	0	0	0	0	0	0	2	0	0
lunging	4	.3740	.3661	35.6	0	0	0	2	2	0	0	0	2	0	0	0	0	0	0	0	0	0	0	0	1	0	0	1	0
lungs	207	.4915	22.223	53.5	26	35	39	31	29	27	16	4	25	1	0	4	0	0	3	139	1	0	0	0	3	12	15	4	0
lunkers	2	.0000	.0243	23.9	0	0	0	0	0	0	0	2	0	0	0	0	0	0	0	0	0	0	0	0	0	0	0	2	0
lunologist	4	.0000	.0789	29.0	0	0	0	4	0	0	0	0	0	0	0	0	0	0	0	4	0	0	0	0	0	0	0	0	0
lunology	2	.0000	.0394	26.0	0	0	0	2	0	0	0	0	0	0	0	0	0	0	0	2	0	0	0	0	0	0	0	0	0
Lupe	20	.0000	.9137	39.6	0	0	0	1	19	0	0	0	20	0	0	0	0	0	0	0	0	0	0	0	0	0	0	0	0
Lupe's	5	.0000	.2284	33.6	0	0	0	0	5	0	0	0	5	0	0	0	0	0	0	0	0	0	0	0	0	0	0	0	0
Lupy	2	.0000	.0234	23.7	0	0	2	0	0	0	0	0	0	0	0	0	0	0	0	0	0	0	0	0	2	0	0	0	0
lurch	4	.3662	.3647	35.6	0	2	0	1	1	0	0	0	2	0	0	0	0	1	0	0	0	0	0	0	0	0	1	0	0
lurched	8	.5358	.9197	39.6	1	1	1	0	3	1	1	0	2	0	0	1	0	0	0	0	0	0	0	0	2	2	0	1	0
lurching	4	.3721	.3657	35.6	0	1	0	1	2	0	0	0	2	0	0	1	0	0	0	0	0	0	0	0	0	1	0	0	0
lure	19	.5042	2.0456	43.1	1	0	1	4	8	1	1	3	3	0	0	3	0	1	0	0	0	0	0	0	1	0	3	8	0
lured	6	.1231	.2155	33.3	0	0	0	3	2	1	0	0	0	0	0	0	0	1	0	0	0	0	0	0	0	0	0	5	0
lures	6	.4291	.5636	37.5	0	1	0	1	2	1	0	1	1	0	0	0	0	0	0	1	0	0	0	1	0	0	2	1	0
lurid	2	.2440	.1132	30.5	0	0	0	0	0	1	1	0	0	0	0	1	0	0	0	0	0	0	0	0	0	0	0	1	0
lurk	3	.3370	.2430	33.9	0	0	0	0	2	1	0	0	1	0	0	1	0	0	0	0	0	0	0	0	0	0	1	0	0
lurked	6	.4863	.6219	37.9	2	0	0	1	2	0	1	0	1	1	1	1	0	0	0	0	0	0	0	0	0	1	1	0	0
lurking	17	.5956	2.1132	43.2	1	3	1	0	7	4	1	0	3	0	0	5	0	1	0	0	0	0	0	0	2	1	2	3	0
Lurvy	9	.2261	.6392	38.1	0	3	6	0	0	0	0	0	6	0	0	0	0	0	0	0	0	0	0	0	3	0	0	0	0
luscious	3	.3399	.2456	33.9	0	0	1	0	2	0	0	0	1	0	0	1	0	0	0	0	0	0	0	0	0	0	0	1	0
lush	16	.6056	2.0012	43.0	3	1	1	2	4	2	0	3	0	0	0	1	0	4	0	3	0	0	0	0	0	2	2	4	0
Lusitania	2	.2306	.1140	30.6	0	0	0	0	0	1	1	0	0	1	0	0	0	1	0	0	0	0	0	0	0	0	0	0	0
Lussurioso	3	.0000	.0434	26.4	0	0	0	0	3	0	0	0	0	0	0	0	0	0	0	0	0	0	0	0	0	3	0	0	0
Lussurioso's	2	.0000	.0290	24.6	0	0	0	0	2	0	0	0	0	0	0	0	0	0	0	0	0	0	0	0	0	2	0	0	0
lust	3	.2332	.1690	32.3	0	0	0	0	2	1	0	0	0	0	0	0	0	0	0	0	0	0	0	0	0	2	0	1	0
luster	22	.5339	2.5278	44.0	3	0	0	3	1	4	5	6	4	1	0	0	0	0	0	12	0	0	2	0	1	0	1	1	0
lustre	2	.2401	.1133	30.5	2	0	0	0	0	0	0	0	0	0	0	0	0	0	0	0	0	0	0	0	0	1	1	0	0
lustrous	7	.1833	.3227	35.1	0	0	0	0	2	2	3	0	1	0	0	0	0	0	0	1	1	0	4	0	0	0	0	0	0
lusty	7	.3866	.5860	37.7	1	2	0	2	0	0	2	0	0	0	0	2	0	0	0	0	0	0	0	0	2	3	0	0	0
lute	14	.2534	.8260	39.2	0	0	0	8	4	1	0	1	1	0	0	1	0	0	0	0	9	0	0	0	0	3	0	0	0
lutes	2	.0000	.0162	22.1	0	0	0	2	0	0	0	0	0	0	0	0	0	0	0	0	2	0	0	0	0	0	0	0	0
luteum	6	.0000	.1183	30.7	0	0	0	0	0	0	6	0	0	0	0	0	0	0	0	6	0	0	0	0	0	0	0	0	0
lutfisk	2	.0000	.0389	25.9	0	2	0	0	0	0	0	0	0	0	0	0	0	2	0	0	0	0	0	0	0	0	0	0	0
Luther	13	.5174	1.3920	41.4	1	0	1	0	7	1	2	1	0	0	0	4	0	0	0	0	1	0	0	0	0	1	3	4	0
Luther's	2	.1698	.1133	30.5	0	0	0	0	2	0	0	0	1	0	0	0	0	0	0	0	0	0	0	0	0	0	1	0	0
Lutheran	7	.1650	.2862	34.6	0	0	1	0	4	1	0	1	0	0	0	0	0	0	0	0	1	0	0	0	0	0	6	0	0
Lutheranism	2	.0000	.0209	23.2	0	0	0	0	1	1	0	0	0	0	0	0	0	0	0	0	0	0	0	0	0	0	2	0	0
luve	8	.1564	.3173	35.0	0	0	7	0	0	0	1	0	0	7	0	0	0	0	0	0	1	0	0	0	0	0	0	0	0
Luxembourg	16	.4550	1.5707	42.0	3	0	4	6	2	0	1	0	0	0	0	0	0	8	0	0	1	0	0	0	0	5	2	0	0
Luxembourgers	2	.0000	.0290	24.6	0	0	2	0	0	0	0	0	0	0	0	0	0	0	0	0	0	0	0	0	0	2	0	0	0
luxuries	6	.3682	.4952	36.9	0	0	0	0	0	3	3	0	0	0	0	1	0	4	1	0	0	0	0	0	0	0	0	0	0
luxurious	17	.6125	2.1680	43.4	3	0	1	4	4	2	2	1	3	0	1	1	0	2	0	0	0	0	0	0	0	3	2	5	0
luxuriously	2	.2285	.1129	30.5	0	1	0	1	0	0	0	0	0	0	0	0	0	1	0	0	0	0	0	0	0	0	1	0	0
luxury	25	.8272	4.1394	46.2	1	2	1	3	7	4	4	3	4	0	0	2	2	3	2	0	2	0	1	0	3	2	2	2	0
Luzon	10	.1285	.3594	35.6	8	1	0	1	0	0	0	0	0	0	0	0	0	2	0	0	0	0	0	0	0	0	8	0	0
LV	3	.0000	.0328	25.2	0	0	0	3	0	0	0	0	0	3	0	0	0	0	0	0	0	0	0	0	0	0	0	0	0
ly	78	.1257	2.5711	44.1	2	13	11	27	12	10	3	0	2	10	0	0	0	0	66	0	0	0	0	0	0	0	0	0	0

6J lulling
7A Lulubelle
7A lumbago
9Q lumbar
5A Lumber
5Q lumber-carrying
8A lumberjacket
9Q luminaries
5Q Luminescence
5H luminesces
8F lummux
3A lun
3P lunar-landing
5N lunch-room
9L luncheons
8L Lunches
7A lunching
6F Lundquists
9R Lundy
7R Lundy's
3J Lune
8F Lung
4P Lunik
8D lunkhead
8D lunkheads
6H luno
8C lupins
9D lurker
6J lurks
4J lusong
9B Luster
4J luster-glossed
8N lustily
7J lute-like
8C lutefisk
9H luteinizing
8A luther
6A Lux'
5P Luxembourgeois
6F Luxemburg
5P luxuriant
5G luz
9J Lvovsky
9E lw
8H Lw
9E lwh
7E LXXV
7N Lybia

Word Type	F	D	U	SFI	3 Gr 3	4 Gr 4	5 Gr 5	6 Gr 6	7 Gr 7	8 Gr 8	9 Gr 9	X UnGr	A Read	B Eng & Gr	C Comp	D Lit	E Math	F Soc Stud	G Spell	H Sci	J Music	K Art	L Home Ec	M Shop	N Lib F	P Lib NF	Q Lib Ref	R Mag	S Rel
Lyda	7	.0000	.1013	30.1	0	7	0	0	0	0	0	0	0	0	0	0	0	0	0	0	0	0	0	0	0	7	0	0	0
Lyda's	3	.0000	.0434	26.4	0	3	0	0	0	0	0	0	0	0	0	0	0	0	0	0	0	0	0	0	0	3	0	0	0
Lydia	30	.4440	3.2340	45.1	13	13	3	0	0	0	1	0	22	0	0	0	0	0	0	0	0	0	0	0	3	4	1	0	0
lye	9	.4118	.8594	39.3	0	7	0	0	0	2	0	0	3	0	0	0	0	0	1	1	0	0	0	0	0	4	0	0	0
lying	275	.8384	46.459	56.7	44	52	41	36	51	25	24	2	110	15	2	30	3	10	1	16	1	2	0	1	41	23	12	8	0
Lyly	2	.0000	.0209	23.2	0	2	0	0	0	0	0	0	0	0	0	0	0	0	0	0	0	0	0	0	0	0	2	0	0
lymph	7	.0000	.1380	31.4	0	0	0	3	2	0	2	0	0	0	0	0	0	0	0	7	0	0	0	0	0	0	0	0	0
Lyndon	10	.3095	.6976	38.4	0	0	1	0	3	2	3	1	0	0	0	0	0	1	0	0	0	0	0	0	0	1	1	7	0
Lynn	5	.2445	.3109	34.9	1	0	0	1	2	1	0	0	1	3	0	0	1	0	0	0	0	0	0	0	0	0	0	0	0
lynx	4	.4447	.3920	35.9	0	0	0	0	2	1	1	0	1	1	0	0	0	0	1	0	0	0	0	0	1	0	0	0	0
Lyon	10	.2580	.6375	38.0	3	0	0	1	0	3	3	0	1	0	0	0	0	4	0	0	0	0	0	0	0	0	5	0	0
Lyons	3	.2197	.2090	33.2	0	0	0	0	1	0	2	0	2	0	0	0	0	0	0	0	0	0	0	0	0	0	1	0	0
lyras	2	.0000	.0162	22.1	0	0	0	0	0	2	0	0	0	0	0	0	0	0	0	0	2	0	0	0	0	0	0	0	0
lyre	9	.5321	1.0352	40.2	0	0	3	1	3	1	0	1	3	1	0	0	0	0	1	0	2	0	0	0	0	2	0	0	0
lyric	21	.5538	2.3744	43.8	0	0	5	1	3	7	3	2	0	1	1	3	0	0	0	0	7	0	0	0	0	0	7	2	0
lyrical	7	.2228	.3586	35.5	0	0	1	0	1	3	1	1	0	0	0	0	0	0	0	0	5	0	0	0	0	1	0	1	0
lyrics	8	.0000	.0647	28.1	0	0	0	2	3	3	0	0	0	0	0	0	0	0	0	0	8	0	0	0	0	0	0	0	0
Lysander	4	.0000	.0429	26.3	0	0	0	0	0	0	4	0	0	0	0	4	0	0	0	0	0	0	0	0	0	0	0	0	0
LYSANDER	6	.0000	.0644	28.1	0	0	0	0	0	0	6	0	0	0	0	6	0	0	0	0	0	0	0	0	0	0	0	0	0
Lyte	10	.0000	.1172	30.7	0	0	0	0	0	10	0	0	0	0	0	0	0	0	0	0	0	0	0	0	10	0	0	0	0
Lytton	2	.2306	.1140	30.6	0	0	0	0	0	2	0	0	0	1	0	0	0	1	0	0	0	0	0	0	0	0	0	0	0
m	420	.6261	54.150	57.3	29	39	51	36	94	93	43	35	26	12	1	2	208	11	42	16	3	0	0	0	3	33	9	54	0
M	159	.7291	23.406	53.7	20	27	16	7	32	42	8	7	4	7	4	8	81	4	4	11	3	0	0	1	2	8	10	12	0
M**	15	.4501	1.4610	41.6	0	1	1	0	1	1	10	1	2	1	0	0	1	1	0	0	0	0	0	0	1	0	8	1	0
MAin	2	.0000	.0914	29.6	0	0	0	0	0	2	0	0	2	0	0	0	0	0	0	0	0	0	0	0	0	0	0	0	0
m-a-r-k	2	.0000	.0914	29.6	0	0	0	0	0	2	0	0	2	0	0	0	0	0	0	0	0	0	0	0	0	0	0	0	0
m-m-m	3	.2261	.2131	33.3	1	0	1	0	1	0	0	0	2	0	0	0	0	0	0	0	0	0	0	0	1	0	0	0	0
M-11	3	.0000	.0365	25.6	0	0	0	0	3	0	0	0	0	0	0	0	0	0	0	0	0	0	0	0	0	0	0	3	0
m'	3	.0000	.0322	25.1	0	0	0	0	0	3	0	0	0	0	0	3	0	0	0	0	0	0	0	0	0	0	0	0	0
M'Gonegal	2	.0000	.0234	23.7	0	0	0	2	0	0	0	0	0	0	0	0	0	0	0	0	0	0	0	0	2	0	0	0	0
m's	6	.2391	.3300	35.2	0	2	2	2	0	0	0	0	0	1	0	0	0	0	4	1	0	0	0	0	0	0	0	0	0
ma	7	.2887	.5193	37.2	0	1	0	4	1	0	0	1	3	0	0	0	0	0	0	0	3	0	0	0	0	0	1	0	0
Ma	198	.4769	20.653	53.1	1	38	101	20	32	6	0	0	49	0	2	20	0	0	0	0	1	0	0	0	97	23	0	6	0
ma'am	48	.5201	5.4272	47.3	2	11	4	7	7	12	5	0	16	0	1	18	0	0	0	0	0	0	0	0	8	2	0	3	0
Ma'am	8	.4508	.8203	39.1	0	2	0	1	4	1	0	0	3	1	0	0	0	0	0	0	0	0	0	0	1	3	0	0	0
Ma'm	3	.0000	.0352	25.5	0	0	3	0	0	0	0	0	0	0	0	0	0	0	0	0	0	0	0	0	3	0	0	0	0
ma'o	2	.0000	.0234	23.7	0	0	0	2	0	0	0	0	0	0	0	0	0	0	0	0	0	0	0	0	2	0	0	0	0
Ma's	11	.2898	.7686	38.9	0	2	8	0	0	1	0	0	2	0	0	0	0	0	0	0	0	0	0	0	7	1	0	1	0
Maarman	3	.0000	.1370	31.4	0	0	0	0	3	0	0	0	3	0	0	0	0	0	0	0	0	0	0	0	0	0	0	0	0
Mab	3	.0000	.0322	25.1	0	1	0	0	0	0	2	0	0	0	0	3	0	0	0	0	0	0	0	0	0	0	0	0	0
Mabel	23	.3651	2.2145	43.5	19	1	0	2	0	1	0	0	18	2	0	0	3	0	0	0	0	0	0	0	0	0	0	0	0
Mac	22	.3768	1.9053	42.8	2	0	4	0	9	7	0	0	6	2	0	12	0	0	1	0	0	0	0	0	0	0	1	0	0
MAC	17	.0803	.4359	36.4	0	0	0	0	16	0	1	0	0	0	0	16	0	0	0	0	0	0	0	0	0	0	1	0	0
MacArt	2	.0000	.0290	24.6	0	0	2	0	0	0	0	0	0	0	0	0	0	0	0	0	0	0	0	0	0	2	0	0	0
MacArthur	7	.0000	.1361	31.3	0	0	1	0	0	6	0	0	0	0	0	0	0	7	0	0	0	0	0	0	0	0	0	0	0
MacDonald	2	.2411	.1091	30.4	0	0	1	0	1	0	0	0	0	0	0	1	0	0	0	0	1	0	0	0	0	0	0	0	0
MacDowell	4	.0000	.0323	25.1	2	0	0	1	0	1	0	0	0	0	0	0	0	0	0	0	4	0	0	0	0	0	0	0	0
MacGregor	6	.1187	.2583	34.1	0	0	2	0	0	0	4	0	2	0	0	4	0	0	0	0	0	0	0	0	0	0	0	0	0
MacGruder	2	.0000	.0299	24.8	0	0	0	0	0	2	0	0	0	0	0	0	2	0	0	0	0	0	0	0	0	0	0	0	0
MacKenzie	2	.2408	.1204	30.8	1	1	0	0	0	0	0	0	0	0	0	0	0	1	0	0	0	0	0	0	0	1	0	0	0
MacLeish	3	.2425	.1816	32.6	0	0	2	1	0	0	0	0	0	0	0	0	0	2	0	0	0	0	0	0	0	0	0	1	0
MacLeod	4	.0000	.1827	32.6	4	0	0	0	0	0	0	0	4	0	0	0	0	0	0	0	0	0	0	0	0	0	0	0	0
MacSparrow	14	.0000	.6396	38.1	0	14	0	0	0	0	0	0	14	0	0	0	0	0	0	0	0	0	0	0	0	0	0	0	0
Mac's	2	.0000	.0215	23.3	0	0	0	0	0	2	0	0	0	0	0	2	0	0	0	0	0	0	0	0	0	0	0	0	0
macabre	2	.2433	.1158	30.6	0	0	0	1	1	0	0	0	0	0	0	0	0	0	0	0	0	0	0	0	0	1	0	1	0
Macabre	2	.0000	.0162	22.1	1	1	0	0	0	0	0	0	0	0	0	0	0	0	0	0	2	0	0	0	0	0	0	0	0
macadam	4	.2986	.2903	34.6	0	1	1	1	0	0	1	0	1	2	0	0	0	0	0	0	0	0	0	0	1	0	0	0	0
macaroni	37	.5516	4.6325	46.7	10	20	1	1	2	3	0	0	28	2	0	0	0	2	0	1	1	0	2	0	0	0	0	1	0
Macaulay's	4	.2201	.2150	33.3	0	0	0	0	0	4	0	0	0	0	0	0	0	0	0	0	0	0	0	0	0	3	1	0	0
Macauley	4	.0000	.1827	32.6	0	0	0	0	0	4	0	0	4	0	0	0	0	0	0	0	0	0	0	0	0	0	0	0	0
Macbeth	9	.1457	.3657	35.6	0	5	0	0	1	2	1	0	0	0	0	1	0	0	0	0	0	0	0	0	0	8	0	0	0
Maccabee	2	.0000	.0162	22.1	0	0	0	0	0	2	0	0	0	0	0	0	0	0	0	0	2	0	0	0	0	0	0	0	0
Macdonald	7	.0000	.0733	28.6	0	0	3	0	0	4	0	0	0	0	0	0	0	0	0	0	0	0	0	0	0	0	7	0	0
mace	2	.2437	.1129	30.5	0	0	0	0	1	0	0	1	0	0	0	0	0	0	0	0	0	0	0	0	0	0	1	1	0
Mace	2	.2446	.1142	30.6	0	0	0	0	1	1	0	0	0	0	0	0	0	0	0	0	0	0	0	0	1	0	0	1	0
Macedon	2	.2446	.1123	30.5	0	0	0	0	0	0	1	1	0	1	0	0	0	0	0	0	0	0	0	0	0	0	1	0	0
Macedonia	13	.2687	.8745	39.4	0	1	0	2	7	0	3	0	1	0	0	0	0	9	0	0	0	0	0	0	0	0	0	3	0
Macedonian	2	.0000	.0389	25.9	0	0	0	0	2	0	0	0	0	0	0	0	0	2	0	0	0	0	0	0	0	0	0	0	0
MACGREGOR	9	.0000	.0966	29.8	0	0	0	0	0	0	9	0	0	0	0	9	0	0	0	0	0	0	0	0	0	0	0	0	0
Mach	3	.3847	.2496	34.0	1	0	0	0	2	0	0	0	0	0	0	0	0	0	0	0	0	0	0	0	0	1	1	1	0
mache	2	.2351	.1166	30.7	0	0	1	0	0	1	0	0	0	0	0	0	0	1	0	0	0	0	0	0	0	0	0	1	0
Machiavelli	7	.2220	.3806	35.8	0	0	5	0	0	0	2	0	0	0	0	0	0	0	0	0	0	0	0	0	0	5	0	2	0
Machiavelli's	3	.2043	.1486	31.7	0	0	3	0	0	0	0	0	0	0	0	0	0	0	0	0	0	0	0	0	0	1	2	0	0
machine	861	.7803	135.34	61.3	127	67	145	85	201	100	110	26	138	19	6	24	166	84	6	70	36	2	60	82	14	53	60	41	0
Machine	13	.5598	1.5389	41.9	0	1	1	0	4	7	0	0	3	0	0	0	3	0	0	0	2	1	0	0	0	0	1	3	0
machine-baste	2	.0000	.0064	18.1	0	0	0	0	1	1	0	0	0	0	0	0	0	0	0	0	0	0	2	0	0	0	0	0	0
machine-gun	5	.3829	.4333	36.4	0	0	1	1	0	3	0	0	1	0	1	1	0	1	0	0	0	0	0	0	0	1	0	0	0
machine-made	3	.2950	.1973	33.0	0	0	0	0	0	0	3	0	0	0	0	0	0	1	0	0	0	0	1	0	0	0	1	0	0
machine-stitch	5	.0000	.0161	22.1	0	0	0	0	0	4	1	0	0	0	0	0	0	0	0	0	0	0	5	0	0	0	0	0	0
machine-tool	3	.2227	.1495	31.7	0	0	0	0	2	0	1	0	0	0	0	0	0	0	0	0	0	0	0	1	0	0	2	0	0
machined	4	.2199	.1933	32.9	0	0	0	0	1	1	2	0	0	0	0	1	0	0	0	0	0	0	0	2	0	0	1	0	0
machinery	221	.6442	29.412	54.7	22	16	43	33	54	23	27	3	20	2	1	5	0	119	4	3	5	0	0	11	1	4	38	8	0
machines	509	.7278	75.137	58.8	65	68	89	59	102	54	59	13	40	8	2	8	18	165	6	68	8	0	9	47	4	27	72	27	0
Machines	3	.3771	.2489	34.0	0	0	0	0	3	0	0	0	0	0	0	1	0	0	0	1	0	0	0	0	0	0	0	1	0
machining	4	.0000	.0101	20.0	0	0	0	0	0	1	3	0	0	0	0	0	0	0	0	0	0	0	0	4	0	0	0	0	0
machinist	5	.4073	.4312	36.3	0	0	0	0	3	0	2	0	0	0	0	0	1	0	0	0	0	0	0	1	0	0	1	2	0
Machu	3	.0000	.0314	25.0	0	0	0	0	0	0	3	0	0	0	0	0	0	0	0	0	0	0	0	0	0	0	3	0	0
Mack	47	.3140	3.9460	46.0	29	6	0	12	0	0	0	0	27	1	0	0	0	1	0	0	0	0	0	0	0	18	0	0	0

8G lyceum
3A Lyceum
7R Lycoming
5P Lydda
5A Lyddy
8R Lydell
3A Lydia's
9D lyin'
9B Lyman
7D lymph-lined
7D lymphatic
8A lynch
8R Lynch
8R Lynchburg
8A lynched
4J Lyndol
6E Lynn's
7H Lynx
5Q lynxes
3K Lyonel
XR Lyonsdale
8Q Lyra
8J lyricist
8J Lyrics
7P Lysistrata's
8N Lyte's
8N Lytes
8N Lytes'
4P Lyttle
7A L12B
7R L4J
7R L5
8A MArket
5A m-e-a-t
3A m-m
6N m-m-mare
6N m-m-maybe
7A m-m-meet
6N m-m-months
3A m-merry
4A m-o-o-n
7R M-1
3B M-1000
7R M/T
9E m/3
3A mlk
7D Ma-ry
8A Ma'll
7A ma'm
6N Ma'o
6J Ma'oz
7N ma's
3A maa-a-a-a
3A maa-a-a-a-a
6A maah
3F Maas
5B MacAdam
9Q MacAlpin
8R MacCartans
5P MacCool
5A MacDermott
9A MacDougall
8E MacGruder's
4P MacKenzie's
5F MacLeish's
8B MacMahon
7D MacMillan's
6A MacPhersons
6A MacPhersons'
7Q macaques
5P Macartney
4R macaws
8P Macbeth's
8Q Macdonald's
8F Macdonough
9R Macedonians
7R macehead
8R Macgillycuddy's
9D mach
3P Mach-2
7P Machiavellian
9M machinability
3P machine-age
7M machine-built
6R machine-gun-like
5N machine-gunning
8D machine-like
9L machine-stitched
8L machine-worked
7J machine's
8R machinelike
3A MACHINERY
9M machinists
8M machinists'
XR Machold
5A Macias
9B macintosh

Word Type	F	D	U	SFI	3 Gr 3	4 Gr 4	5 Gr 5	6 Gr 6	7 Gr 7	8 Gr 8	9 Gr 9	X UnGr	A Read	B Eng & Gr	C Comp	D Lit	E Math	F Soc Stud	G Spell	H Sci	J Music	K Art	L Home Ec	M Shop	N Lib F	P Lib NF	Q Lib Ref	R Mag	S Rel
Mack's	4	.2174	.2134	33.3	2	0	0	1	0	0	1	0	0	1	0	0	0	0	0	0	0	0	0	0	0	3	0	0	0
Mackenzie	2	.2441	.1127	30.5	0	0	1	0	1	0	0	0	0	0	0	0	0	0	0	0	0	0	0	0	1	0	1	0	0
mackerel	15	.6415	1.9680	42.9	3	4	0	2	6	0	0	0	0	3	1	0	0	3	0	3	0	0	0	0	2	2	1	0	0
Mackinac	8	.3706	.6802	38.3	0	0	3	1	0	2	1	1	1	0	0	0	0	3	0	1	0	0	0	0	0	0	3	0	0
mackinaw	2	.0000	.0215	23.3	0	0	0	0	0	0	0	2	0	0	0	2	0	0	0	0	0	0	0	0	0	0	0	0	0
Mackintosh	2	.1698	.1133	30.5	0	0	1	1	0	0	0	0	1	0	0	0	0	0	0	0	0	0	0	0	0	0	1	0	0
Maclay	3	.1277	.1363	31.3	0	0	0	0	3	0	0	0	1	0	0	0	0	0	0	0	0	0	0	0	0	0	0	2	0
Macon	4	.4791	.4053	36.1	1	0	0	0	1	2	0	0	0	0	0	1	0	1	0	0	0	0	0	0	0	1	1	0	0
Macroom	2	.0000	.0290	24.6	0	2	0	0	0	0	0	0	0	0	0	0	0	0	0	0	0	0	0	0	0	2	0	0	0
Macy's	2	.2152	.1357	31.3	0	1	0	0	0	1	0	0	1	0	0	0	0	1	0	0	0	0	0	0	0	0	0	0	0
mad	170	.7910	27.324	54.4	31	32	14	18	40	19	14	2	67	4	2	25	0	10	1	0	4	1	0	0	26	14	5	11	0
Mad	3	.3450	.2505	34.0	0	1	0	1	0	0	0	1	1	0	0	0	0	0	0	0	0	0	0	0	1	1	0	0	0
Madagascar	8	.0908	.2270	33.6	0	0	0	1	7	0	0	0	0	0	0	0	0	1	0	0	0	0	0	0	0	0	7	0	0
madam	34	.5142	3.6771	45.7	1	6	7	1	2	9	8	0	4	0	0	14	0	0	1	0	6	0	0	0	7	1	1	0	0
Madam	21	.5319	2.3668	43.7	1	1	4	0	6	3	6	0	4	1	0	8	0	0	0	0	2	0	0	0	4	0	0	2	0
madame	3	.3380	.2439	33.9	1	0	0	0	0	0	2	0	1	1	0	1	0	0	0	0	0	0	0	0	0	0	0	0	0
Madame	52	.6076	6.6652	48.2	0	16	5	12	8	1	10	0	17	3	0	13	0	0	0	0	2	0	0	0	11	0	3	3	0
Madame's	3	.3394	.2451	33.9	0	2	0	0	0	0	1	0	1	0	0	1	0	0	0	0	0	0	0	0	1	0	0	0	0
maddened	4	.3713	.3634	35.6	0	0	0	1	2	1	0	0	2	0	0	1	0	0	0	0	0	0	0	0	1	0	0	0	0
madder	7	.2177	.3896	35.9	1	3	0	0	3	0	0	0	1	1	0	0	0	0	0	0	0	0	0	0	5	0	0	0	0
maddest	3	.1250	.1342	31.3	1	0	1	1	0	0	0	0	1	0	0	0	0	0	0	0	0	0	0	0	2	0	0	0	0
made	7073	.9482	1325.6	71.2	1315	1125	974	985	1145	775	586	168	1747	285	41	312	218	846	269	922	255	234	157	194	403	512	341	331	6
Made	4	.2975	.2883	34.6	0	2	0	0	2	0	0	0	1	1	0	0	0	0	0	0	0	0	0	0	0	0	2	0	0
made-to-order	2	.0000	.0914	29.6	0	0	2	0	0	0	0	0	2	0	0	0	0	0	0	0	0	0	0	0	0	0	0	0	0
made-up	2	.0000	.0219	23.4	1	0	1	0	0	0	0	0	0	2	0	0	0	0	0	0	0	0	0	0	0	0	0	0	0
Madeleine	3	.3844	.2487	34.0	0	0	1	0	1	0	0	1	0	1	0	0	0	0	0	0	0	0	0	0	0	1	1	0	0
Madeline	5	.1820	.2261	33.5	4	0	0	0	0	1	0	0	0	1	0	0	0	0	0	0	0	0	0	0	4	0	0	0	0
Mademoiselle	7	.3854	.6821	38.3	4	0	0	0	0	3	0	0	5	0	0	1	0	0	0	0	1	0	0	0	0	0	0	0	0
Madero	2	.0000	.0243	23.9	0	0	0	0	2	0	0	0	0	0	0	0	0	0	0	0	0	0	0	0	0	0	0	2	0
Madge	15	.0814	.3888	35.9	0	0	0	0	14	1	0	0	0	0	0	14	0	0	0	0	0	0	0	0	1	0	0	0	0
Madge's	3	.0000	.0322	25.1	0	0	0	0	3	0	0	0	0	0	0	3	0	0	0	0	0	0	0	0	0	0	0	0	0
MADHAV	5	.0000	.0537	27.3	0	0	0	0	0	0	5	0	0	0	0	5	0	0	0	0	0	0	0	0	0	0	0	0	0
madhouse	3	.3465	.2515	34.0	0	0	0	0	2	0	1	0	1	0	0	0	0	0	0	0	0	0	0	0	0	1	0	1	0
Madison	43	.6986	6.1874	47.9	4	5	4	1	9	13	6	1	11	2	1	0	1	9	0	0	0	0	0	1	0	4	2	12	0
Madjapahit	2	.0000	.0243	23.9	0	0	0	2	0	0	0	0	0	0	0	0	0	0	0	0	0	0	0	0	0	0	0	2	0
madly	19	.6069	2.4889	44.0	4	2	2	2	3	3	2	1	10	1	0	1	0	0	0	0	0	0	0	0	3	2	0	2	0
madman	6	.1717	.3427	35.3	0	0	1	1	0	2	2	0	3	0	0	3	0	0	0	0	0	0	0	0	0	0	0	0	0
madmen	4	.2708	.2760	34.4	0	0	1	0	0	2	1	0	1	0	0	2	0	1	0	0	0	0	0	0	0	0	0	0	0
madness	14	.5780	1.6877	42.3	0	2	0	1	2	2	6	1	2	1	0	3	0	0	0	0	0	0	0	0	0	2	3	3	0
Madonna	4	.0250	.0696	28.4	2	2	0	0	0	0	0	0	1	0	0	0	0	0	0	0	0	3	0	0	0	0	0	0	0
Madre	6	.0000	.1167	30.7	0	0	0	3	3	0	0	0	0	0	0	0	0	6	0	0	0	0	0	0	0	0	0	0	0
Madrid	11	.4351	1.1128	40.5	3	1	1	2	4	0	0	0	4	0	0	0	0	5	0	0	0	0	0	0	0	1	1	0	0
madrigal	4	.3627	.3135	35.0	0	0	2	2	0	0	0	0	0	2	0	0	0	0	0	0	1	0	0	0	0	1	0	0	0
madrigals	2	.2407	.1090	30.4	0	0	1	1	0	0	0	0	0	1	0	0	0	0	0	0	1	0	0	0	0	0	0	0	0
Mae	3	.0997	.1145	30.6	0	0	1	1	1	0	0	0	1	0	0	0	0	0	2	0	0	0	0	0	0	0	0	0	0
Maestro	15	.1612	.8154	39.1	0	7	0	0	8	0	0	0	7	0	0	8	0	0	0	0	0	0	0	0	0	0	0	0	0
Maeterlinck	3	.2387	.1708	32.3	0	1	2	0	0	0	0	0	0	0	0	0	0	0	0	0	0	0	0	0	0	2	1	0	0
Mafatu	62	.0837	2.0904	43.2	0	13	0	49	0	0	0	0	13	0	0	0	0	0	0	0	0	0	0	0	49	0	0	0	0
Mafatu's	10	.0804	.3283	35.2	0	2	0	8	0	0	0	0	2	0	0	0	0	0	0	0	0	0	0	0	8	0	0	0	0
Mafia	2	.0000	.0243	23.9	0	0	0	0	0	1	1	0	0	0	0	0	0	0	0	0	0	0	0	0	0	0	0	2	0
mag	2	.0000	.0243	23.9	0	0	0	2	0	0	0	0	0	0	0	0	0	0	0	0	0	0	0	0	0	0	0	2	0
magazine	118	.8561	20.123	53.0	3	21	17	5	30	19	20	3	17	15	4	5	3	6	8	3	1	4	2	4	3	9	4	30	0
Magazine	5	.4702	.4939	36.9	0	0	0	1	1	1	1	1	0	1	0	0	0	0	0	0	0	0	0	0	0	1	1	2	0
magazine's	2	.2442	.1134	30.5	0	0	0	0	0	1	0	1	0	1	0	0	0	0	0	0	0	0	0	0	0	0	0	1	0
magazines	104	.7556	15.843	52.0	5	16	10	10	27	18	14	4	13	11	0	4	5	15	4	8	0	8	10	5	2	6	2	11	0
Magazines'	2	.0000	.0243	23.9	0	0	0	2	0	0	0	0	0	0	0	0	0	0	0	0	0	0	0	0	0	0	0	2	0
Magda	2	.0000	.0215	23.3	0	0	0	0	2	0	0	0	0	0	0	2	0	0	0	0	0	0	0	0	0	0	0	0	0
Magdalena	5	.0000	.0972	29.9	0	0	0	5	0	0	0	0	0	0	0	0	0	5	0	0	0	0	0	0	0	0	0	0	0
Magdalene	2	.2407	.1138	30.6	0	0	0	0	2	0	0	0	0	0	0	1	0	0	0	0	0	0	0	0	0	1	0	0	0
Magdalenian	2	.0000	.0290	24.6	0	0	0	0	0	0	0	2	0	0	0	0	0	0	0	0	0	0	0	0	0	2	0	0	0
Magdeburg	4	.1737	.1745	32.4	1	0	0	0	0	0	3	0	0	0	0	0	0	0	0	0	0	0	0	0	0	1	3	0	0
Magee	2	.0000	.0914	29.6	0	0	0	0	2	0	0	0	2	0	0	0	0	0	0	0	0	0	0	0	0	0	0	0	0
Magellan	41	.5803	5.0136	47.0	7	9	16	6	2	0	1	0	7	0	1	0	0	14	2	1	0	0	0	0	0	1	13	2	0
Magellan's	20	.5042	2.2084	43.4	1	4	9	4	1	0	1	0	4	0	0	0	0	11	1	1	0	0	0	0	0	0	2	1	0
magenta	3	.3870	.2486	34.0	0	0	0	1	0	0	2	0	0	0	0	1	0	0	0	0	0	0	0	0	0	0	1	1	0
Maggie	22	.2070	1.6387	42.1	16	1	0	0	0	3	0	2	20	0	0	0	0	0	0	0	0	0	0	0	0	0	0	2	0
Magi	5	.0000	.2284	33.6	0	0	0	0	0	5	0	0	5	0	0	0	0	0	0	0	0	0	0	0	0	0	0	0	0
magic	279	.8881	49.539	56.9	64	52	49	45	33	17	11	8	120	19	2	16	30	14	3	9	12	1	1	0	4	25	7	16	0
Magic	14	.3686	1.1704	40.7	3	1	8	0	0	1	1	0	2	0	0	0	8	0	0	0	3	0	0	0	0	0	0	1	0
magical	22	.6172	2.8115	44.5	1	4	0	1	12	1	2	1	3	0	0	5	0	1	0	2	1	0	0	0	0	2	6	2	0
magically	6	.3317	.4449	36.5	1	1	1	1	2	0	0	0	0	0	0	0	0	0	0	0	0	0	0	0	0	4	1	1	0
magician	44	.5436	5.1933	47.2	9	5	9	6	8	1	2	4	18	3	6	2	0	0	1	1	2	0	0	0	5	6	0	0	0
Magician	9	.2619	.5387	37.3	1	7	0	0	0	0	1	0	0	0	0	0	0	0	0	0	1	0	0	0	7	0	0	1	0
magician's	3	.0000	.1370	31.4	1	0	0	2	0	0	0	0	3	0	0	0	0	0	0	0	0	0	0	0	0	0	0	0	0
magicians	9	.5580	1.0966	40.4	0	0	1	4	0	1	1	2	4	1	0	0	1	0	0	0	0	0	0	0	0	2	1	0	0
magistrate	6	.4441	.5992	37.8	0	0	2	1	0	2	0	1	2	1	0	2	0	0	0	0	0	0	0	0	0	0	0	1	0
magistrate's	4	.3212	.3104	34.9	2	0	1	0	0	1	0	0	1	0	0	1	0	0	0	0	0	0	0	0	0	2	0	0	0
magistrates	5	.4693	.4986	37.0	0	1	0	0	1	1	2	0	0	0	0	0	0	1	0	0	0	0	0	0	1	2	1	0	0
Maglie	2	.0000	.0290	24.6	2	0	0	0	0	0	0	0	0	0	0	0	0	0	0	0	0	0	0	0	0	2	0	0	0
magma	44	.1683	2.1515	43.3	0	5	18	1	2	2	16	0	0	0	0	0	0	0	1	41	0	0	0	0	0	0	2	0	0
Magna	9	.4649	.9914	40.0	1	0	0	6	0	2	0	0	6	0	0	0	0	1	1	0	0	0	0	0	0	1	0	0	0
magnanimity	2	.2152	.1357	31.3	0	0	0	0	0	2	0	0	1	0	0	0	0	1	0	0	0	0	0	0	0	0	0	0	0
magnanimous	2	.2401	.1133	30.5	0	0	0	1	0	0	1	0	0	0	0	0	0	0	0	0	0	0	0	0	0	1	1	0	0
magnesia	3	.0000	.0591	27.7	0	0	0	0	0	2	0	1	0	0	0	0	0	0	0	3	0	0	0	0	0	0	0	0	0
Magnesia	5	.3157	.3891	35.9	0	0	0	3	1	0	1	0	1	0	0	0	0	0	0	3	0	0	0	0	0	0	1	0	0
magnesite	2	.0000	.0389	25.9	0	0	0	0	2	0	0	0	0	0	0	0	0	2	0	0	0	0	0	0	0	0	0	0	0
magnesium	31	.4902	3.2635	45.1	1	6	2	1	9	5	2	5	2	0	0	0	0	4	0	11	0	0	0	0	0	0	7	7	0
magnet	228	.5807	27.769	54.4	121	10	11	33	24	15	14	0	13	2	1	1	0	3	0	136	4	0	0	12	0	38	15	3	0
magnet's	4	.3647	.3180	35.0	1	0	0	0	3	0	0	0	0	0	0	0	0	0	0	0	0	0	0	0	0	1	1	2	0
Magnete	3	.1813	.1402	31.5	0	0	0	1	2	0	0	0	0	0	0	0	0	0	0	1	0	0	0	0	0	0	2	0	0
Magnetes	2	.0000	.0394	26.0	0	0	0	2	0	0	0	0	0	0	0	0	0	0	0	2	0	0	0	0	0	0	0	0	0
magnetic	164	.5266	18.204	52.6	12	8	6	25	40	27	44	2	6	0	0	0	0	1	1	83	4	0	0	17	0	7	35	10	0
Magnetic	16	.1235	.6566	38.2	0	0	0	15	1	0	0	0	0	0	0	0	0	0	0	15	0	0	0	0	0	0	1	0	0
magnetism	48	.4700	4.8589	46.9	5	3	0	17	11	5	7	0	2	0	0	0	1	0	0	29	1	0	0	6	0	1	6	2	0
magnetite	12	.2025	.6796	38.3	0	0	0	5	1	3	2	1	1	0	0	0	0	0	0	10	0	0	0	0	0	0	1	0	0

4N mackereel
8R Mackey
6A mackintosh
3N Mackrelmint
6H Macmillan
4P Macons
5Q Macquart
7P Macsen
9E Macy
5A MAD
8A maddening
5N Maddox
3A MADE
8A made-over
6F Madeira
XR Madeiras
7P madest
9D Madhav
9D Madhav's
XR Madhukar
4A Madison's
9J madly-moving
4K Madonna's
3A madras
XR Madras
7N madreporical
7R Madsen
7D madwoman
8F madwomen
7J maestoso
7D Maestro's
5P Maffeo
6A Magarac
9Q Magdeburg's
9Q Magdeburgers
XH Magellanic
XR Maggie's
9D maggots
7Q magic-carpet
7D magic-makers
9B Magical
7D magics
6A MAGIQUE
9Q Magister
9R magisterially
7P Magistrate
9F Magistrates'
7N magnates
7Q magnes
7Q Magnes
4Q Magnet
9Q magnetic-extraction
9B magnetisms
7Q magnetization

Word Type	F	D	U	SFI	3 Gr 3	4 Gr 4	5 Gr 5	6 Gr 6	7 Gr 7	8 Gr 8	9 Gr 9	X UnGr	A Read	B Eng & Gr	C Comp	D Lit	E Math	F Soc Stud	G Spell	H Sci	J Music	K Art	L Home Ec	M Shop	N Lib F	P Lib NF	Q Lib Ref	R Mag	S Rel
magnetize	5	.2213	.2870	34.6	0	0	1	0	1	0	3	0	0	0	0	0	0	0	0	4	0	0	0	0	0	0	1	0	0
magnetized	23	.3756	1.8656	42.7	0	2	0	1	12	1	7	0	0	0	0	0	0	0	0	4	1	0	0	1	0	0	16	1	0
magnetizing	2	.2278	.1128	30.5	0	0	0	0	1	1	0	0	0	0	0	0	0	0	0	1	0	0	0	0	0	0	1	0	0
magneto	4	.0000	.0101	20.0	0	0	0	0	4	0	0	0	0	0	0	0	0	0	0	0	0	0	0	4	0	0	0	0	0
magnets	125	.4404	11.942	50.8	49	1	4	30	23	9	9	0	4	0	0	0	0	1	0	63	0	0	0	18	0	27	10	2	0
magnification	9	.3128	.6626	38.2	0	1	0	0	5	1	1	1	0	0	0	1	0	0	0	7	0	0	0	0	0	0	1	0	0
magnifications	2	.0000	.0209	23.2	0	0	0	0	2	0	0	0	0	0	0	0	0	0	0	0	0	0	0	0	0	0	2	0	0
magnificence	3	.3783	.2436	33.9	0	0	0	1	2	0	0	0	0	0	0	0	0	0	1	0	0	0	0	0	0	1	1	0	0
magnificent	73	.7731	11.431	50.6	6	3	7	18	17	8	7	7	17	0	0	5	0	7	2	6	1	3	0	0	7	7	9	9	0
magnificently	4	.3663	.3128	35.0	0	0	1	0	1	2	0	0	0	0	1	0	0	0	0	0	0	0	0	0	0	1	1	1	0
magnificient	2	.2285	.1129	30.5	0	0	0	0	1	1	0	0	0	0	0	0	0	1	0	0	0	0	0	0	0	0	1	0	0
magnifico	2	.0000	.0914	29.6	0	0	0	2	0	0	0	0	2	0	0	0	0	0	0	0	0	0	0	0	0	0	0	0	0
magnified	12	.4908	1.2679	41.0	0	0	1	3	5	3	0	0	1	0	0	3	2	0	0	5	0	0	0	0	0	0	1	0	0
magnifier	9	.1601	.4259	36.3	0	3	0	1	2	1	1	1	0	0	0	0	0	0	0	8	0	0	0	0	0	0	0	1	0
magnifies	4	.4522	.4044	36.1	0	0	0	2	1	0	0	1	1	0	0	0	0	0	0	1	0	0	0	0	1	0	0	1	0
magnify	3	.1847	.1428	31.5	0	0	2	0	0	0	0	1	0	2	0	0	0	0	0	1	0	0	0	0	0	0	0	0	0
magnifying	47	.5819	5.7427	47.6	14	14	9	3	4	3	0	0	2	2	1	1	0	2	0	32	0	1	0	0	0	5	1	0	0
magnitude	47	.4638	4.6950	46.7	0	1	0	1	15	10	14	6	0	1	0	0	17	0	0	21	0	0	0	0	0	0	6	2	0
magnitudes	5	.4394	.4697	36.7	0	0	0	0	3	1	1	0	0	0	0	0	1	0	0	1	0	0	0	0	0	0	2	1	0
magnolia	4	.3755	.3686	35.7	3	0	0	0	1	0	0	0	2	0	0	0	0	0	0	0	0	0	0	0	1	1	0	0	0
Magnolia	2	.2427	.1152	30.6	2	0	0	0	0	0	0	0	0	0	0	0	0	0	0	0	0	0	0	0	1	1	0	0	0
magnum	2	.2437	.1129	30.5	0	0	0	0	2	0	0	0	0	0	0	0	0	0	0	0	0	0	0	0	0	0	1	1	0
magnus	2	.2446	.1123	30.5	0	0	1	0	1	0	0	0	0	1	0	0	0	0	0	0	0	0	0	0	0	0	1	0	0
Magnus	11	.3935	1.0110	40.0	0	0	0	1	5	0	0	5	4	0	0	1	0	0	0	0	0	0	0	0	0	0	1	5	0
Magnus's	2	.0000	.0243	23.9	0	0	0	0	0	0	0	2	0	0	0	0	0	0	0	0	0	0	0	0	0	0	0	2	0
Magog	3	.0000	.0352	25.5	0	0	0	2	1	0	0	0	0	0	0	0	0	0	0	0	0	0	0	0	3	0	0	0	0
Magpie	3	.0000	.1370	31.4	0	3	0	0	0	0	0	0	3	0	0	0	0	0	0	0	0	0	0	0	0	0	0	0	0
Magritte	2	.0000	.0037	15.7	0	0	0	0	2	0	0	0	0	0	0	0	0	0	0	0	0	2	0	0	0	0	0	0	0
Magua	9	.0000	.1055	30.2	0	0	0	0	9	0	0	0	0	0	0	0	0	0	0	0	0	0	0	0	9	0	0	0	0
maguey	6	.0000	.1167	30.7	0	0	0	6	0	0	0	0	0	0	0	0	0	6	0	0	0	0	0	0	0	0	0	0	0
Magyar	2	.0000	.0389	25.9	0	0	0	1	1	0	0	0	0	0	0	0	0	2	0	0	0	0	0	0	0	0	0	0	0
Magyars	4	.0000	.0778	28.9	0	0	0	3	1	0	0	0	0	0	0	0	0	4	0	0	0	0	0	0	0	0	0	0	0
MAH	2	.0000	.0299	24.8	0	0	2	0	0	0	0	0	0	0	0	0	2	0	0	0	0	0	0	0	0	0	0	0	0
Mahatma	3	.2321	.1635	32.1	0	0	0	0	0	3	0	0	0	0	0	0	0	0	0	0	0	0	0	0	0	0	1	2	0
Mahler	2	.2437	.1129	30.5	0	0	0	0	1	0	1	0	0	0	0	0	0	0	0	0	0	0	0	0	0	0	1	1	0
mahn	4	.0000	.0486	26.9	0	0	4	0	0	0	0	0	0	0	0	0	0	0	0	0	0	0	0	0	0	0	0	4	0
mahogany	13	.5046	1.3818	41.4	1	4	1	1	3	0	3	0	0	0	0	4	0	6	0	0	0	0	0	1	0	1	1	0	0
Mahoney	2	.0000	.0215	23.3	0	0	0	0	2	0	0	0	0	0	0	2	0	0	0	0	0	0	0	0	0	0	0	0	0
Mahratta	2	.0000	.0209	23.2	0	0	2	0	0	0	0	0	0	0	0	0	0	0	0	0	0	0	0	0	0	0	2	0	0
Mai	2	.0000	.0209	23.2	0	0	2	0	0	0	0	0	0	0	0	0	0	0	0	0	0	0	0	0	0	0	2	0	0
maid	62	.6018	7.8223	48.9	6	8	5	10	9	7	16	1	16	2	0	22	1	0	1	0	9	0	0	0	2	6	1	2	0
MAID	2	.0000	.0215	23.3	0	0	0	0	0	2	0	0	0	0	0	2	0	0	0	0	0	0	0	0	0	0	0	0	0
maiden	57	.5400	6.7767	48.3	0	11	7	14	13	8	4	0	28	2	0	4	0	0	0	0	13	0	0	0	4	6	0	0	0
Maiden	2	.2303	.1079	30.3	0	0	0	0	1	1	0	0	0	0	0	0	0	0	0	0	1	0	0	0	0	1	0	0	0
maiden's	5	.3087	.3851	35.9	0	0	0	4	0	0	1	0	2	0	0	1	0	0	0	0	2	0	0	0	0	0	0	0	0
maidens	16	.5675	1.9150	42.8	0	5	0	4	4	3	0	0	3	0	0	3	0	2	0	0	3	0	0	0	1	4	0	0	0
maids	21	.5401	2.4345	43.9	0	5	1	3	4	0	8	0	6	1	0	8	0	1	0	0	2	0	0	0	1	2	0	0	0
mail	203	.7697	31.758	55.0	41	33	31	25	34	25	12	2	55	13	11	11	18	41	5	3	2	0	0	0	7	27	2	8	0
Mail	10	.6069	1.2762	41.1	0	2	1	1	5	0	0	1	3	1	0	0	0	0	0	0	1	0	0	0	2	0	2	1	0
mail-order	4	.2393	.3005	34.8	1	0	2	0	1	0	0	0	3	0	0	1	0	0	0	0	0	0	0	0	0	0	0	0	0
mailbag	4	.0290	.0736	28.7	4	0	0	0	0	0	0	0	1	0	3	0	0	0	0	0	0	0	0	0	0	0	0	0	0
mailbags	2	.2152	.1357	31.3	1	0	0	1	0	0	0	0	1	0	0	0	0	1	0	0	0	0	0	0	0	0	0	0	0
mailbox	9	.4628	.9509	39.8	5	1	2	0	0	1	0	0	4	1	1	0	0	2	0	0	0	0	0	0	1	0	0	0	0
mailboxes	5	.4790	.5425	37.3	3	0	0	0	1	1	0	0	2	0	0	0	1	1	0	0	0	0	0	0	0	0	0	1	0
Maile	8	.0000	.3655	35.6	8	0	0	0	0	0	0	0	8	0	0	0	0	0	0	0	0	0	0	0	0	0	0	0	0
mailed	17	.6755	2.3656	43.7	1	2	2	2	3	2	3	2	3	4	0	0	2	2	1	2	0	0	0	0	0	1	0	2	0
mailing	13	.5306	1.4412	41.6	2	0	0	0	5	0	1	5	0	0	0	1	1	0	0	5	0	1	0	0	0	1	4	0	0
mailings	3	.2159	.1532	31.9	0	0	0	0	3	0	0	0	0	0	0	0	0	0	0	0	0	0	0	0	0	0	2	1	0
Maillol	2	.0000	.0037	15.7	0	0	0	0	0	0	2	0	0	0	0	0	0	0	0	0	0	2	0	0	0	0	0	0	0
mailman	24	.4005	2.2837	43.6	16	3	1	0	2	1	1	0	12	7	3	0	1	0	0	0	0	0	0	0	0	0	0	1	0
mailman's	2	.1497	.1046	30.2	1	1	0	0	0	0	0	0	1	0	0	0	0	0	1	0	0	0	0	0	0	0	0	0	0
mailmen	4	.3318	.2887	34.6	1	3	0	0	0	0	0	0	0	1	0	0	0	0	2	0	0	0	0	0	0	1	0	0	0
mails	8	.2535	.4869	36.9	6	0	0	0	1	1	0	0	0	0	0	0	0	1	0	0	0	0	0	0	0	6	0	1	0
maim	2	.1948	.1250	31.0	0	0	0	0	1	0	1	0	1	0	0	0	0	0	0	0	0	0	0	0	0	1	0	0	0
Maimoune	5	.0000	.0586	27.7	0	0	5	0	0	0	0	0	0	0	0	0	0	0	0	0	0	0	0	0	5	0	0	0	0
main	926	.8937	164.78	62.2	74	110	132	136	223	119	112	20	251	124	27	19	10	164	14	73	38	4	30	14	11	40	58	49	0
Main	43	.7747	6.7589	48.3	13	11	9	1	2	2	4	1	11	4	0	2	8	5	0	0	1	0	1	0	1	6	0	4	0
Maine	77	.7799	12.123	50.8	6	3	17	5	14	22	9	1	10	8	2	3	0	29	1	4	2	0	0	0	2	4	6	6	0
mainland	73	.7438	11.043	50.4	8	9	22	11	14	4	2	3	11	1	0	1	0	28	3	2	1	1	0	0	1	11	7	6	0
Mainland	2	.0000	.0914	29.6	0	0	2	0	0	0	0	0	2	0	0	0	0	0	0	0	0	0	0	0	0	0	0	0	0
mainly	163	.8240	26.875	54.3	11	8	30	14	52	22	23	3	11	4	0	2	1	41	2	31	11	1	3	2	3	8	32	11	0
mainmast	7	.3817	.6819	38.3	0	1	0	3	1	2	0	0	5	0	0	1	0	0	0	0	0	0	0	0	0	1	0	0	0
mains	8	.3174	.6481	38.1	4	3	0	0	0	0	1	0	3	0	0	0	0	0	0	4	0	0	0	1	0	0	0	0	0
mainsail	9	.5008	.9928	40.0	0	0	0	4	1	3	1	0	3	0	0	0	0	1	0	0	0	0	0	0	3	0	1	1	0
mainspring	2	.1698	.1133	30.5	0	0	1	0	0	0	1	0	1	0	0	0	0	0	0	0	0	0	0	0	0	0	1	0	0
mainstay	4	.4482	.4009	36.0	1	0	0	1	2	0	0	0	1	0	0	0	0	0	0	1	0	0	0	0	0	0	1	1	0
mainstream	7	.4331	.6456	38.1	1	0	1	0	1	2	2	0	0	0	0	0	0	1	0	0	1	0	0	0	0	2	3	0	0
maintain	96	.8312	15.931	52.0	2	4	9	6	23	26	20	6	5	1	2	1	1	19	1	15	4	0	3	2	2	7	19	14	0
maintained	53	.7122	7.6672	48.8	3	2	4	6	12	13	11	2	6	0	1	0	0	6	1	5	3	0	0	1	1	3	18	8	0
maintaining	23	.6742	3.1485	45.0	3	1	0	2	6	9	1	1	1	0	0	1	0	2	0	3	1	0	2	1	0	3	8	1	0
maintains	16	.7211	2.3246	43.7	0	0	3	1	4	4	4	0	0	2	0	0	1	1	0	2	1	0	1	0	0	2	2	4	0
maintenance	33	.5386	3.7042	45.7	0	0	2	2	10	3	11	5	2	0	0	0	0	2	1	3	0	0	4	0	0	1	6	14	0
Mainz	5	.2778	.2975	34.7	0	0	2	0	0	1	2	0	0	0	0	0	0	0	1	0	0	0	0	2	0	0	2	0	0
maize	8	.3615	.6506	38.1	0	0	0	4	2	0	1	1	0	0	0	1	0	5	0	0	0	0	0	0	0	0	2	0	0
Maj	17	.1171	.5512	37.4	0	0	0	1	12	4	0	0	0	0	0	0	0	0	0	0	0	0	0	0	0	0	15	2	0
Maja	7	.0000	.3198	35.0	0	0	0	7	0	0	0	0	7	0	0	0	0	0	0	0	0	0	0	0	0	0	0	0	0
Maja's	2	.0000	.0914	29.6	0	0	0	2	0	0	0	0	2	0	0	0	0	0	0	0	0	0	0	0	0	0	0	0	0
Majapa	4	.0000	.0778	28.9	0	0	0	0	0	4	0	0	0	0	0	0	0	4	0	0	0	0	0	0	0	0	0	0	0
Majda	16	.0000	.7309	38.6	0	0	0	16	0	0	0	0	16	0	0	0	0	0	0	0	0	0	0	0	0	0	0	0	0
majestic	24	.7569	3.6827	45.7	0	1	3	4	9	4	3	0	5	1	0	1	0	4	0	0	3	0	0	1	1	2	2	4	0
Majestic	2	.1814	.1187	30.7	0	1	0	0	0	0	0	1	1	0	0	0	0	0	0	0	0	0	0	0	0	0	0	1	0
majestically	5	.5550	.5732	37.6	0	0	0	2	3	0	0	0	0	1	0	0	0	0	0	1	1	0	0	0	1	0	0	1	0
majesty	9	.5365	1.0212	40.1	1	1	1	0	2	3	1	0	2	0	1	1	0	0	0	0	2	0	0	0	0	1	2	1	0
Majesty	57	.4726	6.0466	47.8	15	8	7	7	19	1	0	0	22	0	0	8	0	2	0	0	1	0	0	0	21	3	0	0	0
Majesty's	11	.3610	.9541	39.8	0	0	2	1	3	5	0	0	4	1	0	0	0	1	0	0	0	0	0	0	5	0	0	0	0
major	597	.6830	82.576	59.2	26	51	102	78	143	74	98	25	30	15	5	5	5	74	8	28	212	1	4	14	0	17	107	72	0

7Q magnetometer
9J Magnificat
4N magnifying-glass
9F Magnitogorsk
7N magnolias
XR magpies
7F Mahomet
8G Mahon
7G mahout
6J maid's
9P maiden-voyage
7D maidenhair
9D maidenheads
4J Maids
5Q maidservant
8Q Maidservant
9Q Maidstone
7N maigres
4N mail-boat
3P mail-horse
8D mail-opener
7Q mailable
7B Mailed
9K Maillol's
8D maimed
4D Maimie
7Q maiming
7N main-sail
5N main-topsail
6R Maine-built
8R Maine's
5Q Mainichi
7F mainland's
5N mainlander
5Q mainlands
7H Mainsprings
5R Maintenance
8B mair
4E Maisy
6A Maitland
7J maitre
8D Maitre
7Q majesty's

Word Type	F	D	U	SFI	3 Gr 3	4 Gr 4	5 Gr 5	6 Gr 6	7 Gr 7	8 Gr 8	9 Gr 9	X UnGr	A Read	B Eng & Gr	C Comp	D Lit	E Math	F Soc Stud	G Spell	H Sci	J Music	K Art	L Home Ec	M Shop	N Lib F	P Lib NF	Q Lib Ref	R Mag	S Rel
Major	75	.6303	10.031	50.0	9	20	13	7	15	6	2	3	32	0	0	7	0	2	0	0	6	0	0	0	1	20	2	5	0
major-league	7	.2438	.3959	36.0	0	0	3	0	4	0	0	0	0	0	0	0	0	0	0	0	0	0	0	0	0	0	3	4	0
major-minor	2	.0000	.0162	22.1	0	0	0	0	0	1	1	0	0	0	0	0	0	0	0	0	2	0	0	0	0	0	0	0	0
major-scale	2	.0000	.0162	22.1	0	0	2	0	0	0	0	0	0	0	0	0	0	0	0	0	2	0	0	0	0	0	0	0	0
major's	2	.1814	.1187	30.7	0	0	0	1	0	0	0	1	1	0	0	0	0	0	0	0	0	0	0	0	0	0	0	1	0
Major's	2	.1948	.1250	31.0	0	2	0	0	0	0	0	0	1	0	0	0	0	0	0	0	0	0	0	0	0	1	0	0	0
majoring	4	.4804	.4052	36.1	0	0	1	0	1	1	1	0	0	1	0	0	0	1	0	0	0	0	0	0	0	0	1	1	0
majorities	3	.1937	.1495	31.7	0	0	0	0	1	1	1	0	0	0	0	0	0	1	0	0	0	0	0	0	0	0	0	2	0
majority	119	.7603	18.211	52.6	6	1	13	7	32	32	23	5	6	19	4	3	0	31	2	5	1	0	2	0	0	9	21	16	0
majors	5	.2304	.2767	34.4	1	0	0	2	1	0	0	1	0	0	0	0	0	0	0	0	0	0	0	0	0	2	0	3	0
Majors	4	.0000	.0579	27.6	4	0	0	0	0	0	0	0	0	0	0	0	0	0	0	0	0	0	0	0	0	4	0	0	0
mak	2	.0000	.0219	23.4	0	0	0	0	0	2	0	0	0	2	0	0	0	0	0	0	0	0	0	0	0	0	0	0	0
mak'st	2	.0000	.0215	23.3	0	0	0	0	0	0	2	0	0	0	0	2	0	0	0	0	0	0	0	0	0	0	0	0	0
makahiki	3	.0000	.0583	27.7	0	0	3	0	0	0	0	0	0	0	0	0	0	3	0	0	0	0	0	0	0	0	0	0	0
Makassar	2	.2285	.1129	30.5	0	0	0	1	0	1	0	0	0	0	0	0	0	1	0	0	0	0	0	0	0	0	1	0	0
make	8333	.9327	1537.9	71.9	1953	1464	1058	1038	1188	824	665	143	1600	742	107	281	684	783	594	1055	342	351	277	170	299	519	207	316	6
Make	5	.2988	.3268	35.1	0	0	0	3	2	0	0	0	0	1	0	0	0	0	0	0	3	0	0	0	0	0	0	1	0
MAKE	2	.2446	.1257	31.0	0	0	0	1	0	0	1	0	0	0	0	0	0	1	0	1	0	0	0	0	0	0	0	0	0
make-believe	47	.7735	7.3711	48.7	18	21	0	2	3	3	0	0	12	11	1	2	1	4	0	4	2	1	0	0	0	4	0	5	0
make-believes	3	.2357	.2199	33.4	3	0	0	0	0	0	0	0	2	0	0	0	0	0	0	0	0	0	0	0	0	1	0	0	0
make-up	23	.5382	2.7081	44.3	2	0	3	1	12	2	2	1	9	1	0	0	0	0	0	7	0	0	3	1	0	0	0	2	0
maker	36	.7706	5.6122	47.5	4	8	3	6	8	1	4	2	7	0	0	5	0	7	1	2	2	0	0	1	2	0	5	4	0
Maker	6	.3951	.5276	37.2	0	3	0	1	1	1	0	0	1	0	0	1	0	0	0	0	0	0	0	0	3	0	1	0	0
maker's	2	.1621	.0746	28.7	0	0	0	0	1	0	1	0	0	0	1	1	0	0	0	0	0	0	0	0	0	0	0	0	0
makers	50	.6873	7.0265	48.5	6	8	3	5	13	5	7	3	3	2	0	3	0	24	1	3	1	0	1	0	0	0	5	7	0
Makers	4	.1737	.1745	32.4	0	3	1	0	0	0	0	0	0	0	0	0	0	0	0	0	0	0	0	0	0	1	3	0	0
makes	1311	.9520	246.45	63.9	301	196	149	159	207	123	129	47	229	108	16	44	62	96	28	289	63	28	48	20	36	93	62	86	3
Makes	3	.3365	.2489	34.0	0	0	0	0	3	0	0	0	1	0	0	1	0	0	0	1	0	0	0	0	0	0	0	0	0
makeshift	9	.5321	1.0567	40.2	0	0	0	3	5	1	0	0	4	0	0	0	0	1	0	0	0	0	0	0	1	0	2	1	0
maketh	6	.3480	.4603	36.6	3	0	1	0	1	1	0	0	0	0	0	1	0	0	1	0	0	0	0	0	0	4	0	0	0
makeup	15	.4203	1.3538	41.3	2	2	1	2	2	1	1	4	0	1	0	0	0	0	0	3	1	0	0	0	0	0	1	9	0
makin'	3	.1250	.1342	31.3	1	0	0	1	0	1	0	0	1	0	0	0	0	0	0	0	0	0	0	0	2	0	0	0	0
making	1408	.9011	251.98	64.0	193	198	159	212	289	161	164	32	286	66	30	62	36	174	19	154	63	43	90	47	94	101	77	66	0
Making	6	.5055	.6281	38.0	0	1	0	1	3	1	0	0	0	2	0	0	0	1	0	0	1	0	1	0	0	0	0	1	0
makings	6	.3322	.4633	36.7	0	0	0	1	3	2	0	0	2	0	2	0	0	0	0	0	1	0	1	0	0	0	0	0	0
Malabar	4	.4556	.4079	36.1	1	0	1	0	1	1	0	0	1	0	0	0	0	1	0	0	0	0	0	0	1	1	0	0	0
Malacca	2	.0000	.0389	25.9	0	0	1	1	0	0	0	0	0	0	0	0	0	2	0	0	0	0	0	0	0	0	0	0	0
malachite	2	.1717	.1142	30.6	1	0	0	0	0	1	0	0	1	0	0	1	0	0	0	0	0	0	0	0	0	0	0	0	0
maladies	3	.3395	.2468	33.9	0	0	0	0	1	0	2	0	1	0	0	0	0	0	0	0	0	0	0	0	0	1	1	0	0
malady	5	.4183	.4628	36.7	0	0	0	1	1	2	1	0	1	0	0	1	0	0	0	0	0	0	0	0	1	0	2	0	0
malaise	2	.2437	.1129	30.5	0	0	0	0	0	0	1	1	0	0	0	0	0	0	0	0	0	0	0	0	0	0	1	1	0
Malalo	2	.0000	.0290	24.6	0	0	0	0	2	0	0	0	0	0	0	0	0	0	0	0	0	0	0	0	0	2	0	0	0
malaria	33	.5208	3.7260	45.7	4	3	3	9	6	1	2	5	5	0	0	3	0	4	0	17	0	0	0	0	0	3	1	0	0
malarial	3	.3350	.2478	33.9	0	1	0	2	0	0	0	0	1	0	0	0	0	1	0	0	0	0	0	0	0	0	1	0	0
Malawi	3	.1823	.1405	31.5	0	0	0	1	2	0	0	0	0	0	0	0	0	1	0	0	0	0	0	0	0	0	2	0	0
Malay	10	.3352	.7558	38.8	0	0	1	1	7	1	0	0	0	0	2	0	0	6	0	0	0	0	0	0	0	1	1	0	0
Malaya	8	.4548	.7956	39.0	1	0	1	2	0	2	1	1	1	0	0	0	0	2	0	1	0	0	0	0	0	0	3	1	0
Malaysia	11	.4591	1.1097	40.5	1	0	3	3	2	0	1	1	1	0	0	0	0	6	0	1	0	0	0	0	0	0	1	2	0
Malcolm	16	.2541	1.0198	40.1	0	1	1	0	3	0	10	1	3	0	0	0	1	0	0	0	0	0	0	0	0	0	1	11	0
Malcolm's	2	.1814	.1187	30.7	0	0	0	0	1	0	1	0	1	0	0	0	0	0	0	0	0	0	0	0	0	0	0	1	0
male	139	.7195	20.346	53.1	26	12	9	22	46	10	6	8	16	4	2	6	0	4	2	40	5	0	0	0	0	16	35	9	0
male's	2	.0000	.0209	23.2	0	0	0	0	2	0	0	0	0	0	0	0	0	0	0	0	0	0	0	0	0	0	2	0	0
males	44	.4695	4.5404	46.6	17	4	3	2	4	10	2	2	11	0	8	3	0	2	0	8	0	0	0	0	1	6	1	4	0
malformations	3	.3764	.2483	33.9	0	0	0	0	1	1	0	1	0	0	0	0	0	0	0	1	0	0	0	0	0	0	1	1	0
malfunction	4	.2437	.2257	33.5	0	0	0	0	2	0	2	0	0	0	0	0	0	0	0	0	0	0	0	0	0	0	2	2	0
malfunctions	2	.2437	.1129	30.5	0	0	0	0	1	0	1	0	0	0	0	0	0	0	0	0	0	0	0	0	0	0	1	1	0
Malheur	3	.0000	.0583	27.7	0	3	0	0	0	0	0	0	0	0	0	0	0	3	0	0	0	0	0	0	0	0	0	0	0
malice	11	.6819	1.5245	41.8	1	0	1	1	7	1	0	0	1	1	0	1	0	0	2	0	0	0	0	0	2	2	1	1	0
malicious	2	.2297	.1135	30.6	0	0	0	0	1	1	0	0	0	0	0	1	0	1	0	0	0	0	0	0	0	0	0	0	0
malignant	4	.3366	.2993	34.8	0	0	0	0	0	1	2	1	0	0	0	0	0	0	0	1	0	0	0	0	1	0	2	0	0
Mall	3	.3635	.2410	33.8	1	0	0	0	1	1	0	0	0	0	0	0	0	1	0	0	1	0	0	0	0	1	0	0	0
mallard	7	.0869	.2692	34.3	0	7	0	0	0	0	0	0	1	0	0	0	0	0	0	6	0	0	0	0	0	0	0	0	0
mallards	7	.4807	.7781	38.9	4	1	0	0	2	0	0	0	4	0	0	1	0	0	0	1	0	0	0	0	1	0	0	0	0
Mallarme	5	.3304	.3608	35.6	0	0	3	0	1	1	0	0	0	0	0	0	0	0	0	0	1	0	0	0	0	1	3	0	0
malleability	3	.0000	.0076	18.8	0	0	0	0	0	1	2	0	0	0	0	0	0	0	0	0	0	0	0	3	0	0	0	0	0
malleable	6	.3591	.5000	37.0	0	0	1	0	0	4	1	0	1	0	0	0	0	0	0	3	0	0	0	1	0	0	0	1	0
mallee	2	.0000	.0209	23.2	0	0	0	0	2	0	0	0	0	0	0	0	0	0	0	0	0	0	0	0	0	0	2	0	0
mallet	20	.4115	1.7063	42.3	1	3	3	2	4	3	4	0	0	1	0	1	0	0	0	0	7	0	0	6	3	0	1	1	0
Mallie	6	.0000	.2741	34.4	0	0	0	0	6	0	0	0	6	0	0	0	0	0	0	0	0	0	0	0	0	0	0	0	0
Mallory	5	.0000	.2284	33.6	3	0	0	0	0	2	0	0	5	0	0	0	0	0	0	0	0	0	0	0	0	0	0	0	0
Mallorys	2	.0000	.0914	29.6	2	0	0	0	0	0	0	0	2	0	0	0	0	0	0	0	0	0	0	0	0	0	0	0	0
mallow	4	.1999	.1920	32.8	3	0	0	0	0	0	1	0	0	3	0	1	0	0	0	0	0	0	0	0	0	0	0	0	0
mallows	2	.0000	.0215	23.3	0	0	0	0	0	0	2	0	0	0	0	2	0	0	0	0	0	0	0	0	0	0	0	0	0
Mally	12	.0000	.1407	31.5	0	0	0	0	12	0	0	0	0	0	0	0	0	0	0	0	0	0	0	0	12	0	0	0	0
Malmo	3	.0000	.0583	27.7	0	0	0	0	3	0	0	0	0	0	0	0	0	3	0	0	0	0	0	0	0	0	0	0	0
malnourished	2	.2433	.1158	30.6	0	0	0	0	1	1	0	0	0	0	0	0	0	0	0	0	0	0	0	0	0	1	0	1	0
malnutrition	9	.4133	.7999	39.0	0	0	0	0	1	4	4	0	0	0	0	0	0	2	0	0	0	0	1	0	0	1	0	5	0
malocclusion	2	.2346	.1166	30.7	0	0	0	0	2	0	0	0	0	0	0	0	0	0	0	1	0	0	0	0	0	0	0	1	0
Malone	7	.2771	.4435	36.5	1	0	0	5	0	0	1	0	0	1	0	0	0	0	0	0	0	0	0	0	0	1	0	5	0
Maloney	11	.1573	.5869	37.7	0	5	0	0	4	0	2	0	5	0	0	6	0	0	0	0	0	0	0	0	0	0	0	0	0
Malory	4	.0000	.1827	32.6	0	0	0	4	0	0	0	0	4	0	0	0	0	0	0	0	0	0	0	0	0	0	0	0	0
Malory's	3	.0000	.1370	31.4	0	0	0	3	0	0	0	0	3	0	0	0	0	0	0	0	0	0	0	0	0	0	0	0	0
Malpighi	3	.0000	.0591	27.7	0	0	0	0	0	1	2	0	0	0	0	0	0	0	0	3	0	0	0	0	0	0	0	0	0
malt	9	.3172	.6120	37.9	2	1	0	0	2	1	3	0	0	1	0	0	1	0	0	1	2	0	4	0	0	0	0	0	0
Malta	3	.2425	.1816	32.6	0	0	0	2	0	1	0	0	0	0	0	0	0	2	0	0	0	0	0	0	0	0	0	1	0
malted	5	.1865	.3050	34.8	3	0	0	0	0	2	0	0	2	0	0	0	0	3	0	0	0	0	0	0	0	0	0	0	0
maltose	7	.0000	.1380	31.4	0	0	0	0	7	0	0	0	0	0	0	0	0	0	0	7	0	0	0	0	0	0	0	0	0
Maltz	3	.0000	.0365	25.6	0	0	3	0	0	0	0	0	0	0	0	0	0	0	0	0	0	0	0	0	0	0	0	3	0
Malvina	5	.0000	.2284	33.6	0	0	0	0	5	0	0	0	5	0	0	0	0	0	0	0	0	0	0	0	0	0	0	0	0
Malvo	7	.0000	.3198	35.0	7	0	0	0	0	0	0	0	7	0	0	0	0	0	0	0	0	0	0	0	0	0	0	0	0
Malvolia	2	.0000	.0234	23.7	0	0	0	0	2	0	0	0	0	0	0	0	0	0	0	0	0	0	0	0	2	0	0	0	0
mam	2	.0000	.0243	23.9	0	0	0	0	2	0	0	0	0	0	0	0	0	0	0	0	0	0	0	0	0	0	0	2	0
mama	11	.3153	.8837	39.5	4	2	0	4	0	1	0	0	5	0	0	0	0	0	1	0	0	0	0	0	5	0	0	0	0
Mama	425	.4986	48.110	56.8	69	184	2	9	62	90	9	0	237	0	14	15	0	0	0	0	4	0	0	0	140	9	0	6	0
MAMA	23	.0000	.2468	33.9	0	0	0	0	23	0	0	0	0	0	0	23	0	0	0	0	0	0	0	0	0	0	0	0	0

7R major-league-stock-car
7R major-leaguer
8J majorettes
7Q Majorinus
7B majuscule
7B Make-Believe
4B Make-believe
9M make-ready
XR Make-up

5Q makers'
3P makest
5A makhzan
7R mako
9N Mako
6R maktabah
7D malacca
6R malacologists
9R maladie

9R maladroit
8C Malaga
3Q Malays
9R male-female
5A maleman
XR maleness
7Q maleo
8J Maler
6R malevolently

9H malformation
8L malformed
3Q maligayang
7N malignancy
6R Maligne
9B maligned
7N malingering
8R Malinovsky
5Q Malinowski

3A mall
5Q Mallarme's
6A Mallet
7D mallets
XR Mallets
8D malmsey
5F Malo
9D Maloney's
5F malos

9R Malraux
7H maltase
3N Malthace
7R Malthusian
4B maltreat
9F maltreated
9R maltreatment
9L malts
4B Malvern

Word Type	F	D	U	SFI	3 Gr 3	4 Gr 4	5 Gr 5	6 Gr 6	7 Gr 7	8 Gr 8	9 Gr 9	X UnGr	A Read	B Eng & Gr	C Comp	D Lit	E Math	F Soc Stud	G Spell	H Sci	J Music	K Art	L Home Ec	M Shop	N Lib F	P Lib NF	Q Lib Ref	R Mag	S Rel
mama's	5	.0000	.0537	27.3	0	0	0	0	5	0	0	0	0	0	0	5	0	0	0	0	0	0	0	0	0	0	0	0	0
Mama's	48	.4875	5.4052	47.3	2	19	2	6	9	10	0	0	31	0	2	0	0	0	0	0	6	0	0	0	9	0	0	0	0
Mamacita	5	.0000	.0537	27.3	0	5	0	0	0	0	0	0	0	0	0	5	0	0	0	0	0	0	0	0	0	0	0	0	0
Mamie	2	.2433	.1158	30.6	0	1	0	0	0	0	0	1	0	0	0	0	0	0	0	0	0	0	0	0	0	1	0	1	0
Mamita	6	.0000	.2741	34.4	0	2	0	0	4	0	0	0	6	0	0	0	0	0	0	0	0	0	0	0	0	0	0	0	0
mamma	5	.2718	.3338	35.2	0	0	0	3	2	0	0	0	1	0	0	1	0	0	0	0	0	0	0	0	3	0	0	0	0
Mamma	18	.4237	1.7632	42.5	2	10	1	0	4	1	0	0	7	0	0	1	0	0	0	0	0	0	0	0	6	4	0	0	0
mammal	36	.4526	3.5235	45.5	7	1	4	5	18	1	0	0	1	1	0	0	0	0	0	18	0	0	0	0	1	1	12	2	0
Mammalia	2	.0000	.0394	26.0	0	0	0	0	2	0	0	0	0	0	0	0	0	0	0	2	0	0	0	0	0	0	0	0	0
mammalian	6	.0000	.0628	28.0	0	0	0	0	6	0	0	0	0	0	0	0	0	0	0	0	0	0	0	0	0	0	6	0	0
mammals	202	.4645	20.380	53.1	19	10	9	12	123	1	5	23	17	3	0	0	0	0	0	92	0	0	1	0	1	15	68	5	0
Mammals	2	.2433	.1158	30.6	1	0	0	0	0	0	1	0	0	0	0	0	0	0	0	0	0	0	0	0	0	1	0	1	0
mammary	5	.2213	.2870	34.6	0	0	0	0	2	0	1	2	0	0	0	0	0	0	0	4	0	0	0	0	0	0	1	0	0
mammoth	19	.6141	2.4191	43.8	1	5	2	1	4	1	3	2	2	0	0	2	0	1	0	3	0	0	0	0	0	3	3	5	0
Mammoth	4	.3678	.3185	35.0	0	0	0	0	1	1	0	2	0	1	0	0	0	0	0	0	0	0	0	0	2	0	0	1	0
mammoths	6	.3210	.4432	36.5	0	2	0	1	0	1	1	1	0	0	0	0	0	1	0	2	0	0	0	0	0	0	0	3	0
mammy	5	.0804	.1641	32.2	0	4	0	0	1	0	0	0	1	0	0	0	0	0	0	0	0	0	0	0	4	0	0	0	0
Mammy	31	.0646	.9301	39.7	4	27	0	0	0	0	0	0	4	0	0	0	0	0	0	0	0	0	0	0	0	27	0	0	0
Mamzell	2	.0000	.0914	29.6	0	0	0	0	2	0	0	0	2	0	0	0	0	0	0	0	0	0	0	0	0	0	0	0	0
man	5486	.8865	971.39	69.9	978	850	543	618	1274	646	482	95	2047	206	42	638	100	447	51	317	118	36	10	19	430	454	254	298	19
Man	173	.7747	27.489	54.4	43	34	18	17	24	16	14	7	90	3	0	5	1	9	0	2	8	3	0	0	20	6	12	14	0
MAN	16	.1114	.5095	37.1	1	0	0	1	4	2	8	0	0	0	0	14	0	0	0	0	0	0	0	0	0	2	0	0	0
Man-A-Fre	2	.0000	.0243	23.9	0	0	0	0	2	0	0	0	0	0	0	0	0	0	0	0	0	0	0	0	0	0	0	2	0
Man-God	4	.0000	.0486	26.9	0	0	0	4	0	0	0	0	0	0	0	0	0	0	0	0	0	0	0	0	0	0	0	4	0
Man-God's	3	.0000	.0365	25.6	0	0	0	3	0	0	0	0	0	0	0	0	0	0	0	0	0	0	0	0	0	0	0	3	0
Man-Gods	2	.0000	.0243	23.9	0	0	0	2	0	0	0	0	0	0	0	0	0	0	0	0	0	0	0	0	0	0	0	2	0
Man-Gods'	3	.0000	.0365	25.6	0	0	0	3	0	0	0	0	0	0	0	0	0	0	0	0	0	0	0	0	0	0	0	3	0
man-animals	5	.0000	.0586	27.7	0	0	0	0	5	0	0	0	0	0	0	0	0	0	0	0	0	0	0	0	5	0	0	0	0
man-carrying	3	.0000	.1370	31.4	2	0	0	1	0	0	0	0	3	0	0	0	0	0	0	0	0	0	0	0	0	0	0	0	0
man-eating	7	.3691	.6402	38.1	1	0	2	0	3	1	0	0	4	0	1	0	0	0	0	0	0	0	0	0	0	1	1	0	0
man-hours	6	.1870	.2899	34.6	0	0	0	0	6	0	0	0	0	0	0	0	5	0	0	0	0	0	0	0	0	0	1	0	0
man-made	80	.7493	12.189	50.9	17	8	9	11	13	4	12	6	17	1	0	0	0	11	0	12	0	1	5	4	0	13	9	7	0
man-of-all-men	3	.0000	.1370	31.4	0	0	0	3	0	0	0	0	3	0	0	0	0	0	0	0	0	0	0	0	0	0	0	0	0
man-of-war	3	.2197	.2090	33.2	0	0	0	1	1	1	0	0	2	0	0	0	0	0	0	0	0	0	0	0	0	0	1	0	0
man-scent	2	.0000	.0914	29.6	0	1	1	0	0	0	0	0	2	0	0	0	0	0	0	0	0	0	0	0	0	0	0	0	0
man-size	3	.2357	.2199	33.4	1	1	0	0	1	0	0	0	2	0	0	0	0	0	0	0	0	0	0	0	0	1	0	0	0
man's	484	.9146	87.884	59.4	54	63	42	54	152	52	51	16	126	19	4	51	11	41	8	56	10	9	1	4	25	30	57	32	0
Man's	9	.4444	.9012	39.5	4	2	2	0	0	0	1	0	3	0	0	1	0	0	0	0	0	0	0	0	3	0	0	2	0
manage	88	.7572	13.523	51.3	6	21	9	14	22	8	7	1	20	3	0	7	0	12	4	4	0	0	8	0	8	9	5	8	0
manageable	4	.3990	.3412	35.3	0	0	0	0	2	1	1	0	0	1	0	0	0	1	0	0	0	0	1	0	0	0	0	1	0
managed	162	.7783	25.641	54.1	12	26	22	28	37	18	13	6	54	2	1	15	0	13	0	5	0	0	2	0	20	27	6	17	0
management	42	.5970	5.1501	47.1	1	0	4	3	15	2	14	3	2	1	0	2	0	5	0	2	1	0	7	0	1	2	6	13	0
Management	2	.0000	.0243	23.9	0	0	0	0	0	0	0	2	0	0	0	0	0	0	0	0	0	0	0	0	0	0	0	2	0
management's	2	.2437	.1129	30.5	0	0	1	0	0	0	1	0	0	0	0	0	0	0	0	0	0	0	0	0	0	0	1	1	0
manager	85	.7888	13.555	51.3	16	15	5	11	16	10	9	3	23	4	2	3	3	5	1	0	0	0	4	0	9	11	2	18	0
Manager	15	.3989	1.3536	41.3	7	2	0	2	0	3	1	0	3	1	0	0	0	0	0	0	0	0	0	0	0	6	0	5	0
managerial	2	.2351	.1166	30.7	0	0	0	0	0	0	2	0	0	0	0	0	0	1	0	0	0	0	0	0	0	0	0	1	0
managers	25	.5816	3.0657	44.9	1	0	2	5	2	4	10	1	4	0	0	0	0	10	0	1	0	0	2	0	0	1	3	4	0
manages	6	.4544	.6088	37.8	0	0	2	2	1	0	1	0	2	1	0	0	0	0	1	0	0	0	0	0	2	0	0	0	0
managing	22	.5958	2.7058	44.3	0	2	2	1	6	3	6	2	2	1	0	6	0	1	0	1	0	0	3	0	1	4	0	3	0
Managua	4	.0000	.0778	28.9	0	0	0	4	0	0	0	0	0	0	0	0	0	4	0	0	0	0	0	0	0	0	0	0	0
Managua's	2	.0000	.0389	25.9	0	0	0	2	0	0	0	0	0	0	0	0	0	2	0	0	0	0	0	0	0	0	0	0	0
Manaluk	11	.0000	.5025	37.0	11	0	0	0	0	0	0	0	11	0	0	0	0	0	0	0	0	0	0	0	0	0	0	0	0
Manaluk's	5	.0000	.2284	33.6	5	0	0	0	0	0	0	0	5	0	0	0	0	0	0	0	0	0	0	0	0	0	0	0	0
Manassas	3	.1823	.1405	31.5	0	2	0	0	0	1	0	0	0	0	0	0	0	1	0	0	0	0	0	0	0	0	2	0	0
Manaus	6	.0000	.1167	30.7	0	0	1	5	0	0	0	0	0	0	0	0	0	6	0	0	0	0	0	0	0	0	0	0	0
Mance	6	.0000	.0644	28.1	0	0	0	0	6	0	0	0	0	0	0	6	0	0	0	0	0	0	0	0	0	0	0	0	0
Manchester	10	.4310	.9829	39.9	0	1	0	2	2	3	2	0	3	0	0	0	0	3	0	0	0	0	0	0	0	0	3	1	0
Manchu	11	.4185	1.0125	40.1	0	0	2	0	0	7	2	0	0	0	0	0	0	7	0	0	0	0	0	0	0	1	1	2	0
Manchuria	19	.2749	1.2713	41.0	0	1	2	2	0	14	0	0	0	0	0	0	0	15	0	0	0	0	0	0	0	1	3	0	0
Manchurian	5	.3660	.4089	36.1	0	1	0	0	2	2	0	0	0	0	0	0	0	2	0	0	0	0	0	0	0	1	0	2	0
Manchus	12	.1214	.4871	36.9	0	0	1	0	0	11	0	0	0	0	0	0	0	11	0	0	0	0	0	0	0	1	0	0	0
Mandalay	2	.0000	.0215	23.3	0	0	0	0	2	0	0	0	0	0	0	2	0	0	0	0	0	0	0	0	0	0	0	0	0
Mandarin	2	.2446	.1123	30.5	0	0	0	0	0	1	0	1	0	1	0	0	0	0	0	0	0	0	0	0	0	0	1	0	0
mandate	6	.1955	.3185	35.0	0	1	0	1	3	1	0	0	0	0	0	0	0	5	0	0	0	0	0	0	0	0	0	1	0
mandatory	2	.2351	.1166	30.7	0	0	0	0	0	0	2	0	0	0	0	0	0	1	0	0	0	0	0	0	0	0	0	1	0
mandolin	2	.0000	.0162	22.1	0	0	1	1	0	0	0	0	0	0	0	0	0	0	0	0	2	0	0	0	0	0	0	0	0
mane	59	.7156	8.6412	49.4	16	5	5	6	16	6	5	0	17	3	2	12	1	1	2	0	0	3	0	0	13	1	2	2	0
maned	4	.2424	.3036	34.8	3	1	0	0	0	0	0	0	3	0	0	0	0	0	0	0	0	0	0	0	0	0	0	1	0
Maned	3	.0000	.1370	31.4	3	0	0	0	0	0	0	0	3	0	0	0	0	0	0	0	0	0	0	0	0	0	0	0	0
manes	6	.5143	.6574	38.2	1	1	0	1	1	1	1	0	1	0	0	1	0	0	0	0	0	0	0	0	2	1	1	0	0
Manette	9	.0000	.0966	29.8	0	0	0	0	0	0	9	0	0	0	0	9	0	0	0	0	0	0	0	0	0	0	0	0	0
maneuver	17	.5819	2.0720	43.2	0	1	0	0	8	6	2	0	3	1	0	3	0	1	0	0	0	0	0	0	2	0	1	6	0
maneuverability	6	.2437	.3386	35.3	0	0	0	1	5	0	0	0	0	0	0	0	0	0	0	0	0	0	0	0	0	0	3	3	0
maneuvered	2	.1814	.1187	30.7	0	0	0	1	1	0	0	0	1	0	0	0	0	0	0	0	0	0	0	0	0	0	0	1	0
maneuvering	9	.5548	1.0743	40.3	0	0	1	1	3	2	2	0	3	0	0	0	0	1	0	0	0	0	1	0	0	1	1	2	0
maneuvers	7	.4346	.7063	38.5	0	0	0	0	5	1	1	0	3	0	0	0	0	1	0	0	0	0	0	0	0	1	2	0	0
Manfred	2	.2433	.1158	30.6	0	0	0	0	0	0	0	2	0	0	0	0	0	0	0	0	0	0	0	0	0	1	0	1	0
manfully	2	.1787	.1174	30.7	0	0	0	1	1	0	0	0	1	0	0	0	0	0	0	0	0	0	0	0	1	0	0	0	0
manganese	22	.3819	1.9696	42.9	1	0	1	2	11	3	3	1	4	0	0	0	0	13	0	3	0	0	0	0	0	0	2	0	0
manger	21	.6418	2.8023	44.5	3	5	0	5	3	2	1	2	6	0	1	3	1	0	0	0	5	0	0	0	1	2	0	2	0
mangled	2	.2443	.1130	30.5	0	0	0	0	2	0	0	0	0	0	0	1	0	0	0	0	0	0	0	0	1	0	0	0	0
mango	7	.4761	.7121	38.5	1	0	0	4	1	0	0	1	1	0	0	0	0	0	1	0	0	0	0	0	1	0	3	1	0
mangoes	3	.2143	.1568	32.0	0	0	1	0	0	0	0	2	0	0	0	0	0	0	0	0	0	0	0	0	0	1	0	2	0
mangrove	5	.2857	.3274	35.2	1	1	0	2	1	0	0	0	0	0	0	0	0	1	0	0	0	0	0	0	0	1	3	0	0
mangroves	3	.0000	.0322	25.1	0	0	0	0	3	0	0	0	0	0	0	3	0	0	0	0	0	0	0	0	0	0	0	0	0
mangy	2	.2407	.1138	30.6	0	1	0	0	0	1	0	0	0	0	0	1	0	0	0	0	0	0	0	0	0	1	0	0	0
Manhattan	55	.4802	5.6476	47.5	9	7	4	2	15	6	9	3	3	2	0	0	0	16	0	0	1	0	0	0	0	3	4	26	0
Manhattan's	3	.2143	.1568	32.0	0	0	1	0	0	1	1	0	0	0	0	0	0	0	0	0	0	0	0	0	0	1	0	2	0
Manheim	4	.0000	.0429	26.3	0	0	0	0	0	0	4	0	0	0	0	4	0	0	0	0	0	0	0	0	0	0	0	0	0
manhole	7	.0000	.3198	35.0	7	0	0	0	0	0	0	0	7	0	0	0	0	0	0	0	0	0	0	0	0	0	0	0	0
manhood	13	.6316	1.7117	42.3	2	0	1	2	3	2	3	0	3	0	0	2	0	1	0	0	1	0	0	0	0	4	1	1	0
mania	2	.2446	.1142	30.6	0	1	0	0	0	0	0	1	0	0	0	0	0	0	0	0	0	0	0	0	1	0	0	1	0
Maniago	3	.0000	.0365	25.6	0	0	0	0	3	0	0	0	0	0	0	0	0	0	0	0	0	0	0	0	0	0	0	3	0
manicure	2	.2444	.1132	30.5	0	0	0	0	2	0	0	0	0	1	0	0	0	0	0	0	0	0	0	0	1	0	0	0	0

5D mamas
7R Mamas
7P mambises
6J Mambron
9Q Mameluke
XR Mamie's
7A Mamita's
4P mamma's
5A Mammal
7H mammal's
6N mammas
4N Mammoths
4N mammy's
7N man-animal
7A man-destroyer
7Q man-dominated
5A man-eater
7N man-fashion
3P man-grown
7N man-hole
9F man-hour
7R man-powered
4A man-shaped
8A man-to-man
9F man-types
4N Man-who-does-not-put-hi**
8R management-consultant
6R manager's
8G manana
XR mananaesque
3P manatee
XH manatees
7P Manawydan
5P Mancha
8F Manchukuo
3P mandamus
8F Mandan
8G mandarin
5B mandoline
9R Mandragora
9M mandrel
7N maneater
3Q Manet
9D Manette's
7A manfish
6F mangels
8R Mangelsen
3K mangers
9F mangles
4F Mangrove
5A manhood's
7B manhoods
7R maniacal
9R manic

Word Type	F	D	U	SFI	3 Gr 3	4 Gr 4	5 Gr 5	6 Gr 6	7 Gr 7	8 Gr 8	9 Gr 9	X UnGr	A Read	B Eng & Gr	C Comp	D Lit	E Math	F Soc Stud	G Spell	H Sci	J Music	K Art	L Home Ec	M Shop	N Lib F	P Lib NF	Q Lib Ref	R Mag	S Rel
manifest	7	.6188	.9106	39.6	0	0	0	0	2	2	2	1	2	0	0	1	0	1	0	0	0	0	0	0	1	0	1	1	0
manifestation	4	.3498	.3059	34.9	0	0	1	0	1	0	2	0	0	0	0	0	0	0	0	0	0	0	0	0	0	1	2	1	0
manifestations	2	.2278	.1128	30.5	0	0	0	0	2	0	0	0	0	0	0	0	0	0	0	1	0	0	0	0	0	0	1	0	0
manifested	8	.5296	.8732	39.4	0	1	0	1	3	3	0	0	0	1	0	0	0	0	0	0	1	0	0	0	1	0	3	2	0
manifesto	3	.3769	.2484	34.0	0	0	1	0	0	1	0	1	0	0	0	0	0	1	0	0	0	0	0	0	0	0	1	1	0
Manifesto	2	.2351	.1166	30.7	0	0	0	0	0	2	0	0	0	0	0	0	0	1	0	0	0	0	0	0	0	0	0	1	0
manifold	11	.3583	.9052	39.6	1	0	1	0	7	1	1	0	2	0	0	0	0	0	0	0	0	0	0	0	0	2	1	6	0
manifolds	2	.0000	.0243	23.9	0	0	0	0	2	0	0	0	0	0	0	0	0	0	0	0	0	0	0	0	0	0	0	2	0
Manila	22	.2625	1.2862	41.1	15	2	0	3	0	2	0	0	0	0	0	0	0	2	0	0	0	5	0	0	0	0	15	0	0
manioc	11	.1903	.5765	37.6	0	5	0	4	2	0	0	0	0	0	0	0	0	9	0	0	0	0	0	0	0	2	0	0	0
manipulate	4	.3884	.3278	35.2	0	0	2	0	0	1	1	0	0	0	1	0	0	0	0	1	0	0	1	0	1	0	0	0	0
manipulated	6	.4886	.5980	37.8	0	0	0	0	1	3	1	0	0	0	1	0	0	0	0	0	2	1	0	0	0	0	1	1	0
manipulating	2	.2417	.1091	30.4	0	0	0	1	1	0	0	0	0	0	0	0	0	0	0	0	1	0	0	0	0	0	1	0	0
manipulation	11	.5295	1.1986	40.8	1	0	0	0	3	1	2	4	0	0	1	0	0	0	0	0	0	1	0	0	0	2	2	5	0
manipulator	2	.0000	.0389	25.9	0	0	0	0	0	2	0	0	0	0	0	0	0	2	0	0	0	0	0	0	0	0	0	0	0
Manitoba	2	.2285	.1129	30.5	0	0	0	1	1	0	0	0	0	0	0	0	0	1	0	0	0	0	0	0	0	0	1	0	0
mankind	78	.8118	12.761	51.1	3	2	4	13	11	18	21	6	18	1	0	3	1	15	1	11	0	2	0	1	4	3	12	6	0
Mankind	3	.1937	.1495	31.7	0	0	0	0	0	1	0	2	0	0	0	0	0	1	0	0	0	0	0	0	0	0	0	2	0
mankind's	6	.4608	.5786	37.6	0	1	0	0	3	1	1	0	0	0	1	1	0	1	0	0	0	0	0	0	0	0	2	1	0
Manley	2	.2446	.1125	30.5	0	0	0	0	1	0	1	0	0	1	0	1	0	0	0	0	0	0	0	0	0	0	0	0	0
manlike	6	.4505	.5815	37.6	0	0	0	0	5	0	1	0	0	0	0	0	0	1	0	2	0	0	0	0	1	0	2	0	0
manliness	2	.2433	.1158	30.6	0	0	1	0	0	0	0	1	0	0	0	0	0	0	0	0	0	0	0	0	0	1	0	1	0
manly	9	.4279	.8600	39.3	0	1	1	0	2	1	4	0	2	0	0	4	0	1	0	0	0	0	0	0	0	1	0	1	0
manmade	3	.3766	.2497	34.0	2	1	0	0	0	0	0	0	0	0	0	0	0	1	0	0	0	0	0	0	0	1	1	0	0
Mann	5	.3850	.4834	36.8	1	0	1	1	1	1	0	0	3	0	0	0	0	1	0	0	0	0	0	0	0	1	0	0	0
manned	31	.6752	4.2897	46.3	2	3	2	1	13	7	2	1	2	1	0	1	3	7	0	5	0	0	0	0	0	3	1	8	0
Manned	4	.3359	.2989	34.8	0	0	2	1	1	0	0	0	0	0	0	0	0	1	0	0	0	0	0	0	0	0	2	1	0
manner	279	.8949	49.507	56.9	3	16	21	32	90	53	50	14	38	24	9	19	6	13	4	17	26	5	17	20	23	16	20	21	1
mannered	2	.1787	.1174	30.7	1	0	0	0	1	0	0	0	1	0	0	0	0	0	0	0	0	0	0	0	1	0	0	0	0
manners	97	.6096	12.391	50.9	8	14	13	18	12	12	20	0	22	5	0	4	0	6	1	22	0	0	16	0	8	6	3	4	0
Mannheim	2	.0000	.0209	23.2	0	2	0	0	0	0	0	0	0	0	0	0	0	0	0	0	0	0	0	0	0	0	2	0	0
Manny	9	.0829	.2993	34.8	1	0	0	0	0	8	0	0	2	0	0	7	0	0	0	0	0	0	0	0	0	0	0	0	0
manoeuvres	2	.2152	.1357	31.3	0	0	0	0	1	0	1	0	1	0	0	0	0	1	0	0	0	0	0	0	0	0	0	0	0
manometer	2	.2441	.1127	30.5	0	0	0	1	1	0	0	0	0	0	0	0	0	0	0	0	0	0	0	0	1	0	1	0	0
Manon	2	.2417	.1091	30.4	0	0	1	0	0	1	0	0	0	0	0	0	0	0	0	0	1	0	0	0	0	0	1	0	0
manor	15	.4891	1.5779	42.0	0	4	1	9	0	1	0	0	1	0	0	0	0	6	0	0	1	0	0	0	2	5	0	0	0
Manor	3	.3815	.2534	34.0	0	1	0	1	0	0	0	1	0	0	0	0	0	1	0	0	0	0	0	0	0	1	0	0	0
manors	3	.1639	.1674	32.2	0	0	0	2	1	0	0	0	1	0	0	0	0	2	0	0	0	0	0	0	0	0	0	1	0
Manowar	9	.0000	.4111	36.1	0	0	6	0	3	0	0	0	9	0	0	0	0	0	0	0	0	0	0	0	0	0	0	0	0
manpower	4	.3359	.2989	34.8	0	0	1	0	1	0	2	0	0	0	0	0	0	1	0	0	0	0	0	0	0	0	2	1	0
MANSERVANT	4	.0000	.0429	26.3	0	0	0	0	4	0	0	0	0	0	0	4	0	0	0	0	0	0	0	0	0	0	0	0	0
Mansfield	4	.3215	.3104	34.9	0	0	1	0	1	0	2	0	1	0	0	0	0	0	0	0	0	0	0	0	0	2	1	0	0
mansion	24	.6021	2.9895	44.8	3	4	2	3	5	3	1	3	3	1	3	2	0	2	1	0	0	0	0	0	3	4	0	5	0
mansions	7	.4761	.7091	38.5	3	0	1	2	1	0	0	0	0	0	0	0	0	2	0	0	0	0	0	0	2	2	0	1	0
Manson	2	.0000	.0394	26.0	0	0	0	0	0	0	0	2	0	0	0	0	0	0	0	2	0	0	0	0	0	0	0	0	0
manta	2	.2285	.1129	30.5	0	0	0	1	1	0	0	0	0	0	0	0	0	1	0	0	0	0	0	0	0	0	1	0	0
mantel	7	.5265	.7953	39.0	0	2	0	1	1	1	2	0	2	1	0	2	0	0	0	0	0	0	0	0	1	1	0	0	0
Mantell	14	.0702	.4397	36.4	11	0	1	0	2	0	0	0	2	0	0	0	0	0	0	0	0	0	0	0	0	12	0	0	0
Mantell's	2	.1948	.1250	31.0	1	0	0	0	1	0	0	0	1	0	0	0	0	0	0	0	0	0	0	0	0	1	0	0	0
mantelpiece	7	.5651	.8583	39.3	0	4	0	2	1	0	0	0	3	0	0	1	0	0	0	0	0	0	0	0	1	1	0	1	0
mantelshelf	3	.1409	.1472	31.7	0	3	0	0	0	0	0	0	1	0	0	0	0	0	0	0	0	0	0	0	0	2	0	0	0
Manteo	8	.0000	.1158	30.6	0	8	0	0	0	0	0	0	0	0	0	0	0	0	0	0	0	0	0	0	0	8	0	0	0
mantis	2	.2346	.1166	30.7	1	0	0	0	0	1	0	0	0	0	0	0	0	0	0	1	0	0	0	0	0	0	0	1	0
mantises	2	.2278	.1128	30.5	1	0	0	1	0	0	0	0	0	0	0	0	0	0	0	1	0	0	0	0	0	0	1	0	0
mantle	51	.7096	7.4198	48.7	0	8	6	9	11	6	11	0	10	3	1	0	0	0	0	19	0	1	0	0	5	1	8	3	0
Mantle	12	.1729	.5475	37.4	1	0	0	9	0	1	1	0	0	0	0	0	0	0	0	0	0	0	0	0	0	10	0	2	0
Mantle's	3	.2332	.1690	32.3	0	0	0	2	0	1	0	0	0	0	0	0	0	0	0	0	0	0	0	0	0	2	0	1	0
mantles	4	.2248	.2112	33.2	0	0	0	3	0	1	0	0	0	0	0	0	0	0	0	0	1	0	0	0	0	0	0	3	0
Manton	6	.0000	.2741	34.4	0	6	0	0	0	0	0	0	6	0	0	0	0	0	0	0	0	0	0	0	0	0	0	0	0
Mantua	2	.0000	.0215	23.3	0	0	0	0	0	0	2	0	0	0	0	2	0	0	0	0	0	0	0	0	0	0	0	0	0
manual	23	.6470	3.0333	44.8	0	0	1	3	8	3	8	0	2	1	0	6	0	0	0	0	4	0	1	0	0	1	3	5	0
Manual	4	.3214	.2811	34.5	0	2	0	0	1	0	1	0	0	0	0	0	0	0	0	0	0	0	0	1	0	2	1	0	0
manually	4	.3996	.3354	35.3	0	0	1	0	1	0	2	0	0	0	0	0	0	0	0	0	1	0	0	1	0	1	1	0	0
manuals	4	.1622	.1743	32.4	0	0	0	0	2	1	0	1	0	0	0	0	0	1	0	0	0	0	0	0	0	0	0	3	0
Manuel	34	.5583	4.2602	46.3	8	0	12	8	4	2	0	0	23	0	0	0	0	4	0	0	3	0	0	0	1	1	2	0	0
Manuela	8	.0000	.3655	35.6	8	0	0	0	0	0	0	0	8	0	0	0	0	0	0	0	0	0	0	0	0	0	0	0	0
Manuela's	2	.0000	.0914	29.6	2	0	0	0	0	0	0	0	2	0	0	0	0	0	0	0	0	0	0	0	0	0	0	0	0
manufacture	101	.7309	14.954	51.7	5	3	26	17	22	13	12	3	7	3	0	1	1	28	3	18	2	0	3	6	0	3	23	3	0
manufactured	112	.5680	13.281	51.2	5	9	28	16	24	14	12	4	3	0	0	0	1	60	1	7	1	0	1	12	1	5	16	4	0
manufacturer	38	.7873	5.9961	47.8	3	4	4	1	13	9	4	0	1	1	1	0	3	8	0	5	0	0	2	2	1	4	7	3	0
manufacturer's	6	.2941	.3731	35.7	0	0	0	0	3	0	3	0	0	0	0	0	0	0	0	0	0	0	1	3	0	1	0	1	0
manufacturers	50	.6961	7.0944	48.5	0	2	13	1	11	12	9	2	3	2	0	0	0	20	0	4	2	0	1	1	0	1	11	5	0
manufactures	18	.5510	2.0819	43.2	1	1	2	2	8	1	3	0	0	0	1	0	0	10	0	2	0	0	0	0	0	1	2	2	0
manufacturing	199	.5396	22.652	53.6	10	15	53	48	38	16	16	3	3	1	1	0	0	131	1	5	0	0	0	10	2	9	31	7	0
manure	12	.5474	1.3799	41.4	1	3	0	0	3	1	1	3	1	0	0	3	0	1	0	2	0	0	0	0	0	0	0	3	0
Manus	2	.0000	.0219	23.4	0	0	0	0	0	2	0	0	0	2	0	0	0	0	0	0	0	0	0	0	0	0	0	0	0
manuscript	29	.6753	3.9770	46.0	1	3	0	3	13	3	4	2	3	5	3	1	0	0	4	2	3	0	0	0	1	1	5	1	0
manuscripts	18	.5753	2.1248	43.3	0	1	2	2	7	2	4	0	1	6	0	0	0	0	1	0	2	0	0	2	0	2	4	0	0
Manwick	14	.0000	.6396	38.1	14	0	0	0	0	0	0	0	14	0	0	0	0	0	0	0	0	0	0	0	0	0	0	0	0
Manx	6	.0000	.2741	34.4	0	0	0	0	6	0	0	0	6	0	0	0	0	0	0	0	0	0	0	0	0	0	0	0	0
many	12158	.9415	2262.6	73.5	2702	1923	1729	1710	1848	1151	894	201	1592	561	93	269	2658	2268	456	1338	554	168	132	109	168	670	641	474	7
Many	11	.4634	1.1691	40.7	1	8	1	1	0	0	0	0	5	0	0	0	0	2	0	0	1	0	0	0	0	0	0	3	0
many-celled	8	.3589	.6526	38.1	3	0	2	1	1	0	0	1	0	0	0	0	0	0	0	5	0	0	0	0	0	2	1	0	0
many-colored	7	.4584	.6946	38.4	1	2	1	0	2	1	0	0	1	0	0	0	0	1	0	0	0	1	0	0	1	2	1	0	0
many-sided	3	.1796	.1398	31.5	0	0	0	0	1	1	2	0	0	0	0	0	0	2	0	0	0	0	0	1	0	0	0	0	0
many's	4	.4339	.3907	35.9	0	2	2	0	0	0	0	0	1	0	0	0	0	1	0	0	1	0	0	0	0	1	0	0	0
Manya	2	.0000	.0290	24.6	0	0	0	0	0	0	0	2	0	0	0	0	0	0	0	0	0	0	0	0	0	2	0	0	0
Manye	2	.0000	.0215	23.3	0	2	0	0	0	0	0	0	0	0	0	2	0	0	0	0	0	0	0	0	0	0	0	0	0
Manygoats	3	.0000	.0583	27.7	0	3	0	0	0	0	0	0	0	0	0	0	0	3	0	0	0	0	0	0	0	0	0	0	0
manzanita	2	.0000	.0209	23.2	0	0	0	2	0	0	0	0	0	0	0	0	0	0	0	0	0	0	0	0	0	0	2	0	0
Manzoni	3	.0000	.0434	26.4	0	0	3	0	0	0	0	0	0	0	0	0	0	0	0	0	0	0	0	0	0	3	0	0	0
Mao	14	.4379	1.3348	41.3	0	0	5	0	0	9	0	0	0	0	0	0	0	8	0	0	0	0	0	0	0	2	1	3	0
Mao's	8	.3513	.6420	38.1	0	0	2	0	1	5	0	0	0	0	0	0	0	5	0	0	0	0	0	0	0	2	0	1	0
Maori	10	.0000	.1448	31.6	0	0	10	0	0	0	0	0	0	0	0	0	0	0	0	0	0	0	0	0	0	10	0	0	0

5R manicured
8F Manifest
8R Manifesto's
9Q manifestoes
XH manifests
7N manikin
5K manila
8H manipulates
8L manipulative
6H manipulators
5J Manitou
XR Mankind's
5A manliest
XR manlihood
7G mann
9Q Mann's
7R Mannean
4D Mannering
7A mannerisms
6R Manners
8A manning
5R mannish
7Q mannishness
8N manoeuvre
8F manorial
6R manos
3A mans
7R Mans
5Q manservant
XH Manson's
7G mant
7R Manteuffel
7Q mantids
3N mantilla
3P Mantis
8Q mantled
6R mantlepiece
6A Manuel's
7M Manufactured
9R Manufacturers
9Q Manufactures
4Q Manufacturing
8F manured
8D manuring
7G manus
5K manxome
7J many-a
9Q many-bladed
7H many-complexioned
7H many-eyed
7Q many-faced
3J many-headed
6R many-layered
6A many-ribbed
3A many-seeded
6A many-shaped
8N many-tined
6J many-voiced
6F many-windowed
7Q many-year
4F Manygoats'
5Q Manzoni's
9J Manzuoli

Word Type	F	D	U	SFI	3 Gr 3	4 Gr 4	5 Gr 5	6 Gr 6	7 Gr 7	8 Gr 8	9 Gr 9	X UnGr	A Read	B Eng & Gr	C Comp	D Lit	E Math	F Soc Stud	G Spell	H Sci	J Music	K Art	L Home Ec	M Shop	N Lib F	P Lib NF	Q Lib Ref	R Mag	S Rel
Maoris	12	.2995	.8318	39.2	0	0	8	2	0	0	2	0	0	0	0	0	0	2	0	0	0	0	0	0	0	8	0	2	0
map	1223	.5925	152.42	61.8	193	324	199	234	95	89	59	30	99	21	4	3	41	801	8	103	9	0	0	11	6	16	66	35	0
Map	15	.2550	.9820	39.9	0	10	3	0	0	1	0	1	1	0	0	0	0	12	0	1	0	0	0	0	0	0	1	0	0
map-making	2	.0000	.0914	29.6	0	1	1	0	0	0	0	0	2	0	0	0	0	0	0	0	0	0	0	0	0	0	0	0	0
Mapai	2	.0000	.0290	24.6	0	0	2	0	0	0	0	0	0	0	0	0	0	0	0	0	0	0	0	0	0	0	0	0	0
maple	94	.8554	16.067	52.1	28	21	20	6	9	6	3	1	18	4	1	6	2	3	0	17	2	0	1	1	11	9	16	3	0
Maple	4	.2446	.3071	34.9	0	4	0	0	0	0	0	0	3	0	0	0	1	0	0	0	0	0	0	0	0	0	0	0	0
Maple-Leaf	4	.0000	.0429	26.3	4	0	0	0	0	0	0	0	0	0	0	4	0	0	0	0	0	0	0	0	0	0	0	0	0
maple-sugar	2	.0000	.0243	23.9	0	2	0	0	0	0	0	0	0	0	0	0	0	0	0	0	0	0	0	0	0	0	0	2	0
maples	14	.4923	1.4754	41.7	0	2	3	3	4	0	1	1	3	1	3	2	0	0	0	1	1	0	0	0	1	0	1	1	0
Maplewood	5	.0000	.0972	29.9	5	0	0	0	0	0	0	0	0	0	0	0	0	5	0	0	0	0	0	0	0	0	0	0	0
mapmaker	2	.0000	.0389	25.9	0	0	2	0	0	0	0	0	0	0	0	0	0	2	0	0	0	0	0	0	0	0	0	0	0
mapmakers	4	.3623	.3223	35.1	2	0	0	0	2	0	0	0	0	0	0	0	0	1	0	0	0	0	0	0	0	2	1	0	0
mapmaking	2	.2285	.1129	30.5	0	0	1	1	0	0	0	0	0	0	0	0	0	1	0	0	0	0	0	0	0	0	1	0	0
mapped	16	.5385	1.8462	42.7	1	2	2	3	6	2	0	0	3	0	0	0	0	1	0	4	0	0	0	0	0	1	2	5	0
mapping	7	.4136	.6511	38.1	1	2	0	0	2	1	1	0	1	0	0	0	0	0	0	3	0	0	0	0	0	1	2	0	0
maps	428	.6453	57.151	57.6	76	110	67	68	28	25	31	23	33	5	1	2	13	242	3	41	0	2	0	19	2	6	51	8	0
Mapuche	2	.0000	.0209	23.2	0	0	0	0	2	0	0	0	0	0	0	0	0	0	0	0	0	0	0	0	0	0	2	0	0
Maquas	2	.0000	.0234	23.7	0	0	0	0	2	0	0	0	0	0	0	0	0	0	0	0	0	0	0	0	2	0	0	0	0
maquis	6	.0000	.0644	28.1	0	0	0	0	0	6	0	0	0	0	0	6	0	0	0	0	0	0	0	0	0	0	0	0	0
mar	7	.5229	.7753	38.9	0	1	0	0	2	1	1	2	1	0	0	0	0	0	1	0	0	0	0	0	0	2	1	2	0
Mar	8	.0000	.0837	29.2	0	0	0	0	6	1	1	0	0	0	0	0	0	0	0	0	0	0	0	0	0	0	8	0	0
Maracaibo	6	.1822	.3062	34.9	0	0	4	2	0	0	0	0	0	0	0	0	0	5	0	0	0	0	0	0	0	1	0	0	0
maracas	13	.0000	.1051	30.2	2	4	2	0	5	0	0	0	0	0	0	0	0	0	0	0	13	0	0	0	0	0	0	0	0
Marat	8	.0000	.0837	29.2	0	0	8	0	0	0	0	0	0	0	0	0	0	0	0	0	0	0	0	0	0	0	8	0	0
Marat's	2	.0000	.0209	23.2	0	0	2	0	0	0	0	0	0	0	0	0	0	0	0	0	0	0	0	0	0	0	2	0	0
marathon	5	.0000	.2284	33.6	0	0	0	5	0	0	0	0	5	0	0	0	0	0	0	0	0	0	0	0	0	0	0	0	0
Marathon	3	.0000	.0314	25.0	0	0	3	0	0	0	0	0	0	0	0	0	0	0	0	0	0	0	0	0	0	0	3	0	0
marauding	3	.2304	.1619	32.1	0	0	0	0	3	0	0	0	0	0	0	0	0	0	0	0	0	0	0	0	2	0	1	0	0
marble	60	.6519	8.0633	49.1	12	2	14	15	8	6	3	0	7	1	0	2	0	8	0	12	0	4	0	0	3	13	9	1	0
Marble	2	.2437	.1129	30.5	0	0	0	1	1	0	0	0	0	0	0	0	0	0	0	0	0	0	0	0	0	0	1	1	0
marbleizing	2	.0000	.0037	15.7	0	0	2	0	0	0	0	0	0	0	0	0	0	0	0	0	0	2	0	0	0	0	0	0	0
marbles	168	.3939	14.932	51.7	40	65	35	3	16	6	3	0	23	9	0	2	113	0	1	6	0	0	0	0	3	10	0	1	0
Marbury	2	.0000	.0290	24.6	2	0	0	0	0	0	0	0	0	0	0	0	0	0	0	0	0	0	0	0	0	2	0	0	0
marc	3	.2197	.2090	33.2	0	0	0	1	2	0	0	0	2	0	0	0	0	0	0	0	0	0	0	0	0	0	1	0	0
Marc	116	.3181	10.723	50.3	27	4	0	0	83	1	1	0	110	0	0	0	2	0	0	0	0	1	0	0	1	0	0	2	0
Marc's	4	.0000	.1827	32.6	2	0	0	0	2	0	0	0	4	0	0	0	0	0	0	0	0	0	0	0	0	0	0	0	0
marcato	2	.0000	.0162	22.1	0	0	0	0	0	0	2	0	0	0	0	0	0	0	0	0	2	0	0	0	0	0	0	0	0
Marcel	2	.1814	.1187	30.7	0	0	0	1	0	0	1	0	1	0	0	0	0	0	0	0	0	0	0	0	0	0	0	1	0
Marcello	2	.0000	.0394	26.0	0	0	0	0	0	1	1	0	0	0	0	0	0	0	0	2	0	0	0	0	0	0	0	0	0
march	130	.5715	15.750	52.0	23	18	32	8	15	18	11	5	35	2	1	10	0	18	1	0	37	1	0	0	6	9	2	6	2
March	215	.8628	37.094	55.7	37	38	22	17	35	42	14	10	55	11	1	8	7	30	4	11	14	0	0	0	11	19	21	23	0
MARCH	2	.1814	.1187	30.7	1	0	0	1	0	0	0	0	1	0	0	0	0	0	0	0	0	0	0	0	0	0	0	1	0
marched	123	.7568	18.990	52.8	22	28	15	13	14	24	6	1	39	2	3	5	0	12	0	0	3	0	0	0	18	24	8	9	0
marchers	2	.2346	.1166	30.7	0	0	0	0	2	0	0	0	0	0	0	0	0	0	0	1	0	0	0	0	0	0	0	1	0
marches	29	.4534	2.8318	44.5	4	0	10	2	4	6	1	2	4	2	0	1	0	4	0	0	14	0	0	0	0	1	2	1	0
marching	115	.5613	13.592	51.3	13	30	22	8	11	24	6	1	24	4	0	7	3	5	1	0	45	0	0	0	3	13	2	8	0
Marching	10	.0000	.0808	29.1	0	1	2	3	4	0	0	0	0	0	0	0	0	0	0	0	10	0	0	0	0	0	0	0	0
Marcia	5	.1531	.1872	32.7	0	0	0	4	1	0	0	0	0	1	0	0	0	0	4	0	0	0	0	0	0	0	0	0	0
Marcia's	2	.0000	.0299	24.8	0	0	2	0	0	0	0	0	0	0	0	0	2	0	0	0	0	0	0	0	0	0	0	0	0
Marco	57	.4876	6.3881	48.1	28	0	9	5	2	12	1	0	29	0	0	1	0	18	0	0	0	0	0	0	0	7	2	0	0
Marco's	3	.0000	.1370	31.4	3	0	0	0	0	0	0	0	3	0	0	0	0	0	0	0	0	0	0	0	0	0	0	0	0
Marconi	6	.3079	.4501	36.5	1	0	1	0	1	1	1	1	1	0	0	0	0	0	0	3	0	0	0	0	0	0	2	0	0
Marcos	4	.3454	.3075	34.9	0	2	0	1	1	0	0	0	0	0	0	0	0	1	0	0	0	0	0	0	2	0	0	1	0
Marcus	32	.5654	4.0138	46.0	4	0	2	18	0	5	1	2	19	0	0	0	4	3	0	0	0	0	0	0	0	1	4	1	0
Marcy	57	.2033	2.9316	44.7	0	0	50	0	5	0	2	0	4	0	0	2	0	0	0	0	0	0	0	0	5	0	0	46	0
Marcy's	5	.1794	.2258	33.5	0	0	4	0	1	0	0	0	0	0	0	0	0	0	0	0	0	0	0	0	1	0	0	4	0
Mardi	4	.3782	.3355	35.3	0	2	1	0	1	0	0	0	0	0	0	0	0	2	0	0	1	0	0	0	0	1	0	0	0
mare	54	.6807	7.5342	48.8	5	13	4	15	11	5	1	0	10	3	1	7	0	0	0	0	2	0	0	0	17	10	2	2	0
Mare	2	.0000	.0219	23.4	0	0	0	0	2	0	0	0	0	2	0	0	0	0	0	0	0	0	0	0	0	0	0	0	0
mare's	11	.5049	1.1828	40.7	1	2	0	3	2	2	1	0	1	0	0	2	0	2	0	0	0	0	0	0	3	3	0	0	0
mares	12	.2755	.7903	39.0	1	7	3	0	1	0	0	0	1	0	0	0	0	0	0	0	0	0	0	0	4	7	0	0	0
Marfa	4	.0000	.1827	32.6	0	0	4	0	0	0	0	0	4	0	0	0	0	0	0	0	0	0	0	0	0	0	0	0	0
Margaret	53	.7308	7.9183	49.0	2	15	7	8	7	6	6	2	14	9	0	4	3	2	1	0	0	0	0	0	3	12	2	3	0
Margaret's	3	.3780	.2437	33.9	1	1	0	0	0	0	1	0	0	1	0	0	0	0	1	0	0	0	0	0	0	1	0	0	0
margarine	30	.1931	1.4073	41.5	1	1	4	0	10	7	5	1	3	0	0	0	0	1	2	4	0	0	18	0	1	0	0	1	0
Margarita	4	.0000	.1827	32.6	4	0	0	0	0	0	0	0	4	0	0	0	0	0	0	0	0	0	0	0	0	0	0	0	0
marge	2	.0000	.0914	29.6	0	0	0	0	2	0	0	0	2	0	0	0	0	0	0	0	0	0	0	0	0	0	0	0	0
Marge	8	.4496	.7992	39.0	2	1	3	0	2	0	0	0	2	0	0	0	3	0	1	0	0	0	0	0	2	0	0	0	0
Marget	7	.0000	.0751	28.8	0	0	0	0	0	7	0	0	0	0	0	7	0	0	0	0	0	0	0	0	0	0	0	0	0
Marghuerite	2	.0000	.0243	23.9	0	0	0	0	2	0	0	0	0	0	0	0	0	0	0	0	0	0	0	0	0	0	0	2	0
Margie	10	.1134	.3182	35.0	0	0	0	0	1	9	0	0	0	1	0	9	0	0	0	0	0	0	0	0	0	0	0	0	0
Margie's	3	.0000	.0322	25.1	0	0	0	0	0	3	0	0	0	0	0	3	0	0	0	0	0	0	0	0	0	0	0	0	0
margin	59	.7868	9.3190	49.7	0	11	3	5	20	11	8	1	7	17	3	4	3	5	3	3	0	1	0	1	2	2	8	0	0
marginal	10	.5235	1.0911	40.4	0	2	1	0	5	1	1	0	0	1	0	0	0	1	0	1	0	0	0	0	0	1	4	2	0
marginally	2	.0000	.0243	23.9	0	0	0	0	0	0	1	1	0	0	0	0	0	0	0	0	0	0	0	0	0	0	0	2	0
margins	37	.7002	5.2821	47.2	5	4	5	1	11	1	10	0	5	8	3	0	0	4	2	7	1	0	0	1	0	2	4	0	0
Margot	4	.2174	.2134	33.3	0	1	0	0	0	3	0	0	0	1	0	0	0	0	0	0	0	0	0	0	0	3	0	0	0
margraves	2	.0000	.0209	23.2	0	0	0	0	0	1	1	0	0	0	0	0	0	0	0	0	0	0	0	0	0	0	2	0	0
Margrethe	3	.0000	.0434	26.4	0	0	3	0	0	0	0	0	0	0	0	0	0	0	0	0	0	0	0	0	0	3	0	0	0
Margrethe's	4	.0000	.0579	27.6	0	0	4	0	0	0	0	0	0	0	0	0	0	0	0	0	0	0	0	0	0	4	0	0	0
Margriet	5	.0000	.0972	29.9	0	5	0	0	0	0	0	0	0	0	0	0	0	5	0	0	0	0	0	0	0	0	0	0	0
Marguerite	4	.4441	.3916	35.9	0	1	0	0	2	0	1	0	1	0	0	0	0	0	0	0	1	0	0	0	0	0	1	1	0
Maria	199	.6013	25.433	54.1	61	94	4	10	3	13	13	1	60	12	0	11	2	33	0	1	0	0	0	0	1	70	3	6	0
Maria's	13	.4727	1.3794	41.4	4	6	0	1	0	2	0	0	4	2	0	0	0	4	0	0	0	0	0	0	0	3	0	0	0
Mariah	4	.0000	.0486	26.9	4	0	0	0	0	0	0	0	0	0	0	0	0	0	0	0	0	0	0	0	0	0	0	4	0
Marian	15	.2991	1.0000	40.0	0	7	0	4	0	4	0	0	0	1	0	0	0	0	0	0	7	0	0	0	0	7	0	0	0
Marianas	10	.3652	.8329	39.2	0	0	0	7	1	0	2	0	0	0	0	0	3	5	0	2	0	0	0	0	0	0	0	0	0
Mariano	2	.2351	.1166	30.7	0	0	0	1	0	1	0	0	0	0	0	0	0	1	0	0	0	0	0	0	0	0	0	1	0
Marichal	2	.0000	.0243	23.9	0	0	0	1	0	1	0	0	0	0	0	0	0	0	0	0	0	0	0	0	0	0	0	2	0
Marie	77	.7051	11.155	50.5	27	0	10	16	5	9	7	3	22	3	2	2	1	2	0	10	21	1	0	0	0	6	6	1	0
Marie-Joseph	2	.0000	.0234	23.7	0	2	0	0	0	0	0	0	0	0	0	0	0	0	0	0	0	0	0	0	2	0	0	0	0
Marie-Joseph's	2	.0000	.0234	23.7	0	2	0	0	0	0	0	0	0	0	0	0	0	0	0	0	0	0	0	0	2	0	0	0	0
Marie-Louise	17	.0000	.7766	38.9	17	0	0	0	0	0	0	0	17	0	0	0	0	0	0	0	0	0	0	0	0	0	0	0	0
Marie's	6	.4630	.6208	37.9	3	0	0	0	1	0	0	2	2	1	0	0	0	0	0	0	1	0	0	0	0	2	0	0	0
Marietta	6	.3582	.4750	36.8	0	0	5	1	0	0	0	0	0	0	0	0	0	2	0	0	1	0	0	0	3	0	0	0	0

7A map-makers
8E map-to-child
3F map's
6N mape
5P Mapes
3E Mapledale
5G mappa
9H Maps
7Q marabou
6N marae
6J Marais
7P Maran
8Q Maranhao
5Q Marathi
6R Maravich's
5A maravilla
5P Marbella
5A marble-playing
3A marble-topped
5H marble's
6P marbled
9H marblelike
7F march-ins
8J march-like
7N March's
7Q Marches
7D marchin'
XH Marconi's
9D Marcum
6F Marduk
6F Marduk's
5A Marfa's
XH Marfak
8L margarines
3A Margarita's
7N margaritifera
3A Marge's
6H Margery
8D Marget's
4F Margo
7R Margolis
7P Margrave
4F Margriet's
7Q mari
6B Marian's
4R maribou
3A Marie-Louise's
6N marigold

Word Type	F	D	U	SFI	3 Gr 3	4 Gr 4	5 Gr 5	6 Gr 6	7 Gr 7	8 Gr 8	9 Gr 9	X UnGr	A Read	B Eng & Gr	C Comp	D Lit	E Math	F Soc Stud	G Spell	H Sci	J Music	K Art	L Home Ec	M Shop	N Lib F	P Lib NF	Q Lib Ref	R Mag	S Rel
marijuana	36	.1551	1.5113	41.8	0	0	2	0	19	2	11	2	0	0	0	0	0	1	0	6	0	0	0	0	0	0	0	29	0
Marilyn	10	.4712	1.1137	40.5	8	0	0	0	1	1	0	0	7	0	0	0	1	0	1	0	0	0	0	0	0	0	0	1	0
marimba	2	.0000	.0162	22.1	0	0	0	1	1	0	0	0	0	0	0	0	0	0	0	0	2	0	0	0	0	0	0	0	0
Marin	2	.1493	.0692	28.4	0	0	0	0	0	2	0	0	0	0	0	0	0	0	0	0	0	1	0	0	0	0	1	0	0
marina	2	.0000	.0243	23.9	0	0	0	1	0	0	0	1	0	0	0	0	0	0	0	0	0	0	0	0	0	0	0	2	0
marine	57	.7017	8.1416	49.1	1	3	2	10	20	3	14	4	3	3	0	2	1	13	0	11	1	0	0	0	1	2	13	7	0
Marine	21	.5895	2.5821	44.1	7	0	1	3	4	4	1	1	3	0	0	0	0	2	0	1	3	0	0	0	0	2	4	6	0
Marineland	8	.3196	.6960	38.4	0	6	0	1	0	1	0	0	6	0	1	0	0	0	1	0	0	0	0	0	0	0	0	0	0
mariner	3	.3125	.2347	33.7	0	0	0	2	0	1	0	0	1	0	0	0	0	0	0	1	1	0	0	0	0	0	0	0	0
Mariner	22	.5177	2.4065	43.8	1	10	0	1	1	7	2	0	1	0	0	0	7	1	0	3	0	0	0	0	4	0	0	6	0
mariners	8	.4412	.7546	38.8	0	1	1	0	4	2	0	0	0	0	0	0	0	2	0	0	0	0	0	0	0	1	3	2	0
Mariners	2	.0000	.0243	23.9	0	2	0	0	0	0	0	0	0	0	0	0	0	0	0	0	0	0	0	0	0	0	0	2	0
Mariners'	2	.0000	.0243	23.9	0	2	0	0	0	0	0	0	0	0	0	0	0	0	0	0	0	0	0	0	0	0	0	2	0
marines	9	.5436	1.0184	40.1	1	0	2	0	2	2	2	0	0	0	0	1	0	3	0	0	2	0	0	0	0	2	1	0	0
Marines	13	.4015	1.1909	40.8	3	0	1	2	0	7	0	0	2	0	0	0	0	8	0	0	1	0	0	0	0	0	2	0	0
Marinoff	3	.0000	.0328	25.2	0	0	0	0	0	0	3	0	0	3	0	0	0	0	0	0	0	0	0	0	0	0	0	0	0
Mario	17	.1718	1.1892	40.8	6	7	0	3	0	0	0	1	16	0	0	0	0	0	0	0	0	0	0	0	0	0	0	1	0
Mario's	3	.0000	.1370	31.4	2	0	0	1	0	0	0	0	3	0	0	0	0	0	0	0	0	0	0	0	0	0	0	0	0
Marion	6	.4507	.5790	37.6	0	3	2	0	0	1	0	0	0	0	0	0	1	1	0	0	0	0	0	0	2	2	0	0	0
marionette	3	.0000	.1370	31.4	1	0	2	0	0	0	0	0	3	0	0	0	0	0	0	0	0	0	0	0	0	0	0	0	0
Mariquita	14	.0000	.6396	38.1	0	14	0	0	0	0	0	0	14	0	0	0	0	0	0	0	0	0	0	0	0	0	0	0	0
Maris	2	.2433	.1158	30.6	1	1	0	0	0	0	0	0	0	0	0	0	0	0	0	0	0	0	0	0	0	1	0	1	0
maritime	7	.5379	.7793	38.9	1	0	2	0	3	1	0	0	0	0	0	0	0	1	0	0	0	0	0	1	1	2	1	1	0
Maritime	4	.0000	.0419	26.2	0	0	3	0	1	0	0	0	0	0	0	0	0	0	0	0	0	0	0	0	0	0	4	0	0
marjoram	3	.1386	.0963	29.8	0	0	0	1	0	0	2	0	0	0	0	0	0	0	0	0	0	0	2	0	0	0	1	0	0
Marjorie	12	.5413	1.4499	41.6	8	0	0	1	0	3	0	0	7	0	0	1	0	0	0	0	0	0	0	0	0	1	2	1	0
mark	980	.7643	150.57	61.8	142	192	158	109	195	90	85	9	104	137	10	17	186	34	284	50	15	3	40	31	10	23	18	18	0
Mark	275	.8000	44.803	56.5	146	54	14	5	23	28	3	2	124	16	0	8	10	58	1	3	0	2	1	6	26	11	0	9	0
MARK	2	.1787	.1174	30.7	0	0	0	0	2	0	0	0	1	0	0	0	0	0	0	0	0	0	0	0	1	0	0	0	0
Mark's	28	.4854	2.9789	44.7	6	12	0	5	3	2	0	0	8	3	0	1	1	0	0	0	1	0	0	0	13	1	0	0	0
Markab	2	.0000	.0394	26.0	0	0	0	0	0	0	0	2	0	0	0	0	0	0	0	2	0	0	0	0	0	0	0	0	0
markdown	4	.0000	.0599	27.8	0	0	0	0	0	1	3	0	0	0	0	0	4	0	0	0	0	0	0	0	0	0	0	0	0
marked	370	.9389	68.661	58.4	30	53	58	45	84	43	43	14	51	24	2	8	59	32	10	44	27	3	12	7	15	19	32	25	0
markedly	6	.5586	.7010	38.5	0	0	1	0	2	0	2	1	0	0	0	0	0	1	0	2	0	0	0	0	0	1	1	1	0
marker	46	.5007	5.0216	47.0	3	11	14	10	5	3	0	0	13	20	0	3	5	2	1	0	0	0	0	0	0	1	1	0	0
Marker	2	.0000	.0914	29.6	0	0	0	2	0	0	0	0	2	0	0	0	0	0	0	0	0	0	0	0	0	0	0	0	0
markers	25	.3747	2.1083	43.2	1	1	8	5	8	1	1	0	4	14	0	2	4	0	0	0	0	0	0	0	0	0	1	0	0
market	383	.8381	64.546	58.1	71	63	47	54	73	43	24	8	110	4	1	10	2	127	5	9	13	2	14	1	19	18	25	23	0
Market	45	.6881	6.3890	48.1	15	7	3	2	8	1	8	1	11	0	1	1	0	12	0	0	5	0	0	0	0	4	3	8	0
market-place	5	.3536	.4328	36.4	3	1	0	1	0	0	0	0	2	0	0	0	0	0	0	0	0	0	0	0	1	2	0	0	0
marketed	3	.2867	.1938	32.9	0	0	0	1	0	0	1	1	0	0	0	0	0	1	0	0	0	0	1	0	0	0	0	1	0
marketing	20	.6004	2.5299	44.0	3	5	1	3	2	2	3	1	5	0	0	0	0	5	0	0	0	0	2	0	1	1	3	3	0
marketplace	5	.4143	.4656	36.7	0	1	0	0	2	1	1	0	1	0	0	0	0	1	0	0	0	0	0	0	0	0	1	2	0
markets	90	.6278	11.701	50.7	10	10	22	18	13	6	6	5	4	0	0	0	0	55	0	3	1	2	2	0	1	5	9	8	0
marking	68	.5620	7.8811	49.0	7	8	3	2	19	14	15	0	6	2	0	1	7	5	0	3	3	0	16	11	1	5	3	5	0
markings	44	.7292	6.4768	48.1	7	5	8	4	6	6	6	2	5	1	0	0	0	0	3	6	11	1	5	1	1	6	3	1	0
Markland	2	.2446	.1123	30.5	0	0	0	1	1	0	0	0	0	1	0	0	0	0	0	0	0	0	0	0	0	0	1	0	0
Markovna	3	.0000	.1370	31.4	3	0	0	0	0	0	0	0	3	0	0	0	0	0	0	0	0	0	0	0	0	0	0	0	0
marks	469	.7877	73.941	58.7	64	78	112	43	78	44	44	6	35	128	20	14	65	15	102	22	13	5	10	4	7	10	10	9	0
Marks	2	.2446	.1184	30.7	0	1	0	0	0	0	1	0	0	0	0	0	1	0	0	0	0	0	0	0	0	1	0	0	0
marksman	3	.3408	.2477	33.9	0	1	0	1	0	1	0	0	1	0	0	1	0	0	0	0	0	0	0	0	0	1	0	0	0
markup	5	.0000	.0748	28.7	0	0	0	0	0	0	5	0	0	0	0	0	5	0	0	0	0	0	0	0	0	0	0	0	0
Marlene	2	.2427	.1159	30.6	1	0	0	0	1	0	0	0	0	0	0	0	1	0	0	0	0	0	0	0	0	0	0	1	0
Marley	11	.3312	.9379	39.7	0	5	0	0	4	2	0	0	6	1	0	0	0	0	0	0	0	0	0	0	4	0	0	0	0
Marley's	4	.1787	.2347	33.7	0	2	0	0	0	2	0	0	2	0	0	0	0	0	0	0	0	0	0	0	2	0	0	0	0
marlin	4	.2065	.1985	33.0	0	0	0	0	1	0	3	0	0	0	0	0	0	0	0	0	0	0	0	0	3	0	1	0	0
Marlon	3	.1937	.1495	31.7	0	0	0	0	1	1	1	0	0	0	0	0	0	1	0	0	0	0	0	0	0	0	0	2	0
Marlowe	4	.2446	.2246	33.5	0	1	1	0	1	0	1	0	0	2	0	0	0	0	0	0	0	0	0	0	0	0	2	0	0
marmalade	4	.2278	.2911	34.6	3	0	0	1	0	0	0	0	3	0	0	0	0	0	0	0	1	0	0	0	0	0	0	0	0
Marmara	7	.1679	.3402	35.3	0	0	1	2	4	0	0	0	0	0	0	0	0	6	0	0	0	0	0	0	0	1	0	0	0
Marmee	2	.0000	.0234	23.7	0	0	0	0	2	0	0	0	0	0	0	0	0	0	0	0	0	0	0	0	2	0	0	0	0
marmosas	2	.0000	.0209	23.2	0	0	0	0	2	0	0	0	0	0	0	0	0	0	0	0	0	0	0	0	0	0	2	0	0
marmot	2	.1948	.1250	31.0	0	0	1	0	1	0	0	0	1	0	0	0	0	0	0	0	0	0	0	0	0	1	0	0	0
Marmot	5	.0000	.0586	27.7	0	0	0	5	0	0	0	0	0	0	0	0	0	0	0	0	0	0	0	0	5	0	0	0	0
Marne	3	.0000	.0583	27.7	0	0	0	0	0	3	0	0	0	0	0	0	0	3	0	0	0	0	0	0	0	0	0	0	0
maroon	2	.2440	.1132	30.5	0	0	0	0	1	1	0	0	0	0	0	1	0	0	0	0	0	0	0	0	0	0	0	1	0
marooned	3	.2357	.2199	33.4	0	0	0	0	3	0	0	0	2	0	0	0	0	0	0	0	0	0	0	0	0	1	0	0	0
marquee	2	.2440	.1132	30.5	0	0	0	0	1	0	1	0	0	0	0	1	0	0	0	0	0	0	0	0	0	0	0	1	0
Marques	2	.0000	.0389	25.9	0	0	0	2	0	0	0	0	0	0	0	0	0	2	0	0	0	0	0	0	0	0	0	0	0
Marquette	2	.2351	.1166	30.7	0	0	1	1	0	0	0	0	0	0	0	0	0	1	0	0	0	0	0	0	0	0	0	1	0
Marquis	10	.5248	1.0938	40.4	0	1	1	0	3	2	3	0	0	0	0	3	0	3	0	0	2	0	0	0	0	1	1	0	0
Marquise	2	.2387	.1089	30.4	0	1	0	0	1	0	0	0	0	0	0	0	0	0	0	0	1	0	0	0	1	0	0	0	0
marred	7	.4236	.6487	38.1	0	0	0	1	4	0	2	0	1	0	1	1	0	1	0	0	0	0	0	0	0	0	0	3	0
marriage	85	.6993	12.077	50.8	2	7	12	10	29	11	10	4	8	9	0	14	0	3	1	1	2	0	0	0	1	20	10	16	0
Marriage	4	.1534	.1534	31.9	0	0	1	0	0	3	0	0	0	0	0	0	0	0	0	0	3	0	0	0	0	1	0	0	0
marriageable	2	.1717	.1142	30.6	0	0	0	1	1	0	0	0	1	0	0	1	0	0	0	0	0	0	0	0	0	0	0	0	0
marriages	7	.5184	.7825	38.9	0	1	2	0	0	3	1	0	1	0	0	1	0	2	0	1	0	0	0	0	0	2	0	0	0
married	184	.8396	30.947	54.9	25	26	31	22	24	29	20	7	41	12	0	23	2	18	4	0	5	1	1	0	14	31	17	15	0
Married	2	.1494	.1045	30.2	0	0	0	0	2	0	0	0	1	0	0	0	0	0	0	0	1	0	0	0	0	0	0	0	0
marries	5	.3602	.3954	36.0	0	1	0	0	4	0	0	0	0	1	0	0	0	0	0	0	0	0	0	0	0	3	1	0	0
marrow	12	.4995	1.3018	41.1	0	0	1	3	2	5	1	0	2	0	0	0	0	0	0	5	0	0	0	0	3	0	1	1	0
marry	141	.6845	20.038	53.0	36	21	9	20	25	13	17	0	52	1	0	19	1	7	4	0	25	0	0	0	2	19	4	7	0
mars	2	.2278	.1128	30.5	0	0	2	0	0	0	0	0	0	0	0	0	0	0	0	1	0	0	0	0	0	0	1	0	0
Mars	176	.7482	26.940	54.3	17	37	24	37	22	18	14	7	47	1	1	6	24	8	0	52	0	0	0	0	3	9	10	15	0
Mars'	3	.2437	.2277	33.6	0	0	2	0	0	0	1	0	2	0	0	0	0	0	0	1	0	0	0	0	0	0	0	0	0
Marsden	4	.0000	.1827	32.6	0	0	0	0	4	0	0	0	4	0	0	0	0	0	0	0	0	0	0	0	0	0	0	0	0
Marseillaise	4	.1534	.1534	31.9	0	0	1	0	2	1	0	0	0	0	0	0	0	0	0	0	3	0	0	0	0	1	0	0	0
Marseille	6	.1125	.1964	32.9	5	0	0	1	0	0	0	0	0	0	0	0	0	1	0	0	0	0	0	0	0	0	5	0	0
marsh	52	.6995	7.4831	48.7	13	7	8	10	3	3	3	5	12	0	2	6	1	1	0	10	0	0	0	0	4	13	2	1	0
Marsh	18	.5227	2.0782	43.2	2	1	5	0	4	6	0	0	8	0	0	2	0	0	0	0	0	0	0	0	5	0	1	2	0
Marsh's	2	.0000	.0243	23.9	0	0	0	0	2	0	0	0	0	0	0	0	0	0	0	0	0	0	0	0	0	0	0	2	0
marshal	6	.4316	.5770	37.6	0	0	2	1	1	1	1	0	1	1	0	0	0	2	0	0	0	0	0	0	0	0	0	2	0
Marshal	16	.5241	1.7929	42.5	0	0	0	0	5	6	5	0	2	0	0	1	0	6	0	0	0	0	0	0	0	1	1	5	0
marshaled	4	.4866	.4069	36.1	0	1	0	1	0	0	2	0	0	0	0	1	0	0	0	0	0	0	0	0	1	1	1	0	0

4B Marigold
8K Marin's
5R Marina
7P mariner-merchants
7A mariner's
8J Marines'
7Q Maringer
5Q Marino
9R Marinos
7Q marinus
8F Mariposa
7Q Marismas
6F Maritsa
7A market's
7F marketability
7C Marketbasket
XR Marketing
XR Markets
7G markhzan
5N markin'
3A Markle
8Q Marko
3A Marks's
8B marksmanship
8P marksmen's
9Q Markt
5P marl
4E Marla's
7R Marlik
7N marlinspike
8D Marlow
9Q Marlowe's
7A Marlton's
5N MARMALADE
7H Marmet
7Q Marmosa
7R marmots
6R Marner
9Q Maronite
3A marozhenoye
8P Marquesas
4N marquis
8D Marquis's
9D marriage-day
7P marriageble
6R Marriner
9L marring
6J Marry
4R marry-go-round
4A marrying
6A MarsCity
5P Marse
9B marsh-mist
4E Marsha
7D marshal's
8N marshaling
8B marshall

Word Type	F	D	U	SFI	3 Gr 3	4 Gr 4	5 Gr 5	6 Gr 6	7 Gr 7	8 Gr 8	9 Gr 9	X UnGr	A Read	B Eng & Gr	C Comp	D Lit	E Math	F Soc Stud	G Spell	H Sci	J Music	K Art	L Home Ec	M Shop	N Lib F	P Lib NF	Q Lib Ref	R Mag	S Rel
Marshall	25	.5994	3.1964	45.0	3	3	1	0	0	12	3	3	8	0	0	3	1	7	0	0	0	0	0	0	0	3	0	3	0
Marshalls	2	.0000	.0389	25.9	0	0	0	2	0	0	0	0	0	0	0	0	0	2	0	0	0	0	0	0	0	0	0	0	0
marshals	4	.3603	.3219	35.1	0	1	0	0	1	1	0	1	0	0	0	0	0	1	0	0	0	0	0	0	0	2	0	1	0
marshes	33	.6924	4.6794	46.7	3	3	2	12	6	2	4	1	4	0	0	5	0	5	0	7	0	0	0	0	5	2	3	2	0
marshland	4	.2433	.2315	33.6	0	2	0	1	0	0	0	1	0	0	0	0	0	0	0	0	0	0	0	0	0	2	0	2	0
marshlands	3	.3427	.2477	33.9	0	0	0	0	1	1	0	1	1	0	0	0	0	0	0	0	0	0	0	0	1	0	0	1	0
marshmallow	4	.4525	.3990	36.0	0	0	1	1	1	0	1	0	1	1	0	1	0	0	0	0	0	0	0	0	1	0	0	0	0
marshmallows	10	.1951	.4600	36.6	0	1	3	0	3	0	3	0	1	2	0	0	0	0	1	0	0	0	6	0	0	0	0	0	0
marshy	20	.6134	2.5887	44.1	0	3	2	3	9	2	1	0	6	0	0	2	0	4	0	0	1	0	0	0	0	1	5	1	0
Marson	3	.0000	.0449	26.5	0	0	3	0	0	0	0	0	0	0	0	0	3	0	0	0	0	0	0	0	0	0	0	0	0
Marston	2	.0000	.0045	16.5	0	0	0	0	0	2	0	0	0	0	2	0	0	0	0	0	0	0	0	0	0	0	0	0	0
marsupialis	3	.0000	.0314	25.0	0	0	0	0	3	0	0	0	0	0	0	0	0	0	0	0	0	0	0	0	0	0	3	0	0
marsupials	7	.3672	.6359	38.0	0	0	0	3	2	0	0	2	3	0	0	0	0	0	0	3	0	0	0	0	0	0	1	0	0
mart	2	.2440	.1132	30.5	0	0	0	0	0	0	1	1	0	0	0	1	0	0	0	0	0	0	0	0	0	0	0	1	0
Mart	10	.3598	.7788	38.9	1	0	1	7	0	1	0	0	0	2	0	5	0	0	0	0	0	0	0	0	0	0	0	3	0
Martha	71	.7852	11.281	50.5	10	9	9	6	8	14	7	8	17	8	1	2	3	11	2	0	1	0	0	0	1	15	1	9	0
Martha's	6	.3444	.5197	37.2	1	1	3	0	1	0	0	0	3	2	0	0	0	0	0	0	0	0	0	0	0	1	0	0	0
Marthe	12	.0000	.1288	31.1	0	0	0	0	0	0	12	0	0	0	0	12	0	0	0	0	0	0	0	0	0	0	0	0	0
Marti	2	.0000	.0290	24.6	0	0	0	0	2	0	0	0	0	0	0	0	0	0	0	0	0	0	0	0	0	2	0	0	0
martial	5	.4492	.4760	36.8	0	0	0	0	2	3	0	0	0	0	0	1	0	1	0	0	0	0	0	0	1	0	2	0	0
Martian	12	.4458	1.3027	41.1	1	0	0	9	2	0	0	0	9	0	0	0	0	0	0	1	0	0	0	0	0	0	1	1	0
Martin	193	.5893	23.760	53.8	7	48	78	23	13	9	9	6	32	8	0	19	5	12	0	4	6	0	0	0	89	1	9	8	0
Martin's	14	.4964	1.5338	41.9	1	5	3	1	1	0	3	0	5	0	0	0	1	0	0	0	0	0	0	0	4	0	3	1	0
Martina	2	.0000	.0914	29.6	2	0	0	0	0	0	0	0	2	0	0	0	0	0	0	0	0	0	0	0	0	0	0	0	0
Martinez	3	.0000	.0365	25.6	0	0	0	0	1	2	0	0	0	0	0	0	0	0	0	0	0	0	0	0	0	0	0	3	0
martins	2	.0000	.0209	23.2	0	0	0	1	1	0	0	0	0	0	0	0	0	0	0	0	0	0	0	0	0	0	2	0	0
Marty	19	.4255	1.9490	42.9	0	0	18	1	0	0	0	0	12	0	0	0	0	0	1	0	0	0	0	0	5	0	0	1	0
martyr	3	.3265	.2369	33.7	0	0	0	1	1	0	1	0	1	0	0	0	0	0	1	0	0	0	0	0	0	0	0	1	0
martyred	2	.2440	.1132	30.5	0	0	0	0	0	0	2	0	0	0	0	1	0	0	0	0	0	0	0	0	0	0	0	1	0
martyrs	2	.1948	.1250	31.0	1	0	0	0	1	0	0	0	1	0	0	0	0	0	0	0	0	0	0	0	0	1	0	0	0
marvel	23	.7385	3.4794	45.4	0	2	0	3	9	4	2	3	8	1	0	0	0	1	1	1	1	0	0	1	0	2	4	3	0
Marvel	2	.0000	.0243	23.9	0	0	0	0	2	0	0	0	0	0	0	0	0	0	0	0	0	0	0	0	0	0	0	2	0
marveled	17	.4473	1.7763	42.5	1	5	4	0	3	2	2	0	9	0	0	5	0	1	0	0	0	0	0	0	1	1	0	0	0
marveling	2	.0000	.0914	29.6	1	0	1	0	0	0	0	0	2	0	0	0	0	0	0	0	0	0	0	0	0	0	0	0	0
Marvello	23	.0000	1.0507	40.2	0	0	0	23	0	0	0	0	23	0	0	0	0	0	0	0	0	0	0	0	0	0	0	0	0
Marvello's	3	.0000	.1370	31.4	0	0	0	3	0	0	0	0	3	0	0	0	0	0	0	0	0	0	0	0	0	0	0	0	0
marvellously	2	.0000	.0243	23.9	0	0	0	0	0	0	0	2	0	0	0	0	0	0	0	0	0	0	0	0	0	0	0	2	0
marvelous	56	.7891	8.9498	49.5	3	9	6	6	9	4	5	14	15	1	1	3	0	2	1	12	2	0	0	0	10	2	1	6	0
Marvelous	2	.0000	.0234	23.7	0	2	0	0	0	0	0	0	0	0	0	0	0	0	0	0	0	0	0	0	2	0	0	0	0
marvelously	10	.5482	1.1630	40.7	0	2	1	1	3	1	1	1	2	0	0	0	0	1	2	0	0	0	0	0	1	1	0	3	0
marvels	17	.5911	2.0894	43.2	0	2	1	3	5	3	0	3	2	3	0	0	0	1	1	2	0	0	0	0	0	1	6	1	0
Marvin	3	.2121	.1560	31.9	1	0	0	2	0	0	0	0	0	0	0	0	1	0	0	0	0	0	0	0	0	0	0	2	0
Marx	3	.2425	.1816	32.6	0	0	0	0	1	1	1	0	0	0	0	0	0	2	0	0	0	0	0	0	0	0	0	1	0
Marxist	3	.3815	.2534	34.0	0	0	1	0	0	0	2	0	0	0	0	0	0	1	0	0	0	0	0	0	0	1	0	1	0
Mary	675	.7745	105.90	60.2	129	217	144	50	71	21	35	8	163	73	0	22	93	25	18	8	15	0	5	0	108	125	7	10	3
MARY	11	.0000	.1180	30.7	0	0	0	0	1	5	5	0	0	0	0	11	0	0	0	0	0	0	0	0	0	0	0	0	0
Mary's	55	.7922	8.7317	49.4	13	18	12	5	5	0	2	0	3	5	0	4	9	4	3	1	0	1	2	0	3	17	0	3	0
Marya	9	.0000	.4111	36.1	9	0	0	0	0	0	0	0	9	0	0	0	0	0	0	0	0	0	0	0	0	0	0	0	0
Maryark	6	.0000	.2741	34.4	0	0	6	0	0	0	0	0	6	0	0	0	0	0	0	0	0	0	0	0	0	0	0	0	0
Marybeth	2	.0000	.0914	29.6	0	0	0	0	0	2	0	0	2	0	0	0	0	0	0	0	0	0	0	0	0	0	0	0	0
Marygold	7	.1889	.4840	36.8	6	0	1	0	0	0	0	0	6	0	1	0	0	0	0	0	0	0	0	0	0	0	0	0	0
Maryland	52	.6573	7.0241	48.5	12	7	5	6	4	14	3	1	4	1	0	1	0	15	0	1	0	0	0	1	1	17	7	4	0
Maryland's	3	.2321	.1635	32.1	0	0	0	0	2	0	1	0	0	0	0	0	0	0	0	0	0	0	0	0	0	0	1	2	0
Marylou	13	.0000	.5939	37.7	0	0	13	0	0	0	0	0	13	0	0	0	0	0	0	0	0	0	0	0	0	0	0	0	0
Marys	5	.5536	.5695	37.6	0	0	0	0	2	2	1	0	0	1	0	1	0	1	1	0	1	0	0	0	0	0	0	0	0
Maryville	5	.3008	.3635	35.6	0	3	1	1	0	0	0	0	1	0	0	0	0	0	1	0	0	0	0	0	0	3	0	0	0
mas	3	.2143	.1568	32.0	0	0	0	1	0	0	0	2	0	0	0	0	0	0	0	0	0	0	0	0	0	1	0	2	0
Masai	12	.3362	.9192	39.6	1	8	0	1	1	0	1	0	1	0	0	0	0	2	0	0	0	0	0	0	0	0	2	7	0
Masbate	3	.0000	.0314	25.0	3	0	0	0	0	0	0	0	0	0	0	0	0	0	0	0	0	0	0	0	0	0	3	0	0
masculine	7	.4207	.6235	37.9	0	0	1	1	1	0	1	3	0	1	0	0	0	0	0	0	0	0	1	0	0	1	0	4	0
maser	3	.0000	.0352	25.5	0	3	0	0	0	0	0	0	0	0	0	0	0	0	0	0	0	0	0	0	3	0	0	0	0
mash	15	.5982	1.9065	42.8	5	0	0	2	6	0	1	1	5	0	0	0	0	1	0	1	0	0	1	0	4	1	0	2	0
mashed	20	.5530	2.2786	43.6	1	3	0	0	8	3	5	0	1	3	0	3	0	0	1	2	0	0	5	0	2	1	1	1	0
mask	57	.6859	8.1856	49.1	10	15	1	12	8	5	2	4	26	0	1	2	0	4	1	6	0	3	0	0	1	4	0	9	0
masked	9	.3617	.8207	39.1	1	1	4	0	3	0	0	0	5	0	0	0	0	0	0	0	0	0	0	0	1	3	0	0	0
masking	4	.3675	.3176	35.0	0	0	0	0	2	0	0	2	0	1	0	0	0	0	0	1	0	0	0	1	0	0	0	1	0
masks	33	.6402	4.4171	46.5	4	10	2	0	4	10	1	2	11	1	3	0	0	3	1	3	2	3	0	0	0	1	3	2	0
mason	6	.4206	.5711	37.6	2	0	2	1	0	1	0	0	2	0	0	0	0	0	0	0	2	0	0	0	1	0	1	0	0
Mason	17	.5266	1.9065	42.8	0	0	3	2	4	6	2	0	2	0	0	0	0	6	0	0	0	0	0	0	3	0	3	3	0
Mason-Dixon	2	.1494	.1045	30.2	0	0	1	0	1	0	0	0	1	0	0	0	0	0	0	0	1	0	0	0	0	0	0	0	0
masonry	13	.4959	1.3950	41.4	0	0	0	0	9	1	3	0	3	0	0	0	0	0	0	0	0	0	0	1	0	3	1	5	0
masons	7	.4640	.6973	38.4	2	1	1	1	0	1	0	1	0	1	0	1	0	4	0	0	0	0	0	0	0	0	1	0	0
Masons	2	.0000	.0209	23.2	0	0	2	0	0	0	0	0	0	0	0	0	0	0	0	0	0	0	0	0	0	0	2	0	0
masque	3	.2233	.1562	31.9	0	0	0	0	0	2	1	0	0	0	0	1	0	0	0	0	0	0	0	0	0	0	2	0	0
masquerade	4	.4814	.4018	36.0	0	0	1	0	2	1	0	0	0	0	0	1	0	0	0	0	1	0	0	0	1	1	0	0	0
Masquers	2	.0000	.0219	23.4	0	0	0	0	0	0	2	0	0	2	0	0	0	0	0	0	0	0	0	0	0	0	0	0	0
mass	371	.7504	56.440	57.5	22	11	37	31	87	82	88	13	30	3	2	9	19	38	0	165	5	0	0	5	13	19	50	13	0
Mass	29	.3743	2.3513	43.7	4	0	4	1	8	4	8	0	1	0	0	7	1	0	0	0	1	0	0	0	0	2	11	5	0
mass-energy	3	.0000	.0591	27.7	0	0	0	2	0	0	0	1	0	0	0	0	0	0	0	3	0	0	0	0	0	0	0	0	1
mass-produced	2	.2407	.1138	30.6	0	0	0	0	1	0	1	0	0	0	0	1	0	0	0	0	0	0	0	0	0	1	0	0	0
massa	2	.0000	.0290	24.6	0	0	0	0	2	0	0	0	0	0	0	0	0	0	0	0	0	0	0	0	0	2	0	0	0
Massachusetts	131	.7126	19.236	52.8	10	15	39	6	18	32	11	0	32	2	2	0	2	65	1	1	6	1	0	0	3	8	4	4	0
massacre	9	.5039	.9652	39.8	0	1	0	2	5	0	1	0	1	0	0	0	0	1	0	0	0	0	0	0	4	1	1	1	0
Massacre	4	.3647	.3180	35.0	1	0	1	1	1	0	0	0	0	0	0	0	0	0	0	0	0	0	0	0	0	1	1	2	0
massacred	5	.1534	.2162	33.3	0	0	0	0	4	1	0	0	0	0	0	0	0	1	0	0	0	0	0	0	0	4	0	0	0
massage	8	.5504	.9514	39.8	0	0	1	1	2	2	1	1	3	0	0	0	0	0	1	0	0	0	0	0	1	0	1	2	0
massaging	2	.1717	.1142	30.6	0	0	0	0	0	2	0	0	1	0	0	1	0	0	0	0	0	0	0	0	0	0	0	0	0
Massasoit	4	.2424	.3036	34.8	2	1	0	0	0	0	0	1	3	0	0	0	0	0	0	0	0	0	0	0	0	0	0	1	0
Massasoit's	2	.0000	.0914	29.6	2	0	0	0	0	0	0	0	2	0	0	0	0	0	0	0	0	0	0	0	0	0	0	0	0
massed	4	.3104	.2995	34.8	0	0	0	1	3	0	0	0	1	0	0	0	0	0	0	0	0	0	0	0	0	0	1	2	0
masses	142	.7440	21.449	53.3	14	10	23	9	22	28	28	8	12	0	2	3	0	19	1	67	2	5	0	1	2	11	10	7	0
Masses	4	.3518	.3077	34.9	0	0	0	0	3	0	1	0	0	0	0	2	0	0	0	0	0	0	0	0	0	1	0	1	0
Massie	2	.0000	.0290	24.6	0	2	0	0	0	0	0	0	0	0	0	0	0	0	0	0	0	0	0	0	0	2	0	0	0
Massif	2	.0000	.0209	23.2	2	0	0	0	0	0	0	0	0	0	0	0	0	0	0	0	0	0	0	0	0	0	2	0	0

8A Marshall's
9R marshalled
7A Marshes
6A marshlander
3P Marshmallow
6A marshman
5E Marson's
XP Marspiter
7D Marta
5P Marteaux
7Q Martel
7N marten
9D Marthe's
3R Martian's
7F Martians
8D MARTIN
5P Martini
8F Martinique
9E Martins'
5H Martinus
5J Martinville
5A Marty's
5P martyrdom
8Q Marulic
9N marvelling
7R Marx's
3R Maryann
3R Maryann's
7Q Marye's
3A marygold
8F Marylanders
3P Marysville
5P Mascagni
7R mascara
7P Mascara
7B masculinity
9R Maserati
4N masers
4P Mashed
9C mashie
5P Mashonaland
8Q Masjumi
9D Mask
8A masklike
7R Maslowski
8R Masonic
9K Masons'
XP Maspiter
XR Masque
9B masqueraded
7D masquerades
9R masquerading
7P mass-produce
7Q mass-produced-parts
7F mass-producing
8A Massac
8B massachusetts
7R Massachusetts'
7R Massachusetts's
6N massacree
8F massacres
7A massaged
7A masse
9D Massey
7Q Massine's

Word Type	F	D	U	SFI	3 Gr 3	4 Gr 4	5 Gr 5	6 Gr 6	7 Gr 7	8 Gr 8	9 Gr 9	X UnGr	A Read	B Eng & Gr	C Comp	D Lit	E Math	F Soc Stud	G Spell	H Sci	J Music	K Art	L Home Ec	M Shop	N Lib F	P Lib NF	Q Lib Ref	R Mag	S Rel
massing	4	.3786	.3298	35.2	0	0	0	0	2	0	1	1	0	0	0	1	0	0	0	0	0	0	0	0	0	2	0	1	0
massive	66	.8003	10.589	50.2	1	3	2	11	23	11	13	2	6	2	1	2	0	8	1	6	1	1	0	1	2	3	12	20	0
massively	2	.0000	.0243	23.9	0	0	0	0	1	0	1	0	0	0	0	0	0	0	0	0	0	0	0	0	0	0	0	2	0
mast	41	.7921	6.6055	48.2	4	2	4	14	5	7	5	0	17	1	1	3	0	2	0	1	2	0	0	0	4	6	2	2	0
mastadons	2	.0000	.0215	23.3	0	0	0	0	0	0	2	0	0	0	0	2	0	0	0	0	0	0	0	0	0	0	0	0	0
master	335	.8440	56.673	57.5	46	42	26	60	89	36	29	7	93	21	1	26	1	20	23	4	25	1	2	0	58	32	6	22	0
Master	67	.6417	8.9467	49.5	4	17	3	15	21	1	5	1	17	1	0	11	0	0	0	0	1	0	1	0	14	18	1	3	0
master's	25	.6258	3.3042	45.2	5	0	2	5	7	1	5	0	9	0	0	2	1	2	0	0	0	0	0	0	6	0	2	3	0
Master's	2	.0000	.0162	22.1	0	0	1	0	1	0	0	0	0	0	0	0	0	0	0	0	2	0	0	0	0	0	0	0	0
mastered	20	.7473	3.0073	44.8	3	2	1	0	4	4	5	1	2	4	1	0	2	0	1	0	2	0	1	0	0	2	4	1	0
masterful	2	.2427	.1152	30.6	0	0	0	0	2	0	0	0	0	0	0	0	0	0	0	0	0	0	0	0	1	1	0	0	0
mastering	9	.5453	1.0126	40.1	0	0	0	0	3	1	5	0	0	4	0	1	0	1	0	0	1	0	0	0	1	0	0	1	0
masterly	7	.4587	.6816	38.3	0	0	0	0	4	2	0	1	0	0	0	0	0	1	0	0	0	0	0	0	0	2	2	2	0
masterpiece	14	.5645	1.6393	42.1	0	0	2	1	2	4	3	2	1	0	0	2	0	1	0	0	1	0	0	0	0	1	5	3	0
masterpieces	9	.4819	.8970	39.5	0	0	2	0	2	3	2	0	0	0	0	0	0	0	0	0	2	1	0	0	0	1	4	1	0
masters	54	.7361	8.0650	49.1	5	1	8	10	12	9	6	3	8	1	2	3	0	8	0	0	6	0	0	0	3	14	2	7	0
Masters	2	.0000	.0243	23.9	0	0	0	0	2	0	0	0	0	0	0	0	0	0	0	0	0	0	0	0	0	0	0	2	0
masters'	3	.3772	.2437	33.9	1	0	0	0	1	1	0	0	0	0	0	0	0	0	0	0	1	0	0	0	1	1	0	0	0
Mastersingers	3	.0000	.0243	23.8	0	0	0	3	0	0	0	0	0	0	0	0	0	0	0	0	3	0	0	0	0	0	0	0	0
mastery	18	.6840	2.4828	43.9	0	0	1	1	6	4	6	0	1	4	1	1	1	0	2	0	2	2	0	0	1	1	2	0	0
Mastery	4	.0000	.0325	25.1	0	0	0	0	0	4	0	0	0	0	0	0	0	0	4	0	0	0	0	0	0	0	0	0	0
masthead	8	.5734	.9603	39.8	0	0	0	1	0	2	4	1	1	0	0	2	0	0	0	1	0	0	0	0	1	2	1	0	0
mastication	2	.2278	.1128	30.5	0	0	0	0	1	0	0	1	0	0	0	0	0	0	0	1	0	0	0	0	0	0	1	0	0
mastiff	2	.1948	.1250	31.0	0	0	1	0	1	0	0	0	1	0	0	0	0	0	0	0	0	0	0	0	0	1	0	0	0
mastodon	5	.3810	.4789	36.8	1	0	3	0	1	0	0	0	3	0	0	0	0	0	0	1	0	0	0	0	0	0	0	1	0
mastodons	5	.4455	.4788	36.8	2	0	0	0	2	1	0	0	0	0	0	0	0	1	0	1	0	0	0	0	0	0	1	2	0
masts	46	.6147	6.0276	47.8	4	9	1	9	6	6	11	0	20	2	0	1	0	1	0	0	1	0	0	0	2	6	12	1	0
mat	47	.4986	5.4300	47.3	21	4	2	1	10	9	0	0	31	0	0	8	0	3	0	3	0	0	0	0	0	1	1	0	0
Mata	2	.0000	.0234	23.7	0	0	0	2	0	0	0	0	0	0	0	0	0	0	0	0	0	0	0	0	2	0	0	0	0
matador	4	.3863	.3417	35.3	0	0	0	3	1	0	0	0	0	1	0	0	0	2	0	0	0	0	0	0	0	0	0	1	0
Matanuska	3	.0000	.0583	27.7	0	1	2	0	0	0	0	0	0	0	0	0	0	3	0	0	0	0	0	0	0	0	0	0	0
Matasaip	2	.0000	.0234	23.7	0	0	0	2	0	0	0	0	0	0	0	0	0	0	0	0	0	0	0	0	2	0	0	0	0
match	353	.8866	62.224	57.9	62	52	58	47	82	26	20	6	60	11	1	15	78	7	50	36	15	4	10	4	11	17	10	24	0
match-box	2	.0000	.0234	23.7	0	0	2	0	0	0	0	0	0	0	0	0	0	0	0	0	0	0	0	0	2	0	0	0	0
matchbox	7	.0000	.3198	35.0	0	1	5	1	0	0	0	0	7	0	0	0	0	0	0	0	0	0	0	0	0	0	0	0	0
matchboxes	4	.3709	.3633	35.6	0	0	2	0	1	0	1	0	2	0	0	0	0	0	0	0	0	0	0	0	0	0	1	1	0
matched	86	.6411	11.361	50.6	16	11	21	7	10	13	8	0	8	2	0	2	49	4	2	3	2	0	0	1	2	2	6	3	0
matches	93	.9212	16.986	52.3	23	19	9	10	9	13	7	3	20	4	1	3	7	8	5	15	2	0	2	3	5	8	2	8	0
matching	60	.6424	7.8987	49.0	7	4	9	7	10	8	13	2	6	0	0	2	25	0	0	4	1	1	10	2	2	2	2	3	0
matchings	2	.0000	.0299	24.8	2	0	0	0	0	0	0	0	0	0	0	0	2	0	0	0	0	0	0	0	0	0	0	0	0
matchlock	3	.0000	.0352	25.5	0	3	0	0	0	0	0	0	0	0	0	0	0	0	0	0	0	0	0	0	3	0	0	0	0
matchmaker	2	.0000	.0219	23.4	0	0	0	0	0	2	0	0	0	2	0	0	0	0	0	0	0	0	0	0	0	0	0	0	0
matchsticks	3	.1650	.1684	32.3	0	0	2	0	1	0	0	0	1	0	0	0	0	0	0	2	0	0	0	0	0	0	0	0	0
mate	112	.8056	18.363	52.6	12	18	5	29	33	8	7	0	55	0	0	8	1	9	3	4	1	0	0	1	7	6	10	7	0
Mate	5	.2110	.3346	35.2	0	0	0	1	4	0	0	0	3	0	0	0	0	0	0	0	0	0	0	0	0	0	0	2	0
mate's	3	.3394	.2451	33.9	0	0	0	2	1	0	0	0	1	0	0	1	0	0	0	0	0	0	0	0	1	0	0	0	0
Mateo	10	.0000	.1073	30.3	0	0	0	0	8	2	0	0	0	0	0	10	0	0	0	0	0	0	0	0	0	0	0	0	0
mater	4	.3741	.3712	35.7	0	0	1	1	2	0	0	0	2	0	0	0	0	0	0	1	0	0	0	0	0	0	0	1	0
Mater	2	.2442	.1134	30.5	0	0	0	0	1	0	1	0	0	1	0	0	0	0	0	0	0	0	0	0	0	0	0	1	0
material	651	.8348	108.58	60.4	32	61	82	79	148	109	121	19	70	39	8	6	28	35	8	186	29	17	21	47	5	31	87	34	0
Material	2	.2437	.1129	30.5	0	0	1	0	0	0	0	1	0	0	0	0	0	0	0	0	0	0	0	0	0	0	1	1	0
materialize	3	.3863	.2513	34.0	0	0	1	1	0	0	0	1	0	0	0	0	0	0	0	0	0	0	0	0	1	1	0	1	0
materially	2	.2285	.1129	30.5	0	0	0	0	0	2	0	0	0	0	0	0	0	1	0	0	0	0	0	0	0	0	1	0	0
materials	612	.7115	88.124	59.5	50	89	109	70	111	67	90	26	17	7	2	5	4	107	0	193	22	46	27	50	2	26	78	26	0
maternal	11	.5710	1.3183	41.2	0	0	0	2	2	2	2	3	1	0	0	0	0	0	0	4	0	0	0	0	1	1	2	2	0
Maternite	2	.0000	.0243	23.9	0	0	0	0	0	0	0	2	0	0	0	0	0	0	0	0	0	0	0	0	0	0	0	2	0
mates	20	.4486	2.0018	43.0	6	3	0	3	7	0	0	1	5	0	0	0	0	0	0	1	0	0	0	0	5	8	1	0	0
matey	3	.2347	.1695	32.3	1	1	0	0	1	0	0	0	0	0	0	0	0	0	0	0	0	0	0	0	1	2	0	0	0
mateys	3	.0000	.1370	31.4	0	0	0	3	0	0	0	0	3	0	0	0	0	0	0	0	0	0	0	0	0	0	0	0	0
math	18	.5386	2.0824	43.2	1	3	3	3	5	0	2	1	5	2	0	1	2	0	1	0	0	0	0	0	0	0	0	7	0
Math	4	.1960	.2010	33.0	0	1	0	0	3	0	0	0	0	0	0	0	1	0	0	0	0	0	0	0	0	3	0	0	0
MATH	2	.0000	.0299	24.8	0	0	2	0	0	0	0	0	0	0	0	0	2	0	0	0	0	0	0	0	0	0	0	0	0
Math's	2	.0000	.0290	24.6	0	0	0	0	2	0	0	0	0	0	0	0	0	0	0	0	0	0	0	0	0	2	0	0	0
mathematical	121	.4495	11.765	50.7	3	6	16	14	24	32	24	2	7	2	0	2	89	1	1	3	1	1	0	0	1	4	9	0	0
Mathematical	3	.1434	.1493	31.7	0	0	0	1	0	2	0	0	1	0	0	0	2	0	0	0	0	0	0	0	0	0	0	0	0
mathematically	6	.2594	.3518	35.5	0	1	0	0	0	5	0	0	0	0	0	0	3	0	0	0	0	0	0	2	0	0	0	1	0
mathematician	33	.5428	3.7393	45.7	0	1	2	3	4	16	5	2	0	0	0	0	22	1	0	4	0	1	0	1	0	1	2	1	0
mathematicians	38	.2868	2.5678	44.1	1	0	0	2	12	19	3	1	1	0	0	0	29	2	0	0	0	0	0	0	0	4	2	0	0
mathematics	185	.5992	23.122	53.6	3	10	10	16	32	70	36	8	22	5	0	2	106	8	1	9	0	0	2	3	0	8	17	2	0
Mathematics	5	.0000	.0748	28.7	0	0	0	0	0	3	2	0	0	0	0	0	5	0	0	0	0	0	0	0	0	0	0	0	0
Mather	9	.4119	.8739	39.4	0	0	4	1	0	4	0	0	4	3	0	0	0	1	0	0	0	0	0	0	0	0	0	1	0
Mather's	2	.0000	.0914	29.6	0	0	1	0	1	0	0	0	2	0	0	0	0	0	0	0	0	0	0	0	0	0	0	0	0
Mathew	3	.0000	.1370	31.4	0	0	3	0	0	0	0	0	3	0	0	0	0	0	0	0	0	0	0	0	0	0	0	0	0
Mathewson	3	.0000	.0434	26.4	0	2	0	1	0	0	0	0	0	0	0	0	0	0	0	0	0	0	0	0	0	3	0	0	0
Mathilde	7	.0000	.3198	35.0	0	0	0	7	0	0	0	0	7	0	0	0	0	0	0	0	0	0	0	0	0	0	0	0	0
Matholwch	3	.0000	.0434	26.4	0	0	0	0	3	0	0	0	0	0	0	0	0	0	0	0	0	0	0	0	0	3	0	0	0
Matilda	8	.2351	.6222	37.9	0	0	5	2	0	1	0	0	7	0	0	0	0	0	0	0	0	0	0	0	0	0	1	0	0
mating	13	.4383	1.2596	41.0	0	0	2	2	7	0	0	2	2	0	0	0	0	0	0	4	0	0	0	0	0	1	5	1	0
Matisse	6	.1700	.2344	33.7	3	0	1	0	1	1	0	0	0	0	0	0	0	0	0	0	0	3	0	0	0	1	2	0	0
Matjan	2	.0000	.0914	29.6	0	0	0	0	2	0	0	0	2	0	0	0	0	0	0	0	0	0	0	0	0	0	0	0	0
Matoaka	3	.0000	.1370	31.4	3	0	0	0	0	0	0	0	3	0	0	0	0	0	0	0	0	0	0	0	0	0	0	0	0
matoke	2	.0000	.0243	23.9	0	2	0	0	0	0	0	0	0	0	0	0	0	0	0	0	0	0	0	0	0	0	0	2	0
Matrena	10	.0000	.1073	30.3	0	0	0	0	0	10	0	0	0	0	0	10	0	0	0	0	0	0	0	0	0	0	0	0	0
matrimonial	2	.0000	.0290	24.6	0	0	0	0	2	0	0	0	0	0	0	0	0	0	0	0	0	0	0	0	0	2	0	0	0
matrix	5	.0000	.0523	27.2	0	0	0	0	0	0	5	0	0	0	0	0	0	0	0	0	0	0	0	0	0	0	5	0	0
Matrix	15	.0000	.1641	32.2	0	0	0	0	0	15	0	0	0	15	0	0	0	0	0	0	0	0	0	0	0	0	0	0	0
matron	3	.2450	.1650	32.2	0	0	1	0	0	1	1	0	0	1	0	0	0	0	0	0	0	1	0	0	0	1	0	0	0
matrons	2	.1814	.1187	30.7	0	0	0	0	0	1	1	0	1	0	0	0	0	0	0	0	0	0	0	0	0	0	0	1	0
mats	35	.6268	4.5521	46.6	5	9	3	8	5	1	4	0	5	1	0	0	0	14	0	0	0	1	4	0	6	1	1	2	0
Matt	34	.5353	3.8778	45.9	5	12	0	1	9	7	0	0	6	0	0	5	0	3	0	0	0	0	0	0	9	10	0	1	0
matted	13	.4098	1.2309	40.9	3	3	0	2	3	0	1	1	5	0	2	0	0	1	0	0	0	0	0	0	3	0	0	2	0
matter	1132	.9249	207.51	63.2	116	186	137	108	246	190	112	37	233	38	21	74	22	39	16	340	19	2	27	11	73	73	82	61	1
matter-of-fact	8	.6018	1.0081	40.0	0	0	1	1	1	3	2	0	2	2	0	1	0	0	0	0	1	0	0	0	1	0	0	1	0
matter-of-factly	2	.0000	.0914	29.6	1	0	1	0	0	0	0	0	2	0	0	0	0	0	0	0	0	0	0	0	0	0	0	0	0
mattered	14	.5920	1.7369	42.4	3	1	1	3	4	1	1	0	3	1	0	2	0	0	0	0	0	0	0	0	5	1	1	1	0
Matterhorn	3	.3350	.2478	33.9	0	3	0	0	0	0	0	0	1	0	0	0	0	1	0	0	0	0	0	0	0	0	1	0	0
matters	97	.8029	15.646	51.9	8	4	4	10	31	22	16	2	14	2	3	9	1	24	0	1	3	0	2	0	9	4	16	9	0

4R Masson
9N mast-head
9Q mastaba
7N masted
4A master-fiddler
9N masterminded
6J Mastersinger's
6A Masterson
7H masticated
7D Mastodonic
9R masturbation
9P Mat
4P Matachanna
7F Matadi
7Q Matamoros
7D match'd
4G matchless
8H matchstick
7R mate-selection
6H mated
7R Mateos
8F mater's
8R materialistic
XR materialized
8M Materials
7Q materiel
8H Mathematike
7D Mathiesen
8J Mathis
7P Mathonwy
8G matinee
XH matings
7B matko
6N matlike
8D Matrena's
4N matrimony
7R Matsushita
4A Matsuyama
4F Matt's
XH matter-galaxies
7Q matter's

Word Type	F	D	U	SFI	3 Gr 3	4 Gr 4	5 Gr 5	6 Gr 6	7 Gr 7	8 Gr 8	9 Gr 9	X UnGr	A Read	B Eng & Gr	C Comp	D Lit	E Math	F Soc Stud	G Spell	H Sci	J Music	K Art	L Home Ec	M Shop	N Lib F	P Lib NF	Q Lib Ref	R Mag	S Rel
Matthew	38	.5622	4.5785	46.6	0	1	7	17	9	2	1	1	12	0	0	0	0	2	0	0	2	0	0	0	14	3	2	3	0
Matthias	31	.1850	1.7511	42.4	6	20	5	0	0	0	0	0	10	0	0	0	0	0	0	1	0	0	0	0	0	20	0	0	0
Matthiessen	2	.0000	.0243	23.9	0	0	0	0	2	0	0	0	0	0	0	0	0	0	0	0	0	0	0	0	0	0	0	2	0
matting	3	.3380	.2439	33.9	0	0	0	1	1	0	1	0	1	1	0	1	0	0	0	0	0	0	0	0	0	0	0	0	0
mattress	26	.4920	2.8910	44.6	2	6	0	1	10	6	0	1	13	0	0	2	1	3	0	0	0	0	4	0	0	2	0	1	0
mattresses	9	.4339	.8868	39.5	1	1	0	2	1	1	3	0	3	0	0	0	0	0	0	0	0	0	0	0	3	1	0	2	0
maturation	7	.4119	.6269	38.0	0	0	1	0	2	1	2	1	0	0	0	0	0	1	0	2	0	0	0	0	0	0	3	1	0
mature	42	.6797	5.8042	47.6	0	0	5	4	11	5	11	6	2	0	1	0	0	1	0	15	0	1	6	1	0	2	7	6	0
matured	2	.2417	.1091	30.4	0	0	0	0	0	1	1	0	0	0	0	0	0	0	0	0	1	0	0	0	0	0	1	0	0
matures	4	.4737	.3981	36.0	0	0	0	0	1	2	1	0	0	0	0	1	0	0	0	1	1	0	0	0	0	0	1	0	0
maturing	3	.2292	.1672	32.2	0	0	0	0	2	1	0	0	0	0	0	0	0	1	0	1	0	0	0	1	0	0	0	0	0
maturity	33	.4980	3.4114	45.3	0	0	5	3	14	1	10	0	0	0	6	1	0	1	0	10	0	0	7	0	1	3	3	1	0
Mau	2	.0000	.0243	23.9	0	0	0	2	0	0	0	0	0	0	0	0	0	0	0	0	0	0	0	0	0	0	0	2	0
Maud	7	.2444	.4065	36.1	0	3	1	3	0	0	0	0	0	0	0	0	0	0	0	0	0	0	0	0	3	4	0	0	0
Maude	7	.4349	.6502	38.1	0	4	1	0	0	1	1	0	0	1	0	0	1	0	1	0	0	0	0	0	0	4	0	0	0
Maudslay	2	.0000	.0209	23.2	0	0	0	0	2	0	0	0	0	0	0	0	0	0	0	0	0	0	0	0	0	0	2	0	0
Maui	6	.0000	.0703	28.5	0	0	0	6	0	0	0	0	0	0	0	0	0	0	0	0	0	0	0	0	6	0	0	0	0
maul	2	.2440	.1132	30.5	0	0	0	0	0	1	1	0	0	0	0	1	0	0	0	0	0	0	0	0	0	0	0	1	0
mauling	2	.1948	.1250	31.0	0	1	0	0	0	0	1	0	1	0	0	0	0	0	0	0	0	0	0	0	0	1	0	0	0
Mauna	10	.3624	.9037	39.6	0	6	4	0	0	0	0	0	4	0	0	0	0	2	0	4	0	0	0	0	0	0	0	0	0
Maureen	25	.0665	.7271	38.6	0	4	21	0	0	0	0	0	4	0	0	0	0	0	0	0	0	0	0	0	21	0	0	0	0
Maurice	19	.4664	1.8713	42.7	1	1	3	1	8	5	0	0	1	0	0	0	1	0	0	0	7	0	0	0	0	5	4	1	0
Mauritania	7	.2361	.4176	36.2	0	0	0	6	0	1	0	0	0	0	0	0	0	5	0	0	0	0	0	0	0	0	0	2	0
Maury	11	.3854	1.0608	40.3	2	0	0	7	0	2	0	0	7	2	0	0	0	0	0	0	0	0	0	0	0	2	0	0	0
mausoleum	2	.0000	.0243	23.9	0	0	0	2	0	0	0	0	0	0	0	0	0	0	0	0	0	0	0	0	0	0	0	2	0
maverick	5	.2407	.2808	34.5	0	0	0	0	1	2	2	0	0	2	0	0	0	0	0	0	0	0	0	0	0	0	0	3	0
Maverick	23	.2097	1.1649	40.7	0	0	0	0	8	0	3	12	0	3	0	1	0	0	0	0	0	0	0	0	0	0	0	19	0
MAVERICK	7	.0000	.0751	28.8	0	0	0	0	7	0	0	0	0	0	0	7	0	0	0	0	0	0	0	0	0	0	0	0	0
Mawia	3	.0000	.0434	26.4	0	3	0	0	0	0	0	0	0	0	0	0	0	0	0	0	0	0	0	0	0	3	0	0	0
Mawr	3	.2357	.2199	33.4	1	2	0	0	0	0	0	0	2	0	0	0	0	0	0	0	0	0	0	0	0	1	0	0	0
max	2	.0000	.0219	23.4	0	0	0	0	0	2	0	0	0	2	0	0	0	0	0	0	0	0	0	0	0	0	0	0	0
Max	52	.6364	7.1706	48.6	1	4	6	4	4	5	28	0	35	3	0	0	4	1	0	2	0	0	0	0	0	2	3	2	0
Max's	2	.1733	.1149	30.6	0	0	1	0	0	0	1	0	1	1	0	0	0	0	0	0	0	0	0	0	0	0	0	0	0
maxim	6	.3819	.5160	37.1	0	1	1	1	0	1	2	0	1	1	0	0	0	0	0	0	0	0	0	0	3	1	0	0	0
Maxim	2	.0000	.0243	23.9	0	0	0	2	0	0	0	0	0	0	0	0	0	0	0	0	0	0	0	0	0	0	0	2	0
Maximilien	2	.0000	.0209	23.2	0	0	1	0	0	1	0	0	0	0	0	0	0	0	0	0	0	0	0	0	0	0	2	0	0
maxims	6	.1680	.2556	34.1	0	5	1	0	0	0	0	0	0	0	0	0	0	0	0	0	0	0	0	0	5	0	1	0	0
maximum	64	.7375	9.5168	49.8	0	1	3	2	22	10	20	6	3	1	0	1	11	3	0	10	1	0	5	4	0	8	10	7	0
Maxwell	11	.5825	1.3404	41.3	0	4	1	1	0	1	3	1	1	0	0	0	2	0	0	3	0	0	0	0	0	1	2	2	0
Maxwell's	5	.2424	.2988	34.8	0	0	0	0	0	2	1	2	0	0	0	0	0	0	0	3	0	0	0	0	0	0	2	0	0
may	6635	.9269	1216.8	70.9	965	844	759	741	1247	922	986	171	878	583	88	219	422	546	321	1224	293	112	488	156	91	372	498	340	4
May	278	.8507	47.343	56.8	47	49	26	41	58	28	17	12	66	15	4	13	12	35	5	5	8	0	0	0	12	36	35	32	0
May-June	2	.0000	.0243	23.9	0	0	0	0	0	0	2	0	0	0	0	0	0	0	0	0	0	0	0	0	0	0	0	2	0
May's	3	.0000	.0449	26.5	0	3	0	0	0	0	0	0	0	0	0	0	3	0	0	0	0	0	0	0	0	0	0	0	0
Maya	21	.3005	1.4788	41.7	0	1	1	13	4	1	0	1	0	0	0	0	1	13	0	0	0	0	0	0	0	0	7	0	0
Mayaguez	10	.0000	.4568	36.6	10	0	0	0	0	0	0	0	10	0	0	0	0	0	0	0	0	0	0	0	0	0	0	0	0
Mayan	5	.2078	.2673	34.3	0	0	0	4	0	1	0	0	0	0	0	0	0	4	0	0	0	1	0	0	0	0	0	0	0
Mayans	2	.1033	.0599	27.8	0	0	1	0	0	1	0	0	0	0	0	0	0	0	0	1	0	1	0	0	0	0	0	0	0
Mayapan	3	.0000	.0314	25.0	0	0	0	0	3	0	0	0	0	0	0	0	0	0	0	0	0	0	0	0	0	0	3	0	0
Mayas	11	.3411	.8246	39.2	0	3	3	0	5	0	0	0	0	0	0	0	0	2	0	0	1	0	0	0	0	0	7	1	0
maybe	779	.8217	129.76	61.1	217	158	80	81	132	58	42	11	380	18	3	69	5	12	9	24	3	3	10	3	104	85	2	49	0
Maycomb	17	.0000	.1824	32.6	0	0	0	0	0	0	17	0	0	0	0	17	0	0	0	0	0	0	0	0	0	0	0	0	0
mayday	2	.0000	.0914	29.6	0	2	0	0	0	0	0	0	2	0	0	0	0	0	0	0	0	0	0	0	0	0	0	0	0
Mayer	4	.2932	.2861	34.6	0	0	1	0	3	0	0	0	1	0	0	0	0	0	0	0	0	0	0	0	0	0	2	1	0
mayflies	2	.2437	.1129	30.5	0	0	0	0	1	0	0	1	0	0	0	0	0	0	0	0	0	0	0	0	0	0	1	1	0
Mayflower	25	.5672	3.1156	44.9	7	0	7	0	3	3	5	0	12	2	0	0	0	8	0	0	1	0	0	0	1	1	0	0	0
mayfly	7	.0000	.0733	28.6	0	0	0	0	7	0	0	0	0	0	0	0	0	0	0	0	0	0	0	0	0	0	7	0	0
mayhem	2	.2291	.1135	30.5	0	0	0	0	2	0	0	0	0	0	0	1	0	0	0	1	0	0	0	0	0	0	0	0	0
mayn't	2	.2446	.1125	30.5	0	0	1	0	0	0	1	0	0	1	0	1	0	0	0	0	0	0	0	0	0	0	0	0	0
Mayo	20	.2603	1.2129	40.8	0	0	2	0	13	0	5	0	1	1	0	15	0	0	0	0	0	0	0	0	0	1	0	2	0
mayonnaise	11	.0991	.2608	34.2	0	1	0	0	1	1	8	0	0	0	0	0	0	0	1	0	0	0	9	0	0	1	0	0	0
mayor	95	.7357	14.349	51.6	27	5	34	6	6	6	11	0	31	5	0	1	0	26	3	0	5	0	0	0	11	1	7	5	0
Mayor	49	.5320	5.8661	47.7	16	5	2	4	15	2	4	1	29	0	0	4	0	4	0	0	0	0	0	0	1	0	1	10	0
mayor-council	3	.0000	.0583	27.7	0	0	0	0	0	0	3	0	0	0	0	0	0	3	0	0	0	0	0	0	0	0	0	0	0
mayor's	8	.4418	.8012	39.0	0	1	5	0	0	2	0	0	3	0	0	1	0	0	0	0	1	0	0	0	3	0	0	0	0
Mayor's	3	.3454	.2542	34.1	0	0	0	0	2	0	1	0	1	0	0	0	0	1	0	0	0	0	0	0	0	0	0	1	0
Maypole	8	.1787	.4695	36.7	7	0	0	0	1	0	0	0	4	0	0	0	0	0	0	0	0	0	0	0	4	0	0	0	0
Mays	7	.0000	.0851	29.3	0	0	0	0	4	3	0	0	0	0	0	0	0	0	0	0	0	0	0	0	0	0	0	7	0
Mazar	4	.0000	.0486	26.9	0	0	0	0	0	4	0	0	0	0	0	0	0	0	0	0	0	0	0	0	0	0	0	4	0
maze	17	.5591	2.0125	43.0	1	0	1	1	11	2	1	0	2	0	0	0	0	5	0	3	0	0	0	0	0	1	4	2	0
mazurka	3	.0000	.0243	23.8	0	0	1	2	0	0	0	0	0	0	0	0	0	0	0	0	3	0	0	0	0	0	0	0	0
Mazurka	4	.0000	.0323	25.1	0	0	0	3	0	1	0	0	0	0	0	0	0	0	0	0	4	0	0	0	0	0	0	0	0
MC	6	.0000	.0657	28.2	0	0	6	0	0	0	0	0	0	6	0	0	0	0	0	0	0	0	0	0	0	0	0	0	0
McAdam	2	.2412	.1141	30.6	0	1	0	0	0	0	1	0	0	1	0	0	0	0	0	0	0	0	0	0	0	1	0	0	0
McAlastair	3	.0000	.0434	26.4	0	3	0	0	0	0	0	0	0	0	0	0	0	0	0	0	0	0	0	0	0	3	0	0	0
McBrier	2	.0000	.0290	24.6	0	2	0	0	0	0	0	0	0	0	0	0	0	0	0	0	0	0	0	0	0	2	0	0	0
McCann	3	.1409	.1472	31.7	0	2	1	0	0	0	0	0	1	0	0	0	0	0	0	0	0	0	0	0	0	2	0	0	0
McCardell	10	.1351	.3877	35.9	0	9	0	0	0	0	1	0	0	1	0	0	0	0	0	0	0	0	0	0	0	9	0	0	0
McCarroll	2	.0000	.0234	23.7	2	0	0	0	0	0	0	0	0	0	0	0	0	0	0	0	0	0	0	0	2	0	0	0	0
McCarthy	18	.5865	2.2033	43.4	1	1	2	3	2	9	0	0	1	0	0	0	1	7	0	0	0	0	0	0	1	3	1	4	0
McCarthy's	4	.2183	.2285	33.6	1	0	1	0	0	2	0	0	0	0	0	0	0	3	0	0	0	0	0	0	0	1	0	0	0
McCawley	5	.0000	.0724	28.6	0	0	0	0	5	0	0	0	0	0	0	0	0	0	0	0	0	0	0	0	0	5	0	0	0
McClellan	10	.3318	.7364	38.7	0	5	0	0	0	5	0	0	0	0	0	0	0	2	0	0	0	0	0	0	3	0	5	0	0
McClelland	9	.0000	.0966	29.8	0	0	0	0	9	0	0	0	0	0	0	9	0	0	0	0	0	0	0	0	0	0	0	0	0
McClung	2	.0000	.0914	29.6	0	2	0	0	0	0	0	0	2	0	0	0	0	0	0	0	0	0	0	0	0	0	0	0	0
McCormick	25	.4269	2.3955	43.8	0	15	4	0	1	5	0	0	4	0	0	0	0	8	0	0	0	0	0	0	0	11	1	1	0
McCormick's	5	.3684	.4519	36.6	0	0	0	0	0	4	0	1	2	0	0	0	0	2	0	0	0	0	0	0	0	0	0	1	0
McCormicks	2	.0000	.0389	25.9	0	0	2	0	0	0	0	0	0	0	0	0	0	2	0	0	0	0	0	0	0	0	0	0	0
McCoul	5	.0000	.2284	33.6	0	5	0	0	0	0	0	0	5	0	0	0	0	0	0	0	0	0	0	0	0	0	0	0	0
McCovey	6	.0000	.0729	28.6	0	0	0	0	0	6	0	0	0	0	0	0	0	0	0	0	0	0	0	0	0	0	0	6	0
McCrae	2	.0000	.0234	23.7	0	0	2	0	0	0	0	0	0	0	0	0	0	0	0	0	0	0	0	0	2	0	0	0	0

7A Matthew's
3P Matthews
8N Matthewson
4P Matthias'
9J Matthison
7D Mattie
7L maturities
8F Maturity
8R matzo-ball
4A matzoth
7R Mau-Mau
8E Maude's
9D Maudie
7B Maugham
7D mauled
7N maunders
6A Maung
8E Mauritian
6K Maurits
8Q Mauritshuis
XP Maurs
6A Maury's
8Q Maurya
7D mauve
7P Mavis
XP Mavors
7A maw
6A Maw
7N mawnin'
3P maws
3P mawses
8R Mawson
8R Maxey
6R maxima
5E Maxine
4A MAY
8Q May-Day
6P May-pole
7R MAYBE
4R Mayberry
9D Maycomb's
9D Mayella's
5P mayest
6A Mayflowers
7Q mayfly's
5Q Mayling
9R Maynard
5P Maynooth
7Q Mayon
8F mayors
9D mayst
XR Mazatzal
XR Maze
7Q mazes
7R Maziere
7R Maziere's
7R Mazmanian
6P Mazo's
XH Mazon
8Q Mazuranic
7Q Mazzini
3F Mazzone
8G mb
5G mbx
8E mc
4A McCORMICK
XR McAfee
5A McAllen
6G McArthur
4P McBriers
7Q McC
XR McCaffrey
4P McCann's
5A McCantry
8F McCarthyism
7R McCay
9R McChesney
8N McClellan's
5A McCloud
4A McClung's
7D McConnellsburg
8A McCormick-Manny
6A McCoy
8F McCrae's

Word Type	F	D	U	SFI	3 Gr 3	4 Gr 4	5 Gr 5	6 Gr 6	7 Gr 7	8 Gr 8	9 Gr 9	X UnGr	A Read	B Eng & Gr	C Comp	D Lit	E Math	F Soc Stud	G Spell	H Sci	J Music	K Art	L Home Ec	M Shop	N Lib F	P Lib NF	Q Lib Ref	R Mag	S Rel
McDaniel	2	.0000	.0243	23.9	0	0	0	0	0	0	0	2	0	0	0	0	0	0	0	0	0	0	0	0	0	0	0	2	0
McDivitt	3	.0000	.0328	25.2	0	0	3	0	0	0	0	0	0	3	0	0	0	0	0	0	0	0	0	0	0	0	0	0	0
McDonald	2	.2437	.1129	30.5	0	1	0	0	0	1	0	0	0	0	0	0	0	0	0	0	0	0	0	0	0	0	1	1	0
McDougal	11	.0000	.1337	31.3	11	0	0	0	0	0	0	0	0	0	0	0	0	0	0	0	0	0	0	0	0	0	0	11	0
McDowell	3	.2444	.1814	32.6	0	1	0	0	0	2	0	0	0	0	0	0	0	2	0	0	0	0	0	0	0	0	1	0	0
McGarity	2	.0000	.0914	29.6	0	0	2	0	0	0	0	0	2	0	0	0	0	0	0	0	0	0	0	0	0	0	0	0	0
McGarrity	17	.0000	.7766	38.9	17	0	0	0	0	0	0	0	17	0	0	0	0	0	0	0	0	0	0	0	0	0	0	0	0
McGee	5	.2445	.3875	35.9	0	0	0	0	4	0	1	0	4	0	0	0	0	0	0	0	0	0	0	0	0	0	0	1	0
McGill	2	.0000	.0209	23.2	0	0	2	0	0	0	0	0	0	0	0	0	0	0	0	0	0	0	0	0	0	0	2	0	0
McGinley	2	.2446	.1125	30.5	0	0	1	0	1	0	0	0	0	1	0	1	0	0	0	0	0	0	0	0	0	0	0	0	0
McGoogle	10	.0000	.4568	36.6	0	0	0	0	10	0	0	0	10	0	0	0	0	0	0	0	0	0	0	0	0	0	0	0	0
McGoogle's	2	.0000	.0914	29.6	0	0	0	0	2	0	0	0	2	0	0	0	0	0	0	0	0	0	0	0	0	0	0	0	0
McGrannery	13	.0000	.5939	37.7	13	0	0	0	0	0	0	0	13	0	0	0	0	0	0	0	0	0	0	0	0	0	0	0	0
McGrath	6	.3509	.5242	37.2	1	0	3	0	2	0	0	0	3	0	0	2	0	0	0	0	0	0	0	0	1	0	0	0	0
McGraw	2	.0000	.0290	24.6	0	0	0	2	0	0	0	0	0	0	0	0	0	0	0	0	0	0	0	0	0	2	0	0	0
McGraw's	2	.0000	.0290	24.6	1	0	0	1	0	0	0	0	0	0	0	0	0	0	0	0	0	0	0	0	0	2	0	0	0
McGregor	5	.3599	.3906	35.9	1	1	0	1	2	0	0	0	0	2	0	2	0	0	0	0	0	0	0	0	0	1	0	0	0
McHenry	3	.2270	.1588	32.0	0	0	0	1	2	0	0	0	0	2	0	0	0	0	0	0	0	0	0	0	0	0	1	0	0
McIlhenny	6	.2432	.4679	36.7	0	5	0	0	0	0	1	0	5	1	0	0	0	0	0	0	0	0	0	0	0	0	0	0	0
McKay	5	.4788	.5421	37.3	1	0	0	2	0	2	0	0	2	0	0	0	0	1	0	0	0	0	0	0	0	1	0	1	0
McKenna	2	.2351	.1166	30.7	1	0	0	0	0	0	0	1	0	0	0	0	0	1	0	0	0	0	0	0	0	0	0	1	0
McKinley	13	.5774	1.5751	42.0	2	1	5	1	1	2	1	0	1	0	0	0	2	5	0	0	0	0	0	0	0	2	1	2	0
McKinley's	3	.0000	.0434	26.4	3	0	0	0	0	0	0	0	0	0	0	0	0	0	0	0	0	0	0	0	0	3	0	0	0
McLane	2	.0000	.0389	25.9	0	0	0	0	0	2	0	0	0	0	0	0	0	2	0	0	0	0	0	0	0	0	0	0	0
McLane's	2	.0000	.0389	25.9	0	0	0	0	0	2	0	0	0	0	0	0	0	2	0	0	0	0	0	0	0	0	0	0	0
McLaughlin	5	.3300	.4080	36.1	0	0	2	0	0	2	0	1	2	0	0	2	0	0	0	0	0	0	0	0	0	0	0	1	0
McLean	3	.2292	.1615	32.1	2	0	0	0	0	0	1	0	0	0	0	1	0	0	0	0	0	0	0	0	2	0	0	0	0
McLendon	3	.0000	.0365	25.6	0	0	0	0	0	3	0	0	0	0	0	0	0	0	0	0	0	0	0	0	0	0	0	3	0
McLeod	5	.2326	.3837	35.8	0	4	1	0	0	0	0	0	4	0	0	0	0	1	0	0	0	0	0	0	0	0	0	0	0
McLeods	3	.0000	.1370	31.4	0	1	0	2	0	0	0	0	3	0	0	0	0	0	0	0	0	0	0	0	0	0	0	0	0
McNary	3	.0000	.0365	25.6	0	0	0	0	0	0	0	3	0	0	0	0	0	0	0	0	0	0	0	0	0	0	0	3	0
McNeil	5	.0000	.0724	28.6	0	4	0	0	1	0	0	0	0	0	0	0	0	0	0	0	0	0	0	0	0	5	0	0	0
McPhale	3	.0000	.1370	31.4	0	3	0	0	0	0	0	0	3	0	0	0	0	0	0	0	0	0	0	0	0	0	0	0	0
McQuiston	11	.0000	.1180	30.7	0	0	0	0	11	0	0	0	0	0	0	11	0	0	0	0	0	0	0	0	0	0	0	0	0
McVey	5	.0000	.2284	33.6	0	0	0	5	0	0	0	0	5	0	0	0	0	0	0	0	0	0	0	0	0	0	0	0	0
Mcgrath	2	.2443	.1130	30.5	1	0	0	0	1	0	0	0	0	0	0	1	0	0	0	0	0	0	0	0	1	0	0	0	0
Mckinley	5	.2260	.2870	34.6	0	3	1	1	0	0	0	0	0	0	0	0	3	2	0	0	0	0	0	0	0	0	0	0	0
mc2	3	.2445	.1818	32.6	0	0	1	1	1	0	0	0	0	0	0	0	0	0	0	2	0	0	0	0	0	0	1	0	0
Md	3	.1937	.1495	31.7	1	0	0	1	0	0	1	0	0	0	0	0	0	1	0	0	0	0	0	0	0	0	0	2	0
MDXVI	2	.0000	.0299	24.8	0	2	0	0	0	0	0	0	0	0	0	0	2	0	0	0	0	0	0	0	0	0	0	0	0
me	6180	.7816	983.63	69.9	1162	901	523	940	1233	666	676	79	2538	369	83	923	36	86	58	13	214	7	7	0	887	487	16	433	23
Me	23	.1096	.8406	39.2	6	5	3	2	4	3	0	0	6	1	0	1	0	0	0	0	10	0	0	0	0	0	1	0	4
ME	3	.2401	.1655	32.2	2	0	0	1	0	0	0	0	0	0	0	0	0	0	0	0	1	0	0	0	2	0	0	0	0
me-oww	2	.0000	.0914	29.6	0	0	0	2	0	0	0	0	2	0	0	0	0	0	0	0	0	0	0	0	0	0	0	0	0
mea	2	.0000	.0914	29.6	0	0	0	2	0	0	0	0	2	0	0	0	0	0	0	0	0	0	0	0	0	0	0	0	0
Mead	2	.0000	.0209	23.2	0	0	1	0	0	0	1	0	0	0	0	0	0	0	0	0	0	0	0	0	0	0	2	0	0
Meade	5	.3683	.4064	36.1	0	0	0	0	2	3	0	0	0	0	0	1	0	2	0	0	0	0	0	0	0	0	2	0	0
meadow	100	.7706	15.690	52.0	28	16	9	21	19	1	5	1	32	2	2	17	0	4	1	15	0	0	0	0	10	8	4	5	0
Meadow	3	.2223	.2106	33.2	0	3	0	0	0	0	0	0	2	1	0	0	0	0	0	0	0	0	0	0	0	0	0	0	0
meadowlands	2	.0000	.0914	29.6	0	0	0	0	1	1	0	0	2	0	0	0	0	0	0	0	0	0	0	0	0	0	0	0	0
meadowlark	3	.3776	.2493	34.0	1	0	0	0	1	0	0	1	0	1	0	0	0	0	0	1	0	0	0	0	0	0	0	1	0
Meadowlark	16	.0000	.7309	38.6	16	0	0	0	0	0	0	0	16	0	0	0	0	0	0	0	0	0	0	0	0	0	0	0	0
meadows	54	.8085	8.8014	49.4	8	6	7	9	10	12	0	2	13	1	0	5	0	10	0	3	4	1	0	0	4	6	5	2	0
Meadows	5	.3926	.4468	36.5	0	1	2	0	1	1	0	0	1	0	0	0	0	1	0	0	0	0	0	0	0	1	2	0	0
meager	15	.6255	1.9410	42.9	3	1	3	0	2	1	3	2	2	0	0	1	0	1	0	0	0	0	0	0	3	4	2	2	0
meagerly	2	.1698	.1133	30.5	0	0	0	1	1	0	0	0	1	0	0	0	0	0	0	0	0	0	0	0	0	0	1	0	0
meal	286	.6031	35.988	55.6	38	57	35	28	51	23	48	6	59	10	5	16	3	32	6	25	0	0	63	0	11	34	7	15	0
meals	147	.5977	18.279	52.6	27	24	18	11	25	13	22	7	24	4	1	5	8	10	4	18	0	0	33	0	6	17	5	12	0
Meals	3	.3086	.2017	33.0	1	0	0	0	1	0	1	0	0	1	0	0	0	0	0	0	0	0	1	0	0	1	0	0	0
mealtime	11	.1869	.5307	37.2	0	1	0	2	3	3	2	0	2	1	0	0	0	0	0	1	0	0	6	0	0	1	0	0	0
mealtimes	12	.3909	1.0653	40.3	5	1	2	1	1	2	0	0	1	0	0	0	0	0	0	8	0	0	1	0	0	2	0	0	0
mean	1266	.9116	229.22	63.6	201	223	194	175	203	125	120	25	350	150	5	91	129	74	135	69	19	3	6	4	100	58	27	45	1
Mean	4	.3717	.3640	35.6	2	0	0	0	1	0	1	0	2	0	0	1	0	0	0	0	0	0	0	0	0	0	0	1	0
meandering	9	.6001	1.1398	40.6	1	0	0	0	4	4	0	0	2	1	0	1	0	1	0	2	0	0	0	0	0	0	0	2	0
meanders	2	.0000	.0394	26.0	0	0	0	0	0	2	0	0	0	0	0	0	0	0	0	2	0	0	0	0	0	0	0	0	0
meanest	3	.2437	.2277	33.6	0	0	0	0	0	1	1	1	2	0	0	0	0	0	0	1	0	0	0	0	0	0	0	0	0
meanin'	2	.2427	.1152	30.6	0	0	0	0	2	0	0	0	0	0	0	0	0	0	0	0	0	0	0	0	1	1	0	0	0
meaning	1376	.6822	192.60	62.8	114	190	194	225	273	199	159	22	325	340	69	41	72	31	342	39	35	7	1	0	11	23	26	14	0
Meaning	4	.1310	.1410	31.5	0	0	0	0	1	3	0	0	0	0	0	0	0	1	3	0	0	0	0	0	0	0	0	0	0
meaningful	38	.8506	6.4338	48.1	1	0	6	3	11	6	8	3	3	5	1	2	1	2	3	4	5	1	0	0	1	2	2	6	0
meaningfully	3	.2028	.1988	33.0	0	0	1	0	1	1	0	0	2	0	0	0	0	0	0	0	1	0	0	0	0	0	0	0	0
meaningless	22	.7819	3.4630	45.4	1	2	0	2	5	3	8	1	2	1	0	2	4	3	0	2	1	0	0	0	0	3	2	2	0
meanings	419	.4657	41.481	56.2	49	60	74	74	69	55	35	3	55	94	11	6	7	3	222	5	1	1	1	0	0	5	7	1	0
meanly	2	.0000	.0914	29.6	0	0	0	0	1	1	0	0	2	0	0	0	0	0	0	0	0	0	0	0	0	0	0	0	0
meanness	5	.4281	.4726	36.7	0	1	0	1	2	0	0	1	1	1	0	1	0	0	0	0	0	0	0	0	2	0	0	0	0
means	1962	.9165	356.14	65.5	346	286	231	277	371	225	174	52	267	192	16	38	245	179	328	221	108	19	31	39	22	74	106	72	5
Means	12	.4494	1.2696	41.0	1	0	0	0	8	0	3	0	7	0	0	0	0	0	0	0	0	0	0	0	0	1	1	3	0
meant	539	.9410	100.31	60.0	60	88	88	80	104	72	33	14	127	60	5	45	15	54	41	24	8	4	4	2	50	55	14	30	1
meantime	40	.7238	5.9483	47.7	2	3	5	8	13	5	4	0	13	2	0	5	0	2	0	2	0	0	1	0	7	3	0	5	0
meanwhile	132	.8248	21.920	53.4	6	14	15	19	28	24	20	6	36	2	1	9	0	22	2	9	3	0	0	0	7	12	10	19	0
Meany	5	.3837	.4754	36.8	0	0	4	0	0	0	1	0	3	0	0	0	0	0	0	0	0	0	0	0	0	0	1	1	0
Meares	3	.0000	.1370	31.4	0	0	0	0	0	0	3	0	3	0	0	0	0	0	0	0	0	0	0	0	0	0	0	0	0
measles	37	.4966	3.8922	45.9	6	16	0	5	7	3	0	0	2	6	1	0	0	1	0	7	0	0	0	0	1	0	0	19	0
measurable	5	.3753	.4154	36.2	0	0	1	0	2	1	0	1	0	1	0	0	0	0	0	2	0	0	0	0	0	0	0	2	0
measure	1056	.6747	145.25	61.6	131	141	160	132	157	167	149	19	51	6	2	13	520	28	13	150	157	0	34	20	3	15	24	20	0
Measure	2	.2287	.1077	30.3	0	1	0	1	0	0	0	0	0	0	0	0	1	0	0	0	1	0	0	0	0	0	0	0	0
measured	204	.8405	34.286	55.4	12	22	38	24	35	35	31	7	26	4	0	3	43	10	6	52	7	1	5	10	5	7	14	11	0
measurement	164	.5547	19.013	52.8	4	12	29	26	42	25	24	2	5	2	0	0	100	5	0	26	0	0	8	4	0	2	11	1	0
Measurement	2	.1648	.0800	29.0	0	1	0	0	1	0	0	0	0	0	0	0	1	0	0	0	0	0	1	0	0	0	0	0	0
measurements	150	.5482	17.199	52.4	3	8	18	19	32	31	35	4	6	0	0	0	64	2	0	41	0	0	6	17	0	1	6	7	0
measures	399	.5302	44.321	56.5	20	25	81	64	76	72	59	2	20	2	0	0	190	13	0	29	113	1	1	2	3	3	16	6	0
measuring	221	.6172	28.158	54.5	17	18	27	26	43	49	35	6	22	0	0	2	73	9	4	42	1	0	30	18	1	4	11	4	0
meat	617	.6902	87.552	59.4	135	91	80	67	112	24	99	9	140	28	2	13	16	103	24	50	1	0	90	0	29	69	29	23	0
Meat	9	.2322	.4788	36.8	1	0	0	0	4	1	0	3	0	0	0	0	0	0	0	2	0	0	4	0	0	0	0	3	0

6R McCready
8Q McCulloch
8R McCullough
3R McDougal's
6P McDougald
9P McElroy
7R McEwen
7R McFarland
3A McGarrity's
9Q McGeorge
9P McGhee
9P McGhee's
5R McGillicutty
6P McGinnity
3A McGrannery's
7R McGraw-Hill
7D McGurn
XR McIlhenney
7J McIntire
5A McIvor
5P McKee
9D McKenney
9D McKenneys
5K McKnight
7R McLains
7R McLaren
3N McLean's
3N McLeans
XR McLeave
4A McLeod's
8R McMahon
5G McManus
4P McMullen's
4P McNeil's
4A McPhales
XR McQueen
3P McQuinn
4P Mcmullen
7E MCVII
7P MD'S**
6A MDCCLXXVI
4E MDLXVI
4N me-e-e
7N me'll
5N me's
7D Meachachtinny
4P meadowland
7Q meagerness
7P meal-beer
4H meal-times
3A mealy
8Q mean-fowt
7D mean-souled
5A mean-tempered
8E meandered
6A meanderings
8A meaner
6R Meanies
8B meanw'ile
9A Meares'
4N measly
9D measuredly
6A measureless
8L measurement-line
3P MEASURING
7Q meat-cleaver

Word Type	F	D	U	SFI	3 Gr 3	4 Gr 4	5 Gr 5	6 Gr 6	7 Gr 7	8 Gr 8	9 Gr 9	X UnGr	A Read	B Eng & Gr	C Comp	D Lit	E Math	F Soc Stud	G Spell	H Sci	J Music	K Art	L Home Ec	M Shop	N Lib F	P Lib NF	Q Lib Ref	R Mag	S Rel
meat-eater	5	.3683	.4536	36.6	3	0	0	2	0	0	0	0	2	0	0	0	0	0	0	2	0	0	0	0	0	1	0	0	0
meat-eaters	6	.1833	.3085	34.9	1	0	0	2	2	1	0	0	0	0	0	0	0	0	0	5	0	0	0	0	0	1	0	0	0
meat-eating	8	.3215	.6209	37.9	5	0	0	0	3	0	0	0	2	0	0	0	0	0	0	0	0	0	0	0	0	4	2	0	0
meat-hook	4	.0000	.1827	32.6	0	0	0	4	0	0	0	0	4	0	0	0	0	0	0	0	0	0	0	0	0	0	0	0	0
meat-packing	16	.1813	.8101	39.1	3	0	8	1	2	1	1	0	0	0	0	0	0	14	0	0	0	0	0	0	0	0	2	0	0
meatball	4	.0000	.1827	32.6	4	0	0	0	0	0	0	0	4	0	0	0	0	0	0	0	0	0	0	0	0	0	0	0	0
meatballs	6	.2435	.4680	36.7	6	0	0	0	0	0	0	0	5	0	0	1	0	0	0	0	0	0	0	0	0	0	0	0	0
meatpacking	2	.0000	.0389	25.9	1	0	1	0	0	0	0	0	0	0	0	0	0	2	0	0	0	0	0	0	0	0	0	0	0
meats	52	.5008	5.5592	47.5	14	5	3	4	11	7	8	0	9	1	0	0	1	7	0	3	2	0	13	0	3	6	7	0	0
meaty	3	.2332	.1690	32.3	2	0	0	0	0	0	0	1	0	0	0	0	0	0	0	0	0	0	0	0	0	2	0	1	0
Meazles	5	.0000	.2284	33.6	0	0	0	0	5	0	0	0	5	0	0	0	0	0	0	0	0	0	0	0	0	0	0	0	0
mebbe	5	.2579	.3199	35.0	0	0	0	0	3	2	0	0	1	0	0	3	0	0	0	0	0	0	0	0	1	0	0	0	0
mebee	2	.0000	.0234	23.7	0	0	0	0	2	0	0	0	0	0	0	0	0	0	0	0	0	0	0	0	2	0	0	0	0
Mecca	9	.3618	.7594	38.8	0	0	1	6	1	0	1	0	1	0	0	0	0	6	0	0	0	0	0	0	0	1	1	0	0
mechanic	28	.6057	3.4708	45.4	2	5	2	4	8	3	3	1	2	2	3	0	1	2	1	0	1	0	0	5	1	7	1	2	0
mechanic's	2	.0000	.0050	17.0	0	0	0	0	0	0	2	0	0	0	0	0	0	0	0	0	0	0	0	2	0	0	0	0	0
mechanical	131	.6628	17.861	52.5	5	21	23	7	23	20	26	6	22	3	0	4	3	8	0	24	7	0	0	15	3	7	25	10	0
Mechanical	10	.2244	.7618	38.8	9	0	0	0	0	0	1	0	9	0	0	0	0	0	0	0	0	0	0	1	0	0	0	0	0
mechanically	12	.5123	1.3203	41.2	0	1	0	1	3	4	3	0	3	0	0	1	2	0	0	0	0	0	0	2	1	1	2	0	0
mechanics	49	.7326	7.2538	48.6	1	4	5	5	13	8	13	0	5	4	4	2	2	8	1	2	1	0	0	3	0	3	11	3	0
Mechanics	2	.2446	.1123	30.5	0	0	0	0	0	0	2	0	0	1	0	0	0	0	0	0	0	0	0	0	0	0	1	0	0
mechanism	31	.6101	3.8776	45.9	0	1	3	2	12	8	2	3	2	2	0	1	1	0	0	4	3	0	0	3	0	0	11	4	0
mechanisms	11	.1134	.3866	35.9	0	0	0	1	8	1	1	0	1	0	0	0	0	0	0	1	0	0	0	0	0	0	9	0	0
mechanistic	2	.0000	.0209	23.2	0	0	0	0	1	0	1	0	0	0	0	0	0	0	0	0	0	0	0	0	0	0	2	0	0
mechanization	2	.2433	.1158	30.6	0	0	1	1	0	0	0	0	0	0	0	0	0	0	0	0	0	0	0	0	0	1	0	1	0
mechanized	5	.3997	.4312	36.3	0	0	0	0	3	0	2	0	0	0	0	0	0	2	0	0	0	0	0	1	0	0	1	1	0
Mechano	5	.0000	.2284	33.6	0	0	0	0	0	5	0	0	5	0	0	0	0	0	0	0	0	0	0	0	0	0	0	0	0
Mecklenburg	4	.3215	.3104	34.9	0	0	2	1	0	0	1	0	1	0	0	0	0	0	0	0	0	0	0	0	0	2	1	0	0
medal	28	.6610	3.9286	45.9	6	4	3	5	2	4	3	1	15	2	0	1	0	2	0	1	0	0	0	0	0	2	4	1	0
Medal	11	.5818	1.3573	41.3	1	2	2	0	1	5	0	0	3	0	0	1	0	2	0	0	1	0	0	0	0	0	3	1	0
medal's	2	.0000	.0914	29.6	2	0	0	0	0	0	0	0	2	0	0	0	0	0	0	0	0	0	0	0	0	0	0	0	0
medallion	2	.1948	.1250	31.0	0	1	1	0	0	0	0	0	1	0	0	0	0	0	0	0	0	0	0	0	0	1	0	0	0
medals	12	.5531	1.4489	41.6	0	2	0	3	1	3	3	0	5	1	0	0	0	2	0	0	0	0	0	0	0	0	2	2	0
Medano	2	.0000	.0243	23.9	0	0	0	0	0	0	0	2	0	0	0	0	0	0	0	0	0	0	0	0	0	0	0	2	0
MEDBOURNE	10	.0000	.1073	30.3	0	0	0	0	10	0	0	0	0	0	0	10	0	0	0	0	0	0	0	0	0	0	0	0	0
meddle	2	.1717	.1142	30.6	0	0	0	1	0	0	1	0	1	0	0	1	0	0	0	0	0	0	0	0	0	0	0	0	0
meddling	2	.1698	.1133	30.5	0	1	0	0	0	0	1	0	1	0	0	0	0	0	0	0	0	0	0	0	0	0	1	0	0
Medea	6	.0000	.2741	34.4	0	0	0	6	0	0	0	0	6	0	0	0	0	0	0	0	0	0	0	0	0	0	0	0	0
Medellin	3	.2063	.1600	32.0	0	0	2	1	0	0	0	0	0	0	0	0	0	1	0	0	0	0	0	0	0	2	0	0	0
Medes	3	.1983	.1396	31.4	0	0	0	0	3	0	0	0	0	0	0	0	0	0	0	0	2	0	0	0	0	0	0	1	0
media	15	.3164	1.0154	40.1	0	0	0	5	0	6	3	1	0	0	0	0	0	0	0	1	3	5	0	0	0	0	3	3	0
median	13	.1680	.5863	37.7	0	0	3	1	2	5	2	0	0	0	0	0	11	0	0	0	0	0	0	0	0	0	0	2	0
Median	2	.0000	.0243	23.9	0	0	0	0	2	0	0	0	0	0	0	0	0	0	0	0	0	0	0	0	0	0	0	2	0
medians	3	.0000	.0449	26.5	0	0	1	0	0	0	2	0	0	0	0	0	3	0	0	0	0	0	0	0	0	0	0	0	0
Mediation	2	.0000	.0209	23.2	0	0	2	0	0	0	0	0	0	0	0	0	0	0	0	0	0	0	0	0	0	0	2	0	0
mediator	4	.2420	.3089	34.9	0	0	3	0	0	0	1	0	3	0	0	0	0	1	0	0	0	0	0	0	0	0	0	0	0
mediators	2	.0000	.0209	23.2	0	0	2	0	0	0	0	0	0	0	0	0	0	0	0	0	0	0	0	0	0	0	2	0	0
medical	149	.6939	21.154	53.3	8	11	16	8	37	21	40	8	17	2	1	2	0	23	4	33	0	0	0	0	1	11	36	19	0
Medical	23	.4610	2.2625	43.5	0	0	2	2	4	2	6	7	1	0	0	0	0	0	0	4	0	0	1	0	0	1	3	13	0
Medici	3	.1783	.1304	31.2	0	0	1	1	0	0	1	0	0	0	0	0	0	0	0	0	0	1	0	0	0	2	0	0	0
medicinal	2	.0000	.0914	29.6	0	0	1	1	0	0	0	0	2	0	0	0	0	0	0	0	0	0	0	0	0	0	0	0	0
medicine	202	.8481	34.346	55.4	20	34	40	28	33	24	19	4	49	5	3	8	5	16	6	51	2	1	4	0	8	14	23	6	1
Medicine	16	.6067	2.0461	43.1	0	2	1	3	6	1	0	3	3	0	0	1	0	1	0	7	1	0	0	0	0	1	0	2	0
medicine-bag	2	.0000	.0234	23.7	0	2	0	0	0	0	0	0	0	0	0	0	0	0	0	0	0	0	0	0	2	0	0	0	0
medicines	49	.4735	5.0653	47.0	5	8	8	6	6	11	5	0	11	0	0	0	0	7	0	6	0	0	10	0	0	3	10	2	0
Medico	2	.0000	.0290	24.6	0	0	0	0	0	0	2	0	0	0	0	0	0	0	0	0	0	0	0	0	0	2	0	0	0
MEDICO	2	.0000	.0209	23.2	0	0	2	0	0	0	0	0	0	0	0	0	0	0	0	0	0	0	0	0	0	0	2	0	0
medieval	43	.5944	5.2850	47.2	1	3	2	4	9	4	14	6	4	6	0	1	1	1	0	4	5	0	0	0	0	3	17	1	0
Medina	3	.2378	.1809	32.6	0	0	1	2	0	0	0	0	0	0	0	0	0	2	0	0	0	0	0	0	0	1	0	0	0
Medio	6	.0000	.2741	34.4	6	0	0	0	0	0	0	0	6	0	0	0	0	0	0	0	0	0	0	0	0	0	0	0	0
mediocre	5	.3317	.3672	35.6	0	0	0	0	4	0	1	0	0	1	0	0	0	0	0	0	0	0	0	0	0	1	0	3	0
meditate	2	.0000	.0209	23.2	0	2	0	0	0	0	0	0	0	0	0	0	0	0	0	0	0	0	0	0	0	0	2	0	0
meditating	5	.3206	.3937	36.0	0	0	0	2	2	0	0	1	2	0	0	0	0	0	0	0	0	1	0	0	0	0	1	1	0
meditation	2	.1814	.1187	30.7	0	0	0	0	1	0	1	0	1	0	0	0	0	0	0	0	0	0	0	0	0	0	0	1	0
mediterranean	4	.0000	.0778	28.9	0	0	0	0	4	0	0	0	0	0	0	0	0	4	0	0	0	0	0	0	0	0	0	0	0
Mediterranean	157	.6200	20.143	53.0	13	14	19	39	48	12	9	3	4	4	0	1	0	94	1	2	4	2	0	0	5	8	26	6	0
medium	95	.7480	14.241	51.5	8	7	4	14	19	17	24	2	1	5	1	2	0	2	1	25	7	7	12	6	1	6	10	9	0
Medium	6	.2412	.3329	35.2	0	0	0	0	1	0	5	0	0	0	0	0	0	0	0	0	0	0	1	0	0	0	0	5	0
medium-hard	2	.0000	.0050	17.0	0	0	0	0	0	0	2	0	0	0	0	0	0	0	0	0	0	0	0	2	0	0	0	0	0
medium-sized	20	.6693	2.7370	44.4	3	1	4	2	5	3	1	1	1	0	0	2	0	3	0	3	0	0	0	0	1	3	2	5	0
medium-soft	2	.0000	.0050	17.0	0	0	0	0	0	0	2	0	0	0	0	0	0	0	0	0	0	0	0	2	0	0	0	0	0
medium-weight	3	.0945	.0794	29.0	0	1	0	0	0	1	1	0	0	0	0	0	0	0	0	1	0	0	2	0	0	0	0	0	0
mediums	2	.2128	.1055	30.2	0	0	0	0	1	0	1	0	0	0	0	0	0	0	0	1	1	0	0	0	0	0	0	0	0
medley	7	.6602	.9469	39.8	1	0	0	3	0	2	0	1	1	1	0	1	0	0	0	0	1	0	0	0	1	1	0	1	0
Medora	2	.0000	.0914	29.6	0	0	0	0	2	0	0	0	2	0	0	0	0	0	0	0	0	0	0	0	0	0	0	0	0
medulla	10	.1626	.4769	36.8	0	0	0	4	0	5	1	0	0	0	0	0	0	0	0	9	0	0	0	0	0	0	1	0	0
Medusae	3	.0000	.0055	17.4	0	0	0	0	3	0	0	0	0	0	0	0	0	0	0	0	0	3	0	0	0	0	0	0	0
mee-ow	2	.0000	.0914	29.6	1	1	0	0	0	0	0	0	2	0	0	0	0	0	0	0	0	0	0	0	0	0	0	0	0
Meecham	7	.0000	.3198	35.0	7	0	0	0	0	0	0	0	7	0	0	0	0	0	0	0	0	0	0	0	0	0	0	0	0
meek	5	.4273	.4800	36.8	1	1	2	1	0	0	0	0	1	1	0	0	0	1	0	0	0	0	0	0	0	2	0	0	0
meeker	2	.2411	.1091	30.4	1	0	1	0	0	0	0	0	0	0	0	1	0	0	0	0	1	0	0	0	0	0	0	0	0
Meeker	3	.0000	.1370	31.4	3	0	0	0	0	0	0	0	3	0	0	0	0	0	0	0	0	0	0	0	0	0	0	0	0
meekly	13	.5397	1.5740	42.0	0	2	1	2	2	5	1	0	8	1	0	2	0	0	0	0	0	0	0	0	1	1	0	0	0
meekness	2	.2443	.1130	30.5	0	0	1	0	1	0	0	0	0	0	0	1	0	0	0	0	0	0	0	0	1	0	0	0	0
Meeling	3	.0000	.1370	31.4	0	0	0	3	0	0	0	0	3	0	0	0	0	0	0	0	0	0	0	0	0	0	0	0	0
meet	627	.9342	115.98	60.6	107	116	76	71	137	53	59	8	156	25	5	45	21	93	21	24	13	3	22	4	60	67	24	44	0
Meet	2	.1926	.0867	29.4	1	0	0	0	1	0	0	0	0	0	0	0	0	0	0	0	0	0	1	0	0	0	1	0	0
meeting	293	.8877	51.830	57.1	44	41	38	26	51	36	50	7	76	33	2	12	10	51	2	5	5	4	4	0	19	30	8	32	0
Meeting	5	.3854	.4790	36.8	0	1	3	1	0	0	0	0	3	0	0	0	0	0	0	0	0	0	0	0	1	1	0	0	0
meetinghouse	2	.0000	.0290	24.6	0	0	0	0	2	0	0	0	0	0	0	0	0	0	0	0	0	0	0	0	0	2	0	0	0
meetings	71	.7688	11.040	50.4	6	10	10	5	11	13	15	1	11	6	0	1	1	20	0	3	5	0	1	0	1	4	11	7	0
meets	71	.8652	12.238	50.9	8	16	11	7	10	6	11	2	8	3	2	4	7	8	0	11	4	0	1	0	1	8	7	7	0
Meg	39	.3129	2.7541	44.4	0	16	3	0	20	0	0	0	2	0	0	11	1	0	0	0	0	0	0	0	24	0	0	1	0
megalopolis	3	.2425	.1816	32.6	0	0	2	1	0	0	0	0	0	0	0	0	0	2	0	0	0	0	0	0	0	0	0	1	0
megaphone	6	.4667	.6287	38.0	0	1	0	2	1	2	0	0	2	0	0	0	0	0	1	2	1	0	0	0	0	0	0	0	0

5N meat's
5P Meath
9Q mecca
5N Meccano
9Q Mechanick
8F mechanicks
7F mechanize
7D Mechelit
8F Mechi-Kuwi
7R med
8A medallions
9Q Medawar
7N meddled
7J Mede
6F Medellin's
7G mediate
5Q mediation
XR Medicare
XR Medicated
6A medications
9Q medicine's
9Q Medicine's
7A medico
9Q mediocrities
5N meditated
7N meditatively
3K medium-
8M medium-carbon
6A medium-done
XH medium-intensity
3A medium-rare
8L mediumweight
6F medius
8A Medusa
6Q medusa-like
3A Meecham's
7N meed
7R Meehanite
3A Meeker's
6B meeny
7R Meer
7N meetcha
9D meetest
4P Meeting-House
3A meeting-house
5Q Meetings
7N Meg's
7E mega
5Q Megaceros
7Q megadeaths
5Q Megalithic
9Q Megalopolis
7A megalopolitan
8N Megara

Word Type	F	D	U	SFI	3 Gr 3	4 Gr 4	5 Gr 5	6 Gr 6	7 Gr 7	8 Gr 8	9 Gr 9	X UnGr	A Read	B Eng & Gr	C Comp	D Lit	E Math	F Soc Stud	G Spell	H Sci	J Music	K Art	L Home Ec	M Shop	N Lib F	P Lib NF	Q Lib Ref	R Mag	S Rel
megaton	2	.2427	.1159	30.6	0	0	0	0	1	1	0	0	0	0	0	0	1	0	0	0	0	0	0	0	0	0	0	1	0
megawatts	4	.0000	.0486	26.9	0	0	0	0	4	0	0	0	0	0	0	0	0	0	0	0	0	0	0	0	0	0	0	4	0
Megwa	2	.0000	.0914	29.6	0	0	0	0	2	0	0	0	2	0	0	0	0	0	0	0	0	0	0	0	0	0	0	0	0
Mehitable	4	.0000	.0579	27.6	0	4	0	0	0	0	0	0	0	0	0	0	0	0	0	0	0	0	0	0	0	4	0	0	0
Mehmet	4	.0000	.0579	27.6	0	0	4	0	0	0	0	0	0	0	0	0	0	0	0	0	0	0	0	0	0	4	0	0	0
Mehrer	2	.0000	.0243	23.9	0	0	2	0	0	0	0	0	0	0	0	0	0	0	0	0	0	0	0	0	0	0	0	2	0
Meigs	9	.0000	.4111	36.1	0	4	4	0	0	1	0	0	9	0	0	0	0	0	0	0	0	0	0	0	0	0	0	0	0
mein	4	.3865	.3376	35.3	0	1	0	1	0	2	0	0	0	0	0	0	0	2	1	0	1	0	0	0	0	0	0	0	0
meiosis	5	.2424	.2988	34.8	0	0	0	2	3	0	0	0	0	0	0	0	0	0	0	3	0	0	0	0	0	0	2	0	0
Meir	4	.2352	.2332	33.7	0	0	0	0	0	2	2	0	0	0	0	0	0	2	0	0	0	0	0	0	0	0	0	2	0
Meister	4	.2417	.3089	34.9	0	3	0	1	0	0	0	0	3	0	0	0	0	0	0	1	0	0	0	0	0	0	0	0	0
Meitner	3	.0000	.0591	27.7	0	0	0	0	3	0	0	0	0	0	0	0	0	0	0	3	0	0	0	0	0	0	0	0	0
Mekong	15	.1616	.7127	38.5	0	0	1	5	7	0	2	0	0	0	0	0	0	13	0	0	0	0	0	0	0	2	0	0	0
Mel	46	.2060	3.4569	45.4	0	0	12	0	0	33	1	0	43	0	0	0	0	1	0	0	0	0	0	0	0	0	0	2	0
Mel's	2	.0000	.0914	29.6	0	0	2	0	0	0	0	0	2	0	0	0	0	0	0	0	0	0	0	0	0	0	0	0	0
melancholy	28	.6508	3.7459	45.7	0	1	2	5	6	9	4	1	5	0	2	6	0	1	0	0	5	0	0	0	3	4	1	1	0
Melanesians	2	.0000	.0290	24.6	0	0	0	0	2	0	0	0	0	0	0	0	0	0	0	0	0	0	0	0	0	2	0	0	0
Melanie	6	.0000	.0729	28.6	0	0	0	0	0	6	0	0	0	0	0	0	0	0	0	0	0	0	0	0	0	0	0	6	0
Melanie's	2	.0000	.0243	23.9	0	0	0	0	0	2	0	0	0	0	0	0	0	0	0	0	0	0	0	0	0	0	0	2	0
Melanthios	4	.0000	.0429	26.3	0	0	0	0	0	0	4	0	0	0	0	4	0	0	0	0	0	0	0	0	0	0	0	0	0
Melbourne	18	.4564	1.9368	42.9	0	3	0	3	2	9	0	1	10	0	0	0	1	5	0	0	0	0	0	0	0	0	0	2	0
Melinda	8	.2177	.5495	37.4	3	4	0	1	0	0	0	0	5	0	0	0	0	0	0	0	0	0	0	0	0	0	0	3	0
Melindy	12	.0000	.5482	37.4	12	0	0	0	0	0	0	0	12	0	0	0	0	0	0	0	0	0	0	0	0	0	0	0	0
Melindy's	4	.0000	.1827	32.6	4	0	0	0	0	0	0	0	4	0	0	0	0	0	0	0	0	0	0	0	0	0	0	0	0
Melisande	13	.3595	1.2521	41.0	0	1	11	0	0	1	0	0	11	0	0	0	0	0	0	0	1	0	0	0	0	0	1	0	0
Melissa	16	.1336	.7559	38.8	5	10	0	0	1	0	0	0	5	0	0	0	0	0	0	0	0	0	0	0	0	11	0	0	0
Mellen	20	.0000	.9137	39.6	0	0	0	20	0	0	0	0	20	0	0	0	0	0	0	0	0	0	0	0	0	0	0	0	0
mellitus	2	.0000	.0209	23.2	0	0	0	0	0	0	2	0	0	0	0	0	0	0	0	0	0	0	0	0	0	0	2	0	0
mellow	18	.5715	2.1581	43.3	3	0	1	5	3	3	2	1	4	0	0	0	0	0	0	0	6	0	1	0	3	1	1	2	0
mellowed	4	.0000	.0486	26.9	0	0	0	1	2	0	1	0	0	0	0	0	0	0	0	0	0	0	0	0	0	0	0	4	0
mellowness	2	.0000	.0243	23.9	0	0	0	0	0	0	1	1	0	0	0	0	0	0	0	0	0	0	0	0	0	0	0	2	0
melodic	60	.0433	.9828	39.9	3	6	11	11	15	7	6	1	0	0	0	0	0	0	0	0	58	0	0	0	0	1	1	0	0
melodic-rhythmic	2	.0000	.0162	22.1	0	0	0	0	0	0	2	0	0	0	0	0	0	0	0	0	2	0	0	0	0	0	0	0	0
melodie	2	.2407	.1090	30.4	0	0	1	0	0	0	1	0	0	1	0	0	0	0	0	0	1	0	0	0	0	0	0	0	0
melodies	173	.0822	4.2264	46.3	13	11	39	44	42	19	4	1	4	1	1	0	0	0	0	0	164	0	0	0	0	1	1	1	0
melodious	10	.4940	1.0343	40.1	3	1	3	0	1	2	0	0	1	2	1	0	0	0	0	0	3	0	0	0	0	0	3	0	0
melodramatic	2	.2437	.1129	30.5	0	0	0	1	0	0	1	0	0	0	0	0	0	0	0	0	0	0	0	0	0	0	1	1	0
melody	721	.0439	12.066	50.8	103	141	164	133	94	53	29	4	6	2	1	3	0	1	0	0	701	0	0	0	0	4	0	3	0
Melody	2	.0000	.0162	22.1	0	0	0	0	1	1	0	0	0	0	0	0	0	0	0	0	2	0	0	0	0	0	0	0	0
melon	16	.5256	1.7847	42.5	0	5	0	1	8	1	1	0	3	1	0	3	0	0	0	1	0	2	0	0	1	1	0	4	0
melons	10	.4651	1.0182	40.1	2	2	0	1	4	0	1	0	1	0	0	0	0	5	0	1	0	0	1	0	0	2	0	0	0
melt	100	.8407	16.880	52.3	28	20	14	6	9	11	11	1	29	2	1	2	0	9	4	21	2	2	8	3	1	8	5	3	0
melted	152	.7985	24.463	53.9	24	31	23	12	17	10	25	10	31	4	1	9	0	21	0	30	0	4	13	7	5	16	7	4	0
melting	115	.8130	18.806	52.7	10	13	22	27	10	14	17	2	18	2	1	2	17	16	0	33	3	0	1	4	2	1	12	3	0
melts	69	.6324	9.1278	49.6	15	13	9	8	3	7	14	0	14	6	0	0	3	6	1	27	0	0	0	5	0	3	4	0	0
meltwater	2	.0000	.0394	26.0	0	0	0	0	0	0	2	0	0	0	0	0	0	0	0	2	0	0	0	0	0	0	0	0	0
Melvil	2	.0000	.0219	23.4	0	0	0	0	1	1	0	0	0	2	0	0	0	0	0	0	0	0	0	0	0	0	0	0	0
Melville	5	.2590	.3349	35.2	0	0	1	0	2	2	0	0	1	0	0	0	0	1	0	0	0	0	0	0	0	3	0	0	0
Melvin	24	.1557	.9581	39.8	0	0	0	0	0	22	2	0	0	21	0	1	0	0	0	0	0	0	0	0	0	0	0	2	0
member	357	.8842	62.746	58.0	27	51	33	44	78	56	63	5	44	25	2	10	87	38	5	15	6	1	8	8	8	29	49	22	0
member's	4	.3269	.2809	34.5	0	0	1	0	1	0	1	1	0	0	0	0	0	0	0	0	0	0	0	1	0	0	2	1	0
members	837	.8528	142.42	61.5	93	135	87	76	192	125	110	19	94	46	4	9	249	122	8	51	23	2	31	15	5	51	75	52	0
Members	2	.1698	.1133	30.5	0	0	0	0	1	1	0	0	1	0	0	0	0	0	0	0	0	0	0	0	0	0	1	0	0
members'	2	.0000	.0209	23.2	0	0	0	0	2	0	0	0	0	0	0	0	0	0	0	0	0	0	0	0	0	0	2	0	0
membership	30	.6428	3.9414	46.0	1	2	5	2	10	3	7	0	2	1	0	0	1	3	1	0	1	0	1	0	0	3	12	5	0
membrane	81	.4174	7.5735	48.8	0	7	12	11	33	6	8	4	6	0	0	0	0	0	0	57	4	0	0	0	0	4	9	1	0
membranes	20	.3952	1.7415	42.4	0	0	3	2	5	4	4	2	0	0	0	0	0	0	0	10	0	0	0	0	1	2	7	0	0
membranophones	2	.0000	.0162	22.1	0	0	0	0	2	0	0	0	0	0	0	0	0	0	0	0	2	0	0	0	0	0	0	0	0
membranous	2	.2278	.1128	30.5	0	0	0	1	0	1	0	0	0	0	0	0	0	0	0	1	0	0	0	0	0	0	1	0	0
mementos	2	.0000	.0243	23.9	0	0	0	0	2	0	0	0	0	0	0	0	0	0	0	0	0	0	0	0	0	0	0	2	0
memo	2	.2440	.1132	30.5	0	0	0	0	2	0	0	0	0	0	0	1	0	0	0	0	0	0	0	0	0	0	0	1	0
memoirs	8	.4481	.7775	38.9	0	0	0	1	2	1	2	2	1	0	0	0	0	1	0	0	1	0	0	0	0	0	1	4	0
memorable	18	.6960	2.5506	44.1	1	0	3	2	5	4	3	0	3	3	1	3	0	2	0	0	3	1	0	0	0	0	1	1	0
memorial	17	.6594	2.3037	43.6	0	1	6	2	1	5	2	0	3	1	0	2	0	3	1	0	2	1	0	0	0	0	4	0	0
Memorial	23	.7317	3.4342	45.4	5	3	7	3	3	2	0	0	5	3	1	2	2	5	0	0	0	0	0	0	0	2	2	1	0
memorials	2	.2437	.1129	30.5	0	0	0	0	1	0	1	0	0	0	0	0	0	0	0	0	0	0	0	0	0	0	1	1	0
memories	44	.7080	6.3792	48.0	0	8	2	5	10	7	8	4	11	2	1	7	0	3	0	1	2	2	0	0	3	0	0	12	0
Memories	2	.2337	.1157	30.6	0	0	0	0	1	1	0	0	0	0	0	0	0	1	0	0	0	0	0	0	1	0	0	0	0
memorization	2	.0000	.0219	23.4	0	0	0	0	1	0	1	0	0	2	0	0	0	0	0	0	0	0	0	0	0	0	0	0	0
memorize	40	.6904	5.6201	47.5	1	4	5	6	15	5	4	0	3	7	0	4	4	8	8	2	1	0	0	0	1	2	0	0	0
memorized	19	.6356	2.5014	44.0	2	1	4	1	8	0	3	0	4	5	0	0	0	1	1	0	3	0	0	0	1	1	0	3	0
memorizing	8	.5347	.9025	39.6	0	1	2	0	2	1	0	2	1	3	0	0	1	1	1	0	0	0	0	0	0	0	0	1	0
memory	139	.8683	24.100	53.8	12	13	25	18	34	21	13	3	36	11	3	10	1	12	7	4	2	5	0	1	11	20	4	12	0
Memory	4	.4448	.3914	35.9	0	0	3	0	0	1	0	0	1	1	0	0	0	0	0	0	1	0	0	0	0	0	1	0	0
Memphis	28	.6208	3.5716	45.5	9	0	4	1	8	5	1	0	1	0	1	1	1	5	0	0	1	0	0	0	1	6	0	11	0
men	4067	.8292	680.61	68.3	610	805	655	464	693	531	246	63	1475	109	17	285	41	807	29	141	90	14	5	11	219	400	198	208	18
Men	23	.7048	3.3332	45.2	2	2	2	6	3	3	4	1	7	0	0	1	0	1	0	1	3	1	0	0	1	1	4	3	0
men-at-arms	5	.3751	.4035	36.1	2	0	0	2	0	1	0	0	0	2	0	0	0	0	0	0	0	0	0	0	2	0	1	0	0
men's	50	.8730	8.7102	49.4	4	4	7	4	16	7	7	1	13	3	1	7	1	5	1	1	4	0	1	0	4	5	2	2	0
Men's	2	.0000	.0914	29.6	0	0	0	0	0	2	0	0	2	0	0	0	0	0	0	0	0	0	0	0	0	0	0	0	0
menace	14	.6394	1.8510	42.7	0	0	2	0	5	5	2	0	2	1	0	3	0	3	0	0	0	0	0	0	0	2	2	1	0
menaced	6	.4273	.5787	37.6	0	0	0	0	1	3	2	0	1	0	0	0	0	3	0	0	0	0	0	0	0	1	0	1	0
menacing	8	.5243	.8776	39.4	0	1	2	0	1	2	2	0	0	0	0	1	0	2	0	0	0	0	0	0	1	1	0	3	0
menacingly	5	.2312	.2828	34.5	0	0	0	0	3	2	0	0	1	0	2	0	0	0	0	0	0	0	0	0	1	0	1	0	0
menage	2	.2446	.1142	30.6	1	0	0	0	0	0	0	1	0	0	0	0	0	0	0	0	0	0	0	0	1	0	0	1	0
menagerie	5	.3228	.4034	36.1	0	1	1	1	1	0	1	0	2	0	0	2	0	0	0	0	0	0	0	0	0	1	0	0	0
mend	29	.7834	4.5956	46.6	8	7	4	4	3	1	2	0	8	0	1	1	0	2	0	1	4	0	1	0	4	2	2	3	0
mended	23	.6951	3.2669	45.1	1	6	5	3	1	4	3	0	4	2	1	2	0	2	0	2	5	0	0	0	3	2	0	0	0
Mendel	7	.0000	.1380	31.4	0	0	0	5	0	1	1	0	0	0	0	0	0	0	0	7	0	0	0	0	0	0	0	0	0
Mendeleyeff	2	.0000	.0394	26.0	0	0	0	0	0	2	0	0	0	0	0	0	0	0	0	2	0	0	0	0	0	0	0	0	0
Mendelssohn	15	.3116	1.0389	40.2	0	0	1	2	9	3	0	0	0	0	0	1	0	0	0	0	6	0	0	0	0	8	0	0	0
Mendelssohn's	5	.2433	.2841	34.5	0	0	1	1	2	1	0	0	0	0	0	0	0	0	0	0	2	0	0	0	0	3	0	0	0
mender	11	.2838	.6920	38.4	0	0	0	1	2	0	8	0	0	0	2	8	0	1	0	0	0	0	0	0	0	0	0	0	0
Mendi	2	.0000	.0914	29.6	0	0	0	2	0	0	0	0	2	0	0	0	0	0	0	0	0	0	0	0	0	0	0	0	0

9H megatons
XP Mege
7A Megistias
6J Meh-nah-tee
6A Meharry
4P Meherrin
8F Mei
5Q Mei-ling
XR Meier
5Q Meiji
XR Meinhardt
9Q Meinhof
XQ meiotic
4Q Meissen
8Q Mej
7D Meknes
7F Mekong's
5G mel
9Q melancholia
XR melancholic
7N Melancholy
7P melancholy-minded
6R melange
9P melanoma
7L melba
8A Melbourne's
7R Melburn
5J Melchior
XR meld
7N Meleagrina
8D melee
6A Mellens
8J mellophone
8B mellowest
8Q Melnikov
4N Meloche
7P melodrama
8R melodramatically
9R melodrame
7R Melon
7Q melopomene
9D Melora
6R Melrakkasletta
8A melter
8B melvin
XR Member
8Q memberships
7Q membrane-lined
7D Memedhakemo
6R memento
9P memoir
7D memorably
7P memorandum
5A Memorandum
6R memorialized
4D memory's
9R memos
9D MEN
5D menagerie-keepers
7A Menam
3A Menches
3A Menches'
8R mendacity
6H Mendel's
8H Mendeleyeff's
7H Mendeleyev

Word Type	F	D	U	SFI	3 Gr 3	4 Gr 4	5 Gr 5	6 Gr 6	7 Gr 7	8 Gr 8	9 Gr 9	X UnGr	A Read	B Eng & Gr	C Comp	D Lit	E Math	F Soc Stud	G Spell	H Sci	J Music	K Art	L Home Ec	M Shop	N Lib F	P Lib NF	Q Lib Ref	R Mag	S Rel
Mendi's	2	.0000	.0914	29.6	0	0	0	2	0	0	0	0	2	0	0	0	0	0	0	0	0	0	0	0	0	0	0	0	0
mending	14	.5593	1.7248	42.4	5	3	0	2	4	0	0	0	7	0	0	0	0	0	0	2	0	0	0	0	2	2	1	0	0
mends	3	.2254	.1785	32.5	1	1	0	1	0	0	0	0	0	0	0	0	0	1	0	2	0	0	0	0	0	0	0	0	0
Mene	2	.0000	.0162	22.1	0	0	0	0	2	0	0	0	0	0	0	0	0	0	0	0	2	0	0	0	0	0	0	0	0
meneer	3	.1187	.1291	31.1	0	0	0	0	1	2	0	0	1	0	0	2	0	0	0	0	0	0	0	0	0	0	0	0	0
Menelaos	5	.0000	.0537	27.3	0	0	0	0	0	0	5	0	0	0	0	5	0	0	0	0	0	0	0	0	0	0	0	0	0
Menelaus	4	.2971	.2896	34.6	0	0	0	3	0	0	0	1	1	2	0	0	0	0	0	0	0	0	0	0	0	0	0	1	0
Meng	2	.0000	.0162	22.1	0	0	2	0	0	0	0	0	0	0	0	0	0	0	0	0	2	0	0	0	0	0	0	0	0
menial	4	.0000	.0438	26.4	0	0	2	0	0	1	1	0	0	4	0	0	0	0	0	0	0	0	0	0	0	0	0	0	0
Menlo	6	.3173	.4157	36.2	0	0	0	0	2	0	4	0	0	1	0	0	0	0	0	0	1	0	0	0	0	0	4	0	0
menorah	2	.0000	.0162	22.1	0	0	1	0	0	1	0	0	0	0	0	0	0	0	0	0	2	0	0	0	0	0	0	0	0
Menotomy	3	.0000	.0352	25.5	0	2	0	0	0	1	0	0	0	0	0	0	0	0	0	0	0	0	0	0	3	0	0	0	0
Menotti	5	.0000	.0404	26.1	0	0	0	4	0	1	0	0	0	0	0	0	0	0	0	0	5	0	0	0	0	0	0	0	0
menstruation	6	.2427	.3643	35.6	0	0	0	0	0	0	4	2	0	0	0	0	0	0	0	4	0	0	0	0	0	0	0	2	0
ment	22	.0869	.6098	37.9	2	0	0	7	9	3	1	0	2	1	0	0	0	0	19	0	0	0	0	0	0	0	0	0	0
mental	157	.8107	25.625	54.1	12	3	16	31	34	32	25	4	30	7	2	7	5	7	2	48	0	0	7	0	3	8	9	22	0
Mental	3	.2427	.1822	32.6	0	0	0	0	0	2	1	0	0	0	0	0	0	0	0	2	0	0	0	0	0	0	0	1	0
mentally	48	.7295	7.1192	48.5	5	2	8	4	9	16	4	0	5	1	0	0	16	3	1	12	0	1	2	0	0	3	1	3	0
mention	92	.8145	15.065	51.8	13	10	4	13	21	9	16	6	20	7	2	14	0	5	1	8	0	0	0	1	12	6	3	13	0
Mention	3	.2227	.1589	32.0	0	0	0	1	0	2	0	0	0	0	0	0	0	0	0	0	0	0	0	0	2	0	0	1	0
mentioned	147	.9087	26.518	54.2	3	9	8	27	42	19	27	12	33	17	4	11	5	12	1	13	7	0	3	1	9	8	11	12	0
mentioning	5	.4001	.4447	36.5	0	0	0	1	2	1	1	0	1	1	1	0	1	0	0	0	0	0	0	0	0	0	0	1	0
mentions	15	.2377	.8922	39.5	2	1	1	2	3	2	4	0	4	2	6	2	0	0	0	0	0	0	0	0	1	0	0	0	0
menu	29	.4261	2.7043	44.3	2	2	2	4	4	4	7	4	6	2	0	1	2	1	0	0	0	0	9	0	0	1	2	5	0
menus	11	.1502	.4156	36.2	0	0	1	0	2	5	2	1	1	0	0	0	0	0	0	0	0	0	7	0	0	1	0	2	0
Meo	2	.0000	.0290	24.6	0	0	0	0	0	0	2	0	0	0	0	0	0	0	0	0	0	0	0	0	0	2	0	0	0
meow	6	.3966	.5283	37.2	4	1	0	0	0	1	0	0	1	0	0	0	0	0	0	0	2	0	0	0	0	1	0	2	0
meowch	2	.1948	.1250	31.0	1	0	1	0	0	0	0	0	1	0	0	0	0	0	0	0	0	0	0	0	0	1	0	0	0
meowed	3	.1187	.1291	31.1	3	0	0	0	0	0	0	0	1	0	0	2	0	0	0	0	0	0	0	0	0	0	0	0	0
meowing	3	.2261	.2131	33.3	2	1	0	0	0	0	0	0	2	0	0	0	0	0	0	0	0	0	0	0	1	0	0	0	0
Mer	3	.1852	.1342	31.3	0	0	0	0	1	2	0	0	0	0	0	0	0	0	0	0	2	0	0	0	0	1	0	0	0
mercantile	2	.0000	.0290	24.6	0	0	2	0	0	0	0	0	0	0	0	0	0	0	0	0	0	0	0	0	0	2	0	0	0
Mercantile	6	.4408	.5601	37.5	0	0	0	1	1	0	4	0	0	0	0	1	0	0	0	0	0	0	0	0	0	1	1	3	0
Mercator	5	.2205	.2855	34.6	0	1	1	0	0	0	3	0	0	0	0	0	0	4	0	0	0	0	0	0	0	0	1	0	0
Merced	2	.2446	.1257	31.0	0	0	0	0	0	1	1	0	0	0	0	0	0	1	0	1	0	0	0	0	0	0	0	0	0
Mercedes	10	.4374	.9200	39.6	0	0	0	0	0	9	0	1	0	2	0	0	0	0	0	0	3	0	0	0	4	1	0	0	0
Mercedes-Benz	3	.2332	.1690	32.3	0	0	0	0	1	0	0	2	0	0	0	0	0	0	0	0	0	0	0	0	0	2	0	1	0
mercenaries	2	.0000	.0290	24.6	0	0	2	0	0	0	0	0	0	0	0	0	0	0	0	0	0	0	0	0	0	2	0	0	0
merchandise	26	.3486	1.9783	43.0	0	1	1	1	5	7	11	0	2	1	0	4	1	3	0	0	0	0	11	0	2	1	1	0	0
Merchandise	3	.2300	.1627	32.1	0	0	1	2	0	0	0	0	0	1	0	0	0	0	0	0	0	0	0	0	0	0	0	2	0
merchant	102	.8349	17.124	52.3	12	22	12	19	9	16	12	0	28	6	0	6	6	29	1	0	2	1	1	0	7	6	8	1	0
Merchant	11	.2437	.8555	39.3	0	8	1	0	0	2	0	0	9	0	0	0	0	0	0	0	0	0	0	0	2	0	0	0	0
merchant's	7	.5602	.8555	39.3	1	3	1	1	0	1	0	0	3	0	0	0	0	1	0	0	0	0	0	0	1	1	1	0	0
merchants	77	.6195	9.9401	50.0	2	12	17	10	18	13	5	0	8	0	0	1	2	40	1	0	3	0	0	0	3	9	9	1	0
merciful	2	.0665	.0708	28.5	0	0	0	0	2	0	0	0	1	0	1	0	0	0	0	0	0	0	0	0	0	0	0	0	0
merciless	13	.6208	1.7401	42.4	1	0	2	2	3	4	1	0	7	0	0	1	0	2	0	0	0	0	0	0	0	1	1	1	0
mercilessly	5	.3325	.3809	35.8	0	1	0	1	1	1	1	0	1	2	0	0	0	0	0	0	0	1	0	0	1	0	0	0	0
mercuric	9	.0000	.1774	32.5	0	0	1	0	1	4	3	0	0	0	0	0	0	0	0	9	0	0	0	0	0	0	0	0	0
mercury	99	.5018	10.836	50.3	20	4	13	15	11	22	13	1	16	0	0	0	3	6	0	58	0	0	7	0	0	0	8	1	0
Mercury	106	.6363	14.187	51.5	22	16	16	27	11	3	9	2	27	4	0	0	10	0	0	47	0	0	0	1	0	6	7	4	0
Mercutio	20	.0000	.2146	33.3	0	0	0	0	0	0	20	0	0	0	0	20	0	0	0	0	0	0	0	0	0	0	0	0	0
mercy	49	.3587	4.0414	46.1	3	4	4	9	11	9	8	1	10	1	0	10	0	6	1	1	6	0	0	0	7	3	1	1	2
Mercy	8	.3185	.5839	37.7	1	6	0	0	0	0	1	0	0	1	0	0	0	2	0	0	0	0	0	0	0	5	0	0	0
mere	79	.8647	13.594	51.3	1	2	9	9	23	14	12	9	8	5	1	9	0	8	1	7	1	2	1	0	7	6	11	12	0
Meredith	13	.1487	.5105	37.1	0	0	0	1	12	0	0	0	0	0	0	0	0	0	0	0	0	0	0	0	11	0	0	2	0
Meredith's	3	.0000	.0352	25.5	0	0	0	0	3	0	0	0	0	0	0	0	0	0	0	0	0	0	0	0	3	0	0	0	0
merely	205	.9176	37.257	55.7	9	6	15	19	59	30	55	12	30	22	4	19	6	17	0	18	10	5	4	2	14	15	25	14	0
merest	3	.3826	.2445	33.9	0	0	0	0	3	0	0	0	0	0	0	0	0	0	0	0	1	0	0	0	0	0	1	1	0
merge	9	.5923	1.0982	40.4	1	0	0	0	2	2	2	2	0	0	0	0	0	0	0	3	2	0	0	0	1	1	1	1	0
merged	9	.4879	.9707	39.9	1	1	3	1	1	2	0	0	3	0	0	0	0	1	0	0	1	0	0	0	0	1	3	0	0
merger	5	.1882	.2328	33.7	0	0	1	0	0	0	0	4	0	0	0	0	0	0	0	0	0	0	0	0	0	0	1	4	0
merging	4	.3060	.2924	34.7	0	0	1	0	2	1	0	0	1	0	0	0	0	0	0	0	1	0	0	0	0	0	2	0	0
meridian	49	.5109	5.3408	47.3	1	3	3	0	0	33	3	6	1	0	0	0	15	3	2	24	0	0	0	0	0	0	3	1	0
Meridian	3	.2037	.1491	31.7	0	1	0	0	0	0	2	0	0	0	0	2	1	0	0	0	0	0	0	0	0	0	0	0	0
meridians	37	.3939	3.1894	45.0	1	20	0	0	4	12	0	0	0	0	0	0	7	8	0	5	0	0	0	0	0	0	17	0	0
meridiem	6	.2060	.2861	34.6	0	0	0	0	4	0	2	0	0	2	0	0	0	0	4	0	0	0	0	0	0	0	0	0	0
meringue	9	.1618	.3307	35.2	0	2	0	0	7	0	0	0	0	0	0	0	0	0	0	0	0	0	6	0	2	0	1	0	0
MERINGUE	2	.0000	.0064	18.1	0	0	0	0	2	0	0	0	0	0	0	0	0	0	0	0	0	0	2	0	0	0	0	0	0
meristematic	2	.0000	.0394	26.0	0	0	0	0	1	0	1	0	0	0	0	0	0	0	0	2	0	0	0	0	0	0	0	0	0
merit	15	.6542	1.9897	43.0	1	0	0	1	6	3	3	1	0	0	0	2	1	1	3	0	0	0	0	0	2	1	1	4	0
Merit	2	.2351	.1166	30.7	0	0	0	0	0	2	0	0	0	0	0	0	0	1	0	0	0	0	0	0	0	0	0	1	0
merits	7	.5204	.7884	39.0	1	1	0	1	0	3	1	0	2	1	0	2	0	1	0	0	1	0	0	0	0	0	0	0	0
Meriwether	3	.1639	.1674	32.2	0	0	3	0	0	0	0	0	1	0	0	0	0	2	0	0	0	0	0	0	0	0	0	0	0
Merle	28	.1906	2.0291	43.1	2	0	0	0	26	0	0	0	26	0	0	0	0	0	0	0	0	0	0	0	2	0	0	0	0
Merle's	4	.0000	.1827	32.6	0	0	0	0	4	0	0	0	4	0	0	0	0	0	0	0	0	0	0	0	0	0	0	0	0
Merlin	29	.3289	2.6050	44.2	0	0	0	22	1	1	1	4	22	0	0	0	0	0	0	0	0	0	0	0	0	0	1	6	0
Merlin's	2	.0000	.0914	29.6	0	0	0	2	0	0	0	0	2	0	0	0	0	0	0	0	0	0	0	0	0	0	0	0	0
Merlyn	3	.0000	.0365	25.6	0	0	0	0	0	0	3	0	0	0	0	0	0	0	0	0	0	0	0	0	0	0	0	3	0
mermaid	10	.6272	1.3048	41.2	2	0	3	1	1	1	0	2	2	1	0	1	0	1	0	0	0	0	0	0	0	1	1	3	0
Mermaid	4	.2386	.2998	34.8	1	0	0	3	0	0	0	0	3	0	0	0	0	0	0	0	0	0	0	0	0	0	1	0	0
mermaids	7	.1491	.3582	35.5	0	1	0	2	3	0	1	0	3	0	0	4	0	0	0	0	0	0	0	0	0	0	0	0	0
Merovingians	2	.0000	.0209	23.2	0	0	0	0	2	0	0	0	0	0	0	0	0	0	0	0	0	0	0	0	0	0	2	0	0
Merrill	3	.1621	.1254	31.0	1	0	1	0	0	0	1	0	0	0	0	0	0	1	0	0	2	0	0	0	0	0	0	0	0
merrily	28	.6557	3.9183	45.9	10	4	7	2	4	1	0	0	17	2	0	2	0	0	0	0	2	0	0	0	1	2	0	2	0
Merrimac	4	.3334	.2895	34.6	0	1	0	0	2	1	0	0	0	0	0	0	0	0	0	0	2	0	0	0	0	1	1	0	0
merriment	11	.3532	.8772	39.4	1	3	2	2	1	0	2	0	2	0	0	3	0	0	0	0	5	0	0	0	1	0	0	0	0
Merriweather	3	.0000	.0322	25.1	0	0	0	0	0	0	3	0	0	0	0	3	0	0	0	0	0	0	0	0	0	0	0	0	0
merry	97	.6999	14.091	51.5	28	20	16	12	9	4	5	3	42	5	2	11	0	1	2	1	18	0	0	0	2	10	0	3	0
Merry	18	.6339	2.3440	43.7	1	0	1	3	10	2	1	0	3	0	0	1	0	0	0	0	4	1	1	0	6	0	1	1	0
Merry-Go-Round	2	.0000	.0162	22.1	2	0	0	0	0	0	0	0	0	0	0	0	0	0	0	0	2	0	0	0	0	0	0	0	0
merry-go-round	23	.6240	3.0473	44.8	11	6	0	0	0	2	4	0	10	5	0	3	0	0	1	1	1	0	0	0	0	0	0	2	0
merry-go-rounds	2	.2375	.1088	30.4	1	1	0	0	0	0	0	0	0	0	0	0	0	0	0	0	1	0	0	0	0	0	0	1	0
Merrylegs	12	.0000	.1407	31.5	0	0	0	0	12	0	0	0	0	0	0	0	0	0	0	0	0	0	0	0	12	0	0	0	0

8A mendicancy
4Q mendicant
7D Mendota
3Q Mendoza
4N mendy-bag
7A Meneer
7P Menendez
7A menfish
7D Mengue
7F menhaden
8A menials
4P Menie
6A Mennonite
9B Mennonites
6N Menomonie
7J Menorah
9R mental-hospital
8F mentalities
9R mentality
7P mentor
7P Mentor
7P Menuet
6A Menuhin
7P mepacrine
9Q Mephistopheles
6P mephitic
7B mer
4J Mercadante
4F Mercator's
9D mercenary
7R Mercer
4P Mercer's
4N merchandises
7J merchandising
3P MERCHANT
9D merchantmen
9Q Merchiston
3P mercies
9R Mercilessly
8H mercurochrome
4H mercury-lead
XH mercury-vapor
XB mercy**
7D Mercyless
9J merges
9L Meringue
6F Merino
6F merinos
6F Merinos
8F merited
6A Meriweather
8A Merki
8A Merki's
4J merle
8Q Merope
7Q Merovingian
8B Merriam
8G Merriam-Webster's
7Q Merriam's
7R Merrick
7D merrier
8N merriest
6R Merrifield
8Q Merrimack
9D Merriweather's
9H merry-go
6H Merry-go-round
7N merry-makers
7N Merry's

Word Type	F	D	U	SFI	3 Gr 3	4 Gr 4	5 Gr 5	6 Gr 6	7 Gr 7	8 Gr 8	9 Gr 9	X UnGr	A Read	B Eng & Gr	C Comp	D Lit	E Math	F Soc Stud	G Spell	H Sci	J Music	K Art	L Home Ec	M Shop	N Lib F	P Lib NF	Q Lib Ref	R Mag	S Rel
merrymakers	2	.0000	.0162	22.1	0	0	0	0	0	0	2	0	0	0	0	0	0	0	0	0	2	0	0	0	0	0	0	0	0
merrymaking	7	.5373	.8037	39.1	0	2	0	3	1	1	0	0	2	0	0	2	0	0	1	0	1	0	0	0	0	0	1	0	0
Mertons	2	.0000	.0219	23.4	0	0	0	0	0	0	2	0	0	2	0	0	0	0	0	0	0	0	0	0	0	0	0	0	0
Meru	2	.0000	.0209	23.2	0	0	0	0	2	0	0	0	0	0	0	0	0	0	0	0	0	0	0	0	0	0	2	0	0
mesa	12	.3373	1.1165	40.5	3	6	2	0	1	0	0	0	10	0	0	0	0	1	1	0	0	0	0	0	0	0	0	0	0
Mesa	7	.3869	.5963	37.8	0	0	1	2	2	2	0	0	0	2	0	0	0	3	0	0	0	0	0	0	0	0	0	2	0
Mesabi	5	.0743	.1541	31.9	0	0	0	0	0	1	4	0	1	0	0	0	0	0	0	0	0	0	0	0	0	0	4	0	0
mesas	8	.2284	.6152	37.9	1	6	0	1	0	0	0	0	7	0	0	0	0	0	0	0	0	0	0	0	0	0	0	1	0
meseta	7	.0000	.1361	31.3	0	0	0	7	0	0	0	0	0	0	0	0	0	7	0	0	0	0	0	0	0	0	0	0	0
Meseta	4	.0000	.0778	28.9	0	0	0	0	4	0	0	0	0	0	0	0	0	4	0	0	0	0	0	0	0	0	0	0	0
mesh	15	.6814	2.0701	43.2	0	2	1	1	7	2	2	0	1	0	1	0	0	0	0	3	0	1	1	1	0	1	5	1	0
meshes	2	.2446	.1123	30.5	0	0	0	1	1	0	0	0	0	1	0	0	0	0	0	0	0	0	0	0	0	0	1	0	0
mesons	5	.2213	.2870	34.6	0	0	0	0	0	1	4	0	0	0	0	0	0	0	0	4	0	0	0	0	0	0	1	0	0
Mesopotamia	20	.3922	1.6906	42.3	1	3	1	2	6	3	4	0	1	0	0	0	0	4	0	0	0	5	0	1	0	4	5	0	0
Mesopotamian	3	.0994	.0714	28.5	0	0	0	0	1	1	1	0	0	0	0	0	0	0	0	0	0	2	0	0	0	0	1	0	0
Mesopotamians	4	.2709	.2503	34.0	0	0	0	0	2	1	1	0	0	0	0	0	0	2	0	0	0	1	0	0	0	0	1	0	0
Mesozoic	9	.3377	.6991	38.4	0	1	0	5	1	1	1	0	0	0	0	0	0	0	0	6	0	0	0	0	0	1	2	0	0
mesquite	8	.3428	.6878	38.4	0	2	5	0	1	0	0	0	3	0	0	0	0	4	0	0	0	0	0	0	1	0	0	0	0
mess	38	.5418	4.6106	46.6	13	2	5	4	9	2	3	0	23	0	0	4	0	1	0	0	1	0	0	0	7	2	0	0	0
message	253	.7902	40.538	56.1	28	44	38	41	46	32	21	3	81	31	2	14	3	15	5	27	8	2	0	2	10	27	13	11	2
message-carrying	2	.0000	.0394	26.0	0	0	0	2	0	0	0	0	0	0	0	0	0	0	0	2	0	0	0	0	0	0	0	0	0
messages	162	.7790	25.597	54.1	28	19	52	24	12	16	9	2	33	12	0	8	0	15	1	63	3	1	1	1	1	16	7	0	0
messenger	56	.7258	8.4100	49.2	6	8	7	8	9	7	10	1	25	3	0	10	0	2	2	3	1	0	0	0	1	7	1	1	0
Messenger	2	.2337	.1157	30.6	0	0	1	0	0	1	0	0	0	0	0	0	0	1	0	0	0	0	0	0	1	0	0	0	0
messenger's	2	.0000	.0914	29.6	0	1	1	0	0	0	0	0	2	0	0	0	0	0	0	0	0	0	0	0	0	0	0	0	0
messengers	19	.3116	1.4129	41.5	4	3	5	2	3	1	1	0	4	1	0	3	0	2	1	1	1	0	0	0	1	2	2	0	1
Messiah	12	.4594	1.1727	40.7	0	1	1	3	4	1	1	1	1	0	0	0	0	0	0	1	5	0	0	0	0	1	2	2	0
Messina	2	.2446	.1142	30.6	0	0	0	1	1	0	0	0	0	0	0	0	0	0	0	0	0	0	0	0	1	0	0	1	0
messmates	3	.0000	.1370	31.4	0	0	0	0	3	0	0	0	3	0	0	0	0	0	0	0	0	0	0	0	0	0	0	0	0
Messrs	3	.2347	.1695	32.3	0	1	0	0	1	1	0	0	0	0	0	0	0	0	0	0	0	0	0	0	1	2	0	0	0
messy	12	.5140	1.3614	41.3	3	1	1	3	2	2	0	0	5	3	0	0	0	1	0	0	0	0	1	0	2	0	0	0	0
mestizo	5	.3742	.4184	36.2	1	0	0	3	1	0	0	0	0	0	0	0	0	3	0	0	0	0	0	0	0	0	1	1	0
mestizos	5	.2426	.2985	34.7	2	0	0	2	1	0	0	0	0	0	0	0	0	3	0	0	0	0	0	0	0	0	2	0	0
Mestrovich	2	.0000	.0290	24.6	2	0	0	0	0	0	0	0	0	0	0	0	0	0	0	0	0	0	0	0	0	2	0	0	0
Meszar	2	.0000	.0914	29.6	0	0	0	0	0	2	0	0	2	0	0	0	0	0	0	0	0	0	0	0	0	0	0	0	0
met	433	.8380	72.997	58.6	80	76	51	62	59	57	41	7	146	30	0	33	2	49	6	6	10	0	4	0	31	46	26	44	0
Met	3	.2411	.1667	32.2	1	2	0	0	0	0	0	0	0	0	0	0	0	0	0	0	1	0	0	0	0	0	0	2	0
metabolic	4	.2278	.2257	33.5	0	0	0	1	0	1	1	1	0	0	0	0	0	0	0	2	0	0	0	0	0	0	2	0	0
metabolism	12	.2408	.7124	38.5	0	0	0	3	6	2	1	0	0	0	0	0	0	0	0	7	0	0	0	0	0	0	5	0	0
metal	782	.4443	75.658	58.8	118	78	58	64	147	148	146	23	156	4	3	12	10	44	9	113	15	5	8	248	22	42	53	38	0
metal-working	2	.1934	.0846	29.3	0	0	0	0	0	1	1	0	0	0	0	0	0	0	1	0	0	0	0	1	0	0	0	0	0
metallic	44	.7264	6.5022	48.1	4	0	2	5	8	14	3	8	6	1	0	1	0	0	0	16	1	1	3	0	1	2	5	7	0
metalloids	2	.0000	.0394	26.0	0	0	0	0	0	2	0	0	0	0	0	0	0	0	0	2	0	0	0	0	0	0	0	0	0
metallurgist	3	.0000	.1370	31.4	3	0	0	0	0	0	0	0	3	0	0	0	0	0	0	0	0	0	0	0	0	0	0	0	0
metallurgists	6	.3591	.5323	37.3	3	0	0	0	0	0	2	1	3	0	0	0	0	0	0	1	0	0	0	1	0	0	1	0	0
metals	255	.4128	23.736	53.8	60	21	17	18	33	55	43	8	63	0	0	0	1	16	0	66	2	1	0	58	2	5	39	2	0
metalwork	4	.0935	.0899	29.5	1	0	0	0	0	0	3	0	0	0	0	0	0	0	0	0	0	0	0	3	0	0	1	0	0
metalworking	10	.1173	.2857	34.6	1	0	2	0	0	0	7	0	0	1	0	0	0	1	0	0	0	0	0	7	0	1	0	0	0
metamorphic	7	.3311	.5381	37.3	1	1	0	1	0	1	3	0	0	0	0	0	0	0	0	5	0	0	0	0	0	1	1	0	0
metamorphosed	3	.3762	.2496	34.0	1	0	0	1	0	1	1	0	0	0	0	0	0	0	0	1	0	0	0	0	0	1	1	0	0
metamorphosis	18	.2945	1.2363	40.9	5	0	0	2	9	0	1	1	0	0	0	0	0	0	0	9	0	0	0	0	0	1	8	0	0
metaphase	2	.0000	.0209	23.2	0	0	0	2	0	0	0	0	0	0	0	0	0	0	0	0	0	0	0	0	0	0	2	0	0
metaphor	11	.4024	.9450	39.8	0	0	2	0	4	1	4	0	0	7	0	1	0	0	1	1	0	0	0	0	0	0	1	0	0
metaphors	12	.2234	.6595	38.2	0	0	3	0	3	2	4	0	1	9	0	0	0	0	0	0	0	0	0	0	0	1	0	1	0
metaphysical	2	.2437	.1129	30.5	0	0	0	0	0	1	0	1	0	0	0	0	0	0	0	0	0	0	0	0	0	0	1	1	0
metate	3	.0000	.1370	31.4	3	0	0	0	0	0	0	0	3	0	0	0	0	0	0	0	0	0	0	0	0	0	0	0	0
Metcalf	2	.0000	.0243	23.9	0	0	0	0	0	0	0	2	0	0	0	0	0	0	0	0	0	0	0	0	0	0	0	2	0
meted	2	.1733	.1149	30.6	0	0	0	0	0	1	0	1	1	1	0	0	0	0	0	0	0	0	0	0	0	0	0	0	0
meteor	27	.4015	2.4899	44.0	5	9	2	1	3	1	6	0	4	0	0	1	0	1	0	16	0	0	0	0	0	5	0	0	0
Meteor	3	.0000	.0591	27.7	0	0	0	0	0	0	3	0	0	0	0	0	0	0	0	3	0	0	0	0	0	0	0	0	0
meteoric	4	.2287	.2348	33.7	0	0	0	0	2	1	1	0	0	0	0	0	0	0	0	3	0	0	0	0	0	0	0	1	0
meteorite	21	.1086	.9097	39.6	4	14	2	0	0	0	1	0	4	0	0	0	0	0	0	17	0	0	0	0	0	0	0	0	0
meteorites	23	.3239	1.8641	42.7	6	9	0	0	5	0	2	1	6	0	0	0	0	0	0	15	0	0	0	0	1	0	1	0	0
meteoroids	4	.2348	.2372	33.8	0	0	0	3	1	0	0	0	0	0	0	0	0	3	0	0	0	0	0	0	0	0	1	0	0
meteorological	6	.3306	.4637	36.7	0	0	1	0	2	3	0	0	0	0	0	0	0	1	0	4	0	0	0	0	0	0	0	1	0
meteorologist	12	.2639	.7843	38.9	0	5	2	1	1	3	0	0	0	0	0	1	0	0	0	10	0	0	0	0	0	0	0	1	0
meteorologists	18	.0000	.3549	35.5	0	1	13	0	2	2	0	0	0	0	0	0	0	0	0	18	0	0	0	0	0	0	0	0	0
meteorology	8	.1824	.4081	36.1	0	0	2	0	1	3	2	0	0	0	0	0	0	0	0	7	0	0	0	0	0	0	1	0	0
meteors	39	.4162	3.6144	45.6	5	16	4	4	1	3	5	1	1	0	0	1	0	2	0	27	0	0	0	0	0	4	4	0	0
meter	206	.3138	14.104	51.5	26	28	45	36	36	30	5	0	5	0	0	2	26	0	0	7	151	0	0	14	0	0	1	0	0
meters	55	.4727	5.4880	47.4	0	2	15	11	10	4	13	0	0	0	0	1	31	1	0	4	15	0	0	1	0	0	1	1	0
methane	14	.3951	1.2244	40.9	0	0	0	6	5	1	2	0	0	0	0	1	0	7	0	1	0	0	0	0	0	0	0	5	0
methanol	2	.0000	.0209	23.2	0	0	0	1	0	1	0	0	0	0	0	0	0	0	0	0	0	0	0	0	0	0	2	0	0
methinks	7	.3567	.5464	37.4	0	0	1	0	3	0	3	0	0	1	0	3	0	0	0	0	0	0	0	0	0	3	0	0	0
method	626	.7668	96.518	59.8	34	70	93	88	136	79	99	27	32	14	5	9	260	31	15	85	9	8	16	50	7	18	43	24	0
Method	7	.2793	.4312	36.3	0	0	1	0	0	1	5	0	0	0	0	0	1	0	0	1	0	0	3	0	0	0	2	0	0
methodical	3	.3394	.2451	33.9	0	1	1	0	0	1	0	0	1	0	0	1	0	0	0	0	0	0	0	0	1	0	0	0	0
methodically	5	.5605	.5808	37.6	0	0	0	0	3	0	0	2	0	0	0	0	0	0	0	1	0	0	0	0	1	1	1	1	0
Methodist	4	.3212	.3104	34.9	0	1	1	0	1	1	0	0	1	0	0	1	0	0	0	0	0	0	0	0	0	2	0	0	0
methods	320	.7921	50.881	57.1	23	22	54	35	67	48	66	5	27	15	1	5	57	59	4	43	5	5	11	28	1	7	42	10	0
methyl	4	.1494	.1609	32.1	0	0	0	3	1	0	0	0	0	0	0	0	0	0	0	1	0	0	0	0	0	0	3	0	0
meticulous	6	.3498	.4833	36.8	0	0	0	1	1	1	3	0	1	0	0	0	0	0	0	1	0	0	0	0	0	0	3	1	0
meticulously	3	.2181	.1541	31.9	0	0	0	0	2	0	1	0	0	0	0	0	0	0	0	0	0	0	0	0	1	0	2	0	0
metric	57	.3025	4.0072	46.0	0	0	7	7	21	17	5	0	0	0	0	0	41	0	0	12	2	0	0	0	0	0	2	0	0
Metro	3	.0000	.1370	31.4	3	0	0	0	0	0	0	0	3	0	0	0	0	0	0	0	0	0	0	0	0	0	0	0	0
metronome	2	.2303	.1079	30.3	1	0	0	0	0	1	0	0	0	0	0	0	0	0	0	0	1	0	0	0	0	1	0	0	0
metropolis	6	.4784	.6081	37.8	0	0	0	1	0	0	4	1	0	0	0	1	0	2	0	0	0	0	0	0	0	0	1	2	0
Metropolis	29	.0000	.5640	37.5	29	0	0	0	0	0	0	0	0	0	0	0	0	29	0	0	0	0	0	0	0	0	0	0	0
metropolitan	28	.5130	3.0252	44.8	3	0	5	2	10	2	3	3	0	0	0	0	0	11	1	1	0	0	0	0	0	1	6	8	0
Metropolitan	16	.4142	1.4083	41.5	1	0	3	1	5	4	1	1	0	0	0	0	0	1	0	0	2	0	0	0	0	1	9	3	0
Mets	4	.0000	.0486	26.9	0	4	0	0	0	0	0	0	0	0	0	0	0	0	0	0	0	0	0	0	0	0	0	4	0
mettle	4	.2969	.2888	34.6	0	2	0	0	0	2	0	0	1	0	0	2	0	0	0	0	0	0	0	0	1	0	0	0	0
mew	21	.2338	1.1655	40.7	19	1	0	0	1	0	0	0	2	0	0	1	0	0	0	0	15	0	0	0	0	1	0	2	0
mewed	3	.2261	.2131	33.3	1	1	0	0	0	1	0	0	2	0	0	0	0	0	0	0	0	0	0	0	1	0	0	0	0

9B Merryweather
8H merthiolate
7H Merychippus
3A mesdames
5A meself
7J Meshach
9B Mesmer
9B mesmerism
7H Mesohippus
9Q mesometeorology
7Q mesophyll
7Q mesosaur
7Q mesosaurs
5N Mesrour
7A mess-attendant
XN messed
5N Messengers
9R Messer
7D messes
5P messiah
3N messier
7R Messier
6R Messieurs
3P messin'
8Q Mestrovic
7M metal-cutting
7F metal-detection
8M metal-foil
8Q metal's
6R metallastic
8H metallic-looking
4N Metallumai
9Q metallurgical
9Q metallurgy
7Q metalmarks
9F metalware
9M metalworker's
9M metalworkers
6P metamorphism
XH metamorphose
8G Metaphor
9B metaphorical
9Q Metaphysics
3A metates
7D mete
3A meteorite's
3A meteoritic
7H meteorology's
8A Meter
7P methink
8Q Methodism
5H methylene
9Q Metraux
5G metre
8Q metre-making
9E metrei
8Q metres
9Q metrical
8D Metro-Goldwyn
7R Metromedia
7Q metropolises
7R Meuse-Argonne

Word Type	F	D	U	SFI	3 Gr 3	4 Gr 4	5 Gr 5	6 Gr 6	7 Gr 7	8 Gr 8	9 Gr 9	X UnGr	A Read	B Eng & Gr	C Comp	D Lit	E Math	F Soc Stud	G Spell	H Sci	J Music	K Art	L Home Ec	M Shop	N Lib F	P Lib NF	Q Lib Ref	R Mag	S Rel
middle	706	.9231	129.21	61.1	144	114	105	94	110	79	50	10	175	34	11	32	19	65	25	75	83	7	0	4	47	50	36	41	2
Middle	210	.7031	30.039	54.8	13	13	44	38	42	27	31	2	14	9	0	0	1	82	7	4	29	1	1	0	0	16	36	10	0
middle-aged	14	.6333	1.8341	42.6	0	1	1	1	3	1	7	0	2	0	0	1	0	1	0	1	0	0	0	0	3	1	1	4	0
middle-class	10	.3750	.8146	39.1	2	0	1	0	1	2	3	1	0	1	0	0	0	1	0	0	0	0	0	0	0	0	2	6	0
middle-distance	4	.0000	.0579	27.6	0	0	0	0	4	0	0	0	0	0	0	0	0	0	0	0	0	0	0	0	0	4	0	0	0
middle-latitude	5	.2205	.2855	34.6	0	0	1	0	0	0	4	0	0	0	0	0	0	4	0	0	0	0	0	0	0	0	1	0	0
middle-sized	8	.5644	.9785	39.9	2	3	1	1	0	0	1	0	3	1	0	1	0	2	0	0	0	0	0	0	1	0	0	0	0
middlemen	2	.0000	.0243	23.9	0	0	0	0	1	1	0	0	0	0	0	0	0	0	0	0	0	0	0	0	0	0	0	2	0
Middletown	48	.0181	1.1130	40.5	48	0	0	0	0	0	0	0	1	0	0	0	0	47	0	0	0	0	0	0	0	0	0	0	0
Middleville	3	.0000	.0365	25.6	3	0	0	0	0	0	0	0	0	0	0	0	0	0	0	0	0	0	0	0	0	0	0	3	0
middy	6	.2212	.4538	36.6	1	0	0	0	0	5	0	0	5	0	0	0	0	1	0	0	0	0	0	0	0	0	0	0	0
Mide	2	.0000	.0215	23.3	0	0	0	0	0	2	0	0	0	0	0	2	0	0	0	0	0	0	0	0	0	0	0	0	0
midfield	2	.0000	.0243	23.9	0	0	0	1	0	1	0	0	0	0	0	0	0	0	0	0	0	0	0	0	0	0	2	0	0
Midge	23	.1333	1.4860	41.7	0	3	0	5	0	15	0	0	22	0	0	0	0	0	0	0	0	0	0	0	0	1	0	0	0
Midge's	3	.0000	.1370	31.4	0	1	0	0	0	2	0	0	3	0	0	0	0	0	0	0	0	0	0	0	0	0	0	0	0
midget	8	.4511	.8411	39.2	3	0	0	1	3	1	0	0	4	0	0	0	0	0	0	1	0	0	0	0	2	1	0	0	0
midline	3	.1813	.1402	31.5	0	0	0	0	0	2	1	0	0	0	0	0	0	0	0	1	0	0	0	0	0	0	2	0	0
midmorning	5	.1599	.2478	33.9	0	1	0	1	2	0	0	1	2	0	2	0	0	0	0	0	0	0	0	0	0	0	0	1	0
midnight	139	.7387	21.075	53.2	10	25	25	19	22	25	10	3	51	3	10	16	4	8	3	14	2	0	0	0	9	6	4	9	0
Midnight	36	.2463	2.0677	43.2	28	1	0	1	3	3	0	0	0	1	0	5	0	2	0	0	0	0	0	0	28	0	0	0	0
midpoint	10	.2839	.6885	38.4	0	0	2	0	1	6	0	1	1	0	0	0	7	0	0	1	0	0	0	0	0	0	0	1	0
midpoints	2	.0000	.0299	24.8	1	0	0	0	0	0	1	0	0	0	0	0	2	0	0	0	0	0	0	0	0	0	0	0	0
midrib	2	.0000	.0394	26.0	0	0	2	0	0	0	0	0	0	0	0	0	0	0	0	2	0	0	0	0	0	0	0	0	0
midseason	2	.1814	.1187	30.7	0	0	0	1	0	0	1	0	1	0	0	0	0	0	0	0	0	0	0	0	0	0	0	1	0
midshipmen	2	.0000	.0914	29.6	0	0	0	0	0	2	0	0	2	0	0	0	0	0	0	0	0	0	0	0	0	0	0	0	0
midst	67	.8343	11.205	50.5	9	6	5	11	9	14	11	2	16	0	2	8	0	6	0	1	1	1	1	2	13	7	2	7	0
midstream	3	.0000	.1370	31.4	0	0	0	2	1	0	0	0	3	0	0	0	0	0	0	0	0	0	0	0	0	0	0	0	0
midsummer	13	.7029	1.8717	42.7	2	2	1	1	6	0	1	0	2	0	0	1	0	3	0	1	0	0	0	0	1	2	1	2	0
Midsummer	2	.2411	.1091	30.4	0	1	1	0	1	0	0	0	0	0	0	1	0	0	0	0	1	0	0	0	0	0	0	0	0
Midtown	4	.0000	.0599	27.8	0	0	0	0	0	4	0	0	0	0	0	0	4	0	0	0	0	0	0	0	0	0	0	0	0
midway	21	.6740	2.9274	44.7	3	2	0	4	6	3	3	0	5	0	0	1	4	2	0	1	0	0	0	0	2	0	4	2	0
Midway	2	.2351	.1166	30.7	0	0	1	0	0	0	0	1	0	0	0	0	0	1	0	0	0	0	0	0	0	0	0	1	0
midwest	2	.0000	.0389	25.9	0	0	1	0	1	0	0	0	0	0	0	0	0	2	0	0	0	0	0	0	0	0	0	0	0
Midwest	52	.3470	4.2381	46.3	1	2	41	2	3	2	0	1	4	2	0	0	0	40	0	1	0	0	0	0	0	0	2	3	0
midwestern	10	.5570	1.1728	40.7	1	0	2	2	4	1	1	0	1	0	0	0	0	1	0	3	2	0	0	0	1	0	0	2	0
Midwestern	2	.1972	.1262	31.0	0	0	0	1	0	0	1	0	1	0	0	0	1	0	0	0	0	0	0	0	0	0	0	0	0
Midwesterners	2	.2152	.1357	31.3	0	0	0	0	1	1	0	0	1	0	0	0	0	1	0	0	0	0	0	0	0	0	0	0	0
midwife	2	.2441	.1127	30.5	0	0	0	0	0	1	1	0	0	0	0	0	0	0	0	0	0	0	0	0	1	0	1	0	0
midwinter	5	.4244	.4508	36.5	0	1	3	0	0	0	0	1	0	1	0	0	0	1	0	0	2	0	0	0	0	0	0	1	0
midwives	3	.3873	.2495	34.0	0	0	0	0	2	1	0	0	0	0	0	1	0	0	0	0	0	0	0	0	1	0	0	1	0
mien	4	.2048	.1975	33.0	0	1	0	0	2	0	1	0	0	0	0	1	0	0	0	0	0	0	0	0	3	0	0	0	0
Miep	3	.1409	.1472	31.7	0	0	0	0	0	3	0	0	1	0	0	0	0	0	0	0	0	0	0	0	0	2	0	0	0
Miesje	4	.0000	.1827	32.6	0	0	0	4	0	0	0	0	4	0	0	0	0	0	0	0	0	0	0	0	0	0	0	0	0
might	2824	.9551	532.70	67.3	396	481	302	397	590	339	242	77	675	208	46	243	113	273	51	286	123	35	45	13	219	222	91	181	0
mightier	2	.1494	.1045	30.2	1	0	0	1	0	0	0	0	1	0	0	0	0	0	0	0	1	0	0	0	0	0	0	0	0
mighties	3	.0000	.0365	25.6	3	0	0	0	0	0	0	0	0	0	0	0	0	0	0	0	0	0	0	0	0	0	0	3	0
mightiest	7	.5033	.7501	38.8	1	2	1	1	0	0	2	0	1	0	0	1	0	0	0	0	0	0	0	0	0	1	2	2	0
mightily	4	.2816	.2744	34.4	1	0	0	0	1	0	2	0	1	0	0	0	0	0	0	0	0	1	0	0	1	1	0	0	0
mightly	2	.0000	.0290	24.6	1	1	0	0	0	0	0	0	0	0	0	0	0	0	0	0	0	0	0	0	0	2	0	0	0
mightn't	3	.1200	.1302	31.1	0	0	0	1	0	0	2	0	1	2	0	0	0	0	0	0	0	0	0	0	0	0	0	0	0
mighty	247	.6209	32.214	55.1	40	45	24	31	48	32	23	4	73	6	1	42	0	21	0	3	19	0	0	0	24	28	9	18	3
Mighty	6	.2632	.3947	36.0	0	0	0	2	1	3	0	0	1	1	0	0	0	0	0	0	0	0	0	0	0	4	0	0	0
migrant	5	.3651	.4127	36.2	1	0	3	0	0	1	0	0	0	0	0	0	0	3	0	0	0	0	0	0	0	1	0	1	0
migrants	9	.3053	.6244	38.0	0	0	1	0	5	3	0	0	0	1	0	0	0	3	0	0	0	0	0	0	0	0	5	0	0
migrate	35	.5393	3.9738	46.0	2	2	3	11	12	3	1	1	0	1	0	1	0	2	0	19	0	0	0	0	0	2	7	3	0
migrated	12	.3298	.9088	39.6	0	2	5	2	3	0	0	0	1	0	0	0	0	5	0	0	5	0	0	0	0	0	0	1	0
migrates	5	.4510	.5045	37.0	0	1	1	1	2	0	0	0	1	0	0	0	0	0	0	2	0	0	0	0	0	1	0	1	0
migrating	24	.6582	3.2656	45.1	3	1	1	9	7	0	1	2	4	0	0	1	0	2	0	5	0	0	0	0	1	2	5	4	0
migration	49	.5144	5.4450	47.4	1	8	6	16	12	3	3	0	6	0	0	0	0	4	0	25	0	0	0	0	0	2	4	8	0
migrations	14	.4639	1.4214	41.5	2	1	2	3	5	0	1	0	2	0	0	0	0	2	0	3	0	0	0	0	0	2	5	0	0
migratory	5	.4702	.4939	36.9	0	0	1	0	2	1	0	1	0	1	0	0	0	0	0	0	0	0	0	0	0	1	1	2	0
Migratory	2	.0000	.0209	23.2	0	0	2	0	0	0	0	0	0	0	0	0	0	0	0	0	0	0	0	0	0	0	2	0	0
Miguel	5	.5244	.5603	37.5	1	2	0	0	1	1	0	0	1	1	0	0	0	1	1	0	0	0	0	0	0	0	1	0	0
Mihailovna	3	.0000	.1370	31.4	3	0	0	0	0	0	0	0	3	0	0	0	0	0	0	0	0	0	0	0	0	0	0	0	0
Mij	8	.0000	.1556	31.9	8	0	0	0	0	0	0	0	0	0	0	0	0	8	0	0	0	0	0	0	0	0	0	0	0
Mijbil	3	.2279	.2143	33.3	0	0	0	0	2	0	0	1	2	0	0	0	0	0	0	0	0	0	0	0	0	0	0	0	0
Mikado	2	.1494	.1045	30.2	0	0	0	1	0	1	0	0	1	0	0	0	0	0	0	0	1	0	0	0	0	0	0	1	0
mike	18	.3658	1.5223	41.8	4	0	0	3	10	0	1	0	4	0	0	2	0	0	0	1	0	0	0	0	0	1	0	10	0
Mike	461	.6254	62.840	58.0	74	37	13	278	15	42	1	1	325	13	10	5	7	10	1	1	0	0	0	0	9	17	0	63	0
Mike's	21	.5409	2.5772	44.1	2	4	0	12	1	2	0	0	15	1	1	0	1	0	0	0	0	0	0	0	2	1	0	0	0
mikes	3	.0000	.0365	25.6	0	0	0	0	3	0	0	0	0	0	0	0	0	0	0	0	0	0	0	0	0	0	0	3	0
Mikey	8	.0000	.3655	35.6	0	0	8	0	0	0	0	0	8	0	0	0	0	0	0	0	0	0	0	0	0	0	0	0	0
Mikimoto	3	.0000	.0583	27.7	0	3	0	0	0	0	0	0	0	0	0	0	0	3	0	0	0	0	0	0	0	0	0	0	0
Mikko	5	.0000	.2284	33.6	0	5	0	0	0	0	0	0	5	0	0	0	0	0	0	0	0	0	0	0	0	0	0	0	0
Miklos	17	.0000	.7766	38.9	0	17	0	0	0	0	0	0	17	0	0	0	0	0	0	0	0	0	0	0	0	0	0	0	0
Milan	17	.5173	1.8463	42.7	8	0	2	1	1	1	4	0	0	2	0	0	0	4	0	0	0	0	0	0	0	7	3	1	0
Milankovitch	3	.0000	.0314	25.0	0	0	0	0	3	0	0	0	0	0	0	0	0	0	0	0	0	0	0	0	0	0	3	0	0
mild	115	.7725	17.944	52.5	5	10	24	26	24	11	11	4	14	1	0	8	0	45	0	7	4	0	5	4	2	8	8	9	0
milder	8	.3692	.6896	38.4	0	0	4	1	3	0	0	0	1	0	0	0	0	5	0	1	0	0	0	0	0	0	1	0	0
mildly	6	.3639	.4739	36.8	1	0	0	0	1	2	1	1	0	0	0	0	0	0	0	0	0	0	0	0	2	0	1	3	0
Mildred	35	.4781	3.5504	45.5	8	5	2	0	0	3	1	16	2	8	0	1	0	1	0	0	0	0	0	0	1	6	0	16	0
Mildred's	4	.3545	.3097	34.9	3	1	0	0	0	0	0	0	0	2	0	0	0	0	0	0	0	0	0	0	1	1	0	0	0
mile	344	.8287	57.301	57.6	35	64	48	59	68	44	24	2	81	10	2	15	80	34	13	27	0	0	0	0	18	22	18	24	0
Mile	7	.5020	.7522	38.8	1	2	1	1	1	0	0	1	1	0	0	2	0	1	0	0	1	0	0	0	0	2	0	0	0
mile-long	2	.2440	.1132	30.5	0	0	0	0	1	1	0	0	0	0	0	1	0	0	0	0	0	0	0	0	0	0	0	1	0
mile-wide	2	.2437	.1129	30.5	0	0	0	1	1	0	0	0	0	0	0	0	0	0	0	0	0	0	0	0	0	0	1	1	0
mileage	16	.5243	1.8108	42.6	3	4	0	0	6	3	0	0	3	0	0	0	4	5	0	0	0	0	0	0	0	0	1	3	0
miler	2	.0000	.0290	24.6	0	0	0	0	2	0	0	0	0	0	0	0	0	0	0	0	0	0	0	0	0	2	0	0	0
miles	2146	.8187	353.01	65.5	289	379	314	351	404	211	150	48	324	38	13	44	468	381	9	283	7	1	0	11	42	177	182	166	0
Miles	24	.5689	2.9128	44.6	6	1	2	0	12	1	2	0	8	0	0	2	0	0	1	0	1	1	0	0	10	0	1	0	0
milestone	9	.6564	1.2274	40.9	1	1	0	0	2	4	1	0	2	0	0	0	2	1	1	1	0	0	0	0	0	1	1	0	0
milestones	4	.4835	.4115	36.1	0	0	1	1	0	1	1	0	0	0	0	0	1	0	0	1	0	0	0	0	1	1	0	0	0

8R middle-career
9H middle-ear
3Q middle-income
5P middle-of-the-road
7P middle-rail
3G middles
XR Middlesex
7R middleweight
3P Middlewest
7R middling
8A Middy
8R Mideast
7Q midges
4A midgets
5Q Midianite
5P midland
7B Midland
3A Midlands
XR midnight-blue
3N Midnight's
8Q Midsayap
6A midsection
6A midship
7A midshipman
8A Midshipman
8A midshipman's
7P midships
7A midtown
4E Midvale
6E Midville
8A midwatch
6R Midwesterner
8N midwifery
8R midyear
7Q Miers
9K Mies
5B Mifflin
8R Might
6A might's
7A might've
4A Mightiness
6A mighty-statured
XP Miglia
XR mignon
3P mignonette
9Q migraine
7R migrant-worker
7Q migrators
8F Mihiel
8F Miiko
3F Mij's
7D MIKE
7R miked
4A Mikko's
8F Mikoyan
6J Mikrokosmos
6E Milady
9B Milano
9L mild-flavored
9L mild-fruit
6R mild-mannered
4F mildew
8L mildew-resistant
9D mildewed
7Q mildness
4P mile-and-a-half
XR mile-and-a-half-long
6R mile-deep
7A mile-high
7Q mile-round
3R mile-thick
4G milepost
6J miles'
7N Miles's

Word Type	F	D	U	SFI	3 Gr 3	4 Gr 4	5 Gr 5	6 Gr 6	7 Gr 7	8 Gr 8	9 Gr 9	X UnGr	A Read	B Eng & Gr	C Comp	D Lit	E Math	F Soc Stud	G Spell	H Sci	J Music	K Art	L Home Ec	M Shop	N Lib F	P Lib NF	Q Lib Ref	R Mag	S Rel
Milette	2	.0000	.0914	29.6	0	0	0	0	2	0	0	0	2	0	0	0	0	0	0	0	0	0	0	0	0	0	0	0	0
Milhous	2	.2437	.1129	30.5	0	0	0	0	1	1	0	0	0	0	0	0	0	0	0	0	0	0	0	0	0	0	1	1	0
milia	2	.0000	.0162	22.1	0	0	2	0	0	0	0	0	0	0	0	0	0	0	2	0	0	0	0	0	0	0	0	0	0
militant	8	.3817	.6874	38.4	0	0	0	0	3	3	2	0	1	0	0	0	0	2	1	0	0	0	0	0	0	0	0	4	0
militants	7	.0000	.0851	29.3	0	0	1	0	0	3	3	0	0	0	0	0	0	0	0	0	0	0	0	0	0	0	0	7	0
military	209	.6981	29.652	54.7	14	16	29	14	38	54	36	8	10	1	1	4	1	55	3	5	10	0	0	0	4	26	35	54	0
Military	16	.5022	1.7299	42.4	1	2	4	0	3	3	2	1	2	0	0	0	0	6	0	0	0	0	0	0	0	2	4	2	0
militated	2	.0000	.0162	22.1	0	0	0	0	2	0	0	0	0	0	0	0	0	0	2	0	0	0	0	0	0	0	0	0	0
militia	23	.6429	3.0407	44.8	0	10	2	2	2	6	1	0	2	0	0	0	0	4	0	0	1	1	0	0	2	9	2	2	0
Militia	3	.0000	.0434	26.4	0	3	0	0	0	0	0	0	0	0	0	0	0	0	0	0	0	0	0	0	0	3	0	0	0
milk	849	.7243	125.56	61.0	241	103	89	83	135	62	124	12	184	35	7	28	74	108	15	129	5	1	123	2	57	39	16	26	0
Milk	13	.3866	1.1791	40.7	5	0	0	0	3	1	2	2	5	0	0	0	0	0	0	2	0	0	3	0	0	0	1	2	0
milk-toast	3	.0000	.0352	25.5	0	0	0	3	0	0	0	0	0	0	0	0	0	0	0	0	0	0	0	0	3	0	0	0	0
milk-white	4	.2417	.3028	34.8	2	0	0	2	0	0	0	0	3	0	0	0	0	0	0	0	0	0	0	0	1	0	0	0	0
milked	22	.6031	2.8367	44.5	13	3	2	1	1	2	0	0	9	1	2	0	1	1	0	2	1	0	0	0	1	4	0	0	0
milker	3	.0000	.1370	31.4	1	0	0	0	2	0	0	0	3	0	0	0	0	0	0	0	0	0	0	0	0	0	0	0	0
milking	34	.6434	4.6494	46.7	14	4	4	6	1	3	2	0	16	0	2	2	0	5	0	2	1	0	0	0	2	4	0	0	0
milkmaids	2	.0000	.0914	29.6	0	0	0	1	1	0	0	0	2	0	0	0	0	0	0	0	0	0	0	0	0	0	0	0	0
milkman	11	.5367	1.2806	41.1	6	0	0	0	4	0	1	0	3	1	0	1	0	4	0	0	0	0	0	0	2	0	0	0	0
milks	4	.1855	.2376	33.8	0	2	1	0	0	1	0	0	2	0	0	0	0	1	0	0	0	1	0	0	0	0	0	0	0
milkweed	6	.3228	.4570	36.6	1	1	2	1	0	1	0	0	0	0	0	0	0	1	0	4	0	0	0	0	0	1	0	0	0
milky	13	.3710	1.0802	40.3	0	3	5	1	2	1	1	0	0	0	0	2	0	0	0	8	0	0	0	0	0	0	3	0	0
Milky	74	.3452	5.9556	47.7	25	9	15	3	10	9	1	2	2	2	0	1	1	1	0	61	0	0	0	0	1	1	4	0	0
mill	149	.7438	22.640	53.5	30	29	23	14	15	21	16	1	47	3	1	12	1	22	2	5	7	1	0	16	8	10	9	5	0
Mill	25	.5368	2.8543	44.6	1	3	12	0	7	0	0	2	5	0	0	2	3	0	0	0	0	0	0	0	0	3	9	3	0
MillCreekValley	4	.0000	.0778	28.9	4	0	0	0	0	0	0	0	0	0	0	0	0	4	0	0	0	0	0	0	0	0	0	0	0
Mill-wheel	3	.0000	.0352	25.5	0	0	0	0	3	0	0	0	0	0	0	0	0	0	0	0	0	0	0	0	3	0	0	0	0
Millais	2	.0000	.0209	23.2	0	0	2	0	0	0	0	0	0	0	0	0	0	0	0	0	0	0	0	0	0	0	2	0	0
Millard	5	.2351	.3077	34.9	0	0	0	0	1	1	3	0	1	0	0	0	0	1	0	0	0	0	0	0	3	0	0	0	0
Millay	2	.0000	.0215	23.3	0	0	0	0	0	0	2	0	0	0	0	2	0	0	0	0	0	0	0	0	0	0	0	0	0
mille	2	.0000	.0162	22.1	0	2	0	0	0	0	0	0	0	0	0	0	0	0	2	0	0	0	0	0	0	0	0	0	0
milled	5	.4004	.4526	36.6	1	1	0	0	1	0	2	0	1	0	0	2	0	1	0	0	0	0	0	0	0	0	0	1	0
millennia	2	.0000	.0209	23.2	0	0	0	0	1	1	0	0	0	0	0	0	0	0	0	0	0	0	0	0	0	0	2	0	0
millennium	3	.3847	.2496	34.0	0	0	1	0	1	1	0	0	0	0	0	0	0	0	0	0	0	0	0	0	0	1	1	1	0
miller	15	.4778	1.6505	42.2	3	6	3	2	0	1	0	0	9	0	0	0	0	0	0	0	3	1	0	0	1	1	0	0	0
Miller	60	.6214	7.9416	49.0	4	23	8	7	12	0	4	2	27	2	0	10	0	2	0	0	0	0	0	0	7	0	3	9	0
miller's	7	.2445	.5495	37.4	5	1	1	0	0	0	0	0	6	0	0	0	0	0	0	0	1	0	0	0	0	0	0	0	0
Miller's	9	.4243	.8931	39.5	1	3	1	2	0	3	0	0	4	0	0	0	0	1	0	0	0	0	0	0	3	0	1	0	0
Millerbird	3	.0000	.0365	25.6	0	0	0	0	3	0	0	0	0	0	0	0	0	0	0	0	0	0	0	0	0	0	0	3	0
millers	3	.1823	.1405	31.5	0	0	2	0	1	0	0	0	0	0	0	0	0	1	0	0	0	0	0	0	0	0	2	0	0
Millers	3	.2266	.1614	32.1	0	1	0	2	0	0	0	0	0	0	0	0	0	0	0	0	0	0	0	0	1	0	0	2	0
millet	14	.3920	1.2327	40.9	0	1	4	4	4	0	1	0	1	0	0	4	0	7	0	0	0	0	0	0	0	2	0	0	0
Millet	3	.0994	.0714	28.5	0	0	1	0	0	1	1	0	0	0	0	0	0	0	0	0	0	2	0	0	0	0	1	0	0
millibars	2	.0000	.0394	26.0	0	0	0	0	0	2	0	0	0	0	0	0	0	0	0	2	0	0	0	0	0	0	0	0	0
Millie	2	.1733	.1149	30.6	0	1	0	1	0	0	0	0	1	1	0	0	0	0	0	0	0	0	0	0	0	0	0	0	0
Milligan	13	.0000	.5939	37.7	0	0	13	0	0	0	0	0	13	0	0	0	0	0	0	0	0	0	0	0	0	0	0	0	0
milligrams	8	.0000	.0837	29.2	0	0	4	4	0	0	0	0	0	0	0	0	0	0	0	0	0	0	0	0	0	0	8	0	0
Millikan	5	.1882	.2328	33.7	0	0	0	4	0	1	0	0	0	0	0	0	0	0	0	0	0	0	0	0	0	0	1	4	0
millimeter	7	.3375	.5381	37.3	0	0	0	0	4	1	1	1	0	0	0	0	4	0	0	2	0	0	0	0	0	0	0	1	0
millimeters	15	.4521	1.4444	41.6	0	0	1	5	6	0	2	1	0	1	0	0	10	0	0	1	0	0	0	1	0	0	2	0	0
millimicrons	3	.0000	.0591	27.7	0	0	0	0	0	0	0	3	0	0	0	0	0	0	0	3	0	0	0	0	0	0	0	0	0
milliner	2	.2444	.1132	30.5	0	1	1	0	0	0	0	0	0	1	0	0	0	0	0	0	0	0	0	0	1	0	0	0	0
millinery	2	.1839	.0845	29.3	0	0	1	0	0	0	1	0	0	0	0	0	0	0	0	0	0	0	1	0	1	0	0	0	0
milling	24	.3583	1.9108	42.8	2	1	3	3	3	2	10	0	4	0	0	0	0	3	0	0	0	0	2	9	0	2	2	2	0
million	662	.7552	101.08	60.0	62	70	123	73	145	78	86	25	51	11	0	10	64	156	3	72	2	1	0	3	3	87	83	116	0
million-dollar	3	.3815	.2534	34.0	0	0	1	0	0	0	2	0	0	0	0	0	0	1	0	0	0	0	0	0	0	1	0	1	0
millionaire	10	.5932	1.2597	41.0	0	2	1	1	3	1	1	1	3	1	0	0	0	1	0	0	1	0	0	0	0	3	0	1	0
millionaires	3	.3350	.2478	33.9	0	0	0	0	0	2	1	0	1	0	0	0	0	1	0	0	0	0	0	0	0	0	1	0	0
millions	416	.8035	67.156	58.3	68	44	70	61	85	38	37	13	32	11	0	9	16	74	6	116	6	2	0	4	5	54	40	39	2
millionth	3	.0000	.0591	27.7	0	0	0	0	3	0	0	0	0	0	0	0	0	0	0	3	0	0	0	0	0	0	0	0	0
millionths	4	.2672	.2733	34.4	1	0	0	0	0	0	2	1	1	0	0	0	0	0	0	1	0	0	0	0	0	0	2	0	0
millpond	8	.4090	.7291	38.6	1	1	0	3	0	1	2	0	2	1	0	1	0	1	1	0	0	0	0	2	0	0	0	0	0
mills	175	.4805	18.372	52.6	24	19	50	26	35	14	7	0	18	0	0	7	0	124	0	4	1	0	0	9	0	1	7	4	0
Mills	14	.5186	1.6130	42.1	1	3	1	5	3	0	1	0	6	0	0	1	0	0	0	1	0	0	0	0	0	4	0	2	0
millstones	3	.2357	.2199	33.4	1	1	0	0	1	0	0	0	2	0	0	0	0	0	0	0	0	0	0	0	0	1	0	0	0
Millway	2	.0000	.0914	29.6	0	2	0	0	0	0	0	0	2	0	0	0	0	0	0	0	0	0	0	0	0	0	0	0	0
Milly	9	.0000	.4111	36.1	0	3	0	0	6	0	0	0	9	0	0	0	0	0	0	0	0	0	0	0	0	0	0	0	0
Milly's	2	.0000	.0914	29.6	0	0	0	0	2	0	0	0	2	0	0	0	0	0	0	0	0	0	0	0	0	0	0	0	0
Milne	2	.2130	.1056	30.2	1	0	0	1	0	0	0	0	0	0	0	0	0	0	1	1	0	0	0	0	0	0	0	0	0
Milo	13	.1573	.8803	39.4	0	0	9	1	2	1	0	0	12	0	0	0	0	1	0	0	0	0	0	0	0	0	0	0	0
Milo's	3	.0000	.1370	31.4	0	0	3	0	0	0	0	0	3	0	0	0	0	0	0	0	0	0	0	0	0	0	0	0	0
Milrow	4	.0000	.0486	26.9	0	0	0	0	0	4	0	0	0	0	0	0	0	0	0	0	0	0	0	0	0	0	0	4	0
milt	2	.0000	.0394	26.0	0	0	2	0	0	0	0	0	0	0	0	0	0	0	0	2	0	0	0	0	0	0	0	0	0
Milt	16	.4509	1.7295	42.4	0	9	3	2	2	0	0	0	11	0	0	2	0	1	0	0	0	0	0	0	0	0	0	2	0
Milton	25	.5530	2.8738	44.6	1	8	0	2	1	10	2	1	1	0	0	0	0	0	0	1	2	0	0	0	8	9	2	2	0
Milton's	5	.3681	.3974	36.0	0	0	0	0	1	2	2	0	0	0	0	0	0	0	0	0	0	0	0	0	2	0	2	1	0
Milwaukee	20	.5860	2.4238	43.8	2	6	1	2	5	4	0	0	1	0	0	1	4	1	0	0	0	0	0	0	2	1	2	8	0
mimeograph	3	.3346	.2478	33.9	0	0	1	0	2	0	0	0	1	0	0	0	0	0	0	1	0	0	0	0	0	0	1	0	0
mimeographed	3	.2187	.1555	31.9	0	0	0	0	0	2	1	0	0	2	0	0	0	0	0	0	0	0	0	0	0	0	0	1	0
Mimi	5	.0000	.0608	27.8	1	0	0	4	0	0	0	0	0	0	0	0	0	0	0	0	0	0	0	0	0	0	0	5	0
mimic	5	.5615	.5763	37.6	0	1	1	0	1	2	0	0	0	1	0	0	0	0	0	0	1	0	0	0	0	1	1	1	0
mimicked	6	.5562	.7174	38.6	1	1	1	0	2	0	1	0	2	0	0	1	0	0	0	0	0	0	0	0	1	1	1	0	0
mimicry	4	.2278	.2257	33.5	0	0	0	2	2	0	0	0	0	0	0	0	0	0	0	2	0	0	0	0	0	0	2	0	0
mimics	4	.3648	.3138	35.0	0	0	0	0	2	1	1	0	0	1	0	1	0	0	0	0	0	0	0	0	0	0	2	0	0
mimosa	2	.2331	.1157	30.6	0	1	0	0	1	0	0	0	0	0	0	0	0	0	0	1	0	0	0	0	1	0	0	0	0
mimsy	2	.1458	.0682	28.3	0	0	1	1	0	0	0	0	0	1	0	0	0	0	0	0	0	1	0	0	0	0	0	0	0
min	19	.3709	1.5525	41.9	2	2	8	0	0	1	6	0	0	0	0	0	13	0	1	2	3	0	0	0	0	0	0	0	0
Mina	4	.2424	.3036	34.8	0	0	0	0	4	0	0	0	3	0	0	0	0	0	0	0	0	0	0	0	0	0	0	1	0
Minakami	2	.0000	.0209	23.2	0	0	0	0	0	0	2	0	0	0	0	0	0	0	0	0	0	0	0	0	0	0	2	0	0
minaret	2	.0000	.0389	25.9	0	2	0	0	0	0	0	0	0	0	0	0	0	2	0	0	0	0	0	0	0	0	0	0	0
minarets	2	.1042	.0600	27.8	0	1	0	0	0	1	0	0	0	0	0	0	0	1	0	0	0	1	0	0	0	0	0	0	0
mince	8	.2445	.6134	37.9	1	6	1	0	0	0	0	0	6	0	0	0	0	0	0	0	0	0	0	0	0	2	0	0	0
minced	4	.1799	.1929	32.9	0	0	0	0	2	1	1	0	1	0	0	1	0	0	0	0	0	0	2	0	0	0	0	0	0

7R Milford
8J Milhaud
8R milieu
7R milieus
9R militancy
8R militants'
7G militare
8R military-industrial
7R military-rocket
8F militiamen
9L Milium
9L milk-and-egg
7P milk-and-honey
7C milk-jug
7N milk-shake
6F milkers
7N milkgourd
3F milkhouse
4A milking-stool
8A milkman's
7D milkmen
3A milkshake
6D milkwhite
7A milky-white
XR mill's
9Q Mill's
5Q Millais'
7D Millay's
9B Millbrook
7D milldam
6E milleniums
8F Millers'
8A Millford
6E milli-
6E milligram
XH millimicron
5P Millin
8J millin'
5P Millin's
7D milliner's
4D million-dot
7H million-megaton
8A million-miler
5A million-to-one
9P Millions
7P milliped
3H millipede
8H millipedes
7R milliseconds
7P millman
9F millowner
6N millrace
3N millstone
7R Millward
5A millwheel
8R Milne's
8M milo
8Q Milosavljevic
7Q Milutin
7R Mime
6R Mimi's
7H mimicking
7N mimosas
7F Min
9P Minahan
8D Minas

Word Type	F	D	U	SFI	3 Gr 3	4 Gr 4	5 Gr 5	6 Gr 6	7 Gr 7	8 Gr 8	9 Gr 9	X UnGr	A Read	B Eng & Gr	C Comp	D Lit	E Math	F Soc Stud	G Spell	H Sci	J Music	K Art	L Home Ec	M Shop	N Lib F	P Lib NF	Q Lib Ref	R Mag	S Rel
mind	1046	.8886	185.36	62.7	99	178	128	153	204	135	130	19	355	74	20	151	8	34	10	36	33	6	12	4	117	84	32	70	0
Mind	17	.1097	.5013	37.0	0	1	1	0	6	9	0	0	0	0	0	0	0	1	15	0	0	0	0	0	0	0	1	0	0
mind's	20	.6475	2.7093	44.3	3	3	5	2	3	3	1	0	7	4	0	2	0	0	0	0	0	0	0	1	2	3	0	1	0
Mindanao	8	.0908	.2270	33.6	6	0	0	1	0	1	0	0	0	0	0	0	0	1	0	0	0	0	0	0	0	0	7	0	0
minded	14	.5546	1.7177	42.3	1	1	1	3	7	0	1	0	8	0	0	2	0	0	0	0	1	0	0	0	2	0	0	1	0
minding	4	.3713	.3634	35.6	0	1	0	2	1	0	0	0	2	0	0	1	0	0	0	0	0	0	0	0	1	0	0	0	0
mindless	3	.2266	.1614	32.1	0	0	0	0	2	0	1	0	0	0	0	0	0	0	0	0	0	0	0	0	1	0	0	2	0
Mindoro	2	.0000	.0209	23.2	2	0	0	0	0	0	0	0	0	0	0	0	0	0	0	0	0	0	0	0	0	0	2	0	0
minds	110	.7179	16.153	52.1	4	9	15	18	30	14	17	3	25	2	1	15	0	12	0	8	3	0	1	0	7	8	13	14	1
Mindszenty	2	.0000	.0243	23.9	0	0	0	0	0	2	0	0	0	0	0	0	0	0	0	0	0	0	0	0	0	0	0	2	0
mine	378	.8204	62.708	58.0	73	69	51	36	66	32	45	6	152	21	2	52	2	41	12	9	21	0	0	0	17	24	5	20	0
Mine	6	.4741	.6397	38.1	0	0	3	0	0	0	0	3	2	0	0	0	0	0	0	2	0	0	0	0	0	0	1	1	0
MINE	2	.0000	.0914	29.6	2	0	0	0	0	0	0	0	2	0	0	0	0	0	0	0	0	0	0	0	0	0	0	0	0
mine's	2	.1733	.1149	30.6	0	0	1	0	0	1	0	0	1	1	0	0	0	0	0	0	0	0	0	0	0	0	0	0	0
mined	58	.5331	6.6150	48.2	5	7	17	4	16	7	2	0	7	1	0	0	0	30	0	6	0	0	0	4	0	2	8	0	0
Minelli	6	.0000	.2741	34.4	6	0	0	0	0	0	0	0	6	0	0	0	0	0	0	0	0	0	0	0	0	0	0	0	0
miner	22	.6123	2.8640	44.6	3	1	4	2	7	4	1	0	7	2	0	0	0	9	1	0	1	0	0	0	0	1	0	1	0
Miner	4	.0904	.1412	31.5	0	1	3	0	0	0	0	0	1	0	0	0	0	0	0	0	0	0	0	0	0	0	3	0	0
miner's	8	.3870	.7788	38.9	2	0	2	0	3	1	0	0	5	0	0	1	0	2	0	0	0	0	0	0	0	0	0	0	0
mineral	182	.6180	23.444	53.7	8	7	45	17	31	26	30	18	15	0	0	1	0	46	0	74	0	0	6	1	0	7	29	3	0
mineralogically	2	.2278	.1128	30.5	0	0	0	0	0	0	1	1	0	0	0	0	0	0	0	1	0	0	0	0	0	0	1	0	0
mineralogists	3	.1650	.1684	32.3	0	0	0	0	1	0	0	2	1	0	0	0	0	0	0	2	0	0	0	0	0	0	0	0	0
mineralogy	4	.0000	.0789	29.0	0	0	0	0	0	0	0	4	0	0	0	0	0	0	0	4	0	0	0	0	0	0	0	0	0
minerals	341	.5855	42.045	56.2	40	31	61	40	52	43	57	17	34	0	0	0	2	66	1	169	1	1	25	0	0	9	29	4	0
miners	46	.6671	6.3816	48.0	12	5	8	3	7	5	6	0	10	2	0	1	0	21	1	3	1	0	0	0	0	2	4	1	0
miners'	5	.4004	.4526	36.6	1	1	0	0	1	2	0	0	1	0	0	2	0	1	0	0	0	0	0	0	0	0	0	1	0
mines	170	.5514	20.298	53.1	23	37	30	30	31	8	7	4	42	1	0	0	0	92	1	7	4	0	0	0	1	10	8	4	0
Ming	5	.2011	.2522	34.0	0	0	5	0	0	0	0	0	0	0	0	0	0	0	0	0	0	0	0	0	0	4	1	0	0
mingle	6	.4359	.5521	37.4	1	0	0	0	2	0	3	0	0	0	0	1	0	0	0	1	2	0	0	0	0	0	2	0	0
mingled	20	.6466	2.6623	44.3	0	3	0	3	6	4	3	1	3	1	0	3	0	0	1	1	0	0	0	0	6	3	2	0	0
mingles	2	.2375	.1088	30.4	0	1	0	0	1	0	0	0	0	0	0	0	0	0	0	0	1	0	0	0	0	0	0	1	0
mingling	2	.2306	.1140	30.6	0	0	0	2	0	0	0	0	0	1	0	0	0	1	0	0	0	0	0	0	0	0	0	0	0
Mingo	3	.2304	.1619	32.1	0	0	0	0	2	1	0	0	0	0	0	0	0	0	0	0	0	0	0	0	2	0	1	0	0
Minh	4	.3829	.3404	35.3	0	0	0	0	2	1	1	0	0	0	0	0	0	2	0	0	0	0	0	0	0	1	1	0	0
miniature	38	.7469	5.7787	47.6	0	2	3	8	13	3	5	4	10	0	0	5	0	1	1	4	1	0	0	2	1	2	5	6	0
miniatures	5	.2132	.2403	33.8	0	0	0	0	1	4	0	0	0	0	0	0	0	0	0	0	0	2	0	0	0	1	2	0	0
miniaturist	2	.0000	.0209	23.2	0	0	0	0	0	2	0	0	0	0	0	0	0	0	0	0	0	0	0	0	0	0	2	0	0
minibike	2	.0000	.0243	23.9	0	0	0	0	2	0	0	0	0	0	0	0	0	0	0	0	0	0	0	0	0	0	0	2	0
minimal	8	.1444	.3087	34.9	0	0	0	0	1	1	0	6	0	0	0	0	0	0	0	0	0	0	0	0	0	0	1	7	0
minimize	5	.3184	.3581	35.5	0	0	2	0	1	1	1	0	0	0	0	0	0	1	0	0	0	0	0	0	0	0	1	3	0
minimized	3	.3824	.2446	33.9	0	0	0	0	1	1	1	0	0	0	0	1	0	0	0	0	1	0	0	0	0	0	0	1	0
minimum	59	.6428	7.6901	48.9	0	2	3	2	22	13	11	6	0	0	1	0	10	4	0	4	1	0	11	2	0	3	10	13	0
minimum-care	3	.0000	.0097	19.8	0	0	0	0	0	3	0	0	0	0	0	0	0	0	0	0	0	0	3	0	0	0	0	0	0
minimum-energy	3	.0000	.0591	27.7	0	0	0	0	0	0	3	0	0	0	0	0	0	0	0	3	0	0	0	0	0	0	0	0	0
mining	125	.5415	14.433	51.6	9	11	31	22	30	8	14	0	13	0	1	2	0	69	0	5	0	0	0	0	0	9	22	4	0
Mining	3	.0000	.0449	26.5	0	0	0	0	0	0	3	0	0	0	0	0	3	0	0	0	0	0	0	0	0	0	0	0	0
minister	95	.6569	12.932	51.1	4	14	28	5	20	15	8	1	21	2	0	0	0	13	1	3	3	0	0	0	2	16	26	8	0
Minister	42	.5453	4.8585	46.9	0	2	10	1	5	12	10	2	6	1	0	0	0	9	0	0	0	0	0	0	0	8	5	13	0
minister's	9	.4507	.9147	39.6	0	4	2	1	2	1	0	0	3	0	0	2	0	0	0	0	0	0	0	0	0	3	0	1	0
ministers	24	.4720	2.4136	43.8	1	1	4	1	5	7	5	0	1	0	0	0	0	4	0	0	0	0	0	0	0	6	8	5	0
Ministers	13	.3851	1.1074	40.4	0	0	3	1	9	0	0	0	0	0	0	0	0	5	0	0	0	0	0	0	0	5	3	0	0
ministries	3	.3847	.2496	34.0	0	0	1	0	0	1	1	0	0	0	0	0	0	0	0	0	0	0	0	0	0	1	1	1	0
ministry	5	.3022	.3399	35.3	0	0	2	0	1	1	1	0	0	0	0	1	0	1	0	0	0	0	0	0	0	0	3	0	0
Ministry	8	.5024	.8358	39.2	0	0	1	1	3	1	1	1	0	0	0	1	0	0	0	0	1	0	0	0	0	1	1	4	0
mink	15	.6218	1.9964	43.0	0	2	7	1	4	0	1	0	7	1	0	1	0	2	0	0	0	0	0	0	2	2	0	0	0
Mink	18	.0000	.2606	34.2	18	0	0	0	0	0	0	0	0	0	0	0	0	0	0	0	0	0	0	0	0	18	0	0	0
Minkowski's	2	.0000	.0299	24.8	0	0	0	0	0	2	0	0	0	0	0	0	2	0	0	0	0	0	0	0	0	0	0	0	0
minks	7	.4474	.7002	38.5	0	1	2	0	0	1	1	2	2	0	0	2	0	0	0	0	0	0	0	0	1	2	0	0	0
Minks	4	.0000	.0579	27.6	4	0	0	0	0	0	0	0	0	0	0	0	0	0	0	0	0	0	0	0	0	4	0	0	0
Minn	3	.2321	.1635	32.1	0	0	0	0	1	0	0	2	0	0	0	0	0	0	0	0	0	0	0	0	0	0	1	2	0
Minneapolis	8	.4825	.8227	39.2	0	2	0	0	3	2	1	0	1	0	0	1	0	0	0	0	0	0	0	0	1	0	3	2	0
Minnesota	46	.6489	6.1962	47.9	3	6	8	6	7	5	6	5	9	3	0	0	0	8	0	4	1	0	0	0	0	3	5	13	0
Minnie	20	.5341	2.3810	43.8	9	4	0	3	1	2	1	0	11	4	0	1	0	0	0	0	0	0	0	0	2	0	0	2	0
minnow	7	.3808	.6813	38.3	5	1	0	0	1	0	0	0	5	1	0	0	1	0	0	0	0	0	0	0	0	0	0	0	0
Minnow	31	.0000	1.4162	41.5	30	0	0	0	0	1	0	0	31	0	0	0	0	0	0	0	0	0	0	0	0	0	0	0	0
Minnow's	3	.0000	.1370	31.4	3	0	0	0	0	0	0	0	3	0	0	0	0	0	0	0	0	0	0	0	0	0	0	0	0
minnows	6	.6013	.7500	38.8	3	3	0	0	0	0	0	0	1	0	0	1	0	0	0	0	1	0	0	0	1	1	0	1	0
Minny	3	.0000	.1370	31.4	3	0	0	0	0	0	0	0	3	0	0	0	0	0	0	0	0	0	0	0	0	0	0	0	0
minor	223	.3963	18.693	52.7	1	20	35	54	42	38	27	6	5	2	2	4	1	3	1	6	162	0	3	2	0	5	14	13	0
Minor	26	.5594	3.0212	44.8	1	2	2	3	9	4	5	0	1	0	0	0	0	9	0	0	8	1	0	0	0	2	4	1	0
minorities	6	.3567	.4852	36.9	0	0	0	0	4	2	0	0	0	0	0	0	0	4	0	0	0	0	0	0	0	0	1	1	0
minority	27	.4864	2.7957	44.5	0	0	1	2	7	12	4	1	2	1	4	0	0	10	0	0	0	0	0	0	1	0	5	4	0
minors	3	.2143	.1568	32.0	0	0	0	1	2	0	0	0	0	0	0	0	0	0	0	0	0	0	0	0	0	1	0	2	0
Minsk	2	.0000	.0389	25.9	0	2	0	0	0	0	0	0	0	0	0	0	0	2	0	0	0	0	0	0	0	0	0	0	0
minstrel	25	.3092	1.8292	42.6	0	1	4	13	4	1	1	1	6	2	0	1	0	0	0	0	14	0	0	0	0	2	0	0	0
Minstrel	3	.0000	.0243	23.8	0	0	0	3	0	0	0	0	0	0	0	0	0	0	0	0	3	0	0	0	0	0	0	0	0
minstrels	11	.4296	1.0194	40.1	0	1	4	2	3	1	0	0	1	3	0	0	0	1	0	0	4	0	0	0	0	2	0	0	0
Minstrels	3	.1852	.1342	31.3	0	0	1	1	1	0	0	0	0	0	0	0	0	0	0	0	2	0	0	0	0	1	0	0	0
mint	23	.5769	2.8258	44.5	5	3	1	2	9	0	3	0	7	2	0	0	0	4	0	0	0	0	3	0	0	3	3	1	0
Mint	6	.2435	.4680	36.7	0	0	0	0	3	3	0	0	5	0	0	1	0	0	0	0	0	0	0	0	0	0	0	0	0
minted	4	.4504	.4035	36.1	1	0	0	1	1	0	1	0	1	0	0	0	0	1	0	0	0	0	0	0	0	1	1	0	0
minting	2	.0000	.0914	29.6	0	0	1	1	0	0	0	0	2	0	0	0	0	0	0	0	0	0	0	0	0	0	0	0	0
mints	3	.2228	.1655	32.2	2	0	0	1	0	0	0	0	0	0	0	0	1	0	0	0	0	0	0	0	0	2	0	0	0
Mintzer	7	.0000	.3198	35.0	0	0	0	0	0	7	0	0	7	0	0	0	0	0	0	0	0	0	0	0	0	0	0	0	0
minuend	3	.0000	.0449	26.5	1	0	0	0	2	0	0	0	0	0	0	0	3	0	0	0	0	0	0	0	0	0	0	0	0
minuet	26	.0844	.6321	38.0	5	3	10	3	2	3	0	0	0	0	0	1	0	0	0	0	24	0	0	0	0	1	0	0	0
Minuet	6	.0000	.0485	26.9	0	3	3	0	0	0	0	0	0	0	0	0	0	0	0	0	6	0	0	0	0	0	0	0	0
minuets	4	.2578	.2593	34.1	0	0	2	1	1	0	0	0	1	0	0	0	0	0	0	0	2	0	0	0	0	1	0	0	0
minus	53	.5875	6.5040	48.1	6	6	12	9	5	6	8	1	6	0	0	0	31	1	0	3	0	0	2	1	3	1	1	4	0
Minus	9	.0987	.2636	34.2	0	0	1	0	0	0	8	0	0	0	0	0	1	0	0	0	0	0	0	0	0	0	8	0	0
minuscule	4	.4458	.3985	36.0	0	0	0	0	3	0	1	0	1	1	0	0	0	0	0	1	0	0	0	0	0	0	1	0	0
minute	663	.8761	116.22	60.7	123	157	88	60	102	70	49	14	242	18	0	43	69	13	11	80	2	0	12	8	57	53	22	33	0
minute's	2	.2443	.1130	30.5	0	0	0	0	1	0	1	0	0	0	0	1	0	0	0	0	0	0	0	0	1	0	0	0	0
minutemen	3	.0000	.0434	26.4	3	0	0	0	0	0	0	0	0	0	0	0	0	0	0	0	0	0	0	0	0	3	0	0	0

4A mincemeat
9D mincing
5P mind-picture
7H mind-pictures
7R mind-set
7N mindin'
8A mindlessness
9R minefield
4A Miner's
7P Mineral
5P mineral-bearing
5Q mineral-processing
7F mineral-rich
XH mineralogical
XR mineralogist
7H Minerology
7R minesweeper
7Q mingaco
7D Mingoes
7N Mingos
XR Mini-Cooper
XR mini-golf
4R mini-kite
5R mini-loaves
3R mini-parks
XR mini-sanctuary
6R mini-skirt
9R mini-skirts
7A mini-world
XR Miniatures
5A Miniken
9D minim
XR Minimals
9C Minimum
6A minions
9R minirecession
6A miniscule
8R miniskirted
8R miniskirts
4N Minister's
6R Minkegizis
7H Minkowski
5Q Minnehaha
6R Minnesotan
9D minor-league
7J minor-modal
8G Minorca
8F Minoru
9K Minos
9K Minos'
9K Minotaur
7N Minquon
6J minstrel-show
7F mint's
3J Mintie
XR Minto
6N mintral
3P Minty
8A Mintz
8E minuends
8F Minuit
5J Minute
6R minute-by-minute

Word Type	F	D	U	SFI	3 Gr 3	4 Gr 4	5 Gr 5	6 Gr 6	7 Gr 7	8 Gr 8	9 Gr 9	X UnGr	A Read	B Eng & Gr	C Comp	D Lit	E Math	F Soc Stud	G Spell	H Sci	J Music	K Art	L Home Ec	M Shop	N Lib F	P Lib NF	Q Lib Ref	R Mag	S Rel
Minutemen	10	.0000	.4568	36.6	0	1	5	0	4	0	0	0	10	0	0	0	0	0	0	0	0	0	0	0	0	0	0	0	0
minutes	819	.8168	134.84	61.3	119	157	79	91	153	98	94	28	240	25	6	49	121	32	1	76	2	0	61	6	57	66	14	63	0
minutes'	5	.4419	.4853	36.9	0	0	1	1	3	0	0	0	1	0	0	1	0	0	0	1	0	0	1	0	0	0	0	1	0
Mioshi	10	.0000	.4568	36.6	10	0	0	0	0	0	0	0	10	0	0	0	0	0	0	0	0	0	0	0	0	0	0	0	0
miracle	55	.7737	8.6630	49.4	0	6	10	6	15	7	4	7	20	6	0	3	0	1	0	3	3	2	0	0	3	4	3	7	0
Miracle	4	.3374	.3006	34.8	0	0	0	1	0	0	3	0	0	0	0	2	0	0	0	1	0	0	0	0	0	0	0	1	0
miracles	13	.5942	1.6233	42.1	0	0	4	2	3	2	1	1	3	1	0	1	0	0	0	0	0	0	0	0	0	3	2	3	0
Miracles	3	.2304	.1619	32.1	0	0	0	2	0	1	0	0	0	0	0	0	0	0	0	0	0	0	0	0	2	0	1	0	0
miraculous	12	.6674	1.6646	42.2	0	1	3	3	4	0	1	0	4	2	0	1	0	0	0	0	1	0	0	0	0	1	1	2	0
miraculously	11	.5802	1.3455	41.3	0	0	1	2	4	2	2	0	3	0	0	1	0	0	0	0	2	1	0	0	0	2	1	1	0
mirage	5	.4506	.5021	37.0	0	0	1	0	1	0	2	1	1	0	0	1	0	0	0	2	0	0	0	0	0	0	0	1	0
mirages	2	.1814	.1187	30.7	0	0	0	0	2	0	0	0	1	0	0	0	0	0	0	0	0	0	0	0	0	0	0	1	0
Miranda	29	.3702	2.7041	44.3	4	0	8	4	12	0	1	0	16	0	0	0	0	5	0	0	0	0	0	0	0	8	0	0	0
Miranda's	3	.0000	.0434	26.4	0	0	3	0	0	0	0	0	0	0	0	0	0	0	0	0	0	0	0	0	0	3	0	0	0
mire	5	.4701	.4988	37.0	1	1	0	0	1	1	1	0	0	0	0	1	0	1	0	0	0	0	0	0	0	2	1	0	0
mired	5	.3468	.4167	36.2	0	0	2	0	2	0	1	0	2	0	1	0	0	0	0	0	0	0	0	0	0	0	1	1	0
Miriam	3	.2300	.1627	32.1	0	0	0	0	0	1	0	2	0	1	0	0	0	0	0	0	0	0	0	0	0	0	0	2	0
Miroirs	2	.0000	.0290	24.6	0	0	0	1	1	0	0	0	0	0	0	0	0	0	0	0	0	0	0	0	0	2	0	0	0
mirror	209	.7648	32.513	55.1	29	36	13	53	25	6	16	31	47	1	0	13	5	9	1	80	2	7	2	0	14	13	8	7	0
Mirror	4	.0000	.0486	26.9	0	0	0	0	0	0	0	4	0	0	0	0	0	0	0	0	0	0	0	0	0	0	0	4	0
mirror's	3	.3553	.2609	34.2	1	0	0	2	0	0	0	0	1	0	0	0	0	0	0	1	0	0	0	0	0	1	0	0	0
mirrored	4	.3499	.2985	34.7	0	1	0	0	1	0	1	1	0	0	0	0	0	0	0	0	0	1	0	0	1	0	1	1	0
mirrors	61	.7893	9.7642	49.9	8	7	6	21	8	3	2	6	17	1	0	1	0	8	0	15	2	0	2	1	2	0	5	7	0
Mirrors	2	.1948	.1250	31.0	0	0	0	1	0	1	0	0	1	0	0	0	0	0	0	0	0	0	0	0	0	1	0	0	0
mirth	10	.2992	.7159	38.5	1	1	0	2	1	0	4	1	2	0	0	6	0	0	0	0	0	0	0	0	0	1	0	1	0
mirthless	2	.0000	.0234	23.7	0	0	0	1	1	0	0	0	0	0	0	0	0	0	0	0	0	0	0	0	2	0	0	0	0
mis	3	.0997	.1145	30.6	0	0	0	1	2	0	0	0	1	0	0	0	0	0	2	0	0	0	0	0	0	0	0	0	0
Mis'	3	.0000	.0352	25.5	0	0	1	0	0	2	0	0	0	0	0	0	0	0	0	0	0	0	0	0	3	0	0	0	0
misadventure	2	.1717	.1142	30.6	0	0	0	0	0	1	1	0	1	0	0	1	0	0	0	0	0	0	0	0	0	0	0	0	0
misbehaves	2	.0857	.0784	28.9	0	0	0	1	0	0	1	0	1	0	0	0	0	0	0	0	0	0	1	0	0	0	0	0	0
misbehavior	3	.1386	.0963	29.8	0	0	1	0	0	0	2	0	0	0	0	0	0	0	0	0	0	0	2	0	0	0	1	0	0
miscalculated	2	.1948	.1250	31.0	0	0	0	0	1	0	1	0	1	0	0	0	0	0	0	0	0	0	0	0	0	1	0	0	0
miscalculation	2	.1814	.1187	30.7	0	0	1	0	1	0	0	0	1	0	0	0	0	0	0	0	0	0	0	0	0	0	0	1	0
miscellaneous	3	.3877	.2482	33.9	0	0	0	0	0	2	1	0	0	1	0	1	0	0	0	0	0	0	0	0	0	0	1	0	0
mischief	29	.6663	4.1024	46.1	6	4	4	6	4	3	2	0	17	0	0	2	0	1	0	0	0	0	1	0	4	1	2	1	0
mischievous	12	.6417	1.6120	42.1	0	3	1	2	6	0	0	0	4	1	0	0	0	1	1	0	2	0	0	0	2	1	0	0	0
mischievously	3	.3399	.2456	33.9	1	1	0	0	1	0	0	0	1	0	0	1	0	0	0	0	0	0	0	0	0	0	0	1	0
misconception	3	.2159	.1532	31.9	0	0	0	0	0	0	2	1	0	0	0	0	0	0	0	0	0	0	0	0	0	0	2	1	0
misconceptions	2	.2437	.1129	30.5	0	0	0	0	1	0	1	0	0	0	0	0	0	0	0	0	0	0	0	0	0	0	1	1	0
misconduct	4	.3071	.2675	34.3	0	0	3	1	0	0	0	0	0	0	1	0	0	0	0	0	0	0	0	0	0	1	2	0	0
misdemeanor	2	.2351	.1166	30.7	0	0	0	0	1	1	0	0	0	0	0	0	0	1	0	0	0	0	0	0	0	0	0	1	0
misdemeanors	3	.2444	.1814	32.6	0	0	1	0	0	0	2	0	0	0	0	0	0	2	0	0	0	0	0	0	0	0	1	0	0
miser	3	.2012	.1409	31.5	0	0	0	0	1	2	0	0	0	0	0	0	0	0	2	0	0	0	0	0	1	0	0	0	0
miserable	53	.6323	7.1355	48.5	2	6	6	12	13	6	7	1	25	0	1	7	0	1	0	1	0	0	0	0	8	9	0	1	0
miserably	15	.3620	1.3079	41.2	0	1	4	3	2	4	1	0	6	0	0	1	0	0	0	0	0	0	0	0	7	0	1	0	0
miseries	4	.4870	.4078	36.1	0	0	1	1	0	1	1	0	0	0	0	0	0	0	0	0	0	0	0	0	1	1	1	1	0
miserly	6	.5437	.7053	38.5	2	0	0	0	0	1	1	2	2	1	0	1	0	0	1	1	0	0	0	0	0	0	0	0	0
misery	30	.7590	4.6339	46.7	2	0	3	6	6	8	5	0	8	1	0	3	0	5	1	1	1	0	0	0	5	2	3	0	0
Misery	2	.1698	.1133	30.5	0	0	0	0	2	0	0	0	1	0	0	0	0	0	0	0	0	0	0	0	0	0	1	0	0
misfortune	23	.6457	3.1228	44.9	3	0	2	6	6	1	5	0	9	1	0	5	0	1	0	0	0	0	0	0	2	1	3	1	0
misfortunes	4	.3755	.3686	35.7	0	0	2	2	0	0	0	0	2	0	0	0	0	0	0	0	0	0	0	0	1	1	0	0	0
misgivings	3	.3851	.2497	34.0	0	0	1	0	0	1	1	0	0	0	0	1	0	0	0	0	0	0	0	0	1	1	0	0	0
misguided	2	.0000	.0914	29.6	0	0	2	0	0	0	0	0	2	0	0	0	0	0	0	0	0	0	0	0	0	0	0	0	0
mishap	3	.2279	.2143	33.3	0	0	0	1	0	1	0	1	2	0	0	0	0	0	0	0	0	0	0	0	0	0	1	0	0
mishaps	3	.2784	.1822	32.6	0	0	1	0	1	0	1	0	0	0	1	1	0	0	0	0	0	0	0	0	0	0	0	1	0
misinterpret	3	.3780	.2511	34.0	0	0	0	0	1	2	0	0	0	1	0	0	1	1	0	0	0	0	0	0	0	0	0	0	0
misjudged	3	.2212	.2099	33.2	0	0	1	1	1	0	0	0	2	0	0	1	0	0	0	0	0	0	0	0	0	0	0	0	0
mislaid	2	.1717	.1142	30.6	0	1	0	0	0	1	0	0	1	0	0	1	0	0	0	0	0	0	0	0	0	0	0	0	0
mislead	3	.3776	.2489	34.0	0	0	0	0	1	1	0	1	0	0	0	1	0	1	0	0	0	0	0	0	0	0	0	1	0
misleading	13	.5634	1.5462	41.9	0	1	0	0	5	1	6	0	1	1	0	0	0	3	0	4	0	0	0	0	0	1	0	3	0
misled	4	.2971	.2896	34.6	0	0	0	1	0	0	3	0	1	2	0	0	0	0	0	0	0	0	0	0	0	0	0	1	0
mismanagement	2	.2376	.1088	30.4	0	0	0	0	1	1	0	0	0	0	0	0	0	0	1	0	0	0	0	0	0	0	0	1	0
misplaced	4	.2445	.3067	34.9	0	1	1	0	0	1	1	0	3	0	0	0	0	0	0	0	0	0	0	0	0	1	0	0	0
mispronounced	4	.3698	.3173	35.0	0	0	0	0	2	1	1	0	0	2	0	0	0	0	1	0	0	0	0	0	0	0	0	1	0
mispronunciations	2	.2418	.1091	30.4	0	0	1	0	0	1	0	0	0	0	0	0	0	0	1	0	0	0	0	0	0	0	1	0	0
misread	2	.1717	.1142	30.6	0	0	0	0	2	0	0	0	1	0	0	1	0	0	0	0	0	0	0	0	0	0	0	0	0
miss	191	.8493	32.494	55.1	36	50	22	18	25	18	15	7	52	14	0	12	3	14	26	11	7	3	1	0	10	25	2	11	0
Miss	1056	.7639	165.75	62.2	384	167	176	128	85	51	62	3	527	53	3	67	20	64	8	2	6	12	1	0	208	42	8	35	0
MISS	2	.0000	.0215	23.3	0	0	0	0	2	0	0	0	0	0	0	2	0	0	0	0	0	0	0	0	0	0	0	0	0
missed	257	.5816	31.482	55.0	81	52	37	37	31	9	10	0	69	13	3	9	3	3	100	2	2	0	0	0	22	17	1	13	0
misses	20	.6508	2.7568	44.4	7	3	2	2	6	0	0	0	9	0	0	1	0	0	0	4	0	0	1	0	1	3	1	0	0
Misses	4	.0000	.0469	26.7	0	0	0	4	0	0	0	0	0	0	0	0	0	0	0	0	0	0	0	0	4	0	0	0	0
misshapen	2	.0000	.0914	29.6	0	0	0	0	1	1	0	0	2	0	0	0	0	0	0	0	0	0	0	0	0	0	0	0	0
missile	43	.7602	6.6348	48.2	1	1	5	2	15	4	13	2	11	11	1	1	3	2	2	2	0	0	0	1	0	0	5	4	0
Missile	5	.3474	.3866	35.9	0	0	1	2	0	0	2	0	0	0	0	0	0	1	0	0	0	0	0	0	0	2	2	0	0
missiles	24	.6789	3.3489	45.2	3	4	2	2	7	1	5	0	5	1	0	0	2	1	0	2	0	1	0	1	0	0	5	6	0
missing	852	.5259	95.482	59.8	252	140	125	137	104	57	31	6	138	26	3	11	465	1	150	13	10	0	1	0	9	7	9	9	0
mission	165	.6680	22.757	53.6	6	69	15	21	23	17	10	4	23	1	0	8	0	73	1	2	1	0	1	1	1	13	7	33	0
Mission	21	.4154	1.9606	42.9	0	13	0	2	4	2	0	0	2	0	0	2	0	14	0	0	0	0	0	0	1	0	0	2	0
mission's	2	.0000	.0243	23.9	0	0	0	1	1	0	0	0	0	0	0	0	0	0	0	0	0	0	0	0	0	0	0	2	0
missionaries	48	.6080	6.0281	47.8	1	9	13	8	7	6	4	0	0	1	1	0	0	21	0	0	0	0	0	0	2	13	4	6	0
missionary	24	.7047	3.4399	45.4	1	6	1	3	5	5	3	0	3	1	0	1	0	3	3	0	1	0	0	0	0	3	5	4	0
Missionary	4	.2401	.2266	33.6	1	1	0	0	2	0	0	0	0	0	0	0	0	0	0	0	0	0	0	0	0	2	2	0	0
missions	57	.3542	4.6372	46.7	5	10	7	7	11	14	2	1	1	0	0	0	0	42	0	1	0	0	0	0	0	1	3	9	0
missis	2	.0000	.0914	29.6	0	0	0	0	2	0	0	0	2	0	0	0	0	0	0	0	0	0	0	0	0	0	0	0	0
Mississippi	242	.6438	32.652	55.1	26	37	60	28	38	33	16	4	57	3	0	1	2	114	4	9	5	0	0	0	1	15	21	10	0
Missouri	148	.6837	20.939	53.2	7	12	42	10	23	42	10	2	33	5	0	2	2	62	1	3	3	0	0	0	3	5	19	10	0
Missouri's	2	.2152	.1357	31.3	0	0	0	0	1	1	0	0	1	0	0	0	0	1	0	0	0	0	0	0	0	0	0	0	0
misspell	14	.3709	1.1106	40.5	2	1	0	3	4	2	2	0	0	2	0	0	2	0	8	0	0	0	0	0	0	1	0	1	0
misspelled	218	.1117	6.4711	48.1	24	36	32	33	80	8	5	0	1	9	0	0	4	0	197	0	0	0	0	0	0	4	0	3	0
misspelling	4	.2744	.2686	34.3	0	0	1	0	1	2	0	0	1	1	0	0	0	0	2	0	0	0	0	0	0	0	0	0	0

7A Minutes
5G minute1**
XR minutiae
5G minutus
7P Minwax
XR minx
7D minxes
6B miny
6A mio
7Q miocene
8H Miocene
3A Mioshi's
XR Miquelle
7Q Miquelon
XH Mira
XH Mirach
7A miracle-worker
5F Miraflores
6H MIRROR
8B mirry
8B Mirzah
9Q misanthrope
4Q Misanthrope
9B misapplied
7N misbecoming
9R Misbegotten
5A misbehaved
7P miscall
5P miscegenation
7A mischief-makers
5Q mischiefmaker
7D misconstrue
XR misconstrued
7N miscreant
7B miscues
8L misdeed
7F misdeeds
6A Misenum
5Q Miserables
9R misfire
9N misfits
7A Misfortune
7D misgave
9D misgives
7L mishandling
6R Mishe-Nahma
4F Mishima
5P misinformed
9B misinterpretation
9R misinterpretations
7B misinterpreted
8F misjudging
3A mislay
9B mislaying
9D mislike
7R mismatches
6P mispelled
7B mispronounce
7B mispronouncing
XB mispronunciation
7R misquotation
7R misquoted
XB misreading
7Q misrepresent
9D misrepresentation
9R misrepresented
7A misrepresents
7R misshapened
7A missile's
6N missin'
3D mission-house
4F Missionaries
9F Mississippi's
4N missive
7A Missoula
9B missouri
6R Missouri-Kansas-Texas
9B Missourian
9B Misspelled

Word Type	F	D	U	SFI	3 Gr 3	4 Gr 4	5 Gr 5	6 Gr 6	7 Gr 7	8 Gr 8	9 Gr 9	X UnGr	A Read	B Eng & Gr	C Comp	D Lit	E Math	F Soc Stud	G Spell	H Sci	J Music	K Art	L Home Ec	M Shop	N Lib F	P Lib NF	Q Lib Ref	R Mag	S Rel
misspellings	3	.0000	.0243	23.9	0	0	0	0	3	0	0	0	0	0	0	0	0	0	3	0	0	0	0	0	0	0	0	0	0
misspells	2	.2408	.1091	30.4	0	1	0	0	0	0	1	0	0	1	0	0	0	0	1	0	0	0	0	0	0	0	0	0	0
missus	7	.2586	.4493	36.5	4	0	0	2	1	0	0	0	1	0	0	0	0	0	1	0	0	0	0	0	0	5	0	0	0
Missus	6	.2464	.3696	35.7	4	0	0	0	2	0	0	0	1	0	0	1	0	0	0	0	0	0	0	0	0	0	0	4	0
Missy	22	.2012	1.2706	41.0	15	0	0	0	7	0	0	0	7	0	0	0	0	0	0	0	0	0	0	0	1	0	0	14	0
mist	57	.7818	9.0400	49.6	5	3	12	9	16	6	3	3	18	0	1	10	0	1	0	4	1	0	0	1	8	5	4	4	0
mistake	160	.8911	28.426	54.5	31	28	18	19	36	15	12	1	55	12	3	13	8	6	14	6	7	0	0	2	11	8	4	11	0
mistaken	42	.8825	7.3964	48.7	7	5	2	1	6	14	6	1	14	2	1	4	0	2	1	1	1	0	1	1	2	4	5	3	0
mistakenly	7	.4893	.7194	38.6	0	0	0	0	2	3	1	1	0	1	1	0	0	0	0	3	1	0	0	0	0	0	1	0	0
mistakes	164	.5333	18.243	52.6	45	21	26	34	20	11	6	1	13	78	0	2	12	2	37	5	0	1	0	0	3	3	1	7	0
mistaking	2	.2441	.1127	30.5	0	0	0	0	1	0	1	0	0	0	0	0	0	0	0	0	0	0	0	0	1	0	1	0	0
misted	2	.1948	.1250	31.0	1	1	0	0	0	0	0	0	1	0	0	0	0	0	0	0	0	0	0	0	0	1	0	0	0
mister	17	.4179	1.6038	42.1	2	2	1	1	7	1	3	0	5	0	0	8	0	0	2	0	0	0	0	0	1	1	0	0	0
Mister	45	.5607	5.3257	47.3	15	10	2	14	4	0	0	0	10	1	0	1	0	0	2	0	10	0	0	0	15	5	0	1	0
Misti	2	.1698	.1133	30.5	0	0	1	0	1	0	0	0	1	0	0	0	0	0	0	0	0	0	0	0	0	0	1	0	0
mistiness	2	.0000	.0914	29.6	0	0	0	0	2	0	0	0	2	0	0	0	0	0	0	0	0	0	0	0	0	0	0	0	0
mistletoe	12	.4750	1.2170	40.9	2	1	2	4	3	0	0	0	0	0	0	0	0	0	0	6	2	0	0	0	0	2	2	0	0
mistook	2	.2442	.1134	30.5	0	0	0	1	0	1	0	0	0	1	0	0	0	0	0	0	0	0	0	0	0	0	0	1	0
mistreated	2	.2443	.1130	30.5	0	0	0	1	1	0	0	0	0	0	0	1	0	0	0	0	0	0	0	0	1	0	0	0	0
mistreatment	3	.2197	.2090	33.2	0	1	1	1	0	0	0	0	2	0	0	0	0	0	0	0	0	0	0	0	0	0	1	0	0
mistress	30	.6186	3.9002	45.9	1	5	0	6	6	4	8	0	9	0	0	7	0	1	0	0	2	0	0	0	2	4	0	5	0
Mistress	11	.5540	1.2674	41.0	3	3	0	4	0	0	1	0	1	0	0	1	0	0	2	0	1	0	0	0	4	2	0	0	0
mistress'	2	.2433	.1158	30.6	1	0	1	0	0	0	0	0	0	0	0	0	0	0	0	0	0	0	0	0	0	1	0	1	0
mistress's	3	.1250	.1342	31.3	0	1	0	0	2	0	0	0	1	0	0	0	0	0	0	0	0	0	0	0	2	0	0	0	0
mistrust	3	.3766	.2497	34.0	1	0	1	0	0	1	0	0	0	0	0	0	0	1	0	0	0	0	0	0	0	1	1	0	0
mistrusted	2	.2440	.1132	30.5	0	0	0	0	2	0	0	0	0	0	0	1	0	0	0	0	0	0	0	0	0	0	0	1	0
mists	25	.6972	3.6013	45.6	0	2	7	5	6	2	3	0	8	0	0	5	0	1	0	1	1	0	0	0	2	4	2	1	0
misty	19	.6145	2.4542	43.9	0	4	3	3	1	3	5	0	6	1	2	1	0	0	0	2	3	0	0	0	1	1	0	2	0
Misty	12	.0000	.1407	31.5	0	0	10	0	2	0	0	0	0	0	0	0	0	0	0	0	0	0	0	0	12	0	0	0	0
misunderstand	7	.4097	.6191	37.9	0	0	1	0	1	2	3	0	1	1	2	0	0	1	0	0	0	0	1	0	0	0	1	0	0
misunderstanding	16	.6797	2.2242	43.5	0	0	2	1	7	4	2	0	3	3	1	1	1	1	0	0	0	0	2	0	2	1	1	0	0
misunderstandings	4	.4415	.3910	35.9	0	0	0	0	3	0	1	0	1	0	0	0	0	0	0	0	1	0	0	0	0	1	1	0	0
misunderstood	10	.6069	1.2351	40.9	0	1	0	0	2	1	4	2	0	2	1	1	0	0	0	0	0	0	0	0	1	1	1	3	0
misuse	7	.5208	.7559	38.8	1	0	1	0	4	1	0	0	0	1	1	0	1	1	0	0	0	0	0	0	0	0	1	2	0
misused	8	.4634	.7867	39.0	0	0	1	3	1	3	0	0	0	0	0	1	0	1	3	2	0	0	0	0	0	1	0	0	0
mit	3	.3829	.2430	33.9	0	1	0	1	1	0	0	0	0	0	0	0	0	0	1	0	1	0	0	0	1	0	0	0	0
Mit	17	.0000	.2461	33.9	0	17	0	0	0	0	0	0	0	0	0	0	0	0	0	0	0	0	0	0	0	17	0	0	0
Mitchell	18	.4970	1.8822	42.7	1	7	2	0	4	4	0	0	0	0	0	0	1	3	0	0	2	0	0	0	0	5	0	7	0
mite	15	.6992	2.1554	43.3	4	3	0	2	3	2	0	1	4	1	0	1	0	0	0	0	1	0	0	0	3	3	1	1	0
miter	6	.0986	.1514	31.8	0	0	0	0	3	3	0	0	0	0	0	0	0	0	0	0	0	0	0	4	0	2	0	0	0
mites	5	.3691	.4157	36.2	0	0	0	1	4	0	0	0	0	0	0	0	0	0	0	3	0	0	0	0	0	1	1	0	0
Mitford	3	.0000	.0365	25.6	0	0	0	0	0	3	0	0	0	0	0	0	0	0	0	0	0	0	0	0	0	0	0	3	0
mitigate	2	.2441	.1127	30.5	0	0	0	0	1	1	0	0	0	0	0	0	0	0	0	0	0	0	0	0	1	0	1	0	0
mitochondria	3	.0000	.0591	27.7	0	0	0	0	0	0	3	0	0	0	0	0	0	0	0	3	0	0	0	0	0	0	0	0	0
mitosis	6	.1813	.2803	34.5	0	0	0	1	5	0	0	0	0	0	0	0	0	0	0	2	0	0	0	0	0	0	4	0	0
Mitsu	6	.0000	.2741	34.4	6	0	0	0	0	0	0	0	6	0	0	0	0	0	0	0	0	0	0	0	0	0	0	0	0
Mitsu's	2	.0000	.0914	29.6	2	0	0	0	0	0	0	0	2	0	0	0	0	0	0	0	0	0	0	0	0	0	0	0	0
mitt	14	.5230	1.6206	42.1	3	2	3	0	4	1	1	0	6	2	0	0	1	0	0	0	0	0	0	0	0	4	0	1	0
mitten	3	.3234	.2368	33.7	1	1	1	0	0	0	0	0	1	0	0	0	0	0	1	0	0	0	0	0	0	1	0	0	0
mittened	3	.2261	.2131	33.3	0	0	0	1	0	2	0	0	2	0	0	0	0	0	0	0	0	0	0	0	1	0	0	0	0
mittens	32	.6745	4.4608	46.5	8	3	11	5	5	0	0	0	8	0	2	2	4	1	0	3	0	0	0	0	8	1	1	2	0
Mittens	3	.0000	.1370	31.4	0	0	3	0	0	0	0	0	3	0	0	0	0	0	0	0	0	0	0	0	0	0	0	0	0
Mitty	9	.3828	.8707	39.4	0	2	0	0	0	7	0	0	6	0	0	1	0	0	0	0	0	0	0	0	0	2	0	0	0
Mitzi	2	.0000	.0234	23.7	0	0	0	0	2	0	0	0	0	0	0	0	0	0	0	0	0	0	0	0	2	0	0	0	0
mix	129	.6007	15.944	52.0	20	30	4	10	26	17	19	3	16	2	0	3	0	3	3	25	2	15	29	10	3	9	1	8	0
mix-up	3	.2257	.1583	32.0	0	0	1	0	0	1	1	0	0	2	0	1	0	0	0	0	0	0	0	0	0	0	0	0	0
Mixcoatl's	2	.0000	.0389	25.9	0	0	0	2	0	0	0	0	0	0	0	0	0	2	0	0	0	0	0	0	0	0	0	0	0
mixed	324	.8632	55.740	57.5	42	42	46	66	55	38	32	3	39	8	1	8	106	33	8	32	4	6	7	12	16	15	16	13	0
mixed-fraction	4	.0000	.0599	27.8	0	0	4	0	0	0	0	0	0	0	0	0	4	0	0	0	0	0	0	0	0	0	0	0	0
mixed-numeral	2	.0000	.0299	24.8	0	0	2	0	0	0	0	0	0	0	0	0	2	0	0	0	0	0	0	0	0	0	0	0	0
mixed-up	5	.1712	.2142	33.3	3	1	0	0	1	0	0	0	0	4	0	0	0	0	0	0	0	0	0	0	1	0	0	0	0
mixer	9	.3212	.6747	38.3	2	2	1	0	1	0	3	0	2	2	0	0	0	0	0	1	0	0	3	0	0	1	0	0	0
mixers	5	.4297	.4602	36.6	0	1	1	0	2	1	0	0	0	0	0	0	0	1	0	1	0	0	0	1	0	1	1	0	0
mixes	16	.6035	2.0474	43.1	4	6	2	2	1	1	0	0	4	1	0	0	0	2	0	6	0	0	0	1	0	1	1	0	0
mixing	69	.5963	8.4150	49.3	8	10	5	7	13	6	20	0	7	2	1	1	0	1	1	7	2	7	22	3	3	5	3	4	0
Mixing	2	.0000	.0243	23.9	0	0	0	0	0	0	0	2	0	0	0	0	0	0	0	0	0	0	0	0	0	0	0	2	0
Mixtec	2	.0000	.0389	25.9	0	0	0	2	0	0	0	0	0	0	0	0	0	2	0	0	0	0	0	0	0	0	0	0	0
mixture	259	.4515	24.857	54.0	25	23	32	17	40	32	87	3	20	3	1	1	5	14	2	59	2	0	96	11	2	22	10	11	0
mixtures	16	.4829	1.6525	42.2	0	0	3	2	5	2	4	0	1	0	0	0	0	0	0	9	0	0	2	2	0	1	1	0	0
Miz	3	.3394	.2451	33.9	1	0	0	0	2	0	0	0	1	0	0	1	0	0	0	0	0	0	0	0	1	0	0	0	0
Mizar	4	.0000	.0486	26.9	0	0	0	0	4	0	0	0	0	0	0	0	0	0	0	0	0	0	0	0	0	0	0	4	0
mizzen	2	.1698	.1133	30.5	0	0	0	1	0	0	1	0	1	0	0	0	0	0	0	0	0	0	0	0	0	0	1	0	0
mizzenmast	2	.0000	.0914	29.6	0	0	0	2	0	0	0	0	2	0	0	0	0	0	0	0	0	0	0	0	0	0	0	0	0
ml	3	.0000	.0591	27.7	0	0	0	0	1	0	2	0	0	0	0	0	0	0	0	3	0	0	0	0	0	0	0	0	0
Mlle	2	.0000	.0162	22.1	0	0	0	0	0	0	2	0	0	0	0	0	0	0	0	0	2	0	0	0	0	0	0	0	0
mm	23	.5259	2.5281	44.0	0	0	3	0	12	2	4	2	0	0	0	0	14	0	2	2	1	0	0	1	0	3	0	0	0
mm-mm	37	.0000	1.6903	42.3	0	0	0	0	37	0	0	0	37	0	0	0	0	0	0	0	0	0	0	0	0	0	0	0	0
Mme	11	.4439	1.0320	40.1	0	0	0	0	2	0	5	4	0	0	0	2	0	0	0	0	3	0	0	0	0	5	0	1	0
mmm	4	.4446	.3917	35.9	2	0	1	1	0	0	0	0	1	0	0	0	0	0	1	0	0	0	0	0	1	0	1	0	0
mmmm	2	.0000	.0243	23.9	0	0	1	0	0	0	1	0	0	0	0	0	0	0	0	0	0	0	0	0	0	0	0	2	0
mn	3	.0000	.0243	23.9	0	0	1	0	0	2	0	0	0	0	0	0	0	0	3	0	0	0	0	0	0	0	0	0	0
MN	25	.0741	.7067	38.5	1	0	2	1	1	14	6	0	0	1	0	0	24	0	0	0	0	0	0	0	0	0	0	0	0
mnemonic	3	.1855	.1344	31.3	1	0	0	0	0	0	2	0	0	0	0	0	0	0	2	0	0	0	0	0	0	1	0	0	0
MNO	6	.0000	.0898	29.5	0	1	0	1	2	2	0	0	0	0	0	0	6	0	0	0	0	0	0	0	0	0	0	0	0
MNOP	5	.0000	.0748	28.7	0	1	0	1	0	3	0	0	0	0	0	0	5	0	0	0	0	0	0	0	0	0	0	0	0
MNQ	2	.0000	.0299	24.8	0	0	0	0	0	2	0	0	0	0	0	0	2	0	0	0	0	0	0	0	0	0	0	0	0
mo	5	.2443	.2905	34.6	0	0	0	2	3	0	0	0	0	2	0	0	3	0	0	0	0	0	0	0	0	0	0	0	0
Mo	5	.3461	.3825	35.8	0	0	0	1	1	2	1	0	0	0	0	0	0	0	0	1	0	0	0	0	0	0	2	2	0
Moab	3	.2212	.2099	33.2	0	0	2	0	0	1	0	0	2	0	0	1	0	0	0	0	0	0	0	0	0	0	0	0	0
moan	29	.6510	3.9350	45.9	2	9	0	4	11	2	1	0	9	5	0	4	0	0	1	0	1	0	0	0	4	5	0	0	0
Moana	5	.0000	.0586	27.7	0	0	0	5	0	0	0	0	0	0	0	0	0	0	0	0	0	0	0	0	5	0	0	0	0
moaned	25	.6316	3.3292	45.2	1	4	7	3	5	4	1	0	10	1	1	5	0	0	0	0	1	0	0	0	5	0	0	2	0
moaning	16	.7028	2.3477	43.7	3	1	3	1	3	2	2	1	8	1	0	2	0	0	0	1	1	0	0	0	1	1	0	1	0
moans	3	.3764	.2475	33.9	0	0	0	1	1	0	1	0	0	1	0	1	0	1	0	0	0	0	0	0	0	0	0	0	0
moat	12	.6195	1.5822	42.0	4	0	0	6	0	0	2	0	4	0	0	0	0	3	0	2	0	0	0	0	1	1	0	1	0
mob	18	.5398	2.0431	43.1	0	2	0	2	4	5	5	0	2	0	0	5	0	2	0	0	0	0	0	0	3	0	1	5	0

5A Missss
3R Missy's
4P mist-filled
7Q mist-shrouded
4A Mistah
9J mistempered
7D mistreat
5N Misty's
8R MIT
9Q MIT'S**
9B Mitch
8Q Mitchel
9R Mitchell-Finch
3P Mitchell's
4A Mitek
7P mitered
3P MITES
8Q Mithridatic
7B mitre
9R Mitsubishi
3P mitten-like
5N mittered
8R Mitterrand
6A mitts
9Q mitzvah
7L mix-matches
3A mix-mux
3N mix-ups
6F Mixcoatl
5H Mixer
7F mixing-bowl
5J mixolydian
8F Miyoshi
7R Mizar's
3J mizzle
5E ML
9B mlle
7P MLTD
7E MMCCCX
7D mmmmm-hmmmm
4N mmph
8E Mnq
8E MO
7Q moa
7N moanings
9Q moats

Word Type	F	D	U	SFI	3 Gr 3	4 Gr 4	5 Gr 5	6 Gr 6	7 Gr 7	8 Gr 8	9 Gr 9	X UnGr	A Read	B Eng & Gr	C Comp	D Lit	E Math	F Soc Stud	G Spell	H Sci	J Music	K Art	L Home Ec	M Shop	N Lib F	P Lib NF	Q Lib Ref	R Mag	S Rel
mobbed	7	.5596	.8535	39.3	2	0	0	0	2	2	1	0	3	1	0	0	0	1	0	0	0	0	0	0	0	0	1	1	0
mobile	25	.5105	2.6487	44.2	1	7	4	3	7	0	2	1	0	0	0	0	0	0	1	1	0	2	0	0	0	4	5	12	0
Mobile	3	.3395	.2468	33.9	0	0	0	0	2	0	1	0	1	0	0	0	0	0	0	0	0	0	0	0	0	1	1	0	0
mobile-home	2	.0000	.0243	23.9	0	2	0	0	0	0	0	0	0	0	0	0	0	0	0	0	0	0	0	0	0	0	0	2	0
mobiles	3	.1918	.1342	31.3	0	2	0	1	0	0	0	0	0	0	0	0	0	0	0	0	0	1	0	0	0	0	0	2	0
mobility	7	.4559	.6863	38.4	1	1	1	0	2	1	1	0	0	0	0	0	0	1	0	2	0	0	0	0	0	2	2	0	0
mobilized	3	.2425	.1816	32.6	0	0	0	0	1	2	0	0	0	0	0	0	0	2	0	0	0	0	0	0	0	0	0	1	0
Mobius	3	.0000	.0591	27.7	0	0	0	0	3	0	0	0	0	0	0	0	0	0	0	3	0	0	0	0	0	0	0	0	0
mobs	6	.3703	.4939	36.9	0	0	2	0	0	4	0	0	0	0	0	0	0	3	0	0	0	0	0	0	1	0	2	0	0
Moby	3	.3781	.2493	34.0	0	0	0	0	1	2	0	0	0	1	0	0	0	1	0	0	0	0	0	0	0	0	0	1	0
moccasin	13	.5227	1.5282	41.8	4	4	3	1	1	0	0	0	7	2	0	0	0	1	0	1	0	0	0	0	2	0	0	0	0
moccasined	2	.1814	.1187	30.7	0	1	0	1	0	0	0	0	1	0	0	0	0	0	0	0	0	0	0	0	0	0	0	1	0
moccasins	42	.6522	5.8035	47.6	11	6	9	2	10	1	0	3	21	1	1	8	0	2	0	0	0	0	0	0	5	2	0	2	0
Mocha	9	.3385	.7914	39.0	3	0	0	6	0	0	0	0	5	0	0	0	0	1	0	0	0	0	0	0	0	3	0	0	0
mock	13	.5976	1.6073	42.1	0	1	5	0	2	2	3	0	1	4	0	2	0	2	0	0	0	0	0	0	1	1	0	2	0
Mock	21	.0000	.2298	33.6	0	0	21	0	0	0	0	0	0	21	0	0	0	0	0	0	0	0	0	0	0	0	0	0	0
mocked	8	.3729	.6853	38.4	0	0	1	6	0	0	1	0	2	4	0	1	0	0	0	0	0	0	0	0	0	0	0	1	0
mocking	12	.5313	1.4124	41.5	2	1	1	2	4	0	1	1	6	0	0	0	0	0	0	0	2	0	0	0	2	1	0	1	0
mockingbird	4	.4445	.3917	35.9	1	0	0	1	1	1	0	0	1	0	0	1	0	0	0	0	1	0	0	0	1	0	0	0	0
mockingly	2	.2306	.1140	30.6	0	0	0	0	2	0	0	0	0	1	0	0	0	1	0	0	0	0	0	0	0	0	0	0	0
mocks	4	.4419	.3922	35.9	0	0	0	0	2	0	2	0	1	0	0	0	0	0	0	0	1	0	0	0	0	1	0	1	0
mod	2	.0000	.0243	23.9	0	1	1	0	0	0	0	0	0	0	0	0	0	0	0	0	0	0	0	0	0	0	0	2	0
modal	8	.3269	.5695	37.6	0	2	0	1	3	1	0	1	0	4	0	0	0	0	0	0	3	0	0	0	0	1	0	0	0
Modcom	9	.0000	.1094	30.4	0	0	0	0	0	0	9	0	0	0	0	0	0	0	0	0	0	0	0	0	0	0	0	9	0
mode	50	.4665	4.8368	46.8	0	3	2	9	15	8	11	2	0	0	0	3	6	1	0	0	32	1	1	0	1	1	3	1	0
model	332	.7676	51.336	57.1	48	58	37	38	67	36	40	8	30	15	29	1	59	31	4	77	6	16	4	6	1	11	14	28	0
Model	31	.5268	3.4792	45.4	0	4	1	4	9	11	2	0	5	0	4	0	0	10	0	0	0	0	0	1	0	2	1	8	0
Model-A	6	.0000	.0729	28.6	0	0	0	6	0	0	0	0	0	0	0	0	0	0	0	0	0	0	0	0	0	0	0	6	0
Model-T	2	.0000	.0243	23.9	0	0	0	2	0	0	0	0	0	0	0	0	0	0	0	0	0	0	0	0	0	0	0	2	0
modeled	20	.3449	1.5872	42.0	3	4	2	3	5	3	0	0	5	1	0	0	0	1	1	1	1	6	0	0	0	1	2	1	0
modeling	20	.3956	1.6850	42.3	2	6	0	1	7	2	2	0	1	0	0	0	4	0	0	2	0	6	0	3	0	2	1	1	0
models	114	.8400	19.118	52.8	16	21	7	11	29	18	8	4	10	6	0	1	17	10	6	21	2	4	3	0	2	6	15	11	0
moderate	58	.6062	7.1555	48.5	5	2	7	2	9	13	18	2	1	0	0	2	0	7	0	4	8	0	14	3	3	3	6	7	0
moderate-sized	3	.2540	.1940	32.9	0	0	0	1	0	2	0	0	1	0	0	0	0	0	0	0	0	0	1	0	0	0	1	0	0
moderately	15	.6493	1.9785	43.0	3	0	0	1	3	2	4	2	1	2	1	2	0	0	0	0	0	0	2	0	0	2	2	3	0
moderates	8	.4494	.7725	38.9	0	0	0	0	1	5	2	0	0	0	0	0	0	3	0	0	0	0	0	0	0	1	1	3	0
moderating	2	.2446	.1257	31.0	0	0	1	0	1	0	0	0	0	0	0	0	0	1	0	1	0	0	0	0	0	0	0	0	0
moderation	4	.3603	.3219	35.1	1	0	1	2	0	0	0	0	0	0	0	0	0	1	0	0	0	0	0	0	0	2	0	1	0
modern	731	.8348	121.84	60.9	40	48	103	117	178	111	102	32	53	32	3	15	12	201	9	56	65	15	4	21	1	46	146	52	0
Modern	16	.5199	1.7129	42.3	1	2	0	1	3	5	0	4	0	8	0	0	0	0	0	0	2	1	0	0	0	0	2	3	0
modern-day	4	.3751	.3220	35.1	1	0	0	0	2	0	0	1	0	0	0	1	0	0	0	1	0	0	0	1	0	0	1	0	0
modernity	2	.2437	.1129	30.5	0	0	0	0	0	0	2	0	0	0	0	0	0	0	0	0	0	0	0	0	0	0	1	1	0
modernization	8	.2669	.4971	37.0	4	1	1	0	2	0	0	0	0	0	0	0	0	2	0	0	0	0	0	0	0	1	5	0	0
modernize	3	.2444	.1814	32.6	1	0	0	0	1	0	1	0	0	0	0	0	0	2	0	0	0	0	0	0	0	0	1	0	0
modernized	7	.4914	.7205	38.6	0	0	2	2	0	2	1	0	0	0	0	1	0	2	0	0	0	0	0	1	0	1	2	0	0
modernizing	3	.2063	.1600	32.0	0	0	1	0	1	1	0	0	0	0	0	0	0	1	0	0	0	0	0	0	0	2	0	0	0
modes	19	.1914	.8795	39.4	0	0	2	5	3	5	4	0	1	0	0	0	0	0	0	0	15	0	0	0	0	1	1	1	0
modest	37	.7518	5.6353	47.5	3	4	2	2	7	11	5	3	7	3	1	3	0	4	0	0	0	0	2	0	2	3	2	10	0
Modest	2	.0000	.0162	22.1	0	0	0	2	0	0	0	0	0	0	0	0	0	0	0	0	2	0	0	0	0	0	0	0	0
modestly	4	.3816	.3310	35.2	0	1	0	0	2	1	0	0	0	0	0	1	0	0	0	0	0	0	0	0	0	2	1	0	0
modesty	3	.2175	.1545	31.9	0	0	0	0	1	1	1	0	0	0	0	2	0	0	0	0	0	0	0	0	0	0	0	1	0
modification	10	.4933	1.0301	40.1	0	1	0	0	5	3	1	0	0	2	1	0	0	0	0	2	0	0	0	0	0	1	4	0	0
modifications	6	.3493	.4587	36.6	1	0	0	0	4	0	1	0	0	0	0	0	0	0	0	0	0	0	0	0	0	1	2	3	0
modified	62	.6776	8.4581	49.3	0	0	6	5	22	12	15	2	1	15	8	1	0	1	3	2	3	0	2	2	0	3	17	4	0
modifier	32	.3120	2.2364	43.5	0	0	1	5	8	8	10	0	2	26	2	0	0	0	1	0	0	0	0	0	0	0	1	0	0
modifiers	77	.2530	4.4536	46.5	0	0	0	8	34	16	19	0	1	68	3	0	0	0	5	0	0	0	0	0	0	0	0	0	0
modifies	62	.2847	3.9204	45.9	0	0	2	16	16	13	15	0	2	45	13	0	0	0	1	0	0	0	0	0	0	0	1	0	0
modify	68	.3862	5.5867	47.5	0	1	2	14	24	17	10	0	0	48	9	0	0	1	4	3	0	0	0	0	1	1	1	0	0
modifying	31	.3861	2.5103	44.0	0	1	0	3	9	13	5	0	0	14	7	0	0	0	8	0	0	0	0	0	1	0	0	1	0
Modjeska	3	.1101	.0785	28.9	0	0	0	0	1	2	0	0	0	0	2	1	0	0	0	0	0	0	0	0	0	0	0	0	0
modulate	2	.0000	.0162	22.1	0	0	0	0	0	2	0	0	0	0	0	0	0	0	0	0	2	0	0	0	0	0	0	0	0
modulated	6	.2092	.2810	34.5	0	0	0	0	0	5	1	0	0	0	0	0	0	0	0	1	2	0	0	3	0	0	0	0	0
modulation	11	.3165	.7650	38.8	0	0	0	0	2	3	6	0	0	0	0	0	0	0	0	3	7	0	0	1	0	0	0	0	0
Modulation	2	.0000	.0162	22.1	0	0	0	0	0	2	0	0	0	0	0	0	0	0	0	0	2	0	0	0	0	0	0	0	0
module	16	.1444	.6174	37.9	4	0	4	3	4	0	1	0	0	0	0	0	0	0	0	0	0	0	0	0	0	0	2	14	0
Module	10	.1007	.3097	34.9	0	0	0	0	9	0	1	0	0	0	0	0	1	0	0	0	0	0	0	0	0	0	0	9	0
Moebius	2	.0000	.0299	24.8	0	0	0	0	0	2	0	0	0	0	0	0	2	0	0	0	0	0	0	0	0	0	0	0	0
Moffat	9	.3778	.8803	39.4	0	6	3	0	0	0	0	0	7	0	0	1	0	0	0	0	0	0	0	0	0	0	1	0	0
Moffats	3	.1187	.1291	31.1	0	1	2	0	0	0	0	0	1	0	0	2	0	0	0	0	0	0	0	0	0	0	0	0	0
Mogo	6	.0000	.2741	34.4	0	6	0	0	0	0	0	0	6	0	0	0	0	0	0	0	0	0	0	0	0	0	0	0	0
mohair	3	.0000	.0583	27.7	0	0	2	1	0	0	0	0	0	0	0	0	0	3	0	0	0	0	0	0	0	0	0	0	0
Mohammed	16	.3955	1.4104	41.5	2	0	0	5	4	3	2	0	0	0	0	0	0	11	0	0	0	0	0	0	0	2	2	1	0
Mohammedan	8	.5445	.9103	39.6	1	0	0	1	3	3	0	0	0	0	0	1	0	4	1	0	1	0	0	0	0	1	0	0	0
Mohammedanism	4	.2425	.2409	33.8	0	0	0	0	3	1	0	0	0	0	0	0	0	3	0	0	1	0	0	0	0	0	0	0	0
Mohammedans	7	.3439	.5391	37.3	0	0	0	0	0	7	0	0	0	0	0	0	0	4	0	0	0	1	0	0	0	0	2	0	0
Mohawk	12	.4576	1.2505	41.0	4	1	3	0	2	1	0	1	4	0	0	0	0	4	0	0	0	0	0	0	0	3	0	1	0
Mohawks	2	.2443	.1130	30.5	0	0	0	0	2	0	0	0	0	0	0	1	0	0	0	0	0	0	0	0	1	0	0	0	0
Mohee	6	.0000	.0485	26.9	0	0	0	0	6	0	0	0	0	0	0	0	0	0	0	0	6	0	0	0	0	0	0	0	0
Mohenjo-Daro	2	.0000	.0209	23.2	0	0	0	0	0	2	0	0	0	0	0	0	0	0	0	0	0	0	0	0	0	0	2	0	0
Mohican	2	.2443	.1130	30.5	0	0	0	0	2	0	0	0	0	0	0	1	0	0	0	0	0	0	0	0	1	0	0	0	0
Mohicans	2	.0000	.0234	23.7	0	0	0	0	2	0	0	0	0	0	0	0	0	0	0	0	0	0	0	0	2	0	0	0	0
mohney	2	.0000	.0914	29.6	0	0	0	0	2	0	0	0	2	0	0	0	0	0	0	0	0	0	0	0	0	0	0	0	0
Moho	3	.0000	.0314	25.0	0	2	0	0	1	0	0	0	0	0	0	0	0	0	0	0	0	0	0	0	0	0	3	0	0
Mohole	3	.0000	.0314	25.0	0	1	0	0	2	0	0	0	0	0	0	0	0	0	0	0	0	0	0	0	0	0	3	0	0
Mohorovicic	2	.0000	.0209	23.2	0	1	0	0	1	0	0	0	0	0	0	0	0	0	0	0	0	0	0	0	0	0	2	0	0
Mohr	2	.0000	.0162	22.1	0	0	0	2	0	0	0	0	0	0	0	0	0	0	0	0	2	0	0	0	0	0	0	0	0
moil	2	.0000	.0914	29.6	0	0	0	0	2	0	0	0	2	0	0	0	0	0	0	0	0	0	0	0	0	0	0	0	0
Moines	2	.0000	.0914	29.6	0	0	2	0	0	0	0	0	2	0	0	0	0	0	0	0	0	0	0	0	0	0	0	0	0
Moingona	4	.0000	.1827	32.6	0	0	4	0	0	0	0	0	4	0	0	0	0	0	0	0	0	0	0	0	0	0	0	0	0
moist	135	.6275	17.660	52.5	25	24	27	14	25	1	14	5	12	0	0	2	0	27	0	67	0	0	3	0	3	7	8	6	0
moist-heat	2	.0000	.0064	18.1	0	0	0	0	0	0	2	0	0	0	0	0	0	0	0	0	0	0	2	0	0	0	0	0	0
moisten	9	.4552	.8645	39.4	1	0	0	0	3	3	1	1	1	0	0	0	0	0	0	1	1	0	2	2	0	0	0	2	0
moistened	12	.0959	.3210	35.1	0	0	1	0	2	3	6	0	1	0	0	0	0	0	0	1	0	0	9	0	0	0	1	0	0
moistens	2	.2446	.1123	30.5	0	0	0	0	1	0	1	0	0	1	0	0	0	0	0	0	0	0	0	0	0	0	1	0	0
moisture	136	.7369	20.331	53.1	14	17	22	17	28	14	16	8	10	0	1	2	0	26	1	52	0	0	10	4	4	6	11	9	0
moisture-laden	4	.3869	.3419	35.3	1	0	0	1	1	0	1	0	0	0	0	0	0	0	0	2	0	0	0	0	1	0	1	0	0

8A Mobil
8F mobilization
9R mobilize
5R mobsman's
9P mockery
8A Mocking
6F Moctezuma
8R Mod
XR modacrylic
9B modals
XR model-A
6R Model-As
4C model-makers'
8F modelled
7C Models
7Q Modena
9L moderate-priced
8F moderated
6A modernistic
9P modicum
8B modifer
9A modifers
7R Modified
8J Modiste
8C Modjeska's
9J modulating
8J modulations
9H modulator
7M modules
8B modus
7P moe
7A Moeder
7A Moeder's
8R Moeller
8Q Moewe
5D Moffats'
XR Mogollon
8F Mohammed's
8N Mohawks'
6A moidores
XB moisseron
7F moister
6R moistly
8M moisture-
6F moisture-bearing
8L moisture-proof

Word Type	F	D	U	SFI	3 Gr 3	4 Gr 4	5 Gr 5	6 Gr 6	7 Gr 7	8 Gr 8	9 Gr 9	X UnGr	A Read	B Eng & Gr	C Comp	D Lit	E Math	F Soc Stud	G Spell	H Sci	J Music	K Art	L Home Ec	M Shop	N Lib F	P Lib NF	Q Lib Ref	R Mag	S Rel
moistureproof	2	.0000	.0064	18.1	0	0	0	0	0	0	2	0	0	0	0	0	0	0	0	0	0	0	2	0	0	0	0	0	0
Mojave	7	.2989	.5441	37.4	0	4	1	1	1	0	0	0	2	0	0	0	0	1	0	4	0	0	0	0	0	0	0	0	0
Molali	2	.0000	.0389	25.9	0	2	0	0	0	0	0	0	0	0	0	0	0	2	0	0	0	0	0	0	0	0	0	0	0
molar	3	.2445	.1818	32.6	0	0	0	0	1	1	1	0	0	0	0	0	0	0	0	2	0	0	0	0	0	0	1	0	0
molars	7	.2412	.4224	36.3	0	0	2	0	5	0	0	0	0	0	0	0	0	0	0	5	0	0	0	0	0	0	2	0	0
molasses	44	.7217	6.5665	48.2	7	7	6	5	7	5	5	2	19	1	1	1	0	6	0	0	1	0	4	0	3	5	1	2	0
molasses-sweet	2	.1621	.0746	28.7	0	0	0	0	1	1	0	0	0	0	1	1	0	0	0	0	0	0	0	0	0	0	0	0	0
mold	171	.4125	15.567	51.9	42	11	7	22	29	15	42	3	14	0	0	2	0	2	0	91	2	0	0	33	1	5	16	5	0
mold's	2	.2130	.1056	30.2	0	0	1	0	0	1	0	0	0	0	0	0	0	0	1	1	0	0	0	0	0	0	0	0	0
moldable	3	.0000	.0076	18.8	0	0	0	0	3	0	0	0	0	0	0	0	0	0	0	0	0	0	0	3	0	0	0	0	0
Moldau	5	.0000	.0404	26.1	0	0	0	2	0	3	0	0	0	0	0	0	0	0	0	0	5	0	0	0	0	0	0	0	0
molded	15	.6066	1.8831	42.7	1	0	3	1	5	2	1	2	2	0	0	0	0	1	0	2	1	0	1	1	0	1	6	0	0
moldering	2	.1814	.1187	30.7	0	0	0	1	1	0	0	0	1	0	0	0	0	0	0	0	0	0	0	0	0	0	0	1	0
molders	2	.2337	.1157	30.6	0	1	0	0	0	1	0	0	0	0	0	0	0	1	0	0	0	0	0	0	1	0	0	0	0
molding	19	.5592	2.1825	43.4	1	0	5	1	5	4	2	1	1	0	0	0	0	1	0	0	0	1	1	4	0	4	5	2	0
moldings	4	.3214	.2811	34.5	0	0	1	0	2	0	1	0	0	0	0	0	0	0	0	0	0	0	0	1	0	2	1	0	0
Moldoveanu	2	.0000	.0243	23.9	0	0	0	2	0	0	0	0	0	0	0	0	0	0	0	0	0	0	0	0	0	0	0	2	0
molds	63	.5049	6.8775	48.4	13	3	4	22	5	3	7	6	5	0	0	0	0	4	1	46	0	0	3	1	0	0	2	1	0
moldy	5	.3056	.3513	35.5	2	0	1	2	0	0	0	0	0	0	1	0	0	0	0	3	0	0	0	0	0	0	0	1	0
mole	36	.6640	4.9622	47.0	9	2	0	13	8	3	1	0	8	0	0	3	0	0	1	12	1	0	0	0	0	5	5	1	0
Mole	16	.3903	1.4643	41.7	7	1	0	6	2	0	0	0	6	2	0	1	0	0	0	0	0	0	0	0	7	0	0	0	0
mole's	4	.2353	.2382	33.8	2	0	0	1	1	0	0	0	0	0	0	0	0	0	0	3	0	0	0	0	0	0	1	0	0
Mole's	2	.1787	.1174	30.7	1	0	0	1	0	0	0	0	1	0	0	0	0	0	0	0	0	0	0	0	1	0	0	0	0
molecular	20	.3953	1.7408	42.4	1	5	1	1	7	4	1	0	0	0	0	0	0	0	0	10	0	0	0	0	0	1	7	2	0
molecularly	2	.0000	.0209	23.2	0	0	0	2	0	0	0	0	0	0	0	0	0	0	0	0	0	0	0	0	0	0	2	0	0
molecule	160	.3845	13.853	51.4	19	24	16	9	52	5	33	2	0	0	0	0	0	0	0	124	0	0	0	2	0	14	18	2	0
molecules	474	.3349	37.088	55.7	40	193	51	55	57	42	35	1	1	3	0	0	3	0	2	409	4	0	0	2	1	22	23	4	0
molehill	2	.0000	.0209	23.2	0	0	0	0	2	0	0	0	0	0	0	0	0	0	0	0	0	0	0	0	0	0	2	0	0
molehills	2	.0000	.0914	29.6	0	0	2	0	0	0	0	0	2	0	0	0	0	0	0	0	0	0	0	0	0	0	0	0	0
moles	10	.4730	1.0728	40.3	5	0	0	2	3	0	0	0	4	0	0	0	0	0	0	2	0	0	0	0	0	2	2	0	0
molest	2	.2128	.1055	30.2	0	0	0	2	0	0	0	0	0	0	0	0	0	0	0	1	1	0	0	0	0	0	0	0	0
Moliere	6	.2629	.3642	35.6	0	2	1	0	0	1	2	0	0	0	0	0	0	1	0	0	0	0	0	0	0	0	4	1	0
Molinas	4	.0000	.0486	26.9	0	0	0	0	0	4	0	0	0	0	0	0	0	0	0	0	0	0	0	0	0	0	0	4	0
Moll	3	.2197	.2090	33.2	0	0	1	0	2	0	0	0	2	0	0	0	0	0	0	0	0	0	0	0	0	0	1	0	0
Mollendo	2	.0000	.0389	25.9	0	0	0	0	2	0	0	0	0	0	0	0	0	2	0	0	0	0	0	0	0	0	0	0	0
Moller	2	.0000	.0215	23.3	0	0	0	0	2	0	0	0	0	0	0	2	0	0	0	0	0	0	0	0	0	0	0	0	0
Mollet	2	.0000	.0243	23.9	0	0	0	0	0	2	0	0	0	0	0	0	0	0	0	0	0	0	0	0	0	0	0	2	0
Molli	3	.0000	.0243	23.8	3	0	0	0	0	0	0	0	0	0	0	0	0	0	0	0	3	0	0	0	0	0	0	0	0
mollies	2	.1698	.1133	30.5	0	1	0	0	1	0	0	0	1	0	0	0	0	0	0	0	0	0	0	0	0	0	1	0	0
mollusk	8	.5380	.9264	39.7	0	0	0	1	5	0	2	0	2	0	0	0	0	0	0	2	1	0	0	0	2	0	0	1	0
mollusks	19	.4059	1.7423	42.4	0	0	1	4	9	2	3	0	3	0	0	0	0	0	0	8	0	0	0	0	0	0	6	2	0
Mollweide	2	.0000	.0209	23.2	0	2	0	0	0	0	0	0	0	0	0	0	0	0	0	0	0	0	0	0	0	0	2	0	0
Molly	36	.3310	3.2966	45.2	6	15	0	0	13	2	0	0	29	0	0	0	2	0	0	0	0	0	0	0	0	5	0	0	0
Molly's	2	.0000	.0914	29.6	0	1	0	0	1	0	0	0	2	0	0	0	0	0	0	0	0	0	0	0	0	0	0	0	0
Mols	13	.0000	.5939	37.7	0	0	13	0	0	0	0	0	13	0	0	0	0	0	0	0	0	0	0	0	0	0	0	0	0
molt	9	.3453	.7140	38.5	4	0	0	4	1	0	0	0	0	0	0	0	0	0	0	6	0	0	0	0	0	2	1	0	0
molten	53	.4897	5.6387	47.5	5	10	11	2	9	3	11	2	7	0	0	0	0	2	0	29	0	0	0	5	0	1	7	2	0
molting	11	.2677	.7270	38.6	2	2	1	4	2	0	0	0	0	0	0	0	0	0	0	9	0	0	0	0	0	1	1	0	0
molts	9	.1464	.4059	36.1	5	0	2	0	2	0	0	0	0	0	0	0	0	0	0	8	0	0	0	0	0	1	0	0	0
molybdenum	2	.1814	.1187	30.7	1	0	0	1	0	0	0	0	1	0	0	0	0	0	0	0	0	0	0	0	0	0	0	1	0
mom	13	.5836	1.6420	42.2	2	0	3	1	1	3	3	0	6	1	0	1	0	0	0	1	0	0	0	0	3	0	0	1	0
Mom	127	.6662	18.076	52.6	23	24	5	22	40	6	6	1	83	5	0	5	0	5	0	0	0	0	2	0	14	7	0	6	0
Mom's	5	.0000	.2284	33.6	0	0	0	2	3	0	0	0	5	0	0	0	0	0	0	0	0	0	0	0	0	0	0	0	0
mome	2	.1458	.0682	28.3	0	0	1	1	0	0	0	0	0	1	0	0	0	0	0	0	0	1	0	0	0	0	0	0	0
moment	834	.8339	140.16	61.5	69	142	101	139	194	91	83	15	324	44	18	112	4	20	1	38	10	0	4	2	135	65	13	43	1
moment's	11	.6023	1.3946	41.4	2	3	0	1	2	1	2	0	3	1	0	2	0	0	1	0	0	0	0	0	1	3	0	0	0
momentarily	10	.4447	.9398	39.7	1	2	0	2	1	2	2	0	0	0	0	3	0	0	0	0	0	0	0	0	2	1	0	4	0
momentary	9	.4630	.9671	39.9	0	0	0	0	5	1	3	0	5	0	0	2	0	0	0	0	0	0	0	0	1	1	0	0	0
momentous	10	.5120	1.0928	40.4	0	0	2	1	2	3	1	1	1	1	1	0	0	4	0	1	0	0	0	0	0	0	2	0	0
moments	100	.7687	15.599	51.9	8	13	6	13	34	11	8	7	29	15	2	11	0	0	0	3	1	0	2	0	17	4	3	13	0
momentum	22	.6001	2.7748	44.4	1	1	0	0	4	4	12	0	3	0	0	0	0	1	0	10	0	0	0	0	2	2	2	2	0
Momma	7	.0566	.1818	32.6	0	0	0	0	1	6	0	0	1	0	0	6	0	0	0	0	0	0	0	0	0	0	0	0	0
mommy	2	.1717	.1142	30.6	0	0	0	0	2	0	0	0	1	0	0	1	0	0	0	0	0	0	0	0	0	0	0	0	0
Mommy	8	.5422	.8933	39.5	3	2	1	1	0	1	0	0	0	1	1	0	0	1	0	0	0	0	0	0	2	0	2	1	0
mon	3	.2031	.1990	33.0	0	0	1	0	1	0	1	0	2	0	0	0	0	0	1	0	0	0	0	0	0	0	0	0	0
Mon	2	.2411	.1091	30.4	0	2	0	0	0	0	0	0	0	0	0	1	0	0	0	0	1	0	0	0	0	0	0	0	0
Mona	12	.3662	1.0499	40.2	4	5	0	0	0	0	3	0	5	0	0	0	1	0	0	0	0	2	0	0	0	0	1	3	0
Monaco	6	.2629	.3642	35.6	0	0	4	1	1	0	0	0	0	0	0	0	0	1	0	0	0	0	0	0	0	0	4	1	0
Monaghan	5	.0000	.0537	27.3	0	0	0	0	5	0	0	0	0	0	0	5	0	0	0	0	0	0	0	0	0	0	0	0	0
MONAGHAN	42	.0000	.4507	36.5	0	0	0	0	42	0	0	0	0	0	0	42	0	0	0	0	0	0	0	0	0	0	0	0	0
monarch	21	.6965	3.0015	44.8	2	4	6	1	3	1	3	1	4	1	0	2	0	2	1	4	0	0	0	0	1	1	5	0	0
Monarch	3	.2043	.1486	31.7	3	0	0	0	0	0	0	0	0	0	0	0	0	0	0	0	0	0	0	0	0	1	2	0	0
monarchs	13	.6188	1.6618	42.2	2	2	2	0	3	2	1	1	1	1	0	1	0	3	0	0	0	0	0	0	1	3	3	0	0
monarchy	14	.4779	1.4164	41.5	0	0	6	1	3	1	3	0	0	0	0	1	0	2	0	0	0	0	0	0	0	7	3	1	0
monasteries	16	.6519	2.1486	43.3	1	1	1	3	6	2	0	2	2	1	0	0	0	5	1	0	1	0	0	0	0	1	4	1	0
monastery	18	.5914	2.3027	43.6	0	0	9	0	5	1	2	1	9	2	0	0	0	0	0	1	0	1	0	0	0	1	1	3	0
monazite	2	.0000	.0209	23.2	0	0	0	0	2	0	0	0	0	0	0	0	0	0	0	0	0	0	0	0	0	0	2	0	0
Monday	107	.7837	17.030	52.3	26	33	10	8	10	15	3	2	34	4	0	4	25	6	6	5	0	0	1	0	9	5	0	8	0
Monday's	4	.0931	.1444	31.6	3	1	0	0	0	0	0	0	1	3	0	0	0	0	0	0	0	0	0	0	0	0	0	0	0
Mondrian	3	.0994	.0714	28.5	0	1	1	0	0	1	0	0	0	0	0	0	0	0	0	0	0	2	0	0	0	0	1	0	0
Monet	5	.3441	.3659	35.6	0	0	1	0	0	2	0	2	0	0	0	0	0	0	0	0	2	1	0	0	0	0	0	2	0
Monet's	2	.2375	.1088	30.4	0	0	1	0	0	0	0	1	0	0	0	0	0	0	0	0	1	0	0	0	0	0	0	1	0
monetary	7	.0000	.0733	28.6	0	1	0	0	1	5	0	0	0	0	0	0	0	0	0	0	0	0	0	0	0	0	7	0	0
money	1694	.9136	307.57	64.9	367	316	185	169	262	207	160	28	516	66	11	96	186	267	17	15	14	2	48	3	109	175	51	117	1
Money	5	.1865	.3050	34.8	2	1	0	0	0	0	2	0	2	0	0	0	0	3	0	0	0	0	0	0	0	0	0	0	0
money-lender	2	.2139	.1057	30.2	0	0	0	0	0	1	1	0	0	0	0	0	0	1	1	0	0	0	0	0	0	0	0	0	0
money-making	4	.4529	.3998	36.0	1	1	0	0	2	0	0	0	1	0	0	0	0	0	1	0	0	0	0	0	1	0	1	1	0
money's	6	.5444	.7070	38.5	0	1	0	1	2	2	0	0	2	0	0	0	0	1	0	0	1	0	0	0	1	0	0	1	0
Moneybags	2	.0000	.0290	24.6	2	0	0	0	0	0	0	0	0	0	0	0	0	0	0	0	0	0	0	0	0	2	0	0	0
moneyed	4	.0000	.0778	28.9	0	0	0	0	0	4	0	0	0	0	0	0	0	4	0	0	0	0	0	0	0	0	0	0	0
Moneymore	4	.0000	.1827	32.6	0	0	0	0	4	0	0	0	4	0	0	0	0	0	0	0	0	0	0	0	0	0	0	0	0
moneys	2	.2306	.1140	30.6	0	0	0	0	0	1	1	0	0	1	0	0	0	1	0	0	0	0	0	0	0	0	0	0	0
Monge	2	.0000	.0209	23.2	0	0	0	0	0	0	2	0	0	0	0	0	0	0	0	0	0	0	0	0	0	0	2	0	0
Mongol	12	.3571	.9538	39.8	1	1	2	3	0	3	2	0	0	0	0	0	0	4	0	0	0	0	0	0	0	3	5	0	0
Mongolia	14	.5659	1.6422	42.2	3	0	2	1	5	1	2	0	0	0	0	0	0	2	0	1	0	0	0	0	4	4	2	1	0

8L Mold
9H mold-like
9M molder
8M molder's
8F Molders'
9R moldlike
4H Molecu
6H Molecules
7A moleskin
8N molestation
7P molested
7Q molesters
8N Mollie
7C mollified
7C mollify
4Q molluscs
7N molluska
3A molly
7A Molokai
6H molted
7D Molting
5J molto
XH molybdate
8B mom's
6F Mombasa
8Q momenta
9R momento
7E MON
7D MONAGAN
7D MONAHAN
5Q monarch's
8J monarchies
9Q monarchists
9A Monarchs
5A Monarchy
5P monastic
3E Mondays
4K Mondrian's
8Q Monetary
XR Monets
5R MONEY
6A money-back
XR money-bearing
4N money-box
5N money-boxes
7P money-printing
7N money-sack
3P money'
8A moneybags
3P Moneys
6R mongeese

Word Type	F	D	U	SFI	3 Gr 3	4 Gr 4	5 Gr 5	6 Gr 6	7 Gr 7	8 Gr 8	9 Gr 9	X UnGr	A Read	B Eng & Gr	C Comp	D Lit	E Math	F Soc Stud	G Spell	H Sci	J Music	K Art	L Home Ec	M Shop	N Lib F	P Lib NF	Q Lib Ref	R Mag	S Rel
Mongolian	4	.2408	.2408	33.8	0	1	2	0	1	0	0	0	0	0	0	0	0	2	0	0	0	0	0	0	0	2	0	0	0
Mongolians	3	.3454	.2542	34.1	0	0	0	2	1	0	0	0	1	0	0	0	0	1	0	0	0	0	0	0	0	0	0	1	0
Mongols	14	.4620	1.3878	41.4	2	0	2	5	2	3	0	0	0	0	0	1	0	6	0	0	0	0	0	0	0	4	3	0	0
mongoose	16	.3441	1.4465	41.6	0	7	0	3	6	0	0	0	11	0	0	4	0	0	0	0	0	0	0	0	0	0	1	0	0
mongoose's	2	.0000	.0914	29.6	0	1	0	1	0	0	0	0	2	0	0	0	0	0	0	0	0	0	0	0	0	0	0	0	0
mongooses	3	.2279	.2143	33.3	0	1	0	1	1	0	0	0	2	0	0	0	0	0	0	0	0	0	0	0	0	0	0	1	0
mongrel	4	.2427	.2305	33.6	0	0	1	2	1	0	0	0	0	0	0	0	0	0	0	0	0	0	0	0	2	2	0	0	0
Monica	5	.0000	.0748	28.7	0	1	0	0	0	0	0	4	0	0	0	0	5	0	0	0	0	0	0	0	0	0	0	0	0
monitor	12	.5069	1.2921	41.1	2	0	1	4	3	1	1	0	1	0	0	0	0	0	0	3	0	0	0	0	2	0	3	3	0
Monitor	5	.3577	.3868	35.9	0	0	0	3	2	0	0	0	0	0	0	0	0	0	0	0	1	0	0	0	0	0	1	3	0
monitoring	2	.0000	.0243	23.9	0	0	0	0	2	0	0	0	0	0	0	0	0	0	0	0	0	0	0	0	0	0	0	2	0
monitors	2	.2437	.1129	30.5	0	0	0	0	2	0	0	0	0	0	0	0	0	0	0	0	0	0	0	0	0	0	1	1	0
monk	14	.6350	1.8391	42.6	0	2	0	5	5	0	1	1	1	2	0	0	0	5	1	3	1	0	0	0	0	0	0	1	0
Monk	12	.0000	.5482	37.4	0	0	0	0	12	0	0	0	12	0	0	0	0	0	0	0	0	0	0	0	0	0	0	0	0
Monkees	2	.0000	.0243	23.9	0	0	1	0	0	0	0	1	0	0	0	0	0	0	0	0	0	0	0	0	0	0	0	2	0
monkey	144	.8129	23.728	53.8	65	28	15	11	23	2	0	0	64	2	2	12	0	5	3	4	2	1	0	2	31	9	5	2	0
Monkey	11	.3154	.9272	39.7	10	0	0	1	0	0	0	0	7	0	0	0	0	0	0	0	3	0	0	0	0	1	0	0	0
monkey-eating	2	.0000	.0209	23.2	0	0	0	0	2	0	0	0	0	0	0	0	0	0	0	0	0	0	0	0	0	0	2	0	0
monkey's	11	.4430	1.1313	40.5	3	3	1	1	3	0	0	0	5	0	0	3	0	0	0	2	0	0	0	0	1	0	0	0	0
monkeys	124	.8349	20.786	53.2	29	29	18	11	31	1	4	1	33	9	1	5	5	13	1	5	1	2	0	0	10	9	25	5	0
Monkeys	2	.0000	.0234	23.7	0	2	0	0	0	0	0	0	0	0	0	0	0	0	0	0	0	0	0	0	2	0	0	0	0
monkeys'	3	.2346	.1705	32.3	0	2	0	0	0	0	0	1	0	0	0	0	2	0	0	0	0	0	0	0	0	0	0	1	0
monkeyshines	3	.0000	.1370	31.4	2	0	0	0	0	1	0	0	3	0	0	0	0	0	0	0	0	0	0	0	0	0	0	0	0
monks	22	.7190	3.2024	45.1	0	6	5	3	4	2	1	1	2	6	0	1	0	2	2	1	2	0	0	0	1	3	2	0	0
Monmouth	4	.2351	.2146	33.3	0	0	1	0	1	1	0	1	0	0	0	0	0	0	0	0	0	0	0	1	0	0	0	3	0
Mono	2	.2152	.1357	31.3	0	0	1	0	0	1	0	0	1	0	0	0	0	1	0	0	0	0	0	0	0	0	0	0	0
Monocacy	2	.0000	.0209	23.2	0	0	0	0	0	2	0	0	0	0	0	0	0	0	0	0	0	0	0	0	0	0	2	0	0
monochromatic	7	.2951	.4374	36.4	0	0	0	0	1	3	1	2	0	0	0	0	0	0	0	1	2	3	1	0	0	0	0	0	0
monoclinic	3	.2445	.1818	32.6	0	0	0	0	0	0	1	2	0	0	0	0	0	0	0	2	0	0	0	0	0	0	1	0	0
monologue	5	.2844	.3617	35.6	0	0	0	0	2	3	0	0	2	0	1	2	0	0	0	0	0	0	0	0	0	0	0	0	0
monomial	4	.0000	.0599	27.8	0	0	0	0	0	0	4	0	0	0	0	0	4	0	0	0	0	0	0	0	0	0	0	0	0
monomials	3	.0000	.0449	26.5	0	0	0	0	0	0	3	0	0	0	0	0	3	0	0	0	0	0	0	0	0	0	0	0	0
Monongahela	4	.3354	.3295	35.2	0	1	1	1	0	1	0	0	1	0	0	0	0	2	0	0	0	0	0	0	0	1	0	0	0
monopolies	3	.3766	.2497	34.0	0	0	1	0	0	2	0	0	0	0	0	0	0	1	0	0	0	0	0	0	0	1	1	0	0
monopolistic	2	.2433	.1158	30.6	0	0	1	0	0	0	0	1	0	0	0	0	0	0	0	0	0	0	0	0	0	1	0	1	0
monopoly	17	.4240	1.6019	42.0	0	0	3	0	5	9	0	0	1	0	0	0	0	11	0	0	0	0	0	0	0	2	2	1	0
Monopoly	5	.1848	.2301	33.6	0	0	0	0	2	1	2	0	0	1	0	0	0	0	0	0	0	0	0	0	0	0	0	4	0
monoprinting	2	.0000	.0037	15.7	0	0	0	1	1	0	0	0	0	0	0	0	0	0	0	0	0	2	0	0	0	0	0	0	0
monoprints	2	.0000	.0037	15.7	0	0	0	1	1	0	0	0	0	0	0	0	0	0	0	0	0	2	0	0	0	0	0	0	0
monorail	2	.0000	.0299	24.8	1	0	0	0	1	0	0	0	0	0	0	0	2	0	0	0	0	0	0	0	0	0	0	0	0
monotheism	3	.2444	.1814	32.6	0	0	0	0	2	1	0	0	0	0	0	0	0	2	0	0	0	0	0	0	0	0	1	0	0
monotone	2	.1494	.1045	30.2	0	0	0	1	1	0	0	0	1	0	0	0	0	0	0	0	1	0	0	0	0	0	0	0	0
monotonous	16	.6067	1.9891	43.0	1	1	2	3	3	3	3	0	2	1	1	0	0	1	0	1	3	1	4	0	0	1	1	0	0
monotonously	3	.3764	.2483	33.9	0	0	1	0	1	1	0	0	0	0	0	0	0	0	0	1	0	0	0	0	0	0	1	1	0
monotony	7	.4860	.7257	38.6	0	0	0	1	3	2	1	0	1	0	0	2	0	0	0	0	0	0	1	0	1	2	0	0	0
monotremes	4	.0000	.0789	29.0	0	0	0	0	2	0	0	2	0	0	0	0	0	0	0	4	0	0	0	0	0	0	0	0	0
monoxide	15	.2343	.9042	39.6	0	0	0	0	11	4	0	0	0	0	0	0	0	0	0	13	0	0	0	0	0	0	1	1	0
Monroe	13	.4312	1.2264	40.9	1	1	5	0	2	3	1	0	0	0	0	0	0	8	0	0	0	0	0	0	0	2	1	2	0
Monrovia	3	.2425	.1816	32.6	0	1	0	0	1	1	0	0	0	0	0	0	0	2	0	0	0	0	0	0	0	0	0	1	0
Monseigneur	12	.0000	.1288	31.1	0	0	0	0	0	0	12	0	0	0	0	12	0	0	0	0	0	0	0	0	0	0	0	0	0
monsieur	5	.1400	.2438	33.9	2	0	0	0	0	0	3	0	2	0	0	3	0	0	0	0	0	0	0	0	0	0	0	0	0
Monsieur	33	.5063	3.7933	45.8	3	2	8	10	7	1	1	1	19	0	0	5	0	0	0	0	0	0	0	0	6	2	0	1	0
monsoon	13	.2709	.8904	39.5	0	0	1	8	2	1	1	0	1	0	0	0	0	10	0	1	0	0	0	0	0	0	0	1	0
monsoons	4	.0000	.0778	28.9	0	0	0	4	0	0	0	0	0	0	0	0	0	4	0	0	0	0	0	0	0	0	0	0	0
monster	100	.8461	16.972	52.3	10	7	4	10	31	19	10	9	31	5	3	10	0	3	2	8	2	2	0	0	14	6	5	9	0
Monster	7	.0000	.3198	35.0	7	0	0	0	0	0	0	0	7	0	0	0	0	0	0	0	0	0	0	0	0	0	0	0	0
monster's	2	.0000	.0045	16.5	0	0	0	0	0	0	2	0	0	0	2	0	0	0	0	0	0	0	0	0	0	0	0	0	0
monsters	21	.5831	2.5964	44.1	6	1	2	4	4	2	2	0	6	0	0	1	0	2	0	1	0	2	0	0	1	3	4	1	0
monstrous	18	.6047	2.3159	43.6	0	2	1	7	4	1	2	1	7	2	1	0	0	0	0	0	0	0	0	0	2	3	0	3	0
Mont	6	.2861	.3871	35.9	0	0	0	0	4	1	0	1	0	0	0	0	0	0	0	1	1	0	0	0	0	0	4	0	0
Montagu	2	.2408	.1091	30.4	0	1	1	0	0	0	0	0	0	1	0	0	0	0	1	0	0	0	0	0	0	0	0	0	0
Montague	10	.2561	.6126	37.9	0	1	0	0	0	2	7	0	1	0	0	7	0	0	0	0	0	0	0	0	1	1	0	0	0
Montague's	2	.0000	.0215	23.3	0	0	0	0	0	0	2	0	0	0	0	2	0	0	0	0	0	0	0	0	0	0	0	0	0
Montagues	4	.2751	.2689	34.3	0	0	0	0	0	1	3	0	1	0	0	1	0	0	0	0	2	0	0	0	0	0	0	0	0
Montana	52	.6297	6.8117	48.3	6	4	8	6	7	12	5	4	8	0	0	13	3	16	0	1	0	0	0	0	1	3	2	5	0
Montana's	2	.2137	.1056	30.2	1	0	1	0	0	0	0	0	0	0	0	0	0	1	0	0	1	0	0	0	0	0	0	0	0
montane	3	.0000	.0314	25.0	0	0	0	0	3	0	0	0	0	0	0	0	0	0	0	0	0	0	0	0	0	0	3	0	0
Montcalm	7	.4530	.7194	38.6	0	1	0	4	1	1	0	0	2	0	0	0	0	3	0	0	0	0	0	0	1	1	0	0	0
Montclair	6	.4858	.6625	38.2	0	0	0	0	5	1	0	0	3	0	0	1	0	0	0	0	0	0	0	0	0	1	0	1	0
Monte	14	.1604	.6877	38.4	1	11	0	1	0	1	0	0	1	0	0	0	0	12	0	0	0	0	0	0	0	1	0	0	0
Monte's	4	.0000	.0778	28.9	0	4	0	0	0	0	0	0	0	0	0	0	0	4	0	0	0	0	0	0	0	0	0	0	0
Montenegro	5	.2316	.2703	34.3	0	0	0	0	0	3	2	0	0	0	0	0	0	0	0	0	0	0	0	0	0	0	3	2	0
Monterey	12	.3788	1.0361	40.2	0	7	0	3	0	2	0	0	1	0	0	0	0	7	0	0	0	0	0	0	1	0	0	3	0
Monterrey	15	.2435	1.1369	40.6	0	0	10	0	5	0	0	0	10	0	0	0	0	5	0	0	0	0	0	0	0	0	0	0	0
Monteverdi	7	.1929	.3149	35.0	0	2	0	0	0	5	0	0	0	0	0	0	0	0	0	0	5	0	0	0	0	0	2	0	0
Montevideo	6	.2352	.3498	35.4	0	0	0	5	1	0	0	0	0	0	0	0	0	3	0	0	0	0	0	0	0	0	0	3	0
Montezuma	12	.1661	.5768	37.6	0	0	11	0	0	1	0	0	0	0	0	0	0	11	0	0	1	0	0	0	0	0	0	0	0
Montgomery	13	.4554	1.3223	41.2	0	1	1	0	1	7	2	1	3	0	0	0	0	5	0	0	0	0	0	0	0	0	2	3	0
month	403	.8940	71.635	58.6	70	69	49	46	62	45	42	20	80	23	4	17	47	31	23	30	5	0	14	1	24	27	10	67	0
Month	5	.3125	.3478	35.4	0	0	0	0	3	0	1	1	0	0	0	3	1	0	0	0	0	0	0	0	0	0	0	1	0
month's	11	.5868	1.3491	41.3	0	1	1	2	3	2	1	1	2	1	0	0	1	0	0	0	0	0	1	0	1	1	0	4	0
monthly	28	.6767	3.8503	45.9	2	3	1	1	12	2	7	0	2	2	1	0	9	0	0	0	0	0	2	0	2	1	7	2	0
Monthly	2	.0000	.0209	23.2	0	0	1	0	0	1	0	0	0	0	0	0	0	0	0	0	0	0	0	0	0	0	2	0	0
months	658	.8777	115.15	60.6	84	101	91	85	120	74	79	24	129	14	4	17	35	122	15	63	10	1	9	0	31	57	34	117	0
Months	2	.0000	.0914	29.6	0	2	0	0	0	0	0	0	2	0	0	0	0	0	0	0	0	0	0	0	0	0	0	0	0
months'	7	.5517	.8444	39.3	3	0	0	1	2	0	1	0	3	0	0	0	0	1	0	0	1	0	0	0	1	1	0	0	0
Monticello	8	.4186	.7605	38.8	2	1	3	1	1	0	0	0	2	2	0	0	0	1	0	0	0	0	0	0	0	3	0	0	0
Montreal	22	.5281	2.5006	44.0	0	3	7	1	1	4	6	0	4	0	0	0	0	9	0	0	0	0	0	0	1	1	5	2	0
monument	31	.7648	4.7885	46.8	5	4	6	7	3	4	2	0	4	2	0	2	0	8	1	0	2	1	0	0	0	6	3	2	0
Monument	24	.5975	3.0470	44.8	9	5	2	1	3	0	1	3	6	0	0	1	0	6	0	3	0	0	0	0	0	5	0	3	0
monumental	6	.3343	.4455	36.5	0	0	0	1	1	0	4	0	0	0	0	0	0	0	0	1	0	0	0	0	0	0	2	3	0
monuments	29	.5538	3.4140	45.3	3	2	4	0	6	4	9	1	5	2	0	0	0	8	0	2	0	0	0	0	0	1	9	2	0
Monuments	3	.3390	.2450	33.9	0	1	1	0	0	0	1	0	1	0	0	0	0	0	0	0	0	0	0	0	0	0	1	1	0
Monza	5	.3562	.3925	35.9	0	0	1	0	1	0	0	3	0	0	0	0	0	0	0	0	0	0	0	0	0	3	1	1	0
moo	7	.4664	.7388	38.7	4	2	0	0	1	0	0	0	3	1	0	1	0	0	0	0	0	0	0	0	2	0	0	0	0

7R Mongolian-Chinese
6P mongrels
5D Mongrels
7H monitored
4J monkey-baby's
3A monkey-faced
4R monkey-like
9D monkey-puzzle
7R Monkey's
6A monkeying
6G monkeyish
3P Monoclonius
6Q monocotyledon
XJ monodic
8J monody
7R monofilament
5Q monogamy
5B monogram
8F Monogram
5P monolithic
XR monoliths
5P monologues
9F Monomakh
8F monoplane
5H monopolize
7R monopolized
9Q monotheistic
8B monroe
8B monroe's
8F Monroe's
5A Monsen
5A Monsen's
9D Monsieur's
7F Monsoon
7D montage
9D Montala
5A Monterrey's
8J Monteverdi's
6R Montevideo's
5F Montezuma's
9D Montferrat
5H Montgolfier
8F Montgomery's
6A Montignac
8R Montini
8Q montmorillonite
9R Montreat
7A monts
3R Monts-deserts
7F Montt
5R Monty
8R MONY'S
3N moo-oo-oo

Word Type	F	D	U	SFI	3 Gr 3	4 Gr 4	5 Gr 5	6 Gr 6	7 Gr 7	8 Gr 8	9 Gr 9	X UnGr	A Read	B Eng & Gr	C Comp	D Lit	E Math	F Soc Stud	G Spell	H Sci	J Music	K Art	L Home Ec	M Shop	N Lib F	P Lib NF	Q Lib Ref	R Mag	S Rel
mood	220	.6261	28.336	54.5	10	7	20	24	62	54	42	1	39	15	14	20	0	6	0	1	96	5	3	0	4	5	1	11	0
moodily	3	.2292	.1615	32.1	0	0	0	0	1	2	0	0	0	0	0	1	0	0	0	0	0	0	0	0	2	0	0	0	0
moods	32	.4982	3.3288	45.2	2	1	0	3	10	14	2	0	3	1	0	4	0	1	0	1	15	4	1	0	0	2	0	0	0
moody	6	.5293	.6616	38.2	0	0	1	0	3	0	2	0	0	0	0	2	0	0	0	1	0	0	0	0	1	1	0	1	0
Moody	2	.2412	.1141	30.6	1	0	0	0	1	0	0	0	0	1	0	0	0	0	0	0	0	0	0	0	0	1	0	0	0
mooed	2	.0000	.0914	29.6	0	0	1	0	0	1	0	0	2	0	0	0	0	0	0	0	0	0	0	0	0	0	0	0	0
Moog	2	.0000	.0914	29.6	0	0	0	0	2	0	0	0	2	0	0	0	0	0	0	0	0	0	0	0	0	0	0	0	0
mooing	5	.2579	.3658	35.6	0	2	1	1	0	1	0	0	3	0	1	0	0	0	0	0	0	0	0	0	0	0	0	1	0
moon	1046	.8919	185.69	62.7	293	200	81	126	146	57	75	68	194	26	14	60	25	69	24	326	25	1	0	6	27	118	35	95	1
Moon	94	.5992	11.901	50.8	36	25	12	2	8	1	5	5	17	0	0	8	0	3	0	49	3	0	0	0	1	2	4	7	0
MOON	2	.2346	.1166	30.7	1	0	1	0	0	0	0	0	0	0	0	0	0	0	0	1	0	0	0	0	0	0	0	1	0
moon-landing	5	.1398	.1959	32.9	0	0	0	0	5	0	0	0	0	0	0	0	0	1	0	0	0	0	0	0	0	0	0	4	0
moon's	44	.6296	5.7236	47.6	9	5	6	6	5	0	8	5	2	1	0	1	2	6	0	15	2	0	0	0	1	1	0	13	0
Moon's	11	.3663	.9536	39.8	3	2	5	1	0	0	0	0	2	1	0	0	1	0	0	7	0	0	0	0	0	0	0	0	0
moonbeams	3	.3272	.2363	33.7	1	0	1	0	0	0	1	0	1	0	0	1	0	0	0	0	1	0	0	0	0	0	0	0	0
Mooneen	2	.0000	.0914	29.6	0	0	0	0	0	2	0	0	2	0	0	0	0	0	0	0	0	0	0	0	0	0	0	0	0
Mooney	5	.0000	.2284	33.6	0	0	0	5	0	0	0	0	5	0	0	0	0	0	0	0	0	0	0	0	0	0	0	0	0
moonfish	2	.1787	.1174	30.7	0	2	0	0	0	0	0	0	1	0	0	0	0	0	0	0	0	0	0	0	1	0	0	0	0
mooning	2	.0000	.0914	29.6	0	0	0	1	1	0	0	0	2	0	0	0	0	0	0	0	0	0	0	0	0	0	0	0	0
moonless	3	.3365	.2489	34.0	0	0	0	0	1	0	0	2	1	0	0	1	0	0	0	1	0	0	0	0	0	0	0	0	0
moonlight	105	.6962	15.170	51.8	14	20	10	12	9	23	17	0	42	4	1	31	0	2	1	2	1	1	0	0	8	8	0	4	0
Moonlight	3	.2638	.1735	32.4	1	1	1	0	0	0	0	0	0	0	0	0	0	0	0	0	1	1	0	0	0	1	0	0	0
moonlike	2	.0000	.0243	23.9	0	1	0	1	0	0	0	0	0	0	0	0	0	0	0	0	0	0	0	0	0	0	0	2	0
moonlit	8	.5131	.8994	39.5	0	2	2	2	0	1	1	0	3	1	0	0	0	0	0	0	2	0	0	0	1	1	0	0	0
moonrise	3	.2443	.1820	32.6	0	0	0	0	1	0	0	2	0	0	0	1	0	0	0	2	0	0	0	0	0	0	0	0	0
moons	59	.6923	8.4525	49.3	13	11	6	13	6	3	6	1	14	2	0	1	6	3	0	23	1	0	0	0	1	1	6	1	0
moonshine	5	.1794	.2258	33.5	0	0	0	0	1	0	0	4	0	0	0	0	0	0	0	0	0	0	0	0	1	0	0	4	0
moonship	3	.1927	.1491	31.7	0	3	0	0	0	0	0	0	0	0	0	0	0	0	0	1	0	0	0	0	0	0	0	2	0
moonstones	2	.1787	.1174	30.7	0	0	0	1	1	0	0	0	1	0	0	0	0	0	0	0	0	0	0	0	1	0	0	0	0
moor	5	.4755	.5341	37.3	0	1	0	1	0	2	1	0	2	1	0	1	0	0	0	0	0	0	0	0	0	1	0	0	0
Moor	24	.2918	1.7377	42.4	0	4	1	8	8	0	3	0	8	0	0	0	0	0	0	0	12	0	0	0	1	0	0	3	0
Moore	33	.5127	3.5637	45.5	3	9	1	8	2	8	2	0	3	0	0	0	1	0	0	2	4	4	0	0	3	14	2	0	0
Moore's	5	.3094	.3425	35.3	0	1	0	2	0	1	1	0	0	0	0	0	0	0	0	0	0	1	0	0	0	3	1	0	0
moored	5	.3832	.4743	36.8	1	0	1	1	1	0	1	0	3	1	0	0	0	0	0	0	0	0	0	0	0	0	1	0	0
mooring	4	.3696	.3616	35.6	0	0	0	1	1	1	1	0	2	1	0	0	0	0	0	0	0	0	0	0	0	0	1	0	0
moorings	3	.3553	.2608	34.2	0	1	1	0	0	1	0	0	1	0	0	0	0	1	0	0	0	0	0	0	0	1	0	0	0
Moorish	4	.3676	.3150	35.0	0	0	1	2	1	0	0	0	0	0	0	0	0	0	0	0	1	0	0	0	0	0	2	1	0
moors	4	.3287	.2952	34.7	0	1	0	1	2	0	0	0	0	0	0	0	0	1	0	0	0	0	0	0	0	1	2	0	0
Moors	15	.4863	1.5415	41.9	0	0	1	3	5	0	6	0	0	0	0	0	0	5	0	0	2	0	0	0	6	1	0	1	0
moose	52	.6467	7.1420	48.5	1	23	12	2	9	1	0	4	26	2	0	2	4	3	0	0	1	0	0	0	0	0	10	4	0
Moose	11	.4095	1.0587	40.2	4	0	2	2	0	0	1	2	5	0	1	0	0	0	0	0	0	0	0	0	0	1	0	4	0
mop	16	.4980	1.7247	42.4	2	3	1	4	1	2	0	3	4	0	0	0	0	0	0	0	3	0	0	0	5	1	0	3	0
moped	2	.2407	.1138	30.6	0	1	0	0	1	0	0	0	0	0	0	1	0	0	0	0	0	0	0	0	0	1	0	0	0
mopped	3	.2261	.2131	33.3	0	0	0	2	0	0	0	1	2	0	0	0	0	0	0	0	0	0	0	0	1	0	0	0	0
mopping	5	.3311	.4118	36.1	1	2	0	0	0	2	0	0	2	0	0	0	0	0	0	0	0	0	0	0	2	1	0	0	0
mops	7	.5645	.8570	39.3	0	1	0	0	2	3	1	0	3	1	0	1	0	0	0	0	0	0	0	0	1	1	0	0	0
Mor	4	.0000	.1827	32.6	4	0	0	0	0	0	0	0	4	0	0	0	0	0	0	0	0	0	0	0	0	0	0	0	0
moraine	10	.0000	.1972	32.9	0	0	5	0	0	0	5	0	0	0	0	0	0	0	0	10	0	0	0	0	0	0	0	0	0
moraines	7	.1941	.3707	35.7	0	0	3	0	0	0	4	0	0	0	0	0	0	0	0	6	0	0	0	0	0	0	1	0	0
moral	53	.7236	7.8041	48.9	2	0	3	1	16	22	6	3	10	1	1	12	0	2	0	2	2	0	0	0	2	3	6	12	0
morale	7	.5201	.7640	38.8	1	1	0	0	2	1	2	0	0	0	0	0	0	1	0	1	0	0	0	0	0	2	2	1	0
morality	12	.3202	.8607	39.3	0	0	0	0	2	5	2	3	0	0	0	0	0	2	0	0	0	0	0	0	0	0	3	7	0
morally	2	.2440	.1132	30.5	0	0	0	0	0	0	1	1	0	0	0	1	0	0	0	0	0	0	0	0	0	0	0	1	0
morals	8	.5110	.8510	39.3	1	0	1	0	1	3	2	0	0	1	0	3	0	1	0	0	0	0	0	0	0	0	1	2	0
Moran	4	.2954	.2881	34.6	0	1	1	0	0	0	1	1	1	0	0	2	0	0	0	0	0	0	0	0	0	0	0	1	0
morass	2	.2427	.1152	30.6	0	0	1	0	1	0	0	0	0	0	0	0	0	0	0	0	0	0	0	0	1	1	0	0	0
moratorium	3	.0000	.0365	25.6	0	0	0	0	0	1	2	0	0	0	0	0	0	0	0	0	0	0	0	0	0	0	0	3	0
Moravia	2	.2137	.1056	30.2	0	0	1	1	0	0	0	0	0	0	0	0	0	1	0	0	1	0	0	0	0	0	0	0	0
Moravian	8	.1872	.3959	36.0	0	0	5	2	1	0	0	0	1	0	0	0	0	2	0	0	5	0	0	0	0	0	0	0	0
Moravians	5	.0000	.0404	26.1	0	0	4	0	0	1	0	0	0	0	0	0	0	0	0	0	5	0	0	0	0	0	0	0	0
more	9992	.9917	1948.8	72.9	1554	1344	1252	1233	1995	1232	1100	282	1938	623	79	420	752	1288	400	1123	322	108	216	101	465	740	669	742	6
More	19	.3901	1.6322	42.1	5	1	4	0	3	5	0	1	3	2	0	0	0	0	9	0	0	0	0	0	0	1	4	0	0
MORE	2	.2285	.1129	30.5	0	0	0	0	0	0	2	0	0	0	0	0	0	1	0	0	0	0	0	0	0	0	1	0	0
more'n	3	.3408	.2477	33.9	1	0	0	0	1	1	0	0	1	0	0	1	0	0	0	0	0	0	0	0	0	1	0	0	0
Morehead	4	.0000	.0486	26.9	0	0	0	0	4	0	0	0	0	0	0	0	0	0	0	0	0	0	0	0	0	0	0	4	0
Morely	15	.0000	.2917	34.6	15	0	0	0	0	0	0	0	0	0	0	0	0	15	0	0	0	0	0	0	0	0	0	0	0
Morenci	7	.0000	.1361	31.3	0	0	7	0	0	0	0	0	0	0	0	0	0	7	0	0	0	0	0	0	0	0	0	0	0
moreover	110	.8480	18.630	52.7	1	5	8	12	36	22	21	5	12	9	0	5	1	24	3	16	3	0	2	0	3	10	11	11	0
Moreover	7	.0000	.0751	28.8	0	0	0	0	0	0	7	0	0	0	0	7	0	0	0	0	0	0	0	0	0	0	0	0	0
mores	5	.2418	.2811	34.5	0	0	0	0	1	1	1	2	0	0	0	0	0	0	0	0	0	0	0	0	0	0	2	3	0
Moresby	2	.0000	.0209	23.2	0	0	0	0	0	2	0	0	0	0	0	0	0	0	0	0	0	0	0	0	0	0	2	0	0
Morgan	123	.6241	16.525	52.2	27	8	62	2	18	4	2	0	68	0	0	13	0	8	0	0	0	0	0	0	6	9	2	17	0
Morgan's	14	.3123	1.2569	41.0	0	1	13	0	0	0	0	0	12	0	0	0	0	1	0	0	0	0	0	0	0	0	1	0	0
Morgiana	31	.3039	2.2552	43.5	0	15	0	16	0	0	0	0	7	15	0	9	0	0	0	0	0	0	0	0	0	0	0	0	0
Morgiana's	2	.0000	.0215	23.3	0	0	0	2	0	0	0	0	0	0	0	2	0	0	0	0	0	0	0	0	0	0	0	0	0
Mori	3	.0000	.0365	25.6	0	0	0	0	0	0	0	3	0	0	0	0	0	0	0	0	0	0	0	0	0	0	0	3	0
Morin	2	.0000	.0243	23.9	0	0	0	0	2	0	0	0	0	0	0	0	0	0	0	0	0	0	0	0	0	0	0	2	0
Mormon	5	.2138	.2693	34.3	0	0	2	1	2	0	0	0	0	0	0	0	0	2	0	0	0	0	0	0	0	0	0	3	0
Mormons	9	.5222	.9862	39.9	0	0	6	1	0	2	0	0	0	0	0	0	0	4	0	0	2	0	0	0	0	1	1	1	0
morn	15	.4843	1.5831	42.0	3	0	1	2	6	1	2	0	4	0	0	5	0	0	0	0	3	0	0	0	0	2	0	1	0
mornin'	9	.5060	.9955	40.0	1	1	2	0	3	2	0	0	3	0	0	3	0	0	0	0	1	0	0	0	1	1	0	0	0
morning	1736	.8676	302.23	64.8	484	333	145	232	301	134	85	22	763	57	34	152	30	97	11	61	50	0	5	1	190	177	17	89	2
Morning	9	.3407	.6873	38.4	2	0	2	4	1	0	0	0	1	1	0	0	0	0	0	1	5	0	0	0	1	0	0	0	0
morning-glory	2	.1972	.1262	31.0	0	1	0	0	1	0	0	0	1	0	0	0	1	0	0	0	0	0	0	0	0	0	0	0	0
morning's	9	.5201	1.0151	40.1	1	1	1	2	1	0	2	1	3	0	0	2	0	0	0	0	2	0	0	0	1	0	0	1	0
mornings	37	.6797	5.2113	47.2	6	7	2	7	8	1	3	3	11	3	0	5	0	0	1	5	0	0	0	0	7	1	0	4	0
morns	3	.3272	.2363	33.7	1	0	2	0	0	0	0	0	1	0	0	1	0	0	0	0	1	0	0	0	0	0	0	0	0
Moro	2	.0000	.0209	23.2	1	0	0	0	0	1	0	0	0	0	0	0	0	0	0	0	0	0	0	0	0	0	2	0	0
Moroccan	2	.2152	.1357	31.3	0	0	0	1	0	0	1	0	1	0	0	0	0	1	0	0	0	0	0	0	0	0	0	0	0
Morocco	41	.6325	5.3548	47.3	2	2	0	19	7	3	8	0	2	0	0	6	0	23	2	1	1	1	0	0	2	0	3	0	0
moron	2	.1733	.1149	30.6	0	0	0	0	0	2	0	0	1	1	0	0	0	0	0	0	0	0	0	0	0	0	0	0	0

9D Mood
XQ moodier
7J Moods
4A Mool
5Q moom
6N moon-dappled
5B moon-flecked
3P moon-god
6A moon-light
7R moon-magnet
5F moon-shaped
3F moon-shot
9J moon-silvered
8F moon-struck
5A moon-washed
6N moon-white
3A moonbus
8B moone
XH moonfull
9D moonlighting
5C Moonmen
5A moonpath
6R moonquake
4R moonquakes
7H moonscapes
9D moonshines
8G moonstruck
3R moonwalk
8R moonward
6E moonweight
3J moony
7Q moorhens
7A moorish
XH Moorth
8P Moortje
4A moos
7N moose-meat
5Q mooselike
5N moostrap
4A mope
3B mopes
9D moping
7A moppets
8A moppings
5R moppy-haired
6A mor
3A Mor's
9H morainal
8J Morales
5P moralists
9A moralized
9Q Moralls
7Q morasses
8R Moratorium
7B moray
7A morbid
6R morbidly
8Q Mordvinov
7R more-conservative
7R more-elaborate
5R more-or-less
7R more-than-liberal
4J more's
6J Moreen
8J Morelia
7P Morell
7R Morelos
6F Moreno
6F Moreno's
9D Moreover's
9H morganite
5A Morgans'
3R Morgen
6A Morgina
8J Morley
7F Mormonism
4J Morn
8B morne
5R Morne
9R morning-staff
6F Moroccans

Word Type	F	D	U	SFI	3 Gr 3	4 Gr 4	5 Gr 5	6 Gr 6	7 Gr 7	8 Gr 8	9 Gr 9	X UnGr	A Read	B Eng & Gr	C Comp	D Lit	E Math	F Soc Stud	G Spell	H Sci	J Music	K Art	L Home Ec	M Shop	N Lib F	P Lib NF	Q Lib Ref	R Mag	S Rel
Moros	5	.0000	.0523	27.2	4	0	0	0	0	1	0	0	0	0	0	0	0	0	0	0	0	0	0	0	0	0	5	0	0
morpheme	93	.2422	5.1019	47.1	0	0	21	29	31	6	6	0	0	48	0	0	0	0	45	0	0	0	0	0	0	0	0	0	0
morphemes	32	.2185	1.6302	42.1	0	0	5	12	3	9	3	0	0	24	0	0	0	0	8	0	0	0	0	0	0	0	0	0	0
morphine	3	.3870	.2486	34.0	0	0	1	0	0	0	2	0	0	0	0	1	0	0	0	0	0	0	0	0	0	0	1	1	0
Morrall	6	.0000	.0729	28.6	0	0	0	2	2	2	0	0	0	0	0	0	0	0	0	0	0	0	0	0	0	0	0	6	0
Morris	17	.5355	1.9073	42.8	0	0	2	0	4	7	1	3	0	0	0	3	3	4	0	2	0	0	0	0	0	0	0	5	0
Morrison	8	.3174	.6556	38.2	0	1	4	0	3	0	0	0	4	0	0	3	0	0	0	0	0	0	0	0	0	1	0	0	0
Morrissey	2	.1948	.1250	31.0	0	1	0	1	0	0	0	0	1	0	0	0	0	0	0	0	0	0	0	0	0	1	0	0	0
morrow	15	.5573	1.7950	42.5	0	0	1	8	2	0	4	0	5	1	0	4	0	0	0	0	0	0	0	0	3	1	0	1	0
Mors	3	.0000	.0434	26.4	0	0	0	0	0	0	0	3	0	0	0	0	0	0	0	0	0	0	0	0	0	3	0	0	0
Morse	41	.5086	4.5996	46.6	0	20	5	1	12	2	1	0	14	0	0	0	0	1	3	3	1	0	0	0	0	18	1	0	0
morsel	9	.5013	.9892	40.0	0	0	0	4	0	2	3	0	3	0	0	3	0	0	0	0	0	0	0	0	1	1	1	0	0
morsels	5	.3217	.3548	35.5	0	0	0	0	2	1	2	0	0	0	0	3	0	0	0	0	0	0	0	0	0	1	1	0	0
Mort	5	.2341	.2687	34.3	4	0	0	0	1	0	0	0	0	0	0	0	0	0	0	0	0	1	0	0	0	0	0	4	0
Mortain	5	.0000	.2284	33.6	0	0	0	5	0	0	0	0	5	0	0	0	0	0	0	0	0	0	0	0	0	0	0	0	0
mortal	32	.5073	3.5025	45.4	2	3	2	4	4	5	10	2	8	1	0	13	0	0	0	0	3	0	0	0	0	4	0	3	0
mortality	7	.2635	.4293	36.3	0	1	0	1	4	1	0	0	0	0	0	0	0	1	0	0	0	0	0	0	0	0	1	5	0
mortally	5	.3682	.4515	36.5	0	0	2	2	0	0	1	0	2	0	0	0	0	2	0	0	0	0	0	0	1	0	0	0	0
mortals	8	.4624	.7781	38.9	2	0	0	1	3	0	2	0	0	0	0	3	0	0	0	0	0	0	0	0	2	2	1	0	0
mortar	28	.6952	3.9872	46.0	16	1	0	1	3	2	4	1	6	0	0	1	0	2	1	2	2	0	0	2	1	0	4	7	0
mortars	4	.2420	.3089	34.9	0	0	0	0	3	1	0	0	3	0	0	0	0	1	0	0	0	0	0	0	0	0	0	0	0
Morten	2	.0000	.0290	24.6	0	0	0	0	2	0	0	0	0	0	0	0	0	0	0	0	0	0	0	0	0	2	0	0	0
mortgage	8	.5888	.9857	39.9	0	0	1	0	2	2	3	0	1	0	0	0	1	2	0	0	0	0	0	0	1	0	1	2	0
Mortgage	2	.2351	.1166	30.7	0	0	0	0	0	1	1	0	0	0	0	0	0	1	0	0	0	0	0	0	0	0	0	1	0
mortgages	4	.1505	.1615	32.1	0	0	1	0	2	1	0	0	0	0	0	0	0	1	0	0	0	0	0	0	0	0	3	0	0
mortified	4	.3030	.2949	34.7	0	1	1	0	2	0	0	0	1	0	0	0	0	0	0	0	0	0	0	0	2	0	0	1	0
Mortimer	5	.0000	.0608	27.8	0	5	0	0	0	0	0	0	0	0	0	0	0	0	0	0	0	0	0	0	0	0	0	5	0
MORTIMER	3	.0000	.0365	25.6	0	3	0	0	0	0	0	0	0	0	0	0	0	0	0	0	0	0	0	0	0	0	0	3	0
Morton	10	.4394	.9242	39.7	0	1	3	1	3	1	1	0	0	0	0	0	0	0	0	0	3	0	0	0	0	1	2	4	0
Morvidd	4	.0000	.1827	32.6	0	0	0	0	4	0	0	0	4	0	0	0	0	0	0	0	0	0	0	0	0	0	0	0	0
mos'	3	.0000	.0352	25.5	0	0	0	0	3	0	0	0	0	0	0	0	0	0	0	0	0	0	0	0	3	0	0	0	0
mosaic	8	.4324	.7243	38.6	0	0	0	3	2	2	0	1	0	0	0	0	2	0	0	1	0	2	0	1	0	0	1	1	0
Mosaic	2	.0000	.0209	23.2	0	0	0	0	0	2	0	0	0	0	0	0	0	0	0	0	0	0	0	0	0	0	2	0	0
mosaics	5	.1812	.2068	33.2	1	0	0	2	1	0	0	1	0	0	0	0	0	0	0	0	0	2	0	0	0	0	3	0	0
Mosby	11	.0000	.1337	31.3	11	0	0	0	0	0	0	0	0	0	0	0	0	0	0	0	0	0	0	0	0	0	0	11	0
Moscow	43	.5541	4.9806	47.0	0	2	0	15	1	13	12	0	0	0	0	5	2	22	0	0	2	0	0	0	0	0	3	9	0
Moses	61	.2526	3.6473	45.6	14	17	11	1	11	3	4	0	4	0	0	10	0	4	0	0	2	2	0	0	3	20	11	0	5
Moses-Poses	2	.0000	.0290	24.6	0	2	0	0	0	0	0	0	0	0	0	0	0	0	0	0	0	0	0	0	0	2	0	0	0
Moshe	2	.2351	.1166	30.7	0	0	0	0	0	1	1	0	0	0	0	0	0	1	0	0	0	0	0	0	0	0	0	1	0
Moslem	33	.4503	3.1988	45.0	7	3	3	5	10	1	1	3	0	3	0	0	0	17	0	0	0	0	0	0	0	1	10	2	0
Moslems	34	.3716	2.8752	44.6	2	2	4	7	16	1	0	2	1	2	0	0	0	25	0	0	0	0	0	0	0	2	4	0	0
mosque	9	.3208	.6691	38.3	0	3	1	2	2	1	0	0	0	0	0	0	0	7	0	0	0	1	0	0	1	0	0	0	0
mosques	6	.4921	.6367	38.0	0	0	1	1	3	0	1	0	1	0	0	1	0	1	0	0	0	0	0	0	0	1	2	0	0
mosquito	67	.6934	9.7108	49.9	21	9	7	7	15	3	0	5	27	0	1	4	0	5	1	21	0	0	0	0	1	3	4	0	0
mosquito's	2	.0000	.0209	23.2	0	0	0	0	1	0	1	0	0	0	0	0	0	0	0	0	0	0	0	0	0	0	2	0	0
mosquitoes	121	.6647	16.883	52.3	38	6	28	19	10	7	3	10	41	2	0	3	0	5	0	44	0	0	0	0	9	8	5	4	0
moss	81	.7489	12.373	50.9	10	17	4	10	23	6	8	3	21	2	1	9	0	1	1	25	3	4	0	0	7	3	1	3	0
moss-covered	2	.0000	.0389	25.9	0	0	0	0	0	2	0	0	0	0	0	0	0	2	0	0	0	0	0	0	0	0	0	0	0
mosses	44	.3926	3.9066	45.9	6	11	2	5	14	2	3	1	2	0	0	0	0	2	0	31	0	0	0	0	2	1	6	0	0
mossy	12	.6975	1.7101	42.3	2	1	2	1	4	1	0	1	2	1	0	2	0	0	0	1	1	0	0	0	2	2	0	1	0
most	5785	.9431	1078.2	70.3	734	579	819	851	1269	701	668	164	797	293	67	200	81	1247	203	725	210	33	102	107	148	427	676	468	1
Most	11	.5058	1.2229	40.9	1	0	0	4	1	2	0	3	4	1	0	0	0	0	0	0	1	0	0	0	1	0	0	4	0
mostest	3	.2197	.2090	33.2	1	0	0	0	2	0	0	0	2	0	0	0	0	0	0	0	0	0	0	0	0	0	1	0	0
mostly	252	.8832	44.329	56.5	33	34	44	29	56	26	24	6	43	13	3	15	1	47	1	47	6	0	2	2	11	16	27	18	0
Mosul	2	.0000	.0389	25.9	0	0	0	2	0	0	0	0	0	0	0	0	0	2	0	0	0	0	0	0	0	0	0	0	0
mot	2	.2444	.1132	30.5	0	1	0	0	0	0	1	0	0	1	0	0	0	0	0	0	0	0	0	0	1	0	0	0	0
Mote	2	.0000	.0209	23.2	0	0	0	0	1	0	1	0	0	0	0	0	0	0	0	0	0	0	0	0	0	0	2	0	0
motel	34	.5577	4.2329	46.3	5	0	1	22	2	1	2	1	21	0	0	0	0	4	2	1	0	0	0	0	1	0	0	5	0
Motel	7	.0000	.3198	35.0	0	0	0	7	0	0	0	0	7	0	0	0	0	0	0	0	0	0	0	0	0	0	0	0	0
motels	9	.4823	.9332	39.7	1	0	5	1	0	0	0	2	1	0	0	0	4	0	0	0	0	0	0	0	0	1	1	2	0
motes	2	.2440	.1132	30.5	0	1	0	0	0	0	1	0	0	0	0	1	0	0	0	0	0	0	0	0	0	0	0	1	0
moth	60	.5974	7.5368	48.8	25	7	3	7	15	2	1	0	7	0	0	1	0	4	0	30	0	0	1	0	2	10	5	0	0
Moth	12	.2879	.7867	39.0	3	0	0	0	8	0	1	0	0	0	0	1	0	0	0	0	0	0	0	0	0	3	0	8	0
MOTH	3	.0000	.0322	25.1	0	0	0	0	0	0	3	0	0	0	0	3	0	0	0	0	0	0	0	0	0	0	0	0	0
moth's	4	.4502	.4038	36.1	2	0	0	0	1	1	0	0	1	0	0	0	1	0	0	1	0	0	0	0	0	0	1	0	0
mothball	2	.2346	.1166	30.7	1	0	0	0	0	1	0	0	0	0	0	0	0	0	0	1	0	0	0	0	0	0	0	1	0
mother	2343	.8928	417.67	66.2	758	504	169	283	329	147	93	60	964	84	42	201	60	120	34	89	38	9	28	3	246	274	40	111	0
Mother	1005	.8183	166.23	62.2	362	261	79	116	79	41	60	7	387	52	12	104	9	69	34	1	19	1	4	0	115	160	3	35	0
MOTHER	36	.0000	.3863	35.9	0	0	0	0	10	26	0	0	0	0	0	36	0	0	0	0	0	0	0	0	0	0	0	0	0
mother-in-law	2	.2412	.1141	30.6	0	0	0	0	2	0	0	0	0	1	0	0	0	0	0	0	0	0	0	0	0	1	0	0	0
mother-of-pearl	7	.5590	.8526	39.3	0	0	2	1	1	2	0	1	3	0	0	1	0	0	0	1	0	0	0	0	1	0	1	0	0
mother'd	2	.0000	.0914	29.6	0	1	0	1	0	0	0	0	2	0	0	0	0	0	0	0	0	0	0	0	0	0	0	0	0
mother's	202	.7886	32.325	55.1	34	44	23	33	33	16	10	9	71	4	8	22	0	3	1	12	4	0	4	0	23	32	3	15	0
Mother's	52	.6840	7.5199	48.8	11	15	6	9	6	2	1	2	31	1	1	3	0	1	1	0	0	0	0	0	3	9	0	2	0
Mothergooseville	2	.0000	.0243	23.9	2	0	0	0	0	0	0	0	0	0	0	0	0	0	0	0	0	0	0	0	0	0	0	2	0
motherhood	3	.1277	.1363	31.3	0	0	0	1	0	0	1	1	1	0	0	0	0	0	0	0	0	0	0	0	0	0	0	2	0
motherless	6	.2223	.4212	36.2	0	0	1	2	2	0	1	0	4	2	0	0	0	0	0	0	0	0	0	0	0	0	0	0	0
motherly	3	.1250	.1342	31.3	0	1	0	0	2	0	0	0	1	0	0	0	0	0	0	0	0	0	0	0	2	0	0	0	0
mothers	126	.8681	21.857	53.4	41	20	8	14	22	8	10	3	34	5	2	14	2	13	2	6	4	0	3	0	13	17	1	10	0
Mothers	7	.2083	.3739	35.7	1	1	0	0	5	0	0	0	1	1	0	5	0	0	0	0	0	0	0	0	0	0	0	0	0
mothers'	8	.5123	.8772	39.4	6	1	0	1	0	0	0	0	1	0	0	0	0	0	0	2	0	0	0	0	0	2	2	1	0
moths	58	.5420	6.6066	48.2	30	7	1	9	10	0	0	1	1	0	0	1	1	6	0	18	0	0	0	0	0	17	13	1	0
Moths	5	.2183	.2661	34.3	5	0	0	0	0	0	0	0	0	0	0	0	0	0	0	0	1	0	0	0	0	4	0	0	0
motif	3	.0902	.0676	28.3	0	0	0	0	3	0	0	0	0	0	0	0	0	0	0	0	0	2	0	0	0	0	0	1	0
motion	393	.8643	67.657	58.3	27	39	36	69	71	82	50	19	38	43	4	7	5	19	4	127	32	5	4	7	7	18	58	15	0
Motion	5	.3617	.4606	36.6	0	0	1	3	0	1	0	0	3	0	0	0	0	0	0	1	1	0	0	0	0	0	0	0	0
motion-picture	9	.6080	1.1293	40.5	0	1	1	1	3	2	1	0	0	0	0	0	2	2	0	1	0	0	0	0	0	1	1	2	0
motioned	24	.5806	3.0171	44.8	2	3	3	3	5	6	2	0	11	0	0	4	0	1	0	0	0	0	0	0	4	2	0	2	0
motioning	6	.3598	.5339	37.3	0	1	0	2	2	0	1	0	3	0	0	1	0	0	0	0	0	0	0	0	2	0	0	0	0
motionless	43	.7280	6.4348	48.1	3	5	5	9	5	8	4	4	15	2	1	8	0	1	1	4	0	0	0	0	6	4	0	1	0
motions	66	.7528	10.053	50.0	7	12	9	5	12	9	9	3	7	3	0	6	2	3	0	20	9	0	0	0	3	7	4	2	0
motivate	2	.2437	.1129	30.5	1	0	1	0	0	0	0	0	0	0	0	0	0	0	0	0	0	0	0	0	0	0	1	1	0
motivated	9	.3543	.7082	38.5	0	0	1	0	4	4	0	0	1	0	0	0	0	0	0	0	2	0	0	0	0	0	5	1	0
motivating	4	.3676	.3150	35.0	0	0	0	1	0	2	0	1	0	0	0	0	0	0	0	0	1	0	0	0	0	0	2	1	0
motivation	5	.2418	.2811	34.5	0	0	0	0	1	1	3	0	0	0	0	0	0	0	0	0	0	0	0	0	0	0	2	3	0
motive	34	.3362	2.5515	44.1	0	7	3	2	17	2	2	1	4	1	0	1	0	1	0	0	21	0	0	0	0	0	4	2	0

8D morose
8D morrah
7A Morrell
7A Morrell's
XR Morrill
4P Morrison's
XR Morrow
8A Morshead
8G mort
7D mortal's
7Q mortalities
7D mortared
6A Morte
7P Morten's
8N mortgaged
9D mortify
8R mortis
7P mortiser
7N morts
7A Morvidd's
7Q mos
XR Mosca
6P Moscheles
6F Moscow's
5F Moses'
7F Mosque
5A mosquito-bitten
5F mosquitoes'
9D moss-greened
6A moss-hung
5J most-loved
7A mosta
7D Mosten's
6B motch
6G motel**
8L moth-resistant
7R Moth's
3H mothballs
6Q mother-inherited
6A mother-of-pearl-colored
3Q mother-substitute
7R mothers-in-law
3P moths'
7H motifs
5G motio
7R motivates
3J Motive

Word Type	F	D	U	SFI	3 Gr 3	4 Gr 4	5 Gr 5	6 Gr 6	7 Gr 7	8 Gr 8	9 Gr 9	X UnGr	A Read	B Eng & Gr	C Comp	D Lit	E Math	F Soc Stud	G Spell	H Sci	J Music	K Art	L Home Ec	M Shop	N Lib F	P Lib NF	Q Lib Ref	R Mag	S Rel
motives	18	.2181	.9860	39.9	0	7	1	1	5	4	0	0	3	0	0	0	0	1	0	0	12	0	0	0	0	0	2	0	0
motley	3	.3765	.2537	34.0	0	1	0	0	1	1	0	0	0	0	0	0	0	1	0	1	0	0	0	0	1	0	0	0	0
motor	198	.8178	32.613	55.1	23	29	14	22	70	19	18	3	57	10	5	9	3	8	1	30	11	0	0	12	7	8	15	22	0
Motor	6	.3776	.4985	37.0	0	0	0	0	1	2	2	1	0	2	0	0	0	0	0	2	0	0	0	0	0	0	0	2	0
motor-driven	2	.0000	.0914	29.6	0	0	0	2	0	0	0	0	2	0	0	0	0	0	0	0	0	0	0	0	0	0	0	0	0
motor-vehicle	2	.0000	.0299	24.8	0	0	0	0	2	0	0	0	0	0	0	0	2	0	0	0	0	0	0	0	0	0	0	0	0
motor's	2	.1497	.1046	30.2	0	1	0	0	0	1	0	0	1	0	0	0	0	0	1	0	0	0	0	0	0	0	0	2	0
motorbike	2	.0000	.0243	23.9	0	0	0	1	0	0	0	1	0	0	0	0	0	0	0	0	0	0	0	0	0	0	0	0	0
motorboat	6	.4536	.5939	37.7	2	1	1	0	1	1	0	0	1	1	1	0	1	0	0	1	0	0	0	0	0	1	0	0	0
motorboats	3	.2256	.1788	32.5	1	0	0	1	0	0	1	0	1	1	0	0	0	0	0	0	0	0	0	1	0	0	0	0	0
motorcade	3	.3815	.2534	34.0	0	0	0	0	1	2	0	0	0	0	0	0	0	1	0	0	0	0	0	0	0	1	0	1	0
motorcycle	18	.5484	2.1383	43.3	1	1	11	1	2	0	2	0	6	2	0	0	0	1	0	1	0	0	0	0	0	3	0	5	0
motorcycles	9	.4564	.8849	39.5	1	4	0	1	1	1	1	0	0	1	0	0	0	5	0	0	0	0	0	0	0	0	1	2	0
motoring	2	.0000	.0243	23.9	0	0	0	0	1	0	0	1	0	0	0	0	0	0	0	0	0	0	0	0	0	0	0	2	0
motorist	8	.3496	.6249	38.0	0	0	2	1	0	0	3	2	1	2	2	0	0	1	0	0	0	0	0	0	0	0	0	2	0
motorists	15	.4450	1.4249	41.5	0	4	1	1	3	4	0	2	0	2	0	0	0	1	0	1	0	0	0	0	0	4	0	7	0
motorized	4	.3104	.2995	34.8	0	0	0	1	2	1	0	0	1	0	0	0	0	0	0	0	0	0	0	0	0	0	1	2	0
motors	76	.6923	10.918	50.4	6	29	4	10	12	10	3	2	26	1	3	0	0	8	2	18	1	0	0	6	0	2	6	3	0
Motors	13	.4677	1.2966	41.1	0	0	1	1	4	2	5	0	1	0	1	0	0	2	0	0	0	0	0	0	0	0	3	6	0
mottled	4	.1613	.1522	31.8	0	0	1	1	1	0	1	0	0	0	0	0	0	0	0	0	0	2	0	0	0	1	0	1	0
motto	17	.5952	2.1756	43.4	3	3	3	5	3	0	0	0	8	1	0	0	0	0	0	0	2	0	0	0	0	1	3	2	0
Motuan	2	.0000	.0914	29.6	0	0	0	2	0	0	0	0	2	0	0	0	0	0	0	0	0	0	0	0	0	0	0	0	0
mought	4	.1826	.1841	32.7	1	0	0	0	3	0	0	0	0	0	0	0	0	0	0	0	0	0	0	0	3	1	0	0	0
moujik	4	.0000	.0579	27.6	4	0	0	0	0	0	0	0	0	0	0	0	0	0	0	0	0	0	0	0	0	4	0	0	0
mould	2	.2407	.1138	30.6	0	0	0	0	2	0	0	0	0	0	0	1	0	0	0	0	0	0	0	0	0	1	0	0	0
Moultrie	2	.0000	.0209	23.2	0	2	0	0	0	0	0	0	0	0	0	0	0	0	0	0	0	0	0	0	0	0	2	0	0
mound	51	.7811	8.1128	49.1	8	9	10	11	6	2	3	2	20	2	1	1	0	0	0	4	4	0	0	0	5	7	3	4	0
Mound	7	.1702	.3149	35.0	6	0	0	0	0	1	0	0	0	0	0	0	0	0	0	0	0	0	0	0	0	6	1	0	0
mounds	28	.7026	4.0184	46.0	8	3	4	3	4	3	2	1	4	1	1	1	0	2	0	4	0	0	0	0	0	6	5	4	0
mount	42	.7835	6.6626	48.2	5	3	4	7	17	6	0	0	10	1	0	5	1	2	0	6	1	0	0	1	3	8	0	4	0
Mount	151	.7772	23.795	53.8	27	8	25	27	28	19	17	0	32	3	1	1	14	35	2	17	1	0	0	0	0	10	19	16	0
mountain	838	.8599	144.44	61.6	158	122	151	119	188	40	51	9	251	17	5	62	14	163	2	108	14	2	1	0	34	43	86	34	2
Mountain	150	.7873	23.965	53.8	9	20	25	32	38	11	6	9	47	2	0	14	0	24	0	8	13	1	0	0	2	13	9	17	0
mountain-ash	3	.0000	.1370	31.4	0	0	0	3	0	0	0	0	3	0	0	0	0	0	0	0	0	0	0	0	0	0	0	0	0
mountain-building	2	.0000	.0394	26.0	0	0	0	0	0	1	1	0	0	0	0	0	0	0	0	2	0	0	0	0	0	0	0	0	0
mountain-like	2	.1948	.1250	31.0	1	1	0	0	0	0	0	0	1	0	0	0	0	0	0	0	0	0	0	0	0	1	0	0	0
mountain's	5	.3667	.3948	36.0	0	0	0	0	3	0	2	0	0	0	0	2	0	0	0	0	0	0	0	0	0	0	2	1	0
mountaineer	5	.3838	.4772	36.8	1	1	0	2	0	0	1	0	3	1	0	0	0	0	0	0	0	0	0	0	0	1	0	0	0
mountaineer's	2	.2407	.1138	30.6	1	0	0	0	0	0	1	0	0	0	0	1	0	0	0	0	0	0	0	0	0	1	0	0	0
mountaineering	2	.2407	.1138	30.6	0	0	1	0	0	1	0	0	0	0	0	1	0	0	0	0	0	0	0	0	0	1	0	0	0
mountaineers	5	.4642	.4852	36.9	0	0	1	1	3	0	0	0	0	0	0	1	0	0	0	0	1	0	0	0	0	1	2	0	0
mountainous	87	.5098	9.5083	49.8	7	7	15	21	21	4	11	1	4	0	1	0	0	57	0	5	1	0	0	0	1	4	13	1	0
mountains	1081	.8358	181.41	62.6	199	171	187	152	229	67	59	17	210	11	4	50	5	356	5	145	31	12	0	0	21	89	103	38	1
Mountains	208	.6917	29.570	54.7	12	24	58	27	39	22	18	8	27	1	0	5	0	89	1	23	4	0	0	1	3	15	28	11	0
mountainside	31	.6404	4.2163	46.2	4	1	8	5	11	1	1	0	14	1	0	6	0	1	0	5	1	0	0	0	0	1	2	0	0
mountainsides	14	.4016	1.3123	41.2	5	3	2	1	2	0	0	1	3	0	0	0	0	7	0	3	0	0	0	0	0	1	0	0	0
mountaintop	19	.6229	2.5366	44.0	7	5	2	1	2	1	1	0	9	0	0	2	0	3	0	2	1	0	0	0	0	0	2	0	0
mountaintops	10	.4569	1.0420	40.2	1	2	2	2	2	0	1	0	3	0	0	1	0	2	0	4	0	0	0	0	0	0	0	0	0
mounted	132	.8196	21.733	53.4	5	16	19	17	36	21	12	6	30	3	2	10	0	5	0	11	5	0	0	6	14	16	11	19	0
Mounted	2	.1814	.1187	30.7	0	1	0	0	1	0	0	0	1	0	0	0	0	0	0	0	0	0	0	0	0	0	0	1	0
mounting	42	.6986	6.0085	47.8	2	0	6	4	14	6	8	2	8	0	0	1	0	5	0	2	0	0	1	2	3	4	2	14	0
mounts	15	.5702	1.8058	42.6	0	0	3	3	5	3	1	0	3	0	0	2	0	0	0	1	0	0	0	0	3	2	0	4	0
Mourad	6	.0000	.0644	28.1	0	0	0	0	0	6	0	0	0	0	0	6	0	0	0	0	0	0	0	0	0	0	0	0	0
mourn	14	.6353	1.8453	42.7	0	0	2	1	6	4	1	0	3	1	0	2	0	0	0	0	2	0	0	0	1	4	0	1	0
mourned	12	.4994	1.3298	41.2	2	2	1	1	2	2	1	1	5	0	1	3	0	0	0	0	0	0	0	0	0	2	0	1	0
mourner	2	.0000	.0234	23.7	1	1	0	0	0	0	0	0	0	0	0	0	0	0	0	0	0	0	0	0	2	0	0	0	0
mourners	4	.4815	.4019	36.0	1	0	0	0	2	0	1	0	0	0	0	1	0	0	1	0	0	0	0	0	1	1	0	0	0
mournful	26	.6599	3.5578	45.5	3	4	2	6	7	2	2	0	8	3	1	2	0	0	0	0	5	0	0	0	5	1	0	1	0
mournfully	4	.2995	.2902	34.6	0	0	0	1	1	1	1	0	1	1	0	2	0	0	0	0	0	0	0	0	0	0	0	0	0
mourning	14	.6518	1.9012	42.8	1	1	1	6	2	2	1	0	4	0	0	2	0	0	0	2	2	0	0	0	1	1	0	2	0
mouse	207	.7804	32.778	55.2	61	40	24	22	35	14	4	7	64	11	9	33	1	0	8	29	5	0	0	0	14	19	6	8	0
Mouse	42	.4777	4.4021	46.4	25	5	1	0	10	1	0	0	12	0	0	11	0	1	0	0	6	0	0	0	0	0	0	12	0
mouse-catching	2	.0000	.0914	29.6	2	0	0	0	0	0	0	0	2	0	0	0	0	0	0	0	0	0	0	0	0	0	0	0	0
mouse's	8	.1564	.4149	36.2	1	0	4	0	3	0	0	0	4	1	3	0	0	0	0	0	0	0	0	0	0	0	0	0	0
Mouse's	2	.2411	.1091	30.4	1	0	0	0	1	0	0	0	0	0	0	1	0	0	0	0	1	0	0	0	0	0	0	0	0
mouseholed	2	.1948	.1250	31.0	1	0	1	0	0	0	0	0	1	0	0	0	0	0	0	0	0	0	0	0	0	1	0	0	0
mouselike	2	.2405	.1205	30.8	0	0	0	0	1	0	0	1	0	0	0	0	0	0	0	1	0	0	0	0	0	1	0	0	0
Mousetail	2	.0000	.0394	26.0	0	0	0	0	0	0	0	2	0	0	0	0	0	0	0	2	0	0	0	0	0	0	0	0	0
mousetrap	9	.2212	.6853	38.4	9	0	0	0	0	0	0	0	8	0	0	0	0	0	0	0	0	0	0	0	0	0	0	1	0
Mousey	2	.0000	.0914	29.6	0	0	0	0	2	0	0	0	2	0	0	0	0	0	0	0	0	0	0	0	0	0	0	0	0
Mousey's	2	.0000	.0914	29.6	0	0	0	0	2	0	0	0	2	0	0	0	0	0	0	0	0	0	0	0	0	0	0	0	0
mousie	2	.0000	.0162	22.1	2	0	0	0	0	0	0	0	0	0	0	0	0	0	0	0	2	0	0	0	0	0	0	0	0
moustache	8	.4753	.8182	39.1	0	3	1	0	2	0	2	0	1	0	0	1	0	1	0	0	0	0	0	0	3	0	0	2	0
moustached	2	.2408	.1204	30.8	0	0	1	0	1	0	0	0	0	0	0	0	0	1	0	0	0	0	0	0	0	1	0	0	0
mouth	725	.8946	129.21	61.1	145	101	93	82	174	71	48	11	214	22	7	69	0	42	9	111	10	4	9	1	85	57	47	38	0
mouth-watering	2	.2442	.1134	30.5	0	0	0	0	0	0	1	1	0	1	0	0	0	0	0	0	0	0	0	0	0	0	0	1	0
mouthful	22	.6398	2.9989	44.8	5	2	1	6	4	2	1	1	11	1	1	0	0	0	0	2	0	0	0	0	2	3	0	2	0
mouthfuls	4	.3706	.3628	35.6	0	0	1	3	0	0	0	0	2	0	0	0	0	0	0	0	0	0	0	0	1	0	1	0	0
mouthing	2	.1717	.1142	30.6	0	0	1	0	0	1	0	0	1	0	0	1	0	0	0	0	0	0	0	0	0	0	0	0	0
mouthparts	5	.0000	.0986	29.9	0	0	0	0	5	0	0	0	0	0	0	0	0	0	0	5	0	0	0	0	0	0	0	0	0
mouthpiece	31	.3467	2.5095	44.0	6	5	6	4	8	0	2	0	8	1	0	0	0	0	0	4	15	0	0	0	0	0	3	0	0
mouths	96	.7736	15.064	51.8	20	14	16	14	24	6	2	0	24	3	0	8	0	5	0	11	3	0	0	0	11	16	10	5	0
Mouvement	2	.0000	.0290	24.6	0	0	1	0	1	0	0	0	0	0	0	0	0	0	0	0	0	0	0	0	0	2	0	0	0
movable	36	.6454	4.7393	46.8	12	0	1	4	6	5	7	1	0	4	0	2	0	2	4	15	0	0	1	4	0	0	3	1	0
movable-type	3	.1101	.0802	29.0	0	0	0	0	1	0	2	0	0	0	0	0	0	0	0	0	0	0	0	2	0	0	0	1	0
move	1592	.9238	291.59	64.6	388	284	198	209	232	136	101	44	342	41	14	49	85	125	23	415	108	29	15	28	53	123	52	90	0
moved	994	.9116	180.20	62.6	167	165	152	122	187	114	74	13	326	52	9	80	22	145	8	70	20	1	2	8	76	72	38	65	0
movement	507	.7575	77.259	58.9	22	48	101	52	104	110	59	11	43	3	5	16	0	53	5	80	135	32	8	10	17	17	58	25	0
Movement	10	.5062	1.0529	40.2	0	0	2	0	2	3	0	3	0	0	0	0	0	1	0	0	2	0	0	0	0	1	3	3	0
movements	197	.7892	31.279	55.0	11	21	34	19	47	30	31	4	27	4	1	17	0	13	0	46	38	6	3	0	8	8	19	7	0
Movements	2	.0000	.0162	22.1	0	0	2	0	0	0	0	0	0	0	0	0	0	0	0	0	2	0	0	0	0	0	0	0	0
mover	5	.3577	.3868	35.9	1	0	1	0	3	0	0	0	0	0	0	0	0	0	0	0	1	0	0	0	0	0	1	3	0
movers	4	.4501	.4035	36.1	0	2	0	0	2	0	0	0	1	0	0	0	0	0	0	1	0	0	0	0	0	1	1	0	0
moves	485	.8041	78.365	58.9	112	70	65	55	90	46	37	10	50	8	3	15	21	34	1	186	60	11	0	12	0	41	21	22	0

9N Motley
4P Motobloc
XR motorcars
7A motorcycling's
XR motorcyclists
XR Motordrome
5A motorist's
8A motormen
7R MOTORS
5F motorscooters
3P mottles
4Q Mottley
7R mottling
6G motus
4R Mougins
3P moujiks
6A Moulay
5A moulded
7M mouldings
7N mouldy
7Q Moulins
9H Moulton
6P moundsman
5Q MountVernon
6R MountWashington
7A mountain-laurel
5A mountain-lion
7N mountain-peak
7P mountain-rocks
8R Mountaineers
8A mountaineers'
7Q mountainlike
7Q mountains'
7H mountings
8D Mourad's
5A Mourning
3N mouse-cry
8D mouse-haired
7P mouse-tailed
3J Mousehawk's
5B mousehole
8B mouser
7D mousers
3R mousery
3A mousetraps
7D mousie-men
XB mousseron
XR moustaches
7D Mouth
9D mouthed
5J mouthpieces
5R mouthwash
7B movability
4B movables
6B moveless
7Q Mover
9D movers'-talk

Word Type	F	D	U	SFI	3 Gr 3	4 Gr 4	5 Gr 5	6 Gr 6	7 Gr 7	8 Gr 8	9 Gr 9	X UnGr	A Read	B Eng & Gr	C Comp	D Lit	E Math	F Soc Stud	G Spell	H Sci	J Music	K Art	L Home Ec	M Shop	N Lib F	P Lib NF	Q Lib Ref	R Mag	S Rel
moveth	2	.1948	.1250	31.0	1	0	0	0	0	1	0	0	1	0	0	0	0	0	0	0	0	0	0	0	0	1	0	0	0
movie	151	.8572	25.791	54.1	18	23	11	16	34	16	23	10	19	29	4	5	13	18	2	4	6	1	4	1	4	3	4	34	0
Movie-Drome	2	.0000	.0243	23.9	0	0	0	0	0	0	0	2	0	0	0	0	0	0	0	0	0	0	0	0	0	0	0	2	0
movie-making	2	.0000	.0389	25.9	0	0	0	0	0	2	0	0	0	0	0	0	0	2	0	0	0	0	0	0	0	0	0	0	0
moviegoers	2	.1523	.0721	28.6	0	0	0	0	1	0	1	0	0	0	1	0	0	0	0	0	0	0	0	0	0	0	0	1	0
moviegoing	2	.2351	.1166	30.7	0	0	0	0	1	1	0	0	0	0	0	0	0	1	0	0	0	0	0	0	0	0	0	1	0
movies	100	.8419	16.813	52.3	10	20	9	10	22	16	9	4	13	13	3	8	3	21	0	3	6	4	2	0	4	3	4	13	0
movin'	5	.3410	.4178	36.2	0	1	0	0	4	0	0	0	2	0	0	1	0	0	0	0	0	0	0	0	2	0	0	0	0
moving	871	.9129	157.90	62.0	150	174	88	105	161	105	59	29	197	19	9	41	12	66	4	225	38	10	4	15	54	86	46	45	0
moving-picture	3	.3772	.2437	33.9	0	1	0	1	0	1	0	0	0	0	0	0	0	0	0	0	1	0	0	0	1	1	0	0	0
mow	23	.5179	2.5354	44.0	0	5	5	1	6	1	5	0	3	1	1	2	14	0	0	0	0	0	0	0	1	0	1	0	0
mowed	15	.2434	.9050	39.6	1	2	4	1	2	2	3	0	1	1	0	0	12	0	0	0	0	0	0	0	1	0	0	0	0
mower	13	.6467	1.7460	42.4	1	0	0	5	5	0	2	0	3	2	0	0	3	1	0	1	1	0	0	1	1	0	0	0	0
mowers	3	.2292	.1672	32.2	0	0	2	0	0	0	1	0	0	0	0	0	0	1	0	1	0	0	0	1	0	0	0	0	0
mowing	12	.4884	1.2492	41.0	2	3	2	2	1	1	1	0	1	2	0	0	6	1	0	0	0	1	0	0	1	0	0	0	0
mows	6	.4234	.5624	37.5	0	2	1	0	0	1	1	1	1	2	0	0	2	0	0	0	0	0	0	0	0	0	0	1	0
Moynihan	3	.0000	.0365	25.6	0	0	0	0	0	3	0	0	0	0	0	0	0	0	0	0	0	0	0	0	0	0	0	3	0
Mozambique	9	.2931	.6326	38.0	0	0	0	8	0	1	0	0	0	0	0	0	1	7	0	0	0	0	0	0	0	0	1	0	0
Mozart	55	.0603	1.1099	40.5	6	9	6	4	4	16	10	0	1	0	0	1	0	0	0	0	52	0	0	0	0	0	1	0	0
Mozart's	17	.0000	.1374	31.4	0	1	3	2	3	7	1	0	0	0	0	0	0	0	0	0	17	0	0	0	0	0	0	0	0
MP	2	.0000	.0299	24.8	0	0	0	0	0	2	0	0	0	0	0	0	2	0	0	0	0	0	0	0	0	0	0	0	0
mpg	2	.0000	.0243	23.9	0	0	0	0	1	0	0	1	0	0	0	0	0	0	0	0	0	0	0	0	0	0	0	2	0
mph	42	.5026	4.4154	46.4	0	1	4	1	22	8	4	2	0	0	0	0	16	0	0	1	0	0	0	3	0	3	2	17	0
mr	4	.3599	.3543	35.5	2	0	0	0	0	2	0	0	2	0	0	0	0	0	1	0	0	0	0	0	0	0	0	1	0
Mr	3748	.8046	612.22	67.9	986	1026	353	415	363	323	246	36	1569	194	21	296	181	255	35	26	21	3	5	4	521	452	2	163	0
MR	27	.0524	.5535	37.4	0	0	0	0	27	0	0	0	0	0	0	26	0	0	0	0	0	0	0	0	1	0	0	0	0
mrs	2	.0000	.0234	23.7	0	0	2	0	0	0	0	0	0	0	0	0	0	0	0	0	0	0	0	0	2	0	0	0	0
Mrs	1619	.7572	251.76	64.0	545	397	144	143	171	124	84	11	725	96	13	86	59	98	4	6	0	0	4	0	272	177	6	73	0
MRS	16	.0758	.3983	36.0	1	0	0	0	0	10	5	0	0	0	0	15	0	0	0	0	0	0	0	0	0	0	0	1	0
Mt	58	.6063	7.3114	48.6	6	22	2	9	9	2	7	1	3	2	0	0	22	11	0	8	0	0	0	0	0	6	1	5	0
much	5386	.9746	1034.3	70.1	960	830	680	777	995	558	467	119	1124	175	40	224	714	795	56	713	150	36	73	49	265	429	259	279	5
Much	2	.0000	.0243	23.9	0	0	1	0	1	0	0	0	0	0	0	0	0	0	0	0	0	0	0	0	0	0	0	2	0
much-needed	3	.2425	.1816	32.6	0	0	0	0	1	1	1	0	0	0	0	0	0	2	0	0	0	0	0	0	0	0	0	1	0
much-publicized	2	.2278	.1128	30.5	0	0	1	0	0	0	0	1	0	0	0	0	0	0	0	1	0	0	0	0	0	0	1	0	0
much-used	2	.0000	.0914	29.6	0	0	1	0	1	0	0	0	2	0	0	0	0	0	0	0	0	0	0	0	0	0	0	0	0
mucilage	4	.3134	.2876	34.6	0	2	2	0	0	0	0	0	0	0	0	0	0	1	0	1	0	0	0	0	0	0	2	0	0
muck	4	.2991	.2943	34.7	1	0	0	2	0	1	0	0	1	0	0	0	0	0	0	0	0	0	0	0	0	1	0	2	0
mucous	13	.1401	.5705	37.6	0	3	3	1	0	0	5	1	0	0	0	0	0	0	0	12	0	0	0	0	0	0	1	0	0
mucus	19	.1671	.9206	39.6	0	8	1	0	0	1	9	0	0	0	0	0	0	0	0	17	0	0	0	0	0	0	2	0	0
mud	324	.8156	53.432	57.3	108	62	28	55	36	13	17	5	106	7	2	9	0	35	3	53	0	2	0	0	13	56	21	17	0
Mud	4	.2048	.1975	33.0	0	3	0	0	1	0	0	0	0	0	0	1	0	0	0	0	0	0	0	0	3	0	0	0	0
mud-colored	2	.2291	.1135	30.5	1	0	0	0	1	0	0	0	0	0	0	1	0	0	0	1	0	0	0	0	0	0	0	0	0
mud-mixing	2	.0000	.0215	23.3	1	1	0	0	0	0	0	0	0	0	0	2	0	0	0	0	0	0	0	0	0	0	0	0	0
mud-rock	2	.0000	.0914	29.6	2	0	0	0	0	0	0	0	2	0	0	0	0	0	0	0	0	0	0	0	0	0	0	0	0
muddied	2	.2427	.1152	30.6	1	0	0	0	1	0	0	0	0	0	0	0	0	0	0	0	0	0	0	0	1	1	0	0	0
muddier	2	.2346	.1166	30.7	0	0	0	1	1	0	0	0	0	0	0	0	0	0	0	1	0	0	0	0	0	0	0	1	0
muddle	3	.3629	.2409	33.8	0	0	0	0	3	0	0	0	0	0	0	0	0	0	0	1	1	0	0	0	0	1	0	0	0
muddled	3	.2279	.2143	33.3	0	1	0	0	2	0	0	0	2	0	0	0	0	0	0	0	0	0	0	0	0	0	0	1	0
muddy	89	.8054	14.481	51.6	25	20	15	17	8	1	2	1	23	3	1	3	0	7	2	16	0	0	0	0	5	16	4	9	0
Mudhen	7	.0000	.0851	29.3	0	0	0	7	0	0	0	0	0	0	0	0	0	0	0	0	0	0	0	0	0	0	0	7	0
Mudville	2	.0000	.0914	29.6	0	0	0	0	2	0	0	0	2	0	0	0	0	0	0	0	0	0	0	0	0	0	0	0	0
Muff	6	.0000	.0729	28.6	6	0	0	0	0	0	0	0	0	0	0	0	0	0	0	0	0	0	0	0	0	0	0	6	0
Muffet	2	.2443	.1130	30.5	0	1	0	0	1	0	0	0	0	0	0	1	0	0	0	0	0	0	0	0	1	0	0	0	0
muffin	16	.2435	.8151	39.1	1	2	0	0	2	2	9	0	0	1	0	0	0	0	0	0	0	2	12	0	0	0	0	1	0
muffins	14	.2168	.6774	38.3	1	1	0	0	6	2	4	0	1	1	1	0	0	0	0	0	0	0	10	0	0	0	0	1	0
muffled	31	.7278	4.6440	46.7	3	4	2	7	5	5	4	1	12	2	0	5	0	1	0	0	2	0	0	0	3	3	1	2	0
muffler	10	.4248	.9229	39.7	3	3	0	0	3	1	0	0	1	0	0	0	1	0	0	1	0	0	0	2	0	3	0	2	0
mufflers	5	.4490	.5022	37.0	2	1	0	2	0	0	0	0	1	0	0	1	1	0	0	2	0	0	0	0	0	0	0	0	0
mug	8	.2130	.4217	36.3	0	6	0	0	0	0	1	1	0	0	0	0	0	0	0	0	0	0	0	0	2	6	0	0	0
Mug	7	.0000	.1013	30.1	7	0	0	0	0	0	0	0	0	0	0	0	0	0	0	0	0	0	0	0	0	7	0	0	0
mugger	2	.0000	.0243	23.9	0	0	0	1	0	1	0	0	0	0	0	0	0	0	0	0	0	0	0	0	0	0	0	2	0
Muggins	17	.0000	.7766	38.9	2	15	0	0	0	0	0	0	17	0	0	0	0	0	0	0	0	0	0	0	0	0	0	0	0
muggy	8	.5434	.9382	39.7	0	2	0	0	4	1	1	0	2	0	0	1	0	0	0	3	0	0	0	0	0	0	1	1	0
mugs	6	.4377	.5583	37.5	0	3	0	2	0	1	0	0	0	0	0	0	0	1	0	0	2	0	0	0	0	2	1	0	0
Muh-koons	8	.0000	.0972	29.9	0	0	0	8	0	0	0	0	0	0	0	0	0	0	0	0	0	0	0	0	0	0	0	8	0
Muhler	2	.0000	.0243	23.9	0	0	0	0	2	0	0	0	0	0	0	0	0	0	0	0	0	0	0	0	0	0	0	2	0
Muir	18	.2212	1.3706	41.4	2	10	4	1	0	0	0	1	16	0	0	0	0	0	0	0	0	0	0	0	0	0	0	2	0
muktuk	2	.0000	.0162	22.1	0	0	0	2	0	0	0	0	0	0	0	0	0	0	0	0	2	0	0	0	0	0	0	0	0
Mul	9	.0000	.4111	36.1	9	0	0	0	0	0	0	0	9	0	0	0	0	0	0	0	0	0	0	0	0	0	0	0	0
mulatto	3	.3454	.2542	34.1	0	0	0	0	2	0	1	0	1	0	0	0	0	1	0	0	0	0	0	0	0	0	0	1	0
mulattoes	3	.0000	.0583	27.7	0	0	1	1	0	1	0	0	0	0	0	0	0	3	0	0	0	0	0	0	0	0	0	0	0
mulberry	9	.4446	.9022	39.6	4	3	0	1	0	0	1	0	2	0	0	0	0	4	0	0	0	0	0	0	0	2	1	0	0
Mulberry	7	.2273	.5357	37.3	0	5	2	0	0	0	0	0	6	0	0	0	0	0	0	0	0	0	0	0	0	1	0	0	0
Muldoon	5	.0000	.0586	27.7	3	0	0	0	0	0	0	2	0	0	0	0	0	0	0	0	0	0	0	0	5	0	0	0	0
Muldoon's	2	.0000	.0234	23.7	1	0	0	0	0	0	0	1	0	0	0	0	0	0	0	0	0	0	0	0	2	0	0	0	0
mule	76	.8045	12.298	50.9	15	18	7	17	9	7	1	2	17	3	2	8	0	0	2	0	6	0	1	0	5	18	6	8	0
muleback	3	.0000	.1370	31.4	0	0	1	1	1	0	0	0	3	0	0	0	0	0	0	0	0	0	0	0	0	0	0	0	0
mules	51	.6783	7.1997	48.6	16	3	5	15	7	4	0	1	16	2	2	3	0	13	0	1	2	0	0	0	0	11	1	0	0
mulled	2	.1814	.1187	30.7	0	0	2	0	0	0	0	0	1	0	0	0	0	0	0	0	0	0	0	0	0	0	0	1	0
Mullen's	2	.0000	.0914	29.6	0	0	2	0	0	0	0	0	2	0	0	0	0	0	0	0	0	0	0	0	0	0	0	0	0
mullet	5	.2115	.2662	34.3	0	0	2	2	1	0	0	0	0	0	0	0	0	2	0	0	0	0	0	0	3	0	0	0	0
Mullet	2	.0000	.0234	23.7	0	0	0	0	2	0	0	0	0	0	0	0	0	0	0	0	0	0	0	0	2	0	0	0	0
Mulligan	2	.0000	.0234	23.7	1	0	0	0	0	0	0	1	0	0	0	0	0	0	0	0	0	0	0	0	2	0	0	0	0
Mullins	2	.1494	.1045	30.2	0	0	1	1	0	0	0	0	1	0	0	0	0	0	0	0	1	0	0	0	0	0	0	0	0
mulsh	2	.0000	.0234	23.7	0	0	0	0	2	0	0	0	0	0	0	0	0	0	0	0	0	0	0	0	2	0	0	0	0
multi-colored	2	.2437	.1129	30.5	1	0	0	0	0	0	0	1	0	0	0	0	0	0	0	0	0	0	0	0	0	0	1	1	0
multi-syllabic	2	.0000	.0162	22.1	0	0	0	0	2	0	0	0	0	0	0	0	0	0	2	0	0	0	0	0	0	0	0	0	0
multicellular	6	.2071	.3307	35.2	0	0	0	1	4	0	0	1	0	0	0	0	0	0	0	5	0	0	0	0	0	0	1	0	0
multicolored	3	.3815	.2534	34.0	0	0	1	0	1	0	1	0	0	0	0	0	0	1	0	0	0	0	0	0	0	1	0	1	0

XR movie-book
XR movie-dromes
9B movie-goers
5R movie-mag
4F movie-maker
XR movie-mural
7R movie's
6B moviegoers'
9R Movies
8H Moving
3H MOVING
8M moving-coil
8D moving-slow
5A movingly
4A Mowat
5A Mowgli
4N mown
7R Moynahan
8Q mozo
7L mozzarella
7P mpanga
6E MRN
9D Mrunas
6A much-enduring
8R much-feared
7R much-maligned
9D much-nourishing
7N much-prized
7A mucho
XH mucin
7N muck-rakin'
7A muckrakers
XH mucopolysaccharide
4A mud-brick
4N mud-cap
7F mud-daubed
3N mud-roofed
8A mud-spattered
7N mud-stripes
3A mud-walled
7D mudbank
6A mudflats
4A mudhole
3P mudholes
7Q mudskippers
4P mudwalk
7L Muenster
3R Muff's
9L Muffins
4A muffle
4A Mufraw
5A Mugg
7H mugginess
8F Muggletonians
6R Mugur
6R Muh-koons'
6R muh-zay
7P Muhlhausen
4A Muir's
3A Muirs
8F Mukden
3D mukluks
6N Mulai
9D mulberries
3P Muldrow
3P Mule
9R mule-drawn
7A mule-ears
6A mule's
6R muleriders
7D muleteers
5N mullein
5A Mullen
6H Muller
XH Mullica
7R mulling
8H multi-flash
7R multi-lane
3Q multi-million-dollar
7L multi-purpose
9M multi-story
5P multibarreled
7Q multibillion-dollar
7H multicelled
7R multiethnic
8A multifaceted
5Q multifamily
8L multifilament
XH multiflora
9R multilateral
5Q multilaterally
8M multimeters

Word Type	F	D	U	SFI	3 Gr 3	4 Gr 4	5 Gr 5	6 Gr 6	7 Gr 7	8 Gr 8	9 Gr 9	X UnGr	A Read	B Eng & Gr	C Comp	D Lit	E Math	F Soc Stud	G Spell	H Sci	J Music	K Art	L Home Ec	M Shop	N Lib F	P Lib NF	Q Lib Ref	R Mag	S Rel
multimillion-dollar	2	.2446	.1257	31.0	0	0	0	0	2	0	0	0	0	0	0	0	0	1	0	1	0	0	0	0	0	0	0	0	0
multimillionaire	2	.0000	.0243	23.9	0	0	0	0	0	1	0	1	0	0	0	0	0	0	0	0	0	0	0	0	0	0	0	2	0
multiple	158	.2742	10.190	50.1	2	9	34	27	37	23	23	3	0	0	0	0	141	0	0	6	3	0	0	4	0	0	1	3	0
Multiple	2	.2391	.1133	30.5	0	0	0	1	0	0	1	0	0	0	0	0	1	0	0	0	0	0	0	0	0	0	1	0	0
multiples	184	.1162	6.6182	48.2	5	18	70	20	17	42	12	0	0	0	0	0	178	1	0	1	2	0	0	1	0	0	1	0	0
multiplicand	14	.1140	.4954	36.9	0	1	0	3	1	2	7	0	0	0	0	0	13	0	0	0	0	0	0	0	0	0	1	0	0
multiplication	488	.0603	12.678	51.0	45	76	66	67	86	103	38	7	1	0	0	0	475	0	0	5	1	0	0	0	0	2	3	1	0
Multiplication	12	.0000	.1796	32.5	1	1	4	0	4	0	2	0	0	0	0	0	12	0	0	0	0	0	0	0	0	0	0	0	0
multiplication-addition	4	.0000	.0599	27.8	1	0	1	0	0	2	0	0	0	0	0	0	4	0	0	0	0	0	0	0	0	0	0	0	0
multiplications	14	.0000	.2096	33.2	1	3	3	2	1	0	4	0	0	0	0	0	14	0	0	0	0	0	0	0	0	0	0	0	0
multiplicative	27	.0000	.4041	36.1	0	0	0	0	9	17	1	0	0	0	0	0	27	0	0	0	0	0	0	0	0	0	0	0	0
multiplicity	2	.1698	.1133	30.5	0	0	0	0	2	0	0	0	1	0	0	0	0	0	0	0	0	0	0	0	0	0	1	0	0
multiplied	96	.3259	7.1786	48.6	6	7	8	13	18	27	12	5	3	0	0	0	74	3	1	5	0	0	0	0	0	3	6	1	0
multiplier	10	.3276	.7331	38.7	0	1	1	3	2	1	2	0	0	0	0	0	8	0	0	0	0	0	0	1	0	0	1	0	0
multiplies	6	.2076	.3235	35.1	0	0	1	3	0	1	1	0	0	0	0	0	4	0	0	2	0	0	0	0	0	0	0	0	0
multiply	337	.1925	16.967	52.3	17	26	34	82	73	61	42	2	6	1	0	1	304	0	2	12	0	0	2	0	0	5	0	4	0
multiplying	109	.1901	5.3761	47.3	2	3	15	32	20	20	17	0	0	0	0	0	102	0	0	2	0	0	0	2	0	1	0	2	0
multistage	2	.0000	.0394	26.0	0	2	0	0	0	0	0	0	0	0	0	0	0	0	0	2	0	0	0	0	0	0	0	0	0
multitude	21	.6490	2.7895	44.5	2	3	3	0	5	2	5	1	2	1	0	2	0	1	0	1	0	0	0	1	3	3	7	0	0
multitudes	5	.4412	.4709	36.7	1	0	0	0	2	0	1	1	0	0	0	0	0	0	0	1	0	0	0	0	1	1	2	0	0
mumble	6	.4862	.6610	38.2	1	2	1	0	2	0	0	0	3	1	0	1	0	0	0	0	0	0	0	0	0	0	0	1	0
mumble-peg	2	.0000	.0290	24.6	0	2	0	0	0	0	0	0	0	0	0	0	0	0	0	0	0	0	0	0	0	2	0	0	0
mumbled	27	.4534	2.8586	44.6	5	8	3	4	4	2	1	0	15	0	0	1	0	0	0	0	0	0	0	0	8	1	0	2	0
mumbles	5	.2445	.3864	35.9	1	2	1	0	0	0	1	0	4	0	0	1	0	0	0	0	0	0	0	0	0	0	0	0	0
mumbling	6	.2895	.4416	36.4	1	0	1	0	4	0	0	0	2	0	0	0	0	0	0	0	0	0	0	0	3	1	0	0	0
Mumford	2	.0000	.0243	23.9	0	0	0	0	2	0	0	0	0	0	0	0	0	0	0	0	0	0	0	0	0	0	0	2	0
mummies	3	.2043	.1486	31.7	0	1	0	0	2	0	0	0	0	0	0	0	0	0	0	0	0	0	0	0	0	1	2	0	0
mummy	14	.5395	1.6506	42.2	4	0	2	2	2	3	0	1	5	0	0	1	0	1	0	1	0	0	0	0	0	5	1	0	0
Mummy	12	.2825	.7838	38.9	0	1	0	2	0	9	0	0	0	2	0	0	0	0	0	0	0	0	0	0	1	9	0	0	0
Mummy's	2	.2427	.1152	30.6	0	1	0	0	0	1	0	0	0	0	0	0	0	0	0	0	0	0	0	0	1	1	0	0	0
mumps	15	.6122	1.9345	42.9	2	5	0	2	2	1	0	3	3	2	0	0	0	1	0	6	0	0	0	0	1	1	0	1	0
munch	3	.3406	.2461	33.9	1	0	1	1	0	0	0	0	1	1	0	0	0	0	0	0	0	0	0	0	0	0	0	1	0
munched	2	.0000	.0914	29.6	1	0	0	0	1	0	0	0	2	0	0	0	0	0	0	0	0	0	0	0	0	0	0	0	0
munching	10	.5438	1.2021	40.8	1	3	1	2	1	1	0	1	5	0	0	1	0	0	0	1	0	0	0	0	2	0	1	0	0
Munda	5	.0000	.0724	28.6	0	0	0	0	5	0	0	0	0	0	0	0	0	0	0	0	0	0	0	0	0	5	0	0	0
mundane	2	.0000	.0243	23.9	0	0	0	0	0	0	1	1	0	0	0	0	0	0	0	0	0	0	0	0	0	0	0	2	0
Munich	8	.4533	.8281	39.2	0	1	1	1	1	3	1	0	3	0	0	0	0	2	0	0	0	0	0	0	0	1	2	0	0
municipal	11	.4703	1.1554	40.6	2	0	1	0	4	3	1	0	4	0	0	1	0	0	0	0	0	0	0	0	0	1	4	1	0
Municipal	5	.2956	.3348	35.2	0	0	4	0	0	0	1	0	0	0	0	0	0	1	0	0	0	0	0	0	0	0	3	1	0
municipalities	2	.0000	.0290	24.6	0	0	2	0	0	0	0	0	0	0	0	0	0	0	0	0	0	0	0	0	0	2	0	0	0
municipality	4	.3831	.3415	35.3	1	0	0	0	1	2	0	0	0	0	0	0	0	2	0	0	0	0	0	0	0	1	0	1	0
munitions	6	.4626	.5911	37.7	1	0	0	1	0	2	1	1	0	0	0	1	0	2	0	0	0	0	0	0	0	1	2	0	0
Munson	2	.0000	.0243	23.9	0	0	0	0	0	0	1	1	0	0	0	0	0	0	0	0	0	0	0	0	0	0	0	2	0
muoi	2	.0000	.0243	23.9	0	0	0	0	2	0	0	0	0	0	0	0	0	0	0	0	0	0	0	0	0	0	0	2	0
Muong	9	.0000	.1303	31.1	0	0	0	0	0	0	9	0	0	0	0	0	0	0	0	0	0	0	0	0	0	9	0	0	0
Murad	2	.0000	.0290	24.6	0	0	2	0	0	0	0	0	0	0	0	0	0	0	0	0	0	0	0	0	0	2	0	0	0
mural	5	.1419	.2314	33.6	0	2	0	1	0	1	0	1	2	0	0	0	0	0	0	0	0	2	0	0	0	0	0	1	0
murals	6	.5093	.6249	38.0	0	0	2	0	2	1	1	0	0	0	0	1	0	0	0	0	0	0	1	1	0	0	2	1	0
murder	40	.6971	5.7353	47.6	1	1	3	2	20	8	4	1	9	1	0	7	0	4	0	3	0	0	0	0	2	8	1	5	0
murdered	15	.6154	1.9550	42.9	1	0	3	0	5	5	1	0	5	0	0	1	0	2	0	0	0	0	0	0	0	3	2	2	0
murderer	12	.4436	1.1329	40.5	0	0	1	0	4	3	4	0	0	0	0	6	0	2	0	0	0	0	0	0	1	2	0	1	0
murderers	6	.4478	.6013	37.8	0	0	0	0	4	0	2	0	2	0	0	2	0	0	1	0	0	0	0	0	1	0	0	0	0
murdering	2	.2433	.1158	30.6	0	0	0	0	1	0	1	0	0	0	0	0	0	0	0	0	0	0	0	0	0	1	0	1	0
murderous	5	.4880	.5173	37.1	0	0	1	0	1	0	0	3	0	0	0	0	0	0	0	2	0	0	0	0	1	0	1	1	0
Murdle	6	.0000	.0644	28.1	0	6	0	0	0	0	0	0	0	0	0	6	0	0	0	0	0	0	0	0	0	0	0	0	0
Murdle's	4	.0000	.0429	26.3	0	4	0	0	0	0	0	0	0	0	0	4	0	0	0	0	0	0	0	0	0	0	0	0	0
murex	2	.0000	.0243	23.9	0	0	0	2	0	0	0	0	0	0	0	0	0	0	0	0	0	0	0	0	0	0	0	2	0
Muriel	6	.3555	.4681	36.7	0	1	0	0	0	1	4	0	0	1	0	0	2	0	0	0	0	0	0	0	3	0	0	0	0
murk	2	.2407	.1138	30.6	1	1	0	0	0	0	0	0	0	0	0	1	0	0	0	0	0	0	0	0	0	1	0	0	0
murky	11	.5157	1.1668	40.7	0	0	1	0	3	0	6	1	0	1	1	5	0	0	0	0	2	0	0	0	0	0	0	2	0
murmur	16	.6649	2.2049	43.4	0	2	2	2	5	2	2	1	5	0	1	3	0	0	1	0	1	0	0	0	3	1	0	1	0
murmured	47	.6004	5.9747	47.8	7	7	6	8	13	2	3	1	16	1	2	8	0	0	0	0	0	0	0	0	13	2	0	5	0
murmuring	9	.4694	.9177	39.6	0	1	1	1	4	1	1	0	2	1	0	4	0	0	0	0	1	0	0	0	1	0	0	0	0
murmurings	2	.1948	.1250	31.0	0	1	0	0	1	0	0	0	1	0	0	0	0	0	0	0	0	0	0	0	0	1	0	0	0
murmurs	5	.4652	.4865	36.9	0	0	0	0	3	2	0	0	0	1	0	2	0	0	0	0	1	0	0	0	0	1	0	0	0
Murphy	35	.6792	4.8968	46.9	4	16	8	1	5	0	1	0	8	4	1	1	4	0	0	0	0	0	0	0	8	7	0	2	0
Murphy's	7	.4534	.7275	38.6	0	4	2	0	1	0	0	0	3	0	0	0	1	0	0	0	0	0	0	0	2	1	0	0	0
Murphys	2	.0000	.0215	23.3	0	0	0	0	0	0	2	0	0	0	0	2	0	0	0	0	0	0	0	0	0	0	0	0	0
Murray	30	.5915	3.7515	45.7	0	7	4	6	5	5	2	1	7	0	0	4	0	5	0	0	0	0	0	0	0	9	2	3	0
Murrow	4	.2399	.3011	34.8	0	0	0	0	0	0	4	0	3	1	0	0	0	0	0	0	0	0	0	0	0	0	0	0	0
muscle	133	.6891	18.729	52.7	15	14	13	9	22	17	27	16	6	3	1	9	0	5	1	74	0	0	4	1	1	3	21	4	0
Muscle	2	.0000	.0290	24.6	2	0	0	0	0	0	0	0	0	0	0	0	0	0	0	0	0	0	0	0	0	2	0	0	0
muscles	360	.6987	51.435	57.1	57	60	46	57	53	35	40	12	24	7	2	15	1	4	0	217	4	2	5	1	12	12	43	11	0
muscular	48	.6997	6.8352	48.3	0	1	10	5	16	3	10	3	3	7	1	3	0	0	0	16	0	0	0	0	1	6	8	3	0
muse	2	.2297	.1135	30.6	0	0	0	0	1	1	0	0	0	0	0	1	0	1	0	0	0	0	0	0	0	0	0	0	0
Muse	2	.2297	.1135	30.6	0	0	0	0	0	1	1	0	0	0	0	1	0	1	0	0	0	0	0	0	0	0	0	0	0
mused	6	.2896	.4379	36.4	0	1	0	1	1	1	2	0	2	0	0	3	0	0	0	0	0	0	0	0	0	0	0	1	0
Muses	2	.0000	.0162	22.1	0	2	0	0	0	0	0	0	0	0	0	0	0	0	2	0	0	0	0	0	0	0	0	0	0
musette	2	.2375	.1088	30.4	0	0	1	0	0	1	0	0	0	0	0	0	0	0	0	0	1	0	0	0	0	0	0	1	0
musettes	2	.0000	.0162	22.1	0	0	0	2	0	0	0	0	0	0	0	0	0	0	0	0	2	0	0	0	0	0	0	0	0
museum	103	.6853	14.475	51.6	29	25	12	8	9	17	2	1	17	5	0	1	4	17	2	6	0	7	0	0	0	14	15	15	0
Museum	61	.6727	8.3837	49.2	5	9	11	3	10	13	6	4	7	4	0	1	0	5	0	2	2	3	0	0	0	10	16	11	0
museum's	7	.2364	.3850	35.9	0	0	0	0	3	4	0	0	0	0	0	0	0	0	0	0	0	0	0	0	0	0	4	3	0
museums	51	.5794	6.0968	47.9	9	7	12	1	1	14	3	4	2	4	0	0	0	9	1	6	2	7	1	0	0	5	13	1	0
mush	21	.4865	2.3143	43.6	4	8	0	3	3	2	0	1	10	2	0	0	0	1	0	0	0	0	0	0	6	2	0	0	0
musher	12	.0000	.5482	37.4	0	9	3	0	0	0	0	0	12	0	0	0	0	0	0	0	0	0	0	0	0	0	0	0	0
mushers	4	.0000	.1827	32.6	0	0	4	0	0	0	0	0	4	0	0	0	0	0	0	0	0	0	0	0	0	0	0	0	0
mushroom	43	.4890	4.6113	46.6	6	0	7	20	6	1	2	1	6	1	0	1	0	0	1	30	0	0	1	0	0	1	0	2	0
mushrooms	49	.4984	5.3724	47.3	14	2	5	15	5	1	7	0	12	0	0	3	0	0	0	25	0	0	5	0	1	2	0	1	0
mushy	4	.1409	.1725	32.4	0	1	0	0	1	1	0	1	1	0	0	0	0	0	0	1	0	0	2	0	0	0	0	0	0
music	2100	.3273	151.38	61.8	182	277	319	296	385	461	157	23	146	29	9	56	16	36	10	15	1556	8	5	0	31	98	38	47	0
Music	58	.2951	3.9025	45.9	1	2	5	7	24	9	9	1	7	0	1	0	0	0	0	0	41	0	0	0	0	3	3	3	0
MUSIC	5	.1813	.3036	34.8	0	0	0	3	0	0	2	0	3	0	0	0	0	0	0	0	2	0	0	0	0	0	0	0	0

7R multiple-stage
3E MULTIPLICATION
XR multipurpose
5P multiracialism
9M multitooth
6A Mulvaney
6A mum
6N Mum
7B mumbler
7N mummeries
8N Mummers'
4N mummy's
XH mumpish
4R Mumy
7R munch-and-crunch
4Q Munchen
5G mundi
9D mundo
7A munition
4A Munoz
8F Munroe
XR Munson's
5P Munster
5G munth
XR murder-stoppers
8R Murderers'
XR murderously
9P Murdoch
6R Murex
8Q murexes
9H muriatic
5F Murray-Darling
4P Murray's
9B Murrays
7N Murrel's
5P Murrumbidgee
5B Murry
7P murthered
7B mus
7N mus'
7A Muscarello
XB muscheron
8A muscle-bound
4N muscle-building
7Q muscle-powered
8D muscle-shredding
8N muscled
9D Muscovite
9D Muscovites
7R Muscovy
9A musculature
9Q musculoskeletal
5B musculus
9R Musee
5J Musette
8F museum-watgurwa
8Q Museum's
8Q Museums
8N MUSH
8D mushiness
7A Musial
6P music-drama

Word Type	F	D	U	SFI	3 Gr 3	4 Gr 4	5 Gr 5	6 Gr 6	7 Gr 7	8 Gr 8	9 Gr 9	X UnGr	A Read	B Eng & Gr	C Comp	D Lit	E Math	F Soc Stud	G Spell	H Sci	J Music	K Art	L Home Ec	M Shop	N Lib F	P Lib NF	Q Lib Ref	R Mag	S Rel
music-loving	3	.0000	.0243	23.8	0	0	0	0	2	1	0	0	0	0	0	0	0	0	0	0	3	0	0	0	0	0	0	0	0
music's	4	.3408	.2936	34.7	0	0	1	0	0	1	2	0	0	0	0	1	0	0	0	0	2	0	0	0	0	0	0	1	0
musical	460	.3516	34.777	55.4	19	47	71	85	95	110	30	3	14	7	2	2	1	9	6	13	360	4	6	1	7	12	5	11	0
Musical	7	.0859	.2387	33.8	1	0	0	2	1	2	1	0	2	0	0	0	0	0	0	0	5	0	0	0	0	0	0	0	0
musically	6	.0526	.1436	31.6	0	0	0	3	0	2	1	0	1	0	0	0	0	0	0	0	5	0	0	0	0	0	0	0	0
musicals	9	.0956	.2386	33.8	0	0	0	0	4	4	1	0	0	0	0	0	0	0	0	0	8	0	0	0	0	0	0	1	0
musician	52	.6015	6.5280	48.1	3	7	9	12	6	9	5	1	13	1	1	3	0	0	1	3	24	1	1	0	1	2	0	1	0
musician's	2	.1717	.1142	30.6	0	0	1	0	1	0	0	0	1	0	0	1	0	0	0	0	0	0	0	0	0	0	0	0	0
musicians	87	.5223	9.4772	49.8	6	7	11	19	17	21	6	0	8	0	0	2	1	2	0	2	48	2	0	0	0	10	3	8	1
Musicians	2	.1458	.0682	28.3	1	0	0	0	0	1	0	0	0	1	0	0	0	0	0	0	0	1	0	0	0	0	0	0	0
musicianship	2	.0000	.0162	22.1	0	0	0	0	0	0	2	0	0	0	0	0	0	0	0	0	2	0	0	0	0	0	0	0	0
musing	5	.3841	.4756	36.8	0	0	0	1	3	0	1	0	3	0	0	1	0	0	0	0	0	0	0	0	1	0	0	0	0
musk	3	.3399	.2456	33.9	0	0	0	0	1	0	1	1	1	0	0	1	0	0	0	0	0	0	0	0	0	0	0	1	0
musk-oxen	2	.2346	.1166	30.7	0	0	0	0	0	0	0	2	0	0	0	0	0	0	0	1	0	0	0	0	0	0	0	1	0
musket	32	.6230	4.1751	46.2	0	18	1	2	4	5	2	0	8	0	0	3	0	2	0	0	0	0	0	0	6	9	2	2	0
musketeers	3	.0000	.0322	25.1	0	0	0	0	0	0	3	0	0	0	0	3	0	0	0	0	0	0	0	0	0	0	0	0	0
musketry	2	.2440	.1132	30.5	0	0	0	0	1	1	0	0	0	0	0	1	0	0	0	0	0	0	0	0	0	0	0	1	0
muskets	11	.4816	1.2159	40.8	0	1	2	0	5	2	1	0	6	0	0	1	0	0	0	0	0	0	0	0	2	2	0	0	0
Muskiejump	2	.0000	.0243	23.9	0	0	0	2	0	0	0	0	0	0	0	0	0	0	0	0	0	0	0	0	0	0	0	2	0
Muskingum	2	.0000	.0215	23.3	0	0	0	0	2	0	0	0	0	0	0	2	0	0	0	0	0	0	0	0	0	0	0	0	0
muskrat	10	.5047	1.1074	40.4	1	3	2	0	3	0	0	1	3	1	0	3	0	2	0	0	0	0	0	0	0	1	0	0	0
Muskrat	10	.1273	.3745	35.7	9	0	0	0	0	0	0	1	0	0	0	0	0	0	0	0	0	0	0	0	0	9	0	1	0
muskrats	13	.5738	1.6010	42.0	1	1	3	2	3	1	0	2	4	0	0	3	0	1	0	3	0	0	0	0	1	0	0	1	0
Muskrats	14	.0000	.2027	33.1	14	0	0	0	0	0	0	0	0	0	0	0	0	0	0	0	0	0	0	0	0	14	0	0	0
musky	2	.2443	.1130	30.5	0	0	1	1	0	0	0	0	0	0	0	1	0	0	0	0	0	0	0	0	1	0	0	0	0
Musky	11	.0000	.5025	37.0	11	0	0	0	0	0	0	0	11	0	0	0	0	0	0	0	0	0	0	0	0	0	0	0	0
Muslim	14	.2665	.8543	39.3	0	4	.0	0	2	4	4	0	0	0	0	0	0	1	0	0	0	0	0	0	0	2	10	1	0
Muslims	17	.2712	1.0773	40.3	0	0	0	1	12	1	3	0	0	0	0	0	0	1	0	0	0	0	0	0	0	12	4	0	0
muslin	6	.5170	.6604	38.2	0	1	0	3	0	2	0	0	1	0	0	1	0	1	0	0	0	0	1	0	1	1	0	0	0
mussed	5	.3796	.4256	36.3	0	3	0	0	0	0	2	0	1	0	0	2	0	0	0	0	0	0	1	0	0	1	0	0	0
mussel	3	.1169	.1277	31.1	0	1	0	0	2	0	0	0	1	0	0	0	0	0	0	0	0	0	0	0	0	0	2	0	0
mussels	11	.4798	1.2043	40.8	1	4	0	0	4	0	2	0	5	0	0	0	0	0	0	3	0	0	0	0	2	0	1	0	0
Mussolini	10	.3803	.8699	39.4	2	0	1	0	2	3	2	0	1	0	0	0	0	6	0	0	0	0	0	0	0	1	2	0	0
Mussolini's	3	.0000	.0314	25.0	3	0	0	0	0	0	0	0	0	0	0	0	0	0	0	0	0	0	0	0	0	0	3	0	0
Mussorgsky	4	.0000	.0323	25.1	0	0	0	3	0	1	0	0	0	0	0	0	0	0	0	0	4	0	0	0	0	0	0	0	0
must	4307	.9768	828.95	69.2	762	695	523	529	807	461	434	96	1137	237	92	220	297	362	102	533	113	33	87	107	270	336	182	197	2
must've	2	.2443	.1130	30.5	0	0	1	0	1	0	0	0	0	0	0	1	0	0	0	0	0	0	0	0	1	0	0	0	0
mustache	27	.5715	3.2915	45.2	6	3	4	1	2	10	1	0	8	0	0	7	0	1	0	0	1	0	0	0	2	7	0	1	0
mustaches	3	.3394	.2451	33.9	0	1	1	0	1	0	0	0	1	0	0	1	0	0	0	0	0	0	0	0	1	0	0	0	0
Mustafa	5	.0000	.0972	29.9	0	0	0	0	5	0	0	0	0	0	0	0	0	5	0	0	0	0	0	0	0	0	0	0	0
mustang	20	.4003	1.8975	42.8	5	4	0	1	5	5	0	0	9	1	0	7	0	0	0	0	0	0	0	0	0	3	0	0	0
Mustang	9	.1963	.4328	36.4	0	0	0	0	7	2	0	0	0	0	0	2	0	0	0	0	0	0	0	0	0	0	0	7	0
mustangs	11	.3646	1.0012	40.0	0	2	1	0	6	2	0	0	6	0	0	3	0	0	0	0	0	0	0	0	0	2	0	0	0
Mustangs	4	.2427	.2319	33.7	0	0	0	0	2	0	2	0	0	0	0	0	2	0	0	0	0	0	0	0	0	0	0	2	0
Mustapha	6	.1748	.3964	36.0	0	5	1	0	0	0	0	0	5	0	1	0	0	0	0	0	0	0	0	0	0	0	0	0	0
mustard	24	.6568	3.2488	45.1	3	4	0	8	4	1	1	3	4	1	0	0	2	1	0	3	0	0	3	0	1	4	1	4	0
Mustard	14	.1948	.8749	39.4	7	0	7	0	0	0	0	0	7	0	0	0	0	0	0	0	0	0	0	0	0	7	0	0	0
Mustardseed	4	.0000	.0429	26.3	0	0	0	0	0	0	4	0	0	0	0	4	0	0	0	0	0	0	0	0	0	0	0	0	0
MUSTARDSEED	4	.0000	.0429	26.3	0	0	0	0	0	0	4	0	0	0	0	4	0	0	0	0	0	0	0	0	0	0	0	0	0
muster	6	.5323	.6630	38.2	1	1	0	0	1	0	1	2	0	1	0	0	0	0	0	1	0	0	0	0	1	0	2	1	0
mustered	3	.3408	.2477	33.9	1	0	1	0	0	1	0	0	1	0	0	1	0	0	0	0	0	0	0	0	0	1	0	0	0
mustn't	29	.5959	3.7072	45.7	3	5	4	4	7	3	2	1	13	2	1	6	0	0	0	0	0	0	0	0	5	2	0	0	0
musty	10	.6003	1.2524	41.0	0	3	1	0	3	2	1	0	2	2	0	1	0	0	0	0	0	0	0	0	2	0	1	2	0
mutant	3	.2445	.1818	32.6	0	0	0	0	0	0	2	1	0	0	0	0	0	0	0	2	0	0	0	0	0	0	1	0	0
mutated	4	.0000	.0789	29.0	0	0	0	0	0	0	3	1	0	0	0	0	0	0	0	4	0	0	0	0	0	0	0	0	0
mutation	9	.2445	.5455	37.4	0	0	0	2	3	0	1	3	0	0	0	0	0	0	0	6	0	0	0	0	0	0	3	0	0
mutations	17	.3128	1.2447	41.0	0	1	0	1	4	0	2	9	0	0	0	0	0	0	0	12	0	0	0	0	0	0	4	1	0
mute	9	.5312	1.0060	40.0	1	0	0	2	2	3	1	0	1	0	0	1	0	0	0	1	2	0	0	0	3	1	0	0	0
muted	10	.5084	1.0538	40.2	0	1	1	1	2	0	5	0	0	1	0	1	0	1	0	0	4	0	0	0	2	1	0	0	0
mutes	3	.0000	.0243	23.8	0	0	0	0	0	3	0	0	0	0	0	0	0	0	0	0	3	0	0	0	0	0	0	0	0
mutilated	3	.2292	.1615	32.1	0	0	0	0	3	0	0	0	0	0	0	1	0	0	0	0	0	0	0	0	2	0	0	0	0
mutineers	2	.1551	.0728	28.6	0	0	0	0	2	0	0	0	0	0	1	0	0	0	0	0	0	0	0	0	1	0	0	0	0
mutiny	7	.3710	.5793	37.6	0	0	1	1	2	0	3	0	0	0	0	2	0	4	0	0	0	0	0	0	0	0	1	0	0
mutt	2	.2444	.1132	30.5	1	1	0	0	0	0	0	0	0	1	0	0	0	0	0	0	0	0	0	0	1	0	0	0	0
Mutt	10	.0804	.3283	35.2	5	2	0	0	0	3	0	0	2	0	0	0	0	0	0	0	0	0	0	0	8	0	0	0	0
mutter	8	.2155	.5456	37.4	0	0	2	2	3	1	0	0	5	0	0	0	0	0	0	0	0	0	0	0	3	0	0	0	0
muttered	68	.6351	9.1585	49.6	14	11	7	5	19	4	4	4	30	3	0	11	0	1	0	1	0	0	0	0	10	7	0	5	0
muttering	29	.4506	2.9244	44.7	4	5	4	5	7	1	2	1	9	1	0	4	0	0	0	0	0	0	0	0	12	3	0	0	0
mutterings	2	.1787	.1174	30.7	0	1	1	0	0	0	0	0	1	0	0	0	0	0	0	0	0	0	0	0	1	0	0	0	0
mutters	4	.2445	.3067	34.9	2	1	1	0	0	0	0	0	3	0	0	0	0	0	0	0	0	0	0	0	0	1	0	0	0
Mutti	5	.0000	.0724	28.6	0	0	0	0	0	0	5	0	0	0	0	0	0	0	0	0	0	0	0	0	0	5	0	0	0
mutton	14	.5865	1.7163	42.3	2	2	1	7	1	0	1	0	2	0	0	0	0	3	0	0	0	0	1	0	5	1	1	1	0
mutual	25	.6530	3.3281	45.2	2	0	2	1	6	8	5	1	1	1	0	2	0	3	0	2	0	0	2	0	0	2	7	5	0
mutually	7	.4799	.7263	38.6	0	0	0	0	4	1	2	0	1	0	0	0	0	2	0	0	0	0	1	0	0	2	1	0	0
mutuels	3	.0000	.0434	26.4	0	0	0	3	0	0	0	0	0	0	0	0	0	0	0	0	0	0	0	0	0	3	0	0	0
muzzle	27	.6037	3.4052	45.3	1	6	5	5	6	3	0	1	5	0	0	2	0	0	0	1	0	0	0	0	7	7	2	3	0
muzzles	2	.1787	.1174	30.7	0	0	0	1	1	0	0	0	1	0	0	0	0	0	0	0	0	0	0	0	1	0	0	0	0
my	7898	.8356	1328.3	71.2	1517	1141	716	1185	1544	739	940	116	2974	558	125	1254	63	137	140	24	395	25	17	2	922	579	35	627	21
My	228	.4308	20.734	53.2	83	42	41	33	6	13	9	1	7	5	0	5	43	2	128	0	25	0	1	0	2	6	0	4	0
MY	4	.2446	.3071	34.9	1	1	1	1	0	0	0	0	3	0	0	0	1	0	0	0	0	0	0	0	0	0	0	0	0
myalgia	2	.0000	.0209	23.2	0	0	0	0	0	0	2	0	0	0	0	0	0	0	0	0	0	0	0	0	0	0	2	0	0
mycelium	2	.0000	.0394	26.0	0	0	0	2	0	0	0	0	0	0	0	0	0	0	0	2	0	0	0	0	0	0	0	0	0
Mycenae	4	.2223	.2556	34.1	0	0	0	0	0	2	2	0	2	0	0	1	0	0	0	0	0	1	0	0	0	0	0	0	0
Myer	10	.0000	.4568	36.6	0	0	10	0	0	0	0	0	10	0	0	0	0	0	0	0	0	0	0	0	0	0	0	0	0
Myers	14	.4381	1.4916	41.7	0	0	7	0	5	0	0	2	10	0	0	0	0	0	0	1	0	0	0	0	0	0	2	1	0
Myers'	2	.0000	.0914	29.6	0	0	2	0	0	0	0	0	2	0	0	0	0	0	0	0	0	0	0	0	0	0	0	0	0
Mynderse	5	.0000	.0586	27.7	0	5	0	0	0	0	0	0	0	0	0	0	0	0	0	0	0	0	0	0	5	0	0	0	0
Myoux	6	.0000	.2741	34.4	0	6	0	0	0	0	0	0	6	0	0	0	0	0	0	0	0	0	0	0	0	0	0	0	0
Myra	9	.3748	.8547	39.3	0	0	0	6	1	0	2	0	6	2	0	1	0	0	0	0	0	0	0	0	0	0	0	0	0
myriad	10	.5760	1.2135	40.8	1	0	0	0	4	1	2	2	2	0	1	0	0	0	0	2	0	0	0	0	1	1	2	1	0
myriads	5	.3011	.3700	35.7	0	0	0	0	4	0	0	1	1	0	0	0	0	0	0	2	0	0	0	0	0	0	2	0	0
myrrh	5	.2254	.2851	34.5	0	1	0	2	1	0	0	1	1	0	0	0	0	0	0	0	3	0	0	0	0	0	0	1	0
Myrrhine	2	.0000	.0290	24.6	0	0	0	0	2	0	0	0	0	0	0	0	0	0	0	0	0	0	0	0	0	2	0	0	0
myrtle	3	.3374	.2433	33.9	0	0	2	1	0	0	0	0	1	1	0	0	0	0	0	0	0	0	0	0	0	0	1	0	0

5J musicales
9D Musician
9J Musicianship
9D musings
7R muskeg
6Q Muskegon
7N musket-shot
3Q Musketeers
6R Muskiejump's
3A muskrat's
3P Muskrat's
3P Muskrats'
6A muslin's
3N mussed-up
5A mussel-man
5A mussel-man's
XH Musset
6J Mussorgsky's
5N Mussulman
7P mustachios
8D mustang-running
7Q mustards
9B mustering-out
5J musters
3P mutants
6B mutch
9D mutely
8D mutilations
9F Mutiny
5Q Mutsuhito
9P Mutti's
4N mutton-bone
8R Mutual
5G muv'e**
4R muzzle-loader
4R muzzle-loaders
7N muzzle-loadin'
8F muzzled
8Q MV
7N My-Son-Ralph's
4A my-uh-children
7P Mycenaean
XH mycological
8G mykes
8M Mylar
3G myna
5F Myna
4R mynah
3Q mynahs
8D Mynheer
4N Mynheers
9D myopic
XH Myosurus
6A Myra's
6R myrmidons

Word Type	F	D	U	SFI	3 Gr 3	4 Gr 4	5 Gr 5	6 Gr 6	7 Gr 7	8 Gr 8	9 Gr 9	X UnGr	A Read	B Eng & Gr	C Comp	D Lit	E Math	F Soc Stud	G Spell	H Sci	J Music	K Art	L Home Ec	M Shop	N Lib F	P Lib NF	Q Lib Ref	R Mag	S Rel
Myrtle	6	.1425	.2307	33.6	6	0	0	0	0	0	0	0	0	0	0	0	0	0	0	0	0	0	0	0	5	1	0	0	0
myself	465	.7034	67.637	58.3	60	67	42	76	110	42	62	6	174	32	2	81	2	1	7	3	5	0	0	0	83	35	1	39	0
Myself	2	.2376	.1088	30.4	1	0	1	0	0	0	0	0	0	0	0	0	0	0	1	0	0	0	0	0	0	0	0	1	0
mysteries	26	.8086	4.2158	46.2	1	1	3	3	11	4	1	2	3	1	1	1	1	3	1	4	0	1	0	0	1	1	4	4	0
mysterious	140	.8130	22.990	53.6	19	9	22	21	34	14	12	9	48	6	7	7	0	7	0	14	9	3	0	0	10	13	7	9	0
mysteriously	20	.6545	2.7346	44.4	2	3	1	2	7	4	1	0	7	0	0	3	0	0	0	1	2	1	0	0	0	4	1	1	0
mystery	121	.6646	16.579	52.2	14	13	8	18	31	14	16	7	27	13	2	10	2	2	5	9	2	6	0	0	10	11	6	14	2
Mystery	6	.1733	.3447	35.4	2	1	3	0	0	0	0	0	3	3	0	0	0	0	0	0	0	0	0	0	0	0	0	0	0
mystic	8	.5223	.8691	39.4	0	0	1	2	2	1	0	2	0	0	0	0	0	0	0	0	1	0	0	0	1	4	1	1	0
Mystic	2	.2407	.1138	30.6	1	0	0	0	1	0	0	0	0	0	0	1	0	0	0	0	0	0	0	0	0	1	0	0	0
mystical	4	.4529	.3998	36.0	0	2	0	0	0	1	1	0	1	0	0	0	0	0	0	0	0	0	0	0	1	0	1	1	0
mysticism	5	.4821	.5109	37.1	0	0	1	0	2	1	0	1	0	0	0	0	0	2	0	0	1	0	0	0	0	1	1	0	0
mystified	2	.1787	.1174	30.7	0	1	0	1	0	0	0	0	1	0	0	0	0	0	0	0	0	0	0	0	1	0	0	0	0
mystify	3	.3467	.2520	34.0	0	0	0	1	1	1	0	0	1	0	0	0	1	0	0	0	0	0	0	0	0	0	0	1	0
mystifying	3	.3871	.2488	34.0	0	0	0	1	1	0	0	1	0	1	0	0	0	0	0	0	0	0	0	0	0	0	1	1	0
mystique	4	.1622	.1743	32.4	0	0	0	0	3	0	1	0	0	0	0	0	0	1	0	0	0	0	0	0	0	0	0	3	0
myth	29	.6692	3.9932	46.0	2	4	5	3	8	5	1	1	5	6	0	2	0	1	0	3	0	0	0	0	0	4	4	4	0
mythical	4	.2797	.2732	34.4	0	0	0	1	0	0	1	2	1	0	0	0	0	0	0	0	0	1	0	0	0	1	0	1	0
mythological	6	.3641	.4780	36.8	0	0	1	0	0	1	0	4	0	0	0	0	0	0	0	0	0	0	0	0	0	3	2	1	0
mythologists	2	.0000	.0914	29.6	0	0	0	0	0	2	0	0	2	0	0	0	0	0	0	0	0	0	0	0	0	0	0	0	0
mythology	13	.5285	1.4385	41.6	1	0	2	1	1	2	2	4	1	4	0	1	0	0	0	1	0	0	0	0	0	0	3	3	0
Mythology	2	.0000	.0209	23.2	0	0	2	0	0	0	0	0	0	0	0	0	0	0	0	0	0	0	0	0	0	0	2	0	0
myths	36	.7261	5.3589	47.3	1	6	6	8	5	8	2	0	11	6	0	2	0	1	1	4	1	2	0	0	0	4	2	2	0
Mzee	3	.0000	.0365	25.6	0	0	0	3	0	0	0	0	0	0	0	0	0	0	0	0	0	0	0	0	0	0	0	3	0
M1	5	.0000	.0724	28.6	0	0	5	0	0	0	0	0	0	0	0	0	0	0	0	0	0	0	0	0	0	5	0	0	0
M18	3	.0000	.0434	26.4	0	0	3	0	0	0	0	0	0	0	0	0	0	0	0	0	0	0	0	0	0	3	0	0	0
M4	3	.0000	.0434	26.4	0	0	3	0	0	0	0	0	0	0	0	0	0	0	0	0	0	0	0	0	0	3	0	0	0
n	572	.3509	44.575	56.5	64	83	103	59	110	72	80	1	7	20	1	0	423	1	107	0	3	0	0	0	2	2	3	3	0
N	235	.6781	32.332	55.1	16	23	54	33	47	23	33	6	3	67	4	1	108	6	0	5	4	2	1	2	1	8	9	14	0
N**	33	.5067	3.4880	45.4	0	0	5	4	7	5	7	5	1	1	0	0	0	0	1	0	0	0	0	1	0	3	10	16	0
N-V	7	.0000	.0766	28.8	0	0	1	0	6	0	0	0	0	7	0	0	0	0	0	0	0	0	0	0	0	0	0	0	0
N-V-N	5	.0000	.0547	27.4	0	0	1	0	4	0	0	0	0	5	0	0	0	0	0	0	0	0	0	0	0	0	0	0	0
N-lv-adj	4	.0000	.0438	26.4	0	0	0	0	0	4	0	0	0	4	0	0	0	0	0	0	0	0	0	0	0	0	0	0	0
N-lv-n	2	.0000	.0219	23.4	0	0	0	0	0	2	0	0	0	2	0	0	0	0	0	0	0	0	0	0	0	0	0	0	0
N-pole	2	.0000	.0394	26.0	0	0	0	1	0	0	1	0	0	0	0	0	0	0	0	2	0	0	0	0	0	0	0	0	0
N-type	2	.0000	.0394	26.0	0	0	0	0	0	2	0	0	0	0	0	0	0	0	0	2	0	0	0	0	0	0	0	0	0
N-v	3	.0000	.0328	25.2	0	0	0	0	0	3	0	0	0	3	0	0	0	0	0	0	0	0	0	0	0	0	0	0	0
N-v-n	4	.0000	.0438	26.4	0	0	0	0	0	4	0	0	0	4	0	0	0	0	0	0	0	0	0	0	0	0	0	0	0
N-v-n-n	2	.0000	.0219	23.4	0	0	0	0	0	2	0	0	0	2	0	0	0	0	0	0	0	0	0	0	0	0	0	0	0
N-v-ns-n	2	.0000	.0219	23.4	0	0	0	0	0	2	0	0	0	2	0	0	0	0	0	0	0	0	0	0	0	0	0	0	0
n-2	5	.0000	.0748	28.7	0	0	0	0	0	5	0	0	0	0	0	0	5	0	0	0	0	0	0	0	0	0	0	0	0
n/25	3	.0000	.0449	26.5	0	0	0	3	0	0	0	0	0	0	0	0	3	0	0	0	0	0	0	0	0	0	0	0	0
n/4	2	.0000	.0299	24.8	0	0	0	0	0	2	0	0	0	0	0	0	2	0	0	0	0	0	0	0	0	0	0	0	0
N/9	3	.0000	.0449	26.5	0	0	0	0	0	0	3	0	0	0	0	0	3	0	0	0	0	0	0	0	0	0	0	0	0
n's	7	.2810	.4398	36.4	0	1	2	2	1	0	1	0	0	2	0	0	0	0	4	1	0	0	0	0	0	0	0	0	0
n't	4	.0000	.0438	26.4	0	2	0	0	1	0	1	0	0	4	0	0	0	0	0	0	0	0	0	0	0	0	0	0	0
na	4	.1733	.2298	33.6	2	0	0	0	0	2	0	0	2	2	0	0	0	0	0	0	0	0	0	0	0	0	0	0	0
Na	7	.1990	.3456	35.4	2	5	0	0	0	0	0	0	0	0	0	0	0	0	0	0	0	0	0	0	0	2	0	5	0
NaCl	5	.3691	.4157	36.2	1	0	0	1	0	1	2	0	0	0	0	0	0	0	0	3	0	0	0	0	0	1	1	0	0
NaMukonda	3	.0000	.0434	26.4	0	0	0	0	3	0	0	0	0	0	0	0	0	0	0	0	0	0	0	0	0	3	0	0	0
naaah	2	.0000	.0045	16.5	0	0	0	0	0	2	0	0	0	0	2	0	0	0	0	0	0	0	0	0	0	0	0	0	0
Nace	4	.0000	.0429	26.3	0	0	0	0	0	4	0	0	0	0	0	4	0	0	0	0	0	0	0	0	0	0	0	0	0
Nacht	2	.0000	.0162	22.1	0	0	0	0	0	2	0	0	0	0	0	0	0	0	2	0	0	0	0	0	0	0	0	0	0
Nacogdoches	4	.2183	.2285	33.6	0	1	0	0	3	0	0	0	0	0	0	0	0	3	0	0	0	0	0	0	0	1	0	0	0
nacreous	2	.2441	.1127	30.5	0	0	0	0	1	1	0	0	0	0	0	0	0	0	0	0	0	0	0	0	1	0	1	0	0
Nader	3	.0000	.0365	25.6	0	0	0	0	3	0	0	0	0	0	0	0	0	0	0	0	0	0	0	0	0	0	0	3	0
Nadine	6	.0000	.0657	28.2	0	0	0	6	0	0	0	0	0	6	0	0	0	0	0	0	0	0	0	0	0	0	0	0	0
nag	11	.5412	1.2688	41.0	0	1	3	4	1	0	2	0	3	0	1	1	0	0	0	0	1	0	0	0	4	0	1	0	0
Nag	21	.2212	1.4693	41.7	0	6	0	6	9	0	0	0	14	0	0	7	0	0	0	0	0	0	0	0	0	0	0	0	0
Nag's	4	.2393	.3005	34.8	0	1	0	2	1	0	0	0	3	0	0	1	0	0	0	0	0	0	0	0	0	0	0	0	0
Nagaina	13	.2420	.9890	40.0	0	1	0	5	7	0	0	0	10	0	0	3	0	0	0	0	0	0	0	0	0	0	0	0	0
Nagasaki	7	.5231	.7838	38.9	0	0	1	2	1	2	1	0	1	0	0	1	0	3	1	0	0	0	0	0	1	0	0	0	0
Nagel	3	.2223	.2106	33.2	0	0	0	0	3	0	0	0	2	1	0	0	0	0	0	0	0	0	0	0	0	0	0	0	0
nagged	2	.2446	.1142	30.6	1	0	0	0	0	1	0	0	0	0	0	0	0	0	0	0	0	0	0	0	1	0	0	1	0
nagging	4	.3679	.3346	35.2	0	0	0	0	0	2	2	0	1	0	0	1	0	0	0	0	0	0	1	0	0	0	0	1	0
nags	2	.2427	.1152	30.6	0	1	0	1	0	0	0	0	0	0	0	0	0	0	0	0	0	0	0	0	1	1	0	0	0
Naguib	2	.0000	.0389	25.9	0	0	0	0	2	0	0	0	0	0	0	0	0	2	0	0	0	0	0	0	0	0	0	0	0
nah	4	.1814	.2373	33.8	1	0	0	0	1	0	2	0	2	0	0	0	0	0	0	0	0	0	0	0	0	0	0	2	0
nail	153	.6917	21.644	53.4	48	19	17	11	30	16	7	5	21	11	1	4	4	1	1	52	0	1	4	19	3	18	2	11	0
nailed	30	.6660	4.1464	46.2	9	3	5	3	4	3	3	0	8	0	0	1	4	0	0	4	0	0	0	2	3	3	0	5	0
nailing	6	.3346	.4428	36.5	0	1	0	0	4	0	0	1	0	0	0	0	0	0	0	0	0	0	0	1	0	4	0	1	0
Nailles	2	.0000	.0243	23.9	0	0	0	0	0	0	0	2	0	0	0	0	0	0	0	0	0	0	0	0	0	0	0	2	0
nails	168	.8017	27.049	54.3	42	26	12	8	42	10	10	18	26	1	1	7	21	4	1	23	2	3	5	16	14	15	5	24	0
Nairobi	6	.2886	.3962	36.0	0	1	0	2	1	0	2	0	0	0	0	0	0	1	0	0	0	0	0	0	0	0	1	4	0
naive	6	.4644	.5827	37.7	0	0	0	0	1	3	2	0	0	1	0	2	0	0	0	0	0	0	0	0	0	0	2	1	0
naked	54	.7073	7.7599	48.9	3	1	5	6	21	6	7	5	6	2	1	13	0	0	0	6	0	0	0	0	9	6	7	4	0
Nam	23	.4278	2.1284	43.3	0	0	1	4	5	0	11	2	0	1	0	0	0	6	0	0	0	0	0	0	0	8	0	8	0
Nam's	2	.2351	.1166	30.7	0	0	0	0	0	0	2	0	0	0	0	0	0	1	0	0	0	0	0	0	0	0	0	1	0
nama	2	.0000	.0162	22.1	0	0	0	0	2	0	0	0	0	0	0	0	0	0	2	0	0	0	0	0	0	0	0	0	0
namastey	2	.0000	.0914	29.6	0	2	0	0	0	0	0	0	2	0	0	0	0	0	0	0	0	0	0	0	0	0	0	0	0
Namath	10	.0000	.1215	30.8	0	0	0	2	5	2	1	0	0	0	0	0	0	0	0	0	0	0	0	0	0	0	0	10	0
Namath's	2	.0000	.0243	23.9	0	0	0	0	0	2	0	0	0	0	0	0	0	0	0	0	0	0	0	0	0	0	0	2	0
name	3766	.8360	629.90	68.0	759	725	578	618	443	332	244	67	557	304	47	137	1368	231	236	193	113	19	13	30	116	171	105	108	18
Name	2	.2306	.1140	30.6	0	0	0	0	0	2	0	0	0	1	0	0	0	1	0	0	0	0	0	0	0	0	0	0	0
name-tape	3	.0000	.0352	25.5	0	0	3	0	0	0	0	0	0	0	0	0	0	0	0	0	0	0	0	0	3	0	0	0	0
name's	9	.3588	.7881	39.0	0	1	2	1	1	3	1	0	4	0	0	2	0	0	0	0	0	0	0	0	3	0	0	0	0
named	946	.8662	163.68	62.1	173	167	132	173	137	93	44	27	200	42	4	20	244	144	27	49	29	2	1	4	20	62	52	46	0
nameless	9	.5087	.9835	39.9	0	0	0	3	3	1	2	0	2	0	0	2	0	0	0	0	0	0	0	0	3	0	1	1	0
namely	16	.7041	2.2619	43.5	0	1	0	4	5	0	5	1	0	1	0	2	2	0	0	0	2	0	1	1	4	0	3	0	0
names	1016	.8370	169.95	62.3	222	185	130	129	183	92	63	12	144	126	26	22	251	59	135	64	65	3	8	5	13	49	18	23	5

5F MyrtleBeach
7A mysel'
7L mysost
5Q Mysteries
5P mystic-minded
8E mystification
7R mythmaking
7Q mythologies
7A mythos
8P Myths
7Q myxomatosis
5P M19A1
5P M1917A1
5P M1919A4
5P M1919A6

5P M2
5P M2's
5P M20
5P M3
4R NASA's
8B NP's
4R NY
8R NYC
8B N-LV-N
7B N-Lv-N
9E N-factorial
8B N-lnv-n
4A n-n-nothing
4A n-necklace
6D n-no

8B N-v-ns
7R N-10Y
9E n/10
7E n/100
7E n/2200
6E n/48
8E n/6
7E n%
7A n'est-ce
XH N's
5H NaHCO3
6Q NaNO3
9H NaC1
7P NaMutale
7P NaMutale's

6Q NaOH
4A naaw
XR NAB
XR Nabarro
5R nabbed
8J Nachtmusik
3J Nacimiento
7R Nacionales
8Q nacre
8K Nadelman
9Q Nadia
4N Nadie
8J nae
6R Nagafuchi
6A Nagaina's

4F Nagoya
7D Nahar
5A Nahum
8R NAIA
8J naiads
3P NAIL
3Q nail-biting
6P nail's
7D nailed-down
6A Nailer
6A Nailer's
4N nailfile
XR Nailles's
4R Naismith
9R naisty

8D naively
7R naivete
5R Nakamura's
5B Nakashi
3B nakedness
6J nakuba
7P nam
8Q Nama
4B NAME
7R namecalling
9R Named
4A nameplate

Word Type	F	D	U	SFI	3 Gr 3	4 Gr 4	5 Gr 5	6 Gr 6	7 Gr 7	8 Gr 8	9 Gr 9	X UnGr	A Read	B Eng & Gr	C Comp	D Lit	E Math	F Soc Stud	G Spell	H Sci	J Music	K Art	L Home Ec	M Shop	N Lib F	P Lib NF	Q Lib Ref	R Mag	S Rel
mewing	4	.2393	.3005	34.8	1	1	0	0	2	0	0	0	3	0	0	1	0	0	0	0	0	0	0	0	0	0	0	0	0
mews	3	.2804	.1831	32.6	0	0	1	0	0	1	1	0	0	0	1	1	0	0	0	0	0	0	0	0	1	0	0	0	0
Mexican	154	.6851	21.744	53.4	7	20	29	31	36	26	5	0	29	4	0	4	0	67	1	3	10	8	0	0	9	5	7	7	0
Mexican-American	6	.2425	.3632	35.6	0	1	3	0	1	0	1	0	0	0	0	0	0	4	0	0	0	0	0	0	0	0	0	2	0
Mexican-Americans	3	.2425	.1816	32.6	0	2	0	0	0	1	0	0	0	0	0	0	0	2	0	0	0	0	0	0	0	0	0	1	0
Mexican's	2	.1814	.1187	30.7	0	0	1	0	1	0	0	0	1	0	0	0	0	0	0	0	0	0	0	0	0	0	0	1	0
Mexicans	44	.4814	4.7164	46.7	6	7	7	8	8	8	0	0	11	0	0	0	0	20	0	0	1	0	0	0	1	10	0	1	0
Mexico	432	.6694	59.840	57.8	32	63	87	107	79	40	19	5	68	7	1	1	3	229	2	19	18	11	0	0	0	20	38	15	0
MexicoCity	13	.1547	.6975	38.4	0	1	4	6	0	2	0	0	4	0	0	0	0	9	0	0	0	0	0	0	0	0	0	0	0
Mexico's	16	.1696	.7796	38.9	0	0	1	13	2	0	0	0	0	0	0	0	0	14	0	0	0	0	0	0	0	0	0	2	0
Meyer	4	.4572	.4096	36.1	1	0	0	1	1	1	0	0	1	0	0	0	1	0	0	1	0	0	0	0	0	0	0	1	0
Meyerbeer	2	.0000	.0162	22.1	0	0	0	0	1	1	0	0	0	0	0	0	0	0	0	0	2	0	0	0	0	0	0	0	0
Meyers	4	.1907	.1863	32.7	0	1	0	0	0	3	0	0	0	3	0	0	0	0	0	0	0	0	0	0	0	0	0	1	0
mezzo-soprano	2	.0000	.0162	22.1	0	0	0	0	1	1	0	0	0	0	0	0	0	0	0	0	2	0	0	0	0	0	0	0	0
MG	47	.1547	3.1843	45.0	0	0	0	0	0	45	2	0	45	0	0	2	0	0	0	0	0	0	0	0	0	0	0	0	0
MGM	2	.0000	.0243	23.9	0	0	0	0	1	1	0	0	0	0	0	0	0	0	0	0	0	0	0	0	0	0	0	2	0
mi	61	.3459	4.6781	46.7	1	18	6	0	6	28	2	0	1	0	0	0	39	0	0	0	15	0	0	0	0	0	6	0	0
Mi	32	.0000	.3752	35.7	0	0	0	0	32	0	0	0	0	0	0	0	0	0	0	0	0	0	0	0	32	0	0	0	0
Miami	29	.7014	4.1355	46.2	10	2	2	3	7	3	2	0	1	0	1	1	6	8	0	1	0	0	0	0	1	3	1	6	0
miasmas	2	.2407	.1138	30.6	0	1	0	0	1	0	0	0	0	0	0	1	0	0	0	0	0	0	0	0	0	1	0	0	0
mica	18	.2855	1.1578	40.6	0	0	1	7	0	8	1	1	0	0	0	0	0	1	0	3	0	0	0	6	0	7	0	1	0
micaceous	4	.2353	.2382	33.8	0	0	0	0	0	1	0	3	0	0	0	0	0	0	0	3	0	0	0	0	0	0	1	0	0
mice	202	.8318	33.730	55.3	56	25	35	26	25	14	4	17	44	11	2	14	3	3	4	46	8	0	0	0	29	21	11	6	0
Mice	2	.1494	.1045	30.2	0	0	0	0	1	1	0	0	1	0	0	0	0	0	0	0	1	0	0	0	0	0	0	0	0
Mich	6	.1708	.2605	34.2	0	0	0	1	2	1	0	2	0	0	0	0	0	0	0	0	0	0	0	0	0	0	1	5	0
Michael	103	.5616	12.289	50.9	1	2	47	20	20	9	0	4	27	3	1	13	1	0	1	0	0	0	0	0	44	1	1	11	0
Michael's	3	.3872	.2490	34.0	0	2	0	0	1	0	0	0	0	1	0	1	0	0	0	0	0	0	0	0	0	0	0	1	0
Michailovitch	2	.0000	.0215	23.3	0	0	0	0	0	0	2	0	0	0	0	2	0	0	0	0	0	0	0	0	0	0	0	0	0
Michel	8	.5861	.9635	39.8	0	0	0	0	1	2	4	1	0	0	0	2	0	1	0	1	1	0	0	0	0	0	2	1	0
Michelangelo	11	.1548	.4303	36.3	1	0	0	0	2	1	6	1	1	0	0	0	0	1	0	0	0	6	0	0	0	1	1	1	0
Michele	2	.2391	.1133	30.5	0	1	0	0	1	0	0	0	0	0	0	0	1	0	0	0	0	0	0	0	0	0	1	0	0
Michelle	7	.0000	.3198	35.0	7	0	0	0	0	0	0	0	7	0	0	0	0	0	0	0	0	0	0	0	0	0	0	0	0
Michelmore	2	.0000	.0209	23.2	0	0	0	0	2	0	0	0	0	0	0	0	0	0	0	0	0	0	0	0	0	0	2	0	0
Michigan	103	.6578	13.954	51.4	10	9	26	16	8	25	5	4	10	4	0	0	5	32	0	10	1	0	0	0	1	3	21	16	0
Michigan's	6	.3567	.4852	36.9	0	0	4	1	0	1	0	0	0	0	0	0	0	4	0	0	0	0	0	0	0	0	1	1	0
Michigania	3	.2444	.1814	32.6	0	0	0	0	0	3	0	0	0	0	0	0	0	2	0	0	0	0	0	0	0	0	1	0	0
Michot	3	.0000	.0352	25.5	3	0	0	0	0	0	0	0	0	0	0	0	0	0	0	0	0	0	0	0	3	0	0	0	0
Mickey	20	.3082	1.3916	41.4	2	1	0	6	4	2	5	0	0	0	0	1	0	1	0	0	0	0	0	0	0	5	0	13	0
Mickey's	3	.2332	.1690	32.3	0	0	0	3	0	0	0	0	0	0	0	0	0	0	0	0	0	0	0	0	0	2	0	1	0
micro-organisms	6	.3623	.4910	36.9	0	0	0	0	0	2	0	4	0	0	0	1	0	0	0	4	0	0	0	0	0	0	1	0	0
microbe	20	.1231	.8481	39.3	1	1	0	0	2	0	0	16	1	0	0	0	1	0	0	18	0	0	0	0	0	0	0	0	0
microbes	54	.2936	4.5793	46.6	39	4	0	0	2	0	0	9	39	0	0	0	1	0	0	14	0	0	0	0	0	0	0	0	0
microbiologists	2	.0000	.0394	26.0	0	0	0	0	2	0	0	0	0	0	0	0	0	0	0	2	0	0	0	0	0	0	0	0	0
microcosm	4	.1611	.1738	32.4	0	0	0	0	1	2	0	1	0	0	0	0	0	0	0	1	0	0	0	0	0	0	0	3	0
microfarad	3	.0000	.0076	18.8	0	0	0	0	0	3	0	0	0	0	0	0	0	0	0	0	0	0	0	3	0	0	0	0	0
micrometer	18	.1736	.7195	38.6	0	0	0	0	7	0	11	0	0	0	0	0	1	0	0	0	0	0	0	10	0	1	0	6	0
micrometers	6	.1620	.2279	33.6	0	0	0	0	3	0	3	0	0	0	0	0	0	0	0	0	0	0	0	3	0	0	0	3	0
micromicrofarad	2	.0000	.0050	17.0	0	0	0	0	0	2	0	0	0	0	0	0	0	0	0	0	0	0	0	2	0	0	0	0	0
micron	8	.2160	.5447	37.4	0	0	4	0	2	0	0	2	4	0	0	0	0	0	0	4	0	0	0	0	0	0	0	0	0
microns	5	.2365	.3671	35.6	0	0	3	0	1	0	0	1	3	0	0	0	0	0	0	2	0	0	0	0	0	0	0	0	0
microorganism	2	.0000	.0394	26.0	0	0	1	0	1	0	0	0	0	0	0	0	0	0	0	2	0	0	0	0	0	0	0	0	0
microorganisms	26	.2196	1.5085	41.8	0	0	2	11	9	0	4	0	0	0	0	0	0	1	0	23	0	0	0	0	0	0	1	1	0
microphone	27	.4826	2.7879	44.5	3	3	0	2	13	4	2	0	4	1	0	0	0	0	0	3	11	0	0	0	0	3	4	1	0
microphones	5	.3013	.3288	35.2	0	1	0	0	3	0	0	1	0	0	0	0	0	0	0	0	3	0	0	0	0	0	1	1	0
microscope	171	.4389	16.551	52.2	20	25	40	20	37	12	7	10	3	2	1	1	2	1	1	140	0	0	0	2	0	7	11	0	0
microscopes	19	.2607	1.2394	40.9	5	1	1	5	4	0	1	2	0	0	0	0	0	1	0	16	0	0	0	0	0	1	1	0	0
microscopic	33	.3688	2.7287	44.4	0	2	6	6	6	3	9	1	0	1	0	0	0	0	0	20	0	0	0	0	0	0	10	2	0
microscopists	2	.0000	.0209	23.2	0	0	0	0	2	0	0	0	0	0	0	0	0	0	0	0	0	0	0	0	0	0	2	0	0
microwave	2	.1698	.1133	30.5	1	0	0	0	0	0	1	0	1	0	0	0	0	0	0	0	0	0	0	0	0	0	1	0	0
microwaves	4	.3348	.3267	35.1	1	0	0	0	1	0	0	2	1	0	0	0	0	0	0	2	0	0	0	0	0	0	1	0	0
mid	2	.1497	.1046	30.2	1	0	1	0	0	0	0	0	1	0	0	0	0	0	1	0	0	0	0	0	0	0	0	0	0
mid-April	2	.2446	.1142	30.6	0	0	0	0	1	1	0	0	0	0	0	0	0	0	0	0	0	0	0	0	1	0	0	1	0
Mid-Atlantic	2	.2437	.1129	30.5	0	0	0	0	1	0	0	1	0	0	0	0	0	0	0	0	0	0	0	0	0	0	1	1	0
mid-August	2	.2437	.1129	30.5	0	0	0	0	2	0	0	0	0	0	0	0	0	0	0	0	0	0	0	0	0	0	1	1	0
mid-December	3	.3845	.2448	33.9	0	0	0	0	1	1	1	0	0	1	0	0	0	0	0	0	1	0	0	0	0	0	1	0	0
Mid-East	4	.0000	.0778	28.9	0	0	0	0	0	0	4	0	0	0	0	0	0	4	0	0	0	0	0	0	0	0	0	0	0
mid-July	2	.0000	.0243	23.9	0	0	0	0	0	0	0	2	0	0	0	0	0	0	0	0	0	0	0	0	0	0	0	2	0
mid-March	2	.1494	.1045	30.2	0	0	0	1	0	1	0	0	1	0	0	0	0	0	0	0	1	0	0	0	0	0	0	0	0
mid-May	4	.0000	.0486	26.9	0	0	0	2	0	0	0	2	0	0	0	0	0	0	0	0	0	0	0	0	0	0	0	4	0
mid-November	3	.0000	.1370	31.4	0	1	1	1	0	0	0	0	3	0	0	0	0	0	0	0	0	0	0	0	0	0	0	0	0
Mid-Ocean	5	.2424	.2988	34.8	0	0	0	3	2	0	0	0	0	0	0	0	0	0	0	3	0	0	0	0	0	0	2	0	0
mid-October	2	.2375	.1088	30.4	0	0	1	0	1	0	0	0	0	0	0	0	0	0	0	0	1	0	0	0	0	0	0	1	0
mid-afternoon	3	.3553	.2608	34.2	1	0	1	1	0	0	0	0	1	0	0	0	0	1	0	0	0	0	0	0	0	1	0	0	0
mid-air	8	.6637	1.0935	40.4	1	0	0	3	3	0	0	1	1	0	0	1	1	0	0	2	0	0	0	0	1	1	0	1	0
mid-autumn	2	.2278	.1128	30.5	0	0	1	0	1	0	0	0	0	0	0	0	0	0	0	1	0	0	0	0	0	0	1	0	0
mid-day	3	.3777	.2489	34.0	0	0	1	0	1	0	1	0	0	1	0	0	0	1	0	0	0	0	0	0	1	0	0	0	0
mid-fifteenth	2	.1042	.0600	27.8	0	0	1	1	0	0	0	0	0	0	0	0	0	1	0	0	0	1	0	0	0	0	0	0	0
mid-latitudes	2	.2285	.1129	30.5	0	0	0	0	1	0	1	0	0	0	0	0	0	1	0	0	0	0	0	0	0	0	1	0	0
mid-nineteenth	2	.2442	.1134	30.5	0	0	0	0	0	1	0	1	0	1	0	0	0	0	0	0	0	0	0	0	0	0	0	1	0
mid-ocean	2	.2278	.1128	30.5	0	1	0	0	0	0	1	0	0	0	0	0	0	0	0	1	0	0	0	0	0	0	1	0	0
mid-thwart	2	.0000	.0234	23.7	0	0	0	2	0	0	0	0	0	0	0	0	0	0	0	0	0	0	0	0	2	0	0	0	0
mid-17th	2	.0000	.0209	23.2	0	0	0	0	0	0	2	0	0	0	0	0	0	0	0	0	0	0	0	0	0	0	2	0	0
mid-1800's	2	.2278	.1128	30.5	0	0	1	1	0	0	0	0	0	0	0	0	0	0	0	1	0	0	0	0	0	0	1	0	0
mid-19th	2	.2437	.1129	30.5	0	0	1	1	0	0	0	0	0	0	0	0	0	0	0	0	0	0	0	0	0	0	1	1	0
mid-1950's	2	.2437	.1129	30.5	0	0	1	1	0	0	0	0	0	0	0	0	0	0	0	0	0	0	0	0	0	0	1	1	0
mid-1966	2	.0000	.0389	25.9	0	0	1	0	0	1	0	0	0	0	0	0	0	2	0	0	0	0	0	0	0	0	0	0	0
midafternoon	3	.3450	.2505	34.0	0	0	0	0	0	1	2	0	1	0	0	0	0	0	0	0	0	0	0	0	1	1	0	0	0
midair	3	.2212	.2099	33.2	0	0	0	2	1	0	0	0	2	0	0	1	0	0	0	0	0	0	0	0	0	0	0	0	0
Midas	26	.4924	3.0265	44.8	21	0	1	2	1	1	0	0	21	2	1	0	0	0	1	0	0	0	0	0	0	1	0	0	0
midcontinent	2	.2351	.1166	30.7	0	0	0	0	0	1	0	1	0	0	0	0	0	1	0	0	0	0	0	0	0	0	0	1	0
midday	24	.7162	3.5594	45.5	3	1	3	8	6	2	0	1	10	2	0	0	0	2	0	0	1	0	0	0	2	3	1	3	0

5P mewling
5F Mex'ico**
5F Mexican-Spanish
5F Mexicanos
5A Mexicans'
XH MgO
9D MG'S
XP Mi-Careme
7N Mi's
5F MiamiBeach
4P miasma
9H micas
5R Michelle's
XH Michelson
XH Michelson-Twyman
5J Michie
6Q MICHIGAN
9Q Michigan-Canadian
5N micical
7A mickeys
8Q Mickiewicz
6F Micmac
XH micro-organism
XH micro-organsims
6H Microbes
7Q microbial
7H microbiologist
8H microcrystalline
8J Microgroove
XH microgrooved
XH microlite
7H micrometric
6F Micronesia
7Q microphotographs
7H microprojector
6H Microscope
7E microseconds
9M microstructural
9B Microteknic
7Q microworld
6F mid-Asia
5P mid-Bosporus
5F Mid-Continent
XQ mid-Europe
8F mid-January
6F mid-Pacific
7R mid-September
9Q mid-Victorian
XR mid-Winter
9P mid-block
8F mid-century
7R mid-channel
7H mid-continent
7Q mid-continental
XR mid-country
XR mid-course
7P mid-court
7F mid-eighteenth
8J mid-eighth
9H mid-latitude
7D mid-leap
3A mid-morning
9B mid-season
6B mid-sentence
XR mid-state
7N mid-stream
4A mid-winter
5Q mid-1400's
3Q mid-1600's
7F mid-1600s
8F mid-1700s
9Q mid-18th
9F mid-1850's
7R mid-1930's
7Q mid-1960's
9Q mid-1960s
8Q mid-20th
9H midblock
5Q Midcontinent
7R midcourse
6H middens

Word Type	F	D	U	SFI	3 Gr 3	4 Gr 4	5 Gr 5	6 Gr 6	7 Gr 7	8 Gr 8	9 Gr 9	X UnGr	A Read	B Eng & Gr	C Comp	D Lit	E Math	F Soc Stud	G Spell	H Sci	J Music	K Art	L Home Ec	M Shop	N Lib F	P Lib NF	Q Lib Ref	R Mag	S Rel
namesake	3	.3773	.2505	34.0	0	0	0	0	0	1	2	0	0	0	0	1	1	1	0	0	0	0	0	0	0	0	0	0	0
Namese	3	.0000	.0583	27.7	0	0	0	0	0	0	3	0	0	0	0	0	0	3	0	0	0	0	0	0	0	0	0	0	0
naming	98	.5377	11.022	50.4	11	14	19	19	16	12	6	1	3	3	8	2	63	6	3	5	0	0	1	0	1	1	2	0	0
Nan	10	.2446	.7732	38.9	8	0	0	0	0	0	2	0	8	2	0	0	0	0	0	0	0	0	0	0	0	0	0	0	0
Nan's	4	.0000	.0599	27.8	4	0	0	0	0	0	0	0	0	0	0	0	4	0	0	0	0	0	0	0	0	0	0	0	0
Nana	28	.3747	2.5828	44.1	0	0	0	15	7	0	6	0	15	0	0	7	0	0	0	0	0	0	0	0	0	0	0	6	0
NANA	17	.0000	.1824	32.6	0	0	0	0	0	0	17	0	0	0	0	17	0	0	0	0	0	0	0	0	0	0	0	0	0
Nana's	5	.3842	.4760	36.8	0	0	0	3	2	0	0	0	3	0	0	1	0	0	0	0	0	0	0	0	0	0	0	1	0
Nance	2	.1787	.1174	30.7	0	0	0	0	2	0	0	0	1	0	0	0	0	0	0	0	0	0	0	0	1	0	0	0	0
Nancy	126	.6130	16.432	52.2	21	44	27	6	9	19	0	0	47	2	0	0	11	5	7	0	1	0	0	0	3	44	0	6	0
Nancy's	10	.3183	.7896	39.0	2	5	0	0	1	2	0	0	3	0	0	0	5	0	0	0	0	0	0	0	0	2	0	0	0
nankeen	2	.1948	.1250	31.0	0	1	0	1	0	0	0	0	1	0	0	0	0	0	0	0	0	0	0	0	0	1	0	0	0
Nanki-Poo	6	.0000	.0485	26.9	0	0	0	0	0	6	0	0	0	0	0	0	0	0	0	0	6	0	0	0	0	0	0	0	0
Nanking	4	.2285	.2258	33.5	0	0	2	1	0	1	0	0	0	0	0	0	0	2	0	0	0	0	0	0	0	0	2	0	0
Nanko	6	.0000	.0703	28.5	0	0	0	6	0	0	0	0	0	0	0	0	0	0	0	0	0	0	0	0	6	0	0	0	0
Nanna	2	.0000	.0234	23.7	0	0	2	0	0	0	0	0	0	0	0	0	0	0	0	0	0	0	0	0	2	0	0	0	0
Nannerl	6	.2440	.4665	36.7	0	0	6	0	0	0	0	0	5	0	0	0	0	0	0	0	1	0	0	0	0	0	0	0	0
Nannerl's	2	.0000	.0914	29.6	0	0	2	0	0	0	0	0	2	0	0	0	0	0	0	0	0	0	0	0	0	0	0	0	0
Nansen	2	.2405	.1205	30.8	0	0	1	1	0	0	0	0	0	0	0	0	0	0	0	1	0	0	0	0	0	1	0	0	0
Nantaqua	8	.0000	.1158	30.6	0	8	0	0	0	0	0	0	0	0	0	0	0	0	0	0	0	0	0	0	0	8	0	0	0
Nantes	8	.0000	.0837	29.2	3	0	5	0	0	0	0	0	0	0	0	0	0	0	0	0	0	0	0	0	0	0	8	0	0
Nantucket	21	.2193	1.1849	40.7	1	15	0	3	1	0	1	0	2	0	0	1	0	0	0	0	0	0	0	0	0	17	1	0	0
nap	37	.6510	5.0512	47.0	13	7	1	4	7	4	1	0	14	0	0	0	0	2	1	0	1	0	2	0	9	3	0	5	0
nape	2	.2346	.1166	30.7	0	0	0	0	0	0	0	2	0	0	0	0	0	0	0	1	0	0	0	0	0	0	0	1	0
naphtha	3	.1169	.1277	31.1	1	0	2	0	0	0	0	0	1	0	0	0	0	0	0	0	0	0	0	0	0	0	2	0	0
Napier	6	.3261	.4417	36.5	0	0	0	0	0	4	1	1	0	0	0	0	4	0	0	0	0	0	0	0	0	1	1	0	0
napkin	27	.6064	3.3905	45.3	5	3	3	0	3	7	5	1	5	1	1	7	1	0	2	1	0	0	5	0	0	3	0	1	0
napkins	9	.1843	.4095	36.1	1	2	1	0	1	0	4	0	1	0	0	0	0	0	0	0	0	0	5	0	1	2	0	0	0
Naples	24	.4422	2.3397	43.7	8	1	6	3	3	1	2	0	4	1	0	0	0	1	0	0	0	0	0	0	0	13	4	1	0
Napoleon	84	.6740	11.560	50.6	4	8	23	6	16	10	13	4	4	4	0	1	0	25	0	1	6	0	0	0	14	18	10	1	0
Napoleon's	18	.5629	2.0924	43.2	0	1	2	1	2	3	9	0	0	0	0	0	0	5	0	0	1	1	0	0	4	1	6	0	0
Napoleonic	5	.2226	.2657	34.2	0	0	1	0	1	1	2	0	0	0	0	0	0	0	0	0	0	0	0	0	0	2	3	0	0
napped	6	.2622	.3436	35.4	0	2	0	0	0	3	1	0	0	0	0	1	0	0	0	0	0	0	3	0	1	1	0	0	0
napping	8	.4748	.8341	39.2	1	1	1	1	2	0	2	0	2	0	0	3	0	1	0	0	0	0	0	0	1	0	0	1	0
naps	10	.6260	1.3369	41.3	3	4	1	1	1	0	0	0	5	0	0	0	0	0	0	0	1	0	0	0	1	1	1	1	0
Naquin	3	.0000	.1370	31.4	0	0	3	0	0	0	0	0	3	0	0	0	0	0	0	0	0	0	0	0	0	0	0	0	0
Nara	2	.0000	.0389	25.9	0	2	0	0	0	0	0	0	0	0	0	0	0	2	0	0	0	0	0	0	0	0	0	0	0
Narcissus	9	.1245	.3063	34.9	0	0	7	1	0	0	1	0	0	8	0	1	0	0	0	0	0	0	0	0	0	0	0	0	0
narcotic	6	.0000	.1183	30.7	0	0	0	0	6	0	0	0	0	0	0	0	0	0	0	6	0	0	0	0	0	0	0	0	0
narcotics	11	.2041	.6018	37.8	0	0	0	2	6	2	0	1	0	0	0	0	0	0	0	9	0	0	0	0	0	0	0	2	0
Narraganset	3	.2442	.1815	32.6	0	0	2	0	0	0	0	1	0	0	0	1	0	2	0	0	0	0	0	0	0	0	0	0	0
Narragansett	3	.2431	.1816	32.6	0	0	2	1	0	0	0	0	0	0	0	0	0	2	0	0	0	0	0	0	1	0	0	0	0
narrate	2	.1523	.0721	28.6	0	0	0	1	0	0	1	0	0	0	1	0	0	0	0	0	0	0	0	0	0	0	0	1	0
narrates	2	.0000	.0243	23.9	0	0	0	1	0	0	1	0	0	0	0	0	0	0	0	0	0	0	0	0	0	0	0	2	0
narration	10	.3617	.7700	38.9	0	0	0	0	6	2	2	0	0	6	2	0	0	0	0	0	1	0	0	0	0	1	0	0	0
narrative	39	.3056	2.5568	44.1	0	0	1	0	20	6	10	2	0	13	15	3	0	1	0	0	0	0	0	0	4	0	1	2	0
narratives	13	.4509	1.2422	40.9	0	0	0	0	10	0	3	0	0	1	1	1	0	0	0	0	0	0	0	0	0	9	1	0	0
narrator	17	.4629	1.7186	42.4	0	4	0	0	7	0	6	0	4	0	0	6	0	0	0	0	4	0	0	0	0	2	0	1	0
Narrator	31	.5103	3.4967	45.4	0	11	1	13	4	2	0	0	13	4	0	2	0	0	0	0	2	0	0	0	10	0	0	0	0
NARRATOR	4	.0000	.0429	26.3	0	0	0	0	4	0	0	0	0	0	0	4	0	0	0	0	0	0	0	0	0	0	0	0	0
narrow	426	.8941	75.782	58.8	58	54	62	75	90	43	33	11	93	18	9	29	2	108	2	25	4	7	15	6	23	35	38	12	0
narrowed	19	.5665	2.2409	43.5	0	0	4	1	8	5	1	0	2	4	0	5	0	0	0	1	0	0	0	0	5	0	1	1	0
narrower	21	.6896	2.9558	44.7	1	2	3	3	6	4	0	2	3	3	0	0	0	3	0	3	2	2	1	1	0	2	0	1	0
narrowest	4	.4154	.3497	35.4	0	1	1	0	0	1	1	0	0	1	0	0	1	0	0	0	0	0	1	0	0	0	1	0	0
narrowing	7	.5302	.7695	38.9	0	0	1	1	4	1	0	0	0	2	0	2	0	1	0	0	0	0	0	0	0	0	1	1	0
narrowly	11	.5490	1.3350	41.3	0	1	1	3	4	2	0	0	6	1	0	1	0	0	0	0	0	0	0	0	0	0	2	1	0
narrowness	2	.2401	.1133	30.5	0	0	1	0	0	1	0	0	0	0	0	0	0	0	0	0	0	0	0	0	0	1	1	0	0
narrows	4	.4799	.4040	36.1	0	0	0	0	3	0	1	0	0	1	0	1	0	1	0	0	0	0	0	0	0	0	1	0	0
Narrows	2	.2446	.1122	30.5	0	0	0	0	1	0	1	0	0	0	0	1	0	0	0	0	0	0	0	0	0	0	1	0	0
Narvik	2	.0000	.0389	25.9	0	0	0	2	0	0	0	0	0	0	0	0	0	2	0	0	0	0	0	0	0	0	0	0	0
narwhal	7	.0000	.0851	29.3	0	7	0	0	0	0	0	0	0	0	0	0	0	0	0	0	0	0	0	0	0	0	0	7	0
nary	3	.3814	.2446	33.9	2	0	0	1	0	0	0	0	0	0	0	0	0	0	0	0	1	0	0	0	1	0	0	1	0
NASA	14	.4183	1.2808	41.1	1	0	2	4	7	0	0	0	1	0	0	0	0	2	0	0	0	0	0	0	0	3	1	7	0
nasal	22	.4660	2.1900	43.4	0	0	2	0	5	5	10	0	1	0	0	0	0	0	0	7	6	0	0	0	2	0	0	6	0
NASCAR	3	.0000	.0365	25.6	0	0	0	0	3	0	0	0	0	0	0	0	0	0	0	0	0	0	0	0	0	0	0	3	0
nascent	4	.1873	.1827	32.6	0	0	0	0	1	2	1	0	0	0	0	0	0	0	0	0	0	0	0	0	0	0	3	1	0
Nascimento	3	.0000	.0365	25.6	0	0	0	0	3	0	0	0	0	0	0	0	0	0	0	0	0	0	0	0	0	0	0	3	0
Nash	2	.0000	.0219	23.4	0	0	0	0	0	2	0	0	0	2	0	0	0	0	0	0	0	0	0	0	0	0	0	0	0
Nashville	9	.3831	.7393	38.7	0	1	0	0	3	2	3	0	0	1	0	0	0	0	0	0	0	1	0	0	0	1	0	6	0
Nashville's	2	.1814	.1187	30.7	0	0	0	1	0	1	0	0	1	0	0	0	0	0	0	0	0	0	0	0	0	0	0	1	0
Nasmyth	2	.0000	.0209	23.2	0	0	0	0	2	0	0	0	0	0	0	0	0	0	0	0	0	0	0	0	0	0	2	0	0
Nasr-ed-Din	2	.0000	.0914	29.6	0	2	0	0	0	0	0	0	2	0	0	0	0	0	0	0	0	0	0	0	0	0	0	0	0
Nassau	2	.0000	.0209	23.2	0	0	0	0	0	2	0	0	0	0	0	0	0	0	0	0	0	0	0	0	0	0	2	0	0
Nasser	19	.3007	1.3521	41.3	0	0	1	2	7	4	5	0	0	0	0	0	0	13	0	0	0	0	0	0	0	1	0	5	0
Nasser's	6	.2425	.3632	35.6	0	0	0	0	3	1	2	0	0	0	0	0	0	4	0	0	0	0	0	0	0	0	0	2	0
Nast	4	.0000	.0778	28.9	0	0	0	0	0	4	0	0	0	0	0	0	0	4	0	0	0	0	0	0	0	0	0	0	0
nastily	3	.3851	.2497	34.0	0	1	1	0	0	1	0	0	0	0	0	1	0	0	0	0	0	0	0	0	1	1	0	0	0
nasty	19	.5798	2.3615	43.7	2	2	3	1	7	2	2	0	7	1	0	2	0	0	0	0	0	0	0	0	1	3	0	5	0
Nat	63	.1409	3.0904	44.9	0	15	0	25	23	0	0	0	21	0	0	0	0	0	0	0	0	0	0	0	0	42	0	0	0
Nat's	5	.0926	.1850	32.7	0	1	0	3	1	0	0	0	1	0	0	0	0	0	0	0	0	0	0	0	0	4	0	0	0
natal	2	.0000	.0243	23.9	0	0	0	0	2	0	0	0	0	0	0	0	0	0	0	0	0	0	0	0	0	0	0	2	0
Natal	3	.3766	.2497	34.0	0	0	1	0	1	1	0	0	0	0	0	0	0	1	0	0	0	0	0	0	0	1	1	0	0
Natchez	2	.2152	.1357	31.3	0	1	0	0	1	0	0	0	1	0	0	0	0	1	0	0	0	0	0	0	0	0	0	0	0
Natchitoches	2	.0000	.0389	25.9	0	0	0	0	2	0	0	0	0	0	0	0	0	2	0	0	0	0	0	0	0	0	0	0	0
Nate	26	.3509	2.3442	43.7	11	3	1	4	7	0	0	0	16	0	0	7	0	0	0	0	0	0	0	0	0	3	0	0	0
Nate's	3	.0000	.0322	25.1	0	0	0	0	3	0	0	0	0	0	0	3	0	0	0	0	0	0	0	0	0	0	0	0	0
Nathan	75	.2640	6.0685	47.8	48	2	0	0	19	2	4	0	62	0	1	4	1	0	0	0	0	0	0	0	0	2	0	3	2
Nathanael	4	.1505	.1615	32.1	0	2	1	0	0	1	0	0	0	0	0	0	0	0	0	0	0	0	0	0	0	0	3	0	0
Nathaniel	24	.6300	3.2651	45.1	0	1	3	0	16	3	1	0	15	0	0	1	0	1	0	0	2	0	0	0	0	2	2	1	0
nation	510	.7216	74.960	58.7	52	51	78	62	98	114	43	12	44	6	1	11	3	271	5	2	22	0	0	2	6	36	57	43	1
Nation	13	.5130	1.3986	41.5	0	0	1	4	4	2	1	1	1	0	0	1	0	0	0	0	2	0	0	0	0	1	2	6	0
nation-state	2	.0000	.0209	23.2	0	0	0	0	0	2	0	0	0	0	0	0	0	0	0	0	0	0	0	0	0	0	2	0	0
nation-wide	3	.2159	.1532	31.9	1	0	0	0	0	0	1	1	0	0	0	0	0	0	0	0	0	0	0	0	0	0	2	1	0
nation's	91	.5620	10.744	50.3	6	11	12	10	20	14	18	0	6	1	0	0	0	41	1	1	2	0	0	0	0	4	14	21	0
Nation's	5	.3558	.3854	35.9	0	0	0	3	1	1	0	0	0	1	0	0	0	0	0	0	1	0	0	0	0	0	0	3	0
national	327	.7214	47.916	56.8	15	21	48	37	62	89	42	13	31	5	2	4	3	102	6	9	26	0	0	1	5	20	70	48	0
National	234	.7638	35.925	55.6	19	26	34	25	41	38	40	11	12	5	5	2	3	39	0	8	6	0	5	3	5	23	57	61	0

4Q Names
3A Nancy'd
3A Nanette
5N Nannie
5N Nannies
7P nanny-goats
4A Nanook's
7D Nanticokes
4P Nantucketer
7F Nanyang
8E Napier's
9Q NAPOLEONITE
9B Napoli
9N nappy
8F Narcissa
9R narcissism
5B narcissus
5Q Narcotics
7J narrating
XR narrator's
3E narrow-hand
7P narrow-minded
3J narrow-necked
4A narrow-walled
7R NASA'S
7A nasally
7R Naselle
9J Nassau-Weilburg
9R Nasser-oriented
9D nastiest
7P nastiness
3B Nasturtium
8Q Nasution
7A Natalie
7D Nate'd
8B nathaniel
7R Natick
7F nation-building

Word Type	F	D	U	SFI	3 Gr 3	4 Gr 4	5 Gr 5	6 Gr 6	7 Gr 7	8 Gr 8	9 Gr 9	X UnGr	A Read	B Eng & Gr	C Comp	D Lit	E Math	F Soc Stud	G Spell	H Sci	J Music	K Art	L Home Ec	M Shop	N Lib F	P Lib NF	Q Lib Ref	R Mag	S Rel
NATIONAL	2	.0000	.0243	23.9	0	0	0	2	0	0	0	0	0	0	0	0	0	0	0	0	0	0	0	0	0	0	0	2	0
nationalism	15	.5469	1.7147	42.3	0	0	2	0	3	3	7	0	0	0	0	0	0	7	0	0	2	0	0	0	0	2	2	2	0
nationalist	5	.4720	.4941	36.9	0	0	2	2	0	1	0	0	0	0	0	0	0	0	0	0	1	0	0	0	0	1	1	2	0
Nationalist	15	.3547	1.2082	40.8	0	0	2	6	3	4	0	0	0	0	0	0	0	10	0	0	0	0	0	0	0	0	2	3	0
nationalistic	10	.3580	.7794	38.9	0	0	1	1	2	5	1	0	0	0	0	0	0	2	0	0	5	0	0	0	0	1	0	2	0
nationalists	3	.2425	.1816	32.6	0	0	1	0	0	0	2	0	0	0	0	0	0	2	0	0	0	0	0	0	0	0	0	1	0
Nationalists	6	.1955	.3185	35.0	0	0	0	3	0	3	0	0	0	0	0	0	0	5	0	0	0	0	0	0	0	0	0	1	0
nationalities	11	.5452	1.2603	41.0	0	1	2	0	2	0	5	1	1	0	1	0	0	3	1	0	0	0	0	0	0	2	0	3	0
nationality	11	.5934	1.3423	41.3	0	0	2	0	4	2	2	1	0	0	1	0	0	3	0	1	1	0	0	0	0	1	3	1	0
nationalized	4	.3863	.3414	35.3	0	0	0	0	1	1	2	0	0	0	0	0	0	2	0	0	0	0	0	0	0	0	1	1	0
nationally	3	.1277	.1363	31.3	1	0	0	0	1	1	0	0	1	0	0	0	0	0	0	0	0	0	0	0	0	0	0	2	0
nationals	4	.0000	.0778	28.9	0	0	0	0	0	4	0	0	0	0	0	0	0	4	0	0	0	0	0	0	0	0	0	0	0
nations	337	.6692	46.430	56.7	29	13	75	65	41	62	50	2	28	4	1	2	2	191	3	7	9	0	1	0	0	24	46	18	1
Nations	109	.6231	14.218	51.5	6	5	17	18	31	16	16	0	17	3	2	3	1	61	1	1	0	0	0	0	0	6	11	3	0
nationwide	8	.5352	.8948	39.5	1	0	1	0	3	2	1	0	0	1	0	0	0	2	0	1	0	0	0	0	0	0	2	2	0
native	219	.8363	36.673	55.6	21	8	18	34	57	45	25	11	41	21	2	8	3	33	4	11	24	0	1	0	6	14	35	16	0
Native	2	.0000	.0243	23.9	0	0	0	0	0	0	0	2	0	0	0	0	0	0	0	0	0	0	0	0	0	0	0	2	0
native-born	6	.4790	.6112	37.9	1	0	1	1	0	3	0	0	0	0	0	0	0	3	0	0	1	0	0	0	0	0	1	1	0
natively	3	.0000	.0328	25.2	0	0	0	0	2	1	0	0	0	3	0	0	0	0	0	0	0	0	0	0	0	0	0	0	0
natives	72	.7007	10.395	50.2	9	3	20	8	28	1	2	1	16	2	1	2	0	27	0	0	1	0	0	0	4	13	5	1	0
nativity	2	.1378	.0662	28.2	1	0	0	0	0	0	0	1	0	0	0	0	0	0	0	0	0	1	0	0	0	0	0	1	0
NATO	10	.3759	.8160	39.1	2	0	0	0	2	1	5	0	0	0	0	1	0	1	0	0	0	0	0	0	0	0	2	6	0
nats	2	.0000	.0914	29.6	0	0	0	2	0	0	0	0	2	0	0	0	0	0	0	0	0	0	0	0	0	0	0	0	0
Natty	4	.0000	.0438	26.4	0	0	0	0	4	0	0	0	0	4	0	0	0	0	0	0	0	0	0	0	0	0	0	0	0
Natua	9	.0000	.4111	36.1	0	0	0	9	0	0	0	0	9	0	0	0	0	0	0	0	0	0	0	0	0	0	0	0	0
Natua's	3	.0000	.1370	31.4	0	0	0	3	0	0	0	0	3	0	0	0	0	0	0	0	0	0	0	0	0	0	0	0	0
natural	739	.9193	134.47	61.3	63	57	92	85	201	113	107	21	54	29	5	23	113	149	7	77	33	9	24	11	20	42	89	54	0
Natural	21	.5906	2.5752	44.1	2	3	0	3	10	3	0	0	2	1	0	0	0	2	0	0	0	0	0	1	0	6	2	7	0
naturalist	23	.6028	2.8619	44.6	2	3	1	3	9	3	2	0	3	1	2	0	0	0	2	1	0	0	0	0	4	1	8	1	0
naturalistic	2	.0580	.0676	28.3	0	0	0	0	0	2	0	0	1	0	0	0	0	0	0	0	0	1	0	0	0	0	0	0	0
naturalists	8	.5366	.9027	39.6	0	1	0	0	2	0	0	5	0	0	0	0	0	0	0	4	0	0	0	0	1	1	1	1	0
naturalization	4	.0000	.0778	28.9	0	0	0	0	0	1	3	0	0	0	0	0	0	4	0	0	0	0	0	0	0	0	0	0	0
Naturalization	4	.0000	.0778	28.9	0	0	0	0	0	2	2	0	0	0	0	0	0	4	0	0	0	0	0	0	0	0	0	0	0
naturalized	6	.3343	.4660	36.7	0	1	0	0	1	1	2	1	0	0	0	0	0	4	0	1	0	0	0	0	0	0	1	0	0
naturally	159	.8845	27.974	54.5	13	11	11	29	36	30	21	8	27	21	1	10	1	15	1	18	5	4	6	0	12	17	10	11	0
naturalness	2	.1698	.1133	30.5	0	0	0	0	0	2	0	0	1	0	0	0	0	0	0	0	0	0	0	0	0	0	1	0	0
nature	462	.8306	76.710	58.8	35	44	53	41	134	68	60	27	58	17	5	30	3	34	14	77	17	30	3	9	18	34	76	37	0
Nature	41	.7515	6.2992	48.0	1	8	1	4	12	4	2	9	14	3	1	1	2	1	1	0	0	0	0	0	1	11	2	4	0
nature-writing	2	.0000	.0243	23.9	0	0	0	0	2	0	0	0	0	0	0	0	0	0	0	0	0	0	0	0	0	0	0	2	0
nature's	29	.7709	4.5113	46.5	2	8	3	1	6	5	3	1	5	0	0	2	0	5	0	1	2	1	1	1	0	1	7	3	0
Nature's	4	.3199	.3102	34.9	0	1	0	0	3	0	0	0	1	0	0	0	0	0	0	0	0	0	0	0	1	2	0	0	0
natured	3	.2279	.2143	33.3	0	1	1	1	0	0	0	0	2	0	0	0	0	0	0	0	0	0	0	0	0	0	0	1	0
natures	4	.3289	.3049	34.8	0	0	0	0	3	1	0	0	1	0	1	1	0	0	0	0	0	0	0	0	0	0	1	0	0
naught	11	.3952	.9682	39.9	0	0	0	4	2	1	4	0	2	0	0	5	0	0	0	0	1	0	0	0	3	0	0	0	0
naughty	10	.4120	.9419	39.7	2	4	1	0	2	1	0	0	3	0	0	0	0	0	0	0	0	0	0	0	4	2	0	1	0
Naughty	2	.2137	.1056	30.2	0	1	0	1	0	0	0	0	0	0	0	0	0	1	0	0	1	0	0	0	0	0	0	0	0
nauplius	4	.0000	.0789	29.0	0	0	4	0	0	0	0	0	0	0	0	0	0	0	0	4	0	0	0	0	0	0	0	0	0
nausea	6	.2870	.4107	36.1	0	0	3	1	0	1	0	1	1	0	0	0	0	0	0	0	0	0	0	0	0	0	3	2	0
nautes	3	.2379	.1631	32.1	0	0	0	2	0	1	0	0	0	2	0	0	0	0	1	0	0	0	0	0	0	0	0	0	0
nautical	16	.7930	2.5409	44.0	0	2	0	5	2	6	0	1	1	1	0	2	2	1	2	1	1	0	0	0	2	0	1	2	0
Nautilus	37	.3754	3.4651	45.4	0	11	2	1	20	2	1	0	22	1	0	0	0	0	0	0	0	0	0	0	12	0	2	0	0
Navaho	22	.4541	2.2555	43.5	7	7	0	0	7	1	0	0	6	0	0	0	3	8	0	0	0	0	0	0	0	0	0	5	0
Navaholand	6	.0000	.0729	28.6	0	6	0	0	0	0	0	0	0	0	0	0	0	0	0	0	0	0	0	0	0	0	0	6	0
Navahos	13	.0912	.5104	37.1	12	0	0	0	1	0	0	0	2	0	0	0	0	11	0	0	0	0	0	0	0	0	0	0	0
Navajo	3	.3078	.2027	33.1	0	2	0	0	1	0	0	0	0	0	0	0	0	1	0	0	1	0	1	0	0	0	0	0	0
naval	50	.6936	7.0854	48.5	2	3	5	3	20	6	7	4	7	3	0	1	2	7	0	1	1	0	0	0	2	4	14	8	0
Naval	16	.6184	2.0899	43.2	2	1	2	4	3	2	2	0	5	0	0	0	0	3	0	0	1	0	0	0	0	2	2	3	0
navel	3	.3870	.2486	34.0	0	1	0	1	0	0	1	0	0	0	0	1	0	0	0	0	0	0	0	0	0	0	1	1	0
navies	2	.2408	.1204	30.8	1	0	0	0	1	0	0	0	0	0	0	0	0	1	0	0	0	0	0	0	0	1	0	0	0
navigable	12	.4038	1.0708	40.3	1	0	0	1	7	1	0	2	0	0	0	0	0	7	0	1	0	0	0	0	1	0	3	0	0
navigate	8	.5321	.9049	39.6	1	0	0	2	3	1	0	1	1	0	0	0	0	1	0	1	0	0	0	0	0	1	1	3	0
navigated	3	.2270	.1588	32.0	0	0	0	1	2	0	0	0	0	2	0	0	0	0	0	0	0	0	0	0	0	0	1	0	0
navigating	2	.0000	.0914	29.6	0	0	2	0	0	0	0	0	2	0	0	0	0	0	0	0	0	0	0	0	0	0	0	0	0
navigation	34	.7061	4.8976	46.9	1	0	3	9	11	4	4	2	4	1	0	1	1	5	0	4	0	0	0	0	1	4	7	6	0
Navigation	3	.2227	.1589	32.0	0	0	0	0	3	0	0	0	0	0	0	0	0	0	0	0	0	0	0	0	2	0	0	1	0
navigational	8	.3426	.6158	37.9	1	0	0	0	4	3	0	0	0	0	0	0	0	3	0	0	0	0	0	0	0	0	1	4	0
navigator	18	.6297	2.3525	43.7	2	0	5	2	6	3	0	0	2	1	0	0	0	5	0	2	0	0	0	0	0	2	2	4	0
Navigator	7	.4389	.6967	38.4	0	0	4	0	2	1	0	0	2	0	0	0	0	2	0	0	0	0	0	0	0	1	2	0	0
navigators	10	.5128	1.1368	40.6	1	0	4	3	0	0	1	1	3	0	0	0	1	1	0	4	0	0	0	0	0	1	0	0	0
navy	43	.7214	6.3143	48.0	5	0	10	5	7	12	3	1	6	1	1	1	0	16	4	0	0	0	3	0	2	4	5	0	0
Navy	125	.6488	17.285	52.4	11	51	14	9	19	9	7	5	66	1	0	0	0	12	1	1	2	0	0	0	0	18	10	14	0
NAVY	3	.0000	.0449	26.5	0	0	3	0	0	0	0	0	0	0	0	0	3	0	0	0	0	0	0	0	0	0	0	0	0
navy-blue	3	.1250	.1342	31.3	1	0	0	1	1	0	0	0	1	0	0	0	0	0	0	0	0	0	0	0	2	0	0	0	0
Navy's	2	.1814	.1187	30.7	0	1	0	0	1	0	0	0	1	0	0	0	0	0	0	0	0	0	0	0	0	0	0	1	0
naw	4	.4538	.4007	36.0	0	0	0	1	2	1	0	0	1	1	0	0	0	0	0	0	0	0	0	0	1	0	0	1	0
nay	34	.5323	3.8297	45.8	5	4	1	9	2	2	11	0	6	1	0	14	0	1	0	0	4	0	0	0	6	1	0	1	0
Nazaire	2	.0000	.0209	23.2	0	0	2	0	0	0	0	0	0	0	0	0	0	0	0	0	0	0	0	0	0	0	2	0	0
Nazareth	4	.0761	.0988	29.9	3	0	0	0	1	0	0	0	0	0	0	0	0	1	0	0	1	0	0	0	0	1	0	0	1
Nazi	29	.5538	3.4103	45.3	0	3	3	1	8	7	7	0	4	1	0	0	0	10	0	0	0	0	0	0	0	8	4	2	0
Nazis	15	.5017	1.6184	42.1	0	1	2	3	1	3	5	0	2	0	0	0	0	4	0	0	0	0	0	0	0	2	2	5	0
NBA	6	.0000	.0729	28.6	0	0	0	0	1	5	0	0	0	0	0	0	0	0	0	0	0	0	0	0	0	0	0	6	0
NBC	10	.1449	.3852	35.9	0	0	1	0	0	1	8	0	0	0	0	0	0	0	0	0	1	0	0	0	0	0	0	9	0
NBC-TV	2	.0000	.0243	23.9	0	0	0	2	0	0	0	0	0	0	0	0	0	0	0	0	0	0	0	0	0	0	0	2	0
NC	4	.1989	.1812	32.6	1	0	0	0	0	0	3	0	0	1	0	0	1	0	0	0	0	0	0	2	0	0	0	0	0
NCBC	4	.0000	.0486	26.9	0	0	0	0	0	4	0	0	0	0	0	0	0	0	0	0	0	0	0	0	0	0	0	4	0
nce	2	.2446	.1125	30.5	0	0	0	0	0	1	1	0	0	1	0	1	0	0	0	0	0	0	0	0	0	0	0	0	0
NC1234	9	.0000	.4111	36.1	0	0	0	9	0	0	0	0	9	0	0	0	0	0	0	0	0	0	0	0	0	0	0	0	0
nd	2	.2408	.1091	30.4	0	0	0	0	1	0	1	0	0	1	0	0	0	0	1	0	0	0	0	0	0	0	0	0	0
ne	2	.2440	.1132	30.5	0	0	0	0	0	0	2	0	0	0	0	1	0	0	0	0	0	0	0	0	0	0	0	1	0
Ne'eman	2	.0000	.0209	23.2	0	0	0	0	0	0	2	0	0	0	0	0	0	0	0	0	0	0	0	0	0	0	2	0	0
ne'er	16	.5646	1.8840	42.8	1	0	3	2	7	0	3	0	2	2	0	4	0	0	0	0	3	0	0	0	1	4	0	0	0
Neal	4	.3504	.3070	34.9	0	1	0	0	3	0	0	0	0	0	0	2	1	0	0	0	0	0	0	0	0	0	0	1	0
Neanderthal	15	.0675	.3496	35.4	0	0	0	0	15	0	0	0	0	0	0	0	1	0	0	0	0	0	0	0	0	0	14	0	0
Neanderthaler	2	.0000	.0209	23.2	0	0	0	0	2	0	0	0	0	0	0	0	0	0	0	0	0	0	0	0	0	0	2	0	0
Neanderthalers	8	.0000	.0837	29.2	0	0	0	0	8	0	0	0	0	0	0	0	0	0	0	0	0	0	0	0	0	0	8	0	0

8R national-security
8F Nationalism
9L Nationality
5P nationalize
5P nationhood
7F nations'
5J Nativity
9Q natrolite
8A natty
7N natur'
9L natural-fiber
5F natural-gas
8L natural-looking
7A natural-wood
5P naturalism
3A Naturalists
3A Naturalists'
8G naturalize
7R nature-watching
6A naturellement
6P Naturelles
7H Naturwissenschaften
7R Naugahyde
3P naughtiness
6A Nauplius
9B nauseam
7N nauseated
6R nauseous
7Q nautiloids
7Q nautilus
4R Navaholand's
7R Navarro
6A Navesink
7R navigates
4R navy-bean
7D Nayarit
7P Nazi-ruled
9Q Naziism
8R Nazionale
5P Nazis'
7P Nazism
4R NBC'S
7R NCAA
8R NCBC'S
6R Ne
4F NE
4G ne-brath-ka
XH neads
5F Neale

Word Type	F	D	U	SFI	3 Gr 3	4 Gr 4	5 Gr 5	6 Gr 6	7 Gr 7	8 Gr 8	9 Gr 9	X UnGr	A Read	B Eng & Gr	C Comp	D Lit	E Math	F Soc Stud	G Spell	H Sci	J Music	K Art	L Home Ec	M Shop	N Lib F	P Lib NF	Q Lib Ref	R Mag	S Rel
neap	8	.1824	.4081	36.1	0	4	0	2	0	0	2	0	0	0	0	0	0	0	0	7	0	0	0	0	0	0	1	0	0
Neapolitans	2	.0000	.0290	24.6	1	0	1	0	0	0	0	0	0	0	0	0	0	0	0	0	0	0	0	0	0	2	0	0	0
near	1985	.9378	368.56	65.7	433	381	290	266	312	158	111	34	463	51	32	95	11	469	31	285	32	16	18	12	85	168	98	118	1
Near	13	.5236	1.4331	41.6	1	0	0	2	4	2	4	0	0	1	0	0	0	7	1	0	2	0	0	0	0	2	0	0	0
near-by	12	.4541	1.1716	40.7	2	3	0	3	3	1	0	0	0	0	0	1	0	4	0	0	0	0	0	0	2	5	0	0	0
near-collision	4	.2353	.2382	33.8	0	0	0	0	1	0	3	0	0	0	0	0	0	0	0	3	0	0	0	0	0	0	1	0	0
near-perfect	2	.2437	.1129	30.5	0	0	0	0	2	0	0	0	0	0	0	0	0	0	0	0	0	0	0	0	0	0	1	1	0
near-sighted	6	.2437	.4554	36.6	0	1	0	2	1	2	0	0	4	0	0	0	0	0	0	2	0	0	0	0	0	0	0	0	0
nearby	335	.8239	55.688	57.5	61	57	72	39	57	26	15	8	103	8	8	5	2	82	2	31	1	2	1	0	8	21	27	34	0
neared	22	.5095	2.5560	44.1	2	6	1	6	4	3	0	0	13	0	0	0	0	1	0	1	0	0	0	0	1	1	0	5	0
nearer	146	.8770	25.606	54.1	25	30	13	23	23	21	9	2	52	4	2	10	6	10	1	13	2	2	0	1	23	11	8	1	0
nearest	429	.6112	54.324	57.3	47	63	78	59	87	40	53	2	27	7	2	8	262	24	1	36	10	0	0	6	8	18	9	11	0
nearing	15	.5188	1.7504	42.4	1	5	2	2	1	2	1	1	8	0	0	0	0	1	0	0	0	0	0	0	2	1	0	3	0
nearly	769	.9212	140.46	61.5	93	117	101	101	172	74	84	27	170	28	2	52	3	119	20	65	21	3	7	8	49	78	77	67	0
nearness	6	.3385	.4619	36.6	2	0	0	2	0	1	1	0	1	0	0	0	0	0	0	0	3	0	0	0	0	1	1	0	0
nears	8	.5287	.8869	39.5	0	2	2	2	2	0	0	0	0	0	0	0	0	2	0	1	0	0	0	0	0	1	2	2	0
nearsighted	4	.2872	.2840	34.5	1	1	0	0	2	0	0	0	1	0	0	2	0	0	0	0	0	0	0	0	0	1	0	0	0
neat	113	.7792	17.815	52.5	24	21	5	11	23	19	8	2	33	10	5	11	3	4	3	2	0	0	12	3	9	11	1	6	0
neat's-foot	2	.1621	.0746	28.7	0	0	0	0	1	1	0	0	0	0	1	1	0	0	0	0	0	0	0	0	0	0	0	0	0
neater	2	.2433	.1158	30.6	0	1	0	0	1	0	0	0	0	0	0	0	0	0	0	0	0	0	0	0	0	1	0	1	0
neatest	3	.3660	.2695	34.3	1	1	0	1	0	0	0	0	1	0	0	0	0	1	0	1	0	0	0	0	0	0	0	0	0
neatly	81	.7795	12.753	51.1	7	19	7	6	21	9	9	3	20	10	7	3	2	3	1	5	1	1	4	0	7	1	7	9	0
neatness	6	.3214	.4359	36.4	0	1	0	0	3	1	1	0	1	1	0	0	0	0	0	0	0	0	2	0	0	0	2	0	0
Neb	2	.0000	.0243	23.9	0	0	0	0	0	2	0	0	0	0	0	0	0	0	0	0	0	0	0	0	0	0	0	2	0
Nebeker	6	.0000	.0869	29.4	0	6	0	0	0	0	0	0	0	0	0	0	0	0	0	0	0	0	0	0	0	6	0	0	0
Nebraska	49	.7060	7.0670	48.5	0	6	22	2	6	8	3	2	4	1	1	1	0	26	1	3	2	0	0	0	1	1	3	5	0
Nebraska's	3	.0000	.0583	27.7	0	0	3	0	0	0	0	0	0	0	0	0	0	3	0	0	0	0	0	0	0	0	0	0	0
Nebuchadnezzar	16	.4348	1.6670	42.2	10	1	0	2	3	0	0	0	10	0	0	0	0	2	0	0	3	0	0	0	0	0	1	0	0
nebula	2	.2278	.1128	30.5	0	0	0	1	1	0	0	0	0	0	0	0	0	0	0	1	0	0	0	0	0	0	1	0	0
Nebula	4	.2391	.2266	33.6	0	0	0	0	0	4	0	0	0	0	0	0	2	0	0	0	0	0	0	0	0	0	2	0	0
nebulae	5	.2849	.3268	35.1	0	0	0	0	1	3	1	0	0	0	0	0	0	0	0	1	0	0	0	0	0	1	3	0	0
nebulium	2	.0000	.0209	23.2	0	0	0	0	0	2	0	0	0	0	0	0	0	0	0	0	0	0	0	0	0	0	2	0	0
necessarily	66	.7991	10.538	50.2	0	0	4	4	16	20	18	4	3	4	3	1	7	6	1	5	2	0	6	2	0	3	12	11	0
necessary	679	.8423	113.89	60.6	11	35	63	73	180	145	151	21	53	63	17	18	63	58	30	86	30	9	64	56	17	26	47	42	0
necessities	20	.7228	2.9275	44.7	0	1	2	3	4	4	6	0	3	0	0	1	1	3	0	0	1	1	3	1	1	1	3	1	0
necessity	41	.8195	6.7085	48.3	3	0	3	6	10	6	9	4	2	1	1	3	0	5	1	3	2	0	1	0	2	6	10	4	0
Necessity	2	.0000	.0389	25.9	0	0	0	0	0	2	0	0	0	0	0	0	0	2	0	0	0	0	0	0	0	0	0	0	0
neck	373	.8392	62.901	58.0	63	61	52	59	60	27	40	11	126	7	4	35	2	9	3	29	7	10	21	1	61	32	9	17	0
Neck	2	.2427	.1152	30.6	1	0	0	0	0	1	0	0	0	0	0	0	0	0	0	0	0	0	0	0	1	1	0	0	0
neck-and-neck	2	.0000	.0290	24.6	1	0	0	1	0	0	0	0	0	0	0	0	0	0	0	0	0	0	0	0	0	2	0	0	0
neck-and-opening	2	.0000	.0064	18.1	0	0	0	0	0	0	2	0	0	0	0	0	0	0	0	0	0	0	2	0	0	0	0	0	0
neck-string	2	.0000	.0215	23.3	0	0	0	0	2	0	0	0	0	0	0	2	0	0	0	0	0	0	0	0	0	0	0	0	0
neckerchief	2	.1948	.1250	31.0	0	0	0	0	1	0	0	1	1	0	0	0	0	0	0	0	0	0	0	0	0	1	0	0	0
necklace	69	.4532	7.5606	48.8	13	22	25	4	5	0	0	0	49	2	0	1	0	15	0	0	0	0	0	0	1	1	0	0	0
necklaces	7	.4530	.7194	38.6	1	2	1	1	1	1	0	0	2	0	0	0	0	3	0	0	0	0	0	0	1	1	0	0	0
neckline	18	.0000	.0580	27.6	0	0	0	0	7	6	5	0	0	0	0	0	0	0	0	0	0	0	18	0	0	0	0	0	0
necklines	4	.0000	.0129	21.1	0	0	0	0	2	1	1	0	0	0	0	0	0	0	0	0	0	0	4	0	0	0	0	0	0
necks	37	.7043	5.3747	47.3	15	6	1	2	6	5	1	1	12	1	1	1	0	2	0	4	0	3	1	0	3	7	1	1	0
necktie	6	.4235	.5619	37.5	2	1	0	1	1	0	1	0	1	0	0	0	0	0	0	1	0	0	0	1	1	2	0	0	0
neckties	2	.0000	.0389	25.9	1	0	0	1	0	0	0	0	0	0	0	0	0	2	0	0	0	0	0	0	0	0	0	0	0
nectar	69	.5097	7.6277	48.8	25	8	1	13	19	1	1	1	14	0	0	0	0	0	0	19	0	0	0	0	0	16	16	4	0
Ned	125	.5648	15.541	51.9	74	27	3	0	19	1	1	0	67	0	2	1	4	3	0	0	0	0	0	0	21	27	0	0	0
Ned's	5	.2422	.3874	35.9	4	1	0	0	0	0	0	0	4	0	0	0	0	0	0	0	0	0	0	0	0	1	0	0	0
need	2281	.9384	423.47	66.3	575	390	272	248	348	224	187	37	439	161	24	64	183	243	92	518	28	43	86	36	68	138	53	99	6
needed	1131	.9348	209.22	63.2	178	165	163	143	195	141	130	16	224	80	33	19	101	200	22	133	26	9	47	40	31	68	55	42	1
Needham	4	.1995	.2197	33.4	0	0	0	0	0	1	0	3	0	0	0	0	0	1	0	3	0	0	0	0	0	0	0	0	0
Needham's	2	.0000	.0394	26.0	0	0	0	0	0	0	0	2	0	0	0	0	0	0	0	2	0	0	0	0	0	0	0	0	0
needing	12	.6426	1.5847	42.0	0	0	1	1	6	3	1	0	2	0	1	0	0	0	0	2	0	1	0	1	2	0	2	1	0
needle	228	.6789	31.487	55.0	36	12	18	39	46	44	33	0	27	3	16	2	3	7	2	54	22	2	48	11	8	12	8	3	0
needled	3	.3394	.2451	33.9	0	0	1	1	0	0	1	0	1	0	0	1	0	0	0	0	0	0	0	0	1	0	0	0	0
needlefish	2	.0000	.0243	23.9	0	0	0	0	2	0	0	0	0	0	0	0	0	0	0	0	0	0	0	0	0	0	0	2	0
needlelike	5	.3674	.4504	36.5	1	1	1	1	0	0	1	0	2	0	0	0	0	0	0	2	0	0	0	0	0	0	1	0	0
needles	84	.8850	14.855	51.7	28	16	8	12	12	3	4	1	31	4	1	3	4	5	0	11	3	1	1	0	4	9	7	0	0
needless	11	.6117	1.3715	41.4	1	0	0	0	3	5	1	1	0	4	0	1	0	0	1	1	0	0	1	0	0	2	0	1	0
needlessly	6	.2451	.3685	35.7	0	0	0	1	2	1	1	1	1	1	0	0	0	0	0	0	0	0	0	0	0	0	0	4	0
needlework	10	.2326	.5297	37.2	0	2	0	0	8	0	0	0	0	0	0	1	0	2	0	0	0	0	5	0	0	2	0	0	0
needn't	26	.6438	3.5052	45.4	5	4	3	5	4	4	0	1	9	1	0	3	0	0	0	0	2	0	0	0	6	2	0	3	0
needs	616	.8745	107.24	60.3	127	90	80	59	74	68	105	13	83	22	17	13	27	99	9	124	8	14	62	9	16	46	35	31	1
Needs	2	.1812	.0838	29.2	0	0	0	0	2	0	0	0	0	0	0	0	0	0	0	0	0	0	1	0	0	0	0	1	0
needy	10	.6172	1.3024	41.1	0	4	2	0	0	3	1	0	3	1	0	1	0	2	0	0	0	0	0	0	1	0	0	2	0
Neeley	4	.0000	.1827	32.6	0	0	0	0	4	0	0	0	4	0	0	0	0	0	0	0	0	0	0	0	0	0	0	0	0
negative	210	.6625	28.315	54.5	2	6	16	11	37	62	71	5	0	22	1	0	113	0	3	28	3	0	2	11	3	5	9	10	0
negatively	17	.3947	1.5101	41.8	0	0	9	0	7	1	0	0	1	0	0	0	0	0	0	12	0	0	0	1	0	0	3	0	0
negatively-charged	7	.0000	.1380	31.4	0	0	7	0	0	0	0	0	0	0	0	0	0	0	0	7	0	0	0	0	0	0	0	0	0
negatives	22	.3534	1.7382	42.4	0	0	0	8	7	2	4	1	2	14	0	0	1	0	0	0	0	0	0	0	0	3	1	1	0
Negev	10	.4473	.9665	39.9	0	0	4	0	5	1	0	0	0	0	0	0	0	4	0	0	0	0	0	0	0	4	1	1	0
neglect	17	.7368	2.5515	44.1	0	0	2	2	5	4	4	0	3	1	0	0	0	4	2	2	0	0	0	0	1	1	1	2	0
neglected	31	.7687	4.8079	46.8	1	1	4	3	7	4	11	0	4	2	0	0	1	5	0	1	1	0	2	0	3	6	3	3	0
neglecting	3	.3844	.2487	34.0	0	0	0	1	2	0	0	0	0	1	0	0	0	0	0	0	0	0	0	0	0	1	1	0	0
negligent	3	.3394	.2451	33.9	0	0	0	0	2	0	1	0	1	0	0	1	0	0	0	0	0	0	0	0	1	0	0	0	0
negligible	9	.4548	.8793	39.4	1	0	0	0	1	0	0	7	0	0	0	0	0	0	0	4	0	0	0	0	1	0	1	3	0
Negoro	3	.0000	.0365	25.6	0	0	0	0	0	0	0	3	0	0	0	0	0	0	0	0	0	0	0	0	0	0	0	3	0
negotiate	8	.4118	.7394	38.7	0	0	1	1	3	1	2	0	1	0	0	0	0	4	0	0	0	0	0	0	0	0	2	1	0
negotiated	7	.3579	.5531	37.4	0	0	3	0	0	2	2	0	0	0	0	0	0	2	0	0	0	0	0	0	0	0	3	2	0
negotiating	4	.3605	.3115	34.9	0	0	0	1	0	1	2	0	0	1	0	0	0	0	0	0	0	0	0	0	0	0	2	1	0
negotiation	5	.3184	.3581	35.5	0	0	1	0	2	1	1	0	0	0	0	0	0	1	0	0	0	0	0	0	0	0	1	3	0
negotiations	21	.3580	1.6549	42.2	0	1	2	0	3	6	8	1	0	0	0	0	0	3	0	0	0	0	0	0	0	2	3	13	0
negotiators	2	.2351	.1166	30.7	0	0	0	0	0	1	1	0	0	0	0	0	0	1	0	0	0	0	0	0	0	0	0	1	0
Negritos	3	.1823	.1405	31.5	2	0	0	0	1	0	0	0	0	0	0	0	0	1	0	0	0	0	0	0	0	0	2	0	0
negro	3	.2379	.1705	32.3	0	0	0	0	2	1	0	0	0	0	0	1	0	0	0	0	0	0	0	0	0	2	0	0	0
Negro	264	.6830	37.070	55.7	15	17	41	22	39	69	55	6	41	1	0	9	0	91	4	0	29	0	0	0	5	38	10	36	0
Negro's	5	.4808	.5107	37.1	0	0	0	1	0	2	1	1	0	0	0	0	0	2	0	0	1	0	0	0	0	1	0	1	0
negroes	2	.2408	.1204	30.8	0	0	0	0	1	1	0	0	0	0	0	0	0	1	0	0	0	0	0	0	0	1	0	0	0
Negroes	154	.4981	16.563	52.2	12	4	32	12	20	33	39	2	11	0	0	2	0	99	1	0	9	0	0	0	2	22	1	7	0

5P Neapolitan
9D Neapolitan's
8R near-Pentecostal
XP near-certainty
7A near-fanatical
5F near-freezing
XR near-mink
7H near-natural
6E near-record
7R near-stock
8F near-tragic
8K near-vertical
7Q Nearctic
7R Neave
8Q nebiim
4A Nebri
7J Nebuchadnezzar's
6F Nebuchadrezzar
8Q nebula's
8Q nebular
7H Necator
9L necessitate
XQ necessitates
XH necessitating
7F Neches
9L neck-and-armhole
9L neck-and-sleeve
9L neck-opening
4J neck's
8R neckbones
8D neckcurls
7L neckedge
5A Necker
7D neckerchiefs
XR necking
9L Neckline
8Q necrosis
6Q nectaries
6A nectarines
9A Nedick's
8F Nee-say
3A Need
9D need'st
9R needful
4F Needle
7R needle-bearing
9M needle-case
XH needle-fine
5H needle-like
7D needle's
7R needleful
7D needlepoints
6A Needleton
7D neet
8A negation
9E negative/positive/zero
7G neglectful
9B negotiator
7R negotiators'
7Q Negras
7R negritude

Word Type	F	D	U	SFI	3 Gr 3	4 Gr 4	5 Gr 5	6 Gr 6	7 Gr 7	8 Gr 8	9 Gr 9	X UnGr	A Read	B Eng & Gr	C Comp	D Lit	E Math	F Soc Stud	G Spell	H Sci	J Music	K Art	L Home Ec	M Shop	N Lib F	P Lib NF	Q Lib Ref	R Mag	S Rel
Negroid	5	.3830	.4247	36.3	0	1	2	0	2	0	0	0	0	0	0	0	0	2	0	0	0	0	0	0	0	2	1	0	0
Negros	5	.0000	.0523	27.2	5	0	0	0	0	0	0	0	0	0	0	0	0	0	0	0	0	0	0	0	0	0	5	0	0
neigh	4	.0974	.1495	31.7	0	0	3	1	0	0	0	0	1	0	0	0	0	0	0	0	0	0	0	0	3	0	0	0	0
neighbor	178	.7944	28.690	54.6	48	27	21	22	30	7	19	4	66	11	12	11	8	18	8	10	1	1	1	0	6	9	7	8	1
Neighbor	3	.3783	.2509	34.0	0	1	0	1	0	0	1	0	0	1	0	0	0	1	0	0	0	0	0	0	0	1	0	0	0
neighbor's	44	.7715	6.9367	48.4	17	2	7	8	4	2	3	1	19	2	2	1	1	2	0	2	3	0	0	0	4	1	4	3	0
neighborhood	150	.7808	23.747	53.8	40	28	12	17	20	15	15	3	41	10	8	8	0	28	3	8	0	0	2	0	8	10	3	21	0
neighborhoods	22	.3585	1.8015	42.6	15	0	1	1	1	4	0	0	0	1	0	1	0	18	0	0	1	0	0	0	0	0	0	1	0
neighboring	60	.7917	9.5852	49.8	7	2	11	12	14	11	3	0	10	1	0	2	1	22	2	1	0	1	0	1	2	6	8	3	0
neighborliness	2	.2440	.1132	30.5	0	0	0	1	0	1	0	0	0	0	0	1	0	0	0	0	0	0	0	0	0	0	0	1	0
neighborly	7	.3865	.5785	37.6	0	0	0	1	4	0	2	0	0	0	1	4	0	1	0	0	0	0	0	0	1	0	0	0	0
neighbors	248	.8684	43.046	56.3	42	39	30	48	51	22	10	6	63	8	5	29	7	62	2	6	6	1	3	0	13	22	4	17	0
NEIGHBORS	2	.0000	.0215	23.3	0	0	0	0	0	0	2	0	0	0	0	2	0	0	0	0	0	0	0	0	0	0	0	0	0
neighbors'	10	.5535	1.1673	40.7	1	4	0	0	3	2	0	0	2	0	0	3	0	0	0	0	2	0	0	0	1	1	0	1	0
neighbour	4	.2445	.3067	34.9	1	0	0	0	3	0	0	0	3	0	0	0	0	0	0	0	0	0	0	0	0	1	0	0	0
neighbours	8	.3550	.6897	38.4	3	0	1	3	0	0	1	0	3	0	0	0	0	0	0	0	0	0	0	0	2	3	0	0	0
neighed	6	.2426	.3643	35.6	0	0	1	2	2	1	0	0	1	0	0	1	0	0	0	0	0	0	0	0	4	0	0	0	0
neighing	2	.1787	.1174	30.7	0	1	1	0	0	0	0	0	1	0	0	0	0	0	0	0	0	0	0	0	1	0	0	0	0
Neil	15	.3668	1.2240	40.9	6	0	1	2	4	0	2	0	0	0	0	0	5	4	0	0	0	0	0	0	0	0	0	6	0
neither	402	.9163	73.088	58.6	36	52	56	51	95	49	48	15	92	30	1	41	19	39	3	38	8	2	3	1	36	35	18	36	0
Nell	22	.3104	1.9659	42.9	18	1	0	0	1	0	2	0	19	2	0	0	1	0	0	0	0	0	0	0	0	0	0	0	0
Nell's	2	.0000	.0914	29.6	2	0	0	0	0	0	0	0	2	0	0	0	0	0	0	0	0	0	0	0	0	0	0	0	0
Nellie	12	.5062	1.3119	41.2	1	3	0	0	1	4	0	3	3	1	0	0	0	0	0	0	1	0	0	0	4	0	0	3	0
Nelly	68	.1746	4.8229	46.8	65	0	0	1	0	2	0	0	65	0	0	0	0	2	0	0	1	0	0	0	0	0	0	0	0
Nelly's	6	.0000	.2741	34.4	6	0	0	0	0	0	0	0	6	0	0	0	0	0	0	0	0	0	0	0	0	0	0	0	0
Nels	23	.2068	1.2818	41.1	0	0	0	0	7	16	0	0	5	0	0	2	0	0	0	0	0	0	0	0	16	0	0	0	0
NELS	4	.0000	.0429	26.3	0	0	0	0	4	0	0	0	0	0	0	4	0	0	0	0	0	0	0	0	0	0	0	0	0
Nelsen	13	.0000	.1580	32.0	0	0	0	0	13	0	0	0	0	0	0	0	0	0	0	0	0	0	0	0	0	0	0	13	0
Nelson	23	.6817	3.2256	45.1	4	4	4	1	1	5	4	0	5	3	0	0	1	1	0	0	0	0	0	0	3	3	3	4	0
Nelson's	5	.3851	.4791	36.8	2	0	0	1	1	1	0	0	3	0	0	0	1	0	0	0	0	0	0	0	1	0	0	0	0
Nemacolin	6	.0000	.1167	30.7	6	0	0	0	0	0	0	0	0	0	0	0	0	6	0	0	0	0	0	0	0	0	0	0	0
nematodes	3	.1813	.1402	31.5	0	0	0	0	3	0	0	0	0	0	0	0	0	0	0	1	0	0	0	0	0	0	2	0	0
Nemeth	2	.0000	.0914	29.6	2	0	0	0	0	0	0	0	2	0	0	0	0	0	0	0	0	0	0	0	0	0	0	0	0
Nemo	6	.3159	.4192	36.2	0	0	0	1	4	0	1	0	0	1	0	0	0	0	0	0	0	0	0	0	4	0	1	0	0
Nenana	3	.0000	.1370	31.4	0	0	3	0	0	0	0	0	3	0	0	0	0	0	0	0	0	0	0	0	0	0	0	0	0
Neolithic	4	.1901	.1843	32.7	0	1	0	0	2	0	1	0	0	0	0	0	0	0	0	0	0	0	0	0	1	0	3	0	0
neon	18	.5515	2.1228	43.3	1	1	0	3	4	3	6	0	3	0	0	0	0	1	0	9	0	1	0	0	0	1	2	1	0
neoprene	3	.0000	.0365	25.6	0	0	0	1	2	0	0	0	0	0	0	0	0	0	0	0	0	0	0	0	0	0	0	3	0
Neosho	5	.0000	.2284	33.6	5	0	0	0	0	0	0	0	5	0	0	0	0	0	0	0	0	0	0	0	0	0	0	0	0
Neotropical	4	.0000	.0419	26.2	0	0	0	0	4	0	0	0	0	0	0	0	0	0	0	0	0	0	0	0	0	0	4	0	0
Nepal	4	.3730	.3365	35.3	0	0	0	0	3	0	0	1	0	0	0	0	0	2	0	1	0	0	0	0	0	0	1	0	0
Nephele	2	.0000	.0914	29.6	0	0	0	0	0	2	0	0	2	0	0	0	0	0	0	0	0	0	0	0	0	0	0	0	0
nephew	28	.2087	1.6458	42.2	4	2	5	2	6	7	1	1	9	0	0	7	0	2	0	1	0	0	0	0	1	1	2	3	2
nephews	6	.4649	.5887	37.7	0	3	1	0	2	0	0	0	0	0	0	2	1	0	0	0	0	0	0	0	0	2	1	0	0
Neptune	37	.4955	4.0479	46.1	4	15	7	5	1	2	0	3	10	0	0	1	5	0	0	13	0	0	0	0	0	0	8	0	0
ner	3	.2031	.1990	33.0	0	0	1	0	1	1	0	0	2	0	0	0	0	0	1	0	0	0	0	0	0	0	0	0	0
Nereus	2	.0000	.0914	29.6	0	0	0	2	0	0	0	0	2	0	0	0	0	0	0	0	0	0	0	0	0	0	0	0	0
Nerissa	17	.0000	.1824	32.6	0	0	0	0	0	0	17	0	0	0	0	17	0	0	0	0	0	0	0	0	0	0	0	0	0
Nero	10	.2368	.5542	37.4	0	0	0	8	1	0	0	1	0	0	0	0	0	0	0	0	1	0	0	0	8	1	0	0	0
nerve	121	.5472	14.075	51.5	0	15	17	35	18	16	17	3	8	1	0	5	0	3	1	84	1	1	0	0	4	1	11	1	0
nerve-racking	2	.2407	.1138	30.6	0	0	0	0	1	0	1	0	0	0	0	1	0	0	0	0	0	0	0	0	0	1	0	0	0
nerve-shattering	2	.1948	.1250	31.0	1	0	0	0	1	0	0	0	1	0	0	0	0	0	0	0	0	0	0	0	0	1	0	0	0
nerved	2	.2443	.1130	30.5	0	0	0	0	2	0	0	0	0	0	0	1	0	0	0	0	0	0	0	0	1	0	0	0	0
nerveless	2	.1787	.1174	30.7	0	0	0	0	1	1	0	0	1	0	0	0	0	0	0	0	0	0	0	0	1	0	0	0	0
nerves	120	.5754	14.497	51.6	7	5	34	25	17	11	17	4	7	0	0	6	0	0	2	76	1	0	4	0	2	2	17	3	0
nervous	150	.8433	25.281	54.0	4	6	16	34	33	18	37	2	20	4	2	16	3	1	1	47	3	2	6	0	11	7	20	7	0
nervously	41	.6156	5.3717	47.3	2	9	6	8	7	4	5	0	17	2	0	5	0	0	0	1	0	0	0	0	9	4	0	3	0
nervousness	10	.4447	.9553	39.8	1	1	0	2	2	1	3	0	1	0	0	0	0	0	0	1	0	0	2	0	1	1	0	4	0
ness	25	.1128	.8057	39.1	2	11	0	4	5	3	0	0	2	2	0	0	0	0	21	0	0	0	0	0	0	0	0	0	0
Ness	7	.3871	.6753	38.3	0	0	0	0	6	1	0	0	4	0	0	1	0	0	0	2	0	0	0	0	0	0	0	0	0
Nessie	13	.2145	.9737	39.9	0	0	0	0	13	0	0	0	11	0	0	0	0	0	0	2	0	0	0	0	0	0	0	0	0
nest	333	.8386	56.305	57.5	137	38	14	62	43	19	8	12	130	13	0	8	1	7	6	65	10	1	2	0	14	28	32	16	0
nested	5	.2320	.3834	35.8	1	1	0	2	1	0	0	0	4	0	0	0	0	0	0	1	0	0	0	0	0	0	0	0	0
nesting	44	.4451	4.2576	46.3	11	1	2	7	13	0	0	10	5	0	0	0	0	1	0	5	0	0	0	0	0	3	10	20	0
nestle	2	.2285	.1129	30.5	1	0	0	1	0	0	0	0	0	0	0	0	0	1	0	0	0	0	0	0	0	0	1	0	0
nestled	6	.5538	.7178	38.6	2	0	1	0	2	0	0	1	2	0	0	1	0	1	0	0	0	0	0	0	1	0	0	1	0
nestlings	2	.2401	.1133	30.5	1	0	0	0	1	0	0	0	0	0	0	0	0	0	0	0	0	0	0	0	0	1	1	0	0
Nestor	8	.0919	.2859	34.6	0	0	0	2	0	0	6	0	2	0	0	6	0	0	0	0	0	0	0	0	0	0	0	0	0
nests	110	.7122	16.119	52.1	49	15	10	20	6	7	3	0	25	3	0	2	0	5	2	39	0	0	0	0	4	15	6	9	0
net	157	.5752	18.962	52.8	26	23	9	16	28	42	11	2	29	3	24	22	11	9	0	20	0	0	0	0	5	11	9	14	0
NET	7	.1314	.2567	34.1	0	0	0	1	0	0	6	0	0	0	0	0	0	0	0	0	0	0	0	0	0	1	0	6	0
Netherland	4	.0000	.0778	28.9	0	0	4	0	0	0	0	0	0	0	0	0	0	4	0	0	0	0	0	0	0	0	0	0	0
Netherlanders	2	.2285	.1129	30.5	0	1	0	0	0	0	1	0	0	0	0	0	0	1	0	0	0	0	0	0	0	0	1	0	0
Netherlands	127	.4127	11.764	50.7	13	46	14	24	10	8	11	1	7	0	0	0	0	98	1	1	1	0	1	0	0	9	6	3	0
nets	67	.8607	11.537	50.6	13	15	8	10	13	1	3	4	15	1	1	4	0	18	3	8	2	1	0	0	3	6	2	3	0
Netta	9	.0000	.4111	36.1	0	0	9	0	0	0	0	0	9	0	0	0	0	0	0	0	0	0	0	0	0	0	0	0	0
Netta's	2	.0000	.0914	29.6	0	0	2	0	0	0	0	0	2	0	0	0	0	0	0	0	0	0	0	0	0	0	0	0	0
netted	6	.6031	.7561	38.8	0	2	2	0	1	0	1	0	1	0	0	1	0	0	0	1	0	0	0	0	0	1	1	1	0
Nettie	7	.0000	.0821	29.1	0	0	0	7	0	0	0	0	0	0	0	0	0	0	0	0	0	0	0	0	7	0	0	0	0
netting	3	.2387	.1708	32.3	0	0	2	0	1	0	0	0	0	0	0	0	0	0	0	0	0	0	0	0	0	2	1	0	0
nettled	5	.2110	.3346	35.2	1	0	0	2	0	0	2	0	3	0	0	0	0	0	0	0	0	0	0	0	0	0	0	2	0
network	74	.7170	10.731	50.3	2	4	9	14	14	15	15	1	3	0	0	3	10	9	0	6	0	1	1	1	0	6	26	8	0
networks	13	.5115	1.3993	41.5	0	1	0	1	1	5	5	0	0	0	0	0	3	1	0	3	0	0	0	0	0	0	4	2	0
neuron	24	.0000	.4732	36.8	0	0	0	24	0	0	0	0	0	0	0	0	0	0	0	24	0	0	0	0	0	0	0	0	0
neurones	2	.0000	.0209	23.2	0	0	0	0	0	0	2	0	0	0	0	0	0	0	0	0	0	0	0	0	0	0	2	0	0
neurons	20	.1069	.7642	38.8	0	0	0	19	0	0	1	0	0	0	0	0	0	0	0	19	0	0	0	0	0	0	1	0	0
neuroses	10	.0000	.1047	30.2	0	0	10	0	0	0	0	0	0	0	0	0	0	0	0	0	0	0	0	0	0	0	10	0	0
neurosis	7	.2009	.3376	35.3	0	0	5	0	2	0	0	0	0	0	0	0	0	0	0	0	0	0	0	0	0	0	5	2	0
Neurospora	7	.0000	.1380	31.4	0	0	0	0	0	0	7	0	0	0	0	0	0	0	0	7	0	0	0	0	0	0	0	0	0
neurotic	2	.0000	.0243	23.9	0	0	0	0	1	0	0	1	0	0	0	0	0	0	0	0	0	0	0	0	0	0	0	2	0
neutral	52	.7251	7.6312	48.8	2	1	11	7	8	16	6	1	2	1	0	1	0	14	1	8	6	1	0	0	0	1	10	7	0
neutrality	9	.3990	.7760	38.9	0	0	1	1	3	2	2	0	0	0	0	0	0	1	0	0	0	0	0	0	0	3	4	1	0
neutralize	5	.2424	.2988	34.8	0	0	0	0	0	3	1	1	0	0	0	0	0	0	0	3	0	0	0	0	0	0	2	0	0

5Q negundo
3P Nehf
8R Nehru
4J neighb'ring
5R Neighborhood
9R neighborhood-size
8A neighbourhood
9N neighbouring
9N neighbourly
4P neighings
6A neighs
7D Neilberry
7B neisan
6F Neisse
7G nekename
7A nelson
5F Nelsons
6Q nematocysts
7Q nematode
9R nemesis
4N nenni
8K Neo-Classical
XQ Neo-Classicism
8R neo-Dada
8K Neo-Stoic
9J neoclassical
3A neodymium
XB neologism
9H neon-filled
3Q neon-lighted
4F neophytes
8F nephew-caretaker
7D nephew's
9Q nephrons
6N Nepos
7A nerfing
9D Neritos
7Q Nerva
7Q nerve-frazzling
9R nerve-jangling
3A nerve-wracking
8K Nervi's
9Q nervous-system
5G nes
5N Nes
3P nest-building
7Q nest-mound
7D nesters
XB nestling
7Q nestmates
7H net-veined
4A Neteland
6N Nettie's
7C nettle
7N nettles
6R networks'
9P Neua
4P Neuberger
5Q Neuchatel
7J neumes
6J neuralgia
9P Neurological
5Q Neuroses
7Q Neustria
7Q Neustrians
5Q Neutra
5Q neutralization

Word Type	F	D	U	SFI	3 Gr 3	4 Gr 4	5 Gr 5	6 Gr 6	7 Gr 7	8 Gr 8	9 Gr 9	X UnGr	A Read	B Eng & Gr	C Comp	D Lit	E Math	F Soc Stud	G Spell	H Sci	J Music	K Art	L Home Ec	M Shop	N Lib F	P Lib NF	Q Lib Ref	R Mag	S Rel
neutralizing	2	.2346	.1166	30.7	0	0	0	0	1	0	0	1	0	0	0	0	0	0	0	1	0	0	0	0	0	0	0	1	0
neutrals	6	.2997	.3976	36.0	0	0	4	0	0	2	0	0	0	0	0	0	0	1	0	0	0	1	0	0	0	0	4	0	0
neutrino	2	.0000	.0394	26.0	0	0	0	0	1	0	0	1	0	0	0	0	0	0	0	2	0	0	0	0	0	0	0	0	0
neutron	10	.2424	.5976	37.8	0	0	2	2	6	0	0	0	0	0	0	0	0	0	0	6	0	0	0	0	0	0	4	0	0
neutrons	45	.2435	2.7265	44.4	0	0	7	21	14	2	1	0	0	0	0	0	0	0	0	31	0	0	0	0	0	0	14	0	0
Nevada	60	.5604	7.1916	48.6	4	8	15	6	14	8	4	1	9	0	0	0	0	28	0	12	1	0	0	0	0	5	3	2	0
Nevatim	2	.0000	.0914	29.6	2	0	0	0	0	0	0	0	2	0	0	0	0	0	0	0	0	0	0	0	0	0	0	0	0
never	3115	.9008	559.08	67.5	525	553	340	404	629	354	256	54	1146	126	34	321	22	182	43	133	68	11	26	17	378	318	82	208	0
Never	7	.4847	.7768	38.9	0	0	1	4	1	0	1	0	4	0	0	0	0	0	0	0	1	0	0	0	0	0	1	1	0
NEVER	2	.0857	.0784	28.9	0	1	0	0	1	0	0	0	1	0	0	0	0	0	0	0	0	0	1	0	0	0	0	0	0
never-ending	8	.6596	1.0887	40.4	0	2	1	1	2	2	0	0	1	1	0	1	0	2	0	1	0	0	0	0	1	1	0	0	0
Neverland	2	.0000	.0914	29.6	0	0	0	2	0	0	0	0	2	0	0	0	0	0	0	0	0	0	0	0	0	0	0	0	0
nevermore	2	.2443	.1130	30.5	0	0	0	0	1	0	1	0	0	0	0	1	0	0	0	0	0	0	0	0	1	0	0	0	0
nevertheless	114	.7685	17.673	52.5	9	5	8	15	40	24	11	2	16	9	8	8	1	17	2	6	4	0	0	0	4	16	15	8	0
Neville	6	.2028	.3284	35.2	0	0	0	0	4	1	1	0	1	0	0	0	0	1	0	0	0	0	0	0	4	0	0	0	0
Nevin	4	.0000	.0579	27.6	0	4	0	0	0	0	0	0	0	0	0	0	0	0	0	0	0	0	0	0	0	4	0	0	0
new	5448	.9245	997.29	70.0	1115	795	709	775	892	600	396	166	932	296	48	127	150	863	922	424	226	68	67	32	174	311	301	499	8
New	688	.7431	103.90	60.2	73	91	187	73	118	83	51	12	97	23	1	17	5	278	46	11	31	0	0	0	8	61	77	33	0
NewAmsterdam	2	.2137	.1056	30.2	0	0	0	0	1	1	0	0	0	0	0	0	0	1	0	0	1	0	0	0	0	0	0	0	0
NewBritain	2	.0000	.0299	24.8	0	2	0	0	0	0	0	0	0	0	0	0	2	0	0	0	0	0	0	0	0	0	0	0	0
NewCastle	2	.0000	.0209	23.2	0	0	2	0	0	0	0	0	0	0	0	0	0	0	0	0	0	0	0	0	0	0	2	0	0
NewEngland	15	.5552	1.7680	42.5	0	2	7	0	0	3	2	1	2	0	0	0	0	7	0	0	2	0	0	0	0	2	1	1	0
NewHampshire	29	.7563	4.4830	46.5	2	1	7	6	7	4	2	0	10	2	0	1	0	6	1	0	0	0	0	1	2	1	4	1	0
NewHaven	8	.4506	.7692	38.9	1	0	2	0	2	1	1	1	0	0	0	0	0	2	0	0	0	0	0	0	0	1	2	3	0
NewJersey	66	.8174	10.822	50.3	10	7	12	4	15	10	4	4	8	2	0	2	0	16	1	6	3	0	0	1	3	9	5	10	0
NewJersey's	3	.2143	.1568	32.0	1	0	0	0	1	0	0	1	0	0	0	0	0	0	0	0	0	0	0	0	0	1	0	2	0
NewLondon	3	.2435	.2274	33.6	0	2	0	0	0	1	0	0	2	0	0	0	0	1	0	0	0	0	0	0	0	0	0	0	0
NewMexico	46	.6832	6.4607	48.1	3	4	10	5	11	12	0	1	7	3	1	2	1	17	0	1	0	0	0	0	0	1	9	4	0
NewOrleans	120	.5224	13.334	51.2	7	27	38	10	13	22	3	0	9	1	0	2	1	62	0	5	27	0	0	0	0	1	8	4	0
NewSalem	3	.2379	.1705	32.3	0	0	0	0	2	1	0	0	0	0	0	1	0	0	0	0	0	0	0	0	0	2	0	0	0
NewWorld	6	.2378	.3617	35.6	0	1	3	2	0	0	0	0	0	0	0	0	0	4	0	0	0	0	0	0	0	2	0	0	0
NewYork	677	.8194	111.54	60.5	99	96	104	62	100	128	66	22	139	22	6	12	38	143	3	22	20	0	0	2	9	85	70	106	0
NewYorkCity	167	.6954	23.927	53.8	24	38	37	19	15	25	8	1	35	3	0	1	4	61	1	4	8	0	0	0	1	8	18	23	0
NewYorkCity's	2	.1698	.1133	30.5	0	0	0	1	0	0	1	0	1	0	0	0	0	0	0	0	0	0	0	0	0	0	1	0	0
NewYorkState	8	.5626	.9477	39.8	0	3	2	1	2	0	0	0	1	0	0	1	1	1	0	0	0	0	0	0	0	3	1	0	0
NewYork's	15	.5297	1.6701	42.2	2	1	0	1	5	2	3	1	1	2	0	0	0	3	0	0	0	0	0	0	1	0	2	6	0
NewYorker	3	.1858	.1432	31.6	1	0	0	0	1	0	1	0	0	2	0	0	0	1	0	0	0	0	0	0	0	0	0	0	0
NewYorkers	3	.3395	.2468	33.9	1	2	0	0	0	0	0	0	1	0	0	0	0	0	0	0	0	0	0	0	0	1	1	0	0
new-born	7	.5170	.7761	38.9	2	1	1	0	0	1	0	2	1	0	0	0	0	0	0	2	0	0	0	0	0	1	1	2	0
new-fallen	3	.2028	.1988	33.0	2	0	0	1	0	0	0	0	2	0	0	0	0	0	0	0	1	0	0	0	0	0	0	0	0
new-fangled	3	.3395	.2468	33.9	1	0	0	0	2	0	0	0	1	0	0	0	0	0	0	0	0	0	0	0	0	1	1	0	0
new-found	3	.3370	.2430	33.9	0	0	0	1	2	0	0	0	1	0	0	1	0	0	0	0	0	0	0	0	0	0	1	0	0
new-sawn	3	.0000	.0067	18.3	0	0	0	0	0	3	0	0	0	0	3	0	0	0	0	0	0	0	0	0	0	0	0	0	0
new-style	3	.0000	.0365	25.6	0	0	0	0	3	0	0	0	0	0	0	0	0	0	0	0	0	0	0	0	0	0	0	3	0
Newark	8	.4987	.8538	39.3	1	0	2	0	3	1	1	0	1	0	0	0	0	1	0	0	0	0	0	0	0	2	2	2	0
Newbery	4	.2386	.2998	34.8	0	0	4	0	0	0	0	0	3	0	0	0	0	0	0	0	0	0	0	0	0	0	1	0	0
Newbold	2	.0000	.0914	29.6	0	0	0	2	0	0	0	0	2	0	0	0	0	0	0	0	0	0	0	0	0	0	0	0	0
newborn	24	.5925	3.0119	44.8	1	2	3	4	4	4	0	6	5	0	1	1	0	2	0	10	0	0	0	0	0	1	4	0	0
Newbury	2	.0000	.0290	24.6	0	0	0	1	0	1	0	0	0	0	0	0	0	0	0	0	0	0	0	0	0	2	0	0	0
Newcastle	13	.3738	1.0687	40.3	0	5	0	8	0	0	0	0	0	0	0	4	0	4	0	0	0	0	0	0	0	0	0	5	0
Newcomb	2	.0000	.0394	26.0	2	0	0	0	0	0	0	0	0	0	0	0	0	0	0	2	0	0	0	0	0	0	0	0	0
Newcomen	3	.0000	.0314	25.0	0	0	0	0	1	0	2	0	0	0	0	0	0	0	0	0	0	0	0	0	0	0	3	0	0
newcomer	19	.6936	2.7453	44.4	1	4	3	1	4	3	3	0	8	1	0	1	0	2	0	0	0	0	0	0	1	1	3	2	0
newcomers	27	.7077	3.8820	45.9	6	2	8	4	3	3	0	1	2	1	1	1	0	6	0	0	0	0	0	0	5	6	2	3	0
newer	30	.8194	4.9129	46.9	4	2	2	3	6	7	5	1	2	0	0	1	1	9	1	1	5	1	1	1	1	2	1	3	0
Newer	3	.0000	.0314	25.0	0	0	0	0	0	3	0	0	0	0	0	0	0	0	0	0	0	0	0	0	0	0	3	0	0
newest	35	.7750	5.4741	47.4	6	2	4	4	6	3	3	7	4	1	0	0	2	10	0	3	2	0	0	1	2	1	3	6	0
newfangled	4	.3677	.3659	35.6	0	1	0	1	1	1	0	0	2	0	0	1	0	1	0	0	0	0	0	0	0	0	0	0	0
Newfoundland	33	.5132	3.6035	45.6	1	2	7	10	6	5	2	0	2	1	0	0	0	17	0	1	6	0	0	0	0	0	5	1	0
newly	90	.8336	15.049	51.8	15	7	13	8	27	6	12	2	18	5	2	3	0	13	1	13	5	0	0	0	2	9	10	9	0
newly-formed	2	.2446	.1257	31.0	0	0	0	1	1	0	0	0	0	0	0	0	0	1	0	1	0	0	0	0	0	0	0	0	0
Newman	5	.3530	.4326	36.4	0	4	0	0	1	0	0	0	2	0	0	0	0	0	0	0	0	0	0	0	0	2	0	1	0
newpapers	2	.1733	.1149	30.6	0	0	0	1	0	0	1	0	1	1	0	0	0	0	0	0	0	0	0	0	0	0	0	0	0
Newport	5	.2444	.2887	34.6	0	5	0	0	0	0	0	0	0	0	0	0	0	0	0	0	0	0	0	0	0	3	2	0	0
news	410	.7835	65.057	58.1	83	73	48	50	54	53	41	8	110	64	13	33	1	57	1	10	10	0	0	0	28	44	8	29	2
News	23	.6079	2.8982	44.6	1	5	1	2	4	5	5	0	3	3	0	5	0	1	1	0	0	0	0	0	0	5	0	5	0
NewsTime	2	.0000	.0389	25.9	0	0	2	0	0	0	0	0	0	0	0	0	0	2	0	0	0	0	0	0	0	0	0	0	0
newsboy	7	.4832	.7238	38.6	0	1	0	1	1	2	2	0	1	1	1	2	0	0	0	1	0	0	0	0	0	1	0	0	0
newsboy's	2	.2407	.1138	30.6	0	1	0	0	1	0	0	0	0	0	0	1	0	0	0	0	0	0	0	0	0	1	0	0	0
newscast	2	.2300	.1140	30.6	0	0	0	0	1	1	0	0	0	1	0	0	0	0	0	1	0	0	0	0	0	0	0	0	0
newsmagazine	3	.0000	.0365	25.6	0	0	0	0	3	0	0	0	0	0	0	0	0	0	0	0	0	0	0	0	0	0	0	3	0
newsman	2	.1717	.1142	30.6	0	0	0	1	0	0	1	0	1	0	0	1	0	0	0	0	0	0	0	0	0	0	0	0	0
newsmen	8	.4067	.7624	38.8	2	2	0	0	1	3	0	0	3	0	0	0	0	1	0	0	0	0	0	0	0	1	0	3	0
newspaper	308	.8365	51.748	57.1	51	49	44	35	57	41	22	9	94	38	5	21	12	26	8	15	3	18	2	3	13	14	9	27	0
newspaperman	5	.4662	.5254	37.2	0	0	2	2	1	0	0	0	2	0	0	0	0	0	0	0	1	0	0	0	0	1	0	1	0
newspapermen	3	.3815	.2534	34.0	1	1	0	0	1	0	0	0	0	0	0	0	0	1	0	0	0	0	0	0	0	1	0	1	0
newspapers	198	.8832	34.855	55.4	24	31	25	27	29	41	14	7	45	11	1	4	14	41	2	18	0	6	4	6	7	13	8	18	0
newspaperwoman	2	.0000	.0215	23.3	0	0	0	0	2	0	0	0	0	0	0	2	0	0	0	0	0	0	0	0	0	0	0	0	0
newsstand	5	.4733	.5356	37.3	0	1	0	0	1	3	0	0	2	1	0	0	0	1	0	0	0	0	0	0	0	0	0	1	0
newsstands	2	.0000	.0243	23.9	0	0	0	0	1	0	0	1	0	0	0	0	0	0	0	0	0	0	0	0	0	0	0	2	0
Newsweek	5	.0000	.0608	27.8	0	0	0	0	0	4	1	0	0	0	0	0	0	0	0	0	0	0	0	0	0	0	0	5	0
newsy	2	.0000	.0219	23.4	2	0	0	0	0	0	0	0	0	2	0	0	0	0	0	0	0	0	0	0	0	0	0	0	0
Newton	45	.5399	5.3191	47.3	1	1	4	14	2	20	3	0	14	1	0	0	6	0	0	20	0	0	0	0	2	1	1	0	0
Newton's	22	.2073	1.3394	41.3	0	0	5	9	0	7	1	0	5	0	0	0	1	0	0	16	0	0	0	0	0	0	0	0	0
Newtown	4	.1800	.1826	32.6	1	0	0	0	0	0	0	3	0	0	0	0	1	0	0	0	0	0	0	0	3	0	0	0	0
next	2727	.9795	526.21	67.2	629	538	329	318	419	242	219	33	890	128	46	128	154	210	110	202	87	21	28	20	206	228	69	199	1
next-door	4	.4538	.4007	36.0	0	1	1	1	0	0	1	0	1	1	0	0	0	0	0	0	0	0	0	0	1	0	0	1	0
next-higher	3	.0000	.0243	23.8	0	0	0	3	0	0	0	0	0	0	0	0	0	0	0	0	3	0	0	0	0	0	0	0	0
Nez	9	.3535	.7173	38.6	1	0	1	5	2	0	0	0	1	0	0	2	0	0	0	0	0	0	0	0	0	1	0	5	0
NF	2	.1703	.0781	28.9	0	0	1	0	0	0	1	0	0	1	0	0	0	0	0	0	0	0	0	1	0	0	0	0	0
NFL	6	.0000	.0729	28.6	0	0	0	3	2	1	0	0	0	0	0	0	0	0	0	0	0	0	0	0	0	0	0	6	0
ng•	33	.0943	.8883	39.5	12	11	5	2	2	1	0	0	1	0	0	0	0	0	30	0	2	0	0	0	0	0	0	0	0

XH neutrinos
7R neutron-activation
3A nev
9H Nevadas
5A never-endin'
7A never-never
8B never-questioned
9D never-rose
7A never-satisfied
6A never-to-be-forgotten
9D Nevermore
8K NEW
7Q NewAlbany
8R NewBethel's
5Q NewBrunswick
7F NewCaledonia
5F NewEngland's
8F NewEnglanders
6A NewGuinea
7H NewHampshire's
5N NewIpswich
7Q NewMexico-Texas-Mexico
8F NewNetherland
XR NewSeabury
4F NewSmyrna
8F NewSpain
5A NewYear
5Q NewYear's
8R NewYorkCrusade
7A NewYork-Pennsylvania
6F NewYorks
5A NewZealand
7Q New-Mexico
3A new-laid
4A new-made
9H new-moon
6A new-mown
XR new-old
9D new-washed
4A Newberry
6A Newburgh
8P Newburyport
3A newel
7Q Newell
8D newes
8R Newfield
7F newly-arrived
6A newly-built
5A newly-come
5P newly-emerged
3A newlyweds
7D newness
4P Newport's
5A NEWS
5F NewsTime's
6R newsboys
4P Newsboys'
7A newscasters
7Q newsletters
4A newsmen's
4F NEWSPAPERS
7D newsreel
8R Newsweek's
9B newsworthy
7H Newtonian
5N Next
7H next-inner
7H next-to-last
7N next's
3P NF-104A
6R NFL'S
6R ngamia

Word Type	F	D	U	SFI	3 Gr 3	4 Gr 4	5 Gr 5	6 Gr 6	7 Gr 7	8 Gr 8	9 Gr 9	X UnGr	A Read	B Eng & Gr	C Comp	D Lit	E Math	F Soc Stud	G Spell	H Sci	J Music	K Art	L Home Ec	M Shop	N Lib F	P Lib NF	Q Lib Ref	R Mag	S Rel
NGC	3	.0000	.0314	25.0	0	0	0	0	0	3	0	0	0	0	0	0	0	0	0	0	0	0	0	0	0	0	3	0	0
ngk	3	.0000	.0243	23.9	1	0	1	1	0	0	0	0	0	0	0	0	0	0	3	0	0	0	0	0	0	0	0	0	0
Ngo	2	.0000	.0209	23.2	0	0	0	0	0	2	0	0	0	0	0	0	0	0	0	0	0	0	0	0	0	0	2	0	0
Nguyen	2	.0000	.0243	23.9	0	0	0	0	0	1	1	0	0	0	0	0	0	0	0	0	0	0	0	0	0	0	0	2	0
NH4NO2	2	.0000	.0209	23.2	0	0	0	2	0	0	0	0	0	0	0	0	0	0	0	0	0	0	0	0	0	0	2	0	0
niacin	7	.0814	.1630	32.1	0	0	2	0	0	3	2	0	0	0	0	0	0	0	0	2	0	0	5	0	0	0	0	0	0
Niagara	21	.4685	2.1504	43.3	6	3	6	3	0	2	0	1	3	1	0	0	0	5	0	2	0	0	0	0	0	1	0	9	0
Niall	2	.0000	.0290	24.6	0	0	2	0	0	0	0	0	0	0	0	0	0	0	0	0	0	0	0	0	0	2	0	0	0
Niall's	2	.0000	.0290	24.6	0	0	2	0	0	0	0	0	0	0	0	0	0	0	0	0	0	0	0	0	0	2	0	0	0
nibble	23	.5907	2.9390	44.7	7	4	1	4	5	0	1	1	12	2	2	0	0	0	0	0	0	0	1	0	1	3	0	2	0
nibble-nibble	2	.0000	.0914	29.6	2	0	0	0	0	0	0	0	2	0	0	0	0	0	0	0	0	0	0	0	0	0	0	0	0
nibbled	23	.5512	2.7670	44.4	11	7	0	1	2	1	0	1	10	0	0	4	0	0	0	0	0	0	0	0	4	3	0	2	0
nibbles	3	.3395	.2468	33.9	1	0	0	2	0	0	0	0	1	0	0	0	0	0	0	0	0	0	0	0	0	1	1	0	0
nibbling	19	.4249	1.9035	42.8	7	6	0	3	2	1	0	0	10	0	2	0	0	1	0	0	0	0	0	0	5	0	0	1	0
Nibel	2	.0000	.0290	24.6	0	0	0	0	0	0	0	2	0	0	0	0	0	0	0	0	0	0	0	0	0	2	0	0	0
Nibelungen	2	.2417	.1091	30.4	0	0	0	1	1	0	0	0	0	0	0	0	0	0	0	0	1	0	0	0	0	0	1	0	0
Nibs	13	.0000	.5939	37.7	0	0	0	13	0	0	0	0	13	0	0	0	0	0	0	0	0	0	0	0	0	0	0	0	0
Nicaragua	7	.0000	.1361	31.3	0	0	0	7	0	0	0	0	0	0	0	0	0	7	0	0	0	0	0	0	0	0	0	0	0
Nicaragua's	2	.0000	.0389	25.9	0	0	0	2	0	0	0	0	0	0	0	0	0	2	0	0	0	0	0	0	0	0	0	0	0
Nicci	2	.0000	.0914	29.6	0	0	0	2	0	0	0	0	2	0	0	0	0	0	0	0	0	0	0	0	0	0	0	0	0
Niccolo	17	.4436	1.8410	42.7	0	0	3	13	0	0	1	0	13	0	0	0	0	0	0	0	0	0	0	0	0	2	1	1	0
nice	422	.7902	67.725	58.3	136	83	30	52	59	34	22	6	163	51	1	39	0	8	5	3	12	5	1	0	73	30	3	28	0
Nice	2	.0000	.0209	23.2	1	0	0	0	1	0	0	0	0	0	0	0	0	0	0	0	0	0	0	0	0	0	2	0	0
nice-looking	4	.3729	.3664	35.6	1	0	1	0	1	1	0	0	2	1	0	0	0	0	0	0	0	0	0	0	0	1	0	0	0
nicely	37	.7755	5.7585	47.6	7	11	5	1	6	2	2	3	4	2	0	5	0	1	2	2	4	3	1	1	4	5	0	3	0
nicer	11	.4806	1.1962	40.8	6	2	0	1	0	1	1	0	5	0	1	0	0	0	0	1	0	0	0	0	2	2	0	0	0
nicest	17	.6065	2.2125	43.4	5	2	1	3	1	2	3	0	8	1	0	1	0	0	0	0	1	0	0	0	3	3	0	0	0
niche	10	.3805	.8799	39.4	0	0	0	2	4	4	0	0	1	0	0	0	0	2	0	6	0	0	0	0	0	0	1	0	0
niches	6	.2622	.3635	35.6	0	0	0	0	5	0	0	1	0	0	0	0	0	0	0	1	0	0	0	0	0	0	4	1	0
Nicholas	18	.6643	2.5121	44.0	1	2	3	1	5	1	4	1	8	0	0	1	0	0	0	1	3	0	0	0	1	2	1	1	0
Nicholas'	2	.0580	.0676	28.3	0	1	0	0	1	0	0	0	1	0	0	0	0	0	0	0	0	1	0	0	0	0	0	0	0
Nicholl	2	.0000	.0394	26.0	0	0	0	0	0	0	0	2	0	0	0	0	0	0	0	2	0	0	0	0	0	0	0	0	0
Nichols	2	.1698	.1133	30.5	0	0	0	1	0	0	1	0	1	0	0	0	0	0	0	0	0	0	0	0	0	0	1	0	0
nick	7	.4554	.7228	38.6	1	0	2	0	2	1	1	0	3	0	0	1	0	0	0	0	0	0	0	1	0	1	0	1	0
Nick	81	.2234	6.3271	48.0	20	1	8	2	18	32	0	0	77	0	0	0	2	0	0	0	1	0	0	0	0	0	0	1	0
Nick's	11	.1920	.7962	39.0	3	0	3	0	2	3	0	0	10	0	0	0	1	0	0	0	0	0	0	0	0	0	0	0	0
nickel	93	.8168	15.379	51.9	15	26	5	11	25	3	4	4	36	1	0	6	16	8	2	9	1	0	0	2	2	3	6	1	0
nickel-iron	2	.2278	.1128	30.5	0	1	0	0	0	0	1	0	0	0	0	0	0	0	0	1	0	0	0	0	0	0	1	0	0
nickel's	2	.0000	.0215	23.3	0	2	0	0	0	0	0	0	0	0	0	2	0	0	0	0	0	0	0	0	0	0	0	0	0
nickelodeons	2	.0000	.0389	25.9	0	0	0	0	0	2	0	0	0	0	0	0	0	2	0	0	0	0	0	0	0	0	0	0	0
nickels	91	.2590	5.7419	47.6	29	13	16	9	7	1	7	9	5	1	0	1	75	2	0	0	0	0	0	0	4	1	0	2	0
Nickels	2	.0000	.0914	29.6	0	2	0	0	0	0	0	0	2	0	0	0	0	0	0	0	0	0	0	0	0	0	0	0	0
nicker	3	.0000	.0352	25.5	0	3	0	0	0	0	0	0	0	0	0	0	0	0	0	0	0	0	0	0	3	0	0	0	0
nickered	3	.2120	.1548	31.9	0	3	0	0	0	0	0	0	0	0	0	0	0	0	0	0	0	0	0	0	2	1	0	0	0
nickering	6	.3765	.5074	37.1	0	2	0	1	3	0	0	0	1	0	0	3	0	0	0	0	0	0	0	0	1	0	0	1	0
nickname	35	.7267	5.2695	47.2	2	9	5	4	9	3	3	0	16	2	0	0	3	2	2	1	0	0	0	0	1	5	0	3	0
nicknamed	11	.5636	1.3370	41.3	0	2	4	1	2	0	2	0	4	0	0	1	0	1	0	0	0	0	1	0	0	3	0	1	0
nicknames	3	.1409	.1472	31.7	0	1	0	1	1	0	0	0	1	0	0	0	0	0	0	0	0	0	0	0	0	2	0	0	0
nicks	3	.0000	.0076	18.8	0	0	0	0	1	0	2	0	0	0	0	0	0	0	0	0	0	0	0	3	0	0	0	0	0
Nicky	3	.3380	.2439	33.9	0	0	0	0	1	0	2	0	1	1	0	1	0	0	0	0	0	0	0	0	0	0	0	0	0
Nico	13	.0000	.1395	31.4	0	0	0	0	0	0	13	0	0	0	0	13	0	0	0	0	0	0	0	0	0	0	0	0	0
Nicola	14	.0000	.6396	38.1	14	0	0	0	0	0	0	0	14	0	0	0	0	0	0	0	0	0	0	0	0	0	0	0	0
Nicola's	8	.0000	.3655	35.6	8	0	0	0	0	0	0	0	8	0	0	0	0	0	0	0	0	0	0	0	0	0	0	0	0
Nicolai	2	.0000	.0162	22.1	0	1	0	1	0	0	0	0	0	0	0	0	0	0	0	0	2	0	0	0	0	0	0	0	0
Nicolas	4	.2988	.2894	34.6	0	1	1	0	0	0	2	0	1	0	1	0	0	1	0	0	0	0	0	0	0	0	1	0	0
Nicolaus	2	.2446	.1257	31.0	0	0	0	1	0	0	1	0	0	0	0	0	0	1	0	1	0	0	0	0	0	0	0	0	0
Nicolaysen	4	.0000	.1827	32.6	0	0	0	0	4	0	0	0	4	0	0	0	0	0	0	0	0	0	0	0	0	0	0	0	0
Nicole	2	.0000	.0914	29.6	2	0	0	0	0	0	0	0	2	0	0	0	0	0	0	0	0	0	0	0	0	0	0	0	0
nicotinic	2	.0000	.0209	23.2	0	0	2	0	0	0	0	0	0	0	0	0	0	0	0	0	0	0	0	0	0	0	2	0	0
niece	17	.2457	1.0579	40.2	2	2	0	2	5	1	4	1	4	1	0	7	0	0	2	0	0	0	0	0	0	2	0	0	1
Niels	4	.1494	.1609	32.1	0	0	0	0	3	1	0	0	0	0	0	0	0	0	0	1	0	0	0	0	0	0	3	0	0
Nifty	3	.0000	.0328	25.2	0	0	0	3	0	0	0	0	0	3	0	0	0	0	0	0	0	0	0	0	0	0	0	0	0
Niger	5	.3148	.3877	35.9	0	1	0	1	3	0	0	0	1	0	0	0	0	3	0	0	0	0	0	0	0	0	1	0	0
Nigeria	57	.2127	3.2473	45.1	1	39	4	2	10	1	0	0	1	0	0	0	0	50	0	0	0	0	0	0	0	4	1	1	0
Nigeria's	2	.2351	.1166	30.7	0	1	0	0	0	1	0	0	0	0	0	0	0	1	0	0	0	0	0	0	0	0	0	1	0
Nigerian	6	.0000	.1167	30.7	0	6	0	0	0	0	0	0	0	0	0	0	0	6	0	0	0	0	0	0	0	0	0	0	0
Nigerians	16	.0000	.3112	34.9	0	16	0	0	0	0	0	0	0	0	0	0	0	16	0	0	0	0	0	0	0	0	0	0	0
nigger	4	.4873	.4082	36.1	0	0	0	0	2	0	2	0	0	0	0	1	0	0	0	0	0	0	0	0	1	1	0	1	0
Nigger	3	.2143	.1568	32.0	0	0	0	0	2	0	1	0	0	0	0	0	0	0	0	0	0	0	0	0	0	1	0	2	0
nigger-lover	3	.0000	.0322	25.1	0	0	0	0	0	0	3	0	0	0	0	3	0	0	0	0	0	0	0	0	0	0	0	0	0
niggers	7	.3343	.5174	37.1	0	0	0	0	6	0	1	0	0	0	0	1	0	0	0	0	0	0	0	0	4	2	0	0	0
nigh	21	.5460	2.4796	43.9	1	1	3	2	12	2	0	0	8	1	0	3	0	0	0	0	5	0	0	0	3	1	0	0	0
night	2307	.8706	402.27	66.0	536	378	229	329	418	204	168	45	879	70	27	255	12	140	28	165	109	4	8	4	240	216	30	113	7
Night	33	.6077	4.1286	46.2	5	2	1	13	4	5	2	1	4	0	0	1	0	0	1	0	12	1	0	0	6	5	1	2	0
night-lights	3	.0000	.1370	31.4	0	0	0	3	0	0	0	0	3	0	0	0	0	0	0	0	0	0	0	0	0	0	0	0	0
night-shirt	2	.0000	.0234	23.7	0	0	2	0	0	0	0	0	0	0	0	0	0	0	0	0	0	0	0	0	2	0	0	0	0
night-time	4	.4335	.3906	35.9	2	1	0	0	0	0	1	0	1	0	0	0	0	0	0	1	1	0	0	0	0	1	0	0	0
night-writing	6	.0000	.0644	28.1	0	0	0	0	6	0	0	0	0	0	0	6	0	0	0	0	0	0	0	0	0	0	0	0	0
night's	16	.6607	2.2356	43.5	2	1	1	3	4	2	3	0	8	1	0	2	0	0	0	1	1	0	0	0	1	2	0	0	0
Night's	4	.3075	.2938	34.7	1	0	1	0	1	0	1	0	1	0	0	2	0	0	0	0	1	0	0	0	0	0	0	0	0
nightcap	6	.3509	.5242	37.2	0	0	0	1	2	3	0	0	3	0	0	2	0	0	0	0	0	0	0	0	1	0	0	0	0
Nightcrawlers	2	.0000	.0243	23.9	0	0	0	2	0	0	0	0	0	0	0	0	0	0	0	0	0	0	0	0	0	0	0	2	0
nightfall	27	.5796	3.3346	45.2	4	4	3	6	3	6	1	0	9	1	0	7	0	0	0	0	1	0	0	0	6	2	0	1	0
nightgown	10	.4187	.9160	39.6	1	5	1	0	1	2	0	0	1	0	0	2	0	0	0	0	0	0	0	0	3	4	0	0	0
nightgowns	5	.4022	.4433	36.5	1	0	2	0	0	1	1	0	1	0	0	0	0	0	0	0	1	0	1	0	2	0	0	0	0
nighthawks	2	.0000	.0394	26.0	0	0	0	2	0	0	0	0	0	0	0	0	0	0	0	2	0	0	0	0	0	0	0	0	0
nightingale	14	.3312	1.1232	40.5	0	2	1	5	1	2	3	0	5	0	0	6	0	0	0	0	3	0	0	0	0	0	0	0	0
Nightingale	14	.2165	1.0672	40.3	0	8	5	0	0	1	0	0	13	0	0	0	0	0	0	0	1	0	0	0	0	0	0	0	0
nightly	15	.5505	1.7659	42.5	1	1	3	5	2	1	2	0	4	5	0	2	0	0	0	2	1	0	0	0	0	0	0	1	0
nightmare	14	.5487	1.6224	42.1	0	2	1	2	3	5	1	0	2	1	0	2	0	1	0	0	0	0	0	0	0	4	0	4	0
Nightmare	2	.2412	.1141	30.6	0	1	0	0	0	1	0	0	0	1	0	0	0	0	0	0	0	0	0	0	0	1	0	0	0
nightmares	3	.2357	.2199	33.4	0	0	1	1	1	0	0	0	2	0	0	0	0	0	0	0	0	0	0	0	0	1	0	0	0
nightmarish	4	.4482	.4009	36.0	0	0	0	1	2	1	0	0	1	0	0	0	0	0	0	1	0	0	0	0	0	0	1	1	0
nights	167	.7999	27.072	54.3	26	31	15	21	36	14	16	8	55	4	4	10	1	15	0	24	3	1	1	0	12	21	3	12	1

6R Ngamia
8Q nh/(2p)**
7R NHL
7R NHRA
6Q NH3
6Q NH4Cl
3P ni-tro-gen
6R NiagaraFalls
7Q Niagara's
5K nib
4A Nibelungenlied
7N Nibley's
6J Niblock
5P Niccolo's
3D nice-smelling
5A niceness
7Q nicety
5H nichrome
8R nick-name
6A nicked
XR Nickel
5A nickel-plated
3E nickels'
6A Nickie
9M nicking
4G Nickname
6R Nicks
7F Nicobar
7A Nicolaysen's
5F Nicoll
4P niece's
9D nieces
9R Nielsen
XD Nielson
6B nifty
4F NIGERIA
7A nigger-lovers
7N nigger-traders
9C niggerhead
7R Niggers
6A night-air
7P night-and-day
4Q night-blooming
6R night-flier
3R night-flying
5N night-goin'
6R night-hidden
4N night-watchman
3J nightcaps
7R nightclub
7P nightflying
6A nightie
7Q nightingales
9D Nightly
7Q nightmarishly

Word Type	F	D	U	SFI	3 Gr 3	4 Gr 4	5 Gr 5	6 Gr 6	7 Gr 7	8 Gr 8	9 Gr 9	X UnGr	A Read	B Eng & Gr	C Comp	D Lit	E Math	F Soc Stud	G Spell	H Sci	J Music	K Art	L Home Ec	M Shop	N Lib F	P Lib NF	Q Lib Ref	R Mag	S Rel
Nights	9	.4436	.9348	39.7	1	6	1	0	0	1	0	0	5	0	0	0	1	0	0	0	2	0	0	0	0	0	1	0	0
nightshade	3	.1650	.1684	32.3	0	1	0	2	0	0	0	0	1	0	0	0	0	0	0	2	0	0	0	0	0	0	0	0	0
nightshirt	4	.2958	.2914	34.6	1	1	2	0	0	0	0	0	1	0	0	0	0	0	0	0	0	0	0	0	2	1	0	0	0
nighttime	18	.3920	1.6258	42.1	7	5	0	0	2	1	2	1	3	0	0	1	0	0	0	10	0	0	0	0	0	0	0	4	0
Nike	2	.1378	.0662	28.2	0	0	0	0	1	0	1	0	0	0	0	0	0	0	0	0	0	1	0	0	0	0	0	1	0
Nikita	4	.2090	.2014	33.0	0	0	0	1	1	0	2	0	0	0	0	0	0	0	0	0	0	0	0	0	0	0	1	3	0
Nikolai	3	.0000	.0322	25.1	0	0	0	0	0	0	3	0	0	0	0	3	0	0	0	0	0	0	0	0	0	0	0	0	0
Nikon	2	.2437	.1129	30.5	0	0	0	0	1	1	0	0	0	0	0	0	0	0	0	0	0	0	0	0	0	0	1	1	0
Nile	96	.5138	10.503	50.2	2	18	15	17	33	3	7	1	2	1	0	0	5	64	0	2	0	4	0	0	0	2	14	2	0
Niles	2	.0000	.0162	22.1	0	0	0	2	0	0	0	0	0	0	0	0	0	0	0	0	2	0	0	0	0	0	0	0	0
Nils	26	.0000	1.1877	40.7	17	0	0	9	0	0	0	0	26	0	0	0	0	0	0	0	0	0	0	0	0	0	0	0	0
Nils'	2	.0000	.0914	29.6	2	0	0	0	0	0	0	0	2	0	0	0	0	0	0	0	0	0	0	0	0	0	0	0	0
Nilsson	6	.0000	.0703	28.5	6	0	0	0	0	0	0	0	0	0	0	0	0	0	0	0	0	0	0	0	6	0	0	0	0
Nilsson's	2	.2443	.1130	30.5	1	1	0	0	0	0	0	0	0	0	0	1	0	0	0	0	0	0	0	0	1	0	0	0	0
nim	2	.0000	.0219	23.4	0	0	0	0	0	0	0	2	0	2	0	0	0	0	0	0	0	0	0	0	0	0	0	0	0
nimble	15	.6987	2.1696	43.4	4	3	0	1	3	3	0	1	5	1	0	1	0	1	0	1	1	0	0	0	0	3	0	2	0
nimbly	2	.1717	.1142	30.6	0	0	1	0	0	0	1	0	1	0	0	1	0	0	0	0	0	0	0	0	0	0	0	0	0
Nimbus	3	.2427	.1822	32.6	0	0	1	0	2	0	0	0	0	0	0	0	0	0	0	2	0	0	0	0	0	0	0	1	0
Nina	5	.0000	.0972	29.9	1	0	2	1	0	1	0	0	0	0	0	0	0	5	0	0	0	0	0	0	0	0	0	0	0
nine	417	.9136	75.633	58.8	72	83	50	38	76	45	37	16	100	21	4	25	52	39	24	36	14	0	2	0	23	27	18	32	0
Nine	10	.3649	.9635	39.8	0	7	2	1	0	0	0	0	8	0	0	0	0	0	0	0	1	0	0	0	0	1	0	0	0
nine-fifteen	2	.0000	.0914	29.6	0	2	0	0	0	0	0	0	2	0	0	0	0	0	0	0	0	0	0	0	0	0	0	0	0
nine-room	2	.2351	.1166	30.7	0	1	0	1	0	0	0	0	0	0	0	0	0	1	0	0	0	0	0	0	0	0	0	1	0
nine-tenths	6	.3929	.5186	37.1	0	0	0	3	1	0	1	1	0	0	0	0	2	2	0	1	0	0	0	1	0	0	0	0	0
nine-thirty	3	.2357	.2199	33.4	1	2	0	0	0	0	0	0	2	0	0	0	0	0	0	0	0	0	0	0	0	1	0	0	0
nine-year-old	7	.3859	.5868	37.7	0	3	1	2	0	1	0	0	0	0	0	0	0	0	0	0	0	0	0	0	2	3	0	2	0
Niner	2	.0000	.0290	24.6	2	0	0	0	0	0	0	0	0	0	0	0	0	0	0	0	0	0	0	0	0	2	0	0	0
nines	6	.3282	.4857	36.9	0	2	2	1	0	1	0	0	2	0	0	1	3	0	0	0	0	0	0	0	0	0	0	0	0
nineteen	40	.8690	6.9347	48.4	1	7	5	4	11	5	5	2	9	3	1	4	4	3	3	1	2	0	0	0	3	3	1	3	0
nineteenth	63	.5479	7.1387	48.5	2	4	2	3	24	25	1	2	3	4	0	0	1	4	2	3	30	0	1	0	0	8	5	2	0
nineteenth-century	14	.5120	1.4977	41.8	0	0	1	0	5	5	3	0	1	1	1	0	0	1	0	0	6	0	0	0	0	3	0	1	0
ninetieth	2	.1497	.1046	30.2	1	1	0	0	0	0	0	0	1	0	0	0	0	0	1	0	0	0	0	0	0	0	0	0	0
ninety	33	.8415	5.5695	47.5	4	3	6	3	6	6	2	3	8	2	0	1	5	4	2	2	1	0	0	0	3	1	1	3	0
ninety-eight	6	.3853	.5830	37.7	0	3	0	2	0	0	1	0	4	0	0	0	1	0	0	0	0	0	0	0	1	0	0	0	0
ninety-five	2	.2420	.1154	30.6	0	1	0	0	0	0	1	0	0	0	0	0	1	0	0	0	0	0	0	0	1	0	0	0	0
ninety-four	2	.2152	.1357	31.3	0	2	0	0	0	0	0	0	1	0	0	0	0	1	0	0	0	0	0	0	0	0	0	0	0
ninety-nine	3	.3772	.2488	34.0	0	0	0	0	1	2	0	0	0	1	0	0	0	0	0	1	0	0	0	0	1	0	0	0	0
ninety-seven	7	.3216	.5790	37.6	2	2	1	1	0	1	0	0	3	0	0	0	3	1	0	0	0	0	0	0	0	0	0	0	0
ninety-six	2	.1972	.1262	31.0	0	0	0	0	1	1	0	0	1	0	0	0	1	0	0	0	0	0	0	0	0	0	0	0	0
ninety-two	2	.2152	.1357	31.3	0	0	1	1	0	0	0	0	1	0	0	0	0	1	0	0	0	0	0	0	0	0	0	0	0
Ninian	7	.2446	.4046	36.1	0	3	0	0	1	3	0	0	0	0	0	3	0	0	0	0	0	0	0	0	0	4	0	0	0
NINIAN	2	.0000	.0215	23.3	0	0	0	0	0	2	0	0	0	0	0	2	0	0	0	0	0	0	0	0	0	0	0	0	0
ninth	41	.7647	6.2997	48.0	11	4	1	8	7	6	1	3	3	8	0	1	3	2	6	1	2	0	0	0	1	5	5	4	0
Ninth	4	.2424	.3036	34.8	2	0	0	0	1	0	0	1	3	0	0	0	0	0	0	0	0	0	0	0	0	0	0	1	0
ninth-grade	3	.2187	.1555	31.9	0	0	0	0	0	0	3	0	0	2	0	0	0	0	0	0	0	0	0	0	0	0	0	1	0
ninth-grader	2	.0000	.0219	23.4	0	0	0	0	0	0	2	0	0	2	0	0	0	0	0	0	0	0	0	0	0	0	0	0	0
niobium	2	.1814	.1187	30.7	1	0	0	0	1	0	0	0	1	0	0	0	0	0	0	0	0	0	0	0	0	0	0	1	0
nip	4	.4810	.4063	36.1	0	0	1	1	0	1	1	0	0	0	0	1	0	0	0	1	0	0	0	0	1	0	0	1	0
nip-cat	2	.0000	.0914	29.6	0	2	0	0	0	0	0	0	2	0	0	0	0	0	0	0	0	0	0	0	0	0	0	0	0
nipped	9	.4998	.9715	39.9	2	2	3	1	0	0	1	0	2	2	0	0	0	0	0	0	0	0	0	0	3	1	0	1	0
Nipper	5	.0000	.0608	27.8	0	0	0	5	0	0	0	0	0	0	0	0	0	0	0	0	0	0	0	0	0	0	0	5	0
nipping	2	.2441	.1127	30.5	0	0	0	0	2	0	0	0	0	0	0	0	0	0	0	0	0	0	0	0	1	0	1	0	0
Nippon	6	.1937	.2989	34.8	0	2	0	0	1	0	3	0	0	0	0	0	0	2	0	0	0	0	0	0	0	0	0	4	0
Nisei	16	.0000	.3112	34.9	0	0	0	0	0	16	0	0	0	0	0	0	0	16	0	0	0	0	0	0	0	0	0	0	0
Nisei's	2	.0000	.0389	25.9	0	0	0	0	0	2	0	0	0	0	0	0	0	2	0	0	0	0	0	0	0	0	0	0	0
Nissen	3	.0000	.0243	23.8	0	3	0	0	0	0	0	0	0	0	0	0	0	0	0	0	3	0	0	0	0	0	0	0	0
Nita-san	2	.0000	.0914	29.6	0	2	0	0	0	0	0	0	2	0	0	0	0	0	0	0	0	0	0	0	0	0	0	0	0
nitrate	16	.3071	1.1091	40.4	0	1	2	9	3	0	0	1	0	0	0	0	0	3	0	1	0	0	0	0	0	0	10	2	0
nitrates	5	.3829	.4249	36.3	2	0	0	1	0	0	2	0	0	0	0	0	0	0	0	2	0	0	0	0	0	2	1	0	0
nitric	12	.2736	.8023	39.0	0	0	0	5	1	1	1	4	1	0	0	0	0	0	0	6	0	0	0	0	0	0	5	0	0
nitrogen	151	.3684	12.567	51.0	18	12	11	46	27	34	2	1	0	0	0	0	5	0	1	105	0	0	0	0	0	3	34	3	0
nitrogen-containing	2	.0000	.0394	26.0	0	0	0	0	0	0	2	0	0	0	0	0	0	0	0	2	0	0	0	0	0	0	0	0	0
nitrogen-fixing	4	.2353	.2382	33.8	0	0	0	2	1	1	0	0	0	0	0	0	0	0	0	3	0	0	0	0	0	0	1	0	0
nitrous	3	.1813	.1402	31.5	0	0	0	2	1	0	0	0	0	0	0	0	0	0	0	1	0	0	0	0	0	0	2	0	0
nix	5	.2445	.3875	35.9	4	0	0	0	1	0	0	0	4	0	0	0	0	0	0	0	0	0	0	0	0	0	0	1	0
Nixon	115	.1424	4.4730	46.5	4	0	8	2	29	21	51	0	0	0	0	0	0	9	0	1	0	0	0	0	0	0	4	101	0
Nixon's	31	.1203	1.0961	40.4	0	0	0	0	7	8	16	0	0	0	0	0	0	5	0	0	0	0	0	0	0	0	0	26	0
Njoki	6	.0000	.2741	34.4	0	6	0	0	0	0	0	0	6	0	0	0	0	0	0	0	0	0	0	0	0	0	0	0	0
nk	2	.0000	.0162	22.1	0	0	1	1	0	0	0	0	0	0	0	0	0	0	2	0	0	0	0	0	0	0	0	0	0
NL	4	.0000	.0599	27.8	0	4	0	0	0	0	0	0	0	0	0	0	4	0	0	0	0	0	0	0	0	0	0	0	0
NMO	2	.0000	.0299	24.8	0	0	2	0	0	0	0	0	0	0	0	0	2	0	0	0	0	0	0	0	0	0	0	0	0
NMP	2	.0000	.0299	24.8	0	0	2	0	0	0	0	0	0	0	0	0	2	0	0	0	0	0	0	0	0	0	0	0	0
no	8483	.9584	1605.9	72.1	1489	1264	976	1144	1724	908	783	195	2690	354	71	721	274	669	123	694	225	25	109	52	776	775	380	543	2
No	148	.6946	20.848	53.2	13	10	17	23	27	21	23	14	14	4	1	1	4	2	12	16	35	0	0	14	2	21	2	20	0
NO	12	.6515	1.6225	42.1	5	2	0	3	1	1	0	0	3	1	0	0	2	0	0	0	2	0	0	0	1	2	0	1	0
No-Ears	2	.0000	.0914	29.6	2	0	0	0	0	0	0	0	2	0	0	0	0	0	0	0	0	0	0	0	0	0	0	0	0
No-Hair	2	.0000	.0290	24.6	0	0	0	0	0	0	2	0	0	0	0	0	0	0	0	0	0	0	0	0	0	2	0	0	0
no-good	5	.0824	.1675	32.2	0	1	0	0	0	0	0	4	1	0	0	0	0	0	0	0	0	0	0	0	0	0	0	4	0
no-hitter	4	.0000	.0579	27.6	4	0	0	0	0	0	0	0	0	0	0	0	0	0	0	0	0	0	0	0	0	4	0	0	0
no-hitters	2	.0000	.0290	24.6	1	0	0	1	0	0	0	0	0	0	0	0	0	0	0	0	0	0	0	0	0	2	0	0	0
no-oo	2	.2443	.1130	30.5	0	0	1	0	0	0	1	0	0	0	0	1	0	0	0	0	0	0	0	0	1	0	0	0	0
no-word	3	.0000	.0328	25.2	0	3	0	0	0	0	0	0	0	3	0	0	0	0	0	0	0	0	0	0	0	0	0	0	0
no-words	2	.0000	.0219	23.4	0	2	0	0	0	0	0	0	0	2	0	0	0	0	0	0	0	0	0	0	0	0	0	0	0
no'm	4	.0000	.1827	32.6	0	1	0	0	3	0	0	0	4	0	0	0	0	0	0	0	0	0	0	0	0	0	0	0	0
Noah	25	.5070	2.7225	44.3	2	10	0	0	12	0	0	1	6	0	0	0	0	0	4	1	8	0	0	0	0	4	2	0	0
Noah's	6	.3838	.5766	37.6	0	0	0	1	5	0	0	0	4	0	0	0	0	0	0	0	1	0	0	0	0	0	1	0	0
Nobel	31	.3779	2.5716	44.1	0	1	4	2	6	1	17	0	2	2	0	1	0	2	0	1	0	0	0	0	0	2	20	1	0
nobility	20	.4962	2.0748	43.2	3	0	4	2	4	6	1	0	0	1	0	0	0	4	0	0	6	0	0	0	0	4	5	0	0

7Q Nigrae
7R Nihoa
8F Niigata
5F Niihau
8J Nijinsky
7P Nijmegen
4F Nik
4F Nik's
7Q nikau
3A Niki
5H Nikolaus
9Q Nikos
3P nil
4D Nilssons
7E Nim
XR nimble-footed
9D nimble-wittedness
6R nimbleness
7H nimbostratus
7H nimbus
8G Nimes
5F Nimitz
XR nimrods
8F Nina's
8A nine-and-a-half
8F nine-day
4A nine-going-on-ten
XR nine-hole
8F nine-hour
XR nine-hours
7A nine-inning
XB nine-line
5H nine-month
8N nine-o'clock
7J nine-tail
5R nine-thrity
4R nine-volt
8D ninepins
7R nineteen-sixties
8E nineteen-year-old
8F Nineteenth
7P nineties
8J Nineties
7N Ninety-Mile-Curve
8D ninety-degree
6F ninety-eighth
4A ninety-one
8A ninety-three
7G ninth-century
9D ninth-inning
6E ninths
7R niobate
3P Nip-nip-nip
6A nipa
6B nipp'd
6R Nipper's
5C nippers
XH nipples
8A nippy
5Q nips
9R Nipsey
7P nipt
7H nirvana
7P Nishuane
XR nitpickers
6Q nitration
7H nitrocellulose
7Q nitrogen-poor
7H nitrogenous
6Q nitroglycerin
6Q nitron
8R Nittany
7N nitwit
9R Nixons
9B NJ
8Q Njegos
4A Njoki's
5Q NLF
5Q NLRB
8R No-Cal
6R no-ball
7R no-go
7R no-hit
9Q no-knock
7R no-loss
7R no-man's
6R no-man's-land
7A no-muscle
9R no-nonsense
5A no-o-o
6N no-o-o-o
9D no-o-o-o-o
3A no-parking
8L no-sift
3F no-smoking
8F Nob
4J Nobby
9Q nobiliary
6R nobilis

Word Type	F	D	U	SFI	3 Gr 3	4 Gr 4	5 Gr 5	6 Gr 6	7 Gr 7	8 Gr 8	9 Gr 9	X UnGr	A Read	B Eng & Gr	C Comp	D Lit	E Math	F Soc Stud	G Spell	H Sci	J Music	K Art	L Home Ec	M Shop	N Lib F	P Lib NF	Q Lib Ref	R Mag	S Rel
noble	57	.7170	8.3195	49.2	0	3	7	8	18	9	11	1	9	2	0	13	0	7	0	1	2	0	0	0	9	4	6	4	0
Noble	7	.4809	.7744	38.9	0	4	1	1	0	1	0	0	4	0	0	0	0	0	0	0	1	0	0	0	0	1	0	1	0
nobleman	11	.5498	1.2578	41.0	2	1	1	3	0	3	1	0	0	0	0	1	0	4	0	0	1	1	0	0	0	3	0	1	0
noblemen	15	.6165	1.9441	42.9	4	1	3	3	3	1	0	0	4	0	0	0	0	3	0	0	2	0	0	0	2	2	2	0	0
noblemen's	3	.1910	.1473	31.7	2	0	0	1	0	0	0	0	0	0	0	0	0	1	0	0	0	0	0	0	2	0	0	0	0
nobler	4	.3755	.3686	35.7	0	0	1	0	2	1	0	0	2	0	0	0	0	0	0	0	0	0	0	0	1	1	0	0	0
nobles	60	.7318	8.9588	49.5	5	4	4	20	19	6	1	1	11	2	0	2	0	24	0	0	5	1	0	0	2	3	6	4	0
noblest	7	.3354	.5666	37.5	1	1	1	0	1	3	0	0	2	0	0	0	0	0	0	0	0	0	0	0	2	3	0	0	0
nobly	6	.3770	.5771	37.6	0	0	0	1	1	4	0	0	4	0	0	1	0	1	0	0	0	0	0	0	0	0	0	0	0
nobody	335	.7505	51.558	57.1	69	50	36	45	64	29	31	11	136	15	0	44	0	10	6	3	3	2	0	0	53	26	3	34	0
Nobody	4	.0000	.1827	32.6	1	3	0	0	0	0	0	0	4	0	0	0	0	0	0	0	0	0	0	0	0	0	0	0	0
nobody's	10	.4813	1.0613	40.3	1	1	0	3	3	1	1	0	3	0	0	1	0	0	0	0	0	0	0	0	1	1	0	4	0
nocturnal	8	.3462	.6353	38.0	0	0	0	0	7	1	0	0	1	0	0	0	0	0	0	2	0	0	0	0	0	0	4	1	0
Nocturne	2	.2411	.1091	30.4	0	0	0	0	0	1	1	0	0	0	0	1	0	0	0	0	1	0	0	0	0	0	0	0	0
nod	23	.7130	3.4406	45.4	1	4	1	6	6	2	2	1	14	1	0	1	0	1	0	1	1	0	0	0	1	1	0	2	0
nodal	3	.0000	.0591	27.7	0	0	0	0	0	0	0	3	0	0	0	0	0	0	0	3	1	0	0	0	0	0	0	0	0
nodded	240	.6088	31.481	55.0	44	73	24	33	40	14	11	1	121	3	0	23	0	9	0	1	0	0	0	0	38	36	0	9	0
nodding	18	.5518	2.1922	43.4	2	2	1	5	4	2	1	1	9	0	0	2	0	0	0	2	0	0	0	0	3	2	0	0	0
nods	12	.3556	1.0368	40.2	3	0	1	4	1	2	1	0	5	0	0	3	0	0	0	0	0	0	0	0	4	0	0	0	0
nodules	7	.3672	.6359	38.0	0	0	2	0	4	1	0	0	3	0	0	0	0	0	0	3	0	0	0	0	0	0	1	0	0
noise	411	.8279	68.680	58.4	130	84	35	53	57	27	19	6	163	32	5	25	1	9	8	24	19	0	1	0	58	41	3	22	0
noiseless	2	.2446	.1125	30.5	0	0	0	0	1	0	1	0	0	1	0	1	0	0	0	0	0	0	0	0	0	0	0	0	0
noiselessly	9	.5485	1.0654	40.3	1	2	0	1	3	1	0	1	3	1	0	1	0	0	0	0	0	0	0	0	2	2	0	0	0
noises	104	.7033	15.095	51.8	17	14	10	10	34	13	5	1	36	32	3	8	0	1	0	6	2	0	1	0	4	4	1	6	0
noisier	3	.2261	.2131	33.3	2	0	0	0	1	0	0	0	2	0	0	0	0	0	0	0	0	0	0	0	1	0	0	0	0
noisiest	5	.2445	.3100	34.9	2	0	1	0	0	0	2	0	1	0	0	3	0	0	0	0	0	0	0	0	0	1	0	0	0
noisily	16	.5209	1.8329	42.6	1	5	2	1	4	2	1	0	7	2	2	1	0	0	0	0	0	0	0	0	2	1	0	1	0
noisome	3	.1119	.0792	29.0	0	0	0	0	3	0	0	0	0	0	2	0	0	0	0	0	0	0	0	0	0	0	1	0	0
noisy	94	.8340	15.745	52.0	34	15	8	8	18	6	3	2	29	11	3	9	0	3	3	2	9	0	2	0	6	8	1	8	0
Noisy	3	.0000	.0322	25.1	3	0	0	0	0	0	0	0	0	0	0	3	0	0	0	0	0	0	0	0	0	0	0	0	0
Nokomis	3	.0397	.0716	28.5	2	0	1	0	0	0	0	0	1	0	2	0	0	0	0	0	0	0	0	0	0	0	0	0	0
Nolan	24	.3369	2.1720	43.4	0	0	0	0	8	16	0	0	16	0	0	0	0	7	0	0	0	0	0	0	0	0	0	1	0
Noland	7	.0000	.0851	29.3	0	0	7	0	0	0	0	0	0	0	0	0	0	0	0	0	0	0	0	0	0	0	0	7	0
Nolde	2	.0000	.0037	15.7	0	0	0	0	1	1	0	0	0	0	0	0	0	0	0	0	0	2	0	0	0	0	0	0	0
Nole	4	.0000	.1827	32.6	0	4	0	0	0	0	0	0	4	0	0	0	0	0	0	0	0	0	0	0	0	0	0	0	0
Nole's	3	.0000	.1370	31.4	0	3	0	0	0	0	0	0	3	0	0	0	0	0	0	0	0	0	0	0	0	0	0	0	0
nom	2	.0000	.0162	22.1	0	0	0	0	2	0	0	0	0	0	0	0	0	0	2	0	0	0	0	0	0	0	0	0	0
nomad	6	.2590	.4115	36.1	0	1	1	1	2	0	1	0	1	0	0	0	0	4	0	1	0	0	0	0	0	0	0	0	0
nomadic	10	.5323	1.1183	40.5	0	0	0	4	0	2	3	1	0	0	0	1	0	5	0	0	0	0	0	0	1	0	1	2	0
nomads	32	.3172	2.5564	44.1	2	15	1	4	6	3	1	0	9	0	0	0	0	19	0	0	0	0	0	0	0	0	4	0	0
Nome	17	.4003	1.7457	42.4	1	6	5	1	0	4	0	0	14	0	0	0	1	0	0	0	0	0	0	0	0	1	0	1	0
nomenclature	4	.4756	.4063	36.1	0	0	0	0	1	1	2	0	0	0	0	0	0	1	0	1	0	0	0	0	0	0	1	1	0
nominal	15	.4020	1.2704	41.0	0	0	1	0	0	1	12	1	0	8	0	0	0	0	0	0	0	0	0	3	0	1	2	1	0
nominally	4	.3422	.3073	34.9	0	0	0	1	3	0	0	0	0	0	0	0	0	1	0	0	0	0	0	0	0	1	0	2	0
nominals	7	.0000	.0766	28.8	0	0	0	0	0	0	7	0	0	7	0	0	0	0	0	0	0	0	0	0	0	0	0	0	0
nominate	14	.5381	1.6811	42.3	0	0	1	7	1	2	3	0	7	0	0	0	0	4	0	0	0	0	0	0	0	1	1	1	0
nominated	11	.3522	.8598	39.3	0	0	3	0	1	6	1	0	0	2	0	0	0	4	0	0	0	0	0	0	0	0	5	0	0
nominating	3	.2378	.1809	32.6	0	0	0	0	0	0	3	0	0	0	0	0	0	2	0	0	0	0	0	0	0	1	0	0	0
nomination	17	.4421	1.6482	42.2	1	0	4	2	5	1	4	0	3	1	0	0	0	1	0	0	0	0	0	0	0	3	8	1	0
nominations	6	.2270	.3462	35.4	0	0	0	2	0	4	0	0	1	4	0	0	0	0	0	0	0	0	0	0	0	0	0	1	0
nominative	8	.1605	.2966	34.7	0	0	0	3	1	0	4	0	0	4	4	0	0	0	0	0	0	0	0	0	0	0	0	0	0
nominee	14	.1929	.6821	38.3	0	0	9	0	4	0	1	0	1	0	0	0	0	0	0	0	0	0	0	0	0	1	11	1	0
non	6	.5484	.7056	38.5	0	1	0	3	1	0	1	0	2	1	0	0	0	0	1	0	1	0	0	0	0	0	0	1	0
non-Communist	9	.4259	.8289	39.2	1	0	1	6	1	0	0	0	0	0	0	0	0	3	0	0	0	0	0	0	0	1	1	4	0
non-Euclidean	3	.0000	.0449	26.5	0	0	0	0	0	3	0	0	0	0	0	0	3	0	0	0	0	0	0	0	0	0	0	0	0
non-living	4	.2353	.2382	33.8	0	2	0	1	0	1	0	0	0	0	0	0	0	0	0	3	0	0	0	0	0	0	1	0	0
non-metric	2	.0000	.0299	24.8	0	0	0	0	0	0	2	0	0	0	0	0	2	0	0	0	0	0	0	0	0	0	0	0	0
non-negative	6	.0000	.0898	29.5	0	0	0	0	3	3	0	0	0	0	0	0	6	0	0	0	0	0	0	0	0	0	0	0	0
non-objective	2	.1378	.0662	28.2	0	0	0	0	1	0	0	1	0	0	0	0	0	0	0	0	0	1	0	0	0	0	0	1	0
non-porous	3	.0000	.0591	27.7	0	0	0	0	0	0	3	0	0	0	0	0	0	0	0	3	0	0	0	0	0	0	0	0	0
non-stop	2	.2440	.1132	30.5	0	0	0	0	0	0	1	1	0	0	0	1	0	0	0	0	0	0	0	0	0	0	0	1	0
non-terminating	2	.0000	.0299	24.8	0	0	0	1	0	0	1	0	0	0	0	0	2	0	0	0	0	0	0	0	0	0	0	0	0
non-verbal	2	.0000	.0243	23.9	0	0	0	0	0	0	0	2	0	0	0	0	0	0	0	0	0	0	0	0	0	0	0	2	0
non-zero	4	.0000	.0599	27.8	0	0	0	0	1	3	0	0	0	0	0	0	4	0	0	0	0	0	0	0	0	0	0	0	0
nonadjustable	2	.0000	.0243	23.9	0	0	0	0	2	0	0	0	0	0	0	0	0	0	0	0	0	0	0	0	0	0	0	2	0
nonchalant	3	.2332	.1690	32.3	1	0	0	0	0	1	0	1	0	0	0	0	0	0	0	0	0	0	0	0	0	2	0	1	0
noncircular	2	.2278	.1128	30.5	0	0	0	0	0	1	0	1	0	0	0	0	0	0	0	1	0	0	0	0	0	0	1	0	0
nonconductor	2	.2437	.1129	30.5	0	0	0	0	1	1	0	0	0	0	0	0	0	0	0	0	0	0	0	0	0	0	1	1	0
nonconductors	4	.4013	.3370	35.3	0	0	1	0	0	1	2	0	0	0	0	0	0	0	0	1	0	0	1	1	0	0	1	0	0
nonconformist	3	.2445	.1818	32.6	0	0	0	2	0	1	0	0	0	0	0	0	0	0	0	2	0	0	0	0	0	0	1	0	0
nonconformists	3	.1813	.1402	31.5	0	0	0	1	1	0	1	0	0	0	0	0	0	0	0	1	0	0	0	0	0	0	2	0	0
noncoplanar	2	.0000	.0299	24.8	0	0	0	0	2	0	0	0	0	0	0	0	2	0	0	0	0	0	0	0	0	0	0	0	0
noncount	2	.0000	.0219	23.4	0	0	0	0	2	0	0	0	0	2	0	0	0	0	0	0	0	0	0	0	0	0	0	0	0
nondescript	2	.2441	.1127	30.5	0	0	0	1	1	0	0	0	0	0	0	0	0	0	0	0	0	0	0	0	1	0	1	0	0
none	406	.9004	72.704	58.6	48	38	36	51	110	52	56	15	107	20	4	58	12	22	8	28	12	2	2	0	38	33	24	36	0
nonessential	3	.0000	.0328	25.2	0	0	0	0	0	0	3	0	0	3	0	0	0	0	0	0	0	0	0	0	0	0	0	0	0
nonetheless	17	.5555	1.9641	42.9	1	0	2	1	7	4	1	1	1	3	0	1	0	0	0	1	0	0	0	0	0	2	2	7	0
nonexistent	4	.2346	.2332	33.7	0	0	0	0	0	1	3	0	0	0	0	0	0	0	0	2	0	0	0	0	0	0	0	2	0
nonfarm	2	.2351	.1166	30.7	0	0	0	0	0	0	1	1	0	0	0	0	0	1	0	0	0	0	0	0	0	0	0	1	0
nonferrous	5	.1135	.1695	32.3	1	0	0	0	0	0	4	0	1	0	0	0	0	0	0	0	0	0	0	3	0	0	0	1	0
nonfiction	23	.1126	.8096	39.1	0	0	9	7	6	1	0	0	2	19	0	0	0	0	0	2	0	0	0	0	0	0	0	0	0
nonliving	39	.1303	1.6512	42.2	18	0	5	1	10	5	0	0	0	0	0	1	0	0	0	37	0	0	0	0	0	0	1	0	0
nonmaterial	2	.2376	.1088	30.4	0	0	0	0	0	1	1	0	0	0	0	0	0	0	1	0	0	0	0	0	0	0	0	1	0
nonmetal	2	.2160	.1362	31.3	1	0	0	0	0	1	0	0	1	0	0	0	0	0	0	1	0	0	0	0	0	0	0	0	0
nonmetallic	9	.4465	.8847	39.5	1	0	2	0	0	6	0	0	1	0	0	0	0	0	0	5	0	0	0	1	0	1	1	0	0

8D nobleman's
6J nobleness
7F nobles'
9Q noblesse
4N noblewoman
5N nobody'd
8J nocturne
8K nocturnes
7P Nocturnes
7R noddies
9Q node
4P Noey
7N noggin
9B noire
3A noise-maker
7A noise-makers
XR noisemakers
8A Nolan's
4N Noll's
7Q Nollet

9F Nomadic
6F nomads'
9F nominates
6P Nominating
5Q nominee's
5J nominees
5A non-Alaskans
7R non-Alpine
5P non-Arab
5F non-British
XR non-Catholic
8F non-Chinese
7P non-Communists
8F non-English
6F non-Europeans
5R non-Scouts
8F non-Western
9E non-collinear
8B non-criminals
7F non-demonstrators

7Q non-electrical
7A non-existent
5H non-exploding
XR non-farm
8L non-fat
7Q non-fathers
5F non-fiction
9H non-glacial
XH non-green
4H non-hunters
8M non-magnetic
9E non-measurement
9F non-member
7M non-metallic
9Q non-military
5Q non-moving
XH non-mutated
8H non-nutritive
8J non-pentatonic
6H non-permeable

7R non-physical
8E non-positive
6P non-professional
5R non-profit
6E non-repeating
7H non-smokers
7G non-spelling
7R non-stock
8C non-voting
9L non-woven
8E non
6K nonabsorbent
9B nonaction
5Q nonaggression
9E nonagon
4Q nonagricultural
8A nonautomatic
8R nonchalance
8D nonchalantly
XH noncharacteristic

9R nonchurched
9G noncitizens
7E noncollinear
9F noncombat
9Q noncommercial
7D noncommittal
3A nonconducting
8Q nonconformity
7R noncontroversial
7A noncotton-growing
6B noncountable
5Q noncrystalline
7H nondangerous
7R nondealer
8Q nondecorative
7B nondefinite
9M nondevelopable
6J None
7A none-too-keen
7Q nonelectrical

6Q nonembryonic
9Q nonengineers
9Q nonfamilial
5B Nonfiction
6A nonfighters
8C nonfirearms
7R nonflammability
XQ nonfunctional
7Q nongame
6H nongreen
XQ nonhomologous
7R noninterference
XR noninvolvement
7H noniodized
3A noniron
9L nonirritating
XJ nonliturgical
6H nonluminous
6H nonmagnetized
9M nonmarring

Word Type	F	D	U	SFI	3 Gr 3	4 Gr 4	5 Gr 5	6 Gr 6	7 Gr 7	8 Gr 8	9 Gr 9	X UnGr	A Read	B Eng & Gr	C Comp	D Lit	E Math	F Soc Stud	G Spell	H Sci	J Music	K Art	L Home Ec	M Shop	N Lib F	P Lib NF	Q Lib Ref	R Mag	S Rel
nonmetals	15	.2323	.9175	39.6	1	2	0	0	0	12	0	0	1	0	0	0	0	0	0	12	0	0	0	0	0	0	2	0	0
nonnegative	11	.0000	.1647	32.2	0	0	0	0	0	9	2	0	0	0	0	0	11	0	0	0	0	0	0	0	0	0	0	0	0
nonobjective	2	.1493	.0692	28.4	0	0	1	1	0	0	0	0	0	0	0	0	0	0	0	0	0	1	0	0	0	0	1	0	0
nonofficial	2	.2278	.1128	30.5	0	0	0	0	0	2	0	0	0	0	0	0	0	0	0	1	0	0	0	0	0	0	1	0	0
nonparallel	2	.0000	.0299	24.8	0	0	0	0	0	0	2	0	0	0	0	0	2	0	0	0	0	0	0	0	0	0	0	0	0
nonpartisan	2	.1814	.1187	30.7	0	0	0	0	1	1	0	0	1	0	0	0	0	0	0	0	0	0	0	0	0	0	0	1	0
nonpoisonous	2	.2278	.1128	30.5	0	0	0	0	2	0	0	0	0	0	0	0	0	0	0	1	0	0	0	0	0	0	1	0	0
nonporous	4	.0000	.0789	29.0	0	0	4	0	0	0	0	0	0	0	0	0	0	0	0	4	0	0	0	0	0	0	0	0	0
nonprimes	2	.0000	.0299	24.8	0	0	0	0	0	0	2	0	0	0	0	0	2	0	0	0	0	0	0	0	0	0	0	0	0
nonprofessional	3	.0000	.0243	23.8	0	0	0	0	1	0	0	2	0	0	0	0	0	0	0	0	3	0	0	0	0	0	0	0	0
nonprofit	2	.0000	.0209	23.2	0	0	0	0	1	0	1	0	0	0	0	0	0	0	0	0	0	0	0	0	0	0	2	0	0
nonscientist	4	.0000	.0419	26.2	0	0	0	0	0	0	4	0	0	0	0	0	0	0	0	0	0	0	0	0	0	0	4	0	0
nonsense	66	.7447	10.035	50.0	9	12	10	14	9	7	2	3	21	8	0	7	0	1	1	1	7	0	0	0	9	6	1	4	0
nonsingers	2	.0000	.0209	23.2	0	0	0	0	2	0	0	0	0	0	0	0	0	0	0	0	0	0	0	0	0	0	2	0	0
nonskid	2	.0000	.0394	26.0	0	0	2	0	0	0	0	0	0	0	0	0	0	0	0	2	0	0	0	0	0	0	0	0	0
nonstandard	9	.0000	.0985	29.9	0	0	0	0	0	5	4	0	0	9	0	0	0	0	0	0	0	0	0	0	0	0	0	0	0
nonstop	8	.6377	1.0538	40.2	0	0	1	0	4	3	0	0	1	1	0	1	0	1	0	1	0	0	0	0	0	0	1	2	0
nonvascular	2	.0000	.0394	26.0	0	0	0	0	2	0	0	0	0	0	0	0	0	0	0	2	0	0	0	0	0	0	0	0	0
nonverbal	3	.0000	.0328	25.2	0	0	0	0	1	0	2	0	0	3	0	0	0	0	0	0	0	0	0	0	0	0	0	0	0
nonviolence	4	.3097	.2992	34.8	0	0	0	0	1	3	0	0	1	0	0	1	0	0	0	0	0	0	0	0	0	0	0	2	0
nonviolent	6	.0000	.0729	28.6	0	0	0	0	0	6	0	0	0	0	0	0	0	0	0	0	0	0	0	0	0	0	0	6	0
nonwhite	3	.1823	.1405	31.5	0	0	1	0	0	0	2	0	0	0	0	0	0	1	0	0	0	0	0	0	0	0	2	0	0
nonwhites	3	.2378	.1809	32.6	0	0	3	0	0	0	0	0	0	0	0	0	0	2	0	0	0	0	0	0	0	1	0	0	0
nonwoven	2	.0000	.0064	18.1	0	0	0	0	0	0	2	0	0	0	0	0	0	0	0	0	0	0	2	0	0	0	0	0	0
nonzero	16	.0000	.2395	33.8	0	0	0	3	2	4	7	0	0	0	0	0	16	0	0	0	0	0	0	0	0	0	0	0	0
noodles	3	.0524	.0803	29.0	0	0	1	0	1	1	0	0	1	0	0	0	0	0	0	0	0	0	2	0	0	0	0	0	0
nook	5	.5534	.5720	37.6	0	3	0	0	2	0	0	0	0	0	0	1	0	1	0	0	1	0	0	0	0	1	1	0	0
nooks	2	.0857	.0784	28.9	1	0	0	0	1	0	0	0	1	0	0	0	0	0	0	0	0	0	1	0	0	0	0	0	0
noon	198	.9046	35.647	55.5	26	50	18	25	26	33	18	2	62	13	4	11	22	19	8	19	2	1	2	0	11	12	0	12	0
noonday	9	.6033	1.1527	40.6	1	2	0	2	3	1	0	0	3	1	0	1	0	1	0	0	0	0	0	0	2	1	0	0	0
noontime	7	.4335	.6689	38.3	4	0	0	1	1	0	0	1	1	0	1	0	0	0	0	2	0	0	0	0	1	2	0	0	0
noose	7	.4137	.6534	38.2	0	0	1	1	3	2	0	0	2	0	0	3	0	0	1	0	0	0	0	0	0	0	0	1	0
Nooz-hak	4	.0000	.0486	26.9	0	0	0	4	0	0	0	0	0	0	0	0	0	0	0	0	0	0	0	0	0	0	0	4	0
nope	6	.3427	.4955	37.0	0	2	2	0	1	1	0	0	2	0	0	0	0	0	0	0	0	0	0	0	2	0	0	2	0
nor	585	.9180	106.46	60.3	51	58	75	72	148	79	77	25	115	38	3	64	16	55	5	47	19	2	10	2	73	46	36	54	0
Nora	4	.2185	.2038	33.1	2	0	1	1	0	0	0	0	0	3	0	0	0	0	1	0	0	0	0	0	0	0	0	0	0
Norah	3	.0000	.1370	31.4	0	3	0	0	0	0	0	0	3	0	0	0	0	0	0	0	0	0	0	0	0	0	0	0	0
Norbert	3	.0000	.0449	26.5	0	0	0	0	0	0	3	0	0	0	0	0	3	0	0	0	0	0	0	0	0	0	0	0	0
Nordal	3	.0000	.1370	31.4	0	0	0	3	0	0	0	0	3	0	0	0	0	0	0	0	0	0	0	0	0	0	0	0	0
Nordic	3	.2378	.1809	32.6	0	0	1	1	0	0	1	0	0	0	0	0	0	2	0	0	0	0	0	0	0	1	0	0	0
Norfolk	8	.4040	.7171	38.6	0	0	0	0	5	2	1	0	1	0	0	3	0	2	0	0	0	0	0	0	0	0	2	0	0
Noriko	4	.0000	.0778	28.9	0	4	0	0	0	0	0	0	0	0	0	0	0	4	0	0	0	0	0	0	0	0	0	0	0
norm	2	.2437	.1129	30.5	0	0	0	0	1	0	1	0	0	0	0	0	0	0	0	0	0	0	0	0	0	0	1	1	0
Norm	11	.3521	.9557	39.8	0	0	0	2	3	6	0	0	5	0	0	0	0	0	0	0	0	0	0	0	2	0	0	4	0
Norm's	4	.0000	.1827	32.6	0	0	0	0	0	4	0	0	4	0	0	0	0	0	0	0	0	0	0	0	0	0	0	0	0
normal	179	.8353	29.858	54.8	2	5	23	19	48	27	39	16	18	7	3	5	8	4	4	41	3	0	12	3	6	7	26	32	0
Normal	2	.2437	.1129	30.5	0	0	1	0	0	1	0	0	0	0	0	0	0	0	0	0	0	0	0	0	0	0	1	1	0
normality	4	.1611	.1738	32.4	0	0	0	0	2	0	1	1	0	0	0	0	0	0	0	1	0	0	0	0	0	0	0	3	0
normally	76	.7696	11.795	50.7	1	4	6	11	27	11	7	9	9	1	2	1	1	2	1	20	0	1	0	3	1	4	17	13	0
Norman	30	.6226	3.9106	45.9	0	1	2	8	11	6	1	1	9	11	0	0	0	1	3	1	2	1	0	0	0	0	1	1	0
Normandy	23	.5761	2.7341	44.4	3	0	2	3	4	6	4	1	0	5	0	0	0	6	1	0	0	0	0	0	0	1	5	5	0
Normans	13	.3423	.9984	40.0	0	1	0	4	1	5	0	2	1	8	0	0	0	1	2	1	0	0	0	0	0	0	0	0	0
Norris	11	.2432	.8553	39.3	0	0	0	0	11	0	0	0	9	0	0	0	0	0	0	0	0	0	0	0	0	0	0	2	0
Norris-LaGuardia	2	.0000	.0209	23.2	0	0	0	0	2	0	0	0	0	0	0	0	0	0	0	0	0	0	0	0	0	0	2	0	0
Norris'	2	.0000	.0914	29.6	0	0	0	0	2	0	0	0	2	0	0	0	0	0	0	0	0	0	0	0	0	0	0	0	0
Norse	24	.4631	2.3350	43.7	0	4	3	5	11	0	1	0	1	10	0	0	0	1	7	0	1	0	0	0	0	0	4	0	0
Norsemen	11	.4772	1.1396	40.6	0	0	1	2	2	5	0	1	1	2	0	0	0	6	0	0	1	0	0	0	0	1	0	0	0
north	793	.7802	125.12	61.0	129	121	124	144	152	61	37	25	105	11	1	13	16	317	4	103	13	0	1	11	23	66	69	40	0
North	926	.7408	139.84	61.5	124	154	135	142	176	113	65	17	158	14	1	21	21	326	1	91	14	1	0	0	28	59	137	54	0
NorthAmerica	14	.3645	1.2148	40.8	0	1	3	4	0	4	0	2	3	1	0	0	0	9	0	0	0	0	0	0	0	0	1	0	0
NorthAtlantic	2	.1698	.1133	30.5	0	0	1	1	0	0	0	0	1	0	0	0	0	0	0	0	0	0	0	0	0	0	1	0	0
NorthCarolina	50	.6995	7.1955	48.6	4	8	12	1	4	11	6	4	11	1	0	1	0	12	1	4	1	0	0	0	1	4	12	2	0
NorthDakota	14	.5009	1.5532	41.9	2	3	3	2	3	1	0	0	4	0	0	2	0	6	0	1	0	0	0	0	0	0	1	0	0
NorthPole	7	.0861	.2668	34.3	1	0	0	0	0	0	0	6	1	0	0	0	0	6	0	0	0	0	0	0	0	0	0	0	0
north-central	4	.0000	.0419	26.2	1	1	0	0	1	1	0	0	0	0	0	0	0	0	0	0	0	0	0	0	0	0	4	0	0
north-east	2	.0000	.0234	23.7	0	0	0	1	0	0	1	0	0	0	0	0	0	0	0	0	0	0	0	0	2	0	0	0	0
north-flowing	3	.0000	.0583	27.7	0	0	0	3	0	0	0	0	0	0	0	0	0	3	0	0	0	0	0	0	0	0	0	0	0
north-northwest	2	.0000	.0209	23.2	0	0	0	0	0	2	0	0	0	0	0	0	0	0	0	0	0	0	0	0	0	0	2	0	0
north-seeking	16	.1942	.8520	39.3	15	0	0	0	0	0	1	0	0	0	0	0	0	0	0	13	0	0	0	0	0	3	0	0	0
north-south	18	.4838	1.8867	42.8	2	2	0	3	4	1	5	1	1	0	0	0	0	5	0	7	0	0	0	0	0	0	1	4	0
North's	4	.3717	.3640	35.6	0	1	1	0	2	0	0	0	2	0	0	1	0	0	0	0	0	0	0	0	0	0	0	1	0
northbound	2	.2160	.1362	31.3	0	0	0	0	0	2	0	0	1	0	0	0	0	0	0	1	0	0	0	0	0	0	0	0	0
northeast	84	.6243	10.931	50.4	9	6	14	16	17	17	3	2	10	4	0	1	0	34	0	10	0	0	0	0	0	7	13	5	0
Northeast	26	.2084	1.4463	41.6	3	0	6	1	0	12	3	1	0	0	0	0	0	23	0	0	0	0	0	0	0	0	1	2	0
northeastern	47	.4387	4.6084	46.6	2	5	12	6	11	4	4	3	5	0	0	0	0	30	0	4	0	0	0	0	0	4	3	1	0
Northeastern	5	.1966	.2677	34.3	0	3	0	0	0	2	0	0	0	0	0	0	1	4	0	0	0	0	0	0	0	0	0	0	0
northeastward	3	.2239	.1775	32.5	0	0	0	1	1	1	0	0	0	0	0	0	0	2	0	1	0	0	0	0	0	0	0	0	0
norther	4	.2417	.3028	34.8	0	3	1	0	0	0	0	0	3	0	0	0	0	0	0	0	0	0	0	0	1	0	0	0	0
northerly	8	.3270	.6008	37.8	0	0	1	3	2	1	1	0	0	0	0	0	0	4	0	1	0	0	0	0	0	0	3	0	0
northern	470	.6793	65.702	58.2	56	44	81	88	113	31	40	17	50	9	3	3	2	213	2	54	2	0	1	0	4	26	67	34	0
Northern	125	.6153	16.038	52.1	8	14	17	16	23	33	9	5	9	2	0	0	1	71	0	10	3	0	0	1	0	10	10	8	0
northerners	4	.2281	.2337	33.7	0	0	3	0	0	0	1	0	0	0	0	0	0	3	0	0	0	0	0	0	0	0	0	1	0
Northerners	20	.2315	1.2081	40.8	0	0	5	0	2	13	0	0	1	0	0	0	0	16	0	0	0	0	0	0	0	0	3	0	0
northernmost	14	.5508	1.6093	42.1	4	0	2	1	3	1	2	1	0	0	0	1	0	5	0	0	0	0	0	0	0	3	2	3	0
northland	7	.3788	.5924	37.7	0	0	6	1	0	0	0	0	0	0	0	0	0	4	0	0	1	0	0	0	0	2	0	0	0
Northland	4	.3689	.3191	35.0	0	0	0	0	2	1	0	1	0	0	0	0	0	0	0	0	0	0	0	0	2	0	1	1	0
northlands	3	.3427	.2477	33.9	0	0	0	0	1	1	0	1	1	0	0	0	0	0	0	0	0	0	0	0	1	0	0	1	0
Northman	2	.0000	.0914	29.6	0	0	1	0	1	0	0	0	2	0	0	0	0	0	0	0	0	0	0	0	0	0	0	0	0
Northmen	2	.0000	.0389	25.9	0	0	0	2	0	0	0	0	0	0	0	0	0	2	0	0	0	0	0	0	0	0	0	0	0
Northridge	2	.0000	.0243	23.9	0	0	0	0	2	0	0	0	0	0	0	0	0	0	0	0	0	0	0	0	0	0	0	2	0

7E nonmetric
7Q nonmigratory
7Q nonmoving
9J nonmusician
7R nonnative
7H nonparasitic
4P Nonpareil
7N nonparticipating
7G nonper
XH nonperiodic
8Q nonpetroleum
XQ nonpigmented
7D nonplussed
5B nonpoetic
8R nonpolitical
9E nonpositive
5A nonprecious
4H nonpressurized
8Q nonpurulent
9R nonrelatives
8Q nonreligious
8E nonrepeating
5Q nonrepresentational
8B nonrestrictive
6R nonsanctioned
9Q nonscriptural
7A nonsectional
4N nonsensical
9Q nonsleeping
9L nonslippery
6H nonsmoker
5P nonsocialist
7Q nonsongbirds
9Q nonspecialized
8E nonsquare
9L nonstretch
9Q nonteaching
9E nontechnical
9E nonterminating
7R nontoxic
7R nontoxicity
6Q nonuniform
9Q nonuniformity
8R Nonviolent
7Q nonvolcanic
3P noodle-seller
8D Noon
5N noontide
7J noontide's
9R noooo
4A Noordzee
7Q nooses
5E NOPQ
8R NORAD
3Q Nord
XH Norddeutscher-Lloyd
5P Norden
6A Nordland
6A Nordmore
XR Norelco-built
XR Norelco's
5D Norfield
7H Norkay
8J Norma
XH normal-sized
XH normals
7A Norman's
9A Norseman
6J Norseman's
5P NorthAmericans
9A NorthCarolina's
9A NorthCarolinian
7R NorthHollywood
5B North-Easter
7N north-bound
XR north-country
9Q north-eastern
7F north-facing
7R north-to-south
XR Northcliffe
3P northeast-to-southwest
6H northeasterly
5F northerner
5J Northerner
XR northerns
4A northers
6R northing
6J Northland's
7Q Northlands

Word Type	F	D	U	SFI	3 Gr 3	4 Gr 4	5 Gr 5	6 Gr 6	7 Gr 7	8 Gr 8	9 Gr 9	X UnGr	A Read	B Eng & Gr	C Comp	D Lit	E Math	F Soc Stud	G Spell	H Sci	J Music	K Art	L Home Ec	M Shop	N Lib F	P Lib NF	Q Lib Ref	R Mag	S Rel
Northumbria	3	.0000	.0314	25.0	0	0	0	0	3	0	0	0	0	0	0	0	0	0	0	0	0	0	0	0	0	0	3	0	0
northward	57	.6341	7.5296	48.8	2	4	8	10	16	9	8	0	8	0	0	2	0	21	0	8	0	0	0	0	1	5	9	3	0
northwest	78	.7279	11.509	50.6	10	7	15	12	16	11	7	0	4	2	1	5	0	31	1	4	1	0	0	1	0	8	17	3	0
Northwest	61	.7266	9.0384	49.6	3	14	14	5	12	7	4	2	9	0	2	2	0	26	1	1	1	1	0	0	0	4	5	9	0
northwestern	43	.4389	4.1300	46.2	4	3	13	8	14	1	0	0	1	0	0	1	0	29	0	0	1	0	0	0	0	1	8	2	0
Northwestern	2	.0000	.0389	25.9	0	0	0	1	0	1	0	0	0	0	0	0	0	2	0	0	0	0	0	0	0	0	0	0	0
Norton	11	.3438	.9860	39.9	0	0	2	0	6	3	0	0	7	0	0	0	1	0	0	0	0	0	0	0	3	0	0	0	0
Norton's	2	.1787	.1174	30.7	0	0	0	0	2	0	0	0	1	0	0	0	0	0	0	0	0	0	0	0	1	0	0	0	0
Norway	179	.6357	23.838	53.8	35	44	20	49	12	8	10	1	37	3	1	5	0	88	1	2	8	0	0	0	1	23	10	0	0
Norway's	9	.3757	.7534	38.8	0	2	2	5	0	0	0	0	0	0	0	0	0	5	0	0	2	0	0	0	0	2	0	0	0
Norwegian	42	.7142	6.1155	47.9	9	7	7	9	7	3	0	0	7	1	0	0	0	8	0	2	8	0	2	0	3	6	4	1	0
Norwegians	13	.4591	1.3940	41.4	6	1	3	3	0	0	0	0	7	0	0	0	0	3	0	0	2	0	0	0	0	1	0	0	0
nos	2	.1703	.0781	28.9	0	0	0	0	1	0	1	0	0	1	0	0	0	0	0	0	0	0	0	1	0	0	0	0	0
Nos	2	.0000	.0050	17.0	0	0	0	0	1	1	0	0	0	0	0	0	0	0	0	0	0	0	0	2	0	0	0	0	0
nose	544	.8328	91.432	59.6	125	128	52	51	105	56	19	8	218	15	7	64	1	9	6	78	2	4	2	1	66	41	3	27	0
nosebleed	4	.0857	.1568	32.0	0	0	0	2	0	2	0	0	2	0	0	0	0	0	0	0	0	0	2	0	0	0	0	0	0
nosed	5	.2446	.3872	35.9	0	0	1	1	3	0	0	0	4	0	0	0	0	0	0	0	0	0	0	0	1	0	0	0	0
nosepiece	2	.0000	.0394	26.0	0	0	0	0	2	0	0	0	0	0	0	0	0	0	0	2	0	0	0	0	0	0	0	0	0
noses	56	.7289	8.3699	49.2	12	10	5	8	14	3	1	3	17	1	0	8	1	2	0	2	1	0	0	0	7	10	1	6	0
nosewheel	2	.0000	.0290	24.6	2	0	0	0	0	0	0	0	0	0	0	0	0	0	0	0	0	0	0	0	0	2	0	0	0
nosing	9	.4081	.8226	39.2	0	3	0	2	4	0	0	0	2	0	0	2	0	0	0	0	0	0	0	0	4	0	1	0	0
nostalgia	5	.1398	.1959	32.9	0	0	0	1	1	1	1	1	0	0	0	0	0	1	0	0	0	0	0	0	0	0	0	4	0
nostalgic	5	.3475	.3790	35.8	0	0	0	1	0	3	0	1	0	0	0	1	0	0	0	0	0	0	0	0	0	0	1	3	0
nostril	4	.3718	.3639	35.6	0	0	1	2	0	1	0	0	2	1	0	0	0	0	0	0	0	0	0	0	1	0	0	0	0
nostrils	48	.5807	5.8775	47.7	7	4	8	9	11	4	5	0	9	0	0	2	0	0	0	9	0	0	0	0	16	7	3	2	0
not	18645	.9898	3630.8	75.6	3260	2611	2033	2533	3650	2167	1945	446	4954	1124	204	1229	865	1851	567	2086	402	131	372	162	1440	1432	811	998	17
Not	15	.7577	2.3055	43.6	3	4	2	1	3	1	1	0	3	1	0	1	2	2	1	0	0	0	0	0	2	1	0	2	0
NOT	6	.2411	.4668	36.7	1	2	2	1	0	0	0	0	5	0	0	0	0	0	0	0	0	0	0	0	0	0	0	1	0
not-word	3	.0000	.0328	25.2	0	3	0	0	0	0	0	0	0	3	0	0	0	0	0	0	0	0	0	0	0	0	0	0	0
not-words	5	.0000	.0547	27.4	0	5	0	0	0	0	0	0	0	5	0	0	0	0	0	0	0	0	0	0	0	0	0	0	0
notable	18	.4189	1.6160	42.1	1	1	3	1	4	2	6	0	1	0	0	0	0	1	0	2	1	3	0	0	0	2	8	0	0
notables	2	.1948	.1250	31.0	0	0	0	1	1	0	0	0	1	0	0	0	0	0	0	0	0	0	0	0	0	1	0	0	0
notably	19	.5969	2.3251	43.7	0	0	2	2	7	5	3	0	0	0	0	1	0	2	0	1	0	0	1	0	0	3	6	5	0
notary	2	.0000	.0215	23.3	0	0	0	0	0	2	0	0	0	0	0	2	0	0	0	0	0	0	0	0	0	0	0	0	0
notate	7	.0000	.0566	27.5	0	0	3	3	1	0	0	0	0	0	0	0	0	0	0	0	7	0	0	0	0	0	0	0	0
notated	27	.0360	.4076	36.1	0	0	8	4	12	3	0	0	0	0	0	0	0	0	0	0	26	0	0	0	0	1	0	0	0
notating	3	.1826	.1331	31.2	0	0	0	1	2	0	0	0	0	0	0	0	1	0	0	0	2	0	0	0	0	0	0	0	0
notation	240	.2645	14.696	51.7	3	24	30	14	59	93	16	1	1	0	0	0	151	0	0	0	86	0	0	0	0	0	1	1	0
notatum	2	.0000	.0394	26.0	0	0	0	0	0	0	2	0	0	0	0	0	0	0	0	2	0	0	0	0	0	0	0	0	0
notch	27	.6771	3.7593	45.8	3	1	3	7	6	3	4	0	6	0	0	4	2	2	3	3	0	0	1	3	2	0	0	1	0
Notch	6	.2953	.4429	36.5	0	0	0	2	0	1	3	0	2	1	0	3	0	0	0	0	0	0	0	0	0	0	0	0	0
notched	6	.5517	.6871	38.4	0	1	1	0	3	0	0	1	0	0	0	1	0	0	0	1	0	0	0	0	1	2	1	0	0
notches	25	.6103	3.2337	45.1	5	2	2	5	4	5	2	0	9	0	0	0	6	2	0	0	0	0	3	1	0	2	1	1	0
notching	2	.1814	.1187	30.7	1	0	0	0	1	0	0	0	1	0	0	0	0	0	0	0	0	0	0	0	0	0	0	1	0
note	713	.7333	105.45	60.2	86	113	74	96	128	93	111	12	75	43	11	20	41	17	42	84	276	4	9	30	15	18	4	24	0
NOTE	4	.1648	.1599	32.0	0	0	0	0	1	0	3	0	0	0	0	0	2	0	0	0	0	0	2	0	0	0	0	0	0
note-taking	2	.0580	.0676	28.3	0	1	0	0	0	1	0	0	1	0	0	0	0	0	0	0	0	1	0	0	0	0	0	0	0
notebook	123	.5451	14.233	51.5	18	27	16	12	17	18	14	1	27	15	4	4	10	1	24	15	3	0	3	0	5	6	0	3	3
Notebook	20	.0236	.3405	35.3	0	10	4	5	1	0	0	0	1	19	0	0	0	0	0	0	0	0	0	0	0	0	0	0	0
notebooks	24	.6359	3.2172	45.1	3	5	5	1	4	0	5	1	8	1	0	1	8	2	0	0	0	0	0	0	1	2	0	1	0
noted	145	.8771	25.300	54.0	2	5	23	19	47	22	23	4	16	3	3	5	9	16	2	26	11	1	0	1	4	8	25	15	0
notes	534	.5084	56.481	57.5	95	107	84	88	75	40	37	8	40	39	4	15	0	9	8	19	338	4	3	12	2	14	7	20	0
Notes	3	.3822	.2446	33.9	0	0	0	2	1	0	0	0	0	1	0	0	0	0	0	0	1	0	0	0	0	0	0	1	0
notetaking	4	.2000	.0914	29.6	0	1	0	0	0	1	0	0	2	0	0	0	0	0	0	0	0	0	0	0	0	0	0	0	0
noteworthy	4	.3582	.3103	34.9	0	0	0	0	2	2	0	0	0	0	0	0	0	0	0	0	0	0	0	0	1	0	2	1	0
nothin'	15	.5197	1.7103	42.3	0	2	2	0	5	3	3	0	6	1	0	4	0	0	0	0	1	0	0	0	3	0	0	0	0
nothing	1420	.8746	248.57	64.0	235	224	155	202	289	149	134	32	539	65	17	157	7	69	7	81	18	1	7	2	192	144	34	78	2
nothing's	10	.5122	1.1148	40.5	1	1	0	2	3	1	2	0	3	0	0	3	0	0	0	0	0	0	0	0	1	2	0	1	0
nothingness	2	.2152	.1357	31.3	0	0	2	0	0	0	0	0	1	0	0	0	0	1	0	0	0	0	0	0	0	0	0	0	0
notice	1274	.8257	210.06	63.2	133	269	210	226	224	102	104	6	135	165	49	28	117	105	174	139	217	47	9	19	22	20	7	21	0
noticeable	26	.7903	4.1288	46.2	2	1	6	0	4	7	6	0	4	0	1	0	0	3	3	3	3	0	2	1	0	2	2	2	0
noticeably	3	.3845	.2449	33.9	0	0	0	0	2	1	0	0	0	1	0	0	0	0	1	0	0	0	0	0	0	0	1	0	0
noticed	324	.8806	57.016	57.6	47	68	37	45	62	30	27	8	114	17	10	20	10	14	4	31	3	5	1	1	26	41	3	24	0
notices	18	.7043	2.6371	44.2	3	1	2	1	5	4	2	0	8	0	0	1	0	0	1	1	0	0	0	0	2	3	1	1	0
noticing	22	.6308	2.9295	44.7	4	3	1	4	8	0	2	0	9	2	2	2	0	1	0	0	1	0	0	0	3	1	0	1	0
notified	3	.3815	.2534	34.0	0	0	0	0	1	0	2	0	0	0	0	0	0	1	0	0	0	0	0	0	0	1	0	1	0
notify	5	.3497	.3771	35.8	0	0	3	0	1	0	1	0	0	3	0	0	0	0	1	0	0	0	0	0	0	0	1	0	0
noting	22	.6898	3.1014	44.9	0	1	4	2	7	5	3	0	4	3	0	1	0	0	4	3	1	1	0	0	0	1	4	0	0
notion	42	.7307	6.2521	48.0	6	1	1	6	13	5	7	3	9	4	0	4	4	2	0	1	0	0	0	0	4	1	8	5	0
notions	16	.6177	2.0326	43.1	0	2	1	1	7	5	0	0	2	1	0	0	1	1	0	1	0	1	3	0	3	0	2	1	0
notochord	5	.0000	.0986	29.9	0	0	0	0	0	0	4	1	0	0	0	0	0	0	0	5	0	0	0	0	0	0	0	0	0
notorious	4	.3720	.3216	35.1	0	1	0	0	0	3	0	0	0	0	0	0	0	0	0	0	0	0	0	0	1	0	1	2	0
notoriously	5	.4768	.4980	37.0	0	0	0	1	3	1	0	0	0	1	0	1	0	0	0	0	0	0	0	0	0	0	1	2	0
Notre	12	.4138	1.0816	40.3	1	0	1	5	1	1	3	0	1	1	0	0	0	1	0	0	0	0	0	0	0	0	3	6	0
Nottingham	11	.3341	.9222	39.6	0	2	0	4	5	0	0	0	5	0	0	4	0	0	0	0	0	0	0	0	0	2	0	0	0
notwithstanding	6	.4513	.6075	37.8	0	0	0	0	4	0	2	0	2	0	0	0	0	0	0	0	0	0	0	0	2	0	1	1	0
nought	6	.4639	.6235	37.9	0	3	0	0	3	0	0	0	2	0	0	1	0	0	0	0	0	0	0	0	1	2	0	0	0
Noumea	2	.0000	.0389	25.9	0	0	0	0	2	0	0	0	0	0	0	0	0	2	0	0	0	0	0	0	0	0	0	0	0
noun	776	.3964	65.660	58.2	66	151	110	105	107	127	110	0	32	503	56	3	1	0	177	2	1	0	0	0	0	0	1	0	0
noun-verb	3	.2060	.1430	31.6	0	0	0	0	1	2	0	0	0	1	0	0	0	0	2	0	0	0	0	0	0	0	0	0	0
nouns	530	.3867	43.495	56.4	44	72	68	68	108	92	77	1	8	290	31	2	0	0	199	0	0	0	0	0	0	0	0	0	0
Nouns	2	.0000	.0162	22.1	0	0	1	1	0	0	0	0	0	0	0	0	0	0	2	0	0	0	0	0	0	0	0	0	0
nourish	6	.5159	.6438	38.1	0	0	2	1	1	0	1	1	0	0	0	0	0	0	0	2	1	0	1	0	0	0	1	1	0
nourished	14	.6394	1.8576	42.7	1	1	2	3	2	2	3	0	2	0	0	2	0	1	0	4	0	0	0	0	0	2	2	1	0
nourishing	15	.6380	1.9902	43.0	0	2	3	3	4	0	3	0	3	0	0	2	0	2	0	3	0	0	1	0	1	0	3	0	0
nourishment	11	.2416	.6643	38.2	1	0	1	1	7	0	0	1	1	0	0	0	0	0	0	4	0	0	0	0	0	0	6	0	0
Nov	16	.3099	1.0982	40.4	1	0	2	1	5	6	1	0	0	1	0	0	0	0	0	0	0	0	0	0	0	2	11	2	0
nova	3	.2429	.1792	32.5	0	0	0	0	0	1	2	0	0	0	0	0	0	0	0	2	1	0	0	0	0	0	0	0	0
Nova	18	.6268	2.3221	43.7	0	1	5	2	8	1	1	0	1	0	0	0	3	4	0	1	3	0	0	0	0	1	4	1	0
Novalis	2	.0000	.0209	23.2	0	0	0	0	0	0	2	0	0	0	0	0	0	0	0	0	0	0	0	0	0	0	2	0	0
novel	71	.6940	9.9828	50.0	0	1	20	4	10	14	14	8	5	11	0	4	2	0	2	0	1	1	0	0	1	7	19	18	0
novelist	11	.4413	1.0429	40.2	0	0	1	1	5	3	1	0	1	2	0	0	1	0	0	0	0	0	0	0	0	0	5	2	0
novelists	8	.4749	.8099	39.1	0	0	6	0	0	1	1	0	0	0	0	0	0	3	0	0	0	0	0	0	0	2	2	1	0
novels	44	.5858	5.2956	47.2	0	1	19	2	8	5	6	3	1	6	0	4	0	3	0	0	1	0	0	0	0	4	16	9	0
novelties	5	.3455	.3922	35.9	0	0	0	2	1	0	1	1	0	2	0	0	0	2	0	1	0	0	0	0	0	0	0	0	0

7Q northward-flowing
6N northwards
5F northwestward
6R northwoods
7N Nortons'
8C Norvay
8C Norvegian
5A Norwalk
6J Norwegians'
9D Norwood
3P Nose
7D nose-to-concrete
3E nose-to-fingertip
9R nosedive
3N nosey
4Q nost
7A nosy
7R not-fully-seated
7H not-so-dashing
XR not-so-lean
7A not-so-nice
5F not-so-smart
9F not-so-thin
3A not-too-big
7Q not-too-distant
3A not-too-old
7H not-too-stylish
XH not-vaccinated
6R not-yet-born
7J Notation
4N note-books
7Q note-issuing
8J note-reading
7H notebook-size
5A nothin's
3A NOTHING
7F nothing-at-all
7P nothings
9Q notification
5Q notoriety
8G Nots
6P Notus
3A nougat
6N nougats
5B Noun
8G noun-forming
4B noun-signal
7B noun-verb-noun
3A Novac
7Q Novara
9H novas
6G novel**
9R novel's
7R Novelist

Word Type	F	D	U	SFI	3 Gr 3	4 Gr 4	5 Gr 5	6 Gr 6	7 Gr 7	8 Gr 8	9 Gr 9	X UnGr	A Read	B Eng & Gr	C Comp	D Lit	E Math	F Soc Stud	G Spell	H Sci	J Music	K Art	L Home Ec	M Shop	N Lib F	P Lib NF	Q Lib Ref	R Mag	S Rel
novelty	11	.5236	1.1949	40.8	0	1	2	1	1	2	3	1	1	0	0	0	0	0	0	0	0	0	2	1	1	0	4	2	0
November	136	.7596	20.869	53.2	9	17	13	24	31	19	22	1	15	2	0	7	4	30	2	2	2	1	0	0	4	16	18	33	0
Noverre	2	.0000	.0209	23.2	0	0	0	0	0	2	0	0	0	0	0	0	0	0	0	0	0	0	0	0	0	0	2	0	0
Noverre's	2	.0000	.0209	23.2	0	0	0	0	0	2	0	0	0	0	0	0	0	0	0	0	0	0	0	0	0	0	2	0	0
novice	4	.3651	.3122	34.9	0	0	0	0	1	1	2	0	0	0	1	1	0	0	0	0	0	0	0	0	0	1	0	1	0
Novotny	2	.0000	.0243	23.9	0	0	0	0	2	0	0	0	0	0	0	0	0	0	0	0	0	0	0	0	0	0	0	2	0
now	7457	.9264	1370.5	71.4	1465	1357	802	1017	1344	764	569	139	2355	352	54	629	332	595	195	562	272	13	33	19	701	641	181	523	0
Now	4	.4526	.3993	36.0	1	1	1	0	1	0	0	0	1	1	0	1	0	0	0	0	0	0	0	0	0	0	0	1	0
NOW	4	.3721	.3657	35.6	4	0	0	0	0	0	0	0	2	0	0	1	0	0	0	0	0	0	0	0	0	1	0	0	0
now-famous	2	.2437	.1129	30.5	0	0	0	0	1	0	0	1	0	0	0	0	0	0	0	0	0	0	0	0	0	0	1	1	0
now's	2	.2303	.1079	30.3	1	1	0	0	0	0	0	0	0	0	0	0	0	0	0	0	1	0	0	0	0	1	0	0	0
nowadays	41	.8091	6.6559	48.2	5	3	2	6	8	5	7	5	6	4	0	4	0	3	0	4	4	0	1	0	1	5	5	4	0
Nowell	5	.0000	.0404	26.1	0	0	0	5	0	0	0	0	0	0	0	0	0	0	0	0	5	0	0	0	0	0	0	0	0
nowhere	73	.8036	11.825	50.7	7	9	9	10	19	9	10	0	19	3	2	9	0	1	1	3	3	0	0	0	10	11	4	7	0
Nowhere	2	.2297	.1135	30.6	0	0	0	0	1	1	0	0	0	0	0	1	0	1	0	0	0	0	0	0	0	0	0	0	0
noxious	3	.2197	.2090	33.2	0	0	0	2	0	1	0	0	2	0	0	0	0	0	0	0	0	0	0	0	0	0	1	0	0
nozzle	17	.3937	1.4781	41.7	0	5	3	1	3	1	3	1	1	0	0	0	0	0	0	6	0	0	0	3	0	6	1	0	0
nozzles	2	.0000	.0243	23.9	0	0	0	0	2	0	0	0	0	0	0	0	0	0	0	0	0	0	0	0	0	0	0	2	0
NP	30	.0697	.7237	38.6	1	0	0	1	3	17	8	0	0	28	0	0	2	0	0	0	0	0	0	0	0	0	0	0	0
NP'S	3	.0000	.0328	25.2	0	0	0	0	0	3	0	0	0	3	0	0	0	0	0	0	0	0	0	0	0	0	0	0	0
NPN	2	.0000	.0394	26.0	0	0	0	0	0	2	0	0	0	0	0	0	0	0	0	2	0	0	0	0	0	0	0	0	0
Ngong	5	.0000	.2284	33.6	0	5	0	0	0	0	0	0	5	0	0	0	0	0	0	0	0	0	0	0	0	0	0	0	0
NS	8	.3703	.6394	38.1	0	0	0	1	2	3	2	0	0	4	1	0	3	0	0	0	0	0	0	0	0	0	0	0	0
nt	5	.0000	.0406	26.1	0	0	0	0	5	0	0	0	0	0	0	0	0	0	5	0	0	0	0	0	0	0	0	0	0
nu	2	.0000	.0215	23.3	0	2	0	0	0	0	0	0	0	0	0	2	0	0	0	0	0	0	0	0	0	0	0	0	0
nuance	2	.0000	.0162	22.1	0	0	0	0	0	0	2	0	0	0	0	0	0	0	0	0	2	0	0	0	0	0	0	0	0
nubbly	3	.2266	.1614	32.1	0	1	0	0	0	0	0	2	0	0	0	0	0	0	0	0	0	0	0	0	1	0	0	2	0
nuclear	124	.6646	16.815	52.3	0	6	3	19	34	33	22	7	0	1	5	1	5	6	2	56	0	0	0	4	0	0	24	20	0
nuclear-powered	4	.3990	.3412	35.3	0	0	1	0	2	1	0	0	0	1	0	0	0	1	0	0	0	0	1	0	0	0	0	1	0
nuclei	43	.3459	3.3933	45.3	0	0	0	10	15	4	9	5	0	0	0	0	0	0	0	30	0	0	0	1	0	0	12	0	0
nucleic	6	.2071	.3307	35.2	0	0	0	0	1	1	3	1	0	0	0	0	0	0	0	5	0	0	0	0	0	0	1	0	0
nucleotide	2	.0000	.0394	26.0	0	0	0	0	0	0	2	0	0	0	0	0	0	0	0	2	0	0	0	0	0	0	0	0	0
nucleus	104	.3944	9.1575	49.6	2	0	29	20	39	8	5	1	0	0	0	0	0	0	1	79	0	0	0	2	0	2	19	1	0
nude	2	.0000	.0243	23.9	0	0	0	0	0	0	1	1	0	0	0	0	0	0	0	0	0	0	0	0	0	0	0	2	0
nudge	17	.6294	2.2739	43.6	9	0	0	0	5	1	2	0	8	1	1	2	0	0	0	0	0	0	0	0	2	1	0	2	0
nudged	17	.6261	2.2346	43.5	2	5	1	3	3	1	2	0	5	1	0	2	0	1	0	0	0	0	0	0	4	3	0	1	0
nudging	7	.3960	.6161	37.9	1	2	1	0	1	1	1	0	1	0	0	2	0	0	0	0	0	0	0	0	0	1	0	3	0
nugful	2	.0000	.0219	23.4	0	0	0	2	0	0	0	0	0	2	0	0	0	0	0	0	0	0	0	0	0	0	0	0	0
nugget	3	.2197	.2090	33.2	1	0	0	0	0	1	1	0	2	0	0	0	0	0	0	0	0	0	0	0	0	0	1	0	0
nuggets	11	.4357	1.1099	40.5	2	2	1	1	2	2	1	0	4	0	0	0	0	1	0	3	0	0	0	0	0	0	0	3	0
Nui	4	.0000	.0469	26.7	0	0	0	4	0	0	0	0	0	0	0	0	0	0	0	0	0	0	0	0	4	0	0	0	0
nuisance	30	.6746	4.1811	46.2	3	6	2	7	5	3	3	1	7	4	1	2	0	0	0	6	0	0	0	0	7	1	0	2	0
nuisances	2	.0000	.0914	29.6	1	0	1	0	0	0	0	0	2	0	0	0	0	0	0	0	0	0	0	0	0	0	0	0	0
Nuit	2	.0000	.0290	24.6	0	0	0	1	1	0	0	0	0	0	0	0	0	0	0	0	0	0	0	0	0	2	0	0	0
null	8	.3403	.6008	37.8	0	0	1	0	2	2	2	1	0	5	0	0	1	0	0	1	0	0	0	0	0	0	1	0	0
nullified	2	.1787	.1174	30.7	0	0	0	0	2	0	0	0	1	0	0	0	0	0	0	0	0	0	0	0	1	0	0	0	0
num	3	.0000	.0328	25.2	0	0	0	0	0	0	0	3	0	3	0	0	0	0	0	0	0	0	0	0	0	0	0	0	0
Numa	12	.2264	.6714	38.3	8	2	0	0	0	0	0	2	0	0	0	0	8	0	0	0	0	0	0	0	0	4	0	0	0
numb	17	.6916	2.4349	43.9	1	2	2	2	5	2	0	3	5	3	0	1	0	1	0	3	0	0	0	0	1	2	0	1	0
numbed	4	.3018	.2919	34.7	0	0	1	1	1	0	1	0	1	2	0	1	0	0	0	0	0	0	0	0	0	0	0	0	0
number	6059	.5550	704.34	68.5	772	845	887	776	953	964	777	85	334	215	37	30	4254	212	194	261	71	2	15	69	29	105	131	100	0
Number	67	.6009	8.5308	49.3	19	4	15	1	10	10	8	0	22	0	0	9	15	0	0	0	0	0	0	3	15	2	0	1	0
number-line	31	.0000	.4640	36.7	0	13	8	3	4	3	0	0	0	0	0	0	31	0	0	0	0	0	0	0	0	0	0	0	0
number-naming	2	.0000	.0299	24.8	0	2	0	0	0	0	0	0	0	0	0	0	2	0	0	0	0	0	0	0	0	0	0	0	0
number-one	3	.2357	.2199	33.4	0	2	0	1	0	0	0	0	2	0	0	0	0	0	0	0	0	0	0	0	0	1	0	0	0
numbered	105	.7882	16.737	52.2	12	17	18	10	19	17	10	2	29	16	0	1	7	11	10	7	7	0	1	6	4	1	5	0	0
numbering	13	.6436	1.7158	42.3	0	2	1	0	4	2	2	2	1	0	0	0	2	1	0	2	1	0	0	1	0	0	3	2	0
numberless	7	.4024	.6477	38.1	0	0	0	0	4	3	0	0	2	1	0	0	0	2	0	0	0	1	0	0	0	1	0	0	0
numbers	2582	.3433	200.75	63.0	227	359	372	272	526	485	319	22	80	41	1	7	2155	59	34	57	41	0	3	13	2	27	45	17	0
Numbers	5	.4693	.4933	36.9	0	0	1	1	0	1	0	2	0	1	0	0	1	0	0	0	0	0	0	0	0	0	1	2	0
numbing	3	.3272	.2361	33.7	0	0	0	0	3	0	0	0	1	0	0	0	0	0	0	0	1	0	0	0	0	0	1	0	0
numbly	3	.1277	.1363	31.3	0	0	0	0	2	0	1	0	1	0	0	0	0	0	0	0	0	0	0	0	0	0	0	2	0
numbness	6	.4965	.6412	38.1	0	0	1	1	1	2	1	0	1	0	0	2	0	0	0	1	0	0	0	0	1	0	0	1	0
numeral	911	.0818	27.584	54.4	165	117	70	133	226	153	40	7	17	11	0	0	870	5	0	0	4	0	0	0	2	2	0	0	0
numerals	840	.1291	32.601	55.1	201	152	66	86	182	104	38	11	16	19	0	1	785	3	4	4	3	0	0	0	0	3	2	0	0
numeration	42	.0000	.6287	38.0	0	0	2	3	25	10	2	0	0	0	0	0	42	0	0	0	0	0	0	0	0	0	0	0	0
numerator	142	.0000	2.1255	43.3	0	26	7	42	30	20	17	0	0	0	0	0	142	0	0	0	0	0	0	0	0	0	0	0	0
numerators	63	.0000	.9430	39.7	0	8	8	16	16	7	8	0	0	0	0	0	63	0	0	0	0	0	0	0	0	0	0	0	0
numerical	24	.5146	2.5955	44.1	0	1	1	1	3	4	13	1	1	1	0	0	15	0	0	1	1	0	0	2	0	0	2	1	0
numerous	120	.7834	18.849	52.8	6	5	5	14	44	19	18	9	6	5	0	6	0	13	2	16	3	3	1	2	2	9	40	12	0
Numo	13	.0000	.1946	32.9	13	0	0	0	0	0	0	0	0	0	0	0	13	0	0	0	0	0	0	0	0	0	0	0	0
numpire	2	.0000	.0162	22.1	0	0	0	0	2	0	0	0	0	0	0	0	0	0	2	0	0	0	0	0	0	0	0	0	0
numskull	2	.2444	.1132	30.5	0	0	0	0	1	0	0	1	0	1	0	0	0	0	0	0	0	0	0	0	1	0	0	0	0
nun	7	.2727	.4310	36.3	0	0	0	0	1	0	6	0	0	1	0	5	0	0	0	0	0	0	0	0	0	0	0	1	0
nuns	27	.3007	1.8423	42.7	0	3	1	0	1	1	21	0	1	0	0	18	0	1	0	0	0	0	0	0	0	4	0	3	0
nuoc	2	.0000	.0243	23.9	0	0	0	0	2	0	0	0	0	0	0	0	0	0	0	0	0	0	0	0	0	0	0	2	0
nuovo	2	.0000	.0209	23.2	0	0	2	0	0	0	0	0	0	0	0	0	0	0	0	0	0	0	0	0	0	0	2	0	0
nuptial	2	.0000	.0209	23.2	0	0	0	0	2	0	0	0	0	0	0	0	0	0	0	0	0	0	0	0	0	0	2	0	0
Nuremberg	2	.2401	.1133	30.5	0	0	1	0	1	0	0	0	0	0	0	0	0	0	0	0	0	0	0	0	0	1	1	0	0
nuri	2	.0000	.0243	23.9	0	0	0	0	0	0	0	2	0	0	0	0	0	0	0	0	0	0	0	0	0	0	0	2	0
Nurry	2	.0000	.0234	23.7	0	0	2	0	0	0	0	0	0	0	0	0	0	0	0	0	0	0	0	0	2	0	0	0	0
nurse	85	.8370	14.309	51.6	20	15	9	7	9	12	13	0	30	8	1	5	2	1	6	3	0	0	3	0	7	13	3	3	0
Nurse	16	.0978	.4972	37.0	0	0	0	0	2	1	13	0	1	0	0	14	0	0	0	0	0	0	0	0	0	1	0	0	0
nurse's	6	.5385	.6783	38.3	0	1	2	0	1	1	1	0	1	0	0	1	0	0	1	0	0	0	1	0	1	1	0	0	0
nursed	10	.4860	1.0945	40.4	0	3	0	1	3	2	1	0	4	0	0	0	0	1	0	1	0	0	0	0	3	1	0	0	0
nursemaids	2	.0000	.0162	22.1	0	1	0	0	0	0	1	0	0	0	0	0	0	0	0	0	2	0	0	0	0	0	0	0	0
nurseries	2	.2405	.1205	30.8	0	0	1	0	1	0	0	0	0	0	0	0	0	0	0	1	0	0	0	0	0	1	0	0	0
nursery	38	.8163	6.2364	47.9	3	11	4	8	8	3	0	1	10	1	1	5	0	0	1	1	3	0	1	0	1	5	3	6	0
Nursery	2	.2443	.1130	30.5	0	0	1	0	1	0	0	0	0	0	0	1	0	0	0	0	0	0	0	0	1	0	0	0	0
nurses	52	.6916	7.4762	48.7	6	8	9	2	6	15	5	1	16	1	0	1	0	14	1	7	0	0	0	0	0	5	1	6	0
nursing	18	.6084	2.2963	43.6	0	4	5	1	4	1	2	1	4	0	0	2	0	0	0	3	0	0	0	0	1	2	5	1	0
nurtured	6	.5083	.6542	38.2	0	0	0	0	2	2	1	1	1	0	0	0	0	1	0	0	0	0	0	0	1	0	1	2	0

3J November's
8Q Novgorod
8Q Novi
6F Novokuznetsk
XP Novolipki
6F Novosibirsk
8B Novotny's
8R now-dead
7R now-expendable
7D now-familiar
7F now-feeble
7R now-forgotten
7Q now-or-never
5P now-revered
6A noways
3N nowheres
8D nowise
6J Noye's
4A Noyes
7R noys
6Q NO2
6Q NO3
8M Np**
XR NPPC
8M Nprimary/Nsecondary**
7E NQL
8C NRA
7G ns
8M Ns**
8B NS-V
8L nth
8K Nuages
9J nub
7N nubbins
7Q nubs
9E Nuclear
8H nuclear-bomb
7R nuclear-electric
5N nuclear-electronic
8R nuclear-nonproliferation
9H nucleotides
9R Nudge
9R nudity
7Q Nuevo
7R nukes
6A nullah
3P nullify
4G num-ber
3E number-explainer
7E number-pair
6E number-ray
8E numbers-positive
4E Numeral
8E numerating
5Q Numeration
3A numerically
7Q numerously
9B numismatists
8A nummies
7N numnah
3E Numo's
5Q Nunez
7P nunnery
9R Nuns
6P nuptials
XP Nurburgring
7N Nurmi
7N Nurmis
4P nurse-mare
7D nurse-midwives
8A Nurses
5G nurses'
8L Nursing
7P nursling
3Q nurture
7P Nuru

Word Type	F	D	U	SFI	3 Gr 3	4 Gr 4	5 Gr 5	6 Gr 6	7 Gr 7	8 Gr 8	9 Gr 9	X UnGr	A Read	B Eng & Gr	C Comp	D Lit	E Math	F Soc Stud	G Spell	H Sci	J Music	K Art	L Home Ec	M Shop	N Lib F	P Lib NF	Q Lib Ref	R Mag	S Rel
nut	59	.4547	5.9168	47.7	13	2	5	6	18	4	10	1	19	0	2	1	0	3	2	3	2	0	1	18	3	2	0	3	0
nutcracker	6	.2210	.3124	34.9	4	0	1	0	0	0	0	1	0	0	0	0	0	0	0	1	4	0	0	0	0	1	0	0	0
Nutcracker	19	.0000	.1536	31.9	9	0	0	2	4	1	3	0	0	0	0	0	0	0	0	0	19	0	0	0	0	0	0	0	0
nuthatch	2	.2130	.1056	30.2	1	0	0	0	0	0	0	1	0	0	0	0	0	0	1	1	0	0	0	0	0	0	0	0	0
nuthin'	2	.0000	.0914	29.6	0	0	0	0	2	0	0	0	2	0	0	0	0	0	0	0	0	0	0	0	0	0	0	0	0
nutmeg	11	.4604	1.0868	40.4	0	2	1	0	5	1	0	2	2	0	1	0	0	1	0	0	0	0	3	0	0	0	1	3	0
Nutmeg	3	.0000	.1370	31.4	0	0	3	0	0	0	0	0	3	0	0	0	0	0	0	0	0	0	0	0	0	0	0	0	0
nutmegs	2	.1733	.1149	30.6	0	1	1	0	0	0	0	0	1	1	0	0	0	0	0	0	0	0	0	0	0	0	0	0	0
nutrient	17	.2414	1.0233	40.1	4	1	2	3	2	2	2	1	0	0	0	0	0	0	0	14	0	0	3	0	0	0	0	0	0
nutrients	103	.2208	5.3931	47.3	11	11	13	6	30	16	14	2	0	0	0	0	0	0	0	47	0	0	46	0	0	0	6	4	0
nutrition	29	.1528	1.0838	40.3	0	3	2	0	8	10	6	0	0	0	0	0	1	0	0	8	0	0	18	0	0	0	2	0	0
nutritional	7	.0618	.1146	30.6	0	0	0	0	0	1	6	0	0	0	0	0	0	0	0	0	0	0	6	0	0	0	0	1	0
nutritionists	2	.0000	.0064	18.1	0	0	0	0	1	1	0	0	0	0	0	0	0	0	0	0	0	0	2	0	0	0	0	0	0
nutritious	10	.2446	.5476	37.4	0	0	0	1	3	1	4	1	0	0	0	0	0	0	0	2	0	0	5	0	0	0	2	1	0
nutritive	3	.0000	.0097	19.8	0	0	0	0	0	1	2	0	0	0	0	0	0	0	0	0	0	0	3	0	0	0	0	0	0
nuts	143	.8167	23.502	53.7	23	16	17	25	28	12	20	2	36	5	2	9	10	17	1	16	2	0	8	8	5	7	8	8	1
nutshell	3	.2445	.1818	32.6	0	0	0	0	3	0	0	0	0	0	0	0	0	0	0	2	0	0	0	0	0	0	1	0	0
Nuttel	2	.0000	.0215	23.3	0	0	0	0	0	0	2	0	0	0	0	2	0	0	0	0	0	0	0	0	0	0	0	0	0
nutting	2	.0000	.0234	23.7	0	0	0	1	1	0	0	0	0	0	0	0	0	0	0	0	0	0	0	0	2	0	0	0	0
nutty	3	.1277	.1363	31.3	0	0	0	1	0	0	0	2	1	0	0	0	0	0	0	0	0	0	0	0	0	0	0	2	0
nuzzled	4	.2958	.2914	34.6	0	2	1	1	0	0	0	0	1	0	0	0	0	0	0	0	0	0	0	0	2	1	0	0	0
nuzzling	6	.3677	.5353	37.3	0	1	1	2	1	1	0	0	3	1	1	1	0	0	0	0	0	0	0	0	0	0	0	0	0
NV	2	.2404	.1142	30.6	0	1	0	1	0	0	0	0	0	1	0	0	1	0	0	0	0	0	0	0	0	0	0	0	0
Nyari	5	.0000	.2284	33.6	0	5	0	0	0	0	0	0	5	0	0	0	0	0	0	0	0	0	0	0	0	0	0	0	0
Nye	2	.2351	.1166	30.7	0	0	0	1	0	1	0	0	0	0	0	0	0	1	0	0	0	0	0	0	0	0	0	1	0
nylon	58	.4948	6.4540	48.1	0	3	35	4	3	5	7	1	28	1	1	0	0	9	0	2	0	0	11	0	2	0	1	3	0
Nylon	2	.0000	.0290	24.6	2	0	0	0	0	0	0	0	0	0	0	0	0	0	0	0	0	0	0	0	0	2	0	0	0
nylons	5	.0308	.0871	29.4	0	0	1	0	0	1	3	0	1	0	0	0	0	0	0	0	0	0	4	0	0	0	0	0	0
nymph	22	.5865	2.6826	44.3	4	2	2	4	7	0	3	0	2	4	0	3	0	0	0	5	0	0	0	0	0	1	6	1	0
nymphs	30	.6229	3.9733	46.0	1	6	3	12	5	2	1	0	12	3	0	2	0	0	0	7	2	0	0	0	0	0	4	0	0
Nymphs	2	.0000	.0914	29.6	0	0	0	0	0	2	0	0	2	0	0	0	0	0	0	0	0	0	0	0	0	0	0	0	0
N2	2	.0000	.0209	23.2	0	0	0	2	0	0	0	0	0	0	0	0	0	0	0	0	0	0	0	0	0	0	2	0	0
n4	4	.0000	.0486	26.9	0	0	0	4	0	0	0	0	0	0	0	0	0	0	0	0	0	0	0	0	0	0	0	4	0
o	333	.4579	32.474	55.1	56	76	57	54	38	21	29	2	40	45	3	14	14	7	185	2	6	0	0	0	6	6	1	4	0
O	342	.7657	52.821	57.2	44	44	40	31	84	34	57	8	55	14	5	75	31	8	2	23	69	0	0	3	15	17	18	5	2
O**	56	.6291	7.4418	48.7	12	5	1	8	11	4	9	6	22	14	0	5	1	0	0	0	1	0	0	0	6	4	0	3	0
O-me-me	10	.0000	.4568	36.6	0	10	0	0	0	0	0	0	10	0	0	0	0	0	0	0	0	0	0	0	0	0	0	0	0
o/	5	.1531	.1872	32.7	0	0	3	2	0	0	0	0	0	1	0	0	0	0	4	0	0	0	0	0	0	0	0	0	0
o'	73	.5627	8.6988	49.4	6	2	8	22	25	6	4	0	18	9	0	8	0	0	0	0	6	0	0	0	28	2	2	0	0
O'Brien	9	.2864	.6022	37.8	1	0	0	0	4	1	2	1	1	0	0	6	0	0	0	0	0	0	0	0	1	0	0	1	0
O'Connor	2	.2297	.1135	30.6	0	1	0	0	0	0	1	0	0	0	0	1	0	1	0	0	0	0	0	0	0	0	0	0	0
O'Day	11	.0000	.1290	31.1	0	0	0	0	11	0	0	0	0	0	0	0	0	0	0	0	0	0	0	0	11	0	0	0	0
O'Grumpity	5	.1415	.2456	33.9	0	0	3	2	0	0	0	0	2	3	0	0	0	0	0	0	0	0	0	0	0	0	0	0	0
O'Higgins	9	.0000	.1750	32.4	0	0	0	9	0	0	0	0	0	0	0	0	0	9	0	0	0	0	0	0	0	0	0	0	0
O'Linn	6	.0000	.2741	34.4	0	0	0	0	6	0	0	0	6	0	0	0	0	0	0	0	0	0	0	0	0	0	0	0	0
O'Malley	15	.1822	1.0700	40.3	0	0	0	14	1	0	0	0	14	0	0	0	0	0	0	0	0	0	0	0	0	0	1	0	0
O'Malley's	3	.0000	.1370	31.4	0	0	0	3	0	0	0	0	3	0	0	0	0	0	0	0	0	0	0	0	0	0	0	0	0
O'Neil	2	.0000	.0243	23.9	0	0	0	0	0	0	0	2	0	0	0	0	0	0	0	0	0	0	0	0	0	0	0	2	0
O'Neill	6	.2955	.3942	36.0	1	0	0	0	4	0	1	0	0	1	0	0	0	0	0	0	0	0	0	0	0	0	4	1	0
O'Rourke	2	.0000	.0243	23.9	0	2	0	0	0	0	0	0	0	0	0	0	0	0	0	0	0	0	0	0	0	0	0	2	0
O'Toole	5	.3317	.3672	35.6	0	1	1	3	0	0	0	0	0	1	0	0	0	0	0	0	0	0	0	0	0	1	0	3	0
o'clock	255	.8176	42.268	56.3	68	43	29	27	44	20	20	4	116	20	8	13	17	24	4	6	1	0	1	0	18	10	1	16	0
o'coffee	2	.0000	.0215	23.3	0	0	0	2	0	0	0	0	0	0	0	2	0	0	0	0	0	0	0	0	0	0	0	0	0
o'er	61	.5074	6.5523	48.2	4	7	1	5	21	9	12	2	10	5	1	21	0	0	0	0	20	0	0	0	0	2	0	2	0
O'er	2	.0000	.0162	22.1	0	0	0	2	0	0	0	0	0	0	0	0	0	0	0	0	2	0	0	0	0	0	0	0	0
o's	16	.1114	.4708	36.7	1	5	2	3	3	1	1	0	0	2	0	0	0	0	14	0	0	0	0	0	0	0	0	0	0
O's	2	.1494	.1045	30.2	1	0	0	1	0	0	0	0	1	0	0	0	0	0	0	0	1	0	0	0	0	0	0	0	0
oa	4	.0000	.0325	25.1	0	2	2	0	0	0	0	0	0	0	0	0	0	0	4	0	0	0	0	0	0	0	0	0	0
OA	17	.2119	.8595	39.3	1	0	1	1	3	6	5	0	0	0	0	0	12	0	0	0	0	0	0	5	0	0	0	0	0
Oahu	10	.3197	.7737	38.9	0	0	8	2	0	0	0	0	1	0	0	0	0	7	0	1	0	0	0	0	0	0	0	1	0
oak	117	.8333	19.573	52.9	20	18	14	15	24	13	10	3	27	11	4	6	0	8	1	24	1	0	0	2	7	13	10	3	0
Oak	19	.6206	2.4764	43.9	3	4	4	5	0	2	1	0	5	1	0	0	0	6	2	0	0	1	0	0	3	0	1	0	0
oak-tree	2	.0000	.0215	23.3	0	0	0	0	2	0	0	0	0	0	0	2	0	0	0	0	0	0	0	0	0	0	0	0	0
Oakana	7	.0000	.3198	35.0	0	0	0	0	7	0	0	0	7	0	0	0	0	0	0	0	0	0	0	0	0	0	0	0	0
oaken	6	.2435	.4680	36.7	0	0	0	3	2	1	0	0	5	0	0	1	0	0	0	0	0	0	0	0	0	0	0	0	0
Oakes	2	.0000	.0234	23.7	0	0	0	0	2	0	0	0	0	0	0	0	0	0	0	0	0	0	0	0	2	0	0	0	0
Oakland	16	.3169	1.1758	40.7	0	0	1	7	6	0	1	1	1	0	0	0	0	5	0	0	0	0	0	0	0	0	1	9	0
oaks	16	.6086	1.9944	43.0	0	1	4	2	4	3	0	2	1	1	1	1	0	0	0	3	1	2	0	0	0	0	4	2	0
Oaks	5	.3779	.4755	36.8	3	2	0	0	0	0	0	0	3	1	0	0	0	1	0	0	0	0	0	0	0	0	0	0	0
oar	35	.6299	4.7302	46.7	1	6	5	10	5	2	4	2	19	0	0	4	0	1	1	0	0	0	0	0	1	7	1	1	0
oarlocks	2	.2446	.1125	30.5	0	0	0	0	0	1	1	0	0	1	0	1	0	0	0	0	0	0	0	0	0	0	0	0	0
oars	59	.7391	8.9490	49.5	8	13	5	10	11	4	5	3	20	1	0	5	0	6	0	4	1	0	0	0	10	5	1	6	0
oarsman	5	.2422	.3874	35.9	0	0	0	4	1	0	0	0	4	0	0	0	0	0	0	0	0	0	0	0	0	1	0	0	0
oarsmen	11	.2434	.8355	39.2	0	0	2	5	2	1	1	0	8	0	0	0	0	0	0	0	0	0	0	0	0	3	0	0	0
OAS	9	.1824	.4216	36.2	0	0	6	1	1	0	1	0	0	0	0	0	0	3	0	0	0	0	0	0	0	0	6	0	0
oases	22	.3192	1.7070	42.3	0	12	3	4	3	0	0	0	3	1	0	0	0	16	0	0	0	0	0	0	0	0	2	0	0
oasis	27	.3912	2.4092	43.8	0	18	1	1	1	3	3	0	2	0	0	0	0	18	0	3	0	0	0	0	0	0	1	3	0
oat	3	.2292	.1615	32.1	2	0	0	0	1	0	0	0	0	0	0	1	0	0	0	0	0	0	0	0	2	0	0	0	0
oath	42	.6649	5.7491	47.6	1	1	4	7	9	10	10	0	5	1	2	6	0	18	0	0	0	0	0	0	3	2	2	3	0
Oath	2	.0000	.0389	25.9	0	0	0	0	0	0	2	0	0	0	0	0	0	2	0	0	0	0	0	0	0	0	0	0	0
oaths	12	.3988	1.0856	40.4	0	1	4	0	3	1	3	0	3	0	0	4	0	0	0	0	0	0	0	0	4	1	0	0	0
oatmeal	17	.6126	2.2375	43.5	10	3	0	1	2	0	1	0	8	2	0	0	3	2	0	0	0	0	0	0	1	0	1	0	0
oats	71	.7420	10.675	50.3	7	10	8	14	18	7	6	1	7	1	1	9	6	20	0	7	0	0	3	0	13	0	4	0	0
Oats	2	.2444	.1132	30.5	0	1	0	0	1	0	0	0	0	1	0	0	0	0	0	0	0	0	0	0	1	0	0	0	0
Oaxaca	2	.1042	.0600	27.8	0	1	0	1	0	0	0	0	0	0	0	0	0	1	0	0	0	1	0	0	0	0	0	0	0
Ob	2	.0000	.0389	25.9	0	0	0	0	0	0	2	0	0	0	0	0	0	2	0	0	0	0	0	0	0	0	0	0	0
OB	11	.1894	.5026	37.0	1	0	1	1	4	0	4	0	0	0	0	0	7	0	0	0	0	0	0	4	0	0	0	0	0
ob-	2	.0000	.0162	22.1	0	0	0	0	1	1	0	0	0	0	0	0	0	0	2	0	0	0	0	0	0	0	0	0	0

7H nut-bearing
7N nut-brown
3A nut-eater
3N nut-errant
3P nut-growing
XN nut's
3P nutcrackers
6Q nuthatches
6Q nutlets
4D Nutley
5A nutlike
8L NUTRIENTS
9L Nutrition
7L nutritionally
7L nutritionist
8F Nuts
7R nuts-and-bolts
5F Nuuanu
8D nuzzle
4F NW
5E nxn
5E nx0
5E nx3
8E nx3/7
6E nx7
9P Nyantara
4A Nyari's
7Q Nyasaland
9L nylon-cotton
7G nym
7Q nymph's
7Q Nymphalidae
5J Nyu
9B NYU
5J Nyu's
7F Nyun
9E nOn-terminating
9H N2H4
7A N6A
8A N91457
8R OFallon
3R OOOOOOoooo
9D O-U-T
9H o-bead
7G o-ending
3P O-hi-o
5J O-lulu
4A O-me-me's
5A o-o-oh
XP o-oh-oh
4N o-r-r-r-h
4N o-r-r-r-r-h
7R O-ring-sealed
6A O'Bannon
8E O'Boye's
7R O'Boyle
7B O'Brian
8R O'Casey
7R O'Casey's
8P O'Connor's
7N O'Day's
7B O'Dell
8C O'Farrell
5B O'Grumpity's
5B O'Hara
6R O'Hare
5A O'Keefe
3R O'Leary
3R O'Learys'
9P O'Loughlin
8F O'Neale
XR O'Neil's
5P O'Neills
7A o'erheard
8B o'erlooking
5P o'erspreads
9D o'erstare
7N o'erwrought
3A o'fairies
6A o'nights
8J o'wakin'
3A OakCity
9F OakPark
6A oak-covered
7R Oakland's
6A Oakway
8N oakwood
8N oar-blade
3P oar-feet
5A oar-handle
6A oarlock
6R oarmen
8D Oars
6A oarsman's
6P oarsmanship
8F oath-taking
9Q oath's
3A Oatmeal
5G ob
9R OB'S**

Word Type	F	D	U	SFI	3 Gr 3	4 Gr 4	5 Gr 5	6 Gr 6	7 Gr 7	8 Gr 8	9 Gr 9	X UnGr	A Read	B Eng & Gr	C Comp	D Lit	E Math	F Soc Stud	G Spell	H Sci	J Music	K Art	L Home Ec	M Shop	N Lib F	P Lib NF	Q Lib Ref	R Mag	S Rel
Obadiah	2	.2387	.1089	30.4	0	0	0	0	1	1	0	0	0	0	0	0	0	0	0	0	1	0	0	0	1	0	0	0	0
Obed	2	.0000	.0290	24.6	0	2	0	0	0	0	0	0	0	0	0	0	0	0	0	0	0	0	0	0	0	2	0	0	0
Obediah	10	.0000	.1172	30.7	0	0	0	10	0	0	0	0	0	0	0	0	0	0	0	0	0	0	0	0	10	0	0	0	0
obedience	17	.6471	2.2751	43.6	0	1	0	1	8	6	1	0	3	0	0	0	0	3	0	0	1	0	1	0	4	3	0	2	0
obedient	18	.6503	2.4220	43.8	3	3	1	4	6	0	1	0	4	2	0	3	0	1	1	0	0	0	0	0	5	1	1	0	0
obediently	10	.5814	1.2347	40.9	0	1	2	2	3	1	0	1	3	0	0	1	0	0	0	0	0	0	0	0	3	1	1	1	0
obeisance	4	.2048	.1975	33.0	0	0	2	0	1	0	1	0	0	0	0	1	0	0	0	0	0	0	0	0	3	0	0	0	0
Oberlin	3	.1277	.1363	31.3	1	0	0	1	1	0	0	0	1	0	0	0	0	0	0	0	0	0	0	0	0	0	0	2	0
obese	2	.2440	.1132	30.5	0	0	0	0	0	1	1	0	0	0	0	1	0	0	0	0	0	0	0	0	0	0	0	1	0
Obet	15	.0000	.2917	34.6	0	15	0	0	0	0	0	0	0	0	0	0	0	15	0	0	0	0	0	0	0	0	0	0	0
obey	89	.4033	8.2677	49.2	23	13	9	11	12	11	10	0	26	1	0	6	0	16	8	8	1	0	2	0	7	5	2	4	3
obeyed	39	.6562	5.3716	47.3	6	1	8	7	12	1	4	0	14	1	0	7	0	8	0	1	0	0	0	0	5	1	1	1	0
obeying	7	.5116	.7810	38.9	1	0	0	0	3	2	1	0	2	0	0	0	0	1	0	0	0	0	0	0	0	1	2	1	0
obeys	6	.4190	.5518	37.4	1	0	2	0	0	1	2	0	1	1	1	0	0	0	0	1	0	0	0	0	0	0	2	0	0
obi	3	.0000	.1370	31.4	0	0	0	3	0	0	0	0	3	0	0	0	0	0	0	0	0	0	0	0	0	0	0	0	0
Obie	3	.0000	.1370	31.4	0	3	0	0	0	0	0	0	3	0	0	0	0	0	0	0	0	0	0	0	0	0	0	0	0
obituary	2	.1717	.1142	30.6	0	0	0	0	0	2	0	0	1	0	0	1	0	0	0	0	0	0	0	0	0	0	0	0	0
obj	2	.0000	.0219	23.4	0	2	0	0	0	0	0	0	0	2	0	0	0	0	0	0	0	0	0	0	0	0	0	0	0
object	718	.8176	117.35	60.7	21	114	83	94	137	136	123	10	43	163	17	15	81	21	11	203	18	15	4	41	16	20	39	11	0
objected	25	.6076	3.1734	45.0	3	8	1	1	6	5	1	0	4	4	0	0	0	5	0	0	0	0	0	0	3	5	0	4	0
objection	13	.6163	1.6948	42.3	1	0	1	3	3	3	2	0	4	0	0	2	0	3	0	0	0	0	0	0	1	2	1	0	0
objectionable	6	.5377	.6676	38.2	0	0	0	0	1	3	2	0	0	2	0	1	0	0	0	1	1	0	0	0	0	0	0	1	0
objections	12	.6076	1.4894	41.7	1	2	1	0	2	2	4	0	0	2	0	1	0	1	0	0	0	0	0	0	2	1	4	1	0
objective	78	.5977	9.7046	49.9	0	2	2	13	28	11	10	12	8	6	9	0	0	4	0	29	1	0	1	0	0	5	11	4	0
objectively	3	.3780	.2436	33.9	1	0	0	0	0	1	1	0	0	0	0	1	0	0	0	0	1	0	0	0	0	1	0	0	0
objectives	9	.2846	.5799	37.6	0	0	0	0	3	3	2	1	0	0	0	0	0	3	0	0	0	0	0	3	0	2	0	1	0
objectors	2	.2346	.1166	30.7	0	0	0	0	1	0	0	1	0	0	0	0	0	0	0	1	0	0	0	0	0	0	0	1	0
objects	568	.6942	80.180	59.0	74	80	67	87	100	97	49	14	32	37	4	9	148	14	8	171	2	52	4	24	2	11	37	13	0
obligated	2	.2417	.1091	30.4	0	0	0	0	1	0	1	0	0	0	0	0	0	0	0	0	1	0	0	0	0	0	1	0	0
obligation	18	.6296	2.3164	43.6	0	0	1	2	4	7	3	1	1	0	2	2	0	2	0	2	0	0	1	0	2	0	5	1	0
obligations	8	.5294	.8957	39.5	0	1	0	0	2	2	3	0	1	0	1	0	0	1	0	1	0	0	0	0	0	1	2	1	0
obligatory	4	.3501	.2980	34.7	0	0	1	0	2	0	1	0	0	1	0	0	0	0	0	0	0	0	1	0	0	0	2	0	0
oblige	6	.2031	.3980	36.0	0	1	0	3	1	1	0	0	4	0	0	0	0	0	2	0	0	0	0	0	0	0	0	0	0
obliged	17	.6401	2.2518	43.5	1	1	1	3	6	1	3	1	3	1	0	3	0	2	0	0	0	0	0	0	5	1	1	1	0
obliging	3	.1060	.1461	31.6	0	0	0	1	1	1	0	0	2	0	1	0	0	0	0	0	0	0	0	0	0	0	0	0	0
obligingly	5	.3975	.4517	36.5	1	1	2	0	0	1	0	0	1	2	0	0	0	1	0	0	0	0	0	0	0	1	0	0	0
oblique	14	.2617	.8324	39.2	0	0	0	0	2	6	4	2	0	0	0	0	6	0	0	2	0	0	0	5	0	0	1	0	0
obliquely	3	.2071	.1434	31.6	0	0	0	2	0	0	1	0	0	0	0	1	0	0	0	0	2	0	0	0	0	0	0	0	0
obliterate	2	.1814	.1187	30.7	0	0	0	0	0	0	2	0	1	0	0	0	0	0	0	0	0	0	0	0	0	0	0	1	0
obliterated	2	.2401	.1133	30.5	0	0	0	1	1	0	0	0	0	0	0	0	0	0	0	0	0	0	0	0	0	1	1	0	0
oblivion	6	.4520	.6163	37.9	0	0	1	2	3	0	0	0	2	0	0	0	0	0	0	1	0	0	0	0	0	2	0	1	0
oblivious	4	.3641	.3177	35.0	1	0	0	1	1	1	0	0	0	0	0	1	0	0	0	0	0	0	0	0	0	1	0	2	0
oblong	8	.3240	.5797	37.6	0	2	0	1	2	1	2	0	1	0	0	1	0	0	0	0	0	0	3	0	2	1	0	0	0
obloquy	2	.1717	.1142	30.6	0	0	0	0	1	1	0	0	1	0	0	1	0	0	0	0	0	0	0	0	0	0	0	0	0
oboe	32	.0000	.2587	34.1	1	5	5	4	10	7	0	0	0	0	0	0	0	0	0	0	32	0	0	0	0	0	0	0	0
oboes	9	.0851	.2230	33.5	0	0	2	2	2	3	0	0	0	0	0	0	0	0	0	0	8	0	0	0	0	1	0	0	0
Obregon	2	.0000	.0243	23.9	0	0	0	0	2	0	0	0	0	0	0	0	0	0	0	0	0	0	0	0	0	0	0	2	0
obscure	22	.6786	3.0332	44.8	0	0	0	2	7	6	3	4	1	1	1	4	0	1	1	4	0	0	0	0	0	0	5	4	0
obscured	6	.3819	.5342	37.3	0	0	0	3	2	1	0	0	2	0	0	1	0	0	0	1	0	1	0	0	0	0	0	1	0
obscurely	2	.1551	.0728	28.6	0	0	0	0	1	1	0	0	0	0	1	0	0	0	0	0	0	0	0	0	1	0	0	0	0
obscurity	4	.4866	.4064	36.1	0	1	0	0	1	2	0	0	0	1	0	1	0	0	0	0	0	0	0	0	0	1	1	0	0
obsequious	2	.1605	.0742	28.7	0	0	0	0	1	0	1	0	0	1	1	0	0	0	0	0	0	0	0	0	0	0	0	0	0
observable	3	.2445	.1818	32.6	0	0	0	0	1	1	1	0	0	0	0	0	0	0	0	2	0	0	0	0	0	0	1	0	0
observance	8	.3710	.6377	38.0	1	1	2	1	1	0	2	0	0	0	0	0	0	0	0	0	1	0	0	0	1	1	5	0	0
observances	4	.3856	.3384	35.3	0	0	0	1	2	0	1	0	0	0	0	0	0	2	0	0	1	0	0	0	0	0	1	0	0
observant	6	.4180	.5515	37.4	2	0	0	0	2	0	2	0	1	2	0	2	0	0	0	0	0	0	0	0	1	0	0	0	0
observation	98	.8338	16.310	52.1	2	17	5	16	28	6	19	5	4	7	3	7	0	2	1	38	0	1	2	2	3	5	12	11	0
observational	4	.2287	.2348	33.7	0	0	0	0	2	0	0	2	0	0	0	0	0	0	0	3	0	0	0	0	0	0	0	1	0
observations	123	.5061	13.293	51.2	3	20	9	21	31	16	13	10	1	8	1	0	0	0	0	89	0	1	0	0	3	2	17	1	0
observatories	6	.1991	.3231	35.1	0	1	0	1	2	1	1	0	0	0	0	0	0	0	0	5	0	0	0	0	1	0	0	0	0
observatory	23	.4288	2.2698	43.6	0	5	3	4	6	0	3	2	6	0	0	0	0	0	0	13	0	0	0	0	2	1	0	1	0
Observatory	18	.3911	1.5845	42.0	0	3	0	3	6	4	1	1	3	0	0	0	0	0	0	3	0	0	0	0	0	0	7	5	0
observe	349	.7886	55.327	57.4	37	72	57	32	72	32	37	10	16	20	4	5	26	7	19	187	9	14	9	3	5	7	12	6	0
observed	181	.8598	31.016	54.9	6	24	16	29	42	32	22	10	13	8	1	8	7	4	1	77	5	2	3	4	15	5	19	9	0
observer	43	.7434	6.4654	48.1	2	0	2	6	17	5	5	6	5	7	0	2	0	3	1	9	0	2	0	2	0	1	7	4	0
Observer	3	.1250	.1342	31.3	0	0	0	0	0	3	0	0	1	0	0	0	0	0	0	0	0	0	0	0	2	0	0	0	0
observers	28	.5434	3.2146	45.1	0	0	0	7	13	4	2	2	3	1	0	0	0	3	0	5	0	0	0	0	1	0	4	11	0
observes	21	.4209	1.9824	43.0	1	6	4	3	3	2	2	0	2	2	0	0	0	0	0	14	0	0	0	0	0	0	1	2	0
observing	59	.8529	10.057	50.0	1	8	6	6	19	8	9	2	10	6	1	4	3	4	1	17	3	2	1	0	4	0	1	2	0
obsessed	3	.3795	.2506	34.0	0	1	0	0	1	1	0	0	0	0	0	0	0	1	0	0	0	0	0	0	1	0	0	1	0
obsession	7	.3675	.5786	37.6	0	0	1	0	1	2	2	1	1	0	0	1	0	0	0	0	0	0	0	0	0	0	1	4	0
obsidian	7	.3953	.6372	38.0	0	3	0	0	1	2	1	0	1	0	0	0	0	1	0	4	0	0	0	0	0	0	1	0	0
obsolescence	2	.2433	.1158	30.6	0	0	1	0	0	1	0	0	0	0	0	0	0	0	0	0	0	0	0	0	0	1	0	1	0
obsolete	7	.4938	.7247	38.6	0	0	0	0	2	3	1	1	0	3	0	0	1	1	0	0	0	0	0	0	0	0	1	1	0
obstacle	13	.6388	1.7247	42.4	1	0	2	1	3	1	5	0	2	0	0	2	0	3	0	1	0	0	0	0	1	3	1	0	0
obstacles	20	.6231	2.5323	44.0	3	0	1	1	7	0	7	1	0	1	1	3	1	0	0	0	0	0	0	0	1	2	8	3	0
obstinate	3	.2261	.2131	33.3	1	0	0	2	0	0	0	0	2	0	0	0	0	0	0	0	0	0	0	0	1	0	0	0	0
obstinately	3	.2222	.1558	31.9	1	0	0	0	1	1	0	0	0	1	0	0	0	0	0	0	0	0	0	0	0	0	2	0	0
obstruct	4	.2672	.2733	34.4	0	1	2	0	0	0	1	0	1	0	0	0	0	0	0	1	0	0	0	0	0	0	2	0	0
obstruction	2	.2441	.1127	30.5	0	0	0	0	2	0	0	0	0	0	0	0	0	0	0	0	0	0	0	0	1	0	1	0	0
obstructionist	2	.0000	.0914	29.6	0	0	0	0	1	1	0	0	2	0	0	0	0	0	0	0	0	0	0	0	0	0	0	0	0
obstructions	5	.4663	.4872	36.9	0	0	2	1	1	1	0	0	0	1	0	1	0	0	0	0	0	0	0	0	1	0	2	0	0
obsurity	2	.2331	.1157	30.6	0	0	0	0	1	0	0	1	0	0	0	0	0	0	0	1	0	0	0	0	1	0	0	0	0
obtain	207	.7006	29.576	54.7	2	14	17	32	64	31	44	3	16	0	0	2	79	22	1	43	1	0	5	9	2	4	18	5	0
obtainable	4	.3450	.2950	34.7	0	1	0	0	1	0	1	1	0	0	0	0	0	0	0	0	0	0	1	0	0	0	2	1	0
obtained	180	.7782	28.205	54.5	7	10	29	16	34	45	28	11	17	2	1	4	27	22	0	41	2	1	4	13	3	4	33	6	0
obtaining	31	.7276	4.5930	46.6	0	1	6	3	11	6	3	1	4	1	0	1	1	5	0	9	1	0	0	2	0	1	3	3	0
obtains	6	.4816	.6138	37.9	0	0	0	0	5	0	1	0	0	1	0	0	0	0	0	3	1	0	0	0	0	0	1	0	0
obtuse	5	.0000	.0748	28.7	0	0	0	0	1	4	0	0	0	0	0	0	5	0	0	0	0	0	0	0	0	0	0	0	0
obverse	3	.0000	.0243	23.9	0	0	0	0	0	3	0	0	0	0	0	0	0	0	3	0	0	0	0	0	0	0	0	0	0
obvious	81	.7848	12.733	51.0	1	0	9	4	32	12	18	5	3	10	3	5	1	6	0	8	7	0	0	0	2	10	11	15	0
obviously	96	.8381	16.057	52.1	1	2	3	9	42	19	15	5	11	10	5	7	4	3	0	9	1	1	2	0	7	10	16	10	0
OC	8	.1457	.2888	34.6	1	0	2	1	0	0	4	0	0	0	0	0	4	0	0	0	0	0	0	4	0	0	0	0	0
Ocala	2	.0000	.0243	23.9	0	0	0	0	0	0	0	2	0	0	0	0	0	0	0	0	0	0	0	0	0	0	0	2	0

7G obcur
7R Obed's
6N Obediah's
7A Obedience
6A Obedient
9R Ober
6J Oberndorf
7P Obersalzberg
9H object's
8G objectionably
9R objectivity
6A Objects
XR objets
8Q oblast
8Q Oblast
7P Oblate
3P obleege
8B oblig'd
6D obligin'
7Q obliterating
XR obliteration
7Q obliterative
8Q Oblomov
9Q oblongata
5Q oblongifolia
7L oblongs
XR obnoxious
7J oboist
XR obolinqui
8Q Obradovic
8Q Obras
7B obs
7P obscene
9R obscenities
9R obscenity
8P Obscura
7Q obscures
9B obscuring
7N obsequies
8B observ'd
8F Observation
9F OBSERVER
8N Observers
5Q obsesses
5Q obsessional
5Q obsessive-compulsive
7Q obstetrical
7R obstetrician
XH obstinacy
7R obstreperous
6A obstructed
9Q obstructing
9F obstructive
XR obtrusive
7R obviate
7L obviates
8Q Obyknovennaya
7G oc-

Word Type	F	D	U	SFI	3 Gr 3	4 Gr 4	5 Gr 5	6 Gr 6	7 Gr 7	8 Gr 8	9 Gr 9	X UnGr	A Read	B Eng & Gr	C Comp	D Lit	E Math	F Soc Stud	G Spell	H Sci	J Music	K Art	L Home Ec	M Shop	N Lib F	P Lib NF	Q Lib Ref	R Mag	S Rel
occasion	118	.8088	19.153	52.8	2	6	8	21	34	23	21	3	24	13	5	6	0	7	1	0	4	3	11	0	9	13	8	14	0
occasional	57	.7605	8.7451	49.4	2	0	5	5	21	12	10	2	8	1	0	6	0	4	0	3	2	0	1	4	3	5	8	12	0
occasionally	143	.8586	24.463	53.9	4	14	16	8	42	26	27	6	24	14	6	13	1	5	1	7	7	5	6	1	5	6	21	21	0
occasions	83	.7463	12.467	51.0	2	7	10	15	25	12	11	1	7	4	3	3	0	12	1	6	12	6	9	0	6	10	0	4	0
Occidentals	2	.2278	.1128	30.5	0	0	0	0	0	0	1	1	0	0	0	0	0	0	0	1	0	0	0	0	0	0	1	0	0
occupant	4	.3135	.2965	34.7	0	0	1	0	1	0	2	0	1	0	1	0	0	0	0	0	0	0	0	0	0	1	1	0	0
occupants	10	.5410	1.1736	40.7	0	0	2	1	3	3	1	0	3	1	0	2	0	0	0	3	0	0	0	0	0	0	0	1	0
occupation	64	.8041	10.335	50.1	2	5	5	13	19	8	11	1	7	5	1	5	0	24	0	0	1	0	1	2	1	6	6	5	0
Occupation	3	.2432	.1790	32.5	0	1	0	0	0	2	0	0	0	0	0	0	0	2	1	0	0	0	0	0	0	0	0	0	0
occupational	4	.3280	.2948	34.7	0	0	0	0	2	1	1	0	0	0	0	0	0	0	0	1	0	0	0	0	0	1	2	0	0
occupations	33	.5276	3.6707	45.6	0	1	3	6	6	7	9	1	3	1	0	2	2	13	2	0	1	0	0	6	0	1	2	0	0
occupied	104	.7419	15.618	51.9	5	4	11	16	29	15	18	6	10	3	0	9	3	28	2	1	2	0	0	0	7	10	23	6	0
occupies	25	.5562	2.9135	44.6	2	4	1	5	7	4	2	0	0	0	1	0	1	9	0	7	0	0	0	0	0	1	6	0	0
occupy	49	.7906	7.7952	48.9	1	0	6	5	16	12	7	2	4	1	0	3	5	12	1	8	0	0	0	1	0	3	4	7	0
occupying	19	.6989	2.7247	44.4	3	0	3	1	5	3	2	2	3	2	0	1	0	5	0	2	0	0	0	0	1	3	2	0	0
occur	215	.8588	36.770	55.7	6	8	19	22	54	53	46	7	16	33	1	2	27	3	11	60	15	2	1	4	3	4	23	10	0
occurred	129	.8837	22.691	53.6	3	6	14	14	33	30	26	3	24	7	4	8	2	13	3	19	7	0	0	1	10	8	14	9	0
occurrence	19	.5810	2.3223	43.7	0	0	0	4	4	1	3	7	3	2	1	0	0	0	0	7	0	0	0	0	0	0	4	2	0
occurrences	8	.4668	.7988	39.0	0	1	0	1	1	0	3	2	0	1	0	2	0	0	0	4	0	0	0	0	0	0	1	0	0
occurring	25	.6712	3.4004	45.3	0	1	1	2	6	6	8	1	0	2	1	0	3	0	1	5	2	0	0	0	0	1	9	1	0
occurs	154	.8184	25.213	54.0	5	3	22	21	43	22	31	7	8	14	2	1	9	11	9	53	9	0	4	1	0	3	26	4	0
Oceaan	2	.0000	.0914	29.6	0	2	0	0	0	0	0	0	2	0	0	0	0	0	0	0	0	0	0	0	0	0	0	0	0
ocean	843	.7859	134.14	61.3	182	156	129	151	105	39	66	15	148	15	2	19	6	186	7	275	15	5	0	0	14	47	53	51	0
Ocean	314	.6330	41.389	56.2	40	67	72	53	35	21	19	7	31	1	1	3	9	173	1	35	6	0	0	0	3	14	26	11	0
ocean-going	10	.1363	.4315	36.4	2	1	0	4	3	0	0	0	0	0	0	0	0	9	0	0	0	0	0	0	0	1	0	0	0
ocean's	13	.4338	1.2097	40.8	0	0	0	4	5	0	3	1	0	0	0	0	0	0	0	4	0	0	0	0	1	0	5	3	0
oceangoing	5	.1865	.3050	34.8	0	2	2	0	0	1	0	0	2	0	0	0	0	3	0	0	0	0	0	0	0	0	0	0	0
oceanic	8	.3141	.5649	37.5	0	0	0	0	4	1	1	2	0	0	0	0	0	1	0	1	0	0	0	0	0	0	5	1	0
Oceanic	2	.0000	.0234	23.7	0	2	0	0	0	0	0	0	0	0	0	0	0	0	0	0	0	0	0	0	0	0	0	0	0
oceanographer	2	.0000	.0394	26.0	0	0	0	0	1	1	0	0	0	0	0	0	0	0	0	2	0	0	0	0	2	0	0	0	0
oceanographers	22	.2661	1.4700	41.7	0	1	4	4	2	4	6	1	1	0	0	0	0	0	0	18	0	0	0	0	0	0	1	2	0
oceanographic	5	.0000	.0986	29.9	0	0	2	2	0	0	1	0	0	0	0	0	0	0	0	5	0	0	0	0	0	0	0	0	0
Oceanographic	3	.3764	.2483	33.9	0	0	0	1	1	1	0	0	0	0	0	0	0	0	0	1	0	0	0	0	0	0	1	1	0
oceanography	21	.3128	1.5222	41.8	0	0	4	3	4	2	2	6	0	0	0	0	0	0	0	11	0	0	0	0	0	0	1	9	0
Oceanography	2	.2278	.1128	30.5	0	0	0	0	1	1	0	0	0	0	0	0	0	0	0	1	0	0	0	0	0	0	1	0	0
oceans	265	.6279	34.587	55.4	62	27	55	23	44	20	25	9	15	3	0	1	1	59	0	123	0	0	0	0	2	24	27	9	1
Oceans	4	.3750	.3392	35.3	1	0	0	1	0	0	2	0	0	0	0	0	0	1	0	2	0	0	0	0	0	0	0	1	0
ochre	2	.1259	.0687	28.4	0	0	0	0	1	0	1	0	0	0	0	0	0	1	0	0	0	0	0	0	0	0	0	0	0
Ocmulgee	4	.2107	.2095	33.2	3	0	0	1	0	0	0	0	0	0	0	0	0	0	0	0	0	0	0	1	0	3	0	1	0
Ocracoke	3	.2279	.2143	33.3	2	0	0	1	0	0	0	0	2	0	0	0	0	0	0	0	0	0	0	0	0	0	0	1	0
Oct	11	.1998	.5548	37.4	0	0	2	0	3	6	0	0	1	0	0	0	0	0	0	0	0	0	0	0	0	0	8	2	0
octagon	3	.0000	.0449	26.5	0	0	0	0	0	1	2	0	0	0	0	0	3	0	0	0	0	0	0	0	0	0	0	0	0
octave	70	.0442	1.1735	40.7	9	13	17	9	13	9	0	0	0	0	0	1	0	0	0	2	67	0	0	0	0	0	0	0	0
octaves	18	.0846	.4692	36.7	3	4	1	2	5	1	2	0	1	0	0	1	0	0	0	0	16	0	0	0	0	0	0	0	0
Octavian	2	.0000	.0389	25.9	0	0	0	0	2	0	0	0	0	0	0	0	0	2	0	0	0	0	0	0	0	0	0	0	0
October	156	.7970	25.043	54.0	23	23	13	30	26	20	16	5	24	4	1	6	7	40	1	4	5	0	0	0	5	17	12	30	0
October's	2	.1843	.0808	29.1	1	0	1	0	0	0	0	0	0	0	1	0	0	0	0	0	0	0	0	0	0	0	0	0	0
octopus	19	.5769	2.4430	43.9	8	1	1	3	3	1	1	1	13	0	0	1	1	0	0	2	1	0	0	0	1	0	0	1	0
Octopus	2	.0000	.0914	29.6	0	0	0	2	0	0	0	0	2	0	0	0	0	0	0	0	0	0	0	0	0	0	0	0	0
octopuses	9	.4837	1.0071	40.0	1	2	0	0	5	0	1	0	5	0	0	1	1	0	0	2	0	0	0	0	0	0	0	0	0
ocular	2	.0000	.0394	26.0	0	0	0	0	1	0	0	1	0	0	0	0	0	0	0	2	0	0	0	0	0	0	0	0	0
OD	8	.1457	.2888	34.6	1	0	2	1	0	0	4	0	0	0	0	0	4	0	0	0	0	0	0	4	0	0	0	0	0
odd	249	.6469	33.497	55.3	63	47	25	33	52	19	7	3	55	4	3	4	142	2	2	3	0	2	1	2	9	7	5	8	0
odd-looking	6	.5493	.7092	38.5	0	0	1	1	3	0	1	0	2	0	0	0	0	0	0	0	1	0	0	0	0	1	1	1	0
odd-numbered	3	.0000	.0591	27.7	0	0	3	0	0	0	0	0	0	0	0	0	0	0	0	3	0	0	0	0	0	0	0	0	0
odd-shaped	4	.3525	.3212	35.1	0	0	0	0	1	2	1	0	1	0	0	0	0	0	0	0	1	0	0	1	1	0	0	0	0
odd-toed	2	.0000	.0394	26.0	0	0	0	0	2	0	0	0	0	0	0	0	0	0	0	2	0	0	0	0	0	0	0	0	0
odder	2	.2391	.1133	30.5	0	0	0	0	2	0	0	0	0	0	0	0	1	0	0	0	0	0	0	0	0	0	1	0	0
oddest	2	.0000	.0914	29.6	0	0	0	1	1	0	0	0	2	0	0	0	0	0	0	0	0	0	0	0	0	0	0	0	0
oddities	2	.0000	.0290	24.6	0	0	1	0	1	0	0	0	0	0	0	0	0	0	0	0	0	0	0	0	0	2	0	0	0
oddity	3	.3764	.2483	33.9	0	1	0	0	2	0	0	0	0	0	0	0	0	0	0	1	0	0	0	0	0	0	1	1	0
oddly	28	.7234	4.1111	46.1	2	1	2	1	16	0	6	0	4	0	1	4	1	1	0	1	0	1	0	0	0	6	4	5	0
odds	41	.8092	6.6865	48.3	1	4	3	6	8	9	9	1	11	1	1	5	4	4	0	0	0	1	0	0	5	2	4	3	0
Ode	2	.2417	.1091	30.4	0	0	0	0	0	1	1	0	0	0	0	0	0	0	0	0	1	0	0	0	0	0	1	0	0
Odense	5	.2443	.3861	35.9	1	0	0	4	0	0	0	0	4	0	0	0	0	0	0	0	0	0	0	0	0	0	1	0	0
Odette	20	.1468	1.0088	40.0	0	20	0	0	0	0	0	0	8	0	0	0	0	0	0	0	0	0	0	0	12	0	0	0	0
Odette's	2	.1787	.1174	30.7	0	2	0	0	0	0	0	0	1	0	0	0	0	0	0	0	0	0	0	0	1	0	0	0	0
Odile	11	.0000	.5025	37.0	11	0	0	0	0	0	0	0	11	0	0	0	0	0	0	0	0	0	0	0	0	0	0	0	0
Odile's	2	.0000	.0914	29.6	2	0	0	0	0	0	0	0	2	0	0	0	0	0	0	0	0	0	0	0	0	0	0	0	0
odin	2	.1733	.1149	30.6	1	0	0	0	0	0	1	0	1	1	0	0	0	0	0	0	0	0	0	0	0	0	0	0	0
Odin	3	.0000	.0314	25.0	0	0	2	0	0	0	1	0	0	0	0	0	0	0	0	0	0	0	0	0	0	0	3	0	0
odious	3	.3847	.2490	34.0	0	0	0	0	2	1	0	0	0	1	0	1	0	0	0	0	0	0	0	0	0	1	0	0	0
Odoacer	2	.0000	.0209	23.2	0	0	0	0	0	2	0	0	0	0	0	0	0	0	0	0	0	0	0	0	0	0	2	0	0
odometer	10	.0000	.1497	31.8	0	1	1	0	7	1	0	0	0	0	0	0	10	0	0	0	0	0	0	0	0	0	0	0	0
odor	84	.6937	12.035	50.8	11	6	15	7	23	11	10	1	26	1	7	5	1	2	0	16	0	0	5	0	2	5	8	6	0
odorless	10	.3851	.8526	39.3	0	2	1	2	5	0	0	0	0	0	0	0	0	0	0	5	0	0	0	0	0	0	2	3	0
odorous	4	.2995	.2902	34.6	0	0	0	0	3	1	0	0	1	1	0	2	0	0	0	0	0	0	0	0	0	0	0	0	0
odors	37	.7084	5.3857	47.3	2	9	1	3	14	4	3	1	10	0	3	3	0	1	0	9	0	1	1	0	4	2	3	0	0
Odysseus	45	.4671	4.5050	46.5	0	0	0	5	4	8	27	1	6	5	0	26	0	2	0	0	0	1	0	0	0	0	4	1	0
Odysseus'	9	.1767	.4205	36.2	0	0	0	0	1	1	7	0	1	0	0	7	0	0	0	0	0	0	0	0	0	0	1	0	0
Odysseus's	3	.0000	.1370	31.4	0	0	0	0	0	3	0	0	3	0	0	0	0	0	0	0	0	0	0	0	0	0	0	0	0
Odyssey	8	.4663	.7975	39.0	0	0	0	1	4	1	2	0	0	1	0	2	0	4	0	0	0	0	0	0	0	0	1	0	0
Oe	2	.0000	.0162	22.1	0	0	0	0	2	0	0	0	0	0	0	0	0	0	0	0	2	0	0	0	0	0	0	0	0
Oedipus	8	.2482	.4548	36.6	0	0	0	0	0	7	1	0	0	1	0	0	0	0	0	0	0	0	0	0	0	0	6	1	0
Oersted	15	.1756	.7752	38.9	1	0	0	13	1	0	0	0	1	0	0	0	0	0	0	13	0	0	0	0	0	0	1	0	0
oestrous	2	.0000	.0209	23.2	0	0	0	0	2	0	0	0	0	0	0	0	0	0	0	0	0	0	0	0	0	0	2	0	0
oestrus	2	.0000	.0209	23.2	0	0	0	0	2	0	0	0	0	0	0	0	0	0	0	0	0	0	0	0	0	0	2	0	0
Oeuvres	2	.0000	.0209	23.2	0	0	0	0	0	2	0	0	0	0	0	0	0	0	0	0	0	0	0	0	0	0	2	0	0
of	146001	.9912	28461	84.5	18241	18408	18861	19534	29402	20095	17042	4418	24365	7466	1682	6309	14747	17840	4618	18793	7220	1749	2252	2148	6021	9876	11934	8855	126
Of	5	.1446	.1801	32.6	2	0	0	0	0	1	1	0	0	0	0	0	0	0	0	0	4	0	0	0	0	0	0	1	0
OF	2	.1432	.0759	28.8	1	0	0	0	1	0	0	0	0	0	0	0	0	0	0	1	0	0	1	0	0	0	0	0	0
off	3873	.9248	710.92	68.5	760	665	441	529	725	378	294	81	1293	108	36	295	114	225	26	416	68	14	36	58	414	353	106	311	0
Off	2	.2375	.1088	30.4	0	0	0	1	0	1	0	0	0	0	0	0	0	0	0	0	1	0	0	0	0	0	0	1	0
Off-Off	2	.0000	.0243	23.9	0	0	0	0	0	0	0	2	0	0	0	0	0	0	0	0	0	0	0	0	0	0	0	2	0
off-farm	3	.0000	.0365	25.6	0	0	0	0	0	0	0	3	0	0	0	0	0	0	0	0	0	0	0	0	0	0	0	3	0

7J occasioned
7J Occasions
6P occult
9Q Occupations
9F Occupied
5P occupiers
6A ocean-bosom
6E oceanliner
7R Oceanographer

7H oceans'
7B Oceanside
7Q ocellaris
3P ocelli
7R ocelots
5P ochered
9B ochestvo
3G oclock
7A ocotillo

8E octahedron
XH octahedrons
9E octant
7R Octavio
7J Octet
9D octopi
3E ODD
8R odd-job
7D oddments

6J ode
8A Odenwald
8Q Odessa
8Q ODOACER
7N odontognathes
7R odor-causing
3P odor-message
7A odorant
XR odoriferous

XR odour
8Q ODOVACAR
4G oe
9R Oedipe
7R OEM
XR oenologists
XQ Oenothera
7Q Oersted's
3P Oestre

4H OFF
9N off-Broadway
6R off-balance
5J off-beat
9R off-camera
7D off-center
7P off-color

Word Type	F	D	U	SFI	3 Gr 3	4 Gr 4	5 Gr 5	6 Gr 6	7 Gr 7	8 Gr 8	9 Gr 9	X UnGr	A Read	B Eng & Gr	C Comp	D Lit	E Math	F Soc Stud	G Spell	H Sci	J Music	K Art	L Home Ec	M Shop	N Lib F	P Lib NF	Q Lib Ref	R Mag	S Rel
off-guard	2	.0000	.0914	29.6	1	0	0	0	1	0	0	0	2	0	0	0	0	0	0	0	0	0	0	0	0	0	0	0	0
off-off-off	3	.0000	.1370	31.4	0	3	0	0	0	0	0	0	3	0	0	0	0	0	0	0	0	0	0	0	0	0	0	0	0
off-shore	3	.2239	.1775	32.5	0	0	0	0	1	1	1	0	0	0	0	0	0	2	0	1	0	0	0	0	0	0	0	0	0
off-spring	2	.2440	.1132	30.5	0	0	0	1	0	0	1	0	0	0	0	1	0	0	0	0	0	0	0	0	0	0	0	1	0
offen	2	.2443	.1130	30.5	0	0	1	0	0	1	0	0	0	0	0	1	0	0	0	0	0	0	0	0	1	0	0	0	0
Offenbach	2	.0000	.0162	22.1	0	1	0	0	1	0	0	0	0	0	0	0	0	0	0	0	2	0	0	0	0	0	0	0	0
offence	3	.2400	.1655	32.2	0	0	0	0	3	0	0	0	0	0	0	0	0	0	1	0	0	0	0	0	2	0	0	0	0
offend	9	.5844	1.0981	40.4	2	0	0	0	3	1	3	0	1	0	0	0	0	0	0	2	1	0	0	0	2	1	0	2	0
offended	20	.6381	2.6676	44.3	0	0	4	3	10	2	0	1	5	1	0	1	0	5	0	0	0	0	0	0	3	0	1	4	0
offender	3	.3370	.2430	33.9	0	0	0	0	2	0	1	0	1	0	0	1	0	0	0	0	0	0	0	0	0	0	1	0	0
offenders	8	.3917	.6819	38.3	0	0	1	3	1	1	2	0	0	0	0	0	0	1	0	1	0	0	0	0	0	0	2	4	0
offending	5	.4753	.5377	37.3	1	0	0	0	2	1	0	1	2	0	0	0	0	1	0	0	0	0	0	0	1	0	0	1	0
offends	2	.2351	.1166	30.7	0	0	0	0	0	2	0	0	0	0	0	0	0	1	0	0	0	0	0	0	0	0	0	1	0
offense	21	.6304	2.7324	44.4	1	0	0	4	8	6	2	0	3	3	0	0	0	2	4	0	0	0	0	0	0	3	2	4	0
offenses	5	.4161	.4629	36.7	0	0	0	2	2	0	1	0	1	2	0	0	0	0	0	0	0	0	0	0	0	1	1	0	0
offensive	33	.5246	3.6739	45.7	0	1	2	3	11	11	5	0	4	1	0	1	0	5	0	0	0	0	0	0	1	3	2	16	0
offer	185	.8495	31.396	55.0	14	6	16	25	49	44	26	5	33	11	2	15	0	22	1	14	7	0	11	2	20	15	10	21	1
offered	219	.8286	36.524	55.6	31	25	26	39	38	29	25	6	67	12	2	16	1	23	1	3	2	0	2	1	16	32	12	28	1
offering	65	.8013	10.470	50.2	8	3	6	9	14	6	13	6	11	2	0	4	0	7	0	1	0	1	1	2	3	11	7	15	0
offerings	11	.6045	1.3913	41.4	0	0	0	4	3	1	2	1	2	0	0	2	0	3	0	0	1	0	0	0	0	0	1	2	0
offers	77	.7520	11.655	50.7	7	5	11	5	19	9	9	12	4	4	0	2	1	9	0	6	3	1	0	2	1	4	18	22	0
officals	3	.3781	.2493	34.0	0	0	0	0	1	1	1	0	0	1	0	0	0	1	0	0	0	0	0	0	0	0	0	1	0
office	469	.8598	80.580	59.1	51	60	69	46	84	83	71	5	96	40	11	30	16	103	15	12	0	1	1	1	9	45	40	49	0
Office	47	.6619	6.3716	48.0	5	7	8	2	7	8	9	1	4	0	0	1	4	8	0	1	2	0	0	0	1	6	14	6	0
officer	167	.7791	26.462	54.2	18	27	14	15	32	35	22	4	57	1	2	21	1	19	4	0	2	0	0	0	9	24	5	22	0
Officer	42	.6457	5.7415	47.6	10	4	4	5	9	3	7	0	19	3	0	1	1	0	0	0	0	0	0	0	1	9	2	6	0
OFFICER	17	.0000	.7766	38.9	0	0	0	17	0	0	0	0	17	0	0	0	0	0	0	0	0	0	0	0	0	0	0	0	0
officer's	5	.2025	.3254	35.1	0	0	1	0	0	4	0	0	3	0	0	2	0	0	0	0	0	0	0	0	0	0	0	0	0
officers	153	.7319	22.871	53.6	9	10	9	16	35	56	12	6	29	4	0	7	6	55	0	0	1	3	0	0	3	18	5	22	0
Officers	4	.4535	.4021	36.0	0	0	0	2	1	0	1	0	1	0	0	1	1	0	0	0	0	0	0	0	0	0	0	1	0
offices	93	.7163	13.553	51.3	17	12	13	10	17	9	12	3	7	3	0	3	0	40	0	2	3	0	0	2	2	6	11	14	0
Offices	2	.2401	.1133	30.5	1	1	0	0	0	0	0	0	0	0	0	0	0	0	0	0	0	0	0	0	0	1	1	0	0
official	153	.7438	23.077	53.6	5	8	18	22	37	30	31	2	19	4	0	7	0	42	2	4	5	0	1	0	1	19	22	27	0
officialdom	2	.2433	.1158	30.6	0	0	1	0	0	0	0	1	0	0	0	0	0	0	0	0	0	0	0	0	0	1	0	1	0
officially	34	.7201	4.9771	47.0	1	1	6	5	9	7	4	1	4	1	1	0	2	6	1	1	0	0	0	0	0	5	5	8	0
officials	139	.6445	18.504	52.7	3	5	10	18	26	26	47	4	11	1	0	3	0	63	5	4	0	1	0	0	1	12	6	32	0
officious	2	.0000	.0219	23.4	0	0	0	0	0	0	2	0	0	2	0	0	0	0	0	0	0	0	0	0	0	0	0	0	0
offset	23	.4549	2.2169	43.5	0	1	1	2	4	2	8	5	1	0	0	1	0	0	0	7	0	0	1	6	0	1	3	3	0
offsets	2	.1698	.1133	30.5	0	1	0	1	0	0	0	0	1	0	0	0	0	0	0	0	0	0	0	0	0	0	1	0	0
offshore	25	.4781	2.5901	44.1	1	5	0	1	8	3	5	2	3	0	0	0	0	7	0	2	0	0	0	0	0	0	5	8	0
offspring	30	.5128	3.2738	45.2	3	0	1	10	11	1	4	0	2	0	0	3	0	0	0	13	0	0	0	0	0	1	8	3	0
offstage	15	.3066	1.0708	40.3	0	0	1	10	3	0	1	0	2	0	0	0	0	0	0	0	1	0	0	0	10	0	0	2	0
oft	12	.4893	1.2538	41.0	0	0	2	2	3	3	2	0	2	0	0	4	0	0	1	0	3	0	0	0	0	2	0	0	0
often	2611	.9698	499.15	67.0	379	387	360	373	521	269	261	61	520	245	26	82	89	318	155	307	181	42	54	32	83	170	194	112	1
oftener	6	.3108	.4295	36.3	1	2	0	0	0	0	3	0	0	3	0	0	0	2	0	1	0	0	0	0	0	0	0	0	0
oftentimes	4	.4050	.3384	35.3	0	1	0	0	0	1	1	1	0	1	0	0	0	0	0	0	1	0	0	1	0	0	0	1	0
OG	3	.0000	.0449	26.5	0	0	0	1	0	0	2	0	0	0	0	0	3	0	0	0	0	0	0	0	0	0	0	0	0
Ogden	7	.4410	.6603	38.2	1	2	3	1	0	0	0	0	0	0	0	0	0	1	0	0	0	0	0	0	0	3	2	1	0
Ogowe	2	.0000	.0914	29.6	0	0	2	0	0	0	0	0	2	0	0	0	0	0	0	0	0	0	0	0	0	0	0	0	0
ogre	29	.1444	1.4478	41.6	4	24	0	0	1	0	0	0	12	0	0	17	0	0	0	0	0	0	0	0	0	0	0	0	0
Ogre	4	.2393	.3005	34.8	0	4	0	0	0	0	0	0	3	0	0	1	0	0	0	0	0	0	0	0	0	0	0	0	0
ogre's	3	.0000	.0322	25.1	0	3	0	0	0	0	0	0	0	0	0	3	0	0	0	0	0	0	0	0	0	0	0	0	0
oh	1489	.7096	219.30	63.4	430	332	183	202	185	100	46	11	683	30	21	143	2	16	11	9	144	0	1	0	297	88	1	43	0
Oh	19	.3984	1.5985	42.0	5	3	5	4	0	0	0	2	0	1	0	1	0	0	0	0	11	0	0	0	3	1	0	2	0
OH	7	.3517	.5491	37.4	0	0	0	3	0	1	3	0	0	0	0	0	2	0	0	2	0	0	0	0	0	0	3	0	0
oh-h	2	.1717	.1142	30.6	0	1	0	1	0	0	0	0	1	0	0	1	0	0	0	0	0	0	0	0	0	0	0	0	0
oh-h-h	3	.0000	.1370	31.4	1	0	1	0	1	0	0	0	3	0	0	0	0	0	0	0	0	0	0	0	0	0	0	0	0
oh-oh	4	.1717	.2284	33.6	2	0	0	0	2	0	0	0	2	0	0	2	0	0	0	0	0	0	0	0	0	0	0	0	0
ohayo	2	.0000	.0914	29.6	2	0	0	0	0	0	0	0	2	0	0	0	0	0	0	0	0	0	0	0	0	0	0	0	0
ohe	2	.0000	.0162	22.1	0	2	0	0	0	0	0	0	0	0	0	0	0	0	0	0	2	0	0	0	0	0	0	0	0
ohhh	2	.1814	.1187	30.7	0	1	0	0	1	0	0	0	1	0	0	0	0	0	0	0	0	0	0	0	0	0	0	1	0
ohhhh	2	.1814	.1187	30.7	0	0	1	0	0	0	1	0	1	0	0	0	0	0	0	0	0	0	0	0	0	0	0	1	0
Ohio	165	.7657	25.584	54.1	14	26	46	13	22	31	10	3	21	6	2	11	7	66	1	6	4	0	0	0	0	22	9	10	0
Ohio's	5	.0000	.0972	29.9	0	0	4	0	0	1	0	0	0	0	0	0	0	5	0	0	0	0	0	0	0	0	0	0	0
Ohiyesa	16	.0000	.7309	38.6	0	16	0	0	0	0	0	0	16	0	0	0	0	0	0	0	0	0	0	0	0	0	0	0	0
Ohlendorf	5	.0000	.0724	28.6	0	0	0	0	5	0	0	0	0	0	0	0	0	0	0	0	0	0	0	0	0	5	0	0	0
ohm	2	.0000	.0394	26.0	0	0	0	0	0	2	0	0	0	0	0	0	0	0	0	2	0	0	0	0	0	0	0	0	0
Ohm	2	.1249	.0685	28.4	0	0	0	0	0	2	0	0	0	0	0	0	0	0	0	1	0	0	0	1	0	0	0	0	0
Ohm's	4	.0000	.0101	20.0	0	0	0	0	0	4	0	0	0	0	0	0	0	0	0	0	0	0	0	4	0	0	0	0	0
ohms	5	.0254	.0794	29.0	0	0	0	1	0	4	0	0	1	0	0	0	0	0	0	0	0	0	0	4	0	0	0	0	0
oho	2	.0000	.0914	29.6	0	1	0	0	1	0	0	0	2	0	0	0	0	0	0	0	0	0	0	0	0	0	0	0	0
oi	32	.1192	1.1511	40.6	3	11	8	5	3	2	0	0	5	0	0	0	0	0	25	0	0	0	0	0	0	0	0	2	0
OI	2	.0000	.0299	24.8	0	0	0	0	0	0	2	0	0	0	0	0	2	0	0	0	0	0	0	0	0	0	0	0	0
oil	731	.8344	122.13	60.9	108	130	99	64	157	69	94	10	80	24	2	7	14	294	6	66	15	14	25	7	7	47	41	82	0
Oil	22	.4550	2.1526	43.3	2	0	7	6	2	1	3	1	3	0	0	0	0	1	0	0	6	0	0	0	0	0	6	6	0
oil-bearing	3	.2239	.1775	32.5	0	1	0	0	1	0	1	0	0	0	0	0	0	2	0	1	0	0	0	0	0	0	0	0	0
oil-drilling	2	.2351	.1166	30.7	0	0	1	0	0	0	1	0	0	0	0	0	0	1	0	0	0	0	0	0	0	0	0	1	0
oil-filled	2	.2346	.1166	30.7	0	0	0	0	2	0	0	0	0	0	0	0	0	0	0	1	0	0	0	0	0	0	0	1	0
oil-level	2	.0000	.0243	23.9	0	0	0	0	2	0	0	0	0	0	0	0	0	0	0	0	0	0	0	0	0	0	0	2	0
oil-producing	2	.0000	.0389	25.9	0	0	1	0	0	0	1	0	0	0	0	0	0	2	0	0	0	0	0	0	0	0	0	0	0
oil-rich	2	.2437	.1129	30.5	0	1	0	0	0	0	1	0	0	0	0	0	0	0	0	0	0	0	0	0	0	0	1	1	0
oil-soluble	2	.0000	.0394	26.0	0	0	0	0	0	0	2	0	0	0	0	0	0	0	0	2	0	0	0	0	0	0	0	0	0
oilcloth	7	.4796	.7457	38.7	1	1	0	0	2	3	0	0	3	0	0	1	0	0	0	0	0	0	1	1	1	0	0	0	0
oiled	18	.7708	2.8108	44.5	3	1	5	2	4	1	2	0	4	1	1	1	0	2	0	3	0	0	1	0	2	1	1	1	0
oiling	2	.2443	.1130	30.5	0	1	0	1	0	0	0	0	0	0	0	1	0	0	0	0	0	0	0	0	1	0	0	0	0
oilmen	10	.1820	.4749	36.8	5	2	0	0	0	3	0	0	0	0	0	0	0	3	0	0	0	0	0	0	0	0	0	7	0
oils	42	.6293	5.4473	47.4	2	1	8	7	10	8	5	1	6	1	0	1	0	7	2	5	0	0	6	4	0	0	8	2	0
oily	15	.6366	1.9911	43.0	0	2	2	1	3	2	5	0	4	0	1	1	0	1	0	3	0	0	2	0	1	0	1	1	0
oinka	6	.0000	.0485	26.9	0	6	0	0	0	0	0	0	0	0	0	0	0	0	0	0	6	0	0	0	0	0	0	0	0
ointment	4	.4538	.4020	36.0	1	0	0	0	1	1	0	1	1	0	0	1	0	0	0	0	0	0	0	0	0	1	0	1	0
ointments	2	.0000	.0394	26.0	0	0	0	0	1	0	1	0	0	0	0	0	0	0	0	2	0	0	0	0	0	0	0	0	0
Oj	2	.0000	.0162	22.1	0	0	2	0	0	0	0	0	0	0	0	0	0	0	0	0	2	0	0	0	0	0	0	0	0
Ojibway	2	.0000	.0914	29.6	0	0	0	0	2	0	0	0	2	0	0	0	0	0	0	0	0	0	0	0	0	0	0	0	0

8L off-hand
7D off-handedly
9R off-limits
9Q off-normal
4A off-off-off-off
7D off-scene
4B off-schedule
9R off-season
7D off-stage
6A off-the-cuff
XR off-the-farm
XR off-trail
7A off'n
5J off'ring
7D offa
8P offal
7N Offal
4A offat
6J offbeats
9D offend'st
XP Offenhauser-powered
7Q offensively
9F offensives
7R OFFER
7N offhand
3A offhandedly
8N office-safe
7A officeholder
8F officeholders
9F officer-training
3A Officer's
5A officers'
3R Official
8P official-looking
XQ Officials
6R offscreen
9Q offsetting
9C offsprings'
5P oft-quoted
9D oft-repeated
9B Often
9L often-asked
XB oftenest
9D ofttimes
6A Ogburn's
9E OGIH
7A Oglala
8R Ogle
4P oh-oh-oh
6R ohboyohboy
3A ohhhhh
7D ohhhhhh
5A ohhhhhhh
9L ohing
8B ohio
7Q Ohmer
7R ohmic
6P OICURMT
7R oil-base
9D oil-cloth-covered
5F oil-field
9D oil-lamp
7F oil-palms
8L oil-plugged
9R oil-powered
3N oil-room
7R oil-well
6J Oil's
8Q oilseeds
6A oilskin
9F oink
7A Ojibways

Word Type	F	D	U	SFI	3 Gr 3	4 Gr 4	5 Gr 5	6 Gr 6	7 Gr 7	8 Gr 8	9 Gr 9	X UnGr	A Read	B Eng & Gr	C Comp	D Lit	E Math	F Soc Stud	G Spell	H Sci	J Music	K Art	L Home Ec	M Shop	N Lib F	P Lib NF	Q Lib Ref	R Mag	S Rel
Ok	2	.0000	.0914	29.6	0	2	0	0	0	0	0	0	2	0	0	0	0	0	0	0	0	0	0	0	0	0	0	0	0
OK	37	.4644	4.1378	46.2	19	1	1	9	2	2	3	0	29	2	0	0	1	0	0	0	0	0	0	0	0	0	1	4	0
Okaro	17	.0000	.7766	38.9	0	0	0	0	17	0	0	0	17	0	0	0	0	0	0	0	0	0	0	0	0	0	0	0	0
okay	76	.5952	9.6290	49.8	11	9	3	6	29	13	4	1	27	3	0	18	0	3	0	0	0	0	0	0	8	4	0	13	0
Okeechobee	5	.2423	.2894	34.6	3	0	0	0	0	0	0	2	0	0	0	0	0	0	0	0	0	0	0	0	0	3	0	2	0
Okinawa	4	.3647	.3180	35.0	0	0	2	0	0	1	1	0	0	0	0	0	0	0	0	0	0	0	0	0	0	1	1	2	0
Okishgon	2	.0000	.0290	24.6	0	2	0	0	0	0	0	0	0	0	0	0	0	0	0	0	0	0	0	0	0	2	0	0	0
Oklahoma	49	.6897	6.9547	48.4	3	3	12	8	11	4	5	3	9	1	0	0	3	14	0	2	3	0	0	0	0	3	4	10	0
OklahomaCity	4	.2843	.2875	34.6	0	1	0	0	2	0	0	1	1	0	0	0	0	1	0	0	0	0	0	0	0	0	0	2	0
okra	4	.1783	.1776	32.5	0	0	0	2	2	0	0	0	0	0	0	0	0	1	0	1	0	0	2	0	0	0	0	0	0
Okracoke	2	.0000	.0243	23.9	0	2	0	0	0	0	0	0	0	0	0	0	0	0	0	0	0	0	0	0	0	0	0	2	0
okrug	2	.0000	.0209	23.2	0	0	0	0	0	2	0	0	0	0	0	0	0	0	0	0	0	0	0	0	0	0	2	0	0
ol'	9	.3494	.7771	38.9	0	0	4	3	2	0	0	0	4	3	0	0	0	0	0	0	0	0	0	0	0	2	0	0	0
Ol'	4	.1919	.1864	32.7	0	0	0	0	3	1	0	0	0	0	0	3	0	0	0	0	0	0	0	0	1	0	0	0	0
Ola	6	.1852	.2683	34.3	0	0	0	4	2	0	0	0	0	0	0	0	0	0	0	0	4	0	0	0	0	2	0	0	0
Olaf	3	.0000	.0583	27.7	0	3	0	0	0	0	0	0	0	0	0	0	0	3	0	0	0	0	0	0	0	0	0	0	0
old	3894	.9153	708.84	68.5	896	658	436	521	657	348	272	106	1532	164	50	370	69	257	53	125	178	23	17	2	394	309	93	257	1
Old	537	.8250	89.237	59.5	113	92	72	71	104	45	29	11	171	28	3	31	1	77	22	2	54	0	0	0	46	46	37	19	0
OLD	14	.0000	.1502	31.8	0	0	0	0	9	0	5	0	0	0	0	14	0	0	0	0	0	0	0	0	0	0	0	0	0
OldLyme	2	.0000	.0243	23.9	0	0	0	2	0	0	0	0	0	0	0	0	0	0	0	0	0	0	0	0	0	0	0	2	0
old-fashioned	53	.7883	8.4525	49.3	7	4	8	8	16	2	4	4	14	2	2	9	1	3	0	5	2	0	0	0	4	7	1	3	0
old-style	3	.3390	.2450	33.9	0	0	1	0	2	0	0	0	1	0	0	0	0	0	0	0	0	0	0	0	0	0	1	1	0
old-time	28	.5422	3.4401	45.4	0	9	3	1	1	12	1	1	20	0	0	2	0	0	0	0	0	0	0	1	3	0	0	2	0
Old-time	2	.0000	.0914	29.6	0	0	0	0	0	2	0	0	2	0	0	0	0	0	0	0	0	0	0	0	0	0	0	0	0
old-timer	2	.2433	.1158	30.6	0	0	0	1	0	0	0	1	0	0	0	0	0	0	0	0	0	0	0	0	0	1	0	1	0
old-timers	4	.2991	.2943	34.7	0	1	0	2	0	1	0	0	1	0	0	0	0	0	0	0	0	0	0	0	0	1	0	2	0
old-world	4	.4819	.4016	36.0	1	0	2	0	1	0	0	0	0	1	0	0	0	0	0	0	1	0	0	0	0	1	1	0	0
olden	10	.5670	1.2152	40.8	1	2	3	2	1	1	0	0	3	0	1	0	1	2	0	1	1	0	0	0	0	0	0	1	0
older	404	.9017	72.434	58.6	78	94	51	41	55	36	41	8	99	24	2	21	11	48	0	24	9	2	14	2	28	65	16	39	0
Older	3	.0000	.0314	25.0	0	0	0	0	0	3	0	0	0	0	0	0	0	0	0	0	0	0	0	0	0	0	3	0	0
oldest	182	.9062	32.791	55.2	40	37	25	16	34	17	10	3	51	4	0	11	6	24	3	9	8	2	2	2	9	17	26	8	0
Olds	3	.0000	.0365	25.6	0	0	0	0	3	0	0	0	0	0	0	0	0	0	0	0	0	0	0	0	0	0	0	3	0
Oldsmobile	7	.2445	.5383	37.3	0	5	1	0	0	1	0	0	5	0	0	0	0	2	0	0	0	0	0	0	0	0	0	0	0
oldsters	2	.2427	.1152	30.6	0	0	0	1	0	0	0	1	0	0	0	0	0	0	0	0	0	0	0	0	1	1	0	0	0
ole	15	.3413	1.2316	40.9	5	1	3	1	4	0	1	0	5	0	0	0	0	0	0	0	1	0	0	0	8	0	0	1	0
Ole	23	.5531	2.8130	44.5	2	1	3	2	9	3	3	0	13	0	0	2	0	1	0	0	4	0	0	0	0	0	2	1	0
Olema	5	.0000	.0586	27.7	0	0	5	0	0	0	0	0	0	0	0	0	0	0	0	0	0	0	0	0	5	0	0	0	0
oleomargarine	5	.3688	.3935	35.9	2	0	2	0	1	0	0	0	0	0	0	0	2	0	2	0	0	0	1	0	0	0	0	0	0
olfactory	3	.2321	.1635	32.1	0	0	0	0	3	0	0	0	0	0	0	0	0	0	0	0	0	0	0	0	0	0	1	2	0
Olga	11	.1178	.3711	35.7	0	8	0	0	2	1	0	0	0	0	0	0	0	0	0	0	0	0	0	0	0	0	1	10	0
oligarchy	3	.2378	.1809	32.6	0	0	1	0	0	2	0	0	0	0	0	0	0	2	0	0	0	0	0	0	0	1	0	0	0
Oligocene	2	.0000	.0209	23.2	0	0	0	0	2	0	0	0	0	0	0	0	0	0	0	0	0	0	0	0	0	0	2	0	0
Olinos	4	.0000	.1827	32.6	0	0	0	0	4	0	0	0	4	0	0	0	0	0	0	0	0	0	0	0	0	0	0	0	0
olive	65	.8071	10.563	50.2	12	19	3	8	14	4	2	3	11	0	0	3	2	17	1	10	4	0	3	0	2	6	3	3	0
Olive	8	.4682	.7883	39.0	0	0	2	0	3	2	1	0	0	2	0	1	0	0	0	0	0	0	0	0	0	2	0	3	0
olive-green	2	.2278	.1128	30.5	0	0	0	0	1	0	0	1	0	0	0	0	0	0	0	1	0	0	0	0	0	0	1	0	0
olive-jar	2	.0000	.0394	26.0	0	2	0	0	0	0	0	0	0	0	0	0	0	0	0	2	0	0	0	0	0	0	0	0	0
Oliver	31	.6180	4.0131	46.0	1	4	4	3	12	1	1	5	8	1	0	1	0	1	0	0	0	0	0	0	8	3	2	7	0
olives	42	.7076	6.1540	47.9	7	15	5	2	9	2	1	1	15	1	0	2	2	9	0	3	0	0	3	0	1	2	4	0	0
Olmecs	2	.0000	.0389	25.9	0	0	0	2	0	0	0	0	0	0	0	0	0	2	0	0	0	0	0	0	0	0	0	0	0
Olmsted	2	.0000	.0394	26.0	0	0	0	0	2	0	0	0	0	0	0	0	0	0	0	2	0	0	0	0	0	0	0	0	0
Olsen	7	.2909	.5146	37.1	2	0	2	2	0	0	1	0	2	0	0	0	0	0	0	0	0	0	0	0	0	4	0	1	0
Olu	7	.0000	.1361	31.3	0	7	0	0	0	0	0	0	0	0	0	0	0	7	0	0	0	0	0	0	0	0	0	0	0
Olu's	4	.0000	.0778	28.9	0	4	0	0	0	0	0	0	0	0	0	0	0	4	0	0	0	0	0	0	0	0	0	0	0
Olympia	2	.0000	.0389	25.9	0	1	0	0	1	0	0	0	0	0	0	0	0	2	0	0	0	0	0	0	0	0	0	0	0
Olympian	5	.4770	.5360	37.3	0	0	0	3	0	1	1	0	2	0	0	1	0	0	0	0	0	0	0	0	0	1	0	1	0
Olympic	55	.6458	7.4550	48.7	3	5	7	13	17	4	6	0	18	1	0	0	3	7	0	1	0	0	0	0	0	7	8	10	0
Olympics	12	.3733	1.1598	40.6	0	1	1	4	5	1	0	0	9	0	0	0	0	0	0	0	0	0	0	0	0	0	1	2	0
Olympus	13	.7125	1.9049	42.8	0	0	1	4	3	4	0	1	4	2	0	1	0	1	1	0	0	0	0	0	0	2	1	1	0
Omaha	17	.4077	1.5317	41.9	0	3	12	0	0	0	0	2	0	2	0	0	0	11	0	0	0	0	0	0	0	1	0	3	0
Omalia	3	.0000	.0322	25.1	0	0	0	3	0	0	0	0	0	0	0	3	0	0	0	0	0	0	0	0	0	0	0	0	0
Oman	3	.0000	.0583	27.7	0	0	0	3	0	0	0	0	0	0	0	0	0	3	0	0	0	0	0	0	0	0	0	0	0
Omar	6	.0000	.2741	34.4	0	0	0	6	0	0	0	0	6	0	0	0	0	0	0	0	0	0	0	0	0	0	0	0	0
Omar's	2	.0000	.0914	29.6	0	0	0	2	0	0	0	0	2	0	0	0	0	0	0	0	0	0	0	0	0	0	0	0	0
Omega	8	.1194	.2524	34.0	0	1	0	0	0	0	7	0	0	0	0	0	0	0	0	0	0	0	0	0	0	0	7	0	1
omen	7	.4819	.7802	38.9	2	0	0	1	1	1	0	2	4	0	0	0	0	0	0	1	0	0	0	0	1	0	0	1	0
omens	7	.2395	.5461	37.4	4	0	0	0	2	0	1	0	6	0	0	1	0	0	0	0	0	0	0	0	0	0	0	0	0
ominous	20	.7298	2.9668	44.7	0	0	1	3	10	4	2	0	4	1	1	3	0	1	0	0	1	0	0	0	4	1	1	3	0
ominously	4	.4492	.4017	36.0	0	0	0	2	0	0	1	1	1	0	0	1	0	0	0	1	0	0	0	0	0	0	0	1	0
omission	5	.3329	.3577	35.5	0	0	0	0	1	0	4	0	0	3	1	1	0	0	0	0	0	0	0	0	0	0	0	0	0
omit	36	.7188	5.1959	47.2	1	2	0	6	9	10	8	0	0	9	0	1	9	0	2	1	3	0	4	1	3	1	0	2	0
omits	5	.3186	.3543	35.5	0	0	0	0	0	3	2	0	0	3	0	0	0	0	0	1	1	0	0	0	0	0	0	0	0
omitted	45	.6935	6.2557	48.0	0	3	6	11	6	11	7	1	0	16	4	0	3	0	12	0	4	1	1	1	1	0	1	1	0
omitting	10	.5216	1.0717	40.3	0	0	0	4	0	2	4	0	0	5	1	0	2	0	0	0	1	0	0	1	0	0	0	0	0
omnibus	2	.0000	.0162	22.1	0	0	2	0	0	0	0	0	0	0	0	0	0	0	2	0	0	0	0	0	0	0	0	0	0
omnipotent	2	.2444	.1132	30.5	0	0	0	1	0	0	1	0	0	1	0	0	0	0	0	0	0	0	0	0	1	0	0	0	0
omnipresent	3	.3395	.2468	33.9	0	0	0	0	3	0	0	0	1	0	0	0	0	0	0	0	0	0	0	0	0	1	1	0	0
omnivore	2	.0000	.0209	23.2	0	0	0	0	2	0	0	0	0	0	0	0	0	0	0	0	0	0	0	0	0	0	2	0	0
omnivores	3	.1813	.1402	31.5	0	0	0	0	2	1	0	0	0	0	0	0	0	0	0	1	0	0	0	0	0	0	2	0	0
on	36482	.9948	7135.8	78.5	6349	6211	4582	4852	6648	3901	3122	817	8996	1607	396	1944	2278	4099	1278	3411	1903	402	632	506	2289	2671	1575	2476	19
On	30	.4192	2.7044	44.3	1	3	6	4	5	9	2	0	3	1	0	2	1	0	0	1	17	0	0	0	0	1	2	2	0
ON	3	.2053	.1597	32.0	1	0	0	2	0	0	0	0	0	0	0	0	0	0	0	1	0	0	0	0	0	2	0	0	0
on-going	2	.0000	.0914	29.6	0	0	0	0	2	0	0	0	2	0	0	0	0	0	0	0	0	0	0	0	0	0	0	0	0
on-off	2	.2391	.1133	30.5	0	0	0	0	1	1	0	0	0	0	0	0	1	0	0	0	0	0	0	0	0	0	1	0	0
on-the-job	2	.2405	.1205	30.8	0	0	0	0	0	0	2	0	0	0	0	0	0	0	0	1	0	0	0	0	0	1	0	0	0
on-the-spot	5	.3122	.3872	35.9	0	0	0	1	2	0	1	1	1	0	0	0	0	0	0	3	0	0	0	0	0	0	0	1	0
on'y	3	.0000	.0352	25.5	0	0	0	0	3	0	0	0	0	0	0	0	0	0	0	0	0	0	0	0	3	0	0	0	0
Onak	22	.0000	1.0050	40.0	22	0	0	0	0	0	0	0	22	0	0	0	0	0	0	0	0	0	0	0	0	0	0	0	0
Onassis	5	.0000	.0608	27.8	0	0	0	0	0	0	0	5	0	0	0	0	0	0	0	0	0	0	0	0	0	0	0	5	0
once	2435	.9407	453.74	66.6	436	413	290	318	443	269	198	68	881	103	27	204	44	192	52	182	63	5	22	9	209	172	89	176	5
once-great	3	.1639	.1674	32.2	0	0	1	1	1	0	0	0	1	0	0	0	0	2	0	0	0	0	0	0	0	0	0	0	0

6R ok
3N OK**
3P ok-a-leek
3P ok-a-leek-
6A okapi
7A Okaro's
XR okayed
6D oke
8Q Okeford
XB okeh
5Q okey
4F Okhotsk
5Q Okla
7R Oklahoman
XR Oklawaha
6A okto
4G ol
7P Ola's
4F Olaf's
8F old-age
7N old-country
7Q old-man's
7R OLDSMOBILE
6A oldtime
7R oldtimer
9F Olduvai
8R oleaginous
5J Oleana
3N oleander
6Q olefins
9D Olegna
7P oligarchic
6A Olimpico
6A Olipai
7Q olive-drab
3Q olive-growing
8F olive-skinned
8B Olive's
6N olivella
9H olivine
XB Oll
7R Ollan
6F Olmec
8N Olney
9Q ologies
7R Olsen's
6A Olsens
8A Olson
5P Oluf
5P Oluf's
6A Olympians
9D Olympos
4G ombrella
8Q Omdurman
6A Omi
5Q omissions
5E OMN
4A omnibuses
6N omnipotence
8J Omnipotent
6Q omnivorous
5E OMP
XR On-Heliopolis
XR on-her-toes
3J on-ly
3N on-run
8A on-stage
4R on-the-road
8R on-the-roader
9B on-the-scene
7H on-your-own
6G on'ist**
3A Onak's
3P Onandaga
7D Onandagos
7R onboard
3A onc't
9H onca
7A once-a-season
XR once-a-week
6R once-arrogant
6R once-big
5A once-fat
9Q once-for-all

Word Type	F	D	U	SFI	3 Gr 3	4 Gr 4	5 Gr 5	6 Gr 6	7 Gr 7	8 Gr 8	9 Gr 9	X UnGr	A Read	B Eng & Gr	C Comp	D Lit	E Math	F Soc Stud	G Spell	H Sci	J Music	K Art	L Home Ec	M Shop	N Lib F	P Lib NF	Q Lib Ref	R Mag	S Rel
oncoming	16	.5351	1.9009	42.8	1	1	1	5	2	5	1	0	8	0	0	0	1	0	0	2	0	1	0	0	1	0	0	3	0
Ondine	7	.0000	.3198	35.0	0	0	0	7	0	0	0	0	7	0	0	0	0	0	0	0	0	0	0	0	0	0	0	0	0
one	19976	.9949	3907.7	75.9	3687	3260	2431	2708	3424	2257	1730	479	4834	1268	259	960	1679	1806	1037	2074	887	139	231	209	1065	1532	836	1147	13
One	152	.4204	15.097	51.8	23	30	15	6	65	7	3	3	76	5	2	4	2	5	1	4	10	0	0	0	10	20	1	8	4
ONE	5	.4751	.5383	37.3	0	2	0	1	0	0	2	0	2	1	0	0	0	1	0	0	0	0	0	0	0	1	0	0	0
one-	4	.3803	.3253	35.1	0	0	0	0	2	0	0	2	0	0	0	0	0	0	1	1	0	0	0	1	0	0	0	1	0
one-act	5	.3329	.3577	35.5	0	0	0	0	2	3	0	0	0	3	1	1	0	0	0	0	0	0	0	0	0	0	0	0	0
one-celled	20	.4112	1.8175	42.6	3	0	3	2	5	2	5	0	0	1	0	0	0	0	0	13	0	0	0	0	0	3	3	0	0
one-crust	2	.0000	.0064	18.1	0	0	0	0	0	0	2	0	0	0	0	0	0	0	0	0	0	0	2	0	0	0	0	0	0
one-cup	2	.0000	.0064	18.1	0	0	0	0	0	2	0	0	0	0	0	0	0	0	0	0	0	0	2	0	0	0	0	0	0
one-day	3	.2051	.1687	32.3	1	0	0	2	0	0	0	0	1	0	1	0	0	0	0	0	0	0	0	0	0	0	0	1	0
one-digit	2	.0000	.0299	24.8	2	0	0	0	0	0	0	0	0	0	0	0	2	0	0	0	0	0	0	0	0	0	0	0	0
one-dimensional	2	.0000	.0299	24.8	0	0	0	0	2	0	0	0	0	0	0	0	2	0	0	0	0	0	0	0	0	0	0	0	0
one-dollar	3	.3467	.2520	34.0	0	2	0	1	0	0	0	0	1	0	0	0	1	0	0	0	0	0	0	0	0	0	0	1	0
one-dot	2	.0000	.0162	22.1	0	0	0	0	2	0	0	0	0	0	0	0	0	0	2	0	0	0	0	0	0	0	0	0	0
one-eighth	7	.4596	.6847	38.4	2	0	1	0	0	1	2	1	0	0	0	0	3	1	0	1	0	0	0	1	0	0	1	0	0
one-engine	2	.0000	.0914	29.6	1	0	0	0	1	0	0	0	2	0	0	0	0	0	0	0	0	0	0	0	0	0	0	0	0
one-eyed	2	.2408	.1091	30.4	0	0	0	0	2	0	0	0	0	1	0	0	0	0	1	0	0	0	0	0	0	0	0	0	0
one-fifth	9	.4835	.9367	39.7	0	2	0	4	3	0	0	0	0	0	0	0	2	3	0	3	0	0	0	0	0	0	1	0	0
one-foot	5	.4443	.4720	36.7	0	2	0	0	1	1	1	0	0	0	0	0	1	0	1	1	0	0	0	0	0	0	2	0	0
one-fourth	34	.7738	5.3149	47.3	8	3	4	6	8	2	3	0	5	0	0	1	8	6	0	4	0	1	1	1	0	1	5	1	0
one-half	94	.7772	14.716	51.7	11	17	6	6	25	12	13	4	10	8	0	2	16	17	0	14	3	0	7	5	1	2	4	5	0
one-hand	5	.2811	.3645	35.6	0	1	1	0	3	0	0	0	2	0	0	0	0	0	0	0	0	0	0	1	0	2	0	0	0
one-hole	5	.0000	.0986	29.9	0	0	1	0	3	1	0	0	0	0	0	0	0	0	0	5	0	0	0	0	0	0	0	0	0
one-holed	2	.0000	.0394	26.0	0	0	1	1	0	0	0	0	0	0	0	0	0	0	0	2	0	0	0	0	0	0	0	0	0
one-horse	3	.3427	.2477	33.9	0	0	1	1	1	0	0	0	1	0	0	0	0	0	0	0	0	0	0	0	1	0	0	1	0
one-hot-dish	4	.0000	.0129	21.1	0	0	0	0	0	0	4	0	0	0	0	0	0	0	0	0	0	0	4	0	0	0	0	0	0
one-hour	5	.2392	.3123	34.9	0	1	0	1	1	1	1	0	1	0	0	0	0	1	0	0	0	0	0	0	0	0	0	3	0
one-hundred	2	.0000	.0389	25.9	0	0	1	0	0	1	0	0	0	0	0	0	0	2	0	0	0	0	0	0	0	0	0	0	0
one-hundredth	6	.3212	.4556	36.6	0	0	1	0	4	0	1	0	0	0	0	0	1	1	0	4	0	0	0	0	0	0	0	0	0
one-inch	9	.5562	1.0312	40.1	0	0	0	0	3	1	5	0	0	1	0	0	4	0	0	1	0	0	1	1	0	0	1	0	0
one-legged	4	.0000	.1827	32.6	1	2	0	1	0	0	0	0	4	0	0	0	0	0	0	0	0	0	0	0	0	0	0	0	0
one-man	11	.5193	1.2417	40.9	1	0	0	3	1	1	4	1	3	0	0	0	0	2	0	0	0	0	0	0	0	1	2	3	0
one-measure	2	.0000	.0162	22.1	0	1	0	1	0	0	0	0	0	0	0	0	0	0	0	0	2	0	0	0	0	0	0	0	0
one-millionth	2	.0000	.0050	17.0	0	0	0	0	0	2	0	0	0	0	0	0	0	0	0	0	0	0	0	2	0	0	0	0	0
one-paragraph	4	.0000	.0438	26.4	0	1	0	0	0	2	1	0	0	4	0	0	0	0	0	0	0	0	0	0	0	0	0	0	0
one-party	3	.2378	.1809	32.6	0	0	1	0	0	1	1	0	0	0	0	0	0	2	0	0	0	0	0	0	0	1	0	0	0
one-piece	5	.3005	.3447	35.4	2	1	0	0	0	0	2	0	1	0	0	0	0	0	1	0	0	0	2	0	0	0	1	0	0
one-pint	2	.2413	.1212	30.8	0	1	1	0	0	0	0	0	0	0	0	0	1	0	0	1	0	0	0	0	0	0	0	0	0
one-point	4	.0000	.0074	18.7	0	0	2	0	2	0	0	0	0	0	0	0	0	0	0	0	0	4	0	0	0	0	0	0	0
one-quarter	12	.6020	1.5014	41.8	1	2	3	0	3	1	0	2	1	2	0	0	1	5	0	0	0	0	1	0	0	0	1	1	0
one-room	18	.5805	2.3142	43.6	4	6	2	1	3	1	1	0	12	0	0	2	0	1	0	0	1	0	0	0	0	1	1	0	0
one-seeded	4	.0000	.0789	29.0	0	0	0	1	3	0	0	0	0	0	0	0	0	0	0	4	0	0	0	0	0	0	0	0	0
one-sentence	6	.0655	.1711	32.3	0	1	0	0	5	0	0	0	1	5	0	0	0	0	0	0	0	0	0	0	0	0	0	0	0
one-shot	2	.0000	.0243	23.9	0	0	0	0	1	1	0	0	0	0	0	0	0	0	0	0	0	0	0	0	0	0	0	2	0
one-sided	9	.6465	1.2046	40.8	1	1	1	1	2	2	1	0	1	0	0	0	0	1	0	3	0	0	0	0	1	1	1	1	0
one-sixteenth	2	.0725	.0732	28.6	0	0	0	1	1	0	0	0	1	0	0	0	0	0	0	0	0	0	0	1	0	0	0	0	0
one-sixth	7	.4675	.7138	38.5	1	2	0	1	2	1	0	0	1	0	0	0	1	3	0	0	0	0	1	0	0	0	1	0	0
one-story	7	.4602	.7333	38.7	2	3	0	1	1	0	0	0	3	0	0	1	0	0	0	0	0	0	0	0	2	1	0	0	0
one-string	2	.2446	.1257	31.0	1	0	0	0	1	0	0	0	0	0	0	0	0	1	0	1	0	0	0	0	0	0	0	0	0
one-syllable	61	.0874	1.6782	42.2	15	6	11	16	6	3	4	0	5	3	0	0	0	0	53	0	0	0	0	0	0	0	0	0	0
one-tenth	18	.7000	2.5577	44.1	0	2	3	0	9	0	4	0	0	0	0	1	2	5	1	4	0	0	0	1	0	0	2	2	0
one-third	40	.7257	5.9009	47.7	4	7	3	6	9	5	5	1	3	0	0	0	6	14	0	5	0	0	1	1	1	1	6	2	0
one-thirty	2	.0000	.0234	23.7	0	1	0	0	1	0	0	0	0	0	0	0	0	0	0	0	0	0	0	0	2	0	0	0	0
one-thousandth	2	.0000	.0243	23.9	0	0	0	0	2	0	0	0	0	0	0	0	0	0	0	0	0	0	0	0	0	0	0	2	0
one-to-one	25	.0000	.3742	35.7	9	1	4	2	2	2	5	0	0	0	0	0	25	0	0	0	0	0	0	0	0	0	0	0	0
one-two	2	.2128	.1055	30.2	0	0	1	1	0	0	0	0	0	0	0	0	0	0	0	1	1	0	0	0	0	0	0	0	0
one-two-three	2	.1494	.1045	30.2	0	1	1	0	0	0	0	0	1	0	0	0	0	0	0	0	1	0	0	0	0	0	0	0	0
one-view	3	.0000	.0076	18.8	0	0	0	0	0	0	3	0	0	0	0	0	0	0	0	0	0	0	0	3	0	0	0	0	0
one-vowel	2	.0000	.0162	22.1	2	0	0	0	0	0	0	0	0	0	0	0	0	0	2	0	0	0	0	0	0	0	0	0	0
one-way	10	.4590	.9776	39.9	1	0	2	2	2	1	2	0	0	1	0	0	0	2	0	3	0	0	2	0	0	0	0	2	0
one-word	14	.2748	.9285	39.7	4	1	0	2	4	2	1	0	3	4	0	0	0	0	7	0	0	0	0	0	0	0	0	0	0
one-year	3	.2321	.1635	32.1	0	0	1	0	0	0	2	0	0	0	0	0	0	0	0	0	0	0	0	0	0	0	1	2	0
one's	80	.8296	13.269	51.2	2	10	8	7	25	15	7	6	11	11	0	12	1	2	0	5	5	0	1	1	4	9	9	9	0
Oneida	2	.2433	.1158	30.6	1	0	0	0	1	0	0	0	0	0	0	0	0	0	0	0	0	0	0	0	0	1	0	1	0
ones	902	.9202	164.53	62.2	218	152	108	107	142	83	68	24	177	43	8	34	201	59	18	93	25	21	27	6	41	66	37	46	0
Ones	6	.1981	.3210	35.1	0	0	0	0	0	6	0	0	0	0	0	0	0	5	0	0	0	0	0	0	1	0	0	0	0
ones'	27	.0000	.4041	36.1	11	1	10	2	1	0	0	2	0	0	0	0	27	0	0	0	0	0	0	0	0	0	0	0	0
oneself	10	.6177	1.2993	41.1	0	1	3	1	2	3	0	0	3	0	0	1	0	0	0	1	0	0	1	0	1	2	0	1	0
onion	42	.3606	3.3357	45.2	6	4	11	0	4	3	13	1	5	1	0	2	0	0	0	6	2	0	17	0	5	2	0	2	0
onions	52	.4600	5.4092	47.3	8	7	18	2	4	0	11	2	22	0	0	1	0	4	0	0	0	0	10	0	8	3	0	4	0
onlooker	3	.2335	.1566	31.9	0	0	0	0	2	0	1	0	0	0	0	2	0	0	0	0	0	0	1	0	0	0	0	0	0
onlookers	14	.6031	1.8035	42.6	2	2	0	3	4	2	1	0	6	0	1	1	0	1	0	0	2	0	0	0	1	2	0	0	0
only	6583	.9885	1280.4	71.1	900	957	812	898	1371	744	666	235	1581	302	107	336	344	746	144	711	214	48	80	83	360	570	482	471	4
Only	4	.4887	.4068	36.1	0	0	2	0	2	0	0	0	0	1	0	1	0	0	0	0	0	0	0	0	0	0	1	1	0
onrush	2	.0000	.0290	24.6	0	0	1	0	0	0	1	0	0	0	0	0	0	0	0	0	0	0	0	0	0	2	0	0	0
onrushing	4	.2240	.2565	34.1	0	0	0	0	3	0	1	0	2	0	0	0	0	0	0	0	0	1	0	0	0	0	1	0	0
onset	8	.3630	.6708	38.3	0	0	0	2	2	3	1	0	2	0	0	0	0	0	0	0	0	0	0	0	1	0	4	1	0
onslaught	4	.4504	.4035	36.1	0	0	0	2	1	1	0	0	1	0	0	0	0	1	0	0	0	0	0	0	0	1	1	0	0
onstage	5	.2753	.3378	35.3	0	0	0	2	0	3	0	0	1	0	0	1	0	0	0	0	0	0	0	0	0	0	0	3	0
Ont	2	.0000	.0209	23.2	0	0	2	0	0	0	0	0	0	0	0	0	0	0	0	0	0	0	0	0	0	0	2	0	0
Ontario	20	.6363	2.6205	44.2	1	5	5	1	3	1	2	2	1	0	0	0	4	4	0	3	1	0	0	0	1	1	5	0	0
onto	401	.8767	70.310	58.5	83	85	52	51	62	30	27	11	147	5	2	26	7	22	5	31	2	12	4	7	50	37	14	30	0
onward	18	.5913	2.3168	43.6	0	6	2	5	2	2	1	0	10	1	0	0	0	1	1	0	0	0	0	0	3	0	2	0	0
onym	4	.2408	.2182	33.4	0	3	0	0	0	0	0	1	0	2	0	0	0	0	2	0	0	0	0	0	0	0	0	0	0
onyma	2	.0000	.0162	22.1	0	1	0	1	0	0	0	0	0	0	0	0	0	0	2	0	0	0	0	0	0	0	0	0	0
oo	30	.1980	1.5490	41.9	7	12	2	4	3	1	1	0	6	0	0	0	0	0	21	0	1	0	0	0	2	0	0	0	0
Oo	14	.0000	.6396	38.1	0	0	0	14	0	0	0	0	14	0	0	0	0	0	0	0	0	0	0	0	0	0	0	0	0
Oo-loo-te-ka	2	.0000	.0290	24.6	0	2	0	0	0	0	0	0	0	0	0	0	0	0	0	0	0	0	0	0	0	2	0	0	0
oogrug	9	.0000	.4111	36.1	0	1	8	0	0	0	0	0	9	0	0	0	0	0	0	0	0	0	0	0	0	0	0	0	0

8F once-handsome
5A once-living
5F once-vast
7N oncet
8D onct
4P One-B
8L one-and-a-half
8F one-and-a-half-story
6F one-and-only
5E one-another
6P one-cent
8H one-cylinder
7R one-degree
7L one-dish
9B one-family
5A one-fifteen
7R one-for-four
6A one-for-the-money
7E one-four
5H one-fourteenth
3A one-fourth-inch
7A one-goal
3P one-god
8L one-half-inch
6E one-handed
3P one-hitters
4A one-horned
8L one-hundred-and-eight
3P one-hundred-fifty
7A one-hundred-foot
7R one-hundred-million
5A one-hundred-pound
9Q one-in-a-million
7H one-inch-square
9Q one-inch-wide
6A one-l
8M one-lane
8E one-mile
3E one-million
5E one-millions'
6R one-minute
7P one-ness
7J one-of-a-kind
7R one-pound
4E one-quart
6P one-run
3P one-seven
6E one-seventh
3R one-sixth-mile
9E one-sixtieth
6G one-space
6H one-strand
6A one-street
7P one-stringed
7R one-thirtieth
5E one-thousands'
9H one-tube
8H one-twentieth
9Q one-up
7R one-upmanship
6J one-voiced
9L one-wall
6A one-wheeled
4A one-year-old
3H one-year-olds
3A One's
9J Onegin
7D Oneidas
3A oneness
8E ones-tens-hundreds
7Q onesided
7D onetime
7P ong
7R Ongais
7R ongoing
6R Onion
6N onliest
XR Ono
XB onoma
9N onwards
4P Oo-loo-te-ka's
5N oo-oo
6A oo-oo-oo
7A ooey
3A oof

Word Type	F	D	U	SFI	3 Gr 3	4 Gr 4	5 Gr 5	6 Gr 6	7 Gr 7	8 Gr 8	9 Gr 9	X UnGr	A Read	B Eng & Gr	C Comp	D Lit	E Math	F Soc Stud	G Spell	H Sci	J Music	K Art	L Home Ec	M Shop	N Lib F	P Lib NF	Q Lib Ref	R Mag	S Rel
ooh	7	.2697	.4994	37.0	3	3	1	0	0	0	0	0	3	0	0	0	0	0	0	0	3	0	0	0	0	1	0	0	0
ook-ook	3	.0000	.1370	31.4	0	0	3	0	0	0	0	0	3	0	0	0	0	0	0	0	0	0	0	0	0	0	0	0	0
ook-ook-ook	2	.0000	.0914	29.6	0	0	2	0	0	0	0	0	2	0	0	0	0	0	0	0	0	0	0	0	0	0	0	0	0
Ookie	14	.0000	.6396	38.1	0	0	14	0	0	0	0	0	14	0	0	0	0	0	0	0	0	0	0	0	0	0	0	0	0
oom	2	.0000	.0914	29.6	0	0	0	2	0	0	0	0	2	0	0	0	0	0	0	0	0	0	0	0	0	0	0	0	0
oomiak	6	.0000	.1167	30.7	0	6	0	0	0	0	0	0	0	0	0	0	0	6	0	0	0	0	0	0	0	0	0	0	0
Oompa-Loompas	6	.0000	.0703	28.5	0	0	0	0	0	0	0	6	0	0	0	0	0	0	0	0	0	0	0	0	6	0	0	0	0
oompah	5	.0000	.0404	26.1	5	0	0	0	0	0	0	0	0	0	0	0	0	0	0	0	5	0	0	0	0	0	0	0	0
oooooh	2	.0000	.0914	29.6	0	0	0	0	2	0	0	0	2	0	0	0	0	0	0	0	0	0	0	0	0	0	0	0	0
ooze	6	.4605	.5896	37.7	0	2	2	0	1	1	0	0	0	0	0	0	0	0	0	2	0	0	0	0	1	1	2	0	0
oozed	6	.4292	.5878	37.7	1	0	1	0	2	1	1	0	2	1	0	2	0	1	0	0	0	0	0	0	0	0	0	0	0
oozes	3	.2479	.1736	32.4	1	0	0	1	0	0	1	0	0	0	0	0	0	1	0	0	0	0	0	1	0	1	0	0	0
oozie	13	.0000	.5939	37.7	0	0	0	13	0	0	0	0	13	0	0	0	0	0	0	0	0	0	0	0	0	0	0	0	0
oozies	10	.0000	.4568	36.6	0	0	0	10	0	0	0	0	10	0	0	0	0	0	0	0	0	0	0	0	0	0	0	0	0
oozing	3	.2266	.1614	32.1	0	0	0	0	1	1	1	0	0	0	0	0	0	0	0	0	0	0	0	0	1	0	0	2	0
op	5	.4753	.4954	36.9	0	2	1	0	0	1	1	0	0	0	0	0	0	0	1	0	0	0	0	0	2	0	1	1	0
Op	5	.0000	.0404	26.1	0	2	0	0	2	1	0	0	0	0	0	0	0	0	0	0	5	0	0	0	0	0	0	0	0
opal	6	.4859	.6604	38.2	0	0	5	0	1	0	0	0	3	1	0	0	0	0	0	0	0	0	0	0	1	0	1	0	0
opals	4	.0000	.1827	32.6	0	1	2	0	1	0	0	0	4	0	0	0	0	0	0	0	0	0	0	0	0	0	0	0	0
opaque	18	.4402	1.7421	42.4	3	0	0	4	3	2	4	2	4	0	0	0	0	0	0	5	0	3	0	3	1	0	0	2	0
open	1416	.9567	267.63	64.3	250	235	145	160	289	187	116	34	435	25	14	90	101	84	43	117	37	15	33	15	123	130	56	94	4
Open	15	.4843	1.6776	42.2	0	0	0	3	6	5	0	1	9	0	0	0	0	2	0	0	0	1	0	0	0	0	2	1	0
open-air	10	.5156	1.1092	40.5	0	3	2	2	2	1	0	0	2	0	0	1	0	2	0	0	0	0	0	0	0	0	2	3	0
open-end	3	.1980	.1505	31.8	0	0	0	0	0	3	0	0	0	0	0	0	0	2	0	0	0	0	1	0	0	0	0	0	0
open-hearth	6	.1639	.3347	35.2	2	4	0	0	0	0	0	0	2	0	0	0	0	4	0	0	0	0	0	0	0	0	0	0	0
open-minded	2	.2285	.1129	30.5	0	0	0	0	1	0	1	0	0	0	0	0	0	1	0	0	0	0	0	0	0	0	1	0	0
open-mouthed	3	.3663	.2410	33.8	1	0	0	1	1	0	0	0	0	0	0	0	0	0	0	1	1	0	0	0	1	0	0	0	0
open-pit	6	.1823	.2810	34.5	0	0	4	0	2	0	0	0	0	0	0	0	0	2	0	0	0	0	0	0	0	0	4	0	0
open-water	2	.2437	.1129	30.5	0	0	0	0	1	0	0	1	0	0	0	0	0	0	0	0	0	0	0	0	0	0	1	1	0
opened	728	.8735	127.43	61.1	183	154	81	84	114	65	35	12	313	27	3	68	3	53	5	16	17	2	3	4	81	64	21	46	2
opener	8	.4497	.8000	39.0	1	2	0	2	0	2	1	0	2	0	0	0	0	1	0	0	0	0	0	1	0	3	0	1	0
openin'	2	.1733	.1149	30.6	0	0	0	0	1	1	0	0	1	1	0	0	0	0	0	0	0	0	0	0	0	0	0	0	0
opening	380	.8507	64.635	58.1	55	46	32	39	83	50	62	13	91	16	6	30	8	13	6	43	38	0	31	13	19	24	12	30	0
openings	78	.6185	9.9842	50.0	22	4	7	9	9	8	15	4	6	3	0	1	1	5	0	36	0	0	7	8	1	4	2	4	0
openly	16	.5769	2.0023	43.0	0	0	5	2	4	2	2	1	7	0	1	0	0	3	0	0	0	0	0	0	1	2	0	2	0
openmouthed	2	.1814	.1187	30.7	1	0	0	1	0	0	0	0	1	0	0	0	0	0	0	0	0	0	0	0	0	0	0	1	0
openpit	2	.0000	.0209	23.2	0	0	2	0	0	0	0	0	0	0	0	0	0	0	0	0	0	0	0	0	0	0	2	0	0
opens	82	.8450	13.866	51.4	21	7	7	13	17	10	6	1	17	3	0	8	2	6	0	12	9	2	2	0	10	5	4	2	0
openwork	2	.2346	.1166	30.7	0	0	0	0	2	0	0	0	0	0	0	0	0	0	0	1	0	0	0	0	0	0	0	1	0
opera	177	.2611	10.322	50.1	6	9	12	39	33	61	17	0	2	2	0	0	0	2	3	1	132	0	0	0	0	11	22	2	0
Opera	14	.3265	.9880	39.9	1	0	1	5	1	5	1	0	0	0	0	0	0	0	0	0	8	0	0	0	0	1	4	1	0
opera's	2	.0000	.0162	22.1	0	0	0	1	0	1	0	0	0	0	0	0	0	0	0	0	2	0	0	0	0	0	0	0	0
operas	35	.1416	1.2414	40.9	1	0	4	8	8	13	1	0	0	0	0	0	0	1	0	0	30	0	0	0	0	2	2	0	0
operate	96	.7881	15.224	51.8	5	8	10	11	29	11	17	5	10	3	1	2	2	17	0	20	1	0	1	7	3	7	10	12	0
operated	61	.7743	9.5362	49.8	5	4	8	6	14	14	8	2	7	2	0	1	2	15	0	9	1	0	0	2	1	4	7	10	0
operates	38	.5509	4.3657	46.4	0	2	13	1	13	3	6	0	1	1	0	0	7	9	0	5	0	0	0	6	0	3	3	3	0
operatic	16	.2108	.7787	38.9	0	0	4	3	1	7	1	0	0	0	0	0	0	0	0	0	12	0	0	0	0	2	2	0	0
operating	61	.7600	9.3540	49.7	3	0	5	9	16	10	15	3	6	3	0	2	0	8	1	10	0	0	2	4	1	6	4	14	0
operation	251	.6240	32.180	55.1	5	14	18	9	96	59	38	12	11	4	0	7	110	17	2	20	2	0	0	25	3	8	16	26	0
Operation	9	.5295	1.0386	40.2	0	2	2	1	2	1	1	0	3	0	0	1	0	1	0	0	0	0	0	0	0	2	2	0	0
operational	3	.3811	.2536	34.0	0	1	0	0	0	1	0	1	0	0	0	0	1	0	0	1	0	0	0	0	0	0	0	1	0
operations	155	.6452	20.411	53.1	5	5	18	7	53	18	45	4	5	1	1	1	70	11	1	3	1	0	2	16	2	6	17	18	0
Operations	6	.2978	.4235	36.3	0	1	0	1	4	0	0	0	1	0	0	0	0	0	0	0	0	0	0	0	0	0	2	3	0
operative	2	.2437	.1129	30.5	0	0	0	0	1	1	0	0	0	0	0	0	0	0	0	0	0	0	0	0	0	0	1	1	0
operator	54	.7719	8.4343	49.3	1	3	13	8	11	7	7	4	11	1	0	6	11	5	1	3	3	0	0	3	0	3	1	6	0
OPERATOR	11	.0000	.1180	30.7	0	0	0	0	0	11	0	0	0	0	0	11	0	0	0	0	0	0	0	0	0	0	0	0	0
operators	27	.5537	3.1406	45.0	1	0	3	3	7	6	6	1	3	1	0	0	0	4	0	3	0	0	0	1	0	2	12	1	0
operetta	14	.1843	.6111	37.9	0	4	1	4	3	2	0	0	0	0	0	0	0	0	0	0	10	0	0	0	4	0	0	0	0
operettas	11	.0000	.0889	29.5	0	0	0	3	6	2	0	0	0	0	0	0	0	0	0	0	11	0	0	0	0	0	0	0	0
ophthalmologist	2	.0000	.0394	26.0	0	0	2	0	0	0	0	0	0	0	0	0	0	0	0	2	0	0	0	0	0	0	0	0	0
ophthalmologists	3	.0000	.0591	27.7	0	0	1	0	0	2	0	0	0	0	0	0	0	0	0	3	0	0	0	0	0	0	0	0	0
opinion	182	.6559	24.685	53.9	3	4	14	16	50	47	45	3	44	32	23	14	1	23	1	3	1	1	2	0	5	10	5	17	0
opinion-forming	2	.0000	.0914	29.6	0	0	0	0	0	2	0	0	2	0	0	0	0	0	0	0	0	0	0	0	0	0	0	0	0
opinions	72	.7505	11.003	50.4	1	8	7	3	16	21	14	2	20	17	3	1	0	8	0	1	2	0	2	0	2	5	2	9	0
opium	5	.5597	.5840	37.7	0	0	1	0	2	1	1	0	0	0	0	0	0	1	0	1	0	0	0	0	1	1	0	1	0
opossum	16	.4050	1.4927	41.7	1	2	5	0	7	0	0	1	5	0	0	0	0	1	1	2	0	0	0	0	0	0	7	0	0
opossums	13	.4418	1.2938	41.1	2	1	3	0	6	1	0	0	4	0	0	0	0	0	0	1	0	0	0	0	0	2	5	1	0
Oppenheimer	8	.0000	.0972	29.9	0	0	0	0	0	8	0	0	0	0	0	0	0	0	0	0	0	0	0	0	0	0	0	8	0
Oppenheimer's	3	.0000	.0365	25.6	0	0	0	0	0	3	0	0	0	0	0	0	0	0	0	0	0	0	0	0	0	0	0	3	0
Opperman's	2	.0000	.0243	23.9	0	0	0	0	0	2	0	0	0	0	0	0	0	0	0	0	0	0	0	0	0	0	0	2	0
opponent	24	.6707	3.3453	45.2	1	0	1	8	6	5	3	0	7	2	0	2	0	3	0	0	0	0	0	0	3	5	0	2	0
opponent's	3	.2435	.2274	33.6	0	0	0	0	3	0	0	0	2	0	0	0	0	1	0	0	0	0	0	0	0	0	0	0	0
opponents	25	.5613	2.9752	44.7	0	0	4	1	8	6	4	2	5	1	0	1	0	1	0	1	0	0	0	0	0	6	1	9	0
opportune	4	.3553	.3095	34.9	0	0	0	1	0	0	2	1	0	1	0	2	0	0	0	0	0	0	0	0	0	1	0	0	0
opportunism	2	.2446	.1122	30.5	0	0	0	0	1	0	1	0	0	0	0	1	0	0	0	0	0	0	0	0	0	0	1	0	0
opportunities	64	.7614	9.8111	49.9	1	2	8	2	17	14	14	6	3	2	0	2	2	18	1	5	3	0	5	0	1	4	7	11	0
opportunity	139	.9169	25.261	54.0	2	5	15	19	40	33	19	6	22	6	2	13	0	26	4	13	4	2	1	3	4	11	8	20	0
oppose	8	.3603	.6510	38.1	0	0	0	0	0	3	5	0	0	0	0	1	0	5	0	0	0	0	0	0	0	0	0	2	0
opposed	52	.6863	7.2735	48.6	0	1	5	3	14	14	13	2	4	2	0	2	2	10	1	3	1	0	0	0	1	2	17	7	0
opposes	4	.1882	.1766	32.5	0	0	0	0	0	3	1	0	0	0	0	0	0	0	0	1	0	0	0	2	0	0	1	0	0
opposing	26	.6633	3.5162	45.5	1	0	3	2	5	5	10	0	1	1	3	4	0	3	0	6	0	0	0	1	1	4	1	1	0
opposite	591	.8617	101.42	60.1	72	58	73	91	121	90	70	16	66	19	2	19	138	39	61	83	21	25	12	17	14	19	43	13	0
oppositely	2	.1738	.0790	29.0	0	0	0	0	1	1	0	0	0	0	0	0	0	0	0	0	0	0	0	1	0	0	1	0	0
opposites	30	.2903	1.9512	42.9	8	3	5	1	3	8	1	1	0	2	0	0	13	0	15	0	0	0	0	0	0	0	0	0	0
opposition	40	.6560	5.3981	47.3	3	0	3	2	10	15	4	3	5	1	0	1	0	8	0	1	0	0	0	1	0	5	10	8	0
oppressed	7	.5026	.7622	38.8	0	0	0	0	4	2	1	0	2	1	1	0	0	1	0	0	1	0	0	0	0	0	1	0	0
oppressing	2	.1494	.1045	30.2	0	0	0	2	0	0	0	0	1	0	0	0	0	0	0	0	1	0	0	0	0	0	0	0	0
oppression	5	.1380	.2415	33.8	0	2	0	0	1	2	0	0	2	0	0	0	0	0	0	0	0	0	0	0	0	0	3	0	0
oppressive	7	.5193	.7598	38.8	1	1	0	1	4	0	0	0	0	0	0	2	0	1	0	1	0	0	0	0	2	0	1	0	0
oppressors	2	.2408	.1204	30.8	0	0	1	0	0	1	0	0	0	0	0	0	0	1	0	0	0	0	0	0	0	1	0	0	0
optic	3	.0000	.0591	27.7	0	0	0	1	1	1	0	0	0	0	0	0	0	0	0	3	0	0	0	0	0	0	0	0	0
optical	31	.4314	2.9234	44.7	1	3	0	1	7	3	3	13	0	0	0	0	0	0	0	20	0	0	0	0	4	0	4	3	0
optics	9	.3608	.7311	38.6	0	0	0	1	2	0	1	5	0	0	0	0	0	0	0	5	0	0	0	0	0	0	1	3	0
optimism	7	.4085	.6495	38.1	0	0	0	1	2	3	1	0	1	0	0	0	0	3	0	1	0	0	0	0	0	0	0	2	0

3P Ooh
9L oolong
6J oom-pa
6J oom-pah
6J oom-pah-pah
8A oomp
7R oomph
7A ooo
3A ooo-ooo
8D oop
7G oops
4B OOPSA
3Q oozy
9B OP
7P op'd
7Q Opaiva
5B opalways
XH opaqueness
5B opare
5B opdid
8F Opechancanough
6P OPEN
3A open-clawed
XR Open-ended
3A open-faced
7R open-header
9H open-heart
9L open-mesh
7M open-mouth
9F open-row
XR open-up
4R openness
8Q opera-ballets
5P opera-loving
9Q operable
8F operatives
7D opes
9J Opferlied
5B opforks
5Q Ophelia
3A Ophir
8H ophthalmology
9R opiate
9R opiates
3R Opie
5F opihi
8B Opinion
9Q opinionated
3R Opossum
5A opossums'
8R Opperman
6H opponents'
7R opposers
XR oppress
6A oppressions
8F Oppressions
7N oppressiveness
4N oppressor's
5B opput
8R OPPY
9R Opry
5B opthe
5B opthey
XR optically
7H optick
4H optik

Word Type	F	D	U	SFI	3 Gr 3	4 Gr 4	5 Gr 5	6 Gr 6	7 Gr 7	8 Gr 8	9 Gr 9	X UnGr	A Read	B Eng & Gr	C Comp	D Lit	E Math	F Soc Stud	G Spell	H Sci	J Music	K Art	L Home Ec	M Shop	N Lib F	P Lib NF	Q Lib Ref	R Mag	S Rel
optimist	3	.2197	.2090	33.2	0	0	1	2	0	0	0	0	2	0	0	0	0	0	0	0	0	0	0	0	0	0	1	0	0
optimistic	15	.5909	1.8818	42.7	1	0	1	1	2	4	5	1	5	0	0	2	0	0	1	0	0	0	0	0	0	1	2	4	0
optimum	2	.0000	.0209	23.2	0	1	0	0	0	0	1	0	0	0	0	0	0	0	0	0	0	0	0	0	0	0	2	0	0
option	6	.0000	.0729	28.6	0	0	0	1	4	0	1	0	0	0	0	0	0	0	0	0	0	0	0	0	0	0	0	6	0
optional	26	.4749	2.5636	44.1	0	0	3	0	13	6	3	1	0	18	2	1	0	0	0	0	0	0	0	1	0	0	1	3	0
options	3	.0000	.0365	25.6	0	0	0	0	3	0	0	0	0	0	0	0	0	0	0	0	0	0	0	0	0	0	0	3	0
opulent	2	.0000	.0234	23.7	0	1	0	0	1	0	0	0	0	0	0	0	0	0	0	0	0	0	0	0	2	0	0	0	0
Opus	7	.0000	.0566	27.5	1	0	0	2	0	0	4	0	0	0	0	0	0	0	0	0	7	0	0	0	0	0	0	0	0
opwhere	2	.0000	.0219	23.4	0	0	2	0	0	0	0	0	0	2	0	0	0	0	0	0	0	0	0	0	0	0	0	0	0
or	21283	.9502	3991.8	76.0	2570	2774	2531	2570	4272	3040	2955	571	2750	2069	403	764	1766	1934	1254	2764	1076	401	119	682	560	1250	1437	1043	11
Or	3	.3845	.2448	33.9	1	0	0	0	1	0	0	1	0	1	0	0	0	0	0	0	1	0	0	0	0	0	1	0	0
OR	6	.4623	.6240	38.0	0	2	2	1	1	0	0	0	2	1	0	0	2	0	0	0	0	0	0	0	0	1	0	0	0
oracle	4	.3540	.3081	34.9	0	0	0	1	0	2	1	0	0	0	0	1	0	0	0	0	0	0	0	0	0	1	2	0	0
oracular	2	.2412	.1141	30.6	0	0	2	0	0	0	0	0	0	1	0	0	0	0	0	0	0	0	0	0	0	1	0	0	0
oral	41	.6928	5.7752	47.6	2	3	2	9	14	6	5	0	4	18	0	2	1	4	2	2	0	0	1	1	0	2	2	2	0
Oral	9	.1409	.3489	35.4	7	0	0	0	0	2	0	0	0	7	0	0	0	0	0	2	0	0	0	0	0	0	0	0	0
Oralee	24	.0000	.2814	34.5	24	0	0	0	0	0	0	0	0	0	0	0	0	0	0	0	0	0	0	0	24	0	0	0	0
Oralee's	2	.0000	.0234	23.7	2	0	0	0	0	0	0	0	0	0	0	0	0	0	0	0	0	0	0	0	2	0	0	0	0
orally	11	.4706	1.1448	40.6	0	2	0	0	4	3	2	0	3	4	0	1	2	1	0	0	0	0	0	0	0	0	0	0	0
Oramel	2	.0000	.0243	23.9	0	0	0	2	0	0	0	0	0	0	0	0	0	0	0	0	0	0	0	0	0	0	0	2	0
orange	221	.8267	36.574	55.6	68	26	20	29	40	21	11	6	32	19	1	11	17	28	7	27	2	14	12	1	13	7	7	23	0
Orange	12	.5698	1.4240	41.5	0	2	1	2	5	1	1	0	0	1	0	0	0	5	0	1	0	0	1	0	0	3	0	1	0
orange-colored	3	.2261	.2131	33.3	2	0	0	0	1	0	0	0	2	0	0	0	0	0	0	0	0	0	0	0	1	0	0	0	0
orange-red	5	.4696	.4985	37.0	0	2	0	1	1	0	1	0	0	0	0	1	0	0	0	1	0	0	0	0	0	2	1	0	0
orangeade	2	.0000	.0064	18.1	0	0	0	0	0	0	2	0	0	0	0	0	0	0	0	0	0	0	2	0	0	0	0	0	0
oranges	102	.7618	15.784	52.0	40	18	12	10	13	1	6	2	18	2	0	3	23	32	0	7	0	1	1	0	6	3	5	1	0
oration	3	.2236	.1570	32.0	0	0	0	0	2	0	1	0	0	1	0	2	0	0	0	0	0	0	0	0	0	0	0	0	0
orations	2	.2446	.1125	30.5	0	0	0	0	1	0	1	0	0	1	0	1	0	0	0	0	0	0	0	0	0	0	0	0	0
orator	5	.4713	.5334	37.3	0	0	0	1	2	2	0	0	2	0	0	0	0	1	0	0	0	0	0	0	1	0	1	0	0
oratorical	2	.1814	.1187	30.7	0	0	0	0	0	1	1	0	1	0	0	0	0	0	0	0	0	0	0	0	0	0	0	1	0
oratorio	20	.0786	.4696	36.7	0	1	2	6	6	5	0	0	0	0	0	0	0	0	0	0	18	0	0	0	0	2	0	0	0
oratorios	3	.0000	.0243	23.8	0	0	1	0	2	0	0	0	0	0	0	0	0	0	0	0	3	0	0	0	0	0	0	0	0
orators	6	.5573	.7191	38.6	0	1	0	1	3	0	1	0	2	0	0	0	0	0	0	0	0	0	0	0	1	1	1	1	0
oratory	4	.1112	.1666	32.2	0	0	0	0	4	0	0	0	1	0	0	0	0	0	0	0	0	0	0	0	0	3	0	0	0
orb	4	.2405	.2410	33.8	2	0	0	1	1	0	0	0	0	0	0	0	0	0	0	2	0	0	0	0	0	2	0	0	0
orbicules	2	.0000	.0209	23.2	0	0	0	0	0	0	2	0	0	0	0	0	0	0	0	0	0	0	0	0	0	0	2	0	0
orbit	233	.6360	30.797	54.9	41	26	39	23	37	34	30	3	20	2	0	1	16	10	3	135	0	0	0	3	1	13	15	14	0
orbital	17	.5238	1.8701	42.7	1	0	0	1	6	5	2	2	0	0	0	0	2	0	0	8	0	0	0	2	0	1	2	2	0
orbited	9	.5215	1.0107	40.0	0	1	3	3	0	1	1	0	1	0	0	0	0	3	0	2	0	0	0	0	0	2	0	1	0
Orbiter	2	.0000	.0290	24.6	0	0	0	2	0	0	0	0	0	0	0	0	0	0	0	0	0	0	0	0	0	2	0	0	0
orbiting	25	.5808	3.0329	44.8	2	3	1	5	10	1	1	2	1	1	0	0	2	1	0	10	0	0	0	0	0	2	1	7	0
orbits	68	.4418	6.6241	48.2	13	7	9	2	17	12	4	4	4	0	0	0	1	3	0	43	0	0	0	0	1	1	13	2	0
orchard	47	.7285	7.0130	48.5	14	9	2	7	6	7	2	0	12	2	0	3	9	2	2	8	0	0	1	0	8	0	0	0	0
Orchard	2	.0000	.0234	23.7	2	0	0	0	0	0	0	0	0	0	0	0	0	0	0	0	0	0	0	0	2	0	0	0	0
orchard-owners	2	.0000	.0394	26.0	0	0	0	0	2	0	0	0	0	0	0	0	0	0	0	2	0	0	0	0	0	0	0	0	0
orchards	50	.6104	6.4251	48.1	3	7	14	11	6	6	0	3	8	0	0	3	0	25	0	7	2	0	0	0	1	1	2	1	0
orchestra	251	.3131	17.174	52.3	15	30	22	27	72	63	22	0	6	6	1	0	2	7	3	1	188	1	0	0	0	16	17	3	0
Orchestra	20	.2110	.9878	39.9	2	2	3	3	4	5	1	0	0	1	0	0	0	3	0	0	15	0	0	0	0	0	1	0	0
orchestral	55	.1365	1.8858	42.8	0	6	5	3	9	24	8	0	0	0	0	0	0	0	0	0	48	0	0	0	0	3	3	1	0
orchestras	30	.0974	.8082	39.1	1	2	3	2	9	13	0	0	0	0	0	0	0	0	0	0	27	0	0	0	1	2	0	0	0
orchestrated	2	.0000	.0162	22.1	0	0	0	1	0	1	0	0	0	0	0	0	0	0	0	0	2	0	0	0	0	0	0	0	0
orchestration	5	.1563	.1897	32.8	0	1	0	0	1	2	1	0	0	0	0	0	0	0	0	0	4	0	0	0	0	0	1	0	0
orchestrion	3	.0000	.0243	23.8	0	0	0	0	0	0	3	0	0	0	0	0	0	0	0	0	3	0	0	0	0	0	0	0	0
orchid	16	.3085	1.2227	40.9	0	0	0	7	8	0	1	0	3	0	0	0	0	0	0	10	0	0	0	0	0	0	3	0	0
orchids	20	.5466	2.3731	43.8	3	1	1	11	4	0	0	0	5	0	0	0	0	2	0	9	0	0	0	0	1	2	1	0	0
ordain	2	.0000	.0389	25.9	0	0	0	0	0	2	0	0	0	0	0	0	0	2	0	0	0	0	0	0	0	0	0	0	0
ordained	3	.3756	.2468	33.9	0	0	0	0	0	2	1	0	0	0	0	1	0	1	0	0	0	0	0	0	0	0	1	0	0
ordeal	17	.7446	2.5881	44.1	0	1	2	0	6	4	4	0	5	1	0	0	0	2	0	1	1	0	0	0	1	2	1	3	0
ordeals	2	.1717	.1142	30.6	0	0	0	0	0	0	2	0	1	0	0	1	0	0	0	0	0	0	0	0	0	0	0	0	0
order	1507	.8959	267.97	64.3	227	223	192	165	317	168	185	30	209	241	38	28	261	105	193	116	48	17	22	19	40	59	58	53	0
Order	15	.5724	1.8073	42.6	0	2	1	3	2	2	4	1	2	1	0	3	0	4	0	0	0	0	0	0	0	4	1	0	0
ordered	294	.7981	47.526	56.8	23	39	54	47	42	50	36	3	89	11	1	14	76	36	3	3	1	2	0	0	10	17	4	27	0
ordering	10	.5464	1.1606	40.6	1	0	0	1	2	5	1	0	2	1	0	0	4	0	0	0	0	0	1	0	1	1	0	0	0
orderlies	2	.0000	.0215	23.3	0	0	0	0	0	2	0	0	0	0	0	2	0	0	0	0	0	0	0	0	0	0	0	0	0
orderliness	2	.2421	.0995	30.0	0	0	0	0	1	0	1	0	0	0	0	0	0	0	0	0	0	0	1	1	0	0	0	0	0
orderly	49	.8044	7.8994	49.0	2	2	5	4	18	7	9	2	7	7	1	0	1	2	0	7	2	1	4	3	2	0	8	4	0
orders	161	.8776	28.248	54.5	14	25	17	24	33	24	21	3	53	4	1	6	1	21	2	16	8	0	1	0	11	15	13	9	0
Orders	3	.2444	.1814	32.6	0	0	0	0	0	2	1	0	0	0	0	0	0	2	0	0	0	0	0	0	0	0	1	0	0
ordinal	15	.2348	.8273	39.2	0	9	2	0	4	0	0	0	0	0	0	0	8	0	7	0	0	0	0	0	0	0	0	0	0
Ordinance	4	.3344	.3261	35.1	0	0	0	0	1	3	0	0	1	0	0	0	0	2	0	0	0	0	0	0	0	0	1	0	0
ordinances	5	.0000	.0972	29.9	0	0	0	0	1	1	3	0	0	0	0	0	0	5	0	0	0	0	0	0	0	0	0	0	0
ordinaries	2	.0000	.0290	24.6	0	0	0	0	2	0	0	0	0	0	0	0	0	0	0	0	0	0	0	0	0	2	0	0	0
ordinarily	52	.8574	8.8603	49.5	2	1	4	6	18	11	10	0	4	7	2	2	4	3	6	5	3	1	3	3	0	1	7	1	0
ordinary	282	.8926	50.086	57.0	17	40	34	38	68	46	31	8	59	16	6	13	17	19	3	62	3	4	0	10	9	20	26	15	0
ore	199	.5925	24.966	54.0	36	17	31	43	23	25	18	6	32	7	0	3	0	102	2	31	0	0	0	2	0	3	17	0	0
oregon	2	.0000	.0219	23.4	0	0	0	0	0	0	2	0	0	2	0	0	0	0	0	0	0	0	0	0	0	0	0	0	0
Oregon	106	.5861	13.164	51.2	4	12	35	8	9	29	8	1	16	0	0	5	0	59	1	9	2	0	0	0	0	5	4	5	0
Oregon's	3	.0000	.0365	25.6	0	0	0	3	0	0	0	0	0	0	0	0	0	0	0	0	0	0	0	0	0	0	0	3	0
Oreille	2	.0000	.0243	23.9	0	0	0	2	0	0	0	0	0	0	0	0	0	0	0	0	0	0	0	0	0	0	0	2	0
ores	37	.5495	4.4069	46.4	7	1	8	7	6	5	3	0	10	0	1	0	0	12	0	8	0	0	0	0	0	0	6	0	0
Orestes	7	.2446	.4046	36.1	0	0	0	0	4	0	3	0	0	0	0	3	0	0	0	0	0	0	0	0	0	4	0	0	0
Oresund	2	.0000	.0209	23.2	2	0	0	0	0	0	0	0	0	0	0	0	0	0	0	0	0	0	0	0	0	0	2	0	0
Orfeo	3	.2088	.1442	31.6	0	1	0	0	0	2	0	0	0	0	0	0	0	0	0	0	2	0	0	0	0	0	1	0	0
organ	90	.5948	11.009	50.4	6	8	15	13	21	12	13	2	3	4	0	1	0	2	2	20	32	0	0	0	2	6	12	6	0
Organ	2	.2401	.1133	30.5	0	0	0	0	1	1	0	0	0	0	0	0	0	0	0	0	0	0	0	0	0	1	1	0	0
organdy	2	.2316	.0949	29.8	0	1	0	0	0	1	0	0	0	0	0	0	0	0	0	0	0	1	1	0	0	0	0	0	0
organic	59	.4069	5.2649	47.2	0	0	6	7	14	5	21	6	0	0	0	0	0	5	0	27	0	0	0	0	0	1	22	4	0
organism	67	.2129	3.7560	45.7	0	1	4	4	45	1	8	4	0	0	0	0	0	0	0	55	0	0	0	0	0	0	12	0	0
organisms	96	.4033	8.6030	49.3	0	2	4	10	47	4	26	3	0	0	1	0	0	1	0	72	0	0	1	0	0	0	19	2	0
organist	14	.0687	.2982	34.7	0	0	0	8	5	1	0	0	0	0	0	0	0	0	0	0	13	0	0	0	0	0	0	1	0
organists	2	.0000	.0162	22.1	0	0	0	0	0	0	2	0	0	0	0	0	0	0	0	0	2	0	0	0	0	0	0	0	0
organization	161	.8084	26.017	54.2	4	3	20	11	54	32	32	5	8	18	6	2	0	34	1	11	16	6	2	0	1	12	25	19	0
Organization	18	.4726	1.8051	42.6	2	0	6	1	4	0	4	1	0	1	0	0	0	5	0	1	0	0	0	0	0	2	8	1	0
organizational	5	.3974	.4198	36.2	0	0	2	0	2	0	1	0	0	1	1	0	0	0	0	0	0	0	0	0	0	1	2	0	0
organizations	70	.6863	9.7688	49.9	3	1	11	6	16	14	19	0	3	2	1	1	0	21	1	4	1	1	2	0	0	3	28	2	0

7H optimistically
9R optimological
5H optometrist
5H optometrists
5B opyou
6A Oquawka
9J Orah
9F Oran
8F orang-outang
5N ORANGE
8D orange-crate
7H orange-growers
7H orange-growing
3R ORANGE-peel
9L orange-pekoe
7F orange-robed
4D orange-yellowy
6J Oranges
7D orating
5F Orator
6H orb-web
9Q orbicular
4Q Orbis
8D Orbitville
3N Orchard's
6A orchestra's
3B Orchid
7J ordaining
7N ordainment
7R Ordaz
XR order's
4G ordinals
9H ordinance
9F ordinance-making
8E ordinate
5P ordnance
6F Ore
9Q ore-bearing
6R Oregonians
6R Oreille's
6A orf
4K organ-grinder
4K organ-grinder's
9J organ-man
9R organ's
9D organdie
9N organisation
7Q organism's
5Q organization's
XR Organizations

Word Type	F	D	U	SFI	3 Gr 3	4 Gr 4	5 Gr 5	6 Gr 6	7 Gr 7	8 Gr 8	9 Gr 9	X UnGr	A Read	B Eng & Gr	C Comp	D Lit	E Math	F Soc Stud	G Spell	H Sci	J Music	K Art	L Home Ec	M Shop	N Lib F	P Lib NF	Q Lib Ref	R Mag	S Rel
organize	66	.8063	10.658	50.3	2	5	8	5	19	15	11	1	6	10	5	1	5	12	0	4	4	1	2	0	1	6	4	5	0
organized	199	.8218	32.723	55.1	11	9	36	12	61	40	27	3	17	19	1	1	2	41	0	23	18	2	1	3	0	25	37	9	0
Organized	2	.2401	.1133	30.5	0	0	0	1	0	0	1	0	0	0	0	0	0	0	0	0	0	0	0	0	0	1	1	0	0
organizer	6	.6013	.7500	38.8	0	1	0	0	3	1	1	0	1	0	0	1	0	0	0	0	1	0	0	0	1	1	0	1	0
organizers	5	.1318	.1844	32.7	0	0	0	0	4	1	0	0	0	4	0	0	0	1	0	0	0	0	0	0	0	0	0	0	0
organizes	6	.5516	.6859	38.4	0	2	0	0	1	1	2	0	0	1	0	0	2	0	0	1	1	0	0	0	0	0	1	0	0
organizing	36	.7248	5.3307	47.3	2	2	1	5	11	10	5	0	8	7	1	0	4	7	0	0	2	0	0	0	0	1	4	2	0
organs	121	.6058	15.184	51.8	5	5	14	17	30	22	25	3	1	0	1	2	0	1	1	75	5	0	4	0	0	3	22	6	0
organum	3	.0000	.0243	23.8	0	0	0	0	0	2	1	0	0	0	0	0	0	0	0	0	3	0	0	0	0	0	0	0	0
orgies	2	.0000	.0215	23.3	0	0	0	0	0	0	2	0	0	0	0	2	0	0	0	0	0	0	0	0	0	0	0	0	0
orgy	2	.0000	.0234	23.7	0	0	0	0	1	1	0	0	0	0	0	0	0	0	0	0	0	0	0	0	2	0	0	0	0
Orient	32	.5702	3.7901	45.8	2	1	8	1	5	10	3	2	1	0	0	0	2	11	0	2	5	1	0	0	0	0	10	0	0
oriental	6	.3410	.4524	36.6	0	0	2	2	2	0	0	0	0	0	0	0	0	3	0	0	2	1	0	0	0	0	0	0	0
Oriental	28	.7069	4.0084	46.0	0	3	2	1	12	6	1	3	2	0	0	2	0	3	0	2	4	2	1	0	0	6	3	3	0
Orientals	4	.3134	.2876	34.6	0	0	0	0	0	1	2	1	0	0	0	0	0	1	0	1	0	0	0	0	0	0	2	0	0
Oriente	2	.2433	.1158	30.6	0	0	0	0	2	0	0	0	0	0	0	0	0	0	0	0	0	0	0	0	0	1	0	1	0
oriented	4	.2437	.2257	33.5	1	0	0	0	2	0	1	0	0	0	0	0	0	0	0	0	0	0	0	0	0	0	2	2	0
orifices	2	.0000	.0209	23.2	0	0	0	0	1	1	0	0	0	0	0	0	0	0	0	0	0	0	0	0	0	0	2	0	0
origami	4	.0000	.0486	26.9	4	0	0	0	0	0	0	0	0	0	0	0	0	0	0	0	0	0	0	0	0	0	0	4	0
origin	185	.7828	28.991	54.6	4	8	23	26	38	40	38	8	7	16	1	5	31	6	44	20	15	0	1	2	1	9	23	4	0
Origin	3	.2159	.1532	31.9	0	0	0	1	2	0	0	0	0	0	0	0	0	0	0	0	0	0	0	0	0	0	2	1	0
original	403	.8858	70.746	58.5	10	33	40	32	129	83	59	17	20	36	4	17	37	21	27	32	78	10	9	15	5	22	39	31	0
originality	12	.6525	1.5982	42.0	0	0	2	2	3	2	3	0	2	1	0	1	0	0	0	0	1	1	2	1	0	2	1	0	0
originally	145	.8200	23.706	53.7	5	11	26	16	37	25	17	8	8	12	0	7	9	10	15	6	31	1	3	1	0	8	20	14	0
originals	2	.1703	.0781	28.9	0	0	0	0	1	0	1	0	0	1	0	0	0	0	0	0	0	0	0	1	0	0	0	0	0
originate	12	.6655	1.6201	42.1	0	0	0	2	3	3	4	0	0	1	0	1	0	1	0	3	2	0	0	1	0	0	1	0	0
originated	49	.6960	6.8832	48.4	1	1	8	11	10	9	8	1	2	3	0	2	1	2	1	3	18	1	0	1	0	5	8	2	0
originating	6	.4808	.6097	37.9	0	0	1	1	1	0	3	0	0	0	0	0	0	0	0	2	1	0	0	0	0	0	1	2	0
origins	48	.5623	5.5211	47.4	1	2	9	4	15	11	5	1	0	3	2	0	0	3	20	1	1	0	0	0	0	5	12	1	0
Orinoco	5	.3474	.3866	35.9	0	1	1	0	2	0	1	0	0	0	0	0	0	1	0	0	0	0	0	0	0	2	2	0	0
oriole	3	.2429	.1792	32.5	2	0	0	1	0	0	0	0	0	0	0	0	0	0	0	2	1	0	0	0	0	0	0	0	0
Oriole	2	.2152	.1357	31.3	1	1	0	0	0	0	0	0	1	0	0	0	0	1	0	0	0	0	0	0	0	0	0	0	0
orioles	5	.4428	.4992	37.0	1	0	0	3	1	0	0	0	1	0	0	0	0	1	0	2	0	0	0	0	0	0	1	0	0
Orioles	3	.2357	.2199	33.4	3	0	0	0	0	0	0	0	2	0	0	0	0	0	0	0	0	0	0	0	0	1	0	0	0
Orioles'	2	.0000	.0389	25.9	2	0	0	0	0	0	0	0	0	0	0	0	0	2	0	0	0	0	0	0	0	0	0	0	0
Orion	6	.4730	.6083	37.8	0	0	0	3	2	0	0	1	0	0	0	1	0	0	0	3	0	0	0	0	1	1	0	0	0
ork	7	.1560	.3699	35.7	3	4	0	0	0	0	0	0	3	0	0	0	0	0	0	0	0	0	0	0	4	0	0	0	0
Orlando	6	.1221	.2146	33.3	0	0	0	0	3	1	0	2	0	0	0	0	0	0	0	1	0	0	0	0	0	0	0	5	0
Orleans	9	.5387	1.0175	40.1	0	1	0	1	5	1	0	1	1	1	0	0	0	1	0	0	2	0	0	0	1	0	0	3	0
Orlick	3	.0000	.1370	31.4	3	0	0	0	0	0	0	0	3	0	0	0	0	0	0	0	0	0	0	0	0	0	0	0	0
Orlon	6	.0927	.1313	31.2	0	0	0	0	0	3	3	0	0	0	0	0	0	0	1	0	0	0	5	0	0	0	0	0	0
Orlov	6	.0000	.0703	28.5	0	0	0	6	0	0	0	0	0	0	0	0	0	0	0	0	0	0	0	0	6	0	0	0	0
Ormin	2	.0000	.0162	22.1	0	0	0	0	2	0	0	0	0	0	0	0	0	0	2	0	0	0	0	0	0	0	0	0	0
Ormsby	2	.0000	.0290	24.6	2	0	0	0	0	0	0	0	0	0	0	0	0	0	0	0	0	0	0	0	0	2	0	0	0
ornament	16	.6380	2.0661	43.2	0	1	1	1	5	2	5	1	1	1	2	3	0	0	1	0	0	2	1	0	1	1	3	0	0
ornamental	15	.4660	1.4873	41.7	1	0	0	3	5	0	5	1	2	1	0	0	0	0	0	1	2	0	0	0	0	1	5	0	0
ornamentation	7	.3731	.5692	37.6	0	2	0	0	1	2	2	0	1	0	0	0	0	0	1	0	4	0	1	3	0	0	0	0	0
ornamented	6	.4201	.5370	37.3	0	1	0	2	0	2	1	0	0	0	0	3	0	1	0	0	1	0	0	0	0	0	0	1	0
ornaments	18	.6557	2.4152	43.8	5	1	3	3	3	0	0	3	2	0	0	0	0	3	0	0	1	1	0	0	3	2	5	0	0
ornate	5	.5608	.5810	37.6	0	0	2	0	1	0	0	2	0	0	1	0	0	1	0	0	0	0	0	0	1	1	1	1	0
ornery	5	.3326	.4068	36.1	3	1	0	0	0	1	0	0	2	0	1	0	0	0	0	0	0	0	0	0	1	1	0	0	0
ornithine	2	.0000	.0394	26.0	0	0	0	0	0	0	2	0	0	0	0	0	0	0	0	2	0	0	0	0	0	0	0	0	0
ornitholestes	2	.0000	.0290	24.6	0	2	0	0	0	0	0	0	0	0	0	0	0	0	0	0	0	0	0	0	0	2	0	0	0
Ornitholestes	2	.0000	.0290	24.6	2	0	0	0	0	0	0	0	0	0	0	0	0	0	0	0	0	0	0	0	0	2	0	0	0
ornithologists	2	.2437	.1129	30.5	0	0	0	0	1	0	0	1	0	0	0	0	0	0	0	0	0	0	0	0	0	0	1	1	0
ornithology	9	.2379	.4963	37.0	7	0	0	1	0	0	1	0	0	7	0	0	0	0	0	0	0	0	0	0	0	0	1	1	0
ORNITHOLOGY	2	.0000	.0219	23.4	2	0	0	0	0	0	0	0	0	2	0	0	0	0	0	0	0	0	0	0	0	0	0	0	0
Oroville	2	.2351	.1166	30.7	0	0	2	0	0	0	0	0	0	0	0	0	0	1	0	0	0	0	0	0	0	0	0	1	0
orphan	14	.5758	1.7584	42.5	3	0	2	4	2	3	0	0	7	0	0	0	0	1	2	1	0	0	0	0	2	0	0	1	0
Orphan	2	.1814	.1187	30.7	1	1	0	0	0	0	0	0	1	0	0	0	0	0	0	0	0	0	0	0	0	0	0	1	0
orphanage	6	.2419	.4673	36.7	4	0	0	1	0	1	0	0	5	0	0	0	0	0	0	0	0	0	0	0	1	0	0	0	0
orphans	6	.4490	.5744	37.6	0	2	2	0	2	0	0	0	0	0	0	1	0	1	0	0	1	0	0	0	0	3	0	0	0
Orpheus	16	.3243	1.4672	41.7	0	0	12	2	0	1	0	1	14	0	0	0	0	0	0	0	1	0	0	0	0	1	0	0	0
Ortelius	3	.0000	.0314	25.0	0	3	0	0	0	0	0	0	0	0	0	0	0	0	0	0	0	0	0	0	0	0	3	0	0
orthicon	2	.1249	.0685	28.4	0	0	0	0	1	1	0	0	0	0	0	0	0	0	0	1	0	0	0	1	0	0	0	0	0
orthoclase	3	.0000	.0591	27.7	0	0	0	0	0	1	2	0	0	0	0	0	0	0	0	3	0	0	0	0	0	0	0	0	0
orthodontist	2	.0000	.0394	26.0	0	0	1	0	1	0	0	0	0	0	0	0	0	0	0	2	0	0	0	0	0	0	0	0	0
orthodox	5	.2948	.3343	35.2	0	0	0	1	0	2	1	1	0	0	0	0	0	0	0	1	0	0	0	0	0	0	3	1	0
Orthodox	11	.2832	.7022	38.5	0	0	3	1	1	1	5	0	0	0	0	0	0	1	1	0	0	0	0	0	0	1	8	0	0
orthopedist	2	.0000	.0243	23.9	0	0	0	0	0	2	0	0	0	0	0	0	0	0	0	0	0	0	0	0	0	0	0	2	0
Orthoptera	3	.0000	.0591	27.7	0	0	0	1	2	0	0	0	0	0	0	0	0	0	0	3	0	0	0	0	0	0	0	0	0
Orville	42	.4855	4.8641	46.9	5	12	0	15	7	1	2	0	34	2	0	2	0	1	0	2	0	0	0	0	0	0	1	0	0
Orwell	2	.0000	.0243	23.9	0	0	0	0	1	1	0	0	0	0	0	0	0	0	0	0	0	0	0	0	0	0	0	2	0
ory	2	.0000	.0162	22.1	0	0	0	0	0	2	0	0	0	0	0	0	0	0	2	0	0	0	0	0	0	0	0	0	0
Osaka	9	.3545	.8322	39.2	0	1	0	6	1	1	0	0	6	0	0	0	0	1	0	0	0	0	0	0	0	0	0	2	0
Osawatomie	2	.2152	.1357	31.3	0	0	0	1	0	1	0	0	1	0	0	0	0	1	0	0	0	0	0	0	0	0	0	0	0
Osborn	8	.3857	.6901	38.4	0	2	1	0	0	4	1	0	1	0	0	3	1	0	0	0	0	0	0	0	0	3	0	0	0
Osburn	4	.0000	.0579	27.6	0	0	0	0	0	0	4	0	0	0	0	0	0	0	0	0	0	0	0	0	0	4	0	0	0
Oscar	84	.5447	10.296	50.1	50	7	0	4	8	4	10	1	56	2	0	8	0	0	0	0	4	0	0	0	0	0	1	13	0
oscillating	2	.0000	.0209	23.2	0	0	0	0	1	1	0	0	0	0	0	0	0	0	0	0	0	0	0	0	0	0	2	0	0
oscillation	4	.0000	.0789	29.0	0	0	0	0	1	0	1	2	0	0	0	0	0	0	0	4	0	0	0	0	0	0	0	0	0
oscillations	2	.0000	.0394	26.0	0	0	0	0	0	0	0	2	0	0	0	0	0	0	0	2	0	0	0	0	0	0	0	0	0
oscillator	8	.0318	.0861	29.4	0	0	0	0	0	7	1	0	0	0	0	0	0	0	0	1	0	0	0	7	0	0	0	0	0
oscillograph	3	.2088	.1442	31.6	0	0	0	0	1	2	0	0	0	0	0	0	0	0	0	0	2	0	0	0	0	0	1	0	0
oscilloscope	4	.3406	.2870	34.6	0	0	0	0	0	3	1	0	0	0	0	0	0	0	0	0	2	0	0	1	0	0	1	0	0
Oskaloosa	2	.0000	.0215	23.3	0	2	0	0	0	0	0	0	0	0	0	2	0	0	0	0	0	0	0	0	0	0	0	0	0
Osler	3	.2260	.1580	32.0	0	0	0	0	2	0	1	0	0	0	0	2	0	0	0	0	0	0	0	0	0	0	1	0	0
Oslo	22	.4455	2.3561	43.7	7	4	0	3	6	2	0	0	14	1	0	0	0	6	0	0	1	0	0	0	0	0	0	0	0
osmium	4	.2391	.2266	33.6	0	2	0	2	0	0	0	0	0	0	0	0	2	0	0	0	0	0	0	0	0	0	2	0	0
osmosis	2	.0000	.0209	23.2	0	0	0	0	2	0	0	0	0	0	0	0	0	0	0	0	0	0	0	0	0	0	2	0	0
osmotic	2	.0000	.0209	23.2	0	0	0	0	2	0	0	0	0	0	0	0	0	0	0	0	0	0	0	0	0	0	2	0	0
Osocan	3	.0000	.0434	26.4	0	3	0	0	0	0	0	0	0	0	0	0	0	0	0	0	0	0	0	0	0	3	0	0	0
osprey	6	.1673	.2570	34.1	0	0	0	5	0	0	1	0	0	1	0	0	0	0	0	0	0	0	0	0	0	0	0	5	0
Osprey	2	.0000	.0914	29.6	0	0	0	0	2	0	0	0	2	0	0	0	0	0	0	0	0	0	0	0	0	0	0	0	0
ospreys	7	.1529	.2814	34.5	0	0	0	6	1	0	0	0	0	1	0	0	0	0	0	0	0	0	0	0	0	0	0	6	0

9R orgiastic
7Q orient
8J Oriental-sounding
8R orientation
7Q orienting
8G orig/i/nal
3R Origami
8Q originates
8R originator
6R Orinda
6R Orinda's
6P Orithyia
6F Orizaba
7F Orkneys
8B orleans
5F orlon
9L Orlons
8R Orlu
8R Orly
7G Orm
XP ornamenting
9D ornerier
4N orneriness
8Q orogeny
4P Oropeza
7Q Orosius
5R Orpington
8R Orr
6J Orrego-Salas
4G orse
7A Orson
4G ort
3J Orth
7H ortho
7H orthodontia
9Q ORTHODOX
9R orthodoxy
9M orthographic
XH orthorhombic
5Q Ortler
7A Orv
7D Orville's
8R Orwell's
7A Orycteropus
4J os
8Q OsTimbiras
3D Osa's
7A Osceola
8R oscillates
8Q oscillators
6K Osgood's
7J Osiris
9R Oskar
6F Ossetians

Word Type	F	D	U	SFI	3 Gr 3	4 Gr 4	5 Gr 5	6 Gr 6	7 Gr 7	8 Gr 8	9 Gr 9	X UnGr	A Read	B Eng & Gr	C Comp	D Lit	E Math	F Soc Stud	G Spell	H Sci	J Music	K Art	L Home Ec	M Shop	N Lib F	P Lib NF	Q Lib Ref	R Mag	S Rel
Ostade	2	.0000	.0209	23.2	0	0	0	0	0	2	0	0	0	0	0	0	0	0	0	0	0	0	0	0	0	0	2	0	0
Osten-Sacken	2	.0000	.0209	23.2	0	0	0	0	0	2	0	0	0	0	0	0	0	0	0	0	0	0	0	0	0	0	2	0	0
Ostend	5	.3652	.4043	36.1	0	1	0	2	0	2	0	0	0	0	0	0	0	2	0	0	0	0	0	0	1	0	2	0	0
ostensibly	2	.2285	.1129	30.5	0	0	0	0	0	2	0	0	0	0	0	0	0	1	0	0	0	0	0	0	0	0	1	0	0
ostentatious	3	.3272	.2361	33.7	0	0	0	0	1	0	2	0	1	0	0	0	0	0	0	0	1	0	0	0	0	0	1	0	0
ostinato	3	.0000	.0243	23.8	0	0	1	1	1	0	0	0	0	0	0	0	0	0	0	0	3	0	0	0	0	0	0	0	0
ostracod	2	.0000	.0290	24.6	2	0	0	0	0	0	0	0	0	0	0	0	0	0	0	0	0	0	0	0	0	2	0	0	0
ostrich	33	.7211	4.9008	46.9	16	3	1	4	5	3	1	0	11	0	1	1	7	0	0	4	0	1	0	0	1	5	2	0	0
Ostrich	3	.3851	.2497	34.0	1	1	1	0	0	0	0	0	0	0	0	1	0	0	0	0	0	0	0	0	1	1	0	0	0
ostriches	14	.5958	1.7283	42.4	9	2	0	1	2	0	0	0	1	4	0	0	1	0	0	2	0	0	0	0	0	3	2	1	0
Ostrom	7	.0000	.1013	30.1	7	0	0	0	0	0	0	0	0	0	0	0	0	0	0	0	0	0	0	0	0	7	0	0	0
ot	3	.2031	.1990	33.0	1	0	0	1	0	1	0	0	2	0	0	0	0	0	1	0	0	0	0	0	0	0	0	0	0
Otah	7	.0000	.3198	35.0	0	0	0	0	7	0	0	0	7	0	0	0	0	0	0	0	0	0	0	0	0	0	0	0	0
Otah's	5	.0000	.2284	33.6	0	0	0	0	5	0	0	0	5	0	0	0	0	0	0	0	0	0	0	0	0	0	0	0	0
Othello	2	.0000	.0162	22.1	0	0	0	0	1	1	0	0	0	0	0	0	0	0	0	0	2	0	0	0	0	0	0	0	0
other	10729	.9816	2073.4	73.2	1867	1534	1464	1402	1911	1290	1008	253	1920	621	100	394	609	1686	368	1652	450	150	208	185	401	723	746	511	5
Other	26	.2519	1.4983	41.8	0	0	10	4	7	5	0	0	1	1	0	0	0	2	19	0	0	0	0	0	1	0	2	0	0
other's	58	.7434	8.7681	49.4	6	1	5	8	12	18	4	4	14	3	0	7	0	3	11	3	0	2	0	0	5	5	1	4	0
others	1903	.9587	360.10	65.6	307	294	233	232	401	225	175	36	400	135	20	83	30	263	48	253	95	32	55	24	73	160	132	95	5
Others	2	.2160	.1362	31.3	0	1	0	0	1	0	0	0	1	0	0	0	0	0	0	1	0	0	0	0	0	0	0	0	0
others'	4	.2280	.2913	34.6	1	0	0	0	2	1	0	0	3	0	0	0	0	0	1	0	0	0	0	0	0	0	0	0	0
otherwise	130	.8400	21.866	53.4	4	17	10	16	32	13	35	3	28	12	3	11	6	8	0	15	1	0	10	2	2	9	9	14	0
Othman's	2	.0000	.0290	24.6	0	0	2	0	0	0	0	0	0	0	0	0	0	0	0	0	0	0	0	0	0	2	0	0	0
Otis	55	.0321	1.0116	40.0	53	0	1	1	0	0	0	0	1	0	0	0	0	0	0	1	0	0	0	0	53	0	0	0	0
Otonia	2	.0000	.0914	29.6	0	0	2	0	0	0	0	0	2	0	0	0	0	0	0	0	0	0	0	0	0	0	0	0	0
Otranto	2	.0000	.0209	23.2	0	0	1	0	0	0	1	0	0	0	0	0	0	0	0	0	0	0	0	0	0	0	2	0	0
Ottawa	7	.3409	.5398	37.3	0	4	0	0	0	3	0	0	0	0	0	1	0	2	0	0	0	0	0	0	0	4	0	0	0
Ottawas	3	.0000	.0434	26.4	0	3	0	0	0	0	0	0	0	0	0	0	0	0	0	0	0	0	0	0	0	3	0	0	0
otter	29	.5635	3.5223	45.5	5	2	4	8	8	1	0	1	9	0	0	0	0	7	0	1	0	0	0	0	8	2	1	1	0
Otter	25	.0000	.3619	35.6	24	1	0	0	0	0	0	0	0	0	0	0	0	0	0	0	0	0	0	0	0	25	0	0	0
otters	12	.4552	1.3023	41.1	1	0	1	0	8	1	0	1	8	0	0	1	0	1	0	0	0	0	0	0	0	0	0	2	0
Otto	51	.5981	6.3309	48.0	0	19	12	2	13	1	2	2	5	3	0	0	0	0	0	3	1	0	0	0	10	21	5	3	0
Otto's	2	.2427	.1152	30.6	0	1	1	0	0	0	0	0	0	0	0	0	0	0	0	0	0	0	0	0	1	1	0	0	0
Ottoman	15	.3056	1.0662	40.3	0	0	9	0	5	0	1	0	0	0	0	0	0	5	0	0	0	0	0	0	0	9	1	0	0
Ottomans	6	.0000	.0869	29.4	0	0	6	0	0	0	0	0	0	0	0	0	0	0	0	0	0	0	0	0	0	6	0	0	0
ou	104	.0800	2.5004	44.0	13	35	15	29	7	5	0	0	2	3	0	0	0	0	96	0	0	0	0	0	0	0	0	3	0
Ouachita	5	.2426	.2985	34.7	0	0	3	2	0	0	0	0	0	0	0	0	0	3	0	0	0	0	0	0	0	0	2	0	0
Ouachitas	2	.0000	.0389	25.9	0	0	2	0	0	0	0	0	0	0	0	0	0	2	0	0	0	0	0	0	0	0	0	0	0
ouch	21	.4533	2.2397	43.5	7	9	2	1	0	1	1	0	13	1	2	0	0	0	1	0	0	0	0	0	0	4	0	0	0
ough	6	.2661	.3545	35.5	0	3	1	1	0	1	0	0	0	1	0	0	0	0	4	0	0	0	0	0	0	0	0	1	0
ought	220	.8083	35.947	55.6	22	34	22	33	47	26	27	9	74	8	1	34	0	11	4	8	2	0	0	1	26	28	8	15	0
oughta	4	.1919	.1864	32.7	0	0	1	0	1	0	2	0	0	0	0	3	0	0	0	0	0	0	0	0	1	0	0	0	0
oughtn't	2	.0000	.0914	29.6	0	0	0	0	2	0	0	0	2	0	0	0	0	0	0	0	0	0	0	0	0	0	0	0	0
ounce	48	.6188	6.1878	47.9	2	9	8	4	16	4	4	1	7	1	1	1	19	2	0	8	0	0	0	0	0	0	8	1	0
ounces	104	.4721	10.543	50.2	23	21	10	8	27	8	5	2	7	0	0	0	67	0	0	6	0	0	0	2	1	2	14	5	0
our	5777	.8607	993.57	70.0	772	812	668	787	1065	835	655	183	1203	422	92	333	202	1135	234	541	274	53	40	37	203	349	179	441	39
Our	30	.4300	2.7990	44.5	3	4	3	1	5	8	6	0	3	2	0	3	0	6	6	0	2	0	0	0	1	3	1	2	1
ours	97	.8124	15.861	52.0	13	16	19	13	17	9	8	2	22	15	0	4	0	13	2	6	3	3	0	0	7	12	3	7	0
ourselves	142	.7714	22.286	53.5	11	17	10	23	32	29	16	4	43	11	0	10	2	15	1	15	3	1	2	0	4	10	3	21	1
ous	29	.1564	1.1042	40.4	0	0	0	2	16	5	6	0	0	6	0	0	0	0	23	0	0	0	0	0	0	0	0	0	0
ousted	5	.3468	.3830	35.8	0	0	0	1	2	1	0	1	0	0	0	0	0	1	0	0	0	0	0	0	0	0	2	2	0
ouster	2	.0000	.0243	23.9	0	0	0	0	1	1	0	0	0	0	0	0	0	0	0	0	0	0	0	0	0	0	0	2	0
out	12252	.9655	2334.8	73.7	2507	2167	1411	1493	2226	1242	947	259	4098	446	106	1008	307	785	217	1194	223	78	130	112	1236	1105	374	824	9
Out	20	.4783	2.1519	43.3	10	0	2	2	4	0	0	2	8	0	0	0	0	1	0	2	3	0	0	0	0	0	0	6	0
OUT	6	.2515	.3690	35.7	1	0	0	1	0	4	0	0	1	0	0	4	0	0	0	0	1	0	0	0	0	0	0	0	0
out-feed	5	.0000	.0126	21.0	0	0	0	0	0	0	5	0	0	0	0	0	0	0	0	0	0	0	0	5	0	0	0	0	0
out-of-bounds	2	.1442	.0761	28.8	0	0	0	0	1	1	0	0	0	0	0	0	0	1	0	0	0	0	1	0	0	0	0	0	0
out-of-doors	28	.7630	4.3274	46.4	7	5	2	3	3	8	0	0	6	1	0	3	0	4	1	1	5	0	0	1	1	3	0	2	0
out-of-state	2	.0000	.0389	25.9	0	0	2	0	0	0	0	0	0	0	0	0	0	2	0	0	0	0	0	0	0	0	0	0	0
out-of-the-way	7	.5489	.8287	39.2	1	4	0	0	2	0	0	0	2	0	0	0	0	2	1	0	0	0	0	0	0	1	1	0	0
outback	4	.3831	.3415	35.3	0	0	3	0	1	0	0	0	0	0	0	0	0	2	0	0	0	0	0	0	0	1	0	1	0
outboard	8	.4538	.7511	38.8	0	0	0	0	6	0	2	0	0	0	1	1	0	0	0	0	0	0	0	2	0	1	0	3	0
outbound	2	.2285	.1129	30.5	0	0	1	0	1	0	0	0	0	0	0	0	0	1	0	0	0	0	0	0	0	0	1	0	0
outbreak	20	.5078	2.1197	43.3	0	3	0	4	5	6	2	0	0	0	0	1	0	3	1	0	0	0	0	0	0	1	6	8	0
outbreaks	5	.3468	.3830	35.8	0	0	0	0	2	2	1	0	0	0	0	0	0	1	0	0	0	0	0	0	0	0	2	2	0
outbuildings	5	.4110	.4623	36.6	0	1	0	0	2	1	1	0	1	0	0	1	0	1	0	0	0	0	0	0	2	0	0	0	0
outburst	7	.4826	.7678	38.9	0	0	1	3	0	3	0	0	3	0	0	0	0	2	0	0	0	0	0	0	0	1	1	0	0
outbursts	3	.3771	.2489	34.0	0	0	0	0	2	1	0	0	0	0	0	1	0	0	0	1	0	0	0	0	0	0	0	1	0
outcast	4	.4817	.4082	36.1	0	0	1	0	0	3	0	0	0	1	0	0	0	1	0	0	0	0	0	0	0	1	0	1	0
outcasts	2	.2440	.1132	30.5	0	0	0	0	0	1	1	0	0	0	0	1	0	0	0	0	0	0	0	0	0	0	0	1	0
outclassed	2	.2401	.1133	30.5	0	0	0	1	1	0	0	0	0	0	0	0	0	0	0	0	0	0	0	0	0	1	1	0	0
outcome	32	.8103	5.2332	47.2	0	2	6	6	6	7	5	0	10	2	1	3	1	2	1	1	0	1	0	0	0	5	2	3	0
outcomes	4	.2060	.1991	33.0	0	0	0	3	0	0	1	0	0	0	0	0	3	0	0	0	0	1	0	0	0	0	0	0	0
outcries	2	.2446	.1142	30.6	0	0	0	2	0	0	0	0	0	0	0	0	0	0	0	0	0	0	0	0	1	0	0	1	0
outcropping	3	.3427	.2477	33.9	0	0	1	0	2	0	0	0	1	0	0	0	0	0	0	0	0	0	0	0	1	0	0	1	0
outcroppings	3	.3795	.2506	34.0	0	1	0	0	1	1	0	0	0	0	0	0	0	1	0	0	0	0	0	0	1	0	0	1	0
outcrops	6	.1833	.3085	34.9	0	0	0	0	1	0	5	0	0	0	0	0	0	0	0	5	0	0	0	0	0	1	0	0	0
outcry	5	.4396	.4862	36.9	1	0	1	0	3	0	0	0	1	0	0	0	0	0	0	0	0	0	0	0	1	2	1	0	0
outdated	3	.3769	.2484	34.0	0	1	0	0	0	1	1	0	0	0	0	0	0	1	0	0	0	0	0	0	0	0	1	1	0
outdid	3	.3776	.2504	34.0	0	0	0	0	0	1	2	0	0	0	0	1	0	1	0	0	0	0	0	0	0	1	0	0	0
outdistanced	2	.2446	.1142	30.6	0	0	0	1	1	0	0	0	0	0	0	0	0	0	0	0	0	0	0	0	1	0	0	1	0
outdo	5	.4385	.4861	36.9	0	0	1	0	2	1	1	0	1	0	0	0	0	0	0	0	0	0	0	0	1	2	0	1	0
outdoor	38	.7737	5.9322	47.7	5	8	5	5	7	4	1	3	6	0	2	2	1	8	0	2	2	0	1	2	2	2	0	8	0
outdoors	118	.8161	19.408	52.9	39	26	23	11	9	3	5	2	28	1	4	5	1	8	1	32	3	1	1	0	9	19	0	5	0
outdoorsman	2	.1733	.1149	30.6	0	0	0	0	1	0	1	0	1	1	0	0	0	0	0	0	0	0	0	0	0	0	0	0	0
outen	3	.0000	.0352	25.5	0	0	3	0	0	0	0	0	0	0	0	0	0	0	0	0	0	0	0	0	3	0	0	0	0
outer	252	.8514	42.902	56.3	27	34	23	34	57	41	27	9	43	14	1	8	4	13	1	82	2	3	13	5	7	18	29	9	0
Outer	12	.5242	1.3036	41.2	1	2	4	1	2	2	0	0	0	1	0	0	0	1	0	0	1	0	0	0	0	1	5	3	0
outer-edge	2	.0000	.0064	18.1	0	0	0	0	0	0	2	0	0	0	0	0	0	0	0	0	0	0	2	0	0	0	0	0	0
outer-space	2	.1249	.0685	28.4	0	1	0	0	0	0	1	0	0	0	0	0	0	0	0	1	0	0	0	1	0	0	0	0	0
outermost	10	.4182	.9260	39.7	0	1	0	1	4	1	3	0	1	0	0	0	0	0	0	5	0	0	1	0	0	0	3	0	0
outfeed	3	.0000	.0434	26.4	0	0	0	0	3	0	0	0	0	0	0	0	0	0	0	0	0	0	0	0	0	3	0	0	0

8H ossified
9Q ossuaries
4N Ostand
9Q Ostarrichi
8R Osteen
8Q osteitis
7D ostentation
7Q Osteoglossidae
7A ostracism
7A ostracize
3P OSTRACOD
7Q ostracoderms
7Q ostrich-like
7Q ostrichlike
8Q Ostrogoths
XR Ostwald
5A ot-choeck
7R other-wordly
7Q Othere
7D OTHERS
6A otherside
3B otherwhere
5P Othman
3N Otis's
5G ots
7R Otsego
6R otter's
3P Otter's
7N otterlike
3P Otters
9N ottoman
8Q Ottonians
8J Ottorino
8D Ou-dis-sun
6G ou's
8Q Oudewater
9R oui
8P Ouia
8D oul
3A Ouri
XR ourself
7D Oursler
6R ousting
7A out-a
7N out-a-condition
5A out-and-out
6F out-bound
3Q out-dated
7D out-of-beat
9D out-of-control
4D out-of-focusness
7H out-of-school
9L out-of-season
4A out-of-sorts
7R out-of-staters
7A out-of-the-ordinary
9Q out-of-town
9F out-produce
9J out-ring
8C out-roar
7N out-run
4N out-stretched
6B out-talked
7R outasight
8D outbid
8A outbluff
9D outbrave
6P outclass
7A outcrop
5Q outdistance
9K outdistances
9D outdoes
5A outdone
3G Outdoors
7A outdoorsmen
3P OUTER
6K outerspace
7P outfeed-roll

Word Type	F	D	U	SFI	3 Gr 3	4 Gr 4	5 Gr 5	6 Gr 6	7 Gr 7	8 Gr 8	9 Gr 9	X UnGr	A Read	B Eng & Gr	C Comp	D Lit	E Math	F Soc Stud	G Spell	H Sci	J Music	K Art	L Home Ec	M Shop	N Lib F	P Lib NF	Q Lib Ref	R Mag	S Rel
outfield	9	.4199	.8695	39.4	3	2	1	1	1	1	0	0	3	0	0	0	0	0	0	0	0	0	0	0	1	4	0	1	0
outfielder	3	.2143	.1568	32.0	0	0	0	1	2	0	0	0	0	0	0	0	0	0	0	0	0	0	0	0	0	1	0	2	0
outfielders	2	.2412	.1141	30.6	1	0	0	1	0	0	0	0	0	1	0	0	0	0	0	0	0	0	0	0	0	1	0	0	0
outfit	59	.6886	8.3930	49.2	9	1	8	8	14	11	8	0	21	0	2	8	0	4	1	0	0	1	10	1	2	4	1	4	0
outfits	14	.5426	1.6225	42.1	3	0	1	1	3	2	3	1	3	0	0	2	1	2	0	0	0	0	0	0	0	0	1	5	0
outfitted	4	.4817	.4082	36.1	0	0	2	0	2	0	0	0	0	1	0	0	0	1	0	0	0	0	0	0	0	1	0	1	0
outfitters	2	.0000	.0243	23.9	0	0	0	0	0	0	0	2	0	0	0	0	0	0	0	0	0	0	0	0	0	0	0	2	0
outgoing	6	.6210	.7638	38.8	0	0	0	1	2	1	2	0	0	1	0	1	0	1	0	1	0	0	0	0	0	0	1	1	0
outgrabe	2	.1458	.0682	28.3	0	0	1	1	0	0	0	0	0	1	0	0	0	0	0	0	0	1	0	0	0	0	0	0	0
outgrow	4	.4800	.4066	36.1	1	2	0	0	0	0	1	0	0	0	0	0	0	0	0	1	0	0	0	0	1	1	1	0	0
outgrown	6	.4647	.6211	37.9	0	0	1	0	1	2	1	1	2	0	0	0	0	1	0	0	0	0	1	0	0	0	1	1	0
outgrowth	4	.2389	.2497	34.0	0	0	0	1	1	2	0	0	1	0	0	0	0	1	0	0	2	0	0	0	0	0	0	0	0
outhouse	3	.2309	.1631	32.1	0	0	0	0	0	0	3	0	0	0	0	1	0	0	0	0	0	0	0	0	0	0	0	2	0
outhouses	3	.2196	.1554	31.9	0	0	0	0	0	1	2	0	0	0	0	2	0	0	0	0	0	0	0	0	1	0	0	0	0
outing	8	.4282	.7316	38.6	0	2	4	1	0	1	0	0	0	0	0	1	0	0	0	1	0	0	0	0	3	0	0	3	0
outings	3	.2147	.1591	32.0	0	0	0	0	1	2	0	0	0	0	1	0	0	1	0	1	0	0	0	0	0	0	0	0	0
outlandish	6	.5496	.7091	38.5	0	1	1	2	0	1	1	0	2	1	0	1	0	0	0	0	1	0	0	0	0	1	0	0	0
outlaw	23	.5566	2.7833	44.4	0	7	7	0	6	2	1	0	10	0	0	2	0	0	0	0	1	0	0	0	7	0	1	2	0
outlawed	8	.4978	.8634	39.4	0	0	1	1	2	2	2	0	1	0	0	1	0	4	0	0	0	0	0	0	0	1	0	1	0
outlaws	11	.4492	1.1397	40.6	2	3	3	0	3	0	0	0	5	0	0	0	0	0	0	0	1	0	0	0	1	4	0	0	0
outlet	19	.5331	2.1786	43.4	1	1	3	3	8	1	1	1	4	0	0	0	0	6	0	3	1	0	0	2	0	0	3	0	0
outlets	4	.3436	.2981	34.7	0	1	2	0	0	1	0	0	0	0	0	0	0	0	0	0	0	0	1	0	0	2	1	0	0
outline	200	.7501	30.452	54.8	6	18	36	41	44	24	26	5	51	62	10	3	1	17	3	6	9	3	2	15	2	5	4	7	0
Outline	2	.2442	.1134	30.5	0	0	0	0	1	1	0	0	0	1	0	0	0	0	0	0	0	0	0	0	0	0	0	1	0
outlined	30	.8461	5.0687	47.0	0	0	2	7	7	8	5	1	5	1	1	1	4	0	1	5	3	1	1	1	1	0	0	5	0
outlines	40	.6723	5.5079	47.4	5	3	3	6	13	7	2	1	8	5	0	1	0	1	0	2	5	5	1	1	2	4	4	1	0
outlining	8	.4878	.9008	39.5	0	0	4	1	1	1	1	0	5	1	0	0	0	0	0	0	0	0	0	0	1	0	1	0	0
outlived	3	.3370	.2430	33.9	0	1	1	0	0	1	0	0	1	0	0	1	0	0	0	0	0	0	0	0	0	0	1	0	0
outlook	19	.6162	2.3983	43.8	0	0	2	1	7	2	5	2	1	0	0	0	0	2	1	1	1	0	3	0	1	2	1	6	0
outlying	12	.6321	1.5651	41.9	0	2	2	1	3	1	3	0	1	0	0	1	0	3	0	0	0	0	0	0	1	2	1	3	0
outmoded	3	.3553	.2608	34.2	0	0	2	0	1	0	0	0	1	0	0	0	0	1	0	0	0	0	0	0	0	1	0	0	0
outnumber	4	.2348	.2372	33.8	0	0	0	3	1	0	0	0	0	0	0	0	0	3	0	0	0	0	0	0	0	0	1	0	0
outnumbered	13	.5774	1.5645	41.9	0	1	3	1	3	4	1	0	2	1	0	5	0	0	0	0	1	0	0	0	0	1	2	1	0
outnumbering	2	.2285	.1129	30.5	0	0	0	0	1	0	1	0	0	0	0	0	0	1	0	0	0	0	0	0	0	0	1	0	0
outpost	11	.5722	1.3395	41.3	1	1	2	0	2	3	1	1	3	2	0	1	0	1	0	0	0	0	0	0	0	1	0	3	0
outposts	5	.3475	.3790	35.8	0	0	0	2	3	0	0	0	0	0	0	1	0	0	0	0	0	0	0	0	0	0	1	3	0
outpouring	2	.1814	.1187	30.7	0	0	0	1	0	1	0	0	1	0	0	0	0	0	0	0	0	0	0	0	0	0	0	1	0
output	84	.6079	10.530	50.2	5	5	24	15	17	11	7	0	1	1	0	0	45	10	0	8	0	0	1	3	0	1	8	6	0
outputs	3	.3394	.2470	33.9	0	0	0	1	1	1	0	0	1	0	0	0	1	0	0	0	0	0	0	0	0	0	1	0	0
outrage	8	.3426	.6158	37.9	0	0	1	0	2	3	1	1	0	0	0	0	0	3	0	0	0	0	0	0	0	0	1	4	0
outraged	10	.4684	1.0229	40.1	0	0	2	1	5	1	0	1	2	0	0	1	0	1	0	0	0	0	0	0	4	0	0	2	0
outrageous	3	.2443	.1696	32.3	0	0	0	1	0	1	1	0	0	0	1	0	0	1	0	0	0	0	0	0	0	0	0	1	0
outran	5	.3410	.4178	36.2	1	1	0	2	1	0	0	0	2	0	0	1	0	0	0	0	0	0	0	0	2	0	0	0	0
outrigger	5	.3943	.4530	36.6	0	2	1	2	0	0	0	0	1	0	0	0	0	1	0	1	0	0	0	0	2	0	0	0	0
outright	11	.5006	1.1810	40.7	1	1	1	0	4	2	2	0	1	0	0	0	0	4	0	0	0	0	0	0	3	2	1	0	0
outrun	13	.5356	1.5112	41.8	2	0	0	6	3	1	0	1	4	0	0	0	0	1	0	1	0	0	0	0	4	1	0	2	0
outs	7	.4427	.6891	38.4	1	2	1	0	2	1	0	0	2	0	1	0	0	0	0	0	0	0	0	0	2	1	0	1	0
outset	11	.6540	1.4909	41.7	0	0	0	0	2	6	2	1	2	0	0	1	0	3	0	1	1	0	0	0	0	0	1	2	0
outshone	2	.2440	.1132	30.5	0	0	0	0	2	0	0	0	0	0	0	1	0	0	0	0	0	0	0	0	0	0	0	1	0
outside	1008	.9267	185.22	62.7	252	180	102	92	166	94	99	23	282	37	4	72	27	90	7	118	16	7	26	29	78	94	54	67	0
outsider	9	.5170	1.0412	40.2	0	3	0	0	3	1	1	1	5	0	0	1	0	0	0	0	1	0	1	0	0	0	0	1	0
outsiders	13	.6032	1.6276	42.1	1	2	1	2	3	1	3	0	1	0	0	1	0	5	0	0	0	0	1	0	0	1	1	3	0
outskirts	19	.6964	2.7318	44.4	1	5	2	3	5	0	3	0	6	0	1	0	0	1	1	1	0	0	0	0	2	3	3	1	0
outspoken	3	.2054	.1422	31.5	0	0	0	1	1	0	0	1	0	0	1	0	0	0	0	0	0	0	0	0	0	0	0	2	0
outspread	4	.2393	.3005	34.8	0	1	1	0	1	1	0	0	3	0	0	1	0	0	0	0	0	0	0	0	0	0	0	0	0
outstanding	83	.8331	13.822	51.4	3	2	10	10	17	16	17	8	10	3	1	0	2	17	2	5	8	2	3	0	0	5	13	12	0
outstandingly	2	.0857	.0784	28.9	0	0	0	1	0	1	0	0	1	0	0	0	0	0	0	0	0	0	1	0	0	0	0	0	0
outstretched	19	.5685	2.3066	43.6	2	4	4	2	1	3	2	1	5	0	0	1	4	0	0	2	0	0	0	0	5	2	0	0	0
outstrip	2	.2437	.1129	30.5	1	0	0	0	0	0	0	1	0	0	0	0	0	0	0	0	0	0	0	0	0	0	1	1	0
outward	63	.8432	10.618	50.3	2	8	3	7	18	13	12	0	7	2	0	4	1	5	1	18	4	0	0	1	3	7	5	5	0
outwardly	6	.3855	.5426	37.3	2	0	1	0	0	2	1	0	2	0	0	0	0	0	0	1	0	0	1	0	0	2	0	0	0
outwash	8	.0000	.1577	32.0	0	0	0	0	0	0	8	0	0	0	0	0	0	0	0	8	0	0	0	0	0	0	0	0	0
outwit	5	.4718	.5341	37.3	1	1	0	0	0	2	0	1	2	0	0	0	0	1	0	0	0	0	0	0	0	0	1	1	0
outwitted	8	.5352	.9173	39.6	0	1	2	0	1	2	1	1	2	2	0	1	0	0	0	0	0	0	0	0	0	2	1	0	0
oval	41	.7669	6.3050	48.0	9	3	1	6	7	6	8	1	4	0	3	1	0	0	1	4	1	2	4	3	2	6	7	3	0
Oval	2	.0000	.0243	23.9	0	0	0	0	0	0	2	0	0	0	0	0	0	0	0	0	0	0	0	0	0	0	0	2	0
oval-shaped	4	.2278	.2257	33.5	1	0	2	0	0	0	1	0	0	0	0	0	0	0	0	2	0	0	0	0	0	0	2	0	0
ovals	4	.3809	.3242	35.1	1	1	0	0	1	0	1	0	0	1	0	0	0	0	0	0	0	0	0	1	0	1	0	1	0
ovaries	6	.0000	.1183	30.7	0	1	0	0	0	0	5	0	0	0	0	0	0	0	0	6	0	0	0	0	0	0	0	0	0
ovary	29	.1312	1.2285	40.9	3	4	6	1	8	0	6	1	0	0	0	0	0	0	0	27	0	0	0	0	0	0	2	0	0
ovation	2	.2401	.1133	30.5	0	0	0	0	0	0	1	1	0	0	0	0	0	0	0	0	0	0	0	0	0	1	1	0	0
ovations	3	.0000	.0365	25.6	0	0	0	0	0	1	2	0	0	0	0	0	0	0	0	0	0	0	0	0	0	0	0	3	0
oven	128	.5843	15.700	52.0	27	29	6	8	20	13	23	2	32	7	0	3	1	7	4	9	1	0	31	4	14	8	2	5	0
ovenbird	3	.0000	.1370	31.4	3	0	0	0	0	0	0	0	3	0	0	0	0	0	0	0	0	0	0	0	0	0	0	0	0
ovens	11	.5028	1.2076	40.8	5	3	0	0	2	1	0	0	2	0	0	0	0	4	0	1	0	0	0	0	0	3	1	0	0
over	6882	.9679	1314.2	71.2	1256	1209	828	901	1317	710	519	142	2243	212	61	481	152	671	109	549	185	66	94	70	642	643	269	433	2
over-all	28	.7099	4.0241	46.0	0	0	3	6	6	3	7	3	3	0	1	2	1	0	0	3	0	0	3	2	0	4	6	3	0
over-cooked	2	.0000	.0064	18.1	0	0	0	0	1	0	1	0	0	0	0	0	0	0	0	0	0	0	2	0	0	0	0	0	0
over-used	2	.0000	.0219	23.4	0	0	0	2	0	0	0	0	0	2	0	0	0	0	0	0	0	0	0	0	0	0	0	0	0
overactivity	2	.2278	.1128	30.5	0	0	0	0	1	0	1	0	0	0	0	0	0	0	0	1	0	0	0	0	0	0	1	0	0
overall	27	.6180	3.4004	45.3	0	2	1	3	9	4	7	1	0	0	0	1	2	4	0	3	2	0	1	5	1	1	2	5	0
overalls	32	.6009	4.1708	46.2	12	9	4	2	1	2	2	0	18	0	0	2	0	0	0	0	0	0	1	0	6	2	0	3	0
overanxious	2	.2346	.1166	30.7	0	0	0	1	0	0	1	0	0	0	0	0	0	0	0	1	0	0	0	0	0	0	0	1	0
overbearing	2	.0000	.0914	29.6	0	0	0	1	1	0	0	0	2	0	0	0	0	0	0	0	0	0	0	0	0	0	0	0	0
overblouse	2	.1892	.0858	29.3	1	0	0	0	0	1	0	0	0	1	0	0	0	0	0	0	0	0	1	0	0	0	0	0	0
overboard	25	.6446	3.3743	45.3	4	3	4	2	8	3	1	0	8	0	0	0	0	1	1	1	1	0	0	0	6	3	0	4	0
overburden	4	.0000	.0419	26.2	0	0	4	0	0	0	0	0	0	0	0	0	0	0	0	0	0	0	0	0	0	0	4	0	0
overcame	13	.5502	1.5865	42.0	1	0	1	2	6	1	2	0	7	0	0	1	0	2	0	0	0	0	0	0	1	0	2	0	0
overcast	8	.4673	.8165	39.1	1	1	1	0	3	1	1	0	2	0	1	2	0	0	0	0	0	0	0	0	0	1	0	2	0

6B outfeilders
5A Outfield
5Q Outfielders
7A outfighting
XR outfitter
XR outfitters-guides
3Q outfitting
9R outflow
4A outflung
7H outflying
XP outfoxed
9R outgo
7A outgrin
5H outgrows
XH outgrowths
4A outholler
6A outjump
9L outlast
5A Outlaw
7D outlaw's
9Q outlay
8B outlive
7B outlives
7N outmaneuver
5A outmatched
XR outpatient
7A outpointing
8R outpoll
8J outpourings
4Q outproduced
8F outrace
6R outrageously
8F outrages
8R outraging
5F outranked
8R outreach
4A outride
5A outriggers
4A outrope
3P outsail
3A outshouted
9D outsi
8J Outside
9L OUTSIDE
7D Outsider
7F outsider's
9R outsize
7P outsmart
4P outsmarted
7P outsoared
9R outspokenly
7F outswim
9R outta
8D outtrick
6N outwards
3Q outweighed
8A outweighs
7A outwits
7N outwitting
7R ouzel
6Q ovalbumin
9H ovarian
7A oven's
4Q Over
XR over-anxious
9D over-clean
9L over-cooking
6A over-crédulous
3P over-crowded
9B over-generalization
6F over-grazed
7R over-long
5Q over-represented
6N over-ruling
6F over-run
8N over-sized
7R over-the-counter
7R over-the-road
XR overabundant
9Q overactive
7N overanxiousness
5N overbalanced
9D overbear
7L overbeat
8L overblouses
6R overblown
7H overbright
9L overcasting
4Q overcharge
8D overcharged
8D overcharging
9D overclouded

Word Type	F	D	U	SFI	3 Gr 3	4 Gr 4	5 Gr 5	6 Gr 6	7 Gr 7	8 Gr 8	9 Gr 9	X UnGr	A Read	B Eng & Gr	C Comp	D Lit	E Math	F Soc Stud	G Spell	H Sci	J Music	K Art	L Home Ec	M Shop	N Lib F	P Lib NF	Q Lib Ref	R Mag	S Rel
overcoat	15	.6281	1.9678	42.9	1	4	3	1	2	1	3	0	4	3	0	3	0	1	1	0	0	0	0	0	2	1	0	0	0
overcoats	6	.3785	.4921	36.9	1	3	0	1	1	0	0	0	0	0	0	0	0	1	0	0	0	1	0	0	2	2	0	0	0
overcome	95	.7814	14.953	51.7	6	9	10	14	25	12	17	2	12	7	0	6	1	12	4	20	3	2	2	2	4	4	11	4	1
overcomes	3	.0319	.0772	28.9	2	0	0	0	1	0	0	0	1	0	0	0	0	0	0	0	0	0	0	0	0	1	0	0	1
overcoming	10	.5490	1.1755	40.7	1	0	0	2	4	2	1	0	2	1	0	0	0	1	0	4	0	0	1	0	0	0	1	0	0
overcrowded	3	.3452	.2543	34.1	0	0	1	0	1	1	0	0	1	0	0	0	0	0	0	1	0	0	0	0	0	0	0	1	0
overdeveloped	3	.3465	.2515	34.0	0	1	0	0	1	1	0	0	1	0	0	0	0	0	0	0	0	0	0	0	0	1	0	1	0
overdo	3	.3764	.2475	33.9	0	0	0	0	1	1	1	0	0	1	0	1	0	1	0	0	0	0	0	0	0	0	0	0	0
overdone	3	.3772	.2437	33.9	0	1	0	0	1	0	1	0	0	0	0	0	0	0	0	0	1	0	0	0	1	1	0	0	0
overdue	2	.1733	.1149	30.6	0	0	0	0	1	1	0	0	1	1	0	0	0	0	0	0	0	0	0	0	0	0	0	0	0
overeat	2	.2300	.1140	30.6	0	0	0	0	0	1	1	0	0	1	0	0	0	0	0	1	0	0	0	0	0	0	0	0	0
overemphasis	2	.1926	.0867	29.4	0	0	0	0	0	1	1	0	0	0	0	0	0	0	0	0	0	0	1	0	0	0	1	0	0
overemphasized	2	.1033	.0599	27.8	0	0	0	0	1	0	1	0	0	0	0	0	0	0	0	1	0	1	0	0	0	0	0	0	0
overfalls	2	.0000	.0243	23.9	0	0	0	2	0	0	0	0	0	0	0	0	0	0	0	0	0	0	0	0	0	0	0	2	0
overflow	17	.6702	2.3329	43.7	3	4	4	2	3	0	1	0	1	0	0	0	0	5	2	3	0	0	0	1	0	2	1	2	0
overflowed	6	.4853	.6619	38.2	1	2	0	1	1	0	0	1	3	0	0	0	0	0	0	0	0	0	0	0	0	1	1	1	0
overflowing	13	.5775	1.6061	42.1	0	2	2	6	2	0	0	1	4	0	0	3	0	2	0	1	0	0	0	0	1	0	0	2	0
overflows	7	.4753	.7226	38.6	0	0	2	1	3	1	0	0	1	0	0	0	0	2	0	1	2	0	0	0	0	0	1	0	0
overgrown	11	.6857	1.5525	41.9	3	2	1	3	0	1	0	1	2	1	0	0	1	1	0	1	0	0	0	0	1	3	0	1	0
overhand	6	.0873	.1744	32.4	0	1	1	0	3	0	1	0	1	0	0	0	0	0	0	1	0	0	4	0	0	0	0	0	0
overhanging	9	.4801	.9838	39.9	1	2	1	1	3	0	1	0	5	0	1	1	0	0	0	0	0	0	1	0	0	1	0	0	0
overhaul	7	.3546	.5508	37.4	0	0	0	0	5	1	1	0	1	1	0	0	0	0	0	0	0	0	0	2	1	0	0	2	0
overhauled	7	.1922	.3686	35.7	0	0	6	0	0	0	1	0	0	0	0	1	0	0	0	6	0	0	0	0	0	0	0	0	0
overhauling	2	.2346	.1166	30.7	0	0	1	0	0	0	1	0	0	0	0	0	0	0	0	1	0	0	0	0	0	0	0	1	0
overhead	122	.8311	20.423	53.1	18	17	15	19	27	10	12	4	43	5	4	9	6	6	0	7	6	0	1	0	18	5	2	10	0
overhear	3	.2212	.2099	33.2	0	1	0	1	0	1	0	0	2	0	0	1	0	0	0	0	0	0	0	0	0	0	0	0	0
overheard	15	.2480	.9789	39.9	1	0	3	5	1	1	3	1	5	0	0	1	1	0	0	0	0	0	1	0	2	0	0	4	1
overheat	3	.1205	.0847	29.3	0	0	1	0	0	2	0	0	0	0	0	0	0	0	0	0	0	0	0	2	0	0	1	0	0
overheated	4	.3766	.3696	35.7	1	0	2	0	1	0	0	0	2	0	0	0	0	0	0	0	0	0	0	0	0	1	0	1	0
overhung	4	.2969	.2888	34.6	0	1	1	0	1	1	0	0	1	0	0	2	0	0	0	0	0	0	0	0	1	0	0	0	0
overhunting	3	.1813	.1402	31.5	0	0	0	0	2	1	0	0	0	0	0	0	0	0	0	1	0	0	0	0	0	0	2	0	0
overjoyed	13	.6077	1.7057	42.3	3	2	2	2	3	0	1	0	7	1	0	2	0	0	0	0	0	0	0	0	1	1	0	1	0
overlaid	2	.1483	.0728	28.6	0	0	0	0	1	0	0	1	0	0	0	0	0	0	0	0	0	0	0	1	0	1	0	0	0
overlain	2	.0000	.0394	26.0	0	0	0	0	0	0	2	0	0	0	0	0	0	0	0	2	0	0	0	0	0	0	0	0	0
overland	19	.5962	2.4061	43.8	3	1	5	2	4	2	1	1	5	0	0	0	0	6	1	0	0	0	0	0	0	4	1	2	0
Overland	4	.3813	.3772	35.8	1	1	0	1	0	1	0	0	2	0	0	0	0	1	0	0	0	0	0	0	0	1	0	0	0
overlap	27	.4443	2.5059	44.0	4	2	1	1	11	2	3	3	1	0	0	3	1	0	0	3	0	7	5	0	0	2	2	3	0
overlapping	25	.5255	2.7024	44.3	2	3	2	3	10	4	1	0	1	0	0	0	1	2	0	1	4	6	2	1	0	2	4	1	0
overlaps	2	.2427	.1152	30.6	1	0	0	0	0	0	1	0	0	0	0	0	0	0	0	0	0	0	0	0	1	1	0	0	0
overlies	2	.0000	.0394	26.0	0	0	0	0	0	0	2	0	0	0	0	0	0	0	0	2	0	0	0	0	0	0	0	0	0
overload	2	.1620	.0760	28.8	0	0	0	0	0	1	1	0	0	0	0	0	0	0	0	0	0	0	0	1	0	0	0	1	0
overloaded	4	.4856	.4085	36.1	0	0	0	1	2	1	0	0	0	0	0	0	1	0	0	0	0	0	0	0	0	1	1	1	0
overloading	3	.3234	.2368	33.7	0	1	1	0	0	0	1	0	1	0	0	0	0	0	1	0	0	0	0	0	0	1	0	0	0
overlook	22	.7905	3.4679	45.4	1	0	1	1	11	5	3	0	0	6	1	3	0	1	1	1	1	0	1	1	1	4	1	0	0
overlooked	21	.7603	3.2364	45.1	0	3	2	2	6	5	2	1	5	2	1	2	0	1	0	0	0	0	1	0	2	4	1	2	0
overlooking	26	.8024	4.2037	46.2	4	3	3	5	5	2	4	0	6	2	1	3	0	3	0	1	1	0	0	0	3	2	2	2	0
overlooks	5	.3973	.4497	36.5	1	0	1	0	2	0	0	1	1	0	0	0	0	0	0	1	0	0	0	0	0	0	2	1	0
overlords	5	.2418	.3070	34.9	2	0	1	1	0	1	0	0	1	0	0	0	0	0	0	0	0	0	0	0	0	1	3	0	0
overly	8	.4843	.8095	39.1	0	0	1	0	2	1	3	1	0	0	0	0	0	1	0	0	0	0	1	0	1	0	1	4	0
overlying	7	.0000	.1380	31.4	0	0	0	1	0	1	5	0	0	0	0	0	0	0	0	7	0	0	0	0	0	0	0	0	0
overnight	52	.8774	9.1105	49.6	11	7	11	5	8	4	4	2	14	4	1	2	0	8	1	6	1	0	1	0	4	6	2	2	0
overpass	3	.2279	.2143	33.3	0	0	0	1	2	0	0	0	2	0	0	0	0	0	0	0	0	0	0	0	0	0	0	1	0
overpopulation	3	.1823	.1405	31.5	0	0	0	0	3	0	0	0	0	0	0	0	0	1	0	0	0	0	0	0	0	0	2	0	0
overpower	4	.4209	.3528	35.5	1	0	1	0	1	0	1	0	0	0	0	0	0	0	1	0	0	0	1	0	0	1	0	1	0
overpowered	7	.5529	.8448	39.3	0	0	0	2	4	0	1	0	3	0	0	0	0	1	0	0	1	0	0	0	1	0	0	1	0
overpowering	9	.5856	1.1157	40.5	0	0	0	0	2	4	3	0	3	1	1	1	0	0	0	0	1	0	0	0	1	0	0	1	0
overran	8	.5450	.9147	39.6	0	1	0	0	4	0	3	0	0	0	0	0	0	3	1	1	0	0	0	0	0	2	0	1	0
overrated	2	.1787	.1174	30.7	0	0	0	0	1	1	0	0	1	0	0	0	0	0	0	0	0	0	0	0	1	0	0	0	0
overriding	4	.3447	.3156	35.0	1	0	1	0	1	1	0	0	0	0	0	0	0	1	0	1	0	0	0	0	0	2	0	0	0
overruled	2	.2285	.1129	30.5	0	0	1	0	0	1	0	0	0	0	0	0	0	1	0	0	0	0	0	0	0	0	1	0	0
overrun	8	.4552	.8196	39.1	0	2	0	4	2	0	0	0	2	0	0	0	0	3	0	0	0	0	0	0	0	2	0	1	0
overrunning	2	.1814	.1187	30.7	1	0	0	0	0	0	1	0	1	0	0	0	0	0	0	0	0	0	0	0	0	0	0	1	0
overseas	28	.5701	3.3558	45.3	2	3	4	5	3	5	4	2	2	2	0	2	0	15	0	0	0	0	0	0	0	1	3	3	0
overseer	16	.5103	1.7434	42.4	6	1	3	1	2	1	2	0	1	0	0	1	0	6	0	0	0	0	0	0	1	6	0	1	0
overseers	3	.0000	.0583	27.7	0	1	0	1	1	0	0	0	0	0	0	0	0	3	0	0	0	0	0	0	0	0	0	0	0
oversees	2	.2418	.1091	30.4	0	0	1	0	1	0	0	0	0	0	0	0	0	0	1	0	0	0	0	0	0	0	1	0	0
overshadows	2	.2160	.1362	31.3	1	0	0	0	0	0	0	1	1	0	0	0	0	0	0	1	0	0	0	0	0	0	0	0	0
overshoes	5	.3836	.4751	36.8	0	1	1	2	0	1	0	0	3	0	0	0	0	0	0	0	0	0	0	0	1	0	1	0	0
overside	3	.2028	.1988	33.0	0	1	1	0	1	0	0	0	2	0	0	0	0	0	0	0	1	0	0	0	0	0	0	0	0
oversight	2	.2130	.1056	30.2	0	0	0	1	1	0	0	0	0	0	0	0	0	0	1	1	0	0	0	0	0	0	0	0	0
oversimplified	2	.0000	.0243	23.9	0	0	0	0	0	0	1	1	0	0	0	0	0	0	0	0	0	0	0	0	0	0	0	2	0
oversize	6	.1813	.2558	34.1	0	1	0	0	2	0	3	0	0	0	0	0	0	1	0	0	0	0	0	3	0	0	0	2	0
oversized	6	.6031	.7561	38.8	2	0	0	1	1	1	0	1	1	0	0	1	0	0	0	1	0	0	0	0	0	1	1	1	0
overslept	2	.1387	.0689	28.4	1	0	0	0	0	1	0	0	0	0	1	0	0	0	0	0	0	0	0	0	0	1	0	0	0
overstitching	4	.0000	.0129	21.1	0	0	0	0	0	0	4	0	0	0	0	0	0	0	0	0	0	0	4	0	0	0	0	0	0
Overstreet	2	.0000	.0389	25.9	2	0	0	0	0	0	0	0	0	0	0	0	0	2	0	0	0	0	0	0	0	0	0	0	0
overt	2	.2437	.1129	30.5	0	0	0	0	2	0	0	0	0	0	0	0	0	0	0	0	0	0	0	0	0	0	1	1	0
overtake	11	.5846	1.3670	41.4	0	0	3	0	4	3	1	0	3	0	0	0	1	1	0	0	0	0	0	0	2	3	1	0	0
overtaken	7	.5640	.8563	39.3	0	2	1	1	1	0	2	0	3	0	0	1	0	0	0	0	0	0	0	0	1	1	1	0	0
overtakes	3	.2283	.1611	32.1	0	1	0	1	1	0	0	0	0	1	0	0	0	0	0	0	0	0	0	0	2	0	0	0	0
overtaking	5	.4499	.4773	36.8	0	0	0	2	2	0	1	0	0	1	0	2	0	1	0	0	0	0	0	0	0	0	0	1	0
overthrew	3	.1639	.1674	32.2	0	0	1	1	0	1	0	0	1	0	0	0	0	2	0	0	0	0	0	0	0	0	0	0	0
overthrow	8	.4651	.8215	39.1	1	0	2	2	3	0	0	0	2	0	0	0	0	1	0	0	0	0	0	0	0	1	3	1	0
overthrown	16	.6019	1.9764	43.0	2	0	2	1	6	3	2	0	0	0	0	3	0	5	1	0	1	0	0	0	2	0	4	0	0
overtime	7	.4770	.7344	38.7	0	0	0	3	2	0	1	1	2	1	0	0	0	0	0	1	0	0	1	0	0	0	0	2	0
overtired	3	.1970	.1504	31.8	0	0	1	0	0	1	1	0	0	0	0	0	0	0	0	2	0	0	1	0	0	0	0	0	0
overtone	5	.1528	.1868	32.7	0	0	2	0	0	2	1	0	0	1	0	0	0	0	0	0	4	0	0	0	0	0	0	0	0
overtones	11	.3589	.8426	39.3	0	0	2	0	3	2	4	0	0	3	0	1	0	0	0	0	6	0	0	0	0	0	0	1	0
overtook	10	.5039	1.1203	40.5	1	2	1	2	0	3	1	0	4	0	0	0	0	1	0	0	0	0	0	0	3	1	1	0	0
overture	15	.2440	.8240	39.2	0	0	3	0	5	5	2	0	0	0	0	1	0	0	0	0	11	0	0	0	0	1	0	2	0
Overture	10	.0000	.0808	29.1	0	3	0	0	5	1	1	0	0	0	0	0	0	0	0	0	10	0	0	0	0	0	0	0	0
overtures	3	.0000	.0243	23.8	0	0	0	0	2	0	1	0	0	0	0	0	0	0	0	0	3	0	0	0	0	0	0	0	0

8R Overcome
9L overcook
7A Overcrowded
9M overdisplay
9G overdoing
7P overdose
8K overdressed
6R overdrive
6R overdriving
XH overemphasize
8L overemphasizing
6A overestimated
6E overexposed
9Q overexposure
8L overfill
7Q overfishing
8A overflights
7N overflowings
9B overgoing
XH overgraze
XH overgrazed
7Q overgrazing
7D overgrow
8Q overgrowth
XR overhang
3A overhearing
7C overhears
7A overlaced
7A overlapped
XQ overleapt
6Q overloads
XH overlong
3Q overlord
5P overlordship
8A overmastered
6A overmastering
9L overmix
9L overmixed
7B overoil
7P overpast
9D overpeer
9R overplayed
7R overpopulated
6A overpowers
9D overpraise
7H overproduction
6N overreach
8F overreached
7Q overridden
XR overriders
8F overrode
9H overruns
5Q Overseas
7F overseas-tutored
4P oversee
4A overseeing
4R overseer's
9R overshadow
7A overshadowed
9D oversocks
7Q overspreading
6A oversprinkle
7H overstated
8F overstatement
7L overstays
6N overstepped
9L overstitch
XH overstretching
7N overstrung
3Q overstuffed
9Q overtaxed
7R overtaxing
9D overthrows
8Q overthrust
7M overtighten
9D overtrusting
9J Overture-Fantasie

Word Type	F	D	U	SFI	3 Gr 3	4 Gr 4	5 Gr 5	6 Gr 6	7 Gr 7	8 Gr 8	9 Gr 9	X UnGr	A Read	B Eng & Gr	C Comp	D Lit	E Math	F Soc Stud	G Spell	H Sci	J Music	K Art	L Home Ec	M Shop	N Lib F	P Lib NF	Q Lib Ref	R Mag	S Rel
overturn	6	.4682	.6381	38.0	1	0	1	0	3	1	0	0	2	0	0	0	0	2	0	1	0	0	0	0	1	0	0	0	0
overturned	15	.5440	1.8186	42.6	2	6	3	2	0	2	0	0	8	0	0	2	0	3	0	0	0	0	0	0	1	1	0	0	0
overturning	4	.3366	.3291	35.2	0	1	0	0	1	0	2	0	1	0	0	0	0	0	0	2	0	0	0	0	0	0	0	1	0
overuse	3	.2222	.1558	31.9	0	0	0	0	0	0	3	0	0	1	0	0	0	0	0	0	0	0	0	0	0	0	2	0	0
overweight	10	.2869	.6813	38.3	0	0	2	2	3	1	2	0	1	1	0	0	0	0	0	5	0	0	3	0	0	0	0	0	0
overwhelm	4	.3641	.3147	35.0	2	0	1	0	1	0	0	0	0	2	0	1	0	0	0	0	0	0	0	0	0	0	0	1	0
overwhelmed	16	.7172	2.3137	43.6	2	0	2	2	4	3	3	0	1	1	1	1	0	1	1	0	1	0	0	0	4	0	3	2	0
overwhelming	33	.7327	4.9174	46.9	0	1	6	3	10	8	5	0	4	0	0	2	0	9	0	3	2	0	0	0	3	5	1	4	0
overwhelmingly	10	.6239	1.2800	41.1	0	0	1	0	3	2	4	0	1	1	0	1	0	0	0	0	2	0	0	0	0	1	2	2	0
overwork	4	.4516	.4046	36.1	0	0	0	1	1	2	0	0	1	0	0	1	0	1	0	0	0	0	0	0	0	1	0	0	0
overworked	12	.1584	.5455	37.4	2	0	7	0	1	2	0	0	2	9	0	0	0	0	0	0	0	0	0	0	0	1	0	0	0
oviduct	8	.0900	.2261	33.5	0	0	1	0	7	0	0	0	0	0	0	0	0	0	0	1	0	0	0	0	0	0	7	0	0
oviducts	3	.0000	.0591	27.7	0	0	1	0	0	0	2	0	0	0	0	0	0	0	0	3	0	0	0	0	0	0	0	0	0
ovulation	2	.0000	.0394	26.0	0	0	0	0	0	0	2	0	0	0	0	0	0	0	0	2	0	0	0	0	0	0	0	0	0
ovule	2	.0000	.0394	26.0	0	2	0	0	0	0	0	0	0	0	0	0	0	0	0	2	0	0	0	0	0	0	0	0	0
ovules	13	.0000	.2563	34.1	0	3	1	4	2	0	3	0	0	0	0	0	0	0	0	13	0	0	0	0	0	0	0	0	0
ovum	16	.1235	.6566	38.2	0	0	0	1	0	0	13	2	0	0	0	0	0	0	0	15	0	0	0	0	0	0	1	0	0
ow	69	.0718	1.7097	42.3	20	22	5	17	2	2	1	0	6	0	0	0	0	0	61	0	0	0	0	0	1	0	0	1	0
owe	32	.6805	4.5078	46.5	2	6	3	9	7	2	2	1	8	0	0	2	1	4	0	2	0	0	0	0	4	7	0	4	0
owed	29	.3905	2.5887	44.1	5	2	2	7	4	6	3	0	7	2	0	3	2	4	1	0	0	0	0	0	2	2	4	1	1
Owen	8	.6293	1.0362	40.2	1	0	0	0	1	2	2	2	0	1	0	0	0	2	0	2	0	0	0	0	0	1	1	1	0
Owen's	2	.2388	.1089	30.4	0	2	0	0	0	0	0	0	0	0	0	0	0	0	1	0	0	0	0	0	1	0	0	0	0
Owens	12	.5329	1.3633	41.3	0	1	1	1	2	4	3	0	1	0	0	0	0	6	0	1	0	0	0	0	1	0	1	2	0
owes	22	.7002	3.1512	45.0	3	0	1	4	5	1	7	1	4	3	0	2	0	4	0	0	1	0	0	0	1	1	5	1	0
owing	20	.7461	3.0135	44.8	0	1	1	1	8	6	0	3	2	1	0	3	0	1	0	2	1	0	0	0	2	2	4	2	0
owl	137	.7745	21.906	53.4	58	30	8	15	23	2	0	1	91	5	2	13	0	0	4	5	3	1	0	0	4	5	1	3	0
Owl	21	.6638	2.9518	44.7	13	3	0	2	1	2	0	0	12	1	1	0	0	0	1	0	1	1	0	0	2	2	0	0	0
owl's	9	.2926	.7527	38.8	2	3	0	2	2	0	0	0	7	0	0	1	0	0	0	0	0	1	0	0	0	0	0	0	0
Owl's	3	.2031	.1990	33.0	3	0	0	0	0	0	0	0	2	0	0	0	0	0	1	0	0	0	0	0	0	0	0	0	0
owlish	2	.0000	.0914	29.6	2	0	0	0	0	0	0	0	2	0	0	0	0	0	0	0	0	0	0	0	0	0	0	0	0
owls	47	.6560	6.4851	48.1	14	9	4	4	9	4	2	1	19	0	2	5	0	0	0	8	0	0	0	0	0	3	6	4	0
Owls	5	.0000	.2284	33.6	0	3	0	0	0	2	0	0	5	0	0	0	0	0	0	0	0	0	0	0	0	0	0	0	0
own	3006	.9708	575.23	67.6	447	441	380	390	576	405	292	75	661	177	41	208	36	356	182	243	212	55	51	15	153	237	186	190	3
Own	24	.4127	2.0868	43.2	8	3	4	5	2	0	0	2	0	0	0	0	0	0	13	1	2	0	0	0	5	1	0	2	0
owned	198	.8033	32.118	55.1	37	32	20	22	37	28	16	6	46	7	1	10	3	59	1	0	5	1	0	0	10	32	6	17	0
owner	172	.8008	27.915	54.5	38	28	21	26	28	19	9	3	65	14	7	4	1	11	7	2	3	0	0	0	9	22	13	14	0
Owner	3	.2309	.1631	32.1	0	1	0	0	2	0	0	0	0	0	0	1	0	0	0	0	0	0	0	0	0	0	0	2	0
owner's	5	.5333	.5702	37.6	1	0	2	0	0	0	0	2	1	1	0	0	0	0	0	1	0	0	0	0	0	0	1	1	0
owners	108	.7525	16.498	52.2	13	15	18	13	25	13	9	2	19	3	0	3	0	29	2	0	1	0	0	1	6	12	14	18	0
ownership	46	.6098	5.7572	47.6	12	5	8	6	6	5	4	0	2	19	1	2	0	9	5	0	0	0	0	0	0	1	6	1	0
owning	20	.4915	2.1549	43.3	5	2	1	3	4	1	3	1	4	0	0	1	0	8	0	0	0	0	0	0	0	2	0	5	0
owns	60	.7857	9.5514	49.8	18	5	10	11	7	2	4	3	15	3	0	0	5	15	4	1	1	0	0	0	6	3	2	5	0
owre	3	.0000	.0328	25.2	0	0	0	0	0	3	0	0	0	3	0	0	0	0	0	0	0	0	0	0	0	0	0	0	0
ox	57	.6149	7.5265	48.8	22	9	6	4	7	7	2	0	30	2	0	2	0	2	10	0	0	0	0	0	6	0	4	1	0
Ox	5	.2025	.3254	35.1	0	1	1	0	3	0	0	0	3	0	0	2	0	0	0	0	0	0	0	0	0	0	0	0	0
ox-drawn	3	.2063	.1600	32.0	0	2	0	1	0	0	0	0	0	0	0	0	0	1	0	0	0	0	0	0	0	2	0	0	0
oxcart	5	.3852	.4868	36.9	1	3	0	1	0	0	0	0	3	0	0	0	0	1	0	1	0	0	0	0	0	0	0	0	0
oxcarts	7	.3633	.6318	38.0	2	0	0	4	1	0	0	0	3	0	0	0	0	3	0	0	0	0	0	0	0	0	0	1	0
oxen	73	.6874	10.467	50.2	10	19	16	10	11	4	2	1	27	0	2	1	0	23	2	0	3	0	0	0	4	10	1	0	0
Oxenthorpe	4	.2417	.3028	34.8	0	1	3	0	0	0	0	0	3	0	0	0	0	0	0	0	0	0	0	0	1	0	0	0	0
Oxford	16	.5808	1.9083	42.8	0	1	4	2	1	4	4	0	0	0	0	0	2	0	0	1	2	0	0	0	1	3	6	1	0
oxidation	20	.4525	1.9662	42.9	1	0	1	1	9	3	4	1	1	0	0	0	0	0	0	12	0	0	0	2	0	0	3	2	0
oxide	51	.4041	4.5825	46.6	2	6	9	3	6	12	13	0	2	0	0	2	0	0	0	36	0	0	0	6	0	1	4	0	0
oxides	12	.4691	1.2236	40.9	1	0	1	0	2	3	4	1	1	0	0	0	0	0	0	7	0	0	0	1	0	0	1	2	0
oxidize	3	.1785	.1397	31.5	0	0	0	1	2	0	0	0	0	0	0	0	0	0	0	2	0	0	0	1	0	0	0	0	0
oxidized	7	.2980	.5238	37.2	0	0	1	1	2	0	2	1	2	0	0	0	0	0	0	2	0	0	0	0	0	0	3	0	0
oxidizer	8	.2014	.4333	36.4	0	0	0	1	1	1	5	0	0	0	0	0	0	0	1	7	0	0	0	0	0	0	0	0	0
oxtail	2	.2446	.1142	30.6	0	0	0	0	1	0	0	1	0	0	0	0	0	0	0	0	0	0	0	0	1	0	0	1	0
oxyacetylene	2	.0000	.0050	17.0	0	0	0	0	0	0	2	0	0	0	0	0	0	0	0	0	0	0	0	2	0	0	0	0	0
oxygen	625	.4359	60.366	57.8	127	82	105	56	137	71	41	6	26	5	0	0	9	0	0	500	2	0	2	10	1	17	42	11	0
oy	17	.0555	.4221	36.3	3	4	4	3	1	2	0	0	3	0	0	0	0	0	14	0	0	0	0	0	0	0	0	0	0
oyez	3	.0000	.0583	27.7	0	0	0	0	0	3	0	0	0	0	0	0	0	3	0	0	0	0	0	0	0	0	0	0	0
oyster	42	.7574	6.4571	48.1	3	9	0	7	20	1	1	1	9	2	0	7	0	5	1	5	5	0	0	0	5	1	1	1	0
Oyster	3	.2187	.1555	31.9	0	0	0	0	3	0	0	0	0	2	0	0	0	0	0	0	0	0	0	0	0	0	0	1	0
oysters	33	.6893	4.7342	46.8	4	2	2	6	10	4	5	0	11	3	0	2	0	2	0	9	1	0	0	0	0	4	1	0	0
Oysters	11	.2508	.6578	38.2	0	0	0	0	11	0	0	0	1	7	0	3	0	0	0	0	0	0	0	0	0	0	0	0	0
oz	12	.2485	.7136	38.5	0	0	1	3	4	3	0	1	0	0	0	0	10	0	1	0	0	0	0	0	0	0	0	1	0
Oz	2	.2446	.1123	30.5	0	1	0	0	0	0	1	0	0	1	0	0	0	0	0	0	0	0	0	0	0	0	1	0	0
Ozark	6	.0971	.2435	33.9	0	0	6	0	0	0	0	0	1	0	0	0	0	5	0	0	0	0	0	0	0	0	0	0	0
Ozerov	2	.0000	.0914	29.6	0	0	0	2	0	0	0	0	2	0	0	0	0	0	0	0	0	0	0	0	0	0	0	0	0
Ozma	2	.0000	.0243	23.9	0	0	0	0	2	0	0	0	0	0	0	0	0	0	0	0	0	0	0	0	0	0	0	2	0
ozone	2	.2278	.1128	30.5	0	0	0	0	1	0	1	0	0	0	0	0	0	0	0	1	0	0	0	0	0	0	1	0	0
Ozymandias	3	.0000	.0328	25.2	0	0	0	3	0	0	0	0	0	3	0	0	0	0	0	0	0	0	0	0	0	0	0	0	0
p	259	.8028	41.606	56.2	19	25	14	26	69	33	31	42	14	9	0	2	70	10	34	20	15	7	1	4	0	32	4	37	0
P	188	.5898	22.952	53.6	11	9	7	12	71	48	26	4	6	6	2	3	131	3	1	8	0	1	0	5	2	3	8	9	0
P**	73	.6815	10.223	50.1	13	21	4	3	7	18	7	0	10	3	0	5	23	3	0	13	0	0	0	0	3	4	0	9	0
pH	4	.2287	.2348	33.7	0	0	0	0	0	3	0	1	0	0	0	0	0	0	0	3	0	0	0	0	0	0	0	1	0
P'an	6	.0000	.0869	29.4	6	0	0	0	0	0	0	0	0	0	0	0	0	0	0	0	0	0	0	0	0	6	0	0	0
p'ison	2	.0000	.0162	22.1	2	0	0	0	0	0	0	0	0	0	0	0	0	0	0	0	2	0	0	0	0	0	0	0	0
pa	10	.4411	1.0282	40.1	2	2	1	0	2	3	0	0	5	0	0	1	0	0	0	0	0	0	0	0	3	1	0	0	0
Pa	290	.4831	31.007	54.9	5	74	128	29	27	9	18	0	95	0	0	30	0	0	0	0	1	0	0	0	107	50	5	2	0
PA	7	.0000	.1048	30.2	0	2	0	0	3	2	0	0	0	0	0	0	7	0	0	0	0	0	0	0	0	0	0	0	0
pa's	3	.3394	.2451	33.9	0	1	0	0	2	0	0	0	1	0	0	1	0	0	0	0	0	0	0	0	1	0	0	0	0
Pa's	19	.3487	1.6440	42.2	0	3	7	6	2	1	0	0	9	0	0	3	0	0	0	0	0	0	0	0	7	0	0	0	0
Pablito	2	.0000	.0914	29.6	0	1	0	0	1	0	0	0	2	0	0	0	0	0	0	0	0	0	0	0	0	0	0	0	0
Pablo	42	.4886	4.9052	46.9	17	11	0	0	10	3	1	0	36	1	0	2	0	0	0	0	0	1	0	0	0	1	0	1	0
Pablo's	2	.1717	.1142	30.6	1	0	0	0	0	1	0	0	1	0	0	1	0	0	0	0	0	0	0	0	0	0	0	0	0
pace	99	.8258	16.420	52.2	7	15	12	10	17	18	14	6	25	1	2	8	4	6	0	2	5	3	0	0	7	11	7	18	0
paced	15	.6964	2.1767	43.4	4	1	2	6	0	1	0	1	7	1	0	0	1	0	1	0	2	0	0	0	1	1	0	1	0
pacemaker	6	.1116	.1956	32.9	0	0	0	0	0	2	4	0	0	0	0	0	0	0	0	1	0	0	0	0	0	0	5	0	0
pacer	6	.3824	.5759	37.6	0	0	5	0	0	1	0	0	4	0	0	0	0	0	0	0	1	0	0	0	1	0	0	0	0
paces	22	.6368	2.9041	44.6	0	4	2	8	5	1	2	0	5	0	0	3	0	1	3	0	2	0	0	0	5	0	0	3	0
pacific	6	.4424	.5970	37.8	0	0	0	0	3	3	0	0	2	0	0	1	0	0	0	0	0	0	0	0	0	0	2	1	0

5B overused
7A overviewing
9R overweening
8L overwhelms
7L overwhip
5B overworking
9Q ovipositor
5P Oviraptor
7Q ovoviviparous
5A Owens-Adair
4R owl-like
3C owlet
3A owlets
7P own-ness
5Q owner-operated
5A owners'
8N ownin'
7P Owuo
XH OX
9D ox-beef
4A ox-carts
4N oxblood
7R oxbow
4H oxen's
5F oxhides
9H oxidizers
9Q oxidizing
7Q oxpecker
7D oxsters
4N oxygen-hydrogen-carbon
9Q oxygenated
9Q oxygenates
9H oxymuriatic
7H oxytocin
XH OY
4F oy**
8A oyster-fishermen
8A oyster-fishing
9D oyster-stew
7A oyster's
5N oysterer
4P oystermen
3N Oysterville
7R Ozarks
7N Ozell
7H O2
7P PTs
6N p-p-performance
6N p-p-pop
6N p-paddock
5Q P-shaped
8H P-type
4P P-u-m-p
8F p-47
7E p%
3A prk
3A pt
7N p'r'aps
9B p's
9D Pa'd
6R PA'S
5R Paar
8Q Paardeberg
7Q pablum
7E PAC
7Q pacas
7Q Paccard
6A pacemakers
7R Pachacamac
4N Pachyderm

Word Type	F	D	U	SFI	3 Gr 3	4 Gr 4	5 Gr 5	6 Gr 6	7 Gr 7	8 Gr 8	9 Gr 9	X UnGr	A Read	B Eng & Gr	C Comp	D Lit	E Math	F Soc Stud	G Spell	H Sci	J Music	K Art	L Home Ec	M Shop	N Lib F	P Lib NF	Q Lib Ref	R Mag	S Rel
Pacific	386	.7332	57.662	57.6	23	58	70	74	81	44	25	11	45	4	6	6	6	165	2	50	7	0	0	0	6	16	37	36	0
pacifist	3	.1277	.1363	31.3	0	0	0	0	1	1	1	0	1	0	0	0	0	0	0	0	0	0	0	0	0	0	0	2	0
pacing	10	.4694	1.0947	40.4	0	2	4	1	3	0	0	0	6	0	0	0	0	0	0	0	0	0	0	0	1	1	0	2	0
pack	197	.8953	35.149	55.5	34	36	23	43	33	12	13	3	66	4	2	17	12	16	9	5	1	0	5	2	25	18	4	11	0
Pack	2	.2408	.1091	30.4	1	0	0	0	1	0	0	0	0	1	0	0	0	0	1	0	0	0	0	0	0	0	0	0	0
pack-horse	2	.1814	.1187	30.7	0	0	0	1	1	0	0	0	1	0	0	0	0	0	0	0	0	0	0	0	0	0	0	1	0
package	159	.8364	26.666	54.3	34	31	20	13	28	18	11	4	40	11	2	5	31	2	3	10	0	2	13	2	15	8	1	14	0
Package	2	.0000	.0243	23.9	0	0	0	0	2	0	0	0	0	0	0	0	0	0	0	0	0	0	0	0	0	0	0	2	0
packaged	20	.4220	1.8080	42.6	2	0	5	0	7	3	2	1	1	0	0	0	0	3	0	2	0	0	5	0	0	0	6	3	0
packages	86	.7199	12.648	51.0	19	7	21	11	13	10	3	2	15	1	1	1	36	12	1	3	0	0	3	0	2	4	2	5	0
packaging	6	.2881	.3805	35.8	0	0	1	0	0	0	4	1	0	0	0	0	0	0	0	0	0	0	2	0	0	1	0	3	0
Packard	3	.2257	.1583	32.0	0	0	0	0	2	0	1	0	0	2	0	1	0	0	0	0	0	0	0	0	0	0	0	0	0
packed	162	.8205	26.765	54.3	26	34	20	20	36	15	8	3	44	6	1	8	19	21	0	10	0	1	12	0	14	12	4	10	0
packer	5	.3529	.4006	36.0	1	0	0	0	1	1	0	2	0	0	0	0	0	1	0	2	0	0	0	0	0	0	0	2	0
Packer	2	.0000	.0243	23.9	0	0	0	2	0	0	0	0	0	0	0	0	0	0	0	0	0	0	0	0	0	0	0	2	0
packers	3	.1639	.1674	32.2	2	0	0	1	0	0	0	0	1	0	0	0	0	2	0	0	0	0	0	0	0	0	0	0	0
Packers	10	.0000	.1215	30.8	0	0	0	8	0	1	1	0	0	0	0	0	0	0	0	0	0	0	0	0	0	0	0	10	0
packet	26	.4407	2.5784	44.1	11	4	1	2	7	1	0	0	7	0	0	0	0	0	0	1	0	0	0	0	4	12	0	2	0
packets	14	.6882	1.9679	42.9	4	0	2	2	2	3	1	0	1	1	0	0	2	0	0	4	1	0	0	0	0	3	1	1	0
packing	56	.7905	8.9199	49.5	14	11	5	7	11	4	4	0	8	0	0	5	5	16	0	2	0	0	3	1	4	4	3	5	0
packs	25	.7220	3.7132	45.7	7	6	2	2	3	3	2	0	8	1	0	0	4	1	0	1	0	0	0	0	2	2	2	4	0
packsack	4	.2424	.3036	34.8	0	0	0	3	1	0	0	0	3	0	0	0	0	0	0	0	0	0	0	0	0	0	0	1	0
Paco	2	.0000	.0389	25.9	0	2	0	0	0	0	0	0	0	0	0	0	0	2	0	0	0	0	0	0	0	0	0	0	0
pact	10	.1236	.3733	35.7	0	0	7	0	1	0	2	0	1	0	0	0	0	1	0	0	0	0	0	0	0	0	8	0	0
Pact	9	.2975	.6022	37.8	0	0	3	0	3	3	0	0	0	0	0	0	0	1	0	0	0	0	0	0	0	0	5	3	0
pacts	2	.0000	.0243	23.9	0	0	1	1	0	0	0	0	0	0	0	0	0	0	0	0	0	0	0	0	0	0	0	2	0
pacus	3	.0000	.0314	25.0	0	0	0	0	3	0	0	0	0	0	0	0	0	0	0	0	0	0	0	0	0	0	3	0	0
pad	86	.7644	13.341	51.3	4	16	7	8	20	15	12	4	25	4	0	2	5	1	0	8	2	2	9	6	10	5	2	5	0
padded	20	.6451	2.7115	44.3	2	4	1	4	7	0	1	1	8	0	0	3	0	1	0	0	1	1	0	0	4	0	1	1	0
paddies	6	.3545	.5377	37.3	0	3	1	0	1	0	1	0	3	0	0	0	0	1	0	0	0	0	0	0	0	2	0	0	0
padding	6	.3393	.4626	36.7	1	1	0	0	2	0	2	0	1	0	0	1	0	0	0	1	0	0	2	0	0	0	0	1	0
paddle	62	.8030	10.108	50.0	18	12	6	9	14	2	1	0	26	1	0	2	1	5	2	1	4	0	0	0	8	5	3	4	0
Paddle	3	.0000	.1370	31.4	3	0	0	0	0	0	0	0	3	0	0	0	0	0	0	0	0	0	0	0	0	0	0	0	0
paddle-wheel	4	.3829	.3404	35.3	0	1	1	1	1	0	0	0	0	0	0	0	0	2	0	0	0	0	0	0	0	1	1	0	0
paddled	32	.6320	4.3328	46.4	4	3	8	7	8	2	0	0	16	0	0	2	0	8	0	0	2	0	0	0	1	1	0	2	0
paddles	39	.6954	5.5808	47.5	13	4	5	10	6	0	1	0	9	1	0	10	0	7	0	3	1	1	0	1	0	6	0	0	0
paddling	26	.6918	3.7183	45.7	3	7	3	6	6	0	1	0	9	2	1	1	0	0	0	0	4	0	0	0	3	4	0	2	0
paddock	8	.3278	.6009	37.8	0	0	0	2	5	1	0	0	1	0	0	1	0	0	0	0	0	0	0	0	5	0	0	1	0
Paddock	2	.0000	.0234	23.7	0	0	0	0	2	0	0	0	0	0	0	0	0	0	0	0	0	0	0	0	2	0	0	0	0
paddocks	2	.0000	.0234	23.7	0	0	0	0	1	1	0	0	0	0	0	0	0	0	0	0	0	0	0	0	2	0	0	0	0
paddy	16	.3884	1.4651	41.7	2	6	0	2	2	3	1	0	4	0	0	0	0	9	0	0	0	0	0	0	0	2	0	1	0
Paddy	8	.2333	.4457	36.5	0	1	6	1	0	0	0	0	0	0	0	0	0	0	0	0	2	0	0	0	0	6	0	0	0
padlock	3	.2212	.2099	33.2	0	0	2	0	1	0	0	0	2	0	0	1	0	0	0	0	0	0	0	0	0	0	0	0	0
padlocked	2	.1814	.1187	30.7	0	1	0	0	0	0	1	0	1	0	0	0	0	0	0	0	0	0	0	0	0	0	0	1	0
padlocks	2	.1717	.1142	30.6	0	0	0	0	1	1	0	0	1	0	0	1	0	0	0	0	0	0	0	0	0	0	0	0	0
padre	6	.2045	.3270	35.1	0	5	0	0	0	0	1	0	0	0	0	1	0	5	0	0	0	0	0	0	0	0	0	0	0
Padre	2	.0000	.0389	25.9	0	2	0	0	0	0	0	0	0	0	0	0	0	2	0	0	0	0	0	0	0	0	0	0	0
padres	10	.0000	.1945	32.9	1	9	0	0	0	0	0	0	0	0	0	0	0	10	0	0	0	0	0	0	0	0	0	0	0
Padres	2	.0000	.0243	23.9	0	1	0	0	0	1	0	0	0	0	0	0	0	0	0	0	0	0	0	0	0	0	0	2	0
padres’	2	.0000	.0389	25.9	0	2	0	0	0	0	0	0	0	0	0	0	0	2	0	0	0	0	0	0	0	0	0	0	0
pads	26	.7426	3.9161	45.9	4	4	2	6	5	1	4	0	4	0	0	0	1	1	0	4	2	0	1	0	1	4	5	3	0
Padua	8	.4811	.8411	39.2	1	0	0	0	3	1	3	0	2	0	0	3	1	0	0	0	0	0	0	0	0	1	1	0	0
Paducah	2	.2407	.1138	30.6	0	2	0	0	0	0	0	0	0	0	0	1	0	0	0	0	0	0	0	0	0	1	0	0	0
pagan	13	.6574	1.7368	42.4	2	0	1	1	3	1	3	2	0	1	0	2	0	2	0	1	1	0	0	0	1	1	4	0	0
pagans	3	.0000	.0314	25.0	2	0	0	0	0	0	1	0	0	0	0	0	0	0	0	0	0	0	0	0	0	0	3	0	0
page	2831	.7528	429.67	66.3	402	549	458	522	420	294	171	15	276	258	16	21	232	459	679	358	171	156	97	7	8	37	15	41	0
Page	21	.3862	2.1131	43.2	4	5	0	8	1	1	0	2	17	0	0	1	0	1	0	2	0	0	0	0	0	0	0	0	0
pageant	12	.5413	1.3309	41.2	1	1	1	0	6	0	3	0	0	2	2	3	0	1	1	0	0	0	0	0	1	0	2	0	0
Pageant	2	.0000	.0234	23.7	0	0	2	0	0	0	0	0	0	0	0	0	0	0	0	0	0	0	0	0	2	0	0	0	0
pageantry	4	.3160	.2709	34.3	1	1	0	0	0	1	1	0	0	0	1	0	0	0	0	0	2	0	0	0	0	1	0	0	0
pageants	3	.3852	.2500	34.0	0	1	1	0	0	0	1	0	0	0	0	1	0	0	0	0	0	0	0	0	0	1	0	1	0
pages	723	.8648	124.57	61.0	93	120	106	159	128	51	55	11	85	131	4	11	86	173	37	57	26	19	20	4	5	11	24	30	0
Pages	3	.2223	.2106	33.2	1	1	1	0	0	0	0	0	2	1	0	0	0	0	0	0	0	0	0	0	0	0	0	0	0
pagoda	5	.2086	.3320	35.2	0	1	0	2	2	0	0	0	3	0	0	0	0	0	0	0	0	0	0	0	2	0	0	0	0
pah	3	.0000	.1370	31.4	2	0	0	0	0	1	0	0	3	0	0	0	0	0	0	0	0	0	0	0	0	0	0	0	0
Pah-Utes	2	.0000	.0290	24.6	2	0	0	0	0	0	0	0	0	0	0	0	0	0	0	0	0	0	0	0	0	2	0	0	0
paid	392	.8632	67.663	58.3	63	50	45	51	80	55	39	9	97	13	2	22	71	57	4	6	4	0	8	0	33	33	16	26	0
Paige	4	.3097	.2992	34.8	0	0	0	0	3	1	0	0	1	0	0	1	0	0	0	0	0	0	0	0	0	0	0	2	0
pail	78	.7628	12.274	50.9	20	27	0	13	8	7	2	1	45	6	0	1	0	2	5	3	3	0	0	1	5	6	0	1	0
pails	22	.5373	2.5876	44.1	10	7	1	1	2	1	0	0	10	0	2	2	0	0	0	0	0	0	0	2	1	5	0	0	0
Paimpol	2	.0000	.0914	29.6	0	0	0	2	0	0	0	0	2	0	0	0	0	0	0	0	0	0	0	0	0	0	0	0	0
pain	198	.7835	31.496	55.0	14	31	22	25	57	28	17	4	62	9	0	35	0	4	1	34	2	0	4	0	10	13	10	14	0
Pain-Killer	5	.0000	.2284	33.6	0	0	0	0	5	0	0	0	5	0	0	0	0	0	0	0	0	0	0	0	0	0	0	0	0
pain-filled	2	.0000	.0914	29.6	0	1	1	0	0	0	0	0	2	0	0	0	0	0	0	0	0	0	0	0	0	0	0	0	0
pain-killer	2	.2440	.1132	30.5	0	0	0	0	1	0	1	0	0	0	0	1	0	0	0	0	0	0	0	0	0	0	0	1	0
pained	4	.1717	.2284	33.6	1	0	0	0	2	1	0	0	2	0	0	2	0	0	0	0	0	0	0	0	0	0	0	0	0
painful	36	.6639	4.9665	47.0	1	5	3	4	15	3	1	4	10	0	0	2	0	1	0	4	1	0	0	0	3	2	2	11	0
painfully	25	.5736	3.0465	44.8	0	0	6	2	6	6	2	3	6	0	0	1	0	3	0	1	0	0	0	0	4	2	0	8	0
painless	3	.2143	.1568	32.0	0	1	0	0	1	1	0	0	0	0	0	0	0	0	0	0	0	0	0	0	0	1	0	2	0
painlessly	3	.3811	.2534	34.0	0	1	1	1	0	0	0	0	0	0	0	0	0	0	0	1	0	0	0	0	0	1	0	1	0
pains	33	.7785	5.2070	47.2	0	0	1	10	6	10	5	1	8	0	0	5	0	6	1	3	1	0	1	0	3	2	0	3	0
painstaking	8	.5635	.9452	39.8	0	1	0	1	0	0	4	2	1	0	0	1	0	0	0	1	0	0	0	0	0	1	2	2	0
painstakingly	5	.3973	.4497	36.5	1	0	0	0	2	0	1	1	1	0	0	0	0	0	0	1	0	0	0	0	0	0	2	1	0
paint	437	.4126	39.625	56.0	123	99	32	59	56	26	30	12	102	13	6	5	38	12	7	11	11	145	3	23	12	22	7	20	0
Paint	5	.5392	.5735	37.6	1	2	0	0	0	1	0	1	1	0	0	1	0	0	0	0	0	0	0	0	1	1	0	1	0
paintbox	3	.0000	.1370	31.4	3	0	0	0	0	0	0	0	3	0	0	0	0	0	0	0	0	0	0	0	0	0	0	0	0
paintbrush	3	.3231	.2367	33.7	3	0	0	0	0	0	0	0	1	0	0	0	0	0	0	0	1	0	0	0	0	1	0	0	0
paintbrushes	4	.4514	.3996	36.0	1	2	1	0	0	0	0	0	1	1	0	0	0	0	0	0	0	0	0	0	0	1	1	0	0
painted	294	.5173	32.533	55.1	85	69	19	27	59	14	14	7	73	3	2	22	25	16	1	2	11	61	1	3	13	25	13	23	0
Painted	4	.2297	.2271	33.6	0	0	2	0	2	0	0	0	0	0	0	2	0	2	0	0	0	0	0	0	0	0	0	0	0
painter	70	.3391	5.2407	47.2	6	12	3	3	15	17	11	3	9	0	0	4	2	0	2	0	3	23	0	0	2	3	17	5	0
Painter	2	.2437	.1129	30.5	0	0	0	0	0	1	1	0	0	0	0	0	0	0	0	0	0	0	0	0	0	0	1	1	0
painter’s	2	.2417	.1091	30.4	0	0	1	0	0	1	0	0	0	0	0	0	0	0	0	0	1	0	0	0	0	0	1	0	0
painters	44	.2806	2.7283	44.4	6	1	9	1	3	13	9	2	2	2	0	1	0	4	0	0	3	17	0	0	1	1	13	0	0
painting	244	.3072	16.536	52.2	29	36	20	33	53	33	24	16	23	13	0	9	4	12	3	3	27	103	0	3	1	9	18	16	0
Painting	2	.0000	.0209	23.2	0	0	1	0	0	0	1	0	0	0	0	0	0	0	0	0	0	0	0	0	0	0	2	0	0

7A Pacificator
4N pacified
9B pacifier
3P Packet
XR Packing
6H packing-boxes
6H packing-cases
8Q pacta
7N paddle-steamer
7N paddle-wheels
7Q paddlefish
6A paddlelike
6R paddlewheels
5P Paddy’s
7J Paderewski
9Q paeans
7L Paese
3P Paestum
5B paff
9D page’s
9L pageboy
8F pagodalike
7N pagodas
7D Pagosa
9H pah-ree-koo-teen
6N pahua
8D paid-for
6R Paihia
6A paijaik
XR Paik
XR Paik’s
5N pailful
7A pain-crazed
7R pain-killers
5A pain-relieving
7F Paine
7N Painkiller
XR paint-by-the-number
4N paint-can
6A paint-spotted
3K paint’s
8R painterliness
6A paintin’

Word Type	F	D	U	SFI	3 Gr 3	4 Gr 4	5 Gr 5	6 Gr 6	7 Gr 7	8 Gr 8	9 Gr 9	X UnGr	A Read	B Eng & Gr	C Comp	D Lit	E Math	F Soc Stud	G Spell	H Sci	J Music	K Art	L Home Ec	M Shop	N Lib F	P Lib NF	Q Lib Ref	R Mag	S Rel
paintings	145	.3197	10.420	50.2	31	32	10	12	20	22	10	8	18	2	0	5	0	21	2	2	8	52	0	1	0	4	12	18	0
paints	62	.4494	5.9854	47.8	24	14	8	1	8	3	4	0	10	4	0	1	4	4	0	0	1	16	0	5	0	11	3	3	0
pair	724	.7503	110.01	60.4	86	136	111	114	127	97	46	7	103	48	4	28	329	6	53	36	13	1	2	2	31	23	14	31	0
paired	50	.2307	2.8309	44.5	4	4	4	17	4	4	13	0	0	1	0	0	44	0	1	1	0	0	0	0	0	1	2	0	0
pairing	12	.2342	.6800	38.3	4	3	0	1	1	1	2	0	0	0	1	0	11	0	0	0	0	0	0	0	0	0	0	0	0
pairings	11	.0000	.1647	32.2	0	5	5	1	0	0	0	0	0	0	0	0	11	0	0	0	0	0	0	0	0	0	0	0	0
pairs	455	.5747	54.429	57.4	54	76	89	84	51	58	36	7	26	40	2	0	259	3	53	42	4	0	0	1	6	5	8	6	0
paisano	7	.0000	.0851	29.3	0	7	0	0	0	0	0	0	0	0	0	0	0	0	0	0	0	0	0	0	0	0	0	7	0
paisley	2	.2388	.1089	30.4	0	0	0	0	0	2	0	0	0	0	0	0	0	0	1	0	0	0	0	0	1	0	0	0	0
pajama	2	.1733	.1149	30.6	0	0	0	1	0	0	1	0	1	1	0	0	0	0	0	0	0	0	0	0	0	0	0	0	0
pajamas	46	.5608	5.8737	47.7	4	1	2	32	2	1	3	1	38	1	0	1	0	0	0	1	0	0	1	0	1	1	0	2	0
Pakaa	24	.0000	1.0964	40.4	24	0	0	0	0	0	0	0	24	0	0	0	0	0	0	0	0	0	0	0	0	0	0	0	0
pakehas	2	.0000	.0290	24.6	0	0	2	0	0	0	0	0	0	0	0	0	0	0	0	0	0	0	0	0	0	2	0	0	0
Pakistan	33	.3233	2.4838	44.0	0	0	1	13	13	5	1	0	0	1	0	0	0	25	0	0	0	0	0	0	0	0	6	1	0
pal	31	.5491	3.6912	45.7	10	2	5	3	6	3	1	1	12	10	0	1	0	0	0	1	1	0	0	0	2	0	0	4	0
Pal	4	.1757	.1672	32.2	3	0	0	0	0	1	0	0	0	1	0	0	0	0	3	0	0	0	0	0	0	0	0	0	0
pal's	2	.2442	.1134	30.5	0	1	0	0	0	1	0	0	0	1	0	0	0	0	0	0	0	0	0	0	0	0	0	1	0
palace	159	.7261	24.002	53.8	58	21	21	31	13	8	7	0	86	5	0	6	0	13	3	0	11	2	0	0	13	5	6	8	1
Palace	34	.6616	4.7112	46.7	6	7	11	1	1	5	2	1	14	0	0	0	0	0	0	0	2	1	0	0	5	2	4	6	0
palaces	34	.5583	4.0401	46.1	4	4	5	9	6	4	1	1	5	3	0	0	0	19	1	0	2	0	0	0	0	1	3	0	0
palanquin	2	.0000	.0234	23.7	0	0	0	0	2	0	0	0	0	0	0	0	0	0	0	0	0	0	0	0	2	0	0	0	0
palatable	2	.1432	.0759	28.8	0	0	0	0	0	1	0	1	0	0	0	0	0	0	0	1	0	0	1	0	0	0	0	0	0
palate	3	.3668	.2405	33.8	0	0	0	0	0	0	1	2	0	0	0	0	0	0	0	1	1	0	0	0	0	0	1	0	0
Palatine	4	.4858	.4029	36.1	0	1	0	1	0	1	1	0	0	0	0	1	0	0	1	0	0	0	0	0	1	0	1	0	0
Palatium	2	.0000	.0162	22.1	0	0	0	2	0	0	0	0	0	0	0	0	0	0	2	0	0	0	0	0	0	0	0	0	0
Palawan	2	.0000	.0209	23.2	2	0	0	0	0	0	0	0	0	0	0	0	0	0	0	0	0	0	0	0	0	0	2	0	0
pale	167	.7852	26.608	54.3	28	17	16	17	55	10	20	4	57	1	1	35	0	3	4	12	3	1	7	0	23	12	1	7	0
pale-face	2	.0000	.0234	23.7	0	0	0	0	2	0	0	0	0	0	0	0	0	0	0	0	0	0	0	0	2	0	0	0	0
pale-faced	4	.2174	.2134	33.3	0	3	0	0	0	1	0	0	0	1	0	0	0	0	0	0	0	0	0	0	0	3	0	0	0
paled	6	.4195	.5713	37.6	1	1	1	2	1	0	0	0	2	0	1	0	0	0	0	0	0	0	0	0	1	1	0	1	0
paleface	7	.5587	.8485	39.3	0	1	2	1	2	1	0	0	3	1	0	1	0	0	1	0	0	0	0	0	0	1	0	0	0
palefaces	6	.0000	.0869	29.4	0	6	0	0	0	0	0	0	0	0	0	0	0	0	0	0	0	0	0	0	0	6	0	0	0
Paleocene	2	.0000	.0209	23.2	0	0	0	0	2	0	0	0	0	0	0	0	0	0	0	0	0	0	0	0	0	0	2	0	0
Paleolithic	5	.2316	.2703	34.3	0	0	0	0	4	0	1	0	0	0	0	0	0	0	0	0	0	0	0	0	0	0	3	2	0
paleontologist	6	.3256	.5038	37.0	0	0	0	3	2	1	0	0	3	0	0	0	0	0	0	1	0	0	0	0	0	0	2	0	0
paleontologists	10	.3914	.8632	39.4	0	0	1	2	3	3	0	1	0	0	0	0	0	1	0	4	0	0	0	0	0	1	4	0	0
paleontology	4	.3874	.3418	35.3	0	0	0	0	2	1	1	0	0	1	0	0	0	0	0	2	0	0	0	0	0	0	1	0	0
Paleozoic	18	.2445	1.0910	40.4	0	0	0	2	1	4	11	0	0	0	0	0	0	0	0	12	0	0	0	0	0	0	6	0	0
paler	4	.4514	.4045	36.1	1	0	0	1	0	1	0	1	1	0	0	1	0	0	0	1	0	0	0	0	0	1	0	0	0
Palestine	58	.4099	5.2474	47.2	3	4	5	16	16	10	4	0	0	0	0	0	0	40	2	0	0	0	0	0	1	5	7	2	1
Palestinian	2	.2375	.1088	30.4	0	0	0	1	0	0	1	0	0	0	0	0	0	0	0	0	1	0	0	0	0	0	0	1	0
Palestrina	3	.2088	.1442	31.6	0	0	0	1	0	1	1	0	0	0	0	0	0	0	0	0	2	0	0	0	0	0	1	0	0
palette	3	.2120	.1548	31.9	0	0	0	0	3	0	0	0	0	0	0	0	0	0	0	0	0	0	0	0	2	1	0	0	0
Pali	2	.2152	.1357	31.3	0	1	1	0	0	0	0	0	1	0	0	0	0	1	0	0	0	0	0	0	0	0	0	0	0
palindrome	7	.2133	.3751	35.7	0	0	0	2	0	5	0	0	0	0	0	0	5	0	0	0	0	0	0	0	0	2	0	0	0
palindromes	4	.2009	.2054	33.1	0	0	0	1	0	3	0	0	0	0	0	0	3	0	0	0	0	0	0	0	0	1	0	0	0
paling	2	.2407	.1138	30.6	0	0	0	1	1	0	0	0	0	0	0	1	0	0	0	0	0	0	0	0	0	1	0	0	0
palisade	2	.2412	.1141	30.6	0	1	0	0	1	0	0	0	0	1	0	0	0	0	0	0	0	0	0	0	0	1	0	0	0
Palisades	2	.1160	.0650	28.1	0	0	0	0	0	0	2	0	0	0	1	0	0	0	0	1	0	0	0	0	0	0	0	0	0
pall	4	.4538	.4020	36.0	0	0	0	0	1	2	1	0	1	0	0	1	0	0	0	0	0	0	0	0	0	1	0	1	0
palladium	8	.1494	.3218	35.1	0	3	0	3	2	0	0	0	0	0	0	0	0	0	0	2	0	0	0	0	0	0	6	0	0
Palladium	3	.0000	.1370	31.4	0	0	0	0	0	3	0	0	3	0	0	0	0	0	0	0	0	0	0	0	0	0	0	0	0
Pallas	2	.0000	.0215	23.3	0	0	0	0	0	0	2	0	0	0	0	2	0	0	0	0	0	0	0	0	0	0	0	0	0
pallet	11	.3487	1.0386	40.2	9	1	1	0	0	0	0	0	9	0	0	0	0	0	0	0	0	0	0	0	1	1	0	0	0
pallid	4	.3518	.3077	34.9	0	0	0	0	1	3	0	0	0	0	0	2	0	0	0	0	0	0	0	0	0	1	0	1	0
palm	119	.7960	19.097	52.8	15	29	8	25	27	8	4	3	22	1	0	10	4	26	2	10	1	0	1	7	4	14	13	4	0
Palm	3	.3406	.2461	33.9	0	0	0	2	1	0	0	0	1	1	0	0	0	0	0	0	0	0	0	0	0	0	0	1	0
PalmBeach	2	.2346	.1166	30.7	0	0	0	0	1	0	0	1	0	0	0	0	0	0	0	1	0	0	0	0	0	0	0	1	0
PalmSprings	2	.1814	.1187	30.7	0	0	0	0	1	0	0	1	1	0	0	0	0	0	0	0	0	0	0	0	0	0	0	1	0
palm-clad	5	.2442	.2889	34.6	0	0	0	0	0	3	2	0	0	0	0	2	0	0	0	0	0	0	0	0	0	3	0	0	0
palm-leaf	2	.2152	.1357	31.3	0	0	0	1	1	0	0	0	1	0	0	0	0	1	0	0	0	0	0	0	0	0	0	0	0
palm-shaded	2	.2408	.1204	30.8	0	0	2	0	0	0	0	0	0	0	0	0	0	1	0	0	0	0	0	0	0	1	0	0	0
palm-width	3	.0000	.0449	26.5	0	3	0	0	0	0	0	0	0	0	0	0	3	0	0	0	0	0	0	0	0	0	0	0	0
Palma	3	.2378	.1809	32.6	0	0	0	2	1	0	0	0	0	0	0	0	0	2	0	0	0	0	0	0	0	1	0	0	0
Palmellococcus	3	.0000	.0365	25.6	0	0	0	0	0	0	3	0	0	0	0	0	0	0	0	0	0	0	0	0	0	0	0	3	0
Palmer	2	.2297	.1135	30.6	0	1	0	0	0	1	0	0	0	0	0	1	0	1	0	0	0	0	0	0	0	0	0	0	0
palmetto	5	.3640	.4065	36.1	1	0	2	0	1	1	0	0	0	0	0	0	0	2	0	0	0	0	0	0	2	1	0	0	0
palmettos	3	.1250	.1342	31.3	0	0	1	0	2	0	0	0	1	0	0	0	0	0	0	0	0	0	0	0	2	0	0	0	0
palms	55	.7288	8.1444	49.1	6	3	6	15	17	4	4	0	9	0	0	8	0	4	1	2	2	0	1	0	8	10	10	0	0
Palms	2	.0000	.0209	23.2	0	0	0	0	2	0	0	0	0	0	0	0	0	0	0	0	0	0	0	0	0	0	2	0	0
PaloAlto	2	.0000	.0209	23.2	0	0	0	0	0	0	2	0	0	0	0	0	0	0	0	0	0	0	0	0	0	0	2	0	0
Paloma	3	.3263	.2368	33.7	1	1	0	1	0	0	0	0	1	0	0	0	0	0	0	0	1	0	0	0	0	0	0	1	0
Palomar	9	.3203	.7159	38.5	0	2	1	2	2	1	1	0	2	0	0	0	2	0	0	5	0	0	0	0	0	0	0	0	0
Palomar's	4	.0000	.0789	29.0	0	0	0	0	4	0	0	0	0	0	0	0	0	0	0	4	0	0	0	0	0	0	0	0	0
palomino	4	.1733	.2298	33.6	2	0	0	0	0	2	0	0	2	2	0	0	0	0	0	0	0	0	0	0	0	0	0	0	0
Palos	13	.2393	1.0033	40.0	0	0	12	0	1	0	0	0	10	0	0	0	0	3	0	0	0	0	0	0	0	0	0	0	0
palpable	2	.2291	.1135	30.5	0	0	0	0	1	0	0	1	0	0	0	1	0	0	0	1	0	0	0	0	0	0	0	0	0
pals	13	.4584	1.4212	41.5	8	0	2	0	2	1	0	0	9	0	0	0	0	0	0	0	0	0	0	0	1	1	0	2	0
palsy	2	.2446	.1122	30.5	0	0	0	0	0	1	1	0	0	0	0	1	0	0	0	0	0	0	0	0	0	0	1	0	0
paltry	2	.2441	.1127	30.5	1	0	0	0	1	0	0	0	0	0	0	0	0	0	0	0	0	0	0	0	1	0	1	0	0
Pam	13	.2272	.9206	39.6	4	2	0	7	0	0	0	0	8	0	0	0	5	0	0	0	0	0	0	0	0	0	0	0	0
Pam's	2	.0000	.0914	29.6	0	0	0	2	0	0	0	0	2	0	0	0	0	0	0	0	0	0	0	0	0	0	0	0	0
Pamela	14	.2433	1.0734	40.3	7	0	3	3	1	0	0	0	11	0	0	0	0	0	0	0	0	0	0	0	0	0	3	0	0
Pampa	8	.0000	.1556	31.9	0	0	0	8	0	0	0	0	0	0	0	0	0	8	0	0	0	0	0	0	0	0	0	0	0
pampas	17	.4915	1.9151	42.8	9	0	1	2	3	1	1	0	10	0	0	1	0	1	0	0	1	0	0	0	0	0	4	0	0
Pampas	9	.1792	.4594	36.6	7	0	0	0	2	0	0	0	2	0	0	0	0	1	0	0	0	0	0	0	0	0	6	0	0
pamper	2	.0000	.0914	29.6	0	0	0	1	1	0	0	0	2	0	0	0	0	0	0	0	0	0	0	0	0	0	0	0	0
pampered	3	.3874	.2497	34.0	1	0	0	0	0	0	1	1	0	1	0	0	0	0	0	0	0	0	0	0	1	0	0	1	0
pampering	4	.2011	.1965	32.9	0	0	0	0	1	0	1	2	0	0	0	0	0	0	0	0	0	0	0	0	1	0	0	3	0
pamphlet	4	.3802	.3314	35.2	0	0	0	0	1	3	0	0	0	0	0	0	2	0	0	0	0	0	0	0	0	0	1	1	0
pamphlets	7	.4807	.7029	38.5	0	0	0	0	0	4	2	1	0	0	1	0	0	0	0	1	0	0	0	0	2	0	1	2	0
pan	240	.6575	32.574	55.1	66	35	25	21	27	30	35	1	49	4	11	8	0	2	4	75	8	5	43	0	3	18	2	8	0
Pan	37	.5043	3.9237	45.9	3	5	3	7	9	2	7	1	3	0	0	0	0	6	2	0	14	0	0	0	0	1	8	3	0
Pan-American	2	.1698	.1133	30.5	0	0	1	0	1	0	0	0	1	0	0	0	0	0	0	0	0	0	0	0	0	0	1	0	0

5J Pairs
4R paisano's
8G Paisley
6R Paiute
8J Pajama
8F Pajarito
5P pakeha
5F Pakistan's
5Q Pakistanis
8B Pal's
4B palabra
XP Palaeolithic
8Q Palamedes
7N palanquins
5Q Palaquium
7Q palates
6R palatial
7Q Palatines
XR Palatka
5P Palaty
8Q Palavicini
XR palazzi
XR palazzo
5R pale-faces
7B pale-gray
4P pale-lipped
7A pale-pink
5P pale-skinned
5P palefaced
4A palely
6F Palenque
7Q paleoanthropological
7Q paleoanthropology
7Q Paleontologists
5P paleontologists'
5Q Palermo
8P pales
6P palindromic
7Q palintonon
9H palisades
7N palki-garis
6N pallets
7N pallor
7D palls
3Q palm-fringed
4Q palm-like
6Q palm's
6Q palmate
6Q palmately
7C palmed
9R Palmellococcus'
7N palmistry
6Q Palmyra
9Q PaloAlto's
5P Palomares
6J Palomita
6H palpi
6A palpitate
7N palter
4J paly
3A Pamela's
5J Pamina
7R Pamir
9L pan-broiling
9L pan-fried
9L pan-frying

Word Type	F	D	U	SFI	3 Gr 3	4 Gr 4	5 Gr 5	6 Gr 6	7 Gr 7	8 Gr 8	9 Gr 9	X UnGr	A Read	B Eng & Gr	C Comp	D Lit	E Math	F Soc Stud	G Spell	H Sci	J Music	K Art	L Home Ec	M Shop	N Lib F	P Lib NF	Q Lib Ref	R Mag	S Rel
Pan's	4	.0000	.0323	25.1	0	4	0	0	0	0	0	0	0	0	0	0	0	0	0	0	4	0	0	0	0	0	0	0	0
Panama	50	.6445	6.7463	48.3	1	10	20	8	7	1	3	0	11	2	0	0	2	24	1	1	0	0	0	0	2	4	2	1	0
Panamanians	2	.0000	.0389	25.9	0	0	2	0	0	0	0	0	0	0	0	0	0	2	0	0	0	0	0	0	0	0	0	0	0
Panay	5	.0000	.0523	27.2	5	0	0	0	0	0	0	0	0	0	0	0	0	0	0	0	0	0	0	0	0	0	5	0	0
pancake	18	.6885	2.5414	44.1	2	4	1	3	2	3	2	1	4	1	2	1	1	1	0	2	0	1	1	0	2	2	0	0	0
pancakes	17	.5273	2.0386	43.1	10	2	3	1	0	0	1	0	11	0	0	1	2	0	0	1	0	0	0	0	2	0	0	0	0
Pancho	17	.1718	1.1892	40.8	0	0	9	4	4	0	0	0	16	0	0	0	0	0	0	0	0	0	0	0	0	0	0	1	0
pancreas	9	.2445	.5455	37.4	0	0	0	3	2	2	2	0	0	0	0	0	0	0	0	6	0	0	0	0	0	0	3	0	0
pancreatic	3	.0000	.0591	27.7	0	0	0	0	1	2	0	0	0	0	0	0	0	0	0	3	0	0	0	0	0	0	0	0	0
panda	9	.0000	.4111	36.1	9	0	0	0	0	0	0	0	9	0	0	0	0	0	0	0	0	0	0	0	0	0	0	0	0
panda's	2	.0000	.0914	29.6	2	0	0	0	0	0	0	0	2	0	0	0	0	0	0	0	0	0	0	0	0	0	0	0	0
pandas	10	.0000	.4568	36.6	10	0	0	0	0	0	0	0	10	0	0	0	0	0	0	0	0	0	0	0	0	0	0	0	0
pandemonium	4	.2048	.1975	33.0	0	0	0	1	1	1	1	0	0	0	0	1	0	0	0	0	0	0	0	0	3	0	0	0	0
Pandora	12	.2076	.8965	39.5	0	1	6	0	0	5	0	0	11	1	0	0	0	0	0	0	0	0	0	0	0	0	0	0	0
pane	22	.7308	3.2897	45.2	6	3	3	2	5	1	1	1	6	3	0	1	0	1	1	3	1	1	0	0	0	4	0	1	0
panel	49	.6361	6.5059	48.1	8	6	3	3	17	7	5	0	13	1	0	2	0	3	0	4	0	0	4	0	6	2	0	14	0
paneled	3	.2332	.1690	32.3	0	1	0	0	2	0	0	0	0	0	0	0	0	0	0	0	0	0	0	0	0	2	0	1	0
paneling	19	.2457	1.1142	40.5	0	1	0	0	17	0	1	0	0	0	0	0	0	0	0	0	0	0	1	0	1	17	0	0	0
panels	22	.6602	2.9688	44.7	0	4	1	1	10	1	4	1	3	1	0	1	0	1	0	2	0	2	1	2	1	0	1	7	0
panes	18	.4917	1.9065	42.8	6	1	0	1	8	1	1	0	3	2	0	0	4	0	0	4	0	0	0	3	1	0	0	1	0
pangs	10	.5215	1.0980	40.4	0	0	0	2	4	1	1	2	1	0	0	2	0	0	0	1	0	0	1	0	0	1	0	4	0
panhandle	4	.2183	.2285	33.6	1	0	3	0	0	0	0	0	0	0	0	0	0	3	0	0	0	0	0	0	0	1	0	0	0
Panhandle	4	.1325	.1944	32.9	0	1	1	0	2	0	0	0	1	0	0	0	0	3	0	0	0	0	0	0	0	0	0	0	0
Panhard	6	.0000	.0869	29.4	0	0	0	0	0	0	0	6	0	0	0	0	0	0	0	0	0	0	0	0	0	6	0	0	0
Panhards	3	.0000	.0434	26.4	0	0	0	0	0	0	0	3	0	0	0	0	0	0	0	0	0	0	0	0	0	3	0	0	0
panic	44	.5924	5.5655	47.5	2	9	4	5	16	4	4	0	16	0	0	4	0	3	0	0	0	0	0	0	6	2	1	12	0
panicked	2	.2351	.1166	30.7	0	0	0	0	0	1	1	0	0	0	0	0	0	1	0	0	0	0	0	0	0	0	0	1	0
panicky	6	.3617	.5364	37.3	0	1	0	2	1	2	0	0	3	1	0	0	0	0	0	0	0	0	0	0	0	0	0	2	0
panned	3	.2435	.2274	33.6	1	0	1	0	0	1	0	0	2	0	0	0	0	1	0	0	0	0	0	0	0	0	0	0	0
panorama	11	.5319	1.2384	40.9	0	2	2	1	5	1	0	0	2	0	0	0	0	0	0	0	0	1	0	0	2	2	3	1	0
panoramas	2	.1698	.1133	30.5	1	0	0	0	1	0	0	0	1	0	0	0	0	0	0	0	0	0	0	0	0	0	1	0	0
pans	77	.7275	11.386	50.6	14	15	9	7	8	8	16	0	14	0	1	2	0	8	1	11	1	1	13	2	10	7	3	3	0
pansies	23	.3479	1.7675	42.5	20	0	1	0	2	0	0	0	0	0	0	1	6	0	0	1	0	0	0	0	14	1	0	0	0
pansy	10	.1325	.3985	36.0	8	1	1	0	0	0	0	0	1	0	0	0	0	0	0	1	0	0	0	0	8	0	0	0	0
Pansy	3	.2223	.2106	33.2	1	0	0	0	2	0	0	0	2	1	0	0	0	0	0	0	0	0	0	0	0	0	0	0	0
pant	4	.2805	.2842	34.5	1	0	2	0	1	0	0	0	1	0	0	0	0	1	0	0	0	0	0	0	2	0	0	0	0
pantaloon	2	.2412	.1141	30.6	0	0	1	0	0	0	0	1	0	1	0	0	0	0	0	0	0	0	0	0	0	1	0	0	0
Pantaloon	6	.2223	.4212	36.2	0	0	0	4	0	0	0	2	4	2	0	0	0	0	0	0	0	0	0	0	0	0	0	0	0
pantaloons	5	.5370	.5704	37.6	1	1	1	0	1	0	0	1	1	1	0	1	0	0	0	0	0	0	0	0	0	1	1	0	0
Pantanal	4	.0000	.0419	26.2	0	0	4	0	0	0	0	0	0	0	0	0	0	0	0	0	0	0	0	0	0	0	4	0	0
panted	20	.6619	2.7918	44.5	2	2	4	5	4	1	1	1	10	1	1	3	0	0	0	0	0	0	0	0	2	1	1	1	0
Pantelleria	2	.0000	.0209	23.2	0	2	0	0	0	0	0	0	0	0	0	0	0	0	0	0	0	0	0	0	0	0	2	0	0
panteth	2	.0000	.0290	24.6	2	0	0	0	0	0	0	0	0	0	0	0	0	0	0	0	0	0	0	0	0	2	0	0	0
panther	21	.6219	2.7751	44.4	3	2	6	0	7	2	1	0	9	0	1	3	0	0	0	1	0	0	0	0	4	2	1	0	0
Panther	6	.1277	.2726	34.4	0	0	0	0	1	1	0	4	2	0	0	0	0	0	0	0	0	0	0	0	0	0	0	4	0
panther's	2	.0000	.0914	29.6	2	0	0	0	0	0	0	0	2	0	0	0	0	0	0	0	0	0	0	0	0	0	0	0	0
panthers	5	.4718	.5341	37.3	0	0	2	0	0	1	1	1	2	0	0	0	0	1	0	0	0	0	0	0	0	0	1	1	0
Panthers	2	.0000	.0914	29.6	0	0	0	0	0	2	0	0	2	0	0	0	0	0	0	0	0	0	0	0	0	0	0	0	0
panting	35	.4837	3.7679	45.8	3	7	5	7	10	3	0	0	13	0	0	3	0	0	0	0	1	0	0	0	14	3	0	1	0
pantomime	10	.3128	.7531	38.8	3	1	0	2	2	1	0	1	3	0	0	0	0	0	0	0	5	0	0	0	1	0	0	1	0
pantomime-ballet	2	.0000	.0209	23.2	0	0	0	0	0	2	0	0	0	0	0	0	0	0	0	0	0	0	0	0	0	0	2	0	0
pantomiming	3	.3874	.2497	34.0	0	0	0	1	1	0	1	0	0	1	0	0	0	0	0	0	0	0	0	0	1	0	0	1	0
pantry	25	.4246	2.4440	43.9	2	3	2	1	13	2	1	1	10	0	0	10	0	0	0	0	0	0	0	0	3	0	1	1	0
pants	77	.6609	10.570	50.2	13	15	1	2	28	5	9	4	25	4	1	8	0	3	0	0	1	0	11	0	5	8	1	10	0
Pantycelyn	2	.0000	.0243	23.9	0	0	0	0	2	0	0	0	0	0	0	0	0	0	0	0	0	0	0	0	0	0	0	2	0
Panza	6	.0000	.2741	34.4	0	0	0	0	6	0	0	0	6	0	0	0	0	0	0	0	0	0	0	0	0	0	0	0	0
Pao	2	.0000	.0215	23.3	0	0	0	0	2	0	0	0	0	0	0	2	0	0	0	0	0	0	0	0	0	0	0	0	0
Pap	5	.1620	.2493	34.0	0	0	0	0	1	2	2	0	2	0	2	0	0	0	0	0	0	0	0	0	1	0	0	0	0
papa	30	.4009	2.8369	44.5	6	3	7	8	3	1	2	0	13	0	0	2	0	0	1	0	0	0	0	0	13	1	0	0	0
Papa	321	.5812	40.997	56.1	51	173	10	5	44	34	4	0	193	2	4	14	0	0	0	0	2	0	0	0	68	33	0	5	0
PAPA	7	.0000	.0751	28.8	0	0	0	0	7	0	0	0	0	0	0	7	0	0	0	0	0	0	0	0	0	0	0	0	0
Papa's	38	.6132	5.0649	47.0	5	23	3	0	3	4	0	0	24	0	1	2	0	0	0	0	2	0	0	0	4	5	0	0	0
papacy	3	.0000	.0583	27.7	0	0	0	0	0	0	3	0	0	0	0	0	0	3	0	0	0	0	0	0	0	0	0	0	0
papal	11	.4654	1.0989	40.4	0	0	5	0	0	1	5	0	0	0	0	0	0	5	0	0	0	0	0	0	0	3	2	1	0
Papal	9	.3773	.7527	38.8	4	0	0	0	2	0	3	0	0	0	0	0	0	3	0	0	0	0	0	0	0	4	2	0	0
Papapoulos	3	.0000	.1370	31.4	0	3	0	0	0	0	0	0	3	0	0	0	0	0	0	0	0	0	0	0	0	0	0	0	0
Papeete	3	.0000	.1370	31.4	0	0	0	0	3	0	0	0	3	0	0	0	0	0	0	0	0	0	0	0	0	0	0	0	0
paper	2372	.7825	373.94	65.7	488	432	346	297	365	190	217	37	431	274	71	57	287	107	167	330	8	214	49	79	74	115	30	79	0
Paper	17	.4304	1.8203	42.6	5	0	1	0	11	0	0	0	14	0	0	0	0	0	0	0	1	0	0	0	1	0	0	1	0
paper-thin	2	.2405	.1205	30.8	0	1	0	1	0	0	0	0	0	0	0	0	0	0	0	1	0	0	0	0	0	1	0	0	0
paper's	3	.1277	.1363	31.3	0	0	0	1	2	0	0	0	1	0	0	0	0	0	0	0	0	0	0	0	0	0	0	2	0
paperback	3	.3815	.2447	33.9	0	0	0	0	0	1	1	1	0	0	0	0	0	0	1	0	0	0	0	0	1	0	0	1	0
papered	2	.2443	.1130	30.5	1	0	0	0	0	0	1	0	0	0	0	1	0	0	0	0	0	0	0	0	1	0	0	0	0
papermakers	2	.1698	.1133	30.5	0	1	0	0	1	0	0	0	1	0	0	0	0	0	0	0	0	0	0	0	0	0	1	0	0
papermaking	4	.2351	.2146	33.3	0	0	0	0	2	0	2	0	0	0	0	0	0	0	0	0	0	0	0	1	0	0	0	3	0
papers	244	.8669	42.325	56.3	65	32	26	21	46	30	21	3	81	25	6	9	32	15	8	7	1	8	0	3	19	15	5	10	0
Papers	6	.2680	.3527	35.5	0	0	0	2	0	2	2	0	0	0	2	0	0	0	0	0	0	0	0	0	3	0	1	0	0
paperweight	2	.1839	.0845	29.3	1	0	0	0	0	0	1	0	0	0	0	0	0	0	0	0	0	0	1	0	1	0	0	0	0
papier	2	.2351	.1166	30.7	0	0	1	0	0	1	0	0	0	0	0	0	0	1	0	0	0	0	0	0	0	0	0	1	0
papier-mache	14	.0494	.1787	32.5	0	5	3	2	2	2	0	0	0	0	0	1	0	0	0	0	0	12	0	0	0	0	0	1	0
papillae	2	.0000	.0394	26.0	0	0	0	0	0	0	0	2	0	0	0	0	0	0	0	2	0	0	0	0	0	0	0	0	0
papoose	6	.2894	.4192	36.2	0	3	2	0	1	0	0	0	1	0	0	0	0	0	0	0	0	0	0	0	3	2	0	0	0
Pappas	3	.1277	.1363	31.3	1	0	0	0	0	0	0	2	1	0	0	0	0	0	0	0	0	0	0	0	0	0	0	2	0
Pappy	10	.2805	.7336	38.7	4	0	0	0	5	0	1	0	4	0	0	0	0	0	0	0	0	0	0	0	5	0	0	1	0
paprika	3	.2277	.1555	31.9	0	0	0	0	2	0	0	1	0	0	0	0	0	0	0	0	0	0	1	0	0	0	0	2	0
Papua	2	.2285	.1129	30.5	0	0	1	0	0	1	0	0	0	0	0	0	0	1	0	0	0	0	0	0	0	0	1	0	0
Papuan	5	.3836	.4751	36.8	0	0	0	3	2	0	0	0	3	0	0	0	0	0	0	0	0	0	0	0	1	0	1	0	0
papyrus	16	.5261	1.7722	42.5	0	0	2	3	2	2	3	4	2	2	0	0	0	3	0	0	0	1	0	3	0	4	1	0	0
par	7	.5609	.8270	39.2	0	0	1	1	3	0	1	1	1	0	0	0	0	1	1	1	0	0	0	0	0	0	2	1	0
para	5	.3804	.4222	36.3	0	1	0	1	0	3	0	0	0	1	0	0	0	0	1	3	0	0	0	0	0	0	0	0	0
parable	3	.0168	.0208	23.2	2	0	0	0	0	0	1	0	0	0	0	1	0	0	0	0	0	0	0	0	0	0	0	0	2
Parable	2	.0000	.0004	5.5	2	0	0	0	0	0	0	0	0	0	0	0	0	0	0	0	0	0	0	0	0	0	0	0	2
parabola	3	.0000	.0449	26.5	0	0	0	0	0	0	3	0	0	0	0	0	3	0	0	0	0	0	0	0	0	0	0	0	0
Paracelsus	2	.0000	.0209	23.2	0	0	0	1	0	0	1	0	0	0	0	0	0	0	0	0	0	0	0	0	0	0	2	0	0

XH pan-germ
XR panaceas
9R panache
6P PANAMA
7R Panasonic
9D panatela
8A Panchatantra
6N pandanus
9P Pandit
8G Pandora's
7N panful
7N pang
7Q pangolin
XR Panic
8A panic-stricken
8A panic-struck
8D panicstricken
7A panin
9Q Panini's
5F paniolos
8R panjandrum
7D panoramic
5J panpipe
3J Panpipes
4P Pantagraph
XB Pantaleone
6A pantalettes
8Q pantheistic
3N panties
8Q pantomime-ballets
8D pantomimed
7N pantouffles
3P pantries
7R pants-leg
7B pantsandshirt
4Q Panzer
8F Paoli
8Q Papacy
5J Papageno
7R Papas
5P papaws
5J papaya
9F Pape
7Q paper-devourers
8D paper-doily
9R paperboard
3Q papery
XH papilla
9Q Papin
5Q Papineau
9D Papists
3A papooses
XR Pappas'
9Q Pappenheim
9Q Pappenheim's
7A pappy
7A pappy's
6A Papua's
6A Papuans
3A Paquita
5A Para
8A parables
8H parabolic
XH parabolize

Word Type	F	D	U	SFI	3 Gr 3	4 Gr 4	5 Gr 5	6 Gr 6	7 Gr 7	8 Gr 8	9 Gr 9	X UnGr	A Read	B Eng & Gr	C Comp	D Lit	E Math	F Soc Stud	G Spell	H Sci	J Music	K Art	L Home Ec	M Shop	N Lib F	P Lib NF	Q Lib Ref	R Mag	S Rel
parachute	35	.4979	3.8788	45.9	7	3	15	5	2	1	1	1	12	0	0	2	0	1	0	13	0	3	0	0	0	2	0	2	0
parachutes	14	.5045	1.5994	42.0	4	2	5	1	0	2	0	0	7	0	0	0	0	1	0	3	0	1	0	0	0	1	0	1	0
parade	125	.6515	17.023	52.3	22	35	23	10	10	9	15	1	43	6	14	6	1	10	5	10	9	0	0	0	3	11	0	7	0
Parade	9	.3764	.8143	39.1	4	0	1	0	3	1	0	0	4	0	0	0	0	1	0	0	3	0	0	0	1	0	0	0	0
paraded	6	.2406	.3642	35.6	1	0	0	2	0	0	3	0	1	0	0	0	0	0	0	0	0	0	0	0	1	0	0	4	0
parades	30	.6219	3.8696	45.9	6	6	7	1	3	5	0	2	4	0	2	0	0	9	0	0	3	0	0	0	0	4	2	6	0
parading	3	.3267	.2367	33.7	1	0	0	1	0	1	0	0	1	0	0	0	0	0	0	0	1	0	0	0	1	0	0	0	0
paradise	17	.7004	2.4339	43.9	2	1	1	6	1	0	2	4	3	1	0	2	0	2	0	0	1	0	0	0	1	1	1	5	0
Paradise	8	.5082	.8501	39.3	0	0	0	1	2	2	1	2	0	2	0	0	0	1	0	0	0	0	0	0	1	1	0	3	0
paradox	7	.5050	.7601	38.8	0	0	0	1	2	3	1	0	1	0	0	0	0	2	0	0	0	0	0	0	0	1	2	1	0
paradoxes	2	.2408	.1204	30.8	0	0	1	0	0	1	0	0	0	0	0	0	0	1	0	0	0	0	0	0	0	1	0	0	0
paradoxical	2	.2285	.1129	30.5	0	0	0	0	0	2	0	0	0	0	0	0	0	1	0	0	0	0	0	0	0	0	1	0	0
paradoxically	3	.3769	.2484	34.0	0	0	0	0	0	1	2	0	0	0	0	0	0	1	0	0	0	0	0	0	0	0	1	1	0
paraffin	21	.5012	2.2599	43.5	0	10	2	2	3	3	0	1	1	0	0	0	3	0	0	13	0	1	0	0	0	1	2	0	0
paragon	2	.2437	.1129	30.5	0	0	0	1	0	0	1	0	0	0	0	0	0	0	0	0	0	0	0	0	0	0	1	1	0
paragraph	839	.3793	73.180	58.6	84	98	100	87	231	99	137	3	271	314	167	14	7	6	47	8	0	0	0	1	1	0	0	3	0
Paragraph	11	.2444	.8555	39.3	0	0	0	8	1	0	2	0	9	2	0	0	0	0	0	0	0	0	0	0	0	0	0	0	0
paragraphing	2	.0000	.0219	23.4	0	0	0	0	1	0	1	0	0	2	0	0	0	0	0	0	0	0	0	0	0	0	0	0	0
paragraphs	214	.3973	19.441	52.9	9	17	22	31	61	22	52	0	72	89	36	7	1	0	4	2	0	0	0	1	0	1	0	1	0
Paragraphs	2	.1733	.1149	30.6	0	1	0	1	0	0	0	0	1	1	0	0	0	0	0	0	0	0	0	0	0	0	0	0	0
Paraguay	51	.2258	2.9547	44.7	6	0	4	26	14	1	0	0	0	0	0	0	0	40	0	0	0	0	0	0	0	0	11	0	0
Paraguayans	2	.0000	.0389	25.9	0	0	0	2	0	0	0	0	0	0	0	0	0	2	0	0	0	0	0	0	0	0	0	0	0
parakeet	21	.5319	2.4499	43.9	13	1	0	0	3	0	0	4	8	0	0	0	0	0	0	2	0	0	0	0	0	4	2	5	0
parakeets	20	.4648	2.0116	43.0	6	0	0	1	1	2	0	10	3	1	0	0	2	0	0	0	0	0	0	0	0	1	3	10	0
parallax	4	.0000	.0789	29.0	0	0	1	0	3	0	0	0	0	0	0	0	0	0	0	4	0	0	0	0	0	0	0	0	0
parallel	322	.6658	43.556	56.4	23	25	38	25	90	67	41	13	7	2	13	2	166	12	4	30	5	2	10	37	2	6	19	5	0
paralleled	3	.2435	.1694	32.3	0	0	1	0	1	1	0	0	0	0	1	0	0	0	0	1	0	0	0	0	0	0	0	1	0
parallelogram	50	.0279	1.0060	40.0	3	1	9	5	10	10	11	1	0	0	0	0	49	0	0	1	0	0	0	0	0	0	0	0	0
parallelograms	27	.0000	.4041	36.1	0	0	1	5	2	19	0	0	0	0	0	0	27	0	0	0	0	0	0	0	0	0	0	0	0
parallels	48	.4491	4.6257	46.7	1	25	1	2	7	5	5	2	1	1	0	0	3	14	0	2	0	0	0	0	0	2	23	2	0
paralysis	18	.4574	1.8132	42.6	0	0	0	3	6	3	6	0	4	0	0	1	0	0	0	3	0	0	0	0	1	0	8	1	0
paralytic	6	.0000	.1183	30.7	0	0	0	0	6	0	0	0	0	0	0	0	0	0	0	6	0	0	0	0	0	0	0	0	0
paralyze	8	.4055	.7326	38.6	1	0	0	2	5	0	0	0	1	0	0	0	0	0	0	4	0	0	0	0	0	1	2	0	0
paralyzed	19	.7134	2.7626	44.4	1	2	3	5	4	3	1	0	2	1	0	0	0	1	1	6	0	0	0	0	3	2	2	1	0
Paramaribo	2	.0000	.0290	24.6	0	0	2	0	0	0	0	0	0	0	0	0	0	0	0	0	0	0	0	0	0	2	0	0	0
paramecia	5	.0000	.0986	29.9	0	0	0	1	4	0	0	0	0	0	0	0	0	0	0	5	0	0	0	0	0	0	0	0	0
paramecium	17	.2302	1.0348	40.1	4	0	0	0	12	0	1	0	1	0	0	0	0	0	0	13	0	0	0	0	0	3	0	0	0
Paramecium	3	.0000	.0591	27.7	0	0	0	0	3	0	0	0	0	0	0	0	0	0	0	3	0	0	0	0	0	0	0	0	0
paramilitary	2	.0000	.0209	23.2	0	0	0	0	0	2	0	0	0	0	0	0	0	0	0	0	0	0	0	0	0	0	2	0	0
paramount	3	.0000	.0314	25.0	0	0	1	0	0	2	0	0	0	0	0	0	0	0	0	0	0	0	0	0	0	0	3	0	0
Parana	6	.1125	.1964	32.9	3	0	2	0	1	0	0	0	0	0	0	0	0	1	0	0	0	0	0	0	0	0	5	0	0
parapet	5	.1468	.2522	34.0	0	0	2	3	0	0	0	0	2	0	0	0	0	0	0	0	0	0	0	0	3	0	0	0	0
paraphernalia	4	.2445	.3067	34.9	0	0	3	0	0	1	0	0	3	0	0	0	0	0	0	0	0	0	0	0	0	1	0	0	0
paraphrase	7	.2040	.3436	35.4	0	0	0	0	1	0	5	1	0	5	0	0	0	0	0	0	0	0	0	0	0	0	0	2	0
paraplegia	2	.0000	.0209	23.2	0	0	0	0	0	0	2	0	0	0	0	0	0	0	0	0	0	0	0	0	0	0	2	0	0
parasite	16	.3016	1.1274	40.5	0	0	0	0	10	2	3	1	0	0	0	0	0	0	0	12	0	0	3	0	0	0	1	0	0
parasite-chain	4	.0000	.0789	29.0	0	0	0	0	0	4	0	0	0	0	0	0	0	0	0	4	0	0	0	0	0	0	0	0	0
parasites	24	.3057	1.8102	42.6	4	0	1	1	12	4	0	2	4	0	0	0	0	0	0	15	0	0	0	0	0	0	5	0	0
parasitic	18	.1146	.7112	38.5	0	0	1	0	13	0	2	2	0	0	0	0	0	0	0	17	0	0	0	0	0	0	1	0	0
parasitism	2	.0000	.0394	26.0	0	0	0	0	2	0	0	0	0	0	0	0	0	0	0	2	0	0	0	0	0	0	0	0	0
parasitizes	2	.0000	.0394	26.0	0	0	0	0	2	0	0	0	0	0	0	0	0	0	0	2	0	0	0	0	0	0	0	0	0
parasitizing	2	.0000	.0394	26.0	0	0	0	0	2	0	0	0	0	0	0	0	0	0	0	2	0	0	0	0	0	0	0	0	0
parasol	9	.5120	.9901	40.0	1	2	0	4	2	0	0	0	1	0	0	0	0	0	1	4	0	0	0	0	1	2	0	0	0
parasols	2	.2408	.1204	30.8	1	0	0	1	0	0	0	0	0	0	0	0	0	1	0	0	0	0	0	0	0	1	0	0	0
paratrooper	3	.3465	.2515	34.0	1	0	1	1	0	0	0	0	1	0	0	0	0	0	0	0	0	0	0	0	0	1	0	1	0
parcel	32	.7144	4.6378	46.7	2	5	1	3	10	3	8	0	3	3	0	1	1	4	0	0	1	0	0	0	9	3	4	3	0
parcels	14	.5877	1.7471	42.4	2	0	2	5	3	2	0	0	4	0	0	0	2	1	0	0	0	0	0	0	2	2	3	0	0
parched	16	.7017	2.3218	43.7	2	3	0	2	8	1	0	0	5	1	0	2	0	1	0	2	0	0	0	0	1	3	0	1	0
parchment	18	.6063	2.2879	43.6	0	4	2	2	3	2	2	3	5	0	0	1	1	1	1	0	0	0	3	1	0	4	0	1	0
pard	2	.2427	.1152	30.6	0	0	1	0	1	0	0	0	0	0	0	0	0	0	0	0	0	0	0	0	1	1	0	0	0
pardon	33	.5718	4.0162	46.0	0	2	3	7	8	3	9	1	10	1	0	10	0	1	2	0	0	0	0	0	7	1	0	1	0
pardoned	5	.3536	.4328	36.4	2	0	2	0	1	0	0	0	2	0	0	0	0	0	0	0	0	0	0	0	1	2	0	0	0
pare	3	.3265	.2061	33.1	0	1	0	0	1	0	1	0	0	0	0	0	0	0	0	0	0	0	1	1	0	1	0	0	0
parent	56	.7458	8.4686	49.3	8	7	8	3	16	4	10	0	8	1	0	3	0	4	1	10	0	0	1	0	2	4	10	12	0
Parent	3	.2227	.1589	32.0	1	1	0	0	0	0	1	0	0	0	0	0	0	0	0	0	0	0	0	0	2	0	0	1	0
parent's	2	.2444	.1132	30.5	0	2	0	0	0	0	0	0	0	1	0	0	0	0	0	0	0	0	0	0	1	0	0	0	0
parentage	2	.2401	.1133	30.5	0	0	1	1	0	0	0	0	0	0	0	0	0	0	0	0	0	0	0	0	0	1	1	0	0
parental	8	.4923	.8381	39.2	1	0	0	1	1	2	1	2	1	0	1	1	0	1	0	0	0	0	0	0	1	0	0	3	0
parentheses	151	.4873	15.288	51.8	10	12	15	22	41	17	32	2	0	45	9	0	46	0	50	0	0	0	0	0	0	0	1	0	0
parenthetical	3	.2124	.1442	31.6	0	0	0	0	0	0	3	0	0	2	1	0	0	0	0	0	0	0	0	0	0	0	0	0	0
parentis	2	.2442	.1134	30.5	0	0	0	0	0	1	1	0	0	1	0	0	0	0	0	0	0	0	0	0	0	0	0	1	0
parents	490	.7728	76.814	58.9	85	70	56	62	105	50	47	15	131	29	6	29	2	43	5	46	5	2	33	0	27	54	14	60	4
parents'	26	.6330	3.4104	45.3	1	0	0	5	7	3	5	5	5	1	1	6	0	1	0	1	0	0	0	0	2	1	0	8	0
pari-mutuel	4	.0000	.0579	27.6	0	0	0	4	0	0	0	0	0	0	0	0	0	0	0	0	0	0	0	0	0	4	0	0	0
Paricutin	14	.4771	1.5388	41.9	0	0	2	10	1	0	1	0	7	0	0	0	0	0	0	3	0	0	0	0	0	3	1	0	0
parietal	2	.0000	.0209	23.2	0	0	0	0	0	2	0	0	0	0	0	0	0	0	0	0	0	0	0	0	0	0	2	0	0
Parin	2	.1717	.1142	30.6	1	1	0	0	0	0	0	0	1	0	0	1	0	0	0	0	0	0	0	0	0	0	0	0	0
paring	3	.2445	.1903	32.8	1	0	0	0	2	0	1	0	1	0	0	0	0	0	0	0	0	0	1	0	0	0	0	1	0
paris	3	.1650	.1684	32.3	0	0	0	0	1	1	1	0	1	0	0	0	0	0	0	2	0	0	0	0	0	0	0	0	0
Paris	258	.8288	42.916	56.3	29	27	21	31	36	47	58	9	60	7	1	28	5	29	0	9	24	2	0	1	4	20	42	26	0
parish	16	.5633	1.9230	42.8	0	2	6	3	2	1	2	0	4	1	0	1	0	1	0	0	0	0	0	0	0	7	1	1	0
parishes	2	.2285	.1129	30.5	0	0	0	0	2	0	0	0	0	0	0	0	0	1	0	0	0	0	0	0	0	0	1	0	0
parishioners	2	.2433	.1158	30.6	0	0	0	0	1	0	1	0	0	0	0	0	0	0	0	0	0	0	0	0	0	1	0	1	0
Parisian	4	.3192	.2719	34.3	1	0	1	0	1	1	0	0	0	0	0	0	0	0	0	0	1	1	0	0	0	0	2	0	0
parity	2	.0000	.0209	23.2	0	0	0	0	0	2	0	0	0	0	0	0	0	0	0	0	0	0	0	0	0	0	2	0	0
park	281	.7801	44.514	56.5	101	51	49	32	24	14	5	5	83	22	12	3	7	66	6	6	9	0	0	0	9	8	12	38	0
Park	148	.7163	21.645	53.4	22	23	23	11	31	18	17	3	31	13	9	0	3	21	0	3	5	0	0	0	10	4	22	27	0
parka	4	.3097	.2992	34.8	2	0	0	0	1	0	0	1	1	0	0	1	0	0	0	0	0	0	0	0	0	0	0	2	0
parkas	3	.1277	.1363	31.3	0	0	0	1	2	0	0	0	1	0	0	0	0	0	0	0	0	0	0	0	0	0	0	2	0
parked	77	.7190	11.518	50.6	17	13	6	5	26	2	7	1	39	3	1	7	7	3	0	2	0	0	0	0	5	0	0	10	0
Parker	45	.6139	5.9669	47.8	20	1	5	4	7	7	1	0	25	1	0	0	1	1	0	0	1	0	0	0	8	3	0	5	0
Parker's	7	.2366	.5437	37.4	2	2	2	0	0	1	0	0	6	0	0	0	0	0	0	0	0	0	0	0	1	0	0	0	0
Parkers	3	.0000	.1370	31.4	3	0	0	0	0	0	0	0	3	0	0	0	0	0	0	0	0	0	0	0	0	0	0	0	0

6R parachuted
XH parachutelike
9C parade's
XH paraffined
7N paragons
4B paragraphein
6F Paraguay's
6A Paraguayan
3P parakeet's
7H parallactic
9M parallel-line
7R paralleling
9Q paralysed
7H paralyzes
7R paralyzing
3P PARAMECIUM
7H parameciums
9Q paranoia
9Q paranoid
7Q Paraphrase
9Q PARAPLEGIA
9Q Parapsychology
9Q PARAPSYCHOLOGY
4G parare
7H parasitize
7Q parasitized
7H parathormone
7H Parathyroids
8F paratroopers
5P paratroops
5N parboil
4F parch
7D parcheesi
4N parchesi
4P parching
9D parchment-yellow
5A parchments
8A Pard
7G pard-ner
8D pardner
9D pardon-me's
7N pardonable
8D Pardoned
7F pardons
5N pared
7N parenchyma
9R Parent-Teacher
7A parenthesis
5Q Parents
4P parer
9F Pares
6N pareu
XR Parhart
XH parhelic
6P pari-mutuels
6A Paricutin's
7R ParisIsland
XP Paris-to-Berlin
XP Paris-to-Bordeaux
XP Paris-to-Madrid
XP Paris-to-Toulouse
XR Parisians
7Q Parisienne
5N Parizade
7A park-like
3A park
5Q park's
4P Parke
3P Parker-Browne
5Q Parkes

Word Type	F	D	U	SFI	3 Gr 3	4 Gr 4	5 Gr 5	6 Gr 6	7 Gr 7	8 Gr 8	9 Gr 9	X UnGr	A Read	B Eng & Gr	C Comp	D Lit	E Math	F Soc Stud	G Spell	H Sci	J Music	K Art	L Home Ec	M Shop	N Lib F	P Lib NF	Q Lib Ref	R Mag	S Rel
Parkesine	2	.0000	.0209	23.2	0	0	2	0	0	0	0	0	0	0	0	0	0	0	0	0	0	0	0	0	0	0	2	0	0
parking	51	.7341	7.6776	48.9	16	5	10	3	9	2	5	1	15	3	1	1	9	8	0	2	0	0	0	0	0	1	2	9	0
Parking	2	.1523	.0721	28.6	1	0	0	0	1	0	0	0	0	0	1	0	0	0	0	0	0	0	0	0	0	0	0	1	0
parks	92	.7407	13.856	51.4	24	11	15	10	13	7	9	3	12	3	1	1	1	37	0	6	1	1	0	0	1	3	14	11	0
Parks	11	.4554	1.1656	40.7	5	0	3	0	1	1	1	0	5	0	0	0	0	4	0	0	0	0	0	0	0	1	0	1	0
parkway	2	.2408	.1204	30.8	1	1	0	0	0	0	0	0	0	0	0	0	0	1	0	0	0	0	0	0	0	1	0	0	0
parlance	2	.2405	.1205	30.8	0	0	1	0	1	0	0	0	0	0	0	0	0	0	0	1	0	0	0	0	0	1	0	0	0
parley	2	.1787	.1174	30.7	0	1	1	0	0	0	0	0	1	0	0	0	0	0	0	0	0	0	0	0	1	0	0	0	0
parliament	13	.4603	1.2907	41.1	1	0	7	3	1	1	0	0	1	0	0	0	0	4	1	0	0	0	0	0	0	2	5	0	0
Parliament	61	.6330	8.0185	49.0	4	3	24	7	7	8	3	5	8	4	0	1	0	22	0	0	0	0	0	0	2	7	4	13	0
parliamentary	13	.4581	1.2727	41.0	0	0	2	0	2	2	7	0	1	6	0	0	0	1	0	0	0	0	0	0	0	1	3	1	0
Parliamentary	2	.0000	.0389	25.9	0	0	0	0	1	1	0	0	0	0	0	0	0	2	0	0	0	0	0	0	0	0	0	0	0
parlor	48	.7066	6.9697	48.4	9	11	6	5	7	6	4	0	14	0	0	7	0	0	1	0	2	0	1	0	9	10	1	3	0
Parlormaid	3	.0000	.1370	31.4	0	0	3	0	0	0	0	0	3	0	0	0	0	0	0	0	0	0	0	0	0	0	0	0	0
parlors	2	.2408	.1204	30.8	1	0	0	0	0	1	0	0	0	0	0	0	0	1	0	0	0	0	0	0	0	1	0	0	0
parlour	2	.2412	.1141	30.6	1	0	0	0	1	0	0	0	0	1	0	0	0	0	0	0	0	0	0	0	0	1	0	0	0
Parmesan	2	.1442	.0761	28.8	0	0	0	1	1	0	0	0	0	0	0	0	0	1	0	0	0	0	1	0	0	0	0	0	0
Parnassos	2	.0000	.0215	23.3	0	0	0	0	0	0	2	0	0	0	0	2	0	0	0	0	0	0	0	0	0	0	0	0	0
parodies	4	.1789	.1692	32.3	0	0	3	0	1	0	0	0	0	0	0	0	0	0	0	0	3	0	0	0	0	0	1	0	0
parody	7	.3765	.6521	38.1	0	0	0	0	2	0	3	2	4	0	0	0	0	0	0	0	1	0	0	0	0	0	0	2	0
parole	3	.2159	.1532	31.9	0	0	2	1	0	0	0	0	0	0	0	0	0	0	0	0	0	0	0	0	0	0	2	1	0
Parole	2	.0000	.0209	23.2	0	0	2	0	0	0	0	0	0	0	0	0	0	0	0	0	0	0	0	0	0	0	2	0	0
paroxysm	3	.2227	.1589	32.0	0	0	0	0	2	1	0	0	0	0	0	0	0	0	0	0	0	0	0	0	2	0	0	1	0
Parris	3	.0000	.0434	26.4	0	0	0	0	0	0	3	0	0	0	0	0	0	0	0	0	0	0	0	0	0	3	0	0	0
parrot	94	.7101	14.023	51.5	25	40	8	1	8	6	1	5	58	5	1	1	0	5	1	0	0	0	0	0	7	12	2	2	0
Parrot	3	.2279	.2143	33.3	1	0	2	0	0	0	0	0	2	0	0	0	0	0	0	0	0	0	0	0	0	0	0	1	0
parrot's	3	.2279	.2143	33.3	1	0	0	0	2	0	0	0	2	0	0	0	0	0	0	0	0	0	0	0	0	0	0	1	0
parrots	16	.6219	2.0531	43.1	4	7	1	1	1	1	1	0	1	0	0	2	0	4	0	0	1	0	0	0	0	5	2	1	0
Parry	2	.0000	.0914	29.6	0	2	0	0	0	0	0	0	2	0	0	0	0	0	0	0	0	0	0	0	0	0	0	0	0
Parseghian	2	.0000	.0243	23.9	0	0	0	2	0	0	0	0	0	0	0	0	0	0	0	0	0	0	0	0	0	0	0	2	0
parsley	23	.3755	1.8212	42.6	10	1	0	1	3	1	6	1	0	0	0	1	0	0	1	0	0	0	8	0	10	1	1	1	0
Parsley	2	.0000	.0234	23.7	0	2	0	0	0	0	0	0	0	0	0	0	0	0	0	0	0	0	0	0	2	0	0	0	0
parsnip	2	.0000	.0290	24.6	2	0	0	0	0	0	0	0	0	0	0	0	0	0	0	0	0	0	0	0	0	2	0	0	0
parsnips	2	.2412	.1141	30.6	1	0	0	1	0	0	0	0	0	1	0	0	0	0	0	0	0	0	0	0	0	1	0	0	0
parson	10	.5332	1.1316	40.5	0	0	2	1	6	0	1	0	2	1	0	4	0	0	0	0	1	0	0	0	1	1	0	0	0
Parson	5	.3233	.3595	35.6	0	2	2	0	1	0	0	0	0	0	0	0	0	0	0	0	0	0	0	0	3	1	0	1	0
parson's	2	.2446	.1125	30.5	0	0	0	1	0	0	1	0	0	1	0	1	0	0	0	0	0	0	0	0	0	0	0	0	0
parsonage	2	.0000	.0290	24.6	0	2	0	0	0	0	0	0	0	0	0	0	0	0	0	0	0	0	0	0	0	2	0	0	0
Parsons	6	.1133	.1987	33.0	0	0	0	0	6	0	0	0	0	0	0	5	0	0	0	1	0	0	0	0	0	0	0	0	0
Parsons'	3	.0000	.0322	25.1	0	0	0	0	3	0	0	0	0	0	0	3	0	0	0	0	0	0	0	0	0	0	0	0	0
part	4285	.9587	810.56	69.1	731	670	664	630	648	440	434	68	633	284	51	115	403	772	165	624	347	55	85	81	71	212	212	174	1
Part	39	.5944	4.7733	46.8	3	6	1	1	0	7	19	2	4	4	0	0	7	1	15	0	3	0	2	0	0	0	1	2	0
part-singing	2	.0000	.0162	22.1	0	0	0	1	0	1	0	0	0	0	0	0	0	0	0	0	2	0	0	0	0	0	0	0	0
part-time	12	.5442	1.3591	41.3	1	0	0	0	1	5	4	1	0	0	0	0	1	4	0	1	0	0	2	0	0	1	2	1	0
partake	6	.2284	.3735	35.7	1	4	1	0	0	0	0	0	2	0	0	0	0	1	0	0	3	0	0	0	0	0	0	0	0
partakers	2	.0000	.0243	23.9	0	0	0	0	0	0	0	2	0	0	0	0	0	0	0	0	0	0	0	0	0	0	0	2	0
partaking	2	.2446	.1142	30.6	0	0	0	1	1	0	0	0	0	0	0	0	0	0	0	0	0	0	0	0	1	0	0	1	0
parted	26	.6738	3.6547	45.6	3	4	5	7	3	3	1	0	10	0	0	3	0	1	0	0	2	0	0	0	5	3	1	1	0
Parthenon	14	.1099	.4114	36.1	0	1	0	1	3	8	1	0	0	0	0	0	0	5	0	0	0	8	0	0	0	0	1	0	0
partial	59	.6883	8.2323	49.2	2	18	2	1	11	6	16	3	1	4	3	1	26	1	0	7	1	0	0	4	0	4	3	4	0
partially	30	.6856	4.1431	46.2	2	1	1	1	2	4	13	6	0	2	0	2	0	1	0	3	1	1	5	0	2	2	7	4	0
partials	2	.0000	.0162	22.1	2	0	0	0	0	0	0	0	0	0	0	0	0	0	0	0	2	0	0	0	0	0	0	0	0
participant	4	.4711	.3990	36.0	0	0	0	1	0	1	2	0	0	0	0	0	0	1	0	0	1	0	0	0	0	1	0	1	0
participants	14	.5654	1.6545	42.2	0	0	0	2	7	1	4	0	1	1	0	0	0	3	0	0	0	0	0	0	0	3	2	4	0
participate	18	.6624	2.4251	43.8	0	1	4	2	3	3	5	0	1	0	1	1	0	0	0	3	1	0	1	1	0	1	0	8	0
participated	12	.5326	1.3433	41.3	1	0	0	1	1	6	2	1	0	0	0	0	0	6	0	0	1	0	0	0	0	2	2	1	0
participating	5	.4495	.4906	36.9	0	0	0	1	0	3	0	1	1	0	0	0	0	0	0	1	1	0	1	0	0	0	0	1	0
participation	30	.6700	4.0863	46.1	0	0	1	1	13	6	7	2	1	1	0	3	0	5	0	1	6	0	0	0	0	4	5	4	0
participial	12	.1869	.5121	37.1	0	0	0	0	0	2	10	0	0	7	5	0	0	0	0	0	0	0	0	0	0	0	0	0	0
participle	39	.2363	2.1204	43.3	0	0	7	2	9	11	9	1	0	30	0	0	0	0	8	0	0	0	0	0	0	0	0	1	0
participles	4	.2408	.2182	33.4	0	0	0	0	0	3	1	0	0	2	0	0	0	0	2	0	0	0	0	0	0	0	0	0	0
particle	59	.5099	6.4253	48.1	0	2	3	9	8	18	11	8	2	4	0	1	0	0	0	40	0	0	0	2	2	0	8	0	0
particles	290	.6381	38.224	55.8	1	40	28	49	45	67	42	18	14	7	5	0	0	2	1	183	2	0	4	11	0	12	42	7	0
particular	406	.9100	73.188	58.6	6	25	52	49	129	57	71	17	45	53	19	28	20	23	17	61	17	6	7	5	17	13	47	28	0
particularly	252	.9251	46.136	56.6	12	10	33	30	71	47	34	15	34	13	5	15	3	30	5	28	23	2	8	3	6	20	31	26	0
particulars	8	.4302	.7299	38.6	0	1	0	0	5	1	0	1	0	0	0	3	0	0	0	0	0	0	0	0	3	1	0	1	0
parties	132	.7180	19.280	52.9	14	5	19	11	24	30	26	3	18	2	0	3	2	30	0	2	6	0	12	0	4	22	17	14	0
parting	15	.6201	1.9525	42.9	1	1	3	2	5	0	3	0	5	0	0	4	0	0	0	0	1	0	0	1	2	0	1	1	0
partisan	5	.2320	.3834	35.8	0	0	0	0	4	0	1	0	4	0	0	0	0	0	0	1	0	0	0	0	0	0	0	0	0
partisans	3	.3769	.2484	34.0	0	0	0	0	0	1	2	0	0	0	0	0	0	1	0	0	0	0	0	0	0	0	1	1	0
partition	17	.4389	1.6277	42.1	1	2	5	1	4	2	2	0	1	0	0	0	10	2	0	1	0	0	0	0	2	0	1	0	0
Partition	2	.2408	.1204	30.8	0	0	1	0	0	0	1	0	0	0	0	0	0	1	0	0	0	0	0	0	0	1	0	0	0
partitioned	12	.2078	.6322	38.0	0	0	1	8	1	1	1	0	0	0	0	0	10	1	0	0	0	0	0	0	0	0	1	0	0
partitions	8	.3727	.6310	38.0	0	0	0	1	3	2	2	0	0	0	0	0	0	2	0	0	0	2	0	2	0	0	0	2	0
Partlet	4	.0000	.1827	32.6	0	0	4	0	0	0	0	0	4	0	0	0	0	0	0	0	0	0	0	0	0	0	0	0	0
partly	201	.8567	34.384	55.4	12	14	28	19	46	51	20	11	27	6	2	13	3	42	3	41	6	0	8	0	5	14	21	10	0
partner	112	.7318	16.650	52.2	22	18	23	11	22	11	3	2	22	7	0	3	4	2	1	11	29	0	4	0	15	3	6	5	0
partner's	5	.5527	.5722	37.6	2	0	2	0	0	0	1	0	0	0	0	1	1	0	0	1	1	0	0	0	1	0	0	0	0
partners	74	.6311	9.6515	49.8	4	9	15	31	7	1	6	1	6	5	0	1	2	2	0	30	16	0	0	0	3	6	1	2	0
partnership	29	.5346	3.3530	45.3	0	3	6	15	5	0	0	0	6	3	0	0	0	1	0	14	0	0	0	0	0	0	3	2	0
partnerships	10	.1777	.5109	37.1	0	0	0	8	0	0	2	0	0	0	0	0	0	2	0	8	0	0	0	0	0	0	0	0	0
partridge	11	.5462	1.2752	41.1	1	1	2	1	2	3	1	0	3	0	1	1	0	0	0	0	3	0	0	0	2	0	1	0	0
parts	2331	.8865	410.45	66.1	457	324	370	288	335	243	283	31	214	217	25	27	237	358	136	439	202	64	20	98	13	95	113	73	0
partway	4	.2085	.2127	33.3	2	0	0	0	1	0	1	0	0	0	0	0	0	0	0	3	0	0	0	1	0	0	0	0	0
party	625	.8921	111.06	60.5	120	90	74	61	100	87	79	14	177	53	6	31	31	96	16	2	11	2	26	0	30	63	38	43	0
Party	52	.5431	5.9061	47.7	2	0	8	3	7	28	2	2	1	0	0	0	0	19	0	0	1	0	0	0	4	2	13	12	0
party's	10	.4700	1.0198	40.1	0	0	2	0	4	2	2	0	1	0	0	0	0	4	0	0	0	0	0	0	0	1	3	1	0
Party's	4	.4525	.4044	36.1	0	0	0	0	0	2	2	0	1	0	0	0	0	1	0	0	0	0	0	0	1	0	0	1	0
parunts	2	.0000	.0290	24.6	0	2	0	0	0	0	0	0	0	0	0	0	0	0	0	0	0	0	0	0	0	2	0	0	0
pas	2	.1494	.1045	30.2	0	0	0	0	2	0	0	0	1	0	0	0	0	0	0	0	1	0	0	0	0	0	0	0	0
Pasadena	7	.3722	.6752	38.3	0	0	1	2	4	0	0	0	5	0	0	0	0	1	0	0	0	0	0	0	0	0	0	1	0
Pascal	8	.2194	.4321	36.4	2	1	0	0	0	5	0	0	0	2	0	0	6	0	0	0	0	0	0	0	0	0	0	0	0
Pascual	9	.2292	.6951	38.4	0	0	0	0	8	0	1	0	8	0	0	0	0	0	0	0	0	0	0	0	0	0	1	0	0
Pascual's	2	.0000	.0914	29.6	0	0	0	0	2	0	0	0	2	0	0	0	0	0	0	0	0	0	0	0	0	0	0	0	0

5N Parkin's
5R Parkinson
7Q parklands
5F parklike
7Q Parkman
6A Parkson
8M parkways
3A Parl
5A parleys
8Q parliamentarian
9Q parliaments
7J Parlour
7Q Parma
9J Parnassian
5Q Parnassians
5Q Parnassus
5P parochialisms
5P parodied
XR parodist
7Q paroled
8A paroles
8J Paroo
7D paroquets
9E parquet
5Q Parr
6A parried
7D Parrish
9Q parsimonious
8A parsimony
6B parsing
6A parsons
7D parsons'
7H Parsonstown
9M part-assembly
7G part-ner
7Q partakes
7R Parthenia
6P parti-colored
5N partiality
XR participates
XR participatory
8H particle-wave
9Q particle's
7R particulates
5A Partidge
8Q Parties
7R partified
8F Partisan
3Q partly-finished
8A Partridge
6A partridges
9G Parts
XH parturition
7Q party-hat
3Q Pas-de-Calais
XR Pasadella
6E Pascal's
4A paschal
4K Pascin
5F Pascua

Word Type	F	D	U	SFI	3 Gr 3	4 Gr 4	5 Gr 5	6 Gr 6	7 Gr 7	8 Gr 8	9 Gr 9	X UnGr	A Read	B Eng & Gr	C Comp	D Lit	E Math	F Soc Stud	G Spell	H Sci	J Music	K Art	L Home Ec	M Shop	N Lib F	P Lib NF	Q Lib Ref	R Mag	S Rel
Paso	2	.2375	.1088	30.4	1	0	0	0	1	0	0	0	0	0	0	0	0	0	0	0	1	0	0	0	0	0	0	1	0
pass	480	.9125	86.988	59.4	80	59	63	54	114	59	37	14	117	15	2	33	30	44	8	64	18	0	3	1	24	60	30	31	0
Pass	28	.7055	4.1115	46.1	0	1	6	2	15	2	1	1	13	1	0	2	0	3	0	0	2	0	0	0	1	0	3	3	0
passable	4	.4556	.4079	36.1	0	0	1	1	1	1	0	0	1	0	0	0	0	1	0	0	0	0	0	0	1	1	0	0	0
passacaglia	4	.0000	.0323	25.1	0	0	0	0	4	0	0	0	0	0	0	0	0	0	0	0	4	0	0	0	0	0	0	0	0
Passacaglia	2	.0000	.0162	22.1	0	0	0	0	2	0	0	0	0	0	0	0	0	0	0	0	2	0	0	0	0	0	0	0	0
passage	172	.8190	28.233	54.5	10	10	22	19	48	25	32	6	29	30	8	11	0	16	7	12	7	0	1	0	12	7	22	10	0
Passage	17	.4298	1.5952	42.0	0	4	8	0	3	1	1	0	0	0	1	0	0	11	0	0	0	0	0	0	0	1	0	4	0
passages	66	.6088	8.3565	49.2	3	5	9	8	13	9	19	0	12	8	0	1	0	2	0	8	21	0	0	0	3	3	6	2	0
passageway	13	.4610	1.3755	41.4	5	2	2	3	0	0	1	0	6	0	0	1	0	0	0	0	0	0	0	0	0	4	0	2	0
passageways	6	.3365	.4978	37.0	2	1	0	0	2	0	1	0	2	0	0	2	0	0	0	2	0	0	0	0	0	0	0	0	0
passed	813	.9143	147.76	61.7	84	131	107	119	164	114	69	25	260	29	7	52	19	130	3	45	12	2	5	6	73	76	49	45	0
passenger	116	.7683	18.055	52.6	17	17	9	27	11	17	14	4	16	5	0	1	13	27	0	21	2	0	0	0	3	9	4	15	0
passenger-car	2	.2433	.1158	30.6	0	0	0	0	1	0	0	1	0	0	0	0	0	0	0	0	0	0	0	0	0	1	0	1	0
passenger-miles	6	.0000	.0898	29.5	0	0	0	0	6	0	0	0	0	0	0	0	6	0	0	0	0	0	0	0	0	0	0	0	0
passengers	146	.8264	24.265	53.8	19	23	23	20	34	7	18	2	33	4	1	6	12	30	0	8	3	0	0	0	8	21	4	16	0
passengers'	2	.2433	.1158	30.6	0	0	0	0	1	0	1	0	0	0	0	0	0	0	0	0	0	0	0	0	0	1	0	1	0
Passepartout	22	.0685	.5359	37.3	0	0	0	1	21	0	0	0	0	1	0	0	0	0	0	0	0	0	0	0	21	0	0	0	0
passer	8	.0554	.2106	33.2	0	0	0	7	1	0	0	0	1	0	0	0	0	0	0	0	0	0	0	0	0	0	0	7	0
passers	2	.0000	.0243	23.9	0	0	0	1	0	1	0	0	0	0	0	0	0	0	0	0	0	0	0	0	0	0	0	2	0
passers-by	8	.4992	.8452	39.3	1	0	2	1	2	2	0	0	1	1	1	0	0	0	0	0	0	0	0	0	3	1	0	1	0
passersby	4	.3755	.3686	35.7	0	1	0	1	0	1	0	1	2	0	0	0	0	0	0	0	0	0	0	0	1	1	0	0	0
passes	216	.8450	36.468	55.6	28	21	28	31	46	29	30	3	22	5	1	5	11	17	3	67	8	0	2	9	4	23	23	16	0
Passes	2	.0000	.0243	23.9	0	0	0	0	0	1	0	1	0	0	0	0	0	0	0	0	0	0	0	0	0	0	0	2	0
passing	231	.8836	40.746	56.1	17	34	24	41	64	26	17	8	72	3	1	19	9	18	0	24	4	0	3	3	30	20	14	11	0
passion	32	.6904	4.4977	46.5	0	3	5	3	6	9	6	0	4	1	1	7	0	1	0	0	1	0	0	0	8	2	1	6	0
Passion	7	.2409	.3937	36.0	0	0	1	1	3	0	1	1	0	0	0	0	0	0	0	0	3	0	0	0	0	4	0	0	0
passionate	12	.4974	1.2385	40.9	0	0	0	1	4	3	4	0	0	0	0	2	0	1	0	0	5	0	0	0	0	1	1	2	0
passionately	6	.3390	.4900	36.9	0	0	0	1	2	1	2	0	2	0	0	0	0	0	0	0	0	0	0	0	0	0	2	2	0
passions	9	.5541	1.0397	40.2	0	1	1	4	2	0	1	0	1	3	0	1	0	0	0	0	0	0	0	0	1	0	2	1	0
passive	16	.2904	1.0363	40.2	0	0	0	0	5	4	7	0	0	10	0	0	0	0	0	0	0	0	0	0	0	0	5	1	0
Passover	6	.1169	.2555	34.1	0	2	4	0	0	0	0	0	2	0	0	0	0	0	0	0	0	0	0	0	0	0	4	0	0
passport	6	.4529	.6086	37.8	0	0	0	2	2	1	1	0	2	1	0	1	0	0	0	0	0	0	0	0	2	0	0	0	0
passports	3	.3762	.2479	33.9	0	1	0	0	1	1	0	0	0	0	0	0	0	0	0	1	0	0	0	0	1	0	1	0	0
past	1109	.8888	195.97	62.9	140	128	165	173	218	131	132	22	206	118	11	68	22	94	171	70	34	4	3	6	65	78	61	98	0
Past	4	.3604	.3538	35.5	0	0	0	1	2	0	1	0	2	0	0	1	0	0	0	0	1	0	0	0	0	0	0	0	0
past-tense	4	.0000	.0325	25.1	0	0	0	1	1	0	2	0	0	0	0	0	0	0	4	0	0	0	0	0	0	0	0	0	0
paste	96	.5652	11.168	50.5	20	22	25	9	11	6	2	1	8	1	5	4	13	3	2	10	0	26	1	5	2	4	1	9	2
pasteboard	5	.4707	.5371	37.3	1	0	1	0	2	1	0	0	2	0	0	0	0	1	0	1	0	0	0	0	0	0	1	0	0
pasted	22	.3251	1.5295	41.8	5	5	3	1	2	4	2	0	0	1	0	0	3	1	0	1	0	9	0	2	2	3	0	0	0
pastel	2	.1247	.0633	28.0	0	0	0	1	0	1	0	0	0	0	0	0	0	0	0	0	0	1	0	0	0	1	0	0	0
pastels	3	.0978	.0707	28.5	1	0	0	0	1	1	0	0	0	0	0	1	0	0	0	0	0	2	0	0	0	0	0	0	0
Pasteur	52	.4389	5.2535	47.2	2	6	2	23	2	2	4	11	15	3	0	0	2	2	0	29	0	0	0	0	0	0	1	0	0
Pasteur's	2	.2160	.1362	31.3	0	0	0	2	0	0	0	0	1	0	0	0	0	0	0	1	0	0	0	0	0	0	0	0	0
pasteurization	7	.4777	.7248	38.6	0	0	0	2	2	1	2	0	1	1	0	0	0	0	0	3	0	0	1	0	0	0	1	0	0
pasteurized	9	.3861	.7922	39.0	0	0	1	4	2	1	1	0	1	1	0	0	0	0	0	6	0	0	1	0	0	0	0	0	0
pasteurizing	2	.0000	.0299	24.8	1	0	0	0	1	0	0	0	0	0	0	0	2	0	0	0	0	0	0	0	0	0	0	0	0
pastime	8	.3047	.5871	37.7	1	2	0	2	2	0	1	0	2	0	0	0	0	0	0	0	0	0	1	0	0	0	0	5	0
pastimes	3	.1927	.1608	32.1	0	0	1	0	0	1	1	0	1	1	0	0	0	0	0	0	0	1	0	0	0	0	0	0	0
pasting	14	.4276	1.2712	41.0	2	0	7	0	3	1	1	0	1	0	0	1	2	0	0	1	0	4	1	0	1	1	1	1	0
pastor	4	.4350	.3902	35.9	0	1	0	0	0	1	2	0	1	0	0	0	0	1	1	0	0	0	0	0	0	0	0	1	0
pastoral	6	.4377	.5583	37.5	0	0	2	1	3	0	0	0	0	0	0	0	0	1	0	0	2	0	0	0	0	2	1	0	0
pastors	3	.3756	.2468	33.9	0	0	0	0	0	1	2	0	0	0	0	1	0	1	0	0	0	0	0	0	0	0	1	0	0
pastries	5	.3757	.4735	36.8	0	0	4	0	1	0	0	0	3	0	0	0	0	0	0	1	0	0	0	0	0	0	1	0	0
pastry	17	.1533	.8886	39.5	3	5	1	0	1	0	7	0	9	1	0	0	0	0	0	0	0	0	7	0	0	0	0	0	0
pasturage	2	.2285	.1129	30.5	0	0	1	0	1	0	0	0	0	0	0	0	0	1	0	0	0	0	0	0	0	0	1	0	0
pasture	153	.7996	24.819	53.9	49	20	26	27	11	10	8	2	55	4	5	13	3	32	2	0	2	1	0	0	11	19	1	5	0
Pasture	2	.0000	.0243	23.9	0	0	0	0	0	1	0	1	0	0	0	0	0	0	0	0	0	0	0	0	0	0	0	2	0
pastured	5	.4498	.5001	37.0	0	1	1	1	1	1	0	0	1	0	0	1	0	2	0	0	0	0	0	0	0	0	1	0	0
pastureland	2	.0000	.0389	25.9	0	0	1	0	1	0	0	0	0	0	0	0	0	2	0	0	0	0	0	0	0	0	0	0	0
pastures	69	.5664	8.2913	49.2	4	15	17	18	10	4	0	1	7	0	1	2	0	48	0	1	0	1	0	0	2	2	1	4	0
Pastures	3	.0000	.1370	31.4	0	0	0	3	0	0	0	0	3	0	0	0	0	0	0	0	0	0	0	0	0	0	0	0	0
pasturing	3	.2378	.1809	32.6	0	0	2	1	0	0	0	0	0	0	0	0	0	2	0	0	0	0	0	0	0	1	0	0	0
pasty-faced	3	.2279	.2143	33.3	0	0	0	1	1	1	0	0	2	0	0	0	0	0	0	0	0	0	0	0	0	0	0	1	0
pat	29	.6978	4.1463	46.2	8	8	1	3	7	1	1	0	7	2	0	1	0	0	3	0	1	0	2	0	6	6	0	1	0
Pat	53	.6532	7.4463	48.7	15	9	3	15	2	7	1	1	36	2	2	2	3	2	0	0	0	0	0	0	1	2	0	3	0
Pat's	3	.2261	.2131	33.3	1	2	0	0	0	0	0	0	2	0	0	0	0	0	0	0	0	0	0	0	1	0	0	0	0
Patagonia	9	.0449	.2030	33.1	6	1	0	0	2	0	0	0	1	0	0	0	0	0	0	0	0	0	0	0	0	0	8	0	0
Patagonian	4	.0000	.0419	26.2	2	0	0	0	2	0	0	0	0	0	0	0	0	0	0	0	0	0	0	0	0	0	4	0	0
patapon	3	.0000	.0243	23.8	3	0	0	0	0	0	0	0	0	0	0	0	0	0	0	0	3	0	0	0	0	0	0	0	0
patch	97	.8504	16.552	52.2	12	21	9	18	15	10	6	6	33	3	2	6	0	5	2	5	0	0	4	1	9	10	3	14	0
Patch	2	.2106	.0917	29.6	0	0	1	0	0	0	1	0	0	0	0	0	0	0	1	0	0	0	1	0	0	0	0	0	0
patched	14	.4606	1.5045	41.8	1	3	5	2	1	1	1	0	8	0	0	0	0	0	0	0	0	0	0	0	2	1	0	3	0
patches	54	.7877	8.5907	49.3	6	10	8	11	14	3	1	1	11	2	1	1	0	12	0	2	1	2	0	0	7	7	6	2	0
patchwork	13	.7368	1.9405	42.9	0	2	4	2	2	1	2	0	1	1	0	1	0	3	0	1	0	0	0	0	1	2	1	2	0
patent	47	.5318	5.4141	47.3	0	20	7	4	7	6	1	2	16	0	0	0	0	1	3	2	4	0	0	0	0	1	18	2	0
Patent	15	.5120	1.6448	42.2	0	6	2	0	2	4	1	0	3	0	0	0	1	2	1	0	2	0	0	0	0	0	6	0	0
patented	18	.4749	1.8412	42.7	0	6	2	0	4	2	2	2	3	0	0	0	0	1	0	0	2	0	0	0	0	1	8	3	0
patents	21	.4737	2.1081	43.2	0	9	1	0	5	4	1	1	1	0	0	1	0	4	0	0	2	0	0	0	0	0	10	3	0
pater	2	.2412	.1141	30.6	0	0	0	0	1	0	0	1	0	1	0	0	0	0	0	0	0	0	0	0	0	1	0	0	0
path	436	.8728	76.094	58.8	100	90	45	54	82	35	22	8	123	6	2	46	34	16	4	105	5	3	1	1	25	37	13	15	0
Path	4	.1135	.1696	32.3	0	1	0	3	0	0	0	0	1	0	0	0	3	0	0	0	0	0	0	0	0	0	0	0	0
pathetic	8	.5427	.9424	39.7	0	0	0	5	3	0	0	0	3	0	0	0	0	0	0	0	1	0	0	0	2	1	0	1	0
pathetically	2	.1641	.0751	28.8	0	0	0	0	1	0	1	0	0	0	1	0	0	0	0	0	0	0	0	0	0	0	1	0	0
pathfinder	2	.2446	.1257	31.0	1	0	0	1	0	0	0	0	0	0	0	0	0	1	0	1	0	0	0	0	0	0	0	0	0
pathless	2	.0000	.0234	23.7	0	1	0	0	1	0	0	0	0	0	0	0	0	0	0	0	0	0	0	0	2	0	0	0	0
pathology	6	.2879	.3956	36.0	0	0	0	0	2	1	2	1	0	0	0	0	0	0	0	1	0	0	0	0	0	0	1	4	0
paths	73	.8121	11.914	50.8	13	9	6	12	13	13	4	3	11	1	0	4	4	5	0	21	7	0	0	2	3	6	5	4	0
pathway	15	.5736	1.8185	42.6	0	2	2	5	3	2	0	1	2	0	0	1	0	2	0	6	2	0	0	0	0	0	0	2	0
pathways	6	.4539	.5761	37.6	0	0	0	0	4	1	1	0	0	0	0	0	0	1	0	1	0	0	0	1	0	0	2	1	0
Pati	3	.0000	.0434	26.4	0	0	0	0	3	0	0	0	0	0	0	0	0	0	0	0	0	0	0	0	0	3	0	0	0
patience	58	.7936	9.3287	49.7	6	5	12	8	12	8	4	3	20	1	2	5	0	3	0	2	1	0	0	1	8	4	2	9	0
patient	126	.7020	18.040	52.6	10	12	19	7	29	16	29	4	23	1	2	5	2	1	3	17	2	0	19	0	3	14	20	13	1
patient's	13	.3133	.9030	39.6	0	0	2	0	1	3	6	1	1	0	0	0	0	0	0	1	0	0	5	0	0	0	3	3	0

7R Paseo
3Q Pasig
3Q pasko
9Q pasqueflower
7R pass-receiving
7P pass'd
9D passado
7J passar
4R passbook
3P Passeau
9P Passenger
6P passenger-carrying
7G passenger's
9E passer-by
8B passerby
7P passeth
7P passion-winged
9R passionless
4G passus
4G passuum
9B password
5A passwords
4N Passy
XR past-due
5P pasta
9M paste-up
9L pastel-colored
6R pastel-hued
5Q pastes
XH Pasteur-baiters
6A pasteurize
6J pastorals
7R Pastore
7R Pastrengo
7L pastry-lined
5P pasturelands
5G pastus
7D pasuke
4E PAT
4J pat-a-pat-a
4J pat-a-pat-a-pan
4A pat-pats
9L patching
9Q Patchogue
4N patchy-blatchy
7D pate
7D patens
4P patent-leather
9F Patents
8G patere
XH paternal
7A paternalism
5P paternalistic
4P Paterson
5F Paterson's
6P path-breaker
9J Pathetic
5F pathfinders
9H pathogens
9A pathological
9P pathologist
8H pathologists
9D pathos
7D pathway's

Word Type	F	D	U	SFI	3 Gr 3	4 Gr 4	5 Gr 5	6 Gr 6	7 Gr 7	8 Gr 8	9 Gr 9	X UnGr	A Read	B Eng & Gr	C Comp	D Lit	E Math	F Soc Stud	G Spell	H Sci	J Music	K Art	L Home Ec	M Shop	N Lib F	P Lib NF	Q Lib Ref	R Mag	S Rel
patiently	51	.6856	7.1930	48.6	5	6	4	9	17	5	4	1	12	3	1	9	0	2	0	1	0	0	0	0	11	4	0	8	0
patients	52	.7275	7.7595	48.9	3	4	9	2	8	6	16	4	15	0	1	1	0	1	0	10	0	0	1	0	1	5	9	8	0
patients'	2	.0000	.0914	29.6	0	0	2	0	0	0	0	0	2	0	0	0	0	0	0	0	0	0	0	0	0	0	0	0	0
patio	8	.1325	.3888	35.9	0	3	1	4	0	0	0	0	2	0	0	0	0	6	0	0	0	0	0	0	0	0	0	0	0
patios	4	.3457	.3009	34.8	0	0	0	2	2	0	0	0	0	0	0	0	0	2	0	0	0	0	1	1	0	0	0	0	0
pato	4	.0000	.1827	32.6	0	0	0	0	4	0	0	0	4	0	0	0	0	0	0	0	0	0	0	0	0	0	0	0	0
patriarch	5	.4662	.4904	36.9	0	0	1	0	3	0	1	0	0	0	0	0	0	0	0	0	0	0	0	0	2	1	1	1	0
Patricia	40	.2506	2.3144	43.6	35	0	1	1	1	0	0	2	0	0	1	0	0	0	0	0	0	0	0	0	35	0	1	3	0
Patricia's	3	.0000	.0352	25.5	3	0	0	0	0	0	0	0	0	0	0	0	0	0	0	0	0	0	0	0	3	0	0	0	0
patrician	2	.2437	.1129	30.5	1	0	0	0	1	0	0	0	0	0	0	0	0	0	0	0	0	0	0	0	0	0	1	1	0
patricians	2	.0000	.0389	25.9	0	0	0	2	0	0	0	0	0	0	0	0	0	2	0	0	0	0	0	0	0	0	0	0	0
Patrick	58	.7028	8.4868	49.3	23	6	10	2	5	11	0	1	27	7	3	2	0	5	0	1	4	0	0	0	0	4	1	4	0
Patrick's	4	.1948	.2500	34.0	0	2	1	0	0	1	0	0	2	0	0	0	0	0	0	0	0	0	0	0	0	2	0	0	0
patriot	17	.6501	2.2523	43.5	3	1	3	3	2	3	2	0	0	2	0	1	0	5	0	0	3	0	0	0	1	3	2	0	0
Patriot	2	.0000	.0914	29.6	0	1	1	0	0	0	0	0	2	0	0	0	0	0	0	0	0	0	0	0	0	0	0	0	0
patriotic	22	.4743	2.2139	43.5	0	2	5	3	3	8	1	0	3	2	1	1	0	1	0	0	12	0	0	0	0	0	1	1	0
patriotism	18	.5716	2.1482	43.3	1	0	3	1	3	7	3	0	2	0	0	1	0	3	0	0	5	0	0	0	1	4	0	2	0
patriots	13	.6276	1.6860	42.3	0	2	2	3	1	5	0	0	1	2	0	0	0	5	0	0	1	0	0	0	0	1	1	2	0
Patriots	5	.0000	.2284	33.6	0	5	0	0	0	0	0	0	5	0	0	0	0	0	0	0	0	0	0	0	0	0	0	0	0
patrol	46	.7841	7.2802	48.6	2	7	6	13	6	7	4	1	9	1	1	2	2	3	2	3	0	0	0	0	3	4	3	13	0
Patrol	10	.3765	.9649	39.8	0	1	1	5	1	0	0	2	7	0	0	0	0	0	0	0	0	0	0	0	0	2	0	1	0
patrolled	7	.3318	.5130	37.1	0	0	1	2	4	0	0	0	0	0	0	2	0	0	0	0	0	0	0	0	0	1	0	4	0
patrolling	3	.1187	.1291	31.1	0	0	0	0	2	0	1	0	1	0	0	2	0	0	0	0	0	0	0	0	0	0	0	0	0
patrolman	3	.2292	.1615	32.1	0	0	0	0	2	0	1	0	0	0	0	1	0	0	0	0	0	0	0	0	2	0	0	0	0
Patrolman	5	.2086	.3320	35.2	0	0	0	2	3	0	0	0	3	0	0	0	0	0	0	0	0	0	0	0	2	0	0	0	0
patrols	8	.5027	.8581	39.3	1	1	0	2	2	1	0	1	1	0	0	0	1	0	1	0	0	0	0	0	0	3	0	2	0
patron	12	.4900	1.2808	41.1	0	1	2	1	6	2	0	0	3	0	0	0	0	2	0	0	2	0	0	0	1	0	4	0	0
patronage	7	.5819	.8505	39.3	0	0	0	0	2	2	1	2	1	0	0	0	0	1	0	0	1	0	0	0	1	0	1	2	0
patrons	6	.5517	.6872	38.4	0	0	0	0	2	2	2	0	0	0	0	1	0	1	0	0	0	0	0	0	0	2	1	1	0
patronyms	2	.0000	.0243	23.9	0	0	0	0	2	0	0	0	0	0	0	0	0	0	0	0	0	0	0	0	0	0	0	2	0
pats	9	.5029	1.0230	40.1	3	2	1	0	3	0	0	0	5	0	0	1	0	0	0	0	0	0	1	0	1	1	0	0	0
Patsy	64	.4074	5.6345	47.5	1	51	0	0	0	8	4	0	1	4	0	0	0	1	2	0	0	0	6	0	2	48	0	0	0
Patsy's	6	.3646	.4739	36.8	0	5	0	0	0	1	0	0	0	0	0	0	0	0	1	0	0	0	1	0	0	4	0	0	0
patted	70	.6104	9.1178	49.6	14	19	7	10	8	10	2	0	30	3	0	4	0	0	0	0	2	0	0	0	18	9	0	4	0
patter	8	.5175	.8804	39.4	1	3	2	0	2	0	0	0	1	2	0	0	0	0	0	2	1	0	0	0	2	0	0	0	0
pattered	2	.0000	.0914	29.6	1	0	1	0	0	0	0	0	2	0	0	0	0	0	0	0	0	0	0	0	0	0	0	0	0
pattering	5	.2280	.2804	34.5	1	0	0	0	2	2	0	0	1	0	2	1	0	0	0	0	0	0	0	0	0	0	0	1	0
pattern	1057	.7853	165.67	62.2	99	145	146	139	188	176	156	8	40	87	5	19	191	16	129	56	244	27	96	55	7	20	41	24	0
Pattern	58	.1945	2.7026	44.3	0	0	0	0	29	11	18	0	0	47	0	0	0	0	11	0	0	0	0	0	0	0	0	0	0
PATTERN	2	.0000	.0219	23.4	0	2	0	0	0	0	0	0	0	2	0	0	0	0	0	0	0	0	0	0	0	0	0	0	0
patterned	13	.5270	1.3923	41.4	1	0	1	2	2	4	3	0	0	0	1	3	0	0	0	0	1	3	1	0	0	1	3	0	0
patterning	5	.3343	.3654	35.6	0	0	1	0	4	0	0	0	0	3	0	0	0	0	0	0	1	0	0	0	0	1	0	0	0
Patterning	3	.0000	.0243	23.9	0	0	0	0	0	3	0	0	0	0	0	0	0	0	3	0	0	0	0	0	0	0	0	0	0
patternmaker	3	.0986	.0757	28.8	0	0	0	0	1	0	2	0	0	0	0	0	0	0	0	0	0	0	0	2	0	1	0	0	0
patterns	583	.7631	88.985	59.5	44	79	98	61	114	116	63	8	24	62	5	7	77	7	99	25	184	17	16	17	2	11	21	9	0
Patterns	31	.0315	.4420	36.5	13	1	0	0	0	16	1	0	0	0	0	0	1	0	30	0	0	0	0	0	0	0	0	0	0
Patterson	4	.0000	.0486	26.9	0	0	0	0	3	0	0	1	0	0	0	0	0	0	0	0	0	0	0	0	0	0	0	4	0
Patti	7	.1117	.2888	34.6	0	0	1	6	0	0	0	0	2	0	0	0	0	0	0	0	0	0	0	0	0	0	0	5	0
Pattie's	2	.0000	.0299	24.8	0	0	0	2	0	0	0	0	0	0	0	0	2	0	0	0	0	0	0	0	0	0	0	0	0
patties	4	.2376	.2223	33.5	0	3	0	0	0	0	1	0	0	0	0	0	0	0	0	0	0	0	1	0	0	3	0	0	0
patting	20	.5795	2.4445	43.9	3	4	1	2	6	3	1	0	5	1	0	2	0	0	0	1	5	0	0	0	4	2	0	0	0
Patton	8	.2958	.5435	37.4	0	1	0	0	5	2	0	0	0	0	0	0	0	2	0	0	0	0	0	0	1	0	0	5	0
Patton's	2	.2408	.1204	30.8	0	0	1	0	0	1	0	0	0	0	0	0	0	1	0	0	0	0	0	0	0	1	0	0	0
patty	2	.1674	.0805	29.1	0	1	0	0	0	0	1	0	0	0	0	0	0	0	0	0	0	0	1	0	0	1	0	0	0
Patty	34	.7430	5.1885	47.2	14	1	10	2	0	4	3	0	14	5	1	1	4	0	1	0	0	0	1	0	3	4	0	0	0
patty-cakes	2	.0000	.0243	23.9	2	0	0	0	0	0	0	0	0	0	0	0	0	0	0	0	0	0	0	0	0	0	0	2	0
Patty's	6	.4161	.5557	37.4	2	1	2	0	0	1	0	0	1	2	0	0	1	0	0	0	0	0	0	0	0	2	0	0	0
Paul	507	.8050	83.268	59.2	36	84	117	54	56	135	14	11	289	18	12	13	14	9	5	5	8	9	0	0	63	29	11	22	0
Paul-Marc	2	.0000	.0243	23.9	0	0	0	0	0	0	0	2	0	0	0	0	0	0	0	0	0	0	0	0	0	0	0	2	0
Paul's	46	.6164	6.1868	47.9	1	6	8	4	10	14	0	3	31	1	0	0	2	0	0	0	0	0	0	0	4	3	3	2	0
Paula	5	.0000	.0748	28.7	2	0	0	3	0	0	0	0	0	0	0	0	5	0	0	0	0	0	0	0	0	0	0	0	0
Paulette	2	.1814	.1187	30.7	1	0	0	0	1	0	0	0	1	0	0	0	0	0	0	0	0	0	0	0	0	0	0	1	0
Pauli	2	.0000	.0394	26.0	0	0	0	0	0	0	0	2	0	0	0	0	0	0	0	2	0	0	0	0	0	0	0	0	0
Paulo	5	.2205	.2855	34.6	0	0	2	2	1	0	0	0	0	0	0	0	0	4	0	0	0	0	0	0	0	0	1	0	0
Paulossie	9	.0000	.4111	36.1	9	0	0	0	0	0	0	0	9	0	0	0	0	0	0	0	0	0	0	0	0	0	0	0	0
Pauls	2	.0000	.0290	24.6	0	2	0	0	0	0	0	0	0	0	0	0	0	0	0	0	0	0	0	0	0	2	0	0	0
pause	109	.6683	14.828	51.7	8	17	2	22	33	17	8	2	11	29	7	25	0	3	2	0	5	0	0	0	18	4	2	3	0
paused	72	.6075	9.3509	49.7	6	14	3	9	19	12	7	2	31	1	0	12	0	3	0	0	0	0	0	0	11	5	0	9	0
pauses	19	.5197	2.0750	43.2	2	3	3	3	5	2	1	0	2	9	0	3	0	0	1	0	0	0	0	0	2	1	0	1	0
pausing	11	.5492	1.2884	41.1	1	0	0	1	2	3	4	0	3	2	0	2	0	0	0	0	0	0	0	0	2	0	2	0	0
pavane	2	.0000	.0215	23.3	0	0	0	0	2	0	0	0	0	0	0	2	0	0	0	0	0	0	0	0	0	0	0	0	0
paved	45	.6397	5.9712	47.8	4	11	5	6	6	6	6	1	7	2	4	1	0	19	2	1	1	0	0	0	0	2	3	3	0
pavement	33	.6353	4.4174	46.5	4	10	1	4	6	3	5	0	12	1	2	1	1	1	1	4	0	0	0	0	9	1	0	0	0
pavements	6	.4693	.6062	37.8	0	1	1	1	0	1	1	1	0	0	0	0	0	1	0	2	0	0	0	0	1	2	0	0	0
pavilion	4	.3498	.3059	34.9	0	0	1	1	1	1	0	0	0	0	0	0	0	0	0	0	0	0	0	0	0	1	2	1	0
Pavilion	4	.3429	.3033	34.8	0	0	0	0	0	2	2	0	0	0	0	2	0	1	0	0	0	0	0	0	0	0	1	0	0
paving	2	.2446	.1142	30.6	0	0	0	1	1	0	0	0	0	0	0	0	0	0	0	0	0	0	0	0	1	0	0	1	0
Pavlov	9	.2302	.5579	37.5	0	0	0	1	7	0	1	0	1	0	0	0	0	0	0	7	0	0	0	0	0	0	0	1	0
paw	77	.5965	9.7868	49.9	22	21	8	6	19	1	0	0	29	0	0	10	0	1	0	1	5	0	0	0	23	5	2	1	0
Paw	7	.2353	.5425	37.3	1	0	0	5	0	0	0	1	6	0	0	0	0	0	0	0	0	0	0	0	0	0	0	1	0
pawed	7	.3768	.5716	37.6	1	2	0	0	4	0	0	0	0	0	0	2	0	0	0	0	0	0	0	0	3	2	0	0	0
pawing	13	.3679	1.1312	40.5	1	4	1	4	3	0	0	0	4	0	0	1	0	2	0	0	0	0	0	0	6	0	0	0	0
pawn	2	.2444	.1132	30.5	0	0	0	0	1	0	1	0	0	1	0	0	0	0	0	0	0	0	0	0	1	0	0	0	0
Pawn	2	.0000	.0234	23.7	0	0	2	0	0	0	0	0	0	0	0	0	0	0	0	0	0	0	0	0	2	0	0	0	0
pawnbroker's	2	.1717	.1142	30.6	0	0	0	0	1	1	0	0	1	0	0	1	0	0	0	0	0	0	0	0	0	0	0	0	0
Pawnee	12	.2440	.9330	39.7	2	9	0	1	0	0	0	0	10	0	0	0	0	0	0	0	2	0	0	0	0	0	0	0	0
paws	73	.7032	10.726	50.3	26	12	9	7	14	0	4	1	38	4	0	6	0	0	0	1	0	0	1	0	9	5	1	8	0
Paxton	3	.2060	.1500	31.8	0	1	0	0	2	0	0	0	0	0	0	2	0	0	0	0	0	0	0	0	0	1	0	0	0
pay	677	.9158	123.18	60.9	155	97	74	77	91	89	69	25	207	15	8	42	65	125	13	16	17	2	20	2	27	57	15	46	0
payable	2	.2401	.1133	30.5	0	0	0	0	2	0	0	0	0	0	0	0	0	0	0	0	0	0	0	0	0	1	1	0	0
payah	2	.0000	.0234	23.7	0	2	0	0	0	0	0	0	0	0	0	0	0	0	0	0	0	0	0	0	2	0	0	0	0
paycheck	4	.3863	.3417	35.3	0	0	1	0	0	2	1	0	0	1	0	0	0	2	0	0	0	0	0	0	0	0	0	1	0
paying	92	.8086	14.984	51.8	13	4	13	8	17	17	13	7	23	6	1	5	7	13	2	3	1	0	8	0	11	2	3	7	0
Payless	3	.0000	.0352	25.5	3	0	0	0	0	0	0	0	0	0	0	0	0	0	0	0	0	0	0	0	3	0	0	0	0
payload	5	.4850	.5162	37.1	0	0	0	0	2	2	1	0	0	0	0	0	1	0	0	2	0	0	0	0	0	0	1	1	0

3A patina
5P Patje
5R patois
7F Patras
5P patria
6R patriarchal
5Q patriarchs
5P Patrice
8R patricidal
9B Patrickovna
XH Patriofelis
8Q Patriotic
6A PATRIOTIC
7D patrolmen
8A Patrolmen
7D Patron
9P patronize
8F patroon
8F patroons
7C pattens
3A patter-patter
5H patters
6A Patti's
6E Pattie
7J patting-stamping
5N patty-pans
4N Pau
3A Paul-Louis-Toussaint
6E Paula's
7A Paulie
5Q Paulina
3A Paulossie's
8R Paulsen
9R pauperized
7P Pavan
6P Pavane
9D Pavel
8A Pavlova
7R Pavlovich
7A paw-licking
3P paweth
4A pawful
4R Pawnees
7Q pawns
3P pawses
4P pay-shakes-see
9R paychecks
8F payed
7R Payload
7R payload's
8H payloads
6D paymaster

Word Type	F	D	U	SFI	3 Gr 3	4 Gr 4	5 Gr 5	6 Gr 6	7 Gr 7	8 Gr 8	9 Gr 9	X UnGr	A Read	B Eng & Gr	C Comp	D Lit	E Math	F Soc Stud	G Spell	H Sci	J Music	K Art	L Home Ec	M Shop	N Lib F	P Lib NF	Q Lib Ref	R Mag	S Rel
payment	55	.5846	6.7352	48.3	8	7	3	5	8	16	7	1	11	1	0	1	5	7	1	0	0	0	11	0	4	6	4	4	0
payments	31	.5181	3.3862	45.3	4	0	2	3	5	7	6	4	3	0	0	0	6	5	0	0	0	0	5	0	0	0	5	7	0
Payne	2	.2412	.1141	30.6	0	1	0	0	0	0	1	0	0	1	0	0	0	0	0	0	0	0	0	0	0	1	0	0	0
payroll	4	.3518	.3077	34.9	1	0	0	0	2	0	1	0	0	0	0	2	0	0	0	0	0	0	0	0	0	1	0	1	0
payrolls	5	.3726	.4014	36.0	0	0	0	1	1	0	3	0	0	1	0	0	0	0	0	0	0	0	0	0	0	0	2	2	0
pays	56	.8431	9.5038	49.8	19	9	2	5	6	6	5	4	21	2	0	4	6	6	1	1	1	0	1	0	1	7	1	4	0
Payton	2	.0000	.0243	23.9	0	0	0	0	0	0	0	2	0	0	0	0	0	0	0	0	0	0	0	0	0	0	0	2	0
Paz	8	.4363	.7941	39.0	2	0	0	4	2	0	0	0	2	0	0	1	0	4	0	0	0	0	0	0	0	0	0	1	0
PB	6	.0000	.0898	29.5	0	2	0	0	1	3	0	0	0	0	0	0	6	0	0	0	0	0	0	0	0	0	0	0	0
PBP	2	.0000	.0209	23.2	0	0	0	0	0	0	2	0	0	0	0	0	0	0	0	0	0	0	0	0	0	0	2	0	0
PC	3	.0000	.0449	26.5	0	1	0	0	0	2	0	0	0	0	0	0	3	0	0	0	0	0	0	0	0	0	0	0	0
pea	51	.4960	5.5570	47.4	9	13	4	16	6	1	2	0	9	1	0	0	1	0	0	34	2	0	1	0	0	1	2	0	0
pea-green	2	.1717	.1142	30.6	1	1	0	0	0	0	0	0	1	0	0	1	0	0	0	0	0	0	0	0	0	0	0	0	0
Peabody	6	.3530	.5299	37.2	3	0	0	0	0	1	0	2	3	0	0	0	0	0	0	0	0	0	0	0	0	1	0	2	0
peace	343	.7656	53.310	57.3	28	33	29	53	65	65	64	6	71	4	0	28	0	116	7	5	24	0	0	0	11	26	10	40	1
Peace	42	.5397	4.7800	46.8	4	4	4	0	7	14	9	0	3	1	0	1	0	16	0	0	0	0	1	0	0	0	5	15	0
peace-loving	2	.2152	.1357	31.3	0	0	0	1	1	0	0	0	1	0	0	0	0	1	0	0	0	0	0	0	0	0	0	0	0
peaceable	8	.4845	.8983	39.5	0	1	3	1	1	2	0	0	5	0	0	0	0	0	0	0	0	0	0	0	1	1	1	0	0
peaceably	4	.3354	.3295	35.2	1	0	1	1	0	1	0	0	1	0	0	0	0	2	0	0	0	0	0	0	0	1	0	0	0
peaceful	107	.8444	18.103	52.6	16	13	20	11	17	18	8	4	25	4	1	13	1	20	2	2	0	3	1	0	5	16	7	7	0
peacefully	26	.7322	3.9178	45.9	1	6	2	8	6	1	2	0	9	1	0	1	0	6	0	0	1	0	0	0	1	4	2	1	0
peacetime	12	.5657	1.4610	41.6	2	0	2	1	1	5	0	1	3	0	0	0	0	5	0	1	0	0	0	0	1	1	0	1	0
peach	76	.7138	11.182	50.5	19	4	10	23	10	6	4	0	19	2	1	1	7	6	5	32	0	0	1	0	1	0	0	1	0
Peach	5	.3211	.4073	36.1	2	0	1	0	0	0	0	2	2	0	0	0	0	1	0	0	0	0	0	0	0	0	0	2	0
peaches	106	.8346	17.898	52.5	53	6	8	24	7	2	4	2	51	7	2	0	9	10	3	9	0	0	2	0	2	4	3	4	0
Peaches	2	.0000	.0914	29.6	2	0	0	0	0	0	0	0	2	0	0	0	0	0	0	0	0	0	0	0	0	0	0	0	0
Peachtree	3	.0000	.0365	25.6	0	0	0	3	0	0	0	0	0	0	0	0	0	0	0	0	0	0	0	0	0	0	0	3	0
peacock	33	.4057	3.3627	45.3	18	0	0	15	0	0	0	0	25	0	0	0	0	0	0	0	1	0	0	0	6	0	1	0	0
Peacock	5	.1313	.1696	32.3	0	1	0	3	0	1	0	0	0	0	0	0	0	0	0	0	4	0	0	0	0	1	0	0	0
peacock's	4	.2278	.2911	34.6	2	0	0	2	0	0	0	0	3	0	0	0	0	0	0	0	1	0	0	0	0	0	0	0	0
peacocks	7	.5999	.8727	39.4	2	2	0	1	1	1	0	0	1	1	0	1	0	0	0	0	0	0	0	0	1	2	1	0	0
peak	88	.7968	14.104	51.5	8	12	8	14	20	12	13	1	13	3	0	6	2	12	0	6	2	1	0	0	5	8	18	12	0
Peak	26	.6921	3.7534	45.7	0	1	12	2	7	2	2	0	11	0	1	3	0	3	0	3	1	0	0	0	1	0	3	0	0
peaked	4	.3869	.3841	35.8	1	0	2	0	0	1	0	0	2	0	0	0	0	1	0	1	0	0	0	0	0	0	0	0	0
peaks	102	.6583	13.816	51.4	18	9	21	11	26	5	12	0	10	0	0	3	5	33	0	11	0	0	7	0	2	6	23	2	0
Peaks	13	.3860	1.2522	41.0	0	3	8	0	0	0	0	2	8	0	0	0	0	0	0	0	0	0	0	0	0	3	0	2	0
peal	6	.5193	.6609	38.2	0	2	1	1	0	1	1	0	1	1	0	1	0	0	0	0	0	0	0	0	2	0	1	0	0
pealed	2	.2303	.1079	30.3	1	0	0	0	1	0	0	0	0	0	0	0	0	0	0	0	1	0	0	0	0	1	0	0	0
pealing	4	.1789	.1692	32.3	2	0	0	2	0	0	0	0	0	0	0	0	0	0	0	0	3	0	0	0	0	0	1	0	0
peanut	42	.7737	6.6455	48.2	9	10	5	3	9	3	3	0	19	1	1	3	2	2	0	3	0	0	3	0	1	2	3	2	0
Peanut	9	.0000	.4111	36.1	8	0	0	0	1	0	0	0	9	0	0	0	0	0	0	0	0	0	0	0	0	0	0	0	0
peanut-butter	2	.2446	.1125	30.5	0	0	1	0	1	0	0	0	0	1	0	1	0	0	0	0	0	0	0	0	0	0	0	0	0
peanuts	79	.8265	13.204	51.2	21	11	19	4	13	5	3	3	33	9	1	3	10	10	0	3	1	0	1	0	1	3	3	1	0
pear	32	.6826	4.4796	46.5	1	3	5	4	15	1	3	0	6	1	0	1	1	2	0	4	1	0	4	0	7	1	3	1	0
pear-shaped	2	.2446	.1257	31.0	0	0	0	0	0	0	1	1	0	0	0	0	0	1	0	1	0	0	0	0	0	0	0	0	0
Pearce	2	.0000	.0243	23.9	0	0	0	0	2	0	0	0	0	0	0	0	0	0	0	0	0	0	0	0	0	0	0	2	0
pearl	85	.2896	5.9047	47.7	0	8	5	3	62	2	2	3	16	2	0	58	0	2	2	1	0	0	0	0	2	2	0	0	0
Pearl	27	.5978	3.4021	45.3	2	3	6	2	0	11	3	0	5	0	0	1	0	12	0	0	3	0	0	0	0	2	1	3	0
pearls	59	.6729	8.3379	49.2	4	8	6	13	20	5	3	0	26	0	2	7	0	7	0	4	0	0	0	0	9	2	2	0	0
pearly	11	.6208	1.4125	41.5	0	2	0	2	3	0	1	3	1	1	0	0	0	0	0	4	2	0	0	0	1	0	1	1	0
pears	31	.6972	4.3839	46.4	9	6	6	0	5	0	5	0	1	2	0	0	11	3	1	1	0	0	2	0	0	4	2	4	0
Pearson	8	.3052	.5475	37.4	1	3	0	0	2	0	2	0	0	0	0	0	0	0	0	0	0	0	0	0	5	1	0	2	0
Pearsons	2	.0000	.0234	23.7	0	1	0	0	0	0	1	0	0	0	0	0	0	0	0	0	0	0	0	0	2	0	0	0	0
Peary	12	.2369	.7970	39.0	4	1	0	1	6	0	0	0	5	0	0	6	0	1	0	0	0	0	0	0	0	0	0	0	0
Peary's	2	.0000	.0914	29.6	0	2	0	0	0	0	0	0	2	0	0	0	0	0	0	0	0	0	0	0	0	0	0	0	0
peas	70	.5147	7.6772	48.9	13	8	3	11	18	5	11	1	10	5	0	0	0	5	0	20	1	0	15	0	8	3	1	2	0
peasant	42	.7536	6.4474	48.1	5	7	5	8	6	8	2	1	11	0	0	1	0	8	2	1	5	0	0	0	2	6	3	3	0
Peasant	3	.0000	.0243	23.8	0	0	1	1	0	0	1	0	0	0	0	0	0	0	0	0	3	0	0	0	0	0	0	0	0
peasantry	4	.4530	.4014	36.0	0	0	2	0	2	0	0	0	1	0	0	0	0	0	0	0	0	0	0	0	0	1	1	1	0
peasants	59	.6891	8.3290	49.2	9	5	11	10	14	7	2	1	8	0	0	2	0	15	0	0	3	0	0	0	6	12	8	5	0
peasants'	2	.0000	.0243	23.9	0	0	0	0	1	0	0	1	0	0	0	0	0	0	0	0	0	0	0	0	0	0	0	2	0
Peaseblossom	3	.0000	.0322	25.1	0	0	0	0	0	0	3	0	0	0	0	3	0	0	0	0	0	0	0	0	0	0	0	0	0
PEASEBLOSSOM	4	.0000	.0429	26.3	0	0	0	0	0	0	4	0	0	0	0	4	0	0	0	0	0	0	0	0	0	0	0	0	0
Peasley	26	.0000	1.1877	40.7	26	0	0	0	0	0	0	0	26	0	0	0	0	0	0	0	0	0	0	0	0	0	0	0	0
peat	24	.3984	2.2171	43.5	6	6	1	0	3	2	0	6	5	0	0	0	0	0	0	12	0	0	0	0	0	6	1	0	0
pebble	40	.6902	5.6782	47.5	8	4	1	5	12	8	1	1	7	0	0	3	0	5	1	11	6	0	0	0	1	5	1	0	0
pebbled	2	.1387	.0689	28.4	0	0	1	0	0	0	1	0	0	0	1	0	0	0	0	0	0	0	0	0	0	1	0	0	0
pebbles	60	.7442	9.0765	49.6	15	4	2	5	13	11	7	3	9	1	3	2	9	6	0	16	0	2	0	0	3	7	0	2	0
pebbly	2	.2160	.1362	31.3	1	0	0	0	1	0	0	0	1	0	0	0	0	0	0	1	0	0	0	0	0	0	0	0	0
pecan	6	.3250	.4406	36.4	4	1	0	0	0	1	0	0	0	0	0	1	4	0	0	0	0	0	0	0	0	1	0	0	0
pecans	8	.5873	.9836	39.9	2	1	0	1	0	0	4	0	1	1	0	1	2	0	0	1	0	0	0	0	0	2	0	0	0
peccary	23	.3903	2.3084	43.6	18	1	0	0	4	0	0	0	18	0	0	0	0	1	0	0	0	0	0	0	0	1	0	3	0
Peccary	2	.0000	.0914	29.6	2	0	0	0	0	0	0	0	2	0	0	0	0	0	0	0	0	0	0	0	0	0	0	0	0
peck	14	.5324	1.6325	42.1	5	1	0	1	4	1	0	2	5	0	0	3	0	0	0	3	0	0	0	0	0	1	0	2	0
Peck	5	.3098	.3448	35.4	0	0	4	1	0	0	0	0	0	0	0	0	1	0	0	0	0	0	0	0	0	0	3	1	0
pecked	6	.2438	.4681	36.7	3	0	1	0	1	1	0	0	5	0	0	0	0	0	0	0	0	0	0	0	0	0	1	0	0
pecking	14	.3780	1.3303	41.2	3	1	1	0	7	0	0	2	9	0	0	0	0	0	0	0	0	0	0	0	0	0	3	2	0
pecks	8	.2826	.5234	37.2	0	5	0	0	0	0	0	3	0	0	0	0	2	0	0	1	0	0	0	0	0	0	0	5	0
Pecos	29	.5141	3.2693	45.1	5	3	3	7	1	9	0	1	11	0	0	12	0	1	0	0	0	1	0	0	2	0	1	1	0
pectorals	3	.2181	.1541	31.9	0	0	0	0	3	0	0	0	0	0	0	0	0	0	0	0	0	0	0	0	1	0	2	0	0
peculiar	83	.8586	14.239	51.5	4	3	11	14	30	8	11	2	19	2	1	8	1	3	1	7	3	0	1	0	11	8	11	7	0
peculiarities	5	.4699	.4891	36.9	0	0	0	0	4	1	0	0	0	1	0	0	0	0	1	0	0	0	0	0	1	0	2	0	0
peculiarity	2	.2441	.1127	30.5	0	0	0	0	2	0	0	0	0	0	0	0	0	0	0	0	0	0	0	0	1	0	1	0	0
peculiarly	8	.6182	1.0165	40.1	0	0	2	0	1	4	1	0	0	0	0	1	0	2	0	1	1	0	0	0	0	2	1	0	0
pedal	39	.7322	5.8838	47.7	11	4	3	4	9	5	3	0	17	1	0	2	1	0	0	1	7	0	1	0	1	3	2	3	0
pedaled	5	.4769	.5345	37.3	0	0	1	1	2	1	0	0	2	0	0	1	0	0	0	0	0	0	0	0	1	0	0	1	0
pedalfers	3	.0000	.0591	27.7	0	0	0	0	0	0	3	0	0	0	0	0	0	0	0	3	0	0	0	0	0	0	0	0	0
pedals	13	.5664	1.5544	41.9	3	3	0	1	5	0	1	0	3	0	0	1	0	0	0	0	3	0	0	0	0	2	1	3	0
peddle	2	.2387	.1089	30.4	0	0	0	0	1	1	0	0	0	0	0	0	0	0	0	0	1	0	0	0	1	0	0	0	0
peddler	40	.2438	3.2218	45.1	29	2	1	6	2	0	0	0	37	0	0	2	0	0	0	0	0	0	0	0	0	1	0	0	0
Peddler	8	.2426	.6298	38.0	3	0	0	5	0	0	0	0	7	0	0	0	0	0	0	0	1	0	0	0	0	0	0	0	0
peddler's	5	.0000	.2284	33.6	5	0	0	0	0	0	0	0	5	0	0	0	0	0	0	0	0	0	0	0	0	0	0	0	0
peddlers	8	.4693	.8814	39.5	0	5	1	1	0	1	0	0	5	0	0	0	0	1	0	0	1	0	0	0	0	1	0	0	0
peddles	2	.1814	.1187	30.7	0	1	0	0	0	0	1	0	1	0	0	0	0	0	0	0	0	0	0	0	0	0	0	1	0

8Q Payne-Aldrich
8A payoffs
XR Payson
XR Payson-Pine
XR Payton's
3A Pazians
6Q Pb
9H PbS
4R PBA
7E PBC

6Q Pd
8Q Pea
6A pea-jacket
6N pea-shellers
8H pea-sized
7R pea-vine
8B peabody
8Q Peace-Loving
8F peace-through-appeasement
9F peace-time

5Q peaceffully
5F Peaceful
6A peaceful-like
8F peacemakers
4A peacock-feather
7F peak-hatted
5P peak-load
6R peaking
7J Peale
4A peanutbutter

4F PEANUTS
XR Pear
7A pearl-gray
7N pearl-oyster
3A pearl-white
7D pearl's
7D pearlers
7Q pearlfish
3P pearlike
6R Pearls

3J Peas
5D peasant's
9D Peascod
7H peashooter
3A Peasley's
7R peccaries
9F Pechenegs
5Q Peck's
6P peckety-peck-peck
8Q Pecourt

7Q pectoral
9Q pectoralis
7A peculiar-looking
4N peculiar-shaped
6A peculiarsome
8A pedagogy
9H pedalfer
8R pedaling
7P pedantic

Word Type	F	D	U	SFI	3 Gr 3	4 Gr 4	5 Gr 5	6 Gr 6	7 Gr 7	8 Gr 8	9 Gr 9	X UnGr	A Read	B Eng & Gr	C Comp	D Lit	E Math	F Soc Stud	G Spell	H Sci	J Music	K Art	L Home Ec	M Shop	N Lib F	P Lib NF	Q Lib Ref	R Mag	S Rel
peddling	3	.2435	.2274	33.6	1	1	0	0	0	1	0	0	2	0	0	0	0	1	0	0	0	0	0	0	0	0	0	0	0
Peder	4	.0000	.0469	26.7	0	0	0	0	0	4	0	0	0	0	0	0	0	0	0	0	0	0	0	0	4	0	0	0	0
Peder's	2	.0000	.0234	23.7	0	0	0	0	0	2	0	0	0	0	0	0	0	0	0	0	0	0	0	0	2	0	0	0	0
pedestal	10	.3836	.9495	39.8	0	0	3	4	1	1	1	0	6	2	0	2	0	0	0	0	0	0	0	0	0	0	0	0	0
pedestrian	18	.4208	1.6880	42.3	0	0	0	0	6	4	8	0	2	1	2	0	0	0	0	11	0	0	0	0	0	0	2	0	0
pedestrians	11	.3511	.9281	39.7	1	0	0	0	1	1	8	0	2	0	0	0	0	1	0	7	0	0	0	0	1	0	0	0	0
pediatrician	2	.2437	.1129	30.5	0	0	0	0	2	0	0	0	0	0	0	0	0	0	0	0	0	0	0	0	0	0	1	1	0
pediatrics	3	.3764	.2483	33.9	0	0	0	0	0	3	0	0	0	0	0	0	0	0	0	1	0	0	0	0	0	0	1	1	0
pedigree	4	.3771	.3293	35.2	1	1	0	1	1	0	0	0	0	0	0	0	0	0	0	0	0	0	0	0	1	2	0	1	0
pedipalps	3	.0000	.0591	27.7	0	0	0	3	0	0	0	0	0	0	0	0	0	0	0	3	0	0	0	0	0	0	0	0	0
Pedrito	5	.0000	.2284	33.6	0	0	2	3	0	0	0	0	5	0	0	0	0	0	0	0	0	0	0	0	0	0	0	0	0
Pedro	102	.5110	11.740	50.7	25	27	24	10	4	12	0	0	54	0	0	24	0	7	0	0	0	0	0	0	0	1	4	12	0
Pedro's	15	.3703	1.3479	41.3	1	7	5	2	0	0	0	0	7	1	0	6	0	0	0	0	0	0	0	0	0	0	0	1	0
Pee-Wee	15	.0318	.2969	34.7	0	0	1	14	0	0	0	0	1	0	0	0	0	0	0	0	0	0	0	0	14	0	0	0	0
Pee-wee	2	.0000	.0234	23.7	0	0	0	2	0	0	0	0	0	0	0	0	0	0	0	0	0	0	0	0	2	0	0	0	0
peek	9	.4519	.9261	39.7	2	2	1	1	1	1	0	1	4	1	0	0	0	0	0	0	0	1	0	0	1	0	0	2	0
peeked	11	.4893	1.2224	40.9	5	3	0	1	1	1	0	0	6	0	1	1	0	0	0	0	0	0	0	0	2	0	0	1	0
peeking	8	.4844	.8991	39.5	4	1	0	1	1	0	0	1	5	0	0	0	0	0	0	0	0	0	0	0	1	1	0	1	0
peeks	2	.2128	.1055	30.2	1	0	1	0	0	0	0	0	0	0	0	0	0	0	0	1	1	0	0	0	0	0	0	0	0
Peekskill	3	.1277	.1363	31.3	0	0	1	1	0	1	0	0	1	0	0	0	0	0	0	0	0	0	0	0	0	0	0	2	0
peel	27	.6543	3.6629	45.6	4	1	6	3	4	2	6	1	7	1	1	1	0	4	2	2	0	0	4	0	0	1	0	4	0
peeled	16	.6681	2.2089	43.4	1	3	0	3	3	1	5	0	4	1	0	4	0	0	1	1	0	0	0	0	1	2	2	0	0
peeling	21	.4953	2.2974	43.6	5	2	3	4	3	0	4	0	8	1	0	0	0	1	0	1	0	0	4	0	3	1	0	2	0
peelings	5	.1859	.3341	35.2	1	0	0	0	3	0	1	0	4	0	0	0	0	0	0	0	0	0	1	0	0	0	0	0	0
peen	4	.0000	.0101	20.0	0	0	0	0	2	2	0	0	0	0	0	0	0	0	0	0	0	0	0	4	0	0	0	0	0
peening	2	.0000	.0050	17.0	0	0	0	0	2	0	0	0	0	0	0	0	0	0	0	0	0	0	0	2	0	0	0	0	0
peep	15	.6652	2.1133	43.2	3	1	3	3	2	1	1	1	8	1	0	1	0	0	0	1	1	0	0	0	1	2	0	0	0
Peep	3	.0000	.1370	31.4	1	2	0	0	0	0	0	0	3	0	0	0	0	0	0	0	0	0	0	0	0	0	0	0	0
peeped	18	.5644	2.2419	43.5	5	3	2	5	1	1	0	1	10	0	0	3	0	1	0	1	0	0	0	0	2	0	0	1	0
peeper	3	.0000	.0591	27.7	0	0	0	3	0	0	0	0	0	0	0	0	0	0	0	3	0	0	0	0	0	0	0	0	0
peepers	4	.4419	.3920	35.9	3	0	1	0	0	0	0	0	1	0	0	0	0	0	0	0	1	0	0	0	1	1	0	0	0
peephole	8	.4898	.8338	39.2	2	2	0	0	1	0	3	0	1	0	0	2	0	0	0	0	0	0	0	0	3	0	1	1	0
peeping	14	.5980	1.7922	42.5	4	3	1	2	3	0	0	1	6	0	0	2	0	0	0	0	1	0	0	0	3	1	0	1	0
peer	20	.5938	2.4710	43.9	3	0	0	4	8	3	0	2	2	0	0	2	0	1	0	2	0	0	0	0	3	4	0	6	0
Peer	13	.2117	.6296	38.0	2	6	0	1	3	1	0	0	0	0	0	1	0	0	0	0	10	0	0	0	0	0	2	0	0
peered	76	.6965	10.972	50.4	15	20	9	6	17	1	8	0	29	6	1	10	0	0	0	0	0	0	0	0	11	9	1	9	0
peering	40	.6110	5.1977	47.2	4	6	5	8	9	3	4	1	15	1	0	8	0	2	0	3	0	0	0	0	8	2	0	1	0
peerless	3	.2054	.1422	31.5	0	0	0	0	2	1	0	0	0	0	1	0	0	0	0	0	0	0	0	0	0	0	0	2	0
peers	8	.4469	.7721	38.9	0	0	1	2	2	1	2	0	1	2	1	0	0	1	0	0	0	0	0	0	0	0	0	3	0
Peerson	6	.0000	.2741	34.4	0	0	0	6	0	0	0	0	6	0	0	0	0	0	0	0	0	0	0	0	0	0	0	0	0
Peewee	2	.0000	.0243	23.9	0	0	0	2	0	0	0	0	0	0	0	0	0	0	0	0	0	0	0	0	0	0	0	2	0
peg	18	.6722	2.5052	44.0	2	4	0	5	1	5	1	0	5	1	1	2	4	0	0	0	0	0	0	0	0	3	1	1	0
Peg	36	.2913	3.1097	44.9	32	0	0	0	4	0	0	0	31	0	0	0	1	0	0	0	0	0	0	0	0	0	0	4	0
Peg's	3	.0000	.1370	31.4	3	0	0	0	0	0	0	0	3	0	0	0	0	0	0	0	0	0	0	0	0	0	0	0	0
Pegasus	7	.3047	.5207	37.2	0	0	0	1	0	2	1	3	1	0	0	2	0	0	0	4	0	0	0	0	0	0	0	0	0
pegged	2	.0000	.0243	23.9	1	0	0	0	0	1	0	0	0	0	0	0	0	0	0	0	0	0	0	0	0	0	0	2	0
Peggy	48	.5014	5.6519	47.5	38	1	0	1	4	2	1	1	37	1	0	0	1	4	1	0	0	0	0	0	0	0	0	4	0
Peggy's	3	.1937	.1495	31.7	0	0	0	0	2	1	0	0	0	0	0	0	0	1	0	0	0	0	0	0	0	0	0	2	0
Pegleg	5	.0000	.2284	33.6	5	0	0	0	0	0	0	0	5	0	0	0	0	0	0	0	0	0	0	0	0	0	0	0	0
pegmatite	5	.0000	.0986	29.9	0	0	0	0	0	0	1	4	0	0	0	0	0	0	0	5	0	0	0	0	0	0	0	0	0
pegmatites	5	.0000	.0986	29.9	0	0	0	0	0	0	0	5	0	0	0	0	0	0	0	5	0	0	0	0	0	0	0	0	0
pegs	21	.6511	2.8363	44.5	4	3	2	1	4	7	0	0	5	2	0	0	5	0	0	0	0	0	0	1	4	2	0	2	0
Peindo	8	.0000	.3655	35.6	8	0	0	0	0	0	0	0	8	0	0	0	0	0	0	0	0	0	0	0	0	0	0	0	0
Peiping	2	.1698	.1133	30.5	0	0	1	0	0	0	0	1	1	0	0	0	0	0	0	0	0	0	0	0	0	0	1	0	0
Peisistratos	2	.0000	.0215	23.3	0	0	0	0	0	0	2	0	0	0	0	2	0	0	0	0	0	0	0	0	0	0	0	0	0
Pekinese	2	.0000	.0914	29.6	0	0	0	2	0	0	0	0	2	0	0	0	0	0	0	0	0	0	0	0	0	0	0	0	0
Peking	32	.4588	3.1226	44.9	0	4	15	2	3	8	0	0	0	0	0	0	2	8	0	0	0	0	0	0	0	4	14	4	0
Pele	4	.0000	.0486	26.9	0	0	0	0	4	0	0	0	0	0	0	0	0	0	0	0	0	0	0	0	0	0	0	4	0
Pelias	11	.2353	.8127	39.1	0	0	0	8	3	0	0	0	8	0	0	3	0	0	0	0	0	0	0	0	0	0	0	0	0
pelican	17	.5330	2.0345	43.1	3	0	8	3	1	1	1	0	9	0	0	0	0	1	0	3	0	0	0	0	0	3	1	0	0
Pelican	2	.1698	.1133	30.5	1	0	1	0	0	0	0	0	1	0	0	0	0	0	0	0	0	0	0	0	0	0	1	0	0
pelicans	8	.4969	.8740	39.4	3	1	0	1	3	0	0	0	2	0	0	0	0	1	0	1	0	0	0	0	0	3	1	0	0
Pelion	3	.0000	.1370	31.4	0	0	0	3	0	0	0	0	3	0	0	0	0	0	0	0	0	0	0	0	0	0	0	0	0
pell-mell	2	.2152	.1357	31.3	0	1	0	0	0	1	0	0	1	0	0	0	0	1	0	0	0	0	0	0	0	0	0	0	0
pellagra	7	.1941	.3707	35.7	0	1	3	0	1	1	0	1	0	0	0	0	0	0	0	6	0	0	0	0	0	0	1	0	0
Pelleas	2	.2417	.1091	30.4	0	1	0	0	0	1	0	0	0	0	0	0	0	0	0	0	1	0	0	0	0	0	1	0	0
pellet	2	.1787	.1174	30.7	1	0	0	0	0	0	1	0	1	0	0	0	0	0	0	0	0	0	0	0	1	0	0	0	0
pellets	5	.1468	.2522	34.0	2	0	0	0	1	0	2	0	2	0	0	0	0	0	0	0	0	0	0	0	3	0	0	0	0
pellicle	3	.0000	.0591	27.7	0	0	0	0	3	0	0	0	0	0	0	0	0	0	0	3	0	0	0	0	0	0	0	0	0
Pelly	2	.2446	.1142	30.6	0	0	1	0	0	0	1	0	0	0	0	0	0	0	0	0	0	0	0	0	1	0	0	1	0
pelt	8	.3809	.7811	38.9	1	0	1	1	4	0	0	1	6	0	0	0	0	0	0	0	1	0	0	0	0	0	0	1	0
pelted	5	.4755	.5341	37.3	2	0	0	1	1	0	0	1	2	1	0	1	0	0	0	0	0	0	0	0	0	1	0	0	0
Peltier	2	.0000	.0209	23.2	0	0	0	0	0	0	2	0	0	0	0	0	0	0	0	0	0	0	0	0	0	0	2	0	0
pelting	6	.4740	.6118	37.9	0	1	1	1	2	1	0	0	1	0	1	1	0	0	0	1	0	0	0	0	1	0	1	0	0
Pelton	2	.0000	.0394	26.0	0	0	0	2	0	0	0	0	0	0	0	0	0	0	0	2	0	0	0	0	0	0	0	0	0
pelts	15	.5863	1.8750	42.7	0	2	4	6	2	1	0	0	4	0	0	0	0	4	0	1	0	0	0	0	3	2	1	0	0
pelvic	3	.2799	.1829	32.6	0	0	0	0	1	0	2	0	0	0	1	0	0	0	0	0	0	0	0	0	0	0	1	1	0
pelvics	2	.0000	.0209	23.2	0	0	0	0	2	0	0	0	0	0	0	0	0	0	0	0	0	0	0	0	0	0	2	0	0
pelvis	6	.3688	.4931	36.9	0	0	3	0	0	1	2	0	0	0	0	0	0	0	0	3	0	0	0	0	0	0	2	1	0
Pelz	2	.0000	.0243	23.9	0	0	0	0	2	0	0	0	0	0	0	0	0	0	0	0	0	0	0	0	0	0	0	2	0
Pemaquid	2	.0000	.0394	26.0	0	0	0	0	0	2	0	0	0	0	0	0	0	0	0	2	0	0	0	0	0	0	0	0	0
pembo	7	.0000	.0851	29.3	0	0	0	0	0	0	0	7	0	0	0	0	0	0	0	0	0	0	0	0	0	0	0	7	0
pemmican	7	.0000	.1361	31.3	4	3	0	0	0	0	0	0	0	0	0	0	0	7	0	0	0	0	0	0	0	0	0	0	0
pen	194	.8118	31.670	55.0	39	30	34	17	37	18	17	2	53	22	12	12	10	2	8	5	5	4	1	13	27	12	1	7	0
pen-knife	2	.0000	.0394	26.0	0	0	2	0	0	0	0	0	0	0	0	0	0	0	0	2	0	0	0	0	0	0	0	0	0
penalties	8	.5472	.9036	39.6	0	1	1	1	0	3	2	0	0	1	1	1	0	2	0	0	0	0	0	0	0	0	2	1	0
penalty	18	.5836	2.2526	43.5	1	1	5	3	3	2	3	0	7	1	0	1	0	1	0	0	0	0	0	0	0	1	5	2	0
penance	2	.1698	.1133	30.5	0	0	1	0	1	0	0	0	1	0	0	0	0	0	0	0	0	0	0	0	0	0	1	0	0
Penang	7	.0000	.0733	28.6	0	0	0	0	0	7	0	0	0	0	0	0	0	0	0	0	0	0	0	0	0	0	7	0	0
pence	4	.3605	.3148	35.0	0	0	1	2	1	0	0	0	0	0	0	1	1	0	0	0	0	0	0	0	2	0	0	0	0
penchant	2	.2433	.1158	30.6	1	0	0	0	0	1	0	0	0	0	0	0	0	0	0	0	0	0	0	0	0	1	0	1	0
pencil	331	.7372	49.390	56.9	74	57	44	48	36	32	37	3	41	18	4	7	92	5	16	56	2	21	2	30	9	17	2	9	0
pencil-sharpening	2	.0000	.0234	23.7	0	0	0	0	0	2	0	0	0	0	0	0	0	0	0	0	0	0	0	0	2	0	0	0	0

9D Pederek's
6A Pedestal
7N pedestals
9H pedestrian-vehicle
8H pediatricians
8R pedicab
6R pedicabs
9H pedicel
XP pediment
7G pedis
8Q Pedja
9H pedocals
9F pedologists
9H pedon
3P Pee
6N Pee-Wee's
5A Peel
5H peels
3P PEEN
7M peened
9Q Peenemunde
4A peep-peeping
3N peeper-frogs
6H peeper's
9D peepers'
7R peepin'
7R Peeples
8A peer's
7N peerage
9J Peerce
XH peerings
4A Peerless
6A Peerson's
5A peeved
8D peevish
3P peg-leg
4Q peg-tops
6A Pegae
4P Pegg
6A pegging
3A Peindo's
7P Pekin
5Q Peking's
9P Pekingese
XR pelagic
9H Pelecypoda
8Q pelecypods
7Q Pelee
5G pelere
XR Pelham
7A Pell
5Q Peloponnesian
7F peloponnesus
7F Peloponnesus
4P peltries
8R Pelvis
7Q pelvises
7Q Pemberton
3R Pemetic
6F pen-like
XR pen-pals
6H pen-sized
5K pen's
7Q penal
8C penalize
5B penalized
7E pencil-and-paper
7B pencil-drawn
7H pencil-like
8H pencil-shaped
9Q pencil-thick
4H pencil's

Word Type	F	D	U	SFI	3 Gr 3	4 Gr 4	5 Gr 5	6 Gr 6	7 Gr 7	8 Gr 8	9 Gr 9	X UnGr	A Read	B Eng & Gr	C Comp	D Lit	E Math	F Soc Stud	G Spell	H Sci	J Music	K Art	L Home Ec	M Shop	N Lib F	P Lib NF	Q Lib Ref	R Mag	S Rel
penciled	5	.3234	.3742	35.7	1	1	0	0	2	1	0	0	1	0	0	2	0	0	0	0	0	1	0	0	0	1	0	0	0
pencils	111	.5708	13.186	51.2	29	16	34	4	15	4	9	0	5	6	0	4	78	4	1	1	0	2	1	2	3	4	0	0	0
Pend	4	.0000	.0486	26.9	0	0	0	4	0	0	0	0	0	0	0	0	0	0	0	0	0	0	0	0	0	0	0	4	0
pendants	2	.2446	.1142	30.6	0	0	0	0	1	0	0	1	0	0	0	0	0	0	0	0	0	0	0	0	1	0	0	1	0
pending	5	.4626	.4880	36.9	0	0	1	0	2	1	1	0	0	0	0	0	0	1	1	0	0	0	0	0	0	0	1	2	0
Pendragon	3	.0000	.1370	31.4	0	0	0	3	0	0	0	0	3	0	0	0	0	0	0	0	0	0	0	0	0	0	0	0	0
pendulum	24	.6246	3.1501	45.0	3	0	3	5	1	11	1	0	6	0	0	0	7	0	0	5	1	0	0	0	1	0	0	3	0
Penelope	12	.4488	1.2465	41.0	3	0	0	2	2	3	2	0	6	0	0	2	0	0	0	0	0	0	0	0	0	1	3	0	0
penetrate	28	.6624	3.7785	45.8	1	1	2	3	10	2	6	3	0	0	0	4	1	2	0	8	0	0	0	1	0	2	7	3	0
penetrated	16	.6003	1.9992	43.0	1	0	0	1	6	5	3	0	3	0	2	1	0	1	0	2	0	0	0	2	1	2	1	1	0
penetrates	7	.5362	.7954	39.0	0	0	2	1	1	1	1	1	1	0	0	0	0	1	0	1	0	0	0	1	0	1	1	1	0
penetrating	23	.6190	2.9191	44.7	0	1	0	3	9	7	3	0	2	0	1	1	0	1	0	3	1	0	0	4	1	2	5	2	0
penetration	13	.3305	.9355	39.7	0	1	1	0	3	5	3	0	0	0	0	0	0	3	0	0	0	0	0	4	0	0	3	3	0
Penfield	3	.2212	.2099	33.2	0	0	0	0	2	0	1	0	2	0	0	1	0	0	0	0	0	0	0	0	0	0	0	0	0
penguin	32	.3685	2.8597	44.6	8	22	0	0	2	0	0	0	14	1	0	0	0	0	0	1	0	0	0	0	14	0	0	2	0
Penguin	4	.2417	.3028	34.8	0	4	0	0	0	0	0	0	3	0	0	0	0	0	0	0	0	0	0	0	1	0	0	0	0
penguin's	2	.0000	.0234	23.7	0	2	0	0	0	0	0	0	0	0	0	0	0	0	0	0	0	0	0	0	2	0	0	0	0
penguins	48	.4293	4.7768	46.8	7	22	1	0	18	0	0	0	20	0	0	0	1	1	0	1	0	0	0	0	19	5	0	1	0
Penguins	7	.1984	.3681	35.7	2	5	0	0	0	0	0	0	1	0	0	0	0	0	0	0	0	0	0	0	5	1	0	0	0
penicillin	28	.2932	2.1000	43.2	1	3	0	3	4	7	8	2	6	0	0	0	0	0	1	20	0	0	0	0	0	0	0	1	0
Penicillium	5	.0000	.0986	29.9	0	0	0	0	3	0	2	0	0	0	0	0	0	0	0	5	0	0	0	0	0	0	0	0	0
peninsula	86	.4569	8.4767	49.3	18	17	10	26	9	3	3	0	0	0	0	0	0	51	2	0	0	0	0	0	0	6	19	8	0
Peninsula	61	.5251	6.7957	48.3	2	2	16	28	6	4	2	1	2	0	0	0	0	36	2	1	1	0	0	0	0	2	9	8	0
peninsulas	26	.1934	1.3803	41.4	3	8	4	8	3	0	0	0	0	0	0	0	0	23	0	0	0	0	0	0	0	1	0	2	0
penknife	6	.3501	.5265	37.2	0	3	0	0	2	0	1	0	3	0	0	0	0	0	0	0	0	0	0	0	2	1	0	0	0
penmanship	7	.2394	.4594	36.6	1	1	1	1	3	0	0	0	3	0	2	0	1	0	0	0	0	0	0	0	0	1	0	0	0
Penn	40	.5792	4.8720	46.9	4	8	9	1	3	7	5	3	5	0	0	2	0	13	1	0	0	0	0	0	0	8	1	10	0
Penn's	2	.0000	.0389	25.9	0	0	1	0	0	0	1	0	0	0	0	0	0	2	0	0	0	0	0	0	0	0	0	0	0
pennant	15	.3768	1.2855	41.1	3	0	0	9	2	1	0	0	2	0	0	0	1	1	0	0	0	0	0	0	0	9	0	2	0
pennants	3	.2179	.1536	31.9	0	1	1	0	0	0	1	0	0	0	0	0	0	0	0	0	0	0	1	0	0	2	0	0	0
penned	6	.4103	.5499	37.4	1	4	0	0	0	0	1	0	1	0	0	1	0	0	0	0	0	0	0	0	0	3	0	1	0
Pennell	2	.0000	.0234	23.7	2	0	0	0	0	0	0	0	0	0	0	0	0	0	0	0	0	0	0	0	2	0	0	0	0
pennies	181	.4014	16.438	52.2	60	46	23	26	8	4	4	10	30	2	0	3	118	3	0	4	1	0	0	0	4	14	0	2	0
penniless	3	.2357	.2199	33.4	3	0	0	0	0	0	0	0	2	0	0	0	0	0	0	0	0	0	0	0	0	1	0	0	0
Pennines	3	.2444	.1814	32.6	0	0	0	0	3	0	0	0	0	0	0	0	0	2	0	0	0	0	0	0	0	0	1	0	0
Penning	2	.1787	.1174	30.7	0	1	1	0	0	0	0	0	1	0	0	0	0	0	0	0	0	0	0	0	1	0	0	0	0
Pennsylvania	153	.7381	22.975	53.6	26	18	36	14	24	26	7	2	23	7	0	8	6	45	0	3	10	0	0	0	0	29	11	11	0
penny	134	.7964	21.568	53.3	20	33	9	23	15	16	12	6	33	3	3	12	22	3	3	16	1	0	0	1	2	30	0	5	0
Penny	72	.3266	5.5016	47.4	7	15	2	1	47	0	0	0	14	15	0	1	0	0	0	0	0	0	0	0	41	0	0	1	0
penny-winkle	2	.0000	.0914	29.6	0	2	0	0	0	0	0	0	2	0	0	0	0	0	0	0	0	0	0	0	0	0	0	0	0
Penny's	5	.1468	.2522	34.0	1	0	0	0	4	0	0	0	2	0	0	0	0	0	0	0	0	0	0	0	3	0	0	0	0
Pennycuff	13	.2318	.9441	39.8	0	13	0	0	0	0	0	0	9	0	0	0	0	0	0	0	0	0	0	0	4	0	0	0	0
Pennyroyal	5	.0000	.0537	27.3	0	5	0	0	0	0	0	0	0	0	0	5	0	0	0	0	0	0	0	0	0	0	0	0	0
Penobscot	2	.2433	.1158	30.6	1	0	0	0	0	0	0	1	0	0	0	0	0	0	0	0	0	0	0	0	0	1	0	1	0
pens	33	.6501	4.4160	46.5	8	2	9	5	4	2	2	1	5	1	0	1	3	5	0	1	0	3	0	1	9	0	1	3	0
Pensacola	2	.1948	.1250	31.0	1	0	0	0	1	0	0	0	1	0	0	0	0	0	0	0	0	0	0	0	0	1	0	0	0
pension	9	.5802	1.0916	40.4	0	0	1	1	2	2	3	0	1	2	0	0	0	2	0	0	0	0	0	0	0	1	1	2	0
pensions	3	.3769	.2484	34.0	0	0	0	0	2	0	1	0	0	0	0	0	0	1	0	0	0	0	0	0	0	0	1	1	0
pensive	5	.2440	.2763	34.4	0	1	0	0	1	1	2	0	0	0	0	3	0	0	0	0	2	0	0	0	0	0	0	0	0
pensively	2	.1717	.1142	30.6	0	0	0	0	2	0	0	0	1	0	0	1	0	0	0	0	0	0	0	0	0	0	0	0	0
pent-up	2	.2433	.1158	30.6	0	0	0	1	0	0	1	0	0	0	0	0	0	0	0	0	0	0	0	0	0	1	0	1	0
pentagon	7	.0000	.1048	30.2	0	0	0	0	0	3	4	0	0	0	0	0	7	0	0	0	0	0	0	0	0	0	0	0	0
Pentagon	19	.3677	1.5723	42.0	3	0	0	1	2	0	12	1	1	0	0	0	12	2	0	0	0	0	0	0	0	1	0	3	0
pentagonal	3	.0000	.0449	26.5	0	0	1	2	0	0	0	0	0	0	0	0	3	0	0	0	0	0	0	0	0	0	0	0	0
pentameters	3	.0000	.0328	25.2	0	0	0	0	0	0	0	3	0	3	0	0	0	0	0	0	0	0	0	0	0	0	0	0	0
pentatonic	47	.0000	.3800	35.8	0	13	12	12	5	4	1	0	0	0	0	0	0	0	0	0	47	0	0	0	0	0	0	0	0
Pentland	3	.0000	.0322	25.1	0	0	3	0	0	0	0	0	0	0	0	3	0	0	0	0	0	0	0	0	0	0	0	0	0
peonage	3	.2444	.1814	32.6	0	0	0	0	1	2	0	0	0	0	0	0	0	2	0	0	0	0	0	0	0	0	1	0	0
peonies	2	.2405	.1205	30.8	0	0	0	0	1	1	0	0	0	0	0	0	0	0	0	1	0	0	0	0	0	1	0	0	0
peons	2	.0000	.0209	23.2	2	0	0	0	0	0	0	0	0	0	0	0	0	0	0	0	0	0	0	0	0	0	2	0	0
people	7989	.8385	1344.1	71.3	1704	1312	1187	1082	1243	842	528	91	1689	417	49	328	201	2553	112	529	327	110	91	25	173	562	310	467	46
People	45	.6979	6.5107	48.1	9	8	5	1	6	15	1	0	15	5	0	6	0	12	0	1	0	0	1	0	0	2	2	1	0
people's	66	.8458	11.174	50.5	14	10	9	6	15	6	3	3	13	4	0	5	1	14	1	3	3	0	0	2	4	7	2	7	0
People's	15	.4767	1.5179	41.8	1	0	3	2	2	5	2	0	1	0	0	2	0	2	0	0	0	0	0	0	1	0	7	2	0
peopled	3	.2053	.1597	32.0	0	0	1	0	1	0	0	1	0	0	0	0	0	0	0	1	0	0	0	0	0	2	0	0	0
peoples	166	.7266	24.451	53.9	8	7	22	27	57	22	20	3	9	14	0	7	2	68	3	3	5	2	0	0	2	15	33	3	0
peoplish	2	.0000	.0037	15.7	0	0	0	0	0	2	0	0	0	0	0	0	0	0	0	0	0	2	0	0	0	0	0	0	0
Peoria	3	.3872	.2490	34.0	0	1	0	0	0	0	1	1	0	1	0	1	0	0	0	0	0	0	0	0	0	0	0	1	0
pep	8	.3543	.6546	38.2	0	0	1	1	4	1	1	0	2	0	0	0	0	0	0	0	0	0	2	0	0	2	0	2	0
Pepe	21	.1620	1.3267	41.2	0	0	17	0	0	0	4	0	17	0	4	0	0	0	0	0	0	0	0	0	0	0	0	0	0
Pepin	3	.0000	.0314	25.0	0	0	0	0	3	0	0	0	0	0	0	0	0	0	0	0	0	0	0	0	0	0	3	0	0
pepper	45	.7547	6.8793	48.4	2	9	7	4	12	4	2	5	7	2	0	1	0	9	3	5	1	0	4	0	1	5	1	6	0
Pepper	7	.1506	.3607	35.6	6	0	0	1	0	0	0	0	3	4	0	0	0	0	0	0	0	0	0	0	0	0	0	0	0
peppercorns	2	.0000	.0914	29.6	0	0	0	2	0	0	0	0	2	0	0	0	0	0	0	0	0	0	0	0	0	0	0	0	0
peppered	2	.2433	.1158	30.6	0	1	0	0	0	1	0	0	0	0	0	0	0	0	0	0	0	0	0	0	0	1	0	1	0
peppermint	9	.5244	1.0079	40.0	2	1	1	1	2	0	2	0	2	1	1	2	0	0	0	1	0	0	0	0	2	0	0	0	0
peppers	18	.5022	1.9249	42.8	2	3	0	5	3	0	3	2	3	0	0	3	2	1	0	1	0	0	4	0	0	0	1	3	0
Peppi	10	.0000	.4568	36.6	8	0	0	2	0	0	0	0	10	0	0	0	0	0	0	0	0	0	0	0	0	0	0	0	0
Peppi's	4	.0000	.1827	32.6	3	0	0	1	0	0	0	0	4	0	0	0	0	0	0	0	0	0	0	0	0	0	0	0	0
pepsin	3	.2442	.1820	32.6	0	0	0	0	2	0	1	0	0	1	0	0	0	0	0	2	0	0	0	0	0	0	0	0	0
peptic	3	.0000	.0314	25.0	0	0	0	0	0	0	3	0	0	0	0	0	0	0	0	0	0	0	0	0	0	0	3	0	0
per	933	.7632	143.29	61.6	18	50	109	162	245	105	209	35	29	16	4	4	353	76	8	141	9	0	21	31	6	29	93	113	0
Per	2	.0000	.0290	24.6	0	0	0	0	2	0	0	0	0	0	0	0	0	0	0	0	0	0	0	0	0	2	0	0	0
per-acre	2	.0000	.0243	23.9	0	0	0	0	0	0	0	2	0	0	0	0	0	0	0	0	0	0	0	0	0	0	0	2	0
Peralta	2	.0000	.0914	29.6	0	0	2	0	0	0	0	0	2	0	0	0	0	0	0	0	0	0	0	0	0	0	0	0	0
perambulator	3	.0000	.0352	25.5	0	0	3	0	0	0	0	0	0	0	0	0	0	0	0	0	0	0	0	0	3	0	0	0	0
Perce	2	.2407	.1138	30.6	1	0	0	0	1	0	0	0	0	0	0	1	0	0	0	0	0	0	0	0	0	1	0	0	0
perceive	31	.5880	3.8348	45.8	0	0	3	1	21	2	2	2	3	1	1	0	1	0	0	19	0	0	0	0	1	1	1	3	0
perceived	20	.5753	2.3834	43.8	0	0	1	3	7	5	2	2	2	0	2	6	0	0	0	1	0	0	0	0	4	1	1	3	0
perceiver	2	.0000	.0394	26.0	0	0	0	0	2	0	0	0	0	0	0	0	0	0	0	2	0	0	0	0	0	0	0	0	0
perceiving	8	.4349	.7602	38.8	0	1	0	0	5	1	1	0	0	0	0	1	0	0	0	5	0	0	0	0	1	1	0	0	0
Perceiving	2	.0000	.0394	26.0	0	0	0	0	2	0	0	0	0	0	0	0	0	0	0	2	0	0	0	0	0	0	0	0	0

6A pendant
7A pendulous
6A Pendulous
6A pendulums
9D Penelope's
9M penetrator
4N penguins'
4A Penhale
4C penholder
6R peninsula's
9Q Peninsular
7Q penis
XP penknives
7H penlights
7Q penlike
7D PENNA-30
3N Pennell's
7R Penney
3J Pennies
3E pennies'
7F Pennine
5N penning
XR Pennmarva
3P Pennock
6A pennon
4P Penns
4Q Pennsylvania-born
9F Pennsylvania's
9H Pennsylvanian
5P penny-counting
9Q penny-pinching
4D penny-wide
4A penny's
7A Pennys
9D pennyworth
6B Pennyworth
3A penquin
8F Pensions
XR penstocks
5N pent
6J penta
XH pentagons
8M pentagrid
7Q Pentateuch
6A pentathlon
6A Pentathlon
8R Pentecostal
5R penthouses
8Q pentothal
8G Penurious
7R peon
8B peony
4R people-eaters
7R people'd
9Q peoplehood
7F Peoples
5F peoples's
8A pep-talk
7D Pepallistank
9C Pepe's
7Q Pepin's
4N Pepito
3A pepp
4A Pepper's
5Q pepperation
6R Pepperland
6A peppery
9R Peppiatt
8B per-
9R per-capita
5G per'fect**
7P Per's
5P Pera
5G perad'**
7N peradventure
5A Peraltas
7N perambulating
7H perceives

Word Type	F	D	U	SFI	3 Gr 3	4 Gr 4	5 Gr 5	6 Gr 6	7 Gr 7	8 Gr 8	9 Gr 9	X UnGr	A Read	B Eng & Gr	C Comp	D Lit	E Math	F Soc Stud	G Spell	H Sci	J Music	K Art	L Home Ec	M Shop	N Lib F	P Lib NF	Q Lib Ref	R Mag	S Rel
percent	198	.7340	29.299	54.7	2	3	4	35	67	53	22	12	4	10	9	0	79	20	6	14	0	0	4	6	0	1	9	36	0
percentage	46	.7147	6.6721	48.2	3	0	1	1	17	11	8	5	4	5	0	1	2	8	2	5	0	0	4	0	0	1	3	11	0
percentages	6	.2745	.3691	35.7	0	0	0	0	3	1	1	1	0	0	0	0	0	0	0	1	0	0	2	0	0	0	0	3	0
percentile	11	.0000	.1647	32.2	0	0	0	0	0	11	0	0	0	0	0	0	11	0	0	0	0	0	0	0	0	0	0	0	0
percents	11	.0000	.1647	32.2	0	0	0	2	9	0	0	0	0	0	0	0	11	0	0	0	0	0	0	0	0	0	0	0	0
perceptible	8	.4207	.7084	38.5	0	0	0	0	6	1	1	0	0	1	2	0	0	0	0	1	0	0	0	0	2	0	1	1	0
perceptibly	2	.0000	.0234	23.7	0	0	0	0	0	1	1	0	0	0	0	0	0	0	0	0	0	0	0	0	2	0	0	0	0
perception	18	.5241	2.0361	43.1	0	1	0	3	10	2	1	1	3	0	0	1	0	0	0	9	0	0	0	0	1	1	3	0	0
perceptions	2	.0000	.0394	26.0	0	0	0	0	2	0	0	0	0	0	0	0	0	0	0	2	0	0	0	0	0	0	0	0	0
perceptive	7	.4727	.7007	38.5	1	0	1	0	2	1	2	0	0	1	0	0	0	0	0	2	0	0	0	0	0	0	2	2	0
Perces	7	.2228	.3976	36.0	0	0	1	5	1	0	0	0	1	0	0	1	0	0	0	0	0	0	0	0	0	0	0	5	0
perch	36	.7615	5.5739	47.5	5	7	4	5	7	4	3	1	10	1	1	1	0	2	1	5	1	2	0	2	1	8	0	1	0
perched	52	.7792	8.2510	49.2	6	7	8	9	6	6	9	1	20	0	1	11	0	2	0	4	1	1	1	0	4	4	0	3	0
perches	13	.5194	1.4435	41.6	1	4	0	5	2	1	0	0	2	0	0	1	0	0	0	1	0	0	0	0	2	6	1	0	0
perching	6	.4220	.5651	37.5	3	0	0	0	2	0	1	0	1	0	0	1	0	0	0	2	0	0	0	0	0	0	2	0	0
Percival	13	.3388	1.1998	40.8	10	1	1	0	1	0	0	0	10	0	0	0	0	0	0	1	0	0	0	0	0	2	0	0	0
percussion	85	.1702	3.5449	45.5	8	21	12	18	17	9	0	0	3	0	0	0	0	0	0	0	68	0	0	0	0	3	11	0	0
percussions	2	.0000	.0162	22.1	0	0	0	0	2	0	0	0	0	0	0	0	0	0	0	0	2	0	0	0	0	0	0	0	0
percussive	9	.0000	.0728	28.6	0	0	0	3	2	3	1	0	0	0	0	0	0	0	0	0	9	0	0	0	0	0	0	0	0
Percy	4	.3671	.3157	35.0	0	0	0	1	0	2	1	0	0	1	0	2	0	0	0	0	0	0	0	0	0	0	1	0	0
Pere	4	.0000	.1827	32.6	4	0	0	0	0	0	0	0	4	0	0	0	0	0	0	0	0	0	0	0	0	0	0	0	0
Peregil	7	.0000	.3198	35.0	0	0	0	7	0	0	0	0	7	0	0	0	0	0	0	0	0	0	0	0	0	0	0	0	0
perennial	5	.3468	.3830	35.8	0	0	0	1	1	1	0	2	0	0	0	0	0	1	0	0	0	0	0	0	0	0	2	2	0
perennials	8	.2440	.4492	36.5	1	0	0	5	1	0	0	1	0	0	0	0	0	0	0	0	0	0	0	0	1	0	6	1	0
perfect	249	.9431	46.452	56.7	41	27	23	25	56	36	25	16	69	21	3	16	10	16	9	14	7	1	8	3	19	12	10	31	0
perfected	13	.6065	1.6227	42.1	0	0	1	1	6	3	1	1	2	0	1	0	0	0	0	1	2	1	0	1	0	0	5	0	0
perfecting	4	.3266	.2865	34.6	0	0	0	1	0	0	2	1	0	0	0	0	0	0	0	1	0	1	0	0	0	0	1	1	0
perfection	34	.7230	4.9848	47.0	0	1	3	3	8	7	9	3	5	0	0	4	0	3	0	4	4	2	3	0	2	1	5	1	0
perfectly	156	.8821	27.490	54.4	11	27	18	26	35	19	15	5	57	5	7	11	2	7	2	12	4	1	3	1	18	12	6	8	0
Perfidy	3	.0000	.1370	31.4	0	0	0	0	3	0	0	0	3	0	0	0	0	0	0	0	0	0	0	0	0	0	0	0	0
perforated	5	.4875	.5081	37.1	0	1	1	1	0	0	2	0	0	1	0	1	0	0	0	1	0	0	1	0	0	0	0	1	0
perforation	3	.1274	.0913	29.6	0	0	0	0	1	0	2	0	0	0	0	0	0	0	0	0	0	0	2	0	0	0	0	1	0
perforations	2	.1674	.0805	29.1	0	0	0	0	1	0	1	0	0	0	0	0	0	0	0	0	0	0	1	0	0	1	0	0	0
perform	168	.8658	28.949	54.6	6	15	19	25	36	25	40	2	17	9	1	4	34	11	2	20	25	0	3	4	5	8	15	10	0
performance	149	.6940	20.970	53.2	8	11	8	20	45	24	30	3	17	7	2	6	2	2	0	2	51	0	6	1	7	11	3	32	0
performances	35	.4478	3.3126	45.2	1	2	6	5	3	11	6	1	2	0	1	0	1	1	0	2	21	0	0	0	1	1	2	3	0
performed	182	.6891	25.470	54.1	8	15	19	19	45	51	19	6	15	8	2	5	13	11	0	23	67	3	0	0	3	5	11	16	0
performer	44	.3155	3.0250	44.8	1	7	3	5	10	16	1	1	1	0	0	2	0	1	0	0	32	0	1	0	0	1	1	5	0
performers	32	.5088	3.4546	45.4	4	6	4	2	7	7	1	1	5	3	0	0	0	1	1	0	12	0	0	0	0	5	0	5	0
performing	54	.8060	8.7294	49.4	2	3	4	7	15	12	9	2	8	2	1	4	5	3	0	5	11	1	0	2	1	2	0	9	0
Performing	5	.3551	.3836	35.8	0	3	1	0	0	1	0	0	0	0	0	0	0	0	0	0	1	0	0	0	3	0	1	0	0
performs	18	.6356	2.3718	43.8	1	1	1	0	7	3	4	1	3	1	0	2	1	2	0	3	1	0	0	2	0	3	0	0	0
perfume	59	.7533	8.9841	49.5	3	8	5	14	5	1	4	19	8	1	1	4	0	2	2	9	1	0	1	0	3	0	8	19	0
perfumed	4	.4525	.4044	36.1	0	1	1	0	2	0	0	0	1	0	0	0	0	1	0	0	0	0	0	0	1	0	0	1	0
perfumes	14	.3832	1.2399	40.9	2	0	0	8	3	1	0	0	3	0	0	0	0	5	0	0	0	0	0	0	0	1	5	0	0
perfuming	2	.1494	.1045	30.2	0	1	0	0	1	0	0	0	1	0	0	0	0	0	0	0	1	0	0	0	0	0	0	0	0
perhaps	1235	.9318	227.83	63.6	144	204	148	172	270	138	124	35	259	75	21	92	26	124	10	167	46	32	21	8	63	126	79	86	0
peri	7	.0000	.0851	29.3	0	0	0	0	0	0	0	7	0	0	0	0	0	0	0	0	0	0	0	0	0	0	0	7	0
Peri	4	.0000	.0579	27.6	0	0	0	4	0	0	0	0	0	0	0	0	0	0	0	0	0	0	0	0	0	4	0	0	0
periagua	2	.0000	.0234	23.7	0	0	0	2	0	0	0	0	0	0	0	0	0	0	0	0	0	0	0	0	2	0	0	0	0
pericardial	2	.0000	.0209	23.2	0	0	0	0	0	2	0	0	0	0	0	0	0	0	0	0	0	0	0	0	0	0	2	0	0
pericardium	3	.0000	.0314	25.0	0	0	0	0	0	3	0	0	0	0	0	0	0	0	0	0	0	0	0	0	0	0	3	0	0
Pericles	9	.3401	.6917	38.4	0	0	0	2	6	0	0	1	0	0	0	0	0	4	0	0	0	0	0	0	4	0	0	1	0
Perico	4	.0000	.1827	32.6	4	0	0	0	0	0	0	0	4	0	0	0	0	0	0	0	0	0	0	0	0	0	0	0	0
perigee	5	.0000	.0986	29.9	1	0	0	0	0	4	0	0	0	0	0	0	0	0	0	5	0	0	0	0	0	0	0	0	0
peril	16	.6232	2.0817	43.2	0	1	1	2	8	3	1	0	4	1	0	3	0	1	1	0	0	0	0	0	4	0	0	2	0
Peril	3	.0000	.0322	25.1	0	0	0	0	0	0	3	0	0	0	0	3	0	0	0	0	0	0	0	0	0	0	0	0	0
perilous	10	.7077	1.4397	41.6	2	0	1	0	3	3	0	1	1	1	0	1	0	0	0	2	1	0	0	0	1	2	0	1	0
perilously	2	.2160	.1362	31.3	0	0	1	0	0	0	0	1	1	0	0	0	0	0	0	1	0	0	0	0	0	0	0	0	0
perils	6	.4701	.6472	38.1	2	0	0	0	2	2	0	0	3	0	0	1	0	1	0	0	1	0	0	0	0	0	0	0	0
perimeter	140	.0585	3.5806	45.5	0	19	17	20	36	22	26	0	0	0	0	0	136	1	0	0	0	0	0	0	0	1	0	2	0
perimeters	7	.1611	.3071	34.9	0	0	1	3	0	2	1	0	0	0	0	0	6	0	0	0	0	0	0	0	0	0	0	1	0
period	601	.8933	106.42	60.3	42	44	59	69	130	141	83	33	29	69	8	17	32	98	16	66	87	3	14	9	9	29	84	31	0
Period	12	.5708	1.4177	41.5	0	2	0	3	0	3	2	2	0	0	0	0	2	2	0	3	2	1	0	0	0	0	2	0	0
periodic	11	.4977	1.1574	40.6	0	2	1	1	0	2	4	1	0	0	0	0	2	2	0	2	0	0	0	0	0	0	4	1	0
Periodic	7	.3410	.5426	37.3	0	1	0	0	1	5	0	0	0	0	0	0	0	0	0	5	0	0	0	0	0	0	1	0	0
periodical	5	.1511	.1963	32.9	0	1	1	0	2	1	0	0	0	0	0	0	0	0	0	0	0	0	0	1	0	1	4	0	0
Periodical	3	.3406	.2461	33.9	0	0	0	0	2	0	0	1	1	1	0	0	0	0	0	0	0	0	0	0	0	0	0	1	0
periodically	7	.4481	.6882	38.4	0	0	1	0	2	1	3	0	1	0	0	0	0	0	0	3	0	0	0	1	0	0	1	1	0
periodicals	12	.5601	1.3927	41.4	1	2	1	0	4	2	2	0	1	1	0	1	0	0	0	0	0	0	0	1	0	2	5	1	0
periods	190	.8368	31.709	55.0	29	18	20	19	53	24	22	5	10	49	3	2	11	21	14	35	12	2	2	0	1	10	13	5	0
periosteum	2	.0000	.0394	26.0	0	0	0	0	0	2	0	0	0	0	0	0	0	0	0	2	0	0	0	0	0	0	0	0	0
periscope	5	.3850	.4834	36.8	0	1	0	0	1	3	0	0	3	0	0	0	0	1	0	0	0	0	0	0	0	1	0	0	0
perish	11	.6214	1.4090	41.5	0	1	0	2	1	4	3	0	1	1	0	2	0	1	0	0	0	0	0	0	1	3	2	0	0
perishable	8	.5138	.8691	39.4	1	2	1	0	2	0	2	0	0	0	0	0	0	2	0	3	0	0	1	0	0	1	1	0	0
perished	11	.7157	1.6104	42.1	0	1	0	2	4	3	0	1	2	1	0	1	0	1	0	2	0	0	0	0	1	2	1	0	0
periwinkle	2	.2401	.1133	30.5	1	0	0	0	1	0	0	0	0	0	0	0	0	0	0	0	0	0	0	0	0	1	1	0	0
Periwinkle	7	.0000	.3198	35.0	7	0	0	0	0	0	0	0	7	0	0	0	0	0	0	0	0	0	0	0	0	0	0	0	0
Periwinkle's	2	.0000	.0914	29.6	2	0	0	0	0	0	0	0	2	0	0	0	0	0	0	0	0	0	0	0	0	0	0	0	0
periwinkles	4	.0000	.0789	29.0	0	0	0	0	3	1	0	0	0	0	0	0	0	0	0	4	0	0	0	0	0	0	0	0	0
perk	3	.3427	.2477	33.9	1	0	0	0	1	1	0	0	1	0	0	0	0	0	0	0	0	0	0	0	1	0	0	1	0
perked	4	.2417	.3028	34.8	3	1	0	0	0	0	0	0	3	0	0	0	0	0	0	0	0	0	0	0	1	0	0	0	0
Perkins	10	.4629	1.0680	40.3	1	3	4	0	2	0	0	0	5	1	0	0	0	0	0	0	0	0	0	0	0	3	0	1	0
Perley	8	.0000	.1158	30.6	0	8	0	0	0	0	0	0	0	0	0	0	0	0	0	0	0	0	0	0	0	8	0	0	0
Perm	2	.2351	.1166	30.7	0	0	0	0	0	0	1	1	0	0	0	0	0	1	0	0	0	0	0	0	0	0	0	1	0
permanence	3	.2053	.1597	32.0	0	0	0	0	2	0	1	0	0	0	0	0	0	0	0	1	0	0	0	0	0	2	0	0	0
permanent	110	.8211	18.062	52.6	9	4	14	10	26	22	15	10	9	4	1	3	0	22	0	19	3	2	5	6	2	2	21	11	0
permanent-press	8	.2423	.4411	36.4	0	0	0	0	0	2	0	6	0	0	0	0	0	0	0	0	0	0	2	0	0	0	0	6	0
permanently	29	.6749	3.9799	46.0	2	0	6	4	5	2	6	4	1	0	0	1	0	4	0	5	0	0	3	1	0	3	6	5	0
permanganate	4	.0000	.0789	29.0	0	0	3	0	0	1	0	0	0	0	0	0	0	0	0	4	0	0	0	0	0	0	0	0	0
permeable	2	.2278	.1128	30.5	0	0	0	1	1	0	0	0	0	0	0	0	0	0	0	1	0	0	0	0	0	0	1	0	0
permeated	5	.4040	.4228	36.3	0	0	1	0	1	0	2	1	0	0	1	0	0	0	0	0	2	0	0	0	0	1	1	0	0
Permian	7	.0000	.0733	28.6	0	0	0	0	7	0	0	0	0	0	0	0	0	0	0	0	0	0	0	0	0	0	7	0	0
permissible	8	.4526	.7724	38.9	0	0	1	0	4	1	1	1	1	1	0	0	1	0	0	0	0	0	2	0	0	0	2	1	0

5Q Percentage
9N percenter
8E percentiles
7R perceptiveness
8D perchance
3P Percheron
7Q perchlike
7R percolate
9H percolating
7J Percussion
8F perdition
5A perdiz
3A Pere's
6A Peregil's
6A peregrine
7N Pereire
8D peremptory
7Q perennially
4A PERFECT
5G perfect'**
5C perfecter
8F Perfectionists
6A perfections
6A perfidious
8M perforating
9D perforce
8F performe
3J Performers
4P performers'
3Q perfume-making
8A perfunctorily
5R Pergament
3R Perhaps
6B peridinians
9H peridotite
7R Perigron
7E Perimeter
3E PERIMETER
3E PERIMETERS
7R period-luminosity
8J Periods
8Q periostracum
7C peripatetic
4Q peripherally
XR periphery
7F Perisan
8A periscopes
7Q Perish
7J perish-ed
3P Perished
7N perishing
7H peristaltic
9D perjur'd
9D perjured
7A perjury
7N Perk
4P Perkinses
8B perky
7J Perla
4P Perley's
6F permafrost
7P permanency
8M permanent-magnet
8L permanents
9P permeating

Word Type	F	D	U	SFI	3 Gr 3	4 Gr 4	5 Gr 5	6 Gr 6	7 Gr 7	8 Gr 8	9 Gr 9	X UnGr	A Read	B Eng & Gr	C Comp	D Lit	E Math	F Soc Stud	G Spell	H Sci	J Music	K Art	L Home Ec	M Shop	N Lib F	P Lib NF	Q Lib Ref	R Mag	S Rel
permission	87	.8603	14.980	51.8	9	15	9	18	16	8	7	5	24	7	1	4	0	17	2	2	0	0	2	2	4	9	2	11	0
permit	72	.8581	12.290	50.9	4	3	7	7	26	11	12	2	5	5	1	5	0	10	5	8	1	1	6	1	0	6	8	10	0
permits	27	.6128	3.3914	45.3	0	1	1	3	7	5	8	2	1	3	0	0	2	0	0	8	0	0	3	3	0	0	4	3	0
permitted	78	.7971	12.503	51.0	2	4	10	12	19	20	10	1	10	3	0	4	4	20	2	2	0	1	1	0	1	7	17	6	0
permitting	12	.6334	1.5606	41.9	0	1	1	0	5	2	3	0	0	0	0	0	1	3	0	2	0	0	0	0	1	1	3	1	0
pernicious	3	.3826	.2445	33.9	0	0	0	0	0	1	1	1	0	0	0	0	0	0	0	0	1	0	0	0	0	0	1	1	0
Peron	11	.0712	.2691	34.3	10	0	0	0	1	0	0	0	0	0	0	0	0	1	0	0	0	0	0	0	0	0	10	0	0
Peron's	5	.0000	.0523	27.2	5	0	0	0	0	0	0	0	0	0	0	0	0	0	0	0	0	0	0	0	0	0	5	0	0
peroxide	7	.3311	.5381	37.3	1	1	0	0	3	1	1	0	0	0	0	0	0	0	0	5	0	0	0	0	0	1	1	0	0
perpendicular	120	.4008	10.457	50.2	1	4	15	15	20	43	19	3	2	0	0	0	96	0	0	2	1	0	2	11	0	1	4	1	0
perpetrated	2	.2285	.1129	30.5	0	0	1	0	0	1	0	0	0	0	0	0	0	1	0	0	0	0	0	0	0	0	1	0	0
perpetual	17	.6062	2.1349	43.3	0	1	5	1	5	5	0	0	1	1	0	0	0	5	0	1	0	0	0	0	1	2	5	1	0
Perpetual	3	.0000	.1370	31.4	0	0	0	3	0	0	0	0	3	0	0	0	0	0	0	0	0	0	0	0	0	0	0	0	0
perpetually	6	.3923	.5015	37.0	1	1	1	0	2	1	0	0	0	0	1	1	0	0	0	1	0	0	0	0	0	0	3	0	0
perpetuate	3	.3777	.2489	34.0	0	0	0	1	1	1	0	0	0	1	0	0	0	1	0	0	0	0	0	0	1	0	0	0	0
perpetuity	2	.2446	.1123	30.5	0	0	0	0	1	1	0	0	0	1	0	0	0	0	0	0	0	0	0	0	0	0	1	0	0
perplex	3	.3805	.2526	34.0	0	0	0	1	1	1	0	0	0	0	0	0	0	1	0	0	0	0	0	0	1	1	0	0	0
perplexed	16	.5248	1.8096	42.6	1	0	2	1	10	0	2	0	4	0	0	5	0	1	0	1	0	0	0	0	2	0	0	3	0
perplexing	5	.4854	.5160	37.1	1	0	1	0	2	1	0	0	0	0	0	0	0	2	0	0	0	0	0	0	0	1	1	1	0
perplexities	3	.1187	.1291	31.1	0	0	0	0	1	2	0	0	1	0	0	2	0	0	0	0	0	0	0	0	0	0	0	0	0
perplexity	3	.2261	.2131	33.3	0	0	0	1	1	1	0	0	2	0	0	0	0	0	0	0	0	0	0	0	1	0	0	0	0
Perrault	6	.2261	.4261	36.3	1	0	0	0	3	2	0	0	4	0	0	0	0	0	0	0	0	0	0	0	2	0	0	0	0
Perrik	12	.0000	.5482	37.4	0	0	0	12	0	0	0	0	12	0	0	0	0	0	0	0	0	0	0	0	0	0	0	0	0
Perry	15	.5204	1.7305	42.4	1	8	1	3	1	1	0	0	6	0	0	0	0	4	0	0	0	0	0	0	0	1	3	1	0
persecuted	5	.3684	.4146	36.2	1	0	0	1	1	0	2	0	0	0	0	0	0	3	0	0	0	0	0	0	0	1	1	0	0
persecution	14	.5044	1.5446	41.9	1	1	0	1	7	2	2	0	4	0	0	1	0	2	0	1	0	0	0	0	0	0	5	1	0
persecutions	4	.2285	.2258	33.5	0	0	0	0	2	2	0	0	0	0	0	0	0	2	0	0	0	0	0	0	0	0	2	0	0
Persephone	11	.1859	.6687	38.3	0	0	6	0	0	5	0	0	6	0	0	5	0	0	0	0	0	0	0	0	0	0	0	0	0
Persepolis	5	.0000	.0608	27.8	0	0	0	0	5	0	0	0	0	0	0	0	0	0	0	0	0	0	0	0	0	0	0	5	0
Perseus	18	.3824	1.7098	42.3	0	0	0	4	0	11	3	0	11	4	0	3	0	0	0	0	0	0	0	0	0	0	0	0	0
perseverance	7	.3710	.6235	37.9	2	0	0	1	2	1	1	0	3	0	1	0	0	0	0	1	0	0	0	0	0	0	2	0	0
persevered	2	.2346	.1166	30.7	0	0	0	0	1	0	0	1	0	0	0	0	0	0	0	1	0	0	0	0	0	0	0	1	0
Pershing	4	.0000	.0778	28.9	0	0	0	0	0	4	0	0	0	0	0	0	0	4	0	0	0	0	0	0	0	0	0	0	0
Persia	32	.5941	3.9601	46.0	2	2	6	2	14	4	1	1	2	4	0	0	0	15	0	0	1	0	0	0	4	2	4	0	0
Persian	56	.7344	8.2970	49.2	1	3	8	9	19	6	9	1	1	5	0	1	1	20	3	0	1	2	0	0	1	4	10	7	0
Persians	18	.4761	1.8140	42.6	0	0	3	4	7	2	1	1	0	1	0	0	0	9	0	0	2	2	0	0	0	0	4	0	0
persimmon	6	.4087	.5613	37.5	0	1	3	0	0	1	1	0	2	0	0	0	0	0	2	0	0	0	0	0	0	1	0	1	0
Persimmon	3	.0000	.0352	25.5	0	0	3	0	0	0	0	0	0	0	0	0	0	0	0	0	0	0	0	0	3	0	0	0	0
persimmons	3	.2357	.2199	33.4	0	1	2	0	0	0	0	0	2	0	0	0	0	0	0	0	0	0	0	0	0	1	0	0	0
Persinger	3	.0000	.1370	31.4	0	0	0	3	0	0	0	0	3	0	0	0	0	0	0	0	0	0	0	0	0	0	0	0	0
persist	9	.4844	.9101	39.6	0	0	1	1	4	2	0	1	0	0	0	0	0	0	0	1	0	0	1	0	0	1	4	2	0
persisted	16	.6391	2.0721	43.2	0	0	1	1	7	4	3	0	0	0	1	2	0	0	0	0	0	0	1	0	6	3	2	1	0
persistence	2	.0000	.0209	23.2	0	0	0	1	0	0	1	0	0	0	0	0	0	0	0	0	0	0	0	0	0	0	2	0	0
persistent	29	.7645	4.4566	46.5	4	0	5	3	10	4	1	2	2	1	1	3	0	2	1	3	1	0	0	0	1	2	8	4	0
persistently	4	.3745	.3228	35.1	1	0	0	0	3	0	0	0	0	0	0	1	0	0	0	0	0	0	0	0	0	0	1	2	0
persists	6	.2916	.3904	35.9	2	1	0	1	1	0	1	0	0	0	0	0	0	0	0	0	0	0	0	0	1	0	4	1	0
person	1196	.9245	218.94	63.4	146	146	144	155	274	156	152	23	202	221	22	54	35	110	58	188	38	10	64	10	34	51	46	52	1
Person	2	.0000	.0004	5.5	0	2	0	0	0	0	0	0	0	0	0	0	0	0	0	0	0	0	0	0	0	0	0	0	2
person-to-person	3	.3452	.2543	34.1	0	1	0	0	0	1	0	1	1	0	0	0	0	0	0	1	0	0	0	0	0	0	0	1	0
person's	79	.8425	13.316	51.2	6	12	11	8	16	12	13	1	14	12	2	1	1	9	6	17	2	2	3	0	1	0	6	3	0
Person's	4	.0000	.0323	25.1	0	0	0	1	3	0	0	0	0	0	0	0	0	0	0	0	4	0	0	0	0	0	0	0	0
personage	4	.3625	.3158	35.0	0	1	0	0	2	0	0	1	0	0	0	0	0	0	0	0	0	0	0	0	2	1	1	0	0
personages	4	.3799	.3303	35.2	0	1	0	0	0	0	0	3	0	0	0	0	0	0	0	0	0	0	0	0	1	2	1	0	0
personal	255	.8373	42.588	56.3	16	16	13	16	57	72	53	12	29	58	5	12	4	19	1	8	18	10	9	1	4	14	21	42	0
Personal	6	.0000	.0487	26.9	0	0	0	0	6	0	0	0	0	0	0	0	0	0	6	0	0	0	0	0	0	0	0	0	0
personalities	15	.4596	1.4569	41.6	0	1	3	0	5	4	1	1	1	0	0	4	0	1	0	0	0	0	3	0	0	0	1	5	0
personality	97	.7335	14.363	51.6	6	1	10	3	25	28	20	4	12	6	2	8	0	6	1	11	4	4	18	1	0	6	12	6	0
personalized	4	.3715	.3171	35.0	0	0	0	0	2	1	1	0	0	1	0	0	0	0	0	0	1	0	0	0	0	0	2	0	0
personally	27	.7675	4.1803	46.2	0	4	1	3	8	4	6	1	4	2	1	2	0	3	0	0	3	0	0	0	1	5	2	4	0
personified	2	.2433	.1158	30.6	0	0	0	2	0	0	0	0	0	0	0	0	0	0	0	0	0	0	0	0	0	1	0	1	0
personnel	27	.7190	3.9394	46.0	1	1	3	1	6	8	6	1	2	0	0	1	0	5	0	4	1	0	1	0	1	1	4	7	0
persons	304	.8367	50.733	57.1	21	26	57	25	61	51	58	5	23	35	8	4	16	57	17	21	2	1	22	3	1	17	56	21	0
persons'	2	.1483	.0728	28.6	0	0	0	1	0	0	1	0	0	0	0	0	0	0	0	0	0	0	0	1	0	1	0	0	0
perspective	50	.2511	2.8381	44.5	0	5	6	0	30	3	6	0	1	2	0	0	0	7	0	2	0	21	0	0	2	7	5	3	0
Perspective	6	.2795	.3790	35.8	0	4	0	0	1	0	0	1	0	0	0	0	0	0	0	0	0	0	0	0	0	1	4	1	0
perspectives	3	.3801	.2525	34.0	0	0	0	1	2	0	0	0	0	0	0	0	0	0	0	1	0	0	0	0	1	1	0	0	0
perspicacious	3	.3374	.2433	33.9	0	0	1	0	2	1	0	0	1	1	0	0	0	0	0	0	0	0	0	0	0	0	1	0	0
perspiration	41	.6544	5.5362	47.4	3	14	3	2	10	3	5	1	4	2	0	1	0	0	0	21	1	0	1	1	2	0	0	8	0
perspire	12	.4542	1.1744	40.7	1	4	2	0	3	1	1	0	0	0	0	0	0	0	0	7	0	0	1	0	0	0	0	3	0
perspiring	4	.3849	.3440	35.4	0	1	0	0	1	1	1	0	1	0	0	0	0	0	0	0	1	0	1	0	0	0	1	0	0
persuade	40	.7666	6.2032	47.9	2	3	11	5	5	3	11	0	7	3	1	2	0	6	1	0	1	0	0	0	2	12	4	1	0
persuaded	47	.7170	6.9056	48.4	1	0	11	6	13	5	10	1	11	3	0	2	0	9	0	0	1	0	0	0	1	8	7	5	0
persuades	2	.2346	.1166	30.7	0	1	0	0	0	0	0	1	0	0	0	0	0	0	0	1	0	0	0	0	0	0	0	1	0
persuading	8	.4673	.8081	39.1	0	0	1	0	0	4	2	1	1	2	0	0	0	1	0	0	0	0	0	0	0	1	0	3	0
persuasion	11	.4574	1.0796	40.3	0	0	2	0	1	1	4	3	1	0	0	0	0	3	0	2	0	0	0	0	0	0	2	4	0
persuasions	2	.2446	.1142	30.6	0	0	0	1	0	1	0	0	0	0	0	0	0	0	0	0	0	0	0	0	1	0	0	1	0
persuasive	7	.4782	.7025	38.5	0	0	0	0	0	4	3	0	0	1	0	2	0	0	0	0	0	0	0	0	0	2	0	2	0
persuasively	2	.1733	.1149	30.6	0	0	0	1	0	1	0	0	1	1	0	0	0	0	0	0	0	0	0	0	0	0	0	0	0
pert	4	.1892	.1847	32.7	0	0	0	1	1	2	0	0	0	0	0	3	0	0	0	0	0	0	0	0	0	0	0	1	0
pertained	2	.0000	.0243	23.9	0	0	0	0	1	0	0	1	0	0	0	0	0	0	0	0	0	0	0	0	0	0	0	2	0
pertaining	7	.4314	.6664	38.2	0	1	0	3	0	1	1	1	1	0	0	0	0	1	0	1	0	0	0	0	0	0	3	1	0
pertains	3	.2309	.1631	32.1	0	0	0	0	0	0	2	1	0	0	0	1	0	0	0	0	0	0	0	0	0	0	0	2	0
Perth	8	.2348	.4745	36.8	0	3	0	2	1	0	2	0	0	0	0	0	0	6	0	0	0	0	0	0	0	0	2	0	0
pertinent	4	.4826	.4094	36.1	0	0	1	1	2	0	0	0	0	0	0	0	0	0	0	1	0	0	0	0	1	1	0	1	0
perturbed	5	.3701	.4012	36.0	0	0	1	1	2	1	0	0	0	0	1	0	0	1	0	0	0	0	0	0	2	1	0	0	0
Peru	63	.6192	8.0709	49.1	5	10	7	15	11	3	10	2	4	0	0	0	0	24	0	1	4	0	0	0	3	5	8	14	0
Peru's	5	.1398	.1959	32.9	0	0	0	1	1	0	3	0	0	0	0	0	0	1	0	0	0	0	0	0	0	0	0	4	0
Peruvian	11	.3010	.7422	38.7	0	0	0	7	2	1	1	0	0	0	0	0	0	0	0	0	0	0	0	0	0	1	3	7	0
Peruvians	5	.0000	.0608	27.8	0	0	0	5	0	0	0	0	0	0	0	0	0	0	0	0	0	0	0	0	0	0	0	5	0
pervades	3	.2609	.1751	32.4	0	0	0	0	2	0	1	0	0	0	1	0	0	0	0	0	0	0	0	0	0	1	0	1	0
pervading	2	.2337	.1157	30.6	0	0	0	0	1	1	0	0	0	0	0	0	0	1	0	0	0	0	0	0	1	0	0	0	0
pervasive	3	.1277	.1363	31.3	0	0	0	0	1	1	1	0	1	0	0	0	0	0	0	0	0	0	0	0	0	0	0	2	0
perverse	3	.3553	.2608	34.2	0	0	1	1	0	1	0	0	1	0	0	0	0	1	0	0	0	0	0	0	0	1	0	0	0
pesetas	2	.0000	.0234	23.7	0	2	0	0	0	0	0	0	0	0	0	0	0	0	0	0	0	0	0	0	2	0	0	0	0
pesky	2	.2160	.1362	31.3	0	0	0	0	1	1	0	0	1	0	0	0	0	0	0	1	0	0	0	0	0	0	0	0	0

9R permissiveness
XR permless
8E permutation
XR permutations
8J Pernambuco
3Q Perons
9N perpendicularity
8D perpendicularly
9R perpetrator
7N perpetrators
3P perpetual-motion
7Q perpetuated
9Q perpetuator
5Q perplexes
7R perquisites
5A perr-rr-fect
6A Perrik's
6B Perrin
8G persecute
7Q persecutor
6N persecutors
8D Persephone's
7R Persepolitan
9Q persevere
8F persevering
8B persia
8B persian
8Q Persian-speaking
8D persistency
6G personable
8B personalize
8D personification
7B Personification
8D personifies
7P Personnel
3H perspires
7A persuader
8B Persuasion
XR persulphate
9Q Perthshire
7G peruke
4Q perusal
5P perusing
7D pervaded
8Q perversions
7Q perversity
5P perverted
XQ pervious
5N Perviz
7D Peshtank
7R Peskay
4J peskily

Word Type	F	D	U	SFI	3 Gr 3	4 Gr 4	5 Gr 5	6 Gr 6	7 Gr 7	8 Gr 8	9 Gr 9	X UnGr	A Read	B Eng & Gr	C Comp	D Lit	E Math	F Soc Stud	G Spell	H Sci	J Music	K Art	L Home Ec	M Shop	N Lib F	P Lib NF	Q Lib Ref	R Mag	S Rel
peso	2	.1972	.1262	31.0	1	0	0	1	0	0	0	0	1	0	0	0	1	0	0	0	0	0	0	0	0	0	0	0	0
pesos	9	.5408	1.0110	40.0	0	2	1	2	4	0	0	0	0	0	0	2	2	2	0	0	2	0	0	0	0	0	0	1	0
pessimistic	6	.4808	.6097	37.9	0	0	0	0	1	1	2	2	0	0	0	0	0	0	1	2	0	0	0	0	0	0	1	2	0
pest	17	.3499	1.4795	41.7	10	1	1	3	1	0	1	0	8	0	0	0	0	0	0	1	0	0	0	0	7	0	1	0	0
Pest	5	.2360	.3663	35.6	0	0	0	5	0	0	0	0	3	0	0	0	0	2	0	0	0	0	0	0	0	0	0	0	0
Pestalozzi	2	.0000	.0290	24.6	0	0	2	0	0	0	0	0	0	0	0	0	0	0	0	0	0	0	0	0	0	2	0	0	0
pester	4	.3614	.3153	35.0	2	0	1	0	0	0	1	0	0	1	0	0	0	0	0	0	0	0	0	0	2	1	0	0	0
pestered	6	.3823	.5671	37.5	0	0	1	1	2	0	0	2	3	0	0	0	0	0	0	2	0	0	0	0	1	0	0	0	0
pestering	10	.1787	.5869	37.7	6	0	1	0	2	0	0	1	5	0	0	0	0	0	0	0	0	0	0	0	5	0	0	0	0
pesticides	2	.2437	.1129	30.5	0	0	0	0	1	0	1	0	0	0	0	0	0	0	0	0	0	0	0	0	0	0	1	1	0
pestilence	2	.2417	.1091	30.4	0	0	0	1	1	0	0	0	0	0	0	0	0	0	0	0	1	0	0	0	0	0	1	0	0
pestle	7	.3728	.6492	38.1	7	0	0	0	0	0	0	0	4	0	0	0	0	0	0	0	0	0	0	0	0	0	1	2	0
pests	21	.4441	2.0421	43.1	6	3	1	1	3	2	0	5	1	0	0	0	0	0	0	12	0	0	0	0	0	1	3	4	0
pet	196	.8473	33.506	55.3	77	33	15	31	22	9	9	0	97	22	2	5	7	3	3	11	1	3	0	1	6	24	2	9	0
Pet	9	.3732	.8542	39.3	1	2	2	2	1	0	1	0	6	0	0	0	0	0	0	0	0	0	0	0	2	0	0	1	0
pet's	2	.0000	.0914	29.6	1	0	0	1	0	0	0	0	2	0	0	0	0	0	0	0	0	0	0	0	0	0	0	0	0
Petain	2	.0000	.0389	25.9	0	0	0	0	0	0	2	0	0	0	0	0	0	2	0	0	0	0	0	0	0	0	0	0	0
petal	9	.5701	1.0410	40.2	4	2	0	1	0	2	0	0	0	1	1	3	0	0	1	0	0	1	0	0	0	0	2	0	0
petal-like	2	.0000	.0394	26.0	0	0	0	0	0	0	0	2	0	0	0	0	0	0	0	2	0	0	0	0	0	0	0	0	0
petals	45	.5480	5.2533	47.2	6	3	5	16	5	0	1	9	4	0	1	1	0	0	0	32	0	1	0	0	1	2	3	0	0
Petar	3	.0000	.0314	25.0	0	0	0	0	0	3	0	0	0	0	0	0	0	0	0	0	0	0	0	0	0	0	3	0	0
petates	2	.0000	.0389	25.9	0	0	0	2	0	0	0	0	0	0	0	0	0	2	0	0	0	0	0	0	0	0	0	0	0
Pete	143	.5558	16.880	52.3	87	8	8	13	15	9	1	2	34	5	1	4	5	0	1	0	1	0	1	0	72	8	0	11	0
Pete's	18	.5376	2.0848	43.2	4	2	2	2	1	2	0	5	5	0	0	2	5	0	0	0	0	0	0	0	4	0	0	2	0
Peter	455	.7956	74.245	58.7	140	48	31	148	36	28	21	3	286	8	7	10	3	14	3	22	23	1	0	0	38	20	13	7	0
Peter's	29	.6309	3.9491	46.0	3	3	5	12	2	0	4	0	18	0	0	3	0	0	0	2	2	0	0	0	2	1	1	0	0
petered	2	.1787	.1174	30.7	0	1	0	0	1	0	0	0	1	0	0	0	0	0	0	0	0	0	0	0	1	0	0	0	0
Peterkin	2	.0000	.0234	23.7	0	0	0	2	0	0	0	0	0	0	0	0	0	0	0	0	0	0	0	0	2	0	0	0	0
Peters	46	.4971	5.0704	47.1	17	3	1	5	0	17	2	1	18	17	0	0	0	1	0	0	1	0	0	0	5	2	0	2	0
Peters'	6	.3044	.4545	36.6	2	0	0	3	0	1	0	0	2	1	0	0	0	0	0	0	0	0	0	0	3	0	0	0	0
Petersburg	20	.4988	2.0842	43.2	0	4	0	0	1	8	7	0	1	0	0	0	2	0	0	0	6	0	0	0	1	0	6	4	0
Petersen	3	.0000	.1370	31.4	3	0	0	0	0	0	0	0	3	0	0	0	0	0	0	0	0	0	0	0	0	0	0	0	0
Peterson	31	.2535	2.5363	44.0	3	10	2	1	14	0	1	0	28	1	0	0	0	2	0	0	0	0	0	0	0	0	0	0	0
Peterson's	2	.1814	.1187	30.7	1	1	0	0	0	0	0	0	1	0	0	0	0	0	0	0	0	0	0	0	0	0	0	1	0
Petey	7	.2395	.5461	37.4	0	0	0	0	2	5	0	0	6	0	0	1	0	0	0	0	0	0	0	0	0	0	0	0	0
petiole	3	.0000	.0591	27.7	1	0	2	0	0	0	0	0	0	0	0	0	0	0	0	3	0	0	0	0	0	0	0	0	0
petit	3	.0000	.0243	23.8	3	0	0	0	0	0	0	0	0	0	0	0	0	0	0	0	3	0	0	0	0	0	0	0	0
Petit	15	.0756	.4687	36.7	3	0	0	0	0	12	0	0	3	0	0	12	0	0	0	0	0	0	0	0	0	0	0	0	0
petite	2	.1812	.0838	29.2	0	0	1	0	1	0	0	0	0	0	0	0	0	0	0	0	0	0	1	0	0	0	0	1	0
Petite	2	.0000	.0243	23.9	0	0	0	0	0	0	0	2	0	0	0	0	0	0	0	0	0	0	0	0	0	0	0	2	0
petition	35	.6105	4.5872	46.6	0	0	11	6	2	12	3	1	16	0	0	4	0	6	0	0	0	0	0	0	4	0	1	4	0
petitioned	2	.0000	.0389	25.9	0	0	0	0	1	1	0	0	0	0	0	0	0	2	0	0	0	0	0	0	0	0	0	0	0
petitions	6	.3559	.4844	36.9	0	0	0	0	1	4	1	0	0	0	0	1	0	4	0	0	0	0	0	0	0	0	0	1	0
Petrarch	5	.3179	.3510	35.5	1	0	3	0	0	0	1	0	0	0	0	1	0	0	0	0	0	0	0	0	0	1	3	0	0
petrels	4	.0996	.1523	31.8	0	0	0	1	1	0	2	0	1	0	0	0	0	0	0	0	0	0	0	0	0	0	0	3	0
Petri	3	.0000	.0591	27.7	0	0	0	2	0	0	0	1	0	0	0	0	0	0	0	3	0	0	0	0	0	0	0	0	0
petrified	8	.4286	.7506	38.8	0	2	1	3	1	1	0	0	1	2	0	0	0	0	0	0	0	0	0	0	2	3	0	0	0
Petrified	4	.0000	.0778	28.9	0	3	1	0	0	0	0	0	0	0	0	0	0	4	0	0	0	0	0	0	0	0	0	0	0
Petrina	6	.0000	.2741	34.4	0	0	0	6	0	0	0	0	6	0	0	0	0	0	0	0	0	0	0	0	0	0	0	0	0
petroleum	95	.5715	11.404	50.6	6	3	26	14	15	15	16	0	3	0	0	0	0	43	0	24	0	0	0	2	0	4	15	4	0
Petroleum	6	.4196	.5417	37.3	0	0	1	0	3	0	2	0	0	0	0	0	0	1	0	0	0	0	0	0	0	1	1	3	0
Petromin	2	.0000	.0290	24.6	0	0	0	0	2	0	0	0	0	0	0	0	0	0	0	0	0	0	0	0	0	2	0	0	0
Petros	18	.0000	.8223	39.2	0	18	0	0	0	0	0	0	18	0	0	0	0	0	0	0	0	0	0	0	0	0	0	0	0
Petrouchka	27	.0956	.7157	38.5	0	6	0	0	9	0	12	0	0	0	0	0	0	0	0	0	24	0	0	0	0	0	0	3	0
Petrouchka's	3	.0000	.0243	23.8	0	0	0	0	0	0	3	0	0	0	0	0	0	0	0	0	3	0	0	0	0	0	0	0	0
pets	88	.7829	14.041	51.5	37	16	3	17	11	1	2	1	37	5	0	5	1	1	2	1	0	0	1	0	8	15	7	5	0
Petsamo	3	.0000	.0583	27.7	0	0	0	3	0	0	0	0	0	0	0	0	0	3	0	0	0	0	0	0	0	0	0	0	0
petted	14	.6186	1.8567	42.7	4	3	3	0	4	0	0	0	7	1	0	1	0	0	0	0	0	0	0	0	2	2	0	1	0
petticoat	18	.2592	1.0142	40.1	0	2	0	1	1	1	13	0	1	0	1	1	0	0	0	0	1	0	12	0	1	1	0	0	0
petticoats	7	.3703	.6459	38.1	0	1	1	4	1	0	0	0	4	0	0	1	0	0	0	0	0	0	0	0	2	0	0	0	0
Pettigrew	3	.2270	.1588	32.0	0	0	0	0	1	2	0	0	0	2	0	0	0	0	0	0	0	0	0	0	0	0	1	0	0
petting	4	.1787	.2347	33.7	1	2	0	0	1	0	0	0	2	0	0	0	0	0	0	0	0	0	0	0	2	0	0	0	0
petty	7	.4515	.6819	38.3	0	0	0	0	2	2	3	0	1	0	0	3	0	1	0	0	0	0	1	0	0	0	1	0	0
Petty	2	.0000	.0243	23.9	0	0	0	0	1	1	0	0	0	0	0	0	0	0	0	0	0	0	0	0	0	0	0	2	0
Petula	2	.0000	.0243	23.9	0	0	0	2	0	0	0	0	0	0	0	0	0	0	0	0	0	0	0	0	0	0	0	2	0
petulant	4	.1892	.1847	32.7	0	0	1	0	3	0	0	0	0	0	0	3	0	0	0	0	0	0	0	0	0	0	0	1	0
petulantly	2	.1717	.1142	30.6	0	0	0	0	1	1	0	0	1	0	0	1	0	0	0	0	0	0	0	0	0	0	0	0	0
petunia	2	.0000	.0394	26.0	0	0	0	1	0	0	1	0	0	0	0	0	0	0	0	2	0	0	0	0	0	0	0	0	0
Petunia	22	.2305	1.1793	40.7	14	8	0	0	0	0	0	0	0	8	0	14	0	0	0	0	0	0	0	0	0	0	0	0	0
petunias	3	.2433	.1822	32.6	1	0	0	1	1	0	0	0	0	0	0	0	0	0	0	2	0	0	0	0	1	0	0	0	0
pew	6	.2129	.3322	35.2	0	1	0	1	0	0	4	0	1	0	0	4	0	0	0	0	0	0	0	0	0	1	0	0	0
Pew	7	.0000	.0821	29.1	0	0	0	0	7	0	0	0	0	0	0	0	0	0	0	0	0	0	0	0	7	0	0	0	0
pews	3	.3851	.2497	34.0	0	2	0	0	0	0	1	0	0	0	0	1	0	0	0	0	0	0	0	0	1	1	0	0	0
pewter	8	.5376	.9217	39.6	1	2	1	2	2	0	0	0	2	1	0	1	0	0	0	0	0	0	0	0	2	2	0	0	0
Peyton	2	.0000	.0215	23.3	0	0	0	0	0	2	0	0	0	0	0	2	0	0	0	0	0	0	0	0	0	0	0	0	0
Pfungst	9	.0000	.0966	29.8	0	0	0	0	0	0	9	0	0	0	0	9	0	0	0	0	0	0	0	0	0	0	0	0	0
PGA	2	.0000	.0209	23.2	0	0	0	0	2	0	0	0	0	0	0	0	0	0	0	0	0	0	0	0	0	0	2	0	0
ph	31	.2802	2.0454	43.1	0	10	4	5	6	6	0	0	5	6	0	0	2	0	18	0	0	0	0	0	0	0	0	0	0
Ph	8	.5134	.8610	39.3	0	0	3	2	0	0	2	1	0	0	0	0	2	1	0	0	0	0	0	0	0	1	1	3	0
Phaeacians	2	.0000	.0215	23.3	0	0	0	0	0	0	2	0	0	0	0	2	0	0	0	0	0	0	0	0	0	0	0	0	0
Phaethon	4	.0000	.0429	26.3	0	0	0	0	4	0	0	0	0	0	0	4	0	0	0	0	0	0	0	0	0	0	0	0	0
phalanges	2	.0000	.0394	26.0	0	0	0	2	0	0	0	0	0	0	0	0	0	0	0	2	0	0	0	0	0	0	0	0	0
phantom	5	.3828	.4244	36.3	0	0	1	0	0	2	2	0	1	2	0	0	0	0	1	0	0	0	0	1	0	0	0	0	0
Phantom	21	.0429	.4778	36.8	0	2	19	0	0	0	0	0	2	0	0	0	0	0	0	0	0	0	0	0	19	0	0	0	0
Phantom's	7	.0000	.0821	29.1	0	0	7	0	0	0	0	0	0	0	0	0	0	0	0	0	0	0	0	0	7	0	0	0	0
phantoms	3	.3847	.2494	34.0	0	0	0	0	2	1	0	0	0	0	0	0	0	0	0	0	0	0	0	0	1	1	1	0	0
pharaoh	6	.2062	.3286	35.2	0	1	0	1	4	0	0	0	0	0	0	0	0	5	0	0	0	0	0	0	0	0	1	0	0
Pharaoh	20	.4620	2.0118	43.0	1	0	5	6	5	0	3	0	2	0	0	0	4	7	0	0	0	0	0	0	0	1	6	0	0
Pharaoh's	8	.2708	.5520	37.4	0	4	0	0	4	0	0	0	2	0	0	4	0	2	0	0	0	0	0	0	0	0	0	0	0
pharaohs	7	.3870	.5941	37.7	0	1	0	3	1	1	1	0	0	0	0	0	0	3	0	1	0	1	0	0	0	0	2	0	0
Pharaohs	2	.2391	.1133	30.5	0	0	0	2	0	0	0	0	0	0	0	0	1	0	0	0	0	0	0	0	0	0	1	0	0
Pharisees	2	.0000	.0004	5.5	2	0	0	0	0	0	0	0	0	0	0	0	0	0	0	0	0	0	0	0	0	0	0	0	2
pharmaceutical	2	.0000	.0243	23.9	0	0	0	0	1	0	1	0	0	0	0	0	0	0	0	0	0	0	0	0	0	0	0	2	0
pharmacist	2	.0000	.0299	24.8	0	0	0	0	0	2	0	0	0	0	0	0	2	0	0	0	0	0	0	0	0	0	0	0	0
pharmacy	4	.2158	.2006	33.0	0	0	2	0	0	1	1	0	0	0	0	0	0	0	1	0	0	0	0	0	0	0	3	0	0

8F pessimism
7B pessimist
8A pessimists
6A Pest's
3A pesters
6A pestilential
5R Pests
9R pet-food
9F Petain's
7Q Peten
7Q Peterborough
7R peters
4A Petersons
8F Petitioned
5R petitioning
8F Petitions
9R petrel
7A Petrel
9Q petro-chemical
9B Petrograd
9Q petrographical
XR petrol
7P Petromin's
7N petromyzons-pricka
7L Petroni
8Q Petrovic
3B Pets
6A PETS
8A pettier
4A Pettingill's
4A Pettingills
4R Petton
5Q Peuple
7N Pew's
7Q Peyrere
5G pez
6E PF
7R Pfc
7H pfft
9Q PhD
9Q PhD's**
9B Ph-i-i-i-t-t
9D Phaistos
5Q Phalerum
7R phantasmagoric
5N Phantom'll
8K pharaoh-god
7F pharaoh's
3N Pharisee
XH pharmaceuticals
9Q pharmacology
XQ pharoahs

Word Type	F	D	U	SFI	3 Gr 3	4 Gr 4	5 Gr 5	6 Gr 6	7 Gr 7	8 Gr 8	9 Gr 9	X UnGr	A Read	B Eng & Gr	C Comp	D Lit	E Math	F Soc Stud	G Spell	H Sci	J Music	K Art	L Home Ec	M Shop	N Lib F	P Lib NF	Q Lib Ref	R Mag	S Rel
pharynx	7	.2412	.4224	36.3	0	0	0	0	2	0	4	1	0	0	0	0	0	0	0	5	0	0	0	0	0	0	2	0	0
phase	37	.6853	5.1896	47.2	0	0	3	1	10	5	8	10	3	0	1	1	0	1	0	17	1	0	1	0	0	1	4	7	0
phases	24	.5665	2.8529	44.6	0	0	0	0	4	4	12	4	1	0	1	0	0	0	0	16	1	0	0	1	0	0	3	1	0
Phasis	2	.0000	.0914	29.6	0	0	0	2	0	0	0	0	2	0	0	0	0	0	0	0	0	0	0	0	0	0	0	0	0
pheasant	14	.5790	1.6859	42.3	0	0	2	2	3	2	2	3	2	2	0	3	0	0	2	0	0	0	0	0	0	0	1	4	0
Pheasant	2	.0000	.0914	29.6	2	0	0	0	0	0	0	0	2	0	0	0	0	0	0	0	0	0	0	0	0	0	0	0	0
pheasants	10	.5097	1.1132	40.5	2	2	0	2	0	0	1	3	3	0	0	1	0	0	0	1	0	0	0	0	2	0	0	3	0
phenolphthalein	2	.0000	.0394	26.0	0	0	0	0	2	0	0	0	0	0	0	0	0	0	0	2	0	0	0	0	0	0	0	0	0
phenomena	25	.5160	2.7484	44.4	0	1	0	3	4	8	5	4	2	0	0	0	0	1	0	12	0	0	0	2	0	0	5	3	0
phenomenal	4	.2090	.2014	33.0	0	0	0	0	2	0	2	0	0	0	0	0	0	0	0	0	0	0	0	0	0	0	1	3	0
phenomenon	42	.5507	4.8590	46.9	2	0	1	4	20	5	7	3	5	0	0	0	1	0	0	6	1	0	0	0	3	3	17	6	0
phew	3	.2437	.2277	33.6	1	0	1	0	0	0	0	1	2	0	0	0	0	0	0	1	0	0	0	0	0	0	0	0	0
Phidias	4	.2408	.2408	33.8	0	0	0	2	0	0	0	2	0	0	0	0	0	2	0	0	0	0	0	0	0	2	0	0	0
Phil	32	.5941	4.0126	46.0	1	8	1	2	2	7	11	0	9	10	0	4	3	0	1	0	0	0	0	0	0	2	0	3	0
Phil's	5	.3094	.3714	35.7	1	1	1	1	0	0	1	0	1	2	0	0	2	0	0	0	0	0	0	0	0	0	0	0	0
Philadelphia	152	.7512	23.159	53.6	16	29	20	17	23	33	11	3	21	5	0	7	6	45	0	1	7	0	0	0	5	28	15	12	0
Philadelphian	2	.0000	.0389	25.9	0	0	0	0	0	2	0	0	0	0	0	0	0	2	0	0	0	0	0	0	0	0	0	0	0
philanthropic	2	.0000	.0209	23.2	0	0	1	0	1	0	0	0	0	0	0	0	0	0	0	0	0	0	0	0	0	0	2	0	0
philanthropies	2	.2446	.1123	30.5	0	0	1	0	1	0	0	0	0	1	0	0	0	0	0	0	0	0	0	0	0	0	1	0	0
Phileas	26	.0605	.5947	37.7	0	0	0	1	25	0	0	0	0	1	0	0	0	0	0	0	0	0	0	0	25	0	0	0	0
Philharmonic	6	.3374	.4350	36.4	0	0	3	0	0	3	0	0	0	1	0	0	0	0	0	0	3	0	0	0	0	0	2	0	0
Philip	128	.4988	13.518	51.3	4	77	11	4	7	7	11	7	3	5	0	2	2	17	1	1	6	0	0	0	0	80	1	10	0
Philip's	6	.3060	.4219	36.3	0	4	0	0	2	0	0	0	0	0	0	1	0	1	0	0	0	0	0	0	0	4	0	0	0
Philippe	12	.3733	1.1598	40.6	0	0	0	9	2	1	0	0	9	0	0	0	0	0	0	0	0	0	0	0	0	0	1	2	0
Philippine	44	.4280	4.0580	46.1	16	0	5	7	4	12	0	0	0	0	0	1	2	18	1	0	2	0	0	0	0	0	20	0	0
Philippines	77	.3943	6.6434	48.2	30	4	14	14	12	3	0	0	2	0	0	1	0	26	0	1	4	0	0	0	0	1	40	2	0
Philips	4	.0996	.1523	31.8	1	1	0	0	0	0	0	2	1	0	0	0	0	0	0	0	0	0	0	0	0	0	0	3	0
Philistine	7	.3567	.5488	37.4	4	0	0	0	2	0	0	1	0	1	0	2	0	0	0	0	0	0	0	0	0	4	0	0	0
Philistines	9	.2831	.5729	37.6	0	0	0	0	7	0	0	2	0	2	0	6	0	0	0	0	0	0	0	0	0	0	1	0	0
Philleo	2	.0000	.0290	24.6	0	0	0	0	2	0	0	0	0	0	0	0	0	0	0	0	0	0	0	0	0	0	2	0	0
Phillip	2	.2375	.1088	30.4	0	1	0	0	1	0	0	0	0	0	0	0	0	0	0	0	1	0	0	0	0	0	0	1	0
Phillips	14	.5107	1.5503	41.9	0	1	4	1	3	3	2	0	4	0	0	0	1	0	0	1	0	0	0	2	2	1	0	3	0
Philo	8	.2275	.5677	37.5	0	3	5	0	0	0	0	0	5	0	0	0	0	0	0	0	0	0	0	0	0	3	0	0	0
Philo's	2	.0000	.0914	29.6	0	0	2	0	0	0	0	0	2	0	0	0	0	0	0	0	0	0	0	0	0	0	0	0	0
philosopher	27	.7573	4.1342	46.2	1	0	1	2	8	7	5	3	3	2	0	1	3	4	2	4	0	0	0	0	0	1	5	2	0
philosopher-scientists	2	.0000	.0394	26.0	0	0	0	0	1	1	0	0	0	0	0	0	0	0	0	2	0	0	0	0	0	0	0	0	0
Philosopher's	4	.0000	.1827	32.6	0	0	4	0	0	0	0	0	4	0	0	0	0	0	0	0	0	0	0	0	0	0	0	0	0
philosophers	23	.6636	3.1143	44.9	3	0	2	6	4	5	3	0	1	0	0	1	0	8	1	0	2	1	0	0	0	2	6	1	0
philosophic	2	.2387	.1089	30.4	0	0	0	0	1	1	0	0	0	0	0	0	0	0	0	0	1	0	0	0	1	0	0	0	0
philosophical	10	.5138	1.0638	40.3	0	1	1	0	2	3	3	0	0	1	0	1	0	0	0	0	0	0	0	0	2	0	4	2	0
Philosophical	2	.0000	.0234	23.7	0	2	0	0	0	0	0	0	0	0	0	0	0	0	0	0	0	0	0	0	2	0	0	0	0
philosophically	3	.3777	.2489	34.0	0	0	0	0	0	2	1	0	0	1	0	0	0	1	0	0	0	0	0	0	1	0	0	0	0
philosophies	6	.3462	.5138	37.1	0	0	0	0	2	2	2	0	2	0	0	0	0	3	0	0	0	0	0	0	1	0	0	0	0
philosophy	45	.7084	6.4623	48.1	0	0	8	6	14	4	9	4	3	1	1	2	1	8	0	1	2	0	0	0	1	3	14	8	0
Phineas	6	.1361	.2398	33.8	0	5	0	0	0	1	0	0	0	0	0	0	0	1	0	0	0	0	0	0	0	5	0	0	0
Phipps	2	.0000	.0914	29.6	0	0	2	0	0	0	0	0	2	0	0	0	0	0	0	0	0	0	0	0	0	0	0	0	0
phlegm	2	.2285	.1129	30.5	0	0	0	0	0	1	1	0	0	0	0	0	0	1	0	0	0	0	0	0	0	0	1	0	0
phlegmatic	2	.1814	.1187	30.7	0	0	0	1	1	0	0	0	1	0	0	0	0	0	0	0	0	0	0	0	0	0	0	1	0
phoebe	15	.2208	.8177	39.1	0	0	0	2	1	12	0	0	1	1	0	11	0	0	0	2	0	0	0	0	0	0	0	0	0
Phoebe	35	.4641	3.8333	45.8	0	3	1	24	0	6	1	0	23	0	0	7	0	0	0	1	1	0	0	0	0	3	0	0	0
Phoebe's	4	.0000	.1827	32.6	0	0	0	4	0	0	0	0	4	0	0	0	0	0	0	0	0	0	0	0	0	0	0	0	0
phoebes	5	.0000	.2284	33.6	0	0	0	5	0	0	0	0	5	0	0	0	0	0	0	0	0	0	0	0	0	0	0	0	0
Phoenicia	2	.2433	.1158	30.6	0	0	0	0	1	0	0	1	0	0	0	0	0	0	0	0	0	0	0	0	0	1	0	1	0
Phoenician	22	.3396	1.6126	42.1	1	11	1	1	8	0	0	0	0	6	0	0	0	0	12	0	0	0	0	0	0	3	0	1	0
Phoenicians	19	.5579	2.2217	43.5	4	5	2	4	3	0	1	0	3	3	0	0	0	2	7	1	0	1	0	0	0	1	0	1	0
Phoenix	36	.2985	2.4429	43.9	0	3	0	1	3	3	6	20	1	4	0	0	2	0	0	0	0	0	0	0	0	1	1	27	0
Phoenix'	2	.0000	.0243	23.9	0	0	0	0	0	0	0	2	0	0	0	0	0	0	0	0	0	0	0	0	0	0	0	2	0
phone	73	.7853	11.587	50.6	10	0	9	11	15	11	6	3	19	5	1	13	1	3	7	3	0	1	0	0	5	2	0	13	0
phoned	15	.4972	1.6929	42.3	3	8	3	0	2	0	0	1	8	0	0	0	0	1	1	0	0	0	0	0	4	0	0	1	0
phoneme	15	.2379	.8156	39.1	0	0	4	0	1	10	0	0	0	10	0	0	0	0	5	0	0	0	0	0	0	0	0	0	0
phonemes	43	.1803	1.8933	42.8	0	0	5	4	7	18	9	0	0	36	0	0	0	0	7	0	0	0	0	0	0	0	0	0	0
phonemic	3	.0000	.0328	25.2	0	0	0	0	2	1	0	0	0	3	0	0	0	0	0	0	0	0	0	0	0	0	0	0	0
phones	4	.4445	.3916	35.9	1	1	0	0	1	1	0	0	1	0	0	0	0	0	0	0	1	0	0	0	1	0	1	0	0
phonetic	4	.3606	.3540	35.5	0	0	2	0	2	0	0	0	2	1	0	0	0	0	1	0	0	0	0	0	0	0	0	0	0
phonics	2	.0000	.0162	22.1	0	0	0	1	0	1	0	0	0	0	0	0	0	0	2	0	0	0	0	0	0	0	0	0	0
phonies	2	.2446	.1142	30.6	0	0	0	0	0	1	1	0	0	0	0	0	0	0	0	0	0	0	0	0	1	0	0	1	0
phoning	2	.1814	.1187	30.7	2	0	0	0	0	0	0	0	1	0	0	0	0	0	0	0	0	0	0	0	0	0	0	1	0
phonograph	62	.4443	5.7890	47.6	2	4	2	6	34	8	4	2	0	1	0	1	2	3	3	8	35	0	0	0	2	1	6	0	0
Phonograph	5	.0000	.0404	26.1	0	0	0	0	5	0	0	0	0	0	0	0	0	0	0	0	5	0	0	0	0	0	0	0	0
phonographs	9	.0688	.2002	33.0	0	0	0	1	7	1	0	0	0	0	0	0	0	0	0	1	8	0	0	0	0	0	0	0	0
phonological	2	.0000	.0219	23.4	0	0	0	0	0	0	2	0	0	2	0	0	0	0	0	0	0	0	0	0	0	0	0	0	0
phormium	2	.0000	.0209	23.2	0	0	0	0	2	0	0	0	0	0	0	0	0	0	0	0	0	0	0	0	0	0	2	0	0
phosphate	21	.3802	1.8155	42.6	1	0	2	3	1	1	8	5	0	0	0	0	0	7	0	12	0	0	0	0	0	1	1	0	0
phosphates	8	.3342	.6265	38.0	0	0	2	0	0	1	2	3	0	0	0	0	0	2	0	5	0	0	0	0	0	1	0	0	0
phosphor	4	.2401	.2145	33.3	0	0	3	0	1	0	0	0	0	0	0	0	0	0	0	0	0	0	0	1	0	0	3	0	0
phosphorescence	2	.0000	.0394	26.0	0	0	0	0	0	0	0	2	0	0	0	0	0	0	0	2	0	0	0	0	0	0	0	0	0
phosphorescent	3	.1250	.1342	31.3	0	0	1	0	2	0	0	0	1	0	0	0	0	0	0	0	0	0	0	0	2	0	0	0	0
phosphorous	4	.2640	.2261	33.5	0	0	0	0	3	1	0	0	0	0	0	1	0	0	1	0	0	0	2	0	0	0	0	0	0
phosphors	2	.0000	.0394	26.0	0	0	2	0	0	0	0	0	0	0	0	0	0	0	0	2	0	0	0	0	0	0	0	0	0
phosphorus	22	.4968	2.2963	43.6	0	4	3	1	5	8	1	0	0	0	0	0	0	2	4	9	0	0	4	0	0	0	2	1	0
photo	50	.5925	6.1786	47.9	4	14	10	2	4	3	1	12	1	0	0	0	0	29	0	5	0	2	0	1	0	8	2	2	0
photoelectric	11	.1839	.5853	37.7	0	0	1	3	0	5	2	0	3	0	0	0	0	0	0	1	0	0	0	0	0	0	7	0	0
photogenic	2	.2433	.1158	30.6	0	0	1	1	0	0	0	0	0	0	0	0	0	0	0	0	0	0	0	0	0	1	0	1	0
photograph	105	.5296	11.660	50.7	12	9	6	11	30	18	17	2	11	1	0	6	5	3	3	26	1	21	0	8	1	4	5	10	0
photographed	23	.6721	3.1703	45.0	1	4	2	3	4	1	7	1	3	0	1	1	1	0	0	7	0	0	0	2	0	2	3	3	0
photographer	25	.4361	2.4105	43.8	0	1	3	5	6	2	4	4	5	1	0	3	0	0	0	0	0	0	0	0	0	4	0	12	0
photographer's	3	.2578	.1701	32.3	0	1	1	0	1	0	0	0	0	0	0	0	0	0	0	0	0	1	0	0	0	0	1	1	0
photographers	16	.4479	1.5612	41.9	0	1	6	1	4	2	1	1	2	0	0	0	1	0	0	1	0	0	0	0	0	3	1	8	0
photographic	37	.6183	4.7933	46.8	0	1	8	5	3	2	16	3	6	1	0	1	0	0	0	21	0	1	0	1	0	0	4	2	0
photographing	6	.2768	.4686	36.7	0	0	2	1	1	1	0	1	4	0	1	0	0	0	0	0	0	0	0	0	1	0	0	0	0
photographs	102	.5527	11.849	50.7	14	9	6	18	28	10	12	5	13	2	0	2	1	6	0	31	3	17	1	2	2	2	9	11	0
photography	26	.6703	3.5396	45.5	0	1	9	4	4	5	1	2	1	3	0	1	1	0	1	3	0	1	0	0	0	0	4	10	0

7Q phasmids
7Q pheasant-like
4P Phebe
7R Phelps
7N Phelps's
XH Phenocodus
5Q Phenomena
7H phenomenally
XQ phenotype
3N Phewie
7F Phi
8B Philad'a

3P Philadelphia-born
8F Philadelphia's
8R philanderer
5P Philanthropic
5P Philanthropique
5A Philanthropist
XR philanthropy
9B philatelist
5A philatelists
5Q Philbrook
5J Phile
8Q Philipp

8A Philippi
9Q philistine
8Q Philistinism
7R Phillies
5H Phillippine
5A Phillips'
7N Philly
5P philologist
4Q Philon
4Q Philon's
7A philoprogenitiveness
8K Philosopher

8R philosopher-activist
6Q philosopher's
8F Philosophers
7R philosophize
9F Philosophy
7H phloem
4Q phlox
7B Phncn
7Q Phoberomys
5Q phobia
5Q Phobia
6A phoebes'

8A Phoebus
9D Phoebus'
8A Pholus
8G phon
7B phonac
XQ phonation
9Q phonemics
9P Phong
6J phonic
9R phoniness
8G phono
7A phonogram

7A phonograms
7A phony
5D phooey
7Q phosphoglyceric
5Q Phosphorescence
9H phosphoric
XH photo-sphere
8Q photoelectrons
7P photoengraved
9M photofilm
9M photogelatin
9R Photography

					3	4	5	6	7	8	9	X	A	B	C	D	E	F	G	H	J	K	L	M	N	P	Q	R	S
Word Type	F	D	U	SFI	Gr 3	Gr 4	Gr 5	Gr 6	Gr 7	Gr 8	Gr 9	UnGr	Read	Eng & Gr	Comp	Lit	Math	Soc Stud	Spell	Sci	Music	Art	Home Ec	Shop	Lib F	Lib NF	Lib Ref	Mag	Rel
photon	7	.2395	.4133	36.2	0	0	0	0	0	6	1	0	0	0	0	0	0	0	0	4	0	0	0	0	0	0	3	0	0
photons	9	.0000	.0942	29.7	0	0	0	0	5	4	0	0	0	0	0	0	0	0	0	0	0	0	0	0	0	0	9	0	0
photos	27	.4514	2.6072	44.2	3	2	3	1	11	3	1	3	1	0	0	0	3	2	0	4	0	3	0	0	0	1	0	13	0
photosphere	10	.0000	.1972	32.9	0	0	0	1	0	0	0	9	0	0	0	0	0	0	0	10	0	0	0	0	0	0	0	0	0
photosynthesis	42	.3798	3.5752	45.5	2	0	10	13	14	1	2	0	0	0	0	0	0	0	0	30	0	0	0	1	0	0	10	1	0
phototube	3	.0000	.0591	27.7	0	0	0	0	0	0	0	3	0	0	0	0	0	0	0	3	0	0	0	0	0	0	0	0	0
phrase	589	.5114	62.523	58.0	40	94	69	84	101	98	97	6	40	234	82	9	30	4	32	3	144	0	0	0	2	1	2	6	0
phrased	2	.2303	.1079	30.3	0	0	0	0	1	0	1	0	0	0	0	0	0	0	0	0	1	0	0	0	0	1	0	0	0
phrases	390	.5248	42.420	56.3	38	60	46	50	69	68	58	1	31	125	52	5	24	4	24	0	116	0	0	0	4	1	3	1	0
phrasing	14	.2749	.8632	39.4	0	2	2	1	0	2	7	0	0	0	0	0	0	0	0	0	8	0	0	0	0	5	1	0	0
Phrixus	3	.0000	.1370	31.4	0	0	0	1	0	2	0	0	3	0	0	0	0	0	0	0	0	0	0	0	0	0	0	0	0
Phyl	3	.0000	.0365	25.6	0	0	0	0	0	0	0	3	0	0	0	0	0	0	0	0	0	0	0	0	0	0	0	3	0
phyla	5	.2213	.2870	34.6	0	0	0	0	4	0	1	0	0	0	0	0	0	0	0	4	0	0	0	0	0	0	1	0	0
Phyllis	3	.3380	.2439	33.9	0	0	1	1	1	0	0	0	1	1	0	1	0	0	0	0	0	0	0	0	0	0	0	0	0
phylum	17	.0000	.3352	35.3	0	0	0	0	9	0	8	0	0	0	0	0	0	0	0	17	0	0	0	0	0	0	0	0	0
physical	240	.8000	38.468	55.9	14	7	39	25	50	43	51	11	12	4	7	4	11	29	3	62	2	2	21	1	1	20	41	20	0
Physical	3	.2321	.1635	32.1	0	0	0	0	1	0	1	1	0	0	0	0	0	0	0	0	0	0	0	0	0	0	1	2	0
physical-political	2	.0000	.0389	25.9	2	0	0	0	0	0	0	0	0	0	0	0	0	2	0	0	0	0	0	0	0	0	0	0	0
physically	41	.6504	5.4998	47.4	2	3	6	2	11	9	8	0	3	0	0	3	0	7	0	13	0	0	0	0	1	2	4	8	0
physician	40	.6072	5.0103	47.0	0	1	5	2	9	11	11	1	3	0	0	4	0	2	1	9	0	0	4	0	0	1	13	3	0
PHYSICIAN	8	.0000	.0859	29.3	0	0	0	0	0	0	8	0	0	0	0	8	0	0	0	0	0	0	0	0	0	0	0	0	0
physician's	2	.0000	.0209	23.2	0	0	1	0	0	0	1	0	0	0	0	0	0	0	0	0	0	0	0	0	0	0	2	0	0
physicians	23	.6355	3.0011	44.8	0	0	1	1	13	1	6	1	1	1	0	1	0	5	0	3	0	0	0	1	0	0	4	7	0
Physicians	2	.0000	.0209	23.2	0	0	0	0	0	0	2	0	0	0	0	0	0	0	0	0	0	0	0	0	0	0	2	0	0
physicist	45	.4852	4.6374	46.7	0	5	0	2	10	10	11	7	0	1	1	0	3	0	0	21	0	0	0	0	0	0	17	2	0
physicist's	2	.2437	.1129	30.5	0	0	0	0	0	1	1	0	0	0	0	0	0	0	0	0	0	0	0	0	0	0	1	1	0
physicists	24	.4770	2.4293	43.9	3	0	2	1	9	1	5	3	0	0	1	0	3	0	0	9	0	0	0	0	0	1	10	0	0
physics	95	.5645	11.079	50.4	1	2	9	7	17	16	39	4	0	5	0	0	3	5	2	23	0	0	1	3	0	1	48	4	0
Physics	2	.1698	.1133	30.5	0	0	1	0	0	1	0	0	1	0	0	0	0	0	0	0	0	0	0	0	0	0	1	0	0
physiographic	2	.2446	.1257	31.0	0	0	0	0	0	1	1	0	0	0	0	0	0	1	0	1	0	0	0	0	0	0	0	0	0
physiological	9	.4541	.8808	39.4	0	0	0	0	6	0	3	0	1	0	0	0	0	0	0	2	0	0	1	0	0	0	4	1	0
physiologist	3	.1813	.1402	31.5	0	0	0	0	1	0	2	0	0	0	0	0	0	0	0	1	0	0	0	0	0	0	2	0	0
physiology	7	.3466	.5320	37.3	0	0	1	0	1	2	2	1	0	0	0	0	0	0	0	2	0	0	1	0	0	0	4	0	0
pi	9	.2878	.6074	37.8	2	0	0	5	0	0	2	0	0	0	0	0	6	1	0	0	0	0	0	0	0	2	0	0	0
Pi-tin-tin	2	.0000	.0914	29.6	0	0	2	0	0	0	0	0	2	0	0	0	0	0	0	0	0	0	0	0	0	0	0	0	0
Pian'	2	.0000	.0162	22.1	0	0	0	0	2	0	0	0	0	0	0	0	0	0	0	0	2	0	0	0	0	0	0	0	0
pianist	21	.4123	1.8683	42.7	0	2	2	6	5	4	2	0	2	1	0	3	0	1	0	0	11	0	0	0	0	2	0	1	0
pianistic	2	.2303	.1079	30.3	0	0	0	0	1	0	1	0	0	0	0	0	0	0	0	0	1	0	0	0	0	1	0	0	0
pianists	4	.0000	.0323	25.1	0	0	0	0	3	1	0	0	0	0	0	0	0	0	0	0	4	0	0	0	0	0	0	0	0
piano	418	.3575	32.601	55.1	49	88	53	48	73	55	47	5	33	10	3	16	4	1	8	14	294	0	2	0	6	17	2	8	0
Piano	6	.2071	.2869	34.6	0	0	0	0	2	0	4	0	0	0	0	2	0	0	0	0	4	0	0	0	0	0	0	0	0
piano's	2	.0000	.0162	22.1	0	0	0	0	0	0	2	0	0	0	0	0	0	0	0	0	2	0	0	0	0	0	0	0	0
pianoforte	6	.1587	.2280	33.6	0	2	1	0	1	0	2	0	0	0	0	0	0	0	1	0	5	0	0	0	0	0	0	0	0
pianos	3	.3820	.2427	33.9	0	2	0	0	1	0	0	0	0	0	0	0	0	0	1	0	1	0	0	0	0	0	0	1	0
Piato	3	.0000	.0434	26.4	0	0	0	0	3	0	0	0	0	0	0	0	0	0	0	0	0	0	0	0	0	3	0	0	0
piazza	3	.2300	.1627	32.1	0	0	0	0	2	0	1	0	0	1	0	0	0	0	0	0	0	0	0	0	0	0	0	2	0
picada	2	.0000	.0243	23.9	0	0	0	0	0	0	0	2	0	0	0	0	0	0	0	0	0	0	0	0	0	0	0	2	0
Picardy	2	.2303	.1079	30.3	0	1	1	0	0	0	0	0	0	0	0	0	0	0	0	0	1	0	0	0	0	1	0	0	0
picaresque	3	.2159	.1532	31.9	0	0	2	0	1	0	0	0	0	0	0	0	0	0	0	0	0	0	0	0	0	0	2	1	0
Picasso	14	.2981	.9088	39.6	0	6	3	0	1	4	0	0	0	0	0	0	0	0	0	0	0	4	0	0	0	1	3	6	0
Picasso's	2	.0000	.0243	23.9	0	1	0	0	0	0	0	1	0	0	0	0	0	0	0	0	0	0	0	0	0	0	0	2	0
Piccard	2	.0000	.0394	26.0	0	0	1	1	0	0	0	0	0	0	0	0	0	0	0	2	0	0	0	0	0	0	0	0	0
Picchu	3	.0000	.0314	25.0	0	0	0	0	0	0	3	0	0	0	0	0	0	0	0	0	0	0	0	0	0	0	3	0	0
piccolo	9	.0000	.0728	28.6	0	1	2	1	2	1	2	0	0	0	0	0	0	0	0	0	9	0	0	0	0	0	0	0	0
pick	459	.9373	85.231	59.3	135	65	45	55	88	39	28	4	154	22	4	23	14	21	11	49	23	3	5	1	45	35	10	39	0
Pick	2	.0000	.0914	29.6	2	0	0	0	0	0	0	0	2	0	0	0	0	0	0	0	0	0	0	0	0	0	0	0	0
pick-up	5	.4138	.4637	36.7	0	1	1	0	2	0	1	0	1	0	0	0	0	1	0	0	1	0	0	0	0	0	0	2	0
pickaxe	3	.0000	.1370	31.4	0	0	0	3	0	0	0	0	3	0	0	0	0	0	0	0	0	0	0	0	0	0	0	0	0
picked	538	.8712	94.052	59.7	130	129	69	54	87	34	28	7	249	8	3	36	10	32	7	18	9	0	3	3	72	51	6	30	1
picker	5	.3814	.4791	36.8	0	4	1	0	0	0	0	0	3	0	0	0	0	1	0	0	0	0	0	0	0	0	0	1	0
pickerel	4	.4886	.4071	36.1	0	0	0	0	3	1	0	0	0	0	0	1	0	0	0	0	0	0	0	0	1	0	1	1	0
Pickering	4	.3104	.2995	34.8	0	0	1	0	3	0	0	0	1	0	0	0	0	0	0	0	0	0	0	0	0	0	1	2	0
pickers	19	.4487	1.9392	42.9	6	4	3	1	4	1	0	0	8	0	1	0	0	3	0	0	0	3	0	0	3	0	0	1	0
picket	8	.5660	.9906	40.0	1	2	0	3	1	0	0	1	4	0	0	1	1	0	0	0	0	0	0	0	1	0	0	1	0
picketed	2	.1814	.1187	30.7	0	1	0	0	0	1	0	0	1	0	0	0	0	0	0	0	0	0	0	0	0	0	0	1	0
picketing	2	.2437	.1129	30.5	0	0	0	0	1	0	0	1	0	0	0	0	0	0	0	0	0	0	0	0	0	0	1	1	0
pickets	6	.2302	.3676	35.7	1	0	0	4	0	1	0	0	1	0	0	0	4	1	0	0	0	0	0	0	0	0	0	0	0
Pickett	13	.3604	1.2445	40.9	0	10	0	0	1	2	0	0	10	0	0	0	0	2	0	0	0	0	0	0	0	0	1	0	0
pickety	6	.0000	.0869	29.4	6	0	0	0	0	0	0	0	0	0	0	0	0	0	0	0	0	0	0	0	0	6	0	0	0
pickin'	4	.2228	.2087	33.2	3	1	0	0	0	0	0	0	0	0	0	0	0	0	0	0	1	0	0	0	3	0	0	0	0
picking	103	.8261	17.141	52.3	20	30	7	8	18	8	10	2	33	4	1	5	1	8	0	3	1	0	2	0	16	15	4	10	0
pickings	3	.1250	.1342	31.3	0	0	1	0	1	1	0	0	1	0	0	0	0	0	0	0	0	0	0	0	2	0	0	0	0
pickle	12	.4885	1.3034	41.2	0	4	2	2	2	0	2	0	5	0	0	1	0	0	2	1	0	0	2	0	0	1	0	0	0
pickled	7	.5233	.7662	38.8	2	1	1	0	1	1	1	0	1	0	0	1	0	0	0	0	2	0	0	1	1	0	1	0	0
pickles	17	.5939	2.1355	43.3	2	1	6	4	1	0	3	0	6	1	2	1	0	0	0	0	1	0	1	0	4	1	0	0	0
pickling	3	.1856	.1648	32.2	0	1	0	0	0	1	1	0	1	0	0	0	0	0	0	1	0	0	0	1	0	0	0	0	0
picks	70	.7937	11.238	50.5	21	13	4	8	8	9	4	3	18	1	0	6	0	5	0	14	5	0	0	2	5	5	1	8	0
pickup	14	.4347	1.3645	41.3	1	1	2	4	3	1	0	2	4	0	0	0	0	0	0	0	1	0	0	0	1	0	1	7	0
picky	2	.0000	.0243	23.9	0	0	0	0	0	2	0	0	0	0	0	0	0	0	0	0	0	0	0	0	0	0	0	2	0
picnic	128	.7770	20.069	53.0	37	33	14	13	9	7	12	3	27	30	8	6	11	4	10	1	2	1	1	0	12	10	0	5	0
Picnic	2	.0000	.0914	29.6	1	1	0	0	0	0	0	0	2	0	0	0	0	0	0	0	0	0	0	0	0	0	0	0	0
picnickers	2	.1948	.1250	31.0	0	0	1	0	1	0	0	0	1	0	0	0	0	0	0	0	0	0	0	0	0	1	0	0	0
picnicking	2	.2331	.1157	30.6	0	0	0	1	0	1	0	0	0	0	0	0	0	0	0	1	0	0	0	0	1	0	0	0	0
picnics	18	.7045	2.5961	44.1	7	2	1	2	4	2	0	0	4	1	0	0	0	2	2	2	1	0	2	0	2	1	0	1	0
picofarad	4	.0000	.0101	20.0	0	0	0	0	0	4	0	0	0	0	0	0	0	0	0	0	0	0	0	4	0	0	0	0	0
pictograms	2	.0000	.0162	22.1	0	0	0	0	1	1	0	0	0	0	0	0	0	0	2	0	0	0	0	0	0	0	0	0	0
pictographs	3	.2138	.1698	32.3	0	0	0	1	1	1	0	0	1	0	0	0	0	0	1	0	0	1	0	0	0	0	0	0	0
pictorial	7	.3318	.5273	37.2	0	0	0	1	3	0	3	0	1	0	0	0	0	1	0	1	2	0	0	2	0	0	0	0	0
pictorially	2	.0000	.0050	17.0	0	0	0	0	2	0	0	0	0	0	0	0	0	0	0	0	0	0	0	2	0	0	0	0	0
picture	2500	.7824	394.01	66.0	739	582	293	374	243	162	84	23	298	128	28	52	445	395	198	473	40	208	8	21	36	62	65	40	3
Picture	10	.3557	.8030	39.0	7	0	0	0	2	1	0	0	2	0	0	2	0	0	5	0	1	0	0	0	0	0	0	0	0
picture-map	2	.0000	.0389	25.9	0	2	0	0	0	0	0	0	0	0	0	0	0	2	0	0	0	0	0	0	0	0	0	0	0
pictured	202	.7765	31.665	55.0	31	35	28	31	34	25	18	0	29	3	0	3	76	10	15	33	11	5	2	1	3	1	6	4	0

8Q photojournalism
5R photojournalists
8Q photomaterials
9Q photomechanical
9H photometer
7H photometry
8Q photosensitive
XH photospheric
XH photosynthetic
6R phoughsleoti
6E phramid
4Q Phramid
9B Phrase
6C Phrases
7Q Phyllobates
7H phylums
6Q Physalia
7N physetera
7B physic
9R physical-education
9D Physician
9Q physician-naturalists
9Q physicists'
8Q physiographically
7R physiography
XR Physiologist
9Q physiologists
8D physique
5H phytoplankton
8J pianissimo
8J pianist-composer
4Q pianist's
8F Piao
9D piblokto
4J Picardie
XR picaresques
9Q picayune
5C piccalilli
6A Piccaninnies
8J piccolo's
7D pick-a-back
7R pick-me-up
7P pick-up-arm
5A picked-over
4N pickereel
7A Pickering's
9R pickers'
7N Pickett's
7N Picketts
6R Pickford
5N Pickhatchet
8R pickie
7R Pickup
7R pickup-camper
4B picnic-supper
6A Pico
9Q Pictavia
8G pictogram
5E pictograph
7A pictographic
8G pictography
4R pictoral
9Q Picts
6R picture-book
5B picture-drawings
5G picture-like
3B picnic-making
8F picture-scroll
7D picture's

Word Type	F	D	U	SFI	3 Gr 3	4 Gr 4	5 Gr 5	6 Gr 6	7 Gr 7	8 Gr 8	9 Gr 9	X UnGr	A Read	B Eng & Gr	C Comp	D Lit	E Math	F Soc Stud	G Spell	H Sci	J Music	K Art	L Home Ec	M Shop	N Lib F	P Lib NF	Q Lib Ref	R Mag	S Rel
Pictured	3	.0000	.0328	25.2	0	0	2	0	0	0	1	0	0	3	0	0	0	0	0	0	0	0	0	0	0	0	0	0	0
pictures	1168	.7170	171.02	62.3	368	241	141	188	114	72	31	13	230	78	2	25	123	157	100	174	21	114	8	9	20	40	23	44	0
Pictures	4	.3743	.3712	35.7	2	0	0	1	0	1	0	0	2	0	0	0	0	1	0	0	0	0	0	0	0	0	0	1	0
picturesque	27	.7386	4.0243	46.0	3	0	3	2	5	8	3	3	2	4	1	2	0	2	0	1	0	0	0	0	2	4	3	6	0
picturing	9	.5193	.9757	39.9	0	3	0	0	4	1	1	0	0	0	0	1	4	1	0	0	1	0	0	0	0	0	2	0	0
Picunche	8	.0000	.0837	29.2	0	0	0	0	8	0	0	0	0	0	0	0	0	0	0	0	0	0	0	0	0	0	8	0	0
Piddy	7	.0000	.0851	29.3	0	7	0	0	0	0	0	0	0	0	0	0	0	0	0	0	0	0	0	0	0	0	0	7	0
Pidgeon	2	.0000	.0914	29.6	2	0	0	0	0	0	0	0	2	0	0	0	0	0	0	0	0	0	0	0	0	0	0	0	0
Pidgin	9	.0000	.0201	23.0	0	0	0	0	9	0	0	0	0	0	9	0	0	0	0	0	0	0	0	0	0	0	0	0	0
pie	249	.8045	40.364	56.1	81	42	31	15	38	12	25	5	63	17	4	5	50	0	14	20	7	0	20	2	28	14	0	5	0
Pie	11	.2425	.6438	38.1	9	2	0	0	0	0	0	0	0	1	0	0	9	0	0	0	0	0	0	0	0	0	0	1	0
pie-shaped	2	.1483	.0728	28.6	0	1	0	0	0	0	1	0	0	0	0	0	0	0	0	0	0	0	0	1	0	1	0	0	0
piebald	4	.3740	.3661	35.6	0	0	0	3	1	0	0	0	2	0	0	0	0	0	0	0	0	0	0	0	1	0	0	1	0
piebalds	2	.0000	.0290	24.6	2	0	0	0	0	0	0	0	0	0	0	0	0	0	0	0	0	0	0	0	0	2	0	0	0
piece	1198	.8607	205.90	63.1	236	188	159	155	177	142	113	28	268	40	17	40	113	45	24	202	73	42	45	82	63	92	25	27	0
Piece	2	.2411	.1091	30.4	0	0	0	0	1	1	0	0	0	0	0	1	0	0	0	0	1	0	0	0	0	0	0	0	0
pieced	13	.6990	1.8427	42.7	1	2	2	2	3	1	2	0	0	0	0	1	0	2	1	2	0	0	0	0	1	4	1	1	0
piecemeal	3	.3637	.2412	33.8	0	1	1	0	1	0	0	0	0	0	0	0	0	1	1	0	0	0	0	0	0	1	0	0	0
pieces	814	.8074	132.01	61.2	171	157	99	84	113	94	67	29	146	16	2	20	132	36	6	128	39	28	44	69	31	59	30	28	0
Pieces	5	.3623	.3866	35.9	0	2	0	0	2	1	0	0	0	1	0	0	0	0	0	0	2	0	0	0	0	0	2	0	0
piecing	4	.3799	.3303	35.2	0	0	1	1	1	1	0	0	0	0	0	0	0	0	0	0	0	0	0	0	1	2	1	0	0
pied	2	.1787	.1174	30.7	0	0	0	1	1	0	0	0	1	0	0	0	0	0	0	0	0	0	0	0	1	0	0	0	0
Pied	17	.2227	.9169	39.6	3	0	13	0	1	0	0	0	1	0	0	0	0	0	0	0	3	0	0	0	13	0	0	0	0
Piedmont	31	.3562	2.5226	44.0	4	2	22	1	1	1	0	0	0	0	0	0	0	22	0	0	0	0	0	0	0	6	2	1	0
Piedras	3	.2260	.1580	32.0	0	0	0	0	1	0	2	0	0	0	0	2	0	0	0	0	0	0	0	0	0	0	1	0	0
pieman	3	.0000	.0434	26.4	3	0	0	0	0	0	0	0	0	0	0	0	0	0	0	0	0	0	0	0	0	3	0	0	0
pier	40	.6684	5.5956	47.5	4	9	3	12	10	2	0	0	15	1	0	1	0	5	1	0	0	0	0	0	1	6	1	9	0
Pier	21	.1948	.9941	40.0	0	0	20	0	0	1	0	0	0	0	0	0	0	0	0	0	0	1	0	0	20	0	0	0	0
pierce	11	.6680	1.5204	41.8	1	1	0	2	5	0	2	0	3	1	0	1	0	0	0	1	0	0	1	0	2	1	1	0	0
Pierce	12	.6096	1.5898	42.0	1	7	1	0	2	1	0	0	7	0	0	1	1	1	0	0	0	0	0	0	0	1	1	0	0
pierced	19	.6923	2.6931	44.3	1	0	2	2	7	2	4	1	4	2	1	4	0	0	0	1	0	0	0	0	1	1	3	2	0
piercing	24	.6737	3.3485	45.2	0	4	6	6	3	4	1	0	7	0	0	3	0	1	0	0	3	0	0	0	1	4	1	4	0
piercingly	2	.0665	.0708	28.5	0	0	0	0	1	1	0	0	1	0	1	0	0	0	0	0	0	0	0	0	0	0	0	0	0
Pierpont	2	.0000	.0914	29.6	0	1	0	1	0	0	0	0	2	0	0	0	0	0	0	0	0	0	0	0	0	0	0	0	0
Pierre	122	.6719	17.378	52.4	25	32	8	13	7	7	23	7	66	3	0	0	0	20	0	6	0	0	0	0	8	3	9	7	0
Pierre's	3	.2435	.2274	33.6	1	1	0	0	0	0	1	0	2	0	0	0	0	1	0	0	0	0	0	0	0	0	0	0	0
piers	10	.5754	1.1815	40.7	2	3	0	2	0	1	2	0	0	0	0	1	0	1	0	0	0	1	0	0	1	2	1	3	0
Piers	3	.2222	.1558	31.9	0	0	0	0	0	2	0	1	0	1	0	0	0	0	0	0	0	0	0	0	0	0	2	0	0
Pierson	7	.2423	.5283	37.2	0	2	0	5	0	0	0	0	5	0	0	0	0	0	0	0	0	0	0	0	0	2	0	0	0
pies	74	.7244	11.016	50.4	11	19	13	11	10	4	5	1	25	2	1	4	25	1	1	0	1	0	4	0	6	2	2	0	0
Piet	3	.2027	.1376	31.4	0	0	1	0	0	2	0	0	0	0	0	0	0	0	0	0	0	1	0	0	0	0	2	0	0
Pieta	2	.1247	.0633	28.0	1	0	0	0	0	0	1	0	0	0	0	0	0	0	0	0	0	1	0	0	0	1	0	0	0
Pieter	21	.3340	1.9474	42.9	0	13	0	5	3	0	0	0	18	0	0	2	0	0	0	0	0	0	0	0	0	0	1	0	0
piety	5	.4689	.4884	36.9	0	0	1	0	0	1	3	0	0	1	0	0	0	0	0	0	1	0	0	0	0	0	2	1	0
Piezo	2	.0000	.0394	26.0	0	0	0	0	0	0	0	2	0	0	0	0	0	0	0	2	0	0	0	0	0	0	0	0	0
piezo-electric	3	.0000	.0591	27.7	0	0	0	0	0	0	0	3	0	0	0	0	0	0	0	3	0	0	0	0	0	0	0	0	0
Piezo-electric	2	.0000	.0394	26.0	0	0	0	0	0	0	0	2	0	0	0	0	0	0	0	2	0	0	0	0	0	0	0	0	0
pig	142	.7422	21.873	53.4	47	38	18	13	14	5	4	3	81	7	0	4	1	8	3	5	1	0	0	0	19	4	2	7	0
Pig	16	.2097	1.0714	40.3	6	2	2	3	3	0	0	0	10	0	0	6	0	0	0	0	0	0	0	0	0	0	0	0	0
pig-headed	2	.0000	.0215	23.3	0	0	0	0	0	1	1	0	0	0	0	2	0	0	0	0	0	0	0	0	0	0	0	0	0
pig-nuts	2	.0000	.0234	23.7	0	0	0	0	2	0	0	0	0	0	0	0	0	0	0	0	0	0	0	0	2	0	0	0	0
pig's	5	.4174	.4631	36.7	1	0	0	0	2	0	1	1	1	0	0	2	0	0	0	0	0	0	0	0	1	0	0	1	0
Pig's	5	.2445	.3864	35.9	0	0	0	4	1	0	0	0	4	0	0	1	0	0	0	0	0	0	0	0	0	0	0	0	0
pigeon	44	.6727	6.0629	47.8	13	1	1	15	9	2	1	2	5	0	0	1	7	1	1	10	9	0	0	0	1	0	6	3	0
Pigeon	10	.4794	1.0882	40.4	0	3	3	1	3	0	0	0	4	0	0	0	0	3	0	0	0	0	0	0	0	2	1	0	0
pigeon-toed	2	.1814	.1187	30.7	0	0	0	0	0	0	2	0	1	0	0	0	0	0	0	0	0	0	0	0	0	0	0	1	0
pigeon-wing	2	.0000	.0215	23.3	0	0	0	0	0	0	2	0	0	0	0	2	0	0	0	0	0	0	0	0	0	0	0	0	0
pigeons	89	.6812	12.556	51.0	36	4	3	31	8	6	1	0	28	1	6	1	1	1	0	14	14	0	0	0	10	5	6	2	0
Pigg	2	.0000	.0215	23.3	0	2	0	0	0	0	0	0	0	0	0	2	0	0	0	0	0	0	0	0	0	0	0	0	0
piggy	5	.3497	.3894	35.9	2	0	0	3	0	0	0	0	0	1	0	0	3	0	0	0	0	0	0	0	0	1	0	0	0
Piggy	4	.2969	.2888	34.6	3	0	0	1	0	0	0	0	1	0	0	2	0	0	0	0	0	0	0	0	1	0	0	0	0
piggy-back	3	.2051	.1687	32.3	0	1	1	0	0	0	0	1	1	0	1	0	0	0	0	0	0	0	0	0	0	0	0	1	0
piglets	7	.3446	.6113	37.9	1	6	0	0	0	0	0	0	4	0	0	0	0	0	0	0	2	0	0	0	0	0	1	0	0
pigment	15	.3980	1.2995	41.1	0	5	0	0	7	0	1	2	0	1	0	0	0	0	0	8	0	0	3	0	0	0	3	0	0
pigmented	2	.0000	.0209	23.2	0	0	0	0	0	0	0	2	0	0	0	0	0	0	0	0	0	0	0	0	0	0	2	0	0
pigments	6	.1493	.2075	33.2	0	0	0	1	2	3	0	0	0	0	0	0	0	0	0	0	0	3	0	0	0	0	3	0	0
pigmy	2	.2291	.1135	30.5	1	0	0	0	0	0	1	0	0	0	0	1	0	0	0	1	0	0	0	0	0	0	0	0	0
Pignier's	2	.0000	.0215	23.3	0	0	0	0	2	0	0	0	0	0	0	2	0	0	0	0	0	0	0	0	0	0	0	0	0
pigpen	5	.3841	.4756	36.8	2	1	1	0	0	1	0	0	3	0	0	1	0	0	0	0	0	0	0	0	1	0	0	0	0
pigpens	3	.3369	.2489	34.0	0	0	0	1	0	2	0	0	1	0	0	1	0	1	0	0	0	0	0	0	0	0	0	0	0
pigs	189	.7877	30.319	54.8	69	40	9	25	28	5	12	1	74	4	2	4	7	28	2	6	2	0	0	0	36	13	5	6	0
pigskin	2	.1733	.1149	30.6	0	0	2	0	0	0	0	0	1	1	0	0	0	0	0	0	0	0	0	0	0	0	0	0	0
pigsty	2	.2412	.1091	30.4	0	1	0	0	1	0	0	0	0	0	0	1	0	0	1	0	0	0	0	0	0	0	0	0	0
pigtail	4	.1787	.2347	33.7	0	0	1	0	1	2	0	0	2	0	0	0	0	0	0	0	0	0	0	0	2	0	0	0	0
pigtails	10	.5119	1.1135	40.5	5	1	1	2	1	0	0	0	3	0	0	2	0	0	0	0	0	0	0	0	3	1	0	1	0
pike	14	.4922	1.4656	41.7	2	3	0	0	7	0	0	2	1	2	0	0	3	1	0	0	0	0	0	0	0	1	0	6	0
Pike	19	.4581	1.8611	42.7	0	1	3	1	9	5	0	0	0	0	0	0	0	8	0	0	2	0	0	0	0	0	2	7	0
Pike's	4	.4341	.3887	35.9	0	0	3	0	0	1	0	0	1	0	0	1	0	1	0	0	1	0	0	0	0	0	0	0	0
pikes	4	.4521	.3985	36.0	0	0	0	1	2	1	0	0	1	1	0	0	0	0	0	0	0	0	0	0	1	0	1	0	0
Pikes	6	.3527	.4914	36.9	0	0	3	0	1	2	0	0	1	0	1	0	0	3	0	0	0	0	0	0	0	0	1	0	0
pile	189	.8856	33.346	55.2	40	34	25	11	34	21	19	5	45	6	0	20	16	11	2	17	3	1	5	0	21	18	9	15	0
piled	90	.7915	14.491	51.6	22	21	12	7	14	5	6	3	35	3	0	7	0	10	1	4	2	0	0	0	10	10	2	6	0
piled-up	2	.1814	.1187	30.7	0	0	0	1	1	0	0	0	1	0	0	0	0	0	0	0	0	0	0	0	0	0	0	1	0
piles	67	.7414	10.171	50.1	7	20	16	7	6	7	3	1	17	1	2	3	5	8	0	20	0	0	0	0	4	2	0	5	0
pilgrim	4	.4341	.3887	35.9	0	0	2	0	1	1	0	0	1	0	0	1	0	1	0	0	1	0	0	0	0	0	0	0	0
Pilgrim	23	.6007	2.9994	44.8	11	5	5	0	0	1	1	0	12	1	0	0	0	5	2	0	0	0	0	0	0	2	1	0	0
pilgrimage	3	.3842	.2485	34.0	0	0	0	0	1	0	2	0	0	0	0	1	0	0	0	0	0	0	0	0	0	1	1	0	0
pilgrimages	6	.2521	.3540	35.5	0	2	1	0	2	1	0	0	0	0	0	0	0	1	0	0	0	0	0	0	0	1	4	0	0
pilgrims	11	.5701	1.3194	41.2	3	2	0	2	2	0	2	0	2	0	0	0	1	1	0	0	1	0	0	0	0	1	4	1	0
Pilgrims	86	.7030	12.549	51.0	36	9	23	1	14	3	0	0	32	2	0	3	0	24	5	0	7	0	0	0	0	8	1	4	0
Pilgrims'	3	.2028	.1988	33.0	1	1	1	0	0	0	0	0	2	0	0	0	0	0	0	0	1	0	0	0	0	0	0	0	0
pilin'	2	.0000	.0914	29.6	0	0	0	0	2	0	0	0	2	0	0	0	0	0	0	0	0	0	0	0	0	0	0	0	0
piling	13	.5135	1.4024	41.5	0	2	4	1	2	0	3	1	1	0	2	2	0	2	0	0	0	0	0	0	0	2	1	3	0
pilings	5	.3699	.3993	36.0	0	1	0	3	0	0	1	0	0	0	0	0	0	0	0	0	0	0	0	0	1	0	2	2	0
Pilkington	3	.0000	.0352	25.5	0	0	0	0	0	0	3	0	0	0	0	0	0	0	0	0	0	0	0	0	3	0	0	0	0

5R Pictures'
8Q picturesquely
5G pid
7P Pider
7C pidgin
4R pie-eating
3N piecy
9Q pied-billed
5F piedmont
7D Piedra
3N Pieface
7P pierces
7A Piermont
9J Pierrette
9J Pierrot
6A Pierson's
3P Piety
8Q Pieve
XH piezo
XH piezo-electricity
XH Piezo-electricity
XH piezotronics
5B piff
9D pig-trails
4A pigeon-eggs
7H pigeon-holed
4A Pigeon's
6A pigeonhole
8A pigeonholes
7N pigeons's
7A pigging
8A piggish
3A Piggy-wig
7D pigheaded
3G Piglet
3P piglike
9R pigmentation
4A Pigs
9N pigs'
9D pigtailed
6J pike-poles
5A pikemen
3P Pilate
8R Pilate-like
7Q pilchards
7R pile-driver
4A Pileated
XP pileup
9D pilferer
7A pilfering
6N Pilgrim's

Word Type	F	D	U	SFI	3 Gr 3	4 Gr 4	5 Gr 5	6 Gr 6	7 Gr 7	8 Gr 8	9 Gr 9	X UnGr	A Read	B Eng & Gr	C Comp	D Lit	E Math	F Soc Stud	G Spell	H Sci	J Music	K Art	L Home Ec	M Shop	N Lib F	P Lib NF	Q Lib Ref	R Mag	S Rel
Pilkington's	2	.0000	.0234	23.7	0	0	0	0	0	0	2	0	0	0	0	0	0	0	0	0	0	0	0	0	2	0	0	0	0
pill	12	.3899	1.0505	40.2	0	1	2	0	2	1	2	4	2	0	0	1	0	1	1	0	0	0	0	0	0	0	0	7	0
pillaged	3	.2378	.1809	32.6	1	0	0	0	0	1	1	0	0	0	0	0	0	2	0	0	0	0	0	0	0	1	0	0	0
pillar	5	.4751	.5383	37.3	2	0	1	2	0	0	0	0	2	1	0	0	0	1	0	0	0	0	0	0	0	1	0	0	0
pillars	16	.6877	2.2693	43.6	1	1	1	1	8	1	1	2	5	2	0	2	0	1	0	0	1	1	0	1	0	1	0	2	0
pillboxes	2	.0000	.0290	24.6	0	0	2	0	0	0	0	0	0	0	0	0	0	0	0	0	0	0	0	0	0	2	0	0	0
pilloried	2	.1814	.1187	30.7	0	0	0	0	1	1	0	0	1	0	0	0	0	0	0	0	0	0	0	0	0	0	0	1	0
pillow	70	.8002	11.395	50.6	26	9	6	15	4	3	4	3	33	1	1	6	0	2	2	2	3	0	1	0	11	3	0	5	0
pillowcase	5	.3106	.3872	35.9	2	2	0	0	0	0	1	0	2	0	0	0	0	0	0	0	0	0	1	0	0	0	0	2	0
pillowed	2	.1948	.1250	31.0	0	1	0	1	0	0	0	0	1	0	0	0	0	0	0	0	0	0	0	0	0	1	0	0	0
pillows	27	.4772	2.8270	44.5	6	1	2	3	5	0	5	5	7	0	0	0	0	1	0	5	0	0	5	0	2	1	0	6	0
pills	18	.5217	2.0111	43.0	1	1	1	3	5	2	4	1	3	0	0	2	1	0	0	3	0	0	0	0	0	2	0	7	0
pilot	167	.8106	27.463	54.4	29	33	18	29	28	15	11	4	66	10	0	3	7	14	3	26	0	0	1	2	0	19	1	15	0
Pilot	6	.3626	.5119	37.1	1	0	0	2	2	0	1	0	2	0	1	0	0	0	0	0	0	0	0	0	0	1	0	2	0
pilot's	6	.3629	.5312	37.3	1	1	0	2	1	0	0	1	3	0	1	1	0	0	0	0	0	0	0	0	0	0	0	1	0
piloted	4	.3354	.3295	35.2	0	0	1	1	0	1	1	0	1	0	0	0	0	2	0	0	0	0	0	0	0	1	0	0	0
pilothouse	2	.0000	.0914	29.6	0	0	0	0	0	2	0	0	2	0	0	0	0	0	0	0	0	0	0	0	0	0	0	0	0
piloting	4	.4442	.3918	35.9	1	0	0	0	1	1	1	0	1	0	0	1	0	0	0	0	1	0	0	0	0	0	0	1	0
pilots	87	.7050	12.749	51.1	22	9	10	11	13	9	5	8	33	4	0	0	0	11	0	14	0	0	0	1	0	12	2	10	0
Pima	3	.0524	.0803	29.0	0	0	0	0	1	0	2	0	1	0	0	0	0	0	0	0	0	0	2	0	0	0	0	0	0
pimiento	2	.0000	.0290	24.6	0	2	0	0	0	0	0	0	0	0	0	0	0	0	0	0	0	0	0	0	0	2	0	0	0
Pimlico	2	.2303	.1079	30.3	0	1	0	1	0	0	0	0	0	0	0	0	0	0	0	0	1	0	0	0	0	1	0	0	0
pimple	3	.2445	.1818	32.6	0	0	0	0	3	0	0	0	0	0	0	0	0	0	0	2	0	0	0	0	0	0	1	0	0
pimples	7	.3356	.5604	37.5	0	0	0	0	5	1	1	0	2	0	0	0	0	1	0	1	0	0	2	0	1	0	0	0	0
pin	160	.5535	18.376	52.6	28	15	11	16	24	35	28	3	20	2	2	2	5	7	2	17	0	3	56	8	13	10	4	9	0
pin-baste	10	.0000	.0322	25.1	0	0	0	0	1	4	5	0	0	0	0	0	0	0	0	0	0	0	10	0	0	0	0	0	0
pin-striped	3	.0000	.1370	31.4	0	0	0	3	0	0	0	0	3	0	0	0	0	0	0	0	0	0	0	0	0	0	0	0	0
pin-the-tail	2	.0000	.0914	29.6	0	0	0	2	0	0	0	0	2	0	0	0	0	0	0	0	0	0	0	0	0	0	0	0	0
pinacoid	2	.0000	.0394	26.0	0	0	0	0	0	0	0	2	0	0	0	0	0	0	0	2	0	0	0	0	0	0	0	0	0
pinafore	4	.3071	.2967	34.7	0	1	0	2	1	0	0	0	1	0	0	1	0	0	0	0	0	0	0	0	2	0	0	0	0
Pinal	3	.1187	.1291	31.1	0	0	1	0	2	0	0	0	1	0	0	2	0	0	0	0	0	0	0	0	0	0	0	0	0
Pinals	9	.1541	.4726	36.7	0	0	4	0	5	0	0	0	4	0	0	5	0	0	0	0	0	0	0	0	0	0	0	0	0
Pinamar	2	.0000	.0243	23.9	0	0	0	0	0	0	0	2	0	0	0	0	0	0	0	0	0	0	0	0	0	0	0	2	0
pinata	13	.4105	1.2646	41.0	9	1	3	0	0	0	0	0	7	0	0	0	0	0	0	0	4	1	0	0	0	0	0	1	0
pinatas	2	.0580	.0676	28.3	0	1	1	0	0	0	0	0	1	0	0	0	0	0	0	0	0	1	0	0	0	0	0	0	0
pincers	4	.2982	.2887	34.6	0	0	0	1	1	0	2	0	1	0	0	1	0	0	0	0	0	0	0	0	0	0	2	0	0
pinch	30	.6794	4.2400	46.3	6	2	3	7	4	3	4	1	11	0	0	2	0	1	0	4	0	0	2	2	3	1	0	4	0
Pinch's	2	.0000	.0914	29.6	0	0	0	2	0	0	0	0	2	0	0	0	0	0	0	0	0	0	0	0	0	0	0	0	0
pinched	18	.7313	2.6984	44.3	4	5	1	0	4	2	1	1	6	1	0	1	0	1	0	0	1	0	1	0	3	2	0	2	0
pinches	2	.2278	.1128	30.5	0	0	1	0	1	0	0	0	0	0	0	0	0	0	0	1	0	0	0	0	0	0	1	0	0
pinching	5	.4020	.4505	36.5	0	0	0	1	2	1	1	0	1	0	0	0	0	0	0	1	0	0	0	1	0	1	1	0	0
pincushion	4	.1738	.1893	32.8	0	0	1	0	1	0	2	0	1	0	0	0	0	0	0	0	0	0	2	0	1	0	0	0	0
pine	195	.8719	33.915	55.3	38	29	35	29	34	16	11	3	42	2	5	14	7	25	0	16	2	2	0	6	25	17	19	13	0
Pine	10	.4459	.9337	39.7	1	0	0	2	4	1	2	0	0	0	2	2	2	0	0	0	0	0	0	0	2	0	0	2	0
pine-forested	2	.2401	.1133	30.5	1	0	1	0	0	0	0	0	0	0	0	0	0	0	0	0	0	0	0	0	0	1	1	0	0
pineapple	39	.5435	4.3941	46.4	2	5	11	2	12	0	6	1	1	1	0	1	1	11	0	2	0	2	10	0	0	4	1	5	0
Pineapple	2	.1812	.0838	29.2	0	0	0	0	1	0	1	0	0	0	0	0	0	0	0	0	0	0	1	0	0	0	0	1	0
pineapples	28	.4099	2.5583	44.1	6	3	10	3	2	1	2	1	1	0	0	1	0	22	1	0	0	0	2	0	0	1	0	0	0
Pinelli	3	.1277	.1363	31.3	0	0	0	2	1	0	0	0	1	0	0	0	0	0	0	0	0	0	0	0	0	0	0	2	0
pines	37	.8035	6.0017	47.8	5	4	9	3	12	2	0	2	10	1	1	4	2	2	0	3	0	0	0	0	5	3	3	3	0
Pines	3	.3244	.2330	33.7	1	1	1	0	0	0	0	0	1	0	0	0	0	0	1	0	1	0	0	0	0	0	0	0	0
piney	5	.3377	.3703	35.7	0	2	2	1	0	0	0	0	0	0	0	1	0	0	0	0	0	0	0	0	3	0	0	1	0
Piney	2	.0000	.0914	29.6	0	0	0	2	0	0	0	0	2	0	0	0	0	0	0	0	0	0	0	0	0	0	0	0	0
ping	3	.3528	.2566	34.1	0	1	1	1	0	0	0	0	1	0	0	0	1	0	0	0	0	0	0	0	0	1	0	0	0
Ping	5	.0000	.2284	33.6	5	0	0	0	0	0	0	0	5	0	0	0	0	0	0	0	0	0	0	0	0	0	0	0	0
PING	2	.0000	.0243	23.9	2	0	0	0	0	0	0	0	0	0	0	0	0	0	0	0	0	0	0	0	0	0	0	2	0
ping-pong	2	.1473	.0686	28.4	0	0	0	1	0	1	0	0	0	0	0	1	0	0	0	0	0	1	0	0	0	0	0	0	0
pinhead	3	.3762	.2496	34.0	1	1	0	1	0	0	0	0	0	0	0	0	0	0	0	1	0	0	0	0	0	1	1	0	0
pinhead-sized	2	.2300	.1140	30.6	0	0	0	1	0	0	0	1	0	1	0	0	0	0	0	1	0	0	0	0	0	0	0	0	0
pinholes	3	.2602	.1785	32.5	0	0	1	0	0	1	1	0	0	0	0	0	0	0	0	1	0	0	0	1	1	0	0	0	0
pinion	3	.2184	.1759	32.5	0	0	0	0	2	1	0	0	1	0	0	0	0	0	0	0	0	0	0	1	0	0	0	1	0
pink	219	.8384	36.942	55.7	61	28	31	28	26	10	14	21	73	5	1	11	9	5	2	34	0	5	4	0	35	15	3	17	0
Pink	7	.3492	.6279	38.0	0	1	0	3	0	0	0	3	4	0	0	0	0	0	0	1	0	0	0	0	0	0	0	2	0
pinked	2	.1812	.0838	29.2	0	0	0	0	1	0	1	0	0	0	0	0	0	0	0	0	0	0	1	0	0	0	0	1	0
Pinkerton	16	.2445	1.2218	40.9	0	0	0	8	3	5	0	0	11	0	0	0	0	5	0	0	0	0	0	0	0	0	0	0	0
Pinkie	14	.0000	.6396	38.1	0	14	0	0	0	0	0	0	14	0	0	0	0	0	0	0	0	0	0	0	0	0	0	0	0
Pinkie's	5	.0000	.2284	33.6	0	5	0	0	0	0	0	0	5	0	0	0	0	0	0	0	0	0	0	0	0	0	0	0	0
pinkish	3	.1650	.1684	32.3	0	1	2	0	0	0	0	0	1	0	0	0	0	0	0	2	0	0	0	0	0	0	0	0	0
pinks	3	.2321	.1635	32.1	0	1	0	1	1	0	0	0	0	0	0	0	0	0	0	0	0	0	0	0	0	0	1	2	0
Pinky	3	.0000	.0352	25.5	3	0	0	0	0	0	0	0	0	0	0	0	0	0	0	0	0	0	0	0	3	0	0	0	0
pinnacle	4	.3741	.3712	35.7	0	0	0	2	0	1	1	0	2	0	0	0	0	0	0	1	0	0	0	0	0	0	0	1	0
pinned	35	.5712	4.2737	46.3	7	5	0	6	4	10	3	0	12	0	0	1	1	1	0	0	0	0	5	0	5	7	1	2	0
pinning	17	.2129	.8606	39.3	1	2	0	0	2	6	6	0	2	0	0	0	0	0	1	1	0	0	10	0	1	1	0	1	0
Pino	3	.0000	.1370	31.4	0	0	0	0	3	0	0	0	3	0	0	0	0	0	0	0	0	0	0	0	0	0	0	0	0
Pinocchio	37	.0478	.8897	39.5	0	0	4	33	0	0	0	0	4	0	0	0	0	0	0	0	0	0	0	0	33	0	0	0	0
Pinocchio's	2	.0000	.0234	23.7	0	0	0	2	0	0	0	0	0	0	0	0	0	0	0	0	0	0	0	0	2	0	0	0	0
pinon	5	.3211	.4073	36.1	0	2	1	2	0	0	0	0	2	0	0	0	0	1	0	0	0	0	0	0	0	0	0	2	0
pinpoint	9	.5151	.9867	39.9	1	1	1	4	1	1	0	0	1	0	1	0	0	0	0	3	0	0	0	0	0	1	1	2	0
pinpointed	2	.2437	.1129	30.5	0	0	0	0	2	0	0	0	0	0	0	0	0	0	0	0	0	0	0	0	0	0	1	1	0
pinpoints	2	.1551	.0728	28.6	0	0	0	0	1	0	1	0	0	0	1	0	0	0	0	0	0	0	0	0	1	0	0	0	0
pinprick	2	.2433	.1158	30.6	1	0	0	0	0	1	0	0	0	0	0	0	0	0	0	0	0	0	0	0	0	1	0	1	0
pins	93	.5592	11.054	50.4	32	12	2	8	8	12	17	2	29	4	1	5	4	4	1	4	0	1	26	3	0	9	1	1	0
pint	55	.4105	4.9852	47.0	16	19	4	3	5	7	1	0	3	0	0	1	36	2	0	6	0	0	0	0	1	1	0	5	0
Pinta	8	.0000	.1556	31.9	1	0	2	2	0	3	0	0	0	0	0	0	0	8	0	0	0	0	0	0	0	0	0	0	0
pintadines	2	.0000	.0234	23.7	0	0	0	0	2	0	0	0	0	0	0	0	0	0	0	0	0	0	0	0	2	0	0	0	0
pinto	17	.4736	1.8815	42.7	3	13	0	1	0	0	0	0	10	0	0	1	0	4	0	0	0	0	0	0	2	0	0	0	0
Pinto	3	.3272	.2363	33.7	2	1	0	0	0	0	0	0	1	0	0	1	0	0	0	0	1	0	0	0	0	0	0	0	0
pinto's	2	.0000	.0914	29.6	0	1	0	1	0	0	0	0	2	0	0	0	0	0	0	0	0	0	0	0	0	0	0	0	0
pints	49	.4118	4.4745	46.5	26	13	1	2	4	2	1	0	5	0	1	0	35	0	0	2	0	0	0	0	0	1	2	3	0
Pinus	3	.0000	.0591	27.7	0	0	0	0	0	0	3	0	0	0	0	0	0	0	0	3	0	0	0	0	0	0	0	0	0
pinwheel	16	.2730	1.0664	40.3	5	5	6	0	0	0	0	0	1	0	0	0	0	0	0	9	0	0	0	0	0	0	6	0	0
pinwheels	6	.3416	.4760	36.8	2	0	4	0	0	0	0	0	1	0	0	0	0	0	0	1	0	0	0	0	0	1	3	0	0
Pinzon	6	.0000	.2741	34.4	0	0	6	0	0	0	0	0	6	0	0	0	0	0	0	0	0	0	0	0	0	0	0	0	0
pioneer	100	.8088	16.343	52.1	21	12	20	12	23	10	0	2	29	8	1	3	0	26	1	4	6	0	0	0	2	6	9	5	0

7A pillaging
8F pillories
5A pillowcases
4N pilot-bread
3P pilot-training
9D pilotage
4R Pilots
4P pimiento-stuffed
4F Pimwe
4F Pimwe's
3R Pin
9L pin-
6R pin-oak
9F pin-point
7E pin-prick
7A pin-ups
6H pin's
8A Pinar
6A Pinch
7N pinchers
7R Pinchot
3P Pinckney
9L pincushions
7F Pindus
3A pine-covered
XR pine-lined
5N pine-needle
3A pined
5A Pinetree
6A piney-woods
3A Ping's
4R pinged
7A pinging
7R pinheads
8A pinions
7C pink-and-white
5A pink-blossomed
7A pink-cheeked
3P pink-faced
7K pink-robbed
4N Pink-toed
6A Pinkerton's
8B Pinkham
6R pinna
5P Pinnacle
6F pinnacles
6Q pinnately
6A pinned-up
7A Pino's
7H pinpoint-sharp
7Q pinpointing
7H pinpricks
3J Pins
7R Pinson
7N pintadine
3P pintos
5Q PinusCaribaea
5Q PinusPalustris
7Q pinwheel-like
8D pinwheel-shaped
8Q pinworms
XR pinyons
5A Pinzon's

Word Type	F	D	U	SFI	3 Gr 3	4 Gr 4	5 Gr 5	6 Gr 6	7 Gr 7	8 Gr 8	9 Gr 9	X UnGr	A Read	B Eng & Gr	C Comp	D Lit	E Math	F Soc Stud	G Spell	H Sci	J Music	K Art	L Home Ec	M Shop	N Lib F	P Lib NF	Q Lib Ref	R Mag	S Rel
Pioneer	10	.3679	.9197	39.6	1	7	1	0	1	0	0	0	5	0	0	0	0	0	0	2	0	0	0	0	0	3	0	0	0
pioneer's	2	.2160	.1362	31.3	0	0	1	0	0	0	1	0	1	0	0	0	0	0	0	1	0	0	0	0	0	0	0	0	0
pioneered	10	.4825	1.0390	40.2	0	1	1	0	0	3	5	0	1	0	0	0	1	2	0	1	0	0	0	0	0	1	4	0	0
pioneering	11	.5961	1.3452	41.3	0	0	0	1	6	1	2	1	0	0	0	1	1	1	0	1	2	0	0	0	0	0	1	4	0
pioneers	145	.7084	21.097	53.2	35	17	53	8	14	13	2	3	30	2	1	2	0	62	1	3	18	1	0	0	1	6	14	4	0
pioneers'	3	.0000	.1370	31.4	0	2	1	0	0	0	0	0	3	0	0	0	0	0	0	0	0	0	0	0	0	0	0	0	0
Piotr	2	.0000	.0219	23.4	0	0	0	0	0	0	2	0	0	2	0	0	0	0	0	0	0	0	0	0	0	0	0	0	0
pious	7	.5890	.8614	39.4	0	0	3	1	1	2	0	0	1	0	0	1	0	1	0	0	1	0	0	0	1	2	0	0	0
pip	2	.2346	.1166	30.7	0	0	0	1	0	0	0	1	0	0	0	0	0	0	0	1	0	0	0	0	0	0	0	1	0
Pip	3	.0000	.0322	25.1	0	0	0	0	0	0	3	0	0	0	0	3	0	0	0	0	0	0	0	0	0	0	0	0	0
pipe	232	.8392	39.029	55.9	57	31	29	15	63	28	8	1	56	4	0	20	9	25	6	21	18	1	0	13	25	11	15	8	0
piped	22	.6435	2.9274	44.7	4	5	5	1	5	1	1	0	4	0	0	0	0	3	0	0	4	0	0	0	2	3	3	3	0
pipeline	19	.3996	1.7061	42.3	1	2	1	4	4	2	5	0	1	1	0	0	0	13	0	0	0	0	0	0	0	0	1	3	0
pipelines	16	.0446	.4625	36.7	2	0	4	4	4	1	1	0	1	0	0	0	0	15	0	0	0	0	0	0	0	0	0	0	0
piper	4	.2303	.2158	33.3	0	2	2	0	0	0	0	0	0	0	0	0	0	0	0	0	2	0	0	0	0	2	0	0	0
Piper	29	.4804	2.9298	44.7	11	1	11	1	5	0	0	0	2	0	0	4	0	0	0	0	9	0	0	0	11	0	2	1	0
Piper's	6	.2426	.3643	35.6	1	0	4	0	1	0	0	0	1	0	0	1	0	0	0	0	0	0	0	0	4	0	0	0	0
pipers	2	.0000	.0162	22.1	0	0	0	1	0	0	1	0	0	0	0	0	0	0	0	0	2	0	0	0	0	0	0	0	0
pipes	117	.8062	18.953	52.8	22	10	26	19	21	8	9	2	17	0	1	5	1	14	2	30	19	1	0	5	7	5	9	1	0
Pipes	2	.0000	.0162	22.1	1	1	0	0	0	0	0	0	0	0	0	0	0	0	0	0	2	0	0	0	0	0	0	0	0
piping	14	.6058	1.7602	42.5	1	3	3	3	3	1	0	0	2	1	0	1	0	1	0	1	4	0	0	0	2	2	0	0	0
pipkin	2	.0000	.0219	23.4	2	0	0	0	0	0	0	0	0	2	0	0	0	0	0	0	0	0	0	0	0	0	0	0	0
Pipp	4	.0000	.1827	32.6	0	0	0	0	4	0	0	0	4	0	0	0	0	0	0	0	0	0	0	0	0	0	0	0	0
Pippi	67	.1332	3.1409	45.0	55	12	0	0	0	0	0	0	24	0	0	0	0	0	0	0	0	0	0	0	43	0	0	0	0
Pippi's	5	.0804	.1641	32.2	4	1	0	0	0	0	0	0	1	0	0	0	0	0	0	0	0	0	0	0	4	0	0	0	0
Pippilotta	2	.0000	.0234	23.7	2	0	0	0	0	0	0	0	0	0	0	0	0	0	0	0	0	0	0	0	2	0	0	0	0
pique	2	.1839	.0845	29.3	0	0	0	0	1	1	0	0	0	0	0	0	0	0	0	0	0	0	1	0	1	0	0	0	0
piqued	3	.1277	.1363	31.3	0	0	0	0	1	0	1	1	1	0	0	0	0	0	0	0	0	0	0	0	0	0	0	2	0
piracy	4	.3215	.3104	34.9	1	0	1	0	2	0	0	0	1	0	0	0	0	0	0	0	0	0	0	0	0	2	1	0	0
Piraeus	2	.0000	.0389	25.9	0	1	0	0	1	0	0	0	0	0	0	0	0	2	0	0	0	0	0	0	0	0	0	0	0
Pirana	2	.0000	.0290	24.6	0	0	0	0	0	2	0	0	0	0	0	0	0	0	0	0	0	0	0	0	0	2	0	0	0
Pirandello	2	.2401	.1133	30.5	0	1	1	0	0	0	0	0	0	0	0	0	0	0	0	0	0	0	0	0	0	1	1	0	0
piranha	6	.1473	.2287	33.6	0	1	0	0	5	0	0	0	0	0	0	0	0	0	0	0	0	0	0	0	0	0	5	1	0
pirarucu	2	.0000	.0209	23.2	0	0	0	0	2	0	0	0	0	0	0	0	0	0	0	0	0	0	0	0	0	0	2	0	0
pirate	62	.5422	7.7065	48.9	15	19	12	8	7	1	0	0	48	0	0	1	1	4	0	0	0	0	0	0	1	5	1	1	0
Pirate	5	.0000	.2284	33.6	0	0	5	0	0	0	0	0	5	0	0	0	0	0	0	0	0	0	0	0	0	0	0	0	0
pirate's	3	.2279	.2143	33.3	0	2	1	0	0	0	0	0	2	0	0	0	0	0	0	0	0	0	0	0	0	0	0	1	0
pirates	70	.7399	10.649	50.3	8	17	9	18	5	13	0	0	26	6	0	0	1	15	1	0	3	0	0	0	8	4	1	5	0
Pirates	8	.2912	.5377	37.3	5	0	0	0	2	0	1	0	0	0	0	1	6	0	0	0	0	0	0	0	0	0	0	1	0
pirates'	2	.2407	.1090	30.4	0	0	1	0	0	1	0	0	0	1	0	0	0	0	0	0	1	0	0	0	0	0	0	0	0
pirating	2	.1787	.1174	30.7	0	0	1	0	1	0	0	0	1	0	0	0	0	0	0	0	0	0	0	0	1	0	0	0	0
Piri	2	.0000	.0914	29.6	0	0	0	0	2	0	0	0	2	0	0	0	0	0	0	0	0	0	0	0	0	0	0	0	0
Pirulero	6	.0000	.0485	26.9	6	0	0	0	0	0	0	0	0	0	0	0	0	0	0	0	6	0	0	0	0	0	0	0	0
Pisa	6	.3681	.4847	36.9	2	0	0	0	1	2	1	0	0	0	0	0	2	1	0	0	0	1	0	0	0	2	0	0	0
Pisces	2	.0000	.0394	26.0	0	0	0	0	0	0	0	2	0	0	0	0	0	0	0	2	0	0	0	0	0	0	0	0	0
Pish-Tush	3	.0000	.0243	23.8	0	0	0	0	0	3	0	0	0	0	0	0	0	0	0	0	3	0	0	0	0	0	0	0	0
pistil	29	.0000	.5718	37.6	5	3	8	11	0	0	2	0	0	0	0	0	0	0	0	29	0	0	0	0	0	0	0	0	0
pistils	18	.0000	.3549	35.5	0	1	0	16	0	0	0	1	0	0	0	0	0	0	0	18	0	0	0	0	0	0	0	0	0
pistol	50	.5844	6.2908	48.0	3	6	13	4	15	2	7	0	21	0	0	10	0	0	0	1	0	0	0	0	6	9	2	1	0
Pistol	2	.2433	.1158	30.6	1	0	0	1	0	0	0	0	0	0	0	0	0	0	0	0	0	0	0	0	0	1	0	1	0
pistol-shot	2	.0000	.0234	23.7	0	0	0	0	1	1	0	0	0	0	0	0	0	0	0	0	0	0	0	0	2	0	0	0	0
pistols	15	.4637	1.6416	42.2	1	1	5	1	5	2	0	0	10	0	0	1	0	0	0	0	1	0	0	0	0	0	0	3	0
piston	37	.6370	4.8355	46.8	2	1	11	0	6	9	8	0	0	2	2	0	0	0	0	21	1	0	0	2	0	2	4	3	0
Piston	2	.0000	.0162	22.1	0	0	0	0	0	2	0	0	0	0	0	0	0	0	0	0	2	0	0	0	0	0	0	0	0
piston-and-cylinder	2	.0000	.0394	26.0	0	0	0	0	0	2	0	0	0	0	0	0	0	0	0	2	0	0	0	0	0	0	0	0	0
pistons	12	.5518	1.3777	41.4	3	1	2	0	5	0	1	0	0	0	0	1	0	0	0	3	0	0	0	0	0	3	2	3	0
pit	67	.7337	10.148	50.1	2	3	3	13	30	8	7	1	30	1	0	13	0	3	0	4	1	0	1	0	5	2	5	2	0
Pit	2	.2331	.1157	30.6	0	0	0	0	0	2	0	0	0	0	0	0	0	0	0	1	0	0	0	0	1	0	0	0	0
Pitcairn	4	.2393	.3005	34.8	0	0	3	0	1	0	0	0	3	0	0	1	0	0	0	0	0	0	0	0	0	0	0	0	0
Pitcairn's	2	.0000	.0914	29.6	0	0	2	0	0	0	0	0	2	0	0	0	0	0	0	0	0	0	0	0	0	0	0	0	0
pitch	273	.6522	36.508	55.6	55	50	27	25	60	44	8	4	38	39	0	8	0	4	4	32	98	1	0	3	12	19	9	6	0
pitch-black	2	.0000	.0914	29.6	0	1	1	0	0	0	0	0	2	0	0	0	0	0	0	0	0	0	0	0	0	0	0	0	0
pitch-dark	3	.3553	.2609	34.2	0	1	0	1	1	0	0	0	1	0	0	0	0	0	0	1	0	0	0	0	0	1	0	0	0
Pitch-pine	2	.0000	.0914	29.6	0	0	2	0	0	0	0	0	2	0	0	0	0	0	0	0	0	0	0	0	0	0	0	0	0
pitch-producing	2	.0000	.0162	22.1	0	0	0	0	2	0	0	0	0	0	0	0	0	0	0	0	2	0	0	0	0	0	0	0	0
pitch	2	.0000	.0914	29.6	2	0	0	0	0	0	0	0	2	0	0	0	0	0	0	0	0	0	0	0	0	0	0	0	0
pitchblende	11	.4458	1.1314	40.5	0	0	1	2	1	3	1	3	4	1	0	0	0	0	0	5	0	0	0	0	0	0	1	0	0
pitched	52	.7566	8.0127	49.0	7	3	10	9	5	12	6	0	15	2	1	6	0	3	0	1	3	0	0	0	4	11	0	6	0
pitcher	114	.8090	18.693	52.7	31	17	27	13	16	4	6	0	47	12	1	10	5	2	2	4	0	0	0	0	3	13	9	6	0
Pitcher	2	.2437	.1129	30.5	0	0	1	1	0	0	0	0	0	0	0	0	0	0	0	0	0	0	0	0	0	0	1	1	0
pitcher's	14	.5885	1.7577	42.4	2	3	5	2	1	0	1	0	5	1	0	1	0	0	0	0	0	0	0	0	0	3	3	1	0
pitchers	28	.6403	3.7728	45.8	6	5	7	3	6	1	0	0	10	0	0	1	1	0	0	1	0	0	0	0	1	7	4	3	0
pitches	46	.4544	4.4950	46.5	9	9	6	8	8	3	3	0	7	2	0	1	0	0	0	1	23	0	0	0	1	5	3	3	0
pitchfork	3	.3418	.2483	33.9	0	1	0	1	1	0	0	0	1	1	0	0	0	0	0	0	0	0	0	0	0	1	0	0	0
pitchforks	4	.2393	.3005	34.8	0	0	1	0	0	2	1	0	3	0	0	1	0	0	0	0	0	0	0	0	0	0	0	0	0
pitching	51	.6304	6.7893	48.3	19	10	3	9	3	5	2	0	19	1	0	5	0	0	1	1	0	0	0	0	3	11	0	10	0
piteous	5	.1697	.2121	33.3	0	0	0	0	1	0	4	0	0	0	0	4	0	0	0	0	0	0	0	0	1	0	0	0	0
piteously	5	.4769	.5345	37.3	0	1	0	2	1	1	0	0	2	0	0	1	0	0	0	0	0	0	0	0	1	0	0	1	0
pitfalls	4	.1772	.1782	32.5	0	0	0	0	1	3	0	0	0	3	0	0	0	0	0	0	0	0	0	0	0	1	0	0	0
pith	4	.2921	.2600	34.1	0	0	1	1	1	1	0	0	0	0	1	0	0	0	0	1	0	0	0	0	0	0	2	0	0
Pithecanthropus	2	.2278	.1128	30.5	0	0	0	0	2	0	0	0	0	0	0	0	0	0	0	1	0	0	0	0	0	0	1	0	0
pithecoid	2	.0000	.0209	23.2	0	0	0	0	2	0	0	0	0	0	0	0	0	0	0	0	0	0	0	0	0	0	2	0	0
pithy	2	.2442	.1134	30.5	0	0	0	1	1	0	0	0	0	1	0	0	0	0	0	0	0	0	0	0	0	0	0	1	0
pitiable	2	.2443	.1130	30.5	0	0	0	0	1	0	1	0	0	0	0	1	0	0	0	0	0	0	0	0	1	0	0	0	0
pitied	4	.1919	.1864	32.7	0	0	0	0	2	1	1	0	0	0	0	3	0	0	0	0	0	0	0	0	1	0	0	0	0
pitiful	13	.6095	1.7026	42.3	1	4	0	2	2	3	1	0	7	0	1	1	0	0	1	0	1	0	0	0	1	0	0	1	0
pitifully	4	.1814	.2373	33.8	0	1	0	2	1	0	0	0	2	0	0	0	0	0	0	0	0	0	0	0	0	0	0	2	0
pitilessly	2	.1717	.1142	30.6	0	0	0	1	0	0	1	0	1	0	0	1	0	0	0	0	0	0	0	0	0	0	0	0	0
Pitman	3	.2332	.1690	32.3	0	0	0	0	0	0	2	1	0	0	0	0	0	0	0	0	0	0	0	0	0	2	0	1	0
pits	33	.6973	4.7848	46.8	2	3	7	2	7	7	4	1	12	0	0	2	0	7	0	4	0	0	0	1	0	1	4	2	0
Pitt	18	.3736	1.6130	42.1	0	0	8	0	7	0	3	0	7	0	0	7	0	3	0	0	0	0	0	0	0	0	0	1	0
pitted	8	.5756	.9552	39.8	0	1	0	0	3	3	1	0	1	1	0	1	0	0	0	1	0	1	1	0	1	1	0	0	0
pitting	6	.4800	.6533	38.2	0	2	0	0	1	2	0	1	3	0	0	1	0	0	0	0	1	0	0	0	0	0	0	1	0
Pittsburg	4	.2090	.2014	33.0	0	0	1	0	2	1	0	0	0	0	0	0	0	0	0	0	0	0	0	0	0	0	1	3	0
Pittsburgh	60	.6760	8.3694	49.2	11	16	7	11	3	7	5	0	9	2	2	1	4	26	0	1	2	0	0	0	0	10	0	3	0
pituitary	11	.3800	.9347	39.7	0	3	0	0	4	0	4	0	0	0	0	0	0	0	0	6	0	0	0	0	0	3	2	0	0
pity	56	.6844	7.9699	49.0	7	4	8	6	20	3	8	0	22	1	1	11	0	1	0	0	3	0	0	0	11	4	1	1	0

7Q Pious
6R pipe-rack
9R pipe-smoking
8D pipe's
7G pipelayer
6H pipelike
3A Pipestone
7D Pippa's
9R piquant
5Q Pirandello's
4J pirated
6A pirates-to-be
8D Pirates'
3P pirouette
6F Pisa's
6R piscatorial
XH Piscis
6A Pisgah
8Q Pisistratus
7N pison
5A pistareens
7Q piston-cylinder
5H piston-driven
8H piston-engine
6H piston-propeller
7N piston-rod
6J pit-sih-kah-toh
XH pitch-like
5F pitchblack
3Q pitchforked
3P Pitching
6N pities
8D pitiless
5A Pits
9F Pitt's
3A Pitter
5N pitter-pattering
7Q Pittman
7R Pittsfield
7H Pituitary
7A pityin'
9D pitying

Word Type	F	D	U	SFI	3 Gr 3	4 Gr 4	5 Gr 5	6 Gr 6	7 Gr 7	8 Gr 8	9 Gr 9	X UnGr	A Read	B Eng & Gr	C Comp	D Lit	E Math	F Soc Stud	G Spell	H Sci	J Music	K Art	L Home Ec	M Shop	N Lib F	P Lib NF	Q Lib Ref	R Mag	S Rel
pityingly	2	.0000	.0914	29.6	0	0	0	0	1	1	0	0	2	0	0	0	0	0	0	0	0	0	0	0	0	0	0	0	0
Pius	2	.1948	.1250	31.0	1	0	0	0	1	0	0	0	1	0	0	0	0	0	0	0	0	0	0	0	0	1	0	0	0
pivot	23	.7311	3.4169	45.3	0	0	4	2	10	6	0	1	3	0	0	1	1	0	1	6	0	0	0	1	1	3	1	5	0
pivotal	4	.3641	.3177	35.0	0	0	1	0	0	0	1	2	0	0	0	1	0	0	0	0	0	0	0	0	0	1	0	2	0
pivoted	10	.5514	1.1577	40.6	0	0	2	1	5	0	0	2	1	0	0	1	0	0	0	2	0	0	0	0	2	1	3	0	0
pixies	3	.0000	.1370	31.4	3	0	0	0	0	0	0	0	3	0	0	0	0	0	0	0	0	0	0	0	0	0	0	0	0
Pizarro	27	.1708	1.3195	41.2	1	9	13	1	3	0	0	0	0	0	0	0	0	24	0	0	0	0	0	0	0	0	3	0	0
pizza	16	.6074	1.9905	43.0	2	2	2	2	6	1	1	0	0	4	0	0	4	1	0	0	1	0	0	0	1	1	0	4	0
pizzicato	8	.0000	.0647	28.1	0	3	0	3	1	1	0	0	0	0	0	0	0	0	0	0	8	0	0	0	0	0	0	0	0
pl	14	.0252	.2167	33.4	1	3	5	5	0	0	0	0	1	0	0	0	0	0	13	0	0	0	0	0	0	0	0	0	0
placard	4	.3683	.3188	35.0	0	0	0	1	1	1	0	1	0	0	0	1	0	0	0	0	0	0	0	0	2	0	0	1	0
placate	3	.0000	.0365	25.6	0	0	0	0	0	1	0	2	0	0	0	0	0	0	0	0	0	0	0	0	0	0	0	3	0
place	4240	.9540	798.93	69.0	810	773	499	614	713	385	353	93	944	267	43	169	472	442	107	571	145	40	141	103	193	286	141	176	0
Place	17	.7251	2.5070	44.0	2	4	1	2	0	5	3	0	3	2	1	3	0	1	0	1	0	0	0	0	2	2	1	1	0
PLACE	7	.0000	.0821	29.1	0	0	0	7	0	0	0	0	0	0	0	0	0	0	0	0	0	0	0	0	7	0	0	0	0
Place-Value	4	.0000	.0599	27.8	0	4	0	0	0	0	0	0	0	0	0	0	4	0	0	0	0	0	0	0	0	0	0	0	0
place-value	23	.0000	.3443	35.4	3	3	1	1	14	1	0	0	0	0	0	0	23	0	0	0	0	0	0	0	0	0	0	0	0
place-values	2	.0000	.0299	24.8	0	0	0	0	2	0	0	0	0	0	0	0	2	0	0	0	0	0	0	0	0	0	0	0	0
placed	640	.9250	117.27	60.7	73	85	76	81	125	88	85	27	133	48	4	28	49	62	6	89	33	7	31	33	21	33	36	26	1
placeholder	9	.0000	.1347	31.3	0	2	0	0	2	5	0	0	0	0	0	0	9	0	0	0	0	0	0	0	0	0	0	0	0
placeholders	11	.0000	.1647	32.2	0	3	1	0	0	7	0	0	0	0	0	0	11	0	0	0	0	0	0	0	0	0	0	0	0
placement	16	.6310	2.0428	43.1	0	0	0	1	7	5	2	1	0	2	0	0	3	0	0	1	0	1	3	1	0	0	1	4	0
placenta	3	.2445	.1818	32.6	0	0	0	0	2	0	0	1	0	0	0	0	0	0	0	2	0	0	0	0	0	0	1	0	0
placental	2	.2278	.1128	30.5	0	0	0	0	1	0	0	1	0	0	0	0	0	0	0	1	0	0	0	0	0	0	1	0	0
placentalike	2	.0000	.0209	23.2	0	0	0	0	2	0	0	0	0	0	0	0	0	0	0	0	0	0	0	0	0	0	2	0	0
placer	5	.3320	.3590	35.6	0	0	1	3	0	1	0	0	0	0	1	0	0	0	0	0	0	0	0	0	0	0	1	3	0
places	1337	.9046	240.19	63.8	321	223	160	237	201	93	77	25	195	62	15	39	175	330	14	209	42	25	6	7	29	77	68	44	0
Places	3	.2233	.1562	31.9	0	0	2	0	0	1	0	0	0	0	0	1	0	0	0	0	0	0	0	0	0	0	2	0	0
placid	13	.7041	1.8350	42.6	0	2	0	3	5	1	2	0	0	1	1	1	0	0	1	0	1	1	0	0	2	0	2	3	0
Placid	2	.0000	.0914	29.6	0	0	0	2	0	0	0	0	2	0	0	0	0	0	0	0	0	0	0	0	0	0	0	0	0
placing	76	.8672	13.092	51.2	5	4	11	12	7	14	19	4	6	11	2	3	7	5	2	9	4	3	7	3	3	3	4	4	0
placket	20	.0000	.0644	28.1	0	0	0	0	7	8	5	0	0	0	0	0	0	0	0	0	0	0	20	0	0	0	0	0	0
plackets	5	.0000	.0161	22.1	0	0	0	0	1	4	0	0	0	0	0	0	0	0	0	0	0	0	5	0	0	0	0	0	0
plagioclase	3	.1813	.1402	31.5	0	0	0	0	0	0	3	0	0	0	0	0	0	0	0	1	0	0	0	0	0	0	2	0	0
plague	31	.6785	4.3099	46.3	1	0	10	9	5	2	4	0	5	2	0	3	0	1	0	2	0	0	0	0	4	2	8	4	0
plagued	16	.6345	2.1042	43.2	0	0	2	4	4	1	5	0	3	1	1	0	0	1	0	2	1	0	0	0	0	0	2	5	0
plagues	7	.5370	.7863	39.0	0	0	0	2	2	1	1	1	0	0	0	2	0	1	0	2	0	0	0	0	0	0	1	1	0
plaguing	3	.3766	.2497	34.0	0	0	1	0	2	0	0	0	0	0	0	0	0	1	0	0	0	0	0	0	0	1	1	0	0
plaid	15	.2831	1.0464	40.2	1	1	2	3	2	3	3	0	5	1	0	1	0	0	0	0	0	0	6	0	1	1	0	0	0
plaids	3	.1300	.0925	29.7	0	0	0	1	1	0	1	0	0	0	0	0	0	0	0	0	0	0	2	0	1	0	0	0	0
plain	338	.8672	58.523	57.7	35	43	55	64	70	33	34	4	68	15	0	21	0	95	5	17	5	3	14	3	24	27	26	15	0
Plain	31	.2185	1.7804	42.5	1	5	9	2	7	5	2	0	0	0	0	0	0	27	0	0	0	0	0	0	0	2	2	0	0
plain-colored	2	.1033	.0599	27.8	2	0	0	0	0	0	0	0	0	0	0	0	0	0	0	1	0	1	0	0	0	0	0	0	0
plainer	3	.0000	.1370	31.4	0	1	0	2	0	0	0	0	3	0	0	0	0	0	0	0	0	0	0	0	0	0	0	0	0
plainest	3	.3269	.2368	33.7	1	0	0	1	1	0	0	0	1	0	0	0	0	0	1	0	0	0	0	0	1	0	0	0	0
plainly	48	.7588	7.4449	48.7	6	6	7	6	17	3	3	0	18	2	0	6	0	1	0	2	0	1	1	0	6	7	0	4	0
plainness	2	.1934	.0846	29.3	0	0	0	1	0	0	1	0	0	0	0	0	0	0	1	0	0	0	0	1	0	0	0	0	0
plains	358	.6363	47.455	56.8	60	73	84	37	70	13	17	4	48	2	1	7	0	173	0	24	9	0	0	0	4	50	34	6	0
Plains	87	.3634	7.5263	48.8	9	16	53	4	1	3	1	0	16	1	0	0	0	60	0	4	0	0	0	0	0	3	2	1	0
plainsman	2	.0000	.0290	24.6	0	2	0	0	0	0	0	0	0	0	0	0	0	0	0	0	0	0	0	0	0	2	0	0	0
plainsmen	3	.0000	.0434	26.4	0	2	1	0	0	0	0	0	0	0	0	0	0	0	0	0	0	0	0	0	0	3	0	0	0
plainsong	6	.0000	.0485	26.9	0	0	0	4	0	2	0	0	0	0	0	0	0	0	0	0	6	0	0	0	0	0	0	0	0
plainsongs	3	.0000	.0243	23.8	0	0	0	3	0	0	0	0	0	0	0	0	0	0	0	0	3	0	0	0	0	0	0	0	0
plaintiff	10	.4843	1.1247	40.5	0	0	1	6	0	0	3	0	6	1	0	0	0	2	0	0	0	0	0	0	1	0	0	0	0
plaintive	22	.3756	1.7544	42.4	0	2	3	3	5	4	3	2	0	1	0	2	0	0	0	0	13	0	0	0	3	0	0	3	0
plaintively	6	.4467	.6018	37.8	0	2	0	2	1	1	0	0	2	2	0	1	0	0	0	0	0	0	0	0	1	0	0	0	0
plaited	4	.4519	.3985	36.0	1	0	0	1	2	0	0	0	1	0	0	1	0	0	0	0	0	0	0	0	0	0	1	1	0
plan	834	.8235	137.57	61.4	120	124	100	82	140	133	111	24	149	74	13	26	32	130	67	53	14	12	107	19	12	41	24	61	0
Plan	19	.5942	2.3402	43.7	0	1	2	0	2	5	7	2	1	1	0	0	0	7	4	0	0	0	0	0	0	2	2	2	0
planaria	3	.0000	.0434	26.4	3	0	0	0	0	0	0	0	0	0	0	0	0	0	0	0	0	0	0	0	0	3	0	0	0
Planck	9	.2428	.5182	37.1	0	0	0	0	0	8	1	0	0	0	0	0	1	0	0	2	0	0	0	0	0	0	6	0	0
Planck's	2	.2278	.1128	30.5	0	0	0	0	1	1	0	0	0	0	0	0	0	0	0	1	0	0	0	0	0	0	1	0	0
plane	990	.6442	132.29	61.2	124	185	114	134	235	105	79	14	200	26	6	16	352	69	14	90	4	6	0	115	18	24	6	44	0
plane's	9	.4789	1.0094	40.0	0	3	1	2	1	0	2	0	6	1	0	0	0	0	0	0	0	0	0	0	0	1	0	1	0
planed	8	.0516	.1077	30.3	0	0	1	0	3	2	2	0	0	0	0	0	0	0	0	0	0	0	0	7	0	0	1	0	0
planer	8	.0404	.0943	29.7	0	0	0	0	2	0	6	0	0	0	0	0	0	0	0	0	0	0	0	7	0	1	0	0	0
planes	364	.7449	55.226	57.4	67	84	46	41	80	20	23	3	75	4	1	5	144	39	4	16	1	3	0	10	2	27	6	27	0
planet	323	.6918	46.069	56.6	51	71	58	26	51	27	33	6	52	7	0	4	15	25	3	159	2	0	0	3	2	6	29	16	0
Planet	13	.5193	1.5366	41.9	2	0	6	1	2	0	2	0	8	2	0	0	0	1	0	1	0	0	0	0	0	0	1	0	0
planet's	13	.3688	1.0922	40.4	2	1	2	1	4	0	3	0	1	0	0	0	0	0	0	7	0	0	0	0	0	0	4	1	0
planetarium	9	.4061	.8204	39.1	3	3	1	0	2	0	0	0	1	1	0	0	0	0	0	4	0	0	0	0	0	0	0	3	0
Planetarium	2	.2346	.1166	30.7	0	1	0	0	0	1	0	0	0	0	0	0	0	0	0	1	0	0	0	0	0	0	0	1	0
planetary	13	.3629	1.0717	40.3	0	0	0	0	1	8	1	3	1	0	0	1	0	0	0	6	0	0	0	0	0	0	5	0	0
planetoid	2	.0000	.0394	26.0	0	0	0	0	0	2	0	0	0	0	0	0	0	0	0	2	0	0	0	0	0	0	0	0	0
planetoids	5	.3569	.4079	36.1	1	0	0	2	0	2	0	0	0	0	0	0	0	1	0	3	0	0	0	0	0	0	1	0	0
planets	345	.6921	49.086	56.9	58	63	61	39	42	31	35	16	37	6	1	8	11	23	7	202	4	1	0	4	0	13	25	3	0
Planets	8	.3306	.5742	37.6	1	1	2	0	4	0	0	0	0	5	0	0	0	0	0	0	2	0	0	0	0	0	1	0	0
planing	19	.0958	.4338	36.4	1	0	2	0	6	1	9	0	0	1	0	0	0	0	0	0	0	0	0	15	0	1	2	0	0
planishing	2	.0000	.0050	17.0	0	0	0	0	2	0	0	0	0	0	0	0	0	0	0	0	0	0	0	2	0	0	0	0	0
plank	35	.6798	4.9445	46.9	2	3	3	11	12	1	3	0	13	1	0	3	0	1	2	0	4	0	0	0	8	2	0	1	0
planking	3	.0000	.1370	31.4	0	0	0	3	0	0	0	0	3	0	0	0	0	0	0	0	0	0	0	0	0	0	0	0	0
planks	21	.6847	2.9925	44.8	1	6	3	4	4	0	1	2	8	0	0	0	0	1	0	1	1	1	0	0	1	4	2	2	0
plankton	68	.3653	5.6490	47.5	0	32	8	19	4	0	5	0	1	13	0	0	0	0	0	49	0	0	0	0	1	0	3	1	0
planktonburgers	2	.0000	.0394	26.0	0	2	0	0	0	0	0	0	0	0	0	0	0	0	0	2	0	0	0	0	0	0	0	0	0
planned	252	.9142	45.723	56.6	36	39	35	32	42	36	24	8	59	13	2	13	14	47	5	9	4	3	14	3	9	23	10	24	0
planner	5	.4705	.4940	36.9	0	1	1	0	1	2	0	0	0	0	0	1	0	0	0	0	0	0	0	0	0	1	1	2	0
planners	17	.4500	1.6362	42.1	2	1	3	3	4	1	1	2	0	0	0	0	0	4	0	0	0	0	0	0	0	4	2	7	0
planning	207	.7542	31.542	55.0	23	27	23	17	44	36	33	4	37	20	0	6	7	19	1	9	2	5	29	14	9	16	11	22	0
plans	308	.8966	54.855	57.4	44	39	30	44	44	48	43	16	56	17	5	13	11	43	15	14	4	0	17	10	16	33	8	45	1
plant	1051	.7365	157.95	62.0	280	156	129	164	189	44	42	47	142	7	1	8	10	101	12	545	1	3	6	5	10	69	103	27	1
Plant	4	.3730	.3365	35.3	1	1	1	1	0	0	0	0	0	0	0	0	0	2	0	1	0	0	0	0	0	0	1	0	0
plant-animal	7	.0000	.1380	31.4	0	0	0	0	0	7	0	0	0	0	0	0	0	0	0	7	0	0	0	0	0	0	0	0	0
plant-eating	6	.3412	.4577	36.6	2	1	0	1	1	1	0	0	0	0	0	0	0	0	0	1	0	0	0	0	0	3	2	0	0
plant-like	2	.2446	.1257	31.0	0	0	0	1	1	0	0	0	0	0	0	0	0	1	0	1	0	0	0	0	0	0	0	0	0

7A pivot-swing
8N pivoting
8R pivots
7D Piwitak
9D pizened
4F Pizzaro
5E pizzas
6R PL
4A pla-ty
8R placards
5N placatingly
XH placentals
4A Placer
3P Placerville
7N placidly
7Q placoderms
9R plagiarism
8R plagiarize
8R plagiarizing
9Q Plagioclases
8F plague-ridden
5P Plagues
4J plaguey
7J plaguy
4N plaice
6R Plaid
9D plain-song
6R plainclothesmen
7R Plaines
7A plains-dwelling
7P plaint
9F plaintiff's
5A Plainville
6N plait
8A plaiting
7A plaits
6P PLAN
7H Planaria
3P PLANARIA
3P planarias
8M plane-iron
9D plane-tree
9M planer-type
7Q planers
7D planesmen
7H planetai
9H planetesimal
5Q planets'
6P Plank
8A planked
4H plankton-gathering
4H plankton-rich
7Q planktonic
6B Planning
9M planographic
3J Planquette
8H plant-eaters
7Q plant-feeding

Word Type	F	D	U	SFI	3 Gr 3	4 Gr 4	5 Gr 5	6 Gr 6	7 Gr 7	8 Gr 8	9 Gr 9	X UnGr	A Read	B Eng & Gr	C Comp	D Lit	E Math	F Soc Stud	G Spell	H Sci	J Music	K Art	L Home Ec	M Shop	N Lib F	P Lib NF	Q Lib Ref	R Mag	S Rel
plant's	10	.2028	.5114	37.1	1	0	1	0	7	1	0	0	0	0	0	0	0	0	0	4	0	0	0	0	0	0	6	0	0
plantain	2	.2297	.1135	30.6	0	0	0	1	0	0	1	0	0	0	0	1	0	1	0	0	0	0	0	0	0	0	0	0	0
plantains	2	.0000	.0389	25.9	0	0	0	2	0	0	0	0	0	0	0	0	0	2	0	0	0	0	0	0	0	0	0	0	0
plantation	66	.6024	8.3309	49.2	11	4	11	10	16	6	7	1	8	0	0	1	0	27	2	1	0	0	0	0	3	17	1	6	0
Plantation	2	.0000	.0290	24.6	0	2	0	0	0	0	0	0	0	0	0	0	0	0	0	0	0	0	0	0	0	2	0	0	0
plantations	68	.4869	7.1622	48.6	8	4	21	13	14	6	2	0	3	0	0	0	0	50	0	0	2	0	0	1	1	5	4	2	0
planted	220	.8379	36.986	55.7	64	28	33	34	31	16	6	8	41	5	1	10	26	67	4	19	1	0	0	1	8	10	15	12	0
planter	19	.5416	2.1631	43.4	1	0	2	1	7	6	2	0	0	1	0	1	0	11	0	0	0	0	0	1	1	4	0	0	0
planter's	2	.2433	.1158	30.6	0	1	0	0	1	0	0	0	0	0	0	0	0	0	0	0	0	0	0	0	0	1	0	1	0
planters	33	.4470	3.2386	45.1	1	3	12	3	6	5	3	0	1	0	0	1	0	26	0	0	0	0	1	0	1	1	1	1	0
planting	73	.6508	9.9310	50.0	9	14	12	14	5	9	3	7	19	0	0	1	0	17	0	8	1	0	0	0	4	3	2	18	0
plantings	5	.1398	.1959	32.9	0	0	1	1	0	1	0	2	0	0	0	0	0	1	0	0	0	0	0	0	0	0	0	4	0
plants	1886	.7261	279.37	64.5	610	193	247	340	302	89	55	50	171	22	4	10	21	203	14	1059	1	31	5	5	19	108	180	30	3
PLAP-nothing	3	.0000	.1370	31.4	3	0	0	0	0	0	0	0	3	0	0	0	0	0	0	0	0	0	0	0	0	0	0	0	0
PLAP-plap	6	.0000	.2741	34.4	6	0	0	0	0	0	0	0	6	0	0	0	0	0	0	0	0	0	0	0	0	0	0	0	0
plaque	6	.3621	.5367	37.3	3	0	0	0	3	0	0	0	3	0	0	1	0	0	0	0	0	0	0	0	0	0	0	2	0
plaques	3	.2184	.1759	32.5	1	0	0	0	1	1	0	0	1	0	0	0	0	0	0	0	0	0	0	1	0	0	0	1	0
plasma	16	.2165	.9061	39.6	0	0	0	1	4	9	2	0	0	0	0	0	0	0	0	13	0	0	0	0	0	0	3	0	0
plasmodium	3	.0000	.0591	27.7	0	0	0	1	2	0	0	0	0	0	0	0	0	0	0	3	0	0	0	0	0	0	0	0	0
plaster	53	.6841	7.4345	48.7	1	5	7	4	23	8	5	0	9	0	0	6	0	4	0	13	1	3	0	5	3	1	2	6	0
plastered	12	.5743	1.4351	41.6	2	2	1	1	4	0	2	0	1	0	0	2	0	2	0	0	0	0	0	0	2	2	3	0	0
plastic	152	.8249	25.167	54.0	17	28	16	12	23	24	16	16	31	10	1	1	2	1	3	43	6	1	9	7	2	7	6	22	0
plasticine	4	.0000	.0074	18.7	0	4	0	0	0	0	0	0	0	0	0	0	0	0	0	0	0	4	0	0	0	0	0	0	0
plastics	44	.5529	5.0966	47.1	2	1	22	7	6	2	4	0	4	1	0	1	0	4	0	10	0	1	0	2	0	0	21	0	0
plastid	2	.0000	.0394	26.0	0	0	0	0	2	0	0	0	0	0	0	0	0	0	0	2	0	0	0	0	0	0	0	0	0
plastids	2	.2278	.1128	30.5	0	0	0	1	1	0	0	0	0	0	0	0	0	0	0	1	0	0	0	0	0	0	1	0	0
plat	2	.0000	.0050	17.0	0	0	0	0	0	0	2	0	0	0	0	0	0	0	0	0	0	0	0	2	0	0	0	0	0
Plata	10	.1703	.4438	36.5	7	0	0	3	0	0	0	0	0	0	0	0	0	3	0	0	0	0	0	0	0	0	7	0	0
plate	346	.7492	52.738	57.2	53	54	38	22	68	29	62	20	91	15	1	13	6	9	2	61	2	3	25	36	25	28	10	19	0
Plate	10	.1294	.3633	35.6	0	0	0	0	8	2	0	0	0	0	0	8	0	0	0	2	0	0	0	0	0	0	0	0	0
plateau	110	.5475	12.791	51.1	9	5	18	38	25	8	7	0	10	1	0	4	0	65	2	0	0	0	0	0	6	4	16	2	0
Plateau	44	.3388	3.5192	45.5	2	1	22	13	2	4	0	0	3	0	0	0	0	34	0	1	0	0	0	0	0	2	2	2	0
plateaus	33	.1532	1.5144	41.8	1	1	6	10	12	1	2	0	0	0	0	0	0	30	0	0	0	0	0	0	0	0	3	0	0
plated	2	.1738	.0790	29.0	0	0	0	0	2	0	0	0	0	0	0	0	0	0	0	0	0	0	0	1	0	0	1	0	0
plateful	2	.0000	.0234	23.7	1	0	1	0	0	0	0	0	0	0	0	0	0	0	0	0	0	0	0	0	2	0	0	0	0
platen	3	.0000	.0314	25.0	0	0	3	0	0	0	0	0	0	0	0	0	0	0	0	0	0	0	0	0	0	0	3	0	0
plates	175	.6313	22.892	53.6	37	19	30	9	25	20	25	10	36	2	0	6	5	5	1	24	0	1	8	30	19	23	9	6	0
platform	121	.8207	20.119	53.0	17	27	14	16	24	8	9	6	53	3	1	6	2	7	1	11	0	0	0	0	10	12	5	10	0
Platform	2	.2446	.1257	31.0	0	0	0	0	2	0	0	0	0	0	0	0	0	1	0	1	0	0	0	0	0	0	0	0	0
platforms	12	.6192	1.5491	41.9	2	2	1	2	1	0	4	0	2	1	0	0	0	2	0	1	0	0	0	0	0	2	3	1	0
plating	3	.3390	.2450	33.9	1	0	0	0	2	0	0	0	1	0	0	0	0	0	0	0	0	0	0	0	0	0	1	1	0
platinum	25	.5040	2.6937	44.3	2	6	1	5	3	1	3	4	2	0	0	0	2	2	0	8	0	0	0	0	0	1	9	1	0
platitos	2	.0000	.0243	23.9	0	0	0	0	0	0	0	2	0	0	0	0	0	0	0	0	0	0	0	0	0	0	0	2	0
Plato	6	.2031	.3257	35.1	0	0	0	4	2	0	0	0	0	1	0	0	0	5	0	0	0	0	0	0	0	0	0	0	0
Plato's	2	.2408	.1204	30.8	0	0	1	1	0	0	0	0	0	0	0	0	0	1	0	0	0	0	0	0	0	1	0	0	0
platoon	3	.3836	.2486	34.0	0	0	0	0	1	1	1	0	0	1	0	0	1	0	0	0	0	0	0	0	0	0	1	0	0
Platt	5	.3141	.3764	35.8	0	0	0	0	4	0	1	0	1	0	0	0	0	0	0	0	0	0	0	0	0	2	0	2	0
Platte	6	.4770	.6097	37.9	0	0	3	0	1	1	0	1	0	0	0	0	0	3	0	0	1	0	0	0	1	0	0	1	0
platter	15	.4761	1.5928	42.0	3	1	3	0	2	2	4	0	6	0	0	4	0	0	0	0	0	0	2	0	2	1	0	0	0
platters	3	.2124	.1716	32.3	0	1	1	0	0	0	1	0	1	1	1	0	0	0	0	0	0	0	0	0	0	0	0	0	0
platy	2	.0000	.0914	29.6	0	2	0	0	0	0	0	0	2	0	0	0	0	0	0	0	0	0	0	0	0	0	0	0	0
platypus	4	.4800	.4050	36.1	0	1	0	1	1	0	0	1	0	1	0	0	0	0	0	1	0	0	0	0	0	0	1	1	0
platypuses	3	.2321	.1635	32.1	0	0	0	2	1	0	0	0	0	0	0	0	0	0	0	0	0	0	0	0	0	0	1	2	0
plausible	4	.1698	.2267	33.6	0	0	2	0	1	1	0	0	2	0	0	0	0	0	0	0	0	0	0	0	0	0	2	0	0
play	2113	.7224	310.19	64.9	514	546	270	242	229	173	111	28	406	149	14	126	51	70	59	93	731	5	27	2	104	135	34	107	0
Play	7	.3734	.5796	37.6	2	1	0	2	2	0	0	0	1	1	0	0	0	0	0	0	3	0	0	0	0	0	0	2	0
PLAY	2	.0000	.0914	29.6	0	2	0	0	0	0	0	0	2	0	0	0	0	0	0	0	0	0	0	0	0	0	0	0	0
Play-Doh	2	.0000	.0243	23.9	0	0	2	0	0	0	0	0	0	0	0	0	0	0	0	0	0	0	0	0	0	0	0	2	0
play-acting	4	.2742	.2720	34.3	0	1	0	0	3	0	0	0	1	0	0	0	0	0	0	0	0	0	1	0	0	2	0	0	0
play-off	2	.0000	.0914	29.6	0	0	2	0	0	0	0	0	2	0	0	0	0	0	0	0	0	0	0	0	0	0	0	0	0
play-offs	2	.0000	.0914	29.6	0	0	2	0	0	0	0	0	2	0	0	0	0	0	0	0	0	0	0	0	0	0	0	0	0
play-parties	2	.0000	.0162	22.1	0	0	2	0	0	0	0	0	0	0	0	0	0	0	0	0	2	0	0	0	0	0	0	0	0
play-party	2	.0000	.0162	22.1	0	0	2	0	0	0	0	0	0	0	0	0	0	0	0	0	2	0	0	0	0	0	0	0	0
play'd	2	.0000	.0219	23.4	0	0	2	0	0	0	0	0	0	2	0	0	0	0	0	0	0	0	0	0	0	0	0	0	0
playback	5	.2238	.2558	34.1	0	0	0	1	3	1	0	0	0	2	0	0	0	0	0	0	3	0	0	0	0	0	0	0	0
played	810	.6088	102.23	60.1	142	148	122	111	139	105	38	5	143	51	3	20	17	33	16	29	340	1	0	1	33	59	22	42	0
player	247	.7984	39.714	56.0	29	58	35	30	52	34	9	0	44	18	3	7	18	0	4	60	39	0	1	0	6	15	5	27	0
Player	3	.1983	.1396	31.4	0	1	0	2	0	0	0	0	0	0	0	0	0	0	0	0	2	0	0	0	0	0	0	1	0
player's	6	.2625	.3960	36.0	0	0	1	0	3	2	0	0	1	0	0	0	4	0	0	0	0	0	0	0	1	0	0	0	0
players	234	.8148	38.276	55.8	34	59	31	33	34	34	9	0	39	13	1	8	24	4	4	41	36	2	0	0	3	18	5	36	0
Players	2	.2303	.1079	30.3	0	0	1	1	0	0	0	0	0	0	0	0	0	0	0	0	1	0	0	0	0	1	0	0	0
players'	4	.3766	.3696	35.7	0	1	1	1	1	0	0	0	2	0	0	0	0	0	0	0	0	0	0	0	0	1	0	1	0
playful	29	.7520	4.4287	46.5	6	6	3	4	7	1	1	1	7	3	2	1	0	2	2	1	1	0	0	0	1	3	1	5	0
Playful	5	.0000	.0724	28.6	0	5	0	0	0	0	0	0	0	0	0	0	0	0	0	0	0	0	0	0	0	5	0	0	0
playfully	9	.3940	.8366	39.2	2	2	2	0	2	1	0	0	4	1	0	0	0	0	0	0	0	1	0	0	3	0	0	0	0
playfulness	2	.0000	.0914	29.6	0	1	0	0	0	1	0	0	2	0	0	0	0	0	0	0	0	0	0	0	0	0	0	0	0
playground	84	.8365	14.022	51.5	30	19	6	12	12	3	2	0	8	16	2	8	6	5	3	8	1	3	0	0	9	3	2	10	0
playgrounds	22	.4940	2.3541	43.7	3	7	2	3	2	4	0	1	4	0	0	0	0	6	0	0	0	1	0	0	0	0	2	9	0
playhouse	3	.3380	.2498	34.0	1	1	0	0	0	1	0	0	1	1	0	0	0	0	0	1	0	0	0	0	0	0	0	0	0
Playhouse	2	.2440	.1132	30.5	0	0	0	0	0	0	2	0	0	0	0	1	0	0	0	0	0	0	0	0	0	0	0	1	0
playin'	4	.0974	.1495	31.7	0	2	0	0	2	0	0	0	1	0	0	0	0	0	0	0	0	0	0	0	3	0	0	0	0
playing	624	.7503	94.844	59.8	138	112	73	75	105	75	43	3	132	27	5	32	23	20	11	19	201	6	4	1	46	52	10	35	0
playmate	7	.4296	.6895	38.4	3	1	0	1	1	1	0	0	3	1	0	2	0	0	0	0	0	0	1	0	0	0	1	0	0
playmates	10	.4775	1.0895	40.4	2	3	1	2	2	0	0	0	5	0	0	2	0	0	0	0	0	0	0	0	0	2	1	0	0
playpen	6	.3852	.5105	37.1	3	0	0	0	1	0	2	0	0	0	0	0	0	0	1	3	0	0	0	0	0	0	0	2	0
playroom	4	.1948	.2500	34.0	0	4	0	0	0	0	0	0	2	0	0	0	0	0	0	0	0	0	0	0	0	2	0	0	0
plays	304	.8026	48.782	56.9	54	56	41	29	47	35	36	6	25	35	1	18	14	17	5	15	87	4	4	2	8	10	22	37	0
plaything	3	.2197	.2090	33.2	1	0	1	1	0	0	0	0	2	0	0	0	0	0	0	0	0	0	0	0	0	0	1	0	0
playthings	9	.2947	.6495	38.1	0	2	0	1	3	2	0	1	3	0	0	1	0	0	0	0	0	0	3	0	0	0	0	2	0
playtime	3	.1187	.1291	31.1	1	0	0	0	1	1	0	0	1	0	0	2	0	0	0	0	0	0	0	0	0	0	0	0	0
playwright	20	.5627	2.3192	43.7	1	2	2	0	2	6	6	1	1	1	0	9	0	0	1	0	2	0	0	0	0	1	4	1	0
playwrights	6	.2425	.3632	35.6	0	0	1	0	3	0	1	1	0	0	0	0	0	4	0	0	0	0	0	0	0	0	0	2	0
plaza	12	.3477	.9500	39.8	1	0	5	5	1	0	0	0	0	0	0	0	0	6	0	0	0	0	0	0	0	5	1	0	0
Plaza	4	.3104	.2995	34.8	0	0	1	1	0	0	1	1	1	0	0	0	0	0	0	0	0	0	0	0	0	0	1	2	0

8F planter-scalawags
6A plantin'
7Q plantlike
7D Plants
3P PLANTS
7D Plantscheman
8N planty
7B plashless
8A plashy
XR plasm
9F Plassey
5H plast
7H plaster-cracking
8M plasterboard
5K plasterer's
3A plastering
7A plasters
4R plastic-like
9H plasticene
5Q Plastics
5Q plastics-like
7Q plastron
5Q Plataeans
3A plate-glass
5F plateau's
XD plateglass
9M platemakers
9M platemaking
8H Plates
4A platies
7H platinums
9D platitude
9D plats
5A platter's
7H Platyhelminthes
7R plaudits
6A play-actor
7M play-by-play
8F play-soldier
5J play-song
8B playd
5A Played
6R Players'
9D playfellow
9R playgoer
8C Playground
3G Playing
7J playings
4F playland
4A Playland
3A playmaking
5A Playmate
7R playoff
8R playoffs
4P playroom's
9B playwright's
XR playwrighting

Word Type	F	D	U	SFI	3 Gr 3	4 Gr 4	5 Gr 5	6 Gr 6	7 Gr 7	8 Gr 8	9 Gr 9	X UnGr	A Read	B Eng & Gr	C Comp	D Lit	E Math	F Soc Stud	G Spell	H Sci	J Music	K Art	L Home Ec	M Shop	N Lib F	P Lib NF	Q Lib Ref	R Mag	S Rel
plazas	4	.3831	.3415	35.3	0	2	1	1	0	0	0	0	0	0	0	0	0	2	0	0	0	0	0	0	0	1	0	1	0
plea	10	.4718	1.0473	40.2	0	0	0	3	4	2	1	0	3	0	0	0	0	1	0	0	1	0	0	0	0	1	0	4	0
plead	7	.5607	.8553	39.3	0	0	1	0	3	1	1	1	3	0	0	1	0	1	0	0	0	0	0	0	1	0	0	1	0
pleaded	39	.6518	5.3535	47.3	1	8	10	8	5	6	1	0	16	1	0	1	0	3	0	0	0	0	0	0	9	3	3	3	0
pleading	16	.5268	1.8388	42.6	1	3	1	1	4	3	2	1	6	0	0	3	0	0	0	0	2	0	0	0	0	1	0	4	0
pleadingly	5	.0804	.1641	32.2	1	2	0	0	1	0	1	0	1	0	0	0	0	0	0	0	0	0	0	0	4	0	0	0	0
pleas	3	.3776	.2489	34.0	0	0	0	1	0	1	1	0	0	0	0	1	0	1	0	0	0	0	0	0	0	0	0	1	0
pleasant	281	.8569	48.179	56.8	52	44	39	42	54	25	18	7	75	24	12	21	0	27	2	29	10	1	12	0	22	21	12	13	0
pleasanter	6	.5427	.6813	38.3	1	0	0	2	2	1	0	0	0	0	0	1	0	1	0	1	0	0	0	0	1	2	0	0	0
pleasantest	6	.4293	.5878	37.7	1	1	0	1	2	1	0	0	2	0	0	2	0	0	0	1	0	0	0	0	0	0	1	0	0
pleasantly	26	.7500	3.9909	46.0	2	4	3	7	3	5	1	1	9	1	1	3	0	3	0	1	0	0	0	0	3	3	1	1	0
please	501	.8736	87.553	59.4	133	106	49	52	73	29	49	10	189	50	6	43	23	7	24	2	19	1	4	1	54	37	2	39	0
Please	3	.2380	.1632	32.1	0	0	0	1	1	0	1	0	0	2	0	0	0	0	0	0	1	0	0	0	0	0	0	0	0
pleased	224	.6419	30.479	54.8	45	53	23	40	28	20	11	4	101	9	3	16	0	20	1	2	1	0	0	0	33	24	1	11	2
pleases	12	.3433	.9971	40.0	1	2	0	2	4	2	1	0	4	0	0	0	1	2	0	2	0	0	3	0	0	0	0	0	0
pleasing	54	.6243	6.8847	48.4	0	4	8	7	9	16	9	1	7	2	1	3	1	2	0	4	3	9	11	3	2	2	2	2	0
pleasurable	6	.3918	.5204	37.2	0	0	0	0	1	0	2	3	1	0	0	1	0	0	0	0	0	0	1	0	0	0	0	3	0
pleasure	166	.8774	29.022	54.6	11	19	22	18	31	26	31	8	40	14	1	26	1	10	3	2	13	3	3	0	16	13	8	13	0
Pleasure	7	.3815	.6823	38.3	5	0	1	1	0	0	0	0	5	0	0	0	0	0	0	0	0	0	0	0	1	1	0	0	0
pleasures	29	.7996	4.6423	46.7	0	2	4	1	13	4	4	1	3	3	1	4	0	3	0	0	2	0	2	0	3	2	3	3	0
pleat	12	.0000	.0386	25.9	0	0	0	0	0	11	1	0	0	0	0	0	0	0	0	0	0	0	12	0	0	0	0	0	0
pleated	4	.2865	.3001	34.8	0	1	0	1	1	0	1	0	2	0	0	0	0	0	0	0	0	0	1	0	0	0	1	0	0
pleats	11	.0000	.0354	25.5	0	0	0	0	0	8	3	0	0	0	0	0	0	0	0	0	0	0	11	0	0	0	0	0	0
plebeian	2	.2437	.1129	30.5	1	0	0	0	0	0	0	1	0	0	0	0	0	0	0	0	0	0	0	0	0	0	1	1	0
plebeians	2	.0000	.0389	25.9	0	0	0	2	0	0	0	0	0	0	0	0	0	2	0	0	0	0	0	0	0	0	0	0	0
plectra	3	.0000	.0243	23.8	0	0	0	0	3	0	0	0	0	0	0	0	0	0	0	0	3	0	0	0	0	0	0	0	0
plectrum	2	.0000	.0162	22.1	0	0	0	0	2	0	0	0	0	0	0	0	0	0	0	0	2	0	0	0	0	0	0	0	0
pledge	22	.6718	3.0516	44.8	4	4	1	2	4	3	4	0	6	2	0	0	0	1	3	0	3	0	0	0	0	1	2	4	0
Pledge	4	.2278	.2911	34.6	0	3	0	0	0	0	1	0	3	0	0	0	0	0	0	0	1	0	0	0	0	0	0	0	0
pledged	11	.5385	1.2402	40.9	0	0	2	0	4	4	1	0	0	1	0	0	0	5	0	0	0	0	0	0	1	0	2	2	0
pledges	2	.2152	.1357	31.3	0	0	0	0	1	0	1	0	1	0	0	0	0	1	0	0	0	0	0	0	0	0	0	0	0
Pleistocene	5	.0000	.0523	27.2	0	0	0	0	4	1	0	0	0	0	0	0	0	0	0	0	0	0	0	0	0	0	5	0	0
plentie	2	.0000	.0243	23.9	0	0	0	0	0	0	0	2	0	0	0	0	0	0	0	0	0	0	0	0	0	0	0	2	0
plentiful	56	.7906	8.9624	49.5	6	2	7	14	13	9	5	0	13	1	0	0	0	17	0	6	2	0	1	1	3	2	6	4	0
plentifully	2	.2285	.1129	30.5	0	0	1	0	1	0	0	0	0	0	0	0	0	1	0	0	0	0	0	0	0	0	1	0	0
plenty	320	.8700	55.677	57.5	55	51	44	51	64	33	14	8	92	9	5	23	2	40	4	41	2	0	5	0	32	35	11	19	0
plesiosaurus	3	.0000	.1370	31.4	0	0	0	0	3	0	0	0	3	0	0	0	0	0	0	0	0	0	0	0	0	0	0	0	0
pleura	3	.1813	.1402	31.5	0	0	1	0	0	2	0	0	0	0	0	0	0	0	0	1	0	0	0	0	0	0	2	0	0
pleural	10	.1070	.3048	34.8	0	0	0	0	0	9	1	0	0	0	0	0	0	0	0	0	0	0	0	0	1	0	9	0	0
pleurisy	3	.2159	.1532	31.9	0	1	1	0	0	1	0	0	0	0	0	0	0	0	0	0	0	0	0	0	0	0	2	1	0
Plexiglas	2	.2376	.1088	30.4	0	0	0	1	0	1	0	0	0	0	0	0	0	0	1	0	0	0	0	0	0	0	0	1	0
plexiglass	2	.0000	.0914	29.6	0	0	0	2	0	0	0	0	2	0	0	0	0	0	0	0	0	0	0	0	0	0	0	0	0
plexus	2	.2417	.1091	30.4	1	0	0	0	0	0	1	0	0	0	0	0	0	0	0	0	1	0	0	0	0	0	1	0	0
pliable	3	.2824	.2034	33.1	0	0	0	0	2	0	1	0	1	0	0	0	0	0	0	0	0	0	1	1	0	0	0	0	0
pliant	2	.2440	.1132	30.5	0	0	0	0	1	0	1	0	0	0	0	1	0	0	0	0	0	0	0	0	0	0	0	1	0
plied	8	.4988	.8677	39.4	0	0	2	3	1	2	0	0	2	0	0	1	0	1	0	0	2	0	0	0	0	2	0	0	0
pliers	14	.3496	1.0434	40.2	1	0	2	2	2	5	2	0	1	0	0	0	0	0	1	2	0	3	0	6	1	0	0	0	0
plies	3	.2332	.1690	32.3	0	0	0	0	2	0	0	1	0	0	0	0	0	0	0	0	0	0	0	0	0	2	0	1	0
plight	9	.4085	.8095	39.1	0	1	1	2	1	2	2	0	1	1	0	0	0	1	0	0	0	0	0	0	0	0	1	5	0
Pliny	10	.3608	.9586	39.8	1	0	0	4	1	0	4	0	8	0	0	0	0	0	0	0	0	0	0	0	0	1	1	0	0
plod	4	.4533	.4015	36.0	1	1	0	0	1	0	1	0	1	0	0	1	0	0	0	0	0	0	0	0	1	1	0	0	0
plodded	7	.4642	.7439	38.7	2	2	0	1	0	1	0	1	3	1	0	0	0	0	0	1	0	0	0	0	0	2	0	0	0
plodding	6	.4236	.5749	37.6	1	1	1	0	2	0	1	0	2	1	1	0	0	0	0	0	0	0	0	0	1	1	0	0	0
plods	2	.1814	.1187	30.7	0	0	0	1	0	0	0	1	1	0	0	0	0	0	0	0	0	0	0	0	0	0	0	1	0
plop	12	.4243	1.1986	40.8	2	0	0	8	1	0	1	0	6	0	0	1	0	0	0	0	0	0	0	0	4	0	0	1	0
plop-plop	2	.0000	.0290	24.6	0	2	0	0	0	0	0	0	0	0	0	0	0	0	0	0	0	0	0	0	0	2	0	0	0
plopped	6	.2411	.4668	36.7	2	0	0	2	0	2	0	0	5	0	0	0	0	0	0	0	0	0	0	0	0	0	0	1	0
plot	90	.7308	13.311	51.2	10	4	8	4	17	17	25	5	10	8	1	8	5	5	1	9	11	0	0	1	3	3	8	16	1
plots	19	.5989	2.3818	43.8	3	1	1	2	7	0	5	0	3	3	0	0	0	6	0	0	2	0	0	0	0	2	3	0	0
plotted	16	.2514	1.0432	40.2	1	2	2	2	4	0	4	1	4	0	0	1	1	1	0	2	1	0	0	0	0	2	2	1	1
plotting	9	.5165	.9995	40.0	0	0	2	2	3	2	0	0	2	0	0	1	0	0	0	0	0	0	0	0	0	2	1	3	0
plough	4	.2847	.2818	34.5	1	0	0	1	0	2	0	0	1	0	0	0	0	0	0	0	0	0	0	0	0	1	2	0	0
ploughed	3	.3399	.2456	33.9	0	1	0	0	1	0	1	0	1	0	0	1	0	0	0	0	0	0	0	0	0	0	0	1	0
ploughing	8	.2107	.4245	36.3	1	0	0	0	1	6	0	0	1	0	0	6	0	0	0	0	1	0	0	0	0	0	0	0	0
plover	24	.2399	1.7873	42.5	15	0	0	9	0	0	0	0	15	0	0	0	0	0	0	9	0	0	0	0	0	0	0	0	0
plovers	7	.3871	.6751	38.3	5	0	0	1	1	0	0	0	4	0	0	0	0	0	0	2	0	0	0	0	0	0	1	0	0
plow	75	.7657	11.703	50.7	12	18	11	11	12	8	2	1	22	0	2	7	0	22	2	2	3	0	0	0	5	7	2	1	0
plowed	51	.7397	7.6536	48.8	11	12	7	6	2	8	1	4	5	1	2	2	2	16	0	3	0	0	0	0	6	8	1	5	0
plowing	36	.7075	5.2938	47.2	2	8	5	11	4	2	2	2	14	1	0	0	0	5	1	5	0	0	0	0	3	5	0	2	0
plowman	2	.2337	.1157	30.6	0	0	0	0	0	2	0	0	0	0	0	0	0	1	0	0	0	0	0	0	1	0	0	0	0
plows	31	.6472	4.1578	46.2	8	6	1	4	7	5	0	0	4	0	1	0	0	16	0	1	0	1	0	0	1	1	4	2	0
plowshares	2	.2337	.1157	30.6	0	0	0	0	1	1	0	0	0	0	0	0	0	1	0	0	0	0	0	0	1	0	0	0	0
pluck	50	.4495	4.8543	46.9	10	5	9	6	10	7	3	0	6	0	0	6	0	2	0	8	22	0	0	0	2	4	0	0	0
plucked	40	.4769	4.0819	46.1	2	10	3	8	12	4	0	1	6	0	0	4	0	0	0	4	18	0	0	0	4	1	1	2	0
plucking	15	.4110	1.3466	41.3	1	2	3	3	2	1	2	1	2	0	0	1	0	0	0	1	7	0	0	0	0	1	0	3	0
plucks	4	.0000	.0323	25.1	1	3	0	0	0	0	0	0	0	0	0	0	0	0	0	0	4	0	0	0	0	0	0	0	0
plug	48	.6738	6.7392	48.3	9	6	7	3	16	5	2	0	18	0	1	3	0	2	0	5	0	1	0	5	1	4	0	8	0
plugged	15	.5520	1.8012	42.6	5	2	1	1	2	3	0	1	6	0	0	0	0	1	0	1	2	0	0	0	0	0	1	4	0
plugging	2	.1620	.0760	28.8	0	0	0	0	1	0	0	1	0	0	0	0	0	0	0	0	0	0	0	1	0	0	0	1	0
plugs	14	.4737	1.4342	41.6	2	0	4	1	7	0	0	0	2	1	0	0	0	0	0	2	0	0	0	0	1	0	1	7	0
plum	32	.7727	5.0200	47.0	8	8	1	2	4	5	2	2	9	0	0	3	2	2	4	2	0	0	0	0	2	3	2	3	0
Plum	12	.1754	.5008	37.0	11	0	0	0	1	0	0	0	0	3	0	0	0	0	0	0	9	0	0	0	0	0	0	0	0
plumage	9	.4471	.9010	39.5	3	0	0	3	2	0	0	1	2	0	0	0	0	0	0	4	1	0	0	0	0	0	2	0	0
plumb	15	.6032	1.8852	42.8	0	1	9	1	2	2	0	0	1	0	0	1	1	0	0	7	1	0	0	0	2	2	0	0	0
plumber	9	.3737	.8756	39.4	7	0	0	1	0	1	0	0	7	1	0	0	0	0	0	0	0	0	0	0	0	0	0	1	0
plumber's	3	.3553	.2608	34.2	3	0	0	0	0	0	0	0	1	0	0	0	0	1	0	0	0	0	0	0	0	1	0	0	0
plumbers	2	.2285	.1129	30.5	0	0	2	0	0	0	0	0	0	0	0	0	0	1	0	0	0	0	0	0	0	0	1	0	0
plumbing	13	.5286	1.4744	41.7	1	1	4	0	3	2	2	0	2	0	0	0	0	5	0	0	0	0	0	0	0	2	2	2	0
plume	10	.6300	1.3376	41.3	1	2	1	1	3	1	1	0	4	1	0	1	0	0	0	2	0	0	0	0	0	1	1	0	0
plumed	2	.0000	.0914	29.6	1	0	0	1	0	0	0	0	2	0	0	0	0	0	0	0	0	0	0	0	0	0	0	0	0
plumes	19	.6342	2.5422	44.1	6	3	1	3	3	1	2	0	7	0	0	2	0	1	0	1	0	0	0	0	5	1	1	1	0
plummeted	3	.2309	.1631	32.1	0	0	0	2	0	0	1	0	0	0	0	1	0	0	0	0	0	0	0	0	0	0	0	2	0
plump	37	.6524	5.0139	47.0	8	6	2	6	6	2	7	0	11	0	2	0	0	0	0	1	2	0	4	0	5	9	2	1	0
plumper	4	.4442	.3918	35.9	1	0	2	0	0	0	0	1	1	0	0	1	0	0	0	0	1	0	0	0	0	0	0	1	0

7J pleads
4P pleasant-looking
6A pleasant-tasting
5Q Pleasantburg
7R pleasantries
6E Pleasanttown
8L pleasingly
7Q Pleasonton
8G pleasurability
4A pleasure-filled
7A pleasure-seekers
8F pleasure-seeking
7P pleasure's
8Q plebiscites
3Q pledging
9H pleistocene
7Q plenitude
9Q plenties
7Q plentifull
7R plenum
4A plesent
7Q plesiosaurs
9Q plexuses
9L pliability
8H Plicocene
6R plink-plink
7Q pliocene
7Q Pliocene
7H Pliohippus
3D plip
3R plippty-plop
7R PLISS
5R pliz
5P plo-y
5P Plomer
4D Plop
3P PLOP
7H plopping
XQ plosives
9R plotless
3P Plotsky's
5J ploughboy's
6A ploughin'
8D ploughman
XB Ploughman
3J plowin'
8Q Plowman
3N plowshare
7R ploy
6G plsnt
5P pluck'd
3P pluckt
7N plucky
7R Plug
7R plugcasting
7J plugger
5N plum-cake
5Q Plumbing
7H Plumier
5N pluming
9Q plummet
3A plump's
6R plumping
5R plumpish

Word Type	F	D	U	SFI	3 Gr 3	4 Gr 4	5 Gr 5	6 Gr 6	7 Gr 7	8 Gr 8	9 Gr 9	X UnGr	A Read	B Eng & Gr	C Comp	D Lit	E Math	F Soc Stud	G Spell	H Sci	J Music	K Art	L Home Ec	M Shop	N Lib F	P Lib NF	Q Lib Ref	R Mag	S Rel
plums	25	.8204	4.1028	46.1	9	2	5	1	2	4	2	0	2	2	0	2	5	4	0	1	1	0	1	0	1	1	2	3	0
plunder	13	.5791	1.5487	41.9	3	0	2	1	7	0	0	0	1	0	0	3	0	0	4	0	1	0	0	0	2	0	1	1	0
plundered	7	.4231	.6756	38.3	1	0	1	0	3	2	0	0	2	0	0	0	0	1	0	0	1	0	0	0	0	3	0	0	0
plundering	4	.4448	.3914	35.9	0	0	0	0	3	0	1	0	1	1	0	0	0	0	0	0	1	0	0	0	0	0	1	0	0
plunge	30	.7800	4.7440	46.8	4	4	2	8	5	5	2	0	8	1	1	1	0	2	1	3	0	0	0	0	5	5	1	2	0
plunged	67	.6385	9.0156	49.5	6	8	10	13	12	8	10	0	27	0	4	10	0	3	0	0	0	0	0	0	12	4	4	3	0
plunger	5	.3667	.3948	36.0	0	0	0	0	3	0	2	0	0	0	0	2	0	0	0	0	0	0	0	0	0	0	2	1	0
plungers	2	.2401	.1133	30.5	0	0	1	0	0	1	0	0	0	0	0	0	0	0	0	0	0	0	0	0	0	1	1	0	0
plunges	7	.4882	.7347	38.7	1	1	0	0	2	0	3	0	1	1	1	1	0	0	0	2	0	0	0	0	0	1	0	0	0
plunging	26	.6423	3.4941	45.4	0	4	5	4	6	1	5	1	9	0	2	4	0	1	0	0	1	0	0	0	5	1	1	2	0
plunked	5	.2110	.3346	35.2	1	0	1	0	2	1	0	0	3	0	0	0	0	0	0	0	0	0	0	0	0	0	0	2	0
plural	517	.2458	28.875	54.6	89	110	91	76	61	26	62	2	10	193	0	0	4	0	307	2	0	0	0	0	0	1	0	0	0
plurality	4	.1540	.1653	32.2	0	0	0	0	0	4	0	0	0	3	0	0	0	1	0	0	0	0	0	0	0	0	0	0	0
pluralize	3	.2060	.1430	31.6	0	0	0	0	1	0	2	0	0	1	0	0	0	0	2	0	0	0	0	0	0	0	0	0	0
plurals	107	.2032	5.0694	47.0	7	27	18	18	14	6	17	0	1	33	0	0	0	0	73	0	0	0	0	0	0	0	0	0	0
plus	185	.7926	29.397	54.7	11	16	20	22	49	33	24	10	12	17	0	3	62	9	12	12	5	0	7	2	1	4	9	30	0
plush	5	.5352	.5723	37.6	0	0	0	2	1	1	0	1	1	0	0	1	0	1	0	0	0	0	0	0	1	0	0	1	0
Pluto	54	.5473	6.3335	48.0	12	18	13	5	3	2	0	1	8	0	0	1	3	2	0	31	0	0	0	1	0	1	7	0	0
plutonic	3	.0000	.0591	27.7	0	0	0	0	0	1	1	1	0	0	0	0	0	0	0	3	0	0	0	0	0	0	0	0	0
plutonium	4	.3286	.3009	34.8	0	0	0	0	1	2	1	0	0	0	0	0	0	1	0	1	0	0	0	0	0	0	0	2	0
ply	8	.4162	.7243	38.6	1	0	0	1	0	4	2	0	1	0	0	0	0	2	0	0	1	0	2	0	0	0	2	0	0
plying	5	.3416	.4181	36.2	0	3	0	0	2	0	0	0	2	0	0	0	0	0	0	0	0	0	0	0	2	0	1	0	0
Plymouth	50	.5973	6.3679	48.0	13	2	11	2	13	8	1	0	16	0	0	0	2	15	0	0	4	0	0	0	7	0	0	6	0
plywood	27	.6103	3.3668	45.3	0	7	0	0	11	2	2	5	0	0	1	0	0	6	0	0	0	1	0	3	0	4	1	11	0
PM	2	.2442	.1134	30.5	0	0	0	0	1	0	1	0	0	1	0	0	0	0	0	0	0	0	0	0	0	0	0	1	0
PMA	4	.2437	.2257	33.5	0	0	0	0	0	0	2	2	0	0	0	0	0	0	0	0	0	0	0	0	0	0	2	2	0
pneumatic	7	.3765	.6520	38.1	0	1	0	2	2	1	1	0	4	0	0	0	0	0	1	0	0	0	0	0	0	0	0	2	0
pneumonia	20	.6336	2.6354	44.2	3	3	2	3	1	5	2	1	4	0	0	2	0	0	1	4	0	0	0	0	2	2	5	0	0
PNP	2	.0000	.0394	26.0	0	0	0	0	0	2	0	0	0	0	0	0	0	0	0	2	0	0	0	0	0	0	0	0	0
Po	42	.4794	4.5459	46.6	4	0	3	34	0	0	1	0	14	1	0	0	0	21	0	0	0	0	0	0	0	2	3	1	0
poached	2	.1733	.1149	30.6	0	0	2	0	0	0	0	0	1	1	0	0	0	0	0	0	0	0	0	0	0	0	0	0	0
poaching	3	.2387	.1708	32.3	0	1	0	0	2	0	0	0	0	0	0	0	0	0	0	0	0	0	0	0	0	2	1	0	0
pocahontas	2	.0000	.0914	29.6	2	0	0	0	0	0	0	0	2	0	0	0	0	0	0	0	0	0	0	0	0	0	0	0	0
Pocahontas	39	.3033	3.0298	44.8	14	21	1	0	1	2	0	0	14	1	0	0	0	3	0	0	0	0	0	0	0	21	0	0	0
Pocahontas'	3	.2063	.1600	32.0	0	2	0	0	0	1	0	0	0	0	0	0	0	1	0	0	0	0	0	0	0	2	0	0	0
pock-marked	3	.2427	.1822	32.6	0	0	1	0	2	0	0	0	0	0	0	0	0	0	0	2	0	0	0	0	0	0	0	1	0
pocket	305	.7181	45.092	56.5	65	60	19	44	42	40	32	3	113	7	1	30	8	7	2	4	1	0	34	3	32	42	3	18	0
Pocket	4	.1597	.1815	32.6	0	0	2	0	0	0	2	0	1	0	0	0	0	0	0	0	0	0	2	0	0	1	0	0	0
pocket-handkerchief	2	.2446	.1125	30.5	0	0	0	0	1	0	1	0	0	1	0	1	0	0	0	0	0	0	0	0	0	0	0	0	0
pocketbook	10	.4827	1.0319	40.1	3	0	1	1	4	1	0	0	2	1	2	0	0	0	1	0	0	0	0	0	2	0	1	1	0
pocketbooks	2	.2285	.1129	30.5	0	1	0	0	0	1	0	0	0	0	0	0	0	1	0	0	0	0	0	0	0	0	1	0	0
pocketed	4	.3011	.2909	34.6	1	0	1	0	1	1	0	0	1	0	0	2	0	0	0	0	0	0	0	0	0	0	1	0	0
Pocketful	3	.0000	.1370	31.4	0	0	0	3	0	0	0	0	3	0	0	0	0	0	0	0	0	0	0	0	0	0	0	0	0
pocketknife	3	.2051	.1687	32.3	0	0	0	1	1	0	0	1	1	0	1	0	0	0	0	0	0	0	0	0	0	0	0	1	0
pockets	99	.7524	15.305	51.8	30	12	15	12	13	9	7	1	47	1	2	8	0	2	0	3	2	0	9	1	10	7	2	5	0
pockmarked	2	.0000	.0243	23.9	0	0	0	0	0	1	1	0	0	0	0	0	0	0	0	0	0	0	0	0	0	0	0	2	0
poco	2	.0000	.0162	22.1	0	0	0	0	2	0	0	0	0	0	0	0	0	0	0	0	2	0	0	0	0	0	0	0	0
pod	7	.5514	.8310	39.2	2	2	1	0	2	0	0	0	2	1	0	0	0	0	1	2	0	0	0	0	1	0	0	0	0
Pod	34	.0000	.3986	36.0	0	0	34	0	0	0	0	0	0	0	0	0	0	0	0	0	0	0	0	0	34	0	0	0	0
pods	17	.5594	2.0812	43.2	3	6	4	1	0	0	3	0	7	0	0	0	0	2	0	4	0	0	0	0	2	0	2	0	0
podzols	2	.0000	.0394	26.0	0	0	0	0	0	0	2	0	0	0	0	0	0	0	0	2	0	0	0	0	0	0	0	0	0
poem	575	.4983	60.348	57.8	71	101	53	47	147	75	75	6	56	243	0	184	0	3	11	0	54	1	0	0	1	6	12	4	0
poems	156	.6126	19.875	53.0	13	23	18	24	23	33	21	1	33	52	0	30	0	4	0	0	18	2	0	0	0	7	10	0	0
Poems	4	.2446	.2243	33.5	0	0	1	0	0	1	2	0	0	0	0	2	0	0	0	0	0	0	0	0	0	0	2	0	0
poet	233	.5925	28.459	54.5	12	31	23	26	63	37	34	7	21	76	1	86	0	5	1	2	13	2	0	0	0	5	17	4	0
Poet	2	.1717	.1142	30.6	0	0	1	0	0	0	1	0	1	0	0	1	0	0	0	0	0	0	0	0	0	0	0	0	0
poet's	19	.3342	1.4046	41.5	0	0	1	0	6	5	7	0	1	1	0	13	0	0	0	0	1	0	0	0	0	0	3	0	0
poetic	44	.6126	5.5355	47.4	0	3	5	8	6	8	9	5	4	12	0	6	0	0	0	1	7	0	0	0	0	3	9	2	0
poetical	2	.1494	.1045	30.2	0	0	0	1	0	0	1	0	1	0	0	0	0	0	0	0	1	0	0	0	0	0	0	0	0
poetically	2	.0000	.0162	22.1	0	0	0	0	2	0	0	0	0	0	0	0	0	0	2	0	0	0	0	0	0	0	0	0	0
poetry	158	.7405	23.587	53.7	6	29	18	27	23	24	31	0	17	43	2	12	1	6	2	2	26	1	1	0	1	9	31	4	0
Poetry	3	.1858	.1432	31.6	0	1	0	0	1	1	0	0	0	2	0	0	0	1	0	0	0	0	0	0	0	0	0	0	0
poets	79	.7230	11.532	50.6	6	6	14	16	13	10	10	4	6	17	0	10	0	6	0	0	6	2	0	0	1	8	17	6	0
Poher	2	.0000	.0243	23.9	0	0	0	0	0	2	0	0	0	0	0	0	0	0	0	0	0	0	0	0	0	0	0	2	0
poi	6	.2419	.4673	36.7	0	5	0	1	0	0	0	0	5	0	0	0	0	0	0	0	0	0	0	0	1	0	0	0	0
point	1904	.8211	312.86	65.0	145	204	196	251	389	332	338	49	162	68	26	57	847	81	16	220	27	24	34	56	38	70	73	105	0
Point	73	.6860	10.477	50.2	6	2	20	18	9	15	2	1	30	1	0	0	0	13	0	5	0	0	0	0	3	6	6	9	0
pointed	397	.8658	68.985	58.4	94	86	47	44	65	33	24	4	171	8	7	22	3	19	4	30	4	12	2	2	28	47	11	27	0
pointedly	5	.3132	.3542	35.5	0	0	1	1	0	3	0	0	0	0	0	0	0	1	0	0	0	0	0	0	1	0	0	3	0
pointer	23	.3729	1.9413	42.9	3	0	8	0	0	7	5	0	3	1	0	0	6	1	0	7	0	0	0	5	0	0	0	0	0
pointers	7	.1689	.3060	34.9	0	0	1	0	3	0	2	1	1	0	0	0	0	0	0	1	0	0	4	0	0	0	1	0	0
Pointers	2	.2160	.1362	31.3	0	0	0	0	0	1	0	1	1	0	0	0	0	0	0	1	0	0	0	0	0	0	0	0	0
pointing	146	.8363	24.604	53.9	27	32	14	18	23	14	15	3	58	11	1	20	0	5	0	7	4	0	1	2	16	11	2	8	0
points	1115	.6637	151.39	61.8	145	122	131	147	243	154	146	27	60	52	4	11	685	41	11	83	3	4	15	35	12	29	33	37	0
Points	4	.3726	.3390	35.3	0	0	1	0	1	1	1	0	0	0	0	0	1	2	0	1	0	0	0	0	0	0	0	0	0
pointy	3	.1277	.1363	31.3	2	0	0	1	0	0	0	0	1	0	0	0	0	0	0	0	0	0	0	0	0	0	0	2	0
poise	14	.3212	1.0197	40.1	0	1	2	0	5	1	5	0	2	0	0	1	0	0	0	0	0	0	5	0	0	4	0	2	0
poised	18	.6787	2.5192	44.0	5	2	1	4	4	0	2	0	5	1	1	2	0	0	0	0	0	0	1	0	4	3	0	1	0
poison	76	.7386	11.483	50.6	12	1	10	8	23	10	8	4	20	2	1	11	0	2	0	21	0	0	0	0	7	2	5	5	0
poisoned	20	.4717	2.1429	43.3	1	1	0	7	8	3	0	0	9	0	0	2	0	0	0	0	0	0	0	0	0	5	4	0	0
poisoning	11	.5179	1.2382	40.9	1	1	1	2	5	0	1	0	3	0	0	0	0	0	0	3	0	0	1	0	0	0	1	3	0
poisonous	77	.6334	10.159	50.1	30	1	7	6	16	5	7	5	13	3	0	1	0	1	0	28	0	0	1	0	1	10	17	2	0
poisons	10	.5535	1.1648	40.7	1	2	0	2	2	0	3	0	1	0	0	0	0	0	0	4	0	0	1	0	1	0	2	1	0
Poitier	2	.0000	.0389	25.9	0	0	2	0	0	0	0	0	0	0	0	0	0	2	0	0	0	0	0	0	0	0	0	0	0
poke	21	.7044	3.0276	44.8	5	6	2	5	2	1	0	0	4	1	0	2	0	2	0	3	4	0	0	0	2	1	0	2	0
pokeberry	2	.0000	.0914	29.6	0	0	0	2	0	0	0	0	2	0	0	0	0	0	0	0	0	0	0	0	0	0	0	0	0
poked	42	.6273	5.6556	47.5	13	13	4	1	5	1	4	1	23	2	0	5	0	0	0	0	0	0	0	0	4	6	1	1	0
poker	9	.4190	.8239	39.2	0	0	0	4	1	3	1	0	1	1	0	1	0	0	0	0	0	0	0	0	0	1	0	5	0
pokes	8	.3872	.7793	38.9	2	2	1	2	0	0	0	1	5	0	0	0	0	0	0	2	0	0	0	0	0	0	1	0	0
poking	16	.6148	2.0843	43.2	1	4	1	3	4	2	1	0	6	0	0	2	0	2	0	0	0	1	0	0	2	0	2	1	0
Polack	2	.0000	.0914	29.6	0	2	0	0	0	0	0	0	2	0	0	0	0	0	0	0	0	0	0	0	0	0	0	0	0
Poland	58	.5423	6.6728	48.2	1	0	8	23	16	5	5	0	4	1	0	0	0	34	0	0	4	0	0	0	0	6	5	4	0
Poland's	7	.0000	.1361	31.3	0	0	0	6	1	0	0	0	0	0	0	0	0	7	0	0	0	0	0	0	0	0	0	0	0
Polanski	2	.0000	.0243	23.9	0	0	0	0	1	0	1	0	0	0	0	0	0	0	0	0	0	0	0	0	0	0	0	2	0

8F Plums
7A Plumtree
4A plumy
3A plunk
8R Plunkett's
7A plunking
4B Plural
5E Plus
7R plusher
4R Plutarch
7A plutocratic
9D Plutonian
3N pluttifikation
7H plyboard
7R PM'S
5E PMO
8B pn
7J pneu-mo-ni-a
8G pneuma
9Q pneumatically
8G pneumograph
8G pneumon
7D pneumothorax
8E PNO
8E PNQ
7L po'boy
5A poacher
4P poachers
5R Pocatello
4N pocket-knife
7N pocket-money
6R pocket-passing
9L pocket's
3J pocketful
9B pocketsful
7D Pockhapockink
5N Pocomoke
7R Pocono
6A Podarces
7J podium
8F Poe
9Q Poem
5P poet-novelist
8D poet-teacher
8Q Poetical
3A Pogo
4P Pogranichaya
8P poignancy
9R poignant
5P Poignees
6A Poinsett
6A point-blank
8F Point's
8K pointillism
6K pointless
3A Poirion
XH poises
3A poising
8H poisonings
5N pokeberries
3J pokers
5N Pokes
3A poky
7R Polacks

Word Type	F	D	U	SFI	3 Gr 3	4 Gr 4	5 Gr 5	6 Gr 6	7 Gr 7	8 Gr 8	9 Gr 9	X UnGr	A Read	B Eng & Gr	C Comp	D Lit	E Math	F Soc Stud	G Spell	H Sci	J Music	K Art	L Home Ec	M Shop	N Lib F	P Lib NF	Q Lib Ref	R Mag	S Rel
polar	85	.6358	11.351	50.6	8	15	5	12	26	4	13	2	20	0	0	1	0	12	2	32	0	0	0	0	2	1	11	4	0
Polar	13	.5024	1.4418	41.6	1	6	0	5	0	0	1	0	4	0	1	0	0	2	0	3	0	0	0	0	3	0	0	0	0
Polaris	10	.3966	.9195	39.6	0	1	0	5	3	0	0	1	2	0	0	0	0	0	0	6	0	0	0	0	0	0	1	1	0
polarity	11	.2772	.6756	38.3	0	0	1	0	2	4	4	0	0	0	0	0	0	0	0	2	0	0	0	4	0	1	4	0	0
polarized	12	.0826	.3589	35.6	11	0	0	0	0	0	0	1	0	0	0	0	0	0	0	1	0	0	0	0	0	11	0	0	0
Polaski	5	.0000	.2284	33.6	5	0	0	0	0	0	0	0	5	0	0	0	0	0	0	0	0	0	0	0	0	0	0	0	0
polder	9	.0000	.1750	32.4	5	1	0	3	0	0	0	0	0	0	0	0	0	9	0	0	0	0	0	0	0	0	0	0	0
polders	6	.0000	.1167	30.7	3	1	0	2	0	0	0	0	0	0	0	0	0	6	0	0	0	0	0	0	0	0	0	0	0
pole	234	.8083	38.237	55.8	85	26	27	19	52	12	9	4	70	4	0	8	7	12	4	52	6	0	0	10	9	29	16	7	0
Pole	181	.6574	24.901	54.0	29	65	9	34	24	10	8	2	44	1	0	1	11	53	1	48	0	0	0	0	6	2	12	2	0
pole-vault	3	.2384	.1717	32.3	0	0	0	2	0	0	1	0	0	1	0	0	2	0	0	0	0	0	0	0	0	0	0	0	0
poled	4	.1814	.2373	33.8	0	0	0	1	2	0	0	1	2	0	0	0	0	0	0	0	0	0	0	0	0	0	0	2	0
poles	264	.8314	43.991	56.4	69	40	33	26	48	20	15	13	39	6	1	7	5	36	0	63	10	2	0	12	5	32	28	18	0
Poles	30	.5825	3.6540	45.6	4	3	4	8	6	3	2	0	1	0	0	1	1	17	1	1	0	0	0	0	1	3	4	0	0
poli	2	.0000	.0162	22.1	0	0	0	0	2	0	0	0	0	0	0	0	0	0	2	0	0	0	0	0	0	0	0	0	0
police	270	.8236	44.864	56.5	49	12	34	26	55	60	31	3	95	11	2	16	2	22	4	8	0	2	1	0	19	19	10	59	0
Police	9	.5293	1.0542	40.2	0	0	3	0	3	1	2	0	4	0	0	2	1	1	0	0	0	0	0	0	0	0	0	1	0
policeman	155	.7468	24.018	53.8	58	12	15	8	49	8	5	0	95	12	2	10	7	0	5	1	0	0	1	0	15	5	0	2	0
Policeman	2	.2446	.1142	30.6	0	1	1	0	0	0	0	0	0	0	0	0	0	0	0	0	0	0	0	0	1	0	0	1	0
policeman's	8	.4629	.7835	38.9	1	1	2	2	1	0	1	0	0	3	0	0	0	0	1	2	0	0	0	0	2	0	0	0	0
policemen	45	.8008	7.2937	48.6	16	4	5	1	7	8	4	0	14	3	1	3	0	9	1	1	2	0	0	0	2	3	0	6	0
policies	46	.5093	4.9548	47.0	1	4	7	2	9	11	11	1	2	0	0	0	0	14	1	0	0	0	0	0	0	4	11	14	0
policy	102	.5871	12.396	50.9	3	2	6	7	17	33	31	3	6	3	0	1	0	21	0	1	0	0	2	0	5	3	37	23	0
Policy	4	.2352	.2332	33.7	0	0	0	0	0	3	1	0	0	0	0	0	0	2	0	0	0	0	0	0	0	0	0	2	0
Polina	4	.0000	.0323	25.1	0	0	4	0	0	0	0	0	0	0	0	0	0	0	0	0	4	0	0	0	0	0	0	0	0
poling	3	.0000	.0434	26.4	1	0	0	0	0	0	2	0	0	0	0	0	0	0	0	0	0	0	0	0	0	3	0	0	0
polio	57	.3311	4.4366	46.5	2	14	1	8	25	5	2	0	0	1	0	0	2	8	0	44	0	0	0	0	1	0	0	1	0
polish	38	.8270	6.3445	48.0	6	13	4	6	1	4	2	2	15	4	0	1	1	2	2	2	1	0	0	1	2	4	0	3	0
Polish	22	.4913	2.2871	43.6	0	1	1	6	5	6	2	1	1	0	4	1	0	8	0	1	1	0	0	0	0	1	2	3	0
polished	80	.8964	14.260	51.5	9	12	8	8	23	10	5	5	20	3	3	5	1	6	2	3	1	1	1	3	5	10	6	10	0
polishes	4	.3356	.2901	34.6	1	0	0	0	2	0	1	0	0	2	0	0	0	0	0	0	0	0	1	0	0	1	0	0	0
polishing	17	.6025	2.1373	43.3	3	5	1	1	5	0	2	0	4	0	0	2	0	0	0	0	0	1	0	2	2	4	2	0	0
Politburo	2	.0000	.0243	23.9	0	0	0	0	0	2	0	0	0	0	0	0	0	0	0	0	0	0	0	0	0	0	0	2	0
polite	64	.8016	10.380	50.2	15	13	6	5	11	9	5	0	21	4	2	7	0	3	2	5	2	0	0	0	6	9	0	3	0
politely	63	.7647	9.8817	49.9	17	12	8	8	9	4	3	2	30	1	2	5	0	3	2	2	0	0	2	0	9	5	0	2	0
politeness	5	.4583	.4827	36.8	0	1	0	0	3	1	0	0	0	0	0	2	0	0	0	0	0	0	0	0	1	1	0	1	0
political	356	.6516	47.760	56.8	13	24	58	11	81	96	65	8	36	7	2	4	0	110	4	2	6	0	0	0	0	41	81	63	0
Political	9	.3626	.7162	38.6	0	2	4	0	2	1	0	0	0	0	0	0	0	2	0	0	0	0	0	0	1	1	5	0	0
politically	12	.5667	1.4298	41.6	0	0	2	0	3	4	3	0	1	0	0	1	0	5	0	0	0	0	0	0	0	2	2	1	0
politicans	2	.2351	.1166	30.7	0	0	0	0	1	1	0	0	0	0	0	0	0	1	0	0	0	0	0	0	0	0	0	1	0
politician	18	.7098	2.6240	44.2	0	0	2	0	10	2	4	0	5	2	0	2	0	2	1	0	0	0	0	0	0	1	2	3	0
politicians	32	.6313	4.2300	46.3	0	2	2	1	8	13	6	0	8	0	2	1	0	10	0	0	1	0	0	0	1	1	1	7	0
politics	67	.6722	9.2219	49.6	1	0	14	4	19	14	14	1	7	4	0	7	1	13	0	0	1	0	0	0	0	8	8	18	0
Polk	9	.2443	.5514	37.4	1	0	0	0	0	7	1	0	0	0	1	0	0	8	0	0	0	0	0	0	0	0	0	0	0
polka	12	.0287	.1985	33.0	3	1	2	4	0	2	0	0	1	0	0	0	0	0	0	0	11	0	0	0	0	0	0	0	0
Polka	6	.0000	.0485	26.9	0	0	0	6	0	0	0	0	0	0	0	0	0	0	0	0	6	0	0	0	0	0	0	0	0
poll	13	.4568	1.2771	41.1	0	1	0	2	5	2	3	0	1	1	0	1	0	2	0	0	0	0	0	0	1	0	0	7	0
Poll	2	.0000	.0243	23.9	0	0	0	0	1	0	1	0	0	0	0	0	0	0	0	0	0	0	0	0	0	0	0	2	0
polled	4	.3498	.3059	34.9	1	0	0	0	2	1	0	0	0	0	0	0	0	0	0	0	0	0	0	0	0	1	2	1	0
pollen	119	.3594	9.8554	49.9	15	25	8	62	6	1	2	0	3	0	0	0	0	0	1	96	3	0	0	0	0	8	6	2	0
pollen-carriers	2	.0000	.0394	26.0	0	0	0	2	0	0	0	0	0	0	0	0	0	0	0	2	0	0	0	0	0	0	0	0	0
Pollie	3	.0000	.0434	26.4	3	0	0	0	0	0	0	0	0	0	0	0	0	0	0	0	0	0	0	0	0	3	0	0	0
pollinate	2	.0000	.0209	23.2	1	0	0	0	0	0	1	0	0	0	0	0	0	0	0	0	0	0	0	0	0	0	2	0	0
pollinated	2	.0000	.0209	23.2	0	2	0	0	0	0	0	0	0	0	0	0	0	0	0	0	0	0	0	0	0	0	2	0	0
Pollito	6	.0000	.2741	34.4	6	0	0	0	0	0	0	0	6	0	0	0	0	0	0	0	0	0	0	0	0	0	0	0	0
polliwog	2	.0000	.0215	23.3	2	0	0	0	0	0	0	0	0	0	0	2	0	0	0	0	0	0	0	0	0	0	0	0	0
Polliwog	4	.0000	.1827	32.6	0	4	0	0	0	0	0	0	4	0	0	0	0	0	0	0	0	0	0	0	0	0	0	0	0
Pollock	3	.1304	.0878	29.4	0	0	1	0	0	0	2	0	0	0	2	0	0	0	0	0	1	0	0	0	0	0	0	0	0
polls	8	.3681	.6330	38.0	0	0	1	0	1	4	2	0	0	0	2	0	1	1	0	0	0	0	0	0	0	0	1	3	0
pollute	6	.3454	.5132	37.1	0	0	1	0	4	0	1	0	2	0	0	0	0	3	0	0	0	0	0	0	0	0	0	1	0
polluted	29	.4021	2.6101	44.2	13	1	8	2	2	2	1	0	0	1	0	0	0	20	0	5	0	0	0	0	0	0	1	2	0
polluting	4	.2287	.2348	33.7	0	0	0	1	1	1	1	0	0	0	0	0	0	0	0	3	0	0	0	0	0	0	0	1	0
pollution	25	.4152	2.2774	43.6	0	1	8	0	8	5	2	1	0	0	0	0	0	7	0	7	0	0	0	0	0	0	1	10	0
Polly	72	.5684	8.8780	49.5	13	14	10	3	27	4	1	0	33	1	0	7	0	0	0	0	11	0	0	0	13	7	0	0	0
Polly-wolly-doodle	4	.0000	.0323	25.1	4	0	0	0	0	0	0	0	0	0	0	0	0	0	0	0	4	0	0	0	0	0	0	0	0
Polly's	4	.2393	.3005	34.8	0	0	0	0	3	1	0	0	3	0	0	1	0	0	0	0	0	0	0	0	0	0	0	0	0
polnena	2	.0000	.0290	24.6	2	0	0	0	0	0	0	0	0	0	0	0	0	0	0	0	0	0	0	0	0	2	0	0	0
polo	2	.1787	.1174	30.7	0	0	0	0	2	0	0	0	1	0	0	0	0	0	0	0	0	0	0	0	1	0	0	0	0
Polo	22	.3774	1.8917	42.8	0	0	3	6	2	10	1	0	1	0	0	1	0	16	0	0	0	0	0	0	0	2	2	0	0
Polo's	2	.0000	.0389	25.9	0	0	0	0	0	2	0	0	0	0	0	0	0	2	0	0	0	0	0	0	0	0	0	0	0
polonium	25	.0000	.4929	36.9	0	0	0	0	0	0	25	0	0	0	0	0	0	0	0	25	0	0	0	0	0	0	0	0	0
Polonius	5	.0000	.0972	29.9	0	0	5	0	0	0	0	0	0	0	0	0	0	5	0	0	0	0	0	0	0	0	0	0	0
Polos	3	.0000	.0434	26.4	0	0	3	0	0	0	0	0	0	0	0	0	0	0	0	0	0	0	0	0	0	3	0	0	0
Polski	3	.0000	.0328	25.2	0	0	0	0	0	3	0	0	0	3	0	0	0	0	0	0	0	0	0	0	0	0	0	0	0
Polybus	3	.0000	.0314	25.0	0	0	0	0	0	3	0	0	0	0	0	0	0	0	0	0	0	0	0	0	0	0	3	0	0
Polydeuces	4	.2445	.3067	34.9	0	0	0	3	1	0	0	0	3	0	0	0	0	0	0	0	0	0	0	0	0	1	0	0	0
polyglot	2	.2351	.1166	30.7	0	0	0	0	1	1	0	0	0	0	0	0	0	1	0	0	0	0	0	0	0	0	0	1	0
polygon	57	.0000	.8532	39.3	0	1	20	6	10	4	16	0	0	0	0	0	57	0	0	0	0	0	0	0	0	0	0	0	0
polygons	33	.0000	.4940	36.9	0	2	7	5	7	5	7	0	0	0	0	0	33	0	0	0	0	0	0	0	0	0	0	0	0
polyhedron	2	.0000	.0394	26.0	0	0	0	0	2	0	0	0	0	0	0	0	0	0	0	2	0	0	0	0	0	0	0	0	0
polymer	2	.0000	.0394	26.0	0	0	0	0	2	0	0	0	0	0	0	0	0	0	0	2	0	0	0	0	0	0	0	0	0
polymerization	2	.2278	.1128	30.5	0	0	0	0	1	0	1	0	0	0	0	0	0	0	0	1	0	0	0	0	0	0	1	0	0
polymers	3	.2445	.1818	32.6	0	0	0	1	2	0	0	0	0	0	0	0	0	0	0	2	0	0	0	0	0	0	1	0	0
Polynesia	13	.0643	.3705	35.7	0	11	1	0	1	0	0	0	2	0	0	0	0	0	0	0	0	0	0	0	11	0	0	0	0
Polynesian	6	.4805	.6608	38.2	0	0	1	0	3	2	0	0	3	0	0	0	0	1	0	0	0	0	0	0	0	1	1	0	0
Polynesians	6	.4518	.5726	37.6	0	0	0	2	1	2	1	0	0	0	1	0	0	1	0	1	1	0	0	0	2	0	0	0	0
polynomial	29	.0000	.4341	36.4	0	0	0	0	5	8	16	0	0	0	0	0	29	0	0	0	0	0	0	0	0	0	0	0	0
polynomials	20	.0000	.2994	34.8	0	0	0	0	0	12	8	0	0	0	0	0	20	0	0	0	0	0	0	0	0	0	0	0	0
polynya	2	.0000	.0914	29.6	0	2	0	0	0	0	0	0	2	0	0	0	0	0	0	0	0	0	0	0	0	0	0	0	0
polyp	7	.0000	.3198	35.0	0	0	0	0	7	0	0	0	7	0	0	0	0	0	0	0	0	0	0	0	0	0	0	0	0
polyphemus	2	.0000	.0290	24.6	2	0	0	0	0	0	0	0	0	0	0	0	0	0	0	0	0	0	0	0	0	2	0	0	0
polyphonic	12	.1151	.3686	35.7	0	0	0	7	2	3	0	0	0	0	0	0	0	0	0	0	10	0	0	0	0	2	0	0	0
polyps	8	.2989	.6337	38.0	0	0	0	3	5	0	0	0	4	0	0	0	0	1	0	0	0	0	0	0	0	0	3	0	0

6G polar**
9H polarization
8R polarize
7R polarizes
9H Polaroid
3A Polaskis
3A pole-and-safety-pin
6J pole-holders
8R pole-vaulting
6H Pole's
6A polestar
9F poleward
8A POLICE
8F policing
9R policy-committee
8C policy-holders
8R Polident
6P Polido
5J Polina's
7H polio-causing
8A polio-crippled
7H polio-fighting
7H poliomyelitis
8E Polish-American
7R Polish-Americans
3A polished-looking
9D Polites
7R politic
5P political-minded
6F political-physical
7A politician's
8R politicking
9Q Politicks
8Q Politics
8Q Politika
8Q Politische
8A Polizei
3E POLK
8F Polk's
4G polka-dotted
9J polkas
7K Pollaiuolo
5R Pollak
4F Pollard
6H pollen-carrier
8H pollen-carrying
7Q pollination
7Q pollinators
7R polling
4A polliwogs
8R pollsters
XR pollutants
3F pollutes
8G Pollyanna
4B pollywog
6H pollywogs
8J Polonaise
9J Polovtzian
7F poly-
7L poly-unsaturated
8G polyester
XH polyestrous
9Q Polyglotta
6E polygonal
8J polyharmony
9D Polyktor
9M polymetals
4N Polynesia's
8Q Polynices
9J polyphonically
6J polyphony

Word Type	F	D	U	SFI	3 Gr 3	4 Gr 4	5 Gr 5	6 Gr 6	7 Gr 7	8 Gr 8	9 Gr 9	X UnGr	A Read	B Eng & Gr	C Comp	D Lit	E Math	F Soc Stud	G Spell	H Sci	J Music	K Art	L Home Ec	M Shop	N Lib F	P Lib NF	Q Lib Ref	R Mag	S Rel
Polytechnic	2	.0000	.0209	23.2	0	0	1	0	0	0	1	0	0	0	0	0	0	0	0	0	0	0	0	0	0	0	2	0	0
polyurethane	2	.1812	.0838	29.2	0	0	0	0	1	0	1	0	0	0	0	0	0	0	0	0	0	0	1	0	0	0	0	1	0
pomegranate	2	.2440	.1132	30.5	0	0	0	1	0	0	1	0	0	0	0	1	0	0	0	0	0	0	0	0	0	0	0	1	0
Pomerania	5	.2226	.2657	34.2	0	0	2	0	0	0	3	0	0	0	0	0	0	0	0	0	0	0	0	0	0	2	3	0	0
Pomeranian	2	.2418	.1091	30.4	0	0	0	0	0	2	0	0	0	0	0	0	0	0	1	0	0	0	0	0	0	0	1	0	0
pommel	4	.1919	.1864	32.7	0	0	0	1	2	1	0	0	0	0	0	3	0	0	0	0	0	0	0	0	1	0	0	0	0
Pomona	4	.0000	.0486	26.9	0	0	0	0	3	1	0	0	0	0	0	0	0	0	0	0	0	0	0	0	0	0	0	4	0
pomp	13	.5683	1.5471	41.9	0	0	0	3	2	5	2	1	2	0	0	1	0	0	0	0	2	0	0	0	0	3	1	4	0
Pompeii	4	.2386	.2998	34.8	1	0	0	3	0	0	0	0	3	0	0	0	0	0	0	0	0	0	0	0	0	0	1	0	0
Pompey	2	.2408	.1204	30.8	0	0	1	0	1	0	0	0	0	0	0	0	0	1	0	0	0	0	0	0	0	1	0	0	0
Pompidou	14	.0000	.1701	32.3	0	0	0	0	0	11	3	0	0	0	0	0	0	0	0	0	0	0	0	0	0	0	0	14	0
Pompilius	2	.0000	.0290	24.6	0	2	0	0	0	0	0	0	0	0	0	0	0	0	0	0	0	0	0	0	0	2	0	0	0
pompous	5	.4459	.4746	36.8	0	0	1	0	2	1	1	0	0	0	0	2	0	1	0	0	0	0	0	0	0	1	1	0	0
pon	3	.0000	.0243	23.9	0	0	0	0	3	0	0	0	0	0	0	0	0	0	3	0	0	0	0	0	0	0	0	0	0
Ponca	7	.0000	.3198	35.0	0	7	0	0	0	0	0	0	7	0	0	0	0	0	0	0	0	0	0	0	0	0	0	0	0
Ponce	16	.3235	1.2019	40.8	0	0	14	1	1	0	0	0	0	0	0	0	0	12	1	0	0	0	0	0	0	0	3	0	0
poncho	2	.1814	.1187	30.7	0	0	0	2	0	0	0	0	1	0	0	0	0	0	0	0	0	0	0	0	0	0	0	1	0
ponchos	4	.2348	.2372	33.8	1	2	0	1	0	0	0	0	0	0	0	0	0	3	0	0	0	0	0	0	0	0	1	0	0
pond	267	.7584	41.252	56.2	119	39	20	25	36	20	5	3	67	9	14	14	0	9	8	95	11	0	0	2	3	20	6	9	0
Pond	45	.3893	4.0395	46.1	30	8	4	1	1	1	0	0	11	0	1	0	2	0	0	0	0	0	0	0	0	29	1	1	0
Pond's	4	.1112	.1666	32.2	0	4	0	0	0	0	0	0	1	0	0	0	0	0	0	0	0	0	0	0	0	3	0	0	0
ponder	3	.3390	.2450	33.9	0	1	0	0	0	0	1	1	1	0	0	0	0	0	0	0	0	0	0	0	0	0	1	1	0
pondered	15	.5627	1.8168	42.6	0	0	1	2	8	2	1	1	5	0	0	4	1	0	0	2	0	0	0	0	1	0	0	2	0
pondering	3	.3781	.2548	34.1	0	0	0	0	2	1	0	0	0	0	0	0	0	1	0	1	0	0	0	0	0	0	0	1	0
ponderosa	4	.3519	.3117	34.9	0	1	0	0	0	0	1	2	0	0	0	0	0	1	0	0	0	0	0	0	0	0	1	2	0
ponderous	6	.4406	.5957	37.8	1	0	0	0	3	1	0	1	2	0	0	0	0	0	0	0	0	0	0	0	1	0	2	1	0
pondo	4	.0000	.0325	25.1	0	4	0	0	0	0	0	0	0	0	0	0	0	0	4	0	0	0	0	0	0	0	0	0	0
ponds	70	.6872	9.9451	50.0	19	5	6	20	12	2	2	4	14	1	1	1	0	9	0	26	0	0	0	0	0	5	5	8	0
pone	2	.1733	.1149	30.6	0	0	0	2	0	0	0	0	1	1	0	0	0	0	0	0	0	0	0	0	0	0	0	0	0
ponere	2	.0000	.0219	23.4	0	0	0	1	0	1	0	0	0	2	0	0	0	0	0	0	0	0	0	0	0	0	0	0	0
PONG	3	.0000	.1370	31.4	3	0	0	0	0	0	0	0	3	0	0	0	0	0	0	0	0	0	0	0	0	0	0	0	0
pongee	2	.0000	.0234	23.7	0	0	0	2	0	0	0	0	0	0	0	0	0	0	0	0	0	0	0	0	2	0	0	0	0
ponies	62	.7402	9.3830	49.7	18	15	17	5	6	1	0	0	19	2	1	1	2	3	2	0	1	0	0	0	17	10	2	2	0
Pons	2	.0000	.0290	24.6	0	2	0	0	0	0	0	0	0	0	0	0	0	0	0	0	0	0	0	0	0	2	0	0	0
Pontiac	38	.1830	1.8052	42.6	0	32	0	2	3	0	1	0	0	0	0	0	0	0	0	0	0	0	0	0	0	33	1	4	0
Pontiac's	3	.2332	.1690	32.3	0	2	0	0	1	0	0	0	0	0	0	0	0	0	0	0	0	0	0	0	0	2	0	1	0
pontoon	3	.2357	.2199	33.4	1	1	0	1	0	0	0	0	2	0	0	0	0	0	0	0	0	0	0	0	0	1	0	0	0
pontoons	6	.3396	.5199	37.2	0	1	0	2	2	0	0	1	3	0	0	0	0	0	0	1	0	0	0	0	0	0	0	2	0
pony	210	.7565	32.500	55.1	47	64	15	31	22	22	9	0	83	11	8	22	5	4	7	0	2	1	0	0	35	29	3	0	0
Pony	58	.5646	7.0484	48.5	10	34	6	0	2	6	0	0	21	5	1	16	0	1	0	0	0	0	0	0	1	13	0	0	0
pony's	20	.5447	2.4143	43.8	1	10	2	3	2	1	1	0	11	0	1	3	0	0	0	0	0	0	0	0	3	2	0	0	0
poodle	16	.4329	1.6798	42.3	4	3	0	6	2	1	0	0	11	3	0	0	0	0	0	0	0	0	0	0	0	1	0	1	0
poodles	16	.3442	1.4991	41.8	1	6	2	7	0	0	0	0	13	0	0	0	2	0	0	0	0	0	0	0	1	0	0	0	0
pooh	4	.0974	.1495	31.7	3	1	0	0	0	0	0	0	1	0	0	0	0	0	0	0	0	0	0	0	3	0	0	0	0
Pooh	44	.2889	3.8223	45.8	33	10	0	0	1	0	0	0	40	0	0	1	0	0	3	0	0	0	0	0	0	0	0	0	0
Pooh-Bah	9	.0000	.0728	28.6	0	0	0	0	0	9	0	0	0	0	0	0	0	0	0	0	9	0	0	0	0	0	0	0	0
pool	197	.8653	34.114	55.3	32	23	21	36	33	25	20	7	65	15	5	24	21	4	6	10	9	1	0	0	6	10	3	18	0
Pool	17	.2248	1.3010	41.1	11	1	0	3	0	0	0	2	15	0	0	0	0	0	0	0	0	0	0	0	0	0	0	2	0
pooling	2	.2337	.1157	30.6	0	0	0	0	1	1	0	0	0	0	0	0	0	1	0	0	0	0	0	0	1	0	0	0	0
pools	57	.7475	8.7039	49.4	10	4	8	15	15	4	1	0	17	1	1	9	0	4	0	5	0	0	0	0	4	4	2	10	0
Pooneno	2	.0000	.0290	24.6	0	2	0	0	0	0	0	0	0	0	0	0	0	0	0	0	0	0	0	0	0	2	0	0	0
poop	3	.3669	.2412	33.8	0	0	2	0	0	1	0	0	0	0	0	0	0	1	0	0	1	0	0	0	1	0	0	0	0
poor	851	.8988	152.46	61.8	163	120	88	133	163	113	58	13	318	34	11	83	1	100	16	38	32	4	17	2	70	51	25	46	3
Poor	9	.5148	1.0267	40.1	0	4	1	1	0	2	1	0	4	0	0	1	0	1	0	0	2	0	0	0	0	0	1	0	0
Poore	3	.0000	.0352	25.5	0	0	0	0	0	0	0	3	0	0	0	0	0	0	0	0	0	0	0	0	3	0	0	0	0
poorer	21	.6568	2.8809	44.6	7	3	1	3	1	3	1	2	7	0	0	2	0	2	0	1	1	0	0	0	1	0	5	2	0
poorest	12	.6228	1.5557	41.9	2	0	4	1	2	2	1	0	2	0	1	0	1	1	0	2	1	0	0	0	0	3	0	1	0
poorly	25	.5805	3.0356	44.8	3	6	2	2	3	4	4	1	4	1	0	0	0	4	0	0	0	0	3	0	0	4	6	3	0
Poozy	6	.0000	.0729	28.6	0	6	0	0	0	0	0	0	0	0	0	0	0	0	0	0	0	0	0	0	0	0	0	6	0
pop	118	.8498	20.022	53.0	27	22	22	6	14	19	6	2	18	2	1	14	9	5	2	12	4	0	1	0	13	4	11	22	0
Pop	50	.6203	6.5678	48.2	12	10	5	5	3	7	8	0	20	0	0	11	0	0	0	0	2	0	0	0	3	3	8	3	0
Pop's	3	.2279	.2143	33.3	1	0	2	0	0	0	0	0	2	0	0	0	0	0	0	0	0	0	0	0	0	0	0	1	0
popcorn	44	.7956	7.0698	48.5	12	17	3	1	4	1	4	2	12	6	0	5	7	1	4	1	1	0	1	0	1	2	0	3	0
pope	18	.3036	1.2621	41.0	2	0	4	1	1	2	8	0	0	0	0	0	0	9	0	0	0	0	0	0	1	0	8	0	0
Pope	27	.5873	3.2639	45.1	1	0	4	0	7	5	9	1	0	1	0	0	0	4	1	1	0	0	0	0	1	3	5	11	0
Pope's	6	.4567	.5841	37.7	2	0	0	0	2	2	0	0	0	0	0	0	0	1	0	0	0	0	0	0	2	2	0	1	0
popes	6	.3492	.4786	36.8	1	0	1	0	0	0	4	0	0	0	0	0	0	4	0	0	0	0	0	0	0	1	1	0	0
popgun	3	.1650	.1684	32.3	1	0	2	0	0	0	0	0	1	0	0	0	0	0	0	2	0	0	0	0	0	0	0	0	0
popinjay	2	.0000	.0215	23.3	0	0	0	0	2	0	0	0	0	0	0	2	0	0	0	0	0	0	0	0	0	0	0	0	0
poplar	17	.5070	1.8699	42.7	4	3	1	1	0	3	4	1	5	1	0	2	2	1	0	0	0	0	0	3	0	2	1	0	0
Poplar	3	.0000	.0434	26.4	0	3	0	0	0	0	0	0	0	0	0	0	0	0	0	0	0	0	0	0	0	3	0	0	0
poplars	6	.4380	.5945	37.7	0	0	1	2	1	1	1	0	2	0	0	2	0	0	0	0	0	0	0	0	1	1	0	0	0
Popocatepetl	3	.3732	.2514	34.0	0	0	0	1	0	0	2	0	0	1	0	0	0	1	0	1	0	0	0	0	0	0	0	0	0
POPOV	5	.0000	.0537	27.3	0	0	0	0	0	0	5	0	0	0	0	5	0	0	0	0	0	0	0	0	0	0	0	0	0
popped	49	.6984	7.0915	48.5	14	11	5	3	9	2	5	0	19	5	0	4	0	0	0	0	0	0	1	0	8	4	1	7	0
Popper	95	.1434	4.7070	46.7	14	81	0	0	0	0	0	0	37	0	0	0	0	0	0	0	0	0	0	0	58	0	0	0	0
Popper's	9	.0880	.3138	35.0	1	8	0	0	0	0	0	0	2	0	0	0	0	0	0	0	0	0	0	0	7	0	0	0	0
Poppers	6	.0000	.0703	28.5	0	6	0	0	0	0	0	0	0	0	0	0	0	0	0	0	0	0	0	0	6	0	0	0	0
poppies	8	.2839	.6516	38.1	5	1	0	0	0	2	0	0	6	0	0	1	0	0	0	0	0	1	0	0	0	0	0	0	0
popping	25	.6569	3.4351	45.4	7	3	6	2	5	1	1	0	9	4	0	1	0	0	0	1	0	0	0	0	4	1	1	4	0
Poppins	38	.1019	1.1589	40.6	0	3	35	0	0	0	0	0	0	3	0	0	0	0	0	0	0	0	0	0	35	0	0	0	0
Poppins's	2	.0000	.0234	23.7	0	0	2	0	0	0	0	0	0	0	0	0	0	0	0	0	0	0	0	0	2	0	0	0	0
poppy	15	.6215	1.9990	43.0	8	0	0	2	1	1	0	3	7	0	0	1	0	0	0	3	0	0	0	0	0	2	1	1	0
Poppy	2	.0000	.0234	23.7	0	0	0	0	2	0	0	0	0	0	0	0	0	0	0	0	0	0	0	0	2	0	0	0	0
poppycock	2	.0000	.0914	29.6	0	0	0	0	2	0	0	0	2	0	0	0	0	0	0	0	0	0	0	0	0	0	0	0	0
pops	10	.5031	1.0804	40.3	4	1	0	0	2	1	1	1	1	0	0	2	0	0	0	4	0	0	0	0	0	1	0	2	0
Pops	4	.0000	.1827	32.6	0	2	0	0	2	0	0	0	4	0	0	0	0	0	0	0	0	0	0	0	0	0	0	0	0
popsicles	6	.0000	.0898	29.5	6	0	0	0	0	0	0	0	0	0	0	0	6	0	0	0	0	0	0	0	0	0	0	0	0
Popsipetels	4	.0000	.0469	26.7	0	4	0	0	0	0	0	0	0	0	0	0	0	0	0	0	0	0	0	0	4	0	0	0	0
populace	3	.2143	.1568	32.0	0	0	0	1	0	0	2	0	0	0	0	0	0	0	0	0	0	0	0	0	0	1	0	2	0
popular	393	.7166	56.888	57.6	11	28	67	62	79	89	43	14	35	24	2	7	2	49	3	7	148	3	13	6	2	20	48	24	0
Popular	3	.1937	.1495	31.7	0	1	0	0	0	0	1	1	0	0	0	0	0	1	0	0	0	0	0	0	0	0	0	2	0
popularity	37	.5930	4.5364	46.6	0	2	1	8	6	11	8	1	4	0	0	2	1	5	0	0	13	0	0	1	0	3	7	1	0

7F polytheism
9J polytonality
4R polyunsaturated
7D pomander
4G pome
7F pomegranates
6R pomes
4N Pomfret
9J Pomilui
8N pompadour
9L pompadours
XQ Pompeiian
4P pompons
8A pomposity
8D pompously
7Q pond's
XR ponderosas
7Q ponderosity
7Q ponders
6A Ponds
7H ponente
6E pong
8Q Ponkapog
4P Pons'
5P pontiff
3P Pontius
6R pontoon-type
3C Pontoosuc
6A Pontus
7N pony-carts
4A pony-face
8A ponytail
3J poo-ee-lee
6J Poo-poo
6A poochie-pies
4A poodle-sitting
7A POOF
7G poofreader
8R pooh-bah
3P pooh-poohed
4A Pooh's
3A pool's
4P Poole
7F pooled
8B poolroom
7A Pools
6G poolside
4G poom
7R pooped
6P POOR
5N poor-box
9L poor-boy
5A poor-dog
8D poore
7N pooty
7A pop-out
3A pop-up
8M pop-up-type
XB Popes
6R Popescu
8K Popeye
5H popguns
8F popinjays
6N Popish
7L poplin
7A Poppa
3A popper
4A poppers
8Q Popple
6H poppy-seed
9Q popularization
8J popularize

Word Type	F	D	U	SFI	3 Gr 3	4 Gr 4	5 Gr 5	6 Gr 6	7 Gr 7	8 Gr 8	9 Gr 9	X UnGr	A Read	B Eng & Gr	C Comp	D Lit	E Math	F Soc Stud	G Spell	H Sci	J Music	K Art	L Home Ec	M Shop	N Lib F	P Lib NF	Q Lib Ref	R Mag	S Rel
popularized	4	.3334	.2895	34.6	0	0	1	2	0	0	1	0	0	0	0	0	0	0	0	0	2	0	0	0	0	1	1	0	0
popularly	6	.4247	.5835	37.7	2	0	1	0	2	1	0	0	2	0	0	0	0	1	0	0	0	0	0	0	0	0	2	1	0
populate	5	.4365	.4591	36.6	0	0	1	2	1	0	0	1	0	0	0	1	0	0	2	0	0	0	0	0	0	1	0	1	0
populated	54	.5174	5.9051	47.7	1	2	13	4	17	5	11	1	0	1	0	0	3	27	0	2	0	0	0	0	0	3	14	4	0
population	449	.6599	60.805	57.8	19	60	66	69	112	54	56	13	18	5	1	5	47	187	2	23	2	0	1	0	1	21	91	45	0
populations	45	.6304	5.8520	47.7	1	5	6	1	19	5	3	5	2	0	1	0	2	11	0	10	0	0	0	0	0	2	12	5	0
Populist	5	.1285	.1797	32.5	0	0	0	0	4	0	1	0	0	0	0	0	0	1	0	0	0	0	0	0	0	0	4	0	0
populous	12	.5995	1.4995	41.8	1	0	1	1	4	4	0	1	2	0	0	1	0	0	0	0	0	0	0	0	2	3	2	2	0
porcelain	21	.4264	1.9190	42.8	3	2	2	3	10	1	0	0	0	0	0	0	0	2	0	0	0	0	0	1	0	12	6	0	0
porch	168	.8045	27.375	54.4	31	39	18	11	31	18	14	6	64	8	2	27	1	7	2	4	0	2	1	0	24	8	1	17	0
porches	9	.5801	1.0931	40.4	1	1	3	1	2	0	1	0	1	0	0	2	0	3	0	0	1	0	0	0	1	1	0	0	0
porcupine	27	.6742	3.8383	45.8	11	2	1	3	3	3	1	3	15	4	1	1	0	0	0	0	0	1	0	0	1	0	2	2	0
porcupines	7	.5124	.7817	38.9	2	1	0	1	2	0	1	0	2	1	0	0	0	0	0	1	0	0	0	0	0	1	2	0	0
pore	13	.5150	1.4093	41.5	0	4	2	0	4	0	3	0	1	0	0	2	0	0	1	2	1	0	0	0	6	0	0	0	0
pored	3	.3429	.2528	34.0	0	0	0	2	1	0	0	0	1	0	0	0	0	0	0	1	0	0	0	0	1	0	0	0	0
pores	17	.5446	1.9321	42.9	0	4	2	0	6	0	3	2	0	0	0	2	0	0	0	8	0	0	0	1	0	0	4	2	0
Porgy	4	.0000	.0323	25.1	0	0	0	0	3	1	0	0	0	0	0	0	0	0	0	0	4	0	0	0	0	0	0	0	0
poring	3	.2279	.2143	33.3	0	0	0	2	1	0	0	0	2	0	0	0	0	0	0	0	0	0	0	0	0	0	0	1	0
pork	74	.4192	6.6708	48.2	6	7	6	7	8	1	26	13	7	4	0	0	1	7	1	3	0	0	25	0	4	6	1	15	0
Pork	8	.2011	.3931	35.9	0	0	2	0	0	0	0	6	0	0	0	0	0	0	0	0	0	0	0	0	2	0	0	6	0
Porkey	8	.0000	.0938	29.7	8	0	0	0	0	0	0	0	0	0	0	0	0	0	0	0	0	0	0	0	8	0	0	0	0
Porklet	2	.0000	.0243	23.9	0	0	0	0	0	0	0	2	0	0	0	0	0	0	0	0	0	0	0	0	0	0	0	2	0
Porky	2	.0000	.0215	23.3	0	2	0	0	0	0	0	0	0	0	0	2	0	0	0	0	0	0	0	0	0	0	0	0	0
porous	27	.4231	2.4791	43.9	1	1	11	3	5	1	5	0	0	0	0	0	0	0	0	16	0	0	0	4	0	1	4	2	0
porphyries	3	.2383	.1815	32.6	0	0	0	1	0	0	1	1	0	0	0	0	0	0	0	2	0	0	0	0	0	1	0	0	0
porphyry	3	.0000	.0434	26.4	0	0	0	3	0	0	0	0	0	0	0	0	0	0	0	0	0	0	0	0	0	3	0	0	0
porpoise	15	.5759	1.8891	42.8	9	1	1	2	2	0	0	0	8	0	0	0	1	0	2	1	0	0	0	0	0	1	2	0	0
Porpoise	5	.0000	.2284	33.6	5	0	0	0	0	0	0	0	5	0	0	0	0	0	0	0	0	0	0	0	0	0	0	0	0
porpoises	11	.3533	.8680	39.4	3	5	0	1	0	0	1	1	0	0	0	0	0	0	0	3	0	0	0	0	5	3	0	0	0
porridge	21	.5839	2.6180	44.2	1	8	0	9	1	1	1	0	6	0	0	1	0	5	1	0	0	0	0	0	2	6	0	0	0
porringer	7	.0000	.3198	35.0	1	6	0	0	0	0	0	0	7	0	0	0	0	0	0	0	0	0	0	0	0	0	0	0	0
port	193	.6569	26.310	54.2	26	28	32	36	36	21	11	3	33	3	0	3	0	88	1	3	6	0	0	0	7	15	26	8	0
Port	19	.5039	2.0532	43.1	0	0	3	4	4	7	1	0	3	0	0	3	0	4	0	0	0	0	0	0	0	0	6	3	0
PortHuron	2	.0000	.0389	25.9	0	2	0	0	0	0	0	0	0	0	0	0	0	2	0	0	0	0	0	0	0	0	0	0	0
Port-au-Prince	2	.2446	.1122	30.5	0	0	0	0	0	1	1	0	0	0	0	1	0	0	0	0	0	0	0	0	0	0	1	0	0
portable	19	.6056	2.3603	43.7	1	2	0	1	5	4	4	2	2	0	0	0	0	0	0	2	3	0	2	3	1	1	3	2	0
portage	7	.3698	.6466	38.1	0	0	3	3	1	0	0	0	4	0	0	0	0	0	0	0	0	0	0	0	1	0	0	2	0
Portage	2	.2440	.1132	30.5	0	0	1	1	0	0	0	0	0	0	0	1	0	0	0	0	0	0	0	0	0	0	0	1	0
portages	3	.2279	.2143	33.3	0	0	0	1	2	0	0	0	2	0	0	0	0	0	0	0	0	0	0	0	0	0	0	1	0
portal	5	.4281	.4726	36.7	0	1	2	0	1	1	0	0	1	1	0	1	0	0	0	0	0	0	0	0	2	0	0	0	0
Portal	7	.0000	.3198	35.0	7	0	0	0	0	0	0	0	7	0	0	0	0	0	0	0	0	0	0	0	0	0	0	0	0
portals	5	.2443	.3861	35.9	3	0	1	0	0	0	0	1	4	0	0	0	0	0	0	0	0	0	0	0	0	0	1	0	0
Porte	2	.0000	.0914	29.6	2	0	0	0	0	0	0	0	2	0	0	0	0	0	0	0	0	0	0	0	0	0	0	0	0
portenos	2	.0000	.0209	23.2	2	0	0	0	0	0	0	0	0	0	0	0	0	0	0	0	0	0	0	0	0	0	2	0	0
portents	2	.2446	.1257	31.0	0	0	0	0	1	1	0	0	0	0	0	0	0	1	0	1	0	0	0	0	0	0	0	0	0
porter	13	.2731	.8826	39.5	1	2	0	0	9	0	1	0	3	8	0	0	0	1	0	0	0	0	0	0	0	0	1	0	0
Porter	30	.5684	3.7212	45.7	16	7	0	1	4	2	0	0	15	0	0	0	0	0	0	0	2	0	0	0	5	1	1	6	0
Porter's	3	.3269	.2368	33.7	1	1	0	0	0	1	0	0	1	0	0	0	0	0	0	0	0	0	0	0	1	1	0	0	0
porters	3	.2357	.2199	33.4	1	0	0	0	0	2	0	0	2	0	0	0	0	0	1	0	0	0	0	0	0	0	0	0	0
portfolio	3	.2143	.1568	32.0	0	0	0	0	1	1	0	1	0	0	0	0	0	0	0	0	0	0	0	0	0	1	0	2	0
porthole	12	.4799	1.2923	41.1	1	2	0	2	0	2	5	0	5	1	0	4	0	0	0	0	0	0	0	0	0	1	0	1	0
portholes	3	.3399	.2456	33.9	0	1	0	0	1	0	1	0	1	0	0	1	0	0	0	0	0	0	0	0	0	0	0	1	0
Portia	22	.0000	.2361	33.7	0	0	0	0	0	0	22	0	0	0	0	22	0	0	0	0	0	0	0	0	0	0	0	0	0
portion	121	.7916	19.191	52.8	4	3	4	13	34	30	25	8	9	1	5	3	14	9	0	21	7	0	9	9	6	5	18	5	0
portions	53	.8366	8.8476	49.5	0	4	3	6	15	10	11	4	3	1	0	2	4	7	0	9	1	1	1	3	1	7	7	6	0
Portland	7	.4589	.7241	38.6	0	1	0	1	2	1	2	0	2	1	0	1	0	3	0	0	0	0	0	0	0	0	0	0	0
portly	4	.3394	.3015	34.8	0	0	0	0	1	1	2	0	0	0	0	2	0	1	0	0	0	0	0	0	1	0	0	0	0
Porto	4	.3519	.3117	34.9	0	0	1	1	0	0	2	0	0	0	0	0	0	1	0	0	0	0	0	0	0	0	1	2	0
Porto-Vecchio	2	.0000	.0215	23.3	0	0	0	0	0	2	0	0	0	0	0	2	0	0	0	0	0	0	0	0	0	0	0	0	0
Portola	11	.2443	.6677	38.2	0	6	0	4	0	1	0	0	0	0	0	0	0	7	0	0	0	0	0	0	0	0	0	4	0
portrait	39	.4068	3.4803	45.4	5	5	6	4	9	6	1	3	7	2	0	1	0	1	1	0	0	9	0	0	0	4	8	6	0
Portrait	3	.0994	.0714	28.5	0	0	0	0	2	0	1	0	0	0	0	0	0	0	0	0	0	2	0	0	0	0	1	0	0
portraits	13	.2984	.8706	39.4	3	2	2	0	3	1	1	1	1	1	0	0	0	1	0	0	0	4	0	0	0	2	4	0	0
portray	14	.4783	1.3978	41.5	0	1	0	4	3	3	1	2	1	2	0	0	0	0	0	0	5	2	0	0	0	0	2	2	0
portrayal	3	.3824	.2446	33.9	0	1	0	0	1	0	1	0	0	0	0	1	0	0	0	0	1	0	0	0	0	0	0	1	0
portrayed	7	.4731	.7090	38.5	1	2	1	0	1	1	1	0	1	0	0	1	0	0	0	0	1	0	0	0	0	1	3	0	0
portraying	2	.2411	.1091	30.4	0	0	0	0	1	1	0	0	0	0	0	1	0	0	0	0	1	0	0	0	0	0	0	0	0
portrays	3	.3826	.2445	33.9	0	0	1	0	0	0	1	1	0	0	0	0	0	0	0	0	1	0	0	0	0	0	1	1	0
ports	79	.5609	9.2872	49.7	8	3	7	21	18	14	8	0	3	0	0	2	1	42	0	0	2	0	0	2	0	6	20	1	0
Portsmouth	4	.3287	.2952	34.7	0	0	0	0	2	2	0	0	0	0	0	0	0	1	0	0	0	0	0	0	0	1	2	0	0
Portugal	68	.3692	5.7186	47.6	2	4	20	28	5	7	2	0	3	0	0	0	0	47	0	0	1	0	0	0	0	1	14	2	0
Portugal's	4	.2285	.2258	33.5	0	0	3	1	0	0	0	0	0	0	0	0	0	2	0	0	0	0	0	0	0	0	2	0	0
Portuguese	62	.6083	7.8469	48.9	3	1	14	18	15	8	3	0	4	1	1	0	0	37	3	0	4	0	0	0	1	3	8	0	0
pos	4	.0000	.0325	25.1	0	1	0	0	3	0	0	0	0	0	0	0	0	0	4	0	0	0	0	0	0	0	0	0	0
pose	17	.2785	1.0175	40.1	1	1	1	1	4	2	6	1	0	1	0	1	0	1	0	0	0	8	1	0	0	1	1	3	0
posed	14	.6291	1.7954	42.5	1	1	0	1	1	7	3	0	0	2	0	1	1	2	0	1	0	1	0	0	0	0	4	2	0
Poseidon	9	.0000	.0966	29.8	0	0	0	0	0	7	2	0	0	0	0	9	0	0	0	0	0	0	0	0	0	0	0	0	0
Poseidon's	5	.0000	.2284	33.6	0	0	0	5	0	0	0	0	5	0	0	0	0	0	0	0	0	0	0	0	0	0	0	0	0
poses	9	.3291	.6501	38.1	0	0	0	3	5	1	0	0	1	0	0	0	0	0	0	0	0	3	1	0	0	0	1	3	0
Posey	3	.2279	.2143	33.3	2	0	0	0	1	0	0	0	2	0	0	0	0	0	0	0	0	0	0	0	0	0	0	1	0
posing	9	.4246	.8013	39.0	1	1	0	0	4	2	1	0	0	1	0	1	0	0	0	0	0	2	0	0	0	2	2	1	0
position	540	.8954	96.016	59.8	21	48	61	76	129	87	90	28	78	43	10	13	39	33	8	97	17	4	15	32	15	38	48	50	0
positional	2	.2391	.1133	30.5	0	0	0	0	1	0	1	0	0	0	0	0	1	0	0	0	0	0	0	0	0	0	1	0	0
positioned	7	.4255	.6430	38.1	0	0	1	1	5	0	0	0	0	0	0	0	0	0	0	3	0	0	0	1	0	1	0	2	0
positions	155	.8585	26.515	54.2	6	14	15	26	40	12	25	17	11	24	0	3	13	14	4	41	2	2	1	2	2	8	19	9	0
positive	204	.5775	24.474	53.9	2	2	28	6	49	49	65	3	4	4	5	1	131	0	4	35	1	0	0	4	2	2	4	7	0
positively	35	.7231	5.1408	47.1	0	1	9	2	13	6	3	1	3	2	0	6	0	1	0	14	0	0	1	1	1	0	3	3	0
positively-charged	9	.0000	.1774	32.5	0	0	7	2	0	0	0	0	0	0	0	0	0	0	0	9	0	0	0	0	0	0	0	0	0
positives	2	.0000	.0209	23.2	0	0	0	0	0	0	2	0	0	0	0	0	0	0	0	0	0	0	0	0	0	0	2	0	0
posse	5	.3161	.3505	35.4	0	2	0	0	3	0	0	0	0	0	0	3	0	0	0	0	0	0	0	0	1	1	0	0	0
possess	38	.7123	5.4819	47.4	1	1	2	6	12	7	6	3	1	2	0	3	0	5	2	9	2	0	0	0	0	2	10	2	0
possessed	41	.7304	6.1464	47.9	1	1	2	5	16	10	6	0	14	1	0	4	0	2	0	3	1	2	0	0	3	4	6	1	0
possesses	15	.6782	2.0631	43.1	0	2	1	1	4	3	3	1	1	2	1	1	0	0	1	1	0	0	0	0	1	1	5	1	0
possessing	8	.5407	.9372	39.7	0	0	0	0	4	1	3	0	3	0	0	0	0	0	0	0	1	0	0	0	1	0	2	1	0
possession	86	.8097	13.971	51.5	4	13	7	16	19	16	9	2	12	15	0	3	0	16	6	2	3	0	1	0	8	8	9	3	0

3A por
7R porbeagle
7P porcelains
XB porcine
7A porcupine-quill
3A porcupine's
7Q porcupinefish
7Q porcupinefishes
5F Porcupines
XB porcus
7P porecelain
XR porgy
3N pork-chop
9B pork-chops
9D porkeaters
XR porker
7A porkers
3N Porkey's
XR Porklets
9R pornography
6A porosus
7D Porpoises'
3J Porridge
XP Porsche
XP Porsche's
7R Porsches
9D PortArthur
4B porta
7R portability
7J portaged
6A portcullis
7N porte-cochere
7R ported
8F portended
7R portentous
4A porter's
9B Porterfield
9B portioned
6R Portman
8F portolani
5P Portolu
XR portrayals
4B portus
3J Posada
5B posies
3P Positano
7Q Position
6P POSITION
7R positioning
8P positiveness
7Q positron

Word Type	F	D	U	SFI	3 Gr 3	4 Gr 4	5 Gr 5	6 Gr 6	7 Gr 7	8 Gr 8	9 Gr 9	X UnGr	A Read	B Eng & Gr	C Comp	D Lit	E Math	F Soc Stud	G Spell	H Sci	J Music	K Art	L Home Ec	M Shop	N Lib F	P Lib NF	Q Lib Ref	R Mag	S Rel
possessions	57	.7046	8.1935	49.1	4	6	5	7	13	6	14	2	6	2	0	10	0	17	1	3	0	0	0	0	2	6	8	2	0
possessive	104	.3529	7.8626	49.0	0	22	31	24	11	5	11	0	0	65	4	0	0	0	35	0	0	0	0	0	0	0	0	0	0
possessives	12	.1757	.5017	37.0	0	1	0	4	1	4	2	0	0	3	0	0	0	0	9	0	0	0	0	0	0	0	0	0	0
possessor	6	.4771	.6524	38.1	0	0	2	1	0	2	0	1	3	0	0	0	0	0	0	0	1	0	0	0	0	1	0	1	0
possibilites	2	.2440	.1132	30.5	0	0	1	0	1	0	0	0	0	0	0	1	0	0	0	0	0	0	0	0	0	0	0	1	0
possibilities	54	.8613	9.2548	49.7	1	1	5	5	18	12	8	4	5	3	1	0	4	6	1	7	8	2	2	1	0	2	5	7	0
possibility	53	.8115	8.6285	49.4	1	5	5	12	11	8	7	4	6	3	0	1	1	5	0	8	3	0	1	0	3	11	3	8	0
possible	930	.9271	170.61	62.3	45	89	130	96	202	187	150	31	115	59	11	26	137	89	15	149	43	9	43	26	25	52	79	52	0
possibly	129	.8666	22.306	53.5	7	7	19	19	34	17	20	6	28	4	2	7	2	7	1	8	1	0	2	2	12	13	21	19	0
possum	15	.5552	1.7484	42.4	3	6	0	1	3	1	0	1	2	0	0	3	0	0	0	0	1	0	0	0	1	6	2	0	0
Possum	2	.2407	.1138	30.6	0	2	0	0	0	0	0	0	0	0	0	1	0	0	0	0	0	0	0	0	0	1	0	0	0
possums	2	.2401	.1133	30.5	0	1	0	0	1	0	0	0	0	0	0	0	0	0	0	0	0	0	0	0	0	1	1	0	0
Possy	10	.0000	.4568	36.6	0	0	10	0	0	0	0	0	10	0	0	0	0	0	0	0	0	0	0	0	0	0	0	0	0
Possy's	5	.0000	.2284	33.6	0	0	5	0	0	0	0	0	5	0	0	0	0	0	0	0	0	0	0	0	0	0	0	0	0
post	253	.8874	44.686	56.5	38	42	29	31	42	28	32	11	50	17	1	14	5	48	11	16	3	0	2	10	16	25	15	20	0
Post	34	.7711	5.3100	47.3	8	2	0	1	10	6	7	0	7	2	1	3	1	9	0	0	2	0	0	0	0	2	3	4	0
Post-Impressionist	2	.0000	.0037	15.7	0	0	0	0	0	2	0	0	0	0	0	0	0	0	0	0	0	2	0	0	0	0	0	0	0
post-office	3	.0000	.0328	25.2	0	1	2	0	0	0	0	0	0	3	0	0	0	0	0	0	0	0	0	0	0	0	0	0	0
post-war	2	.2401	.1133	30.5	0	1	1	0	0	0	0	0	0	0	0	0	0	0	0	0	0	0	0	0	0	1	1	0	0
postage	21	.6345	2.7572	44.4	3	0	6	0	7	3	2	0	3	4	1	0	5	1	0	1	0	0	0	0	0	5	1	0	0
postage-stamp	3	.0000	.1370	31.4	0	0	3	0	0	0	0	0	3	0	0	0	0	0	0	0	0	0	0	0	0	0	0	0	0
postal	12	.4902	1.2453	41.0	0	0	0	0	6	6	0	0	0	1	0	1	0	5	0	0	0	0	0	0	0	1	4	0	0
Postal	3	.2444	.1814	32.6	0	0	0	0	1	0	2	0	0	0	0	0	0	2	0	0	0	0	0	0	0	0	1	0	0
postcard	5	.4291	.4660	36.7	0	1	2	0	2	0	0	0	1	1	1	1	0	0	1	0	0	0	0	0	0	0	0	0	0
postcards	3	.2257	.1583	32.0	0	0	0	0	1	0	2	0	0	2	0	1	0	0	0	0	0	0	0	0	0	0	0	0	0
posted	12	.4762	1.2965	41.1	3	0	2	1	0	4	2	0	6	0	0	1	1	0	0	0	0	0	2	0	0	1	1	0	0
poster	55	.2398	3.0233	44.8	17	12	10	5	5	3	3	0	4	3	0	0	8	0	2	3	0	26	1	0	3	4	0	1	0
posterior	3	.1813	.1402	31.5	0	0	0	0	1	1	0	1	0	0	0	0	0	0	0	1	0	0	0	0	0	0	2	0	0
posterity	6	.4347	.5911	37.7	0	2	0	0	0	0	3	1	2	0	0	0	1	0	0	0	0	0	0	0	1	0	2	0	0
posters	45	.5620	5.2246	47.2	9	9	2	11	4	2	6	2	4	2	1	0	4	2	0	4	0	10	4	2	4	7	0	1	0
postgraduate	2	.2408	.1204	30.8	1	0	0	0	0	1	0	0	0	0	0	0	0	1	0	0	0	0	0	0	0	1	0	0	0
posting	2	.2407	.1138	30.6	0	0	0	0	1	1	0	0	0	0	0	1	0	0	0	0	0	0	0	0	0	1	0	0	0
postman	27	.3231	2.0686	43.2	13	2	3	4	1	1	3	0	7	3	8	0	0	5	1	2	1	0	0	0	0	0	0	0	0
postmaster	12	.5133	1.3385	41.3	4	0	1	0	4	1	1	1	3	0	0	0	0	2	0	0	0	0	0	0	0	3	3	1	0
Postmaster	11	.1284	.4597	36.6	0	0	0	0	1	6	4	0	0	0	0	0	0	10	0	0	0	0	0	0	0	1	0	0	0
postmasters	2	.2401	.1133	30.5	0	0	0	0	2	0	0	0	0	0	0	0	0	0	0	0	0	0	0	0	0	1	1	0	0
postmen	2	.1717	.1142	30.6	0	1	0	0	0	0	1	0	1	0	0	1	0	0	0	0	0	0	0	0	0	0	0	0	0
postpone	6	.5026	.6254	38.0	0	1	0	0	1	3	1	0	0	2	0	1	0	1	0	0	0	0	1	0	0	0	1	0	0
postponed	7	.5178	.7773	38.9	0	2	0	0	2	3	0	0	2	1	1	0	0	0	0	0	1	0	0	0	1	0	1	0	0
postponement	4	.3689	.3351	35.3	0	0	0	0	3	0	1	0	1	0	0	0	0	0	0	0	0	0	1	0	0	0	1	1	0
postponing	3	.3086	.2017	33.0	0	0	1	0	0	2	0	0	0	1	0	0	0	0	0	0	0	0	1	0	0	1	0	0	0
postriders	2	.0000	.0290	24.6	0	0	0	0	2	0	0	0	0	0	0	0	0	0	0	0	0	0	0	0	0	2	0	0	0
posts	75	.8196	12.335	50.9	5	10	20	12	8	9	8	3	10	1	0	5	3	17	2	10	1	2	0	0	1	8	6	9	0
postulated	3	.0000	.0314	25.0	0	0	0	0	1	2	0	0	0	0	0	0	0	0	0	0	0	0	0	0	0	0	3	0	0
postulates	3	.0000	.0314	25.0	0	0	0	3	0	0	0	0	0	0	0	0	0	0	0	0	0	0	0	0	0	0	3	0	0
posture	47	.3908	4.0593	46.1	22	4	10	0	2	3	6	0	0	0	1	0	0	0	0	34	0	0	9	0	0	1	1	1	0
postured	2	.0000	.0243	23.9	0	0	0	2	0	0	0	0	0	0	0	0	0	0	0	0	0	0	0	0	0	0	0	2	0
postures	2	.0000	.0215	23.3	0	0	0	0	0	2	0	0	0	0	0	2	0	0	0	0	0	0	0	0	0	0	0	0	0
postwar	10	.3743	.8368	39.2	0	0	0	0	0	7	2	1	0	0	0	0	0	6	0	0	0	0	0	0	0	0	2	2	0
Posy	10	.0000	.4568	36.6	10	0	0	0	0	0	0	0	10	0	0	0	0	0	0	0	0	0	0	0	0	0	0	0	0
Posy's	3	.0000	.1370	31.4	3	0	0	0	0	0	0	0	3	0	0	0	0	0	0	0	0	0	0	0	0	0	0	0	0
pot	155	.8847	27.409	54.4	41	37	21	9	29	6	7	5	59	6	2	9	2	8	2	19	7	0	2	0	5	18	4	12	0
pot-bellied	6	.4699	.5926	37.7	0	0	1	0	4	0	1	0	0	1	0	0	0	0	0	0	0	0	0	0	1	2	2	0	0
potash	7	.4223	.6451	38.1	1	0	0	1	1	0	2	2	0	0	0	0	0	2	0	3	0	0	0	1	0	0	1	0	0
potassium	23	.3045	1.6350	42.1	0	4	5	1	3	6	1	3	0	0	0	0	0	0	0	14	0	0	0	0	0	0	8	1	0
potato	122	.8677	21.177	53.3	16	29	16	20	23	8	7	3	37	6	1	6	10	4	7	22	1	1	6	0	11	8	1	1	0
potatoes	274	.7971	44.166	56.5	42	59	35	37	62	10	24	5	76	7	3	8	9	57	5	14	2	1	24	0	34	19	8	7	0
Potatoes	2	.2303	.1079	30.3	0	1	1	0	0	0	0	0	0	0	0	0	0	0	0	0	1	0	0	0	0	1	0	0	0
Potawatomies	4	.0000	.0579	27.6	0	4	0	0	0	0	0	0	0	0	0	0	0	0	0	0	0	0	0	0	0	4	0	0	0
potbellied	4	.0919	.1430	31.6	0	0	0	0	1	1	2	0	1	0	0	3	0	0	0	0	0	0	0	0	0	0	0	0	0
Potemkin	2	.0000	.0209	23.2	0	0	0	0	0	2	0	0	0	0	0	0	0	0	0	0	0	0	0	0	0	0	2	0	0
potent	10	.3761	.8565	39.3	0	0	1	0	2	1	5	1	2	0	0	2	0	0	0	0	0	0	0	0	0	1	0	5	0
potentate	2	.2446	.1122	30.5	0	0	0	0	0	1	1	0	0	0	0	1	0	0	0	0	0	0	0	0	0	0	1	0	0
potential	64	.6401	8.4277	49.3	3	1	1	10	22	10	13	4	5	1	1	0	0	3	0	19	0	0	0	4	1	1	9	20	0
potentialities	3	.2387	.1708	32.3	0	0	1	0	1	0	1	0	0	0	0	0	0	0	0	0	0	0	0	0	0	2	1	0	0
potentially	5	.3211	.3600	35.6	0	0	0	2	1	2	0	0	0	0	1	0	0	2	0	0	0	0	0	0	0	0	0	2	0
potholes	2	.1814	.1187	30.7	1	0	0	0	1	0	0	0	1	0	0	0	0	0	0	0	0	0	0	0	0	0	0	1	0
potion	5	.3343	.4151	36.2	0	1	0	2	1	0	0	1	2	0	0	0	0	0	0	0	0	0	0	0	0	1	0	2	0
potlatch	5	.0000	.2284	33.6	0	5	0	0	0	0	0	0	5	0	0	0	0	0	0	0	0	0	0	0	0	0	0	0	0
Potomac	32	.6507	4.2588	46.3	7	8	3	1	6	4	3	0	1	3	0	0	1	7	0	0	0	0	0	0	2	7	6	5	0
pots	88	.7339	13.305	51.2	27	10	7	15	17	8	3	1	31	0	0	3	0	17	0	9	0	0	1	0	10	11	2	4	0
pottage	2	.2441	.1127	30.5	0	0	0	0	2	0	0	0	0	0	0	0	0	0	0	0	0	0	0	0	1	0	1	0	0
Pottapetal	8	.0000	.0875	29.4	0	8	0	0	0	0	0	0	0	8	0	0	0	0	0	0	0	0	0	0	0	0	0	0	0
potted	8	.5220	.9085	39.6	5	1	0	1	1	0	0	0	3	1	1	0	1	0	0	0	1	0	0	0	0	0	1	0	0
potter	4	.2420	.3089	34.9	3	1	0	0	0	0	0	0	3	0	0	0	0	1	0	0	0	0	0	0	0	0	0	0	0
Potter	4	.2246	.2111	33.2	0	0	1	0	2	0	0	1	0	0	0	0	0	0	1	0	0	0	0	0	0	0	0	3	0
Potter's	2	.2407	.1138	30.6	1	0	1	0	0	0	0	0	0	0	0	1	0	0	0	0	0	0	0	0	0	1	0	0	0
pottering	2	.1621	.0746	28.7	0	0	0	0	1	1	0	0	0	0	1	1	0	0	0	0	0	0	0	0	0	0	0	0	0
potters	3	.3350	.2478	33.9	1	1	1	0	0	0	0	0	1	0	0	0	0	1	0	0	0	0	0	0	0	0	1	0	0
pottery	74	.6351	9.6710	49.9	13	25	7	7	12	5	4	1	8	5	0	2	0	22	0	1	3	7	0	2	2	2	19	1	0
Pottleby	7	.0000	.3198	35.0	7	0	0	0	0	0	0	0	7	0	0	0	0	0	0	0	0	0	0	0	0	0	0	0	0
Potts	5	.0000	.2284	33.6	0	0	0	0	5	0	0	0	5	0	0	0	0	0	0	0	0	0	0	0	0	0	0	0	0
pouch	35	.6288	4.7001	46.7	3	6	5	11	3	5	1	1	16	0	1	3	0	2	0	4	0	0	0	0	1	8	0	0	0
pouches	11	.5770	1.3429	41.3	3	0	3	1	2	1	0	1	2	0	0	0	0	1	0	2	0	0	0	0	1	3	2	0	0
pouf	3	.3394	.2451	33.9	0	1	1	0	1	0	0	0	1	0	0	1	0	0	0	0	0	0	0	0	1	0	0	0	0
Poulenc's	2	.0000	.0162	22.1	0	0	0	0	0	2	0	0	0	0	0	0	0	0	0	0	2	0	0	0	0	0	0	0	0
poultice	4	.2443	.2260	33.5	0	0	0	0	4	0	0	0	0	0	0	2	0	0	0	0	0	0	0	0	2	0	0	0	0
poultry	45	.4961	4.7946	46.8	5	1	11	8	6	3	11	0	6	0	0	1	0	14	0	6	0	0	9	0	2	0	2	5	0
poultrymen	4	.2281	.2337	33.7	0	0	3	0	0	0	0	1	0	0	0	0	0	3	0	0	0	0	0	0	0	0	0	1	0
pounce	5	.4504	.5012	37.0	1	0	1	1	0	0	1	1	1	1	0	1	0	0	0	2	0	0	0	0	0	0	0	0	0
pounced	5	.4789	.5381	37.3	0	1	1	1	1	1	0	0	2	0	0	0	0	0	0	0	0	0	0	0	1	1	0	1	0
pounces	3	.3365	.2489	34.0	0	0	0	2	0	0	1	0	1	0	0	1	0	0	0	1	0	0	0	0	0	0	0	0	0

5R possessiveness
7N possessors
5A Possible
7R possibles
8Q post-Homeric
8K Post-Impressionists
8F Post-Reconstruction
8Q post-apostolic
7R post-fledging
7H post-hurricane
8Q post-impressionist
XH post-mortem
5Q post-romantic
7R post-season
7A post's
6F Postage
7P postdebutantes
XR posterish
8F Posterity
8Q postern
7Q posthole
8Q posthumas
8Q posthumes
8Q posthumous
8Q Posthumous
5Q posthumously
9D postilions
4P postmark
7P Postmasters
XR postmistress
7R postpaid
9R postprandial
7P postrider
7P postrider's
8Q postulating
4R Pot
7N pot-lid
9L pot-roasting
9B pot's
8H potable
6J Potato
4N potato-picking
7N potencies
7N potency
7E potentiometer
5P potestas
6N potful
5Q pothooks
4A potlatches
XR potlicker
6F Potosi
4Q Potowomut
9D Potpan
XB potpourri
7D potroast
8F Potsdam
3F Pottery
5N potting
6A potting-shed
3A Pottlebys
7A Potts'
XH pouch-bearers
8N pouch-strings
7H pouched
XH Pouchet
8F pouchful
6H pouchlike
4R Poughkeepsie
XH Pouilly-le-Fort
8Q poular
8J Poulenc
6N poulticed
3F Poultry
6B poultry-yard

Word Type	F	D	U	SFI	3 Gr 3	4 Gr 4	5 Gr 5	6 Gr 6	7 Gr 7	8 Gr 8	9 Gr 9	X UnGr	A Read	B Eng & Gr	C Comp	D Lit	E Math	F Soc Stud	G Spell	H Sci	J Music	K Art	L Home Ec	M Shop	N Lib F	P Lib NF	Q Lib Ref	R Mag	S Rel
pouncing	2	.0000	.0914	29.6	0	0	2	0	0	0	0	0	2	0	0	0	0	0	0	0	0	0	0	0	0	0	0	0	0
pound	227	.7590	34.835	55.4	28	43	22	40	39	24	24	7	27	12	0	2	98	8	6	21	1	0	6	2	10	13	8	13	0
Pound-Sweet	6	.0000	.2741	34.4	6	0	0	0	0	0	0	0	6	0	0	0	0	0	0	0	0	0	0	0	0	0	0	0	0
pounded	64	.7969	10.390	50.2	8	18	8	8	12	6	3	1	31	1	1	6	0	3	0	0	2	0	1	0	7	7	2	3	0
pounding	83	.7954	13.376	51.3	8	20	7	10	15	14	6	3	28	0	0	9	0	2	0	6	6	1	0	1	9	11	1	9	0
pounds	562	.7826	88.693	59.5	65	77	95	59	132	60	52	22	76	12	3	15	210	15	2	66	0	0	5	10	28	47	19	54	0
Pounds	3	.1910	.1473	31.7	0	0	2	0	0	1	0	0	0	0	0	0	0	1	0	0	0	0	0	0	2	0	0	0	0
pour	190	.6247	24.661	53.9	34	40	19	12	27	27	27	4	32	3	1	9	6	4	3	70	3	0	35	4	5	5	2	8	0
poured	189	.8356	31.749	55.0	36	28	29	21	35	16	22	2	54	6	0	27	5	18	0	21	2	0	1	3	22	16	6	8	0
pouring	57	.7949	9.1662	49.6	7	8	9	9	10	3	8	3	16	1	0	5	1	5	0	9	1	0	3	3	3	6	1	3	0
pours	40	.3795	3.5387	45.5	2	9	12	6	5	3	2	1	8	1	0	3	0	4	0	17	0	0	0	0	0	2	2	2	1
pout	5	.2007	.3235	35.1	0	0	0	0	5	0	0	0	3	0	0	0	0	0	0	0	0	0	0	0	0	0	2	0	0
pouted	4	.0000	.1827	32.6	1	2	0	0	1	0	0	0	4	0	0	0	0	0	0	0	0	0	0	0	0	0	0	0	0
poverty	54	.6914	7.6017	48.8	4	0	8	5	13	12	9	3	2	0	0	2	0	18	0	1	2	1	0	0	2	10	3	13	0
Poverty	2	.2433	.1158	30.6	0	0	0	1	0	1	0	0	0	0	0	0	0	0	0	0	0	0	0	0	0	1	0	1	0
poverty-stricken	3	.3676	.2407	33.8	0	0	1	0	0	0	2	0	0	0	0	0	0	1	1	0	0	0	0	0	0	0	1	0	0
pow	2	.1814	.1187	30.7	0	0	2	0	0	0	0	0	1	0	0	0	0	0	0	0	0	0	0	0	0	0	0	1	0
Pow	3	.0000	.0365	25.6	0	1	0	0	1	0	1	0	0	0	0	0	0	0	0	0	0	0	0	0	0	0	0	3	0
powder	189	.7075	27.280	54.4	10	39	20	19	30	36	28	7	35	11	0	10	0	9	7	27	1	0	29	4	7	28	8	13	0
Powder	2	.1814	.1187	30.7	0	1	0	0	0	0	0	1	1	0	0	0	0	0	0	0	0	0	0	0	0	0	0	1	0
powdered	38	.6938	5.3680	47.3	1	8	3	5	7	4	8	2	2	0	0	2	0	1	0	16	1	0	2	3	1	5	2	3	0
powders	8	.4362	.7432	38.7	0	1	1	0	1	0	2	3	0	0	0	1	0	0	0	2	0	0	1	0	0	0	0	4	0
powdery	11	.4653	1.1822	40.7	2	3	1	1	2	1	0	1	5	0	0	0	0	0	0	4	0	0	0	0	0	0	1	1	0
Powell	22	.3015	1.5853	42.0	0	1	3	15	3	0	0	0	4	0	0	2	0	0	0	0	0	0	0	0	0	2	0	14	0
power	1065	.8717	184.82	62.7	71	65	127	135	268	226	139	34	109	25	19	18	99	299	14	78	20	7	0	53	18	76	131	97	2
Power	17	.5499	1.9638	42.9	0	1	3	2	4	4	2	1	2	0	0	0	0	3	0	0	2	0	0	0	1	0	3	6	0
power-driven	4	.2336	.2503	34.0	0	0	0	1	3	0	0	0	1	0	0	0	0	2	0	0	0	0	0	1	0	0	0	0	0
powerboat	3	.0000	.1370	31.4	0	0	2	0	1	0	0	0	3	0	0	0	0	0	0	0	0	0	0	0	0	0	0	0	0
powered	26	.5966	3.2733	45.1	1	7	1	2	8	1	3	3	7	0	0	0	1	1	0	3	0	0	0	2	0	1	5	6	0
powerful	357	.7119	52.095	57.2	31	41	58	57	87	44	31	8	77	8	5	15	2	68	6	39	10	5	0	0	12	35	40	31	4
powerfully	9	.5531	1.0852	40.4	1	0	1	2	2	2	1	0	4	0	0	1	0	0	0	0	0	0	0	0	2	0	1	1	0
powerhouse	8	.3286	.6018	37.8	0	1	3	1	0	0	0	3	0	0	0	0	0	2	0	2	0	0	0	0	0	0	0	4	0
powerhouses	2	.2351	.1166	30.7	0	0	1	0	1	0	0	0	0	0	0	0	0	1	0	0	0	0	0	0	0	0	0	1	0
powering	3	.2433	.1822	32.6	0	0	0	1	0	0	2	0	0	0	0	0	0	0	0	2	0	0	0	0	1	0	0	0	0
powerless	6	.4271	.5864	37.7	0	0	0	1	5	0	0	0	2	0	0	2	0	1	0	0	0	0	0	0	0	0	0	1	0
powerlessness	2	.2446	.1142	30.6	0	0	0	0	2	0	0	0	0	0	0	0	0	0	0	0	0	0	0	0	1	0	0	1	0
powers	155	.7539	23.617	53.7	7	6	13	6	37	45	36	5	13	4	4	4	33	39	2	5	2	0	0	0	0	16	26	7	0
Powers	15	.4921	1.5839	42.0	4	2	1	0	0	4	2	2	1	0	0	0	0	6	0	0	0	0	0	0	4	2	0	2	0
Powhatan	14	.2383	.9325	39.7	5	8	0	0	0	1	0	0	5	0	0	0	0	1	0	0	0	0	0	0	0	8	0	0	0
Powhatan's	2	.1948	.1250	31.0	1	1	0	0	0	0	0	0	1	0	0	0	0	0	0	0	0	0	0	0	0	1	0	0	0
powwow	4	.4714	.3990	36.0	0	0	1	1	1	1	0	0	0	0	0	0	0	1	1	0	0	0	0	0	1	1	0	0	0
pox	4	.2344	.2377	33.8	0	2	0	1	0	0	1	0	0	0	0	1	0	0	0	3	0	0	0	0	0	0	0	0	0
pp	14	.6159	1.7598	42.5	0	2	0	0	1	7	3	1	1	1	0	0	4	0	2	1	1	2	1	1	0	0	0	0	0
PQ	26	.0000	.3892	35.9	1	0	9	0	0	13	3	0	0	0	0	0	26	0	0	0	0	0	0	0	0	0	0	0	0
PQR	3	.0000	.0449	26.5	0	1	1	0	1	0	0	0	0	0	0	0	3	0	0	0	0	0	0	0	0	0	0	0	0
PQRS	2	.0000	.0299	24.8	0	0	1	0	0	1	0	0	0	0	0	0	2	0	0	0	0	0	0	0	0	0	0	0	0
pr	4	.0000	.0325	25.1	0	1	2	1	0	0	0	0	0	0	0	0	0	0	4	0	0	0	0	0	0	0	0	0	0
PR	2	.0000	.0299	24.8	0	1	0	0	0	1	0	0	0	0	0	0	2	0	0	0	0	0	0	0	0	0	0	0	0
practicable	5	.4159	.4502	36.5	1	0	0	0	0	1	2	1	0	0	0	0	1	1	0	1	0	0	0	1	0	1	0	0	0
practical	140	.8200	22.981	53.6	6	4	9	23	32	19	34	13	20	9	4	6	7	8	0	14	3	0	4	8	1	9	29	18	0
practically	110	.8889	19.425	52.9	5	5	12	8	34	14	21	11	12	7	1	9	0	15	1	16	3	0	1	2	8	9	13	13	0
practice	601	.9231	109.86	60.4	60	105	76	68	121	54	111	6	119	66	10	16	53	27	37	43	72	6	21	17	10	38	34	32	0
Practice	7	.3527	.5433	37.4	0	0	0	0	4	1	1	1	0	3	0	0	3	0	0	0	0	0	0	0	0	0	0	1	0
practiced	79	.8464	13.404	51.3	11	8	9	11	16	11	12	1	21	4	0	7	3	9	0	4	5	0	0	2	3	8	8	5	0
practices	53	.7217	7.7271	48.9	0	4	12	3	6	6	16	6	2	1	0	0	4	7	0	11	3	0	5	3	0	2	10	5	0
practicing	73	.9113	13.225	51.2	9	18	14	5	11	11	5	0	23	7	0	5	4	6	1	7	3	0	1	1	4	5	3	3	0
practised	4	.3757	.3182	35.0	0	0	0	1	2	0	1	0	0	0	1	0	0	0	0	0	0	0	0	0	1	0	1	1	0
Pragmatic	2	.0000	.0389	25.9	0	0	0	0	0	0	2	0	0	0	0	0	0	2	0	0	0	0	0	0	0	0	0	0	0
Prague	14	.4358	1.2964	41.1	0	0	0	1	4	2	7	0	0	1	0	0	0	1	0	0	1	0	0	0	0	1	1	9	0
prairie	134	.7914	21.508	53.3	20	31	25	8	30	9	9	2	44	4	2	23	0	7	2	15	1	0	0	0	16	9	7	4	0
Prairie	19	.5874	2.3291	43.7	0	4	2	5	6	2	0	0	2	0	0	3	0	5	0	0	0	0	0	0	2	3	4	0	0
PrairieCity	2	.0000	.0914	29.6	2	0	0	0	0	0	0	0	2	0	0	0	0	0	0	0	0	0	0	0	0	0	0	0	0
prairie-dog	3	.3847	.2490	34.0	0	1	0	0	2	0	0	0	0	1	0	1	0	0	0	0	0	0	0	0	0	1	0	0	0
prairie's	2	.1717	.1142	30.6	0	1	0	0	0	1	0	0	1	0	0	1	0	0	0	0	0	0	0	0	0	0	0	0	0
prairies	45	.7521	6.8668	48.4	5	5	11	6	7	7	2	2	6	1	0	3	0	14	0	5	3	0	0	0	1	4	4	4	0
praise	73	.4485	7.1928	48.6	4	7	12	12	22	4	11	1	18	2	0	8	0	2	0	1	24	1	0	0	2	5	1	7	2
Praise	5	.3013	.3288	35.2	0	0	1	0	0	1	3	0	0	0	0	0	0	0	0	0	3	0	0	0	0	0	1	1	0
praise-singer's	2	.0000	.0290	24.6	0	0	0	0	2	0	0	0	0	0	0	0	0	0	0	0	0	0	0	0	0	2	0	0	0
praised	27	.7042	3.9115	45.9	2	8	1	8	5	1	1	1	8	0	1	1	0	4	0	0	5	1	0	0	2	4	0	1	0
praises	8	.4333	.7397	38.7	1	2	3	1	0	1	0	0	1	0	0	0	0	0	0	0	4	0	1	0	1	0	1	0	0
praising	3	.2028	.1988	33.0	0	1	1	0	1	0	0	0	2	0	0	0	0	0	0	0	1	0	0	0	0	0	0	0	0
prance	6	.3416	.4646	36.7	2	2	0	2	0	0	0	0	1	0	0	0	0	0	0	0	3	0	0	0	1	0	0	1	0
pranced	8	.2304	.4888	36.9	1	1	1	2	2	0	0	1	2	0	0	0	0	0	0	0	0	0	0	0	5	1	0	0	0
prancing	9	.5572	1.0775	40.3	2	3	0	1	3	0	0	0	3	0	1	1	0	1	0	0	0	0	0	0	1	1	0	1	0
pranks	5	.3734	.4245	36.3	0	2	2	0	0	0	1	0	1	0	0	1	0	1	0	0	2	0	0	0	0	0	0	0	0
Pranks	2	.0000	.0162	22.1	0	0	0	1	0	1	0	0	0	0	0	0	0	0	0	0	2	0	0	0	0	0	0	0	0
Pratt	4	.2445	.3067	34.9	0	1	0	3	0	0	0	0	3	0	0	0	0	0	0	0	0	0	0	0	0	1	0	0	0
prawns	3	.2437	.2277	33.6	0	0	1	0	2	0	0	0	2	0	0	0	0	0	0	1	0	0	0	0	0	0	0	0	0
pray	85	.4818	8.7814	49.4	8	17	9	14	9	7	21	0	15	6	0	24	0	3	3	0	15	0	0	0	9	1	1	6	2
prayed	44	.7003	6.3599	48.0	7	13	4	3	6	6	5	0	15	3	0	8	0	2	1	0	6	0	0	0	2	4	0	3	0
prayer	58	.7734	9.1033	49.6	5	7	6	9	12	7	10	2	18	3	0	11	0	3	2	0	4	1	0	0	4	1	2	9	0
Prayer	3	.2249	.1514	31.8	0	1	0	0	1	0	1	0	0	0	0	0	0	0	2	0	1	0	0	0	0	0	0	0	0
prayer-books	3	.0000	.0352	25.5	0	2	0	1	0	0	0	0	0	0	0	0	0	0	0	0	0	0	0	0	3	0	0	0	0
prayer-place	2	.0000	.0389	25.9	0	0	0	0	0	2	0	0	0	0	0	0	0	2	0	0	0	0	0	0	0	0	0	0	0
prayerful	3	.1983	.1396	31.4	0	0	0	1	0	0	1	1	0	0	0	0	0	0	0	0	2	0	0	0	0	0	0	1	0
prayers	47	.7607	7.2448	48.6	6	4	6	11	11	1	7	1	11	2	2	7	0	4	1	0	3	2	0	0	6	8	0	1	0
prayeth	2	.1551	.0728	28.6	0	0	1	0	1	0	0	0	0	0	1	0	0	0	0	0	0	0	0	0	1	0	0	0	0
praying	29	.1835	1.4744	41.7	6	3	1	3	6	3	7	0	6	1	0	5	0	1	0	2	1	0	0	0	4	1	2	3	3
prays	3	.3272	.2361	33.7	0	0	1	0	1	0	1	0	1	0	0	0	0	0	0	0	1	0	0	0	0	0	1	0	0
pre	5	.0000	.0406	26.1	0	1	2	2	0	0	0	0	0	0	0	0	0	0	5	0	0	0	0	0	0	0	0	0	0
Pre-Cambrian	4	.1494	.1609	32.1	0	0	0	0	0	3	1	0	0	0	0	0	0	0	0	1	0	0	0	0	0	0	3	0	0
pre-Christian	3	.0000	.0314	25.0	0	0	0	0	1	1	1	0	0	0	0	0	0	0	0	0	0	0	0	0	0	0	3	0	0
pre-Columbian	2	.0000	.0209	23.2	0	0	0	0	2	0	0	0	0	0	0	0	0	0	0	0	0	0	0	0	0	0	2	0	0

5N Pounds'
XH Poupet
6A POUR
8Q Pouring
6A pous
7H pousse-cafe
8A poverty-ridden
6J Poverty's
8P pow-wow
3P powder-charged
7Q powder-down
9L powder-like
8F Powderly
5R powed
6R Powell's
XR power-assisted
5A power-hungry
5P power-operated
7R power-producing
7R power-train
6J Powerful
XR Powers'
7R POWS
9R Powys
7F Poznan
7P Pozzi
7Q Pozzuoli
7E PQL
7E PQN
3A prce
8F practicability
XR practical-minded
9L practicality
9L practice-plan
3P practise
9P practising
XR practitioners
3A Pradesh
4F Prado's
5P Praetorian
9R pragmatist's
9R Prague's
7Q prairieland
3P Prairies
7D prairieside
7P praise-singer
7P praise-singing
5Q Praises
8B praiseworthy
5A Praiseworthy
9D Pramnian
9J prances
6A Prancing
5B pranksters
5J Praties
3C prattles
8L prattling
5N Prawns
8J pray'rs
3S prayer-songs
3P Praying
8D Pre
3A pre-Aztec
5P pre-Civil
6F Pre-Classic
8Q pre-Communist

Word Type	F	D	U	SFI	3 Gr 3	4 Gr 4	5 Gr 5	6 Gr 6	7 Gr 7	8 Gr 8	9 Gr 9	X UnGr	A Read	B Eng & Gr	C Comp	D Lit	E Math	F Soc Stud	G Spell	H Sci	J Music	K Art	L Home Ec	M Shop	N Lib F	P Lib NF	Q Lib Ref	R Mag	S Rel
pre-Greek	2	.0000	.0037	15.7	0	0	0	0	0	0	2	0	0	0	0	0	0	0	0	0	0	2	0	0	0	0	0	0	0
Pre-Raphaelite	2	.0000	.0209	23.2	0	0	2	0	0	0	0	0	0	0	0	0	0	0	0	0	0	0	0	0	0	0	2	0	0
pre-eminence	2	.2433	.1158	30.6	0	0	1	0	0	0	1	0	0	0	0	0	0	0	0	0	0	0	0	0	0	1	0	1	0
pre-season	2	.0000	.0243	23.9	0	0	0	1	1	0	0	0	0	0	0	0	0	0	0	0	0	0	0	0	0	0	0	2	0
pre-war	2	.2441	.1127	30.5	0	0	0	0	2	0	0	0	0	0	0	0	0	0	0	0	0	0	0	0	1	0	1	0	0
preach	5	.3676	.4527	36.6	0	1	1	2	0	1	0	0	2	0	0	0	0	2	0	0	0	0	0	0	0	1	0	0	0
preached	13	.6905	1.8271	42.6	2	0	2	1	3	1	4	0	1	0	0	1	0	2	1	0	0	0	0	0	1	3	2	2	0
preacher	17	.4116	1.5373	41.9	0	8	0	2	3	3	0	1	1	2	0	0	0	2	0	0	0	0	0	0	0	10	0	2	0
preacher's	3	.3852	.2500	34.0	0	1	0	0	0	1	1	0	0	0	0	1	0	0	0	0	0	0	0	0	0	1	0	1	0
preachers	3	.3766	.2497	34.0	0	1	0	0	1	1	0	0	0	0	0	0	0	1	0	0	0	0	0	0	0	1	1	0	0
preaching	8	.5923	.9930	40.0	0	2	2	0	0	2	2	0	1	0	0	1	0	3	0	0	0	0	0	0	0	1	1	1	0
preachy	2	.1948	.1250	31.0	0	1	0	0	0	1	0	0	1	0	0	0	0	0	0	0	0	0	0	0	0	1	0	0	0
Preakness	2	.0000	.0234	23.7	0	0	0	1	1	0	0	0	0	0	0	0	0	0	0	0	0	0	0	0	2	0	0	0	0
Preamble	3	.0000	.0583	27.7	0	0	0	0	0	3	0	0	0	0	0	0	0	3	0	0	0	0	0	0	0	0	0	0	0
Prean	2	.0000	.0914	29.6	0	0	0	2	0	0	0	0	2	0	0	0	0	0	0	0	0	0	0	0	0	0	0	0	0
Preble	17	.0000	.7766	38.9	0	0	2	15	0	0	0	0	17	0	0	0	0	0	0	0	0	0	0	0	0	0	0	0	0
Preble's	3	.0000	.1370	31.4	0	0	1	2	0	0	0	0	3	0	0	0	0	0	0	0	0	0	0	0	0	0	0	0	0
Precambrian	3	.2445	.1818	32.6	0	0	0	0	1	0	2	0	0	0	0	0	0	0	0	2	0	0	0	0	0	0	1	0	0
precarious	4	.4538	.4020	36.0	0	0	0	1	0	1	2	0	1	0	0	1	0	0	0	0	0	0	0	0	0	1	0	1	0
precariously	4	.1854	.1872	32.7	0	1	0	0	2	0	1	0	0	0	0	0	0	0	0	0	0	0	0	0	0	1	0	3	0
precaution	8	.4795	.8500	39.3	0	0	1	0	3	1	2	1	3	0	0	2	0	0	0	0	0	0	0	1	1	0	0	1	0
precautions	22	.6281	2.8276	44.5	0	1	0	4	4	8	4	1	1	1	0	4	0	1	0	5	0	0	1	3	0	1	1	4	0
precede	10	.6167	1.2688	41.0	0	0	0	2	1	3	2	2	1	3	0	0	1	0	1	0	1	0	0	0	0	1	0	2	0
preceded	67	.5541	7.5922	48.8	1	1	3	8	25	12	17	0	1	10	2	1	0	2	34	1	2	0	0	0	3	1	8	1	1
precedent	7	.4241	.6392	38.1	0	0	1	0	1	2	3	0	0	0	0	0	0	2	0	0	0	0	0	0	0	1	3	1	0
precedents	4	.2285	.2258	33.5	0	0	0	0	0	2	2	0	0	0	0	0	0	2	0	0	0	0	0	0	0	0	2	0	0
precedes	14	.5360	1.5568	41.9	0	2	0	3	2	5	2	0	1	5	2	1	1	0	2	1	0	0	0	0	0	0	1	0	0
preceding	93	.7072	13.299	51.2	0	2	5	10	35	20	20	1	3	26	1	2	30	3	8	5	2	0	0	0	2	2	7	2	0
precinct	6	.4719	.6068	37.8	0	0	1	0	0	1	4	0	0	0	0	0	0	3	0	0	0	0	0	0	0	1	1	1	0
precious	136	.8493	23.251	53.7	19	21	26	22	20	14	10	4	56	8	1	3	0	22	1	4	0	1	0	1	14	10	6	9	0
precipice	6	.2953	.4429	36.5	0	0	0	0	1	4	1	0	2	1	0	3	0	0	0	0	0	0	0	0	0	0	0	0	0
precipices	2	.1387	.0689	28.4	1	0	1	0	0	0	0	0	0	0	1	0	0	0	0	0	0	0	0	0	0	1	0	0	0
precipitate	22	.3147	1.6338	42.1	0	0	0	1	15	2	2	2	0	0	0	2	0	0	0	18	0	0	0	0	0	0	1	1	0
precipitated	2	.2278	.1128	30.5	0	0	1	0	0	1	0	0	0	0	0	0	0	0	0	1	0	0	0	0	0	0	1	0	0
precipitation	26	.3280	2.0200	43.1	0	7	2	5	4	3	5	0	1	0	0	0	0	2	0	20	0	0	0	0	0	0	2	1	0
precipitous	4	.3498	.3059	34.9	0	0	1	1	2	0	0	0	0	0	0	0	0	0	0	0	0	0	0	0	0	1	2	1	0
precise	99	.5359	10.912	50.4	2	0	3	4	41	21	23	5	4	12	28	4	14	1	2	4	2	2	1	1	1	4	13	6	0
precisely	58	.8463	9.8056	49.9	1	4	8	5	22	7	9	2	10	5	1	5	9	0	0	3	2	0	1	0	4	4	8	6	0
precision	50	.7951	7.9753	49.0	3	0	2	1	18	5	16	5	4	1	0	2	9	3	0	11	2	1	2	4	0	4	4	3	0
predation	2	.0000	.0209	23.2	0	0	0	0	2	0	0	0	0	0	0	0	0	0	0	0	0	0	0	0	0	0	2	0	0
predator	13	.2096	.6366	38.0	0	0	0	0	12	1	0	0	0	0	1	0	0	0	0	0	0	0	0	0	0	0	12	0	0
predators	28	.2896	1.8274	42.6	0	0	0	1	26	1	0	0	0	0	0	1	0	0	0	3	0	0	0	0	0	0	19	5	0
predatory	6	.2307	.3476	35.4	0	0	1	0	4	0	1	0	1	0	0	1	0	0	0	0	0	0	0	0	0	0	4	0	0
predawn	2	.2297	.1135	30.6	0	0	0	0	1	1	0	0	0	0	0	1	0	1	0	0	0	0	0	0	0	0	0	0	0
predecessor	9	.4263	.8253	39.2	0	0	0	0	2	2	2	3	0	0	0	0	0	1	0	0	0	0	0	0	0	4	1	3	0
predecessors	13	.5013	1.3776	41.4	0	0	0	1	6	1	4	1	1	0	0	0	0	2	0	1	1	2	0	0	0	3	1	2	0
predestination	3	.0000	.0314	25.0	0	0	0	0	0	3	0	0	0	0	0	0	0	0	0	0	0	0	0	0	0	0	3	0	0
predetermined	5	.3943	.4207	36.2	0	1	0	0	3	1	0	0	0	0	0	0	0	1	0	0	0	0	0	1	0	0	2	1	0
predicament	5	.4188	.4411	36.4	0	0	0	0	2	2	1	0	0	0	0	1	0	0	0	0	0	1	0	0	1	1	0	1	0
predicate	248	.3123	16.856	52.3	20	34	59	38	55	20	22	0	2	188	42	0	0	0	13	0	0	0	0	0	0	0	3	0	0
predicates	28	.1692	1.2069	40.8	4	4	10	3	4	1	2	0	1	26	1	0	0	0	0	0	0	0	0	0	0	0	0	0	0
predict	66	.7024	9.4759	49.8	0	9	9	9	10	13	15	1	5	3	0	2	7	8	2	28	1	0	0	0	0	0	7	3	0
predictable	7	.3243	.4912	36.9	0	1	0	1	2	2	1	0	0	0	1	0	0	0	0	0	0	0	0	0	0	0	5	1	0
predicted	27	.6983	3.8632	45.9	0	6	1	0	3	6	5	6	3	0	0	0	2	2	0	11	0	0	1	0	1	2	2	3	0
predicting	5	.3049	.3828	35.8	0	0	1	1	0	2	1	0	1	0	0	0	1	0	0	3	0	0	0	0	0	0	0	0	0
prediction	21	.6008	2.6542	44.2	0	4	3	2	3	2	5	2	3	1	0	2	1	0	0	11	0	0	0	0	0	1	1	1	0
predictions	22	.5006	2.3755	43.8	0	3	0	3	4	6	5	1	1	1	0	1	2	2	0	14	0	0	0	0	0	0	1	0	0
predicts	2	.2278	.1128	30.5	0	1	0	0	0	1	0	0	0	0	0	0	0	0	0	1	0	0	0	0	0	0	1	0	0
predisposition	2	.0000	.0914	29.6	0	0	0	0	0	0	2	0	2	0	0	0	0	0	0	0	0	0	0	0	0	0	0	0	0
predominance	4	.3573	.2975	34.7	0	0	0	0	3	0	1	0	0	0	0	0	0	0	0	0	0	1	1	0	0	0	2	0	0
predominant	9	.5153	.9560	39.8	0	0	0	0	3	5	1	0	0	0	0	0	0	1	0	0	3	0	1	0	0	0	2	2	0
predominantly	11	.5398	1.2226	40.9	0	0	3	0	3	2	1	2	0	0	0	0	0	0	0	0	1	0	1	0	0	3	4	2	0
predominate	4	.3175	.2812	34.5	0	0	0	0	2	2	0	0	0	0	0	0	0	0	0	1	2	0	0	0	0	0	1	0	0
predominated	2	.2128	.1055	30.2	0	0	0	0	0	0	1	1	0	0	0	0	0	0	0	1	1	0	0	0	0	0	0	0	0
predominates	2	.1674	.0805	29.1	0	0	0	0	0	0	2	0	0	0	0	0	0	0	0	0	0	0	1	0	0	1	0	0	0
predominating	2	.1698	.1133	30.5	0	0	0	0	1	1	0	0	1	0	0	0	0	0	0	0	0	0	0	0	0	0	1	0	0
preeminence	2	.2285	.1129	30.5	0	0	0	0	0	1	1	0	0	0	0	0	0	1	0	0	0	0	0	0	0	0	1	0	0
preeminently	2	.0000	.0215	23.3	0	0	0	0	0	2	0	0	0	0	0	2	0	0	0	0	0	0	0	0	0	0	0	0	0
preen	3	.1169	.1277	31.1	0	1	0	0	2	0	0	0	1	0	0	0	0	0	0	0	0	0	0	0	0	0	2	0	0
preened	2	.1787	.1174	30.7	0	1	1	0	0	0	0	0	1	0	0	0	0	0	0	0	0	0	0	0	1	0	0	0	0
preening	3	.3369	.2489	34.0	0	1	0	0	1	1	0	0	1	0	0	1	0	1	0	0	0	0	0	0	0	0	0	0	0
prefab	4	.0000	.1827	32.6	0	0	4	0	0	0	0	0	4	0	0	0	0	0	0	0	0	0	0	0	0	0	0	0	0
prefabricated	5	.2007	.3235	35.1	0	0	3	0	0	0	2	0	3	0	0	0	0	0	0	0	0	0	0	0	0	0	2	0	0
prefabs	3	.0000	.1370	31.4	0	0	3	0	0	0	0	0	3	0	0	0	0	0	0	0	0	0	0	0	0	0	0	0	0
preface	7	.4506	.6751	38.3	0	0	1	0	2	3	1	0	1	0	0	0	0	0	1	0	3	0	0	0	0	0	1	1	0
prefer	110	.8721	19.063	52.8	8	3	12	20	24	20	17	6	12	6	2	6	6	4	7	13	4	2	11	2	2	5	13	15	0
preferable	3	.2754	.1835	32.6	0	0	0	0	2	0	1	0	0	0	0	0	0	0	0	0	0	0	0	1	0	1	0	1	0
preferably	12	.5079	1.2626	41.0	1	0	0	1	1	4	4	1	0	2	1	0	0	0	0	3	0	0	3	0	0	1	0	2	0
preference	14	.4709	1.3713	41.4	0	0	2	3	2	4	2	1	0	0	0	1	1	1	0	0	0	0	4	0	1	1	1	4	0
preferences	3	.3255	.2085	33.2	0	0	0	0	1	1	1	0	0	1	0	0	0	0	0	0	0	0	1	0	0	0	1	0	0
preferred	73	.8952	12.967	51.1	5	7	7	9	24	5	11	5	11	6	1	3	1	4	8	2	3	0	3	2	7	9	5	8	0
preferring	6	.5454	.6762	38.3	0	0	0	0	2	2	1	1	0	0	0	1	0	1	0	0	1	0	0	0	0	0	1	2	0
prefers	20	.5779	2.3743	43.8	1	1	0	2	7	3	5	1	1	3	0	1	0	2	1	0	0	0	4	0	0	1	3	4	0
prefix	200	.2226	10.702	50.3	5	13	40	40	49	43	9	1	21	13	1	2	2	2	154	1	0	0	0	0	1	2	1	0	0
prefixes	98	.1565	3.9844	46.0	0	5	10	23	33	26	0	1	8	7	0	0	5	0	78	0	0	0	0	0	0	0	0	0	0
preflight	4	.0000	.0579	27.6	4	0	0	0	0	0	0	0	0	0	0	0	0	0	0	0	0	0	0	0	0	4	0	0	0
preformed	2	.2128	.1055	30.2	0	0	0	0	0	1	0	1	0	0	0	0	0	0	0	1	1	0	0	0	0	0	0	0	0
pregnancy	9	.4001	.7761	38.9	0	0	0	0	6	1	1	1	0	0	0	0	0	0	0	1	0	0	0	0	0	1	3	4	0
pregnant	12	.5080	1.2719	41.0	0	0	0	0	10	1	0	1	0	0	0	1	0	0	0	1	0	0	0	0	1	1	2	6	0
prehensile	2	.2437	.1129	30.5	0	1	0	0	1	0	0	0	0	0	0	0	0	0	0	0	0	0	0	0	0	0	1	1	0
prehistoric	53	.7523	8.0849	49.1	3	1	6	7	8	13	13	2	9	2	0	1	0	12	0	3	1	2	2	0	0	6	10	5	0
prehistory	6	.3498	.4833	36.8	0	0	0	0	5	0	1	0	1	0	0	0	0	0	0	1	0	0	0	0	0	0	3	1	0
prejudging	3	.0000	.0591	27.7	0	0	0	0	3	0	0	0	0	0	0	0	0	0	0	3	0	0	0	0	0	0	0	0	0
prejudice	24	.6687	3.3250	45.2	0	0	7	1	7	4	5	0	6	0	0	5	1	2	0	2	0	0	1	0	0	3	0	4	0

7Q pre-European	7Q pre-man	7N preamble	9F precipitously	7R predator-prey	9D prefixed
9K pre-Hellenic	8N pre-med	8J preamplifier	7J preciseness	7Q predator's	7G prefixing
6A pre-Olympic	XR pre-order	8D prearranged	7Q precisioned-machined	7R predestined	8R pregame
7R pre-World	6P pre-race	7H precedence	4Q preclude	9R predicaments	8E Preger
7P pre-arranged	7J pre-recorded	8R precedency	9E precocious	9B Predicate	7Q prehatched
9L pre-cooked	7B pre-scientific	7D precepts	9Q precognitive	9Q predicated	9L preheat
XR pre-determine	9L pre-shrink	XH precession	7H preconceived	4N predisposed	9M preheats
7Q pre-eminent	7N Preacher	XH precessional	6F preconquest	8Q predisposing	7Q prehistorian
7N pre-game	7D Preacher's	8D precincts	9L precooked	4Q predominately	7Q prehuman
XR pre-heated	9Q preaches	9D precipated	7H precursor	8Q Predrag	9J Preis
3Q pre-historic	8Q preachments	7H precipitating	9Q precursors	7Q preengineering	5A prejudged

Word Type	F	D	U	SFI	3 Gr 3	4 Gr 4	5 Gr 5	6 Gr 6	7 Gr 7	8 Gr 8	9 Gr 9	X UnGr	A Read	B Eng & Gr	C Comp	D Lit	E Math	F Soc Stud	G Spell	H Sci	J Music	K Art	L Home Ec	M Shop	N Lib F	P Lib NF	Q Lib Ref	R Mag	S Rel
Prejudice	2	.2437	.1129	30.5	0	0	2	0	0	0	0	0	0	0	0	0	0	0	0	0	0	0	0	0	0	0	1	1	0
prejudiced	12	.6820	1.6824	42.3	0	1	3	0	3	3	2	0	2	1	0	1	0	1	0	2	0	0	0	0	0	1	1	3	0
prejudices	11	.6636	1.5015	41.8	0	0	0	0	3	1	4	3	2	1	0	0	0	0	0	1	1	0	1	0	0	3	1	1	0
prelates	2	.2437	.1129	30.5	1	0	0	0	0	0	1	0	0	0	0	0	0	0	0	0	0	0	0	0	0	0	1	1	0
preliminaries	3	.3427	.2477	33.9	0	1	0	0	1	1	0	0	1	0	0	0	0	0	0	0	0	0	0	0	1	0	0	1	0
preliminary	28	.7134	4.0059	46.0	0	1	2	2	7	3	11	2	1	2	1	0	0	1	0	2	2	2	4	4	1	2	3	3	0
prelude	6	.0956	.1668	32.2	0	1	2	0	0	2	1	0	0	0	0	0	0	1	0	0	5	0	0	0	0	0	0	0	0
Prelude	11	.0000	.0889	29.5	0	0	1	1	1	8	0	0	0	0	0	0	0	0	0	0	11	0	0	0	0	0	0	0	0
preludes	3	.2088	.1442	31.6	0	0	0	0	0	2	1	0	0	0	0	0	0	0	0	0	2	0	0	0	0	0	1	0	0
Preludes	5	.1313	.1696	32.3	0	0	0	0	1	4	0	0	0	0	0	0	0	0	0	0	4	0	0	0	0	1	0	0	0
premarital	2	.0000	.0243	23.9	0	0	0	0	1	0	0	1	0	0	0	0	0	0	0	0	0	0	0	0	0	0	0	2	0
premature	2	.2440	.1132	30.5	0	0	0	0	0	0	1	1	0	0	0	1	0	0	0	0	0	0	0	0	0	0	0	1	0
prematurely	2	.2331	.1157	30.6	0	0	0	0	1	1	0	0	0	0	0	0	0	0	0	1	0	0	0	0	1	0	0	0	0
premier	10	.3913	.8503	39.3	0	0	0	1	2	6	1	0	0	0	0	1	0	3	0	0	0	0	0	0	0	0	5	1	0
Premier	7	.3085	.4949	36.9	0	0	1	0	0	4	2	0	0	0	0	0	0	2	0	0	0	0	0	0	0	1	0	4	0
premiere	4	.3399	.2931	34.7	0	0	0	1	0	1	2	0	0	1	0	0	0	0	0	0	2	0	0	0	0	0	0	1	0
premieres	3	.2043	.1486	31.7	0	0	1	0	1	0	0	1	0	0	0	0	0	0	0	0	0	0	0	0	0	1	2	0	0
premise	5	.2418	.2811	34.5	0	1	0	0	1	0	1	2	0	0	0	0	0	0	0	0	0	0	0	0	0	0	2	3	0
premises	4	.4519	.3985	36.0	0	0	0	1	1	1	1	0	1	0	0	1	0	0	0	0	0	0	0	0	0	0	1	1	0
premium	9	.5871	1.1009	40.4	0	1	0	0	2	1	5	0	1	0	0	0	3	1	1	1	0	0	1	0	0	0	1	0	0
premiums	7	.3684	.5608	37.5	0	2	1	0	0	0	2	2	0	0	0	0	2	0	0	0	0	0	0	0	0	0	3	2	0
premolars	2	.0000	.0209	23.2	0	0	0	0	2	0	0	0	0	0	0	0	0	0	0	0	0	0	0	0	0	0	2	0	0
prenatal	2	.0000	.0243	23.9	0	0	0	0	0	0	0	2	0	0	0	0	0	0	0	0	0	0	0	0	0	0	0	2	0
preoccupation	7	.5897	.8591	39.3	0	0	1	0	0	2	3	1	1	1	0	1	0	0	0	0	0	0	0	0	0	1	1	2	0
preoccupied	7	.3957	.6154	37.9	0	0	1	1	3	1	1	0	1	0	0	0	0	0	0	0	0	0	0	0	0	1	2	3	0
prep	5	.3428	.3717	35.7	0	1	0	0	0	1	2	1	0	3	0	0	0	0	1	0	0	0	0	0	0	0	0	1	0
Prep	2	.1733	.1149	30.6	0	0	0	0	1	0	1	0	1	1	0	0	0	0	0	0	0	0	0	0	0	0	0	0	0
preparation	66	.7286	9.7093	49.9	4	3	3	7	17	9	20	3	6	8	0	5	0	7	1	3	1	1	9	0	1	6	11	7	0
preparations	32	.6945	4.6285	46.7	3	5	4	7	7	3	3	0	14	1	0	4	0	2	0	0	2	0	0	0	3	2	4	0	0
preparatory	6	.4530	.5817	37.6	0	1	1	0	1	0	3	0	1	0	0	0	0	0	0	0	2	0	0	1	0	0	1	1	0
prepare	224	.7683	34.729	55.4	17	17	35	23	62	28	39	3	30	22	0	8	4	37	5	38	7	0	27	5	6	8	9	18	0
prepared	282	.8430	47.510	56.8	14	36	33	50	49	38	60	2	50	41	0	12	3	33	12	15	0	1	24	6	17	27	26	14	1
prepares	10	.3856	.8251	39.2	0	0	2	2	1	3	2	0	0	1	3	0	1	2	0	1	1	0	0	0	0	0	1	0	0
preparing	105	.7911	16.748	52.2	5	14	17	9	22	18	18	2	22	12	1	3	2	14	0	8	2	0	11	1	8	4	5	12	0
preposition	71	.2711	4.2490	46.3	0	21	1	10	9	8	22	0	0	54	15	0	0	0	2	0	0	0	0	0	0	0	0	0	0
prepositional	88	.3056	5.8504	47.7	0	20	11	2	13	20	22	0	0	67	15	0	0	0	6	0	0	0	0	0	0	0	0	0	0
prepositions	32	.2638	1.8634	42.7	0	4	3	7	2	3	13	0	0	23	8	0	0	0	1	0	0	0	0	0	0	0	0	0	0
preposterous	2	.2441	.1127	30.5	0	0	0	1	1	0	0	0	0	0	0	0	0	0	0	0	0	0	0	0	1	0	1	0	0
pres	2	.0000	.0219	23.4	0	0	1	0	0	1	0	0	0	2	0	0	0	0	0	0	0	0	0	0	0	0	0	0	0
Pres	4	.1966	.1884	32.8	0	0	0	0	4	0	0	0	0	0	0	1	0	0	0	0	0	0	0	0	0	0	3	0	0
Presbyterian	3	.2159	.1532	31.9	0	0	1	1	1	0	0	0	0	0	0	0	0	0	0	0	0	0	0	0	0	0	2	1	0
Prescott	3	.2261	.2131	33.3	0	0	3	0	0	0	0	0	2	0	0	0	0	0	0	0	0	0	0	0	1	0	0	0	0
prescribe	2	.1442	.0761	28.8	0	0	0	0	0	2	0	0	0	0	0	0	0	1	0	0	0	0	1	0	0	0	0	0	0
prescribed	22	.5184	2.3712	43.7	0	0	0	1	4	8	9	0	0	0	0	0	1	4	0	3	2	0	5	0	0	1	1	5	0
prescribing	2	.1698	.1133	30.5	0	0	1	0	0	0	1	0	1	0	0	0	0	0	0	0	0	0	0	0	0	0	1	0	0
prescription	4	.3233	.3124	34.9	0	0	1	2	1	0	0	0	1	0	0	0	2	0	0	0	0	0	0	0	0	0	1	0	0
prescriptions	3	.2942	.1970	32.9	0	0	0	0	0	1	2	0	0	0	0	0	0	0	0	1	0	0	1	0	0	0	1	0	0
preseason	2	.1812	.0838	29.2	0	0	0	0	0	2	0	0	0	0	0	0	0	0	0	0	0	0	1	0	0	0	0	1	0
presence	125	.8362	20.883	53.2	6	6	9	11	33	23	28	9	13	4	3	15	0	5	1	28	3	0	3	0	9	10	13	18	0
present	732	.9543	137.90	61.4	84	87	60	90	152	116	111	32	133	90	8	30	22	54	45	99	28	1	16	4	28	52	66	55	1
Present	4	.3212	.3104	34.9	0	2	0	0	0	1	1	0	1	0	0	1	0	0	0	0	0	0	0	0	0	2	0	0	0
present-day	39	.7875	6.1394	47.9	0	8	5	4	10	6	5	1	1	4	0	0	1	6	2	4	8	1	2	2	0	3	5	0	0
present-tense	2	.0000	.0219	23.4	0	0	2	0	0	0	0	0	0	2	0	0	0	0	0	0	0	0	0	0	0	0	0	0	0
presentable	3	.1250	.1342	31.3	0	0	0	1	1	1	0	0	1	0	0	0	0	0	0	0	0	0	0	0	2	0	0	0	0
presentation	16	.6130	2.0117	43.0	0	0	1	2	3	2	8	0	2	1	0	0	2	0	0	0	5	0	1	2	0	1	1	1	0
presented	139	.9370	25.761	54.1	6	11	11	15	32	39	22	3	31	18	3	7	9	8	5	3	11	1	3	1	8	12	11	8	0
presentiment	3	.0000	.0352	25.5	0	0	0	1	2	0	0	0	0	0	0	0	0	0	0	0	0	0	0	0	3	0	0	0	0
presenting	31	.6534	4.1546	46.2	2	3	1	5	5	6	8	1	6	6	4	2	0	1	0	0	3	2	0	0	2	2	2	1	0
presently	84	.6539	11.493	50.6	7	13	5	13	20	12	13	1	30	3	0	19	2	0	0	2	2	0	0	0	15	8	1	2	0
presents	130	.8988	23.239	53.7	31	21	9	10	23	12	18	6	37	12	3	11	1	10	5	2	13	1	2	0	7	10	9	7	0
Presents	2	.0000	.0243	23.9	0	0	0	0	0	0	2	0	0	0	0	0	0	0	0	0	0	0	0	0	0	0	0	2	0
preservation	21	.6528	2.7931	44.5	0	0	2	1	7	2	6	3	1	0	0	1	0	1	0	2	2	0	1	0	0	2	7	4	0
preservatives	3	.2445	.1818	32.6	0	0	0	0	0	1	1	1	0	0	0	0	0	0	0	2	0	0	0	0	0	0	1	0	0
preserve	61	.6455	8.0962	49.1	2	3	12	4	14	7	15	4	9	1	0	2	3	7	3	1	1	0	6	1	2	7	12	5	1
preserved	58	.7067	8.3223	49.2	2	4	13	10	8	8	7	6	5	2	1	1	0	10	0	3	8	0	0	0	0	6	14	8	0
preserver	2	.2152	.1357	31.3	0	0	0	1	0	0	1	0	1	0	0	0	0	1	0	0	0	0	0	0	0	0	0	0	0
preserves	17	.6869	2.4134	43.8	2	2	2	0	5	1	5	0	5	1	0	2	2	0	0	2	0	0	1	0	0	1	3	0	0
preserving	19	.5622	2.2667	43.6	1	1	3	0	6	5	3	0	3	0	0	0	0	6	0	1	0	0	0	0	0	3	4	2	0
preshrinking	2	.0000	.0064	18.1	0	0	0	0	0	0	2	0	0	0	0	0	0	0	0	0	0	0	2	0	0	0	0	0	0
preshrunk	5	.1070	.1239	30.9	0	0	0	0	0	3	2	0	0	0	0	0	0	0	1	0	0	0	4	0	0	0	0	0	0
preside	9	.5869	1.1143	40.5	0	1	1	2	3	2	0	0	2	0	0	0	0	1	0	0	0	0	0	0	1	2	2	1	0
presided	10	.5496	1.1574	40.6	0	0	1	0	2	3	4	0	1	1	0	1	0	3	0	0	0	0	0	0	0	1	3	0	0
presidency	11	.1597	.4647	36.7	0	0	5	0	0	4	2	0	0	0	0	0	0	3	0	0	0	0	0	0	0	0	8	0	0
Presidency	17	.2639	1.1165	40.5	1	1	2	0	3	4	6	0	3	0	0	0	0	1	0	0	0	0	0	0	0	2	0	11	0
president	198	.7655	30.629	54.9	15	15	39	21	41	35	27	5	29	10	1	1	6	37	7	2	4	0	0	0	5	27	38	31	0
President	602	.6884	84.933	59.3	60	46	86	38	107	154	98	13	72	17	2	1	2	201	6	4	7	0	0	2	14	74	49	151	0
President-elect	11	.4194	1.0158	40.1	0	0	0	0	3	7	1	0	0	1	0	0	0	7	0	0	0	0	0	0	0	2	0	1	0
president's	4	.1814	.2373	33.8	1	0	0	1	2	0	0	0	2	0	0	0	0	0	0	0	0	0	0	0	0	0	0	2	0
President's	45	.4661	4.6223	46.6	7	4	1	2	10	11	9	1	9	0	0	0	0	9	0	0	0	0	0	0	0	11	1	15	0
presidential	32	.5607	3.7298	45.7	1	0	11	1	5	7	7	0	1	1	0	0	0	9	1	0	1	0	0	0	0	1	10	8	0
Presidential	22	.4942	2.3493	43.7	0	0	1	1	14	3	3	0	4	0	0	0	0	3	0	0	0	0	0	0	0	4	7	4	0
presidents	18	.6638	2.4275	43.9	2	1	4	0	1	1	6	3	0	2	0	0	4	2	2	0	1	0	0	0	0	3	0	4	0
Presidents	24	.4026	2.1744	43.4	0	1	6	0	3	6	8	0	4	0	0	0	0	5	0	0	0	0	0	0	0	1	2	12	0
Presidents'	2	.0000	.0243	23.9	2	0	0	0	0	0	0	0	0	0	0	0	0	0	0	0	0	0	0	0	0	0	0	2	0
presides	2	.2408	.1204	30.8	0	0	0	0	0	0	2	0	0	0	0	0	0	1	0	0	0	0	0	0	0	1	0	0	0
presiding	7	.4332	.6741	38.3	3	0	0	0	1	2	1	0	1	0	0	0	0	2	0	0	0	0	0	0	0	2	0	2	0
presidio	2	.0000	.0243	23.9	0	0	0	2	0	0	0	0	0	0	0	0	0	0	0	0	0	0	0	0	0	0	0	2	0
Presidio	2	.1698	.1133	30.5	0	0	0	0	1	1	0	0	1	0	0	0	0	0	0	0	0	0	0	0	0	0	1	0	0
Presley	7	.1529	.2814	34.5	0	0	0	0	1	6	0	0	0	1	0	0	0	0	0	0	0	0	0	0	0	0	0	6	0
presocial	2	.0000	.0243	23.9	0	0	0	0	2	0	0	0	0	0	0	0	0	0	0	0	0	0	0	0	0	0	0	2	0
press	247	.7020	35.121	55.5	31	28	21	17	49	36	58	7	32	9	0	12	3	12	3	16	19	5	51	16	8	12	16	33	0
Press	9	.4661	.9698	39.9	1	0	0	1	1	6	0	0	5	0	0	0	1	0	0	0	1	0	0	0	0	0	2	0	0
pressed	134	.7870	21.312	53.3	16	18	14	12	27	23	19	5	36	0	0	24	1	11	1	5	2	7	7	3	8	15	6	8	0
presser	21	.0246	.1762	32.5	0	0	0	0	1	15	4	1	0	0	0	0	0	0	0	0	0	0	20	0	0	0	0	1	0
presses	57	.6906	8.0057	49.0	18	8	6	8	7	3	5	2	0	0	0	2	2	6	2	27	5	0	0	4	2	1	2	4	0

9R prejudicing
XB prelate
7R prelaunch
7R premed
9Q premedical
7R premeds
XH premie
8Q premiership
7R Preminger
7A premixed
7Q premolar
8F premonition
5Q Prendergast
3A Prentice
XR prepackaged
4A prepaid
3P Prepare
7R preparedness
8D preparest
8F prepayment
6A prepoceros
5P preponderance
8A preponderant
3P preponderantly
6B prepose
9B preposition-shifting
3P prepotency
9D prereading
XP prerogative
7A Pres-l-dent
5G pres'ent**
9D presage
4R preschool
7R preschoolers
8R prescience
9M presensitized
5G present**
8Q Presern
XR Preservation
8G preservationist
7R preservative
4F preservers
4P Presiding
4F presidios
8R Presley's
7M press-like
8L press-on
7P press'd
3A Presser
8L presser-bar

Word Type	F	D	U	SFI	3 Gr 3	4 Gr 4	5 Gr 5	6 Gr 6	7 Gr 7	8 Gr 8	9 Gr 9	X UnGr	A Read	B Eng & Gr	C Comp	D Lit	E Math	F Soc Stud	G Spell	H Sci	J Music	K Art	L Home Ec	M Shop	N Lib F	P Lib NF	Q Lib Ref	R Mag	S Rel
pressing	92	.6026	11.372	50.6	15	9	11	7	11	19	18	2	8	0	1	9	0	2	1	17	6	2	27	2	5	3	1	8	0
pressure	499	.7077	72.207	58.6	59	55	69	66	100	70	69	11	63	3	1	7	7	15	5	240	10	0	10	34	4	28	40	32	0
pressured	2	.0000	.0243	23.9	0	0	0	0	1	0	1	0	0	0	0	0	0	0	0	0	0	0	0	0	0	0	0	2	0
pressures	33	.6016	4.1402	46.2	1	1	1	3	7	3	16	1	3	0	0	0	0	2	0	12	0	0	0	1	0	3	3	9	0
pressuring	3	.2051	.1687	32.3	0	0	0	0	2	1	0	0	1	0	1	0	0	0	0	0	0	0	0	0	0	0	0	1	0
pressurized	13	.2349	.7864	39.0	1	3	2	1	2	3	1	0	0	0	0	0	0	0	0	11	0	0	0	0	0	1	0	1	0
presswork	2	.0000	.0050	17.0	0	0	0	0	0	0	2	0	0	0	0	0	0	0	0	0	0	0	0	2	0	0	0	0	0
prestidigitator	2	.0000	.0219	23.4	0	0	0	0	0	0	2	0	0	2	0	0	0	0	0	0	0	0	0	0	0	0	0	0	0
prestige	20	.7179	2.9178	44.7	0	0	3	1	4	4	5	3	3	2	0	0	0	3	1	0	1	0	1	0	0	1	4	4	0
prestigious	3	.2321	.1635	32.1	0	0	0	0	3	0	0	0	0	0	0	0	0	0	0	0	0	0	0	0	0	0	1	2	0
presto	5	.3567	.3860	35.9	1	1	0	0	0	1	1	1	0	0	0	1	0	0	0	0	1	0	0	0	0	0	0	3	0
Preston	4	.3624	.3169	35.0	0	0	0	1	0	0	3	0	0	1	0	0	1	0	0	0	0	0	0	0	0	0	0	2	0
Preston's	2	.0000	.0243	23.9	0	0	0	0	2	0	0	0	0	0	0	0	0	0	0	0	0	0	0	0	0	0	0	2	0
presumably	16	.5756	1.9065	42.8	0	0	1	3	3	5	2	2	1	1	0	1	0	1	0	1	0	1	0	0	1	0	1	8	0
presume	7	.4188	.6411	38.1	0	0	0	1	1	3	2	0	1	0	1	3	0	1	0	0	0	0	0	0	0	0	0	1	0
presumed	4	.4890	.4068	36.1	0	0	0	0	1	3	0	0	0	1	0	1	0	0	0	0	0	0	0	0	1	0	1	0	0
presumptuous	3	.0000	.0322	25.1	0	0	0	0	1	0	2	0	0	0	0	3	0	0	0	0	0	0	0	0	0	0	0	0	0
pretence	3	.2120	.1548	31.9	1	0	0	1	1	0	0	0	0	0	0	0	0	0	0	0	0	0	0	0	2	1	0	0	0
pretend	115	.8722	20.007	53.0	39	18	15	9	18	8	6	2	29	18	2	6	5	4	5	11	15	2	3	0	7	5	1	2	0
pretended	67	.6474	9.1632	49.6	18	24	4	9	6	5	1	0	29	3	0	7	0	2	0	0	0	0	1	0	8	16	0	1	0
pretending	46	.6644	6.4338	48.1	16	9	5	3	6	4	3	0	21	1	0	2	2	0	1	1	0	0	0	0	10	5	0	3	0
pretends	9	.7146	1.3138	41.2	3	3	2	1	0	0	0	0	2	1	0	1	0	1	1	0	1	0	0	0	1	1	0	0	0
pretense	7	.5100	.7447	38.7	0	0	2	0	2	2	1	0	0	0	0	1	0	1	0	0	0	0	0	0	3	0	1	1	0
pretentious	3	.3768	.2437	33.9	0	0	0	0	1	1	0	1	0	0	0	0	0	0	0	0	1	0	0	0	0	1	0	1	0
pretext	4	.3024	.3033	34.8	0	0	0	0	3	1	0	0	1	0	0	0	0	1	0	0	0	0	0	0	0	2	0	0	0
Pretoria	4	.3182	.2816	34.5	0	1	0	2	0	1	0	0	0	0	0	0	0	1	0	0	2	0	0	0	0	0	1	0	0
prettier	13	.5715	1.5352	41.9	3	0	2	1	2	1	3	1	1	5	0	3	0	0	1	0	1	0	0	0	0	1	0	1	0
prettiest	25	.7419	3.8062	45.8	10	5	3	2	4	1	0	0	9	1	1	1	0	2	0	2	2	0	0	0	0	5	1	1	0
prettily	8	.3598	.7349	38.7	1	2	0	1	3	1	0	0	5	0	0	2	0	0	0	0	0	0	0	0	0	1	0	0	0
pretty	573	.8556	98.344	59.9	147	111	57	74	95	48	31	10	212	42	9	45	1	14	16	9	24	3	5	0	94	45	6	48	0
Pretty	2	.0000	.0162	22.1	0	0	0	0	1	1	0	0	0	0	0	0	0	0	0	0	2	0	0	0	0	0	0	0	0
pretzel	4	.4098	.3465	35.4	0	0	0	0	0	1	2	1	0	1	0	0	1	0	0	0	0	0	1	0	0	0	0	1	0
Pretzie	5	.0000	.0586	27.7	5	0	0	0	0	0	0	0	0	0	0	0	0	0	0	0	0	0	0	0	5	0	0	0	0
Pretzie's	2	.0000	.0234	23.7	2	0	0	0	0	0	0	0	0	0	0	0	0	0	0	0	0	0	0	0	2	0	0	0	0
prevail	7	.5131	.7434	38.7	0	0	0	0	3	0	3	1	0	0	1	0	0	0	0	2	1	0	1	0	0	0	0	2	0
prevailed	12	.6283	1.5622	41.9	0	0	2	3	1	1	3	2	2	0	0	0	0	1	0	0	2	0	0	0	1	3	1	2	0
prevailing	26	.5194	2.8288	44.5	2	2	5	4	5	3	3	2	0	1	0	0	0	6	0	3	0	0	0	0	1	1	11	3	0
prevalent	11	.5177	1.1832	40.7	0	1	0	0	5	2	2	1	0	0	0	0	0	0	0	2	0	0	1	0	1	0	4	3	0
prevent	248	.7219	36.276	55.6	13	14	40	25	63	43	42	8	23	6	1	10	0	29	3	61	2	0	34	14	12	10	25	18	0
preventable	2	.0000	.0394	26.0	0	0	1	0	0	1	0	0	0	0	0	0	0	0	0	2	0	0	0	0	0	0	0	0	0
prevented	27	.7545	4.1477	46.2	1	1	5	5	8	3	4	0	6	0	1	2	2	2	0	7	0	0	0	0	1	1	2	3	0
preventing	22	.6797	3.0935	44.9	0	2	4	1	9	3	1	2	5	0	0	0	0	3	0	6	0	0	1	1	0	1	1	4	0
prevention	15	.4579	1.4733	41.7	1	0	0	0	3	6	1	4	0	0	0	0	0	2	0	5	0	0	0	0	0	0	4	4	0
Prevention	6	.3627	.5371	37.3	4	0	0	0	1	1	0	0	3	0	0	0	0	0	0	0	0	0	0	0	0	0	1	2	0
preventive	4	.2287	.2348	33.7	0	0	0	0	2	0	2	0	0	0	0	0	0	0	0	3	0	0	0	0	0	0	0	1	0
Preventive	2	.2433	.1158	30.6	0	0	0	0	2	0	0	0	0	0	0	0	0	0	0	0	0	0	0	0	0	1	0	1	0
prevents	39	.6231	5.0331	47.0	3	1	6	3	10	4	10	2	5	1	0	0	1	1	0	14	0	0	6	2	1	2	2	4	0
preview	16	.5117	1.9012	42.8	0	0	1	0	13	2	0	0	12	0	0	1	0	1	0	0	1	0	0	0	0	0	0	1	0
previewing	8	.0000	.3655	35.6	0	0	0	0	8	0	0	0	8	0	0	0	0	0	0	0	0	0	0	0	0	0	0	0	0
previous	150	.9244	27.424	54.4	4	4	8	14	42	37	36	5	13	9	3	3	22	9	8	14	10	1	3	1	3	16	11	24	0
previously	52	.8001	8.3298	49.2	2	0	6	3	16	12	10	3	4	1	0	3	3	7	1	3	2	0	5	2	1	6	6	8	0
prewar	3	.2425	.1816	32.6	0	0	0	0	1	2	0	0	0	0	0	0	0	2	0	0	0	0	0	0	0	0	0	1	0
prey	109	.4889	11.508	50.6	16	4	7	17	62	0	3	0	20	1	0	4	0	4	0	12	1	0	0	0	3	6	54	4	0
preyed	8	.3298	.6306	38.0	0	2	0	2	3	1	0	0	2	0	0	0	0	0	0	1	0	0	0	0	0	1	4	0	0
preying	2	.1698	.1133	30.5	0	0	0	0	2	0	0	0	1	0	0	0	0	0	0	0	0	0	0	0	0	0	1	0	0
preys	2	.1698	.1133	30.5	0	0	1	0	1	0	0	0	1	0	0	0	0	0	0	0	0	0	0	0	0	0	1	0	0
Priam	10	.2048	.7309	38.6	0	0	0	3	0	6	1	0	9	0	0	0	0	0	0	0	0	1	0	0	0	0	0	0	0
Priam's	3	.0000	.1370	31.4	0	0	0	0	0	3	0	0	3	0	0	0	0	0	0	0	0	0	0	0	0	0	0	0	0
price	289	.7837	45.750	56.6	47	22	31	25	54	34	66	10	56	1	1	9	78	36	4	3	2	0	13	0	13	19	17	37	0
Price	33	.5172	3.9541	46.0	10	0	14	3	3	1	2	0	25	0	0	3	1	1	0	0	0	0	0	0	0	0	1	2	0
priced	13	.4035	1.1507	40.6	0	0	2	1	10	0	0	0	1	0	0	0	2	1	0	0	0	0	0	0	0	0	2	7	0
priceless	6	.4274	.5610	37.5	0	0	1	1	0	2	1	1	1	0	1	0	0	1	0	0	1	0	0	0	0	0	0	2	0
prices	100	.7349	14.884	51.7	8	7	9	11	14	22	22	7	9	1	1	2	5	27	0	1	0	1	4	0	2	4	11	32	0
prick	9	.5410	1.0280	40.1	2	1	0	1	1	1	1	2	1	0	0	1	0	0	0	3	1	0	0	1	0	2	0	0	0
prick'd	3	.0000	.0434	26.4	0	0	0	0	3	0	0	0	0	0	0	0	0	0	0	0	0	0	0	0	0	3	0	0	0
pricked	21	.4301	2.0123	43.0	4	3	7	1	5	0	1	0	5	1	0	2	0	0	0	0	0	0	0	0	11	1	0	1	0
pricking	3	.2227	.1589	32.0	0	1	1	0	1	0	0	0	0	0	0	0	0	0	0	0	0	0	0	0	2	0	0	1	0
prickle	3	.3833	.2447	33.9	0	0	0	2	1	0	0	0	0	0	0	0	0	0	0	0	1	0	0	0	1	0	1	0	0
prickles	4	.1750	.1896	32.8	2	1	0	1	0	0	0	0	0	0	0	0	0	0	0	1	0	0	0	0	0	3	0	0	0
prickly	24	.6405	3.2614	45.1	2	5	3	5	8	0	1	0	12	0	1	1	0	0	0	0	0	1	0	0	3	2	4	0	0
prickly-pear	3	.2120	.1548	31.9	1	0	0	0	2	0	0	0	0	0	0	0	0	0	0	0	0	0	0	0	2	1	0	0	0
pricks	2	.0000	.0290	24.6	0	1	0	0	1	0	0	0	0	0	0	0	0	0	0	0	0	0	0	0	0	2	0	0	0
pride	145	.8233	24.035	53.8	10	15	15	25	42	24	10	4	43	4	0	17	0	14	2	2	2	0	1	3	20	17	5	15	0
Pride	2	.2417	.1091	30.4	0	0	2	0	0	0	0	0	0	0	0	0	0	0	0	0	1	0	0	0	0	0	1	0	0
prided	3	.1910	.1473	31.7	0	1	1	0	0	1	0	0	0	0	0	0	0	1	0	0	0	0	0	0	2	0	0	0	0
pried	10	.5449	1.1812	40.7	2	0	0	1	3	1	2	1	3	0	0	1	0	0	0	3	0	0	0	0	2	0	0	1	0
pries	2	.0000	.0209	23.2	0	0	0	0	2	0	0	0	0	0	0	0	0	0	0	0	0	0	0	0	0	0	2	0	0
priest	86	.5238	9.5586	49.8	6	10	6	22	15	12	14	1	12	1	0	15	0	11	1	2	2	2	0	0	9	12	2	15	2
Priest	4	.1210	.2172	33.4	0	0	0	3	0	0	1	0	3	0	0	0	0	0	0	0	0	1	0	0	0	0	0	0	0
priest's	3	.3399	.2456	33.9	0	0	0	2	0	0	1	0	1	0	0	1	0	0	0	0	0	0	0	0	0	0	0	1	0
priesthood	4	.1737	.1745	32.4	0	0	2	0	1	0	1	0	0	0	0	0	0	0	0	0	0	0	0	0	0	1	3	0	0
Priestley	13	.0000	.2563	34.1	0	5	2	1	5	0	0	0	0	0	0	0	0	0	0	13	0	0	0	0	0	0	0	0	0
Priestley's	3	.0000	.0591	27.7	0	0	1	0	2	0	0	0	0	0	0	0	0	0	0	3	0	0	0	0	0	0	0	0	0
Priestly	3	.0000	.0591	27.7	0	0	2	1	0	0	0	0	0	0	0	0	0	0	0	3	0	0	0	0	0	0	0	0	0
priests	67	.6653	9.1802	49.6	0	4	11	29	11	6	3	3	8	2	0	0	0	27	0	0	3	1	0	0	0	7	9	10	0
Priests	3	.0000	.1370	31.4	0	0	0	3	0	0	0	0	3	0	0	0	0	0	0	0	0	0	0	0	0	0	0	0	0
prim	7	.4418	.7057	38.5	0	0	0	1	4	1	1	0	3	0	1	1	1	0	0	0	0	0	0	0	0	0	1	0	0
Prim	4	.0000	.1827	32.6	4	0	0	0	0	0	0	0	4	0	0	0	0	0	0	0	0	0	0	0	0	0	0	0	0
primacy	2	.2441	.1127	30.5	0	0	0	0	2	0	0	0	0	0	0	0	0	0	0	0	0	0	0	0	1	0	1	0	0
primaeval	2	.2437	.1129	30.5	0	0	0	0	1	0	0	1	0	0	0	0	0	0	0	0	0	0	0	0	0	0	1	1	0
primal	2	.2407	.1138	30.6	0	0	1	0	0	1	0	0	0	0	0	1	0	0	0	0	0	0	0	0	0	1	0	0	0
primaries	3	.0902	.0676	28.3	0	0	0	0	1	2	0	0	0	0	0	0	0	0	0	0	0	2	0	0	0	0	0	1	0
primarily	70	.7829	10.960	50.4	3	1	2	3	21	11	24	5	2	3	3	0	0	5	1	6	8	1	1	1	0	6	21	12	0
primary	126	.7550	19.079	52.8	12	6	10	8	31	36	21	2	8	1	0	1	3	11	21	8	11	6	4	13	1	6	22	10	0
primate	3	.0000	.0314	25.0	0	0	0	0	3	0	0	0	0	0	0	0	0	0	0	0	0	0	0	0	0	0	3	0	0
primates	16	.0900	.4521	36.6	0	0	0	0	16	0	0	0	0	0	0	0	0	0	0	2	0	0	0	0	0	0	14	0	0

8K pressing-down
9M pressman
6Q pressure-and-catalysis
XH pressure-electricity
7D pressure's
7N presuming
7C presumption
7R presupposed
5Q presupposes
7R pretechnological
5G pretekt'**
7A pretelevision
XR pretender
6J Pretender
8A pretendin'
7D Pretense
6P preternatural
5Q pretexts
8B prettied
7R prettified
8N prettiness
7A pretty-please
4P prettying
5B pretzels
7H Prevailing
7A Preview
7A previewed
5Q Prevost
6A prexie
6F PRI
5F Pribilof
9R price-wage
9M prick-punch
9D pricksong
7A prid'near
7A pride's
5R prideful
9K prides
6F priest-architect
4Q priest-teacher
6A priestess
8A priestesses
5A priestly
9D Prig
9B prima
3K PRIMARY

Word Type	F	D	U	SFI	3 Gr 3	4 Gr 4	5 Gr 5	6 Gr 6	7 Gr 7	8 Gr 8	9 Gr 9	X UnGr	A Read	B Eng & Gr	C Comp	D Lit	E Math	F Soc Stud	G Spell	H Sci	J Music	K Art	L Home Ec	M Shop	N Lib F	P Lib NF	Q Lib Ref	R Mag	S Rel
prime	335	.3316	25.106	54.0	26	34	25	38	96	79	31	6	1	0	1	1	274	4	0	4	2	0	0	0	3	9	21	15	0
Prime	27	.5537	3.1545	45.0	0	1	5	0	5	7	5	4	3	1	0	0	0	7	0	0	0	0	0	0	0	5	3	8	0
primer	16	.1130	.4406	36.4	0	5	0	0	0	5	6	0	0	0	0	0	0	0	0	0	0	0	0	11	0	4	1	0	0
Primer	4	.3677	.3659	35.6	0	0	2	0	1	0	1	0	2	0	0	1	0	1	0	0	0	0	0	0	0	0	0	0	0
primes	27	.0000	.4041	36.1	0	4	1	9	5	4	4	0	0	0	0	0	27	0	0	0	0	0	0	0	0	0	0	0	0
Primes	2	.0000	.0299	24.8	0	0	0	2	0	0	0	0	0	0	0	0	2	0	0	0	0	0	0	0	0	0	0	0	0
primeval	11	.2810	.6966	38.4	0	0	0	1	8	0	0	2	0	0	0	0	0	0	0	0	0	0	0	0	0	1	7	3	0
Primeval	3	.0000	.0365	25.6	0	0	0	0	0	0	0	3	0	0	0	0	0	0	0	0	0	0	0	0	0	0	0	3	0
priming	7	.2748	.4860	36.9	0	5	0	0	0	1	1	0	2	0	0	1	0	0	0	0	0	0	0	0	4	0	0	0	0
primitive	174	.8131	28.302	54.5	5	10	17	22	63	17	27	13	11	6	1	3	4	31	5	25	19	5	0	3	0	13	41	7	0
Primitive	7	.4009	.5985	37.8	0	1	0	0	5	0	1	0	0	4	0	1	0	0	0	0	0	0	0	0	1	0	0	1	0
primitives	7	.2749	.4505	36.5	0	0	0	6	0	1	0	0	1	0	0	0	0	0	0	0	0	1	0	0	0	0	5	0	0
primly	4	.3740	.3661	35.6	0	2	0	0	0	0	2	0	2	0	0	0	0	0	0	0	0	0	0	0	1	0	0	1	0
primordial	3	.0000	.0314	25.0	0	1	0	0	1	0	1	0	0	0	0	0	0	0	0	0	0	0	0	0	0	0	3	0	0
primrose	2	.2411	.1091	30.4	1	0	0	0	0	0	1	0	0	0	0	1	0	0	0	0	1	0	0	0	0	0	0	0	0
primus	3	.2441	.1719	32.4	0	0	0	0	0	3	0	0	0	0	0	0	0	0	1	0	0	0	0	0	0	2	0	0	0
Primus	2	.0000	.0914	29.6	0	0	0	0	2	0	0	0	2	0	0	0	0	0	0	0	0	0	0	0	0	0	0	0	0
prince	106	.7368	16.180	52.1	46	5	11	11	16	8	3	6	55	3	0	9	0	8	2	0	5	0	0	0	6	8	0	10	0
Prince	180	.6910	25.774	54.1	33	18	40	51	15	13	8	2	63	0	0	17	0	11	1	1	25	0	0	0	3	28	9	22	0
prince's	5	.3833	.4767	36.8	5	0	0	0	0	0	0	0	3	0	0	1	0	0	0	0	0	0	0	0	0	1	0	0	0
Prince's	12	.4627	1.2084	40.8	1	2	3	5	1	0	0	0	2	0	0	0	0	0	0	0	2	0	0	0	1	6	0	1	0
princely	6	.4163	.5544	37.4	0	2	1	1	1	1	0	0	1	0	0	0	0	0	0	0	1	0	0	0	1	3	0	0	0
princes	28	.6770	3.9138	45.9	2	2	4	6	4	1	6	3	7	0	0	1	0	2	0	0	1	0	0	0	3	4	5	5	0
Princes	4	.4519	.3985	36.0	0	0	0	1	2	0	1	0	1	0	0	1	0	0	0	0	0	0	0	0	0	0	1	1	0
princess	116	.7121	17.349	52.4	55	12	17	9	9	9	1	4	75	3	1	10	1	1	4	0	2	0	0	0	14	1	1	3	0
Princess	115	.5486	14.380	51.6	36	37	14	18	2	6	1	1	89	0	0	3	0	0	0	0	1	0	0	0	3	11	4	4	0
Princess'	3	.2212	.2099	33.2	0	2	0	0	0	1	0	0	2	0	0	1	0	0	0	0	0	0	0	0	0	0	0	0	0
princess's	2	.1717	.1142	30.6	1	0	0	0	0	1	0	0	1	0	0	1	0	0	0	0	0	0	0	0	0	0	0	0	0
Princess's	8	.0000	.3655	35.6	6	1	0	1	0	0	0	0	8	0	0	0	0	0	0	0	0	0	0	0	0	0	0	0	0
princesses	6	.2212	.4198	36.2	1	4	0	1	0	0	0	0	4	0	0	2	0	0	0	0	0	0	0	0	0	0	0	0	0
Princeton	24	.6385	3.2080	45.1	1	1	3	7	5	4	3	0	6	3	0	0	0	5	0	2	0	0	0	0	0	2	1	5	0
principal	208	.7893	32.909	55.2	3	6	16	30	81	35	31	6	15	41	13	9	12	19	6	18	7	0	0	1	3	14	32	18	0
Principal	5	.4688	.4931	36.9	0	1	2	0	0	2	0	0	0	0	0	1	0	0	0	0	0	0	0	0	1	1	0	2	0
principal's	11	.5106	1.1666	40.7	0	0	0	2	4	1	4	0	0	3	0	4	2	0	1	0	0	0	0	0	0	1	0	0	0
principalities	2	.1698	.1133	30.5	0	0	0	0	1	0	1	0	1	0	0	0	0	0	0	0	0	0	0	0	0	0	1	0	0
principality	2	.2433	.1158	30.6	0	0	0	1	1	0	0	0	0	0	0	0	0	0	0	0	0	0	0	0	0	1	0	1	0
principally	18	.5343	1.9855	43.0	0	0	2	0	7	6	3	0	0	0	0	0	0	2	1	2	4	0	0	1	0	0	8	0	0
principals	8	.4114	.7135	38.5	0	1	0	1	1	0	5	0	0	1	0	0	1	2	0	0	0	0	0	0	0	0	0	4	0
Principia	4	.0000	.1827	32.6	0	0	0	0	0	4	0	0	4	0	0	0	0	0	0	0	0	0	0	0	0	0	0	0	0
principle	178	.7536	27.024	54.3	4	8	24	31	32	47	28	4	7	3	1	1	72	12	3	23	10	0	1	7	0	6	21	11	0
principles	169	.8404	28.315	54.5	1	3	22	25	40	39	33	6	11	13	1	2	41	18	4	12	6	1	4	10	0	11	25	10	0
Principles	3	.2181	.1541	31.9	0	1	1	0	0	0	1	0	0	0	0	0	0	0	0	0	0	0	0	0	1	0	2	0	0
print	134	.6020	16.653	52.2	12	28	15	17	27	15	18	2	21	16	1	8	5	10	11	5	1	26	1	8	6	4	4	7	0
printed	277	.8369	46.387	56.7	33	43	36	32	43	31	54	5	63	33	1	8	6	19	34	11	13	8	10	21	3	17	20	10	0
printer	25	.7358	3.7535	45.7	4	2	4	4	3	6	1	1	7	5	0	1	0	1	2	0	0	1	0	0	2	3	1	2	0
printer's	6	.2218	.3534	35.5	0	0	0	3	1	2	0	0	2	1	0	0	0	0	0	0	0	2	0	0	0	0	0	1	0
printers	14	.4479	1.3059	41.2	0	0	1	0	2	10	1	0	0	4	0	1	0	1	7	0	0	0	0	1	0	0	0	0	0
printing	172	.5691	20.023	53.0	11	13	20	23	22	16	63	4	10	14	1	3	8	9	22	1	1	9	0	46	3	6	30	9	0
Printing	3	.2043	.1486	31.7	1	0	1	0	0	0	1	0	0	0	0	0	0	0	0	0	0	0	0	0	0	1	2	0	0
prints	56	.4120	4.9811	47.0	15	10	4	7	6	2	6	6	9	0	1	1	3	2	1	2	1	20	1	4	0	6	1	4	0
Prinz	10	.0000	.1094	30.4	0	0	10	0	0	0	0	0	0	10	0	0	0	0	0	0	0	0	0	0	0	0	0	0	0
prior	19	.6884	2.6768	44.3	0	0	0	3	7	4	5	0	3	0	1	1	0	1	0	2	1	0	0	0	0	3	2	5	0
priorities	2	.0000	.0243	23.9	0	0	0	0	0	1	1	0	0	0	0	0	0	0	0	0	0	0	0	0	0	0	0	2	0
priority	7	.3957	.6154	37.9	1	1	1	0	1	1	2	0	1	0	0	0	0	0	0	0	0	0	0	0	0	1	2	3	0
Priority	2	.0000	.0209	23.2	0	0	0	0	2	0	0	0	0	0	0	0	0	0	0	0	0	0	0	0	0	0	2	0	0
Pris	3	.0000	.0365	25.6	0	0	0	0	0	0	0	3	0	0	0	0	0	0	0	0	0	0	0	0	0	0	0	3	0
Priscilla	19	.2176	1.4390	41.6	6	0	0	11	0	0	0	2	17	0	0	0	0	0	0	0	0	0	0	0	0	0	0	2	0
prism	80	.4179	7.2718	48.6	2	2	4	18	24	24	3	3	0	0	0	0	56	0	0	13	0	0	0	2	1	3	5	0	0
prismatic	3	.2445	.1818	32.6	0	0	0	0	0	1	1	1	0	0	0	0	0	0	0	2	0	0	0	0	0	0	1	0	0
prisms	18	.5526	2.0692	43.2	0	3	0	3	2	7	2	1	0	0	0	0	7	0	0	3	0	0	0	0	2	1	4	1	0
prison	94	.7305	14.052	51.5	12	11	17	5	28	9	11	1	26	1	0	14	0	10	1	1	1	0	0	0	9	13	13	5	0
Prison	2	.1814	.1187	30.7	0	0	0	0	1	0	0	1	1	0	0	0	0	0	0	0	0	0	0	0	0	0	0	1	0
prisoner	48	.7489	7.3346	48.7	5	10	11	3	6	6	6	1	14	2	1	7	0	5	0	0	0	0	0	0	5	7	2	5	0
prisoner-of-war	2	.1494	.1045	30.2	0	0	0	1	1	0	0	0	1	0	0	0	0	0	0	0	1	0	0	0	0	0	0	0	0
prisoners	44	.6917	6.2629	48.0	1	5	9	9	14	3	3	0	10	0	1	5	0	9	0	0	0	0	0	0	5	5	8	1	0
prisons	4	.3429	.3033	34.8	0	0	1	0	1	0	2	0	0	0	0	2	0	1	0	0	0	0	0	0	0	0	1	0	0
Prissy	8	.0000	.3655	35.6	8	0	0	0	0	0	0	0	8	0	0	0	0	0	0	0	0	0	0	0	0	0	0	0	0
prithee	3	.3854	.2500	34.0	0	0	1	0	1	1	0	0	0	1	0	0	0	0	0	0	0	0	0	0	1	1	0	0	0
privacy	18	.6564	2.4279	43.9	0	2	0	2	6	5	1	2	3	2	0	1	0	0	1	1	0	0	1	0	4	0	0	5	0
private	163	.7749	25.426	54.1	10	11	20	13	43	30	27	9	17	5	1	8	0	28	4	5	3	0	1	0	10	12	35	34	0
Private	7	.2070	.3419	35.3	0	0	0	0	1	6	0	0	0	0	0	0	0	1	0	0	5	0	0	0	0	0	0	1	0
privately	23	.7225	3.3876	45.3	1	1	2	1	5	8	5	0	4	0	0	3	0	3	0	2	1	0	0	0	2	1	2	5	0
privilege	35	.3169	2.6369	44.2	0	2	6	4	13	3	6	1	7	0	0	2	1	5	1	1	0	1	0	0	5	4	2	4	2
privileged	10	.5818	1.2006	40.8	1	0	3	0	2	4	0	0	1	0	1	1	0	0	0	0	1	0	0	0	0	1	3	2	0
privileges	32	.5929	3.9249	45.9	3	2	1	1	5	10	9	1	0	0	1	1	0	16	0	2	0	0	2	0	0	2	8	0	0
privy	2	.2440	.1132	30.5	0	0	0	0	1	0	1	0	0	0	0	1	0	0	0	0	0	0	0	0	0	0	0	1	0
Prix	7	.2220	.3806	35.8	0	0	0	2	2	0	0	3	0	0	0	0	0	0	0	0	0	0	0	0	0	5	0	2	0
prize	173	.7884	27.724	54.4	51	22	13	23	22	24	15	3	69	21	2	7	1	4	6	2	3	0	0	0	30	8	14	6	0
Prize	31	.6564	4.1568	46.2	1	1	6	4	5	8	6	0	2	0	0	3	0	4	0	1	2	0	0	0	3	4	10	2	0
prized	33	.6612	4.5635	46.6	5	1	2	6	14	2	1	2	11	1	0	0	0	7	0	1	1	0	0	0	1	1	7	3	0
prizes	51	.7210	7.5331	48.8	16	8	3	11	3	9	1	0	15	2	2	2	1	3	3	0	1	0	0	0	15	3	4	0	0
pro	21	.2612	1.2644	41.0	0	1	4	10	4	2	0	0	1	0	0	0	0	0	9	0	0	0	0	0	0	0	0	11	0
pro-Soviet	2	.0000	.0243	23.9	0	0	0	0	1	1	0	0	0	0	0	0	0	0	0	0	0	0	0	0	0	0	0	2	0
pro-slavery	4	.0000	.0778	28.9	0	0	0	0	0	0	4	0	0	0	0	0	0	4	0	0	0	0	0	0	0	0	0	0	0
probabilistic	2	.0000	.0209	23.2	0	0	0	0	0	0	2	0	0	0	0	0	0	0	0	0	0	0	0	0	0	0	2	0	0
probabilities	2	.2346	.1166	30.7	0	0	0	0	1	0	1	0	0	0	0	0	0	0	0	1	0	0	0	0	0	0	0	1	0
probability	54	.4960	5.6997	47.6	1	0	3	9	3	20	15	3	3	1	0	1	36	0	1	3	0	0	1	0	0	1	1	6	0
probable	28	.7998	4.4809	46.5	0	1	1	2	6	9	5	4	1	1	0	1	1	0	1	8	1	0	1	1	1	1	5	5	0
probably	1123	.9428	209.29	63.2	113	130	140	161	253	156	126	44	188	100	13	47	63	102	25	219	36	13	35	5	29	82	77	89	0
probation	11	.2094	.8231	39.2	0	0	0	0	1	2	8	0	10	0	0	0	0	0	0	0	0	0	0	0	1	0	0	0	0
probe	31	.5384	3.5328	45.5	1	21	2	1	3	1	1	1	1	0	0	0	0	2	1	15	0	0	0	0	0	8	3	1	0
probed	7	.3669	.5663	37.5	0	0	0	1	4	2	0	0	0	0	0	2	0	0	0	2	0	0	0	0	0	0	0	3	0
probes	17	.4906	1.7893	42.5	0	7	1	2	3	2	1	1	0	0	0	2	0	1	0	11	0	0	0	0	0	1	1	1	0
probing	19	.5996	2.3749	43.8	1	0	3	4	5	6	0	0	2	1	0	0	0	1	0	5	0	0	0	0	0	2	4	4	0

8Q Primeiros
6J primitive-sounding
3A primitively
7Q primitiveness
7L primost
8Q Primoz
5Q Primrose
9D primroses
8Q Prince-Bishop
8R Princeton's
9R Principality
9R Principals
9R principals'
4A Pringle
5A Pringle's
6A Printers
7D printers'
6A printin'
9Q PRINTING
5A printing-office
4Q printings
7K printmaker
8E printout
8B printshop
7A Prioli
7N prised
8A prism-fringed
4N prison-bars
8P prison-house
5Q prison-reform
9R prisoners'
9R prisonlike
9D Priss
XR pristine
7D Pritchard
8M pritchel
8D privates
9P privation
5F Privilege
8J Privy
7A prize-fight
9B prize-winning
9Q prizefight
8A prizefighter
8D prizefighters
8A prizemaster
4P Prizes
XR prizewinning
9R Pro
5F pro-Communist
9R pro-European
9R pro-Gaullist
9F pro-Israel
5P pro-Ottoman
8R Pro-Quarterback
9F pro-and-con
9F pro-business
7R pro-concentration
3Q pro-democratic
7P pro-liberation
8F pro-ratification
8E Probability

Word Type	F	D	U	SFI	3 Gr 3	4 Gr 4	5 Gr 5	6 Gr 6	7 Gr 7	8 Gr 8	9 Gr 9	X UnGr	A Read	B Eng & Gr	C Comp	D Lit	E Math	F Soc Stud	G Spell	H Sci	J Music	K Art	L Home Ec	M Shop	N Lib F	P Lib NF	Q Lib Ref	R Mag	S Rel
problem	1117	.8196	183.61	62.6	149	136	150	140	184	156	161	41	139	49	8	18	407	123	11	119	13	1	20	12	9	35	54	99	0
Problem	14	.3389	1.0918	40.4	3	0	0	1	7	1	2	0	2	0	2	0	9	0	0	0	0	0	0	0	0	0	1	0	0
problem-solving	8	.2337	.5029	37.0	0	0	4	0	1	2	1	0	1	0	0	0	0	6	0	0	0	0	0	0	0	1	0	0	0
problems	917	.8818	160.72	62.1	94	86	108	105	160	202	144	18	73	49	6	16	286	153	25	82	7	2	27	15	8	25	67	75	1
Problems	4	.2220	.2176	33.4	1	2	1	0	0	0	0	0	0	0	0	0	3	0	0	0	0	0	0	0	0	0	1	0	0
proboscis	6	.1473	.2287	33.6	0	0	5	1	0	0	0	0	0	0	0	0	0	0	0	0	0	0	0	0	0	0	5	1	0
procaine	3	.1927	.1491	31.7	0	0	0	0	0	0	1	2	0	0	0	0	0	0	0	1	0	0	0	0	0	0	0	2	0
procedure	103	.6712	14.037	51.5	0	1	2	7	20	36	31	6	6	12	0	0	22	2	2	16	4	1	8	16	0	3	5	6	0
procedures	26	.7252	3.7984	45.8	0	0	2	0	9	6	8	1	0	2	0	0	1	2	0	7	5	0	1	1	0	1	5	1	0
proceed	53	.8303	8.7847	49.4	1	1	3	6	16	12	11	3	4	3	0	5	5	4	0	7	2	0	1	3	8	2	6	3	0
proceeded	30	.6702	4.1205	46.1	0	1	3	5	8	10	2	1	5	0	1	7	0	2	1	0	0	0	0	0	6	0	4	4	0
proceeding	12	.5897	1.4622	41.6	0	1	0	1	2	3	5	0	1	0	0	3	4	0	0	0	0	0	0	1	1	0	1	1	0
proceedings	16	.5751	1.9143	42.8	1	0	0	0	5	7	3	0	0	0	0	2	0	8	0	0	0	0	0	0	2	1	1	2	0
proceeds	17	.5910	2.0894	43.2	1	1	0	3	5	4	2	1	1	2	0	0	1	0	0	6	0	0	0	0	0	1	4	2	0
process	468	.8220	76.839	58.9	11	12	35	42	147	91	118	12	20	23	3	8	34	42	8	135	9	5	22	32	3	16	77	31	0
processed	33	.5962	4.0878	46.1	5	0	9	2	6	1	10	0	3	0	0	0	0	11	0	3	0	0	4	1	0	1	8	2	0
processes	134	.5951	16.448	52.2	1	1	9	16	32	26	45	4	6	5	0	0	0	13	0	47	0	1	24	11	0	3	19	5	0
processing	41	.6381	5.3721	47.3	8	0	10	3	8	6	6	0	0	0	0	0	0	19	0	5	0	0	2	2	0	5	6	2	0
procession	57	.7162	8.3707	49.2	15	9	2	11	13	4	2	1	16	3	0	8	0	2	0	1	5	0	0	0	11	7	1	3	0
processional	3	.0000	.0243	23.8	0	2	0	0	1	0	0	0	0	0	0	0	0	0	0	0	3	0	0	0	0	0	0	0	0
processions	8	.5496	.9204	39.6	2	2	0	1	1	0	2	0	1	0	0	2	0	0	0	1	2	0	0	0	1	0	1	0	0
proclaim	8	.6080	1.0237	40.1	1	1	1	1	0	1	2	1	2	0	0	1	0	1	0	0	0	0	0	0	0	2	1	1	0
proclaimed	29	.7264	4.2645	46.3	0	2	5	4	8	9	1	0	2	0	0	2	0	7	1	0	2	0	0	0	2	4	5	4	0
proclaiming	4	.3582	.3103	34.9	0	0	0	0	2	2	0	0	0	0	0	0	0	0	0	0	0	0	0	0	1	0	2	1	0
proclaims	6	.4757	.5970	37.8	0	0	1	1	3	0	1	0	0	0	0	0	0	1	0	0	1	0	0	1	0	1	0	2	0
proclamation	13	.6843	1.8011	42.6	1	1	2	0	7	1	1	0	0	1	0	1	0	3	1	0	1	0	0	0	4	1	1	0	0
Proclamation	9	.2444	.5442	37.4	0	0	4	0	1	4	0	0	0	0	0	0	0	6	0	0	0	0	0	0	0	0	3	0	0
proclamations	2	.2401	.1133	30.5	0	0	1	0	1	0	0	0	0	0	0	0	0	0	0	0	0	0	0	0	0	1	1	0	0
procure	3	.2357	.2199	33.4	0	0	0	1	2	0	0	0	2	0	0	0	0	0	0	0	0	0	0	0	0	1	0	0	0
procured	2	.2401	.1133	30.5	0	0	0	0	0	1	1	0	0	0	0	0	0	0	0	0	0	0	0	0	0	1	1	0	0
procuring	3	.3791	.2506	34.0	0	0	0	1	1	1	0	0	0	0	0	0	0	0	0	1	0	0	0	0	1	0	0	1	0
prodded	5	.3842	.4760	36.8	0	1	1	1	0	1	1	0	3	0	0	1	0	0	0	0	0	0	0	0	0	0	0	1	0
prodding	2	.1948	.1250	31.0	1	0	0	0	0	0	1	0	1	0	0	0	0	0	0	0	0	0	0	0	0	1	0	0	0
prodigal	2	.2440	.1132	30.5	0	0	0	0	1	0	1	0	0	0	0	1	0	0	0	0	0	0	0	0	0	0	0	1	0
prodigies	2	.0000	.0389	25.9	0	0	0	0	0	2	0	0	0	0	0	0	0	2	0	0	0	0	0	0	0	0	0	0	0
prodigious	16	.5492	1.8180	42.6	0	0	0	2	6	3	5	0	0	1	0	3	0	1	0	2	0	0	0	0	5	0	4	0	0
prodigy	2	.1717	.1142	30.6	0	0	0	0	1	1	0	0	1	0	0	1	0	0	0	0	0	0	0	0	0	0	0	0	0
produce	586	.8607	100.37	60.0	45	53	72	86	138	83	85	24	21	21	8	8	15	121	7	147	40	7	13	26	6	30	93	23	0
produced	526	.8452	88.610	59.5	16	28	64	74	126	113	82	23	18	9	5	6	15	96	5	144	61	8	6	22	12	16	74	29	0
producer	30	.5898	3.6971	45.7	4	2	8	1	7	3	4	1	2	0	0	0	1	14	0	1	1	0	0	0	0	2	5	4	0
producers	23	.4439	2.2371	43.5	3	0	4	2	1	2	4	7	2	0	0	0	0	9	0	1	0	0	0	0	0	0	3	8	0
Producers	6	.0000	.0729	28.6	0	0	0	0	1	0	0	5	0	0	0	0	0	0	0	0	0	0	0	0	0	0	0	6	0
produces	213	.8023	34.225	55.3	12	14	30	33	46	41	27	10	6	0	3	1	21	36	4	67	25	2	6	13	0	5	19	5	0
producing	102	.8348	16.998	52.3	2	5	14	14	30	16	16	5	6	2	1	2	1	21	0	22	11	1	2	5	4	2	16	6	0
product	860	.4227	78.905	59.0	92	119	128	146	143	126	97	9	15	8	0	0	707	39	1	13	4	3	7	24	1	6	22	10	0
production	227	.7091	32.622	55.1	7	4	36	24	64	43	41	8	4	2	0	3	4	83	2	15	9	0	1	15	1	24	38	26	0
productions	12	.4233	1.0769	40.3	0	0	1	2	1	1	2	5	0	0	0	0	0	0	0	0	3	0	0	0	0	2	1	6	0
productive	45	.5718	5.3823	47.3	3	2	3	4	16	5	9	3	1	3	0	0	0	25	2	2	0	0	0	0	0	1	5	6	0
productivity	7	.4693	.7027	38.5	0	0	0	0	2	2	3	0	0	0	0	0	0	3	0	0	0	0	0	0	0	1	1	2	0
products	1044	.6447	138.26	61.4	117	176	190	166	174	121	88	12	25	6	0	1	444	324	7	45	4	0	18	28	0	24	93	25	0
Products	5	.4087	.4322	36.4	0	0	1	0	4	0	0	0	0	0	0	0	0	0	0	0	0	0	0	1	0	1	1	2	0
Prof	4	.2073	.2003	33.0	0	0	0	1	3	0	0	0	0	0	0	1	0	0	0	0	0	0	0	0	0	0	0	3	0
profane	7	.5126	.7434	38.7	0	1	0	2	2	2	0	0	0	0	0	3	0	0	0	0	1	0	0	0	1	1	0	1	0
profanely	2	.2443	.1130	30.5	0	0	0	0	1	0	1	0	0	0	0	1	0	0	0	0	0	0	0	0	1	0	0	0	0
profess	3	.3777	.2489	34.0	0	0	0	0	2	0	1	0	0	1	0	0	0	1	0	0	0	0	0	0	1	0	0	0	0
profession	31	.7363	4.6344	46.7	0	2	3	2	11	6	7	0	5	1	0	0	0	8	2	0	2	0	0	1	2	1	7	2	0
professional	122	.8006	19.591	52.9	1	5	17	16	28	20	30	5	14	0	4	3	3	18	0	7	5	0	6	3	1	11	20	27	0
Professional	3	.0000	.0365	25.6	0	3	0	0	0	0	0	0	0	0	0	0	0	0	0	0	0	0	0	0	0	0	0	3	0
professionally	4	.3745	.3228	35.1	0	0	0	0	1	1	1	1	0	0	0	1	0	0	0	0	0	0	0	0	0	0	1	2	0
professionals	12	.4837	1.2374	40.9	0	0	0	7	1	4	0	0	1	0	1	0	0	1	0	0	1	0	0	0	0	7	1	0	0
professions	7	.4283	.6370	38.0	0	1	1	0	0	1	4	0	0	0	0	1	0	2	0	0	0	0	0	1	0	0	3	0	0
professor	60	.6579	8.2514	49.2	2	6	3	10	17	11	8	3	20	2	0	3	1	3	0	4	0	0	0	0	0	9	14	4	0
Professor	80	.7676	12.496	51.0	15	29	12	0	5	9	5	5	25	3	0	2	0	2	1	4	3	0	1	0	16	16	3	4	0
professor's	4	.3766	.3696	35.7	1	1	0	1	0	0	0	1	2	0	0	0	0	0	0	0	0	0	0	0	0	1	0	1	0
Professor's	3	.2261	.2131	33.3	1	1	1	0	0	0	0	0	2	0	0	0	0	0	0	0	0	0	0	0	1	0	0	0	0
professorial	2	.0000	.0209	23.2	0	0	0	0	0	0	2	0	0	0	0	0	0	0	0	0	0	0	0	0	0	0	2	0	0
professors	7	.5515	.8378	39.2	0	1	1	3	1	0	0	1	2	0	0	0	0	2	0	1	0	0	0	0	0	1	0	1	0
proffered	5	.4613	.4845	36.9	0	0	1	0	4	0	0	0	0	0	0	2	0	0	0	0	0	0	0	0	1	1	1	0	0
proficiency	4	.3637	.3175	35.0	1	0	0	1	1	1	0	0	0	1	0	0	0	0	0	0	0	0	0	0	0	1	0	2	0
proficient	3	.3822	.2446	33.9	0	0	0	0	1	0	2	0	0	1	0	0	0	0	0	0	1	0	0	0	0	0	0	1	0
profile	19	.5424	2.1564	43.3	1	1	0	0	2	5	10	0	0	1	0	2	0	3	0	7	0	2	0	0	0	3	1	0	0
profiles	7	.3860	.5946	37.7	0	0	0	1	1	3	2	0	0	0	0	1	0	0	0	4	0	1	0	0	0	0	0	1	0
profit	67	.6427	8.8305	49.5	7	4	12	6	17	13	6	2	3	2	1	2	10	18	5	1	0	0	1	0	1	8	7	7	1
profitable	22	.6318	2.8747	44.6	1	0	2	3	9	3	4	0	2	0	1	1	0	10	0	0	1	0	0	0	1	2	4	0	0
profitably	4	.4484	.4050	36.1	0	0	1	0	0	1	1	1	1	0	0	0	0	1	0	1	0	0	0	0	0	0	1	0	0
profited	3	.2478	.1662	32.2	0	0	0	1	1	0	1	0	0	0	0	0	0	0	0	0	0	1	0	0	0	1	1	0	0
profiting	2	.0000	.0209	23.2	1	0	0	0	0	1	0	0	0	0	0	0	0	0	0	0	0	0	0	0	0	0	2	0	0
profitless	2	.1497	.1046	30.2	0	0	0	0	0	2	0	0	1	0	0	0	0	0	1	0	0	0	0	0	0	0	0	0	0
profits	38	.5678	4.5413	46.6	1	0	4	3	9	19	2	0	2	1	0	0	1	25	0	0	1	0	1	0	0	1	3	3	0
profound	29	.6886	4.0756	46.1	0	1	1	3	11	9	4	0	4	0	0	5	0	1	0	2	2	0	0	0	5	1	5	4	0
profoundly	10	.6636	1.3808	41.4	0	0	1	1	1	5	2	0	3	0	0	1	0	1	0	0	0	0	0	0	1	1	1	2	0
profuse	2	.2285	.1129	30.5	0	0	0	0	1	0	1	0	0	0	0	0	0	1	0	0	0	0	0	0	0	0	1	0	0
profusion	8	.4228	.7193	38.6	0	0	0	0	6	1	1	0	0	0	0	0	0	1	0	1	0	1	0	0	1	0	4	0	0
progeny	2	.1698	.1133	30.5	0	0	0	0	2	0	0	0	1	0	0	0	0	0	0	0	0	0	0	0	0	0	1	0	0
progesterone	4	.0000	.0789	29.0	0	0	0	0	0	0	4	0	0	0	0	0	0	0	0	4	0	0	0	0	0	0	0	0	0
prognosis	2	.2440	.1132	30.5	0	0	0	0	0	2	0	0	0	0	0	1	0	0	0	0	0	0	0	0	0	0	0	1	0
program	296	.8384	49.549	57.0	27	27	32	23	74	45	60	8	36	35	1	5	11	29	2	16	43	1	4	2	5	16	33	57	0
Program	25	.5433	2.7974	44.5	3	2	3	4	6	3	3	1	1	2	0	1	0	0	11	0	2	0	0	0	1	1	1	5	0
programmatic	3	.0000	.0243	23.8	0	0	0	0	2	1	0	0	0	0	0	0	0	0	0	0	3	0	0	0	0	0	0	0	0
programmed	9	.5056	.9620	39.8	0	0	0	1	3	4	1	0	1	2	0	0	3	0	0	0	0	1	0	0	0	0	1	1	0
Programmed	3	.0000	.0449	26.5	0	0	0	0	1	1	1	0	0	0	0	0	3	0	0	0	0	0	0	0	0	0	0	0	0
programmers	2	.0000	.0219	23.4	0	0	0	2	0	0	0	0	0	2	0	0	0	0	0	0	0	0	0	0	0	0	0	0	0
programming	2	.1814	.1187	30.7	0	0	0	1	0	0	0	1	1	0	0	0	0	0	0	0	0	0	0	0	0	0	0	1	0
programs	135	.7678	20.809	53.2	11	17	14	13	24	33	20	3	4	18	0	2	0	26	7	12	10	0	4	0	0	6	22	24	0
progress	228	.8739	39.627	56.0	11	11	26	32	57	48	34	9	21	14	1	8	2	54	24	15	6	0	4	4	6	15	25	29	0
Progress	14	.4524	1.3256	41.2	2	4	2	1	3	2	0	0	0	0	3	0	0	2	2	1	0	0	0	0	3	0	3	0	0

6H problem-questions	9P Proctor	7P production-type	5P professing	8A Proffessor	7Q progenitor
6P problem's	7A procurator	8G productively	7A profession's	6H Profiles	9B prognosticate
4Q problematical	7A Procurator	9B profane/profanity	5R PROFESSORS	9F profit-making	9Q prognosticators
9Q process-color	9D procures	7P profaned	8G professors'	7H profligate	9R program's
8M Processes	5H Procyon	XD profanity	7A professorship	5P profounder	7R programed
5P Procession	3A prod	7R proferring	9R proffer	8R profundity	7R programmer
XR processors	7Q prodigiously	5P professed	7R proffering	7Q profusely	5G progress'**
6A Proclaim	4J prods	XR professes	5A proffessor	5G prog'ress**	

Word Type	F	D	U	SFI	3 Gr 3	4 Gr 4	5 Gr 5	6 Gr 6	7 Gr 7	8 Gr 8	9 Gr 9	X UnGr	A Read	B Eng & Gr	C Comp	D Lit	E Math	F Soc Stud	G Spell	H Sci	J Music	K Art	L Home Ec	M Shop	N Lib F	P Lib NF	Q Lib Ref	R Mag	S Rel
progressed	10	.5641	1.2240	40.9	0	0	1	1	2	5	1	0	4	0	0	0	1	1	0	1	2	0	0	0	1	0	0	0	0
progresses	11	.5108	1.1797	40.7	1	1	0	2	4	1	2	0	1	0	1	0	0	0	0	2	4	0	0	0	0	0	1	2	0
progressing	2	.2407	.1090	30.4	0	0	0	1	0	1	0	0	0	1	0	0	0	0	0	0	1	0	0	0	0	0	0	0	0
progression	20	.5085	2.1344	43.3	0	0	1	3	6	5	4	1	2	0	0	0	2	0	1	0	7	0	0	0	0	0	4	4	0
progressions	2	.0000	.0162	22.1	0	0	0	0	0	2	0	0	0	0	0	0	0	0	0	0	2	0	0	0	0	0	0	0	0
progressive	33	.6878	4.6118	46.6	0	0	3	6	4	5	15	0	2	5	0	0	0	7	1	1	2	0	0	1	0	1	10	3	0
Progressive	3	.2425	.1816	32.6	0	0	0	0	1	2	0	0	0	0	0	0	0	2	0	0	0	0	0	0	0	0	0	1	0
progressively	3	.3847	.2496	34.0	0	0	1	0	2	0	0	0	0	0	0	0	0	0	0	0	0	0	0	0	0	1	1	1	0
prohibited	13	.4309	1.2145	40.8	1	0	2	0	7	2	0	1	1	0	0	0	0	2	0	0	0	0	0	0	0	1	5	4	0
prohibiting	3	.3766	.2497	34.0	0	0	1	0	0	1	1	0	0	0	0	0	0	1	0	0	0	0	0	0	0	1	1	0	0
prohibition	5	.5554	.5732	37.6	0	0	0	0	2	3	0	0	0	0	0	0	0	1	1	0	0	0	0	0	1	0	1	1	0
prohibits	3	.2321	.1635	32.1	0	0	0	0	1	1	0	1	0	0	0	0	0	0	0	0	0	0	0	0	0	0	1	2	0
project	208	.4866	21.216	53.3	7	16	10	20	49	39	45	22	20	9	1	1	5	12	5	12	3	3	4	70	8	6	14	35	0
Project	46	.6074	5.7588	47.6	1	11	6	4	14	5	3	2	1	0	0	0	1	10	0	5	0	0	0	4	0	11	6	8	0
project's	2	.2437	.1129	30.5	0	0	0	0	0	0	1	1	0	0	0	0	0	0	0	0	0	0	0	0	0	0	1	1	0
projected	21	.4641	2.0526	43.1	0	1	1	3	3	3	10	0	1	0	0	1	0	0	0	3	0	0	0	5	3	1	4	3	0
projectile	10	.4473	1.0275	40.1	0	0	8	0	0	0	0	2	3	0	0	0	0	4	0	2	0	0	0	0	0	1	0	0	0
projectiles	3	.3762	.2496	34.0	0	0	0	0	1	0	0	2	0	0	0	0	0	0	0	1	0	0	0	0	0	1	1	0	0
projecting	10	.5741	1.1800	40.7	0	1	0	0	3	1	3	2	0	0	0	1	0	0	0	2	0	0	0	1	1	0	2	3	0
projection	40	.5064	4.2316	46.3	0	23	8	1	1	1	2	4	0	1	0	0	0	9	0	1	1	0	0	1	1	0	21	5	0
Projection	2	.0000	.0389	25.9	1	1	0	0	0	0	0	0	0	0	0	0	0	2	0	0	0	0	0	0	0	0	0	0	0
projections	22	.4195	2.0226	43.1	1	5	5	2	3	0	2	4	0	0	0	0	0	5	0	9	0	0	0	0	0	0	7	1	0
projector	20	.5786	2.4605	43.9	2	3	0	10	1	1	1	2	4	1	1	0	0	0	0	10	0	0	0	0	0	1	1	2	0
projectors	7	.1941	.3707	35.7	0	0	0	6	0	1	0	0	0	0	0	0	0	0	0	6	0	0	0	0	0	0	1	0	0
projects	113	.5364	12.646	51.0	6	5	13	6	36	22	15	10	12	6	1	0	1	14	0	7	2	1	2	30	1	9	16	11	0
Prokofiev	3	.0000	.0243	23.8	0	0	1	1	0	1	0	0	0	0	0	0	0	0	0	0	3	0	0	0	0	0	0	0	0
prolegs	2	.0000	.0290	24.6	2	0	0	0	0	0	0	0	0	0	0	0	0	0	0	0	0	0	0	0	0	2	0	0	0
proletariat	3	.3863	.2513	34.0	0	1	1	0	1	0	0	0	0	0	0	0	0	0	0	0	0	0	0	0	1	1	0	1	0
proliferation	4	.0904	.1412	31.5	0	0	0	0	0	2	2	0	1	0	0	0	0	0	0	0	0	0	0	0	0	0	3	0	0
prolific	8	.4839	.8433	39.3	0	0	3	0	5	0	0	0	2	0	0	1	0	0	0	0	0	0	0	0	0	1	3	1	0
prolong	6	.3755	.4730	36.7	1	2	0	0	0	0	3	0	0	0	0	0	0	0	0	0	3	0	1	0	0	0	2	0	0
prolongation	3	.2443	.1820	32.6	0	0	0	0	0	1	0	2	0	0	0	1	0	0	0	2	0	0	0	0	0	0	0	0	0
prolonged	16	.6629	2.1752	43.4	0	0	0	0	7	2	5	2	2	0	1	2	0	0	0	4	0	1	0	0	0	2	2	2	0
prom	2	.1674	.0805	29.1	0	0	0	0	0	0	2	0	0	0	0	0	0	0	0	0	0	0	1	0	0	1	0	0	0
Prom	11	.0000	.1592	32.0	11	0	0	0	0	0	0	0	0	0	0	0	0	0	0	0	0	0	0	0	0	11	0	0	0
prom'nade	2	.0000	.0162	22.1	0	2	0	0	0	0	0	0	0	0	0	0	0	0	0	0	2	0	0	0	0	0	0	0	0
promenade	9	.2414	.4945	36.9	3	2	3	0	0	1	0	0	0	0	0	0	0	0	0	1	6	0	0	0	0	0	2	0	0
Promenade	6	.3200	.4217	36.3	0	3	0	0	0	0	3	0	0	0	0	0	0	0	0	0	3	0	0	0	0	2	0	1	0
promethea	3	.0000	.0434	26.4	3	0	0	0	0	0	0	0	0	0	0	0	0	0	0	0	0	0	0	0	0	3	0	0	0
prometheas	3	.0000	.0434	26.4	3	0	0	0	0	0	0	0	0	0	0	0	0	0	0	0	0	0	0	0	0	3	0	0	0
Prometheus	26	.3473	2.4338	43.9	0	0	0	18	4	3	1	0	21	0	0	4	0	0	0	0	1	0	0	0	0	0	0	0	0
prominence	9	.5753	1.0689	40.3	1	0	0	0	2	2	4	0	0	0	0	1	0	2	0	1	1	0	0	0	0	0	3	1	0
prominent	55	.8185	8.9977	49.5	1	4	4	7	10	13	8	8	5	3	0	1	0	5	1	7	4	3	2	1	2	5	11	5	0
promise	191	.4349	19.151	52.8	33	25	27	40	23	19	19	5	79	4	1	15	4	17	2	2	3	0	0	0	14	12	14	19	5
promised	236	.4418	23.829	53.8	39	45	35	38	38	27	10	4	89	5	0	17	1	33	4	1	8	0	2	0	21	31	7	11	6
Promised	3	.0589	.0561	27.5	1	0	2	0	0	0	0	0	0	0	0	0	0	0	0	0	1	0	0	0	0	1	0	0	1
promises	46	.3353	3.5844	45.5	6	5	10	5	9	6	3	2	7	2	0	5	0	12	0	0	2	0	0	0	3	1	5	7	2
promising	36	.7108	5.2456	47.2	5	3	3	6	12	4	1	2	8	1	0	1	0	4	0	2	0	0	0	0	3	6	5	6	0
promontory	2	.1717	.1142	30.6	0	0	0	1	0	0	1	0	1	0	0	1	0	0	0	0	0	0	0	0	0	0	0	0	0
Promontory	5	.0824	.1675	32.2	3	1	0	1	0	0	0	0	1	0	0	0	0	0	0	0	0	0	0	0	0	0	0	4	0
promote	25	.5191	2.7297	44.4	1	1	6	3	5	1	6	2	2	0	0	0	0	4	3	1	1	0	0	0	0	0	11	3	0
promoted	14	.5797	1.7032	42.3	0	0	2	2	2	5	3	0	2	0	0	0	0	4	0	0	2	0	0	0	0	2	3	1	0
promoters	6	.5406	.6739	38.3	0	0	0	1	2	2	0	1	0	0	0	1	0	1	0	0	0	0	0	0	0	1	1	2	0
promotes	3	.2445	.1818	32.6	0	0	1	0	1	0	0	1	0	0	0	0	0	0	0	2	0	0	0	0	0	0	1	0	0
promoting	13	.5839	1.5565	41.9	1	0	3	0	4	1	3	1	0	0	0	1	0	2	0	1	0	0	2	0	1	1	4	1	0
promotion	19	.6929	2.6810	44.3	0	0	3	1	4	1	9	1	2	2	0	2	0	2	1	0	0	0	0	0	1	2	1	6	0
prompt	12	.5980	1.4719	41.7	0	1	1	1	6	1	1	1	0	3	0	1	0	1	0	1	0	0	0	0	1	0	1	4	0
prompted	8	.4955	.8405	39.2	0	0	2	2	4	0	0	0	1	0	0	0	0	0	0	0	1	0	0	0	3	0	2	1	0
promptly	57	.7900	9.0629	49.6	3	7	6	8	15	11	6	1	10	7	2	4	0	3	0	2	0	0	1	0	9	5	7	7	0
promptness	2	.0857	.0784	28.9	0	0	1	0	0	1	0	0	1	0	0	0	0	0	0	0	0	0	1	0	0	0	0	0	0
prompts	2	.1926	.0867	29.4	0	0	0	0	0	0	2	0	0	0	0	0	0	0	0	0	0	0	1	0	0	0	1	0	0
promulgated	3	.3847	.2496	34.0	0	0	0	0	1	2	0	0	0	0	0	0	0	0	0	0	0	0	0	0	0	1	1	1	0
pron	2	.2408	.1091	30.4	0	0	0	0	0	1	1	0	0	1	0	0	0	0	1	0	0	0	0	0	0	0	0	0	0
prone	7	.1588	.3746	35.7	0	0	1	1	2	0	1	2	3	0	0	0	0	0	0	0	0	0	0	0	0	0	0	4	0
prong	2	.0000	.0394	26.0	0	0	1	1	0	0	0	0	0	0	0	0	0	0	0	2	0	0	0	0	0	0	0	0	0
pronghorn	4	.0904	.1412	31.5	0	0	1	0	3	0	0	0	1	0	0	0	0	0	0	0	0	0	0	0	0	0	3	0	0
prongs	14	.3712	1.1625	40.7	1	0	2	4	3	4	0	0	0	0	0	0	0	0	0	10	1	0	0	2	0	1	0	0	0
pronoun	179	.3117	12.186	50.9	19	24	25	20	37	23	31	0	6	122	42	0	1	0	5	0	0	0	2	0	0	0	1	0	0
Pronoun	2	.2446	.1123	30.5	0	0	1	1	0	0	0	0	0	1	0	0	0	0	0	0	0	0	0	0	0	0	1	0	0
pronounce	238	.2632	14.611	51.6	10	51	48	47	60	16	4	2	27	40	0	1	0	2	159	1	2	0	0	0	0	3	0	3	0
pronounced	143	.4971	14.895	51.7	5	13	31	24	31	25	10	4	13	36	2	1	3	3	69	1	7	0	0	0	3	3	1	1	0
pronouncement	2	.2152	.1357	31.3	0	0	0	0	1	0	1	0	1	0	0	0	0	1	0	0	0	0	0	0	0	0	0	0	0
pronounces	25	.2636	1.6492	42.2	0	2	2	6	11	3	1	0	7	3	0	0	0	0	14	0	0	0	0	0	0	1	0	0	0
pronouncing	17	.5924	2.0893	43.2	1	0	3	1	8	2	1	1	2	4	0	1	0	2	4	0	0	0	0	0	0	2	0	2	0
pronouns	124	.2320	6.6493	48.2	7	12	29	16	14	20	26	0	0	113	5	0	0	0	6	0	0	0	0	0	0	0	0	0	0
pronunciation	238	.2835	15.531	51.9	6	39	34	32	81	30	14	2	28	54	0	0	0	0	146	0	2	0	0	0	0	4	4	0	0
pronunciations	83	.1267	2.8400	44.5	3	10	20	11	21	16	2	0	5	7	0	0	0	0	70	0	0	0	0	0	0	0	0	1	0
proof	80	.8354	13.379	51.3	1	1	5	16	21	17	15	4	15	3	0	4	11	3	13	7	1	0	1	1	1	4	8	8	0
Proof	2	.1497	.1046	30.2	0	0	0	1	0	1	0	0	1	0	0	0	0	0	1	0	0	0	0	0	0	0	0	0	0
proofed	2	.2376	.1088	30.4	0	0	0	0	1	1	0	0	0	0	0	0	0	0	1	0	0	0	0	0	0	0	0	1	0
proofread	91	.1977	4.1908	46.2	21	24	11	18	11	3	3	0	0	28	0	0	0	0	63	0	0	0	0	0	0	0	0	0	0
Proofread	4	.0000	.0438	26.4	0	0	4	0	0	0	0	0	0	4	0	0	0	0	0	0	0	0	0	0	0	0	0	0	0
proofreader	3	.2060	.1430	31.6	0	0	0	1	1	1	0	0	0	1	0	0	0	0	2	0	0	0	0	0	0	0	0	0	0
proofreaders	5	.1315	.1700	32.3	1	0	0	1	3	0	0	0	0	0	0	0	0	0	4	0	0	0	0	0	0	1	0	0	0
proofreading	14	.2301	.7336	38.7	4	1	2	2	5	0	0	0	0	6	0	0	0	0	8	0	0	0	0	0	0	0	0	0	0
Proofreading	3	.2060	.1430	31.6	0	1	0	0	1	1	0	0	0	1	0	0	0	0	2	0	0	0	0	0	0	0	0	0	0
proofs	8	.5528	.9123	39.6	0	1	0	0	2	2	2	1	0	1	0	0	3	0	1	1	0	0	0	1	0	0	1	0	0
proofsheets	2	.0000	.0209	23.2	0	0	0	0	2	0	0	0	0	0	0	0	0	0	0	0	0	0	0	0	0	0	2	0	0
prop	14	.5754	1.7137	42.3	3	1	1	3	3	0	3	0	4	0	0	1	0	0	0	0	0	0	0	0	1	3	1	4	0
propaganda	12	.5077	1.2730	41.0	0	0	1	0	3	2	5	1	0	0	0	1	0	1	0	0	0	0	0	0	0	3	3	4	0
propagate	2	.0000	.0209	23.2	0	0	0	0	1	0	1	0	0	0	0	0	0	0	0	0	0	0	0	0	0	0	2	0	0
propagated	3	.0000	.0591	27.7	0	0	0	0	1	0	1	1	0	0	0	0	0	0	0	3	0	0	0	0	0	0	0	0	0
propagating	2	.2278	.1128	30.5	0	0	0	0	2	0	0	0	0	0	0	0	0	0	0	1	0	0	0	0	0	0	1	0	0
propagation	2	.2433	.1158	30.6	0	0	1	0	1	0	0	0	0	0	0	0	0	0	0	0	0	0	0	0	0	1	0	1	0
propel	12	.4189	1.1251	40.5	0	2	1	3	3	1	2	0	2	0	0	0	0	0	0	4	0	0	0	0	0	0	4	2	0
propellant	3	.0000	.0591	27.7	0	0	0	0	0	3	0	0	0	0	0	0	0	0	0	3	0	0	0	0	0	0	0	0	0

5P progressivism
6J Proh-koh-fee-ehf
7Q prohibit
9R Prohibited
8F Prohibition
8L prohibitions
5G proj'ect**
5G project'**
9K projectile-hurling
7P Projet
8J Prokofieff
8F Proletarian
9R proliferate
9Q proliferated
8J prologue
6J Prologue
7N prolongations
3P Prom's
8Q promenades
5P Promessi
7D Prometheus'
8Q prominently
7P promiscuity
5R Promise
8B promissory
5A Promote
7R promoter
XR promotional
5A prompting
9Q promulgation
3Q pronged
7Q pronghorns
8G PRONOUNCE
8R pronouncements
5F Pronouncing
9D pronto
6G pronunication
9B proofreads
7D Prop
8K propaganda-style
5P propagandists
6Q propane
7N propaty

Word Type	F	D	U	SFI	3 Gr 3	4 Gr 4	5 Gr 5	6 Gr 6	7 Gr 7	8 Gr 8	9 Gr 9	X UnGr	A Read	B Eng & Gr	C Comp	D Lit	E Math	F Soc Stud	G Spell	H Sci	J Music	K Art	L Home Ec	M Shop	N Lib F	P Lib NF	Q Lib Ref	R Mag	S Rel
propellants	6	.0000	.1183	30.7	0	0	0	0	0	4	2	0	0	0	0	0	0	0	0	6	0	0	0	0	0	0	0	0	0
propelled	10	.6101	1.2625	41.0	0	1	1	3	2	1	1	1	1	0	0	0	0	0	0	2	1	0	0	0	1	1	3	1	0
propeller	40	.6385	5.3971	47.3	5	12	3	10	6	3	1	0	13	0	0	2	6	4	0	11	0	0	0	0	0	1	3	0	0
propeller-driven	3	.3824	.2446	33.9	0	0	0	1	2	0	0	0	0	0	0	1	0	0	0	0	1	0	0	0	0	0	0	1	0
propeller's	3	.0000	.0591	27.7	0	3	0	0	0	0	0	0	0	0	0	0	0	0	0	3	0	0	0	0	0	0	0	0	0
propellers	12	.5569	1.4764	41.7	4	0	0	1	7	0	0	0	6	1	0	0	1	0	0	2	0	0	0	0	0	2	0	0	0
propelling	6	.2456	.3419	35.3	2	0	0	0	3	0	0	1	0	0	0	0	0	0	0	2	0	2	0	0	1	1	0	0	0
propels	2	.2278	.1128	30.5	0	0	0	0	1	0	1	0	0	0	0	0	0	0	0	1	0	0	0	0	0	0	1	0	0
proper	412	.7692	63.604	58.0	23	40	48	42	96	64	83	16	34	99	34	15	22	18	20	56	9	0	14	31	16	15	16	13	0
properly	147	.8396	24.627	53.9	10	14	12	14	47	24	18	8	16	17	2	6	4	5	2	32	3	1	12	9	7	5	13	13	0
properties	217	.5739	25.904	54.1	8	5	12	12	44	75	55	6	6	0	0	0	82	0	0	74	0	1	3	20	1	3	25	2	0
property	419	.5187	45.967	56.6	17	32	57	44	57	112	91	9	16	1	1	4	285	33	1	27	2	0	0	7	8	7	13	14	0
Property	31	.1267	1.1694	40.7	1	6	3	0	6	6	9	0	0	1	0	0	29	0	0	0	0	0	0	0	0	0	1	0	0
prophase	2	.0000	.0209	23.2	0	0	0	2	0	0	0	0	0	0	0	0	0	0	0	0	0	0	0	0	0	0	2	0	0
prophecies	5	.3547	.4331	36.4	0	0	1	0	1	2	1	0	2	0	0	1	0	0	0	0	0	0	0	0	0	2	0	0	0
prophecy	12	.5942	1.5125	41.8	0	0	2	3	3	4	0	0	4	0	0	3	0	0	1	0	0	0	0	0	0	2	1	1	0
prophesied	7	.4366	.6857	38.4	0	1	0	0	2	2	1	1	2	0	0	0	0	0	0	0	0	0	0	0	0	1	2	2	0
prophesy	2	.0000	.0162	22.1	0	0	1	0	0	1	0	0	0	0	0	0	0	0	2	0	0	0	0	0	0	0	0	0	0
prophet	14	.1380	.5755	37.6	3	0	0	1	3	4	3	0	2	0	0	2	0	3	1	0	1	0	0	0	0	2	1	0	2
Prophet	7	.3773	.6081	37.8	0	2	2	1	1	0	1	0	2	0	0	0	0	0	0	0	0	1	0	0	0	2	2	0	0
prophetic	5	.3959	.4162	36.2	0	0	0	0	0	2	3	0	0	0	0	1	0	0	0	0	1	1	0	0	0	0	0	2	0
prophets	12	.5131	1.2915	41.1	0	0	0	6	1	5	0	0	0	0	0	0	0	5	1	0	1	0	0	0	0	0	4	1	0
propitious	3	.3873	.2485	34.0	1	0	0	0	1	0	1	0	0	0	0	1	0	0	0	0	0	0	0	0	1	0	1	0	0
proponents	6	.2437	.3386	35.3	0	0	0	0	4	0	1	1	0	0	0	0	0	0	0	0	0	0	0	0	0	0	3	3	0
proportion	88	.7419	13.138	51.2	3	3	3	2	47	12	17	1	2	2	0	2	38	8	0	5	1	3	5	5	2	3	10	2	0
proportional	21	.3787	1.7528	42.4	0	0	1	0	4	13	3	0	0	0	0	0	12	0	0	3	0	0	0	0	0	1	5	0	0
proportioned	4	.3064	.2566	34.1	1	0	0	0	0	1	2	0	0	0	0	0	0	0	0	0	0	1	2	0	0	1	0	0	0
proportions	72	.5701	8.3899	49.2	0	1	5	3	22	20	19	2	2	0	0	1	16	5	0	5	2	14	7	9	2	1	5	3	0
propos'd	2	.0000	.0219	23.4	0	0	0	0	0	2	0	0	0	2	0	0	0	0	0	0	0	0	0	0	0	0	0	0	0
proposal	22	.6620	2.9866	44.8	0	1	3	3	3	9	1	2	2	2	0	1	0	5	0	1	0	0	0	0	3	0	3	5	0
proposals	4	.1854	.1872	32.7	0	0	0	0	2	0	2	0	0	0	0	0	0	0	0	0	0	0	0	0	0	1	0	3	0
propose	20	.7625	3.0699	44.9	0	2	3	4	7	2	2	0	2	2	0	5	0	1	1	1	1	0	0	0	2	2	2	1	0
proposed	62	.7736	9.6571	49.8	2	0	5	3	10	12	23	7	6	2	0	2	1	8	0	11	1	0	5	1	2	3	10	10	0
proposes	8	.5893	.9659	39.8	0	0	0	0	2	2	2	2	0	1	0	1	0	1	0	0	1	0	0	0	0	0	1	3	0
proposing	2	.1814	.1187	30.7	0	0	0	0	1	0	1	0	1	0	0	0	0	0	0	0	0	0	0	0	0	0	0	1	0
proposition	16	.6420	2.1385	43.3	2	1	2	0	7	3	1	0	4	0	0	3	0	1	0	0	0	0	0	0	1	3	2	2	0
propositions	3	.1169	.1277	31.1	0	0	0	0	1	0	2	0	1	0	0	0	0	0	0	0	0	0	0	0	0	0	2	0	0
propounded	2	.2433	.1158	30.6	0	0	1	0	0	0	0	1	0	0	0	0	0	0	0	0	0	0	0	0	0	1	0	1	0
propped	21	.5705	2.5619	44.1	3	1	4	3	6	1	3	0	7	0	0	2	0	1	0	0	0	0	1	0	6	0	0	4	0
proprietary	2	.2285	.1129	30.5	0	0	0	0	0	2	0	0	0	0	0	0	0	1	0	0	0	0	0	0	0	0	1	0	0
proprietor	12	.5756	1.4502	41.6	2	0	0	1	1	3	5	0	2	0	0	2	0	2	2	0	0	0	0	0	0	1	0	3	0
proprietors	5	.3684	.4146	36.2	1	0	0	0	0	3	1	0	0	0	0	0	0	3	0	0	0	0	0	0	0	1	1	0	0
proprietorships	2	.0000	.0389	25.9	0	0	0	0	0	0	2	0	0	0	0	0	0	2	0	0	0	0	0	0	0	0	0	0	0
props	6	.4471	.6014	37.8	1	0	0	2	2	1	0	0	2	1	0	2	0	0	0	0	0	0	0	0	0	0	1	0	0
propulsion	10	.5172	1.1023	40.4	0	0	2	2	2	0	3	1	1	0	0	0	0	0	1	4	0	0	0	0	0	0	2	2	0
propulsive	3	.0000	.0314	25.0	0	1	0	0	1	0	1	0	0	0	0	0	0	0	0	0	0	0	0	0	0	0	3	0	0
propwash	2	.0000	.0290	24.6	2	0	0	0	0	0	0	0	0	0	0	0	0	0	0	0	0	0	0	0	0	2	0	0	0
pros	6	.1453	.2356	33.7	0	0	0	3	2	0	1	0	0	0	0	0	0	0	0	0	0	0	0	0	0	1	0	5	0
prosaic	3	.2443	.1820	32.6	0	1	0	0	1	0	0	1	0	0	0	1	0	0	0	2	0	0	0	0	0	0	0	0	0
prose	30	.6209	3.8498	45.9	1	1	2	2	9	6	9	0	5	6	0	7	0	0	1	0	1	0	0	0	0	2	7	1	0
prosecute	4	.4713	.3985	36.0	0	0	1	1	0	2	0	0	0	1	0	0	0	1	1	0	0	0	0	0	0	1	0	0	0
prosecuted	3	.3791	.2506	34.0	0	0	0	0	1	2	0	0	0	0	0	0	0	0	0	1	0	0	0	0	1	0	0	1	0
prosecutes	2	.0000	.0389	25.9	0	0	0	0	0	1	1	0	0	0	0	0	0	2	0	0	0	0	0	0	0	0	0	0	0
prosecution	8	.5720	.9559	39.8	0	0	0	2	1	3	2	0	1	2	0	1	0	1	0	0	0	0	0	0	0	0	1	2	0
prosecutor	2	.1698	.1133	30.5	0	0	0	0	1	1	0	0	1	0	0	0	0	0	0	0	0	0	0	0	0	0	1	0	0
prosecutors	3	.3870	.2486	34.0	0	0	0	0	0	2	1	0	0	0	0	1	0	0	0	0	0	0	0	0	0	0	1	1	0
Proserpina	4	.0000	.1827	32.6	0	0	0	0	0	4	0	0	4	0	0	0	0	0	0	0	0	0	0	0	0	0	0	0	0
Proserpine	2	.0000	.0290	24.6	0	0	0	2	0	0	0	0	0	0	0	0	0	0	0	0	0	0	0	0	0	2	0	0	0
proslavery	5	.2426	.2985	34.7	0	0	2	0	0	3	0	0	0	0	0	0	0	3	0	0	0	0	0	0	0	0	2	0	0
prospect	28	.7210	4.1052	46.1	0	0	5	9	6	3	3	2	5	0	1	1	0	1	1	0	1	0	0	0	3	3	4	8	0
Prospect	4	.2352	.2332	33.7	2	0	0	0	2	0	0	0	0	0	0	0	0	2	0	0	0	0	0	0	0	0	0	2	0
prospecting	8	.3704	.7630	38.8	0	0	0	5	2	1	0	0	5	0	0	0	0	2	0	1	0	0	0	0	0	0	0	0	0
prospective	10	.5706	1.2107	40.8	0	0	0	0	4	3	1	2	2	1	0	0	0	1	0	2	0	0	0	0	0	0	1	3	0
prospector	8	.4932	.8747	39.4	1	1	1	2	1	2	0	0	3	0	1	1	0	1	0	0	0	0	0	0	0	1	0	1	0
prospector's	2	.1387	.0689	28.4	1	0	0	0	0	1	0	0	0	0	1	0	0	0	0	0	0	0	0	0	0	1	0	0	0
prospectors	14	.6541	1.8921	42.8	0	0	3	4	2	2	1	2	2	0	0	0	0	3	1	3	2	0	0	0	0	0	1	2	0
prospects	12	.5921	1.4928	41.7	0	0	0	0	6	3	3	0	2	0	0	0	0	4	0	0	1	0	0	0	0	1	2	2	0
prosper	11	.5565	1.2972	41.1	2	2	0	2	3	0	1	1	2	0	0	1	0	1	0	0	0	0	0	0	0	4	2	1	0
prospered	12	.5219	1.3406	41.3	0	0	2	1	2	5	1	1	1	0	0	0	0	6	0	1	0	0	0	0	0	1	2	1	0
prospering	5	.4409	.4707	36.7	0	0	1	1	1	1	1	0	0	0	0	0	0	1	0	0	0	0	0	0	0	1	2	1	0
prosperity	30	.6604	4.0770	46.1	4	0	5	1	7	6	7	0	3	0	0	3	0	11	0	0	1	0	0	0	1	5	4	2	0
prosperous	43	.5334	4.8823	46.9	3	2	10	10	5	4	9	0	3	0	0	1	0	25	0	0	0	0	0	0	2	3	4	5	0
Pross	4	.0000	.0429	26.3	0	0	0	0	0	0	4	0	0	0	0	4	0	0	0	0	0	0	0	0	0	0	0	0	0
prostrate	7	.5861	.8535	39.3	0	1	2	0	3	0	1	0	1	0	0	0	0	0	0	0	1	0	0	0	2	1	1	1	0
prostration	2	.0000	.0209	23.2	0	0	0	0	0	1	1	0	0	0	0	0	0	0	0	0	0	0	0	0	0	0	2	0	0
protagonist	2	.2433	.1158	30.6	0	0	1	0	0	0	0	1	0	0	0	0	0	0	0	0	0	0	0	0	0	1	0	1	0
protect	340	.8660	58.840	57.7	64	61	48	41	61	36	28	1	65	1	2	4	2	73	10	88	7	1	8	4	6	27	26	16	0
protected	129	.8157	21.170	53.3	17	27	21	15	21	17	9	2	25	3	2	3	0	28	0	20	1	0	2	1	4	6	23	11	0
protecting	41	.7133	6.0341	47.8	5	4	8	7	8	7	2	0	11	0	0	0	1	8	1	10	0	0	0	0	3	2	1	4	0
protection	153	.8289	25.446	54.1	11	16	12	21	40	19	26	8	29	3	0	5	0	24	0	26	0	2	5	3	8	10	26	12	0
Protection	5	.2956	.3348	35.2	0	1	0	1	2	1	0	0	0	0	0	0	0	1	0	0	0	0	0	0	0	0	3	1	0
protections	2	.2446	.1257	31.0	0	0	0	0	0	2	0	0	0	0	0	0	0	1	0	1	0	0	0	0	0	0	0	0	0
protective	70	.6421	9.2277	49.7	7	4	5	9	22	9	13	1	3	0	0	2	0	11	2	17	0	0	0	2	0	5	23	5	0
protectively	2	.1698	.1133	30.5	0	0	0	0	2	0	0	0	1	0	0	0	0	0	0	0	0	0	0	0	0	0	1	0	0
protector	8	.3200	.6441	38.1	0	0	1	2	3	2	0	0	3	0	0	0	0	2	0	0	0	0	0	0	0	0	3	0	0
Protector	2	.0000	.0234	23.7	0	0	0	0	2	0	0	0	0	0	0	0	0	0	0	0	0	0	0	0	2	0	0	0	0
protectorate	3	.2444	.1814	32.6	0	0	2	0	1	0	0	0	0	0	0	0	0	2	0	0	0	0	0	0	0	0	1	0	0
Protectorate	2	.2285	.1129	30.5	0	0	1	0	1	0	0	0	0	0	0	0	0	1	0	0	0	0	0	0	0	0	1	0	0
protects	52	.6259	6.8026	48.3	9	8	8	5	7	6	8	1	6	0	0	1	1	10	1	24	0	0	0	0	0	3	3	3	0
protein	121	.3206	9.0992	49.6	4	3	12	32	34	17	15	4	11	0	0	0	1	0	0	76	0	0	27	0	0	1	4	1	0
proteins	81	.2903	5.4951	47.4	4	0	13	12	28	16	7	1	2	1	0	0	0	0	0	51	0	0	22	0	0	0	5	0	0
protest	43	.7330	6.4360	48.1	4	5	6	2	15	6	4	1	10	0	0	2	0	8	1	0	1	0	0	0	4	5	5	7	0
Protestant	26	.4984	2.7215	44.3	0	1	4	3	5	7	5	1	1	0	0	0	0	4	1	0	2	0	0	0	0	2	13	3	0
Protestants	18	.3174	1.2824	41.1	5	2	2	0	1	5	3	0	0	0	0	0	0	4	0	0	0	0	0	0	0	2	11	1	0
protested	45	.6612	6.1404	47.9	3	8	4	4	8	8	8	2	9	2	0	5	1	3	0	0	0	0	0	0	14	5	2	4	0
protesters	4	.1622	.1743	32.4	0	0	0	0	3	1	0	0	0	0	0	0	0	1	0	0	0	0	0	0	0	0	0	3	0
protesting	7	.2215	.3961	36.0	1	0	2	0	2	0	1	1	1	1	0	0	0	0	0	0	0	0	0	0	0	0	0	5	0

4Q propellent
3P propeller-powered
6N propension
7Q propensity
8Q property-owning
8Q prophet-leaders
8R propjet
8Q proportionality
7R proportionally
9M proportionate
9Q proportionately
3A propped-open
9Q Propulsion
9D prorogue
7Q proroguing
8Q proscribed
6B prosecute-prosecution
8Q prosecuting
7R prosecution-fearing
7Q prosimian
7Q prosimians
5B Prospecting
7Q Prospects
7R Prospera
5P prosperous-looking
8F prospers
8Q prostate
8Q prostatis
5P prostitutes
8F prostrated
8R protean
5F protectorates
8P protectors
6N proteges
7Q protein-rich
9E protein-to-carbohydrate
9H Proterozoic
8Q Protestantism

Word Type	F	D	U	SFI	3 Gr 3	4 Gr 4	5 Gr 5	6 Gr 6	7 Gr 7	8 Gr 8	9 Gr 9	X UnGr	A Read	B Eng & Gr	C Comp	D Lit	E Math	F Soc Stud	G Spell	H Sci	J Music	K Art	L Home Ec	M Shop	N Lib F	P Lib NF	Q Lib Ref	R Mag	S Rel
protests	23	.5152	2.5527	44.1	1	0	3	0	4	11	2	2	4	0	0	2	0	7	0	0	0	0	0	0	0	1	1	8	0
prothallium	6	.0000	.1183	30.7	0	0	0	0	0	0	6	0	0	0	0	0	0	0	0	6	0	0	0	0	0	0	0	0	0
Protist	2	.0000	.0394	26.0	0	0	0	0	0	0	2	0	0	0	0	0	0	0	0	2	0	0	0	0	0	0	0	0	0
protists	11	.0000	.2169	33.4	0	0	3	0	1	1	6	0	0	0	0	0	0	0	0	11	0	0	0	0	0	0	0	0	0
proton	7	.1941	.3707	35.7	0	0	1	3	2	1	0	0	0	0	0	0	0	0	0	6	0	0	0	0	0	0	1	0	0
protons	31	.3172	2.3016	43.6	0	0	14	5	6	5	1	0	0	0	0	0	0	0	0	26	0	0	0	3	0	0	2	0	0
protoplasm	66	.1004	2.4476	43.9	0	0	25	2	36	0	1	2	0	0	0	0	0	0	0	63	0	0	0	0	0	0	3	0	0
Protos	14	.0000	.2027	33.1	0	14	0	0	0	0	0	0	0	0	0	0	0	0	0	0	0	0	0	0	0	14	0	0	0
prototype	9	.3532	.7019	38.5	0	0	0	0	4	2	2	1	0	0	0	0	0	0	0	2	0	0	0	0	0	0	3	4	0
protozoa	20	.1626	.9539	39.8	0	0	2	9	8	0	1	0	0	0	0	0	0	0	0	18	0	0	0	0	0	0	2	0	0
Protozoa	2	.0000	.0394	26.0	0	0	0	0	0	0	0	2	0	0	0	0	0	0	0	2	0	0	0	0	0	0	0	0	0
protozoan	12	.2025	.6796	38.3	1	2	0	2	7	0	0	0	1	0	0	0	0	0	0	10	0	0	0	0	0	0	1	0	0
protozoans	33	.0439	.9566	39.8	2	8	0	16	6	0	1	0	2	0	0	0	0	0	0	31	0	0	0	0	0	0	0	0	0
protracted	2	.2446	.1142	30.6	0	0	0	0	1	1	0	0	0	0	0	0	0	0	0	0	0	0	0	0	1	0	0	1	0
protractor	57	.3072	4.0265	46.0	0	0	16	9	11	5	12	4	0	0	0	0	48	0	1	5	0	0	0	2	0	1	0	0	0
protruded	6	.4433	.5977	37.8	0	0	0	1	3	1	1	0	2	0	0	1	0	0	0	0	0	0	0	0	1	0	2	0	0
protruding	5	.4228	.4710	36.7	0	1	1	1	2	0	0	0	1	0	0	0	0	0	0	0	0	0	0	0	1	1	0	2	0
proud	361	.8705	62.939	58.0	78	83	32	45	62	35	23	3	143	10	3	45	0	23	4	0	18	5	2	1	26	46	7	27	1
prouder	3	.2374	.1625	32.1	1	0	0	1	0	0	1	0	0	0	0	2	0	0	0	0	1	0	0	0	0	0	0	0	0
proudest	7	.5555	.8368	39.2	1	2	3	0	1	0	0	0	2	0	0	1	0	2	0	0	0	0	0	0	0	0	1	1	0
proudly	122	.7234	18.384	52.6	33	36	12	12	13	8	7	1	68	4	4	5	0	4	0	1	3	0	1	0	11	19	0	2	0
Proutte	8	.0000	.0938	29.7	0	8	0	0	0	0	0	0	0	0	0	0	0	0	0	0	0	0	0	0	8	0	0	0	0
prove	257	.8791	45.072	56.5	29	30	24	26	62	41	37	8	66	20	1	20	54	13	5	13	3	1	2	0	6	18	14	21	0
proved	239	.8653	41.289	56.2	13	18	28	44	66	35	22	13	49	4	3	7	18	22	5	27	6	0	0	3	15	16	26	37	1
proven	11	.5734	1.3391	41.3	0	0	0	3	1	4	1	2	2	0	0	0	0	4	0	1	0	0	0	0	1	0	2	1	0
Provencal	4	.2437	.2257	33.5	0	0	2	0	0	0	0	2	0	0	0	0	0	0	0	0	0	0	0	0	0	0	2	2	0
Provence	4	.1873	.1827	32.6	1	0	0	0	0	0	2	1	0	0	0	0	0	0	0	0	0	0	0	0	0	0	3	1	0
proverb	4	.3277	.3071	34.9	0	0	0	1	1	0	2	0	1	1	0	0	0	0	0	0	0	0	0	1	0	1	0	0	0
proverbial	2	.1839	.0845	29.3	0	0	0	0	2	0	0	0	0	0	0	0	0	0	0	0	0	0	1	0	1	0	0	0	0
proverbs	3	.2063	.1600	32.0	0	1	0	0	2	0	0	0	0	0	0	0	0	1	0	0	0	0	0	0	0	2	0	0	0
Proverbs	2	.0000	.0290	24.6	0	2	0	0	0	0	0	0	0	0	0	0	0	0	0	0	0	0	0	0	0	2	0	0	0
proves	26	.7422	3.9331	45.9	2	2	2	4	7	3	4	2	7	1	0	3	1	0	0	1	1	0	0	0	2	2	5	3	0
provide	361	.8516	61.247	57.9	13	11	52	38	79	74	82	12	23	17	5	4	7	95	4	51	21	4	23	16	4	15	51	21	0
provided	228	.8762	39.716	56.0	4	16	31	21	53	61	27	15	21	5	3	4	10	51	3	18	11	4	5	5	6	6	49	27	0
providence	6	.2822	.3882	35.9	0	0	0	4	1	1	0	0	0	1	0	0	0	1	0	0	0	0	0	0	4	0	0	0	0
Providence	27	.6789	3.8063	45.8	0	2	3	6	10	6	0	0	8	1	0	0	1	5	0	1	0	0	0	0	5	1	4	1	0
Provident	3	.0000	.1370	31.4	0	3	0	0	0	0	0	0	3	0	0	0	0	0	0	0	0	0	0	0	0	0	0	0	0
providers	2	.0000	.0394	26.0	0	0	0	0	0	0	0	2	0	0	0	0	0	0	0	2	0	0	0	0	0	0	0	0	0
provides	117	.7712	18.121	52.6	4	7	9	11	31	19	27	9	7	7	0	3	3	16	1	17	5	0	8	6	0	4	25	15	0
providing	50	.7960	7.9723	49.0	4	1	3	2	17	11	10	2	4	3	0	1	0	3	0	7	1	1	3	2	1	5	12	7	0
Provincale	2	.0000	.0914	29.6	0	0	0	0	0	0	2	0	2	0	0	0	0	0	0	0	0	0	0	0	0	0	0	0	0
province	76	.6396	10.011	50.0	5	3	17	14	16	15	4	2	7	3	0	4	0	23	0	0	5	0	0	0	1	6	22	5	0
Province	12	.4002	1.0523	40.2	1	0	1	2	4	4	0	0	1	0	0	0	0	1	0	0	0	0	0	0	0	2	6	2	0
province's	2	.2285	.1129	30.5	0	0	1	0	1	0	0	0	0	0	0	0	0	1	0	0	0	0	0	0	0	0	1	0	0
provinces	65	.5403	7.3339	48.7	5	6	8	6	25	11	4	0	0	1	1	0	0	24	0	1	0	0	0	0	1	9	24	4	0
Provinces	19	.3681	1.5459	41.9	1	0	2	7	9	0	0	0	0	0	0	0	0	7	0	0	0	0	0	0	0	2	9	1	0
provincial	16	.4867	1.6670	42.2	0	0	6	1	4	4	1	0	2	0	0	0	0	1	0	0	1	0	0	0	0	5	6	1	0
Provincial	2	.1738	.0790	29.0	0	1	0	0	1	0	0	0	0	0	0	0	0	0	0	0	0	0	0	1	0	0	1	0	0
proving	16	.6297	2.0913	43.2	0	1	2	2	5	3	1	2	2	0	0	0	0	2	1	3	0	0	0	0	1	3	0	4	0
provision	13	.4317	1.1838	40.7	0	0	0	1	4	5	2	1	0	0	0	0	0	2	0	0	0	0	2	0	1	0	7	1	0
provisional	5	.2205	.2855	34.6	0	0	0	0	3	1	1	0	0	0	0	0	0	4	0	0	0	0	0	0	0	0	1	0	0
provisions	34	.7505	5.1797	47.1	1	3	6	4	7	7	6	0	6	2	0	3	0	5	0	2	0	0	0	0	3	5	4	4	0
proviso	2	.2446	.1123	30.5	0	0	0	0	0	1	0	1	0	1	0	0	0	0	0	0	0	0	0	0	0	0	1	0	0
Proviso	3	.0000	.0583	27.7	0	0	0	0	0	3	0	0	0	0	0	0	0	3	0	0	0	0	0	0	0	0	0	0	0
provocation	2	.2446	.1123	30.5	0	0	0	1	1	0	0	0	0	1	0	0	0	0	0	0	0	0	0	0	0	0	1	0	0
provocative	7	.4076	.6256	38.0	0	0	1	0	2	2	2	0	1	0	0	0	0	0	0	0	1	0	0	0	0	0	3	2	0
provoke	4	.4495	.4018	36.0	0	0	0	1	1	0	1	1	1	0	0	1	0	1	0	0	0	0	0	0	0	0	0	1	0
provoked	9	.4866	.9130	39.6	1	0	0	1	1	1	4	1	0	0	1	1	0	1	0	0	0	0	0	0	0	0	2	4	0
provoking	6	.4470	.5692	37.6	0	0	3	1	1	0	0	1	0	0	0	0	0	0	0	1	0	0	0	0	2	0	2	1	0
prow	11	.5133	1.2545	41.0	0	0	0	5	5	0	1	0	5	1	0	3	0	0	0	0	0	0	0	0	1	1	0	0	0
prowess	7	.5216	.7672	38.8	0	0	0	1	4	2	0	0	1	0	0	0	0	0	0	0	1	0	0	1	0	1	2	1	0
prowl	10	.3911	.9815	39.9	4	0	0	0	3	3	0	0	7	0	1	0	0	0	1	1	0	0	0	0	0	0	0	0	0
prowled	5	.4296	.4747	36.8	0	1	0	1	3	0	0	0	1	0	0	0	0	0	0	0	0	0	0	0	1	0	1	2	0
prowling	11	.7139	1.6091	42.1	3	3	0	2	2	1	0	0	3	1	0	1	0	1	1	0	1	0	0	0	1	0	0	2	0
prowls	2	.2375	.1088	30.4	0	1	0	0	0	0	1	0	0	0	0	0	0	0	0	0	1	0	0	0	0	0	0	1	0
proxemics	2	.0000	.0243	23.9	0	0	0	0	0	0	0	2	0	0	0	0	0	0	0	0	0	0	0	0	0	0	0	2	0
proximity	4	.3676	.3150	35.0	0	0	0	0	1	1	1	1	0	0	0	0	0	0	0	0	1	0	0	0	0	0	2	1	0
prt	2	.0000	.0299	24.8	0	0	0	0	2	0	0	0	0	0	0	0	2	0	0	0	0	0	0	0	0	0	0	0	0
PRT	2	.0000	.0299	24.8	0	0	0	0	0	2	0	0	0	0	0	0	2	0	0	0	0	0	0	0	0	0	0	0	0
prudence	3	.3815	.2534	34.0	0	0	1	0	0	1	1	0	0	0	0	0	0	1	0	0	0	0	0	0	0	1	0	1	0
Prudence	13	.3319	.9741	39.9	11	0	0	0	2	0	0	0	0	0	0	0	0	5	0	0	0	0	0	0	0	2	6	0	0
prudent	9	.5073	.9656	39.8	0	0	0	0	5	2	2	0	1	1	0	4	0	1	1	0	0	0	0	0	1	0	0	0	0
prudery	2	.0000	.0219	23.4	0	0	0	0	0	0	0	2	0	2	0	0	0	0	0	0	0	0	0	0	0	0	0	0	0
Prudhomme	2	.0000	.0243	23.9	0	0	0	0	2	0	0	0	0	0	0	0	0	0	0	0	0	0	0	0	0	0	0	2	0
prune	8	.4819	.8788	39.4	3	2	1	1	1	0	0	0	4	0	0	0	0	0	0	0	0	0	0	0	1	2	1	0	0
Prune	2	.0000	.0243	23.9	0	0	0	0	0	0	0	2	0	0	0	0	0	0	0	0	0	0	0	0	0	0	0	2	0
pruned	5	.0000	.0523	27.2	0	0	0	5	0	0	0	0	0	0	0	0	0	0	0	0	0	0	0	0	0	0	5	0	0
prunes	7	.5420	.7953	39.0	1	0	1	2	2	0	1	0	1	1	0	1	0	0	0	0	0	0	1	0	2	1	0	0	0
pruning	10	.2355	.5782	37.6	0	0	1	8	0	0	0	1	1	0	0	0	0	0	0	1	0	0	0	0	0	0	7	1	0
Prussia	29	.2115	1.6288	42.1	0	0	0	0	8	2	19	0	0	0	0	0	0	25	0	1	0	0	0	0	0	0	3	0	0
Prussia's	4	.0000	.0778	28.9	0	0	0	0	1	0	3	0	0	0	0	0	0	4	0	0	0	0	0	0	0	0	0	0	0
Prussian	10	.3423	.7773	38.9	0	0	0	0	1	2	5	2	0	0	0	0	0	4	0	2	0	0	0	0	0	0	4	0	0
Prussians	2	.2408	.1204	30.8	1	0	0	0	0	0	1	0	0	0	0	0	0	1	0	0	0	0	0	0	0	1	0	0	0
Prutenicae	3	.0000	.0591	27.7	0	0	0	0	0	0	0	3	0	0	0	0	0	0	0	3	0	0	0	0	0	0	0	0	0
pry	19	.6043	2.4126	43.8	2	5	1	6	3	0	1	1	3	0	0	0	0	2	0	8	0	0	0	1	1	0	1	3	0
Pryderi	2	.0000	.0290	24.6	0	0	0	0	2	0	0	0	0	0	0	0	0	0	0	0	0	0	0	0	0	2	0	0	0
prying	6	.5187	.6677	38.2	2	0	0	2	2	0	0	0	1	0	0	0	0	0	0	1	0	0	0	0	1	2	1	0	0
Pryor	2	.0000	.0299	24.8	0	0	0	0	2	0	0	0	0	0	0	0	2	0	0	0	0	0	0	0	0	0	0	0	0
psalm	6	.5155	.6547	38.2	0	1	1	0	2	1	1	0	1	1	0	2	0	0	1	0	0	0	0	0	0	0	1	0	0
Psalm	11	.3856	.9162	39.6	1	0	5	0	3	1	1	0	1	1	0	2	0	0	1	0	6	0	0	0	0	0	0	0	0
psalms	3	.0171	.0207	23.2	2	0	0	0	0	0	1	0	0	0	0	0	0	0	0	0	0	0	0	0	0	0	1	0	2
Psalms	3	.1852	.1342	31.3	0	1	2	0	0	0	0	0	0	0	0	0	0	0	0	0	2	0	0	0	0	0	0	0	0
pseudopods	2	.0000	.0394	26.0	0	0	0	0	1	0	1	0	0	0	0	0	0	0	0	2	0	0	0	0	0	1	0	0	0

7Q Protests
9H prothallia
5H protist
7Q protistans
9H Protists
6H protium
4P protoceratops
6Q Protococcus
9H protonema
4P Protos's
7P protractors
7F protrude
5H protrudes
7Q protrusion
7N protuberances
6R protuberant
3A Proudfoot
3N proudfully
7Q Proustian
4N Prouttes
7P Provet
6N providentially
6A provider
4F Provincetown
8F provincial-minded
5P provincialism
5P Proving
9D Provis
XR Provision
9F Provisional
9D provisioned
8B provocations
6B provoke-provocation
3P provokes
7C provokingly
7L provolone
4P prowler
7A Prowler
4Q prowlers
7N prowlin'
6A prowlishly
4P prows
XR proxemic
8H Proxima
7P Prudence's
9E Prudent
7D prudently
7F Prudhoe
XB prudish
3P prune-jack
6A Pryce
7P Pryderi's
7E Pryor's
8G ps
8E PS
5J psalm-tunes
7C psalmody
5J Psalter
7J psaltery
XQ Pseudoalleles
XQ pseudoallelism
9Q pseudonym
6Q pseudopodia
XH pseudopregnant
6R pshaw
3P pshaws

Word Type	F	D	U	SFI	3 Gr 3	4 Gr 4	5 Gr 5	6 Gr 6	7 Gr 7	8 Gr 8	9 Gr 9	X UnGr	A Read	B Eng & Gr	C Comp	D Lit	E Math	F Soc Stud	G Spell	H Sci	J Music	K Art	L Home Ec	M Shop	N Lib F	P Lib NF	Q Lib Ref	R Mag	S Rel
psi	7	.2425	.3907	35.9	0	0	0	0	6	0	1	0	0	0	0	0	0	0	0	0	0	0	0	1	0	0	0	6	0
psittacosis	2	.2401	.1133	30.5	1	0	0	0	0	1	0	0	0	0	0	0	0	0	0	0	0	0	0	0	0	1	1	0	0
PSQ	2	.0000	.0299	24.8	0	0	0	0	2	0	0	0	0	0	0	0	2	0	0	0	0	0	0	0	0	0	0	0	0
pss	2	.0000	.0914	29.6	0	0	0	0	2	0	0	0	2	0	0	0	0	0	0	0	0	0	0	0	0	0	0	0	0
psst	5	.0000	.2284	33.6	1	4	0	0	0	0	0	0	5	0	0	0	0	0	0	0	0	0	0	0	0	0	0	0	0
Psyche	10	.0000	.1448	31.6	0	0	0	10	0	0	0	0	0	0	0	0	0	0	0	0	0	0	0	0	0	10	0	0	0
psychedelic	4	.0000	.0486	26.9	0	0	0	0	0	3	0	1	0	0	0	0	0	0	0	0	0	0	0	0	0	0	0	4	0
psychiatric	7	.3249	.5134	37.1	0	0	1	0	2	2	2	0	0	0	0	0	0	0	0	2	0	0	0	0	0	0	1	4	0
psychiatrist	6	.2879	.3956	36.0	0	0	0	0	3	1	1	1	0	0	0	0	0	0	0	1	0	0	0	0	0	0	1	4	0
psychiatrists	9	.4295	.8271	39.2	0	0	4	0	1	1	1	2	0	0	0	0	0	0	0	1	0	0	0	0	0	2	2	4	0
psychiatry	3	.0000	.0365	25.6	0	0	0	1	1	0	1	0	0	0	0	0	0	0	0	0	0	0	0	0	0	0	0	3	0
psychic	2	.1698	.1133	30.5	0	0	0	0	0	0	2	0	1	0	0	0	0	0	0	0	0	0	0	0	0	0	1	0	0
Psychical	2	.0000	.0209	23.2	0	0	0	0	0	0	2	0	0	0	0	0	0	0	0	0	0	0	0	0	0	0	2	0	0
psychoanalytic	2	.0000	.0243	23.9	0	0	0	0	0	2	0	0	0	0	0	0	0	0	0	0	0	0	0	0	0	0	0	2	0
psychological	28	.5980	3.4239	45.3	1	1	8	1	9	3	4	1	0	0	1	1	0	0	0	3	0	0	1	0	0	3	10	9	0
psychologically	3	.2321	.1635	32.1	0	0	0	0	2	0	0	1	0	0	0	0	0	0	0	0	0	0	0	0	0	0	1	2	0
psychologist	11	.3726	.9033	39.6	1	0	1	0	7	2	0	0	0	0	0	1	0	0	0	1	0	0	0	0	0	7	0	2	0
Psychologist	2	.0000	.0243	23.9	0	0	0	0	0	0	2	0	0	0	0	0	0	0	0	0	0	0	0	0	0	0	0	2	0
psychologists	17	.5798	2.0384	43.1	2	0	1	2	7	2	3	0	1	1	0	0	1	0	0	1	0	0	1	0	0	2	2	8	0
psychology	22	.3161	1.5842	42.0	0	0	3	6	3	5	5	0	2	0	0	0	2	1	1	0	0	0	0	0	0	0	15	1	0
psychoses	2	.0000	.0209	23.2	0	0	2	0	0	0	0	0	0	0	0	0	0	0	0	0	0	0	0	0	0	0	2	0	0
psychosis	7	.2366	.4193	36.2	0	0	0	0	0	0	7	0	0	0	0	0	0	0	0	5	0	0	0	0	0	0	0	2	0
psychotherapy	2	.2278	.1128	30.5	0	0	1	0	0	0	1	0	0	0	0	0	0	0	0	1	0	0	0	0	0	0	1	0	0
pt	2	.0000	.0162	22.1	0	0	1	0	0	1	0	0	0	0	0	0	0	0	2	0	0	0	0	0	0	0	0	0	0
PT	10	.2434	.5851	37.7	0	0	0	1	8	1	0	0	0	0	0	0	1	0	0	0	0	0	0	0	0	8	1	0	0
PT-59	2	.0000	.0290	24.6	0	0	0	0	2	0	0	0	0	0	0	0	0	0	0	0	0	0	0	0	0	2	0	0	0
PTA	8	.3483	.6153	37.9	1	5	0	0	1	1	0	0	0	1	0	0	1	1	0	0	0	0	0	0	5	0	0	0	0
ptarmigan	2	.0000	.0209	23.2	0	0	0	0	2	0	0	0	0	0	0	0	0	0	0	0	0	0	0	0	0	0	2	0	0
ptero	3	.0000	.0591	27.7	0	0	0	0	3	0	0	0	0	0	0	0	0	0	0	3	0	0	0	0	0	0	0	0	0
Ptolemaic	7	.0000	.1380	31.4	0	0	0	0	0	6	0	1	0	0	0	0	0	0	0	7	0	0	0	0	0	0	0	0	0
Ptolemy	7	.0000	.1380	31.4	0	0	0	0	0	4	2	1	0	0	0	0	0	0	0	7	0	0	0	0	0	0	0	0	0
Ptolemy's	5	.0000	.0986	29.9	0	0	0	0	0	3	1	1	0	0	0	0	0	0	0	5	0	0	0	0	0	0	0	0	0
public	447	.8467	75.617	58.8	33	21	50	34	88	104	99	18	67	24	3	10	2	88	5	20	27	3	4	2	9	27	89	67	0
Public	16	.5590	1.8722	42.7	2	3	2	1	5	2	0	1	1	1	0	1	0	5	0	0	0	0	0	0	1	0	1	6	0
public-address	2	.1733	.1149	30.6	0	0	0	0	1	1	0	0	1	1	0	0	0	0	0	0	0	0	0	0	0	0	0	0	0
public-relations	4	.1622	.1743	32.4	0	0	0	0	0	1	1	2	0	0	0	0	0	1	0	0	0	0	0	0	0	0	0	3	0
public-school	2	.2440	.1132	30.5	0	0	0	0	1	0	1	0	0	0	0	1	0	0	0	0	0	0	0	0	0	0	0	1	0
public's	4	.3397	.3024	34.8	0	0	0	0	1	3	0	0	0	2	0	0	0	1	0	0	0	0	0	0	0	0	0	1	0
publication	16	.5744	1.8806	42.7	0	3	2	0	4	3	4	0	0	3	1	0	1	0	0	1	1	0	0	0	0	0	7	2	0
publications	9	.5768	1.0566	40.2	0	0	1	0	6	1	0	1	0	0	1	0	0	0	1	0	2	0	0	0	0	1	2	2	0
Publications	3	.2398	.1721	32.4	0	0	0	0	0	3	0	0	0	0	0	0	2	0	0	0	0	0	0	0	0	0	1	0	0
publicity	21	.2499	1.2561	41.0	0	2	0	3	9	4	0	3	1	1	0	0	0	1	0	0	0	0	0	0	0	2	0	16	0
publicize	4	.4485	.4009	36.0	0	0	0	3	0	1	0	0	1	0	0	0	0	1	0	0	0	0	0	0	0	0	1	1	0
publicized	5	.3742	.4184	36.2	0	0	0	0	2	2	1	0	0	0	0	0	0	3	0	0	0	0	0	0	0	0	1	1	0
publicly	21	.7415	3.1404	45.0	0	2	1	3	5	4	5	1	1	1	0	2	0	4	1	1	2	0	0	0	0	2	2	5	0
publish	23	.7236	3.3963	45.3	2	3	4	1	3	6	4	0	4	2	0	2	0	5	0	2	0	0	0	0	1	1	4	2	0
published	141	.7476	21.263	53.3	1	15	13	17	35	32	22	6	13	13	1	9	3	3	4	18	10	0	0	0	0	9	40	18	0
publisher	17	.6513	2.2931	43.6	1	4	4	2	3	1	2	0	4	2	0	0	2	0	0	0	0	0	0	1	0	3	3	2	0
publishers	16	.5096	1.7306	42.4	1	5	1	1	2	1	5	0	3	1	0	0	0	1	1	0	1	0	0	2	0	0	7	0	0
publishes	5	.3053	.3370	35.3	0	0	2	0	2	1	0	0	0	0	1	0	0	0	0	1	0	0	0	0	0	0	3	0	0
publishing	14	.5255	1.5294	41.8	2	2	2	0	5	1	2	0	0	1	0	0	0	2	0	0	1	0	0	0	0	3	6	1	0
Publishing	2	.2391	.1133	30.5	0	0	0	0	1	1	0	0	0	0	0	0	1	0	0	0	0	0	0	0	0	0	1	0	0
Puccini	4	.0000	.0323	25.1	0	0	0	0	1	3	0	0	0	0	0	0	0	0	0	0	4	0	0	0	0	0	0	0	0
puck	10	.1814	.5933	37.7	0	0	0	0	10	0	0	0	5	0	0	0	0	0	0	0	0	0	0	0	0	0	0	5	0
pucker	3	.2330	.1860	32.7	0	1	1	0	0	1	0	0	1	0	0	0	0	0	0	0	0	0	1	0	0	1	0	0	0
puckered	5	.2445	.3100	34.9	1	2	0	0	2	0	0	0	1	0	0	3	0	0	0	0	0	0	0	0	0	1	0	0	0
puckering	2	.0000	.0064	18.1	0	0	0	0	1	0	1	0	0	0	0	0	0	0	0	0	0	0	2	0	0	0	0	0	0
Pud	11	.0386	.2305	33.6	0	0	0	0	10	1	0	0	1	0	0	10	0	0	0	0	0	0	0	0	0	0	0	0	0
pudding	33	.5721	3.9461	46.0	10	8	0	4	7	2	2	0	6	1	0	2	0	1	1	4	4	0	7	0	3	0	0	4	0
puddings	5	.3767	.4319	36.4	0	1	0	1	1	2	0	0	1	0	0	1	0	0	0	2	0	0	1	0	0	0	0	0	0
puddle	21	.6141	2.7133	44.3	7	4	3	3	3	1	0	0	6	2	0	0	0	0	1	3	0	1	0	0	6	2	0	0	0
Puddleby	6	.1660	.2536	34.0	0	5	1	0	0	0	0	0	0	0	0	1	0	0	0	0	0	0	0	0	5	0	0	0	0
Puddleby-on-the-Marsh	2	.0000	.0234	23.7	0	2	0	0	0	0	0	0	0	0	0	0	0	0	0	0	0	0	0	0	2	0	0	0	0
puddles	10	.4433	.9896	40.0	2	3	2	0	1	1	0	1	3	0	2	0	0	1	0	2	0	1	0	0	0	0	1	0	0
Pudge	4	.2399	.3011	34.8	0	3	0	0	0	1	0	0	3	1	0	0	0	0	0	0	0	0	0	0	0	0	0	0	0
pudgy	2	.0000	.0234	23.7	1	0	0	0	0	0	0	1	0	0	0	0	0	0	0	0	0	0	0	0	2	0	0	0	0
Puebla	2	.1042	.0600	27.8	0	1	0	1	0	0	0	0	0	0	0	0	0	1	0	0	0	1	0	0	0	0	0	0	0
pueblo	21	.4140	2.0084	43.0	1	12	1	6	1	0	0	0	6	0	0	0	0	11	1	0	0	2	0	0	0	0	0	1	0
Pueblo	25	.3725	2.0851	43.2	14	1	1	0	4	0	5	0	0	0	0	0	0	15	0	0	0	0	0	0	0	0	4	6	0
pueblos	10	.4548	.9820	39.9	2	3	3	0	0	2	0	0	0	1	0	0	0	5	0	0	0	0	0	0	0	3	1	0	0
Pueblos	10	.3368	.7697	38.9	7	3	0	0	0	0	0	0	0	0	0	0	0	6	0	0	0	0	0	0	0	1	3	0	0
puerta	2	.0000	.0162	22.1	0	0	2	0	0	0	0	0	0	0	0	0	0	0	0	0	2	0	0	0	0	0	0	0	0
Puerto	57	.6208	7.3344	48.7	18	5	17	4	5	3	5	0	7	3	0	0	0	13	1	1	4	0	0	0	1	2	3	22	0
puff	45	.7483	6.9454	48.4	17	6	6	4	5	6	1	0	22	2	0	6	0	3	3	3	0	0	0	1	1	3	0	1	0
puffball	4	.0000	.0789	29.0	0	0	0	4	0	0	0	0	0	0	0	0	0	0	0	4	0	0	0	0	0	0	0	0	0
puffballs	5	.0000	.0986	29.9	0	0	0	5	0	0	0	0	0	0	0	0	0	0	0	5	0	0	0	0	0	0	0	0	0
puffed	35	.6386	4.6694	46.7	5	6	6	4	2	8	3	1	10	0	3	5	0	2	0	3	0	0	0	0	5	4	1	2	0
Puffer	3	.0000	.1370	31.4	3	0	0	0	0	0	0	0	3	0	0	0	0	0	0	0	0	0	0	0	0	0	0	0	0
puffing	30	.6692	4.2748	46.3	7	9	1	2	8	0	2	1	19	0	1	2	0	1	0	0	1	0	0	0	2	2	0	2	0
puffs	27	.7842	4.2813	46.3	4	6	3	1	6	4	3	0	7	2	1	4	0	1	0	1	0	0	1	0	3	4	1	2	0
puffy	4	.3387	.3012	34.8	3	0	0	0	1	0	0	0	0	0	0	2	0	0	0	1	0	0	0	0	1	0	0	0	0
pug	3	.2292	.1615	32.1	1	0	0	0	0	2	0	0	0	0	0	1	0	0	0	0	0	0	0	0	2	0	0	0	0
Puget	14	.6205	1.7846	42.5	4	0	5	0	2	2	1	0	0	0	0	2	0	4	0	1	0	0	0	0	1	1	1	4	0
pugilist	2	.0000	.0215	23.3	0	0	0	0	0	2	0	0	0	0	0	2	0	0	0	0	0	0	0	0	0	0	0	0	0
pugilistic	4	.1757	.1766	32.5	0	0	0	1	0	3	0	0	0	0	0	3	0	0	0	0	0	0	0	0	0	1	0	0	0
pugilists	2	.0000	.0290	24.6	0	0	0	2	0	0	0	0	0	0	0	0	0	0	0	0	0	0	0	0	0	2	0	0	0
pugnacious	2	.0000	.0215	23.3	0	0	0	0	0	2	0	0	0	0	0	2	0	0	0	0	0	0	0	0	0	0	0	0	0
puili	3	.0000	.0243	23.8	1	0	2	0	0	0	0	0	0	0	0	0	0	0	0	0	3	0	0	0	0	0	0	0	0
puking	2	.2433	.1158	30.6	0	0	1	0	1	0	0	0	0	0	0	0	0	0	0	0	0	0	0	0	0	1	0	1	0
Pulaski	3	.3350	.2478	33.9	0	0	1	1	0	1	0	0	1	0	0	0	0	1	0	0	0	0	0	0	0	0	1	0	0
Pulitzer	13	.5473	1.5497	41.9	0	0	7	2	1	3	0	0	5	0	0	2	0	3	0	0	2	0	0	0	0	0	1	0	0
pull	558	.9032	100.34	60.0	139	116	67	83	67	49	31	6	179	5	2	25	4	26	11	109	12	5	19	8	39	66	18	30	0
pulled	770	.8485	131.85	61.2	189	213	88	74	114	53	32	7	397	6	9	64	5	31	5	28	10	2	4	3	76	79	13	38	0
puller	5	.2557	.2895	34.6	1	0	0	1	3	0	0	0	0	0	0	0	0	0	0	1	0	0	0	2	0	1	0	1	0

3P pshawses
6A pssst
XR psyche
7R psychiatrist's
9Q psychical
8R psyching
5R psycho-cybernetics
8R psychoanalysis
8R psychoanalyst
8R psychoanalyst's
8Q psychogenic
9Q psychokinesis
9R Psychologists
5Q psychoneuroses
5Q Psychotherapy
9R psychotic
7R psychotics
9H psychrometer
8H Pt
7P PT-109
7P PT-114
7P PT-187
8R PT-76
9R Ptakovina
7H ptera
4P pterosaurs
8G ptomaine
8F Pub
7R puberty
3Q public-health
7B public-house
9R public-maintenance
8F public-spirited
3S publicans
4Q Publication
6P publicist
7Q publicists
6R publicizing
8B publick
7A publishment
XR Pucci
7L puckers
3A puckery
6A pudding-face
3J pudding-string
8F puddlers
3A puddling
9R Pueblo's
3F PuertoRico
4P puff-puff-puff
7Q puffers
9A puffiness
6R Pugh
7P pugmarks
8D pugnus
5J puilis
5P Pukekohe
5P pukka
8Q Pulangi
5P Pulcinella
9B pull-a-button
3P pulldown
6P puller-downers

Word Type	F	D	U	SFI	3 Gr 3	4 Gr 4	5 Gr 5	6 Gr 6	7 Gr 7	8 Gr 8	9 Gr 9	X UnGr	A Read	B Eng & Gr	C Comp	D Lit	E Math	F Soc Stud	G Spell	H Sci	J Music	K Art	L Home Ec	M Shop	N Lib F	P Lib NF	Q Lib Ref	R Mag	S Rel
pulley	52	.4136	4.8213	46.8	22	2	1	21	0	0	3	3	2	0	1	0	0	2	0	43	0	0	0	2	0	2	0	0	0
pulleys	21	.3947	1.8617	42.7	5	0	2	10	2	1	0	1	0	0	0	0	1	2	0	15	0	0	0	0	0	1	2	0	0
pulling	221	.8765	38.826	55.9	42	54	37	29	28	12	19	0	97	1	1	15	1	9	1	31	2	1	4	3	18	21	4	12	0
Pullman	32	.0950	1.0188	40.1	0	30	0	0	1	1	0	0	0	0	0	0	0	1	0	0	0	0	0	0	0	30	0	1	0
Pullmans	2	.1523	.0721	28.6	0	0	0	1	0	0	1	0	0	0	1	0	0	0	0	0	0	0	0	0	0	0	0	1	0
pulls	134	.7797	21.138	53.3	33	23	31	24	7	5	9	2	18	2	1	2	7	8	3	63	4	0	1	0	3	12	4	6	0
pulmonary	10	.2426	.6051	37.8	0	0	0	6	0	2	2	0	0	0	0	0	0	0	0	7	0	0	0	0	0	0	3	0	0
pulp	49	.6899	6.9089	48.4	0	2	24	8	8	3	3	1	1	2	0	1	0	25	0	10	0	0	2	1	1	2	2	2	0
pulpit	8	.6130	1.0267	40.1	0	1	1	1	4	1	0	0	2	0	0	0	0	0	0	0	1	0	0	0	1	2	1	1	0
pulpit-voice	2	.0000	.0243	23.9	0	0	0	0	0	2	0	0	0	0	0	0	0	0	0	0	0	0	0	0	0	0	0	2	0
pulpwood	2	.2152	.1357	31.3	0	0	1	0	1	0	0	0	1	0	0	0	0	1	0	0	0	0	0	0	0	0	0	0	0
pulpy	2	.2160	.1362	31.3	0	0	0	1	1	0	0	0	1	0	0	0	0	0	0	1	0	0	0	0	0	0	0	0	0
pulque	2	.0000	.0215	23.3	0	0	0	0	2	0	0	0	0	0	0	2	0	0	0	0	0	0	0	0	0	0	0	0	0
pulsar	2	.0000	.0243	23.9	0	0	0	0	0	0	0	2	0	0	0	0	0	0	0	0	0	0	0	0	0	0	0	2	0
pulsars	2	.0000	.0243	23.9	0	0	0	0	0	0	0	2	0	0	0	0	0	0	0	0	0	0	0	0	0	0	0	2	0
pulsate	4	.2305	.2357	33.7	0	0	0	0	1	0	3	0	0	0	0	0	0	0	0	3	0	0	0	0	1	0	0	0	0
pulsating	6	.3350	.4562	36.6	0	0	0	0	3	0	3	0	0	0	0	1	0	0	0	4	0	0	0	1	0	0	0	0	0
pulsation	3	.3768	.2437	33.9	1	0	0	0	2	0	0	0	0	0	0	0	0	0	0	0	1	0	0	0	0	1	0	1	0
pulsations	3	.0000	.0243	23.8	0	0	0	0	3	0	0	0	0	0	0	0	0	0	0	0	3	0	0	0	0	0	0	0	0
pulse	53	.7830	8.2995	49.2	9	7	1	7	11	4	9	5	0	1	0	3	4	1	0	12	7	2	2	0	4	1	9	7	0
pulses	9	.4080	.8000	39.0	0	0	1	0	2	0	5	1	1	0	0	0	0	0	0	1	0	0	0	1	0	0	5	1	0
pulsing	7	.4250	.6746	38.3	0	0	1	0	4	1	1	0	2	0	0	0	0	0	0	1	0	0	0	0	0	0	2	2	0
pulverized	2	.2437	.1129	30.5	0	0	0	0	1	1	0	0	0	0	0	0	0	0	0	0	0	0	0	0	0	0	1	1	0
puma	3	.2437	.2277	33.6	0	0	2	0	0	0	1	0	2	0	0	0	0	0	0	1	0	0	0	0	0	0	0	0	0
pumas	3	.3870	.2486	34.0	0	0	0	0	3	0	0	0	0	0	0	1	0	0	0	0	0	0	0	0	0	0	1	1	0
pumice	15	.5672	1.7872	42.5	0	4	2	1	1	2	5	0	1	2	0	0	0	0	0	8	0	0	0	1	1	1	0	1	0
pump	117	.7288	17.464	52.4	22	28	18	12	24	3	8	2	32	0	0	5	0	11	5	22	3	0	0	9	2	7	10	11	0
pumped	66	.6387	8.8189	49.5	11	12	12	10	9	6	3	3	13	0	0	0	0	11	0	22	0	0	0	0	4	3	5	8	0
pumpernickel	2	.1497	.1046	30.2	0	1	0	0	0	1	0	0	1	0	0	0	0	0	1	0	0	0	0	0	0	0	0	0	0
pumpers	2	.0000	.0914	29.6	0	2	0	0	0	0	0	0	2	0	0	0	0	0	0	0	0	0	0	0	0	0	0	0	0
pumping	28	.7495	4.2734	46.3	1	4	2	5	5	6	4	1	6	0	0	1	0	3	1	7	0	0	0	1	1	1	4	3	0
pumpkin	57	.8402	9.6494	49.8	19	13	8	5	7	1	3	1	24	2	1	2	2	1	2	5	2	0	3	0	6	1	1	5	0
Pumpkin	5	.2086	.3320	35.2	1	0	0	2	0	2	0	0	3	0	0	0	0	0	0	0	0	0	0	0	2	0	0	0	0
pumpkins	38	.4344	3.6883	45.7	25	3	4	5	0	0	0	1	9	1	0	0	0	2	1	2	1	0	0	0	0	1	0	21	0
pumps	51	.6558	6.9212	48.4	12	9	6	4	11	5	2	2	6	0	0	0	0	9	0	20	0	0	0	2	5	1	4	4	0
pun	7	.3154	.5582	37.5	0	0	5	0	1	1	0	0	3	3	0	0	0	0	0	0	0	0	0	0	1	0	0	0	0
punch	54	.5034	5.7600	47.6	15	4	3	2	9	5	15	1	9	0	0	0	2	1	0	8	1	0	10	11	3	5	0	4	0
Punch	10	.4294	.8943	39.5	0	0	1	2	3	0	4	0	0	0	1	0	0	0	0	0	5	0	0	0	3	0	1	0	0
punched	24	.7127	3.4978	45.4	2	2	2	3	10	2	2	1	5	3	0	3	3	2	0	0	0	0	0	0	2	3	3	0	0
punchers	2	.0000	.0162	22.1	0	1	0	0	0	1	0	0	0	0	0	0	0	0	0	0	2	0	0	0	0	0	0	0	0
punches	10	.5414	1.1923	40.8	4	0	0	0	4	1	0	1	5	0	0	0	0	0	0	0	0	0	0	1	1	1	1	1	0
punching	15	.5551	1.8236	42.6	5	3	2	2	2	0	1	0	7	2	0	0	0	0	0	0	0	0	0	0	1	3	0	2	0
punctuality	2	.0857	.0784	28.9	0	0	0	0	0	2	0	0	1	0	0	0	0	0	0	0	0	0	1	0	0	0	0	0	0
punctually	3	.1250	.1342	31.3	0	0	0	2	0	1	0	0	1	0	0	0	0	0	0	0	0	0	0	0	2	0	0	0	0
punctuate	27	.2400	1.4878	41.7	0	3	5	9	3	2	5	0	0	21	0	0	0	0	5	0	0	0	0	0	1	0	0	0	0
punctuated	19	.2596	1.1799	40.7	0	0	3	4	4	2	6	0	2	13	0	0	0	0	0	0	0	0	0	0	0	1	0	3	0
punctuating	4	.1772	.1782	32.5	0	0	1	0	1	1	1	0	0	3	0	0	0	0	0	0	0	0	0	0	0	1	0	0	0
punctuation	165	.4234	14.676	51.7	12	27	30	22	40	16	18	0	2	105	23	4	5	0	21	0	0	0	0	0	1	2	1	1	0
puncture	7	.3736	.5903	37.7	0	1	0	1	5	0	0	0	1	0	0	3	0	0	0	1	0	0	0	0	0	0	0	2	0
puncture-proof	3	.3670	.2406	33.8	1	0	0	2	0	0	0	0	0	0	0	0	0	0	1	1	0	0	0	0	0	0	1	0	0
punctures	7	.3717	.6748	38.3	0	5	0	1	1	0	0	0	5	0	0	0	0	0	0	1	0	0	0	0	0	0	0	1	0
pungent	9	.5521	1.0414	40.2	0	0	0	1	3	0	3	2	1	2	0	1	0	0	0	1	0	0	0	0	0	0	1	3	0
punish	29	.7407	4.3857	46.4	6	3	10	5	3	2	0	0	8	1	0	3	0	3	1	0	1	0	0	0	4	5	3	0	0
punishable	2	.1494	.1045	30.2	0	0	0	1	0	1	0	0	1	0	0	0	0	0	0	0	1	0	0	0	0	0	0	0	0
punished	38	.6324	5.0675	47.0	4	4	10	2	8	7	3	0	12	1	0	0	0	9	0	0	0	0	0	0	6	6	1	3	0
punishing	6	.4699	.5926	37.7	0	1	1	0	3	0	1	0	0	1	0	0	0	0	0	0	0	0	0	0	1	2	2	0	0
punishment	45	.7613	6.9653	48.4	0	0	8	7	9	15	3	3	13	4	0	2	0	4	0	1	1	0	3	0	7	2	4	4	0
punishments	2	.2408	.1204	30.8	0	0	0	0	0	1	0	1	0	0	0	0	0	1	0	0	0	0	0	0	0	1	0	0	0
punk	3	.0000	.1370	31.4	2	0	0	0	1	0	0	0	3	0	0	0	0	0	0	0	0	0	0	0	0	0	0	0	0
Punky	2	.0000	.0914	29.6	0	0	0	0	2	0	0	0	2	0	0	0	0	0	0	0	0	0	0	0	0	0	0	0	0
Punta	4	.3360	.3283	35.2	0	0	1	1	1	1	0	0	1	0	0	0	0	2	0	0	0	0	0	0	0	0	0	1	0
punting	2	.1814	.1187	30.7	0	0	0	0	0	0	2	0	1	0	0	0	0	0	0	0	0	0	0	0	0	0	0	1	0
puny	9	.4212	.8685	39.4	0	0	4	1	1	0	2	1	3	0	0	2	0	0	0	1	0	0	0	0	3	0	0	0	0
pup	30	.5487	3.6854	45.7	4	8	4	4	9	1	0	0	19	3	0	3	0	0	0	0	0	0	0	0	0	2	0	3	0
pupa	17	.2560	1.0687	40.3	2	0	1	2	11	0	1	0	1	0	0	0	0	0	0	8	0	0	0	0	0	0	8	0	0
pupae	19	.3258	1.4670	41.7	11	3	1	4	0	0	0	0	1	0	0	0	0	0	0	14	0	0	0	0	0	2	2	0	0
pupil	95	.6934	13.370	51.3	11	14	7	28	22	9	3	1	7	26	3	2	8	1	6	19	0	8	0	0	7	2	3	3	0
pupil's	2	.2408	.1091	30.4	1	0	0	1	0	0	0	0	0	1	0	0	0	0	1	0	0	0	0	0	0	0	0	0	0
pupils	173	.7719	26.859	54.3	20	69	22	26	17	6	12	1	12	19	3	1	71	7	6	15	1	7	4	0	5	12	1	9	0
pupils'	7	.4875	.7121	38.5	2	2	1	0	1	0	1	0	0	1	1	0	3	0	0	1	0	0	1	0	0	0	0	0	0
puppet	39	.7603	5.9454	47.7	5	11	2	13	3	2	3	0	3	2	1	3	1	1	3	0	4	3	1	0	12	1	1	3	0
puppet's	3	.2400	.1655	32.2	0	1	0	2	0	0	0	0	0	0	0	0	0	0	1	0	0	0	0	0	2	0	0	0	0
puppets	25	.5448	2.8760	44.6	4	6	1	2	7	0	3	2	6	0	0	1	0	0	2	0	11	1	0	0	1	0	1	2	0
puppies	32	.7610	4.9968	47.0	7	8	2	9	2	1	3	0	14	2	0	0	5	1	2	3	0	0	1	0	1	1	0	2	0
puppy	87	.6996	12.485	51.0	24	20	4	30	7	0	1	1	19	12	7	2	3	3	7	16	0	0	0	0	6	8	0	4	0
puppyhood	2	.1787	.1174	30.7	1	0	0	0	1	0	0	0	1	0	0	0	0	0	0	0	0	0	0	0	1	0	0	0	0
pups	16	.4789	1.7225	42.4	2	6	5	0	2	0	0	1	6	0	0	0	0	1	0	0	0	0	0	0	2	6	0	1	0
Purcell	7	.0000	.0566	27.5	0	1	0	5	1	0	0	0	0	0	0	0	0	0	0	0	7	0	0	0	0	0	0	0	0
Purcell's	3	.0000	.0243	23.8	1	0	0	2	0	0	0	0	0	0	0	0	0	0	0	0	3	0	0	0	0	0	0	0	0
purchase	87	.6746	12.014	50.8	8	4	17	7	16	17	12	6	12	3	0	2	9	18	0	3	0	0	14	3	3	4	6	10	0
Purchase	15	.0000	.2917	34.6	0	1	2	0	2	10	0	0	0	0	0	0	0	15	0	0	0	0	0	0	0	0	0	0	0
purchased	51	.6331	6.6191	48.2	3	3	4	7	13	13	8	0	7	1	2	1	4	8	1	0	0	0	8	8	0	2	4	5	0
purchaser	6	.3898	.5368	37.3	1	0	1	3	1	0	0	0	2	0	0	0	0	0	0	0	0	0	0	1	1	0	2	0	0
purchases	26	.4302	2.3763	43.8	3	1	1	2	3	10	4	2	2	0	0	0	6	2	0	0	0	0	9	2	0	0	1	4	0
purchasing	13	.4971	1.3455	41.3	0	0	1	2	2	3	5	0	1	0	0	0	0	1	1	0	0	0	4	1	0	1	1	3	0
Purdue	4	.0000	.0486	26.9	0	0	0	2	2	0	0	0	0	0	0	0	0	0	0	0	0	0	0	0	0	0	0	4	0
Purdue's	2	.0000	.0243	23.9	0	0	0	1	1	0	0	0	0	0	0	0	0	0	0	0	0	0	0	0	0	0	0	2	0
purdy	4	.0000	.1827	32.6	0	0	0	4	0	0	0	0	4	0	0	0	0	0	0	0	0	0	0	0	0	0	0	0	0
Purdy	25	.2428	1.4193	41.5	14	0	0	0	11	0	0	0	0	0	0	0	0	0	0	0	0	0	0	0	11	0	0	14	0
Purdy's	4	.0000	.0486	26.9	4	0	0	0	0	0	0	0	0	0	0	0	0	0	0	0	0	0	0	0	0	0	0	4	0
Purdys'	2	.0000	.0234	23.7	0	0	0	0	2	0	0	0	0	0	0	0	0	0	0	0	0	0	0	0	2	0	0	0	0
pure	202	.8638	34.831	55.4	22	17	34	28	41	24	25	11	32	1	1	4	4	12	4	71	15	2	2	2	5	8	20	19	0
pure-blooded	3	.2444	.1814	32.6	1	0	0	2	0	0	0	0	0	0	0	0	0	2	0	0	0	0	0	0	0	0	1	0	0
purebred	4	.1112	.1666	32.2	1	0	0	3	0	0	0	0	1	0	0	0	0	0	0	0	0	0	0	0	0	3	0	0	0
puree	2	.1812	.0838	29.2	0	0	0	0	0	0	1	1	0	0	0	0	0	0	0	0	0	0	1	0	0	0	0	1	0

7N pullin'
7K Pullock
8R pullout
9B pullover
7N pullulate
7M Pulsa-Jet
7D pulsed
8D pulseless
XH pulverulent
5Q pulvilli
4G pum
4A pummeled
5Q Pump
9F pump's
4D Pumpkin-eater
7L pumpkin-egg
8N Pumpkin's
XB punch-marks
6P puncher
6B punctual
7H punctured
8R pundits
9P punh
XP punishes
5Q Punishment
7N punkin-heads
7N punks
5B punner
5A puns
8B punster
9B punt
7G punters
9D punto
3Q pupal
7Q pupas
7Q pupation
XF Pupil
9B pupil-teacher
6P PUPIL'S
5A Pupin
8K Puppet
9J puppet-clown
3A Puppets
3A puppies'
4N Puppy
9A puppy-belly
5B puppy's
6A Purari
5Q purchasers
XD Purdey's
3R PURDY'S
3A PURE
5R pure-bred

Word Type	F	D	U	SFI	3 Gr 3	4 Gr 4	5 Gr 5	6 Gr 6	7 Gr 7	8 Gr 8	9 Gr 9	X UnGr	A Read	B Eng & Gr	C Comp	D Lit	E Math	F Soc Stud	G Spell	H Sci	J Music	K Art	L Home Ec	M Shop	N Lib F	P Lib NF	Q Lib Ref	R Mag	S Rel
purely	22	.7494	3.3167	45.2	1	0	2	3	3	5	4	4	1	1	0	0	0	1	1	3	2	1	0	0	1	3	4	4	0
purer	4	.2582	.2544	34.1	0	0	1	0	0	1	2	0	1	0	1	2	0	0	0	0	0	0	0	0	0	0	0	0	0
purest	3	.2074	.1511	31.8	0	0	1	0	1	1	0	0	0	2	0	0	0	0	0	0	0	0	0	0	0	1	0	0	0
purge	4	.4799	.4062	36.1	0	0	0	0	2	1	1	0	0	1	0	1	0	1	0	0	0	0	0	0	0	1	0	0	0
purification	7	.4863	.7149	38.5	1	1	1	1	1	1	1	0	0	0	0	0	0	0	0	1	0	0	0	0	1	1	3	1	0
purified	8	.4055	.7326	38.6	1	0	1	1	3	0	1	1	1	0	0	0	0	0	0	4	0	0	0	0	0	1	2	0	0
purify	8	.4484	.8101	39.1	0	1	3	2	0	1	1	0	2	0	0	0	0	2	0	2	0	0	0	0	0	0	2	0	0
purifying	13	.5223	1.4362	41.6	0	3	2	1	3	3	0	1	0	0	0	1	0	3	0	5	0	0	0	0	0	1	3	0	0
Purim	6	.2028	.3977	36.0	0	4	0	0	0	2	0	0	4	0	0	0	0	0	0	0	2	0	0	0	0	0	0	0	0
purine	2	.0000	.0394	26.0	0	0	0	0	0	0	2	0	0	0	0	0	0	0	0	2	0	0	0	0	0	0	0	0	0
Purist	2	.2446	.1125	30.5	0	0	0	0	0	1	1	0	0	1	0	1	0	0	0	0	0	0	0	0	0	0	0	0	0
purists	2	.2437	.1129	30.5	0	0	0	0	1	0	1	0	0	0	0	0	0	0	0	0	0	0	0	0	0	0	1	1	0
Puritan	13	.3712	1.1087	40.4	0	1	5	0	2	5	0	0	1	0	0	0	0	8	0	0	0	0	0	0	0	3	1	0	0
puritanical	2	.2285	.1129	30.5	0	0	0	0	0	2	0	0	0	0	0	0	0	1	0	0	0	0	0	0	0	0	1	0	0
Puritans	23	.4111	2.1112	43.2	0	0	11	2	2	8	0	0	1	0	0	0	0	17	0	0	2	0	0	0	0	1	1	1	0
purity	11	.5319	1.2544	41.0	2	1	0	0	5	2	0	1	2	0	0	0	0	2	0	1	0	0	0	0	0	1	1	4	0
purloin	2	.0000	.0914	29.6	0	0	1	1	0	0	0	0	2	0	0	0	0	0	0	0	0	0	0	0	0	0	0	0	0
purple	157	.8907	27.848	54.4	37	20	16	29	22	11	19	3	47	7	2	20	8	5	3	5	9	6	4	1	16	11	4	9	0
Purple	4	.4574	.4121	36.2	0	0	0	1	1	1	0	1	1	0	0	0	0	1	0	1	0	0	0	0	0	0	0	1	0
purples	2	.1042	.0600	27.8	0	1	1	0	0	0	0	0	0	0	0	0	0	1	0	0	0	1	0	0	0	0	0	0	0
purplish	3	.3772	.2503	34.0	0	1	0	0	1	0	0	1	0	0	0	1	0	0	0	1	0	0	0	0	0	1	0	0	0
purport	2	.2441	.1127	30.5	0	1	0	0	0	0	1	0	0	0	0	0	0	0	0	0	0	0	0	0	1	0	1	0	0
purpose	360	.8919	63.764	58.0	13	26	34	39	89	58	84	17	59	51	15	37	7	30	3	27	11	5	11	16	13	29	24	22	0
purposed	2	.2405	.1205	30.8	0	0	0	1	1	0	0	0	0	0	0	0	0	0	0	1	0	0	0	0	0	1	0	0	0
purposeful	5	.5375	.5712	37.6	0	0	1	0	3	0	1	0	1	0	0	1	0	0	0	0	0	0	0	0	1	1	1	0	0
purposely	14	.6313	1.8487	42.7	0	0	2	3	5	3	1	0	4	3	1	1	0	1	0	1	0	0	0	0	1	0	0	2	0
purposes	132	.7581	20.143	53.0	6	8	17	15	36	24	20	6	10	9	0	3	3	23	1	20	7	1	10	14	1	7	12	11	0
purr	17	.6434	2.2828	43.6	7	4	3	1	0	2	0	0	5	3	0	2	0	0	0	1	2	0	0	0	1	3	0	0	0
purred	8	.5455	.9478	39.8	3	2	0	1	1	0	0	1	3	1	0	0	0	0	0	0	0	0	0	0	1	1	0	2	0
purring	19	.5793	2.4012	43.8	6	3	1	1	8	0	0	0	10	1	0	1	0	0	0	0	0	0	0	0	4	2	0	1	0
purse	59	.7325	8.7951	49.4	12	5	2	9	11	5	14	1	15	8	1	3	6	2	2	0	0	0	8	2	6	1	0	5	0
pursed	3	.2279	.2143	33.3	0	0	1	0	2	0	0	0	2	0	0	0	0	0	0	0	0	0	0	0	0	0	0	1	0
Purser	2	.0000	.0290	24.6	0	0	0	0	0	0	2	0	0	0	0	0	0	0	0	0	0	0	0	0	0	2	0	0	0
purses	9	.4102	.8620	39.4	1	0	2	4	1	1	0	0	3	0	0	0	0	3	0	1	0	1	0	0	0	1	0	0	0
pursue	27	.5782	3.2247	45.1	0	1	0	2	14	2	7	1	1	0	0	1	0	4	0	1	0	0	1	0	1	1	11	6	0
pursued	26	.7287	3.8785	45.9	0	2	1	2	9	7	4	1	8	1	1	3	0	1	0	0	1	0	0	0	1	4	5	1	0
pursuer	2	.2437	.1129	30.5	0	0	0	1	1	0	0	0	0	0	0	0	0	0	0	0	0	0	0	0	0	0	1	1	0
pursuers	9	.5024	.9744	39.9	0	0	2	1	5	1	0	0	2	0	0	1	0	0	0	0	0	0	0	0	3	1	2	0	0
pursuing	16	.6052	1.9931	43.0	0	1	2	1	5	2	3	2	1	0	0	4	0	1	0	0	0	0	0	0	2	2	3	3	0
pursuit	41	.7097	5.9579	47.8	0	1	5	2	16	10	6	1	9	0	0	7	0	4	0	2	1	0	0	0	7	3	5	3	0
Pursuit	3	.1639	.1674	32.2	0	0	0	1	0	2	0	0	1	0	0	0	0	2	0	0	0	0	0	0	0	0	0	0	0
pursuits	8	.5207	.8676	39.4	0	0	0	0	2	3	2	1	0	0	0	0	0	2	0	0	1	0	0	0	1	0	3	1	0
purty	3	.2196	.1554	31.9	0	0	0	1	0	2	0	0	0	0	0	2	0	0	0	0	0	0	0	0	1	0	0	0	0
pus	8	.3419	.6196	37.9	0	0	0	3	0	4	1	0	0	0	0	0	0	0	0	4	0	0	0	0	0	1	3	0	0
push	339	.8239	56.055	57.5	109	67	39	35	42	23	19	5	50	2	1	13	3	15	6	130	7	2	11	15	14	43	8	19	0
PUSH	2	.1814	.1187	30.7	0	2	0	0	0	0	0	0	1	0	0	0	0	0	0	0	0	0	0	0	0	0	0	1	0
push-button	3	.3764	.2483	33.9	0	0	0	0	1	0	1	1	0	0	0	0	0	0	0	1	0	0	0	0	0	0	1	1	0
push-up	5	.0000	.0748	28.7	0	5	0	0	0	0	0	0	0	0	0	0	5	0	0	0	0	0	0	0	0	0	0	0	0
push-ups	17	.0000	.2545	34.1	0	15	2	0	0	0	0	0	0	0	0	0	17	0	0	0	0	0	0	0	0	0	0	0	0
pushcart	3	.2279	.2143	33.3	0	0	0	1	2	0	0	0	2	0	0	0	0	0	0	0	0	0	0	0	0	0	0	1	0
pushed	401	.8542	68.894	58.4	92	80	42	53	80	35	14	5	165	6	1	22	5	28	1	42	3	0	2	7	39	43	10	27	0
pushers	3	.2277	.1555	31.9	0	0	0	0	1	2	0	0	0	0	0	0	0	0	0	0	0	0	1	0	0	0	0	2	0
pushes	107	.7183	15.822	52.0	34	15	19	13	13	8	3	2	27	0	1	3	0	4	0	47	3	0	0	3	2	10	5	2	0
pushing	165	.8601	28.438	54.5	36	36	17	16	30	11	19	0	51	2	2	14	0	8	0	29	3	0	3	1	12	20	6	14	0
pushmi-pullyu	6	.2196	.3108	34.9	0	2	4	0	0	0	0	0	0	0	0	4	0	0	0	0	0	0	0	0	2	0	0	0	0
pushups	5	.0000	.0986	29.9	1	1	0	3	0	0	0	0	0	0	0	0	0	0	0	5	0	0	0	0	0	0	0	0	0
Pushups	2	.0000	.0394	26.0	0	2	0	0	0	0	0	0	0	0	0	0	0	0	0	2	0	0	0	0	0	0	0	0	0
Puss	9	.3317	.7406	38.7	6	0	0	0	2	0	1	0	4	0	0	0	0	0	0	0	3	0	0	0	2	0	0	0	0
Puss-in-Boots	4	.0000	.1827	32.6	4	0	0	0	0	0	0	0	4	0	0	0	0	0	0	0	0	0	0	0	0	0	0	0	0
puss-in-boots	3	.0000	.1370	31.4	3	0	0	0	0	0	0	0	3	0	0	0	0	0	0	0	0	0	0	0	0	0	0	0	0
Pussick	2	.2407	.1138	30.6	1	0	0	0	0	1	0	0	0	0	0	1	0	0	0	0	0	0	0	0	0	1	0	0	0
pussy	8	.4181	.7647	38.8	4	1	0	1	2	0	0	0	3	2	1	0	0	0	0	0	0	0	0	0	2	0	0	0	0
Pussy	7	.2423	.5283	37.2	7	0	0	0	0	0	0	0	5	0	0	0	0	0	0	0	0	0	0	0	0	2	0	0	0
Pussy-Cat	2	.1733	.1149	30.6	1	1	0	0	0	0	0	0	1	1	0	0	0	0	0	0	0	0	0	0	0	0	0	0	0
pussy-cat	4	.0000	.0579	27.6	4	0	0	0	0	0	0	0	0	0	0	0	0	0	0	0	0	0	0	0	0	4	0	0	0
pussywillows	2	.0000	.0914	29.6	0	0	1	0	1	0	0	0	2	0	0	0	0	0	0	0	0	0	0	0	0	0	0	0	0
put	3942	.9477	738.97	68.7	1153	785	454	431	453	361	235	70	1241	213	21	236	235	225	241	445	47	39	79	38	343	303	69	167	0
Put	2	.1717	.1142	30.6	1	0	0	0	1	0	0	0	1	0	0	1	0	0	0	0	0	0	0	0	0	0	0	0	0
put-together	3	.0997	.1145	30.6	1	1	1	0	0	0	0	0	1	0	0	0	0	0	2	0	0	0	0	0	0	0	0	0	0
Putnam	17	.0889	.5191	37.2	0	3	0	1	0	0	13	0	0	0	0	0	0	0	0	0	0	0	0	0	0	16	0	1	0
Putnam's	2	.2303	.1079	30.3	0	0	1	0	0	0	1	0	0	0	0	0	0	0	0	0	1	0	0	0	0	1	0	0	0
putrid	2	.2446	.1123	30.5	0	0	0	0	1	1	0	0	0	1	0	0	0	0	0	0	0	0	0	0	0	0	1	0	0
puts	156	.8160	25.665	54.1	41	22	21	20	23	13	10	6	44	6	0	12	5	12	4	22	7	3	1	0	4	13	6	16	1
putt	3	.2223	.2106	33.2	0	0	0	2	0	1	0	0	2	1	0	0	0	0	0	0	0	0	0	0	0	0	0	0	0
putter	4	.4890	.4068	36.1	0	0	1	0	1	2	0	0	0	1	0	1	0	0	0	0	0	0	0	0	1	0	1	0	0
Putter	2	.0000	.0234	23.7	0	0	2	0	0	0	0	0	0	0	0	0	0	0	0	0	0	0	0	0	2	0	0	0	0
puttin'	3	.3394	.2451	33.9	1	0	0	1	1	0	0	0	1	0	0	1	0	0	0	0	0	0	0	0	1	0	0	0	0
putting	347	.9225	63.495	58.0	85	53	35	35	57	42	33	7	101	35	5	25	15	15	21	27	1	6	11	3	33	23	5	21	0
putty	10	.4350	.9758	39.9	0	3	1	0	1	5	0	0	3	0	1	1	0	0	0	3	0	0	0	2	0	0	0	0	0
putz	2	.0000	.0162	22.1	0	0	2	0	0	0	0	0	0	0	0	0	0	0	0	0	2	0	0	0	0	0	0	0	0
puzzle	156	.5027	16.588	52.2	39	18	25	24	18	18	11	3	19	2	0	2	16	1	75	13	4	0	0	0	3	8	5	8	0
Puzzle	9	.2274	.4957	37.0	0	0	7	0	0	2	0	0	0	0	0	0	7	0	2	0	0	0	0	0	0	0	0	0	0
puzzled	116	.7246	17.401	52.4	24	30	15	13	13	14	6	1	51	3	1	8	1	3	0	7	0	0	0	0	15	19	0	8	0
puzzlement	4	.0996	.1523	31.8	1	0	0	0	2	1	0	0	1	0	0	0	0	0	0	0	0	0	0	0	0	0	0	3	0
puzzles	32	.6302	4.1889	46.2	9	1	11	6	3	2	0	0	5	1	0	0	12	0	3	4	0	0	0	0	0	2	1	4	0
Puzzles	2	.2427	.1159	30.6	0	0	1	1	0	0	0	0	0	0	0	0	1	0	0	0	0	0	0	0	0	0	0	1	0
puzzling	24	.6943	3.4360	45.4	0	1	1	7	8	3	2	2	6	2	1	2	0	0	0	7	0	0	0	0	2	0	1	3	0
Puzzling	4	.0000	.0438	26.4	0	0	0	0	4	0	0	0	0	4	0	0	0	0	0	0	0	0	0	0	0	0	0	0	0
Pwyll	2	.0000	.0290	24.6	0	0	0	0	2	0	0	0	0	0	0	0	0	0	0	0	0	0	0	0	0	2	0	0	0
PX	2	.0000	.0243	23.9	0	0	0	0	2	0	0	0	0	0	0	0	0	0	0	0	0	0	0	0	0	0	0	2	0
PY	9	.0000	.1347	31.3	0	0	0	9	0	0	0	0	0	0	0	0	9	0	0	0	0	0	0	0	0	0	0	0	0
Pygmalion	4	.3683	.3188	35.0	0	0	0	2	0	1	1	0	0	0	0	1	0	0	0	0	0	0	0	0	2	0	0	1	0
pygmies	2	.2285	.1129	30.5	1	1	0	0	0	0	0	0	0	0	0	0	0	1	0	0	0	0	0	0	0	0	1	0	0
Pygmies	11	.2251	.6407	38.1	0	8	3	0	0	0	0	0	0	0	0	0	0	8	0	0	0	0	0	0	0	3	0	0	0

5J pureta
8P purged
9R Purina
9R Purina-Taiyo
9H purines
8B purist
5A Puritan's
XR Puritanical
8D purled
8L purls
3J purple-blue
4A purple-colored
8N purple-like
9D purple-tinted
5N purpleblack
6R purpler
6A purplish-brown
9D purpos'd
7A purposefully
8J Purse
9R purser
6R purserettes
4D pursing
9Q pursues
9N Purvis
9B push-a-button
9Q push-button-controlled
4N push-push-push
7R push/pull
7R pushbutton
6F pushcarts
6A pushin'
3P pushing-up
5D pushmi-pullyus
3H pushpins
7R pushrod
3A puss
4A puss-in-the-corner
6P PUT
6A Put-in-Bay
6A put-out
8A put-put
XR putable-in
6A Putah
4P Putnams
7R Putney
5P putrefying
5A putt-putt-putt
6H Putting
5J putzes
7R puzzlers
7P Pwyll's
6J py
3A pyatj
3A pyatnashki
8R Pycope
5P pygmoid

Word Type	F	D	U	SFI	3 Gr 3	4 Gr 4	5 Gr 5	6 Gr 6	7 Gr 7	8 Gr 8	9 Gr 9	X UnGr	A Read	B Eng & Gr	C Comp	D Lit	E Math	F Soc Stud	G Spell	H Sci	J Music	K Art	L Home Ec	M Shop	N Lib F	P Lib NF	Q Lib Ref	R Mag	S Rel
pygmy	5	.4169	.4619	36.6	1	0	1	1	2	0	0	0	1	1	0	0	0	0	0	0	0	0	0	0	0	0	2	1	0
Pygmy	3	.2378	.1809	32.6	0	2	1	0	0	0	0	0	0	0	0	0	0	2	0	0	0	0	0	0	0	1	0	0	0
Pyle	2	.0000	.0219	23.4	0	0	0	0	2	0	0	0	0	2	0	0	0	0	0	0	0	0	0	0	0	0	0	0	0
pylon	2	.1247	.0633	28.0	0	0	2	0	0	0	0	0	0	0	0	0	0	0	0	0	0	1	0	0	0	1	0	0	0
pyramid	72	.6393	9.4283	49.7	0	11	5	16	10	16	14	0	2	0	1	2	39	9	1	5	0	2	0	5	0	0	6	0	0
Pyramid	23	.3473	1.8055	42.6	1	2	0	9	0	0	11	0	1	0	0	0	13	3	0	0	0	0	0	0	0	0	6	0	0
pyramidal	2	.1378	.0662	28.2	0	0	0	0	0	0	1	1	0	0	0	0	0	0	0	0	0	1	0	0	0	0	0	1	0
pyramids	38	.5601	4.4586	46.5	0	3	5	11	5	8	6	0	1	0	0	0	13	17	0	1	0	2	0	1	0	0	3	0	0
pyre	2	.2437	.1129	30.5	0	0	0	0	0	0	1	1	0	0	0	0	0	0	0	0	0	0	0	0	0	0	1	1	0
Pyrenees	13	.3319	.9741	39.9	3	0	2	1	7	0	0	0	0	0	0	0	0	5	0	0	0	0	0	0	0	2	6	0	0
Pyrex	4	.2427	.2417	33.8	0	0	0	0	2	1	1	0	0	0	0	0	0	0	1	3	0	0	0	0	0	0	0	0	0
pyrimidine	3	.0000	.0591	27.7	0	0	0	0	0	0	3	0	0	0	0	0	0	0	0	3	0	0	0	0	0	0	0	0	0
pyrite	14	.1733	.8124	39.1	5	0	0	0	0	9	0	0	5	0	0	0	0	0	0	9	0	0	0	0	0	0	0	0	0
pyrosoma	2	.0000	.0394	26.0	0	0	2	0	0	0	0	0	0	0	0	0	0	0	0	2	0	0	0	0	0	0	0	0	0
Pyrotector	2	.0000	.0243	23.9	0	0	0	0	2	0	0	0	0	0	0	0	0	0	0	0	0	0	0	0	0	0	0	2	0
pyroxene	2	.0000	.0394	26.0	0	0	0	0	0	0	1	1	0	0	0	0	0	0	0	2	0	0	0	0	0	0	0	0	0
pyroxenes	3	.0000	.0591	27.7	0	0	0	0	0	0	1	2	0	0	0	0	0	0	0	3	0	0	0	0	0	0	0	0	0
pyroxylin	2	.0000	.0209	23.2	0	0	2	0	0	0	0	0	0	0	0	0	0	0	0	0	0	0	0	0	0	0	2	0	0
pyruvic	3	.0000	.0591	27.7	0	0	0	0	0	0	3	0	0	0	0	0	0	0	0	3	0	0	0	0	0	0	0	0	0
Pythagoras	10	.1392	.3987	36.0	0	0	1	4	0	3	2	0	0	0	0	1	9	0	0	0	0	0	0	0	0	0	0	0	0
Pythagorean	16	.0682	.4419	36.5	0	0	0	1	1	9	5	0	0	0	0	0	15	0	0	1	0	0	0	0	0	0	0	0	0
python	11	.4280	1.0750	40.3	0	1	0	2	5	3	0	0	4	3	0	0	1	0	0	0	0	0	0	0	0	0	3	0	0
pythons	2	.0000	.0209	23.2	0	0	0	0	2	0	0	0	0	0	0	0	0	0	0	0	0	0	0	0	0	0	2	0	0
q	43	.5309	4.7241	46.7	1	3	4	4	9	16	5	1	0	1	2	0	20	0	9	0	0	0	0	0	0	1	10	0	0
Q	63	.5478	7.1283	48.5	1	11	2	1	11	10	27	0	0	2	2	25	28	0	3	0	0	0	0	1	0	0	0	2	0
QP	2	.0000	.0299	24.8	0	0	0	0	0	2	0	0	0	0	0	0	2	0	0	0	0	0	0	0	0	0	0	0	0
qt	4	.3844	.3320	35.2	0	0	2	0	1	1	0	0	0	0	0	0	2	0	1	0	0	0	0	0	0	0	1	0	0
qu	15	.0621	.4029	36.1	0	4	7	1	2	1	0	0	3	0	0	0	0	0	12	0	0	0	0	0	0	0	0	0	0
quack	23	.2433	1.7810	42.5	17	4	0	0	1	0	0	1	19	0	0	0	0	0	0	0	4	0	0	0	0	0	0	0	0
quacked	2	.0000	.0914	29.6	2	0	0	0	0	0	0	0	2	0	0	0	0	0	0	0	0	0	0	0	0	0	0	0	0
quacking	14	.0000	.6396	38.1	11	1	0	2	0	0	0	0	14	0	0	0	0	0	0	0	0	0	0	0	0	0	0	0	0
quacks	2	.0000	.0914	29.6	0	0	0	0	0	2	0	0	2	0	0	0	0	0	0	0	0	0	0	0	0	0	0	0	0
quadrangle	3	.2445	.1818	32.6	0	1	0	0	0	2	0	0	0	0	0	0	0	0	0	2	0	0	0	0	0	0	1	0	0
quadrates	2	.0000	.0394	26.0	0	0	0	0	2	0	0	0	0	0	0	0	0	0	0	2	0	0	0	0	0	0	0	0	0
quadratic	11	.0000	.1647	32.2	0	0	0	0	0	0	11	0	0	0	0	0	11	0	0	0	0	0	0	0	0	0	0	0	0
quadrilateral	18	.0000	.2694	34.3	0	1	1	4	2	4	6	0	0	0	0	0	18	0	0	0	0	0	0	0	0	0	0	0	0
quadrilaterals	21	.0000	.3143	35.0	1	0	1	4	0	15	0	0	0	0	0	0	21	0	0	0	0	0	0	0	0	0	0	0	0
quadruple	7	.2604	.3895	35.9	0	0	0	0	4	0	3	0	0	0	0	0	0	0	0	0	3	0	0	3	0	0	1	0	0
quagmire	3	.3427	.2477	33.9	0	0	0	1	0	2	0	0	1	0	0	0	0	0	0	0	0	0	0	0	1	0	0	1	0
quail	22	.5887	2.8453	44.5	1	12	0	4	2	1	0	2	13	0	0	1	0	2	0	2	0	0	0	0	0	0	1	3	0
quaint	17	.6891	2.3978	43.8	1	1	0	3	5	3	3	1	3	1	1	4	0	2	0	1	1	0	0	0	2	0	0	2	0
quaintly	2	.2407	.1138	30.6	0	0	1	0	0	0	1	0	0	0	0	1	0	0	0	0	0	0	0	0	0	1	0	0	0
quake	9	.5151	1.0085	40.0	3	1	2	0	2	1	0	0	3	0	0	2	0	0	0	0	2	0	0	0	1	1	0	0	0
quaked	2	.2443	.1130	30.5	0	0	0	0	1	1	0	0	0	0	0	1	0	0	0	0	0	0	0	0	1	0	0	0	0
Quaker	23	.5474	2.6969	44.3	1	9	3	2	3	1	4	0	5	2	0	1	0	4	0	0	0	0	0	0	2	9	0	0	0
Quakers	23	.5088	2.4968	44.0	1	7	8	0	2	1	4	0	1	0	0	2	0	11	0	0	1	0	0	0	0	7	1	0	0
quaking	5	.4122	.4599	36.6	0	1	1	0	1	2	0	0	1	0	0	2	0	0	0	0	0	0	0	0	1	1	0	0	0
qualifications	20	.6435	2.6765	44.3	0	0	0	0	8	4	8	0	4	1	0	0	0	6	0	0	1	0	1	0	0	3	0	4	0
qualified	19	.5751	2.2714	43.6	0	0	4	1	7	3	3	1	1	3	0	0	0	2	0	2	0	0	0	0	0	2	2	7	0
qualifiers	2	.0000	.0243	23.9	0	0	0	0	2	0	0	0	0	0	0	0	0	0	0	0	0	0	0	0	0	0	0	2	0
qualifies	4	.3705	.3360	35.3	0	0	0	1	2	0	1	0	1	0	0	0	0	0	0	0	0	0	1	0	1	0	1	0	0
qualify	13	.5907	1.5803	42.0	3	0	2	1	3	2	1	1	0	2	0	0	1	2	0	0	0	0	0	0	0	2	2	4	0
qualifying	3	.0000	.0365	25.6	0	0	0	0	3	0	0	0	0	0	0	0	0	0	0	0	0	0	0	0	0	0	0	3	0
qualitative	2	.0000	.0209	23.2	0	0	0	0	0	1	1	0	0	0	0	0	0	0	0	0	0	0	0	0	0	0	2	0	0
qualities	108	.7388	16.091	52.1	3	1	10	12	24	23	33	2	18	4	2	13	0	5	1	1	13	9	16	5	2	7	8	4	0
quality	259	.7524	39.091	55.9	13	9	15	26	63	67	53	13	19	18	0	6	5	18	4	11	77	13	25	7	8	11	20	17	0
quandary	3	.0000	.0067	18.3	0	0	0	0	3	0	0	0	0	0	3	0	0	0	0	0	0	0	0	0	0	0	0	0	0
quanta	11	.1543	.5092	37.1	0	0	1	0	0	3	0	7	0	0	0	0	0	0	0	10	0	0	0	0	0	0	1	0	0
quantitative	3	.2445	.1818	32.6	0	0	0	0	1	0	2	0	0	0	0	0	0	0	0	2	0	0	0	0	0	0	1	0	0
quantitatively	2	.0000	.0209	23.2	0	0	0	0	0	2	0	0	0	0	0	0	0	0	0	0	0	0	0	0	0	0	2	0	0
quantities	113	.7941	18.033	52.6	3	2	15	15	28	25	17	8	8	2	2	0	11	30	0	26	1	1	4	5	0	3	18	2	0
quantity	74	.7938	11.790	50.7	2	2	7	8	16	19	16	4	6	1	0	3	12	6	0	14	2	0	3	3	4	4	15	1	0
quantum	21	.2861	1.3816	41.4	0	0	1	0	1	13	6	0	0	0	0	0	1	0	0	6	0	0	0	0	0	0	13	1	0
Quantum	2	.0000	.0209	23.2	0	0	1	0	0	0	1	0	0	0	0	0	0	0	0	0	0	0	0	0	0	0	2	0	0
quarantine	4	.3658	.3646	35.6	1	2	0	0	0	1	0	0	2	0	0	0	0	0	0	1	0	0	0	0	0	0	1	0	0
quarantined	2	.2405	.1205	30.8	1	0	0	0	0	0	0	1	0	0	0	0	0	0	0	1	0	0	0	0	0	1	0	0	0
quarantines	2	.0000	.0394	26.0	0	0	0	2	0	0	0	0	0	0	0	0	0	0	0	2	0	0	0	0	0	0	0	0	0
quarrel	53	.7881	8.4326	49.3	5	1	8	6	11	10	12	0	11	3	1	8	0	8	3	1	0	0	0	0	4	10	2	2	0
quarreled	21	.6344	2.7688	44.4	6	1	4	1	3	4	2	0	4	0	0	2	0	5	0	0	0	0	1	0	1	3	5	0	0
quarreling	21	.4683	2.2351	43.5	5	1	4	0	2	3	5	1	10	1	0	0	0	3	0	0	1	0	4	0	1	0	1	0	0
quarrels	14	.4257	1.3275	41.2	2	3	2	1	1	4	0	1	1	0	0	0	0	9	0	0	0	0	0	0	0	2	1	1	0
quarrelsome	7	.4224	.7014	38.5	0	1	0	3	2	0	1	0	4	0	0	1	0	0	0	0	0	0	1	0	1	0	0	0	0
quarried	6	.2521	.3540	35.5	1	0	1	1	1	0	2	0	0	0	0	0	0	1	0	0	0	0	0	0	0	1	4	0	0
quarries	7	.1931	.3682	35.7	1	1	2	2	0	1	0	0	0	0	0	0	0	6	0	0	0	0	0	0	0	0	1	0	0
quarry	22	.6561	3.0133	44.8	1	7	0	1	9	1	1	2	7	1	0	1	0	1	0	2	0	0	0	0	1	1	6	2	0
quarrying	4	.4866	.4070	36.1	1	0	1	0	1	1	0	0	0	0	0	1	0	0	0	0	0	0	0	0	0	1	1	1	0
quart	85	.4811	8.8291	49.5	29	17	11	2	11	12	2	1	9	0	0	0	54	2	3	10	0	0	4	0	1	0	1	1	0
quarter	275	.7695	42.702	56.3	76	34	25	25	45	33	27	10	48	4	0	11	36	7	4	18	70	0	2	6	23	16	8	22	0
Quarter	7	.4121	.6390	38.1	4	0	0	0	0	1	2	0	1	0	0	2	0	0	0	0	0	0	0	0	0	3	0	1	0
quarter-century	3	.3781	.2493	34.0	0	0	0	0	2	0	0	1	0	1	0	0	0	1	0	0	0	0	0	0	0	0	0	1	0
quarter-inch	4	.3709	.3633	35.6	0	0	1	1	1	0	0	1	2	0	0	0	0	0	0	0	0	0	0	0	0	0	1	1	0
quarter-less	2	.0000	.0914	29.6	0	0	0	0	0	2	0	0	2	0	0	0	0	0	0	0	0	0	0	0	0	0	0	0	0
quarter-mile	4	.1611	.1738	32.4	0	0	0	1	2	0	1	0	0	0	0	0	0	0	0	1	0	0	0	0	0	0	0	3	0
quarter-pound	4	.0000	.0129	21.1	0	0	0	0	2	1	1	0	0	0	0	0	0	0	0	0	0	0	4	0	0	0	0	0	0
quarter-tones	2	.0000	.0162	22.1	0	0	0	1	0	1	0	0	0	0	0	0	0	0	0	0	2	0	0	0	0	0	0	0	0
quarter's	3	.0000	.0449	26.5	0	0	3	0	0	0	0	0	0	0	0	0	3	0	0	0	0	0	0	0	0	0	0	0	0
quarterback	40	.4359	3.7475	45.7	0	0	3	15	12	4	6	0	3	7	2	0	4	0	0	0	0	0	0	0	0	0	0	24	0
Quarterback	4	.0000	.0486	26.9	0	0	0	0	1	2	1	0	0	0	0	0	0	0	0	0	0	0	0	0	0	0	0	4	0
quarterbacks	4	.0000	.0486	26.9	0	0	0	3	0	1	0	0	0	0	0	0	0	0	0	0	0	0	0	0	0	0	0	4	0
quartered	4	.3488	.3091	34.9	0	0	0	1	3	0	0	0	0	0	0	1	0	1	0	0	0	0	0	0	2	0	0	0	0
quartermaster	2	.1948	.1250	31.0	0	0	0	0	1	1	0	0	1	0	0	0	0	0	0	0	0	0	0	0	0	1	0	0	0
quarters	115	.8147	18.805	52.7	12	10	15	12	25	12	20	9	18	2	1	6	37	8	0	3	7	0	2	0	7	9	9	6	0
quartet	28	.2243	1.4298	41.6	1	6	4	2	4	8	2	1	0	0	0	1	0	0	0	0	22	0	0	0	0	2	1	2	0

4A pyjamas
7P Pylades
8G Pyle's
9D Pylos
8G pyr
9N pyramid-shaped
9Q Pyramid's
8F pyramided
6F Pyramids
3P pyrate
9H pyrimidines
7F pyrites

8A pyrometer
5H pyrosomas
4R Pyrrhus
8B Python
7Q python's
XH P1
6G q-z
8Q q's
5Q qat
6F Qatar
4E QR
7E QRS

6R qu'est-ce
8H Quadrangle
8H quadrangles
8M quadrangular
4H quadrant
7H quadrate
7R quadrennial
9Q quadriceps
9E Quadrilaterals
3B Quadruped
9F Quadruple
9M quads

4N Quagga
9R Quai
6A Quail
3J Quail's
6A quails
7A quaint-looking
3A quainter
5P quaintness
4N quakingly
7B qualification
XB quality**
3P Qualla

9E quantifier
9E quantifiers
8Q quantized
7N quare
8A Quarrels
4H quart-size
7P quarter-
6A quarter-acre
7D quarter-blood
7R quarter-miling
4J quarter-note
5A quarter-turn

7E quarter-units
7R quarterback's
7A quarterdeck
9R quarterlies
9J quarterly
9P Quartermaster
7R quartermile

Word Type	F	D	U	SFI	3 Gr 3	4 Gr 4	5 Gr 5	6 Gr 6	7 Gr 7	8 Gr 8	9 Gr 9	X UnGr	A Read	B Eng & Gr	C Comp	D Lit	E Math	F Soc Stud	G Spell	H Sci	J Music	K Art	L Home Ec	M Shop	N Lib F	P Lib NF	Q Lib Ref	R Mag	S Rel
Quartet	7	.0000	.0566	27.5	0	1	1	1	3	1	0	0	0	0	0	0	0	0	0	0	7	0	0	0	0	0	0	0	0
quartets	7	.0000	.0566	27.5	0	0	4	0	0	3	0	0	0	0	0	0	0	0	0	0	7	0	0	0	0	0	0	0	0
quartile	7	.0000	.1048	30.2	0	0	0	0	0	7	0	0	0	0	0	0	7	0	0	0	0	0	0	0	0	0	0	0	0
quarts	95	.3163	7.0575	48.5	29	23	12	7	8	7	8	1	9	0	0	2	72	2	0	3	0	0	0	0	1	0	4	2	0
quartz	43	.4466	4.1601	46.2	0	0	18	3	3	8	4	7	0	0	0	0	0	0	0	29	0	0	0	4	0	2	6	2	0
quartzite	6	.3187	.4303	36.3	0	0	1	3	0	0	2	0	0	0	0	0	0	0	0	1	0	0	0	0	0	2	3	0	0
quasars	2	.0000	.0394	26.0	0	0	0	0	2	0	0	0	0	0	0	0	0	0	0	2	0	0	0	0	0	0	0	0	0
quaternions	2	.0000	.0299	24.8	0	0	0	0	2	0	0	0	0	0	0	0	2	0	0	0	0	0	0	0	0	0	0	0	0
quay	2	.0000	.0234	23.7	0	0	0	0	2	0	0	0	0	0	0	0	0	0	0	0	0	0	0	0	2	0	0	0	0
quays	3	.2347	.1695	32.3	0	2	0	0	1	0	0	0	0	0	0	0	0	0	0	0	0	0	0	0	1	2	0	0	0
que	6	.4134	.5451	37.4	0	1	1	3	1	0	0	0	1	0	0	0	0	0	1	0	1	0	0	0	0	0	0	3	0
Quebec	29	.5131	3.2191	45.1	2	4	7	10	3	2	1	0	5	0	0	0	0	14	0	0	2	0	0	0	4	0	4	0	0
Quechan	2	.0000	.0389	25.9	0	2	0	0	0	0	0	0	0	0	0	0	0	2	0	0	0	0	0	0	0	0	0	0	0
queeck	2	.0000	.0234	23.7	0	0	0	0	0	2	0	0	0	0	0	0	0	0	0	0	0	0	0	0	2	0	0	0	0
queen	206	.8780	36.119	55.6	81	34	23	24	22	11	8	3	58	8	2	15	6	13	9	30	8	1	0	0	3	37	10	6	0
Queen	203	.8042	33.051	55.2	16	33	82	27	15	18	8	4	69	4	0	6	3	35	3	1	10	2	0	0	36	11	12	11	0
queen-king	5	.0000	.0748	28.7	0	5	0	0	0	0	0	0	0	0	0	0	5	0	0	0	0	0	0	0	0	0	0	0	0
queen's	6	.3721	.5495	37.4	4	1	1	0	0	0	0	0	3	0	0	0	0	0	0	0	0	0	0	0	0	2	1	0	0
Queen's	14	.5861	1.7342	42.4	2	2	3	4	1	2	0	0	4	0	1	0	0	1	0	0	2	0	0	0	4	1	0	1	0
Queenie	8	.1550	.4207	36.2	0	8	0	0	0	0	0	0	3	0	0	0	0	0	0	0	0	0	0	0	0	5	0	0	0
Queenie's	5	.1634	.2733	34.4	0	5	0	0	0	0	0	0	2	0	0	0	0	0	0	0	0	0	0	0	0	3	0	0	0
queenly	2	.0000	.0215	23.3	0	0	0	0	0	0	2	0	0	0	0	2	0	0	0	0	0	0	0	0	0	0	0	0	0
queens	21	.6102	2.6967	44.3	12	3	1	3	2	0	0	0	4	1	0	0	0	2	1	6	0	0	0	0	1	6	0	0	0
Queens	3	.2332	.1690	32.3	2	0	0	0	1	0	0	0	0	0	0	0	0	0	0	0	0	0	0	0	0	2	0	1	0
Queensberry	3	.0000	.0434	26.4	0	0	0	3	0	0	0	0	0	0	0	0	0	0	0	0	0	0	0	0	0	3	0	0	0
Queensborough	2	.0000	.0234	23.7	0	2	0	0	0	0	0	0	0	0	0	0	0	0	0	0	0	0	0	0	2	0	0	0	0
Queensland	5	.3343	.3773	35.8	0	0	3	1	0	1	0	0	0	0	0	0	0	1	0	0	0	0	0	0	0	3	1	0	0
queer	102	.7368	15.522	51.9	14	21	20	22	12	8	3	2	45	6	0	8	0	4	1	13	1	0	0	0	12	10	2	0	0
queer-looking	5	.2320	.3834	35.8	1	2	0	2	0	0	0	0	4	0	0	0	0	0	0	1	0	0	0	0	0	0	0	0	0
queerest	5	.2445	.3864	35.9	1	0	0	1	2	0	1	0	4	0	0	1	0	0	0	0	0	0	0	0	0	0	0	0	0
quench	4	.4814	.4018	36.0	1	1	0	1	0	0	1	0	0	1	0	0	0	0	0	0	1	0	0	0	1	1	0	0	0
quenched	3	.3805	.2526	34.0	0	1	0	1	0	1	0	0	0	0	0	0	0	1	0	0	0	0	0	0	1	1	0	0	0
Quentin	9	.0000	.4111	36.1	0	6	0	0	0	3	0	0	9	0	0	0	0	0	0	0	0	0	0	0	0	0	0	0	0
querulous	2	.2152	.1357	31.3	0	0	0	0	1	1	0	0	1	0	0	0	0	1	0	0	0	0	0	0	0	0	0	0	0
query	3	.0000	.0365	25.6	0	0	0	0	0	0	1	2	0	0	0	0	0	0	0	0	0	0	0	0	0	0	0	3	0
quest	18	.6252	2.3826	43.8	3	1	0	4	7	2	1	0	7	1	0	4	0	0	0	1	0	0	0	0	2	2	1	0	0
question	895	.9068	161.17	62.1	132	136	111	112	172	120	95	17	193	156	14	36	118	62	38	94	23	2	5	6	34	37	24	53	0
Question	4	.4784	.4100	36.1	0	1	0	0	0	2	1	0	0	1	0	0	1	1	0	1	0	0	0	0	0	0	0	0	0
questionable	7	.4909	.7516	38.8	0	0	1	1	3	1	1	0	2	1	0	0	0	1	0	0	2	0	0	0	0	0	0	1	0
questioned	39	.4187	3.7430	45.7	4	4	3	5	5	8	10	0	13	1	0	4	0	2	0	1	0	0	0	0	3	5	3	6	1
questioner	4	.1971	.1895	32.8	0	0	0	0	0	1	3	0	0	1	0	3	0	0	0	0	0	0	0	0	0	0	0	0	0
questioners	8	.0506	.1942	32.9	0	1	0	0	0	1	6	0	1	0	0	7	0	0	0	0	0	0	0	0	0	0	0	0	0
questioning	19	.6940	2.7083	44.3	0	2	1	1	5	5	5	0	5	0	0	3	0	1	2	0	0	1	0	0	2	1	1	3	0
questioningly	3	.2212	.2099	33.2	0	1	1	0	0	1	0	0	2	0	0	1	0	0	0	0	0	0	0	0	0	0	0	0	0
questionnaire	2	.2437	.1129	30.5	0	0	0	1	1	0	0	0	0	0	0	0	0	0	0	0	0	0	0	0	0	0	1	1	0
questionnaires	2	.0000	.0209	23.2	0	0	1	0	0	0	1	0	0	0	0	0	0	0	0	0	0	0	0	0	0	0	2	0	0
questions	1135	.8544	193.88	62.9	170	215	194	153	172	120	97	14	228	202	5	31	225	95	86	107	16	3	9	5	14	42	27	40	0
quests	2	.2446	.1184	30.7	1	0	0	0	0	0	1	0	0	0	0	0	1	0	0	0	0	0	0	0	0	1	0	0	0
queue	4	.3394	.3015	34.8	0	0	1	0	0	1	2	0	0	0	0	2	0	1	0	0	0	0	0	0	1	0	0	0	0
Quezon	4	.0000	.0419	26.2	4	0	0	0	0	0	0	0	0	0	0	0	0	0	0	0	0	0	0	0	0	0	4	0	0
quick	394	.8917	70.047	58.5	58	72	46	45	91	46	28	8	137	12	11	30	8	15	7	11	9	4	11	0	38	49	20	32	0
quick-drying	4	.2199	.2615	34.2	2	0	0	0	0	0	1	1	2	0	0	0	0	0	0	1	0	0	0	1	0	0	0	0	0
quick-frozen	3	.2444	.1814	32.6	1	0	0	1	1	0	0	0	0	0	0	0	0	2	0	0	0	0	0	0	0	0	1	0	0
quick-quick	3	.0000	.1370	31.4	0	3	0	0	0	0	0	0	3	0	0	0	0	0	0	0	0	0	0	0	0	0	0	0	0
quick-tempered	5	.4238	.4714	36.7	0	0	1	2	2	0	0	0	1	1	0	0	0	0	0	0	0	0	0	0	0	1	0	2	0
quick-witted	2	.2446	.1125	30.5	0	0	0	1	1	0	0	0	0	1	0	1	0	0	0	0	0	0	0	0	0	0	0	0	0
quicken	2	.2440	.1132	30.5	0	0	0	0	0	1	0	1	0	0	0	1	0	0	0	0	0	0	0	0	0	0	0	1	0
quickened	19	.5844	2.3789	43.8	0	2	5	3	4	2	3	0	7	0	0	4	0	1	0	1	0	0	0	0	4	1	1	0	0
quickening	3	.2319	.1611	32.1	0	0	0	0	1	2	0	0	0	0	0	0	0	1	0	0	0	1	0	0	0	0	1	0	0
quicker	36	.6596	4.8973	46.9	5	7	6	3	5	3	5	2	7	0	0	2	2	1	3	5	0	0	0	4	4	5	0	3	0
quickest	11	.6792	1.5331	41.9	4	0	2	1	4	0	0	0	2	0	0	1	1	1	0	0	0	0	0	1	1	2	1	1	0
quickly	1063	.9495	199.62	63.0	182	253	128	117	200	100	73	10	345	47	12	74	49	82	36	96	17	12	35	8	60	110	28	52	0
quickness	4	.3710	.3211	35.1	0	0	0	1	3	0	0	0	0	1	0	0	0	0	0	0	0	0	0	0	1	0	0	2	0
quicksand	5	.4789	.5381	37.3	1	0	1	1	2	0	0	0	2	0	0	0	0	0	0	0	0	0	0	0	1	1	0	1	0
quicksilver	9	.3929	.8598	39.3	1	0	0	4	3	0	1	0	5	0	1	2	0	1	0	0	0	0	0	0	0	0	0	0	0
Quicksilver	5	.0000	.2284	33.6	0	0	0	0	0	5	0	0	5	0	0	0	0	0	0	0	0	0	0	0	0	0	0	0	0
quiet	533	.8623	92.130	59.6	136	91	58	52	86	54	48	8	201	44	7	59	1	14	4	23	29	6	2	0	54	51	8	30	0
Quiet	2	.0000	.0243	23.9	0	0	0	0	0	0	0	2	0	0	0	0	0	0	0	0	0	0	0	0	0	0	0	2	0
quieted	17	.6614	2.3832	43.8	5	2	2	3	4	0	1	0	9	0	0	1	0	0	0	1	1	0	0	0	2	2	1	0	0
quieter	18	.6943	2.5842	44.1	1	2	1	2	9	1	2	0	6	1	0	2	0	0	0	1	2	0	0	0	1	2	0	3	0
quietest	3	.2357	.2199	33.4	1	0	1	1	0	0	0	0	2	0	0	0	0	0	0	0	0	0	0	0	0	1	0	0	0
quietly	344	.8456	58.531	57.7	70	76	42	44	60	27	20	5	139	21	5	27	0	12	2	13	15	0	2	0	40	38	7	22	1
quietness	5	.2357	.3471	35.4	0	0	1	1	2	0	0	1	3	0	0	0	0	0	0	0	0	1	0	0	0	0	0	1	0
quiets	2	.2433	.1158	30.6	1	0	0	0	0	0	1	0	0	0	0	0	0	0	0	0	0	0	0	0	0	1	0	1	0
quill	17	.7571	2.6316	44.2	1	2	3	3	6	1	0	1	6	0	0	1	0	1	1	2	1	0	0	0	1	2	2	0	0
quills	26	.5983	3.3774	45.3	15	2	3	1	4	0	1	0	15	2	0	0	0	0	0	0	3	0	0	0	2	0	3	1	0
quilt	34	.7991	5.4609	47.4	3	6	6	7	6	3	3	0	6	4	1	4	2	3	2	0	0	0	1	0	7	2	0	2	0
quilted	4	.2424	.3036	34.8	0	0	1	1	1	1	0	0	3	0	0	0	0	0	0	0	0	0	0	0	0	0	0	1	0
quilting	11	.4486	1.0976	40.4	0	2	0	5	3	1	0	0	3	1	0	1	0	0	0	0	0	0	0	0	5	1	0	0	0
quilts	7	.3858	.6848	38.4	0	2	3	0	0	1	1	0	5	0	0	1	0	0	0	0	0	0	0	0	1	0	0	0	0
Quimby	12	.1522	.6221	37.9	12	0	0	0	0	0	0	0	5	0	0	0	0	0	0	0	0	0	0	0	7	0	0	0	0
Quimbys'	2	.1787	.1174	30.7	2	0	0	0	0	0	0	0	1	0	0	0	0	0	0	0	0	0	0	0	1	0	0	0	0
QUINCE	3	.0000	.0322	25.1	0	0	0	0	0	0	3	0	0	0	0	3	0	0	0	0	0	0	0	0	0	0	0	0	0
Quincy	10	.5510	1.2022	40.8	1	0	1	0	4	4	0	0	4	2	0	0	0	2	0	0	0	0	0	0	1	0	1	0	0
quinine	6	.1717	.3427	35.3	0	0	0	3	0	0	0	3	3	0	0	3	0	0	0	0	0	0	0	0	0	0	0	0	0
Quinn	5	.0000	.0608	27.8	0	0	0	0	0	0	5	0	0	0	0	0	0	0	0	0	0	0	0	0	0	0	0	5	0
Quinn's	2	.0000	.0243	23.9	0	0	0	0	0	0	2	0	0	0	0	0	0	0	0	0	0	0	0	0	0	0	0	2	0
quintessence	2	.0000	.0243	23.9	0	0	0	0	1	1	0	0	0	0	0	0	0	0	0	0	0	0	0	0	0	0	0	2	0
quintet	5	.0000	.0404	26.1	0	1	1	1	2	0	0	0	0	0	0	0	0	0	0	0	5	0	0	0	0	0	0	0	0
quipu	6	.1494	.3134	35.0	0	0	3	3	0	0	0	0	3	0	0	0	0	0	0	0	3	0	0	0	0	0	0	0	0
quipus	2	.2375	.1088	30.4	0	0	0	1	1	0	0	0	0	0	0	0	0	0	0	0	1	0	0	0	0	0	0	1	0
quire	2	.2408	.1091	30.4	0	0	0	1	0	1	0	0	0	1	0	0	0	0	1	0	0	0	0	0	0	0	0	0	0
quirk	4	.4538	.4020	36.0	1	0	0	0	0	1	1	1	1	0	0	1	0	0	0	0	0	0	0	0	0	1	0	1	0
quirks	3	.3346	.2478	33.9	0	0	0	0	2	1	0	0	1	0	0	0	0	0	0	1	0	0	0	0	0	0	1	0	0

9Q quasi-public
XR quasi-queasy
7H quasi-stellar
7R quasifederal
7J quatre
6E quatrilaterals
7D quavered
8D quavering
5N quavery
XB que'que
7F quebracho

6R Quechuan
9A queenlike
5H queerer
8A quell
5P quelled
XB quelque
4P Quemados
4A Quentin's
4Q queries
7N questing
4J question-answer

9D question's
6F Quetzalcoatl
7Q queues
XR queuing
XR quibble
7D quibbled
9A quick-action
7L quick-change
7A quick-moving
7P quick-running
7R quick-to-make

4K quickdrying
XR quickens
7N quicker'n
7R quickie
9E quickies
8A Quicksilver's
5N quid
6R Quidley
9B quien
4Q quiescence
7Q quiescent

3A QUIET
3P quiet-appearing
8D quieting
7N quietude
6A quietus
3P quilt-making
8Q Quinault
3A quince
9B Quince
6A quinking
XD quinquina

5J Quinten
4Q Quintero
6J Quintet
6R Quintor
7A Quintus
6J Quipu
8R Quirinale

Word Type	F	D	U	SFI	3 Gr 3	4 Gr 4	5 Gr 5	6 Gr 6	7 Gr 7	8 Gr 8	9 Gr 9	X UnGr	A Read	B Eng & Gr	C Comp	D Lit	E Math	F Soc Stud	G Spell	H Sci	J Music	K Art	L Home Ec	M Shop	N Lib F	P Lib NF	Q Lib Ref	R Mag	S Rel
quirt	2	.1717	.1142	30.6	0	0	1	0	1	0	0	0	1	0	0	1	0	0	0	0	0	0	0	0	0	0	0	0	0
quit	69	.7040	10.087	50.0	11	9	10	5	15	7	11	1	29	3	0	7	0	3	2	1	1	0	0	0	2	7	0	14	0
quite	967	.9010	173.43	62.4	110	164	91	147	216	109	91	39	296	70	9	79	17	67	13	77	30	0	4	2	87	85	62	69	0
Quito	15	.1242	.6143	37.9	13	0	0	0	1	0	1	0	0	1	0	0	0	14	0	0	0	0	0	0	0	0	0	0	0
quits	2	.2442	.1134	30.5	0	1	0	1	0	0	0	0	0	1	0	0	0	0	0	0	0	0	0	0	0	0	0	1	0
quitting	6	.3427	.4955	37.0	2	1	0	0	2	0	0	1	2	0	0	0	0	0	0	0	0	0	0	0	2	0	0	2	0
quiver	23	.5552	2.8086	44.5	4	8	5	2	4	0	0	0	12	3	0	0	0	0	0	0	2	0	0	0	4	2	0	0	0
quivered	13	.3559	1.0720	40.3	1	1	4	1	5	1	0	0	3	0	0	2	0	0	0	0	0	0	0	0	7	0	0	1	0
quivering	25	.5642	2.9566	44.7	1	4	3	2	7	3	5	0	4	2	0	4	0	0	0	0	1	0	0	0	10	1	0	3	0
quivers	2	.1787	.1174	30.7	0	0	0	1	1	0	0	0	1	0	0	0	0	0	0	0	0	0	0	0	1	0	0	0	0
Quixote	11	.3785	1.0838	40.3	0	0	0	0	9	2	0	0	9	0	0	0	0	0	1	0	1	0	0	0	0	0	0	0	0
quixotic	2	.2418	.1091	30.4	0	0	0	0	1	1	0	0	0	0	0	0	0	0	1	0	0	0	0	0	0	0	1	0	0
quiz	13	.4203	1.2736	41.1	5	4	1	0	1	2	0	0	5	2	0	0	5	0	0	1	0	0	0	0	0	0	0	0	0
Quiz	2	.0000	.0299	24.8	0	0	0	0	0	0	2	0	0	0	0	0	2	0	0	0	0	0	0	0	0	0	0	0	0
quizzical	3	.3852	.2500	34.0	0	1	0	0	0	0	2	0	0	0	0	1	0	0	0	0	0	0	0	0	0	1	0	1	0
Quonset	3	.0000	.0434	26.4	0	0	0	0	3	0	0	0	0	0	0	0	0	0	0	0	0	0	0	0	0	3	0	0	0
quota	12	.5588	1.4909	41.7	7	0	1	0	1	3	0	0	7	1	0	0	0	2	0	0	0	0	0	0	0	0	1	1	0
quotas	4	.1737	.1745	32.4	0	0	1	0	3	0	0	0	0	0	0	0	0	0	0	0	0	0	0	0	0	1	3	0	0
quotation	104	.4205	9.2460	49.7	13	2	33	4	18	18	15	1	1	74	9	4	9	0	3	0	0	0	0	0	1	0	1	2	0
quotations	20	.4577	1.9551	42.9	0	0	3	0	7	6	4	0	3	9	3	1	0	0	3	0	0	0	0	0	0	0	1	0	0
quote	13	.5137	1.3992	41.5	0	1	3	0	1	1	7	0	0	2	0	0	0	2	0	1	0	0	0	0	0	1	1	6	0
quoted	20	.5289	2.2362	43.5	0	2	5	1	6	0	6	0	3	8	0	0	0	0	0	0	0	0	0	0	3	2	2	2	0
quotes	3	.3769	.2484	34.0	0	0	0	0	1	0	1	1	0	0	0	0	0	1	0	0	0	0	0	0	0	0	1	1	0
quoth	7	.2930	.4888	36.9	0	0	3	1	1	0	2	0	1	0	0	3	0	0	0	0	0	0	0	0	0	3	0	0	0
quotient	314	.0090	5.2132	47.2	20	66	68	80	38	29	13	0	0	0	0	0	313	0	0	0	0	0	0	0	0	0	0	1	0
quotients	225	.0000	3.3679	45.3	14	41	56	69	16	15	14	0	0	0	0	0	225	0	0	0	0	0	0	0	0	0	0	0	0
quoting	8	.5920	.9989	40.0	0	0	1	0	4	0	2	1	2	2	0	1	0	1	0	0	0	0	0	0	1	0	0	1	0
qx0	2	.0000	.0299	24.8	0	0	0	2	0	0	0	0	0	0	0	0	2	0	0	0	0	0	0	0	0	0	0	0	0
r	303	.4127	26.658	54.3	35	57	45	57	50	23	30	6	12	15	5	1	64	9	178	1	0	0	0	0	0	5	6	7	0
R	135	.6173	17.130	52.3	11	10	18	7	18	46	23	2	7	6	2	2	72	4	3	7	1	0	0	14	3	0	6	8	0
R**	12	.4938	1.2925	41.1	0	0	2	0	3	1	5	1	3	4	0	0	0	2	0	0	0	0	0	0	0	0	2	1	0
r-f	2	.1249	.0685	28.4	0	0	0	0	0	1	1	0	0	0	0	0	0	0	0	1	0	0	0	1	0	0	0	0	0
r-r-r-r-rrring	2	.0000	.0215	23.3	2	0	0	0	0	0	0	0	0	0	0	2	0	0	0	0	0	0	0	0	0	0	0	0	0
R-80	39	.0000	1.7816	42.5	0	0	0	0	39	0	0	0	39	0	0	0	0	0	0	0	0	0	0	0	0	0	0	0	0
R/N	2	.0000	.0050	17.0	0	0	0	0	0	2	0	0	0	0	0	0	0	0	0	0	0	0	0	2	0	0	0	0	0
r/s	3	.0000	.0449	26.5	0	0	0	0	0	1	2	0	0	0	0	0	3	0	0	0	0	0	0	0	0	0	0	0	0
r's	4	.1757	.1672	32.2	0	1	1	2	0	0	0	0	0	1	0	0	0	0	3	0	0	0	0	0	0	0	0	0	0
R's	5	.3672	.4527	36.6	1	0	0	0	1	1	2	0	2	0	0	0	1	2	0	0	0	0	0	0	0	0	0	0	0
Rab	21	.3447	1.7587	42.5	0	0	0	0	0	21	0	0	8	0	0	5	0	0	0	0	0	0	0	0	8	0	0	0	0
Rab's	2	.1787	.1174	30.7	0	0	0	0	0	2	0	0	1	0	0	0	0	0	0	0	0	0	0	0	1	0	0	0	0
rabbet	16	.0000	.0404	26.1	0	0	0	0	0	3	13	0	0	0	0	0	0	0	0	0	0	0	0	16	0	0	0	0	0
rabbi	5	.4860	.5169	37.1	1	0	1	0	1	2	0	0	0	1	0	0	0	0	0	2	0	0	0	0	1	1	0	0	0
rabbis	3	.2425	.1816	32.6	0	2	0	0	1	0	0	0	0	0	0	0	0	2	0	0	0	0	0	0	0	0	0	1	0
rabbit	209	.8271	35.025	55.4	56	40	47	19	36	6	1	4	105	15	3	5	4	2	9	13	1	0	0	0	12	19	10	11	0
Rabbit	92	.5831	11.930	50.8	33	32	4	1	13	8	1	0	67	2	0	8	0	0	0	0	5	0	0	0	5	1	0	4	0
rabbit-hole	2	.0000	.0234	23.7	0	0	2	0	0	0	0	0	0	0	0	0	0	0	0	0	0	0	0	0	2	0	0	0	0
rabbit's	12	.5339	1.3983	41.5	5	3	2	1	1	0	0	0	5	0	0	0	0	0	2	0	2	0	0	0	2	1	0	0	0
Rabbit's	2	.0000	.0914	29.6	0	2	0	0	0	0	0	0	2	0	0	0	0	0	0	0	0	0	0	0	0	0	0	0	0
rabbits	160	.8677	27.798	54.4	44	24	28	23	26	8	4	3	53	6	3	8	10	4	4	25	2	0	1	0	6	22	13	3	0
rabbitskin	3	.0000	.0583	27.7	0	0	0	0	0	3	0	0	0	0	0	0	0	3	0	0	0	0	0	0	0	0	0	0	0
Rabdologia	3	.0000	.0449	26.5	0	0	0	0	0	3	0	0	0	0	0	0	3	0	0	0	0	0	0	0	0	0	0	0	0
rabies	21	.5433	2.4445	43.9	1	3	0	11	2	3	1	0	3	2	0	1	0	0	0	12	0	0	0	0	0	1	1	1	0
raccoon	64	.7315	9.7022	49.9	15	23	3	2	4	12	0	5	33	3	0	2	0	1	2	0	1	0	0	0	8	3	3	8	0
Raccoon	8	.2659	.5472	37.4	7	1	0	0	0	0	0	0	2	0	0	0	0	0	0	0	0	0	0	0	0	5	0	1	0
raccoon's	2	.2411	.1091	30.4	0	1	0	0	1	0	0	0	0	0	0	1	0	0	0	0	1	0	0	0	0	0	0	0	0
raccoons	25	.5269	2.9587	44.7	10	6	1	3	5	0	0	0	14	0	0	2	0	0	0	0	0	0	0	0	0	6	1	2	0
Raccoons	3	.2379	.1705	32.3	2	0	0	0	1	0	0	0	0	0	0	1	0	0	0	0	0	0	0	0	0	2	0	0	0
race	638	.8107	105.19	60.2	92	88	41	66	181	122	27	21	315	14	4	18	22	37	8	11	5	0	1	0	50	104	17	32	0
Race	17	.6008	2.1869	43.4	2	2	1	1	6	2	0	3	7	0	0	0	0	1	0	0	1	0	0	0	3	3	0	2	0
racecourse	2	.0000	.0914	29.6	0	0	2	0	0	0	0	0	2	0	0	0	0	0	0	0	0	0	0	0	0	0	0	0	0
raced	181	.7330	27.618	54.4	43	44	20	21	28	17	6	2	106	8	1	12	2	4	1	1	1	0	0	0	15	19	0	11	0
racer	10	.6425	1.3320	41.2	0	1	3	0	4	1	1	0	2	2	0	0	1	1	0	0	0	0	0	0	1	0	1	2	0
racers	16	.3279	1.2626	41.0	2	7	0	0	5	0	0	2	4	0	0	0	0	0	0	0	0	0	0	0	0	7	0	5	0
races	109	.7751	17.222	52.4	24	10	13	8	23	22	5	4	39	4	1	1	2	16	0	0	2	0	0	0	13	17	5	9	0
Races	3	.0000	.0243	23.8	0	0	1	2	0	0	0	0	0	0	0	0	0	0	0	0	3	0	0	0	0	0	0	0	0
racetrack	15	.3289	1.3832	41.4	0	0	0	0	0	14	1	0	13	0	0	0	0	0	0	0	0	0	0	0	0	0	1	1	0
Rachel	15	.5275	1.6807	42.3	0	8	1	0	1	2	3	0	2	1	1	2	0	2	0	0	0	0	0	0	0	7	0	0	0
Rachmaninoff	2	.2411	.1091	30.4	0	0	0	1	0	0	1	0	0	0	0	1	0	0	0	0	1	0	0	0	0	0	0	0	0
racial	31	.5058	3.2997	45.2	0	0	5	0	6	4	16	0	1	0	0	1	0	5	0	0	0	0	0	0	0	6	10	8	0
racing	173	.7581	26.818	54.3	34	18	11	31	53	9	3	14	65	3	1	5	10	4	0	0	3	0	0	0	21	21	11	29	0
Racing	2	.0000	.0243	23.9	0	0	0	0	2	0	0	0	0	0	0	0	0	0	0	0	0	0	0	0	0	0	0	2	0
racism	2	.2351	.1166	30.7	0	0	0	0	0	0	1	1	0	0	0	0	0	1	0	0	0	0	0	0	0	0	0	1	0
racist	4	.1622	.1743	32.4	0	0	0	0	1	1	2	0	0	0	0	0	0	1	0	0	0	0	0	0	0	0	0	3	0
racists	2	.2351	.1166	30.7	0	0	0	0	0	0	2	0	0	0	0	0	0	1	0	0	0	0	0	0	0	0	0	1	0
rack	50	.6788	7.0678	48.5	14	14	2	0	7	2	8	3	20	3	1	5	2	1	0	2	0	0	6	0	1	4	0	5	0
racked	5	.4788	.5421	37.3	0	0	1	1	2	0	0	1	2	0	0	0	0	1	0	0	0	0	0	0	0	1	0	1	0
racket	24	.6710	3.3531	45.3	5	4	5	2	1	4	2	1	8	1	0	2	3	0	0	0	0	0	0	0	3	4	0	3	0
racks	9	.5665	1.0825	40.3	2	0	0	3	2	2	0	0	2	0	0	1	2	1	0	1	0	0	0	1	0	0	0	1	0
Racky	13	.0000	.5939	37.7	0	13	0	0	0	0	0	0	13	0	0	0	0	0	0	0	0	0	0	0	0	0	0	0	0
Racky's	3	.0000	.1370	31.4	0	3	0	0	0	0	0	0	3	0	0	0	0	0	0	0	0	0	0	0	0	0	0	0	0
racquet	2	.1733	.1149	30.6	0	0	0	1	1	0	0	0	1	1	0	0	0	0	0	0	0	0	0	0	0	0	0	0	0
racquets	2	.0000	.0914	29.6	0	0	0	2	0	0	0	0	2	0	0	0	0	0	0	0	0	0	0	0	0	0	0	0	0
Radames	2	.0000	.0162	22.1	0	0	0	0	0	0	2	0	0	0	0	0	0	0	0	0	2	0	0	0	0	0	0	0	0
radar	70	.5969	8.7042	49.4	1	9	2	15	21	15	6	1	3	1	0	1	1	2	1	36	0	0	0	1	0	2	4	18	0
Radcliffe	2	.0000	.0914	29.6	0	0	2	0	0	0	0	0	2	0	0	0	0	0	0	0	0	0	0	0	0	0	0	0	0
radial	8	.5068	.8486	39.3	0	0	0	0	3	4	0	1	0	0	0	0	2	0	0	2	0	0	0	1	0	0	2	1	0
radial-arm	2	.0000	.0290	24.6	0	0	0	0	2	0	0	0	0	0	0	0	0	0	0	0	0	0	0	0	0	2	0	0	0
radiance	4	.4445	.3917	35.9	0	0	1	1	0	1	1	0	1	0	0	1	0	0	0	0	1	0	0	0	1	0	0	0	0
radiant	26	.7641	3.9902	46.0	0	2	2	5	4	7	3	3	1	2	1	3	0	0	0	8	3	0	0	1	2	0	3	2	0
Radiant	2	.0000	.0243	23.9	0	0	0	0	0	0	0	2	0	0	0	0	0	0	0	0	0	0	0	0	0	0	0	2	0
radiate	14	.4786	1.4240	41.5	0	1	0	3	4	1	4	1	0	1	0	0	0	1	0	5	0	0	0	0	0	0	5	2	0
radiated	2	.1738	.0790	29.0	0	0	0	0	2	0	0	0	0	0	0	0	0	0	0	0	0	0	0	1	0	0	1	0	0
radiates	9	.5065	.9583	39.8	0	0	0	2	2	3	2	0	0	0	1	0	0	0	0	5	0	0	1	0	0	0	1	1	0

4N Quite
3F Quito's
6B quitted
7A quitter
7Q Quivira
6R Quizword
8B quizzed
9R quotes-within-quotes
7P Qur'anic
8G quy
8D qvick
6N R-R-Roxana
3B r-adders
3B r-droppers
3J R-i-n-g-o
9B r-o-u-g-h
3A r-r-rip
6N r-r-rising
4A r-r-rumbled
8D r-right
4A R-u-f
8B R-339-40
8B R-340
9E r/t
3A r
7R Raab
9M rabbet-and-dado
9M rabbeting
9Q Rabbinical
9Q Rabbis
8N rabbit-eared
6H rabbit-proof
5N rabbit-skin
3D rabbity
4N rabble
7Q Rabelais
7P Rabelaisian
3R Raccoon's
7R race-car
6A race-horse
9C racehorse
7R racer's
7R Raceway
8B rachel
9D Rachel's
7J Rachmaninoff's
9Q Racial
9F racially
4Q Racine
7R racing-power
7B Racket
9B racketeer
8D racketing
5A rackets
4N rackety
6A racking
5G racoon
3Q Radar
6H radar-equipped
6R radar-navigator
6Q radar-wind
8B Radbourne
5Q Radcliffe-Brown
5Q Radcliffe's
5Q raddiator
9M radial-line
9Q radially
9E radians
5A radiantly

					3	4	5	6	7	8	9	X	A	B	C	D	E	F	G	H	J	K	L	M	N	P	Q	R	S
Word Type	F	D	U	SFI	Gr 3	Gr 4	Gr 5	Gr 6	Gr 7	Gr 8	Gr 9	UnGr	Read	Eng & Gr	Comp	Lit	Math	Soc Stud	Spell	Sci	Music	Art	Home Ec	Shop	Lib F	Lib NF	Lib Ref	Mag	Rel
radiating	12	.4351	1.1118	40.5	0	3	0	0	3	1	2	3	0	0	0	0	0	0	0	2	0	0	0	0	2	0	5	3	0
radiation	119	.2972	8.3915	49.2	4	0	11	25	10	33	25	11	0	0	0	0	0	1	0	85	0	0	0	0	0	2	30	1	0
Radiation	5	.2948	.3343	35.2	0	0	2	1	2	0	0	0	0	0	0	0	0	0	0	1	0	0	0	0	0	0	3	1	0
radiations	19	.4038	1.7286	42.4	0	0	0	4	3	4	5	3	1	0	0	0	0	0	0	14	0	0	0	0	1	1	1	1	0
radiator	25	.5892	3.0786	44.9	7	6	2	1	7	1	1	0	3	1	0	1	0	0	0	4	0	0	0	0	0	8	2	6	0
radiators	6	.4357	.5848	37.7	1	1	3	0	1	0	0	0	1	0	0	1	0	0	0	3	0	0	0	0	0	0	1	0	0
radical	31	.5652	3.6274	45.6	0	2	1	4	5	5	14	0	1	2	0	1	10	0	0	0	0	0	0	0	2	0	6	9	0
Radical	7	.2373	.4228	36.3	0	0	0	0	1	2	4	0	1	0	0	0	0	2	0	0	0	0	0	0	0	0	4	0	0
radically	5	.4612	.4831	36.8	0	0	0	0	2	1	2	0	0	0	0	0	0	0	0	0	1	0	0	0	0	1	2	1	0
radicals	10	.3319	.7349	38.7	0	0	0	1	3	3	2	1	0	0	0	0	2	0	0	0	0	0	0	0	0	0	2	6	0
radii	7	.2446	.4063	36.1	0	0	3	0	3	0	1	0	0	0	0	0	6	0	0	0	0	0	0	1	0	0	0	0	0
radio	587	.8177	96.570	59.8	77	75	85	83	101	111	41	14	119	26	1	13	11	69	12	166	30	0	5	33	8	36	32	26	0
Radio	6	.2886	.3962	36.0	1	0	1	1	3	0	0	0	0	0	0	0	0	1	0	0	0	0	0	0	0	0	1	4	0
radio-active	3	.0000	.1370	31.4	0	0	0	3	0	0	0	0	3	0	0	0	0	0	0	0	0	0	0	0	0	0	0	0	0
radio-frequency	6	.0412	.0796	29.0	0	0	0	0	0	5	1	0	0	0	0	0	0	0	0	1	0	0	0	5	0	0	0	0	0
radioactive	70	.3892	6.1134	47.9	0	3	6	8	16	22	11	4	2	1	0	1	1	1	0	46	0	0	0	0	0	0	17	1	0
radioactivity	22	.4766	2.2901	43.6	1	0	3	0	3	7	5	3	2	0	1	0	0	0	0	15	0	0	0	0	0	1	1	2	0
radiocarbon	3	.3848	.2601	34.2	0	0	0	0	0	2	1	0	0	0	0	0	1	1	0	1	0	0	0	0	0	0	0	0	0
radioed	7	.2988	.5465	37.4	0	1	1	3	1	1	1	0	3	0	0	0	0	0	0	1	0	0	0	0	0	0	0	3	0
radioisotope	2	.0000	.0394	26.0	0	0	0	1	0	1	0	0	0	0	0	0	0	0	0	2	0	0	0	0	0	0	0	0	0
radioisotopes	4	.0000	.0789	29.0	0	0	0	3	0	1	0	0	0	0	0	0	0	0	0	4	0	0	0	0	0	0	0	0	0
radioman	10	.1364	.4083	36.1	8	0	0	2	0	0	0	0	1	0	0	0	0	1	0	0	0	0	0	0	0	0	0	8	0
radiometer	4	.0000	.0789	29.0	4	0	0	0	0	0	0	0	0	0	0	0	0	0	0	4	0	0	0	0	0	0	0	0	0
radiophone	3	.0000	.0583	27.7	0	0	3	0	0	0	0	0	0	0	0	0	0	3	0	0	0	0	0	0	0	0	0	0	0
radios	54	.7905	8.6424	49.4	6	5	6	10	13	6	8	0	14	1	0	0	3	12	1	5	3	0	0	2	3	0	5	5	0
radiosonde	5	.2213	.2870	34.6	0	0	1	1	3	0	0	0	0	0	0	0	0	0	0	4	0	0	0	0	0	0	1	0	0
radiosondes	3	.2427	.1822	32.6	0	0	0	0	3	0	0	0	0	0	0	0	0	0	0	2	0	0	0	0	0	0	0	1	0
radiotelephone	4	.0000	.0778	28.9	0	1	3	0	0	0	0	0	0	0	0	0	0	4	0	0	0	0	0	0	0	0	0	0	0
radish	14	.6431	1.8467	42.7	4	5	1	1	3	0	0	0	0	1	0	1	0	2	1	5	0	0	0	0	3	1	0	0	0
radishes	19	.6179	2.4297	43.9	8	3	2	1	4	0	1	0	2	2	0	0	2	2	0	3	0	0	2	0	5	1	0	0	0
radium	17	.5041	1.8704	42.7	1	0	0	6	5	1	2	2	4	5	0	0	0	2	0	4	0	0	0	0	0	0	2	0	0
radius	118	.3215	8.5546	49.3	4	20	13	11	21	33	16	0	1	0	0	0	95	0	0	3	0	0	0	14	0	0	2	3	0
Radius	4	.0000	.0429	26.3	0	0	0	0	0	0	4	0	0	0	0	4	0	0	0	0	0	0	0	0	0	0	0	0	0
Radley	2	.0000	.0215	23.3	0	0	0	0	0	0	2	0	0	0	0	2	0	0	0	0	0	0	0	0	0	0	0	0	0
Rado	2	.0000	.0243	23.9	0	0	0	0	0	0	2	0	0	0	0	0	0	0	0	0	0	0	0	0	0	0	0	2	0
Rado's	2	.0000	.0243	23.9	0	0	0	0	0	0	2	0	0	0	0	0	0	0	0	0	0	0	0	0	0	0	0	2	0
raf'	3	.0000	.0352	25.5	0	0	0	0	3	0	0	0	0	0	0	0	0	0	0	0	0	0	0	0	3	0	0	0	0
Rafael	15	.0000	.6852	38.4	12	3	0	0	0	0	0	0	15	0	0	0	0	0	0	0	0	0	0	0	0	0	0	0	0
raffia	2	.1926	.0867	29.4	0	0	0	1	0	0	1	0	0	0	0	0	0	0	0	0	0	0	1	0	0	0	1	0	0
rafflesias	2	.0000	.0394	26.0	0	0	0	2	0	0	0	0	0	0	0	0	0	0	0	2	0	0	0	0	0	0	0	0	0
Raffy	15	.0000	.6852	38.4	0	15	0	0	0	0	0	0	15	0	0	0	0	0	0	0	0	0	0	0	0	0	0	0	0
raft	105	.7237	15.802	52.0	11	18	4	19	19	19	8	7	54	4	1	7	0	2	0	6	0	0	0	0	9	13	0	9	0
rafter	2	.1717	.1142	30.6	1	0	0	0	1	0	0	0	1	0	0	1	0	0	0	0	0	0	0	0	0	0	0	0	0
rafters	11	.6317	1.4399	41.6	0	3	0	5	1	0	1	1	2	0	0	1	0	1	0	0	2	0	0	0	2	2	0	1	0
rafts	16	.5155	1.7828	42.5	6	1	2	5	1	1	0	0	3	0	0	0	0	4	0	0	0	0	0	0	0	5	1	3	0
rag	35	.6978	5.1015	47.1	9	12	2	2	4	4	1	1	17	1	0	2	0	0	0	1	1	0	0	1	4	7	0	1	0
rage	77	.6782	10.919	50.4	12	10	10	11	19	7	5	3	34	1	0	13	0	0	0	1	4	1	0	0	14	5	0	4	0
raged	25	.6275	3.2975	45.2	1	5	3	1	9	5	1	0	7	0	0	5	0	6	0	0	0	0	0	0	3	2	1	1	0
rages	5	.3102	.3964	36.0	0	0	2	0	2	1	0	0	2	2	0	0	0	1	0	0	0	0	0	0	0	0	0	0	0
ragged	56	.8065	9.1480	49.6	5	11	8	6	13	6	6	1	22	2	2	5	0	3	0	2	2	1	0	0	7	3	1	6	0
Raggletaggletown	5	.0000	.0404	26.1	5	0	0	0	0	0	0	0	0	0	0	0	0	0	0	0	5	0	0	0	0	0	0	0	0
raging	37	.6121	4.8643	46.9	4	10	2	4	9	1	3	4	18	0	0	0	0	0	0	1	1	0	0	0	2	6	2	7	0
ragman	3	.0000	.1370	31.4	0	0	3	0	0	0	0	0	3	0	0	0	0	0	0	0	0	0	0	0	0	0	0	0	0
Ragnhild	2	.0000	.0290	24.6	0	0	0	0	0	2	0	0	0	0	0	0	0	0	0	0	0	0	0	0	0	2	0	0	0
rags	27	.6198	3.5273	45.5	4	8	2	6	3	3	1	0	9	1	0	2	0	2	0	0	5	0	0	0	4	4	0	0	0
Rags	11	.1030	.3312	35.2	10	1	0	0	0	0	0	0	0	10	0	0	0	0	0	0	0	0	0	0	1	0	0	0	0
ragtime	19	.0477	.3304	35.2	0	0	0	6	1	10	2	0	0	0	0	0	0	0	0	0	18	0	0	0	0	1	0	0	0
ragweed	3	.0000	.0591	27.7	0	0	0	3	0	0	0	0	0	0	0	0	0	0	0	3	0	0	0	0	0	0	0	0	0
rah	6	.0000	.0485	26.9	6	0	0	0	0	0	0	0	0	0	0	0	0	0	0	0	6	0	0	0	0	0	0	0	0
raid	34	.6522	4.6222	46.6	2	2	4	10	5	7	3	1	10	2	0	6	0	3	0	0	0	0	0	0	0	4	5	4	0
raided	8	.4416	.7536	38.8	0	0	1	2	3	1	1	0	0	0	0	2	0	2	0	0	0	0	0	0	0	1	3	0	0
raider	3	.3766	.2480	33.9	0	1	0	0	0	2	0	0	0	0	0	0	0	1	0	0	0	0	0	0	1	0	1	0	0
Raider	5	.0000	.0586	27.7	0	0	0	0	5	0	0	0	0	0	0	0	0	0	0	0	0	0	0	0	5	0	0	0	0
raiders	18	.6844	2.5294	44.0	4	2	2	4	3	2	1	0	3	1	0	1	0	5	2	0	0	0	0	0	1	2	3	0	0
Raiders	5	.0000	.0608	27.8	0	0	0	1	4	0	0	0	0	0	0	0	0	0	0	0	0	0	0	0	0	0	0	5	0
raiding	6	.4286	.5793	37.6	0	1	0	1	1	2	0	1	1	1	0	0	0	3	0	0	0	0	0	0	0	1	0	0	0
raids	19	.6387	2.5026	44.0	3	2	2	3	1	5	3	0	2	2	0	0	0	4	0	0	0	0	0	0	1	3	3	4	0
rail	81	.8394	13.683	51.4	4	13	10	17	22	6	8	1	30	5	1	10	0	8	1	1	1	0	0	2	8	7	4	3	0
Rail	3	.2321	.1635	32.1	0	0	0	0	2	1	0	0	0	0	0	0	0	0	0	0	0	0	0	0	0	0	1	2	0
railed	2	.2297	.1135	30.6	0	0	0	0	0	0	2	0	0	0	0	1	0	1	0	0	0	0	0	0	0	0	0	0	0
railing	30	.6820	4.2337	46.3	4	8	2	7	0	7	1	1	8	0	1	6	0	2	0	5	0	0	0	0	2	2	0	4	0
railings	5	.4505	.4809	36.8	0	3	0	0	2	0	0	0	0	0	0	0	0	1	0	0	0	0	0	0	2	1	0	1	0
railroad	335	.8193	55.178	57.4	49	73	60	43	44	44	16	6	57	11	2	10	3	137	5	7	16	1	0	4	5	30	24	23	0
Railroad	28	.5222	3.1618	45.0	5	4	3	3	3	8	1	1	6	0	0	0	0	10	0	0	5	0	0	0	0	4	0	3	0
railroaders	7	.0000	.1013	30.1	0	7	0	0	0	0	0	0	0	0	0	0	0	0	0	0	0	0	0	0	0	7	0	0	0
railroading	3	.3390	.2450	33.9	0	1	0	1	0	1	0	0	1	0	0	0	0	0	0	0	0	0	0	0	0	0	1	1	0
railroads	173	.6165	22.104	53.4	21	21	42	21	24	33	8	3	6	4	4	1	0	107	0	2	5	0	0	2	0	9	28	5	0
railroads'	2	.2351	.1166	30.7	0	0	0	1	0	1	0	0	0	0	0	0	0	1	0	0	0	0	0	0	0	0	0	1	0
rails	59	.7735	9.2548	49.7	11	7	18	4	12	4	2	1	15	2	2	1	2	10	0	2	9	0	0	0	3	8	2	3	0
railway	45	.6964	6.4036	48.1	4	12	8	5	11	5	0	0	6	0	0	3	0	9	1	1	0	0	0	0	5	4	7	9	0
Railway	10	.4195	.9114	39.6	0	1	3	0	3	2	0	1	1	0	0	0	0	1	0	0	1	0	0	0	0	0	5	2	0
railways	14	.4459	1.3392	41.3	2	2	3	3	2	1	1	0	0	0	0	0	0	5	0	0	0	0	0	0	0	2	5	2	0
raiment	2	.2427	.1152	30.6	1	0	0	0	1	0	0	0	0	0	0	0	0	0	0	0	0	0	0	0	1	1	0	0	0
rain	938	.9004	168.02	62.3	240	205	109	128	135	63	46	12	205	38	15	46	3	217	24	164	29	4	2	1	37	91	33	27	2
Rain	7	.3867	.6852	38.4	0	0	1	5	0	0	1	0	5	1	0	0	0	0	0	0	0	0	0	0	0	0	1	0	0
Rain-Mount	2	.0000	.0162	22.1	0	2	0	0	0	0	0	0	0	0	0	0	0	0	0	0	2	0	0	0	0	0	0	0	0
rain-forest	4	.2285	.2258	33.5	0	0	0	0	1	1	2	0	0	0	0	0	0	2	0	0	0	0	0	0	0	0	2	0	0
rain-soaked	2	.1247	.0633	28.0	0	1	1	0	0	0	0	0	0	0	0	0	0	0	0	0	0	1	0	0	0	1	0	0	0
rain's	2	.1787	.1174	30.7	0	0	1	0	1	0	0	0	1	0	0	0	0	0	0	0	0	0	0	0	1	0	0	0	0
rainbow	76	.7287	11.252	50.5	14	15	3	32	5	6	1	0	8	9	4	0	0	6	0	30	0	2	3	0	2	5	7	0	0
Rainbow	3	.1548	.1479	31.7	0	0	1	1	0	0	1	0	1	0	0	0	0	1	0	0	0	1	0	0	0	0	0	0	0
rainbow-colored	2	.2401	.1133	30.5	1	0	0	1	0	0	0	0	0	0	0	0	0	0	0	0	0	0	0	0	0	1	1	0	0
rainbows	8	.4936	.8557	39.3	0	1	1	4	2	0	0	0	1	0	0	0	0	1	0	3	0	0	0	0	0	0	2	1	0

7R radiator-related
9Q Radicals
6H radio-activity
9H radio-frequencies
8J radio-phonographs
9B radio-sending
9P radio-shack
4F radio-telephone
7R radio-telescope
7A radiogram
7R radioing
9H radiolarians
7R Radiophysics
5A radiotelescope
5A radiotelescopes
8A Radium
6R radjas
XR Radman
9Q radome
9Q radomes
8H radon
7P Rae
9Q Raeburn
5G Raeder
7Q Raffaele
7D raffish
8A raft's
7D rafted
5J raftsmen
5J Raftsmen
5A Rag
9D rag-bag
7N rag-money
7P raga
6A ragamuffin
8Q Ragang
7P ragas
XR ragazza
8A ragged-looking
5B raggeder
9D raggedly
3R raggedy
5A ragman's
XR ragouts
6N Rags-an'-Bottles
6J Ragshag
8J Ragtime
8J ragtime-blues
6J Rah-coh-tsee
6J Rahck-mah-nee-nawf
6R Rahman
7N Raider's
6R rail-backed
7F rail-river-rail
5A rail-splitter
3P railhead
XQ railraods
4J railroad's
5Q railway-signal
5N Rain-Pipes
3J rain-bringers
4N rain-butt
6A rain-doors
9D rain-receptive
3A rain-rutted
5N rain-washed
3A rain-wet
6F rainbearing
6R rainbow-hued
6H rainbow-like
6R rainbow-ribboned
9D rainbow's

Word Type	F	D	U	SFI	3 Gr 3	4 Gr 4	5 Gr 5	6 Gr 6	7 Gr 7	8 Gr 8	9 Gr 9	X UnGr	A Read	B Eng & Gr	C Comp	D Lit	E Math	F Soc Stud	G Spell	H Sci	J Music	K Art	L Home Ec	M Shop	N Lib F	P Lib NF	Q Lib Ref	R Mag	S Rel
raincoat	18	.6566	2.5021	44.0	4	3	7	2	1	0	1	0	9	2	0	0	0	0	1	1	0	0	0	0	2	1	0	2	0
raincoats	7	.4378	.6999	38.5	2	2	3	0	0	0	0	0	2	0	0	0	0	1	0	2	0	0	0	0	2	0	0	0	0
raindrop	28	.1138	1.1302	40.5	1	3	0	20	2	0	2	0	1	0	0	0	0	0	0	26	0	0	0	0	0	0	1	0	0
raindrops	28	.6902	3.9644	46.0	9	3	0	8	4	2	1	1	4	1	1	1	0	0	0	12	1	1	0	0	0	3	4	0	0
rained	49	.7242	7.3586	48.7	13	17	5	3	5	5	0	1	22	3	0	0	0	8	2	3	4	0	0	0	0	5	1	1	0
Rainey	2	.0000	.0209	23.2	0	0	2	0	0	0	0	0	0	0	0	0	0	0	0	0	0	0	0	0	0	0	2	0	0
rainfall	166	.4824	17.374	52.4	11	34	26	38	31	15	9	2	6	0	0	0	7	96	1	33	0	0	0	0	0	4	18	1	0
rainforest	2	.0000	.0389	25.9	0	0	0	1	1	0	0	0	0	0	0	0	0	2	0	0	0	0	0	0	0	0	0	0	0
Rainier	12	.6340	1.5750	42.0	2	0	2	1	3	0	4	0	1	0	0	0	1	2	0	3	0	0	0	0	0	1	2	2	0
rainiest	2	.0000	.0389	25.9	0	0	0	2	0	0	0	0	0	0	0	0	0	2	0	0	0	0	0	0	0	0	0	0	0
raining	58	.6978	8.3223	49.2	23	9	11	1	4	4	4	2	15	15	0	9	0	1	2	6	1	0	0	0	2	2	1	4	0
rainless	3	.2444	.1814	32.6	1	0	0	1	0	0	1	0	0	0	0	0	0	2	0	0	0	0	0	0	0	0	1	0	0
rainmaker	3	.0000	.1370	31.4	0	0	0	0	0	3	0	0	3	0	0	0	0	0	0	0	0	0	0	0	0	0	0	0	0
rainmakers	8	.2275	.5677	37.5	5	0	0	0	0	2	1	0	5	0	0	0	0	0	0	0	0	0	0	0	0	3	0	0	0
rains	121	.7004	17.414	52.4	26	28	16	28	14	2	5	2	17	1	0	2	0	43	0	25	3	0	0	0	4	10	7	9	0
Rainsford	10	.1134	.3182	35.0	0	0	0	1	0	0	0	9	0	1	0	9	0	0	0	0	0	0	0	0	0	0	0	0	0
Rainsford's	2	.0000	.0219	23.4	0	0	0	2	0	0	0	0	0	2	0	0	0	0	0	0	0	0	0	0	0	0	0	0	0
rainstorm	10	.2298	.6358	38.0	1	4	1	1	3	0	0	0	4	1	3	0	0	2	0	0	0	0	0	0	0	0	0	0	0
rainstorms	3	.2321	.1635	32.1	1	0	0	0	1	0	0	1	0	0	0	0	0	0	0	0	0	0	0	0	0	0	1	2	0
rainwater	10	.3467	.8038	39.1	0	2	6	0	0	0	1	1	0	1	0	0	0	3	0	6	0	0	0	0	0	0	0	0	0
rainy	122	.7391	18.373	52.6	22	23	20	27	16	6	6	2	17	4	2	9	0	59	1	11	0	2	0	0	2	5	7	3	0
raise	344	.8526	58.713	57.7	66	57	56	51	39	37	32	6	63	17	0	11	9	112	8	43	13	0	4	1	11	18	17	17	0
raised	518	.8987	92.656	59.7	77	73	65	95	102	49	47	10	132	17	4	45	14	117	7	27	17	1	0	4	36	42	24	31	0
raiser	3	.2444	.1814	32.6	0	0	0	0	2	0	1	0	0	0	0	0	0	2	0	0	0	0	0	0	0	0	1	0	0
raises	63	.8071	10.227	50.1	7	9	6	13	8	4	15	1	11	5	1	0	0	9	0	10	5	0	0	2	1	4	5	10	0
raisin	10	.5226	1.1092	40.5	1	2	0	1	2	0	4	0	2	1	0	2	0	0	0	1	0	0	2	0	1	0	1	0	0
raisin'	2	.0000	.0914	29.6	0	0	0	2	0	0	0	0	2	0	0	0	0	0	0	0	0	0	0	0	0	0	0	0	0
raising	134	.8548	22.867	53.6	8	14	30	30	30	9	11	2	16	3	1	7	7	39	2	8	7	0	1	0	12	17	11	3	0
raisins	20	.4419	1.9741	43.0	3	5	0	3	5	1	3	0	5	0	0	0	0	5	0	1	0	0	4	0	2	3	0	0	0
Raja	4	.2183	.2285	33.6	1	3	0	0	0	0	0	0	0	0	0	0	0	3	0	0	0	0	0	0	0	1	0	0	0
Rajasthan	2	.0000	.0209	23.2	0	0	0	0	0	2	0	0	0	0	0	0	0	0	0	0	0	0	0	0	0	0	2	0	0
rake	37	.6490	5.0420	47.0	13	6	8	3	2	5	0	0	15	5	2	3	0	0	2	0	0	0	0	0	6	4	0	0	0
raked	18	.5566	2.1799	43.4	8	3	1	0	1	5	0	0	8	0	1	1	0	0	0	0	0	0	0	0	5	1	0	2	0
raking	10	.5499	1.1715	40.7	4	1	0	1	1	3	0	0	3	0	1	1	0	0	0	0	2	0	0	0	2	0	0	1	0
rakishly	2	.1814	.1187	30.7	0	0	0	0	2	0	0	0	1	0	0	0	0	0	0	0	0	0	0	0	0	0	0	1	0
Rakoczy	2	.0000	.0162	22.1	0	0	0	1	0	1	0	0	0	0	0	0	0	0	0	0	2	0	0	0	0	0	0	0	0
Rakumi	5	.0000	.2284	33.6	0	0	0	5	0	0	0	0	5	0	0	0	0	0	0	0	0	0	0	0	0	0	0	0	0
Raleigh	14	.6187	1.7993	42.6	1	6	2	0	3	2	0	0	2	0	0	1	0	2	0	0	1	0	0	0	0	5	2	1	0
rallied	7	.4725	.7030	38.5	3	1	1	0	0	2	0	0	0	0	0	0	0	2	0	0	0	0	0	0	0	2	2	0	0
rallies	8	.5956	.9712	39.9	0	0	1	0	1	3	2	1	0	1	1	1	0	1	0	0	1	0	0	0	0	0	1	2	0
rally	63	.5761	8.1514	49.1	0	3	3	2	49	2	3	1	49	0	2	2	0	2	0	0	0	0	0	0	1	2	1	4	0
Rally	5	.0000	.2284	33.6	0	0	0	0	5	0	0	0	5	0	0	0	0	0	0	0	0	0	0	0	0	0	0	0	0
rallying	6	.5368	.6876	38.4	0	0	0	0	2	3	0	1	1	1	0	0	0	2	0	0	0	0	0	0	0	0	1	1	0
Ralph	117	.7302	17.600	52.5	20	23	20	8	18	24	2	2	46	12	0	3	5	2	0	0	5	0	0	0	5	26	4	9	0
Ralph's	5	.3126	.3746	35.7	1	2	0	0	2	0	0	0	1	0	0	0	0	0	0	0	0	0	0	0	2	2	0	0	0
ram	40	.5842	5.1929	47.2	2	21	1	1	6	7	2	0	29	0	1	1	0	0	0	1	0	0	0	2	0	4	0	2	0
Ram	4	.2248	.2112	33.2	0	1	1	0	1	0	1	0	0	0	0	0	0	0	0	0	1	0	0	0	0	0	0	3	0
ram's	2	.1814	.1187	30.7	0	0	0	0	1	1	0	0	1	0	0	0	0	0	0	0	0	0	0	0	0	0	0	1	0
Rama	4	.0000	.0778	28.9	0	4	0	0	0	0	0	0	0	0	0	0	0	4	0	0	0	0	0	0	0	0	0	0	0
Raman	4	.0000	.1827	32.6	4	0	0	0	0	0	0	0	4	0	0	0	0	0	0	0	0	0	0	0	0	0	0	0	0
rambled	4	.1349	.2265	33.6	0	0	1	3	0	0	0	0	3	0	1	0	0	0	0	0	0	0	0	0	0	0	0	0	0
Rambler	4	.0996	.1523	31.8	0	1	0	0	3	0	0	0	1	0	0	0	0	0	0	0	0	0	0	0	0	0	0	3	0
rambles	2	.2446	.1142	30.6	0	0	0	0	0	1	0	1	0	0	0	0	0	0	0	0	0	0	0	0	1	0	0	1	0
rambling	12	.5276	1.3389	41.3	0	0	1	3	3	2	2	1	2	0	0	2	0	2	0	0	1	0	0	2	2	0	0	1	0
Rameau	7	.2977	.4571	36.6	0	2	3	0	1	1	0	0	0	0	0	0	0	0	0	0	4	0	0	0	0	1	2	0	0
ramekins	2	.0000	.0243	23.9	0	0	0	0	0	0	0	2	0	0	0	0	0	0	0	0	0	0	0	0	0	0	0	2	0
ramifications	2	.0000	.0243	23.9	0	0	0	0	0	1	1	0	0	0	0	0	0	0	0	0	0	0	0	0	0	0	0	2	0
Ramirez	2	.0000	.0914	29.6	2	0	0	0	0	0	0	0	2	0	0	0	0	0	0	0	0	0	0	0	0	0	0	0	0
ramjet	2	.0000	.0394	26.0	0	0	0	0	0	0	1	1	0	0	0	0	0	0	0	2	0	0	0	0	0	0	0	0	0
rammed	16	.4299	1.5273	41.8	1	2	1	1	4	3	4	0	4	0	0	0	0	0	0	1	0	0	0	3	3	1	0	4	0
Ramo	6	.0000	.0703	28.5	0	0	0	6	0	0	0	0	0	0	0	0	0	0	0	0	0	0	0	0	6	0	0	0	0
Ramon	73	.2127	4.6722	46.7	69	0	0	0	0	4	0	0	35	0	0	1	0	0	0	0	0	0	0	0	0	0	0	37	0
Ramon's	12	.2411	.9337	39.7	12	0	0	0	0	0	0	0	10	0	0	0	0	0	0	0	0	0	0	0	0	0	0	2	0
Ramona	77	.1006	2.9454	44.7	77	0	0	0	0	0	0	0	20	0	0	0	0	0	0	0	0	0	0	0	57	0	0	0	0
Ramona's	6	.0688	.1783	32.5	6	0	0	0	0	0	0	0	1	0	0	0	0	0	0	0	0	0	0	0	5	0	0	0	0
ramp	12	.4914	1.2605	41.0	4	0	1	5	2	0	0	0	1	0	0	0	0	2	0	0	0	0	0	0	2	3	0	4	0
rampage	4	.2835	.2871	34.6	0	0	1	0	2	1	0	0	1	0	0	0	0	0	0	1	0	0	0	0	0	0	0	2	0
rampaging	2	.1948	.1250	31.0	1	0	0	1	0	0	0	0	1	0	0	0	0	0	0	0	0	0	0	0	0	1	0	0	0
rampant	2	.2285	.1129	30.5	0	0	0	0	0	1	1	0	0	0	0	0	0	1	0	0	0	0	0	0	0	0	1	0	0
ramparts	10	.5354	1.1339	40.5	0	1	0	1	4	1	3	0	2	0	0	1	0	0	0	0	1	0	0	0	1	0	4	1	0
ramping	4	.0000	.1827	32.6	0	0	0	4	0	0	0	0	4	0	0	0	0	0	0	0	0	0	0	0	0	0	0	0	0
rampion	11	.2152	.8321	39.2	11	0	0	0	0	0	0	0	10	0	0	1	0	0	0	0	0	0	0	0	0	0	0	0	0
ramrod	4	.2186	.2141	33.3	0	3	0	0	1	0	0	0	0	0	0	1	0	0	0	0	0	0	0	0	0	3	0	0	0
rams	6	.3960	.5320	37.3	0	1	0	1	1	1	2	0	1	0	0	2	0	0	0	1	0	0	0	0	0	0	2	0	0
Rams	14	.2314	.8984	39.5	5	1	0	0	2	2	4	0	5	0	0	0	1	0	0	0	0	0	0	0	0	0	0	8	0
Rams'	2	.1814	.1187	30.7	1	0	0	0	0	0	1	0	1	0	0	0	0	0	0	0	0	0	0	0	0	0	0	1	0
Ramsay	2	.0000	.0234	23.7	0	0	0	0	2	0	0	0	0	0	0	0	0	0	0	0	0	0	0	0	2	0	0	0	0
ramshackle	5	.3085	.3664	35.6	0	0	2	1	1	0	1	0	1	0	0	2	0	0	0	0	0	0	0	0	0	0	0	2	0
ran	1374	.7883	221.26	63.4	403	319	132	146	210	94	52	18	680	58	13	105	19	52	9	13	21	1	0	0	182	148	12	61	0
Rana	2	.0000	.0394	26.0	0	0	0	0	2	0	0	0	0	0	0	0	0	0	0	2	0	0	0	0	0	0	0	0	0
ranch	243	.7316	36.371	55.6	119	29	33	23	23	12	2	2	62	7	0	13	7	54	3	2	1	1	2	2	75	4	2	8	0
Ranch	33	.6265	4.3847	46.4	10	7	2	5	0	7	0	2	11	1	0	2	8	6	0	4	0	0	0	0	0	0	0	1	0
ranch-hand	4	.0000	.0469	26.7	0	0	0	0	0	4	0	0	0	0	0	0	0	0	0	0	0	0	0	0	4	0	0	0	0
ranch's	2	.0000	.0914	29.6	0	0	0	0	2	0	0	0	2	0	0	0	0	0	0	0	0	0	0	0	0	0	0	0	0
rancher	23	.6563	3.0932	44.9	7	2	4	1	4	3	1	1	2	2	2	1	0	7	0	1	0	1	0	0	4	0	0	3	0
rancher's	3	.3431	.2528	34.0	1	0	0	1	0	1	0	0	1	0	0	0	0	1	0	0	0	0	0	0	1	0	0	0	0
Ranchera	2	.0000	.0914	29.6	2	0	0	0	0	0	0	0	2	0	0	0	0	0	0	0	0	0	0	0	0	0	0	0	0
ranchers	44	.6050	5.5855	47.5	11	5	6	8	5	3	1	5	5	2	0	1	0	24	0	4	1	0	0	0	4	0	1	2	0
ranches	87	.5528	10.233	50.1	21	13	27	12	5	4	2	3	9	3	0	1	0	57	0	2	0	2	0	0	4	0	7	2	0
ranching	11	.5702	1.3091	41.2	3	0	2	2	2	0	1	1	1	0	0	0	0	2	0	1	1	0	0	0	1	0	4	1	0
Rancho	2	.2152	.1357	31.3	0	0	1	0	0	1	0	0	1	0	0	0	0	1	0	0	0	0	0	0	0	0	0	0	0
rancid	3	.0524	.0803	29.0	0	0	0	0	1	0	2	0	1	0	0	0	0	0	0	0	0	0	2	0	0	0	0	0	0
Rand	3	.2279	.2143	33.3	1	1	0	1	0	0	0	0	2	0	0	0	0	0	0	0	0	0	0	0	0	0	0	1	0
Randal	4	.0000	.0429	26.3	0	0	0	0	0	0	4	0	0	0	0	4	0	0	0	0	0	0	0	0	0	0	0	0	0
Randall	8	.3157	.6233	37.9	0	1	0	2	3	0	2	0	3	0	0	0	0	0	0	0	3	0	0	0	0	0	0	2	0
Randall's	2	.1787	.1174	30.7	0	0	0	2	0	0	0	0	1	0	0	0	0	0	0	0	0	0	0	0	1	0	0	0	0

XH Raindrop
7R raindrop-shaped
7F rainforests
4D rainingest
XR rainsuit
4G Rainy
7F raisers
7P Raising
3Q Rajah
7F rajahs
4P rakers
6A rakin'
9B rakish
XR raky
4P Raleigh's
8B Ralphie
9R Ralston
6N ramblings
5G rambunctious
7D rambunctiousness
XQ Rameses
8L ramie
4N ramming
6N Ramo's
6R rampaged
6N rampart
9P Rampart
7A ramped
6A ramping-performance
6R ramps
9R rampway
9F Ramsey
6A Ran
9H Rance
8N ranch-cup
8D ranch-house
7D ranchhouse
7A ranchman
8G rancho
8F ranchos
8E Ranchville
5N rancor
9J rancour
6R rand
5P Randazzo

Word Type	F	D	U	SFI	3 Gr 3	4 Gr 4	5 Gr 5	6 Gr 6	7 Gr 7	8 Gr 8	9 Gr 9	X UnGr	A Read	B Eng & Gr	C Comp	D Lit	E Math	F Soc Stud	G Spell	H Sci	J Music	K Art	L Home Ec	M Shop	N Lib F	P Lib NF	Q Lib Ref	R Mag	S Rel
Randers	3	.0000	.0314	25.0	3	0	0	0	0	0	0	0	0	0	0	0	0	0	0	0	0	0	0	0	0	0	3	0	0
Randolph	13	.5146	1.4063	41.5	0	1	1	1	0	8	2	0	0	1	0	5	1	4	0	1	0	0	0	0	1	0	0	0	0
random	31	.7807	4.8583	46.9	2	0	1	1	15	2	9	1	3	1	2	2	4	0	0	3	1	0	0	1	3	2	6	3	0
Random	2	.2437	.1129	30.5	0	0	1	0	0	0	0	1	0	0	0	0	0	0	0	0	0	0	0	0	0	0	1	1	0
randomly	3	.2445	.1818	32.6	0	0	0	0	1	0	2	0	0	0	0	0	0	0	0	2	0	0	0	0	0	0	1	0	0
Randy	35	.4397	3.6177	45.6	10	12	8	0	1	3	1	0	20	4	0	0	0	0	8	0	0	0	0	0	0	0	0	3	0
Randy's	7	.0000	.0568	27.5	0	0	7	0	0	0	0	0	0	0	0	0	0	0	7	0	0	0	0	0	0	0	0	0	0
rang	138	.7296	20.841	53.2	45	30	14	11	20	11	7	0	65	13	0	12	0	5	1	5	0	0	0	0	17	8	3	9	0
range	351	.8293	58.176	57.6	15	36	42	40	121	48	36	13	34	4	1	15	18	36	0	53	43	0	11	5	6	24	66	35	0
Range	39	.6913	5.4904	47.4	3	4	6	8	6	5	6	1	2	0	0	2	0	10	1	5	3	0	0	0	0	2	8	6	0
ranged	18	.7156	2.6427	44.2	2	0	3	2	3	5	2	1	5	0	0	1	0	1	0	1	1	0	0	0	2	1	3	3	0
Rangeley	2	.0000	.0914	29.6	0	0	0	2	0	0	0	0	2	0	0	0	0	0	0	0	0	0	0	0	0	0	0	0	0
ranger	15	.6151	1.9908	43.0	1	4	0	3	1	5	1	0	8	0	0	1	0	2	0	0	1	0	0	0	0	1	0	2	0
Ranger	9	.5106	.9837	39.9	0	5	0	1	2	0	1	0	2	3	0	0	0	0	0	0	1	0	0	0	1	0	2	0	0
rangers	13	.6510	1.7718	42.5	0	6	2	0	2	3	0	0	4	2	0	2	0	2	0	1	0	0	0	0	0	1	0	1	0
Rangers	7	.1738	.3196	35.0	0	0	0	0	5	2	0	0	0	0	0	0	0	2	0	0	0	0	0	0	5	0	0	0	0
ranges	105	.6863	14.762	51.7	6	5	32	17	24	7	13	1	9	0	0	0	2	37	0	16	4	0	0	2	1	6	21	7	0
Ranges	8	.3723	.6780	38.3	0	0	3	0	1	0	4	0	0	0	0	0	0	3	0	4	0	0	0	0	0	0	1	0	0
ranging	39	.6698	5.3413	47.3	1	1	2	2	14	7	6	6	4	0	0	1	1	3	0	7	0	2	0	3	0	2	6	10	0
rank	76	.7990	12.189	50.9	3	2	7	10	15	26	13	0	9	1	0	3	14	11	2	2	7	0	0	2	4	2	15	4	0
Rank	5	.0000	.2284	33.6	0	0	5	0	0	0	0	0	5	0	0	0	0	0	0	0	0	0	0	0	0	0	0	0	0
rank-and-file	2	.2351	.1166	30.7	0	0	0	0	0	1	1	0	0	0	0	0	0	1	0	0	0	0	0	0	0	0	0	1	0
ranked	6	.5046	.6517	38.1	0	0	2	0	3	1	0	0	1	0	0	0	0	0	0	1	0	0	0	0	0	1	1	2	0
Rankin	6	.1361	.2398	33.8	5	0	0	0	0	1	0	0	0	0	0	0	0	1	0	0	0	0	0	0	0	5	0	0	0
ranking	6	.3946	.5204	37.2	0	0	0	1	1	2	2	0	0	0	0	0	0	3	0	1	0	0	0	1	0	0	1	0	0
ranks	51	.7588	7.8072	48.9	1	3	7	8	12	16	2	2	4	0	1	2	3	13	0	2	3	0	0	0	6	1	5	11	0
Ranse	9	.0000	.0966	29.8	0	0	0	0	9	0	0	0	0	0	0	9	0	0	0	0	0	0	0	0	0	0	0	0	0
ransom	9	.4536	.9562	39.8	0	0	0	1	4	3	0	1	5	2	0	0	0	1	0	0	0	0	0	0	0	0	0	1	0
rant	2	.1733	.1149	30.6	0	0	0	1	0	0	0	1	1	1	0	0	0	0	0	0	0	0	0	0	0	0	0	0	0
Ranta	2	.0000	.0914	29.6	0	2	0	0	0	0	0	0	2	0	0	0	0	0	0	0	0	0	0	0	0	0	0	0	0
Raoul	2	.0000	.0037	15.7	2	0	0	0	0	0	0	0	0	0	0	0	0	0	0	0	0	2	0	0	0	0	0	0	0
rap	8	.5479	.9088	39.6	0	3	0	1	0	2	1	1	1	2	0	1	0	0	1	0	2	0	0	1	0	0	0	0	0
rape	2	.2407	.1138	30.6	0	0	0	0	1	0	1	0	0	0	0	1	0	0	0	0	0	0	0	0	0	1	0	0	0
raped	2	.0000	.0290	24.6	0	0	0	0	2	0	0	0	0	0	0	0	0	0	0	0	0	0	0	0	0	2	0	0	0
Raphael	2	.0000	.0209	23.2	0	0	1	0	0	0	1	0	0	0	0	0	0	0	0	0	0	0	0	0	0	0	2	0	0
rapid	107	.8594	18.321	52.6	3	5	14	11	32	28	11	3	12	2	1	9	3	18	3	14	10	3	0	2	2	3	20	5	0
rapid-fire	4	.4538	.4020	36.0	0	0	2	1	1	0	0	0	1	0	0	1	0	0	0	0	0	0	0	0	0	1	0	1	0
rapid-traverse	2	.0000	.0050	17.0	0	0	0	0	0	0	2	0	0	0	0	0	0	0	0	0	0	0	0	2	0	0	0	0	0
rapidity	13	.6471	1.7367	42.4	0	1	1	1	6	2	2	0	2	0	0	0	0	1	0	1	1	0	0	0	4	2	1	1	0
rapidly	300	.9196	54.656	57.4	25	24	34	44	78	47	36	12	38	14	2	12	8	49	5	68	12	6	4	9	12	15	28	18	0
rapids	43	.6046	5.4902	47.4	1	7	15	7	9	1	1	2	10	0	0	0	0	16	0	0	2	0	0	0	4	1	2	8	0
Rapids	8	.4402	.7981	39.0	0	0	4	1	0	2	1	0	2	0	0	0	0	4	0	0	1	0	0	0	0	0	0	1	0
rapier	4	.4447	.3919	35.9	0	0	1	0	0	3	0	0	1	0	0	1	0	0	1	0	0	0	0	0	1	0	0	0	0
Rappahannock	3	.2444	.1814	32.6	0	0	0	0	1	2	0	0	0	0	0	0	0	2	0	0	0	0	0	0	0	0	1	0	0
rapped	11	.3752	1.0607	40.3	3	0	1	2	4	0	1	0	8	0	0	1	0	0	0	0	0	0	0	0	2	0	0	0	0
rapping	6	.1187	.2583	34.1	2	0	0	0	0	0	4	0	2	0	0	4	0	0	0	0	0	0	0	0	0	0	0	0	0
rapport	3	.2143	.1568	32.0	0	0	0	1	1	1	0	0	0	0	0	0	0	0	0	0	0	0	0	0	0	1	0	2	0
rapprochement	2	.0000	.0243	23.9	0	0	0	0	0	0	2	0	0	0	0	0	0	0	0	0	0	0	0	0	0	0	0	2	0
raps	4	.3717	.3640	35.6	0	0	0	1	0	1	2	0	2	0	0	1	0	0	0	0	0	0	0	0	0	0	0	1	0
rapscallion	2	.1787	.1174	30.7	0	2	0	0	0	0	0	0	1	0	0	0	0	0	0	0	0	0	0	0	1	0	0	0	0
rapscallions	2	.0000	.0234	23.7	0	0	0	0	2	0	0	0	0	0	0	0	0	0	0	0	0	0	0	0	2	0	0	0	0
rapture	5	.4748	.4951	36.9	0	1	0	0	2	0	1	1	0	0	0	1	0	0	0	0	1	0	0	0	2	0	0	1	0
Rapunzel	14	.1034	.5445	37.4	14	0	0	0	0	0	0	0	4	0	0	10	0	0	0	0	0	0	0	0	0	0	0	0	0
rare	126	.7643	19.503	52.9	12	13	13	10	36	19	14	9	25	3	0	7	0	11	0	13	7	0	3	0	3	13	30	11	0
rarefied	7	.2361	.3891	35.9	0	0	0	4	2	1	0	0	0	0	0	0	0	0	0	1	0	0	0	0	0	0	5	1	0
rarely	85	.8651	14.642	51.7	2	5	8	12	21	20	12	5	11	5	3	4	0	8	2	9	4	0	2	1	2	7	15	12	0
rarer	5	.2365	.3671	35.6	2	1	0	0	0	0	0	2	3	0	0	0	0	0	0	2	0	0	0	0	0	0	0	0	0
rarest	6	.4535	.6090	37.8	0	2	1	0	2	1	0	0	2	0	0	1	0	0	0	0	0	0	0	0	2	0	1	0	0
rarity	4	.3060	.2670	34.3	1	0	0	0	2	0	1	0	0	0	1	2	0	0	0	0	0	0	0	0	0	1	0	0	0
Raroia	5	.3087	.3698	35.7	0	0	0	0	1	2	2	0	1	0	0	2	0	0	0	0	0	0	0	0	0	2	0	0	0
Ras	3	.0000	.0583	27.7	0	0	0	2	1	0	0	0	0	0	0	0	0	3	0	0	0	0	0	0	0	0	0	0	0
rascal	10	.5546	1.2157	40.8	1	2	1	3	2	0	1	0	5	0	0	0	0	0	1	0	1	0	0	0	2	1	0	0	0
Rascal	15	.2417	.8422	39.3	0	7	0	0	8	0	0	0	0	0	0	8	0	0	0	0	0	0	0	0	0	0	0	7	0
Rascal's	2	.0000	.0215	23.3	0	0	0	0	2	0	0	0	0	0	0	2	0	0	0	0	0	0	0	0	0	0	0	0	0
rascally	2	.2443	.1130	30.5	0	0	0	2	0	0	0	0	0	0	0	1	0	0	0	0	0	0	0	0	1	0	0	0	0
rascals	10	.3653	.9450	39.8	2	2	1	4	1	0	0	0	7	0	0	0	0	0	0	0	0	0	0	0	2	1	0	0	0
rash	8	.6165	1.0396	40.2	0	0	2	0	3	1	2	0	2	1	0	0	0	2	0	1	0	0	0	0	0	0	1	1	0
rashly	2	.2443	.1130	30.5	0	1	0	0	1	0	0	0	0	0	0	1	0	0	0	0	0	0	0	0	1	0	0	0	0
Raskin	3	.0000	.0365	25.6	0	0	0	0	0	3	0	0	0	0	0	0	0	0	0	0	0	0	0	0	0	0	0	3	0
rasp	11	.2418	.5933	37.7	0	0	0	0	1	3	6	1	1	0	0	0	0	0	0	1	1	1	0	7	0	0	0	0	0
raspberries	14	.5406	1.5808	42.0	7	0	0	5	1	0	0	1	0	1	1	0	0	6	0	1	0	0	0	0	0	0	4	1	0
raspberry	14	.6335	1.8721	42.7	7	0	0	4	0	0	2	1	5	1	0	1	0	1	0	2	0	0	0	0	0	0	3	1	0
rasping	8	.4320	.7672	38.8	0	0	1	1	3	2	1	0	2	0	0	3	0	0	0	0	1	0	0	0	2	0	0	0	0
rat	85	.7460	13.010	51.1	50	11	2	7	13	1	0	1	33	2	0	3	0	1	1	6	3	0	0	0	16	6	9	5	0
Rat	20	.4276	2.0005	43.0	4	0	6	6	4	0	0	0	10	6	0	0	0	0	0	0	3	0	0	0	0	0	0	1	0
rat-a-tat-tat	3	.2437	.2277	33.6	0	2	0	1	0	0	0	0	2	0	0	0	0	0	0	1	0	0	0	0	0	0	0	0	0
rat's	3	.2332	.1690	32.3	1	1	0	0	0	0	0	1	0	0	0	0	0	0	0	0	0	0	0	0	0	2	0	1	0
Rat's	2	.0000	.0914	29.6	0	0	0	0	2	0	0	0	2	0	0	0	0	0	0	0	0	0	0	0	0	0	0	0	0
ratchet	3	.0000	.0076	18.8	0	0	0	0	0	0	3	0	0	0	0	0	0	0	0	0	0	0	0	3	0	0	0	0	0
rate	359	.8247	59.200	57.7	11	30	43	37	84	58	69	27	22	9	1	10	88	20	2	77	3	0	12	8	9	13	36	49	0
rated	17	.5390	1.9094	42.8	1	0	1	4	3	3	2	3	0	0	0	1	0	1	0	2	0	0	0	0	0	5	2	6	0
Ratendon	2	.0000	.0914	29.6	0	0	0	0	0	2	0	0	2	0	0	0	0	0	0	0	0	0	0	0	0	0	0	0	0
rates	86	.6299	11.084	50.4	0	8	8	3	32	15	14	6	1	4	0	0	12	6	0	13	0	0	3	0	0	1	23	23	0
Rathbun	4	.0000	.1827	32.6	0	4	0	0	0	0	0	0	4	0	0	0	0	0	0	0	0	0	0	0	0	0	0	0	0
rather	734	.9437	136.89	61.4	55	76	85	86	190	97	120	25	147	50	18	70	16	52	11	72	38	10	18	8	41	48	67	68	0
Rathmann	3	.0000	.0434	26.4	0	0	0	0	0	0	0	3	0	0	0	0	0	0	0	0	0	0	0	0	0	3	0	0	0
raths	2	.1458	.0682	28.3	0	0	1	1	0	0	0	0	0	1	0	0	0	0	0	0	0	1	0	0	0	0	0	0	0
ratification	5	.1990	.2695	34.3	0	0	1	0	0	4	0	0	0	0	0	0	0	4	0	0	0	0	0	0	0	1	0	0	0
ratified	7	.2924	.4696	36.7	1	2	1	0	0	2	1	0	0	0	0	0	0	2	0	0	0	0	0	0	0	1	4	0	0
ratify	3	.3766	.2497	34.0	1	0	1	0	0	1	0	0	0	0	0	0	0	1	0	0	0	0	0	0	0	1	1	0	0
rating	20	.6910	2.8582	44.6	7	0	1	1	3	6	2	0	7	1	0	0	2	0	0	2	1	0	1	2	1	0	2	1	0
ratings	6	.4284	.5426	37.3	0	0	0	0	1	3	2	0	0	1	0	0	1	0	0	0	0	0	1	0	0	0	0	3	0
ratio	111	.2664	7.0213	48.5	0	0	4	14	27	36	29	1	0	0	1	0	98	0	0	6	0	0	0	1	0	0	0	5	0
ration	5	.4228	.4710	36.7	0	1	0	1	1	2	0	0	1	0	0	0	0	0	0	0	0	0	0	0	1	1	0	2	0
rational	332	.0565	8.3516	49.2	0	9	26	22	63	173	39	0	0	0	0	0	324	0	0	0	0	0	0	0	0	0	3	5	0
rationale	6	.3047	.4104	36.1	0	0	0	0	0	0	3	3	0	0	0	0	0	0	0	0	0	0	0	0	0	1	1	4	0

5A rangeland
6R rangelands
6R ranger-naturalists
6P ranger's
7N Rangoon
9D rangy
9P rankling
5Q rankness
8Q Rann
7R Rano
9R ransacked
5F Ransom
7D Ransome
8F ranting
7R rantings
5F RapidCity
5P rapid-firing
XR rapid's
6A rapine
8R rapist
7N rapt
7Q raptorial
8D raptured
7D rapturous
7R Raraku
7Q rare-earth
6Q rarefaction
XH Rasalague
6R Rascals
6P Raschi
7J rasgueado
9D rasher
8F rashness
8R Raskin's
7R Rasmussen
7R raspberry-flavored
7Q rasps
6C raspy
3R rat-killing
7N rat-racing
8D rat-tat
7Q ratchets
7Q ratel
4J rath-er
8G rathskeller
7L Rating
6E rational-number
5Q rationalism

Word Type	F	D	U	SFI	3 Gr 3	4 Gr 4	5 Gr 5	6 Gr 6	7 Gr 7	8 Gr 8	9 Gr 9	X UnGr	A Read	B Eng & Gr	C Comp	D Lit	E Math	F Soc Stud	G Spell	H Sci	J Music	K Art	L Home Ec	M Shop	N Lib F	P Lib NF	Q Lib Ref	R Mag	S Rel
rationality	4	.0000	.0486	26.9	0	0	0	0	0	4	0	0	0	0	0	0	0	0	0	0	0	0	0	0	0	0	0	4	0
rationalize	3	.3394	.2470	33.9	0	0	0	0	2	0	1	0	1	0	0	0	1	0	0	0	0	0	0	0	0	0	1	0	0
rationalized	4	.0996	.1523	31.8	0	0	0	0	2	0	0	2	1	0	0	0	0	0	0	0	0	0	0	0	0	0	0	3	0
rationally	2	.1698	.1133	30.5	0	0	0	0	1	1	0	0	1	0	0	0	0	0	0	0	0	0	0	0	0	0	1	0	0
rationed	4	.3512	.3114	34.9	1	0	0	0	2	0	1	0	0	0	0	0	0	0	0	1	0	0	0	0	0	0	1	2	0
rations	16	.6104	2.0724	43.2	0	1	4	1	6	2	2	0	6	0	0	1	0	0	0	0	0	0	0	0	2	2	3	2	0
ratios	18	.1387	.7177	38.6	0	0	0	5	8	2	2	1	0	0	0	0	16	0	0	0	0	0	0	0	0	0	0	2	0
ratlines	2	.0000	.0914	29.6	0	0	0	2	0	0	0	0	2	0	0	0	0	0	0	0	0	0	0	0	0	0	0	0	0
Raton	2	.0000	.0243	23.9	0	0	0	0	2	0	0	0	0	0	0	0	0	0	0	0	0	0	0	0	0	0	0	2	0
ratproof	2	.0000	.0394	26.0	0	0	0	2	0	0	0	0	0	0	0	0	0	0	0	2	0	0	0	0	0	0	0	0	0
rats	122	.7402	18.482	52.7	41	10	13	15	29	13	1	0	38	0	0	3	0	2	0	17	5	0	3	0	25	6	12	11	0
ratted	2	.0000	.0914	29.6	0	1	0	0	1	0	0	0	2	0	0	0	0	0	0	0	0	0	0	0	0	0	0	0	0
rattle	43	.7525	6.5616	48.2	9	5	9	4	7	3	3	3	9	3	2	2	0	2	0	4	6	0	0	0	8	3	1	3	0
rattle-trap	2	.0000	.0914	29.6	2	0	0	0	0	0	0	0	2	0	0	0	0	0	0	0	0	0	0	0	0	0	0	0	0
rattled	32	.6546	4.3426	46.4	9	5	3	4	8	0	3	0	8	1	0	4	0	0	0	0	1	0	0	0	8	6	1	3	0
rattler	9	.5201	.9816	39.9	1	4	1	0	3	0	0	0	0	0	0	0	0	2	0	1	0	0	0	0	3	0	1	2	0
Rattler	3	.2357	.2199	33.4	0	0	0	0	2	0	1	0	2	0	0	0	0	0	0	0	0	0	0	0	0	1	0	0	0
rattlers	4	.0904	.1412	31.5	1	0	0	0	3	0	0	0	1	0	0	0	0	0	0	0	0	0	0	0	0	0	3	0	0
rattles	25	.6018	3.1382	45.0	12	0	3	3	6	0	1	0	6	2	1	0	0	2	0	0	10	1	0	0	1	1	1	0	0
rattlesnake	23	.7405	3.5048	45.4	4	3	7	4	3	0	2	0	10	1	0	2	1	0	0	1	2	0	0	0	2	0	2	2	0
rattlesnakes	26	.6534	3.5585	45.5	10	3	6	0	5	2	0	0	8	0	1	0	0	0	0	8	0	0	0	0	2	2	2	3	0
rattlin'	4	.0000	.0323	25.1	0	4	0	0	0	0	0	0	0	0	0	0	0	0	0	0	4	0	0	0	0	0	0	0	0
rattling	26	.6217	3.3688	45.3	3	6	1	6	4	4	2	0	6	1	0	4	0	0	0	2	4	0	0	0	7	1	0	1	0
raucous	4	.2417	.3028	34.8	0	0	0	2	1	1	0	0	3	0	0	0	0	0	0	0	0	0	0	0	1	0	0	0	0
ravage	3	.3873	.2485	34.0	0	0	0	0	2	0	1	0	0	0	0	1	0	0	0	0	0	0	0	0	1	0	1	0	0
ravaged	3	.2143	.1568	32.0	0	0	1	2	0	0	0	0	0	0	0	0	0	0	0	0	0	0	0	0	0	1	0	2	0
ravages	4	.4516	.4046	36.1	0	0	1	0	1	1	1	0	1	0	0	1	0	1	0	0	0	0	0	0	0	1	0	0	0
ravaging	2	.2291	.1135	30.5	0	0	0	0	1	0	0	1	0	0	0	1	0	0	0	1	0	0	0	0	0	0	0	0	0
rave	2	.1733	.1149	30.6	0	0	0	1	0	0	0	1	1	1	0	0	0	0	0	0	0	0	0	0	0	0	0	0	0
ravel	2	.0000	.0064	18.1	0	0	0	0	0	1	1	0	0	0	0	0	0	0	0	0	0	0	2	0	0	0	0	0	0
Ravel	22	.2797	1.3851	41.4	2	0	0	6	8	6	0	0	0	0	0	0	0	0	0	0	11	0	0	0	0	10	1	0	0
Ravel's	4	.2303	.2158	33.3	0	0	0	1	3	0	0	0	0	0	0	0	0	0	0	0	2	0	0	0	0	2	0	0	0
raven	4	.4538	.4020	36.0	1	1	1	0	0	0	1	0	1	0	0	1	0	0	0	0	0	0	0	0	0	1	0	1	0
Raven	14	.2410	.8027	39.0	0	9	0	0	0	2	3	0	0	0	0	5	0	0	0	0	0	0	0	0	0	9	0	0	0
Ravenna	4	.2277	.2047	33.1	0	0	1	1	0	2	0	0	0	0	0	0	0	0	0	0	0	1	0	0	0	0	3	0	0
ravenous	5	.3087	.3698	35.7	2	0	0	1	1	0	1	0	1	0	0	2	0	0	0	0	0	0	0	0	0	2	0	0	0
ravens	7	.5919	.8666	39.4	2	0	1	0	2	1	0	1	1	0	0	0	0	1	0	0	0	0	0	0	1	2	1	1	0
Ravenwood	2	.0000	.0219	23.4	0	0	0	0	0	2	0	0	0	2	0	0	0	0	0	0	0	0	0	0	0	0	0	0	0
raves	2	.1494	.1045	30.2	0	0	0	0	1	1	0	0	1	0	0	0	0	0	0	0	1	0	0	0	0	0	0	0	0
ravine	26	.6177	3.3647	45.3	3	5	1	8	2	6	1	0	8	1	1	3	0	0	0	0	1	2	0	0	8	2	0	0	0
ravines	7	.4577	.6690	38.3	0	0	1	2	2	2	0	0	0	0	0	1	0	0	0	0	0	1	0	0	3	1	1	0	0
ravishing	2	.2387	.1089	30.4	0	0	0	0	1	0	1	0	0	0	0	0	0	0	0	0	1	0	0	0	1	0	0	0	0
raw	188	.7676	29.170	54.6	16	22	37	33	42	10	25	3	19	6	0	7	0	77	3	19	0	0	8	3	5	12	22	7	0
raw-boned	4	.4560	.4041	36.1	0	2	0	0	1	1	0	0	1	0	0	0	0	0	0	0	0	0	0	0	1	1	0	1	0
Raw-hunt	3	.0000	.0434	26.4	0	3	0	0	0	0	0	0	0	0	0	0	0	0	0	0	0	0	0	0	0	3	0	0	0
rawhide	5	.3987	.4506	36.5	1	0	2	0	2	0	0	0	1	0	0	0	0	1	0	0	0	0	0	0	1	0	2	0	0
Rawlings	2	.0000	.0215	23.3	0	0	0	0	2	0	0	0	0	0	0	2	0	0	0	0	0	0	0	0	0	0	0	0	0
Rawlins	5	.0000	.0608	27.8	0	0	0	0	0	0	0	5	0	0	0	0	0	0	0	0	0	0	0	0	0	0	0	5	0
ray	146	.3955	12.783	51.1	24	19	37	18	33	10	4	1	8	2	0	2	109	0	1	8	3	0	0	0	4	0	7	2	0
Ray	41	.5975	5.3679	47.3	10	3	13	3	4	4	3	1	25	1	0	1	6	0	0	3	0	0	0	0	0	1	0	4	0
Ray's	3	.2427	.1822	32.6	0	0	0	0	2	1	0	0	0	0	0	0	0	0	0	2	0	0	0	0	0	0	0	1	0
Raymond	6	.3657	.5386	37.3	0	1	0	3	2	0	0	0	3	0	0	0	0	0	0	0	1	0	0	0	0	0	0	2	0
rayon	47	.4338	4.3651	46.4	1	1	12	5	1	10	17	0	0	0	0	0	0	16	0	12	0	0	13	3	0	1	2	0	0
rayons	2	.1432	.0759	28.8	0	0	0	0	0	1	1	0	0	0	0	0	0	0	0	1	0	0	1	0	0	0	0	0	0
rays	291	.6645	39.823	56.0	48	23	24	44	90	33	18	11	25	2	0	5	75	16	2	113	0	0	1	4	3	4	39	2	0
razor	20	.5476	2.3702	43.7	3	4	2	3	5	3	0	0	7	0	0	1	0	1	0	3	0	2	0	0	2	1	3	0	0
razor-sharp	5	.4599	.4875	36.9	0	1	0	2	1	0	1	0	0	0	0	0	0	1	0	0	0	0	0	0	1	0	1	2	0
RCA	3	.2411	.1667	32.2	0	0	0	1	0	1	0	1	0	0	0	0	0	0	0	0	1	0	0	0	0	0	0	2	0
rd	2	.2418	.1091	30.4	0	1	0	0	1	0	0	0	0	0	0	0	0	0	1	0	0	0	0	0	0	0	1	0	0
re	34	.3833	2.7716	44.4	1	8	9	3	8	3	1	1	1	3	0	0	0	0	18	1	9	0	0	0	0	0	0	2	0
re-	3	.0000	.0328	25.2	0	0	1	0	0	2	0	0	0	3	0	0	0	0	0	0	0	0	0	0	0	0	0	0	0
re-birth	2	.0000	.0290	24.6	0	0	0	0	0	0	0	2	0	0	0	0	0	0	0	0	0	0	0	0	0	2	0	0	0
re-born	4	.0000	.0579	27.6	0	0	0	0	0	0	0	4	0	0	0	0	0	0	0	0	0	0	0	0	0	4	0	0	0
re-create	4	.2417	.2182	33.4	0	0	0	0	4	0	0	0	0	0	0	0	0	0	0	0	2	0	0	0	0	0	2	0	0
re-dedication	2	.0000	.0162	22.1	0	0	0	0	0	2	0	0	0	0	0	0	0	0	0	0	2	0	0	0	0	0	0	0	0
re-echoed	2	.1948	.1250	31.0	0	1	0	1	0	0	0	0	1	0	0	0	0	0	0	0	0	0	0	0	0	1	0	0	0
re-education	2	.2408	.1204	30.8	0	0	0	0	1	1	0	0	0	0	0	0	0	1	0	0	0	0	0	0	0	1	0	0	0
re-elected	6	.4622	.5828	37.7	0	1	1	0	1	2	1	0	0	0	0	1	0	0	0	0	0	0	0	0	0	1	2	2	0
re-election	6	.1937	.2989	34.8	0	0	0	0	0	3	3	0	0	0	0	0	0	2	0	0	0	0	0	0	0	0	0	4	0
re-enter	2	.0000	.0215	23.3	0	0	0	0	0	2	0	0	0	0	0	2	0	0	0	0	0	0	0	0	0	0	0	0	0
re-entered	2	.0000	.0389	25.9	0	0	0	0	1	1	0	0	0	0	0	0	0	2	0	0	0	0	0	0	0	0	0	0	0
re-entry	3	.1169	.1277	31.1	0	0	2	1	0	0	0	0	1	0	0	0	0	0	0	0	0	0	0	0	0	0	2	0	0
re-established	2	.2437	.1129	30.5	1	0	0	0	1	0	0	0	0	0	0	0	0	0	0	0	0	0	0	0	0	0	1	1	0
re-route	2	.0000	.0914	29.6	0	0	0	2	0	0	0	0	2	0	0	0	0	0	0	0	0	0	0	0	0	0	0	0	0
reabsorbed	2	.0000	.0209	23.2	0	0	0	0	0	0	2	0	0	0	0	0	0	0	0	0	0	0	0	0	0	0	2	0	0
reach	648	.9328	119.71	60.8	86	115	86	109	119	60	61	12	138	22	4	27	24	101	3	120	12	8	10	4	31	57	38	49	0
reached	886	.8754	155.29	61.9	144	192	122	129	157	82	43	17	349	17	6	61	13	88	2	33	16	3	4	1	98	92	46	57	0
Reacher	6	.0000	.2741	34.4	6	0	0	0	0	0	0	0	6	0	0	0	0	0	0	0	0	0	0	0	0	0	0	0	0
reaches	195	.8118	31.811	55.0	23	27	28	42	41	17	11	6	20	3	0	7	2	33	0	72	12	2	1	1	3	14	13	12	0
reaching	132	.8753	23.080	53.6	11	22	18	21	23	13	17	7	36	4	3	9	0	18	0	20	3	0	2	1	4	10	11	11	0
react	45	.6467	6.0187	47.8	1	5	9	5	13	5	6	1	5	2	0	6	0	5	0	16	0	0	0	0	1	0	7	3	0
reacted	10	.4844	1.0358	40.2	0	0	1	0	3	4	2	0	1	0	0	0	0	0	0	2	1	0	0	0	0	0	2	4	0
reacting	9	.5913	1.0819	40.3	0	0	2	0	1	1	3	2	0	1	0	1	0	0	0	0	0	1	1	0	0	1	1	3	0
reaction	135	.7452	20.378	53.1	2	8	7	31	39	19	25	4	12	5	2	2	3	3	0	55	3	0	0	3	2	3	20	22	0
Reaction	3	.2076	.1618	32.1	0	0	3	0	0	0	0	0	0	0	0	0	2	0	0	1	0	0	0	0	0	0	0	0	0
reactions	51	.6502	6.8161	48.3	0	0	8	6	15	11	10	1	4	0	1	2	0	0	0	24	0	0	2	3	0	1	12	2	0
reactive	5	.3636	.4034	36.1	0	0	0	0	3	1	1	0	0	0	0	0	0	0	0	2	0	0	0	0	0	0	2	1	0
reactor	19	.4128	1.7332	42.4	0	0	0	11	6	2	0	0	0	0	0	0	0	1	0	13	0	0	0	1	0	0	0	4	0
reactors	7	.2430	.4215	36.2	0	0	0	2	4	1	0	0	0	0	0	0	0	0	0	4	0	0	0	0	0	0	0	3	0
reacts	19	.4332	1.7942	42.5	0	1	1	5	7	2	3	0	0	1	0	0	0	1	0	11	0	0	0	0	0	0	5	1	0
read	3057	.9250	561.18	67.5	604	541	341	387	609	288	254	33	1071	528	47	132	247	220	196	115	84	30	20	33	99	127	23	83	2
Read	11	.4452	1.1210	40.5	4	0	0	0	2	1	2	2	4	3	0	0	0	3	0	0	0	0	0	0	0	0	0	1	0
readable	3	.3811	.2534	34.0	0	0	0	0	2	0	0	1	0	0	0	0	0	0	0	1	0	0	0	0	0	1	0	1	0

8E rationals
3R rats'
9M rattail
6R Ratterree
7R Rattle
5D rattlesnake-skin
8A rattletrap
4J Rattlin'
7A ratty
6A Ratty
7P Raubal
9F Raul
4J rauschpfeife
5N raveled
9L raveling
9L ravels
6J Ravens
4N raving
7B ravioli
7Q ravished
5F raw-fur
7H rawins
7H rawinsonde
3P Rawlings'
7N ray-fish
4A rayed
9L Rayon
5Q Rays
7R razed
7Q razor-thin
3P razors
7N razzed
3P razzle-dazzler
7E RBC
9B Rd
3J re-animated
8J re-appear
6J re-arrange
9N re-baited
9H re-converted
9H re-converts
8A re-created
8M re-drawn
9H re-emit
7N re-enforced
5P re-enforcements
8F re-enslaved
6P re-entering
6N re-enters
6E re-equip
9F re-equipped
8G re-examine
8F re-examined
7R re-form
4K re-making
8E re-name
8E re-named
7R re-run
5A re-spon-si-bil-i-ty
4N re-union
6J re-write
9Q reabsorb
4J reach'd
6H REACT
8M reactance
3P reaction-control
7R reactor's
7R Reactors

Word Type	F	D	U	SFI	3 Gr 3	4 Gr 4	5 Gr 5	6 Gr 6	7 Gr 7	8 Gr 8	9 Gr 9	X UnGr	A Read	B Eng & Gr	C Comp	D Lit	E Math	F Soc Stud	G Spell	H Sci	J Music	K Art	L Home Ec	M Shop	N Lib F	P Lib NF	Q Lib Ref	R Mag	S Rel
reader	256	.5417	29.512	54.7	22	51	15	8	51	43	56	10	65	89	33	12	3	13	2	2	2	0	0	0	2	8	15	10	0
Reader	4	.2417	.3028	34.8	1	3	0	0	0	0	0	0	3	0	0	0	0	0	0	0	0	0	0	0	1	0	0	0	0
reader's	24	.2726	1.4256	41.5	0	4	0	0	1	9	10	0	1	10	11	1	0	0	0	0	0	1	0	0	0	0	0	0	0
Reader's	3	.2257	.1583	32.0	0	0	0	0	2	0	1	0	0	2	0	1	0	0	0	0	0	0	0	0	0	0	0	0	0
readers	86	.5896	10.738	50.3	4	6	12	5	15	18	18	8	29	14	11	5	0	1	1	1	0	1	0	0	3	2	1	17	0
Readers'	3	.3406	.2461	33.9	0	0	0	0	2	0	0	1	1	1	0	0	0	0	0	0	0	0	0	0	0	0	0	1	0
readily	69	.7303	10.227	50.1	3	2	4	7	22	12	15	4	11	3	0	4	1	3	2	17	0	1	4	8	3	1	9	2	0
readiness	12	.4321	1.1692	40.7	0	2	2	1	3	2	2	0	4	0	0	2	0	0	0	0	0	0	0	2	1	3	0	0	0
reading	850	.9003	152.63	61.8	121	122	95	84	205	103	106	14	366	126	8	59	36	36	18	46	37	4	5	7	24	30	11	37	0
Reading	14	.5153	1.5655	41.9	4	2	4	0	4	0	0	0	4	5	0	2	1	1	0	0	0	0	0	0	1	0	0	0	0
readings	22	.5894	2.7533	44.4	0	3	7	0	5	4	2	1	5	0	0	0	5	0	0	7	0	0	0	0	2	0	1	2	0
readjust	3	.0000	.0076	18.8	0	0	0	0	1	1	1	0	0	0	0	0	0	0	0	0	0	0	0	3	0	0	0	0	0
readjusting	3	.1927	.1491	31.7	0	0	1	0	1	1	0	0	0	0	0	0	0	0	0	1	0	0	0	0	0	0	0	2	0
readmission	4	.2090	.2014	33.0	0	0	0	0	3	0	0	1	0	0	0	0	0	0	0	0	0	0	0	0	0	0	1	3	0
readmitted	2	.0000	.0389	25.9	0	0	0	0	0	1	1	0	0	0	0	0	0	2	0	0	0	0	0	0	0	0	0	0	0
reads	120	.6902	16.864	52.3	35	24	13	15	13	7	13	0	17	46	2	5	5	7	20	2	4	0	0	2	0	2	3	4	1
ready	1207	.9372	224.13	63.5	300	283	134	145	161	103	62	19	421	119	10	60	9	98	24	71	35	5	24	6	120	127	16	60	2
Ready	2	.1698	.1133	30.5	1	0	0	0	1	0	0	0	1	0	0	0	0	0	0	0	0	0	0	0	0	0	1	0	0
ready-made	13	.4770	1.3225	41.2	0	1	2	1	2	3	4	0	2	1	1	1	0	2	0	1	0	0	4	0	0	0	0	1	0
ready-mount	4	.0000	.0789	29.0	0	0	0	0	0	4	0	0	0	0	0	0	0	0	0	4	0	0	0	0	0	0	0	0	0
ready-to-eat	4	.0000	.0129	21.1	0	0	0	0	0	1	3	0	0	0	0	0	0	0	0	0	0	0	4	0	0	0	0	0	0
readying	7	.5106	.7604	38.8	0	0	1	0	5	1	0	0	1	1	0	0	0	0	0	0	0	0	0	0	0	2	2	1	0
readymade	2	.0000	.0064	18.1	0	0	0	0	0	2	0	0	0	0	0	0	0	0	0	0	0	0	2	0	0	0	0	0	0
Readywell	5	.0000	.2284	33.6	5	0	0	0	0	0	0	0	5	0	0	0	0	0	0	0	0	0	0	0	0	0	0	0	0
reaffirm	2	.1698	.1133	30.5	1	0	0	0	0	1	0	0	1	0	0	0	0	0	0	0	0	0	0	0	0	0	1	0	0
reaffirmed	2	.0000	.0243	23.9	0	0	0	0	1	0	0	1	0	0	0	0	0	0	0	0	0	0	0	0	0	0	0	2	0
Reagan	4	.0000	.0486	26.9	0	0	0	0	1	1	0	2	0	0	0	0	0	0	0	0	0	0	0	0	0	0	0	4	0
real	910	.9343	168.40	62.3	159	142	95	80	144	131	122	37	259	46	5	61	94	61	15	52	16	20	12	6	76	71	31	85	0
Real	2	.0000	.0389	25.9	0	1	0	0	0	1	0	0	0	0	0	0	0	2	0	0	0	0	0	0	0	0	0	0	0
real-life	4	.3863	.3417	35.3	0	2	0	1	0	1	0	0	0	1	0	0	0	2	0	0	0	0	0	0	0	0	0	1	0
realio	7	.1726	.3988	36.0	4	0	3	0	0	0	0	0	3	0	0	0	0	0	0	0	0	0	0	0	0	4	0	0	0
realism	17	.5302	1.8563	42.7	0	0	3	0	8	6	0	0	0	0	0	0	0	1	0	0	3	2	0	0	0	3	4	4	0
Realism	4	.0758	.0744	28.7	0	0	0	0	0	4	0	0	0	0	0	0	0	0	0	0	0	3	0	0	0	0	1	0	0
realist	5	.4684	.5253	37.2	0	0	1	0	2	0	1	1	2	0	0	1	0	0	0	0	1	0	0	0	0	0	0	1	0
realistic	25	.4879	2.5156	44.0	0	3	2	2	7	6	5	0	1	4	0	2	0	1	0	0	5	6	2	0	0	0	3	1	0
realistically	9	.5183	.9768	39.9	0	0	2	0	3	3	1	0	1	0	0	0	0	0	0	0	1	1	0	0	1	0	2	3	0
realists	3	.2063	.1600	32.0	0	0	2	0	0	1	0	0	0	0	0	0	0	1	0	0	0	0	0	0	0	2	0	0	0
realities	12	.5554	1.4196	41.5	0	0	1	0	5	1	4	1	3	0	0	2	1	0	0	0	0	0	0	0	0	1	1	4	0
reality	56	.8024	9.0079	49.5	1	1	7	3	18	15	10	1	5	1	1	8	0	7	0	7	2	2	0	0	2	7	9	5	0
realization	14	.5780	1.7084	42.3	0	0	1	4	3	3	3	0	4	0	1	1	0	0	0	0	1	0	0	0	1	0	5	1	0
realize	183	.8835	32.165	55.1	10	13	17	17	57	31	32	6	31	8	2	20	5	21	5	22	6	0	12	2	4	13	13	19	0
realized	226	.8374	38.127	55.8	18	33	32	28	50	27	33	5	87	6	2	24	1	19	0	7	3	0	3	0	21	18	17	18	0
realizes	16	.6600	2.1971	43.4	1	1	4	2	5	2	1	0	4	0	0	1	0	2	0	2	0	0	0	0	0	2	2	3	0
realizing	25	.6443	3.3514	45.3	1	4	0	0	12	3	3	2	6	0	0	2	0	1	0	3	0	0	0	0	2	1	6	4	0
really	1414	.9428	263.96	64.2	277	237	156	215	255	119	116	39	491	61	9	88	26	93	25	135	22	9	15	9	124	142	34	128	3
realm	26	.5942	3.2467	45.1	2	2	2	4	10	3	3	0	6	0	0	1	0	0	0	1	1	0	0	0	2	6	8	1	0
realms	3	.3769	.2484	34.0	0	0	0	1	1	0	1	0	0	0	0	0	0	1	0	0	0	0	0	0	0	0	1	1	0
realskole	3	.0000	.0314	25.0	3	0	0	0	0	0	0	0	0	0	0	0	0	0	0	0	0	0	0	0	0	0	3	0	0
ream	3	.2797	.1854	32.7	0	1	0	0	1	1	0	0	0	1	0	0	1	0	0	0	0	0	0	1	0	0	0	0	0
reams	3	.3856	.2526	34.0	0	1	1	0	0	1	0	0	0	0	0	0	1	0	0	0	0	0	0	0	1	1	0	0	0
reap	8	.5299	.9267	39.7	1	0	0	3	3	1	0	0	3	0	0	0	1	0	0	0	0	0	0	0	1	1	2	0	0
reaper	19	.5482	2.2419	43.5	0	7	5	0	1	5	0	1	4	0	0	0	0	9	1	0	0	0	0	0	0	3	1	1	0
reapers	5	.3704	.4149	36.2	1	0	0	0	0	4	0	0	0	0	0	0	0	3	0	0	1	0	0	0	0	1	0	0	0
reaping	4	.2338	.2367	33.7	0	0	3	0	1	0	0	0	0	0	0	1	0	3	0	0	0	0	0	0	0	0	0	0	0
reappear	5	.3836	.4751	36.8	1	0	0	2	2	0	0	0	3	0	0	0	0	0	0	0	0	0	0	0	1	0	1	0	0
reappeared	12	.4019	1.1161	40.5	4	0	1	2	4	0	1	0	4	0	0	0	0	0	0	0	0	0	0	0	2	1	0	5	0
reappearing	2	.2437	.1129	30.5	0	0	0	1	1	0	0	0	0	0	0	0	0	0	0	0	0	0	0	0	0	0	1	1	0
reappears	2	.2446	.1257	31.0	0	0	0	0	1	0	1	0	0	0	0	0	0	1	0	1	0	0	0	0	0	0	0	0	0
reappraisal	3	.1169	.1277	31.1	0	0	0	0	1	1	1	0	1	0	0	0	0	0	0	0	0	0	0	0	0	0	2	0	0
rear	162	.7794	25.474	54.1	12	18	5	18	64	23	16	6	30	2	3	18	0	2	1	17	1	0	0	8	19	20	9	32	0
Rear	4	.3709	.3633	35.6	0	0	1	1	1	0	1	0	2	0	0	0	0	0	0	0	0	0	0	0	0	0	1	1	0
rear-view	2	.0000	.0914	29.6	0	0	0	2	0	0	0	0	2	0	0	0	0	0	0	0	0	0	0	0	0	0	0	0	0
rear-vision	2	.1787	.1174	30.7	0	0	0	0	2	0	0	0	1	0	0	0	0	0	0	0	0	0	0	0	1	0	0	0	0
rear'd	2	.0000	.0290	24.6	0	0	0	0	2	0	0	0	0	0	0	0	0	0	0	0	0	0	0	0	0	2	0	0	0
reared	35	.6326	4.6567	46.7	4	4	1	8	12	4	1	1	12	0	0	6	0	2	0	0	0	0	0	0	6	2	2	5	0
rearing	8	.3958	.7063	38.5	1	2	2	1	2	0	0	0	1	0	0	0	0	0	0	0	0	0	0	0	2	4	0	1	0
rearrange	24	.4592	2.3674	43.7	0	1	3	5	9	5	1	0	2	7	1	0	13	0	0	0	1	0	0	0	0	0	0	0	0
rearranged	7	.4846	.7321	38.6	0	1	0	2	1	2	1	0	1	1	0	0	0	0	0	3	1	0	1	0	0	0	0	0	0
rearrangement	7	.3517	.5491	37.4	0	0	2	0	1	0	1	3	0	0	0	0	2	0	0	2	0	0	0	0	0	0	3	0	0
rearrangements	2	.2391	.1133	30.5	0	0	1	0	0	0	0	1	0	0	0	0	1	0	0	0	0	0	0	0	0	0	1	0	0
rearranging	10	.5265	1.1074	40.4	0	2	1	1	3	1	1	1	1	4	0	0	2	0	0	0	0	0	0	0	1	0	1	1	0
rearward	3	.2159	.1532	31.9	0	1	0	0	1	0	1	0	0	0	0	0	0	0	0	0	0	0	0	0	0	0	2	1	0
reason	701	.9440	130.86	61.2	63	103	68	103	157	93	97	17	152	47	10	43	27	102	11	94	16	2	10	3	36	49	34	65	0
Reason	4	.3806	.3303	35.2	0	0	0	0	0	1	3	0	0	0	0	0	2	0	0	0	1	0	0	0	0	0	0	1	0
reasonable	67	.7938	10.707	50.3	0	5	10	2	14	14	18	4	11	7	0	5	6	8	0	8	0	0	6	1	5	3	3	4	0
reasonably	26	.6853	3.6447	45.6	1	2	1	4	7	4	7	0	4	1	2	5	0	1	0	3	1	0	0	0	0	5	2	2	0
reasoned	18	.5993	2.3166	43.6	1	1	2	2	5	3	4	0	7	0	1	1	0	1	1	6	0	0	0	0	0	0	0	1	0
reasoning	43	.6144	5.4396	47.4	0	0	5	5	9	13	10	1	0	3	0	2	21	1	1	9	0	0	0	0	1	1	3	1	0
reasons	367	.8310	61.043	57.9	32	35	36	60	77	66	57	4	51	52	19	17	8	85	5	33	4	2	17	0	11	18	20	25	0
reassemble	4	.3231	.3124	34.9	0	0	0	0	3	0	1	0	1	0	0	1	2	0	0	0	0	0	0	0	0	0	0	0	0
reassurance	3	.2197	.2090	33.2	1	0	1	1	0	0	0	0	2	0	0	0	0	0	0	0	0	0	0	0	0	0	1	0	0
reassure	5	.5396	.5739	37.6	0	2	1	1	0	1	0	0	1	1	0	0	0	0	0	0	0	0	0	0	1	1	0	1	0
reassured	11	.4780	1.1747	40.7	0	2	0	2	3	1	3	0	4	1	0	1	0	0	0	1	0	0	0	0	4	0	0	0	0
reassuring	11	.5857	1.3765	41.4	1	0	1	5	1	3	0	0	4	0	0	1	0	1	0	0	1	0	0	0	3	0	1	0	0
reassuringly	7	.5373	.8076	39.1	1	0	0	2	3	0	1	0	2	0	0	1	0	0	0	0	0	0	0	0	2	0	1	1	0
reawakening	2	.0000	.0162	22.1	0	0	0	0	0	2	0	0	0	0	0	0	0	0	0	0	2	0	0	0	0	0	0	0	0
Reb	5	.3181	.3528	35.5	1	0	0	0	0	4	0	0	0	3	0	0	0	0	0	0	0	0	0	0	1	1	0	0	0
Reba	2	.0000	.0914	29.6	2	0	0	0	0	0	0	0	2	0	0	0	0	0	0	0	0	0	0	0	0	0	0	0	0
rebec	2	.0000	.0162	22.1	0	0	0	0	2	0	0	0	0	0	0	0	0	0	0	0	2	0	0	0	0	0	0	0	0
Rebecca	11	.4003	.9904	40.0	4	3	1	0	1	0	1	1	2	3	0	0	0	0	0	0	0	0	0	0	0	5	0	1	0
rebel	23	.6430	3.0981	44.9	0	1	4	4	10	3	1	0	6	0	0	1	0	8	0	1	3	0	0	0	1	2	0	1	0
Rebel	2	.2408	.1204	30.8	0	1	0	0	0	1	0	0	0	0	0	0	0	1	0	0	0	0	0	0	0	1	0	0	0
rebelled	13	.3772	1.1373	40.6	0	0	2	7	1	0	3	0	2	0	0	0	0	7	0	1	0	0	0	0	0	0	3	0	0
rebelling	3	.2425	.1816	32.6	0	0	0	1	0	1	1	0	0	0	0	0	0	2	0	0	0	0	0	0	0	0	0	1	0
rebellion	29	.5711	3.4403	45.4	1	1	7	3	1	8	6	2	2	0	0	0	0	4	0	0	1	0	0	0	4	2	9	7	0
Rebellion	9	.2159	.4839	36.8	0	0	4	0	2	3	0	0	0	0	0	0	0	4	0	0	0	0	0	0	0	0	5	0	0
rebellions	3	.2425	.1816	32.6	0	0	0	0	0	1	2	0	0	0	0	0	0	2	0	0	0	0	0	0	0	0	0	1	0

7A readied
7D readier
4A readin'
9H readjusted
8F readjustment
7R readmit
7R ready-to-go
8R reaffirmation
9R reaffirms
8R Reagan's
7A REAL
9Q real-estate
9F realignment
6N realising
XR realtor
9M reamed
8M reaming
4A REAPER
9J reappearance
9M reapply
4R reappointed
5Q reapportion
XP rear-engined
7Q rear-guard
7R rear-spring
9R rearmament
5E rearrangments
8A rearview
9D reason's
4D reasonableness
7Q reassert
3N reasserted
8F reasserting
9R reassessing
8R reattached
7P reaver
XQ reawakened
7J rebab
5Q Rebate
5Q rebates

Word Type	F	D	U	SFI	3 Gr 3	4 Gr 4	5 Gr 5	6 Gr 6	7 Gr 7	8 Gr 8	9 Gr 9	X UnGr	A Read	B Eng & Gr	C Comp	D Lit	E Math	F Soc Stud	G Spell	H Sci	J Music	K Art	L Home Ec	M Shop	N Lib F	P Lib NF	Q Lib Ref	R Mag	S Rel
rebellious	8	.5618	.9356	39.7	0	0	1	0	5	1	1	0	1	0	1	2	0	1	1	0	0	0	0	0	0	0	1	1	0
rebels	14	.4885	1.4614	41.6	0	1	2	0	3	4	2	2	1	0	0	2	0	3	0	0	0	0	0	0	0	3	0	5	0
Reber	2	.0000	.0394	26.0	0	0	0	0	0	2	0	0	0	0	0	0	0	0	0	2	0	0	0	0	0	0	0	0	0
rebirth	10	.4629	.9658	39.8	0	2	0	0	2	3	2	1	0	0	0	1	0	1	0	1	2	2	0	0	0	0	1	2	0
reborn	5	.4500	.5011	37.0	1	0	0	1	1	0	1	1	1	0	0	0	0	2	0	0	0	0	0	0	0	0	1	1	0
rebound	6	.2414	.3167	35.0	0	0	0	1	2	0	3	0	0	0	0	0	0	0	0	0	1	0	0	3	0	1	0	1	0
rebounded	4	.3723	.3645	35.6	0	0	1	1	1	1	0	0	2	1	0	0	0	0	0	0	0	0	0	0	0	0	0	1	0
rebounding	2	.0000	.0914	29.6	0	0	0	0	0	2	0	0	2	0	0	0	0	0	0	0	0	0	0	0	0	0	0	0	0
rebounds	2	.1620	.0760	28.8	0	1	0	0	0	0	1	0	0	0	0	0	0	0	0	0	0	0	0	1	0	0	0	1	0
rebozos	2	.1042	.0600	27.8	0	1	0	1	0	0	0	0	0	0	0	0	0	1	0	0	0	1	0	0	0	0	0	0	0
Rebs	3	.2120	.1548	31.9	1	0	0	0	0	2	0	0	0	0	0	0	0	0	0	0	0	0	0	0	2	1	0	0	0
rebuff	2	.2337	.1157	30.6	0	0	0	0	1	1	0	0	0	0	0	0	0	1	0	0	0	0	0	0	1	0	0	0	0
rebuffed	2	.2408	.1204	30.8	0	0	0	0	1	0	1	0	0	0	0	0	0	1	0	0	0	0	0	0	0	1	0	0	0
rebuild	12	.5804	1.4739	41.7	1	1	2	3	3	0	2	0	2	0	0	1	0	5	0	0	0	0	0	0	0	2	1	1	0
rebuilding	19	.6408	2.5462	44.1	5	3	2	2	3	2	2	0	5	0	1	0	0	5	0	0	0	0	0	0	2	3	2	1	0
rebuilt	27	.5223	3.0536	44.8	5	2	3	10	4	2	1	0	6	0	0	0	0	10	0	0	1	0	0	0	0	2	7	1	0
rebuked	4	.3266	.3036	34.8	0	0	0	0	2	2	2	0	1	1	1	1	0	0	0	0	0	0	0	0	0	0	0	1	0
recalcitrant	2	.2433	.1158	30.6	0	0	0	0	1	0	1	0	0	0	0	0	0	0	0	0	0	0	0	0	0	1	0	1	0
recall	138	.8333	23.051	53.6	0	16	16	27	41	19	18	1	21	6	5	4	25	15	3	36	4	1	0	0	3	2	8	5	0
recalled	38	.7431	5.7491	47.6	1	4	1	7	8	8	7	2	8	2	0	2	0	7	0	2	0	1	0	0	2	2	3	9	0
recalling	7	.4661	.7289	38.6	1	1	1	2	0	0	2	0	3	0	1	0	0	0	0	0	1	0	0	1	0	1	0	0	0
recalls	27	.5473	3.1170	44.9	1	1	4	2	4	10	3	2	5	0	1	1	0	0	0	0	1	1	0	0	0	1	1	16	0
recapitulation	4	.0000	.0323	25.1	0	0	0	0	0	4	0	0	0	0	0	0	0	0	0	0	4	0	0	0	0	0	0	0	0
recapture	6	.5374	.6888	38.4	0	0	1	0	2	3	0	0	1	1	0	0	0	2	0	0	0	0	0	0	1	0	0	1	0
recaptured	4	.3418	.2942	34.7	1	0	0	0	1	2	0	0	0	0	0	0	0	0	0	0	2	0	0	0	0	0	1	1	0
recaptures	2	.2411	.1091	30.4	0	0	0	0	2	0	0	0	0	0	0	1	0	0	0	0	1	0	0	0	0	0	0	0	0
recede	5	.4236	.4585	36.6	0	0	1	1	0	1	2	0	1	0	0	0	0	0	0	0	0	1	1	0	0	0	1	1	0
receded	7	.5043	.7573	38.8	1	0	0	1	5	0	0	0	1	0	0	1	0	1	0	0	0	0	0	0	2	2	0	0	0
recedes	2	.1948	.1250	31.0	0	0	1	0	1	0	0	0	1	0	0	0	0	0	0	0	0	0	0	0	0	1	0	0	0
receding	17	.7320	2.5010	44.0	0	0	0	0	12	1	4	0	0	0	0	2	1	1	0	2	0	1	1	0	3	1	2	3	0
receipt	14	.6212	1.8085	42.6	0	4	2	0	6	0	2	0	3	0	1	2	0	0	1	0	0	0	0	0	2	4	0	1	0
receipts	7	.3122	.4965	37.0	0	0	4	0	0	0	3	0	0	1	0	0	5	0	0	0	0	0	0	0	1	0	0	0	0
receive	246	.6803	34.259	55.3	28	22	43	31	47	33	30	12	29	8	7	6	54	31	3	27	6	1	2	5	8	18	24	13	4
received	370	.9280	67.979	58.3	37	39	52	50	74	54	54	10	62	26	4	20	62	46	1	22	14	1	3	5	18	24	29	33	0
receiver	82	.5630	9.7047	49.9	4	4	17	20	13	17	5	2	9	5	0	4	0	0	0	36	0	0	0	10	3	2	10	3	0
receiver's	2	.2433	.1158	30.6	0	0	0	1	1	0	0	0	0	0	0	0	0	0	0	0	0	0	0	0	0	1	0	1	0
receivers	13	.5155	1.3950	41.4	1	2	1	2	5	1	1	0	0	0	0	0	0	0	0	3	2	0	0	1	0	0	1	6	0
receives	113	.8340	18.783	52.7	3	10	21	15	13	9	36	6	3	7	1	0	8	25	2	15	22	1	5	3	0	3	10	8	0
receiving	66	.7751	10.303	50.1	4	4	7	9	16	10	15	1	5	2	2	7	2	6	0	18	2	0	0	0	0	6	9	7	0
recent	246	.8541	41.873	56.2	9	7	26	36	69	33	54	12	15	15	3	6	9	65	3	28	7	1	2	1	4	8	39	40	0
recently	211	.8397	35.392	55.5	5	16	20	33	64	23	32	18	20	13	2	6	1	37	4	25	1	1	1	3	7	13	19	58	0
receptacle	5	.3749	.4195	36.2	0	0	0	0	1	1	2	1	0	0	0	0	0	0	0	3	0	0	0	0	0	0	1	1	0
reception	25	.5610	2.9473	44.7	0	1	3	0	12	5	4	0	5	0	0	4	0	0	0	1	0	0	0	3	2	0	5	5	0
receptions	6	.3784	.4853	36.9	0	0	2	0	2	2	0	0	0	0	0	0	0	1	0	0	0	0	2	0	0	1	1	1	0
receptive	4	.4806	.4072	36.1	0	0	1	0	2	0	1	0	0	0	0	0	0	1	0	0	0	0	0	0	0	1	1	1	0
receptors	4	.2278	.2257	33.5	0	0	0	0	2	0	2	0	0	0	0	0	0	0	0	2	0	0	0	0	0	0	2	0	0
recess	38	.7345	5.7221	47.6	14	8	3	4	4	1	1	3	13	1	2	2	1	0	1	2	0	0	0	0	6	4	1	5	0
recesses	4	.3771	.3227	35.1	0	1	0	0	2	1	0	0	0	0	0	1	0	0	1	0	0	0	0	0	2	0	0	0	0
recession	4	.3286	.3009	34.8	0	0	0	0	0	1	2	1	0	0	0	0	0	1	0	1	0	0	0	0	0	0	0	2	0
recessive	6	.0000	.1183	30.7	0	0	0	5	0	1	0	1	0	0	0	0	0	0	0	6	0	0	0	0	0	0	0	0	0
Recife	3	.0000	.0583	27.7	0	0	2	0	1	0	0	0	0	0	0	0	0	3	0	0	0	0	0	0	0	0	0	0	0
recipe	49	.5162	5.2426	47.2	2	4	10	6	4	9	11	3	1	3	1	1	18	1	1	1	0	0	13	0	0	2	1	6	0
Recipe	2	.0000	.0299	24.8	0	0	2	0	0	0	0	0	0	0	0	0	2	0	0	0	0	0	0	0	0	0	0	0	0
recipes	21	.2004	.9495	39.8	0	1	1	0	5	7	5	2	0	1	0	0	2	0	0	1	0	0	13	0	0	1	0	3	0
recipient	2	.2300	.1140	30.6	0	0	0	0	0	0	2	2	0	1	0	0	0	0	0	1	0	0	0	0	0	0	0	0	0
recipients	6	.3788	.5050	37.0	0	0	0	0	0	1	1	4	0	0	0	0	0	0	0	3	0	0	0	0	0	0	1	2	0
reciprocal	67	.0617	1.7445	42.4	0	2	6	16	4	30	8	1	0	0	0	0	65	0	0	0	0	0	0	0	0	0	2	0	0
reciprocals	18	.0000	.2694	34.3	0	2	1	8	2	4	1	0	0	0	0	0	18	0	0	0	0	0	0	0	0	0	0	0	0
reciprocating	3	.2227	.1495	31.7	0	2	0	0	0	1	1	0	0	0	0	0	0	0	0	0	0	0	0	1	0	0	2	0	0
recital	4	.3279	.3043	34.8	0	0	0	2	1	0	1	0	1	1	1	0	0	0	0	0	0	0	0	0	0	0	1	0	0
recitals	4	.0000	.0323	25.1	0	0	2	0	2	0	0	0	0	0	0	0	0	0	0	0	4	0	0	0	0	0	0	0	0
recitation	2	.1717	.1142	30.6	0	0	1	0	0	0	1	0	1	0	0	1	0	0	0	0	0	0	0	0	0	0	0	0	0
recitations	3	.3271	.2364	33.7	0	0	0	1	1	0	1	0	1	1	0	0	0	0	0	0	1	0	0	0	0	0	0	0	0
recitative	5	.2063	.2450	33.9	0	0	0	2	0	3	0	0	0	0	0	0	0	0	0	0	3	0	0	0	0	2	0	0	0
recitatives	5	.1313	.1696	32.3	0	0	0	2	0	3	0	0	0	0	0	0	0	0	0	0	4	0	0	0	0	1	0	0	0
recite	21	.5959	2.6395	44.2	1	3	1	1	11	2	2	0	6	1	0	3	1	1	0	1	6	0	0	0	1	1	0	0	0
recited	18	.6214	2.3280	43.7	0	0	3	0	10	2	2	1	4	0	1	5	0	1	0	1	1	0	0	0	4	0	1	0	0
reciting	4	.2431	.2111	33.2	0	0	1	0	1	1	1	0	0	0	1	0	0	0	0	0	3	0	0	0	0	0	0	0	0
reckless	13	.5623	1.5620	41.9	0	1	4	2	2	2	1	1	4	0	0	0	0	1	1	0	2	0	0	0	1	0	0	4	0
recklessly	6	.4124	.5480	37.4	0	4	1	0	2	1	1	0	1	0	0	2	0	0	0	0	0	0	0	0	2	1	0	0	0
recklessness	4	.2954	.2881	34.6	0	0	0	0	0	0	4	0	1	0	0	2	0	0	0	0	0	0	0	0	0	0	0	1	0
reckon	63	.5611	7.5483	48.8	6	7	10	7	21	6	5	1	18	2	0	15	1	3	0	0	0	0	0	0	18	4	0	2	0
reckoned	17	.6225	2.1876	43.4	1	1	2	7	7	3	1	0	3	1	1	2	0	0	0	0	0	0	0	0	5	0	3	2	0
reckoning	12	.4908	1.2519	41.0	0	0	0	1	2	2	1	0	1	0	0	1	0	1	0	0	0	0	0	0	5	1	0	3	0
reclaim	5	.3806	.4395	36.4	0	0	0	0	4	0	0	0	1	0	0	0	0	1	0	1	0	0	0	0	0	0	2	0	0
reclaimed	10	.3912	.8821	39.5	1	0	0	2	6	0	1	0	1	0	0	0	0	5	0	0	0	0	0	0	1	0	3	0	0
reclamation	8	.2585	.4790	36.8	1	0	1	0	0	0	0	6	0	0	0	0	0	0	0	0	0	0	0	0	0	1	1	6	0
Reclamation	5	.0824	.1675	32.2	0	0	0	1	0	0	0	4	1	0	0	0	0	0	0	0	0	0	0	0	0	0	0	4	0
recline	2	.0000	.0219	23.4	0	0	0	0	1	1	0	0	0	2	0	0	0	0	0	0	0	0	0	0	0	0	0	0	0
reclining	5	.5384	.5724	37.6	0	1	0	0	2	1	0	1	1	1	0	1	0	0	0	0	0	0	0	0	0	1	0	1	0
recognition	56	.8216	9.2342	49.7	1	0	7	4	16	17	10	1	11	1	1	2	1	9	0	3	7	0	1	0	2	4	9	5	0
recognizable	13	.6757	1.7895	42.5	1	0	0	1	5	2	3	1	1	2	0	1	0	0	1	3	1	1	0	0	0	2	1	0	0
recognize	234	.9005	41.890	56.2	24	21	29	26	56	40	30	8	60	35	7	8	8	10	5	28	16	5	8	1	4	13	14	12	0
recognized	169	.8730	29.405	54.7	11	8	19	17	44	36	28	6	32	16	1	12	5	20	3	13	6	0	2	0	9	9	28	13	0
recognizes	22	.7500	3.3243	45.2	0	1	1	2	5	7	6	0	1	4	0	1	0	2	0	4	1	0	1	0	0	2	2	4	0
recognizing	24	.8064	3.8929	45.9	1	0	2	1	7	6	5	2	6	5	1	2	0	1	1	1	1	1	0	1	0	2	1	1	0
recoil	5	.4509	.5024	37.0	0	0	0	0	2	0	3	0	1	1	0	0	0	0	0	2	0	0	0	0	0	0	0	1	0
recollect	3	.3408	.2477	33.9	1	1	0	0	0	1	0	0	1	0	0	1	0	0	0	0	0	0	0	0	0	1	0	0	0
recollected	2	.0000	.0914	29.6	0	0	0	1	1	0	0	0	2	0	0	0	0	0	0	0	0	0	0	0	0	0	0	0	0
recollection	8	.4702	.8579	39.3	0	0	0	1	3	3	1	0	4	0	0	2	0	0	1	0	0	0	0	0	1	0	0	0	0
recollections	2	.1948	.1250	31.0	0	1	1	0	0	0	0	0	1	0	0	0	0	0	0	0	0	0	0	0	0	1	0	0	0
recombination	2	.0000	.0209	23.2	0	0	0	0	2	0	0	0	0	0	0	0	0	0	0	0	0	0	0	0	0	0	2	0	0
recombined	2	.0000	.0394	26.0	0	0	0	2	0	0	0	0	0	0	0	0	0	0	0	2	0	0	0	0	0	0	0	0	0
recommend	16	.6443	2.1008	43.2	1	2	0	1	5	3	3	1	0	2	0	0	0	3	0	2	0	0	2	0	2	1	1	3	0
recommendation	7	.5684	.8352	39.2	0	0	1	0	2	1	2	1	1	0	0	1	0	0	0	1	0	0	0	0	1	1	2	1	0

8N rebelliously
5R rebelliousness
8F Rebels
3Q Rebild
7P rebounder
4K rebozo
7H rebranch
6C rebuilds
5P rebuke
9D rebukes
8Q rebus
5G rec'ord**
7R recalibrating
9D recant
9R recapitalize
XH Recent
6R receptionist
7Q receptionists
7R receptor
9M recessed
XH recessivity
6R recharged
8A recheck
6A rechinked
7R rechristened
9Q reciprocate
5Q recirculate
8H recirculated
5Q recirculates
6J recitare
7D reciter
8D recites
7N reck'ned
9D reck'ning
4R Recker
8N reckonin'
7R reclaimable
7A reclined
8B reclines
8K Reclining
8M reclose
4Q recluse
9D recognise
7N recognised
5P recognizably
9D recoiled
8F recollecting
9H recombines
8M recomended
9D recommence
6N recommenced

Word Type	F	D	U	SFI	3 Gr 3	4 Gr 4	5 Gr 5	6 Gr 6	7 Gr 7	8 Gr 8	9 Gr 9	X UnGr	A Read	B Eng & Gr	C Comp	D Lit	E Math	F Soc Stud	G Spell	H Sci	J Music	K Art	L Home Ec	M Shop	N Lib F	P Lib NF	Q Lib Ref	R Mag	S Rel
recommendations	11	.6193	1.4348	41.6	0	1	1	2	0	2	4	1	3	1	0	1	0	1	0	3	0	0	1	0	0	0	0	1	0
recommended	40	.6479	5.2575	47.2	0	1	2	4	9	10	12	2	2	1	2	0	0	3	0	4	1	0	8	4	3	1	2	9	0
recommends	8	.4187	.7209	38.6	0	0	0	1	5	0	2	0	0	1	0	0	0	2	0	2	0	0	2	0	0	0	0	1	0
recompense	4	.1349	.2265	33.6	0	0	0	3	0	0	1	0	3	0	1	0	0	0	0	0	0	0	0	0	0	0	0	0	0
reconcile	8	.4711	.7976	39.0	0	0	0	1	0	3	4	0	0	0	1	0	0	2	0	1	0	0	0	0	0	0	1	3	0
reconciliation	3	.2309	.1631	32.1	0	0	1	0	1	0	1	0	0	0	0	1	0	0	0	0	0	0	0	0	0	0	0	2	0
reconnaissance	3	.2143	.1568	32.0	0	0	0	2	0	0	1	0	0	0	0	0	0	0	0	0	0	0	0	0	0	1	0	2	0
reconnoiter	2	.2446	.1142	30.6	0	0	1	0	1	0	0	0	0	0	0	0	0	0	0	0	0	0	0	0	1	0	0	1	0
reconnoitre	2	.1787	.1174	30.7	0	0	0	1	1	0	0	0	1	0	0	0	0	0	0	0	0	0	0	0	1	0	0	0	0
reconsider	2	.2413	.1212	30.8	0	0	0	0	1	0	1	0	0	0	0	0	1	0	0	1	0	0	0	0	0	0	0	0	0
reconstruct	10	.5531	1.1588	40.6	0	2	0	1	2	3	1	1	0	0	0	0	2	3	0	2	0	0	0	0	0	0	2	1	0
reconstructed	4	.3676	.3150	35.0	0	0	1	0	2	1	0	0	0	0	0	0	0	0	0	0	1	0	0	0	0	0	2	1	0
reconstructing	4	.2278	.2257	33.5	0	0	0	0	1	1	2	0	0	0	0	0	0	0	0	2	0	0	0	0	0	0	2	0	0
reconstruction	13	.2815	.8938	39.5	0	0	0	0	4	5	4	0	1	0	0	0	0	8	0	0	0	0	0	0	0	0	4	0	0
Reconstruction	12	.2798	.8273	39.2	0	0	0	0	1	8	3	0	1	0	0	0	0	8	0	0	0	0	0	0	0	0	3	0	0
record	662	.8812	115.97	60.6	77	90	54	90	157	97	74	23	76	20	2	13	92	33	63	142	77	5	14	5	4	24	30	62	0
Record	47	.3851	3.8676	45.9	22	10	0	1	6	8	0	0	0	0	3	0	20	0	23	0	0	0	0	0	0	0	0	1	0
record-breaking	7	.5608	.8567	39.3	0	0	1	3	0	2	0	1	3	0	0	1	0	0	0	1	0	0	0	0	0	1	0	1	0
record-makers	2	.0000	.0162	22.1	0	0	0	0	2	0	0	0	0	0	0	0	0	0	0	0	2	0	0	0	0	0	0	0	0
record-making	3	.3125	.2347	33.7	0	0	0	2	1	0	0	0	1	0	0	0	0	0	0	1	1	0	0	0	0	0	0	0	0
record-playing	2	.2128	.1055	30.2	0	0	0	1	1	0	0	0	0	0	0	0	0	0	0	1	1	0	0	0	0	0	0	0	0
recorded	134	.8620	22.986	53.6	0	17	8	16	51	24	10	8	10	3	3	3	21	12	0	15	12	2	0	2	3	8	19	21	0
recorder	40	.2753	2.4888	44.0	2	12	4	6	12	2	1	1	2	3	0	0	0	1	1	2	29	0	0	0	0	0	1	1	0
Recorder	2	.2137	.1056	30.2	0	0	0	0	0	2	0	0	0	0	0	0	0	1	0	0	1	0	0	0	0	0	0	0	0
recorders	18	.2030	.8948	39.5	3	4	2	2	6	1	0	0	1	0	0	0	0	1	0	2	13	0	0	0	0	0	0	1	0
recording	193	.2628	11.324	50.5	3	28	16	38	74	26	7	1	2	5	1	1	3	3	5	8	153	0	0	0	0	0	2	10	0
Recording	2	.2375	.1088	30.4	0	0	0	0	1	1	0	0	0	0	0	0	0	0	0	0	1	0	0	0	0	0	0	1	0
recordings	40	.1841	1.7431	42.4	6	2	2	3	10	12	4	1	0	2	0	0	0	2	0	0	33	0	0	0	0	0	1	2	0
records	253	.7961	40.437	56.1	24	28	22	29	79	44	18	9	30	9	0	4	24	21	3	37	58	1	10	1	3	10	15	27	0
Records	6	.3285	.4276	36.3	2	0	0	1	0	3	0	0	0	0	0	0	0	0	0	0	3	0	0	0	2	0	0	1	0
recount	3	.1187	.1291	31.1	0	0	0	1	0	0	2	0	1	0	0	2	0	0	0	0	0	0	0	0	0	0	0	0	0
recounted	7	.4202	.6600	38.2	0	0	0	0	4	1	2	0	2	0	0	2	0	0	0	0	0	1	0	0	0	1	0	1	0
recounting	2	.2440	.1132	30.5	0	0	0	0	0	1	1	0	0	0	0	1	0	0	0	0	0	0	0	0	0	0	0	1	0
recounts	4	.3513	.3115	34.9	0	0	1	0	2	0	1	0	0	0	0	1	0	1	0	0	0	0	0	0	0	0	0	2	0
recourse	4	.3488	.3091	34.9	0	0	2	0	1	0	0	1	0	0	0	0	0	0	0	1	0	0	0	0	2	0	1	0	0
recover	37	.7461	5.6403	47.5	5	6	5	6	8	4	3	0	11	0	1	0	0	4	2	2	0	0	0	0	3	6	5	3	0
recovered	50	.7834	7.9559	49.0	1	6	6	9	11	7	7	3	15	1	0	4	1	5	1	5	0	0	0	0	3	10	3	2	0
recoveries	3	.1277	.1363	31.3	0	1	0	0	2	0	0	0	1	0	0	0	0	0	0	0	0	0	0	0	0	0	0	2	0
recovering	6	.5594	.6895	38.4	1	0	0	0	3	1	0	1	0	0	0	1	0	0	0	1	0	0	1	0	1	0	1	1	0
recovery	27	.7429	4.0700	46.1	0	1	1	5	7	9	2	2	4	0	0	3	0	4	0	5	0	1	1	0	2	0	3	4	0
Recovery	8	.4713	.8566	39.3	0	3	0	0	2	0	0	3	3	0	0	0	0	0	0	3	0	0	0	0	0	0	1	1	0
recreation	47	.8214	7.7172	48.9	4	4	2	2	7	16	10	2	4	2	2	1	2	13	0	2	7	1	3	1	0	6	2	1	0
Recreation	2	.2351	.1166	30.7	1	0	1	0	0	0	0	0	0	0	0	0	0	1	0	0	0	0	0	0	0	0	0	1	0
recreational	13	.5717	1.5346	41.9	1	0	1	0	3	4	1	3	1	0	0	0	0	0	0	1	4	0	1	0	0	1	2	3	0
Recreations	2	.0000	.0299	24.8	0	0	0	0	0	2	0	0	0	0	0	0	2	0	0	0	0	0	0	0	0	0	0	0	0
recrossed	2	.1948	.1250	31.0	0	1	0	1	0	0	0	0	1	0	0	0	0	0	0	0	0	0	0	0	0	1	0	0	0
recruit	5	.4539	.4841	36.8	0	0	1	0	2	1	1	0	0	0	0	0	0	1	0	0	0	0	0	0	1	1	0	2	0
recruited	6	.5649	.7037	38.5	0	0	1	0	1	1	3	0	0	0	0	1	0	2	0	0	0	0	0	0	0	1	1	1	0
recruiting	5	.4270	.4804	36.8	0	0	2	0	2	0	1	0	1	0	0	0	0	1	0	0	0	0	0	0	0	2	0	1	0
recruitment	2	.2346	.1166	30.7	0	0	0	0	1	0	1	0	0	0	0	0	0	0	0	1	0	0	0	0	0	0	0	1	0
recruits	7	.5557	.8376	39.2	0	0	1	2	2	1	1	0	2	0	0	0	0	2	0	0	0	0	0	0	1	0	1	1	0
rectangle	170	.2444	10.179	50.1	17	11	36	13	27	40	26	0	5	0	0	0	153	1	0	4	0	0	1	3	0	1	0	2	0
rectangles	32	.2806	2.0776	43.2	2	0	9	7	1	11	2	0	0	0	0	0	28	0	0	0	0	3	0	0	0	0	1	0	0
Rectangles	2	.0000	.0299	24.8	0	0	0	0	0	0	2	0	0	0	0	0	2	0	0	0	0	0	0	0	0	0	0	0	0
rectangular	101	.5006	10.662	50.3	11	8	16	14	23	12	14	3	3	0	0	1	75	2	0	4	0	1	4	8	0	0	2	1	0
rectangular-shaped	2	.0725	.0732	28.6	1	0	0	0	0	0	1	0	1	0	0	0	0	0	0	0	0	0	0	1	0	0	0	0	0
rectory	3	.0000	.1370	31.4	0	0	3	0	0	0	0	0	3	0	0	0	0	0	0	0	0	0	0	0	0	0	0	0	0
rectum	2	.0000	.0394	26.0	0	0	0	0	0	2	0	0	0	0	0	0	0	0	0	2	0	0	0	0	0	0	0	0	0
recumbent	2	.1387	.0689	28.4	0	0	0	1	1	0	0	0	0	0	1	0	0	0	0	0	0	0	0	0	0	1	0	0	0
recuperate	2	.2412	.1141	30.6	0	0	0	0	0	0	2	0	0	1	0	0	0	0	0	0	0	0	0	0	0	1	0	0	0
recur	4	.2353	.2382	33.8	0	0	0	0	0	0	2	2	0	0	0	0	0	0	0	3	0	0	0	0	0	0	1	0	0
recurrence	3	.3407	.2479	33.9	0	0	0	0	1	2	0	0	1	0	0	1	1	0	0	0	0	0	0	0	0	0	0	0	0
recurrent	3	.3871	.2488	34.0	0	0	0	0	0	2	0	1	0	1	0	0	0	0	0	0	0	0	0	0	0	0	1	1	0
recurring	4	.3175	.2812	34.5	0	0	0	0	2	1	1	0	0	0	0	0	0	0	0	1	2	0	0	0	0	0	1	0	0
red	1557	.9121	282.24	64.5	347	301	183	233	255	121	89	28	474	51	24	94	214	69	22	162	26	41	21	4	128	105	42	80	0
Red	393	.8198	65.252	58.1	59	30	53	63	140	34	9	5	171	8	1	17	2	52	0	2	11	3	3	0	59	16	15	33	0
red-and-green	2	.0000	.0914	29.6	2	0	0	0	0	0	0	0	2	0	0	0	0	0	0	0	0	0	0	0	0	0	0	0	0
red-and-white	6	.3786	.5797	37.6	3	0	0	1	1	1	0	0	4	0	0	0	0	0	0	1	0	0	0	0	0	0	0	1	0
red-and-white-striped	2	.2337	.1157	30.6	0	1	1	0	0	0	0	0	0	0	0	0	0	1	0	0	0	0	0	0	1	0	0	0	0
red-bearded	2	.1698	.1133	30.5	0	0	0	0	1	0	1	0	1	0	0	0	0	0	0	0	0	0	0	0	0	0	1	0	0
red-brick	5	.2422	.3874	35.9	4	1	0	0	0	0	0	0	4	0	0	0	0	0	0	0	0	0	0	0	0	1	0	0	0
red-brown	6	.3492	.4613	36.6	1	0	3	0	0	1	0	1	0	0	0	0	0	1	0	1	0	1	0	0	3	0	0	0	0
red-coated	2	.2433	.1158	30.6	1	0	1	0	0	0	0	0	0	0	0	0	0	0	0	0	0	0	0	0	0	1	0	1	0
red-coats	2	.1717	.1142	30.6	0	0	0	0	0	1	1	0	1	0	0	1	0	0	0	0	0	0	0	0	0	0	0	0	0
red-eyed	8	.3219	.6016	37.8	1	0	0	6	1	0	0	0	0	1	0	0	0	0	0	6	0	0	0	0	1	0	0	0	0
red-faced	10	.4746	1.1011	40.4	2	1	2	0	3	1	1	0	6	0	0	1	0	0	0	0	0	0	0	0	2	0	0	1	0
Red-footed	2	.0000	.0243	23.9	0	0	0	0	2	0	0	0	0	0	0	0	0	0	0	0	0	0	0	0	0	0	0	2	0
red-gold	5	.3126	.3746	35.7	1	1	0	2	0	1	0	0	1	0	0	0	0	0	0	0	0	0	0	0	2	2	0	0	0
red-haired	9	.5031	.9702	39.9	1	3	1	1	0	1	2	0	1	0	0	2	0	2	0	0	0	0	0	0	0	3	0	1	0
red-headed	6	.4279	.5869	37.7	0	0	2	1	3	0	0	0	2	0	0	2	0	1	0	0	0	0	0	0	1	0	0	0	0
red-hot	12	.5924	1.5274	41.8	3	3	0	2	0	2	2	0	5	0	0	1	0	1	0	1	0	0	0	1	0	2	1	0	0
red-orange	2	.1812	.0838	29.2	0	0	0	0	2	0	0	0	0	0	0	0	0	0	0	0	0	0	1	0	0	0	0	1	0
red-purple	2	.0857	.0784	28.9	0	0	1	0	1	0	0	0	1	0	0	0	0	0	0	0	0	0	1	0	0	0	0	0	0
red-rimmed	2	.0000	.0914	29.6	1	0	0	0	1	0	0	0	2	0	0	0	0	0	0	0	0	0	0	0	0	0	0	0	0
red-white-and-blue	3	.1187	.1291	31.1	0	0	1	0	1	1	0	0	1	0	0	2	0	0	0	0	0	0	0	0	0	0	0	0	0
red-winged	4	.3362	.3304	35.2	3	0	1	0	0	0	0	0	1	0	0	0	0	0	0	2	0	0	0	0	0	1	0	0	0
Red's	11	.3444	.8954	39.5	0	2	1	1	6	0	0	1	3	0	0	1	0	0	0	0	0	0	0	0	6	0	0	1	0
redbird	2	.0000	.0215	23.3	0	0	0	0	2	0	0	0	0	0	0	2	0	0	0	0	0	0	0	0	0	0	0	0	0
redbirds	2	.0000	.0234	23.7	1	0	0	0	1	0	0	0	0	0	0	0	0	0	0	0	0	0	0	0	2	0	0	0	0
redbud	2	.2427	.1152	30.6	0	1	0	0	0	1	0	0	0	0	0	0	0	0	0	0	0	0	0	0	1	1	0	0	0
redcoats	20	.4677	2.1750	43.4	7	9	1	0	1	2	0	0	11	0	0	0	0	1	0	0	0	0	0	0	1	6	0	1	0

8Q recomment
XR reconciled
5Q recondition
7Q reconnoitering
8Q reconquest
8Q reconsideration
7R reconstitute
7R reconstituted
9Q Reconstructionist
7Q reconstructions
8Q reconstructs
7H recontamination
8F reconversion
8F reconvert
8F reconverted
7E recopying
9Q record-buying
9F record-keeping
7E record-player
6R record-setting
5G record'**
XB Recorded
8R recorder's
8F Recorder's
7A recreant
7K recreate
8D recreations
5A recrossing
3P Recruiting
9Q Recruitment
6Q recrystallized
6P recrystallizes
5Q rectified
8H rectifier
7N rectilinear
8F rectitude
8D Rector
9Q recuperated
8Q recuperates
8R recuperation
9R recuperative
4P recurred
8Q recurrently
8J recurs
XH recurved
XR recycling
5F RedCross
3A Red-Face
6A Red-Handed
6A red-and-blue
6R red-and-gold
7R red-and-yellow
6N red-beaked
3H red-bellied
7Q red-billed
7N red-bird
3N red-cheeked
6A red-circled
9D red-coat
5N red-flannel
3A red-handled
6N red-head
7R red-lined
9D red-lipped
3P red-painted
4R red-roofed
7A red-shirted
7Q red-shouldered
9F red-sleeved
4A red-striped
7Q red-tailed
7R Red-tailed
6A red-throat
3A red-topped
9L red-violet
4A red-wheeled
9L red-wine
3J red-wing
3P red-winger
6R Redbirds
6A Redbreast
4P redbrick
7A redcap
8F redcoat

Word Type	F	D	U	SFI	3 Gr 3	4 Gr 4	5 Gr 5	6 Gr 6	7 Gr 7	8 Gr 8	9 Gr 9	X UnGr	A Read	B Eng & Gr	C Comp	D Lit	E Math	F Soc Stud	G Spell	H Sci	J Music	K Art	L Home Ec	M Shop	N Lib F	P Lib NF	Q Lib Ref	R Mag	S Rel
Redcoats	5	.2395	.3804	35.8	0	0	3	0	2	0	0	0	4	0	0	0	0	0	0	0	1	0	0	0	0	0	0	0	0
redden	2	.2331	.1157	30.6	0	0	0	0	1	0	0	1	0	0	0	0	0	0	0	1	0	0	0	0	1	0	0	0	0
reddened	6	.2877	.4366	36.4	0	0	3	1	1	0	0	1	1	0	0	0	0	0	0	4	0	0	0	0	0	0	0	1	0
redder	12	.3472	1.0898	40.4	5	0	5	2	0	0	0	0	8	0	0	0	0	0	0	0	0	0	0	0	3	1	0	0	0
reddest	5	.3349	.4111	36.1	1	0	1	0	1	1	1	0	2	0	0	2	0	0	0	0	0	0	0	0	0	0	1	0	0
reddish	21	.6203	2.7453	44.4	2	6	3	2	2	3	2	1	5	0	0	1	0	2	0	7	0	0	0	1	1	4	0	0	0
reddish-brown	10	.5841	1.2429	40.9	1	2	3	2	1	0	1	0	3	0	0	0	0	1	1	1	0	0	0	0	2	0	2	0	0
redecorating	2	.0000	.0299	24.8	0	0	0	2	0	0	0	0	0	0	0	0	2	0	0	0	0	0	0	0	0	0	0	0	0
redeem	2	.2408	.1204	30.8	0	0	0	0	1	1	0	0	0	0	0	0	0	1	0	0	0	0	0	0	0	1	0	0	0
Redeemer	3	.2444	.1814	32.6	0	0	0	1	0	2	0	0	0	0	0	0	0	2	0	0	0	0	0	0	0	0	1	0	0
redemption	3	.1937	.1495	31.7	0	0	0	0	1	0	2	0	0	0	0	0	0	1	0	0	0	0	0	0	0	0	0	2	0
redesigned	2	.2433	.1158	30.6	0	0	0	0	1	0	0	1	0	0	0	0	0	0	0	0	0	0	0	0	0	1	0	1	0
Redfield	3	.0000	.0591	27.7	0	0	0	0	3	0	0	0	0	0	0	0	0	0	0	3	0	0	0	0	0	0	0	0	0
redfish	2	.0000	.0209	23.2	0	0	0	0	2	0	0	0	0	0	0	0	0	0	0	0	0	0	0	0	0	0	2	0	0
redhead	7	.3626	.6400	38.1	0	1	2	2	2	0	0	0	4	0	0	0	0	0	0	0	0	0	0	0	0	1	0	2	0
redheads	3	.3814	.2537	34.0	0	0	0	1	1	0	1	0	0	0	0	0	1	1	0	0	0	0	0	0	0	0	0	1	0
Redhorse	4	.0000	.0778	28.9	4	0	0	0	0	0	0	0	0	0	0	0	0	4	0	0	0	0	0	0	0	0	0	0	0
rediscover	2	.2407	.1090	30.4	0	0	0	0	1	0	0	1	0	1	0	0	0	0	0	0	1	0	0	0	0	0	0	0	0
rediscovered	8	.5036	.8503	39.3	0	1	1	0	2	0	1	3	1	1	0	0	0	0	0	0	2	0	0	0	0	0	2	2	0
redistribution	2	.2401	.1133	30.5	1	0	1	0	0	0	0	0	0	0	0	0	0	0	0	0	0	0	0	0	0	1	1	0	0
redness	6	.3765	.5074	37.1	0	0	0	0	3	1	1	1	1	0	0	3	0	0	0	0	0	0	0	0	1	0	0	1	0
redolent	2	.1733	.1149	30.6	0	0	0	0	1	0	1	0	1	1	0	0	0	0	0	0	0	0	0	0	0	0	0	0	0
Redonda	3	.0000	.0583	27.7	0	0	0	0	3	0	0	0	0	0	0	0	0	3	0	0	0	0	0	0	0	0	0	0	0
redoubled	3	.3873	.2485	34.0	0	0	0	0	1	0	2	0	0	0	0	1	0	0	0	0	0	0	0	0	1	0	1	0	0
redoubts	2	.0000	.0215	23.3	0	0	0	0	2	0	0	0	0	0	0	2	0	0	0	0	0	0	0	0	0	0	0	0	0
redraw	2	.1674	.0805	29.1	0	0	0	0	1	1	0	0	0	0	0	0	0	0	0	0	0	0	1	0	0	1	0	0	0
redress	2	.2408	.1204	30.8	0	0	0	0	1	1	0	0	0	0	0	0	0	1	0	0	0	0	0	0	0	1	0	0	0
reds	11	.4953	1.1656	40.7	3	1	1	4	1	1	0	0	2	1	0	0	0	1	1	1	1	2	0	0	0	1	0	1	0
Reds	5	.1398	.1959	32.9	0	0	0	0	1	3	1	0	0	0	0	0	0	1	0	0	0	0	0	0	0	0	0	4	0
redskin	2	.0000	.0914	29.6	0	0	0	1	0	1	0	0	2	0	0	0	0	0	0	0	0	0	0	0	0	0	0	0	0
Redskin	2	.0000	.0215	23.3	0	0	0	0	2	0	0	0	0	0	0	2	0	0	0	0	0	0	0	0	0	0	0	0	0
redskins	3	.0000	.1370	31.4	0	1	0	2	0	0	0	0	3	0	0	0	0	0	0	0	0	0	0	0	0	0	0	0	0
Redskins	3	.0000	.0365	25.6	0	0	0	3	0	0	0	0	0	0	0	0	0	0	0	0	0	0	0	0	0	0	0	3	0
Redstone	2	.2405	.1205	30.8	0	0	0	1	0	0	0	1	0	0	0	0	0	0	0	1	0	0	0	0	0	1	0	0	0
reduce	90	.7050	12.852	51.1	1	9	1	10	28	14	25	2	3	2	0	2	31	3	3	16	1	0	9	1	0	1	8	10	0
reduced	101	.8912	17.871	52.5	3	6	8	13	16	23	24	8	9	6	0	3	15	10	3	16	3	2	1	1	2	4	14	12	0
reduces	19	.5877	2.2948	43.6	1	1	2	1	4	7	8	1	1	0	1	0	0	0	0	5	0	0	2	2	0	0	7	1	0
reducing	21	.6621	2.8349	44.5	0	1	0	2	7	4	7	0	2	1	0	0	7	1	0	1	0	1	3	1	0	0	3	1	0
reduction	29	.6420	3.8247	45.8	0	0	2	4	2	2	11	8	1	0	0	1	1	1	0	11	0	0	1	0	0	3	7	3	0
reductions	2	.2391	.1133	30.5	0	1	0	0	1	0	0	0	0	0	0	0	1	0	0	0	0	0	0	0	0	0	1	0	0
redwood	18	.7278	2.6592	44.2	4	3	2	3	1	3	2	0	2	3	0	0	1	5	1	1	0	0	0	1	1	0	2	1	0
Redwood	11	.2005	.6266	38.0	3	0	0	0	0	0	0	8	3	0	0	0	0	0	0	1	0	0	0	0	0	0	0	7	0
redwoods	11	.5882	1.3694	41.4	3	2	2	2	0	0	1	1	2	0	0	0	1	3	0	1	0	0	0	0	0	2	0	2	0
Redwoods	2	.2442	.1134	30.5	0	0	0	1	0	0	1	0	0	1	0	0	0	0	0	0	0	0	0	0	0	0	0	1	0
ree	3	.0995	.1144	30.6	0	3	0	0	0	0	0	0	1	0	0	0	0	0	0	0	2	0	0	0	0	0	0	0	0
reed	28	.6207	3.5766	45.5	2	5	2	6	10	2	1	0	3	2	0	2	0	4	0	0	9	1	0	0	0	3	0	4	0
Reed	83	.4831	9.0073	49.5	34	22	6	1	11	4	1	4	25	2	0	0	1	36	0	5	0	0	0	0	0	14	0	0	0
Reed's	7	.3579	.6270	38.0	2	3	0	0	1	1	0	0	3	0	0	0	0	3	0	0	0	0	0	0	0	1	0	0	0
reeds	70	.7140	10.191	50.1	13	17	9	10	17	3	0	1	14	5	0	12	0	6	0	3	13	3	0	0	1	6	1	6	0
Reeds	2	.0000	.0290	24.6	0	2	0	0	0	0	0	0	0	0	0	0	0	0	0	0	0	0	0	0	0	2	0	0	0
reedy	3	.1983	.1396	31.4	0	0	0	0	2	1	0	0	0	0	0	0	0	0	0	0	2	0	0	0	0	0	0	1	0
reef	51	.6247	6.6240	48.2	5	1	0	28	5	5	7	0	10	0	1	6	0	3	0	0	0	0	0	0	14	7	0	10	0
Reef	4	.2843	.2875	34.6	3	0	0	0	1	0	0	0	1	0	0	0	0	1	0	0	0	0	0	0	0	0	0	2	0
reef-passage	2	.0000	.0234	23.7	0	0	0	2	0	0	0	0	0	0	0	0	0	0	0	0	0	0	0	0	2	0	0	0	0
reefs	17	.6109	2.1719	43.4	3	0	0	5	4	1	4	0	4	0	1	2	0	0	0	1	0	0	0	0	0	2	2	5	0
reeked	3	.1187	.1291	31.1	0	0	1	0	1	0	1	0	1	0	0	2	0	0	0	0	0	0	0	0	0	0	0	0	0
reeking	2	.2446	.1142	30.6	0	0	0	0	1	0	1	0	0	0	0	0	0	0	0	0	0	0	0	0	1	0	0	1	0
reel	12	.3601	.9716	39.9	2	2	2	1	4	0	1	0	2	1	0	0	0	0	0	0	5	0	0	0	0	0	0	4	0
reeled	7	.4447	.7199	38.6	1	0	1	1	4	0	0	0	3	0	0	0	0	0	0	1	0	0	0	0	2	1	0	0	0
reeling	3	.2212	.2099	33.2	0	0	1	1	1	0	0	0	2	0	0	1	0	0	0	0	0	0	0	0	0	0	0	0	0
reels	5	.4208	.4637	36.7	0	0	1	1	3	0	0	0	1	0	0	0	0	0	0	0	1	0	0	0	0	0	2	1	0
reentrant	2	.0000	.0394	26.0	0	0	0	0	0	0	0	2	0	0	0	0	0	0	0	2	0	0	0	0	0	0	0	0	0
Reese	2	.0000	.0290	24.6	2	0	0	0	0	0	0	0	0	0	0	0	0	0	0	0	0	0	0	0	0	2	0	0	0
reet	2	.0000	.0215	23.3	0	0	0	0	2	0	0	0	0	0	0	2	0	0	0	0	0	0	0	0	0	0	0	0	0
Reeves	8	.1382	.2974	34.7	7	0	0	0	0	0	1	0	0	1	0	0	0	0	0	0	0	0	0	0	7	0	0	0	0
refer	202	.7921	32.007	55.1	4	12	21	21	54	39	46	5	7	57	1	2	37	11	16	26	14	0	9	6	3	0	6	7	0
referee	6	.3836	.5176	37.1	0	0	0	1	3	1	0	1	1	0	0	0	0	0	2	1	0	0	0	0	0	0	0	2	0
referee's	2	.0000	.0914	29.6	0	0	0	0	1	1	0	0	2	0	0	0	0	0	0	0	0	0	0	0	0	0	0	0	0
referees	2	.2152	.1357	31.3	0	0	0	0	1	0	1	0	1	0	0	0	0	1	0	0	0	0	0	0	0	0	0	0	0
reference	118	.8210	19.408	52.9	2	19	7	6	37	19	16	12	18	30	2	5	16	8	2	9	2	0	1	4	0	2	10	9	0
Reference	5	.2178	.2834	34.5	0	0	1	1	3	0	0	0	0	1	0	0	0	4	0	0	0	0	0	0	0	0	0	0	0
references	22	.6066	2.7161	44.3	0	0	0	0	6	5	10	1	0	6	0	3	0	1	0	3	0	0	2	3	0	0	1	3	0
referendum	10	.3436	.7612	38.8	0	0	2	0	1	1	6	0	0	0	0	0	0	2	0	0	0	0	0	0	0	0	3	5	0
referred	108	.8275	17.810	52.5	1	2	7	15	27	22	28	6	2	20	1	3	6	14	1	18	9	0	7	5	1	4	11	6	0
referring	45	.8432	7.5721	48.8	0	2	5	6	13	10	9	0	5	8	1	3	7	1	3	8	0	0	1	2	2	1	2	1	0
refers	94	.7821	14.694	51.7	1	8	5	8	24	27	20	1	4	19	5	2	7	3	4	11	15	4	0	6	0	1	11	2	0
refill	7	.4628	.6964	38.4	1	2	1	1	2	0	0	0	1	1	0	0	1	0	0	0	0	0	1	0	0	0	0	3	0
refilled	4	.3401	.3205	35.1	0	1	1	0	2	0	0	0	1	0	0	0	0	1	0	0	0	0	1	0	0	0	0	1	0
refine	12	.5986	1.4981	41.8	0	0	2	4	5	1	0	0	2	0	0	0	0	2	3	1	1	0	0	0	0	0	2	1	0
refined	38	.7354	5.7104	47.6	2	0	1	7	13	11	4	0	10	0	0	2	0	10	1	1	2	0	2	1	0	2	7	0	0
refinement	10	.1692	.4425	36.5	0	0	0	0	2	1	4	3	0	0	0	0	0	0	0	3	0	0	0	0	0	0	7	0	0
refinements	5	.4374	.4530	36.6	0	0	1	0	2	1	1	0	0	0	0	0	0	0	0	0	0	0	1	1	0	1	2	0	0
refineries	37	.2107	2.0794	43.2	6	0	13	6	6	2	3	1	0	0	0	0	0	32	0	2	0	0	0	0	0	0	3	0	0
refinery	20	.4671	2.0454	43.1	1	2	2	3	4	3	5	0	2	0	0	0	0	11	0	1	0	0	0	0	0	1	4	1	0
refining	16	.5299	1.8128	42.6	0	0	5	2	1	4	4	0	2	0	0	0	0	7	0	2	0	1	0	0	0	0	3	1	0
refinished	2	.0000	.0215	23.3	0	1	0	0	1	0	0	0	0	0	0	2	0	0	0	0	0	0	0	0	0	0	0	0	0
reflect	77	.8487	13.028	51.1	3	11	7	20	11	11	10	4	7	6	1	4	0	9	0	16	12	1	1	3	0	4	6	7	0
reflected	132	.8250	21.799	53.4	8	16	9	35	19	20	15	10	10	4	2	4	1	10	0	52	10	2	0	2	7	6	18	4	0
reflecting	30	.5655	3.6564	45.6	1	1	4	12	5	3	2	2	9	0	0	0	0	2	0	9	0	0	0	0	0	1	5	4	0
reflection	35	.7621	5.4156	47.3	2	1	1	15	7	3	5	1	7	2	1	2	0	0	0	12	1	0	0	0	3	2	2	3	0
reflections	18	.4818	1.8250	42.6	0	0	2	1	8	2	3	2	1	0	1	1	0	1	0	4	0	4	0	0	2	0	2	2	0
reflective	8	.5045	.8554	39.3	0	0	0	0	2	2	2	2	1	0	0	0	0	0	0	0	2	0	0	0	0	2	1	2	0
reflectively	2	.2427	.1152	30.6	0	0	0	0	0	0	2	0	0	0	0	0	0	0	0	0	0	0	0	0	1	1	0	0	0

9D reddening
7R reddens
5J Redding
XR reddish-bronze
7M reddish-colored
XR reddish-purple
7L redecorate
3P redeemed
3P redeemeth
9E redefinition
9R Redemptoristine
9Q redesign
XR redevelopment
7A redeyed
7H Redfield's
4P Redhead
7N redheaded
5A Redheaded
7L redirect
9Q redirecting
7L redirection
7R redirects
9Q rediscovering
9H redistilled
8R redlight
9D redly
6R Redmond-Bend
9L redo
7R redone
7N redoubling
7D redoubt
7P redoubtable
7Q redpolls
7P redrawing
9F redrawn
8F Redress
8A redshanks
7E Redtown
7R redundant
7D redwings
6R RedwoodCity
7N reed-fringed
4P Reeds'
5Q Reedy
7A reek
8R Reeks
3J Reel
6F reelected
5B Reeling
XR reenlistment
4R reentered
8G reenters
XH reentrants
3P Reese's
5R reestablish
7Q reestablishment
7R reexamination
7R ref
6F refaced
7R refectory
4Q referenced
5Q Referendum
XH refigure
9H refiner
6F refines
5A refinish
9D refinisher
6A refit
XR reflectance
6H REFLECTED
XR Reflection

Word Type	F	D	U	SFI	3 Gr 3	4 Gr 4	5 Gr 5	6 Gr 6	7 Gr 7	8 Gr 8	9 Gr 9	X UnGr	A Read	B Eng & Gr	C Comp	D Lit	E Math	F Soc Stud	G Spell	H Sci	J Music	K Art	L Home Ec	M Shop	N Lib F	P Lib NF	Q Lib Ref	R Mag	S Rel
reflector	20	.3664	1.7214	42.4	1	1	1	10	3	3	1	0	3	0	0	0	2	0	0	13	0	0	0	0	0	0	2	0	0
reflectors	4	.4574	.4121	36.2	0	0	1	0	1	1	1	0	1	0	0	0	0	1	0	1	0	0	0	0	0	0	0	1	0
reflects	52	.7618	7.9574	49.0	1	6	2	12	9	8	9	5	2	5	1	1	0	4	0	13	10	0	3	1	0	0	4	8	0
reflex	23	.1863	1.1964	40.8	0	0	8	7	2	5	1	0	0	0	0	1	0	0	0	21	0	0	0	0	0	0	1	0	0
reflexes	15	.3942	1.3111	41.2	1	0	2	5	2	1	4	0	0	0	0	0	0	0	0	9	0	0	0	0	0	1	4	1	0
reflexive	6	.0000	.0657	28.2	0	0	2	0	4	0	0	0	0	6	0	0	0	0	0	0	0	0	0	0	0	0	0	0	0
reform	41	.6040	5.0794	47.1	2	2	6	3	7	8	13	0	0	1	0	0	0	8	1	1	3	0	0	0	0	4	11	12	0
Reform	7	.2034	.3402	35.3	0	0	0	0	2	0	5	0	0	0	0	0	0	0	0	0	0	0	0	0	2	0	5	0	0
Reformation	12	.1507	.4732	36.8	0	0	4	1	5	1	1	0	0	0	0	0	0	1	0	0	0	0	0	0	0	1	10	0	0
reformatory	7	.3588	.6102	37.9	0	0	0	0	3	3	1	0	3	0	0	2	0	0	0	0	0	0	0	0	2	0	0	0	0
reformed	3	.3874	.2497	34.0	0	0	0	0	2	0	1	0	0	1	0	0	0	0	0	0	0	0	0	0	1	0	0	1	0
Reformed	5	.1649	.2071	33.2	0	0	0	1	0	3	1	0	0	0	0	0	0	0	0	0	0	0	0	0	0	0	4	1	0
reformer	4	.3603	.3219	35.1	0	1	1	0	0	2	0	0	0	0	0	0	0	1	0	0	0	0	0	0	0	2	0	1	0
reformers	11	.4892	1.1736	40.7	0	0	3	0	3	5	0	0	2	0	0	0	0	4	0	0	0	0	0	0	0	1	3	1	0
reforming	3	.2444	.1814	32.6	0	0	1	0	0	2	0	0	0	0	0	0	0	2	0	0	0	0	0	0	0	0	1	0	0
reforms	25	.6124	3.1785	45.0	0	1	7	2	5	5	5	0	2	0	0	0	0	8	0	1	1	0	0	0	1	6	5	1	0
refracted	4	.3658	.3646	35.6	0	0	0	4	0	0	0	0	2	0	0	0	0	0	0	1	0	0	0	0	0	0	1	0	0
refracting	9	.3558	.8547	39.3	0	1	0	7	0	0	0	1	7	0	0	0	0	0	0	1	0	0	0	0	0	0	1	0	0
refraction	3	.0000	.0591	27.7	0	0	0	1	0	0	1	1	0	0	0	0	0	0	0	3	0	0	0	0	0	0	0	0	0
refractor-reflector	2	.0000	.0914	29.6	0	0	0	2	0	0	0	0	2	0	0	0	0	0	0	0	0	0	0	0	0	0	0	0	0
refrain	71	.1368	2.5692	44.1	2	16	21	16	6	8	2	0	4	1	0	3	0	0	0	2	60	0	0	0	0	1	0	0	0
Refrain	9	.0000	.0728	28.6	2	5	0	2	0	0	0	0	0	0	0	0	0	0	0	0	9	0	0	0	0	0	0	0	0
refrained	2	.2291	.1135	30.5	0	0	0	0	1	1	0	0	0	0	0	1	0	0	0	1	0	0	0	0	0	0	0	0	0
refraining	2	.2160	.1362	31.3	0	0	0	1	1	0	0	0	1	0	0	0	0	0	0	1	0	0	0	0	0	0	0	0	0
refresh	8	.5584	.9326	39.7	0	0	1	2	0	2	1	2	1	1	0	0	1	0	0	0	2	0	0	0	1	0	0	2	0
refreshed	9	.5452	1.0155	40.1	0	1	0	1	2	2	2	1	0	1	1	1	3	0	0	1	0	0	0	0	0	0	0	2	0
refreshes	2	.2285	.1129	30.5	0	0	0	0	0	1	1	0	0	0	0	0	0	1	0	0	0	0	0	0	0	0	1	0	0
refreshing	11	.6443	1.4471	41.6	0	1	0	2	3	2	3	0	1	1	1	1	0	0	0	2	2	0	1	0	0	0	0	2	0
refreshment	11	.5886	1.3769	41.4	0	1	0	5	2	0	2	1	4	1	0	2	0	0	0	0	0	0	1	0	1	0	0	2	0
refreshments	22	.6268	2.8334	44.5	0	6	1	2	2	4	6	1	3	2	1	3	4	0	0	0	0	0	4	0	2	2	0	1	0
refrigerant	2	.2437	.1129	30.5	0	0	0	0	1	1	0	0	0	0	0	0	0	0	0	0	0	0	0	0	0	0	1	1	0
refrigerated	9	.3760	.7421	38.7	1	0	0	1	2	2	3	0	1	0	0	0	0	1	0	1	1	0	3	0	0	0	2	0	0
refrigeration	13	.5959	1.5696	42.0	0	2	1	0	4	1	5	0	0	0	1	0	0	2	0	0	1	0	3	1	0	0	3	2	0
refrigerator	107	.4911	11.321	50.5	24	28	8	11	7	3	26	0	18	5	0	0	3	14	0	22	0	0	25	0	11	5	3	1	0
refrigerators	29	.6836	4.0428	46.1	5	2	6	2	4	4	6	0	2	1	1	0	1	10	1	2	0	0	0	3	0	2	4	2	0
refuel	4	.4502	.4024	36.0	0	0	2	1	1	0	0	0	1	1	0	0	0	1	0	0	0	0	0	0	0	0	0	1	0
refueling	3	.2346	.1705	32.3	0	1	0	0	0	0	2	0	0	0	0	0	2	0	0	0	0	0	0	0	0	0	0	1	0
refuge	44	.6593	6.0047	47.8	2	2	10	4	15	8	2	1	11	0	1	0	0	3	1	0	1	0	0	0	3	4	14	6	0
Refuge	3	.2445	.1818	32.6	0	0	1	0	0	0	0	2	0	0	0	0	0	0	0	2	0	0	0	0	0	0	1	0	0
refugee	12	.5200	1.3062	41.2	1	0	1	1	6	0	3	0	0	0	0	0	0	2	1	0	0	0	0	0	0	5	1	3	0
refugees	20	.5899	2.4320	43.9	2	2	1	1	10	3	1	0	1	0	0	5	0	1	1	0	0	0	0	0	0	4	3	5	0
refuges	11	.0976	.4103	36.1	0	3	5	0	2	0	1	0	3	0	0	0	0	0	0	0	0	0	0	0	0	0	8	0	0
refund	4	.2442	.2268	33.6	0	0	0	0	0	0	2	2	0	2	0	0	0	0	0	0	0	0	0	0	0	0	0	2	0
refunded	2	.2442	.1134	30.5	0	0	0	0	0	0	2	0	0	1	0	0	0	0	0	0	0	0	0	0	0	0	0	1	0
refusal	16	.6219	2.0558	43.1	0	0	4	1	8	0	3	0	2	0	0	1	0	0	1	0	0	0	0	0	2	6	2	2	0
refuse	57	.7805	8.9941	49.5	4	5	4	11	13	7	11	2	14	3	2	9	0	2	3	5	0	0	3	0	3	4	0	9	0
refused	166	.7823	26.317	54.2	16	12	26	21	44	25	18	4	42	3	0	11	0	34	0	2	4	1	0	0	12	23	13	21	0
refuses	13	.5870	1.5877	42.0	1	1	2	0	1	5	1	2	2	0	0	0	0	1	0	0	2	0	1	0	1	0	1	5	0
refusing	21	.6460	2.8449	44.5	2	1	6	2	6	2	2	0	7	1	0	0	0	2	0	0	0	0	0	0	3	4	3	1	0
reg'ment	3	.0000	.0322	25.1	0	0	0	0	0	3	0	0	0	0	0	3	0	0	0	0	0	0	0	0	0	0	0	0	0
regain	18	.7046	2.6069	44.2	1	0	4	2	5	4	2	0	4	1	0	2	0	5	0	0	0	0	0	0	2	2	1	1	0
regained	22	.5955	2.7604	44.4	1	2	2	3	9	1	4	0	4	0	0	1	0	8	0	0	0	0	0	0	5	2	1	1	0
regaining	4	.4799	.4062	36.1	1	0	0	0	2	1	0	0	0	1	0	1	0	1	0	0	0	0	0	0	0	1	0	0	0
regal	5	.3254	.3979	36.0	1	1	1	1	1	0	0	0	2	0	0	0	0	0	0	0	1	1	0	0	0	1	0	0	0
Regan	2	.0000	.0914	29.6	0	0	0	2	0	0	0	0	2	0	0	0	0	0	0	0	0	0	0	0	0	0	0	0	0
regard	69	.8674	11.912	50.8	2	0	6	7	27	10	13	4	7	3	2	3	2	14	1	5	2	0	1	2	3	5	14	5	0
regarded	94	.8192	15.394	51.9	3	3	9	3	25	29	19	3	8	4	1	9	2	13	2	6	5	1	0	0	5	4	26	8	0
regarding	17	.6951	2.4099	43.8	1	1	0	2	6	3	4	0	2	0	0	1	1	3	1	2	0	0	2	0	2	1	2	0	0
regardless	52	.7905	8.2490	49.2	0	0	2	7	11	11	21	0	8	2	1	2	2	1	3	5	2	0	6	4	2	3	7	4	0
regards	7	.3780	.6159	37.9	0	1	0	1	2	1	2	0	2	0	0	0	0	1	0	0	0	0	0	0	0	0	3	1	0
regatta	3	.0000	.0434	26.4	0	0	0	3	0	0	0	0	0	0	0	0	0	0	0	0	0	0	0	0	0	3	0	0	0
regattas	2	.2433	.1158	30.6	0	0	0	1	0	0	0	1	0	0	0	0	0	0	0	0	0	0	0	0	0	1	0	1	0
regency	2	.2285	.1129	30.5	0	0	0	0	1	1	0	0	0	0	0	0	0	1	0	0	0	0	0	0	0	0	1	0	0
regent	2	.2401	.1133	30.5	0	0	2	0	0	0	0	0	0	0	0	0	0	0	0	0	0	0	0	0	0	1	1	0	0
regicide	2	.2442	.1134	30.5	0	0	0	0	1	0	1	0	0	1	0	0	0	0	0	0	0	0	0	0	0	0	0	1	0
regime	17	.4067	1.4868	41.7	0	0	2	1	1	8	5	0	0	0	0	0	0	2	0	0	0	0	0	0	0	2	6	7	0
regiment	24	.5110	2.6321	44.2	1	2	0	3	2	14	2	0	4	0	0	9	0	5	0	0	0	0	0	0	2	3	1	0	0
Regiment	3	.3395	.2468	33.9	0	0	1	2	0	0	0	0	1	0	0	0	0	0	0	0	0	0	0	0	0	1	1	0	0
regimentation	3	.2379	.1705	32.3	0	0	0	0	3	0	0	0	0	0	0	1	0	0	0	0	0	0	0	0	0	2	0	0	0
regiments	19	.5368	2.1805	43.4	0	0	0	4	1	9	1	4	4	0	0	5	0	3	0	0	0	0	0	0	0	1	1	5	0
regimes	2	.2351	.1166	30.7	0	0	0	0	0	1	1	0	0	0	0	0	0	1	0	0	0	0	0	0	0	0	0	1	0
Regina	2	.1733	.1149	30.6	0	0	0	0	0	1	1	0	1	1	0	0	0	0	0	0	0	0	0	0	0	0	0	0	0
Reginald	3	.3231	.2367	33.7	0	0	0	0	2	0	1	0	1	0	0	0	0	0	0	0	1	0	0	0	0	1	0	0	0
region	825	.6265	106.94	60.3	54	105	193	140	149	121	47	16	30	2	3	10	277	305	6	64	3	0	0	1	1	27	77	19	0
Region	19	.2016	1.0347	40.1	0	8	9	0	0	1	0	1	0	0	0	0	0	17	0	0	0	0	0	0	0	0	1	1	0
region's	4	.3863	.3414	35.3	0	0	0	1	1	0	1	1	0	0	0	0	0	2	0	0	0	0	0	0	0	0	1	1	0
regional	24	.4435	2.2991	43.6	4	0	3	1	8	3	1	4	1	0	0	1	0	8	0	1	0	0	0	0	0	0	10	3	0
regionals	2	.0000	.0243	23.9	0	0	0	0	0	0	0	2	0	0	0	0	0	0	0	0	0	0	0	0	0	0	0	2	0
regions	355	.6560	47.864	56.8	19	40	63	71	74	53	30	5	11	1	0	2	86	106	0	71	6	0	1	1	1	8	54	7	0
register	52	.7286	7.7062	48.9	7	12	1	7	11	8	6	0	10	3	0	1	2	1	0	7	12	0	0	2	1	5	6	2	0
registered	25	.7114	3.6207	45.6	0	2	5	1	8	6	2	1	2	1	0	1	4	6	0	2	0	0	0	0	0	2	4	3	0
registering	2	.2346	.1166	30.7	0	0	1	0	0	0	0	1	0	0	0	0	0	0	0	1	0	0	0	0	0	0	0	1	0
registers	8	.5740	.9427	39.7	0	0	0	2	2	2	1	1	0	0	0	1	0	0	0	2	2	0	1	0	0	1	1	0	0
registrant	2	.0000	.0209	23.2	0	0	0	0	2	0	0	0	0	0	0	0	0	0	0	0	0	0	0	0	0	0	2	0	0
registration	7	.2635	.4293	36.3	0	1	0	0	4	2	0	0	0	0	0	0	0	1	0	0	0	0	0	0	0	0	1	5	0
regret	40	.6913	5.6663	47.5	2	1	2	7	16	5	6	1	9	3	2	10	0	2	4	0	0	0	0	0	5	3	0	2	0
regretful	2	.0665	.0708	28.5	0	0	1	0	0	1	0	0	1	0	1	0	0	0	0	0	0	0	0	0	0	0	0	0	0
regretfully	7	.4673	.7408	38.7	1	1	0	0	5	0	0	0	3	0	0	1	0	0	0	0	0	0	0	0	1	0	0	2	0
regrets	9	.5144	.9917	40.0	0	0	1	1	3	3	1	0	2	2	0	0	0	0	0	0	1	0	0	0	3	0	0	1	0
regretted	9	.5427	1.0265	40.1	0	1	0	1	3	1	3	0	1	0	0	1	0	1	0	0	0	0	1	0	2	3	0	0	0
regretting	2	.2440	.1132	30.5	0	1	0	0	1	0	0	0	0	0	0	1	0	0	0	0	0	0	0	0	0	0	0	1	0
regroup	22	.0000	.3293	35.2	5	1	3	11	2	0	0	0	0	0	0	0	22	0	0	0	0	0	0	0	0	0	0	0	0
regrouped	8	.0645	.2421	33.8	4	3	0	1	0	0	0	0	1	0	0	0	7	0	0	0	0	0	0	0	0	0	0	0	0
regrouping	11	.0000	.1647	32.2	6	0	0	4	0	1	0	0	0	0	0	0	11	0	0	0	0	0	0	0	0	0	0	0	0
regular	359	.9107	64.763	58.1	7	52	41	45	84	51	69	10	40	33	2	19	33	20	27	50	16	1	22	9	11	22	21	33	0

5Q Reflector
9L refold
8E refolded
3Q reforestation
9Q REFORM
7R Reforma
9B reformate
9B reformation
5Q Reformers
9R reformism
6Q refract
6H REFRACTING
7R refractive
7R refresher
7B refreshingly
8R refried
8Q refrigerants
7L refrigerate
7H refrigerates
9F refrigerating
5Q Refrigeration
9L refrozen
7D refueled
7P refugee-camp-building
XR refunds
8B refurnish
8F refutations
7R refuted
8Q refutes
8D regalia
7A regaling
3P regardeth
7A regenerate
9H regenerated
4R regeneration
9Q regents
7Q regimen
8D regimental
6J Regimental
XR regimented
4A Regional
5P regionalist
3F Regions
6A Regis
4P Register
9C Registrar's
7R registrations
7G regrettable
XR regrowth

Word Type	F	D	U	SFI	3 Gr 3	4 Gr 4	5 Gr 5	6 Gr 6	7 Gr 7	8 Gr 8	9 Gr 9	X UnGr	A Read	B Eng & Gr	C Comp	D Lit	E Math	F Soc Stud	G Spell	H Sci	J Music	K Art	L Home Ec	M Shop	N Lib F	P Lib NF	Q Lib Ref	R Mag	S Rel
Regular	2	.0000	.0243	23.9	0	0	1	0	0	0	0	1	0	0	0	0	0	0	0	0	0	0	0	0	0	0	0	2	0
regularity	11	.6382	1.4454	41.6	0	0	0	1	3	2	3	2	1	0	0	1	3	0	0	2	1	0	0	0	0	0	2	1	0
regularly	88	.8582	15.056	51.8	3	7	10	10	26	12	15	5	8	12	0	2	2	11	2	20	2	1	1	0	4	4	8	11	0
regulars	5	.3585	.4002	36.0	1	0	0	0	0	0	4	0	0	0	0	2	0	2	0	0	0	0	0	0	0	1	0	0	0
regulate	27	.6340	3.4950	45.4	1	2	6	1	7	3	7	0	0	0	0	0	0	5	0	6	1	0	3	1	0	1	8	2	0
regulated	17	.6742	2.3426	43.7	0	0	3	0	6	6	1	1	2	0	0	0	0	0	0	2	1	0	1	0	1	3	3	4	0
regulates	15	.5422	1.6900	42.3	0	0	6	2	4	0	3	0	0	0	0	0	0	1	0	4	1	0	0	1	0	2	6	0	0
regulating	10	.3759	.8167	39.1	0	0	1	0	5	4	0	0	0	0	0	0	0	1	0	2	0	0	1	0	0	0	6	0	0
regulation	19	.4841	1.9608	42.9	0	1	5	0	4	7	2	0	2	0	0	0	0	1	0	3	0	0	2	0	0	1	9	1	0
regulations	35	.5896	4.2879	46.3	2	1	3	1	8	8	10	2	2	0	0	0	0	8	1	2	0	0	0	0	0	7	7	8	0
regulator	3	.3255	.2085	33.2	0	0	1	0	0	1	1	0	0	1	0	0	0	0	0	0	0	0	1	0	0	0	1	0	0
regulators	3	.2942	.1970	32.9	0	0	1	0	0	0	2	0	0	0	0	0	0	0	0	1	0	0	1	0	0	0	1	0	0
regulatory	5	.2316	.2703	34.3	0	0	3	0	1	0	1	0	0	0	0	0	0	0	0	0	0	0	0	0	0	0	3	2	0
rehabilitate	3	.3870	.2486	34.0	0	0	2	0	0	1	0	0	0	0	0	1	0	0	0	0	0	0	0	0	0	0	1	1	0
rehabilitation	3	.2043	.1486	31.7	0	0	2	0	0	0	1	0	0	0	0	0	0	0	0	0	0	0	0	0	0	1	2	0	0
rehearsal	16	.6063	2.0584	43.1	0	3	1	6	0	1	4	1	6	2	0	0	0	0	0	0	2	0	0	0	3	1	0	2	0
rehearsals	3	.3267	.2367	33.7	1	0	0	1	0	0	1	0	1	0	0	0	0	0	0	0	1	0	0	0	1	0	0	0	0
rehearse	6	.4653	.5882	37.7	0	1	0	1	3	1	0	0	0	1	0	0	0	0	0	0	1	0	0	0	1	3	0	0	0
rehearsed	9	.4815	.9215	39.6	0	0	2	3	0	2	2	0	1	3	0	1	0	0	0	0	0	0	0	0	3	0	1	0	0
rehearsing	8	.6018	1.0129	40.1	1	0	2	1	2	1	1	0	2	1	0	0	1	0	0	0	0	0	0	0	1	1	0	2	0
reheat	2	.2421	.0995	30.0	0	0	0	0	0	2	0	0	0	0	0	0	0	0	0	0	0	0	1	1	0	0	0	0	0
Reich	2	.2405	.1205	30.8	0	0	0	0	2	0	0	0	0	0	0	0	0	0	0	1	0	0	0	0	0	1	0	0	0
reign	30	.6631	4.0896	46.1	2	1	8	7	6	3	2	1	5	1	0	0	0	4	3	0	2	0	0	0	0	4	8	3	0
reigned	13	.7248	1.9153	42.8	2	1	3	1	4	2	0	0	2	0	0	2	0	1	0	1	1	0	0	0	2	1	2	1	0
reigning	4	.4525	.3990	36.0	0	0	0	0	1	2	1	0	1	1	0	1	0	0	0	0	0	0	0	0	1	0	0	0	0
reigns	9	.5974	1.1139	40.5	0	0	0	2	3	1	2	1	1	1	0	0	0	1	0	0	1	0	0	0	0	1	3	1	0
rein	19	.6531	2.5477	44.1	1	3	0	6	5	2	2	0	3	0	1	3	0	0	2	0	0	0	0	0	3	3	0	4	0
reincarnation	2	.0000	.0243	23.9	0	0	0	0	2	0	0	0	0	0	0	0	0	0	0	0	0	0	0	0	0	0	0	2	0
reindeer	51	.6212	6.9078	48.4	5	31	4	5	3	1	0	2	35	0	0	0	0	1	0	1	3	0	0	0	4	3	1	3	0
Reindeer	3	.0000	.0352	25.5	0	0	0	0	0	3	0	0	0	0	0	0	0	0	0	0	0	0	0	0	3	0	0	0	0
reined	4	.2872	.2840	34.5	0	2	0	0	1	1	0	0	1	0	0	2	0	0	0	0	0	0	0	0	0	1	0	0	0
reinforce	14	.3577	1.0574	40.2	0	1	0	0	4	4	4	1	0	2	0	0	0	0	0	0	1	0	6	0	1	2	0	2	0
reinforced	13	.5386	1.4346	41.6	0	0	0	0	4	4	5	0	0	0	0	0	0	2	0	0	1	2	2	0	0	1	3	2	0
reinforcement	9	.4290	.8115	39.1	0	0	0	0	1	1	7	0	0	0	0	0	0	0	0	0	0	1	1	0	0	1	0	6	0
reinforcements	8	.5625	.9440	39.7	1	0	0	0	2	3	2	0	1	0	0	0	0	1	0	0	0	0	0	0	1	1	2	2	0
reinforcing	2	.1926	.0867	29.4	0	0	0	0	0	1	1	0	0	0	0	0	0	0	0	0	0	0	1	0	0	0	1	0	0
Reino	3	.0000	.0352	25.5	0	0	0	0	3	0	0	0	0	0	0	0	0	0	0	0	0	0	0	0	3	0	0	0	0
reins	53	.6642	7.3906	48.7	11	13	7	10	5	3	4	0	23	0	2	5	0	1	0	0	1	0	0	0	8	9	0	4	0
reintroduced	3	.2321	.1635	32.1	0	0	0	0	1	0	0	2	0	0	0	0	0	0	0	0	0	0	0	0	0	0	1	2	0
reinvaded	2	.0000	.0209	23.2	0	0	0	0	2	0	0	0	0	0	0	0	0	0	0	0	0	0	0	0	0	0	2	0	0
Reiser	3	.2332	.1690	32.3	2	0	0	0	1	0	0	0	0	0	0	0	0	0	0	0	0	0	0	0	0	2	0	1	0
reiterated	3	.2465	.1705	32.3	0	0	0	1	0	2	0	0	0	0	1	0	0	1	0	0	0	0	0	0	1	0	0	0	0
reject	8	.5276	.9193	39.6	0	0	0	1	3	2	2	0	3	0	0	1	0	1	1	0	0	0	0	1	0	0	0	1	0
rejected	25	.6456	3.2983	45.2	1	0	5	0	4	5	8	2	1	1	0	1	1	1	0	2	2	0	0	0	0	4	2	10	0
rejecting	4	.3771	.3293	35.2	0	0	2	0	1	0	0	1	0	0	0	0	0	0	0	0	0	0	0	0	1	2	0	1	0
rejection	10	.5092	1.0787	40.3	0	0	4	0	2	0	2	2	0	0	0	0	0	1	0	3	0	0	0	0	0	4	1	1	0
rejects	5	.4599	.4875	36.9	0	0	1	0	0	1	2	1	0	0	0	0	0	1	0	0	0	0	0	0	1	0	1	2	0
rejoice	11	.4387	1.0244	40.1	0	3	2	2	1	0	2	1	1	0	2	2	0	1	0	0	4	0	0	0	0	0	0	1	0
rejoiced	16	.6520	2.2003	43.4	1	0	2	5	2	4	1	1	7	0	0	2	0	1	0	0	0	0	0	0	2	1	2	1	0
rejoices	3	.1983	.1396	31.4	1	0	0	1	0	0	0	1	0	0	0	0	0	0	0	0	2	0	0	0	0	0	0	1	0
rejoicing	15	.5295	1.7340	42.4	3	2	2	4	2	2	0	0	6	0	1	1	0	1	0	0	4	0	0	0	0	2	0	0	0
rejoicings	2	.1787	.1174	30.7	0	0	0	1	1	0	0	0	1	0	0	0	0	0	0	0	0	0	0	0	1	0	0	0	0
rejoin	4	.3223	.3041	34.8	0	2	0	0	1	1	0	0	1	0	0	0	0	0	0	0	0	0	0	1	0	1	0	1	0
rejoined	10	.4130	.9133	39.6	1	0	0	1	3	4	1	0	2	0	2	1	0	1	0	0	0	0	0	0	3	0	0	1	0
rejoining	3	.3870	.2492	34.0	0	0	0	0	2	0	0	1	0	0	0	0	0	0	0	0	0	0	0	0	1	0	1	1	0
rejoyce	2	.0000	.0243	23.9	0	0	0	0	0	0	0	2	0	0	0	0	0	0	0	0	0	0	0	0	0	0	0	2	0
Relais	2	.0000	.0914	29.6	2	0	0	0	0	0	0	0	2	0	0	0	0	0	0	0	0	0	0	0	0	0	0	0	0
relapse	3	.0000	.0322	25.1	0	0	0	0	0	0	3	0	0	0	0	3	0	0	0	0	0	0	0	0	0	0	0	0	0
relate	38	.7284	5.5808	47.5	1	5	3	1	11	4	11	2	4	4	3	6	0	0	0	4	5	3	1	0	1	1	2	4	0
related	371	.8378	61.962	57.9	26	55	45	62	79	51	42	11	28	53	9	3	71	10	70	53	16	5	6	5	0	12	26	4	0
relates	22	.4639	2.1131	43.2	0	0	1	3	9	4	3	2	1	2	7	0	0	0	0	1	4	2	0	0	0	2	2	1	0
relating	19	.5958	2.3133	43.6	0	0	1	2	7	5	3	1	1	0	1	0	0	1	1	0	1	3	0	0	2	2	4	3	0
relation	100	.8285	16.521	52.2	2	5	11	11	27	23	17	4	5	6	3	0	15	6	0	17	6	6	4	2	2	5	15	8	0
Relation	2	.2391	.1133	30.5	0	0	1	0	0	0	1	0	0	0	0	0	1	0	0	0	0	0	0	0	0	0	1	0	0
relations	97	.7764	15.171	51.8	6	3	12	4	22	21	25	4	11	1	0	2	4	21	4	2	2	0	0	2	3	9	20	16	0
Relations	8	.3703	.6659	38.2	0	0	3	0	2	1	2	0	1	0	0	0	0	1	0	0	0	0	0	0	0	0	3	3	0
relationship	153	.7836	23.995	53.8	0	9	12	9	53	39	27	4	9	30	14	5	18	5	9	14	10	0	2	4	1	3	17	12	0
relationships	84	.8237	13.794	51.4	0	2	7	5	33	12	15	10	1	12	4	1	11	5	0	18	4	3	1	1	0	3	12	8	0
relative	149	.6795	20.465	53.1	3	7	8	15	45	31	35	5	4	26	20	5	7	1	0	27	12	1	0	8	1	6	27	4	0
relatively	125	.7474	18.798	52.7	2	2	9	4	42	25	32	9	4	1	1	2	2	11	0	24	3	1	8	2	0	8	42	16	0
relatives	87	.5567	10.286	50.1	11	14	12	7	22	11	6	4	18	9	1	4	1	8	0	11	0	1	3	0	1	13	9	6	2
relativity	16	.3470	1.2607	41.0	0	0	2	3	0	2	9	0	0	0	0	0	2	0	0	9	0	0	0	0	0	0	5	0	0
Relativity	2	.1698	.1133	30.5	0	0	1	0	0	1	0	0	1	0	0	0	0	0	0	0	0	0	0	0	0	0	1	0	0
relax	40	.7567	6.1533	47.9	3	2	4	2	13	8	5	3	9	2	0	4	0	3	0	9	2	0	2	0	0	1	2	6	0
relaxation	12	.5984	1.4944	41.7	0	0	3	1	2	2	3	1	2	0	0	1	0	0	0	1	0	0	1	0	0	1	3	3	0
relaxed	42	.8408	7.0621	48.5	1	5	6	3	13	5	8	1	9	4	1	6	0	0	0	2	4	1	1	0	6	3	2	3	0
relaxes	4	.3352	.2986	34.8	0	0	0	0	2	0	1	1	0	0	0	0	0	0	0	1	0	0	0	0	0	0	2	1	0
relaxing	9	.5062	.9590	39.8	0	1	0	0	3	2	1	2	1	0	0	1	0	0	0	1	0	0	2	0	1	0	1	2	0
relay	44	.6374	5.9912	47.8	7	4	4	17	6	5	1	0	22	0	0	1	3	0	0	5	0	0	0	0	0	4	2	7	0
Relay	2	.0000	.0914	29.6	0	0	0	2	0	0	0	0	2	0	0	0	0	0	0	0	0	0	0	0	0	0	0	0	0
relayed	8	.3459	.6435	38.1	2	1	0	0	0	3	2	0	2	2	0	0	0	0	0	1	0	0	0	2	0	1	0	0	0
relays	14	.5216	1.6090	42.1	0	2	0	6	3	3	0	0	5	0	0	0	0	0	0	4	0	0	0	1	0	3	1	0	0
release	94	.7837	14.858	51.7	4	4	16	11	36	7	15	1	15	1	0	3	1	3	1	26	6	0	1	4	3	4	18	8	0
released	103	.7996	16.586	52.2	2	10	12	12	35	12	15	5	16	3	0	7	1	8	0	25	2	0	0	1	6	7	10	17	0
releases	20	.5404	2.2726	43.6	0	0	0	3	8	4	4	1	0	1	0	2	0	0	0	12	1	0	0	0	0	0	1	3	0
releasing	21	.7141	3.0377	44.8	2	1	1	0	11	4	0	2	1	1	0	0	0	1	0	5	1	0	0	1	1	3	5	2	0
relentless	18	.5651	2.1356	43.3	0	2	1	4	8	1	1	1	3	0	0	1	0	0	0	0	0	0	0	0	3	2	4	5	0
relentlessly	8	.5851	.9904	40.0	0	0	0	1	5	1	1	0	2	0	0	0	0	1	0	0	0	0	0	0	1	1	2	1	0
relevance	5	.4085	.4628	36.7	0	0	1	0	1	0	2	1	1	0	0	0	0	1	0	0	0	0	0	0	0	1	0	2	0
relevant	4	.3647	.3180	35.0	0	0	0	0	1	0	3	0	0	0	0	0	0	0	0	0	0	0	0	0	0	1	1	2	0
reliability	7	.4954	.7456	38.7	0	2	0	0	1	1	2	1	1	0	0	0	0	1	0	0	0	0	0	0	0	2	2	1	0
reliable	36	.6473	4.8130	46.8	4	4	4	0	12	5	6	1	6	0	0	1	0	5	0	3	0	0	4	0	1	5	6	5	0
reliably	3	.1277	.1363	31.3	0	0	0	0	1	1	0	1	1	0	0	0	0	0	0	0	0	0	0	0	0	0	0	2	0
reliance	12	.6264	1.5524	41.9	0	0	1	1	5	2	3	0	1	0	0	0	0	4	1	0	1	0	0	0	0	1	1	3	0

8H regularities
9A regularized
9B regulate/regulation
7Q regurgitate
7R regurgitated
5Q rehabilitated
7D rehash
7R rehashed
7R rehashes
7Q rehashing
7R reheated
8F rehire
8R rehired
7P Reichstag's
5R Reid
5Q Reign
8A Reilly
6A Reillys'
9R reimburse
4A reindeer-keeping
3B reindeer-sled
7H reinfected
6H Reinfeld
7R reinforces
7R Reinhart
XH Reinhold
9Q reinserted
9Q reinsertion
6P reinsmen
5P reintergrated
9Q reinterpreted
8A reinterpreting
3P Reiser's
8F reiterate
9Q rejections
7R rejetting
3P rejoiceth
6A rejoicingly
7A rejuvenate
9L rejuvenating
XR rekindle
4A reklektion
7P relapses
6B Relative
8Q relativistic
7R relaxers
7F relaying
XQ relearning
7R releasible
9D relegate
8C relegated
6A relent
5A relented
9D relevancy
4A Reliability

Word Type	F	D	U	SFI	3 Gr 3	4 Gr 4	5 Gr 5	6 Gr 6	7 Gr 7	8 Gr 8	9 Gr 9	X UnGr	A Read	B Eng & Gr	C Comp	D Lit	E Math	F Soc Stud	G Spell	H Sci	J Music	K Art	L Home Ec	M Shop	N Lib F	P Lib NF	Q Lib Ref	R Mag	S Rel
Reliance	2	.0000	.0209	23.2	0	0	0	0	0	0	2	0	0	0	0	0	0	0	0	0	0	0	0	0	0	0	2	0	0
relic	4	.2441	.2254	33.5	0	1	0	0	2	0	1	0	0	0	0	0	0	0	0	0	0	0	0	0	2	0	2	0	0
relics	10	.4846	1.0378	40.2	0	1	2	1	2	2	0	2	1	0	0	0	0	1	0	0	0	0	0	0	0	3	2	3	0
relied	14	.6345	1.8369	42.6	0	0	1	0	2	6	4	1	2	2	1	1	0	3	0	1	0	0	0	0	0	1	3	0	0
relief	110	.7856	17.490	52.4	13	21	14	8	24	14	14	2	29	1	0	10	0	16	0	2	1	3	0	1	10	7	12	18	0
relies	7	.3667	.5777	37.6	0	0	0	2	4	1	0	0	1	1	0	0	0	0	0	0	0	0	0	0	0	0	1	4	0
relieve	24	.7476	3.6334	45.6	2	1	1	2	9	4	5	0	3	1	0	3	0	1	0	5	1	0	0	0	1	2	4	3	0
relieved	40	.6876	5.6802	47.5	6	5	7	7	6	3	4	2	11	2	0	0	0	2	0	3	1	0	1	0	11	4	0	5	0
relieving	4	.4466	.3993	36.0	0	0	0	0	1	0	3	0	1	1	0	1	0	0	0	1	0	0	0	0	0	0	0	0	0
religion	179	.5312	20.058	53.0	20	8	35	17	41	32	24	2	8	3	0	2	2	78	3	3	5	2	0	0	0	22	39	9	3
Religion	4	.4873	.4082	36.1	0	0	1	0	2	0	1	0	0	0	0	1	0	0	0	0	0	0	0	0	1	1	0	1	0
religions	38	.5683	4.5252	46.6	1	9	6	3	11	6	1	1	1	0	1	0	0	23	0	0	1	0	0	0	1	5	5	1	0
religious	202	.7609	30.888	54.9	7	17	30	19	44	48	30	7	7	4	1	6	4	55	1	2	25	5	0	1	2	22	57	9	1
Religious	3	.3870	.2486	34.0	0	1	0	0	1	0	1	0	0	0	0	1	0	0	0	0	0	0	0	0	0	0	1	1	0
relish	6	.4866	.6618	38.2	1	0	0	0	1	1	3	0	3	0	0	1	0	0	0	0	0	0	0	0	1	0	0	1	0
relishes	3	.1274	.0913	29.6	0	0	0	0	1	0	1	1	0	0	0	0	0	0	0	0	0	0	2	0	0	0	0	1	0
reload	3	.1409	.1472	31.7	0	2	1	0	0	0	0	0	1	0	0	0	0	0	0	0	0	0	0	0	0	2	0	0	0
reloaded	2	.1698	.1133	30.5	0	0	1	1	0	0	0	0	1	0	0	0	0	0	0	0	0	0	0	0	0	0	1	0	0
relocate	2	.2391	.1133	30.5	0	0	0	0	2	0	0	0	0	0	0	0	1	0	0	0	0	0	0	0	0	0	1	0	0
relocated	2	.0000	.0914	29.6	0	0	0	0	2	0	0	0	2	0	0	0	0	0	0	0	0	0	0	0	0	0	0	0	0
reluctance	11	.5633	1.2774	41.1	2	0	1	1	4	2	1	0	0	0	0	1	0	1	0	0	0	0	0	0	4	1	2	2	0
reluctant	18	.6538	2.4272	43.9	0	1	0	4	8	2	2	1	3	1	0	3	0	2	0	1	1	0	0	0	2	0	0	5	0
reluctantly	36	.5160	3.9186	45.9	2	4	2	6	12	9	1	0	5	1	3	10	0	0	0	0	0	0	0	0	13	0	0	4	0
rely	42	.7628	6.4364	48.1	0	3	5	4	17	4	7	2	3	5	1	3	0	3	1	3	0	0	3	0	1	3	11	5	0
relying	4	.4804	.4052	36.1	0	0	1	0	0	0	3	0	0	1	0	0	0	1	0	0	0	0	0	0	0	0	1	1	0
remain	271	.9142	49.117	56.9	12	25	41	48	63	42	33	7	41	12	4	13	6	33	10	52	8	2	7	1	5	18	37	21	1
remainder	130	.3972	11.357	50.6	5	16	21	25	42	13	8	0	4	0	0	1	103	4	0	3	1	0	2	1	0	0	9	2	0
remainders	102	.0237	1.9624	42.9	14	13	27	32	7	5	4	0	0	0	0	0	101	0	0	0	0	0	0	0	1	0	0	0	0
remained	241	.8688	41.747	56.2	17	23	26	34	63	36	31	11	41	13	3	15	9	33	3	19	8	1	0	0	21	25	33	16	1
remaining	157	.9007	28.056	54.5	11	13	17	19	34	30	26	7	17	4	0	8	28	22	4	19	3	3	6	2	7	5	13	16	0
remains	213	.8335	35.467	55.5	12	19	31	32	42	32	37	8	11	7	3	3	5	26	3	66	8	0	3	3	2	11	39	23	0
remark	47	.7843	7.4229	48.7	4	5	6	7	10	6	9	0	9	6	1	9	0	2	4	0	0	0	2	0	6	5	1	2	0
remarkable	141	.8320	23.497	53.7	9	17	16	17	38	20	19	5	23	5	2	9	0	14	2	21	2	3	0	0	9	13	29	9	0
remarkably	19	.6398	2.5115	44.0	1	1	1	1	7	4	4	0	3	1	0	3	0	1	0	1	0	0	0	0	0	2	3	5	0
remarked	62	.7020	8.8969	49.5	2	11	8	8	18	9	2	4	12	4	2	12	2	2	0	1	0	0	0	0	14	7	0	6	0
remarks	47	.7759	7.3717	48.7	3	1	10	3	7	9	12	2	10	6	3	6	1	3	3	6	0	0	1	0	3	3	0	2	0
rembo-chari	7	.0000	.0851	29.3	0	0	0	0	0	0	0	7	0	0	0	0	0	0	0	0	0	0	0	0	0	0	0	7	0
Rembrandt	17	.1724	.6694	38.3	0	0	0	0	1	8	0	8	0	0	0	0	0	0	0	0	0	8	0	0	0	1	8	0	0
Rembrandt's	4	.1493	.1383	31.4	0	0	0	0	0	2	0	2	0	0	0	0	0	0	0	0	0	2	0	0	0	0	2	0	0
remedied	3	.3345	.2080	33.2	0	0	0	0	0	0	3	0	0	0	1	1	0	0	0	0	0	0	1	0	0	0	0	0	0
remedies	13	.5324	1.5283	41.8	0	0	1	9	1	1	1	0	6	0	0	0	0	1	0	0	2	0	0	0	0	2	2	0	0
remedy	19	.6285	2.4611	43.9	0	0	2	0	8	3	5	1	2	0	0	4	0	2	0	1	0	0	1	0	0	2	1	6	0
remember	1423	.9254	260.75	64.2	211	248	178	199	299	169	100	19	276	165	9	101	125	101	210	121	53	24	19	17	73	75	3	50	1
Remember	29	.2639	1.8254	42.6	23	0	0	2	2	2	0	0	5	0	0	1	0	1	19	0	3	0	0	0	0	0	0	0	0
REMEMBER	3	.0000	.0243	23.9	3	0	0	0	0	0	0	0	0	0	0	0	0	0	3	0	0	0	0	0	0	0	0	0	0
remembered	331	.8343	55.758	57.5	63	76	42	50	48	34	16	2	148	8	1	30	3	16	1	5	10	8	1	1	37	37	6	19	0
remembering	68	.7544	10.415	50.2	7	15	9	8	12	8	8	1	16	3	0	8	3	0	4	9	0	4	0	1	9	5	0	6	0
remembers	25	.7832	3.9645	46.0	2	4	5	3	2	3	3	3	7	1	0	4	0	1	1	1	2	0	0	0	1	3	1	3	0
remembrance	10	.5499	1.1715	40.7	1	1	2	1	2	1	2	0	3	0	1	1	0	0	0	0	2	0	0	0	2	0	0	1	0
remind	101	.8413	17.007	52.3	11	14	16	19	13	12	14	2	20	4	1	11	16	12	6	6	8	4	0	0	4	3	1	5	0
reminded	86	.8371	14.465	51.6	11	20	14	15	15	6	5	0	26	2	1	10	0	8	0	1	1	1	1	1	9	16	0	9	0
reminder	23	.5664	2.7802	44.4	4	5	1	2	6	2	1	2	7	0	0	0	0	1	4	1	1	0	0	0	2	0	0	7	0
reminders	9	.4915	.9567	39.8	2	0	1	3	1	1	0	1	1	0	0	0	0	2	0	1	0	0	0	0	0	3	0	2	0
reminding	14	.5464	1.6602	42.2	1	2	0	2	6	2	0	1	5	0	0	1	0	0	0	3	0	1	0	0	3	0	1	0	0
reminds	42	.6620	5.7373	47.6	4	4	9	7	6	5	7	0	10	3	0	5	2	6	6	0	0	4	0	1	3	0	0	2	0
Remington	10	.4695	1.0913	40.4	0	6	2	1	0	1	0	0	6	0	0	1	0	0	0	0	0	0	0	0	0	0	2	1	0
reminiscence	2	.2411	.1091	30.4	0	0	0	0	1	1	0	0	0	0	0	1	0	0	0	0	1	0	0	0	0	0	0	0	0
reminiscences	2	.0000	.0243	23.9	0	0	0	0	2	0	0	0	0	0	0	0	0	0	0	0	0	0	0	0	0	0	0	2	0
reminiscent	8	.3553	.6142	37.9	1	0	0	1	3	3	0	0	0	0	0	0	0	0	0	0	1	0	0	0	0	0	4	3	0
reminiscing	2	.0000	.0394	26.0	0	0	0	0	2	0	0	0	0	0	0	0	0	0	0	2	0	0	0	0	0	0	0	0	0
remitted	2	.0000	.0234	23.7	0	0	0	1	1	0	0	0	0	0	0	0	0	0	0	0	0	0	0	0	2	0	0	0	0
remnant	10	.5656	1.1968	40.8	0	0	0	1	5	3	1	0	2	0	0	1	0	2	0	0	0	0	0	0	1	0	3	1	0
remnants	18	.5317	1.9757	43.0	0	0	2	1	14	1	0	0	0	0	3	2	0	2	0	1	1	0	0	0	0	3	5	1	0
remodeled	2	.1674	.0805	29.1	0	0	1	0	0	1	0	0	0	0	0	0	0	0	0	0	0	0	1	0	0	1	0	0	0
remodeling	5	.4815	.5043	37.0	0	0	0	1	3	0	0	1	0	1	0	0	0	0	1	0	0	0	0	0	0	2	0	1	0
remolding	2	.2285	.1129	30.5	0	0	0	0	1	1	0	0	0	0	0	0	0	1	0	0	0	0	0	0	0	0	1	0	0
remonstrance	3	.2196	.1554	31.9	0	0	0	0	1	2	0	0	0	0	0	2	0	0	0	0	0	0	0	0	1	0	0	0	0
Remonstrance	3	.0000	.0314	25.0	0	0	0	0	0	3	0	0	0	0	0	0	0	0	0	0	0	0	0	0	0	0	3	0	0
remonstrances	2	.2285	.1129	30.5	0	0	0	0	0	1	1	0	0	0	0	0	0	1	0	0	0	0	0	0	0	0	1	0	0
remorse	7	.3858	.6848	38.4	0	1	0	2	3	1	0	0	5	0	0	1	0	0	0	0	0	0	0	0	1	0	0	0	0
remorseless	2	.2427	.1152	30.6	0	0	1	0	1	0	0	0	0	0	0	0	0	0	0	0	0	0	0	0	1	1	0	0	0
remorselessly	2	.2433	.1158	30.6	0	0	0	1	0	0	1	0	0	0	0	0	0	0	0	0	0	0	0	0	0	1	0	1	0
remote	61	.8290	10.133	50.1	2	0	8	10	18	11	8	4	9	4	0	3	0	13	1	8	1	2	0	1	1	5	8	5	0
remotely	4	.4491	.4015	36.0	0	0	0	0	1	1	0	2	1	1	0	0	0	0	0	1	0	0	0	0	1	0	0	0	0
remoteness	4	.3494	.3094	34.9	0	0	0	0	4	0	0	0	0	0	0	0	0	1	0	0	0	0	0	0	2	0	1	0	0
remotest	4	.2440	.2264	33.5	0	0	0	1	0	1	1	1	0	0	0	2	0	0	0	0	0	0	0	0	0	0	0	2	0
removable	3	.2754	.1835	32.6	0	0	0	1	2	0	0	0	0	0	0	0	0	0	0	0	0	0	0	1	0	1	0	1	0
removal	28	.7650	4.3044	46.3	0	0	1	0	9	11	6	1	1	1	0	1	0	3	1	5	0	0	1	1	0	3	6	5	0
remove	215	.6569	28.724	54.6	12	22	17	16	54	52	32	10	14	4	1	5	10	8	10	50	1	3	43	26	3	13	7	17	0
removed	247	.7300	36.474	55.6	17	17	27	19	63	45	46	13	27	4	1	12	11	10	5	53	3	0	21	28	11	10	28	23	0
removes	13	.6325	1.6710	42.2	0	0	3	0	7	1	2	0	0	1	0	1	0	1	0	2	0	0	1	1	1	0	5	0	0
removing	56	.5884	6.7403	48.3	5	3	2	1	13	13	17	2	2	3	0	4	5	6	1	4	0	0	14	6	0	4	3	4	0
remuda	4	.2443	.2260	33.5	0	2	0	0	2	0	0	0	0	0	0	2	0	0	0	0	0	0	0	0	2	0	0	0	0
Remus	6	.2827	.4100	36.1	1	0	0	0	1	3	0	1	1	0	0	3	0	0	0	0	0	0	0	0	0	2	0	0	0
renaissance	3	.3665	.2412	33.8	0	0	0	0	0	2	0	1	0	0	0	0	0	1	0	0	1	0	0	0	0	0	0	1	0
Renaissance	49	.4511	4.5809	46.6	2	2	8	0	5	15	7	10	0	3	0	0	0	0	0	1	13	8	0	0	0	1	20	3	0
Renaldo	3	.0000	.1370	31.4	3	0	0	0	0	0	0	0	3	0	0	0	0	0	0	0	0	0	0	0	0	0	0	0	0
Renaldo's	5	.0000	.2284	33.6	5	0	0	0	0	0	0	0	5	0	0	0	0	0	0	0	0	0	0	0	0	0	0	0	0
rename	96	.0000	1.4370	41.6	23	34	15	17	5	2	0	0	0	0	0	0	96	0	0	0	0	0	0	0	0	0	0	0	0
renamed	21	.3647	1.7376	42.4	8	4	5	0	2	2	0	0	2	0	0	0	15	1	0	0	1	0	0	0	0	0	1	1	0
renaming	17	.0657	.4615	36.6	7	2	3	2	1	2	0	0	0	0	0	0	16	1	0	0	0	0	0	0	0	0	0	0	0
Renard	3	.0000	.0352	25.5	0	0	0	0	3	0	0	0	0	0	0	0	0	0	0	0	0	0	0	0	3	0	0	0	0
render	16	.6921	2.2338	43.5	0	1	1	1	6	4	3	0	0	1	0	3	0	2	1	0	2	0	0	0	1	0	2	4	0
rendered	21	.6414	2.7780	44.4	0	1	0	2	12	4	2	0	4	1	0	4	0	1	0	1	0	2	1	0	1	2	4	0	0
rendering	5	.4137	.4607	36.6	0	0	1	0	2	0	0	2	1	1	0	2	0	0	0	0	0	0	0	0	0	1	0	0	0
rendezvous	15	.6349	1.9575	42.9	2	1	3	0	5	3	1	0	1	0	1	1	0	3	0	1	0	0	0	0	0	2	2	4	0

7N relict
7N relicts
7P relief-etched
XR relief's
7R reliefs
7N relinquish
9L reliquefied
6B relive
XQ relocating
9D relocation
7Q remade
8A remainer
5R remaking
7R remanufactured
9D remarkin'
4N remarking
7R remarriage
9L remedying
7B remember'd
3A Remember's
4Q Remembrance
9D remembrances
8J Remendado
7R reminisces
6N remission
8G remits
8G remittance
5P remittances
8G remitting
7A remonstrated
7D remonstrating
9J remorseful
6A remorsefully
XR remote-controlled
7N remoter
3F remover
7N remunerations
7R Remy
5P Renaissance-style
6B rend
9Q renderings
5P renders
6A rendezvousing
6N rending

Word Type	F	D	U	SFI	3 Gr 3	4 Gr 4	5 Gr 5	6 Gr 6	7 Gr 7	8 Gr 8	9 Gr 9	X UnGr	A Read	B Eng & Gr	C Comp	D Lit	E Math	F Soc Stud	G Spell	H Sci	J Music	K Art	L Home Ec	M Shop	N Lib F	P Lib NF	Q Lib Ref	R Mag	S Rel
rendition	2	.2407	.1090	30.4	0	0	0	0	1	0	0	1	0	1	0	0	0	0	0	0	1	0	0	0	0	0	0	0	0
Rendova	6	.0000	.0869	29.4	0	0	0	0	6	0	0	0	0	0	0	0	0	0	0	0	0	0	0	0	0	6	0	0	0
Rene	8	.4521	.8200	39.1	0	3	1	0	2	1	1	0	3	0	0	0	1	1	0	0	0	1	0	0	1	1	0	0	0
renegade	3	.2175	.1545	31.9	0	0	0	0	2	0	1	0	0	0	0	2	0	0	0	0	0	0	0	0	0	0	0	1	0
renew	12	.5545	1.4151	41.5	1	0	1	2	3	5	0	0	3	1	0	1	0	2	1	0	0	0	2	0	0	2	0	0	0
renewal	3	.3870	.2492	34.0	0	0	1	0	1	0	1	0	0	0	0	0	0	0	0	0	0	0	0	0	1	0	1	1	0
renewed	15	.6708	2.0374	43.1	1	0	1	2	5	4	2	0	0	0	0	2	0	3	0	0	2	1	0	0	3	1	1	2	0
renews	2	.2433	.1158	30.6	0	0	0	0	1	0	1	0	0	0	0	0	0	0	0	0	0	0	0	0	0	1	0	1	0
Renfrew	2	.2346	.1166	30.7	0	0	0	1	0	0	0	1	0	0	0	0	0	0	0	1	0	0	0	0	0	0	0	1	0
Renner	5	.0000	.2284	33.6	1	0	0	4	0	0	0	0	5	0	0	0	0	0	0	0	0	0	0	0	0	0	0	0	0
Rennes	2	.0000	.0209	23.2	0	0	2	0	0	0	0	0	0	0	0	0	0	0	0	0	0	0	0	0	0	0	2	0	0
Rennie	2	.0000	.0215	23.3	0	2	0	0	0	0	0	0	0	0	0	2	0	0	0	0	0	0	0	0	0	0	0	0	0
Reno	2	.2408	.1204	30.8	0	0	0	0	0	1	1	0	0	0	0	0	0	1	0	0	0	0	0	0	0	1	0	0	0
Renoir	4	.4734	.3985	36.0	1	1	0	0	0	1	1	0	0	0	0	0	0	1	0	0	1	0	0	0	0	0	1	1	0
renounced	3	.3795	.2506	34.0	0	0	0	0	1	1	1	0	0	0	0	0	0	1	0	0	0	0	0	0	1	0	0	1	0
renown	5	.3767	.4001	36.0	0	0	0	0	2	0	3	0	0	0	0	1	0	0	0	0	0	1	0	0	0	1	2	0	0
renowned	16	.5683	1.8979	42.8	1	3	3	0	3	3	3	0	2	2	0	3	0	0	0	0	0	0	0	0	0	4	4	1	0
rent	71	.7874	11.405	50.6	28	6	9	6	10	3	8	1	31	2	0	3	7	9	2	0	0	0	0	0	5	3	4	5	0
rental	4	.4806	.4072	36.1	0	0	1	1	0	1	0	1	0	0	0	0	0	1	0	0	0	0	0	0	0	1	1	1	0
rentals	2	.2427	.1159	30.6	0	0	0	1	0	0	0	1	0	0	0	0	1	0	0	0	0	0	0	0	0	0	0	1	0
rented	30	.7706	4.6978	46.7	8	1	1	5	6	4	4	1	9	4	1	2	1	3	0	0	0	0	0	0	2	2	2	4	0
renter	5	.2443	.3861	35.9	5	0	0	0	0	0	0	0	4	0	0	0	0	0	0	0	0	0	0	0	0	0	1	0	0
renters	9	.3471	.8192	39.1	7	0	1	1	0	0	0	0	6	0	0	0	0	1	0	0	0	0	0	0	0	0	2	0	0
renters'	2	.0000	.0914	29.6	2	0	0	0	0	0	0	0	2	0	0	0	0	0	0	0	0	0	0	0	0	0	0	0	0
rents	7	.5387	.8161	39.1	3	0	1	0	1	1	1	0	2	0	0	1	0	1	0	0	0	0	0	0	0	2	0	1	0
reopened	4	.4843	.4123	36.2	0	0	1	2	0	0	0	1	0	0	0	0	1	0	0	1	0	0	0	0	0	1	0	1	0
reopening	2	.2417	.1211	30.8	0	0	0	1	0	1	0	0	0	0	0	0	1	1	0	0	0	0	0	0	0	0	0	0	0
reorganization	3	.3847	.2496	34.0	0	0	0	0	2	0	0	1	0	0	0	0	0	0	0	0	0	0	0	0	0	1	1	1	0
reorganized	6	.5649	.7039	38.5	0	1	2	0	0	0	2	1	0	1	0	0	0	2	0	0	0	0	0	0	0	1	1	1	0
Rep	2	.0000	.0243	23.9	0	0	0	0	0	0	2	0	0	0	0	0	0	0	0	0	0	0	0	0	0	0	0	2	0
repackaged	2	.0000	.0243	23.9	0	0	0	0	0	0	0	2	0	0	0	0	0	0	0	0	0	0	0	0	0	0	0	2	0
repacked	2	.2408	.1204	30.8	0	0	1	0	0	0	1	0	0	0	0	0	0	1	0	0	0	0	0	0	0	1	0	0	0
repaid	9	.4578	.9269	39.7	0	0	1	1	4	0	3	0	3	0	0	1	3	0	0	0	0	0	0	0	2	0	0	0	0
repainted	3	.0000	.0449	26.5	0	1	0	1	0	0	1	0	0	0	0	0	3	0	0	0	0	0	0	0	0	0	0	0	0
repair	81	.7577	12.396	50.9	9	10	5	10	16	15	13	3	12	3	3	1	1	14	1	7	0	0	8	5	0	7	10	9	0
repaired	42	.7769	6.5924	48.2	5	9	6	7	7	3	4	1	7	7	2	1	3	7	0	5	0	0	1	0	0	4	2	3	0
repairing	19	.6396	2.4885	44.0	1	6	0	1	2	8	1	0	2	0	0	1	1	2	1	1	0	0	3	2	0	4	1	1	0
repairman	5	.3088	.3650	35.6	0	1	1	1	0	0	2	0	1	2	0	0	0	0	0	1	0	1	0	0	0	0	0	0	0
repairmen	4	.3344	.3261	35.1	0	0	2	1	1	0	0	0	1	0	0	0	0	2	0	0	0	0	0	0	0	0	1	0	0
repairs	31	.7799	4.8908	46.9	1	1	4	4	9	6	5	1	7	4	1	0	0	5	0	4	0	0	2	1	1	1	1	4	0
repast	5	.4293	.4745	36.8	0	0	0	3	2	0	0	0	1	0	0	1	0	0	0	0	0	0	0	0	1	0	0	2	0
repay	15	.5552	1.7934	42.5	0	3	2	2	6	0	2	0	5	0	1	3	4	1	0	0	0	0	0	0	0	0	1	0	0
repayment	2	.0000	.0209	23.2	0	0	1	0	1	0	0	0	0	0	0	0	0	0	0	0	0	0	0	0	0	0	2	0	0
repays	2	.2287	.1077	30.3	0	0	0	0	0	2	0	0	0	0	0	0	1	0	0	0	1	0	0	0	0	0	0	0	0
repeal	10	.4201	.9769	39.9	0	0	3	0	4	3	0	0	3	0	0	0	0	5	0	0	0	0	0	0	0	1	0	1	0
repealed	3	.2321	.1635	32.1	0	0	1	0	0	0	0	2	0	0	0	0	0	0	0	0	0	0	0	0	0	0	1	2	0
repeat	199	.7965	31.693	55.0	18	26	18	38	37	29	33	0	15	16	2	7	21	7	4	25	60	8	10	5	4	3	4	8	0
repeated	270	.7368	40.274	56.1	20	44	39	30	63	42	24	8	44	10	1	30	28	7	0	21	67	17	0	4	14	8	8	11	0
repeatedly	19	.7062	2.7449	44.4	0	2	2	1	8	3	2	1	4	0	0	1	3	0	0	1	0	0	0	1	2	1	2	4	0
repeating	111	.5989	13.738	51.4	2	6	8	6	15	49	25	0	6	4	0	3	71	2	1	1	12	2	0	1	4	2	0	2	0
repeats	34	.6563	4.5425	46.6	3	1	1	2	8	9	9	1	1	1	0	7	12	0	0	3	6	1	0	0	0	1	1	1	0
repel	22	.2977	1.4959	41.7	3	0	6	0	4	7	2	0	0	0	0	0	0	0	0	12	0	0	0	6	0	1	3	0	0
repelled	17	.6519	2.2606	43.5	0	1	9	0	4	2	1	0	0	1	0	3	0	0	0	8	1	1	0	1	0	1	1	0	0
repelling	2	.0000	.0209	23.2	0	0	0	0	2	0	0	0	0	0	0	0	0	0	0	0	0	0	0	0	0	0	2	0	0
repent	6	.0958	.2271	33.6	1	0	0	0	3	0	2	0	2	0	0	1	0	0	0	0	0	0	0	0	1	0	0	1	1
repentance	11	.4594	1.1440	40.6	0	0	0	5	3	1	1	1	4	0	0	0	0	1	0	1	0	0	0	0	4	0	1	0	0
repented	2	.1717	.1142	30.6	0	0	0	0	1	0	0	1	1	0	0	1	0	0	0	0	0	0	0	0	0	0	0	0	0
repertoire	8	.3875	.6574	38.2	0	0	0	0	2	3	3	0	0	0	0	2	0	0	0	0	4	0	0	0	0	1	1	0	0
repertory	6	.3912	.4986	37.0	0	0	1	1	0	3	1	0	0	0	0	0	0	0	0	0	3	0	0	0	0	1	1	1	0
repetend	8	.0000	.1197	30.8	0	0	0	0	0	8	0	0	0	0	0	0	8	0	0	0	0	0	0	0	0	0	0	0	0
repetition	78	.5453	8.6900	49.4	3	7	10	17	19	11	8	3	2	10	0	8	1	1	4	1	31	12	2	0	0	2	1	3	0
repetitions	12	.4455	1.1035	40.4	0	2	0	0	3	4	2	1	0	1	0	3	0	0	1	0	5	2	0	0	0	0	0	0	0
repetitive	7	.5004	.7607	38.8	0	2	1	1	2	1	0	0	2	0	0	1	0	0	0	0	2	0	0	0	0	1	0	1	0
replace	349	.5210	38.219	55.8	74	87	45	63	39	20	19	2	8	20	0	3	255	9	11	6	2	0	2	6	2	8	6	11	0
replaceable	2	.1249	.0685	28.4	0	0	0	0	0	0	2	0	0	0	0	0	0	0	0	1	0	0	0	1	0	0	0	0	0
replaced	143	.8941	25.370	54.0	9	12	23	17	37	28	13	4	14	9	2	4	14	19	7	13	6	0	1	5	6	5	23	15	0
replacement	136	.1386	5.5102	47.4	0	9	9	39	21	33	24	1	2	0	0	0	124	1	0	3	0	0	0	0	0	0	1	5	0
replacements	23	.0804	.7123	38.5	0	10	0	2	0	7	4	0	1	0	0	0	21	1	0	0	0	0	0	0	0	0	0	0	0
replaces	27	.6225	3.4621	45.4	0	8	4	3	4	5	2	1	1	6	0	1	10	2	1	4	0	0	0	0	1	0	0	1	0
replacing	46	.6227	5.8701	47.7	0	2	12	3	14	6	7	2	1	6	0	0	20	3	2	0	0	0	0	1	0	0	4	9	0
replanted	3	.3350	.2478	33.9	0	1	0	2	0	0	0	0	1	0	0	0	0	1	0	0	0	0	0	0	0	0	1	0	0
replanting	2	.2152	.1357	31.3	0	0	1	1	0	0	0	0	1	0	0	0	0	1	0	0	0	0	0	0	0	0	0	0	0
replay	3	.3824	.2447	33.9	0	1	0	0	2	0	0	0	0	1	0	0	0	0	1	0	0	0	0	0	0	0	0	1	0
replenish	5	.3995	.4278	36.3	0	0	1	1	1	1	1	0	0	0	0	1	0	1	0	0	0	1	0	0	0	1	0	1	0
replenished	2	.2441	.1127	30.5	0	0	0	0	2	0	0	0	0	0	0	0	0	0	0	0	0	0	0	0	1	0	1	0	0
replenishing	3	.0000	.0314	25.0	0	1	0	0	2	0	0	0	0	0	0	0	0	0	0	0	0	0	0	0	0	0	3	0	0
replica	3	.2197	.2090	33.2	0	0	0	1	1	1	0	0	2	0	0	0	0	0	0	0	0	0	0	0	0	0	1	0	0
replicas	3	.3847	.2496	34.0	1	0	0	0	1	0	1	0	0	0	0	0	0	0	0	0	0	0	0	0	0	1	1	1	0
replied	439	.7356	66.378	58.2	78	112	61	61	77	28	20	2	168	21	9	42	3	19	2	0	0	0	1	0	84	64	4	22	0
replies	11	.6678	1.4899	41.7	0	0	2	0	5	3	1	0	0	2	0	2	0	2	0	0	1	0	0	0	0	1	1	2	0
reply	96	.7906	15.353	51.9	7	9	12	12	19	19	16	2	27	10	0	11	1	7	5	1	1	0	0	0	9	8	3	13	0
replying	6	.5538	.7178	38.6	0	0	1	1	1	1	1	1	2	0	0	1	0	1	0	0	0	0	0	0	1	0	0	1	0
report	457	.7842	72.202	58.6	42	92	62	63	83	56	50	9	68	146	10	8	14	47	17	56	3	0	7	1	12	19	10	39	0
Report	6	.4022	.5125	37.1	0	0	0	0	2	1	2	1	0	1	1	0	0	0	0	0	0	0	0	0	0	1	0	3	0
reported	147	.7838	23.349	53.7	11	5	21	16	44	27	20	3	39	9	1	3	10	13	2	11	0	0	0	0	1	13	15	30	0
reportedly	9	.1342	.3305	35.2	0	0	0	0	5	1	3	0	0	0	0	0	0	0	0	0	0	0	0	0	0	0	1	8	0
reporter	62	.7109	9.0502	49.6	11	8	3	6	14	6	14	0	18	13	3	9	2	6	1	0	0	0	0	0	3	1	1	5	0
Reporter	3	.0000	.1370	31.4	0	3	0	0	0	0	0	0	3	0	0	0	0	0	0	0	0	0	0	0	0	0	0	0	0
reporter's	5	.1599	.2478	33.9	1	0	0	0	2	1	1	0	2	0	2	0	0	0	0	0	0	0	0	0	0	0	0	1	0
reporters	34	.6097	4.3260	46.4	3	6	1	4	8	5	6	1	7	5	0	0	0	1	2	0	0	0	0	0	1	4	2	12	0
reporting	25	.5978	3.0819	44.9	0	4	1	1	11	3	3	2	2	7	2	0	2	0	0	1	1	0	0	0	0	4	0	6	0
Reporting	2	.2446	.1125	30.5	0	0	0	0	1	1	0	0	0	1	0	1	0	0	0	0	0	0	0	0	0	0	0	0	0
reports	167	.7923	26.665	54.3	10	13	29	30	31	23	22	9	32	41	2	4	1	22	1	14	1	0	4	3	0	3	17	22	0
repose	8	.5920	.9993	40.0	0	1	1	0	0	2	3	1	2	0	0	0	0	1	0	1	0	0	1	0	1	0	1	1	0
reposed	2	.2152	.1357	31.3	0	0	0	1	0	1	0	0	1	0	0	0	0	1	0	0	0	0	0	0	0	0	0	0	0

8J renditions
3A Renee
XR renewable
6R renewing
5Q Reni
7H rennin
4R Renoir's
9R renomination
8F renounce
5P renovate
3P renovated
XR Renshaw
9E Rent
5A renting
8G reoccurrence
8F reorganize
4Q reorganizing
XR reorient
7A rep
7P repainting
4F Repair
7R repair-cost
7R repairable
6H repairman's
8R reparations
8D repassing
9R repatriate
XR repave
9F repaying
8H repels
XH repentant
XH repenteth
7P repents
5P repercussions
4J repetions
7H repetitious
9B rephrases
9P rephrasing
7N repine
7N repinings
4A replant
5R Replay
9R replaying
7Q replenishes
9R replete
6A repletion
9H replication
5A repointed
8N report-card
8R report's
7R Report's
7B Reports
7N reposeful

Word Type	F	D	U	SFI	3 Gr 3	4 Gr 4	5 Gr 5	6 Gr 6	7 Gr 7	8 Gr 8	9 Gr 9	X UnGr	A Read	B Eng & Gr	C Comp	D Lit	E Math	F Soc Stud	G Spell	H Sci	J Music	K Art	L Home Ec	M Shop	N Lib F	P Lib NF	Q Lib Ref	R Mag	S Rel
reposes	2	.2411	.1091	30.4	0	1	0	0	1	0	0	0	0	0	0	1	0	0	0	0	1	0	0	0	0	0	0	0	0
represent	442	.7227	64.645	58.1	6	24	41	47	113	144	59	8	23	27	0	3	215	28	54	33	16	3	3	8	0	7	14	8	0
representation	20	.6443	2.6178	44.2	1	2	3	1	6	6	1	0	0	1	0	0	3	3	0	0	2	0	0	2	0	2	5	2	0
representations	14	.5123	1.4847	41.7	0	0	0	1	7	6	0	0	0	0	0	0	6	0	5	1	0	1	0	1	0	0	0	0	0
representative	53	.8228	8.7265	49.4	2	3	5	1	12	16	6	8	5	2	0	2	1	10	5	6	1	0	2	0	1	6	8	4	0
Representative	8	.4264	.7719	38.9	0	0	0	1	2	2	3	0	2	0	0	0	0	2	0	0	0	0	0	0	0	0	1	3	0
representatives	72	.5389	8.2230	49.2	5	5	8	5	21	16	10	2	5	2	0	0	1	35	0	2	0	0	0	0	0	5	16	6	0
Representatives	27	.5491	3.1452	45.0	9	1	1	1	3	9	3	0	3	1	0	0	0	9	0	0	0	0	0	0	1	10	1	2	0
represented	242	.7650	37.235	55.7	3	12	24	13	67	71	44	8	13	24	0	4	101	19	20	9	13	4	1	0	3	9	16	6	0
representing	75	.7664	11.545	50.6	2	5	1	6	21	24	15	1	4	1	1	0	31	1	3	3	6	2	0	1	1	3	13	5	0
represents	303	.7091	43.504	56.4	7	24	32	32	59	98	49	2	10	16	0	6	158	10	35	23	12	2	2	3	0	4	13	9	0
repressed	3	.3395	.2468	33.9	0	1	1	0	1	0	0	0	1	0	0	0	0	0	0	0	0	0	0	0	0	1	1	0	0
repression	5	.3336	.3687	35.7	0	0	1	0	1	2	1	0	0	0	0	0	0	0	0	0	0	0	0	0	0	1	1	3	0
repressive	2	.0000	.0243	23.9	0	0	0	0	0	1	1	0	0	0	0	0	0	0	0	0	0	0	0	0	0	0	0	2	0
reprieve	2	.0000	.0215	23.3	0	0	0	0	0	1	1	0	0	0	0	2	0	0	0	0	0	0	0	0	0	0	0	0	0
reprinted	7	.5891	.8587	39.3	0	0	1	0	2	3	0	1	1	1	0	0	0	0	0	0	0	0	0	0	1	1	1	2	0
reprisal	3	.2309	.1631	32.1	0	0	0	0	1	2	0	0	0	0	0	1	0	0	0	0	0	0	0	0	0	0	0	2	0
reprisals	2	.2285	.1129	30.5	1	0	0	0	0	1	0	0	0	0	0	0	0	1	0	0	0	0	0	0	0	0	1	0	0
reproach	9	.4228	.8319	39.2	0	1	1	1	4	1	1	0	1	0	0	2	0	0	0	0	0	0	0	0	3	3	0	0	0
reproached	4	.4518	.3982	36.0	1	0	0	0	3	0	0	0	1	0	0	1	0	0	0	0	0	0	0	0	1	0	1	0	0
reproaches	2	.0000	.0234	23.7	0	0	0	0	2	0	0	0	0	0	0	0	0	0	0	0	0	0	0	0	2	0	0	0	0
reproachfully	4	.1787	.2347	33.7	0	1	1	1	1	0	0	0	2	0	0	0	0	0	0	0	0	0	0	0	2	0	0	0	0
reproduce	66	.4824	6.8404	48.4	17	6	9	5	20	4	5	0	1	1	0	0	0	0	1	46	1	0	0	3	0	1	12	0	0
reproduced	14	.5697	1.6327	42.1	0	1	1	0	7	5	0	0	0	1	1	1	1	0	0	2	6	0	0	0	0	1	1	0	0
reproduces	6	.0000	.1183	30.7	1	0	2	0	3	0	0	0	0	0	0	0	0	0	0	6	0	0	0	0	0	0	0	0	0
reproducing	6	.4659	.5937	37.7	1	1	0	1	1	2	0	0	0	0	0	0	0	0	0	2	1	0	0	0	0	1	2	0	0
reproduction	44	.5130	4.7930	46.8	4	1	7	0	12	7	10	3	0	1	0	0	0	0	2	31	0	0	0	2	0	0	4	4	0
reproductions	3	.2321	.1635	32.1	0	0	0	0	0	0	1	2	0	0	0	0	0	0	0	0	0	0	0	0	0	0	1	2	0
reproductive	15	.2445	.9092	39.6	0	0	0	1	9	1	4	0	0	0	0	0	0	0	0	10	0	0	0	0	0	0	5	0	0
reps	3	.0000	.0365	25.6	0	0	0	0	0	0	0	3	0	0	0	0	0	0	0	0	0	0	0	0	0	0	0	3	0
reptile	43	.4437	4.0822	46.1	4	7	5	2	24	0	1	0	0	0	1	0	0	1	0	12	0	0	0	0	0	9	20	0	0
Reptile	2	.0000	.0914	29.6	0	0	2	0	0	0	0	0	2	0	0	0	0	0	0	0	0	0	0	0	0	0	0	0	0
reptiles	215	.4782	22.083	53.4	50	31	5	31	89	0	6	3	9	1	1	0	1	0	1	91	0	0	0	0	0	49	61	1	0
Reptiles	15	.3483	1.1679	40.7	1	7	2	1	4	0	0	0	0	0	0	0	0	0	0	3	0	0	0	0	0	8	4	0	0
reptilian	9	.3023	.5974	37.8	0	0	1	0	7	0	1	0	0	0	1	0	0	0	0	0	0	0	0	0	0	1	7	0	0
republic	67	.5010	7.1878	48.6	11	1	11	13	13	14	4	0	5	0	0	0	0	29	0	0	2	0	0	0	0	12	17	2	0
Republic	103	.5202	11.391	50.6	11	4	13	21	38	11	5	0	3	1	0	2	0	65	0	1	4	0	0	0	0	3	14	10	0
republican	5	.5599	.5798	37.6	1	0	0	0	1	1	2	0	0	0	0	1	0	1	0	0	0	0	0	0	0	1	1	1	0
Republican	56	.5085	6.1248	47.9	0	0	9	0	14	26	7	0	7	0	0	1	0	25	0	0	0	0	0	0	1	1	13	8	0
Republicans	34	.5317	3.8928	45.9	2	0	2	0	8	13	8	1	6	0	0	0	0	16	0	0	0	0	0	0	1	2	5	4	0
republics	27	.4519	2.6429	44.2	0	0	5	4	9	6	3	0	0	0	0	1	0	17	0	0	0	0	0	0	0	2	5	2	0
Republics	3	.1823	.1405	31.5	0	0	1	1	0	0	1	0	0	0	0	0	0	1	0	0	0	0	0	0	0	0	2	0	0
repudiated	8	.3876	.7088	38.5	0	0	0	0	5	1	2	0	2	0	0	1	0	0	0	0	0	0	0	0	1	0	0	4	0
repudiation	2	.2401	.1133	30.5	0	0	0	0	1	0	1	0	0	0	0	0	0	0	0	0	0	0	0	0	0	1	1	0	0
repugnance	3	.1250	.1342	31.3	0	0	0	0	2	1	0	0	1	0	0	0	0	0	0	0	0	0	0	0	2	0	0	0	0
repugnant	2	.0000	.0243	23.9	0	0	0	0	0	0	0	2	0	0	0	0	0	0	0	0	0	0	0	0	0	0	0	2	0
repulsed	3	.3833	.2447	33.9	0	0	0	0	2	0	1	0	0	0	0	0	0	0	0	0	1	0	0	0	1	0	1	0	0
repulsion	7	.4285	.6532	38.2	0	0	1	0	3	3	0	0	1	0	0	0	0	0	0	1	0	0	0	1	0	0	3	1	0
repulsive	8	.3015	.5595	37.5	0	0	0	1	2	1	4	0	0	4	0	0	0	1	0	3	0	0	0	0	0	0	0	0	0
reputable	3	.2043	.1486	31.7	1	1	0	0	0	0	1	0	0	0	0	0	0	0	0	0	0	0	0	0	0	1	2	0	0
reputation	65	.7555	9.9519	50.0	2	6	11	5	16	10	11	4	13	2	0	6	0	3	0	2	1	0	1	0	7	8	13	9	0
reputations	6	.4809	.6604	38.2	0	0	0	1	4	0	0	1	3	1	0	0	0	0	0	1	0	0	0	0	0	0	0	1	0
reputed	2	.2285	.1129	30.5	0	0	0	0	0	2	0	0	0	0	0	0	0	1	0	0	0	0	0	0	0	0	1	0	0
request	46	.8004	7.4297	48.7	2	4	6	4	16	6	5	3	13	7	1	5	0	3	3	0	0	0	1	0	1	3	2	7	0
requested	16	.5300	1.7936	42.5	0	1	0	3	3	4	4	1	2	0	0	3	0	2	0	0	0	0	0	0	0	1	2	6	0
requesting	8	.4961	.8469	39.3	0	0	0	1	3	3	0	1	1	2	0	2	0	0	0	1	0	0	0	0	0	0	0	2	0
requests	17	.5691	2.0429	43.1	0	1	1	1	5	4	5	0	3	3	0	3	0	3	0	1	0	0	0	0	0	0	0	4	0
require	151	.8063	24.367	53.9	4	3	11	15	34	28	48	8	14	12	1	6	13	20	3	19	4	2	17	11	1	8	15	5	0
required	236	.7658	36.302	55.6	5	13	18	20	51	46	72	11	14	17	1	5	12	39	2	29	6	1	18	25	3	13	34	17	0
requirement	20	.7021	2.8611	44.6	1	0	0	3	4	5	5	2	1	0	0	1	2	4	0	7	0	0	1	1	0	0	2	1	0
requirements	63	.8140	10.228	50.1	0	1	6	2	15	13	22	4	2	3	1	2	4	5	1	6	1	1	6	1	0	5	16	9	0
requires	139	.8474	23.448	53.7	3	5	8	20	38	25	32	8	10	17	6	3	10	10	2	22	9	1	10	8	0	8	13	10	0
requiring	22	.7301	3.2316	45.1	2	0	0	0	7	6	7	0	0	1	0	3	1	3	0	1	1	0	1	0	0	3	6	2	0
requisite	2	.2285	.1129	30.5	0	0	1	0	0	1	0	0	0	0	0	0	0	1	0	0	0	0	0	0	0	0	1	0	0
reradiate	3	.0000	.0314	25.0	0	0	3	0	0	0	0	0	0	0	0	0	0	0	0	0	0	0	0	0	0	0	3	0	0
reread	49	.4573	5.2442	47.2	3	4	12	8	12	7	3	0	31	5	6	3	0	0	3	0	1	0	0	0	0	0	0	0	0
rereading	2	.0665	.0708	28.5	0	1	0	0	0	0	1	0	1	0	1	0	0	0	0	0	0	0	0	0	0	0	0	0	0
rescind	2	.2351	.1166	30.7	0	0	0	0	0	1	1	0	0	0	0	0	0	1	0	0	0	0	0	0	0	0	0	1	0
rescinded	2	.1948	.1250	31.0	0	0	1	0	1	0	0	0	1	0	0	0	0	0	0	0	0	0	0	0	0	1	0	0	0
rescue	78	.7337	11.904	50.8	1	6	30	8	18	6	6	3	44	4	2	4	0	5	0	5	1	0	0	0	0	4	1	8	0
Rescue	7	.0000	.3198	35.0	0	4	1	0	0	2	0	0	7	0	0	0	0	0	0	0	0	0	0	0	0	0	0	0	0
rescued	29	.6367	3.9243	45.9	5	8	4	2	9	0	1	0	14	3	2	2	0	2	0	0	0	0	0	0	2	2	0	2	0
rescuer	2	.0000	.0914	29.6	0	0	1	1	0	0	0	0	2	0	0	0	0	0	0	0	0	0	0	0	0	0	0	0	0
rescuers	7	.4848	.7687	38.9	0	0	0	0	2	2	1	2	3	0	0	1	0	0	0	2	0	0	0	0	0	0	1	0	0
rescues	3	.3845	.2497	34.0	0	0	1	0	1	1	0	0	0	0	0	1	1	0	0	0	0	0	0	0	1	0	0	0	0
rescuing	3	.2437	.2277	33.6	0	0	0	1	0	1	0	1	2	0	0	0	0	0	0	1	0	0	0	0	0	0	0	0	0
research	215	.7605	32.977	55.2	8	14	17	33	46	36	41	20	14	12	0	1	2	16	2	67	5	1	5	2	0	13	55	20	0
Research	21	.5351	2.3489	43.7	0	2	4	2	5	0	5	3	2	1	0	0	0	0	0	0	0	0	1	0	1	1	7	8	0
researched	3	.2277	.1555	31.9	0	0	1	0	2	0	0	0	0	0	0	0	0	0	0	0	0	0	1	0	0	0	0	2	0
researcher	4	.3750	.3392	35.3	0	0	0	0	3	1	0	0	0	0	0	0	0	1	0	2	0	0	0	0	0	0	0	1	0
researchers	11	.3651	.8841	39.5	0	0	1	0	3	2	3	2	0	0	0	0	0	0	0	3	0	0	0	0	0	0	4	4	0
researches	3	.0000	.0314	25.0	0	0	0	0	2	0	1	0	0	0	0	0	0	0	0	0	0	0	0	0	0	0	3	0	0
researching	2	.2441	.1127	30.5	0	0	0	0	0	0	2	0	0	0	0	0	0	0	0	0	0	0	0	0	1	0	1	0	0
reseed	2	.0000	.0914	29.6	0	0	1	1	0	0	0	0	2	0	0	0	0	0	0	0	0	0	0	0	0	0	0	0	0
resemblance	22	.7492	3.3429	45.2	1	0	2	3	4	5	2	5	4	1	0	1	1	0	0	5	0	0	1	1	1	1	5	1	0
resemblances	7	.3247	.4924	36.9	0	0	0	0	3	1	3	0	0	0	0	0	0	0	0	0	0	0	1	0	0	0	5	1	0
resemble	57	.7991	9.1594	49.6	4	3	7	8	14	11	8	2	8	0	1	4	0	7	2	14	3	1	4	0	0	6	7	0	0
resembled	24	.7525	3.6450	45.6	3	3	2	1	7	4	2	2	3	0	1	4	0	0	0	3	2	1	0	0	2	5	2	1	0
resembles	38	.7509	5.7803	47.6	1	2	4	6	13	6	5	1	6	3	1	2	0	4	0	5	3	0	0	0	0	3	9	2	0
resembling	20	.7337	2.9588	44.7	0	3	0	2	8	2	4	1	2	1	1	1	0	0	2	2	1	1	0	0	0	1	6	2	0
resent	11	.6258	1.4185	41.5	0	1	0	0	4	2	2	2	1	1	0	2	0	2	1	0	0	0	0	0	0	1	0	3	0
resented	8	.3356	.6130	37.9	0	0	1	2	4	0	0	1	1	0	0	0	0	0	0	0	0	0	0	0	1	0	1	5	0
resentful	13	.3999	1.1410	40.6	1	0	8	0	2	1	0	1	1	0	0	0	0	1	0	0	0	0	0	0	1	1	1	8	0
resenting	2	.1787	.1174	30.7	0	0	0	0	2	0	0	0	1	0	0	0	0	0	0	0	0	0	0	0	1	0	0	0	0
resentment	19	.6461	2.5074	44.0	1	0	1	1	7	3	5	1	1	0	0	2	0	2	0	0	0	0	1	0	4	2	1	6	0
resentments	2	.2351	.1166	30.7	0	0	0	0	0	0	2	0	0	0	0	0	0	1	0	0	0	0	0	0	0	0	0	1	0

7H repositioned
7H repositioning
9R repository
8F reprehensible
3P representare
7D repress
7P repressions
8J reprieved
8L reprimand
6C reprimanded
8A reprints
6N reproachful-like
5N reproaching
7Q reprogram
7A reprove
4N reproved
4A reprovingly
5A REPTILE
5P reptile's
7Q reptiles'
5F REPUBLIC
8F republic's
5P republicanism
8Q Republika
7N repudiate
8F repudiating
4P repulsing
9B repulsively
7Q repurchases
8R Requiem
7N requireth
9D requisition
9D requite
3A rereads
8J rerecord
7R rerunning
5Q resale
7P rescrubbing
4A RESCUE
3N reseeding
9F resell
9R resenter
8A resentfully

Word Type	F	D	U	SFI	3 Gr 3	4 Gr 4	5 Gr 5	6 Gr 6	7 Gr 7	8 Gr 8	9 Gr 9	X UnGr	A Read	B Eng & Gr	C Comp	D Lit	E Math	F Soc Stud	G Spell	H Sci	J Music	K Art	L Home Ec	M Shop	N Lib F	P Lib NF	Q Lib Ref	R Mag	S Rel
resents	2	.2412	.1141	30.6	0	1	0	0	1	0	0	0	0	1	0	0	0	0	0	0	0	0	0	0	0	1	0	0	0
reservation	48	.6884	6.8355	48.3	15	20	4	1	6	0	1	1	13	0	0	3	1	10	0	0	0	0	0	0	7	6	2	6	0
Reservation	12	.4067	1.0931	40.4	1	3	1	0	5	0	0	2	2	0	0	0	3	0	0	0	0	0	0	0	0	2	0	5	0
reservations	19	.5719	2.3158	43.6	5	5	1	0	2	4	2	0	4	0	0	0	0	7	0	0	0	0	0	0	1	4	2	1	0
reserve	25	.7539	3.8079	45.8	1	1	3	0	11	4	4	1	4	0	0	1	0	1	2	1	1	0	1	0	3	1	5	5	0
Reserve	29	.3438	2.2079	43.4	1	0	1	1	21	2	3	0	2	1	0	0	0	0	0	0	0	0	1	0	0	2	21	2	0
reserved	26	.6996	3.6768	45.7	1	2	3	0	8	8	4	0	0	4	0	2	1	5	0	0	2	0	0	0	0	4	5	3	0
reserves	16	.5856	1.9553	42.9	2	1	0	1	4	2	6	0	1	0	0	1	0	6	0	1	0	0	0	0	0	1	3	3	0
reservoir	28	.6907	3.9499	46.0	7	6	4	2	2	3	0	4	1	1	0	0	2	7	0	8	1	0	0	0	0	1	3	4	0
Reservoir	2	.0000	.0389	25.9	2	0	0	0	0	0	0	0	0	0	0	0	0	2	0	0	0	0	0	0	0	0	0	0	0
reservoirs	16	.5066	1.7443	42.4	0	1	4	3	3	2	1	2	1	0	0	0	0	2	0	9	0	0	0	0	1	0	2	1	0
reset	3	.0965	.0750	28.7	0	0	0	0	1	1	1	0	0	0	0	0	1	0	0	0	0	0	0	2	0	0	0	0	0
reshape	2	.1442	.0761	28.8	0	0	0	0	0	2	0	0	0	0	0	0	0	1	0	0	0	0	1	0	0	0	0	0	0
reshaped	3	.2929	.1965	32.9	0	0	0	0	0	1	2	0	0	0	0	1	0	0	0	1	0	0	1	0	0	0	0	0	0
reshaping	3	.1813	.1402	31.5	0	1	0	0	0	1	1	0	0	0	0	0	0	0	0	1	0	0	0	0	0	0	2	0	0
reside	3	.1639	.1674	32.2	0	0	0	0	1	0	2	0	1	0	0	0	0	2	0	0	0	0	0	0	0	0	0	0	0
resided	4	.3372	.2996	34.8	0	0	0	0	0	1	3	0	0	0	0	0	0	1	0	0	0	0	0	0	1	0	2	0	0
residence	27	.6868	3.7762	45.8	1	0	5	4	6	5	6	0	2	2	0	3	0	6	1	0	0	0	0	0	1	1	5	6	0
residences	6	.4769	.6522	38.1	0	0	0	1	1	3	1	0	3	0	0	0	1	0	1	0	0	0	0	0	1	0	0	0	0
resident	11	.4752	1.1425	40.6	0	1	0	1	4	0	3	2	2	0	0	0	0	1	0	2	0	0	0	0	0	0	2	4	0
residential	11	.4963	1.1592	40.6	2	0	0	1	1	4	3	0	0	1	0	0	0	5	0	1	0	0	0	0	0	0	3	1	0
residents	23	.5966	2.8584	44.6	0	1	4	5	6	4	2	1	2	0	0	0	1	5	0	2	0	0	0	0	0	3	4	6	0
resides	4	.3618	.3223	35.1	0	0	1	0	1	0	2	0	0	1	0	0	0	1	0	0	0	0	0	0	0	2	0	0	0
residual	3	.3811	.2534	34.0	0	0	1	0	0	0	1	1	0	0	0	0	0	0	0	1	0	0	0	0	0	1	0	1	0
residue	9	.5048	.9587	39.8	0	1	0	2	1	4	0	1	0	1	0	0	0	1	0	3	0	0	0	0	0	0	3	1	0
resign	16	.6761	2.1934	43.4	1	0	5	3	1	4	2	0	0	1	0	1	0	4	2	1	1	0	0	0	2	0	4	0	0
resignation	13	.5439	1.4810	41.7	0	0	2	1	2	7	1	0	1	2	0	0	0	2	0	0	0	0	0	0	0	1	3	4	0
resigned	17	.4818	1.7524	42.4	2	2	3	2	3	3	2	0	3	1	2	0	0	1	0	0	1	0	0	0	0	0	8	1	0
resigning	4	.3465	.3040	34.8	0	0	1	1	0	2	0	0	0	0	0	0	0	1	0	0	1	0	0	0	0	0	2	0	0
resilient	2	.1641	.0751	28.8	0	0	0	0	1	0	1	0	0	0	1	0	0	0	0	0	0	0	0	0	0	0	1	0	0
resin	17	.4344	1.5430	41.9	0	3	6	1	1	3	3	0	0	0	0	0	0	2	0	0	0	0	1	4	1	1	8	0	0
resinous	4	.4119	.3390	35.3	0	0	1	0	2	0	1	0	0	0	1	1	0	0	0	0	0	0	0	1	0	0	1	0	0
resins	5	.2857	.3274	35.2	0	1	2	1	1	0	0	0	0	0	0	0	0	1	0	0	0	0	0	0	0	1	3	0	0
resist	47	.7395	7.0491	48.5	4	2	4	8	12	8	7	2	10	0	0	1	0	3	3	1	0	1	3	5	4	6	6	4	0
resistance	134	.3738	10.715	50.3	4	7	2	4	23	65	19	10	4	1	0	0	1	7	2	15	1	0	4	52	0	17	15	15	0
resistant	15	.6010	1.8442	42.7	1	0	0	2	6	4	2	0	0	0	0	0	0	0	1	4	0	0	1	2	0	3	3	1	0
resisted	18	.6130	2.3244	43.7	0	1	0	3	6	4	2	2	4	1	0	1	0	7	0	0	0	0	0	0	1	1	0	3	0
resisting	6	.5219	.6628	38.2	0	0	1	0	1	1	1	2	1	0	0	1	0	0	0	0	1	0	0	0	0	0	1	2	0
resistivity	4	.0000	.0101	20.0	0	0	0	0	0	4	0	0	0	0	0	0	0	0	0	0	0	0	0	4	0	0	0	0	0
resistor	3	.1101	.0802	29.0	0	0	0	0	1	2	0	0	0	0	0	0	0	0	0	0	0	0	0	2	0	0	0	1	0
resistors	5	.1220	.1758	32.5	0	0	0	1	0	3	1	0	1	0	0	0	0	0	0	0	0	0	0	3	0	0	1	0	0
resists	6	.3097	.4182	36.2	0	1	0	0	0	2	3	0	1	0	0	0	0	0	0	1	0	0	2	2	0	0	0	0	0
resolute	7	.4871	.7278	38.6	0	1	0	2	2	1	1	0	1	0	1	2	0	1	0	0	0	0	0	0	1	0	0	1	0
resolutely	11	.5169	1.1954	40.8	0	1	0	3	1	4	1	1	1	1	0	4	0	0	0	0	0	0	0	0	3	1	0	1	0
resolution	13	.5831	1.5762	42.0	0	1	2	0	1	5	2	2	0	0	0	1	0	5	0	2	0	0	0	0	3	1	1	0	0
resolutions	18	.5281	2.1452	43.3	1	1	1	0	10	5	0	0	10	0	0	0	0	5	1	0	0	0	0	0	0	1	1	0	0
resolve	17	.6415	2.2878	43.6	0	1	1	4	1	3	6	1	5	1	0	3	0	4	0	1	0	0	0	0	0	0	1	2	0
resolved	41	.6495	5.5107	47.4	0	3	4	9	9	10	6	0	8	0	0	6	0	6	0	0	2	0	0	0	12	3	2	2	0
resolves	2	.2297	.1135	30.6	0	0	0	0	0	2	0	0	0	0	0	1	0	1	0	0	0	0	0	0	0	0	0	0	0
resolving	3	.3763	.2435	33.9	0	0	0	1	0	0	2	0	0	0	0	0	1	0	0	0	1	0	0	0	1	0	0	0	0
resonance	6	.3781	.4872	36.9	0	1	0	1	0	1	2	1	0	0	0	0	0	0	0	1	3	0	0	0	0	0	1	1	0
resonant	5	.2177	.2519	34.0	0	0	1	0	1	2	1	0	0	0	0	0	0	0	0	0	3	0	0	0	0	0	0	2	0
resonator	6	.0000	.0485	26.9	1	0	1	1	3	0	0	0	0	0	0	0	0	0	0	0	6	0	0	0	0	0	0	0	0
resort	29	.6013	3.5944	45.6	2	0	5	6	7	7	0	2	1	0	2	1	0	6	0	1	0	0	0	0	0	5	4	9	0
resorted	3	.2431	.1816	32.6	0	0	0	0	1	2	0	0	0	0	0	0	0	2	0	0	0	0	0	0	1	0	0	0	0
resorts	11	.6275	1.4312	41.6	2	0	4	1	2	0	1	1	1	1	0	0	0	3	0	1	0	0	0	0	0	3	1	1	0
resound	2	.1494	.1045	30.2	0	0	0	0	1	1	0	0	1	0	0	0	0	0	0	0	1	0	0	0	0	0	0	0	0
resounded	3	.3427	.2477	33.9	0	2	1	0	0	0	0	0	1	0	0	0	0	0	0	0	0	0	0	0	1	0	0	1	0
resounding	5	.4264	.4716	36.7	1	0	0	0	1	1	1	1	1	0	0	0	0	0	0	0	0	0	0	0	2	0	1	1	0
resounds	3	.3811	.2534	34.0	0	0	0	1	1	0	0	1	0	0	0	0	0	0	0	1	0	0	0	0	0	1	0	1	0
resource	29	.5390	3.3075	45.2	9	4	5	4	4	3	0	0	1	0	0	0	0	19	1	1	0	0	1	0	1	0	4	1	0
resourceful	5	.4272	.4803	36.8	0	3	0	0	2	0	0	0	1	0	0	0	0	1	0	0	0	0	0	0	1	2	0	0	0
resourcefulness	2	.2446	.1257	31.0	0	0	0	0	1	1	0	0	0	0	0	0	0	1	0	1	0	0	0	0	0	0	0	0	0
resources	232	.6423	30.718	54.9	26	17	47	29	56	24	29	4	8	3	1	0	1	131	1	13	7	0	6	0	0	11	36	14	0
Resources	8	.2535	.4869	36.9	0	0	0	1	7	0	0	0	0	0	0	0	0	1	0	0	0	0	0	0	0	6	0	1	0
respect	185	.8730	32.160	55.1	14	18	17	16	33	41	42	4	25	8	2	10	20	20	5	21	5	0	2	1	8	18	19	20	1
respectability	4	.4870	.4076	36.1	0	0	1	0	0	1	2	0	0	1	0	1	0	0	0	0	0	0	0	0	0	1	0	1	0
respectable	23	.7129	3.3730	45.3	1	1	0	6	6	2	3	4	7	0	0	1	0	0	3	4	1	0	0	0	4	1	1	1	0
respected	37	.7320	5.5654	47.5	3	5	4	3	12	7	2	1	12	0	0	5	0	6	0	2	0	0	1	0	2	6	1	2	0
respectful	16	.6131	2.0432	43.1	2	2	0	4	6	2	0	0	3	0	0	5	0	2	1	0	1	0	0	0	2	2	0	0	0
respectfully	12	.6684	1.6555	42.2	1	2	2	2	3	2	0	0	3	0	0	2	0	0	1	0	1	0	0	0	2	2	0	1	0
respecting	5	.5597	.5840	37.7	0	0	1	0	2	1	1	0	0	0	0	0	0	1	0	1	0	0	0	0	1	1	0	1	0
respective	14	.6630	1.8775	42.7	0	1	0	1	2	4	5	1	0	1	0	0	1	1	1	0	0	0	0	1	1	1	5	2	0
respectively	28	.5122	3.0262	44.8	0	0	0	0	8	13	7	0	1	1	0	0	17	0	0	2	1	0	0	0	1	0	3	2	0
respects	32	.6912	4.5141	46.5	1	1	4	3	7	8	8	0	5	2	0	6	0	3	0	1	0	0	3	0	2	2	6	2	0
respell	4	.0000	.0325	25.1	0	0	0	3	1	0	0	0	0	0	0	0	0	0	4	0	0	0	0	0	0	0	0	0	0
respelled	30	.0527	.7195	38.6	6	4	5	2	8	5	0	0	5	0	0	0	0	0	25	0	0	0	0	0	0	0	0	0	0
respelling	70	.1812	3.6158	45.6	19	11	8	9	8	8	7	0	21	5	0	0	0	0	44	0	0	0	0	0	0	0	0	0	0
respellings	38	.0895	1.0567	40.2	4	7	6	6	10	4	1	0	3	2	0	0	0	0	33	0	0	0	0	0	0	0	0	0	0
Respighi	2	.0000	.0162	22.1	1	0	0	0	0	1	0	0	0	0	0	0	0	0	0	0	2	0	0	0	0	0	0	0	0
respiration	41	.4311	3.8967	45.9	0	2	0	2	14	6	17	0	1	0	0	0	1	0	0	31	0	0	2	0	0	0	4	2	0
respiratory	16	.3322	1.2243	40.9	0	0	0	0	5	5	5	1	1	0	0	0	0	0	0	7	0	0	0	0	0	0	7	1	0
respire	2	.2413	.1212	30.8	0	0	0	0	1	0	1	0	0	0	0	0	1	0	0	1	0	0	0	0	0	0	0	0	0
respite	4	.4478	.4002	36.0	0	0	0	1	1	1	1	0	1	0	0	0	0	1	0	0	0	0	0	0	1	0	1	0	0
resplendent	7	.6597	.9526	39.8	0	0	0	0	4	1	2	0	1	1	0	1	0	1	0	1	0	0	0	0	1	1	0	0	0
respond	54	.7794	8.5015	49.3	1	2	7	3	17	10	9	5	9	5	1	3	1	0	0	17	6	0	0	0	3	3	2	4	0
responded	40	.6780	5.5475	47.4	1	3	3	5	10	11	6	1	4	0	0	1	0	6	0	4	3	0	0	0	2	3	5	12	0
responding	6	.3990	.5294	37.2	0	0	0	3	1	1	1	0	1	0	0	0	0	0	0	0	0	1	0	0	1	1	0	2	0
responds	9	.4875	.9405	39.7	1	0	1	3	3	1	0	0	1	0	0	0	0	0	0	3	0	0	0	1	0	0	2	2	0
response	74	.8419	12.415	50.9	2	3	7	11	17	14	16	4	4	5	1	2	0	1	2	15	5	1	0	1	7	5	5	20	0
responses	25	.5057	2.6815	44.3	0	4	0	13	5	1	2	0	0	0	0	0	3	0	0	14	4	0	0	0	0	0	2	2	0
responsibilities	25	.7367	3.7601	45.8	0	1	2	3	6	3	10	0	6	4	0	0	0	4	0	2	0	0	1	0	1	2	3	2	0
responsibility	110	.8595	18.888	52.8	0	6	16	11	34	16	25	2	22	0	2	5	2	7	1	21	4	0	5	1	3	12	10	15	0
responsibilty	3	.2357	.2199	33.4	0	0	0	1	1	0	1	0	2	0	0	0	0	0	0	0	0	0	0	0	0	1	0	0	0
responsible	137	.7838	21.601	53.3	4	8	13	17	29	27	36	3	11	2	1	3	0	27	0	28	2	0	8	1	6	12	27	9	0
responsive	9	.5108	.9872	39.9	0	0	0	0	5	1	2	1	2	0	0	1	0	0	0	0	0	0	0	0	1	0	2	3	0
rest	1183	.9789	228.12	63.6	204	215	140	178	202	122	104	18	328	41	19	72	49	114	27	106	82	7	21	9	95	111	40	61	1
restate	4	.0778	.0786	29.0	0	0	0	1	0	0	3	0	0	0	3	0	0	0	0	0	0	0	0	0	0	0	0	1	0

7E Reservations
7A reservers
7Q resets
8F resettled
5P resettlement
7Q resettling
3A residing
4N residuary
7L resift
9R resignations
7N resignedly
7P resin-coated
9H resinosa
8Q Resistant
8Q resistible
7R resized
8J resonators
6R resort-studded
6A Resort's
9A resorting
9J Resound
7R resoundingly
7R Respect
7L RESPECT
6G respells
9L respinning
5H respirator
9L respun
5Q Rest
9P rest-room
7R restaining
4A restart
8B restated

Word Type	F	D	U	SFI	3 Gr 3	4 Gr 4	5 Gr 5	6 Gr 6	7 Gr 7	8 Gr 8	9 Gr 9	X UnGr	A Read	B Eng & Gr	C Comp	D Lit	E Math	F Soc Stud	G Spell	H Sci	J Music	K Art	L Home Ec	M Shop	N Lib F	P Lib NF	Q Lib Ref	R Mag	S Rel
restatement	4	.0000	.0089	19.5	0	0	0	0	0	0	4	0	0	0	4	0	0	0	0	0	0	0	0	0	0	0	0	0	0
restatements	2	.1843	.0808	29.1	0	0	0	0	1	0	1	0	0	0	1	0	0	0	0	0	1	0	0	0	0	0	0	0	0
restaurant	77	.8425	13.022	51.1	10	10	5	10	20	7	13	2	23	7	0	10	4	7	4	5	1	0	3	0	2	3	2	6	0
Restaurant	5	.4631	.4896	36.9	0	1	0	1	2	0	0	1	0	0	0	1	1	0	0	0	0	0	0	0	0	1	0	2	0
restaurants	45	.6278	5.8725	47.7	5	4	5	6	6	10	7	2	7	0	0	2	0	10	1	3	0	0	0	0	1	1	6	14	0
rested	88	.8152	14.490	51.6	15	15	12	13	18	9	3	3	29	5	1	7	0	6	1	11	1	1	0	0	16	6	0	4	0
restful	6	.3900	.5089	37.1	0	1	2	0	0	0	2	1	1	0	0	0	0	0	1	0	1	0	2	0	0	0	0	1	0
resting	100	.7856	15.982	52.0	18	11	12	14	22	9	11	3	34	0	1	10	1	7	0	21	2	2	0	0	3	10	0	9	0
Restitution	2	.0000	.0209	23.2	0	0	0	0	0	0	2	0	0	0	0	0	0	0	0	0	0	0	0	0	0	0	2	0	0
restive	3	.3369	.2489	34.0	0	0	0	0	1	2	0	0	1	0	0	1	0	1	0	0	0	0	0	0	0	0	0	0	0
restless	71	.7503	10.836	50.3	2	17	10	7	13	13	8	1	18	0	2	8	0	6	0	1	6	0	0	0	13	10	3	4	0
restlessly	11	.5372	1.3197	41.2	0	2	2	2	4	1	0	0	6	1	0	0	0	1	0	0	0	0	0	0	2	1	0	0	0
restlessness	6	.2197	.4180	36.2	1	0	0	2	3	0	0	0	4	0	0	0	0	0	0	0	0	0	0	0	0	0	2	0	0
restoration	9	.4856	.9500	39.8	0	0	0	0	4	0	5	0	2	0	0	1	0	1	0	0	0	0	0	0	0	0	3	2	0
restorative	3	.0000	.0365	25.6	0	0	0	0	3	0	0	0	0	0	0	0	0	0	0	0	0	0	0	0	0	0	0	3	0
restore	34	.7497	5.1424	47.1	0	1	2	4	8	7	9	3	2	0	0	1	0	9	1	2	1	0	2	0	2	3	4	7	0
restored	39	.7411	5.8767	47.7	3	1	3	8	10	7	3	4	7	1	0	2	0	6	0	4	0	0	1	0	2	2	8	6	0
restores	2	.2433	.1158	30.6	0	0	0	0	2	0	0	0	0	0	0	0	0	0	0	0	0	0	0	0	0	1	0	1	0
restoring	7	.6185	.8865	39.5	0	0	2	1	2	0	2	0	0	0	0	1	0	1	0	0	0	0	0	0	1	2	1	1	0
restrain	9	.5245	1.0179	40.1	1	1	3	0	0	2	1	1	2	0	0	2	0	2	0	0	0	0	0	0	2	1	0	0	0
restrained	15	.5971	1.8340	42.6	0	0	0	1	4	8	2	0	0	2	0	0	0	3	0	0	4	0	1	0	0	3	0	2	0
restraint	11	.4926	1.1447	40.6	0	0	1	1	3	2	4	0	1	0	0	1	0	0	0	0	0	0	1	0	0	1	1	6	0
restraints	5	.2648	.3286	35.2	0	0	0	0	4	0	1	0	1	0	0	0	0	0	0	0	0	0	0	0	3	0	0	1	0
restrict	7	.3162	.4966	37.0	0	0	0	1	4	0	1	1	0	2	0	0	0	0	0	1	0	0	0	0	0	0	0	4	0
restricted	25	.6098	3.1549	45.0	0	3	2	0	6	5	6	3	2	0	1	0	0	4	0	3	0	0	0	0	0	3	7	5	0
restricting	2	.1698	.1133	30.5	0	0	0	1	0	1	0	0	1	0	0	0	0	0	0	0	0	0	0	0	0	0	1	0	0
restriction	7	.6175	.8845	39.5	0	0	0	0	3	2	2	0	0	0	0	0	2	1	1	0	0	0	0	0	1	0	1	1	0
restrictions	21	.6105	2.6231	44.2	1	0	4	1	10	2	2	1	0	0	0	3	1	3	0	0	0	0	0	0	3	1	6	4	0
restrictive	4	.4741	.3984	36.0	0	0	0	0	0	3	1	0	0	1	0	0	0	1	0	0	1	0	0	0	0	0	1	0	0
rests	49	.6436	6.4337	48.1	10	6	5	4	7	4	10	3	2	0	0	4	1	2	0	9	16	0	2	0	0	5	5	3	0
result	594	.8837	104.25	60.2	22	23	72	58	135	128	121	35	38	39	2	8	117	84	6	88	36	4	7	17	7	22	74	45	0
resultant	6	.4449	.5729	37.6	0	0	0	0	1	1	4	0	0	0	0	0	3	1	0	0	0	0	0	0	0	0	1	1	0
resulted	53	.7179	7.7204	48.9	2	5	5	4	17	8	11	1	4	2	2	1	0	9	0	9	4	0	0	0	0	6	13	3	0
resulting	54	.7396	8.0437	49.1	0	2	2	2	17	13	16	2	1	0	1	0	16	2	0	12	6	0	3	2	0	0	7	4	0
results	324	.8522	55.016	57.4	14	21	41	38	79	67	52	12	15	11	2	7	88	19	4	89	9	6	13	10	2	11	21	17	0
resume	6	.4923	.6054	37.8	0	0	1	2	0	1	2	0	0	0	1	0	0	0	2	0	1	0	0	0	0	0	1	1	0
resumed	15	.6023	1.8857	42.8	1	0	2	2	5	2	3	0	3	0	0	2	0	1	0	0	1	0	0	0	5	0	2	1	0
resumption	2	.2446	.1122	30.5	0	0	0	0	0	1	1	0	0	0	0	1	0	0	0	0	0	0	0	0	0	0	1	0	0
resurgent	3	.2159	.1532	31.9	0	0	0	0	1	0	0	2	0	0	0	0	0	0	0	0	0	0	0	0	0	0	2	1	0
resurrected	2	.2427	.1152	30.6	0	0	0	1	1	0	0	0	0	0	0	0	0	0	0	0	0	0	0	0	1	1	0	0	0
resurrection	3	.2321	.1635	32.1	0	0	0	0	1	1	1	0	0	0	0	0	0	0	0	0	0	0	0	0	0	0	1	2	0
resuscitation	3	.0000	.0314	25.0	0	0	0	0	0	3	0	0	0	0	0	0	0	0	0	0	0	0	0	0	0	0	3	0	0
Resuscitation	2	.0000	.0394	26.0	0	0	0	0	0	2	0	0	0	0	0	0	0	0	0	2	0	0	0	0	0	0	0	0	0
retail	14	.4362	1.2992	41.1	0	1	5	0	2	0	5	1	0	0	0	0	2	1	0	0	0	0	0	0	0	2	7	2	0
retailer	3	.2321	.1635	32.1	0	0	1	0	0	0	1	1	0	0	0	0	0	0	0	0	0	0	0	0	0	0	1	2	0
retailing	2	.2285	.1129	30.5	0	0	0	0	1	1	0	0	0	0	0	0	0	1	0	0	0	0	0	0	0	0	1	0	0
retain	32	.7244	4.6496	46.7	0	0	1	1	3	6	18	3	0	2	0	2	3	4	1	3	2	1	5	3	0	1	5	0	0
retained	26	.7571	3.9610	46.0	0	1	0	0	9	6	7	3	2	2	0	0	2	1	0	2	4	0	1	0	1	2	4	5	0
retainers	5	.0743	.1541	31.9	0	0	0	1	0	4	0	0	1	0	0	0	0	0	0	0	0	0	0	0	0	0	4	0	0
retaining	9	.3400	.6654	38.2	0	0	0	0	6	1	2	0	0	0	0	0	1	1	0	1	0	0	0	3	0	1	2	0	0
retains	5	.5475	.5690	37.6	0	0	0	1	2	2	0	0	0	1	0	0	0	1	1	1	0	0	0	0	0	0	1	0	0
retake	3	.3454	.2542	34.1	0	0	0	1	0	2	0	0	1	0	0	0	0	1	0	0	0	0	0	0	0	0	0	1	0
retaliate	2	.2440	.1132	30.5	0	0	0	0	1	0	1	0	0	0	0	1	0	0	0	0	0	0	0	0	0	0	0	1	0
retaliated	4	.3647	.3180	35.0	0	0	1	0	1	2	0	0	0	0	0	0	0	0	0	0	0	0	0	0	0	1	1	2	0
retaliation	3	.0000	.0365	25.6	0	0	0	0	0	0	3	0	0	0	0	0	0	0	0	0	0	0	0	0	0	0	0	3	0
retard	3	.2254	.1785	32.5	0	0	0	1	1	0	1	0	0	0	0	0	0	1	0	2	0	0	0	0	0	0	0	0	0
retardation	2	.2346	.1166	30.7	0	0	0	0	1	0	0	1	0	0	0	0	0	0	0	1	0	0	0	0	0	0	0	1	0
retarded	6	.2511	.3618	35.6	0	0	1	1	0	0	3	1	0	0	0	0	0	1	0	1	0	0	0	0	0	0	0	4	0
retell	6	.2354	.3541	35.5	0	0	1	0	1	3	1	0	1	4	0	1	0	0	0	0	0	0	0	0	0	0	0	0	0
retellings	2	.0000	.0914	29.6	0	0	0	0	0	2	0	0	2	0	0	0	0	0	0	0	0	0	0	0	0	0	0	0	0
retention	7	.5072	.7395	38.7	0	0	2	0	1	2	0	2	0	0	0	0	0	0	0	1	0	0	1	0	0	2	2	1	0
retied	2	.0000	.0234	23.7	1	1	0	0	0	0	0	0	0	0	0	0	0	0	0	0	0	0	0	0	2	0	0	0	0
retina	20	.2366	1.3013	41.1	1	0	0	9	6	3	0	1	4	0	0	0	0	0	1	15	0	0	0	0	0	0	0	0	0
retinas	2	.2278	.1128	30.5	0	0	0	1	1	0	0	0	0	0	0	0	0	0	0	1	0	0	0	0	0	0	1	0	0
retire	12	.7320	1.7745	42.5	0	1	1	3	4	1	2	0	1	1	0	2	0	1	1	0	0	0	0	0	2	2	1	1	0
retired	37	.6313	4.8294	46.8	1	2	4	2	15	3	7	3	6	0	3	2	0	4	0	0	0	0	0	0	6	4	3	9	0
retirement	22	.5441	2.5398	44.0	0	1	3	0	2	5	6	5	4	0	0	0	0	2	1	1	0	0	1	0	0	1	1	11	0
retires	3	.2530	.1734	32.4	0	0	0	0	1	0	1	1	0	0	1	0	0	0	0	1	0	0	0	0	0	0	1	0	0
retiring	11	.5961	1.3841	41.4	0	0	0	2	5	2	2	0	3	0	0	2	0	0	0	1	0	0	0	0	2	0	1	2	0
retold	8	.3808	.7824	38.9	1	1	1	0	2	3	0	0	6	0	0	0	0	0	0	0	0	0	0	0	0	0	1	1	0
retort	3	.1187	.1291	31.1	0	1	0	0	1	0	1	0	1	0	0	2	0	0	0	0	0	0	0	0	0	0	0	0	0
retorted	15	.5140	1.7853	42.5	1	4	2	3	3	2	0	0	11	0	0	0	1	0	0	0	0	0	0	0	1	1	0	1	0
retouching	5	.0000	.0986	29.9	0	0	0	0	0	0	0	5	0	0	0	0	0	0	0	5	0	0	0	0	0	0	0	0	0
retrace	15	.2754	.8944	39.5	0	8	0	3	1	2	0	1	1	0	8	0	0	0	1	0	0	0	2	0	1	0	0	2	0
retraced	3	.3385	.2445	33.9	0	0	1	1	1	0	0	0	1	0	0	0	0	0	0	0	0	0	0	0	1	0	1	0	0
retracing	4	.1135	.1696	32.3	0	0	0	0	0	3	1	0	1	0	0	0	3	0	0	0	0	0	0	0	0	0	0	0	0
retract	2	.2433	.1158	30.6	1	0	0	0	0	0	0	1	0	0	0	0	0	0	0	0	0	0	0	0	0	1	0	1	0
retreat	50	.8019	8.0792	49.1	2	6	4	4	12	12	9	1	11	1	1	5	0	9	3	0	1	0	0	0	2	6	7	4	0
retreated	15	.5157	1.6551	42.2	0	2	2	0	10	0	1	0	3	0	1	0	0	2	0	0	0	0	0	0	2	1	6	0	0
retreating	5	.3752	.4067	36.1	0	1	1	0	1	1	1	0	0	0	0	2	0	0	0	0	0	0	0	0	0	2	1	0	0
retreats	3	.2143	.1568	32.0	0	0	1	0	0	0	1	1	0	0	0	0	0	0	0	0	0	0	0	0	0	1	0	2	0
retrieve	2	.2412	.1091	30.4	0	0	0	0	0	1	1	0	0	0	0	1	0	0	1	0	0	0	0	0	0	0	0	0	0
retrieved	3	.2120	.1548	31.9	0	1	1	0	1	0	0	0	0	0	0	0	0	0	0	0	0	0	0	0	2	1	0	0	0
retriever	2	.1523	.0721	28.6	0	0	0	0	1	0	0	1	0	0	1	0	0	0	0	0	0	0	0	0	0	0	0	1	0
retrieving	3	.3771	.2489	34.0	0	0	0	1	1	0	0	1	0	0	0	1	0	0	0	1	0	0	0	0	0	0	0	1	0
retro	2	.2289	.1077	30.3	0	0	0	0	0	1	1	0	0	0	0	0	1	0	1	0	0	0	0	0	0	0	0	0	0
retrograde	5	.0000	.0404	26.1	0	0	0	0	0	5	0	0	0	0	0	0	0	0	0	0	5	0	0	0	0	0	0	0	0
retrorockets	2	.1497	.1046	30.2	0	0	0	1	0	1	0	0	1	0	0	0	0	0	1	0	0	0	0	0	0	0	0	0	0
retrospect	2	.2433	.1158	30.6	0	0	0	0	0	1	1	0	0	0	0	0	0	0	0	0	0	0	0	0	0	1	0	1	0
retting	2	.1926	.0867	29.4	0	0	0	1	0	1	0	0	0	0	0	0	0	0	0	0	0	0	1	0	0	0	1	0	0
return	532	.9107	96.276	59.8	51	77	76	68	131	52	66	11	148	13	5	44	10	74	1	42	30	0	9	8	25	42	38	43	0
returnable	4	.0000	.0129	21.1	0	0	0	0	0	0	4	0	0	0	0	0	0	0	0	0	0	0	4	0	0	0	0	0	0
returned	489	.8894	86.720	59.4	42	68	72	74	117	58	47	11	147	18	6	35	6	70	3	18	12	0	2	4	55	54	27	32	0
returning	108	.8859	19.044	52.8	14	11	13	9	39	17	5	0	20	6	1	12	2	19	0	7	3	0	1	1	7	11	12	6	0
returns	66	.8818	11.582	50.6	4	8	6	6	19	11	11	1	10	1	1	5	2	7	2	13	6	0	1	0	2	7	6	3	0

9C restates
XR restaurant-tearoom
8F restaurateur
6A resting-place
8Q restiveness
XR restorer
8D restoreth
7A restraining
9B restricts
5A restringing
XR resubmitted
8B Result
7P resumes
9Q Resumption
5P resurgence
8D resurrect
3N Resurrection
9R resurveyed
7D Retail
9F retailers
XR retails
7M retainer
8Q retaken
8R retaliating
9R retaliatory
9F retards
7N retched
7N retchings
7P retentive
7P reticular
7Q reticulate
6A retinal
9D retinue
9R retiree
XR retirees
4A retorts
4C retraces
7R retractable
XR retraction
8F retrain
9P retransmitted
XR retrenchment
8F retribution
7R retrieval
5N Retriever
9E retro-rockets
XR retroactively
5Q retrofire
8H retrolental
7Q retromorphosis
3K Returning

Word Type	F	D	U	SFI	3 Gr 3	4 Gr 4	5 Gr 5	6 Gr 6	7 Gr 7	8 Gr 8	9 Gr 9	X UnGr	A Read	B Eng & Gr	C Comp	D Lit	E Math	F Soc Stud	G Spell	H Sci	J Music	K Art	L Home Ec	M Shop	N Lib F	P Lib NF	Q Lib Ref	R Mag	S Rel
Reuben	2	.0857	.0784	28.9	0	0	0	0	1	1	0	0	1	0	0	0	0	0	0	0	0	0	1	0	0	0	0	0	0
reunion	10	.6051	1.2480	41.0	0	0	1	1	4	1	1	2	1	2	0	0	0	1	0	0	0	0	1	0	2	1	2	0	0
reunite	2	.0000	.0243	23.9	0	0	0	0	2	0	0	0	0	0	0	0	0	0	0	0	0	0	0	0	0	0	0	2	0
reused	4	.3231	.2911	34.6	0	0	0	1	1	0	2	0	0	0	0	0	0	0	0	2	0	0	1	0	0	0	0	1	0
Reuther	2	.2437	.1129	30.5	0	0	1	0	0	0	1	0	0	0	0	0	0	0	0	0	0	0	0	0	0	0	1	1	0
rev	2	.0000	.0243	23.9	0	0	0	0	1	0	0	1	0	0	0	0	0	0	0	0	0	0	0	0	0	0	0	2	0
Rev	4	.2932	.2861	34.6	0	0	1	0	2	1	0	0	1	0	0	0	0	0	0	0	0	0	0	0	0	0	2	1	0
reveal	73	.6144	9.1807	49.6	2	0	3	7	23	17	18	3	5	12	4	8	0	4	4	5	1	1	2	2	1	2	10	10	2
revealed	73	.7894	11.562	50.6	3	3	4	10	20	17	16	0	7	4	2	10	0	5	0	5	4	0	0	0	5	7	12	12	0
revealing	14	.5977	1.7556	42.4	0	2	3	1	5	0	1	2	3	0	0	0	0	0	0	2	0	1	0	0	1	2	2	3	0
reveals	34	.7552	5.1669	47.1	0	0	1	2	12	5	11	3	4	4	3	2	0	2	1	2	2	2	1	0	0	1	3	7	0
reveille	3	.2266	.1614	32.1	0	0	2	1	0	0	0	0	0	0	0	0	0	0	0	0	0	0	0	0	1	0	0	2	0
revel	3	.3408	.2477	33.9	0	0	0	0	1	1	1	0	1	0	0	1	0	0	0	0	0	0	0	0	0	1	0	0	0
Revel	2	.0000	.0914	29.6	0	0	0	2	0	0	0	0	2	0	0	0	0	0	0	0	0	0	0	0	0	0	0	0	0
revelation	16	.5512	1.8362	42.6	0	0	0	3	4	4	4	1	2	1	2	1	0	0	0	0	1	0	0	0	0	2	6	1	0
revelations	3	.3870	.2486	34.0	0	0	0	0	1	0	2	0	0	0	0	1	0	0	0	0	0	0	0	0	0	0	1	1	0
revelry	2	.1787	.1174	30.7	0	0	0	1	1	0	0	0	1	0	0	0	0	0	0	0	0	0	0	0	1	0	0	0	0
revenge	26	.5919	3.2035	45.1	0	0	5	2	10	3	5	1	4	2	0	11	0	1	1	0	0	0	0	0	2	3	1	1	0
revengeful	2	.2306	.1140	30.6	0	0	0	0	0	1	1	0	0	1	0	0	0	1	0	0	0	0	0	0	0	0	0	0	0
revenue	10	.5182	1.0879	40.4	0	0	0	0	3	0	7	0	0	0	0	0	1	4	1	0	0	0	0	0	0	0	3	1	0
Revenue	5	.2288	.2760	34.4	0	0	0	0	2	0	3	0	0	0	0	0	2	0	0	0	0	0	0	0	0	0	0	3	0
revenues	4	.2090	.2014	33.0	0	0	0	1	0	0	2	1	0	0	0	0	0	0	0	0	0	0	0	0	0	0	1	3	0
reverberated	2	.1551	.0728	28.6	0	0	0	1	1	0	0	0	0	0	1	0	0	0	0	0	0	0	0	0	1	0	0	0	0
reverberating	3	.3263	.2368	33.7	0	0	1	1	0	1	0	0	1	0	0	0	0	0	0	0	1	0	0	0	0	0	0	1	0
reverberations	2	.2441	.1127	30.5	0	0	0	0	0	1	1	0	0	0	0	0	0	0	0	0	0	0	0	0	1	0	1	0	0
Revere	22	.6251	2.9536	44.7	2	6	6	2	2	3	1	0	12	3	0	0	0	1	0	0	1	0	0	0	3	1	0	1	0
Revere's	3	.3418	.2486	34.0	0	2	0	0	1	0	0	0	1	1	0	0	1	0	0	0	0	0	0	0	0	0	0	0	0
revered	4	.2978	.2918	34.7	0	0	1	0	2	1	0	0	1	0	0	0	0	1	0	0	0	0	0	1	0	1	0	0	0
reverence	11	.5256	1.1993	40.8	0	0	3	1	3	2	2	0	0	1	0	1	0	0	0	0	0	0	0	0	4	3	2	0	0
reverend	4	.3721	.3657	35.6	1	0	0	1	1	0	1	0	2	0	0	1	0	0	0	0	0	0	0	0	0	1	0	0	0
Reverend	20	.6005	2.5434	44.1	1	3	2	1	4	4	4	1	6	0	0	4	0	2	0	0	0	0	0	0	3	3	0	2	0
reverent	5	.1563	.1897	32.8	0	0	0	1	0	1	3	0	0	0	0	0	0	0	0	0	4	0	0	0	0	0	1	0	0
reverently	4	.4348	.3900	35.9	0	0	0	1	0	1	1	1	1	0	0	0	0	1	0	0	1	0	0	0	0	0	0	1	0
reverse	63	.6594	8.4389	49.3	2	1	9	7	16	14	11	3	2	6	0	1	12	4	2	5	4	0	0	9	0	4	9	5	0
reversed	25	.7390	3.7248	45.7	1	2	0	3	11	3	5	0	1	1	0	2	3	3	0	3	1	0	0	2	0	2	4	3	0
reversely	3	.0000	.0314	25.0	0	0	0	0	3	0	0	0	0	0	0	0	0	0	0	0	0	0	0	0	0	0	3	0	0
reverses	4	.4408	.3908	35.9	0	0	0	1	2	0	1	0	1	0	0	0	1	0	0	0	1	0	0	0	0	0	1	0	0
reversing	8	.4097	.7042	38.5	0	0	0	1	0	3	1	3	0	1	0	0	1	1	0	2	0	0	0	2	0	0	0	1	0
revert	2	.2437	.1129	30.5	0	0	0	0	2	0	0	0	0	0	0	0	0	0	0	0	0	0	0	0	0	0	1	1	0
review	312	.4703	30.781	54.9	56	45	40	44	63	33	31	0	19	29	2	5	27	4	180	8	27	0	2	0	0	1	2	6	0
Review	83	.0664	1.7245	42.4	6	23	32	13	6	1	0	2	0	1	0	0	0	0	79	0	0	0	0	0	0	0	1	2	0
reviewed	12	.6055	1.5248	41.8	0	1	0	2	2	5	2	0	3	2	0	2	3	0	1	0	0	0	0	0	0	0	0	1	0
reviewer	3	.0000	.0365	25.6	0	0	0	0	1	2	0	0	0	0	0	0	0	0	0	0	0	0	0	0	0	0	0	3	0
reviewers	2	.2440	.1132	30.5	0	0	0	0	0	1	1	0	0	0	0	1	0	0	0	0	0	0	0	0	0	0	0	1	0
reviewing	11	.5594	1.3493	41.3	1	0	1	0	4	4	0	1	5	0	0	1	0	3	0	0	1	0	0	0	0	0	0	1	0
reviews	10	.5440	1.1433	40.6	0	0	1	0	3	2	4	0	1	1	0	1	0	2	0	0	1	0	0	0	0	0	0	4	0
revile	2	.2346	.1166	30.7	0	0	0	0	1	0	1	0	0	0	0	0	0	0	0	1	0	0	0	0	0	0	0	1	0
revise	31	.3994	2.6505	44.2	0	1	13	5	6	4	2	0	1	22	3	0	1	1	1	0	0	0	0	0	0	1	0	1	0
Revise	3	.0000	.0328	25.2	0	0	3	0	0	0	0	0	0	3	0	0	0	0	0	0	0	0	0	0	0	0	0	0	0
revised	13	.4606	1.2542	41.0	0	4	1	0	2	3	1	2	0	3	0	0	0	0	0	0	1	0	0	0	0	0	4	5	0
Revised	3	.0000	.0314	25.0	0	3	0	0	0	0	0	0	0	0	0	0	0	0	0	0	0	0	0	0	0	0	3	0	0
revising	3	.0000	.0328	25.2	0	0	1	0	2	0	0	0	0	3	0	0	0	0	0	0	0	0	0	0	0	0	0	0	0
revision	13	.5049	1.3605	41.3	0	4	1	0	2	3	3	0	0	4	0	0	0	0	0	1	0	0	0	1	0	0	5	2	0
revival	7	.4300	.6338	38.0	0	1	2	1	1	1	1	0	0	0	0	0	0	0	0	0	2	0	0	0	0	1	3	1	0
revive	11	.5871	1.3756	41.4	0	0	3	2	3	1	2	0	4	0	0	0	0	0	0	0	2	0	0	0	1	1	2	1	0
revived	16	.5994	1.9718	42.9	0	3	3	2	3	2	3	0	1	1	0	0	0	1	0	0	4	0	0	0	1	3	4	1	0
revocation	2	.2401	.1133	30.5	0	0	1	0	0	0	1	0	0	0	0	0	0	0	0	0	0	0	0	0	0	1	1	0	0
revoked	3	.3769	.2484	34.0	1	0	0	0	1	1	0	0	0	0	0	0	0	1	0	0	0	0	0	0	0	0	1	1	0
revolt	33	.5754	3.9365	46.0	2	0	5	1	12	4	3	6	2	0	0	1	0	5	0	0	2	0	0	0	1	2	10	10	0
revolted	12	.5179	1.3115	41.2	1	0	4	1	2	4	0	0	1	0	0	0	0	4	0	0	1	1	0	0	1	0	4	0	0
revolting	2	.2351	.1166	30.7	0	0	0	0	0	1	1	0	0	0	0	0	0	1	0	0	0	0	0	0	0	0	0	1	0
revolts	2	.2408	.1204	30.8	0	0	0	0	2	0	0	0	0	0	0	0	0	1	0	0	0	0	0	0	0	1	0	0	0
revolution	111	.7556	16.898	52.3	6	9	15	10	33	24	10	4	3	0	0	3	4	33	1	15	5	1	0	6	1	4	12	23	0
Revolution	107	.6688	14.658	51.7	9	2	18	12	23	25	17	1	8	0	0	3	0	42	0	1	7	3	0	0	1	7	22	13	0
revolutionaries	11	.3929	.9357	39.7	1	0	2	1	5	1	1	0	0	0	0	0	0	1	0	0	0	0	0	0	0	2	2	6	0
revolutionary	35	.6835	4.8461	46.9	1	0	2	2	12	9	6	3	0	0	0	3	0	4	1	2	2	0	0	0	1	6	5	11	0
Revolutionary	49	.5488	5.6718	47.5	3	7	19	3	8	9	0	0	5	1	0	0	0	19	0	0	8	0	0	0	0	4	11	1	0
revolutionists	2	.2446	.1142	30.6	0	1	0	0	1	0	0	0	0	0	0	0	0	0	0	0	0	0	0	0	1	0	0	1	0
revolutionize	5	.4169	.4619	36.6	1	0	0	0	2	0	1	1	1	1	0	0	0	0	0	0	0	0	0	0	0	0	2	1	0
revolutionized	11	.5694	1.3067	41.2	0	0	2	0	4	2	3	0	2	1	0	0	0	1	1	0	0	1	0	1	0	0	4	0	0
revolutions	26	.6609	3.4996	45.4	2	2	7	4	4	6	1	0	0	0	0	0	3	8	0	0	2	0	0	1	0	3	6	3	0
revolve	26	.6407	3.4745	45.4	0	12	4	2	2	5	1	0	5	0	0	0	0	3	2	11	2	0	0	1	0	0	2	0	0
revolved	23	.5190	2.5053	44.0	1	0	1	3	4	6	8	0	1	0	0	0	0	3	0	7	3	0	0	4	1	0	3	1	0
revolver	10	.5550	1.2175	40.9	0	1	3	1	4	0	1	0	5	0	0	1	0	0	0	0	0	0	0	0	2	0	1	1	0
revolvers	3	.2357	.2199	33.4	1	0	1	0	1	0	0	0	2	0	0	0	0	0	0	0	0	0	0	0	0	1	0	0	0
revolves	26	.4750	2.6554	44.2	2	3	9	2	2	3	5	0	0	0	0	1	0	8	0	12	0	0	0	3	0	1	1	0	0
revolving	20	.6614	2.7070	44.3	1	0	4	5	5	3	1	1	2	1	0	2	0	1	0	6	0	0	2	2	1	0	2	1	0
revue	3	.1983	.1396	31.4	0	0	0	0	2	0	0	1	0	0	0	0	0	0	0	0	2	0	0	0	0	0	0	1	0
revulsion	3	.2387	.1708	32.3	0	0	0	0	0	0	3	0	0	0	0	0	0	0	0	0	0	0	0	0	0	2	1	0	0
reward	84	.4314	8.2720	49.2	18	8	11	16	18	7	4	2	28	0	0	6	0	5	1	6	0	0	0	0	9	14	6	7	2
rewarded	25	.3658	2.1722	43.4	2	3	3	4	5	4	2	2	9	1	1	2	0	1	0	0	1	0	0	0	1	4	0	4	1
rewarding	16	.6357	2.1103	43.2	0	0	2	2	8	0	1	3	3	0	0	0	1	0	0	2	0	0	0	1	1	2	1	5	0
rewards	16	.5323	1.8166	42.6	0	1	0	2	4	3	3	3	3	0	0	0	0	1	0	2	2	0	0	0	0	0	2	6	0
reword	3	.3273	.2365	33.7	0	1	1	0	1	0	0	0	1	1	0	0	0	0	1	0	0	0	0	0	0	0	0	0	0
rework	2	.1812	.0838	29.2	0	0	0	0	1	1	0	0	0	0	0	0	0	0	0	0	0	0	1	0	0	0	0	1	0
reworked	5	.3275	.3650	35.6	0	0	0	0	3	1	0	1	0	0	0	0	0	0	0	1	1	0	0	0	0	0	0	3	0
rewoven	2	.1432	.0759	28.8	0	1	0	0	0	0	1	0	0	0	0	0	0	0	0	1	0	0	1	0	0	0	0	0	0
rewrite	125	.4242	11.266	50.5	6	17	32	23	17	19	10	1	4	51	1	0	23	0	44	0	0	0	0	0	0	0	0	2	0
rewriting	7	.4503	.6656	38.2	1	1	1	3	1	0	0	0	0	3	0	1	2	0	0	0	0	0	0	0	0	0	1	0	0
rewritten	13	.5735	1.5771	42.0	0	3	4	1	3	0	2	0	3	3	0	0	4	0	0	0	1	0	0	0	0	1	1	0	0
rewrote	4	.3693	.3613	35.6	0	1	0	0	1	0	2	0	2	0	0	1	0	0	0	0	0	0	0	0	0	0	1	0	0
rex	3	.0909	.0708	28.5	1	0	0	0	0	0	2	0	0	0	2	0	0	0	0	0	0	0	0	0	0	1	0	0	0
Rex	22	.4212	2.1012	43.2	3	10	1	0	0	4	4	0	6	4	0	2	0	0	0	0	0	0	0	0	0	10	0	0	0
Rexy	2	.0000	.0914	29.6	0	0	0	0	0	2	0	0	2	0	0	0	0	0	0	0	0	0	0	0	0	0	0	0	0
Rey	2	.0000	.0209	23.2	0	0	0	0	2	0	0	0	0	0	0	0	0	0	0	0	0	0	0	0	0	0	2	0	0
Reynard	4	.2333	.2229	33.5	0	1	3	0	0	0	0	0	0	0	0	0	0	0	0	0	1	0	0	0	0	3	0	0	0
Reynaud	2	.0000	.0290	24.6	0	0	0	0	2	0	0	0	0	0	0	0	0	0	0	0	0	0	0	0	0	2	0	0	0

3P Reulbach
8Q reunification
3K reunions
6J rev'rently
8B reve
5P Revelation
4A revelled
XB revellers
9D revels
8D revenged
7D reverberation
5Q revere
7D reverenced
9D reverso
9D reverted
7H revisions
8D revisit
8F revitalizing
9R Revival
9R Revivals
7A reviver
8Q revives
3R revoir
5Q revolutionist
7R revs
8Q Revulgo
4H reweaving
7L rewhipped
4B reworded
5R reworking
4P Rex's
7Q Rey's
6A Reyburn
8Q reyes
5P Reynaert
8D Reynard's
XR Reynold

Word Type	F	D	U	SFI	3 Gr 3	4 Gr 4	5 Gr 5	6 Gr 6	7 Gr 7	8 Gr 8	9 Gr 9	X UnGr	A Read	B Eng & Gr	C Comp	D Lit	E Math	F Soc Stud	G Spell	H Sci	J Music	K Art	L Home Ec	M Shop	N Lib F	P Lib NF	Q Lib Ref	R Mag	S Rel
Reynolds	10	.5564	1.2075	40.8	0	0	3	1	3	0	1	2	4	0	0	1	0	0	0	0	0	0	0	0	0	2	1	2	0
rh	3	.3770	.2435	33.9	1	0	0	0	0	1	1	0	0	1	0	0	1	0	1	0	0	0	0	0	0	0	0	0	0
Rhadan	2	.0000	.0914	29.6	0	0	0	2	0	0	0	0	2	0	0	0	0	0	0	0	0	0	0	0	0	0	0	0	0
rhapsodies	4	.0000	.0323	25.1	0	0	0	0	3	1	0	0	0	0	0	0	0	0	0	0	4	0	0	0	0	0	0	0	0
rhapsody	2	.0000	.0162	22.1	0	0	0	1	1	0	0	0	0	0	0	0	0	0	0	0	2	0	0	0	0	0	0	0	0
Rhapsody	4	.0000	.0323	25.1	0	0	0	3	0	1	0	0	0	0	0	0	0	0	0	0	4	0	0	0	0	0	0	0	0
Rheingold	2	.0000	.0162	22.1	0	0	0	2	0	0	0	0	0	0	0	0	0	0	0	0	2	0	0	0	0	0	0	0	0
Rhenish	2	.0000	.0215	23.3	0	0	0	0	0	0	2	0	0	0	0	2	0	0	0	0	0	0	0	0	0	0	0	0	0
rhetoric	5	.3786	.4118	36.1	0	0	1	0	1	1	2	0	0	0	0	1	0	0	0	0	0	0	0	0	0	2	0	2	0
rhetorical	3	.0000	.0067	18.3	0	0	0	0	3	0	0	0	0	0	3	0	0	0	0	0	0	0	0	0	0	0	0	0	0
rhetorically	2	.1551	.0728	28.6	0	0	0	0	1	1	0	0	0	0	1	0	0	0	0	0	0	0	0	0	1	0	0	0	0
Rhett	2	.0000	.0914	29.6	0	0	2	0	0	0	0	0	2	0	0	0	0	0	0	0	0	0	0	0	0	0	0	0	0
rheumatic	10	.4995	1.0737	40.3	0	1	2	1	1	2	3	0	1	0	0	1	0	0	1	5	0	0	0	0	0	0	2	0	0
rheumatism	14	.5882	1.7651	42.5	0	2	2	2	5	3	0	0	6	0	0	3	0	0	2	0	1	0	0	0	1	1	0	0	0
Rhiannon	3	.0000	.0434	26.4	0	0	0	0	3	0	0	0	0	0	0	0	0	0	0	0	0	0	0	0	0	3	0	0	0
Rhine	37	.4090	3.3542	45.3	3	12	0	13	1	2	6	0	0	1	0	0	0	30	0	0	2	2	0	0	0	2	0	0	0
rhino	14	.2273	1.0714	40.3	2	12	0	0	0	0	0	0	12	0	0	0	0	0	0	0	0	0	0	0	0	2	0	0	0
rhinoceros	20	.4913	2.0878	43.2	5	5	0	1	7	2	0	0	3	1	1	0	0	1	0	1	1	4	0	0	0	5	3	0	0
rhinos	2	.2433	.1158	30.6	0	1	0	0	1	0	0	0	0	0	0	0	0	0	0	0	0	0	0	0	0	1	0	1	0
Rhinos	2	.0000	.0914	29.6	0	2	0	0	0	0	0	0	2	0	0	0	0	0	0	0	0	0	0	0	0	0	0	0	0
rhizoids	3	.0000	.0591	27.7	0	0	0	0	0	0	3	0	0	0	0	0	0	0	0	3	0	0	0	0	0	0	0	0	0
rhizopods	2	.0000	.0394	26.0	0	0	0	0	0	0	2	0	0	0	0	0	0	0	0	2	0	0	0	0	0	0	0	0	0
Rhoda	5	.2443	.3861	35.9	4	0	0	0	0	0	1	0	4	0	0	0	0	0	0	0	0	0	0	0	0	0	1	0	0
Rhode	6	.4364	.5565	37.5	1	3	2	0	0	0	0	0	0	0	0	0	0	1	0	0	1	0	0	0	0	0	1	3	0
RhodeIsland	34	.6666	4.6526	46.7	0	6	7	3	7	8	1	2	2	0	1	0	2	17	1	1	0	0	0	0	2	1	5	2	0
Rhodes	14	.6141	1.7784	42.5	0	1	5	0	3	1	4	0	1	1	0	0	0	3	1	0	0	0	0	0	0	5	1	2	0
Rhodesia	4	.2183	.2285	33.6	0	1	1	2	0	0	0	0	0	0	0	0	0	3	0	0	0	0	0	0	0	1	0	0	0
rhodium	2	.0000	.0209	23.2	0	2	0	0	0	0	0	0	0	0	0	0	0	0	0	0	0	0	0	0	0	0	2	0	0
rhododendrons	2	.2441	.1127	30.5	1	0	0	0	0	1	0	0	0	0	0	0	0	0	0	0	0	0	0	0	1	0	1	0	0
Rhododendrons	2	.0000	.0394	26.0	0	0	0	0	0	0	0	2	0	0	0	0	0	0	0	2	0	0	0	0	0	0	0	0	0
Rhodora	2	.2278	.1128	30.5	0	0	0	0	0	1	0	1	0	0	0	0	0	0	0	1	0	0	0	0	0	0	1	0	0
Rhody	3	.0000	.0243	23.8	0	0	0	0	3	0	0	0	0	0	0	0	0	0	0	0	3	0	0	0	0	0	0	0	0
rhombi	6	.0000	.0898	29.5	0	0	0	0	0	6	0	0	0	0	0	0	6	0	0	0	0	0	0	0	0	0	0	0	0
rhombus	5	.0000	.0748	28.7	0	0	0	2	0	3	0	0	0	0	0	0	5	0	0	0	0	0	0	0	0	0	0	0	0
rhombuses	2	.0000	.0299	24.8	0	0	0	0	0	2	0	0	0	0	0	0	2	0	0	0	0	0	0	0	0	0	0	0	0
Rhone	6	.3367	.4508	36.5	3	0	0	2	0	0	1	0	0	1	0	0	0	2	0	0	0	0	0	0	0	0	3	0	0
rhubarb	3	.3847	.2494	34.0	0	1	1	1	0	0	0	0	0	0	0	0	0	0	0	0	0	0	0	0	1	1	1	0	0
rhyme	226	.4641	22.342	53.5	102	38	23	25	12	13	11	2	32	53	2	15	0	0	111	0	7	0	1	0	1	2	1	1	0
Rhyme	2	.0000	.0162	22.1	0	2	0	0	0	0	0	0	0	0	0	0	0	0	0	0	2	0	0	0	0	0	0	0	0
rhymed	3	.1200	.1302	31.1	0	2	0	0	1	0	0	0	1	2	0	0	0	0	0	0	0	0	0	0	0	0	0	0	0
rhymes	87	.4503	8.6224	49.4	51	10	5	8	4	4	5	0	24	14	0	8	0	0	36	0	2	0	0	0	1	0	0	2	0
rhyming	35	.2970	2.2778	43.6	19	9	2	1	1	2	1	0	0	16	0	2	0	0	17	0	0	0	0	0	0	0	0	0	0
Rhyne	2	.0000	.0243	23.9	0	0	0	0	2	0	0	0	0	0	0	0	0	0	0	0	0	0	0	0	0	0	0	2	0
rhythm	574	.3252	40.189	56.0	101	82	102	78	113	57	38	3	12	15	1	25	1	0	1	5	474	19	3	2	1	9	1	5	0
Rhythm	13	.0000	.1051	30.2	12	0	0	0	0	1	0	0	0	0	0	0	0	0	0	0	13	0	0	0	0	0	0	0	0
rhythmic	87	.3030	5.7455	47.6	4	4	11	16	23	15	14	0	2	0	0	1	0	0	0	1	70	3	0	0	3	2	4	1	0
rhythmical	3	.2088	.1442	31.6	1	0	0	0	1	0	1	0	0	0	0	0	0	0	0	0	2	0	0	0	0	0	1	0	0
rhythmically	8	.2856	.5257	37.2	0	0	0	1	5	2	0	0	1	0	0	1	0	0	0	0	5	0	0	0	0	0	1	0	0
rhythms	100	.2244	5.1260	47.1	3	16	18	19	24	12	8	0	2	2	0	0	0	1	0	0	86	2	0	0	0	4	2	1	0
ri	2	.0000	.0162	22.1	0	2	0	0	0	0	0	0	0	0	0	0	0	0	0	0	2	0	0	0	0	0	0	0	0
rib	40	.4686	3.9576	46.0	4	1	6	1	4	5	18	1	2	1	0	1	1	0	0	13	0	0	3	11	1	1	3	3	0
Ribaut	5	.0000	.0972	29.9	0	0	5	0	0	0	0	0	0	0	0	0	0	5	0	0	0	0	0	0	0	0	0	0	0
ribbed	5	.4158	.4213	36.2	0	0	0	1	1	0	3	0	0	0	0	0	0	0	0	0	0	1	1	2	1	0	0	0	0
ribbing	2	.2444	.1132	30.5	0	0	0	0	0	1	1	0	0	1	0	0	0	0	0	0	0	0	0	0	1	0	0	0	0
ribbon	121	.7708	18.875	52.8	40	17	16	18	7	11	11	1	25	5	0	6	25	7	3	5	1	0	5	0	27	3	1	8	0
Ribbon	5	.4143	.4656	36.7	1	0	1	1	0	0	0	2	1	0	0	0	0	1	0	0	0	0	0	0	0	0	1	2	0
ribbon-shaped	2	.1249	.0685	28.4	0	0	0	0	1	1	0	0	0	0	0	0	0	0	0	1	0	0	0	1	0	0	0	0	0
ribbons	65	.8818	11.451	50.6	13	15	5	16	6	7	2	1	23	1	1	5	5	6	0	1	0	1	1	1	8	6	1	5	0
riboflavin	14	.2618	.8495	39.3	0	0	5	1	3	3	2	0	0	0	0	0	0	0	0	7	0	0	5	0	0	0	2	0	0
ribonucleic	2	.0000	.0394	26.0	0	0	0	0	1	0	1	0	0	0	0	0	0	0	0	2	0	0	0	0	0	0	0	0	0
ribs	94	.8323	15.716	52.0	11	13	22	7	18	11	10	2	22	1	0	8	6	2	0	25	3	0	1	2	11	3	5	5	0
Ribs	3	.0000	.1370	31.4	0	3	0	0	0	0	0	0	3	0	0	0	0	0	0	0	0	0	0	0	0	0	0	0	0
Ribsy	32	.1488	1.6309	42.1	2	22	8	0	0	0	0	0	13	0	0	0	0	0	0	0	0	0	0	0	19	0	0	0	0
Rica	5	.2360	.3663	35.6	0	0	1	4	0	0	0	0	3	0	0	0	0	2	0	0	0	0	0	0	0	0	0	0	0
Rican	10	.0460	.2382	33.8	3	0	3	0	2	1	1	0	1	0	0	0	0	0	0	0	0	0	0	0	0	0	0	9	0
Ricans	3	.2425	.1816	32.6	0	0	3	0	0	0	0	0	0	0	0	0	0	2	0	0	0	0	0	0	0	0	0	1	0
Ricardo	23	.0000	1.0507	40.2	11	12	0	0	0	0	0	0	23	0	0	0	0	0	0	0	0	0	0	0	0	0	0	0	0
Ricco	9	.0000	.0966	29.8	0	0	0	0	0	0	9	0	0	0	0	9	0	0	0	0	0	0	0	0	0	0	0	0	0
Ricco's	2	.0000	.0215	23.3	0	0	0	0	0	0	2	0	0	0	0	2	0	0	0	0	0	0	0	0	0	0	0	0	0
rice	264	.6721	36.920	55.7	38	66	32	58	33	22	12	3	69	0	0	12	0	108	1	8	0	0	8	0	4	12	29	13	0
Rice	10	.4790	1.0875	40.4	6	2	1	0	1	0	0	0	4	0	0	1	0	3	0	0	0	0	0	0	0	2	0	0	0
rice-balls	2	.0000	.0290	24.6	2	0	0	0	0	0	0	0	0	0	0	0	0	0	0	0	0	0	0	0	0	2	0	0	0
Rice's	3	.2379	.1705	32.3	0	2	1	0	0	0	0	0	0	0	0	1	0	0	0	0	0	0	0	0	0	2	0	0	0
rich	584	.9168	106.25	60.3	88	77	111	72	108	71	47	10	136	20	2	43	1	144	10	35	24	11	17	1	30	48	37	24	1
Rich	5	.2414	.3872	35.9	2	1	1	1	0	0	0	0	4	0	0	0	1	0	0	0	0	0	0	0	0	0	0	0	0
Rich-ard	2	.0000	.0243	23.9	0	0	2	0	0	0	0	0	0	0	0	0	0	0	0	0	0	0	0	0	0	0	0	2	0
Richard	254	.7719	39.580	56.0	13	27	73	41	34	49	12	5	45	30	1	2	22	8	1	7	18	0	2	0	4	19	29	66	0
Richard's	23	.5040	2.4668	43.9	2	5	6	5	2	2	0	1	2	4	0	0	6	2	0	1	0	0	0	0	0	0	0	8	0
Richards	19	.6222	2.4479	43.9	0	2	10	3	3	0	1	0	1	3	0	2	0	7	0	3	0	0	0	0	0	0	1	2	0
Richardson	15	.4915	1.5499	41.9	0	0	10	1	1	1	2	0	1	0	0	1	0	0	0	0	0	1	0	0	8	0	1	3	0
Richardson's	4	.2441	.2254	33.5	0	0	4	0	0	0	0	0	0	0	0	0	0	0	0	0	0	0	0	0	2	0	2	0	0
Richelieu	2	.0000	.0243	23.9	0	0	0	2	0	0	0	0	0	0	0	0	0	0	0	0	0	0	0	0	0	0	0	2	0
richer	33	.7644	5.1074	47.1	3	7	0	5	6	6	5	1	5	0	0	2	1	8	2	4	1	0	1	0	0	4	5	0	0
riches	58	.6265	7.6394	48.8	11	7	16	6	10	5	2	1	15	0	0	3	0	20	0	0	3	0	0	0	0	6	9	2	0
richest	43	.6419	5.7599	47.6	8	3	13	4	6	7	2	0	10	1	0	2	0	13	0	0	0	0	1	0	1	6	9	0	0
richly	17	.6787	2.3669	43.7	1	1	1	4	5	2	1	2	3	0	0	2	0	2	0	0	1	0	0	0	2	1	4	2	0
Richmond	22	.5816	2.6712	44.3	1	1	5	1	3	9	2	0	1	3	1	1	0	12	0	0	0	0	0	0	0	2	2	0	0
richness	15	.7433	2.2414	43.5	2	0	3	0	5	3	2	0	1	1	0	1	0	1	1	1	1	1	1	0	1	1	4	0	0
richt	3	.0000	.0328	25.2	0	0	0	0	0	3	0	0	0	3	0	0	0	0	0	0	0	0	0	0	0	0	0	0	0
Rick	34	.3240	2.8760	44.6	12	0	0	13	4	5	0	0	19	1	0	0	1	0	0	0	0	0	0	0	0	0	0	13	0
Rick's	3	.2279	.2143	33.3	1	0	0	1	1	0	0	0	2	0	0	0	0	0	0	0	0	0	0	0	0	0	0	1	0
rickets	8	.2439	.4902	36.9	0	1	2	0	3	0	2	0	0	0	0	0	0	0	0	7	0	0	1	0	0	0	0	0	0
rickety	16	.6629	2.1899	43.4	5	1	2	0	4	1	3	0	4	3	1	1	0	0	0	0	0	0	0	0	3	1	1	2	0
Rickey	6	.0000	.2741	34.4	0	0	0	0	0	0	6	0	6	0	0	0	0	0	0	0	0	0	0	0	0	0	0	0	0

6E Reynolds'
7A Reynow
9Q Rh
9M RH
9Q Rh-negative
9Q Rh-positive
6P Rhapsodie
6J Rhapsodies
7Q rhea
XP Rhea
4Q Rheims
4Q Rheims-Challoner
4Q Rheims-Douay
3J Rheinhold
8Q Rheneia
7Q rhesus
9Q Rhetorick
5A Rhett's
5A Rhetts
5A Rhetts'
8G rheum
8G rheuma
9D rheumatiz
8G rheumy
8F Rhinebeck
6J Rhinegold
6R Rhinelanders
6A Rhino
3P rhino's
6F rhinoceroses
7Q rhizome
4Q RhodeIsland's
5P Rhodes's
6H Rhodesian
6F Rhodesias
XH Rhododendron
8B Rhonda
9H rhyolite
9H rhyolitic
9Q rhythm-keeper
5P Ri
8J RIAA
9D Rialto
8N riata
XR Rib
9P rib-cage
7H ribbon-like
XR ribbon-tied
8L ribbonlike
8D RIBBY
7N ribcage
3Q Ribe
9D Riblov
9H ribose
7R RIBS
4A Ricardo's
3P rice-plants
7Q rice's
6A ricebucket
5D Rices
8Q ricewater
XR rich-with-protein
5F Richards's
7D richly-carved
8R Richter
3E Richy

Word Type	F	D	U	SFI	3 Gr 3	4 Gr 4	5 Gr 5	6 Gr 6	7 Gr 7	8 Gr 8	9 Gr 9	X UnGr	A Read	B Eng & Gr	C Comp	D Lit	E Math	F Soc Stud	G Spell	H Sci	J Music	K Art	L Home Ec	M Shop	N Lib F	P Lib NF	Q Lib Ref	R Mag	S Rel
Rickover	5	.2110	.3346	35.2	0	3	0	0	2	0	0	0	3	0	0	0	0	0	0	0	0	0	0	0	0	0	0	2	0
Ricky	170	.2491	13.850	51.4	0	21	0	0	149	0	0	0	159	0	0	0	0	0	8	0	0	0	0	0	0	0	0	3	0
Ricky's	26	.2765	2.2206	43.5	0	3	0	0	23	0	0	0	24	0	0	0	0	0	1	0	0	0	0	0	0	0	0	1	0
Rico	42	.6660	5.7532	47.6	15	5	10	4	2	2	4	0	6	3	0	0	0	10	1	1	4	0	0	0	0	2	3	12	0
rid	139	.5203	15.857	52.0	38	18	30	15	18	14	4	2	41	1	0	7	0	9	2	43	1	0	0	0	10	12	1	10	2
riddance	2	.1787	.1174	30.7	1	0	0	1	0	0	0	0	1	0	0	0	0	0	0	0	0	0	0	0	1	0	0	0	0
ridden	41	.7249	6.1208	47.9	8	15	3	5	6	2	2	0	16	8	1	1	0	0	1	1	0	0	0	0	6	3	2	2	0
ridding	2	.2160	.1362	31.3	1	0	0	0	0	0	0	1	1	0	0	0	0	0	0	1	0	0	0	0	0	0	0	0	0
riddle	53	.5514	6.6043	48.2	3	7	4	0	34	5	0	0	39	5	0	0	0	0	5	1	0	0	1	0	0	0	2	0	0
Riddle	2	.1787	.1174	30.7	0	0	0	1	1	0	0	0	1	0	0	0	0	0	0	0	0	0	0	0	1	0	0	0	0
riddled	3	.2181	.1541	31.9	0	0	0	0	3	0	0	0	0	0	0	0	0	0	0	0	0	0	0	0	1	0	2	0	0
Riddler	26	.0000	1.1877	40.7	0	0	0	0	26	0	0	0	26	0	0	0	0	0	0	0	0	0	0	0	0	0	0	0	0
riddles	26	.6199	3.4469	45.4	6	7	1	3	8	1	0	0	13	2	0	1	0	0	5	1	0	0	0	0	0	1	1	2	0
ride	617	.8648	106.96	60.3	208	151	59	54	79	45	16	5	228	28	8	31	22	54	9	23	16	2	0	0	78	71	5	42	0
Ride	4	.0759	.1243	30.9	1	1	0	1	0	1	0	0	1	0	0	0	0	0	0	0	3	0	0	0	0	0	0	0	0
rider	112	.7162	16.525	52.2	27	20	1	29	17	8	10	0	37	1	1	8	0	4	0	10	1	0	0	0	29	10	3	8	0
Rider	4	.3689	.3191	35.0	0	0	1	2	1	0	0	0	0	0	0	0	0	0	0	0	0	0	0	0	2	0	1	1	0
rider's	7	.4041	.6290	38.0	0	2	0	4	1	0	0	0	1	0	0	0	0	0	0	0	0	0	0	0	1	2	0	3	0
Rider's	4	.0000	.0469	26.7	0	0	0	4	0	0	0	0	0	0	0	0	0	0	0	0	0	0	0	0	4	0	0	0	0
riders	81	.7829	12.838	51.1	23	12	8	18	8	8	4	0	20	4	2	3	0	6	1	5	1	0	0	0	9	16	1	13	0
Riders	8	.3872	.7790	38.9	3	0	1	0	1	2	1	0	5	0	0	0	0	2	0	0	0	0	0	0	0	0	1	0	0
rides	86	.8170	14.242	51.5	27	7	9	18	12	6	3	4	39	2	2	5	3	3	1	7	9	0	0	0	4	5	1	5	0
ridge	82	.7309	12.256	50.9	17	7	13	8	8	14	15	0	20	5	0	11	0	6	0	8	0	0	0	0	9	16	3	4	0
Ridge	36	.5970	4.4949	46.5	2	3	14	2	9	6	0	0	5	0	0	4	1	10	0	1	0	0	0	0	0	3	10	2	0
ridges	80	.7984	12.826	51.1	18	3	15	11	13	8	8	4	6	1	0	2	0	19	1	17	1	4	3	1	3	11	6	5	0
Ridges	2	.0000	.0389	25.9	0	0	2	0	0	0	0	0	0	0	0	0	0	2	0	0	0	0	0	0	0	0	0	0	0
ridicule	14	.6503	1.9129	42.8	0	0	0	2	5	4	3	0	5	1	0	0	0	1	0	2	2	0	0	0	0	2	1	0	0
ridiculed	7	.5371	.7820	38.9	0	0	1	0	3	2	1	0	0	2	0	1	0	1	0	0	0	0	0	0	0	2	0	1	0
ridiculous	34	.7675	5.3209	47.3	2	7	6	5	2	8	3	1	13	3	1	2	2	0	0	0	0	1	0	0	5	2	1	4	0
ridiculously	2	.1907	.0862	29.4	0	0	0	0	0	1	1	0	0	0	0	1	0	0	0	0	0	0	1	0	0	0	0	0	0
ridin'	3	.2374	.1625	32.1	0	0	0	0	2	0	1	0	0	0	0	2	0	0	0	0	1	0	0	0	0	0	0	0	0
riding	297	.8296	49.633	57.0	87	52	31	26	49	38	12	2	105	17	9	35	0	20	4	5	9	1	1	0	40	31	5	15	0
Riding	17	.3742	1.6218	42.1	1	3	0	11	0	2	0	0	12	0	0	2	0	0	0	0	3	0	0	0	0	0	0	0	0
ridley	3	.0000	.0314	25.0	0	0	0	0	3	0	0	0	0	0	0	0	0	0	0	0	0	0	0	0	0	0	3	0	0
rife	2	.2446	.1122	30.5	0	0	0	0	1	0	1	0	0	0	0	1	0	0	0	0	0	0	0	0	0	0	1	0	0
riffles	3	.3390	.2450	33.9	0	0	1	1	1	0	0	0	1	0	0	0	0	0	0	0	0	0	0	0	0	0	1	1	0
rifle	140	.7150	20.564	53.1	5	23	30	18	49	12	1	2	43	2	3	37	1	1	2	5	1	0	0	0	13	20	3	9	0
Rifle	2	.1551	.0728	28.6	0	0	0	0	1	1	0	0	0	0	1	0	0	0	0	0	0	0	0	0	1	0	0	0	0
rifleman	2	.2433	.1158	30.6	0	0	1	0	1	0	0	0	0	0	0	0	0	0	0	0	0	0	0	0	0	1	0	1	0
riflemen	6	.2378	.3617	35.6	0	0	4	0	0	2	0	0	0	0	0	0	0	4	0	0	0	0	0	0	0	2	0	0	0
rifles	34	.6578	4.6372	46.7	3	4	5	4	11	5	2	0	8	2	0	6	1	3	0	0	1	0	0	0	0	7	0	6	0
rift	10	.4241	.9829	39.9	0	0	1	7	1	1	0	0	3	0	0	1	0	5	0	0	0	0	0	0	0	1	0	0	0
Rift	7	.3415	.5477	37.4	0	0	0	4	2	0	1	0	0	0	0	0	0	4	0	1	0	0	0	0	0	0	2	0	0
rig	17	.5879	2.1213	43.3	2	0	3	2	3	3	4	0	5	0	0	1	0	2	0	0	0	0	0	0	2	0	3	4	0
Riga	2	.0000	.0209	23.2	0	0	2	0	0	0	0	0	0	0	0	0	0	0	0	0	0	0	0	0	0	0	2	0	0
Rigby	10	.0756	.3125	34.9	0	0	2	0	4	4	0	0	2	0	0	8	0	0	0	0	0	0	0	0	0	0	0	0	0
RIGBY	11	.0000	.1180	30.7	0	0	0	0	0	11	0	0	0	0	0	11	0	0	0	0	0	0	0	0	0	0	0	0	0
rigged	11	.5071	1.2281	40.9	0	1	1	1	4	2	2	0	4	0	0	1	0	1	0	0	0	0	0	0	2	0	3	0	0
rigging	21	.5943	2.6661	44.3	2	1	1	7	3	4	3	0	8	1	2	1	0	3	0	0	0	0	0	0	0	3	2	1	0
Riggs	20	.3721	1.8286	42.6	3	12	0	0	5	0	0	0	10	0	0	5	0	0	0	0	0	0	0	0	0	5	0	0	0
right	4815	.9615	914.23	69.6	1064	808	469	507	893	587	425	62	1642	205	27	312	587	246	124	239	160	18	118	65	424	320	99	227	2
Right	38	.2526	2.3025	43.6	2	0	5	29	0	1	1	0	3	3	0	0	1	1	0	0	0	0	0	0	29	0	0	1	0
RIGHT	2	.2109	.0918	29.6	1	0	0	0	1	0	0	0	0	0	0	0	0	0	0	0	1	0	1	0	0	0	0	0	0
right-	2	.1387	.0689	28.4	0	1	0	1	0	0	0	0	0	0	1	0	0	0	0	0	0	0	0	0	0	1	0	0	0
Right-Distributive	4	.0000	.0599	27.8	0	0	0	0	0	0	4	0	0	0	0	0	4	0	0	0	0	0	0	0	0	0	0	0	0
right-about	2	.2427	.1152	30.6	0	0	1	0	0	1	0	0	0	0	0	0	0	0	0	0	0	0	0	0	1	1	0	0	0
right-angle	4	.3123	.2739	34.4	0	0	0	0	3	1	0	0	0	0	0	0	0	0	0	0	0	0	0	1	0	1	0	2	0
right-center	2	.0000	.0215	23.3	0	0	0	0	0	2	0	0	0	0	0	2	0	0	0	0	0	0	0	0	0	0	0	0	0
right-cut	2	.0000	.0050	17.0	0	0	0	0	0	0	2	0	0	0	0	0	0	0	0	0	0	0	0	2	0	0	0	0	0
right-hand	45	.7278	6.6162	48.2	3	7	6	7	7	2	13	0	4	3	0	4	8	3	8	5	1	2	0	4	1	2	0	0	0
right-handed	8	.4519	.7806	38.9	3	3	1	0	0	0	1	0	1	0	1	0	0	0	0	1	0	0	0	1	0	4	0	0	0
right-hander	5	.2390	.2808	34.5	4	0	0	0	0	0	1	0	0	0	0	0	0	0	0	0	0	0	0	1	0	4	0	0	0
right-of-way	3	.3826	.2445	33.9	0	0	2	0	0	0	0	1	0	0	0	0	0	0	0	0	1	0	0	0	0	0	1	1	0
right-side	4	.0000	.0101	20.0	0	0	0	0	0	0	4	0	0	0	0	0	0	0	0	0	0	0	0	4	0	0	0	0	0
righted	9	.0000	.4111	36.1	0	2	0	4	1	2	0	0	9	0	0	0	0	0	0	0	0	0	0	0	0	0	0	0	0
righteous	2	.0000	.0234	23.7	0	1	0	1	0	0	0	0	0	0	0	0	0	0	0	0	0	0	0	0	2	0	0	0	0
righteousness	4	.4711	.3982	36.0	0	0	1	0	0	3	0	0	0	0	0	1	0	1	0	0	1	0	0	0	0	1	0	0	0
rightful	12	.5213	1.3475	41.3	0	1	0	3	4	4	0	0	2	0	0	0	0	5	0	0	0	0	0	0	2	0	1	2	0
rightfully	5	.5251	.5620	37.5	0	1	0	2	0	0	2	0	1	0	0	0	0	1	0	0	1	0	0	0	1	0	0	1	0
rightly	14	.5824	1.7601	42.5	0	1	0	5	3	1	3	1	6	0	0	2	0	1	0	0	0	0	0	0	1	1	0	3	0
rightness	2	.2408	.1204	30.8	0	0	1	0	0	0	1	0	0	0	0	0	0	1	0	0	0	0	0	0	0	1	0	0	0
rights	225	.6915	32.079	55.1	8	16	23	28	37	82	27	4	38	1	1	4	0	105	3	22	2	0	1	0	2	9	24	13	0
Rights	24	.5689	2.8939	44.6	1	0	1	1	2	11	8	0	3	1	0	1	0	13	0	1	0	0	0	0	0	1	3	1	0
rigid	49	.7622	7.5335	48.8	1	2	3	7	20	7	7	2	6	1	0	3	1	4	0	5	2	0	0	3	3	5	10	6	0
rigidity	5	.2043	.2298	33.6	0	0	0	0	3	0	2	0	0	0	0	0	0	0	0	0	0	0	0	2	0	0	3	0	0
rigidly	4	.3225	.3013	34.8	0	0	1	0	1	1	1	0	1	0	1	0	0	0	0	0	0	0	0	0	0	0	1	1	0
Rigoletto	3	.0000	.0243	23.8	0	0	0	1	1	1	0	0	0	0	0	0	0	0	0	0	3	0	0	0	0	0	0	0	0
rigor	2	.1523	.0721	28.6	0	0	0	0	0	2	0	0	0	0	1	0	0	0	0	0	0	0	0	0	0	0	0	1	0
rigorous	3	.1169	.1277	31.1	0	0	0	1	1	0	1	0	1	0	0	0	0	0	0	0	0	0	0	0	0	0	2	0	0
rigors	8	.4159	.7122	38.5	0	0	0	1	2	3	2	0	0	0	0	1	0	0	0	1	0	0	0	0	0	0	2	4	0
rigs	6	.2307	.3476	35.4	0	0	0	1	0	0	5	0	1	0	0	1	0	0	0	0	0	0	0	0	0	0	4	0	0
Rikki	20	.2445	1.5455	41.9	12	3	0	0	5	0	0	0	16	0	0	4	0	0	0	0	0	0	0	0	0	0	0	0	0
Rikki-tikki	37	.2404	2.7927	44.5	0	11	0	9	17	0	0	0	28	0	0	9	0	0	0	0	0	0	0	0	0	0	0	0	0
Rikki-tikki-tavi	5	.2445	.3864	35.9	0	3	0	1	1	0	0	0	4	0	0	1	0	0	0	0	0	0	0	0	0	0	0	0	0
Rikki's	2	.0000	.0914	29.6	2	0	0	0	0	0	0	0	2	0	0	0	0	0	0	0	0	0	0	0	0	0	0	0	0
riled	2	.2411	.1091	30.4	0	1	0	0	0	0	1	0	0	0	0	1	0	0	0	0	1	0	0	0	0	0	0	0	0
Riley	25	.4503	2.4164	43.8	2	18	3	1	0	0	1	0	1	3	0	0	0	2	0	0	3	0	0	0	0	15	0	1	0
rills	2	.0000	.0389	25.9	0	0	2	0	0	0	0	0	0	0	0	0	0	2	0	0	0	0	0	0	0	0	0	0	0
rim	75	.7795	11.828	50.7	9	9	7	16	13	12	7	2	18	2	6	2	0	13	0	6	3	0	3	1	7	4	4	6	0
Rim	8	.3009	.5810	37.6	1	0	1	5	0	0	0	1	2	0	1	0	0	0	0	0	0	0	0	0	0	0	0	5	0
Rimac	2	.0000	.0389	25.9	0	2	0	0	0	0	0	0	0	0	0	0	0	2	0	0	0	0	0	0	0	0	0	0	0
Rimbaud	2	.0000	.0209	23.2	0	0	2	0	0	0	0	0	0	0	0	0	0	0	0	0	0	0	0	0	0	0	2	0	0
rime	3	.3385	.2445	33.9	1	1	0	0	1	0	0	0	1	0	0	0	0	0	0	0	0	0	0	0	1	0	1	0	0
rimmed	4	.3713	.3634	35.6	0	0	1	1	1	0	1	0	2	0	0	1	0	0	0	0	0	0	0	0	1	0	0	0	0
rimrock	2	.0000	.0914	29.6	0	0	0	2	0	0	0	0	2	0	0	0	0	0	0	0	0	0	0	0	0	0	0	0	0

7R Rickover's
8L rickrack
4N Ricky-ticky
7A Rickyyyyy
9P ricocheted
7Q ricocheting
7L ricotta
3J riddle-ma-ree
7A riddle-me-that
7A riddle-me-this
4A Riddles
4D ridge-pole
6A ridge-shaped
5Q ridged
7R ridgetop
9D ridgetops
6N ridging
7A ridiculing
4A ridingest
8A Ridinghood
9D Ridley
7Q ridleys
6H Riedman
8J Riegger
4A Riehls
8E Riemann
8J Rienzi
8D Rieseberg
6F Rif
5A rifle's
3P rifled
7N rifts
4J Rig-A-Jig-Jig
7D Rigby's
5H Rigel
7A riggings
4P right-field
7P right-footed
9Q right-thinking
7F Righteous
6A righteously
7A righthand
5H righthanded
7R righthander
7R righting
XR rights-of-way
7F rigidities
4P Rih
8Q Rijksmuseum
8K Rijn
3N rile
7N rimed

Word Type	F	D	U	SFI	3 Gr 3	4 Gr 4	5 Gr 5	6 Gr 6	7 Gr 7	8 Gr 8	9 Gr 9	X UnGr	A Read	B Eng & Gr	C Comp	D Lit	E Math	F Soc Stud	G Spell	H Sci	J Music	K Art	L Home Ec	M Shop	N Lib F	P Lib NF	Q Lib Ref	R Mag	S Rel
rims	11	.6232	1.4587	41.6	3	1	2	1	3	1	0	0	5	0	0	1	0	1	0	0	1	0	1	0	1	1	0	0	0
Rimsky-Korsakov	5	.0000	.0404	26.1	0	1	0	1	1	0	2	0	0	0	0	0	0	0	0	0	5	0	0	0	0	0	0	0	0
Rinaldo	6	.0000	.2741	34.4	6	0	0	0	0	0	0	0	6	0	0	0	0	0	0	0	0	0	0	0	0	0	0	0	0
rind	8	.3301	.5872	37.7	0	1	2	1	1	1	2	0	1	1	0	0	0	0	0	0	0	0	3	0	2	0	0	1	0
rinds	2	.1839	.0845	29.3	0	1	0	0	1	0	0	0	0	0	0	0	0	0	0	0	0	0	1	0	1	0	0	0	0
ring	516	.9098	93.291	59.7	183	88	44	69	60	40	26	6	151	29	2	29	76	14	41	30	25	2	2	3	48	26	8	30	0
Ring	18	.7030	2.5612	44.1	2	5	1	5	1	3	0	1	0	1	0	0	1	4	0	1	3	0	0	0	1	4	2	1	0
ring-like	2	.0000	.0394	26.0	0	0	0	0	0	0	2	0	0	0	0	0	0	0	0	2	0	0	0	0	0	0	0	0	0
ring-necked	4	.3864	.3418	35.3	2	0	0	0	0	0	1	1	0	0	0	0	0	0	0	2	0	0	0	0	0	0	1	1	0
ring-toss	2	.0000	.0299	24.8	0	0	0	2	0	0	0	0	0	0	0	0	2	0	0	0	0	0	0	0	0	0	0	0	0
ringed	15	.6302	1.9452	42.9	7	1	0	0	4	1	1	1	2	2	0	2	1	0	0	0	1	0	0	0	0	1	5	1	0
ringer	3	.0000	.1370	31.4	1	2	0	0	0	0	0	0	3	0	0	0	0	0	0	0	0	0	0	0	0	0	0	0	0
ringers	4	.0000	.1827	32.6	0	4	0	0	0	0	0	0	4	0	0	0	0	0	0	0	0	0	0	0	0	0	0	0	0
ringing	70	.7396	10.537	50.2	6	13	11	8	7	16	8	1	15	2	1	13	0	6	0	8	9	0	0	0	9	5	0	2	0
ringlets	4	.2445	.3067	34.9	1	0	0	1	0	2	0	0	3	0	0	0	0	0	0	0	0	0	0	0	0	1	0	0	0
Ringling	9	.3194	.6434	38.1	0	8	0	0	0	1	0	0	0	0	0	0	0	0	0	0	0	1	0	0	0	7	0	1	0
ringmaster	7	.2362	.5173	37.1	4	1	0	0	2	0	0	0	5	0	0	0	0	0	0	0	0	0	0	0	2	0	0	0	0
ringo	2	.0000	.0162	22.1	2	0	0	0	0	0	0	0	0	0	0	0	0	0	0	0	2	0	0	0	0	0	0	0	0
rings	158	.8844	27.872	54.5	28	25	11	17	23	40	10	4	44	7	0	12	18	8	4	23	2	0	6	3	3	11	6	11	0
ringside	2	.2443	.1130	30.5	0	0	0	0	1	0	1	0	0	0	0	1	0	0	0	0	0	0	0	0	1	0	0	0	0
ringtail	2	.2446	.1142	30.6	0	0	0	0	1	0	0	1	0	0	0	0	0	0	0	0	0	0	0	0	1	0	0	1	0
rink	6	.3204	.4906	36.9	3	0	1	0	1	1	0	0	3	0	0	0	1	0	0	0	0	1	0	0	0	0	0	1	0
rinse	22	.5655	2.6797	44.3	10	1	2	1	1	4	0	3	8	0	1	0	0	0	0	4	0	0	2	0	0	1	0	6	0
rinsed	11	.5716	1.3571	41.3	3	0	2	2	1	2	1	0	4	0	0	0	0	0	0	3	0	0	1	0	1	1	0	1	0
rinsing	4	.3686	.3286	35.2	1	0	0	0	1	1	1	0	1	0	1	0	0	0	0	0	0	0	1	0	0	0	1	0	0
Rinty	7	.0000	.3198	35.0	7	0	0	0	0	0	0	0	7	0	0	0	0	0	0	0	0	0	0	0	0	0	0	0	0
Rinuccini	2	.0000	.0290	24.6	0	0	0	2	0	0	0	0	0	0	0	0	0	0	0	0	0	0	0	0	0	2	0	0	0
Rio	74	.5815	9.0162	49.6	4	12	5	17	26	8	0	2	9	2	0	2	0	27	0	1	7	0	0	0	0	1	21	4	0
riot	13	.5858	1.5582	41.9	0	0	0	2	3	5	3	0	0	2	0	2	0	2	0	0	2	1	0	0	0	0	0	4	0
rioted	3	.3553	.2608	34.2	0	0	1	0	1	1	0	0	1	0	0	0	0	1	0	0	0	0	0	0	0	1	0	0	0
rioting	8	.4596	.7912	39.0	1	0	1	0	2	2	2	0	0	0	0	0	0	4	0	0	0	0	0	0	0	1	1	2	0
riotous	3	.3773	.2485	34.0	0	0	0	1	0	2	0	0	0	0	0	1	0	1	0	0	0	0	0	0	1	0	0	0	0
riots	15	.3473	1.1539	40.6	2	0	2	1	2	3	2	3	0	0	0	0	0	2	0	1	0	0	0	0	0	0	3	9	0
rip	17	.6718	2.3836	43.8	8	1	3	2	2	0	1	0	7	1	1	1	0	0	0	0	0	0	1	0	1	2	0	3	0
Rip	30	.4963	3.2412	45.1	0	0	2	1	19	6	2	0	9	2	2	11	0	0	0	0	0	0	0	0	6	0	0	0	0
ripe	104	.8372	17.510	52.4	25	16	11	24	11	8	9	0	33	5	4	10	1	12	6	12	0	0	1	0	6	6	4	4	0
ripen	15	.4020	1.4099	41.5	3	3	3	4	2	0	0	0	4	0	0	0	0	8	0	0	0	0	0	0	2	1	0	0	0
ripened	22	.6702	3.0366	44.8	2	4	2	4	7	2	0	1	3	0	0	2	0	3	0	7	0	0	2	0	2	1	1	1	0
ripening	10	.5675	1.2046	40.8	0	2	1	1	1	3	1	1	2	0	0	1	0	1	0	2	0	0	0	0	3	0	1	0	0
ripens	4	.3813	.3772	35.8	2	0	1	0	1	0	0	0	2	0	0	0	0	1	0	0	0	0	0	0	0	1	0	0	0
ripieno	3	.0000	.0243	23.8	0	0	0	0	0	3	0	0	0	0	0	0	0	0	0	0	3	0	0	0	0	0	0	0	0
ripped	44	.7685	6.8795	48.4	7	6	4	6	11	6	3	1	14	4	0	1	0	2	0	2	1	0	2	0	5	5	1	7	0
ripping	25	.3777	2.0614	43.1	0	3	0	1	14	5	2	0	5	0	1	2	0	0	0	0	0	0	2	11	1	0	2	1	0
ripple	8	.5544	.9290	39.7	2	0	1	1	2	1	1	0	1	0	0	1	0	0	0	0	0	0	0	0	3	1	1	1	0
Ripple	2	.0000	.0162	22.1	0	0	0	2	0	0	0	0	0	0	0	0	0	0	0	0	2	0	0	0	0	0	0	0	0
rippled	11	.6769	1.5605	41.9	0	1	3	2	2	2	1	0	5	0	0	1	0	1	0	0	1	0	0	0	1	0	1	1	0
ripples	11	.5239	1.2189	40.9	1	1	0	1	4	2	1	1	1	0	0	0	0	1	0	3	3	0	0	0	0	0	2	1	0
rippling	15	.6431	2.0023	43.0	3	1	1	3	4	2	1	0	4	2	1	0	0	1	0	0	3	0	0	0	2	1	1	0	0
rips	7	.4444	.7125	38.5	2	1	0	0	4	0	0	0	3	0	0	1	0	0	0	1	0	0	0	1	0	0	0	1	0
rise	375	.9338	69.320	58.4	34	57	59	53	67	27	62	16	74	14	4	19	7	44	4	70	16	3	3	3	13	24	43	33	1
risen	44	.1825	2.2377	43.5	6	7	4	7	13	3	3	1	9	3	1	6	1	2	0	3	0	0	0	0	2	7	2	3	5
riser	7	.2451	.3774	35.8	0	0	0	0	2	3	2	0	0	0	0	2	0	0	0	0	0	0	0	3	0	0	0	2	0
risers	2	.0000	.0243	23.9	0	0	0	0	2	0	0	0	0	0	0	0	0	0	0	0	0	0	0	0	0	0	0	2	0
rises	174	.8208	28.667	54.6	18	23	22	33	31	20	21	6	22	9	3	7	3	26	0	57	9	1	0	0	4	5	19	9	0
rising	215	.8328	35.947	55.6	15	36	21	42	42	27	25	7	52	9	3	19	0	12	0	29	10	1	0	0	17	24	18	20	1
Rising	4	.3348	.3266	35.1	0	1	0	1	1	0	1	0	1	0	0	1	0	2	0	0	0	0	0	0	0	0	0	0	0
risk	68	.7851	10.839	50.4	4	10	7	9	17	12	7	2	22	2	0	6	0	7	0	4	0	0	2	0	4	6	6	9	0
risked	12	.6673	1.6708	42.2	1	1	3	1	3	1	2	0	4	1	0	2	0	2	0	0	0	0	0	0	1	1	0	1	0
risking	5	.3855	.4777	36.8	0	1	0	0	3	1	0	0	3	0	0	0	0	0	0	0	0	0	0	0	1	0	0	1	0
risks	21	.6562	2.8704	44.6	1	1	3	2	7	2	5	0	6	0	0	3	0	2	0	0	0	0	0	0	1	4	2	3	0
risky	16	.5215	1.7567	42.4	0	2	0	2	6	2	3	1	1	0	0	2	1	1	0	1	0	0	0	0	1	1	0	8	0
Rit	3	.0000	.0434	26.4	3	0	0	0	0	0	0	0	0	0	0	0	0	0	0	0	0	0	0	0	0	3	0	0	0
Rita	17	.4156	1.6147	42.1	1	11	0	1	0	0	4	0	5	1	0	4	7	0	0	0	0	0	0	0	0	0	0	0	0
Rita's	2	.0000	.0914	29.6	0	2	0	0	0	0	0	0	2	0	0	0	0	0	0	0	0	0	0	0	0	0	0	0	0
ritard	3	.0000	.0243	23.8	0	2	1	0	0	0	0	0	0	0	0	0	0	0	0	0	3	0	0	0	0	0	0	0	0
Ritchie	23	.1773	1.1281	40.5	0	0	0	1	21	0	1	0	4	0	0	17	0	0	0	1	0	0	0	0	0	0	0	1	0
RITCHIE	32	.0000	.3434	35.4	0	0	0	0	32	0	0	0	0	0	0	32	0	0	0	0	0	0	0	0	0	0	0	0	0
Ritchie's	8	.0506	.1942	32.9	0	0	0	0	8	0	0	0	1	0	0	7	0	0	0	0	0	0	0	0	0	0	0	0	0
rite	2	.2306	.1140	30.6	0	0	0	1	0	1	0	0	0	1	0	0	0	1	0	0	0	0	0	0	0	0	0	0	0
Rite	8	.1143	.2390	33.8	0	0	0	0	2	4	2	0	0	0	0	0	0	0	0	0	7	0	0	0	0	0	1	0	0
rites	10	.5136	1.0841	40.4	0	0	0	3	4	0	2	1	1	2	0	0	0	0	0	0	0	0	0	0	0	2	2	3	0
Ritter	5	.1294	.1816	32.6	0	0	0	0	0	0	4	1	0	0	0	4	0	0	0	1	0	0	0	0	0	0	0	0	0
ritual	22	.5950	2.7163	44.3	0	0	1	4	10	4	3	0	3	6	0	0	0	1	0	0	2	0	0	0	2	0	2	6	0
ritualistic	4	.0000	.0419	26.2	0	0	0	0	2	2	0	0	0	0	0	0	0	0	0	0	0	0	0	0	0	0	4	0	0
rituals	5	.4180	.4632	36.7	0	0	1	1	3	0	0	0	1	2	0	0	0	0	0	0	1	0	0	0	0	1	0	0	0
rival	34	.7070	4.9248	46.9	2	4	5	1	8	6	7	1	7	0	0	2	0	5	1	1	0	0	0	0	2	4	5	7	0
rivaled	7	.3795	.5833	37.7	0	0	0	2	1	3	0	1	0	0	0	0	0	3	0	0	2	0	0	0	0	0	0	2	0
rivalries	7	.4057	.6463	38.1	0	0	0	0	2	2	3	0	1	0	0	0	0	4	0	0	0	0	0	0	0	1	1	0	0
rivalry	6	.4533	.5866	37.7	0	0	1	1	0	1	2	1	1	0	0	1	0	0	0	0	0	1	0	0	0	1	1	1	0
rivals	22	.6113	2.7886	44.5	1	1	2	1	5	5	7	0	1	0	0	0	0	10	0	1	1	0	0	0	1	2	4	2	0
river	1170	.8659	202.80	63.1	239	252	180	178	187	72	36	26	334	23	8	72	14	284	16	64	46	2	0	2	50	126	55	74	0
River	761	.7435	115.18	60.6	85	121	172	125	124	71	36	27	119	7	2	16	10	315	6	22	24	2	0	0	13	76	78	71	0
river-barge	2	.0000	.0243	23.9	0	0	0	0	0	0	0	2	0	0	0	0	0	0	0	0	0	0	0	0	0	0	0	2	0
river-wall	2	.0000	.0234	23.7	0	2	0	0	0	0	0	0	0	0	0	0	0	0	0	0	0	0	0	0	2	0	0	0	0
river's	19	.7149	2.8144	44.5	3	1	5	1	5	2	1	1	8	0	0	0	1	1	0	1	1	0	0	0	2	1	3	2	0
River's	3	.3668	.2405	33.8	0	0	0	0	2	0	1	0	0	0	0	0	0	0	0	1	1	0	0	0	0	0	1	0	0
Rivera	2	.0000	.0914	29.6	2	0	0	0	0	0	0	0	2	0	0	0	0	0	0	0	0	0	0	0	0	0	0	0	0
riverbank	20	.6232	2.6563	44.2	3	7	0	5	3	0	0	2	9	1	0	4	0	1	0	0	0	0	0	0	2	2	0	1	0
Riverbank	3	.0000	.0322	25.1	0	0	0	0	0	0	3	0	0	0	0	3	0	0	0	0	0	0	0	0	0	0	0	0	0
riverbanks	5	.3016	.3700	35.7	0	0	0	3	2	0	0	0	1	0	0	0	0	2	0	0	0	0	0	0	0	0	2	0	0
riverbed	3	.0000	.1370	31.4	0	2	1	0	0	0	0	0	3	0	0	0	0	0	0	0	0	0	0	0	0	0	0	0	0
riverboat	8	.4632	.8051	39.1	1	4	2	0	1	0	0	0	1	0	0	0	0	1	0	0	1	0	0	0	0	4	0	1	0
riverboats	6	.3616	.4807	36.8	0	0	2	0	2	2	0	0	0	0	0	1	0	3	0	0	2	0	0	0	0	0	0	0	0
riverlike	2	.0000	.0290	24.6	2	0	0	0	0	0	0	0	0	0	0	0	0	0	0	0	0	0	0	0	0	2	0	0	0

6B Rin
8P Rin-Tin-Tin
3A Rinaldos
3A ring-a-ring
7R ring-around-a-rosy
5C ring'd
6R ring's
XH Ringer-Locke's
5N ringingly
5H ringlike
4P Ringling's
6R Ringo
7H ringstand
9Q Ringstrasse
3B rinks
XR rinses
3A Rinty's
6F RIO
7Q RioGrande
7P Rios
8F rioters
7C riotously
3P RIP
7C Rip's
7E ripcord
6Q ripener
6R Ripening
7N ripped-open
9J ripplin'
7M ripsaw
6A riptide
4E RIS
7A Rise
8F risings
5N risk's
9R riskier
5P Risorgimento
6G rist
3P Rit's
9B Rite-Spot
3P ritten
7R ritualized
7R Ritz
8J Rival
7N rivaling
3Q Rivals
5P river-bend
5A river-boat
6J river-boatmen
6A river-bound
9Q river-craft
6N river-front
6J river-snow
3A Riveras
3A Riveras'
5Q riverbeds
6J riverboatman
7R riverboatmen
5Q riverfront
3Q riverless

Word Type	F	D	U	SFI	3 Gr 3	4 Gr 4	5 Gr 5	6 Gr 6	7 Gr 7	8 Gr 8	9 Gr 9	X UnGr	A Read	B Eng & Gr	C Comp	D Lit	E Math	F Soc Stud	G Spell	H Sci	J Music	K Art	L Home Ec	M Shop	N Lib F	P Lib NF	Q Lib Ref	R Mag	S Rel
riverman	4	.1349	.2265	33.6	1	0	0	2	0	1	0	0	3	0	1	0	0	0	0	0	0	0	0	0	0	0	0	0	0
rivers	524	.6951	74.916	58.7	123	76	126	70	85	20	19	5	70	7	1	7	1	245	4	71	7	0	0	1	1	41	46	21	0
Rivers	13	.6185	1.6531	42.2	3	1	4	1	1	1	1	1	0	2	0	0	2	4	0	0	0	0	0	0	0	2	2	1	0
Riverside	9	.4066	.8246	39.2	0	0	0	1	3	5	0	0	1	0	0	0	0	5	0	0	0	0	0	0	0	0	1	2	0
Rivertown	3	.0000	.0328	25.2	0	0	0	3	0	0	0	0	0	3	0	0	0	0	0	0	0	0	0	0	0	0	0	0	0
rivet	22	.0168	.1392	31.4	0	0	0	0	9	12	1	0	0	0	0	0	0	0	0	0	0	0	0	21	0	1	0	0	0
riveted	6	.2669	.4019	36.0	0	0	0	2	1	3	0	0	2	0	0	1	0	0	0	0	0	0	0	2	1	0	0	0	0
riveting	5	.0000	.0126	21.0	0	0	0	0	0	2	3	0	0	0	0	0	0	0	0	0	0	0	0	5	0	0	0	0	0
rivets	28	.1078	.8110	39.1	0	3	0	0	5	14	6	0	3	0	0	0	0	0	0	0	0	0	0	20	1	0	2	2	0
Riviera	2	.1948	.1250	31.0	1	0	0	0	1	0	0	0	1	0	0	0	0	0	0	0	0	0	0	0	0	1	0	0	0
Riyadh	2	.0000	.0389	25.9	0	0	0	0	2	0	0	0	0	0	0	0	0	2	0	0	0	0	0	0	0	0	0	0	0
Rizk	2	.1717	.1142	30.6	0	0	0	0	0	1	1	0	1	0	0	1	0	0	0	0	0	0	0	0	0	0	0	0	0
RLD	2	.0000	.0219	23.4	0	0	2	0	0	0	0	0	0	2	0	0	0	0	0	0	0	0	0	0	0	0	0	0	0
RNA	6	.0000	.1183	30.7	0	0	0	0	3	0	3	0	0	0	0	0	0	0	0	6	0	0	0	0	0	0	0	0	0
roach	3	.0000	.0322	25.1	0	0	1	0	2	0	0	0	0	0	0	3	0	0	0	0	0	0	0	0	0	0	0	0	0
roaches	2	.0000	.0215	23.3	0	0	0	0	1	1	0	0	0	0	0	2	0	0	0	0	0	0	0	0	0	0	0	0	0
road	1106	.8757	194.34	62.9	243	192	99	99	246	157	54	16	554	32	20	85	22	69	10	23	5	1	1	12	110	77	10	74	1
Road	89	.7996	14.508	51.6	8	12	15	3	21	24	1	5	45	3	2	4	4	6	1	0	1	0	0	0	4	6	2	11	0
road's	2	.1717	.1142	30.6	0	0	0	1	1	0	0	0	1	0	0	1	0	0	0	0	0	0	0	0	0	0	0	0	0
roadbed	4	.3709	.3633	35.6	0	0	1	1	1	0	1	0	2	0	0	0	0	0	0	0	0	0	0	0	0	0	1	1	0
Roadeo	5	.1468	.2522	34.0	0	0	0	2	3	0	0	0	2	0	0	0	0	0	0	0	0	0	0	0	3	0	0	0	0
Roadeos	2	.0000	.0914	29.6	0	0	0	2	0	0	0	0	2	0	0	0	0	0	0	0	0	0	0	0	0	0	0	0	0
roadhouses	2	.2152	.1357	31.3	0	0	2	0	0	0	0	0	1	0	0	0	0	1	0	0	0	0	0	0	0	0	0	0	0
roadmaster	6	.0655	.1711	32.3	1	0	5	0	0	0	0	0	1	5	0	0	0	0	0	0	0	0	0	0	0	0	0	0	0
Roadmaster	17	.0000	.7766	38.9	12	0	0	0	5	0	0	0	17	0	0	0	0	0	0	0	0	0	0	0	0	0	0	0	0
roadrunner	8	.0000	.0972	29.9	0	8	0	0	0	0	0	0	0	0	0	0	0	0	0	0	0	0	0	0	0	0	0	8	0
roadrunners	2	.0000	.0243	23.9	0	2	0	0	0	0	0	0	0	0	0	0	0	0	0	0	0	0	0	0	0	0	0	2	0
roads	359	.8322	59.851	57.8	72	51	48	54	47	44	36	7	45	13	8	21	4	136	4	16	3	2	0	5	7	42	36	17	0
Roads	6	.5041	.6459	38.1	2	1	0	0	1	2	0	0	1	0	0	1	0	0	0	0	0	0	0	0	0	1	2	1	0
roadside	29	.7626	4.5136	46.5	6	6	2	1	8	4	1	1	10	0	1	3	0	3	0	3	0	1	0	0	2	1	2	3	0
roadsides	5	.4790	.5126	37.1	0	0	0	1	0	1	0	3	0	1	0	1	0	1	0	2	0	0	0	0	0	0	0	0	0
roadster	21	.4729	2.3354	43.7	0	1	0	1	4	14	0	1	14	0	0.	0	0	0	0	0	0	0	0	0	2	2	0	3	0
roadsters	2	.0000	.0290	24.6	0	0	0	0	0	0	0	2	0	0	0	0	0	0	0	0	0	0	0	0	0	2	0	0	0
roadway	21	.4983	2.1868	43.4	0	0	0	2	4	5	10	0	2	0	1	6	0	0	0	1	0	0	0	5	2	1	3	0	0
roadways	5	.5473	.5689	37.6	1	0	1	2	1	0	0	0	0	1	0	0	0	1	0	1	1	0	0	0	0	0	1	0	0
Roald	3	.2425	.1816	32.6	0	1	0	1	1	0	0	0	0	0	0	0	0	2	0	0	0	0	0	0	0	0	0	1	0
roam	45	.7783	7.1043	48.5	13	5	9	2	9	5	2	0	13	5	2	2	0	5	1	3	5	0	0	0	1	6	1	1	0
roamed	45	.4544	4.4902	46.5	9	3	14	11	3	2	1	2	6	1	0	1	0	12	0	4	2	0	0	0	1	10	1	6	1
roaming	16	.7056	2.3496	43.7	1	3	1	3	6	0	2	0	7	1	0	1	0	1	0	1	0	0	0	0	1	2	0	2	0
roan	15	.3204	1.0766	40.3	6	1	0	0	7	1	0	0	0	1	0	0	0	0	0	0	0	0	0	0	7	7	0	0	0
Roanoke	14	.4117	1.2846	41.1	0	8	1	0	2	2	1	0	2	1	0	0	0	1	0	0	0	0	0	0	0	8	2	0	0
Roanokes	3	.0000	.0434	26.4	0	3	0	0	0	0	0	0	0	0	0	0	0	0	0	0	0	0	0	0	0	3	0	0	0
Roany	2	.0000	.0234	23.7	0	0	0	0	2	0	0	0	0	0	0	0	0	0	0	0	0	0	0	0	2	0	0	0	0
roar	167	.7450	25.614	54.1	21	29	25	24	35	22	8	3	78	4	10	13	0	8	0	5	13	1	0	0	14	11	4	6	0
roared	135	.6603	18.859	52.8	32	21	6	12	28	25	9	2	71	3	6	18	0	0	0	1	2	0	0	0	15	11	0	8	0
roaring	72	.8055	11.803	50.7	8	18	6	11	16	7	5	1	36	1	1	9	0	2	0	4	3	1	0	0	5	4	1	5	0
roars	17	.6385	2.2904	43.6	1	3	2	3	3	0	2	3	7	0	1	1	0	0	0	1	1	0	0	0	1	1	0	4	0
roast	55	.7713	8.6239	49.4	12	12	3	8	11	1	5	3	19	4	0	3	1	1	4	2	2	0	4	0	9	1	1	4	0
roasted	27	.7150	3.9574	46.0	5	2	3	6	7	0	4	0	7	2	0	2	0	2	0	2	0	0	2	0	4	4	2	0	0
roaster	4	.2780	.2956	34.7	0	0	1	0	1	1	1	0	2	0	0	0	0	0	0	0	0	0	1	0	0	0	0	1	0
roasting	14	.3108	1.0346	40.1	1	0	3	2	1	2	5	0	4	0	0	0	0	0	0	0	0	0	5	0	1	2	2	0	0
roasts	6	.1582	.2814	34.5	2	0	0	0	1	0	3	0	2	0	0	0	0	0	0	0	0	0	3	0	1	0	0	0	0
rob	14	.7448	2.1093	43.2	1	2	1	3	4	0	3	0	2	1	0	2	0	0	1	1	1	0	0	0	2	2	0	2	0
Rob	18	.3683	1.7387	42.4	0	15	1	0	1	1	0	0	14	0	0	2	0	0	0	0	0	0	0	0	0	2	0	0	0
robb'st	2	.0000	.0290	24.6	0	0	0	0	2	0	0	0	0	0	0	0	0	0	0	0	0	0	0	0	0	2	0	0	0
robbed	25	.6612	3.4352	45.4	4	2	3	5	4	3	4	0	7	3	0	4	0	2	0	0	0	0	0	0	3	4	0	2	0
robber	38	.7009	5.5725	47.5	10	2	3	12	10	0	1	0	21	1	1	3	0	0	1	0	3	0	0	0	6	1	1	0	0
Robber	3	.1200	.1302	31.1	1	2	0	0	0	0	0	0	1	2	0	0	0	0	0	0	0	0	0	0	0	0	0	0	0
robbers	67	.6714	9.5475	49.8	16	4	5	26	12	2	2	0	39	6	0	2	0	5	0	0	2	0	0	0	5	7	0	1	0
robbers'	3	.0000	.1370	31.4	0	0	0	2	1	0	0	0	3	0	0	0	0	0	0	0	0	0	0	0	0	0	0	0	0
robbery	21	.5176	2.4377	43.9	6	1	4	2	7	0	1	0	11	0	0	0	0	1	1	0	0	0	0	0	6	1	1	0	0
Robbie	27	.2419	1.5204	41.8	0	0	0	0	11	0	4	12	0	0	0	11	0	0	0	0	0	0	0	0	0	0	0	16	0
Robbie's	2	.2440	.1132	30.5	0	0	0	0	1	0	0	1	0	0	0	1	0	0	0	0	0	0	0	0	0	0	0	1	0
robbing	5	.4587	.5207	37.2	0	0	2	0	1	1	1	0	2	0	0	0	0	1	0	0	1	0	0	0	0	0	1	0	0
Robbins	2	.2387	.1089	30.4	0	0	0	0	0	1	1	0	0	0	0	0	0	0	0	0	1	0	0	0	1	0	0	0	0
Robby	2	.0000	.0243	23.9	0	0	0	0	0	0	0	2	0	0	0	0	0	0	0	0	0	0	0	0	0	0	0	2	0
robe	38	.6521	5.1488	47.1	7	8	3	8	7	1	2	2	11	1	0	8	0	3	1	0	2	3	0	0	2	3	0	4	0
Robe	5	.0000	.2284	33.6	0	0	5	0	0	0	0	0	5	0	0	0	0	0	0	0	0	0	0	0	0	0	0	0	0
robed	3	.3274	.2364	33.7	0	0	1	2	0	0	0	0	1	0	0	1	0	0	1	0	0	0	0	0	0	0	0	0	0
Robert	257	.7854	40.866	56.1	26	92	35	22	23	27	25	7	64	9	2	7	2	34	2	8	9	0	0	0	4	61	23	32	0
Robert's	14	.6022	1.7569	42.4	3	9	0	1	0	1	0	0	2	2	0	0	1	0	0	1	0	0	0	0	1	3	0	4	0
Roberta	7	.3592	.5444	37.4	2	1	2	0	0	0	2	0	0	2	0	0	0	0	0	0	1	0	0	0	0	0	0	4	0
Roberto	14	.0000	.2723	34.4	0	14	0	0	0	0	0	0	0	0	0	0	0	14	0	0	0	0	0	0	0	0	0	0	0
Roberts	14	.5844	1.7256	42.4	4	2	0	1	0	7	0	0	3	1	0	0	0	2	0	0	0	0	0	0	0	2	3	3	0
Roberts's	2	.2433	.1158	30.6	1	0	0	0	0	1	0	0	0	0	0	0	0	0	0	0	0	0	0	0	0	1	0	1	0
Robertson	17	.3722	1.3673	41.4	0	0	10	1	1	5	0	0	0	5	0	0	0	0	0	0	0	0	0	0	8	0	0	4	0
robes	33	.7442	4.9665	47.0	1	8	6	6	5	4	2	1	3	4	1	3	0	10	1	0	1	0	0	0	6	3	1	0	0
Robie	4	.0000	.0429	26.3	0	0	0	0	4	0	0	0	0	0	0	4	0	0	0	0	0	0	0	0	0	0	0	0	0
robin	57	.6147	7.5223	48.8	35	6	5	5	6	0	0	0	27	0	0	2	0	0	7	9	0	0	0	0	1	9	2	0	0
Robin	219	.3082	16.361	52.1	7	19	28	150	12	2	1	0	56	2	1	2	0	1	1	0	1	0	0	0	144	8	0	3	0
robin's	3	.2430	.1792	32.5	3	0	0	0	0	0	0	0	0	0	0	0	0	0	1	2	0	0	0	0	0	0	0	0	0
Robin's	9	.1957	.5675	37.5	0	0	1	5	3	0	0	0	5	0	0	0	0	0	0	0	0	0	0	0	4	0	0	0	0
robin's-egg-blue	3	.0000	.0352	25.5	0	0	3	0	0	0	0	0	0	0	0	0	0	0	0	0	0	0	0	0	3	0	0	0	0
robins	54	.6817	7.6241	48.8	25	8	6	3	5	1	1	5	15	1	2	1	1	0	2	9	0	0	0	0	1	16	6	0	0
robins'	3	.0000	.0434	26.4	0	3	0	0	0	0	0	0	0	0	0	0	0	0	0	0	0	0	0	0	0	3	0	0	0
Robinson	47	.6938	6.8940	48.4	2	5	5	5	12	4	14	0	30	2	0	3	0	3	1	0	0	0	0	0	4	1	1	2	0
Robinson's	4	.2446	.3071	34.9	0	0	1	1	2	0	0	0	3	0	0	0	1	0	0	0	0	0	0	0	0	0	0	0	0
Robinsons	4	.0000	.1827	32.6	0	1	0	0	3	0	0	0	4	0	0	0	0	0	0	0	0	0	0	0	0	0	0	0	0
robot	71	.4575	7.7408	48.9	46	2	2	2	3	3	13	0	49	0	0	15	1	0	1	2	0	0	0	0	0	2	0	1	0
Robot	2	.0000	.0914	29.6	0	0	1	1	0	0	0	0	2	0	0	0	0	0	0	0	0	0	0	0	0	0	0	0	0
robots	32	.2937	2.6078	44.2	16	0	3	0	1	2	10	0	21	0	0	10	0	0	0	0	0	0	0	0	0	0	1	0	0
Robots	2	.1717	.1142	30.6	0	0	1	0	0	0	1	0	1	0	0	1	0	0	0	0	0	0	0	0	0	0	0	0	0
robs	4	.3428	.3131	35.0	0	0	1	0	1	1	1	0	1	0	1	0	0	0	1	0	0	0	0	0	0	0	1	0	0
robust	8	.4989	.8547	39.3	1	1	2	0	0	4	0	0	1	0	0	1	0	2	0	0	2	0	0	0	0	2	0	0	0
roc	2	.0000	.0914	29.6	0	0	0	0	2	0	0	0	2	0	0	0	0	0	0	0	0	0	0	0	0	0	0	0	0
Roc	2	.2427	.1152	30.6	1	0	0	0	0	0	0	1	0	0	0	0	0	0	0	0	0	0	0	0	1	1	0	0	0
Rochambeau	4	.0000	.0469	26.7	0	0	0	0	0	0	0	4	0	0	0	0	0	0	0	0	0	0	0	0	4	0	0	0	0

4A rivermen
4A Rivington
8A rivulet
3A rivulets
3P Rizzuto
6E RL
8Q Roach
8J road-
7H road-builders
7R road-building
7R road-racing
7R road-trips
9Q roadbeds
6B roadblock
5B roadbuilder
6A roadeo
5A roadhouse
5A Roadhouse
XH roadless
3A ROADMASTER
3A Roadmaster's
4R roadrunner's
7N roadstead
7F roams
7P roarer
6A Roaring
9Q Roash
3N ROBBED
6N robber-crab
9D robberies
8F Robbery
5A Robe's
4N Roberge
4N Roberge's
9B Roberta's
5Q Robespierre
7D robin's-egg
6A robio
XR Roblee
4A robot's
4Q Roby
6B Robyn

Word Type	F	D	U	SFI	3 Gr 3	4 Gr 4	5 Gr 5	6 Gr 6	7 Gr 7	8 Gr 8	9 Gr 9	X UnGr	A Read	B Eng & Gr	C Comp	D Lit	E Math	F Soc Stud	G Spell	H Sci	J Music	K Art	L Home Ec	M Shop	N Lib F	P Lib NF	Q Lib Ref	R Mag	S Rel
Rochelle	3	.2445	.1818	32.6	0	0	0	0	0	1	0	2	0	0	0	0	0	0	0	2	0	0	0	0	0	0	1	0	0
Rochester	9	.3840	.8120	39.1	0	0	7	0	2	0	0	0	3	0	0	0	0	1	0	0	0	0	0	0	0	0	1	4	0
Rociada	2	.0000	.0914	29.6	0	0	0	0	2	0	0	0	2	0	0	0	0	0	0	0	0	0	0	0	0	0	0	0	0
rock	925	.8439	156.61	61.9	181	135	158	139	129	67	92	24	207	27	5	41	8	62	7	288	6	3	0	5	41	95	68	62	0
Rock	69	.6934	10.053	50.0	17	11	7	3	14	13	1	3	37	1	0	1	0	8	0	0	4	0	0	0	2	5	2	9	0
rock-eater	2	.0000	.0914	29.6	2	0	0	0	0	0	0	0	2	0	0	0	0	0	0	0	0	0	0	0	0	0	0	0	0
rock-hard	3	.3346	.2478	33.9	0	0	0	1	2	0	0	0	1	0	0	0	0	0	0	1	0	0	0	0	0	0	1	0	0
rock's	2	.2278	.1128	30.5	0	0	0	2	0	0	0	0	0	0	0	0	0	0	0	1	0	0	0	0	0	0	1	0	0
rocked	39	.7409	5.9987	47.8	11	8	4	5	8	3	0	0	23	1	1	2	0	1	1	0	1	0	0	0	4	3	0	2	0
Rockefeller	25	.2960	1.7203	42.4	2	0	17	1	0	4	1	0	2	0	0	0	0	4	0	0	0	0	0	0	0	2	16	1	0
Rockefeller's	2	.0000	.0209	23.2	0	0	2	0	0	0	0	0	0	0	0	0	0	0	0	0	0	0	0	0	0	0	2	0	0
Rockefellers	3	.0000	.0365	25.6	0	0	0	0	0	1	2	0	0	0	0	0	0	0	0	0	0	0	0	0	0	0	0	3	0
rocker	19	.6503	2.5750	44.1	2	6	1	1	6	2	1	0	6	4	0	2	0	0	0	0	0	0	1	0	1	2	0	3	0
rockers	2	.2376	.1088	30.4	0	0	1	1	0	0	0	0	0	0	0	0	0	0	1	0	0	0	0	0	0	0	0	1	0
rocket	242	.7610	37.645	55.8	38	31	60	31	26	32	20	4	71	8	1	0	21	10	4	86	0	1	0	2	0	27	4	7	0
Rocket	13	.3492	1.1929	40.8	7	3	1	1	1	0	0	0	9	0	0	0	0	0	0	0	0	0	0	0	0	1	0	3	0
rocket's	2	.2160	.1362	31.3	0	0	1	0	0	1	0	0	1	0	0	0	0	0	0	1	0	0	0	0	0	0	0	0	0
rocketed	2	.2408	.1091	30.4	0	0	0	0	1	1	0	0	0	1	0	0	0	0	1	0	0	0	0	0	0	0	0	0	0
rocketing	2	.0000	.0162	22.1	1	1	0	0	0	0	0	0	0	0	0	0	0	0	0	0	2	0	0	0	0	0	0	0	0
rocketry	3	.3128	.2349	33.7	0	0	1	0	0	2	0	0	1	0	0	0	0	0	1	1	0	0	0	0	0	0	0	0	0
rockets	136	.7488	20.805	53.2	17	13	22	39	15	9	17	4	31	6	0	0	15	7	0	51	0	1	0	2	1	12	3	7	0
Rockets	3	.2437	.2277	33.6	0	2	0	1	0	0	0	0	2	0	0	0	0	0	0	1	0	0	0	0	0	0	0	0	0
Rockford	3	.2279	.2143	33.3	0	0	0	0	0	2	0	1	2	0	0	0	0	0	0	0	0	0	0	0	0	0	0	1	0
Rockies	50	.6266	6.5283	48.1	1	10	11	5	14	5	3	1	7	0	2	1	0	24	0	1	1	0	0	0	0	2	6	6	0
rocking	47	.7633	7.3638	48.7	13	7	5	3	9	2	8	0	22	1	1	3	0	0	0	4	1	0	0	0	5	4	1	5	0
Rockne	9	.2269	.6923	38.4	0	0	0	9	0	0	0	0	8	1	0	0	0	0	0	0	0	0	0	0	0	0	0	0	0
Rockne's	2	.0000	.0914	29.6	0	0	0	2	0	0	0	0	2	0	0	0	0	0	0	0	0	0	0	0	0	0	0	0	0
Rockport	15	.1167	.5953	37.7	14	0	0	0	0	0	0	1	0	0	0	0	0	14	0	0	0	0	0	0	0	0	0	1	0
rocks	740	.8316	123.71	60.9	173	131	91	83	79	70	95	18	155	15	5	22	22	34	6	288	6	7	0	1	22	74	40	41	2
Rocks	2	.1717	.1142	30.6	1	0	0	0	1	0	0	0	1	0	0	1	0	0	0	0	0	0	0	0	0	0	0	0	0
rockslides	4	.0000	.0486	26.9	4	0	0	0	0	0	0	0	0	0	0	0	0	0	0	0	0	0	0	0	0	0	0	4	0
rockweed	2	.0000	.0914	29.6	0	0	0	2	0	0	0	0	2	0	0	0	0	0	0	0	0	0	0	0	0	0	0	0	0
Rockwell	3	.1101	.0802	29.0	0	0	0	0	0	1	2	0	0	0	0	0	0	0	0	0	0	0	0	2	0	0	0	1	0
rocky	144	.8182	23.752	53.8	30	28	30	21	20	6	5	4	35	1	3	10	0	36	1	24	1	1	0	0	6	6	11	9	0
Rocky	88	.6510	11.933	50.8	8	16	25	9	14	8	6	2	16	0	0	4	0	34	0	12	0	0	0	0	2	6	9	5	0
Rococo	3	.0994	.0714	28.5	0	0	0	0	0	2	0	1	0	0	0	0	0	0	0	0	0	2	0	0	0	0	1	0	0
rod	259	.7255	38.623	55.9	22	23	35	12	85	52	12	18	77	4	2	3	33	5	0	67	3	0	0	17	6	14	3	25	0
Rod	39	.5813	4.7464	46.8	0	18	1	6	12	2	0	0	6	0	0	2	2	0	0	0	0	0	0	0	8	10	1	10	0
Rod's	3	.2292	.1615	32.1	0	2	0	0	1	0	0	0	0	0	0	1	0	0	0	0	0	0	0	0	2	0	0	0	0
Roddenberry	4	.0000	.0469	26.7	0	0	4	0	0	0	0	0	0	0	0	0	0	0	0	0	0	0	0	0	4	0	0	0	0
rodding	2	.0000	.0243	23.9	0	0	0	0	2	0	0	0	0	0	0	0	0	0	0	0	0	0	0	0	0	0	0	2	0
rode	425	.7894	68.080	58.3	116	103	42	48	64	30	20	2	147	34	7	37	6	31	10	2	9	0	0	0	65	61	0	16	0
rodent	5	.0000	.0523	27.2	0	0	0	4	1	0	0	0	0	0	0	0	0	0	0	0	0	0	0	0	0	0	5	0	0
rodents	23	.3610	1.9211	42.8	1	0	3	5	12	1	1	0	5	0	0	1	0	0	0	3	0	0	0	0	0	2	12	0	0
rodeo	52	.3951	4.7795	46.8	33	4	3	4	5	2	1	0	18	1	0	2	0	2	1	0	1	0	0	0	27	0	0	0	0
Rodeo	4	.2703	.2662	34.3	1	2	0	0	1	0	0	0	1	0	0	0	0	0	0	0	2	0	0	0	1	0	0	0	0
rodeos	9	.4549	.9024	39.6	3	4	0	1	0	1	0	0	2	1	0	1	0	1	0	0	0	0	0	0	4	0	0	0	0
Rodgers	6	.1304	.1990	33.0	0	0	0	2	1	2	1	0	0	0	0	0	0	0	0	0	5	0	0	0	1	0	0	0	0
Rodin	5	.0722	.1365	31.4	0	0	0	0	1	0	4	0	1	0	0	0	0	1	0	0	0	3	0	0	0	0	0	0	0
rodlike	2	.2278	.1128	30.5	0	0	1	0	0	0	1	0	0	0	0	0	0	0	0	1	0	0	0	0	0	0	1	0	0
Rodmika	7	.0000	.3198	35.0	0	0	0	7	0	0	0	0	7	0	0	0	0	0	0	0	0	0	0	0	0	0	0	0	0
Rodolfo	6	.0000	.0485	26.9	0	6	0	0	0	0	0	0	0	0	0	0	0	0	0	0	6	0	0	0	0	0	0	0	0
Rodriguez	4	.0000	.1827	32.6	4	0	0	0	0	0	0	0	4	0	0	0	0	0	0	0	0	0	0	0	0	0	0	0	0
rods	90	.6441	12.070	50.8	14	9	9	11	24	12	11	0	20	2	1	1	20	2	0	22	0	0	0	9	7	4	1	1	0
roe	3	.2309	.1631	32.1	0	0	0	0	0	2	1	0	0	0	0	1	0	0	0	0	0	0	0	0	0	0	0	2	0
Roe	2	.0000	.0243	23.9	0	0	0	0	1	0	0	1	0	0	0	0	0	0	0	0	0	0	0	0	0	0	0	2	0
Roebling	6	.0000	.2741	34.4	0	0	0	6	0	0	0	0	6	0	0	0	0	0	0	0	0	0	0	0	0	0	0	0	0
roebuck	2	.1717	.1142	30.6	0	0	1	0	0	1	0	0	1	0	0	1	0	0	0	0	0	0	0	0	0	0	0	0	0
Roehr	2	.0000	.0243	23.9	0	0	0	0	2	0	0	0	0	0	0	0	0	0	0	0	0	0	0	0	0	0	0	2	0
Roentgen	8	.0000	.1577	32.0	0	0	0	0	0	7	0	1	0	0	0	0	0	0	0	8	0	0	0	0	0	0	0	0	0
Roentgen's	8	.0000	.1577	32.0	0	0	0	0	1	7	0	0	0	0	0	0	0	0	0	8	0	0	0	0	0	0	0	0	0
Roethke	2	.1473	.0686	28.4	0	0	0	0	1	1	0	0	0	0	0	1	0	0	0	0	0	1	0	0	0	0	0	0	0
Rofelia	4	.0000	.0469	26.7	0	0	4	0	0	0	0	0	0	0	0	0	0	0	0	0	0	0	0	0	4	0	0	0	0
roger	2	.2442	.1134	30.5	0	0	0	1	0	1	0	0	0	1	0	0	0	0	0	0	0	0	0	0	0	0	0	1	0
Roger	82	.8535	14.032	51.5	18	3	31	11	6	11	1	1	21	3	1	1	5	13	2	15	2	0	0	0	1	9	3	6	0
Roger's	4	.3359	.3305	35.2	1	0	2	1	0	0	0	0	1	0	0	0	1	0	0	2	0	0	0	0	0	0	0	0	0
Rogers	71	.5045	8.0131	49.0	17	27	12	2	3	5	5	0	29	0	0	1	0	10	0	1	0	0	0	0	0	22	0	8	0
Rogers'	2	.1948	.1250	31.0	0	1	1	0	0	0	0	0	1	0	0	0	0	0	0	0	0	0	0	0	0	1	0	0	0
rogue	3	.3394	.2451	33.9	0	1	0	0	0	1	1	0	1	0	0	1	0	0	0	0	0	0	0	0	1	0	0	0	0
rogues	6	.0000	.2741	34.4	0	0	0	6	0	0	0	0	6	0	0	0	0	0	0	0	0	0	0	0	0	0	0	0	0
Rohde	3	.0000	.0322	25.1	0	0	0	0	3	0	0	0	0	0	0	3	0	0	0	0	0	0	0	0	0	0	0	0	0
rol	2	.0000	.0162	22.1	0	0	0	0	2	0	0	0	0	0	0	0	0	0	0	0	2	0	0	0	0	0	0	0	0
Roland	25	.2855	2.1497	43.3	0	13	0	9	2	1	0	0	22	0	0	0	0	0	0	1	0	0	0	0	0	0	2	0	0
Roland's	2	.0000	.0914	29.6	0	1	0	1	0	0	0	0	2	0	0	0	0	0	0	0	0	0	0	0	0	0	0	0	0
role	124	.8063	19.997	53.0	5	4	10	5	40	29	24	7	7	4	0	5	6	17	3	8	9	2	3	0	0	7	28	25	0
roles	25	.6396	3.2565	45.1	0	2	2	1	11	4	5	0	0	1	0	2	1	5	0	0	3	0	0	0	0	1	7	5	0
Rolfe	12	.4158	1.0900	40.4	0	6	0	0	2	3	0	1	0	0	0	0	0	4	0	0	0	0	0	0	0	6	1	1	0
roll	266	.9095	48.067	56.8	66	41	29	33	41	29	23	4	73	7	1	11	21	13	6	28	4	5	10	9	10	32	8	28	0
Roll	4	.0000	.0789	29.0	4	0	0	0	0	0	0	0	0	0	0	0	0	0	0	4	0	0	0	0	0	0	0	0	0
rolled	315	.8897	55.975	57.5	53	62	29	51	61	29	22	8	128	11	3	23	4	15	1	13	4	5	4	5	42	31	3	23	0
rolled-up	6	.4520	.6163	37.9	4	1	0	0	1	0	0	0	2	0	0	0	0	0	0	1	0	0	0	0	0	2	0	1	0
roller	37	.6809	5.1135	47.1	6	11	5	8	3	2	1	1	3	1	4	1	4	1	1	5	0	4	0	1	6	2	1	3	0
roller-coaster	2	.1378	.0662	28.2	0	0	0	1	0	0	1	0	0	0	0	0	0	0	0	0	0	1	0	0	0	0	0	1	0
roller-skate	2	.0000	.0914	29.6	1	0	0	1	0	0	0	0	2	0	0	0	0	0	0	0	0	0	0	0	0	0	0	0	0
roller-skating	3	.3383	.2498	34.0	2	1	0	0	0	0	0	0	1	1	0	0	0	1	0	0	0	0	0	0	0	0	0	0	0
rollers	33	.5787	4.0010	46.0	1	7	6	9	2	6	2	0	4	0	0	0	0	3	0	11	0	0	1	4	1	3	6	0	0
rollicking	8	.5039	.8506	39.3	0	2	1	1	3	1	0	0	1	1	0	2	0	0	0	0	2	0	0	0	2	0	0	0	0
Rollin	4	.0000	.0486	26.9	0	0	0	0	0	0	4	0	0	0	0	0	0	0	0	0	0	0	0	0	0	0	0	4	0
rolling	206	.8918	36.563	55.6	34	29	39	18	44	20	17	5	49	4	4	15	1	33	0	9	5	4	6	7	10	31	11	17	0
Rollins's	2	.0000	.0299	24.8	0	0	0	0	2	0	0	0	0	0	0	0	2	0	0	0	0	0	0	0	0	0	0	0	0
Rollo	11	.1272	.3758	35.7	0	0	0	0	10	1	0	0	0	0	0	10	0	0	1	0	0	0	0	0	0	0	0	0	0
rolls	113	.7226	16.572	52.2	37	13	12	7	22	15	7	0	17	4	0	8	12	4	0	12	1	2	6	15	5	19	2	6	0
Rolls	3	.0000	.1370	31.4	0	1	0	0	0	0	2	0	3	0	0	0	0	0	0	0	0	0	0	0	0	0	0	0	0

XN Rochambeau's
8R Rochet
9J Rochlitz
6J Rock-a
XR rock-and-brush
4A rock-and-roll
6B rock-beating
5A rock-bound
6N rock-cod
XQ rock-fill
7H rock-floored
8R rock-group
6F rock-like
4N rock-rabbits
7A rock-slide
7R rock-steady
4P rockaway
6F rockcovered
4A rocker's
3P rocket-augmented
XH rocket-type
9B rocketeer
7Q rocketeers
9R rocketings
5Q Rockhill
5Q Rockhurst
4N Rocking
6P Rocking-Horse
7P rocklike
4P Rockridge
6A rockslide
9M Rockwell-C
6R Rocky's
5Q rococo
7R rod-handling
7R rod-like
5H rod-shaped
8H rod's
7A rodders
XR Rodehaver
4A rodeo's
5Q Roderick
XP Rodger
8R Rodion
6A Rodmika's
5A Rodney
8Q Rodrigo
4F Rodriquez
6A Roebling's
XH roentgen
8R roes
3A roguishly
6J Roh-see-nee
9K Rohe
6P roil
7L role-playing
4F Rolf
XR Rolfe's
5Q roll-call
8J Roll-off
3A roll-over
3D roll-the-shoe-button
6A roll-top
9Q rollability
4Q Rolland
4A Rollick
5N rolling-pin
3A rollover
9D rollrock

Word Type	F	D	U	SFI	3 Gr 3	4 Gr 4	5 Gr 5	6 Gr 6	7 Gr 7	8 Gr 8	9 Gr 9	X UnGr	A Read	B Eng & Gr	C Comp	D Lit	E Math	F Soc Stud	G Spell	H Sci	J Music	K Art	L Home Ec	M Shop	N Lib F	P Lib NF	Q Lib Ref	R Mag	S Rel
Rolls-Royce	10	.0000	.4568	36.6	0	0	0	0	0	0	10	0	10	0	0	0	0	0	0	0	0	0	0	0	0	0	0	0	0
roly-poly	3	.1539	.1476	31.7	0	0	2	0	1	0	0	0	1	0	0	0	0	0	0	1	0	1	0	0	0	0	0	0	0
Roma	2	.2446	.1125	30.5	0	0	0	0	0	0	2	0	0	1	0	1	0	0	0	0	0	0	0	0	0	0	0	0	0
Roman	327	.7567	49.835	57.0	65	47	36	35	65	36	34	9	23	21	0	6	65	39	24	2	5	0	0	0	6	26	87	22	1
Roman's	2	.0000	.0243	23.9	0	0	0	0	2	0	0	0	0	0	0	0	0	0	0	0	0	0	0	0	0	0	0	2	0
romance	15	.5788	1.8234	42.6	1	1	1	2	4	3	2	1	2	0	0	2	0	4	0	0	0	0	0	0	0	2	1	4	0
romances	3	.3863	.2513	34.0	0	0	1	0	1	1	0	0	0	0	0	0	0	0	0	0	0	0	0	0	1	1	0	1	0
Romanesque	5	.1439	.1655	32.2	1	0	0	0	1	0	3	0	0	0	0	0	0	0	0	0	1	3	0	0	0	1	0	0	0
Romania	2	.0000	.0389	25.9	0	0	0	0	0	1	1	0	0	0	0	0	0	2	0	0	0	0	0	0	0	0	0	0	0
Romanov	2	.2351	.1166	30.7	0	0	0	0	1	1	0	0	0	0	0	0	0	1	0	0	0	0	0	0	0	0	0	1	0
Romans	129	.7675	19.890	53.0	18	13	18	19	28	9	21	3	6	13	0	0	13	26	20	4	1	1	2	1	0	11	29	2	0
romantic	56	.7417	8.3587	49.2	3	3	3	4	9	21	11	2	5	1	0	7	0	5	0	0	16	2	1	1	3	3	9	3	0
Romantic	34	.2377	1.8062	42.6	0	0	1	1	2	25	2	3	0	0	0	0	0	0	0	0	29	1	0	0	0	2	2	0	0
romantic-period	2	.0000	.0162	22.1	0	0	0	0	0	2	0	0	0	0	0	0	0	0	0	0	2	0	0	0	0	0	0	0	0
romanticism	2	.2417	.1091	30.4	0	0	1	0	0	1	0	0	0	0	0	0	0	0	0	0	1	0	0	0	0	0	1	0	0
Romanticism	3	.2088	.1442	31.6	0	0	0	0	0	0	1	2	0	0	0	0	0	0	0	0	2	0	0	0	0	0	1	0	0
Romanticist	4	.2385	.2074	33.2	0	0	0	0	0	3	0	1	0	0	0	0	0	0	0	0	3	1	0	0	0	0	0	0	0
Romanticists	2	.1696	.0749	28.7	0	0	0	0	0	0	1	1	0	0	0	0	0	0	0	0	1	1	0	0	0	0	0	0	0
Romberg	2	.0000	.0162	22.1	0	0	0	0	2	0	0	0	0	0	0	0	0	0	0	0	2	0	0	0	0	0	0	0	0
Rome	162	.7941	25.787	54.1	31	18	12	25	33	17	21	5	6	9	0	3	5	46	2	2	5	2	0	3	3	30	32	14	0
Rome's	7	.3271	.5268	37.2	1	2	0	1	0	0	2	1	1	0	0	0	0	0	0	0	0	0	0	0	0	1	4	1	0
Romeo	93	.2556	5.5944	47.5	0	0	0	1	1	11	80	0	8	0	0	69	0	0	1	0	14	0	0	0	1	0	0	0	0
Romeo's	6	.2411	.3272	35.1	0	0	0	0	0	0	6	0	0	0	0	3	0	0	0	0	3	0	0	0	0	0	0	0	0
Romero	6	.2212	.4198	36.2	0	2	0	0	4	0	0	0	4	0	0	2	0	0	0	0	0	0	0	0	0	0	0	0	0
Romeros	3	.0000	.1370	31.4	0	0	0	0	3	0	0	0	3	0	0	0	0	0	0	0	0	0	0	0	0	0	0	0	0
Rommel	2	.0000	.0209	23.2	0	2	0	0	0	0	0	0	0	0	0	0	0	0	0	0	0	0	0	0	0	0	2	0	0
Romney	2	.2401	.1133	30.5	0	1	0	0	1	0	0	0	0	0	0	0	0	0	0	0	0	0	0	0	0	1	1	0	0
romp	7	.4520	.7275	38.6	0	0	2	2	1	0	1	1	3	0	0	0	0	0	0	1	0	0	0	0	1	0	0	2	0
romped	4	.2405	.2474	33.9	0	2	1	1	0	0	0	0	1	0	1	0	0	0	0	0	0	0	0	0	0	2	0	0	0
Romulus	5	.2011	.2522	34.0	1	0	0	0	0	1	0	3	0	0	0	0	0	0	0	0	0	0	0	0	0	4	1	0	0
ron	15	.0000	.1213	30.8	15	0	0	0	0	0	0	0	0	0	0	0	0	0	0	0	15	0	0	0	0	0	0	0	0
Ron	15	.4386	1.4094	41.5	0	3	0	5	3	3	1	0	1	0	0	0	5	0	6	0	0	0	0	0	1	1	0	1	0
Ron's	13	.0628	.2659	34.2	0	0	0	12	0	1	0	0	0	0	0	0	1	0	12	0	0	0	0	0	0	0	0	0	0
Ronald	10	.4988	1.0461	40.2	1	1	0	0	1	1	2	4	0	1	1	0	0	0	0	3	0	0	0	0	0	0	1	4	0
Roncesvalles	2	.0000	.0209	23.2	0	0	0	0	2	0	0	0	0	0	0	0	0	0	0	0	0	0	0	0	0	0	2	0	0
Roncole	3	.0000	.1370	31.4	0	0	0	3	0	0	0	0	3	0	0	0	0	0	0	0	0	0	0	0	0	0	0	0	0
Rondaro	4	.0000	.1827	32.6	0	4	0	0	0	0	0	0	4	0	0	0	0	0	0	0	0	0	0	0	0	0	0	0	0
Rondaros'	2	.0000	.0914	29.6	0	2	0	0	0	0	0	0	2	0	0	0	0	0	0	0	0	0	0	0	0	0	0	0	0
rondeau	3	.0000	.0243	23.8	0	0	3	0	0	0	0	0	0	0	0	0	0	0	0	0	3	0	0	0	0	0	0	0	0
rondo	27	.0000	.2183	33.4	5	11	4	0	5	2	0	0	0	0	0	0	0	0	0	0	27	0	0	0	0	0	0	0	0
Rondo	3	.0000	.0243	23.8	2	1	0	0	0	0	0	0	0	0	0	0	0	0	0	0	3	0	0	0	0	0	0	0	0
Ronkonkoma	2	.0000	.0219	23.4	0	0	0	0	0	2	0	0	0	2	0	0	0	0	0	0	0	0	0	0	0	0	0	0	0
Ronny	3	.0000	.0352	25.5	0	3	0	0	0	0	0	0	0	0	0	0	0	0	0	0	0	0	0	0	3	0	0	0	0
Rontu	17	.0924	.6129	37.9	0	0	0	17	0	0	0	0	4	0	0	0	0	0	0	0	0	0	0	0	13	0	0	0	0
roof	276	.8778	48.479	56.9	82	39	29	32	41	20	23	10	113	6	5	24	0	22	5	7	6	8	1	5	23	21	8	22	0
roofed	2	.1787	.1174	30.7	0	1	0	0	1	0	0	0	1	0	0	0	0	0	0	0	0	0	0	0	1	0	0	0	0
roofing	8	.5492	.8990	39.5	0	1	0	1	4	1	1	0	0	1	0	0	0	0	0	0	0	1	0	1	0	2	1	2	0
roofs	63	.6928	9.0721	49.6	12	15	8	16	7	4	1	0	20	0	1	3	0	23	0	2	2	0	0	0	2	7	0	3	0
rooftop	4	.2780	.2956	34.7	1	1	0	1	0	1	0	0	2	0	0	0	0	0	0	0	0	0	1	0	0	0	0	1	0
rooftops	11	.5413	1.2836	41.1	3	2	3	1	0	0	0	2	3	0	1	0	0	0	0	3	0	0	0	0	0	1	1	2	0
rooked	2	.1717	.1142	30.6	0	0	0	0	2	0	0	0	1	0	0	1	0	0	0	0	0	0	0	0	0	0	0	0	0
rookeries	2	.2278	.1128	30.5	0	0	0	0	1	0	0	1	0	0	0	0	0	0	0	1	0	0	0	0	0	0	1	0	0
rookie	9	.3480	.6833	38.3	0	0	1	2	4	2	0	0	0	0	1	0	0	0	0	0	0	0	0	0	0	2	0	6	0
rookies	3	.0000	.0365	25.6	0	0	0	1	0	2	0	0	0	0	0	0	0	0	0	0	0	0	0	0	0	0	0	3	0
room	1801	.9069	324.86	65.1	375	335	193	190	306	208	164	30	577	85	20	153	75	97	21	140	38	23	87	9	175	190	18	93	0
Room	31	.5627	3.7494	45.7	10	9	5	1	3	2	1	0	11	1	0	0	1	0	2	0	1	0	0	0	12	2	0	1	0
roomers	2	.0000	.0914	29.6	0	0	0	0	2	0	0	0	2	0	0	0	0	0	0	0	0	0	0	0	0	0	0	0	0
roomful	6	.4741	.6397	38.1	3	2	0	0	1	0	0	0	2	0	0	0	0	0	0	2	0	0	0	0	0	0	1	1	0
roommate	11	.5203	1.2049	40.8	1	5	0	0	2	1	2	0	1	1	0	0	0	0	1	0	0	0	1	0	0	6	0	1	0
roommates	2	.2433	.1158	30.6	0	1	0	0	0	0	1	0	0	0	0	0	0	0	0	0	0	0	0	0	0	1	0	1	0
rooms	209	.9297	38.471	55.9	45	22	30	27	24	32	16	13	43	6	3	12	10	31	2	15	8	4	10	5	15	13	11	21	0
roomy	5	.4773	.5129	37.1	1	1	0	1	2	0	0	0	0	1	0	0	0	2	0	1	0	0	0	0	0	1	0	0	0
Roop	15	.0000	.1759	32.5	0	15	0	0	0	0	0	0	0	0	0	0	0	0	0	0	0	0	0	0	15	0	0	0	0
Roosevelt	146	.6660	20.391	53.1	14	30	17	3	34	31	12	5	53	2	0	2	2	37	1	1	0	0	0	0	0	18	14	16	0
Roosevelt's	12	.2152	.8141	39.1	1	1	0	1	2	4	3	0	6	0	0	0	0	6	0	0	0	0	0	0	0	0	0	0	0
Roosevelts	2	.0000	.0914	29.6	0	2	0	0	0	0	0	0	2	0	0	0	0	0	0	0	0	0	0	0	0	0	0	0	0
roost	14	.5395	1.6606	42.2	4	2	0	3	3	1	0	1	6	0	0	2	0	0	0	1	0	0	0	0	0	3	0	2	0
roosted	4	.4758	.4063	36.1	1	0	0	2	0	0	1	0	0	0	0	1	0	1	0	1	0	0	0	0	1	0	0	0	0
rooster	54	.6631	7.4976	48.7	14	17	5	9	3	6	0	0	23	5	2	5	0	1	0	2	5	4	0	0	0	6	0	1	0
Rooster	19	.2374	1.4911	41.7	2	15	0	2	0	0	0	0	17	0	0	0	0	0	0	0	2	0	0	0	0	0	0	0	0
rooster's	2	.2160	.1362	31.3	0	0	1	1	0	0	0	0	1	0	0	0	0	0	0	1	0	0	0	0	0	0	0	0	0
roosters	11	.2790	.7581	38.8	3	1	0	0	4	0	3	0	3	0	3	3	0	2	0	0	0	0	0	0	0	0	0	0	0
Roosters	2	.1494	.1045	30.2	1	1	0	0	0	0	0	0	1	0	0	0	0	0	0	0	1	0	0	0	0	0	0	0	0
roosting	2	.1814	.1187	30.7	1	1	0	0	0	0	0	0	1	0	0	0	0	0	0	0	0	0	0	0	0	0	0	1	0
roosts	3	.3465	.2515	34.0	1	0	0	2	0	0	0	0	1	0	0	0	0	0	0	0	0	0	0	0	0	1	0	1	0
root	568	.4838	58.060	57.6	76	72	87	92	89	104	37	11	49	28	0	3	49	12	308	63	13	1	1	2	8	8	14	9	0
Root	10	.4442	.9947	40.0	3	0	1	1	2	3	0	0	3	0	0	0	0	0	2	0	1	0	0	0	0	4	0	0	0
rooted	29	.7274	4.2996	46.3	3	6	1	3	7	5	4	0	6	0	0	2	0	3	0	2	3	1	0	0	0	3	4	5	0
rooters	7	.4761	.7075	38.5	1	0	0	1	1	2	2	0	0	0	0	2	0	0	0	2	0	0	0	0	0	2	1	0	0
rooting	15	.4420	1.6083	42.1	3	6	0	2	2	1	1	0	10	0	0	0	0	1	0	3	0	0	0	0	0	0	0	1	0
roots	444	.8082	71.976	58.6	109	53	53	67	83	40	28	11	37	3	1	9	32	32	79	142	12	3	0	0	14	35	33	11	1
rope	451	.8615	78.156	58.9	94	87	64	107	50	21	14	14	213	11	3	29	18	16	9	54	3	4	0	1	51	24	4	11	0
roped	13	.6147	1.6700	42.2	3	2	4	1	1	1	1	0	3	0	0	3	0	1	0	0	1	0	0	0	3	1	0	1	0
roped-off	2	.0000	.0243	23.9	0	0	0	0	1	0	1	0	0	0	0	0	0	0	0	0	0	0	0	0	0	0	0	2	0
ropelike	2	.0665	.0708	28.5	0	0	0	1	1	0	0	0	1	0	1	0	0	0	0	0	0	0	0	0	0	0	0	0	0
roper	3	.3408	.2477	33.9	0	2	0	0	1	0	0	0	1	0	0	1	0	0	0	0	0	0	0	0	0	1	0	0	0
ropers	2	.2152	.1357	31.3	0	1	1	0	0	0	0	0	1	0	0	0	0	1	0	0	0	0	0	0	0	0	0	0	0
ropes	99	.8656	17.174	52.3	19	19	7	16	18	10	4	6	36	5	2	6	3	9	0	5	4	1	0	0	4	16	5	3	0
roping	17	.5113	1.9452	42.9	7	2	4	1	2	1	0	0	8	0	0	4	0	2	0	0	0	0	0	0	2	1	0	0	0
Roquefort	3	.0000	.0097	19.8	0	0	0	0	1	0	2	0	0	0	0	0	0	0	0	0	0	0	3	0	0	0	0	0	0
Roquerre	3	.0000	.0434	26.4	0	0	0	0	3	0	0	0	0	0	0	0	0	0	0	0	0	0	0	0	0	3	0	0	0
Rosa	39	.4781	4.2789	46.3	6	28	1	3	1	0	0	0	18	0	0	1	0	14	0	0	0	0	0	0	1	0	0	5	0
Rosa's	3	.0000	.1370	31.4	0	3	0	0	0	0	0	0	3	0	0	0	0	0	0	0	0	0	0	0	0	0	0	0	0
Rosal	2	.0000	.0234	23.7	0	0	0	0	2	0	0	0	0	0	0	0	0	0	0	0	0	0	0	0	2	0	0	0	0
Rosalie	20	.0000	.9137	39.6	0	0	20	0	0	0	0	0	20	0	0	0	0	0	0	0	0	0	0	0	0	0	0	0	0

3D roly
7Q Romagna
4Q Romain
7L romaine
8G Romance
9R Romani
8B romanian
3Q Romanized
8Q Romanovich
XP Romans'
9Q romanticist
7Q romanticized
5P romantics
3A Romona
7C romping
6A Romsdal
9F Romulo
7R Rona
4A Rondaros
5J Rondeau
7R Ronnie
6N Rontu's
4N roof-board
4H roofers
4N rookery
9R Rookie
5Q Rookwood
5A room-sized
6P room's
7R roomiest
9R rooming
6A Rooms
7Q root-hair
7D root-hold
6D rootingest
8R rootless
5H rootlike
7A Roots
7Q rootstock
6Q rootstocks
4B rope-jumping
7A rope's
3B Roper
7D ropes'
6A ropewalk
8R ropework
4A ropingest
7Q ropy
7P Roquerre's

Word Type	F	D	U	SFI	3 Gr 3	4 Gr 4	5 Gr 5	6 Gr 6	7 Gr 7	8 Gr 8	9 Gr 9	X UnGr	A Read	B Eng & Gr	C Comp	D Lit	E Math	F Soc Stud	G Spell	H Sci	J Music	K Art	L Home Ec	M Shop	N Lib F	P Lib NF	Q Lib Ref	R Mag	S Rel
Rosalind	3	.2228	.1655	32.2	0	3	0	0	0	0	0	0	0	0	0	0	1	0	0	0	0	0	0	0	0	2	0	0	0
Rosaline	2	.0000	.0914	29.6	0	0	0	0	0	2	0	0	2	0	0	0	0	0	0	0	0	0	0	0	0	0	0	0	0
Rosamond	3	.0000	.1370	31.4	0	0	0	3	0	0	0	0	3	0	0	0	0	0	0	0	0	0	0	0	0	0	0	0	0
Rosario	9	.3564	.8554	39.3	1	0	7	1	0	0	0	0	7	0	0	0	0	1	0	0	0	0	0	0	0	0	1	0	0
rose	461	.8477	78.465	58.9	55	64	51	84	103	47	49	8	155	26	5	70	7	30	6	21	3	1	0	1	55	37	19	25	0
Rose	55	.5783	6.7612	48.3	26	10	0	5	3	2	4	5	15	0	0	1	2	1	1	5	1	0	0	0	23	4	1	1	0
Rose-Red	3	.0000	.1370	31.4	3	0	0	0	0	0	0	0	3	0	0	0	0	0	0	0	0	0	0	0	0	0	0	0	0
rose-colored	3	.3350	.2478	33.9	0	0	1	0	1	1	0	0	1	0	0	0	0	1	0	0	0	0	0	0	0	0	1	0	0
rose-purple	3	.0000	.0591	27.7	0	0	0	0	0	0	0	3	0	0	0	0	0	0	0	3	0	0	0	0	0	0	0	0	0
rosebud	2	.0000	.0219	23.4	0	0	1	0	0	1	0	0	0	2	0	0	0	0	0	0	0	0	0	0	0	0	0	0	0
Rosebud	9	.1550	.3885	35.9	1	1	0	0	0	0	7	0	1	0	0	7	0	0	0	0	0	0	0	0	0	1	0	0	0
rosebush	14	.4689	1.4107	41.5	5	1	2	2	3	1	0	0	1	0	0	3	0	0	0	4	0	0	0	0	5	0	0	1	0
rosebushes	7	.1473	.2916	34.6	6	0	0	0	0	0	0	1	0	0	0	0	6	0	0	0	0	0	0	0	0	1	0	0	0
Rosecrans	2	.0000	.0209	23.2	0	0	0	0	2	0	0	0	0	0	0	0	0	0	0	0	0	0	0	0	0	0	2	0	0
rosemary	6	.1699	.2286	33.6	0	0	0	0	1	0	5	0	0	0	0	1	0	0	0	0	0	0	4	0	0	0	1	0	0
Rosemary	5	.2824	.3832	35.8	0	0	1	1	3	0	0	0	3	0	1	0	0	0	0	0	1	0	0	0	0	0	0	0	0
Rosemary's	2	.1814	.1187	30.7	0	0	0	0	2	0	0	0	1	0	0	0	0	0	0	0	0	0	0	0	0	0	0	1	0
Rosemont	3	.0000	.0352	25.5	3	0	0	0	0	0	0	0	0	0	0	0	0	0	0	0	0	0	0	0	3	0	0	0	0
Rosenberg	3	.0000	.0365	25.6	0	0	0	0	0	0	2	1	0	0	0	0	0	0	0	0	0	0	0	0	0	0	0	3	0
roses	82	.6990	11.769	50.7	19	11	13	8	16	10	5	0	22	13	7	8	9	2	0	3	6	0	0	0	5	4	2	1	0
Roses	4	.3611	.3119	34.9	0	0	2	1	0	0	1	0	0	0	0	1	0	0	0	0	0	0	0	0	0	0	2	1	0
rosettes	2	.2300	.1140	30.6	0	0	0	0	1	1	0	0	0	1	0	0	0	0	0	1	0	0	0	0	0	0	0	0	0
Rosie	29	.1884	1.6339	42.1	27	1	0	1	0	0	0	0	10	0	0	0	0	0	0	0	0	0	0	0	0	1	0	18	0
Rosie's	6	.0706	.1822	32.6	4	0	0	2	0	0	0	0	1	0	0	0	0	0	0	0	0	0	0	0	0	0	0	5	0
rosin	9	.3086	.6316	38.0	0	0	3	2	1	3	0	0	1	0	0	2	0	2	0	0	0	0	0	3	0	0	1	0	0
rosin-core	2	.0000	.0050	17.0	0	0	0	0	0	2	0	0	0	0	0	0	0	0	0	0	0	0	0	2	0	0	0	0	0
Rosita	3	.0000	.1370	31.4	3	0	0	0	0	0	0	0	3	0	0	0	0	0	0	0	0	0	0	0	0	0	0	0	0
Ross	72	.4919	7.5343	48.8	16	3	1	4	34	6	2	6	6	1	0	7	0	1	0	7	0	0	0	0	37	10	1	2	0
Ross's	2	.1787	.1174	30.7	0	0	0	1	1	0	0	0	1	0	0	0	0	0	0	0	0	0	0	0	1	0	0	0	0
Rossi	8	.0000	.3655	35.6	0	0	0	8	0	0	0	0	8	0	0	0	0	0	0	0	0	0	0	0	0	0	0	0	0
Rossini	8	.0000	.0647	28.1	0	1	0	3	2	2	0	0	0	0	0	0	0	0	0	0	8	0	0	0	0	0	0	0	0
Rossini's	3	.0000	.0243	23.8	0	0	0	2	0	1	0	0	0	0	0	0	0	0	0	0	3	0	0	0	0	0	0	0	0
Rostand	2	.2418	.1091	30.4	0	1	0	0	0	1	0	0	0	0	0	0	0	0	1	0	0	0	0	0	0	0	1	0	0
roster	8	.4099	.7219	38.6	0	0	1	2	4	0	1	0	1	0	0	0	2	0	0	0	0	0	0	0	0	0	3	2	0
Rostron	9	.0000	.1303	31.1	0	0	0	0	0	0	9	0	0	0	0	0	0	0	0	0	0	0	0	0	0	9	0	0	0
rosy	21	.6187	2.7489	44.4	4	5	0	2	4	4	1	1	8	0	0	1	0	0	0	0	1	0	1	0	6	3	0	1	0
Rosy	16	.3335	1.4322	41.6	12	0	0	0	0	1	3	0	12	0	2	1	0	0	0	0	0	0	0	0	0	0	0	1	0
rosy-faced	2	.0000	.0914	29.6	0	0	1	0	1	0	0	0	2	0	0	0	0	0	0	0	0	0	0	0	0	0	0	0	0
rot	8	.6018	1.0188	40.1	0	1	1	2	0	1	2	1	2	0	0	1	0	1	0	1	0	0	0	0	0	2	0	1	0
rotary	20	.2834	1.2372	40.9	0	0	1	0	6	2	11	0	1	0	0	0	1	0	0	2	1	0	12	1	0	0	1	1	0
Rotary	3	.2435	.2274	33.6	0	2	0	0	0	1	0	0	2	0	0	0	0	1	0	0	0	0	0	0	0	0	0	0	0
rotate	32	.6066	4.0215	46.0	4	6	2	5	5	6	3	1	2	1	0	0	0	5	1	12	0	0	1	4	0	0	3	3	0
rotated	11	.5261	1.2094	40.8	2	2	2	1	2	0	2	0	0	0	0	0	0	4	0	0	0	0	0	1	0	1	2	3	0
rotates	39	.4253	3.6841	45.7	7	14	9	4	1	3	1	0	1	0	0	0	1	19	0	13	0	0	0	0	0	0	5	0	0
rotating	28	.4694	2.7855	44.4	0	9	4	1	2	5	4	3	1	0	0	0	1	4	0	5	0	0	0	5	0	0	8	4	0
rotation	46	.4237	4.1782	46.2	2	5	1	5	13	10	3	7	0	0	0	0	0	6	0	15	0	0	0	10	1	0	9	5	0
Rotation	2	.0000	.0394	26.0	0	0	0	2	0	0	0	0	0	0	0	0	0	0	0	2	0	0	0	0	0	0	0	0	0
rotations	2	.2278	.1128	30.5	0	1	0	0	1	0	0	0	0	0	0	0	0	0	0	1	0	0	0	0	0	0	1	0	0
Roth	4	.1529	.1647	32.2	3	0	0	0	0	1	0	0	0	3	0	0	0	0	0	1	0	0	0	0	0	0	0	0	0
rotifer	7	.0000	.1013	30.1	7	0	0	0	0	0	0	0	0	0	0	0	0	0	0	0	0	0	0	0	0	7	0	0	0
rotor	20	.5105	2.3218	43.7	2	1	0	9	6	0	1	1	12	0	0	0	0	0	0	2	0	0	0	1	0	0	4	1	0
rotor's	3	.0000	.0314	25.0	0	0	0	0	3	0	0	0	0	0	0	0	0	0	0	0	0	0	0	0	0	0	3	0	0
rotors	5	.0000	.2284	33.6	3	0	0	2	0	0	0	0	5	0	0	0	0	0	0	0	0	0	0	0	0	0	0	0	0
rots	2	.0000	.0389	25.9	0	1	1	0	0	0	0	0	0	0	0	0	0	2	0	0	0	0	0	0	0	0	0	0	0
rotted	8	.6081	1.0241	40.1	2	0	0	2	2	0	2	0	2	1	0	1	0	1	0	0	0	0	0	0	0	2	0	1	0
rotten	19	.5971	2.4179	43.8	5	1	1	0	4	0	2	6	7	1	0	4	0	0	0	1	0	0	0	0	1	1	0	4	0
Rotterdam	27	.3194	2.0688	43.2	12	9	1	0	1	1	3	0	2	0	0	1	0	21	0	0	0	0	0	0	0	2	1	0	0
Rotterdam's	4	.2338	.2367	33.7	3	0	0	0	0	0	1	0	0	0	0	1	0	3	0	0	0	0	0	0	0	0	0	0	0
rotting	10	.7139	1.4424	41.6	1	1	2	2	4	0	0	0	0	0	0	1	0	1	0	2	1	0	0	0	2	1	1	1	0
Rouault	2	.1493	.0692	28.4	0	0	1	0	0	1	0	0	0	0	0	0	0	0	0	0	0	1	0	0	0	0	1	0	0
Rouen	4	.4820	.4132	36.2	0	0	0	1	0	1	0	2	0	0	0	0	1	1	0	1	0	0	0	0	0	0	0	1	0
rouge	4	.2320	.2087	33.2	0	0	0	0	0	3	0	1	0	0	0	0	0	0	1	1	0	0	2	0	0	0	0	0	0
rough	292	.8555	49.871	57.0	31	57	39	43	57	37	23	5	53	9	8	19	2	55	7	19	6	16	5	13	15	30	14	21	0
Rough	8	.4485	.8019	39.0	0	2	2	0	1	2	1	0	2	0	0	0	0	2	0	0	0	0	0	0	0	0	2	2	0
rough-and-ready	3	.3408	.2477	33.9	0	0	0	0	3	0	0	0	1	0	0	1	0	0	0	0	0	0	0	0	0	1	0	0	0
rough-hewn	2	.2376	.1088	30.4	0	0	1	0	0	0	0	1	0	0	0	0	0	0	1	0	0	0	0	0	0	0	0	1	0
roughage	9	.3739	.7250	38.6	1	0	3	2	0	1	2	0	0	0	0	0	0	0	1	3	0	0	3	0	0	1	1	0	0
roughed	3	.2880	.1944	32.9	0	0	0	0	2	1	0	0	0	0	0	0	0	0	0	1	0	0	1	0	1	0	0	0	0
roughened	4	.4482	.4009	36.0	1	0	0	0	2	0	0	1	1	0	0	0	0	0	0	1	0	0	0	0	0	0	1	1	0
rougher	7	.5065	.7775	38.9	0	3	0	0	1	1	2	0	2	0	0	2	0	1	0	1	0	0	0	0	1	0	0	0	0
roughest	7	.3304	.5199	37.2	0	1	0	0	4	2	0	0	1	0	2	0	0	0	0	0	0	0	0	0	0	1	2	1	0
roughing	3	.0000	.0076	18.8	0	0	0	0	1	1	1	0	0	0	0	0	0	0	0	0	0	0	0	3	0	0	0	0	0
roughly	51	.8399	8.5556	49.3	2	2	4	5	19	8	6	5	4	1	1	4	0	7	0	12	0	0	1	1	3	6	6	5	0
roughness	10	.3720	.8134	39.1	0	1	1	3	2	2	1	0	1	1	0	0	0	0	0	2	0	3	1	0	1	1	0	0	0
roun'	4	.1787	.2347	33.7	0	0	0	0	4	0	0	0	2	0	0	0	0	0	0	0	0	0	0	0	2	0	0	0	0
round	1076	.9217	196.62	62.9	223	206	156	184	144	81	59	23	259	19	7	66	160	81	23	66	125	9	13	18	94	68	32	36	0
Round	16	.4497	1.7364	42.4	0	1	2	12	1	0	0	0	12	1	0	0	0	0	0	0	2	0	0	0	0	0	1	0	0
round-faced	2	.1948	.1250	31.0	1	0	0	0	1	0	0	0	1	0	0	0	0	0	0	0	0	0	0	0	0	1	0	0	0
round-head	3	.0000	.0076	18.8	0	0	0	0	0	3	0	0	0	0	0	0	0	0	0	0	0	0	0	3	0	0	0	0	0
round-the-clock	3	.2054	.1422	31.5	0	0	0	0	3	0	0	0	0	0	1	0	0	0	0	0	0	0	0	0	0	0	0	2	0
round-trip	5	.4501	.5037	37.0	0	0	0	2	1	2	0	0	1	0	0	0	1	2	0	0	0	0	0	0	0	0	0	1	0
round-up	3	.3394	.2451	33.9	0	1	0	0	2	0	0	0	1	0	0	1	0	0	0	0	0	0	0	0	1	0	0	0	0
roundabout	5	.3854	.4790	36.8	1	0	2	1	1	0	0	0	3	0	0	0	0	0	0	0	0	0	0	0	1	1	0	0	0
rounded	162	.8606	27.801	54.4	16	17	31	26	28	20	15	9	24	5	6	4	48	7	5	19	0	4	3	5	7	11	5	9	0
roundelay	2	.0000	.0914	29.6	0	0	0	2	0	0	0	0	2	0	0	0	0	0	0	0	0	0	0	0	0	0	0	0	0
rounder	2	.2441	.1127	30.5	0	0	0	1	1	0	0	0	0	0	0	0	0	0	0	0	0	0	0	0	1	0	1	0	0
rounders	11	.1891	.5322	37.3	0	2	0	8	0	0	1	0	0	2	0	0	0	0	0	0	0	0	0	0	0	9	0	0	0
rounding	46	.3971	4.0768	46.1	3	9	6	15	8	4	1	0	5	0	2	1	34	0	0	1	0	0	0	0	1	0	0	2	0
roundly	5	.4110	.4623	36.6	1	0	0	0	3	1	0	0	1	0	0	1	0	1	0	0	0	0	0	0	2	0	0	0	0
roundness	7	.2061	.3638	35.6	2	0	0	0	0	2	3	0	0	0	0	0	0	4	0	1	0	2	0	0	0	0	0	0	0
roundnose	4	.0000	.0101	20.0	0	0	0	0	3	0	1	0	0	0	0	0	0	0	0	0	0	0	0	4	0	0	0	0	0
roundout	2	.0000	.0290	24.6	2	0	0	0	0	0	0	0	0	0	0	0	0	0	0	0	0	0	0	0	0	2	0	0	0

5J Rosamunde
9P rosary
7N rose-leafy
5P rose-moles
7R rose-pink
9L rose-red
5E Rose's
3A rosebeds
9D Rosebud's
5A Rosella
8R Rosen
7R Rosenbloom
6J Rosenkavalier
7B Rosetta
7H rosette
6F rosewood
3N Rosh
7B Rosi
7N rosily
5Q Rosin
8M rosin-
8M rosin-type
9D Rosina
9A Roslyn
7H Rosse
7K Rosselli
5Q Rossetti
6A Rossis
9D Rossum
9D Rossum's
XH Rostand's
9E Rostvold
7C rosy-cheeked
7Q rotational
9J rote
9Q Rotenturmstrasse
6R Rothesay
7Q Rothschild
3P ROTIFER
XR rotisserie
5P Rotorua
XR rotund
7R Rouge
3Q rough-and-tumble
4R rough-cut
7R rough-house
6R rough-poured
6R rough-riding
9R rough-shod
7K roughen
8P roughhouse
4Q roughs
5Q Rougon
7R roulade
8J Roumania
6N round-about-ways
8H round-and-round
9Q round-bottom
7L round-bowled
3N round-eyed
7N round-log
5K round-nib
5E round-number
9M round-split
4A round-topped
7D round-ups
6B Roundabout
8D rounde
7A rounded-to
9P rounder's
7A Roundeyed
4N roundheaded
XR Roundheads
7A roundish
3A roundrock

Word Type	F	D	U	SFI	3 Gr 3	4 Gr 4	5 Gr 5	6 Gr 6	7 Gr 7	8 Gr 8	9 Gr 9	X UnGr	A Read	B Eng & Gr	C Comp	D Lit	E Math	F Soc Stud	G Spell	H Sci	J Music	K Art	L Home Ec	M Shop	N Lib F	P Lib NF	Q Lib Ref	R Mag	S Rel
rounds	58	.7429	8.7260	49.4	3	3	18	11	11	3	5	4	9	1	1	1	5	2	0	2	12	0	1	0	1	12	1	10	0
roundup	17	.5684	2.0908	43.2	1	6	4	0	4	0	0	2	7	1	0	1	0	1	0	0	0	0	0	0	3	0	0	4	0
roundups	3	.3776	.2489	34.0	0	1	0	1	0	0	0	1	0	0	0	1	0	1	0	0	0	0	0	0	0	0	0	1	0
roundworm	4	.0000	.0789	29.0	0	0	0	0	4	0	0	0	0	0	0	0	0	0	0	4	0	0	0	0	0	0	0	0	0
roundworms	5	.2213	.2870	34.6	0	0	0	0	3	1	1	0	0	0	0	0	0	0	0	4	0	0	0	0	0	0	1	0	0
rouse	12	.4136	1.0774	40.3	0	1	0	1	6	1	3	0	1	4	0	5	0	1	0	0	0	0	0	0	1	0	0	0	0
roused	21	.6793	2.9529	44.7	2	3	2	4	4	2	3	1	6	3	0	2	0	0	0	1	0	0	0	0	2	5	1	1	0
rouses	2	.2417	.1091	30.4	0	0	0	0	0	1	1	0	0	0	0	0	0	0	0	0	1	0	0	0	0	0	1	0	0
rousing	9	.6094	1.1346	40.5	1	1	0	1	4	1	0	1	1	0	0	0	0	1	0	0	1	0	0	0	3	1	1	1	0
Rousseau	6	.3041	.3897	35.9	1	0	1	0	0	2	2	0	0	0	0	0	0	0	0	0	1	2	0	0	0	0	2	1	0
Rousseau's	2	.0000	.0209	23.2	0	0	0	0	0	2	0	0	0	0	0	0	0	0	0	0	0	0	0	0	0	0	2	0	0
rout	10	.5270	1.1147	40.5	0	2	1	3	1	2	1	0	1	0	0	1	0	2	0	0	0	0	0	0	4	1	1	0	0
route	196	.8226	32.431	55.1	18	22	45	23	46	23	17	2	41	7	2	7	4	67	1	5	2	0	0	2	12	15	19	12	0
Route	12	.4618	1.2234	40.9	0	1	0	3	4	1	0	3	3	1	0	2	0	1	0	0	0	0	0	0	0	0	0	5	0
routed	6	.4908	.6144	37.9	0	0	1	1	1	2	1	0	0	0	1	0	0	1	0	1	0	0	0	1	1	1	0	0	0
router	2	.0000	.0050	17.0	0	0	0	0	1	0	1	0	0	0	0	0	0	0	0	0	0	0	0	2	0	0	0	0	0
routes	95	.6316	12.438	50.9	4	10	15	22	18	10	13	3	10	2	0	2	1	42	0	0	1	1	0	0	0	4	18	14	0
routine	55	.7554	8.3971	49.2	1	2	5	8	18	9	11	1	10	0	2	6	0	3	0	1	9	0	2	0	1	5	6	10	0
routines	8	.4391	.7393	38.7	0	0	2	1	2	1	2	0	0	0	0	0	0	1	0	0	2	0	1	0	0	0	0	4	0
Roux	7	.0000	.1380	31.4	0	0	0	0	0	0	0	7	0	0	0	0	0	0	0	7	0	0	0	0	0	0	0	0	0
Roved	2	.0000	.0162	22.1	0	0	0	0	2	0	0	0	0	0	0	0	0	0	0	0	2	0	0	0	0	0	0	0	0
rover	5	.1993	.2508	34.0	0	0	5	0	0	0	0	0	0	0	0	1	0	0	0	0	0	0	0	0	0	4	0	0	0
Rover	24	.6719	3.3933	45.3	8	3	2	3	5	0	1	2	12	1	1	1	0	0	0	0	1	0	0	0	1	3	0	4	0
Rover's	2	.0000	.0162	22.1	0	2	0	0	0	0	0	0	0	0	0	0	0	0	0	0	2	0	0	0	0	0	0	0	0
roving	4	.2708	.2760	34.4	0	1	0	1	0	1	1	0	1	0	0	2	0	1	0	0	0	0	0	0	0	0	0	0	0
row	510	.7845	80.466	59.1	134	76	57	71	72	67	22	11	66	7	4	15	208	14	32	7	69	3	15	1	16	26	8	19	0
Row	22	.2792	1.3704	41.4	6	0	0	4	10	2	0	0	0	0	0	0	2	0	0	2	15	0	0	0	1	0	0	2	0
rowboat	29	.7018	4.2638	46.3	7	10	3	3	2	1	1	2	16	3	1	2	1	0	0	1	0	0	0	0	2	2	0	1	0
rowboats	5	.1534	.2162	33.3	1	2	0	1	0	0	1	0	0	0	0	0	0	1	0	0	0	0	0	0	0	4	0	0	0
rowdy	4	.4417	.3913	35.9	0	1	0	0	1	1	1	0	1	0	0	1	0	0	0	0	1	0	0	0	0	1	0	0	0
Rowdy	5	.0000	.2284	33.6	5	0	0	0	0	0	0	0	5	0	0	0	0	0	0	0	0	0	0	0	0	0	0	0	0
rowed	43	.6078	5.6664	47.5	12	11	4	4	6	5	1	0	24	2	0	1	0	3	0	0	0	0	0	0	7	5	1	0	0
rowing	27	.6589	3.7201	45.7	4	3	1	13	4	1	0	1	10	0	1	2	0	0	0	0	2	0	0	0	3	7	0	2	0
rows	277	.7228	40.940	56.1	92	44	30	20	43	31	11	6	58	3	1	11	131	16	0	12	8	2	7	1	9	12	0	6	0
Roxanne	14	.0000	.6396	38.1	0	0	0	14	0	0	0	0	14	0	0	0	0	0	0	0	0	0	0	0	0	0	0	0	0
Roxbury	3	.3427	.2477	33.9	0	0	0	0	0	2	1	0	1	0	0	0	0	0	0	0	0	0	0	0	1	0	0	1	0
Roy	38	.6815	5.3954	47.3	0	18	3	3	4	7	2	1	15	1	0	2	4	0	1	0	4	0	0	0	0	4	0	7	0
Roy's	5	.3574	.3946	36.0	0	4	0	1	0	0	0	0	0	0	0	0	3	0	1	0	0	0	0	0	0	1	0	0	0
royal	105	.8109	17.132	52.3	23	8	12	11	24	20	6	1	23	0	0	8	2	15	1	2	8	2	0	0	7	16	12	9	0
Royal	82	.6532	11.142	50.5	14	7	7	9	15	10	15	5	23	0	0	2	1	6	0	4	6	0	0	0	10	0	21	9	0
Royale	2	.2152	.1357	31.3	1	0	1	0	0	0	0	0	1	0	0	0	0	1	0	0	0	0	0	0	0	0	0	0	0
royalties	5	.2138	.2693	34.3	0	0	0	0	3	0	2	0	0	0	0	0	0	2	0	0	0	0	0	0	0	0	0	3	0
royalty	18	.3898	1.5732	42.0	0	1	5	4	4	4	0	0	4	0	0	1	0	0	0	0	8	0	0	0	1	0	0	4	0
Rozinante	2	.0000	.0914	29.6	0	0	0	0	2	0	0	0	2	0	0	0	0	0	0	0	0	0	0	0	0	0	0	0	0
RP	3	.0000	.0449	26.5	0	0	3	0	0	0	0	0	0	0	0	0	3	0	0	0	0	0	0	0	0	0	0	0	0
rpm	26	.3663	2.0279	43.1	0	0	0	1	19	0	6	0	0	0	0	1	0	0	0	0	0	1	0	6	0	0	0	18	0
RPM	2	.2446	.1142	30.6	0	0	0	0	2	0	0	0	0	0	0	0	0	0	0	0	0	0	0	0	1	0	0	1	0
rr	2	.0000	.0234	23.7	0	2	0	0	0	0	0	0	0	0	0	0	0	0	0	0	0	0	0	0	2	0	0	0	0
RR	4	.0000	.0789	29.0	0	0	0	4	0	0	0	0	0	0	0	0	0	0	0	4	0	0	0	0	0	0	0	0	0
RS	17	.0000	.2545	34.1	1	0	3	2	1	4	6	0	0	0	0	0	17	0	0	0	0	0	0	0	0	0	0	0	0
RST	7	.0000	.1048	30.2	0	1	0	1	2	3	0	0	0	0	0	0	7	0	0	0	0	0	0	0	0	0	0	0	0
RSW	2	.0000	.0299	24.8	0	0	2	0	0	0	0	0	0	0	0	0	2	0	0	0	0	0	0	0	0	0	0	0	0
RT	11	.1318	.3630	35.6	0	0	2	0	0	9	0	0	0	0	0	0	5	0	0	0	0	0	0	6	0	0	0	0	0
RTV	2	.0000	.0299	24.8	0	0	2	0	0	0	0	0	0	0	0	0	2	0	0	0	0	0	0	0	0	0	0	0	0
rub	83	.7885	13.178	51.2	25	18	7	11	12	2	8	0	11	2	0	7	0	2	2	27	1	3	5	2	6	13	2	0	0
rubato	3	.0000	.0243	23.8	0	0	0	0	0	0	3	0	0	0	0	0	0	0	0	0	3	0	0	0	0	0	0	0	0
rubbed	134	.8385	22.571	53.5	20	26	19	18	23	20	6	2	41	2	1	16	0	3	1	16	0	4	2	2	21	15	5	5	0
rubber	337	.8573	57.891	57.6	46	94	71	31	46	25	22	2	84	5	2	3	10	35	3	114	10	2	2	8	7	11	28	13	0
Rubber	3	.2159	.1532	31.9	0	0	2	0	1	0	0	0	0	0	0	0	0	0	0	0	0	0	0	0	0	0	2	1	0
rubber-covered	2	.0000	.0050	17.0	0	0	0	0	0	2	0	0	0	0	0	0	0	0	0	0	0	0	0	2	0	0	0	0	0
rubber-sheet	2	.0000	.0299	24.8	0	0	0	0	0	2	0	0	0	0	0	0	2	0	0	0	0	0	0	0	0	0	0	0	0
rubberlike	3	.1205	.0847	29.3	0	0	1	0	0	1	1	0	0	0	0	0	0	0	0	0	0	0	0	2	0	0	1	0	0
rubbers	6	.3514	.5082	37.1	3	1	0	2	0	0	0	0	2	0	1	0	0	0	0	2	0	0	0	0	1	0	0	0	0
rubbery	4	.0000	.1827	32.6	1	2	0	0	1	0	0	0	4	0	0	0	0	0	0	0	0	0	0	0	0	0	0	0	0
rubbing	92	.7182	13.509	51.3	14	19	14	11	13	12	6	3	25	0	3	8	0	0	1	13	0	9	3	3	14	7	3	3	0
rubbings	9	.0000	.0166	22.2	0	4	4	0	0	1	0	0	0	0	0	0	0	0	0	0	0	9	0	0	0	0	0	0	0
rubbish	28	.7086	4.0584	46.1	3	9	3	3	5	4	1	0	5	1	2	2	0	3	0	5	0	0	0	0	2	4	3	1	0
rubble	8	.3856	.7620	38.8	0	0	5	1	1	0	0	1	5	0	1	1	0	0	0	0	0	0	0	0	0	0	0	1	0
rubbly	2	.0000	.0215	23.3	0	0	0	0	2	0	0	0	0	0	0	2	0	0	0	0	0	0	0	0	0	0	0	0	0
Rube	2	.2427	.1152	30.6	1	0	0	0	0	0	0	1	0	0	0	0	0	0	0	0	0	0	0	0	1	1	0	0	0
Rubens	2	.0000	.0209	23.2	0	0	0	0	0	0	0	2	0	0	0	0	0	0	0	0	0	0	0	0	0	0	2	0	0
rubidium	4	.0904	.1412	31.5	1	2	0	0	1	0	0	0	1	0	0	0	0	0	0	0	0	0	0	0	0	0	3	0	0
rubies	18	.2744	1.5238	41.8	0	2	0	2	14	0	0	0	16	0	0	0	0	0	0	1	0	0	0	0	1	0	0	0	0
Rubinstein	7	.0000	.0566	27.5	0	1	0	0	1	0	5	0	0	0	0	0	0	0	0	0	7	0	0	0	0	0	0	0	0
Rubinstein's	2	.0000	.0162	22.1	0	0	0	0	0	0	2	0	0	0	0	0	0	0	0	0	2	0	0	0	0	0	0	0	0
Rubio	11	.0000	.1290	31.1	0	0	0	0	0	0	11	0	0	0	0	0	0	0	0	0	0	0	0	0	11	0	0	0	0
rubs	10	.4014	.9271	39.7	4	1	2	1	0	0	2	0	2	0	0	1	0	0	0	6	0	0	0	0	0	0	1	0	0
ruby	11	.5539	1.2846	41.1	3	0	4	1	1	2	0	0	2	2	0	0	0	1	1	0	1	0	0	0	4	0	0	0	0
Ruby	16	.3498	1.5095	41.8	11	2	1	0	0	0	0	2	13	0	0	0	0	0	0	0	0	0	0	0	1	0	0	2	0
Ruby-Throat	2	.0000	.0914	29.6	2	0	0	0	0	0	0	0	2	0	0	0	0	0	0	0	0	0	0	0	0	0	0	0	0
ruchi-pip	7	.0000	.0851	29.3	0	0	0	0	0	0	0	7	0	0	0	0	0	0	0	0	0	0	0	0	0	0	0	7	0
ruck	2	.1717	.1142	30.6	0	0	0	0	1	1	0	0	1	0	0	1	0	0	0	0	0	0	0	0	0	0	0	0	0
ruckus	4	.4538	.4007	36.0	0	1	2	0	0	0	0	1	1	1	0	0	0	0	0	0	0	0	0	0	1	0	0	1	0
rudder	27	.5709	3.3183	45.2	3	3	5	7	8	0	1	0	9	0	1	0	0	1	0	5	0	0	0	0	0	4	0	7	0
ruddy	6	.6023	.7576	38.8	1	0	0	2	1	1	1	0	1	0	0	1	0	1	0	1	0	0	0	0	1	0	0	1	0
rude	36	.7256	5.3191	47.3	3	2	4	6	13	6	2	0	9	3	2	7	0	1	1	0	1	0	3	0	5	1	0	3	0
rudely	16	.6417	2.1461	43.3	5	1	4	1	1	3	1	0	5	1	1	1	0	1	0	0	0	0	0	0	4	2	1	0	0
rudeness	8	.4610	.7921	39.0	0	0	2	1	3	2	0	0	1	0	1	2	0	0	0	0	0	0	0	0	0	3	0	1	0
Rudi	5	.0000	.2284	33.6	0	0	0	0	0	5	0	0	5	0	0	0	0	0	0	0	0	0	0	0	0	0	0	0	0
Rudi's	2	.0000	.0914	29.6	0	0	0	0	0	2	0	0	2	0	0	0	0	0	0	0	0	0	0	0	0	0	0	0	0
rudimentary	3	.3395	.2468	33.9	0	0	1	0	1	1	0	0	1	0	0	0	0	0	0	0	0	0	0	0	0	1	1	0	0
Rudolf	3	.3452	.2543	34.1	0	0	0	2	0	0	0	1	1	0	0	0	0	0	0	1	0	0	0	0	0	0	0	1	0
Rudolph	15	.4348	1.4463	41.6	0	1	0	5	3	6	0	0	4	0	0	1	0	1	0	1	7	1	0	0	0	0	0	0	0
Rudy	14	.1255	.5188	37.2	11	1	0	0	1	1	0	0	1	0	0	0	0	0	0	0	0	0	0	0	12	0	0	1	0

7N roundtailed
3G Roundup
3A Rourke
8Q Rousseauist
6R roustabout
8A roustabouts
6A Routes
6N routs
XH Roux's
6J rove
8F Rovere
3A Rovers
4Q roves
4J rovin'
8J roving's
4K row-type
XR rowan
9P Rowe
XR rowels
XR Rowland
8G Roxane
5N Roxie
9Q royalist
7F royalists
7A royalities
4R Royals
4A Royce
7R Royce's
7R Royersford
XD Roylott
XD Roylott's
9D Roylotts
8D roysterers
7R Rozelle
7E RPS
8E RQ
6R Rs
6R RS'S
5E RSO
8E RSP
4E RSTU
9E rt
5E RTVX
7E RU
5R rub-a-dub-dub
4G rub-ber
7N rubbage
7C rubber-heeled
7N rubber-neck
7Q rubber-producing
6A rubber-soled
6R rubberized
4N rubbery-looking
6J Rubbly
7N rubdown
4R rubella
XQ Rubens'
7D rubicund
XR Ruby's
4A ruching
5A ruckuses
7Q rudiments
8A Rudisberg
6A Rudolph's

Word Type	F	D	U	SFI	3 Gr 3	4 Gr 4	5 Gr 5	6 Gr 6	7 Gr 7	8 Gr 8	9 Gr 9	X UnGr	A Read	B Eng & Gr	C Comp	D Lit	E Math	F Soc Stud	G Spell	H Sci	J Music	K Art	L Home Ec	M Shop	N Lib F	P Lib NF	Q Lib Ref	R Mag	S Rel
rue	4	.2445	.3067	34.9	2	0	0	0	2	0	0	0	3	0	0	0	0	0	0	0	0	0	0	0	0	1	0	0	0
Rue	2	.2405	.1205	30.8	0	0	0	0	0	0	0	2	0	0	0	0	0	0	0	1	0	0	0	0	0	1	0	0	0
ruefully	5	.4022	.4242	36.3	0	0	0	3	2	0	0	0	0	0	1	1	0	0	0	0	0	0	0	0	2	0	0	1	0
Rufe	8	.2155	.5456	37.4	0	0	2	5	0	0	1	0	5	0	0	0	0	0	0	0	0	0	0	0	3	0	0	0	0
ruff	8	.5474	.9485	39.8	2	0	1	1	2	1	1	0	3	1	0	1	0	0	0	0	0	0	0	0	2	0	0	1	0
ruffed	2	.2401	.1133	30.5	1	0	0	0	1	0	0	0	0	0	0	0	0	0	0	0	0	0	0	0	0	1	1	0	0
ruffians	6	.3871	.5823	37.7	0	0	2	3	0	1	0	0	4	0	0	0	0	0	0	0	0	0	0	0	0	0	1	1	0
Ruffing	2	.2433	.1158	30.6	1	0	0	0	1	0	0	0	0	0	0	0	0	0	0	0	0	0	0	0	0	1	0	1	0
ruffle	17	.2510	1.0057	40.0	1	0	1	4	3	0	8	0	3	0	0	1	0	0	0	0	1	0	9	0	1	1	0	1	0
ruffled	12	.6049	1.5664	41.9	3	5	0	2	1	1	0	0	6	0	0	1	0	1	0	0	0	0	0	0	2	1	0	1	0
ruffles	12	.3741	1.0790	40.3	3	0	0	5	1	0	3	0	6	0	0	1	0	0	0	0	1	0	3	0	1	0	0	0	0
Ruffles	16	.0000	.7309	38.6	0	0	0	16	0	0	0	0	16	0	0	0	0	0	0	0	0	0	0	0	0	0	0	0	0
Rufus	78	.3641	6.4759	48.1	0	21	18	0	0	1	38	0	15	0	1	13	0	0	0	0	0	0	0	0	47	2	0	0	0
RUFUS	2	.1717	.1142	30.6	0	2	0	0	0	0	0	0	1	0	0	1	0	0	0	0	0	0	0	0	0	0	0	0	0
Rufus's	4	.2048	.1975	33.0	0	1	0	0	0	0	3	0	0	0	0	1	0	0	0	0	0	0	0	0	3	0	0	0	0
rug	82	.8504	14.012	51.5	35	14	2	13	9	2	5	2	30	6	0	3	4	6	2	8	1	3	1	0	4	6	2	6	0
rugby	2	.2446	.1123	30.5	0	0	1	0	0	1	0	0	0	1	0	0	0	0	0	0	0	0	0	0	0	0	1	0	0
Rugby	4	.3831	.3415	35.3	0	0	1	2	0	1	0	0	0	0	0	0	0	2	0	0	0	0	0	0	0	1	0	1	0
Rugg	9	.0000	.1055	30.2	0	9	0	0	0	0	0	0	0	0	0	0	0	0	0	0	0	0	0	0	9	0	0	0	0
Rugg's	2	.0000	.0234	23.7	0	2	0	0	0	0	0	0	0	0	0	0	0	0	0	0	0	0	0	0	2	0	0	0	0
rugged	79	.6828	11.062	50.4	2	7	22	10	22	3	5	8	7	1	0	3	0	36	0	2	1	1	0	0	1	7	7	13	0
Rugiati	4	.0000	.0486	26.9	0	0	0	0	4	0	0	0	0	0	0	0	0	0	0	0	0	0	0	0	0	0	0	4	0
rugs	43	.6681	5.9225	47.7	7	5	7	7	13	2	1	1	7	2	0	0	3	14	0	4	0	3	3	0	3	0	1	3	0
ruh	2	.0000	.0162	22.1	0	0	0	0	0	2	0	0	0	0	0	0	0	0	2	0	0	0	0	0	0	0	0	0	0
Ruhr	7	.1464	.3624	35.6	1	0	0	5	0	0	1	0	2	0	0	0	0	5	0	0	0	0	0	0	0	0	0	0	0
ruin	43	.8184	7.0728	48.5	5	4	4	7	7	10	5	1	9	0	1	5	0	9	0	2	1	0	1	2	4	5	1	3	0
ruined	55	.7440	8.3247	49.2	5	6	12	12	10	8	0	2	11	1	0	11	0	3	0	9	0	1	0	0	7	5	2	5	0
ruining	5	.2324	.2701	34.3	0	0	0	1	1	1	2	0	0	0	2	1	0	1	0	1	0	0	0	0	0	0	0	0	0
ruins	56	.6439	7.4866	48.7	2	5	6	11	16	8	6	2	11	2	0	3	0	18	1	2	1	4	0	0	0	1	10	3	0
rule	618	.8171	100.94	60.0	55	74	123	106	106	75	72	7	43	52	2	5	194	58	124	30	3	3	4	13	10	30	31	15	1
Rule	37	.5744	4.4253	46.5	7	0	9	0	8	9	4	0	3	11	0	1	14	0	1	1	0	0	0	0	2	3	0	1	0
rule-of-thumb	2	.2391	.1133	30.5	0	0	0	0	0	0	2	0	0	0	0	0	1	0	0	0	0	0	0	0	0	0	1	0	0
ruled	130	.7494	19.734	53.0	12	10	18	30	28	17	11	4	12	6	0	2	1	58	1	3	3	1	0	2	4	8	23	6	0
Rulefinder's	8	.0000	.0649	28.1	0	8	0	0	0	0	0	0	0	0	0	0	0	0	8	0	0	0	0	0	0	0	0	0	0
Rulemaker's	5	.0000	.0406	26.1	0	0	0	5	0	0	0	0	0	0	0	0	0	0	5	0	0	0	0	0	0	0	0	0	0
ruler	260	.7479	39.341	55.9	46	44	47	27	25	36	33	2	21	6	2	4	129	30	5	22	8	1	4	0	2	10	14	1	1
rulers	89	.6834	12.427	50.9	4	11	28	12	18	6	9	1	3	2	0	2	12	39	1	2	0	0	1	0	0	11	12	4	0
Rulers	3	.0000	.1370	31.4	0	0	3	0	0	0	0	0	3	0	0	0	0	0	0	0	0	0	0	0	0	0	0	0	0
rules	444	.8839	78.045	58.9	44	55	51	51	84	77	72	10	78	82	6	7	34	27	49	49	6	3	12	19	12	21	18	21	0
Rules	49	.2542	3.0563	44.9	39	3	2	5	0	0	0	0	3	0	0	0	37	0	0	0	0	0	0	0	2	7	0	0	0
Rulescouter's	8	.0000	.0649	28.1	0	0	8	0	0	0	0	0	0	0	0	0	0	0	8	0	0	0	0	0	0	0	0	0	0
ruling	32	.6195	4.0815	46.1	3	3	4	3	7	4	8	0	0	0	0	1	0	15	0	0	2	0	0	0	2	4	5	3	0
rulings	4	.2183	.2285	33.6	0	0	1	0	0	0	3	0	0	0	0	0	0	3	0	0	0	0	0	0	0	1	0	0	0
rum	22	.5537	2.5985	44.1	0	0	1	4	12	5	0	0	5	0	0	3	0	5	0	0	1	0	0	0	7	0	1	0	0
rum-tum-tiddle-um-tum	2	.0000	.0914	29.6	1	1	0	0	0	0	0	0	2	0	0	0	0	0	0	0	0	0	0	0	0	0	0	0	0
rum-tum-tum-tiddle-um	2	.0000	.0914	29.6	1	1	0	0	0	0	0	0	2	0	0	0	0	0	0	0	0	0	0	0	0	0	0	0	0
Rumania	11	.2217	.6468	38.1	2	0	0	6	0	1	1	1	2	0	0	0	0	2	0	0	0	0	0	0	0	0	0	7	0
Rumanians	5	.2445	.3026	34.8	0	0	0	3	1	0	1	0	0	0	0	0	0	3	0	0	0	0	0	0	0	0	0	2	0
rumble	20	.6959	2.8396	44.5	2	3	2	3	0	6	3	1	3	1	2	2	0	1	0	3	2	0	0	0	1	2	1	2	0
rumbled	16	.4880	1.7259	42.4	6	3	2	2	2	1	0	0	5	1	2	0	0	4	0	0	0	0	0	0	2	2	0	0	0
rumbles	3	.0744	.0660	28.2	0	2	1	0	0	0	0	0	0	0	2	0	0	1	0	0	0	0	0	0	0	0	0	0	0
rumbling	22	.5606	2.6434	44.2	5	1	4	2	6	3	0	1	7	0	2	1	0	1	0	1	0	0	0	0	6	3	0	1	0
Rumford	9	.1719	.4433	36.5	0	0	2	5	1	0	0	1	0	0	0	0	0	0	0	8	0	0	0	0	0	0	1	0	0
Rumley	3	.0000	.0434	26.4	0	3	0	0	0	0	0	0	0	0	0	0	0	0	0	0	0	0	0	0	0	3	0	0	0
rummage	3	.2283	.1611	32.1	0	0	1	0	0	1	0	1	0	1	0	0	0	0	0	0	0	0	0	0	2	0	0	0	0
rummaged	5	.3410	.4178	36.2	0	2	1	1	0	0	1	0	2	0	0	1	0	0	0	0	0	0	0	0	2	0	0	0	0
rummaging	3	.2279	.2143	33.3	1	1	0	0	1	0	0	0	2	0	0	0	0	0	0	0	0	0	0	0	0	0	0	1	0
rumor	10	.4529	1.0117	40.1	0	0	1	0	2	6	1	0	3	1	0	4	0	1	0	0	0	0	0	0	0	0	0	1	0
rumored	4	.4485	.4009	36.0	0	0	0	1	1	1	1	0	1	0	0	0	0	1	0	0	0	0	0	0	0	0	1	1	0
rumors	17	.6209	2.1783	43.4	4	0	1	0	7	1	4	0	2	1	0	3	0	0	0	0	0	0	0	0	1	5	3	2	0
rump	10	.4718	.9992	40.0	1	1	1	0	4	2	1	0	1	0	1	4	0	0	0	0	0	0	0	0	3	0	1	0	0
Rumpelstiltskin	2	.0580	.0676	28.3	1	0	0	0	0	1	0	0	1	0	0	0	0	0	0	0	0	1	0	0	0	0	0	0	0
rumpled	4	.4519	.3985	36.0	0	1	0	1	1	0	0	1	1	0	0	1	0	0	0	0	0	0	0	0	0	0	1	1	0
rumps	4	.4866	.4069	36.1	0	1	0	0	3	0	0	0	0	0	0	1	0	0	0	0	0	0	0	0	1	1	1	0	0
rumpus	2	.1733	.1149	30.6	0	1	0	0	0	0	1	0	1	1	0	0	0	0	0	0	0	0	0	0	0	0	0	0	0
rumtum	3	.0000	.0243	23.8	3	0	0	0	0	0	0	0	0	0	0	0	0	0	0	0	3	0	0	0	0	0	0	0	0
run	1473	.9311	271.96	64.3	357	262	169	167	268	135	90	25	494	71	14	96	18	144	18	93	34	8	10	13	144	144	42	130	0
Run	22	.5892	2.7453	44.4	1	7	0	8	3	3	0	0	6	0	0	2	0	1	0	0	0	0	0	0	1	7	4	1	0
run-down	7	.1464	.3624	35.6	4	0	1	1	0	1	0	0	2	0	0	0	0	5	0	0	0	0	0	0	0	0	0	0	0
run-of-the-mill	2	.1814	.1187	30.7	0	1	0	0	0	0	0	1	1	0	0	0	0	0	0	0	0	0	0	0	0	0	0	1	0
run-off	2	.2300	.1140	30.6	0	1	0	0	0	1	0	0	0	1	0	0	0	0	0	1	0	0	0	0	0	0	0	0	0
run-on	10	.0000	.1094	30.4	0	0	0	0	7	0	3	0	0	10	0	0	0	0	0	0	0	0	0	0	0	0	0	0	0
run-ons	2	.0000	.0219	23.4	0	0	0	0	1	0	1	0	0	2	0	0	0	0	0	0	0	0	0	0	0	0	0	0	0
runaway	44	.6386	5.9547	47.7	5	15	5	5	5	7	1	1	18	1	2	0	0	8	1	1	0	0	0	0	0	8	0	5	0
Runaway	5	.2055	.2584	34.1	0	0	0	0	4	0	1	0	0	0	0	3	0	2	0	0	0	0	0	0	0	0	0	0	0
runaways	6	.2407	.3413	35.3	0	1	0	0	5	0	0	0	0	0	0	3	0	0	0	0	0	0	0	0	0	3	0	0	0
rundown	4	.3740	.3380	35.3	0	1	0	0	0	1	2	0	0	0	0	0	0	2	0	1	0	0	0	0	1	0	0	0	0
runes	2	.0000	.0162	22.1	0	0	0	0	2	0	0	0	0	0	0	0	0	0	2	0	0	0	0	0	0	0	0	0	0
rung	29	.6023	3.6581	45.6	0	9	6	2	6	4	2	0	7	10	2	3	0	1	0	1	0	0	0	0	2	1	0	2	0
rungs	4	.3483	.3141	35.0	0	1	0	0	3	0	0	0	1	0	1	0	0	0	0	0	0	1	0	0	0	0	0	1	0
runic	3	.0000	.0243	23.9	0	0	0	0	3	0	0	0	0	0	0	0	0	0	3	0	0	0	0	0	0	0	0	0	0
runned	3	.0000	.1370	31.4	0	0	3	0	0	0	0	0	3	0	0	0	0	0	0	0	0	0	0	0	0	0	0	0	0
runner	50	.6591	6.9754	48.4	7	12	8	7	15	0	1	0	24	0	0	5	6	1	0	2	0	0	0	0	1	9	1	1	0
Runner	3	.1277	.1363	31.3	0	1	0	0	0	0	1	1	1	0	0	0	0	0	0	0	0	0	0	0	0	0	0	2	0
runner's	2	.1717	.1142	30.6	0	0	1	1	0	0	0	0	1	0	0	1	0	0	0	0	0	0	0	0	0	0	0	0	0
runners	53	.7108	7.8128	48.9	7	10	8	10	12	4	2	0	22	0	0	5	0	1	1	3	0	0	0	0	4	10	3	4	0
runnin'	6	.3544	.5269	37.2	0	0	1	0	4	0	1	0	3	0	0	2	0	0	0	0	0	0	0	0	0	0	1	0	0
running	797	.9004	143.03	61.6	162	137	74	93	179	79	53	20	304	24	4	51	7	31	10	55	12	8	7	5	109	68	25	77	0
Running	3	.3791	.2506	34.0	0	2	0	1	0	0	0	0	0	0	0	0	0	0	0	1	0	0	0	0	1	0	0	1	0
Runnymede	2	.1733	.1149	30.6	0	0	0	1	0	0	1	0	1	1	0	0	0	0	0	0	0	0	0	0	0	0	0	0	0
runoff	6	.2879	.3956	36.0	0	0	0	1	3	0	0	2	0	0	0	0	0	0	0	1	0	0	0	0	0	0	1	4	0
runs	312	.9208	57.012	57.6	64	42	36	34	61	26	39	10	85	18	1	15	11	35	3	33	7	2	1	8	13	24	19	37	0
runt	6	.3394	.4902	36.9	0	3	0	1	1	0	1	0	2	0	0	2	0	0	0	0	0	0	0	0	2	0	0	0	0
runts	2	.0000	.0914	29.6	0	1	1	0	0	0	0	0	2	0	0	0	0	0	0	0	0	0	0	0	0	0	0	0	0

5A rued
9J ruehmen
9D RUFE
6N ruffian
9L ruffler
7N Ruffler
7N Ruffler's
5A ruffling
7D ruffs
7H rufus
3P rug-making
7Q rug's
7R Ruger
4Q ruggedness
7R Rugiati's
5H Ruhle
3A Ruida
3A Ruida's
9D ruinin'
7D Ruler
7P ruler-and-compass
9R ruling-class
4A Rum
9B rum-colored
8F rum-molasses-slave
6R Rumania's
7B Rumanian
7D Rumbles
7A rumblings
6H rumford
5Q ruminants
XR rumination
3A rummages
8R Rumor
9N rumours
7R rumples
7D rumpling
4P Run-Sheep-Run
7P run-in
9R run-it-up-the-flagpole
9B run-togethers
9D run'st
4A runabouts
9D runagate
3A runcible
4B rune
6A Runic
9D Runkleman's
8D runn
3D runn'th
7R runner-up
7R Runners
8D runneth
6N running-away
7D running-down
XP runnings
7L runny
9B Runs
4N runty

Word Type	F	D	U	SFI	3 Gr 3	4 Gr 4	5 Gr 5	6 Gr 6	7 Gr 7	8 Gr 8	9 Gr 9	X UnGr	A Read	B Eng & Gr	C Comp	D Lit	E Math	F Soc Stud	G Spell	H Sci	J Music	K Art	L Home Ec	M Shop	N Lib F	P Lib NF	Q Lib Ref	R Mag	S Rel
runway	37	.5648	4.4829	46.5	8	4	0	8	14	0	1	2	12	1	0	7	1	1	0	0	0	0	0	0	0	6	0	9	0
runways	15	.6232	1.9775	43.0	7	0	0	5	2	1	0	0	5	0	0	0	0	3	0	1	0	0	0	1	0	2	1	2	0
rupees	3	.2369	.2208	33.4	0	2	0	1	0	0	0	0	2	0	0	0	1	0	0	0	0	0	0	0	0	0	0	0	0
Rupert	14	.4473	1.4795	41.7	2	7	3	0	1	0	1	0	8	0	1	0	0	3	0	0	0	0	0	0	0	0	0	2	0
rupture	4	.3395	.3008	34.8	0	0	0	0	2	0	2	0	0	0	0	1	0	0	0	1	0	0	0	0	0	0	2	0	0
ruptured	4	.2835	.2871	34.6	0	1	0	0	0	2	1	0	1	0	0	0	0	0	0	1	0	0	0	0	0	0	0	2	0
rural	59	.6913	8.3174	49.2	0	1	13	7	17	9	12	0	3	3	0	3	0	25	2	1	4	0	0	0	0	4	3	11	0
ruse	2	.0000	.0914	29.6	0	0	0	0	1	1	0	0	2	0	0	0	0	0	0	0	0	0	0	0	0	0	0	0	0
rush	132	.8376	22.238	53.5	24	16	19	14	31	16	11	1	44	2	0	19	0	8	1	10	5	2	1	0	12	10	5	13	0
Rush	10	.2756	.6594	38.2	0	2	4	2	2	0	0	0	2	0	0	0	0	0	0	0	6	0	0	0	0	0	1	1	0
rushed	200	.7777	31.738	55.0	49	51	16	24	27	15	12	6	80	11	0	14	0	16	1	6	4	0	1	0	22	31	1	13	0
rushes	48	.6821	6.7726	48.3	13	6	9	4	9	3	4	0	12	0	1	9	0	1	0	11	0	0	0	0	1	8	4	1	0
rushing	92	.8284	15.388	51.9	24	12	13	13	12	10	6	2	35	1	0	6	0	13	0	6	4	2	1	0	5	10	2	7	0
Rushmore	2	.2417	.1211	30.8	0	0	1	0	0	0	1	0	0	0	0	0	1	1	0	0	0	0	0	0	0	0	0	0	0
Rusk	2	.2351	.1166	30.7	0	0	0	0	0	0	2	0	0	0	0	0	0	1	0	0	0	0	0	0	0	0	0	1	0
Russ	11	.2070	.8193	39.1	0	0	0	1	10	0	0	0	10	0	0	0	0	0	0	0	0	0	0	0	0	0	0	1	0
Russe	4	.3418	.2942	34.7	0	0	1	0	2	1	0	0	0	0	0	0	0	0	0	0	2	0	0	0	0	0	1	1	0
Russell	25	.6174	3.1759	45.0	8	2	1	3	7	0	4	0	2	2	1	0	0	0	0	0	0	0	0	0	2	9	3	6	0
Russia	194	.6559	26.120	54.2	7	9	29	56	25	39	27	2	5	4	0	7	2	110	0	1	17	1	1	0	0	14	20	12	0
Russia's	9	.3854	.7818	38.9	0	0	1	2	2	2	2	0	1	0	0	0	0	3	0	0	0	0	0	0	0	0	1	4	0
Russian	175	.7164	25.412	54.1	8	10	13	34	39	40	28	3	16	9	0	14	3	32	3	9	41	0	0	0	3	9	25	11	0
Russians	63	.6883	8.8405	49.5	2	5	11	15	15	7	8	0	4	1	0	4	0	19	1	0	2	0	0	0	2	7	7	16	0
Russo	3	.2283	.1611	32.1	0	1	0	0	2	0	0	0	0	1	0	0	0	0	0	0	0	0	0	0	2	0	0	0	0
rust	39	.6771	5.4778	47.4	6	10	3	5	9	3	2	1	11	1	0	4	0	2	0	8	0	0	0	2	2	1	0	8	0
rusted	15	.6855	2.1361	43.3	3	5	1	0	1	4	1	0	5	2	0	0	1	1	0	2	2	0	0	0	0	1	0	1	0
rustic	9	.5487	1.0339	40.1	0	1	0	2	2	1	3	0	1	1	0	3	0	1	0	0	1	0	0	0	0	0	0	2	0
rusting	9	.3992	.8089	39.1	1	1	3	1	2	0	1	0	1	0	0	0	0	0	0	5	0	0	0	1	0	0	0	2	0
rustle	16	.6292	2.1181	43.3	2	3	2	1	7	1	0	0	5	0	0	3	0	1	0	2	1	0	0	0	3	1	0	0	0
rustled	10	.5147	1.1178	40.5	0	2	1	3	3	1	0	0	3	1	0	2	0	0	0	0	0	0	0	0	3	1	0	0	0
rustlers	2	.2337	.1157	30.6	1	0	1	0	0	0	0	0	0	0	0	0	0	1	0	0	0	0	0	0	1	0	0	0	0
rustles	2	.2442	.1134	30.5	1	0	0	0	1	0	0	0	0	1	0	0	0	0	0	0	0	0	0	0	0	0	0	1	0
rustling	35	.7007	5.0204	47.0	5	5	5	2	13	4	1	0	8	2	3	5	0	2	0	2	2	1	0	0	6	4	0	0	0
rustlings	2	.1717	.1142	30.6	0	0	1	0	1	0	0	0	1	0	0	1	0	0	0	0	0	0	0	0	0	0	0	0	0
rustproof	2	.0000	.0064	18.1	0	0	0	0	0	1	1	0	0	0	0	0	0	0	0	0	0	0	2	0	0	0	0	0	0
rusts	4	.0000	.0789	29.0	0	3	1	0	0	0	0	0	0	0	0	0	0	0	0	4	0	0	0	0	0	0	0	0	0
Rustum	6	.0000	.0869	29.4	0	0	0	0	6	0	0	0	0	0	0	0	0	0	0	0	0	0	0	0	0	6	0	0	0
Rustum's	6	.0000	.0869	29.4	0	0	0	0	6	0	0	0	0	0	0	0	0	0	0	0	0	0	0	0	0	6	0	0	0
rusty	55	.7313	8.2024	49.1	7	10	7	1	23	6	1	0	13	7	2	9	0	1	0	5	1	0	0	0	9	4	0	4	0
Rusty	6	.2249	.3433	35.4	4	1	0	0	0	0	1	0	1	0	0	4	0	0	0	0	0	0	0	0	0	0	0	1	0
rut	5	.2445	.3100	34.9	0	0	0	0	5	0	0	0	1	0	0	3	0	0	0	0	0	0	0	0	0	1	0	0	0
Rutgers	5	.3487	.4032	36.1	1	0	0	0	0	1	3	0	0	0	0	0	0	1	0	3	0	0	0	0	0	1	0	0	0
Ruth	59	.6239	7.7900	48.9	16	19	8	3	3	6	4	0	21	2	0	3	17	0	0	0	0	1	0	0	0	12	0	3	0
Ruth's	8	.5497	.9115	39.6	1	1	3	1	0	1	0	1	0	1	0	0	3	0	1	0	0	0	0	0	0	2	0	1	0
ruther	3	.2120	.1548	31.9	0	1	0	0	2	0	0	0	0	0	0	0	0	0	0	0	0	0	0	0	2	1	0	0	0
Rutherford	7	.4249	.6411	38.1	0	0	1	3	1	2	0	0	0	0	0	0	0	1	0	2	1	0	0	0	0	0	3	0	0
Rutherford's	2	.2278	.1128	30.5	0	0	0	1	1	0	0	0	0	0	0	0	0	0	0	1	0	0	0	0	0	0	1	0	0
ruthless	7	.5438	.7910	39.0	1	0	0	1	3	2	0	0	0	1	0	0	0	1	0	0	0	0	0	0	0	2	1	2	0
ruthlessly	3	.3851	.2497	34.0	0	0	1	0	0	1	1	0	0	0	0	1	0	0	0	0	0	0	0	0	1	1	0	0	0
Ruthven	2	.0000	.0243	23.9	0	0	0	0	0	0	0	2	0	0	0	0	0	0	0	0	0	0	0	0	0	0	0	2	0
Rutledge	4	.1948	.2500	34.0	0	0	0	0	1	2	1	0	2	0	0	0	0	0	0	0	0	0	0	0	0	2	0	0	0
ruts	16	.6129	2.0978	43.2	2	3	0	4	2	5	0	0	7	0	1	1	0	3	0	0	0	0	0	0	2	1	0	1	0
rutted	7	.6556	.9439	39.7	2	0	0	2	2	1	0	0	1	0	0	1	0	1	1	0	0	0	0	0	1	1	0	1	0
Ruwenzori	5	.1285	.1797	32.5	0	0	0	0	5	0	0	0	0	0	0	0	0	1	0	0	0	0	0	0	0	0	4	0	0
Ruzhonka	15	.0000	.6852	38.4	15	0	0	0	0	0	0	0	15	0	0	0	0	0	0	0	0	0	0	0	0	0	0	0	0
RV	3	.0000	.0449	26.5	0	0	0	1	0	2	0	0	0	0	0	0	3	0	0	0	0	0	0	0	0	0	0	0	0
Rw	3	.2442	.1820	32.6	0	0	0	2	0	0	1	0	0	1	0	0	0	0	0	2	0	0	0	0	0	0	0	0	0
RW	12	.2076	.6470	38.1	0	0	0	11	0	1	0	0	0	0	0	0	8	0	0	4	0	0	0	0	0	0	0	0	0
Ryan	21	.3401	1.7774	42.5	0	0	0	13	5	0	2	1	9	0	0	0	0	0	0	0	0	0	0	0	0	4	0	8	0
rye	33	.6233	4.3221	46.4	0	5	1	15	7	0	5	0	6	2	0	0	0	15	0	6	0	0	1	0	1	0	1	1	0
Rye	6	.0000	.0485	26.9	0	3	0	0	0	3	0	0	0	0	0	0	0	0	0	0	6	0	0	0	0	0	0	0	0
Ryrie	3	.1200	.1302	31.1	0	0	3	0	0	0	0	0	1	2	0	0	0	0	0	0	0	0	0	0	0	0	0	0	0
Rysavy's	2	.0000	.0243	23.9	0	0	0	0	0	0	0	2	0	0	0	0	0	0	0	0	0	0	0	0	0	0	0	2	0
R1	3	.0000	.0076	18.8	0	0	0	0	0	3	0	0	0	0	0	0	0	0	0	0	0	0	0	3	0	0	0	0	0
R10	2	.0000	.0243	23.9	0	0	0	0	2	0	0	0	0	0	0	0	0	0	0	0	0	0	0	0	0	0	0	2	0
r2	2	.0000	.0299	24.8	0	0	0	0	0	0	2	0	0	0	0	0	2	0	0	0	0	0	0	0	0	0	0	0	0
R2	3	.0000	.0076	18.8	0	0	0	0	0	3	0	0	0	0	0	0	0	0	0	0	0	0	0	3	0	0	0	0	0
R300	2	.0000	.0914	29.6	2	0	0	0	0	0	0	0	2	0	0	0	0	0	0	0	0	0	0	0	0	0	0	0	0
s	1002	.6507	132.99	61.2	172	172	144	130	115	92	152	25	73	113	5	11	110	70	348	28	1	0	3	4	2	21	60	153	0
S	262	.7855	41.383	56.2	23	31	26	18	57	60	38	9	23	7	3	1	71	36	8	9	4	0	0	2	4	16	22	56	0
S**	23	.5498	2.6373	44.2	2	2	1	2	8	5	2	1	1	1	0	1	4	0	0	0	0	0	0	0	0	8	1	7	0
SOS	2	.0000	.0914	29.6	2	0	0	0	0	0	0	0	2	0	0	0	0	0	0	0	0	0	0	0	0	0	0	0	0
S-IVB	2	.0000	.0243	23.9	0	0	0	2	0	0	0	0	0	0	0	0	0	0	0	0	0	0	0	0	0	0	0	2	0
s'pose	6	.3875	.4978	37.0	0	0	1	0	2	3	0	0	0	2	0	2	0	0	0	0	0	0	0	0	2	0	0	0	0
s's	11	.0886	.2756	34.4	0	4	0	5	1	1	0	0	0	1	0	0	0	0	10	0	0	0	0	0	0	0	0	0	0
sa	5	.0000	.0608	27.8	0	0	0	0	0	0	0	5	0	0	0	0	0	0	0	0	0	0	0	0	0	0	0	5	0
Sa'ud	5	.0000	.0724	28.6	0	0	0	0	5	0	0	0	0	0	0	0	0	0	0	0	0	0	0	0	0	5	0	0	0
Sa'udi	4	.0000	.0579	27.6	0	0	0	0	4	0	0	0	0	0	0	0	0	0	0	0	0	0	0	0	0	4	0	0	0
Saar	4	.0000	.0778	28.9	0	0	0	4	0	0	0	0	0	0	0	0	0	4	0	0	0	0	0	0	0	0	0	0	0
sabbath	2	.2437	.1129	30.5	0	0	1	0	0	0	0	1	0	0	0	0	0	0	0	0	0	0	0	0	0	0	1	1	0
Sabbath	14	.0666	.4781	36.8	4	4	0	1	4	1	0	0	5	2	0	0	0	2	0	0	0	0	0	0	1	1	0	0	3
saber	6	.3894	.5190	37.2	0	1	0	1	3	1	0	0	1	0	0	3	0	0	0	0	1	0	0	0	0	0	0	1	0
sabers	2	.0000	.0914	29.6	0	0	0	1	1	0	0	0	2	0	0	0	0	0	0	0	0	0	0	0	0	0	0	0	0
Sabin	7	.0000	.1380	31.4	0	1	0	1	5	0	0	0	0	0	0	0	0	0	0	7	0	0	0	0	0	0	0	0	0
Sabine	3	.2378	.1809	32.6	0	0	0	0	2	0	0	1	0	0	0	0	0	2	0	0	0	0	0	0	0	1	0	0	0
Sabor	4	.0000	.1827	32.6	0	0	0	0	0	4	0	0	4	0	0	0	0	0	0	0	0	0	0	0	0	0	0	0	0
sabotage	5	.3184	.3581	35.5	1	0	0	0	0	2	2	0	0	0	0	0	0	1	0	0	0	0	0	0	0	0	1	3	0
sabre	2	.0000	.0234	23.7	0	0	0	0	2	0	0	0	0	0	0	0	0	0	0	0	0	0	0	0	2	0	0	0	0
sabre-toothed	2	.0000	.0394	26.0	0	2	0	0	0	0	0	0	0	0	0	0	0	0	0	2	0	0	0	0	0	0	0	0	0
sac	32	.4493	3.1125	44.9	0	1	1	15	8	6	1	0	1	0	0	0	0	0	0	17	0	1	0	0	2	0	11	0	0
Sac	3	.0000	.0434	26.4	0	3	0	0	0	0	0	0	0	0	0	0	0	0	0	0	0	0	0	0	0	3	0	0	0

4A Rupert's
7R Rupp
4B Rural
XR Ruritanian
9R rusher
8Q Ruslan
XR Ruspoli
3P Russell's
7N russet
8B russian
7A Russian-American
9B Russian-Japanese
6F Russian-controlled
7R Russias
9C rust-brown
8F rust-caked
9Q rust-colored
8P rust-red
3A rust'y
5R rusted-out
5P Rusticana
7N rustlin'
3R rustly
7A Rusty's
4A rutabaga
6F rutabagas
4Q ruthenium
9B Ruthie
8F ruthlessness
3A rutile
3A Rutile
7E RUV
7Q Ruwenzori's
8Q Ruy
7P Ruysdael
7Q Ry
6D Rychit
9P Ryersons
6R Ryland
4P Rysdyk's
8D Ryuho
8Q Ryukyu
6E R5
7R R9
XR S&M
XR S&M's
3D S-
7R S-cast
9H S-pole
4A s-s-s-s-sound
4R s-s-sir
4A s-s-stand
9Q S-shaped
9E s-square
3A s-surprise
4A s-t-r-e-t-c-h-e-d
4A s-t-r-e-t-c-h-i-n-g
7N S-turn
7R s-90
XB s'en
3A s'matter
8A s'picious
7D s'prise
7A S's
7D sa-a-ay
9L Saaba
5N Saala
5N Saala's
7C Saardam
7A sab'ring
6F Sabah
8N Sabbath-breaking
XP sabbatical
9B sabe
9Q Sabellicus
5A saber-toothed
XH sabertoothed
7Q Sabi
7Q Sable
XP Sablons
9F sabotaged
9F saboteurs
3A sabots
6A Sabour
3A sabra
9Q SABRA
6J Sabre

Word Type	F	D	U	SFI	3 Gr 3	4 Gr 4	5 Gr 5	6 Gr 6	7 Gr 7	8 Gr 8	9 Gr 9	X UnGr	A Read	B Eng & Gr	C Comp	D Lit	E Math	F Soc Stud	G Spell	H Sci	J Music	K Art	L Home Ec	M Shop	N Lib F	P Lib NF	Q Lib Ref	R Mag	S Rel
Sacagawea	7	.0000	.3198	35.0	0	0	7	0	0	0	0	0	7	0	0	0	0	0	0	0	0	0	0	0	0	0	0	0	0
Sacajawea	10	.0000	.4568	36.6	0	5	5	0	0	0	0	0	10	0	0	0	0	0	0	0	0	0	0	0	0	0	0	0	0
Sachs	8	.0910	.2081	33.2	0	0	0	7	0	1	0	0	0	0	0	0	1	0	0	0	7	0	0	0	0	0	0	0	0
sack	99	.7032	14.490	51.6	27	19	9	12	14	8	10	0	45	5	0	11	6	2	0	1	1	1	0	0	18	9	0	0	0
sacked	5	.4642	.4852	36.9	0	0	0	0	2	1	2	0	0	0	0	1	0	0	0	0	1	0	0	0	0	1	2	0	0
sacking	5	.3596	.3917	35.9	0	0	0	0	3	1	1	0	0	0	0	2	1	0	0	0	0	0	0	0	2	0	0	0	0
Sackman	6	.0000	.2741	34.4	6	0	0	0	0	0	0	0	6	0	0	0	0	0	0	0	0	0	0	0	0	0	0	0	0
sacks	35	.7197	5.1483	47.1	5	10	4	6	2	6	2	0	7	0	0	4	5	5	1	0	0	0	0	0	6	5	1	1	0
Sacramento	24	.7015	3.4541	45.4	2	2	6	3	3	3	3	2	4	2	0	0	2	6	0	2	0	0	0	0	0	2	3	3	0
sacred	70	.7314	10.387	50.2	6	1	14	9	13	14	11	2	11	2	0	4	0	9	0	0	11	3	0	0	3	12	9	6	0
Sacred	9	.5377	1.0454	40.2	0	1	0	4	0	3	1	0	3	0	0	1	0	0	0	0	0	0	0	0	2	0	2	1	0
sacrifice	35	.3436	2.7998	44.5	6	0	4	7	7	5	5	1	8	3	1	3	0	2	0	0	1	0	0	1	2	7	2	3	2
sacrificed	9	.5305	1.0411	40.2	0	0	1	0	4	3	1	0	3	2	0	0	0	1	0	0	0	0	0	0	1	2	0	0	0
sacrifices	9	.1233	.3808	35.8	1	0	0	3	1	3	1	0	2	0	0	0	0	2	0	0	0	0	0	0	1	3	0	0	1
sacrificing	2	.1812	.0838	29.2	0	0	0	0	1	0	1	0	0	0	0	0	0	0	0	0	0	0	1	0	0	0	0	1	0
sacrilege	2	.0580	.0676	28.3	0	0	0	0	0	2	0	0	1	0	0	0	0	0	0	0	0	1	0	0	0	0	0	0	0
sacrosanct	2	.2441	.1127	30.5	0	0	0	0	0	1	1	0	0	0	0	0	0	0	0	0	0	0	0	0	1	0	1	0	0
sacs	35	.3016	2.5685	44.1	3	0	15	9	6	2	0	0	2	0	0	0	0	0	0	28	0	0	0	0	0	2	1	2	0
sad	309	.8477	52.751	57.2	99	55	24	38	44	25	24	0	143	15	3	42	1	14	14	3	21	3	2	0	21	17	1	8	1
sad-looking	3	.2197	.2090	33.2	2	0	1	0	0	0	0	0	2	0	0	0	0	0	0	0	0	0	0	0	0	0	1	0	0
saddened	12	.6092	1.5169	41.8	1	0	1	2	2	2	3	1	2	3	0	3	0	0	0	0	0	0	0	0	1	1	1	1	0
sadder	12	.5807	1.5125	41.8	4	4	0	2	1	1	0	0	6	1	1	1	0	1	0	0	0	0	0	0	1	0	0	1	0
saddest	4	.2393	.3005	34.8	1	2	0	0	0	1	0	0	3	0	0	1	0	0	0	0	0	0	0	0	0	0	0	0	0
saddle	184	.7025	26.477	54.2	22	41	13	27	43	20	18	0	46	0	13	33	0	8	1	1	8	0	0	5	38	22	2	7	0
Saddle	2	.2440	.1132	30.5	0	0	0	0	2	0	0	0	0	0	0	1	0	0	0	0	0	0	0	0	0	0	0	1	0
saddlebag	3	.3847	.2490	34.0	0	1	0	0	0	2	0	0	0	1	0	1	0	0	0	0	0	0	0	0	0	1	0	0	0
saddlebags	5	.2240	.2676	34.3	0	1	0	0	3	0	1	0	0	0	0	3	0	0	0	0	0	0	0	0	0	2	0	0	0
saddled	22	.4742	2.2986	43.6	4	4	2	3	6	0	3	0	6	0	0	5	0	1	0	0	0	0	0	0	7	3	0	0	0
saddles	8	.4371	.8099	39.1	3	2	2	1	0	0	0	0	4	0	1	0	0	1	0	0	0	1	0	0	1	0	0	0	0
saddling	4	.3071	.2967	34.7	1	1	0	1	1	0	0	0	1	0	0	1	0	0	0	0	0	0	0	0	2	0	0	0	0
sadly	109	.6704	15.496	51.9	33	27	13	12	16	4	2	2	63	3	0	12	0	3	0	0	1	0	0	0	10	9	1	7	0
sadness	36	.6958	5.1792	47.1	3	5	3	2	16	4	3	0	13	2	1	7	0	2	0	0	2	2	0	0	3	4	0	0	0
sae	2	.2407	.1090	30.4	0	0	0	1	0	1	0	0	0	1	0	0	0	0	0	0	1	0	0	0	0	0	0	0	0
saeters	2	.0000	.0389	25.9	0	2	0	0	0	0	0	0	0	0	0	0	0	2	0	0	0	0	0	0	0	0	0	0	0
Safad	2	.0000	.0389	25.9	0	0	0	0	2	0	0	0	0	0	0	0	0	2	0	0	0	0	0	0	0	0	0	0	0
safari	3	.3374	.2433	33.9	0	0	0	1	2	0	0	0	1	1	0	0	0	0	0	0	0	0	0	0	0	0	1	0	0
safaris	3	.1409	.1472	31.7	0	0	0	1	2	0	0	0	1	0	0	0	0	0	0	0	0	0	0	0	0	2	0	0	0
safe	474	.8874	83.933	59.2	108	96	61	65	65	36	37	6	146	9	2	31	1	49	13	67	2	0	10	5	44	51	15	29	0
safe-kept	2	.0000	.0914	29.6	0	0	1	1	0	0	0	0	2	0	0	0	0	0	0	0	0	0	0	0	0	0	0	0	0
safeguard	12	.4716	1.2375	40.9	0	0	3	0	0	3	5	1	1	0	0	0	0	6	0	2	0	0	0	0	0	1	2	0	0
safeguarded	4	.4632	.3973	36.0	0	0	0	0	2	2	0	0	0	0	0	0	0	1	1	1	0	0	0	0	0	1	0	0	0
safeguarding	2	.1170	.0651	28.1	0	0	0	0	0	2	0	0	0	0	1	0	0	1	0	0	0	0	0	0	0	0	0	0	0
safeguards	7	.2989	.5441	37.4	0	0	0	2	3	1	1	0	2	0	0	0	0	1	0	4	0	0	0	0	0	0	0	0	0
safekeeping	3	.2212	.2099	33.2	0	1	1	1	0	0	0	0	2	0	0	1	0	0	0	0	0	0	0	0	0	0	0	0	0
safely	202	.8860	35.679	55.5	44	38	14	26	37	24	13	6	53	6	1	11	0	20	7	29	3	0	4	6	8	22	7	25	0
Safely	2	.2446	.1257	31.0	0	0	0	0	0	2	0	0	0	0	0	0	0	1	0	1	0	0	0	0	0	0	0	0	0
safer	50	.8076	8.1680	49.1	6	13	7	9	8	3	4	0	16	0	1	1	1	4	0	6	0	0	1	0	5	7	3	5	0
safest	10	.6588	1.3511	41.3	0	0	1	1	4	1	3	0	1	0	0	1	0	2	0	1	1	0	1	0	0	2	1	0	0
safety	245	.8498	41.710	56.2	28	38	18	17	60	56	23	5	56	8	3	10	0	35	4	51	0	0	4	9	4	18	21	22	0
Safety	12	.5684	1.4260	41.5	0	1	1	0	7	3	0	0	1	4	0	0	1	1	0	3	0	0	1	0	0	0	0	1	0
saffron	3	.2159	.1532	31.9	0	0	0	1	1	0	0	1	0	0	0	0	0	0	0	0	0	0	0	0	0	0	2	1	0
sag	7	.4553	.7110	38.5	0	1	2	0	2	0	0	2	2	0	0	1	0	0	0	0	0	0	0	0	0	2	0	2	0
saga	2	.2285	.1129	30.5	0	0	0	0	0	1	1	0	0	0	0	0	0	1	0	0	0	0	0	0	0	0	1	0	0
sagacity	6	.4141	.5315	37.3	0	0	0	0	1	2	3	0	0	0	0	3	0	1	0	0	0	0	0	0	1	0	1	0	0
sagas	3	.2444	.1814	32.6	2	0	0	0	1	0	0	0	0	0	0	0	0	2	0	0	0	0	0	0	0	0	1	0	0
sage	16	.5652	1.9463	42.9	2	0	0	1	7	2	3	1	6	0	0	3	0	0	0	2	0	0	2	0	0	1	1	1	0
sagebrush	12	.5353	1.4012	41.5	2	5	1	1	2	0	0	1	4	0	0	0	0	2	0	0	0	0	0	0	1	2	0	3	0
sagged	10	.5023	1.0931	40.4	0	3	1	0	5	0	1	0	3	0	1	2	0	0	0	0	0	0	0	0	2	2	0	0	0
sagging	11	.5025	1.2015	40.8	0	4	0	2	2	2	1	0	3	0	0	0	0	0	0	0	1	0	0	0	2	1	0	4	0
Sagittarius	2	.2160	.1362	31.3	0	0	0	0	0	1	0	1	1	0	0	0	0	0	0	1	0	0	0	0	0	0	0	0	0
sagu	2	.0000	.0219	23.4	0	0	0	2	0	0	0	0	0	2	0	0	0	0	0	0	0	0	0	0	0	0	0	0	0
saguaro	2	.0000	.0394	26.0	2	0	0	0	0	0	0	0	0	0	0	0	0	0	0	2	0	0	0	0	0	0	0	0	0
Sahara	76	.4228	7.1471	48.5	3	12	7	20	21	1	12	0	2	0	1	0	0	59	0	5	0	0	0	0	1	1	5	2	0
Saharan	2	.0000	.0389	25.9	0	0	0	1	1	0	0	0	0	0	0	0	0	2	0	0	0	0	0	0	0	0	0	0	0
sahibs	2	.1948	.1250	31.0	0	0	1	1	0	0	0	0	1	0	0	0	0	0	0	0	0	0	0	0	0	1	0	0	0
Sai	12	.2445	.9201	39.6	0	9	0	0	0	0	3	0	9	0	0	0	0	0	0	0	0	0	0	0	0	3	0	0	0
said	15309	.7898	2468.9	73.9	4451	3387	1674	1757	2182	1084	641	133	7511	384	82	1272	245	637	71	112	113	7	14	9	2661	1437	66	672	16
Saigon	9	.1501	.3708	35.7	0	0	1	2	0	2	4	0	0	0	0	0	0	2	0	0	0	0	0	0	0	0	0	7	0
sail	312	.8373	52.548	57.2	69	62	41	61	38	24	14	3	94	14	2	11	2	70	7	8	10	0	0	0	24	39	14	17	0
Sail	2	.1733	.1149	30.6	1	0	0	0	0	1	0	0	1	1	0	0	0	0	0	0	0	0	0	0	0	0	0	0	0
sail-away	2	.0000	.0914	29.6	0	2	0	0	0	0	0	0	2	0	0	0	0	0	0	0	0	0	0	0	0	0	0	0	0
sailboat	30	.6627	4.1484	46.2	8	3	3	6	4	3	2	1	11	1	3	0	5	0	1	1	0	1	0	0	1	4	1	1	0
sailboats	15	.6088	1.9226	42.8	4	1	2	3	1	1	3	0	4	0	1	0	1	2	0	1	0	0	0	0	0	1	4	1	0
sailed	282	.7678	44.288	56.5	50	47	54	36	65	23	5	2	103	9	2	6	1	89	2	4	15	0	0	0	10	23	11	7	0
sailing	203	.8472	34.506	55.4	41	35	37	31	29	13	15	2	57	7	7	9	1	42	3	11	9	1	0	0	6	22	15	13	0
sailing-ship	2	.2417	.1091	30.4	0	0	1	0	1	0	0	0	0	0	0	0	0	0	0	0	1	0	0	0	0	0	1	0	0
sailing-ships	2	.0000	.0234	23.7	0	2	0	0	0	0	0	0	0	0	0	0	0	0	0	0	0	0	0	0	2	0	0	0	0
sailor	96	.8065	15.737	52.0	12	15	16	18	22	8	2	3	44	5	2	8	0	14	3	1	2	0	0	0	7	6	1	3	0
Sailor	4	.3559	.3535	35.5	0	4	0	0	0	0	0	0	2	0	0	0	1	0	0	0	1	0	0	0	0	0	0	0	0
sailor's	4	.2389	.2497	34.0	0	1	1	1	1	0	0	0	1	0	0	0	0	1	0	0	2	0	0	0	0	0	0	0	0
sailors	200	.8788	35.100	55.5	44	33	36	31	24	20	8	4	57	10	2	14	2	41	4	14	15	0	0	1	10	14	9	7	0
sailors'	2	.0000	.0914	29.6	0	1	0	1	0	0	0	0	2	0	0	0	0	0	0	0	0	0	0	0	0	0	0	0	0
sailplane	3	.0000	.1370	31.4	0	0	3	0	0	0	0	0	3	0	0	0	0	0	0	0	0	0	0	0	0	0	0	0	0
sailplanes	2	.1814	.1187	30.7	0	0	1	0	1	0	0	0	1	0	0	0	0	0	0	0	0	0	0	0	0	0	0	1	0
sails	110	.8559	18.857	52.8	27	16	17	19	10	12	8	1	32	5	2	5	0	17	4	1	6	2	0	0	13	14	7	2	0
sainak	2	.0000	.0914	29.6	0	0	2	0	0	0	0	0	2	0	0	0	0	0	0	0	0	0	0	0	0	0	0	0	0
saint	17	.6018	2.1186	43.3	0	3	1	1	3	3	6	0	2	0	0	5	0	2	0	0	1	0	0	0	1	0	3	3	0
Saint	52	.6703	7.2612	48.6	2	6	10	16	7	3	8	0	19	3	0	11	0	1	0	0	1	0	0	0	3	4	8	2	0
SaintLouis	2	.0000	.0914	29.6	2	0	0	0	0	0	0	0	2	0	0	0	0	0	0	0	0	0	0	0	0	0	0	0	0
Saint-Moritz	3	.0000	.1370	31.4	0	0	0	3	0	0	0	0	3	0	0	0	0	0	0	0	0	0	0	0	0	0	0	0	0
Saint-Saens	9	.0000	.0728	28.6	7	1	0	0	1	0	0	0	0	0	0	0	0	0	0	0	9	0	0	0	0	0	0	0	0
Saint's	2	.0000	.0914	29.6	0	0	0	2	0	0	0	0	2	0	0	0	0	0	0	0	0	0	0	0	0	0	0	0	0
saintly	3	.3851	.2497	34.0	1	0	0	0	1	0	1	0	0	0	0	1	0	0	0	0	0	0	0	0	1	1	0	0	0

7Q SAC
7N sachem
7D sachet
7H sackful
9D Saco
4S sacrament
7N Sacrament
7Q sacraments
5Q sacredly
9Q sacrificial
7N sacrilegious
7D Sad
7N sadden
7N saddens
4N saddle-blanket
6A saddle-bow
6A saddle-bronc
9M saddle-clamp
5A saddlemaker
4R saddler
8B Sadducism
9Q Sadi
9B Sadie
5N sadiron
8F sadists
8D Sadler
8J Saens
7R Saf-Guard
8A Safari
9Q Safawid
3A SAFE
8D safe-cracker
3A safe-folded
8R Safeguard
8D safes
8F safety-glass
7H safety-minded
6A safety's
9D Safeway
7B Saffron
8R Safka
7A sagacious
6A Sagamon
3A sagely
6Q Saginaw
6Q sago
7F Sagres
7B sags
XR Saguaro
6J Sagwa
7D Sahib
XR Saidenberg
9R Saigon's
3P Sail-Back
4A sail-aways
4J sail'd
3A sailbag
7L sailcloth
5A Sailed
6R Sailing
6A sailmaker
5R sailmaster
8J Sailor's
5A sailplaning
5J SaintNicholas
6R Saint-Jean
8Q Saint-Leon
7F saint's
7J Sainte
4R Sainte-Marie
8R sainthood

Word Type	F	D	U	SFI	3 Gr 3	4 Gr 4	5 Gr 5	6 Gr 6	7 Gr 7	8 Gr 8	9 Gr 9	X UnGr	A Read	B Eng & Gr	C Comp	D Lit	E Math	F Soc Stud	G Spell	H Sci	J Music	K Art	L Home Ec	M Shop	N Lib F	P Lib NF	Q Lib Ref	R Mag	S Rel
saints	12	.5317	1.3718	41.4	0	1	1	2	6	1	1	0	3	0	0	3	0	3	0	0	1	1	0	0	0	1	0	0	0
Saints	8	.4085	.6957	38.4	0	0	0	3	2	2	1	0	0	0	0	0	0	1	0	0	3	0	0	0	0	0	1	3	0
saith	4	.2130	.2109	33.2	1	1	0	0	2	0	0	0	0	0	0	0	0	0	0	0	0	0	0	0	1	3	0	0	0
sake	69	.7252	10.264	50.1	1	8	5	19	11	8	14	3	22	3	0	14	0	1	0	2	4	0	0	0	7	8	3	5	0
sakes	19	.4206	1.8557	42.7	1	4	1	1	5	1	6	0	8	0	0	5	0	0	0	0	0	0	0	0	5	1	0	0	0
Sakura	2	.0000	.0162	22.1	0	2	0	0	0	0	0	0	0	0	0	0	0	0	0	0	2	0	0	0	0	0	0	0	0
Sal	8	.3670	.6511	38.1	1	4	0	2	1	0	0	0	1	3	0	0	0	0	0	0	3	0	0	0	0	1	0	0	0
salable	2	.2441	.1127	30.5	0	0	0	0	2	0	0	0	0	0	0	0	0	0	0	0	0	0	0	0	1	0	1	0	0
salad	84	.1666	3.4748	45.4	3	6	4	3	49	5	13	1	9	2	0	1	3	1	1	5	0	0	56	0	2	1	0	3	0
Saladin	8	.0000	.0837	29.2	0	8	0	0	0	0	0	0	0	0	0	0	0	0	0	0	0	0	0	0	0	0	8	0	0
salads	38	.0603	.5977	37.8	0	0	0	2	19	5	10	2	0	0	0	0	0	0	0	0	0	0	34	0	0	1	2	1	0
salamander	3	.3346	.2478	33.9	0	0	0	2	1	0	0	0	1	0	0	0	0	0	0	1	0	0	0	0	0	0	1	0	0
salamanders	14	.4528	1.3685	41.4	4	2	0	5	3	0	0	0	0	0	0	0	0	0	0	7	0	0	0	0	1	3	3	0	0
salaries	10	.5381	1.1292	40.5	0	0	2	1	1	2	4	0	0	0	0	0	2	4	0	0	0	0	0	0	0	1	2	1	0
salary	37	.6512	4.9813	47.0	4	1	8	5	7	5	6	1	6	0	0	0	11	5	2	1	0	0	2	0	0	3	0	7	0
saldu	24	.0000	.4668	36.7	0	0	0	0	0	24	0	0	0	0	0	0	0	24	0	0	0	0	0	0	0	0	0	0	0
sale	147	.8244	24.361	53.9	32	19	18	23	21	14	17	3	32	6	1	2	39	30	6	3	4	0	4	0	5	4	3	8	0
Sale	14	.2973	.9553	39.8	5	0	8	0	1	0	0	0	0	0	0	1	10	0	0	0	0	0	0	0	3	0	0	0	0
salem	2	.0000	.0219	23.4	0	0	0	0	0	2	0	0	0	2	0	0	0	0	0	0	0	0	0	0	0	0	0	0	0
Salem	29	.4877	3.0358	44.8	0	2	4	3	1	7	10	2	2	0	0	1	0	8	0	0	2	0	0	0	0	14	0	2	0
Salerio	12	.0000	.1288	31.1	0	0	0	0	0	0	12	0	0	0	0	12	0	0	0	0	0	0	0	0	0	0	0	0	0
sales	100	.6439	13.339	51.3	11	14	10	5	24	7	24	5	18	2	0	0	30	11	0	0	2	0	4	0	0	1	7	25	0
Sales	2	.2427	.1159	30.6	0	0	1	0	0	0	1	0	0	0	0	0	1	0	0	0	0	0	0	0	0	0	0	1	0
salesgirl	9	.2307	.6917	38.4	8	0	0	0	0	0	1	0	8	0	0	0	0	0	0	0	0	0	1	0	0	0	0	0	0
salesman	46	.7193	6.8009	48.3	23	9	0	3	4	3	4	0	15	2	2	0	7	2	0	1	2	0	0	0	9	0	4	2	0
salesmen	4	.3401	.3205	35.1	2	1	0	0	0	1	0	0	1	0	0	0	0	1	0	0	0	0	1	0	0	0	0	1	0
Salih	3	.0000	.0434	26.4	0	0	0	0	0	0	0	3	0	0	0	0	0	0	0	0	0	0	0	0	0	3	0	0	0
Salinas	2	.2443	.1130	30.5	0	0	0	0	0	2	0	0	0	0	0	1	0	0	0	0	0	0	0	0	1	0	0	0	0
saline	2	.2278	.1128	30.5	0	0	0	0	1	0	0	1	0	0	0	0	0	0	0	1	0	0	0	0	0	0	1	0	0
salinity	11	.3248	.8310	39.2	0	0	6	0	2	1	2	0	0	0	0	0	0	0	0	8	0	0	0	0	0	0	2	1	0
Salisbury	4	.3813	.3309	35.2	0	2	0	0	2	0	0	0	0	1	0	0	0	0	0	0	0	0	0	0	0	2	1	0	0
saliva	21	.3886	1.8920	42.8	3	0	4	3	6	0	2	3	4	0	0	1	0	0	0	12	0	0	0	0	0	0	4	0	0
salivary	3	.2445	.1818	32.6	0	0	1	0	0	1	1	0	0	0	0	0	0	0	0	2	0	0	0	0	0	0	1	0	0
salivating	2	.2346	.1166	30.7	0	0	1	0	0	0	1	0	0	0	0	0	0	0	0	1	0	0	0	0	0	0	0	1	0
Salk	19	.3502	1.5436	41.9	0	10	0	2	5	2	0	0	0	0	0	0	2	8	0	9	0	0	0	0	0	0	0	0	0
Salle	3	.3756	.2468	33.9	1	0	0	0	0	1	1	0	0	0	0	1	0	1	0	0	0	0	0	0	0	0	1	0	0
sallied	2	.0580	.0676	28.3	0	0	0	0	0	2	0	0	1	0	0	0	0	0	0	0	0	1	0	0	0	0	0	0	0
sallow	2	.2446	.1125	30.5	0	0	0	0	0	0	2	0	0	1	0	1	0	0	0	0	0	0	0	0	0	0	0	0	0
sally	3	.3874	.2497	34.0	1	0	1	1	0	0	0	0	0	1	0	0	0	0	0	0	0	0	0	0	1	0	0	1	0
Sally	338	.5939	42.050	56.2	208	67	26	14	11	9	2	1	69	15	1	0	31	3	1	0	1	3	9	0	161	41	0	3	0
Sally's	26	.4890	2.9123	44.6	10	6	2	4	2	0	2	0	14	1	0	0	7	1	0	0	0	0	0	0	3	0	0	0	0
Salmagundi	2	.0000	.0045	16.5	0	0	0	0	0	0	2	0	0	0	2	0	0	0	0	0	0	0	0	0	0	0	0	0	0
salmon	205	.6875	29.043	54.6	24	58	40	22	53	4	2	2	32	1	1	1	0	33	3	75	0	0	1	0	7	1	16	34	0
Salmon	5	.3023	.3461	35.4	1	0	2	1	0	1	0	0	0	0	0	0	0	1	0	0	0	0	0	0	0	1	0	3	0
salmon-pink	2	.2160	.1362	31.3	0	0	0	0	1	0	1	0	1	0	0	0	0	0	0	1	0	0	0	0	0	0	0	0	0
salol	3	.0000	.0591	27.7	0	0	0	0	0	3	0	0	0	0	0	0	0	0	0	3	0	0	0	0	0	0	0	0	0
salon	4	.3784	.3243	35.1	0	0	2	0	0	0	2	0	0	0	0	1	0	0	0	0	1	0	0	0	0	0	0	2	0
Salon	2	.2417	.1091	30.4	0	0	1	1	0	0	0	0	0	0	0	0	0	0	0	0	1	0	0	0	0	0	1	0	0
Salonika	2	.0000	.0389	25.9	0	0	0	0	2	0	0	0	0	0	0	0	0	2	0	0	0	0	0	0	0	0	0	0	0
saloon	13	.4507	1.3268	41.2	0	0	0	6	6	1	0	0	5	0	0	4	0	0	0	0	0	0	0	0	2	0	0	2	0
saloons	4	.2440	.2264	33.5	0	0	0	1	0	2	0	1	0	0	0	2	0	0	0	0	0	0	0	0	0	0	0	2	0
SALPAC	2	.0000	.0209	23.2	0	0	0	0	2	0	0	0	0	0	0	0	0	0	0	0	0	0	0	0	0	0	2	0	0
salt	497	.7419	75.279	58.8	103	75	81	57	73	31	68	9	113	5	5	9	2	26	3	183	7	3	45	0	15	40	20	21	0
Salt	33	.5533	3.8436	45.8	0	3	7	2	8	3	0	10	4	0	0	0	0	5	0	1	1	0	0	0	9	1	1	11	0
SaltLakeCity	14	.4861	1.4729	41.7	2	3	5	0	4	0	0	0	1	0	0	0	3	7	0	0	1	0	0	0	0	2	0	0	0
salt-and-peppers	2	.0000	.0064	18.1	0	0	0	0	2	0	0	0	0	0	0	0	0	0	0	0	0	0	2	0	0	0	0	0	0
salt-camp	2	.0000	.0290	24.6	0	0	2	0	0	0	0	0	0	0	0	0	0	0	0	0	0	0	0	0	0	2	0	0	0
salt-makers	2	.0000	.0914	29.6	0	0	2	0	0	0	0	0	2	0	0	0	0	0	0	0	0	0	0	0	0	0	0	0	0
salt-marsh	2	.2401	.1133	30.5	1	0	1	0	0	0	0	0	0	0	0	0	0	0	0	0	0	0	0	0	0	1	1	0	0
salt-water	9	.6146	1.1656	40.7	2	2	0	1	0	3	0	1	3	0	0	0	1	0	0	0	0	0	1	0	1	1	1	1	0
salted	21	.5970	2.6617	44.3	1	3	5	4	5	1	2	0	7	0	1	1	0	5	0	0	0	0	3	0	0	2	1	1	0
saltin'	2	.0000	.0914	29.6	0	0	0	0	2	0	0	0	2	0	0	0	0	0	0	0	0	0	0	0	0	0	0	0	0
saltiness	3	.0000	.0591	27.7	0	0	3	0	0	0	0	0	0	0	0	0	0	0	0	3	0	0	0	0	0	0	0	0	0
salting	3	.2435	.2274	33.6	1	0	0	0	0	2	0	0	2	0	0	0	0	1	0	0	0	0	0	0	0	0	0	0	0
saltings	2	.0000	.0914	29.6	0	0	0	0	0	2	0	0	2	0	0	0	0	0	0	0	0	0	0	0	0	0	0	0	0
Salton	2	.2152	.1357	31.3	1	0	0	0	1	0	0	0	1	0	0	0	0	1	0	0	0	0	0	0	0	0	0	0	0
saltpeter	4	.0000	.0419	26.2	0	1	0	3	0	0	0	0	0	0	0	0	0	0	0	0	0	0	0	0	0	0	4	0	0
salts	14	.3396	1.0945	40.4	0	1	3	0	7	1	2	0	0	0	0	0	0	0	0	10	0	0	0	0	0	0	2	2	0
salty	54	.7550	8.2687	49.2	14	12	5	8	6	7	2	0	6	5	0	1	0	7	2	21	0	1	0	0	3	5	2	1	0
Salty	38	.0000	1.7359	42.4	0	38	0	0	0	0	0	0	38	0	0	0	0	0	0	0	0	0	0	0	0	0	0	0	0
salubrious	2	.2437	.1129	30.5	0	0	0	0	1	0	0	1	0	0	0	0	0	0	0	0	0	0	0	0	0	0	1	1	0
salutation	15	.3034	1.0146	40.1	1	1	0	1	9	1	2	0	1	10	3	1	0	0	0	0	0	0	0	0	0	0	0	0	0
salutations	8	.0000	.0178	22.5	1	5	0	2	0	0	0	0	0	0	8	0	0	0	0	0	0	0	0	0	0	0	0	0	0
salute	27	.7126	3.9772	46.0	4	2	4	7	4	4	1	1	11	0	0	1	0	1	4	0	2	0	0	0	2	3	1	2	0
Salute	4	.0000	.0323	25.1	0	0	0	0	4	0	0	0	0	0	0	0	0	0	0	0	4	0	0	0	0	0	0	0	0
saluted	8	.3545	.7108	38.5	1	3	1	1	0	1	0	1	4	0	0	0	0	0	0	0	0	0	0	0	1	3	0	0	0
salutes	4	.3606	.3539	35.5	0	0	0	3	0	1	0	0	2	0	0	1	0	0	1	0	0	0	0	0	0	0	0	0	0
saluting	2	.2388	.1089	30.4	1	0	0	1	0	0	0	0	0	0	0	0	0	0	1	0	0	0	0	0	1	0	0	0	0
Salvador	13	.3604	1.0607	40.3	0	0	9	2	1	1	0	0	0	0	0	0	0	10	0	0	0	0	1	0	0	0	2	0	0
salvage	40	.5978	5.2768	47.2	3	25	1	4	6	1	0	0	29	0	0	0	0	0	1	0	0	1	1	0	1	1	0	6	0
salvaged	5	.3124	.3537	35.5	0	0	0	2	2	0	0	1	0	0	0	0	0	0	0	1	0	0	0	0	1	0	0	3	0
salvaging	3	.2266	.1614	32.1	0	0	0	0	3	0	0	0	0	0	0	0	0	0	0	0	0	0	0	0	1	0	0	2	0
salvation	13	.2389	.7241	38.6	2	0	1	3	2	3	1	1	0	0	0	0	0	1	0	0	1	0	0	0	2	2	2	4	1
Salvation	2	.0000	.0243	23.9	0	0	0	0	0	0	2	0	0	0	0	0	0	0	0	0	0	0	0	0	0	0	0	2	0
salvo	2	.0000	.0290	24.6	0	0	2	0	0	0	0	0	0	0	0	0	0	0	0	0	0	0	0	0	0	2	0	0	0
Salzburg	3	.0995	.1144	30.6	0	0	1	0	0	1	1	0	1	0	0	0	0	0	0	0	2	0	0	0	0	0	0	0	0
Sam	604	.6144	77.506	58.9	320	150	30	27	36	15	4	22	129	24	2	8	30	12	1	1	0	7	0	0	244	114	1	31	0
Sam's	58	.5951	7.2963	48.6	33	11	1	2	6	1	1	3	17	3	0	0	1	2	1	0	0	2	0	0	23	6	0	3	0
Samantha	4	.2424	.3036	34.8	0	0	0	3	0	0	0	1	3	0	0	0	0	0	0	0	0	0	0	0	0	0	0	1	0
Samar	2	.0000	.0209	23.2	2	0	0	0	0	0	0	0	0	0	0	0	0	0	0	0	0	0	0	0	0	0	2	0	0
Samarai	4	.0000	.1827	32.6	0	0	0	4	0	0	0	0	4	0	0	0	0	0	0	0	0	0	0	0	0	0	0	0	0
Samaria	6	.2062	.3286	35.2	0	0	0	2	3	1	0	0	0	0	0	0	0	5	0	0	0	0	0	0	0	0	1	0	0
Samaritan	2	.0000	.0215	23.3	0	0	0	0	1	0	1	0	0	0	0	2	0	0	0	0	0	0	0	0	0	0	0	0	0
Samarkand	9	.0449	.2030	33.1	0	1	0	0	0	7	1	0	1	0	0	0	0	0	0	0	0	0	0	0	0	0	8	0	0

6A saints-and-dragons
7Q saints'
6N Saints'
6J sairly
5R Sajid
7D Sakes
6F Sakhalin
XH saki
8A Saki
5H sal
8L Salad
7L salad-maker
XR Salada
4Q SALADIN
7P Salaga
4Q Salah-al-Din
4Q SALAMANDER
7L salami
8N Salamis
9N salao
5R salaried
5A salarium
8F saldu's
6R sales-order
9B salesclerk
7R salesmanship
8L salesperson
3P salesrooms
8Q Salic
8F salient
XP Salih's
7R salinities
7D Salish
7D Salishan
7N Sallie
3D Sallyann
4F salmon-canning
7R salmon's
5R Salmon's
7R salmons'
4F Salonica
3A salons
9D Saloon
5P salt-boilers
3A salt-clay
5P salt-kettles
6F salt-mining
4A salt-pan
4A salt-pans
5N salt-rising
9H saltation
XR saltbox
7A saltbush
9L saltines
5Q saltmaking
3F saltwater
3A salvagin'
4P salve
5P Salvemini
3N salvia
9P Saly
7Q Salzburgers
9Q Salzgries
9D sam
7H samara
7H samaras

Word Type	F	D	U	SFI	3 Gr 3	4 Gr 4	5 Gr 5	6 Gr 6	7 Gr 7	8 Gr 8	9 Gr 9	X UnGr	A Read	B Eng & Gr	C Comp	D Lit	E Math	F Soc Stud	G Spell	H Sci	J Music	K Art	L Home Ec	M Shop	N Lib F	P Lib NF	Q Lib Ref	R Mag	S Rel
samba	2	.0000	.0162	22.1	0	0	0	2	0	0	0	0	0	0	0	0	0	0	0	0	2	0	0	0	0	0	0	0	0
Samboy	3	.0000	.0322	25.1	0	0	0	0	0	0	3	0	0	0	0	3	0	0	0	0	0	0	0	0	0	0	0	0	0
same	5022	.9383	931.59	69.7	914	703	574	659	886	690	496	100	744	303	35	153	1066	318	422	728	298	37	97	85	118	235	196	186	1
Same	2	.2407	.1138	30.6	0	0	0	0	1	0	1	0	0	0	0	1	0	0	0	0	0	0	0	0	0	1	0	0	0
sameness	4	.4629	.4147	36.2	0	0	2	1	0	1	0	0	1	0	0	0	1	1	0	0	0	0	0	0	0	1	0	0	0
samisen	2	.1494	.1045	30.2	0	1	0	0	1	0	0	0	1	0	0	0	0	0	0	0	1	0	0	0	0	0	0	0	0
Sammie	3	.0000	.0434	26.4	0	3	0	0	0	0	0	0	0	0	0	0	0	0	0	0	0	0	0	0	0	3	0	0	0
Sammy	42	.5680	5.2072	47.2	22	8	3	3	0	1	5	0	21	0	2	5	1	1	0	0	0	0	0	0	0	2	0	10	0
Sammy's	6	.3060	.4405	36.4	1	2	0	3	0	0	0	0	1	0	0	0	3	0	0	0	0	0	0	0	0	0	0	2	0
Samoa	2	.0000	.0243	23.9	2	0	0	0	0	0	0	0	0	0	0	0	0	0	0	0	0	0	0	0	0	0	0	2	0
Samos	2	.2446	.1257	31.0	0	0	0	0	0	1	1	0	0	0	0	0	0	1	0	1	0	0	0	0	0	0	0	0	0
Samoset	2	.0000	.0914	29.6	2	0	0	0	0	0	0	0	2	0	0	0	0	0	0	0	0	0	0	0	0	0	0	0	0
sample	128	.6683	17.461	52.4	6	13	18	13	21	24	32	1	7	12	13	1	14	7	17	43	0	0	4	0	1	3	1	5	0
sampled	4	.4568	.4091	36.1	0	1	1	0	1	0	1	0	1	0	0	0	0	0	0	1	0	0	0	0	0	1	0	1	0
sampler	12	.2792	.8204	39.1	2	7	0	2	1	0	0	0	2	0	0	0	0	0	0	0	0	0	1	0	0	9	0	0	0
samplers	3	.0945	.0794	29.0	0	0	0	1	1	0	1	0	0	0	0	0	0	0	0	1	0	0	2	0	0	0	0	0	0
samples	97	.7328	14.406	51.6	3	9	10	17	18	10	22	8	5	1	4	2	2	6	11	48	0	1	0	1	0	1	6	9	0
sampling	32	.4514	3.1800	45.0	0	0	0	11	13	6	2	0	2	0	0	0	5	0	0	20	0	0	0	0	0	1	1	3	0
samplings	2	.2346	.1166	30.7	0	0	0	0	0	1	1	0	0	0	0	0	0	0	0	1	0	0	0	0	0	0	0	1	0
Sampson	16	.0000	.1717	32.3	0	0	0	0	0	0	16	0	0	0	0	16	0	0	0	0	0	0	0	0	0	0	0	0	0
Samson	15	.5441	1.7869	42.5	1	7	0	0	0	3	1	3	7	3	0	0	0	0	0	0	2	0	0	0	1	0	2	0	0
Samsun	3	.0000	.0583	27.7	0	0	0	0	3	0	0	0	0	0	0	0	0	3	0	0	0	0	0	0	0	0	0	0	0
Samuel	63	.7005	9.0007	49.5	1	19	16	3	3	13	7	1	8	4	0	1	1	10	1	0	7	0	0	0	2	18	10	1	0
san	5	.4443	.4745	36.8	0	1	2	0	1	0	0	1	0	2	0	0	0	0	0	1	0	0	0	0	0	1	0	1	0
San	67	.6443	8.9491	49.5	1	10	14	20	15	5	2	0	10	0	0	6	0	25	0	1	4	0	0	0	0	3	7	11	0
SanAntonio	8	.3428	.6878	38.4	0	4	1	0	2	1	0	0	3	0	0	0	0	4	0	0	0	0	0	0	1	0	0	0	0
SanDiego	21	.5860	2.5821	44.1	1	7	2	1	6	3	1	0	2	0	1	0	0	8	0	3	0	0	0	0	1	1	0	5	0
SanFernando	3	.0000	.0583	27.7	0	3	0	0	0	0	0	0	0	0	0	0	0	3	0	0	0	0	0	0	0	0	0	0	0
SanFranciscans	4	.3422	.3073	34.9	0	1	0	1	1	0	0	1	0	0	0	0	0	1	0	0	0	0	0	0	0	1	0	2	0
SanFrancisco	147	.7357	22.010	53.4	15	15	25	22	23	33	11	3	20	3	6	2	16	51	0	9	3	0	0	0	3	5	6	23	0
SanFrancisco-Oakland	2	.0000	.0389	25.9	0	0	0	2	0	0	0	0	0	0	0	0	0	2	0	0	0	0	0	0	0	0	0	0	0
SanFrancisco's	11	.4605	1.0995	40.4	0	0	1	0	2	6	2	0	0	0	0	0	0	7	0	1	0	0	0	0	0	1	1	1	0
SanGabriel	3	.2435	.2274	33.6	0	1	0	0	2	0	0	0	2	0	0	0	0	1	0	0	0	0	0	0	0	0	0	0	0
SanJacinto	2	.2408	.1204	30.8	0	1	1	0	0	0	0	0	0	0	0	0	0	1	0	0	0	0	0	0	0	1	0	0	0
SanJose	6	.2352	.3498	35.4	0	2	0	1	0	1	1	1	0	0	0	0	0	3	0	0	0	0	0	0	0	0	0	3	0
SanJuan	5	.0000	.2284	33.6	2	3	0	0	0	0	0	0	5	0	0	0	0	0	0	0	0	0	0	0	0	0	0	0	0
SanLuisObispo	3	.0000	.0583	27.7	0	3	0	0	0	0	0	0	0	0	0	0	0	3	0	0	0	0	0	0	0	0	0	0	0
SanMartin's	2	.0000	.0209	23.2	2	0	0	0	0	0	0	0	0	0	0	0	0	0	0	0	0	0	0	0	0	0	2	0	0
SanPedro	8	.2708	.5520	37.4	0	0	2	0	5	1	0	0	2	0	0	4	0	2	0	0	0	0	0	0	0	0	0	0	0
Sanborn	3	.2223	.2106	33.2	2	0	0	0	0	0	1	0	2	1	0	0	0	0	0	0	0	0	0	0	0	0	0	0	0
Sancho	8	.0000	.3655	35.6	0	5	0	0	3	0	0	0	8	0	0	0	0	0	0	0	0	0	0	0	0	0	0	0	0
sanction	3	.3465	.2515	34.0	0	1	0	0	2	0	0	0	1	0	0	0	0	0	0	0	0	0	0	0	0	1	0	1	0
Sanction	2	.0000	.0389	25.9	0	0	0	0	0	0	2	0	0	0	0	0	0	2	0	0	0	0	0	0	0	0	0	0	0
sanctioned	5	.4689	.4984	37.0	0	0	0	1	2	2	0	0	0	0	0	0	0	1	0	0	0	0	0	0	0	2	1	1	0
sanctity	3	.3870	.2486	34.0	0	0	0	0	0	1	1	1	0	0	0	1	0	0	0	0	0	0	0	0	0	0	1	1	0
sanctuaries	11	.3063	.8420	39.3	0	4	4	0	1	0	2	0	4	0	0	0	0	0	0	0	0	0	0	0	0	0	5	2	0
sanctuary	14	.5362	1.5886	42.0	0	2	0	1	1	5	5	0	2	2	0	0	0	1	0	0	0	0	0	0	0	4	4	1	0
Sanctuary	5	.0000	.0523	27.2	0	0	3	0	2	0	0	0	0	0	0	0	0	0	0	0	0	0	0	0	0	0	5	0	0
sand	672	.8095	109.77	60.4	135	118	93	89	89	50	78	20	176	13	13	26	9	61	5	158	3	8	1	46	29	80	21	23	0
Sand	9	.5054	.9704	39.9	1	0	4	0	1	0	0	3	1	0	0	0	0	3	0	0	2	0	0	0	0	0	1	2	0
sand-bank	2	.0000	.0234	23.7	0	0	0	0	2	0	0	0	0	0	0	0	0	0	0	0	0	0	0	0	2	0	0	0	0
sand-lot	2	.0000	.0914	29.6	0	0	2	0	0	0	0	0	2	0	0	0	0	0	0	0	0	0	0	0	0	0	0	0	0
sandal	5	.4721	.5342	37.3	1	1	0	2	1	0	0	0	2	0	0	1	0	1	0	0	0	0	0	0	1	0	0	0	0
sandals	22	.6487	2.9914	44.8	1	3	1	13	4	0	0	0	8	4	1	3	0	4	0	0	1	1	0	0	0	0	0	0	0
sandalwood	7	.2310	.5032	37.0	0	1	2	4	0	0	0	0	4	0	0	0	0	3	0	0	0	0	0	0	0	0	0	3	0
sandbar	4	.2073	.2003	33.0	0	0	0	0	4	0	0	0	0	0	0	1	0	0	0	0	0	0	0	0	0	0	0	0	0
sandbox	4	.1999	.1920	32.8	0	0	0	3	0	0	1	0	0	3	0	1	0	0	0	0	0	0	0	0	0	0	0	0	0
Sandburg	10	.5096	1.0675	40.3	0	0	1	1	4	3	1	0	1	2	0	4	0	0	0	0	1	1	0	0	0	1	0	0	0
Sandburg's	2	.0000	.0219	23.4	0	0	0	0	0	0	2	0	0	2	0	0	0	0	0	0	0	0	0	0	0	0	0	0	0
sanded	17	.1333	.6536	38.2	2	1	1	1	1	3	8	0	4	2	0	0	0	0	0	0	0	0	0	10	0	0	1	0	0
sanders	2	.0000	.0050	17.0	0	0	0	0	2	0	0	0	0	0	0	0	0	0	0	0	0	0	0	2	0	0	0	0	0
Sanders	8	.2152	.5428	37.3	0	3	4	1	0	0	0	0	4	0	0	0	0	4	0	0	0	0	0	0	0	0	0	0	0
Sanderson	7	.2489	.4412	36.4	0	0	0	0	5	2	0	0	1	0	0	0	0	2	0	0	0	0	0	0	4	0	0	0	0
sandhill	6	.2279	.4286	36.3	0	4	0	0	0	0	0	2	4	0	0	0	0	0	0	0	0	0	0	0	0	0	0	2	0
sanding	16	.0619	.2933	34.7	0	0	0	0	6	0	10	0	1	0	0	0	0	0	0	0	0	0	0	13	0	1	0	1	0
Sandino	4	.0000	.1827	32.6	4	0	0	0	0	0	0	0	4	0	0	0	0	0	0	0	0	0	0	0	0	0	0	0	0
Sandino's	2	.0000	.0914	29.6	2	0	0	0	0	0	0	0	2	0	0	0	0	0	0	0	0	0	0	0	0	0	0	0	0
sandlot	3	.2187	.1555	31.9	0	0	0	1	2	0	0	0	0	2	0	0	0	0	0	0	0	0	0	0	0	0	0	1	0
sandpaper	29	.3596	2.2601	43.5	3	3	0	1	8	1	10	3	4	0	1	0	0	0	0	4	1	4	0	14	0	1	0	0	0
sandpipers	8	.4055	.7412	38.7	3	0	0	1	3	0	0	1	2	0	0	0	0	0	0	2	0	0	0	0	0	0	3	1	0
Sandra	73	.4128	7.5968	48.8	15	1	0	46	10	0	1	0	59	2	0	0	0	0	1	0	0	0	0	0	10	0	1	0	0
Sandra's	2	.0000	.0234	23.7	0	0	0	0	2	0	0	0	0	0	0	0	0	0	0	0	0	0	0	0	2	0	0	0	0
sands	43	.7503	6.5603	48.2	3	2	10	6	13	2	5	2	8	5	0	5	0	8	0	6	1	0	0	0	0	4	3	3	0
sandspit	2	.0000	.0234	23.7	0	0	0	2	0	0	0	0	0	0	0	0	0	0	0	0	0	0	0	0	2	0	0	0	0
sandstone	39	.4107	3.5366	45.5	8	12	5	10	1	0	2	1	0	0	0	0	0	0	0	21	0	0	0	0	0	13	2	3	0
sandstones	2	.0000	.0394	26.0	0	0	0	0	0	0	2	0	0	0	0	0	0	0	0	2	0	0	0	0	0	0	0	0	0
sandstorm	4	.3869	.3841	35.8	0	1	0	0	2	0	1	0	2	0	0	0	0	1	0	1	0	0	0	0	0	0	0	0	0
sandstorms	3	.2239	.1775	32.5	0	0	0	3	0	0	0	0	0	0	0	0	0	2	0	1	0	0	0	0	0	0	0	0	0
sandwich	90	.5049	9.6685	49.9	15	19	9	7	17	7	15	1	18	5	2	5	9	0	2	4	0	0	27	0	6	10	0	2	0
Sandwich	5	.4063	.4386	36.4	0	1	2	1	0	0	0	1	0	1	0	0	0	1	2	1	0	0	0	0	0	0	0	0	0
sandwiched	4	.4344	.3899	35.9	1	0	0	1	0	2	0	0	1	0	0	0	0	0	0	1	1	0	0	0	0	0	0	1	0
sandwiches	126	.5444	14.606	51.6	43	26	6	4	11	10	23	3	33	13	0	3	31	1	3	0	0	0	25	0	5	3	4	5	0
sandy	117	.8195	19.346	52.9	26	22	16	17	22	4	8	2	35	0	2	8	0	20	1	15	4	0	0	0	7	8	10	7	0
Sandy	64	.6814	9.0789	49.6	28	16	3	7	4	4	1	1	23	13	0	1	2	8	2	0	3	0	0	0	0	10	0	2	0
sandy-haired	2	.1948	.1250	31.0	0	2	0	0	0	0	0	0	1	0	0	0	0	0	0	0	0	0	0	0	0	1	0	0	0
Sandy's	4	.3723	.3645	35.6	2	0	1	1	0	0	0	0	2	1	0	0	0	0	0	0	0	0	0	0	0	0	0	1	0
sane	2	.0000	.0162	22.1	0	0	0	0	2	0	0	0	0	0	0	0	0	2	0	0	0	0	0	0	0	0	0	0	0
sanely	4	.0000	.0325	25.1	0	0	0	0	4	0	0	0	0	0	0	0	0	4	0	0	0	0	0	0	0	0	0	0	0
Sanford	2	.2139	.1057	30.2	0	0	0	0	0	2	0	0	0	0	0	0	1	1	0	0	0	0	0	0	0	0	0	0	0
Sanforized	4	.1272	.1155	30.6	0	0	0	0	0	1	3	0	0	0	0	0	0	1	0	0	0	0	3	0	0	0	0	0	0
sang	267	.7531	40.892	56.1	62	59	52	24	36	21	12	1	78	15	3	26	0	11	10	0	63	0	0	0	25	18	4	13	1
Sangamon	2	.1698	.1133	30.5	0	1	1	0	0	0	0	0	1	0	0	0	0	0	0	0	0	0	0	0	0	0	1	0	0
Sangay	2	.0000	.0209	23.2	0	0	0	0	2	0	0	0	0	0	0	0	0	0	0	0	0	0	0	0	0	0	2	0	0
Sangre	3	.1927	.1491	31.7	0	0	0	0	1	0	1	1	0	0	0	0	0	0	0	1	0	0	0	0	0	0	0	2	0

5Q sambuqs
7H same-sized
6A same's
9Q Samios
6J Samoan
7K Samothrace
5B sampan
6A sampans
XQ Sampling
4P Samuel's
4F samurai
5F SanBernardino
XR SanBernardo
4F SanBuenaventura
8C SanFranciscan
5F SanJoaquin
6R SanLeandro
XR SanLuis
9R SanMarino
3Q SanMartin
6R SanMateo
7B SanNicholas
6R SanPablo
7F SanPedro's
6R SanRafael
5R San-San
4Q sanatana
9R sanatorium
9F Sanctam
4S sanctified
5P sanctions
9D sanctorum
9D sanctum
3A sand-colored
7M sand-like
9M sand-resin
4A sandal-wood
7D sandaled
6A sandbag
5F sandbags
6A sandbank
8P sandbanks
7R sandbars
7E Sandberg
XR sandblasted
9R Sander
4A Sanders'
7H sandglasses
4N sandiest-yellowish
6R Sandoz
9C sandpaper-like
6A Sandpiper
4F SANDWICHES
6A sandwichy
3D sandworm
4N sandy-coloured
7A sandy-land
4N sandy-yellow-brownish
4N sandy-yellowish
8F Sandys
7G saner
7G sanest
9L Sanforizing
9Q Sango
7R sanguinary

Word Type	F	D	U	SFI	3 Gr 3	4 Gr 4	5 Gr 5	6 Gr 6	7 Gr 7	8 Gr 8	9 Gr 9	X UnGr	A Read	B Eng & Gr	C Comp	D Lit	E Math	F Soc Stud	G Spell	H Sci	J Music	K Art	L Home Ec	M Shop	N Lib F	P Lib NF	Q Lib Ref	R Mag	S Rel
sanguine	2	.2442	.1134	30.5	0	0	0	0	0	0	2	0	0	1	0	0	0	0	0	0	0	0	0	0	0	0	0	1	0
Sanguine	4	.0000	.0486	26.9	0	0	0	0	4	0	0	0	0	0	0	0	0	0	0	0	0	0	0	0	0	0	0	4	0
sanitary	12	.4215	1.0858	40.4	1	0	1	2	1	4	3	0	0	0	0	1	0	3	0	3	0	0	3	0	0	0	2	0	0
sanitation	10	.5345	1.1214	40.5	0	0	1	1	1	2	5	0	0	0	0	1	0	2	0	4	0	0	1	0	0	0	2	0	0
sanity	4	.3611	.3119	34.9	0	0	0	0	2	1	1	0	0	0	0	1	0	0	0	0	0	0	0	0	0	0	2	1	0
Sanja	2	.0000	.0389	25.9	0	2	0	0	0	0	0	0	0	0	0	0	0	2	0	0	0	0	0	0	0	0	0	0	0
sank	87	.7061	12.812	51.1	8	20	9	16	21	8	5	0	43	3	0	10	1	1	0	2	0	0	0	0	10	9	4	4	0
Sanne	2	.0000	.0290	24.6	0	0	0	0	0	2	0	0	0	0	0	0	0	0	0	0	0	0	0	0	0	2	0	0	0
sans	4	.0000	.0579	27.6	0	0	4	0	0	0	0	0	0	0	0	0	0	0	0	0	0	0	0	0	0	4	0	0	0
Sanskrit	6	.2767	.4255	36.3	0	0	2	0	2	0	2	0	2	0	0	0	0	0	0	0	0	0	0	0	0	1	3	0	0
Santa	111	.7856	17.782	52.5	23	27	18	12	7	14	9	1	46	3	1	4	0	24	4	0	5	0	0	0	7	4	1	12	0
SantaBarbara	6	.1937	.2989	34.8	0	2	0	0	0	0	4	0	0	0	0	0	0	2	0	0	0	0	0	0	0	0	0	4	0
SantaClara	3	.0000	.0583	27.7	0	3	0	0	0	0	0	0	0	0	0	0	0	3	0	0	0	0	0	0	0	0	0	0	0
SantaCruz	3	.1937	.1495	31.7	0	1	0	2	0	0	0	0	0	0	0	0	0	1	0	0	0	0	0	0	0	0	0	2	0
SantaFe	12	.2754	.8501	39.3	5	4	2	0	0	1	0	0	2	0	0	0	2	8	0	0	0	0	0	0	0	0	0	0	0
Santa-Fe	2	.0000	.0215	23.3	0	0	0	0	2	0	0	0	0	0	0	2	0	0	0	0	0	0	0	0	0	0	0	0	0
Santiago	10	.2731	.6688	38.3	0	0	0	5	3	0	2	0	0	0	0	0	0	8	0	0	0	0	0	0	1	1	0	0	0
Santo	16	.4789	1.6679	42.2	0	0	4	7	3	1	1	0	3	0	0	0	0	3	0	0	0	0	0	0	1	0	3	6	0
Santo's	2	.0000	.0243	23.9	0	0	0	2	0	0	0	0	0	0	0	0	0	0	0	0	0	0	0	0	0	0	0	2	0
Santos	3	.2425	.1816	32.6	0	0	2	0	1	0	0	0	0	0	0	0	0	2	0	0	0	0	0	0	0	0	0	1	0
Santy	8	.0000	.3655	35.6	0	8	0	0	0	0	0	0	8	0	0	0	0	0	0	0	0	0	0	0	0	0	0	0	0
Sao	5	.2205	.2855	34.6	0	0	2	2	1	0	0	0	0	0	0	0	0	4	0	0	0	0	0	0	0	0	1	0	0
sap	49	.6914	6.9695	48.4	11	9	9	2	9	5	3	1	11	1	0	1	0	4	1	9	0	0	0	4	2	4	9	3	0
sapiens	7	.3224	.5180	37.1	0	1	0	0	5	1	0	0	0	0	0	0	0	1	0	3	0	0	0	0	0	0	3	0	0
Sapir	5	.0000	.0523	27.2	0	0	1	0	0	0	4	0	0	0	0	0	0	0	0	0	0	0	0	0	0	0	5	0	0
sapling	3	.3399	.2456	33.9	0	0	0	1	2	0	0	0	1	0	0	1	0	0	0	0	0	0	0	0	0	0	0	1	0
sapped	4	.3287	.2952	34.7	1	0	0	0	3	0	0	0	0	0	0	0	0	1	0	0	0	0	0	0	0	1	2	0	0
sapphire	8	.5067	.8722	39.4	1	0	4	0	1	1	1	0	2	3	0	1	0	0	0	0	1	0	0	0	0	0	1	0	0
sapphires	4	.2918	.2856	34.6	0	0	0	2	2	0	0	0	1	0	1	0	0	0	0	1	0	0	0	0	1	0	0	0	0
saprophytes	3	.2445	.1818	32.6	0	0	0	1	2	0	0	0	0	0	0	0	0	0	0	2	0	0	0	0	0	0	1	0	0
saprophytic	2	.2278	.1128	30.5	0	0	0	1	1	0	0	0	0	0	0	0	0	0	0	1	0	0	0	0	0	0	1	0	0
Sara	45	.4806	5.1167	47.1	32	2	1	2	4	4	0	0	33	1	0	0	7	0	0	0	0	0	0	0	0	0	2	2	0
sarabande	2	.2303	.1079	30.3	0	0	0	0	1	1	0	0	0	0	0	0	0	0	0	0	1	0	0	0	0	1	0	0	0
Saracens	5	.3770	.4201	36.2	0	0	0	0	1	3	0	1	0	1	0	0	0	3	0	0	0	0	0	0	0	0	1	0	0
Sarah	134	.4618	14.562	51.6	31	55	15	13	2	8	10	0	83	0	2	1	17	1	1	1	0	0	0	0	4	17	1	4	2
Sarah's	15	.1872	.9091	39.6	1	5	8	1	0	0	0	0	7	0	0	0	8	0	0	0	0	0	0	0	0	0	0	0	0
Sarasota	3	.2578	.1701	32.3	1	0	0	0	1	1	0	0	0	0	0	0	0	0	0	0	0	1	0	0	0	0	1	1	0
Saratoga	7	.4035	.6340	38.0	0	0	0	0	4	3	0	0	1	0	0	0	0	3	0	0	2	0	0	0	0	0	0	1	0
sarcasm	7	.4852	.7772	38.9	0	0	0	0	6	1	0	0	4	0	0	1	0	0	1	0	0	0	0	0	1	0	0	0	0
sarcastic	9	.4539	.8473	39.3	0	0	0	0	1	3	4	1	0	2	2	3	0	0	0	1	0	0	1	0	0	0	0	0	0
sarcastically	4	.2424	.3036	34.8	0	0	1	1	1	1	0	0	3	0	0	0	0	0	0	0	0	0	0	0	0	0	0	1	0
sardine	6	.3332	.4436	36.5	2	0	0	0	1	0	3	0	0	0	0	2	0	1	0	0	0	0	0	0	3	0	0	0	0
sardines	17	.6162	2.1855	43.4	4	5	1	4	1	0	2	0	2	0	0	1	0	4	0	4	0	0	0	0	4	1	1	0	0
Sardinia	9	.3381	.6843	38.4	2	0	0	3	2	0	2	0	0	0	0	1	0	4	0	0	0	0	0	0	0	0	4	0	0
Sardinian	2	.2401	.1133	30.5	0	0	1	0	1	0	0	0	0	0	0	0	0	0	0	0	0	0	0	0	0	1	1	0	0
Sargasso	4	.3366	.2993	34.8	0	0	3	0	0	0	1	0	0	0	0	0	0	0	0	1	0	0	0	0	1	0	2	0	0
Sargent	14	.3840	1.2089	40.8	0	0	8	0	5	0	1	0	3	0	1	0	0	0	0	0	0	0	0	0	0	0	8	2	0
Sargon	2	.2401	.1133	30.5	0	0	1	0	1	0	0	0	0	0	0	0	0	0	0	0	0	0	0	0	0	1	1	0	0
Sarnoff	11	.2031	.5979	37.8	0	9	0	0	0	0	0	2	0	0	0	0	0	9	0	0	0	0	0	0	0	0	0	2	0
Sarowek	2	.0000	.0219	23.4	0	0	0	0	2	0	0	0	0	2	0	0	0	0	0	0	0	0	0	0	0	0	0	0	0
Saroyan	6	.1717	.3427	35.3	0	0	0	0	3	3	0	0	3	0	0	3	0	0	0	0	0	0	0	0	0	0	0	0	0
sartorius	2	.0000	.0209	23.2	0	0	0	0	0	0	2	0	0	0	0	0	0	0	0	0	0	0	0	0	0	0	2	0	0
SAS	4	.2427	.2319	33.7	0	0	0	0	0	2	0	2	0	0	0	0	2	0	0	0	0	0	0	0	0	0	0	2	0
Sascha	13	.0000	.5939	37.7	0	13	0	0	0	0	0	0	13	0	0	0	0	0	0	0	0	0	0	0	0	0	0	0	0
Sascha's	3	.0000	.1370	31.4	0	3	0	0	0	0	0	0	3	0	0	0	0	0	0	0	0	0	0	0	0	0	0	0	0
sash	22	.4573	2.1919	43.4	4	3	2	3	6	2	0	2	6	1	0	1	0	0	1	0	2	0	0	6	2	1	1	1	0
sashes	9	.3944	.7675	38.9	0	1	1	2	3	1	1	0	1	0	0	0	0	2	1	0	0	0	0	3	0	0	0	1	0
Saskatchewan	13	.4879	1.4443	41.6	0	1	0	0	8	0	4	0	7	0	0	2	0	0	0	0	0	0	1	0	0	0	2	2	0
Saskia	6	.0525	.0806	29.1	0	0	0	0	0	5	0	1	0	0	0	0	0	0	0	0	0	5	0	0	0	0	1	0	0
sass	3	.2279	.2143	33.3	0	0	1	0	2	0	0	0	2	0	0	0	0	0	0	0	0	0	0	0	0	0	0	1	0
sassafras	7	.3994	.6386	38.1	2	1	1	2	0	1	0	0	2	0	0	3	0	0	0	0	0	0	0	0	0	1	1	0	0
Sassafras	2	.0000	.0215	23.3	0	0	0	0	2	0	0	0	0	0	0	2	0	0	0	0	0	0	0	0	0	0	0	0	0
Sassoon	4	.0000	.0486	26.9	0	0	4	0	0	0	0	0	0	0	0	0	0	0	0	0	0	0	0	0	0	0	0	4	0
sassy	8	.3264	.6662	38.2	5	0	0	0	0	3	0	0	4	0	0	3	0	0	0	0	0	0	0	0	0	0	0	1	0
Sassy	22	.0231	.3848	35.9	20	2	0	0	0	0	0	0	1	0	0	0	0	0	0	0	0	0	0	0	21	0	0	0	0
sat	1138	.7277	171.60	62.3	285	256	106	123	180	101	75	12	562	35	26	138	6	30	6	5	13	0	0	0	156	116	2	43	0
Sat	3	.3725	.2432	33.9	1	0	0	1	0	0	1	0	0	0	0	0	1	0	1	0	0	0	0	0	0	1	0	0	0
SAT	2	.0000	.0243	23.9	0	0	0	0	2	0	0	0	0	0	0	0	0	0	0	0	0	0	0	0	0	0	0	2	0
Satan	12	.1850	.5511	37.4	1	5	0	0	2	2	1	1	0	1	0	4	0	0	0	0	0	0	0	0	0	6	0	0	1
satchel	2	.1948	.1250	31.0	0	0	1	0	0	1	0	0	1	0	0	0	0	0	0	0	0	0	0	0	0	1	0	0	0
Satchmo	2	.2411	.1091	30.4	0	0	0	0	0	1	1	0	0	0	0	1	0	0	0	0	1	0	0	0	0	0	0	0	0
satellite	158	.6044	19.929	53.0	30	34	15	28	11	30	8	2	10	1	0	0	11	7	1	73	0	0	0	4	0	43	3	5	0
satellite's	5	.3660	.4140	36.2	0	1	1	0	1	1	1	0	0	0	0	0	0	0	0	3	0	0	0	0	0	1	0	1	0
satellites	191	.5991	23.941	53.8	50	47	20	25	18	18	10	3	10	1	0	2	4	13	1	107	0	1	0	1	0	40	6	5	0
SATELLITES	2	.0000	.0394	26.0	2	0	0	0	0	0	0	0	0	0	0	0	0	0	0	2	0	0	0	0	0	0	0	0	0
satin	17	.7232	2.4840	44.0	4	1	1	3	2	3	2	1	2	0	0	3	0	1	1	1	2	0	2	1	2	1	0	1	0
satins	6	.3225	.4126	36.2	4	0	0	0	0	0	1	1	0	0	0	0	0	0	0	0	4	0	1	0	0	0	0	1	0
satiny	3	.3852	.2500	34.0	2	0	0	0	0	0	0	1	0	0	0	1	0	0	0	0	0	0	0	0	0	1	0	1	0
satire	11	.5446	1.2298	40.9	0	0	1	0	2	2	1	5	0	3	0	1	0	0	0	0	2	0	0	0	0	0	3	2	0
satires	2	.2351	.1166	30.7	0	0	0	0	1	0	1	0	0	0	0	0	0	1	0	0	0	0	0	0	0	0	0	1	0
satiric	2	.0000	.0209	23.2	0	0	0	0	0	2	0	0	0	0	0	0	0	0	0	0	0	0	0	0	0	0	2	0	0
satirical	5	.4593	.4771	36.8	0	0	1	0	0	0	3	1	0	1	1	0	0	0	0	0	1	0	0	0	0	1	0	1	0
satirized	2	.2412	.1141	30.6	0	0	1	0	0	0	0	1	0	1	0	0	0	0	0	0	0	0	0	0	0	1	0	0	0
satisfaction	85	.8543	14.505	51.6	5	5	9	16	23	12	13	2	17	3	2	5	0	10	2	7	5	0	5	1	17	5	2	4	0
satisfactorily	15	.7330	2.2273	43.5	0	0	3	2	3	4	3	0	2	0	0	1	0	2	0	2	1	0	1	1	1	0	3	1	0
satisfactory	51	.7293	7.4960	48.7	1	0	1	9	12	13	15	0	6	5	1	3	1	3	2	3	0	1	9	5	3	1	7	1	0
satisfied	133	.9022	23.851	53.8	13	16	18	19	29	21	13	4	33	8	3	15	2	9	3	13	3	2	2	0	16	12	2	10	0
satisfies	7	.4206	.6157	37.9	1	0	0	0	1	0	5	0	0	0	1	0	3	0	0	0	0	0	2	0	0	0	1	0	0
satisfy	68	.7400	10.216	50.1	3	3	5	12	7	12	24	2	11	3	0	2	12	12	2	3	0	0	7	0	3	4	6	3	0
satisfying	43	.7204	6.2542	48.0	2	4	3	6	3	6	16	3	4	6	0	3	6	4	1	0	4	0	7	1	2	1	2	2	0
satura	2	.0000	.0219	23.4	0	0	0	0	0	0	0	2	0	2	0	0	0	0	0	0	0	0	0	0	0	0	0	0	0
saturated	10	.4109	.9095	39.6	0	0	4	1	0	1	4	0	0	0	0	0	0	1	0	6	0	0	0	0	0	1	2	0	0
saturation	4	.2287	.2348	33.7	0	0	0	0	0	0	4	0	0	0	0	0	0	0	0	3	0	0	0	0	0	0	0	1	0

8Q Sanibel
7A sanitarium
8F Sanitary
7D Sankhicani
8F Sansei
5F SantaAna
3A Santa's
6F Santiago's
9Q Santos-Dumont
3Q Saone
7D Saosquahanaunks
7Q sap-transporting
7J Sapete
7R Sapirstein
7N sapling-Dante
9B sapodilla
5Q Sapotaceae
8F sapping
9D Sappleton
7D sapsucker
3A Sara's
8R Saragat
9F Sarai
7Q saran-plastic
6F sarapes
6F Sarawak
8A sarcophagus
5P Sardauna
9N sardine's
8D sardonic
4Q Sardou
3N Sarepta
7R Sargent's
4F Sarnoffs
7J Saro
5P sarong-wrapped
7A sarongs
3J sarpent
7A Sarpi
8R sartorial
9R Sartres
7A sashayed
9A Saskatchewan's
XQ Saskia's
9Q Sassanian
5N Sassanidae
7D sassed
5R Sassoon's
6J Satan's
7A satang
7P satanic
7D Satch
7R Satchel
7D Satchell
9L sateen
7N satiate
8J Satie
9A sating
XB satira
9Q satirist
5Q satirizes
7D Satisfaction
7N satisfactions
9C Satisfactory
3P satisfieth
7A satrap
7D Sattisfield
7C saturate

Word Type	F	D	U	SFI	3 Gr 3	4 Gr 4	5 Gr 5	6 Gr 6	7 Gr 7	8 Gr 8	9 Gr 9	X UnGr	A Read	B Eng & Gr	C Comp	D Lit	E Math	F Soc Stud	G Spell	H Sci	J Music	K Art	L Home Ec	M Shop	N Lib F	P Lib NF	Q Lib Ref	R Mag	S Rel
Saturday	222	.8295	37.002	55.7	66	45	24	27	24	16	16	4	63	17	10	10	26	14	15	3	4	1	1	0	35	8	1	14	0
Saturday's	2	.1733	.1149	30.6	1	1	0	0	0	0	0	0	1	1	0	0	0	0	0	0	0	0	0	0	0	0	0	0	0
Saturdays	18	.6090	2.2831	43.6	6	1	2	1	0	8	0	0	3	5	1	0	2	3	0	0	0	0	0	0	3	0	0	1	0
Saturn	71	.6811	9.9763	50.0	9	22	4	12	13	7	3	1	14	0	0	2	9	0	2	24	0	0	0	4	0	2	7	7	0
Saturn's	2	.0000	.0209	23.2	0	0	0	0	2	0	0	0	0	0	0	0	0	0	0	0	0	0	0	0	0	0	2	0	0
Satyagraha	2	.0000	.0243	23.9	0	0	0	0	0	2	0	0	0	0	0	0	0	0	0	0	0	0	0	0	0	0	0	2	0
sauce	62	.3489	4.7579	46.8	5	8	5	2	12	2	20	8	7	3	0	1	1	1	1	4	2	0	27	0	1	4	0	10	0
saucepan	26	.3139	1.8749	42.7	5	1	6	1	5	3	3	2	4	0	0	0	0	0	0	5	0	0	10	0	1	0	2	4	0
saucer	53	.7011	7.7498	48.9	11	5	10	11	10	4	2	0	26	1	1	5	0	1	0	1	0	0	2	0	11	3	0	2	0
Saucer	13	.1289	.5460	37.4	0	12	0	0	1	0	0	0	0	0	0	0	0	0	0	12	0	0	0	0	0	0	0	1	0
saucer-shaped	2	.2346	.1166	30.7	0	1	0	0	0	1	0	0	0	0	0	0	0	0	0	1	0	0	0	0	0	0	0	1	0
saucers	20	.5240	2.3616	43.7	8	3	1	1	6	0	0	1	12	0	0	0	0	0	0	0	3	0	0	0	2	1	0	2	0
sauces	8	.0197	.0979	29.9	0	0	0	1	0	1	6	0	1	0	0	0	0	0	0	0	0	0	7	0	0	0	0	0	0
saucy	8	.5915	.9829	39.9	0	3	2	0	0	1	0	2	1	1	0	0	0	0	0	0	1	0	0	0	1	2	0	2	0
Saucy	2	.0000	.0234	23.7	0	2	0	0	0	0	0	0	0	0	0	0	0	0	0	0	0	0	0	0	0	0	0	2	0
Saudi	16	.2730	1.0676	40.3	0	4	0	5	2	1	4	0	0	0	0	1	0	13	0	0	0	0	0	0	2	0	0	0	0
sauerkraut	6	.3665	.4823	36.8	0	1	2	1	0	1	0	1	0	0	0	0	0	0	2	2	0	0	0	0	2	0	0	0	0
Saul	15	.2065	.7529	38.8	5	0	0	1	7	2	0	0	0	0	0	7	0	1	0	0	0	0	0	0	0	6	0	0	1
Sault	3	.2365	.1616	32.1	0	0	0	2	1	0	0	0	0	0	0	0	0	0	0	0	1	0	0	0	0	0	2	0	0
Saunders	5	.0000	.2284	33.6	0	0	0	0	5	0	0	0	5	0	0	0	0	0	0	0	0	0	0	0	0	0	0	0	0
sauntered	10	.4326	.9969	40.0	1	3	1	1	2	1	1	0	4	0	0	2	0	1	0	0	0	0	0	0	3	0	0	0	0
sausage	16	.6500	2.2301	43.5	6	3	0	1	1	3	1	1	10	1	0	1	0	0	1	1	0	0	0	0	1	1	0	0	0
sausages	33	.2981	2.6096	44.2	11	1	4	5	2	6	4	0	19	1	0	0	0	0	0	0	0	0	8	0	5	0	0	0	0
Saussure	2	.0000	.0209	23.2	0	0	0	0	2	0	0	0	0	0	0	0	0	0	0	0	0	0	0	0	0	0	2	0	0
savage	58	.7442	8.7718	49.4	2	7	9	8	19	6	3	4	12	2	0	9	0	5	0	1	2	1	0	0	13	9	1	3	0
savagely	17	.5060	1.8193	42.6	0	0	3	1	6	7	0	0	2	4	0	4	0	0	0	0	0	0	0	0	5	0	0	2	0
savageness	2	.0000	.0234	23.7	0	0	0	0	2	0	0	0	0	0	0	0	0	0	0	0	0	0	0	0	2	0	0	0	0
savagery	5	.3077	.3653	35.6	0	0	3	1	1	0	0	0	1	0	0	0	0	0	0	0	0	0	0	0	0	0	2	2	0
savages	22	.6839	3.0981	44.9	0	3	4	4	6	5	0	0	5	1	0	4	0	2	0	0	0	0	0	0	3	4	2	1	0
savanna	15	.3732	1.2554	41.0	0	2	2	1	9	0	1	0	1	0	0	0	0	5	0	1	0	0	0	0	0	0	7	1	0
savannah	4	.0000	.0486	26.9	0	4	0	0	0	0	0	0	0	0	0	0	0	0	0	0	0	0	0	0	0	0	0	4	0
Savannah	11	.4337	1.0432	40.2	1	4	2	0	0	1	3	0	0	0	0	0	3	6	0	0	0	0	0	0	0	1	1	0	0
savannas	20	.2446	1.2079	40.8	0	1	0	1	10	0	8	0	0	0	0	0	0	13	0	0	0	0	0	0	0	0	7	0	0
savants	2	.2433	.1158	30.6	0	0	1	0	0	0	1	0	0	0	0	0	0	0	0	0	0	0	0	0	0	1	0	1	0
save	396	.6750	55.474	57.4	78	59	55	51	70	37	40	6	128	13	3	34	35	23	3	18	3	2	25	4	29	26	13	31	6
Save	6	.0000	.0485	26.9	0	0	4	2	0	0	0	0	0	0	0	0	0	0	0	0	6	0	0	0	0	0	0	0	0
saved	256	.6588	35.425	55.5	59	65	28	24	40	13	13	14	103	1	5	15	39	9	2	10	1	0	1	3	27	24	4	9	3
saver	4	.3369	.2946	34.7	1	0	2	0	0	0	1	0	0	0	0	0	2	0	0	0	0	0	1	0	1	0	0	0	0
saves	32	.3381	2.4435	43.9	9	0	6	4	3	4	3	3	3	3	2	0	10	0	0	2	0	0	0	1	3	3	1	2	2
saving	81	.7217	12.006	50.8	9	16	8	15	13	10	8	2	26	3	1	5	4	7	1	6	2	0	5	1	7	5	4	3	1
savings	51	.6585	6.8932	48.4	8	4	10	9	6	3	10	1	6	0	0	0	16	6	2	0	0	0	3	0	1	1	10	6	0
Savings	4	.1760	.1902	32.8	3	0	0	0	0	0	1	0	0	0	0	0	0	1	0	0	0	0	0	0	0	3	0	0	0
savior	2	.0299	.0221	23.4	1	0	0	0	0	1	0	0	0	0	0	0	0	0	0	0	0	0	0	0	0	0	1	0	1
Savior	18	.0176	.1455	31.6	10	4	1	1	1	1	0	0	0	0	0	0	0	3	0	0	3	0	0	0	0	0	0	0	12
Saviour	4	.3683	.3188	35.0	0	0	0	2	0	0	1	1	0	0	0	1	0	0	0	0	0	0	0	0	2	0	0	1	0
Savonarola	2	.0000	.0290	24.6	0	0	2	0	0	0	0	0	0	0	0	0	0	0	0	0	0	0	0	0	0	2	0	0	0
savor	3	.3427	.2477	33.9	0	0	0	0	2	0	1	0	1	0	0	0	0	0	0	0	0	0	0	0	1	0	0	1	0
savoring	2	.2331	.1157	30.6	0	0	0	0	2	0	0	0	0	0	0	0	0	0	0	1	0	0	0	0	1	0	0	0	0
savory	7	.3425	.5073	37.1	0	0	0	1	2	0	4	0	0	1	0	0	0	0	0	0	0	0	3	0	1	0	1	1	0
Savoy	3	.0000	.0314	25.0	0	0	0	0	3	0	0	0	0	0	0	0	0	0	0	0	0	0	0	0	0	0	3	0	0
saw	2900	.9012	521.32	67.2	711	554	305	326	530	259	186	29	1271	141	30	283	37	194	43	93	34	24	0	71	321	214	32	109	3
Saw	2	.2411	.1091	30.4	0	0	1	0	0	0	1	0	0	0	0	1	0	0	0	0	1	0	0	0	0	0	0	0	0
SAW	5	.0000	.0724	28.6	4	0	0	1	0	0	0	0	0	0	0	0	0	0	0	0	0	0	0	0	0	5	0	0	0
sawdust	19	.7347	2.8256	44.5	4	8	1	2	2	1	1	0	2	0	0	2	0	2	0	3	1	1	1	1	1	5	0	0	0
sawed	14	.5777	1.7132	42.3	1	1	3	3	2	2	2	0	4	0	1	1	0	2	0	1	0	0	0	2	2	0	1	0	0
sawed-off	2	.0000	.0914	29.6	0	1	1	0	0	0	0	0	2	0	0	0	0	0	0	0	0	0	0	0	0	0	0	0	0
sawhorse	5	.2620	.3230	35.1	1	0	0	0	2	1	1	0	1	1	0	3	0	0	0	0	0	0	0	0	0	0	0	0	0
sawing	20	.2754	1.2873	41.1	0	2	3	2	3	3	7	0	3	0	0	0	0	4	0	1	1	0	1	9	0	1	0	0	0
sawmill	20	.4849	2.1429	43.3	6	1	6	1	5	0	0	1	6	0	0	1	0	6	0	0	0	0	0	3	0	2	1	1	0
sawmills	19	.4378	1.8199	42.6	3	0	6	2	5	2	0	1	1	0	0	0	0	12	0	0	0	0	0	2	0	0	2	2	0
saws	19	.5477	2.1560	43.3	5	1	4	1	2	4	2	0	2	0	2	1	0	2	0	1	0	1	0	5	1	3	1	0	0
Sawyer	17	.5265	1.9778	43.0	0	3	2	3	8	1	0	0	8	1	1	0	0	0	0	0	0	0	0	0	3	0	0	4	0
Sax	2	.1494	.1045	30.2	0	0	0	1	0	1	0	0	1	0	0	0	0	0	0	0	1	0	0	0	0	0	0	0	0
Saxon	5	.5386	.5712	37.6	0	1	0	2	1	1	0	0	1	1	0	0	0	0	0	0	0	0	0	0	1	0	1	1	0
Saxons	18	.5719	2.1162	43.3	0	0	2	5	8	0	3	0	0	5	0	1	2	3	4	0	0	0	0	0	0	0	3	0	0
Saxony	10	.5629	1.1793	40.7	0	0	0	2	1	2	5	0	1	0	0	0	0	3	0	0	2	0	0	0	1	1	2	0	0
saxophone	12	.2926	.7720	38.9	0	1	2	2	0	7	0	0	0	0	0	0	0	0	1	1	8	0	0	0	2	0	0	0	0
saxophones	2	.0000	.0162	22.1	0	0	0	0	0	2	0	0	0	0	0	0	0	0	0	0	2	0	0	0	0	0	0	0	0
say	3916	.8606	673.26	68.3	938	669	454	503	650	358	307	37	983	405	21	305	240	141	785	175	90	17	20	7	306	199	47	171	4
sayids	2	.0000	.0209	23.2	0	0	2	0	0	0	0	0	0	0	0	0	0	0	0	0	0	0	0	0	0	0	2	0	0
sayin'	3	.3394	.2451	33.9	0	0	0	0	2	1	0	0	1	0	0	1	0	0	0	0	0	0	0	0	1	0	0	0	0
saying	524	.8661	90.902	59.6	94	96	61	71	96	63	42	1	192	51	4	50	13	24	19	15	11	3	4	0	59	40	4	33	2
Saying	2	.1042	.0600	27.8	0	1	0	0	0	0	1	0	0	0	0	0	0	1	0	0	0	1	0	0	0	0	0	0	0
sayings	17	.4980	1.8814	42.7	1	5	3	1	3	3	1	0	6	0	0	5	0	3	1	2	0	0	0	0	0	0	0	0	0
Sayonara	3	.0000	.0583	27.7	0	1	0	0	0	2	0	0	0	0	0	0	0	3	0	0	0	0	0	0	0	0	0	0	0
Sayre	2	.2440	.1132	30.5	0	0	0	0	1	1	0	0	0	0	0	1	0	0	0	0	0	0	0	0	0	0	0	1	0
says	1180	.7662	184.15	62.7	336	117	128	125	208	115	106	45	397	73	5	125	19	77	71	17	18	2	7	0	71	97	9	184	8
SAYS	2	.0000	.0004	5.5	2	0	0	0	0	0	0	0	0	0	0	0	0	0	0	0	0	0	0	0	0	0	0	0	2
sc	8	.1114	.2354	33.7	0	0	1	4	3	0	0	0	0	1	0	0	0	0	7	0	0	0	0	0	0	0	0	0	0
SC	2	.1892	.0858	29.3	0	0	0	0	0	0	2	0	0	1	0	0	0	0	0	0	0	0	1	0	0	0	0	0	0
scabbard	8	.3792	.7811	38.9	0	0	0	5	3	0	0	0	6	0	0	0	0	0	0	0	0	0	0	0	1	0	0	1	0
scabbards	2	.0000	.0243	23.9	0	0	0	0	2	0	0	0	0	0	0	0	0	0	0	0	0	0	0	0	0	0	0	2	0
scabbed	2	.1717	.1142	30.6	0	0	1	0	0	1	0	0	1	0	0	1	0	0	0	0	0	0	0	0	0	0	0	0	0
scabs	2	.1717	.1142	30.6	0	0	0	0	2	0	0	0	1	0	0	1	0	0	0	0	0	0	0	0	0	0	0	0	0
scalar	4	.0000	.0599	27.8	0	0	0	0	0	0	4	0	0	0	0	0	4	0	0	0	0	0	0	0	0	0	0	0	0
scalawags	3	.3369	.2489	34.0	0	0	0	0	2	1	0	0	1	0	0	1	0	1	0	0	0	0	0	0	0	0	0	0	0
scalded	2	.0000	.0064	18.1	0	0	0	0	1	0	1	0	0	0	0	0	0	0	0	0	0	0	2	0	0	0	0	0	0
scalding	5	.5389	.5716	37.6	0	0	1	1	1	1	1	0	1	1	0	1	0	0	0	0	0	0	0	0	1	0	0	1	0
scalds	2	.2346	.1166	30.7	0	0	1	0	1	0	0	0	0	0	0	0	0	0	0	1	0	0	0	0	0	0	0	1	0
scale	737	.5602	85.211	59.3	57	165	176	87	79	90	75	8	29	1	1	1	92	60	3	76	379	6	5	27	1	15	26	15	0
Scale	4	.3529	.2948	34.7	0	0	1	0	1	1	1	0	0	0	0	0	0	0	0	1	2	0	0	1	0	0	0	0	0
scale-like	2	.2405	.1205	30.8	1	0	0	0	0	0	1	0	0	0	0	0	0	0	0	1	0	0	0	0	0	1	0	0	0
scale-line	7	.0000	.0566	27.5	0	0	4	3	0	0	0	0	0	0	0	0	0	0	0	0	7	0	0	0	0	0	0	0	0
scaled	9	.5691	1.0619	40.3	0	0	0	2	4	2	1	0	0	0	0	1	4	1	0	0	0	0	0	0	1	1	0	1	0

9B Saturday-night
9L Sauce
3A Saucepan
4H Saucer's
7N saucily
7R SAUCY
4P Sauk
7A Saunders'
4Q Saunderstown
7B saunter
8G Sauria
7L saute
9L sauteed
8G sauterne
8G Sauternes
7F Sava
4P Savage
4A savage-looking
9R savaged
8F Savages
5A savages'
7Q Savery
7N Savile
7D savin'
7A Saving
XH Savinien
6J Savior's
9K Savoie
5P Savonarola's
9R savored
5A savvied
7D savvy
7R saw-duty
7N saw-file
7M saw-table
6A saw-tooth
XN saw-toothed
9M saw's
4P sawbuck
7R sawhorses
5A Sawmills
9D sawn
9M sawyer
7N SAWYER
7P Saxe-Weimar
9D Saxony's
5B Say
7P say'st
6A sayah
7P sayen
3R Saylor
3A Sayor
7R SCAA'S
XR scab-resistant
8D scabby-kneed
8F scaffold
7J scala
3P Scala
7L scald
8J scale-step
6J scale-tones
7H scalelike

Word Type	F	D	U	SFI	3 Gr 3	4 Gr 4	5 Gr 5	6 Gr 6	7 Gr 7	8 Gr 8	9 Gr 9	X UnGr	A Read	B Eng & Gr	C Comp	D Lit	E Math	F Soc Stud	G Spell	H Sci	J Music	K Art	L Home Ec	M Shop	N Lib F	P Lib NF	Q Lib Ref	R Mag	S Rel
scalene	3	.2346	.1705	32.3	0	0	0	0	1	0	2	0	0	0	0	0	2	0	0	0	0	0	0	0	0	0	0	1	0
scales	185	.6659	25.292	54.0	42	13	17	36	45	21	11	0	23	1	0	6	13	3	2	50	48	0	1	0	2	18	15	3	0
Scales	2	.0000	.0234	23.7	0	0	0	0	2	0	0	0	0	0	0	0	0	0	0	0	0	0	0	0	2	0	0	0	0
scaling	5	.4764	.5339	37.3	0	0	1	1	0	1	1	1	2	0	0	0	0	0	0	0	0	0	0	0	1	0	1	1	0
scallop	4	.2386	.2998	34.8	2	0	0	0	2	0	0	0	3	0	0	0	0	0	0	0	0	0	0	0	0	0	1	0	0
scalloped	3	.1386	.0963	29.8	0	0	0	0	1	0	2	0	0	0	0	0	0	0	0	0	0	0	2	0	0	0	1	0	0
scallops	11	.3802	1.0631	40.3	1	0	0	3	4	1	2	0	7	0	0	0	0	0	0	3	0	0	0	0	0	0	1	0	0
scalp	34	.6712	4.6891	46.7	3	4	0	5	9	6	6	1	6	0	0	5	0	3	0	0	0	0	2	0	6	8	3	1	0
scalped	7	.1889	.3522	35.5	1	0	0	1	4	1	0	0	1	0	0	5	0	0	0	0	0	0	0	0	0	1	0	0	0
scalpel	5	.2646	.3249	35.1	0	0	0	0	3	1	1	0	1	0	0	3	0	0	0	0	0	0	0	0	0	0	1	0	0
scalplock	3	.0000	.0352	25.5	0	2	1	0	0	0	0	0	0	0	0	0	0	0	0	0	0	0	0	0	3	0	0	0	0
scalps	10	.3816	.8357	39.2	0	2	0	0	5	3	0	0	0	0	0	5	0	3	0	0	0	0	0	0	0	1	0	1	0
scaly	9	.4942	.9650	39.8	1	1	0	2	2	0	0	3	2	0	0	0	0	0	0	2	0	1	0	0	1	1	2	0	0
Scaly-Skin	3	.0000	.1370	31.4	3	0	0	0	0	0	0	0	3	0	0	0	0	0	0	0	0	0	0	0	0	0	0	0	0
scaly-winged	2	.0000	.0394	26.0	0	0	0	1	1	0	0	0	0	0	0	0	0	0	0	2	0	0	0	0	0	0	0	0	0
scamp	7	.2326	.5117	37.1	1	1	0	3	2	0	0	0	5	0	0	2	0	0	0	0	0	0	0	0	0	0	0	0	0
scamper	5	.4727	.5348	37.3	2	1	1	1	0	0	0	0	2	1	0	0	0	1	0	0	0	0	0	0	1	0	0	0	0
scampered	25	.6774	3.5118	45.5	11	6	1	2	2	2	1	0	8	1	1	3	0	1	0	0	0	0	0	0	3	3	0	5	0
scampering	10	.4645	1.0661	40.3	2	1	2	2	2	1	0	0	5	2	0	2	0	0	0	0	0	0	0	0	0	1	0	0	0
scan	16	.6193	2.1188	43.3	0	0	3	2	8	2	1	0	8	1	0	0	0	0	0	1	2	0	0	1	2	0	0	1	0
scandalous	2	.1733	.1149	30.6	0	0	0	1	0	0	1	0	1	1	0	0	0	0	0	0	0	0	0	0	0	0	0	0	0
scandals	3	.3769	.2484	34.0	0	0	0	0	0	2	1	0	0	0	0	0	0	1	0	0	0	0	0	0	0	0	1	1	0
Scandinavia	25	.6183	3.1654	45.0	2	0	9	3	3	2	5	1	0	3	0	0	0	4	0	1	0	1	0	0	0	8	6	2	0
Scandinavian	54	.6011	6.6414	48.2	7	2	6	20	10	2	3	4	0	13	0	0	0	11	13	0	2	0	0	0	0	5	8	2	0
Scandinavians	8	.2800	.5008	37.0	0	0	1	0	5	2	0	0	0	6	0	0	0	0	1	0	0	0	0	0	0	0	1	0	0
scanned	11	.5643	1.3064	41.2	1	1	0	4	2	3	0	0	2	0	0	1	0	0	0	0	0	0	0	0	3	1	1	3	0
scanning	17	.6525	2.3343	43.7	1	1	1	0	9	4	0	1	6	0	0	1	0	0	0	5	0	0	0	0	1	1	1	2	0
scans	4	.1791	.1711	32.3	0	0	0	0	2	1	0	1	0	0	0	0	0	0	0	1	0	0	0	2	0	0	0	1	0
scant	10	.4299	.9468	39.8	0	1	0	0	5	1	2	1	2	0	0	0	0	0	0	1	0	0	1	0	0	0	5	1	0
scantily	5	.4755	.5327	37.3	0	0	2	0	2	1	0	0	2	0	0	1	0	0	0	0	0	0	0	0	0	0	1	1	0
scanty	9	.6478	1.2048	40.8	1	1	1	1	2	1	2	0	1	1	0	1	0	3	0	1	0	0	0	0	1	0	1	0	0
scapegoat	5	.1751	.2165	33.4	0	0	0	0	4	0	1	0	0	1	0	4	0	0	0	0	0	0	0	0	0	0	0	0	0
scar	29	.5970	3.6706	45.6	4	6	2	1	9	3	4	0	9	0	0	8	0	1	0	1	0	0	0	0	3	5	1	1	0
scarce	66	.7807	10.416	50.2	7	8	6	16	14	5	6	4	13	0	0	7	0	11	2	5	2	0	0	0	9	5	7	5	0
scarcely	118	.8364	19.814	53.0	8	16	7	26	29	18	14	0	34	4	3	13	0	5	1	3	2	1	1	0	17	17	14	3	0
scarcer	4	.1948	.2500	34.0	2	2	0	0	0	0	0	0	2	0	0	0	0	0	0	0	0	0	0	0	0	2	0	0	0
scarcity	6	.4426	.5660	37.5	1	1	0	2	1	0	1	0	0	0	0	0	0	1	0	0	0	0	0	0	0	1	2	2	0
Scard	2	.0000	.0243	23.9	0	0	0	0	2	0	0	0	0	0	0	0	0	0	0	0	0	0	0	0	0	0	0	2	0
scare	55	.6513	7.5585	48.8	16	14	7	4	11	2	1	0	24	0	0	5	0	1	2	0	0	0	0	0	7	12	1	3	0
scare-baby	2	.0000	.0914	29.6	0	0	0	2	0	0	0	0	2	0	0	0	0	0	0	0	0	0	0	0	0	0	0	0	0
scarecrow	30	.5073	3.3973	45.3	20	4	0	0	4	1	0	1	14	1	0	4	0	0	0	0	0	0	0	0	9	1	0	1	0
scarecrow's	2	.2446	.1125	30.5	0	1	0	0	1	0	0	0	0	1	0	1	0	0	0	0	0	0	0	0	0	0	0	0	0
scarecrows	3	.2437	.2277	33.6	0	2	0	0	0	0	0	1	2	0	0	0	0	0	0	1	0	0	0	0	0	0	0	0	0
scared	151	.7363	22.822	53.6	32	36	21	12	21	10	19	0	57	5	1	29	0	0	2	0	5	1	0	0	17	22	0	12	0
scared-cats	3	.0000	.0352	25.5	0	0	0	3	0	0	0	0	0	0	0	0	0	0	0	0	0	0	0	0	3	0	0	0	0
scares	5	.3473	.4170	36.2	2	0	1	0	1	1	0	0	2	0	1	1	0	0	0	0	0	0	0	0	1	0	0	0	0
scarf	50	.7326	7.4668	48.7	16	7	7	8	6	2	3	1	14	5	0	3	5	0	3	0	8	0	4	0	3	2	0	3	0
scarf-skin	2	.0000	.0290	24.6	0	0	0	0	2	0	0	0	0	0	0	0	0	0	0	0	0	0	0	0	0	2	0	0	0
scarfpin	2	.1717	.1142	30.6	0	0	0	0	2	0	0	0	1	0	0	1	0	0	0	0	0	0	0	0	0	0	0	0	0
scarfs	5	.3442	.3806	35.8	1	0	0	2	1	0	1	0	1	0	0	1	0	0	0	0	0	1	2	0	0	0	0	0	0
scaring	2	.1787	.1174	30.7	1	0	0	0	0	0	1	0	1	0	0	0	0	0	0	0	0	0	0	0	1	0	0	0	0
Scarlatti	3	.0000	.0243	23.8	0	1	0	1	0	1	0	0	0	0	0	0	0	0	0	0	3	0	0	0	0	0	0	0	0
scarlet	55	.7437	8.3775	49.2	5	6	8	11	11	3	7	4	19	0	2	5	0	1	0	8	4	0	0	0	8	1	3	4	0
Scarlet	4	.3813	.3772	35.8	0	0	1	0	1	2	0	0	2	0	0	0	0	1	0	0	0	0	0	0	0	1	0	0	0
scarp	3	.3762	.2496	34.0	0	1	1	0	0	0	1	0	0	0	0	0	0	0	0	1	0	0	0	0	0	1	1	0	0
scarred	13	.6289	1.7163	42.3	1	1	0	2	5	2	2	0	4	1	0	3	0	1	0	0	0	0	0	0	1	1	0	2	0
scarring	2	.1787	.1174	30.7	0	0	1	0	0	1	0	0	1	0	0	0	0	0	0	0	0	0	0	0	1	0	0	0	0
scars	18	.6132	2.3612	43.7	2	1	6	1	3	0	5	0	8	1	0	2	0	0	0	2	0	0	0	0	2	0	0	3	0
scarves	15	.6198	1.9440	42.9	5	1	4	3	2	0	0	0	3	0	1	1	3	4	0	0	0	0	0	0	0	0	1	2	0
scary	23	.6722	3.2479	45.1	12	4	3	1	1	2	0	0	11	2	1	0	0	1	0	0	1	0	0	0	3	1	0	3	0
scat	6	.3564	.5313	37.3	4	1	0	0	1	0	0	0	3	0	0	0	0	0	0	0	0	0	0	0	2	0	0	1	0
scatter	27	.7086	3.9273	45.9	6	1	6	10	1	1	2	0	6	0	0	2	0	0	1	7	2	0	0	0	0	5	2	2	0
scatterbrained	2	.1814	.1187	30.7	0	1	0	0	0	0	0	1	1	0	0	0	0	0	0	0	0	0	0	0	0	0	0	1	0
scattered	174	.8393	29.344	54.7	24	21	26	34	36	17	12	4	47	3	1	7	0	37	0	16	2	1	1	0	11	15	21	12	0
scattering	24	.7569	3.6779	45.7	4	4	2	4	5	5	0	0	5	0	1	4	0	0	0	2	1	1	0	0	2	3	3	2	0
scatters	4	.1335	.1958	32.9	1	1	1	0	1	0	0	0	1	0	0	0	0	0	0	3	0	0	0	0	0	0	0	0	0
scavenge	2	.2433	.1158	30.6	0	0	1	0	0	1	0	0	0	0	0	0	0	0	0	0	0	0	0	0	0	1	0	1	0
scavengers	6	.2445	.3637	35.6	0	0	0	0	2	3	1	0	0	0	0	0	0	0	0	4	0	0	0	0	0	0	2	0	0
Sceaux	3	.0000	.0434	26.4	0	0	0	0	0	0	0	3	0	0	0	0	0	0	0	0	0	0	0	0	0	3	0	0	0
scene	302	.7501	45.741	56.6	20	17	24	43	78	51	54	15	48	16	30	48	0	21	3	14	28	11	1	0	12	18	21	31	0
Scene	3	.2411	.1667	32.2	0	0	2	0	0	0	1	0	0	0	0	0	0	0	0	0	1	0	0	0	0	0	0	2	0
SCENE	2	.0000	.0215	23.3	0	0	0	0	2	0	0	0	0	0	0	2	0	0	0	0	0	0	0	0	0	0	0	0	0
scenery	54	.7603	8.3031	49.2	6	11	9	7	15	4	2	0	8	2	1	4	0	17	0	0	8	2	0	0	1	4	3	4	0
scenes	59	.7801	9.2689	49.7	6	7	4	4	11	14	10	3	10	2	2	9	0	10	0	0	10	2	1	0	0	3	4	6	0
Scenes	2	.0000	.0162	22.1	1	0	0	1	0	0	0	0	0	0	0	0	0	0	0	0	2	0	0	0	0	0	0	0	0
scenic	22	.6346	2.8750	44.6	3	3	4	1	2	1	4	4	3	1	0	0	2	0	0	1	1	0	0	2	0	3	2	7	0
scent	69	.6645	9.5250	49.8	5	9	8	9	12	5	4	17	21	2	1	5	0	2	0	0	0	0	0	0	8	3	5	22	0
scented	13	.4310	1.2825	41.1	0	0	2	1	7	2	0	1	5	0	0	4	0	0	0	0	0	0	0	0	3	0	0	1	0
scenting	9	.3534	.6960	38.4	0	1	0	0	2	1	0	5	0	0	0	1	0	0	0	0	0	0	0	0	1	1	0	6	0
scents	9	.4200	.8416	39.3	0	0	2	2	1	0	2	2	2	0	0	3	0	0	0	0	0	0	0	0	0	0	1	3	0
scepter	4	.3011	.2909	34.6	0	1	0	0	2	1	0	0	1	0	0	2	0	0	0	0	0	0	0	0	0	0	1	0	0
Schahriar	3	.0000	.0352	25.5	0	0	3	0	0	0	0	0	0	0	0	0	0	0	0	0	0	0	0	0	3	0	0	0	0
Scheat	2	.0000	.0394	26.0	0	0	0	0	0	0	0	2	0	0	0	0	0	0	0	2	0	0	0	0	0	0	0	0	0
schedule	61	.5701	7.3091	48.6	5	1	0	11	28	2	12	2	12	7	0	0	0	3	0	3	0	0	10	0	1	9	3	13	0
scheduled	24	.7242	3.5253	45.5	0	2	2	1	7	7	5	0	2	2	1	1	2	5	0	1	0	0	0	0	2	2	0	6	0
schedules	9	.6076	1.1433	40.6	0	0	0	2	6	1	0	0	2	0	0	0	0	0	1	0	0	0	0	0	1	2	1	2	0
Scheherazade	4	.3123	.2986	34.8	0	1	2	1	0	0	0	0	1	0	0	0	0	0	0	0	1	0	0	0	2	0	0	0	0
Scheherazade's	2	.0000	.0162	22.1	0	2	0	0	0	0	0	0	0	0	0	0	0	0	0	0	2	0	0	0	0	0	0	0	0
schematic	2	.1249	.0685	28.4	0	0	0	0	2	0	0	0	0	0	0	0	0	0	0	1	0	0	0	1	0	0	0	0	0
scheme	59	.8895	10.426	50.2	0	1	7	4	20	10	12	5	9	8	1	5	3	3	0	6	3	1	3	0	3	6	3	5	0
Scheme	5	.0000	.0724	28.6	0	0	5	0	0	0	0	0	0	0	0	0	0	0	0	0	0	0	0	0	0	5	0	0	0
schemes	10	.5279	1.0973	40.4	1	0	0	0	3	3	2	1	1	0	0	0	0	1	0	1	0	2	1	1	1	0	2	0	0
scheming	3	.3399	.2456	33.9	0	0	1	0	1	0	1	0	1	0	0	1	0	0	0	0	0	0	0	0	0	0	0	1	0

6H scalers
5D scalesome
7J scalewise
8G scallions
5R scallop-edge
7N scalping
5N scalplocks
7H scaly-wings
5B Scamp
5N scamped
5D scamperings
4B scampers
8F scandal
5Q Scandal
8B scandalized
7G scandere
6B Scandinavians'
7P scann'd
9D scanted
4P scantiest
8N scantling
9D scape
8F scapegoats
5H scaphe
XH scapula
6D Scar
4A scarabs
7A Scarborough
7R Scards
8A scared-like
4J scareder
4P scaredy-cats
3N scarerabbit
8R Scarface
4P Scarfoglio
8D scarified
XR scarlet-red
9H scarps
9H scarpside
3J scarum
3J Scat
4A SCAT
7N scathed
XR Scatter
7Q scavenged
7H scavenger
7Q scavenging
7R SCCA
XR scene's
3D scenery's
6A Scent
6F scepters
XN scepticism
7B sceptre
7D Schachachgokhos
9A Schaefer
7R Schaeffer
5N Schahzeman
6J schalmei
6H Schatz
9Q Schechter
7Q scheduling
6Q Scheele
XH Scheelite
7J Schelomo
5H Schematisme
5A schemed
6A schemers

Word Type	F	D	U	SFI	3 Gr 3	4 Gr 4	5 Gr 5	6 Gr 6	7 Gr 7	8 Gr 8	9 Gr 9	X UnGr	A Read	B Eng & Gr	C Comp	D Lit	E Math	F Soc Stud	G Spell	H Sci	J Music	K Art	L Home Ec	M Shop	N Lib F	P Lib NF	Q Lib Ref	R Mag	S Rel
Schenectady	2	.1698	.1133	30.5	0	0	1	1	0	0	0	0	1	0	0	0	0	0	0	0	0	0	0	0	0	0	1	0	0
scherzo	6	.1151	.1843	32.7	0	0	3	0	0	3	0	0	0	0	0	0	0	0	0	0	5	0	0	0	0	1	0	0	0
Scherzo	3	.0000	.0243	23.8	0	0	2	0	1	0	0	0	0	0	0	0	0	0	0	0	3	0	0	0	0	0	0	0	0
Schett	2	.0000	.0243	23.9	0	0	0	2	0	0	0	0	0	0	0	0	0	0	0	0	0	0	0	0	0	0	0	2	0
Schiller	5	.1854	.2289	33.6	0	0	0	0	1	4	0	0	0	0	0	0	0	0	0	0	0	0	0	0	4	0	1	0	0
Schiller's	2	.0000	.0234	23.7	0	0	0	0	0	2	0	0	0	0	0	0	0	0	0	0	0	0	0	0	2	0	0	0	0
schip	3	.0000	.0328	25.2	0	0	0	0	0	3	0	0	0	3	0	0	0	0	0	0	0	0	0	0	0	0	0	0	0
Schirra	3	.0000	.0328	25.2	0	0	3	0	0	0	0	0	0	3	0	0	0	0	0	0	0	0	0	0	0	0	0	0	0
schist	7	.0000	.1013	30.1	0	0	0	7	0	0	0	0	0	0	0	0	0	0	0	0	0	0	0	0	0	7	0	0	0
schists	5	.2235	.2839	34.5	0	0	0	3	0	0	1	1	0	0	0	0	0	0	0	2	0	0	0	0	0	3	0	0	0
schizophrenics	3	.0000	.0365	25.6	0	0	0	0	0	0	1	2	0	0	0	0	0	0	0	0	0	0	0	0	0	0	0	3	0
Schleiden	3	.2445	.1818	32.6	0	0	2	0	1	0	0	0	0	0	0	0	0	0	0	2	0	0	0	0	0	0	1	0	0
Schleimann	4	.0000	.1827	32.6	0	0	4	0	0	0	0	0	4	0	0	0	0	0	0	0	0	0	0	0	0	0	0	0	0
Schliemann	2	.0000	.0914	29.6	0	0	0	0	2	0	0	0	2	0	0	0	0	0	0	0	0	0	0	0	0	0	0	0	0
Schmeling	5	.0000	.2284	33.6	0	0	0	0	5	0	0	0	5	0	0	0	0	0	0	0	0	0	0	0	0	0	0	0	0
Schmidt	13	.2147	.7690	38.9	0	1	0	4	0	0	8	0	4	0	0	8	0	0	0	0	0	0	0	0	0	0	0	1	0
Scho	11	.0000	.5025	37.0	0	0	0	0	11	0	0	0	11	0	0	0	0	0	0	0	0	0	0	0	0	0	0	0	0
Schoeffer	2	.0000	.0209	23.2	0	0	2	0	0	0	0	0	0	0	0	0	0	0	0	0	0	0	0	0	0	0	2	0	0
scholar	26	.6872	3.6483	45.6	0	2	3	6	3	2	9	1	3	3	0	2	1	3	0	0	1	0	0	0	0	7	5	1	0
scholar-bureaucrats	2	.0000	.0389	25.9	0	0	0	0	0	2	0	0	0	0	0	0	0	2	0	0	0	0	0	0	0	0	0	0	0
scholar's	2	.2427	.1152	30.6	0	0	1	0	1	0	0	0	0	0	0	0	0	0	0	0	0	0	0	0	1	1	0	0	0
scholarly	6	.4063	.5388	37.3	0	0	0	0	3	0	3	0	1	0	0	0	0	0	0	0	1	0	0	0	0	0	1	3	0
scholars	56	.7229	8.2131	49.1	1	4	9	5	10	19	7	1	5	5	1	2	0	16	2	1	0	0	0	0	4	5	14	1	0
scholarship	12	.6221	1.5538	41.9	0	1	2	1	3	3	2	0	2	0	0	0	0	1	0	1	0	0	0	0	2	2	1	3	0
scholarships	8	.4387	.7384	38.7	0	0	1	0	2	0	5	0	0	4	0	0	0	0	0	0	1	0	0	0	0	0	1	2	0
scholastic	6	.2437	.3386	35.3	1	0	0	0	2	1	1	1	0	0	0	0	0	0	0	0	0	0	0	0	0	0	3	3	0
Scholastic	2	.0000	.0243	23.9	0	0	0	2	0	0	0	0	0	0	0	0	0	0	0	0	0	0	0	0	0	0	0	2	0
Schonberg	3	.0000	.0243	23.8	0	0	0	0	0	3	0	0	0	0	0	0	0	0	0	0	3	0	0	0	0	0	0	0	0
Schonberg's	3	.0000	.0243	23.8	0	0	0	0	0	3	0	0	0	0	0	0	0	0	0	0	3	0	0	0	0	0	0	0	0
school	2599	.9423	484.43	66.9	663	516	259	214	426	208	268	45	659	227	45	101	195	308	51	123	46	17	78	17	201	204	77	250	0
School	146	.8208	24.004	53.8	40	16	19	9	27	16	15	4	21	14	1	6	34	4	2	0	4	0	2	0	10	12	9	27	0
school-age	2	.2446	.1257	31.0	1	0	0	0	0	1	0	0	0	0	0	0	0	1	0	1	0	0	0	0	0	0	0	0	0
school-bag	5	.0000	.0586	27.7	5	0	0	0	0	0	0	0	0	0	0	0	0	0	0	0	0	0	0	0	5	0	0	0	0
school's	20	.7360	2.9831	44.7	1	4	4	1	2	4	3	1	3	3	1	2	1	0	1	1	0	0	0	0	1	4	0	3	0
schoolbag	2	.0000	.0914	29.6	1	0	0	0	1	0	0	0	2	0	0	0	0	0	0	0	0	0	0	0	0	0	0	0	0
schoolbook	2	.1698	.1133	30.5	0	0	0	1	1	0	0	0	1	0	0	0	0	0	0	0	0	0	0	0	0	0	1	0	0
schoolbooks	15	.5949	1.9312	42.9	2	6	3	0	2	1	1	0	8	1	1	0	0	1	0	0	0	0	0	1	2	1	0	0	0
schoolboy	16	.5713	1.9656	42.9	1	3	3	2	3	4	0	0	6	0	0	4	0	1	0	0	0	0	0	0	2	0	1	2	0
schoolboys	10	.5405	1.1592	40.6	2	2	1	1	1	1	1	1	2	0	0	1	0	1	0	1	0	0	0	0	0	4	0	1	0
schoolchildren	7	.4642	.7067	38.5	3	1	1	1	1	0	0	0	1	1	0	0	0	0	0	1	0	0	0	0	0	1	0	3	0
schoolfellows	2	.2444	.1132	30.5	0	0	0	2	0	0	0	0	0	1	0	0	0	0	0	0	0	0	0	0	1	0	0	0	0
schoolgirl	5	.4789	.5381	37.3	0	0	1	2	1	1	0	0	2	0	0	0	0	0	0	0	0	0	0	0	1	1	0	1	0
schoolhouse	43	.6301	5.7215	47.6	10	10	3	7	8	4	1	0	16	1	0	2	0	1	1	0	1	0	0	0	10	10	0	1	0
schoolhouses	5	.3766	.4670	36.7	1	3	0	0	1	0	0	0	3	0	0	0	0	0	0	0	1	0	0	0	0	0	1	0	0
schooling	26	.6994	3.7981	45.8	3	4	4	4	2	5	4	0	12	1	1	0	0	7	1	0	1	0	0	0	1	0	1	1	0
schoolmaster	24	.5491	2.8917	44.6	0	15	0	1	4	3	1	0	11	0	0	2	0	0	0	0	1	0	0	0	1	8	1	0	0
schoolmaster's	2	.0000	.0914	29.6	0	2	0	0	0	0	0	0	2	0	0	0	0	0	0	0	0	0	0	0	0	0	0	0	0
schoolmate	3	.2330	.1860	32.7	1	0	0	0	1	0	1	0	1	0	0	0	0	0	0	0	0	0	1	0	0	1	0	0	0
schoolmates	4	.2780	.2956	34.7	1	0	1	1	0	0	1	0	2	0	0	0	0	0	0	0	0	0	1	0	0	0	0	1	0
schoolroom	40	.6031	5.1962	47.2	20	4	3	4	0	4	5	0	20	1	2	5	0	2	0	0	0	0	0	0	7	3	0	0	0
schoolrooms	2	.2405	.1205	30.8	1	1	0	0	0	0	0	0	0	0	0	0	0	0	0	1	0	0	0	0	0	1	0	0	0
schools	420	.7523	64.065	58.1	46	44	51	43	90	42	97	7	55	12	4	2	9	146	0	13	9	0	1	3	5	26	51	84	0
Schools	4	.1698	.2267	33.6	1	0	0	0	3	0	0	0	2	0	0	0	0	0	0	0	0	0	0	0	0	0	2	0	0
schoolteacher	8	.5925	.9933	40.0	2	0	1	0	1	0	4	0	1	1	0	1	0	3	0	0	0	0	0	0	1	1	0	0	0
schoolteachers	5	.3380	.4246	36.3	1	1	0	0	2	0	1	0	2	0	0	0	0	1	0	0	0	0	0	0	0	2	0	0	0
schoolwork	14	.5975	1.7792	42.5	1	3	2	1	2	0	5	0	5	3	0	2	0	1	0	1	0	0	0	1	0	0	0	1	0
schoolyard	16	.6019	1.9743	43.0	2	5	4	2	1	1	1	0	0	1	0	2	2	0	0	1	0	0	0	0	6	2	0	2	0
schooner	30	.6842	4.2365	46.3	0	0	6	8	11	2	3	0	9	0	2	2	0	2	1	0	1	0	0	0	6	0	3	4	0
schooner's	3	.2175	.1545	31.9	0	1	1	1	0	0	0	0	0	0	0	2	0	0	0	0	0	0	0	0	0	0	0	1	0
schooners	12	.4733	1.3012	41.1	2	0	1	5	0	1	2	1	6	0	1	0	0	1	0	0	0	0	0	0	0	3	0	1	0
schottische	3	.2009	.1407	31.5	1	0	2	0	0	0	0	0	0	0	0	0	0	0	0	0	2	0	0	0	1	0	0	0	0
Schramm	2	.0000	.0243	23.9	0	0	0	0	2	0	0	0	0	0	0	0	0	0	0	0	0	0	0	0	0	0	0	2	0
Schubert	17	.0387	.3337	35.2	1	0	1	5	4	6	0	0	2	0	0	0	0	0	0	0	15	0	0	0	0	0	0	0	0
Schubert's	4	.0000	.0323	25.1	0	0	0	1	3	0	0	0	0	0	0	0	0	0	0	0	4	0	0	0	0	0	0	0	0
Schuller	4	.0000	.0323	25.1	0	0	0	4	0	0	0	0	0	0	0	0	0	0	0	0	4	0	0	0	0	0	0	0	0
Schulthess	2	.0000	.0215	23.3	0	0	0	0	0	2	0	0	0	0	0	2	0	0	0	0	0	0	0	0	0	0	0	0	0
Schultz	6	.0000	.2741	34.4	0	6	0	0	0	0	0	0	6	0	0	0	0	0	0	0	0	0	0	0	0	0	0	0	0
Schuman	9	.0000	.0728	28.6	0	0	4	0	1	4	0	0	0	0	0	0	0	0	0	0	9	0	0	0	0	0	0	0	0
Schumann	18	.1504	.6685	38.3	1	1	0	6	3	6	1	0	0	0	0	0	0	0	0	0	15	0	0	0	0	2	1	0	0
Schuster	5	.0000	.0724	28.6	0	5	0	0	0	0	0	0	0	0	0	0	0	0	0	0	0	0	0	0	0	5	0	0	0
Schuyler	3	.0000	.0583	27.7	0	0	0	0	0	3	0	0	0	0	0	0	0	3	0	0	0	0	0	0	0	0	0	0	0
Schuylkill	5	.3609	.3959	36.0	0	0	0	3	2	0	0	0	0	0	0	1	0	0	0	0	0	0	0	0	0	3	1	0	0
schwa	79	.0952	2.0776	43.2	0	15	19	13	20	12	0	0	0	6	0	0	0	0	72	0	0	0	0	0	0	0	0	1	0
Schwann	3	.2445	.1818	32.6	0	0	2	0	1	0	0	0	0	0	0	0	0	0	0	2	0	0	0	0	0	0	1	0	0
Schweitzer	4	.2891	.2856	34.6	0	0	2	2	0	0	0	0	1	2	0	0	0	0	0	0	0	0	0	0	0	1	0	0	0
Schwinn	2	.0000	.0243	23.9	0	0	0	0	2	0	0	0	0	0	0	0	0	0	0	0	0	0	0	0	0	0	0	2	0
science	602	.8371	100.93	60.0	41	74	68	67	118	90	121	23	100	44	3	6	39	27	22	166	1	4	3	3	3	9	129	42	1
Science	40	.6752	5.4903	47.4	3	9	4	2	12	3	4	3	1	5	0	1	2	1	0	8	1	0	0	0	3	2	13	3	0
science-fiction	9	.5052	.9652	39.8	0	0	0	1	3	0	4	1	1	0	1	3	1	0	0	2	0	0	0	0	0	0	1	0	0
science-oriented	2	.0000	.0209	23.2	0	0	0	0	0	0	2	0	0	0	0	0	0	0	0	0	0	0	0	0	0	0	2	0	0
science's	2	.2437	.1129	30.5	0	0	0	0	0	0	1	1	0	0	0	0	0	0	0	0	0	0	0	0	0	0	1	1	0
sciences	35	.4373	3.2645	45.1	0	1	6	3	7	3	14	1	0	0	0	0	1	2	2	7	0	0	0	0	1	1	20	1	0
Sciences	9	.2855	.5755	37.6	0	0	4	1	2	0	1	1	0	0	0	0	0	0	0	0	0	0	0	0	1	0	6	2	0
scientific	364	.8072	58.966	57.7	19	29	33	51	67	73	80	12	35	8	1	5	51	17	9	103	2	2	5	5	3	15	86	17	0
Scientific	3	.2143	.1568	32.0	0	0	1	0	1	1	0	0	0	0	0	0	0	0	0	0	0	0	0	0	0	1	0	2	0
scientifically	8	.5254	.8737	39.4	0	1	0	1	1	0	5	0	0	1	0	1	0	0	1	2	0	0	0	0	0	0	3	0	0
scientist	353	.6884	50.244	57.0	62	72	45	66	37	20	47	4	68	8	0	2	11	14	2	181	0	1	1	4	1	20	30	10	0
Scientist	2	.2437	.1129	30.5	0	0	0	1	1	0	0	0	0	0	0	0	0	0	0	0	0	0	0	0	0	0	1	1	0
scientist's	7	.2395	.4133	36.2	0	1	1	1	0	0	4	0	0	0	0	0	0	0	0	4	0	0	0	0	0	0	3	0	0
scientists	1062	.6985	152.40	61.8	184	156	164	235	134	86	86	17	132	13	2	3	12	53	5	588	4	0	8	4	1	61	82	93	1
scientists'	2	.2160	.1362	31.3	0	1	0	1	0	0	0	0	1	0	0	0	0	0	0	1	0	0	0	0	0	0	0	0	0
Scillies	5	.0000	.0608	27.8	0	0	0	0	5	0	0	0	0	0	0	0	0	0	0	0	0	0	0	0	0	0	0	5	0
Scilly	5	.4243	.4716	36.7	1	0	0	0	4	0	0	0	1	0	0	0	0	0	0	0	0	0	0	0	0	1	1	2	0

9J scherzos
5P Scheveningen
6A Schiaparelli
7R Schiefer
XR Schifano
6R Schistocerca
XR schizo's
9R schizophrenic
7D Schka'ak
8D Schlapp
7R Schleidt
5A Schleimann's
XR schlepp
3Q Schleswig-Holstein
XR Schneider
9D schnell
7A Scho's
8J Schoenberg
6B Schoffer
XJ scholasticism
5E SCHOOL
7R school-ager
8J school-band
9F school-board
9R school-bond
5P school-boy
4H school-building
XE school-day
4A school-houses
7P school-master
7N school-time
3N school-yard
7D schoolbell
4F schoolboy's
3A schoolday
8Q schooled
7A schoolhalls
9R schoolman
7N schoolmarm
7A schoolmarms'
6P schoolmasters
4P schooltime
9D schoolyard's
5N schoolyards
8B schoone
9A Schrafft's
5P Schreiner
5P Schreiner's
9Q Schrodinger
7D Schuler
5J Schuman's
7J Schumanns
7D Schwanammek
6J Schwanda
7D schwannack
6R Schwartz
6A Schwartzwalder
9J Schwarzkopf
7G schwas
7R Schweizer
7G sci
9L Science's
7H scientific-supply
5P scientist-explorer
4H scientist-occupants
7J scientist-philosopher
5P Scientists
XN Scientists'

Word Type	F	D	U	SFI	3 Gr 3	4 Gr 4	5 Gr 5	6 Gr 6	7 Gr 7	8 Gr 8	9 Gr 9	X UnGr	A Read	B Eng & Gr	C Comp	D Lit	E Math	F Soc Stud	G Spell	H Sci	J Music	K Art	L Home Ec	M Shop	N Lib F	P Lib NF	Q Lib Ref	R Mag	S Rel
scimitar	2	.2407	.1138	30.6	0	0	1	0	0	0	1	0	0	0	0	1	0	0	0	0	0	0	0	0	0	1	0	0	0
scissor	3	.2687	.2001	33.0	2	0	0	0	1	0	0	0	1	0	0	0	0	0	0	0	1	0	1	0	0	0	0	0	0
scissors	72	.6457	9.6733	49.9	22	9	12	9	14	3	0	3	19	0	0	1	5	1	0	17	3	7	7	1	2	6	0	3	0
Scleroscope	6	.0000	.0151	21.8	0	0	0	0	0	0	6	0	0	0	0	0	0	0	0	0	0	0	0	6	0	0	0	0	0
scoff	7	.5304	.7988	39.0	0	0	0	3	1	1	1	1	2	0	0	2	0	0	0	0	0	0	0	0	1	0	1	1	0
scoffed	9	.5577	1.1129	40.5	1	2	0	4	1	1	0	0	5	0	0	0	0	1	0	0	0	0	0	0	1	1	0	1	0
scoffing	2	.1717	.1142	30.6	0	0	0	1	0	1	0	0	1	0	0	1	0	0	0	0	0	0	0	0	0	0	0	0	0
scold	19	.6382	2.5669	44.1	7	3	4	1	0	4	0	0	8	0	1	1	0	3	1	0	0	0	0	0	3	2	0	0	0
scolded	44	.7217	6.6286	48.2	13	12	5	7	2	2	2	1	26	3	1	3	0	1	0	0	0	1	0	0	2	5	0	2	0
scolding	20	.5234	2.3374	43.7	7	3	0	2	4	2	0	2	11	1	2	3	0	0	0	0	0	0	0	0	1	1	0	1	0
Scone	5	.0000	.0523	27.2	0	0	0	0	0	0	5	0	0	0	0	0	0	0	0	0	0	0	0	0	0	0	5	0	0
scones	2	.1787	.1174	30.7	0	0	1	1	0	0	0	0	1	0	0	0	0	0	0	0	0	0	0	0	1	0	0	0	0
scoop	16	.7307	2.3621	43.7	4	2	4	1	4	1	0	0	1	1	0	1	0	2	1	1	0	0	1	0	0	3	1	4	0
scooped	23	.6987	3.3152	45.2	4	2	7	3	4	3	0	0	7	0	0	4	0	2	0	1	0	0	0	1	4	2	1	1	0
scooping	4	.2680	.2737	34.4	0	0	1	1	1	0	1	0	1	0	0	0	0	1	0	0	0	0	0	0	0	0	2	0	0
scoops	11	.5211	1.2046	40.8	6	1	0	0	3	0	1	0	1	0	0	0	0	0	0	1	0	0	1	0	0	1	3	4	0
scoot	3	.3852	.2500	34.0	1	1	0	0	0	0	1	0	0	0	0	1	0	0	0	0	0	0	0	0	0	1	0	1	0
scooted	3	.2261	.2131	33.3	0	1	0	1	1	0	0	0	2	0	0	0	0	0	0	0	0	0	0	0	1	0	0	0	0
scooter	6	.3922	.5392	37.3	0	2	0	2	2	0	0	0	2	1	0	2	0	0	0	0	0	0	0	1	0	0	0	0	0
Scooter	15	.1029	.5831	37.7	0	11	4	0	0	0	0	0	4	0	0	0	0	0	0	0	0	0	0	0	11	0	0	0	0
scooters	5	.3496	.4069	36.1	1	1	0	1	0	0	2	0	1	0	0	0	0	2	0	0	0	0	0	1	0	0	1	0	0
scooting	2	.2440	.1132	30.5	0	0	0	1	1	0	0	0	0	0	0	1	0	0	0	0	0	0	0	0	0	0	0	1	0
scope	24	.6258	3.0987	44.9	0	0	0	1	4	8	8	3	3	2	0	5	0	1	0	1	0	0	0	0	0	2	5	5	0
scorched	21	.6764	2.9431	44.7	0	7	3	2	7	1	1	0	6	0	1	3	0	1	0	3	0	0	0	0	3	0	1	3	0
scorching	11	.5419	1.3145	41.2	0	1	1	2	3	1	0	3	5	0	0	0	0	1	0	0	0	0	0	0	2	2	0	1	0
score	411	.6273	52.735	57.2	87	65	38	41	94	59	22	5	28	23	1	7	124	4	140	4	36	0	5	0	14	11	5	9	0
Score	9	.4779	.8956	39.5	2	3	0	0	0	1	3	0	0	3	0	0	3	0	2	0	0	0	0	1	0	0	0	0	0
SCORE	2	.0000	.0914	29.6	0	2	0	0	0	0	0	0	2	0	0	0	0	0	0	0	0	0	0	0	0	0	0	0	0
scoreboard	3	.2227	.1589	32.0	0	0	0	1	2	0	0	0	0	0	0	0	0	0	0	0	0	0	0	0	2	0	0	1	0
scored	65	.7732	10.186	50.1	26	5	4	6	6	12	5	1	15	4	0	0	17	2	0	4	2	0	0	1	5	4	2	9	0
Scored	4	.0000	.0599	27.8	0	0	0	0	0	0	4	0	0	0	0	0	4	0	0	0	0	0	0	0	0	0	0	0	0
scorer	2	.2433	.1158	30.6	0	0	0	0	2	0	0	0	0	0	0	0	0	0	0	0	0	0	0	0	0	1	0	1	0
scores	87	.7354	12.954	51.1	13	11	9	9	11	21	8	5	9	2	2	4	34	3	1	4	6	0	0	0	0	3	8	11	0
scoring	26	.7122	3.8240	45.8	0	1	2	4	12	4	3	0	10	3	0	2	0	1	0	0	0	1	0	0	2	2	1	4	0
scorn	18	.5892	2.2036	43.4	0	2	2	2	6	4	2	0	3	0	1	6	0	0	1	0	1	0	0	0	5	0	0	1	0
scorned	7	.5328	.8000	39.0	1	0	0	0	3	0	2	1	2	0	0	2	0	0	0	0	1	0	0	0	0	0	1	1	0
scornful	10	.5114	1.1124	40.5	1	2	1	3	1	1	1	0	3	0	0	0	0	0	0	0	0	0	0	0	3	1	2	1	0
scornfully	23	.5294	2.7139	44.3	0	6	3	5	4	4	1	0	12	1	0	2	0	0	0	0	0	0	0	0	5	3	0	0	0
scorning	2	.2440	.1132	30.5	0	0	0	0	0	0	1	1	0	0	0	1	0	0	0	0	0	0	0	0	0	0	0	1	0
scorns	2	.2411	.1091	30.4	0	0	0	0	1	0	1	0	0	0	0	1	0	0	0	0	1	0	0	0	0	0	0	0	0
Scorpio	2	.0000	.0394	26.0	0	0	0	0	0	0	0	2	0	0	0	0	0	0	0	2	0	0	0	0	0	0	0	0	0
scorpion	8	.0915	.2300	33.6	0	0	0	0	7	0	0	1	0	0	0	7	0	0	0	1	0	0	0	0	0	0	0	0	0
Scorpion	5	.3177	.3576	35.5	0	0	0	0	4	0	0	1	0	0	0	0	0	0	0	1	0	0	0	0	0	0	1	3	0
scorpions	6	.4058	.5461	37.4	3	1	0	0	1	1	0	0	1	0	1	0	0	0	0	2	0	0	0	0	0	1	0	1	0
scort	3	.0000	.0243	23.9	0	3	0	0	0	0	0	0	0	0	0	0	0	0	3	0	0	0	0	0	0	0	0	0	0
Scot	3	.3877	.2482	33.9	0	0	0	0	1	1	1	0	0	1	0	1	0	0	0	0	0	0	0	0	0	0	1	0	0
scotch	2	.2278	.1128	30.5	0	1	0	0	0	1	1	0	0	0	0	0	0	0	0	1	0	0	0	0	0	0	1	0	0
Scotch	13	.5244	1.4474	41.6	3	2	2	1	2	3	0	0	2	0	0	0	0	0	1	2	4	0	0	0	1	3	0	0	0
Scotch-Irish	3	.3769	.2484	34.0	0	0	1	0	0	1	0	1	0	0	0	0	0	1	0	0	0	0	0	0	0	0	1	1	0
Scotchman	2	.2427	.1152	30.6	1	0	0	0	1	0	0	0	0	0	0	0	0	0	0	0	0	0	0	0	1	1	0	0	0
Scotia	12	.4917	1.2458	41.0	0	1	4	2	3	1	1	0	0	0	0	0	0	4	0	1	2	0	0	0	0	1	4	0	0
Scotland	79	.6920	11.206	50.5	6	6	18	12	16	7	12	2	16	4	0	1	0	12	3	0	12	0	0	0	1	7	18	5	0
Scotland's	7	.4559	.6713	38.3	1	0	1	2	1	1	1	0	0	0	0	1	0	1	0	0	3	0	0	0	0	1	0	1	0
Scots	9	.6109	1.1271	40.5	0	0	1	2	2	3	1	0	0	2	0	1	0	2	0	0	0	0	0	0	2	1	1	0	0
Scott	89	.7756	14.084	51.5	2	10	20	21	15	17	3	1	34	8	0	1	7	14	0	0	4	0	0	0	8	6	4	3	0
Scott's	5	.3676	.4527	36.6	1	0	1	2	1	0	0	0	2	0	0	0	0	2	0	0	0	0	0	0	0	1	0	0	0
Scottie	2	.1814	.1187	30.7	1	0	1	0	0	0	0	0	1	0	0	0	0	0	0	0	0	0	0	0	0	0	0	1	0
Scottish	43	.6328	5.5665	47.5	0	3	9	6	5	11	8	1	3	7	0	2	1	3	0	2	12	0	0	0	0	3	8	2	0
Scotts	2	.0000	.0914	29.6	0	0	1	1	0	0	0	0	2	0	0	0	0	0	0	0	0	0	0	0	0	0	0	0	0
Scotty	118	.1528	7.9956	49.0	0	0	0	2	1	115	0	0	114	0	0	3	0	0	0	0	0	0	0	0	0	1	0	0	0
Scotty's	4	.2424	.3036	34.8	0	0	0	2	0	1	0	1	3	0	0	0	0	0	0	0	0	0	0	0	0	0	0	1	0
scoundrel	7	.5198	.7664	38.8	1	1	1	1	2	1	0	0	1	0	0	2	0	0	1	0	1	0	0	0	2	0	0	0	0
scour	2	.2130	.1056	30.2	0	0	0	1	0	0	1	0	0	0	0	0	0	0	1	1	0	0	0	0	0	0	0	0	0
scoured	9	.4664	.9055	39.6	0	0	5	0	2	2	0	0	1	0	0	3	0	1	0	0	0	0	0	0	0	3	1	0	0
scourge	6	.3759	.5761	37.6	0	1	0	4	0	0	0	1	4	0	0	0	0	0	0	1	0	0	0	0	0	0	1	0	0
scouring	9	.4367	.8872	39.5	1	1	1	3	1	0	2	0	2	0	0	2	0	0	0	4	0	0	0	0	0	0	0	1	0
scout	53	.7908	8.3983	49.2	5	9	7	5	25	2	0	0	4	6	1	4	1	3	1	1	1	0	0	0	13	6	7	5	0
Scout	50	.7697	7.7414	48.9	6	7	10	1	2	6	5	13	4	5	1	4	8	0	1	3	1	0	1	0	0	12	0	10	0
scouting	15	.5880	1.8826	42.7	2	3	3	3	1	0	2	1	5	1	0	2	0	0	0	1	0	0	0	0	0	4	0	2	0
Scouting	2	.0000	.0290	24.6	0	0	0	0	0	0	0	2	0	0	0	0	0	0	0	0	0	0	0	0	0	2	0	0	0
scoutmaster	2	.1362	.0684	28.3	1	0	0	0	1	0	0	0	0	0	1	0	1	0	0	0	0	0	0	0	0	0	0	0	0
scouts	47	.6522	6.3047	48.0	10	4	5	5	5	13	2	3	5	1	3	2	19	4	0	2	0	0	0	0	1	3	1	6	0
Scouts	64	.6008	7.9646	49.0	14	10	4	17	4	1	0	14	4	1	1	0	19	2	1	3	0	0	0	0	0	15	0	18	0
scow	7	.3396	.5492	37.4	0	1	1	0	4	1	0	0	1	0	0	0	0	1	0	0	0	0	0	0	0	0	1	4	0
scowl	7	.4046	.6252	38.0	2	1	1	0	2	0	0	1	1	0	0	2	0	0	0	0	0	0	0	0	1	0	0	3	0
scowled	32	.6099	4.1433	46.2	7	9	3	1	9	0	3	0	12	2	0	6	0	0	0	0	0	0	0	0	4	5	0	3	0
scowling	3	.2212	.2099	33.2	0	1	0	1	0	1	0	0	2	0	0	1	0	0	0	0	0	0	0	0	0	0	0	0	0
scows	3	.1937	.1495	31.7	0	0	1	0	2	0	0	0	0	0	0	0	0	1	0	0	0	0	0	0	0	0	0	2	0
scr	2	.0000	.0162	22.1	0	0	1	1	0	0	0	0	0	0	0	0	0	0	2	0	0	0	0	0	0	0	0	0	0
scrabbled	3	.3394	.2451	33.9	0	0	1	0	2	0	0	0	1	0	0	1	0	0	0	0	0	0	0	0	1	0	0	0	0
scraggly	6	.5156	.6598	38.2	5	0	0	0	0	1	0	0	1	0	0	1	0	0	0	0	0	0	0	0	1	1	0	2	0
scram	2	.1733	.1149	30.6	0	0	1	0	0	0	0	1	1	1	0	0	0	0	0	0	0	0	0	0	0	0	0	0	0
scramble	21	.7087	3.0819	44.9	4	6	2	4	3	2	0	0	8	1	0	1	0	2	0	0	0	0	0	0	2	3	1	3	0
scrambled	84	.6492	11.468	50.6	15	20	11	12	14	6	5	1	35	9	0	4	0	1	11	0	0	0	0	0	15	5	0	4	0
scrambling	24	.6400	3.2632	45.1	4	5	2	2	4	3	3	1	12	3	1	1	0	0	0	0	0	0	0	0	3	1	0	3	0
scrap	43	.5780	5.1578	47.1	4	5	5	2	11	13	3	0	7	0	0	4	0	1	1	3	0	3	1	10	3	4	1	5	0
scrapbook	26	.7176	3.8355	45.8	6	3	9	0	1	3	3	1	7	0	0	0	5	4	2	3	0	0	1	0	2	0	0	2	0
scrapbooks	2	.2446	.1142	30.6	0	0	0	0	0	0	1	1	0	0	0	0	0	0	0	0	0	0	0	0	1	0	0	1	0
scrape	41	.8546	6.9958	48.4	10	9	4	4	6	2	5	1	7	1	2	4	0	4	1	8	1	1	2	1	3	5	1	0	0
Scrape	2	.0000	.0389	25.9	0	0	0	0	2	0	0	0	0	0	0	0	0	2	0	0	0	0	0	0	0	0	0	0	0
scraped	41	.7972	6.6082	48.2	7	6	6	10	8	1	3	0	11	1	0	2	0	4	0	5	1	1	0	0	6	2	3	5	0
scraper	12	.0476	.1736	32.4	0	1	0	0	8	1	2	0	0	0	0	0	0	1	0	1	0	0	0	10	0	0	0	0	0
scrapers	7	.2228	.3542	35.5	0	0	0	1	6	0	0	0	0	0	0	0	0	0	0	0	0	0	0	3	0	3	1	0	0
scrapes	8	.6104	1.0093	40.0	2	2	1	1	2	0	0	0	1	1	0	0	0	0	0	1	0	0	0	1	1	1	1	1	0
scraping	19	.4195	1.7382	42.4	0	3	0	3	11	2	0	0	4	0	0	3	0	1	0	0	1	0	1	6	2	0	0	1	0
scrapings	2	.0000	.0394	26.0	0	0	0	0	2	0	0	0	0	0	0	0	0	0	0	2	0	0	0	0	0	0	0	0	0

7N scimitars
8Q scintillant
9R scintillating
7Q scions
7N scissored
6A scissoring
3A Scituate
6H sclera
9Q sclerosis
8B scoffingly
4A scolds
9Q scolecite
9Q SCOLECITE
7N scombrus
6A sconces
9Q SCONE
4N Scoot
7N scootched
7R scoots
3E scorekeeper
9D scoreless
9R scorers'
3G Scores
9E Scoring
3P scorneth
7A scornin'
7R Scorpion's
3P Scotsman
8F Scotsmen
7Q Scottish-born
9F Scottsboro
XR Scottsdale
8A Scotty'll
4N scoundrels
XR scoured-the
7A scourged
4Q scourges
6R Scout-o-rama
6R Scoutmaster
9R scouts'
4J scowly
6N scrabbling
4D scraggy
6R scrambler
9R scramblers
3P scrambles
6P scramblings
7M Scraping

Word Type	F	D	U	SFI	3 Gr 3	4 Gr 4	5 Gr 5	6 Gr 6	7 Gr 7	8 Gr 8	9 Gr 9	X UnGr	A Read	B Eng & Gr	C Comp	D Lit	E Math	F Soc Stud	G Spell	H Sci	J Music	K Art	L Home Ec	M Shop	N Lib F	P Lib NF	Q Lib Ref	R Mag	S Rel
scrapped	2	.1814	.1187	30.7	0	0	0	0	0	1	0	1	1	0	0	0	0	0	0	0	0	0	0	0	0	0	0	1	0
scrappy	2	.0000	.0290	24.6	2	0	0	0	0	0	0	0	0	0	0	0	0	0	0	0	0	0	0	0	0	2	0	0	0
scraps	40	.6225	5.1828	47.1	4	11	4	5	8	4	2	2	11	1	0	1	0	1	0	1	0	5	5	1	3	5	3	3	0
scratch	96	.8472	16.287	52.1	15	19	12	17	16	8	9	0	24	4	1	2	8	7	4	13	3	6	1	3	9	2	4	5	0
Scratch	5	.2579	.3199	35.0	0	1	0	0	1	0	3	0	1	0	0	3	0	0	0	0	0	0	0	0	1	0	0	0	0
scratchboard	2	.0000	.0037	15.7	0	0	0	2	0	0	0	0	0	0	0	0	0	0	0	0	0	2	0	0	0	0	0	0	0
scratched	96	.7521	14.826	51.7	18	21	19	12	15	8	2	1	42	3	2	3	1	3	0	6	3	4	0	0	18	8	2	1	0
scratches	15	.6358	1.9832	43.0	3	2	1	3	2	1	2	1	2	1	0	0	2	2	0	4	0	0	0	0	3	1	0	0	0
scratching	45	.6395	6.1105	47.9	3	12	8	6	9	5	2	0	22	1	0	2	0	0	1	1	0	2	0	0	11	3	1	1	0
scratchy	9	.3890	.7889	39.0	0	2	3	1	3	0	0	0	2	0	0	0	0	0	0	0	3	0	0	0	3	1	0	0	0
scrawl	2	.2407	.1138	30.6	0	0	0	1	1	0	0	0	0	0	0	1	0	0	0	0	0	0	0	0	0	1	0	0	0
scrawled	5	.3456	.4158	36.2	0	2	0	0	2	0	1	0	2	0	1	1	0	0	0	0	0	0	0	0	0	0	0	1	0
scrawny	7	.2607	.4728	36.7	0	2	2	1	1	0	1	0	2	0	0	0	0	0	0	0	0	0	0	0	0	1	0	4	0
scream	51	.7168	7.4771	48.7	12	3	7	5	16	3	4	1	13	4	1	5	0	0	1	0	0	0	0	0	13	6	2	6	0
screamed	99	.6723	14.022	51.5	22	15	12	14	23	4	9	0	51	7	2	18	0	2	0	0	0	0	0	0	10	3	1	5	0
screamer	2	.1160	.0650	28.1	0	0	0	0	0	1	1	0	0	0	1	0	0	0	0	1	0	0	0	0	0	0	0	0	0
screaming	46	.5982	5.8325	47.7	8	7	9	9	4	6	3	0	15	1	0	7	0	0	0	1	0	0	1	0	14	6	0	1	0
screams	26	.6807	3.6819	45.7	5	1	4	3	5	6	1	1	10	0	0	3	0	1	0	1	3	0	1	0	4	0	0	3	0
screech	17	.6345	2.3232	43.7	4	3	0	7	1	0	2	0	10	1	0	0	0	1	0	1	0	0	0	0	2	1	0	1	0
screeched	13	.5966	1.6850	42.3	4	0	1	4	3	1	0	0	7	0	0	2	0	1	0	0	0	0	0	0	1	1	0	1	0
screeches	3	.3400	.2455	33.9	0	0	0	0	2	1	0	0	1	1	0	0	0	0	0	0	0	0	0	0	1	0	0	0	0
screeching	23	.6500	3.1749	45.0	4	7	3	2	4	1	2	0	12	1	0	1	0	0	0	0	2	0	0	0	3	3	0	1	0
screen	174	.8154	28.453	54.5	13	30	34	30	31	23	7	6	24	4	1	12	33	8	1	37	2	7	3	12	5	6	5	14	0
screened	11	.4411	1.0562	40.2	1	0	0	1	4	1	2	2	1	0	0	0	1	2	0	0	0	0	0	0	2	0	0	5	0
screening	8	.5803	.9718	39.9	0	1	1	3	3	0	0	0	1	0	0	0	2	0	0	1	0	0	0	0	1	0	1	2	0
screens	33	.5570	3.9022	45.9	3	3	6	9	8	3	0	1	8	0	0	0	6	1	0	4	0	1	0	6	1	1	2	3	0
screw	100	.3563	7.7259	48.9	4	7	1	30	20	16	19	3	2	0	2	2	0	3	1	33	0	0	2	40	5	2	1	7	0
screwdriver	14	.3975	1.1609	40.6	2	0	3	3	3	3	0	0	0	0	2	0	0	0	0	1	0	0	0	5	1	1	0	4	0
Screwdrivers'	2	.0000	.0914	29.6	0	2	0	0	0	0	0	0	2	0	0	0	0	0	0	0	0	0	0	0	0	0	0	0	0
screwed	22	.5245	2.4575	43.9	5	1	2	1	6	2	1	4	4	0	0	1	0	1	0	2	0	0	0	2	9	0	0	3	0
screwing	2	.0000	.0215	23.3	0	0	0	1	1	0	0	0	0	0	0	2	0	0	0	0	0	0	0	0	0	0	0	0	0
screws	66	.3029	4.3724	46.4	4	5	3	12	19	12	9	2	2	0	0	0	1	0	0	13	0	2	0	32	4	3	6	3	0
Scriabin	2	.0000	.0162	22.1	0	0	0	0	0	2	0	0	0	0	0	0	0	0	0	0	2	0	0	0	0	0	0	0	0
scrib	3	.0000	.0243	23.9	0	0	0	0	3	0	0	0	0	0	0	0	0	0	3	0	0	0	0	0	0	0	0	0	0
scribbled	6	.5430	.7061	38.5	0	0	0	3	1	2	0	0	2	0	0	1	0	1	1	0	0	0	0	0	0	1	0	0	0
scribbling	3	.1187	.1291	31.1	0	0	0	0	1	0	2	0	1	0	0	2	0	0	0	0	0	0	0	0	0	0	0	0	0
scribe	8	.5036	.8478	39.3	1	0	0	2	2	2	1	0	0	0	0	0	1	3	1	0	0	0	0	1	0	2	0	0	0
scribere	3	.0000	.0243	23.9	0	0	0	0	3	0	0	0	0	0	0	0	0	0	3	0	0	0	0	0	0	0	0	0	0
scribes	18	.1282	.6307	38.0	3	0	1	2	4	5	1	2	0	3	0	0	1	3	2	0	0	0	0	0	0	4	1	1	3
Scribes	2	.2306	.1140	30.6	0	0	0	2	0	0	0	0	0	1	0	0	0	1	0	0	0	0	0	0	0	0	0	0	0
scribing	2	.0000	.0050	17.0	0	0	0	0	0	1	1	0	0	0	0	0	0	0	0	0	0	0	0	2	0	0	0	0	0
Scribner's	3	.0000	.0434	26.4	0	3	0	0	0	0	0	0	0	0	0	0	0	0	0	0	0	0	0	0	0	3	0	0	0
scrimmage	9	.4765	.9870	39.9	0	0	0	1	2	4	2	0	5	1	0	0	0	0	0	0	0	0	0	0	1	0	0	2	0
scrimped	2	.1717	.1142	30.6	0	1	0	0	1	0	0	0	1	0	0	1	0	0	0	0	0	0	0	0	0	0	0	0	0
Scripps	2	.2278	.1128	30.5	0	0	0	0	1	1	0	0	0	0	0	0	0	0	0	1	0	0	0	0	0	0	1	0	0
script	20	.4940	2.0480	43.1	0	3	0	0	10	1	5	1	0	6	0	1	0	0	5	0	1	0	0	0	0	0	0	7	0
scripts	4	.3678	.3187	35.0	0	0	1	0	1	1	0	1	0	0	0	0	0	0	1	0	0	0	0	0	0	1	0	2	0
Scripture	5	.3416	.4181	36.2	0	0	0	2	2	1	0	0	2	0	0	0	0	0	0	0	0	0	0	0	2	0	1	0	0
Scriptures	3	.0000	.0314	25.0	0	0	0	0	2	1	0	0	0	0	0	0	0	0	0	0	0	0	0	0	0	0	3	0	0
scroll	28	.3229	2.1120	43.2	3	1	0	9	11	2	2	0	7	0	0	5	0	1	0	0	0	0	0	8	7	0	0	0	0
scrolls	6	.1959	.2916	34.6	1	0	0	1	2	0	1	1	1	0	0	0	0	0	0	0	0	0	0	3	1	0	1	0	0
Scrooby	3	.0000	.0434	26.4	0	3	0	0	0	0	0	0	0	0	0	0	0	0	0	0	0	0	0	0	0	3	0	0	0
scrooched	2	.0000	.0914	29.6	0	2	0	0	0	0	0	0	2	0	0	0	0	0	0	0	0	0	0	0	0	0	0	0	0
Scrooge	48	.5265	5.6446	47.5	0	12	0	0	25	10	1	0	26	2	0	6	0	0	1	0	0	0	0	0	12	0	1	0	0
scrounging	3	.2261	.2131	33.3	0	1	0	0	2	0	0	0	2	0	0	0	0	0	0	0	0	0	0	0	1	0	0	0	0
scrub	36	.6944	5.1326	47.1	3	5	3	8	10	5	2	0	9	2	0	3	0	2	1	1	0	0	3	0	10	1	1	3	0
scrubbed	25	.6292	3.3343	45.2	5	3	1	0	5	7	3	1	11	3	0	2	0	0	0	0	0	0	1	0	6	1	1	0	0
scrubbing	16	.5505	1.9419	42.9	1	4	1	2	2	4	2	0	8	0	0	1	0	1	0	0	0	0	0	0	4	1	0	1	0
scrubby	4	.2152	.2714	34.3	1	0	1	0	1	0	1	0	2	0	0	0	0	2	0	0	0	0	0	0	0	0	0	0	0
scrubwoman	2	.0000	.0215	23.3	0	0	0	0	2	0	0	0	0	0	0	2	0	0	0	0	0	0	0	0	0	0	0	0	0
scruple	2	.2446	.1125	30.5	0	0	0	0	0	0	2	0	0	1	0	1	0	0	0	0	0	0	0	0	0	0	0	0	0
scrupulous	2	.2351	.1166	30.7	0	0	0	0	1	1	0	0	0	0	0	0	0	1	0	0	0	0	0	0	0	0	0	1	0
scrutinized	4	.4529	.3998	36.0	0	0	0	1	3	0	0	0	1	0	0	0	0	0	0	0	0	0	0	0	1	0	1	1	0
scrutiny	5	.4017	.4228	36.3	0	0	0	0	3	1	1	0	0	0	1	0	0	0	0	0	0	0	0	0	1	0	2	1	0
SCS	11	.0000	.2169	33.4	0	0	0	0	0	0	0	11	0	0	0	0	0	0	0	11	0	0	0	0	0	0	0	0	0
scuba	13	.3852	1.2440	40.9	0	3	1	7	2	0	0	0	7	0	0	0	0	0	0	4	0	0	0	0	0	0	0	2	0
scudding	2	.1458	.0682	28.3	1	0	0	0	0	0	1	0	0	1	0	0	0	0	0	0	0	1	0	0	0	0	0	0	0
scuff	5	.2446	.3872	35.9	4	0	1	0	0	0	0	0	4	0	0	0	0	0	0	0	0	0	0	0	1	0	0	0	0
scuffed	6	.3689	.5007	37.0	1	0	0	1	3	0	1	0	1	0	0	3	0	0	0	0	0	0	0	0	1	1	0	0	0
scuffle	6	.5489	.6762	38.3	1	1	0	0	2	2	0	0	0	1	0	2	0	0	0	0	1	0	0	0	1	0	0	1	0
scuffled	2	.2440	.1132	30.5	0	0	1	0	1	0	0	0	0	0	0	1	0	0	0	0	0	0	0	0	0	0	0	1	0
scuffling	7	.3277	.5736	37.6	1	2	0	1	2	1	0	0	3	0	0	0	0	0	0	0	0	0	0	0	3	0	1	0	0
scullery	4	.0000	.0469	26.7	0	0	2	0	2	0	0	0	0	0	0	0	0	0	0	0	0	0	0	0	4	0	0	0	0
sculling	3	.3272	.2361	33.7	0	1	1	0	1	0	0	0	1	0	0	0	0	0	0	0	1	0	0	0	0	0	1	0	0
scullion	2	.0000	.0914	29.6	0	0	0	2	0	0	0	0	2	0	0	0	0	0	0	0	0	0	0	0	0	0	0	0	0
sculptor	44	.3792	3.7487	45.7	2	11	2	7	9	4	8	1	9	3	0	1	0	8	1	0	1	11	0	0	0	0	7	3	0
sculptor's	2	.0580	.0676	28.3	0	0	0	0	0	1	1	0	1	0	0	0	0	0	0	0	0	1	0	0	0	0	0	0	0
sculptors	22	.2030	1.0352	40.2	3	0	3	1	2	9	3	1	0	1	0	0	0	5	0	0	0	10	0	0	0	2	4	0	0
sculptural	8	.0799	.1587	32.0	0	0	1	0	1	4	2	0	0	0	0	0	0	0	0	0	0	6	0	0	0	1	1	0	0
sculpture	72	.1984	3.3070	45.2	5	9	3	5	9	22	10	9	4	2	0	0	0	4	0	1	6	38	0	0	0	2	5	10	0
sculptured	9	.4320	.8483	39.3	0	0	0	0	5	1	3	0	2	0	1	1	0	1	0	0	0	2	0	0	0	0	2	0	0
sculptures	11	.1548	.4303	36.3	2	1	0	1	2	3	0	2	1	0	0	0	0	1	0	0	0	6	0	0	0	1	1	1	0
sculpturing	2	.0000	.0243	23.9	0	0	0	0	1	0	0	1	0	0	0	0	0	0	0	0	0	0	0	0	0	0	0	2	0
scum	8	.3439	.6283	38.0	2	0	2	0	1	1	2	0	0	0	0	0	0	0	0	6	0	0	1	0	0	0	0	1	0
scupper	2	.0000	.0914	29.6	0	0	0	0	2	0	0	0	2	0	0	0	0	0	0	0	0	0	0	0	0	0	0	0	0
scurried	16	.5327	1.8084	42.6	3	3	0	4	5	0	0	1	3	2	2	3	0	0	0	1	0	0	0	0	0	4	0	1	0
scurry	8	.5922	.9977	40.0	1	2	0	2	1	0	0	2	2	2	0	1	0	0	0	1	1	0	0	0	1	0	0	0	0
Scurry	3	.0000	.1370	31.4	0	3	0	0	0	0	0	0	3	0	0	0	0	0	0	0	0	0	0	0	0	0	0	0	0
scurrying	16	.5706	1.9724	43.0	3	4	0	3	3	2	1	0	7	0	1	3	0	0	0	0	0	0	0	0	0	1	1	3	0
scurvy	14	.3798	1.2432	40.9	0	1	9	2	1	0	1	0	2	0	0	0	0	3	0	8	0	0	0	0	0	0	0	1	0
scuttle	6	.4393	.5955	37.7	1	1	1	1	2	0	0	0	2	1	0	2	0	0	0	0	0	0	0	0	0	1	0	0	0
scuttled	10	.4716	1.0776	40.3	2	5	0	0	2	1	0	0	5	0	0	2	0	0	0	0	0	0	0	0	2	0	0	1	0
scuttling	6	.3636	.5318	37.3	2	0	1	1	1	1	0	0	3	1	1	0	0	0	0	0	0	0	0	0	1	0	0	0	0
Scylla	4	.0000	.0429	26.3	0	0	0	0	0	0	4	0	0	0	0	4	0	0	0	0	0	0	0	0	0	0	0	0	0

8C scrapping
6A scratch-scratch
9D Scratch's
9Q scratched-up
7A scrawling
XH scrawls
5N screamin'
7P screamingly
4D screech-owl's
7P screened-in
6R screenplay

7R screenwriter
7N screw-driver
5B screwball
7E screwdrivers
7R screwless
8G scriba
5N scribble
4N scribblers
9N scribbles
4Q Scribe
3N scribe's

7M scribed
9M scriber
4P Scribner
8D scrimmages
XR scrimmaging
9D scrip
9R scriptural
6N scripture
7R scriptwriter
4A scritch-scratched
8B scrivener

6A scriveners
7A• Scrooge's
XN scroonched
4P scrouged
3Q scrubs
4J Scrubs
8D scruff
7A scruffy
XR scrummaging
8L scrumptious
3B Scrumptious

XD scruples
9R scrupulously
7D scrutinizes
7C scrutinizing
6G scssrs
5B scudded
6R Scudder
6P Scudder's
5A scuffed-up
4N scuffing
7R sculled

5A Sculpin
5A Sculpin's
4R sculpted
8J sculpting
9Q Sculpture
7Q scup
8G scuppernongs
5Q scuro
6A scurvy-ridden
8F scutage
7R scuttlebutt

Word Type	F	D	U	SFI	3 Gr 3	4 Gr 4	5 Gr 5	6 Gr 6	7 Gr 7	8 Gr 8	9 Gr 9	X UnGr	A Read	B Eng & Gr	C Comp	D Lit	E Math	F Soc Stud	G Spell	H Sci	J Music	K Art	L Home Ec	M Shop	N Lib F	P Lib NF	Q Lib Ref	R Mag	S Rel
scythe	14	.3960	1.3226	41.2	0	5	3	3	1	2	0	0	6	0	0	0	0	2	0	0	0	0	0	0	5	1	0	0	0
scythes	2	.1948	.1250	31.0	0	2	0	0	0	0	0	0	1	0	0	0	0	0	0	0	0	0	0	0	0	1	0	0	0
SDS	5	.0000	.0608	27.8	0	0	0	0	0	0	4	1	0	0	0	0	0	0	0	0	0	0	0	0	0	0	0	5	0
se	13	.2434	.7187	38.6	1	4	2	0	3	3	0	0	0	8	0	0	0	0	5	0	0	0	0	0	0	0	0	0	0
SE	14	.2884	.9233	39.7	0	1	3	0	0	1	9	0	0	9	0	0	3	1	0	1	0	0	0	0	0	0	0	0	0
sea	1812	.8922	322.28	65.1	372	272	210	326	366	147	89	30	509	58	9	84	22	291	13	256	47	22	1	3	147	150	137	63	0
Sea	473	.7206	70.622	58.5	36	178	45	83	76	37	12	6	186	13	0	1	3	153	1	8	9	4	0	0	9	20	46	20	0
sea-faring	3	.3759	.2471	33.9	0	0	0	1	1	0	1	0	0	1	0	0	0	1	0	0	0	0	0	0	0	0	1	0	0
sea-going	3	.3374	.2433	33.9	2	0	0	0	0	1	0	0	1	1	0	0	0	0	0	0	0	0	0	0	0	0	1	0	0
sea-gull	5	.0000	.2284	33.6	0	5	0	0	0	0	0	0	5	0	0	0	0	0	0	0	0	0	0	0	0	0	0	0	0
sea-gull's	2	.1717	.1142	30.6	0	1	0	0	1	0	0	0	1	0	0	1	0	0	0	0	0	0	0	0	0	0	0	0	0
sea-hunters	2	.2297	.1135	30.6	0	0	0	0	1	1	0	0	0	0	0	1	0	1	0	0	0	0	0	0	0	0	0	0	0
sea-level	4	.2298	.2346	33.7	2	0	1	0	1	0	0	0	0	0	0	0	0	3	0	0	0	0	0	0	1	0	0	0	0
sea-monster	3	.1187	.1291	31.1	0	0	0	0	1	0	2	0	1	0	0	2	0	0	0	0	0	0	0	0	0	0	0	0	0
sea-run	5	.0000	.0608	27.8	0	0	0	0	5	0	0	0	0	0	0	0	0	0	0	0	0	0	0	0	0	0	0	5	0
sea-shine	2	.0000	.0215	23.3	0	0	0	0	2	0	0	0	0	0	0	2	0	0	0	0	0	0	0	0	0	0	0	0	0
sea's	5	.5552	.5731	37.6	0	0	0	2	2	1	0	0	0	0	0	0	0	1	0	0	1	0	0	0	1	0	1	1	0
seabirds	3	.3815	.2534	34.0	0	0	2	0	0	0	0	1	0	0	0	0	0	1	0	0	0	0	0	0	0	1	0	1	0
seaboard	6	.4317	.5817	37.6	2	0	1	0	0	2	1	0	1	0	0	0	0	3	0	0	0	0	0	0	1	0	0	1	0
Seaboard	5	.1927	.2617	34.2	1	0	3	0	1	0	0	0	1	0	0	0	0	0	0	1	3	0	0	0	0	0	0	0	0
Seabold	5	.0000	.2284	33.6	0	5	0	0	0	0	0	0	5	0	0	0	0	0	0	0	0	0	0	0	0	0	0	0	0
seacoast	21	.5811	2.5959	44.1	4	2	5	5	3	1	1	0	4	0	0	1	0	8	0	3	0	0	0	0	0	3	2	0	0
seacoasts	6	.4498	.5952	37.7	1	0	0	1	0	3	1	0	1	0	0	0	0	2	0	1	0	0	1	0	0	0	1	0	0
seafarer	2	.2278	.1128	30.5	0	0	0	0	2	0	0	0	0	0	0	0	0	0	0	1	0	0	0	0	0	0	1	0	0
seafarers	3	.3350	.2478	33.9	0	0	1	1	1	0	0	0	1	0	0	0	0	1	0	0	0	0	0	0	0	0	1	0	0
seafaring	12	.5773	1.4295	41.6	1	1	0	3	3	2	1	1	1	0	0	3	0	1	2	0	0	1	0	0	3	0	1	0	0
seafood	8	.3214	.5998	37.8	1	5	1	0	1	0	0	0	0	0	0	1	0	6	0	0	0	0	0	0	1	0	0	0	0
seagoing	7	.3347	.5099	37.1	1	0	0	0	3	3	0	0	0	2	0	1	0	0	0	0	0	0	0	0	0	0	4	0	0
seagulls	3	.0000	.1370	31.4	1	0	2	0	0	0	0	0	3	0	0	0	0	0	0	0	0	0	0	0	0	0	0	0	0
seahorse	12	.1112	.3903	35.9	0	11	0	0	1	0	0	0	0	0	0	0	0	0	0	0	0	0	0	0	0	0	1	11	0
seahorse's	2	.0000	.0243	23.9	0	2	0	0	0	0	0	0	0	0	0	0	0	0	0	0	0	0	0	0	0	0	0	2	0
seahorses	2	.0000	.0243	23.9	0	2	0	0	0	0	0	0	0	0	0	0	0	0	0	0	0	0	0	0	0	0	0	2	0
seal	84	.8827	14.788	51.7	8	13	18	11	17	10	5	2	22	9	2	7	1	7	2	13	1	1	1	0	2	12	2	2	0
Seal	4	.2010	.2271	33.6	0	3	0	0	1	0	0	0	1	0	0	0	0	2	0	0	0	1	0	0	0	0	0	0	0
Sealab	8	.2284	.6152	37.9	0	0	0	8	0	0	0	0	7	0	0	0	0	0	0	0	0	0	0	0	0	0	0	1	0
Sealacell	2	.1483	.0728	28.6	0	0	0	0	1	1	0	0	0	0	0	0	0	0	0	0	0	0	0	1	0	1	0	0	0
sealed	63	.7641	9.7223	49.9	4	6	5	6	22	7	10	3	7	0	1	5	0	2	0	17	1	0	0	1	2	6	8	13	0
Sealed	2	.2446	.1125	30.5	0	0	0	0	1	1	0	0	0	1	0	1	0	0	0	0	0	0	0	0	0	0	0	0	0
sealed-in	6	.0000	.1183	30.7	0	0	6	0	0	0	0	0	0	0	0	0	0	0	0	6	0	0	0	0	0	0	0	0	0
sealer	9	.1101	.2406	33.8	0	0	0	2	7	0	0	0	0	0	0	0	0	0	0	0	0	0	0	6	0	0	0	3	0
sealing	8	.4824	.8368	39.2	2	0	1	2	0	2	1	0	2	0	1	0	0	0	0	0	1	0	0	0	0	2	2	0	0
seals	49	.8287	8.1581	49.1	15	4	4	4	13	6	2	1	12	1	0	2	1	2	0	6	1	1	0	1	2	9	7	4	0
seals'	2	.0000	.0914	29.6	0	0	0	0	2	0	0	0	2	0	0	0	0	0	0	0	0	0	0	0	0	0	0	0	0
sealskin	8	.4756	.8909	39.5	4	3	0	0	0	1	0	0	5	0	0	1	0	1	0	0	0	0	0	0	0	1	0	0	0
sealskins	6	.4731	.6398	38.1	0	3	0	0	2	0	1	0	2	1	0	0	0	2	0	0	0	0	0	0	0	1	0	0	0
seam	123	.2424	6.2896	48.0	1	0	0	2	24	42	52	2	2	1	0	2	0	2	0	1	0	0	88	24	0	2	0	1	0
seaman	18	.5838	2.2485	43.5	3	7	1	2	4	1	0	0	6	0	0	0	0	2	1	0	0	0	0	0	3	5	0	1	0
Seaman	2	.1948	.1250	31.0	0	0	0	0	1	0	1	0	1	0	0	0	0	0	0	0	0	0	0	0	0	1	0	0	0
seaman's	6	.4858	.6602	38.2	0	2	0	2	1	0	1	0	3	0	0	1	0	0	0	0	0	0	0	0	1	0	1	0	0
seamanship	3	.1930	.1642	32.2	0	0	0	1	2	0	0	0	1	0	1	0	0	0	0	0	0	0	0	0	0	1	0	0	0
seamed	2	.1621	.0746	28.7	0	0	0	0	0	1	1	0	0	0	1	1	0	0	0	0	0	0	0	0	0	0	0	0	0
seamen	34	.6959	4.9170	46.9	4	5	0	8	10	5	2	0	11	0	0	1	0	11	0	3	1	0	0	0	1	2	3	1	0
seamline	9	.0000	.0290	24.6	0	0	0	0	9	0	0	0	0	0	0	0	0	0	0	0	0	0	9	0	0	0	0	0	0
seams	82	.2451	4.3618	46.4	4	0	0	0	19	17	42	0	5	0	0	2	0	2	0	0	0	0	57	12	1	0	3	0	0
seamstress	3	.2540	.1940	32.9	1	0	0	1	0	0	1	0	1	0	0	0	0	0	0	0	0	0	1	0	0	0	1	0	0
Seaography	2	.0000	.0219	23.4	0	0	2	0	0	0	0	0	0	2	0	0	0	0	0	0	0	0	0	0	0	0	0	0	0
seaport	38	.4474	3.7490	45.7	6	8	7	10	4	1	1	1	3	0	0	0	0	24	0	0	0	0	0	0	1	4	5	1	0
seaports	26	.4595	2.5876	44.1	2	2	8	6	6	2	0	0	0	2	0	1	1	18	0	0	0	0	0	0	0	1	3	0	0
search	246	.8937	43.745	56.4	24	30	34	30	66	28	26	8	57	10	3	11	1	27	4	30	9	7	2	1	10	22	27	24	1
Search	3	.2435	.2274	33.6	0	3	0	0	0	0	0	0	2	0	0	0	0	1	0	0	0	0	0	0	0	0	0	0	0
searched	76	.7921	12.213	50.9	10	9	10	14	22	5	2	4	27	4	1	8	1	4	1	1	1	0	0	0	6	7	1	14	0
searchers	6	.2942	.4422	36.5	0	0	2	0	1	0	0	3	1	0	0	0	0	0	0	4	0	0	0	0	0	0	1	0	0
searches	11	.6303	1.4302	41.6	3	2	2	1	1	1	0	1	1	1	0	0	0	0	1	3	1	0	0	0	0	1	0	3	0
searching	106	.7776	16.721	52.2	22	16	11	15	27	10	5	0	30	3	2	5	1	12	1	8	1	2	0	2	7	9	10	12	1
searchingly	2	.1814	.1187	30.7	0	0	1	0	0	0	0	1	1	0	0	0	0	0	0	0	0	0	0	0	0	0	0	1	0
searchlight	5	.2320	.3834	35.8	0	0	0	2	2	0	1	0	4	0	0	0	0	0	0	1	0	0	0	0	0	0	0	0	0
searchlights	5	.1875	.3065	34.9	0	1	2	1	0	0	1	0	2	0	0	0	0	0	0	3	0	0	0	0	0	0	0	0	0
Searcy	8	.0000	.0938	29.7	0	0	0	0	8	0	0	0	0	0	0	0	0	0	0	0	0	0	0	0	8	0	0	0	0
Seares	2	.0000	.0243	23.9	0	0	0	0	2	0	0	0	0	0	0	0	0	0	0	0	0	0	0	0	0	0	0	2	0
searing	4	.3614	.3220	35.1	1	2	0	0	1	0	0	0	0	0	0	1	0	0	0	1	0	0	0	0	0	2	0	0	0
seas	191	.8113	31.173	54.9	36	16	28	29	38	25	17	2	30	9	3	5	0	52	1	27	4	0	0	1	5	17	28	9	0
Seas	16	.5192	1.8893	42.8	4	1	2	3	3	2	1	0	10	0	0	0	0	2	0	0	0	1	0	0	1	1	1	0	0
seashells	4	.4818	.4128	36.2	0	2	0	0	1	0	0	1	0	0	0	0	0	1	0	1	0	0	0	0	0	1	0	1	0
seashore	54	.7736	8.4789	49.3	8	16	7	5	11	4	2	1	12	2	2	0	0	2	1	21	1	1	0	0	3	3	3	3	0
seasick	4	.3303	.3297	35.2	0	1	0	1	0	0	0	2	1	0	0	0	0	1	0	2	0	0	0	0	0	0	0	0	0
seaside	8	.5179	.8581	39.3	2	1	1	0	3	1	0	0	0	0	1	0	0	0	0	1	0	1	0	0	1	3	0	1	0
Seaside	3	.1639	.1674	32.2	0	2	1	0	0	0	0	0	1	0	0	0	0	2	0	0	0	0	0	0	0	0	0	0	0
season	370	.8849	65.131	58.1	49	48	46	75	82	32	28	10	53	10	1	19	4	80	4	35	14	1	13	1	12	29	32	61	1
season-long	2	.0000	.0243	23.9	0	1	0	0	0	0	1	0	0	0	0	0	0	0	0	0	0	0	0	0	0	0	0	2	0
season's	8	.2664	.5122	37.1	0	1	0	1	2	0	2	2	1	0	0	0	0	0	0	0	0	0	0	0	0	0	2	5	0
seasonal	24	.7214	3.4896	45.4	0	0	2	1	8	8	4	1	0	0	0	1	0	2	1	6	1	1	1	0	0	1	7	3	0
seasonally	2	.2278	.1128	30.5	0	1	0	0	0	0	1	0	0	0	0	0	0	0	0	1	0	0	0	0	0	0	1	0	0
seasoned	12	.4327	1.0854	40.4	0	1	1	2	3	0	5	0	0	0	0	2	0	0	0	1	0	0	4	0	2	1	1	1	0
seasoning	14	.4523	1.3061	41.2	0	0	0	2	5	0	5	2	0	0	0	1	0	0	0	1	0	0	5	2	0	1	1	3	0
seasonings	14	.0000	.0451	26.5	0	0	0	0	2	0	12	0	0	0	0	0	0	0	0	0	0	0	14	0	0	0	0	0	0
seasons	175	.5134	19.109	52.8	60	22	16	27	21	19	10	0	12	11	0	9	0	28	9	52	3	0	1	1	1	14	18	12	4
Seasons	3	.0000	.0243	23.8	0	0	2	0	0	1	0	0	0	0	0	0	0	0	0	0	3	0	0	0	0	0	0	0	0
seat	339	.8547	58.179	57.6	63	56	32	31	84	37	32	4	132	25	4	29	1	15	2	7	3	0	1	4	31	30	15	40	0
seated	87	.7404	13.144	51.2	8	13	6	8	27	13	11	1	25	2	4	11	1	6	0	3	1	0	6	0	12	13	0	3	0
seating	7	.5269	.7981	39.0	1	0	0	2	2	2	0	0	2	0	0	0	0	1	0	0	1	0	0	0	1	0	0	2	0
seats	143	.8835	25.179	54.0	24	27	6	13	41	16	14	2	35	6	0	7	32	8	3	2	2	1	2	1	7	17	6	14	0
Seattle	48	.6715	6.5921	48.2	1	8	14	3	12	6	4	0	3	3	0	6	2	15	0	1	1	0	0	0	0	1	4	12	0
seaward	16	.6682	2.2138	43.5	1	1	0	5	6	2	1	0	4	0	0	1	0	1	0	1	0	0	0	0	3	1	2	3	0

7Q scythed
7P Scythian
4N scything
XQ Scyths
4A sea-
9D Sea-Nymphs
7B Sea-Wind
8D sea-beasts
6A sea-bird
5P sea-birds
6A sea-blue
9F sea-borne
6H sea-bottom
4P sea-dyke
9R sea-feeding
8B sea-fight
7Q sea-floor
7D sea-fog
8D Sea-goddess
6D sea-green
8B sea-lice
7N sea-mile
8D sea-otter
7N sea-salute
4A sea-shell
7N sea-song
7Q sea-turtle
7N sea-unicorns
4N sea-voyages
7N sea-water
8D seabag
4P Seabird
7A seacrets
5R Seafair
6A Seafaring
5C seagull
4D seagulls'
4G seal-oil
4P seal's
7R sealed-off
6A sealers
3R sealife
7B sealing-wax
8M seam-welding
9M seamer
5B seamews
9L seamless
7L seamlines
XR seamounts
4J seamstresses
7R Sean
4A seaplanes
3P Seaport
XH searcher
3P searcheth
XH searchings
XH seared
9H Searles
7Q searobins
7R Sears
3R seashell
3J seashores
3B Season
3H SEASONS
5A seasons'
7R seat-belt
7R seater
7D Seathl
9F SEATO
8D Seaton
5R Seattle's

Word Type	F	D	U	SFI	3 Gr 3	4 Gr 4	5 Gr 5	6 Gr 6	7 Gr 7	8 Gr 8	9 Gr 9	X UnGr	A Read	B Eng & Gr	C Comp	D Lit	E Math	F Soc Stud	G Spell	H Sci	J Music	K Art	L Home Ec	M Shop	N Lib F	P Lib NF	Q Lib Ref	R Mag	S Rel
seawater	18	.3141	1.3680	41.4	6	0	0	1	3	1	7	0	1	0	0	0	0	4	0	12	0	0	0	0	0	1	0	0	0
seaway	4	.2285	.2258	33.5	0	0	0	0	0	0	4	0	0	0	0	0	0	2	0	0	0	0	0	0	0	0	2	0	0
Seaway	4	.2680	.2737	34.4	0	0	1	0	3	0	0	0	1	0	0	0	0	1	0	0	0	0	0	0	0	0	2	0	0
seaweed	41	.7449	6.2370	47.9	15	8	4	6	4	3	1	0	12	0	1	8	0	1	0	5	0	1	0	0	1	5	2	5	0
seaweeds	5	.3219	.3937	36.0	3	0	1	1	0	0	0	0	1	0	0	0	0	0	0	2	0	0	0	0	0	2	0	0	0
seaworthy	3	.3769	.2484	34.0	0	0	0	1	0	1	1	0	0	0	0	0	0	1	0	0	0	0	0	0	0	0	1	1	0
Sebastian	25	.2662	1.4922	41.7	3	3	3	7	5	3	1	0	0	0	0	0	0	2	0	0	17	0	0	0	0	3	3	0	0
sec	8	.2588	.4968	37.0	0	1	4	0	1	1	1	0	0	0	0	0	6	0	0	1	0	0	0	0	1	0	0	0	0
Sec	12	.1088	.3367	35.3	0	0	0	0	1	0	11	0	0	0	0	0	0	0	0	3	0	0	0	8	0	0	1	0	0
secare	2	.0000	.0219	23.4	0	0	0	2	0	0	0	0	0	2	0	0	0	0	0	0	0	0	0	0	0	0	0	0	0
secede	6	.3612	.4858	36.9	1	0	5	0	0	0	0	0	0	0	0	0	0	3	0	0	0	0	0	0	0	1	2	0	0
seceded	3	.3766	.2497	34.0	1	1	0	0	0	1	0	0	0	0	0	0	0	1	0	0	0	0	0	0	0	1	1	0	0
seceding	2	.0000	.0389	25.9	0	0	2	0	0	0	0	0	0	0	0	0	0	2	0	0	0	0	0	0	0	0	0	0	0
secession	13	.3756	1.1564	40.6	0	0	3	0	5	4	1	0	3	0	0	0	0	8	0	0	0	0	0	0	0	0	1	1	0
Secession	2	.0000	.0914	29.6	0	0	0	1	1	0	0	0	2	0	0	0	0	0	0	0	0	0	0	0	0	0	0	0	0
secluded	5	.3750	.4036	36.1	0	0	0	0	2	2	0	1	0	0	0	2	0	0	0	0	0	0	0	0	0	0	1	2	0
seclusion	5	.4174	.4631	36.7	0	0	0	0	0	1	4	0	1	0	0	2	0	0	0	0	0	0	0	0	1	0	0	1	0
Seco	3	.0000	.1370	31.4	0	3	0	0	0	0	0	0	3	0	0	0	0	0	0	0	0	0	0	0	0	0	0	0	0
second	2094	.9447	390.80	65.9	287	271	290	344	359	295	213	35	346	247	39	63	308	103	156	183	208	9	23	38	72	100	91	107	1
Second	44	.6945	6.2947	48.0	12	4	7	7	2	7	5	0	10	2	0	1	2	11	0	0	0	0	0	0	8	4	5	1	0
SECOND	4	.0000	.0429	26.3	0	0	0	0	0	1	3	0	0	0	0	4	0	0	0	0	0	0	0	0	0	0	0	0	0
second-best	3	.2435	.2274	33.6	0	0	0	2	0	0	1	0	2	0	0	0	0	1	0	0	0	0	0	0	0	0	0	0	0
second-class	6	.2408	.3612	35.6	0	0	0	0	0	2	1	3	0	0	0	0	0	3	0	0	0	0	0	0	0	3	0	0	0
second-floor	8	.5651	.9906	40.0	4	0	0	1	2	0	0	1	4	0	0	1	1	0	0	0	0	0	0	0	0	1	0	1	0
second-growth	2	.2291	.1135	30.5	0	0	0	0	1	0	0	1	0	0	0	1	0	0	0	1	0	0	0	0	0	0	0	0	0
second-hand	9	.3383	.7786	38.9	3	0	2	1	2	1	0	0	5	0	0	3	0	0	0	0	0	0	0	0	1	0	0	0	0
second-largest	4	.4777	.4091	36.1	0	1	1	0	1	1	0	0	0	0	0	1	0	1	0	1	0	0	0	0	0	1	0	0	0
second-place	2	.2433	.1158	30.6	0	0	0	0	0	1	0	1	0	0	0	0	0	0	0	0	0	0	0	0	0	1	0	1	0
second-story	2	.2446	.1142	30.6	0	0	0	0	0	0	0	2	0	0	0	0	0	0	0	0	0	0	0	0	1	0	0	1	0
second-string	2	.2442	.1134	30.5	0	0	0	0	0	1	1	0	0	1	0	0	0	0	0	0	0	0	0	0	0	0	0	1	0
second-team	2	.1717	.1142	30.6	0	0	0	1	0	1	0	0	1	0	0	1	0	0	0	0	0	0	0	0	0	0	0	0	0
second-year	3	.0000	.0365	25.6	0	0	0	0	2	0	1	0	0	0	0	0	0	0	0	0	0	0	0	0	0	0	0	3	0
secondary	70	.5937	8.4896	49.3	2	1	6	9	14	17	18	3	3	2	1	0	0	2	15	10	1	0	2	14	0	2	13	5	0
seconded	9	.1038	.2749	34.4	0	1	0	0	2	4	2	0	0	8	0	0	0	0	0	0	0	0	0	0	0	1	0	0	0
secondhand	9	.4801	.9679	39.9	1	0	0	3	2	1	2	0	4	0	1	2	0	0	0	0	0	0	0	0	1	0	1	0	0
secondly	4	.2847	.2818	34.5	0	0	0	0	2	1	1	0	1	0	0	0	0	0	0	0	0	0	0	0	0	1	2	0	0
seconds	239	.8228	39.585	56.0	33	24	16	43	58	35	24	6	63	9	1	16	58	5	1	28	0	0	2	6	7	7	8	28	0
secrecy	14	.4849	1.5235	41.8	0	1	0	1	4	6	1	1	6	0	0	1	0	0	0	0	0	0	0	0	1	0	1	5	0
secret	276	.8468	47.098	56.7	53	47	29	49	42	27	25	4	126	9	5	23	5	14	3	7	4	0	1	0	22	24	9	24	0
Secret	34	.3838	3.0504	44.8	3	0	1	0	17	11	1	1	10	1	0	2	0	0	0	0	0	0	0	0	0	19	0	2	0
secretarial	2	.2437	.1129	30.5	0	0	1	0	0	0	1	0	0	0	0	0	0	0	0	0	0	0	0	0	0	0	1	1	0
secretariat	2	.2401	.1133	30.5	0	0	1	0	0	0	0	1	0	0	0	0	0	0	0	0	0	0	0	0	0	1	1	0	0
Secretariat	11	.3767	1.0203	40.1	0	0	0	5	0	1	3	2	5	0	0	0	0	4	0	0	0	0	0	0	0	0	0	2	0
secretaries	13	.5685	1.5118	41.8	0	0	0	3	7	0	3	0	0	1	0	0	0	1	0	0	1	0	2	0	0	1	4	3	0
Secretaries	2	.2408	.1204	30.8	1	0	0	0	0	0	1	0	0	0	0	0	0	1	0	0	0	0	0	0	0	1	0	0	0
secretary	55	.6463	7.3054	48.6	4	8	8	2	14	11	8	0	6	7	0	0	3	9	1	0	0	0	0	0	4	2	17	6	0
Secretary	60	.6087	7.5597	48.8	1	0	6	0	5	24	23	1	3	3	0	0	0	23	0	1	5	0	0	0	1	2	5	17	0
Secretary-General	10	.2391	.6129	37.9	0	0	0	3	1	4	2	0	2	0	3	0	0	4	0	0	0	0	0	0	0	0	0	1	0
secretary-general	4	.1698	.2267	33.6	0	0	2	2	0	0	0	0	2	0	0	0	0	0	0	0	0	0	0	0	0	0	2	0	0
secrete	9	.5341	1.0084	40.0	0	0	0	0	5	1	3	0	0	0	0	1	0	0	0	4	0	0	0	0	1	1	2	0	0
secreted	9	.2926	.6417	38.1	0	0	1	0	4	1	3	0	1	0	0	0	0	0	0	5	0	0	0	0	0	0	3	0	0
secretes	7	.3663	.5745	37.6	0	0	0	0	6	0	1	0	0	0	0	0	0	0	0	4	0	0	0	0	1	0	2	0	0
secretion	7	.3372	.5334	37.3	0	0	0	0	3	1	3	0	0	0	0	0	0	0	0	3	0	0	0	0	0	1	3	0	0
secretions	12	.2076	.6257	38.0	0	0	0	0	3	1	6	2	0	0	0	0	0	0	0	5	0	0	0	0	0	0	7	0	0
secretive	2	.2446	.1122	30.5	0	0	0	0	2	0	0	0	0	0	0	1	0	0	0	0	0	0	0	0	0	0	1	0	0
secretly	45	.6758	6.3473	48.0	5	6	7	5	12	8	2	0	17	1	0	7	0	5	0	0	2	0	0	0	6	6	1	0	0
secrets	40	.7148	5.9341	47.7	4	4	8	8	6	7	0	3	18	1	1	2	0	0	1	5	0	0	0	0	4	0	1	7	0
Secs	2	.0000	.0050	17.0	0	0	0	0	0	0	2	0	0	0	0	0	0	0	0	0	0	0	0	2	0	0	0	0	0
sect	7	.3078	.4868	36.9	0	0	1	1	3	0	2	0	0	1	0	0	0	2	0	0	0	0	0	0	0	0	4	0	0
section	643	.7222	93.670	59.7	32	85	72	75	133	101	132	13	54	43	7	8	34	70	15	49	229	4	25	53	2	15	17	18	0
Section	34	.6299	4.4052	46.4	0	8	1	1	2	10	11	1	0	0	1	2	7	6	0	13	0	0	0	3	0	0	1	1	0
sectional	17	.1862	.8126	39.1	0	0	1	0	3	5	8	0	2	1	0	0	0	5	0	0	0	0	0	8	0	1	0	0	0
sectionalism	2	.0000	.0914	29.6	0	0	0	0	2	0	0	0	2	0	0	0	0	0	0	0	0	0	0	0	0	0	0	0	0
sectioned	2	.0000	.0050	17.0	0	0	0	0	0	0	2	0	0	0	0	0	0	0	0	0	0	0	0	2	0	0	0	0	0
sectioning	7	.0000	.0177	22.5	0	0	0	0	0	0	7	0	0	0	0	0	0	0	0	0	0	0	0	7	0	0	0	0	0
sections	266	.7374	39.506	56.0	18	34	42	37	47	52	33	3	19	9	3	1	10	38	1	20	98	4	14	6	0	15	20	8	0
sector	18	.5667	2.0999	43.2	0	1	0	1	1	4	11	0	0	0	0	2	5	2	0	0	0	0	0	2	0	0	3	4	0
sectors	4	.1828	.1857	32.7	0	0	0	1	1	0	1	1	0	0	0	0	1	0	0	0	0	0	0	0	0	0	0	3	0
sects	8	.4112	.7301	38.6	0	0	0	0	4	2	2	0	1	0	0	0	0	2	0	0	0	0	0	0	0	0	2	3	0
secular	17	.4014	1.4442	41.6	0	0	1	1	2	6	5	2	0	0	0	0	0	0	0	0	7	0	0	0	0	2	6	2	0
secure	75	.8091	12.151	50.8	3	7	12	3	19	17	12	2	8	1	0	2	0	12	5	10	2	3	7	4	4	7	5	5	0
secured	33	.7018	4.7201	46.7	0	2	7	6	8	2	7	1	5	0	0	0	2	4	0	0	0	0	1	2	4	2	7	6	0
securely	31	.5236	3.3889	45.3	4	4	0	3	10	5	3	2	4	1	0	0	0	0	0	3	0	1	3	8	7	1	0	3	0
secures	7	.4910	.7234	38.6	1	0	0	0	1	2	3	0	0	0	0	0	0	3	0	1	0	0	1	1	0	0	1	0	0
securing	12	.5712	1.4620	41.6	0	0	3	1	4	4	0	0	3	0	0	0	0	4	0	2	1	0	1	1	0	0	0	0	0
securities	6	.2159	.3065	34.9	0	0	1	0	2	0	2	1	0	0	0	0	0	0	0	0	0	0	0	0	0	0	4	2	0
security	56	.7201	8.1484	49.1	3	0	3	7	10	22	10	1	2	0	1	3	2	12	1	0	0	0	2	0	1	5	10	17	0
Security	18	.5299	2.0375	43.1	1	0	0	2	2	5	8	0	2	0	0	1	0	9	0	0	0	0	0	0	0	1	3	2	0
sedan	6	.5568	.7182	38.6	0	0	0	0	2	3	1	0	2	1	0	1	0	0	0	0	0	0	0	0	1	1	0	0	0
sedans	3	.0000	.0365	25.6	0	0	0	0	2	0	0	1	0	0	0	0	0	0	0	0	0	0	0	0	0	0	0	3	0
sedate	5	.4770	.5360	37.3	0	2	0	1	1	0	1	0	2	0	0	1	0	0	0	0	0	0	0	0	0	1	0	1	0
sedately	4	.3387	.3012	34.8	0	0	1	0	2	1	0	0	0	0	0	2	0	0	0	1	0	0	0	0	1	0	0	0	0
sedentary	4	.2065	.1985	33.0	0	3	0	0	1	0	0	0	0	0	0	0	0	0	0	0	0	0	0	0	3	0	1	0	0
Seder	2	.0000	.0914	29.6	0	2	0	0	0	0	0	0	2	0	0	0	0	0	0	0	0	0	0	0	0	0	0	0	0
sedges	4	.0000	.0419	26.2	0	0	0	0	2	0	2	0	0	0	0	0	0	0	0	0	0	0	0	0	0	0	4	0	0
Sedgwick	2	.0000	.0209	23.2	0	0	0	0	2	0	0	0	0	0	0	0	0	0	0	0	0	0	0	0	0	0	2	0	0
sediment	28	.4409	2.7277	44.4	2	2	10	0	3	3	8	0	2	0	0	0	0	0	0	19	0	0	1	0	0	2	4	0	0
sedimentary	42	.2552	2.6841	44.3	7	4	14	2	2	4	7	2	0	0	0	0	0	0	0	35	0	0	0	0	0	3	4	0	0
sedimentation	4	.0000	.0789	29.0	0	0	0	0	0	3	0	1	0	0	0	0	0	0	0	4	0	0	0	0	0	0	0	0	0
sediments	32	.2275	1.8679	42.7	9	0	0	0	6	14	3	0	0	0	0	0	0	0	0	25	0	0	0	0	0	0	7	0	0
sedition	3	.2304	.1619	32.1	0	0	1	0	0	2	0	0	0	0	0	0	0	0	0	0	0	0	0	0	2	0	1	0	0
Sedition	4	.0000	.0778	28.9	0	0	0	0	0	4	0	0	0	0	0	0	0	4	0	0	0	0	0	0	0	0	0	0	0
see	8518	.9734	1634.3	72.1	1996	1667	1084	1076	1177	758	613	147	2234	384	113	467	434	896	354	1219	210	161	97	106	678	611	281	270	3
See	28	.5314	3.1902	45.0	0	8	7	8	2	0	1	2	8	0	0	1	0	0	5	0	1	0	0	0	0	0	9	4	0
SEE	2	.2420	.1154	30.6	1	0	0	0	0	0	1	0	0	0	0	0	1	0	0	0	0	0	0	0	1	0	0	0	0
see-saw	3	.2086	.1620	32.1	0	0	0	0	1	2	0	0	0	0	0	0	2	1	0	0	0	0	0	0	0	0	0	0	0

7G seaways
9Q sebaceous
8Q Sebastopol
7A seben
4Q Secessionists
8D sech
7G seclude
7R second-autumn
5A second-base
7R second-baseman
6A second-fastest
3A second-from-the-top
7R second-generation
9B second-grade
6J second-line
7R second-rate
4H second-smallest
8P Secondary
7B seconding
6A seconds'
7A secrecy's
7Q secretary-stenographer
9Q secretin
6B sect-
5P sectarian
XH sectile
7M sectional-view
7A sectionalist
8E Sections
7R sects'
9R Secular
4R Secunda
XH Secunderabad
9F Securities
7Q Secy
8D sed
7B sedative
8Q sedatives
9Q seditious
7P seduce
8R seduced
9R sedulous
7L see-through
8D see'
5Q see'uh

Word Type	F	D	U	SFI	3 Gr 3	4 Gr 4	5 Gr 5	6 Gr 6	7 Gr 7	8 Gr 8	9 Gr 9	X UnGr	A Read	B Eng & Gr	C Comp	D Lit	E Math	F Soc Stud	G Spell	H Sci	J Music	K Art	L Home Ec	M Shop	N Lib F	P Lib NF	Q Lib Ref	R Mag	S Rel
Seebeck	2	.0000	.0209	23.2	0	0	0	0	0	0	2	0	0	0	0	0	0	0	0	0	0	0	0	0	0	0	2	0	0
seed	243	.5312	27.834	54.4	61	48	27	54	27	4	4	18	43	0	0	1	12	19	8	107	2	2	1	0	7	13	12	12	4
seed-making	3	.0000	.0591	27.7	0	0	3	0	0	0	0	0	0	0	0	0	0	0	0	3	0	0	0	0	0	0	0	0	0
seedbed	3	.0000	.0583	27.7	0	0	0	0	0	3	0	0	0	0	0	0	0	3	0	0	0	0	0	0	0	0	0	0	0
seeding	6	.2204	.4533	36.6	0	0	4	2	0	0	0	0	5	0	0	0	0	0	0	1	0	0	0	0	0	0	0	0	0
seedling	13	.2260	.7884	39.0	2	10	0	0	1	0	0	0	1	0	0	0	2	0	0	10	0	0	0	0	0	0	0	0	0
seedlings	28	.4655	2.8507	44.5	3	2	1	3	8	5	0	6	1	0	0	1	0	7	0	16	0	0	0	0	0	0	2	1	0
seeds	560	.7793	88.629	59.5	207	88	55	101	61	13	17	18	122	3	1	2	1	66	6	228	2	1	8	0	15	50	29	25	1
seegars	2	.0000	.0234	23.7	0	0	0	0	2	0	0	0	0	0	0	0	0	0	0	0	0	0	0	0	2	0	0	0	0
seein'	2	.1787	.1174	30.7	0	0	0	1	0	1	0	0	1	0	0	0	0	0	0	0	0	0	0	0	1	0	0	0	0
seeing	341	.8427	57.713	57.6	41	55	44	51	75	43	28	4	111	22	4	36	1	13	5	30	4	12	2	0	44	25	9	23	0
Seeing	6	.2438	.4681	36.7	4	0	0	1	0	0	1	0	5	0	0	0	0	0	0	0	0	0	0	0	0	0	1	0	0
seek	110	.8420	18.547	52.7	8	11	14	20	22	16	16	3	22	2	1	7	0	19	0	9	14	1	1	0	3	12	13	6	0
seeked	2	.0000	.0914	29.6	2	0	0	0	0	0	0	0	2	0	0	0	0	0	0	0	0	0	0	0	0	0	0	0	0
seekers	9	.6136	1.1588	40.6	1	0	3	0	1	4	0	0	2	1	0	0	0	2	0	0	1	0	0	0	0	2	0	1	0
seeking	83	.8780	14.519	51.6	2	7	10	12	19	18	12	3	15	4	1	4	3	18	1	4	3	1	0	0	3	6	9	11	0
seeks	25	.6720	3.4700	45.4	1	2	2	4	7	2	7	0	5	1	0	0	0	2	0	6	2	0	0	0	1	1	6	1	0
seem	792	.8940	140.77	61.5	122	109	95	100	164	92	73	37	157	55	14	52	17	58	13	125	38	34	10	3	38	54	55	69	0
seemed	1303	.7979	211.66	63.3	171	234	158	197	247	178	90	28	601	35	24	126	4	87	4	22	16	2	2	0	168	105	13	94	0
seeming	14	.6160	1.7792	42.5	0	2	0	2	2	1	7	0	2	1	0	2	0	0	0	0	0	0	1	0	4	1	3	0	0
seemingly	28	.7338	4.1788	46.2	1	0	3	3	13	1	7	0	5	1	0	4	0	4	0	1	1	0	0	0	1	2	5	4	0
seems	638	.9395	118.56	60.7	95	99	86	78	135	61	69	15	133	47	13	44	13	43	12	104	39	9	7	3	23	52	40	56	0
seen	1663	.9252	305.34	64.8	302	313	192	239	306	155	118	38	515	83	16	116	44	151	14	260	30	25	5	9	125	144	59	67	0
seep	3	.3450	.2505	34.0	0	1	0	1	1	0	0	0	1	0	0	0	0	0	0	0	0	0	0	0	1	1	0	0	0
seepage	2	.2437	.1129	30.5	0	0	0	0	1	0	1	0	0	0	0	0	0	0	0	0	0	0	0	0	0	0	1	1	0
seeped	7	.2326	.5117	37.1	0	2	1	1	3	0	0	0	5	0	0	2	0	0	0	0	0	0	0	0	0	0	0	0	0
seeping	2	.0000	.0914	29.6	0	0	0	2	0	0	0	0	2	0	0	0	0	0	0	0	0	0	0	0	0	0	0	0	0
seeps	11	.4884	1.1458	40.6	0	3	4	1	1	0	1	1	0	0	0	0	0	1	0	5	0	0	0	0	0	1	3	1	0
sees	180	.8494	30.617	54.9	27	21	22	29	35	22	19	5	45	11	8	14	1	17	0	21	7	5	1	0	9	16	10	15	0
Sees	5	.0000	.0586	27.7	0	5	0	0	0	0	0	0	0	0	0	0	0	0	0	0	0	0	0	0	5	0	0	0	0
Seesall	3	.0000	.0365	25.6	0	0	0	0	3	0	0	0	0	0	0	0	0	0	0	0	0	0	0	0	0	0	0	3	0
seesaw	19	.3124	1.3364	41.3	4	4	0	1	0	0	0	10	0	0	0	0	0	0	0	2	6	0	0	0	0	11	0	0	0
seesaws	5	.2890	.3193	35.0	4	1	0	0	0	0	0	0	0	1	0	0	0	0	0	0	3	0	0	0	0	1	0	0	0
seethed	5	.5375	.5712	37.6	1	1	0	1	1	0	1	0	1	0	0	1	0	0	0	0	0	0	0	0	1	1	1	0	0
seething	7	.6578	.9491	39.8	0	0	1	1	3	1	1	0	1	1	0	1	0	1	0	1	0	0	0	0	0	0	1	1	0
segment	329	.0839	9.9102	50.0	41	37	47	24	54	95	29	2	0	0	0	0	318	0	0	2	2	0	0	0	0	1	2	4	0
segmented	6	.0000	.1183	30.7	0	0	0	0	4	1	1	0	0	0	0	0	0	0	0	6	0	0	0	0	0	0	0	0	0
segments	230	.1105	8.0686	49.1	28	15	46	26	51	32	31	1	0	0	0	0	216	0	0	7	0	0	0	0	1	1	1	4	0
segregated	2	.0000	.0389	25.9	0	0	0	0	1	0	1	0	0	0	0	0	0	2	0	0	0	0	0	0	0	0	0	0	0
segregation	17	.4496	1.6443	42.2	0	0	0	0	2	7	5	3	0	0	0	1	0	8	0	0	0	0	0	0	0	0	3	5	0
Seine	6	.3400	.5092	37.1	1	0	0	4	0	0	0	1	2	0	0	0	0	3	0	0	0	0	0	0	0	1	0	0	0
seiners	2	.0000	.0234	23.7	0	2	0	0	0	0	0	0	0	0	0	0	0	0	0	0	0	0	0	0	2	0	0	0	0
seismic	5	.2213	.2870	34.6	0	1	0	0	0	4	0	0	0	0	0	0	0	0	0	4	0	0	0	0	0	0	1	0	0
seismograph	8	.0782	.2923	34.7	0	0	3	0	1	0	1	3	1	0	0	0	0	0	0	7	0	0	0	0	0	0	0	0	0
seize	40	.7726	6.2334	47.9	2	7	4	7	10	4	6	0	5	2	0	1	0	10	0	0	3	0	0	1	4	6	5	3	0
seized	124	.7121	18.138	52.6	6	16	11	31	28	22	10	0	30	0	0	11	0	31	1	0	1	0	0	0	10	16	12	12	0
seizes	2	.2446	.1122	30.5	0	0	0	0	1	0	1	0	0	0	0	1	0	0	0	0	0	0	0	0	0	0	1	0	0
seizing	13	.6249	1.6884	42.3	1	0	3	1	3	4	1	0	2	0	0	1	0	4	1	0	0	0	0	0	1	1	3	0	0
seizure	13	.3555	1.0187	40.1	1	0	0	0	4	1	7	0	0	0	0	0	0	3	0	0	0	0	0	0	0	0	5	5	0
Sejna	2	.0000	.0243	23.9	0	0	0	0	2	0	0	0	0	0	0	0	0	0	0	0	0	0	0	0	0	0	0	2	0
Selassie	5	.0000	.0972	29.9	0	0	0	2	3	0	0	0	0	0	0	0	0	5	0	0	0	0	0	0	0	0	0	0	0
seldom	156	.9068	28.103	54.5	9	18	22	28	39	18	20	2	38	13	1	4	5	14	7	12	10	0	0	3	13	12	12	12	0
select	193	.7380	28.618	54.6	7	5	13	18	47	60	39	4	18	33	6	4	16	5	20	10	6	3	27	24	0	7	5	9	0
selected	123	.8327	20.445	53.1	9	5	14	11	30	25	24	5	14	9	2	1	12	16	1	7	6	2	7	12	6	6	10	12	0
selecting	51	.7037	7.2081	48.6	1	1	5	5	14	13	10	2	3	8	2	2	5	2	0	0	3	5	9	4	1	0	6	1	0
selection	196	.5741	23.965	53.8	0	7	23	17	58	32	52	7	76	14	36	5	3	1	0	5	5	0	15	7	0	3	21	5	0
selections	39	.5575	4.7854	46.8	0	0	7	8	9	10	5	0	22	4	0	3	0	1	0	0	6	0	3	0	0	0	0	0	0
selective	10	.3263	.7258	38.6	0	0	0	0	5	4	0	1	1	0	0	0	0	0	0	0	0	0	0	2	0	0	6	1	0
Selective	10	.2435	.5670	37.5	0	0	0	0	8	2	0	0	0	0	0	0	0	1	0	0	0	0	0	0	0	0	7	2	0
selector	6	.3349	.4497	36.5	0	0	4	0	2	0	0	0	0	0	0	0	4	0	0	0	0	0	0	0	0	0	1	1	0
selects	12	.6387	1.5424	41.9	0	0	3	0	4	1	4	0	0	3	1	0	0	0	1	1	1	0	1	2	0	0	2	0	0
selenium	2	.0000	.0209	23.2	0	1	0	0	0	0	1	0	0	0	0	0	0	0	0	0	0	0	0	0	0	0	2	0	0
self	41	.8194	6.7564	48.3	0	5	7	5	17	4	1	2	11	2	0	2	0	3	4	2	3	0	2	0	5	2	1	4	0
self-assertion	2	.2152	.1357	31.3	0	0	0	0	1	1	0	0	1	0	0	0	0	1	0	0	0	0	0	0	0	0	0	0	0
self-assurance	3	.3772	.2503	34.0	0	0	0	0	3	0	0	0	0	0	0	1	0	0	0	1	0	0	0	0	0	1	0	0	0
self-care	2	.0000	.0394	26.0	0	0	2	0	0	0	0	0	0	0	0	0	0	0	0	2	0	0	0	0	0	0	0	0	0
self-centered	4	.3706	.3628	35.6	0	0	0	1	1	2	0	0	2	0	0	0	0	0	0	0	0	0	0	0	1	0	1	0	0
self-confidence	14	.6536	1.8713	42.7	2	0	1	2	1	5	2	1	1	0	0	1	0	1	0	3	0	1	1	0	1	0	1	4	0
self-confident	4	.3679	.3346	35.2	0	0	1	0	2	0	1	0	1	0	0	1	0	0	0	0	0	0	1	0	0	0	0	1	0
self-conscious	16	.5519	1.8504	42.7	0	0	2	1	9	3	1	0	1	0	0	3	0	0	0	7	0	0	2	0	1	0	1	1	0
self-consciousness	2	.2446	.1142	30.6	0	0	1	0	1	0	0	0	0	0	0	0	0	0	0	0	0	0	0	0	1	0	0	1	0
self-contained	4	.4475	.4001	36.0	0	1	0	2	1	0	0	0	1	0	0	0	0	0	0	1	0	0	0	0	1	0	1	0	0
self-control	5	.5247	.5614	37.5	0	0	1	0	2	1	0	1	1	1	0	0	0	1	0	0	1	0	0	0	0	0	0	1	0
self-controlled	2	.1948	.1250	31.0	0	1	0	1	0	0	0	0	1	0	0	0	0	0	0	0	0	0	0	0	0	1	0	0	0
self-defeating	2	.2285	.1129	30.5	0	0	0	0	2	0	0	0	0	0	0	0	0	1	0	0	0	0	0	0	0	0	1	0	0
self-defense	6	.4424	.5970	37.8	0	1	2	1	1	1	0	0	2	0	0	1	0	0	0	0	0	0	0	0	0	0	2	1	0
self-denial	2	.2388	.1089	30.4	0	0	0	0	1	1	0	0	0	0	0	0	0	0	1	0	0	0	0	0	1	0	0	0	0
self-determination	3	.2321	.1635	32.1	0	0	0	0	0	2	1	0	0	0	0	0	0	0	0	0	0	0	0	0	0	0	1	2	0
self-educated	3	.2197	.2090	33.2	0	0	0	0	1	1	1	0	2	0	0	0	0	0	0	0	0	0	0	0	0	0	1	0	0
self-employed	2	.2285	.1129	30.5	0	0	0	0	1	1	0	0	0	0	0	0	0	1	0	0	0	0	0	0	0	0	1	0	0
self-evident	4	.2708	.2760	34.4	0	0	0	0	2	1	1	0	1	0	0	2	0	1	0	0	0	0	0	0	0	0	0	0	0
self-explanatory	2	.0000	.0290	24.6	0	0	1	0	1	0	0	0	0	0	0	0	0	0	0	0	0	0	0	0	0	2	0	0	0
self-expression	2	.2375	.1088	30.4	0	0	0	0	0	1	0	1	0	0	0	0	0	0	0	0	1	0	0	0	0	0	0	1	0
self-fabric	2	.0000	.0064	18.1	0	0	0	0	1	1	0	0	0	0	0	0	0	0	0	0	0	0	2	0	0	0	0	0	0
self-governing	12	.4555	1.1876	40.7	0	0	1	2	6	1	2	0	0	0	0	0	0	8	1	1	0	0	0	0	0	1	1	0	0
self-government	20	.4784	2.0530	43.1	1	0	3	1	3	8	4	0	0	0	0	0	1	12	1	0	0	0	0	0	0	3	3	0	0
self-help	5	.3241	.3584	35.5	0	0	0	3	1	1	0	0	0	0	0	0	0	1	0	0	0	0	1	0	0	0	0	3	0
self-importance	2	.2407	.1138	30.6	0	0	0	0	2	0	0	0	0	0	0	1	0	0	0	0	0	0	0	0	0	1	0	0	0
self-imposed	2	.2437	.1129	30.5	0	0	0	0	0	1	1	0	0	0	0	0	0	0	0	0	0	0	0	0	0	0	1	1	0
self-knowledge	2	.0000	.0064	18.1	0	0	0	0	2	0	0	0	0	0	0	0	0	0	0	0	0	0	2	0	0	0	0	0	0
self-made	2	.1259	.0687	28.4	0	0	0	0	0	1	1	0	0	0	0	0	0	1	0	0	0	0	0	1	0	0	0	0	0

6A seed-filled
3F seed-gathering
5H seed-makers
6Q seed-pod
3P seed's
8F seedbeds
7R seedless
7H seedling's
XR Seeds
9D seedstitch
7D seedtime
6G seedy
7K Seeganna
8K SEEING
9D seem'd
9D seem'st
7R Seemed
XR Seen
5P seers
5A seersucker
3P seesawses
9R Segal
6G segl
7M segma
3E Segment
9B segmental
5G segonku
5Q Segonzac
4A Segowlee
8F segregationist
7D segue
8Q Segundos
XR Seguret
7D sehe
6A Seid
9R seigneur
4N seining
4H seismographs
9H seismologists
8R seismometers
7P seiz'd
8Q seizures
7R Sejna's
7Q Selection
7J selectively
5A Selectman
5E Selector
7R Selena
9H selenite
9H selenography
9G self-A14**
8K Self-Destroying
3P Self-Initiated
9C self-adjustment
7Q self-advancement
6A self-appointed
5Q self-awareness
6Q self-centeredness
8R self-certainty
5P self-chosen
3N self-consciously
7Q self-correcting
9D self-correction
5P self-deceiving
9R self-deception
9R self-deceptively
8Q self-deprecatory
8F self-described
7R self-destruction
XR self-discipline
7R self-disqualification
9R self-doubt
7Q self-effacing
9Q self-effacingly
4Q self-forgetting
XR self-hatred
8F self-hypnosis
8L self-improvement
8C self-inflicted
9D self-instruction
8L self-interfacing
8Q self-limited
7G self-loading
9R self-loathing

Word Type	F	D	U	SFI	3 Gr 3	4 Gr 4	5 Gr 5	6 Gr 6	7 Gr 7	8 Gr 8	9 Gr 9	X UnGr	A Read	B Eng & Gr	C Comp	D Lit	E Math	F Soc Stud	G Spell	H Sci	J Music	K Art	L Home Ec	M Shop	N Lib F	P Lib NF	Q Lib Ref	R Mag	S Rel
self-pity	3	.3427	.2477	33.9	1	0	0	0	1	1	0	0	1	0	0	0	0	0	0	0	0	0	0	0	1	0	0	1	0
self-possessed	2	.2411	.1091	30.4	0	0	0	0	0	0	2	0	0	0	0	1	0	0	0	0	1	0	0	0	0	0	0	0	0
self-propelled	4	.2405	.2410	33.8	0	1	2	0	0	0	0	1	0	0	0	0	0	0	0	2	0	0	0	0	0	2	0	0	0
self-reliance	2	.2446	.1123	30.5	0	0	0	0	1	1	0	0	0	1	0	0	0	0	0	0	0	0	0	0	0	0	1	0	0
self-respect	9	.5277	1.0302	40.1	0	1	1	2	1	2	2	0	2	0	0	0	0	2	0	2	0	0	0	0	0	1	2	0	0
self-respecting	6	.5516	.7098	38.5	1	0	1	0	1	2	1	0	2	1	0	0	0	0	0	0	1	0	0	0	1	0	1	0	0
self-righteousness	3	.2332	.1690	32.3	0	0	2	0	0	0	1	0	0	0	0	0	0	0	0	0	0	0	0	0	0	2	0	1	0
self-rule	2	.0000	.0389	25.9	0	0	0	1	1	0	0	0	0	0	0	0	0	2	0	0	0	0	0	0	0	0	0	0	0
self-satisfied	2	.1698	.1133	30.5	0	0	0	0	1	1	0	0	1	0	0	0	0	0	0	0	0	0	0	0	0	0	1	0	0
self-sufficiency	3	.3759	.2471	33.9	0	0	0	1	2	0	0	0	0	1	0	0	0	1	0	0	0	0	0	0	0	0	1	0	0
self-sufficient	7	.5284	.7911	39.0	1	0	1	0	3	0	1	1	1	0	0	0	0	2	0	0	0	0	0	0	0	2	1	1	0
self-supporting	6	.4118	.5409	37.3	0	0	1	1	2	0	1	1	1	0	0	0	0	0	0	0	0	0	1	0	0	0	2	2	0
self-sustaining	7	.2258	.3774	35.8	0	0	0	0	5	0	2	0	0	0	0	0	0	1	0	0	0	0	0	0	0	1	5	0	0
self-taught	4	.3875	.3294	35.2	0	0	1	0	0	1	2	0	0	0	0	0	0	1	0	0	1	0	0	1	0	0	1	0	0
self-test	12	.0000	.0974	29.9	0	0	0	0	0	12	0	0	0	0	0	0	0	0	12	0	0	0	0	0	0	0	0	0	0
self-tests	7	.0841	.1784	32.5	0	0	0	0	0	7	0	0	0	0	0	0	0	0	6	1	0	0	0	0	0	0	0	0	0
selfish	30	.6532	4.0663	46.1	1	3	6	3	8	4	1	4	7	2	0	3	0	4	0	1	1	0	0	0	8	0	0	4	0
selfishness	3	.2261	.2131	33.3	0	0	1	0	1	0	1	0	2	0	0	0	0	0	0	0	0	0	0	0	1	0	0	0	0
Selkirk	7	.1226	.2619	34.2	0	6	0	0	1	0	0	0	0	0	0	0	0	1	0	0	0	0	0	0	0	6	0	0	0
sell	462	.8461	78.600	59.0	146	97	47	52	65	25	23	7	152	12	0	16	29	120	8	5	15	1	4	0	26	41	9	24	0
seller	9	.4334	.8342	39.2	1	4	1	0	0	3	0	0	0	2	0	0	5	1	0	0	0	0	1	0	0	0	0	0	0
Seller	10	.2415	.7512	38.8	0	3	7	0	0	0	0	0	7	0	0	0	3	0	0	0	0	0	0	0	0	0	0	0	0
sellers	5	.3525	.4000	36.0	2	0	1	0	0	0	0	2	0	0	0	0	0	2	0	1	0	0	0	0	0	0	0	2	0
selling	133	.7615	20.649	53.1	25	16	17	14	33	11	12	5	37	0	0	4	16	33	1	1	4	0	1	0	4	10	2	20	0
sells	66	.7722	10.346	50.1	25	5	2	6	17	2	7	2	16	5	0	0	5	17	3	0	1	0	2	0	0	8	2	7	0
Selma	4	.0000	.1827	32.6	4	0	0	0	0	0	0	0	4	0	0	0	0	0	0	0	0	0	0	0	0	0	0	0	0
Selman	2	.0000	.0394	26.0	0	0	0	1	0	0	1	0	0	0	0	0	0	0	0	2	0	0	0	0	0	0	0	0	0
selvage	4	.0000	.0129	21.1	0	0	0	0	0	4	0	0	0	0	0	0	0	0	0	0	0	0	4	0	0	0	0	0	0
selvages	4	.0000	.0129	21.1	0	0	0	0	0	4	0	0	0	0	0	0	0	0	0	0	0	0	4	0	0	0	0	0	0
selves	3	.2175	.1545	31.9	0	0	0	0	1	0	2	0	0	0	0	2	0	0	0	0	0	0	0	0	0	0	0	1	0
semantics	6	.1823	.2810	34.5	0	0	3	0	1	2	0	0	0	0	0	0	0	2	0	0	0	0	0	0	0	0	4	0	0
semaphore	6	.0000	.2741	34.4	6	0	0	0	0	0	0	0	6	0	0	0	0	0	0	0	0	0	0	0	0	0	0	0	0
semaphores	2	.2446	.1122	30.5	0	0	1	0	0	0	1	0	0	0	0	1	0	0	0	0	0	0	0	0	0	0	1	0	0
semblance	5	.4122	.4599	36.6	0	0	0	1	2	0	2	0	1	0	0	2	0	0	0	0	0	0	0	0	1	1	0	0	0
semester	13	.6323	1.6764	42.2	1	1	0	1	5	0	3	2	1	0	0	0	0	0	1	0	2	0	1	0	2	0	2	4	0
semesters	2	.2437	.1129	30.5	0	0	0	0	1	0	1	0	0	0	0	0	0	0	0	0	0	0	0	0	0	0	1	1	0
semi-automatic	3	.0000	.0434	26.4	0	0	3	0	0	0	0	0	0	0	0	0	0	0	0	0	0	0	0	0	0	3	0	0	0
semi-circle	5	.1953	.2495	34.0	0	0	0	0	0	5	0	0	0	0	0	0	4	0	0	0	0	0	0	0	1	0	0	0	0
semi-circular	3	.2611	.1753	32.4	0	0	1	0	1	1	0	0	0	0	1	0	1	0	0	0	0	0	0	0	1	0	0	0	0
semi-darkness	2	.2411	.1091	30.4	0	0	0	0	1	0	1	0	0	0	0	1	0	0	0	0	1	0	0	0	0	0	0	0	0
semi-desert	2	.0000	.0243	23.9	0	2	0	0	0	0	0	0	0	0	0	0	0	0	0	0	0	0	0	0	0	0	0	2	0
semiarid	12	.1787	.6305	38.0	0	0	0	5	7	0	0	0	1	0	0	0	0	10	0	0	0	0	0	0	0	1	0	0	0
semicircle	22	.5143	2.4285	43.9	1	1	0	5	10	3	2	0	4	0	0	2	12	1	0	0	2	0	0	1	0	0	0	0	0
semicircles	3	.2346	.1705	32.3	0	1	0	1	0	1	0	0	0	0	0	0	2	0	0	0	0	0	0	0	0	0	0	1	0
semicolon	8	.3608	.6396	38.1	0	0	0	0	4	2	2	0	1	5	1	1	0	0	0	0	0	0	0	0	0	0	0	0	0
semicolons	2	.0000	.0914	29.6	0	0	0	0	2	0	0	0	2	0	0	0	0	0	0	0	0	0	0	0	0	0	0	0	0
semiconductor	8	.3000	.6132	37.9	2	0	0	0	1	5	0	0	2	0	0	0	0	0	0	5	0	0	0	0	0	0	0	1	0
semiconductors	3	.0000	.0314	25.0	0	3	0	0	0	0	0	0	0	0	0	0	0	0	0	0	0	0	0	0	0	0	3	0	0
semidarkness	2	.1733	.1149	30.6	0	0	2	0	0	0	0	0	1	1	0	0	0	0	0	0	0	0	0	0	0	0	0	0	0
semidiurnal	4	.0000	.0789	29.0	0	0	0	0	0	0	0	4	0	0	0	0	0	0	0	4	0	0	0	0	0	0	0	0	0
semifinals	2	.0000	.0914	29.6	0	0	1	1	0	0	0	0	2	0	0	0	0	0	0	0	0	0	0	0	0	0	0	0	0
semimetals	2	.1698	.1133	30.5	1	1	0	0	0	0	0	0	1	0	0	0	0	0	0	0	0	0	0	0	0	0	1	0	0
semimonthly	2	.0000	.0299	24.8	0	0	0	2	0	0	0	0	0	0	0	0	2	0	0	0	0	0	0	0	0	0	0	0	0
seminar	2	.0000	.0243	23.9	0	0	0	0	1	1	0	0	0	0	0	0	0	0	0	0	0	0	0	0	0	0	0	2	0
Seminary	7	.3324	.5133	37.1	0	1	0	2	2	1	1	0	0	0	0	0	0	0	0	0	0	0	0	0	0	1	2	4	0
Seminole	3	.2357	.2199	33.4	0	1	0	0	2	0	0	0	2	0	0	0	0	0	0	0	0	0	0	0	0	1	0	0	0
Seminoles	5	.1634	.2733	34.4	3	0	0	0	2	0	0	0	2	0	0	0	0	0	0	0	0	0	0	0	0	3	0	0	0
semiskilled	2	.0000	.0050	17.0	0	0	0	0	0	0	2	0	0	0	0	0	0	0	0	0	0	0	0	2	0	0	0	0	0
Semites	6	.2218	.3387	35.3	0	0	0	2	3	1	0	0	0	0	0	0	0	5	0	0	0	1	0	0	0	0	0	0	0
Semitic	11	.2816	.6957	38.4	0	0	1	2	8	0	0	0	0	1	0	0	0	2	7	0	0	0	0	0	0	1	0	0	0
semitransparent	2	.2160	.1362	31.3	1	0	1	0	0	0	0	0	1	0	0	0	0	0	0	1	0	0	0	0	0	0	0	0	0
semitropical	4	.2405	.2410	33.8	1	0	1	0	1	0	1	0	0	0	0	0	0	0	0	2	0	0	0	0	0	2	0	0	0
sempervirens	3	.2159	.1532	31.9	0	0	2	1	0	0	0	0	0	0	0	0	0	0	0	0	0	0	0	0	0	0	2	1	0
Sen	5	.3726	.4014	36.0	0	0	0	0	3	1	1	0	0	1	0	0	0	0	0	0	0	0	0	0	0	0	2	2	0
senate	3	.1823	.1405	31.5	1	1	0	1	0	0	0	0	0	0	0	0	0	1	0	0	0	0	0	0	0	0	2	0	0
Senate	138	.5849	17.265	52.4	16	3	7	4	63	22	19	4	44	1	0	0	0	30	1	0	0	0	0	0	0	17	15	30	0
Senate's	2	.0000	.0243	23.9	0	0	0	0	1	0	1	0	0	0	0	0	0	0	0	0	0	0	0	0	0	0	0	2	0
senator	15	.4948	1.5923	42.0	1	1	2	0	1	8	2	0	1	3	0	0	0	7	0	0	0	0	0	0	0	2	2	0	0
Senator	62	.6355	8.3945	49.2	0	2	3	1	35	10	9	2	28	1	0	4	0	14	0	0	0	0	0	0	0	3	4	8	0
senator's	4	.4713	.3985	36.0	0	0	1	0	1	1	1	0	0	1	0	0	0	1	1	0	0	0	0	0	0	1	0	0	0
senatorial	3	.3374	.2433	33.9	0	0	1	0	2	0	0	0	1	1	0	0	0	0	0	0	0	0	0	0	0	0	1	0	0
senators	18	.3782	1.5160	41.8	1	3	3	1	3	4	1	2	0	0	0	0	0	10	0	0	0	0	0	0	0	0	3	5	0
Senators	53	.4848	5.7965	47.6	15	1	0	0	23	12	2	0	20	1	0	0	0	14	0	0	0	0	0	0	0	15	0	3	0
Senators'	2	.2433	.1158	30.6	1	0	0	0	1	0	0	0	0	0	0	0	0	0	0	0	0	0	0	0	0	1	0	1	0
send	485	.9193	88.498	59.5	94	92	56	69	74	55	39	6	129	24	9	47	6	59	8	71	13	3	2	2	24	51	11	26	0
Send	2	.2303	.1079	30.3	2	0	0	0	0	0	0	0	0	0	0	0	0	0	0	0	1	0	0	0	0	1	0	0	0
Sendall	6	.0000	.0869	29.4	0	6	0	0	0	0	0	0	0	0	0	0	0	0	0	0	0	0	0	0	0	6	0	0	0
Sendall's	3	.0000	.0434	26.4	0	3	0	0	0	0	0	0	0	0	0	0	0	0	0	0	0	0	0	0	0	3	0	0	0
sender	13	.5649	1.5229	41.8	0	1	7	0	3	0	2	0	0	2	1	0	1	0	0	5	0	0	0	0	0	1	3	0	0
sender's	2	.1605	.0742	28.7	0	0	1	1	0	0	0	0	0	1	1	0	0	0	0	0	0	0	0	0	0	0	0	0	0
senders	3	.2445	.1818	32.6	2	0	0	0	1	0	0	0	0	0	0	0	0	0	0	2	0	0	0	0	0	0	1	0	0
sendeth	2	.2427	.1152	30.6	1	0	0	0	1	0	0	0	0	0	0	0	0	0	0	0	0	0	0	0	1	1	0	0	0
sending	110	.8316	18.395	52.6	12	16	22	19	19	12	8	2	28	3	0	2	0	8	2	25	4	0	0	1	9	11	9	8	0
sends	82	.3551	6.7327	48.3	22	11	10	10	12	7	5	5	10	0	0	3	1	9	1	28	4	0	0	0	2	10	4	7	3
Seneca	8	.3270	.6293	38.0	2	1	0	1	1	0	1	2	2	0	0	0	0	0	0	0	0	0	0	0	0	3	0	3	0
Senecas	6	.3850	.5818	37.6	0	1	0	0	5	0	0	0	4	0	0	1	0	0	0	0	0	0	0	0	0	1	0	0	0
Senegal	2	.1674	.0805	29.1	0	0	1	0	1	0	0	0	0	0	0	0	0	0	0	0	0	0	1	0	0	1	0	0	0
senile	2	.2346	.1166	30.7	0	0	0	0	0	0	1	1	0	0	0	0	0	0	0	1	0	0	0	0	0	0	0	1	0
senility	2	.0000	.0394	26.0	0	0	0	0	1	0	0	1	0	0	0	0	0	0	0	2	0	0	0	0	0	0	0	0	0
senior	26	.6158	3.3537	45.3	0	0	0	3	8	7	8	0	7	3	0	0	1	0	1	0	0	0	1	0	0	2	1	10	0
Senior	9	.5074	1.0026	40.0	0	0	1	4	2	0	1	1	3	0	0	1	1	0	0	0	0	0	0	0	0	1	0	3	0

8Q self-medication
7G self-movable
9H self-perpetuating
XH self-photographs
5R self-portrait
7R self-preservation
9L self-regard
8F self-reliant
9Q self-repair
5N self-sacrificing
5A self-sealing
8F self-seekers
6E self-service
7R self-serving
9R self-sorrow
9Q self-stabilizing
7R self-tapping
8P self-termed
6H self-understanding
6J selfishly
9P selflessness
4A selfsame
5P Selim
7G selinon
9Q Seljuk
7F Selkirk's
7R Selkirks
XR seller's
5A Seller's
8R sellout
3A Selma's
5A Selo
6R semaphoring
7F semi-arid
9R semi-autobiography
3Q semi-feudal
6R semi-finals
9M semi-finished
8M semi-gloss
9H semi-invalids
5P semi-male
XH semi-molten
7A semi-precious
8R semi-religious
8R semi-suicidal
5Q semiannual
7C semiannually
7Q semiaquatic
7P semicircular
7P semicolonial
9Q semiconducting
8D semifantastic
9L semifermented
7M semigloss
7R semikit
5N Semina's
7R seminaries
6R seminars
5Q seminary
8Q seminomadic
9P semiobscene
7Q semiparasites
7Q semipermeable
7H semiporous
6R semipro
7Q semiprocessed
5Q semiprofessional
6H semirigid
7L semiripened
7Q semirotary
7A semirural
9Q semita
9H semitropics
7G semivowels
5P Sempre
5Q senates
7A Senatorial
8A sence
XR send-off
8F Sendai

Word Type	F	D	U	SFI	3 Gr 3	4 Gr 4	5 Gr 5	6 Gr 6	7 Gr 7	8 Gr 8	9 Gr 9	X UnGr	A Read	B Eng & Gr	C Comp	D Lit	E Math	F Soc Stud	G Spell	H Sci	J Music	K Art	L Home Ec	M Shop	N Lib F	P Lib NF	Q Lib Ref	R Mag	S Rel
seniors	6	.2050	.3004	34.8	0	0	0	0	0	0	6	0	0	4	0	0	2	0	0	0	0	0	0	0	0	0	0	0	0
Sennacharib	4	.0000	.0438	26.4	0	0	0	4	0	0	0	0	0	4	0	0	0	0	0	0	0	0	0	0	0	0	0	0	0
sennit	2	.0000	.0234	23.7	0	0	0	2	0	0	0	0	0	0	0	0	0	0	0	0	0	0	0	0	2	0	0	0	0
senor	5	.2445	.3864	35.9	4	0	0	0	0	0	1	0	4	0	0	1	0	0	0	0	0	0	0	0	0	0	0	0	0
Senor	19	.4632	2.0518	43.1	6	0	4	7	0	1	1	0	10	0	0	1	0	6	0	0	2	0	0	0	0	0	0	0	0
senora	2	.0000	.0914	29.6	0	0	2	0	0	0	0	0	2	0	0	0	0	0	0	0	0	0	0	0	0	0	0	0	0
Senora	3	.0000	.1370	31.4	0	0	3	0	0	0	0	0	3	0	0	0	0	0	0	0	0	0	0	0	0	0	0	0	0
senorita	2	.1497	.1046	30.2	1	0	0	0	0	1	0	0	1	0	0	0	0	0	1	0	0	0	0	0	0	0	0	0	0
Senorita	2	.0000	.0914	29.6	2	0	0	0	0	0	0	0	2	0	0	0	0	0	0	0	0	0	0	0	0	0	0	0	0
sensation	43	.7571	6.5672	48.2	3	1	3	8	12	4	4	8	2	1	0	0	0	2	0	15	3	1	1	0	1	8	3	6	0
sensational	5	.3307	.3580	35.5	0	0	0	1	2	0	1	1	0	0	1	1	0	0	0	0	0	0	0	0	0	0	0	3	0
sensations	14	.4480	1.3746	41.4	0	0	1	2	5	4	1	1	1	2	0	0	0	0	0	9	0	1	0	0	0	0	1	0	0
sense	556	.9197	101.32	60.1	41	70	47	57	136	87	102	16	102	51	18	37	8	28	16	80	13	4	11	4	19	51	59	55	0
Sense	2	.0000	.0162	22.1	0	0	0	0	2	0	0	0	0	0	0	0	0	0	2	0	0	0	0	0	0	0	0	0	0
sensed	25	.7017	3.6136	45.6	1	0	3	4	9	4	3	1	7	0	0	4	0	3	0	1	1	0	0	0	2	1	1	5	0
senseless	9	.5506	1.0833	40.3	0	1	1	3	3	1	0	0	4	0	0	0	0	0	0	0	0	0	0	0	1	1	1	2	0
senses	151	.4350	14.167	51.5	17	11	17	29	33	14	24	6	9	13	33	9	0	0	0	60	0	0	0	0	5	4	8	10	0
sensibilities	2	.2160	.1362	31.3	0	0	0	1	0	0	0	1	1	0	0	0	0	0	0	1	0	0	0	0	0	0	0	0	0
sensible	57	.8191	9.3798	49.7	2	9	3	11	14	7	7	4	14	5	2	2	9	1	4	2	1	0	4	0	2	4	1	6	0
sensibly	5	.3550	.4331	36.4	0	0	1	2	1	0	1	0	2	0	0	0	0	0	0	0	0	0	0	0	0	2	1	0	0
sensing	11	.3351	.8503	39.3	0	0	0	5	4	1	0	1	1	0	0	0	0	0	0	3	0	0	0	0	1	0	0	6	0
sensitive	86	.7534	13.107	51.2	1	7	10	12	25	15	12	4	8	1	0	1	1	5	0	32	7	1	0	3	0	5	10	12	0
sensitivity	14	.5334	1.5729	42.0	0	0	0	4	4	2	2	2	1	4	0	0	0	2	0	3	0	1	0	0	0	0	0	3	0
sensitized	6	.0000	.0151	21.8	0	0	0	0	0	0	6	0	0	0	0	0	0	0	0	0	0	0	0	6	0	0	0	0	0
sensor	7	.2353	.5425	37.3	5	0	1	0	1	0	0	0	6	0	0	0	0	0	0	0	0	0	0	0	0	0	0	1	0
sensors	4	.3512	.3114	34.9	0	0	0	1	3	0	0	0	0	0	0	0	0	0	0	1	0	0	0	0	0	0	1	2	0
sensory	32	.3555	2.5181	44.0	0	0	4	9	9	1	8	1	0	1	7	0	0	0	0	17	0	0	0	0	0	0	5	2	0
sensuous	2	.2375	.1088	30.4	0	0	0	0	0	1	0	1	0	0	0	0	0	0	0	0	1	0	0	0	0	0	0	1	0
sent	835	.8189	137.90	61.4	141	169	99	115	142	93	59	17	238	36	11	45	9	161	11	62	10	2	0	9	47	108	33	48	5
sentence	3122	.5529	362.78	65.6	529	421	452	379	523	425	377	16	545	1272	243	19	602	14	367	21	0	0	1	0	11	4	11	11	1
Sentence	41	.4178	3.6512	45.6	6	9	1	3	1	19	2	0	0	11	0	0	18	0	11	0	0	0	0	0	0	0	1	0	0
sentenced	3	.3263	.2368	33.7	1	0	0	0	0	1	1	0	1	0	0	0	0	0	0	0	1	0	0	0	0	0	0	1	0
sentences	2611	.5210	284.46	64.5	520	381	361	347	422	273	298	9	253	1271	185	15	325	8	523	11	2	0	1	0	2	6	0	8	1
Sentences	7	.2809	.4424	36.5	0	2	0	1	2	0	2	0	0	5	0	0	1	0	1	0	0	0	0	0	0	0	0	0	0
sentiment	15	.6294	1.9223	42.8	0	0	1	1	3	7	3	0	0	1	0	2	0	3	1	0	4	0	0	0	0	2	2	0	0
sentimental	24	.5724	2.8491	44.5	2	1	3	4	0	5	7	2	2	2	0	1	0	1	0	0	7	0	0	0	1	7	0	3	0
sentiments	11	.5966	1.3872	41.4	0	0	0	1	5	3	1	1	3	1	0	0	0	2	0	0	1	0	0	0	0	0	1	3	0
sentinel	3	.1042	.0759	28.8	0	0	0	1	2	0	0	0	0	0	2	0	0	0	0	0	0	0	0	0	1	0	0	0	0
Sentinel	2	.2446	.1123	30.5	0	0	1	0	0	1	0	0	0	1	0	0	0	0	0	0	0	0	0	0	0	0	1	0	0
sentinels	3	.2261	.2131	33.3	0	1	0	0	1	1	0	0	2	0	0	0	0	0	0	0	0	0	0	0	1	0	0	0	0
sentries	5	.3747	.4028	36.1	0	1	0	1	2	0	1	0	0	0	0	2	0	0	0	0	0	0	0	0	2	0	1	0	0
sentry	6	.3662	.4912	36.9	0	0	1	3	0	1	1	0	1	0	1	1	0	0	0	0	0	0	0	0	3	0	0	0	0
Sentry	10	.0000	.1172	30.7	0	0	0	10	0	0	0	0	0	0	0	0	0	0	0	0	0	0	0	0	10	0	0	0	0
Seoul	8	.1646	.3366	35.3	0	0	0	6	0	0	2	0	0	0	0	0	0	0	0	0	1	0	0	0	0	0	0	7	0
Seoul's	2	.0000	.0243	23.9	0	0	0	0	0	0	2	0	0	0	0	0	0	0	0	0	0	0	0	0	0	0	0	2	0
sepals	16	.0000	.3155	35.0	0	0	3	3	0	0	3	7	0	0	0	0	0	0	0	16	0	0	0	0	0	0	0	0	0
separable	2	.0000	.0219	23.4	0	0	0	0	0	0	2	0	0	2	0	0	0	0	0	0	0	0	0	0	0	0	0	0	0
separate	416	.8927	73.658	58.7	25	47	53	60	78	73	68	12	33	55	13	6	28	59	44	61	16	3	14	15	5	10	39	15	0
separated	198	.9109	35.748	55.5	16	23	22	27	45	28	30	7	21	17	1	8	18	39	4	28	7	1	3	9	11	10	14	7	0
separately	63	.7590	9.5853	49.8	6	8	13	8	11	11	5	1	3	3	0	0	8	5	9	6	7	2	9	1	2	1	6	1	0
separates	71	.7117	10.215	50.1	5	6	13	7	18	8	14	0	1	2	1	0	18	10	1	13	2	0	10	1	0	2	6	4	0
separating	30	.8236	4.9396	46.9	2	2	4	8	7	2	4	1	2	1	0	2	3	5	1	4	1	0	2	0	1	3	4	1	0
separation	18	.6798	2.5053	44.0	0	2	0	0	10	4	2	0	2	1	0	0	0	3	0	4	0	0	1	1	0	0	2	4	0
separatism	2	.2351	.1166	30.7	0	0	0	0	1	1	0	0	0	0	0	0	0	1	0	0	0	0	0	0	0	0	0	1	0
separatists	3	.2143	.1568	32.0	0	0	1	2	0	0	0	0	0	0	0	0	0	0	0	0	0	0	0	0	0	1	0	2	0
separator	4	.3444	.3047	34.8	1	0	0	0	0	1	2	0	0	2	0	0	0	1	0	0	0	0	0	0	0	0	1	0	0
separators	2	.2306	.1140	30.6	1	0	0	0	0	1	0	0	0	1	0	0	0	1	0	0	0	0	0	0	0	0	0	0	0
Sepia	3	.0000	.0434	26.4	0	0	0	0	0	0	3	0	0	0	0	0	0	0	0	0	0	0	0	0	0	3	0	0	0
Sepp	4	.0000	.1827	32.6	3	1	0	0	0	0	0	0	4	0	0	0	0	0	0	0	0	0	0	0	0	0	0	0	0
Sepp's	2	.0000	.0914	29.6	0	2	0	0	0	0	0	0	2	0	0	0	0	0	0	0	0	0	0	0	0	0	0	0	0
Seppala	7	.0000	.3198	35.0	0	0	7	0	0	0	0	0	7	0	0	0	0	0	0	0	0	0	0	0	0	0	0	0	0
Sept	11	.0978	.3168	35.0	0	0	2	1	5	3	0	0	0	0	0	0	0	0	0	0	0	0	0	0	0	0	10	1	0
September	172	.8179	28.280	54.5	12	37	27	21	29	18	20	8	31	6	1	3	15	38	2	10	3	0	0	0	12	12	7	32	0
septic	3	.2445	.1818	32.6	0	0	1	1	1	0	0	0	0	0	0	0	0	0	0	2	0	0	0	0	0	0	1	0	0
septum	2	.0000	.0394	26.0	0	0	0	0	0	0	2	0	0	0	0	0	0	0	0	2	0	0	0	0	0	0	0	0	0
sequel	2	.1948	.1250	31.0	0	0	1	0	1	0	0	0	1	0	0	0	0	0	0	0	0	0	0	0	0	1	0	0	0
sequence	82	.7397	12.259	50.9	2	11	2	9	29	8	18	3	10	6	1	1	8	1	0	13	19	0	1	2	0	0	16	4	0
sequences	17	.4958	1.7438	42.4	0	3	1	2	6	2	2	1	0	1	1	0	1	0	0	2	9	0	0	0	0	0	2	1	0
sequins	3	.0939	.1398	31.5	0	3	0	0	0	0	0	0	2	0	0	0	0	0	0	0	0	1	0	0	0	0	0	0	0
sequoia	18	.4028	1.5866	42.0	4	0	0	1	10	0	3	0	0	0	0	0	3	0	0	7	0	0	0	0	0	1	7	0	0
Sequoia	6	.4880	.6272	38.0	0	0	2	3	1	0	0	0	0	0	0	1	0	2	0	2	0	0	0	0	0	0	0	1	0
sequoias	4	.3544	.3197	35.0	2	0	0	0	0	0	1	1	0	0	0	0	1	0	0	1	0	0	0	0	0	2	0	0	0
Sequoyah	23	.1333	1.4860	41.7	13	0	0	10	0	0	0	0	22	0	0	0	0	0	0	0	0	0	0	0	0	1	0	0	0
Sequoyah's	4	.0000	.1827	32.6	3	0	0	1	0	0	0	0	4	0	0	0	0	0	0	0	0	0	0	0	0	0	0	0	0
Serafina	17	.0000	.7766	38.9	17	0	0	0	0	0	0	0	17	0	0	0	0	0	0	0	0	0	0	0	0	0	0	0	0
Serafina's	3	.0000	.1370	31.4	3	0	0	0	0	0	0	0	3	0	0	0	0	0	0	0	0	0	0	0	0	0	0	0	0
Serafine	2	.0000	.0243	23.9	0	0	0	0	0	0	0	2	0	0	0	0	0	0	0	0	0	0	0	0	0	0	0	2	0
serape	3	.0000	.1370	31.4	1	0	0	0	0	0	2	0	3	0	0	0	0	0	0	0	0	0	0	0	0	0	0	0	0
serapes	2	.0000	.0037	15.7	0	2	0	0	0	0	0	0	0	0	0	0	0	0	0	0	0	2	0	0	0	0	0	0	0
Serapis	7	.2402	.5467	37.4	0	0	0	2	5	0	0	0	6	0	0	0	0	0	0	0	0	0	0	0	0	0	1	0	0
Serbia	5	.3639	.4034	36.1	0	0	0	0	0	4	1	0	0	0	0	0	0	2	0	0	0	0	0	0	0	0	2	1	0
Serbian	7	.2435	.3975	36.0	0	0	0	0	2	5	0	0	0	1	0	0	0	1	0	0	0	0	0	0	0	0	5	0	0
Serbo-Croatian	3	.2159	.1532	31.9	0	0	0	0	0	2	1	0	0	0	0	0	0	0	0	0	0	0	0	0	0	0	2	1	0
Serbs	2	.0000	.0389	25.9	0	0	0	0	2	0	0	0	0	0	0	0	0	2	0	0	0	0	0	0	0	0	0	0	0
serenade	4	.0759	.1243	30.9	0	0	1	2	0	1	0	0	1	0	0	0	0	0	0	0	3	0	0	0	0	0	0	0	0
serene	13	.5881	1.6190	42.1	0	2	2	1	2	4	1	1	4	0	0	1	0	0	0	0	0	1	0	0	1	2	1	3	0
serenely	6	.4700	.6094	37.8	0	0	2	0	1	2	1	0	1	0	0	1	0	1	0	0	2	0	0	0	0	0	0	1	0
Sereni	2	.0000	.0162	22.1	0	2	0	0	0	0	0	0	0	0	0	0	0	0	0	0	2	0	0	0	0	0	0	0	0
serenity	8	.1507	.3149	35.0	0	0	1	0	3	2	1	1	1	0	0	0	0	0	0	0	0	4	0	0	0	1	0	2	0
serf	4	.3344	.3261	35.1	0	0	0	3	0	1	0	0	1	0	0	0	0	2	0	0	0	0	0	0	0	0	1	0	0
serfs	14	.5143	1.5854	42.0	1	1	1	9	2	0	0	0	4	0	0	0	0	6	0	0	0	0	0	0	0	2	1	1	0
Serge	5	.3638	.3894	35.9	0	0	1	2	0	1	1	0	0	0	0	0	0	0	0	0	2	0	0	0	2	0	1	0	0
sergeant	30	.6256	4.0352	46.1	5	8	4	4	2	5	2	0	17	1	0	4	0	0	1	0	0	0	0	0	4	2	0	1	0
Sergeant	19	.5333	2.3000	43.6	0	0	8	6	3	2	0	0	13	1	0	0	0	0	0	0	0	0	0	0	1	0	2	2	0
Sergeant-at-Arms	2	.0000	.0914	29.6	0	0	0	2	0	0	0	0	2	0	0	0	0	0	0	0	0	0	0	0	0	0	0	0	0

7P Senir
6A Sensational
3A sensei
7A senselessly
6R Sensenbrenner
6H Senses
7P sensitively
4F Sensoji
6R Sensory
XR sensuously
5P sensuousness
9C sentence's
9D sentencing
6P sentimentales
9R sentimentalism
3G sents
6G seolc
6B seon
7D Seon
9Q separateness
8F Separation
9Q separations
5P separatist
5F Separatists
9E septagon
8B september
3J September's
9R septuagenarians
8A sepulchral
7N sepulchre
7F Sepulchre
7R sequential
5R sequined
7A Sequoya
4Q Serafin
7F Seraglio
6A Seraphine
9R Serb
8F Serbia's
8Q Serbians
6R sere
6A Serena
3Q serenaded
8J serenades
6A serenading
8J Serene
5F Serenity
6F serfdom
4N serge
7D Sergeant-Major

Word Type	F	D	U	SFI	3 Gr 3	4 Gr 4	5 Gr 5	6 Gr 6	7 Gr 7	8 Gr 8	9 Gr 9	X UnGr	A Read	B Eng & Gr	C Comp	D Lit	E Math	F Soc Stud	G Spell	H Sci	J Music	K Art	L Home Ec	M Shop	N Lib F	P Lib NF	Q Lib Ref	R Mag	S Rel
sergeant-major	6	.1493	.2320	33.7	0	0	0	1	5	0	0	0	0	0	0	5	0	0	0	0	0	0	0	0	0	0	0	1	0
Sergeant's	2	.0000	.0914	29.6	0	0	1	1	0	0	0	0	2	0	0	0	0	0	0	0	0	0	0	0	0	0	0	0	0
Sergey	2	.0000	.0162	22.1	0	0	0	2	0	0	0	0	0	0	0	0	0	0	0	0	2	0	0	0	0	0	0	0	0
serial	3	.1174	.0833	29.2	0	1	0	0	0	0	2	0	0	1	0	0	0	0	0	0	0	0	0	2	0	0	0	0	0
series	303	.8276	50.047	57.0	8	11	30	37	88	68	43	18	18	22	2	10	8	23	3	60	34	0	5	15	3	15	57	28	0
Series	41	.4720	4.2488	46.3	20	2	4	8	5	0	2	0	9	2	1	0	1	0	0	0	1	0	0	0	0	25	0	2	0
Serilda	12	.0000	.5482	37.4	0	0	0	12	0	0	0	0	12	0	0	0	0	0	0	0	0	0	0	0	0	0	0	0	0
serious	278	.9262	50.997	57.1	19	27	28	26	65	54	45	14	53	20	9	15	2	31	4	36	13	2	4	2	15	24	22	26	0
seriously	92	.8581	15.785	52.0	7	6	8	15	18	16	17	5	23	7	2	5	1	6	0	5	3	0	0	1	8	9	9	13	0
seriousness	11	.6705	1.5220	41.8	0	0	4	2	1	1	2	1	2	0	0	1	0	2	0	2	0	0	1	0	1	1	1	0	0
sermon	21	.6646	2.8660	44.6	0	3	2	2	8	1	3	2	3	0	0	1	0	2	1	0	1	0	0	0	5	4	0	4	0
sermons	12	.5461	1.3788	41.4	0	3	2	2	4	1	0	0	2	0	0	1	0	1	0	0	1	1	0	0	5	0	1	0	0
serpent	21	.5034	2.2386	43.5	4	0	0	2	10	2	3	0	3	1	3	6	0	0	0	0	1	0	0	0	0	6	1	0	0
Serpent	2	.2337	.1157	30.6	0	0	0	1	1	0	0	0	0	0	0	0	0	1	0	0	0	0	0	0	1	0	0	0	0
serpent's	2	.1717	.1142	30.6	0	0	0	1	1	0	0	0	1	0	0	1	0	0	0	0	0	0	0	0	0	0	0	0	0
serpentine	3	.3390	.2450	33.9	0	0	0	2	1	0	0	0	1	0	0	0	0	0	0	0	0	0	0	0	0	0	1	1	0
serpents	6	.4780	.6160	37.9	1	0	0	2	1	1	1	0	1	0	0	0	0	0	2	0	0	0	0	0	1	1	0	1	0
Serpicos	2	.0000	.0389	25.9	2	0	0	0	0	0	0	0	0	0	0	0	0	2	0	0	0	0	0	0	0	0	0	0	0
Serra	38	.2314	2.2397	43.5	0	13	12	10	0	3	0	0	0	0	0	0	0	28	0	0	0	0	0	0	0	0	0	10	0
serum	10	.2213	.5740	37.6	1	0	0	3	0	0	0	6	0	0	0	0	0	0	0	8	0	0	0	0	0	0	2	0	0
servant	98	.4002	9.0761	49.6	18	16	5	13	31	8	6	1	30	1	0	7	0	8	0	7	2	1	0	0	13	21	2	3	3
Servant	3	.0000	.0322	25.1	0	0	0	0	0	0	3	0	0	0	0	3	0	0	0	0	0	0	0	0	0	0	0	0	0
servants	93	.6370	12.483	51.0	13	25	7	6	24	14	3	1	33	2	0	10	0	14	0	1	1	1	0	0	8	12	5	5	1
serve	317	.7788	49.654	57.0	11	24	33	40	90	46	59	14	46	10	9	12	8	40	3	23	11	2	51	8	10	23	31	30	0
served	275	.7011	39.312	55.9	17	23	43	25	63	49	46	9	44	9	0	11	2	50	2	10	11	1	43	1	12	19	37	23	0
serves	103	.8830	18.040	52.6	4	10	6	17	30	13	19	4	5	6	3	3	2	14	2	15	7	2	6	4	3	2	15	14	0
service	298	.8870	52.561	57.2	27	26	30	23	79	42	52	19	46	9	2	11	7	51	2	11	10	1	7	2	15	38	44	42	0
Service	77	.6170	9.8615	49.9	3	9	7	3	28	7	5	15	9	0	0	2	2	5	0	10	0	0	0	0	0	18	13	18	0
serviceable	5	.4755	.5327	37.3	0	0	0	1	2	0	2	0	2	0	0	1	0	0	0	0	0	0	0	0	0	0	1	1	0
servicemen	4	.2296	.2103	33.2	0	0	0	0	2	0	1	1	0	0	1	0	0	0	0	0	0	0	0	0	0	0	0	3	0
services	166	.7339	24.715	53.9	23	9	29	13	24	28	37	3	13	1	0	4	1	75	3	7	8	1	6	0	1	9	29	8	0
Services	3	.3465	.2515	34.0	1	0	0	1	1	0	0	0	1	0	0	0	0	0	0	0	0	0	0	0	0	1	0	1	0
serving	78	.3638	6.1858	47.9	0	8	2	9	27	10	18	4	6	0	0	1	1	10	0	2	3	0	31	0	0	7	4	13	0
Servingman	3	.0000	.0322	25.1	0	0	0	0	0	0	3	0	0	0	0	3	0	0	0	0	0	0	0	0	0	0	0	0	0
servings	10	.1637	.3848	35.9	0	0	0	1	4	2	3	0	0	0	0	0	0	0	0	1	0	0	6	0	0	0	0	3	0
servitude	6	.2431	.3633	35.6	0	0	2	0	2	2	0	0	0	0	0	0	0	4	0	0	0	0	0	0	2	0	0	0	0
Sesamaul	2	.0000	.0914	29.6	0	0	0	2	0	0	0	0	2	0	0	0	0	0	0	0	0	0	0	0	0	0	0	0	0
sesame	5	.4592	.5222	37.2	0	0	0	2	1	0	1	1	2	0	0	0	0	0	0	1	1	0	0	0	0	0	0	1	0
Sesame	6	.0000	.2741	34.4	0	5	0	1	0	0	0	0	6	0	0	0	0	0	0	0	0	0	0	0	0	0	0	0	0
session	48	.8071	7.7942	48.9	5	3	5	1	18	11	5	0	10	2	0	3	1	7	2	0	5	0	1	0	0	7	4	6	0
sessions	12	.4313	1.1239	40.5	1	0	3	3	3	1	1	0	1	0	0	0	0	2	0	0	0	0	0	0	0	1	5	3	0
set	3572	.8141	583.67	67.7	492	568	480	486	649	499	323	75	504	125	28	103	1702	182	50	159	65	6	34	60	116	178	111	146	3
Set	4	.1511	.1521	31.8	0	0	0	0	0	4	0	0	0	0	0	0	1	0	3	0	0	0	0	0	0	0	0	0	0
set-in	2	.0000	.0064	18.1	0	0	0	0	1	0	1	0	0	0	0	0	0	0	0	0	0	0	2	0	0	0	0	0	0
set-to	2	.0000	.0243	23.9	0	0	0	1	1	0	0	0	0	0	0	0	0	0	0	0	0	0	0	0	0	0	0	2	0
set-up	3	.0000	.0591	27.7	0	3	0	0	0	0	0	0	0	0	0	0	0	0	0	3	0	0	0	0	0	0	0	0	0
setback	4	.3024	.3033	34.8	2	0	0	0	1	0	1	0	1	0	0	0	0	1	0	0	0	0	0	0	0	2	0	0	0
setbacks	2	.2433	.1158	30.6	1	0	0	0	0	1	0	0	0	0	0	0	0	0	0	0	0	0	0	0	0	1	0	1	0
Seth	28	.5460	3.4475	45.4	8	4	1	9	5	1	0	0	19	1	0	4	2	0	0	0	0	0	0	0	0	1	1	0	0
sets	915	.5050	97.804	59.9	203	126	144	131	140	97	53	21	26	19	1	14	662	26	27	52	14	0	1	6	4	13	24	26	0
setscrew	2	.0000	.0050	17.0	0	0	0	0	0	0	2	0	0	0	0	0	0	0	0	0	0	0	0	2	0	0	0	0	0
Setsu	4	.0000	.0429	26.3	0	0	0	0	4	0	0	0	0	0	0	4	0	0	0	0	0	0	0	0	0	0	0	0	0
SETSU	4	.0000	.0429	26.3	0	0	0	0	4	0	0	0	0	0	0	4	0	0	0	0	0	0	0	0	0	0	0	0	0
setter	7	.3659	.5721	37.6	0	1	3	1	0	1	1	0	1	4	0	1	0	0	1	0	0	0	0	0	0	0	0	0	0
Setter	3	.2196	.1554	31.9	1	1	1	0	0	0	0	0	0	0	0	2	0	0	0	0	0	0	0	0	1	0	0	0	0
setters	2	.1717	.1142	30.6	0	0	1	0	1	0	0	0	1	0	0	1	0	0	0	0	0	0	0	0	0	0	0	0	0
settin'	5	.4218	.4665	36.7	1	0	0	1	1	2	0	0	1	2	0	1	0	0	0	0	0	0	0	0	1	0	0	0	0
setting	222	.9219	40.571	56.1	23	21	28	33	42	43	26	6	55	9	5	16	9	25	1	6	23	3	7	2	15	15	10	21	0
settings	19	.6844	2.6540	44.2	1	2	1	1	7	6	0	1	3	0	0	0	3	1	0	1	5	1	1	0	2	0	1	1	0
settle	164	.8008	26.553	54.2	25	28	35	22	19	21	13	1	37	3	0	7	0	55	3	20	0	1	2	0	8	12	11	5	0
settled	399	.8059	64.827	58.1	41	67	79	69	64	52	25	2	87	6	6	23	2	113	6	6	27	0	0	0	20	45	41	17	0
settlement	140	.6773	19.560	52.9	15	16	33	18	18	21	19	0	22	6	0	2	1	62	1	0	2	0	0	0	5	12	15	12	0
settlements	80	.6352	10.571	50.2	7	5	22	14	10	18	4	0	12	0	1	0	0	35	0	0	3	0	0	0	1	8	12	8	0
settler	20	.6169	2.6385	44.2	3	4	3	5	3	1	0	1	8	0	0	2	0	4	0	2	0	0	0	0	0	3	1	0	0
settler's	2	.1948	.1250	31.0	1	1	0	0	0	0	0	0	1	0	0	0	0	0	0	0	0	0	0	0	0	1	0	0	0
settlers	369	.6350	49.079	56.9	62	52	107	44	50	48	4	2	77	7	0	3	0	178	2	7	25	0	0	0	6	29	28	7	0
settlers'	4	.2412	.2282	33.6	1	1	0	0	1	0	1	0	0	2	0	0	0	0	0	0	0	0	0	0	0	2	0	0	0
settles	30	.7241	4.4368	46.5	5	3	6	6	6	2	0	2	5	0	0	1	0	2	0	8	1	0	0	0	4	5	2	2	0
settling	55	.8116	8.9797	49.5	3	7	11	12	10	7	3	2	10	2	1	2	0	12	0	6	5	0	0	0	5	5	5	2	0
setup	7	.2205	.3670	35.6	0	0	0	0	3	1	2	1	0	0	0	0	0	0	0	0	0	0	0	0	0	0	2	5	0
sev'n	2	.0000	.0162	22.1	0	2	0	0	0	0	0	0	0	0	0	0	0	0	0	0	2	0	0	0	0	0	0	0	0
Sevastopol	2	.0000	.0209	23.2	0	1	0	0	0	1	0	0	0	0	0	0	0	0	0	0	0	0	0	0	0	0	2	0	0
seven	687	.9149	124.75	61.0	145	107	77	83	108	73	71	23	170	39	3	37	93	61	46	33	27	0	0	1	31	60	30	55	1
Seven	22	.7540	3.3774	45.3	1	2	0	4	9	1	5	0	6	1	0	0	0	3	0	1	1	0	1	0	2	1	4	2	0
seven-day	2	.1523	.0721	28.6	0	1	0	0	0	1	0	0	0	0	1	0	0	0	0	0	0	0	0	0	0	0	0	1	0
seven-digit	2	.0000	.0914	29.6	0	0	0	0	0	2	0	0	2	0	0	0	0	0	0	0	0	0	0	0	0	0	0	0	0
seven-eighths	2	.2413	.1212	30.8	0	1	0	1	0	0	0	0	0	0	0	0	1	0	0	1	0	0	0	0	0	0	0	0	0
seven-thirty	2	.1948	.1250	31.0	0	2	0	0	0	0	0	0	1	0	0	0	0	0	0	0	0	0	0	0	0	1	0	0	0
seven-year-old	14	.3987	1.2396	40.9	0	9	2	1	1	0	1	0	1	0	0	0	0	1	0	1	0	0	0	0	1	9	1	0	0
sevens	15	.0000	.2245	33.5	1	6	7	0	0	0	0	1	0	0	0	0	15	0	0	0	0	0	0	0	0	0	0	0	0
seventeen	59	.7808	9.3650	49.7	2	10	9	5	19	5	9	0	20	3	2	7	4	4	1	2	0	0	0	0	3	9	0	4	0
Seventeen	4	.0000	.0469	26.7	0	0	4	0	0	0	0	0	0	0	0	0	0	0	0	0	0	0	0	0	4	0	0	0	0
seventeen-thousand-mile	2	.0000	.0290	24.6	0	2	0	0	0	0	0	0	0	0	0	0	0	0	0	0	0	0	0	0	0	2	0	0	0
seventeen-year-old	3	.2332	.1690	32.3	0	2	1	0	0	0	0	0	0	0	0	0	0	0	0	0	0	0	0	0	0	2	0	1	0
seventeenth	41	.7680	6.3224	48.0	2	2	3	9	11	9	2	3	2	2	2	2	1	6	1	5	10	1	0	0	0	5	1	3	0
Seventeenth	4	.2445	.3067	34.9	4	0	0	0	0	0	0	0	3	0	0	0	0	0	0	0	0	0	0	0	0	1	0	0	0
seventeenth-century	11	.5774	1.3197	41.2	0	0	0	1	5	2	1	2	1	0	0	3	2	0	0	0	1	0	0	0	0	2	0	2	0
seventh	71	.6066	8.8749	49.5	8	12	11	11	11	13	5	0	7	7	0	2	3	9	3	1	28	0	0	0	2	3	2	4	0
Seventh	11	.4508	1.1390	40.6	0	0	2	1	6	0	2	0	5	1	0	0	0	0	0	0	0	0	0	0	0	2	3	0	0
seventh-grade	9	.2364	.4940	36.9	0	0	0	1	5	1	2	0	0	7	0	1	0	0	0	0	0	0	0	0	0	0	0	1	0
seventh-grader	2	.2433	.1158	30.6	1	0	0	1	0	0	0	0	0	0	0	0	0	0	0	0	0	0	0	0	0	1	0	1	0
sevenths	2	.2287	.1077	30.3	0	0	1	0	1	0	0	0	0	0	0	0	1	0	0	0	1	0	0	0	0	0	0	0	0
seventies	2	.1523	.0721	28.6	0	0	0	0	1	0	1	0	0	0	1	0	0	0	0	0	0	0	0	0	0	0	0	1	0

5N sergeant's
XR serialized
8F serials
9D Seribriakov
5A seringero's
5A seringueiro's
7D serious-looking
7L serious-minded
6R Seronera
7H serpent-like
3F Serpico
5F Serra's
7R serrated
6H serums
7Q serval
8Q servanda
7F servant's
8N servants'
XH Servetus
7R service/repair
7F Serviceable
6A serving-men
5G servire
7N servitors
5G servus
8D ses
XR sessile
8J Sessions
8F Sessue
3P SET
5D set-gun
8G Sets
7D SETS
7D Setsu's
7N setter's
4A Setting
7Q seuerall
8K Seurat
4P seven-and-a-half
8N seven-dollar
7J seven-eleven
7Q seven-foot
4A seven-letter
XR seven-member
7H seven-month-old
6E seven-ninths
7J seven-note
7B seven-pound
9B seven-sentence
7P seven-story
6E seven-tenths
6F seven-year
6D sevenscore
7Q seventeen-year
8F Seventh-Day
7A seventh-graders

Word Type	F	D	U	SFI	3 Gr 3	4 Gr 4	5 Gr 5	6 Gr 6	7 Gr 7	8 Gr 8	9 Gr 9	X UnGr	A Read	B Eng & Gr	C Comp	D Lit	E Math	F Soc Stud	G Spell	H Sci	J Music	K Art	L Home Ec	M Shop	N Lib F	P Lib NF	Q Lib Ref	R Mag	S Rel
seventy	47	.7794	7.4449	48.7	3	4	12	5	13	4	3	3	15	2	0	2	2	6	2	1	0	0	0	0	9	3	2	3	0
Seventy	4	.0000	.0438	26.4	0	0	0	0	3	1	0	0	0	4	0	0	0	0	0	0	0	0	0	0	0	0	0	0	0
seventy-eight	2	.2160	.1362	31.3	0	0	1	0	0	1	0	0	1	0	0	0	0	0	0	1	0	0	0	0	0	0	0	0	0
seventy-five	35	.7537	5.3964	47.3	9	6	1	3	8	3	4	1	12	1	0	3	1	3	0	2	2	0	0	0	5	5	0	1	0
seventy-four	4	.2446	.3071	34.9	0	3	0	0	0	0	1	0	3	0	0	0	1	0	0	0	0	0	0	0	0	0	0	0	0
seventy-nine	4	.2305	.2357	33.7	0	1	0	3	0	0	0	0	0	0	0	0	0	0	0	3	0	0	0	0	1	0	0	0	0
seventy-one	2	.2398	.1138	30.6	0	0	1	0	0	0	1	0	0	0	0	1	1	0	0	0	0	0	0	0	0	0	0	0	0
seventy-six	4	.4802	.4072	36.1	0	0	0	0	2	0	1	1	0	0	0	1	1	0	0	1	0	0	0	0	1	0	0	0	0
seventy-two	7	.3356	.5665	37.5	1	2	0	2	1	0	1	0	2	0	0	2	3	0	0	0	0	0	0	0	0	0	0	0	0
sever	4	.4485	.4009	36.0	0	1	0	1	0	1	0	1	1	0	0	0	0	1	0	0	0	0	0	0	0	0	1	1	0
several	1801	.9476	337.18	65.3	161	276	273	262	375	219	191	44	317	127	23	54	67	274	41	246	97	35	43	46	59	126	126	120	0
severe	88	.7751	13.771	51.4	2	4	10	12	21	20	17	2	15	0	4	1	0	10	2	10	2	0	2	0	3	8	15	16	0
severed	3	.2304	.1619	32.1	0	0	0	1	1	1	0	0	0	0	0	0	0	0	0	0	0	0	0	0	2	0	1	0	0
severely	23	.7020	3.3476	45.2	3	1	3	4	4	5	2	1	8	0	0	2	0	5	0	1	0	0	0	0	2	1	2	2	0
severest	2	.2152	.1357	31.3	0	0	0	0	0	2	0	0	1	0	0	0	0	1	0	0	0	0	0	0	0	0	0	0	0
severing	3	.3272	.2363	33.7	0	0	0	0	1	0	2	0	1	0	0	1	0	0	0	0	1	0	0	0	0	0	0	0	0
severity	4	.0974	.1495	31.7	0	2	2	0	0	0	0	0	1	0	0	0	0	0	0	0	0	0	0	0	3	0	0	0	0
Severn	3	.0000	.1370	31.4	0	0	1	0	2	0	0	0	3	0	0	0	0	0	0	0	0	0	0	0	0	0	0	0	0
Seville	9	.1294	.3305	35.2	0	1	1	4	2	1	0	0	1	0	0	0	0	0	0	0	7	0	0	0	0	1	0	0	0
sew	57	.5296	6.4354	48.1	13	10	5	8	16	4	1	0	15	0	1	0	3	7	5	1	1	1	17	0	1	2	1	2	0
sewage	31	.6059	3.8794	45.9	1	0	8	12	2	2	6	0	0	1	0	0	1	4	0	12	0	0	1	0	0	0	7	5	0
sewage-disposal	2	.0000	.0394	26.0	0	0	0	1	0	1	0	0	0	0	0	0	0	0	0	2	0	0	0	0	0	0	0	0	0
Seward	9	.4769	.9814	39.9	0	0	7	0	1	1	0	0	4	0	0	0	0	3	0	0	0	0	0	0	0	0	1	1	0
Seward's	3	.1639	.1674	32.2	0	0	3	0	0	0	0	0	1	0	0	0	0	2	0	0	0	0	0	0	0	0	0	0	0
sewed	33	.5705	4.0176	46.0	9	5	6	2	3	7	1	0	12	0	2	0	0	5	2	0	0	1	7	0	3	1	0	0	0
Sewell	2	.0000	.0914	29.6	0	0	2	0	0	0	0	0	2	0	0	0	0	0	0	0	0	0	0	0	0	0	0	0	0
sewer	8	.4965	.8368	39.2	0	1	3	0	3	0	1	0	0	0	0	0	0	0	0	3	0	0	0	1	2	1	0	1	0
sewerage	3	.1823	.1405	31.5	0	0	2	0	0	1	0	0	0	0	0	0	0	1	0	0	0	0	0	0	0	0	2	0	0
sewers	8	.5549	.9577	39.8	0	0	0	3	4	0	1	0	2	0	0	0	0	2	0	2	0	0	0	0	1	0	1	0	0
sewing	130	.3969	11.294	50.5	16	10	11	14	32	20	26	1	23	3	2	2	1	10	1	6	2	1	57	0	8	7	6	1	0
sewn	10	.3881	.9008	39.5	1	0	3	2	2	1	1	0	4	0	0	0	0	1	0	0	0	1	3	0	0	0	0	1	0
sex	83	.5057	8.8126	49.5	0	0	6	5	35	4	28	5	1	5	0	1	0	3	0	11	0	0	1	0	0	9	5	47	0
Sex	6	.0000	.0729	28.6	0	0	0	0	0	0	5	1	0	0	0	0	0	0	0	0	0	0	0	0	0	0	0	6	0
sex-education	5	.0000	.0608	27.8	0	0	0	0	5	0	0	0	0	0	0	0	0	0	0	0	0	0	0	0	0	0	0	5	0
sexes	8	.4400	.7500	38.8	0	0	0	1	4	2	0	1	0	1	0	0	0	1	0	1	0	0	0	0	0	0	4	1	0
sextant	5	.1901	.2435	33.9	0	0	0	4	0	1	0	0	0	0	0	0	0	0	0	0	0	0	0	0	0	4	0	1	0
sexton	2	.0000	.0219	23.4	0	0	0	0	0	2	0	0	0	2	0	0	0	0	0	0	0	0	0	0	0	0	0	0	0
Sextus	2	.0000	.0290	24.6	0	2	0	0	0	0	0	0	0	0	0	0	0	0	0	0	0	0	0	0	0	2	0	0	0
sexual	20	.4370	1.8716	42.7	0	0	1	0	12	2	2	3	0	0	0	0	0	0	0	5	0	0	0	0	0	2	7	6	0
sexuality	2	.0000	.0243	23.9	0	0	0	0	1	1	0	0	0	0	0	0	0	0	0	0	0	0	0	0	0	0	0	2	0
sexually	2	.2437	.1129	30.5	0	0	0	1	0	0	1	0	0	0	0	0	0	0	0	0	0	0	0	0	0	0	1	1	0
Seybold	5	.0000	.0608	27.8	0	0	0	5	0	0	0	0	0	0	0	0	0	0	0	0	0	0	0	0	0	0	0	5	0
Seymour	5	.3681	.3974	36.0	0	0	1	0	2	0	2	0	0	0	0	0	0	0	0	0	0	0	0	0	2	0	2	1	0
SF	2	.2446	.1125	30.5	0	0	0	0	1	1	0	0	0	1	0	1	0	0	0	0	0	0	0	0	0	0	0	0	0
sferics	2	.0000	.0394	26.0	0	0	0	0	0	2	0	0	0	0	0	0	0	0	0	2	0	0	0	0	0	0	0	0	0
sh	145	.1783	6.3118	48.0	22	36	23	22	31	9	2	0	6	7	0	0	0	0	118	0	0	0	0	0	2	9	0	3	0
sh-h	2	.0000	.0215	23.3	0	0	0	0	0	0	2	0	0	0	0	2	0	0	0	0	0	0	0	0	0	0	0	0	0
sh-h-h	3	.2212	.2099	33.2	0	1	0	0	0	1	1	0	2	0	0	1	0	0	0	0	0	0	0	0	0	0	0	0	0
shabbiness	2	.0000	.0290	24.6	0	0	1	1	0	0	0	0	0	0	0	0	0	0	0	0	0	0	0	0	0	2	0	0	0
shabby	20	.6535	2.7165	44.3	3	2	3	2	3	5	1	1	5	3	0	2	0	2	0	0	0	0	0	0	1	4	0	3	0
shack	40	.6432	5.4869	47.4	6	5	3	7	13	1	5	0	21	1	2	1	0	4	0	0	0	0	0	0	2	5	0	4	0
shackles	2	.2441	.1127	30.5	1	0	0	0	1	0	0	0	0	0	0	0	0	0	0	0	0	0	0	0	1	0	1	0	0
Shackleton	2	.0000	.0914	29.6	0	0	0	2	0	0	0	0	2	0	0	0	0	0	0	0	0	0	0	0	0	0	0	0	0
shacks	9	.3751	.7574	38.8	0	1	4	2	2	0	0	0	0	0	0	0	0	5	0	0	0	0	0	0	0	2	0	2	0
shad	2	.0000	.0243	23.9	0	0	0	0	0	2	0	0	0	0	0	0	0	0	0	0	0	0	0	0	0	0	0	2	0
Shad	2	.0000	.0234	23.7	0	0	2	0	0	0	0	0	0	0	0	0	0	0	0	0	0	0	0	0	2	0	0	0	0
shade	203	.9188	36.991	55.7	43	32	22	33	32	25	5	11	45	2	4	5	36	13	5	20	5	4	5	1	17	23	9	9	0
shaded	121	.5530	14.056	51.5	22	17	15	32	13	12	8	2	8	1	0	2	79	13	1	2	2	1	0	1	3	0	1	7	0
shades	69	.5785	8.2340	49.2	11	14	4	6	20	7	4	3	8	10	0	3	2	6	3	2	2	14	7	1	1	5	2	3	0
Shades	2	.0000	.0243	23.9	0	0	0	0	1	0	1	0	0	0	0	0	0	0	0	0	0	0	0	0	0	0	0	2	0
shading	29	.5134	3.1835	45.0	0	15	2	4	1	1	3	3	4	0	0	1	1	13	0	0	0	4	0	1	1	0	1	3	0
shadoof	2	.0000	.0389	25.9	0	0	0	0	2	0	0	0	0	0	0	0	0	2	0	0	0	0	0	0	0	0	0	0	0
shadow	221	.8237	36.711	55.6	15	21	33	47	46	23	26	10	73	3	2	31	14	10	1	25	1	6	0	0	19	21	5	10	0
Shadow	46	.1055	2.8018	44.5	39	7	0	0	0	0	0	0	45	0	0	0	0	0	0	0	0	0	0	0	0	0	1	0	0
Shadow's	6	.0000	.2741	34.4	6	0	0	0	0	0	0	0	6	0	0	0	0	0	0	0	0	0	0	0	0	0	0	0	0
shadowed	7	.6060	.8862	39.5	0	1	1	1	1	2	1	0	1	0	0	1	0	2	0	0	0	0	0	0	1	1	0	1	0
shadowing	3	.3854	.2500	34.0	0	0	0	1	2	0	0	0	0	1	0	0	0	0	0	0	0	0	0	0	1	1	0	0	0
shadows	147	.6970	21.047	53.2	23	34	18	15	24	20	5	8	40	6	5	24	0	7	0	9	4	13	0	0	17	10	5	7	0
shadowy	30	.7046	4.3052	46.3	4	3	4	7	6	5	0	1	5	2	2	3	0	1	0	2	3	0	0	0	6	0	1	5	0
Shadrach	5	.3541	.3828	35.8	0	0	0	0	2	3	0	0	0	0	0	1	0	0	0	0	1	0	0	0	3	0	0	0	0
Shadrach's	3	.0000	.0352	25.5	0	0	0	0	0	3	0	0	0	0	0	0	0	0	0	0	0	0	0	0	3	0	0	0	0
Shadwell	2	.0000	.0290	24.6	0	2	0	0	0	0	0	0	0	0	0	0	0	0	0	0	0	0	0	0	0	2	0	0	0
shady	30	.7419	4.5758	46.6	6	8	4	2	8	1	0	1	11	1	0	2	0	2	0	6	2	0	0	0	2	1	0	3	0
shaft	69	.7203	10.205	50.1	10	6	9	12	18	11	2	1	21	0	0	1	0	2	0	8	0	0	1	4	6	8	11	7	0
Shafter	5	.0000	.0608	27.8	0	0	0	0	0	0	0	5	0	0	0	0	0	0	0	0	0	0	0	0	0	0	0	5	0
Shafter's	2	.0000	.0243	23.9	0	0	0	0	0	0	0	2	0	0	0	0	0	0	0	0	0	0	0	0	0	0	0	2	0
Shaftesbury	2	.2437	.1129	30.5	0	0	0	0	0	1	0	1	0	0	0	0	0	0	0	0	0	0	0	0	0	0	1	1	0
shafts	31	.6071	4.0238	46.0	8	2	2	6	7	4	2	0	13	0	0	0	0	3	0	3	0	0	0	2	4	0	5	1	0
Shag	10	.0000	.4568	36.6	0	10	0	0	0	0	0	0	10	0	0	0	0	0	0	0	0	0	0	0	0	0	0	0	0
shaggy	34	.6769	4.7419	46.8	5	7	5	2	8	4	2	1	8	1	0	6	0	2	0	1	0	2	0	0	6	4	1	3	0
shaggy-haired	2	.1621	.0746	28.7	0	0	0	0	1	0	1	0	0	0	1	1	0	0	0	0	0	0	0	0	0	0	0	0	0
shah	2	.0000	.0389	25.9	0	0	0	0	2	0	0	0	0	0	0	0	0	2	0	0	0	0	0	0	0	0	0	0	0
shake	143	.8389	24.163	53.8	31	31	19	17	22	11	9	3	55	3	1	7	0	3	1	19	8	0	6	1	15	17	1	6	0
shaken	42	.7414	6.3259	48.0	6	1	6	9	7	9	3	1	9	0	0	6	0	2	0	2	3	0	3	0	4	5	2	6	0
shaker	8	.2700	.5513	37.4	0	0	0	0	8	0	0	0	2	0	0	4	0	0	0	2	0	0	0	0	0	0	0	0	0
shakers	3	.2441	.1719	32.4	3	0	0	0	0	0	0	0	0	0	0	0	0	0	0	0	1	0	0	0	0	2	0	0	0
Shakers	6	.2217	.3130	35.0	0	0	4	1	0	1	0	0	0	0	0	0	0	1	0	0	4	0	0	0	0	1	0	0	0
shakes	39	.7862	6.2466	48.0	9	8	4	9	3	1	5	0	16	3	0	5	1	1	0	5	2	0	1	0	2	2	0	1	0
Shakespeare	33	.7538	5.0025	47.0	1	1	3	7	8	7	5	1	3	9	1	1	0	2	4	0	3	0	0	0	2	2	4	2	0
Shakespeare's	19	.5640	2.2271	43.5	0	1	3	3	5	4	3	0	2	6	0	0	0	1	0	0	4	0	0	0	2	1	3	0	0
shakily	11	.3866	1.0595	40.3	3	2	1	1	4	0	0	0	7	0	0	2	0	0	0	0	0	0	0	0	2	0	0	0	0
shaking	146	.7434	22.360	53.5	30	35	9	18	24	18	11	1	67	2	0	15	0	2	0	6	6	0	3	0	23	12	1	9	0
shaky	19	.6689	2.6670	44.3	2	3	1	1	10	0	1	1	8	0	0	1	0	2	1	0	0	0	0	0	2	2	0	3	0
shale	19	.5761	2.3090	43.6	6	5	0	6	1	1	0	0	2	0	0	0	0	4	0	5	0	0	0	0	1	5	2	0	0

5A seventy-eighth
3N seventy-five-cent
3P seventy-foot-long
5A seventy-ninth
9D seventy-odd
3A seventy-seven
5R seventy-seven-year-old
9C seventy-sixth
3P seventy-ton
7A several-year
8F severally
9H Severe
8F severities
7F Sevres
5Q Sewage
5A Sewell's
7N sewers'
6A sewin'
7L Sewing
5Q sewing-machine
6H sews
6F Sewyne
9R sex-in-class
9R sex-in-school
9R sex-related
7P sextette
XR sexy
6R Seydhisfjordhur
8R Sgt
8D sha'l
8B shabby-looking
6N shackled
7N shad-bellied
7D shade-preserved
6F shadings
5R shadow-box
5A shadow-flecked
9D shadow-papers
3P shadowings
4R Shadows
5Q Shafii
7Q shaftless
7R shag
7Q shagbark
5N shaggy-lookin'
8Q Shah-i-Zind
8K Shahn
6A shake-up
9B shaked
7D Shakespearean
9R Shakespeares
9J Shakespearian
5J Shaking
5P shakos
8A Shakur
7D Shalehaha

Word Type	F	D	U	SFI	3 Gr 3	4 Gr 4	5 Gr 5	6 Gr 6	7 Gr 7	8 Gr 8	9 Gr 9	X UnGr	A Read	B Eng & Gr	C Comp	D Lit	E Math	F Soc Stud	G Spell	H Sci	J Music	K Art	L Home Ec	M Shop	N Lib F	P Lib NF	Q Lib Ref	R Mag	S Rel
shales	4	.0000	.0789	29.0	1	0	0	0	0	0	3	0	0	0	0	0	0	0	0	4	0	0	0	0	0	0	0	0	0
shall	1051	.8386	176.92	62.5	152	110	112	169	172	145	174	17	289	61	12	192	47	111	13	55	52	2	2	0	99	82	17	13	4
Shall	3	.1983	.1396	31.4	0	0	0	2	0	1	0	0	0	0	0	0	0	0	0	0	2	0	0	0	0	0	0	1	0
shallow	136	.8593	23.329	53.7	21	16	14	26	27	13	15	4	23	1	4	8	0	20	1	20	0	3	5	3	2	22	14	10	0
shallow-water	3	.2445	.1818	32.6	0	0	0	0	1	0	2	0	0	0	0	0	0	0	0	2	0	0	0	0	0	0	1	0	0
shallower	3	.3776	.2493	34.0	0	0	1	0	0	1	0	1	0	1	0	0	0	0	0	1	0	0	0	0	0	0	0	1	0
shallows	11	.5831	1.3323	41.2	0	0	2	3	3	0	1	2	1	0	0	2	0	0	0	1	0	0	0	0	1	1	1	4	0
Shalom	4	.0000	.0323	25.1	0	0	3	1	0	0	0	0	0	0	0	0	0	0	0	0	4	0	0	0	0	0	0	0	0
shalt	22	.4993	2.2936	43.6	1	0	9	2	1	2	6	1	1	0	0	7	0	0	0	0	2	0	0	0	1	1	9	1	0
sham	4	.3726	.3697	35.7	0	0	0	1	1	2	0	0	2	0	0	0	0	1	0	0	0	0	0	0	1	0	0	0	0
Sham	31	.0000	.3634	35.6	0	0	0	31	0	0	0	0	0	0	0	0	0	0	0	0	0	0	0	0	31	0	0	0	0
Sham's	12	.1071	.3772	35.8	0	0	0	11	1	0	0	0	0	0	0	1	0	0	0	0	0	0	0	0	11	0	0	0	0
shaman	2	.0000	.0215	23.3	0	0	0	0	0	2	0	0	0	0	0	2	0	0	0	0	0	0	0	0	0	0	0	0	0
shambles	2	.2433	.1158	30.6	0	0	1	0	0	0	0	1	0	0	0	0	0	0	0	0	0	0	0	0	0	1	0	1	0
shambling	2	.2285	.1129	30.5	0	0	0	0	1	1	0	0	0	0	0	0	0	1	0	0	0	0	0	0	0	0	1	0	0
shame	67	.6016	8.5600	49.3	12	3	6	8	18	9	10	1	24	4	0	18	0	2	0	0	0	0	0	0	11	4	2	2	0
shamefaced	2	.2446	.1142	30.6	0	0	0	1	1	0	0	0	0	0	0	0	0	0	0	0	0	0	0	0	1	0	0	1	0
shameful	2	.0000	.0914	29.6	0	0	0	0	1	1	0	0	2	0	0	0	0	0	0	0	0	0	0	0	0	0	0	0	0
shameless	2	.1814	.1187	30.7	0	1	0	0	0	0	1	0	1	0	0	0	0	0	0	0	0	0	0	0	0	0	0	1	0
shamelessly	2	.1814	.1187	30.7	0	0	0	2	0	0	0	0	1	0	0	0	0	0	0	0	0	0	0	0	0	0	0	1	0
shames	2	.2407	.1138	30.6	0	0	1	0	0	1	0	0	0	0	0	1	0	0	0	0	0	0	0	0	0	1	0	0	0
shampoo	2	.1648	.0800	29.0	0	0	0	0	0	1	1	0	0	0	0	0	1	0	0	0	0	0	1	0	0	0	0	0	0
shampoos	2	.1926	.0867	29.4	0	0	0	1	0	1	0	0	0	0	0	0	0	0	0	0	0	0	1	0	0	0	1	0	0
Shan	3	.2435	.2274	33.6	0	0	0	2	1	0	0	0	2	0	0	0	0	1	0	0	0	0	0	0	0	0	0	0	0
shan't	8	.2097	.5357	37.3	0	1	3	2	1	0	1	0	5	0	0	3	0	0	0	0	0	0	0	0	0	0	0	2	0
Shandon	2	.0000	.0243	23.9	0	0	0	2	0	0	0	0	0	0	0	0	0	0	0	0	0	0	0	0	0	0	0	0	0
Shane	24	.3059	1.9909	43.0	0	0	0	0	8	15	1	0	15	0	0	1	0	0	0	0	0	0	0	0	8	0	0	0	0
Shane's	3	.1250	.1342	31.3	0	0	0	0	2	1	0	0	1	0	0	0	0	0	0	0	0	0	0	0	2	0	0	0	0
Shanghai	8	.4689	.7995	39.0	0	0	3	0	2	3	0	0	0	0	0	0	0	3	0	0	0	0	0	0	2	1	2	0	0
Shangri-La	2	.2408	.1204	30.8	0	0	0	0	0	1	1	0	0	0	0	0	0	1	0	0	0	0	0	0	0	1	0	0	0
Shangri-la	7	.1146	.2114	33.3	6	0	0	0	0	0	0	1	0	0	0	0	0	0	0	0	6	0	0	0	0	0	0	1	0
Shanidar	2	.0000	.0209	23.2	0	0	0	0	2	0	0	0	0	0	0	0	0	0	0	0	0	0	0	0	0	0	2	0	0
shank	13	.4754	1.2830	41.1	0	0	4	0	0	2	4	3	0	0	0	0	0	0	0	3	0	0	2	3	1	1	3	0	0
Shankillas	2	.0000	.0389	25.9	0	0	0	0	2	0	0	0	0	0	0	0	0	2	0	0	0	0	0	0	0	0	0	0	0
shanks	4	.3733	.3101	34.9	0	0	0	0	2	1	1	0	0	0	0	0	0	0	0	0	0	0	1	1	0	0	2	0	0
Shannon	4	.4478	.4002	36.0	0	0	1	0	2	0	1	0	1	0	0	0	0	1	0	0	0	0	0	0	1	0	1	0	0
shantey	3	.0000	.0243	23.8	0	0	2	1	0	0	0	0	0	0	0	0	0	0	0	0	3	0	0	0	0	0	0	0	0
shanteyman	2	.0000	.0162	22.1	0	1	1	0	0	0	0	0	0	0	0	0	0	0	0	0	2	0	0	0	0	0	0	0	0
shanteys	2	.0000	.0162	22.1	0	0	1	1	0	0	0	0	0	0	0	0	0	0	0	0	2	0	0	0	0	0	0	0	0
shanties	2	.1494	.1045	30.2	0	0	0	1	0	1	0	0	1	0	0	0	0	0	0	0	1	0	0	0	0	0	0	0	0
shanty	8	.5386	.9406	39.7	0	3	0	1	3	0	1	0	3	1	0	0	0	1	0	0	0	0	0	0	1	0	0	2	0
shape	766	.7703	118.83	60.7	122	131	86	76	130	86	117	18	93	12	7	20	64	58	3	168	21	56	38	66	17	54	60	29	0
shaped	204	.8606	35.024	55.4	42	28	31	24	43	21	13	2	31	2	2	2	11	28	2	37	7	8	12	5	6	26	18	7	0
shapel	2	.0000	.0215	23.3	0	0	0	0	0	0	2	0	0	0	0	2	0	0	0	0	0	0	0	0	0	0	0	0	0
shapeless	2	.2401	.1133	30.5	0	1	1	0	0	0	0	0	0	0	0	0	0	0	0	0	0	0	0	0	0	1	1	0	0
shapely	2	.2446	.1142	30.6	0	0	0	0	1	0	0	1	0	0	0	0	0	0	0	0	0	0	0	0	1	0	0	1	0
shaper	6	.0000	.0151	21.8	0	0	0	0	0	0	6	0	0	0	0	0	0	0	0	0	0	0	0	6	0	0	0	0	0
shapers	4	.3290	.2836	34.5	0	0	0	0	1	0	1	2	0	0	0	0	0	0	0	0	0	0	0	1	0	0	1	2	0
shapes	343	.4332	31.843	55.0	100	50	30	49	45	31	35	3	49	4	10	4	9	11	1	49	3	118	9	21	2	16	18	19	0
shaping	24	.5879	2.9226	44.7	3	1	3	1	2	3	10	1	3	1	1	0	0	3	0	3	0	0	2	5	0	3	2	1	0
Shapiro	5	.1468	.2522	34.0	0	0	0	0	3	2	0	0	2	0	0	0	0	0	0	0	0	0	0	0	3	0	0	0	0
Shapley	11	.0000	.1337	31.3	0	0	0	0	11	0	0	0	0	0	0	0	0	0	0	0	0	0	0	0	0	0	0	11	0
Shapley's	5	.0000	.0608	27.8	0	0	0	0	5	0	0	0	0	0	0	0	0	0	0	0	0	0	0	0	0	0	0	5	0
share	354	.9244	64.806	58.1	43	73	49	45	74	31	31	8	62	43	5	17	29	55	6	13	18	2	13	0	15	23	24	28	1
sharecropper	2	.2441	.1127	30.5	2	0	0	0	0	0	0	0	0	0	0	0	0	0	0	0	0	0	0	0	1	0	1	0	0
sharecroppers	3	.0000	.0314	25.0	1	0	2	0	0	0	0	0	0	0	0	0	0	0	0	0	0	0	0	0	0	0	3	0	0
shared	117	.8679	20.255	53.1	13	15	18	5	37	14	8	7	22	8	1	9	16	16	0	3	2	1	0	1	1	8	12	17	0
shares	29	.6844	4.0815	46.1	2	3	1	6	9	3	4	1	5	1	0	0	5	3	0	2	0	0	0	0	0	5	4	4	0
sharing	51	.6166	6.4781	48.1	7	5	7	3	10	7	10	2	6	2	3	2	0	7	0	3	1	0	7	0	5	3	4	7	1
shark	92	.7258	13.845	51.4	5	19	8	17	23	13	7	0	44	1	1	0	3	1	0	6	0	0	0	0	11	7	10	8	0
Shark	6	.2297	.3406	35.3	0	3	0	0	3	0	0	0	0	0	0	3	0	3	0	0	0	0	0	0	0	0	0	0	0
shark's	11	.5310	1.2237	40.9	0	1	1	2	2	2	3	0	1	0	1	1	0	0	0	1	0	0	0	0	5	1	1	0	0
sharks	75	.6797	10.789	50.3	1	38	3	3	21	7	1	1	45	0	1	1	1	0	1	2	0	0	0	0	7	3	11	3	0
Sharks	7	.0000	.3198	35.0	7	0	0	0	0	0	0	0	7	0	0	0	0	0	0	0	0	0	0	0	0	0	0	0	0
sharks'	4	.1948	.2500	34.0	0	0	0	0	0	4	0	0	2	0	0	0	0	0	0	0	0	0	1	0	0	2	0	0	0
sharkskin	2	.1442	.0761	28.8	0	0	1	0	0	0	1	0	0	0	0	0	0	1	0	0	0	0	0	0	0	0	0	0	0
Sharon	35	.4159	3.4884	45.4	1	7	0	3	22	1	1	0	19	0	0	1	5	0	0	0	0	0	0	0	0	0	0	10	0
Sharon's	3	.1277	.1363	31.3	0	1	0	0	2	0	0	0	1	0	0	0	0	0	0	0	0	0	0	0	0	0	0	2	0
sharp	499	.9049	89.717	59.5	110	89	48	65	97	43	37	10	134	17	16	33	3	14	5	54	36	12	7	25	39	67	17	19	1
Sharp	24	.1300	1.5397	41.9	2	12	0	9	1	0	0	0	23	0	0	0	0	0	0	0	0	0	0	0	0	1	0	0	0
sharp-breaking	2	.1948	.1250	31.0	1	0	0	0	1	0	0	0	1	0	0	0	0	0	0	0	0	0	0	0	0	1	0	0	0
sharp-eyed	3	.2379	.1705	32.3	2	0	0	0	0	0	1	0	0	0	0	1	0	0	0	0	0	0	0	0	0	2	0	0	0
sharp-pointed	6	.4297	.5705	37.6	1	2	0	1	1	0	1	0	1	0	0	0	0	2	0	0	0	0	0	1	0	1	1	0	0
sharped	2	.0000	.0162	22.1	1	1	0	0	0	0	0	0	0	0	0	0	0	0	0	0	2	0	0	0	0	0	0	0	0
sharpen	23	.7358	3.4268	45.3	0	7	1	2	4	5	3	1	5	3	2	1	0	1	2	0	3	0	1	2	1	1	0	1	0
sharpened	22	.5955	2.7200	44.3	1	1	5	4	7	1	3	0	4	2	0	3	0	1	0	2	1	0	1	4	1	0	3	0	0
sharpening	9	.3166	.6358	38.0	0	2	0	1	2	1	3	0	1	0	0	0	0	0	0	0	0	0	0	3	3	0	1	1	0
Sharpening	2	.0000	.0050	17.0	0	0	0	0	2	0	0	0	0	0	0	0	0	0	0	0	0	0	0	2	0	0	0	0	0
sharpens	2	.1812	.0838	29.2	0	0	0	0	0	0	1	1	0	0	0	0	0	0	0	0	0	0	1	0	0	0	0	1	0
sharper	12	.5521	1.3795	41.4	2	0	3	1	4	0	2	0	1	0	0	1	0	0	0	0	2	0	0	0	4	3	1	0	0
sharpest	2	.2152	.1357	31.3	0	0	1	0	1	0	0	0	1	0	0	0	0	1	0	0	0	0	0	0	0	0	0	0	0
sharply	113	.8243	18.764	52.7	12	18	14	13	23	16	15	2	37	1	2	11	0	7	1	4	6	0	1	0	20	7	7	9	0
sharpness	6	.3112	.4907	36.9	0	1	0	4	0	1	0	0	3	0	0	0	0	0	0	2	0	0	1	0	0	0	0	0	0
sharps	23	.2682	1.3501	41.3	10	4	0	0	7	1	1	0	0	2	1	1	0	0	0	0	19	0	0	0	0	0	0	0	0
Shasta	4	.2353	.2382	33.8	0	0	0	0	1	1	2	0	0	0	0	0	0	0	0	3	0	0	0	0	0	0	1	0	0
Shatt-al-Arab	3	.0000	.0583	27.7	0	0	0	2	1	0	0	0	0	0	0	0	0	3	0	0	0	0	0	0	0	0	0	0	0
shatter	2	.0000	.0914	29.6	0	1	0	0	1	0	0	0	2	0	0	0	0	0	0	0	0	0	0	0	0	0	0	0	0
shattered	42	.6832	5.9454	47.7	3	1	4	5	13	9	7	0	13	1	0	8	0	5	0	0	0	0	0	0	5	3	4	3	0
shattering	12	.6491	1.5850	42.0	0	1	1	2	3	2	3	0	0	1	0	3	0	2	0	0	0	0	0	0	2	1	1	2	0
shatters	2	.0000	.0394	26.0	0	0	0	0	1	1	0	0	0	0	0	0	0	0	0	2	0	0	0	0	0	0	0	0	0
shave	15	.5330	1.7501	42.4	5	0	4	1	1	1	1	2	6	0	0	1	0	0	0	0	0	0	0	0	0	2	2	4	0
shaved	11	.5333	1.2757	41.1	3	1	1	1	5	0	0	0	4	0	0	1	0	0	0	0	0	0	0	0	3	0	1	2	0
shaven	4	.1757	.1766	32.5	0	1	0	0	2	0	1	0	0	0	0	3	0	0	0	0	0	0	0	0	0	1	0	0	0
shaver	6	.3427	.4955	37.0	0	2	0	2	0	0	0	2	2	0	0	0	0	0	0	0	0	0	0	0	2	0	0	2	0

4P shallop
9H shallow-
7R shallow-reach
9F shallow-rooted
7F shallowness
8A shamed
7Q shamefacedly
7J shamisen
7F shamma
7D Shammah
5J shammash

5R shampooing
8G shamrock
8P shamrocks
5Q Shandy
5P Shanghainese
5N Shank
7F Shankilla
5Q Shanter
5J shanteyman's
6J shanty-men
4A shantyboat

8F Shao-ch'i
XR Shape
9L shape-holding
5R shape-up
5J shaped-note
5P shapelessness
5F share-croppers
7A sharecrop
5Q Sharecropper
5P shareholders
7P shareholding

9F shareowner
7P Shari
7Q shark-infested
7Q sharklike
3A Sharks'
7Q sharp-clawed
9M sharp-edged
7D sharp-faced
7R sharp-lady-teller
5F sharp-shooting
5P sharp-spoken

9Q sharp-tailed
3P sharp-toed
6Q sharp-toothed
6A Sharp's
9A sharpener
5N sharpenin'
7M sharpenings
3J sharping
XH sharply-toothed
7Q sharpshin
4E sharpshooter

6R sharpshooter's
7A sharpshooters
5F shatter-proof
3Q shatterproof
9K Shattuck
XH Shaula
8D Shave
XR shaver's
5F shavers

Word Type	F	D	U	SFI	3 Gr 3	4 Gr 4	5 Gr 5	6 Gr 6	7 Gr 7	8 Gr 8	9 Gr 9	X UnGr	A Read	B Eng & Gr	C Comp	D Lit	E Math	F Soc Stud	G Spell	H Sci	J Music	K Art	L Home Ec	M Shop	N Lib F	P Lib NF	Q Lib Ref	R Mag	S Rel
shaves	4	.3688	.3163	35.0	0	1	0	1	0	2	0	0	0	0	0	2	0	0	1	0	0	0	0	0	0	0	0	1	0
shaving	11	.6385	1.4336	41.6	2	2	0	1	4	1	0	1	1	0	0	3	0	0	0	0	1	0	0	1	1	1	2	1	0
shavings	18	.3531	1.3551	41.3	0	5	2	2	5	2	2	0	0	0	0	2	0	0	0	0	0	0	0	6	2	5	3	0	0
Shaw	17	.5096	1.8406	42.6	0	9	1	2	2	3	0	0	1	0	0	0	1	2	1	1	0	0	0	0	0	9	0	2	0
Shaw's	3	.3862	.2532	34.0	0	1	0	0	1	0	1	0	0	0	0	0	1	0	0	0	0	0	0	0	0	1	0	1	0
Shawanose	3	.0000	.0322	25.1	0	0	0	0	3	0	0	0	0	0	0	3	0	0	0	0	0	0	0	0	0	0	0	0	0
shawl	40	.6067	5.1843	47.1	3	15	2	2	12	4	2	0	17	2	0	11	0	3	0	0	0	1	0	0	3	3	0	0	0
shawls	2	.2401	.1133	30.5	0	1	0	0	0	0	1	0	0	0	0	0	0	0	0	0	0	0	0	0	0	1	1	0	0
Shawnee	3	.1187	.1291	31.1	0	0	0	1	2	0	0	0	1	0	0	2	0	0	0	0	0	0	0	0	0	0	0	0	0
Shawnees	4	.2186	.2141	33.3	0	0	3	0	1	0	0	0	0	0	0	1	0	0	0	0	0	0	0	0	0	3	0	0	0
Shays	3	.0000	.0583	27.7	0	0	0	0	0	3	0	0	0	0	0	0	0	3	0	0	0	0	0	0	0	0	0	0	0
Shays'	2	.0000	.0389	25.9	0	0	0	0	0	2	0	0	0	0	0	0	0	2	0	0	0	0	0	0	0	0	0	0	0
she	13653	.8238	2274.6	73.6	3763	2758	1685	1497	2084	956	776	134	5917	411	126	1357	545	300	107	178	209	44	68	0	2294	1414	83	599	1
She	4	.2578	.2593	34.1	0	0	1	1	0	0	2	0	1	0	0	0	0	0	0	0	2	0	0	0	0	1	0	0	0
she-bear	2	.2443	.1130	30.5	0	0	0	0	1	0	1	0	0	0	0	1	0	0	0	0	0	0	0	0	1	0	0	0	0
she-wolf	4	.1826	.1841	32.7	1	0	0	0	3	0	0	0	0	0	0	0	0	0	0	0	0	0	0	0	3	1	0	0	0
she'	2	.0000	.0914	29.6	2	0	0	0	0	0	0	0	2	0	0	0	0	0	0	0	0	0	0	0	0	0	0	0	0
she'd	130	.5805	16.490	52.2	26	19	16	14	26	10	18	1	72	3	1	19	0	0	0	0	0	0	0	0	25	8	0	2	0
she'll	65	.6698	9.2229	49.6	25	15	6	7	4	3	4	1	37	1	0	7	0	0	1	0	3	0	0	0	5	8	0	3	0
She'll	2	.0000	.0162	22.1	0	0	0	2	0	0	0	0	0	0	0	0	0	0	0	0	2	0	0	0	0	0	0	0	0
she's	245	.6417	33.212	55.2	35	51	33	26	56	7	32	5	106	8	0	40	0	2	0	0	7	0	0	0	41	16	0	25	0
She's	4	.1112	.1666	32.2	0	0	0	0	1	0	3	0	1	0	0	0	0	0	0	0	0	0	0	0	0	3	0	0	0
Shea	3	.0000	.0365	25.6	0	1	0	1	0	0	0	1	0	0	0	0	0	0	0	0	0	0	0	0	0	0	0	3	0
sheaf	6	.3376	.4505	36.5	0	3	0	0	2	0	1	0	0	0	0	1	0	0	0	0	0	0	0	0	0	4	1	0	0
shear	10	.5616	1.1838	40.7	3	3	0	1	1	0	2	0	1	0	0	0	0	4	0	1	0	0	0	1	0	1	1	1	0
sheared	4	.4485	.4009	36.0	0	0	1	2	1	0	0	0	1	0	0	0	0	1	0	0	0	0	0	0	0	0	1	1	0
shearer	3	.0000	.0583	27.7	0	0	2	1	0	0	0	0	0	0	0	0	0	3	0	0	0	0	0	0	0	0	0	0	0
shearing	21	.2005	1.0332	40.1	2	1	1	3	6	2	6	0	1	0	0	0	0	6	0	0	0	0	0	9	0	5	0	0	0
shears	30	.4847	3.0586	44.9	0	7	2	5	13	0	3	0	1	0	0	0	0	1	0	5	0	0	5	4	0	13	0	1	0
sheath	5	.5531	.5722	37.6	0	1	1	2	1	0	0	0	0	0	0	0	0	0	0	1	1	0	0	0	1	1	1	0	0
sheathed	4	.3883	.3268	35.1	0	0	0	0	2	1	1	0	0	0	1	1	0	0	0	1	0	0	0	1	0	0	0	0	0
sheathing	4	.3662	.3647	35.6	0	0	1	2	0	1	0	0	2	0	0	0	0	1	0	0	0	0	0	0	0	0	1	0	0
sheaths	4	.3741	.3400	35.3	0	0	0	2	1	0	0	1	0	0	0	0	0	1	0	2	0	0	0	0	0	1	0	0	0
sheaves	10	.5009	1.1007	40.4	2	4	3	0	0	1	0	0	3	0	0	0	0	1	0	0	1	0	0	0	0	4	1	0	0
Sheba	4	.0000	.1827	32.6	0	1	0	3	0	0	0	0	4	0	0	0	0	0	0	0	0	0	0	0	0	0	0	0	0
shed	131	.8839	23.164	53.6	23	30	10	21	25	14	6	2	53	3	1	5	6	10	1	13	3	0	2	0	12	14	4	4	0
shedding	11	.3418	.8867	39.5	3	1	1	2	2	1	1	0	1	0	0	1	0	0	0	8	0	0	0	0	0	0	1	0	0
sheds	19	.5704	2.3114	43.6	4	2	2	9	2	0	0	0	3	1	0	1	0	6	0	6	0	0	0	0	0	2	0	0	0
Sheean	5	.0000	.0537	27.3	0	0	0	0	5	0	0	0	0	0	0	5	0	0	0	0	0	0	0	0	0	0	0	0	0
SHEEAN	2	.0000	.0215	23.3	0	0	0	0	2	0	0	0	0	0	0	2	0	0	0	0	0	0	0	0	0	0	0	0	0
sheefish	2	.0000	.0243	23.9	0	0	0	1	0	0	0	1	0	0	0	0	0	0	0	0	0	0	0	0	0	0	0	2	0
Sheela	3	.0000	.1370	31.4	0	3	0	0	0	0	0	0	3	0	0	0	0	0	0	0	0	0	0	0	0	0	0	0	0
sheen	9	.5565	1.0451	40.2	1	0	0	2	2	1	2	1	1	3	0	0	0	0	0	0	1	0	0	0	1	1	0	2	0
sheep	464	.8748	81.030	59.1	120	84	66	85	64	11	16	18	94	30	3	17	9	169	13	29	10	2	2	0	18	32	16	19	1
Sheep	7	.3500	.5537	37.4	4	0	1	0	1	0	0	1	1	0	0	2	0	0	0	1	3	0	0	0	0	0	0	0	0
sheep-herding	2	.2408	.1204	30.8	0	0	1	0	1	0	0	0	0	0	0	0	0	1	0	0	0	0	0	0	0	1	0	0	0
sheep's	6	.4774	.6519	38.1	3	2	0	0	1	0	0	0	3	0	0	1	0	0	0	0	1	0	0	0	0	1	0	0	0
sheepfold	3	.0000	.0434	26.4	0	3	0	0	0	0	0	0	0	0	0	0	0	0	0	0	0	0	0	0	0	3	0	0	0
sheepherders	4	.3270	.3194	35.0	1	0	1	1	1	0	0	0	1	0	0	0	0	2	0	0	1	0	0	0	0	0	0	0	0
sheepish	4	.2424	.3036	34.8	0	1	0	3	0	0	0	0	3	0	0	0	0	0	0	0	0	0	0	0	0	0	0	1	0
sheepishly	8	.4542	.7687	38.9	0	2	0	1	4	1	0	0	0	1	0	1	0	0	0	0	0	0	0	0	3	3	0	0	0
sheepmen	3	.2435	.2274	33.6	1	1	0	0	1	0	0	0	2	0	0	0	0	1	0	0	0	0	0	0	0	0	0	0	0
sheepshearers	3	.0000	.0583	27.7	3	0	0	0	0	0	0	0	0	0	0	0	0	3	0	0	0	0	0	0	0	0	0	0	0
sheepskin	9	.4790	1.0094	40.0	0	4	1	0	2	0	0	2	6	0	0	1	0	0	0	0	0	0	0	0	0	1	0	1	0
sheepskins	9	.2801	.6120	37.9	2	1	0	1	3	0	2	0	1	0	2	0	0	5	0	0	0	0	0	0	0	1	0	0	0
sheer	50	.7185	7.2807	48.6	3	1	2	6	10	13	13	2	7	2	0	7	0	2	0	0	3	0	5	0	5	5	7	7	0
sheet	367	.7661	56.528	57.5	27	52	43	43	70	59	64	9	34	36	1	8	47	10	28	68	4	7	21	45	12	22	4	20	0
Sheet	4	.1432	.1519	31.8	0	0	0	0	2	2	0	0	0	0	0	0	0	0	0	2	0	0	2	0	0	0	0	0	0
sheet-metal	12	.0326	.1154	30.6	0	0	0	0	7	0	5	0	0	0	0	0	0	0	0	0	0	0	0	11	0	0	0	1	0
sheets	193	.7929	30.799	54.9	27	30	36	15	28	18	28	11	29	7	0	3	33	16	3	37	0	6	5	16	11	7	10	10	0
Sheffield	3	.0000	.0583	27.7	0	0	0	0	3	0	0	0	0	0	0	0	0	3	0	0	0	0	0	0	0	0	0	0	0
Sheila	4	.2194	.2161	33.3	1	0	0	3	0	0	0	0	0	1	0	0	3	0	0	0	0	0	0	0	0	0	0	0	0
shekels	2	.0000	.0215	23.3	0	0	0	0	2	0	0	0	0	0	0	2	0	0	0	0	0	0	0	0	0	0	0	0	0
Shelby	16	.1409	.6081	37.8	0	0	0	1	14	1	0	0	0	2	0	0	0	0	0	0	0	0	0	0	0	0	0	14	0
Shelepin	2	.0000	.0243	23.9	0	0	0	0	0	2	0	0	0	0	0	0	0	0	0	0	0	0	0	0	0	0	0	2	0
shelf	150	.8269	25.001	54.0	36	32	16	26	22	13	4	1	50	2	0	11	26	2	7	14	1	0	4	0	13	11	5	4	0
shell	245	.8516	41.822	56.2	56	40	23	33	55	18	15	5	69	3	1	14	0	4	3	55	4	6	8	2	9	30	30	7	0
Shell	2	.2285	.1129	30.5	0	0	2	0	0	0	0	0	0	0	0	0	0	1	0	0	0	0	0	0	0	0	1	0	0
shell-like	3	.3365	.2489	34.0	0	1	1	0	1	0	0	0	1	0	0	1	0	0	0	1	0	0	0	0	0	0	0	0	0
shell-shocked	2	.2437	.1129	30.5	0	0	0	0	2	0	0	0	0	0	0	0	0	0	0	0	0	0	0	0	0	0	1	1	0
shellac	13	.3617	.9873	39.9	2	1	1	0	3	2	4	0	0	0	0	1	0	0	0	1	0	1	0	6	0	2	1	1	0
shellacking	2	.2443	.1130	30.5	0	0	0	0	1	0	1	0	0	0	0	1	0	0	0	0	0	0	0	0	1	0	0	0	0
shelled	11	.3608	.8639	39.4	1	1	0	1	8	0	0	0	0	0	0	0	0	0	0	1	0	0	0	0	1	1	7	1	0
Shelley	6	.4856	.6596	38.2	0	0	3	1	1	0	1	0	3	1	0	1	0	0	0	0	0	0	0	0	0	0	1	0	0
Shelley's	2	.2412	.1091	30.4	0	0	0	0	0	2	0	0	0	0	0	1	0	0	1	0	0	0	0	0	0	0	0	0	0
shellfish	13	.5374	1.5005	41.8	2	2	2	2	4	0	1	0	2	0	0	0	0	3	0	3	0	0	0	0	2	3	0	0	0
shelling	3	.3769	.2484	34.0	0	1	0	1	0	1	0	0	0	0	0	0	0	1	0	0	0	0	0	0	0	0	1	1	0
shells	248	.8237	41.100	56.1	78	32	19	31	46	26	13	3	62	2	1	11	11	8	2	52	2	9	3	0	10	32	30	13	0
shelter	146	.8499	24.827	53.9	9	28	13	20	43	14	16	3	28	1	1	11	1	25	1	13	0	0	2	2	21	19	12	9	0
sheltered	37	.7271	5.5302	47.4	6	7	8	7	3	2	2	2	12	0	0	3	0	6	0	1	1	0	0	0	6	2	3	3	0
sheltering	11	.6029	1.3806	41.4	1	1	0	1	2	2	3	1	2	0	0	2	0	1	0	0	0	1	0	0	2	1	1	1	0
shelters	18	.5531	2.1220	43.3	1	8	0	4	3	1	0	1	4	0	0	0	0	4	0	0	0	1	0	0	0	3	5	1	0
shelved	2	.0000	.0914	29.6	0	0	0	0	2	0	0	0	2	0	0	0	0	0	0	0	0	0	0	0	0	0	0	0	0
shelves	92	.7918	14.667	51.7	20	4	9	19	15	18	5	2	18	9	0	4	18	5	1	1	0	0	6	4	11	2	6	7	0
Shem	2	.0000	.0914	29.6	0	0	0	0	2	0	0	0	2	0	0	0	0	0	0	0	0	0	0	0	0	0	0	0	0
Shenandoah	7	.6549	.9426	39.7	0	0	3	1	0	2	1	0	1	0	0	1	0	1	0	0	1	0	0	0	0	1	1	1	0
Shep	10	.2086	.6640	38.2	3	0	0	0	4	1	0	2	6	0	0	0	0	0	0	0	0	0	0	0	4	0	0	0	0
Shepard	4	.2191	.2297	33.6	0	0	0	1	1	0	0	2	0	0	0	0	0	0	0	3	0	0	0	0	0	1	0	0	0
shepherd	77	.7676	12.085	50.8	22	4	10	22	7	3	0	9	34	11	0	1	2	0	2	1	8	1	0	0	8	5	3	1	0
Shepherd	12	.4017	1.0667	40.3	3	0	0	7	1	0	1	0	2	2	0	0	0	0	0	0	2	0	0	0	6	0	0	0	0
shepherd's	4	.2445	.3067	34.9	0	1	1	2	0	0	0	0	3	0	0	0	0	0	0	0	0	0	0	0	0	1	0	0	0
shepherdess	2	.1948	.1250	31.0	0	0	0	2	0	0	0	0	1	0	0	0	0	0	0	0	0	0	0	0	0	1	0	0	0
shepherds	32	.3903	2.6503	44.2	8	6	2	4	2	7	0	3	1	2	1	4	0	3	0	0	11	4	0	0	0	2	0	2	2
sherbet	4	.0994	.0978	29.9	1	0	0	0	1	0	2	0	0	0	0	0	0	0	0	0	0	0	3	0	0	0	0	1	0
Sheridan	3	.3873	.2495	34.0	0	0	0	0	2	0	1	0	0	0	0	1	0	0	0	0	0	0	0	0	1	0	0	1	0

6A Shaving
6A shaving-lotion
6J Shaw-stah-koh-vitch
XB shaws
9Q Shay
4A shaynicke
5J she-bang
3G sheap
9H shear-like
3J Shearing
4P shearingtime
7R shearwaters
7R sheave
4N shed's
6B shedule
4A sheep-farmer
8Q sheep-stealing
5J sheepherder's
4Q sheepherding
5F sheepshearing
3A sheerest
6F sheet-iron
6N sheeted
7M sheetmetal
4A Shehir
7R Shelbys
4A shelf-displays
4P shelf-fashion
6R shell-bearing
4N shell-fish
8M shell-type
7A shellacked
7P shellbursts
8R shellings
6A shelly
8D shelter-box
7R shelterbelt
4A Shelton
4A Sheltons
8G shen**
9Q shenanigans
9B Shenton's
7N Shep'll
5B shepherd-swains
6A Shepherd's
3A shepherding
9D shepherds'
8R Shepley
7A Sheppard
7R Sher
3R sherbert
8A Sheridan's

Word Type	F	D	U	SFI	3 Gr 3	4 Gr 4	5 Gr 5	6 Gr 6	7 Gr 7	8 Gr 8	9 Gr 9	X UnGr	A Read	B Eng & Gr	C Comp	D Lit	E Math	F Soc Stud	G Spell	H Sci	J Music	K Art	L Home Ec	M Shop	N Lib F	P Lib NF	Q Lib Ref	R Mag	S Rel
sheriff	69	.5781	8.6662	49.4	2	5	15	12	15	18	2	0	34	9	0	8	0	0	0	0	0	0	0	0	12	5	1	0	0
Sheriff	35	.3961	3.3831	45.3	2	3	8	9	4	8	1	0	20	0	0	10	0	0	0	0	0	0	0	0	1	4	0	0	0
sheriff's	14	.2999	1.0176	40.1	0	0	2	0	2	10	0	0	3	8	0	0	0	2	0	0	0	0	0	0	1	0	0	0	0
Sheriff's	3	.2212	.2099	33.2	0	0	2	1	0	0	0	0	2	0	0	1	0	0	0	0	0	0	0	0	0	0	0	0	0
sheriffs	2	.2297	.1135	30.6	0	0	0	0	1	1	0	0	0	0	0	1	0	1	0	0	0	0	0	0	0	0	0	0	0
Sherlock	15	.4450	1.4534	41.6	0	0	1	2	2	3	7	0	3	1	2	7	0	0	1	1	0	0	0	0	0	0	0	0	0
Sherm	8	.0000	.3655	35.6	0	0	0	0	8	0	0	0	8	0	0	0	0	0	0	0	0	0	0	0	0	0	0	0	0
Sherman	24	.6001	2.9700	44.7	1	3	1	0	4	9	5	1	0	0	0	0	5	6	0	0	0	0	0	0	1	4	5	3	0
Sherrill	8	.1814	.4746	36.8	4	0	4	0	0	0	0	0	4	0	0	0	0	0	0	0	0	0	0	0	0	0	0	4	0
Sherring	3	.0000	.1370	31.4	0	0	0	3	0	0	0	0	3	0	0	0	0	0	0	0	0	0	0	0	0	0	0	0	0
sherry	2	.2408	.1091	30.4	0	0	0	0	0	1	1	0	0	1	0	0	0	0	1	0	0	0	0	0	0	0	0	0	0
Sherry	6	.2445	.3343	35.2	0	1	0	5	0	0	0	0	0	0	1	0	0	0	0	0	0	0	0	0	5	0	0	0	0
Sherwood	16	.4638	1.7255	42.4	0	3	8	1	4	0	0	0	9	0	0	3	0	0	0	0	0	0	0	0	1	3	0	0	0
Shetland	5	.4700	.5048	37.0	0	1	0	0	2	1	0	1	0	0	0	0	0	2	1	1	0	0	0	0	0	1	0	0	0
shh	4	.3718	.3639	35.6	3	0	1	0	0	0	0	0	2	1	0	0	0	0	0	0	0	0	0	0	1	0	0	0	0
shhh	5	.2446	.3872	35.9	4	0	0	0	1	0	0	0	4	0	0	0	0	0	0	0	0	0	0	0	1	0	0	0	0
Shi	2	.0000	.0389	25.9	0	0	0	2	0	0	0	0	0	0	0	0	0	2	0	0	0	0	0	0	0	0	0	0	0
ShiMutale	5	.0000	.0724	28.6	0	0	0	0	5	0	0	0	0	0	0	0	0	0	0	0	0	0	0	0	0	5	0	0	0
shied	3	.3776	.2489	34.0	0	1	0	0	1	1	0	0	0	0	0	1	0	1	0	0	0	0	0	0	0	0	0	1	0
shield	46	.7096	6.7971	48.3	8	9	1	10	7	2	8	1	22	0	0	5	0	3	1	2	0	0	2	0	0	7	2	2	0
Shield	3	.0000	.0583	27.7	0	0	2	0	0	0	1	0	0	0	0	0	0	3	0	0	0	0	0	0	0	0	0	0	0
shield-shaped	2	.0000	.0290	24.6	2	0	0	0	0	0	0	0	0	0	0	0	0	0	0	0	0	0	0	0	0	2	0	0	0
shielded	9	.5126	.9884	39.9	0	0	0	2	2	2	3	0	1	0	0	1	0	0	0	4	1	0	0	0	0	0	0	2	0
shields	17	.6896	2.4368	43.9	1	3	0	4	5	0	3	1	6	1	0	3	0	1	0	3	1	0	0	0	0	1	1	0	0
shift	70	.7585	10.713	50.3	2	3	9	8	23	8	14	3	6	4	0	5	0	7	0	15	0	0	4	1	1	5	5	17	0
shifta	2	.0000	.0243	23.9	0	0	0	2	0	0	0	0	0	0	0	0	0	0	0	0	0	0	0	0	0	0	0	2	0
shifted	44	.8110	7.1606	48.5	1	3	3	2	12	15	5	3	6	3	0	6	0	6	0	5	3	0	0	1	2	3	2	7	0
shifting	44	.8354	7.3522	48.7	2	5	8	6	11	6	5	1	8	2	0	5	0	1	0	4	3	1	1	1	1	3	9	5	0
shiftless	3	.2196	.1554	31.9	0	0	0	0	2	1	0	0	0	0	0	2	0	0	0	0	0	0	0	0	1	0	0	0	0
shifts	20	.7440	3.0144	44.8	0	1	2	3	7	5	1	1	3	1	0	2	0	1	1	2	2	0	0	0	0	2	1	5	0
shifty	4	.1772	.1782	32.5	0	0	0	0	1	3	0	0	0	3	0	0	0	0	0	0	0	0	0	0	0	1	0	0	0
Shiite	3	.0000	.0314	25.0	0	0	0	0	0	0	3	0	0	0	0	0	0	0	0	0	0	0	0	0	0	0	3	0	0
Shikara	3	.0000	.0322	25.1	0	0	0	0	3	0	0	0	0	0	0	3	0	0	0	0	0	0	0	0	0	0	0	0	0
shilling	10	.6722	1.3977	41.5	3	1	2	2	2	0	0	0	3	0	0	1	2	1	0	0	0	0	0	0	1	1	1	0	0
shillings	24	.6310	3.2765	45.2	3	6	6	5	1	3	0	0	15	2	0	1	1	3	0	0	0	0	0	0	1	0	0	1	0
Shiloh	4	.3790	.3299	35.2	0	2	1	1	0	0	0	0	0	0	0	0	0	0	0	0	0	0	0	0	0	2	1	1	0
shimmer	3	.2946	.1896	32.8	0	0	0	0	0	0	2	1	0	0	1	0	0	0	0	0	1	0	0	0	0	0	0	1	0
shimmered	6	.3876	.5828	37.7	1	0	2	1	2	0	0	0	4	1	0	0	0	0	0	0	0	0	0	0	1	0	0	0	0
shimmering	15	.5878	1.8302	42.6	0	1	3	2	7	1	1	0	2	1	0	5	0	0	0	2	2	1	0	0	2	0	0	0	0
shin	4	.4487	.4010	36.0	0	1	2	0	0	0	1	0	1	0	0	1	0	1	0	0	0	0	0	0	1	0	0	0	0
Shin	2	.0000	.0243	23.9	0	0	0	2	0	0	0	0	0	0	0	0	0	0	0	0	0	0	0	0	0	0	0	2	0
Shin-n-n-n-ny	2	.0000	.0914	29.6	0	2	0	0	0	0	0	0	2	0	0	0	0	0	0	0	0	0	0	0	0	0	0	0	0
Shin-n-n-ny	4	.0000	.1827	32.6	0	4	0	0	0	0	0	0	4	0	0	0	0	0	0	0	0	0	0	0	0	0	0	0	0
shine	157	.7738	24.760	53.9	49	50	8	18	14	8	5	5	52	3	2	10	0	8	3	38	7	2	0	0	6	18	2	5	1
shined	8	.3407	.6683	38.2	1	4	0	0	3	0	0	0	3	0	0	0	0	0	0	0	0	0	0	0	3	2	0	0	0
shines	75	.6577	10.224	50.1	29	18	7	12	4	2	3	0	14	2	3	3	0	12	1	19	4	1	0	0	0	9	2	4	1
shingle	11	.5032	1.1847	40.7	0	3	2	0	5	1	0	0	2	2	0	2	0	0	0	0	0	0	0	0	1	0	0	4	0
shingled	5	.5384	.5724	37.6	0	1	0	0	2	1	0	1	1	1	0	1	0	0	0	0	0	0	0	0	0	1	0	1	0
shingles	24	.6713	3.2878	45.2	3	4	1	1	12	1	1	1	3	0	1	4	0	1	0	0	1	0	0	1	1	1	1	10	0
shining	269	.8570	46.214	56.6	72	54	22	41	45	14	15	6	87	17	4	27	0	12	1	33	13	3	0	0	25	29	4	14	0
shinny	2	.1717	.1142	30.6	0	0	0	0	1	0	1	0	1	0	0	1	0	0	0	0	0	0	0	0	0	0	0	0	0
Shinny	2	.0000	.0914	29.6	0	2	0	0	0	0	0	0	2	0	0	0	0	0	0	0	0	0	0	0	0	0	0	0	0
shinnying	2	.0665	.0708	28.5	0	0	1	0	1	0	0	0	1	0	1	0	0	0	0	0	0	0	0	0	0	0	0	0	0
shins	3	.2071	.1434	31.6	2	0	1	0	0	0	0	0	0	0	0	1	0	0	0	0	2	0	0	0	0	0	0	0	0
shiny	123	.8028	19.944	53.0	37	29	12	13	11	7	7	7	33	7	2	7	0	9	0	21	2	5	0	0	10	8	3	16	0
Shiny-Shack-on-Wheel	3	.0000	.0365	25.6	0	0	0	3	0	0	0	0	0	0	0	0	0	0	0	0	0	0	0	0	0	0	0	3	0
ship	1021	.8432	173.79	62.4	211	304	128	152	126	49	47	4	465	30	5	30	12	167	16	36	16	1	0	1	63	110	20	49	0
Ship	15	.5222	1.7567	42.4	2	0	7	1	3	0	2	0	7	0	0	1	1	5	0	0	0	0	0	0	0	0	0	1	0
ship's	48	.7994	7.7757	48.9	3	11	13	8	11	0	1	1	16	0	1	2	1	6	2	2	0	0	0	0	4	8	4	2	0
shipboard	4	.4501	.4035	36.1	0	0	0	2	1	0	1	0	1	0	0	0	0	0	0	1	0	0	0	0	0	1	1	0	0
shipbuilders	4	.3350	.3295	35.2	0	0	2	0	0	1	1	0	1	0	0	0	1	2	0	0	0	0	0	0	0	0	0	0	0
shipbuilding	17	.3822	1.4459	41.6	6	1	1	1	1	7	0	0	0	0	0	0	0	10	0	0	0	0	0	0	0	1	5	1	0
shipload	2	.2152	.1357	31.3	1	1	0	0	0	0	0	0	1	0	0	0	0	1	0	0	0	0	0	0	0	0	0	0	0
shiploads	4	.2348	.2372	33.8	1	1	1	1	0	0	0	0	0	0	0	0	0	3	0	0	0	0	0	0	0	0	1	0	0
Shipman	6	.0000	.0869	29.4	0	6	0	0	0	0	0	0	0	0	0	0	0	0	0	0	0	0	0	0	0	6	0	0	0
Shipman's	2	.0000	.0290	24.6	0	2	0	0	0	0	0	0	0	0	0	0	0	0	0	0	0	0	0	0	0	2	0	0	0
shipment	19	.6311	2.4803	43.9	0	2	5	3	7	1	0	1	1	0	0	0	5	7	1	1	0	0	0	0	0	2	1	1	0
shipments	11	.4727	1.1271	40.5	1	0	2	2	1	2	3	0	1	0	0	0	0	6	0	0	0	0	0	1	0	0	1	2	0
shipped	104	.6683	14.357	51.6	16	18	29	13	19	4	4	1	13	2	0	1	3	59	0	2	0	0	2	2	4	6	9	1	0
shippers	5	.5476	.5698	37.6	0	0	0	0	2	1	1	1	0	0	0	1	0	1	0	1	1	0	0	0	0	0	0	1	0
shipping	73	.7403	10.939	50.4	8	9	14	10	18	7	7	0	5	2	1	2	4	28	2	1	0	0	1	0	2	6	17	2	0
ships	731	.7459	111.29	60.5	131	126	134	110	108	80	30	12	148	22	1	14	6	324	5	29	17	1	0	3	10	70	52	29	0
ships'	6	.5313	.6872	38.4	0	0	0	3	3	0	0	0	1	1	0	0	0	2	0	1	0	0	0	0	0	1	0	0	0
shipshape	2	.2440	.1132	30.5	0	0	0	1	1	0	0	0	0	0	0	1	0	0	0	0	0	0	0	0	0	0	0	1	0
shipwreck	5	.3818	.4261	36.3	0	1	0	3	1	0	0	0	1	1	0	0	0	0	0	0	0	1	0	0	1	0	0	1	0
shipwrecked	11	.5441	1.2668	41.0	0	4	2	0	3	1	0	1	2	0	0	0	0	1	1	0	0	0	0	0	4	0	2	1	0
shipyard	5	.2360	.3663	35.6	1	0	3	0	1	0	0	0	3	0	0	0	0	2	0	0	0	0	0	0	0	0	0	0	0
shipyards	13	.3768	1.1385	40.6	2	2	3	3	2	1	0	0	2	0	0	0	0	8	0	0	0	0	0	0	0	1	2	0	0
Shire	3	.3844	.2487	34.0	1	0	0	0	1	1	0	0	0	1	0	0	0	0	0	0	0	0	0	0	0	1	1	0	0
Shirley	43	.5293	5.2567	47.2	7	1	7	0	2	4	22	0	34	3	0	0	1	1	0	0	0	0	0	0	2	0	1	1	0
Shiro	4	.0000	.0778	28.9	0	4	0	0	0	0	0	0	0	0	0	0	0	4	0	0	0	0	0	0	0	0	0	0	0
Shiro's	2	.0000	.0389	25.9	0	2	0	0	0	0	0	0	0	0	0	0	0	2	0	0	0	0	0	0	0	0	0	0	0
shirt	222	.8109	36.401	55.6	36	54	12	20	44	27	27	2	88	12	3	18	4	1	6	1	2	1	18	2	28	26	2	10	0
shirt-tail	2	.2443	.1130	30.5	0	0	0	0	0	1	1	0	0	0	0	1	0	0	0	0	0	0	0	0	1	0	0	0	0
shirts	40	.7424	6.0687	47.8	10	2	3	4	8	9	2	2	12	2	0	5	2	5	0	1	1	0	3	0	1	3	0	5	0
shirza	2	.0000	.0219	23.4	0	0	0	0	0	2	0	0	0	2	0	0	0	0	0	0	0	0	0	0	0	0	0	0	0
Shiseido	2	.0000	.0243	23.9	0	0	0	0	0	0	0	2	0	0	0	0	0	0	0	0	0	0	0	0	0	0	0	2	0
shiver	33	.6544	4.5476	46.6	6	7	4	4	9	2	1	0	15	2	1	5	0	0	0	0	1	0	0	0	7	1	0	1	0
shivered	54	.6554	7.4645	48.7	6	12	10	9	12	3	2	0	25	2	2	9	0	2	0	0	0	0	0	0	8	4	0	2	0
shivering	39	.6764	5.5054	47.4	6	3	5	9	6	7	3	0	16	2	1	9	0	1	0	0	1	0	0	0	5	3	0	1	0
shivers	9	.4601	.8649	39.4	1	1	1	2	2	1	1	0	0	0	1	2	0	0	0	0	0	0	0	0	4	0	0	2	0
Shivery	2	.0000	.0234	23.7	2	0	0	0	0	0	0	0	0	0	0	0	0	0	0	0	0	0	0	0	2	0	0	0	0

4P Sherman's
3A Sherrills
6N Sherry's
7D Sherwood's
9B shes
3A shhh-shhh
9Q Shia
7Q shibboleth
4P Shibe
9D shies
4F Shikoku
6J shill's
7A shillelagh
5R Shilshole
7M shim
3F Shima
7R shimmed
7K shimmers
7Q shimmies
7D shimmy
7P shims
4A Shin-n-ny
5D shindigs
7Q shiners
7J Shines
6C shingling
6R shingly
6A shiniest
7A shinin'
6A shininess
9R Shinjuku
5Q Shinn
7D shinned
5D shinnied
5Q Shinto
9H shiny-faced
8G shion
XD Ship-Trap
8F ship-building
4N ship-rats
3A ship-to-shore
4N ship-wrecked
9F shipbuilder
7Q shipmasts
3Q shipmates
4P shipowner
9B Shippen
7H shipper
3P Shippingport
4R Shiprock
3P Ships
3P SHIPS
4D shipwrecks
8F shipwrights
7R Shirahama
9A shirk
4A shirked
9A Shirl
9A ShirleyKochendorfer
3A Shirleys
7R Shiroma
9L shirring
7A Shirt
XH shirt-front
8N shirt-sleeved
7D shirt-sleeves
9L shirting
3Q shirtless
6A shirtlike
7A shirtsleeves
XP shirttail
4J shirttails
8N shirtwaist
9P Shithead
8A shiverin'
4D shiverings
XR shlocks

Word Type	F	D	U	SFI	3 Gr 3	4 Gr 4	5 Gr 5	6 Gr 6	7 Gr 7	8 Gr 8	9 Gr 9	X UnGr	A Read	B Eng & Gr	C Comp	D Lit	E Math	F Soc Stud	G Spell	H Sci	J Music	K Art	L Home Ec	M Shop	N Lib F	P Lib NF	Q Lib Ref	R Mag	S Rel
Shoaf	2	.0000	.0914	29.6	0	0	0	0	2	0	0	0	2	0	0	0	0	0	0	0	0	0	0	0	0	0	0	0	0
shoal	3	.3267	.2367	33.7	0	0	0	1	0	2	0	0	1	0	0	0	0	0	0	0	1	0	0	0	1	0	0	0	0
shoals	5	.4713	.5334	37.3	0	0	0	2	3	0	0	0	2	0	0	0	0	1	0	0	0	0	0	0	1	0	1	0	0
Shoals	7	.2354	.3942	36.0	2	0	0	4	1	0	0	0	0	0	0	0	0	0	0	0	0	0	0	0	0	3	0	4	0
shock	100	.7438	15.035	51.8	4	12	12	8	31	15	14	4	12	2	0	9	0	1	3	9	1	0	0	2	6	10	17	28	0
shocked	42	.7182	6.2029	47.9	5	8	3	6	10	6	3	1	13	0	0	7	0	4	0	1	1	0	0	0	4	6	3	3	0
shocker	2	.0000	.0243	23.9	0	0	0	1	0	0	0	1	0	0	0	0	0	0	0	0	0	0	0	0	0	0	0	2	0
shocking	16	.6479	2.1306	43.3	1	2	1	1	4	5	2	0	1	0	0	2	0	3	0	3	0	0	0	0	3	0	2	2	0
shockingly	3	.3772	.2503	34.0	0	0	0	0	1	0	2	0	0	0	0	1	0	0	0	1	0	0	0	0	0	1	0	0	0
shocks	29	.5604	3.4088	45.3	2	3	0	2	16	2	3	1	4	0	0	0	0	1	0	2	0	0	0	1	4	0	5	12	0
shod	6	.4382	.5830	37.7	0	1	1	0	0	2	1	1	2	0	1	0	0	0	0	0	1	1	0	0	0	1	0	0	0
shoddy	2	.1787	.1174	30.7	0	0	0	0	0	1	1	0	1	0	0	0	0	0	0	0	0	0	0	0	1	0	0	0	0
shoe	146	.8819	25.683	54.1	58	21	7	8	13	17	20	2	44	3	3	22	19	7	11	4	4	0	3	1	11	5	4	5	0
Shoe	2	.0000	.0243	23.9	0	0	0	0	0	2	0	0	0	0	0	0	0	0	0	0	0	0	0	0	0	0	0	2	0
shoelace	3	.3772	.2488	34.0	0	0	1	1	0	1	0	0	0	1	0	0	0	0	0	1	0	0	0	0	1	0	0	0	0
shoelaces	8	.5341	.9273	39.7	0	2	0	1	2	2	1	0	2	0	0	0	1	0	1	3	0	0	0	0	0	1	0	0	0
shoemaker	15	.4598	1.5380	41.9	2	3	1	3	0	1	5	0	5	0	0	5	0	1	0	0	3	0	0	0	0	0	0	0	0
Shoemaker	2	.0000	.0243	23.9	0	0	0	0	0	2	0	0	0	0	0	0	0	0	0	0	0	0	0	0	0	0	0	1	0
shoemaker's	5	.4769	.5345	37.3	0	2	0	2	0	0	1	0	2	0	0	1	0	0	0	0	0	0	0	0	1	0	0	2	0
shoemakers	3	.0000	.0583	27.7	0	0	2	0	0	1	0	0	0	0	0	0	0	3	0	0	0	0	0	0	0	0	0	1	0
shoes	461	.8759	80.814	59.1	140	70	64	51	67	44	21	4	175	15	9	36	13	57	9	16	8	1	8	0	60	37	7	10	0
Shoes	6	.3532	.4994	37.0	1	0	1	0	0	2	2	0	2	0	0	1	0	0	0	0	0	1	0	0	0	0	0	2	0
shoeshine	7	.3951	.6528	38.1	0	2	0	1	3	0	1	0	3	0	0	0	0	0	0	0	0	0	0	1	0	2	0	1	0
Shoeshine	2	.0000	.0914	29.6	0	2	0	0	0	0	0	0	2	0	0	0	0	0	0	0	0	0	0	0	0	0	0	0	0
shoestring	6	.2435	.4548	36.6	4	0	0	2	0	0	0	0	4	0	0	0	0	2	0	0	0	0	0	0	0	0	0	0	0
Shoestring	11	.0000	.1290	31.1	0	0	11	0	0	0	0	0	0	0	0	0	0	0	0	0	0	0	0	0	11	0	0	0	0
Shoestring's	2	.0000	.0234	23.7	0	0	2	0	0	0	0	0	0	0	0	0	0	0	0	0	0	0	0	0	2	0	0	0	0
shoestrings	3	.0000	.1370	31.4	1	0	0	0	1	1	0	0	3	0	0	0	0	0	0	0	0	0	0	0	0	0	0	0	0
Shoie	7	.0000	.3198	35.0	3	0	0	4	0	0	0	0	7	0	0	0	0	0	0	0	0	0	0	0	0	0	0	0	0
shone	119	.7242	17.843	52.5	19	30	16	20	21	6	5	2	55	10	1	17	0	3	0	3	2	0	0	0	15	8	0	5	0
shoo	20	.2558	1.2505	41.0	7	7	3	0	3	0	0	0	4	0	0	0	0	0	0	0	12	0	0	0	3	1	0	0	0
Shoo	2	.1494	.1045	30.2	1	0	0	0	1	0	0	0	1	0	0	0	0	0	0	0	1	0	0	0	0	0	0	0	0
shooed	4	.3702	.3622	35.6	1	1	0	0	0	0	2	0	2	1	0	1	0	0	0	0	0	0	0	0	0	0	0	0	0
shooing	4	.3017	.3031	34.8	1	2	0	0	0	0	0	1	1	0	0	0	0	0	0	1	0	0	0	0	0	2	0	0	0
shook	420	.6879	60.413	57.8	82	103	50	62	73	27	20	3	195	8	2	62	1	7	1	1	6	0	0	0	63	50	1	23	0
shoot	214	.7898	34.358	55.4	36	74	26	14	44	12	7	1	82	6	1	22	0	3	7	9	2	1	0	0	16	49	4	12	0
shooter	3	.2184	.1759	32.5	0	0	0	1	1	0	1	0	1	0	0	0	0	0	0	0	0	0	0	1	0	0	0	1	0
shooters	2	.2440	.1132	30.5	0	0	0	0	1	1	0	0	0	0	0	1	0	0	0	0	0	0	0	0	0	0	0	1	0
shootin'	5	.1468	.2522	34.0	0	0	0	2	1	2	0	0	2	0	0	0	0	0	0	0	0	0	0	0	3	0	0	0	0
shooting	138	.7981	22.300	53.5	20	29	14	16	28	18	7	6	42	8	0	10	0	4	2	19	3	0	0	0	9	20	5	16	0
shootings	2	.2351	.1166	30.7	0	0	0	1	0	0	1	0	0	0	0	0	0	1	0	0	0	0	0	0	0	0	0	1	0
shoots	58	.7466	8.8416	49.5	11	11	6	7	15	4	1	3	17	2	1	3	0	1	0	10	0	0	0	2	1	5	13	3	0
shop	365	.6821	51.755	57.1	94	63	44	49	37	33	44	1	137	15	2	14	6	44	7	5	0	1	4	46	25	36	5	18	0
Shop	13	.4762	1.4502	41.6	7	3	1	2	0	0	0	0	8	0	0	0	2	2	0	0	0	0	0	0	1	0	0	0	0
shopkeeper	9	.4702	.9696	39.9	2	0	3	1	1	1	1	0	4	0	0	0	0	2	0	0	0	0	0	0	0	1	0	2	0
shopkeepers	13	.4660	1.3420	41.3	3	2	2	3	0	2	1	0	2	0	0	0	2	7	0	0	0	0	0	0	1	1	0	0	0
shopped	2	.0000	.0914	29.6	1	1	0	0	0	0	0	0	2	0	0	0	0	0	0	0	0	0	0	0	0	0	0	0	0
shopper	9	.3286	.6848	38.4	1	0	3	1	0	1	3	0	2	2	0	0	0	1	0	0	0	0	3	0	0	0	0	1	0
shoppers	12	.4836	1.3423	41.3	6	3	0	2	0	0	1	0	7	0	0	0	0	2	0	0	1	0	0	0	0	0	0	2	0
shopping	92	.6756	12.764	51.1	27	15	11	5	16	5	10	3	18	3	5	2	8	16	1	0	0	0	12	0	2	3	3	19	0
shops	126	.7209	18.531	52.7	14	15	17	19	18	16	20	7	23	1	0	4	0	33	2	7	1	1	1	13	5	11	9	15	0
shopwork	2	.2285	.1129	30.5	0	0	0	0	0	1	1	0	0	0	0	0	0	1	0	0	0	0	0	0	0	0	1	0	0
Shora	12	.0000	.1407	31.5	0	0	12	0	0	0	0	0	0	0	0	0	0	0	0	0	0	0	0	0	12	0	0	0	0
shore	447	.8703	77.811	58.9	71	88	56	77	100	31	15	9	141	15	11	32	4	50	3	27	9	4	0	0	49	44	27	31	0
Shore	5	.1622	.2522	34.0	1	2	0	0	0	0	2	0	2	0	0	0	0	0	0	0	0	0	0	2	0	1	0	0	0
shoreline	15	.5551	1.7464	42.4	3	2	1	2	3	2	2	0	1	0	0	0	0	2	0	2	0	0	0	0	0	3	3	4	0
shorelines	2	.2278	.1128	30.5	1	0	0	0	0	0	1	0	0	0	0	0	0	0	0	1	0	0	0	0	0	0	1	0	0
shores	102	.6557	13.831	51.4	19	9	19	11	25	10	5	4	15	1	0	3	0	32	0	9	3	0	0	0	3	8	25	3	0
shoreward	4	.4482	.4009	36.0	0	0	0	0	3	1	0	0	1	0	0	0	0	0	0	1	0	0	0	0	0	0	1	1	0
shorn	4	.4535	.4003	36.0	0	0	0	1	2	0	1	0	1	0	0	1	0	0	0	0	0	0	0	0	1	0	0	1	0
short	1534	.8972	273.37	64.4	314	266	197	195	297	140	91	34	314	99	55	51	121	89	273	109	64	11	31	21	59	94	63	80	0
Short	6	.5134	.6544	38.2	0	0	2	1	3	0	0	0	1	2	0	1	0	0	0	0	0	0	0	0	0	0	1	1	0
short-arc	2	.0000	.0243	23.9	0	0	0	0	2	0	0	0	0	0	0	0	0	0	0	0	0	0	0	0	0	0	0	2	0
short-cut	2	.0000	.0243	23.9	0	0	0	1	0	1	0	0	0	0	0	0	0	0	0	0	0	0	0	0	0	0	0	2	0
short-legged	2	.0000	.0290	24.6	0	0	2	0	0	0	0	0	0	0	0	0	0	0	0	0	0	0	0	0	0	2	0	0	0
short-lived	11	.6335	1.4358	41.6	0	0	2	1	2	3	3	0	1	0	1	0	0	2	0	2	1	0	0	0	1	0	1	2	0
short-order	2	.0000	.0219	23.4	0	0	2	0	0	0	0	0	0	2	0	0	0	0	0	0	0	0	0	0	0	0	0	0	0
short-range	2	.2346	.1166	30.7	0	0	0	0	2	0	0	0	0	0	0	0	0	0	0	1	0	0	0	0	0	0	0	1	0
short-short	2	.0000	.0389	25.9	0	0	2	0	0	0	0	0	0	0	0	0	0	2	0	0	0	0	0	0	0	0	0	0	0
short-story	5	.3822	.4186	36.2	0	0	3	0	2	0	0	0	0	1	0	0	2	0	0	0	0	0	0	0	0	2	0	0	0
short-term	2	.2346	.1166	30.7	0	0	0	0	0	0	1	1	0	0	0	0	0	0	0	1	0	0	0	0	0	0	0	1	0
short-vowel	5	.0621	.1343	31.3	1	1	0	3	0	0	0	0	1	0	0	0	0	0	4	0	0	0	0	0	0	0	0	0	0
short-wave	14	.3406	1.1175	40.5	0	2	1	0	1	0	4	6	1	0	0	0	0	0	2	10	0	0	0	0	0	1	0	0	0
shortage	28	.6231	3.6066	45.6	4	2	2	2	8	5	5	0	2	0	0	2	0	10	2	2	0	0	0	0	1	0	7	2	0
shortages	9	.4756	.9078	39.6	0	0	2	3	2	0	2	0	0	0	0	0	0	1	0	1	0	0	0	0	0	2	1	4	0
shortcake	2	.0000	.0234	23.7	0	0	0	0	2	0	0	0	0	0	0	0	0	0	0	0	0	0	0	0	2	0	0	0	0
shortcoming	2	.2417	.1211	30.8	0	0	0	0	0	1	1	0	0	0	0	0	1	1	0	0	0	0	0	0	0	0	0	0	0
shortcomings	3	.3369	.2489	34.0	0	0	0	1	1	1	0	0	1	0	0	1	0	1	0	0	0	0	0	0	0	0	0	0	0
shortcut	20	.0581	.5144	37.1	0	0	3	0	4	13	0	0	0	0	0	0	19	1	0	0	0	0	0	0	0	0	0	0	0
shortcuts	4	.0000	.0599	27.8	1	0	3	0	0	0	0	0	0	0	0	0	4	0	0	0	0	0	0	0	0	0	0	0	0
shorten	25	.7213	3.6364	45.6	3	1	5	5	5	6	0	0	2	1	0	1	4	0	4	2	1	0	3	2	2	2	0	1	0
shortened	27	.6241	3.4512	45.4	3	3	6	4	5	3	2	1	2	1	0	0	0	3	10	3	1	0	2	0	2	0	2	1	0
shortening	33	.2199	1.5914	42.0	0	5	2	1	4	11	10	0	0	0	0	0	0	1	0	1	4	0	21	0	0	2	3	1	0
shortens	2	.1249	.0685	28.4	0	1	0	0	1	0	0	0	0	0	0	0	0	0	0	1	0	0	0	1	0	0	0	0	0
shorter	192	.9062	34.503	55.4	38	46	24	13	23	18	19	11	25	11	1	1	43	13	13	21	14	1	6	4	3	13	12	11	0
shortest	62	.5841	7.5431	48.8	14	21	3	3	9	4	7	1	3	5	0	3	31	3	1	10	0	0	0	0	0	3	3	0	0
shorthand	12	.5060	1.2686	41.0	3	0	2	1	4	2	0	0	0	2	0	0	6	0	0	0	2	0	0	0	0	1	1	0	0
shortly	102	.8577	17.494	52.4	4	12	13	11	26	21	12	3	24	4	0	8	0	14	2	8	4	2	1	0	3	8	15	9	0
shortness	4	.2056	.2516	34.0	0	0	0	2	1	1	0	0	2	0	1	0	0	0	0	1	0	0	0	0	0	0	0	0	0
shortnin'	7	.0000	.0566	27.5	0	0	0	7	0	0	0	0	0	0	0	0	0	0	0	0	7	0	0	0	0	0	0	0	0
shorts	21	.4762	2.1365	43.3	4	1	0	0	3	7	5	1	4	3	0	2	0	0	0	1	0	0	6	1	0	0	0	4	0
shortsighted	3	.3773	.2505	34.0	0	0	0	0	0	1	2	0	0	0	0	1	1	1	0	0	0	0	0	0	0	0	0	0	0
shortstop	23	.4178	2.0838	43.2	2	0	3	2	3	1	12	0	2	12	0	0	0	0	0	0	0	0	0	0	0	3	2	4	0
shortwave	3	.3732	.2514	34.0	0	0	0	0	1	1	0	1	0	1	0	0	0	1	0	1	0	0	0	0	0	0	0	0	0

7D Shochoh
XH shock-softening
7R shock's
XR shockers
4P shoe-button
8N shoe-leather
6A shoe-off
7A shoehorn
7N shoeless
7J shofar

9R Shoji
3A shokolad
5E shole
5Q Sholes
5B Shona
6A shoofly
8R Shook
6B shoon
9R shoot-the-looters
8C Shooting

6R shop-lines
XR shop-owner
9D shop-window
6F shopkeeper's
9C shopkeepers'
5R shoplifts
7Q shoppers'
5N shopping-list
XR shopping's
9Q shoptalk

9R shopworn
5N Shora's
7R shorebirds
7R Shorebirds
7R ShortHills
7A short-
4A Short-Step
8M short-blade
7R short-changed
5Q short-circuit

6N short-cropped
7R short-cycle
7H short-day
7R short-duration
5A short-handled
4H short-horned
6J short-long
7Q short-necked
6R short-needled
XH short-period

7Q short-tempered
XH short-tubed
8M shorted
4P shorthanded
8F Shorthorn
8F Shorthorns
7A shorthose
5D Shortleg
8R shortlived
XR Shorts

Word Type	F	D	U	SFI	3 Gr 3	4 Gr 4	5 Gr 5	6 Gr 6	7 Gr 7	8 Gr 8	9 Gr 9	X UnGr	A Read	B Eng & Gr	C Comp	D Lit	E Math	F Soc Stud	G Spell	H Sci	J Music	K Art	L Home Ec	M Shop	N Lib F	P Lib NF	Q Lib Ref	R Mag	S Rel
shorty	2	.0000	.0234	23.7	2	0	0	0	0	0	0	0	0	0	0	0	0	0	0	0	0	0	0	0	2	0	0	0	0
Shorty	94	.1724	4.3511	46.4	81	5	6	1	0	1	0	0	9	0	0	1	0	0	0	0	2	0	0	0	78	4	0	0	0
Shoshone	6	.3793	.5819	37.6	1	4	0	0	0	1	0	0	4	0	0	0	0	0	0	1	0	0	0	0	0	1	0	0	0
Shoshoni	2	.0000	.0914	29.6	0	0	2	0	0	0	0	0	2	0	0	0	0	0	0	0	0	0	0	0	0	0	0	0	0
Shostakovitch	2	.0000	.0162	22.1	0	0	0	1	0	1	0	0	0	0	0	0	0	0	0	0	2	0	0	0	0	0	0	0	0
shot	398	.7831	63.327	58.0	45	77	37	42	117	46	28	6	137	11	1	48	1	15	5	15	10	0	0	0	50	45	9	51	0
Shot	2	.0000	.0914	29.6	2	0	0	0	0	0	0	0	2	0	0	0	0	0	0	0	0	0	0	0	0	0	0	0	0
shotgun	13	.6192	1.6739	42.2	0	0	3	1	4	2	3	0	3	1	1	2	0	0	0	0	0	0	0	0	2	0	1	3	0
shotguns	4	.2512	.2516	34.0	0	0	0	1	3	0	0	0	1	0	1	0	0	0	0	0	0	0	0	0	0	0	0	2	0
shots	78	.6830	11.011	50.4	3	19	10	10	22	8	4	2	21	2	0	3	0	1	0	5	0	1	0	0	6	15	2	22	0
Shotton	2	.0000	.0290	24.6	2	0	0	0	0	0	0	0	0	0	0	0	0	0	0	0	0	0	0	0	0	2	0	0	0
should	3470	.9137	628.42	68.0	448	487	360	410	654	462	554	95	622	384	54	168	259	252	120	372	96	40	290	150	162	218	109	170	4
should've	3	.1187	.1291	31.1	0	0	1	0	2	0	0	0	1	0	0	2	0	0	0	0	0	0	0	0	0	0	0	0	0
shoulder	385	.8419	65.216	58.1	48	82	41	61	89	31	30	3	151	6	4	44	0	8	1	16	16	1	16	3	55	39	7	18	0
shoulder-high	2	.1814	.1187	30.7	0	1	0	1	0	0	0	0	1	0	0	0	0	0	0	0	0	0	0	0	0	0	0	1	0
shouldered	8	.2882	.5887	37.7	2	0	1	1	1	1	2	0	3	0	0	4	0	0	0	0	0	0	0	0	0	0	1	0	0
shouldering	5	.3081	.3654	35.6	1	0	0	1	1	0	2	0	1	0	0	2	0	0	0	0	0	0	0	0	2	0	0	0	0
shoulders	259	.8536	44.386	56.5	31	61	36	37	50	23	17	4	98	6	2	25	0	9	0	13	5	8	6	2	28	34	7	16	0
Shoulders	4	.0000	.0486	26.9	0	4	0	0	0	0	0	0	0	0	0	0	0	0	0	0	0	0	0	0	0	0	0	4	0
Shoulders'	2	.0000	.0243	23.9	0	2	0	0	0	0	0	0	0	0	0	0	0	0	0	0	0	0	0	0	0	0	0	2	0
shouldn't	90	.7206	13.415	51.3	20	16	11	15	15	3	7	3	38	5	0	3	0	2	1	3	0	0	0	1	14	10	0	13	0
shout	143	.7869	22.985	53.6	28	30	20	21	21	10	10	3	70	6	1	15	0	7	1	5	11	0	0	0	11	9	1	6	0
shouted	558	.7454	86.226	59.4	169	131	62	85	51	33	18	9	324	7	12	39	0	10	0	4	7	0	1	0	66	65	0	22	1
shoutin'	2	.0000	.0162	22.1	0	0	0	0	0	0	2	0	0	0	0	0	0	0	0	0	2	0	0	0	0	0	0	0	0
shouting	127	.7216	18.850	52.8	23	23	18	18	25	9	7	4	44	0	3	20	0	5	0	3	4	0	0	0	20	13	1	14	0
shoutings	2	.1787	.1174	30.7	0	0	0	1	1	0	0	0	1	0	0	0	0	0	0	0	0	0	0	0	1	0	0	0	0
shouts	46	.7446	7.0356	48.5	5	7	7	13	7	4	3	0	19	1	0	5	0	2	0	2	2	0	2	0	5	2	0	6	0
shove	15	.5532	1.7914	42.5	2	2	3	4	3	0	0	1	5	0	0	0	0	1	0	1	1	0	0	0	3	0	0	4	0
shoved	31	.6369	4.1472	46.2	5	6	4	4	7	3	1	1	10	1	0	3	0	0	0	3	0	0	0	0	7	4	0	3	0
shovel	60	.7438	9.1572	49.6	16	9	11	11	9	2	2	0	22	5	0	2	0	3	6	8	1	0	0	0	8	1	0	4	0
Shovel	7	.0000	.3198	35.0	0	0	0	7	0	0	0	0	7	0	0	0	0	0	0	0	0	0	0	0	0	0	0	0	0
shoveled	12	.5469	1.4607	41.6	6	1	2	1	2	0	0	0	6	0	0	0	2	1	0	2	0	0	0	0	0	1	0	0	0
shoveling	10	.5074	1.1215	40.5	2	2	1	0	1	2	2	0	4	1	0	3	0	0	0	0	0	0	0	0	0	1	0	1	0
shovels	27	.5801	3.3184	45.2	3	3	8	3	3	4	3	0	6	0	0	0	0	5	0	3	1	0	0	0	0	1	8	3	0
shoving	16	.5201	1.8637	42.7	2	4	1	6	1	1	1	0	8	0	0	0	0	0	0	1	0	0	0	0	3	3	0	1	0
show	2734	.9316	503.91	67.0	595	491	363	324	365	293	253	50	451	215	27	93	545	259	252	232	79	81	27	77	99	111	65	117	4
Show	24	.5987	3.0199	44.8	2	9	2	2	4	2	3	0	6	1	0	0	0	4	0	0	2	2	0	0	2	0	1	6	0
show-off	5	.4730	.5355	37.3	1	1	0	1	1	0	1	0	2	1	0	0	0	0	0	1	0	0	0	0	0	0	0	1	0
show's	3	.2054	.1422	31.5	0	0	0	0	0	0	3	0	0	0	1	0	0	0	0	0	0	0	0	0	0	0	0	2	0
showcase	4	.3113	.2711	34.3	0	2	0	1	0	1	0	0	0	0	1	0	0	0	0	0	0	0	0	0	1	0	0	2	0
showdown	4	.3097	.2992	34.8	0	1	0	0	1	0	2	0	1	0	0	1	0	0	0	0	0	0	0	0	0	0	0	2	0
showed	478	.8792	83.979	59.2	92	84	54	60	76	65	38	9	159	18	2	30	15	43	7	30	7	5	1	2	54	40	21	42	2
shower	44	.7759	6.9396	48.4	5	9	3	10	10	2	4	1	13	2	0	6	0	1	1	9	1	0	0	0	4	2	1	4	0
showered	6	.4805	.6598	38.2	1	0	0	1	2	2	0	0	3	1	0	0	0	0	0	1	0	0	0	0	1	0	0	0	0
showers	23	.7265	3.4341	45.4	4	4	1	5	5	2	1	1	7	0	0	2	0	3	1	3	2	0	0	0	0	3	0	2	0
showing	331	.8851	58.298	57.7	50	43	37	54	47	52	42	6	59	21	4	14	56	38	12	40	5	16	4	7	15	15	13	12	0
showman	6	.2401	.3311	35.2	0	2	0	4	0	0	0	0	0	0	0	0	0	0	0	0	2	0	0	0	4	0	0	0	0
Showman	4	.0000	.0323	25.1	0	0	0	0	0	0	4	0	0	0	0	0	0	0	0	0	4	0	0	0	0	0	0	0	0
showmanship	2	.0000	.0162	22.1	0	0	0	0	1	1	0	0	0	0	0	0	0	0	0	0	2	0	0	0	0	0	0	0	0
showmen	2	.2152	.1357	31.3	1	0	0	0	0	1	0	0	1	0	0	0	0	1	0	0	0	0	0	0	0	0	0	0	0
shown	1490	.7673	229.85	63.6	149	248	190	179	258	228	205	33	67	40	4	8	529	144	99	244	40	21	20	142	6	38	47	40	1
showplace	3	.2300	.1627	32.1	0	0	0	2	0	0	1	0	0	1	0	0	0	0	0	0	0	0	0	0	0	0	0	2	0
shows	1184	.9095	213.42	63.3	202	211	166	207	140	116	126	16	89	61	14	21	217	268	68	201	49	27	14	43	8	42	24	37	1
showy	15	.5346	1.7541	42.4	1	0	1	2	1	2	2	6	5	0	0	0	0	0	0	5	1	0	0	0	1	0	0	3	0
shrank	15	.6061	1.9170	42.8	0	2	4	3	3	2	1	0	4	0	0	3	0	0	0	2	0	0	0	0	2	2	0	2	0
shredded	6	.2485	.3321	35.2	0	0	0	1	2	1	2	0	0	0	0	1	0	1	0	0	0	0	3	0	0	0	0	1	0
shreds	7	.5502	.8346	39.2	0	0	2	0	3	1	1	0	2	0	0	0	0	1	0	2	0	0	0	0	0	0	1	1	0
Shreveport	6	.2031	.3257	35.1	0	0	3	0	1	1	1	0	0	1	0	0	0	5	0	0	0	0	0	0	0	0	0	0	0
shrew	4	.3711	.3648	35.6	1	0	1	0	2	0	0	0	2	0	0	0	0	0	0	0	0	0	0	0	0	1	1	0	0
shrewd	9	.5680	1.0630	40.3	0	0	1	0	1	2	4	1	1	0	1	2	0	1	0	0	0	0	0	0	1	0	1	2	0
shrewdly	6	.4640	.6235	37.9	0	1	4	0	0	1	0	0	2	0	0	0	0	0	0	0	0	0	0	0	1	2	1	0	0
shrews	6	.4738	.6387	38.1	0	0	1	0	4	0	0	1	2	0	0	1	0	0	0	2	0	0	0	0	0	0	1	0	0
Shrewsbury	2	.1698	.1133	30.5	0	0	1	1	0	0	0	0	1	0	0	0	0	0	0	0	0	0	0	0	0	0	1	0	0
shriek	17	.6502	2.2566	43.5	2	4	3	1	2	3	1	1	2	1	2	1	0	0	1	0	1	0	0	0	4	1	1	3	0
shrieked	27	.6043	3.4778	45.4	4	6	5	3	4	1	3	1	11	0	1	4	0	0	0	0	0	0	0	0	6	3	0	2	0
shrieking	15	.4500	1.5097	41.8	1	1	1	4	2	3	1	2	5	0	2	0	0	0	0	0	0	0	0	0	4	2	0	2	0
shrieks	6	.5188	.6686	38.3	1	1	0	2	0	0	0	2	1	0	0	0	0	0	0	1	0	0	0	0	1	2	0	1	0
shrill	74	.7505	11.293	50.5	8	7	8	13	22	11	5	0	20	8	3	8	0	1	0	2	7	0	0	0	12	8	1	4	0
shrilled	4	.1787	.2347	33.7	0	0	1	3	0	0	0	0	2	0	0	0	0	0	0	0	0	0	0	0	2	0	0	0	0
shrilling	5	.4167	.4618	36.6	0	0	1	1	2	0	1	0	1	0	0	2	0	0	0	0	1	0	0	0	0	1	0	0	0
shrilly	10	.5057	1.1046	40.4	0	0	3	3	3	1	0	0	3	1	0	2	0	1	0	0	0	0	0	0	3	0	0	0	0
shrimp	29	.6166	3.7827	45.8	2	2	3	8	13	0	0	1	7	1	0	1	0	5	0	11	0	0	0	0	0	0	2	2	0
Shrimp	2	.0000	.0234	23.7	0	2	0	0	0	0	0	0	0	0	0	0	0	0	0	0	0	0	0	0	2	0	0	0	0
shrimps	13	.5300	1.4716	41.7	4	3	1	0	5	0	0	0	2	0	0	0	0	0	0	3	0	0	0	0	3	3	2	0	0
shrine	22	.7194	3.2466	45.1	2	5	3	3	2	4	3	0	6	2	0	2	0	5	1	0	0	1	0	0	0	2	2	1	0
shrines	10	.3043	.6986	38.4	0	3	3	1	0	1	2	0	0	0	0	0	0	4	0	0	0	0	0	0	0	1	5	0	0
shrink	20	.5420	2.2564	43.5	0	1	0	5	3	5	4	2	2	1	0	0	0	0	4	5	0	0	4	2	0	0	0	2	0
shrinkage	6	.3034	.3752	35.7	0	0	0	0	1	1	4	0	0	0	0	0	0	0	0	0	0	0	3	2	0	0	1	0	0
shrinking	14	.5953	1.7615	42.5	1	3	4	2	2	0	2	0	3	0	0	0	0	2	0	4	0	0	1	0	2	0	0	2	0
shrinks	8	.5002	.8291	39.2	0	0	0	1	2	2	3	0	0	0	0	0	1	0	0	2	0	0	2	1	1	0	1	0	0
shriveled	3	.3429	.2528	34.0	0	1	0	0	0	1	0	1	1	0	0	0	0	0	0	1	0	0	0	0	1	0	0	0	0
shroud	3	.2260	.1580	32.0	0	0	0	0	1	0	2	0	0	0	0	2	0	0	0	0	1	0	0	0	0	0	1	0	0
shrouded	7	.3950	.5983	37.8	0	0	0	1	3	1	2	0	0	0	0	0	0	0	0	1	0	0	0	0	0	1	0	4	0
shrouding	2	.1814	.1187	30.7	0	0	0	0	2	0	0	0	1	0	0	0	0	0	0	0	0	0	0	0	0	0	0	1	0
shrouds	3	.3406	.2461	33.9	0	0	1	2	0	0	0	0	1	1	0	0	0	0	0	0	0	0	0	0	0	0	0	1	0
shrub	25	.6126	3.1789	45.0	4	5	2	5	1	2	1	5	2	1	0	0	0	2	0	7	0	0	0	0	5	4	4	0	0
shrubbery	6	.3730	.5104	37.1	0	0	0	1	4	0	0	1	1	0	0	1	0	0	0	1	0	0	0	0	0	0	0	3	0
shrubs	53	.6644	7.2163	48.6	3	11	4	5	11	5	5	9	3	0	1	3	0	10	0	12	0	0	0	0	0	5	13	6	0
shrug	11	.5637	1.3035	41.2	2	1	2	2	2	0	1	1	2	3	0	0	0	0	0	0	1	0	0	0	1	1	0	3	0
shrugged	54	.6358	7.2292	48.6	8	11	7	5	10	8	3	2	20	0	2	5	0	2	0	0	0	0	0	0	12	6	0	7	0
shrugging	3	.3450	.2505	34.0	0	1	0	1	1	0	0	0	1	0	0	0	0	0	0	0	0	0	0	0	1	1	0	0	0
shrugs	6	.4510	.6073	37.8	0	0	1	2	2	1	0	0	2	0	0	1	0	0	0	0	0	0	0	0	2	0	0	1	0
shrunk	13	.6692	1.8415	42.7	3	0	3	2	1	3	1	0	7	0	0	1	0	1	0	0	0	0	1	0	1	1	1	1	0
shrunken	2	.1839	.0845	29.3	0	0	0	0	1	0	1	0	0	0	0	0	0	0	0	0	0	0	0	0	1	0	0	0	0
Shuai	2	.0000	.0914	29.6	0	2	0	0	0	0	0	0	2	0	0	0	0	0	0	0	0	0	0	0	0	0	0	0	0
Shubrick	2	.0000	.0914	29.6	0	0	0	0	0	2	0	0	2	0	0	0	0	0	0	0	0	0	0	0	0	0	0	0	0

3N Shorty's
7R shot-peened
4P shot-put
6A shotput
3P Shotton's
6N shoulder-of-mutton
3A shoulder-to-shoulder
3P shouldest
8B shouldnt
9D shouldst
8C shovelful
4A shovelfuls
3N shovelled
5Q Shovels
3P shoves
4J shovin'
6N SHOW
5Q Show-Off
8R show-biz
7P show'd
9D show'rs
9M showcard
8N showcases
9D showering
7A Showers
4J showman's
9D showoff
3F showrooms
6R Shows
5G shr
9R shrapnel
7Q shred
4R shredders
5F Shreveport's
7Q shrike
7Q shrikes
3A shriller
6H shrimplike
3P SHRIMPS
6R Shrimpy
6R Shrimpy's
5Q Shrine
8A shrine-shaped
9P shrivel
XH shrubby
7Q shrublike
6A shu
8R Shubert

Word Type	F	D	U	SFI	3 Gr 3	4 Gr 4	5 Gr 5	6 Gr 6	7 Gr 7	8 Gr 8	9 Gr 9	X UnGr	A Read	B Eng & Gr	C Comp	D Lit	E Math	F Soc Stud	G Spell	H Sci	J Music	K Art	L Home Ec	M Shop	N Lib F	P Lib NF	Q Lib Ref	R Mag	S Rel
shucked	2	.1787	.1174	30.7	0	0	0	1	0	1	0	0	1	0	0	0	0	0	0	0	0	0	0	0	1	0	0	0	0
shucks	5	.3283	.3632	35.6	0	1	1	0	3	0	0	0	0	1	0	0	0	0	0	0	0	0	0	0	3	1	0	0	0
shudder	18	.5677	2.1813	43.4	0	2	3	2	6	3	1	1	5	0	0	3	0	1	0	0	0	0	0	0	1	5	0	3	0
shuddered	19	.4978	2.0632	43.1	1	5	1	3	5	3	1	0	5	0	0	4	0	1	0	0	0	0	0	0	5	4	0	0	0
shuddering	9	.4540	.9137	39.6	0	1	0	2	4	2	0	0	3	0	0	2	0	0	0	0	1	0	0	0	0	0	0	3	0
shudders	7	.4807	.7179	38.6	0	0	1	0	4	0	2	0	1	1	0	3	0	0	0	0	1	0	0	0	0	0	0	1	0
shuffle	10	.4853	1.0597	40.3	2	0	1	4	1	1	0	1	2	0	1	0	0	0	0	3	0	0	0	0	0	2	0	2	0
shuffled	8	.5277	.9071	39.6	0	3	0	0	3	0	0	2	2	0	0	1	0	0	0	0	0	0	0	0	2	1	0	2	0
shuffles	2	.2413	.1212	30.8	0	0	1	0	0	0	1	0	0	0	0	0	1	0	0	1	0	0	0	0	0	0	0	0	0
shuffling	10	.5932	1.2626	41.0	1	0	3	0	3	1	1	1	4	1	1	0	0	0	0	0	1	0	0	0	1	0	1	1	0
Shula	2	.0000	.0243	23.9	0	0	0	0	0	2	0	0	0	0	0	0	0	0	0	0	0	0	0	0	0	0	0	2	0
Shule	3	.0000	.0243	23.8	0	0	0	3	0	0	0	0	0	0	0	0	0	0	0	0	3	0	0	0	0	0	0	0	0
Shultz	7	.0000	.0851	29.3	0	0	0	0	0	0	7	0	0	0	0	0	0	0	0	0	0	0	0	0	0	0	0	7	0
shun	10	.5332	1.1408	40.6	0	1	1	0	4	2	2	0	3	0	0	2	0	0	2	0	0	1	0	0	0	0	1	1	0
shunned	3	.3465	.2515	34.0	0	1	1	1	0	0	0	0	1	0	0	0	0	0	0	0	0	0	0	0	0	1	0	1	0
shunted	2	.1717	.1142	30.6	0	1	0	0	1	0	0	0	1	0	0	1	0	0	0	0	0	0	0	0	0	0	0	0	0
Shurcliff	2	.0000	.0243	23.9	0	0	0	0	0	0	0	2	0	0	0	0	0	0	0	0	0	0	0	0	0	0	0	2	0
shush	2	.1948	.1250	31.0	1	0	1	0	0	0	0	0	1	0	0	0	0	0	0	0	0	0	0	0	0	1	0	0	0
shut	283	.8066	46.251	56.7	68	50	26	42	62	13	17	5	109	4	4	28	0	11	5	20	0	0	3	0	45	23	8	23	0
shutdown	3	.3871	.2488	34.0	0	0	0	0	0	1	1	1	0	1	0	0	0	0	0	0	0	0	0	0	0	0	1	1	0
shutouts	3	.2143	.1568	32.0	1	0	0	2	0	0	0	0	0	0	0	0	0	0	0	0	0	0	0	0	0	1	0	2	0
shuts	9	.6234	1.1884	40.7	4	0	0	1	2	1	0	1	3	1	0	1	0	1	0	2	0	0	0	0	0	0	1	0	0
shutter	9	.4808	.9339	39.7	1	0	2	1	1	1	3	0	1	0	0	3	0	0	0	3	0	0	0	0	1	0	0	1	0
shuttered	2	.2440	.1132	30.5	0	0	0	0	1	0	1	0	0	0	0	1	0	0	0	0	0	0	0	0	0	0	0	1	0
shutters	22	.6582	3.0266	44.8	5	4	4	1	3	4	0	1	8	4	0	2	0	0	0	0	0	0	0	0	3	2	1	2	0
shutting	3	.2031	.1990	33.0	2	0	0	1	0	0	0	0	2	0	0	0	0	0	1	0	0	0	0	0	0	0	0	0	0
shuttle	6	.2765	.3443	35.4	0	0	0	1	1	3	1	0	0	0	0	0	0	0	0	0	0	1	4	0	0	0	1	0	0
shuttled	2	.1907	.0862	29.4	0	0	0	0	0	2	0	0	0	0	0	1	0	0	0	0	0	0	1	0	0	0	0	0	0
shuttling	3	.3263	.2368	33.7	0	0	0	0	2	1	0	0	1	0	0	0	0	0	0	0	1	0	0	0	0	0	0	1	0
shy	92	.7427	13.976	51.5	11	18	14	9	21	9	8	2	31	13	3	16	0	5	0	2	0	0	1	0	7	3	1	10	0
Shylock	16	.0993	.4644	36.7	0	0	0	0	0	1	15	0	0	0	0	15	0	0	1	0	0	0	0	0	0	0	0	0	0
shyly	19	.5585	2.2739	43.6	2	3	5	1	3	4	1	0	6	0	0	4	0	1	0	0	1	0	0	0	5	0	0	2	0
shyness	5	.4293	.4745	36.8	0	3	1	0	0	0	1	0	1	0	0	1	0	0	0	0	0	0	0	0	1	0	0	2	0
si	14	.5371	1.6072	42.1	2	1	1	5	3	0	2	0	4	0	0	2	0	0	2	0	3	0	0	0	3	0	0	0	0
Si-Ling-Shi	3	.0000	.1370	31.4	0	3	0	0	0	0	0	0	3	0	0	0	0	0	0	0	0	0	0	0	0	0	0	0	0
Siam	3	.3781	.2493	34.0	0	0	0	1	0	1	0	1	0	1	0	0	0	1	0	0	0	0	0	0	0	0	0	1	0
Siamese	4	.3160	.2729	34.4	0	1	0	0	1	2	0	0	0	2	1	0	0	0	0	0	0	0	0	0	1	0	0	0	0
Siata	3	.0000	.0322	25.1	0	0	0	0	0	0	3	0	0	0	0	3	0	0	0	0	0	0	0	0	0	0	0	0	0
Sibelius	5	.0000	.0404	26.1	0	0	0	2	0	3	0	0	0	0	0	0	0	0	0	0	5	0	0	0	0	0	0	0	0
Siberia	31	.5016	3.3246	45.2	2	4	0	11	3	3	7	1	0	0	0	0	0	19	0	3	1	0	0	0	0	3	1	4	0
Siberian	13	.5495	1.5116	41.8	0	2	1	1	3	0	6	0	1	0	0	0	0	5	0	1	0	0	0	0	0	3	2	1	0
Sibiu	3	.0000	.0365	25.6	0	0	0	3	0	0	0	0	0	0	0	0	0	0	0	0	0	0	0	0	0	0	0	3	0
Sibley	11	.0000	.5025	37.0	11	0	0	0	0	0	0	0	11	0	0	0	0	0	0	0	0	0	0	0	0	0	0	0	0
Sibyl	4	.2186	.2141	33.3	0	0	0	3	0	0	1	0	0	0	0	1	0	0	0	0	0	0	0	0	0	3	0	0	0
sic	2	.2441	.1127	30.5	0	0	1	0	0	1	0	0	0	0	0	0	0	0	0	0	0	0	0	0	1	0	1	0	0
sich	5	.3291	.3639	35.6	0	1	0	0	3	1	0	0	0	0	0	1	0	0	0	0	0	0	0	0	3	1	0	0	0
Sicilian	5	.4426	.4717	36.7	0	0	3	0	0	0	1	1	0	1	0	0	0	0	0	1	0	0	0	0	0	1	2	0	0
Sicily	30	.5508	3.4659	45.4	6	2	2	10	5	0	2	3	2	2	0	0	0	9	1	1	0	0	0	0	1	3	11	0	0
sick	334	.5991	42.893	56.3	76	71	35	36	64	23	24	5	141	15	2	25	0	19	10	24	5	0	6	0	31	29	5	17	5
sickbed	2	.1948	.1250	31.0	0	1	1	0	0	0	0	0	1	0	0	0	0	0	0	0	0	0	0	0	0	1	0	0	0
sickened	4	.4887	.4073	36.1	0	0	2	0	1	1	0	0	0	1	0	0	0	0	0	0	0	0	0	0	1	0	1	1	0
sickening	6	.2747	.4669	36.7	0	2	1	2	1	0	0	0	4	0	1	0	0	0	0	0	0	0	0	0	0	0	0	1	0
sickle	3	.3764	.2475	33.9	0	1	0	1	1	0	0	0	0	1	0	1	0	1	0	0	0	0	0	0	0	0	0	0	0
sickles	2	.2152	.1357	31.3	0	0	0	2	0	0	0	0	1	0	0	0	0	1	0	0	0	0	0	0	0	0	0	0	0
sickly	13	.6029	1.6835	42.3	2	0	3	2	5	0	1	0	6	0	0	2	1	0	0	0	0	0	0	0	2	1	0	1	0
sickness	59	.7682	9.2320	49.7	9	9	6	9	12	7	6	1	17	1	0	6	0	11	0	8	0	0	2	0	4	5	4	1	0
sicknesses	2	.2346	.1166	30.7	1	1	0	0	0	0	0	0	0	0	0	0	0	0	0	1	0	0	0	0	0	0	0	1	0
Sid	16	.3158	1.4467	41.6	5	0	0	0	10	1	0	0	14	0	0	0	0	0	0	0	0	0	0	0	1	0	0	1	0
side	2532	.9141	459.47	66.6	455	424	259	240	507	311	284	52	652	50	20	160	261	170	41	301	38	27	108	95	198	226	72	113	0
Side	19	.4832	2.0433	43.1	1	4	1	0	2	10	1	0	7	0	0	0	1	1	0	1	5	0	0	0	0	0	0	4	0
side-by-side	2	.1972	.1262	31.0	0	0	0	0	1	1	0	0	1	0	0	0	1	0	0	0	0	0	0	0	0	0	0	0	0
side-looking	2	.0000	.0243	23.9	0	0	0	2	0	0	0	0	0	0	0	0	0	0	0	0	0	0	0	0	0	0	0	2	0
sideboard	3	.2292	.1615	32.1	0	0	0	0	2	1	0	0	0	0	0	1	0	0	0	0	0	0	0	0	2	0	0	0	0
sideburns	2	.2401	.1133	30.5	1	1	0	0	0	0	0	0	0	0	0	0	0	0	0	0	0	0	0	0	0	1	1	0	0
sided	4	.3344	.3261	35.1	0	1	1	0	0	0	2	0	1	0	0	0	0	2	0	0	0	0	0	0	0	0	1	0	0
sideheads	2	.0000	.0914	29.6	0	2	0	0	0	0	0	0	2	0	0	0	0	0	0	0	0	0	0	0	0	0	0	0	0
sideline	3	.3427	.2477	33.9	0	0	0	1	2	0	0	0	1	0	0	0	0	0	0	0	0	0	0	0	1	0	0	1	0
sidelines	10	.5417	1.1286	40.5	1	2	1	0	5	0	1	0	1	1	1	0	0	0	0	0	0	0	1	0	0	2	0	4	0
sidelong	2	.2407	.1138	30.6	0	0	0	1	0	1	0	0	0	0	0	1	0	0	0	0	0	0	0	0	0	1	0	0	0
Sider	2	.0000	.0234	23.7	0	0	0	0	2	0	0	0	0	0	0	0	0	0	0	0	0	0	0	0	2	0	0	0	0
Siders	3	.0000	.0352	25.5	0	0	0	0	3	0	0	0	0	0	0	0	0	0	0	0	0	0	0	0	3	0	0	0	0
sides	827	.7924	131.89	61.2	95	73	104	91	128	177	153	6	114	17	2	26	331	70	4	66	2	9	43	26	24	39	25	29	0
sideshows	2	.1494	.1045	30.2	0	2	0	0	0	0	0	0	1	0	0	0	0	0	0	0	1	0	0	0	0	0	0	0	0
sidestepped	3	.2187	.1555	31.9	0	0	2	0	0	0	0	1	0	2	0	0	0	0	0	0	0	0	0	0	0	0	0	1	0
sidetrack	2	.2152	.1357	31.3	0	1	0	1	0	0	0	0	1	0	0	0	0	1	0	0	0	0	0	0	0	0	0	0	0
sidetracked	3	.3406	.2461	33.9	0	1	0	0	2	0	0	0	1	1	0	0	0	0	0	0	0	0	0	0	0	0	0	1	0
sidewalk	113	.7981	18.287	52.6	35	21	11	6	19	7	12	2	41	3	6	9	3	8	2	11	1	0	1	0	13	4	2	9	0
sidewalks	42	.5716	5.0206	47.0	8	10	3	7	6	3	3	2	5	0	6	2	2	10	0	2	0	0	0	1	1	3	0	10	0
sideways	47	.7445	7.1593	48.5	8	5	10	6	7	5	2	4	14	1	0	5	0	0	0	11	2	0	0	0	3	4	4	3	0
sidewhiskers	2	.2437	.1129	30.5	0	1	0	1	0	0	0	0	0	0	0	0	0	0	0	0	0	0	0	0	0	0	1	1	0
Sidewinder	2	.0000	.0299	24.8	0	2	0	0	0	0	0	0	0	0	0	0	2	0	0	0	0	0	0	0	0	0	0	0	0
sidewise	9	.5726	1.0717	40.3	1	2	0	1	3	1	1	0	1	2	0	2	0	0	0	1	0	0	0	1	0	1	0	1	0
siding	8	.5706	.9506	39.8	0	1	2	1	4	0	0	0	1	0	0	1	0	1	0	0	0	0	0	1	1	0	1	2	0
Siding	2	.0000	.0914	29.6	0	0	2	0	0	0	0	0	2	0	0	0	0	0	0	0	0	0	0	0	0	0	0	0	0
sidle	2	.2440	.1132	30.5	0	0	0	0	1	1	0	0	0	0	0	1	0	0	0	0	0	0	0	0	0	0	0	1	0
sidled	5	.3175	.4036	36.1	0	0	0	2	1	2	0	0	2	0	0	0	0	1	0	0	0	0	0	0	2	0	0	0	0
Sidney	25	.2698	1.5627	41.9	18	5	1	0	0	1	0	0	0	0	0	0	0	3	0	0	0	0	0	0	18	3	0	1	0
Sidney's	3	.0000	.0352	25.5	3	0	0	0	0	0	0	0	0	0	0	0	0	0	0	0	0	0	0	0	3	0	0	0	0
Sidon	5	.4689	.4984	37.0	1	1	0	1	1	0	1	0	0	0	0	0	0	1	0	0	0	0	0	0	0	2	1	1	0
Siecus	3	.0000	.0365	25.6	0	0	0	0	0	0	3	0	0	0	0	0	0	0	0	0	0	0	0	0	0	0	0	3	0
SIECUS	3	.0000	.0365	25.6	0	0	0	0	3	0	0	0	0	0	0	0	0	0	0	0	0	0	0	0	0	0	0	3	0
siege	12	.4441	1.1815	40.7	0	0	3	1	3	1	4	0	3	2	0	1	0	1	0	0	0	0	0	0	0	0	5	0	0
sieges	2	.2285	.1129	30.5	0	0	0	0	0	2	0	0	0	0	0	0	0	1	0	0	0	0	0	0	0	0	1	0	0
Siegfried	10	.2768	.6444	38.1	0	1	0	2	7	0	0	0	1	0	0	0	0	0	0	0	4	0	0	0	0	0	0	5	0

7D shudderingly
XR shunners
7Q shuns
7A shunt
9Q shunts
6A shur-r-r
4P shure
XR shut-down
9K shut-in
9D shut-ins
6F shut-off

9Q Shutt
8A shuttles
6J Shvet
3A shyer
7A shying
5Q Si
5Q SiO2
5Q Sian
9Q Sibbald
6J Sibelius'
9F Siberia's

7Q Siberians
5A Sibitsky
6R Sibiu's
XR siblings
9D Sibylla
7Q Sicilies
7F Sick
7D sick-bed
3Q sick-benefit
8A sick-leave
7N sick-room

8F sicken
4A sickish
7Q Sickles
8Q Sickness
7A Siddy
8E Side-Angle-Side
9L Side-Seam
8E Side-Side-Side
9M side-facing
8L side-seam
9J side-shows

5A side-stepped
6N side-stepping
9D side-wall
7Q side-wheelers
7N side-whiskers
7R sidearm
7A sideboards
9B sidecar
4A SIDEHEADS
8C sidehill
XH sidereal

4P sidesaddle
5H sideshow
6A sideslipped
XR sidestepping
6H sideward
6R sidewheel
3P sidewinders
6A Sidi
7Q siegecraft
8J Siegmeister

Word Type	F	D	U	SFI	3 Gr 3	4 Gr 4	5 Gr 5	6 Gr 6	7 Gr 7	8 Gr 8	9 Gr 9	X UnGr	A Read	B Eng & Gr	C Comp	D Lit	E Math	F Soc Stud	G Spell	H Sci	J Music	K Art	L Home Ec	M Shop	N Lib F	P Lib NF	Q Lib Ref	R Mag	S Rel
Sieke	2	.0000	.0290	24.6	0	2	0	0	0	0	0	0	0	0	0	0	0	0	0	0	0	0	0	0	0	2	0	0	0
sienna	3	.0000	.0434	26.4	0	3	0	0	0	0	0	0	0	0	0	0	0	0	0	0	0	0	0	0	0	3	0	0	0
Sierra	38	.5135	4.1999	46.2	1	2	7	4	14	2	4	4	3	0	0	0	0	19	0	7	0	0	0	0	0	1	3	5	0
Sierras	14	.3655	1.1682	40.7	0	0	2	2	3	0	7	0	0	0	0	0	0	4	0	8	0	0	0	0	0	0	2	0	0
siesta	5	.2229	.2794	34.5	3	0	0	1	1	0	0	0	1	0	2	0	0	1	0	0	1	0	0	0	0	0	0	0	0
sieve	15	.4370	1.3780	41.4	1	0	0	0	6	4	3	1	0	0	0	1	6	0	0	0	0	0	4	0	2	0	1	1	0
Sieve	5	.1926	.2474	33.9	0	0	0	0	5	0	0	0	0	0	0	0	4	0	0	0	0	0	0	0	0	0	0	1	0
sieved	3	.2359	.1459	31.6	0	0	0	0	1	2	0	0	0	0	0	0	0	0	0	0	0	0	2	1	0	0	0	0	0
sieves	2	.2433	.1158	30.6	1	0	0	0	0	0	0	1	0	0	0	0	0	0	0	0	0	0	0	0	0	1	0	1	0
sift	23	.1014	.5972	37.8	0	0	0	2	1	5	14	1	1	0	0	0	1	0	0	0	0	0	18	0	1	0	0	2	0
sifted	16	.4854	1.6445	42.2	1	2	1	2	6	2	2	0	2	1	0	0	0	2	0	1	0	0	5	1	1	1	0	2	0
sifting	7	.3821	.5732	37.6	0	1	0	1	2	2	1	0	1	1	0	0	0	0	0	0	1	0	3	1	0	0	0	0	0
sifts	2	.2442	.1134	30.5	0	0	0	0	0	0	1	1	0	1	0	0	0	0	0	0	0	0	0	0	0	0	0	1	0
sigh	57	.6302	7.6214	48.8	8	11	10	9	15	3	1	0	25	4	0	9	1	1	0	0	2	0	0	0	11	4	0	0	0
sighed	144	.6882	20.707	53.2	29	46	18	16	21	11	3	0	65	3	1	16	0	3	0	0	2	0	0	0	22	25	1	6	0
sighing	26	.6803	3.6413	45.6	0	1	4	7	5	4	4	1	7	1	2	4	0	0	0	0	2	0	0	0	4	2	1	3	0
sighs	20	.6479	2.7225	44.3	1	3	2	6	5	1	2	0	8	1	0	2	0	0	0	0	2	0	0	0	4	1	0	2	0
sight	565	.8696	98.413	59.9	98	103	64	76	119	49	43	13	215	19	12	55	10	19	0	47	24	2	0	4	62	53	16	27	0
sight-seeing	4	.3743	.3712	35.7	0	1	1	1	1	0	0	0	2	0	0	0	0	1	0	0	0	0	0	0	0	0	0	1	0
sight-singing	4	.0000	.0323	25.1	0	0	0	4	0	0	0	0	0	0	0	0	0	0	0	0	4	0	0	0	0	0	0	0	0
sighted	48	.8142	7.9200	49.0	7	8	5	11	10	4	2	1	20	3	1	5	0	4	0	4	1	0	0	0	2	3	3	2	0
sighted-in	2	.0000	.0243	23.9	0	0	0	0	2	0	0	0	0	0	0	0	0	0	0	0	0	0	0	0	0	0	0	2	0
sighting	4	.3415	.3070	34.9	0	0	1	2	0	0	1	0	0	0	0	0	0	0	0	1	0	0	0	0	0	1	0	2	0
sightings	4	.1611	.1738	32.4	0	0	0	2	2	0	0	0	0	0	0	0	0	0	0	1	0	0	0	0	0	0	0	3	0
sightless	3	.2212	.2099	33.2	0	0	1	1	1	0	0	0	2	0	0	1	0	0	0	0	0	0	0	0	0	0	0	0	0
sights	71	.8051	11.517	50.6	8	12	10	11	18	5	6	1	16	6	4	7	0	15	0	4	1	2	1	0	2	5	2	6	0
sightseeing	6	.4812	.6606	38.2	0	3	1	0	0	1	0	1	3	1	0	0	0	1	0	0	0	0	0	0	0	0	0	1	0
sightseers	4	.2638	.2715	34.3	1	0	0	2	0	1	0	0	1	0	1	0	0	1	0	1	0	0	0	0	0	0	0	0	0
Sigma	2	.0000	.0299	24.8	0	0	2	0	0	0	0	0	0	0	0	0	2	0	0	0	0	0	0	0	0	0	0	0	0
Sigmund	2	.2375	.1088	30.4	0	0	0	0	1	0	1	0	0	0	0	0	0	0	0	0	1	0	0	0	0	0	0	1	0
sign	615	.8824	108.37	60.3	189	92	55	77	107	53	34	8	206	15	4	35	115	32	23	13	29	0	2	3	42	47	10	39	0
Sign	4	.3678	.3185	35.0	0	1	2	0	0	1	0	0	0	1	0	0	0	0	0	0	0	0	0	0	2	0	0	1	0
signal	274	.8614	47.286	56.7	55	57	40	28	43	29	17	5	93	47	2	13	6	9	8	28	5	0	0	6	14	12	14	17	0
Signal	4	.3750	.3392	35.3	0	0	0	0	2	1	1	0	0	0	0	0	0	1	0	2	0	0	0	0	0	0	0	1	0
signaled	45	.7577	6.9605	48.4	2	11	4	8	5	10	5	0	15	7	0	2	6	3	1	0	1	0	0	0	3	2	0	5	0
signaling	16	.6121	2.0822	43.2	0	5	4	1	5	0	0	1	6	0	0	1	0	1	0	1	0	0	0	0	0	1	3	3	0
signalled	2	.2444	.1132	30.5	0	0	1	0	1	0	0	0	0	1	0	0	0	0	0	0	0	0	0	0	1	0	0	0	0
signals	178	.8538	30.335	54.8	41	30	15	15	32	21	22	2	23	31	0	4	12	6	5	45	2	1	1	4	4	11	18	11	0
signature	133	.2162	6.6358	48.2	35	31	25	16	14	5	7	0	4	9	0	0	0	0	2	0	113	2	0	0	0	3	0	0	0
signatures	24	.4506	2.2860	43.6	0	0	5	2	8	7	2	0	2	2	0	0	0	2	0	0	12	3	0	0	1	1	0	1	0
signboards	2	.2297	.1135	30.6	0	0	0	1	1	0	0	0	0	0	0	1	0	1	0	0	0	0	0	0	0	0	0	0	0
signed	113	.7232	16.714	52.2	11	14	17	21	15	17	14	4	23	6	0	3	4	27	0	2	0	0	0	0	3	14	13	18	0
signer	2	.1494	.1045	30.2	0	0	0	0	2	0	0	0	1	0	0	0	0	0	0	0	1	0	0	0	0	0	0	0	0
signers	6	.0000	.1167	30.7	0	0	0	0	0	5	1	0	0	0	0	0	0	6	0	0	0	0	0	0	0	0	0	0	0
signet	9	.1880	.6453	38.1	0	0	1	4	0	1	3	0	8	0	0	0	0	0	0	1	0	0	0	0	0	0	0	0	0
significance	53	.6769	7.3357	48.7	2	1	2	1	16	17	12	2	8	1	5	4	1	5	0	2	1	0	1	0	0	4	13	8	0
significant	92	.8023	14.794	51.7	0	0	3	4	14	40	28	3	7	8	1	3	33	6	0	6	5	1	1	0	0	2	9	10	0
significantly	19	.7493	2.8540	44.6	0	0	0	0	7	3	8	1	0	0	1	2	0	2	0	2	0	0	1	1	1	1	4	4	0
signified	5	.3832	.4308	36.3	0	0	0	2	2	0	0	1	1	0	0	0	0	0	0	0	2	0	0	0	1	1	0	0	0
signifies	4	.4736	.3987	36.0	0	1	0	1	1	1	0	0	0	0	0	0	0	1	1	0	0	0	0	0	0	0	1	1	0
signify	7	.5829	.8530	39.3	0	0	0	0	4	1	2	0	1	0	0	1	0	0	0	1	0	0	0	0	1	0	1	2	0
signifying	3	.0000	.0328	25.2	0	0	0	0	1	0	0	2	0	3	0	0	0	0	0	0	0	0	0	0	0	0	0	0	0
signing	15	.6471	2.0195	43.1	2	1	2	1	1	4	4	0	4	0	0	0	0	1	0	0	0	0	1	0	2	3	2	2	0
Signor	19	.2610	1.1592	40.6	0	0	0	12	7	0	0	0	1	0	0	7	0	0	0	0	0	0	0	0	11	0	0	0	0
signpost	3	.2037	.1491	31.7	0	0	0	0	2	1	0	0	0	0	0	2	1	0	0	0	0	0	0	0	0	0	0	0	0
signposts	7	.4772	.7665	38.8	0	1	3	0	1	0	2	0	3	0	0	0	1	2	0	1	0	0	0	0	0	0	0	0	0
signs	352	.9095	63.544	58.0	76	46	34	37	73	43	36	7	63	13	2	21	32	47	16	46	14	0	2	0	24	22	15	35	0
Signs	2	.2404	.1142	30.6	2	0	0	0	0	0	0	0	0	1	0	0	1	0	0	0	0	0	0	0	0	0	0	0	0
Sigrid	2	.1494	.1045	30.2	0	0	0	0	1	0	1	0	1	0	0	0	0	0	0	0	1	0	0	0	0	0	0	0	0
Sikes	2	.2442	.1134	30.5	0	0	0	1	1	0	0	0	0	1	0	0	0	0	0	0	0	0	0	0	0	0	0	1	0
Sikorsky	2	.0000	.0914	29.6	0	2	0	0	0	0	0	0	2	0	0	0	0	0	0	0	0	0	0	0	0	0	0	0	0
Sikorsky's	2	.0000	.0914	29.6	0	2	0	0	0	0	0	0	2	0	0	0	0	0	0	0	0	0	0	0	0	0	0	0	0
silage	4	.3831	.3415	35.3	0	0	2	2	0	0	0	0	0	0	0	0	0	2	0	0	0	0	0	0	0	1	0	1	0
Silas	6	.4513	.6075	37.8	0	2	1	2	1	0	0	0	2	0	0	0	0	0	0	0	0	0	0	0	2	0	1	1	0
silence	248	.6917	35.507	55.5	19	33	41	31	72	26	23	3	88	11	1	45	0	2	1	2	15	0	1	0	59	11	1	11	0
Silence	4	.2417	.3028	34.8	0	1	0	0	3	0	0	0	3	0	0	0	0	0	0	0	0	0	0	0	1	0	0	0	0
silenced	8	.5576	.9646	39.8	1	0	0	2	2	2	0	1	3	0	0	1	0	0	0	0	0	0	0	0	1	2	1	0	0
silences	8	.4930	.8534	39.3	0	1	0	3	2	1	1	0	2	0	0	0	0	1	0	0	1	1	0	0	2	0	1	0	0
silent	626	.3658	51.077	57.1	132	119	106	111	80	44	28	6	108	21	2	35	0	4	388	1	7	0	0	0	24	16	7	13	0
Silent	7	.3672	.5689	37.5	1	1	0	3	1	1	0	0	1	0	0	0	0	0	2	0	3	0	0	0	0	1	0	0	0
silent-letter	2	.2408	.1091	30.4	0	1	0	0	0	0	0	1	0	1	0	0	0	0	1	0	0	0	0	0	0	0	0	0	0
silently	103	.7504	15.853	52.0	15	16	13	16	28	8	6	1	44	2	1	17	0	0	4	0	5	0	1	0	15	9	0	5	0
Silesia	6	.0000	.1167	30.7	0	0	0	1	0	0	5	0	0	0	0	0	0	6	0	0	0	0	0	0	0	0	0	0	0
silhouette	8	.5510	.9217	39.6	0	1	1	1	1	1	3	0	1	1	0	0	0	0	0	0	1	0	1	0	0	3	0	1	0
silhouetted	5	.3496	.3978	36.0	0	0	1	1	2	0	1	0	1	0	1	0	0	0	0	0	0	0	0	0	2	0	0	1	0
silhouettes	3	.1320	.1599	32.0	1	0	0	1	0	0	1	0	2	0	0	0	0	0	0	0	0	0	1	0	0	0	0	0	0
silica	24	.2614	1.4899	41.7	0	3	14	1	0	4	2	0	0	0	0	0	0	0	0	10	0	0	0	0	0	1	13	0	0
silicate	4	.2672	.2733	34.4	1	0	0	0	0	1	2	0	1	0	0	0	0	0	0	1	0	0	0	0	0	0	2	0	0
silicates	4	.2353	.2382	33.8	0	0	1	0	0	0	2	1	0	0	0	0	0	0	0	3	0	0	0	0	0	0	1	0	0
silicious	3	.0000	.0591	27.7	0	0	0	0	0	0	3	0	0	0	0	0	0	0	0	3	0	0	0	0	0	0	0	0	0
silicon	28	.4021	2.4941	44.0	2	4	10	1	5	1	5	0	4	0	0	0	0	0	0	7	0	0	0	4	0	1	12	0	0
silicone	2	.0000	.0209	23.2	0	0	2	0	0	0	0	0	0	0	0	0	0	0	0	0	0	0	0	0	0	0	2	0	0
silicones	4	.1494	.1609	32.1	0	0	3	1	0	0	0	0	0	0	0	0	0	0	0	1	0	0	0	0	0	0	3	0	0
silk	184	.8790	32.263	55.1	56	22	15	43	22	14	9	3	41	1	4	10	2	42	6	29	3	2	8	1	4	19	10	2	0
silken	21	.7365	3.2036	45.1	5	0	3	4	4	1	2	2	11	1	0	1	0	0	0	1	1	0	0	0	1	1	2	2	0
silks	21	.6747	2.9146	44.6	3	1	3	5	2	3	2	2	3	0	0	2	0	8	0	1	2	1	0	0	0	1	1	2	0
silkworm	5	.4369	.4818	36.8	3	0	1	0	0	1	0	0	1	0	0	0	0	1	0	0	0	0	1	0	0	1	1	0	0
silkworms	11	.3229	.8295	39.2	8	1	0	2	0	0	0	0	0	0	0	0	0	6	0	1	0	0	0	0	0	4	0	0	0
silky	32	.6986	4.6219	46.6	6	1	6	6	8	2	1	2	10	1	0	2	0	1	0	3	2	0	0	0	4	8	0	1	0
sill	25	.7299	3.7264	45.7	6	5	2	3	4	2	2	1	6	0	1	4	0	2	0	3	1	0	0	0	5	1	1	1	0
sillier	3	.3400	.2455	33.9	0	2	0	1	0	0	0	0	1	1	0	0	0	0	0	0	0	0	0	0	1	0	0	0	0
silliest	4	.0000	.1827	32.6	1	1	0	1	0	1	0	0	4	0	0	0	0	0	0	0	0	0	0	0	0	0	0	0	0
silliness	3	.3452	.2543	34.1	1	0	0	0	1	0	0	1	1	0	0	0	0	0	0	1	0	0	0	0	0	0	0	1	0
sills	6	.4802	.6606	38.2	1	4	0	0	0	0	1	0	3	0	0	0	0	0	0	1	0	0	0	0	0	1	1	0	0
silly	150	.7262	22.732	53.6	60	31	9	26	15	7	0	2	91	7	1	4	0	2	1	2	8	0	0	0	22	6	2	4	0
Silly	3	.0000	.1370	31.4	0	1	2	0	0	0	0	0	3	0	0	0	0	0	0	0	0	0	0	0	0	0	0	0	0
silo	5	.4535	.4737	36.8	0	0	1	0	3	1	0	0	0	1	1	1	0	1	1	0	0	0	0	0	0	0	0	0	0

7Q Sierra-Cascades
5P sierras
3A siestas
4N Sieur
9Q Sif
9L sifter
8Q Sigel
6A sighings
3P Sighs
6J sight-sing
6R sightseer
7N signalized
9D signally
7R Signals
7N signboard
9D Signior
9D signiors
7A signless
6N signor's
6N Signor's
6A Sigurdur
6R Sigworth
6Q Sikkeland
8D sil
5A Silbernagle
5G silekt'**
5A SILENCE
5N silencing
3J Silhouette
5Q Silica
8H siliceous
5Q silicic
5Q silicofluoride
5Q Silicon
3F Silk
XR silk-bound
9F silk-manufacturing
3A silkier
6D silkiest
5Q silky-haired
7A Sill
4A sillying

Word Type	F	D	U	SFI	Gr 3	Gr 4	Gr 5	Gr 6	Gr 7	Gr 8	Gr 9	UnGr	Read	Eng & Gr	Comp	Lit	Math	Soc Stud	Spell	Sci	Music	Art	Home Ec	Shop	Lib F	Lib NF	Lib Ref	Mag	Rel
silt	17	.5511	1.9975	43.0	0	4	4	3	1	2	3	0	2	0	0	0	4	0	0	6	0	0	0	0	0	1	3	0	0
silts	2	.0000	.0394	26.0	0	0	0	0	0	0	2	0	0	0	0	0	0	0	0	2	0	0	0	0	0	1	0	0	0
Silurian	2	.0000	.0209	23.2	0	0	0	0	2	0	0	0	0	0	0	0	0	0	0	0	0	0	0	0	0	0	2	0	0
silver	502	.9184	91.545	59.6	96	93	75	75	67	56	28	12	148	22	7	56	18	78	1	31	22	3	3	3	43	24	27	16	0
Silver	48	.4961	5.2144	47.2	1	9	3	2	24	4	4	1	14	0	0	1	0	4	0	0	3	0	0	0	22	2	1	1	0
silver-colored	3	.1650	.1684	32.3	1	1	0	0	1	0	0	0	1	0	0	1	0	0	0	0	0	0	0	0	0	0	0	0	0
silver-gray	3	.2120	.1548	31.9	1	2	0	0	0	0	0	0	1	0	0	0	0	0	0	2	0	0	0	0	0	0	0	0	0
silver-sweet	2	.0000	.0162	22.1	0	0	0	0	0	0	2	0	0	0	0	0	0	0	0	0	0	0	0	0	2	0	0	0	0
silver-white	3	.2828	.1883	32.7	0	0	2	0	0	0	1	0	0	0	0	0	0	0	1	0	0	0	0	0	1	0	0	0	0
silvered	7	.3853	.6286	38.0	0	0	1	0	5	1	0	0	2	0	0	0	0	0	1	0	0	0	0	0	1	0	0	0	0
silverfish	4	.1750	.1896	32.8	3	0	0	0	0	0	0	0	1	0	0	0	0	0	0	1	0	0	0	0	0	3	0	0	0
silvering	2	.1787	.1174	30.7	0	1	0	1	0	0	0	0	1	0	0	0	0	0	0	1	0	0	0	0	0	0	3	0	0
Silverplate	2	.0000	.0243	23.9	2	0	0	0	0	0	0	0	0	0	0	0	0	0	0	0	0	0	0	0	0	0	0	0	0
silversmith	8	.4683	.8477	39.3	0	4	3	0	0	1	0	0	3	0	0	0	0	0	0	0	0	0	0	0	0	0	0	2	0
silversmiths	4	.2152	.2714	34.3	0	2	1	1	0	0	0	0	2	0	0	0	0	0	0	0	0	0	0	0	2	0	1	0	0
Silverspot	11	.0000	.5025	37.0	11	0	0	0	0	0	0	0	11	0	0	0	0	0	0	0	0	0	0	0	0	0	0	0	0
Silverspot's	2	.0000	.0914	29.6	2	0	0	0	0	0	0	0	2	0	0	0	0	0	0	0	0	0	0	0	0	0	0	0	0
Silverspray	2	.0000	.0914	29.6	0	0	0	0	2	0	0	0	2	0	0	0	0	0	0	0	0	0	0	0	0	0	0	0	0
silverware	21	.5604	2.4715	43.9	2	1	2	8	1	4	3	0	2	0	0	0	0	0	0	0	0	0	0	0	0	0	0	2	0
silvery	44	.8007	7.1327	48.5	7	5	2	9	10	4	5	2	14	1	0	4	0	1	0	9	3	0	1	0	3	0	1	2	0
silvery-white	5	.3095	.3959	36.0	0	2	1	1	1	0	0	0	2	2	0	0	0	0	0	1	0	0	0	0	0	0	0	0	0
Silvia	2	.2305	.1080	30.3	0	0	0	0	1	0	0	1	4	0	0	0	0	0	0	0	0	0	0	0	0	1	0	0	0
Simba	4	.0000	.1827	32.6	0	0	0	4	0	0	0	0	4	0	0	0	0	0	0	0	0	0	0	0	0	1	0	0	0
Simbolon	2	.0000	.0209	23.2	0	0	0	0	0	2	0	0	0	0	0	0	0	2	0	0	0	0	0	0	0	0	0	0	0
Simburg	3	.0000	.0365	25.6	0	0	0	0	3	0	0	0	0	0	0	0	0	0	0	0	0	0	0	0	0	0	3	0	0
Simenon	3	.0000	.0434	26.4	0	0	3	0	0	0	0	0	0	0	0	0	0	0	0	0	0	0	0	0	0	0	0	3	0
similar	555	.8741	96.329	59.8	15	27	45	75	131	107	133	22	26	31	17	14	110	32	24	98	49	1	15	27	6	18	53	34	0
similarities	41	.7113	5.8884	47.7	2	0	6	1	16	12	3	1	2	9	1	1	1	0	1	8	9	1	0	7	0	1	7	0	0
similarity	27	.6065	3.3532	45.3	0	0	1	3	9	8	5	1	0	10	1	2	2	0	0	5	0	0	0	1	0	2	5	0	0
similarly	54	.7438	8.0758	49.1	1	1	5	3	13	13	17	1	1	7	4	1	13	0	0	10	0	0	1	2	0	2	5	0	0
simile	17	.1531	.5852	37.7	0	8	7	0	0	0	1	1	0	4	11	1	0	0	0	0	0	0	0	0	0	0	0	0	0
similes	6	.1605	.2225	33.5	0	0	6	0	0	0	0	0	0	3	3	0	0	0	0	0	0	0	0	0	0	0	0	0	0
simmer	10	.1493	.3512	35.5	0	0	0	0	3	2	3	2	0	0	0	0	0	0	0	0	0	0	6	0	0	0	0	4	0
simmered	4	.4574	.4121	36.2	0	0	1	1	1	0	1	1	0	0	0	1	0	0	0	1	0	0	1	0	0	0	0	1	0
simmering	4	.2419	.2121	33.3	0	0	1	0	3	0	1	0	0	0	0	0	0	0	1	0	0	0	1	0	0	0	0	1	0
Simmons	7	.2423	.5283	37.2	0	0	0	2	0	1	0	0	5	0	0	0	0	0	0	0	0	0	0	0	0	0	2	0	0
Simmons'	4	.0000	.1827	32.6	0	0	1	0	0	4	0	0	4	0	0	0	0	0	0	0	0	0	0	0	0	2	0	0	0
Simms	2	.2306	.1140	30.6	0	1	0	0	0	0	0	1	0	0	0	0	0	0	0	0	0	0	0	0	0	0	2	0	0
Simon	107	.5318	12.184	50.9	23	50	4	15	0	10	4	1	21	0	0	1	0	5	0	1	0	0	0	0	1	14	54	4	0
Simon's	11	.2806	.7336	38.7	5	4	0	0	0	0	2	0	1	0	0	0	0	0	0	0	0	0	0	0	5	5	0	0	0
Simons	4	.2445	.3067	34.9	0	1	0	0	0	0	0	3	3	0	0	0	0	1	0	0	0	0	0	0	0	0	0	0	0
simple	956	.8866	168.24	62.3	60	97	107	128	237	141	144	42	99	137	38	31	76	60	14	154	45	21	43	47	15	50	73	53	0
Simple	8	.0000	.0258	24.1	0	0	0	0	0	0	8	0	0	0	0	0	0	0	0	0	0	0	0	0	0	0	0	0	0
simple-minded	2	.1733	.1149	30.6	0	0	0	2	0	0	0	0	0	1	0	0	0	0	0	0	0	0	0	0	0	0	0	0	0
simpler	58	.8398	9.7302	49.9	2	8	5	6	11	9	10	7	6	2	0	1	12	1	1	15	3	1	2	3	1	4	4	2	0
simplest	172	.6370	22.510	53.5	6	11	12	75	34	22	8	4	7	3	1	2	113	3	2	15	1	2	1	2	1	6	8	2	0
simpleton	6	.2223	.4212	36.2	1	1	2	1	1	0	0	0	4	2	0	0	0	0	0	0	0	0	0	0	6	8	5	0	0
Simpleton	3	.0000	.1370	31.4	3	0	0	0	0	0	0	0	3	0	0	0	0	0	0	0	0	0	0	0	0	0	0	0	0
simplicity	30	.6215	3.7559	45.7	1	0	1	1	10	6	11	0	1	0	0	2	0	1	0	0	2	3	6	1	3	2	1	2	0
simplified	49	.6057	6.0655	47.8	1	0	2	6	16	11	13	0	0	4	0	3	19	1	0	6	5	1	6	1	1	4	0	0	0
simplify	97	.1243	3.6297	45.6	0	0	0	4	21	57	15	0	0	1	0	0	92	0	1	1	0	0	0	0	0	0	0	1	0
simplifying	11	.3816	.9026	39.6	0	0	0	0	6	3	2	0	0	0	0	0	6	0	4	0	0	1	0	0	0	0	0	0	0
simply	410	.9360	75.862	58.8	21	31	41	47	131	58	65	16	58	30	11	18	29	18	16	49	13	3	8	5	14	31	49	58	0
Simpson	13	.4933	1.3578	41.3	0	4	0	1	5	2	1	0	1	0	1	0	0	0	0	0	0	0	0	0	0	2	5	4	0
Simpson's	3	.3856	.2526	34.0	0	1	0	0	2	0	0	0	0	0	0	0	0	0	0	0	0	0	2	5	0	4	0	0	0
Sims	3	.3365	.2489	34.0	0	0	0	2	0	1	0	0	1	0	0	0	0	0	0	0	0	0	0	0	0	0	0	0	0
simulate	9	.5229	.9770	39.9	2	0	1	0	3	0	0	3	1	0	0	0	0	0	0	1	0	0	0	0	0	0	0	0	0
simulated	7	.3325	.5074	37.1	0	0	1	0	2	1	2	1	0	0	0	0	0	0	0	1	0	0	1	0	0	2	2	3	0
simulator	2	.2401	.1133	30.5	1	0	0	1	0	0	0	0	0	0	0	0	0	0	0	0	0	0	1	1	0	0	0	5	0
simultaneous	6	.3856	.4890	36.9	0	0	0	0	2	1	0	3	0	0	0	0	0	0	0	0	0	0	0	0	0	0	0	3	0
simultaneously	26	.6307	3.3469	45.2	2	1	1	2	12	2	5	2	1	0	0	2	0	0	2	6	0	0	0	2	3	4	6	0	0
sin	20	.1776	.9642	39.8	2	1	1	2	5	7	2	0	0	3	0	0	0	0	0	0	0	0	0	2	2	3	4	2	0
Sinai	13	.4401	1.2265	40.9	0	0	4	3	1	2	3	0	0	0	0	1	0	0	0	0	0	0	0	2	2	1	4	0	0
Sinatra	2	.2440	.1132	30.5	0	0	1	0	0	0	0	1	0	0	0	0	0	1	0	0	0	0	0	0	0	0	4	4	0
Sinbad	30	.3888	2.7942	44.5	0	17	0	0	13	0	0	0	13	0	0	0	0	1	0	0	3	0	0	0	0	13	0	0	0
since	2041	.9472	381.90	65.8	163	247	234	298	429	344	255	71	320	101	15	93	367	226	41	180	60	22	36	31	57	142	171	179	0
sincere	11	.6156	1.3730	41.4	0	0	1	2	2	2	3	1	2	1	0	1	0	3	0	1	0	1	0	1	1	0	1	1	0
sincerely	7	.6185	.9061	39.6	0	0	1	2	2	0	1	1	2	1	0	0	0	1	0	0	0	1	0	1	0	0	1	0	0
sincerest	2	.1814	.1187	30.7	0	0	0	2	0	0	0	0	0	0	0	0	0	0	0	0	1	0	0	1	0	0	1	0	0
sincerity	7	.5293	.7774	38.9	0	0	0	1	0	3	3	0	1	0	0	0	0	0	0	0	1	0	1	0	0	0	1	0	0
Sind	9	.0000	.0942	29.7	0	0	0	0	0	9	0	0	0	0	0	0	0	0	0	0	0	0	0	0	0	0	9	0	0
Sinda	2	.0000	.0162	22.1	0	0	0	2	0	0	0	0	0	0	0	0	0	0	0	0	0	0	0	0	2	0	0	0	0
Sindbad	3	.0000	.1370	31.4	0	3	0	0	0	0	0	0	3	0	0	0	0	0	0	0	0	0	0	0	0	0	0	0	0
Sindre	10	.0000	.4568	36.6	0	0	10	0	0	0	0	0	0	0	0	0	0	0	0	0	0	0	0	0	10	0	0	0	0
sinew	12	.4203	1.1126	40.5	0	4	0	4	2	1	0	0	1	0	0	0	0	0	0	2	0	0	0	0	1	0	0	0	0
sinews	9	.4264	.8583	39.3	2	2	3	2	0	0	0	0	1	0	0	2	0	0	0	2	0	0	0	0	2	0	0	0	0
sinful	4	.4516	.4046	36.1	1	0	0	1	1	1	0	0	1	0	0	0	0	2	0	0	0	0	0	0	0	0	1	0	0
sing	1014	.3241	73.633	58.7	253	266	143	136	92	44	77	3	120	21	0	41	1	13	8	5	735	0	0	2	0	19	30	9	1
Sing	13	.3749	1.1027	40.4	0	0	0	2	0	2	9	0	2	0	1	0	0	0	0	0	1	0	0	0	0	9	0	0	0
Singapore	8	.3460	.6915	38.4	0	0	3	2	2	1	0	0	3	0	0	1	0	4	0	0	0	0	0	0	0	0	0	0	0
singer	55	.4449	5.2475	47.2	12	4	2	4	17	9	6	1	7	1	0	5	0	0	0	0	29	0	0	0	2	3	4	2	0
Singer	82	.4200	8.6687	49.4	54	14	2	1	10	1	0	0	68	0	0	1	0	2	0	0	2	0	0	0	1	3	1	4	0
singer's	4	.2578	.2593	34.1	0	0	0	0	0	0	4	0	0	0	0	0	0	0	0	0	2	0	0	0	0	0	0	2	0
Singer's	10	.0000	.4568	36.6	8	2	0	0	0	0	0	0	10	0	0	0	0	0	0	0	0	0	0	0	0	0	0	0	0
singers	63	.3023	4.1958	46.2	8	3	10	6	10	12	13	1	0	1	0	3	0	2	0	0	44	0	0	0	0	3	2	6	0
Singers	3	.1983	.1396	31.4	1	0	0	1	1	0	0	0	0	0	0	0	0	0	0	0	3	0	0	0	0	0	0	0	0
Singh	5	.0000	.2284	33.6	4	0	0	0	1	0	0	0	4	0	0	0	0	0	0	0	0	0	0	0	0	0	0	0	0
singin'	5	.2445	.3864	35.9	0	2	0	0	1	0	0	0	4	0	0	0	0	1	0	0	0	0	0	0	0	0	0	0	0
singing	473	.5223	52.238	57.2	110	71	77	71	66	40	31	7	86	16	0	26	1	10	1	7	248	0	0	0	0	20	34	7	1
Singing	9	.3938	.8371	39.2	4	0	0	3	0	1	0	1	4	0	0	0	0	0	0	0	3	0	0	0	0	0	0	0	0
single	817	.9243	149.38	61.7	46	83	93	117	203	124	113	38	100	68	21	34	60	49	104	99	47	6	19	28	20	45	69	48	0
single-bit	2	.0000	.0914	29.6	0	0	0	0	2	0	0	0	0	0	0	0	0	0	0	2	0	0	0	0	0	0	0	0	0
single-cell	2	.0000	.0394	26.0	0	0	0	0	2	0	0	0	0	0	0	0	0	0	0	2	0	0	0	0	0	0	0	0	0
single-celled	8	.2971	.5713	37.6	0	1	0	3	0	2	1	1	0	0	0	0	0	0	0	6	0	0	0	0	0	0	0	0	0

5P Silone
8R silos
8N Silsbee
8N Silsbees
6F silt-laden
7R Silvano
5B silvaticus
7D SilverCity
XR SilverSprings
3R silver-blue
3Q silver-buckled

6B silver-feathered
9D silver-haired
6R silver-handled
4R silver-painted
XH silver-pitchblende
9D silver-studded
5A silver-tipped
5R silver-zinc
3P Silverfish
8A Silvering
7Q silverwork

7N sim
XQ Simbal
8Q Simbirsk
7R Simca
8F Simcoe
8F Simcoe's
9R Simcox
5N Simeon
8G Simile
9E similitude
XH simmers

5J Simoneaux
8G simonize
6P Simonized
9F simony
9B Simpkins
6H SIMPLE
7R simple-lever
XH simple-looking
8A simpleminded
3A Simpleton's
4Q simulates

5Q simulators
5Q simultaneity
4P Sinbad's
3B Sincerely
6R Sinclair
4Q sine
7A sinewy
8J sinfonia
6A Sing's
7J singable
7P Singakademie

7G singe
XJ singers'
7Q singes
7N singing-bird
4A singing-birds
8J singing-school
4A SINGLE
8Q single-electron

Word Type	F	D	U	SFI	3 Gr 3	4 Gr 4	5 Gr 5	6 Gr 6	7 Gr 7	8 Gr 8	9 Gr 9	X UnGr	A Read	B Eng & Gr	C Comp	D Lit	E Math	F Soc Stud	G Spell	H Sci	J Music	K Art	L Home Ec	M Shop	N Lib F	P Lib NF	Q Lib Ref	R Mag	S Rel
single-engine	3	.3454	.2542	34.1	0	0	0	0	0	1	1	1	1	0	0	0	0	1	0	0	0	0	0	0	0	0	0	1	0
single-footing	2	.0000	.0914	29.6	0	0	2	0	0	0	0	0	2	0	0	0	0	0	0	0	0	0	0	0	0	0	0	0	0
single-handed	3	.2261	.2131	33.3	0	1	1	0	0	1	0	0	2	0	0	0	0	0	0	0	0	0	0	0	1	0	0	0	0
single-line	2	.1696	.0749	28.7	0	0	0	1	0	1	0	0	0	0	0	0	0	0	0	0	1	1	0	0	0	0	0	0	0
single-minded	2	.2408	.1204	30.8	0	0	1	0	1	0	0	0	0	0	0	0	0	1	0	0	0	0	0	0	0	1	0	0	0
single-thickness	2	.1249	.0685	28.4	0	0	0	0	0	1	0	1	0	0	0	0	0	0	0	1	0	0	0	1	0	0	0	0	0
single-word	9	.0000	.0985	29.9	0	0	0	2	5	2	0	0	0	9	0	0	0	0	0	0	0	0	0	0	1	0	0	0	0
singled	6	.4683	.6320	38.0	0	0	0	1	0	3	2	0	2	0	0	0	0	2	1	0	0	0	0	0	1	0	0	0	0
singlehanded	3	.2266	.1614	32.1	0	0	1	2	0	0	0	0	0	0	0	0	0	0	0	0	0	0	0	0	0	0	0	2	0
singleness	2	.1907	.0862	29.4	0	0	0	0	0	0	2	0	0	0	0	1	0	0	0	0	0	0	1	0	0	0	0	0	0
singles	2	.0000	.0243	23.9	0	0	0	0	1	1	0	0	0	0	0	0	0	0	0	0	0	0	0	0	0	0	0	2	0
singly	13	.6321	1.6707	42.2	0	0	0	2	8	3	0	0	0	1	1	0	2	1	0	1	2	0	0	0	1	0	4	0	0
sings	127	.3962	11.029	50.4	32	20	11	23	19	12	10	0	19	8	0	11	0	2	1	2	72	0	0	0	3	2	0	7	0
singsong	2	.0000	.0290	24.6	0	0	1	1	0	0	0	0	0	0	0	0	0	0	0	0	0	0	0	0	0	2	0	0	0
singular	240	.3239	17.012	52.3	30	54	32	35	30	13	45	1	5	135	0	6	1	0	88	1	0	0	0	0	2	1	1	0	0
singularly	3	.3873	.2485	34.0	0	1	0	0	2	0	0	0	0	0	0	1	0	0	0	0	0	0	0	0	1	0	1	0	0
singulars	4	.0000	.0325	25.1	0	0	3	1	0	0	0	0	0	0	0	0	0	0	4	0	0	0	0	0	0	0	0	0	0
sinister	11	.4509	1.1794	40.7	0	0	0	5	3	2	1	0	7	0	0	2	0	1	0	0	0	0	0	0	0	0	0	1	0
sink	149	.8342	25.016	54.0	29	26	14	12	26	28	10	4	52	5	8	10	1	7	1	14	7	1	3	0	16	12	2	10	0
sinker	3	.3265	.2369	33.7	0	1	1	1	0	0	0	0	1	0	0	0	0	0	1	0	0	0	0	0	0	0	0	1	0
sinkers	2	.1620	.0760	28.8	0	0	0	1	0	1	0	0	0	0	0	0	0	0	0	0	0	0	0	1	0	0	0	1	0
Sinkfield	4	.0000	.0429	26.3	0	0	0	0	0	0	4	0	0	0	0	4	0	0	0	0	0	0	0	0	0	0	0	0	0
Sinkfield's	2	.0000	.0215	23.3	0	0	0	0	0	0	2	0	0	0	0	2	0	0	0	0	0	0	0	0	0	0	0	0	0
Sinkiang	4	.3422	.3073	34.9	0	0	1	0	2	1	0	0	0	0	0	0	0	1	0	0	0	0	0	0	0	1	0	2	0
sinking	38	.7442	5.8180	47.6	4	1	10	4	11	1	5	2	15	2	1	0	0	3	0	6	0	0	0	0	4	3	3	1	0
sinks	30	.6624	4.0950	46.1	3	5	4	3	4	7	2	2	3	0	1	0	0	4	0	12	3	0	0	0	0	1	2	4	0
sinned	7	.0347	.1063	30.3	4	0	0	1	0	0	1	1	0	0	0	0	0	1	0	0	0	0	0	0	1	2	0	0	3
sinner	5	.3664	.4061	36.1	0	1	0	0	0	0	2	2	0	0	0	2	0	0	0	2	0	0	0	0	1	0	0	0	0
sinners	11	.0214	.0933	29.7	7	0	0	1	0	0	1	2	0	0	0	0	0	0	0	0	1	0	0	0	0	1	0	2	7
Sinon	7	.1953	.4422	36.5	0	0	0	4	0	3	0	0	4	3	0	0	0	0	0	0	0	0	0	0	0	0	0	0	0
sins	10	.1812	.4564	36.6	1	1	0	2	0	3	2	1	0	0	0	3	0	2	0	0	0	0	0	0	1	2	1	0	1
sinuous	2	.2387	.1089	30.4	0	0	0	0	2	0	0	0	0	0	0	0	0	0	0	0	1	0	0	0	1	0	0	0	0
sinusoidal	2	.0000	.0209	23.2	0	2	0	0	0	0	0	0	0	0	0	0	0	0	0	0	0	0	0	0	0	0	2	0	0
sion	21	.0000	.1704	32.3	0	0	0	4	5	12	0	0	0	0	0	0	0	0	21	0	0	0	0	0	0	0	0	0	0
Sioux	41	.6592	5.7413	47.6	6	22	4	3	5	1	0	0	22	1	1	1	0	5	0	0	0	0	0	0	7	2	0	2	0
SiouxFalls	2	.2437	.1129	30.5	1	0	0	0	0	0	1	0	0	0	0	0	0	0	0	0	0	0	0	0	0	0	1	1	0
sip	22	.6437	2.9491	44.7	6	1	9	3	3	0	0	0	6	5	0	2	0	0	0	2	2	0	0	0	0	2	3	0	0
siphon	4	.2287	.2348	33.7	0	0	1	0	0	0	2	1	0	0	0	0	0	0	0	3	0	0	0	0	0	0	0	1	0
siphons	3	.2427	.1822	32.6	0	0	1	1	0	0	1	0	0	0	0	0	0	0	0	2	0	0	0	0	0	0	0	1	0
sipped	6	.3859	.5833	37.7	0	2	1	0	3	0	0	0	4	0	0	0	0	0	0	0	0	0	0	0	1	1	0	0	0
sipping	8	.4871	.9006	39.5	0	0	1	3	2	2	0	0	5	0	0	1	0	0	0	0	0	0	0	0	1	0	0	1	0
sips	4	.2393	.3005	34.8	2	0	0	1	0	0	1	0	3	0	0	1	0	0	0	0	0	0	0	0	0	0	0	0	0
sir	310	.6819	43.943	56.4	27	66	25	39	77	35	39	2	116	2	5	58	0	3	1	0	19	0	0	0	49	45	0	12	0
Sir	241	.7466	36.461	55.6	22	33	22	66	30	41	18	9	40	10	0	17	3	7	3	17	9	0	0	0	69	19	20	27	0
SIR	22	.0664	.5074	37.1	0	0	0	0	0	21	1	0	0	0	0	21	0	0	0	0	0	0	0	0	0	0	1	0	0
Siraj-ed-Din	4	.0000	.1827	32.6	0	4	0	0	0	0	0	0	4	0	0	0	0	0	0	0	0	0	0	0	0	0	0	0	0
sire	12	.4435	1.1610	40.6	1	2	0	2	1	3	2	1	2	0	0	5	0	0	0	0	0	0	0	0	3	1	0	1	0
Sire	14	.2004	.8998	39.5	7	2	3	2	0	0	0	0	8	0	0	0	0	0	0	0	0	0	0	0	6	0	0	0	0
siree	3	.3450	.2505	34.0	0	2	0	1	0	0	0	0	1	0	0	0	0	0	0	0	0	0	0	0	1	1	0	0	0
siren	12	.4921	1.3342	41.3	1	2	1	0	5	1	2	0	6	2	1	0	0	0	0	1	0	0	0	0	0	0	0	2	0
sirenians	3	.0000	.0314	25.0	0	0	0	0	3	0	0	0	0	0	0	0	0	0	0	0	0	0	0	0	0	0	3	0	0
sirens	6	.2434	.3142	35.0	1	0	0	0	1	1	3	0	0	0	3	1	0	0	0	0	1	0	0	0	0	0	1	0	0
Sirius	8	.3737	.6800	38.3	0	2	4	0	2	0	0	0	0	0	0	0	2	2	0	4	0	0	0	0	0	0	0	0	0
sirloin	3	.2277	.1555	31.9	0	0	0	0	0	0	1	2	0	0	0	0	0	0	0	0	0	0	1	0	0	0	0	2	0
sirs	2	.1494	.1045	30.2	1	0	0	0	1	0	0	0	1	0	0	0	0	0	0	0	1	0	0	0	0	0	0	0	0
Sirs	2	.2306	.1140	30.6	0	1	0	0	0	1	0	0	0	1	0	0	0	1	0	0	0	0	0	0	0	0	0	0	0
sirup	10	.0000	.0322	25.1	0	0	0	0	1	1	8	0	0	0	0	0	0	0	0	0	0	0	10	0	0	0	0	0	0
Sis	4	.2840	.2988	34.8	0	0	0	0	1	1	2	0	2	1	0	0	0	0	0	0	0	0	1	0	0	0	0	0	0
sisal	11	.3466	.9469	39.8	0	0	0	3	7	1	0	0	4	0	0	0	0	6	0	0	0	0	1	0	0	0	0	0	0
Sisco	4	.0974	.1495	31.7	0	0	0	0	3	1	0	0	1	0	0	0	0	0	0	0	0	0	0	0	3	0	0	0	0
Sissa	7	.0000	.3198	35.0	0	0	7	0	0	0	0	0	7	0	0	0	0	0	0	0	0	0	0	0	0	0	0	0	0
Sissa's	2	.0000	.0914	29.6	0	0	2	0	0	0	0	0	2	0	0	0	0	0	0	0	0	0	0	0	0	0	0	0	0
sissy	5	.4723	.4943	36.9	2	0	0	0	1	1	1	0	0	1	0	1	0	0	0	0	0	0	0	0	2	0	0	1	0
sister	403	.8724	70.345	58.5	108	105	38	47	42	25	28	10	152	39	11	25	11	10	10	3	19	0	9	0	33	54	6	20	1
Sister	36	.3618	3.2314	45.1	3	11	3	0	6	0	13	0	19	0	0	14	0	0	0	0	1	0	0	0	0	1	0	1	0
sister-in-law	2	.1717	.1142	30.6	0	0	0	0	2	0	0	0	1	0	0	1	0	0	0	0	0	0	0	0	0	0	0	0	0
sister's	21	.4521	2.0932	43.2	5	3	1	2	6	3	1	0	6	4	4	1	0	0	0	0	0	0	0	0	2	3	1	0	0
sisters	182	.7869	29.173	54.6	46	45	28	18	29	9	6	1	80	8	3	13	0	1	1	7	8	0	7	0	14	26	4	9	1
Sisters	5	.4727	.5350	37.3	0	2	0	1	1	0	1	0	2	0	0	1	0	1	0	0	0	0	0	0	0	0	0	1	0
Sistine	2	.2351	.1166	30.7	0	0	0	0	1	0	1	0	0	0	0	0	0	1	0	0	0	0	0	0	0	0	0	1	0
sit	549	.8826	96.863	59.9	136	91	60	72	88	55	42	5	218	34	15	53	11	27	12	28	23	1	5	0	40	42	9	31	0
Sit	4	.2346	.2332	33.7	2	0	0	0	2	0	0	0	0	0	0	0	0	0	0	2	0	0	0	0	0	0	0	2	0
sit-down	2	.1814	.1187	30.7	1	0	0	0	0	0	0	1	1	0	0	0	0	0	0	0	0	0	0	0	0	0	0	1	0
sit-ins	2	.2351	.1166	30.7	0	0	0	0	1	0	0	1	0	0	0	0	0	1	0	0	0	0	0	0	0	0	0	1	0
sit-ups	4	.0000	.0599	27.8	0	0	4	0	0	0	0	0	0	0	0	0	4	0	0	0	0	0	0	0	0	0	0	0	0
site	108	.6656	14.758	51.7	7	3	13	23	27	8	13	14	15	0	1	2	1	12	0	6	0	0	0	2	1	11	32	25	0
Site	4	.3709	.3633	35.6	0	0	0	0	1	3	0	0	2	0	0	0	0	0	0	0	0	0	0	0	0	0	1	1	0
sites	28	.4631	2.7561	44.4	1	3	3	5	10	2	0	4	1	0	0	0	0	3	0	1	0	0	0	0	1	2	12	8	0
sith	2	.2427	.1152	30.6	0	0	0	0	2	0	0	0	0	0	0	0	0	0	0	0	0	0	0	0	1	1	0	0	0
Sitka	5	.3639	.4034	36.1	0	0	2	0	1	0	2	0	0	0	0	0	0	2	0	0	0	0	0	0	0	0	2	1	0
sits	102	.8266	16.921	52.3	21	13	13	11	19	10	12	3	24	7	2	13	0	6	0	5	10	0	3	0	2	13	4	13	0
sitter	8	.3982	.7276	38.6	0	0	1	2	2	1	2	0	3	0	0	0	0	0	0	0	0	1	2	0	2	0	0	0	0
sitters	5	.2010	.2850	34.5	0	0	0	2	2	0	1	0	2	0	0	0	0	0	0	0	0	0	2	0	1	0	0	0	0
sittin'	7	.3703	.6459	38.1	0	0	2	2	2	1	0	0	4	0	0	1	0	0	0	0	0	0	0	0	2	0	0	0	0
sitting	482	.8438	81.887	59.1	103	98	54	63	79	44	34	7	203	17	8	62	3	16	4	6	13	4	7	0	67	48	7	17	0
Sitting	5	.2620	.3230	35.1	0	0	0	1	3	1	0	0	1	1	0	3	0	0	0	0	0	0	0	0	0	0	0	0	0
sitting-room	6	.0688	.1783	32.5	1	0	0	0	5	0	0	0	1	0	0	0	0	0	0	0	0	0	0	0	5	0	0	0	0
situated	22	.3140	1.5602	41.9	4	0	0	1	6	9	2	0	1	0	0	1	0	3	0	0	0	0	0	0	1	0	15	1	0
situation	243	.8282	40.217	56.0	12	11	22	19	72	66	39	2	30	27	18	23	22	22	6	16	1	0	12	4	11	13	13	25	0
situations	73	.8112	11.840	50.7	0	4	7	4	30	14	14	0	6	13	4	4	9	5	4	6	2	0	2	0	0	2	10	6	0
six	1229	.9321	226.91	63.6	249	179	154	159	226	115	84	63	308	55	9	38	157	111	89	93	56	2	7	5	42	105	54	98	0
Six	21	.5920	2.6194	44.2	1	8	1	3	1	1	2	4	5	0	0	1	0	0	0	1	2	0	0	0	1	5	0	6	0

7R single-file
3J single-footer
7R single-four
8D single-headed
9D single-hooved
8H single-letter
XR single-lift
7Q single-manned
7D single-motored
6J single-note
XR single-overhead-camshaft
7Q single-piece
9M single-point
7J single-reed
5Q single-sail
9Q single-ship
7D single-shot
9D single-soled
7M single-story
6R single-wing
7R single-witness
6R singlehandler
7A singleminded
8F Singleton
5R singling
6J Sings
3N singsonging
4B Singular
8P sinister-looking
4F Sink
5N Sinks
9P Sinky
3S Sinless
5P Sinnamary
4N sinner's
7N sinnin'
8F Sino-Japanese
7R Sino-Soviet
8A Sinon's
7N Sintram
9Q sinus
4H sinuses
5A Sion
9R siphoned
8A sir'd
7A sired
7A siren's
8K Sirenes
6P sires
9D sirrah
3A sirree
4P Sirtori
8L Sirup
5A sirupy
4A sis
8N sissies
3N sissiest
3A Sissy
5A sister'll
7N sisterly
3Q sisters'
4A Sisters'
8Q Sisyphus
5R sitar
7A sitch
XR sited
8R Sites
XQ sitter's
XB sitteth
9Q Sittingbourne
7N sittyated
7P situate
7D Sitwell

Word Type	F	D	U	SFI	3 Gr 3	4 Gr 4	5 Gr 5	6 Gr 6	7 Gr 7	8 Gr 8	9 Gr 9	X UnGr	A Read	B Eng & Gr	C Comp	D Lit	E Math	F Soc Stud	G Spell	H Sci	J Music	K Art	L Home Ec	M Shop	N Lib F	P Lib NF	Q Lib Ref	R Mag	S Rel
six-	2	.2300	.1140	30.6	0	0	1	0	0	0	1	0	0	1	0	0	0	0	0	1	0	0	0	0	0	0	0	0	0
six-cylinder	3	.0000	.0365	25.6	0	0	0	0	3	0	0	0	0	0	0	0	0	0	0	0	0	0	0	0	0	0	0	3	0
six-day	6	.1453	.2356	33.7	0	0	1	3	0	2	0	0	0	0	0	0	0	0	0	0	0	0	0	0	0	1	0	5	0
six-feet-four	2	.0000	.0914	29.6	0	2	0	0	0	0	0	0	2	0	0	0	0	0	0	0	0	0	0	0	0	0	0	0	0
six-foot	7	.3715	.6737	38.3	1	1	1	2	1	1	0	0	5	0	0	1	0	0	0	1	0	0	0	0	0	0	0	0	0
six-foot-long	2	.1523	.0721	28.6	0	0	0	0	0	1	0	1	0	0	1	0	0	0	0	0	0	0	0	0	0	0	0	1	0
six-inch	4	.2031	.2455	33.9	1	0	2	1	0	0	0	0	2	0	0	0	0	0	0	0	0	1	0	0	0	1	0	0	0
six-inch-long	2	.2401	.1133	30.5	1	0	0	0	1	0	0	0	0	0	0	0	0	0	0	0	0	0	0	0	0	1	1	0	0
six-month	2	.0000	.0243	23.9	0	0	0	0	1	1	0	0	0	0	0	0	0	0	0	0	0	0	0	0	0	0	0	2	0
six-ounce	2	.0000	.0243	23.9	2	0	0	0	0	0	0	0	0	0	0	0	0	0	0	0	0	0	0	0	0	0	0	2	0
six-sevenths	2	.0000	.0389	25.9	0	0	0	1	0	1	0	0	0	0	0	0	0	2	0	0	0	0	0	0	0	0	0	0	0
six-shooter	3	.2435	.2274	33.6	0	1	1	0	1	0	0	0	2	0	0	0	0	1	0	0	0	0	0	0	0	0	0	0	0
six-shooters	2	.2443	.1130	30.5	0	1	0	0	1	0	0	0	0	0	0	1	0	0	0	0	0	0	0	0	1	0	0	0	0
six-sided	3	.2445	.1818	32.6	0	1	0	1	1	0	0	0	0	0	0	0	0	0	0	2	0	0	0	0	0	0	1	0	0
six-story	2	.1814	.1187	30.7	0	1	1	0	0	0	0	0	1	0	0	0	0	0	0	0	0	0	0	0	0	0	0	1	0
six-thirty	7	.3193	.5099	37.1	2	1	1	0	2	1	0	0	1	0	2	1	0	1	0	0	0	0	0	0	2	0	0	0	0
six-year-old	10	.2905	.7128	38.5	0	8	0	0	0	0	2	0	2	2	0	0	0	0	0	0	0	0	0	0	0	6	0	0	0
sixes	22	.0000	.3293	35.2	9	3	2	5	1	1	1	0	0	0	0	0	22	0	0	0	0	0	0	0	0	0	0	0	0
sixpence	6	.4124	.5480	37.4	1	1	2	0	1	0	1	0	1	0	0	2	0	0	0	0	0	0	0	0	2	1	0	0	0
sixteen	104	.7695	16.347	52.1	14	17	15	16	24	10	7	1	39	2	0	1	6	7	2	6	6	0	0	0	9	20	0	6	0
sixteen-year-old	4	.2073	.2003	33.0	0	0	3	0	0	0	1	0	0	0	0	1	0	0	0	0	0	0	0	0	0	0	0	3	0
sixteenth	36	.7143	5.1976	47.2	1	2	5	6	9	4	7	2	2	6	1	2	2	2	1	6	10	0	0	0	0	1	2	1	0
Sixteenth	3	.2357	.2199	33.4	2	0	0	1	0	0	0	0	2	0	0	0	0	0	0	0	0	0	0	0	0	1	0	0	0
sixteenth-century	4	.3112	.2775	34.4	0	0	0	1	2	1	0	0	0	0	0	0	0	1	0	0	2	0	0	0	0	0	0	1	0
sixteenths	9	.1040	.3090	34.9	0	1	2	0	2	1	3	0	0	0	0	0	8	0	0	1	0	0	0	0	0	0	0	0	0
sixth	99	.7992	15.837	52.0	11	13	12	25	23	11	4	0	7	6	0	4	17	9	8	2	20	1	0	0	3	10	5	7	0
Sixth	11	.3774	.9922	40.0	0	0	1	0	5	1	4	0	5	0	0	0	0	0	1	0	4	0	0	0	0	1	0	0	0
sixth-grade	18	.3246	1.2550	41.0	0	2	1	13	0	1	1	0	0	2	0	1	5	0	2	0	0	6	0	0	2	0	0	0	0
sixth-grader	2	.2404	.1142	30.6	0	0	0	1	0	1	0	0	0	1	0	0	1	0	0	0	0	0	0	0	0	0	0	0	0
sixth-graders	2	.0000	.0299	24.8	0	0	0	2	0	0	0	0	0	0	0	0	2	0	0	0	0	0	0	0	0	0	0	0	0
sixths	15	.2444	.8640	39.4	6	2	3	3	1	0	0	0	0	0	0	0	10	0	0	0	5	0	0	0	0	0	0	0	0
sixtieth	2	.0000	.0914	29.6	0	0	0	0	2	0	0	0	2	0	0	0	0	0	0	0	0	0	0	0	0	0	0	0	0
sixty	108	.8880	19.130	52.8	21	16	14	13	25	10	5	4	30	3	1	6	8	16	4	16	2	0	1	0	8	10	1	2	0
sixty-eight	5	.4833	.5473	37.4	2	0	1	0	2	0	0	0	2	0	0	0	1	1	0	0	0	0	0	0	0	1	0	0	0
sixty-five	9	.6075	1.1555	40.6	0	2	1	1	3	2	0	0	2	0	0	0	2	1	0	2	0	0	0	0	1	1	0	0	0
sixty-four	10	.4577	1.0981	40.4	1	2	4	0	3	0	0	0	7	0	0	0	1	1	0	0	0	0	0	0	0	0	0	1	0
sixty-nine	3	.2261	.2131	33.3	0	2	1	0	0	0	0	0	2	0	0	0	0	0	0	0	0	0	0	0	1	0	0	0	0
sixty-seven	3	.1434	.1493	31.7	0	1	0	2	0	0	0	0	1	0	0	0	2	0	0	0	0	0	0	0	0	0	0	0	0
sixty-six	5	.3487	.4032	36.1	1	2	0	0	1	1	0	0	0	0	0	0	0	1	0	3	0	0	0	0	0	1	0	0	0
sixty-three	5	.0947	.1886	32.8	1	0	2	1	0	1	0	0	1	0	0	0	4	0	0	0	0	0	0	0	0	0	0	0	0
sixty-two	2	.1972	.1262	31.0	0	1	1	0	0	0	0	0	1	0	0	0	1	0	0	0	0	0	0	0	0	0	0	0	0
sizable	15	.6350	1.9549	42.9	1	0	0	3	8	2	0	1	0	1	0	0	1	3	0	3	0	0	0	0	0	1	2	4	0
Sizaire	2	.0000	.0290	24.6	0	2	0	0	0	0	0	0	0	0	0	0	0	0	0	0	0	0	0	0	0	2	0	0	0
size	1057	.7858	166.86	62.2	155	136	119	108	216	114	182	27	98	16	5	23	144	116	26	193	20	10	36	117	27	65	111	50	0
sized	10	.3985	.8682	39.4	0	0	0	1	4	2	3	0	1	0	0	1	0	0	0	2	0	0	3	0	1	0	0	2	0
Sizemore	2	.0000	.0243	23.9	0	0	0	0	0	2	0	0	0	0	0	0	0	0	0	0	0	0	0	0	0	0	0	2	0
sizes	201	.6650	27.222	54.3	35	28	20	18	41	25	31	3	21	2	2	3	11	12	0	37	11	16	12	37	2	12	14	9	0
sizing	4	.2800	.2967	34.7	0	0	1	0	2	0	1	0	2	0	0	0	0	0	0	0	0	0	1	0	1	0	0	0	0
sizzle	6	.4288	.5779	37.6	2	1	0	0	2	1	0	0	2	1	0	0	0	0	1	0	2	0	0	0	0	0	0	0	0
sizzled	5	.3833	.4767	36.8	2	0	0	2	0	0	1	0	3	0	0	1	0	0	0	0	0	0	0	0	0	1	0	0	0
sizzling	6	.4834	.6645	38.2	0	2	1	1	1	0	0	1	3	0	0	0	0	0	0	1	0	0	0	0	1	1	0	0	0
Sjaantje	8	.0000	.3655	35.6	0	0	0	8	0	0	0	0	8	0	0	0	0	0	0	0	0	0	0	0	0	0	0	0	0
Sjaantje's	2	.0000	.0914	29.6	0	0	0	2	0	0	0	0	2	0	0	0	0	0	0	0	0	0	0	0	0	0	0	0	0
Sjaelland	2	.0000	.0209	23.2	2	0	0	0	0	0	0	0	0	0	0	0	0	0	0	0	0	0	0	0	0	0	2	0	0
sk	9	.1025	.2494	34.0	2	2	2	2	0	0	0	1	0	1	0	0	0	0	8	0	0	0	0	0	0	0	0	0	0
Skagerrak	2	.2285	.1129	30.5	1	0	0	1	0	0	0	0	0	0	0	0	0	1	0	0	0	0	0	0	0	0	1	0	0
Skaret	2	.0000	.0290	24.6	0	0	0	0	2	0	0	0	0	0	0	0	0	0	0	0	0	0	0	0	0	2	0	0	0
skate	33	.5476	3.9377	46.0	16	9	1	3	1	2	1	0	14	6	0	0	0	0	6	2	0	0	0	0	4	1	0	0	0
skated	17	.4312	1.6473	42.2	4	3	0	5	1	4	0	0	4	3	0	0	0	4	0	0	0	0	0	0	6	0	0	0	0
skater	10	.4566	1.0650	40.3	3	1	0	1	0	4	1	0	5	0	0	2	0	1	0	2	0	0	0	0	0	0	0	0	0
skaters	18	.6572	2.4814	43.9	2	9	1	2	0	4	0	0	6	1	1	1	0	5	0	2	0	0	0	0	1	0	1	0	0
skates	69	.7807	10.870	50.4	17	25	5	14	4	4	0	0	13	5	3	5	10	0	3	4	2	0	0	0	8	14	2	0	0
Skates	2	.1948	.1250	31.0	0	0	1	0	0	1	0	0	1	0	0	0	0	0	0	0	0	0	0	0	0	1	0	0	0
skating	54	.7721	8.5117	49.3	9	12	3	2	6	19	2	1	22	5	3	4	2	7	0	0	0	1	1	0	2	3	0	4	0
Skeeter	9	.3770	.8786	39.4	1	0	0	0	0	7	0	1	7	0	0	0	0	0	0	0	1	0	0	0	0	0	0	1	0
skein	3	.3870	.2492	34.0	2	0	0	0	1	0	0	0	0	0	0	0	0	0	0	0	0	0	0	0	1	0	1	1	0
skeins	8	.4501	.7628	38.8	3	1	1	0	3	0	0	0	0	0	0	0	0	1	0	0	0	0	0	0	2	0	2	3	0
skeletal	30	.3590	2.4038	43.8	0	0	0	5	7	4	11	3	0	0	0	0	0	1	0	13	0	0	0	0	0	0	13	3	0
skeleton	98	.7716	15.275	51.8	18	14	10	11	25	9	4	7	10	3	1	6	3	3	0	38	3	0	0	2	1	19	8	1	0
skeletons	44	.6078	5.5930	47.5	5	3	8	9	14	3	2	0	6	0	0	1	0	3	0	11	0	0	0	0	1	14	6	2	0
skeptic	2	.2433	.1158	30.6	0	0	1	0	1	0	0	0	0	0	0	0	0	0	0	0	0	0	0	0	0	1	0	1	0
skeptical	10	.4499	.9674	39.9	0	0	0	2	5	1	1	1	1	1	0	0	0	0	0	0	0	0	0	0	2	0	1	5	0
skepticism	2	.0000	.0209	23.2	0	0	0	0	1	1	0	0	0	0	0	0	0	0	0	0	0	0	0	0	0	0	2	0	0
sketch	102	.5977	12.458	51.0	8	11	12	3	26	15	23	4	3	3	6	1	34	3	3	12	5	4	0	23	1	1	1	2	0
sketched	16	.5214	1.7295	42.4	0	1	1	1	7	1	3	2	1	0	1	0	5	0	0	0	0	1	0	4	0	2	0	2	0
sketches	49	.5655	5.7023	47.6	10	6	4	3	11	3	11	1	3	4	0	0	13	1	0	4	1	6	2	10	0	3	1	1	0
sketching	22	.2914	1.3672	41.4	0	4	2	2	9	1	4	0	2	1	0	0	0	0	0	0	1	6	0	12	0	0	0	0	0
sketchy	3	.1937	.1495	31.7	0	0	0	1	0	1	1	0	0	0	0	0	0	1	0	0	0	0	0	0	0	0	0	2	0
skew	16	.2434	.9278	39.7	0	2	0	0	14	0	0	0	0	0	0	0	14	0	0	0	0	0	0	2	0	0	0	0	0
skewbalds	2	.0000	.0290	24.6	2	0	0	0	0	0	0	0	0	0	0	0	0	0	0	0	0	0	0	0	0	2	0	0	0
skewer	3	.3847	.2490	34.0	0	1	0	0	0	1	1	0	0	1	0	1	0	0	0	0	0	0	0	0	0	1	0	0	0
ski	29	.6962	4.1345	46.2	4	5	5	3	6	2	4	0	5	4	0	0	1	4	2	2	0	0	1	0	0	2	0	8	0
Ski	8	.0000	.3655	35.6	4	1	0	1	1	1	0	0	8	0	0	0	0	0	0	0	0	0	0	0	0	0	0	0	0
skid	4	.3721	.3657	35.6	2	0	0	0	0	1	1	0	2	0	0	1	0	0	0	0	0	0	0	0	0	1	0	0	0
skidded	11	.5771	1.3683	41.4	3	1	1	1	3	0	2	0	5	0	1	1	0	1	0	0	0	0	0	1	1	0	1	0	0
skidding	4	.2512	.2516	34.0	1	0	0	1	2	0	0	0	1	0	1	0	0	0	0	0	0	0	0	0	0	0	0	2	0
skied	2	.0000	.0914	29.6	0	2	0	0	0	0	0	0	2	0	0	0	0	0	0	0	0	0	0	0	0	0	0	0	0
skier	11	.4825	1.2184	40.9	0	0	1	1	6	0	3	0	6	0	0	1	2	0	0	0	0	0	0	0	0	0	0	2	0
skiers	12	.2279	.8571	39.3	0	0	3	5	3	0	0	1	8	0	0	0	0	0	0	0	0	0	0	0	0	0	0	4	0
skies	74	.7976	11.928	50.8	6	13	10	13	15	7	5	5	18	1	2	4	0	4	2	19	2	0	0	0	1	5	6	10	0
skiff	14	.1457	.6013	37.8	0	0	0	1	4	4	5	0	2	0	0	0	0	0	0	0	0	0	0	0	11	1	0	0	0
skiffs	2	.1787	.1174	30.7	0	0	0	1	0	1	0	0	1	0	0	0	0	0	0	0	0	0	0	0	1	0	0	0	0
skiing	19	.4616	1.9805	43.0	1	1	2	5	4	3	2	1	7	4	2	0	0	5	0	0	0	0	0	0	0	0	0	1	0

XR Six-Pack
6N six-and-twenty
9Q six-by-eight-inch
7A six-class
9P six-eight-wheeler
·7A six-foot-six
7R six-footer
7D six-guns
XR six-hour
7D six-hundred
4A six-hundred-foot
4F six-lane

8D six-letter
6F Six-mile
4J six-note
3A six-page
5E six-place
7A six-pound
3A six-room
7G six-syllable
6G six-ton
7Q sixpenny
8A Sixteen
XP sixteen-cylinder

7P sixteen-hundreds
7R sixteen-year-olds
6K sixth-century
6R sixth-inning
5E sixtieths
5A sixty-first
3A sixty-five-mile-per-hour
7A sixty-five's
7A Sixty-fourth
9L sixty-inch
5A sixty-one
4F sixty-one-year

5R sixty-year
5R sixtyish
4P Sizaire-Naudin
4P Sizaires
9M Size
7A sizzles
6A Sjanntje
3A skrt
7N sk'yerd
5F Skagway
7R skater's
3J Skating

8A skating's
7A Skavar
7A Skavinsky
5G skedaddle
8D skedaddlin'
4A skedaddling
8F skeered
7Q skeletally
7Q skeleton-key
5J skeleton-like
4J skeletons'
XR skeptically

7R skeptics
9C Sketch
4P sketchbook
9C Sketchbook
6R sketchiest
7K sketchily
7R skewbacks
5A Skidbladner
XB skiddoo
4P Skiko

Word Type	F	D	U	SFI	3 Gr 3	4 Gr 4	5 Gr 5	6 Gr 6	7 Gr 7	8 Gr 8	9 Gr 9	X UnGr	A Read	B Eng & Gr	C Comp	D Lit	E Math	F Soc Stud	G Spell	H Sci	J Music	K Art	L Home Ec	M Shop	N Lib F	P Lib NF	Q Lib Ref	R Mag	S Rel
skilful	3	.3382	.2140	33.3	0	0	0	0	1	0	2	0	0	0	0	1	0	0	0	0	1	0	1	0	0	0	0	0	0
skill	262	.8931	46.506	56.7	4	14	32	31	71	46	51	13	53	27	4	11	8	44	6	11	17	6	18	10	10	14	14	9	0
Skillbook	3	.0000	.1370	31.4	0	0	0	0	3	0	0	0	3	0	0	0	0	0	0	0	0	0	0	0	0	0	0	0	0
skilled	100	.7159	14.598	51.6	5	7	18	8	23	10	28	1	14	3	1	4	0	34	0	9	3	1	0	10	1	8	10	2	0
skillet	30	.4571	2.9322	44.7	0	14	0	4	6	4	2	0	3	1	0	1	0	0	0	0	1	0	6	0	0	14	0	4	0
skillful	79	.7892	12.579	51.0	3	16	5	12	20	11	11	1	17	7	6	7	1	18	2	4	0	1	1	4	3	5	3	0	0
skillfully	21	.6884	2.9443	44.7	0	3	4	1	3	5	5	0	2	2	1	3	0	6	1	0	4	0	0	0	0	1	0	1	0
skills	161	.7973	25.944	54.1	2	15	31	24	47	17	22	3	43	9	8	0	0	46	3	11	8	1	6	8	0	7	3	8	0
Skills	4	.2243	.2241	33.5	0	1	1	0	0	1	0	1	0	0	0	0	0	3	0	0	0	0	1	0	0	0	0	0	0
skim	58	.7443	8.8895	49.5	1	3	15	5	24	3	6	1	25	8	1	2	0	5	0	8	0	0	3	0	2	0	1	3	0
skimmed	17	.5310	1.9479	42.9	1	1	3	9	2	0	1	0	5	0	0	1	0	0	0	0	0	0	0	0	6	1	1	3	0
skimmers	2	.2442	.1134	30.5	0	1	1	0	0	0	0	0	0	1	0	0	0	0	0	0	0	0	0	0	0	0	0	1	0
skimming	47	.6053	6.1864	47.9	2	3	12	4	25	0	1	0	28	7	0	2	0	1	0	0	0	0	0	0	4	2	0	3	0
skimped	2	.2442	.1134	30.5	0	0	0	0	1	0	1	0	0	1	0	0	0	0	0	0	0	0	0	0	0	0	0	1	0
Skimpy	6	.0000	.0644	28.1	0	0	0	0	6	0	0	0	0	0	0	6	0	0	0	0	0	0	0	0	0	0	0	0	0
skims	3	.3759	.2474	33.9	0	1	1	0	1	0	0	0	0	1	0	1	0	0	0	1	0	0	0	0	0	0	0	0	0
skin	677	.8266	112.30	60.5	162	106	84	74	123	45	57	26	106	11	5	36	2	20	7	264	9	9	33	1	34	72	33	35	0
Skin	2	.0000	.0914	29.6	0	0	0	0	2	0	0	0	2	0	0	0	0	0	0	0	0	0	0	0	0	0	0	0	0
skin's	2	.0000	.0243	23.9	0	0	0	0	2	0	0	0	0	0	0	0	0	0	0	0	0	0	0	0	0	0	0	0	0
skink	2	.0000	.0914	29.6	2	0	0	0	0	0	0	0	2	0	0	0	0	0	0	0	0	0	0	0	0	0	0	2	0
skinks	11	.3735	1.0675	40.3	8	0	0	0	1	0	2	0	8	0	0	0	0	0	0	2	0	0	0	0	0	0	1	0	0
skinned	14	.5323	1.5757	42.0	2	0	2	2	3	2	3	0	2	0	1	3	0	2	0	0	0	0	0	0	5	1	0	0	0
Skinner	24	.4298	2.4134	43.8	8	6	0	5	4	0	1	0	11	0	0	0	0	0	0	0	0	0	0	0	4	8	0	1	0
Skinner's	5	.2086	.3320	35.2	0	3	0	0	2	0	0	0	3	0	0	0	0	0	0	0	0	0	0	0	2	0	0	0	0
skinning	7	.5751	.8427	39.3	0	1	0	1	2	1	2	0	1	2	0	0	0	0	0	1	0	0	0	0	1	0	1	1	0
skinny	26	.6927	3.7348	45.7	8	2	3	5	4	2	2	0	10	2	1	2	0	0	0	0	0	0	0	0	5	2	1	3	0
Skinny	7	.2326	.5117	37.1	2	3	0	0	2	0	0	0	5	0	0	2	0	0	0	0	0	0	0	0	0	0	0	0	0
skins	168	.8672	29.132	54.6	43	33	20	26	25	8	12	1	41	3	1	4	5	48	5	13	3	1	6	0	10	18	8	2	0
skip	61	.6547	8.2478	49.2	18	14	6	4	12	1	6	0	15	3	0	3	0	4	2	0	20	0	3	0	4	5	1	1	0
Skip	31	.2516	2.2572	43.5	2	4	24	0	0	0	1	0	19	1	0	0	0	0	0	0	11	0	0	0	0	0	0	0	0
skipped	21	.5522	2.5392	44.0	6	5	2	0	2	3	2	1	10	2	0	4	0	0	0	0	0	0	0	0	3	0	0	2	0
skipper	27	.4980	3.1012	44.9	0	14	2	1	9	1	0	0	17	0	0	0	0	1	0	0	0	0	0	0	1	4	0	4	0
Skipper	20	.4977	2.3448	43.7	9	3	0	1	7	0	0	0	16	0	0	1	0	0	0	0	1	0	0	0	1	0	0	1	0
skipper's	2	.0000	.0914	29.6	0	1	0	0	1	0	0	0	2	0	0	0	0	0	0	0	0	0	0	0	0	0	0	0	0
Skipper's	2	.0000	.0914	29.6	2	0	0	0	0	0	0	0	2	0	0	0	0	0	0	0	0	0	0	0	0	0	0	0	0
skippers	8	.4681	.8346	39.2	0	2	0	1	4	0	0	1	3	0	1	0	0	0	0	0	0	0	0	0	1	0	1	2	0
skipping	45	.6534	6.0346	47.8	12	13	3	3	9	0	5	0	8	0	1	4	1	0	0	0	13	0	1	0	9	2	0	6	0
Skipping	2	.0000	.0162	22.1	2	0	0	0	0	0	0	0	0	0	0	0	0	0	0	0	2	0	0	0	0	0	0	0	0
skips	21	.0561	.3939	36.0	5	3	4	5	1	2	1	0	0	0	0	0	0	0	0	0	20	0	0	0	0	0	1	0	0
skipwise	4	.0000	.0323	25.1	4	0	0	0	0	0	0	0	0	0	0	0	0	0	0	0	4	0	0	0	0	0	0	0	0
skirl	2	.0000	.0219	23.4	0	0	2	0	0	0	0	0	0	2	0	0	0	0	0	0	0	0	0	0	0	0	0	0	0
skirmish	3	.2387	.1708	32.3	1	1	0	0	1	0	0	0	0	0	0	0	0	0	0	0	0	0	0	0	0	2	1	0	0
skirmishers	2	.0000	.0215	23.3	0	0	0	0	0	2	0	0	0	0	0	2	0	0	0	0	0	0	0	0	0	0	0	0	0
skirmishes	4	.3519	.3117	34.9	1	0	0	0	0	3	0	0	0	0	0	0	0	1	0	0	0	0	0	0	0	0	1	2	0
skirmishing	2	.1698	.1133	30.5	0	0	0	1	1	0	0	0	1	0	0	0	0	0	0	0	0	0	0	0	0	0	1	0	0
skirt	123	.3955	10.409	50.2	10	13	6	13	31	27	22	1	14	4	1	12	7	1	4	0	0	2	58	0	7	2	1	10	0
skirted	7	.5369	.8074	39.1	0	1	0	3	1	2	0	0	2	1	0	1	0	0	0	0	0	0	0	0	2	0	0	1	0
skirting	2	.1698	.1133	30.5	0	0	0	0	2	0	0	0	1	0	0	0	0	0	0	0	0	0	0	0	0	0	1	0	0
skirts	78	.5874	9.6062	49.8	10	14	15	12	7	11	8	1	16	1	0	3	15	9	1	0	1	0	14	0	10	6	1	1	0
skis	17	.4474	1.8391	42.6	2	8	3	3	0	0	1	0	12	2	0	0	0	2	0	0	0	0	0	0	0	1	0	0	0
skit	11	.5472	1.2412	40.9	0	0	5	0	5	0	1	0	0	0	0	0	0	0	0	0	0	0	1	0	3	3	1	3	0
skits	2	.2442	.1134	30.5	0	0	0	0	0	1	0	1	0	1	0	0	0	0	0	0	0	0	0	0	0	0	0	1	0
skitter	2	.1717	.1142	30.6	0	0	0	0	1	0	1	0	1	0	0	1	0	0	0	0	0	0	0	0	0	0	0	0	0
skittering	3	.2261	.2131	33.3	0	1	1	1	0	0	0	0	2	0	0	0	0	0	0	0	0	0	0	0	1	0	0	0	0
skittish	3	.2332	.1690	32.3	0	2	0	0	1	0	0	0	0	0	0	0	0	0	0	0	0	0	0	0	0	2	0	1	0
skive	3	.0000	.0076	18.8	0	0	0	0	3	0	0	0	0	0	0	0	0	0	0	0	0	0	0	3	0	0	0	0	0
skived	2	.0000	.0050	17.0	0	0	0	0	2	0	0	0	0	0	0	0	0	0	0	0	0	0	0	2	0	0	0	0	0
Skoal	2	.0000	.0162	22.1	0	2	0	0	0	0	0	0	0	0	0	0	0	0	0	0	2	0	0	0	0	0	0	0	0
Skoplje	2	.0000	.0243	23.9	0	0	0	0	0	0	2	0	0	0	0	0	0	0	0	0	0	0	0	0	0	0	0	2	0
Skorich	2	.0000	.0243	23.9	0	0	0	0	2	0	0	0	0	0	0	0	0	0	0	0	0	0	0	0	0	0	0	2	0
skulked	2	.2337	.1157	30.6	0	0	0	0	1	1	0	0	0	0	0	0	0	1	0	0	0	0	0	0	1	0	0	0	0
skulking	3	.2292	.1615	32.1	0	0	0	1	1	1	0	0	0	0	0	1	0	0	0	0	0	0	0	0	2	0	0	0	0
skull	77	.6585	10.382	50.2	4	7	11	12	19	5	16	3	3	2	0	4	2	0	0	24	0	0	0	0	4	16	15	7	0
skulls	20	.4001	1.7149	42.3	2	1	1	3	11	0	2	0	0	0	0	1	0	0	0	1	0	0	0	0	0	3	11	4	0
skunk	70	.5853	9.0171	49.6	35	15	8	7	2	2	0	1	45	2	1	2	0	0	2	0	0	0	0	0	15	0	0	3	0
Skunk	18	.0000	.8223	39.2	16	2	0	0	0	0	0	0	18	0	0	0	0	0	0	0	0	0	0	0	0	0	0	0	0
Skunk's	2	.0000	.0914	29.6	1	1	0	0	0	0	0	0	2	0	0	0	0	0	0	0	0	0	0	0	0	0	0	0	0
skunks	22	.6673	3.0856	44.9	8	2	4	5	0	3	0	0	10	1	0	2	0	0	0	0	0	0	0	0	2	3	1	3	0
sky	976	.8436	165.45	62.2	276	166	98	127	143	71	42	53	302	38	24	75	1	42	5	221	26	30	0	0	44	111	11	44	2
Sky	32	.4824	3.4453	45.4	4	11	0	12	0	3	0	2	13	2	0	1	0	1	0	1	11	0	0	0	0	2	0	1	0
sky-blue	2	.2137	.1056	30.2	0	0	1	0	1	0	0	0	0	0	0	0	0	1	0	0	1	0	0	0	0	0	0	0	0
sky's	3	.2261	.2131	33.3	0	1	2	0	0	0	0	0	2	0	0	0	0	0	0	0	0	0	0	0	1	0	0	0	0
Skycrane	11	.0000	.1647	32.2	0	0	0	0	0	11	0	0	0	0	0	0	11	0	0	0	0	0	0	0	0	0	0	0	0
Skye	5	.0000	.0404	26.1	0	1	3	0	0	1	0	0	0	0	0	0	0	0	0	0	5	0	0	0	0	0	0	0	0
skylights	2	.0000	.0243	23.9	0	0	0	2	0	0	0	0	0	0	0	0	0	0	0	0	0	0	0	0	0	0	0	2	0
skyline	9	.6074	1.1183	40.5	1	0	2	0	4	0	2	0	0	1	0	2	0	1	0	0	1	0	0	0	2	2	0	0	0
Skyphone	3	.0000	.0365	25.6	3	0	0	0	0	0	0	0	0	0	0	0	0	0	0	0	0	0	0	0	0	0	0	3	0
skyrocket	4	.0000	.0789	29.0	4	0	0	0	0	0	0	0	0	0	0	0	0	0	0	4	0	0	0	0	0	0	0	0	0
skyscraper	27	.7017	3.9460	46.0	10	2	3	3	3	4	2	0	13	1	1	0	0	1	2	1	0	0	0	1	0	0	2	5	0
skyscrapers	28	.6977	4.0299	46.1	7	1	5	7	2	4	1	1	6	1	0	2	1	10	0	2	0	0	0	0	0	2	1	3	0
skyward	6	.4365	.5966	37.8	1	2	0	1	2	0	0	0	2	1	0	0	0	0	0	1	0	0	0	0	2	0	0	0	0
skywriter	2	.1717	.1142	30.6	2	0	0	0	0	0	0	0	1	0	0	1	0	0	0	0	0	0	0	0	0	0	0	0	0
skywriting	2	.0000	.0215	23.3	2	0	0	0	0	0	0	0	0	0	0	2	0	0	0	0	0	0	0	0	0	0	0	0	0
sl	10	.0000	.0812	29.1	4	1	3	2	0	0	0	0	0	0	0	0	0	0	10	0	0	0	0	0	0	0	0	0	0
slab	31	.6458	4.1304	46.2	5	1	9	2	6	2	1	5	7	1	0	1	0	1	1	1	0	2	0	4	5	0	3	5	0
slabs	23	.5827	2.7724	44.4	1	1	4	3	3	4	6	1	4	1	1	2	0	0	0	0	0	4	0	3	2	3	2	1	0
slack	13	.5334	1.4647	41.7	0	0	2	2	4	1	3	1	2	1	0	1	0	0	0	0	0	0	0	0	5	0	1	3	0
slackened	2	.1787	.1174	30.7	0	0	1	0	1	0	0	0	1	0	0	0	0	0	0	0	0	0	0	0	1	0	0	0	0
slackening	2	.0000	.0243	23.9	0	0	0	0	0	0	2	0	0	0	0	0	0	0	0	0	0	0	0	0	0	0	0	2	0
slacks	4	.2486	.2813	34.5	0	0	0	0	3	0	1	0	2	0	0	0	0	0	0	1	0	0	1	0	0	0	0	0	0
Slade	12	.2369	.6606	38.2	0	0	0	5	0	0	7	0	0	0	0	7	0	0	0	0	0	0	0	0	5	0	0	0	0
slag	9	.3088	.7038	38.5	6	0	1	1	0	0	1	0	2	0	0	0	0	5	0	2	0	0	0	0	0	0	0	0	0
Slagle	4	.0000	.1827	32.6	0	0	0	4	0	0	0	0	4	0	0	0	0	0	0	0	0	0	0	0	0	0	0	0	0
slain	27	.6588	3.6783	45.7	1	1	4	7	4	5	5	0	7	0	0	5	0	0	0	0	2	1	0	0	5	3	4	0	0

4P skillets
5N skim-milk
7B skimp
7B skimpy
9L skin-deep
3P skin-made
5R skin-pampering
6A skin-tight
8G skinflint
6H skinlike
3A skip-the-rope
5A Skip's
7D Skippy
7D skirled
6E skirt-blouse
7D skittered
8D skittery
7M skiving
XP Sklodovski
XP Sklodovskis
4J skoal
9F Skokie
8N Skookum
6G skor
XR Skorpios
7R Skorzeny
4J skull-and-bones
5Q skullcaps
4N skunk-cabbage
4A skunk's
XR skunked
6A skurried
8P sky-encircled
7P Sky-god
4R sky-high
7N sky-journey
6A sky-lift
7H sky-mountains
6A sky-travelers
7R skyball
3A skycraper
7E skydiver
6A skyhigh
3J skylark
7R Skylark
7A skylarking
7Q skylarks
8Q Skylax
8N skylight
XR skyrocketed
3A skyrockets
8A Skyscraper
8D Skyward
XH skywards
6A skyways
6R slack-water
8N slacked
7R slags
8D slaine
8H slake

Word Type	F	D	U	SFI	3 Gr 3	4 Gr 4	5 Gr 5	6 Gr 6	7 Gr 7	8 Gr 8	9 Gr 9	X UnGr	A Read	B Eng & Gr	C Comp	D Lit	E Math	F Soc Stud	G Spell	H Sci	J Music	K Art	L Home Ec	M Shop	N Lib F	P Lib NF	Q Lib Ref	R Mag	S Rel
slaked	4	.0000	.0789	29.0	3	0	0	0	0	1	0	0	0	0	0	0	0	0	0	4	0	0	0	0	0	0	0	0	0
slalom	2	.0000	.0914	29.6	0	0	0	0	2	0	0	0	2	0	0	0	0	0	0	0	0	0	0	0	0	0	0	0	0
slaloms	2	.0000	.0243	23.9	0	0	0	0	2	0	0	0	0	0	0	0	0	0	0	0	0	0	0	0	0	0	0	2	0
slam	13	.4829	1.3700	41.4	3	1	0	2	5	1	1	0	4	0	2	3	0	0	0	0	1	0	0	0	1	0	0	2	0
slammed	36	.5866	4.5546	46.6	5	8	6	2	6	7	2	0	17	1	3	1	0	0	0	1	1	0	0	0	1	1	1	9	0
slamming	7	.3929	.6461	38.1	1	0	0	1	3	1	1	0	3	0	1	0	0	0	0	0	0	0	0	0	0	0	1	2	0
slams	6	.2249	.3433	35.4	1	0	0	1	0	4	0	0	1	0	0	4	0	0	0	0	0	0	0	0	0	0	0	1	0
slander	4	.4799	.4040	36.1	0	0	1	0	1	1	1	0	0	1	0	1	0	1	0	0	0	0	0	0	0	0	1	0	0
slang	27	.5529	3.1030	44.9	0	5	6	1	7	1	1	6	2	13	1	2	0	0	0	0	0	0	0	0	1	6	1	1	0
slant	91	.5824	10.813	50.3	10	30	14	13	11	7	6	0	4	5	21	2	3	0	26	15	0	3	3	3	3	2	0	1	0
slanted	32	.5377	3.6651	45.6	6	7	5	2	5	2	5	0	7	3	5	2	0	1	0	9	0	0	0	3	1	0	0	1	0
slanting	40	.6956	5.6324	47.5	0	12	7	6	10	2	3	0	2	14	3	1	1	6	0	5	0	3	1	1	1	1	1	0	0
slants	3	.2537	.1736	32.4	0	1	0	0	1	0	1	0	0	0	1	0	0	1	0	0	0	0	0	0	0	0	1	0	0
slap	39	.5540	4.6219	46.6	13	7	3	7	5	2	2	0	12	1	0	2	0	0	0	1	12	0	0	0	3	6	0	2	0
slapped	38	.5854	4.8146	46.8	3	5	4	9	14	1	1	1	18	0	0	4	0	0	0	0	0	0	0	0	7	6	1	2	0
slapping	17	.5866	2.1148	43.3	4	0	3	0	4	3	2	1	5	0	0	4	0	1	0	1	3	0	0	0	1	2	0	0	0
slaps	11	.5627	1.3358	41.3	2	1	1	1	3	3	0	0	4	0	0	3	0	0	0	1	0	0	0	0	1	1	0	1	0
slapstick	2	.2375	.1088	30.4	0	0	0	0	1	0	0	1	0	0	0	0	0	0	0	0	1	0	0	0	0	0	0	1	0
slash	37	.5202	3.9668	46.0	10	1	3	2	8	11	2	0	1	18	0	1	0	0	7	0	0	0	5	0	2	0	1	2	0
slashed	11	.3645	.9711	39.9	0	2	4	1	2	2	0	0	5	0	2	0	0	1	0	0	0	0	0	0	1	0	0	2	0
slashes	2	.1814	.1187	30.7	0	0	0	1	0	0	1	0	1	0	0	0	0	0	0	0	0	0	0	0	0	0	0	1	0
slashing	5	.5387	.5729	37.6	0	1	0	2	1	1	0	0	1	0	0	0	0	0	0	0	0	0	0	0	1	1	1	1	0
slate	20	.6431	2.6572	44.2	1	2	3	9	1	3	1	0	4	1	1	1	0	0	0	0	0	1	0	0	1	7	4	0	0
slated	3	.3824	.2446	33.9	1	0	0	0	2	0	0	0	0	0	0	1	0	0	0	0	1	0	0	0	0	0	0	1	0
Slater	32	.1669	1.3799	41.4	0	0	30	0	0	0	2	0	0	0	0	2	0	3	0	0	0	0	0	0	27	0	0	0	0
Slater's	4	.2337	.2315	33.6	0	0	4	0	0	0	0	0	0	0	0	0	0	2	0	0	0	0	0	0	2	0	0	0	0
Slaters	3	.0000	.0352	25.5	0	0	3	0	0	0	0	0	0	0	0	0	0	0	0	0	0	0	0	0	3	0	0	0	0
slates	4	.2417	.3028	34.8	0	1	2	1	0	0	0	0	3	0	0	0	0	0	0	0	0	0	0	0	1	0	0	0	0
slats	6	.3718	.5494	37.4	1	4	0	0	1	0	0	0	3	0	0	1	0	0	0	0	0	0	0	0	0	2	0	0	0
Slats	5	.0000	.0724	28.6	0	5	0	0	0	0	0	0	0	0	0	0	0	0	0	0	0	0	0	0	0	5	0	0	0
slaty	2	.1387	.0689	28.4	0	0	0	1	0	1	0	0	0	0	1	0	0	0	0	0	0	0	0	0	0	1	0	0	0
slaughter	18	.6496	2.4312	43.9	0	1	1	3	6	3	2	2	4	0	0	3	0	4	0	0	0	0	0	0	1	2	1	3	0
slaughter-house	3	.0000	.0352	25.5	0	0	0	0	3	0	0	0	0	0	0	0	0	0	0	0	0	0	0	0	3	0	0	0	0
slaughtered	10	.5872	1.2266	40.9	1	0	2	2	1	3	1	0	1	1	0	2	0	3	0	0	0	0	0	0	0	2	1	0	0
slaughterhouses	2	.2408	.1204	30.8	0	0	2	0	0	0	0	0	0	0	0	0	0	1	0	0	0	0	0	0	0	1	0	0	0
slaughtering	4	.3603	.3219	35.1	0	0	1	0	2	0	0	1	0	0	0	0	0	1	0	0	0	0	0	0	0	2	0	1	0
slave	175	.6861	24.735	53.9	31	10	41	15	34	33	8	3	32	3	0	6	0	56	4	0	4	0	0	0	16	41	12	1	0
Slave	11	.5035	1.1847	40.7	0	0	1	0	6	4	0	0	1	0	0	1	0	4	0	0	0	0	0	0	2	0	0	3	0
slaveholding	2	.2152	.1357	31.3	0	0	0	0	1	1	0	0	1	0	0	0	0	1	0	0	0	0	0	0	0	0	0	0	0
slavers	2	.2407	.1138	30.6	0	0	1	0	1	0	0	0	0	0	0	1	0	0	0	0	0	0	0	0	0	1	0	0	0
slavery	160	.5194	17.733	52.5	19	10	34	3	19	62	13	0	7	1	0	3	0	100	0	0	0	0	0	0	4	25	19	0	1
slaves	206	.6010	25.913	54.1	49	14	46	21	34	28	11	3	21	3	0	6	2	91	0	1	1	0	0	1	4	58	16	2	0
Slavic	8	.2370	.4443	36.5	0	0	0	1	6	1	0	0	0	0	0	0	0	2	5	0	0	0	0	0	0	1	0	0	0
slaving	2	.1698	.1133	30.5	0	0	0	0	1	1	0	0	1	0	0	0	0	0	0	0	0	0	0	0	0	0	1	0	0
Slavs	12	.4232	1.0956	40.4	0	0	3	0	5	2	2	0	0	0	0	0	0	5	4	0	0	0	0	0	0	2	1	0	0
slay	12	.5356	1.4120	41.5	1	0	0	6	2	1	2	0	5	0	0	2	0	1	1	0	0	0	0	0	0	3	0	0	0
slayer	4	.2003	.1916	32.8	0	0	0	0	1	0	3	0	0	0	0	3	0	0	0	0	0	0	0	0	0	0	1	0	0
slaying	3	.2261	.2131	33.3	0	0	0	1	1	1	0	0	2	0	0	0	0	0	0	0	0	0	0	0	1	0	0	0	0
sleazy	2	.0000	.0064	18.1	0	0	0	0	0	2	0	0	0	0	0	0	0	0	0	0	0	0	2	0	0	0	0	0	0
sled	104	.6765	14.909	51.7	14	26	26	13	13	11	1	0	61	2	1	0	1	10	4	0	1	0	0	0	18	3	0	3	0
sledding	2	.1787	.1174	30.7	1	0	0	0	1	0	0	0	1	0	0	0	0	0	0	0	0	0	0	0	1	0	0	0	0
sledge	7	.3135	.5813	37.6	0	2	1	0	4	0	0	0	4	0	0	0	0	0	0	1	2	0	0	0	0	0	0	0	0
sledgehammer	2	.2443	.1130	30.5	0	0	0	0	2	0	0	0	0	0	0	1	0	0	0	0	0	0	0	0	1	0	0	0	0
sledges	5	.4223	.4661	36.7	0	1	0	1	0	0	3	0	1	1	0	2	0	0	0	0	0	0	0	0	0	0	1	0	0
sleds	34	.5663	4.2101	46.2	8	8	8	3	5	0	0	2	14	0	0	0	0	10	3	5	0	0	0	0	1	1	0	0	0
sleek	37	.7349	5.5404	47.4	4	5	0	8	15	1	2	2	9	3	1	3	0	0	0	1	0	0	0	0	7	5	4	4	0
sleep	717	.8531	122.95	60.9	227	120	72	67	111	59	55	6	286	20	6	60	4	24	9	73	31	0	12	0	77	83	9	23	0
Sleep	7	.3179	.4930	36.9	0	0	4	0	1	1	0	1	0	0	0	4	0	0	0	0	0	0	0	0	0	1	0	2	0
sleeper	7	.5238	.7781	38.9	0	0	1	1	2	1	1	1	1	1	1	1	0	1	0	1	0	0	0	0	0	0	0	1	0
Sleeper	3	.2378	.1809	32.6	0	2	0	0	0	0	1	0	0	0	0	0	0	2	0	0	0	0	0	0	0	1	0	0	0
sleepers	9	.5252	1.0498	40.2	0	0	1	2	6	0	0	0	4	2	0	1	0	1	0	1	0	0	0	0	0	0	0	0	0
sleepier	2	.0000	.0914	29.6	1	1	0	0	0	0	0	0	2	0	0	0	0	0	0	0	0	0	0	0	0	0	0	0	0
sleepily	18	.6026	2.3060	43.6	2	5	2	2	5	2	0	0	6	2	0	1	0	2	0	0	0	0	0	0	3	4	0	0	0
sleepiness	3	.2212	.2099	33.2	0	0	0	2	0	0	1	0	2	0	0	1	0	0	0	0	0	0	0	0	0	0	0	0	0
sleeping	258	.8762	45.316	56.6	78	38	22	40	43	16	18	3	117	9	1	23	4	23	1	8	8	3	1	0	14	21	7	18	0
Sleeping	5	.1190	.2188	33.4	2	1	0	0	2	0	0	0	2	0	0	0	0	0	0	0	3	0	0	0	0	0	0	0	0
sleepless	5	.4304	.4740	36.8	0	1	1	1	0	2	0	0	1	0	0	0	0	0	0	0	1	0	0	0	1	0	0	2	0
sleeps	46	.7693	7.2071	48.6	15	7	0	6	10	0	6	2	14	2	1	5	1	3	0	6	0	0	0	0	3	8	0	3	0
sleepwalkers	3	.0000	.0322	25.1	0	0	0	0	3	0	0	0	0	0	0	3	0	0	0	0	0	0	0	0	0	0	0	0	0
sleepy	93	.7895	14.963	51.8	29	19	14	10	12	8	1	0	41	9	3	7	1	4	1	7	1	0	0	0	9	7	2	1	0
Sleepy	14	.2571	1.0931	40.4	0	0	8	4	0	0	2	0	11	0	2	0	0	0	0	0	0	0	0	0	0	0	0	1	0
sleepy-eyed	2	.2440	.1132	30.5	1	0	0	0	0	0	1	0	0	0	0	1	0	0	0	0	0	0	0	0	0	0	0	1	0
sleepy-head	2	.2442	.1134	30.5	2	0	0	0	0	0	0	0	0	1	0	0	0	0	0	0	0	0	0	0	0	0	0	1	0
sleepy-looking	2	.1787	.1174	30.7	1	0	0	1	0	0	0	0	1	0	0	0	0	0	0	0	0	0	0	0	1	0	0	0	0
sleet	22	.6677	3.0120	44.8	3	2	2	5	4	4	2	0	2	1	1	3	0	1	0	7	0	0	0	0	5	1	1	0	0
sleets	2	.0000	.0394	26.0	1	1	0	0	0	0	0	0	0	0	0	0	0	0	0	2	0	0	0	0	0	0	0	0	0
sleeve	76	.3931	6.5050	48.1	1	10	1	6	30	10	18	0	13	1	0	7	0	0	0	1	1	0	32	3	6	4	0	8	0
sleeveless	4	.1417	.1728	32.4	0	0	0	0	2	2	0	0	1	0	0	0	0	1	0	0	0	0	2	0	0	0	0	0	0
sleeves	55	.6455	7.4033	48.7	8	4	6	8	14	12	2	1	19	0	0	5	4	1	0	0	2	1	10	1	6	3	0	3	0
sleigh	16	.7039	2.3081	43.6	7	4	0	2	2	0	1	0	4	1	0	0	2	0	2	0	2	0	0	0	2	2	0	1	0
sleigh-bells	2	.0000	.0162	22.1	2	0	0	0	0	0	0	0	0	0	0	0	0	0	0	0	2	0	0	0	0	0	0	0	0
sleighbells	2	.0000	.0914	29.6	0	2	0	0	0	0	0	0	2	0	0	0	0	0	0	0	0	0	0	0	0	0	0	0	0
slender	90	.7922	14.337	51.6	15	8	7	9	25	11	10	5	13	4	0	4	0	7	0	18	3	6	5	2	5	9	8	6	0
slenderer	4	.2278	.2911	34.6	1	2	0	0	0	1	0	0	3	0	0	0	0	0	0	0	1	0	0	0	0	0	0	0	0
slept	200	.7309	30.185	54.8	39	32	21	31	43	15	14	5	85	7	0	29	5	14	4	7	0	0	0	0	23	18	0	8	0
sleuthing	2	.2433	.1158	30.6	0	0	1	0	1	0	0	0	0	0	0	0	0	0	0	0	0	0	0	0	0	1	0	1	0
slew	10	.4810	1.1144	40.5	2	0	1	4	0	1	1	1	6	0	0	1	0	0	0	0	0	0	0	0	0	2	0	1	0
slewed	3	.3450	.2505	34.0	0	0	0	2	1	0	0	0	1	0	0	0	0	0	0	0	0	0	0	0	1	1	0	0	0
slews	2	.2446	.1122	30.5	0	0	0	0	1	0	1	0	0	0	0	1	0	0	0	0	0	0	0	0	0	0	1	0	0
slice	88	.7536	13.438	51.3	25	15	14	4	17	5	7	1	12	2	0	6	5	3	3	24	0	0	6	0	1	17	3	6	0
sliced	24	.2710	1.5853	42.0	4	1	0	1	6	0	9	3	6	1	0	0	0	2	0	0	0	0	10	0	0	2	0	3	0
slices	74	.5258	8.1549	49.1	2	35	4	3	11	4	13	2	7	3	0	2	10	2	2	4	0	0	18	0	1	19	2	4	0
slicing	7	.4849	.7591	38.8	1	1	1	1	0	1	2	0	3	0	0	0	0	0	0	0	0	0	1	0	1	1	0	1	0
slick	28	.7308	4.1656	46.2	6	3	0	5	8	1	5	0	6	2	0	3	0	0	0	3	3	0	1	0	3	1	0	6	0

6P SLAM
4A slam-banging
9A slammings
9D sland'red
8F slanderers
7D slanderous
5Q Slang
9B slantwise
7R slap-shot
6F slap-slapping
9B slat
5N slat-backed
7R slate-gray
9D slaught'red
5G Slav
3P slave-catcher's
4A slave-girls
5A slave's
7D slaveboy
5F slaved
8F slaveholders
5F slaveowners
8N slavered
8F slavery's
7D slavish
8N slavishly
7Q slayings
7A slays
5Q Slayton
7D Sleamish
7N sled-dog
6A sled-trains
7N sledge-hammer
9Q sledgehammers
9D sleekly
7Q sleekness
3A sleep'y**
8J sleepin'
3R sleeping-bag-bed
6A sleeping-bunks
5H sleeplike
7D sleepwalker
6R sleepwalking
3J sleepyhead
9L sleeve-or-armhole
7L sleevecap
7A sleeved
3J Sleigh
6A sleigh-ride
3P sleuth
3P sleuths
7N Slewfoot
7A slewin'
7D slick-talking
6J slick-tongued

Word Type	F	D	U	SFI	3 Gr 3	4 Gr 4	5 Gr 5	6 Gr 6	7 Gr 7	8 Gr 8	9 Gr 9	X UnGr	A Read	B Eng & Gr	C Comp	D Lit	E Math	F Soc Stud	G Spell	H Sci	J Music	K Art	L Home Ec	M Shop	N Lib F	P Lib NF	Q Lib Ref	R Mag	S Rel
slicked	2	.2433	.1158	30.6	0	1	0	0	1	0	0	0	0	0	0	0	0	0	0	0	0	0	0	0	0	1	0	1	0
slicker	8	.3771	.7570	38.8	0	0	0	7	1	0	0	0	5	0	0	1	0	0	0	0	0	0	0	0	0	0	0	2	0
slid	108	.6886	15.439	51.9	20	24	14	17	22	4	6	1	40	4	2	12	0	1	2	0	0	0	0	0	21	20	0	6	0
slide	182	.8962	32.426	55.1	30	32	37	27	33	18	5	0	32	4	2	7	8	2	8	58	13	1	2	5	8	20	6	6	0
Slidell	6	.2444	.3628	35.6	0	0	2	0	0	4	0	0	0	0	0	0	0	4	0	0	0	0	0	0	0	0	2	0	0
slider	19	.1671	.9206	39.6	0	0	2	0	0	0	0	17	0	0	0	0	0	0	0	17	0	0	0	0	0	0	2	0	0
sliders	5	.1127	.2213	33.4	0	0	0	1	0	0	0	4	1	0	0	0	0	0	0	4	0	0	0	0	0	0	0	0	0
slides	44	.7832	6.9507	48.4	3	10	8	6	5	6	4	2	5	0	0	1	1	5	0	14	2	1	0	1	0	6	4	4	0
sliding	75	.7948	12.081	50.8	14	13	8	6	18	6	6	4	25	2	1	7	1	5	1	9	1	0	0	5	5	5	1	7	0
slight	127	.8912	22.493	53.5	8	7	11	18	43	15	21	4	23	4	5	19	0	7	2	15	4	1	4	2	10	8	7	16	0
slightest	37	.7773	5.8391	47.7	3	4	5	3	12	7	2	1	11	2	1	2	0	4	0	1	0	0	0	0	4	4	3	5	0
slightly	247	.8322	41.059	56.1	16	22	21	34	72	25	45	12	32	6	7	11	9	17	4	35	16	2	15	24	14	28	11	16	0
Slightly	6	.0000	.2741	34.4	0	0	0	6	0	0	0	0	6	0	0	0	0	0	0	0	0	0	0	0	0	0	0	0	0
Slightly's	2	.0000	.0914	29.6	0	0	0	2	0	0	0	0	2	0	0	0	0	0	0	0	0	0	0	0	0	0	0	0	0
slim	40	.6788	5.6142	47.5	3	6	2	7	11	7	2	2	11	0	0	6	0	2	0	2	0	0	2	0	5	5	0	7	0
Slim	37	.3315	3.2854	45.2	14	13	7	2	1	0	0	0	26	0	0	9	0	0	0	0	0	0	0	0	0	0	0	2	0
slime	11	.3002	.7558	38.8	0	0	1	0	8	0	2	0	0	1	0	0	0	0	0	4	0	0	0	0	0	0	6	0	0
slimmer	3	.1927	.1491	31.7	0	0	0	1	1	1	0	0	0	0	0	0	0	0	0	1	0	0	0	0	0	0	0	2	0
slimnastics	2	.0000	.0243	23.9	0	0	2	0	0	0	0	0	0	0	0	0	0	0	0	0	0	0	0	0	0	0	0	2	0
slimy	7	.3548	.5543	37.4	1	0	0	3	0	0	1	2	0	3	0	1	0	0	0	3	0	0	0	0	0	0	0	0	0
sling	9	.6347	1.1822	40.7	1	1	1	1	1	2	2	0	1	0	0	2	0	1	0	2	0	0	0	0	0	1	1	1	0
Slinger	3	.0000	.1370	31.4	3	0	0	0	0	0	0	0	3	0	0	0	0	0	0	0	0	0	0	0	0	0	0	0	0
slinging	2	.1787	.1174	30.7	0	1	0	0	1	0	0	0	1	0	0	0	0	0	0	0	0	0	0	0	1	0	0	0	0
slingshot	16	.2865	1.2332	40.9	0	4	9	3	0	0	0	0	6	0	0	0	0	0	0	9	0	0	0	0	0	1	0	0	0
slink	5	.3071	.3634	35.6	0	1	0	0	1	1	2	0	1	2	0	2	0	0	0	0	0	0	0	0	0	0	0	0	0
slinking	4	.2948	.2815	34.5	1	2	0	0	0	1	0	0	1	1	0	0	0	0	0	0	0	1	0	0	0	0	0	1	0
slip	149	.8000	23.990	53.8	12	17	12	13	37	29	25	4	34	10	3	14	4	8	0	15	1	2	18	8	5	12	4	11	0
slip-roll	2	.0000	.0050	17.0	0	0	0	0	0	0	2	0	0	0	0	0	0	0	0	0	0	0	0	2	0	0	0	0	0
slip-stitch	2	.0000	.0064	18.1	0	0	0	0	2	0	0	0	0	0	0	0	0	0	0	0	0	0	2	0	0	0	0	0	0
Slipher	4	.2417	.3089	34.9	0	0	3	0	1	0	0	0	3	0	0	0	0	0	0	1	0	0	0	0	0	0	0	0	0
slippage	4	.2423	.2206	33.4	0	0	0	0	3	0	1	0	0	0	0	0	0	0	0	0	0	0	1	0	0	0	0	3	0
slipped	214	.7864	34.353	55.4	36	50	23	38	39	14	12	2	101	7	3	20	0	7	1	1	1	0	1	1	26	31	2	12	0
slipper	23	.6191	2.9649	44.7	8	5	3	2	1	3	1	0	6	0	2	2	0	0	2	1	6	0	0	0	1	2	0	1	0
slippered	3	.3847	.2490	34.0	0	0	1	0	0	1	0	1	0	1	0	1	0	0	0	0	0	0	0	0	0	1	0	0	0
slipperiness	3	.3365	.2489	34.0	0	0	0	1	1	1	0	0	1	0	0	1	0	0	0	1	0	0	0	0	0	0	0	0	0
slippers	38	.7222	5.6565	47.5	11	9	2	4	5	6	1	0	15	1	0	5	0	1	0	0	4	0	1	0	4	5	0	2	0
slippery	55	.7394	8.3611	49.2	4	11	11	11	11	3	3	1	19	3	1	5	0	4	0	13	0	0	0	0	0	5	4	1	0
slipping	58	.7697	9.1221	49.6	4	16	5	14	9	5	4	1	25	1	0	4	0	1	2	3	0	0	4	1	7	4	1	5	0
Slippy	9	.0000	.4111	36.1	0	0	0	0	9	0	0	0	9	0	0	0	0	0	0	0	0	0	0	0	0	0	0	0	0
slips	34	.7221	5.0417	47.0	6	3	4	6	1	9	5	0	11	4	0	0	5	1	0	2	0	0	2	2	0	3	1	3	0
slit	40	.5099	4.4014	46.4	10	3	3	2	1	11	3	7	5	0	0	0	0	0	0	21	0	0	3	0	0	8	1	2	0
slither	4	.3351	.3269	35.1	0	0	0	4	0	0	0	0	1	1	0	0	0	2	0	0	0	0	0	0	0	0	0	0	0
slithering	2	.1814	.1187	30.7	0	0	1	0	0	0	1	0	1	0	0	0	0	0	0	0	0	0	0	0	0	0	0	1	0
slithy	5	.2380	.2686	34.3	0	0	1	4	0	0	0	0	0	4	0	0	0	0	0	0	0	1	0	0	0	0	0	0	0
slits	24	.5725	2.9008	44.6	8	1	2	1	7	1	2	2	4	0	0	1	0	0	0	11	0	0	1	3	1	1	1	1	0
slitted	2	.2291	.1135	30.5	0	0	0	0	1	0	0	1	0	0	0	1	0	0	0	1	0	0	0	0	0	0	0	0	0
slitting	4	.3436	.2981	34.7	0	0	0	0	3	0	1	0	0	0	0	0	0	0	0	0	0	0	1	0	0	2	1	0	0
sliver	3	.1409	.1472	31.7	0	0	0	0	3	0	0	0	1	0	0	0	0	0	0	0	0	0	0	0	0	2	0	0	0
slivers	3	.1941	.1614	32.1	0	2	0	1	0	0	0	0	1	0	0	1	0	0	0	0	0	1	0	0	0	0	0	0	0
Slivka	3	.0000	.1370	31.4	0	0	0	0	0	3	0	0	3	0	0	0	0	0	0	0	0	0	0	0	0	0	0	0	0
Sloan	6	.2321	.3270	35.1	0	0	1	0	0	4	1	0	0	0	0	0	0	0	0	0	0	0	0	0	0	0	2	4	0
Sloane	2	.0000	.0243	23.9	0	0	1	0	0	1	0	0	0	0	0	0	0	0	0	0	0	0	0	0	0	0	0	2	0
Slocum	2	.2401	.1133	30.5	1	0	0	0	1	0	0	0	0	0	0	0	0	0	0	0	0	0	0	0	0	1	1	0	0
slogan	17	.4994	1.8493	42.7	1	0	7	2	3	3	1	0	3	0	0	0	0	7	0	0	0	0	0	0	0	2	1	4	0
slogans	11	.4486	1.0689	40.3	0	0	3	0	4	2	1	1	1	0	0	0	0	0	0	1	0	0	1	0	0	6	0	2	0
sloop	11	.5012	1.2089	40.8	0	1	0	6	1	3	0	0	4	1	1	3	0	0	0	0	0	0	0	0	2	0	0	0	0
sloops	4	.3743	.3712	35.7	0	0	0	2	0	1	0	1	2	0	0	0	0	1	0	0	0	0	0	0	0	0	0	1	0
slop	3	.2257	.1583	32.0	2	0	0	0	0	0	1	0	0	2	0	1	0	0	0	0	0	0	0	0	0	0	0	0	0
slope	146	.7978	23.570	53.7	18	21	21	15	33	17	19	2	39	2	1	20	0	9	0	39	0	1	0	2	13	7	11	2	0
Slope	3	.2425	.1816	32.6	0	0	2	1	0	0	0	0	0	0	0	0	0	2	0	0	0	0	0	0	0	0	0	1	0
sloped	10	.3707	.9720	39.9	0	3	1	3	2	0	1	0	8	1	0	0	0	0	0	0	0	0	0	0	0	0	1	0	0
slopes	132	.7066	19.140	52.8	6	15	27	23	36	11	12	2	20	2	0	7	0	54	2	16	1	0	0	0	2	8	12	8	0
sloping	36	.6614	4.9496	46.9	1	5	2	8	10	5	5	0	7	0	0	1	0	7	1	13	0	0	0	2	0	2	2	1	0
sloppy	5	.1962	.2531	34.0	0	0	1	0	2	1	1	0	1	0	0	0	0	0	0	0	0	0	0	2	0	0	0	2	0
Sloppy	3	.2143	.1568	32.0	0	0	2	1	0	0	0	0	0	0	0	0	0	0	0	0	0	0	0	0	0	1	0	2	0
slosh	4	.4338	.3908	35.9	0	1	0	0	1	1	1	0	1	0	0	0	0	0	1	1	0	0	0	0	0	1	0	0	0
sloshed	7	.3666	.6426	38.1	0	1	3	1	1	1	0	0	4	0	0	0	0	0	0	0	0	0	0	0	2	0	0	1	0
sloshes	2	.2405	.1205	30.8	0	1	0	0	0	0	1	0	0	0	0	0	0	0	0	1	0	0	0	0	0	1	0	0	0
sloshing	5	.4763	.5353	37.3	0	0	0	3	2	0	0	0	2	0	0	0	0	0	0	0	0	0	0	0	0	1	1	1	0
slot	39	.5351	4.4588	46.5	4	3	5	5	10	1	4	7	8	3	0	1	1	0	0	10	0	0	0	6	1	5	0	4	0
sloth	20	.4784	2.1924	43.4	9	2	4	0	1	4	0	0	10	0	0	5	0	1	0	2	0	0	0	0	0	2	0	0	0
sloths	3	.3769	.2484	34.0	0	0	0	1	1	1	0	0	0	0	0	0	0	1	0	0	0	0	0	0	0	0	1	1	0
slots	17	.6032	2.1188	43.3	6	0	3	1	3	3	1	0	1	2	0	0	1	0	0	6	0	1	0	2	0	2	0	2	0
slotted	4	.0751	.0794	29.0	1	0	0	0	0	1	2	0	0	0	0	0	0	0	0	0	0	0	0	3	0	1	0	0	0
slouch	5	.4281	.4726	36.7	0	0	1	2	0	1	1	0	1	1	0	1	0	0	0	0	0	0	0	0	2	0	0	0	0
slouched	2	.2297	.1135	30.6	0	0	0	0	0	1	1	0	0	0	0	1	0	1	0	0	0	0	0	0	0	0	0	0	0
slouching	4	.1892	.1847	32.7	0	0	1	0	1	1	1	0	0	0	0	3	0	0	0	0	0	0	0	0	0	0	0	1	0
Slovakia	4	.0000	.0778	28.9	0	0	0	4	0	0	1	0	0	0	0	0	0	4	0	0	0	0	0	0	0	0	0	0	0
Slovaks	7	.0000	.1361	31.3	0	0	0	7	0	0	0	0	0	0	0	0	0	7	0	0	0	0	0	0	0	0	0	0	0
Slovenes	2	.0000	.0389	25.9	0	0	0	0	2	0	0	0	0	0	0	0	0	2	0	0	0	0	0	0	0	0	0	0	0
Slovenia	3	.2321	.1635	32.1	0	0	0	0	0	1	2	0	0	0	0	0	0	0	0	0	0	0	0	0	0	0	1	2	0
Slovenian	4	.0000	.0419	26.2	0	0	0	0	0	4	0	0	0	0	0	0	0	0	0	0	0	0	0	0	0	0	4	0	0
slovenly	3	.3350	.2478	33.9	0	0	1	0	1	1	0	0	1	0	0	0	0	1	0	0	0	0	0	0	0	0	1	0	0
slow	396	.8673	68.684	58.4	63	44	54	33	104	56	36	6	118	12	0	34	4	22	5	45	39	1	7	0	26	33	28	22	0
Slow	5	.2278	.2869	34.6	2	1	0	0	0	2	0	0	1	0	0	0	0	0	0	0	3	0	0	0	1	0	0	0	0
slow-growing	5	.1285	.1797	32.5	0	0	2	0	2	1	0	0	0	0	0	0	0	1	0	0	0	0	0	0	0	0	4	0	0
slow-like	2	.2388	.1089	30.4	0	0	0	1	1	0	0	0	0	0	0	0	0	0	1	0	0	0	0	0	1	0	0	0	0
slow-moving	13	.5197	1.4781	41.7	3	1	0	2	2	1	3	0	3	0	0	0	0	2	0	5	0	0	0	0	0	1	0	2	0
slow-thinking	2	.2160	.1362	31.3	0	1	0	1	0	0	0	1	1	0	0	0	0	0	0	1	0	0	0	0	0	0	0	0	0
slow-water	3	.0000	.0365	25.6	0	3	0	0	0	0	0	0	0	0	0	0	0	0	0	0	0	0	0	0	0	0	0	3	0
slowdown	5	.3767	.4160	36.2	0	0	0	0	1	0	4	0	0	0	0	0	0	2	0	0	0	0	0	0	0	0	1	2	0
slowed	71	.7825	11.365	50.6	10	11	5	9	19	9	5	3	33	1	1	5	1	3	0	9	0	0	0	0	5	8	2	3	0
slower	58	.7152	8.4596	49.3	6	9	12	5	15	4	5	2	9	0	0	1	1	2	0	14	11	0	0	2	5	9	2	2	0
slower-moving	2	.0000	.0394	26.0	0	0	0	2	0	0	0	0	0	0	0	0	0	0	0	2	0	0	0	0	0	0	0	0	0

9D slicked-up
5A slickens
5P slickers
7R slicks
7P slide-hopping
9Q sliderule
4D sliding's
4P slighted
7N slighting
9J slightingly
5R slim-down
5A Slim's
7Q slimness
4A sling-shot
9D slinger
7R slip-in
7L slip-stitches
3A slipp
5J Slippers
4N slippery-slidy
8B slippin'
7A slippy
7L slipstitch
4Q slipware
9R slit-eyed
7P slit-throat
7N slithered
9Q Sloan's
3A slob
3A slobby
7R slobs
5A slogging
4N slops
8L slot-seam
3A Sloth
8D sloth's
5A slothful
9M slotter
7Q slotters
9M slotting
7B sloucher
9R slouches
6R slough
9H sloughs
7A Sloughs
9R Slovenia's
7H SLOW
4P slow-burning
7D slow-down
8D slow-paced
3N slow-poke
8D slow-rising
7D slow-speaking
7N slow-tracked
7N slow-trailing
9B slow-up

Word Type	F	D	U	SFI	3 Gr 3	4 Gr 4	5 Gr 5	6 Gr 6	7 Gr 7	8 Gr 8	9 Gr 9	X UnGr	A Read	B Eng & Gr	C Comp	D Lit	E Math	F Soc Stud	G Spell	H Sci	J Music	K Art	L Home Ec	M Shop	N Lib F	P Lib NF	Q Lib Ref	R Mag	S Rel
slowest	7	.3627	.5770	37.6	1	1	2	1	0	2	0	0	1	0	0	0	4	0	0	0	0	0	0	1	0	1	0	0	0
slowing	25	.7878	3.9985	46.0	3	5	0	3	7	2	4	1	8	2	0	2	0	1	0	4	1	0	0	0	2	3	1	1	0
slowly	1112	.9290	204.96	63.1	212	239	125	121	229	102	71	13	388	60	14	70	2	66	28	143	32	3	16	10	96	113	29	42	0
slowness	8	.5479	.9180	39.6	1	0	1	0	3	2	1	0	1	0	1	2	0	1	0	0	0	0	0	0	0	1	1	0	0
slowpoke	4	.3812	.3773	35.8	1	2	0	1	0	0	0	0	2	0	0	0	0	0	0	1	0	0	0	0	0	1	0	0	0
slows	22	.6723	3.0315	44.8	2	1	3	4	4	1	6	1	2	0	1	0	0	0	0	9	1	0	1	0	0	2	2	4	0
slowworm	2	.2401	.1133	30.5	1	0	0	0	1	0	0	0	0	0	0	0	0	0	0	0	0	0	0	0	0	1	1	0	0
sludge	4	.2090	.2014	33.0	0	0	1	0	1	0	2	0	0	0	0	0	0	0	0	0	0	0	0	0	0	0	1	3	0
Slue-foot	3	.0000	.1370	31.4	0	0	0	3	0	0	0	0	3	0	0	0	0	0	0	0	0	0	0	0	0	0	0	0	0
slug	5	.3974	.4472	36.5	2	1	0	0	1	0	1	0	1	0	0	0	0	0	0	1	0	0	0	1	1	1	0	0	0
slugger	4	.2031	.2455	33.9	0	0	0	1	2	1	0	0	2	0	0	0	0	0	0	0	0	1	0	0	0	1	0	0	0
sluggers	2	.2433	.1158	30.6	1	0	0	1	0	0	0	0	0	0	0	0	0	0	0	0	0	0	0	0	0	1	0	1	0
slugging	4	.3513	.3115	34.9	0	0	2	0	0	2	0	0	0	0	0	1	0	1	0	0	0	0	0	0	0	0	0	2	0
sluggish	6	.5160	.6584	38.2	0	1	1	0	1	1	1	1	1	0	0	1	0	0	1	0	0	0	0	0	0	1	0	2	0
slugs	7	.4599	.7241	38.6	4	1	1	0	1	0	0	0	2	0	0	1	0	0	0	3	1	0	0	0	0	0	0	0	0
sluice	4	.3097	.2992	34.8	1	0	1	1	1	0	0	1	1	0	0	1	0	0	0	0	0	0	0	0	0	0	0	2	0
sluicing	2	.0000	.0045	16.5	0	0	0	0	0	2	0	0	0	0	2	0	0	0	0	0	0	0	0	0	0	0	0	0	0
slum	16	.4388	1.5340	41.9	0	1	2	0	2	1	10	0	0	0	0	0	0	11	0	0	0	0	0	0	1	1	1	2	0
slumber	11	.6184	1.4496	41.6	0	1	1	1	6	1	1	0	5	0	0	1	0	0	0	0	1	0	0	0	2	1	1	0	0
slumbered	5	.2445	.3864	35.9	0	1	0	1	3	0	0	0	4	0	0	1	0	0	0	0	0	0	0	0	0	0	0	0	0
slumbering	4	.3726	.3697	35.7	1	0	1	1	1	0	0	0	2	0	0	0	0	1	0	0	0	0	0	0	1	0	0	0	0
slumbers	3	.3346	.2478	33.9	0	0	1	0	0	0	1	1	1	0	0	0	0	0	0	1	0	0	0	0	0	0	1	0	0
slump	4	.4499	.4023	36.0	2	0	0	0	2	0	0	0	1	1	0	0	0	0	0	1	0	0	0	0	0	0	0	1	0
slumped	8	.5384	.9371	39.7	1	1	1	1	1	2	1	0	3	2	0	1	0	0	0	0	0	0	0	0	0	1	0	1	0
slums	22	.4605	2.2856	43.6	4	1	3	2	3	4	5	0	6	0	0	0	0	11	0	0	0	0	0	0	0	1	3	1	0
slung	22	.6757	3.1020	44.9	5	3	4	5	1	2	1	1	9	0	1	2	0	0	0	1	2	0	0	0	4	2	1	0	0
slunk	10	.5125	1.0852	40.4	1	2	1	1	3	2	0	0	1	0	0	2	0	1	0	0	0	0	0	0	4	1	0	1	0
slup-slup	2	.0000	.0914	29.6	0	0	0	2	0	0	0	0	2	0	0	0	0	0	0	0	0	0	0	0	0	0	0	0	0
slur	4	.1754	.1669	32.2	1	0	0	0	2	1	0	0	0	1	0	0	0	0	0	0	3	0	0	0	0	0	0	0	0
slurp	2	.1605	.0742	28.7	0	0	0	0	0	1	1	0	0	1	1	0	0	0	0	0	0	0	0	0	0	0	0	0	0
slurred	4	.3702	.3170	35.0	0	0	0	0	0	2	2	0	0	0	0	2	0	0	0	0	1	0	0	0	1	0	0	0	0
slurry	3	.0000	.0076	18.8	0	0	0	0	3	0	0	0	0	0	0	0	0	0	0	0	0	0	0	3	0	0	0	0	0
slurs	3	.0000	.0243	23.8	0	0	0	2	0	0	1	0	0	0	0	0	0	0	0	0	3	0	0	0	0	0	0	0	0
slush	2	.2446	.1142	30.6	0	1	0	0	1	0	0	0	0	0	0	0	0	0	0	0	0	0	0	0	1	0	0	1	0
slushy	2	.1717	.1142	30.6	0	0	1	1	0	0	0	0	1	0	0	1	0	0	0	0	0	0	0	0	0	0	0	0	0
sly	16	.7032	2.3157	43.6	4	1	4	1	1	3	1	1	5	1	1	2	0	1	1	0	0	0	0	0	2	1	0	2	0
slyly	9	.4354	.8882	39.5	3	1	1	2	0	1	0	1	3	0	0	2	0	0	0	0	0	0	0	0	0	1	0	3	0
sm	3	.0000	.0243	23.9	2	0	0	1	0	0	0	0	0	0	0	0	0	0	3	0	0	0	0	0	0	0	0	0	0
smack	14	.6724	1.9478	42.9	1	2	2	4	3	0	2	0	4	2	0	2	0	0	0	0	1	0	0	0	1	2	0	2	0
smacked	11	.4784	1.2108	40.8	1	3	1	1	4	0	0	1	6	0	0	0	0	0	0	0	0	0	0	0	2	2	0	1	0
smacking	4	.3097	.2992	34.8	1	1	0	0	2	0	0	0	1	0	0	1	0	0	0	0	0	0	0	0	0	0	0	2	0
smacks	2	.2405	.1205	30.8	0	0	0	0	1	0	0	1	0	0	0	0	0	0	0	1	0	0	0	0	0	1	0	0	0
small	3555	.9421	662.52	68.2	629	624	460	480	587	354	300	121	817	96	54	149	105	519	50	604	103	49	102	78	133	301	205	190	0
Small	34	.3861	2.9787	44.7	24	7	2	0	1	0	0	0	4	0	0	0	0	1	0	7	1	0	0	0	0	20	0	1	0
small-scale	6	.4917	.6206	37.9	0	0	3	0	1	2	0	0	0	0	0	0	0	1	0	1	2	0	0	0	0	1	1	0	0
small-sized	3	.2351	.1529	31.8	0	1	0	0	0	2	0	0	0	0	0	0	0	0	0	0	2	0	0	1	0	0	0	0	0
small-town	9	.5775	1.0674	40.3	0	0	3	0	3	2	1	0	0	0	0	3	0	1	0	0	1	0	0	0	0	1	1	2	0
smaller	634	.9011	113.48	60.5	114	99	73	87	104	71	64	22	89	13	2	12	69	97	14	149	7	14	7	14	16	52	42	37	0
smallest	286	.8595	49.047	56.9	46	46	35	37	55	40	19	8	38	5	5	7	101	16	7	44	7	2	2	6	8	17	13	8	0
smallish	3	.3346	.2478	33.9	0	1	0	0	2	0	0	0	1	0	0	0	0	0	0	1	0	0	0	0	0	0	1	0	0
smallpox	22	.5688	2.7171	44.3	5	1	0	0	9	3	4	0	8	1	0	0	0	1	0	8	0	0	0	0	2	0	2	0	0
smart	109	.7677	17.103	52.3	32	14	14	12	14	11	11	1	46	8	4	12	0	4	2	2	0	0	1	0	15	10	1	4	0
Smart	18	.3469	1.6810	42.3	5	9	0	3	0	0	1	0	14	0	0	0	0	0	0	0	0	0	0	0	0	3	0	1	0
smarted	3	.3450	.2505	34.0	0	1	1	0	0	0	1	0	1	0	0	0	0	0	0	0	0	0	0	0	1	1	0	0	0
smarter	11	.3509	1.0274	40.1	8	1	0	1	0	1	0	0	8	0	0	0	0	0	0	1	0	0	0	0	0	2	0	0	0
smartest	7	.4815	.7791	38.9	3	1	1	0	1	0	1	0	4	1	0	0	0	1	0	0	0	0	0	0	0	0	0	1	0
smarting	8	.5456	.9479	39.8	0	2	0	3	2	0	1	0	3	0	0	1	0	0	0	0	0	0	0	0	1	1	0	2	0
smartly	5	.3414	.4194	36.2	0	0	0	4	1	0	0	0	2	0	0	0	0	0	0	0	0	0	0	1	1	0	0	2	0
smarty	2	.1787	.1174	30.7	1	0	0	0	1	0	0	0	1	0	0	0	0	0	0	0	0	0	0	0	1	0	0	0	0
smash	20	.7254	2.9852	44.7	3	1	2	1	4	7	2	0	7	0	0	2	1	0	0	2	1	0	0	0	1	1	1	4	0
smashed	62	.8040	10.153	50.1	8	8	7	2	10	24	3	0	32	2	1	6	0	3	1	1	0	1	0	0	4	4	1	6	0
smasher	2	.2278	.1128	30.5	0	0	0	0	0	0	2	0	0	0	0	0	0	0	0	1	0	0	0	0	0	0	1	0	0
smashes	3	.1060	.1461	31.6	2	0	0	0	0	0	1	0	2	0	1	0	0	0	0	0	0	0	0	0	0	0	0	0	0
smashing	11	.5188	1.2419	40.9	1	0	1	1	6	2	0	0	3	0	0	0	0	0	0	2	0	0	0	0	3	1	0	2	0
smashup	5	.0000	.2284	33.6	0	0	0	0	0	5	0	0	5	0	0	0	0	0	0	0	0	0	0	0	0	0	0	0	0
smeared	7	.5563	.8388	39.2	1	2	1	1	1	0	1	0	2	1	0	0	0	0	0	2	0	0	0	0	1	0	0	1	0
smearing	2	.1605	.0742	28.7	0	0	1	0	1	0	0	0	0	1	1	0	0	0	0	0	0	0	0	0	0	0	0	0	0
smears	3	.2435	.1694	32.3	0	0	0	1	1	0	0	1	0	0	1	0	0	0	0	1	0	0	0	0	0	0	0	1	0
Smedley	3	.0000	.1370	31.4	0	3	0	0	0	0	0	0	3	0	0	0	0	0	0	0	0	0	0	0	0	0	0	0	0
Smee	14	.0000	.6396	38.1	0	0	0	14	0	0	0	0	14	0	0	0	0	0	0	0	0	0	0	0	0	0	0	0	0
Smee's	2	.0000	.0914	29.6	0	0	0	2	0	0	0	0	2	0	0	0	0	0	0	0	0	0	0	0	0	0	0	0	0
smell	378	.7096	55.232	57.4	80	83	47	34	67	36	23	8	121	27	29	33	0	6	4	47	3	0	1	0	51	35	7	14	0
smelled	80	.5928	10.279	50.1	20	23	12	7	8	6	4	0	42	4	5	2	0	3	0	1	0	0	0	0	16	6	1	0	0
smellers	2	.1948	.1250	31.0	1	0	0	0	0	1	0	0	1	0	0	0	0	0	0	0	0	0	0	0	0	1	0	0	0
smelling	35	.6406	4.6109	46.6	5	8	3	2	9	5	2	1	4	2	3	2	0	0	0	7	0	0	0	0	9	1	3	4	0
smells	84	.6954	12.081	50.8	16	15	8	10	15	5	15	0	30	6	7	9	0	1	0	6	0	2	0	0	11	8	2	2	0
smelly	5	.3380	.4246	36.3	0	1	1	0	2	1	0	0	2	0	0	0	0	1	0	0	0	0	0	0	0	2	0	0	0
Smelly	7	.0000	.3198	35.0	0	0	0	0	0	7	0	0	7	0	0	0	0	0	0	0	0	0	0	0	0	0	0	0	0
smelt	7	.6110	.9011	39.5	1	3	1	1	1	0	0	0	2	0	0	0	0	0	0	1	1	0	0	0	1	1	1	0	0
smelted	2	.0000	.0389	25.9	0	0	0	0	2	0	0	0	0	0	0	0	0	2	0	0	0	0	0	0	0	0	0	0	0
smelter	5	.0000	.2284	33.6	5	0	0	0	0	0	0	0	5	0	0	0	0	0	0	0	0	0	0	0	0	0	0	0	0
smelters	7	.3545	.6148	37.9	3	0	0	1	2	0	1	0	3	0	0	0	0	2	0	0	0	0	0	0	0	0	2	0	0
smelting	9	.4551	.8974	39.5	1	0	2	1	3	0	2	0	1	0	0	0	0	3	0	1	0	0	0	0	0	1	3	0	0
Smetana	4	.0000	.0323	25.1	0	0	0	0	0	4	0	0	0	0	0	0	0	0	0	0	4	0	0	0	0	0	0	0	0
Smetana's	2	.0000	.0162	22.1	0	0	0	1	0	1	0	0	0	0	0	0	0	0	0	0	2	0	0	0	0	0	0	0	0
smidgen	3	.1277	.1363	31.3	0	0	1	0	1	0	0	1	1	0	0	0	0	0	0	0	0	0	0	0	0	0	0	2	0
Smiggle	2	.0000	.0215	23.3	2	0	0	0	0	0	0	0	0	0	0	2	0	0	0	0	0	0	0	0	0	0	0	0	0
smile	281	.8158	46.295	56.7	32	67	30	38	62	19	26	7	104	15	6	37	1	6	4	0	6	3	1	0	45	23	3	27	0
smiled	413	.6741	58.478	57.7	106	126	35	40	62	25	15	4	190	9	1	36	0	17	0	2	6	0	0	0	66	70	0	16	0
smiles	58	.7783	9.1949	49.6	10	10	4	8	15	7	3	1	25	4	1	10	0	0	1	0	4	1	2	0	7	0	0	3	0
Smiley	3	.2384	.1717	32.3	2	0	0	0	1	0	0	0	0	1	0	0	2	0	0	0	0	0	0	0	0	0	0	0	0
smiling	148	.6765	20.932	53.2	24	37	23	12	29	14	6	3	61	3	0	21	0	9	0	0	2	0	1	0	27	17	0	7	0
Smiling	3	.0000	.1370	31.4	0	0	0	3	0	0	0	0	3	0	0	0	0	0	0	0	0	0	0	0	0	0	0	0	0
smirk	3	.2357	.2199	33.4	0	1	0	0	1	1	0	0	2	0	0	0	0	0	0	0	0	0	0	0	0	1	0	0	0
Smit	2	.0000	.0914	29.6	0	2	0	0	0	0	0	0	2	0	0	0	0	0	0	0	0	0	0	0	0	0	0	0	0
smite	3	.2137	.1446	31.6	0	0	0	0	1	2	0	0	0	0	1	2	0	0	0	0	0	0	0	0	0	0	0	0	0

4F slowest-moving
5Q slowly-moving
8M sloyd
7A slud
8D Slue-Foot
9D slugfests
9B sluggard
8G sluggards
3A Slugger
6A sluggishly
6R sluiced
5Q sluices
3A slurper
9A slurping
8J slurring
7A slushed
4N slushy-squshy
9D sluttish
3A smrt
7F Smaland
8F smaller-arms
7A small-club
8F small-fisted
7Q small-leafed
6D small-paned
4N Small-person-without-an**
3K small-size
7K smaller-appearing
8B smaller-wheeled
7R smallmouth
9L smallness
5R smart-alecky
4P smartaleck
8A smarter'n
7N smartin'
4A smartness
3P Smarty
7A smash-up
8N Smasher
9Q smashers
8A smatterers
7R Smear
4N smelliest
7A smellin'
3D Smiggles
7P smirch'd

Word Type	F	D	U	SFI	3 Gr 3	4 Gr 4	5 Gr 5	6 Gr 6	7 Gr 7	8 Gr 8	9 Gr 9	X UnGr	A Read	B Eng & Gr	C Comp	D Lit	E Math	F Soc Stud	G Spell	H Sci	J Music	K Art	L Home Ec	M Shop	N Lib F	P Lib NF	Q Lib Ref	R Mag	S Rel
smith	7	.3238	.5078	37.1	0	6	1	0	0	0	0	0	0	0	0	0	0	0	0	0	1	0	0	0	1	5	0	0	0
Smith	206	.8175	33.859	55.3	49	69	11	7	23	21	20	6	44	7	1	13	12	9	8	10	4	0	1	0	10	65	6	16	0
SMITH	5	.0000	.0537	27.3	0	0	0	0	0	5	0	0	0	0	0	5	0	0	0	0	0	0	0	0	0	0	0	0	0
Smith's	24	.7806	3.7897	45.8	5	5	0	3	6	2	2	1	5	1	0	1	6	2	1	1	0	0	0	0	3	2	1	1	0
smithereens	2	.1787	.1174	30.7	1	0	0	0	0	0	0	1	1	0	0	0	0	0	0	0	0	0	0	0	1	0	0	0	0
Smiths	17	.5213	1.9639	42.9	1	0	6	0	0	4	5	1	7	4	0	0	2	0	0	3	0	0	0	0	0	0	0	1	0
Smiths'	4	.3755	.3686	35.7	2	1	1	0	0	0	0	0	2	0	0	0	0	0	0	0	0	0	0	0	1	1	0	0	0
Smithsonian	3	.3847	.2496	34.0	1	0	1	0	0	0	0	1	0	0	0	0	0	0	0	0	0	0	0	0	0	1	1	1	0
smithy	5	.3844	.4760	36.8	1	0	3	0	0	1	0	0	3	1	0	0	0	0	0	0	0	0	0	0	1	0	0	0	0
smitten	3	.1187	.1291	31.1	0	0	0	1	0	1	1	0	1	0	0	2	0	0	0	0	0	0	0	0	0	0	0	0	0
Smitty's	2	.0000	.0914	29.6	0	0	0	0	0	2	0	0	2	0	0	0	0	0	0	0	0	0	0	0	0	0	0	0	0
smock	2	.0000	.0914	29.6	0	0	0	2	0	0	0	0	2	0	0	0	0	0	0	0	0	0	0	0	0	0	0	0	0
smocks	2	.1814	.1187	30.7	0	1	0	0	1	0	0	0	1	0	0	0	0	0	0	0	0	0	0	0	0	0	0	1	0
smog	22	.5281	2.4598	43.9	7	1	5	0	2	3	2	2	0	2	0	0	0	9	0	6	0	0	0	0	0	0	1	4	0
smoke	328	.8466	55.812	57.5	70	48	48	44	56	42	17	3	113	7	7	36	0	28	12	39	6	0	0	1	28	33	8	10	0
smoke-pall	3	.0000	.0322	25.1	0	0	0	0	3	0	0	0	0	0	0	3	0	0	0	0	0	0	0	0	0	0	0	0	0
smoke's	2	.0000	.0914	29.6	0	0	0	0	2	0	0	0	2	0	0	0	0	0	0	0	0	0	0	0	0	0	0	0	0
smoked	33	.6933	4.7125	46.7	0	7	2	3	12	2	4	3	8	0	0	4	0	4	0	1	0	0	0	0	4	5	2	5	0
smokehouse	6	.2226	.3457	35.4	1	0	0	1	4	0	0	0	1	0	0	0	0	0	0	0	0	0	0	0	4	1	0	0	0
smokeless	3	.3762	.2496	34.0	0	1	1	0	0	1	0	0	0	0	0	0	0	0	0	1	0	0	0	0	0	1	1	0	0
smokers	7	.1827	.3580	35.5	0	0	0	0	6	0	1	0	0	0	0	0	0	0	0	6	0	0	0	0	0	0	0	1	0
smokes	2	.2160	.1362	31.3	0	0	0	1	0	1	0	0	1	0	0	0	0	0	0	1	0	0	0	0	0	0	0	0	0
smokestack	10	.3696	.9619	39.8	0	4	5	0	0	1	0	0	7	0	0	0	0	0	0	2	0	0	0	0	0	1	0	0	0
smokestacks	3	.3759	.2471	33.9	0	0	0	1	0	0	2	0	0	1	0	0	0	1	0	0	0	0	0	0	0	0	1	0	0
Smokey	8	.4295	.7526	38.8	5	0	0	2	1	0	0	0	0	0	0	0	0	5	0	0	0	0	0	0	1	1	0	1	0
Smokies	2	.2401	.1133	30.5	0	0	1	0	1	0	0	0	0	0	0	0	0	0	0	0	0	0	0	0	0	1	1	0	0
smoking	51	.7317	7.5917	48.8	4	5	2	5	16	8	9	2	7	3	0	8	0	9	0	8	0	0	0	0	7	2	3	4	0
smoky	12	.5979	1.5238	41.8	0	0	0	6	1	2	2	1	4	2	0	1	0	0	2	2	0	0	0	0	0	0	0	1	0
Smoky	46	.3878	3.8381	45.8	3	31	7	1	2	2	0	0	1	0	0	2	0	1	0	0	10	0	0	0	29	1	2	0	0
Smoky's	6	.0000	.0703	28.5	0	6	0	0	0	0	0	0	0	0	0	0	0	0	0	0	0	0	0	0	6	0	0	0	0
smoldered	3	.1910	.1473	31.7	1	0	0	0	1	0	1	0	0	0	0	0	0	1	0	0	0	0	0	0	2	0	0	0	0
smoldering	8	.4036	.7646	38.8	0	0	0	2	5	1	0	0	4	0	1	2	0	0	0	0	0	0	0	0	1	0	0	0	0
smolders	2	.2437	.1129	30.5	0	0	0	0	1	0	1	0	0	0	0	0	0	0	0	0	0	0	0	0	0	0	1	1	0
Smollett	4	.2441	.2254	33.5	0	0	1	0	2	0	1	0	0	0	0	0	0	0	0	0	0	0	0	0	2	0	2	0	0
smooth	331	.7914	52.729	57.2	60	38	32	39	71	41	41	9	70	9	3	28	2	18	4	39	8	16	30	28	19	27	10	20	0
smooth-flowing	2	.2303	.1079	30.3	1	0	0	0	1	0	0	0	0	0	0	0	0	0	0	0	1	0	0	0	0	1	0	0	0
smoothed	42	.6928	5.9820	47.8	8	9	8	3	9	1	3	1	11	0	0	4	0	3	0	0	1	3	0	1	7	6	1	5	0
smoother	12	.5983	1.4924	41.7	0	1	1	2	2	2	3	1	3	0	0	0	0	0	0	0	1	1	2	1	0	0	1	3	0
smoothest	4	.3415	.3070	34.9	1	1	0	1	1	0	0	0	0	0	0	0	0	0	0	1	0	0	0	0	0	1	0	2	0
smoothing	12	.4388	1.1363	40.6	0	2	2	3	0	3	1	1	2	0	0	0	0	1	0	0	0	0	1	3	3	0	0	2	0
smoothly	94	.8203	15.454	51.9	13	7	14	11	23	13	12	1	16	10	1	4	0	8	1	15	11	3	8	0	4	4	3	6	0
smoothness	12	.5698	1.4219	41.5	1	0	1	4	3	0	3	0	2	0	0	2	0	0	0	2	1	2	1	1	0	0	0	1	0
smooths	3	.3776	.2504	34.0	0	0	0	1	2	0	0	0	0	0	0	1	0	1	0	0	0	0	0	0	0	1	0	0	0
smorrebrod	2	.0000	.0209	23.2	2	0	0	0	0	0	0	0	0	0	0	0	0	0	0	0	0	0	0	0	0	0	2	0	0
smote	8	.5220	.9017	39.6	2	0	2	0	3	0	1	0	2	0	0	1	0	0	0	0	0	0	0	0	1	3	0	1	0
smother	11	.5295	1.2756	41.1	1	2	1	2	2	2	0	1	4	0	0	1	0	0	0	2	0	0	0	0	3	0	1	0	0
smothered	8	.3204	.6115	37.9	1	1	0	2	4	0	0	0	2	0	0	3	0	0	0	0	0	0	0	0	3	0	0	0	0
smothering	3	.2309	.1631	32.1	0	1	0	0	1	1	0	0	0	0	0	1	0	0	0	0	0	0	0	0	0	0	0	2	0
Smothers	4	.1814	.2373	33.8	0	0	2	0	1	0	1	0	2	0	0	0	0	0	0	0	0	0	0	0	0	0	0	2	0
smudge	8	.5175	.8972	39.5	0	4	1	2	1	0	0	0	2	0	0	2	0	0	0	1	0	0	0	0	1	2	0	0	0
smudged	6	.3852	.5822	37.7	1	1	0	1	2	0	1	0	4	1	0	0	0	0	0	0	0	0	0	0	0	1	0	0	0
smudges	4	.2955	.2576	34.1	0	1	0	1	0	1	0	1	0	2	0	0	0	0	0	0	0	1	0	0	0	0	0	1	0
smug	3	.2060	.1500	31.8	1	0	0	0	1	0	1	0	0	0	0	2	0	0	0	0	0	0	0	0	0	1	0	0	0
smuggle	2	.1787	.1174	30.7	0	0	0	0	1	1	0	0	1	0	0	0	0	0	0	0	0	0	0	0	1	0	0	0	0
smuggled	3	.3756	.2468	33.9	1	0	1	0	1	0	0	0	0	0	0	1	0	1	0	0	0	0	0	0	0	0	1	0	0
smuggler	6	.0000	.2741	34.4	0	6	0	0	0	0	0	0	6	0	0	0	0	0	0	0	0	0	0	0	0	0	0	0	0
smugglers	13	.4421	1.3410	41.3	0	7	3	0	1	2	0	0	7	1	0	0	0	0	0	0	3	0	0	0	0	0	0	2	0
Smugglers'	2	.0000	.0243	23.9	0	0	2	0	0	0	0	0	0	0	0	0	0	0	0	0	0	0	0	0	0	0	0	2	0
smuggling	5	.4625	.4880	36.9	0	0	2	0	0	3	0	0	0	0	0	0	0	1	0	0	1	0	0	0	0	0	1	2	0
Smythe	3	.0000	.0328	25.2	0	0	0	0	0	0	3	0	0	3	0	0	0	0	0	0	0	0	0	0	0	0	0	0	0
sn	4	.0000	.0325	25.1	1	0	1	2	0	0	0	0	0	0	0	0	0	0	4	0	0	0	0	0	0	0	0	0	0
snack	29	.4396	2.7754	44.4	4	3	2	4	8	2	5	1	5	3	0	0	1	0	0	4	0	0	8	0	1	2	0	5	0
snacks	20	.4573	1.9885	43.0	1	3	1	4	5	2	4	0	3	1	0	0	0	2	1	6	0	0	5	0	0	0	1	1	0
snag	2	.1787	.1174	30.7	0	0	0	0	2	0	0	0	1	0	0	0	0	0	0	0	0	0	0	0	1	0	0	0	0
snagged	3	.2445	.1903	32.8	0	0	0	1	1	1	0	0	1	0	0	0	0	0	0	0	0	0	1	0	0	0	0	1	0
Snaggs	4	.0000	.0429	26.3	0	0	0	0	0	4	0	0	0	0	0	4	0	0	0	0	0	0	0	0	0	0	0	0	0
SNAGGS	15	.0000	.1610	32.1	0	0	0	0	0	15	0	0	0	0	0	15	0	0	0	0	0	0	0	0	0	0	0	0	0
snags	5	.5380	.5702	37.6	0	0	1	1	2	0	0	1	1	1	0	1	0	0	0	0	0	0	0	0	0	0	1	1	0
snail	47	.6776	6.7242	48.3	25	9	1	2	3	5	0	2	24	0	0	1	5	0	0	6	0	0	0	0	1	6	2	2	0
snail's	3	.3769	.2505	34.0	0	1	1	0	1	0	0	0	0	0	0	1	1	0	0	1	0	0	0	0	0	0	0	0	0
snails	43	.6657	5.9277	47.7	13	8	4	4	9	3	0	2	7	0	0	1	0	1	0	20	0	1	0	0	4	3	3	3	0
snake	226	.7451	34.493	55.4	93	27	20	31	41	6	4	4	66	6	6	10	3	0	3	84	1	0	0	0	11	7	14	15	0
Snake	30	.3925	3.0264	44.8	14	1	1	11	3	0	0	0	24	0	0	0	0	1	0	0	1	0	0	0	0	0	0	4	0
Snake-Eye	11	.0392	.2337	33.7	0	10	0	0	0	1	0	0	1	10	0	0	0	0	0	0	0	0	0	0	0	0	0	0	0
snake-bite	2	.1717	.1142	30.6	0	0	0	0	0	2	0	0	1	0	0	1	0	0	0	0	0	0	0	0	0	0	0	0	0
snake-like	4	.3192	.3100	34.9	0	1	1	0	1	1	0	0	1	0	0	0	0	0	0	0	0	0	0	0	0	2	0	1	0
snake's	21	.4577	2.1640	43.4	11	4	0	3	1	1	1	0	5	1	0	0	0	0	0	11	0	0	0	0	0	1	0	3	0
snakebite	2	.2351	.1166	30.7	0	0	0	0	1	1	0	0	0	0	0	0	0	1	0	0	0	0	0	0	0	0	0	1	0
snaked	4	.3030	.2949	34.7	0	0	1	0	1	1	1	0	1	0	0	0	0	0	0	0	0	0	0	0	2	0	0	1	0
snakefish's	2	.0000	.0215	23.3	0	0	0	0	0	0	2	0	0	0	0	2	0	0	0	0	0	0	0	0	0	0	0	0	0
snakelike	5	.3416	.4181	36.2	0	0	0	0	4	0	0	1	2	0	0	0	0	0	0	0	0	0	0	0	2	0	1	0	0
snakes	210	.5890	26.390	54.2	101	12	13	28	45	4	3	4	54	5	0	3	0	5	1	95	0	0	0	0	7	8	30	2	0
snap	67	.7579	10.282	51.5	9	13	4	10	16	10	3	2	16	3	1	1	2	0	1	7	4	0	8	5	6	4	2	7	0
snapped	98	.6859	14.155	51.5	31	12	13	16	17	6	3	0	55	1	2	8	0	1	1	1	0	0	0	0	17	5	1	6	0
Snapper	12	.0000	.5482	37.4	12	0	0	0	0	0	0	0	12	0	0	0	0	0	0	0	0	0	0	0	0	0	0	0	0
Snapper's	6	.0000	.2741	34.4	6	0	0	0	0	0	0	0	6	0	0	0	0	0	0	0	0	0	0	0	0	0	0	0	0
snappers	2	.0000	.0209	23.2	0	0	0	0	2	0	0	0	0	0	0	0	0	0	0	0	0	0	0	0	0	0	2	0	0
snapping	35	.7135	5.1430	47.1	5	6	7	4	7	3	1	2	13	0	3	1	0	1	1	1	4	0	1	0	2	4	1	3	0
snappy	6	.5200	.6615	38.2	0	0	2	0	1	1	1	1	1	1	0	0	0	0	0	0	1	0	0	0	1	0	0	2	0
snaps	25	.3175	1.8448	42.7	8	1	2	1	3	10	0	0	5	1	0	0	0	1	0	4	1	0	10	0	0	2	1	0	0
snapshot	5	.1801	.2214	33.5	1	1	0	0	3	0	0	0	0	4	0	0	0	0	0	0	0	0	0	0	0	0	1	0	0
snapshots	4	.2571	.2540	34.0	0	1	0	1	0	1	1	0	1	2	1	0	0	0	0	0	0	0	0	0	0	0	0	0	0
snare	26	.4836	2.6332	44.2	2	3	1	4	9	6	1	0	2	1	1	4	0	1	0	0	14	0	0	0	2	0	1	0	0
snares	8	.4955	.8405	39.2	2	0	0	3	3	0	0	0	1	0	0	0	0	0	0	0	1	0	0	0	3	0	2	1	0

9Q Smith-Hughes
4D smiths
5A Smithy
8A Smitty
9L smocked
7Q smog-free
6R smog-shrouded
3F smoggy
7R Smoggy
7P Smoke
3D SMOKE
XR smoke-blackened
8D smoke-curl
8D smoke-infested
8B smoke-jumper
4D smoke-like
8D smoke-wreathed
XR Smoked
7R smoked-pork-rib
8F smokehole
8F smokeholes
4A smokehouses
7A smokelike
4F Smokes
3P smokier
7A smokin'
6F Smoking
7N smoking-den
7R smolts
6A Smooth
6A smooth-looking
7M smooth-textured
4N smooth-tongued
6N Smoothfield
7M Smoothing
7R smoothworking
7N smouldering
8D Smug
7F Smyrna
7H Sn
5A snagging
6N Snail
7H snail-like
7D snail-paced
7D snaith
6A snake-charmer
7A snake-fish
7Q snake-free
3H snakes'
5N snaking
3A snaky
7J snap-clap-pat-stamp
7J snap-clap-stamp
9H snapdragon
7N snapdragons
7R snappily
7R snapping-back
7J snapping-clapping
7J snapping-clapping-thigh
7D snaring

Word Type	F	D	U	SFI	3 Gr 3	4 Gr 4	5 Gr 5	6 Gr 6	7 Gr 7	8 Gr 8	9 Gr 9	X UnGr	A Read	B Eng & Gr	C Comp	D Lit	E Math	F Soc Stud	G Spell	H Sci	J Music	K Art	L Home Ec	M Shop	N Lib F	P Lib NF	Q Lib Ref	R Mag	S Rel
snarl	15	.4978	1.7052	42.3	3	1	4	2	4	1	0	0	9	0	1	1	0	0	0	0	0	0	0	0	3	1	0	0	0
snarled	37	.7535	5.6883	47.5	6	3	3	5	11	3	5	1	12	4	1	3	0	1	0	1	1	0	0	0	5	4	0	5	0
snarling	20	.5617	2.4144	43.8	5	4	0	0	10	1	0	0	7	0	0	3	0	0	0	0	1	0	0	0	6	2	0	1	0
snarls	3	.3764	.2483	33.9	0	1	0	0	1	0	0	1	0	0	0	0	0	0	0	1	0	0	0	0	0	0	1	1	0
snatch	11	.5610	1.2918	41.1	2	2	2	2	2	0	1	0	2	0	1	1	0	0	0	0	2	0	0	0	3	0	0	2	0
snatched	34	.5075	3.8239	45.8	9	2	4	7	6	3	2	1	14	1	0	7	0	0	0	1	0	0	0	0	9	2	0	0	0
snatches	5	.3228	.4034	36.1	1	0	0	0	0	2	2	0	2	0	0	2	0	0	0	0	0	0	0	0	0	1	0	0	0
snatching	4	.3715	.3204	35.1	0	1	1	2	0	0	0	0	0	1	0	1	0	0	0	0	0	0	0	0	2	0	0	0	0
SNCC	7	.0000	.0851	29.3	0	0	0	0	0	7	0	0	0	0	0	0	0	0	0	0	0	0	0	0	0	0	0	7	0
Snead	2	.2412	.1141	30.6	0	0	0	0	1	0	1	0	0	1	0	0	0	0	0	0	0	0	0	0	0	1	0	0	0
sneak	25	.6984	3.5631	45.5	2	2	3	2	7	3	4	2	4	1	1	6	0	0	0	2	0	0	0	0	3	3	1	4	0
sneaked	8	.4993	.8525	39.3	1	3	0	1	1	1	1	0	1	2	0	0	0	0	0	0	0	0	0	0	1	3	0	1	0
sneakers	16	.5382	1.8745	42.7	2	3	5	1	3	2	0	0	6	0	0	0	0	0	0	0	1	0	0	0	3	2	0	4	0
sneaking	11	.5899	1.3715	41.4	1	2	2	0	2	2	2	0	3	1	0	1	0	0	0	0	0	0	0	0	3	2	0	1	0
Sneed	2	.2412	.1091	30.4	0	0	0	0	0	2	0	0	0	0	0	1	0	0	1	0	0	0	0	0	0	0	0	0	0
Sneem	2	.0000	.0243	23.9	0	0	0	0	0	2	0	0	0	0	0	0	0	0	0	0	0	0	0	0	0	0	0	2	0
sneer	5	.4751	.5316	37.3	0	0	0	1	4	0	0	0	2	1	0	1	0	0	0	0	0	0	0	0	0	0	1	0	0
sneered	11	.5201	1.2519	41.0	1	0	1	1	4	2	1	1	4	0	0	2	0	0	0	0	0	0	0	0	3	1	0	1	0
sneering	2	.0000	.0215	23.3	0	0	0	0	1	1	0	0	0	0	0	2	0	0	0	0	0	0	0	0	0	0	0	0	0
sneeringly	2	.1717	.1142	30.6	0	0	0	0	2	0	0	0	1	0	0	1	0	0	0	0	0	0	0	0	0	0	0	0	0
sneeze	35	.6385	4.7673	46.8	9	7	1	4	11	2	1	0	18	0	2	1	0	0	0	5	3	0	0	0	1	3	0	2	0
sneezed	18	.4884	1.9706	42.9	8	2	1	6	1	0	0	0	8	0	0	1	0	0	0	0	2	0	0	0	6	0	0	1	0
sneezes	4	.3470	.3506	35.4	0	1	0	1	2	0	0	0	2	0	0	0	0	0	0	1	1	0	0	0	0	0	0	0	0
sneezing	11	.4823	1.1596	40.6	1	2	2	3	2	0	1	0	2	0	1	0	0	0	0	5	0	0	0	0	2	0	1	0	0
Snick	12	.1989	.7691	38.9	7	0	0	0	0	0	5	0	7	5	0	0	0	0	0	0	0	0	0	0	0	0	0	0	0
snicker	5	.1634	.2733	34.4	2	1	0	0	2	0	0	0	2	0	0	0	0	0	0	0	0	0	0	0	0	3	0	0	0
snickered	5	.3330	.4105	36.1	1	0	1	0	1	2	0	0	2	2	0	0	0	0	0	0	0	0	0	0	1	0	0	0	0
sniff	30	.3500	2.7158	44.3	10	7	4	1	8	0	0	0	19	0	0	1	0	0	0	1	0	0	0	0	9	0	0	0	0
sniffed	63	.6005	8.2016	49.1	21	15	6	8	6	6	0	1	34	1	0	7	0	1	0	0	0	0	0	0	8	9	0	3	0
sniffing	31	.5088	3.6073	45.6	6	12	5	4	1	3	0	0	20	1	1	0	0	0	0	0	0	0	0	0	7	0	0	2	0
sniffle	2	.0000	.0215	23.3	0	0	0	0	0	0	2	0	0	0	0	2	0	0	0	0	0	0	0	0	0	0	0	0	0
sniffled	5	.3833	.4767	36.8	3	1	0	0	0	0	1	0	3	0	0	1	0	0	0	0	0	0	0	0	0	1	0	0	0
sniffles	10	.3712	.9514	39.8	4	0	0	0	1	2	3	0	7	0	0	2	0	0	0	0	0	0	0	0	1	0	0	0	0
sniffling	3	.0000	.1370	31.4	1	0	0	1	0	0	1	0	3	0	0	0	0	0	0	0	0	0	0	0	0	0	0	0	0
sniffs	7	.2088	.5197	37.2	3	1	1	1	0	0	0	1	6	0	0	0	0	0	0	1	0	0	0	0	0	0	0	0	0
Sniggers	6	.0000	.2741	34.4	0	0	0	0	0	6	0	0	6	0	0	0	0	0	0	0	0	0	0	0	0	0	0	0	0
snip	14	.4719	1.4807	41.7	7	2	0	4	1	0	0	0	5	0	1	0	0	0	1	1	0	0	0	0	0	6	0	0	0
snipe	2	.2437	.1129	30.5	0	0	0	0	1	0	0	1	0	0	0	0	0	0	0	0	0	0	0	0	0	0	1	1	0
Snipe	2	.0000	.0215	23.3	0	0	0	0	0	0	2	0	0	0	0	2	0	0	0	0	0	0	0	0	0	0	0	0	0
Snipkin	3	.0000	.0328	25.2	3	0	0	0	0	0	0	0	0	3	0	0	0	0	0	0	0	0	0	0	0	0	0	0	0
snipped	4	.2393	.3005	34.8	2	1	0	0	0	0	1	0	3	0	0	1	0	0	0	0	0	0	0	0	0	0	0	0	0
snips	13	.3820	1.0553	40.2	0	0	1	0	9	0	2	1	0	0	0	0	0	0	0	0	0	1	0	2	0	0	0	10	0
snobbish	4	.3141	.3005	34.8	1	0	0	0	1	2	0	0	1	0	0	0	0	0	0	0	1	0	0	0	0	0	0	2	0
snobs	2	.2305	.1080	30.3	0	0	0	0	0	1	0	1	0	0	0	0	0	0	1	0	0	0	0	0	0	1	0	0	0
Snoodie	3	.0000	.0352	25.5	0	0	0	3	0	0	0	0	0	0	0	0	0	0	0	0	0	0	0	0	3	0	0	0	0
Snooky	10	.0000	.4568	36.6	0	10	0	0	0	0	0	0	10	0	0	0	0	0	0	0	0	0	0	0	0	0	0	0	0
Snooper	2	.0000	.0914	29.6	0	0	2	0	0	0	0	0	2	0	0	0	0	0	0	0	0	0	0	0	0	0	0	0	0
Snoopy	9	.0000	.4111	36.1	9	0	0	0	0	0	0	0	9	0	0	0	0	0	0	0	0	0	0	0	0	0	0	0	0
snooze	4	.0000	.1827	32.6	1	1	0	1	1	0	0	0	4	0	0	0	0	0	0	0	0	0	0	0	0	0	0	0	0
snoozing	4	.4526	.3993	36.0	1	1	1	0	0	1	0	0	1	1	0	1	0	0	0	0	0	0	0	0	0	0	0	1	0
snore	8	.5662	.9902	40.0	2	1	3	1	1	0	0	0	4	1	0	1	0	0	0	0	0	0	0	0	1	1	0	0	0
snored	3	.2279	.2143	33.3	1	1	0	0	1	0	0	0	2	0	0	0	0	0	0	0	0	0	0	0	0	0	0	1	0
snoring	15	.4319	1.4696	41.7	2	1	1	5	4	1	1	0	6	0	3	1	0	0	0	0	2	0	0	0	1	1	0	1	0
snorkel	7	.3596	.6018	37.8	1	0	3	2	0	1	0	0	2	0	1	0	0	0	0	3	0	0	0	0	0	1	0	0	0
snorkels	3	.1930	.1642	32.2	1	0	0	1	0	1	0	0	1	0	1	0	0	0	0	0	0	0	0	0	0	1	0	0	0
snort	14	.4591	1.4146	41.5	1	7	2	1	1	2	0	0	4	0	0	0	0	0	2	0	5	0	0	0	1	2	0	0	0
snorted	42	.4344	4.2435	46.3	6	6	4	7	18	0	1	0	20	0	0	9	0	0	0	0	0	0	0	0	11	0	0	2	0
snorting	15	.3431	1.3089	41.2	1	6	1	0	4	3	0	0	8	0	0	0	0	0	0	0	0	0	0	0	5	2	0	0	0
snorts	4	.1948	.2500	34.0	1	0	0	2	1	0	0	0	2	0	0	0	0	0	0	0	0	0	0	0	0	2	0	0	0
snout	24	.6051	3.1524	45.0	6	4	2	2	7	1	1	1	14	1	0	2	0	0	0	0	0	0	0	0	2	2	3	0	0
snouts	6	.3501	.5265	37.2	3	0	1	0	2	0	0	0	3	0	0	0	0	0	0	0	0	0	0	0	2	1	0	0	0
snow	948	.8863	168.09	62.3	224	209	133	152	109	58	55	8	395	47	10	67	9	114	11	126	15	3	4	0	43	55	25	24	0
Snow	12	.5330	1.3667	41.4	1	2	4	1	0	2	0	2	3	0	0	3	0	1	0	0	1	1	0	0	0	0	0	3	0
Snow-White	3	.0000	.1370	31.4	3	0	0	0	0	0	0	0	3	0	0	0	0	0	0	0	0	0	0	0	0	0	0	0	0
snow-capped	17	.5192	1.9628	42.9	3	1	3	3	5	1	1	0	7	0	0	0	0	5	0	0	0	0	0	0	1	1	3	0	0
snow-clad	2	.2285	.1129	30.5	0	0	0	0	1	1	0	0	0	0	0	0	0	1	0	0	0	0	0	0	0	0	1	0	0
snow-covered	21	.4641	2.2329	43.5	4	5	3	4	4	1	0	0	8	0	0	1	0	10	0	0	0	0	0	0	1	0	1	0	0
snow-topped	2	.2427	.1152	30.6	1	0	0	1	0	0	0	0	0	0	0	0	0	0	0	0	0	0	0	0	1	1	0	0	0
snow-white	5	.4190	.4648	36.7	1	0	3	0	1	0	0	0	1	2	0	0	0	0	0	0	0	0	0	0	1	0	0	1	0
snow's	2	.0000	.0914	29.6	0	0	0	2	0	0	0	0	2	0	0	0	0	0	0	0	0	0	0	0	0	0	0	0	0
Snow's	2	.0000	.0243	23.9	0	0	0	0	0	1	0	1	0	0	0	0	0	0	0	0	0	0	0	0	0	0	0	2	0
snowball	14	.3419	1.2172	40.9	1	4	1	6	2	0	0	0	6	0	0	0	0	0	1	7	0	0	0	0	0	0	0	0	0
Snowball	5	.3560	.3924	35.9	0	3	0	0	0	1	1	0	0	1	0	0	0	0	0	0	0	0	0	0	1	3	0	0	0
Snowball's	3	.2120	.1548	31.9	0	1	0	0	0	0	2	0	0	0	0	0	0	0	0	0	0	0	0	0	2	1	0	0	0
snowballs	6	.3716	.5493	37.4	4	0	0	1	1	0	0	0	3	1	0	0	0	0	0	0	0	0	0	0	0	2	0	0	0
snowbanks	3	.1930	.1642	32.2	0	2	0	0	1	0	0	0	1	0	1	0	0	0	0	0	0	0	0	0	0	1	0	0	0
snowbound	3	.2435	.2274	33.6	0	1	1	0	0	1	0	0	2	0	0	0	0	1	0	0	0	0	0	0	0	0	0	0	0
snowcapped	4	.2352	.2332	33.7	0	0	1	1	1	0	1	0	0	0	0	0	0	2	0	0	0	0	0	0	0	0	0	2	0
Snowden	2	.0000	.0914	29.6	0	0	0	0	2	0	0	0	2	0	0	0	0	0	0	0	0	0	0	0	0	0	0	0	0
snowdrift	6	.3734	.5631	37.5	0	2	0	2	0	2	0	0	3	0	0	0	0	1	0	2	0	0	0	0	0	0	0	0	0
snowdrifts	8	.4760	.8923	39.5	1	2	2	1	2	0	0	0	5	0	0	0	0	0	0	1	0	0	0	0	0	1	0	1	0
snowdrops	2	.2160	.1362	31.3	0	0	0	1	1	0	0	0	1	0	0	0	0	0	0	1	0	0	0	0	0	0	0	0	0
snowed	16	.4694	1.7161	42.3	11	1	1	1	0	1	0	1	8	0	0	1	0	0	0	1	4	0	0	0	0	0	0	2	0
snowfall	17	.5563	2.0483	43.1	2	3	3	1	5	0	3	0	5	0	0	1	0	7	0	1	0	0	0	0	0	0	2	1	0
snowflake	6	.4713	.6085	37.8	0	1	2	0	0	2	1	0	0	1	0	0	2	1	0	2	0	0	0	0	0	0	0	0	0
snowflakes	24	.6587	3.3098	45.2	14	4	0	3	1	2	0	0	7	0	0	1	0	1	0	8	1	0	0	0	1	4	1	0	0
snowing	18	.5906	2.2945	43.6	8	3	2	2	1	1	1	0	7	0	0	0	0	1	0	5	1	0	0	0	0	3	0	1	0
snowman	14	.4481	1.3744	41.4	7	1	0	1	1	4	0	0	3	7	1	0	0	0	0	0	0	0	0	0	1	2	0	0	0
snowmen	2	.2152	.1357	31.3	1	0	0	0	1	0	0	0	1	0	0	0	0	1	0	0	0	0	0	0	0	0	0	0	0
snowmobile	7	.0000	.0851	29.3	0	0	0	0	7	0	0	0	0	0	0	0	0	0	0	0	0	0	0	0	0	0	0	7	0
snowmobiler	2	.0000	.0243	23.9	0	0	0	0	2	0	0	0	0	0	0	0	0	0	0	0	0	0	0	0	0	0	0	2	0
snowplow	6	.3281	.5066	37.0	4	1	0	1	0	0	0	0	3	0	0	2	0	0	0	1	0	0	0	0	0	0	0	0	0
snowplows	2	.2306	.1140	30.6	1	0	0	0	0	0	1	0	0	1	0	0	0	1	0	0	0	0	0	0	0	0	0	0	0
snows	29	.6430	3.9310	45.9	9	7	6	2	1	2	1	1	10	0	0	0	0	4	0	3	2	0	0	0	2	7	0	1	0

6J snaw
9R snazzy
3N sneakin'
8A sneaks
3B sneaky
7D sneerified-like
5A sneers
9B snick
5A Snickasee
5K snicker-snack
8N snickering
XH sniffish
3N sniffly
6A sniffy
9D sniggering
9D snipers
8F snipers'
7N snipping
3N Snipps
7D sniveling
8R snobbism
9B Snood
7A snoofed
6B snoofing
4A Snooky's
8A snooper
6A snooping
5A snoozed
5B snoozes
9Q Snoqualmie
8P snorers
4P snores
8A snorin'
7Q snorkeling
9D SNOUT
4F Snow-Hut
4F snow-bound
7Q snow-choked
6A snow-flakes
3P snow-hidden
6A snow-hung
9D Snow-on-the-Mountain
3J snow-sea's
3A snow-suited
6P snow-wrapped
3J snow-wreaths
4G snowbank
4A Snowbird
4A Snowbird's
5A snowbirds
5F snowclad
5F snowcovered
7A Snowden's
7R Snowdon
7D snowdraped
5B snowfalls
7Q snowfields
3J snowhouse
7F snowless
7A Snowman

Word Type	F	D	U	SFI	3 Gr 3	4 Gr 4	5 Gr 5	6 Gr 6	7 Gr 7	8 Gr 8	9 Gr 9	X UnGr	A Read	B Eng & Gr	C Comp	D Lit	E Math	F Soc Stud	G Spell	H Sci	J Music	K Art	L Home Ec	M Shop	N Lib F	P Lib NF	Q Lib Ref	R Mag	S Rel
snowshoe	4	.3710	.3211	35.1	0	0	0	1	1	0	0	2	0	1	0	0	0	0	0	0	0	0	0	0	1	0	0	2	0
Snowshoe	6	.0000	.2741	34.4	0	5	0	1	0	0	0	0	6	0	0	0	0	0	0	0	0	0	0	0	0	0	0	0	0
snowshoes	18	.5059	2.1154	43.3	1	8	2	0	6	0	0	1	13	0	0	1	0	1	0	0	0	0	0	0	2	0	0	1	0
snowstorm	22	.6238	2.9132	44.6	6	3	5	3	3	0	2	0	9	1	2	1	0	4	0	1	0	1	0	0	0	1	0	2	0
snowstorms	6	.4694	.6407	38.1	1	0	3	1	1	0	0	0	2	0	0	0	0	2	0	1	0	0	0	0	0	1	0	0	0
snowy	56	.6940	8.1405	49.1	14	12	6	11	7	2	3	1	26	2	0	6	0	12	2	3	0	0	0	0	1	1	0	3	0
Snowy	6	.2408	.3612	35.6	0	0	6	0	0	0	0	0	0	0	0	0	0	3	0	0	0	0	0	0	0	3	0	0	0
snub	2	.2427	.1152	30.6	0	1	0	1	0	0	0	0	0	0	0	0	0	0	0	0	0	0	0	0	1	1	0	0	0
snuff	10	.4183	.9256	39.7	0	3	0	2	3	0	1	1	2	0	0	2	0	0	0	0	0	0	0	0	2	0	4	0	0
snuff-box	2	.1717	.1142	30.6	1	0	0	0	0	1	0	0	1	0	0	1	0	0	0	0	0	0	0	0	0	0	0	0	0
snuffed	8	.5074	.8816	39.5	0	2	0	4	0	1	1	0	2	0	0	2	0	1	0	0	0	0	0	0	2	1	0	0	0
snuffle	2	.1948	.1250	31.0	1	1	0	0	0	0	0	0	1	0	0	0	0	0	0	0	0	0	0	0	0	1	0	0	0
snuffled	3	.0000	.1370	31.4	1	2	0	0	0	0	0	0	3	0	0	0	0	0	0	0	0	0	0	0	0	0	0	0	0
snuffling	3	.2357	.2199	33.4	1	1	0	1	0	0	0	0	2	0	0	0	0	0	0	0	0	0	0	0	0	1	0	0	0
snug	30	.6084	3.8842	45.9	8	6	5	2	4	3	2	0	12	1	0	1	0	0	0	1	0	0	2	0	8	4	0	1	0
snuggle	3	.2357	.2199	33.4	2	0	0	0	1	0	0	0	2	0	0	0	0	0	0	0	0	0	0	0	0	1	0	0	0
snuggled	12	.4638	1.2809	41.1	2	4	2	1	3	0	0	0	6	0	0	1	0	0	0	0	0	0	0	0	3	2	0	0	0
snuggling	3	.2468	.1912	32.8	0	1	1	0	0	0	1	0	1	0	0	0	0	0	0	0	0	0	1	0	1	0	0	0	0
snugly	14	.5176	1.6128	42.1	1	3	1	3	0	0	1	5	6	0	0	0	0	0	0	3	0	0	0	1	0	3	0	1	0
Snyder	3	.3847	.2490	34.0	0	0	0	1	0	0	2	0	0	1	0	1	0	0	0	0	0	0	0	0	0	1	0	0	0
so	11543	.9794	2227.1	73.5	1996	1957	1327	1665	2090	1211	1007	290	3443	454	99	958	530	910	207	915	359	85	166	106	1111	1122	415	651	12
So	5	.4699	.4937	36.9	0	0	1	0	2	0	1	1	0	1	0	1	0	0	0	0	0	0	0	0	0	1	0	2	0
so-called	61	.6748	8.4090	49.2	1	2	7	6	23	7	12	3	6	1	0	0	1	5	1	8	3	0	0	1	1	4	23	7	0
so's	10	.4736	1.1181	40.5	1	2	0	3	4	0	0	0	7	1	0	1	0	0	0	0	0	0	0	0	0	1	0	0	0
soak	29	.5439	3.3716	45.3	7	7	3	3	3	3	2	1	5	1	0	0	0	4	0	11	0	0	4	0	0	1	1	2	0
soaked	43	.7588	6.6176	48.2	3	6	6	9	8	3	6	2	10	2	2	1	0	2	0	7	1	0	5	1	4	5	1	2	0
soaking	22	.6249	2.8169	44.5	2	6	5	2	4	1	1	1	1	3	0	0	0	1	0	2	0	0	2	0	4	3	0	6	0
soaks	16	.4041	1.4659	41.7	2	4	6	0	0	2	1	1	1	0	0	0	0	3	0	10	0	0	0	0	0	1	0	1	0
Soames	2	.0000	.0243	23.9	0	0	0	0	0	0	2	0	0	0	0	0	0	0	0	0	0	0	0	0	0	0	0	2	0
soap	134	.8179	22.229	53.5	21	30	23	9	10	33	8	0	58	1	2	1	4	5	5	31	0	0	3	0	5	9	4	6	0
Soap	9	.1513	.3540	35.5	9	0	0	0	0	0	0	0	0	0	0	0	0	0	0	0	1	0	0	0	8	0	0	0	0
soaped	2	.0000	.0914	29.6	0	0	2	0	0	0	0	0	2	0	0	0	0	0	0	0	0	0	0	0	0	0	0	0	0
soapless	4	.0000	.0789	29.0	0	0	0	0	0	0	4	0	0	0	0	0	0	0	0	4	0	0	0	0	0	0	0	0	0
soaps	12	.3768	1.0200	40.1	0	0	0	1	2	2	7	0	1	0	0	0	0	0	0	7	0	0	2	0	0	0	2	0	0
soapsuds	2	.1160	.0650	28.1	0	0	0	0	0	2	0	0	0	0	1	0	0	0	0	1	0	0	0	0	0	0	0	0	0
soapy	8	.2949	.5647	37.5	1	0	0	0	1	5	1	0	2	1	0	0	0	0	0	1	0	0	3	0	1	0	0	0	0
soar	19	.6243	2.5021	44.0	2	6	4	2	3	1	0	1	6	1	0	0	0	0	1	4	1	0	0	0	0	1	0	5	0
soared	29	.6679	4.0889	46.1	2	7	3	5	5	2	4	1	15	3	0	4	0	1	0	0	0	0	0	0	2	1	2	1	0
soaring	31	.6379	4.1530	46.2	2	1	6	5	6	3	4	4	11	0	1	2	0	1	0	0	0	0	0	0	1	2	4	9	0
soars	5	.5242	.5601	37.5	0	1	3	0	0	0	1	0	1	1	0	0	0	1	0	0	1	0	0	0	0	0	1	0	0
sob	15	.5054	1.6954	42.3	3	2	0	4	3	1	1	1	7	0	0	4	0	0	0	0	0	0	0	0	1	2	0	1	0
SOB'S	2	.0000	.0243	23.9	0	0	2	0	0	0	0	0	0	0	0	0	0	0	0	0	0	0	0	0	0	0	0	2	0
sobbed	20	.5683	2.4798	43.9	7	3	1	6	2	1	0	0	10	0	0	2	0	0	0	0	1	0	0	0	5	1	1	0	0
sobbing	23	.6621	3.1643	45.0	2	7	1	2	6	4	1	0	7	2	1	3	0	0	0	0	0	0	0	0	3	5	0	2	0
sober	24	.5681	2.8304	44.5	1	2	1	3	9	4	4	0	2	1	0	7	0	1	1	0	0	0	0	0	8	1	0	3	0
soberly	8	.6263	1.0615	40.3	1	1	0	2	2	1	1	0	3	1	0	0	0	1	0	0	0	0	0	0	1	1	0	1	0
sobriquet	3	.3847	.2496	34.0	0	0	1	0	0	1	0	1	0	0	0	0	0	0	0	0	0	0	0	0	0	1	1	1	0
sobs	22	.5121	2.5048	44.0	1	4	0	8	5	2	2	0	10	0	0	5	0	0	0	0	0	0	0	0	4	1	0	2	0
soccer	11	.6278	1.4399	41.6	2	2	1	0	4	1	1	0	2	1	0	0	0	2	0	1	0	0	0	0	0	1	1	3	0
Soccer	2	.0000	.0394	26.0	0	0	0	2	0	0	0	0	0	0	0	0	0	0	0	2	0	0	0	0	0	0	0	0	0
sociability	2	.2441	.1127	30.5	0	1	0	0	1	0	0	0	0	0	0	0	0	0	0	0	0	0	0	0	1	0	1	0	0
sociable	7	.3889	.5950	37.7	0	1	0	0	4	1	1	0	1	0	0	1	0	0	0	0	0	0	2	0	0	1	2	0	0
Sociable	2	.2407	.1090	30.4	0	0	0	0	1	0	1	0	0	1	0	0	0	0	0	0	1	0	0	0	0	0	0	0	0
social	272	.8249	44.838	56.5	11	4	55	13	87	41	48	13	25	25	0	2	4	31	4	19	13	2	8	2	4	27	64	42	0
Social	17	.5035	1.8468	42.7	1	0	2	1	4	4	5	0	3	1	0	0	0	5	0	0	0	0	0	0	1	0	6	1	0
socialism	8	.3359	.5979	37.8	0	0	0	0	1	3	4	0	0	0	0	0	0	2	0	0	0	0	0	0	0	0	4	2	0
socialist	5	.3687	.4014	36.0	0	0	2	0	0	2	0	1	0	0	0	0	0	0	0	0	0	0	0	0	0	2	2	1	0
Socialist	9	.3144	.6314	38.0	0	0	0	2	1	5	1	0	0	0	0	0	0	1	0	0	0	0	0	0	0	0	4	4	0
socially	18	.5247	1.9849	43.0	0	0	6	2	3	1	6	0	0	3	0	0	0	0	0	7	0	0	0	0	0	2	1	5	0
societies	49	.6519	6.5528	48.2	2	0	11	1	19	9	2	5	4	5	0	0	0	5	0	7	3	0	0	0	0	6	14	5	0
Societies	3	.3783	.2509	34.0	0	0	2	0	0	0	1	0	0	1	0	0	0	1	0	0	0	0	0	0	0	1	0	0	0
society	176	.8454	29.636	54.7	5	6	23	9	51	41	30	11	8	7	2	3	2	33	4	6	10	2	1	1	5	24	36	32	0
Society	70	.7062	10.088	50.0	7	5	16	12	12	8	10	0	11	0	0	1	0	10	0	2	3	0	0	1	11	10	17	4	0
society's	2	.2437	.1129	30.5	0	1	0	0	1	0	0	0	0	0	0	0	0	0	0	0	0	0	0	0	0	0	1	1	0
sociologist	2	.0000	.0243	23.9	0	0	0	0	1	0	0	1	0	0	0	0	0	0	0	0	0	0	0	0	0	0	0	2	0
sociologists	3	.2054	.1422	31.5	0	0	0	0	1	1	1	0	0	0	1	0	0	0	0	0	0	0	0	0	0	0	0	2	0
sociology	7	.5075	.7435	38.7	0	0	1	0	3	1	1	1	0	1	0	0	1	1	0	0	0	0	0	0	0	0	1	3	0
sock	28	.4937	2.9896	44.8	2	12	4	1	1	6	1	1	7	0	0	1	0	5	4	0	0	0	6	0	2	0	0	3	0
socked	3	.1277	.1363	31.3	0	0	1	1	0	0	0	1	1	0	0	0	0	0	0	0	0	0	0	0	0	0	0	2	0
socket	19	.6262	2.4574	43.9	3	0	7	1	4	4	0	0	2	0	1	0	0	2	0	8	0	1	3	1	0	1	0	0	0
sockets	11	.5659	1.2913	41.1	2	2	0	0	1	2	2	2	1	2	0	2	0	0	0	0	0	0	0	1	0	2	0	3	0
socks	73	.7125	10.767	50.3	34	6	6	9	3	3	8	4	29	0	0	0	2	4	1	8	1	0	6	0	7	5	2	8	0
Socks	5	.0756	.1562	31.9	1	0	0	0	2	2	0	0	1	0	0	4	0	0	0	0	0	0	0	0	0	0	0	0	0
Socrates	9	.3961	.7858	39.0	0	0	0	5	1	2	0	1	0	0	0	0	0	6	0	0	0	1	0	0	0	0	1	1	0
Socrates'	3	.0000	.0583	27.7	0	0	0	3	0	0	0	0	0	0	0	0	0	3	0	0	0	0	0	0	0	0	0	0	0
sod	27	.7224	3.9788	46.0	4	4	4	4	7	3	1	0	6	4	0	4	0	3	0	0	3	0	0	0	2	1	3	1	0
soda	112	.7210	16.496	52.2	21	12	9	15	17	19	17	2	19	3	1	3	12	6	4	39	0	0	11	0	4	7	1	2	0
Soda	2	.2420	.1154	30.6	0	0	0	1	1	0	0	0	0	0	0	0	1	0	0	0	0	0	0	0	1	0	0	0	0
SODA	3	.0000	.0322	25.1	0	0	0	0	3	0	0	0	0	0	0	3	0	0	0	0	0	0	0	0	0	0	0	0	0
soda-water	3	.0000	.1370	31.4	0	0	0	0	3	0	0	0	3	0	0	0	0	0	0	0	0	0	0	0	0	0	0	0	0
sodas	5	.4131	.4612	36.6	0	1	0	1	0	2	1	0	1	2	0	0	0	0	0	0	0	0	0	0	0	1	0	1	0
sodden	4	.3097	.2992	34.8	0	0	0	1	2	1	0	0	1	0	0	1	0	0	0	0	0	0	0	0	0	0	0	2	0
sodium	73	.4644	7.3620	48.7	5	5	20	9	2	7	23	2	1	0	0	0	1	1	1	50	0	0	0	0	0	6	7	6	0
sofa	37	.7464	5.6740	47.5	7	8	7	7	6	1	1	0	16	3	1	1	0	3	2	0	0	0	0	2	4	4	0	1	0
sofas	2	.0857	.0784	28.9	0	0	0	1	1	0	0	0	1	0	0	0	0	0	0	0	0	0	1	0	0	0	0	0	0
Sofia	5	.2447	.2801	34.5	0	0	0	2	0	2	0	1	0	0	0	0	0	0	0	0	2	0	0	0	0	0	0	3	0
soft	669	.8888	118.44	60.7	145	111	56	74	156	52	67	8	192	20	6	49	0	25	31	95	33	18	37	23	39	57	20	24	0
Soft	6	.2401	.3156	35.0	0	0	0	0	1	1	4	0	0	0	1	0	0	0	0	0	5	0	0	0	0	0	0	0	0
soft-bodied	7	.2844	.4888	36.9	0	0	0	0	6	0	1	0	1	0	0	0	0	0	0	3	0	0	0	0	0	0	3	0	0
soft-boiled	2	.1787	.1174	30.7	1	0	0	0	1	0	0	0	1	0	0	0	0	0	0	0	0	0	0	0	1	0	0	0	0
soft-shelled	3	.2197	.2090	33.2	0	0	0	0	3	0	0	0	2	0	0	0	0	0	0	0	0	0	0	0	0	0	1	0	0
soft-spoken	5	.4241	.4715	36.7	0	1	0	2	1	0	1	0	1	0	0	1	0	0	0	0	0	0	0	0	0	1	0	2	0
softball	6	.3131	.4579	36.6	0	3	0	2	0	1	0	0	1	0	0	0	0	0	0	3	0	0	0	0	0	0	0	2	0

5A snowslide
7Q snowslides
5D snubbed
5D snubbing
8D snuffbox
8Q snuffboxes
5N snuffing
3P snuffs
9D SNUG
7A snuggles
6A so-and-so's
5G so-ber
9B so-o-o-o
9D so'm
5P Soaks
7P soap-box
3R soap-bubble
6E soapcakes
8H soapflakes
7A soapmaker
6A soapmaking
9Q soapweed
3P soarers
5A Soaring
6R sober-eyed
4A Sobersides
3A Sobo
4G socc
8R soccer-style
8D socialist-hated
8F socialistic
7D socialite
9A socialized
8Q Socinian
7R sociological
5A socker
7Q sockeye
8A Socony
5Q Socotra
5J sod-buster
3A sod-covered
3N soda-pop
5F sodbusters
5N sodded
5Q sodium-aluminum
7A sods
4F soe
7A sof'
7R sofa-bed
7A Sofie
9B soft-and-white
4F soft-coal
3Q soft-cushioned
6A soft-drink
7N soft-eyed
3A soft-feeling
7A soft-footed
9F soft-goods
3A soft-hearted
7D soft-like
4J soft-loud
3R soft-ly
7A soft-nosed
7R soft-pedaled
7Q soft-shells
8A soft-soap
9M soft-soldered
9M soft-soldering
7N soft-tanned
6E Softball

Word Type	F	D	U	SFI	3 Gr 3	4 Gr 4	5 Gr 5	6 Gr 6	7 Gr 7	8 Gr 8	9 Gr 9	X UnGr	A Read	B Eng & Gr	C Comp	D Lit	E Math	F Soc Stud	G Spell	H Sci	J Music	K Art	L Home Ec	M Shop	N Lib F	P Lib NF	Q Lib Ref	R Mag	S Rel
soften	23	.6508	3.0765	44.9	3	1	2	5	1	5	3	3	4	0	0	0	0	2	1	4	1	2	4	1	1	1	0	2	0
softened	26	.5999	3.3025	45.2	4	5	1	4	6	4	2	0	9	0	0	2	0	3	1	2	0	2	4	0	1	1	0	1	0
softeners	2	.0000	.0394	26.0	0	0	0	0	0	1	1	0	0	0	0	0	0	0	0	2	0	0	0	0	0	0	0	0	0
softening	2	.2446	.1123	30.5	0	0	0	0	1	0	1	0	0	1	0	0	0	0	0	0	0	0	0	0	0	0	1	0	0
softens	7	.3862	.5749	37.6	0	0	3	1	1	0	1	1	0	0	0	0	0	0	0	0	0	0	1	0	0	0	3	3	0
softer	58	.7508	8.7763	49.4	11	10	3	4	7	11	12	0	7	3	0	5	0	2	1	8	9	1	4	6	1	9	1	1	0
softest	4	.4730	.3990	36.0	1	1	1	0	0	0	1	0	0	0	0	0	0	0	0	1	1	0	0	0	1	0	0	1	0
Softest-Walker	4	.0000	.1827	32.6	4	0	0	0	0	0	0	0	4	0	0	0	0	0	0	0	0	0	0	0	0	0	0	0	0
softly	308	.7907	49.463	56.9	63	58	33	49	58	25	21	1	126	13	1	34	0	3	39	2	23	1	4	0	33	20	1	8	0
softness	17	.4696	1.7216	42.4	0	2	1	1	4	4	4	1	4	1	0	1	0	0	0	1	2	4	1	0	0	1	1	1	0
softwood	7	.3053	.4716	36.7	0	0	3	0	2	0	2	0	0	0	0	0	0	1	0	0	0	0	0	1	0	0	5	0	0
softwoods	3	.2053	.1597	32.0	1	0	0	0	2	0	0	0	0	0	0	0	0	0	0	1	0	0	0	0	0	2	0	0	0
soggy	16	.5950	1.9423	42.9	3	1	0	0	6	1	3	2	0	0	1	3	0	0	0	3	0	0	3	0	2	2	2	0	0
Sogne	2	.2408	.1204	30.8	0	0	1	1	0	0	0	0	0	0	0	0	0	1	0	0	0	0	0	0	0	1	0	0	0
Sohrab	7	.0000	.1013	30.1	0	0	0	0	7	0	0	0	0	0	0	0	0	0	0	0	0	0	0	0	0	7	0	0	0
soil	921	.6654	126.31	61.0	277	140	130	99	99	76	60	40	40	4	0	0	0	234	8	467	0	1	10	1	9	40	63	43	1
Soil	8	.1340	.3470	35.4	0	0	0	1	0	1	0	6	0	0	0	0	0	1	0	7	0	0	0	0	0	0	0	0	0
soiled	11	.2678	.7157	38.5	0	2	0	1	2	5	0	1	2	0	0	0	0	0	0	3	0	0	4	0	2	0	0	0	0
soils	54	.4403	5.2331	47.2	2	3	9	8	11	5	15	1	0	0	0	0	0	25	0	22	0	0	0	0	0	1	3	3	0
Sokoto	2	.0000	.0290	24.6	0	0	2	0	0	0	0	0	0	0	0	0	0	0	0	0	0	0	0	0	0	2	0	0	0
sol	12	.1958	.5793	37.6	1	4	6	0	1	0	0	0	1	0	0	0	0	0	1	1	9	0	0	0	0	0	0	0	0
Sol	5	.1901	.2435	33.9	0	3	1	0	0	0	0	1	0	0	0	0	0	0	0	0	0	0	0	0	0	4	0	1	0
Sol-leks	5	.0000	.2284	33.6	0	0	0	0	5	0	0	0	5	0	0	0	0	0	0	0	0	0	0	0	0	0	0	0	0
solace	6	.3222	.4215	36.2	1	0	0	0	0	3	2	0	0	0	0	4	0	0	0	0	1	0	0	0	0	0	1	0	0
Solanio	9	.0000	.0966	29.8	0	0	0	0	0	0	9	0	0	0	0	9	0	0	0	0	0	0	0	0	0	0	0	0	0
solar	198	.5341	22.469	53.5	42	35	12	32	33	27	12	5	3	2	0	6	6	11	0	142	1	0	0	3	0	5	15	4	0
Solbakken	2	.0000	.0914	29.6	0	0	0	0	2	0	0	0	2	0	0	0	0	0	0	0	0	0	0	0	0	0	0	0	0
sold	477	.8502	81.325	59.1	120	88	70	58	65	33	36	7	119	10	2	13	98	118	5	13	10	0	5	3	19	32	11	19	0
solder	34	.0311	.3332	35.2	0	1	0	0	2	16	14	1	0	0	0	0	0	0	0	2	0	0	0	31	1	0	0	0	0
soldered	8	.0535	.1604	32.1	0	0	0	1	1	3	2	1	1	0	0	0	0	0	0	1	0	0	0	6	0	0	0	0	0
soldering	40	.0467	.6202	37.9	0	1	2	0	2	21	14	0	3	0	0	0	0	0	0	1	0	0	0	34	0	0	1	1	0
solders	2	.1698	.1133	30.5	1	1	0	0	0	0	0	0	1	0	0	0	0	0	0	0	0	0	0	0	0	0	1	0	0
soldier	216	.5170	24.788	53.9	45	39	22	19	39	43	8	1	97	7	2	34	1	13	4	9	9	0	0	0	8	16	6	6	4
Soldier	8	.3318	.6535	38.2	0	3	1	3	0	1	0	0	3	0	0	0	0	0	0	0	0	0	0	0	0	2	3	0	0
soldier's	12	.4732	1.3303	41.2	1	6	2	0	0	1	2	0	8	0	0	2	0	0	0	0	1	0	0	0	0	0	0	1	0
soldiering	2	.2285	.1129	30.5	0	0	0	0	0	1	1	0	0	0	0	0	0	1	0	0	0	0	0	0	0	0	1	0	0
soldiers	512	.8399	86.471	59.4	93	102	85	52	65	80	14	21	159	15	5	28	11	113	6	5	23	2	0	0	32	57	16	38	2
Soldiers	2	.2417	.1091	30.4	1	0	0	0	1	0	0	0	0	0	0	0	0	0	0	0	1	0	0	0	0	0	1	0	0
soldiers'	3	.3406	.2461	33.9	0	1	0	0	0	1	1	0	1	1	0	0	0	0	0	0	0	0	0	0	0	0	0	1	0
sole	40	.6310	5.1546	47.1	3	9	8	0	6	3	9	2	2	0	0	5	0	1	3	0	1	0	0	0	9	6	12	1	0
solely	16	.6956	2.2564	43.5	1	0	2	0	3	4	4	2	0	1	0	3	0	2	0	4	1	0	1	0	1	3	0	0	0
solemn	53	.7651	8.2585	49.2	9	4	6	9	14	3	7	1	18	3	1	5	0	2	0	0	2	0	0	0	10	4	2	6	0
solemnity	4	.3702	.3170	35.0	0	0	0	0	1	0	3	0	0	0	0	2	0	0	0	0	1	0	0	0	1	0	0	0	0
solemnly	34	.6397	4.5959	46.6	1	8	4	5	8	5	3	0	14	1	0	8	0	3	0	0	0	0	0	0	3	2	1	2	0
soles	18	.6791	2.5614	44.1	3	3	3	3	4	1	0	1	8	0	1	1	0	1	0	3	0	0	0	1	1	1	1	0	0
solicitous	2	.2401	.1133	30.5	0	0	1	0	1	0	0	0	0	0	0	0	0	0	0	0	0	0	0	0	0	1	1	0	0
solicitude	2	.0665	.0708	28.5	0	0	0	0	1	0	1	0	1	0	1	0	0	0	0	0	0	0	0	0	0	0	0	0	0
solid	390	.8436	65.797	58.2	54	68	36	32	65	47	71	17	47	3	4	12	21	20	5	151	4	9	2	16	14	34	26	22	0
Solid	2	.0000	.0394	26.0	0	2	0	0	0	0	0	0	0	0	0	0	0	0	0	2	0	0	0	0	0	0	0	0	0
solid-fuel	5	.3683	.4536	36.6	0	0	2	1	0	0	2	0	2	0	0	0	0	0	0	2	0	0	0	0	0	1	0	0	0
solidarity	4	.3863	.3414	35.3	0	0	1	1	0	1	1	0	0	0	0	0	0	2	0	0	0	0	0	0	0	0	1	1	0
solidified	5	.3691	.4157	36.2	0	0	0	0	1	0	4	0	0	0	0	0	0	0	0	3	0	0	0	0	0	1	1	0	0
solidifies	2	.2278	.1128	30.5	0	0	1	0	0	1	0	0	0	0	0	0	0	0	0	1	0	0	0	0	0	0	1	0	0
solidify	5	.2068	.2673	34.3	0	0	0	0	0	2	3	0	0	0	0	0	0	0	0	4	0	1	0	0	0	0	0	0	0
solidifying	2	.2346	.1166	30.7	0	0	0	0	1	1	0	0	0	0	0	0	0	0	0	1	0	0	0	0	0	0	0	1	0
solidity	5	.3017	.3365	35.3	0	0	0	1	3	0	0	1	0	0	0	0	0	0	0	0	0	1	0	0	0	3	0	1	0
solidly	13	.6459	1.7704	42.5	0	1	2	0	6	1	3	0	5	0	0	2	0	1	0	1	0	0	0	0	1	1	0	2	0
solids	60	.4725	6.1669	47.9	5	9	5	7	4	13	16	1	2	0	0	0	2	0	0	48	0	1	0	3	0	2	1	0	0
solidus	2	.0000	.0162	22.1	0	2	0	0	0	0	0	0	0	0	0	0	0	0	2	0	0	0	0	0	0	0	0	0	0
solitary	28	.6180	3.5963	45.6	0	4	0	8	11	2	3	0	6	1	2	4	0	0	0	1	0	0	0	0	8	0	4	2	0
Solitary	3	.2332	.1690	32.3	3	0	0	0	0	0	0	0	0	0	0	0	0	0	0	0	0	0	0	0	0	2	0	1	0
solitude	10	.4729	1.0096	40.0	0	0	1	1	3	3	1	1	1	0	0	4	0	0	0	0	0	0	0	0	0	2	1	2	0
solitudes	3	.1858	.1432	31.6	0	0	0	0	1	2	0	0	0	2	0	0	0	0	0	0	0	0	0	0	0	0	0	0	0
solo	97	.2901	6.1467	47.9	5	16	15	6	20	21	14	0	0	2	0	9	0	1	3	0	73	0	0	0	1	5	2	1	0
solo-chorus	2	.0000	.0162	22.1	1	0	1	0	0	0	0	0	0	0	0	0	0	0	0	0	2	0	0	0	0	0	0	0	0
solo-dance	2	.0000	.0215	23.3	0	0	0	0	0	0	2	0	0	0	0	2	0	0	0	0	0	0	0	0	0	0	0	0	0
soloist	5	.0000	.0404	26.1	0	0	0	1	2	2	0	0	0	0	0	0	0	0	0	0	5	0	0	0	0	0	0	0	0
soloists	4	.1534	.1534	31.9	0	0	0	1	2	1	0	0	0	0	0	0	0	0	0	0	3	0	0	0	0	1	0	0	0
Solomon	45	.3425	3.9548	46.0	1	10	4	19	5	4	2	0	24	1	0	0	0	8	0	0	0	0	0	0	2	7	2	0	1
Solomon's	7	.2445	.5383	37.3	1	3	0	3	0	0	0	0	5	0	0	0	0	2	0	0	0	0	0	0	0	0	0	0	0
Solomons	2	.2401	.1133	30.5	0	0	0	0	2	0	0	0	0	0	0	0	0	0	0	0	0	0	0	0	0	1	1	0	0
Solon	7	.4629	.6957	38.4	0	0	0	0	5	2	0	0	0	0	0	0	0	4	1	0	0	0	0	0	1	0	0	1	0
solos	10	.0336	.1805	32.6	0	1	1	2	5	1	0	0	1	0	0	0	0	0	0	0	9	0	0	0	0	0	0	0	0
solstice	2	.0000	.0243	23.9	0	0	0	0	0	0	0	2	0	0	0	0	0	0	0	0	0	0	0	0	0	0	0	2	0
solubility	26	.0896	.9160	39.6	0	0	7	0	9	1	9	0	0	0	0	0	0	0	0	25	0	0	0	0	0	0	1	0	0
soluble	21	.3852	1.7992	42.6	1	0	2	2	7	2	6	1	0	0	0	0	0	0	0	14	0	1	0	0	0	0	6	0	0
solute	4	.0000	.0789	29.0	3	0	0	0	1	0	0	0	0	0	0	0	0	0	0	4	0	0	0	0	0	0	0	0	0
solution	516	.5569	60.112	57.8	30	55	43	78	95	102	104	9	9	2	1	2	320	10	1	110	1	1	5	6	6	5	16	21	0
solutions	104	.5561	12.084	50.8	6	7	13	18	22	26	10	2	0	2	0	0	57	10	0	22	1	0	0	3	0	1	5	3	0
solve	874	.3687	72.218	58.6	119	184	152	162	96	103	46	12	32	19	3	3	696	37	8	36	1	2	0	0	3	13	8	13	0
solved	88	.8221	14.516	51.6	11	8	13	9	15	16	14	2	12	4	0	2	20	16	1	10	1	0	2	0	2	4	7	7	0
solvent	18	.2393	1.1021	40.4	3	0	0	5	3	1	5	1	0	0	0	0	0	1	0	15	0	0	0	0	0	0	2	0	0
solvents	2	.0000	.0394	26.0	0	0	0	0	0	0	2	0	0	0	0	0	0	0	0	2	0	0	0	0	0	0	0	0	0
solver	3	.2371	.1813	32.6	0	0	1	1	0	1	0	0	0	0	0	0	1	0	0	2	0	0	0	0	0	0	0	0	0
solves	6	.4749	.5957	37.8	1	0	0	1	1	2	1	0	0	0	1	0	2	0	1	1	1	0	0	0	0	0	0	0	0
solving	71	.5323	8.0215	49.0	4	10	5	5	17	19	10	1	7	3	0	1	39	0	0	11	2	0	0	0	0	1	5	2	0
Somali	4	.2281	.2337	33.7	0	0	0	4	0	0	0	0	0	0	0	0	0	3	0	0	0	0	0	0	0	0	0	1	0
Somaliland	2	.0000	.0389	25.9	0	0	0	0	2	0	0	0	0	0	0	0	0	2	0	0	0	0	0	0	0	0	0	0	0
Somalis	10	.4365	.9967	40.0	0	3	1	4	2	0	0	0	3	0	0	0	0	3	0	0	0	0	0	0	0	1	0	3	0
somatotropin	2	.0000	.0209	23.2	0	0	0	0	0	0	2	0	0	0	0	0	0	0	0	0	0	0	0	0	0	0	2	0	0
somber	14	.7001	2.0169	43.0	2	0	2	4	1	3	1	1	4	0	0	2	0	1	0	0	1	0	0	0	2	1	2	1	0
sombrero	11	.5288	1.2635	41.0	7	1	2	0	1	0	0	0	4	1	0	2	1	0	0	0	0	1	0	0	2	0	0	0	0
sombreros	4	.2386	.2998	34.8	4	0	0	0	0	0	0	0	3	0	0	0	0	0	0	0	0	0	0	0	0	0	1	0	0
some	11534	.9834	2232.7	73.5	2406	1730	1447	1473	1972	1272	956	278	2271	778	123	473	478	1587	406	1967	397	158	229	114	502	799	569	666	17
Some	9	.5681	1.0960	40.4	2	1	2	1	1	2	0	0	3	1	0	0	0	1	1	1	2	0	0	0	0	0	0	0	0

7R softface
3A softies
7P Sohrab's
6R Soichi
9L soil-
9F soil-and-climate
XH soil-and-land-capability
7Q soil-dwelling
9F soil-forming
XH soil-use
5N soil's
7A Soilers
5P sojourn
7B sojourned
4P Sol's
7A solaced
6H SOLAR
5H solar-system
9M Soldering
8J Soldier's
4P soldiers-to-be
8D Soldiers'
7N soldiership
XR soldiery
5N Sole
7Q Solecki's
9D solemnize
4N solemnized
8M solenoid
6C soliciting
9D solicitor
7D solicitously
8D solid-board
7R solid-bushed
7H solid-in-liquid
6A solid-looking
9Q solid-state
9H solidification
8G soliloquy
7J Soliloquy
6F Solis
8D Solly
8G solon
6H Solstice
9H solubilities
XP Solutrean
4P Solway
9D Solyman
5E SOM
8A som'n
7F Somalia
XQ somatic
7D somberly

Word Type	F	D	U	SFI	3 Gr 3	4 Gr 4	5 Gr 5	6 Gr 6	7 Gr 7	8 Gr 8	9 Gr 9	X UnGr	A Read	B Eng & Gr	C Comp	D Lit	E Math	F Soc Stud	G Spell	H Sci	J Music	K Art	L Home Ec	M Shop	N Lib F	P Lib NF	Q Lib Ref	R Mag	S Rel
Some-one	2	.0000	.0219	23.4	0	0	0	0	2	0	0	0	0	2	0	0	0	0	0	0	0	0	0	0	0	0	0	0	0
somebody	179	.7706	28.185	54.5	34	30	24	18	39	19	13	2	76	21	3	18	0	4	2	5	1	0	0	0	25	9	4	11	0
somebody's	17	.6380	2.2890	43.6	1	2	2	3	2	3	3	1	7	1	0	2	0	0	1	0	0	0	0	0	1	1	0	4	0
someday	132	.7003	19.196	52.8	41	25	15	21	13	10	3	4	51	5	0	6	1	12	2	8	0	1	1	1	5	14	1	24	1
somehow	159	.8257	26.498	54.2	15	24	24	31	31	19	11	4	58	4	1	12	1	10	0	12	1	1	0	0	21	16	6	16	0
someone	908	.9132	164.77	62.2	230	163	111	97	149	88	56	14	290	136	9	53	26	47	18	70	33	7	12	7	57	76	5	59	3
Someone	2	.2411	.1091	30.4	0	1	0	1	0	0	0	0	0	0	0	1	0	0	0	0	1	0	0	0	0	0	0	0	0
someone's	26	.7326	3.8625	45.9	8	2	3	2	1	3	5	2	4	1	2	3	0	2	0	2	3	0	0	0	2	3	1	3	0
someplace	7	.5026	.7499	38.8	0	1	0	0	3	1	0	2	1	0	0	2	0	0	0	0	0	0	0	0	1	1	0	2	0
somersault	9	.4935	.9592	39.8	0	3	3	0	2	1	0	0	2	0	0	3	0	0	0	0	0	0	0	0	1	1	2	0	0
somersaulting	3	.2212	.2099	33.2	1	0	0	0	2	0	0	0	2	0	0	1	0	0	0	0	0	0	0	0	0	0	0	0	0
somersaults	9	.4842	1.0002	40.0	4	1	0	1	2	1	0	0	5	1	0	1	0	0	0	0	0	0	0	0	0	2	0	0	0
Somerset	4	.4538	.4007	36.0	0	1	0	0	2	0	0	1	1	1	0	0	0	0	0	0	0	0	0	0	1	0	0	1	0
Somervell	5	.1415	.2456	33.9	0	0	0	3	0	2	0	0	2	3	0	0	0	0	0	0	0	0	0	0	0	0	0	0	0
Somerville	6	.0000	.0729	28.6	0	0	6	0	0	0	0	0	0	0	0	0	0	0	0	0	0	0	0	0	0	0	0	6	0
somethimes	2	.2404	.1142	30.6	0	0	1	1	0	0	0	0	0	1	0	0	1	0	0	0	0	0	0	0	0	0	0	0	0
somethin'	14	.4949	1.4940	41.7	0	1	1	1	4	6	1	0	3	3	0	2	0	0	0	0	0	0	0	0	5	0	0	1	0
something	2761	.9448	516.26	67.1	617	534	320	292	482	260	208	48	945	256	47	215	45	116	68	271	49	36	36	13	255	207	45	156	1
something's	10	.3419	.8849	39.5	0	1	3	2	3	1	0	0	6	0	0	0	0	0	0	0	0	0	0	0	3	1	0	0	0
somethings	2	.2160	.1362	31.3	0	1	0	0	1	0	0	0	1	0	0	0	0	0	0	1	0	0	0	0	0	0	0	0	0
sometime	56	.7988	9.0466	49.6	7	15	5	6	15	3	4	1	17	4	1	7	0	4	1	2	0	0	0	0	8	6	3	3	0
sometimes	2278	.9855	441.78	66.5	448	363	295	277	385	266	185	59	414	191	24	107	92	279	123	302	117	30	52	40	80	191	132	101	3
Sometimes	2	.0000	.0209	23.2	2	0	0	0	0	0	0	0	0	0	0	0	0	0	0	0	0	0	0	0	0	0	2	0	0
someway	5	.4190	.4648	36.7	0	1	2	0	0	0	2	0	1	2	0	0	0	0	0	0	0	0	0	0	1	0	0	1	0
somewhat	224	.9242	41.013	56.1	13	18	27	50	56	24	26	10	42	13	3	11	9	26	4	34	8	0	3	6	12	10	23	20	0
somewhere	213	.8628	36.829	55.7	23	30	26	34	55	21	19	5	74	9	2	19	3	15	3	15	2	0	1	0	24	13	11	22	0
somewheres	3	.2196	.1554	31.9	0	0	1	0	1	1	0	0	0	0	0	2	0	0	0	0	0	0	0	0	1	0	0	0	0
Somme	2	.2285	.1129	30.5	0	0	0	0	1	1	0	0	0	0	0	0	0	1	0	0	0	0	0	0	0	0	1	0	0
Sommers	4	.0000	.0778	28.9	0	0	0	0	4	0	0	0	0	0	0	0	0	4	0	0	0	0	0	0	0	0	0	0	0
Somsak	5	.0000	.2284	33.6	0	0	0	0	5	0	0	0	5	0	0	0	0	0	0	0	0	0	0	0	0	0	0	0	0
son	771	.6134	100.32	60.0	102	147	91	127	164	64	59	17	294	16	7	108	5	36	7	3	26	4	1	0	51	114	46	42	11
Son	94	.1862	4.4685	46.5	6	21	4	3	56	1	1	2	9	0	0	49	0	1	0	0	7	0	0	0	4	10	1	4	9
son-in-law	9	.6484	1.2104	40.8	0	1	0	3	1	0	4	0	2	0	0	2	0	1	0	0	0	0	0	0	1	1	1	1	0
son's	26	.6522	3.5925	45.6	5	3	3	6	5	1	3	0	13	1	0	5	0	1	0	0	1	0	0	0	2	1	0	2	0
Son's	6	.0000	.0644	28.1	0	0	0	0	6	0	0	0	0	0	0	6	0	0	0	0	0	0	0	0	0	0	0	0	0
sonar	25	.4986	2.8129	44.5	1	11	1	2	5	3	1	1	12	2	0	0	0	0	0	3	0	0	0	0	0	0	1	7	0
sonata	23	.0513	.4109	36.1	0	1	0	0	1	21	0	0	0	0	0	1	0	0	0	0	22	0	0	0	0	0	0	0	0
Sonata	5	.0000	.0404	26.1	1	0	0	0	2	2	0	0	0	0	0	0	0	0	0	0	5	0	0	0	0	0	0	0	0
sonata-form	5	.0000	.0404	26.1	0	0	0	0	0	5	0	0	0	0	0	0	0	0	0	0	5	0	0	0	0	0	0	0	0
sonatas	6	.0000	.0485	26.9	0	1	1	0	0	2	2	0	0	0	0	0	0	0	0	0	6	0	0	0	0	0	0	0	0
song	1525	.2784	95.888	59.8	293	348	287	245	152	105	76	19	112	23	4	57	0	11	3	6	1220	3	0	1	23	22	13	26	1
Song	44	.4293	3.9527	46.0	6	2	8	5	12	5	6	0	0	2	0	7	0	2	0	0	27	1	0	0	0	2	0	3	0
song-like	4	.0000	.0323	25.1	0	0	0	0	0	1	3	0	0	0	0	0	0	0	0	0	4	0	0	0	0	0	0	0	0
song-thrush	3	.0000	.1370	31.4	3	0	0	0	0	0	0	0	3	0	0	0	0	0	0	0	0	0	0	0	0	0	0	0	0
song-writing	2	.0000	.0162	22.1	0	0	1	0	0	1	0	0	0	0	0	0	0	0	0	0	2	0	0	0	0	0	0	0	0
song's	2	.0000	.0162	22.1	1	0	0	1	0	0	0	0	0	0	0	0	0	0	0	0	2	0	0	0	0	0	0	0	0
songbirds	10	.3347	.7435	38.7	1	1	0	0	5	0	0	3	0	0	0	0	0	0	0	2	0	0	0	0	0	1	6	1	0
songbook	4	.0000	.0438	26.4	0	0	0	0	0	4	0	0	0	4	0	0	0	0	0	0	0	0	0	0	0	0	0	0	0
songs	658	.2906	42.644	56.3	62	105	160	130	101	80	15	5	33	9	2	15	0	16	3	2	502	1	1	0	10	28	12	24	0
Songs	7	.0000	.0566	27.5	0	0	3	1	1	0	2	0	0	0	0	0	0	0	0	0	7	0	0	0	0	0	0	0	0
Songster	4	.0000	.0579	27.6	0	4	0	0	0	0	0	0	0	0	0	0	0	0	0	0	0	0	0	0	0	4	0	0	0
songwriters	2	.2351	.1166	30.7	0	1	0	0	0	1	0	0	0	0	0	0	0	1	0	0	0	0	0	0	0	0	0	1	0
sonic	8	.2446	.4866	36.9	0	0	2	1	3	0	0	2	0	0	0	0	0	0	0	5	0	0	0	0	0	0	0	3	0
Sonic	3	.0000	.0365	25.6	0	0	0	0	0	0	0	3	0	0	0	0	0	0	0	0	0	0	0	0	0	0	0	3	0
sonnet	7	.0000	.0766	28.8	0	0	0	5	1	1	0	0	0	7	0	0	0	0	0	0	0	0	0	0	0	0	0	0	0
sonnets	5	.2446	.3866	35.9	0	0	1	4	0	0	0	0	4	1	0	0	0	0	0	0	0	0	0	0	0	0	0	0	0
sonny	2	.0000	.0914	29.6	0	2	0	0	0	0	0	0	2	0	0	0	0	0	0	0	0	0	0	0	0	0	0	0	0
Sonny	13	.6154	1.7225	42.4	4	3	1	2	2	0	1	0	7	1	0	1	0	0	0	0	0	0	0	0	0	1	1	2	0
Sonny's	3	.0000	.1370	31.4	3	0	0	0	0	0	0	0	3	0	0	0	0	0	0	0	0	0	0	0	0	0	0	0	0
Sonora	3	.3815	.2534	34.0	1	0	0	1	1	0	0	0	0	0	0	0	0	1	0	0	0	0	0	0	0	1	0	1	0
Sonoran	4	.1698	.2267	33.6	0	0	0	0	4	0	0	0	2	0	0	0	0	0	0	0	0	0	0	0	0	0	2	0	0
sonorous	3	.3779	.2436	33.9	0	0	1	1	1	0	0	0	0	1	0	0	0	0	0	0	1	0	0	0	0	1	0	0	0
sons	156	.4725	16.618	52.2	27	23	23	19	37	15	7	5	61	2	0	16	0	22	0	0	4	0	0	0	9	18	12	9	3
Sons	13	.6759	1.8378	42.6	0	1	9	0	1	2	0	0	5	0	0	1	0	3	0	0	1	0	0	0	0	1	1	1	0
soo	2	.2387	.1089	30.4	0	0	1	0	1	0	0	0	0	0	0	0	0	0	0	0	1	0	0	0	1	0	0	0	0
Soo	4	.2278	.2911	34.6	0	0	3	0	1	0	0	0	3	0	0	0	0	0	0	0	1	0	0	0	0	0	0	0	0
Soo-Pung	16	.0000	.7309	38.6	16	0	0	0	0	0	0	0	16	0	0	0	0	0	0	0	0	0	0	0	0	0	0	0	0
Soo-Pung's	2	.0000	.0914	29.6	2	0	0	0	0	0	0	0	2	0	0	0	0	0	0	0	0	0	0	0	0	0	0	0	0
soon	2129	.9180	388.58	65.9	471	467	283	295	292	172	114	35	786	50	15	102	7	288	18	173	54	5	16	4	199	230	62	119	1
sooner	89	.7794	14.140	51.5	19	14	11	13	15	9	6	2	35	3	1	9	0	6	1	6	1	0	0	0	16	2	2	7	0
Sooner	27	.2433	2.0665	43.2	12	0	5	0	9	0	1	0	21	6	0	0	0	0	0	0	0	0	0	0	0	0	0	0	0
Soong	3	.2159	.1532	31.9	0	0	3	0	0	0	0	0	0	0	0	0	0	0	0	0	0	0	0	0	0	0	2	1	0
soot	14	.6123	1.8513	42.7	3	4	2	3	2	0	0	0	7	1	0	0	0	2	0	1	0	0	0	0	0	2	0	1	0
soothe	9	.4362	.8692	39.4	0	1	2	1	4	0	1	0	2	0	0	0	0	0	0	0	0	0	1	0	3	3	0	0	0
soothed	4	.3713	.3634	35.6	0	0	1	0	2	1	0	0	2	0	0	1	0	0	0	0	0	0	0	0	1	0	0	0	0
soothing	11	.4935	1.1602	40.6	1	1	1	1	3	2	2	0	2	0	0	2	0	0	0	0	3	0	0	0	3	0	0	1	0
soothingly	7	.4760	.7168	38.6	0	1	0	1	3	1	1	0	1	0	0	1	0	0	0	0	0	0	0	0	3	1	0	1	0
sooty	4	.1717	.2284	33.6	0	1	0	0	2	1	0	0	2	0	0	2	0	0	0	0	0	0	0	0	0	0	0	0	0
Sooty	22	.1503	1.4753	41.7	14	0	0	0	8	0	0	0	21	0	0	0	0	0	0	0	0	0	0	0	0	0	0	1	0
Sooty's	5	.0000	.2284	33.6	3	0	0	0	2	0	0	0	5	0	0	0	0	0	0	0	0	0	0	0	0	0	0	0	0
sop	2	.0000	.0243	23.9	0	0	0	0	1	0	1	0	0	0	0	0	0	0	0	0	0	0	0	0	0	0	0	2	0
Soperville	4	.0000	.1827	32.6	0	4	0	0	0	0	0	0	4	0	0	0	0	0	0	0	0	0	0	0	0	0	0	0	0
Sophia	2	.0000	.0389	25.9	0	0	0	1	1	0	0	0	0	0	0	0	0	2	0	0	0	0	0	0	0	0	0	0	0
sophisticated	25	.6112	3.1375	45.0	1	0	0	2	9	2	9	2	1	1	0	0	0	2	0	3	2	0	1	0	0	0	6	9	0
sophistication	6	.3341	.4387	36.4	0	0	0	1	0	2	2	1	0	0	0	0	0	0	0	0	1	0	0	0	0	0	1	4	0
Sophocles	2	.2285	.1129	30.5	0	0	0	0	1	1	0	0	0	0	0	0	0	1	0	0	0	0	0	0	0	0	1	0	0
sophomore	7	.5197	.7557	38.8	1	0	1	0	1	1	3	0	0	1	0	0	1	0	1	0	0	0	0	0	0	1	0	3	0
soprano	35	.1914	1.5746	42.0	0	2	4	3	10	4	12	0	0	0	0	1	0	0	1	2	29	0	0	0	0	1	0	1	0
sopranos	3	.0000	.0243	23.8	0	0	0	0	0	1	2	0	0	0	0	0	0	0	0	0	3	0	0	0	0	0	0	0	0
Sorbonne	4	.2201	.2150	33.3	1	0	0	0	0	0	0	3	0	0	0	0	0	0	0	0	0	0	0	0	0	3	1	0	0
sorcerer	7	.4102	.6279	38.0	0	0	2	1	0	4	0	0	1	2	0	3	0	0	0	0	1	0	0	0	0	0	0	0	0
sorcerer's	3	.0000	.0322	25.1	0	0	0	0	0	3	0	0	0	0	0	3	0	0	0	0	0	0	0	0	0	0	0	0	0
Sorcerer's	2	.1696	.0749	28.7	0	0	0	0	1	1	0	0	0	0	0	0	0	0	0	0	1	1	0	0	0	0	0	0	0
sorcery	2	.1733	.1149	30.6	0	0	0	0	1	1	0	0	1	1	0	0	0	0	0	0	0	0	0	0	0	0	0	0	0
sordid	4	.4543	.4025	36.0	0	0	0	0	3	1	0	0	1	1	0	0	0	0	0	0	0	0	0	0	0	1	0	1	0

6A Somebody-or-other
6R somebody'd
8D someding
8B Someones
3A somersaulted
7N somersets
4A Somethin'
7N somethin's
8Q sometime-editor
8Q Sommerfeld
8B Somnium
7R son-of-a-gun
9H SONAR
5A Sonarman
7A sonars
6P Sonatina
3R song-birds
7G song-chants
9J song-theme
8F song-writer's
7Q songbird
7J songwriter
7A sonita
6A sonnet-thing
8F Sonoma
3P SOON
7D soon's
7R Sooners
7P soonest
6P SOOT
4A soot-blackened
4A soot-smudged
9D sooth
6A soothes
7A soothsayer-priest
5Q soothsayers
9D Sopel
6R soph
4N Sophia's
3B Sophie
9R Sophocles'
9B sophomores
9D Sophy
4N sopping
4R sops
6J sopsorghum
XR Sopwith
3A Sorby
6A Sorcerer-in-Ordinary
5B sorcerers
6A sorcerers'
6P Sorceries

Word Type	F	D	U	SFI	3 Gr 3	4 Gr 4	5 Gr 5	6 Gr 6	7 Gr 7	8 Gr 8	9 Gr 9	X UnGr	A Read	B Eng & Gr	C Comp	D Lit	E Math	F Soc Stud	G Spell	H Sci	J Music	K Art	L Home Ec	M Shop	N Lib F	P Lib NF	Q Lib Ref	R Mag	S Rel
sore	40	.7779	6.3036	48.0	8	6	8	6	4	4	4	0	11	1	2	3	0	2	3	4	4	0	0	0	3	3	0	4	0
sorely	7	.5125	.7679	38.9	0	2	0	0	2	1	2	0	1	1	0	2	0	2	0	0	0	0	0	0	0	0	0	1	0
sores	5	.4858	.5164	37.1	0	1	1	1	1	0	1	0	0	0	0	0	0	0	0	2	0	0	0	0	1	1	1	0	0
sorghum	7	.6001	.8777	39.4	0	0	1	3	2	0	0	1	1	1	0	0	1	2	0	0	1	0	0	0	0	0	0	1	0
sorrel	9	.2967	.6794	38.3	2	3	0	4	0	0	0	0	3	0	0	0	0	0	0	0	0	0	0	0	0	5	1	0	0
Sorrell	64	.1639	3.5118	45.5	0	0	0	0	35	29	0	0	29	0	0	0	0	0	0	0	0	0	0	0	35	0	0	0	0
Sorrell's	4	.1787	.2347	33.7	0	0	0	0	2	2	0	0	2	0	0	0	0	0	0	0	0	0	0	0	2	0	0	0	0
sorrow	63	.5422	7.2791	48.6	6	3	5	11	17	4	11	6	16	0	0	16	0	1	0	1	10	1	0	0	11	5	0	1	1
sorrow's	2	.2446	.1084	30.3	0	0	0	0	1	1	0	0	0	0	0	0	0	0	1	0	1	0	0	0	0	0	0	0	0
sorrowful	13	.6068	1.6630	42.2	2	2	2	1	3	2	1	0	4	0	0	2	0	0	0	0	1	0	0	0	3	2	1	0	0
sorrowfully	8	.5576	.9646	39.8	1	3	0	1	2	0	1	0	3	0	0	1	0	0	0	0	0	0	0	0	1	2	1	0	0
sorrowing	3	.3847	.2448	33.9	0	0	1	0	2	0	0	0	0	0	0	1	0	0	0	0	1	0	0	0	0	0	1	0	0
sorrows	12	.6064	1.5400	41.9	0	3	0	0	4	2	3	0	4	0	0	2	0	0	0	0	1	0	0	0	1	3	0	1	0
sorry	282	.6736	39.703	56.0	71	43	30	34	45	33	24	2	118	11	1	55	0	7	6	0	2	0	4	0	42	26	0	8	2
sort	375	.8750	65.527	58.2	41	42	41	52	106	40	37	16	112	14	4	33	4	7	4	19	6	1	3	2	64	42	23	37	0
sorta	3	.2292	.1615	32.1	0	0	0	0	3	0	0	0	0	0	0	1	0	0	0	0	0	0	0	0	2	0	0	0	0
sorted	20	.6921	2.8388	44.5	9	4	0	0	4	1	2	0	3	1	0	3	2	7	0	0	0	0	0	1	0	1	1	1	0
sortie	3	.2386	.1624	32.1	0	0	1	0	1	1	0	0	0	0	0	0	0	0	0	0	0	1	0	0	0	1	0	1	0
sorting	19	.6876	2.7002	44.3	5	1	3	4	2	1	3	0	5	2	1	0	0	6	0	1	0	0	0	1	1	0	1	1	0
sorts	76	.8776	13.298	51.2	10	9	9	10	20	7	7	4	18	4	1	3	1	9	0	7	1	3	1	1	5	6	9	7	0
SOS	2	.2160	.1362	31.3	0	0	1	1	0	0	0	0	1	0	0	0	0	0	0	1	0	0	0	0	0	0	0	0	0
Soto	6	.0000	.0869	29.4	5	0	0	0	1	0	0	0	0	0	0	0	0	0	0	0	0	0	0	0	0	6	0	0	0
sought	94	.8073	15.278	51.8	6	7	8	12	31	12	16	2	22	1	0	5	0	7	0	5	4	2	0	1	11	6	14	16	0
souks	4	.0000	.1827	32.6	0	0	0	4	0	0	0	0	4	0	0	0	0	0	0	0	0	0	0	0	0	0	0	0	0
soul	125	.7446	18.869	52.8	5	5	16	20	33	12	27	7	23	2	1	31	0	5	2	1	7	0	0	0	16	20	6	11	0
Soul	3	.2411	.1667	32.2	0	0	0	1	2	0	0	0	0	0	0	0	0	0	0	0	1	0	0	0	0	0	0	2	0
souls	25	.7044	3.5721	45.5	1	2	1	2	6	1	6	6	2	0	0	4	0	1	0	1	1	1	0	0	1	7	3	4	0
sound	4667	.5384	525.74	67.2	1056	895	717	759	608	476	135	21	661	433	35	119	10	40	2296	306	448	9	6	2	117	74	38	73	0
Sound	51	.7491	7.7883	48.9	17	7	8	1	11	3	3	1	14	0	0	2	0	5	2	2	1	0	0	0	5	4	8	8	0
SOUND	4	.2393	.3005	34.8	0	0	0	3	1	0	0	0	3	0	0	1	0	0	0	0	0	0	0	0	0	0	0	0	0
sound-maker	2	.0000	.0394	26.0	2	0	0	0	0	0	0	0	0	0	0	0	0	0	0	2	0	0	0	0	0	0	0	0	0
sound-makers	6	.2128	.3166	35.0	3	3	0	0	0	0	0	0	0	0	0	0	0	0	0	3	3	0	0	0	0	0	0	0	0
sound-pictures	2	.0000	.0914	29.6	0	0	0	0	2	0	0	0	2	0	0	0	0	0	0	0	0	0	0	0	0	0	0	0	0
sound-spelling	3	.0000	.0243	23.9	0	0	0	0	0	3	0	0	0	0	0	0	0	0	3	0	0	0	0	0	0	0	0	0	0
sound-spellings	9	.0000	.0730	28.6	0	0	0	0	0	9	0	0	0	0	0	0	0	0	9	0	0	0	0	0	0	0	0	0	0
sound-wave	3	.2442	.1820	32.6	0	0	0	1	0	0	2	0	0	1	0	0	0	0	0	2	0	0	0	0	0	0	0	0	0
sound's	3	.3380	.2439	33.9	0	1	1	0	1	0	0	0	1	1	0	1	0	0	0	0	0	0	0	0	0	0	0	0	0
sounded	242	.7585	37.552	55.7	43	52	28	32	55	18	10	4	100	8	3	20	0	6	19	2	25	0	0	0	35	18	0	6	0
sounder	8	.2890	.5608	37.5	0	0	4	2	0	1	0	1	0	0	0	0	0	1	0	6	0	0	0	0	0	0	0	1	0
Sounder	4	.0000	.1827	32.6	0	0	0	0	4	0	0	0	4	0	0	0	0	0	0	0	0	0	0	0	0	0	0	0	0
sounders	2	.2160	.1362	31.3	0	0	0	1	1	0	0	0	1	0	0	0	0	0	0	1	0	0	0	0	0	0	0	0	0
sounding	56	.6236	7.1777	48.6	4	7	5	10	19	4	7	0	6	1	2	4	1	0	1	10	22	0	0	0	2	1	2	4	0
soundings	10	.3246	.7593	38.8	0	0	1	0	2	4	3	0	0	0	0	0	2	0	0	7	0	0	0	0	1	0	0	0	0
soundless	3	.2754	.1780	32.5	0	1	0	1	0	1	0	0	0	0	0	0	0	0	0	0	1	1	0	0	1	0	0	0	0
soundlessly	3	.3394	.2451	33.9	0	0	0	1	2	0	0	0	1	0	0	1	0	0	0	0	0	0	0	0	1	0	0	0	0
soundly	29	.6887	4.1953	46.2	9	4	1	4	7	4	0	0	15	1	0	1	0	3	1	0	0	0	0	1	3	4	0	0	0
soundproof	3	.3765	.2411	33.8	0	0	0	1	0	2	0	0	0	0	0	0	0	0	1	0	1	0	0	0	0	1	0	0	0
sounds	1606	.6286	207.59	63.2	324	328	232	252	253	157	45	15	248	196	25	41	4	16	646	120	202	15	2	0	22	33	13	23	0
Sounds	8	.3788	.7561	38.8	0	4	1	2	1	0	0	0	5	2	0	0	0	0	0	0	1	0	0	0	0	0	0	0	0
soup	184	.5448	21.681	53.4	29	25	28	16	39	9	21	17	70	6	0	8	7	8	4	10	1	0	38	0	13	2	2	15	0
souped-up	2	.1733	.1149	30.6	0	0	0	0	1	1	0	0	1	1	0	0	0	0	0	0	0	0	0	0	0	0	0	0	0
soups	11	.2260	.6114	37.9	1	0	2	3	1	1	3	0	2	0	0	0	0	0	0	1	0	0	5	0	0	0	3	0	0
soupy	3	.2217	.1569	32.0	0	0	2	0	1	0	0	0	0	0	0	0	0	0	0	1	0	1	0	0	0	0	0	1	0
sour	29	.6270	3.7440	45.7	1	4	7	4	5	2	5	1	4	2	0	2	0	0	4	5	0	0	5	0	3	1	1	2	0
Sour	2	.1839	.0845	29.3	0	1	0	0	0	1	0	0	0	0	0	0	0	0	0	0	0	0	1	0	1	0	0	0	0
source	303	.8555	51.662	57.1	11	14	36	39	97	58	36	12	21	18	5	8	0	49	7	84	9	2	9	6	1	8	57	19	0
sources	161	.7793	25.212	54.0	3	9	30	15	43	38	13	10	12	10	2	1	0	26	2	29	6	0	14	2	1	9	34	13	0
sourdough	2	.0000	.0215	23.3	0	0	0	0	1	1	0	0	0	0	0	2	0	0	0	0	0	0	0	0	0	0	0	0	0
soured	2	.2446	.1122	30.5	0	0	0	0	1	0	1	0	0	0	0	1	0	0	0	0	0	0	0	0	0	0	1	0	0
Sourwood	3	.2071	.1434	31.6	0	0	0	3	0	0	0	0	0	0	0	1	0	0	0	0	2	0	0	0	0	0	0	0	0
Sousa	31	.2418	1.7500	42.4	0	18	11	0	0	2	0	0	0	0	0	0	0	0	0	0	13	0	0	0	0	18	0	0	0
Sousa's	3	.1852	.1342	31.3	0	1	1	0	0	0	1	0	0	0	0	0	0	0	0	0	2	0	0	0	0	1	0	0	0
south	709	.7871	112.70	60.5	110	99	109	125	138	53	47	28	94	10	4	20	3	296	5	76	9	0	1	12	18	62	58	41	0
South	928	.7603	142.91	61.6	104	118	175	130	205	125	62	9	102	13	3	26	9	395	4	59	29	2	1	1	20	79	117	68	0
SouthAmerica	4	.3024	.3033	34.8	0	1	3	0	0	0	0	0	1	0	0	0	0	1	0	0	0	0	0	0	0	2	0	0	0
SouthAmerican	2	.2408	.1204	30.8	0	1	0	0	1	0	0	0	0	0	0	0	0	1	0	0	0	0	0	0	0	1	0	0	0
SouthCarolina	68	.5600	8.0372	49.1	7	7	38	2	3	9	2	0	3	0	0	1	2	44	1	2	2	0	0	0	0	5	5	3	0
SouthCarolina's	8	.1558	.3721	35.7	1	0	7	0	0	0	0	0	0	0	0	0	0	7	0	0	0	0	0	0	0	1	0	0	0
SouthDakota	35	.6252	4.5399	46.6	3	1	14	3	1	1	10	2	3	2	0	0	1	13	0	4	0	0	0	0	1	1	8	2	0
SouthPole	7	.1464	.3624	35.6	0	0	0	1	1	0	0	5	2	0	0	0	0	5	0	0	0	0	0	0	0	0	0	0	0
South-West	2	.0000	.0389	25.9	0	0	0	2	0	0	0	0	0	0	0	0	0	2	0	0	0	0	0	0	0	0	0	0	0
south-central	3	.1823	.1405	31.5	1	0	0	0	2	0	0	0	0	0	0	0	0	1	0	0	0	0	0	0	0	0	2	0	0
south-facing	2	.0000	.0389	25.9	0	0	0	0	2	0	0	0	0	0	0	0	0	2	0	0	0	0	0	0	0	0	0	0	0
south-seeking	13	.2126	.7325	38.6	12	0	0	0	0	0	1	0	0	0	0	0	0	0	0	10	0	0	0	0	0	3	0	0	0
South's	4	.2348	.2372	33.8	0	0	1	0	0	2	1	0	0	0	0	0	0	3	0	0	0	0	0	0	0	0	1	0	0
southeast	66	.6355	8.6629	49.4	10	6	11	9	19	6	5	0	4	2	0	1	0	29	0	2	3	0	0	0	0	10	10	5	0
Southeast	95	.1749	4.7456	46.8	4	1	19	22	46	1	1	1	0	0	0	1	0	87	0	0	0	0	0	0	0	3	0	4	0
southeastern	67	.5186	7.4378	48.7	6	5	16	11	14	5	8	2	4	0	0	0	1	39	0	6	1	0	0	0	0	3	10	3	0
Southeastern	6	.1822	.3062	34.9	0	0	5	0	1	0	0	0	0	0	0	0	0	5	0	0	0	0	0	0	0	1	0	0	0
southeastward	7	.3415	.5477	37.4	0	0	2	1	4	0	0	0	0	0	0	0	0	4	0	1	0	0	0	0	0	0	2	0	0
southerly	5	.3278	.4057	36.1	0	0	0	1	1	2	0	1	2	0	0	0	0	0	0	0	0	0	0	0	0	0	2	1	0
southern	469	.6503	63.088	58.0	58	52	91	84	94	39	39	12	41	6	1	3	2	241	4	43	10	1	0	0	4	25	72	16	0
Southern	175	.7224	25.715	54.1	10	9	39	15	40	43	15	4	12	1	1	5	1	89	0	6	6	0	2	2	0	11	19	20	0
southerner	2	.0000	.0389	25.9	0	0	2	0	0	0	0	0	0	0	0	0	0	2	0	0	0	0	0	0	0	0	0	0	0
Southerner	8	.5132	.8911	39.5	0	2	1	1	3	1	0	0	2	0	0	1	0	1	0	0	1	0	0	0	0	3	0	0	0
southerners	9	.3875	.7725	38.9	3	0	6	0	0	0	0	0	0	0	0	0	0	4	0	0	0	0	0	0	0	3	2	0	0
Southerners	28	.2845	1.9553	42.9	1	0	9	0	2	13	2	1	1	0	0	0	0	23	0	0	0	0	0	0	0	2	1	1	0
southernmost	14	.3509	1.1181	40.5	3	1	3	0	2	4	1	0	0	0	0	0	0	9	0	0	0	0	0	0	0	2	3	0	0
southland	2	.2375	.1088	30.4	0	0	1	1	0	0	0	0	0	0	0	0	0	0	0	0	1	0	0	0	0	0	0	1	0
Southland	6	.2217	.3130	35.0	0	1	4	0	0	1	0	0	0	0	0	0	0	1	0	0	4	0	0	0	0	1	0	0	0
southpaw	4	.3783	.3298	35.2	2	0	1	0	1	0	0	0	0	1	0	0	0	0	0	0	0	0	0	0	0	2	0	1	0
Southpaw	8	.0000	.3655	35.6	0	8	0	0	0	0	0	0	8	0	0	0	0	0	0	0	0	0	0	0	0	0	0	0	0
southward	79	.6351	10.465	50.2	5	12	12	14	18	9	7	2	11	1	1	1	0	36	0	10	0	0	0	0	0	8	9	2	0
Southwark	2	.0000	.0243	23.9	0	2	0	0	0	0	0	0	0	0	0	0	0	0	0	0	0	0	0	0	0	0	0	2	0

9Q soreness
XP Sorghum
6A sorghum-molasses
5P Soria
4P Sorrel
4F Sorrow
4N Sorrowing
XR sorrowless
3D sort-out
7N sorters
8K Sortie
8R sorties
6P Sortileges
XB soth
3P Soto's
8F sotweed
5J Sou'
4J sou'wester
XR souffle
XR souffles
XH sought-after
6A souk
7J soul-stirring
5Q Soule
7J soulful
7R soulmates
8G sound-
9G sound-alike
7R sound-deadening
7P sound-effects
9D sound-minded
7A sound-writing
8F soundness
5R soundtrack
6R soup's
5A soupbone
7R souqs
9B sour-looking
4A Sourdough
8H Souris
3A sourly
3A SouthAfrica
8F SouthCarolinian
9Q SouthDakota's
6A SouthDevon
8H SouthPacific
6N SouthSeas
8R SouthVietnam's
9Q South-African
9R south-side
8H south-southeast
XR south's
7N Southampton
7C southard
8H southcentral
9D Southcott
7A southeasterly
9Q Southend
5J Southerly
3P Southside
5Q southward-flowing
7N southwards

Word Type	F	D	U	SFI	3 Gr 3	4 Gr 4	5 Gr 5	6 Gr 6	7 Gr 7	8 Gr 8	9 Gr 9	X UnGr	A Read	B Eng & Gr	C Comp	D Lit	E Math	F Soc Stud	G Spell	H Sci	J Music	K Art	L Home Ec	M Shop	N Lib F	P Lib NF	Q Lib Ref	R Mag	S Rel
southwest	69	.6365	9.0919	49.6	12	8	7	13	21	7	0	1	6	0	1	0	0	26	0	8	0	0	0	0	1	5	12	10	0
Southwest	42	.6816	5.9138	47.7	8	7	5	4	7	6	0	5	8	2	0	1	0	15	0	3	2	0	0	0	0	3	1	7	0
southwestern	48	.3865	4.2085	46.2	1	6	7	9	10	10	4	1	3	0	0	0	0	31	0	3	0	0	0	0	0	0	9	2	0
Southwestern	4	.2843	.2875	34.6	0	0	0	0	3	0	0	1	1	0	0	0	0	1	0	0	0	0	0	0	0	0	0	2	0
southwestward	2	.2351	.1166	30.7	0	0	1	1	0	0	0	0	0	0	0	0	0	1	0	0	0	0	0	0	0	0	0	1	0
souvenir	5	.5375	.5728	37.6	0	3	1	0	0	0	1	0	1	1	0	0	1	0	0	0	0	0	0	0	0	1	1	0	0
souvenirs	2	.2446	.1184	30.7	1	0	0	1	0	0	0	0	0	0	0	0	1	0	0	0	0	0	0	0	0	1	0	0	0
sovereign	16	.5174	1.7731	42.5	0	6	1	0	5	3	1	0	2	0	0	1	0	4	0	0	0	0	0	0	1	7	1	0	0
sovereigns	17	.1677	.7523	38.8	0	0	0	0	15	2	0	0	1	0	0	0	0	0	0	0	0	0	0	0	14	0	2	0	0
sovereignty	13	.3272	.9828	39.9	0	0	3	1	0	9	0	0	0	0	0	0	0	9	0	0	0	0	0	0	1	0	3	0	0
Soviet	175	.4878	18.270	52.6	2	6	8	54	26	36	41	2	4	0	0	2	0	93	1	2	0	0	0	0	0	7	27	39	0
SovietUnion	3	.1639	.1674	32.2	0	0	0	0	2	0	1	0	1	0	0	0	0	2	0	0	0	0	0	0	0	0	0	0	0
Soviet-made	2	.2285	.1129	30.5	0	0	0	0	0	1	1	0	0	0	0	0	0	1	0	0	0	0	0	0	0	0	1	0	0
Soviets	5	.2445	.3026	34.8	0	0	0	0	1	2	1	1	0	0	0	0	0	3	0	0	0	0	0	0	0	0	0	2	0
sow	21	.5856	2.5459	44.1	3	1	1	7	9	0	0	0	1	0	0	1	0	4	5	2	0	0	0	0	0	1	1	6	0
sowed	6	.5313	.6862	38.4	1	0	1	2	0	1	0	1	1	1	0	0	0	2	0	1	0	0	0	0	0	0	0	1	0
Sower	2	.0000	.0004	5.5	2	0	0	0	0	0	0	0	0	0	0	0	0	0	0	0	0	0	0	0	0	0	0	0	2
sowing	3	.2321	.1635	32.1	0	2	0	0	0	1	0	0	0	0	0	0	0	0	0	0	0	0	0	0	0	0	1	2	0
sown	7	.3659	.5734	37.6	1	1	1	0	2	2	0	0	0	0	0	0	0	4	0	0	0	0	0	0	1	0	2	0	0
sows	3	.2071	.1434	31.6	2	0	0	0	0	1	0	0	0	0	0	1	0	0	0	0	2	0	0	0	0	0	0	0	0
Sox	23	.3605	1.9235	42.8	3	5	0	5	9	0	1	0	5	1	0	0	0	0	0	0	0	0	0	0	0	6	0	11	0
soy	7	.4118	.6533	38.2	0	0	2	0	0	0	0	5	1	1	0	0	0	0	0	4	0	0	0	0	0	0	0	1	0
soya	3	.2540	.1940	32.9	1	0	0	1	0	1	0	0	1	0	0	0	0	0	0	0	0	0	1	0	0	0	1	0	0
soybean	6	.3806	.5671	37.5	1	0	3	0	0	0	0	2	3	0	0	0	0	0	0	2	0	0	0	0	0	1	0	0	0
soybeans	30	.5370	3.5041	45.4	0	5	10	1	1	1	3	9	7	0	0	0	0	11	0	8	0	0	1	0	0	0	0	3	0
Soyuz	4	.0000	.0486	26.9	0	3	0	0	0	0	0	1	0	0	0	0	0	0	0	0	0	0	0	0	0	0	0	4	0
sp	13	.0000	.1055	30.2	4	1	4	4	0	0	0	0	0	0	0	0	0	0	13	0	0	0	0	0	0	0	0	0	0
SP	2	.0000	.0299	24.8	0	0	0	0	0	2	0	0	0	0	0	0	2	0	0	0	0	0	0	0	0	0	0	0	0
space	1499	.8586	256.87	64.1	215	242	196	186	286	188	128	58	208	72	16	23	156	76	41	452	39	73	26	28	17	108	71	93	0
Space	34	.7313	5.0712	47.1	1	3	7	9	6	3	5	0	7	3	1	0	2	4	0	6	1	0	0	3	0	4	1	2	0
space-time	2	.0000	.0209	23.2	0	0	0	0	0	0	2	0	0	0	0	0	0	0	0	0	0	0	0	0	0	0	2	0	0
spacecraft	83	.6895	11.710	50.7	13	11	14	16	14	7	7	1	9	2	0	0	6	1	2	29	0	1	0	3	0	1	5	24	0
Spacecraft	6	.3769	.4968	37.0	0	0	2	2	2	0	0	0	0	0	0	0	0	2	0	0	0	0	0	0	0	0	2	2	0
spacecraft's	4	.2090	.2014	33.0	1	0	0	0	2	0	1	0	0	0	0	0	0	0	0	0	0	0	0	0	0	0	1	3	0
spaced	35	.7086	5.0145	47.0	2	10	5	1	5	2	10	0	3	0	1	2	6	3	1	2	0	1	1	5	0	0	8	2	0
spaceman	7	.3689	.6364	38.0	3	1	0	2	0	1	0	0	3	0	0	0	0	0	1	3	0	0	0	0	0	0	0	0	0
spaceman's	2	.1814	.1187	30.7	2	0	0	0	0	0	0	0	1	0	0	0	0	0	0	0	0	0	0	0	0	0	0	1	0
spacemen	6	.2757	.4319	36.4	5	1	0	0	0	0	0	0	2	0	0	0	0	0	0	1	0	0	0	0	0	0	0	3	0
spaces	227	.6824	31.336	55.0	67	35	35	17	32	10	24	7	14	14	1	1	37	11	57	17	13	27	3	12	2	5	3	10	0
spaceship	34	.6098	4.4615	46.5	8	7	3	5	5	4	2	0	15	4	0	1	0	5	0	6	0	0	0	0	0	0	0	3	0
Spaceship	3	.0000	.0365	25.6	0	0	0	0	0	0	3	0	0	0	0	0	0	0	0	0	0	0	0	0	0	0	0	3	0
spaceships	7	.3414	.5832	37.7	1	0	0	5	1	0	0	0	2	2	0	0	0	0	0	3	0	0	0	0	0	0	0	0	0
spacespeak	2	.0000	.0219	23.4	0	0	2	0	0	0	0	0	0	2	0	0	0	0	0	0	0	0	0	0	0	0	0	0	0
spacing	22	.4992	2.2576	43.5	0	8	1	1	1	6	5	0	1	0	2	1	0	0	6	3	0	1	0	7	0	0	1	0	0
spacious	17	.5748	2.0359	43.1	1	0	2	0	3	9	2	0	3	1	0	2	0	0	0	0	1	2	0	0	1	1	5	1	0
spaciousness	2	.1839	.0845	29.3	0	0	0	1	0	0	1	0	0	0	0	0	0	0	0	0	0	0	1	0	1	0	0	0	0
spade	7	.4683	.7057	38.5	2	0	0	0	0	1	3	1	1	3	0	1	0	0	0	0	0	0	0	0	0	1	0	1	0
spaded	2	.2160	.1362	31.3	1	0	0	1	0	0	0	0	1	0	0	0	0	0	0	1	0	0	0	0	0	0	0	0	0
spades	8	.5610	.9871	39.9	3	1	2	1	1	0	0	0	4	0	0	1	0	1	0	0	0	0	0	0	0	1	0	1	0
spaghetti	29	.5337	3.3244	45.2	7	4	1	2	5	2	8	0	9	6	0	2	0	2	1	2	0	0	6	1	0	0	0	0	0
Spain	325	.6102	41.133	56.1	43	42	79	63	47	40	8	3	15	6	0	0	1	173	5	0	23	2	0	0	0	30	58	12	0
Spain's	13	.4178	1.1878	40.7	0	0	10	3	0	0	0	0	0	0	0	0	0	5	0	0	0	0	0	0	0	6	1	1	0
spak	2	.0000	.0219	23.4	0	0	0	0	0	2	0	0	0	2	0	0	0	0	0	0	0	0	0	0	0	0	0	0	0
spake	8	.4470	.7936	39.0	2	0	0	1	1	2	2	0	2	0	0	2	0	0	0	0	1	0	0	0	0	3	0	0	0
Spalding	3	.2143	.1568	32.0	0	0	0	3	0	0	0	0	0	0	0	0	0	0	0	0	0	0	0	0	0	1	0	2	0
Spallanzani	4	.0000	.0789	29.0	0	0	0	0	0	0	0	4	0	0	0	0	0	0	0	4	0	0	0	0	0	0	0	0	0
span	51	.7618	7.8046	48.9	1	3	1	10	16	4	14	2	1	2	0	2	6	5	0	9	0	1	1	2	0	3	16	3	0
spangle	3	.2437	.2277	33.6	2	0	0	0	1	0	0	0	2	0	0	0	0	0	0	1	0	0	0	0	0	0	0	0	0
spangled	5	.4385	.4861	36.9	0	3	0	2	0	0	0	0	1	0	0	0	0	0	0	0	0	0	0	0	1	2	0	1	0
spangles	4	.2454	.2714	34.3	1	0	2	0	0	0	1	0	2	0	1	0	0	0	0	0	0	0	0	0	0	0	1	0	0
Spaniard	13	.4987	1.3688	41.4	0	4	3	3	2	1	0	0	1	0	0	0	0	1	0	0	3	0	0	0	5	2	0	1	0
Spaniards	91	.6109	11.541	50.6	5	6	32	17	17	10	0	4	4	8	0	1	0	48	0	1	2	0	0	0	2	11	11	3	0
spaniel	8	.4627	.8271	39.2	1	1	5	1	0	0	0	0	3	0	1	1	0	0	0	0	0	0	0	0	0	1	2	0	0
spaniels	4	.3721	.3175	35.0	0	0	2	0	0	1	1	0	0	0	0	1	0	0	1	0	0	0	0	0	0	0	2	0	0
Spanish	476	.7415	71.572	58.5	61	61	99	103	73	52	23	4	57	14	0	18	4	161	13	2	55	0	0	1	11	53	67	20	0
Spanish-American	10	.5011	1.0747	40.3	1	0	2	0	3	3	1	0	1	0	0	2	0	4	0	0	0	0	0	0	0	1	2	0	0
Spanish-speaking	7	.3448	.5223	37.2	2	1	1	2	1	0	0	0	0	1	0	0	0	1	0	0	4	0	0	0	0	0	1	0	0
spank	4	.2703	.2662	34.3	2	0	1	0	1	0	0	0	1	0	0	0	0	0	0	0	2	0	0	0	1	0	0	0	0
Spank	11	.0000	.5025	37.0	11	0	0	0	0	0	0	0	11	0	0	0	0	0	0	0	0	0	0	0	0	0	0	0	0
spanked	16	.4679	1.6072	42.1	3	6	3	1	3	0	0	0	2	0	0	4	0	0	0	0	0	0	0	0	6	1	0	3	0
spanking	3	.3873	.2485	34.0	0	2	0	0	1	0	0	0	0	0	0	1	0	0	0	0	0	0	0	0	1	0	1	0	0
spanned	4	.3267	.2856	34.6	0	0	2	1	0	1	0	0	0	0	0	0	0	0	0	0	2	0	0	0	0	1	0	1	0
spanning	4	.3617	.3220	35.1	0	0	0	0	4	0	0	0	0	0	0	0	0	0	0	1	0	0	0	0	0	2	1	0	0
spans	6	.5576	.7001	38.5	0	1	1	0	3	0	1	0	0	0	0	0	1	2	0	1	0	0	0	0	0	0	1	1	0
spar	13	.6695	1.7812	42.5	0	1	3	0	4	2	3	0	1	0	0	2	0	3	0	1	1	0	0	0	0	1	1	3	0
spare	94	.8162	15.517	51.9	14	12	9	13	19	11	11	5	36	2	2	9	1	5	0	5	1	1	0	0	9	9	1	13	0
Spare	2	.0000	.0162	22.1	0	0	1	1	0	0	0	0	0	0	0	0	0	0	2	0	0	0	0	0	0	0	0	0	0
spared	25	.7309	3.7477	45.7	3	0	2	9	5	3	3	0	8	0	0	2	0	2	0	1	1	0	0	0	3	2	4	2	0
spareribs	4	.2423	.2206	33.4	0	0	0	0	3	0	1	0	0	0	0	0	0	0	0	0	0	0	1	0	0	0	0	3	0
spares	5	.1600	.2088	33.2	0	1	0	0	4	0	0	0	0	0	0	0	0	0	0	0	0	0	0	0	4	1	0	0	0
sparin'	2	.0000	.0234	23.7	0	0	0	0	0	2	0	0	0	0	0	0	0	0	0	0	0	0	0	0	2	0	0	0	0
sparing	2	.2152	.1357	31.3	0	0	0	0	1	1	0	0	1	0	0	0	0	1	0	0	0	0	0	0	0	0	0	0	0
sparingly	6	.4218	.5403	37.3	0	0	0	2	2	1	1	0	1	0	0	0	0	0	0	0	1	0	2	1	1	0	0	0	0
spark	76	.7859	12.015	50.8	9	2	11	12	24	17	1	0	9	1	3	5	0	6	0	16	0	1	0	5	3	9	7	11	0
sparked	6	.4121	.5479	37.4	0	0	0	2	3	0	1	0	1	0	0	0	0	0	0	0	0	0	0	0	0	1	2	2	0
sparkle	15	.6189	1.9910	43.0	4	4	2	2	2	0	1	0	8	0	0	1	0	0	0	1	0	1	1	0	1	1	1	0	0
sparkled	29	.5694	3.6487	45.6	9	11	3	5	1	0	0	0	17	0	0	2	0	0	0	1	0	0	0	0	3	5	0	1	0
Sparkler	2	.0000	.0243	23.9	0	0	0	0	0	0	0	2	0	0	0	0	0	0	0	0	0	0	0	0	0	0	0	2	0
sparkles	6	.3454	.5085	37.1	3	0	1	0	1	0	0	1	2	0	0	0	0	2	0	0	0	0	0	0	0	0	0	2	0
sparkling	67	.8165	11.034	50.4	15	9	12	6	14	5	5	1	23	3	2	4	0	6	0	1	5	3	2	0	4	8	1	5	0
sparkly	3	.2143	.1568	32.0	2	0	1	0	0	0	0	0	0	0	0	0	0	0	0	0	0	0	0	0	0	1	0	2	0
sparks	42	.7308	6.3113	48.0	6	10	6	6	4	7	1	2	13	1	0	1	0	1	0	12	1	0	0	0	5	3	3	2	0
Sparky	6	.2967	.4241	36.3	6	0	0	0	0	0	0	0	1	0	0	0	0	0	0	0	0	0	0	0	2	0	0	3	0
sparrow	19	.5637	2.2277	43.5	6	0	1	2	6	1	1	2	1	4	0	4	0	0	0	4	0	0	0	0	0	2	4	0	0

4R Southwesterners
7R Southworth
7P sovereign's
9R Soviet-American
7R Soviet-Chinese
6P Soviet-Union
8R Soviet-built
8Q Soviet-trained
3P SOW
8D Sowback
7A sowbelly

6B sower
9H SO4
8B SP-1
8B SP-2
5P spa
5P Spaarndam
3P SPACE
7P space-consuming
7A space-ship
6R space-shot
4N space-sick

7H spacebound
3A spaceboy
3P spacecrafts
3F spaceflights
3A spacegirl
8H spacelike
7B Spaceman
7B Spacemen
7B Spacemen's
7R spacers
9R spaceship's

6R spacesuits
3A Spade
6A spade-blade
XB spade-work
8D spadeful
7Q spadelike
8B spadesman
4A Spadina
3A spading
6B spaker
5F Spalding's

9L spandex
5A spang
3J Spangled
5P Spaniard's
5Q Spaniel
5F Spanish-Indian
4R Spanish-born
7A spankin'
5D spanks
3J spanky
5R Spanky

6J sparely
7R Spark
7P spark-plug
3A sparklers
7P sparkless
6H sparkling-clear
6R Sparks
3R Sparky's
6A sparred
6P sparring

Word Type	F	D	U	SFI	3 Gr 3	4 Gr 4	5 Gr 5	6 Gr 6	7 Gr 7	8 Gr 8	9 Gr 9	X UnGr	A Read	B Eng & Gr	C Comp	D Lit	E Math	F Soc Stud	G Spell	H Sci	J Music	K Art	L Home Ec	M Shop	N Lib F	P Lib NF	Q Lib Ref	R Mag	S Rel
sparrow's	2	.1458	.0682	28.3	0	0	0	0	1	1	0	0	0	1	0	0	0	0	0	0	0	1	0	0	0	0	0	0	0
sparrows	20	.6190	2.5684	44.1	13	1	3	1	1	0	0	1	2	0	0	2	1	0	0	6	0	0	0	0	1	1	1	6	0
spars	9	.4469	.8633	39.4	0	2	4	0	0	0	3	0	0	0	0	0	0	4	0	0	1	0	0	0	0	1	3	0	0
sparse	14	.5554	1.6350	42.1	2	1	1	2	3	3	2	0	1	1	0	0	0	5	0	0	0	0	0	0	0	3	3	1	0
sparsely	12	.4162	1.0814	40.3	1	0	2	1	5	1	2	0	0	0	0	0	0	4	0	0	0	0	0	0	0	2	5	1	0
Sparta	9	.5291	1.0293	40.1	0	1	1	4	0	2	1	0	2	0	0	1	0	4	1	0	0	0	0	0	0	0	1	0	0
Spartacus	2	.0000	.0290	24.6	0	2	0	0	0	0	0	0	0	0	0	0	0	0	0	0	0	0	0	0	0	2	0	0	0
Spartan	4	.3215	.3104	34.9	0	1	1	0	2	0	0	0	1	0	0	0	0	0	0	0	0	0	0	0	0	2	1	0	0
Spartans	10	.3208	.8285	39.2	0	5	0	2	0	3	0	0	5	0	0	0	0	2	3	0	0	0	0	0	0	0	0	0	0
spasm	4	.3727	.3210	35.1	0	0	0	1	3	0	0	0	0	0	0	1	0	0	0	0	0	0	0	0	2	0	1	0	0
spasms	3	.3394	.2451	33.9	0	0	0	0	2	1	0	0	1	0	0	1	0	0	0	0	0	0	0	0	1	0	0	0	0
spat	18	.6566	2.4792	43.9	2	2	2	3	5	2	2	0	7	0	0	3	0	1	0	0	1	0	0	0	2	2	0	2	0
spatial	5	.4507	.4762	36.8	0	0	0	0	1	1	1	2	0	0	0	0	0	0	0	1	1	0	0	0	0	0	2	1	0
spatially	2	.0000	.0219	23.4	0	0	0	0	0	0	2	0	0	2	0	0	0	0	0	0	0	0	0	0	0	0	0	0	0
spatter	4	.4865	.4031	36.1	0	1	0	0	1	2	0	0	0	1	0	1	0	0	1	0	0	0	0	0	0	0	1	0	0
spattered	9	.4417	.9154	39.6	1	5	1	1	1	0	0	0	4	0	0	0	0	0	0	0	1	0	0	0	3	1	0	0	0
spattering	6	.2696	.4126	36.2	0	0	1	0	2	1	1	1	2	0	0	0	0	0	0	1	0	0	2	0	0	0	0	1	0
spatters	2	.2407	.1138	30.6	1	0	0	0	1	0	0	0	0	0	0	1	0	0	0	0	0	0	0	0	0	1	0	0	0
spatula	12	.1727	.5087	37.1	0	4	0	0	1	6	1	0	1	1	0	0	0	0	0	0	0	0	7	0	0	3	0	0	0
Spaulding	2	.0000	.0914	29.6	0	0	1	0	0	1	0	0	2	0	0	0	0	0	0	0	0	0	0	0	0	0	0	0	0
spawn	4	.2090	.2014	33.0	0	0	0	0	4	0	0	0	0	0	0	0	0	0	0	0	0	0	0	0	0	0	1	3	0
spawned	5	.3116	.3461	35.4	0	0	0	0	3	0	1	1	0	0	0	0	0	0	0	0	0	0	0	0	0	1	3	1	0
spawning	6	.2321	.3270	35.1	0	0	0	2	3	0	0	1	0	0	0	0	0	0	0	0	0	0	0	0	0	0	2	4	0
speak	661	.9053	118.97	60.8	95	73	95	89	125	81	89	14	187	102	9	70	11	56	18	40	19	2	2	1	55	57	13	18	1
speaker	145	.5519	16.620	52.2	21	22	11	13	25	36	17	0	12	84	4	18	1	2	5	4	7	0	0	0	1	2	2	3	0
Speaker	6	.2952	.4383	36.4	2	1	0	0	1	2	0	0	1	0	0	0	0	2	0	0	0	0	0	0	0	3	0	0	0
speaker's	22	.4838	2.2797	43.6	2	5	1	1	3	7	3	0	4	10	2	4	0	0	0	0	0	0	0	0	0	1	1	0	0
speakers	49	.3725	4.0502	46.1	0	2	4	10	13	13	7	0	5	34	0	2	0	2	2	3	0	0	0	1	0	0	0	0	0
speakin'	2	.1787	.1174	30.7	0	0	0	0	1	1	0	0	1	0	0	0	0	0	0	0	0	0	0	0	1	0	0	0	0
speaking	293	.8136	47.907	56.8	19	33	29	36	84	53	34	5	67	58	5	33	2	18	12	11	17	0	1	5	14	24	11	13	2
speaking-tube	3	.0000	.1370	31.4	3	0	0	0	0	0	0	0	3	0	0	0	0	0	0	0	0	0	0	0	0	0	0	0	0
speaks	86	.3203	6.5351	48.2	10	14	4	9	25	10	13	1	21	17	2	19	0	3	1	3	1	1	0	0	7	3	1	2	5
spear	99	.6631	13.996	51.5	5	16	12	47	17	1	1	0	61	2	0	2	0	3	0	2	0	0	0	2	17	4	5	1	0
Spear	2	.1641	.0751	28.8	0	0	0	0	1	0	1	0	0	0	1	0	0	0	0	0	0	0	0	0	0	0	1	0	0
speared	3	.1250	.1342	31.3	0	0	1	1	1	0	0	0	1	0	0	0	0	0	0	0	0	0	0	0	2	0	0	0	0
spearheads	3	.2378	.1809	32.6	0	1	0	0	2	0	0	0	0	0	0	0	0	2	0	0	0	0	0	0	0	1	0	0	0
spearing	2	.1523	.0721	28.6	0	0	0	0	1	1	0	0	0	0	1	0	0	0	0	0	0	0	0	0	0	0	0	1	0
spearmint	2	.1787	.1174	30.7	1	0	0	1	0	0	0	0	1	0	0	0	0	0	0	0	0	0	0	0	1	0	0	0	0
spears	52	.7928	8.3384	49.2	7	14	4	13	5	4	4	1	14	2	0	6	0	8	1	1	2	0	0	0	7	3	3	5	0
Specht	2	.0000	.0290	24.6	0	0	0	0	2	0	0	0	0	0	0	0	0	0	0	0	0	0	0	0	0	2	0	0	0
special	1192	.9390	221.28	63.4	167	242	155	146	206	134	122	20	201	100	21	24	67	129	56	171	53	17	46	41	16	63	79	104	4
Special	18	.5743	2.1841	43.4	1	2	0	0	8	1	1	5	4	0	0	2	0	0	0	0	1	0	0	0	0	7	2	2	0
specialist	18	.6311	2.3647	43.7	0	0	1	1	3	2	9	2	4	1	0	0	0	1	0	1	1	0	0	0	0	2	5	3	0
specialist's	2	.2437	.1129	30.5	0	0	0	0	0	0	1	1	0	0	0	0	0	0	0	0	0	0	0	0	0	0	1	1	0
specialists	27	.4762	2.8095	44.5	6	0	1	1	6	4	7	2	5	0	0	0	0	5	0	3	0	0	0	0	0	0	9	5	0
specialization	9	.5001	.9419	39.7	0	0	0	1	2	2	4	0	0	3	0	0	0	2	0	1	0	0	0	1	0	0	2	0	0
specializations	5	.0000	.0523	27.2	0	0	0	0	4	0	1	0	0	0	0	0	0	0	0	0	0	0	0	0	0	0	5	0	0
specialize	35	.5215	3.8590	45.9	0	0	14	3	4	5	6	3	0	1	0	0	0	17	0	5	1	0	0	0	0	1	9	1	0
specialized	72	.6466	9.5311	49.8	0	4	9	7	26	9	15	2	3	4	0	1	1	6	0	16	1	0	0	2	0	6	27	5	0
specializes	13	.4583	1.2916	41.1	1	1	1	1	6	1	0	2	0	0	0	0	0	6	0	3	0	0	0	0	0	0	1	3	0
specializing	5	.4882	.5167	37.1	0	0	1	0	2	2	0	0	0	0	0	1	0	2	0	0	0	0	0	0	0	0	1	1	0
specially	43	.6639	5.9029	47.7	0	5	7	7	12	6	6	0	11	1	0	0	2	5	0	2	3	0	1	5	0	3	8	2	0
specially-treated	2	.0000	.0299	24.8	0	0	0	0	2	0	0	0	0	0	0	0	2	0	0	0	0	0	0	0	0	0	0	0	0
specials	6	.3436	.4468	36.5	0	0	2	1	2	0	1	0	0	0	0	0	0	0	0	0	0	0	1	0	1	0	0	4	0
Specials	3	.0000	.1370	31.4	2	0	0	0	1	0	0	0	3	0	0	0	0	0	0	0	0	0	0	0	0	0	0	0	0
specialties	8	.3706	.6802	38.3	1	0	0	3	1	1	2	0	1	0	0	0	0	3	0	1	0	0	0	0	0	0	3	0	0
specialty	27	.6517	3.5750	45.5	5	0	3	6	6	0	5	2	0	0	0	2	0	5	0	1	3	0	0	1	0	2	9	4	0
speciation	2	.0000	.0209	23.2	0	0	0	0	2	0	0	0	0	0	0	0	0	0	0	0	0	0	0	0	0	0	2	0	0
species	276	.3889	23.529	53.7	4	2	7	9	202	2	25	25	12	1	0	1	0	0	0	66	0	0	0	1	7	4	157	27	0
Species	3	.2159	.1532	31.9	0	0	0	1	2	0	0	0	0	0	0	0	0	0	0	0	0	0	0	0	0	0	2	1	0
specific	247	.5586	28.388	54.5	0	12	26	19	65	55	65	5	11	53	60	2	8	6	4	41	9	1	8	5	0	10	21	8	0
specifically	18	.5772	2.1505	43.3	0	0	1	2	5	3	3	4	1	4	0	0	0	1	0	1	1	0	0	0	0	1	2	7	0
specifications	11	.3599	.8459	39.3	0	0	0	0	7	1	3	0	0	0	0	0	0	0	0	0	0	0	0	3	0	2	2	4	0
specifics	3	.2321	.1635	32.1	0	0	1	0	1	0	1	0	0	0	0	0	0	0	0	0	0	0	0	0	0	0	1	2	0
specified	22	.5596	2.5214	44.0	0	0	2	0	6	6	8	0	0	4	0	0	8	0	0	0	0	0	2	3	0	0	4	1	0
specifies	3	.1970	.1504	31.8	0	0	0	0	1	1	1	0	0	0	0	0	0	0	0	2	0	0	1	0	0	0	0	0	0
specify	9	.4386	.8372	39.2	0	0	0	0	1	2	5	1	0	0	0	0	3	1	0	1	1	0	0	2	0	0	0	1	0
specifying	3	.2292	.1672	32.2	0	1	0	0	0	0	2	0	0	0	0	0	0	1	0	1	0	0	0	1	0	0	0	0	0
specimen	43	.6557	5.8209	47.6	2	1	0	2	23	8	2	5	3	0	1	2	0	2	0	26	0	0	0	1	3	2	1	2	0
specimens	52	.6186	6.6890	48.3	3	3	3	0	19	7	4	13	4	0	0	4	0	0	0	28	0	0	0	1	2	5	6	2	0
speck	27	.5355	3.0890	44.9	1	4	2	4	9	5	2	0	6	1	4	0	2	0	0	4	0	0	0	0	3	5	1	1	0
Speck	7	.0000	.3198	35.0	0	7	0	0	0	0	0	0	7	0	0	0	0	0	0	0	0	0	0	0	0	0	0	0	0
Speck's	2	.0000	.0914	29.6	0	2	0	0	0	0	0	0	2	0	0	0	0	0	0	0	0	0	0	0	0	0	0	0	0
speckled	7	.5879	.8562	39.3	0	2	0	1	2	1	0	1	1	1	0	0	0	0	0	0	1	0	0	0	1	1	0	2	0
Speckles	9	.0000	.4111	36.1	9	0	0	0	0	0	0	0	9	0	0	0	0	0	0	0	0	0	0	0	0	0	0	0	0
specks	20	.6323	2.6517	44.2	3	4	2	5	5	0	1	0	4	1	0	1	0	4	0	7	0	0	0	0	1	0	2	0	0
spectacle	22	.6690	2.9829	44.7	1	1	0	4	10	4	0	2	0	0	0	2	0	1	0	2	2	0	0	0	6	2	4	3	0
spectacles	23	.4546	2.2767	43.6	3	6	4	2	8	0	0	0	4	0	0	7	0	0	0	0	0	0	0	0	8	3	0	1	0
spectacular	55	.6921	7.7014	48.9	4	4	3	6	18	8	8	4	2	0	2	2	0	3	0	4	5	1	0	0	0	5	17	14	0
spectacularly	3	.2309	.1631	32.1	0	0	0	0	2	0	0	1	0	0	0	1	0	0	0	0	0	0	0	0	0	0	0	2	0
spectator	12	.6086	1.5284	41.8	0	0	0	2	1	5	4	0	2	1	0	0	0	4	0	1	0	0	1	0	0	1	2	0	0
Spectator	3	.2076	.1697	32.3	0	0	0	0	1	1	1	0	1	0	1	0	0	0	0	0	0	0	0	0	1	0	0	0	0
spectators	44	.7774	6.9412	48.4	0	1	4	17	10	6	3	3	14	3	1	3	1	1	0	1	2	2	0	0	1	6	1	8	0
specter	4	.2440	.2264	33.5	0	0	0	0	0	1	2	1	0	0	0	2	0	0	0	0	0	0	0	0	0	0	0	2	0
spectra	15	.3801	1.2667	41.0	0	0	0	3	1	6	5	0	0	0	0	0	0	0	0	8	0	0	0	0	0	0	4	3	0
spectral	3	.1832	.1417	31.5	0	0	0	0	1	2	0	0	0	0	0	2	0	0	0	1	0	0	0	0	0	0	0	0	0
spectrograph	3	.1927	.1491	31.7	0	0	0	2	0	0	1	0	0	0	0	0	0	0	0	1	0	0	0	0	0	0	0	2	0
spectroscope	18	.0000	.3549	35.5	0	0	0	6	0	6	5	1	0	0	0	0	0	0	0	18	0	0	0	0	0	0	0	0	0
spectroscopy	3	.3764	.2483	33.9	0	0	0	2	1	0	0	0	0	0	0	0	0	0	0	1	0	0	0	0	0	0	1	1	0
spectrum	86	.3978	7.6271	48.8	0	0	7	29	7	11	25	7	1	0	0	0	1	0	0	61	0	1	0	0	0	0	19	3	0
speculate	10	.5939	1.2583	41.0	0	1	1	2	4	2	0	0	3	0	0	1	0	0	0	1	0	0	0	0	1	0	2	2	0
speculated	2	.2437	.1129	30.5	0	0	0	0	1	1	0	0	0	0	0	0	0	0	0	0	0	0	0	0	0	0	1	1	0
speculating	5	.3642	.3974	36.0	0	0	0	0	2	1	1	1	0	0	0	0	0	0	0	0	0	0	0	0	2	1	0	2	0
speculation	18	.4589	1.7471	42.4	1	0	1	0	5	4	5	2	0	0	0	0	0	2	0	0	0	0	0	0	1	2	5	8	0
speculations	7	.5803	.8496	39.3	0	0	0	1	2	1	2	1	1	1	0	0	0	0	0	1	0	0	0	0	2	0	1	1	0
speculatively	2	.1787	.1174	30.7	0	0	0	0	2	0	0	0	1	0	0	0	0	0	0	0	0	0	0	0	1	0	0	0	0

7B sparrows'
7Q sparser
8G spartan
3P Spartanburg
6R spas
7N spasmodic
9Q spastic
8R spate
7R spates
4P spats
9D speak'st
7R Speaks
6R spear-like
7P spear-nosed
9B spear-sharp
7D spear's
6A speargun
XR spearheaded
7R spearlike
4F spearthrowers
7A spec'
9Q special-effects
8R special-forces
3P special-reaction
5R special-summer
5R Specialist
XR specialists'
3F specialities
7H specially-built
8F specie
9Q Specie
9B specific-detail
7R specification
7R specificity
5Q specious
7Q speckle
4D speckles
4N speckly
4N speckly-spickly
XR specs
5R spectaculars
8F specters
8Q spectrograms
6R spectrographic
9H spectrometry
XH spectroscopes
9R speculative

Word Type	F	D	U	SFI	3 Gr 3	4 Gr 4	5 Gr 5	6 Gr 6	7 Gr 7	8 Gr 8	9 Gr 9	X UnGr	A Read	B Eng & Gr	C Comp	D Lit	E Math	F Soc Stud	G Spell	H Sci	J Music	K Art	L Home Ec	M Shop	N Lib F	P Lib NF	Q Lib Ref	R Mag	S Rel
speculators	2	.2437	.1129	30.5	0	0	0	0	0	0	2	0	0	0	0	0	0	0	0	0	0	0	0	0	0	0	1	1	0
sped	38	.6773	5.4030	47.3	4	6	5	7	9	4	3	0	18	2	0	6	0	1	0	1	0	0	0	0	5	2	1	2	0
speech	469	.7986	75.192	58.8	17	27	56	39	134	89	96	11	77	117	8	43	2	22	70	10	13	2	1	0	18	39	26	21	0
Speech	9	.5386	1.0206	40.1	0	0	1	0	0	2	4	2	1	3	0	0	0	1	0	0	0	0	0	0	0	1	1	2	0
speeches	57	.7059	8.3048	49.2	4	8	11	2	9	17	6	0	17	5	0	5	0	12	0	0	0	0	0	0	2	9	2	5	0
speechless	19	.5060	2.1542	43.3	3	6	3	3	2	1	1	0	9	0	0	1	0	0	0	0	0	0	0	0	5	3	0	1	0
speed	750	.9093	135.54	61.3	64	91	66	114	226	111	65	13	196	12	1	23	92	25	9	139	26	4	3	10	46	49	46	69	0
Speed	8	.3437	.6913	38.4	0	3	0	0	4	1	0	0	4	0	0	1	0	0	0	0	0	0	0	0	0	0	0	3	0
speed-limit	2	.0000	.0234	23.7	0	0	0	0	0	2	0	0	0	0	0	0	0	0	0	0	0	0	0	0	2	0	0	0	0
speedboat	2	.1733	.1149	30.6	0	1	0	0	1	0	0	0	1	1	0	0	0	0	0	0	0	0	0	0	0	0	0	0	0
speeded	18	.7025	2.6074	44.2	0	0	5	2	4	3	3	1	4	1	0	0	1	4	0	4	0	0	0	0	2	0	1	1	0
speediest	3	.3795	.2506	34.0	0	0	0	0	2	1	0	0	0	0	0	0	0	1	0	0	0	0	0	0	1	0	0	1	0
speedily	4	.4445	.3917	35.9	0	0	1	1	1	0	1	0	1	0	0	1	0	0	0	0	1	0	0	0	1	0	0	0	0
speeding	45	.6996	6.5917	48.2	2	9	4	4	8	13	5	0	21	0	0	1	0	2	0	11	1	0	0	0	2	3	1	3	0
speedometer	12	.4812	1.3339	41.3	1	4	1	0	3	1	2	0	7	0	0	1	2	0	0	0	0	0	0	0	2	0	0	0	0
speeds	93	.7397	13.956	51.4	6	7	10	20	21	13	8	8	9	1	0	1	11	4	1	32	6	0	0	1	0	2	10	15	0
speedster	2	.2433	.1158	30.6	0	0	0	1	0	0	1	0	0	0	0	0	0	0	0	0	0	0	0	0	0	1	0	1	0
speedway	2	.0000	.0290	24.6	1	0	0	0	0	0	0	1	0	0	0	0	0	0	0	0	0	0	0	0	0	2	0	0	0
Speedway	3	.0000	.1370	31.4	0	0	0	0	0	3	0	0	3	0	0	0	0	0	0	0	0	0	0	0	0	0	0	0	0
Speedwell	5	.1118	.2195	33.4	0	0	4	0	1	0	0	0	1	0	0	0	0	4	0	0	0	0	0	0	0	0	0	0	0
speedy	11	.6568	1.5013	41.8	3	2	1	1	2	1	1	0	3	0	0	1	0	1	0	0	1	0	0	0	0	2	2	1	0
speleologists	2	.0000	.0243	23.9	0	0	0	0	0	1	1	0	0	0	0	0	0	0	0	0	0	0	0	0	0	0	0	2	0
spell	1052	.2174	53.294	57.3	274	220	175	200	105	45	26	7	42	108	2	7	7	5	845	2	4	0	1	0	9	8	5	7	0
spellbound	5	.2422	.3874	35.9	0	0	1	2	1	1	0	0	4	0	0	0	0	0	0	0	0	0	0	0	0	1	0	0	0
spelled	779	.2160	38.692	55.9	165	131	157	153	113	42	14	4	10	124	1	4	2	2	614	0	1	0	0	1	2	9	1	8	0
speller	15	.3500	1.2746	41.1	4	1	3	0	0	0	7	0	6	7	0	0	1	0	1	0	0	0	0	0	0	0	0	0	0
Speller	83	.0054	.7961	39.0	1	16	16	18	32	0	0	0	1	0	0	0	0	0	82	0	0	0	0	0	0	0	0	0	0
spellers	5	.2240	.2560	34.1	0	0	0	0	2	0	3	0	0	2	0	0	0	0	3	0	0	0	0	0	0	0	0	0	0
spelling	1217	.1894	55.008	57.4	402	126	153	145	152	188	42	9	38	128	0	6	19	0	992	4	1	0	0	1	4	10	2	12	0
Spelling	297	.0018	2.5475	44.1	21	62	63	57	83	11	0	0	1	0	0	0	0	0	296	0	0	0	0	0	0	0	0	0	0
spellings	163	.1512	6.0877	47.8	5	18	36	26	40	37	1	0	2	18	0	0	0	0	138	0	0	0	0	0	0	1	4	0	0
Spellman	2	.1378	.0662	28.2	0	0	0	0	1	1	0	0	0	0	0	0	0	0	0	0	0	1	0	0	0	0	0	1	0
spells	352	.0796	8.4029	49.2	45	78	70	93	44	16	3	3	6	5	0	3	0	1	329	0	1	0	0	0	0	1	0	6	0
spelt	5	.3087	.3662	35.6	0	1	0	0	1	1	2	0	1	2	0	0	0	0	0	0	0	0	0	0	2	0	0	0	0
spelunkers	2	.0000	.0243	23.9	0	0	0	0	0	2	0	0	0	0	0	0	0	0	0	0	0	0	0	0	0	0	0	2	0
Spence	3	.2260	.1580	32.0	0	0	0	0	3	0	0	0	0	0	0	2	0	0	0	0	0	0	0	0	0	0	1	0	0
Spencer	7	.2402	.5467	37.4	0	6	0	0	0	0	1	0	6	0	0	0	0	0	0	0	0	0	0	0	0	0	1	0	0
Spencer's	3	.2028	.1988	33.0	0	2	0	0	1	0	0	0	2	0	0	0	0	0	0	0	1	0	0	0	0	0	0	0	0
spend	418	.8906	74.099	58.7	101	67	54	56	66	27	37	10	91	24	4	16	90	35	5	35	3	2	19	2	14	36	10	32	0
spending	84	.6377	11.145	50.5	9	11	10	5	12	16	18	3	23	5	1	2	3	6	0	3	1	0	15	0	3	3	5	14	0
spends	58	.8322	9.6717	49.9	10	10	4	5	8	6	14	1	11	8	2	1	9	4	2	6	0	0	2	0	2	1	4	6	0
spendthrift	3	.3847	.2494	34.0	0	0	0	0	3	0	0	0	0	0	0	0	0	0	0	0	0	0	0	0	1	1	1	0	0
Spens	5	.0000	.0547	27.4	0	0	0	0	1	4	0	0	0	5	0	0	0	0	0	0	0	0	0	0	0	0	0	0	0
spent	522	.9011	93.509	59.7	84	73	72	79	76	76	51	11	120	18	8	24	131	59	4	9	11	4	9	2	32	34	28	29	0
sperm	60	.4178	5.6733	47.5	7	8	7	9	18	0	6	5	11	0	0	0	0	0	0	26	0	0	0	0	0	7	16	0	0
sperms	2	.0000	.0394	26.0	0	0	0	0	2	0	0	0	0	0	0	0	0	0	0	2	0	0	0	0	0	0	0	0	0
spewed	3	.3871	.2488	34.0	0	0	0	0	1	0	1	1	0	1	0	0	0	0	0	0	0	0	0	0	0	0	1	1	0
Speyside	2	.0000	.0243	23.9	0	0	0	2	0	0	0	0	0	0	0	0	0	0	0	0	0	0	0	0	0	0	0	2	0
sphere	115	.7064	16.475	52.2	9	16	4	3	14	52	13	4	1	1	2	2	55	21	3	12	1	1	0	2	0	2	12	0	0
spheres	46	.4529	4.5416	46.6	2	5	0	2	2	9	25	1	0	0	0	3	4	2	0	31	0	0	0	0	0	1	0	5	0
spherical	12	.3909	1.0302	40.1	0	1	1	1	2	2	5	0	0	0	0	0	1	0	0	5	0	0	0	0	0	0	5	1	0
sphincter	2	.0000	.0394	26.0	0	0	0	0	2	0	0	0	0	0	0	0	0	0	0	2	0	0	0	0	0	0	0	0	0
sphinx	8	.0935	.2340	33.7	0	1	0	0	0	7	0	0	0	7	0	0	0	1	0	0	0	0	0	0	0	0	0	0	0
Sphinx	7	.3423	.5200	37.2	1	0	2	1	2	1	0	0	0	0	0	0	1	1	0	0	0	2	0	0	1	1	1	0	0
spic	3	.2765	.1899	32.8	0	2	0	0	0	0	1	0	0	0	0	0	0	1	0	0	0	0	1	0	0	1	0	0	0
spice	19	.7658	2.9277	44.7	3	3	5	2	4	0	0	2	2	2	1	0	0	3	0	1	3	0	1	0	1	1	2	2	0
Spice	6	.4736	.6382	38.0	0	2	1	0	2	1	0	0	2	0	0	1	0	2	0	0	0	0	0	0	0	0	1	0	0
spiced	3	.2124	.1716	32.3	0	0	1	0	1	0	1	0	1	1	1	0	0	0	0	0	0	0	0	0	0	0	0	0	0
spices	56	.6584	7.5740	48.8	5	4	9	7	10	7	6	8	5	0	1	1	0	23	1	1	0	0	5	0	0	3	6	10	0
spicy	10	.5121	1.0984	40.4	1	4	0	1	2	1	1	0	2	3	0	0	0	0	0	0	0	0	0	0	2	2	0	1	0
spider	229	.6151	29.894	54.8	67	13	21	96	21	4	7	0	64	3	0	9	0	0	4	108	0	0	0	2	2	27	1	9	0
Spider	41	.2361	2.7938	44.5	24	0	1	0	0	15	1	0	20	0	0	1	0	0	0	0	0	0	0	0	0	0	0	20	0
spider's	22	.3075	1.7089	42.3	2	1	3	14	2	0	0	0	5	0	0	0	0	0	0	15	0	0	0	0	1	0	0	1	0
Spider's	2	.0000	.0243	23.9	1	0	1	0	0	0	0	0	0	0	0	0	0	0	0	0	0	0	0	0	0	0	0	2	0
spiders	131	.4818	13.903	51.4	50	5	3	51	17	4	1	0	23	1	0	2	0	1	0	58	0	0	0	0	4	40	1	1	0
spiders'	4	.4491	.4015	36.0	0	0	0	1	2	0	1	0	1	1	0	0	0	0	0	1	0	0	0	0	1	0	0	0	0
spidery	3	.3841	.2496	34.0	0	0	0	0	2	0	1	0	0	0	0	0	1	0	0	0	0	0	0	0	0	0	1	1	0
spied	31	.5804	3.9533	46.0	6	7	3	4	8	3	0	0	18	0	0	5	0	3	0	0	1	0	0	0	2	2	0	0	0
spies	15	.6158	1.9580	42.9	0	3	3	0	4	3	2	0	5	0	0	2	0	4	0	0	1	0	0	0	2	0	0	1	0
spike	18	.6465	2.4331	43.9	4	3	3	2	2	1	2	1	6	0	0	4	0	1	0	1	2	0	0	1	0	1	0	2	0
Spike	7	.0000	.0751	28.8	0	0	0	0	0	7	0	0	0	0	0	7	0	0	0	0	0	0	0	0	0	0	0	0	0
Spike's	2	.0000	.0215	23.3	0	0	0	0	0	2	0	0	0	0	0	2	0	0	0	0	0	0	0	0	0	0	0	0	0
spiked	10	.3925	.9033	39.6	0	1	3	3	1	0	0	2	3	0	0	0	0	0	0	1	3	0	0	0	0	0	0	3	0
spikes	23	.6395	3.1190	44.9	6	5	4	4	3	0	0	1	10	1	0	0	0	1	0	1	2	0	0	0	1	6	0	1	0
spiky	4	.2417	.3028	34.8	1	0	0	2	0	1	0	0	3	0	0	0	0	0	0	0	0	0	0	0	1	0	0	0	0
spill	23	.6690	3.2117	45.1	4	7	2	1	4	5	0	0	8	0	0	3	0	4	0	0	0	0	1	0	3	3	1	0	0
spilled	52	.8338	8.7291	49.4	7	10	7	5	10	5	7	1	18	7	1	6	1	3	0	5	0	0	1	1	3	3	0	3	0
spilling	10	.5533	1.2073	40.8	0	0	3	1	2	2	1	1	4	1	0	0	0	0	0	2	0	0	0	0	2	0	0	1	0
spills	8	.3909	.6846	38.4	0	2	1	2	1	0	1	1	1	0	1	4	0	0	0	0	0	0	0	0	0	0	0	2	0
spillways	2	.0000	.0243	23.9	0	0	0	0	1	0	0	1	0	0	0	0	0	0	0	0	0	0	0	0	0	0	0	2	0
spilt	3	.2060	.1500	31.8	0	0	0	2	1	0	0	0	0	0	0	2	0	0	0	0	0	0	0	0	0	1	0	0	0
spin	137	.8438	23.178	53.7	62	13	12	16	16	12	2	4	31	4	1	1	0	10	0	32	7	1	1	1	2	11	11	24	0
spinach	18	.3317	1.3445	41.3	2	1	2	1	5	0	5	2	2	2	0	1	0	2	0	3	0	0	7	0	1	0	0	0	0
spinal	49	.4216	4.5263	46.6	0	1	9	7	8	7	15	2	0	0	0	0	3	0	1	30	0	0	0	0	0	1	13	1	0
spindle	37	.3041	2.6579	44.2	7	0	1	7	8	6	7	1	10	1	0	0	0	0	0	1	0	0	1	14	0	0	3	7	0
spindle-shaped	2	.2441	.1127	30.5	0	0	0	0	2	0	0	0	0	0	0	0	0	0	0	0	0	0	0	0	1	0	1	0	0
Spindler	5	.0000	.0586	27.7	0	0	0	5	0	0	0	0	0	0	0	0	0	0	0	0	0	0	0	0	5	0	0	0	0
spindles	10	.4679	.9992	40.0	1	0	0	1	6	2	0	0	1	0	0	0	0	2	0	0	0	1	0	1	0	0	0	5	0
spindling	2	.0000	.0234	23.7	0	0	1	1	0	0	0	0	0	0	0	0	0	0	0	0	0	0	0	0	2	0	0	0	0
spindly	2	.2405	.1205	30.8	1	0	0	0	1	0	0	0	0	0	0	0	0	0	0	1	0	0	0	0	0	1	0	0	0
spine	35	.7684	5.4149	47.3	1	3	7	5	8	2	7	2	4	8	1	1	3	0	0	4	0	1	0	0	3	2	6	2	0
spine-tingling	2	.0000	.0215	23.3	0	0	0	0	0	0	2	0	0	0	0	2	0	0	0	0	0	0	0	0	0	0	0	0	0
spinel	2	.0000	.0394	26.0	0	0	0	0	0	0	0	2	0	0	0	0	0	0	0	2	0	0	0	0	0	0	0	0	0
spines	24	.6181	3.1002	44.9	5	2	1	4	11	0	1	0	5	1	0	0	0	0	0	5	0	1	0	0	2	4	6	0	0

9R speech-writers
7R speechwriter
9M speed-change
9D speed-mad
7E speed-skating
9M Speedball
5H speedier
8R Speeds
7Q speedsters
7R Speer

9R Speleology
5B spell-bound
7P spellbinder
8A spelldown
8A spelldowns
6A SPELLES
8G spelling-pattern
5F spender
5R spenders
4F Spending

4A spendings
XB Spenser
XH spermatozoon
7R Sperry
9D spets
9H spew
6A spewing
7R spews
9B Speyer's
9H sphere-gas

7Q sphere's
XH sphericity
7A spheroid
8B sphinxlike
7G spicere
3J spicky
4A spicy-smelling
4N Spider-monkey
4N spider-web
7R spider-webbed

4A spider-webs
9Q spiderwort
7P spiel
8R spiffiest
7A spik
7Q spike-toothed
7N spile
4P spilikins
5Q Spill
5R spilleth

5J Spillville
4N Spinach
9M spindle-reverse
9M spindle-reversing
6N Spindlers
6N spindlin'
8H spine-covered
6E spine-tailed

Word Type	F	D	U	SFI	3 Gr 3	4 Gr 4	5 Gr 5	6 Gr 6	7 Gr 7	8 Gr 8	9 Gr 9	X UnGr	A Read	B Eng & Gr	C Comp	D Lit	E Math	F Soc Stud	G Spell	H Sci	J Music	K Art	L Home Ec	M Shop	N Lib F	P Lib NF	Q Lib Ref	R Mag	S Rel
spinet	2	.0000	.0290	24.6	0	2	0	0	0	0	0	0	0	0	0	0	0	0	0	0	0	0	0	0	0	2	0	0	0
spink	8	.0000	.3655	35.6	0	8	0	0	0	0	0	0	8	0	0	0	0	0	0	0	0	0	0	0	0	0	0	0	0
Spink	11	.0000	.5025	37.0	11	0	0	0	0	0	0	0	11	0	0	0	0	0	0	0	0	0	0	0	0	0	0	0	0
spinner	6	.3328	.4478	36.5	0	0	1	1	0	0	4	0	0	1	0	0	4	0	0	0	0	0	0	0	0	0	0	1	0
spinneret	3	.0000	.0591	27.7	0	0	0	0	0	0	3	0	0	0	0	0	0	0	0	3	0	0	0	0	0	0	0	0	0
spinnerets	8	.0782	.2923	34.7	0	0	0	4	1	0	3	0	1	0	0	0	0	0	0	7	0	0	0	0	0	0	0	0	0
spinners	8	.3840	.7425	38.7	0	1	0	1	5	0	1	0	4	0	1	0	0	1	0	0	0	0	0	0	0	0	2	0	0
spinning	112	.8850	19.741	53.0	28	20	12	13	25	8	5	1	23	0	1	1	0	21	1	16	9	1	3	2	8	7	11	8	0
spins	52	.6099	6.6798	48.2	17	15	2	3	6	4	0	5	8	3	0	0	0	21	1	13	0	0	0	0	0	3	2	1	0
spiny	16	.5296	1.8034	42.6	2	0	0	2	6	1	2	3	2	0	0	1	0	0	0	5	0	0	0	0	1	2	5	0	0
spiracles	4	.2353	.2382	33.8	0	0	1	2	1	0	0	0	0	0	0	0	0	0	0	3	0	0	0	0	0	0	1	0	0
spiral	36	.7244	5.2641	47.2	1	3	6	4	13	2	4	3	1	0	0	1	0	2	2	12	4	2	0	2	1	0	3	6	0
spiraled	3	.2279	.2143	33.3	0	0	0	2	0	1	0	0	2	0	0	0	0	0	0	0	0	0	0	0	0	0	0	1	0
spirals	8	.5257	.8863	39.5	2	0	2	2	1	0	1	0	1	0	0	0	0	0	0	2	2	0	0	1	1	0	1	0	0
spire	4	.4556	.4079	36.1	1	2	0	0	1	0	0	0	1	0	0	0	0	1	0	0	0	0	0	0	1	1	0	0	0
spires	9	.3138	.6714	38.3	1	2	0	0	2	0	4	0	2	0	0	0	0	1	0	0	0	2	0	0	1	3	0	0	0
Spiridon	2	.0000	.0914	29.6	0	0	0	2	0	0	0	0	2	0	0	0	0	0	0	0	0	0	0	0	0	0	0	0	0
spirilla	2	.0000	.0394	26.0	0	0	0	1	1	0	0	0	0	0	0	0	0	0	0	2	0	0	0	0	0	0	0	0	0
spirit	241	.8262	39.855	56.0	9	17	30	23	56	55	42	9	44	9	4	38	0	15	0	6	42	6	5	0	15	18	23	16	0
Spirit	16	.1030	.4732	36.7	0	5	1	0	7	1	2	0	0	1	1	2	0	5	0	0	0	0	0	0	2	0	1	0	4
spirit's	3	.2379	.1705	32.3	0	0	0	0	3	0	0	0	0	0	0	1	0	0	0	0	0	0	0	0	0	2	0	0	0
spirited	13	.6029	1.6414	42.2	1	3	0	2	1	4	1	1	3	0	0	1	0	0	0	0	2	0	0	0	2	3	0	2	0
spirits	86	.8146	14.124	51.5	8	17	14	10	17	9	10	1	27	7	2	13	0	6	0	1	3	0	1	0	6	7	10	3	0
Spirits	5	.2395	.3804	35.8	2	0	2	1	0	0	0	0	4	0	0	0	0	0	0	0	1	0	0	0	0	0	0	0	0
spiritual	49	.5868	5.8782	47.7	1	2	8	7	4	9	14	4	0	0	0	3	0	5	0	0	16	0	1	0	0	6	10	8	0
spirituals	17	.0000	.1374	31.4	0	1	6	4	2	2	2	0	0	0	0	0	0	0	0	0	17	0	0	0	0	0	0	0	0
Spiros	9	.0000	.4111	36.1	9	0	0	0	0	0	0	0	9	0	0	0	0	0	0	0	0	0	0	0	0	0	0	0	0
spit	25	.6977	3.5831	45.5	5	0	4	3	6	2	4	1	7	1	1	5	0	0	1	0	0	0	0	0	5	1	1	3	0
spite	173	.8750	30.200	54.8	16	28	16	25	41	22	22	3	43	7	7	15	1	15	3	15	7	1	1	0	13	18	17	10	0
spits	5	.4694	.5313	37.3	0	2	0	1	1	0	1	0	2	0	0	1	0	1	0	0	0	0	0	0	0	0	1	0	0
spitting	9	.4607	.9454	39.8	1	2	1	1	1	2	1	0	4	0	0	2	0	0	0	0	0	0	0	0	2	1	0	0	0
Spitz	12	.3313	.9669	39.9	0	3	0	0	4	5	0	0	4	0	0	0	0	0	0	0	0	0	0	0	5	0	0	3	0
splash	75	.8161	12.370	50.9	22	8	9	12	16	3	3	2	27	3	0	7	0	2	2	8	4	0	0	0	5	7	3	7	0
splashed	44	.6947	6.3876	48.1	12	12	5	5	7	2	0	1	21	2	2	5	0	2	0	2	0	0	0	0	2	4	0	4	0
splashes	13	.5417	1.4834	41.7	2	1	0	1	6	1	2	0	2	5	0	1	0	0	0	1	0	1	0	0	0	1	0	2	0
splashing	39	.7422	5.9589	47.8	10	7	4	5	11	1	0	1	18	5	0	3	0	0	0	0	1	1	0	0	3	2	3	3	0
splatter	2	.2130	.1056	30.2	0	0	0	0	0	2	0	0	0	0	0	0	0	0	1	1	0	0	0	0	0	0	0	0	0
splattered	2	.1814	.1187	30.7	1	0	0	0	0	0	0	1	1	0	0	0	0	0	0	0	0	0	0	0	0	0	0	1	0
splayed-out	2	.1717	.1142	30.6	0	0	1	0	0	1	0	0	1	0	0	1	0	0	0	0	0	0	0	0	0	0	0	0	0
splendid	88	.8095	14.371	51.6	11	8	10	24	12	11	10	2	26	3	0	8	0	10	3	0	2	1	0	0	13	4	8	10	0
splendidly	8	.6244	1.0541	40.2	0	1	1	3	2	1	0	0	3	1	0	1	0	0	0	0	1	0	0	0	1	1	0	0	0
splendor	31	.7454	4.6950	46.7	4	2	3	6	5	7	3	1	7	0	1	3	0	2	0	1	5	0	0	0	2	5	3	2	0
splendors	3	.3870	.2492	34.0	0	1	0	0	0	1	1	0	0	0	0	0	0	0	0	0	0	0	0	0	1	0	1	1	0
splendour	3	.2347	.1695	32.3	0	0	1	0	1	1	0	0	0	0	0	0	0	0	0	0	0	0	0	0	1	2	0	0	0
spliced	2	.2375	.1088	30.4	0	0	0	0	1	0	1	0	0	0	0	0	0	0	0	0	1	0	0	0	0	0	0	1	0
spline	5	.0694	.0889	29.5	0	0	0	0	1	4	0	0	0	0	0	0	0	0	0	0	0	0	0	4	0	0	0	1	0
splined	2	.0000	.0243	23.9	0	0	0	0	2	0	0	0	0	0	0	0	0	0	0	0	0	0	0	0	0	0	0	2	0
splines	5	.1935	.2236	33.5	0	0	0	0	3	2	0	0	0	0	0	0	0	0	0	0	0	0	0	2	0	0	0	3	0
splint	20	.3853	1.7878	42.5	1	2	0	1	6	9	1	0	3	0	0	0	0	0	1	14	0	0	0	0	1	0	0	1	0
splinter	8	.4349	.7439	38.7	0	4	0	2	0	0	1	1	0	0	0	0	0	0	0	2	1	0	0	0	0	0	1	4	0
splintered	14	.5087	1.5952	42.0	0	3	0	4	3	1	3	0	7	0	0	3	0	1	0	0	0	0	0	1	0	0	0	2	0
splintering	6	.2820	.4730	36.7	0	0	1	2	1	2	0	0	4	0	1	1	0	0	0	0	0	0	0	0	0	0	0	0	0
splinters	9	.4468	.9474	39.8	1	0	3	1	3	0	0	1	5	0	0	2	0	0	0	1	0	0	0	0	0	1	0	0	0
splints	3	.3370	.2430	33.9	1	0	0	0	1	0	1	0	1	0	0	1	0	0	0	0	0	0	0	0	0	0	1	0	0
split	159	.8070	25.858	54.1	26	15	16	30	44	19	7	2	36	5	0	6	2	10	7	34	4	0	1	10	5	19	14	6	0
Split	3	.2321	.1635	32.1	0	0	2	0	0	1	0	0	0	0	0	0	0	0	0	0	0	0	0	0	0	0	1	2	0
split-second	3	.1169	.1277	31.1	0	0	0	0	2	0	1	0	1	0	0	0	0	0	0	0	0	0	0	0	0	0	2	0	0
splits	34	.5901	4.2516	46.3	6	1	4	7	11	2	1	2	8	0	0	0	4	0	0	8	0	0	0	0	0	5	7	2	0
splitting	24	.5714	2.8501	44.5	4	0	1	4	8	6	0	1	1	0	0	1	1	1	0	8	0	0	0	3	0	2	5	2	0
splotches	5	.3520	.3895	35.9	3	0	0	1	0	0	1	0	0	0	0	0	0	0	0	0	0	0	0	0	1	3	0	1	0
spluttered	6	.3543	.5046	37.0	1	0	0	0	3	0	2	0	2	0	1	2	0	1	0	0	0	0	0	0	0	0	0	0	0
spluttering	2	.1717	.1142	30.6	0	1	0	0	0	1	0	0	1	0	0	1	0	0	0	0	0	0	0	0	0	0	0	0	0
Spock	8	.1444	.3087	34.9	0	0	0	0	1	7	0	0	0	0	0	0	0	0	0	0	0	0	0	0	0	0	1	7	0
Spofford	17	.0000	.1993	33.0	17	0	0	0	0	0	0	0	0	0	0	0	0	0	0	0	0	0	0	0	17	0	0	0	0
spoil	59	.8317	9.8461	49.9	14	11	7	9	9	4	4	1	12	3	0	6	0	10	2	9	0	1	3	0	4	5	3	1	0
spoiled	53	.8441	8.9781	49.5	13	5	2	13	9	4	7	0	15	5	2	3	2	4	1	7	0	0	0	1	5	5	1	2	0
spoiling	15	.4949	1.6030	42.0	2	4	1	1	1	5	1	0	1	0	0	0	0	7	0	5	0	1	1	0	0	0	0	0	0
spoils	13	.6431	1.7492	42.4	2	2	1	1	2	3	2	0	4	0	0	1	0	2	0	0	0	0	1	0	0	2	2	1	0
spoke	512	.7464	78.176	58.9	59	92	58	73	108	66	52	4	180	44	10	82	4	28	13	1	9	2	0	1	56	48	7	23	4
spoked	2	.0000	.0209	23.2	0	0	0	0	2	0	0	0	0	0	0	0	0	0	0	0	0	0	0	0	0	0	2	0	0
spoken	230	.7434	34.608	55.4	28	16	30	37	48	42	28	1	40	76	2	8	0	17	39	3	6	2	2	0	11	8	12	4	0
SPOKEN	4	.0000	.0323	25.1	0	0	0	4	0	0	0	0	0	0	0	0	0	0	0	0	4	0	0	0	0	0	0	0	0
spokes	22	.6621	3.0143	44.8	3	2	4	2	4	0	7	0	5	0	0	1	5	2	0	1	0	0	0	2	3	1	1	1	0
spokeshave	4	.0000	.0101	20.0	0	0	0	0	1	0	3	0	0	0	0	0	0	0	0	0	0	0	0	4	0	0	0	0	0
spokesman	11	.4220	1.0748	40.3	0	0	2	2	2	2	2	1	4	1	0	0	0	2	0	0	0	0	0	0	0	0	0	4	0
spokesmen	10	.3624	.8239	39.2	0	0	0	0	1	7	1	1	1	0	0	0	0	3	0	0	0	0	0	0	0	0	1	5	0
sponge	64	.6834	8.9643	49.5	14	12	10	11	10	4	3	0	14	2	4	8	1	1	0	10	0	8	1	2	4	3	4	2	0
sponged	2	.2443	.1130	30.5	0	1	0	0	0	1	0	0	0	0	0	1	0	0	0	0	0	0	0	0	1	0	0	0	0
spongelike	4	.4734	.4039	36.1	0	0	0	1	2	0	1	0	0	0	0	1	0	1	0	1	0	0	0	0	0	0	1	0	0
sponges	39	.7066	5.7139	47.6	3	6	19	2	6	0	2	1	14	0	0	3	1	3	0	9	0	1	0	0	1	2	5	0	0
sponging	2	.1787	.1174	30.7	0	0	0	0	2	0	0	0	1	0	0	0	0	0	0	0	0	0	0	0	1	0	0	0	0
spongy	7	.4489	.6700	38.3	1	0	1	0	4	1	0	0	0	0	0	0	0	0	0	3	0	1	0	0	1	0	1	1	0
sponsor	6	.3721	.5495	37.4	0	2	0	2	1	0	1	0	3	0	0	0	0	0	0	0	0	0	0	0	0	2	1	0	0
sponsored	14	.5792	1.6816	42.3	2	2	1	1	2	3	2	1	1	1	0	0	0	3	0	0	0	0	1	0	0	1	5	2	0
sponsoring	3	.3863	.2513	34.0	0	0	2	0	1	0	0	0	0	0	0	0	0	0	0	0	0	0	0	0	1	1	0	1	0
sponsors	4	.3141	.3005	34.8	0	1	0	0	1	2	0	0	1	0	0	0	0	0	0	0	1	0	0	0	0	0	0	2	0
spontaneous	8	.5305	.8833	39.5	0	0	0	0	3	2	1	2	0	0	0	1	0	0	0	2	2	0	0	0	0	1	0	2	0
spontaneously	6	.5324	.6660	38.2	0	1	0	0	2	1	1	1	0	0	0	0	0	1	0	1	1	0	0	0	0	0	1	2	0
spook	4	.2195	.2024	33.1	1	0	0	0	2	0	0	1	0	0	0	0	0	0	0	0	0	1	0	0	0	0	0	3	0
spooks	4	.1696	.1498	31.8	3	1	0	0	0	0	0	0	0	0	0	0	0	0	0	0	2	2	0	0	0	0	0	0	0
spooky	6	.5128	.6531	38.1	2	1	0	0	2	1	0	0	1	2	0	0	0	0	0	0	1	0	0	0	1	0	0	1	0
spool	26	.4765	2.7315	44.4	9	0	2	4	4	3	3	1	6	0	0	0	2	0	0	10	0	0	4	0	0	2	0	2	0
spools	10	.4501	.9535	39.8	2	4	0	0	1	2	0	1	1	1	0	0	0	1	0	0	0	2	0	2	1	2	0	0	0

6J spinets
6B spinge
9C spinnaker
9D spinners'
XR Spinney
6A spinnin'
7N spinning-wheel
XB spinosus
8J Spinoza
3R spinsters
6B spintains
7H spiny-skinned
7A spiraling
4A spiralled
XR Spire
6H spirillum
6A spirit-cliffs
5P spirit-lifting
3P spirit-men
4P spiritedly
9R spirituality
7P spiritually
6J Spirituals
7Q Spiro
5N spit-spot
9D spited
8A spitefully
9A Spitfires
9B spitted
7A spittin'
8B spittoon
6P spitz
3A Spitz-dog
4R Spivenses
3A spl
3P SPLASH
7P splashings
8D splashless
5R splashy
5A splat
3A splattering
9H spleen
7N splendidest
7D splice
XR splinter-proof
6H splintery
7A split-bamboo
4Q split-letter
7N split-rail
6R split-twig
9R Splits
7D splot
7B splotching
9R splotchy
7R splurge
9Q Spohr
9H spoilage
7R spoiler
7R Spoiler
5J Spoken
8Q spoliation
5F sponge-fishing
4A sponge-like
7R Sponheim
5Q sponsorship
5P spontaneity
7R spoofing
7R spooked
3N spookiest

Word Type	F	D	U	SFI	3 Gr 3	4 Gr 4	5 Gr 5	6 Gr 6	7 Gr 7	8 Gr 8	9 Gr 9	X UnGr	A Read	B Eng & Gr	C Comp	D Lit	E Math	F Soc Stud	G Spell	H Sci	J Music	K Art	L Home Ec	M Shop	N Lib F	P Lib NF	Q Lib Ref	R Mag	S Rel
spoon	92	.3838	7.8872	49.0	17	22	7	1	15	18	8	4	16	0	1	1	0	6	0	15	0	0	32	0	5	12	0	4	0
Spoon	3	.1409	.1472	31.7	2	0	1	0	0	0	0	0	1	0	0	0	0	0	0	0	0	0	0	0	0	2	0	0	0
spooned	2	.0000	.0064	18.1	0	0	0	0	0	0	2	0	0	0	0	0	0	0	0	0	0	0	2	0	0	0	0	0	0
spoonful	20	.4620	2.0005	43.0	6	4	3	2	1	4	0	0	2	0	0	0	0	1	0	8	0	0	4	0	2	1	0	2	0
spoonfuls	4	.4255	.3553	35.5	1	0	0	1	1	1	0	0	0	0	0	1	0	0	0	0	0	0	1	0	1	0	1	0	0
spoons	31	.4897	3.2380	45.1	6	2	6	2	4	6	4	1	6	0	0	4	2	1	0	0	5	0	8	0	1	3	0	1	0
spoonsful	2	.0000	.0290	24.6	0	2	0	0	0	0	0	0	0	0	0	0	0	0	0	0	0	0	0	0	0	2	0	0	0
sporadic	3	.3811	.2534	34.0	0	0	1	1	0	0	0	1	0	0	0	0	0	0	0	1	0	0	0	0	0	1	0	1	0
spore	22	.0000	.4338	36.4	4	7	2	4	2	0	3	0	0	0	0	0	0	0	0	22	0	0	0	0	0	0	0	0	0
spores	71	.0847	2.5492	44.1	18	3	10	24	4	0	12	0	4	0	0	0	0	0	0	66	0	0	0	0	0	0	1	0	0
sporophyte	3	.0000	.0591	27.7	0	0	0	0	0	0	3	0	0	0	0	0	0	0	0	3	0	0	0	0	0	0	0	0	0
sport	117	.8609	20.188	53.1	16	14	9	30	15	13	13	7	41	7	4	5	0	9	3	7	1	0	2	1	2	16	6	13	0
Sport	9	.0917	.2682	34.3	0	1	0	0	8	0	0	0	0	0	0	0	0	1	0	0	0	0	0	0	0	0	0	8	0
sported	3	.3465	.2515	34.0	0	1	0	0	0	1	1	0	1	0	0	0	0	0	0	0	0	0	0	0	0	1	0	1	0
sporting	20	.6510	2.6665	44.3	0	2	1	2	5	5	1	4	2	1	0	4	0	1	0	0	0	0	0	1	2	4	0	5	0
Sporting	2	.2398	.1138	30.6	0	0	0	1	0	0	1	0	0	0	0	1	1	0	0	0	0	0	0	0	0	0	0	0	0
sports	160	.8860	28.284	54.5	16	14	19	26	35	33	13	4	50	12	2	5	5	25	2	7	0	1	8	2	3	13	7	18	0
Sports	6	.3206	.4224	36.3	0	0	0	2	2	2	0	0	0	0	1	0	0	0	0	0	0	0	0	0	0	1	0	4	0
sports-car	11	.2432	.8553	39.3	0	0	0	0	1	10	0	0	9	0	0	0	0	0	0	0	0	0	0	0	0	0	0	2	0
sportscaster	2	.0000	.0299	24.8	0	0	0	0	2	0	0	0	0	0	0	0	2	0	0	0	0	0	0	0	0	0	0	0	0
sportsman	7	.4631	.6806	38.3	0	0	0	1	1	1	2	2	0	1	1	0	0	0	0	1	0	0	0	0	1	0	0	3	0
Sportsman	3	.1277	.1363	31.3	0	0	0	1	1	1	0	0	1	0	0	0	0	0	0	0	0	0	0	0	0	0	0	2	0
Sportsman's	3	.1409	.1472	31.7	2	0	0	0	1	0	0	0	1	0	0	0	0	0	0	0	0	0	0	0	0	2	0	0	0
sportsmanlike	2	.1948	.1250	31.0	0	0	0	0	2	0	0	0	1	0	0	0	0	0	0	0	0	0	0	0	0	1	0	0	0
sportsmanship	14	.3880	1.2708	41.0	2	1	0	3	2	1	5	0	3	0	0	0	0	0	0	9	0	0	1	0	0	1	0	0	0
sportsmen	14	.4529	1.4113	41.5	0	0	2	0	6	2	1	3	3	0	0	0	0	5	0	0	0	0	0	0	0	0	3	3	0
sportswear	3	.0000	.0097	19.8	0	0	0	0	1	1	1	0	0	0	0	0	0	0	0	0	0	0	3	0	0	0	0	0	0
sportswriter	4	.0000	.0486	26.9	0	0	0	0	4	0	0	0	0	0	0	0	0	0	0	0	0	0	0	0	0	0	0	4	0
sportswriters	2	.1814	.1187	30.7	0	0	0	1	1	0	0	0	1	0	0	0	0	0	0	0	0	0	0	0	0	0	0	1	0
sporty	3	.0000	.0365	25.6	0	0	0	0	3	0	0	0	0	0	0	0	0	0	0	0	0	0	0	0	0	0	0	3	0
spot	403	.9131	73.140	58.6	86	61	61	38	79	37	24	17	126	13	8	21	2	29	2	58	8	3	2	8	23	45	17	38	0
Spot	48	.4804	5.1169	47.1	26	5	0	9	7	0	1	0	18	1	4	5	0	0	1	0	0	0	0	0	19	0	0	0	0
spot-color	2	.0000	.0209	23.2	0	0	0	0	0	0	2	0	0	0	0	0	0	0	0	0	0	0	0	0	0	0	2	0	0
spot-welded	2	.0000	.0243	23.9	0	0	0	0	2	0	0	0	0	0	0	0	0	0	0	0	0	0	0	0	0	0	0	2	0
Spot's	3	.0000	.1370	31.4	0	0	0	3	0	0	0	0	3	0	0	0	0	0	0	0	0	0	0	0	0	0	0	0	0
spotless	5	.3833	.4767	36.8	1	1	1	0	2	0	0	0	3	0	0	1	0	0	0	0	0	0	0	0	0	1	0	0	0
spotlight	11	.6160	1.3996	41.5	2	0	0	0	4	4	0	1	1	1	0	3	0	2	0	0	0	0	0	0	0	1	1	2	0
spotlights	2	.2128	.1055	30.2	0	0	0	0	2	0	0	0	0	0	0	0	0	0	0	1	1	0	0	0	0	0	0	0	0
spots	157	.7915	25.022	54.0	37	21	13	21	37	9	14	5	29	3	1	7	4	7	2	26	2	13	5	3	11	13	13	18	0
Spotsylvania	4	.2298	.2346	33.7	0	0	0	0	0	4	0	0	0	0	0	0	0	3	0	0	0	0	0	0	1	0	0	0	0
spotted	98	.7791	15.532	51.9	20	19	10	16	21	5	3	4	36	3	5	6	2	2	1	6	0	0	1	1	7	7	1	20	0
spotting	4	.3141	.3005	34.8	0	1	0	2	1	0	0	0	1	0	0	0	0	0	1	0	0	0	0	0	0	0	0	2	0
spotty	5	.3791	.4191	36.2	0	0	1	0	1	1	2	0	1	0	0	0	0	0	0	0	0	1	1	0	0	0	0	2	0
Spotty	13	.0000	.5939	37.7	13	0	0	0	0	0	0	0	13	0	0	0	0	0	0	0	0	0	0	0	0	0	0	0	0
spout	29	.5000	3.3258	45.2	0	11	3	11	4	0	0	0	16	0	0	1	0	0	0	9	0	0	0	0	2	0	1	0	0
spouted	2	.1814	.1187	30.7	0	0	0	2	0	0	0	0	1	0	0	0	0	0	0	0	0	0	0	0	0	0	0	1	0
spouting	8	.2417	.6056	37.8	0	3	0	3	2	0	0	0	6	0	0	0	0	0	0	0	0	0	0	0	2	0	0	0	0
spouts	3	.3273	.2365	33.7	0	0	0	2	0	0	0	1	1	1	0	0	0	0	1	0	0	0	0	0	0	0	0	0	0
spr	2	.0000	.0162	22.1	0	0	1	1	0	0	0	0	0	0	0	0	0	0	2	0	0	0	0	0	0	0	0	0	0
sprang	106	.7279	15.967	52.0	10	16	10	20	27	20	2	1	50	4	2	5	1	5	2	0	2	0	0	0	24	7	4	0	0
sprawl	5	.4483	.4754	36.8	0	0	0	2	3	0	0	0	0	0	0	1	0	1	0	0	0	0	0	0	0	0	2	1	0
sprawled	15	.5214	1.7235	42.4	0	0	5	4	2	1	3	0	6	0	0	3	0	1	0	0	0	0	0	0	3	2	0	0	0
sprawling	16	.5070	1.7582	42.5	2	3	0	2	4	1	3	1	4	0	0	0	0	0	0	1	0	0	0	0	1	1	3	6	0
sprawls	2	.1698	.1133	30.5	1	1	0	0	0	0	0	0	1	0	0	0	0	0	0	0	0	0	0	0	0	0	1	0	0
spray	72	.6037	9.0782	49.6	8	5	4	23	26	1	1	4	15	2	0	0	0	4	1	12	1	1	1	13	4	6	1	11	0
spray-gun	4	.0000	.0101	20.0	0	0	0	0	4	0	0	0	0	0	0	0	0	0	0	0	0	0	0	4	0	0	0	0	0
sprayed	18	.5757	2.2175	43.5	0	2	4	4	4	3	1	0	6	0	0	0	0	2	0	2	0	1	0	2	0	3	0	2	0
spraying	10	.3107	.6934	38.4	2	0	1	0	7	0	0	0	0	0	0	1	0	3	0	0	0	0	0	3	0	3	0	0	0
sprays	16	.5987	2.0158	43.0	7	1	2	2	3	0	1	0	3	0	0	0	0	2	0	3	0	0	0	0	1	1	1	5	0
spread	531	.8977	94.831	59.8	91	84	72	83	104	54	28	15	117	7	4	27	4	83	3	83	12	8	18	1	27	63	39	35	0
spread-out	2	.0000	.0394	26.0	0	0	0	2	0	0	0	0	0	0	0	0	0	0	0	2	0	0	0	0	0	0	0	0	0
spreader	2	.0000	.0064	18.1	0	0	0	0	0	1	1	0	0	0	0	0	0	0	0	0	0	0	2	0	0	0	0	0	0
spreading	73	.8514	12.437	50.9	7	6	12	12	18	8	6	4	17	0	1	5	0	7	0	8	0	2	2	1	11	7	7	5	0
Spreading	2	.0000	.0290	24.6	0	0	0	0	1	1	0	0	0	0	0	0	0	0	0	0	0	0	0	0	0	2	0	0	0
spreads	51	.6580	6.9574	48.4	15	6	5	4	7	8	4	2	9	0	3	3	0	6	0	15	0	0	1	0	0	12	1	1	0
spree	2	.2351	.1166	30.7	0	0	0	0	1	1	0	0	0	0	0	0	0	1	0	0	0	0	0	0	0	0	0	1	0
sprig	2	.1814	.1187	30.7	0	0	0	1	1	0	0	0	1	0	0	0	0	0	0	0	0	0	0	0	0	0	0	1	0
sprigged	2	.0000	.0234	23.7	0	0	1	1	0	0	0	0	0	0	0	0	0	0	0	0	0	0	0	0	2	0	0	0	0
sprightly	10	.4451	.9535	39.8	0	4	0	1	4	1	0	0	1	5	0	2	0	0	0	0	1	0	0	0	0	0	0	1	0
sprigs	3	.1386	.0963	29.8	0	0	1	0	0	0	2	0	0	0	0	0	0	0	0	0	0	0	2	0	0	0	1	0	0
spring	802	.9253	147.22	61.7	170	137	82	134	124	79	36	40	229	16	10	47	6	84	19	122	26	2	3	10	52	77	28	71	0
Spring	58	.7522	8.8960	49.5	17	4	9	3	7	10	4	4	19	4	0	8	4	2	0	0	10	1	0	0	1	3	2	4	0
spring-loaded	3	.0000	.0365	25.6	0	0	0	0	3	0	0	0	0	0	0	0	0	0	0	0	0	0	0	0	0	0	0	3	0
spring's	2	.1160	.0650	28.1	0	1	0	1	0	0	0	0	0	0	1	0	0	0	0	1	0	0	0	0	0	0	0	0	0
springboard	7	.4848	.7687	38.9	0	4	2	0	0	1	0	0	3	0	0	1	0	0	0	2	0	0	0	0	0	0	1	0	0
Springfield	14	.6347	1.8155	42.6	0	3	3	0	2	5	1	0	1	0	1	4	0	1	0	0	2	0	0	0	0	2	1	2	0
springhaas	2	.0000	.0209	23.2	0	0	0	0	2	0	0	0	0	0	0	0	0	0	0	0	0	0	0	0	0	0	2	0	0
springing	13	.5776	1.5754	42.0	1	3	2	0	2	4	1	0	2	0	0	3	0	3	0	0	2	0	0	0	2	1	0	0	0
springs	88	.8598	15.155	51.8	14	11	10	18	21	8	4	2	24	2	0	5	1	15	0	13	2	0	1	1	3	6	6	9	0
Springs	19	.4649	2.0848	43.2	3	0	9	2	2	0	2	1	12	0	0	0	0	2	0	0	0	0	0	0	0	2	0	3	0
springtime	26	.6883	3.7561	45.7	6	6	1	4	5	4	0	0	13	1	0	2	0	1	0	3	2	0	0	0	3	0	0	1	0
Springtime	2	.0000	.0162	22.1	1	0	0	1	0	0	0	0	0	0	0	0	0	0	0	0	2	0	0	0	0	0	0	0	0
springy	8	.5445	.9162	39.6	1	1	2	2	0	1	0	1	1	0	0	0	0	0	0	1	2	0	0	0	1	1	0	2	0
sprinkle	47	.5592	5.4964	47.4	9	9	5	3	9	3	6	3	5	0	0	1	0	2	1	15	0	1	11	1	0	4	0	6	0
sprinkled	23	.7596	3.5330	45.5	4	6	2	4	2	3	2	0	4	0	1	1	0	3	0	2	0	1	2	0	3	3	1	2	0
sprinkler	5	.3132	.3878	35.9	0	2	0	0	1	1	1	0	1	0	0	0	0	0	0	3	0	0	0	0	1	0	0	0	0
sprinklers	3	.2437	.2277	33.6	2	1	0	0	0	0	0	0	2	0	0	0	0	0	0	1	0	0	0	0	0	0	0	0	0
sprinkles	2	.2300	.1140	30.6	0	0	0	0	1	0	0	1	0	1	0	0	0	0	0	1	0	0	0	0	0	0	0	0	0
sprinkling	17	.6152	2.2248	43.5	6	1	4	1	2	2	0	1	6	0	0	0	1	0	0	5	0	0	0	1	1	1	0	2	0
sprint	8	.3017	.6776	38.3	5	0	0	1	1	0	1	0	6	0	0	0	0	0	0	0	0	0	0	1	0	1	0	0	0
sprinted	3	.2212	.2099	33.2	0	0	1	1	0	0	1	0	2	0	0	1	0	0	0	0	0	0	0	0	0	0	0	0	0
sprinter	8	.5160	.8613	39.4	1	0	0	2	3	1	1	0	0	1	0	1	0	0	0	0	0	0	0	0	1	4	0	1	0
sprinters	3	.0000	.0434	26.4	0	0	0	1	2	0	0	0	0	0	0	0	0	0	0	0	0	0	0	0	0	3	0	0	0
sprit	5	.0000	.0523	27.2	0	0	0	0	0	0	5	0	0	0	0	0	0	0	0	0	0	0	0	0	0	0	5	0	0

7A spoon-fed	7R sporting-goods	6A Spot'll	5Q sprains	6R spring-board	7Q springhase
7Q spoonbills	3Q sports-loving	9L spotlessly	3P sprat	3A spring-cleaning	4P springhouse
4N Spooner	6F sports-minded	8R spotlighted	XR spray-throwing	8M spring-driven	7A springless
7P spoor	XB sports-writer's	8P Spotswood	7B Sprayberry	5Q spring-fed	3P Springtail
9H sporangia	7R sportscasters	4R spotters	3A sprayer	3N spring-guns	3P SPRINGTAILS
9H sporangium	8C sportsman-hunter	7R spouse	3P spreadeth	7P spring-head	7A Springwater
6H spore-bearing	9B sportsman's	6R spraddled	7Q spreadings	9Q spring-like	9R SPRINKEL
7R Sport's	9D sportswoman	8R Sprague-Martell	5R sprees	9H spring-summer	7D sprinklings
7R sporters	7R Sportvan	7B sprained	8A sprightliness	4A spring-well	7P sprinting
8F sportier	5P Sposi	9A spraining	6Q spring-blooming	7R Springfields	6A sprints

Word Type	F	D	U	SFI	3 Gr 3	4 Gr 4	5 Gr 5	6 Gr 6	7 Gr 7	8 Gr 8	9 Gr 9	X UnGr	A Read	B Eng & Gr	C Comp	D Lit	E Math	F Soc Stud	G Spell	H Sci	J Music	K Art	L Home Ec	M Shop	N Lib F	P Lib NF	Q Lib Ref	R Mag	S Rel
sprit-end	2	.0000	.0209	23.2	0	0	0	0	0	0	2	0	0	0	0	0	0	0	0	0	0	0	0	0	0	0	2	0	0
sprite	3	.3779	.2436	33.9	2	0	0	0	1	0	0	0	0	1	0	0	0	0	0	0	1	0	0	0	0	1	0	0	0
sprites	4	.2445	.3067	34.9	3	0	0	1	0	0	0	0	3	0	0	0	0	0	0	0	0	0	0	0	0	1	0	0	0
sprocket	2	.0000	.0243	23.9	0	0	0	0	2	0	0	0	0	0	0	0	0	0	0	0	0	0	0	0	0	0	0	2	0
sprockets	3	.2321	.1635	32.1	0	1	0	0	1	0	1	0	0	0	0	0	0	0	0	0	0	0	0	0	0	0	1	2	0
sprout	16	.5988	2.0681	43.2	3	2	3	1	6	0	0	1	7	2	0	0	0	1	0	4	0	0	0	0	1	0	1	0	0
sprouted	12	.5124	1.3653	41.4	1	4	0	2	4	1	0	0	4	0	0	1	0	1	0	5	0	0	0	0	0	0	1	0	0
sprouting	7	.5509	.8357	39.2	1	2	0	0	3	1	0	0	2	1	0	0	0	1	0	2	0	0	0	0	0	0	0	1	0
sprouts	8	.3261	.6433	38.1	2	0	1	0	1	1	2	1	3	1	0	0	0	0	0	2	0	0	2	0	0	0	0	0	0
spruce	39	.7513	5.9455	47.7	5	1	7	5	7	6	7	1	7	0	0	4	0	8	0	2	1	0	0	1	2	2	7	5	0
Spruce	3	.1941	.1614	32.1	0	2	0	1	0	0	0	0	1	0	0	1	0	0	0	0	0	1	0	0	0	0	0	0	0
sprue	4	.0000	.0101	20.0	0	0	0	0	0	4	0	0	0	0	0	0	0	0	0	0	0	0	0	4	0	0	0	0	0
sprung	12	.5916	1.4831	41.7	1	1	2	1	3	1	2	1	2	2	0	0	0	1	0	0	0	0	0	1	1	4	1	0	0
spry	3	.3780	.2436	33.9	1	1	0	0	0	0	1	0	0	0	0	1	0	0	0	0	1	0	0	0	0	1	0	0	0
Spud	21	.0000	.9593	39.8	17	0	0	4	0	0	0	0	21	0	0	0	0	0	0	0	0	0	0	0	0	0	0	0	0
Spuhler	2	.0000	.0290	24.6	0	0	2	0	0	0	0	0	0	0	0	0	0	0	0	0	0	0	0	0	0	2	0	0	0
spumes	2	.0000	.0234	23.7	0	0	1	0	1	0	0	0	0	0	0	0	0	0	0	0	0	0	0	0	2	0	0	0	0
spun	65	.7575	10.022	50.0	16	8	10	4	8	8	9	2	19	2	1	2	2	8	0	2	1	0	7	0	6	6	3	6	0
Spun	6	.0000	.0657	28.2	0	6	0	0	0	0	0	0	0	6	0	0	0	0	0	0	0	0	0	0	0	0	0	0	0
spunk	3	.3863	.2513	34.0	0	1	1	0	0	1	0	0	0	0	0	0	0	0	0	0	0	0	0	0	1	1	0	1	0
Spunk	18	.0000	.8223	39.2	18	0	0	0	0	0	0	0	18	0	0	0	0	0	0	0	0	0	0	0	0	0	0	0	0
spunky	3	.3267	.2367	33.7	0	1	2	0	0	0	0	0	1	0	0	0	0	0	0	0	1	0	0	0	1	0	0	0	0
spur	24	.5627	2.7984	44.5	1	3	2	2	7	5	2	2	2	0	0	1	0	1	0	0	1	0	0	3	1	2	3	10	0
Spurio	3	.0000	.0434	26.4	0	0	0	0	3	0	0	0	0	0	0	0	0	0	0	0	0	0	0	0	0	3	0	0	0
spurred	11	.5818	1.3609	41.3	0	0	1	0	4	5	0	1	3	0	0	1	0	2	0	1	2	0	0	0	0	0	0	2	0
spurring	3	.3452	.2543	34.1	0	0	1	0	0	1	0	1	1	0	0	0	0	0	0	1	0	0	0	0	0	0	0	1	0
spurs	25	.6046	3.1548	45.0	2	1	2	4	10	2	3	1	4	0	0	7	0	4	1	2	0	0	0	0	4	0	0	3	0
spurt	12	.5736	1.4570	41.6	3	1	3	1	3	1	0	0	2	0	0	0	0	1	0	3	0	0	0	0	3	2	1	0	0
spurted	5	.3530	.4326	36.4	0	1	0	2	1	0	0	1	2	0	0	0	0	0	0	0	0	0	0	0	0	2	0	1	0
spurting	4	.4521	.3985	36.0	0	0	0	1	0	1	2	0	1	1	0	0	0	0	0	0	0	0	0	0	1	0	1	0	0
spurts	14	.4400	1.3596	41.3	0	3	2	2	3	4	0	0	1	2	0	1	0	0	0	9	0	0	0	0	0	0	1	0	0
sputnik	4	.2107	.2095	33.2	0	0	0	3	0	1	0	0	0	0	0	0	0	0	0	0	0	0	0	0	0	3	0	1	0
Sputnik	16	.4210	1.4690	41.7	1	6	4	3	0	0	2	0	0	0	0	0	0	1	0	4	0	0	0	0	0	9	1	1	0
sputter	5	.3343	.4151	36.2	1	2	1	0	1	0	0	0	2	0	0	0	0	0	0	0	0	0	0	0	0	1	0	2	0
sputtered	6	.4493	.6074	37.8	3	2	0	0	1	0	0	0	2	0	0	1	0	0	0	0	0	0	0	0	0	1	0	2	0
sputtering	4	.3865	.3420	35.3	0	0	0	0	0	1	1	2	0	0	0	1	0	0	0	2	0	0	0	0	0	0	0	1	0
spy	43	.7405	6.5677	48.2	8	7	6	6	2	3	8	3	20	3	0	7	2	2	1	0	1	0	0	0	2	2	0	3	0
spyglass	4	.3867	.3417	35.3	0	1	1	0	0	1	1	0	0	1	0	0	0	2	0	0	0	0	0	0	1	0	0	0	0
spyglasses	3	.2357	.2199	33.4	0	1	0	0	2	0	0	0	2	0	0	0	0	0	0	0	0	0	0	0	0	1	0	0	0
spying	7	.3626	.6400	38.1	2	1	0	2	2	0	0	0	4	0	0	0	0	0	0	0	0	0	0	0	0	1	0	2	0
sq	23	.1294	.8768	39.4	0	0	0	0	1	16	6	0	0	0	0	0	21	0	0	0	0	0	0	0	0	0	2	0	0
squ	2	.0000	.0162	22.1	0	0	1	1	0	0	0	0	0	0	0	0	0	0	2	0	0	0	0	0	0	0	0	0	0
squabble	2	.0000	.0290	24.6	0	0	1	0	1	0	0	0	0	0	0	0	0	0	0	0	0	0	0	0	0	2	0	0	0
squabbles	3	.3851	.2497	34.0	2	0	0	0	1	0	0	0	0	0	0	1	0	0	0	0	0	0	0	0	1	1	0	0	0
squad	16	.6584	2.2327	43.5	1	2	2	1	4	5	1	0	8	1	0	0	0	2	1	1	0	0	0	0	0	0	2	1	0
squadron	24	.5308	2.7893	44.5	3	0	1	7	6	5	2	0	8	0	0	1	0	5	0	0	0	0	0	0	0	6	0	4	0
Squadron	9	.3948	.8036	39.1	3	0	0	1	1	3	1	0	1	0	0	0	0	3	0	0	0	0	0	0	0	4	0	1	0
squads	2	.1717	.1142	30.6	0	0	0	0	0	2	0	0	1	0	0	1	0	0	0	0	0	0	0	0	0	0	0	0	0
squalid	5	.3547	.4331	36.4	0	0	0	2	1	0	2	0	2	0	0	1	0	0	0	0	0	0	0	0	0	2	0	0	0
squall	11	.4201	1.0263	40.1	1	1	0	2	4	1	2	0	1	0	0	2	0	0	0	4	0	0	0	0	0	4	0	0	0
squalling	3	.2292	.1615	32.1	0	0	0	0	2	1	0	0	0	0	0	1	0	0	0	0	0	0	0	0	2	0	0	0	0
squalor	3	.3350	.2478	33.9	1	0	0	1	0	1	0	0	1	0	0	0	0	1	0	0	0	0	0	0	0	0	1	0	0
Squalus	5	.0000	.2284	33.6	0	0	5	0	0	0	0	0	5	0	0	0	0	0	0	0	0	0	0	0	0	0	0	0	0
Squalus'	3	.0000	.1370	31.4	0	0	3	0	0	0	0	0	3	0	0	0	0	0	0	0	0	0	0	0	0	0	0	0	0
squandered	2	.2440	.1132	30.5	0	0	0	0	1	0	1	0	0	0	0	1	0	0	0	0	0	0	0	0	0	0	0	1	0
Squanto	23	.1564	1.5639	41.9	15	0	0	0	8	0	0	0	22	0	0	1	0	0	0	0	0	0	0	0	0	0	0	0	0
Squanto's	3	.0000	.1370	31.4	1	0	0	1	1	0	0	0	3	0	0	0	0	0	0	0	0	0	0	0	0	0	0	0	0
square	965	.7156	140.32	61.5	109	97	140	144	96	216	145	18	93	8	2	25	502	49	4	61	20	5	18	51	17	40	45	25	0
Square	37	.6787	5.1822	47.1	2	5	9	5	3	7	3	3	8	1	0	0	6	5	0	0	1	0	0	0	2	3	1	10	0
square-faced	2	.2440	.1132	30.5	0	0	0	0	0	1	1	0	0	0	0	1	0	0	0	0	0	0	0	0	0	0	0	1	0
square-jawed	2	.1717	.1142	30.6	0	0	0	0	2	0	0	0	1	0	0	1	0	0	0	0	0	0	0	0	0	0	0	0	0
square-rigged	4	.3567	.3537	35.5	1	1	0	2	0	0	0	0	2	0	0	0	0	0	0	0	1	0	0	0	0	1	0	0	0
square-ruled	2	.0000	.0299	24.8	0	0	2	0	0	0	0	0	0	0	0	0	2	0	0	0	0	0	0	0	0	0	0	0	0
square-shaped	5	.3371	.3808	35.8	4	0	0	0	1	0	0	0	0	0	0	0	3	1	0	0	0	0	0	0	0	0	1	0	0
squared	25	.6353	3.2397	45.1	2	2	5	2	7	1	6	0	1	1	0	3	10	0	0	0	0	0	1	3	1	2	1	2	0
squarely	10	.5289	1.1656	40.7	3	0	2	0	4	1	0	0	4	0	0	0	0	1	0	2	0	0	0	1	1	0	0	1	0
squareness	7	.0000	.0177	22.5	0	0	0	0	6	1	0	0	0	0	0	0	0	0	0	0	0	0	0	7	0	0	0	0	0
squarenose	2	.0000	.0050	17.0	0	0	0	0	2	0	0	0	0	0	0	0	0	0	0	0	0	0	0	2	0	0	0	0	0
squares	183	.6833	25.408	54.0	35	21	25	29	18	27	24	4	7	3	2	0	108	7	6	4	3	4	2	12	2	13	0	10	0
Squares	3	.0000	.0449	26.5	0	0	2	0	0	0	1	0	0	0	0	0	3	0	0	0	0	0	0	0	0	0	0	0	0
squaring	11	.2323	.5767	37.6	0	0	0	2	4	3	2	0	0	0	0	1	3	0	0	0	0	0	0	5	0	2	0	0	0
squarish	2	.1787	.1174	30.7	0	0	0	1	1	0	0	0	1	0	0	0	0	0	0	0	0	0	0	0	1	0	0	0	0
squash	48	.7989	7.7139	48.9	12	11	5	3	9	3	2	3	9	1	2	5	0	6	4	4	0	0	3	0	5	3	5	1	0
squashed	4	.1919	.1864	32.7	0	1	0	0	0	0	3	0	0	0	0	3	0	0	0	0	0	0	0	0	1	0	0	0	0
squashes	7	.4589	.7293	38.6	1	4	0	0	1	1	0	0	3	1	0	2	0	0	0	0	0	0	0	0	1	0	0	0	0
squat	16	.6116	2.0183	43.0	2	1	0	2	4	5	2	0	2	2	1	3	0	1	0	0	0	0	0	0	0	0	4	3	0
Squat	2	.0000	.0394	26.0	2	0	0	0	0	0	0	0	0	0	0	0	0	0	0	2	0	0	0	0	0	0	0	0	0
squatted	24	.5046	2.6638	44.3	1	3	6	4	8	1	1	0	9	0	1	5	0	0	0	0	0	0	0	0	8	0	0	1	0
squatter	4	.3287	.2952	34.7	0	1	1	0	1	1	0	0	0	0	0	0	0	1	0	0	0	0	0	0	0	1	2	0	0
squatting	14	.5886	1.7265	42.4	2	3	1	3	2	1	1	1	3	0	1	3	0	0	0	1	1	0	0	0	4	1	0	0	0
squatty	2	.0000	.0914	29.6	0	1	0	0	1	0	0	0	2	0	0	0	0	0	0	0	0	0	0	0	0	0	0	0	0
squaw	16	.5569	1.9569	42.9	0	10	0	0	3	3	0	0	8	1	0	2	0	0	0	0	0	0	0	0	2	3	0	0	0
squawk	10	.5585	1.2200	40.9	2	3	1	1	1	2	0	0	5	2	0	1	0	0	1	0	1	0	0	0	0	0	0	0	0
squawked	10	.0000	.4568	36.6	3	1	0	6	0	0	0	0	10	0	0	0	0	0	0	0	0	0	0	0	0	0	0	0	0
squawking	9	.2430	.6880	38.4	4	1	1	1	0	2	0	0	7	0	0	2	0	0	0	0	0	0	0	0	0	0	0	0	0
squawkings	2	.0000	.0914	29.6	2	0	0	0	0	0	0	0	2	0	0	0	0	0	0	0	0	0	0	0	0	0	0	0	0
squawks	2	.1787	.1174	30.7	1	0	1	0	0	0	0	0	1	0	0	0	0	0	0	0	0	0	0	0	1	0	0	0	0
squaws	12	.4509	1.2176	40.9	2	4	1	0	5	0	0	0	4	0	0	3	0	0	0	0	1	0	0	0	0	4	0	0	0
squeak	32	.7530	4.9121	46.9	13	6	4	2	2	2	3	0	10	2	1	4	0	2	0	1	4	0	0	0	2	2	0	4	0
squeaked	15	.6059	1.9254	42.8	6	4	1	2	0	0	2	0	5	1	0	1	0	0	0	0	0	0	0	0	2	3	0	3	0
squeaking	7	.4890	.7839	38.9	1	3	1	1	1	0	0	0	4	1	0	0	0	0	0	0	0	0	0	0	1	0	0	1	0
squeaks	2	.2331	.1157	30.6	1	1	0	0	0	0	0	0	0	0	0	0	0	0	0	1	0	0	0	0	1	0	0	0	0
squeaky	11	.5349	1.2795	41.1	4	3	1	1	1	1	0	0	4	0	1	2	0	0	0	1	0	0	0	0	0	1	0	2	0
Squeaky	3	.0000	.1370	31.4	3	0	0	0	0	0	0	0	3	0	0	0	0	0	0	0	0	0	0	0	0	0	0	0	0
squeal	13	.6759	1.8295	42.6	1	3	2	1	4	2	0	0	5	0	0	2	0	0	1	0	1	0	0	0	0	2	1	1	0

9Q sprit-sail
3P spritten
8A sproutin'
5F spruce-tree
7Q spruced-up
6A sprucely
6R sprung-open
7A spss
7E SPT
3A spud
7H spumone
9L spun-bonded
9L Spunized
7D spunkier
5N spunkiness
3N Spur
XR Spur-Rowell
7P Spurio's
6B spurn
7N spurned
8N Spurs
5A sput-sputs
8E SPX
6N Spy
7N spy-glass
7E Spyglass
9R Sp4
9F squab
5P squabbled
9F squabbling
7Q squabs
8R Squad
7R squadrons
5N squalls
3Q squandering
7H squanders
5P square-bodied
9D square-dance
3A square-hewn
7Q square-meter
6A square-rigger
9P square-riggers
7R square-tube
9Q squaresails
7A squaring-off
9D Squash
9P squash-court
6F squats
8A squatters

Word Type	F	D	U	SFI	3 Gr 3	4 Gr 4	5 Gr 5	6 Gr 6	7 Gr 7	8 Gr 8	9 Gr 9	X UnGr	A Read	B Eng & Gr	C Comp	D Lit	E Math	F Soc Stud	G Spell	H Sci	J Music	K Art	L Home Ec	M Shop	N Lib F	P Lib NF	Q Lib Ref	R Mag	S Rel
squealed	11	.4784	1.2108	40.8	5	4	1	0	0	1	0	0	6	0	0	0	0	0	0	0	0	0	0	0	2	2	0	1	0
Squealer	6	.0000	.0703	28.5	0	0	0	0	0	0	6	0	0	0	0	0	0	0	0	0	0	0	0	0	6	0	0	0	0
squealing	19	.6294	2.5732	44.1	1	12	2	1	2	1	0	0	11	0	0	1	0	1	0	0	1	0	0	0	3	1	0	1	0
squeals	6	.4206	.5367	37.3	1	0	0	1	4	0	0	0	0	0	0	3	0	0	0	0	0	0	0	0	1	1	0	1	0
squeeze	52	.7330	7.7722	48.9	18	7	5	6	6	3	4	3	10	0	0	2	0	1	0	16	0	1	0	3	5	5	5	4	0
squeezed	59	.8030	9.5656	49.8	12	9	7	9	11	4	7	0	15	2	1	6	0	3	0	12	1	2	0	0	5	8	3	1	0
squeezes	15	.3754	1.2929	41.1	3	1	3	3	3	1	1	0	1	0	0	1	0	0	0	11	0	0	0	0	0	1	1	0	0
squeezing	26	.7119	3.8087	45.8	1	3	6	4	7	2	3	0	8	0	1	1	0	0	0	7	0	0	2	1	2	1	3	0	0
squid	19	.5197	2.1591	43.3	3	4	1	4	6	0	1	0	6	0	0	2	0	0	0	5	4	0	0	0	0	2	0	0	0
squid-jiggin'	6	.0000	.0485	26.9	0	6	0	0	0	0	0	0	0	0	0	0	0	0	0	0	6	0	0	0	0	0	0	0	0
squids	7	.1963	.4436	36.5	1	1	0	2	3	0	0	0	3	0	0	0	0	0	0	4	0	0	0	0	0	0	0	0	0
Squiles	2	.0000	.0219	23.4	0	0	0	0	0	0	2	0	0	2	0	0	0	0	0	0	0	0	0	0	0	0	0	0	0
squint	3	.1927	.1491	31.7	0	0	1	1	1	0	0	0	0	0	0	0	0	0	0	1	0	0	0	0	0	0	0	0	0
squinted	17	.5367	1.9992	43.0	5	5	4	1	0	0	2	0	7	0	0	1	0	0	0	0	0	0	0	0	4	3	0	2	0
squinting	14	.5317	1.6187	42.1	0	0	2	2	8	0	2	0	5	2	0	1	0	0	0	0	0	0	0	0	2	0	0	4	0
squire	13	.2618	.9070	39.6	0	0	0	3	9	1	0	0	3	0	0	1	0	9	0	0	0	0	0	0	0	0	0	0	0
Squire	8	.3126	.5590	37.5	0	2	1	0	5	0	0	0	0	0	0	1	0	0	0	0	0	0	0	0	5	2	0	0	0
squires	3	.3454	.2542	34.1	0	0	0	1	1	1	0	0	1	0	0	0	0	1	0	0	0	0	0	0	0	0	0	1	0
squirm	5	.5382	.5720	37.6	1	0	1	2	1	0	0	0	1	1	0	1	0	0	0	0	0	0	0	0	1	1	0	0	0
squirmed	14	.4593	1.4999	41.8	2	3	1	0	4	4	0	0	8	2	0	0	0	0	0	0	0	0	0	0	3	1	0	0	0
squirming	7	.5227	.7950	39.0	0	4	0	0	3	0	0	0	2	0	0	0	0	1	0	0	0	0	0	0	2	1	1	0	0
squirrel	88	.8036	14.381	51.6	23	17	9	12	17	6	3	1	41	2	2	4	0	3	4	4	1	0	0	0	7	13	2	5	0
Squirrel	15	.5779	1.8791	42.7	12	1	0	0	1	1	0	0	7	0	0	2	0	0	0	1	0	0	0	0	1	0	3	1	0
squirrel's	7	.4817	.7747	38.9	2	3	0	1	0	0	1	0	4	1	0	0	0	0	1	0	0	0	0	0	0	1	0	0	0
Squirrel's	2	.0000	.0209	23.2	2	0	0	0	0	0	0	0	0	0	0	0	0	0	0	0	0	0	0	0	0	0	2	0	0
squirrels	85	.7679	13.217	51.2	19	12	9	8	24	2	3	8	18	5	3	8	0	1	3	11	0	0	0	0	1	15	11	9	0
squirrels'	2	.0000	.0162	22.1	0	0	0	2	0	0	0	0	0	0	0	0	0	0	2	0	0	0	0	0	0	0	0	0	0
squirt	12	.5394	1.4307	41.6	5	1	2	1	1	1	1	0	5	0	0	1	0	0	0	4	0	0	0	0	0	1	0	1	0
squirted	3	.3365	.2489	34.0	1	0	0	1	1	0	0	0	1	0	0	1	0	0	0	1	0	0	0	0	0	0	0	0	0
squirting	4	.3011	.2909	34.6	3	0	0	0	1	0	0	0	1	0	0	2	0	0	0	0	0	0	0	0	0	0	1	0	0
squirts	3	.2383	.1815	32.6	1	0	0	1	0	0	1	0	0	0	0	0	0	0	0	2	0	0	0	0	0	1	0	0	0
squishy	3	.2261	.2131	33.3	0	0	0	1	0	2	0	0	2	0	0	0	0	0	0	0	0	0	0	0	1	0	0	0	0
Sr	3	.2223	.2106	33.2	0	0	0	1	0	0	2	0	2	1	0	0	0	0	0	0	0	0	0	0	0	0	0	0	0
SR	5	.1602	.2108	33.2	0	0	0	4	0	1	0	0	0	0	0	0	1	0	0	0	0	0	0	0	0	0	0	4	0
SRA	2	.0000	.0389	25.9	0	1	0	0	0	0	0	1	0	0	0	0	0	2	0	0	0	0	0	0	0	0	0	0	0
ss	25	.1647	.9977	40.0	1	2	7	8	4	3	0	0	0	4	0	0	0	0	20	1	0	0	0	0	0	0	0	0	0
SSS	2	.0000	.0299	24.8	0	0	0	0	0	2	0	0	0	0	0	0	2	0	0	0	0	0	0	0	0	0	0	0	0
SST	5	.2129	.2689	34.3	0	0	0	0	2	0	0	3	0	0	0	0	0	0	0	2	0	0	0	0	0	0	0	3	0
SST'S	3	.0000	.0365	25.6	0	0	0	0	0	0	0	3	0	0	0	0	0	0	0	0	0	0	0	0	0	0	0	3	0
st	23	.0425	.4787	36.8	9	5	6	2	1	0	0	0	3	0	0	0	0	0	20	0	0	0	0	0	0	0	0	0	0
St	275	.8300	45.687	56.6	18	35	69	35	46	25	35	12	34	5	1	13	9	72	2	6	24	4	0	0	13	32	37	23	0
ST	2	.0000	.0299	24.8	0	1	0	0	0	1	0	0	0	0	0	0	2	0	0	0	0	0	0	0	0	0	0	0	0
StAndrews	2	.2401	.1133	30.5	0	1	0	0	0	0	1	0	0	0	0	0	0	0	0	0	0	0	0	0	0	1	1	0	0
StElmo's	2	.1698	.1133	30.5	0	0	1	0	1	0	0	0	1	0	0	0	0	0	0	0	0	0	0	0	0	0	1	0	0
StGeorge	43	.0000	1.9644	42.9	0	0	0	43	0	0	0	0	43	0	0	0	0	0	0	0	0	0	0	0	0	0	0	0	0
StJohn	2	.0000	.0209	23.2	0	0	0	0	1	0	1	0	0	0	0	0	0	0	0	0	0	0	0	0	0	0	2	0	0
StJoseph	2	.2152	.1357	31.3	0	0	2	0	0	0	0	0	1	0	0	0	0	1	0	0	0	0	0	0	0	0	0	0	0
StLawrence	8	.4131	.7410	38.7	0	2	3	0	2	0	1	0	1	0	0	0	0	4	0	0	0	0	0	0	1	0	2	0	0
StLouis	28	.4788	2.9316	44.7	6	1	6	2	8	5	0	0	3	1	0	0	4	16	0	1	0	0	0	0	0	0	3	0	0
StMark's	2	.0000	.0234	23.7	0	0	0	2	0	0	0	0	0	0	0	0	0	0	0	0	0	0	0	0	2	0	0	0	0
StMary's	3	.0000	.1370	31.4	0	0	3	0	0	0	0	0	3	0	0	0	0	0	0	0	0	0	0	0	0	0	0	0	0
StNicholas	3	.2261	.2131	33.3	0	0	0	0	1	0	0	2	2	0	0	0	0	0	0	0	0	0	0	0	1	0	0	0	0
StVitus's	2	.2441	.1127	30.5	0	2	0	0	0	0	0	0	0	0	0	0	0	0	0	0	0	0	0	0	1	0	1	0	0
stab	15	.7370	2.2586	43.5	2	0	2	2	6	3	0	0	4	1	0	1	0	1	0	1	1	0	0	0	1	3	2	0	0
stabbed	6	.4988	.6426	38.1	0	0	1	0	1	3	1	0	1	0	0	2	0	1	0	0	0	0	0	0	1	0	1	0	0
stabbing	3	.1250	.1342	31.3	0	1	0	1	1	0	0	0	1	0	0	0	0	0	0	0	0	0	0	0	2	0	0	0	0
stability	21	.5570	2.4202	43.8	1	0	2	0	7	5	5	1	0	0	0	0	0	4	0	2	0	0	2	0	0	2	7	4	0
stabilization	3	.3847	.2496	34.0	0	0	1	0	0	0	1	1	0	0	0	0	0	0	0	0	0	0	0	0	0	1	1	1	0
stabilize	3	.3769	.2484	34.0	1	0	0	0	2	0	0	0	0	0	0	0	0	1	0	0	0	0	0	0	0	0	1	1	0
stabilized	2	.0000	.0394	26.0	0	0	0	2	0	0	0	0	0	0	0	0	0	0	0	2	0	0	0	0	0	0	0	0	0
stable	114	.7553	17.447	52.4	12	15	7	12	47	12	5	4	23	1	3	2	0	2	0	5	4	1	0	0	29	18	13	13	0
stableboys	4	.3755	.3686	35.7	0	2	0	2	0	0	0	0	2	0	0	0	0	0	0	0	0	0	0	0	1	1	0	0	0
stables	25	.3057	1.8736	42.7	0	0	2	10	7	5	1	0	7	0	0	3	0	1	0	0	0	0	0	0	14	0	0	0	0
stabs	3	.0995	.1144	30.6	0	0	0	0	3	0	0	0	1	0	0	0	0	0	0	0	2	0	0	0	0	0	0	0	0
staccato	12	.1962	.5771	37.6	1	1	2	2	3	0	3	0	1	0	0	0	0	0	0	0	9	0	0	0	1	0	0	1	0
stack	41	.8455	6.9332	48.4	12	7	4	1	5	9	2	1	8	1	1	2	10	2	1	2	0	1	2	0	2	3	1	5	0
stacked	36	.6861	5.1146	47.1	4	7	7	3	4	8	3	0	12	2	0	0	6	0	0	2	1	0	0	3	2	1	4	3	0
stacking	7	.4507	.7017	38.5	1	1	1	0	1	1	2	0	2	1	0	0	0	1	0	0	0	0	0	1	0	0	0	2	0
stacks	13	.5100	1.4811	41.7	3	2	2	1	1	4	0	0	6	0	0	0	4	0	0	0	0	0	1	0	0	1	0	1	0
Stacy	2	.1814	.1187	30.7	0	1	0	0	1	0	0	0	1	0	0	0	0	0	0	0	0	0	0	0	0	0	0	1	0
stadium	24	.6182	3.1013	44.9	3	3	4	4	2	2	3	3	5	1	0	1	2	5	0	0	0	2	0	0	0	5	2	1	0
Stadium	12	.3380	.9399	39.7	5	1	1	2	2	1	0	0	2	0	0	0	0	0	0	0	0	0	0	0	0	2	1	7	0
staff	164	.6001	20.331	53.1	24	38	15	12	33	13	26	3	21	9	1	9	2	6	0	2	61	0	0	0	2	8	12	31	0
Staff	10	.5053	1.0675	40.3	1	0	0	2	4	1	2	0	1	0	0	0	0	1	0	0	3	0	0	0	0	1	1	3	0
staffed	2	.2437	.1129	30.5	0	0	0	1	0	1	0	0	0	0	0	0	0	0	0	0	0	0	0	0	0	0	1	1	0
staffs	11	.5128	1.2302	40.9	1	2	1	3	3	1	0	0	3	0	0	1	0	3	0	0	0	0	0	0	0	0	3	1	0
stag	7	.2926	.4905	36.9	0	4	0	1	2	0	0	0	1	0	0	0	0	0	0	0	0	0	0	0	0	4	2	0	0
stage	344	.8818	60.373	57.8	23	46	36	43	101	40	42	13	65	19	5	19	7	12	6	54	40	0	1	11	22	21	26	36	0
Stage	2	.2387	.1089	30.4	0	1	0	0	1	0	0	0	0	0	0	0	0	0	0	0	1	0	0	0	1	0	0	0	0
stagecoach	33	.4470	3.3603	45.3	13	10	2	3	4	0	1	0	11	0	0	1	1	4	0	0	0	0	0	0	1	15	0	0	0
stagecoaches	5	.3850	.4834	36.8	1	1	0	2	0	1	0	0	3	0	0	0	0	1	0	0	0	0	0	0	0	1	0	0	0
staged	13	.5854	1.5907	42.0	0	0	2	2	4	4	0	1	2	0	0	0	0	2	0	0	2	0	1	0	0	3	0	3	0
stagehand	3	.3825	.2447	33.9	0	1	0	0	1	1	0	0	0	0	0	1	0	0	1	0	0	0	0	0	0	0	0	1	0
stages	73	.7398	10.869	50.4	3	5	8	3	27	7	15	5	1	10	0	5	0	0	0	26	2	1	4	3	0	1	16	4	0
Stagg	2	.2285	.1129	30.5	0	0	0	0	2	0	0	0	0	0	0	0	0	1	0	0	0	0	0	0	0	0	1	0	0
stagger	2	.2433	.1158	30.6	0	1	1	0	0	0	0	0	0	0	0	0	0	0	0	0	0	0	0	0	0	1	0	1	0
staggered	25	.7499	3.8305	45.8	1	3	2	6	7	5	1	0	9	1	1	3	0	1	1	0	0	0	1	0	4	1	0	3	0
staggering	19	.7094	2.7365	44.4	1	1	2	1	5	5	3	1	2	1	0	2	0	3	0	0	0	0	0	1	4	1	3	2	0
staggers	2	.1733	.1149	30.6	0	0	1	0	1	0	0	0	1	1	0	0	0	0	0	0	0	0	0	0	0	0	0	0	0
staghorn	5	.2144	.2818	34.5	0	4	0	1	0	0	0	0	0	0	0	0	0	0	0	4	0	0	0	0	1	0	0	0	0
staging	4	.2578	.2593	34.1	0	0	0	3	1	0	0	0	1	0	0	0	0	0	0	0	2	0	0	0	0	1	0	0	0
stagnant	4	.1335	.1958	32.9	1	0	0	3	0	0	0	0	1	0	0	0	0	0	0	3	0	0	0	0	0	0	0	0	0
stags	2	.2440	.1132	30.5	0	0	0	0	1	1	0	0	0	0	0	1	0	0	0	0	0	0	0	0	0	0	0	1	0
Stahl	2	.0000	.0243	23.9	0	0	0	0	2	0	0	0	0	0	0	0	0	0	0	0	0	0	0	0	0	0	0	2	0

8Q squib
4J squiddin'
7D squidging
8D squiggle
7Q squiggling
3R squinchy
8R squirms
9R squirreling
8R SRO
9E SS
6A ssh
8G ssion
3R Ssss
3A ssssss
3R Sssssss
3P sssssssssssst
7B SSSTT
8F Ssuh-chwan
9Q StAmbrose
9Q StBartholomew's
6N StDenis
3N StFrancis
6A StGeorge's
6A StLucy's
6A StMark
5F StMary
8A StMoritz
5A StPaul's
9Q StStephen's
4Q StVitus
6F St-Etienne
5R ST-148
3A stnds
8B stabil
6K stabile
6K stabiles
7R stabilizer
7N stable-men
3P stable-yard
6N stableful
6A stablemen
7Q stably
6A Stacey
7P stadholder
XP stadia
6A Stadio
7R stadiums
6R staffers
7D Stafford
XP stag's
6A stage-manager
7B stage-plank
3N stage-scared
7R stage-whispered
9L Stagecrafter's
9R stageful
8D stagestruck
3Q stagnating
7F stagnation

Word Type	F	D	U	SFI	3 Gr 3	4 Gr 4	5 Gr 5	6 Gr 6	7 Gr 7	8 Gr 8	9 Gr 9	X UnGr	A Read	B Eng & Gr	C Comp	D Lit	E Math	F Soc Stud	G Spell	H Sci	J Music	K Art	L Home Ec	M Shop	N Lib F	P Lib NF	Q Lib Ref	R Mag	S Rel
staid	2	.1814	.1187	30.7	0	0	1	0	0	0	0	1	1	0	0	0	0	0	0	0	0	0	0	0	0	0	0	1	0
stain	19	.6717	2.6242	44.2	1	1	2	1	8	3	1	2	3	0	0	1	0	0	1	4	0	0	1	0	1	3	0	5	0
stained	13	.5656	1.5434	41.9	1	1	2	2	3	2	1	1	3	1	0	1	0	0	0	0	0	2	1	0	1	1	1	2	0
stained-glass	4	.3672	.3092	34.9	0	0	1	1	0	0	2	0	0	0	0	0	0	0	0	0	1	1	0	0	0	0	1	1	0
staining	2	.1717	.1142	30.6	0	0	0	0	1	1	0	0	1	0	0	1	0	0	0	0	0	0	0	0	0	0	0	0	0
stainless	9	.5191	.9960	40.0	1	0	1	2	2	1	2	0	1	1	0	0	0	1	0	3	0	0	0	1	0	0	0	2	0
stainless-steel	2	.2446	.1257	31.0	1	0	1	0	0	0	0	0	0	0	0	0	0	1	0	1	0	0	0	0	0	0	0	0	0
stains	13	.7200	1.8790	42.7	1	0	3	2	1	2	3	1	0	1	1	2	0	0	1	2	0	0	1	0	2	0	2	1	0
stair	18	.6251	2.4002	43.8	3	2	5	3	4	0	1	0	9	0	0	2	0	0	2	0	1	0	0	0	2	0	0	2	0
Stair	2	.1733	.1149	30.6	0	1	0	0	0	1	0	0	1	1	0	0	0	0	0	0	0	0	0	0	0	0	0	0	0
staircase	19	.6505	2.5842	44.1	2	4	4	2	0	3	4	0	6	0	1	2	0	3	0	0	0	0	0	0	3	2	0	2	0
stairs	184	.7801	29.354	54.7	41	36	30	14	34	16	12	1	87	9	0	16	1	2	1	12	1	0	3	0	22	19	3	8	0
stairway	30	.6351	3.9978	46.0	3	5	3	8	3	6	1	1	10	0	0	1	0	1	0	4	0	1	4	0	4	3	0	2	0
stairways	11	.5264	1.2520	41.0	4	0	1	2	2	0	2	0	2	0	0	2	0	2	0	4	0	0	0	0	0	0	1	0	0
stake	47	.5165	5.1588	47.1	10	2	8	1	9	3	13	1	10	3	0	4	0	2	4	1	0	0	0	10	9	1	1	2	0
staked	8	.5014	.8704	39.4	2	0	1	0	3	1	1	0	2	0	0	1	0	0	0	0	0	0	0	0	1	1	0	3	0
stakes	16	.5103	1.7362	42.4	1	1	3	1	3	1	5	1	3	3	0	2	1	1	0	0	0	0	0	3	2	0	0	1	0
stalactites	5	.3490	.3888	35.9	2	0	1	0	2	0	0	0	0	2	0	0	0	0	0	1	0	0	0	0	0	2	0	0	0
stalagmites	2	.2405	.1205	30.8	1	0	1	0	0	0	0	0	0	0	0	0	0	0	0	1	0	0	0	0	0	1	0	0	0
stale	14	.6396	1.8581	42.7	3	0	4	0	4	1	2	0	3	2	0	3	0	0	0	2	0	0	1	0	0	2	1	0	0
Staley	13	.0000	.5939	37.7	13	0	0	0	0	0	0	0	13	0	0	0	0	0	0	0	0	0	0	0	0	0	0	0	0
Stalin	10	.2996	.6754	38.3	0	0	0	5	1	3	1	0	0	0	0	0	0	1	0	0	0	0	0	0	0	0	3	6	0
Stalingrad	2	.2408	.1204	30.8	0	0	0	1	1	0	0	0	0	0	0	0	0	1	0	0	0	0	0	0	0	1	0	0	0
stalk	72	.6724	10.159	50.1	11	9	10	7	25	1	9	0	28	1	0	2	0	1	1	20	0	0	0	0	0	8	6	5	0
stalked	20	.6267	2.6201	44.2	0	4	4	1	6	2	2	1	5	0	0	4	0	1	0	1	0	0	0	0	5	2	1	1	0
stalking	16	.6584	2.1895	43.4	2	3	0	0	7	2	2	0	5	2	0	2	0	0	0	0	1	0	0	0	2	1	3	0	0
stalklike	2	.0000	.0394	26.0	0	0	2	0	0	0	0	0	0	0	0	0	0	0	0	2	0	0	0	0	0	0	0	0	0
stalks	51	.7489	7.7464	48.9	12	7	9	9	5	3	2	4	7	0	2	1	0	7	1	10	0	0	0	0	8	6	4	5	0
stall	95	.5230	10.920	50.4	26	16	3	17	25	5	3	0	38	0	0	5	0	0	0	0	1	0	0	0	33	10	1	7	0
stalled	5	.4770	.5360	37.3	2	0	0	0	0	1	2	0	2	0	0	1	0	0	0	0	0	0	0	0	0	1	0	1	0
stallion	53	.4402	5.0489	47.0	6	10	5	3	23	6	0	0	6	1	0	4	0	0	0	0	2	0	0	0	32	6	1	1	0
stallion's	7	.0000	.0821	29.1	0	0	1	0	6	0	0	0	0	0	0	0	0	0	0	0	0	0	0	0	7	0	0	0	0
stallions	4	.2427	.2305	33.6	0	2	0	2	0	0	0	0	0	0	0	0	0	0	0	0	0	0	0	0	2	2	0	0	0
Stallo	3	.0000	.1370	31.4	0	3	0	0	0	0	0	0	3	0	0	0	0	0	0	0	0	0	0	0	0	0	0	0	0
stalls	18	.6120	2.3582	43.7	2	3	2	7	1	2	0	1	8	0	0	0	0	1	0	1	1	0	0	0	4	1	0	2	0
stalwart	5	.4038	.4473	36.5	0	1	1	1	2	0	0	0	1	0	1	1	0	0	0	0	0	0	0	0	1	1	0	0	0
stamen	5	.0000	.0986	29.9	0	1	2	1	0	0	1	0	0	0	0	0	0	0	0	5	0	0	0	0	0	0	0	0	0
stamens	27	.0000	.5323	37.3	3	2	2	15	0	0	1	4	0	0	0	0	0	0	0	27	0	0	0	0	0	0	0	0	0
stamina	5	.3307	.3683	35.7	2	0	0	1	0	1	1	0	0	0	0	0	0	0	2	1	0	0	0	0	0	2	0	0	0
Stamitz	3	.0000	.0314	25.0	0	3	0	0	0	0	0	0	0	0	0	0	0	0	0	0	0	0	0	0	0	0	3	0	0
stammered	13	.3797	1.1494	40.6	1	2	0	6	1	0	2	1	4	0	0	2	0	0	0	0	0	0	0	0	6	1	0	0	0
stammering	2	.2443	.1130	30.5	0	0	0	1	1	0	0	0	0	0	0	1	0	0	0	0	0	0	0	0	1	0	0	0	0
stamp	76	.8233	12.578	51.0	14	11	13	7	15	11	4	1	20	9	3	0	13	9	5	1	6	0	1	1	0	1	2	5	0
Stamp	15	.3637	1.2747	41.1	0	0	10	2	0	3	0	0	2	2	0	1	0	10	0	0	0	0	0	0	0	0	0	0	0
stamped	62	.7331	9.3014	49.7	10	16	6	4	14	5	6	1	19	1	0	8	0	4	1	0	3	0	0	3	8	11	0	4	0
stampede	12	.4729	1.3218	41.2	0	3	4	1	2	2	0	0	7	0	0	2	0	2	0	0	0	0	0	0	1	0	0	0	0
Stampede	2	.0000	.0389	25.9	0	0	2	0	0	0	0	0	0	0	0	0	0	2	0	0	0	0	0	0	0	0	0	0	0
stampeded	6	.2440	.4665	36.7	0	4	1	0	0	1	0	0	5	0	0	0	0	0	0	0	1	0	0	0	0	0	0	0	0
stampeding	4	.3354	.3295	35.2	0	2	2	0	0	0	0	0	1	0	0	0	0	2	0	0	0	0	0	0	0	1	0	0	0
stamping	32	.6874	4.5727	46.6	5	5	7	4	5	2	3	1	13	0	1	3	0	1	0	1	3	0	0	1	8	0	0	1	0
stamps	132	.6631	18.007	52.6	21	20	36	9	27	11	5	3	16	10	2	0	72	13	1	1	2	1	1	0	1	6	1	5	0
Stamps	2	.2404	.1142	30.6	0	0	0	1	0	1	0	0	0	1	0	0	1	0	0	0	0	0	0	0	0	0	0	0	0
Stan	61	.4719	6.4274	48.1	6	3	4	9	28	5	5	1	22	6	0	3	1	0	0	0	0	0	0	0	25	0	0	4	0
Stan's	17	.0924	.6129	37.9	0	0	0	4	13	0	0	0	4	0	0	0	0	0	0	0	0	0	0	0	13	0	0	0	0
stance	8	.4349	.7360	38.7	0	0	0	1	1	0	5	1	0	1	0	2	0	0	0	0	0	0	0	0	1	0	0	4	0
stanch	3	.3385	.2445	33.9	0	0	0	1	2	0	0	0	1	0	0	0	0	0	0	0	0	0	0	0	1	0	1	0	0
stanchest	2	.1717	.1142	30.6	0	0	0	0	2	0	0	0	1	0	0	1	0	0	0	0	0	0	0	0	0	0	0	0	0
stanchions	3	.3824	.2446	33.9	0	0	1	1	0	0	1	0	0	0	0	1	0	0	0	0	1	0	0	0	0	0	0	1	0
stand	1081	.9731	207.37	63.2	210	212	136	114	208	95	92	14	323	88	17	80	63	83	32	110	37	18	19	4	77	53	25	51	1
stand-up	2	.1814	.1187	30.7	1	0	0	0	0	0	0	1	1	0	0	0	0	0	0	0	0	0	0	0	0	0	0	1	0
standard	242	.7252	35.443	55.5	17	46	23	18	43	58	36	1	13	35	1	0	79	16	0	10	12	0	2	17	0	11	31	15	0
Standard	24	.5364	2.6992	44.3	0	3	8	2	1	5	5	0	2	2	0	0	0	2	0	4	0	0	0	2	0	0	10	2	0
standard-size	2	.1812	.0838	29.2	0	0	0	0	1	0	1	0	0	0	0	0	0	0	0	0	0	0	1	0	0	0	0	1	0
standardized	11	.5735	1.2925	41.1	0	0	0	1	4	4	2	0	0	2	0	0	1	0	0	2	3	0	0	1	0	0	2	0	0
standards	91	.7553	13.811	51.4	5	2	16	4	18	22	21	3	4	9	1	0	1	19	0	4	5	0	9	4	0	8	17	10	0
Standards	8	.4654	.7758	38.9	3	0	0	0	0	2	3	0	0	1	0	0	1	1	0	0	0	0	1	2	0	2	0	0	0
Standby	4	.2437	.2257	33.5	0	0	0	0	2	0	0	2	0	0	0	0	0	0	0	0	0	0	0	0	0	0	2	2	0
standin'	2	.1787	.1174	30.7	0	0	2	0	0	0	0	0	1	0	0	0	0	0	0	0	0	0	0	0	1	0	0	0	0
standing	575	.8846	101.70	60.1	105	100	57	74	129	57	44	9	240	18	7	62	12	23	4	22	9	7	3	2	75	47	16	28	0
Standing	4	.2386	.2998	34.8	3	0	0	0	0	1	0	0	3	0	0	0	0	0	0	0	0	0	0	0	0	0	1	0	0
standings	3	.2279	.2143	33.3	0	1	0	1	1	0	0	0	2	0	0	0	0	0	0	0	0	0	0	0	0	0	0	1	0
Standish	19	.0000	.8680	39.4	18	0	0	0	0	1	0	0	19	0	0	0	0	0	0	0	0	0	0	0	0	0	0	0	0
standpipe	9	.1430	.3905	35.9	0	2	3	0	4	0	0	0	2	0	0	0	0	0	0	3	0	0	0	4	0	0	0	0	0
standpipes	2	.1249	.0685	28.4	0	0	1	0	1	0	0	0	0	0	0	0	0	0	0	1	0	0	0	1	0	0	0	0	0
standpoint	9	.5869	1.0825	40.3	0	0	0	0	2	1	5	1	0	0	0	0	0	0	0	3	1	0	1	1	0	0	1	2	0
stands	473	.9383	87.824	59.4	99	87	48	56	86	53	33	11	108	51	5	26	62	60	20	32	14	4	3	1	14	24	19	30	0
standstill	8	.4291	.7277	38.6	2	1	1	0	2	2	0	0	0	0	0	0	0	0	0	0	0	0	0	0	3	1	3	1	0
Stanet	2	.0000	.0389	25.9	2	0	0	0	0	0	0	0	0	0	0	0	0	2	0	0	0	0	0	0	0	0	0	0	0
Stanford	19	.4480	1.7841	42.5	0	0	0	0	2	5	12	0	0	0	2	1	0	0	0	1	0	0	0	0	0	0	9	6	0
Stanford's	4	.3160	.2725	34.4	0	0	0	0	0	1	3	0	0	0	1	0	0	0	0	0	0	0	0	0	0	0	2	1	0
Stanley	45	.5592	5.3150	47.3	0	15	1	2	10	2	9	6	5	1	1	0	0	19	0	1	0	0	0	0	0	0	6	12	0
Stanley's	7	.1931	.3682	35.7	0	2	0	0	2	0	3	0	0	0	0	0	0	6	0	0	0	0	0	0	0	0	1	0	0
Stanoski	2	.2407	.1138	30.6	1	0	0	0	0	1	0	0	0	0	0	1	0	0	0	0	0	0	0	0	0	1	0	0	0
Stanton	9	.2728	.6324	38.0	0	0	0	0	5	3	1	0	3	0	0	0	0	0	0	0	0	0	0	0	5	0	1	0	0
Stanton's	4	.2386	.2998	34.8	0	0	0	0	0	3	1	0	3	0	0	0	0	0	0	0	0	0	0	0	0	0	1	0	0
stanza	87	.3956	7.4083	48.7	5	7	17	10	25	18	5	0	4	46	0	28	0	0	1	0	6	0	0	0	2	0	0	0	0
stanzas	36	.3996	3.0871	44.9	8	5	3	0	8	8	3	1	2	15	0	9	0	0	0	0	10	0	0	0	0	0	0	0	0
staphylococci	3	.2445	.1818	32.6	0	0	0	0	0	1	2	0	0	0	0	0	0	0	0	2	0	0	0	0	0	0	1	0	0
staple	18	.5629	2.1741	43.4	7	0	3	1	5	1	1	0	6	0	0	0	0	3	0	1	0	2	1	0	0	1	2	2	0
stapled	2	.0725	.0732	28.6	0	0	0	0	1	1	0	0	1	0	0	0	0	0	0	0	0	0	0	1	0	0	0	0	0
staples	7	.4051	.6127	37.9	1	0	0	0	1	5	0	0	0	0	0	0	0	3	0	0	0	1	0	0	0	0	2	1	0
star	398	.8205	65.634	58.2	61	46	58	60	61	43	38	31	66	15	4	24	11	10	5	156	21	1	0	0	11	29	17	28	0
Star	328	.3047	23.534	53.7	42	93	84	88	8	7	6	0	67	3	0	4	5	12	203	14	7	0	0	0	4	8	1	0	0
Star-Spangled	11	.2594	.6861	38.4	0	5	1	1	0	3	1	0	2	1	0	0	0	0	0	0	7	0	0	0	0	0	1	0	0
star-light	3	.2060	.1500	31.8	1	0	0	0	0	0	2	0	0	0	0	2	0	0	0	0	0	0	0	0	0	1	0	0	0

4J stain'd
9K Stained
4A stair-step
6R staircased
4R staircases
7N stairhead
XR Stairs
3N stake-racing
7A staking
9B stalactite
9B stalagmite
6G stalemate
9R stalemated
8R stalemating
3A Staley's
9R Stalinism
5R STALKING
3A Stall
8D stammer
5J stamp-clap
7P stampers
8A stan'
6R stanchion
3A Stand-Like-a-Rock
6A stand-by
9Q stand-in
7F stand-ins
6R stand-outs
9D stand'st
7F standard-gauge
4P Standardbred
8J standardization
3Q standardize
XR standby
6P stander-uppers
7N standeth
3A standoffish
7R standout
6H standpoints
6R Stanfield
9C STANFORD
XR stank
4F Stanleys
7R stannous
7H stannum
8Q stantibus
9H staphylococcus
7B stapler
3P star-bright
9D star-crossed
6R star-detonating
3A star-filled

Word Type	F	D	U	SFI	3 Gr 3	4 Gr 4	5 Gr 5	6 Gr 6	7 Gr 7	8 Gr 8	9 Gr 9	X UnGr	A Read	B Eng & Gr	C Comp	D Lit	E Math	F Soc Stud	G Spell	H Sci	J Music	K Art	L Home Ec	M Shop	N Lib F	P Lib NF	Q Lib Ref	R Mag	S Rel
star-shaped	2	.2412	.1091	30.4	1	0	0	1	0	0	0	0	0	0	0	1	0	0	1	0	0	0	0	0	0	0	0	0	0
star's	10	.4941	1.0672	40.3	1	0	0	1	4	1	2	1	1	1	0	1	0	0	0	5	0	0	0	0	0	0	0	2	0
starboard	28	.5151	3.2798	45.2	0	9	0	7	4	3	4	1	17	1	0	1	0	0	0	0	0	0	0	0	0	5	0	4	0
starch	62	.5353	7.0629	48.5	12	7	19	5	11	1	6	1	6	0	0	0	0	0	0	37	0	1	7	0	3	4	4	0	0
starched	4	.3786	.3298	35.2	1	1	0	0	1	0	1	0	0	0	0	1	0	0	0	0	0	0	0	0	0	2	0	1	0
starches	14	.2702	.8901	39.5	1	2	2	0	6	2	1	0	1	0	0	0	0	0	0	6	0	0	5	0	0	0	2	0	0
starchy	4	.3929	.3379	35.3	1	0	0	1	0	1	1	0	0	0	0	0	0	0	0	1	0	0	1	0	0	1	1	0	0
stardom	3	.3454	.2542	34.1	0	0	0	1	1	1	0	0	1	0	0	0	0	1	0	0	0	0	0	0	0	0	0	1	0
stare	70	.7072	10.280	50.1	7	15	7	8	15	10	7	1	31	3	3	11	1	0	0	4	1	0	0	0	6	7	0	3	0
stared	221	.6341	29.626	54.7	44	53	36	17	47	12	10	2	90	3	2	37	0	5	0	0	0	0	0	0	43	28	0	13	0
stares	15	.4456	1.5971	42.0	5	2	2	0	5	0	1	0	10	1	0	3	0	0	0	0	0	0	0	0	1	0	0	0	0
Starfighter	3	.2264	.1679	32.2	1	0	0	2	0	0	0	0	0	0	0	0	2	0	0	0	0	0	0	0	0	1	0	0	0
Starfighters	2	.0000	.0243	23.9	0	0	0	0	0	0	0	2	0	0	0	0	0	0	0	0	0	0	0	0	0	0	0	2	0
starfish	46	.6376	6.1233	47.9	17	7	4	4	10	3	1	0	10	0	0	3	0	1	0	15	0	1	0	0	1	0	4	11	0
Starfish	13	.0000	.5939	37.7	13	0	0	0	0	0	0	0	13	0	0	0	0	0	0	0	0	0	0	0	0	0	0	0	0
stargazer	2	.0000	.0914	29.6	0	0	0	2	0	0	0	0	2	0	0	0	0	0	0	0	0	0	0	0	0	0	0	0	0
staring	117	.6736	16.492	52.2	19	24	9	18	23	9	13	2	50	3	0	20	0	4	0	0	0	2	0	0	21	6	1	10	0
stark	10	.5348	1.1015	40.4	0	0	0	1	4	4	1	0	0	0	0	2	0	0	0	0	0	1	0	0	1	1	1	4	0
Stark	3	.0995	.1144	30.6	1	0	0	0	2	0	0	0	1	0	0	0	0	0	0	0	2	0	0	0	0	0	0	0	0
Starkey	9	.3652	.8659	39.4	0	0	0	7	0	0	2	0	7	0	0	0	1	0	0	0	0	0	0	0	1	0	0	0	0
starkly	5	.5605	.5805	37.6	0	0	1	0	0	2	2	0	0	1	0	1	0	1	0	0	0	0	0	0	0	1	0	1	0
starlight	12	.5509	1.3998	41.5	0	3	1	1	6	0	1	0	2	1	0	4	0	0	0	3	1	0	0	0	1	0	0	0	0
starling	2	.0000	.0394	26.0	0	0	0	0	0	0	0	2	0	0	0	0	0	0	0	2	0	0	0	0	0	0	0	0	0
starlings	4	.4501	.4035	36.1	2	0	0	1	1	0	0	0	1	0	0	0	0	0	0	1	0	0	0	0	0	1	1	0	0
starlit	6	.5432	.7069	38.5	1	0	0	1	3	1	0	0	2	0	0	0	0	0	0	1	1	0	0	0	1	1	0	0	0
Starr	4	.3785	.3310	35.2	0	0	0	3	1	0	0	0	0	0	0	0	2	0	0	0	0	0	0	0	1	0	0	1	0
starred	6	.3972	.5309	37.3	0	0	1	2	0	1	0	2	1	1	0	1	0	0	0	0	0	0	0	0	0	0	0	3	0
starring	4	.0000	.0486	26.9	0	1	0	1	1	1	0	0	0	0	0	0	0	0	0	0	0	0	0	0	0	0	0	4	0
starry	13	.3782	1.1266	40.5	1	1	3	1	3	3	1	0	4	0	3	0	0	1	0	0	3	0	0	0	0	1	1	0	0
Starry	3	.0000	.1370	31.4	0	3	0	0	0	0	0	0	3	0	0	0	0	0	0	0	0	0	0	0	0	0	0	0	0
stars	713	.8180	117.28	60.7	150	98	75	97	123	65	72	33	103	20	8	46	34	29	5	327	14	1	1	0	12	56	31	25	1
Stars	18	.5984	2.2425	43.5	3	1	6	1	2	3	1	1	3	1	0	1	0	2	0	1	6	0	0	0	0	1	2	1	0
start	1087	.9651	206.96	63.2	246	179	124	115	204	111	81	27	282	41	14	39	69	82	61	95	68	10	21	19	67	89	33	97	0
Start	2	.0000	.0243	23.9	0	0	1	0	1	0	0	0	0	0	0	0	0	0	0	0	0	0	0	0	0	0	0	2	0
started	1409	.8774	247.77	63.9	302	335	173	141	253	117	69	19	632	39	10	94	47	124	17	49	10	1	1	9	113	146	31	86	0
Started	2	.2375	.1088	30.4	0	0	0	0	0	1	0	1	0	0	0	0	0	0	0	0	1	0	0	0	0	0	0	1	0
starter	18	.6494	2.4056	43.8	3	4	0	5	4	1	1	0	3	2	0	0	0	0	0	0	0	0	1	1	2	5	0	4	0
starters	4	.3331	.2899	34.6	0	0	1	0	1	1	0	1	0	0	0	0	0	0	0	0	0	0	1	0	0	1	0	2	0
starting	343	.8945	61.089	57.9	45	72	33	33	66	49	34	11	97	8	2	12	43	20	4	27	41	1	3	10	23	20	6	26	0
Starting	2	.2303	.1079	30.3	1	1	0	0	0	0	0	0	0	0	0	0	0	0	0	0	1	0	0	0	0	1	0	0	0
startle	4	.3721	.3657	35.6	0	1	1	1	0	0	1	0	2	0	0	1	0	0	0	0	0	0	0	0	0	1	0	0	0
startled	78	.6683	10.880	50.4	8	15	14	10	16	7	7	1	30	4	4	14	0	1	0	0	1	0	0	0	7	12	0	5	0
startling	36	.7495	5.4316	47.3	5	2	0	4	11	7	5	2	2	1	1	5	0	2	0	3	1	0	0	0	2	5	8	6	0
startlingly	5	.4427	.4634	36.7	0	1	0	0	2	1	1	0	0	1	0	0	0	0	0	0	2	0	0	0	1	0	0	1	0
starts	273	.8373	45.752	56.6	76	53	32	26	50	18	11	7	55	9	3	15	21	10	31	28	51	0	1	2	8	20	7	12	0
starvation	23	.6768	3.1920	45.0	2	0	3	3	11	2	1	1	3	1	0	2	0	4	0	2	0	0	0	0	1	1	6	3	0
starve	31	.6638	4.2418	46.3	3	3	2	3	8	8	3	1	6	5	0	6	0	1	0	4	1	0	0	0	5	0	3	0	0
starved	26	.6619	3.5926	45.6	0	8	7	2	5	3	1	0	9	0	0	3	0	1	0	1	0	0	1	0	6	3	0	2	0
starveling	2	.1733	.1149	30.6	0	0	0	0	2	0	0	0	1	1	0	0	0	0	0	0	0	0	0	0	0	0	0	0	0
starving	21	.7421	3.2081	45.1	1	5	1	1	8	2	1	2	9	1	0	3	0	0	0	2	1	0	0	0	1	2	1	1	0
state	1281	.8445	216.18	63.3	107	151	239	96	218	266	171	33	109	64	13	36	110	472	20	101	9	1	8	6	22	73	139	98	0
State	193	.7481	29.236	54.7	12	10	32	19	36	34	36	14	25	9	2	12	8	32	1	4	1	0	0	1	2	19	13	64	0
state-owned	2	.0000	.0389	25.9	0	0	0	1	1	0	0	0	0	0	0	0	0	2	0	0	0	0	0	0	0	0	0	0	0
state's	34	.6165	4.3251	46.4	1	1	14	2	3	3	7	3	1	1	1	1	0	14	0	1	0	0	0	0	0	1	5	9	0
State's	9	.2754	.6383	38.0	0	0	0	2	4	1	1	1	3	0	0	1	0	0	0	0	0	0	0	0	0	0	0	5	0
stated	139	.8034	22.426	53.5	1	5	9	14	38	30	38	4	20	14	7	0	40	11	1	12	9	0	4	3	1	1	8	8	0
statehood	6	.1822	.3062	34.9	0	0	4	0	0	2	0	0	0	0	0	0	0	5	0	0	0	0	0	0	0	1	0	0	0
stately	31	.6692	4.2378	46.3	3	3	3	4	7	4	7	0	4	1	0	3	0	3	0	1	7	2	0	0	5	3	2	0	0
statement	507	.6616	68.591	58.4	17	73	70	64	75	100	100	8	36	86	11	11	261	17	27	13	15	0	2	0	2	4	8	14	0
statements	305	.6255	39.375	56.0	17	55	37	57	44	36	55	4	30	52	15	9	151	7	6	18	1	0	2	0	0	0	8	6	0
Staten	9	.4511	.8578	39.3	2	0	0	0	4	0	3	0	0	1	0	0	0	0	0	0	0	0	0	0	0	2	2	4	0
stateroom	4	.3713	.3634	35.6	0	1	0	0	0	2	1	0	2	0	0	1	0	0	0	0	0	0	0	0	1	0	0	0	0
states	683	.7487	103.66	60.2	62	80	169	37	104	156	63	12	51	17	10	7	21	360	12	43	10	2	5	1	1	38	81	24	0
States	114	.6077	14.523	51.6	14	12	40	8	17	13	8	2	15	2	0	1	0	58	0	3	7	0	0	0	0	14	8	6	0
states'	2	.2401	.1133	30.5	1	0	1	0	0	0	0	0	0	0	0	0	0	0	0	0	0	0	0	0	0	1	1	0	0
stateside	2	.2433	.1158	30.6	0	0	0	0	1	1	0	0	0	0	0	0	0	0	0	0	0	0	0	0	0	1	0	1	0
statesman	15	.5715	1.8195	42.6	0	0	3	2	8	2	0	0	4	1	0	1	0	1	0	0	0	0	0	0	0	1	5	2	0
statesmanship	2	.0000	.0914	29.6	0	0	0	0	2	0	0	0	2	0	0	0	0	0	0	0	0	0	0	0	0	0	0	0	0
statesmen	8	.5139	.8891	39.5	0	0	2	1	1	2	2	0	2	1	0	0	0	1	0	0	0	0	0	0	0	0	2	2	0
static	58	.5385	6.4707	48.1	4	3	10	4	12	20	2	3	1	0	0	4	0	0	1	18	2	1	0	12	0	5	12	2	0
static-electricity	2	.0000	.0209	23.2	0	0	0	0	0	0	2	0	0	0	0	0	0	0	0	0	0	0	0	0	0	0	2	0	0
stating	27	.6477	3.5294	45.5	0	1	6	1	10	3	6	0	0	4	4	1	7	0	1	0	3	0	0	2	2	0	1	2	0
station	341	.8919	60.672	57.8	75	59	18	64	62	28	30	5	114	20	5	11	11	22	4	44	4	0	0	5	20	33	14	34	0
Station	20	.6582	2.7341	44.4	1	5	2	1	2	4	5	0	5	4	1	0	0	3	0	2	0	0	0	0	0	1	3	1	0
stationary	33	.5692	3.8484	45.9	0	2	2	3	9	7	8	2	0	2	0	0	0	0	1	9	0	1	1	7	0	1	8	3	0
stationed	26	.7277	3.8725	45.9	1	2	6	3	6	5	3	0	6	1	0	3	0	7	0	1	1	0	0	0	0	2	2	3	0
stationery	9	.5181	.9756	39.9	1	1	3	1	2	0	1	0	1	4	0	1	0	0	1	0	0	0	0	1	0	0	0	1	0
stations	150	.7142	21.964	53.4	18	21	21	27	32	17	10	4	28	1	0	0	0	23	1	38	4	0	0	1	0	14	19	21	0
statistic	2	.2433	.1158	30.6	0	0	1	0	0	1	0	0	0	0	0	0	0	0	0	0	0	0	0	0	0	1	0	1	0
statistical	12	.5321	1.3214	41.2	0	3	0	0	3	3	3	0	0	1	0	0	3	1	0	0	0	0	0	1	0	0	5	1	0
statistically	2	.1160	.0650	28.1	0	0	0	0	0	1	0	1	0	0	1	0	0	0	0	1	0	0	0	0	0	0	0	0	0
statistician	3	.0000	.0449	26.5	0	0	0	0	0	3	0	0	0	0	0	0	3	0	0	0	0	0	0	0	0	0	0	0	0
statistics	47	.7230	6.8656	48.4	2	3	2	2	10	16	11	1	1	0	1	1	15	5	0	2	0	0	1	0	1	4	6	10	0
Statistics	4	.2129	.2122	33.3	0	0	0	0	0	2	2	0	0	0	0	0	3	0	0	0	0	0	0	0	0	0	0	1	0
stator	2	.1620	.0760	28.8	0	0	0	0	2	0	0	0	0	0	0	0	0	0	0	0	0	0	0	1	0	0	0	1	0
statuary	2	.2408	.1204	30.8	1	0	0	0	0	1	0	0	0	0	0	0	0	1	0	0	0	0	0	0	0	1	0	0	0
statue	123	.7376	18.691	52.7	29	17	14	21	18	12	10	2	55	8	1	12	1	13	3	0	1	8	0	1	1	4	9	6	0
Statue	15	.4640	1.5780	42.0	7	1	1	0	5	1	0	0	6	0	0	5	1	2	0	0	0	0	0	0	0	0	1	0	0
statues	34	.4684	3.4369	45.4	12	3	2	5	3	6	3	0	5	1	0	2	0	9	0	1	2	6	0	0	0	3	5	0	0
statuettes	2	.2446	.1122	30.5	0	1	0	0	0	0	1	0	0	0	0	1	0	0	0	0	0	0	0	0	0	0	1	0	0
stature	13	.6386	1.7173	42.3	0	1	1	2	3	4	2	0	2	0	0	3	0	2	0	0	0	0	0	0	1	2	1	2	0
statures	2	.0000	.0914	29.6	0	0	0	0	2	0	0	0	2	0	0	0	0	0	0	0	0	0	0	0	0	0	0	0	0
status	43	.7831	6.7419	48.3	1	2	2	2	15	11	9	1	1	8	1	2	1	7	1	0	0	1	0	0	1	6	7	7	0
statute	7	.3772	.5732	37.6	0	0	1	0	3	2	1	0	0	0	0	0	2	0	0	0	0	0	0	0	0	0	2	3	0
Staubach	3	.0000	.0365	25.6	0	0	0	0	3	0	0	0	0	0	0	0	0	0	0	0	0	0	0	0	0	0	0	3	0
stauncher	2	.2306	.1140	30.6	0	0	0	0	0	1	0	1	0	1	0	0	0	1	0	0	0	0	0	0	0	0	0	0	0

7H star-wound	7B starless	3R Starve	3P StateHouse	9D Stateroom	8E Statistical
6A Star's	XR starlight's	9D Starveling	7R State-designate	6Q states-general	5Q Statuary
4A starburst	9Q Starling	6H starves	8R state-police	7R statewide	9F Statute
3A Starcher	5P starry-eyed	6J starvin'	7F state-run	8M Static	7R statutes
3P stardust	7R Stars'	7Q Starving	5Q state-supported	9H station's	7Q statutory
7B starer	7N Starter	XR stashed	9R State-supported	8B stationers	9D staunch
4N stargazing	4J startin'	5G stat	9R State-wide	3N stationmaster	3P staunched
XR starkers	9A startingly	7D STATE	6J stately-flowing	3P stationmen	7G staunchest

Word Type	F	D	U	SFI	3 Gr 3	4 Gr 4	5 Gr 5	6 Gr 6	7 Gr 7	8 Gr 8	9 Gr 9	X UnGr	A Read	B Eng & Gr	C Comp	D Lit	E Math	F Soc Stud	G Spell	H Sci	J Music	K Art	L Home Ec	M Shop	N Lib F	P Lib NF	Q Lib Ref	R Mag	S Rel
staunchness	2	.1787	.1174	30.7	0	0	0	1	0	1	0	0	1	0	0	0	0	0	0	0	0	0	0	0	1	0	0	0	0
staurolite	2	.0000	.0394	26.0	0	0	0	0	0	0	0	2	0	0	0	0	0	0	0	2	0	0	0	0	0	0	0	0	0
Stavanger	2	.0000	.0914	29.6	0	0	0	2	0	0	0	0	2	0	0	0	0	0	0	0	0	0	0	0	0	0	0	0	0
stave	5	.2445	.3875	35.9	0	0	0	3	1	0	1	0	4	0	0	0	0	0	0	0	0	0	0	0	0	0	0	1	0
staves	6	.0995	.2287	33.6	0	0	0	4	2	0	0	0	2	0	0	0	0	0	0	0	4	0	0	0	0	0	0	0	0
stay	914	.8949	163.08	62.1	270	191	94	95	144	60	46	14	304	21	5	62	2	63	21	135	19	5	17	0	96	84	20	60	0
Stay	6	.3587	.4719	36.7	0	0	0	1	4	1	0	0	0	1	0	0	0	0	0	0	0	0	0	0	0	2	0	3	0
stay-at-home	4	.2595	.2549	34.1	0	0	0	1	1	1	1	0	1	0	1	0	0	0	0	0	0	0	0	0	0	0	2	0	0
stayed	339	.8285	56.887	57.6	91	63	55	38	43	26	15	8	163	17	2	20	3	26	1	19	5	0	1	0	27	37	4	14	0
staying	62	.7377	9.4510	49.8	11	18	4	8	10	4	6	1	29	3	0	1	0	4	0	1	1	0	0	0	5	9	3	6	0
stayline	3	.0000	.0097	19.8	0	0	0	0	0	0	3	0	0	0	0	0	0	0	0	0	0	0	3	0	0	0	0	0	0
stays	90	.8186	14.797	51.7	20	15	13	12	8	6	11	5	11	2	1	4	4	8	1	35	1	0	3	0	3	10	2	5	0
staysail	2	.0665	.0708	28.5	0	0	0	1	1	0	0	0	1	0	1	0	0	0	0	0	0	0	0	0	0	0	0	0	0
staystitch	9	.0000	.0290	24.6	0	0	0	0	3	1	5	0	0	0	0	0	0	0	0	0	0	0	9	0	0	0	0	0	0
staystitch-plus	2	.0000	.0064	18.1	0	0	0	0	0	0	2	0	0	0	0	0	0	0	0	0	0	0	2	0	0	0	0	0	0
staystitched	2	.0000	.0064	18.1	0	0	0	0	0	1	1	0	0	0	0	0	0	0	0	0	0	0	2	0	0	0	0	0	0
staystitching	14	.0000	.0451	26.5	0	0	0	0	7	3	4	0	0	0	0	0	0	0	0	0	0	0	14	0	0	0	0	0	0
SteMarie	2	.0000	.0209	23.2	0	0	0	2	0	0	0	0	0	0	0	0	0	0	0	0	0	0	0	0	0	0	2	0	0
stead	8	.5878	.9939	40.0	1	0	0	2	1	2	2	0	2	0	0	2	0	1	0	0	0	0	0	0	0	1	1	1	0
steadfast	9	.1243	.3516	35.5	4	0	0	0	1	1	3	0	2	0	0	1	0	1	0	0	0	1	0	0	0	1	0	1	2
steadfastly	5	.4140	.4655	36.7	0	0	0	0	2	2	1	0	1	0	0	1	0	1	0	0	0	0	0	0	0	0	0	2	0
steadied	7	.4645	.7371	38.7	0	1	1	3	1	1	0	0	3	0	0	1	0	0	0	0	0	0	0	0	2	0	0	1	0
steadier	4	.2424	.3036	34.8	0	0	1	2	1	0	0	0	3	0	0	0	0	0	0	0	0	0	0	0	0	0	0	1	0
steadily	118	.8831	20.783	53.2	4	15	12	16	36	17	14	4	33	3	1	9	1	7	2	14	7	0	0	2	12	7	12	8	0
steadiness	2	.2401	.1133	30.5	0	1	0	0	0	0	1	0	0	0	0	0	0	0	0	0	0	0	0	0	0	1	1	0	0
steady	243	.8427	41.005	56.1	20	31	38	50	43	27	25	9	55	9	1	19	1	12	4	31	42	0	2	3	20	19	5	20	0
steadying	6	.2279	.4286	36.3	0	0	2	0	2	0	1	1	4	0	0	0	0	0	0	0	0	0	0	0	0	0	0	2	0
steak	30	.6814	4.2088	46.2	5	3	7	5	5	3	2	0	7	4	0	0	4	1	5	1	0	0	0	0	4	1	0	3	0
steaks	18	.5159	1.9435	42.9	1	6	1	1	0	1	6	2	1	2	0	0	0	1	0	0	0	0	3	0	0	7	1	3	0
steal	83	.7404	12.600	51.0	22	17	5	7	18	8	5	1	30	3	0	11	0	0	2	3	4	0	0	0	11	14	2	3	0
stealer	3	.2379	.1705	32.3	1	0	1	0	0	0	1	0	0	0	0	1	0	0	0	0	0	0	0	0	0	2	0	0	0
stealing	46	.6387	6.1792	47.9	7	9	5	5	11	9	0	0	17	1	0	10	0	1	0	0	0	0	0	0	7	4	3	3	0
steals	11	.5857	1.3334	41.2	2	4	2	1	0	0	2	0	1	1	0	1	0	0	0	1	2	0	0	0	0	0	1	4	0
stealth	3	.2260	.1580	32.0	0	0	0	0	1	1	1	0	0	0	0	2	0	0	0	0	0	0	0	0	0	0	1	0	0
stealthily	4	.3740	.3661	35.6	0	0	0	2	1	0	0	1	2	0	0	0	0	0	0	0	0	0	0	0	1	0	0	1	0
stealthy	6	.2212	.4198	36.2	0	0	2	0	2	2	0	0	4	0	0	2	0	0	0	0	0	0	0	0	0	0	0	0	0
steam	340	.8579	58.346	57.7	73	59	54	35	48	33	31	7	69	5	7	6	1	41	8	83	11	0	1	3	15	44	34	12	0
Steam	4	.3689	.3191	35.0	0	0	0	0	3	0	0	1	0	0	0	0	0	0	0	0	0	0	0	0	2	0	1	1	0
steam-driven	4	.4767	.4085	36.1	0	0	1	0	1	1	1	0	0	0	0	0	1	1	0	1	0	0	0	0	0	0	1	0	0
steam-engine	2	.2441	.1127	30.5	0	0	1	0	1	0	0	0	0	0	0	0	0	0	0	0	0	0	0	0	1	0	1	0	0
steam-powered	2	.1698	.1133	30.5	0	0	0	1	1	0	0	0	1	0	0	0	0	0	0	0	0	0	0	0	0	0	1	0	0
steamboat	34	.7263	5.0915	47.1	6	6	3	8	7	3	1	0	12	2	1	0	0	9	0	1	2	0	0	0	2	2	0	3	0
Steamboat	19	.1316	.7260	38.6	17	0	0	0	0	2	0	0	0	0	0	0	0	0	0	0	0	0	0	0	0	17	0	2	0
steamboatman	4	.0000	.0438	26.4	0	0	0	0	4	0	0	0	0	4	0	0	0	0	0	0	0	0	0	0	0	0	0	0	0
steamboats	11	.3306	.8437	39.3	1	1	4	1	1	3	0	0	0	0	0	0	0	8	1	0	0	0	0	0	0	2	0	0	0
steamed	18	.6701	2.4780	43.9	2	3	3	1	5	3	1	0	3	1	1	4	0	3	0	0	1	0	0	0	2	3	0	0	0
steamer	34	.6294	4.4747	46.5	0	1	3	9	18	2	0	1	8	0	0	1	0	7	0	1	1	0	0	0	9	0	2	5	0
Steamer	5	.0000	.2284	33.6	0	4	1	0	0	0	0	0	5	0	0	0	0	0	0	0	0	0	0	0	0	0	0	0	0
steamers	10	.4733	1.0042	40.0	0	1	4	0	3	2	0	0	0	0	0	0	0	4	0	0	1	0	0	0	2	0	3	0	0
steaming	48	.7905	7.6968	48.9	7	13	3	7	8	4	4	2	15	2	1	1	0	7	0	2	1	0	0	0	6	8	3	2	0
steamship	13	.6131	1.6880	42.3	2	1	1	2	3	3	1	0	4	0	0	0	0	3	0	0	0	0	0	0	1	2	2	1	0
Steamship	3	.1900	.1470	31.7	0	0	0	0	2	0	0	1	0	0	0	0	0	0	0	1	0	0	0	0	2	0	0	0	0
steamships	11	.3685	.9200	39.6	1	3	2	2	2	1	0	0	0	0	0	0	1	8	0	0	0	0	0	0	0	1	1	0	0
steamy	8	.5917	.9986	40.0	0	0	2	1	1	1	1	2	2	2	0	1	0	0	0	1	0	0	0	0	1	0	0	1	0
steed	12	.5870	1.4962	41.7	1	2	0	3	1	4	0	1	4	2	0	3	0	0	0	0	1	0	0	0	1	1	0	0	0
steeds	2	.2412	.1141	30.6	0	1	0	1	0	0	0	0	0	1	0	0	0	0	0	0	0	0	0	0	0	1	0	0	0
steel	565	.6450	75.297	58.8	90	75	66	52	103	91	84	4	80	8	5	23	7	161	3	85	16	3	0	84	9	26	32	23	0
Steel	9	.5229	.9750	39.9	0	0	3	1	3	0	2	0	0	0	0	0	0	2	0	0	1	0	0	1	0	0	3	2	0
steel-driving	5	.2445	.3864	35.9	0	0	0	0	5	0	0	0	4	0	0	1	0	0	0	0	0	0	0	0	0	0	0	0	0
steel-making	2	.2160	.1362	31.3	1	0	0	0	1	0	0	0	1	0	0	0	0	0	0	1	0	0	0	0	0	0	0	0	0
steel-tipped	2	.1733	.1149	30.6	0	0	0	1	0	1	0	0	1	1	0	0	0	0	0	0	0	0	0	0	0	0	0	0	0
Steele	5	.3125	.3478	35.4	1	0	0	0	3	0	0	1	0	0	0	3	1	0	0	0	0	0	0	0	0	0	0	1	0
STEELE	11	.0000	.1180	30.7	0	0	0	0	11	0	0	0	0	0	0	11	0	0	0	0	0	0	0	0	0	0	0	0	0
Steelers	2	.0000	.0243	23.9	0	0	0	0	2	0	0	0	0	0	0	0	0	0	0	0	0	0	0	0	0	0	0	2	0
steelhead	2	.0000	.0243	23.9	0	0	0	0	2	0	0	0	0	0	0	0	0	0	0	0	0	0	0	0	0	0	0	2	0
steelmaking	2	.0000	.0389	25.9	0	2	0	0	0	0	0	0	0	0	0	0	0	2	0	0	0	0	0	0	0	0	0	0	0
steels	16	.0886	.3933	35.9	0	1	0	0	1	1	13	0	0	0	0	0	0	2	0	3	0	0	0	11	0	0	0	0	0
steelworkers	2	.0000	.0914	29.6	2	0	0	0	0	0	0	0	2	0	0	0	0	0	0	0	0	0	0	0	0	0	0	0	0
steely	4	.3164	.2806	34.5	0	0	1	1	0	0	1	1	0	0	0	1	0	0	0	1	2	0	0	0	0	0	0	0	0
steep	184	.7983	29.792	54.7	29	34	39	28	27	12	14	1	60	6	0	9	0	39	6	13	3	0	0	0	7	23	13	5	0
steep-sided	5	.2904	.3732	35.7	0	2	1	1	0	1	0	0	1	0	0	0	0	3	0	1	0	0	0	0	0	0	0	0	0
steeped	7	.5630	.8002	39.0	0	1	0	1	2	1	2	0	0	0	1	2	0	0	0	0	1	0	1	0	1	0	0	1	0
steeper	12	.4440	1.2178	40.9	2	3	0	2	1	1	3	0	4	0	0	0	0	0	0	5	0	0	0	1	2	0	0	0	0
steepest	4	.4495	.4018	36.0	0	0	0	1	2	0	1	0	1	0	0	1	0	1	0	0	0	0	0	0	0	0	0	1	0
steeple	16	.6405	2.1267	43.3	5	5	0	2	1	0	0	3	4	0	0	1	0	0	1	0	3	0	0	0	3	2	0	2	0
Steeple	3	.0995	.1144	30.6	2	1	0	0	0	0	0	0	1	0	0	0	0	0	0	0	2	0	0	0	0	0	0	0	0
steeplechase	2	.0000	.0243	23.9	0	0	0	2	0	0	0	0	0	0	0	0	0	0	0	0	0	0	0	0	0	0	0	2	0
steeples	8	.3415	.6303	38.0	2	2	1	0	0	2	1	0	1	0	0	4	0	2	0	0	0	0	0	0	0	1	0	0	0
steeply	12	.4619	1.2522	41.0	1	2	2	4	1	0	2	0	3	0	0	0	1	6	0	1	0	0	0	0	0	1	0	0	0
steepness	2	.2291	.1135	30.5	0	0	1	0	0	0	1	0	0	0	0	1	0	0	0	1	0	0	0	0	0	0	0	0	0
steer	79	.6373	10.626	50.3	14	18	11	11	15	5	3	2	32	1	0	3	0	5	0	5	5	6	0	0	14	3	1	4	0
steer's	7	.0000	.3198	35.0	0	3	0	0	4	0	0	0	7	0	0	0	0	0	0	0	0	0	0	0	0	0	0	0	0
steerage	5	.3737	.4056	36.1	1	0	0	0	0	1	3	0	0	1	0	2	0	0	0	0	0	0	0	0	0	2	0	0	0
steered	21	.6790	3.0172	44.8	2	3	1	1	11	2	1	0	12	0	0	1	0	1	0	1	0	0	0	0	2	1	1	2	0
steering	75	.6706	10.567	50.2	5	9	4	6	32	15	4	0	34	0	1	3	0	1	0	3	0	0	0	0	6	6	3	18	0
steers	28	.4907	3.0119	44.8	3	2	7	2	7	3	4	0	8	0	0	11	0	2	1	0	0	0	0	0	2	4	0	0	0
steersman	2	.2446	.1184	30.7	0	1	0	0	0	0	1	0	0	0	0	0	1	0	0	0	0	0	0	0	0	1	0	0	0
Stefan	3	.0000	.1370	31.4	0	0	0	0	3	0	0	0	3	0	0	0	0	0	0	0	0	0	0	0	0	0	0	0	0
Stefansson	6	.0000	.0869	29.4	6	0	0	0	0	0	0	0	0	0	0	0	0	0	0	0	0	0	0	0	0	6	0	0	0
Stegner	7	.1396	.2274	33.6	0	0	0	0	3	0	4	0	0	0	4	3	0	0	0	0	0	0	0	0	0	0	0	0	0
stegosaurs	2	.0000	.0290	24.6	0	2	0	0	0	0	0	0	0	0	0	0	0	0	0	0	0	0	0	0	0	2	0	0	0
stegosaurus	4	.2009	.2054	33.1	0	1	0	3	0	0	0	0	0	0	0	0	3	0	0	0	0	0	0	0	0	1	0	0	0
Stegosaurus	11	.1647	.4899	36.9	9	0	0	0	0	2	0	0	0	0	0	0	2	0	0	0	0	0	0	0	0	9	0	0	0
Steichen	2	.0000	.0243	23.9	0	0	0	0	2	0	0	0	0	0	0	0	0	0	0	0	0	0	0	0	0	0	0	2	0
Stein	6	.3606	.4737	36.8	0	2	0	0	3	0	1	0	0	0	0	0	0	0	0	0	0	0	0	0	0	2	1	3	0

5P staunchly
8D staving
7Q stay-at-homes
8L stay-stitching
3N stayin'
9L staylines
7A Ste-e-even
6N steadies
7Q steadiest
7B steadiment
6J steady-beat
XR steak-maker
7D stealers
3P steam-basket
6H steam-heating
7Q steam-propelled
7Q steam's
4P steamcars
7N steamer's
4A steaming-hot
7A steamrollered
3B steams
4P Stearns
7R steel-and-glass
9D steel-blue
4R steel-cold
8F steel-frame
9Q steel-gray
5A steel-like
9R steel-mill
7R steel-rimmed
9M steel-rolling
3P Steeldust
7D steeled
3A steelworker
6R steely-eyed
6J Steens
9D steep-roofed
6A steepened
8A steepening
7A steeping
3D steeple-sliding's
7Q steepsided
5B steepy
6A steerer
7R Steering
7A Stefan's
4R Stefanich
8Q Stefano
5J Steffe
9C Steffens
9B Stefferud
9C Stegner's
6H Stehli

Word Type	F	D	U	SFI	3 Gr 3	4 Gr 4	5 Gr 5	6 Gr 6	7 Gr 7	8 Gr 8	9 Gr 9	X UnGr	A Read	B Eng & Gr	C Comp	D Lit	E Math	F Soc Stud	G Spell	H Sci	J Music	K Art	L Home Ec	M Shop	N Lib F	P Lib NF	Q Lib Ref	R Mag	S Rel
Steinbeck	12	.0000	.0268	24.3	0	0	0	0	0	9	3	0	0	0	12	0	0	0	0	0	0	0	0	0	0	0	0	0	0
Steiner	2	.0000	.0234	23.7	0	0	0	0	0	2	0	0	0	0	0	0	0	0	0	0	0	0	0	0	2	0	0	0	0
Steinmetz	10	.0000	.4568	36.6	0	0	0	10	0	0	0	0	10	0	0	0	0	0	0	0	0	0	0	0	0	0	0	0	0
Stella	5	.1781	.2198	33.4	0	0	0	0	4	1	0	0	0	4	0	1	0	0	0	0	0	0	0	0	0	0	0	0	0
stellar	3	.2383	.1815	32.6	0	0	0	0	3	0	0	0	0	0	0	0	0	0	0	2	0	0	0	0	0	1	0	0	0
stem	138	.7962	22.121	53.4	35	12	11	17	44	5	12	2	20	5	4	2	0	4	1	48	3	3	2	0	5	6	27	8	0
stemmed	5	.4625	.4880	36.9	0	0	1	0	1	1	2	0	0	0	0	0	0	1	0	0	1	0	0	0	0	0	1	2	0
stemming	3	.2387	.1708	32.3	0	0	1	0	2	0	0	0	0	0	0	0	0	0	0	0	0	0	0	0	0	2	1	0	0
stems	171	.7555	26.201	54.2	52	13	16	30	48	4	4	4	22	1	1	0	1	4	0	76	10	3	2	0	5	20	18	8	0
stench	3	.3394	.2451	33.9	0	0	0	0	2	0	1	0	1	0	0	1	0	0	0	0	0	0	0	0	1	0	0	0	0
Stengel	10	.0000	.1448	31.6	3	0	0	7	0	0	0	0	0	0	0	0	0	0	0	0	0	0	0	0	0	10	0	0	0
stenographers	8	.2669	.4971	37.0	1	0	0	0	5	2	0	0	0	0	0	0	0	2	0	0	0	0	0	0	0	1	5	0	0
stentor	2	.2405	.1205	30.8	1	0	1	0	0	0	0	0	0	0	0	0	0	0	0	1	0	0	0	0	0	1	0	0	0
step	749	.8621	128.72	61.1	128	133	113	90	118	62	88	17	130	47	11	30	131	42	6	43	148	2	23	13	36	25	18	44	0
Step	16	.4101	1.4398	41.6	2	6	0	0	2	3	3	0	2	0	0	0	8	0	5	0	0	0	1	0	0	0	0	0	0
step-bend	2	.0000	.0162	22.1	2	0	0	0	0	0	0	0	0	0	0	0	0	0	0	0	2	0	0	0	0	0	0	0	0
step-by-step	2	.2300	.1140	30.6	0	0	0	0	1	0	1	0	0	1	0	0	0	0	0	1	0	0	0	0	0	0	0	0	0
step-hop	2	.0000	.0162	22.1	0	2	0	0	0	0	0	0	0	0	0	0	0	0	0	0	2	0	0	0	0	0	0	0	0
step-mother	4	.1948	.2500	34.0	0	1	0	2	1	0	0	0	2	0	0	0	0	0	0	0	0	0	0	0	0	2	0	0	0
stepfather	7	.3179	.4930	36.9	0	3	0	0	3	0	1	0	0	0	0	4	0	0	0	0	0	0	0	0	0	1	0	2	0
Stephan	2	.0000	.0243	23.9	0	1	0	0	0	0	0	1	0	0	0	0	0	0	0	0	0	0	0	0	0	0	0	2	0
Stephanie	7	.1544	.2832	34.5	0	0	6	0	0	0	1	0	0	0	0	1	0	0	0	0	0	0	0	0	0	0	0	6	0
Stephen	81	.2022	5.0520	47.0	9	15	10	19	6	20	2	0	41	0	2	0	1	8	0	0	10	0	0	0	0	8	5	0	6
Stephen's	2	.0231	.0234	23.7	0	2	0	0	0	0	0	0	0	0	0	0	0	0	0	0	0	0	0	0	0	1	0	0	1
Stephenson	19	.2513	1.1359	40.6	1	15	0	0	2	1	0	0	1	1	0	0	0	0	0	0	0	0	0	0	0	1	1	15	0
stepladder	6	.4473	.6033	37.8	3	1	2	0	0	0	0	0	2	0	0	0	0	0	0	0	1	0	0	0	2	1	0	0	0
stepmother	13	.5157	1.5229	41.8	9	0	1	1	0	1	0	1	8	0	0	1	0	0	0	1	2	0	0	0	0	0	0	1	0
steppe	6	.3691	.4960	37.0	0	0	0	3	1	1	1	0	0	0	0	0	0	4	1	0	0	0	0	0	0	0	1	0	0
stepped	257	.7584	40.078	56.0	57	60	23	34	35	27	18	3	123	7	1	21	1	17	1	3	4	0	0	0	38	20	3	18	0
stepper	3	.2060	.1500	31.8	0	1	0	0	0	0	2	0	0	0	0	2	0	0	0	0	0	0	0	0	0	1	0	0	0
steppes	19	.3104	1.4098	41.5	0	2	1	13	1	0	2	0	1	0	0	0	0	14	0	0	0	0	0	0	0	1	3	0	0
stepping	42	.7787	6.6278	48.2	7	7	1	5	14	3	5	0	14	0	1	1	0	1	1	0	1	3	2	1	6	3	4	4	0
steps	747	.8630	128.59	61.1	146	111	118	76	137	79	77	3	167	32	14	51	93	23	22	34	134	1	28	28	49	38	11	22	0
Steps	17	.2133	.8450	39.3	2	3	1	2	1	5	3	0	0	1	0	0	4	0	12	0	0	0	0	0	0	0	0	0	0
stepwise	2	.0000	.0162	22.1	2	0	0	0	0	0	0	0	0	0	0	0	0	0	0	0	2	0	0	0	0	0	0	0	0
stereo	15	.4353	1.4518	41.6	0	0	1	3	5	5	0	1	3	0	0	0	0	0	0	5	5	0	0	0	0	0	1	1	0
stereophonic	2	.2407	.1090	30.4	0	0	0	0	1	0	1	0	0	1	0	0	0	0	0	0	1	0	0	0	0	0	0	0	0
stereoscopic	2	.2278	.1128	30.5	0	0	0	0	1	0	0	1	0	0	0	0	0	0	0	1	0	0	0	0	0	0	1	0	0
stereotyped	3	.3847	.2496	34.0	0	0	1	0	2	0	0	0	0	0	0	0	0	0	0	0	0	0	0	0	0	1	1	1	0
stereotypes	3	.2478	.1662	32.2	0	0	1	0	1	0	1	0	0	0	0	0	0	0	0	0	0	1	0	0	0	1	1	0	0
sterile	12	.5508	1.3792	41.4	0	0	2	0	3	2	2	3	0	0	1	1	0	0	0	6	0	0	0	0	0	1	2	1	0
sterilization	2	.0000	.0394	26.0	0	0	0	0	2	0	0	0	0	0	0	0	0	0	0	2	0	0	0	0	0	0	0	0	0
sterilize	3	.0000	.0591	27.7	0	0	0	1	1	1	0	0	0	0	0	0	0	0	0	3	0	0	0	0	0	0	0	0	0
sterilized	6	.3449	.4757	36.8	0	0	0	0	2	2	1	1	0	0	0	0	0	0	0	4	0	0	0	0	0	1	0	1	0
sterling	7	.5197	.7736	38.9	0	1	0	2	0	2	2	0	1	0	0	0	2	0	0	0	0	0	0	0	1	0	1	2	0
Sterling	23	.5494	2.6998	44.3	0	3	1	6	11	1	0	1	6	1	0	8	0	0	0	2	0	0	0	0	1	0	1	4	0
stern	75	.7433	11.464	50.6	6	11	10	14	20	4	9	1	32	1	2	5	0	2	0	0	2	0	0	0	9	13	3	6	0
Stern	2	.0000	.0243	23.9	0	0	0	0	0	2	0	0	0	0	0	0	0	0	0	0	0	0	0	0	0	0	0	2	0
stern-wheeler	2	.0000	.0243	23.9	0	0	0	0	2	0	0	0	0	0	0	0	0	0	0	0	0	0	0	0	0	0	0	2	0
sternly	35	.6135	4.5343	46.6	7	7	5	8	7	0	1	0	12	0	1	3	0	0	0	0	0	0	0	0	11	3	1	4	0
sternum	2	.0000	.0209	23.2	0	0	0	0	0	2	0	0	0	0	0	0	0	0	0	0	0	0	0	0	0	0	2	0	0
stethoscope	10	.2160	.6809	38.3	2	0	7	0	0	0	1	0	5	0	0	0	0	0	0	5	0	0	0	0	0	0	0	0	0
Stetson	6	.3549	.4614	36.6	0	1	2	1	0	2	0	0	0	1	0	3	0	0	0	0	0	0	0	0	2	0	0	0	0
Stettin	2	.0000	.0389	25.9	0	0	0	2	0	0	0	0	0	0	0	0	0	2	0	0	0	0	0	0	0	0	0	0	0
Steve	136	.6364	18.470	52.7	34	25	23	8	30	11	4	1	68	11	0	4	20	1	0	3	0	0	0	0	0	10	0	19	0
Steve's	12	.4799	1.3003	41.1	3	4	2	1	0	2	0	0	5	2	0	0	3	0	0	0	0	0	0	0	0	2	0	0	0
stevedores	3	.3431	.2528	34.0	0	0	0	0	2	1	0	0	1	0	0	0	0	1	0	0	0	0	0	0	1	0	0	0	0
Steven	11	.3496	1.0400	40.2	0	2	0	7	2	0	0	0	9	1	0	0	1	0	0	0	0	0	0	0	0	0	0	0	0
Steven's	6	.1200	.2605	34.2	0	4	0	2	0	0	0	0	2	4	0	0	0	0	0	0	0	0	0	0	0	0	0	0	0
Stevens	8	.4840	.8583	39.3	0	5	0	1	0	2	0	0	3	0	0	0	0	1	0	0	1	1	0	0	1	0	1	0	0
Stevenson	34	.4865	3.5633	45.5	1	21	1	1	8	0	2	0	5	4	0	0	0	0	0	0	2	0	0	0	0	19	2	2	0
STEVENSON	10	.0000	.1073	30.3	0	0	0	0	0	10	0	0	0	0	0	10	0	0	0	0	0	0	0	0	0	0	0	0	0
Stevenson's	7	.5590	.8056	39.1	1	2	0	0	2	1	1	0	0	1	0	1	0	0	1	0	0	0	0	0	0	2	0	2	0
Stevie	56	.0362	1.1779	40.7	0	55	1	0	0	0	0	0	0	0	0	0	0	0	0	0	0	0	0	0	0	55	0	1	0
Stevie's	2	.0000	.0290	24.6	0	2	0	0	0	0	0	0	0	0	0	0	0	0	0	0	0	0	0	0	0	2	0	0	0
stew	61	.6771	8.6479	49.4	17	27	3	2	6	0	5	1	28	2	2	2	0	3	1	0	0	0	6	0	3	12	1	1	0
steward	18	.5430	2.0595	43.1	0	1	0	10	1	1	1	4	1	4	0	1	0	8	0	0	0	0	0	0	2	0	0	2	0
Steward	7	.4157	.6450	38.1	0	0	0	2	2	0	3	0	1	0	0	0	0	0	0	0	0	0	0	0	1	3	0	2	0
stewardess	15	.5132	1.7374	42.4	4	1	3	0	4	2	0	1	8	1	1	0	0	3	0	0	0	0	0	0	0	0	0	2	0
stewardesses	8	.2424	.6072	37.8	3	0	0	1	0	4	0	0	6	0	0	0	0	0	0	0	0	0	0	0	0	0	0	2	0
stewards	3	.3815	.2534	34.0	0	0	0	1	1	0	1	0	0	0	0	0	0	1	0	0	0	0	0	0	0	1	0	1	0
stewardship	2	.1698	.1133	30.5	0	0	0	0	2	0	0	0	1	0	0	0	0	0	0	0	0	0	0	0	0	0	1	0	0
Stewart	12	.3307	.8873	39.5	5	0	0	0	2	1	4	0	0	0	0	1	0	0	0	0	0	0	0	0	0	7	0	4	0
stewed	7	.3830	.5759	37.6	0	3	0	1	1	2	0	0	0	3	0	0	0	0	0	0	0	0	1	0	0	3	0	0	0
stewing	2	.0000	.0064	18.1	0	0	0	0	0	0	2	0	0	0	0	0	0	0	0	0	0	0	2	0	0	0	0	0	0
stews	3	.1200	.1302	31.1	1	2	0	0	0	0	0	0	1	2	0	0	0	0	0	0	0	0	0	0	0	0	0	0	0
Stewy	6	.0000	.0703	28.5	6	0	0	0	0	0	0	0	0	0	0	0	0	0	0	0	0	0	0	0	6	0	0	0	0
stick	502	.9185	91.647	59.6	147	100	50	63	73	39	20	10	188	14	3	22	17	18	12	74	9	13	5	8	31	43	16	29	0
Stick	3	.2435	.1694	32.3	0	0	0	1	0	1	0	1	0	0	1	0	0	0	0	1	0	0	0	0	0	0	0	1	0
stick-together	2	.0000	.0914	29.6	0	0	2	0	0	0	0	0	2	0	0	0	0	0	0	0	0	0	0	0	0	0	0	0	0
Stickeen	6	.0000	.2741	34.4	0	4	2	0	0	0	0	0	6	0	0	0	0	0	0	0	0	0	0	0	0	0	0	0	0
Stickeen's	2	.0000	.0914	29.6	0	0	2	0	0	0	0	0	2	0	0	0	0	0	0	0	0	0	0	0	0	0	0	0	0
sticker	2	.0000	.0914	29.6	0	0	0	0	2	0	0	0	2	0	0	0	0	0	0	0	0	0	0	0	0	0	0	0	0
stickers	5	.5354	.5726	37.6	0	1	0	1	1	0	2	0	1	1	0	0	0	0	0	1	0	0	0	0	1	0	0	1	0
stickiness	4	.3869	.3419	35.3	0	1	1	0	0	1	0	1	0	0	0	0	0	0	0	2	0	0	0	0	1	0	1	0	0
sticking	65	.8036	10.586	50.2	19	9	7	12	13	1	3	1	26	1	0	5	0	0	0	3	2	0	2	2	6	9	4	5	0
sticks	242	.9068	43.676	56.4	73	49	24	32	44	11	8	1	89	2	1	6	29	10	3	14	17	5	8	3	16	20	10	9	0
sticky	74	.7690	11.644	50.7	22	14	8	5	14	3	5	3	29	2	1	0	0	3	1	19	0	1	0	0	2	3	9	4	0
stiff	138	.8425	23.279	53.7	22	25	12	18	30	16	12	3	33	5	0	16	2	5	2	11	4	6	7	1	14	17	8	7	0
stiff-legged	8	.4700	.8099	39.1	2	1	0	1	4	0	0	0	1	0	0	2	0	1	0	0	0	0	0	0	3	0	0	1	0
stiffen	2	.1698	.1133	30.5	0	1	1	0	0	0	0	0	1	0	0	0	0	0	0	0	0	0	0	0	0	0	1	0	0
stiffened	17	.6530	2.2821	43.6	0	6	0	0	3	4	4	0	3	2	0	5	0	0	0	0	2	0	0	0	1	1	1	2	0

9C Steinbeck's
7Q steinbok
6A Steinmetz'
7B Stella's
XH Stellaeborg
7Q Steller's
7J stem-down
7J stem-up
3P stem-winding
5H stemlike
5Q Stendhal
6P Stengel's
9F Stennis
7H Steno
8G stenographer
7Q stenography
7Q Stenopterygius
7Q stenotype
8G Stentor
3P STENTOR
8G stentorian
7J step-and-a-half
3J step-bends
8M step-down
3J step-pictures
8M step-up
4R stepbrother
7P stepbrothers
XR stepchildren
5P Stepchildren
4R stepfather's
5Q Stephane
7D Stephens
7P stepmother's
9F stepped-up
9D steppers
7R steppin'
5F steppingstone
6F steppingstones
4R stepsister
3J stepsisters
7A stepson
8D stept
XB stercoris
8H stereophonically
7H stereotype
7D sterilizer
7D sterilizes
8H sterilizing
5F stern-faced
6A stern-first
7F stern-minded
8R Stern's
5P Sternberg
5Q Sterne
6R sterner
9D sternest
6A sternness
7Q Steuben
7A stevedore
7R StevensPoint
3A stewardess's
7N Stewards'
9Q Stewart's
9Q stewpan
3N Stewpot
6A sthronshuch
5N stick-and-mud
7R stick-shift
7P stick-to-it-iveness
9D stick-up
7A stickball
7N stickin'
7R STICKS
4A sticktights
5N stid
9D sties

Word Type	F	D	U	SFI	3 Gr 3	4 Gr 4	5 Gr 5	6 Gr 6	7 Gr 7	8 Gr 8	9 Gr 9	X UnGr	A Read	B Eng & Gr	C Comp	D Lit	E Math	F Soc Stud	G Spell	H Sci	J Music	K Art	L Home Ec	M Shop	N Lib F	P Lib NF	Q Lib Ref	R Mag	S Rel
stiffening	6	.3922	.4982	37.0	0	1	1	0	2	0	2	0	0	0	0	1	0	1	0	0	0	0	2	0	1	0	1	0	0
stiffly	31	.6928	4.4516	46.5	6	5	2	1	9	2	5	1	11	2	0	7	0	1	0	2	0	0	1	0	3	3	0	1	0
stiffness	6	.4604	.5940	37.7	1	0	0	1	1	1	2	0	1	0	0	0	0	0	0	1	0	1	0	1	0	1	1	0	0
stifle	5	.4177	.4466	36.5	1	1	0	0	0	2	1	0	0	0	0	0	0	1	0	0	0	0	1	0	0	2	1	0	0
stifled	10	.5550	1.1602	40.6	0	0	3	0	6	0	1	0	1	0	0	1	0	0	0	1	0	0	0	0	3	0	2	2	0
stifling	6	.3598	.5339	37.3	0	0	0	1	4	1	0	0	3	0	0	1	0	0	0	0	0	0	0	0	2	0	0	0	0
stigma	9	.5159	.9700	39.9	0	3	0	0	3	1	2	0	0	0	0	2	0	0	0	2	0	0	0	0	0	1	3	1	0
stil	2	.0000	.0209	23.2	0	0	2	0	0	0	0	0	0	0	0	0	0	0	0	0	0	0	0	0	0	0	2	0	0
stile	5	.2542	.3208	35.1	0	2	0	0	2	1	0	0	1	0	0	0	0	0	0	0	0	0	0	0	3	1	0	0	0
stiletto	2	.0000	.0234	23.7	0	0	0	2	0	0	0	0	0	0	0	0	0	0	0	0	0	0	0	0	2	0	0	0	0
still	3421	.9588	647.85	68.1	574	520	408	467	711	384	286	71	1024	123	17	233	65	374	47	301	93	20	30	13	303	334	208	234	2
Still	3	.0966	.0702	28.5	0	0	0	0	0	3	0	0	0	1	0	0	0	0	0	0	0	2	0	0	0	0	0	0	0
still-larger	2	.0000	.0209	23.2	0	0	0	0	1	0	1	0	0	0	0	0	0	0	0	0	0	0	0	0	0	0	2	0	0
still-life	2	.1717	.1142	30.6	0	0	0	0	2	0	0	0	1	0	0	1	0	0	0	0	0	0	0	0	0	0	0	0	0
stilled	5	.2732	.3348	35.2	1	0	1	0	3	0	0	0	1	0	0	0	0	0	0	0	0	0	0	0	3	0	1	0	0
stillest	2	.1717	.1142	30.6	0	0	0	0	1	0	1	0	1	0	0	1	0	0	0	0	0	0	0	0	0	0	0	0	0
stillness	41	.6943	5.9473	47.7	4	9	6	2	5	10	3	2	20	1	0	8	0	0	0	2	2	1	0	0	3	2	0	2	0
Stillwater	6	.0000	.0703	28.5	0	6	0	0	0	0	0	0	0	0	0	0	0	0	0	0	0	0	0	0	6	0	0	0	0
stilts	11	.5914	1.3445	41.3	2	0	2	2	2	0	2	1	1	0	0	1	0	1	0	0	0	1	0	0	1	2	3	1	0
stimulant	7	.1865	.3084	34.9	0	0	0	0	1	2	4	0	0	0	0	0	0	1	0	1	0	0	4	0	1	0	0	0	0
stimulate	18	.7006	2.5614	44.1	0	1	2	2	5	1	5	2	1	3	0	0	0	1	0	5	1	0	1	0	0	1	3	2	0
stimulated	17	.5647	1.9836	43.0	2	3	1	0	8	1	2	0	0	0	1	0	0	2	0	2	0	0	0	0	0	3	6	3	0
stimulates	8	.3771	.6500	38.1	0	0	0	0	3	3	2	0	0	0	0	0	0	0	0	2	0	0	2	0	0	1	3	0	0
stimulating	8	.5967	.9728	39.9	0	0	1	0	5	1	1	0	0	1	0	0	0	0	0	0	1	0	1	0	0	2	1	2	0
stimulation	3	.2233	.1562	31.9	1	0	0	0	1	0	1	0	0	0	0	1	0	0	0	0	0	0	0	0	0	0	2	0	0
stimuli	15	.4018	1.3912	41.4	0	0	2	0	8	0	5	0	4	0	0	0	0	0	0	5	0	0	0	0	0	0	5	1	0
stimulus	29	.3786	2.4669	43.9	0	1	3	3	14	3	4	1	3	0	0	0	0	0	0	9	1	0	0	0	0	2	14	0	0
Stina	6	.0000	.2741	34.4	6	0	0	0	0	0	0	0	6	0	0	0	0	0	0	0	0	0	0	0	0	0	0	0	0
sting	34	.6806	4.8598	46.9	6	8	1	2	14	2	1	0	17	1	0	4	0	1	0	1	1	0	0	0	1	1	6	1	0
Sting	2	.0000	.0243	23.9	0	0	0	0	2	0	0	0	0	0	0	0	0	0	0	0	0	0	0	0	0	0	0	2	0
stinger	8	.3586	.7155	38.5	7	0	0	0	0	0	1	0	4	0	0	0	0	0	0	0	0	0	0	0	0	3	1	0	0
stingers	5	.2442	.2889	34.6	3	0	0	0	2	0	0	0	0	0	0	2	0	0	0	0	0	0	0	0	0	3	0	0	0
stinging	18	.6313	2.3743	43.8	0	5	1	5	3	3	1	0	5	0	0	1	0	1	0	1	0	1	0	0	4	0	3	2	0
stings	6	.4970	.6404	38.1	1	1	1	0	3	0	0	0	1	1	0	1	0	0	0	1	0	0	0	0	0	0	2	0	0
stingy	6	.5433	.6717	38.3	0	1	1	1	2	0	0	1	0	0	0	2	0	0	1	0	0	0	0	0	1	1	0	1	0
stink	4	.4712	.3983	36.0	0	1	0	0	1	1	1	0	0	0	0	1	0	1	1	0	0	0	0	0	0	1	0	0	0
stinking	3	.3431	.2528	34.0	0	0	0	0	1	1	1	0	1	0	0	0	0	1	0	0	0	0	0	0	1	0	0	0	0
stint	7	.2958	.5054	37.0	0	0	0	1	3	2	0	1	2	0	0	0	0	0	0	0	3	0	0	0	0	0	0	2	0
stipend	2	.1698	.1133	30.5	0	0	0	0	0	0	2	0	1	0	0	0	0	0	0	0	0	0	0	0	0	0	1	0	0
stipulated	3	.2321	.1635	32.1	0	0	0	0	1	1	0	1	0	0	0	0	0	0	0	0	0	0	0	0	0	0	1	2	0
stir	125	.6158	15.897	52.0	19	14	12	9	20	16	29	6	20	6	1	6	0	2	1	21	3	1	32	4	11	11	0	6	0
stirred	88	.8045	14.303	51.6	6	13	19	8	20	11	9	2	27	3	1	12	0	8	0	2	0	1	1	0	18	5	4	6	0
stirring	96	.5438	11.053	50.4	11	7	13	10	18	11	24	2	22	1	1	4	0	6	0	7	7	0	25	0	3	8	5	7	0
stirrup	25	.6673	3.4461	45.4	1	2	5	7	5	2	0	3	4	4	0	2	2	0	0	9	1	0	0	0	1	2	0	0	0
stirrups	14	.4200	1.2551	41.0	1	0	2	0	4	1	4	2	1	2	3	4	0	1	0	0	0	0	0	0	3	0	0	0	0
stirs	10	.5942	1.2757	41.1	2	2	2	1	0	1	2	0	4	1	0	2	0	1	0	1	0	0	0	0	0	0	0	1	0
stitch	105	.1727	3.9696	46.0	1	0	1	3	23	17	59	1	3	1	0	1	0	0	1	0	0	3	91	4	0	1	0	0	0
stitched	28	.3715	2.2245	43.5	2	3	5	1	5	5	7	0	3	0	0	3	0	0	0	0	2	2	14	0	2	2	0	0	0
stitchery	4	.0000	.0074	18.7	0	0	0	3	1	0	0	0	0	0	0	0	0	0	0	0	0	4	0	0	0	0	0	0	0
stitches	66	.2011	2.9640	44.7	1	4	0	6	16	17	22	0	4	0	0	0	0	2	0	0	0	5	51	0	2	1	0	1	0
stitching	77	.0118	.4729	36.7	0	0	1	0	13	27	36	0	1	0	0	1	0	0	0	0	0	0	75	0	0	0	0	0	0
stock	227	.5680	26.468	54.2	12	9	13	10	86	45	45	7	9	10	3	6	25	15	2	1	1	1	3	58	10	26	18	39	0
Stock	7	.4675	.7187	38.6	2	0	2	0	2	0	0	1	2	0	0	0	0	0	0	0	0	1	0	0	1	1	1	1	0
stock-car	2	.0000	.0243	23.9	0	0	0	0	2	0	0	0	0	0	0	0	0	0	0	0	0	0	0	0	0	0	0	2	0
stock-still	4	.1787	.2347	33.7	0	0	2	1	1	0	0	0	2	0	0	0	0	0	0	0	0	0	0	0	2	0	0	0	0
stockade	27	.5533	3.3331	45.2	12	2	6	0	5	1	1	0	16	0	0	2	0	3	0	0	0	0	0	0	3	3	0	0	0
stockades	2	.1717	.1142	30.6	0	0	0	0	2	0	0	0	1	0	0	1	0	0	0	0	0	0	0	0	0	0	0	0	0
stocked	16	.7128	2.3271	43.7	1	4	0	1	5	3	1	1	3	0	0	2	0	1	0	1	0	0	1	0	1	2	2	3	0
stockholder	3	.3844	.2487	34.0	0	0	2	0	0	0	1	0	0	1	0	0	0	0	0	0	0	0	0	0	0	1	1	0	0
stockholders	4	.2330	.2363	33.7	0	0	0	0	1	2	1	0	0	1	0	0	0	3	0	0	0	0	0	0	0	0	0	0	0
Stockholm	13	.5965	1.5898	42.0	0	2	0	4	0	0	7	0	0	3	0	3	0	2	0	0	0	0	0	0	0	1	2	2	0
stocking	44	.4798	4.5446	46.6	4	9	7	1	1	15	5	2	11	1	1	6	0	0	2	0	0	0	13	0	2	1	0	7	0
stockinged	2	.1948	.1250	31.0	0	0	0	0	0	2	0	0	1	0	0	0	0	0	0	0	0	0	0	0	0	1	0	0	0
stockings	42	.6586	5.7517	47.6	2	11	8	5	7	1	7	1	13	2	0	7	1	1	0	0	0	0	3	0	8	6	1	0	0
stockpile	2	.2433	.1158	30.6	0	0	1	1	0	0	0	0	0	0	0	0	0	0	0	0	0	0	0	0	0	1	0	1	0
stocks	38	.7512	5.7621	47.6	2	0	6	2	10	4	12	2	2	1	0	1	0	13	0	2	1	0	1	1	0	4	6	6	0
Stockton	3	.3454	.2542	34.1	0	1	0	1	0	1	0	0	1	0	0	0	0	1	0	0	0	0	0	0	0	0	0	1	0
stocky	12	.5326	1.3437	41.3	1	1	1	3	2	4	0	0	1	0	0	0	0	1	0	2	0	0	1	0	0	0	3	4	0
stockyards	8	.4532	.8135	39.1	0	0	3	0	3	0	1	1	2	0	0	1	0	3	0	0	0	0	0	0	0	0	0	2	0
stoical	2	.1494	.1045	30.2	0	0	0	0	1	0	1	0	1	0	0	0	0	0	0	0	1	0	0	0	0	0	0	0	0
Stoics	2	.1693	.0748	28.7	0	0	0	0	0	2	0	0	0	0	0	0	0	0	1	0	0	1	0	0	0	0	0	0	0
Stoke	2	.0000	.0215	23.3	0	0	0	0	0	0	1	1	0	0	0	2	0	0	0	0	0	0	0	0	0	0	0	0	0
Stoke-on-Trent	2	.0000	.0389	25.9	0	0	0	0	2	0	0	0	0	0	0	0	0	2	0	0	0	0	0	0	0	0	0	0	0
stoked	2	.1814	.1187	30.7	0	0	0	1	1	0	0	0	1	0	0	0	0	0	0	0	0	0	0	0	0	0	0	1	0
Stokes	6	.4862	.6613	38.2	0	2	0	1	2	1	0	0	3	0	0	0	0	0	0	0	0	0	0	0	1	0	1	1	0
stoking	2	.1787	.1174	30.7	0	0	0	0	2	0	0	0	1	0	0	0	0	0	0	0	0	0	0	0	1	0	0	0	0
stole	52	.6885	7.4838	48.7	7	7	6	13	10	6	3	0	24	7	0	7	0	3	1	0	0	0	0	0	5	3	1	1	0
stolen	53	.6982	7.6454	48.8	7	7	4	9	15	7	4	0	17	3	0	9	1	4	0	0	0	0	0	0	8	6	1	4	0
stolid	4	.2954	.2881	34.6	0	1	0	0	1	1	0	1	1	0	0	2	0	0	0	0	0	0	0	0	0	0	0	1	0
stomach	184	.7637	28.624	54.6	21	26	31	17	39	13	27	10	48	2	1	11	0	3	3	62	0	0	1	0	15	10	18	10	0
stomach's	2	.2437	.1129	30.5	0	0	0	0	1	0	1	0	0	0	0	0	0	0	0	0	0	0	0	0	0	0	1	1	0
stomachache	5	.5363	.5746	37.6	1	2	1	0	1	0	0	0	1	0	0	1	0	0	0	1	0	0	0	0	0	1	0	1	0
stomachs	19	.6195	2.5028	44.0	3	3	1	3	6	0	0	3	7	0	0	0	0	0	0	4	0	0	0	0	2	3	2	1	0
stomata	5	.2424	.2988	34.8	3	0	0	0	2	0	0	0	0	0	0	0	0	0	0	3	0	0	0	0	0	0	2	0	0
stomp	8	.3283	.6691	38.3	3	0	1	3	0	0	1	0	4	3	0	0	0	0	0	0	0	0	0	0	0	0	0	1	0
stomped	3	.3408	.2477	33.9	0	1	1	1	0	0	0	0	1	0	0	1	0	0	0	0	0	0	0	0	0	1	0	0	0
stomping	3	.0000	.1370	31.4	1	0	0	0	2	0	0	0	3	0	0	0	0	0	0	0	0	0	0	0	0	0	0	0	0
stone	593	.8709	103.17	60.1	103	93	73	115	104	40	55	10	166	24	12	48	12	75	5	40	20	23	0	4	31	51	52	30	0
Stone	51	.6238	6.7091	48.3	2	4	10	5	5	14	11	0	18	3	6	1	3	9	2	1	0	0	1	0	0	0	5	2	0
STONE	2	.0000	.0215	23.3	0	0	0	0	0	0	2	0	0	0	0	2	0	0	0	0	0	0	0	0	0	0	0	0	0
stone-deaf	2	.0000	.0914	29.6	0	2	0	0	0	0	0	0	2	0	0	0	0	0	0	0	0	0	0	0	0	0	0	0	0
stone-like	2	.0000	.0914	29.6	0	0	1	0	1	0	0	0	2	0	0	0	0	0	0	0	0	0	0	0	0	0	0	0	0
stone-paved	2	.2152	.1357	31.3	0	1	0	1	0	0	0	0	1	0	0	0	0	1	0	0	0	0	0	0	0	0	0	0	0

XH stiffens
7R stiffer
9D stiffest
XB stig
XB stig-
XB stigan
7Q stigmas
8F stigmatized
XB stigrap
XB stigweard
7Q still-active
8A still-breathing
XR still-buried
7F still-dark
4Q still-molten
6R still-plentiful
6R still-wet
8G Stille
6Q stills
9D Stillson
4G stilt
8R Stilt
7P stilted
7L Stilton
5H stimulants
7H Stimulated
6B stinch
7D stingiest
7A stingray
7R Stingray
7N stink's
7Q stinkjims
9N stinks
5P stipple
9D stipulate
9F stipulation
8Q stipulations
9L Stirred
7Q stirrings
7E STK
5N stoat
5Q stock-
5Q stock-share
9D Stockholm's
7F stockier
9L stocking-covered
4R Stockings
7R stockmaker
7R stockmaking
8D stockmen's
9R stockpiles
7Q stockroom
6A stoi
8G stoic
8K Stoic
9A stoically
4J stoke
8R Stokely
7A Stollak
3P stomach-ache
7A stomach-down
3P stomach-hair
7C stomacher
7D stomper
5F stone-age
5A stone-blind
8D stone-blue
4A stone-tipped
4N stone-topped
8D stone-wall

Word Type	F	D	U	SFI	3 Gr 3	4 Gr 4	5 Gr 5	6 Gr 6	7 Gr 7	8 Gr 8	9 Gr 9	X UnGr	A Read	B Eng & Gr	C Comp	D Lit	E Math	F Soc Stud	G Spell	H Sci	J Music	K Art	L Home Ec	M Shop	N Lib F	P Lib NF	Q Lib Ref	R Mag	S Rel
stone's	6	.3875	.5818	37.6	0	3	0	2	0	0	1	0	4	0	0	1	0	0	0	0	0	0	0	0	0	0	1	0	0
Stone's	2	.1362	.0684	28.3	0	0	1	0	0	0	1	0	0	0	1	0	1	0	0	0	0	0	0	0	0	0	0	0	0
stoneboat	2	.0000	.0290	24.6	0	2	0	0	0	0	0	0	0	0	0	0	0	0	0	0	0	0	0	0	0	2	0	0	0
Stonecrop	4	.0000	.1827	32.6	0	0	0	4	0	0	0	0	4	0	0	0	0	0	0	0	0	0	0	0	0	0	0	0	0
stonecutter	2	.0000	.0914	29.6	1	0	0	0	1	0	0	0	2	0	0	0	0	0	0	0	0	0	0	0	0	0	0	0	0
stonecutters	2	.2285	.1129	30.5	0	0	0	0	0	1	0	1	0	0	0	0	0	1	0	0	0	0	0	0	0	0	1	0	0
stoned	2	.1814	.1187	30.7	0	0	0	0	1	1	0	0	1	0	0	0	0	0	0	0	0	0	0	0	0	0	0	1	0
Stonehenge	5	.0000	.0986	29.9	0	0	0	0	0	0	5	0	0	0	0	0	0	0	0	5	0	0	0	0	0	0	0	0	0
stonemason	2	.1698	.1133	30.5	0	0	0	0	1	0	1	0	1	0	0	0	0	0	0	0	0	0	0	0	0	0	1	0	0
stones	269	.8669	46.701	56.7	74	33	26	51	33	19	29	4	91	10	0	19	19	26	0	24	2	7	1	3	20	18	15	13	1
Stonewall	5	.5597	.5840	37.7	0	0	2	0	0	2	0	1	0	0	0	0	0	1	0	1	0	0	0	0	1	1	0	1	0
stoneware	3	.1823	.1405	31.5	0	2	0	0	0	1	0	0	0	0	0	0	0	1	0	0	0	0	0	0	0	0	2	0	0
stonework	3	.2136	.1470	31.7	0	1	0	0	1	0	1	0	0	0	0	0	0	0	0	0	0	0	0	1	0	0	0	2	0
Stoney	2	.2446	.1142	30.6	0	0	0	0	1	0	1	0	0	0	0	0	0	0	0	0	0	0	0	0	1	0	0	1	0
stony	24	.7216	3.5325	45.5	9	3	3	2	6	0	1	0	4	4	1	0	0	5	0	3	1	0	0	0	3	1	2	0	0
stood	1387	.7576	215.75	63.3	294	305	155	177	256	118	76	6	635	32	11	169	3	48	9	3	10	8	1	0	238	154	18	48	0
stooges	2	.0000	.0290	24.6	0	0	0	0	2	0	0	0	0	0	0	0	0	0	0	0	0	0	0	0	0	2	0	0	0
stool	58	.6880	8.2444	49.2	9	11	8	1	10	5	7	7	19	6	3	11	2	0	0	1	0	1	0	0	12	1	0	2	0
stools	10	.6270	1.2786	41.1	0	2	0	1	0	5	1	1	0	0	0	1	0	3	0	0	1	0	0	1	1	0	2	1	0
stoop	29	.6420	3.9238	45.9	5	10	6	2	6	0	0	0	12	2	0	1	0	0	0	0	1	1	0	0	8	3	0	1	0
stooped	40	.6819	5.6996	47.6	6	12	0	3	13	2	4	0	18	1	1	7	0	0	0	0	0	0	1	0	6	5	1	0	0
stooping	15	.4228	1.4344	41.6	1	3	3	0	5	2	1	0	5	0	0	3	0	0	0	0	0	2	0	0	4	1	0	0	0
stoops	3	.2374	.1625	32.1	1	0	0	0	0	0	2	0	0	0	0	2	0	0	0	0	1	0	0	0	0	0	0	0	0
stop	1081	.9328	200.11	63.0	310	205	118	118	162	89	68	11	444	34	5	73	25	81	18	104	27	0	10	6	83	98	18	54	1
Stop	10	.5132	1.1488	40.6	7	1	0	1	1	0	0	0	5	0	0	0	0	0	0	1	2	0	0	0	1	0	0	1	0
stopovers	2	.2306	.1140	30.6	0	0	0	0	0	2	0	0	0	1	0	0	0	1	0	0	0	0	0	0	0	0	0	0	0
stopped	1057	.8126	174.51	62.4	259	230	112	110	177	108	51	10	511	43	5	69	12	66	6	29	4	2	1	3	145	104	7	50	0
stopper	43	.2647	2.8719	44.6	3	11	15	1	4	5	4	0	2	0	0	0	0	0	0	36	0	0	0	0	2	2	1	0	0
stoppers	5	.3759	.4201	36.2	0	0	1	0	2	1	1	0	0	0	0	0	0	0	0	3	0	0	0	0	1	0	1	0	0
stoppin'	2	.0000	.0215	23.3	0	0	0	0	1	1	0	0	0	0	0	2	0	0	0	0	0	0	0	0	0	0	0	0	0
stopping	122	.8771	21.387	53.3	22	22	12	19	17	10	18	2	39	3	2	9	2	8	6	18	4	0	1	0	7	8	1	14	0
stops	132	.8471	22.382	53.5	25	14	13	13	36	9	16	6	27	6	5	13	8	14	4	23	9	0	1	0	1	5	2	14	0
stopwatch	7	.2256	.5342	37.3	0	0	0	0	6	0	1	0	6	0	0	0	1	0	0	0	0	0	0	0	0	0	0	0	0
storage	60	.5750	7.1285	48.5	1	2	6	2	16	10	12	11	4	1	0	0	5	5	0	5	0	0	10	1	0	1	20	8	0
storages	2	.0000	.0209	23.2	0	0	0	0	0	0	2	0	0	0	0	0	0	0	0	0	0	0	0	0	0	0	2	0	0
store	681	.9030	122.42	60.9	222	127	65	45	100	67	48	7	235	40	19	45	45	55	20	45	7	3	34	4	35	55	12	27	0
Store	19	.6518	2.5996	44.1	4	4	0	4	3	0	4	0	7	0	0	1	4	0	1	0	1	0	0	0	1	4	0	0	0
store-bought	2	.2351	.1166	30.7	0	0	0	1	0	1	0	0	0	0	0	0	0	1	0	0	0	0	0	0	0	0	0	1	0
store-ward	2	.0000	.0219	23.4	0	0	2	0	0	0	0	0	0	2	0	0	0	0	0	0	0	0	0	0	0	0	0	0	0
store's	5	.1657	.1954	32.9	1	0	0	0	0	3	1	0	0	0	0	0	1	0	0	0	0	0	3	0	0	1	0	0	0
stored	189	.7574	28.997	54.6	42	15	17	33	39	14	21	8	25	1	1	2	4	26	2	63	1	1	20	4	3	14	14	8	0
storehouse	23	.5331	2.6662	44.3	4	2	4	3	7	1	2	0	8	0	0	2	0	3	6	0	0	0	0	0	0	3	0	1	0
storehouses	8	.4478	.7788	38.9	0	1	1	2	4	0	0	0	1	0	0	2	0	3	1	0	0	1	0	0	0	0	0	0	0
storekeeper	32	.5983	4.1216	46.2	10	6	1	8	5	0	2	0	15	0	2	2	0	1	1	3	0	0	0	0	7	1	0	0	0
storekeeper's	2	.0000	.0290	24.6	0	2	0	0	0	0	0	0	0	0	0	0	0	0	0	0	0	0	0	0	0	2	0	0	0
storekeepers	9	.3202	.7142	38.5	3	0	4	2	0	0	0	0	2	0	0	0	0	5	0	0	0	0	0	0	0	2	0	0	0
storeroom	12	.4044	1.2047	40.8	10	1	0	0	1	0	0	0	8	0	0	0	1	1	0	1	0	1	0	0	0	0	0	0	0
storerooms	4	.2417	.3028	34.8	1	0	1	0	1	0	1	0	3	0	0	0	0	0	0	0	0	0	0	0	1	0	0	0	0
stores	204	.7956	32.725	55.1	64	38	31	15	17	18	19	2	27	4	2	10	2	92	2	18	3	1	9	0	4	15	6	9	0
Stores	3	.3769	.2484	34.0	0	0	1	0	0	2	0	0	0	0	0	0	0	1	0	0	0	0	0	0	0	0	1	1	0
stories	701	.8347	117.75	60.7	126	161	87	98	103	84	36	6	241	136	13	59	10	73	9	25	23	4	2	1	10	39	21	32	3
Stories	4	.3729	.3664	35.6	1	0	0	2	1	0	0	0	2	1	0	0	0	0	0	0	0	0	0	0	0	1	0	0	0
storing	25	.7414	3.7380	45.7	4	5	2	2	3	3	3	3	3	1	1	0	0	1	2	4	2	1	3	0	0	0	5	2	0
stork	7	.4345	.6511	38.1	1	0	4	0	1	0	0	1	0	0	0	0	0	0	0	1	0	0	0	0	3	2	1	0	0
storks	22	.3178	1.5694	42.0	2	1	13	3	3	0	0	0	1	0	0	0	0	0	0	0	0	0	0	0	14	0	5	2	0
storm	319	.8820	56.253	57.5	63	54	49	64	55	16	12	6	121	12	5	8	4	16	8	35	8	0	1	7	40	32	5	17	0
Storm	13	.2047	.9672	39.9	7	5	0	0	0	1	0	0	12	0	0	0	0	0	0	0	0	0	0	0	0	0	1	0	0
storm-swept	3	.1060	.1461	31.6	0	0	2	0	1	0	0	0	2	0	1	0	0	0	0	0	0	0	0	0	0	0	0	0	0
Stormalong	42	.2084	2.7693	44.4	19	3	0	19	1	0	0	0	23	0	0	0	0	0	0	0	0	0	0	0	0	19	0	0	0
stormed	13	.5521	1.5861	42.0	3	3	0	2	3	1	1	0	7	1	0	0	0	0	0	0	0	0	0	0	1	2	2	0	0
Stormie	5	.0000	.2284	33.6	0	0	0	5	0	0	0	0	5	0	0	0	0	0	0	0	0	0	0	0	0	0	0	0	0
storming	8	.3282	.6682	38.2	3	0	1	0	1	3	0	0	4	0	0	3	0	0	0	0	0	0	0	0	1	0	0	0	0
storms	116	.8116	19.017	52.8	16	13	23	22	21	11	5	5	30	1	1	4	0	19	0	29	1	1	0	0	6	7	6	11	0
Storms	3	.2427	.1822	32.6	0	1	0	0	1	0	1	0	0	0	0	0	0	0	0	2	0	0	0	0	0	0	0	1	0
stormy	40	.7923	6.3949	48.1	9	7	6	5	5	6	1	1	10	4	0	1	0	5	0	1	5	2	1	1	4	3	0	3	0
Stormy	12	.2261	.9283	39.7	0	0	1	0	11	0	0	0	11	0	0	0	0	0	0	0	1	0	0	0	0	0	0	0	0
Stormy's	2	.0000	.0914	29.6	0	0	0	0	2	0	0	0	2	0	0	0	0	0	0	0	0	0	0	0	0	0	0	0	0
Storting	2	.0000	.0290	24.6	0	0	2	0	0	0	0	0	0	0	0	0	0	0	0	0	0	0	0	0	0	2	0	0	0
story	2237	.8632	386.62	65.9	529	377	323	303	293	261	130	21	764	379	89	143	61	201	149	88	111	17	5	2	38	77	45	67	1
Story	31	.6833	4.3026	46.3	4	3	3	4	3	11	2	1	3	4	0	0	0	2	5	3	6	2	0	0	0	1	3	2	0
story-poem	2	.0000	.0215	23.3	0	0	0	0	0	0	2	0	0	0	0	2	0	0	0	0	0	0	0	0	0	0	0	0	0
story-poems	2	.0000	.0215	23.3	0	0	0	0	0	0	2	0	0	0	0	2	0	0	0	0	0	0	0	0	0	0	0	0	0
story-teller	2	.2443	.1130	30.5	0	0	0	1	0	1	0	0	0	0	0	1	0	0	0	0	0	0	0	0	1	0	0	0	0
story-telling	3	.3782	.2435	33.9	0	0	1	1	1	0	0	0	0	0	0	0	0	0	0	0	1	0	0	0	0	1	1	0	0
story's	4	.3231	.3016	34.8	0	0	1	0	3	0	0	0	1	0	1	1	0	0	0	0	0	0	0	0	1	0	0	0	0
storybook	5	.3374	.4118	36.1	1	2	0	1	0	1	0	0	2	0	1	0	0	1	0	0	1	0	0	0	0	0	0	0	0
storybooks	5	.2620	.3711	35.7	3	1	0	0	0	0	1	0	3	0	0	0	0	0	0	0	0	0	0	1	0	1	0	0	0
storyteller	28	.6123	3.7173	45.7	4	5	5	7	3	1	2	1	17	3	0	4	0	0	0	0	1	0	0	0	1	1	0	1	0
STORYTELLER	7	.0000	.3198	35.0	0	0	0	7	0	0	0	0	7	0	0	0	0	0	0	0	0	0	0	0	0	0	0	0	0
storytellers	8	.4543	.8406	39.2	0	1	1	3	1	2	0	0	4	0	0	2	0	1	0	0	1	0	0	0	0	0	0	0	0
storytelling	21	.5198	2.4027	43.8	3	1	3	4	6	3	1	0	9	5	0	3	0	0	0	0	3	0	0	0	0	1	0	0	0
stout	48	.7580	7.4235	48.7	6	8	6	10	11	2	4	1	16	1	2	6	0	4	0	1	1	0	0	0	5	7	3	2	0
Stout	7	.2135	.3599	35.6	0	0	0	2	5	0	0	0	0	0	0	0	0	0	0	0	0	0	0	0	2	0	0	5	0
stouter	2	.2446	.1122	30.5	0	0	0	0	1	0	1	0	0	0	0	1	0	0	0	0	0	0	0	0	0	0	1	0	0
stoutest	2	.1948	.1250	31.0	1	0	0	1	0	0	0	0	1	0	0	0	0	0	0	0	0	0	0	0	0	1	0	0	0
stoutly	11	.4787	1.2201	40.9	1	2	0	4	0	1	3	0	7	1	1	0	0	0	1	0	0	0	0	0	0	1	0	0	0
Stoutness	2	.0000	.0914	29.6	1	1	0	0	0	0	0	0	2	0	0	0	0	0	0	0	0	0	0	0	0	0	0	0	0
stove	183	.8074	29.940	54.8	46	38	13	14	28	28	15	1	74	14	2	21	1	11	0	7	1	0	1	8	21	12	3	7	0
Stove	2	.1649	.0767	28.8	0	1	0	0	0	0	1	0	0	0	0	0	0	0	0	0	0	0	0	1	1	0	0	0	0
stovepipe	11	.5391	1.2923	41.1	2	2	1	0	0	4	1	1	4	0	0	1	0	1	0	1	0	1	0	0	0	2	0	1	0
stoves	29	.6617	3.9812	46.0	4	8	3	6	1	4	3	0	7	0	1	3	0	8	1	3	0	0	0	3	1	1	1	0	0
stow	3	.2028	.1988	33.0	1	0	0	2	0	0	0	0	2	0	0	0	0	0	0	0	1	0	0	0	0	0	0	0	0
Stowe	4	.2408	.2408	33.8	2	0	1	0	0	1	0	0	0	0	0	0	0	2	0	0	0	0	0	0	0	2	0	0	0
stowed	8	.5464	.9485	39.8	0	0	1	2	5	0	0	0	3	1	0	0	0	0	0	0	0	0	0	0	0	1	1	2	0
stowing	4	.3097	.2992	34.8	0	1	0	2	0	0	0	1	1	0	0	1	0	0	0	0	0	0	0	0	0	0	0	2	0
str	4	.0000	.0325	25.1	1	1	1	1	0	0	0	0	0	0	0	0	0	0	4	0	0	0	0	0	0	0	0	0	0

7R Stonebreaker
6A Stonecrop's
8R Stoned
9Q stonemasonry
9M stonemasons
7D stonepipe
4P Stoner
4J stoneworker

9K Stoneworkers'
XR StoneyPoint
7D stonily
8F Stony
8D stony-eyed
7N Stood
3P stoodest
3A stop-and-go

3A stoplight
3H stoplights
9Q stoppage
8H stoppered
XH storable
3P storage-jar
9R Storch
3N store-room

7A store'd
9P Storekeeper
4P storekeeping
7Q storied
6A storin'
4N storks'
5A storm-cloud
7H storm-ravaged

7C storm-swelled
5A storm-tossed
3A storm's
3A Storm's
8B storme
4A Story-Writing
7N story-book
3B story-playing

4P Storybook
4N Storyland
7D storyteller's
3R stowaway
3P stows
5A Stoyan
9Q Strachan
8B Strachey

Word Type	F	D	U	SFI	3 Gr 3	4 Gr 4	5 Gr 5	6 Gr 6	7 Gr 7	8 Gr 8	9 Gr 9	X UnGr	A Read	B Eng & Gr	C Comp	D Lit	E Math	F Soc Stud	G Spell	H Sci	J Music	K Art	L Home Ec	M Shop	N Lib F	P Lib NF	Q Lib Ref	R Mag	S Rel
straddle	2	.2411	.1091	30.4	0	0	0	0	2	0	0	0	0	0	0	1	0	0	0	0	1	0	0	0	0	0	0	0	0
straddled	3	.0000	.1370	31.4	0	1	1	1	0	0	0	0	3	0	0	0	0	0	0	0	0	0	0	0	0	0	0	0	0
straddles	3	.1796	.1398	31.5	0	0	1	1	0	0	1	0	0	0	0	0	0	2	0	0	0	0	0	1	0	0	0	0	0
straddling	3	.2197	.2090	33.2	0	0	1	1	1	0	0	0	2	0	0	0	0	0	0	0	0	0	0	0	0	0	1	0	0
Stradivarius	2	.1948	.1250	31.0	1	0	0	0	1	0	0	0	1	0	0	0	0	0	0	0	0	0	0	0	0	1	0	0	0
straggled	3	.3385	.2445	33.9	1	0	0	0	2	0	0	0	1	0	0	0	0	0	0	0	0	0	0	0	1	0	1	0	0
straggler	2	.1787	.1174	30.7	0	0	0	0	0	1	1	0	1	0	0	0	0	0	0	0	0	0	0	0	1	0	0	0	0
stragglers	4	.4516	.4046	36.1	1	0	1	0	1	0	1	0	1	0	0	1	0	1	0	0	0	0	0	0	0	1	0	0	0
straggling	10	.5472	1.2039	40.8	1	4	1	2	0	0	2	0	5	0	0	2	0	0	0	0	1	0	0	0	1	1	0	0	0
straight	797	.9183	145.21	61.6	182	101	76	72	164	92	95	15	215	17	6	51	51	38	5	90	19	13	45	33	64	76	21	52	1
Straight	5	.0000	.2284	33.6	5	0	0	0	0	0	0	0	5	0	0	0	0	0	0	0	0	0	0	0	0	0	0	0	0
straight-line	2	.1249	.0685	28.4	0	0	1	0	0	0	1	0	0	0	0	0	0	0	0	1	0	0	0	1	0	0	0	0	0
straight-winged	2	.0000	.0394	26.0	0	0	0	1	1	0	0	0	0	0	0	0	0	0	0	2	0	0	0	0	0	0	0	0	0
straightaway	2	.1523	.0721	28.6	0	0	0	0	1	0	1	0	0	0	1	0	0	0	0	0	0	0	0	0	0	0	0	1	0
straightedge	22	.2186	1.1440	40.6	1	0	0	3	4	9	5	0	0	0	0	0	16	0	0	0	0	0	0	6	0	0	0	0	0
straighten	21	.5005	2.2549	43.5	2	2	2	3	3	2	6	1	5	1	0	0	0	0	1	3	0	0	6	1	1	2	1	0	0
straightened	57	.7157	8.4240	49.3	4	16	7	4	7	11	7	1	22	3	0	4	0	4	0	2	1	0	3	0	12	2	0	4	0
straightening	11	.7028	1.5902	42.0	0	1	3	2	2	0	2	1	3	1	0	0	0	1	0	1	0	0	1	0	1	1	1	1	0
straightens	9	.4882	.9441	39.8	1	2	0	2	2	0	2	0	1	0	0	2	0	0	0	2	0	0	0	0	0	1	0	3	0
straighter	11	.5921	1.3764	41.4	2	3	0	1	4	0	1	0	3	1	0	1	0	0	0	1	0	0	0	1	0	3	0	1	0
straightforward	6	.4419	.5633	37.5	0	1	1	1	2	1	0	0	0	0	0	0	0	0	0	2	0	0	1	0	0	0	2	1	0
straightway	8	.4736	.8212	39.1	0	1	1	2	0	2	2	0	2	0	1	2	0	0	0	0	2	0	0	0	0	1	0	0	0
strain	74	.6620	10.098	50.0	2	5	4	10	25	8	11	9	16	2	0	4	0	0	0	13	4	0	12	1	8	5	2	7	0
strained	47	.7830	7.4830	48.7	4	8	5	10	7	6	5	2	17	2	1	4	0	2	0	3	0	0	1	0	9	5	1	2	0
strainer	4	.3497	.2980	34.7	0	0	0	0	3	0	1	0	0	1	0	2	0	0	0	0	0	0	1	0	0	0	0	0	0
straining	24	.6226	3.1184	44.9	0	3	2	3	11	3	2	0	6	0	1	4	0	0	0	1	1	0	0	0	8	2	0	1	0
strains	20	.5256	2.2434	43.5	1	0	2	2	2	1	3	9	1	0	0	1	0	1	0	12	1	0	0	0	0	3	1	0	0
strait	13	.4232	1.2042	40.8	0	2	6	2	0	2	1	0	0	0	0	1	0	8	0	0	0	0	0	0	0	0	1	3	0
Strait	31	.3945	2.7508	44.4	1	1	6	9	3	8	2	1	1	0	0	0	0	22	0	1	0	0	0	0	0	1	4	2	0
straits	10	.3395	.8298	39.2	1	0	0	4	1	3	1	0	3	0	0	0	0	4	0	0	0	0	0	0	0	0	3	0	0
Straits	16	.4578	1.5875	42.0	0	1	2	2	9	2	0	0	0	0	0	0	0	10	0	1	0	0	0	0	2	1	2	0	0
strand	12	.5555	1.4011	41.5	0	1	1	1	2	3	2	2	2	1	0	2	0	0	0	2	0	0	2	0	2	0	0	1	0
Strand	3	.2321	.1635	32.1	0	0	1	0	0	0	0	2	0	0	0	0	0	0	0	0	0	0	0	0	0	0	1	2	0
stranded	7	.3940	.6470	38.1	0	0	4	0	1	1	1	0	3	0	1	0	0	0	0	0	0	0	0	0	2	0	1	0	0
strands	49	.7131	7.1265	48.5	5	4	3	13	8	5	8	3	7	0	0	1	0	0	0	19	3	0	4	2	4	3	3	3	0
strange	710	.8957	126.94	61.0	150	144	89	88	119	63	47	10	299	37	9	69	9	48	7	42	19	11	3	1	42	76	16	22	0
Strange	2	.1733	.1149	30.6	0	1	0	0	1	0	0	0	1	1	0	0	0	0	0	0	0	0	0	0	0	0	0	0	0
strange-looking	12	.5976	1.5302	41.8	4	1	2	1	3	0	1	0	5	1	0	2	0	0	0	0	2	0	0	0	1	0	0	1	0
strange-sounding	2	.0580	.0676	28.3	1	0	0	0	0	1	0	0	1	0	0	0	0	0	0	0	0	1	0	0	0	0	0	0	0
strangely	51	.8033	8.2821	49.2	6	4	11	8	12	2	8	0	15	0	0	4	0	3	1	5	1	0	1	0	5	10	3	3	0
strangeness	8	.5055	.8678	39.4	2	0	2	0	3	1	0	0	2	1	0	0	0	0	1	0	0	1	0	0	2	0	0	1	0
stranger	179	.7787	28.401	54.5	32	31	30	19	31	20	15	1	74	6	7	25	0	2	3	3	7	0	1	0	18	18	2	13	0
Stranger	7	.2589	.4496	36.5	1	5	0	0	0	1	0	0	1	0	0	0	0	0	0	0	1	0	0	0	0	5	0	0	0
stranger's	8	.4672	.8336	39.2	1	1	3	1	0	2	0	0	3	0	1	1	0	0	0	0	0	0	0	0	1	0	0	2	0
Stranger's	7	.0000	.1013	30.1	0	7	0	0	0	0	0	0	0	0	0	0	0	0	0	0	0	0	0	0	0	7	0	0	0
strangers	93	.7045	13.757	51.4	18	15	19	15	9	13	4	0	53	4	0	4	0	8	1	1	0	0	0	0	3	14	3	2	0
strangest	23	.5847	2.9079	44.6	11	2	2	4	2	0	2	0	10	0	0	2	0	1	1	1	0	0	0	0	1	7	0	0	0
strangle	5	.4372	.4596	36.6	0	0	3	1	0	1	0	0	0	0	0	0	0	0	2	0	0	0	0	0	0	1	1	1	0
strangled	6	.4180	.5515	37.4	0	0	2	0	1	2	1	0	1	2	0	2	0	0	0	0	0	0	0	0	1	0	0	0	0
Strangler	3	.0000	.0365	25.6	0	0	0	3	0	0	0	0	0	0	0	0	0	0	0	0	0	0	0	0	0	0	0	3	0
strangles	2	.2427	.1152	30.6	1	0	0	0	0	1	0	0	0	0	0	0	0	0	0	0	0	0	0	0	1	1	0	0	0
strangling	3	.1250	.1342	31.3	0	0	0	2	1	0	0	0	1	0	0	0	0	0	0	0	0	0	0	0	2	0	0	0	0
strap	41	.7014	6.0181	47.8	13	12	1	5	6	3	1	0	21	0	0	5	0	4	1	1	1	0	0	0	4	3	0	1	0
strapped	30	.7008	4.3828	46.4	7	6	2	6	7	1	1	0	14	0	1	3	0	1	0	2	1	0	0	0	2	1	0	5	0
straps	30	.5841	3.6959	45.7	3	2	0	5	7	8	4	1	9	0	1	1	0	2	0	2	1	0	7	1	4	0	0	2	0
Strasbourg	2	.1733	.1149	30.6	0	0	0	1	1	0	0	0	1	1	0	0	0	0	0	0	0	0	0	0	0	0	0	0	0
Strassburg	2	.1703	.0781	28.9	0	1	0	0	0	0	1	0	0	1	0	0	0	0	0	0	0	0	0	1	0	0	0	0	0
Strassmann	2	.2278	.1128	30.5	0	0	0	0	2	0	0	0	0	0	0	0	0	0	0	1	0	0	0	0	0	0	1	0	0
Strat-O-Matic	2	.0000	.0243	23.9	0	0	0	0	0	2	0	0	0	0	0	0	0	0	0	0	0	0	0	0	0	0	0	2	0
strata	11	.3895	.9374	39.7	0	1	1	0	5	1	3	0	0	0	0	0	0	4	0	0	0	0	0	0	1	1	5	0	0
stratagem	4	.2891	.2856	34.6	0	0	0	1	1	2	0	0	1	2	0	0	0	0	0	0	0	0	0	0	0	1	0	0	0
strategem	2	.0000	.0209	23.2	0	0	0	0	0	1	1	0	0	0	0	0	0	0	0	0	0	0	0	0	0	0	2	0	0
strategic	24	.5480	2.7536	44.4	2	0	4	3	4	7	4	0	1	0	1	0	0	9	0	0	0	0	0	0	0	2	7	4	0
strategically	4	.3354	.3295	35.2	1	0	1	0	1	1	0	0	1	0	0	0	0	2	0	0	0	0	0	0	0	1	0	0	0
strategist	3	.3847	.2496	34.0	1	0	0	0	0	1	1	0	0	0	0	0	0	0	0	0	0	0	0	0	0	1	1	1	0
strategy	21	.6891	2.9517	44.7	0	2	0	2	3	6	8	0	2	1	0	3	2	3	0	1	0	0	0	0	0	1	4	4	0
stratification	2	.2437	.1129	30.5	0	0	0	0	2	0	0	0	0	0	0	0	0	0	0	0	0	0	0	0	0	0	1	1	0
stratified	3	.0000	.0591	27.7	0	0	0	0	0	0	3	0	0	0	0	0	0	0	0	3	0	0	0	0	0	0	0	0	0
stratosphere	4	.3823	.3406	35.3	0	0	1	1	1	0	1	0	0	0	0	0	1	0	0	2	0	0	0	0	0	0	1	0	0
stratum	2	.2437	.1129	30.5	0	0	0	0	0	0	1	1	0	0	0	0	0	0	0	0	0	0	0	0	0	0	1	1	0
stratus	9	.1464	.4059	36.1	4	0	0	3	2	0	0	0	0	0	0	0	0	0	0	8	0	0	0	0	0	1	0	0	0
Strauss	10	.0885	.2512	34.0	0	0	0	4	2	4	0	0	0	0	0	0	0	0	0	0	9	0	0	0	0	0	0	1	0
Stravinsky	22	.0824	.5270	37.2	1	3	0	1	7	4	6	0	0	0	0	0	0	0	0	0	20	0	0	0	0	0	0	2	0
Stravinsky's	5	.1563	.1897	32.8	0	0	0	0	0	3	2	0	0	0	0	0	0	0	0	0	4	0	0	0	0	0	1	0	0
straw	213	.8369	35.851	55.5	79	35	20	28	25	12	13	1	68	1	6	19	4	20	1	18	12	0	1	0	23	24	10	6	0
Straw	10	.4117	1.0101	40.0	1	1	0	6	1	1	0	0	7	0	1	0	0	0	0	0	1	0	0	0	1	0	0	0	0
straw-colored	2	.0000	.0243	23.9	0	1	0	0	1	0	0	0	0	0	0	0	0	0	0	0	0	0	0	0	0	0	0	2	0
strawberries	42	.7909	6.7153	48.3	9	4	14	6	5	1	3	0	11	3	1	1	3	5	0	2	0	0	3	0	6	2	1	4	0
strawberry	26	.7050	3.7577	45.7	8	1	6	4	3	2	2	0	5	5	0	0	0	1	1	7	0	0	1	0	3	2	0	1	0
Strawberry	4	.2228	.2087	33.2	0	0	2	0	1	0	0	1	0	0	0	0	0	0	0	0	1	0	0	0	3	0	0	0	0
straws	24	.6288	3.1587	45.0	9	4	1	1	4	5	0	0	6	0	1	1	2	0	0	7	0	2	0	0	3	1	0	1	0
stray	38	.7111	5.5643	47.5	6	8	5	3	8	2	4	2	13	2	2	5	0	1	1	2	1	0	0	0	6	0	0	5	0
strayed	13	.4312	1.2309	40.9	0	4	1	0	4	1	3	0	2	0	0	4	0	0	0	0	0	0	0	0	3	4	0	0	0
straying	5	.4614	.5191	37.2	2	0	1	1	0	0	1	0	2	0	0	0	0	0	1	0	1	0	0	0	0	1	0	0	0
strays	6	.5068	.6479	38.1	1	0	2	1	1	0	1	0	1	0	0	2	0	0	1	0	0	0	0	0	0	1	0	1	0
streak	60	.6601	8.2816	49.2	13	8	4	3	12	7	9	4	19	0	2	8	0	0	0	18	1	0	0	0	4	1	0	7	0
Streak	6	.0000	.0644	28.1	0	0	0	0	0	0	6	0	0	0	0	6	0	0	0	0	0	0	0	0	0	0	0	0	0
streaked	24	.7044	3.4916	45.4	8	6	2	0	4	2	0	2	8	1	0	3	0	0	0	2	0	0	0	0	3	3	1	3	0
streaking	2	.1814	.1187	30.7	0	0	0	0	2	0	0	0	1	0	0	0	0	0	0	0	0	0	0	0	0	0	0	1	0
streaks	28	.6525	3.8315	45.8	3	5	2	4	10	1	3	0	11	0	0	2	0	2	0	1	1	1	0	2	7	1	0	0	0
stream	338	.9122	61.268	57.9	50	39	36	57	59	47	38	12	92	13	7	30	5	28	6	67	10	1	1	2	12	23	16	25	0
Stream	38	.6000	4.7548	46.8	3	8	12	3	4	2	6	0	2	0	1	0	0	1	0	22	2	0	0	0	2	4	4	0	0
streamed	23	.6248	3.0655	44.9	0	8	4	5	4	1	1	0	10	0	0	1	0	3	0	1	0	0	0	0	4	1	0	3	0
streamer	6	.5160	.6584	38.2	1	1	1	0	2	0	0	1	1	0	0	1	0	0	0	0	1	0	0	0	0	1	0	2	0
streamers	21	.3665	1.9584	42.9	4	9	4	1	3	0	0	0	13	0	0	0	0	0	0	0	0	0	0	0	2	6	0	0	0

6A strafe
8F strafing
5F straggle
9R straggly
6A straight-ahead
7N straight-away
7R straight-back
5A straight-faced
9Q straight-grained
7M straight-peen
7J straight-tubed
3A straight-up-and-down
8D straightaways
6A straightness
XH strain-specific
7Q strainers
7Q straitened
6A stramash
5R Strang
3A strange-acting
5F strangely-carved
7F strangest-looking
3P stranglehold
3P strangler
7R strangulation
8D Strangways'
8D STRANGWAYS'
7C strap-iron
7P strapless
9Q straplike
XB strapping
6N stratagems
7R strategists
XR Strates
5F Stratford
XR Strathmore
5P stratifications
7H stratocumulus
6A Stratton
7J Straus
9P Strauses
6P STRAW
7A straw-stuffed
7R Strawberries
8R strawberry-blond
6A strawcoated
3P strawses
7Q streaky
9H stream-deposited
7R stream-of-consciousness
6A stream's

Word Type	F	D	U	SFI	3 Gr 3	4 Gr 4	5 Gr 5	6 Gr 6	7 Gr 7	8 Gr 8	9 Gr 9	X UnGr	A Read	B Eng & Gr	C Comp	D Lit	E Math	F Soc Stud	G Spell	H Sci	J Music	K Art	L Home Ec	M Shop	N Lib F	P Lib NF	Q Lib Ref	R Mag	S Rel
streaming	24	.6576	3.2989	45.2	2	4	2	4	8	1	1	2	9	0	0	5	0	1	0	0	2	1	0	0	2	1	0	3	0
streamline	3	.3662	.2412	33.8	1	0	1	0	0	1	0	0	0	0	0	0	0	0	1	1	0	0	0	0	0	0	0	1	0
streamlined	18	.7001	2.5604	44.1	2	1	5	0	6	3	0	1	1	2	0	0	0	3	2	5	0	1	0	1	0	0	1	2	0
streamlining	3	.3769	.2484	34.0	0	0	0	0	2	0	1	0	0	0	0	0	0	1	0	0	0	0	0	0	0	0	1	1	0
streams	267	.7789	42.017	56.2	45	31	46	41	41	27	29	7	26	2	1	8	0	82	1	70	7	1	0	1	3	24	17	24	0
street	748	.8793	131.46	61.2	216	138	71	72	126	57	66	2	272	53	19	69	4	76	21	23	27	8	2	0	71	55	10	38	0
Street	243	.8261	40.496	56.1	44	49	29	22	39	34	23	3	89	29	6	16	19	21	2	0	4	0	0	1	22	17	1	16	0
street-corner	2	.2433	.1158	30.6	0	0	1	0	0	0	1	0	0	0	0	0	0	0	0	0	0	0	0	0	0	1	0	1	0
streetcar	10	.5358	1.1756	40.7	3	0	2	1	0	4	0	0	4	0	0	2	0	1	0	0	0	0	0	0	1	2	0	0	0
streetcars	5	.4485	.5011	37.0	1	2	1	1	0	0	0	0	1	0	0	0	0	2	0	0	0	0	0	0	0	1	1	0	0
streets	452	.8484	76.867	58.9	101	96	44	75	57	39	32	8	99	6	11	22	9	165	3	16	9	3	1	3	18	38	17	32	0
Streets	3	.2121	.1560	31.9	1	1	0	0	1	0	0	0	0	0	0	0	1	0	0	0	0	0	0	0	0	0	0	2	0
strength	354	.8926	62.833	58.0	25	44	45	48	76	65	48	3	82	8	7	23	2	33	4	22	6	14	9	19	24	39	36	25	1
strengthen	43	.7775	6.7319	48.3	2	4	10	8	4	7	6	2	3	2	2	0	0	10	0	13	2	0	2	2	1	2	2	2	0
strengthened	26	.6908	3.6407	45.6	1	0	3	4	9	3	6	0	0	0	0	1	3	6	0	0	1	1	0	0	0	6	4	4	0
strengthening	6	.4365	.5633	37.5	0	1	1	1	1	1	1	0	0	0	1	1	0	1	0	2	0	0	0	0	0	1	0	0	0
strengthens	10	.3253	.6975	38.4	0	2	0	1	4	2	0	1	0	0	0	0	0	0	0	1	1	1	0	2	0	2	1	1	1
strengths	7	.4727	.7007	38.5	1	0	0	0	1	3	2	0	0	1	0	0	0	0	0	2	0	0	0	0	0	0	2	2	0
strenuous	14	.6769	1.9480	42.9	0	0	1	1	5	4	3	0	2	1	1	0	1	2	0	2	0	0	0	0	1	3	0	1	0
strenuously	2	.2446	.1125	30.5	0	0	0	0	0	1	1	0	0	1	0	1	0	0	0	0	0	0	0	0	0	0	0	0	0
strep	2	.2331	.1157	30.6	0	0	0	0	0	0	2	0	0	0	0	0	0	0	0	1	0	0	0	0	1	0	0	0	0
streptococcal	7	.0000	.1380	31.4	0	0	0	0	0	0	7	0	0	0	0	0	0	0	0	7	0	0	0	0	0	0	0	0	0
streptomycin	5	.2340	.2966	34.7	0	0	0	2	0	2	0	1	0	0	0	0	0	0	1	4	0	0	0	0	0	0	0	0	0
stress	120	.5927	14.464	51.6	2	4	25	15	28	16	27	3	0	52	0	0	0	2	36	3	7	0	4	2	0	2	8	4	0
stressed	38	.5038	3.9626	46.0	0	1	9	2	14	9	2	1	1	6	0	0	0	1	16	1	6	0	0	0	0	0	6	1	0
stresses	21	.5962	2.5666	44.1	1	2	3	3	6	4	1	1	1	3	0	0	0	0	0	2	4	0	0	1	0	1	8	1	0
stressing	2	.2446	.1123	30.5	0	0	0	0	0	1	1	0	0	1	0	0	0	0	0	0	0	0	0	0	0	0	1	0	0
stretch	192	.8037	30.991	54.9	32	24	21	24	28	17	37	9	37	4	2	10	3	18	3	15	3	6	30	4	14	17	10	15	1
stretch-out	2	.0000	.0050	17.0	0	0	0	0	2	0	0	0	0	0	0	0	0	0	0	0	0	0	0	2	0	0	0	0	0
stretched	251	.8869	44.391	56.5	45	42	21	40	53	30	16	4	75	5	2	24	5	19	1	25	15	1	2	5	32	22	5	12	1
stretcher	18	.1532	1.2117	40.8	1	1	0	0	1	12	3	0	17	0	0	0	0	0	0	0	0	0	0	0	0	1	0	0	0
stretcher-bearing	2	.0000	.0914	29.6	0	0	0	0	0	2	0	0	2	0	0	0	0	0	0	0	0	0	0	0	0	0	0	0	0
stretchers	2	.2420	.1154	30.6	0	0	0	0	1	0	1	0	0	0	0	0	1	0	0	0	0	0	0	0	1	0	0	0	0
stretches	89	.7705	13.929	51.4	10	15	14	15	21	5	6	3	18	1	1	1	0	35	0	10	0	2	2	0	2	9	4	4	0
stretching	71	.7613	10.905	50.4	8	6	13	10	11	9	14	0	12	2	1	4	4	11	1	4	1	3	12	3	4	2	5	2	0
Stretching	2	.0000	.0219	23.4	0	0	2	0	0	0	0	0	0	2	0	0	0	0	0	0	0	0	0	0	0	0	0	0	0
stretchout	3	.0000	.0076	18.8	0	0	0	0	0	0	3	0	0	0	0	0	0	0	0	0	0	0	0	3	0	0	0	0	0
stretchy	4	.1814	.2373	33.8	2	0	0	0	0	0	0	2	2	0	0	0	0	0	0	0	0	0	0	0	0	0	0	2	0
stretto	4	.0000	.0323	25.1	0	0	0	0	1	3	0	0	0	0	0	0	0	0	0	0	4	0	0	0	0	0	0	0	0
strew	2	.0000	.0219	23.4	0	0	0	2	0	0	0	0	0	2	0	0	0	0	0	0	0	0	0	0	0	0	0	0	0
strewing	3	.3762	.2479	33.9	0	0	0	0	2	0	1	0	0	0	0	0	0	0	0	1	0	0	0	0	1	0	1	0	0
strewn	11	.5759	1.3289	41.2	1	0	1	3	3	2	1	0	2	0	1	1	0	1	0	0	0	0	0	0	2	1	0	3	0
stricken	15	.5413	1.7559	42.4	2	1	1	0	7	2	2	0	5	1	0	1	0	0	0	1	0	0	0	0	5	0	2	0	0
strict	46	.7427	6.9451	48.4	1	4	9	8	9	10	5	0	9	2	0	1	0	6	0	4	6	0	0	0	3	3	8	4	0
stricter	2	.0000	.0914	29.6	0	2	0	0	0	0	0	0	2	0	0	0	0	0	0	0	0	0	0	0	0	0	0	0	0
strictest	3	.2468	.1912	32.8	0	1	0	1	0	0	1	0	1	0	0	0	0	0	0	0	0	0	1	0	1	0	0	0	0
strictly	38	.7932	6.0709	47.8	0	0	1	5	22	3	2	5	7	3	0	1	0	2	1	5	0	1	1	0	1	2	6	8	0
stride	29	.5044	3.1936	45.0	2	1	6	4	10	5	1	0	7	0	0	2	0	0	0	4	0	0	0	0	2	13	0	1	0
strident	4	.3130	.2785	34.4	0	0	0	0	2	1	1	0	0	0	0	0	0	1	0	0	2	0	0	0	1	0	0	0	0
strides	12	.5022	1.3766	41.4	0	0	3	5	1	0	3	0	7	0	1	1	0	1	0	1	0	0	0	0	0	1	0	0	0
striding	10	.5428	1.1465	40.6	2	3	1	0	2	1	1	0	2	0	1	3	0	0	0	0	1	0	0	0	1	2	0	0	0
strife	21	.5597	2.4767	43.9	4	2	0	4	7	1	3	0	4	0	0	2	0	3	0	0	6	0	0	0	0	1	4	1	0
strike	252	.8341	42.147	56.2	46	25	26	38	53	36	22	6	51	7	3	11	1	20	4	52	12	0	0	14	13	20	17	27	0
Strike	4	.3559	.3535	35.5	0	0	0	0	2	1	1	0	2	0	0	0	1	0	0	0	1	0	0	0	0	0	0	0	0
strike-out	2	.0000	.0914	29.6	0	0	0	0	2	0	0	0	2	0	0	0	0	0	0	0	0	0	0	0	0	0	0	0	0
striker	3	.1174	.0833	29.2	0	0	0	0	1	2	0	0	0	1	0	0	0	0	0	0	0	0	0	2	0	0	0	0	0
strikes	91	.8349	15.202	51.8	15	7	12	7	22	13	9	6	10	1	1	3	4	8	1	25	5	0	0	1	1	7	11	13	0
striking	121	.7937	19.242	52.8	7	11	14	15	35	21	17	1	12	1	2	9	0	10	0	9	18	2	0	10	9	12	15	12	0
Striking	3	.2357	.2199	33.4	0	0	2	0	1	0	0	0	2	0	0	0	0	0	0	0	0	0	0	0	0	1	0	0	0
strikingly	6	.3608	.4692	36.7	1	1	1	1	2	0	0	0	0	0	0	0	0	0	0	0	1	0	0	0	0	2	3	0	0
string	483	.7190	70.635	58.5	104	103	78	62	55	63	16	2	84	14	1	20	34	10	4	73	136	27	2	2	31	25	8	12	0
String	2	.0000	.0162	22.1	0	0	1	0	1	0	0	0	0	0	0	0	0	0	0	0	2	0	0	0	0	0	0	0	0
stringed	17	.2154	.8465	39.3	2	3	2	2	3	4	0	1	0	0	0	0	0	0	1	1	13	0	0	0	0	2	0	0	0
stringent	7	.2445	.5383	37.3	0	0	5	0	0	2	0	0	5	0	0	0	0	2	0	0	0	0	0	0	0	0	0	0	0
stringer	2	.0000	.0243	23.9	0	0	0	2	0	0	0	0	0	0	0	0	0	0	0	0	0	0	0	0	0	0	0	2	0
stringing	6	.4635	.6233	37.9	2	1	0	1	0	0	1	1	2	0	0	1	0	0	0	0	0	0	0	0	0	2	0	1	0
strings	212	.3896	18.006	52.6	30	47	33	31	43	19	9	0	23	13	0	1	0	6	0	10	133	1	1	0	3	12	4	5	0
stringy	11	.5218	1.2173	40.9	1	1	5	0	2	1	1	0	2	3	0	0	0	0	0	0	0	0	1	0	3	0	0	2	0
strip	230	.7560	35.170	55.5	39	25	18	29	41	40	24	14	31	8	0	5	35	29	0	48	1	9	11	21	6	9	5	12	0
Strip	7	.1817	.3553	35.5	0	2	0	0	4	0	1	0	0	0	0	0	0	6	0	0	0	0	0	0	0	0	0	1	0
stripe	8	.4929	.8607	39.3	3	2	0	0	2	1	0	0	2	0	0	0	1	0	0	0	0	0	0	0	1	1	0	3	0
striped	62	.7489	9.5168	49.8	7	7	9	25	9	3	2	0	24	4	0	8	5	0	0	3	0	1	0	0	10	1	2	4	0
stripers	2	.1814	.1187	30.7	0	0	0	0	1	1	0	0	1	0	0	0	0	0	0	0	0	0	0	0	0	0	0	1	0
stripes	43	.7883	6.8515	48.4	20	0	6	5	2	6	4	0	10	2	0	0	1	4	1	4	3	1	0	0	9	6	1	1	0
Stripes	14	.3978	1.2509	41.0	2	1	6	1	0	3	1	0	3	0	0	0	0	2	0	0	6	0	0	0	0	1	2	0	0
striping	2	.0000	.0290	24.6	2	0	0	0	0	0	0	0	0	0	0	0	0	0	0	0	0	0	0	0	0	2	0	0	0
stripped	20	.6508	2.6674	44.3	1	0	1	2	11	4	0	1	2	0	0	3	0	3	0	1	0	0	0	2	3	1	2	3	0
stripping	10	.1643	.3817	35.8	0	0	0	2	7	1	0	0	0	0	0	1	2	0	0	0	0	0	0	6	0	1	0	0	0
strips	188	.6593	25.484	54.1	34	32	27	18	34	18	14	11	33	8	0	4	21	11	0	22	2	25	12	4	6	24	7	9	0
stripy	2	.0000	.0234	23.7	0	2	0	0	0	0	0	0	0	0	0	0	0	0	0	0	0	0	0	0	2	0	0	0	0
strive	11	.6271	1.4331	41.6	0	0	1	0	6	1	2	1	2	0	0	2	0	2	0	0	0	0	1	0	1	2	0	1	0
strives	3	.3346	.2478	33.9	0	0	0	0	2	0	1	0	1	0	0	0	0	0	0	1	0	0	0	0	0	0	1	0	0
striving	9	.5951	1.1193	40.5	0	1	1	1	2	1	3	0	2	1	0	2	0	0	0	0	1	0	0	0	0	0	2	1	0
strobe	2	.2446	.1142	30.6	0	0	0	0	1	0	0	1	0	0	0	0	0	0	0	0	0	0	0	0	1	0	0	1	0
stroboscope	2	.0000	.0209	23.2	0	0	0	0	0	0	1	1	0	0	0	0	0	0	0	0	0	0	0	0	0	0	2	0	0
strode	26	.6462	3.5317	45.5	4	4	6	5	7	0	0	0	10	1	0	4	0	0	0	0	0	0	0	0	4	4	1	2	0
stroke	143	.5847	17.373	52.4	5	49	21	13	25	15	13	2	28	2	35	7	0	2	5	18	5	5	1	10	10	3	3	9	0
stroked	41	.5757	5.2556	47.2	12	6	2	8	6	5	2	0	28	2	0	2	0	0	0	2	0	0	0	0	3	4	0	0	0
strokes	88	.6550	11.646	50.7	1	27	10	8	15	8	18	1	8	7	11	3	1	1	2	5	1	13	11	11	1	7	3	3	0
stroking	12	.6359	1.5883	42.0	0	2	1	5	1	2	1	0	3	1	0	1	0	1	0	1	1	0	0	1	3	0	0	0	0
stroll	29	.7523	4.4599	46.5	6	7	2	5	6	3	0	0	11	1	1	2	1	0	0	0	2	0	0	0	5	1	3	2	0
strolled	12	.4564	1.2477	41.0	1	2	0	2	4	1	2	0	5	3	0	1	0	0	0	0	0	0	0	0	0	3	0	0	0
stroller	2	.1787	.1174	30.7	1	0	0	0	0	0	1	0	1	0	0	0	0	0	0	0	0	0	0	0	1	0	0	0	0
strollers	3	.3394	.2470	33.9	1	0	0	1	0	1	0	0	1	0	0	0	1	0	0	0	0	0	0	0	0	0	1	0	0
strolling	11	.5483	1.2884	41.1	2	0	1	4	1	2	1	0	3	0	0	0	0	1	1	0	3	0	0	0	0	2	1	0	0

6R streamliner
8F streamliners
5A Streator
7D STREET
7R street-type
6A Street's
7R streetable
9R Streetcar
5P streetwalkers
8R Streisand
7B Strength
5Q Strengthening
8Q streptococci
5H streptococcus
9H Streptomyces
8G streptos
3P Stresa
7Q stress-resistance
7B stress-shift
7M stretch-outs
4B stretch'd
9L stretchability
XH stretched-out
4H Stretcher
8A stretcher-bearers
5P stretcheth
8A stretchin'
7D strewed
8H striated
XH striations
8R stridency
5H strike-anywhere
8A strike-outs
4A Strikeback
3P strikeout
7A strikers
4Q Strikes
4Q string-propelled
7R stringently
4P Stringer
7J Strings
4J strip-ed
XR strip-mined
9Q strip-mining
3P STRIPS
8Q strivings
9Q stroboscopic
9H strobus
7P strok'd
7R Stroller's

Word Type	F	D	U	SFI	3 Gr 3	4 Gr 4	5 Gr 5	6 Gr 6	7 Gr 7	8 Gr 8	9 Gr 9	X UnGr	A Read	B Eng & Gr	C Comp	D Lit	E Math	F Soc Stud	G Spell	H Sci	J Music	K Art	L Home Ec	M Shop	N Lib F	P Lib NF	Q Lib Ref	R Mag	S Rel
Strolling	3	.0000	.0243	23.8	0	0	2	0	0	1	0	0	0	0	0	0	0	0	0	0	3	0	0	0	0	0	0	0	0
strong	1140	.9299	210.02	63.2	227	202	162	158	181	118	83	9	288	36	10	64	2	127	13	145	97	24	12	11	53	119	78	58	3
Strong	15	.2705	.9649	39.8	1	9	4	0	1	0	0	0	1	0	0	5	0	0	0	0	0	0	0	0	0	9	0	0	0
strong-flavored	2	.0000	.0064	18.1	0	0	0	0	0	0	2	0	0	0	0	0	0	0	0	0	0	0	2	0	0	0	0	0	0
strong-minded	2	.1948	.1250	31.0	0	0	0	2	0	0	0	0	1	0	0	0	0	0	0	0	0	0	0	0	0	1	0	0	0
strong-willed	2	.0000	.0243	23.9	0	0	0	1	1	0	0	0	0	0	0	0	0	0	0	0	0	0	0	0	0	0	0	2	0
stronger	179	.8904	31.757	55.0	34	19	19	38	39	18	10	2	48	8	2	11	0	22	1	23	5	0	4	6	9	21	11	8	0
strongest	54	.8216	8.9108	49.5	14	4	8	10	5	8	5	0	9	1	0	1	0	8	0	9	2	1	0	1	3	12	3	4	0
Strongest-One	4	.0000	.1827	32.6	4	0	0	0	0	0	0	0	4	0	0	0	0	0	0	0	0	0	0	0	0	0	0	0	0
Strongfort	6	.0000	.2741	34.4	0	0	0	0	6	0	0	0	6	0	0	0	0	0	0	0	0	0	0	0	0	0	0	0	0
Strongfort's	3	.0000	.1370	31.4	0	0	0	0	3	0	0	0	3	0	0	0	0	0	0	0	0	0	0	0	0	0	0	0	0
strongholds	5	.5602	.5801	37.6	0	0	1	1	0	0	1	2	0	1	0	0	0	1	0	0	0	0	0	0	0	1	1	1	0
strongly	90	.8711	15.606	51.9	7	15	8	6	27	13	8	6	11	5	1	4	0	13	6	11	3	2	0	0	4	8	12	10	0
strontium	4	.3352	.2986	34.8	0	1	0	0	2	0	0	1	0	0	0	0	0	0	0	1	0	0	0	0	0	0	2	1	0
Stroop	2	.0000	.0914	29.6	0	0	2	0	0	0	0	0	2	0	0	0	0	0	0	0	0	0	0	0	0	0	0	0	0
strouding	2	.0000	.0215	23.3	0	0	0	0	2	0	0	0	0	0	0	2	0	0	0	0	0	0	0	0	0	0	0	0	0
strove	10	.5369	1.1156	40.5	0	0	0	0	4	3	3	0	1	0	0	2	0	0	0	0	2	1	0	0	3	0	1	0	0
strown	2	.0000	.0219	23.4	0	0	0	2	0	0	0	0	0	2	0	0	0	0	0	0	0	0	0	0	0	0	0	0	0
struck	291	.8419	49.190	56.9	27	41	20	49	90	38	20	6	93	9	4	31	0	14	5	11	24	0	0	2	45	21	11	21	0
structural	43	.5582	4.8776	46.9	0	0	2	0	15	6	20	0	1	0	1	0	0	0	2	5	0	7	3	10	0	1	11	2	0
structurally	2	.2278	.1128	30.5	0	0	0	0	1	0	1	0	0	0	0	0	0	0	0	1	0	0	0	0	0	0	1	0	0
structure	343	.8088	55.441	57.4	6	13	25	29	121	71	64	14	12	62	17	1	3	9	9	110	9	11	11	6	2	15	53	13	0
Structure	2	.0000	.0219	23.4	0	0	0	0	1	0	1	0	0	2	0	0	0	0	0	0	0	0	0	0	0	0	0	0	0
structures	110	.7552	16.752	52.2	2	5	6	8	31	20	28	10	5	12	3	0	4	2	0	47	3	2	0	3	0	2	20	7	0
struggle	164	.8336	27.451	54.4	10	11	21	17	50	32	20	3	39	6	1	16	0	38	1	4	4	3	0	0	8	18	17	9	0
struggled	99	.7417	15.092	51.8	6	20	12	17	27	13	4	0	41	1	3	10	0	4	0	0	0	0	0	1	15	10	3	11	0
struggles	24	.7016	3.4296	45.4	3	2	1	3	6	5	4	0	3	0	1	1	0	3	0	0	1	0	0	0	5	4	1	5	0
struggling	48	.7209	7.1679	48.6	6	7	5	9	12	3	6	0	21	2	0	3	0	5	0	0	0	0	0	0	5	4	4	4	0
Struggling	2	.1814	.1187	30.7	0	0	0	1	0	1	0	0	1	0	0	0	0	0	0	0	0	0	0	0	0	0	0	1	0
strum	26	.0867	.6419	38.1	9	9	3	3	2	0	0	0	0	0	0	0	0	0	0	0	24	0	0	0	1	0	0	1	0
strummed	6	.2034	.3105	34.9	0	1	2	0	3	0	0	0	1	0	0	1	0	0	0	0	4	0	0	0	0	0	0	0	0
strumming	9	.0681	.2583	34.1	3	2	1	1	2	0	0	0	2	0	0	0	0	0	0	0	7	0	0	0	0	0	0	0	0
strums	2	.0000	.0162	22.1	1	0	0	0	1	0	0	0	0	0	0	0	0	0	0	0	2	0	0	0	0	0	0	0	0
strung	28	.7948	4.4694	46.5	6	1	0	3	9	3	4	2	3	4	0	1	1	1	1	3	2	0	0	0	1	7	2	2	0
strut	4	.2358	.2662	34.3	0	0	1	0	0	2	1	0	2	0	1	0	0	0	0	0	0	0	0	0	0	0	0	1	0
Struthers	3	.0000	.0434	26.4	0	3	0	0	0	0	0	0	0	0	0	0	0	0	0	0	0	0	0	0	0	3	0	0	0
struts	3	.3265	.2369	33.7	1	0	0	1	1	0	0	0	1	0	0	0	0	0	1	0	0	0	0	0	0	0	0	1	0
strutted	19	.6394	2.5872	44.1	4	7	0	4	2	1	1	0	10	0	1	1	0	0	0	0	1	0	0	0	2	2	0	2	0
strutting	11	.5277	1.2630	41.0	3	3	0	1	2	2	0	0	4	0	0	2	0	0	0	0	0	1	0	0	1	2	0	1	0
Stryver	3	.0000	.0322	25.1	0	0	0	0	0	0	3	0	0	0	0	3	0	0	0	0	0	0	0	0	0	0	0	0	0
STU	2	.0000	.0299	24.8	0	1	0	0	0	1	0	0	0	0	0	0	2	0	0	0	0	0	0	0	0	0	0	0	0
Stuart	66	.3784	5.4057	47.3	2	11	9	14	25	0	3	2	7	5	21	13	1	0	0	0	2	0	0	0	0	7	8	2	0
Stuart's	3	.2197	.2090	33.2	0	1	2	0	0	0	0	0	2	0	0	0	0	0	0	0	0	0	0	0	0	0	1	0	0
stub	11	.6053	1.4175	41.5	1	2	1	2	2	0	3	0	4	0	0	0	3	0	0	0	0	0	0	0	1	1	1	1	0
stubbed	4	.4866	.4064	36.1	1	0	0	0	1	1	1	0	0	1	0	1	0	0	0	0	0	0	0	0	0	1	1	0	0
Stubbins	6	.0000	.0703	28.5	0	6	0	0	0	0	0	0	0	0	0	0	0	0	0	0	0	0	0	0	6	0	0	0	0
stubble	14	.5829	1.7262	42.4	2	0	3	1	5	2	1	0	4	0	1	3	0	0	0	0	0	0	0	0	2	2	0	2	0
stubbled	2	.2442	.1134	30.5	0	0	0	1	1	0	0	0	0	1	0	0	0	0	0	0	0	0	0	0	0	0	0	1	0
stubborn	51	.4688	5.3792	47.3	10	5	6	6	14	8	1	1	19	0	0	7	0	6	1	1	0	0	0	0	4	3	3	6	1
stubbornly	20	.6778	2.8005	44.5	2	3	3	1	5	4	2	0	5	1	0	1	0	3	0	0	0	0	0	0	3	1	4	2	0
stubbornness	4	.1919	.1864	32.7	1	0	0	0	0	3	0	0	0	0	0	3	0	0	0	0	0	0	0	0	1	0	0	0	0
Stubbs	7	.0000	.3198	35.0	0	7	0	0	0	0	0	0	7	0	0	0	0	0	0	0	0	0	0	0	0	0	0	0	0
stubby	16	.4266	1.5915	42.0	0	5	2	3	5	0	0	1	7	0	0	0	0	0	0	1	0	0	0	0	6	1	0	1	0
stubs	6	.3120	.4084	36.1	0	1	0	0	1	0	4	0	0	0	0	0	2	0	0	0	0	0	0	2	1	0	0	1	0
stucco	2	.1259	.0687	28.4	0	0	0	1	1	0	0	0	0	0	0	0	0	1	0	0	0	0	0	1	0	0	0	0	0
stuck	186	.8449	31.673	55.0	45	43	15	10	33	21	12	7	85	6	4	15	0	5	3	5	4	2	0	1	16	26	1	13	0
Stuck	5	.0000	.0724	28.6	4	0	0	0	0	0	0	1	0	0	0	0	0	0	0	0	0	0	0	0	0	5	0	0	0
stuck-up	2	.2152	.1357	31.3	1	0	0	1	0	0	0	0	1	0	0	0	0	1	0	0	0	0	0	0	0	0	0	0	0
stud	8	.3227	.5650	37.5	0	6	0	0	2	0	0	0	0	0	0	0	0	0	0	0	0	0	0	1	6	0	0	1	0
studded	10	.5671	1.2053	40.8	2	1	1	3	3	0	0	0	2	0	0	0	0	1	0	1	0	0	0	0	1	3	0	2	0
student	280	.8708	48.437	56.9	10	17	22	19	60	51	89	12	21	45	7	6	30	16	17	7	7	2	1	7	1	22	21	69	1
Student	11	.5777	1.3106	41.2	2	0	1	0	3	2	3	0	0	3	0	0	0	1	0	1	0	0	0	0	0	2	2	2	0
student's	13	.5969	1.5948	42.0	0	0	0	1	4	1	3	4	0	2	0	0	3	0	0	2	1	0	0	0	0	0	1	4	0
students	475	.8457	80.043	59.0	10	36	46	54	126	81	96	26	36	45	6	15	87	34	5	8	13	2	8	4	4	28	56	124	0
Students	5	.3705	.4043	36.1	0	0	0	0	1	1	3	0	0	2	0	0	2	0	0	0	0	0	0	0	0	0	0	1	0
students'	3	.2043	.1486	31.7	1	1	0	0	0	0	1	0	0	0	0	0	0	0	0	0	0	0	0	0	0	1	2	0	0
studied	432	.9047	77.487	58.9	57	68	58	48	88	60	44	9	48	57	5	14	31	37	54	67	24	5	3	2	7	26	39	13	0
studies	191	.8558	32.650	55.1	12	19	31	20	54	21	29	5	31	13	0	2	3	24	8	38	2	2	4	2	1	12	35	14	0
Studies	3	.1927	.1491	31.7	0	0	0	1	0	1	1	0	0	0	0	0	0	0	0	1	0	0	0	0	0	0	0	2	0
studio	40	.6857	5.5521	47.4	3	7	3	3	12	8	3	1	2	1	0	5	1	1	1	1	4	2	1	0	1	2	0	18	0
Studio	2	.2446	.1122	30.5	0	0	0	0	0	2	0	0	0	0	0	1	0	0	0	0	0	0	0	0	0	0	1	0	0
studios	5	.1398	.1959	32.9	0	1	1	0	1	1	0	1	0	0	0	0	0	1	0	0	0	0	0	0	0	0	0	4	0
studious	7	.5607	.8563	39.3	1	1	1	1	2	0	1	0	3	0	0	1	0	1	0	0	0	0	0	0	1	1	0	0	0
studiously	2	.2444	.1132	30.5	0	0	0	0	0	1	1	0	0	1	0	0	0	0	0	0	0	0	0	0	1	0	0	0	0
studs	8	.5838	.9503	39.8	0	1	1	0	4	1	1	0	0	1	0	0	0	0	1	0	0	0	1	1	0	2	0	2	0
study	2581	.7560	392.34	65.9	276	416	468	398	500	274	209	40	164	238	19	19	479	149	807	296	112	31	22	17	14	44	95	75	0
Study	28	.2314	1.5017	41.8	2	4	4	3	6	3	6	0	1	2	0	0	1	0	21	1	0	0	0	0	0	0	0	2	0
studyin'	2	.0000	.0234	23.7	0	0	1	0	1	0	0	0	0	0	0	0	0	0	0	0	0	0	0	0	2	0	0	0	0
studying	256	.9372	47.453	56.8	23	42	22	37	57	45	26	4	46	22	2	10	11	26	23	39	6	5	4	3	4	15	19	21	0
Stuey	21	.0000	.9593	39.8	20	1	0	0	0	0	0	0	21	0	0	0	0	0	0	0	0	0	0	0	0	0	0	0	0
stuff	129	.7214	19.202	52.8	13	13	20	21	27	14	17	4	50	6	0	13	0	1	1	9	1	0	0	0	18	6	3	21	0
stuffed	45	.7084	6.6331	48.2	9	8	4	5	11	8	0	0	21	1	0	5	0	0	0	3	1	0	1	0	1	5	0	7	0
stuffiness	3	.2212	.2099	33.2	0	0	0	0	1	1	1	0	2	0	0	1	0	0	0	0	0	0	0	0	0	0	0	0	0
stuffing	19	.5864	2.4147	43.8	4	9	0	0	0	2	4	0	10	2	0	1	0	0	0	0	0	0	2	0	2	1	1	0	0
stuffs	3	.2357	.2199	33.4	1	0	1	1	0	0	0	0	2	0	0	0	0	0	0	0	0	0	0	0	0	1	0	0	0
stuffy	5	.4305	.4752	36.8	1	0	0	2	0	1	0	1	1	1	0	1	0	0	0	0	0	0	0	0	0	0	0	2	0
stumble	14	.6623	1.9485	42.9	2	4	0	3	3	1	1	0	6	0	0	1	0	1	1	0	1	0	0	0	0	3	1	0	0
stumbled	53	.6464	7.2094	48.6	6	13	7	12	9	4	2	0	21	3	0	6	0	0	1	0	0	0	0	0	9	9	0	4	0
stumbles	3	.3390	.2450	33.9	0	1	1	0	1	0	0	0	1	0	0	0	0	0	0	0	0	0	0	0	0	0	1	1	0
stumblest	2	.0000	.0215	23.3	0	0	0	0	0	0	2	0	0	0	0	2	0	0	0	0	0	0	0	0	0	0	0	0	0
stumbling	16	.6066	2.0487	43.1	1	1	2	4	3	1	3	1	5	1	0	4	0	0	0	1	0	0	0	0	3	0	1	1	0
stumblingly	2	.2433	.1158	30.6	0	0	2	0	0	0	0	0	0	0	0	0	0	0	0	0	0	0	0	0	0	1	0	1	0
stummick	2	.2443	.1130	30.5	1	0	0	0	0	0	1	0	0	0	0	1	0	0	0	0	0	0	0	0	1	0	0	0	0
stump	39	.6531	5.3681	47.3	5	11	7	2	10	3	1	0	17	2	0	4	0	1	0	0	0	0	0	0	8	4	2	1	0
stumped	3	.3400	.2455	33.9	1	1	0	1	0	0	0	0	1	1	0	0	0	0	0	0	0	0	0	0	1	0	0	0	0

9B strolls
7Q Stromboli
3A Stromeyer
9Q Stromont
4A strong-armed
3A strong-looking
7Q strong-winged
5D strong-withered
4P Strong's
3R strongbox
7D stronghold
6J strongly-accented
4A strongly-built
4P Strongs
4P Strongs'
8R Strongside
7R strontium-rich
8B Strovalone
9M structural-steel
9Q Structuralist
7H structured
8A strudel
3J strum-a-strum-a-strum
7A strummin'
7A struttin'
8D strutworks
8Q Struve
8A Stryker
7F Strymon
6R Stu
4P Stuarts
9B stub-tailed
7A stubbier
XH stubbiness
9R stubble-bearded
5A stubbly
4N stud's
9R student-government
8R student-oriented
4P Studios
7Q Studs
9B study-hall
7R study-time
3A Stuey's
7A Stuff
5R stuff's
XR Stuffed
4B stuffin'
7H Stulka
8R stultifying
8R Stump
6R stumpers
8D Stumpland

Word Type	F	D	U	SFI	3 Gr 3	4 Gr 4	5 Gr 5	6 Gr 6	7 Gr 7	8 Gr 8	9 Gr 9	X UnGr	A Read	B Eng & Gr	C Comp	D Lit	E Math	F Soc Stud	G Spell	H Sci	J Music	K Art	L Home Ec	M Shop	N Lib F	P Lib NF	Q Lib Ref	R Mag	S Rel
stumps	20	.4197	2.0984	43.2	12	2	1	1	2	1	1	0	16	0	1	0	0	1	0	0	0	0	0	0	0	0	2	0	0
stumpy	2	.2433	.1158	30.6	1	0	0	1	0	0	0	0	0	0	0	0	0	0	0	0	0	0	0	0	0	1	0	1	0
stung	27	.6197	3.5320	45.5	1	6	4	5	6	5	0	0	9	1	0	5	0	1	0	1	0	0	0	0	6	3	0	1	0
stunned	15	.6521	2.0304	43.1	0	1	1	4	6	2	1	0	4	0	1	1	0	0	0	1	0	0	0	0	2	1	2	3	0
stunning	4	.3097	.2992	34.8	0	0	0	0	0	1	1	2	1	0	0	1	0	0	0	0	0	0	0	0	0	0	0	2	0
stunt	31	.7202	4.5777	46.6	3	2	2	9	3	9	1	2	7	2	1	2	2	0	0	10	0	0	0	0	0	2	1	4	0
stunted	7	.4273	.6562	38.2	0	2	1	1	1	1	1	0	1	0	0	0	0	1	0	1	0	0	1	0	0	0	3	0	0
stunts	19	.4755	1.9826	43.0	1	4	0	8	3	3	0	0	3	0	0	0	1	0	0	6	0	0	0	0	2	7	0	0	0
stupefied	2	.2401	.1133	30.5	0	0	0	0	0	1	1	0	0	0	0	0	0	0	0	0	0	0	0	0	0	1	1	0	0
stupendous	10	.5665	1.1798	40.7	0	0	1	2	5	1	1	0	1	0	1	1	0	0	0	2	0	0	0	0	1	0	3	1	0
Stupenfeffer	3	.0000	.0352	25.5	0	3	0	0	0	0	0	0	0	0	0	0	0	0	0	0	0	0	0	0	3	0	0	0	0
stupid	69	.6257	9.2135	49.6	18	5	4	11	12	10	2	7	33	0	0	7	0	0	0	0	0	0	0	0	8	10	4	7	0
stupider	2	.2437	.1129	30.5	0	0	0	1	1	0	0	0	0	0	0	0	0	0	0	0	0	0	0	0	0	0	1	1	0
stupidity	6	.5158	.6598	38.2	1	1	0	0	3	0	1	0	1	0	0	0	0	0	0	0	0	0	0	0	1	1	1	2	0
stupidly	3	.0000	.0352	25.5	0	1	0	0	1	1	0	0	0	0	0	0	0	0	0	0	0	0	0	0	3	0	0	0	0
stupor	3	.3429	.2528	34.0	0	0	0	0	3	0	0	0	1	0	0	0	0	0	0	1	0	0	0	0	1	0	0	0	0
sturdiest	2	.1814	.1187	30.7	0	0	0	0	1	0	0	1	1	0	0	0	0	0	0	0	0	0	0	0	0	0	0	1	0
sturdy	54	.8030	8.6878	49.4	8	7	6	3	11	11	7	1	6	1	1	3	1	7	0	1	3	2	5	0	3	12	5	4	0
sturgeon	2	.0000	.0243	23.9	0	0	0	1	0	1	0	0	0	0	0	0	0	0	0	0	0	0	0	0	0	0	0	2	0
Sturgeon	2	.0000	.0243	23.9	0	0	0	2	0	0	0	0	0	0	0	0	0	0	0	0	0	0	0	0	0	0	0	2	0
stuttered	3	.3873	.2495	34.0	0	1	0	0	0	1	1	0	0	0	0	1	0	0	0	0	0	0	0	0	1	0	0	1	0
Stutz	40	.0000	1.8273	42.6	0	0	1	0	0	39	0	0	40	0	0	0	0	0	0	0	0	0	0	0	0	0	0	0	0
STUW	5	.0000	.0748	28.7	0	0	5	0	0	0	0	0	0	0	0	0	5	0	0	0	0	0	0	0	0	0	0	0	0
Stuyvesant	2	.2440	.1132	30.5	0	0	0	0	1	0	0	1	0	0	0	1	0	0	0	0	0	0	0	0	0	0	0	1	0
sty	3	.2380	.1632	32.1	1	0	0	0	0	0	0	2	0	2	0	0	0	0	0	0	1	0	0	0	0	0	0	0	0
style	356	.6639	47.772	56.8	6	21	31	46	92	99	53	8	22	17	2	5	1	21	2	2	163	25	24	9	6	14	25	18	0
style-right	2	.0000	.0064	18.1	0	0	0	0	0	0	2	0	0	0	0	0	0	0	0	0	0	0	2	0	0	0	0	0	0
styled	2	.1674	.0805	29.1	0	0	1	0	0	1	0	0	0	0	0	0	0	0	0	0	0	0	1	0	0	1	0	0	0
styles	77	.5822	9.1458	49.6	1	1	3	11	23	25	11	2	6	1	0	0	0	5	0	0	24	2	16	10	0	1	7	5	0
styling	3	.3164	.1983	33.0	0	0	0	0	1	1	0	1	0	0	0	0	0	0	0	0	0	1	1	0	0	0	0	1	0
stylish	3	.2076	.1697	32.3	1	0	0	2	0	0	0	0	1	0	1	0	0	0	0	0	0	0	0	0	1	0	0	0	0
stylist	3	.0000	.0365	25.6	0	0	3	0	0	0	0	0	0	0	0	0	0	0	0	0	0	0	0	0	0	0	0	3	0
stylistic	3	.1983	.1396	31.4	0	0	0	0	1	1	1	0	0	0	0	0	0	0	0	0	2	0	0	0	0	0	0	1	0
stylized	3	.1168	.0792	29.0	0	0	0	0	0	2	1	0	0	0	0	0	0	0	0	0	1	2	0	0	0	0	0	0	0
stylus	10	.2312	.5290	37.2	0	0	1	0	5	4	0	0	0	0	0	0	2	0	0	0	7	0	0	0	0	0	1	0	0
stymied	2	.0000	.0243	23.9	0	0	0	0	0	1	1	0	0	0	0	0	0	0	0	0	0	0	0	0	0	0	0	2	0
su	3	.2440	.1815	32.6	0	0	0	1	0	2	0	0	0	1	0	0	0	2	0	0	0	0	0	0	0	0	0	0	0
suan-pan	2	.0000	.0299	24.8	0	0	0	1	0	1	0	0	0	0	0	0	2	0	0	0	0	0	0	0	0	0	0	0	0
sub	44	.4085	4.4335	46.5	1	24	3	2	14	1	1	0	30	0	0	0	0	0	8	2	0	0	0	0	0	0	0	4	0
Sub	8	.0000	.0972	29.9	4	0	0	0	0	0	0	4	0	0	0	0	0	0	0	0	0	0	0	0	0	0	0	8	0
sub-	4	.3606	.3540	35.5	0	0	0	0	1	3	0	0	2	1	0	0	0	0	1	0	0	0	0	0	0	0	0	0	0
sub-assemblies	3	.2357	.2199	33.4	0	0	0	0	1	2	0	0	2	0	0	0	0	0	0	0	0	0	0	0	0	1	0	0	0
sub-continent	2	.0000	.0389	25.9	0	0	0	2	0	0	0	0	0	0	0	0	0	2	0	0	0	0	0	0	0	0	0	0	0
sub-zero	4	.3709	.3633	35.6	0	0	1	0	0	1	1	1	2	0	0	0	0	0	0	0	0	0	0	0	0	0	1	1	0
sub's	4	.1814	.2373	33.8	0	0	1	0	2	0	0	1	2	0	0	0	0	0	0	0	0	0	0	0	0	0	0	2	0
subarctic	2	.2285	.1129	30.5	0	0	0	1	1	0	0	0	0	0	0	0	0	1	0	0	0	0	0	0	0	0	1	0	0
subcommittee	5	.1848	.2301	33.6	0	0	0	0	3	0	2	0	0	1	0	0	0	0	0	0	0	0	0	0	0	0	0	4	0
subcompact	5	.0000	.0608	27.8	0	0	0	0	5	0	0	0	0	0	0	0	0	0	0	0	0	0	0	0	0	0	0	5	0
subcompacts	3	.0000	.0365	25.6	0	0	0	0	3	0	0	0	0	0	0	0	0	0	0	0	0	0	0	0	0	0	0	3	0
subconscious	2	.2437	.1129	30.5	0	0	0	0	0	0	1	1	0	0	0	0	0	0	0	0	0	0	0	0	0	0	1	1	0
subconsciously	3	.2300	.1627	32.1	0	0	0	1	0	0	2	0	0	1	0	0	0	0	0	0	0	0	0	0	0	0	0	2	0
subcontinent	13	.1391	.5653	37.5	0	0	1	7	3	1	1	0	0	0	0	0	0	12	0	0	0	0	0	0	0	0	1	0	0
subdivide	5	.3234	.3553	35.5	0	0	0	0	1	4	0	0	0	3	0	0	0	1	0	0	0	0	1	0	0	0	0	0	0
subdivided	7	.4661	.6971	38.4	0	0	0	0	4	1	1	1	0	0	0	0	2	0	0	2	0	0	0	0	0	1	2	0	0
subdivision	10	.4379	.9310	39.7	0	0	0	0	8	0	2	0	0	0	0	0	6	0	0	0	0	0	0	1	0	0	2	1	0
subdivisions	16	.6309	2.0545	43.1	0	3	0	2	4	4	3	0	0	3	1	0	2	2	0	2	0	0	0	2	0	0	3	1	0
subdue	4	.4801	.3989	36.0	0	0	1	0	1	1	1	0	0	0	0	1	0	0	1	0	1	0	0	0	0	1	0	0	0
subdued	12	.5781	1.4475	41.6	0	1	1	1	5	2	2	0	2	0	0	3	0	0	0	0	1	0	0	0	3	0	2	1	0
subduing	2	.0000	.0209	23.2	0	0	0	0	1	1	0	0	0	0	0	0	0	0	0	0	0	0	0	0	0	0	2	0	0
subhead	2	.1698	.1133	30.5	0	0	1	0	1	0	0	0	1	0	0	0	0	0	0	0	0	0	0	0	0	0	1	0	0
subheadings	9	.2269	.6923	38.4	0	2	4	0	3	0	0	0	8	1	0	0	0	0	0	0	0	0	0	0	0	0	0	0	0
subheads	4	.1443	.2329	33.7	0	0	0	0	3	0	1	0	3	0	0	0	0	0	0	0	0	0	0	1	0	0	0	0	0
subhuman	2	.2437	.1129	30.5	0	0	0	0	1	0	1	0	0	0	0	0	0	0	0	0	0	0	0	0	0	0	1	1	0
subject	882	.6270	112.47	60.5	61	74	143	98	193	102	192	19	36	487	82	30	10	17	35	15	38	15	1	4	10	25	47	30	0
Subject	8	.2399	.6021	37.8	5	1	0	0	1	0	1	0	6	2	0	0	0	0	0	0	0	0	0	0	0	0	0	0	0
subject-predicate	2	.0000	.0219	23.4	0	0	0	0	2	0	0	0	0	2	0	0	0	0	0	0	0	0	0	0	0	0	0	0	0
subject's	2	.1621	.0746	28.7	0	0	0	0	0	1	1	0	0	0	1	1	0	0	0	0	0	0	0	0	0	0	0	0	0
subjected	20	.7250	2.9450	44.7	0	0	2	2	6	4	4	2	2	2	0	1	0	3	0	4	3	0	0	0	1	2	2	0	0
subjects	299	.7129	42.985	56.3	26	29	50	36	56	40	51	11	15	116	21	12	3	23	11	12	10	13	0	0	5	21	28	9	0
subjugated	2	.2412	.1141	30.6	0	0	0	0	1	1	0	0	0	1	0	0	0	0	0	0	0	0	0	0	0	1	0	0	0
subjugation	2	.2440	.1132	30.5	0	0	0	0	2	0	0	0	0	0	0	1	0	0	0	0	0	0	0	0	0	0	0	1	0
subkingdom	2	.0000	.0209	23.2	0	0	0	2	0	0	0	0	0	0	0	0	0	0	0	0	0	0	0	0	0	0	2	0	0
Sublette	4	.0000	.0579	27.6	0	4	0	0	0	0	0	0	0	0	0	0	0	0	0	0	0	0	0	0	0	4	0	0	0
sublime	7	.4255	.6242	38.0	0	1	0	0	3	0	2	1	0	0	0	1	0	0	0	0	3	0	0	0	1	0	2	0	0
submarine	122	.7898	19.783	53.0	22	51	4	3	24	6	10	2	76	3	1	6	2	3	0	7	0	1	3	0	2	0	7	11	0
Submarine	2	.0000	.0243	23.9	0	0	1	1	0	0	0	0	0	0	0	0	0	0	0	0	0	0	0	0	0	0	0	2	0
submarines	29	.6876	4.1293	46.2	1	8	2	0	9	6	3	0	8	2	0	0	1	5	0	4	0	0	0	1	0	0	2	6	0
submerge	7	.4431	.7149	38.5	1	2	1	0	2	0	0	1	3	1	0	2	0	0	0	1	0	0	0	0	0	0	0	0	0
submerged	28	.6585	3.7960	45.8	1	1	1	1	14	4	4	2	4	0	1	0	1	1	0	5	0	0	0	0	1	2	6	7	0
submergence	2	.2278	.1128	30.5	0	0	0	0	0	1	1	0	0	0	0	0	0	0	0	1	0	0	0	0	0	0	1	0	0
submetallic	2	.0000	.0394	26.0	0	0	0	0	0	0	0	2	0	0	0	0	0	0	0	2	0	0	0	0	0	0	0	0	0
submission	3	.2227	.1589	32.0	0	0	0	0	2	1	0	0	0	0	0	0	0	0	0	0	0	0	0	0	2	0	0	1	0
submit	14	.6541	1.8857	42.8	0	0	2	3	4	3	1	1	2	0	0	0	0	1	1	1	0	0	0	0	4	2	1	2	0
submitted	16	.6514	2.1462	43.3	2	0	1	0	4	5	3	1	1	0	0	2	0	6	0	1	0	0	0	0	1	3	1	1	0
subordinate	27	.1513	.9375	39.7	0	0	0	0	12	7	8	0	0	6	17	0	0	1	0	0	0	0	0	0	0	1	2	0	0
subordinated	5	.3354	.3513	35.5	0	0	1	0	0	1	3	0	0	0	2	0	0	0	0	0	0	0	1	0	0	1	1	0	0
subordinating	9	.0411	.1003	30.0	0	0	0	0	0	0	9	0	0	1	8	0	0	0	0	0	0	0	0	0	0	0	0	0	0
subordination	6	.0000	.0657	28.2	0	0	0	0	0	6	0	0	0	6	0	0	0	0	0	0	0	0	0	0	0	0	0	0	0
subordinator	7	.0000	.0766	28.8	0	0	0	0	1	6	0	0	0	7	0	0	0	0	0	0	0	0	0	0	0	0	0	0	0
subordinators	4	.0000	.0438	26.4	0	0	0	0	3	1	0	0	0	4	0	0	0	0	0	0	0	0	0	0	0	0	0	0	0
subparticles	2	.0000	.0394	26.0	0	0	0	0	2	0	0	0	0	0	0	0	0	0	0	2	0	0	0	0	0	0	0	0	0

6A stunting
3N Stupid
6P STUPID
6B stupidest
8B Sturbridge
9D sturdier
5N sturdily
7M sturdiness
7Q sturgeons
8A Sturgis
5P Sturzo
8G stutter
8E stutterer
6N stuttering
XB sty-rope
6P Stygian
8J Styles
8J stylistically
8K stylize
9D Styx
8F Su
9F sub-Saharan
7B sub-branch
7B sub-branches
7J sub-dominate
XH sub-fibrils
6Q sub-kingdom
XH sub-microscopic
9A sub-standard
8A sub-sub-
8A sub-sub-sub-contractors
7A sub-systems
XH sub-visible
7R sub-2000-rpm
7Q Subarctic
9M subassemblies
4P subatomic
7Q subbirds
4Q subcaste
4Q subcastes
5R subcategories
6Q subclass
7R Subcommittee
9Q subcommittees
7R SUBCOMPACTS
XH subconchoidal
7R subcontracted
5Q subcooling
7R subcultures
XH subcutaneous
7P subdues
9H subglacial
9Q subgroups
9F subhumid
4B subj
7G subject-predicate-object
9B subject-verb
7B subject-verb-complement
9P subjecting
5Q Subjection
8J subjective
3P subjectively
7R subjectivity
5Q subjects'
XR subjugate
9R sublimate
7R sublimely
9H sublimes
5P Submachine
4Q submarine-infested
5A submarine's
XH submerging
XH submersion
8F Submission
5R submits
XR submitting
9H suborder
7H suborders
9D subornation

Word Type	F	D	U	SFI	3 Gr 3	4 Gr 4	5 Gr 5	6 Gr 6	7 Gr 7	8 Gr 8	9 Gr 9	X UnGr	A Read	B Eng & Gr	C Comp	D Lit	E Math	F Soc Stud	G Spell	H Sci	J Music	K Art	L Home Ec	M Shop	N Lib F	P Lib NF	Q Lib Ref	R Mag	S Rel
subphyla	2	.0000	.0394	26.0	0	0	0	0	0	0	2	0	0	0	0	0	0	0	0	2	0	0	0	0	0	0	0	0	0
subphylum	6	.0000	.1183	30.7	0	0	0	0	0	0	3	3	0	0	0	0	0	0	0	6	0	0	0	0	0	0	0	0	0
subs	8	.0000	.0972	29.9	0	0	0	0	8	0	0	0	0	0	0	0	0	0	0	0	0	0	0	0	0	0	0	8	0
subscribe	8	.4991	.8682	39.4	0	1	0	3	3	1	0	0	2	0	0	1	0	1	2	0	0	0	0	0	0	2	0	0	0
subscribed	5	.4587	.4821	36.8	0	0	1	0	2	1	1	0	0	1	0	0	0	0	0	0	0	0	0	0	1	1	2	0	0
subscriber	3	.2223	.2106	33.2	0	0	0	1	1	1	0	0	2	1	0	0	0	0	0	0	0	0	0	0	0	0	0	0	0
subscribers	4	.3723	.3645	35.6	0	0	0	1	0	3	0	0	2	1	0	0	0	0	0	0	0	0	0	0	0	0	0	1	0
subscript	2	.2413	.1212	30.8	0	0	0	0	0	1	1	0	0	0	0	0	1	0	0	1	0	0	0	0	0	0	0	0	0
subscription	8	.5484	.9029	39.6	0	0	0	0	3	1	3	1	0	2	0	0	1	0	1	0	0	0	0	0	0	0	2	2	0
subscriptions	2	.1641	.0751	28.8	0	0	0	1	1	0	0	0	0	0	1	0	0	0	0	0	0	0	0	0	0	0	1	0	0
subsequent	21	.6102	2.6181	44.2	0	0	1	1	9	3	5	2	1	1	2	1	1	0	0	1	0	1	0	0	0	0	6	7	0
subsequently	17	.4556	1.6391	42.1	0	0	1	2	5	3	4	2	0	0	0	2	0	0	0	3	0	0	0	0	0	1	8	3	0
subset	79	.0096	1.3500	41.3	10	14	18	6	15	8	7	1	1	0	0	0	78	0	0	0	0	0	0	0	0	0	0	0	0
subsets	46	.0151	.8451	39.3	4	6	5	5	15	11	0	0	1	0	0	0	45	0	0	0	0	0	0	0	0	0	0	0	0
subside	2	.2278	.1128	30.5	0	0	0	0	2	0	0	0	0	0	0	0	0	0	0	1	0	0	0	0	0	0	1	0	0
subsided	13	.5858	1.5851	42.0	1	1	0	1	7	1	2	0	2	0	1	3	0	1	1	0	0	0	0	0	1	0	0	4	0
subsidiary	7	.3414	.5239	37.2	0	0	1	0	1	1	4	0	0	0	0	0	0	0	0	0	0	0	0	0	0	1	3	3	0
subsidies	2	.0000	.0243	23.9	0	0	0	0	0	0	1	1	0	0	0	0	0	0	0	0	0	0	0	0	0	0	0	2	0
subsidize	2	.0000	.0243	23.9	0	0	0	0	1	0	0	1	0	0	0	0	0	0	0	0	0	0	0	0	0	0	0	2	0
subsidized	4	.2090	.2014	33.0	0	0	0	0	0	0	3	1	0	0	0	0	0	0	0	0	0	0	0	0	0	0	1	3	0
subsist	3	.2159	.1532	31.9	0	1	0	0	2	0	0	0	0	0	0	0	0	0	0	0	0	0	0	0	0	0	2	1	0
subsistence	6	.4725	.6073	37.8	0	1	2	0	0	1	2	0	0	0	0	0	0	3	0	0	0	0	0	0	1	1	1	0	0
subsoil	5	.2849	.3268	35.1	0	1	1	0	0	0	3	0	0	0	0	0	0	0	0	1	0	0	0	0	0	1	3	0	0
substance	260	.6493	34.761	55.4	18	16	51	32	34	48	52	9	4	2	0	5	2	4	4	178	1	1	3	7	4	10	24	11	0
Substance	5	.0000	.2284	33.6	0	0	5	0	0	0	0	0	5	0	0	0	0	0	0	0	0	0	0	0	0	0	0	0	0
substances	315	.3966	28.140	54.5	32	15	61	40	48	45	62	12	7	0	0	0	1	1	2	263	1	0	4	2	1	2	27	4	0
substandard	4	.1907	.1863	32.7	0	0	0	0	1	2	1	0	0	3	0	0	0	0	0	0	0	0	0	0	0	0	0	1	0
substantial	31	.6483	4.0847	46.1	0	1	4	4	8	2	11	1	1	0	2	1	0	4	1	1	0	0	4	0	0	3	5	9	0
substantially	5	.4169	.4619	36.6	0	0	2	0	1	0	2	0	1	1	0	0	0	0	0	0	0	0	0	0	0	0	2	1	0
substations	2	.0000	.0394	26.0	0	0	0	0	2	0	0	0	0	0	0	0	0	0	0	2	0	0	0	0	0	0	0	0	0
substitute	92	.7405	13.682	51.4	6	5	8	10	13	26	23	1	4	25	0	2	14	1	6	7	3	1	12	1	6	0	7	3	0
substituted	33	.7499	4.9924	47.0	0	1	2	10	6	5	6	3	4	4	0	0	4	1	3	3	3	0	3	0	0	1	4	3	0
substitutes	10	.5052	1.0606	40.3	1	0	6	0	1	0	1	1	1	5	0	1	0	0	0	0	0	0	1	0	0	0	1	1	0
substituting	18	.6991	2.5292	44.0	2	0	4	1	3	6	1	1	0	4	0	1	0	1	5	1	0	0	1	1	0	1	2	1	0
substitution	5	.3724	.4047	36.1	0	0	0	1	0	3	1	0	0	1	0	0	2	0	0	0	0	0	0	0	0	0	2	0	0
substitutions	3	.2208	.1563	31.9	0	0	0	0	2	1	0	0	0	2	0	0	0	0	0	0	0	0	0	0	1	0	0	0	0
subsystems	2	.0000	.0209	23.2	0	0	0	0	0	0	2	0	0	0	0	0	0	0	0	0	0	0	0	0	0	0	2	0	0
subterfuge	2	.1814	.1187	30.7	0	0	0	0	1	1	0	0	1	0	0	0	0	0	0	0	0	0	0	0	0	0	0	1	0
subterranean	7	.2657	.4214	36.2	0	0	0	1	5	0	1	0	0	0	0	0	0	0	0	0	0	0	0	0	1	0	5	1	0
subterraneous	2	.0000	.0209	23.2	0	0	0	0	2	0	0	0	0	0	0	0	0	0	0	0	0	0	0	0	0	0	2	0	0
subtitle	3	.3272	.2363	33.7	0	0	0	0	2	1	0	0	1	0	0	1	0	0	0	0	1	0	0	0	0	0	0	0	0
subtle	33	.6811	4.5334	46.6	0	0	1	2	7	8	9	6	1	2	0	5	0	0	0	1	6	3	1	0	1	2	4	7	0
subtle-minded	2	.0000	.0215	23.3	0	0	0	0	0	0	2	0	0	0	0	2	0	0	0	0	0	0	0	0	0	0	0	0	0
subtler	5	.2418	.3070	34.9	0	0	1	0	3	0	1	0	1	0	0	0	0	0	0	0	0	0	0	0	0	1	3	0	0
subtlety	3	.3811	.2534	34.0	0	0	0	0	2	0	1	0	0	0	0	0	0	0	0	1	0	0	0	0	0	1	0	1	0
subtly	5	.3836	.4069	36.1	0	0	1	1	1	1	0	1	0	0	0	0	0	0	0	0	1	1	0	0	0	1	0	2	0
subtopic	4	.1733	.2298	33.6	0	0	2	2	0	0	0	0	2	2	0	0	0	0	0	0	0	0	0	0	0	0	0	0	0
subtopics	13	.4302	1.3035	41.2	0	2	4	6	1	0	0	0	6	4	1	0	0	2	0	0	0	0	0	0	0	0	0	0	0
subtract	292	.2414	17.200	52.4	77	28	51	40	25	27	37	7	5	10	0	0	262	0	6	3	0	0	0	3	0	2	0	1	0
SUBTRACT	2	.0000	.0299	24.8	2	0	0	0	0	0	0	0	0	0	0	0	2	0	0	0	0	0	0	0	0	0	0	0	0
subtracted	83	.0921	2.6531	44.2	10	21	24	12	5	0	10	1	1	0	0	0	79	1	1	0	0	0	0	0	0	0	0	1	0
subtracting	60	.0481	1.4152	41.5	8	5	5	6	4	20	11	1	0	0	0	0	59	0	0	0	1	0	0	0	0	0	0	0	0
subtraction	227	.0502	5.4480	47.4	36	41	27	20	51	24	20	8	0	0	0	0	223	0	3	0	0	0	0	0	0	1	0	0	0
Subtraction	9	.0000	.1347	31.3	0	0	8	0	1	0	0	0	0	0	0	0	9	0	0	0	0	0	0	0	0	0	0	0	0
subtractions	9	.0000	.1347	31.3	1	0	2	0	3	2	1	0	0	0	0	0	9	0	0	0	0	0	0	0	0	0	0	0	0
subtracts	4	.0000	.0599	27.8	0	0	4	0	0	0	0	0	0	0	0	0	4	0	0	0	0	0	0	0	0	0	0	0	0
subtrahend	7	.0000	.1048	30.2	4	0	0	0	2	1	0	0	0	0	0	0	7	0	0	0	0	0	0	0	0	0	0	0	0
subtropical	4	.1505	.1615	32.1	0	0	1	0	1	1	1	0	0	0	0	0	0	1	0	0	0	0	0	0	0	0	3	0	0
subtropics	2	.2446	.1257	31.0	0	0	0	0	1	0	1	0	0	0	0	0	0	1	0	1	0	0	0	0	0	0	0	0	0
suburb	15	.6074	1.8817	42.7	2	0	4	1	1	3	3	1	1	0	0	1	0	3	0	0	0	0	0	0	2	1	3	4	0
suburban	17	.2520	1.0365	40.2	0	0	0	2	2	3	5	5	1	0	0	0	0	3	0	0	0	0	0	0	0	0	1	12	0
suburbs	24	.5636	2.8299	44.5	3	0	4	1	6	2	8	0	2	0	0	1	0	7	0	1	0	0	1	0	0	0	8	4	0
subversion	2	.0000	.0389	25.9	0	0	0	0	0	2	0	0	0	0	0	0	0	2	0	0	0	0	0	0	0	0	0	0	0
subversive	2	.2337	.1157	30.6	0	0	0	0	0	1	1	0	0	0	0	0	0	1	0	0	0	0	0	0	1	0	0	0	0
subway	37	.7533	5.7170	47.6	10	3	5	1	1	12	5	0	15	5	0	2	0	4	0	2	1	1	0	0	0	1	2	4	0
subways	14	.4026	1.3031	41.1	3	2	2	5	0	2	0	0	3	0	0	0	0	8	0	0	0	0	0	0	0	0	1	2	0
Succah	7	.0000	.3198	35.0	0	7	0	0	0	0	0	0	7	0	0	0	0	0	0	0	0	0	0	0	0	0	0	0	0
succeed	50	.7616	7.7167	48.9	0	5	6	1	13	12	12	1	8	2	0	5	0	13	0	4	0	0	2	0	1	6	5	4	0
succeeded	103	.7622	15.889	52.0	4	6	14	12	34	16	13	4	17	1	0	6	0	16	1	6	2	1	0	0	5	14	24	10	0
succeeding	12	.6886	1.6743	42.2	2	0	1	2	1	3	2	1	0	1	0	1	2	1	0	2	1	0	0	0	0	0	3	1	0
succeeds	7	.5918	.8523	39.3	0	1	1	0	3	1	1	0	0	0	0	2	0	1	1	1	0	0	0	0	0	1	1	0	0
success	242	.9114	43.750	56.4	13	14	34	33	63	43	32	10	45	9	2	7	1	35	8	12	14	3	8	2	7	31	18	40	0
successes	15	.6126	1.9001	42.8	0	1	0	1	4	7	2	0	2	0	0	1	1	1	0	0	2	0	0	0	0	1	5	2	0
successful	236	.9158	42.817	56.3	14	23	36	13	53	46	43	8	32	6	5	6	8	41	5	22	13	5	7	5	3	20	31	27	0
successfully	70	.8631	12.044	50.8	1	4	11	5	26	11	9	3	11	5	1	3	2	6	0	9	3	0	2	3	1	5	11	8	0
succession	49	.8036	7.9021	49.0	1	1	5	8	16	11	5	2	8	1	0	1	2	2	6	2	6	1	0	0	2	5	8	5	0
Succession	5	.2441	.3058	34.9	0	0	2	0	0	0	3	0	0	0	0	0	0	3	0	0	0	0	0	0	0	2	0	0	0
successive	35	.7738	5.4180	47.3	0	1	1	3	15	1	11	3	0	1	2	2	6	2	0	4	1	2	0	1	0	2	6	6	0
successively	3	.3762	.2479	33.9	0	0	0	0	1	0	1	1	0	0	0	0	0	0	0	1	0	0	0	0	1	0	1	0	0
successor	18	.5974	2.2340	43.5	1	1	3	1	2	6	2	2	1	2	0	0	0	5	0	1	0	0	0	0	0	5	3	1	0
successors	7	.2258	.3774	35.8	0	0	1	0	0	4	2	0	0	0	0	0	0	1	0	0	0	0	0	0	0	1	5	0	0
succinctly	2	.2442	.1134	30.5	0	0	0	0	2	0	0	0	0	1	0	0	0	0	0	0	0	0	0	0	0	0	0	1	0
succor	3	.3851	.2497	34.0	0	1	0	0	0	0	2	0	0	0	0	1	0	0	0	0	0	0	0	0	1	1	0	0	0
succotash	8	.4010	.7101	38.5	2	0	3	0	0	0	0	3	1	0	0	3	0	2	0	0	2	0	0	0	0	0	0	0	0
succulent	3	.3553	.2609	34.2	1	0	1	0	0	0	0	1	1	0	0	0	0	0	0	1	0	0	0	0	0	1	0	0	0
succumb	3	.3452	.2543	34.1	0	0	0	0	0	0	2	1	1	0	0	0	0	0	0	1	0	0	0	0	0	0	0	1	0
such	4223	.9537	795.09	69.0	375	457	517	539	907	674	608	146	701	280	40	199	293	453	135	651	161	53	130	107	136	228	406	250	0
suck	31	.6268	4.1128	46.1	11	2	4	4	7	2	1	0	11	0	0	1	0	1	0	6	0	0	0	0	2	2	7	1	0
sucked	26	.5385	3.0131	44.8	4	3	2	3	8	1	3	2	7	0	0	8	0	0	0	3	0	0	0	0	4	3	0	1	0
sucker	3	.2304	.1619	32.1	1	0	0	0	2	0	0	0	0	0	0	0	0	0	0	0	0	0	0	0	2	0	1	0	0
suckers	4	.2353	.2382	33.8	0	0	0	3	1	0	0	0	0	0	0	0	0	0	0	3	0	0	0	0	0	0	1	0	0
sucking	40	.7126	5.8126	47.6	9	2	3	4	12	4	5	1	7	0	1	6	0	1	0	7	0	0	0	2	6	3	7	0	0
sucks	10	.4339	.9977	40.0	3	1	1	1	3	0	0	1	3	0	0	0	0	1	0	4	0	0	0	0	0	0	2	0	0
suction	14	.5405	1.6398	42.1	0	2	4	0	4	2	0	2	4	0	0	0	0	0	0	3	0	0	0	0	0	3	1	3	0
Sudan	11	.5247	1.2587	41.0	2	0	1	2	3	3	0	0	3	0	0	0	0	4	0	0	0	0	0	0	1	1	2	0	0
Sudana	3	.0000	.1370	31.4	0	3	0	0	0	0	0	0	3	0	0	0	0	0	0	0	0	0	0	0	0	0	0	0	0
Sudanese	3	.0000	.0583	27.7	0	0	0	3	0	0	0	0	0	0	0	0	0	3	0	0	0	0	0	0	0	0	0	0	0

9B subpoints
7H Subragmanyan
7F subregion
7F subregions
9E subscribing
8H subscripts
7A subservience
5P subservient
9R subsidiaries
8A subsiding
5P subsidy
6A subsisted
8R subsisting
7Q subsists
9Q subspecies
6H SUBSTANCES
7B substand
7A substantial-looking
6A substantiating
7L Substitute
9Q subsystem
3P subtil
7N Subtil
7Q subtleties
8E subtrahends
7E subunits
7R Suburban
7R suburbanites
8F Subversive
8F subversives
9R subvert
4A SUCCESSFULLY
7Q successions
3P successor's
7R succinct
4A Succos
7Q succumbed
9Q succumbs
9J suck'd
XH suckled
6F Sucre

Word Type	F	D	U	SFI	3 Gr 3	4 Gr 4	5 Gr 5	6 Gr 6	7 Gr 7	8 Gr 8	9 Gr 9	X UnGr	A Read	B Eng & Gr	C Comp	D Lit	E Math	F Soc Stud	G Spell	H Sci	J Music	K Art	L Home Ec	M Shop	N Lib F	P Lib NF	Q Lib Ref	R Mag	S Rel
sudden	235	.8050	38.266	55.8	26	42	24	24	54	32	26	7	82	7	11	30	0	6	2	16	5	1	1	0	30	22	9	13	0
suddenly	993	.8367	167.94	62.3	184	206	147	128	165	89	56	18	488	37	16	73	2	40	2	29	13	4	2	2	116	99	17	53	0
suddenness	2	.1698	.1133	30.5	0	1	1	0	0	0	0	0	1	0	0	0	0	0	0	0	0	0	0	0	0	0	1	0	0
SUDHA	6	.0000	.0644	28.1	0	0	0	0	0	0	6	0	0	0	0	6	0	0	0	0	0	0	0	0	0	0	0	0	0
suds	12	.3842	1.0541	40.2	0	0	3	0	1	7	0	1	2	0	0	0	0	0	0	6	0	0	2	0	0	0	0	2	0
Suds	14	.2148	.9558	39.8	0	0	0	0	9	5	0	0	9	0	0	5	0	0	0	0	0	0	0	0	0	0	0	0	0
sue	10	.4771	1.0793	40.3	1	0	1	1	1	3	3	0	4	2	0	0	0	3	1	0	0	0	0	0	0	0	0	0	0
Sue	138	.6070	17.804	52.5	61	23	10	16	13	5	7	3	48	14	0	1	56	4	5	0	0	0	3	0	1	3	0	3	0
Sue's	20	.3844	1.8593	42.7	9	3	3	1	0	3	1	0	9	0	0	0	9	0	1	0	0	0	0	0	0	0	0	1	0
suede	3	.3319	.2114	33.3	0	0	1	0	0	1	1	0	0	0	0	0	0	0	1	0	0	0	1	0	0	0	0	1	0
suet	10	.6071	1.2464	41.0	2	0	2	4	1	1	0	0	1	2	0	1	0	0	1	0	0	0	1	0	0	1	3	0	0
suey	2	.2408	.1091	30.4	1	0	0	0	0	1	0	0	0	1	0	0	0	0	1	0	0	0	0	0	0	0	0	0	0
Suez	34	.3687	2.8625	44.6	0	0	0	12	11	3	8	0	2	0	0	0	0	21	0	0	0	0	0	0	3	0	0	8	0
suffer	55	.8298	9.1608	49.6	1	5	8	5	17	8	11	0	12	6	0	2	0	10	1	4	4	0	2	0	5	4	4	1	0
suffered	92	.7902	14.668	51.7	8	8	14	8	20	17	13	4	17	2	2	9	0	22	1	1	0	2	0	0	2	16	7	11	0
sufferer	3	.2196	.1554	31.9	0	0	0	0	1	0	2	0	0	0	0	2	0	0	0	0	0	0	0	0	1	0	0	0	0
suffering	64	.7909	10.223	50.1	2	5	8	8	18	13	6	4	14	2	0	4	1	7	1	7	1	3	0	0	4	9	3	8	0
sufferings	4	.4870	.4078	36.1	0	0	0	2	1	0	1	0	0	0	0	0	0	0	0	0	0	0	0	0	1	1	1	1	0
suffers	11	.5966	1.3548	41.3	1	1	0	2	3	2	2	0	0	1	0	3	0	2	1	3	0	0	0	0	0	0	0	1	0
suffice	7	.4780	.6932	38.4	0	0	0	2	3	0	1	1	0	1	1	0	0	0	0	0	0	0	0	0	1	0	3	1	0
suffices	2	.2346	.1166	30.7	0	0	0	0	0	0	0	2	0	0	0	0	0	0	0	1	0	0	0	0	0	0	0	1	0
sufficient	86	.8120	13.956	51.4	1	2	8	10	20	17	20	8	4	3	1	6	3	9	1	15	1	0	9	1	7	7	13	6	0
sufficiently	30	.8101	4.8693	46.9	1	1	2	3	7	6	4	6	3	0	0	1	0	3	0	6	1	1	1	1	2	2	6	3	0
suffix	428	.1031	12.623	51.0	4	46	77	97	80	105	19	0	22	33	0	0	0	0	372	1	0	0	0	0	0	0	0	0	0
suffixes	188	.1095	6.0399	47.8	1	27	27	34	53	43	3	0	18	13	0	0	0	0	157	0	0	0	0	0	0	0	0	0	0
suffocated	3	.2078	.1429	31.5	0	0	0	0	2	0	1	0	0	0	1	0	0	0	0	0	0	0	0	0	2	0	0	0	0
suffocating	2	.2446	.1122	30.5	0	0	0	0	1	1	0	0	0	0	0	1	0	0	0	0	0	0	0	0	0	0	1	0	0
suffocation	2	.1698	.1133	30.5	0	0	0	0	1	1	0	0	1	0	0	0	0	0	0	0	0	0	0	0	0	0	1	0	0
Suffolk	4	.3790	.3299	35.2	2	0	0	0	1	1	0	0	0	0	0	0	0	0	0	0	0	0	0	0	0	2	1	1	0
suffrage	6	.3473	.4627	36.7	0	0	0	0	1	5	0	0	0	0	1	0	0	3	0	0	0	0	0	0	0	0	2	0	0
sugar	574	.6702	79.146	59.0	107	74	104	93	91	32	63	10	70	9	0	12	10	116	9	167	4	0	70	0	20	27	33	27	0
Sugar	13	.2180	.7034	38.5	8	0	0	1	3	1	0	0	2	1	0	0	0	0	0	0	9	0	0	0	0	0	0	1	0
sugar-cane	2	.0000	.0914	29.6	0	1	1	0	0	0	0	0	2	0	0	0	0	0	0	0	0	0	0	0	0	0	0	0	0
sugar-rich	2	.0000	.0394	26.0	0	0	2	0	0	0	0	0	0	0	0	0	0	0	0	2	0	0	0	0	0	0	0	0	0
sugarcane	5	.2037	.2562	34.1	0	0	0	0	2	2	1	0	0	0	0	0	0	2	0	0	0	0	0	0	0	0	3	0	0
sugared	6	.2217	.3822	35.8	0	1	0	3	0	0	2	0	3	0	0	0	0	0	0	0	0	0	2	0	1	0	0	0	0
sugarhouse	2	.2446	.1142	30.6	0	1	0	1	0	0	0	0	0	0	0	0	0	0	0	0	0	0	0	0	1	0	0	1	0
sugars	19	.4509	1.8610	42.7	1	1	2	0	10	0	3	2	1	0	0	0	0	0	0	11	0	0	2	0	0	0	4	1	0
sugary	5	.1511	.1963	32.9	0	1	0	2	1	0	0	1	0	0	0	0	0	0	0	0	0	0	0	0	0	1	4	0	0
suggest	244	.7415	36.375	55.6	16	25	34	28	64	42	32	3	17	50	4	19	34	11	13	12	28	24	10	0	1	5	5	11	0
suggested	305	.9170	55.406	57.4	24	37	40	34	72	48	40	10	52	20	14	13	39	13	10	23	27	5	7	2	16	26	16	22	0
suggesting	28	.5567	3.1741	45.0	0	1	1	2	11	9	3	1	1	4	1	1	0	0	0	0	4	7	1	1	0	3	4	1	0
suggestion	40	.7105	5.8055	47.6	1	4	5	3	10	11	5	1	9	6	0	2	2	1	2	3	0	0	4	1	0	1	0	9	0
suggestions	117	.7611	17.876	52.5	3	12	26	17	15	13	28	3	11	24	4	1	1	18	7	4	4	6	18	5	1	5	3	5	0
suggestive	5	.4326	.4580	36.6	0	0	0	0	1	0	2	2	0	0	1	1	1	0	0	1	0	0	0	1	0	0	1	0	0
suggests	129	.8658	22.216	53.5	10	12	14	13	36	16	24	4	12	16	7	3	25	13	3	13	11	2	2	3	0	2	8	9	0
suh	12	.1358	.4380	36.4	0	2	0	0	1	1	8	0	0	0	0	10	0	0	0	0	0	0	0	0	0	2	0	0	0
suicidal	2	.1814	.1187	30.7	0	0	0	0	1	1	0	0	1	0	0	0	0	0	0	0	0	0	0	0	0	0	0	1	0
suicide	13	.3781	1.0837	40.3	0	0	0	0	3	1	4	5	1	0	0	0	0	0	0	0	0	0	0	0	0	2	4	6	0
suicides	9	.0909	.2671	34.3	0	0	0	0	1	0	1	7	0	0	0	0	0	0	0	1	0	0	0	0	0	0	0	8	0
suing	3	.2435	.2274	33.6	0	0	0	0	0	2	1	0	2	0	0	0	0	1	0	0	0	0	0	0	0	0	0	0	0
suit	292	.8398	49.447	56.9	49	65	28	39	38	34	32	7	132	12	2	21	0	9	5	24	6	5	23	3	12	16	6	16	0
Suit	2	.0000	.0243	23.9	0	0	0	0	0	0	0	2	0	0	0	0	0	0	0	0	0	0	0	0	0	0	0	2	0
suitable	143	.7607	21.823	53.4	1	7	18	13	39	26	34	5	10	16	2	8	2	14	2	17	7	4	27	5	5	3	15	6	0
suitably	2	.1892	.0858	29.3	0	0	0	0	0	0	2	0	0	1	0	0	0	0	0	0	0	0	1	0	0	0	0	0	0
suitcase	36	.6938	5.2556	47.2	4	4	3	14	5	5	1	0	21	0	0	4	1	1	1	0	0	0	1	0	2	1	0	4	0
suitcases	10	.4706	1.0517	40.2	6	1	2	0	1	0	0	0	3	0	1	1	0	4	0	0	0	0	0	0	0	0	1	1	0
suite	26	.4281	2.3204	43.7	4	3	8	0	2	7	1	1	0	0	1	0	1	0	1	0	17	0	0	0	2	0	1	3	0
Suite	18	.0631	.3618	35.6	8	3	0	3	4	0	0	0	0	0	0	0	0	0	0	0	17	0	0	0	0	0	1	0	0
suited	71	.8418	11.921	50.8	5	8	16	8	19	3	11	1	7	1	2	3	0	17	1	4	5	1	6	3	1	8	8	4	0
suites	10	.2063	.4899	36.9	2	0	1	1	4	1	1	0	0	0	0	0	0	0	0	0	6	0	0	0	0	4	0	0	0
suiting	3	.1352	.0947	29.8	0	0	0	1	1	0	1	0	0	1	0	0	0	0	0	0	0	0	2	0	0	0	0	0	0
suitor	11	.4778	1.2268	40.9	0	1	0	7	2	0	1	0	7	0	0	1	0	0	0	0	0	0	0	0	0	2	0	1	0
suitors	13	.3586	1.1181	40.5	0	1	0	4	1	1	6	0	5	0	0	6	0	0	0	0	0	0	0	0	1	0	1	0	0
suits	108	.6597	14.839	51.7	16	29	14	10	12	17	10	0	34	4	0	0	14	7	0	12	2	0	16	3	2	8	1	5	0
Sukarno	6	.1125	.1964	32.9	0	0	1	0	0	5	0	0	0	0	0	0	0	1	0	0	0	0	0	0	0	0	5	0	0
Sukeforth	5	.0000	.2284	33.6	0	0	0	0	0	0	5	0	5	0	0	0	0	0	0	0	0	0	0	0	0	0	0	0	0
Sukey	3	.2261	.2131	33.3	0	2	1	0	0	0	0	0	2	0	0	0	0	0	0	0	0	0	0	0	1	0	0	0	0
sukiyaki	6	.4701	.6471	38.1	0	1	5	0	0	0	0	0	3	0	0	0	0	1	1	0	0	0	0	0	0	0	1	0	0
Sukkah	3	.0000	.0243	23.8	3	0	0	0	0	0	0	0	0	0	0	0	0	0	0	0	3	0	0	0	0	0	0	0	0
Sukkot	2	.0000	.0162	22.1	2	0	0	0	0	0	0	0	0	0	0	0	0	0	0	0	2	0	0	0	0	0	0	0	0
sulfa	2	.0000	.0394	26.0	0	2	0	0	0	0	0	0	0	0	0	0	0	0	0	2	0	0	0	0	0	0	0	0	0
sulfate	15	.1880	.7794	38.9	0	0	0	0	0	10	4	1	0	0	0	0	0	0	0	13	0	0	0	0	0	0	2	0	0
sulfide	9	.0713	.3150	35.0	1	0	3	2	0	1	2	0	1	0	0	0	0	0	0	8	0	0	0	0	0	0	0	0	0
sulfides	4	.2160	.2724	34.4	2	0	0	0	0	1	1	0	2	0	0	0	0	0	0	2	0	0	0	0	0	0	0	0	0
sulfur	49	.3193	3.7006	45.7	0	2	13	10	3	14	7	0	0	0	0	0	0	7	0	37	0	0	0	0	0	0	4	1	0
sulfuric	14	.3761	1.1805	40.7	0	0	3	3	0	2	6	0	0	0	0	0	5	0	0	7	0	0	0	0	0	0	2	0	0
sulid	3	.0000	.0365	25.6	0	0	0	0	3	0	0	0	0	0	0	0	0	0	0	0	0	0	0	0	0	0	0	3	0
Suliram	3	.0000	.0243	23.8	0	0	0	3	0	0	0	0	0	0	0	0	0	0	0	0	3	0	0	0	0	0	0	0	0
sulk	2	.0000	.0914	29.6	1	1	0	0	0	0	0	0	2	0	0	0	0	0	0	0	0	0	0	0	0	0	0	0	0
sulkily	8	.4223	.7747	38.9	1	0	0	1	4	2	0	0	3	1	0	3	0	0	0	0	0	0	0	0	1	0	0	0	0
sulking	5	.2445	.3875	35.9	2	1	0	0	2	0	0	0	4	0	0	0	0	0	0	0	0	0	0	0	0	0	0	1	0
sulky	3	.3271	.2364	33.7	0	1	0	0	1	0	1	0	1	1	0	0	0	0	0	0	1	0	0	0	0	0	0	0	0
sullen	22	.6378	2.9539	44.7	0	0	6	2	8	4	2	0	8	1	0	4	0	0	0	1	0	0	0	0	2	3	0	3	0
sullenly	8	.5479	.9555	39.8	1	1	2	0	2	1	0	1	3	0	0	1	0	0	0	1	0	0	0	0	1	2	0	0	0
Sullivan	47	.6347	6.2873	48.0	0	5	15	6	11	8	2	0	17	4	0	3	0	2	0	0	2	0	0	0	0	11	0	8	0
Sullivan's	6	.5076	.6502	38.1	0	0	2	1	1	0	2	0	1	2	0	1	0	0	0	0	0	0	0	0	0	1	0	1	0
sulphur	17	.6014	2.1245	43.3	5	1	3	5	2	0	1	0	1	0	0	0	0	5	0	3	0	1	0	1	0	5	1	0	0
sultan	3	.0000	.0314	25.0	0	3	0	0	0	0	0	0	0	0	0	0	0	0	0	0	0	0	0	0	0	0	3	0	0
Sultan	41	.4043	3.8349	45.8	0	12	10	6	3	9	1	0	14	0	0	10	0	3	0	0	0	0	0	0	14	0	0	0	0
Sultan's	8	.1998	.4155	36.2	0	1	4	2	0	1	0	0	1	0	0	1	0	0	0	0	0	0	0	0	6	0	0	0	0
Sultana	4	.3391	.3045	34.8	1	0	2	0	1	0	0	0	0	0	0	0	0	1	0	0	0	0	0	0	2	1	0	0	0
Sultans	4	.2183	.2285	33.6	0	0	1	0	3	0	0	0	0	0	0	0	0	3	0	0	0	0	0	0	0	0	0	0	0
sultry	6	.5160	.6584	38.2	0	2	0	0	3	0	0	1	1	0	0	0	0	0	0	0	1	0	0	0	0	1	0	2	0
Sulzer	4	.0000	.0789	29.0	0	0	0	0	0	0	0	4	0	0	0	1	0	0	0	4	0	0	0	0	0	0	0	0	0

6P Sudden
6F Sudetes
9D Sudha
4Q Sudras
8R Suede
9F sues
8F sufferable
8F sufferage
9D sufferance
7H sufficed
9R suffit
8G Suffixes
7Q suffocates
8F suffrages
5Q suffruticosa
7P suffusions
7G sug-
9J Sugar-Plum
6H sugar-box
9R sugar-coated
6R sugar-coating
7N sugar-hogshead
6H sugar-maple
5F sugar-mill
8F sugar-plantation
7F sugar-producing
6A sugar-water
8R sugarfree
7D Suggett
6R Suisun
9L suitability
5P Sukenik
8Q Sukkur
XH Sul
8Q Sulawesi
8Q sulfadiazine
9P Sulivan
3A sulked
8D sulled
4F Sulo
3P sulphur-bottom
6B sulphur-bottomed
XH sulphuric
6P sulphurous
5P sultanate
9F sultans
5R sultry-voiced
3Q Sulu
XH Sulzer's

Word Type	F	D	U	SFI	3 Gr 3	4 Gr 4	5 Gr 5	6 Gr 6	7 Gr 7	8 Gr 8	9 Gr 9	X UnGr	A Read	B Eng & Gr	C Comp	D Lit	E Math	F Soc Stud	G Spell	H Sci	J Music	K Art	L Home Ec	M Shop	N Lib F	P Lib NF	Q Lib Ref	R Mag	S Rel
sum	800	.2056	42.094	56.2	92	127	141	98	94	127	101	20	16	3	0	10	731	3	2	3	0	0	3	1	10	5	5	8	0
Sum	17	.1152	.5971	37.8	0	16	0	1	0	0	0	0	0	0	0	0	0	0	0	0	1	0	0	0	0	16	0	0	0
SUM	3	.0000	.1370	31.4	0	0	0	3	0	0	0	0	3	0	0	0	0	0	0	0	0	0	0	0	0	0	0	0	0
sumac	6	.3709	.5281	37.2	0	2	0	1	3	0	0	0	2	1	0	0	0	0	0	2	0	0	0	1	0	0	0	0	0
sumach	2	.0000	.0394	26.0	0	2	0	0	0	0	0	0	0	0	0	0	0	0	0	2	0	0	0	0	0	0	0	0	0
sumacs	2	.1787	.1174	30.7	0	1	0	0	0	1	0	0	1	0	0	0	0	0	0	0	0	0	0	0	1	0	0	0	0
Sumatra	8	.3129	.5707	37.6	0	0	2	1	2	3	0	0	0	0	0	0	0	3	0	0	0	0	0	0	0	1	4	0	0
Sumer	2	.2285	.1129	30.5	0	0	0	0	1	0	1	0	0	0	0	0	0	1	0	0	0	0	0	0	0	0	1	0	0
Sumerian	4	.2709	.2503	34.0	0	0	0	1	1	1	1	0	0	0	0	0	0	2	0	0	0	1	0	0	0	0	1	0	0
Sumerians	7	.3619	.5540	37.4	0	0	0	0	3	1	0	3	0	3	0	0	0	2	2	0	0	0	0	0	0	0	0	0	0
summaries	2	.1812	.0838	29.2	0	0	0	0	0	0	2	0	0	0	0	0	0	0	0	0	0	0	1	0	0	0	0	1	0
summarily	3	.3350	.2478	33.9	0	0	0	0	1	1	1	0	1	0	0	0	0	1	0	0	0	0	0	0	0	0	1	0	0
summarize	6	.4418	.5909	37.7	0	0	1	1	1	1	2	0	1	1	0	0	2	2	0	0	0	0	0	0	0	0	0	0	0
summarized	9	.6242	1.1498	40.6	0	0	1	0	3	2	3	0	0	1	0	0	0	2	0	1	0	0	1	0	0	1	1	2	0
summarizes	6	.3060	.4399	36.4	0	0	0	2	1	1	2	0	2	0	2	0	1	0	0	0	0	0	1	0	0	0	0	0	0
summary	39	.5422	4.4854	46.5	0	1	2	6	11	14	4	1	7	18	0	1	1	2	2	4	1	0	0	0	0	0	0	3	0
Summary	13	.0794	.3024	34.8	0	3	3	3	3	1	0	0	0	0	0	1	0	0	12	0	0	0	0	0	0	0	0	0	0
summed	13	.5498	1.4759	41.7	3	1	1	3	0	3	2	0	0	4	0	2	0	0	0	1	0	0	0	0	0	1	1	4	0
summer	1048	.8924	186.27	62.7	253	205	154	138	123	66	79	30	251	47	17	54	19	204	16	105	20	0	12	1	54	108	31	109	0
Summer	14	.5236	1.5946	42.0	3	2	1	4	3	0	0	1	5	4	0	1	0	0	0	0	2	0	0	0	0	0	0	2	0
summer's	15	.6793	2.1045	43.2	3	4	2	3	1	0	2	0	4	1	0	1	0	0	0	1	1	0	0	0	3	1	0	3	0
Summer's	3	.1409	.1472	31.7	2	0	0	1	0	0	0	0	1	0	0	0	0	0	0	0	0	0	0	0	0	2	0	0	0
summers	88	.5796	10.780	50.3	9	12	21	25	7	2	12	0	11	2	0	1	0	50	0	3	1	0	0	0	5	1	9	5	0
Summers	5	.0000	.2284	33.6	2	0	3	0	0	0	0	0	5	0	0	0	0	0	0	0	0	0	0	0	0	0	0	0	0
Summerset	2	.0000	.0914	29.6	0	0	0	2	0	0	0	0	2	0	0	0	0	0	0	0	0	0	0	0	0	0	0	0	0
summertime	24	.6701	3.3463	45.2	5	6	3	2	4	0	0	4	7	2	0	0	0	5	0	1	1	0	0	0	5	1	0	2	0
summing	3	.2143	.1568	32.0	0	0	1	1	0	0	0	1	0	0	0	0	0	0	0	0	0	0	0	0	0	1	0	2	0
summit	33	.7259	4.8629	46.9	2	0	2	4	10	7	8	0	5	2	2	5	0	2	0	2	0	0	0	0	3	3	5	4	0
Summit	8	.3856	.7620	38.8	0	1	0	0	5	0	2	0	5	0	1	1	0	0	0	0	0	0	0	0	0	0	0	1	0
summits	10	.4631	1.0073	40.0	1	0	1	1	4	2	1	0	2	0	0	2	0	0	0	0	0	0	0	0	0	1	4	1	0
summon	12	.6063	1.5357	41.9	1	1	0	5	1	3	1	0	3	0	0	1	0	3	0	0	1	0	0	0	1	3	0	0	0
summoned	23	.6999	3.3039	45.2	0	2	4	1	8	4	3	1	5	0	0	2	0	3	0	1	1	0	0	0	5	1	1	4	0
summons	4	.4419	.3922	35.9	1	0	1	0	1	1	0	0	1	0	0	0	0	0	0	0	1	0	0	0	0	1	0	1	0
Sumner	11	.4822	1.2258	40.9	0	2	5	1	1	2	0	0	6	0	0	0	0	2	0	0	0	0	0	0	0	2	0	1	0
sumptuous	2	.1814	.1187	30.7	0	0	0	0	1	1	0	0	1	0	0	0	0	0	0	0	0	0	0	0	0	0	0	1	0
sums	319	.0877	9.9812	50.0	57	85	58	40	49	18	10	2	4	0	0	2	302	8	0	0	0	0	0	0	2	0	1	0	0
Sumter	14	.2391	.8712	39.4	0	3	8	0	1	2	0	0	1	0	0	0	0	11	0	0	0	0	0	0	0	0	2	0	0
sun	1977	.8957	352.58	65.5	568	362	205	260	277	119	115	71	425	47	12	117	38	201	21	631	26	6	3	16	80	211	82	59	2
Sun	124	.6592	16.877	52.3	41	12	22	12	20	4	8	5	12	2	0	14	0	10	0	59	4	0	0	0	6	3	2	12	0
SUN	2	.0000	.0394	26.0	2	0	0	0	0	0	0	0	0	0	0	0	0	0	0	2	0	0	0	0	0	0	0	0	0
SunCity	2	.0000	.0243	23.9	0	0	0	0	0	0	0	2	0	0	0	0	0	0	0	0	0	0	0	0	0	0	0	2	0
Sun-Dance	4	.0000	.1827	32.6	4	0	0	0	0	0	0	0	4	0	0	0	0	0	0	0	0	0	0	0	0	0	0	0	0
sun-baked	3	.3350	.2478	33.9	2	0	0	1	0	0	0	0	1	0	0	0	0	1	0	0	0	0	0	0	0	0	1	0	0
sun-bleached	2	.2152	.1357	31.3	0	0	0	1	1	0	0	0	1	0	0	0	0	1	0	0	0	0	0	0	0	0	0	0	0
sun-browned	2	.1787	.1174	30.7	1	1	0	0	0	0	0	0	1	0	0	0	0	0	0	0	0	0	0	0	1	0	0	0	0
sun-drenched	2	.2285	.1129	30.5	1	0	0	0	1	0	0	0	0	0	0	0	0	1	0	0	0	0	0	0	0	0	1	0	0
sun-dried	4	.3310	.2973	34.7	0	0	0	1	1	1	1	0	0	0	0	2	0	1	0	0	0	0	0	0	0	1	0	0	0
sun-flecked	2	.2433	.1158	30.6	0	0	0	2	0	0	0	0	0	0	0	0	0	0	0	0	0	0	0	0	0	1	0	1	0
sun-god	3	.2028	.1988	33.0	0	2	0	1	0	0	0	0	2	0	0	0	0	0	0	0	1	0	0	0	0	0	0	0	0
sun-up	3	.0000	.1370	31.4	0	1	1	1	0	0	0	0	3	0	0	0	0	0	0	0	0	0	0	0	0	0	0	0	0
sun-warmed	4	.2142	.2512	34.0	0	0	2	1	0	1	0	0	2	0	0	0	0	0	0	0	0	1	0	0	0	0	0	1	0
sun's	88	.6201	11.378	50.6	15	16	6	10	31	2	3	5	11	2	0	1	0	4	0	45	0	0	1	7	2	5	8	2	0
Sun's	5	.0000	.0986	29.9	4	0	1	0	0	0	0	0	0	0	0	0	0	0	0	5	0	0	0	0	0	0	0	0	0
sunai	2	.0000	.0914	29.6	0	0	2	0	0	0	0	0	2	0	0	0	0	0	0	0	0	0	0	0	0	0	0	0	0
sunbaked	2	.1717	.1142	30.6	0	0	0	0	2	0	0	0	1	0	0	1	0	0	0	0	0	0	0	0	0	0	0	0	0
sunbeams	4	.3812	.3773	35.8	2	1	0	1	0	0	0	0	2	0	0	0	0	0	0	1	0	0	0	0	0	1	0	0	0
sunbonnet	4	.4533	.4015	36.0	1	0	1	0	2	0	0	0	1	0	0	1	0	0	0	0	0	0	0	0	1	1	0	0	0
sunburn	14	.4839	1.4851	41.7	1	0	2	1	1	1	2	6	3	0	0	1	0	0	0	4	0	0	0	0	0	0	1	5	0
sunburned	7	.3869	.6852	38.4	0	1	1	3	1	0	1	0	5	0	0	1	0	0	0	0	0	0	0	0	0	0	1	0	0
sunburst	2	.2441	.1127	30.5	0	0	0	1	1	0	0	0	0	0	0	0	0	0	0	0	0	0	0	0	1	0	1	0	0
sundae	6	.4801	.6535	38.2	0	1	0	4	0	0	0	1	3	1	0	0	0	0	1	0	0	0	0	0	0	0	0	1	0
sundaes	4	.2289	.2155	33.3	1	2	1	0	0	0	0	0	0	0	0	0	2	0	2	0	0	0	0	0	0	0	0	0	0
Sunday	209	.8242	34.603	55.4	43	47	21	9	35	28	17	9	50	9	1	15	14	12	5	2	12	0	1	0	25	30	4	28	1
Sunday-school	3	.2283	.1611	32.1	0	0	0	0	3	0	0	0	0	1	0	0	0	0	0	0	0	0	0	0	2	0	0	0	0
Sundays	21	.6515	2.8415	44.5	2	4	4	0	4	2	0	5	5	0	0	1	1	2	0	0	1	0	0	0	6	3	0	2	0
sundial	6	.3674	.5480	37.4	0	1	3	0	2	0	0	0	3	0	0	0	2	0	0	0	0	0	0	0	0	1	0	0	0
sundials	3	.2197	.2090	33.2	0	0	2	0	0	0	1	0	2	0	0	0	0	0	0	0	0	0	0	0	0	0	1	0	0
sundown	24	.7028	3.5022	45.4	1	5	6	4	5	1	2	0	10	3	0	1	0	0	0	2	2	0	0	0	3	2	1	0	0
sundry	2	.0000	.0243	23.9	0	0	0	0	1	0	1	0	0	0	0	0	0	0	0	0	0	0	0	0	0	0	0	2	0
sunfish	10	.3028	.6648	38.2	1	7	0	0	1	0	1	0	0	0	2	0	0	0	0	0	0	0	0	0	0	0	1	7	0
sunflower	23	.4815	2.4281	43.9	4	8	0	9	0	0	1	1	3	0	0	0	0	0	0	14	0	0	0	0	2	1	1	2	0
Sunflower	3	.0000	.1370	31.4	0	0	0	3	0	0	0	0	3	0	0	0	0	0	0	0	0	0	0	0	0	0	0	0	0
sunflowers	11	.4007	1.0221	40.1	0	1	1	7	2	0	0	0	2	0	0	0	0	2	0	6	0	0	0	0	1	0	0	0	0
sung	260	.1630	10.406	50.2	23	45	48	69	32	18	24	1	7	10	0	1	0	1	1	0	223	0	0	0	1	8	6	2	0
SUNG	4	.0000	.0323	25.1	0	0	0	4	0	0	0	0	0	0	0	0	0	0	0	0	4	0	0	0	0	0	0	0	0
sunglasses	8	.3469	.6730	38.3	3	1	1	1	2	0	0	0	3	2	0	0	0	0	0	0	0	0	0	0	0	0	0	3	0
sunk	44	.8307	7.3809	48.7	1	15	3	5	12	5	3	0	19	2	1	4	0	3	2	1	0	0	0	1	4	4	1	2	0
sunken	16	.6563	2.2200	43.5	5	0	4	1	4	1	1	0	7	1	0	1	0	2	0	1	0	0	0	0	1	3	0	0	0
sunless	3	.3875	.2489	34.0	0	0	1	1	0	0	1	0	0	1	0	1	0	0	0	0	0	0	0	0	1	0	0	0	0
sunlight	288	.7955	46.307	56.7	81	68	28	44	37	19	5	6	52	7	6	8	1	17	1	136	1	3	3	1	11	23	8	10	0
sunlit	12	.5266	1.3720	41.4	0	5	1	2	0	0	3	1	3	0	1	1	0	0	0	5	0	0	0	0	0	1	0	1	0
sunned	3	.2120	.1548	31.9	1	0	0	0	1	1	0	0	0	0	0	0	0	0	0	0	0	0	0	0	2	1	0	0	0
sunnies	2	.0000	.0290	24.6	0	2	0	0	0	0	0	0	0	0	0	0	0	0	0	0	0	0	0	0	0	2	0	0	0
sunning	6	.5162	.6598	38.2	1	1	1	1	1	1	0	0	1	0	0	0	0	0	0	1	0	0	1	0	0	1	1	1	0
sunny	116	.8889	20.531	53.1	39	26	6	16	11	11	4	3	23	6	2	9	0	19	1	21	2	2	2	0	4	14	4	7	0
Sunny	9	.0829	.2993	34.8	2	0	0	0	0	7	0	0	2	0	0	7	0	0	0	0	0	0	0	0	0	0	0	0	0
Sunnyside	4	.1170	.1302	31.1	2	0	0	0	0	0	2	0	0	0	2	0	0	2	0	0	0	0	0	0	0	0	0	0	0
sunrise	50	.8280	8.3353	49.2	3	16	12	5	5	5	2	2	14	3	1	3	0	5	1	9	2	0	0	0	5	4	0	3	0
Sunrise	7	.2946	.4911	36.9	2	0	3	0	2	0	0	0	1	0	0	0	4	0	0	0	2	0	0	0	0	0	0	0	0
suns	8	.5647	.9898	40.0	0	1	3	2	1	1	0	0	4	0	0	0	1	0	0	0	0	0	0	0	1	1	1	0	0
Suns	4	.0000	.0486	26.9	0	0	0	0	0	4	0	0	0	0	0	0	0	0	0	0	0	0	0	0	0	0	0	4	0
sunset	75	.8208	12.395	50.9	16	14	9	8	18	2	6	2	19	4	3	4	0	6	0	17	4	1	0	0	4	6	1	6	0
Sunset	5	.2445	.3864	35.9	3	0	0	1	0	0	1	0	4	0	0	1	0	0	0	0	0	0	0	0	0	0	0	0	0
sunsets	9	.3813	.8759	39.4	2	0	2	2	2	0	0	1	6	0	0	0	0	0	0	2	0	0	0	0	0	0	0	1	0

4P Sum'll	8R summerized	7N sun-colored	3P sun-reflecting	4A Sunday-go-to-meeting	7Q sunlike
4P Sum's	8J Summertime	XR sun-cooked	9D sun-seeking	7N Sunday-like	9Q Sunni
4H sumachs	5Q sumo	8B sun-cracked	9D sun-split	6J sunder	7F sunnier
3P Sumbawa	6N sumpin'	9Q sun-diety	3N sun-suit	7A sundered	9Q Sunnite
7N sumfn	3E Sums	7A sun-hardened	4D sun-tan	7Q sunfishes	8D Sunny's
8R summa	8Q Sumual	8A sun-heat	8P sun-worshiping	7D sunflower-crown	8D sunrays
7H summarization	7D sun-and-wind	6R sun-heated	5R sunbathing	8K Sunflowers	7D sunsheen
9H summarizing	5F sun-bathing	XR sun-javelins	4C sunbeam	XQ Sung	7R sunshield
6N summation	8A sun-blackened	6R sun-kilned	5N sunbonnets	7R Sunizona	
6R summer-resident	6P sun-bright	8N sun-kissed	7F Sunda	3A Sunken	
4A summerhouse	6R sun-bronzed	7R sun-measurement	7F Sundanese	6A sunlamps	

Word Type	F	D	U	SFI	3 Gr 3	4 Gr 4	5 Gr 5	6 Gr 6	7 Gr 7	8 Gr 8	9 Gr 9	X UnGr	A Read	B Eng & Gr	C Comp	D Lit	E Math	F Soc Stud	G Spell	H Sci	J Music	K Art	L Home Ec	M Shop	N Lib F	P Lib NF	Q Lib Ref	R Mag	S Rel
sunshine	133	.8223	22.049	53.4	29	28	13	24	18	12	3	6	35	3	0	5	0	22	1	27	4	0	2	0	7	17	4	6	0
Sunshine	4	.3354	.3295	35.2	0	1	3	0	0	0	0	0	1	0	0	0	0	2	0	0	0	0	0	0	0	1	0	0	0
sunshiny	4	.0974	.1495	31.7	0	3	0	0	1	0	0	0	1	0	0	0	0	0	0	0	0	0	0	0	3	0	0	0	0
sunspot	2	.2160	.1362	31.3	0	0	0	1	1	0	0	0	1	0	0	0	0	0	0	1	0	0	0	0	0	0	0	0	0
sunspots	11	.2677	.7270	38.6	0	3	0	0	7	0	0	1	0	0	0	0	0	0	0	9	0	0	0	0	0	1	1	0	0
suntan	6	.3822	.5664	37.5	1	1	0	2	0	2	0	0	3	1	0	0	0	0	0	2	0	0	0	0	0	0	0	0	0
sunup	12	.5949	1.5140	41.8	2	3	3	0	2	2	0	0	4	0	0	3	0	0	0	0	1	0	0	0	1	2	1	0	0
sup	4	.3606	.3539	35.5	0	0	1	0	2	0	1	0	2	0	0	1	0	0	1	0	0	0	0	0	0	0	0	0	0
super	21	.6170	2.6818	44.3	1	2	3	9	2	2	2	0	3	0	0	2	0	2	3	1	0	0	1	0	1	0	0	8	0
Super	9	.2105	.4966	37.0	2	0	0	1	4	1	0	1	1	0	0	0	0	2	0	0	0	0	0	0	0	0	0	6	0
Super-Duper	23	.2110	1.5417	41.9	0	14	9	0	0	0	0	0	14	0	0	0	0	0	0	0	0	0	0	0	9	0	0	0	0
Super-Duper's	2	.0000	.0234	23.7	0	0	2	0	0	0	0	0	0	0	0	0	0	0	0	0	0	0	0	0	2	0	0	0	0
Super-Lite	10	.0000	.1215	30.8	0	0	0	10	0	0	0	0	0	0	0	0	0	0	0	0	0	0	0	0	0	0	0	10	0
superb	18	.5980	2.2177	43.5	1	0	0	1	8	4	4	0	1	0	0	0	0	2	0	0	1	1	0	0	0	4	4	5	0
superbly	6	.3940	.5012	37.0	0	0	1	0	2	1	1	1	0	0	0	0	0	0	0	0	0	1	0	0	1	0	1	3	0
supercold	2	.0000	.0394	26.0	0	0	0	0	2	0	0	0	0	0	0	0	0	0	0	2	0	0	0	0	0	0	0	0	0
superconducting	2	.0000	.0243	23.9	0	0	0	0	2	0	0	0	0	0	0	0	0	0	0	0	0	0	0	0	0	0	0	2	0
superconductors	3	.1277	.1363	31.3	1	0	0	0	2	0	0	0	1	0	0	0	0	0	0	0	0	0	0	0	0	0	0	2	0
superficial	9	.4106	.8102	39.1	0	0	2	0	2	4	0	1	1	0	0	0	0	0	0	0	0	0	0	0	0	2	3	3	0
superficially	3	.2321	.1635	32.1	0	0	0	0	1	0	1	1	0	0	0	0	0	0	0	0	0	0	0	0	0	0	1	2	0
superheated	2	.0000	.0394	26.0	0	0	0	0	0	0	2	0	0	0	0	0	0	0	0	2	0	0	0	0	0	0	0	0	0
superheterodyne	3	.0000	.0076	18.8	0	0	0	0	0	3	0	0	0	0	0	0	0	0	0	0	0	0	0	3	0	0	0	0	0
superhighway	28	.2786	1.9175	42.8	7	15	0	1	2	2	0	1	1	1	0	0	0	22	0	0	0	0	0	0	0	0	2	4	0
superhighways	6	.3105	.4058	36.1	1	1	0	0	1	2	0	1	0	0	0	0	0	1	0	0	0	0	0	2	0	0	0	1	0
superimpose	2	.1259	.0687	28.4	0	0	0	0	1	0	1	0	0	0	0	0	0	1	0	0	0	0	0	1	0	0	0	0	0
superimposed	6	.4311	.5437	37.4	0	0	2	1	1	0	2	0	0	0	0	0	0	0	0	0	0	0	0	1	0	1	2	2	0
superimposing	2	.0000	.0050	17.0	0	0	0	0	0	0	2	0	0	0	0	0	0	0	0	0	0	0	0	2	0	0	0	0	0
superintendent	20	.6131	2.5356	44.0	4	1	0	0	6	2	6	1	2	1	0	0	0	3	1	0	0	0	0	0	4	1	1	7	0
superintendents	4	.2352	.2332	33.7	0	0	0	0	1	0	3	0	0	0	0	0	0	2	0	0	0	0	0	0	0	0	0	2	0
superintends	2	.0000	.0389	25.9	0	0	0	0	0	2	0	0	0	0	0	0	0	2	0	0	0	0	0	0	0	0	0	0	0
superior	53	.8431	8.9233	49.5	1	1	1	6	21	10	10	3	8	1	1	10	0	6	0	2	4	0	1	1	3	3	5	8	0
Superior	36	.4556	3.6333	45.6	3	3	16	3	3	5	2	1	4	0	0	2	2	24	0	1	0	0	0	0	0	0	2	1	0
superiority	24	.5906	2.9381	44.7	0	0	5	0	7	5	7	0	1	0	0	5	0	5	0	1	0	0	0	0	0	7	3	2	0
superiors	4	.1814	.2373	33.8	0	0	0	1	2	1	0	0	2	0	0	0	0	0	0	0	0	0	0	0	0	0	0	2	0
superlative	27	.3911	2.2152	43.5	0	0	7	0	7	0	12	1	0	11	7	2	0	0	5	1	0	0	0	0	0	0	0	1	0
superlatives	5	.4482	.4685	36.7	0	0	2	0	1	2	0	0	0	0	0	1	0	0	1	0	0	0	1	0	0	2	0	0	0
supermarket	26	.7422	3.9399	46.0	9	3	3	3	5	1	1	1	6	1	0	0	4	4	1	3	0	0	0	0	0	1	3	3	0
supermarkets	15	.5213	1.6677	42.2	4	1	3	2	1	2	0	2	1	0	0	0	1	7	0	1	0	0	0	0	0	0	2	3	0
supermen	2	.0000	.0914	29.6	0	0	0	1	0	1	0	0	2	0	0	0	0	0	0	0	0	0	0	0	0	0	0	0	0
supernatural	15	.5792	1.8212	42.6	0	0	2	3	6	1	3	0	3	0	0	4	0	0	0	0	2	0	0	0	3	2	1	0	0
supersaturated	2	.0000	.0045	16.5	0	0	0	0	2	0	0	0	0	0	2	0	0	0	0	0	0	0	0	0	0	0	0	0	0
superseded	3	.0000	.0314	25.0	0	0	0	0	1	0	2	0	0	0	0	0	0	0	0	0	0	0	0	0	0	0	3	0	0
superset	11	.0000	.1647	32.2	0	0	8	3	0	0	0	0	0	0	0	0	11	0	0	0	0	0	0	0	0	0	0	0	0
supersonic	10	.6405	1.3208	41.2	4	0	0	0	4	1	1	0	1	1	0	1	0	0	0	2	0	0	0	0	0	3	1	1	0
superstar	2	.0000	.0243	23.9	0	0	0	0	0	1	0	1	0	0	0	0	0	0	0	0	0	0	0	0	0	0	0	2	0
superstars	2	.0000	.0243	23.9	0	1	0	0	1	0	0	0	0	0	0	0	0	0	0	0	0	0	0	0	0	0	0	2	0
superstition	19	.7301	2.8292	44.5	0	1	0	4	6	3	3	2	4	1	0	3	0	0	0	5	1	0	1	0	1	0	1	2	0
Superstition	3	.0000	.1370	31.4	0	0	3	0	0	0	0	0	3	0	0	0	0	0	0	0	0	0	0	0	0	0	0	0	0
superstitions	16	.5955	2.0106	43.0	1	1	2	6	1	1	2	2	4	3	0	1	0	1	0	2	0	0	0	0	0	1	4	0	0
superstitious	14	.6575	1.9187	42.8	1	3	1	2	2	1	0	4	4	0	0	1	0	0	0	2	0	0	0	0	1	2	1	3	0
superstructure	2	.1698	.1133	30.5	1	0	0	0	0	0	1	0	1	0	0	0	0	0	0	0	0	0	0	0	0	0	1	0	0
supertrees	5	.0000	.0608	27.8	5	0	0	0	0	0	0	0	0	0	0	0	0	0	0	0	0	0	0	0	0	0	0	5	0
supervise	9	.5782	1.1070	40.4	1	0	2	0	4	1	1	0	3	0	0	1	0	0	1	0	0	0	1	0	0	2	0	1	0
supervised	8	.5597	.9387	39.7	1	0	1	0	3	1	2	0	1	2	0	1	0	0	0	1	0	0	0	0	0	1	2	0	0
supervises	6	.3492	.4786	36.8	1	0	2	0	0	3	0	0	0	0	0	0	0	4	0	0	0	0	0	0	0	1	1	0	0
supervising	4	.3624	.3169	35.0	0	0	0	0	2	1	1	0	0	1	0	0	1	0	0	0	0	0	0	0	0	0	0	2	0
supervision	17	.4420	1.6234	42.1	1	0	1	0	9	4	2	0	1	0	0	0	0	2	0	2	0	0	0	0	0	3	8	1	0
supervisor	4	.2412	.2282	33.6	0	0	0	0	4	0	0	0	0	2	0	0	0	0	0	0	0	0	0	0	0	2	0	0	0
Supervisor	2	.0000	.0243	23.9	0	0	1	1	0	0	0	0	0	0	0	0	0	0	0	0	0	0	0	0	0	0	0	2	0
supervisors	5	.4409	.4707	36.7	0	0	0	0	2	1	2	0	0	0	0	0	0	1	0	0	0	0	0	0	0	1	2	1	0
supper	317	.7877	50.884	57.1	94	74	27	37	40	21	19	5	141	8	4	41	2	18	3	1	6	0	8	0	47	27	1	10	0
Supper	2	.1948	.1250	31.0	1	0	0	0	1	0	0	0	1	0	0	0	0	0	0	0	0	0	0	0	0	1	0	0	0
supper-table	2	.2440	.1132	30.5	0	1	0	0	1	0	0	0	0	0	0	1	0	0	0	0	0	0	0	0	0	0	0	1	0
supperless	2	.2441	.1127	30.5	1	0	0	1	0	0	0	0	0	0	0	0	0	0	0	0	0	0	0	0	1	0	1	0	0
suppers	6	.3829	.5026	37.0	2	1	0	0	2	0	1	0	1	0	0	0	0	0	1	0	1	0	2	0	0	1	0	0	0
suppertime	13	.5322	1.4805	41.7	3	1	2	2	2	0	3	0	4	2	2	2	0	0	1	0	1	0	0	0	1	0	0	0	0
supplanted	4	.3603	.3110	34.9	0	0	1	1	1	1	0	0	0	0	0	0	0	0	0	0	1	0	0	0	0	1	2	0	0
supple	6	.2870	.3718	35.7	0	0	0	0	4	2	0	0	0	0	2	2	0	0	0	0	0	0	0	0	0	0	2	0	0
supplement	25	.5913	3.0450	44.8	3	1	0	0	9	6	5	1	1	0	0	1	9	0	0	1	0	0	2	0	0	1	6	4	0
supplementary	17	.1933	.8774	39.4	0	0	0	0	6	3	8	0	1	0	0	0	14	0	0	1	0	0	0	0	0	0	0	1	0
supplemented	4	.3637	.3064	34.9	0	1	0	0	0	2	1	0	0	0	0	0	0	0	0	0	1	0	1	0	0	0	2	0	0
supplements	5	.3465	.3866	35.9	0	1	1	0	1	2	0	0	0	0	0	0	2	0	0	1	0	0	0	0	0	0	2	0	0
supplication	2	.2427	.1152	30.6	0	0	0	1	1	0	0	0	0	0	0	0	0	0	0	0	0	0	0	0	1	1	0	0	0
supplied	83	.8015	13.391	51.3	5	10	11	11	20	5	20	1	15	4	3	2	0	16	1	10	1	0	1	5	1	9	12	3	0
suppliers	2	.0000	.0209	23.2	0	0	1	1	0	0	0	0	0	0	0	0	0	0	0	0	0	0	0	0	0	0	2	0	0
supplies	250	.7966	40.185	56.0	17	36	69	29	37	35	21	6	48	2	1	5	2	85	4	16	6	0	14	3	2	17	30	15	0
supply	404	.8331	67.395	58.3	31	39	63	64	87	59	52	9	46	24	7	4	30	92	2	90	2	1	22	1	6	13	42	22	0
Supply	3	.0000	.0328	25.2	0	0	3	0	0	0	0	0	0	3	0	0	0	0	0	0	0	0	0	0	0	0	0	0	0
supplying	27	.6539	3.6003	45.6	0	1	1	4	10	5	6	0	0	7	1	0	3	9	3	1	0	0	0	0	0	1	2	0	0
support	341	.8451	57.501	57.6	25	17	47	22	70	75	75	10	32	30	13	6	9	62	4	48	0	11	2	9	4	27	53	31	0
supported	83	.7844	13.109	51.2	4	2	12	9	27	15	10	4	9	3	2	4	0	21	0	9	1	0	0	2	1	4	14	13	0
supporter	3	.2043	.1486	31.7	1	0	1	0	1	0	0	0	0	0	0	0	0	0	0	0	0	0	0	0	0	1	2	0	0
supporters	8	.5390	.8937	39.5	0	0	0	0	1	3	2	2	0	2	1	1	0	2	0	0	0	0	0	0	0	1	0	1	0
supporting	59	.7088	8.5766	49.3	4	1	3	1	23	8	15	4	15	7	0	1	0	3	0	9	4	0	0	4	1	0	7	8	0
supports	55	.6727	7.5327	48.8	3	3	6	7	16	4	14	2	4	0	6	2	0	4	0	15	2	2	0	6	0	6	5	3	0
suppose	797	.8428	134.58	61.3	115	123	97	135	142	121	52	12	155	73	11	47	202	29	13	147	3	1	5	5	43	45	3	15	0
supposed	194	.8821	34.168	55.3	25	33	24	36	36	17	17	6	62	12	1	14	2	18	1	9	4	1	0	1	15	18	9	27	0
supposedly	19	.6342	2.4809	43.9	1	1	2	1	7	2	3	2	1	1	0	1	0	5	0	2	0	0	1	0	0	2	0	6	0
supposes	2	.2446	.1122	30.5	0	0	1	0	1	0	0	0	0	0	0	1	0	0	0	0	0	0	0	0	0	0	1	0	0
supposing	10	.5083	1.0709	40.3	0	0	4	1	4	1	0	0	1	0	0	1	1	0	1	0	1	0	0	0	5	0	0	0	0
suppressed	8	.3508	.6185	37.9	0	1	0	1	0	3	3	0	0	0	0	1	0	1	0	0	0	0	0	0	5	1	0	0	0
suppressing	2	.2446	.1142	30.6	0	0	0	0	1	1	0	0	0	0	0	0	0	0	0	0	0	0	0	0	1	0	0	1	0
suppression	5	.3116	.3461	35.4	0	0	1	0	0	2	2	0	0	0	0	0	0	0	0	0	0	0	0	0	0	1	3	1	0

7A sunshine-smelling
8D sunslanting
4A sunstroke
8D sunstruck
5R sunsuit
8Q sunt
9D sunward
5A sunwarmed
7G sup-
7R super-accurate
8K super-beings
6R super-block
6R super-blocks
7R super-car
8R super-cool
8R super-cultured
XH super-elastic
9H super-high
7B super-intelligent
6R super-pitcher
XR super-rich
6R super-ruin
7R super-structure
XR super-subjectivity
9R super-systems
9Q superabundance
5A Superbly
9R supercharged
XR superduper
7R superfecund
7R superfluous
9H superheating
6P superhuman
8A superintendence
6A Superintendent
4P superintendent's
7A superjet
9L Superloft
9Q supermachines
3P Superman
9Q supernaturalism
9D supernaturally
XR supernova
XR superpool
8E superscript
7R superseding
5A supersensitive
6E supersets
XR supersonically
7Q superstition-ridden
9Q superswift
7R supertanker
4R supertankers
7P Supervacuo
7R supervened
8Q supervisory
9R Supervisory
8H supervoltage
9R supine
4A supp-
3G supper**
8R supplant
7R supplemental
7A Support
9B Supporting
XR supportive
9P suppress
8Q suppuration
XQ supralaryngeal

Word Type	F	D	U	SFI	3 Gr 3	4 Gr 4	5 Gr 5	6 Gr 6	7 Gr 7	8 Gr 8	9 Gr 9	X UnGr	A Read	B Eng & Gr	C Comp	D Lit	E Math	F Soc Stud	G Spell	H Sci	J Music	K Art	L Home Ec	M Shop	N Lib F	P Lib NF	Q Lib Ref	R Mag	S Rel
supremacy	12	.4818	1.2235	40.9	0	0	1	0	3	3	4	1	0	0	0	0	0	4	0	0	0	0	0	0	3	0	3	2	0
supreme	27	.6305	3.5378	45.5	1	0	3	2	7	8	5	1	4	1	0	0	0	9	1	1	0	0	0	0	1	1	7	2	0
Supreme	78	.4815	8.1957	49.1	12	0	9	3	11	28	15	0	9	0	0	1	1	44	0	0	0	0	0	0	0	9	12	2	0
supremely	2	.2437	.1129	30.5	0	0	0	0	1	0	0	1	0	0	0	0	0	0	0	0	0	0	0	0	0	0	1	1	0
sure	1956	.9224	357.97	65.5	388	404	215	238	345	203	130	33	607	161	21	125	43	92	145	158	43	3	58	40	177	159	29	95	0
Sure	2	.0000	.0914	29.6	2	0	0	0	0	0	0	0	2	0	0	0	0	0	0	0	0	0	0	0	0	0	0	0	0
sure-enough	3	.2261	.2131	33.3	0	0	2	0	1	0	0	0	2	0	0	0	0	0	0	0	0	0	0	0	1	0	0	0	0
sure-footed	5	.4419	.4983	37.0	3	0	1	0	0	0	1	0	1	0	0	0	0	2	0	1	0	0	0	0	0	0	1	0	0
surefooted	2	.2306	.1140	30.6	0	0	0	1	0	1	0	0	0	1	0	0	0	1	0	0	0	0	0	0	0	0	0	0	0
surely	231	.8556	39.705	56.0	38	48	24	30	38	24	22	7	93	4	1	26	3	9	2	12	11	0	1	1	21	23	5	19	0
sureness	4	.3188	.2956	34.7	0	1	1	0	1	1	0	0	1	0	0	0	0	0	1	0	0	1	0	0	0	0	1	0	0
surer	5	.4721	.5342	37.3	0	0	2	0	1	2	0	0	2	0	0	1	0	1	0	0	0	0	0	0	1	0	0	0	0
surest	11	.5912	1.3312	41.2	1	0	1	0	3	5	1	0	0	2	0	3	0	1	0	0	0	0	1	0	0	2	0	2	0
surf	35	.5585	4.1667	46.2	2	1	9	10	8	0	4	1	12	1	5	1	0	1	0	1	1	4	0	0	2	0	4	3	0
surface	1281	.7887	203.42	63.1	83	172	150	144	272	170	234	56	157	17	12	20	144	95	7	399	19	30	18	110	13	52	122	66	0
Surface	4	.2351	.2146	33.3	0	0	0	0	4	0	0	0	0	0	0	0	0	0	0	0	0	0	0	1	0	0	0	3	0
surfaced	12	.5367	1.3981	41.5	0	4	0	0	5	1	2	0	4	0	0	1	0	0	0	1	0	0	0	1	0	4	0	1	0
surfacer	2	.1483	.0728	28.6	0	0	0	0	1	0	1	0	0	0	0	0	0	0	0	0	0	0	0	1	0	1	0	0	0
surfaces	127	.4970	13.147	51.2	5	12	14	14	26	24	26	6	6	0	1	2	17	0	1	23	0	10	0	37	0	7	17	6	0
surfacing	5	.1179	.1481	31.7	0	0	0	0	2	0	3	0	0	0	0	0	0	0	0	0	0	0	0	3	0	2	0	0	0
surfboard	5	.3111	.3857	35.9	0	0	3	1	1	0	0	0	1	0	0	0	0	3	0	0	0	0	0	0	0	0	0	1	0
surfboarding	4	.2330	.2363	33.7	0	0	3	0	0	1	0	0	0	1	0	0	0	3	0	0	0	0	0	0	0	0	0	0	0
surfboards	2	.2152	.1357	31.3	0	0	1	0	1	0	0	0	1	0	0	0	0	1	0	0	0	0	0	0	0	0	0	0	0
surfer	2	.1814	.1187	30.7	0	0	0	1	1	0	0	0	1	0	0	0	0	0	0	0	0	0	0	0	0	0	0	1	0
surfers	7	.2353	.5425	37.3	0	0	0	1	6	0	0	0	6	0	0	0	0	0	0	0	0	0	0	0	0	0	0	1	0
surfing	12	.3638	.9987	40.0	0	0	1	7	3	0	0	1	2	1	0	0	0	1	0	0	0	0	0	0	0	1	0	7	0
Surfing	5	.2392	.3123	34.9	0	0	1	3	1	0	0	0	1	0	0	0	0	1	0	0	0	0	0	0	0	0	0	3	0
surge	20	.7330	2.9904	44.8	3	1	2	2	5	1	5	1	5	1	1	2	0	0	0	3	1	0	0	0	3	0	2	2	0
surged	17	.5941	2.1133	43.2	0	1	2	3	7	4	0	0	3	0	0	1	0	2	0	0	1	0	0	0	5	1	0	4	0
surgeon	18	.6448	2.3883	43.8	1	1	2	1	2	4	6	1	2	1	0	0	0	1	0	3	1	0	0	0	1	1	6	2	0
Surgeon	3	.2053	.1597	32.0	0	0	0	1	0	0	2	0	0	0	0	0	0	0	0	1	0	0	0	0	0	2	0	0	0
surgeons	9	.4754	.9117	39.6	0	0	1	0	1	3	3	1	0	1	0	0	0	0	0	4	0	0	0	0	0	0	2	2	0
surgery	45	.5019	4.8126	46.8	0	3	7	0	7	13	11	4	2	0	0	0	0	4	0	14	0	0	0	0	0	4	4	17	0
surges	5	.5331	.5710	37.6	0	0	1	0	1	2	0	1	1	0	0	1	0	0	0	1	0	0	0	0	0	1	1	0	0
surgical	13	.4089	1.1450	40.6	0	0	4	0	1	6	2	0	0	0	0	1	0	0	0	3	0	0	0	0	0	1	7	1	0
surging	10	.6024	1.2852	41.1	1	1	0	2	2	2	2	0	4	0	0	0	0	1	0	0	1	0	0	0	1	0	2	1	0
Surinam	5	.3753	.4190	36.2	0	0	0	0	5	0	0	0	0	0	0	0	0	3	0	0	0	0	0	0	1	0	1	0	0
surkus	3	.0000	.0352	25.5	3	0	0	0	0	0	0	0	0	0	0	0	0	0	0	0	0	0	0	0	3	0	0	0	0
surly	3	.3824	.2446	33.9	0	1	0	1	0	0	1	0	0	0	0	1	0	0	0	0	1	0	0	0	0	0	0	1	0
surmise	2	.2285	.1129	30.5	0	0	0	0	1	1	0	0	0	0	0	0	0	1	0	0	0	0	0	0	0	0	1	0	0
surmises	2	.0000	.0209	23.2	0	0	0	0	2	0	0	0	0	0	0	0	0	0	0	0	0	0	0	0	0	0	2	0	0
surmounted	5	.4001	.4514	36.5	0	0	0	0	3	1	0	1	1	0	0	1	0	0	0	1	0	0	0	0	0	0	2	0	0
surname	7	.4774	.6880	38.4	0	4	0	1	0	1	1	0	0	1	1	0	0	0	3	0	0	0	0	0	1	0	1	0	0
surnames	2	.0000	.0162	22.1	0	2	0	0	0	0	0	0	0	0	0	0	0	0	2	0	0	0	0	0	0	0	0	0	0
Surov	2	.0000	.0914	29.6	0	0	0	2	0	0	0	0	2	0	0	0	0	0	0	0	0	0	0	0	0	0	0	0	0
Surov's	4	.0000	.1827	32.6	0	0	0	4	0	0	0	0	4	0	0	0	0	0	0	0	0	0	0	0	0	0	0	0	0
surpass	6	.4993	.6271	38.0	0	0	0	1	1	3	1	0	0	0	0	1	0	1	0	1	2	0	0	0	0	0	1	0	0
surpassed	9	.5502	1.0413	40.2	1	0	0	2	3	2	1	0	1	0	0	0	0	1	0	0	0	0	0	0	3	2	1	1	0
surpassing	2	.2351	.1166	30.7	0	0	0	1	0	1	0	0	0	0	0	0	0	1	0	0	0	0	0	0	0	0	0	1	0
surplus	21	.6644	2.8761	44.6	2	1	2	0	7	4	4	1	3	0	0	2	0	8	0	0	0	0	0	1	1	1	2	3	0
surpluses	2	.2408	.1204	30.8	0	0	1	0	0	1	0	0	0	0	0	0	0	1	0	0	0	0	0	0	0	1	0	0	0
surprise	389	.8534	66.794	58.2	123	65	51	45	47	32	12	14	174	12	7	21	4	17	6	11	4	2	2	1	64	32	4	28	0
Surprise	2	.2375	.1088	30.4	1	0	0	0	0	0	0	1	0	0	0	0	0	0	0	0	1	0	0	0	0	0	0	1	0
surprised	349	.8164	57.863	57.6	98	84	43	46	42	26	7	3	173	14	2	22	5	16	4	11	1	2	1	0	45	31	0	22	0
surprises	36	.7574	5.5438	47.4	7	13	1	3	10	1	0	1	11	0	2	2	0	1	0	1	0	0	2	1	4	2	5	5	0
surprising	111	.8440	18.793	52.7	10	14	17	18	26	12	9	5	28	1	0	5	3	19	3	12	6	3	0	0	4	9	10	8	0
surprisingly	43	.6841	6.0462	47.8	7	1	6	2	13	3	8	3	8	1	2	1	0	5	0	5	0	0	0	0	0	5	8	8	0
surrealist	2	.2433	.1158	30.6	0	0	0	0	1	1	0	0	0	0	0	0	0	0	0	0	0	0	0	0	0	1	0	1	0
surrender	53	.6520	7.1820	48.6	1	5	7	6	9	20	5	0	9	1	1	1	0	27	0	0	1	0	0	0	1	4	6	2	0
surrendered	34	.5946	4.2234	46.3	3	2	10	4	6	7	2	0	4	1	1	0	0	13	0	0	0	0	0	0	1	2	10	2	0
surrendering	3	.2212	.2099	33.2	0	0	0	1	1	1	0	0	2	0	0	1	0	0	0	0	0	0	0	0	0	0	0	0	0
surrey	7	.4612	.7313	38.6	0	3	0	0	1	0	3	0	3	1	0	2	0	0	0	0	0	0	0	0	0	0	1	0	0
Surrey	3	.1169	.1277	31.1	0	1	0	0	0	2	0	0	1	0	0	0	0	0	0	0	0	0	0	0	0	0	2	0	0
surround	36	.8196	5.9076	47.7	4	6	5	7	8	2	3	1	3	1	0	2	0	7	3	6	1	1	0	0	1	4	4	3	0
surrounded	164	.8604	28.200	54.5	17	22	24	31	37	15	16	2	32	8	2	7	2	33	1	19	2	3	0	0	12	16	20	7	0
surrounding	116	.8253	19.163	52.8	5	4	10	18	36	16	19	8	10	3	1	9	2	24	1	24	0	3	0	2	2	4	19	12	0
surroundings	68	.8654	11.741	50.7	4	7	5	11	17	11	10	3	11	0	2	4	1	8	3	17	1	1	0	1	3	4	9	3	0
surrounds	29	.7694	4.5197	46.6	2	2	5	4	6	1	6	3	4	1	0	1	1	5	0	9	1	0	0	0	1	2	3	1	0
surtax	6	.0000	.0729	28.6	0	0	0	0	0	0	5	1	0	0	0	0	0	0	0	0	0	0	0	0	0	0	0	6	0
Surtsey	5	.0000	.2284	33.6	0	0	0	5	0	0	0	0	5	0	0	0	0	0	0	0	0	0	0	0	0	0	0	0	0
surveillance	6	.1708	.2605	34.2	0	0	0	3	3	0	0	0	0	0	0	0	0	0	0	0	0	0	0	0	0	0	1	5	0
survey	60	.7962	9.6180	49.8	5	1	10	5	12	9	11	7	11	6	0	3	1	2	1	7	2	1	0	0	1	3	8	14	0
Survey	13	.5061	1.3996	41.5	0	0	3	2	3	3	2	0	1	2	0	0	0	0	0	4	0	0	0	0	0	0	2	4	0
surveyed	17	.6412	2.2608	43.5	0	3	3	1	7	3	0	0	3	2	1	1	0	4	0	1	0	0	0	0	4	1	0	0	0
surveying	20	.6815	2.7943	44.5	1	2	7	3	3	2	2	0	2	0	0	1	2	6	0	0	0	0	0	0	2	4	2	1	0
surveyor	9	.5287	1.0335	40.1	0	2	2	2	0	1	1	1	2	0	0	0	0	3	0	1	0	0	0	0	0	2	1	0	0
surveyors	5	.4416	.4721	36.7	0	1	0	0	0	0	3	1	0	0	0	2	1	0	0	1	0	0	0	0	0	0	0	1	0
surveyors'	3	.2390	.1719	32.4	0	0	0	3	0	0	0	0	0	0	0	1	2	0	0	0	0	0	0	0	0	0	0	0	0
surveys	13	.5447	1.4990	41.8	0	0	2	2	5	0	2	2	2	1	0	0	0	0	0	3	0	0	1	0	0	0	1	5	0
survival	45	.5859	5.4855	47.4	1	2	4	1	23	7	6	1	5	0	1	2	0	3	0	6	1	0	0	0	0	1	19	7	0
survive	87	.8275	14.433	51.6	3	15	5	15	35	8	6	0	13	3	1	5	0	9	4	22	2	0	1	0	1	4	15	7	0
survived	48	.6805	6.6834	48.2	1	3	3	11	16	4	6	4	6	2	0	3	0	5	1	4	0	0	0	0	1	3	11	12	0
survives	7	.5459	.7971	39.0	0	0	0	0	1	3	2	1	0	0	0	0	0	2	0	1	1	0	0	0	0	0	1	2	0
surviving	13	.3942	1.1554	40.6	0	3	2	0	4	2	1	1	2	0	0	0	0	1	0	3	0	0	0	0	0	0	6	1	0
survivor	5	.4110	.4368	36.4	0	1	1	0	2	0	0	1	0	0	0	0	0	1	1	0	0	1	0	0	0	1	0	1	0
survivors	17	.7434	2.5670	44.1	0	0	3	2	7	2	3	0	3	1	0	2	0	2	1	1	0	0	0	0	0	3	2	2	0
Susan	143	.7302	21.417	53.3	66	24	15	11	12	4	11	0	44	24	4	0	32	4	1	8	2	0	0	0	5	8	0	11	0
Susan's	18	.4016	1.5734	42.0	3	5	1	4	2	1	2	0	0	5	0	0	10	1	0	1	0	0	0	0	0	0	0	1	0
Susanna	11	.0730	.2463	33.9	1	5	3	1	0	1	0	0	0	0	0	0	0	0	0	0	10	0	0	0	0	1	0	0	0
Susannah	11	.0000	.1592	32.0	1	10	0	0	0	0	0	0	0	0	0	0	0	0	0	0	0	0	0	0	0	11	0	0	0
susceptibility	2	.2346	.1166	30.7	0	0	0	0	1	0	1	0	0	0	0	0	0	0	0	1	0	0	0	0	0	0	0	1	0
susceptible	11	.4333	1.0345	40.1	0	1	0	1	3	3	2	1	1	1	0	0	0	0	0	2	0	0	0	0	0	0	5	2	0
Susie	22	.5828	2.7199	44.3	9	11	2	0	0	0	0	0	7	7	1	2	0	0	0	0	2	0	0	0	0	3	0	0	0
suspect	44	.7741	6.8755	48.4	3	6	6	6	9	7	4	3	8	2	2	7	0	0	3	7	1	0	0	0	3	2	2	7	0
suspect's	2	.2412	.1091	30.4	0	0	0	0	0	0	2	0	0	0	0	1	0	0	1	0	0	0	0	0	0	0	0	0	0

5Q Supremacy
6G sur
9D surcease
9R surcharge
8R sure-fingered
7A sure's
9D surety
8B surf-riding
3R surf-swept
6H SURFACE
7R surface-feeding
7D surface-wind
5F surfboarders
7A surfed
7Q surfeit
6R surfers'
7R surficial
6R surfmen
9M surform
6R surge-driven
8J surge's
8H surgeon-barber
7C surgeon-dentist
8N surgeon's
9P Surgeon's
7Q surgeonfish
9Q Surgeons
7F surgeons'
5P surges'
XH surgically
7H surmised
8F surmount
7N surmounting
7N surmullet
6G suronder
5F surpasses
6A surprisin'
4N surprising-
5Q Surrealism
7P surrealists
4P surrenders
7N surreptitiously
8R surrogate
XH surveyor's
5Q Survival
XP Survive
4P Susannah's
3P Susans
7D susceptibilities
3B SUSHES
5F Susitna

Word Type	F	D	U	SFI	3 Gr 3	4 Gr 4	5 Gr 5	6 Gr 6	7 Gr 7	8 Gr 8	9 Gr 9	X UnGr	A Read	B Eng & Gr	C Comp	D Lit	E Math	F Soc Stud	G Spell	H Sci	J Music	K Art	L Home Ec	M Shop	N Lib F	P Lib NF	Q Lib Ref	R Mag	S Rel
suspected	41	.7249	6.0520	47.8	3	2	3	7	12	6	5	3	6	0	0	6	1	2	1	9	0	0	0	0	2	2	5	7	0
suspects	8	.4083	.7313	38.6	0	0	1	0	0	2	5	0	1	0	0	1	0	3	0	0	0	0	0	0	0	0	0	3	0
suspend	6	.4137	.5672	37.5	0	0	0	2	2	1	1	0	2	0	1	0	0	0	0	1	0	0	0	0	1	0	1	0	0
suspended	47	.7340	7.0231	48.5	2	3	10	4	11	7	5	5	8	0	0	3	0	2	0	11	0	1	0	0	5	4	7	6	0
suspender	2	.2443	.1130	30.5	1	0	0	0	0	1	0	0	0	0	0	1	0	0	0	0	0	0	0	0	1	0	0	0	0
suspenders	9	.3296	.6586	38.2	2	6	0	0	1	0	0	0	0	0	0	1	0	0	0	0	0	0	0	0	5	3	0	0	0
suspending	2	.0000	.0243	23.9	0	0	0	0	1	0	1	0	0	0	0	0	0	0	0	0	0	0	0	0	0	0	0	2	0
suspense	36	.5727	4.3224	46.4	0	0	2	10	5	8	10	1	7	5	1	16	0	0	0	0	0	0	0	0	2	2	2	1	0
suspenseful	2	.2446	.1122	30.5	0	0	0	0	1	0	1	0	0	0	0	1	0	0	0	0	0	0	0	0	0	0	1	0	0
suspension	23	.5245	2.5967	44.1	3	0	2	8	8	1	0	1	5	0	0	0	2	1	0	1	0	0	0	0	0	4	1	9	0
suspensions	2	.0000	.0394	26.0	0	0	2	0	0	0	0	0	0	0	0	0	0	0	0	2	0	0	0	0	0	0	0	0	0
suspicion	24	.6569	3.2536	45.1	1	0	1	2	8	3	8	1	4	0	0	5	0	5	1	0	0	0	0	0	1	2	1	5	0
suspicions	7	.4446	.6943	38.4	0	0	0	4	2	0	1	0	2	0	0	2	0	0	0	0	0	0	0	0	1	0	0	2	0
suspicious	38	.6955	5.4849	47.4	1	6	1	9	10	6	5	0	15	2	0	6	0	1	0	0	1	0	0	0	6	2	1	4	0
suspiciously	11	.5441	1.3131	41.2	1	0	3	2	4	0	1	0	5	0	0	2	0	0	0	0	0	0	0	0	1	1	0	2	0
Susquehanna	12	.4390	1.1576	40.6	2	2	2	0	6	0	0	0	2	0	0	3	0	0	0	0	0	0	0	0	0	4	0	3	0
Sussex	4	.3790	.3299	35.2	2	0	0	0	0	1	0	1	0	0	0	0	0	0	0	0	0	0	0	0	0	2	1	1	0
sustain	10	.6393	1.2976	41.1	0	1	1	0	4	0	4	0	0	0	0	2	0	0	0	2	2	0	1	0	1	0	1	1	0
sustained	28	.7257	4.1160	46.1	1	0	3	1	9	6	8	0	4	0	1	1	0	2	1	0	6	0	0	0	2	3	4	4	0
sustaining	2	.2401	.1133	30.5	0	1	1	0	0	0	0	0	0	0	0	0	0	0	0	0	0	0	0	0	0	1	1	0	0
Susy	5	.0000	.2284	33.6	0	0	5	0	0	0	0	0	5	0	0	0	0	0	0	0	0	0	0	0	0	0	0	0	0
Sutherland	2	.0000	.0914	29.6	0	0	0	0	0	0	2	0	2	0	0	0	0	0	0	0	0	0	0	0	0	0	0	0	0
Sutter	11	.2540	.8004	39.0	0	0	0	0	0	10	1	0	6	0	2	0	0	3	0	0	0	0	0	0	0	0	0	0	0
suture	4	.2287	.2348	33.7	0	0	0	3	0	0	0	1	0	0	0	0	0	0	0	3	0	0	0	0	0	0	0	1	0
Suwa	3	.0000	.0583	27.7	0	0	0	0	0	3	0	0	0	0	0	0	0	3	0	0	0	0	0	0	0	0	0	0	0
Suzanne	3	.0000	.0449	26.5	0	0	0	0	0	3	0	0	0	0	0	0	3	0	0	0	0	0	0	0	0	0	0	0	0
Suzuki	7	.1817	.3553	35.5	0	3	0	0	1	3	0	0	0	0	0	0	0	6	0	0	0	0	0	0	0	0	0	1	0
Suzy	4	.0000	.1827	32.6	0	0	0	4	0	0	0	0	4	0	0	0	0	0	0	0	0	0	0	0	0	0	0	0	0
Svatopluk	5	.0000	.2284	33.6	0	0	0	0	5	0	0	0	5	0	0	0	0	0	0	0	0	0	0	0	0	0	0	0	0
Svatopluk's	4	.0000	.1827	32.6	0	0	0	0	4	0	0	0	4	0	0	0	0	0	0	0	0	0	0	0	0	0	0	0	0
svnnch	5	.0000	.2284	33.6	5	0	0	0	0	0	0	0	5	0	0	0	0	0	0	0	0	0	0	0	0	0	0	0	0
Svoboda	2	.0000	.0243	23.9	0	0	0	0	0	1	1	0	0	0	0	0	0	0	0	0	0	0	0	0	0	0	0	2	0
sw	3	.2031	.1990	33.0	0	3	0	0	0	0	0	0	2	0	0	0	0	0	1	0	0	0	0	0	0	0	0	0	0
swabbed	2	.2407	.1138	30.6	0	1	0	0	1	0	0	0	0	0	0	1	0	0	0	0	0	0	0	0	0	1	0	0	0
swagger	4	.3071	.2967	34.7	0	1	0	1	2	0	0	0	1	0	0	1	0	0	0	0	0	0	0	0	2	0	0	0	0
swaggered	2	.1551	.0728	28.6	0	0	1	0	0	1	0	0	0	0	1	0	0	0	0	0	0	0	0	0	1	0	0	0	0
swaggering	4	.4442	.3918	35.9	0	0	1	0	1	0	2	0	1	0	0	1	0	0	0	0	1	0	0	0	0	0	0	1	0
Swahili	6	.2321	.3270	35.1	0	0	0	4	0	0	2	0	0	0	0	0	0	0	0	0	0	0	0	0	0	0	2	4	0
swallow	69	.7531	10.665	50.3	30	8	9	9	7	6	0	0	26	4	1	1	0	2	0	15	0	0	0	0	6	9	2	3	0
swallowed	131	.6850	19.082	52.8	66	22	6	13	11	3	10	0	89	0	2	9	0	1	0	6	0	0	1	0	12	7	1	3	0
swallowing	24	.6618	3.2966	45.2	3	2	4	4	4	4	3	0	5	1	0	1	0	2	0	7	0	0	0	0	3	1	4	0	0
swallows	37	.6843	5.1949	47.2	14	5	1	11	4	1	1	0	5	0	0	2	0	0	0	10	2	0	0	0	2	9	4	3	0
swallowtails	2	.0000	.0209	23.2	0	0	0	0	2	0	0	0	0	0	0	0	0	0	0	0	0	0	0	0	0	0	2	0	0
swam	176	.7667	27.827	54.4	45	77	4	15	15	12	5	3	103	9	1	6	0	4	2	1	4	0	0	0	10	22	3	11	0
swamp	64	.7427	9.7340	49.9	16	17	5	1	16	6	1	2	20	0	1	4	1	5	0	4	1	0	0	0	4	18	5	1	0
Swamp	13	.4991	1.4627	41.7	5	2	1	0	2	1	1	1	6	0	0	3	0	1	0	1	0	0	0	0	0	2	0	0	0
swamped	2	.2446	.1142	30.6	0	0	1	0	1	0	0	0	0	0	0	0	0	0	0	0	0	0	0	0	1	0	0	1	0
swamping	2	.2303	.1079	30.3	0	1	1	0	0	0	0	0	0	0	0	0	0	0	0	0	1	0	0	0	0	1	0	0	0
swamplands	2	.0000	.0243	23.9	0	1	0	0	0	0	0	1	0	0	0	0	0	0	0	0	0	0	0	0	0	0	0	2	0
swamps	66	.6929	9.3713	49.7	12	7	8	7	18	6	2	6	7	0	1	7	0	14	0	14	0	0	0	0	0	15	4	4	0
swampy	28	.6029	3.5314	45.5	2	6	7	6	5	1	0	1	3	1	2	0	0	12	0	4	0	0	0	0	0	2	2	2	0
swan	29	.5137	3.3104	45.2	14	0	2	5	7	0	1	0	15	0	0	0	0	0	0	0	8	2	0	1	0	0	3	0	0
Swan	24	.4223	2.2531	43.5	3	0	1	8	7	1	3	1	6	3	0	0	0	0	0	1	11	0	0	0	1	1	1	0	0
swans	15	.2679	.9771	39.9	7	0	1	3	3	0	0	1	3	0	0	0	0	1	0	0	9	0	0	0	0	1	0	1	0
Swanson	4	.2424	.3036	34.8	0	0	0	0	3	0	0	1	3	0	0	0	0	0	0	0	0	0	0	0	0	0	0	1	0
swap	6	.4195	.5713	37.6	0	1	2	0	2	0	0	0	2	0	1	0	0	0	0	0	0	0	0	0	1	1	0	1	0
swapped	10	.1863	.4374	36.4	8	0	0	1	1	0	0	0	0	0	0	1	0	0	0	0	8	0	0	0	0	0	0	1	0
swapping	4	.4485	.4009	36.0	0	1	0	0	0	0	1	2	1	0	0	0	0	1	0	0	0	0	0	0	0	0	1	1	0
sward	3	.0000	.1370	31.4	0	0	0	3	0	0	0	0	3	0	0	0	0	0	0	0	0	0	0	0	0	0	0	0	0
swarm	24	.7244	3.5109	45.5	3	0	2	5	8	3	2	1	2	1	2	1	0	1	1	1	1	0	0	0	2	3	4	5	0
swarmed	26	.6912	3.7195	45.7	1	4	4	5	8	3	0	1	8	2	1	0	0	4	0	1	0	0	0	0	6	2	1	1	0
swarming	13	.6330	1.6873	42.3	0	3	2	1	3	3	0	1	1	0	1	1	0	0	0	0	0	0	0	0	1	3	2	3	0
swarms	18	.6178	2.3153	43.6	1	2	3	5	2	1	3	1	2	0	0	0	0	1	0	6	0	0	0	0	3	2	1	3	0
swart	2	.1621	.0746	28.7	0	0	0	0	1	0	1	0	0	0	1	1	0	0	0	0	0	0	0	0	0	0	0	0	0
swartgevaar	2	.0000	.0290	24.6	0	0	2	0	0	0	0	0	0	0	0	0	0	0	0	0	0	0	0	0	0	2	0	0	0
swarthy	3	.2212	.2099	33.2	0	1	0	1	0	0	1	0	2	0	0	1	0	0	0	0	0	0	0	0	0	0	0	0	0
swash	4	.3604	.3539	35.5	3	1	0	0	0	0	0	0	2	1	0	0	0	0	0	0	1	0	0	0	0	0	0	0	0
swat	2	.0000	.0209	23.2	0	0	0	0	1	0	1	0	0	0	0	0	0	0	0	0	0	0	0	0	0	0	2	0	0
swath	2	.1698	.1133	30.5	1	0	0	0	1	0	0	0	1	0	0	0	0	0	0	0	0	0	0	0	0	0	1	0	0
sway	27	.7298	4.0189	46.0	7	3	1	3	8	1	3	1	7	1	0	2	0	0	0	1	3	1	0	0	1	2	3	6	0
swayed	26	.5886	3.2971	45.2	1	10	7	1	4	3	0	0	11	0	0	2	0	3	1	0	0	0	0	0	6	3	0	0	0
swaying	23	.6245	3.0418	44.8	7	2	2	3	6	3	0	0	9	1	0	3	0	1	0	0	1	0	0	0	5	3	0	0	0
sways	2	.1696	.0749	28.7	1	0	0	0	1	0	0	0	0	0	0	0	0	0	0	0	1	1	0	0	0	0	0	0	0
swear	34	.5515	3.9461	46.0	0	1	2	7	7	4	12	1	5	0	0	12	0	3	0	1	2	0	0	0	7	0	0	4	0
swearing	6	.2896	.4134	36.2	1	0	0	0	0	3	3	0	1	0	0	3	0	0	0	0	0	0	0	0	2	0	0	0	0
swears	3	.3272	.2363	33.7	1	0	1	0	0	0	1	0	1	0	0	1	0	0	0	0	1	0	0	0	0	0	0	0	0
sweat	105	.8009	16.965	52.3	10	18	8	14	32	9	13	1	25	6	2	11	0	8	1	14	0	0	0	3	21	8	1	5	0
sweat-soldered	2	.0000	.0050	17.0	0	0	0	0	0	1	1	0	0	0	0	0	0	0	0	0	0	0	0	2	0	0	0	0	0
sweated	6	.1717	.3427	35.3	0	0	0	1	3	2	0	0	3	0	0	3	0	0	0	0	0	0	0	0	0	0	0	0	0
sweater	50	.7958	8.0609	49.1	12	8	2	9	9	1	7	2	18	1	1	3	4	0	3	4	1	1	4	0	0	3	0	7	0
sweaterandskirt	2	.0000	.0219	23.4	0	0	0	0	2	0	0	0	0	2	0	0	0	0	0	0	0	0	0	0	0	0	0	0	0
sweaters	30	.4805	3.0397	44.8	3	2	1	6	5	11	2	0	2	2	0	1	7	1	0	1	0	0	7	0	8	1	0	0	0
sweating	10	.4512	1.0122	40.1	0	2	2	1	2	2	1	0	3	0	1	0	0	0	0	1	0	0	0	0	1	4	0	0	0
sweaty	4	.1814	.2373	33.8	0	0	0	2	2	0	0	0	2	0	0	0	0	0	0	0	0	0	0	0	0	0	0	2	0
Swede	8	.3494	.6405	38.1	0	0	0	1	5	0	0	2	1	0	0	4	0	0	0	2	0	0	0	0	0	0	0	1	0
Sweden	101	.7013	14.434	51.6	9	8	20	20	20	7	13	4	7	3	0	1	2	36	2	4	9	0	0	0	0	17	15	5	0
Sweden's	6	.2952	.4383	36.4	0	0	3	1	2	0	0	0	1	0	0	0	0	2	0	0	0	0	0	0	0	3	0	0	0
Swedes	9	.5813	1.0727	40.3	1	2	2	1	2	0	0	1	0	0	0	0	0	1	0	0	2	0	0	0	2	1	2	1	0
Swedish	34	.6698	4.6417	46.7	4	3	10	5	3	4	3	2	2	1	0	0	1	5	0	2	7	0	0	0	1	5	7	3	0
Sweeney	24	.0000	1.0964	40.4	0	0	24	0	0	0	0	0	24	0	0	0	0	0	0	0	0	0	0	0	0	0	0	0	0
Sweeney's	5	.0000	.2284	33.6	0	0	5	0	0	0	0	0	5	0	0	0	0	0	0	0	0	0	0	0	0	0	0	0	0
sweep	81	.7982	12.998	51.1	8	12	10	11	24	9	5	2	13	7	0	10	1	11	2	3	11	0	0	0	7	4	4	8	0
sweeper	12	.4197	1.1108	40.5	2	1	1	6	1	0	1	0	2	6	0	1	0	0	0	0	0	0	0	0	0	2	0	1	0
sweepers	2	.2351	.1166	30.7	1	0	0	0	0	0	1	0	0	0	0	0	0	1	0	0	0	0	0	0	0	0	0	1	0

4F suspecting
9B suspicious/suspicion
9B suspiciousion
9D suspiciousness
7J Susquehan-i-a
9P Sustagen
4A Sustaining
6H sustains
7D susurrus
4J Susyanna
8A suthin'
8A Sutter's
9P sutured
8Q suzerainty
4F Suzuki's
7R Suzy's
7D Sven
9F Sverdlovsk
8Q svet
5Q Svibul
4F SW
7D swaddled
3P swaddling
4A swag
5B swain
5B swains
8A swaller
4A Swallow
5A swallow-shadows
5J swallow-tail
4P swallow-tailed
3H swallow's
XR swallower
3P swallowtail
8H swampland
6H swamplike
7P Swamps
5H swan-neck
6D swan's
5J Swan's
8A swank
7F Swansea
7A Swanson's
7N swaps
5A Swarthmore
9R swastika
XR swatches
7N swathed
6A swaths
7Q swatting
5Q Swayne
6F Swaziland
9Q sweat-soaked
6E sweater-skirt
7R sweats
5R sweatshirt
7A sweatshirts
5P Sweden-Finland
5A Sweep

Word Type	F	D	U	SFI	3 Gr 3	4 Gr 4	5 Gr 5	6 Gr 6	7 Gr 7	8 Gr 8	9 Gr 9	X UnGr	A Read	B Eng & Gr	C Comp	D Lit	E Math	F Soc Stud	G Spell	H Sci	J Music	K Art	L Home Ec	M Shop	N Lib F	P Lib NF	Q Lib Ref	R Mag	S Rel
sweeping	95	.7956	15.228	51.8	4	11	6	11	12	39	10	2	20	1	3	6	26	4	1	4	7	4	0	0	3	3	8	5	0
sweeps	36	.7605	5.5136	47.4	2	4	6	3	6	13	2	0	2	2	1	2	11	1	0	6	3	0	0	0	3	0	1	4	0
sweepstakes	2	.2442	.1134	30.5	0	0	0	0	0	0	1	1	0	1	0	0	0	0	0	0	0	0	0	0	0	0	0	1	0
Sweepstakes	2	.0000	.0290	24.6	0	0	0	0	0	0	0	2	0	0	0	0	0	0	0	0	0	0	0	0	0	2	0	0	0
sweet	319	.8459	54.056	57.3	65	53	39	44	51	33	25	9	85	17	3	38	1	22	5	22	41	0	11	0	30	22	12	10	0
Sweet	17	.3932	1.4819	41.7	1	2	3	3	4	2	2	0	3	1	0	1	0	1	0	0	9	0	0	0	0	1	0	1	0
sweet-potato	2	.0000	.0914	29.6	0	0	0	0	2	0	0	0	2	0	0	0	0	0	0	0	0	0	0	0	0	0	0	0	0
sweet-smelling	15	.6104	1.9712	42.9	5	2	3	4	0	0	1	0	8	1	0	2	0	0	1	0	0	0	0	0	0	1	2	0	0
sweete	2	.0000	.0209	23.2	0	0	0	0	2	0	0	0	0	0	0	0	0	0	0	0	0	0	0	0	0	0	2	0	0
sweeten	4	.3572	.3111	34.9	1	0	0	2	0	0	1	0	0	2	0	1	0	0	0	0	0	0	0	0	0	1	0	0	0
sweetened	4	.2088	.1939	32.9	0	1	0	0	2	0	1	0	0	0	0	0	0	1	0	0	0	0	2	0	1	0	0	0	0
sweeteners	2	.0000	.0394	26.0	0	0	0	0	1	1	0	0	0	0	0	0	0	0	0	2	0	0	0	0	0	0	0	0	0
sweeter	17	.3475	1.3952	41.4	1	2	1	10	1	0	0	2	5	9	0	0	0	0	0	0	1	0	0	0	0	0	0	2	0
sweetest	13	.6375	1.7338	42.4	3	1	0	4	4	0	1	0	4	0	0	2	0	0	0	1	2	0	0	0	2	1	0	1	0
sweetheart	14	.4373	1.2873	41.1	0	0	1	1	7	3	2	0	0	0	0	3	0	1	0	0	6	0	0	0	3	1	0	0	0
Sweetheart	9	.1444	.3358	35.3	0	0	0	1	8	0	0	0	0	0	0	8	0	0	0	0	1	0	0	0	0	0	0	0	0
sweetheart's	2	.0000	.0162	22.1	0	0	0	2	0	0	0	0	0	0	0	0	0	0	0	0	2	0	0	0	0	0	0	0	0
sweeting	2	.2442	.1134	30.5	0	0	0	0	1	1	0	0	0	1	0	0	0	0	0	0	0	0	0	0	0	0	0	1	0
sweetly	9	.4757	.9207	39.6	1	1	3	1	2	0	1	0	2	2	1	0	0	0	0	0	3	0	0	0	1	0	0	0	0
sweetmeats	2	.1717	.1142	30.6	0	0	0	1	0	0	1	0	1	0	0	1	0	0	0	0	0	0	0	0	0	0	0	0	0
sweetness	14	.7170	2.0319	43.1	1	0	3	0	3	3	3	1	1	1	0	2	1	0	0	1	1	0	0	0	2	2	0	3	0
sweetpotatoes	3	.0000	.0097	19.8	0	0	0	0	0	0	3	0	0	0	0	0	0	0	0	0	0	0	3	0	0	0	0	0	0
Sweetree	8	.0000	.3655	35.6	0	0	0	0	0	8	0	0	8	0	0	0	0	0	0	0	0	0	0	0	0	0	0	0	0
sweets	17	.5707	2.1030	43.2	4	2	1	2	2	3	2	1	8	1	0	0	0	0	0	1	2	0	2	0	0	1	0	2	0
Sweets	2	.0000	.0162	22.1	2	0	0	0	0	0	0	0	0	0	0	0	0	0	0	0	2	0	0	0	0	0	0	0	0
swell	49	.7857	7.8304	48.9	13	11	6	7	6	2	3	1	19	2	0	4	0	1	1	2	3	0	0	0	7	5	3	2	0
swelled	25	.5698	2.9882	44.8	2	2	0	4	8	8	1	0	4	0	0	9	0	2	0	0	0	0	0	0	4	2	2	2	0
swelling	21	.6578	2.8683	44.6	1	2	3	3	9	2	1	0	6	1	0	5	0	0	0	1	1	0	0	0	3	0	1	3	0
swellings	2	.0000	.0394	26.0	0	0	0	0	2	0	0	0	0	0	0	0	0	0	0	2	0	0	0	0	0	0	0	0	0
swells	18	.5903	2.2528	43.5	5	2	0	4	3	2	2	0	5	0	0	4	0	0	0	3	2	0	0	0	0	3	0	1	0
sweltered	2	.0000	.0914	29.6	0	0	0	2	0	0	0	0	2	0	0	0	0	0	0	0	0	0	0	0	0	0	0	0	0
sweltering	2	.2160	.1362	31.3	1	0	0	0	1	0	0	0	1	0	0	0	0	0	0	1	0	0	0	0	0	0	0	0	0
Swenson	8	.2393	.6011	37.8	3	0	0	0	3	2	0	0	6	0	0	2	0	0	0	0	0	0	0	0	0	0	0	0	0
swept	161	.8292	26.820	54.3	24	26	12	23	36	29	8	3	41	6	5	18	11	16	3	4	1	0	0	0	18	19	5	14	0
swerve	4	.2393	.3005	34.8	3	0	0	0	0	1	0	0	3	0	0	1	0	0	0	0	0	0	0	0	0	0	0	0	0
swerved	8	.4236	.7572	38.8	0	1	1	3	3	0	0	0	2	0	0	3	0	0	0	0	0	0	0	0	0	0	1	2	0
swift	131	.7377	19.820	53.0	22	14	16	29	27	6	14	3	44	2	0	21	1	8	0	6	2	0	0	0	14	20	8	5	0
Swift	17	.3354	1.5020	41.8	9	2	0	0	0	1	4	1	11	1	0	0	0	0	0	0	0	0	0	0	0	0	0	5	0
swift-flowing	5	.0000	.0972	29.9	0	1	4	0	0	0	0	0	0	0	0	0	0	5	0	0	0	0	0	0	0	0	0	0	0
Swift-goer	5	.0000	.0724	28.6	5	0	0	0	0	0	0	0	0	0	0	0	0	0	0	0	0	0	0	0	0	5	0	0	0
swift-moving	3	.2435	.2274	33.6	1	1	0	0	0	1	0	0	2	0	0	0	0	1	0	0	0	0	0	0	0	0	0	0	0
Swift's	4	.3599	.3543	35.5	2	0	0	0	0	1	1	0	2	0	0	0	0	0	1	0	0	0	0	0	0	0	0	1	0
swifter	4	.3711	.3648	35.6	0	0	1	0	2	1	0	0	2	0	0	0	0	0	0	0	0	0	0	0	0	1	1	0	0
swiftest	3	.2357	.2199	33.4	0	0	1	0	1	1	0	0	2	0	0	0	0	0	0	0	0	0	0	0	0	1	0	0	0
Swifties	2	.0000	.0219	23.4	0	0	0	0	0	2	0	0	0	2	0	0	0	0	0	0	0	0	0	0	0	0	0	0	0
swiftly	112	.8530	19.176	52.8	8	23	15	20	24	11	10	1	35	3	0	8	0	19	2	14	3	1	0	0	8	8	5	6	0
swiftness	11	.4803	1.2144	40.8	1	3	1	3	3	0	0	0	6	0	0	0	0	0	0	0	0	0	0	0	1	2	0	2	0
swifts	11	.3523	.8826	39.5	4	0	1	6	0	0	0	0	0	0	0	1	0	0	0	6	0	0	0	0	0	4	0	0	0
swim	290	.9029	52.187	57.2	84	80	20	36	38	16	9	7	110	9	1	19	6	13	10	39	4	1	3	0	18	32	9	16	0
swimmer	34	.5976	4.2909	46.3	8	10	3	5	4	3	1	0	9	3	3	0	0	0	0	8	1	0	0	0	0	2	1	7	0
swimmerets	4	.0000	.0789	29.0	0	0	0	1	3	0	0	0	0	0	0	0	0	0	0	4	0	0	0	0	0	0	0	0	0
swimmers	24	.6207	3.1176	44.9	5	5	2	6	3	0	2	1	5	1	1	0	0	0	0	6	0	0	0	0	0	4	1	6	0
swimming	270	.8961	48.240	56.8	57	61	27	38	42	25	16	4	94	21	5	19	11	17	4	26	1	1	1	0	14	22	11	23	0
swims	47	.5689	5.6823	47.5	16	9	6	5	6	5	0	0	12	12	4	0	0	0	0	8	0	0	0	0	2	6	0	3	0
swindle	2	.2446	.1125	30.5	0	0	0	0	2	0	0	0	0	1	0	1	0	0	0	0	0	0	0	0	0	0	0	0	0
swine	7	.3250	.5030	37.0	0	0	0	0	2	0	3	2	0	1	0	4	0	0	0	0	0	0	0	0	0	2	0	0	0
swineherd	6	.2796	.4291	36.3	0	0	0	0	3	0	3	0	2	0	0	3	0	0	0	0	0	0	0	0	0	1	0	0	0
swing	189	.8636	32.569	55.1	52	34	29	19	27	12	14	2	40	6	4	12	2	8	5	21	34	3	0	2	9	21	5	17	0
Swing	7	.3192	.4752	36.8	0	0	3	1	1	1	1	0	0	0	0	1	0	0	0	0	5	1	0	0	0	0	0	0	0
swinging	108	.8384	18.272	52.6	11	23	17	17	23	9	6	2	50	5	0	10	1	1	5	4	0	1	1	1	13	3	2	11	0
swings	44	.7460	6.7025	48.3	12	11	2	5	8	4	1	1	13	0	0	3	3	0	2	6	6	0	0	0	0	4	3	4	0
swiped	4	.3619	.3155	35.0	0	1	0	1	1	1	0	0	0	0	0	1	0	0	0	0	0	0	0	0	2	1	0	0	0
swirl	14	.5839	1.7395	42.4	1	2	1	1	5	1	1	2	5	0	1	0	0	0	0	0	1	0	1	0	0	2	0	4	0
swirled	16	.6095	2.0958	43.2	4	1	3	4	0	1	2	1	8	1	1	2	0	0	0	1	0	0	0	0	0	2	1	0	0
swirling	29	.5442	3.4130	45.3	3	8	4	7	3	1	2	1	10	0	0	2	0	0	0	3	0	3	0	0	1	4	1	5	0
swirls	3	.3781	.2493	34.0	1	0	2	0	0	0	0	0	0	1	0	0	0	1	0	0	0	0	0	0	0	0	0	1	0
swish	36	.4131	3.4618	45.4	19	8	4	3	1	0	1	0	16	1	0	1	0	0	0	0	13	0	0	0	4	1	0	0	0
SWISH-swish	2	.0000	.0162	22.1	2	0	0	0	0	0	0	0	0	0	0	0	0	0	0	0	2	0	0	0	0	0	0	0	0
swished	9	.5317	1.0184	40.1	2	3	1	0	3	0	0	0	2	0	1	1	0	0	0	0	0	0	0	0	2	1	0	2	0
swishing	13	.6057	1.6708	42.2	4	3	0	1	2	1	2	0	5	1	0	2	0	0	0	0	2	0	0	0	1	0	0	2	0
swiss	2	.0000	.0389	25.9	0	2	0	0	0	0	0	0	0	0	0	0	0	2	0	0	0	0	0	0	0	0	0	0	0
Swiss	119	.7265	17.623	52.5	9	36	29	20	12	8	3	2	15	0	0	3	5	44	0	4	5	1	1	0	0	27	10	4	0
switch	119	.6714	16.524	52.2	23	17	12	19	22	19	5	2	30	0	0	2	1	1	0	23	4	0	1	12	9	12	5	19	0
switchboard	3	.3272	.2361	33.7	0	0	0	2	0	0	1	0	1	0	0	0	0	0	0	0	1	0	0	0	0	0	1	0	0
switched	40	.6802	5.7155	47.6	9	6	2	7	8	4	4	0	20	0	0	6	1	2	0	0	4	0	0	0	2	3	1	1	0
switches	31	.5771	3.7937	45.8	9	4	7	3	3	5	0	0	6	1	0	0	0	1	0	14	1	0	0	3	0	2	2	1	0
switching	20	.6639	2.7574	44.4	1	3	2	2	7	4	1	0	6	0	0	2	0	1	0	1	2	0	0	0	1	0	4	3	0
swits	2	.0000	.0215	23.3	0	0	0	0	0	0	2	0	0	0	0	2	0	0	0	0	0	0	0	0	0	0	0	0	0
Switzerland	121	.7547	18.522	52.7	11	35	27	19	11	11	4	3	17	2	0	1	3	41	1	4	7	1	1	0	0	24	15	4	0
Switzerland's	9	.2354	.5180	37.1	0	1	7	1	0	0	0	0	0	0	0	0	0	1	0	0	0	0	0	0	0	7	0	1	0
swivel	4	.3018	.2919	34.7	0	1	0	0	1	2	0	0	1	2	0	1	0	0	0	0	0	0	0	0	0	0	0	0	0
swiveled	3	.3873	.2495	34.0	0	0	1	0	0	1	1	0	0	0	0	1	0	0	0	0	0	0	0	0	1	0	0	1	0
swollen	39	.6198	5.0825	47.1	2	0	8	9	10	6	4	0	12	0	0	10	0	1	1	2	0	0	0	0	6	0	2	5	0
swoop	14	.5420	1.6886	42.3	4	4	0	2	3	0	1	0	8	0	0	1	0	0	0	0	1	0	0	0	0	0	1	3	0
swooped	18	.4923	2.0411	43.1	3	5	4	5	1	0	0	0	11	0	0	1	0	1	0	0	0	0	0	0	4	0	1	0	0
swooping	5	.2445	.3864	35.9	2	0	0	1	1	1	0	0	4	0	0	1	0	0	0	0	0	0	0	0	0	0	0	0	0
swoops	5	.4781	.5442	37.4	0	1	1	1	0	1	0	1	2	0	0	0	0	1	0	1	0	0	0	0	0	0	0	1	0
sword	93	.8316	15.601	51.9	4	15	10	27	17	9	8	3	37	4	0	10	0	9	3	3	5	2	0	0	6	7	2	5	0
Sword	2	.1787	.1174	30.7	1	0	0	0	1	0	0	0	1	0	0	0	0	0	0	0	0	0	0	0	1	0	0	0	0
swordfish	7	.2753	.4414	36.4	5	1	0	0	1	0	0	0	0	1	0	0	1	0	0	0	0	0	0	0	0	0	0	5	0
swordplay	2	.2446	.1125	30.5	0	0	0	1	0	1	0	0	0	1	0	1	0	0	0	0	0	0	0	0	0	0	0	0	0
swords	38	.6736	5.3854	47.3	2	6	5	7	8	6	1	3	18	1	0	4	0	6	0	0	1	0	0	0	2	0	5	1	0
swordsman	3	.3128	.2349	33.7	0	0	0	1	0	1	0	1	1	0	0	0	0	0	1	1	0	0	0	0	0	0	0	0	0
swordtails	3	.1434	.1493	31.7	2	1	0	0	0	0	0	0	1	0	0	0	2	0	0	0	0	0	0	0	0	0	0	0	0
swore	28	.7307	4.1767	46.2	1	1	3	5	6	9	3	0	7	1	0	5	0	3	1	0	2	0	0	0	4	2	0	3	0

9L sweet-flavored
8P sweet-natured
4E sweet-pea
7D sweet-sour
5A sweet-talked
9D Sweet's
9J sweethearts
7A sweetie
7D sweetish
8A Sweetree's
7J Swell
4F swept-back
7R swept-wing
4R swerving
7Q swervings
7A swift-footed
4P swift-running
7J swift-slapping
8C swiftest-moving
6G swigglenit
7N swilling
4R Swim
8B swim-bladder
7D swimmin'
6A Swimming
4A swimming's
4G swimsuits
7R swindler
9Q swindlers
XB swinelike
XR swing-wing
XR swinger
5R swingers
5Q swinging-sector
9N swingy
6P swishy-wishy
4P swisssh
XR switch-over
6P switchboards
6R switchers
9P switchman
8D swoon
9B swoons
4A SWOOOOOOOSH
3A swoosh
3P SWOOSH
4A swooshing
7N swop
7R Swope
4F Swordfish
4A swordtail

Word Type	F	D	U	SFI	3 Gr 3	4 Gr 4	5 Gr 5	6 Gr 6	7 Gr 7	8 Gr 8	9 Gr 9	X UnGr	A Read	B Eng & Gr	C Comp	D Lit	E Math	F Soc Stud	G Spell	H Sci	J Music	K Art	L Home Ec	M Shop	N Lib F	P Lib NF	Q Lib Ref	R Mag	S Rel
sworn	9	.5239	1.0206	40.1	0	0	3	2	0	2	2	0	2	0	0	2	0	3	0	0	0	0	0	0	1	1	0	0	0
swum	8	.3263	.6695	38.3	1	0	2	2	2	1	0	0	4	0	0	0	0	0	0	0	0	0	0	0	3	1	0	0	0
swung	164	.6806	23.368	53.7	29	30	19	23	38	17	8	0	73	1	2	14	0	4	0	4	2	0	0	0	34	22	0	8	0
Sy	2	.0000	.0290	24.6	0	0	0	0	2	0	0	0	0	0	0	0	0	0	0	0	0	0	0	0	0	2	0	0	0
sycamore	4	.4500	.4063	36.1	2	0	0	0	1	1	0	0	1	0	0	1	0	1	0	1	0	0	0	0	0	0	0	0	0
sycamores	2	.0000	.0290	24.6	0	0	2	0	0	0	0	0	0	0	0	0	0	0	0	0	0	0	0	0	0	2	0	0	0
Sydney	14	.4573	1.4003	41.5	0	1	1	8	1	1	2	0	1	0	0	2	1	8	0	0	0	0	0	0	0	0	0	2	0
Sykes	3	.0000	.0322	25.1	0	0	0	0	0	0	3	0	0	0	0	3	0	0	0	0	0	0	0	0	0	0	0	0	0
syllabic	54	.0613	1.0697	40.3	15	0	0	0	20	18	1	0	0	3	0	0	0	0	51	0	0	0	0	0	0	0	0	0	0
syllabicated	2	.1497	.1046	30.2	0	1	0	0	1	0	0	0	1	0	0	0	0	0	1	0	0	0	0	0	0	0	0	0	0
syllabication	3	.0000	.0243	23.9	0	0	0	0	2	1	0	0	0	0	0	0	0	0	3	0	0	0	0	0	0	0	0	0	0
syllable	533	.2083	27.024	54.3	66	87	123	88	95	55	18	1	55	53	0	0	0	3	400	0	21	0	0	0	0	1	0	0	0
syllables	706	.1520	27.770	54.4	81	135	171	152	79	64	22	2	53	43	0	1	0	2	593	0	10	1	0	0	0	1	1	1	0
Sylvain	16	.0000	.1876	32.7	0	16	0	0	0	0	0	0	0	0	0	0	0	0	0	0	0	0	0	0	16	0	0	0	0
sylvan	3	.3234	.2368	33.7	0	0	2	0	1	0	0	0	1	0	0	0	0	0	1	0	0	0	0	0	0	1	0	0	0
Sylvanus	3	.0000	.0352	25.5	0	3	0	0	0	0	0	0	0	0	0	0	0	0	0	0	0	0	0	0	3	0	0	0	0
Sylvester	2	.1717	.1142	30.6	0	1	0	0	0	0	1	0	1	0	0	1	0	0	0	0	0	0	0	0	0	0	0	0	0
Sylvia	14	.2199	.7042	38.5	3	0	2	1	0	0	8	0	1	3	0	0	1	0	1	0	0	0	8	0	0	0	0	0	0
Sylvia's	3	.1367	.0954	29.8	0	0	0	0	1	0	2	0	0	0	0	1	0	0	0	0	0	0	2	0	0	0	0	0	0
Sylvie	9	.2212	.6297	38.0	4	2	3	0	0	0	0	0	6	0	0	3	0	0	0	0	0	0	0	0	0	0	0	0	0
Sylvis	2	.0000	.0389	25.9	0	0	0	0	0	2	0	0	0	0	0	0	0	2	0	0	0	0	0	0	0	0	0	0	0
symbiosis	3	.0000	.0591	27.7	0	0	0	0	3	0	0	0	0	0	0	0	0	0	0	3	0	0	0	0	0	0	0	0	0
symbiotic	2	.0000	.0394	26.0	0	0	0	0	2	0	0	0	0	0	0	0	0	0	0	2	0	0	0	0	0	0	0	0	0
symbol	381	.7543	57.855	57.6	21	32	49	44	102	97	34	2	22	40	0	0	165	16	56	12	14	2	0	7	0	18	15	13	1
symbolic	16	.4974	1.6563	42.2	0	0	0	1	8	2	4	1	0	2	0	0	3	1	0	0	0	2	0	0	0	0	2	6	0
symbolism	5	.4538	.4838	36.8	0	0	0	0	2	1	2	0	0	0	0	0	1	0	0	1	0	0	0	0	0	0	1	2	0
symbolize	19	.6055	2.3687	43.7	0	0	2	1	9	2	4	1	1	8	0	0	2	3	0	1	1	1	0	0	0	0	1	1	0
symbolized	12	.5844	1.4431	41.6	1	0	2	2	2	2	3	0	0	2	0	0	3	1	0	0	0	0	0	0	0	1	3	2	0
symbolizes	14	.6141	1.7699	42.5	0	1	3	2	4	3	1	0	1	2	0	2	1	0	0	2	2	0	0	0	0	0	0	4	0
symbolizing	2	.1033	.0599	27.8	0	0	0	0	2	0	0	0	0	0	0	0	0	0	0	1	0	1	0	0	0	0	0	0	0
symbols	451	.7331	66.687	58.2	18	57	44	35	148	95	50	4	20	57	0	3	194	39	39	14	27	7	1	24	0	6	10	10	0
Symi	7	.0000	.3198	35.0	7	0	0	0	0	0	0	0	7	0	0	0	0	0	0	0	0	0	0	0	0	0	0	0	0
symmetric	2	.0000	.0299	24.8	0	0	0	0	0	2	0	0	0	0	0	0	2	0	0	0	0	0	0	0	0	0	0	0	0
symmetrical	20	.4305	1.8131	42.6	0	0	5	0	3	6	5	1	0	0	0	1	11	0	0	0	0	1	0	5	0	0	1	1	0
symmetry	24	.4516	2.3455	43.7	1	0	4	1	7	10	1	0	1	0	0	1	15	0	0	4	1	0	0	0	0	1	1	0	0
sympathetic	19	.6600	2.6136	44.2	1	2	2	2	3	5	2	2	6	0	0	1	0	1	0	0	1	0	0	0	1	3	1	5	0
sympathetically	2	.1787	.1174	30.7	1	0	0	1	0	0	0	0	1	0	0	0	0	0	0	0	0	0	0	0	1	0	0	0	0
sympathies	7	.3085	.4949	36.9	0	0	1	1	1	2	2	0	0	0	0	0	0	2	0	0	0	0	0	0	0	1	0	4	0
sympathize	4	.1717	.2284	33.6	0	0	0	1	1	1	1	0	2	0	0	2	0	0	0	0	0	0	0	0	0	0	0	0	0
sympathized	4	.2982	.2887	34.6	1	0	2	0	0	1	0	0	1	0	0	1	0	0	0	0	0	0	0	0	0	0	2	0	0
sympathizers	3	.3769	.2484	34.0	0	0	1	0	0	2	0	0	0	0	0	0	0	1	0	0	0	0	0	0	0	0	1	1	0
sympathy	45	.7519	6.8482	48.4	4	1	3	5	15	6	11	0	8	1	1	8	0	3	0	0	2	0	0	0	8	4	6	4	0
symphonic	37	.0598	.7218	38.6	0	1	2	1	0	23	10	0	0	2	0	0	0	0	0	0	35	0	0	0	0	0	0	0	0
symphonies	23	.0000	.1859	32.7	0	1	3	5	2	11	1	0	0	0	0	0	0	0	0	0	23	0	0	0	0	0	0	0	0
symphony	86	.2223	4.3439	46.4	2	3	17	9	11	31	13	0	1	3	0	0	0	0	0	1	75	2	0	0	0	1	3	0	0
Symphony	44	.0191	.5250	37.2	2	1	5	5	10	11	10	0	0	0	0	0	0	1	0	0	43	0	0	0	0	0	0	0	0
symptom	7	.3267	.5083	37.1	0	1	0	0	2	2	1	1	0	0	0	0	0	0	0	1	0	0	0	0	0	0	3	3	0
symptoms	20	.5380	2.2417	43.5	1	2	0	2	5	6	2	2	1	0	0	0	0	0	0	2	0	0	2	0	0	5	6	4	0
syn-	2	.2408	.1091	30.4	0	1	0	0	1	0	0	0	0	1	0	0	0	0	1	0	0	0	0	0	0	0	0	0	0
synagogue	4	.0205	.0727	28.6	3	1	0	0	0	0	0	0	1	0	0	0	0	0	0	0	0	0	0	0	1	0	0	0	2
Synagogue	2	.2417	.1091	30.4	1	0	0	0	0	0	1	0	0	0	0	0	0	0	0	0	1	0	0	0	0	0	1	0	0
synapse	2	.2278	.1128	30.5	0	0	0	2	0	0	0	0	0	0	0	0	0	0	0	1	0	0	0	0	0	0	1	0	0
synapsed	2	.0000	.0209	23.2	0	0	0	2	0	0	0	0	0	0	0	0	0	0	0	0	0	0	0	0	0	0	2	0	0
synchrotron	4	.2353	.2382	33.8	0	0	0	1	2	0	1	0	0	0	0	0	0	0	0	3	0	0	0	0	0	0	1	0	0
syncopated	26	.0000	.2102	33.2	1	1	5	11	3	4	1	0	0	0	0	0	0	0	0	0	26	0	0	0	0	0	0	0	0
syncopation	25	.0000	.2021	33.1	0	1	3	10	2	9	0	0	0	0	0	0	0	0	0	0	25	0	0	0	0	0	0	0	0
syndicate	2	.0000	.0215	23.3	0	0	0	0	1	1	0	0	0	0	0	2	0	0	0	0	0	0	0	0	0	0	0	0	0
Syndicate	2	.0000	.0290	24.6	0	2	0	0	0	0	0	0	0	0	0	0	0	0	0	0	0	0	0	0	0	2	0	0	0
syndicated	2	.1948	.1250	31.0	0	1	0	0	1	0	0	0	1	0	0	0	0	0	0	0	0	0	0	0	0	1	0	0	0
synonym	60	.2795	3.8350	45.8	0	14	9	8	13	5	6	5	5	24	0	0	1	0	30	0	0	0	0	0	0	0	0	0	0
synonymous	20	.1689	.7396	38.7	0	0	13	0	1	1	3	2	0	0	14	0	0	0	0	0	0	0	1	0	1	0	2	2	0
synonyms	102	.2408	5.6315	47.5	5	6	16	30	30	10	1	4	3	42	0	0	0	0	57	0	0	0	0	0	0	0	0	0	0
Synonyms	2	.2408	.1091	30.4	0	0	0	0	0	1	0	1	0	1	0	0	0	0	1	0	0	0	0	0	0	0	0	0	0
synopsis	2	.2375	.1088	30.4	0	0	0	0	0	2	0	0	0	0	0	0	0	0	0	0	1	0	0	0	0	0	0	1	0
synthesis	9	.4559	.8844	39.5	1	0	1	2	2	0	3	0	0	0	0	0	0	1	0	4	0	0	0	0	0	0	2	2	0
synthesize	3	.2445	.1818	32.6	0	0	0	0	1	0	2	0	0	0	0	0	0	0	0	2	0	0	0	0	0	0	1	0	0
synthesized	3	.2383	.1815	32.6	0	0	0	0	1	0	2	0	0	0	0	0	0	0	0	2	0	0	0	0	0	1	0	0	0
synthesizer	2	.0000	.0914	29.6	0	0	0	0	2	0	0	0	2	0	0	0	0	0	0	0	0	0	0	0	0	0	0	0	0
synthetic	41	.6534	5.4585	47.4	0	2	11	2	8	6	11	1	2	0	0	0	0	6	2	7	0	1	7	1	0	2	10	3	0
synthetics	4	.2570	.2219	33.5	0	0	0	0	0	1	2	1	0	0	0	0	0	0	1	0	0	0	2	0	0	0	0	1	0
Syracuse	9	.3841	.7716	38.9	0	1	0	1	2	0	1	4	1	0	0	1	0	0	0	0	0	0	0	0	0	5	2	0	0
Syria	41	.3601	3.4286	45.4	3	4	1	21	8	2	2	0	3	0	0	0	0	30	0	0	0	0	0	0	0	4	2	2	0
Syria's	2	.0000	.0389	25.9	0	0	0	2	0	0	0	0	0	0	0	0	0	2	0	0	0	0	0	0	0	0	0	0	0
Syrian	10	.6176	1.2637	41.0	0	0	2	1	1	1	5	0	0	2	0	0	0	2	0	0	1	0	0	0	0	2	2	1	0
Syrians	5	.3704	.4149	36.2	0	0	1	2	1	1	0	0	0	0	0	0	0	3	0	0	1	0	0	0	0	1	0	0	0
syrinx	2	.2417	.1091	30.4	0	1	0	0	1	0	0	0	0	0	0	0	0	0	0	0	1	0	0	0	0	0	1	0	0
Syrinx	2	.0000	.0162	22.1	0	2	0	0	0	0	0	0	0	0	0	0	0	0	0	0	2	0	0	0	0	0	0	0	0
syrup	50	.6989	7.1140	48.5	8	7	15	1	7	4	7	1	6	4	0	4	3	5	1	0	0	0	2	0	17	2	0	6	0
syrups	2	.2446	.1125	30.5	0	0	0	0	0	1	1	0	0	1	0	1	0	0	0	0	0	0	0	0	0	0	0	0	0
syrupy	4	.3869	.3841	35.8	0	0	0	0	2	1	1	0	2	0	0	0	0	1	0	1	0	0	0	0	0	0	0	0	0
system	1110	.8043	179.00	62.5	59	69	110	127	343	199	167	36	48	30	5	32	224	122	13	289	28	1	3	5	1	35	165	109	0
System	56	.5285	6.2191	47.9	0	2	6	4	23	14	4	3	6	13	0	0	2	4	0	0	0	0	1	0	0	0	22	8	0
system's	5	.4478	.4751	36.8	0	0	0	0	3	0	2	0	0	0	0	1	0	0	0	1	0	0	0	0	0	0	2	1	0
System's	2	.0000	.0914	29.6	0	0	0	0	0	2	0	0	2	0	0	0	0	0	0	0	0	0	0	0	0	0	0	0	0
systematic	23	.6455	3.0206	44.8	0	0	2	1	5	3	11	1	0	0	0	0	1	4	1	1	1	0	0	1	0	2	9	3	0
systematically	11	.6227	1.4095	41.5	0	0	0	1	3	0	6	1	1	1	0	0	1	2	0	0	0	0	0	1	1	0	3	1	0
systems	210	.7312	31.094	54.9	6	11	25	24	50	38	46	10	9	10	2	0	22	21	2	65	2	0	0	2	0	3	46	26	0
Systems	4	.3512	.3114	34.9	0	0	1	2	1	0	0	0	0	0	0	0	0	0	0	1	0	0	0	0	0	0	1	2	0
Szilard	2	.0000	.0209	23.2	0	0	0	0	0	0	2	0	0	0	0	0	0	0	0	0	0	0	0	0	0	0	2	0	0
S1	7	.1048	.2062	33.1	0	0	0	0	0	4	0	3	0	0	0	0	0	0	0	3	0	0	0	4	0	0	0	0	0
S2	3	.1785	.1397	31.5	0	0	0	0	0	1	0	2	0	0	0	0	0	0	0	2	0	0	0	1	0	0	0	0	0
t	195	.5588	22.970	53.6	38	48	17	10	39	16	26	1	40	6	1	3	44	1	74	4	0	0	1	0	4	1	11	5	0
T	176	.7806	27.637	54.4	14	37	24	16	39	31	14	1	16	8	4	0	70	14	2	8	2	0	2	7	3	22	11	7	0
TV's	2	.0000	.0243	23.9	0	2	0	0	0	0	0	0	0	0	0	0	0	0	0	0	0	0	0	0	0	0	0	2	0
T-cd	2	.0000	.0219	23.4	0	0	0	0	0	2	0	0	0	2	0	0	0	0	0	0	0	0	0	0	0	0	0	0	0
T-cdSP	2	.0000	.0219	23.4	0	0	0	0	0	2	0	0	0	2	0	0	0	0	0	0	0	0	0	0	0	0	0	0	0

XR Sycamore
7R sycophants
6R Sydney's
9H syenite
8B syle
7G syllabize
3A sylph
3A Sylvie's

8H Symbol
5P symbolically
3A Symi's
7Q symmetrically
8F sympathizer
9J Symphonies
8H symposium
9B Symposium

5P synagogues
8H synchrotrons
3A Syncom
6J syncopate
8R syndrome
7J Syne
8Q synod
9Q synovial

8B syntax
8H Syntaxis
6J Synthesizer
9H synthesizing
9H synthetically
9H syphilis
9Q Syracusans
8D Syringa

7Q syringe
8F SYSTEM
8H systematize
8F Szechwan
7J Szigeti
9M S2S
8M S3
8M S4

7R T-Bird
6N T-T-T-Twickerham
7B T-Yes/No
8E T-bone

Word Type	F	D	U	SFI	3 Gr 3	4 Gr 4	5 Gr 5	6 Gr 6	7 Gr 7	8 Gr 8	9 Gr 9	X UnGr	A Read	B Eng & Gr	C Comp	D Lit	E Math	F Soc Stud	G Spell	H Sci	J Music	K Art	L Home Ec	M Shop	N Lib F	P Lib NF	Q Lib Ref	R Mag	S Rel
T-do	4	.0000	.0438	26.4	0	0	0	0	1	0	3	0	0	4	0	0	0	0	0	0	0	0	0	0	0	0	0	0	0
T-e-a-c-h-e-r	2	.0000	.0290	24.6	0	2	0	0	0	0	0	0	0	0	0	0	0	0	0	0	0	0	0	0	0	2	0	0	0
T-shaped	3	.0000	.0449	26.5	0	0	0	0	0	3	0	0	0	0	0	0	3	0	0	0	0	0	0	0	0	0	0	0	0
T-shirt	4	.3071	.2967	34.7	2	0	0	0	1	1	0	0	1	0	0	1	0	0	0	0	0	0	0	0	2	0	0	0	0
T-wh	2	.0000	.0219	23.4	0	0	0	0	0	0	2	0	0	2	0	0	0	0	0	0	0	0	0	0	0	0	0	0	0
T-37	4	.2107	.2095	33.2	3	0	0	0	0	0	0	1	0	0	0	0	0	0	0	0	0	0	0	0	0	3	0	1	0
t'	11	.0697	.3255	35.1	1	1	0	0	0	9	0	0	2	0	0	9	0	0	0	0	0	0	0	0	0	0	0	0	0
T'ang	9	.0000	.1750	32.4	0	0	0	0	0	9	0	0	0	0	0	0	0	9	0	0	0	0	0	0	0	0	0	0	0
t'other	3	.3400	.2455	33.9	1	0	1	0	1	0	0	0	1	1	0	0	0	0	0	0	0	0	0	0	1	0	0	0	0
t's	8	.4125	.7306	38.6	1	4	0	1	1	0	1	0	2	2	1	0	0	0	3	0	0	0	0	0	0	0	0	0	0
ta	15	.0000	.1213	30.8	10	0	0	4	1	0	0	0	0	0	0	0	0	0	0	0	15	0	0	0	0	0	0	0	0
Ta	3	.0000	.1370	31.4	0	3	0	0	0	0	0	0	3	0	0	0	0	0	0	0	0	0	0	0	0	0	0	0	0
Ta-kuan	6	.0000	.1167	30.7	0	0	0	6	0	0	0	0	0	0	0	0	0	6	0	0	0	0	0	0	0	0	0	0	0
Ta-lin	5	.0000	.0724	28.6	5	0	0	0	0	0	0	0	0	0	0	0	0	0	0	0	0	0	0	0	0	5	0	0	0
ta-rah-ra-ra-rah	2	.0000	.0914	29.6	2	0	0	0	0	0	0	0	2	0	0	0	0	0	0	0	0	0	0	0	0	0	0	0	0
ta-ump	11	.0000	.5025	37.0	11	0	0	0	0	0	0	0	11	0	0	0	0	0	0	0	0	0	0	0	0	0	0	0	0
ta-umps	2	.0000	.0914	29.6	2	0	0	0	0	0	0	0	2	0	0	0	0	0	0	0	0	0	0	0	0	0	0	0	0
ta'en	2	.2446	.1125	30.5	0	0	0	0	1	0	1	0	0	1	0	1	0	0	0	0	0	0	0	0	0	0	0	0	0
tab	3	.0000	.0365	25.6	2	0	0	0	1	0	0	0	0	0	0	0	0	0	0	0	0	0	0	0	0	0	0	3	0
tabasco	2	.0000	.0243	23.9	0	1	0	0	1	0	0	0	0	0	0	0	0	0	0	0	0	0	0	0	0	0	0	2	0
Tabasco	2	.2106	.0917	29.6	0	0	0	0	0	1	1	0	0	0	0	0	0	0	1	0	0	0	1	0	0	0	0	0	0
tabby	2	.2443	.1130	30.5	0	0	0	0	2	0	0	0	0	0	0	1	0	0	0	0	0	0	0	0	1	0	0	0	0
Tabby	7	.3117	.5573	37.5	0	1	4	2	0	0	0	0	3	0	0	0	0	0	0	0	0	0	0	0	3	1	0	0	0
tabi	5	.1865	.3050	34.8	0	3	0	2	0	0	0	0	2	0	0	0	0	3	0	0	0	0	0	0	0	0	0	0	0
table	1502	.8808	263.51	64.2	294	219	171	124	259	208	215	12	315	76	13	105	423	52	29	120	16	6	75	50	84	80	13	44	1
Table	61	.7149	8.9356	49.5	1	8	2	12	7	20	8	3	12	6	0	0	15	7	1	13	0	0	1	3	0	1	2	0	0
table-clamp	2	.0000	.0050	17.0	0	0	0	0	0	0	2	0	0	0	0	0	0	0	0	0	0	0	0	2	0	0	0	0	0
table's	2	.2388	.1089	30.4	0	0	0	0	1	1	0	0	0	0	0	0	0	0	1	0	0	0	0	0	1	0	0	0	0
tablecloth	21	.4699	2.1677	43.4	1	11	0	2	1	2	4	0	6	2	0	5	2	2	0	0	0	0	4	0	0	0	0	0	0
tablecloths	2	.0000	.0914	29.6	1	0	1	0	0	0	0	0	2	0	0	0	0	0	0	0	0	0	0	0	0	0	0	0	0
tableland	7	.0861	.2668	34.3	1	0	0	1	4	1	0	0	1	0	0	0	0	6	0	0	0	0	0	0	0	0	0	0	0
tablelands	4	.3344	.3261	35.1	1	1	1	1	0	0	0	0	1	0	0	0	0	2	0	0	0	0	0	0	0	0	1	0	0
tables	171	.8599	29.366	54.7	46	18	14	18	24	19	23	9	34	4	2	8	46	15	1	11	0	2	5	8	10	11	5	9	0
Tables	3	.2383	.1815	32.6	0	0	1	0	0	0	0	2	0	0	0	0	0	0	0	2	0	0	0	0	0	1	0	0	0
tablespoon	19	.2750	1.1637	40.7	2	4	1	0	5	3	2	2	0	0	0	0	5	0	0	2	0	0	8	0	0	0	0	4	0
tablespoonfuls	3	.1970	.1504	31.8	0	0	1	0	1	1	0	0	0	0	0	0	0	0	0	2	0	0	1	0	0	0	0	0	0
tablespoons	26	.2926	1.7025	42.3	2	7	1	1	4	5	4	2	1	0	0	0	2	0	0	3	0	0	11	0	0	6	0	3	0
tablet	23	.4355	2.1429	43.3	0	7	2	5	7	1	1	0	1	0	5	3	7	3	1	1	0	0	0	0	0	2	0	0	0
tabletop	5	.2431	.2776	34.4	0	0	0	0	1	4	0	0	0	0	0	0	0	0	0	0	0	0	0	1	0	0	0	4	0
tabletops	2	.1698	.1133	30.5	0	0	2	0	0	0	0	0	1	0	0	0	0	0	0	0	0	0	0	0	0	0	1	0	0
tablets	15	.6057	1.8667	42.7	0	3	3	0	2	4	3	0	1	0	0	1	4	1	0	1	0	1	0	2	0	0	3	1	0
tableware	4	.1443	.2329	33.7	3	0	0	0	0	0	1	0	3	0	0	0	0	0	0	0	0	0	0	1	0	0	0	0	0
taboo	3	.2332	.1690	32.3	0	0	0	0	3	0	0	0	0	0	0	0	0	0	0	0	0	0	0	0	0	2	0	1	0
taboos	2	.2437	.1129	30.5	0	0	0	0	0	0	1	1	0	0	0	0	0	0	0	0	0	0	0	0	0	0	1	1	0
tabor	5	.1530	.1990	33.0	0	0	0	4	1	0	0	0	0	0	0	4	0	0	0	0	0	0	0	0	0	1	0	0	0
Tabor	14	.0566	.3635	35.6	0	0	0	2	12	0	0	0	2	0	0	12	0	0	0	0	0	0	0	0	0	0	0	0	0
Tabor's	4	.0000	.0429	26.3	0	0	0	0	4	0	0	0	0	0	0	4	0	0	0	0	0	0	0	0	0	0	0	0	0
tabs	11	.5943	1.3843	41.4	0	3	0	2	3	2	0	1	3	0	0	0	3	1	0	0	1	0	0	0	1	0	0	2	0
Tabulae	2	.0000	.0394	26.0	0	0	0	0	0	0	0	2	0	0	0	0	0	0	0	2	0	0	0	0	0	0	0	0	0
tabular	9	.0803	.2103	33.2	0	0	0	0	0	0	6	3	0	0	0	0	0	0	0	3	0	0	0	6	0	0	0	0	0
tabulate	2	.0000	.0299	24.8	0	0	0	2	0	0	0	0	0	0	0	0	2	0	0	0	0	0	0	0	0	0	0	0	0
tabulated	3	.2823	.1865	32.7	0	0	0	0	2	0	1	0	0	0	0	0	1	0	0	0	0	0	0	1	0	0	1	0	0
tabulating	2	.1457	.0722	28.6	0	0	0	0	1	0	1	0	0	0	0	0	1	0	0	0	0	0	0	1	0	0	0	0	0
tabulation	2	.2413	.1212	30.8	0	0	0	0	1	0	0	1	0	0	0	0	1	0	0	1	0	0	0	0	0	0	0	0	0
tacit	2	.0000	.0243	23.9	0	0	0	0	0	2	0	0	0	0	0	0	0	0	0	0	0	0	0	0	0	0	0	2	0
taciturn	2	.2440	.1132	30.5	0	0	0	0	1	1	0	0	0	0	0	1	0	0	0	0	0	0	0	0	0	0	0	1	0
tack	30	.6839	4.1471	46.2	6	5	2	6	7	1	2	1	1	0	0	1	0	0	1	6	1	1	3	4	6	4	0	2	0
tacked	7	.4407	.6927	38.4	1	4	1	0	1	0	0	0	2	0	0	0	0	0	0	0	1	0	0	0	1	3	0	0	0
tacking	2	.1948	.1250	31.0	0	1	1	0	0	0	0	0	1	0	0	0	0	0	0	0	0	0	0	0	0	1	0	0	0
tackle	48	.7749	7.5480	48.8	16	0	1	8	9	3	7	4	11	4	0	1	0	3	1	14	0	0	0	1	4	2	1	6	0
tackled	16	.6540	2.1915	43.4	3	1	1	3	3	1	4	0	6	2	0	0	1	0	0	0	1	0	0	0	0	1	2	3	0
tackler	2	.0000	.0219	23.4	0	0	2	0	0	0	0	0	0	2	0	0	0	0	0	0	0	0	0	0	0	0	0	0	0
tackles	4	.3606	.3540	35.5	2	0	0	0	0	2	0	0	2	1	0	0	0	0	1	0	0	0	0	0	0	0	0	0	0
tackling	4	.4817	.4082	36.1	0	0	0	0	3	1	0	0	0	1	0	0	0	1	0	0	0	0	0	0	0	1	0	1	0
tacks	25	.4293	2.2823	43.6	8	2	0	4	0	0	10	1	1	0	0	0	0	0	1	9	0	3	8	0	0	2	0	1	0
Tacoma	18	.4165	1.6494	42.2	14	2	0	0	0	0	2	0	0	1	1	0	0	14	0	0	2	0	0	0	0	0	0	0	0
taconite	12	.1952	.5626	37.5	0	0	0	0	0	3	9	0	0	3	0	0	0	0	0	0	0	0	0	0	0	0	9	0	0
tacos	3	.0000	.0322	25.1	0	3	0	0	0	0	0	0	0	0	0	3	0	0	0	0	0	0	0	0	0	0	0	0	0
tact	5	.2350	.2615	34.2	0	0	0	2	0	2	1	0	0	0	2	0	0	0	0	0	0	0	0	0	2	0	0	1	0
tactful	2	.2152	.1357	31.3	0	0	0	0	0	2	0	0	1	0	0	0	0	1	0	0	0	0	0	0	0	0	0	0	0
tactfully	2	.2412	.1141	30.6	0	0	0	0	1	1	0	0	0	1	0	0	0	0	0	0	0	0	0	0	0	1	0	0	0
tactic	3	.1277	.1363	31.3	0	0	0	0	2	1	0	0	1	0	0	0	0	0	0	0	0	0	0	0	0	0	0	2	0
tactical	4	.3192	.3100	34.9	0	0	1	0	3	0	0	0	1	0	0	0	0	0	0	0	0	0	0	0	0	2	0	1	0
tactics	25	.5134	2.7224	44.3	1	0	3	1	9	5	5	1	3	0	0	1	0	1	0	0	0	0	0	0	2	3	3	12	0
Tad	14	.0000	.6396	38.1	0	0	0	14	0	0	0	0	14	0	0	0	0	0	0	0	0	0	0	0	0	0	0	0	0
taddledum	3	.0000	.0243	23.8	3	0	0	0	0	0	0	0	0	0	0	0	0	0	0	0	3	0	0	0	0	0	0	0	0
tadpole	24	.5078	2.6553	44.2	6	4	5	3	4	0	0	2	4	1	0	0	1	0	0	13	0	0	0	0	0	3	2	0	0
tadpoles	40	.4511	4.0567	46.1	15	0	5	12	5	0	0	3	8	0	0	0	0	0	0	23	0	0	0	0	4	3	2	0	0
Tadzhik	2	.2437	.1129	30.5	0	0	0	0	1	1	0	0	0	0	0	0	0	0	0	0	0	0	0	0	0	0	1	1	0
taffeta	4	.2494	.2817	34.5	1	0	0	2	0	0	1	0	2	0	0	0	0	1	0	0	0	0	1	0	0	0	0	0	0
taffy	3	.2212	.2099	33.2	0	1	1	0	0	0	1	0	2	0	0	1	0	0	0	0	0	0	0	0	0	0	0	0	0
Taffy	7	.0000	.0821	29.1	0	7	0	0	0	0	0	0	0	0	0	0	0	0	0	0	0	0	0	0	7	0	0	0	0
Taft	11	.2258	.7756	38.9	0	0	0	0	6	5	0	0	6	0	0	0	0	5	0	0	0	0	0	0	0	0	0	0	0
Taft-Hartley	4	.0000	.0419	26.2	0	0	1	0	3	0	0	0	0	0	0	0	0	0	0	0	0	0	0	0	0	0	4	0	0
tag	51	.8710	8.8762	49.5	15	15	4	4	6	3	3	1	15	4	0	4	2	5	2	3	2	0	2	0	4	2	4	2	0
Tag	28	.2402	2.1867	43.4	24	4	0	0	0	0	0	0	24	0	0	0	0	0	0	0	0	0	0	0	0	0	4	0	0
Tag-end	2	.0000	.0914	29.6	0	0	0	2	0	0	0	0	2	0	0	0	0	0	0	0	0	0	0	0	0	0	0	0	0
Tagalog	3	.2444	.1814	32.6	1	0	0	2	0	0	0	0	0	0	0	0	0	2	0	0	0	0	0	0	0	0	1	0	0
Tagami	5	.0000	.0972	29.9	0	5	0	0	0	0	0	0	0	0	0	0	0	5	0	0	0	0	0	0	0	0	0	0	0
tagboard	2	.0000	.0394	26.0	0	0	2	0	0	0	0	0	0	0	0	0	0	0	0	2	0	0	0	0	0	0	0	0	0
tagged	26	.6344	3.4839	45.4	2	7	5	4	6	1	1	0	9	1	0	2	1	0	0	7	0	0	0	0	0	0	4	2	0
tagging	8	.5336	.9338	39.7	2	2	2	2	0	0	0	0	3	0	0	0	0	0	0	1	1	0	0	0	0	1	0	2	0
tags	25	.5358	2.8414	44.5	4	3	5	1	3	6	2	1	4	1	0	1	3	0	1	7	0	0	5	0	0	1	0	2	0
tah	3	.1983	.1396	31.4	2	1	0	0	0	0	0	0	0	0	0	0	0	0	0	0	2	0	0	0	0	0	0	1	0

9B T-formation
7B T-imp
6R T-minus-2-hours-and-17-**
6R T-minus-9-seconds
9B T-object
4P T-r-e-l-l-i-s
6E t-shaped
7P T-shirts
9M T-square
6N t-t-triumph
9M T-tap
9B T-terminal
6A T-zero
9E T-16
XR T-38
9E t/r
8J T'Lagunna
3A t'ain't
8D t'day
8N t'eef
7A t'ink
4E TA
3P Ta-lin's
3J ta-ta-ta-ta-taa
6G taai
7Q Taal
8R Tab
7E TAB
6G tab-let
5A Tabby's
5F Tabernacle
5P tabernas
5A Tabitha
7R table-desk
9M table-feed
3P table-tennis
7J tableau
9C tableaus
8F tabled
XR tabloid
7F Tabriz
6N tabu
7Q tabulates
7R tach
7N tachometer
9H tachylite
9L Tack
8R Tackle
7M tacky
4D taco
7D Taco
7D TACO
3P Tactical
9Q tactile
9F tactless
4A tad
6A Tad's
XH tadpole's
3A tadpoles'
9L taffetas
4N Taffimai
3N taffy-colored
3A Tagoona
6Q tagua
7F Tagus

Word Type	F	D	U	SFI	3 Gr 3	4 Gr 4	5 Gr 5	6 Gr 6	7 Gr 7	8 Gr 8	9 Gr 9	X UnGr	A Read	B Eng & Gr	C Comp	D Lit	E Math	F Soc Stud	G Spell	H Sci	J Music	K Art	L Home Ec	M Shop	N Lib F	P Lib NF	Q Lib Ref	R Mag	S Rel
Tahiti	9	.3798	.8397	39.2	0	0	0	2	5	2	0	0	5	0	0	0	0	0	0	0	0	1	0	0	1	2	0	0	0
Tahitian	2	.0000	.0243	23.9	0	0	0	1	1	0	0	0	0	0	0	0	0	0	0	0	0	0	0	0	0	0	0	2	0
Tahoe	2	.2152	.1357	31.3	0	1	0	0	0	0	1	0	1	0	0	0	0	1	0	0	0	0	0	0	0	0	0	0	0
taiga	5	.0000	.0972	29.9	0	0	0	0	0	0	5	0	0	0	0	0	0	5	0	0	0	0	0	0	0	0	0	0	0
tail	620	.8845	109.64	60.4	208	109	56	88	96	30	20	13	256	13	7	40	11	7	14	46	18	8	0	1	56	76	27	40	0
Tail	4	.0000	.1827	32.6	3	1	0	0	0	0	0	0	4	0	0	0	0	0	0	0	0	0	0	0	0	0	0	0	0
tail-feathers	3	.2261	.2131	33.3	0	3	0	0	0	0	0	0	2	0	0	0	0	0	0	0	0	0	0	0	1	0	0	0	0
tail's	2	.2411	.1091	30.4	1	0	0	0	1	0	0	0	0	0	0	1	0	0	0	0	1	0	0	0	0	0	0	0	0
tailback	2	.0000	.0243	23.9	0	0	0	2	0	0	0	0	0	0	0	0	0	0	0	0	0	0	0	0	0	0	0	2	0
tailcoat	2	.1787	.1174	30.7	1	1	0	0	0	0	0	0	1	0	0	0	0	0	0	0	0	0	0	0	1	0	0	0	0
tailgate	4	.2073	.2003	33.0	0	1	0	0	3	0	0	0	0	0	0	1	0	0	0	0	0	0	0	0	0	0	0	3	0
tailless	5	.4503	.5015	37.0	0	0	0	2	3	0	0	0	1	0	0	0	0	0	0	2	0	0	0	0	1	0	1	0	0
taillight	3	.2279	.2143	33.3	1	1	0	0	1	0	0	0	2	0	0	0	0	0	0	0	0	0	0	0	0	0	0	1	0
taillights	3	.2279	.2143	33.3	2	0	0	0	1	0	0	0	2	0	0	0	0	0	0	0	0	0	0	0	0	0	0	1	0
tailor	37	.6713	5.2367	47.2	5	18	3	3	0	3	5	0	20	0	2	3	2	0	1	0	4	0	0	0	0	1	1	3	0
tailor-bird	3	.0000	.1370	31.4	0	3	0	0	0	0	0	0	3	0	0	0	0	0	0	0	0	0	0	0	0	0	0	0	0
tailor-made	2	.1698	.1133	30.5	0	1	0	0	0	0	1	0	1	0	0	0	0	0	0	0	0	0	0	0	0	0	1	0	0
tailor's	7	.0000	.0225	23.5	0	0	0	0	0	0	7	0	0	0	0	0	0	0	0	0	0	0	7	0	0	0	0	0	0
tailored	7	.1768	.2898	34.6	0	0	0	0	3	3	1	0	0	0	0	0	0	1	0	0	0	0	4	0	0	0	0	2	0
tailoring	8	.4753	.8906	39.5	1	0	3	2	1	0	1	0	5	0	0	1	0	0	0	1	0	0	0	0	0	1	0	0	0
tailors	8	.5587	.9347	39.7	0	2	3	1	0	0	2	0	1	0	0	2	0	2	0	0	1	0	1	0	0	0	1	0	0
tails	123	.8595	21.179	53.3	34	23	17	17	16	9	7	0	39	2	3	13	3	3	4	18	0	3	1	0	8	14	8	4	0
tailstock	15	.0897	.3341	35.2	0	0	0	0	4	7	4	0	0	0	0	0	0	0	0	0	0	0	0	11	0	0	0	4	0
Tainaron	2	.0000	.0914	29.6	0	0	2	0	0	0	0	0	2	0	0	0	0	0	0	0	0	0	0	0	0	0	0	0	0
taine	2	.0000	.0215	23.3	0	0	0	0	0	2	0	0	0	0	0	2	0	0	0	0	0	0	0	0	0	0	0	0	0
taint	3	.2524	.1934	32.9	0	0	0	0	1	0	1	1	1	0	0	1	0	0	0	0	0	0	1	0	0	0	0	0	0
tainted	2	.0000	.0215	23.3	0	0	0	0	0	0	2	0	0	0	0	2	0	0	0	0	0	0	0	0	0	0	0	0	0
Tainter	5	.0000	.0404	26.1	0	0	0	0	5	0	0	0	0	0	0	0	0	0	0	0	5	0	0	0	0	0	0	0	0
Taipei	4	.3519	.3117	34.9	0	0	1	3	0	0	0	0	0	0	0	0	0	1	0	0	0	0	0	0	0	0	1	2	0
Taiwan	10	.2138	.5386	37.3	0	0	0	8	2	0	0	0	0	0	0	0	0	4	0	0	0	0	0	0	0	0	0	6	0
take	4089	.9797	789.08	69.0	901	723	463	471	739	401	317	74	1163	212	24	262	164	350	235	439	111	22	75	27	331	317	124	228	5
Take	3	.0997	.1145	30.6	1	0	0	2	0	0	0	0	1	0	0	0	0	0	2	0	0	0	0	0	0	0	0	0	0
take-off	24	.5043	2.6214	44.2	0	2	3	6	10	0	3	0	5	0	0	8	3	1	0	2	0	0	0	0	0	5	0	0	0
take-over	2	.0000	.0389	25.9	0	0	1	0	0	0	1	0	0	0	0	0	0	2	0	0	0	0	0	0	0	0	0	0	0
take-up	7	.0000	.0225	23.5	0	0	0	0	1	3	3	0	0	0	0	0	0	0	0	0	0	0	7	0	0	0	0	0	0
taken	1015	.9346	187.88	62.7	130	155	131	140	211	133	95	20	254	40	8	52	20	192	15	100	27	1	16	15	58	80	66	71	0
takened	2	.0000	.0234	23.7	0	0	0	0	2	0	0	0	0	0	0	0	0	0	0	0	0	0	0	0	2	0	0	0	0
takeoff	12	.5061	1.3058	41.2	4	0	0	1	6	1	0	0	2	1	0	0	2	0	0	1	0	0	0	0	0	1	0	5	0
takeoffs	2	.2442	.1134	30.5	0	0	0	0	1	1	0	0	0	1	0	0	0	0	0	0	0	0	0	0	0	0	0	1	0
takeover	2	.0000	.0243	23.9	0	0	0	2	0	0	0	0	0	0	0	0	0	0	0	0	0	0	0	0	0	0	0	2	0
takes	835	.9254	153.09	61.8	194	116	106	91	154	82	69	23	146	45	3	34	50	71	6	213	38	4	9	15	24	71	43	63	0
taketh	4	.4510	.3992	36.0	1	0	1	1	1	0	0	0	1	0	0	1	0	0	0	0	0	0	0	0	0	1	1	0	0
takin'	5	.2342	.2727	34.4	0	0	0	0	4	1	0	0	0	0	0	3	0	0	0	0	0	0	0	0	2	0	0	0	0
taking	719	.9309	132.65	61.2	113	115	89	103	125	94	60	20	211	32	9	49	17	70	5	54	11	9	22	7	80	59	20	64	0
Takume	2	.2407	.1138	30.6	0	0	0	0	0	1	1	0	0	0	0	1	0	0	0	0	0	0	0	0	0	1	0	0	0
Talbot	6	.2432	.4679	36.7	5	0	0	0	1	0	0	0	5	1	0	0	0	0	0	0	0	0	0	0	0	0	0	0	0
Talbot's	3	.0000	.1370	31.4	3	0	0	0	0	0	0	0	3	0	0	0	0	0	0	0	0	0	0	0	0	0	0	0	0
talcum	3	.2950	.1973	33.0	0	1	0	0	0	0	2	0	0	0	0	0	0	1	0	0	0	0	1	0	0	0	1	0	0
tale	95	.7683	14.889	51.7	9	18	13	16	13	15	6	5	38	6	0	11	0	1	3	2	14	1	0	0	5	5	1	8	0
Tale	4	.1999	.1920	32.8	0	2	0	0	1	0	0	1	0	3	0	1	0	0	0	0	0	0	0	0	0	0	0	0	0
talent	43	.7356	6.4324	48.1	0	2	6	5	8	14	7	1	9	2	0	3	1	6	0	0	2	2	2	0	0	2	2	12	0
talented	26	.6965	3.7023	45.7	2	3	4	0	11	4	2	0	5	1	1	0	0	1	1	0	2	0	0	0	0	5	3	7	0
talents	18	.6281	2.3168	43.6	2	4	1	0	1	6	4	0	1	3	0	3	0	3	0	0	1	0	0	0	0	0	4	3	0
tales	140	.7961	22.735	53.6	18	37	28	18	19	11	7	2	71	3	1	12	0	10	0	0	9	2	0	0	2	14	9	7	0
Tales	10	.4389	.9603	39.8	1	1	0	2	2	3	1	0	2	0	1	0	0	1	4	0	0	0	0	0	0	2	0	0	0
talisman	4	.0919	.1430	31.6	0	0	0	1	3	0	0	0	1	0	0	3	0	0	0	0	0	0	0	0	0	0	0	0	0
talk	1133	.8822	199.80	63.0	280	229	148	107	176	112	68	13	434	167	7	80	19	83	33	61	9	4	17	3	88	71	8	49	0
talkative	3	.2468	.1912	32.8	1	0	0	0	2	0	0	0	1	0	0	0	0	0	0	0	0	0	1	0	1	0	0	0	0
talked	415	.8005	67.550	58.3	97	98	55	36	61	43	24	1	179	30	5	32	4	51	2	1	2	0	2	0	41	43	2	21	0
talker	10	.3630	.9402	39.7	5	0	1	1	1	0	0	2	7	2	0	0	0	0	0	0	0	0	0	0	0	1	0	0	0
talkers	3	.3870	.2486	34.0	0	0	2	0	0	0	1	0	0	0	0	1	0	0	0	0	0	0	0	0	0	0	1	1	0
talkin'	5	.2342	.2727	34.4	1	0	0	0	2	1	1	0	0	0	0	3	0	0	0	0	0	0	0	0	2	0	0	0	0
talking	613	.8859	108.53	60.4	138	96	64	85	116	63	39	12	255	65	15	46	4	24	9	19	13	2	8	1	68	55	2	26	1
Talking	6	.4206	.5711	37.6	2	0	0	1	2	1	0	0	2	0	0	0	0	0	0	0	2	0	0	0	1	0	1	0	0
talks	85	.7330	12.780	51.1	21	8	9	4	13	13	13	4	29	6	4	2	1	8	0	1	0	0	2	0	2	5	4	21	0
tall	848	.9268	155.94	61.9	223	181	108	115	96	70	42	13	280	43	18	53	66	87	15	55	24	15	5	2	43	85	14	43	0
Tall	6	.2261	.4261	36.3	4	0	0	2	0	0	0	0	4	0	0	0	0	0	0	0	0	0	0	0	2	0	0	0	0
tall-masted	2	.1948	.1250	31.0	1	0	0	1	0	0	0	0	1	0	0	0	0	0	0	0	0	0	0	0	0	1	0	0	0
Tallahassee	5	.1792	.2371	33.7	1	0	0	4	0	0	0	0	0	0	0	0	4	0	0	0	0	0	0	0	0	1	0	0	0
taller	80	.8377	13.493	51.3	24	21	10	8	4	6	6	1	26	6	0	2	8	6	2	13	2	0	0	0	3	7	1	4	0
tallest	66	.7766	10.389	50.2	16	24	9	5	5	2	3	2	16	3	3	2	15	7	3	3	0	0	0	0	1	7	2	4	0
tallied	2	.2446	.1142	30.6	0	0	0	1	1	0	0	0	0	0	0	0	0	0	0	0	0	0	0	0	1	0	0	1	0
Tallis	3	.0000	.0243	23.8	0	1	0	2	0	0	0	0	0	0	0	0	0	0	0	0	3	0	0	0	0	0	0	0	0
tallness	3	.1650	.1684	32.3	0	0	0	3	0	0	0	0	1	0	0	0	0	0	0	2	0	0	0	0	0	0	0	0	0
tallow	12	.4741	1.2938	41.1	9	0	1	1	0	1	0	0	5	0	0	0	0	2	0	0	0	0	0	0	2	3	0	0	0
tally	16	.0365	.3750	35.7	0	0	8	0	3	0	5	0	1	0	0	0	15	0	0	0	0	0	0	0	0	0	0	0	0
Tallyville	2	.0000	.0299	24.8	0	0	0	2	0	0	0	0	0	0	0	0	2	0	0	0	0	0	0	0	0	0	0	0	0
Talon	2	.0000	.0290	24.6	2	0	0	0	0	0	0	0	0	0	0	0	0	0	0	0	0	0	0	0	0	2	0	0	0
talons	5	.3365	.4127	36.2	0	1	0	1	1	2	0	0	2	2	0	0	0	0	0	0	0	0	0	0	0	0	1	0	0
Talore	4	.0000	.1827	32.6	0	0	0	0	4	0	0	0	4	0	0	0	0	0	0	0	0	0	0	0	0	0	0	0	0
Tam	7	.1253	.2239	33.5	6	0	1	0	0	0	0	0	0	0	0	0	0	0	0	0	6	0	0	0	0	0	1	0	0
tamanu	2	.0000	.0234	23.7	0	0	0	2	0	0	0	0	0	0	0	0	0	0	0	0	0	0	0	0	2	0	0	0	0
Tamanyan	2	.0000	.0209	23.2	0	0	0	0	0	2	0	0	0	0	0	0	0	0	0	0	0	0	0	0	0	0	2	0	0
Tamara	6	.0000	.2741	34.4	3	0	0	0	3	0	0	0	6	0	0	0	0	0	0	0	0	0	0	0	0	0	0	0	0
tambourin	2	.0000	.0162	22.1	0	0	2	0	0	0	0	0	0	0	0	0	0	0	0	0	2	0	0	0	0	0	0	0	0
tambourine	34	.1936	1.5467	41.9	4	4	7	16	3	0	0	0	1	0	1	0	0	0	0	0	30	0	0	0	1	0	0	1	0
tambourines	6	.1389	.2076	33.2	0	0	0	1	3	2	0	0	0	0	0	0	0	0	0	0	5	0	0	0	0	0	1	0	0
tame	58	.7850	9.2814	49.7	5	13	8	17	12	1	1	1	23	2	0	5	1	1	2	11	0	0	0	0	4	3	2	4	0
tamed	32	.6408	4.3060	46.3	5	4	4	8	9	2	0	0	8	1	0	4	0	5	0	11	0	0	0	0	1	1	1	0	0
Tamenund	3	.0000	.0352	25.5	0	0	0	0	3	0	0	0	0	0	0	0	0	0	0	0	0	0	0	0	3	0	0	0	0
Tamerlane	3	.2387	.1708	32.3	0	0	2	0	0	1	0	0	0	0	0	0	0	0	0	0	0	0	0	0	0	2	1	0	0
taming	2	.0000	.0243	23.9	1	0	0	0	1	0	0	0	0	0	0	0	0	0	0	0	0	0	0	0	0	0	0	2	0
tamp	2	.1494	.1045	30.2	0	1	1	0	0	0	0	0	1	0	0	0	0	0	0	0	1	0	0	0	0	0	0	0	0

6R Tahitians
7R Tahuya
4F tai
5R TaiChiChuan
7A tail-end
4D tail-feather
7N tail-holt
7Q tail-lashing
8D tail-light
3A tailboard
8N tailed
7D tailing
3P taillike
6A tailorbird
6A Tailors
7A tailpipe
8B tailspin
6A tailwind
7A tainting
6R Taipei's
9R Taiyo
8Q Tajik
8F Taka
9R Takano
7R take-home
7B Taken
6R takeovers
4A taker
5P takers
9Q Takeshi
4F Taking
8Q Talayan
6P talc
7D talcumed
8Q Talin
3A talk-talk-talk
3A talk-talk-talked
3A talk-talk-talking
9D talk'st
6A talking-to
5A tall-tale
XN tall-windowed
9D tallies
9E Tally
8B Talmud
9C taloned
4P tam-o'-shanter
7J tam-tams
7A Tam's
9B tamada
6A Tamaki
6A Tamakis
8G tamale
3P tamandua
9A Tamarack
XR tamarind
7B tamarisk
3A Tamatomo
8J tamber
6J tambo
7Q Tambora
5J Tambourin
8Q Tamburlaine
7D tameness
3A tamer
8Q Tamerlane's
7B tames
5A tamest
XR Tamil
5J Tamino
8F Tammany
5E Tammy's

Word Type	F	D	U	SFI	3 Gr 3	4 Gr 4	5 Gr 5	6 Gr 6	7 Gr 7	8 Gr 8	9 Gr 9	X UnGr	A Read	B Eng & Gr	C Comp	D Lit	E Math	F Soc Stud	G Spell	H Sci	J Music	K Art	L Home Ec	M Shop	N Lib F	P Lib NF	Q Lib Ref	R Mag	S Rel
Tampa	7	.2909	.5146	37.1	4	0	1	1	0	0	0	1	2	0	0	0	0	0	0	0	0	0	0	0	0	4	0	1	0
tan	51	.8348	8.5968	49.3	24	8	0	7	6	5	0	1	22	1	0	1	3	2	2	7	0	1	2	0	4	2	1	3	0
Tanana	4	.2183	.2285	33.6	1	2	1	0	0	0	0	0	0	0	0	0	0	3	0	0	0	0	0	0	0	1	0	0	0
tanbark	3	.0000	.1370	31.4	0	0	3	0	0	0	0	0	3	0	0	0	0	0	0	0	0	0	0	0	0	0	0	0	0
Tandy	18	.0000	.8223	39.2	18	0	0	0	0	0	0	0	18	0	0	0	0	0	0	0	0	0	0	0	0	0	0	0	0
Taney	25	.3116	2.2388	43.5	21	0	0	0	0	4	0	0	21	0	0	0	0	3	0	0	0	0	0	0	0	0	1	0	0
tang	5	.2052	.2590	34.1	0	2	0	0	2	1	0	0	1	0	0	2	0	0	0	0	0	0	0	2	0	0	0	0	0
Tanganyika	8	.3469	.6925	38.4	0	1	0	3	2	0	2	0	3	0	0	0	0	4	0	0	0	0	0	0	0	0	1	0	0
tangent	8	.3576	.6454	38.1	0	1	0	0	0	4	2	1	0	0	0	0	4	0	0	3	0	0	0	0	0	0	1	0	0
tangerines	4	.2424	.2409	33.8	0	0	0	0	3	1	0	0	0	0	0	0	0	3	1	0	0	0	0	0	0	0	0	0	0
tangible	12	.6230	1.5407	41.9	0	0	1	0	5	0	3	3	1	0	0	2	0	0	0	2	0	0	0	0	1	1	2	3	0
Tangier	2	.1497	.1046	30.2	1	0	0	0	0	1	0	0	1	0	0	0	0	0	1	0	0	0	0	0	0	0	0	0	0
tangle	26	.7220	3.8386	45.8	1	5	1	5	8	3	3	0	7	0	1	2	0	1	0	0	0	1	0	0	5	4	2	3	0
tangled	51	.7129	7.4720	48.7	4	7	8	8	12	9	2	1	15	2	0	8	0	7	0	0	0	2	0	0	7	3	2	5	0
tangles	2	.2152	.1357	31.3	0	0	1	1	0	0	0	0	1	0	0	0	0	1	0	0	0	0	0	0	0	0	0	0	0
tangling	3	.3394	.2451	33.9	0	1	1	0	0	1	0	0	1	0	0	1	0	0	0	0	0	0	0	0	1	0	0	0	0
tango	2	.2446	.1084	30.3	0	0	0	0	1	1	0	0	0	0	0	0	0	0	1	0	1	0	0	0	0	0	0	0	0
tangy	6	.3481	.4452	36.5	0	1	1	0	3	1	0	0	0	0	1	4	0	0	1	0	0	0	0	0	0	0	0	0	0
tank	174	.8247	28.938	54.6	29	38	33	21	26	17	9	1	55	6	2	0	19	7	2	30	0	0	0	6	7	19	9	12	0
Tank	2	.0000	.0389	25.9	0	0	0	0	0	1	1	0	0	0	0	0	0	2	0	0	0	0	0	0	0	0	0	0	0
tankard	2	.1717	.1142	30.6	0	0	1	0	0	1	0	0	1	0	0	1	0	0	0	0	0	0	0	0	0	0	0	0	0
tanker	11	.4300	1.0293	40.1	2	3	0	1	3	1	1	0	0	0	0	0	0	4	0	1	0	0	0	0	0	2	0	4	0
tankers	14	.4582	1.3984	41.5	1	3	1	4	3	0	2	0	1	0	1	0	0	8	0	0	0	0	0	0	0	1	0	3	0
tankful	2	.2346	.1166	30.7	0	0	0	1	0	0	0	1	0	0	0	0	0	0	0	1	0	0	0	0	0	0	0	1	0
tanks	110	.7801	17.547	52.4	26	33	10	9	15	6	10	1	46	0	0	2	2	19	1	12	0	1	0	0	3	12	6	6	0
tanned	17	.6967	2.4538	43.9	2	3	3	3	4	1	1	0	5	1	0	1	0	5	0	1	1	0	0	0	0	2	0	1	0
tanner	10	.3273	.7452	38.7	0	0	7	1	1	0	1	0	1	0	0	0	0	1	0	0	2	0	0	0	6	0	0	0	0
Tanner	21	.1405	1.3776	41.4	0	1	0	0	0	20	0	0	20	0	0	0	0	0	0	0	0	0	0	0	0	1	0	0	0
Tanner's	2	.1787	.1174	30.7	0	0	0	1	0	1	0	0	1	0	0	0	0	0	0	0	0	0	0	0	1	0	0	0	0
tanneries	5	.1990	.2695	34.3	0	0	2	0	3	0	0	0	0	0	0	0	0	4	0	0	0	0	0	0	0	1	0	0	0
tannery	2	.0000	.0914	29.6	0	0	1	1	0	0	0	0	2	0	0	0	0	0	0	0	0	0	0	0	0	0	0	0	0
Tannhauser	2	.0000	.0162	22.1	0	0	0	0	1	1	0	0	0	0	0	0	0	0	0	0	2	0	0	0	0	0	0	0	0
tannic	2	.1442	.0761	28.8	0	0	0	0	1	0	1	0	0	0	0	0	0	1	0	0	0	0	1	0	0	0	0	0	0
tanning	13	.6025	1.6499	42.2	0	1	4	4	3	0	0	1	3	0	0	1	0	2	0	1	0	0	0	0	4	1	1	0	0
tans	2	.1033	.0599	27.8	0	1	0	0	0	1	0	0	0	0	0	0	0	0	0	1	0	1	0	0	0	0	0	0	0
Tanta	3	.0000	.1370	31.4	0	3	0	0	0	0	0	0	3	0	0	0	0	0	0	0	0	0	0	0	0	0	0	0	0
tantalizing	8	.6248	1.0580	40.2	0	0	0	2	3	3	0	0	3	0	0	1	0	0	0	1	0	0	0	0	1	0	1	1	0
Tante	23	.2125	1.4158	41.5	0	23	0	0	0	0	0	0	9	0	0	0	0	0	0	0	0	0	0	0	13	1	0	0	0
tantrum	4	.0000	.0129	21.1	0	0	0	0	0	2	2	0	0	0	0	0	0	0	0	0	0	0	4	0	0	0	0	0	0
tantrums	10	.3242	.7399	38.7	1	1	1	0	3	2	2	0	2	0	0	1	0	0	0	0	0	0	4	0	0	1	1	1	0
Tanura	2	.0000	.0389	25.9	0	0	0	1	1	0	0	0	0	0	0	0	0	2	0	0	0	0	0	0	0	0	0	0	0
Tanya	3	.0000	.1370	31.4	3	0	0	0	0	0	0	0	3	0	0	0	0	0	0	0	0	0	0	0	0	0	0	0	0
Tanzania	4	.3863	.3414	35.3	0	0	0	1	1	1	1	0	0	0	0	0	0	2	0	0	0	0	0	0	0	0	1	1	0
Tao	4	.0000	.0469	26.7	0	0	0	0	4	0	0	0	0	0	0	0	0	0	0	0	0	0	0	0	4	0	0	0	0
Taoism	2	.0000	.0389	25.9	0	0	0	0	1	1	0	0	0	0	0	0	0	2	0	0	0	0	0	0	0	0	0	0	0
Taoist	2	.0000	.0290	24.6	2	0	0	0	0	0	0	0	0	0	0	0	0	0	0	0	0	0	0	0	0	2	0	0	0
tap	133	.5657	15.413	51.9	15	12	31	13	13	26	23	0	5	4	3	3	0	3	1	18	55	0	2	23	5	8	2	1	0
tap-drill	5	.0000	.0126	21.0	0	0	0	0	0	0	5	0	0	0	0	0	0	0	0	0	0	0	0	5	0	0	0	0	0
tap-tapping	4	.1717	.2284	33.6	0	3	0	0	1	0	0	0	2	0	0	2	0	0	0	0	0	0	0	0	0	0	0	0	0
tape	197	.6819	27.376	54.4	25	29	13	24	45	36	20	5	26	7	0	5	18	3	2	31	28	2	36	4	0	11	2	22	0
taped	7	.3804	.6371	38.0	2	2	1	0	0	1	1	0	3	0	0	0	0	0	0	1	0	0	0	1	0	0	0	2	0
taper	10	.2789	.5733	37.6	1	0	0	0	1	6	2	0	0	0	0	0	0	0	0	0	0	1	1	7	0	0	0	1	0
tapered	11	.2589	.6084	37.8	0	0	0	0	5	5	1	0	0	1	0	0	0	0	0	0	0	0	1	6	0	0	0	3	0
tapering	11	.5233	1.1933	40.8	1	0	0	0	5	0	5	0	1	0	0	0	0	2	0	0	0	2	2	1	0	0	2	1	0
tapers	8	.5157	.8693	39.4	1	0	0	1	2	1	2	1	1	1	0	1	0	0	0	0	0	0	0	1	0	1	0	3	0
tapes	18	.5651	2.1005	43.2	1	6	1	2	4	2	2	0	2	1	0	1	0	0	0	0	3	1	3	0	0	0	0	7	0
tapestries	8	.5760	.9482	39.8	0	1	1	1	4	0	0	1	0	0	0	1	0	2	0	0	0	0	1	0	0	1	2	1	0
tapestry	12	.4885	1.2284	40.9	0	0	3	4	1	3	0	1	0	0	0	1	0	4	0	0	1	2	0	0	0	1	1	2	0
tapeworm	3	.0000	.0591	27.7	0	0	0	0	3	0	0	0	0	0	0	0	0	0	0	3	0	0	0	0	0	0	0	0	0
tapeworms	5	.2213	.2870	34.6	0	0	1	0	3	1	0	0	0	0	0	0	0	0	0	4	0	0	0	0	0	0	1	0	0
taping	5	.3842	.4760	36.8	2	0	1	0	0	1	1	0	3	0	0	1	0	0	0	0	0	0	0	0	0	0	0	1	0
tapir	6	.4521	.6155	37.9	2	2	0	0	2	0	0	0	2	0	0	0	0	0	0	1	0	0	0	0	0	2	1	0	0
tapped	46	.6326	6.0687	47.8	9	7	6	5	9	4	6	0	14	0	2	1	0	4	0	0	7	0	0	6	1	3	2	6	0
tapping	32	.4466	3.1171	44.9	6	4	6	4	2	1	8	1	7	0	0	7	0	0	0	0	13	0	0	0	2	0	1	2	0
taproom	2	.1787	.1174	30.7	0	0	0	1	0	1	0	0	1	0	0	0	0	0	0	0	0	0	0	0	1	0	0	0	0
taproot	5	.1127	.2213	33.4	4	1	0	0	0	0	0	0	1	0	0	0	0	0	0	4	0	0	0	0	0	0	0	0	0
taps	13	.5784	1.5391	41.9	1	3	1	0	3	3	2	0	1	0	1	3	0	0	0	0	5	0	0	1	0	0	1	1	0
tar	29	.6815	4.1606	46.2	4	4	9	3	2	2	5	0	14	1	0	1	0	1	0	5	0	0	0	0	0	3	1	3	0
Tar	2	.1814	.1187	30.7	0	0	1	1	0	0	0	0	1	0	0	0	0	0	0	0	0	0	0	0	0	0	0	1	0
tar-baby	4	.0000	.1827	32.6	0	0	0	0	4	0	0	0	4	0	0	0	0	0	0	0	0	0	0	0	0	0	0	0	0
Tara	16	.3867	1.5607	41.9	1	0	13	2	0	0	0	0	11	0	0	0	0	0	0	0	2	0	0	0	0	3	0	0	0
tarantula	12	.4163	1.2072	40.8	8	3	0	1	0	0	0	0	7	0	0	3	0	0	0	1	0	0	0	0	0	1	0	0	0
tarantulas	3	.3452	.2543	34.1	1	1	0	1	0	0	0	0	1	0	0	0	0	0	0	1	0	0	0	0	0	0	0	1	0
tardy	3	.1187	.1291	31.1	0	0	1	0	0	1	1	0	1	0	0	2	0	0	0	0	0	0	0	0	0	0	0	0	0
target	93	.7462	14.157	51.5	3	23	10	12	18	18	9	0	19	4	0	3	1	4	1	33	1	0	0	0	2	13	6	6	0
targets	21	.5649	2.4604	43.9	2	0	3	0	6	5	4	1	0	0	0	1	0	4	0	2	0	0	0	0	0	3	5	6	0
tariff	28	.2998	2.0163	43.0	0	0	3	0	2	17	6	0	1	0	0	0	0	22	1	0	0	0	0	0	0	0	4	0	0
Tariff	2	.2285	.1129	30.5	0	1	0	0	0	0	1	0	0	0	0	0	0	1	0	0	0	0	0	0	0	0	1	0	0
tariffs	13	.3965	1.1225	40.5	0	2	6	0	0	0	5	0	0	0	0	0	0	4	0	0	0	0	0	0	0	2	6	1	0
Tarkenton	7	.0000	.0851	29.3	0	0	0	6	1	0	0	0	0	0	0	0	0	0	0	0	0	0	0	0	0	0	0	7	0
tarnish	5	.1875	.3065	34.9	0	0	0	2	0	2	1	0	2	0	0	0	0	0	0	3	0	0	0	0	0	0	0	0	0
tarnished	6	.2634	.4165	36.2	1	0	2	1	1	1	0	0	2	3	0	0	0	0	0	1	0	0	0	0	0	0	0	0	0
taro	2	.0000	.0389	25.9	0	0	0	0	2	0	0	0	0	0	0	0	0	2	0	0	0	0	0	0	0	0	0	0	0
tarp	2	.1814	.1187	30.7	0	0	0	0	2	0	0	0	1	0	0	0	0	0	0	0	0	0	0	0	0	0	0	1	0
tarpaulin	5	.4302	.4729	36.7	2	0	0	1	2	0	0	0	1	1	0	0	0	0	0	0	1	0	0	0	2	0	0	0	0
Tarpon	6	.2355	.4634	36.7	1	0	5	0	0	0	0	0	5	0	0	0	0	0	0	0	0	0	0	0	0	1	0	0	0
Tarr	5	.0000	.0972	29.9	5	0	0	0	0	0	0	0	0	0	0	0	0	5	0	0	0	0	0	0	0	0	0	0	0
tarragon	4	.1926	.1735	32.4	0	0	0	1	1	0	2	0	0	0	0	0	0	0	0	0	0	0	2	0	0	0	2	0	0
tarried	4	.4494	.4016	36.0	1	0	0	1	2	0	0	0	1	1	0	0	0	1	0	0	0	0	0	0	1	0	0	0	0
Tarriers	3	.0000	.0243	23.8	0	2	1	0	0	0	0	0	0	0	0	0	0	0	0	0	3	0	0	0	0	0	0	0	0

7Q tampering
5J tampers
5Q Tampico
4N tamping
5J Tamping
6F Tana
7Q tanagers
9Q tandem
7R tandems
7A Tane-Matarau
3A Taney's
9M Tang
6B Tanganyikan
6D Tangari
9M tangency
9R tangentially
XR tangents
7D tangibility
6A Tangiers
8D tangled-up
8J Tanglewood
7A tank-house
3P tank-like
7N Tankadere
7N Tankadere's
7R Tanker
4R tanker's
3P TANKERS
7J Tanko
5N tanner's
6F tanners
6A Tanners
4A tannin
XH tantalite
3A tantalum
7Q tantamount
XR Tanya's
5P tao
7N Taocat
8F Taoists
8F Taos
4E TAP
3N tap-dancing
6N tap-room
9M tap's
6N tapa
8J Tape
8J tape-recorder
7R taperground
4H tapioca
XH tapiolite
7R tapirs
8A Tappan
6H tapper
3H taproots
6R Taps
6N Tapu
9R tar-black
4N tar-paper
4J tarantella
3B Tarantula
4D tarantula's
5A Tarascan
5A Tarascans
5A Tarbell
5A tarboosh
5Q tarbooshes
3P tardigrade
3P TARDIGRADE
9D tardiness
9Q Tarentum
8P tares
8R targeting
7A tariff-protected
4Q Tariffs
6R Tarkenton's
6N tarlaton
6A Tarleton
4Q Tarlton
4Q Tarlton's
6R Tarn
4A Tarnish's
3A tarnishes
8Q tarnishing
5F TarponSprings
8D tarred

Word Type	F	D	U	SFI	3 Gr 3	4 Gr 4	5 Gr 5	6 Gr 6	7 Gr 7	8 Gr 8	9 Gr 9	X UnGr	A Read	B Eng & Gr	C Comp	D Lit	E Math	F Soc Stud	G Spell	H Sci	J Music	K Art	L Home Ec	M Shop	N Lib F	P Lib NF	Q Lib Ref	R Mag	S Rel
tarry	8	.5696	.9516	39.8	0	2	0	1	2	1	1	1	1	0	0	2	0	0	0	1	1	0	0	0	2	0	0	1	0
Tarrytown	2	.0665	.0708	28.5	0	0	0	0	0	1	1	0	1	0	1	0	0	0	0	0	0	0	0	0	0	0	0	0	0
tart	9	.2704	.6354	38.0	0	0	2	3	0	2	2	0	4	1	0	0	0	0	0	0	0	0	3	0	0	0	0	1	0
Tartaglia	2	.0000	.0299	24.8	0	0	0	0	0	2	0	0	0	0	0	0	2	0	0	0	0	0	0	0	0	0	0	0	0
tartar	3	.3255	.2085	33.2	0	0	1	0	1	1	0	0	0	1	0	0	0	0	0	0	0	0	1	0	0	0	1	0	0
Tartar	2	.2285	.1129	30.5	0	0	0	0	0	1	1	0	0	0	0	0	0	1	0	0	0	0	0	0	0	0	1	0	0
Tartars	2	.0000	.0389	25.9	0	0	0	0	0	0	2	0	0	0	0	0	0	2	0	0	0	0	0	0	0	0	0	0	0
tarts	10	.5928	1.2438	40.9	3	0	3	1	1	1	1	0	2	1	0	1	3	0	0	0	0	0	0	0	2	0	0	1	0
Tarzan	5	.3254	.3578	35.5	0	0	3	0	0	2	0	0	0	0	1	1	0	0	0	0	0	0	0	0	0	3	0	0	0
Tashkent	2	.2297	.1135	30.6	0	0	0	1	0	0	1	0	0	0	0	1	0	1	0	0	0	0	0	0	0	0	0	0	0
task	181	.9210	33.033	55.2	8	18	26	27	42	31	23	6	32	8	2	12	3	21	2	17	4	1	2	1	11	24	23	18	0
Task	2	.0000	.0290	24.6	0	0	0	1	1	0	0	0	0	0	0	0	0	0	0	0	0	0	0	0	0	2	0	0	0
tasks	63	.8457	10.643	50.3	4	2	7	11	11	13	8	7	9	4	1	5	0	9	0	6	0	0	3	1	3	6	8	8	0
Tasky	3	.0000	.0352	25.5	0	0	0	0	3	0	0	0	0	0	0	0	0	0	0	0	0	0	0	0	3	0	0	0	0
Tasky's	2	.0000	.0234	23.7	0	0	0	0	2	0	0	0	0	0	0	0	0	0	0	0	0	0	0	0	2	0	0	0	0
Tasman	2	.0000	.0389	25.9	0	1	1	0	0	0	0	0	0	0	0	0	0	2	0	0	0	0	0	0	0	0	0	0	0
Tasmania	2	.2306	.1140	30.6	0	0	0	1	0	0	1	0	0	1	0	0	0	1	0	0	0	0	0	0	0	0	0	0	0
tassel	4	.4530	.4014	36.0	2	0	1	0	1	0	0	0	1	0	0	0	0	0	0	0	0	0	0	0	0	1	1	1	0
tasseled	2	.2407	.1138	30.6	0	0	2	0	0	0	0	0	0	0	0	1	0	0	0	0	0	0	0	0	0	1	0	0	0
tassels	3	.0000	.1370	31.4	0	0	0	2	0	1	0	0	3	0	0	0	0	0	0	0	0	0	0	0	0	0	0	0	0
taste	283	.8040	45.790	56.6	38	34	44	46	41	22	40	18	55	28	17	18	1	9	2	69	8	0	13	1	14	21	8	19	0
tasted	75	.7912	12.079	50.8	12	14	16	6	16	5	6	0	32	5	2	5	0	4	0	5	1	0	2	0	11	5	0	3	0
tasteless	9	.5155	1.0003	40.0	0	2	3	2	2	0	0	0	2	0	0	0	0	0	1	3	0	0	1	0	0	0	2	0	0
tastes	58	.7202	8.4604	49.3	7	10	14	4	5	6	11	1	6	14	4	1	0	3	1	11	2	0	4	0	0	1	5	6	0
tasting	24	.6413	3.1761	45.0	2	4	2	2	3	7	1	3	4	2	3	1	0	0	0	6	0	1	1	0	0	2	0	4	0
tastings	2	.0000	.0243	23.9	0	0	0	0	0	0	0	2	0	0	0	0	0	0	0	0	0	0	0	0	0	0	0	2	0
tasty	29	.7629	4.4920	46.5	8	2	4	5	6	2	1	1	8	2	1	2	0	4	0	1	2	0	3	0	1	2	1	2	0
Tata	2	.0000	.0389	25.9	0	0	0	0	0	0	2	0	0	0	0	0	0	2	0	0	0	0	0	0	0	0	0	0	0
Tate	6	.2350	.3529	35.5	1	0	1	0	0	0	4	0	1	0	0	4	0	0	0	0	0	0	0	0	0	0	1	0	0
taters	2	.0000	.0290	24.6	0	2	0	0	0	0	0	0	0	0	0	0	0	0	0	0	0	0	0	0	0	2	0	0	0
Tatius	2	.0000	.0290	24.6	0	0	0	0	0	0	0	2	0	0	0	0	0	0	0	0	0	0	0	0	0	2	0	0	0
tattered	23	.4567	2.3085	43.6	2	2	1	3	5	10	0	0	6	0	2	11	0	0	0	0	0	0	0	0	1	2	0	1	0
tatters	5	.2025	.3254	35.1	1	1	0	1	0	0	2	0	3	0	0	2	0	0	0	0	0	0	0	0	0	0	0	0	0
tattletale	2	.0000	.0914	29.6	0	1	0	1	0	0	0	0	2	0	0	0	0	0	0	0	0	0	0	0	0	0	0	0	0
tattoo	5	.3765	.4671	36.7	0	1	0	1	2	1	0	0	3	0	0	1	0	0	0	0	1	0	0	0	0	0	0	0	0
tattooed	7	.3915	.6042	37.8	0	3	0	0	1	1	0	2	1	0	1	0	0	0	0	0	0	0	0	0	2	0	0	3	0
Tatum	7	.2181	.3829	35.8	0	0	4	0	0	0	3	0	0	0	0	0	0	0	0	3	0	0	0	0	4	0	0	0	0
taught	283	.8902	50.223	57.0	45	39	34	54	47	35	25	4	85	25	2	24	4	40	6	8	7	0	1	1	26	23	17	14	0
Taung	3	.0000	.0314	25.0	0	0	0	0	3	0	0	0	0	0	0	0	0	0	0	0	0	0	0	0	0	0	3	0	0
taunt	3	.2175	.1545	31.9	0	0	0	0	1	1	1	0	0	0	0	2	0	0	0	0	0	0	0	0	0	0	0	1	0
taunted	7	.3626	.6400	38.1	1	0	1	4	1	0	0	0	4	0	0	0	0	0	0	0	0	0	0	0	0	1	0	2	0
taunting	3	.1187	.1291	31.1	0	0	0	0	1	1	1	0	1	0	0	2	0	0	0	0	0	0	0	0	0	0	0	0	0
taunts	2	.2305	.1080	30.3	0	0	0	0	1	1	0	0	0	0	0	0	0	0	1	0	0	0	0	0	0	1	0	0	0
taut	18	.6248	2.3485	43.7	1	0	4	5	4	0	2	2	5	0	0	2	1	0	0	0	0	0	1	0	4	0	4	1	0
Tavana	4	.0000	.0469	26.7	0	0	0	4	0	0	0	0	0	0	0	0	0	0	0	0	0	0	0	0	4	0	0	0	0
tavern	32	.5916	4.1072	46.1	2	7	2	11	1	7	2	0	16	0	0	2	0	2	0	0	0	0	0	0	2	7	3	0	0
Tavern	8	.4734	.8847	39.5	0	0	3	3	0	1	1	0	5	0	0	1	0	1	0	0	1	0	0	0	0	0	0	0	0
taverns	3	.1187	.1291	31.1	0	0	0	0	1	0	2	0	1	0	0	2	0	0	0	0	0	0	0	0	0	0	0	0	0
taw	2	.1717	.1142	30.6	0	0	0	0	2	0	0	0	1	0	0	1	0	0	0	0	0	0	0	0	0	0	0	0	0
Tawik	12	.0000	.1288	31.1	0	0	0	0	0	12	0	0	0	0	0	12	0	0	0	0	0	0	0	0	0	0	0	0	0
tawny	6	.2953	.4429	36.5	1	0	2	0	1	0	2	0	2	1	0	3	0	0	0	0	0	0	0	0	0	0	0	0	0
tax	233	.6398	30.706	54.9	21	6	31	24	26	36	81	8	12	3	0	1	60	84	6	0	1	0	3	0	2	10	19	30	2
Tax	2	.2351	.1166	30.7	0	0	0	0	0	1	0	1	0	0	0	0	0	1	0	0	0	0	0	0	0	0	0	1	0
tax-reform	2	.0000	.0243	23.9	0	0	0	0	0	0	2	0	0	0	0	0	0	0	0	0	0	0	0	0	0	0	0	2	0
taxable	5	.3586	.3956	36.0	0	0	0	0	0	0	5	0	0	0	0	0	3	0	0	0	0	0	0	0	0	0	1	1	0
taxation	17	.4158	1.5506	41.9	1	2	3	1	1	3	6	0	1	0	0	0	0	6	0	0	0	0	0	0	0	2	7	1	0
Taxco	2	.1042	.0600	27.8	0	1	0	1	0	0	0	0	0	0	0	0	0	1	0	0	0	1	0	0	0	0	0	0	0
taxed	10	.4315	.9425	39.7	0	1	2	2	1	2	1	1	0	0	0	0	1	6	0	0	0	0	0	0	0	0	1	2	0
taxes	104	.6166	13.293	51.2	18	6	16	10	11	14	26	3	3	0	1	1	5	61	5	2	0	0	0	0	0	6	11	9	0
taxi	43	.5706	5.4352	47.4	16	7	3	5	12	0	0	0	26	0	0	0	1	6	0	0	4	0	0	0	0	2	0	4	0
taxicab	6	.3774	.5776	37.6	4	0	0	0	1	0	1	0	4	1	0	0	0	1	0	0	0	0	0	0	0	0	0	0	0
taxicabs	6	.3786	.5793	37.6	3	2	1	0	0	0	0	0	4	0	0	0	0	1	0	0	0	0	0	0	1	0	0	0	0
taxied	2	.1717	.1142	30.6	0	0	0	1	1	0	0	0	1	0	0	1	0	0	0	0	0	0	0	0	0	0	0	0	0
taxiing	3	.1409	.1472	31.7	2	0	0	0	0	0	1	0	1	0	0	0	0	0	0	0	0	0	0	0	0	2	0	0	0
taxing	3	.1823	.1405	31.5	1	0	1	1	0	0	0	0	0	0	0	0	0	1	0	0	0	0	0	0	0	0	2	0	0
taxis	21	.5305	2.3605	43.7	11	4	0	3	1	0	1	1	1	5	0	0	0	10	0	1	0	0	0	0	1	1	0	2	0
taxonomic	2	.0000	.0209	23.2	0	0	0	0	2	0	0	0	0	0	0	0	0	0	0	0	0	0	0	0	0	0	2	0	0
taxpayer	10	.3552	.8700	39.4	0	0	0	0	0	4	5	1	4	0	0	0	4	0	0	0	0	0	0	0	0	0	0	2	0
taxpayer's	2	.0000	.0299	24.8	0	0	0	0	0	0	2	0	0	0	0	0	2	0	0	0	0	0	0	0	0	0	0	0	0
taxpayers	6	.3729	.5103	37.1	0	0	0	0	0	1	4	1	1	1	0	0	0	1	0	0	0	0	0	0	0	0	0	3	0
Tay	3	.2260	.1580	32.0	0	0	0	0	0	0	3	0	0	0	0	2	0	0	0	0	0	0	0	0	0	0	1	0	0
Taylor	34	.6634	4.7192	46.7	1	8	2	5	3	12	1	2	11	1	0	1	0	11	0	0	2	0	0	0	3	1	0	4	0
Taylor's	8	.4614	.8294	39.2	0	3	0	1	3	0	1	0	3	2	0	1	0	0	0	0	0	0	0	0	2	0	0	0	0
Tazieff	5	.0000	.2284	33.6	0	0	0	0	5	0	0	0	5	0	0	0	0	0	0	0	0	0	0	0	0	0	0	0	0
TC	2	.2427	.1159	30.6	0	1	0	0	0	0	0	1	0	0	0	0	1	0	0	0	0	0	0	0	0	0	0	1	0
tch	9	.0000	.0730	28.6	3	2	0	3	0	1	0	0	0	0	0	0	0	0	9	0	0	0	0	0	0	0	0	0	0
Tchaikovsky	42	.0749	.9401	39.7	7	1	0	3	3	4	24	0	0	0	0	3	0	0	0	0	39	0	0	0	0	0	0	0	0
Tchaikovsky's	15	.0000	.1213	30.8	0	0	0	0	4	1	10	0	0	0	0	0	0	0	0	0	15	0	0	0	0	0	0	0	0
Tchaikowsky	2	.0000	.0162	22.1	0	0	0	0	0	2	0	0	0	0	0	0	0	0	0	0	2	0	0	0	0	0	0	0	0
TD	3	.2309	.1631	32.1	0	0	0	0	0	1	2	0	0	0	0	1	0	0	0	0	0	0	0	0	0	0	0	2	0
te	2	.2408	.1091	30.4	0	0	0	2	0	0	0	0	0	1	0	0	0	0	1	0	0	0	0	0	0	0	0	0	0
tea	223	.6904	31.813	55.0	25	35	46	28	39	18	32	0	67	3	2	14	5	46	0	3	9	0	28	0	17	21	2	6	0
Tea	10	.4541	.9761	39.9	1	2	2	0	2	3	0	0	1	0	0	0	0	1	0	0	3	0	0	0	3	2	0	0	0
teach	254	.6665	35.311	55.5	57	42	29	35	43	23	21	4	87	11	1	24	2	32	5	1	5	1	0	1	29	23	9	20	3
teacher	836	.8357	139.72	61.5	187	180	119	108	113	68	54	7	155	138	15	33	45	43	191	44	16	1	16	2	36	66	4	29	2
Teacher	54	.5324	6.2411	48.0	1	26	8	3	16	0	0	0	17	0	0	6	0	0	0	0	0	0	0	0	4	22	2	3	0
teacher's	51	.7817	8.0196	49.0	11	5	2	2	13	6	10	2	5	9	1	2	12	7	2	3	5	0	0	0	1	3	0	1	0
Teacher's	8	.3541	.6871	38.4	1	3	0	0	4	0	0	0	3	0	0	2	0	0	0	0	0	0	0	0	0	3	0	0	0
teachers	160	.8406	26.862	54.3	20	25	19	13	36	18	26	3	15	11	3	7	6	42	3	8	1	1	4	1	5	12	9	31	1
teachers'	3	.2432	.1790	32.5	0	0	0	1	1	0	1	0	0	0	0	0	0	2	1	0	0	0	0	0	0	0	0	0	0
teaches	30	.2661	2.0036	43.0	7	7	1	2	4	4	4	1	7	8	1	1	0	5	0	1	1	0	0	0	0	0	1	3	2
teaching	124	.7850	19.635	52.9	18	16	15	19	25	8	18	5	22	8	1	11	0	22	1	5	5	1	1	0	6	12	11	17	1
teachings	14	.4316	1.3250	41.2	1	0	0	6	5	1	1	0	0	1	0	0	0	10	0	0	0	0	0	0	1	1	1	0	0
teacup	5	.3850	.4834	36.8	1	2	0	2	0	0	0	0	3	0	0	0	0	1	0	0	0	0	0	0	0	1	0	0	0

7P Tarshish
7Q tarsier-like
9L tart-fruit
8E Tartalea
7F tartan-kilted
7C Tartar's
5N Tartary
5A tartly
XH tartrate
4A taschen
9L Taslan
4A Tasmanian
8A Tassel
8A Tassel's
7Q tastier
7Q tastiest
4A tat-tat
9R tat-tat-tat
6F Tatra
6F Tatras
4A tattle
8A tattlers
6A tattooing
6A taubada
5Q Tauern
7N tauntingly
XP tautline
9R tax-cutting
9R tax-free
6G taxare
XR taxbreak
6F Taxco's
9Q taxi-laden
3A taxi's
7A taxidermist
7A taxidermist's
9P taxidermy
3P taxiway
9Q taxpaying
4A taylor-bird
6J Tayluer
7P Tayxas
7R Tchikrin
9P tcusk
7R TDC
8R TDS
9Q Te
4P Te-a-o-ga
5A tea-party
6P tea-pots
7R Teach
8R teach-ins
8G teacher-dictated
9J teacher-friend
9Q teacher-training
5A Teaching
8R teaching-technology
4K teacups
9N Teagarden

Word Type	F	D	U	SFI	3 Gr 3	4 Gr 4	5 Gr 5	6 Gr 6	7 Gr 7	8 Gr 8	9 Gr 9	X UnGr	A Read	B Eng & Gr	C Comp	D Lit	E Math	F Soc Stud	G Spell	H Sci	J Music	K Art	L Home Ec	M Shop	N Lib F	P Lib NF	Q Lib Ref	R Mag	S Rel
teak	6	.3476	.5208	37.2	0	1	1	3	1	0	0	0	3	0	0	0	0	0	0	0	0	0	0	0	0	0	2	1	0
teakettle	23	.5544	2.8641	44.6	16	3	1	1	1	1	0	0	15	0	1	0	0	1	0	4	1	0	0	0	0	0	1	0	0
teakwood	2	.0000	.0389	25.9	0	0	0	0	2	0	0	0	0	0	0	0	0	2	0	0	0	0	0	0	0	0	0	0	0
Teal	2	.0000	.0243	23.9	0	0	0	0	2	0	0	0	0	0	0	0	0	0	0	0	0	0	0	0	0	0	0	2	0
team	620	.8520	106.04	60.3	80	121	83	80	120	76	52	8	211	56	5	26	55	16	28	57	4	0	0	1	18	69	7	67	0
Team	13	.3579	1.1539	40.6	5	5	0	2	1	0	0	0	6	0	0	0	5	0	0	0	0	0	0	0	0	0	0	2	0
team-dogs	2	.0000	.0234	23.7	0	0	0	0	0	2	0	0	0	0	0	0	0	0	0	0	0	0	0	0	2	0	0	0	0
team's	5	.3469	.4217	36.2	1	0	2	2	0	0	0	0	2	0	0	0	0	0	1	0	0	0	0	0	0	0	0	2	0
teamed	6	.4764	.6014	37.8	1	0	1	0	4	0	0	0	0	0	0	1	0	0	0	0	0	0	0	0	1	2	0	2	0
teammate	30	.3166	2.3580	43.7	9	10	0	2	4	3	2	0	12	1	0	0	1	0	14	1	0	0	0	0	0	0	0	1	0
teammates	12	.5334	1.4376	41.6	0	2	3	1	2	4	0	0	7	2	0	0	0	0	0	1	0	0	0	0	1	0	0	1	0
teams	150	.8699	26.053	54.2	17	42	24	17	21	10	13	6	34	5	2	5	29	9	6	13	0	1	1	0	2	18	6	19	0
teamster	4	.0919	.1430	31.6	0	0	1	0	1	1	1	0	1	0	0	3	0	0	0	0	0	0	0	0	0	0	0	0	0
teamsters	4	.4570	.4091	36.1	0	1	1	1	1	0	0	0	1	0	0	0	0	1	0	0	0	0	0	0	0	1	0	1	0
teamwork	11	.5497	1.2667	41.0	1	0	0	1	4	0	5	0	2	1	0	0	0	0	0	1	0	0	2	1	1	0	3	0	0
teapot	21	.6787	3.0068	44.8	9	3	2	1	2	0	3	1	11	2	0	1	0	3	0	1	0	0	1	0	0	1	1	0	0
teapots	14	.2361	1.0780	40.3	11	1	0	1	0	1	0	0	11	0	0	0	0	3	0	0	0	0	0	0	0	0	0	0	0
tear	121	.9242	22.162	53.5	13	20	23	20	10	17	15	3	29	11	3	12	5	4	3	15	1	2	4	1	11	7	4	9	0
Tear	2	.0000	.0290	24.6	0	2	0	0	0	0	0	0	0	0	0	0	0	0	0	0	0	0	0	0	0	2	0	0	0
tear-gas	2	.0000	.0243	23.9	0	0	0	0	0	2	0	0	0	0	0	0	0	0	0	0	0	0	0	0	0	0	0	2	0
teardrop	2	.0000	.0209	23.2	0	0	0	0	0	0	2	0	0	0	0	0	0	0	0	0	0	0	0	0	0	0	2	0	0
tearful	6	.1844	.3418	35.3	0	2	0	1	1	2	0	0	3	1	2	0	0	0	0	0	0	0	0	0	0	0	0	0	0
tearing	62	.8826	10.922	50.4	5	15	11	9	12	4	5	1	19	2	0	7	2	3	1	9	0	1	1	1	5	5	5	1	0
tearing-down	2	.0000	.0209	23.2	0	0	0	0	2	0	0	0	0	0	0	0	0	0	0	0	0	0	0	0	0	0	2	0	0
tears	223	.7907	35.786	55.5	33	46	15	41	37	16	32	3	83	8	6	45	0	5	2	10	6	0	3	0	26	15	5	9	0
teas	7	.3617	.5868	37.7	0	1	0	3	2	1	0	0	2	0	0	1	0	1	0	0	0	0	2	0	1	0	0	0	0
tease	28	.6787	3.8861	45.9	5	9	4	4	2	3	1	0	5	1	2	2	0	0	1	0	4	0	0	0	6	5	0	2	0
teased	23	.6206	3.0559	44.9	6	9	1	2	4	1	0	0	11	1	0	1	0	1	0	0	0	0	0	0	3	5	1	0	0
teasing	35	.6845	5.0333	47.0	8	10	5	2	5	3	1	1	18	3	0	2	0	1	0	0	1	0	0	0	2	3	0	5	0
teaspoon	40	.3629	3.1589	45.0	1	5	1	4	9	14	2	4	3	0	1	0	1	0	0	6	0	0	17	0	3	4	0	5	0
teaspoonful	12	.2225	.7449	38.7	1	3	1	1	3	3	0	0	2	0	0	0	0	0	0	9	0	0	0	0	0	1	0	0	0
teaspoonfuls	10	.3388	.7795	38.9	2	1	2	3	0	2	0	0	0	1	0	0	0	0	0	8	0	0	1	0	0	0	0	0	0
teaspoons	10	.4704	1.0070	40.0	0	6	0	0	3	1	0	0	0	0	0	0	2	0	0	5	0	0	1	0	0	0	0	2	0
teatime	4	.1112	.1666	32.2	1	2	0	0	1	0	0	0	1	0	0	0	0	0	0	0	0	0	0	0	0	3	0	0	0
Tebbits	4	.0000	.0469	26.7	4	0	0	0	0	0	0	0	0	0	0	0	0	0	0	0	0	0	0	0	4	0	0	0	0
Tech	6	.2885	.3888	35.9	0	0	1	0	1	4	0	0	0	1	0	4	0	0	0	0	0	0	0	0	0	1	0	0	0
technical	84	.7924	13.324	51.2	1	3	11	8	17	12	20	12	3	2	2	0	3	7	0	15	11	1	0	2	1	4	19	14	0
Technical	3	.0000	.0314	25.0	0	0	2	0	0	0	1	0	0	0	0	0	0	0	0	0	0	0	0	0	0	0	3	0	0
technically	17	.6024	2.1271	43.3	0	0	1	1	4	5	6	0	2	0	0	0	0	2	0	2	3	0	0	0	0	1	3	4	0
technician	3	.2076	.1618	32.1	0	0	0	0	0	0	2	1	0	0	0	0	2	0	0	1	0	0	0	0	0	0	0	0	0
technicians	19	.5666	2.2569	43.5	0	1	2	2	2	4	7	1	2	0	0	0	0	4	0	3	0	0	0	2	0	1	4	3	0
technicolor	3	.3874	.2497	34.0	0	0	1	0	2	0	0	0	0	1	0	0	0	0	0	0	0	0	0	0	1	0	0	1	0
technique	55	.6563	7.2968	48.6	0	2	4	3	21	8	13	4	1	0	1	2	0	1	0	2	10	4	0	1	0	2	19	12	0
Technique	5	.1449	.1805	32.6	0	0	0	0	0	4	0	1	0	0	0	0	0	0	4	0	0	0	0	0	0	0	0	1	0
techniques	90	.8170	14.664	51.7	1	1	4	8	22	16	27	11	3	5	3	0	4	5	0	12	13	2	1	2	0	6	19	15	0
technological	20	.5915	2.4369	43.9	1	0	1	0	5	3	7	3	0	0	0	1	0	4	1	2	0	0	0	0	0	2	7	3	0
technologists	2	.2427	.1159	30.6	0	0	0	0	0	1	1	0	0	0	0	0	1	0	0	0	0	0	0	0	0	0	0	1	0
technology	61	.6674	8.2832	49.2	1	1	4	8	14	10	21	2	0	2	0	0	3	7	2	12	0	0	0	1	0	3	16	15	0
Technology	13	.5119	1.3687	41.4	1	0	2	1	2	2	5	0	0	0	2	0	1	1	0	0	0	2	0	0	0	1	3	3	0
Tecumseh	2	.2408	.1204	30.8	1	0	0	0	0	1	0	0	0	0	0	0	0	1	0	0	0	0	0	0	0	1	0	0	0
Ted	94	.8002	15.267	51.8	30	22	12	4	10	11	5	0	39	16	1	2	12	2	4	0	0	1	1	0	5	2	0	9	0
Ted's	12	.2986	.8890	39.5	6	3	1	0	1	0	1	0	3	2	0	0	7	0	0	0	0	0	0	0	0	0	0	0	0
teddy	4	.0665	.1417	31.5	1	2	0	0	0	1	0	0	2	0	2	0	0	0	0	0	0	0	0	0	0	0	0	0	0
Teddy	86	.3550	7.6046	48.8	5	69	0	3	3	3	3	0	40	0	0	0	0	2	1	0	0	0	0	0	0	39	0	4	0
Teddy's	15	.1685	1.0405	40.2	0	8	0	2	5	0	0	0	14	0	0	0	0	0	0	0	0	0	0	0	0	1	0	0	0
tedious	19	.7412	2.8416	44.5	0	0	2	2	6	5	3	1	2	0	1	1	3	0	1	0	1	0	0	0	1	3	4	2	0
tee	4	.3710	.3211	35.1	0	1	1	0	0	1	1	0	0	1	0	0	0	0	0	0	0	0	0	0	1	0	0	2	0
Tee	16	.1864	1.1524	40.6	0	1	0	15	0	0	0	0	15	0	0	1	0	0	0	0	0	0	0	0	0	0	0	0	0
Teedie	3	.0000	.1370	31.4	0	0	3	0	0	0	0	0	3	0	0	0	0	0	0	0	0	0	0	0	0	0	0	0	0
Teeling	2	.0000	.0914	29.6	0	0	0	2	0	0	0	0	2	0	0	0	0	0	0	0	0	0	0	0	0	0	0	0	0
teemed	5	.1511	.1963	32.9	0	0	0	0	4	0	1	0	0	0	0	0	0	0	0	0	0	0	0	0	0	1	4	0	0
teeming	17	.5133	1.8227	42.6	0	0	0	1	7	3	5	1	1	0	2	4	0	0	0	2	0	0	0	0	0	1	6	1	0
teen	9	.4554	.8692	39.4	0	2	3	0	0	4	0	0	0	0	0	0	0	2	1	2	0	0	2	0	0	0	0	2	0
Teen-Age	2	.2300	.1140	30.6	0	0	0	0	1	1	0	0	0	1	0	0	0	0	0	1	0	0	0	0	0	0	0	0	0
teen-age	15	.4107	1.3892	41.4	0	1	0	0	4	6	3	1	4	0	0	0	0	0	0	2	0	0	3	0	0	0	1	5	0
teen-aged	4	.0996	.1523	31.8	0	0	3	1	0	0	0	0	1	0	0	0	0	0	0	0	0	0	0	0	0	0	0	3	0
teen-ager	11	.4210	.9935	40.0	0	0	2	0	4	1	3	1	1	1	0	0	0	0	0	0	1	0	2	0	0	0	0	6	0
teen-agers	35	.5569	4.0703	46.1	0	5	5	2	5	11	7	0	6	2	1	0	0	1	0	2	0	1	9	0	1	0	2	10	0
teenage	3	.2411	.1667	32.2	0	0	0	2	0	1	0	0	0	0	0	0	0	0	0	0	1	0	0	0	0	0	0	2	0
teenager	6	.3021	.4093	36.1	0	0	1	4	0	1	0	0	0	0	0	0	0	1	0	0	1	0	0	0	0	0	0	4	0
teenagers	23	.5147	2.5004	44.0	0	1	8	3	6	2	3	0	1	1	0	0	0	10	0	0	0	0	3	0	0	1	1	6	0
teens	35	.6307	4.5531	46.6	0	0	21	1	6	4	3	0	2	0	0	3	0	14	0	3	1	0	3	0	0	1	1	7	0
teeny	2	.1717	.1142	30.6	0	0	0	0	0	1	1	0	1	0	0	1	0	0	0	0	0	0	0	0	0	0	0	0	0
Teeny	15	.0000	.6852	38.4	15	0	0	0	0	0	0	0	15	0	0	0	0	0	0	0	0	0	0	0	0	0	0	0	0
teepee	2	.0580	.0676	28.3	1	0	1	0	0	0	0	0	1	0	0	0	0	0	0	0	0	1	0	0	0	0	0	0	0
teepees	3	.0344	.0680	28.3	2	1	0	0	0	0	0	0	1	0	0	0	0	0	0	0	0	2	0	0	0	0	0	0	0
tees	2	.1814	.1187	30.7	0	0	0	1	1	0	0	0	1	0	0	0	0	0	0	0	0	0	0	0	0	0	0	1	0
Teeter	4	.0000	.0486	26.9	0	0	0	0	4	0	0	0	0	0	0	0	0	0	0	0	0	0	0	0	0	0	0	4	0
teetered	2	.2443	.1130	30.5	0	0	1	0	0	0	1	0	0	0	0	1	0	0	0	0	0	0	0	0	1	0	0	0	0
teeth	538	.8567	92.214	59.6	144	46	71	57	148	37	31	4	128	15	5	44	3	3	9	110	4	0	13	13	44	99	30	18	0
Teeth	3	.2181	.1541	31.9	1	1	1	0	0	0	0	0	0	0	0	0	0	0	0	0	0	0	0	0	1	0	2	0	0
Tegumai	10	.0000	.1172	30.7	0	10	0	0	0	0	0	0	0	0	0	0	0	0	0	0	0	0	0	0	10	0	0	0	0
Tehran	2	.2351	.1166	30.7	0	0	0	0	2	0	0	0	0	0	0	0	0	1	0	0	0	0	0	0	0	0	0	1	0
Tehuantepec	2	.2285	.1129	30.5	0	0	1	1	0	0	0	0	0	0	0	0	0	1	0	0	0	0	0	0	0	0	1	0	0
Teichner	3	.0000	.1370	31.4	0	0	0	3	0	0	0	0	3	0	0	0	0	0	0	0	0	0	0	0	0	0	0	0	0
Tejas	3	.0000	.0583	27.7	0	0	0	0	3	0	0	0	0	0	0	0	0	3	0	0	0	0	0	0	0	0	0	0	0
Tekana	21	.0000	.9593	39.8	0	0	0	0	21	0	0	0	21	0	0	0	0	0	0	0	0	0	0	0	0	0	0	0	0
Tel	9	.2444	.5495	37.4	0	0	4	1	4	0	0	0	0	0	0	0	0	5	0	0	0	0	0	0	0	4	0	0	0
tele	2	.1497	.1046	30.2	0	0	1	1	0	0	0	0	1	0	0	0	0	0	1	0	0	0	0	0	0	0	0	0	0
telecast	7	.3399	.5470	37.4	0	0	2	0	1	4	0	0	0	0	0	0	0	2	0	4	0	0	0	1	0	0	0	0	0
telegram	26	.4861	2.8066	44.5	0	8	0	2	6	2	7	1	9	9	0	2	0	1	0	1	0	0	0	0	0	4	0	0	0
telegrams	11	.5447	1.2836	41.1	0	1	1	1	3	2	1	2	2	1	0	0	0	2	0	4	0	0	0	1	0	0	1	0	0
telegraph	84	.7948	13.487	51.3	9	10	17	11	14	14	5	4	17	1	3	4	0	14	2	20	3	0	0	2	1	13	4	0	0
Telegraph	6	.3697	.5371	37.3	0	0	1	0	1	4	0	0	3	0	1	1	0	0	0	0	0	0	0	0	0	0	1	0	0

8A teal
7A teamer
8F teaming
4A Teams
9R Teamster
6R tear-blinded
6A tear-stained
9P tear-streaked
4P Tear's
4B tearfully
5N Tears
9D teary
7A teaser
7D teashop
7N teasin'
9J teasingly
8N teats
XN Teavee
7R Tebbetts
7N teched
7B technicalities
XH technics
8R technocratic
8R technocrats
9Q technologies
9Q technology-oriented
5G tect
6G tectus
9D tediousness
XR tedium
9R tee-ers
6A tee-hee
5A Teedie's
7Q teem
7R teems
8L teen-ager's
9R teenies
4R Teens
3A Teeny's
8A teeter
6A teetering
4N teething
5Q Teflon
5G tegere
4N Tegumai's
5R Teh-chuan
7A Teide
4A Teiglech
8B teir
7A Tekana's
7J Tekel
4Q Tekrit
7N teks
7A tele-
8Q Telegonus

Word Type	F	D	U	SFI	3 Gr 3	4 Gr 4	5 Gr 5	6 Gr 6	7 Gr 7	8 Gr 8	9 Gr 9	X UnGr	A Read	B Eng & Gr	C Comp	D Lit	E Math	F Soc Stud	G Spell	H Sci	J Music	K Art	L Home Ec	M Shop	N Lib F	P Lib NF	Q Lib Ref	R Mag	S Rel
telegraphed	2	.1948	.1250	31.0	1	1	0	0	0	0	0	0	1	0	0	0	0	0	0	0	0	0	0	0	0	1	0	0	0
telegraphy	5	.3816	.4230	36.3	0	0	0	0	0	1	1	3	0	0	0	0	0	0	0	3	1	0	0	0	0	0	1	0	0
Telemachos	8	.0000	.0859	29.3	0	0	0	0	0	0	8	0	0	0	0	8	0	0	0	0	0	0	0	0	0	0	0	0	0
Telemachus	8	.3452	.6691	38.3	0	0	3	0	3	2	0	0	3	0	0	0	0	0	0	0	0	0	0	0	3	0	2	0	0
teleology	2	.0000	.0243	23.9	0	0	0	0	2	0	0	0	0	0	0	0	0	0	0	0	0	0	0	0	0	0	0	2	0
teleosts	6	.0000	.0628	28.0	0	0	0	0	6	0	0	0	0	0	0	0	0	0	0	0	0	0	0	0	0	0	6	0	0
telephone	284	.9291	52.296	57.2	61	41	33	49	47	21	29	3	76	22	5	7	9	16	8	49	2	2	5	5	24	8	28	18	0
Telephone	9	.4333	.8433	39.3	0	0	1	2	2	3	1	0	1	0	0	0	0	0	0	1	2	0	0	0	0	0	4	1	0
telephoned	22	.6230	2.9601	44.7	7	4	3	3	3	1	1	0	13	1	0	2	0	1	0	0	0	0	0	0	3	1	0	1	0
telephones	35	.6497	4.7053	46.7	7	3	8	1	6	2	8	0	5	1	0	0	4	11	0	3	0	0	0	2	0	0	6	3	0
telephoning	2	.1551	.0728	28.6	0	0	0	1	1	0	0	0	0	0	1	0	0	0	0	0	0	0	0	0	1	0	0	0	0
telephony	2	.2417	.1091	30.4	0	0	0	0	0	2	0	0	0	0	0	0	0	0	0	0	1	0	0	0	0	0	1	0	0
telescope	186	.5288	21.657	53.4	9	37	22	50	27	16	16	9	58	0	0	1	7	0	0	94	0	0	0	0	6	8	6	6	0
Telescope	2	.1717	.1142	30.6	0	0	1	0	1	0	0	0	1	0	0	1	0	0	0	0	0	0	0	0	0	0	0	0	0
telescopes	71	.3087	5.4997	47.4	11	6	8	22	10	5	2	7	14	0	0	0	0	1	0	51	0	0	0	0	0	1	2	2	0
telescopic	2	.2401	.1133	30.5	0	0	0	0	1	0	1	0	0	0	0	0	0	0	0	0	0	0	0	0	0	1	1	0	0
telescoping	2	.2346	.1166	30.7	0	0	1	0	0	0	0	1	0	0	0	0	0	0	0	1	0	0	0	0	0	0	0	1	0
teletype	2	.2405	.1205	30.8	0	0	1	0	1	0	0	0	0	0	0	0	0	0	0	1	0	0	0	0	0	1	0	0	0
Teletype	2	.1814	.1187	30.7	0	0	0	1	1	0	0	0	1	0	0	0	0	0	0	0	0	0	0	0	0	0	0	1	0
teletypes	3	.3399	.2456	33.9	0	0	0	1	0	1	1	0	1	0	0	1	0	0	0	0	0	0	0	0	0	0	0	1	0
televised	6	.2321	.3270	35.1	0	2	0	1	2	0	1	0	0	0	0	0	0	0	0	0	0	0	0	0	0	0	2	4	0
television	411	.8850	72.256	58.6	45	54	61	56	80	64	45	6	36	47	8	9	22	63	5	82	19	3	10	20	1	14	36	36	0
Television	6	.5353	.6644	38.2	1	0	1	1	2	1	0	0	0	1	0	0	0	1	0	0	1	0	0	0	0	0	2	1	0
tell	3715	.9321	686.09	68.4	1008	762	405	405	570	264	256	45	1064	569	28	256	418	259	99	263	147	28	23	15	222	191	29	98	6
Tell	48	.2232	3.2132	45.1	12	13	12	7	3	1	0	0	27	0	0	0	0	2	0	0	19	0	0	0	0	0	0	0	0
Tell's	2	.0000	.0914	29.6	0	0	2	0	0	0	0	0	2	0	0	0	0	0	0	0	0	0	0	0	0	0	0	0	0
teller	9	.5772	1.0836	40.3	3	0	0	3	3	0	0	0	1	0	0	1	3	0	0	0	1	0	0	0	0	1	0	2	0
Teller	2	.2375	.1088	30.4	0	0	0	0	1	1	0	0	0	0	0	0	0	0	0	0	1	0	0	0	0	0	0	1	0
tellers	9	.2648	.6170	37.9	0	1	1	2	0	4	1	0	3	5	0	0	0	0	0	0	0	0	0	0	0	0	1	0	0
tellin'	5	.3841	.4756	36.8	0	0	1	1	1	2	0	0	3	0	0	1	0	0	0	0	0	0	0	0	1	0	0	0	0
telling	374	.7642	58.293	57.7	58	69	45	55	77	38	25	7	136	63	9	28	6	13	14	18	5	1	1	2	26	23	2	24	3
tells	808	.7949	129.98	61.1	268	121	88	97	109	79	34	12	250	119	20	15	101	64	33	50	73	8	5	2	4	27	9	22	6
Tellson's	4	.0000	.0429	26.3	0	0	0	0	0	0	4	0	0	0	0	4	0	0	0	0	0	0	0	0	0	0	0	0	0
telltale	9	.5279	1.0295	40.1	2	1	1	2	2	1	0	0	3	0	1	1	0	0	0	0	0	0	0	0	1	2	0	1	0
Telly	3	.0000	.0352	25.5	0	0	3	0	0	0	0	0	0	0	0	0	0	0	0	0	0	0	0	0	3	0	0	0	0
Telstar	19	.3696	1.7903	42.5	16	0	3	0	0	0	0	0	11	0	0	0	2	0	0	6	0	0	0	0	0	0	0	0	0
Telstars	2	.0000	.0914	29.6	2	0	0	0	0	0	0	0	2	0	0	0	0	0	0	0	0	0	0	0	0	0	0	0	0
tembo-no	7	.0000	.0851	29.3	0	0	0	0	0	0	0	7	0	0	0	0	0	0	0	0	0	0	0	0	0	0	0	7	0
temper	67	.6491	9.0286	49.6	5	8	7	10	19	9	9	0	19	3	1	4	0	4	1	1	0	0	10	0	15	3	1	5	0
tempera	21	.0234	.1859	32.7	3	4	2	9	1	1	1	0	1	0	0	1	0	0	0	0	0	19	0	0	0	0	0	0	0
temperament	8	.6134	1.0271	40.1	0	0	1	0	3	3	1	0	2	1	0	1	0	0	0	0	1	0	0	0	0	2	0	1	0
temperamental	8	.4846	.8987	39.5	5	0	0	0	3	0	0	0	5	1	0	0	0	0	0	0	0	0	0	0	1	1	0	0	0
temperate	29	.5367	3.2737	45.2	0	5	4	1	12	2	3	2	0	0	0	0	0	7	1	10	0	0	0	0	0	1	8	2	0
temperature	766	.7039	110.12	60.4	105	106	84	101	134	121	105	10	46	5	2	4	118	39	4	398	0	0	29	8	8	26	52	27	0
temperatures	194	.6754	26.959	54.3	15	28	37	25	38	22	24	5	20	0	0	0	12	30	0	74	0	0	2	5	1	6	37	7	0
tempered	4	.0725	.1464	31.7	0	0	0	1	0	2	1	0	2	0	0	0	0	0	0	0	0	0	0	2	0	0	0	0	0
tempering	3	.1101	.0802	29.0	0	0	0	0	1	0	2	0	0	0	0	0	0	0	0	0	0	0	0	2	0	0	0	1	0
tempers	10	.5944	1.2760	41.1	0	0	2	1	6	1	0	0	4	0	0	2	0	1	0	1	0	0	0	0	0	0	1	1	0
tempest	6	.4342	.5720	37.6	0	2	0	2	1	1	0	0	1	0	0	0	0	0	0	0	1	0	0	0	2	2	0	0	0
Tempest	5	.1738	.2196	33.4	0	0	0	4	1	0	0	0	0	0	0	0	0	0	0	0	0	0	0	0	4	0	0	1	0
tempestuous	2	.2305	.1080	30.3	0	0	1	0	0	0	1	0	0	0	0	0	0	0	1	0	0	0	0	0	0	1	0	0	0
templada	2	.0000	.0389	25.9	0	0	0	1	0	0	1	0	0	0	0	0	0	2	0	0	0	0	0	0	0	0	0	0	0
templates	3	.0000	.0076	18.8	0	0	0	0	0	0	3	0	0	0	0	0	0	0	0	0	0	0	0	3	0	0	0	0	0
temple	85	.5338	9.5800	49.8	9	1	6	28	10	18	5	8	11	3	0	5	0	22	1	0	10	8	0	0	1	14	5	3	2
Temple	27	.5954	3.3299	45.2	0	7	11	0	5	1	2	1	3	1	0	0	0	4	0	0	1	2	0	0	1	3	10	2	0
temples	69	.5863	8.3717	49.2	8	8	15	13	14	6	5	0	2	3	0	1	0	30	1	0	0	6	2	0	0	6	17	1	0
Templeton	6	.0000	.0703	28.5	0	6	0	0	0	0	0	0	0	0	0	0	0	0	0	0	0	0	0	0	6	0	0	0	0
tempo	90	.2508	5.0568	47.0	11	7	29	4	22	13	4	0	1	0	1	2	0	1	0	1	73	0	0	0	2	3	6	0	0
temporal	4	.3623	.3223	35.1	1	0	0	0	1	1	1	0	0	0	0	0	0	1	0	0	0	0	0	0	0	2	1	0	0
temporarily	22	.6186	2.8234	44.5	2	1	0	1	7	6	5	0	3	1	2	0	0	4	0	3	0	0	0	0	3	0	4	2	0
temporary	60	.7577	9.1719	49.6	8	5	5	14	7	10	10	1	5	3	0	3	0	6	0	11	1	0	2	0	2	4	12	11	0
tempos	2	.0000	.0162	22.1	0	1	0	0	0	1	0	0	0	0	0	0	0	0	0	0	2	0	0	0	0	0	0	0	0
tempt	4	.3424	.2974	34.7	0	0	0	1	0	1	2	0	0	0	0	1	0	0	0	0	0	0	1	0	0	2	0	0	0
temptation	14	.1870	.8275	39.2	1	0	2	3	5	2	1	0	7	0	0	2	0	0	0	0	1	0	0	0	2	0	0	1	1
temptations	3	.3833	.2447	33.9	0	0	0	1	1	1	0	0	0	0	0	0	0	0	0	0	1	0	0	0	1	0	1	0	0
tempted	19	.7369	2.8184	44.5	1	0	3	2	6	5	2	0	1	1	0	4	0	1	1	1	0	0	1	0	1	1	4	3	0
tempter	2	.0000	.0215	23.3	0	0	0	0	0	0	2	0	0	0	0	2	0	0	0	0	0	0	0	0	0	0	0	0	0
tempting	18	.6699	2.4900	44.0	1	2	1	3	4	1	6	0	5	3	1	1	0	1	0	0	0	0	2	0	1	2	0	2	0
tempts	2	.2446	.1122	30.5	0	0	0	0	1	0	1	0	0	0	0	1	0	0	0	0	0	0	0	0	0	0	1	0	0
tempus	3	.3773	.2433	33.9	0	0	1	0	0	1	1	0	0	0	0	0	1	0	1	0	0	0	0	0	0	0	1	0	0
ten	1225	.8703	212.74	63.3	246	164	136	177	208	116	108	70	255	97	30	45	316	93	54	98	12	2	7	3	69	78	20	46	0
Ten	16	.6051	1.9768	43.0	2	0	8	4	2	0	0	0	0	0	0	0	0	1	1	0	1	0	0	0	3	1	4	5	0
ten-dollar	3	.3528	.2566	34.1	0	3	0	0	0	0	0	0	1	0	0	0	1	0	0	0	0	0	0	0	0	1	0	0	0
ten-foot	6	.3718	.5494	37.4	1	0	2	0	1	1	1	0	3	0	0	1	0	0	0	0	0	0	0	0	0	2	0	0	0
ten-horse	3	.0000	.0067	18.3	0	0	0	0	0	0	3	0	0	0	3	0	0	0	0	0	0	0	0	0	0	0	0	0	0
ten-mile	2	.2407	.1138	30.6	0	0	0	1	1	0	0	0	0	0	0	1	0	0	0	0	0	0	0	0	0	1	0	0	0
ten-minute	4	.4485	.4009	36.0	2	1	0	0	0	0	0	1	1	0	0	0	0	1	0	0	0	0	0	0	0	0	1	1	0
ten-thirty	2	.2443	.1130	30.5	0	0	0	0	1	0	1	0	0	0	0	1	0	0	0	0	0	0	0	0	1	0	0	0	0
ten-thousand	3	.0000	.0449	26.5	0	3	0	0	0	0	0	0	0	0	0	0	3	0	0	0	0	0	0	0	0	0	0	0	0
ten-thousands'	3	.0000	.0449	26.5	0	0	2	0	0	0	1	0	0	0	0	0	3	0	0	0	0	0	0	0	0	0	0	0	0
ten-thousandth	3	.3811	.2534	34.0	0	0	0	0	2	0	1	0	0	0	0	0	0	0	0	1	0	0	0	0	0	1	0	1	0
ten-thousandths	4	.0000	.0486	26.9	0	0	0	0	4	0	0	0	0	0	0	0	0	0	0	0	0	0	0	0	0	0	0	4	0
ten-yard	2	.1814	.1187	30.7	0	0	0	2	0	0	0	0	1	0	0	0	0	0	0	0	0	0	0	0	0	0	0	1	0
ten-year	8	.5155	.8869	39.5	0	0	1	1	0	5	1	0	2	0	1	1	0	2	0	0	0	0	0	1	0	0	0	1	0
ten-year-old	18	.3293	1.5035	41.8	2	7	2	1	2	3	1	0	8	0	0	0	0	0	0	0	0	0	0	0	2	8	0	0	0
tenacious	3	.1169	.1277	31.1	1	0	0	0	0	0	2	0	1	0	0	0	0	0	0	0	0	0	0	0	0	0	2	0	0
tenacity	2	.2441	.1127	30.5	0	0	0	0	1	1	0	0	0	0	0	0	0	0	0	0	0	0	0	0	1	0	1	0	0
tenant	18	.3449	1.3874	41.4	4	1	4	1	3	2	3	0	0	0	0	1	0	7	0	0	0	0	0	0	0	1	9	0	0
tenants	16	.5198	1.7608	42.5	2	0	2	7	1	4	0	0	0	1	0	1	0	10	0	0	0	0	0	0	1	1	2	0	0
Tenaya	2	.2446	.1123	30.5	0	1	1	0	0	0	0	0	0	1	0	0	0	0	0	0	0	0	0	0	0	0	1	0	0
tend	107	.7695	16.565	52.2	9	5	16	13	27	11	22	4	7	7	1	3	1	9	0	32	3	0	12	2	5	3	11	11	0
tended	38	.7834	5.9903	47.8	4	4	7	3	7	6	6	1	5	1	1	2	0	9	1	0	2	2	0	0	2	4	6	3	0
tendencies	9	.5508	1.0414	40.2	0	0	0	2	3	4	0	0	1	0	0	1	0	0	0	2	1	0	0	0	0	1	3	0	0
tendency	41	.8012	6.5550	48.2	0	0	1	4	9	9	15	3	1	6	1	1	0	2	0	4	5	0	1	2	2	4	10	2	0

8Q telegraphs
5N Telemachus'
9Q telemeter
7Q teleost
9Q telepathic
9Q telepathy
8Q Telephotography
6R teleplay
6Q teleprinter
6H TELESCOPE
5Q telescoped
9Q teletypewriter
5H televise
9R Television-Allen
7Q television-receiving
4R television's
9Q Telford
8D tell-tale
9B teller's
6B Telling
XR tellingly
3A tellurides
4Q tellurium
5N Telly's
6Q telophase
3H Telstar's
7Q temensis
7Q temerity
7N temperaments
7D tempest-tost
5P tempestuously
9M template
7D Templecombe
4N Templeton's
XR tempora
6N tempters
3P temptingly
8Q Temur
6P TEN
7K ten-
XH ten-billionth
3H ten-cent
9R ten-day
9Q ten-decimal-digit
9E ten-digit
XH ten-division
3P ten-gallon
4A ten-going-on-eleven
7A ten-knot
7D ten-league
7R ten-man
5E ten-millions'
8D ten-month
4J ten-note
3R ten-ounce
3J ten-penny
7H ten-percent
4A ten-pound
7N ten-second
5E ten-thousands
6E ten-thousandths'
3P ten-ton
6P ten-volume
4N ten-week
3Q tenant-farming
XR Tend'r

Word Type	F	D	U	SFI	3 Gr 3	4 Gr 4	5 Gr 5	6 Gr 6	7 Gr 7	8 Gr 8	9 Gr 9	X UnGr	A Read	B Eng & Gr	C Comp	D Lit	E Math	F Soc Stud	G Spell	H Sci	J Music	K Art	L Home Ec	M Shop	N Lib F	P Lib NF	Q Lib Ref	R Mag	S Rel
tender	126	.5360	14.251	51.5	9	13	8	14	36	13	28	5	24	4	0	2	0	6	0	4	9	0	31	0	15	15	5	11	0
tenderfoot	3	.0000	.0322	25.1	0	0	0	0	3	0	0	0	0	0	0	3	0	0	0	0	0	0	0	0	0	0	0	0	0
tenderhearted	2	.1814	.1187	30.7	0	0	1	1	0	0	0	0	1	0	0	0	0	0	0	0	0	0	0	0	0	0	0	1	0
tenderized	2	.1812	.0838	29.2	0	0	0	0	0	0	1	1	0	0	0	0	0	0	0	0	0	0	1	0	0	0	0	1	0
tenderly	14	.5938	1.7827	42.5	3	3	1	1	2	1	1	2	6	0	0	2	0	0	0	1	2	0	0	0	2	0	0	1	0
tenderness	8	.4116	.7495	38.7	1	0	1	1	0	2	3	0	3	0	0	1	0	0	0	0	1	0	2	0	1	0	0	0	0
tenders	4	.2287	.2348	33.7	0	0	0	4	0	0	0	0	0	0	0	0	0	0	0	3	0	0	0	0	0	0	0	1	0
tending	22	.6802	3.0945	44.9	1	2	1	4	5	4	5	0	6	0	0	5	0	3	2	2	0	1	0	0	1	1	1	0	0
tendon	5	.2129	.2689	34.3	1	1	0	0	0	2	1	0	0	0	0	0	0	0	0	2	0	0	0	0	0	0	0	3	0
tendons	14	.0869	.5384	37.3	7	4	0	0	1	0	1	1	2	0	0	0	0	0	0	12	0	0	0	0	0	0	0	0	0
tendrils	6	.2679	.4018	36.0	0	0	1	0	3	2	0	0	1	0	0	3	0	0	0	2	0	0	0	0	0	0	0	0	0
tends	62	.7141	8.9638	49.5	3	6	5	3	19	10	15	1	2	1	0	2	0	4	3	23	4	0	1	4	0	1	14	3	0
tenement	8	.5061	.8732	39.4	1	1	0	0	4	1	1	0	2	1	1	0	0	1	0	0	0	0	0	0	0	0	2	1	0
tenements	6	.3456	.4849	36.9	0	0	0	2	0	4	0	0	1	0	1	0	0	3	0	0	0	0	0	0	0	0	0	1	0
Tenerife	3	.0000	.1370	31.4	0	0	0	0	3	0	0	0	3	0	0	0	0	0	0	0	0	0	0	0	0	0	0	0	0
tenfold	2	.2446	.1122	30.5	0	0	0	0	1	1	0	0	0	0	0	1	0	0	0	0	0	0	0	0	0	0	1	0	0
Tenley	5	.0000	.2284	33.6	0	0	0	0	0	5	0	0	5	0	0	0	0	0	0	0	0	0	0	0	0	0	0	0	0
Tenn	2	.2437	.1129	30.5	0	0	0	0	1	1	0	0	0	0	0	0	0	0	0	0	0	0	0	0	0	0	1	1	0
Tennessee	86	.6988	12.363	50.9	23	8	20	7	8	8	4	8	18	1	0	3	2	19	0	3	2	0	0	0	0	22	8	8	0
tennis	76	.8024	12.353	50.9	5	5	16	10	20	14	6	0	29	11	5	1	4	7	1	3	0	1	2	2	0	3	3	4	0
Tennis	3	.0000	.1370	31.4	0	0	3	0	0	0	0	0	3	0	0	0	0	0	0	0	0	0	0	0	0	0	0	0	0
Tennyson	5	.3856	.4325	36.4	1	1	0	1	2	0	0	0	1	1	0	0	0	0	0	0	2	0	0	0	0	1	0	0	0
Tenochtitlan	3	.0000	.0583	27.7	0	0	3	0	0	0	0	0	0	0	0	0	0	3	0	0	0	0	0	0	0	0	0	0	0
tenon	7	.0000	.0177	22.5	0	0	0	0	7	0	0	0	0	0	0	0	0	0	0	0	0	0	0	7	0	0	0	0	0
tenons	2	.0000	.0050	17.0	0	0	0	0	2	0	0	0	0	0	0	0	0	0	0	0	0	0	0	2	0	0	0	0	0
tenor	18	.1822	.7713	38.9	0	2	2	0	9	4	1	0	0	1	0	1	0	0	0	0	15	0	0	0	0	0	0	1	0
tens	306	.1530	13.234	51.2	110	41	47	45	30	17	13	3	7	2	0	0	281	3	2	1	0	0	0	0	0	3	3	4	0
tens'	23	.0000	.3443	35.4	9	2	9	2	0	0	0	1	0	0	0	0	23	0	0	0	0	0	0	0	0	0	0	0	0
tense	194	.4343	17.855	52.5	2	24	27	34	33	43	30	1	8	116	0	7	0	1	44	0	1	0	1	0	7	3	1	5	0
tense-forming	2	.0000	.0162	22.1	0	0	0	0	0	2	0	0	0	0	0	0	0	0	2	0	0	0	0	0	0	0	0	0	0
tensed	4	.3071	.2967	34.7	0	0	2	0	1	0	1	0	1	0	0	1	0	0	0	0	0	0	0	0	2	0	0	0	0
tensely	3	.3370	.2430	33.9	0	0	1	0	1	0	1	0	1	0	0	1	0	0	0	0	0	0	0	0	0	0	1	0	0
tenses	13	.2358	.6960	38.4	0	0	0	1	2	8	2	0	0	6	0	0	0	0	7	0	0	0	0	0	0	0	0	0	0
tensile	6	.1835	.2281	33.6	0	0	0	0	0	2	4	0	0	0	0	0	0	0	0	0	0	1	0	5	0	0	0	0	0
tensing	2	.2427	.1152	30.6	0	1	0	1	0	0	0	0	0	0	0	0	0	0	0	0	0	0	0	0	1	1	0	0	0
tension	56	.6157	7.0038	48.5	3	0	5	3	15	15	14	1	4	0	4	4	0	1	0	2	6	0	16	3	3	4	5	4	0
tensions	11	.4468	1.0320	40.1	0	0	3	0	2	3	3	0	0	0	0	0	0	0	0	0	0	0	2	0	0	3	2	4	0
tent	208	.7114	30.593	54.9	67	48	32	11	23	14	11	2	82	5	2	17	6	7	10	1	0	3	0	1	18	27	1	26	2
tentacle	2	.0000	.0209	23.2	0	0	0	0	2	0	0	0	0	0	0	0	0	0	0	0	0	0	0	0	0	0	2	0	0
tentacles	13	.4822	1.3542	41.3	0	2	0	2	8	0	1	0	1	0	0	1	2	0	0	6	0	0	0	0	0	0	3	0	0
tentative	8	.5379	.8958	39.5	0	0	0	0	5	0	3	0	0	0	0	2	1	0	0	2	0	0	0	0	1	0	2	0	0
tentatively	6	.3588	.4627	36.7	0	2	0	0	3	1	0	0	0	0	1	0	0	0	0	0	0	0	0	0	3	0	0	2	0
tenth	73	.7082	10.552	50.2	4	4	10	8	24	15	4	4	10	1	0	3	30	5	3	3	1	0	0	0	1	5	6	5	0
Tenth	5	.4328	.4755	36.8	0	1	2	1	0	0	0	1	1	0	0	0	0	0	0	0	1	0	0	0	0	0	1	2	0
tenths	45	.1844	2.1705	43.4	0	0	3	22	6	8	6	0	0	0	0	0	42	1	0	0	0	0	1	0	0	0	1	0	0
tenths'	3	.0000	.0449	26.5	0	0	0	2	1	0	0	0	0	0	0	0	3	0	0	0	0	0	0	0	0	0	0	0	0
tents	85	.8054	13.786	51.4	20	21	9	12	13	6	2	2	17	5	0	2	8	15	4	0	4	2	0	0	7	17	0	4	0
tenuous	3	.2445	.1818	32.6	0	0	0	0	1	1	0	1	0	0	0	0	0	0	0	2	0	0	0	0	0	0	1	0	0
tenure	3	.3395	.2468	33.9	0	0	2	0	1	0	0	0	1	0	0	0	0	0	0	0	0	0	0	0	0	1	1	0	0
Tenure	3	.1823	.1405	31.5	0	0	1	0	0	1	1	0	0	0	0	0	0	1	0	0	0	0	0	0	0	1	2	0	0
Tenzing	12	.2988	.8020	39.0	0	0	0	0	6	0	6	0	0	5	0	6	0	0	0	1	0	0	0	0	0	0	0	0	0
Teotihuacan	4	.0000	.0778	28.9	0	0	0	4	0	0	0	0	0	0	0	0	0	4	0	0	0	0	0	0	0	0	0	0	0
Teotihuacanos	5	.0000	.0972	29.9	0	0	0	5	0	0	0	0	0	0	0	0	0	5	0	0	0	0	0	0	0	0	0	0	0
tepee	8	.3810	.7827	38.9	5	2	0	0	1	0	0	0	6	1	0	0	0	0	0	0	0	0	0	0	1	0	0	0	0
tepees	15	.5376	1.7639	42.5	5	2	3	1	4	0	0	0	5	0	0	0	0	5	0	0	0	0	0	0	2	1	0	2	0
tephra	2	.0000	.0914	29.6	0	0	0	2	0	0	0	0	2	0	0	0	0	0	0	0	0	0	0	0	0	0	0	0	0
tepid	2	.2303	.1079	30.3	0	0	0	1	0	0	1	0	0	0	0	0	0	0	0	0	1	0	0	0	0	1	0	0	0
ter	2	.1497	.1046	30.2	0	0	1	0	0	1	0	0	1	0	0	0	0	0	1	0	0	0	0	0	0	0	0	0	0
terciopelo	2	.0000	.0243	23.9	0	0	0	0	2	0	0	0	0	0	0	0	0	0	0	0	0	0	0	0	0	0	0	2	0
Teresa	3	.2197	.2090	33.2	0	0	1	0	0	2	0	0	2	0	0	0	0	0	0	0	0	0	0	0	0	0	1	0	0
term	226	.8348	37.645	55.8	2	8	30	12	61	43	58	12	14	33	0	4	23	32	9	28	22	0	3	3	0	10	35	10	0
Terman	2	.0000	.0209	23.2	0	0	0	0	0	0	2	0	0	0	0	0	0	0	0	0	0	0	0	0	0	0	2	0	0
termed	14	.5604	1.6155	42.1	0	0	1	1	5	4	1	2	0	2	0	0	0	1	0	1	1	0	0	0	1	0	6	2	0
terminal	42	.5878	5.1350	47.1	6	0	6	4	6	7	7	6	2	3	0	0	1	2	1	20	0	0	0	5	1	1	3	3	0
terminals	19	.4349	1.7737	42.5	0	0	4	1	4	6	0	4	1	2	0	0	0	0	0	6	0	0	0	4	0	0	2	4	0
terminate	7	.5290	.7733	38.9	0	0	0	0	0	3	2	2	0	0	0	0	2	1	0	0	0	0	0	0	0	1	2	1	0
terminated	7	.4348	.6444	38.1	0	0	0	0	3	2	2	0	0	0	0	0	0	0	0	0	0	0	0	0	1	1	3	2	0
terminates	2	.0000	.0299	24.8	0	0	0	0	0	0	2	0	0	0	0	0	2	0	0	0	0	0	0	0	0	0	0	0	0
terminating	28	.2231	1.5677	42.0	0	0	0	1	2	14	11	0	1	0	0	1	24	0	0	0	0	0	0	0	0	0	1	0	0
termination	6	.4846	.6011	37.8	0	0	0	0	2	2	2	0	0	0	1	0	0	1	0	0	0	0	1	0	1	0	2	0	0
terminology	3	.3826	.2445	33.9	0	0	0	1	1	0	0	1	0	0	0	0	0	0	0	0	1	0	0	0	0	0	1	1	0
termite	10	.5144	1.1162	40.5	0	0	0	4	4	1	1	0	2	0	0	1	1	0	0	4	0	0	0	0	0	0	2	0	0
termites	28	.5258	3.1747	45.0	5	0	0	13	10	0	0	0	5	0	1	0	0	2	0	12	0	0	0	0	0	1	7	0	0
terms	425	.8447	71.551	58.5	7	12	41	47	112	87	110	9	21	24	6	7	154	47	9	32	12	4	9	3	5	10	61	21	0
tern	8	.4518	.8031	39.0	0	1	0	4	0	2	1	0	2	2	1	0	0	0	0	2	0	0	0	0	0	1	0	0	0
terns	12	.4518	1.1921	40.8	1	0	0	8	3	0	0	0	1	0	0	0	0	0	0	7	0	0	0	0	0	1	2	1	0
terra	3	.3676	.2407	33.8	0	0	0	1	0	2	0	0	0	0	0	0	0	1	1	0	0	0	0	0	0	0	1	0	0
terrace	14	.3425	1.1130	40.5	0	0	0	1	3	3	4	3	3	0	0	2	0	0	0	3	0	3	0	0	0	0	0	3	0
Terrace	4	.1959	.1920	32.8	0	0	1	0	0	0	2	1	0	0	0	0	0	0	0	0	0	0	0	0	3	0	0	1	0
terraced	16	.4924	1.7242	42.7	4	2	2	2	5	1	0	0	4	0	0	2	0	4	0	0	0	0	0	0	0	0	5	1	0
terraces	15	.5943	1.8738	42.7	5	2	0	1	4	1	2	0	2	0	0	1	1	7	0	0	0	0	0	0	1	1	2	0	0
terrain	37	.5565	4.2585	46.3	3	2	2	5	17	0	3	5	1	1	0	0	0	2	0	1	1	0	0	1	0	3	11	16	0
terramycin	5	.4822	.5113	37.1	0	0	0	0	0	3	1	1	0	0	0	0	0	0	1	2	0	0	0	0	0	1	1	0	0
Terrance	4	.0000	.1827	32.6	0	0	0	0	0	4	0	0	4	0	0	0	0	0	0	0	0	0	0	0	0	0	0	0	0
terrarium	12	.0000	.2366	33.7	8	4	0	0	0	0	0	0	0	0	0	0	0	0	0	12	0	0	0	0	0	0	0	0	0
terrere	2	.0000	.0162	22.1	0	0	2	0	0	0	0	0	0	0	0	0	0	0	2	0	0	0	0	0	0	0	0	0	0
terrestrial	10	.0759	.2544	34.1	0	0	0	0	9	0	1	0	0	0	0	0	0	0	0	1	0	0	0	0	0	0	9	0	0
terrible	253	.8047	41.227	56.2	48	38	37	45	41	22	16	6	90	11	2	25	0	19	3	8	3	0	0	0	35	31	7	19	0
Terrible	2	.1948	.1250	31.0	1	0	1	0	0	0	0	0	1	0	0	0	0	0	0	0	0	0	0	0	0	1	0	0	0
terrible-tempered	2	.0000	.0243	23.9	1	0	0	0	0	0	0	1	0	0	0	0	0	0	0	0	0	0	0	0	0	0	0	2	0
terribly	68	.6330	9.0755	49.6	12	9	8	9	11	5	12	2	26	2	0	10	0	0	1	0	1	0	0	0	16	6	0	6	0
terrier	15	.6030	1.9287	42.9	2	1	1	2	8	1	0	0	6	0	1	1	0	0	0	2	0	1	0	0	2	2	0	0	0
terriers	4	.1787	.2347	33.7	0	2	0	0	0	2	0	0	2	0	0	0	0	0	0	0	0	0	0	0	2	0	0	0	0
terrific	32	.5176	3.7094	45.7	5	5	4	7	9	1	1	0	16	0	0	0	0	0	0	1	0	0	0	0	6	5	0	4	0

5G tendere
4P tenderer
3N tenderfeet
3N tenderfoots
9L tenderizer
6A tenderloin
XR Tenderloin
6A tendin'
9D tendril
8A Tenedos
8Q tenesmus
8Q tenet
7A tenets
6R tengo
8D Teniers
8D tenn
3A Tennes
5F Tenneseee-NorthCarolina
6A Tenney
7P tenny-runners
3B Tennyson's
8J tenors
5N tenpence
4N tenpenny
5G tens**
7K tenseness
3N tent-like
7N tent-roof
6R tent-shaded
7A tent-shaped
6Q tentacled
4P tentfolk
9R tentful
5J tenuto
9R Teodoro
XR teonanctatl
6F Teotihuacano
3A Terai
8F Terence
9D tergiversation
9Q Terminal
5P termini
6H termites'
4P tern's
7R Terns
5J Terra
6J terra-cotta
7F terracing
8A Terrance's
8A Terranova
6A Terrapin
7H terrapins
XH terraria
4Q Terrarum
3P Terre
7Q terrestris

Word Type	F	D	U	SFI	3 Gr 3	4 Gr 4	5 Gr 5	6 Gr 6	7 Gr 7	8 Gr 8	9 Gr 9	X UnGr	A Read	B Eng & Gr	C Comp	D Lit	E Math	F Soc Stud	G Spell	H Sci	J Music	K Art	L Home Ec	M Shop	N Lib F	P Lib NF	Q Lib Ref	R Mag	S Rel
Terrific	2	.1405	.0669	28.3	0	1	0	0	0	1	0	0	0	0	0	0	0	0	0	0	0	1	0	0	1	0	0	0	0
terrified	40	.7467	6.1249	47.9	8	8	3	5	4	6	3	3	16	2	2	4	0	0	0	2	0	0	1	0	3	5	1	4	0
terrifies	2	.2437	.1129	30.5	1	0	0	0	1	0	0	0	0	0	0	0	0	0	0	0	0	0	0	0	0	0	1	1	0
terrify	3	.2124	.1716	32.3	0	0	1	0	0	1	1	0	1	1	1	0	0	0	0	0	0	0	0	0	0	0	0	0	0
terrifying	19	.5578	2.2803	43.6	0	4	2	5	2	2	4	0	7	1	2	1	0	0	0	1	1	0	0	0	5	1	0	0	0
territorial	19	.4989	2.0062	43.0	1	0	1	1	2	9	5	0	0	1	0	1	0	9	0	0	0	0	0	0	0	1	6	1	0
territoriality	2	.0000	.0243	23.9	0	0	0	0	0	0	0	2	0	0	0	0	0	0	0	0	0	0	0	0	0	0	0	2	0
territories	44	.3306	3.3562	45.3	3	2	5	6	10	15	3	0	1	0	0	0	0	27	0	0	0	0	0	0	0	1	14	1	0
Territories	7	.5048	.7748	38.9	0	0	1	2	2	1	0	1	2	0	0	1	0	1	0	1	0	0	0	0	0	0	2	0	0
territory	152	.6502	20.369	53.1	9	10	36	17	29	32	17	2	9	2	0	4	3	80	3	2	4	0	0	0	2	11	22	10	0
Territory	42	.6312	5.4604	47.4	4	5	14	3	5	8	2	1	1	4	0	5	0	19	0	0	0	0	0	0	1	6	3	3	0
terror	76	.7682	11.883	50.7	5	9	4	16	24	9	8	1	25	0	2	9	0	6	0	2	4	0	0	0	11	5	4	8	0
Terror	3	.3385	.2445	33.9	1	0	1	1	0	0	0	0	1	0	0	0	0	0	0	0	0	0	0	0	1	0	1	0	0
terror-stricken	3	.0000	.1370	31.4	0	0	0	2	1	0	0	0	3	0	0	0	0	0	0	0	0	0	0	0	0	0	0	0	0
terrorism	2	.0000	.0243	23.9	0	0	0	0	0	0	2	0	0	0	0	0	0	0	0	0	0	0	0	0	0	0	0	2	0
terrorists	2	.0000	.0243	23.9	0	0	0	1	0	1	0	0	0	0	0	0	0	0	0	0	0	0	0	0	0	0	0	2	0
terrorize	2	.2285	.1129	30.5	0	1	0	0	0	1	0	0	0	0	0	0	0	1	0	0	0	0	0	0	0	0	1	0	0
terrorized	5	.2446	.3866	35.9	0	0	1	1	1	2	0	0	4	1	0	0	0	0	0	0	0	0	0	0	0	0	0	0	0
terrorizing	3	.3431	.2528	34.0	0	0	0	1	1	1	0	0	1	0	0	0	0	1	0	0	0	0	0	0	1	0	0	0	0
terrors	12	.5356	1.3537	41.3	0	0	2	2	4	1	3	0	1	0	0	4	0	3	0	0	0	0	0	0	2	1	1	0	0
Terry	75	.6707	10.617	50.3	2	13	3	22	13	17	5	0	39	3	0	8	6	0	0	4	0	0	4	0	0	3	0	8	0
Terry's	3	.2524	.1934	32.9	0	0	0	1	0	1	1	0	1	0	0	1	0	0	0	0	0	0	1	0	0	0	0	0	0
tersely	3	.3873	.2495	34.0	0	0	0	0	2	0	1	0	0	0	0	1	0	0	0	0	0	0	0	0	1	0	0	1	0
Terwilliger	7	.0000	.0821	29.1	0	0	7	0	0	0	0	0	0	0	0	0	0	0	0	0	0	0	0	0	7	0	0	0	0
Teshumai	3	.0000	.0352	25.5	0	3	0	0	0	0	0	0	0	0	0	0	0	0	0	0	0	0	0	0	3	0	0	0	0
Tess	2	.2398	.1138	30.6	0	1	0	0	0	1	0	0	0	0	0	1	1	0	0	0	0	0	0	0	0	0	0	0	0
test	663	.8321	110.41	60.4	64	90	76	73	131	138	64	27	82	43	1	6	73	18	100	205	4	0	13	16	5	23	12	61	1
Test	196	.0352	2.9798	44.7	33	47	32	27	52	5	0	0	2	1	0	0	0	0	190	0	0	0	0	0	0	1	0	2	0
testacea	2	.0000	.0234	23.7	0	0	0	0	2	0	0	0	0	0	0	0	0	0	0	0	0	0	0	0	2	0	0	0	0
testament	3	.3267	.2367	33.7	0	0	1	1	1	0	0	0	1	0	0	0	0	0	0	0	1	0	0	0	1	0	0	0	0
Testament	17	.3781	1.3769	41.4	0	10	1	2	2	1	0	1	0	0	0	0	0	1	0	0	4	0	0	0	1	1	10	0	0
tested	84	.7724	13.133	51.2	10	13	7	11	20	11	9	3	17	1	1	2	3	2	1	22	0	0	4	4	2	1	5	19	0
tester	9	.0859	.2593	34.1	0	0	0	2	0	0	7	0	2	1	0	0	0	0	0	0	0	0	0	6	0	0	0	0	0
Tester	2	.0000	.0050	17.0	0	0	0	0	0	0	2	0	0	0	0	0	0	0	0	0	0	0	0	2	0	0	0	0	0
testers	3	.0437	.0743	28.7	0	0	0	0	0	0	3	0	1	0	0	0	0	0	0	0	0	0	0	2	0	0	0	0	0
Testers	3	.0000	.0076	18.8	0	0	0	0	0	0	3	0	0	0	0	0	0	0	0	0	0	0	0	3	0	0	0	0	0
testes	3	.0000	.0591	27.7	0	0	1	0	0	0	1	1	0	0	0	0	0	0	0	3	0	0	0	0	0	0	0	0	0
testified	2	.2440	.1132	30.5	0	0	0	0	1	0	1	0	0	0	0	1	0	0	0	0	0	0	0	0	0	0	0	1	0
testify	10	.5229	1.0849	40.4	0	0	0	0	4	3	2	1	0	0	1	0	0	2	0	0	0	0	0	0	2	0	3	2	0
testifying	2	.2405	.1205	30.8	0	0	0	0	2	0	0	0	0	0	0	0	0	0	0	1	0	0	0	0	0	1	0	0	0
testimonial	2	.2427	.1152	30.6	0	1	0	1	0	0	0	0	0	0	0	0	0	0	0	0	0	0	0	0	1	1	0	0	0
testimony	17	.6409	2.2301	43.5	0	0	0	1	5	5	5	1	2	2	2	0	0	2	3	1	0	1	0	0	0	0	2	2	0
testing	80	.6106	10.151	50.1	10	5	3	13	13	16	18	2	15	2	0	5	3	3	2	10	0	0	1	14	2	5	7	11	0
tests	185	.7273	27.190	54.3	16	18	17	23	38	38	18	17	13	8	0	1	9	5	42	37	1	0	2	10	0	15	11	31	0
Tests	2	.0000	.0050	17.0	0	0	0	0	0	0	2	0	0	0	0	0	0	0	0	0	0	0	0	2	0	0	0	0	0
Tet	3	.0000	.0365	25.6	0	0	0	0	0	3	0	0	0	0	0	0	0	0	0	0	0	0	0	0	0	0	0	3	0
tetanus	9	.0000	.1774	32.5	0	4	0	5	0	0	0	0	0	0	0	0	0	0	0	9	0	0	0	0	0	0	0	0	0
tether	4	.3072	.2981	34.7	2	0	0	0	0	1	0	1	1	0	0	0	0	0	0	0	0	0	0	0	1	0	0	2	0
tethered	5	.4213	.4686	36.7	0	1	0	3	1	0	0	0	1	0	0	1	0	0	0	0	0	0	0	0	2	1	0	0	0
Teton	4	.0000	.0778	28.9	0	4	0	0	0	0	0	0	0	0	0	0	0	4	0	0	0	0	0	0	0	0	0	0	0
tetrachloride	4	.0000	.0789	29.0	0	0	0	0	0	0	4	0	0	0	0	0	0	0	0	4	0	0	0	0	0	0	0	0	0
tetrad	4	.0000	.0419	26.2	0	0	0	4	0	0	0	0	0	0	0	0	0	0	0	0	0	0	0	0	0	0	4	0	0
tetrads	2	.0000	.0209	23.2	0	0	0	2	0	0	0	0	0	0	0	0	0	0	0	0	0	0	0	0	0	0	2	0	0
tetraethyl	4	.2437	.2257	33.5	0	0	0	2	1	0	1	0	0	0	0	0	0	0	0	0	0	0	0	0	0	0	2	2	0
tetrahedron	4	.0000	.0599	27.8	0	0	1	0	0	3	0	0	0	0	0	0	4	0	0	0	0	0	0	0	0	0	0	0	0
tetrahedrons	3	.0000	.0449	26.5	0	0	0	0	0	3	0	0	0	0	0	0	3	0	0	0	0	0	0	0	0	0	0	0	0
tetrapod	2	.0000	.0209	23.2	0	0	0	0	2	0	0	0	0	0	0	0	0	0	0	0	0	0	0	0	0	0	2	0	0
tetrapods	3	.0000	.0314	25.0	0	0	0	0	3	0	0	0	0	0	0	0	0	0	0	0	0	0	0	0	0	0	3	0	0
Teunis	12	.0000	.1407	31.5	0	12	0	0	0	0	0	0	0	0	0	0	0	0	0	0	0	0	0	0	12	0	0	0	0
Teunis's	2	.0000	.0234	23.7	0	2	0	0	0	0	0	0	0	0	0	0	0	0	0	0	0	0	0	0	2	0	0	0	0
Teutonic	6	.4291	.5437	37.4	0	0	2	1	2	0	1	0	0	0	0	0	0	0	0	0	1	0	0	0	0	1	3	1	0
Tewindrow	2	.0000	.0234	23.7	0	2	0	0	0	0	0	0	0	0	0	0	0	0	0	0	0	0	0	0	2	0	0	0	0
Tex	3	.1277	.1363	31.3	0	0	0	0	2	0	0	1	1	0	0	0	0	0	0	0	0	0	0	0	0	0	0	2	0
Texan	2	.2306	.1140	30.6	0	0	0	0	1	0	1	0	0	1	0	0	0	1	0	0	0	0	0	0	0	0	0	0	0
Texans	31	.5693	3.8462	45.9	0	13	3	0	10	3	1	1	13	0	0	1	0	7	0	0	0	0	0	0	1	7	0	2	0
Texans'	2	.0000	.0914	29.6	0	0	2	0	0	0	0	0	2	0	0	0	0	0	0	0	0	0	0	0	0	0	0	0	0
texas	2	.1787	.1174	30.7	0	0	0	0	1	1	0	0	1	0	0	0	0	0	0	0	0	0	0	0	1	0	0	0	0
Texas	398	.6970	57.343	57.6	36	79	78	30	106	43	12	14	93	3	0	10	3	170	0	17	6	2	0	0	5	44	17	28	0
Texian's	3	.0000	.0583	27.7	0	0	0	0	0	3	0	0	0	0	0	0	0	3	0	0	0	0	0	0	0	0	0	0	0
text	63	.7225	9.1883	49.6	0	2	10	4	10	18	17	2	6	5	0	6	2	4	1	3	20	0	1	3	0	2	7	3	0
Text	7	.2301	.3830	35.8	3	0	0	0	0	0	4	0	0	0	0	4	0	0	0	0	0	0	0	0	0	3	0	0	0
textbook	35	.6533	4.7212	46.7	0	7	8	1	6	7	6	0	4	5	0	0	4	8	0	7	0	0	1	0	0	0	6	0	0
textbooks	26	.6874	3.7378	45.7	0	1	1	2	11	6	5	0	11	2	0	0	3	5	0	1	0	0	0	1	0	0	2	1	0
textile	60	.3101	4.3895	46.4	3	5	24	9	9	2	7	1	0	0	0	0	0	48	1	0	0	0	0	0	0	1	9	1	0
textiles	46	.5561	5.3816	47.3	4	0	12	12	8	3	7	0	2	0	0	0	0	27	1	1	0	0	2	0	0	2	8	3	0
texts	9	.4985	.9299	39.7	0	0	0	0	4	3	1	1	0	1	0	1	0	1	0	0	4	0	0	0	0	0	1	1	0
texture	79	.3973	6.5428	48.2	2	4	9	5	22	16	18	3	2	0	0	1	0	1	0	12	9	31	10	5	0	0	5	3	0
textured	12	.1556	.3891	35.9	0	3	2	2	2	0	3	0	0	0	0	0	0	0	0	0	0	9	3	0	0	0	0	0	0
textures	28	.0758	.4770	36.8	4	5	8	4	2	3	1	1	0	0	0	0	0	0	0	0	0	25	2	0	0	0	0	1	0
th	108	.1208	3.5649	45.5	10	38	22	9	21	2	4	2	6	8	0	0	2	0	92	0	0	0	0	0	0	0	0	0	0
TH	6	.0000	.0487	26.9	0	1	1	2	1	1	0	0	0	0	0	0	0	0	6	0	0	0	0	0	0	0	0	0	0
th'	18	.1801	.7988	39.0	0	4	0	0	0	13	1	0	0	0	0	14	0	0	0	0	0	0	0	0	4	0	0	0	0
Tha	8	.0000	.1158	30.6	0	0	0	0	2	0	6	0	0	0	0	0	0	0	0	0	0	0	0	0	0	8	0	0	0
THA	2	.0000	.0299	24.8	0	0	2	0	0	0	0	0	0	0	0	0	2	0	0	0	0	0	0	0	0	0	0	0	0
Thacia	3	.0000	.0352	25.5	3	0	0	0	0	0	0	0	0	0	0	0	0	0	0	0	0	0	0	0	3	0	0	0	0
Thacia's	3	.0000	.0352	25.5	3	0	0	0	0	0	0	0	0	0	0	0	0	0	0	0	0	0	0	0	3	0	0	0	0
Thad	16	.0845	.4434	36.5	15	0	0	0	0	0	1	0	0	0	0	0	0	0	0	0	0	0	0	0	1	0	0	15	0
Thai	2	.2408	.1204	30.8	0	0	0	0	1	0	1	0	0	0	0	0	0	1	0	0	0	0	0	0	0	1	0	0	0
Thailand	17	.2964	1.1986	40.8	0	0	3	3	6	1	3	1	0	0	0	0	0	13	0	0	0	0	0	0	0	0	3	1	0
thair	3	.0000	.0328	25.2	0	0	0	0	0	3	0	0	0	3	0	0	0	0	0	0	0	0	0	0	0	0	0	0	0
thakin	2	.0000	.0914	29.6	0	0	0	2	0	0	0	0	2	0	0	0	0	0	0	0	0	0	0	0	0	0	0	0	0
Thakin	10	.0000	.4568	36.6	0	0	0	10	0	0	0	0	10	0	0	0	0	0	0	0	0	0	0	0	0	0	0	0	0
Thallophyta	2	.0000	.0209	23.2	0	0	0	2	0	0	0	0	0	0	0	0	0	0	0	0	0	0	0	0	0	0	2	0	0
thallophytes	3	.0000	.0314	25.0	0	0	0	3	0	0	0	0	0	0	0	0	0	0	0	0	0	0	0	0	0	0	3	0	0
Thames	22	.7097	3.1855	45.0	1	1	2	11	2	1	3	1	3	1	0	0	0	4	0	1	1	0	0	0	3	5	3	1	0
than	7982	.9725	1529.6	71.8	1231	1074	993	1082	1600	972	830	200	1351	383	39	328	1174	939	253	990	215	64	142	101	296	628	538	539	2
thank	301	.7454	46.070	56.6	81	64	30	37	32	24	24	9	124	22	3	41	0	8	7	1	5	0	0	0	46	31	0	13	0

5P territory-wide
9R terrorist
7Q terseness
5A terset
5A terset-huk-fo-o-r
5N Terwilliger's
4P Teshura
3N Tessin
9Q test-ban
7F test-drilling
6P test-pilot
7H test-tube
9H test-tubeful
7H testa
8A testaments
6A testily
XH testis
7Q testy
9R tete-a-tete
3N tetrarch's
8D Tewkesbury
7Q Texas-Mexican
4P Texel
8F Texian
7B Textbook
5Q Textile
8R textile-mill
3Q textile-printing
9L Textralized
7K textural
9L texturized
XP Teyjat
6E TFC
6N th-th-there
3A thnks
7J th'unbroken
7R tha's
3R Thad's
7R thalidomide
8B thame
8A Than
8A than's

Word Type	F	D	U	SFI	3 Gr 3	4 Gr 4	5 Gr 5	6 Gr 6	7 Gr 7	8 Gr 8	9 Gr 9	X UnGr	A Read	B Eng & Gr	C Comp	D Lit	E Math	F Soc Stud	G Spell	H Sci	J Music	K Art	L Home Ec	M Shop	N Lib F	P Lib NF	Q Lib Ref	R Mag	S Rel
thank-you	16	.1568	.6968	38.4	3	6	1	4	0	0	2	0	2	13	0	0	0	0	1	0	0	0	0	0	0	0	0	0	0
thanked	54	.4132	5.3812	47.3	12	11	7	11	7	3	3	0	31	1	0	6	0	3	0	0	1	0	0	0	6	4	0	1	1
thankful	45	.3155	3.4236	45.3	19	8	4	5	4	1	3	1	15	1	0	1	0	1	1	0	1	13	0	0	3	6	0	3	0
Thankful	4	.0000	.1827	32.6	0	0	0	4	0	0	0	0	4	0	0	0	0	0	0	0	0	0	0	0	0	0	0	0	0
thankfulness	3	.2196	.1554	31.9	0	0	0	1	0	0	2	0	0	0	0	2	0	0	0	0	0	0	0	0	1	0	0	0	0
thanking	10	.6160	1.3077	41.2	3	2	1	1	1	0	2	0	4	1	0	1	0	1	0	0	0	0	1	0	1	1	0	0	0
thankless	2	.2297	.1135	30.6	0	0	0	1	0	0	1	0	0	0	0	1	0	1	0	0	0	0	0	0	0	0	0	0	0
thanks	180	.7752	28.393	54.5	33	36	15	22	33	14	23	4	64	8	4	16	0	11	0	2	10	0	1	0	21	21	2	19	1
thanksgiving	5	.5304	.5639	37.5	2	0	0	1	0	0	2	0	1	0	0	1	0	0	0	0	1	0	0	0	0	1	0	1	0
Thanksgiving	100	.6582	13.635	51.3	54	19	7	7	8	0	5	0	29	6	0	5	2	5	9	1	7	10	0	0	14	2	1	9	0
Thant	8	.2281	.4674	36.7	0	0	0	2	4	1	1	0	0	0	0	0	0	6	0	0	0	0	0	0	0	0	0	2	0
thar	6	.2261	.4261	36.3	0	0	2	4	0	0	0	0	4	0	0	0	0	0	0	0	0	0	0	0	2	0	0	0	0
that	47443	.9932	9266.4	79.7	7336	7019	5897	6385	9070	5809	4765	1162	11772	2975	545	2657	3191	4188	2722	5227	1471	361	629	399	3037	3149	2173	2887	60
That	17	.6522	2.2912	43.6	3	1	3	3	2	2	3	0	4	2	0	1	0	0	1	0	4	0	0	0	1	3	0	1	0
THAT	2	.0000	.0914	29.6	1	0	1	0	0	0	0	0	2	0	0	0	0	0	0	0	0	0	0	0	0	0	0	0	0
that'd	12	.3496	1.0055	40.0	0	7	0	2	1	1	1	0	4	0	0	1	0	0	0	0	0	0	0	0	6	1	0	0	0
that'll	21	.5176	2.4369	43.9	4	2	3	6	3	2	1	0	11	0	0	2	0	0	0	0	0	0	0	0	5	2	0	1	0
that's	1286	.7860	206.28	63.1	280	301	112	127	236	118	82	30	598	43	4	134	10	25	3	21	22	1	6	4	175	119	2	119	0
thatch	13	.5392	1.5273	41.8	1	3	0	3	4	1	1	0	4	1	0	0	0	4	0	0	0	0	0	0	0	3	1	0	0
thatch-roofed	3	.2435	.2274	33.6	2	0	0	0	1	0	0	0	2	0	0	0	0	1	0	0	0	0	0	0	0	0	0	0	0
thatched	11	.4325	1.0880	40.4	0	1	0	4	4	1	1	0	3	0	0	0	0	5	0	0	0	0	0	0	0	1	2	0	0
Thatcher	9	.3578	.7883	39.0	0	1	0	0	7	1	0	0	4	0	0	0	0	0	0	0	0	0	0	0	3	0	0	2	0
thats	2	.1787	.1174	30.7	0	2	0	0	0	0	0	0	1	0	0	0	0	0	0	0	0	0	0	0	1	0	0	0	0
thaw	13	.4948	1.4223	41.5	1	2	1	2	2	0	3	2	5	1	0	0	0	1	0	0	0	0	2	0	1	0	0	3	0
thawed	12	.4417	1.1453	40.6	3	1	0	1	1	2	4	0	2	0	0	0	0	0	0	0	0	0	3	0	2	1	1	3	0
thaws	7	.5164	.7721	38.9	2	0	1	1	0	0	3	0	1	2	0	1	0	2	0	0	0	0	0	0	0	0	1	0	0
Thayer	3	.2387	.1708	32.3	0	0	0	0	1	0	2	0	0	0	0	0	0	0	0	0	0	0	0	0	0	2	1	0	0
the	373123	.9969	73122	88.6	60660	57013	48724	50209	68874	44281	34762	8600	82275	20310	4597	17339	32221	40305	18484	40224	17978	3063	4915	5680	18695	25175	21382	20186	294
The	833	.7920	132.99	61.2	68	114	114	121	169	130	87	30	196	60	2	40	11	29	14	16	169	7	0	2	22	70	73	122	0
THE	102	.4051	8.8687	49.5	17	3	2	1	22	52	5	0	2	0	0	74	1	1	0	11	0	1	1	0	1	3	0	5	2
theater	74	.8346	12.331	50.9	5	6	9	7	17	18	12	0	10	8	2	1	9	6	4	1	16	1	1	0	1	3	5	6	0
Theater	12	.4862	1.2573	41.0	0	1	1	1	7	0	2	0	2	0	0	0	0	1	0	0	0	0	0	0	3	0	2	4	0
theaters	30	.6725	4.1224	46.2	4	4	8	3	1	8	2	0	1	0	1	1	1	15	0	0	3	0	0	0	2	1	4	1	0
theatre	16	.5370	1.7678	42.5	0	0	2	3	3	1	1	6	0	0	0	1	0	0	2	1	5	0	0	0	2	0	0	5	0
Theatre	13	.4876	1.3375	41.3	1	0	0	1	3	3	1	4	1	0	0	1	1	0	0	0	3	0	0	0	0	0	1	6	0
theatres	5	.2580	.3252	35.1	0	0	0	1	2	0	0	2	1	0	0	0	0	0	0	0	0	0	0	0	0	1	0	3	0
theatrical	13	.4464	1.2390	40.9	0	0	0	3	2	4	3	1	1	0	0	0	0	0	0	0	4	0	0	0	0	2	1	5	0
Theban	2	.2446	.1125	30.5	0	0	0	0	0	1	1	0	0	1	0	1	0	0	0	0	0	0	0	0	0	0	0	0	0
Thebes	7	.3511	.5483	37.4	0	0	0	0	3	4	0	0	0	1	0	0	0	3	0	0	0	0	0	0	0	0	3	0	0
thecodont	3	.0000	.0434	26.4	1	2	0	0	0	0	0	0	0	0	0	0	0	0	0	0	0	0	0	0	0	3	0	0	0
thecodonts	11	.0000	.1592	32.0	5	6	0	0	0	0	0	0	0	0	0	0	0	0	0	0	0	0	0	0	0	11	0	0	0
thee	266	.5917	32.484	55.1	16	93	24	37	28	4	62	2	15	17	1	62	0	2	0	0	18	0	0	0	30	115	2	4	0
Thee	21	.2108	1.0175	40.1	4	5	2	4	1	1	1	3	1	0	0	0	0	0	0	0	16	0	0	0	0	0	2	3	0
theft	11	.5692	1.3413	41.3	1	0	0	2	2	3	3	0	4	1	0	1	1	1	1	0	0	1	0	0	2	0	0	0	0
thefts	2	.0000	.0215	23.3	0	0	0	0	2	0	0	0	1	0	0	2	0	0	0	0	0	0	0	0	0	0	0	0	0
their	13258	.9675	2529.8	74.0	2265	1857	1651	1855	2727	1497	1076	330	2995	475	94	736	231	2141	319	1228	498	137	131	54	793	1410	1074	929	13
theirs	60	.7959	9.6468	49.8	2	10	8	9	15	6	8	2	17	9	1	5	0	5	3	3	1	3	0	0	6	4	1	2	0
Thelma	6	.2411	.4668	36.7	0	5	0	0	0	1	0	0	5	0	0	0	0	0	0	0	0	0	0	0	0	0	0	1	0
them	11997	.9757	2306.6	73.6	2401	2049	1464	1610	2184	1114	925	250	3288	608	104	767	342	1039	580	1122	361	160	196	84	1027	1231	459	607	22
theme	183	.3281	13.053	51.2	3	22	37	24	43	17	34	3	6	18	0	8	0	4	2	1	132	0	3	0	0	4	0	5	0
Theme	9	.2085	.4305	36.3	2	2	0	2	3	0	0	0	0	1	0	0	0	0	0	0	7	0	0	0	0	0	1	0	0
THEME	2	.0000	.0914	29.6	0	0	0	2	0	0	0	0	2	0	0	0	0	0	0	0	0	0	0	0	0	0	0	0	0
themes	77	.4478	7.1551	48.5	0	7	12	15	16	13	13	1	0	6	0	3	0	1	1	0	51	3	0	0	1	1	3	7	0
themselves	962	.9095	173.69	62.4	141	96	107	132	237	113	100	36	192	48	6	57	6	136	16	115	18	7	11	1	48	114	97	87	3
then	12022	.9731	2306.5	73.6	2619	2230	1489	1575	2022	1085	782	220	3835	435	96	767	1185	690	743	909	401	58	88	110	1010	893	228	564	10
Then	2	.2306	.1140	30.6	0	1	1	0	0	0	0	0	0	1	0	0	0	1	0	0	0	0	0	0	0	0	0	0	0
THEN	2	.0000	.0394	26.0	0	2	0	0	0	0	0	0	0	0	0	0	0	0	0	2	0	0	0	0	0	0	0	0	0
then-known	2	.2278	.1128	30.5	1	0	0	0	0	1	0	0	0	0	0	0	0	0	0	1	0	0	0	0	0	0	1	0	0
thence	7	.5490	.7934	39.0	1	0	0	1	0	2	2	1	0	0	0	2	0	0	0	0	0	0	0	0	1	2	1	1	0
thenceforth	2	.2401	.1133	30.5	0	0	1	0	1	0	0	0	0	0	0	0	0	0	0	0	0	0	0	0	0	1	1	0	0
Theo	2	.0000	.0914	29.6	0	0	2	0	0	0	0	0	2	0	0	0	0	0	0	0	0	0	0	0	0	0	0	0	0
Theobald	3	.0000	.0591	27.7	0	0	0	0	0	0	0	3	0	0	0	0	0	0	0	3	0	0	0	0	0	0	0	0	0
Theobold	5	.0000	.2284	33.6	0	0	0	5	0	0	0	0	5	0	0	0	0	0	0	0	0	0	0	0	0	0	0	0	0
theocratic	2	.0000	.0243	23.9	0	0	0	0	2	0	0	0	0	0	0	0	0	0	0	0	0	0	0	0	0	0	0	2	0
Theodor	3	.3840	.2594	34.1	0	0	1	0	2	0	0	0	0	0	0	0	0	1	0	1	0	0	0	0	0	1	0	0	0
Theodore	70	.5939	8.8407	49.5	12	26	3	2	8	11	6	2	22	0	0	0	0	8	0	2	0	3	0	0	0	12	4	19	0
Theodore's	3	.0000	.0434	26.4	0	3	0	0	0	0	0	0	0	0	0	0	0	0	0	0	0	0	0	0	0	3	0	0	0
Theodoric	2	.0000	.0209	23.2	0	0	0	0	0	2	0	0	0	0	0	0	0	0	0	0	0	0	0	0	0	0	2	0	0
theologian	2	.2446	.1123	30.5	0	0	0	1	0	1	0	0	0	1	0	0	0	0	0	0	0	0	0	0	0	0	1	0	0
Theodore	70	.5939	8.8407	49.5	12	26	3	2	8	11	6	2	22	0	0	0	0	8	0	2	0	3	0	0	0	12	4	19	0
Theodore's	3	.0000	.0434	26.4	0	3	0	0	0	0	0	0	0	0	0	0	0	0	0	0	0	0	0	0	0	3	0	0	0
Theodoric	2	.0000	.0209	23.2	0	0	0	0	0	2	0	0	0	0	0	0	0	0	0	0	0	0	0	0	0	0	2	0	0
theologian	2	.2446	.1123	30.5	0	0	0	1	0	1	0	0	0	1	0	0	0	0	0	0	0	0	0	0	0	0	1	0	0
theological	5	.2226	.2657	34.2	0	0	2	0	2	1	0	0	0	0	0	0	0	0	0	0	0	0	0	0	0	2	3	0	0
theology	8	.3741	.6418	38.1	0	0	0	3	1	3	0	1	0	1	0	0	0	0	0	0	1	0	0	0	0	1	5	0	0
theorem	17	.1002	.5595	37.5	0	1	0	0	0	4	12	0	0	0	0	0	16	0	0	0	0	0	0	0	0	0	1	0	0
Theorem	12	.0000	.1796	32.5	0	0	1	3	0	6	2	0	0	0	0	0	12	0	0	0	0	0	0	0	0	0	0	0	0
theorems	9	.3685	.7351	38.7	0	1	0	0	1	2	5	0	0	0	0	0	6	1	0	0	0	0	0	0	0	0	0	1	0
theoretical	18	.2622	1.0906	40.4	0	0	0	1	3	2	10	2	0	0	0	0	0	0	0	3	0	0	0	0	0	1	12	3	0
theoretically	9	.4782	.9267	39.7	0	0	1	1	2	1	1	3	1	0	0	0	0	0	0	2	0	0	0	0	0	1	3	2	0
theories	80	.6498	10.694	50.3	0	12	8	10	12	19	12	7	4	1	0	1	2	0	2	42	1	1	0	1	0	0	16	9	0
theorist	2	.0000	.0243	23.9	0	0	0	0	0	1	1	0	0	0	0	0	0	0	0	0	0	0	0	0	0	0	0	2	0
theorists	4	.3134	.2876	34.6	0	0	0	0	1	2	1	0	0	0	0	0	0	1	0	1	0	0	0	0	0	0	2	0	0
theorized	4	.3864	.3418	35.3	0	0	0	1	1	2	0	0	0	0	0	0	0	0	0	2	0	0	0	0	0	0	1	1	0
theory	240	.6609	32.572	55.1	2	23	22	49	42	46	44	12	19	3	0	4	8	5	3	90	4	0	1	2	0	13	71	17	0
Theory	18	.2509	1.1603	40.6	0	9	1	3	1	3	0	1	1	0	0	0	0	0	0	15	0	0	0	0	0	0	1	1	0
therapeutic	5	.2580	.3252	35.1	0	0	0	1	2	0	1	1	1	0	0	0	0	0	0	0	0	0	0	0	0	1	0	3	0
therapy	14	.3400	1.0742	40.3	0	0	1	1	1	2	6	3	1	0	0	0	0	0	0	1	0	0	0	0	1	1	2	9	0
there	15194	.9738	2916.6	74.6	3279	2516	1861	2044	2604	1463	1101	326	4254	604	110	953	1199	1747	206	1550	434	88	137	103	1100	1393	564	748	4
There	3	.2365	.1616	32.1	0	2	0	0	0	1	0	0	0	0	0	0	0	0	0	0	1	0	0	0	0	0	2	0	0
there'd	12	.4157	1.1153	40.5	3	1	2	0	4	2	0	0	3	0	1	2	0	0	0	0	0	0	0	0	6	0	0	0	0
there'll	28	.6035	3.6430	45.6	4	11	2	4	4	1	0	2	14	0	0	2	0	0	0	0	0	0	1	0	2	7	0	2	0
there're	3	.1277	.1363	31.3	0	1	1	0	1	0	0	0	1	0	0	0	0	0	0	0	0	0	0	0	0	0	0	2	0
there's	624	.8013	101.53	60.1	139	124	50	91	126	56	28	10	270	16	6	67	2	10	3	8	30	2	1	1	82	59	1	66	0

6B Thank-you
9B thank-you-letter
6A Thankful's
9C thankfully
XR thanx
8Q Thar
7R that-this
3A that'
9D thataway
6F thatch-roof
6R thatched-roof
4A thawing
9P Thayers
7H thea
9R theatergoer
9R theatergoers
9Q Theatre-Lyrique
9R theatricality
9D theatrically
4Q Theatrum
8B theayter
9J Thebom
3P thecondonts
7R Theda
6A Theebaw
5R thees
5F Theiler
9L theine
5F Their
9B theirself
4G Thelma's
XR Them
8D them's
8J thematic
8J theme-and-variations
9Q thenceforward
9B Theodora
5A theologian's
9B Theodora
5A theologian's
9Q Theological
5Q Theophile
9B Theophilus
6Q Theophrastus
6P theorbo
8F theoreticians
8Q Theoria
5Q Theories
7Q theorize
8F theorizing
9Q theorizings
5R therapist
9R therapists
4P there-of
7B there-their

Word Type	F	D	U	SFI	3 Gr 3	4 Gr 4	5 Gr 5	6 Gr 6	7 Gr 7	8 Gr 8	9 Gr 9	X UnGr	A Read	B Eng & Gr	C Comp	D Lit	E Math	F Soc Stud	G Spell	H Sci	J Music	K Art	L Home Ec	M Shop	N Lib F	P Lib NF	Q Lib Ref	R Mag	S Rel
thereabouts	4	.3673	.3658	35.6	1	0	1	0	2	0	0	0	2	0	0	1	0	0	0	1	0	0	0	0	0	0	0	0	0
thereafter	31	.7493	4.7089	46.7	2	3	3	1	5	10	5	2	5	0	0	3	3	3	2	1	0	0	0	0	1	6	5	2	0
thereat	2	.2443	.1130	30.5	0	0	0	0	0	1	1	0	0	0	0	1	0	0	0	0	0	0	0	0	1	0	0	0	0
thereby	39	.7682	6.0339	47.8	0	2	2	1	14	11	4	5	3	1	1	2	0	0	0	14	2	0	2	0	4	1	5	4	0
therefore	495	.9270	90.769	59.6	13	24	26	59	129	105	118	21	48	42	8	34	68	69	15	71	14	3	18	17	14	22	39	13	0
therein	4	.3721	.3657	35.6	0	0	1	0	2	0	1	0	2	0	0	1	0	0	0	0	0	0	0	0	0	1	0	0	0
thereof	10	.5178	1.0887	40.4	2	0	0	0	0	4	4	0	0	0	0	0	0	5	1	0	0	0	0	1	0	2	1	0	0
thereon	2	.2401	.1133	30.5	1	1	0	0	0	0	0	0	0	0	0	0	0	0	0	0	0	0	0	0	0	1	1	0	0
theres	3	.0000	.0328	25.2	0	0	0	0	0	0	3	0	0	3	0	0	0	0	0	0	0	0	0	0	0	0	0	0	0
Theresa	20	.3747	1.9327	42.9	0	3	2	0	0	14	1	0	15	0	2	0	1	1	0	0	0	0	0	0	1	0	0	0	0
thereto	2	.2427	.1152	30.6	0	1	0	0	1	0	0	0	0	0	0	0	0	0	0	0	0	0	0	0	1	1	0	0	0
thereupon	7	.5024	.7484	38.7	0	2	1	0	2	2	0	0	1	0	0	1	0	0	0	0	0	0	0	0	2	1	2	0	0
thermal	22	.4790	2.3393	43.7	0	0	6	0	3	3	9	1	5	0	0	0	0	0	0	11	0	0	0	0	0	1	3	2	0
thermals	4	.2424	.3036	34.8	0	0	3	0	1	0	0	0	3	0	0	0	0	0	0	0	0	0	0	0	0	0	0	1	0
thermistor	4	.0000	.0486	26.9	0	0	0	0	4	0	0	0	0	0	0	0	0	0	0	0	0	0	0	0	0	0	0	4	0
thermistor's	2	.0000	.0243	23.9	0	0	0	0	2	0	0	0	0	0	0	0	0	0	0	0	0	0	0	0	0	0	0	2	0
thermo	3	.2197	.2090	33.2	0	0	0	1	2	0	0	0	2	0	0	0	0	0	0	0	0	0	0	0	0	0	1	0	0
thermocouple	2	.0000	.0050	17.0	0	0	0	0	0	2	0	0	0	0	0	0	0	0	0	0	0	0	0	2	0	0	0	0	0
thermodynamics	6	.2655	.3986	36.0	0	0	0	0	1	2	3	0	1	0	0	0	0	0	0	2	0	0	0	0	0	0	3	0	0
thermoelectric	2	.0000	.0209	23.2	0	0	0	0	0	0	2	0	0	0	0	0	0	0	0	0	0	0	0	0	0	0	2	0	0
thermoelement	4	.0000	.0469	26.7	0	4	0	0	0	0	0	0	0	0	0	0	0	0	0	0	0	0	0	0	4	0	0	0	0
thermometer	154	.5863	19.030	52.8	44	19	15	18	22	25	9	2	24	0	0	1	20	2	1	67	0	0	17	0	2	10	6	4	0
thermometers	44	.4503	4.5968	46.6	14	2	7	5	5	4	7	0	17	0	0	0	2	1	0	21	0	0	0	0	0	2	1	0	0
thermonuclear	5	.0000	.0986	29.9	0	0	0	0	3	0	2	0	0	0	0	0	0	0	0	5	0	0	0	0	0	0	0	0	0
thermoplastic	4	.4352	.3558	35.5	0	0	1	0	1	1	1	0	0	0	0	0	0	0	0	0	1	0	1	1	0	0	1	0	0
Thermopylae	4	.2386	.2998	34.8	0	2	0	0	2	0	0	0	3	0	0	0	0	0	0	0	0	0	0	0	0	0	1	0	0
thermos	6	.5526	.7177	38.6	1	0	1	0	1	3	0	0	2	1	0	1	1	0	0	1	0	0	0	0	0	0	0	0	0
thermoscope	2	.1698	.1133	30.5	0	0	0	0	2	0	0	0	1	0	0	0	0	0	0	0	0	0	0	0	0	0	1	0	0
thermostat	24	.3277	1.8332	42.6	0	1	8	2	5	7	1	0	5	0	0	1	0	0	0	5	0	0	0	7	1	0	0	5	0
thermostats	3	.2184	.1759	32.5	0	0	1	0	1	1	0	0	1	0	0	0	0	0	0	0	0	0	0	1	0	0	0	1	0
these	11611	.9361	2148.5	73.3	1979	1763	1701	1521	2060	1323	1009	255	1306	932	126	302	1224	1668	1680	1719	482	170	150	161	183	476	678	347	7
Theseus	3	.1783	.1304	31.2	0	0	0	2	0	0	1	0	0	0	0	0	0	0	0	0	0	1	0	0	0	2	0	0	0
THESEUS	4	.0000	.0429	26.3	0	0	0	0	0	0	4	0	0	0	0	4	0	0	0	0	0	0	0	0	0	0	0	0	0
thesis	7	.5859	.8560	39.3	0	0	1	0	2	2	2	0	1	1	0	0	1	0	0	0	0	0	0	0	0	1	1	2	0
Thessaly	9	.1212	.4142	36.2	0	0	0	1	7	1	0	0	2	0	0	0	0	7	0	0	0	0	0	0	0	0	0	0	0
they	27620	.9702	5284.8	77.2	6018	4924	3422	3886	4567	2374	1896	533	7540	1226	189	1600	533	3754	513	3281	749	276	314	147	1907	2946	1216	1392	37
They	5	.3933	.4378	36.4	0	0	2	1	2	0	0	0	1	0	0	1	0	0	0	0	2	0	0	0	0	0	0	1	0
THEY	2	.0000	.0914	29.6	0	0	2	0	0	0	0	0	2	0	0	0	0	0	0	0	0	0	0	0	0	0	0	0	0
they'd	137	.5666	16.524	52.2	7	30	18	10	45	5	17	5	38	2	0	28	0	1	0	0	0	0	0	0	33	18	0	17	0
they'll	120	.7479	18.433	52.7	27	26	9	19	24	7	6	2	52	3	1	15	0	1	0	0	10	1	0	0	11	18	0	8	0
they're	345	.6892	49.183	56.9	60	67	33	43	78	31	18	15	111	16	0	38	2	6	4	0	8	0	0	0	56	37	0	67	0
they've	53	.5874	6.7094	48.3	8	13	2	11	8	3	4	4	23	0	0	4	0	2	0	0	0	0	0	0	9	6	0	9	0
theyre	2	.0000	.0219	23.4	0	0	0	0	0	2	0	0	0	2	0	0	0	0	0	0	0	0	0	0	0	0	0	0	0
thiamin	3	.1970	.1504	31.8	0	0	2	0	0	1	0	0	0	0	0	0	0	0	0	2	0	0	1	0	0	0	0	0	0
thiamine	11	.2273	.5808	37.6	0	0	2	0	4	2	3	0	0	0	0	0	0	0	0	4	0	0	5	0	0	0	2	0	0
thick	540	.9185	98.442	59.9	109	96	73	66	81	42	58	15	137	14	6	37	10	53	7	107	5	12	14	10	31	55	22	20	0
thick-walled	5	.3426	.3891	35.9	0	0	1	1	2	0	1	0	0	0	0	0	0	1	0	2	0	0	0	0	0	0	2	0	0
thicken	7	.5314	.7840	38.9	1	0	2	1	1	0	2	0	1	2	0	0	0	0	0	1	1	0	1	0	0	1	0	0	0
thickened	10	.2407	.5843	37.7	2	1	1	1	2	0	3	0	1	0	0	0	0	0	0	3	0	0	4	0	0	2	0	0	0
thickening	9	.4689	.9010	39.5	0	0	3	2	2	0	2	0	1	0	0	2	0	0	0	2	0	0	2	0	1	0	1	0	0
thickens	4	.3364	.2938	34.7	2	0	0	1	1	0	0	0	0	0	0	0	0	0	0	0	0	0	1	0	0	2	0	1	0
thicker	44	.6104	5.6393	47.5	7	6	10	3	10	4	4	0	8	1	0	0	0	0	0	19	3	0	0	2	0	8	3	0	0
thickest	10	.6217	1.3350	41.3	1	2	1	3	1	1	1	0	5	0	0	0	1	0	0	1	0	0	0	0	1	1	1	0	0
thicket	31	.7588	4.8491	46.9	3	4	7	3	8	2	2	2	16	0	0	1	0	4	1	1	1	0	0	0	2	1	1	3	0
thickets	20	.6482	2.6902	44.3	3	2	2	1	3	4	2	3	5	0	2	4	0	1	0	3	0	1	0	0	1	1	1	1	0
thickly	26	.6158	3.4084	45.3	2	2	4	5	7	2	3	1	9	0	0	2	0	9	0	2	0	1	0	0	0	0	2	1	0
thickness	81	.6419	10.593	50.3	2	7	7	1	25	21	13	5	4	0	0	1	5	1	0	21	1	3	10	13	1	8	8	5	0
thicknesses	10	.3925	.8128	39.1	0	0	3	1	0	2	4	0	0	0	0	0	1	0	0	0	0	0	4	2	0	1	2	0	0
thief	68	.8225	11.266	50.5	9	7	6	25	7	12	2	0	22	7	1	6	5	2	4	0	3	0	0	0	4	6	0	8	0
thief's	2	.2289	.1077	30.3	0	0	0	1	0	1	0	0	0	0	0	0	1	0	1	0	0	0	0	0	0	0	0	0	0
Thieu	3	.0000	.0365	25.6	0	0	0	0	0	1	2	0	0	0	0	0	0	0	0	0	0	0	0	0	0	0	0	3	0
thieves	34	.7161	5.0507	47.0	2	10	4	8	3	5	2	0	15	3	0	4	0	1	0	2	0	0	0	0	1	4	1	3	0
thieves'	2	.1787	.1174	30.7	0	0	0	0	2	0	0	0	1	0	0	0	0	0	0	0	0	0	0	0	1	0	0	0	0
thieving	2	.1717	.1142	30.6	0	0	1	0	1	0	0	0	1	0	0	1	0	0	0	0	0	0	0	0	0	0	0	0	0
thigh	21	.7749	3.2695	45.1	1	0	2	3	6	1	6	2	2	0	1	4	2	0	0	3	1	0	1	0	1	1	3	2	0
thighs	13	.4886	1.3395	41.3	0	0	1	0	8	0	4	0	1	0	0	6	0	0	0	0	1	0	0	0	3	1	1	0	0
thimble	30	.5208	3.2726	45.1	0	4	1	1	13	1	10	0	4	0	0	1	0	0	2	1	0	0	2	6	2	1	0	11	0
thimbles	2	.2152	.1357	31.3	1	0	0	1	0	0	0	0	1	0	0	0	0	1	0	0	0	0	0	0	0	0	0	0	0
thin	611	.8422	103.19	60.1	108	95	85	70	106	67	66	14	162	9	4	31	4	29	9	126	11	21	25	36	40	53	32	19	0
thin-lipped	2	.2351	.1166	30.7	0	0	0	0	1	0	1	0	0	0	0	0	0	1	0	0	0	0	0	0	0	0	0	1	0
thin-walled	4	.1966	.1884	32.8	0	0	0	0	3	0	1	0	0	0	0	1	0	0	0	0	0	0	0	0	0	0	3	0	0
thine	13	.5440	1.4808	41.7	4	0	2	4	2	0	0	0	1	0	0	2	0	2	0	0	3	0	0	0	1	4	0	0	0
Thine	2	.0000	.0162	22.1	0	0	0	1	1	0	0	0	0	0	0	0	0	0	0	0	2	0	0	0	0	0	0	0	0
thing	1828	.9507	343.71	65.4	366	293	239	235	346	190	120	39	637	122	16	148	33	75	37	213	35	20	17	12	196	117	29	120	1
Thing	9	.4131	.8309	39.2	1	4	0	1	3	0	0	0	2	0	0	3	0	0	0	0	0	0	0	0	3	0	0	1	0
Thing-finder	4	.0000	.1827	32.6	4	0	0	0	0	0	0	0	4	0	0	0	0	0	0	0	0	0	0	0	0	0	0	0	0
thing's	4	.3718	.3639	35.6	0	0	0	1	3	0	0	0	2	1	0	0	0	0	0	0	0	0	0	0	1	0	0	0	0
things	4070	.9367	754.87	68.8	1085	795	517	422	584	325	260	82	1002	310	52	226	87	458	85	864	44	108	76	36	206	271	80	158	7
Things	8	.5596	.9363	39.7	2	1	1	0	3	1	0	0	0	0	0	1	0	3	0	2	1	0	0	0	1	0	0	0	0
think	4746	.9318	876.31	69.4	1047	930	564	597	813	441	281	73	1351	414	36	374	653	282	126	455	100	85	50	9	350	227	34	199	1
Think	3	.3863	.2513	34.0	0	0	0	0	1	1	1	0	0	0	0	0	0	0	0	0	0	0	0	0	1	1	0	1	0
Think-and-Do	15	.0000	.6852	38.4	0	5	3	7	0	0	0	0	15	0	0	0	0	0	0	0	0	0	0	0	0	0	0	0	0
thinker	7	.5917	.8663	39.4	0	1	0	0	2	2	0	2	1	1	0	1	0	0	0	1	0	0	0	0	0	2	0	1	0
thinkers	17	.6495	2.2844	43.6	1	2	2	0	3	4	5	0	3	1	0	1	0	4	0	1	0	1	0	0	0	1	4	1	0
thinkin'	4	.3713	.3634	35.6	1	1	0	0	1	1	0	0	2	0	0	1	0	0	0	0	0	0	0	0	1	0	0	0	0
thinking	694	.9219	127.10	61.0	112	137	93	89	120	76	59	8	258	29	5	48	61	38	7	52	6	8	5	2	64	49	14	48	0
Thinking	2	.2442	.1134	30.5	0	0	1	0	0	0	0	1	0	1	0	0	0	0	0	0	0	0	0	0	0	0	0	1	0
thinks	217	.9054	39.206	55.9	78	23	23	23	33	19	16	2	107	11	4	12	4	14	3	16	1	2	3	1	14	10	2	13	0
Thinkum	22	.0000	.2673	34.3	22	0	0	0	0	0	0	0	0	0	0	0	0	0	0	0	0	0	0	0	0	0	0	22	0
thinly	13	.3540	1.1129	40.5	1	0	4	3	3	2	0	0	3	0	0	0	0	8	0	1	0	0	0	0	0	0	1	0	0
thinned	8	.2345	.4741	36.8	0	3	1	0	2	0	2	0	2	0	0	0	0	0	0	0	0	0	0	3	0	1	0	2	0
thinner	58	.6909	8.2322	49.2	9	11	6	5	18	3	5	1	13	0	0	1	1	2	0	15	3	1	3	7	2	5	5	0	0
thinness	2	.1717	.1142	30.6	0	0	0	1	0	0	1	0	1	0	0	1	0	0	0	0	0	0	0	0	0	0	0	0	0
thinnest	6	.4703	.6421	38.1	0	1	0	1	2	0	1	1	2	0	0	0	1	1	0	2	0	0	0	0	0	0	0	0	0
thinning	5	.3965	.4240	36.3	0	1	0	0	1	2	0	1	0	0	0	0	0	0	0	1	0	0	0	1	0	0	1	2	0

7G therefor
7B therefrom
9F Theresa's
8A thereunto
8C therewith
8M thermocouples
6Q thermoelectrical
9Q Thermoelectricity
8E thermometer's
5R Thermos
5Q thermosetting
8M Thermostat
7Q thermostatic
XR thesaurus
8G thesauruses
3A These
5P theses
7A Thesiger
XR thespian
8A Thetis
3A They're
8B they's
XR They've
8B theyd
8B theyll
3A thick-furred
9D thick-growing
6A thick-headedness
6N thick-leaved
4N thick-set
8D thick-spread
4A thickety
8A thiefs
8F Thierry
9R Thieu's
4E Thieves
9A thievish
7L Thigh
8R thighbone
3F thimbleberry
5H thimbleful
4A thin-as-a-rake
4P thin-faced
3A thin-leafed
4P thin-sliced
XB thincan
3H THINGS
7H things-more
7D things'll
7Q thingumabobs
3N THINK
4N Thinkalot
7Q thinke
3R Thinker

Word Type	F	D	U	SFI	3 Gr 3	4 Gr 4	5 Gr 5	6 Gr 6	7 Gr 7	8 Gr 8	9 Gr 9	X UnGr	A Read	B Eng & Gr	C Comp	D Lit	E Math	F Soc Stud	G Spell	H Sci	J Music	K Art	L Home Ec	M Shop	N Lib F	P Lib NF	Q Lib Ref	R Mag	S Rel
thins	3	.2942	.1970	32.9	0	0	0	0	2	1	0	0	0	0	0	0	0	0	0	1	0	0	1	0	0	0	1	0	0
third	945	.9275	173.50	62.4	168	103	145	144	163	110	103	9	167	91	14	32	143	78	45	64	111	11	4	12	34	48	44	47	0
Third	38	.7596	5.8219	47.7	8	4	4	3	5	10	3	1	5	3	1	1	0	4	1	2	8	0	0	0	7	2	1	3	0
THIRD	3	.0000	.0322	25.1	0	0	0	0	0	2	1	0	0	0	0	3	0	0	0	0	0	0	0	0	0	0	0	0	0
third-class	2	.0000	.0290	24.6	0	0	0	0	0	0	0	2	0	0	0	0	0	0	0	0	0	0	0	0	0	2	0	0	0
third-floor	3	.2357	.2199	33.4	2	0	1	0	0	0	0	0	2	0	0	0	0	0	0	0	0	0	0	0	0	1	0	0	0
third-grade	10	.1621	.4118	36.1	10	0	0	0	0	0	0	0	1	2	0	0	1	1	0	0	0	5	0	0	0	0	0	0	0
thirds	83	.4704	8.2893	49.2	19	6	24	12	11	9	2	0	2	2	0	0	45	4	0	1	20	0	0	0	0	6	2	1	0
thirst	33	.7039	4.7926	46.8	3	5	3	6	9	7	0	0	10	2	0	4	0	5	0	0	0	0	0	0	5	4	1	2	0
thirsty	55	.8078	9.0035	49.5	16	9	2	12	9	6	0	1	21	5	1	5	0	4	2	5	0	0	0	0	2	7	2	1	0
thirteen	116	.8000	18.702	52.7	33	13	25	12	13	17	3	0	21	0	1	4	4	28	7	4	7	0	0	0	12	22	2	4	0
Thirteen	2	.2337	.1157	30.6	1	0	1	0	0	0	0	0	0	0	0	0	0	1	0	0	0	0	0	0	1	0	0	0	0
thirteen-year-old	5	.2684	.3533	35.5	0	1	1	1	1	1	0	0	2	0	1	0	0	0	0	0	0	0	0	0	0	2	0	0	0
thirteenth	17	.6545	2.2440	43.5	1	0	1	1	3	2	6	3	0	4	0	1	1	1	3	0	1	2	0	1	0	1	0	2	0
thirties	6	.3811	.4892	36.9	1	0	0	0	5	0	0	0	0	0	0	1	1	0	0	0	3	0	0	0	0	1	0	0	0
thirty	214	.8823	37.704	55.8	39	23	35	28	40	23	23	3	71	13	6	18	5	22	5	13	9	0	4	0	13	23	3	9	0
Thirty	3	.3847	.2496	34.0	0	0	2	0	0	0	0	1	0	0	0	0	0	0	0	0	0	0	0	0	0	1	1	1	0
thirty-day	2	.1674	.0805	29.1	0	1	0	0	0	1	0	0	0	0	0	0	0	0	0	0	0	0	1	0	0	1	0	0	0
thirty-eight	10	.5625	1.2255	40.9	1	0	4	3	0	1	1	0	4	0	0	1	2	2	0	0	0	0	0	0	0	0	0	1	0
thirty-five	44	.8013	7.1397	48.5	6	4	4	5	9	10	4	2	15	4	0	5	6	3	1	0	1	0	0	0	2	4	1	2	0
thirty-five-year-old	2	.2433	.1158	30.6	0	0	0	0	1	0	1	0	0	0	0	0	0	0	0	0	0	0	0	0	0	1	0	1	0
thirty-four	6	.4620	.6243	38.0	0	2	2	0	1	0	1	0	2	0	0	0	2	0	0	0	0	0	0	0	0	1	0	1	0
thirty-inch	3	.2799	.1829	32.6	1	0	0	0	1	0	0	1	0	0	1	0	0	0	0	0	0	0	0	0	0	0	1	1	0
thirty-minute	2	.0665	.0708	28.5	1	0	0	0	0	0	1	0	1	0	1	0	0	0	0	0	0	0	0	0	0	0	0	0	0
thirty-nine	6	.4224	.5666	37.5	0	0	3	1	1	1	0	0	1	2	0	0	0	2	0	0	0	0	0	0	0	0	0	1	0
thirty-one	8	.6680	1.1069	40.4	0	2	2	1	2	0	0	1	2	0	0	0	1	1	1	0	0	0	0	0	0	1	1	1	0
thirty-seven	18	.6979	2.5757	44.1	5	2	4	1	2	2	2	0	4	1	1	2	4	1	0	0	1	0	0	0	3	1	0	0	0
thirty-six	12	.5542	1.4304	41.6	2	4	1	1	0	3	0	1	3	0	0	1	1	3	0	2	0	1	0	0	0	1	0	0	0
thirty-six-inch	2	.0000	.0914	29.6	0	0	0	0	2	0	0	0	2	0	0	0	0	0	0	0	0	0	0	0	0	0	0	0	0
thirty-three	11	.5084	1.2431	40.9	1	3	2	0	1	2	1	1	4	0	1	0	1	1	0	3	0	0	0	0	0	1	0	0	0
thirty-two	13	.6155	1.6761	42.2	4	2	3	2	0	1	1	0	3	0	1	0	1	1	0	1	1	0	0	0	0	4	1	0	0
this	23301	.9851	4517.4	76.5	3596	3509	2900	3262	4285	2822	2347	580	4523	1210	266	1110	2060	2737	994	2836	1808	376	235	370	954	1457	1129	1213	23
This	13	.4785	1.3119	41.2	0	1	0	3	7	0	2	0	1	0	0	0	1	1	1	0	6	0	0	0	0	0	1	2	0
THIS	2	.2346	.1166	30.7	1	1	0	0	0	0	0	0	0	0	0	0	0	0	0	1	0	0	0	0	0	0	0	1	0
thisaway	2	.1717	.1142	30.6	0	1	0	0	1	0	0	0	1	0	0	1	0	0	0	0	0	0	0	0	0	0	0	0	0
thistle	5	.4755	.5341	37.3	1	1	3	0	0	0	0	0	2	1	0	1	0	0	0	0	0	0	0	0	0	1	0	0	0
thither	9	.4271	.8741	39.4	0	0	0	2	3	3	1	0	3	0	0	3	0	0	0	0	0	0	0	0	2	1	0	0	0
Thitpan	5	.0000	.0537	27.3	0	0	0	0	5	0	0	0	0	0	0	5	0	0	0	0	0	0	0	0	0	0	0	0	0
tho'	2	.0000	.0219	23.4	0	0	2	0	0	0	0	0	0	2	0	0	0	0	0	0	0	0	0	0	0	0	0	0	0
Thoburn	6	.0000	.2741	34.4	0	0	0	0	6	0	0	0	6	0	0	0	0	0	0	0	0	0	0	0	0	0	0	0	0
Thom	2	.0000	.0389	25.9	0	0	0	2	0	0	0	0	0	0	0	0	0	2	0	0	0	0	0	0	0	0	0	0	0
Thomas	244	.7547	37.156	55.7	7	83	33	18	43	26	19	15	22	11	0	20	7	29	3	2	11	0	0	1	2	72	34	30	0
Thomas'	3	.1409	.1472	31.7	0	3	0	0	0	0	0	0	1	0	0	0	0	0	0	0	0	0	0	0	0	2	0	0	0
Thomas's	6	.2274	.3456	35.4	0	1	0	4	1	0	0	0	1	0	0	4	0	0	0	0	0	0	0	0	1	0	0	0	0
Thomases	5	.1668	.2098	33.2	0	1	0	1	3	0	0	0	0	0	0	4	0	0	0	0	0	0	0	0	0	0	0	1	0
Thomases'	2	.0000	.0243	23.9	0	2	0	0	0	0	0	0	0	0	0	0	0	0	0	0	0	0	0	0	0	0	0	2	0
Thomis	8	.0000	.3655	35.6	0	0	0	0	8	0	0	0	8	0	0	0	0	0	0	0	0	0	0	0	0	0	0	0	0
Thompkins	3	.0000	.0449	26.5	0	0	0	0	0	3	0	0	0	0	0	0	3	0	0	0	0	0	0	0	0	0	0	0	0
Thompson	25	.6846	3.5232	45.5	1	4	1	8	4	3	2	2	6	3	0	0	0	0	2	2	2	0	0	0	1	3	0	6	0
Thompson's	2	.1843	.0808	29.1	0	2	0	0	0	0	0	0	0	0	1	0	0	0	0	0	1	0	0	0	0	0	0	0	0
Thomson	11	.2735	.6936	38.4	0	0	3	0	1	2	5	0	1	0	0	0	0	0	0	0	4	0	0	0	0	0	6	0	0
THOMSON	4	.0000	.0419	26.2	0	0	0	0	0	0	4	0	0	0	0	0	0	0	0	0	0	0	0	0	0	0	4	0	0
Thomson's	4	.2764	.2696	34.3	0	0	2	1	1	0	0	0	1	0	0	0	0	0	0	0	2	0	0	0	0	0	1	0	0
thong	6	.3583	.4703	36.7	0	3	1	2	0	0	0	0	0	0	0	0	0	0	0	0	0	0	0	0	3	2	1	0	0
thongs	14	.4451	1.4861	41.7	3	5	3	0	3	0	0	0	9	0	0	1	0	0	0	0	0	0	0	0	3	1	0	0	0
Thor	7	.5514	.8308	39.2	0	3	0	1	1	1	1	0	2	0	0	0	0	0	1	2	0	0	0	0	1	0	1	0	0
thoracic	3	.0000	.0591	27.7	0	0	0	0	0	0	3	0	0	0	0	0	0	0	0	3	0	0	0	0	0	0	0	0	0
Thorarinsson	3	.0000	.1370	31.4	0	0	0	3	0	0	0	0	3	0	0	0	0	0	0	0	0	0	0	0	0	0	0	0	0
thorax	23	.4225	2.1285	43.3	7	1	1	5	3	3	3	0	0	0	0	0	0	0	0	13	0	0	0	0	0	4	5	1	0
Thoreau	11	.1915	.5107	37.1	0	0	1	0	1	9	0	0	0	1	0	0	0	0	0	0	0	0	0	0	0	1	9	0	0
Thoreau's	4	.1737	.1745	32.4	0	0	1	0	0	3	0	0	0	0	0	0	0	0	0	0	0	0	0	0	0	1	3	0	0
Thorfin	13	.0000	.5939	37.7	0	0	0	0	13	0	0	0	13	0	0	0	0	0	0	0	0	0	0	0	0	0	0	0	0
thorium	3	.1813	.1402	31.5	0	0	0	0	2	0	1	0	0	0	0	0	0	0	0	1	0	0	0	0	0	0	2	0	0
thorn	27	.7044	3.9474	46.0	4	3	8	5	5	0	1	1	12	3	0	1	0	0	1	0	4	0	0	0	1	3	1	1	0
thornbush	4	.2107	.2095	33.2	0	0	0	0	3	0	0	1	0	0	0	0	0	0	0	0	0	0	0	0	0	3	0	1	0
thorned	3	.3399	.2456	33.9	0	2	0	0	1	0	0	0	1	0	0	1	0	0	0	0	0	0	0	0	0	0	0	1	0
thornlike	2	.1948	.1250	31.0	1	0	0	1	0	0	0	0	1	0	0	0	0	0	0	0	0	0	0	0	0	1	0	0	0
thorns	28	.7271	4.2012	46.2	11	7	4	2	2	1	1	0	12	0	1	2	0	2	1	0	0	1	0	0	4	3	0	2	0
Thornton	33	.5169	3.8587	45.9	0	0	5	0	20	7	1	0	19	1	0	0	5	0	0	0	0	0	0	0	6	0	0	2	0
Thornton's	4	.1787	.2347	33.7	0	0	0	0	2	2	0	0	2	0	0	0	0	0	0	0	0	0	0	0	2	0	0	0	0
thorny	10	.4140	.9045	39.6	2	2	1	0	4	0	0	1	1	1	0	0	0	3	0	0	0	2	0	0	1	1	1	0	0
thorough	30	.6822	4.1468	46.2	1	1	1	4	5	3	11	4	2	6	0	2	1	0	0	2	0	0	3	3	1	5	1	4	0
thorough-bass	2	.2303	.1079	30.3	0	0	0	1	0	1	0	0	0	0	0	0	0	0	0	0	1	0	0	0	0	1	0	0	0
thoroughbred	8	.4715	.8456	39.3	0	4	0	1	2	1	0	0	3	0	0	0	0	0	0	0	1	0	0	0	2	2	0	0	0
thoroughbreds	2	.1948	.1250	31.0	0	0	0	2	0	0	0	0	1	0	0	0	0	0	0	0	0	0	0	0	0	1	0	0	0
thoroughfare	5	.4224	.4655	36.7	0	0	0	0	4	0	1	0	1	0	0	2	0	0	0	0	1	0	0	0	0	0	0	1	0
thoroughfares	3	.1832	.1417	31.5	0	0	0	0	1	1	1	0	0	0	0	2	0	0	0	1	0	0	0	0	0	0	0	0	0
thoroughgoing	3	.3769	.2484	34.0	0	0	0	0	0	2	1	0	0	0	0	0	0	1	0	0	0	0	0	0	0	0	1	1	0
thoroughly	92	.7216	13.451	51.3	4	4	12	7	16	26	20	3	13	10	0	2	0	3	6	13	0	1	9	10	1	6	4	14	0
thoroughness	4	.2721	.2774	34.4	0	0	0	1	1	0	2	0	1	2	0	0	0	0	0	1	0	0	0	0	0	0	0	0	0
Thorpe	15	.1173	.6476	38.1	0	11	0	4	0	0	0	0	4	0	0	0	0	0	0	0	0	0	0	0	0	11	0	0	0
those	2647	.9774	509.64	67.1	307	348	298	345	602	352	286	109	614	181	24	147	85	299	78	275	84	33	58	14	175	206	170	199	5
Those	4	.4418	.3915	35.9	1	1	0	1	0	1	0	0	1	1	0	0	0	0	0	0	1	0	0	0	0	1	0	0	0
thou	247	.5465	28.074	54.5	22	2	30	23	41	11	116	2	16	16	0	124	0	7	0	0	13	1	0	0	13	46	9	2	0
Thou	14	.2414	.7891	39.0	1	3	2	3	4	0	0	1	1	0	0	0	0	0	0	0	10	0	0	0	1	1	0	1	0
thou'lt	3	.0000	.0352	25.5	0	0	0	3	0	0	0	0	0	0	0	0	0	0	0	0	0	0	0	0	3	0	0	0	0
thou'rt	6	.0000	.0703	28.5	0	0	0	6	0	0	0	0	0	0	0	0	0	0	0	0	0	0	0	0	6	0	0	0	0
thou'st	2	.2427	.1152	30.6	0	0	1	0	1	0	0	0	0	0	0	0	0	0	0	0	0	0	0	0	1	1	0	0	0
though	1339	.9358	248.14	63.9	154	168	168	183	313	148	158	47	383	80	20	135	14	106	11	71	34	7	21	2	152	135	56	111	1
thought	2835	.9088	513.42	67.1	631	555	323	321	458	285	221	41	1263	106	29	212	54	193	21	107	47	16	15	3	342	255	44	126	2
Thought	2	.2152	.1357	31.3	1	0	0	0	0	1	0	0	1	0	0	0	0	1	0	0	0	0	0	0	0	0	0	0	0
thought-provoking	2	.2411	.1091	30.4	0	0	0	0	0	0	2	0	0	0	0	1	0	0	0	0	1	0	0	0	0	0	0	0	0
thoughtful	57	.8163	9.3689	49.7	5	6	9	5	17	10	5	0	17	7	1	5	0	4	0	2	2	1	5	0	3	5	2	3	0
thoughtfully	54	.6535	7.5094	48.8	3	16	9	12	7	5	2	0	30	1	0	5	1	0	0	0	1	0	1	0	7	8	0	0	0

XH thiouracil
5A third-base
3E third-graders
7F third-largest
8R third-party
6B third-person
9H third-quarter
7F third-ranking
8A third-rate
9R third-world
9R third-year
8Q thirdly
3P Thirst
6A thirsting
4A thirteen-day-old
7R thirteen-gun
7A thirteen-inch
8F Thirteenth
8A Thirties
4G thirtieth
4B Thirtieth
6N Thirty-Ninth
6N Thirty-Seventh
6A thirty-fifth
6A thirty-five-foot
5A thirty-footer
3R thirty-ninth
7E thirty-sixes
7N thirty-thirty
7D THIRTYONE
XJ this-worldliness
3A this'n
9D Thisbe
7B thish-yer
3A thist
7A thistledown
3P thitten
XB thocht
9A Thoedore
7A tholes
7A Thomis's
7M thonging
9Q THOR
7A Thor-Able-Star
8Q Thore
4N thorn-bush
7P thorn-covered
7N thorn-tails
6A Thornapple
9G Thorndike-Barnhart
XR Thorney
4A thornless
3P Thoroughbred
9B thoroughful
4A Thorveg
7D THOU
8A thought-out

Word Type	F	D	U	SFI	3 Gr 3	4 Gr 4	5 Gr 5	6 Gr 6	7 Gr 7	8 Gr 8	9 Gr 9	X UnGr	A Read	B Eng & Gr	C Comp	D Lit	E Math	F Soc Stud	G Spell	H Sci	J Music	K Art	L Home Ec	M Shop	N Lib F	P Lib NF	Q Lib Ref	R Mag	S Rel
thoughtfulness	7	.4795	.7426	38.7	1	1	0	2	2	1	0	0	2	1	0	0	0	0	0	2	0	0	1	0	0	1	0	0	0
thoughtless	10	.3432	.8261	39.2	0	2	1	0	4	1	2	0	3	1	2	0	0	1	0	3	0	0	0	0	0	0	0	0	0
thoughtlessly	2	.0857	.0784	28.9	0	0	0	1	1	0	0	0	1	0	0	0	0	0	0	0	0	0	1	0	0	0	0	0	0
thoughts	238	.8440	40.147	56.0	17	30	26	41	51	42	28	3	50	32	13	27	1	8	1	1	14	5	2	1	30	24	5	23	1
thousand	597	.9147	108.38	60.3	63	93	85	103	116	68	40	29	125	26	4	37	109	97	11	46	15	3	1	2	26	47	24	24	0
Thousand	5	.5401	.5759	37.6	1	2	0	1	0	1	0	0	1	1	0	0	1	0	0	0	0	0	0	0	0	1	0	1	0
thousand-dollar	2	.1948	.1250	31.0	0	1	0	0	1	0	0	0	1	0	0	0	0	0	0	0	0	0	0	0	0	1	0	0	0
thousand-mile	2	.2401	.1133	30.5	1	0	0	0	1	0	0	0	0	0	0	0	0	0	0	0	0	0	0	0	0	1	1	0	0
thousands	727	.8902	128.71	61.1	108	95	117	108	123	88	60	28	91	24	3	14	76	189	9	111	21	4	1	6	15	57	64	42	0
thousands'	4	.0000	.0599	27.8	2	1	0	1	0	0	0	0	0	0	0	0	4	0	0	0	0	0	0	0	0	0	0	0	0
thousandth	16	.4697	1.6142	42.1	0	0	4	3	6	2	1	0	1	1	0	1	10	0	0	2	0	0	0	1	0	0	0	0	0
thousandths	35	.3479	2.7191	44.3	0	0	4	15	10	5	1	0	0	0	0	0	28	0	0	1	0	0	0	1	0	0	1	4	0
thousandths'	3	.0000	.0449	26.5	0	0	0	2	1	0	0	0	0	0	0	0	3	0	0	0	0	0	0	0	0	0	0	0	0
thr	5	.0000	.0406	26.1	0	2	2	1	0	0	0	0	0	0	0	0	0	0	5	0	0	0	0	0	0	0	0	0	0
Thrace	9	.0000	.1750	32.4	0	0	0	0	9	0	0	0	0	0	0	0	0	9	0	0	0	0	0	0	0	0	0	0	0
thrall	3	.2143	.1568	32.0	0	0	0	0	1	1	0	1	0	0	0	0	0	0	0	0	0	0	0	0	0	1	0	2	0
thrash	2	.0000	.0914	29.6	0	0	1	1	0	0	0	0	2	0	0	0	0	0	0	0	0	0	0	0	0	0	0	0	0
thrashed	14	.5766	1.7399	42.4	0	3	1	6	1	2	1	0	6	0	1	2	0	0	0	0	0	0	0	0	1	2	0	2	0
thrashes	2	.0665	.0708	28.5	0	0	1	1	0	0	0	0	1	0	1	0	0	0	0	0	0	0	0	0	0	0	0	0	0
thrashing	10	.4413	.9703	39.9	1	2	0	3	2	1	1	0	2	0	0	2	0	0	0	0	0	0	0	0	3	0	0	3	0
thread	317	.5671	37.383	55.7	70	24	29	20	27	41	104	2	56	4	3	5	4	29	0	29	4	9	85	53	10	6	8	12	0
threaded	20	.4367	1.8236	42.6	0	1	1	2	1	3	8	4	1	0	0	0	0	2	0	1	0	1	2	8	3	0	1	1	0
threading	10	.3757	.7998	39.0	0	1	0	1	1	3	4	0	1	0	0	0	0	0	0	0	0	0	4	2	0	0	1	2	0
threadlike	3	.1688	.1341	31.3	2	0	0	0	1	0	0	0	0	0	1	0	0	0	0	2	0	0	0	0	0	0	0	0	0
threads	135	.5355	15.021	51.8	20	5	4	27	17	20	39	3	13	0	0	3	1	3	0	30	4	3	22	34	2	6	8	6	0
threat	48	.7046	6.9106	48.4	4	1	5	4	12	14	7	1	8	0	0	5	0	8	0	1	0	0	1	0	4	3	7	11	0
threaten	17	.6956	2.4249	43.8	1	1	5	1	3	5	1	0	2	1	0	1	0	7	0	1	0	0	0	0	1	2	1	1	0
threatened	79	.7848	12.548	51.0	8	5	10	13	21	15	6	1	19	2	1	5	0	14	0	3	1	0	0	0	5	7	8	14	0
threatening	22	.6879	3.1419	45.0	1	4	4	3	4	1	4	1	7	0	1	0	0	4	0	2	0	0	0	0	3	2	1	2	0
threateningly	3	.2261	.2131	33.3	0	1	1	1	0	0	0	0	2	0	0	0	0	0	0	0	0	0	0	0	1	0	0	0	0
threatens	10	.4862	1.0184	40.1	0	0	0	1	3	0	6	0	0	0	0	1	0	0	0	0	0	0	0	0	1	2	1	5	0
threats	25	.6819	3.5750	45.5	1	1	2	2	11	5	3	0	11	0	0	1	0	5	0	1	0	0	1	0	3	1	0	2	0
three	4413	.9534	830.82	69.2	790	689	554	606	817	487	363	107	884	275	56	168	607	354	354	333	297	27	42	53	194	326	164	279	0
Three	66	.7639	10.230	50.1	20	6	7	4	17	9	2	1	18	10	0	5	2	4	0	2	11	1	0	0	2	1	7	3	0
three-	6	.4492	.5624	37.5	2	0	0	1	1	1	1	0	0	0	0	0	0	0	1	0	1	0	0	0	1	0	3	0	0
three-cell	2	.0000	.0394	26.0	0	0	0	0	0	2	0	0	0	0	0	0	0	0	0	2	0	0	0	0	0	0	0	0	0
three-cornered	6	.1717	.3427	35.3	0	0	1	2	2	1	0	0	3	0	0	3	0	0	0	0	0	0	0	0	0	0	0	0	0
three-day	8	.3876	.7088	38.5	0	2	0	1	2	3	0	0	2	0	0	1	0	0	0	0	0	0	0	0	1	0	0	4	0
three-decker	2	.0000	.0914	29.6	0	2	0	0	0	0	0	0	2	0	0	0	0	0	0	0	0	0	0	0	0	0	0	0	0
three-digit	4	.2009	.2054	33.1	2	0	0	0	0	0	1	1	0	0	0	0	3	0	0	0	0	0	0	0	0	1	0	0	0
three-dimensional	24	.2725	1.4619	41.6	0	2	2	8	6	1	2	3	1	0	0	0	6	0	0	2	0	10	0	1	0	0	1	3	0
three-eighths	3	.2346	.1705	32.3	0	0	0	2	0	0	0	1	0	0	0	0	2	0	0	0	0	0	0	0	0	0	0	1	0
three-fifths	2	.2285	.1129	30.5	1	0	0	1	0	0	0	0	0	0	0	0	0	1	0	0	0	0	0	0	0	0	1	0	0
three-foot	3	.3390	.2450	33.9	0	0	0	2	1	0	0	0	1	0	0	0	0	0	0	0	0	0	0	0	0	0	1	1	0
three-fourths	19	.5698	2.2658	43.6	1	2	3	5	2	3	1	2	1	0	0	0	1	6	0	4	0	0	2	0	0	0	1	4	0
three-headed	2	.2160	.1362	31.3	0	0	0	0	0	1	0	1	1	0	0	0	0	0	0	1	0	0	0	0	0	0	0	0	0
three-hour	2	.0000	.0243	23.9	0	0	0	0	1	0	1	0	0	0	0	0	0	0	0	0	0	0	0	0	0	0	0	2	0
three-inch	4	.4873	.4082	36.1	0	0	0	1	2	1	0	0	0	0	0	1	0	0	0	0	0	0	0	0	1	1	0	1	0
three-layer	2	.0000	.0394	26.0	0	0	0	0	2	0	0	0	0	0	0	0	0	0	0	2	0	0	0	0	0	0	0	0	0
three-legged	7	.2440	.4485	36.5	0	2	3	1	0	1	0	0	2	0	0	4	1	0	0	0	0	0	0	0	0	0	0	0	0
three-letter	5	.2329	.2910	34.6	2	1	0	1	1	0	0	0	1	1	0	0	0	0	3	0	0	0	0	0	0	0	0	0	0
three-man	8	.5124	.8749	39.4	1	2	0	0	3	2	0	0	1	0	0	0	0	1	0	3	0	0	1	1	0	0	0	1	0
three-mile	3	.3406	.2461	33.9	0	0	1	1	0	0	1	0	1	1	0	0	0	0	0	0	0	0	0	0	0	0	0	1	0
three-minute	9	.4211	.8176	39.1	0	1	3	1	3	0	1	0	0	4	0	1	0	0	0	3	0	0	0	0	0	0	0	1	0
three-month	3	.2346	.1705	32.3	0	0	0	2	0	1	0	0	0	0	0	0	2	0	0	0	0	0	0	0	0	0	0	1	0
three-o'clock	2	.0000	.0914	29.6	0	2	0	0	0	0	0	0	2	0	0	0	0	0	0	0	0	0	0	0	0	0	0	0	0
three-part	16	.0224	.2337	33.7	2	2	4	3	3	2	0	0	1	0	0	0	0	0	0	0	15	0	0	0	0	0	0	0	0
three-penny	2	.2297	.1135	30.6	0	1	0	0	0	1	0	0	0	0	0	1	0	1	0	0	0	0	0	0	0	0	0	0	0
three-place	4	.0000	.0599	27.8	1	0	1	0	0	1	1	0	0	0	0	0	4	0	0	0	0	0	0	0	0	0	0	0	0
three-pound	2	.1814	.1187	30.7	0	0	0	0	0	1	0	1	1	0	0	0	0	0	0	0	0	0	0	0	0	0	0	1	0
three-quarters	13	.6215	1.6558	42.2	1	1	1	0	5	1	1	3	0	0	0	3	1	1	0	2	0	0	0	0	3	1	0	2	0
three-sided	4	.2281	.2337	33.7	0	0	1	2	0	1	0	0	0	0	0	0	0	3	0	0	0	0	0	0	0	0	0	1	0
three-speed	2	.2437	.1129	30.5	0	1	0	0	1	0	0	0	0	0	0	0	0	0	0	0	0	0	0	0	0	0	1	1	0
three-stage	4	.3611	.3201	35.1	0	1	0	3	0	0	0	0	0	0	0	0	0	0	1	1	0	0	0	0	0	2	0	0	0
three-strand	2	.2346	.1166	30.7	0	0	0	1	0	0	0	1	0	0	0	0	0	0	0	1	0	0	0	0	0	0	0	1	0
three-stringed	2	.0000	.0162	22.1	0	0	1	1	0	0	0	0	0	0	0	0	0	0	0	0	2	0	0	0	0	0	0	0	0
three-syllable	19	.0352	.3529	35.5	3	5	5	2	2	2	0	0	2	0	0	0	0	0	17	0	0	0	0	0	0	0	0	0	0
three-time	2	.0000	.0389	25.9	0	0	0	0	0	2	0	0	0	0	0	0	0	2	0	0	0	0	0	0	0	0	0	0	0
three-toed	2	.2160	.1362	31.3	1	0	0	0	1	0	0	0	1	0	0	0	0	0	0	1	0	0	0	0	0	0	0	0	0
three-tone	2	.0000	.0162	22.1	0	2	0	0	0	0	0	0	0	0	0	0	0	0	0	0	2	0	0	0	0	0	0	0	0
three-way	6	.1665	.2671	34.3	0	0	1	0	1	4	0	0	1	0	0	0	0	1	0	0	0	0	0	3	0	0	0	1	0
three-wheeled	2	.2401	.1133	30.5	0	1	0	0	1	0	0	0	0	0	0	0	0	0	0	0	0	0	0	0	0	1	1	0	0
three-word	4	.1757	.1672	32.2	0	0	0	0	2	0	2	0	0	1	0	0	0	0	3	0	0	0	0	0	0	0	0	0	0
three-year	8	.5510	.9041	39.6	0	0	0	2	1	3	2	0	0	0	1	1	0	0	0	0	0	0	0	0	1	1	2	2	0
three-year-old	16	.5923	1.9743	43.0	4	7	0	0	2	2	1	0	2	1	0	1	0	0	0	1	0	0	1	0	0	8	1	1	0
three's	2	.1494	.1045	30.2	1	0	1	0	0	0	0	0	1	0	0	0	0	0	0	0	1	0	0	0	0	0	0	0	0
threes	36	.3593	2.8663	44.6	10	6	7	4	4	1	1	3	0	0	0	0	24	1	0	3	7	0	0	0	0	0	0	1	0
threescore	3	.3380	.2439	33.9	0	0	0	1	1	1	0	0	1	1	0	1	0	0	0	0	0	0	0	0	0	0	0	0	0
threshed	8	.4176	.7470	38.7	1	1	2	1	3	0	0	0	1	0	0	2	0	4	0	0	0	0	0	0	0	0	1	0	0
thresher	2	.2351	.1166	30.7	0	0	0	0	1	1	0	0	0	0	0	0	0	1	0	0	0	0	0	0	0	0	0	1	0
threshers	2	.2337	.1157	30.6	1	0	0	0	0	1	0	0	0	0	0	0	0	1	0	0	0	0	0	0	1	0	0	0	0
threshes	2	.2137	.1056	30.2	1	0	0	1	0	0	0	0	0	0	0	0	0	1	0	0	1	0	0	0	0	0	0	0	0
threshing	17	.5838	2.0698	43.2	6	2	2	5	2	0	0	0	1	0	0	1	0	7	0	0	0	0	0	0	4	1	2	1	0
threshold	17	.6482	2.2711	43.6	0	0	1	2	8	2	4	0	3	0	0	3	0	0	0	1	1	0	0	0	3	1	4	1	0
threw	342	.7753	54.046	57.3	71	87	29	44	69	30	10	2	133	8	5	40	6	8	7	5	4	0	0	0	60	39	4	23	0
thrice	6	.5577	.7197	38.6	0	1	1	3	1	0	0	0	2	0	0	1	0	0	0	0	0	0	0	0	1	1	0	1	0
thrift	4	.3416	.3027	34.8	0	0	0	0	1	1	2	0	0	1	0	2	0	1	0	0	0	0	0	0	0	0	0	0	0
thrifty	12	.6884	1.6970	42.3	2	0	0	5	2	3	0	0	3	0	0	2	0	1	2	0	1	0	0	0	1	0	1	1	0
thrill	25	.7046	3.6395	45.6	2	5	2	5	5	4	1	1	9	2	0	5	0	1	1	0	1	0	0	0	0	4	1	1	0
thrilled	22	.4796	2.3030	43.6	3	8	0	3	1	3	3	1	7	0	5	2	0	1	0	0	2	1	0	0	0	1	0	3	0
thrillers	2	.2407	.1138	30.6	0	0	1	0	1	0	0	0	0	0	0	1	0	0	0	0	0	0	0	0	0	1	0	0	0
thrilling	41	.6201	5.3377	47.3	2	9	6	12	5	3	1	3	13	3	5	2	0	2	1	0	0	1	0	0	1	9	0	4	0

7C thoughtlessness
6P Thoughts
4N thousand-pound
9D thousand-year-old
XH thousandfold
9B Thread
8M thread-diameter
XH thread-like
9B THREE
6J Three-Cornered
3P Three-Horned
7M Three-M-Ite
7D three-act
6F three-and
4K three-and-one-half
3N three-base
9R three-button
XR three-by-five-inch
XR three-cabin
7Q three-celled
4E three-cent
9Q three-color
7A three-colored
9D three-corner
6R three-deep
4K three-dimensions
6A three-foot-square
3N three-four
3P three-horn
3P three-horned
8D three-hours'
4P three-hundred
4P Three-hundred
7D three-hundred-mile
7H three-in-one
6A three-l
7P three-lane
5G three-letters
XH three-lobed
6A three-masted
8D three-mile-thick
9L three-months'
5R three-ounce
7R three-piece
8L three-ply
9B three-pronged
6A three-quarter
7R three-rib
9B three-room
7Q three-score
5C three-sentence
6G three-space
6R three-step
7A three-store
4A three-story
6E three-tenths
4N three-thousand
7Q three-to-four-pound
4A three-ton
7R three-unit
9M three-view
6R three-weak
9A three-wheel
5R three-year-olds
9R Threepenny
5N threepenny-bit
5R threesome
8Q Threnody
6F thresh
7R Thresher
7A threwed
5R thriftily
6R thrill-a-minute
3P thriller

Word Type	F	D	U	SFI	3 Gr 3	4 Gr 4	5 Gr 5	6 Gr 6	7 Gr 7	8 Gr 8	9 Gr 9	X UnGr	A Read	B Eng & Gr	C Comp	D Lit	E Math	F Soc Stud	G Spell	H Sci	J Music	K Art	L Home Ec	M Shop	N Lib F	P Lib NF	Q Lib Ref	R Mag	S Rel
thrills	15	.6135	1.9484	42.9	0	0	3	3	4	1	1	3	6	0	1	1	0	0	0	0	1	1	0	0	0	2	0	3	0
thrive	23	.6815	3.2242	45.1	3	2	1	7	4	1	3	2	4	0	0	1	0	3	0	4	1	0	0	0	1	1	6	2	0
thrived	7	.5551	.8091	39.1	0	0	0	1	2	2	2	0	0	0	0	1	0	3	1	0	0	0	0	0	0	1	1	0	0
thrives	7	.4119	.6269	38.0	0	0	2	0	1	0	4	0	0	0	0	0	0	1	0	2	0	0	0	0	0	0	3	1	0
thriving	29	.6099	3.6724	45.6	4	0	4	6	8	4	2	1	2	0	0	1	0	13	0	1	3	0	0	0	0	2	5	2	0
Thro'	2	.0000	.0162	22.1	0	0	0	0	0	2	0	0	0	0	0	0	0	0	0	0	2	0	0	0	0	0	0	0	0
throat	207	.8180	34.179	55.3	26	36	19	37	45	25	14	5	68	9	0	25	0	2	4	33	8	0	2	1	27	18	2	8	0
throatily	3	.3427	.2477	33.9	0	0	0	1	1	0	0	1	1	0	0	0	0	0	0	0	0	0	0	0	1	0	0	1	0
throats	27	.7444	4.1202	46.1	5	0	4	5	7	2	3	1	9	2	0	2	0	1	0	5	0	0	0	0	3	1	2	2	0
throaty	6	.3598	.5339	37.3	0	2	0	1	1	1	1	0	3	0	0	1	0	0	0	0	0	0	0	0	2	0	0	0	0
throb	6	.4797	.6535	38.2	1	0	0	1	2	2	0	0	3	0	0	0	0	0	0	0	1	0	0	0	1	0	0	1	0
throbbed	7	.3621	.6358	38.0	0	2	0	0	2	2	1	0	4	0	0	2	0	0	0	0	0	0	0	0	1	0	0	0	0
throbbing	11	.6703	1.5253	41.8	0	2	2	1	2	2	2	0	3	1	0	1	0	0	0	0	1	0	0	0	2	2	0	1	0
throbs	2	.2442	.1134	30.5	0	0	0	0	0	1	1	0	0	1	0	0	0	0	0	0	0	0	0	0	0	0	0	1	0
throne	74	.7448	11.252	50.5	10	9	17	10	11	10	6	1	21	1	0	12	0	12	1	0	5	0	0	0	7	8	5	2	0
Throne	9	.1915	.4852	36.9	5	1	1	2	0	0	0	0	2	0	0	0	0	1	0	0	0	0	0	0	6	0	0	0	0
throned	2	.1497	.1046	30.2	0	0	0	0	1	1	0	0	1	0	0	0	0	0	1	0	0	0	0	0	0	0	0	0	0
thrones	4	.4456	.3981	36.0	0	0	0	2	0	1	1	0	1	0	0	1	0	1	0	0	0	0	0	0	0	0	1	0	0
throng	17	.6978	2.4459	43.9	0	3	1	5	4	2	1	1	5	0	0	1	0	1	0	0	1	0	0	0	3	3	1	2	0
thronged	12	.5942	1.5126	41.8	1	2	2	2	1	3	1	0	4	0	0	3	0	0	0	0	1	0	0	0	0	2	1	1	0
thronging	5	.3436	.4206	36.2	0	0	1	1	1	0	0	2	2	0	0	1	0	0	0	0	0	0	0	0	0	0	0	2	0
throngs	5	.4683	.5251	37.2	1	0	0	3	0	0	1	0	2	0	0	0	0	0	0	0	1	0	0	0	0	0	1	1	0
throttle	15	.6161	1.9204	42.8	4	1	1	1	5	0	3	0	3	0	1	1	0	0	0	0	0	0	0	1	0	5	1	3	0
throttles	6	.1948	.3750	35.7	3	0	1	2	0	0	0	0	3	0	0	0	0	0	0	0	0	0	0	0	0	3	0	0	0
through	5442	.9862	1056.2	70.2	834	906	672	735	1033	611	473	178	1214	157	61	321	314	466	115	890	184	68	84	74	322	436	339	390	7
Through	9	.5801	1.0954	40.4	0	4	3	1	1	0	0	0	1	1	0	0	0	4	0	0	1	0	0	0	0	0	1	1	0
throughout	458	.8512	77.745	58.9	32	47	66	60	99	74	62	18	49	13	6	12	9	102	5	34	75	3	3	3	5	15	91	32	1
throw	281	.9057	50.699	57.1	54	78	27	30	59	15	14	4	109	16	2	26	4	12	3	26	4	1	1	1	18	28	12	18	0
throwed	3	.1250	.1342	31.3	0	1	0	0	2	0	0	0	1	0	0	0	0	0	0	0	0	0	0	0	2	0	0	0	0
thrower	7	.4450	.6972	38.4	0	1	2	0	3	0	0	1	2	0	0	0	0	0	0	0	0	0	0	0	0	2	2	1	0
throwin'	2	.2440	.1132	30.5	0	0	0	1	1	0	0	0	0	0	0	1	0	0	0	0	0	0	0	0	0	0	0	1	0
throwing	109	.8370	18.407	52.6	22	25	11	10	24	9	6	2	46	4	1	7	0	3	0	12	1	1	1	0	16	6	2	9	0
thrown	175	.8685	30.400	54.8	22	25	24	19	45	19	16	5	55	6	3	18	1	19	2	6	8	0	2	0	20	19	8	8	0
throws	59	.7739	9.2656	49.7	12	3	3	5	22	7	7	0	14	2	1	4	14	1	0	10	2	0	0	0	1	6	0	4	0
thru	13	.2428	.8668	39.4	1	7	1	4	0	0	0	0	5	0	0	0	1	0	0	0	0	0	0	0	7	0	0	0	0
thrush	2	.2407	.1090	30.4	2	0	0	0	0	0	0	0	0	1	0	0	0	0	0	0	1	0	0	0	0	0	0	0	0
thrushes	10	.5892	1.2400	40.9	2	1	0	3	2	2	0	0	2	2	0	0	0	0	0	2	0	0	0	0	1	1	2	0	0
thrust	132	.8029	21.340	53.3	8	28	16	16	26	19	18	1	22	1	0	18	4	4	1	39	1	0	1	3	17	7	6	8	0
thrust-to-weight	2	.0000	.0394	26.0	0	0	0	0	0	2	0	0	0	0	0	0	0	0	0	2	0	0	0	0	0	0	0	0	0
thrusting	9	.4348	.9064	39.6	3	0	0	3	2	1	0	0	4	0	0	1	0	0	0	0	0	0	0	0	3	1	0	0	0
thrusts	4	.4522	.4044	36.1	0	0	1	2	0	1	0	0	1	0	0	0	0	0	0	1	0	0	0	0	1	0	0	1	0
thu'	2	.0000	.0914	29.6	0	0	0	0	2	0	0	0	2	0	0	0	0	0	0	0	0	0	0	0	0	0	0	0	0
Thucydides	2	.0000	.0209	23.2	0	0	2	0	0	0	0	0	0	0	0	0	0	0	0	0	0	0	0	0	0	0	2	0	0
thud	26	.7063	3.8351	45.8	3	11	2	4	5	1	0	0	12	0	0	2	1	3	0	4	1	0	0	0	1	2	0	0	0
thudded	3	.2212	.2099	33.2	0	0	0	0	1	2	0	0	2	0	0	1	0	0	0	0	0	0	0	0	0	0	0	0	0
thudding	3	.2784	.1822	32.6	1	0	1	0	1	0	0	0	0	0	1	1	0	0	0	0	0	0	0	0	0	0	0	1	0
thuds	4	.1717	.2284	33.6	0	0	0	0	0	3	1	0	2	0	0	2	0	0	0	0	0	0	0	0	0	0	0	0	0
Thuillier	2	.0000	.0394	26.0	0	0	0	0	0	0	0	2	0	0	0	0	0	0	0	2	0	0	0	0	0	0	0	0	0
thumb	150	.8123	24.358	53.9	51	23	7	9	21	17	22	0	18	0	3	15	12	0	3	11	24	0	9	10	16	13	9	7	0
Thumb	10	.5479	1.2250	40.9	6	1	0	2	0	1	0	0	6	0	0	0	0	1	1	0	0	0	0	0	1	1	0	0	0
thumb-sucking	4	.0000	.0419	26.2	4	0	0	0	0	0	0	0	0	0	0	0	0	0	0	0	0	0	0	0	0	0	4	0	0
thumb-width	3	.0000	.0449	26.5	0	3	0	0	0	0	0	0	0	0	0	0	3	0	0	0	0	0	0	0	0	0	0	0	0
thumbed	2	.2442	.1134	30.5	0	0	0	0	0	1	1	0	0	1	0	0	0	0	0	0	0	0	0	0	0	0	0	1	0
thumbnail	3	.0000	.0076	18.8	0	0	0	0	2	0	1	0	0	0	0	0	0	0	0	0	0	0	0	3	0	0	0	0	0
thumbs	18	.6076	2.2670	43.6	3	2	1	1	6	1	4	0	3	0	1	2	1	0	0	1	0	0	3	0	0	5	1	1	0
thumbtack	5	.3691	.4157	36.2	4	0	0	0	1	0	0	0	0	0	0	0	0	0	0	3	0	0	0	0	0	1	1	0	0
thumbtacks	11	.3228	.8531	39.3	5	0	0	2	2	0	2	0	1	1	0	0	1	0	0	8	0	0	0	0	0	0	0	0	0
thump	62	.5170	7.1580	48.5	11	22	8	11	6	3	1	0	31	6	0	3	0	0	0	0	0	0	0	0	18	2	0	2	0
thump-thump	10	.0000	.1172	30.7	3	0	0	7	0	0	0	0	0	0	0	0	0	0	0	0	0	0	0	0	10	0	0	0	0
thumped	16	.5832	1.9949	43.0	3	3	1	1	6	1	0	1	6	0	0	1	0	0	0	0	2	0	0	0	4	1	0	2	0
thumping	15	.4944	1.6156	42.1	1	5	3	2	0	3	1	0	4	1	0	6	0	1	0	0	0	0	0	0	2	0	0	1	0
thumps	8	.4695	.8612	39.4	1	1	2	0	3	0	1	0	4	0	0	0	0	0	0	0	0	0	0	0	0	1	1	2	0
thunder	140	.5661	16.848	52.3	31	20	12	34	18	13	5	7	35	4	5	15	0	6	5	21	6	1	0	0	18	16	2	3	3
Thunder	12	.0797	.4053	36.1	10	0	2	0	0	0	0	0	2	0	0	0	0	0	0	0	0	0	0	0	0	10	0	0	0
Thunderbird	3	.1937	.1495	31.7	0	1	0	0	1	0	0	1	0	0	0	0	0	1	0	0	0	0	0	0	0	0	0	2	0
thunderbolt	7	.4635	.6920	38.4	2	0	2	0	1	2	0	0	1	2	1	1	0	0	0	0	0	0	0	0	0	0	2	0	0
Thunderbolt	5	.0000	.2284	33.6	5	0	0	0	0	0	0	0	5	0	0	0	0	0	0	0	0	0	0	0	0	0	0	0	0
thunderbolts	3	.3274	.2364	33.7	0	0	0	0	3	0	0	0	1	0	0	1	0	0	1	0	0	0	0	0	0	0	0	0	0
thundered	21	.6951	3.0670	44.9	2	2	2	5	7	2	1	0	12	2	0	2	0	1	1	0	1	0	0	0	1	0	0	1	0
thunderhead	7	.1690	.3428	35.4	2	0	3	1	0	0	1	0	0	0	0	0	0	0	0	6	0	0	0	0	0	1	0	0	0
thunderheads	3	.3452	.2543	34.1	0	0	1	1	1	0	0	0	1	0	0	0	0	0	0	1	0	0	0	0	0	0	0	1	0
thundering	17	.5547	2.0526	43.1	4	5	1	3	0	2	2	0	7	0	1	1	0	1	0	0	0	0	0	0	2	5	0	0	0
thunderous	17	.5388	1.9983	43.0	0	1	3	3	7	2	1	0	7	0	0	1	0	0	0	0	2	0	0	0	4	0	0	3	0
thunders	7	.5624	.8204	39.1	0	1	0	2	0	0	4	0	1	0	0	1	0	0	0	0	2	0	0	0	1	0	1	1	0
thundershower	2	.0000	.0914	29.6	0	2	0	0	0	0	0	0	2	0	0	0	0	0	0	0	0	0	0	0	0	0	0	0	0
thunderstorm	21	.5447	2.4323	43.9	3	4	1	1	11	0	0	1	3	1	2	0	0	0	0	10	1	0	0	0	2	0	0	2	0
thunderstorms	21	.4077	1.9899	43.0	0	4	1	1	5	1	3	6	6	0	0	0	0	0	0	8	0	0	0	0	0	1	0	6	0
thunderstruck	3	.3431	.2528	34.0	0	0	0	1	1	1	0	0	1	0	0	0	0	1	0	0	0	0	0	0	1	0	0	0	0
Thurber	14	.2646	.8711	39.4	0	0	0	0	3	11	0	0	2	0	3	9	0	0	0	0	0	0	0	0	0	0	0	0	0
Thurber's	7	.2267	.3568	35.5	0	0	0	0	2	5	0	0	0	0	2	5	0	0	0	0	0	0	0	0	0	0	0	0	0
Thursday	70	.7872	11.102	50.5	12	10	6	7	10	10	14	1	14	4	2	16	13	2	3	0	4	0	1	0	4	1	0	6	0
Thursdays	2	.1814	.1187	30.7	1	1	0	0	0	0	0	0	1	0	0	0	0	0	0	0	0	0	0	0	0	0	0	1	0
thus	756	.9418	140.61	61.5	17	44	59	101	226	146	136	27	51	32	11	31	89	70	12	148	23	5	9	17	29	50	130	48	1
Thutmose	2	.2446	.1123	30.5	0	0	1	0	0	0	0	1	0	1	0	0	0	0	0	0	0	0	0	0	0	0	1	0	0
thwap	2	.0000	.0914	29.6	0	0	0	0	0	2	0	0	2	0	0	0	0	0	0	0	0	0	0	0	0	0	0	0	0
thwart	2	.2443	.1130	30.5	0	1	0	0	0	0	1	0	0	0	0	1	0	0	0	0	0	0	0	0	1	0	0	0	0
thwarted	10	.6178	1.2863	41.1	0	0	0	0	4	1	4	1	2	0	0	1	0	0	0	1	0	0	1	0	0	2	1	2	0
thwarts	2	.2444	.1132	30.5	0	0	0	1	0	1	0	0	0	1	0	0	0	0	0	0	0	0	0	0	1	0	0	0	0
thy	198	.6070	24.701	53.9	14	14	27	27	33	11	70	2	14	13	0	64	0	3	0	0	23	0	0	0	19	47	9	4	2
Thy	24	.2612	1.3813	41.4	3	3	3	11	4	0	0	0	0	0	0	0	0	0	0	0	20	0	0	0	1	2	0	0	1
thyme	4	.1092	.1038	30.2	0	0	0	1	0	0	3	0	0	0	0	0	0	0	0	0	0	0	3	0	0	0	1	0	0
thymine	3	.0000	.0591	27.7	0	0	0	0	0	0	3	0	0	0	0	0	0	0	0	3	0	0	0	0	0	0	0	0	0
Thyrker	2	.0000	.0219	23.4	0	0	0	2	0	0	0	0	0	2	0	0	0	0	0	0	0	0	0	0	0	0	0	0	0
thyroid	20	.3600	1.6329	42.1	0	0	0	14	3	2	0	1	0	0	0	0	0	0	0	15	0	0	1	0	0	0	4	0	0
thyroxin	3	.2445	.1818	32.6	0	0	0	1	2	0	0	0	0	0	0	0	0	0	0	2	0	0	0	0	0	0	1	0	0

7R throat-tearing
7P throatless
9Q throes
6R Throop
9D throstle
7A throttled
3P THROUGH
XR through-the-water
3Q throughways
3D throw-away
7P throwback
5F throwers
7A thru'
3J thrum
6N thrummed
3H thrush's
7A Thrust
7R thrusters
5Q Thruway
7B ths
9R thub-thub-thubbing
6A THUD
7P thugs
6N thumb-tacks
8J Thumbelina
7M thumbnails
6A thumbprints
8R thumbs-up
7D thumper
3N Thumpy
7J thund'ring
3P thunder-cart
3P thunder-spirits
7B thunder-stone
5J thunder's
5N thunderation
8B thunderclaps
3R thundercloud
8J Thunderer
8A thundergust
8D thunderin'
4A thundershowers
5B thundersticks
3N thundery
5P Thurgau
8B thursday
3B Thursday's
XR thusly
8A thwacked
6R thwarting
7B Thyangboche
8F Thye
XH thymus
7H Thyroid

Word Type	F	D	U	SFI	3 Gr 3	4 Gr 4	5 Gr 5	6 Gr 6	7 Gr 7	8 Gr 8	9 Gr 9	X UnGr	A Read	B Eng & Gr	C Comp	D Lit	E Math	F Soc Stud	G Spell	H Sci	J Music	K Art	L Home Ec	M Shop	N Lib F	P Lib NF	Q Lib Ref	R Mag	S Rel
thyself	13	.3983	1.1336	40.5	1	0	0	5	2	1	4	0	1	0	0	4	0	1	0	0	0	0	0	0	6	1	0	0	0
ti	21	.3577	1.6260	42.1	1	2	4	3	9	2	0	0	1	1	0	0	0	2	10	0	7	0	0	0	0	0	0	0	0
Ti	2	.0000	.0389	25.9	0	0	0	2	0	0	0	0	0	0	0	0	0	2	0	0	0	0	0	0	0	0	0	0	0
tial	3	.0000	.0243	23.9	0	0	0	0	3	0	0	0	0	0	0	0	0	0	3	0	0	0	0	0	0	0	0	0	0
Tiber	8	.4825	.8217	39.1	2	0	0	3	2	0	1	0	0	0	0	0	0	3	0	0	0	0	0	0	0	2	1	2	0
Tibet	7	.4447	.7116	38.5	1	0	0	0	5	0	1	0	2	0	0	0	0	3	0	1	0	0	0	0	0	0	1	0	0
tibia	2	.2413	.1212	30.8	0	0	0	0	1	0	0	1	0	0	0	0	1	0	0	1	0	0	0	0	0	0	0	0	0
tick	25	.7374	3.7452	45.7	10	5	0	1	6	0	2	1	4	0	0	2	1	0	0	7	4	0	1	0	1	2	2	1	0
Tick	6	.0000	.2741	34.4	0	0	0	0	6	0	0	0	6	0	0	0	0	0	0	0	0	0	0	0	0	0	0	0	0
tick-bird	2	.0000	.0290	24.6	2	0	0	0	0	0	0	0	0	0	0	0	0	0	0	0	0	0	0	0	0	2	0	0	0
tick-birds	6	.0000	.0869	29.4	6	0	0	0	0	0	0	0	0	0	0	0	0	0	0	0	0	0	0	0	0	6	0	0	0
tick-tack-toe	3	.3407	.2479	33.9	0	0	0	0	1	1	1	0	1	0	0	1	1	0	0	0	0	0	0	0	0	0	0	0	0
tick-tick	2	.0000	.0914	29.6	0	0	0	1	1	0	0	0	2	0	0	0	0	0	0	0	0	0	0	0	0	0	0	0	0
ticked	5	.4143	.4656	36.7	1	0	1	2	1	0	0	0	1	0	0	0	0	1	0	0	0	0	0	0	0	0	1	2	0
ticket	100	.7868	16.046	52.1	25	23	22	6	13	4	6	1	43	5	1	2	21	7	3	0	0	0	0	0	5	5	4	4	0
Ticket	9	.2212	.6853	38.4	0	1	8	0	0	0	0	0	8	0	0	1	0	0	0	0	0	0	0	0	0	0	0	1	0
tickets	157	.5245	18.112	52.6	64	37	19	10	7	7	11	2	56	4	1	1	72	10	0	0	0	0	0	0	2	6	0	5	0
Tickets	3	.3873	.2485	34.0	0	0	0	0	2	0	0	1	0	0	0	1	0	0	0	0	0	0	0	0	1	0	1	0	0
Tickie	2	.0000	.0914	29.6	0	0	0	0	2	0	0	0	2	0	0	0	0	0	0	0	0	0	0	0	0	0	0	0	0
ticking	14	.4397	1.3488	41.3	5	0	1	1	5	1	1	0	3	0	2	6	0	0	0	1	1	0	0	0	0	1	0	0	0
tickle	19	.4768	2.0764	43.2	9	2	2	2	0	2	1	1	10	0	0	5	0	0	0	1	0	0	0	0	2	0	0	1	0
tickled	23	.6316	3.1123	44.9	11	0	4	2	4	2	0	0	13	0	1	1	0	0	1	0	1	0	0	0	4	2	0	0	0
tickling	7	.4808	.7784	38.9	0	1	0	1	0	1	3	1	4	0	0	1	0	0	0	1	0	0	0	0	0	0	0	1	0
ticklish	5	.3707	.4004	36.0	0	1	0	0	2	0	1	1	0	0	0	2	0	0	0	0	0	0	0	0	1	0	0	2	0
ticks	18	.4720	1.8316	42.6	3	1	0	0	7	0	0	7	0	0	0	1	1	0	0	11	0	0	0	0	0	3	2	0	0
ticktacktoe	2	.2446	.1123	30.5	0	0	1	0	0	0	1	0	0	1	0	0	0	0	0	0	0	0	0	0	0	0	1	0	0
Ticonderoga	8	.3662	.7294	38.6	0	0	2	0	4	2	0	0	4	0	0	0	0	2	0	0	0	0	0	0	0	0	2	0	0
tidal	59	.4297	5.6822	47.5	0	2	4	2	9	4	18	20	6	0	0	1	0	3	0	39	0	0	0	0	0	0	4	6	0
tidbit	2	.1948	.1250	31.0	0	0	0	0	1	1	0	0	1	0	0	0	0	0	0	0	0	0	0	0	0	1	0	0	0
tidbits	4	.3641	.3324	35.2	0	0	1	1	0	0	1	1	1	0	0	0	0	0	0	0	0	0	1	0	1	0	0	1	0
tiddle-iddle	4	.0000	.1827	32.6	0	4	0	0	0	0	0	0	4	0	0	0	0	0	0	0	0	0	0	0	0	0	0	0	0
tide	158	.8178	25.953	54.1	24	33	10	22	21	15	11	22	24	3	4	11	2	11	0	46	3	0	1	0	19	12	7	15	0
tides	110	.5672	13.177	51.2	7	26	4	15	13	7	19	19	6	3	0	3	2	6	0	71	1	0	0	0	1	7	6	4	0
Tidewater	3	.0000	.0434	26.4	3	0	0	0	0	0	0	0	0	0	0	0	0	0	0	0	0	0	0	0	0	3	0	0	0
tidied	3	.2357	.2199	33.4	0	1	1	1	0	0	0	0	2	0	0	0	0	0	0	0	0	0	0	0	0	1	0	0	0
tidings	8	.5879	.9939	40.0	1	0	0	0	2	3	1	1	2	0	0	2	0	0	0	1	0	0	0	0	1	1	1	0	0
tidy	28	.7409	4.2215	46.3	1	4	5	6	3	3	3	3	7	1	1	2	0	0	0	1	0	0	1	0	7	2	2	4	0
tie	234	.8865	41.417	56.2	77	31	23	29	24	35	12	3	85	19	3	8	12	9	8	22	4	2	13	0	11	18	3	17	0
Tie	2	.1494	.1045	30.2	1	0	1	0	0	0	0	0	1	0	0	0	0	0	0	0	1	0	0	0	0	0	0	0	0
tie-up	2	.2408	.1204	30.8	1	0	0	0	0	1	0	0	0	0	0	0	0	1	0	0	0	0	0	0	0	1	0	0	0
tied	379	.8704	66.196	58.2	87	95	53	48	59	22	11	4	176	10	3	31	3	22	3	12	12	4	3	0	46	32	8	14	0
tier	5	.4578	.4816	36.8	0	0	1	1	1	0	2	0	0	1	0	0	0	0	0	0	0	0	0	0	0	1	2	1	0
tierra	6	.1955	.3185	35.0	0	0	0	2	1	0	3	0	0	0	0	0	0	5	0	0	0	0	0	0	0	0	0	1	0
Tierra	11	.2364	.6401	38.1	3	0	0	2	3	3	0	0	0	0	0	0	0	6	0	0	0	0	0	0	0	0	5	0	0
ties	85	.7014	12.210	50.9	15	7	21	7	9	14	10	2	18	2	0	0	6	15	0	2	9	0	9	0	2	4	7	11	0
Tiflin	9	.2292	.4844	36.9	0	0	0	0	1	8	0	0	0	0	0	3	0	0	0	1	0	0	0	0	6	0	0	0	0
tiger	112	.7627	17.566	52.4	34	16	19	8	23	2	9	1	56	7	2	10	2	0	1	10	0	0	0	0	2	7	2	13	0
Tiger	14	.4772	1.5613	41.9	9	2	0	3	0	0	0	0	9	0	0	1	0	0	0	0	0	0	0	0	0	2	0	2	0
tiger's	8	.2424	.6072	37.8	1	3	2	2	0	0	0	0	6	0	0	0	0	0	0	0	0	0	0	0	0	0	0	2	0
tigers	31	.6835	4.4251	46.5	13	5	4	1	3	2	1	2	13	5	0	0	1	0	1	2	0	0	0	0	3	3	0	3	0
Tigers	14	.3792	1.2644	41.0	6	3	3	1	1	0	0	0	5	1	0	0	7	0	0	0	0	0	0	0	0	0	0	1	0
tight	208	.8703	36.192	55.6	45	34	18	28	47	16	16	4	68	7	4	11	1	3	1	16	4	1	7	7	32	25	4	17	0
tight-fisted	2	.0000	.0234	23.7	0	1	1	0	0	0	0	0	0	0	0	0	0	0	0	0	0	0	0	0	2	0	0	0	0
tight-fitting	5	.1877	.2757	34.4	0	1	0	2	0	1	1	0	2	0	0	0	0	0	0	0	0	0	2	0	0	1	0	0	0
tight-lipped	3	.2212	.2099	33.2	0	0	1	0	1	0	1	0	2	0	0	1	0	0	0	0	0	0	0	0	0	0	0	0	0
tight-rope	2	.2433	.1158	30.6	0	0	0	0	1	0	0	1	0	0	0	0	0	0	0	0	0	0	0	0	0	1	0	1	0
tighten	31	.5092	3.3192	45.2	3	2	4	4	10	4	3	1	4	0	1	1	0	0	0	5	1	0	1	9	2	3	1	3	0
tightened	27	.5025	2.9296	44.7	0	3	2	3	9	5	5	0	8	0	1	6	0	0	0	0	0	0	0	5	5	1	0	1	0
tightening	12	.5497	1.3991	41.5	2	2	0	1	3	2	2	0	3	0	0	0	0	1	1	0	1	0	0	2	1	1	0	2	0
tighter	23	.6742	3.2507	45.1	7	3	3	3	2	3	2	0	10	1	1	3	0	1	0	3	1	0	0	0	3	0	0	0	0
tightly	172	.7781	27.226	54.3	32	37	23	20	27	17	14	2	63	2	1	8	1	4	0	23	7	0	15	7	14	16	5	6	0
tightly-stretched	2	.2128	.1055	30.2	0	0	0	1	1	0	0	0	0	0	0	0	0	0	0	1	1	0	0	0	0	0	0	0	0
tightness	3	.2269	.1793	32.5	0	0	0	1	1	0	1	0	1	0	0	1	0	0	0	0	0	0	0	1	0	0	0	0	0
tightrope	8	.5482	.9559	39.8	1	0	1	1	1	1	3	0	3	1	0	0	0	1	0	0	0	0	0	0	1	2	0	0	0
tights	4	.2991	.2943	34.7	1	1	0	0	0	2	0	0	1	0	0	0	0	0	0	0	0	0	0	0	0	1	0	2	0
Tigreans	3	.0000	.0583	27.7	0	0	0	0	3	0	0	0	0	0	0	0	0	3	0	0	0	0	0	0	0	0	0	0	0
Tigris	7	.3981	.6270	38.0	0	0	0	2	2	1	1	1	1	1	0	0	1	3	0	0	0	1	0	0	0	0	0	0	0
tiki	2	.0000	.0914	29.6	0	0	0	2	0	0	0	0	2	0	0	0	0	0	0	0	0	0	0	0	0	0	0	0	0
Tiki	3	.0000	.0591	27.7	0	3	0	0	0	0	0	0	0	0	0	0	0	0	0	3	0	0	0	0	0	0	0	0	0
tikki	7	.0000	.0851	29.3	0	0	0	0	0	0	0	7	0	0	0	0	0	0	0	0	0	0	0	0	0	0	0	7	0
Tikki	7	.0000	.0851	29.3	0	0	0	0	0	0	0	7	0	0	0	0	0	0	0	0	0	0	0	0	0	0	0	7	0
til	2	.2443	.1130	30.5	0	0	0	0	1	1	0	0	0	0	0	1	0	0	0	0	0	0	0	0	1	0	0	0	0
Tilda	2	.0000	.0914	29.6	0	0	0	1	0	1	0	0	2	0	0	0	0	0	0	0	0	0	0	0	0	0	0	0	0
Tilden	2	.2285	.1129	30.5	0	1	0	0	0	1	0	0	0	0	0	0	0	1	0	0	0	0	0	0	0	0	1	0	0
Tildy	6	.0000	.0644	28.1	0	0	0	0	0	6	0	0	0	0	0	6	0	0	0	0	0	0	0	0	0	0	0	0	0
tile	30	.5572	3.4910	45.4	0	3	11	5	5	2	4	0	2	1	0	0	7	9	0	1	0	4	0	2	0	2	1	1	0
tiled	7	.4826	.7678	38.9	2	0	0	2	2	1	0	0	3	0	0	0	0	2	0	0	0	0	0	0	0	1	1	0	0
tiles	44	.4990	4.7570	46.8	15	11	13	0	2	0	1	2	9	0	0	0	22	5	0	0	0	4	0	1	0	0	1	2	0
till	414	.7327	62.267	57.9	53	74	49	53	104	41	37	3	146	11	2	65	0	11	0	10	21	0	1	0	79	48	5	15	0
Till	4	.0000	.0323	25.1	0	0	0	1	2	1	0	0	0	0	0	0	0	0	0	0	4	0	0	0	0	0	0	0	0
tillage	2	.2408	.1204	30.8	0	0	1	0	0	0	1	0	0	0	0	0	0	1	0	0	0	0	0	0	0	1	0	0	0
Tillamook	3	.1250	.1342	31.3	2	0	1	0	0	0	0	0	1	0	0	0	0	0	0	0	0	0	0	0	2	0	0	0	0
tilled	5	.4500	.5011	37.0	1	1	0	1	0	2	1	0	1	0	0	0	0	2	0	0	0	0	0	0	0	0	1	1	0
tiller	17	.3300	1.3958	41.4	1	1	4	2	6	1	2	0	8	0	4	0	0	0	0	0	0	0	0	0	1	2	1	1	0
Tillie	3	.0000	.1370	31.4	0	3	0	0	0	0	0	0	3	0	0	0	0	0	0	0	0	0	0	0	0	0	0	0	0
tilling	3	.2425	.1816	32.6	0	0	0	0	2	0	0	1	0	0	0	0	0	2	0	0	0	0	0	0	0	0	0	1	0
Tilly	7	.2241	.4269	36.3	2	0	0	0	0	0	4	1	2	0	0	0	0	0	0	1	0	0	0	0	0	0	4	0	0
tilt	27	.6168	3.4869	45.4	6	1	5	2	11	0	2	0	5	0	0	1	1	1	0	8	0	0	0	0	0	1	5	5	0
tilted	51	.5700	6.1606	47.9	25	5	9	2	5	3	2	0	5	0	0	1	2	3	0	30	0	0	0	0	3	3	3	1	0
tilting	6	.2972	.4165	36.2	0	1	0	1	3	1	0	0	1	0	0	0	0	1	0	0	0	0	0	2	1	0	1	0	0
tilts	7	.3259	.5325	37.3	3	0	2	1	0	0	1	0	0	0	0	0	0	0	0	5	0	0	0	0	1	1	0	0	0
Tim	194	.6707	27.457	54.4	94	55	11	15	13	5	1	0	99	12	1	8	23	3	1	0	0	0	0	0	4	5	0	38	0
tim-ber	2	.0000	.0162	22.1	0	0	1	1	0	0	0	0	0	0	0	0	0	0	2	0	0	0	0	0	0	0	0	0	0

XH thyroxine
4A thzt
7N ti-ti
8D ti-tum-tum-tum
7A Tia
6F Tiahuanaco
3R Tibbar
6J Tibbo
4P Tibbs
3N Tiberias
3N Tiberius
5P Tibetans
3A Tiby
7Q tic
XR Tic-Tac-Toe
5A tick-ets
3A tick
7A Tick's
7B ticker
4N ticket-window
6R ticketed
3F tickles
8C tickly
7D tiddlywinks
6A Tide
XH tide-prediction
8N tide-water
5N tide's
5F Tidelands
9R tideline
4A tidewater
4N Tidy
4A tidying
7B tie-in
7R tie-ins
XH Tie-ko
9Q Tiefer
5Q Tientsin
3A tiepin
5Q Tiepolo
4J Tierce
7D tiewig
3P Tiger-Cat
7N tiger-eyed
4A tiger-striped
3A Tiger's
8A Tight
9R tight-clenched
3P tight-throated
6N tight-waisted
7R tightens
7F tightly-woven
4N tightly-wrapped
4A Tightness
5P tights-covered
6F Tigrais
XB Tigris-Euphrates
6R Tijuana
6J tikling
5J Tikling
6G tilde
3Q tile-roofed
9B Tiles
8Q tilework
7J Till's
3Q tillable
9D tillers
9H tillites
9Q Tilly's
XR tilth

Word Type	F	D	U	SFI	3 Gr 3	4 Gr 4	5 Gr 5	6 Gr 6	7 Gr 7	8 Gr 8	9 Gr 9	X UnGr	A Read	B Eng & Gr	C Comp	D Lit	E Math	F Soc Stud	G Spell	H Sci	J Music	K Art	L Home Ec	M Shop	N Lib F	P Lib NF	Q Lib Ref	R Mag	S Rel
Tim's	21	.3777	1.8780	42.7	5	11	3	2	0	0	0	0	7	0	0	0	3	2	0	0	0	0	0	0	0	0	0	9	0
Timawi	5	.0000	.0972	29.9	0	0	0	0	0	5	0	0	0	0	0	0	0	5	0	0	0	0	0	0	0	0	0	0	0
timbales	2	.0000	.0064	18.1	0	0	0	0	0	0	2	0	0	0	0	0	0	0	0	0	0	0	2	0	0	0	0	0	0
timber	98	.8315	16.355	52.1	5	2	23	11	36	11	5	5	22	2	1	6	0	22	5	3	1	0	0	2	5	5	16	8	0
Timber	3	.0000	.0434	26.4	0	3	0	0	0	0	0	0	0	0	0	0	0	0	0	0	0	0	0	0	0	3	0	0	0
timbered	2	.2297	.1135	30.6	0	0	1	0	0	1	0	0	0	0	0	1	0	1	0	0	0	0	0	0	0	0	0	0	0
timberland	3	.3390	.2450	33.9	0	1	1	0	1	0	0	0	1	0	0	0	0	0	0	0	0	0	0	0	0	0	1	1	0
timberlands	2	.0725	.0732	28.6	0	0	1	0	1	0	0	0	1	0	0	0	0	0	0	0	0	0	0	1	0	0	0	0	0
timbers	14	.4797	1.5060	41.8	0	0	4	5	4	1	0	0	6	0	2	2	0	1	0	0	0	0	0	0	1	1	0	1	0
timbre	36	.0000	.2911	34.6	5	0	1	1	14	15	0	0	0	0	0	0	0	0	0	0	36	0	0	0	0	0	0	0	0
timbres	5	.0000	.0404	26.1	0	0	0	0	0	5	0	0	0	0	0	0	0	0	0	0	5	0	0	0	0	0	0	0	0
Timbuctoo	4	.0000	.1827	32.6	0	4	0	0	0	0	0	0	4	0	0	0	0	0	0	0	0	0	0	0	0	0	0	0	0
Timbuktu	2	.1494	.1045	30.2	0	1	0	1	0	0	0	0	1	0	0	0	0	0	0	0	1	0	0	0	0	0	0	0	0
time	8441	.9833	1634.3	72.1	1580	1393	992	1149	1473	899	746	209	2479	412	89	453	243	838	174	842	403	48	150	64	672	686	339	544	5
Time	41	.7218	6.0052	47.8	2	2	1	2	6	22	5	1	5	3	1	2	0	1	0	6	2	0	1	0	2	0	2	16	0
TIME	8	.1303	.2868	34.6	0	0	0	7	0	1	0	0	0	0	0	0	0	0	0	0	0	0	0	0	7	0	0	1	0
time-consuming	4	.3711	.3648	35.6	0	0	0	0	3	1	0	0	2	0	0	0	0	0	0	0	0	0	0	0	0	1	1	0	0
time-honored	2	.0000	.0389	25.9	0	0	0	0	0	2	0	0	0	0	0	0	0	2	0	0	0	0	0	0	0	0	0	0	0
time's	4	.3713	.3634	35.6	0	1	0	1	1	1	0	0	2	0	0	1	0	0	0	0	0	0	0	0	1	0	0	0	0
Time's	2	.0000	.0243	23.9	0	0	0	0	0	0	2	0	0	0	0	0	0	0	0	0	0	0	0	0	0	0	0	2	0
timed	17	.6589	2.3709	43.7	1	1	1	5	5	2	2	0	8	0	0	2	1	0	0	3	0	0	0	0	1	1	1	0	0
timekeeper	3	.2212	.2099	33.2	0	0	0	0	2	1	0	0	2	0	0	1	0	0	0	0	0	0	0	0	0	0	0	0	0
timeless	4	.2031	.2455	33.9	0	0	0	1	1	0	2	0	2	0	0	0	0	0	0	0	0	1	0	0	0	1	0	0	0
Timeless	2	.1814	.1187	30.7	0	0	0	2	0	0	0	0	1	0	0	0	0	0	0	0	0	0	0	0	0	0	0	1	0
timelessness	2	.2351	.1166	30.7	0	0	0	1	1	0	0	0	0	0	0	0	0	1	0	0	0	0	0	0	0	0	0	1	0
timely	3	.3779	.2436	33.9	0	0	0	0	1	1	1	0	0	1	0	0	0	0	0	0	1	0	0	0	0	1	0	0	0
Timely	2	.0000	.0162	22.1	0	2	0	0	0	0	0	0	0	0	0	0	0	0	0	0	2	0	0	0	0	0	0	0	0
timer	7	.1035	.2277	33.6	1	0	0	2	0	4	0	0	1	0	0	0	0	0	0	2	0	0	0	4	0	0	0	0	0
Timer	24	.0000	.4668	36.7	24	0	0	0	0	0	0	0	0	0	0	0	0	24	0	0	0	0	0	0	0	0	0	0	0
times	2051	.9579	387.76	65.9	312	321	272	245	360	265	219	57	360	74	14	74	344	191	26	321	156	19	25	20	66	154	119	87	1
Times	30	.6056	3.7988	45.8	0	6	0	2	5	11	2	4	5	3	0	1	0	5	0	1	0	0	0	0	1	4	0	10	0
timetable	9	.3051	.6329	38.0	1	0	1	0	2	1	4	0	0	0	0	0	0	0	0	3	0	0	0	0	0	1	0	5	0
timid	23	.7316	3.4151	45.3	1	4	3	2	7	5	1	0	4	2	1	5	0	1	0	0	1	0	0	0	3	4	1	1	0
timidly	12	.4599	1.2685	41.0	0	3	1	3	1	3	1	0	6	1	0	3	0	0	0	0	0	0	0	0	2	0	0	0	0
timing	26	.4887	2.8129	44.5	0	4	3	3	14	1	1	0	8	0	0	0	0	1	0	4	0	0	0	0	1	0	2	10	0
Timing	2	.0000	.0914	29.6	0	0	0	0	2	0	0	0	2	0	0	0	0	0	0	0	0	0	0	0	0	0	0	0	0
Timken	2	.0000	.0299	24.8	0	0	0	0	0	0	2	0	0	0	0	0	2	0	0	0	0	0	0	0	0	0	0	0	0
Timmie	2	.0000	.0290	24.6	0	2	0	0	0	0	0	0	0	0	0	0	0	0	0	0	0	0	0	0	0	2	0	0	0
Timmy	25	.4337	2.6439	44.2	22	0	1	0	0	1	1	0	18	2	0	0	1	0	0	0	0	0	0	0	4	0	0	0	0
Timor	2	.0000	.0389	25.9	0	0	1	0	1	0	0	0	0	0	0	0	0	2	0	0	0	0	0	0	0	0	0	0	0
timothy	2	.2331	.1157	30.6	1	0	0	0	1	0	0	0	0	0	0	0	0	0	0	1	0	0	0	0	1	0	0	0	0
Timothy	80	.2474	6.5157	48.1	75	0	2	0	0	0	1	2	75	0	0	1	0	0	0	0	0	0	0	0	0	2	0	2	0
Timothy's	6	.0000	.2741	34.4	6	0	0	0	0	0	0	0	6	0	0	0	0	0	0	0	0	0	0	0	0	0	0	0	0
timpani	16	.0000	.1294	31.1	1	2	0	4	6	3	0	0	0	0	0	0	0	0	0	0	16	0	0	0	0	0	0	0	0
Timur	7	.0000	.0733	28.6	0	0	0	0	0	7	0	0	0	0	0	0	0	0	0	0	0	0	0	0	0	0	7	0	0
tin	203	.8886	36.008	55.6	62	23	25	16	31	15	28	3	69	5	3	12	3	16	1	41	8	5	1	6	10	11	8	4	0
Tin	10	.1952	.4835	36.8	2	0	0	2	5	0	1	0	1	2	0	0	0	0	0	0	7	0	0	0	0	0	0	0	0
Tina	15	.3838	1.4497	41.6	12	0	3	0	0	0	0	0	10	0	0	0	0	0	0	0	0	0	0	0	2	0	0	3	0
Tindell	6	.0000	.0729	28.6	0	0	0	6	0	0	0	0	0	0	0	0	0	0	0	0	0	0	0	0	0	0	0	6	0
tinder	9	.5321	1.0567	40.2	3	1	2	1	0	2	0	0	4	0	0	0	0	1	0	0	0	0	0	0	1	0	2	1	0
tinderbox	12	.2090	.8987	39.5	10	0	0	1	0	0	1	0	11	0	0	1	0	0	0	0	0	0	0	0	0	0	0	0	0
tines	5	.1072	.1241	30.9	0	1	0	0	0	4	0	0	0	0	0	0	0	0	0	0	1	0	4	0	0	0	0	0	0
tinfoil	6	.4746	.6402	38.1	2	1	1	0	0	1	0	2	2	1	0	0	0	0	0	2	0	0	0	0	1	0	0	0	0
ting	2	.0000	.0162	22.1	2	0	0	0	0	0	0	0	0	0	0	0	0	0	0	0	2	0	0	0	0	0	0	0	0
Ting	2	.0000	.0290	24.6	0	0	0	0	0	0	2	0	0	0	0	0	0	0	0	0	0	0	0	0	0	2	0	0	0
tinge	2	.2337	.1157	30.6	0	0	1	0	1	0	0	0	0	0	0	0	0	1	0	0	0	0	0	0	1	0	0	0	0
tingle	2	.1814	.1187	30.7	1	0	0	0	0	0	0	1	1	0	0	0	0	0	0	0	0	0	0	0	0	0	0	1	0
tingled	4	.1717	.2284	33.6	2	0	0	1	1	0	0	0	2	0	0	2	0	0	0	0	0	0	0	0	0	0	0	0	0
tingling	6	.5580	.7201	38.6	2	1	0	1	1	1	0	0	2	1	0	0	0	0	0	0	0	0	0	0	1	1	0	1	0
tinier	3	.3395	.2468	33.9	0	2	0	1	0	0	0	0	1	0	0	0	0	0	0	0	0	0	0	0	0	1	1	0	0
tiniest	16	.5611	1.9185	42.8	6	2	0	4	1	1	1	1	3	1	0	0	0	0	0	7	0	0	0	0	1	3	1	0	0
Tink	11	.0000	.5025	37.0	0	0	0	11	0	0	0	0	11	0	0	0	0	0	0	0	0	0	0	0	0	0	0	0	0
tinker	5	.5631	.5751	37.6	1	0	0	1	1	1	1	0	0	1	0	1	0	0	1	0	1	0	0	0	0	0	0	1	0
Tinker	24	.1550	1.2607	41.0	13	0	0	11	0	0	0	0	10	0	0	0	0	0	0	0	0	0	0	0	0	0	0	14	0
Tinker's	6	.1688	.2585	34.1	5	1	0	0	0	0	0	0	0	0	0	1	0	0	0	0	0	0	0	0	0	0	0	5	0
tinkered	2	.0000	.0914	29.6	0	0	0	1	0	1	0	0	2	0	0	0	0	0	0	0	0	0	0	0	0	0	0	0	0
tinkering	6	.5437	.7050	38.5	0	0	1	0	4	1	0	0	2	0	0	1	0	1	1	0	0	0	0	0	0	0	1	0	0
tinkers	4	.3784	.3243	35.1	0	1	1	2	0	0	0	0	0	0	0	1	0	0	0	0	1	0	0	0	0	0	0	2	0
tinkle	13	.4545	1.3423	41.3	2	2	1	4	1	2	1	0	6	0	2	1	0	0	2	0	0	0	0	0	0	1	0	1	0
tinkled	4	.2417	.3028	34.8	1	2	0	0	0	1	0	0	3	0	0	0	0	0	0	0	0	0	0	0	1	0	0	0	0
tinkling	7	.3816	.6609	38.2	1	1	1	1	1	1	1	0	4	0	0	0	0	0	0	0	1	0	0	0	0	2	0	0	0
tinned	3	.0000	.0076	18.8	0	0	0	0	0	3	0	0	0	0	0	0	0	0	0	0	0	0	0	3	0	0	0	0	0
Tinnie	2	.0000	.0290	24.6	0	2	0	0	0	0	0	0	0	0	0	0	0	0	0	0	0	0	0	0	0	2	0	0	0
tinny	4	.2431	.2111	33.2	0	0	0	0	3	1	0	0	0	0	1	0	0	0	0	0	3	0	0	0	0	0	0	0	0
tins	7	.4474	.7002	38.5	1	0	1	0	1	2	2	0	2	0	0	2	0	0	0	0	0	0	0	0	1	2	0	0	0
tinsel	6	.4347	.5510	37.4	2	1	0	1	0	0	0	2	0	0	0	0	0	0	0	1	0	1	0	0	1	0	1	2	0
tint	4	.4739	.3988	36.0	0	0	1	0	2	0	1	0	0	0	0	1	0	1	1	0	0	0	0	0	1	0	0	0	0
tinted	7	.4559	.6925	38.4	0	0	1	0	4	1	0	1	1	0	0	3	0	0	0	1	0	0	0	0	0	0	1	1	0
Tintin	2	.0000	.0243	23.9	0	0	0	0	0	0	0	2	0	0	0	0	0	0	0	0	0	0	0	0	0	0	0	2	0
tinting	2	.2421	.0995	30.0	0	0	0	0	0	1	1	0	0	0	0	0	0	0	0	0	0	0	1	1	0	0	0	0	0
Tinto	2	.2152	.1357	31.3	0	0	1	1	0	0	0	0	1	0	0	0	0	1	0	0	0	0	0	0	0	0	0	0	0
tints	7	.3105	.4732	36.8	0	0	2	0	4	0	0	1	0	0	0	1	0	0	0	1	0	0	3	0	0	1	0	1	0
tiny	904	.8862	159.67	62.0	210	166	94	154	145	66	42	27	189	21	22	26	1	67	11	311	7	5	10	4	36	93	52	48	1
Tiny	9	.4014	.7623	38.8	4	1	0	0	4	0	0	0	0	1	0	3	0	0	0	0	4	0	0	0	0	0	0	1	0
Tioga	7	.5361	.8078	39.1	0	2	1	2	2	0	0	0	2	1	0	0	0	0	0	0	0	0	0	0	0	1	1	2	0
tion	39	.0105	.4305	36.3	0	6	2	11	6	14	0	0	1	0	0	0	0	0	38	0	0	0	0	0	0	0	0	0	0
tious	2	.0000	.0162	22.1	0	0	0	0	2	0	0	0	0	0	0	0	0	0	2	0	0	0	0	0	0	0	0	0	0
tip	243	.9161	44.142	56.4	51	45	23	23	64	14	13	10	38	4	1	11	17	31	4	52	3	2	8	3	9	22	27	11	0
Tip	8	.3302	.6646	38.2	0	0	1	0	0	7	0	0	4	0	1	3	0	0	0	0	0	0	0	0	0	0	0	0	0
tip-toe	3	.2187	.1555	31.9	1	0	0	0	2	0	0	0	0	2	0	0	0	0	0	0	0	0	0	0	0	0	0	1	0
Tippecanoe	2	.2306	.1140	30.6	0	0	0	0	0	1	1	0	0	1	0	0	0	1	0	0	0	0	0	0	0	0	0	0	0
tipped	31	.6004	4.0331	46.1	8	5	9	3	5	0	1	0	16	0	0	3	0	0	0	3	0	0	0	0	4	4	0	1	0
tippet	2	.1814	.1187	30.7	0	0	0	1	0	0	0	1	1	0	0	0	0	0	0	0	0	0	0	0	0	0	0	1	0
tipping	11	.5500	1.2517	41.0	1	1	1	0	6	1	0	1	0	1	0	1	0	0	0	1	0	0	0	0	3	1	0	4	0
Tippy	3	.0000	.0328	25.2	3	0	0	0	0	0	0	0	0	3	0	0	0	0	0	0	0	0	0	0	0	0	0	0	0
tips	84	.8440	14.183	51.5	9	13	12	10	27	7	4	2	15	2	0	4	0	1	1	23	3	1	4	3	3	7	7	10	0

9L timbale
6G timber-workers
3A Timberlake
7Q timberline
8J timbrels
8J Timbres
4J Timbucktoo
4H time-a
8A time-and-a-half
5B time-saver
7R time-to-time
7A timekeeper's
7A timepiece
XR Timers'
4P times'
XR timetables
7D timeworn
6N Timi
3A Timmm-berr
4D Timpie
8Q Timur-i-leng
9Q Timurid
4A tin-bottomed
6H tin-can
4D tinder-box
4N tine
3J ting-a-ling-a-ling
3J tinga
8A tinged
4D tingles
5R tingly
7N Tingou
8K Tinguely's
7P tinker's
4P Tinnie's
8M tinning
5A Tinsley
6A tintinnabulation
7P Tintoretto's
3A tio
3A Tio
4P tip-cart
8F tip-off
3R tip-top
7H tipping-bucket
3N Tipple
6R tippling
3A tipsy-toeing

Word Type	F	D	U	SFI	3 Gr 3	4 Gr 4	5 Gr 5	6 Gr 6	7 Gr 7	8 Gr 8	9 Gr 9	X UnGr	A Read	B Eng & Gr	C Comp	D Lit	E Math	F Soc Stud	G Spell	H Sci	J Music	K Art	L Home Ec	M Shop	N Lib F	P Lib NF	Q Lib Ref	R Mag	S Rel
tiptoe	16	.5951	2.0334	43.1	1	2	1	2	3	1	4	2	6	0	0	3	0	0	0	2	1	0	0	0	3	0	0	1	0
tiptoed	16	.5758	2.0041	43.0	5	5	2	2	0	1	1	0	8	1	1	1	0	0	0	0	0	0	0	0	2	3	0	0	0
tiptoeing	2	.2440	.1132	30.5	0	0	0	0	1	0	0	1	0	0	0	1	0	0	0	0	0	0	0	0	0	0	0	1	0
tiptoes	4	.3567	.3537	35.5	2	2	0	0	0	0	0	0	2	0	0	0	0	0	0	0	1	0	0	0	0	1	0	0	0
tiptop	2	.2411	.1091	30.4	1	0	0	0	0	0	1	0	0	0	0	1	0	0	0	0	1	0	0	0	0	0	0	0	0
tire	88	.8297	14.705	51.7	8	16	10	6	17	21	8	2	30	5	2	1	3	1	8	14	1	0	4	0	3	4	2	10	0
Tire	2	.2437	.1129	30.5	0	0	1	0	1	0	0	0	0	0	0	0	0	0	0	0	0	0	0	0	0	0	1	1	0
tired	461	.8246	76.910	58.9	127	90	62	52	57	37	32	4	202	31	2	38	1	26	5	23	7	0	5	0	61	42	7	11	0
Tired	3	.3271	.2364	33.7	1	1	0	0	0	1	0	0	1	1	0	0	0	0	0	0	1	0	0	0	0	0	0	0	0
tired-looking	3	.2357	.2199	33.4	1	0	0	1	0	0	1	0	2	0	0	0	0	0	0	0	0	0	0	0	0	1	0	0	0
tiredly	4	.2445	.3067	34.9	0	1	0	0	3	0	0	0	3	0	0	0	0	0	0	0	0	0	0	0	0	1	0	0	0
tiredness	3	.3465	.2515	34.0	0	1	0	1	1	0	0	0	1	0	0	0	0	0	0	0	0	0	0	0	0	1	0	1	0
tireless	6	.6006	.7554	38.8	0	0	0	1	2	2	0	1	1	1	0	1	0	1	0	1	0	0	0	0	1	0	0	0	0
tires	85	.8098	13.908	51.4	12	13	7	4	26	15	6	2	26	1	2	1	12	8	0	6	1	0	0	1	2	5	4	16	0
Tiresias	2	.0000	.0215	23.3	0	0	0	0	0	0	2	0	0	0	0	2	0	0	0	0	0	0	0	0	0	0	0	0	0
tiresome	14	.6693	1.9467	42.9	3	3	2	0	4	1	1	0	4	1	0	2	0	2	0	0	0	0	0	0	2	2	0	1	0
Tirilira	3	.0000	.0243	23.8	3	0	0	0	0	0	0	0	0	0	0	0	0	0	0	0	3	0	0	0	0	0	0	0	0
Tirilirala	4	.0000	.0323	25.1	4	0	0	0	0	0	0	0	0	0	0	0	0	0	0	0	4	0	0	0	0	0	0	0	0
tiring	18	.6402	2.4182	43.8	1	5	2	3	4	0	2	1	6	0	1	2	0	2	1	0	0	0	0	0	0	4	0	2	0
Tiros	12	.2395	.7317	38.6	1	0	3	0	2	6	0	0	0	0	0	0	0	0	0	11	0	0	0	1	0	0	0	0	0
tissue	130	.5409	14.761	51.7	5	5	6	19	33	24	33	5	3	0	0	1	0	0	0	73	0	9	4	0	1	3	31	5	0
tissues	71	.4995	7.5533	48.8	1	1	6	8	20	14	17	4	2	1	0	1	0	0	0	43	0	0	7	0	2	0	13	2	0
Titan	14	.4721	1.5655	41.9	2	0	0	6	1	1	3	1	10	0	0	0	2	0	0	0	1	0	0	0	0	0	1	0	0
TITANIA	6	.0000	.0644	28.1	0	0	0	0	0	0	6	0	0	0	0	6	0	0	0	0	0	0	0	0	0	0	0	0	0
titanic	3	.1813	.1402	31.5	0	0	0	0	3	0	0	0	0	0	0	0	0	0	0	1	0	0	0	0	0	0	2	0	0
Titanic	6	.1826	.2832	34.5	0	0	0	0	0	0	6	0	0	0	0	1	0	0	0	0	0	0	0	0	0	5	0	0	0
Titanic's	6	.0000	.0869	29.4	0	0	0	0	0	0	6	0	0	0	0	0	0	0	0	0	0	0	0	0	0	6	0	0	0
titanium	14	.5120	1.6036	42.1	7	2	0	2	2	1	0	0	7	0	0	0	0	0	0	1	0	0	0	1	0	0	2	3	0
Titans	4	.3606	.3539	35.5	1	0	0	1	0	2	0	0	2	0	0	1	0	0	1	0	0	0	0	0	0	0	0	0	0
Tithers	2	.0000	.0290	24.6	0	0	0	0	0	2	0	0	0	0	0	0	0	0	0	0	0	0	0	0	0	2	0	0	0
tithery	2	.0000	.0162	22.1	0	0	2	0	0	0	0	0	0	0	0	0	0	0	0	0	2	0	0	0	0	0	0	0	0
Titipu	2	.0000	.0162	22.1	0	0	0	0	0	2	0	0	0	0	0	0	0	0	0	0	2	0	0	0	0	0	0	0	0
title	302	.8053	48.882	56.9	40	39	34	31	68	34	46	10	65	88	3	12	11	14	7	7	23	2	0	14	4	11	15	26	0
Title	2	.2442	.1134	30.5	0	1	0	0	0	0	0	1	0	1	0	0	0	0	0	0	0	0	0	0	0	0	0	1	0
titled	8	.4567	.7650	38.8	0	1	3	1	3	0	0	0	0	0	0	0	0	1	0	0	3	1	0	0	0	2	0	1	0
titles	97	.7019	13.894	51.4	17	9	14	13	15	18	10	1	20	40	2	2	0	6	10	0	7	1	0	1	0	1	3	4	0
Tito	3	.1937	.1495	31.7	0	0	0	0	2	0	1	0	0	0	0	0	0	1	0	0	0	0	0	0	0	0	0	2	0
Tituba	8	.0000	.1158	30.6	0	0	0	0	0	0	8	0	0	0	0	0	0	0	0	0	0	0	0	0	0	8	0	0	0
titular	2	.2401	.1133	30.5	0	0	1	0	0	0	1	0	0	0	0	0	0	0	0	0	0	0	0	0	0	1	1	0	0
Titus	9	.5528	1.0850	40.4	0	1	3	2	3	0	0	0	4	1	0	0	0	0	0	0	0	0	0	0	2	0	1	1	0
Tiziano	4	.0000	.1827	32.6	0	0	0	4	0	0	0	0	4	0	0	0	0	0	0	0	0	0	0	0	0	0	0	0	0
Tlingit	7	.0000	.1361	31.3	0	0	7	0	0	0	0	0	0	0	0	0	0	7	0	0	0	0	0	0	0	0	0	0	0
tlot-tlot	10	.2025	.6507	38.1	0	0	0	0	0	6	4	0	6	0	0	4	0	0	0	0	0	0	0	0	0	0	0	0	0
tluth	2	.0000	.0914	29.6	0	2	0	0	0	0	0	0	2	0	0	0	0	0	0	0	0	0	0	0	0	0	0	0	0
TNT	10	.3097	.7729	38.9	0	1	2	1	2	0	2	2	3	0	0	0	0	0	0	3	0	0	0	0	0	0	4	0	0
to	121347	.9909	23653	83.7	20509	19280	14518	15353	22488	14623	11705	2871	31302	6437	1241	6511	7589	12184	4320	10588	4609	1112	2416	1646	7829	9793	5718	7833	219
To	15	.4212	1.3662	41.4	3	1	1	1	1	0	0	8	1	0	0	0	0	1	0	0	2	0	0	0	0	1	1	9	0
TO	10	.2994	.6964	38.4	0	0	2	2	5	1	0	0	1	0	0	6	0	0	0	1	0	0	0	0	0	0	0	2	0
to-and-fro	3	.0000	.0591	27.7	0	0	0	0	2	0	1	0	0	0	0	0	0	0	0	3	0	0	0	0	0	0	0	0	0
to-day	18	.4581	1.8223	42.6	4	2	2	4	3	0	1	2	4	0	0	0	0	0	0	2	0	0	0	0	7	4	1	0	0
to-do	2	.2443	.1130	30.5	0	0	0	0	2	0	0	0	0	0	0	1	0	0	0	0	0	0	0	0	1	0	0	0	0
to-morrow	9	.2261	.6392	38.1	0	2	0	7	0	0	0	0	6	0	0	0	0	0	0	0	0	0	0	0	3	0	0	0	0
to-night	6	.3908	.5203	37.2	0	0	0	2	1	1	2	0	1	0	0	3	0	0	0	0	1	0	0	0	1	0	0	0	0
toad	85	.6540	11.758	50.7	32	13	0	28	6	4	2	0	35	0	0	4	0	0	0	27	0	1	0	0	2	10	5	1	0
Toad	6	.2355	.4634	36.7	1	0	0	5	0	0	0	0	5	0	0	0	0	0	0	0	0	0	0	0	0	1	0	0	0
toad's	4	.3685	.3667	35.6	2	0	0	1	0	0	0	1	2	1	0	0	0	0	0	1	0	0	0	0	0	0	0	0	0
toads	89	.4419	8.8882	49.5	20	10	0	50	5	1	2	1	17	3	0	2	0	0	0	55	0	0	0	0	0	9	3	0	0
toadstool	4	.2995	.2902	34.6	0	0	1	0	0	2	0	1	1	1	0	2	0	0	0	0	0	0	0	0	0	0	0	0	0
toadstools	3	.3668	.2407	33.8	1	0	1	0	0	1	0	0	0	0	0	1	0	0	0	1	1	0	0	0	0	0	0	0	0
toast	57	.6565	7.6137	48.8	7	11	6	6	11	8	8	0	6	11	1	2	0	0	4	4	8	0	11	0	3	4	1	2	0
Toast	5	.2218	.3471	35.4	2	0	3	0	0	0	0	0	3	0	0	0	0	0	0	0	0	0	0	0	0	2	0	0	0
toasted	16	.3679	1.2647	41.0	2	2	3	1	1	0	6	1	1	0	0	3	0	0	0	0	1	0	6	0	0	2	0	3	0
toaster	16	.2257	.8497	39.3	6	0	4	0	0	6	0	0	0	0	0	0	0	0	0	4	0	0	0	6	0	6	0	0	0
toasters	9	.4069	.7754	38.9	1	0	1	2	0	5	0	0	0	0	1	1	0	1	0	2	0	0	0	3	0	1	0	0	0
toasting	4	.2342	.2025	33.1	0	1	1	0	0	2	0	0	0	1	0	0	0	0	1	0	0	0	0	2	0	0	0	0	0
toastmaster	2	.2412	.1141	30.6	0	0	0	0	0	1	1	0	0	1	0	0	0	0	0	0	0	0	0	0	0	1	0	0	0
toasts	4	.3442	.2950	34.7	0	0	0	0	0	0	3	1	0	2	0	0	0	0	0	0	0	0	1	0	0	0	0	1	0
Toba	3	.1843	.1420	31.5	0	1	0	0	0	2	0	0	0	0	0	2	0	1	0	0	0	0	0	0	0	0	0	0	0
tobacco	172	.6557	23.325	53.7	12	26	35	31	31	21	9	7	18	0	0	8	0	82	4	11	0	0	0	0	11	21	10	7	0
Tobacco	2	.2297	.1135	30.6	0	0	0	0	1	1	0	0	0	0	0	1	0	1	0	0	0	0	0	0	0	0	0	0	0
Tobacconist	2	.0000	.0389	25.9	0	0	0	0	0	2	0	0	0	0	0	0	0	2	0	0	0	0	0	0	0	0	0	0	0
Tobby	4	.0000	.0429	26.3	0	0	0	0	0	0	4	0	0	0	0	4	0	0	0	0	0	0	0	0	0	0	0	0	0
Tobe	11	.0000	.5025	37.0	0	0	11	0	0	0	0	0	11	0	0	0	0	0	0	0	0	0	0	0	0	0	0	0	0
Tobey	2	.1042	.0600	27.8	0	0	0	0	1	1	0	0	0	0	0	0	0	1	0	0	0	1	0	0	0	0	0	0	0
Tobey's	2	.0000	.0037	15.7	0	0	0	0	2	0	0	0	0	0	0	0	0	0	0	0	0	2	0	0	0	0	0	0	0
Tobias	18	.2292	1.3902	41.4	0	16	1	0	0	0	1	0	16	0	0	0	0	0	0	0	0	0	0	0	0	0	2	0	0
toboggan	4	.3619	.3167	35.0	1	0	0	1	1	0	0	1	0	0	0	0	0	0	0	0	0	0	0	0	1	1	0	2	0
Toby	51	.2952	4.4115	46.4	30	14	0	0	0	1	0	6	43	0	0	0	0	0	0	0	0	0	0	0	1	0	0	7	0
Toby's	6	.2279	.4286	36.3	3	1	0	0	0	0	0	2	4	0	0	0	0	0	0	0	0	0	0	0	0	0	0	2	0
toccata	3	.0000	.0243	23.8	0	0	0	0	0	3	0	0	0	0	0	0	0	0	0	0	3	0	0	0	0	0	0	0	0
Toccata	2	.2303	.1079	30.3	0	0	0	0	1	1	0	0	0	0	0	0	0	0	0	0	1	0	0	0	0	1	0	0	0
tock	2	.0000	.0215	23.3	2	0	0	0	0	0	0	0	0	0	0	2	0	0	0	0	0	0	0	0	0	0	0	0	0
Tock	2	.0000	.0914	29.6	0	0	2	0	0	0	0	0	2	0	0	0	0	0	0	0	0	0	0	0	0	0	0	0	0
Tocqueville	3	.0000	.0328	25.2	0	0	0	0	0	0	3	0	0	3	0	0	0	0	0	0	0	0	0	0	0	0	0	0	0
Tod	3	.2300	.1627	32.1	0	1	0	0	1	1	0	0	0	1	0	0	0	0	0	0	0	0	0	0	0	0	0	2	0
today	1923	.9501	361.02	65.6	362	317	261	245	336	202	155	45	424	112	15	59	38	388	92	140	101	14	11	14	66	149	173	123	4
Today	6	.2861	.3938	36.0	1	1	0	0	0	3	1	0	0	1	0	0	0	1	0	0	0	0	0	0	0	0	0	4	0
today's	201	.6973	28.255	54.5	20	18	43	51	24	21	17	7	8	4	4	2	6	9	89	15	8	6	0	5	1	10	15	19	0
Today's	3	.2435	.2274	33.6	2	0	1	0	0	0	0	0	2	0	0	0	0	1	0	0	0	0	0	0	0	0	0	0	0
Todd	15	.3234	1.1131	40.5	3	9	0	0	1	2	0	0	1	0	0	1	0	0	0	0	0	0	0	0	3	10	0	0	0
toddle	2	.2160	.1362	31.3	0	0	0	1	0	0	0	1	1	0	0	0	0	0	0	1	0	0	0	0	0	0	0	0	0
toddler	4	.3587	.3096	34.9	2	0	1	1	0	0	0	0	0	0	1	1	0	0	0	1	0	0	0	0	0	0	1	0	0
toddlers	4	.3485	.3103	34.9	0	0	1	0	1	1	0	1	0	0	0	0	0	0	0	1	0	0	0	0	1	0	0	2	0
toddling	2	.2427	.1152	30.6	0	1	0	0	1	0	0	0	0	0	0	0	0	0	0	0	0	0	0	0	1	1	0	0	0
Todds	2	.0000	.0290	24.6	0	2	0	0	0	0	0	0	0	0	0	0	0	0	0	0	0	0	0	0	0	2	0	0	0
toe	84	.8977	15.019	51.8	21	12	4	15	15	7	8	2	27	2	0	5	2	6	5	7	3	0	2	1	9	8	2	5	0

7F tirade
8F tirades
9F Tiran
4A Tired-Dog
3J Tirilita
5G tis
3P Tishbite
8G titan
8M titanate
7R titans
9D tithe
7P Titian
8P Titicaca
9N title-deeds
7A titleholder
7B titlts
3H titmouse
8F Tito's
6P Titov
7A tittered
6N tittle
4R Titusville
4Q Tiverton
7E TK
9M TL
9P TLC
7A tle
8B to-daeg
4N to-morrow's
7B to-too
7N to-wit
6A to't
3R Toadstool
8F tobacco-growing
6F tobacco-producing
5N Tobacconist's
9B tobaccos
7N tobacker
5A Tobe's
4N tobogganed
XD toboggans
4J tocar
4P Todd,/
7P Todd's
5Q Todi
9D todo

Word Type	F	D	U	SFI	3 Gr 3	4 Gr 4	5 Gr 5	6 Gr 6	7 Gr 7	8 Gr 8	9 Gr 9	X UnGr	A Read	B Eng & Gr	C Comp	D Lit	E Math	F Soc Stud	G Spell	H Sci	J Music	K Art	L Home Ec	M Shop	N Lib F	P Lib NF	Q Lib Ref	R Mag	S Rel
toenails	5	.3656	.3946	36.0	1	0	0	0	2	0	1	1	0	0	0	0	0	0	0	0	0	0	1	0	2	2	0	0	0
toes	169	.8332	28.351	54.5	56	25	15	16	36	8	7	6	54	3	1	20	4	7	0	27	5	0	3	0	15	22	5	3	0
Toff	13	.0000	.5939	37.7	0	0	0	0	0	13	0	0	13	0	0	0	0	0	0	0	0	0	0	0	0	0	0	0	0
Toffy	7	.0000	.3198	35.0	0	0	0	0	0	7	0	0	7	0	0	0	0	0	0	0	0	0	0	0	0	0	0	0	0
Tog	4	.0000	.0323	25.1	4	0	0	0	0	0	0	0	0	0	0	0	0	0	0	0	4	0	0	0	0	0	0	0	0
together	2629	.9617	498.81	67.0	569	426	277	364	424	274	244	51	563	119	21	105	156	254	135	322	135	65	114	68	128	207	102	131	4
Together	2	.2351	.1166	30.7	1	0	1	0	0	0	0	0	0	0	0	0	0	1	0	0	0	0	0	0	0	0	0	1	0
togetherness	2	.0000	.0243	23.9	0	0	0	0	0	1	0	1	0	0	0	0	0	0	0	0	0	0	0	0	0	0	0	2	0
toggle	2	.0000	.0243	23.9	0	0	0	2	0	0	0	0	0	0	0	0	0	0	0	0	0	0	0	0	0	0	0	2	0
Togo	5	.2326	.3837	35.8	0	1	4	0	0	0	0	0	4	0	0	0	0	1	0	0	0	0	0	0	0	0	0	0	0
toh	2	.0000	.0162	22.1	0	0	0	0	0	2	0	0	0	0	0	0	0	0	2	0	0	0	0	0	0	0	0	0	0
toil	26	.7264	3.8250	45.8	0	0	0	2	12	10	2	0	3	1	1	7	0	4	1	0	1	0	0	0	4	2	2	0	0
Toil	2	.1948	.1250	31.0	0	0	0	2	0	0	0	0	1	0	0	0	0	0	0	0	0	0	0	0	0	1	0	0	0
toiled	13	.4552	1.3104	41.2	2	0	0	2	6	1	2	0	3	0	0	0	0	1	0	0	0	0	0	0	5	3	0	1	0
toilet	17	.5100	1.8170	42.6	1	1	2	1	2	2	6	2	0	0	0	2	0	0	0	7	0	0	3	0	2	1	0	2	0
toiling	6	.4858	.6602	38.2	0	2	0	2	1	1	0	0	3	0	0	1	0	0	0	0	0	0	0	0	1	0	1	0	0
toils	3	.3772	.2437	33.9	0	0	0	1	1	0	1	0	0	0	0	0	0	0	0	0	1	0	0	0	1	1	0	0	0
toilsome	2	.2411	.1091	30.4	0	0	0	1	0	1	0	0	0	0	0	1	0	0	0	0	1	0	0	0	0	0	0	0	0
Tokay	3	.2432	.1790	32.5	0	0	0	2	0	1	0	0	0	0	0	0	0	2	1	0	0	0	0	0	0	0	0	0	0
token	18	.7276	2.6367	44.2	0	2	3	1	1	4	6	1	0	2	0	2	0	1	1	2	0	0	0	0	1	2	3	4	0
tokens	2	.0000	.0243	23.9	0	0	0	0	0	0	2	0	0	0	0	0	0	0	0	0	0	0	0	0	0	0	0	2	0
Toklug-Timur	2	.0000	.0209	23.2	0	0	0	0	0	2	0	0	0	0	0	0	0	0	0	0	0	0	0	0	0	0	2	0	0
tokonoma	6	.0000	.1167	30.7	0	4	0	0	0	2	0	0	0	0	0	0	0	6	0	0	0	0	0	0	0	0	0	0	0
Tokyo	69	.5288	7.7995	48.9	1	28	24	5	5	1	5	0	8	2	1	0	2	36	0	0	0	0	0	0	0	0	16	4	0
Tokyo's	5	.2956	.3348	35.2	0	1	3	0	0	0	1	0	0	0	0	0	0	1	0	0	0	0	0	0	0	0	3	1	0
Toland	2	.0000	.0914	29.6	0	0	0	0	2	0	0	0	2	0	0	0	0	0	0	0	0	0	0	0	0	0	0	0	0
told	2028	.8716	354.49	65.5	424	466	229	245	324	207	106	27	889	73	9	178	27	131	17	56	29	5	5	1	196	255	18	137	2
tole	7	.1093	.2839	34.5	1	0	4	0	2	0	0	0	2	0	0	0	0	0	0	0	0	0	0	0	5	0	0	0	0
Toledo	3	.3847	.2496	34.0	0	2	0	0	0	1	0	0	0	0	0	0	0	0	0	0	0	0	0	0	0	1	1	1	0
tolerable	2	.2446	.1122	30.5	0	0	0	0	2	0	0	0	0	0	0	1	0	0	0	0	0	0	0	0	0	0	1	0	0
tolerance	6	.5356	.6706	38.3	0	0	1	1	1	0	2	1	0	0	0	1	1	0	0	1	0	0	0	0	0	1	0	2	0
tolerances	3	.1101	.0802	29.0	0	0	0	0	1	0	2	0	0	0	0	0	0	0	0	0	0	0	0	2	0	0	0	1	0
tolerant	9	.5628	1.0515	40.2	1	0	0	0	3	4	1	0	0	0	0	0	0	2	0	1	0	0	0	0	1	1	3	1	0
tolerantly	2	.0000	.0914	29.6	0	0	0	1	1	0	0	0	2	0	0	0	0	0	0	0	0	0	0	0	0	0	0	0	0
tolerate	5	.4860	.5175	37.1	0	0	0	0	2	1	0	2	0	0	0	0	0	0	0	2	0	0	0	0	1	1	0	1	0
tolerated	7	.5375	.7723	38.9	0	0	0	2	0	4	1	0	0	1	1	0	0	1	0	0	0	0	1	0	0	1	2	0	0
toleration	3	.2444	.1814	32.6	0	0	0	0	0	1	2	0	0	0	0	0	0	2	0	0	0	0	0	0	0	0	1	0	0
Toleration	5	.1285	.1797	32.5	0	0	0	0	0	3	2	0	0	0	0	0	0	1	0	0	0	0	0	0	0	0	4	0	0
toll	33	.6412	4.4396	46.5	4	3	3	1	15	5	1	1	11	0	1	0	0	3	0	2	1	0	0	0	0	1	6	8	0
tolled	4	.0000	.1827	32.6	0	2	0	1	1	0	0	0	4	0	0	0	0	0	0	0	0	0	0	0	0	0	0	0	0
tolling	2	.1717	.1142	30.6	0	0	0	1	1	0	0	0	1	0	0	1	0	0	0	0	0	0	0	0	0	0	0	0	0
tolls	8	.4582	.8336	39.2	0	1	1	2	3	0	1	0	3	0	0	0	0	2	0	0	0	0	0	0	0	0	2	1	0
Tolman	7	.0000	.3198	35.0	0	0	7	0	0	0	0	0	7	0	0	0	0	0	0	0	0	0	0	0	0	0	0	0	0
Toltec	6	.0000	.1167	30.7	0	0	0	6	0	0	0	0	0	0	0	0	0	6	0	0	0	0	0	0	0	0	0	0	0
Toltecs	10	.3120	.7330	38.7	0	1	1	8	0	0	0	0	0	0	0	0	0	8	0	0	1	0	0	0	0	0	1	0	0
Tolya	2	.0000	.0914	29.6	2	0	0	0	0	0	0	0	2	0	0	0	0	0	0	0	0	0	0	0	0	0	0	0	0
tom	2	.2376	.1088	30.4	1	0	0	0	1	0	0	0	0	0	0	0	0	0	1	0	0	0	0	0	0	0	0	1	0
Tom	906	.8084	148.80	61.7	234	243	103	95	143	57	28	3	421	52	11	26	83	66	50	0	3	1	1	0	116	53	4	19	0
TOM	2	.1649	.0767	28.8	0	0	0	0	1	0	1	0	0	0	0	0	0	0	0	0	0	0	0	1	1	0	0	0	0
tom-tit	2	.0000	.0219	23.4	2	0	0	0	0	0	0	0	0	2	0	0	0	0	0	0	0	0	0	0	0	0	0	0	0
tom-tom	3	.2058	.1429	31.5	3	0	0	0	0	0	0	0	0	1	0	0	0	0	0	0	2	0	0	0	0	0	0	0	0
tom-toms	4	.3838	.3309	35.2	0	0	2	0	2	0	0	0	0	0	0	0	0	0	0	0	1	0	0	0	0	2	1	0	0
Tom'	4	.0000	.1827	32.6	0	4	0	0	0	0	0	0	4	0	0	0	0	0	0	0	0	0	0	0	0	0	0	0	0
Tom's	106	.7123	15.565	51.9	22	31	11	11	19	7	5	0	34	4	1	0	22	11	8	0	0	0	0	0	18	5	0	3	0
tomahawk	15	.6289	1.9730	43.0	3	5	3	0	3	0	0	1	4	0	0	3	0	1	0	0	0	0	0	0	3	2	1	1	0
Tomahawk	12	.1594	.5136	37.1	0	12	0	0	0	0	0	0	0	0	0	0	0	3	0	0	0	0	0	0	9	0	0	0	0
tomahawks	3	.3873	.2485	34.0	1	0	0	0	2	0	0	0	0	0	0	1	0	0	0	0	0	0	0	0	1	0	1	0	0
Tomahawks	4	.0000	.0469	26.7	0	4	0	0	0	0	0	0	0	0	0	0	0	0	0	0	0	0	0	0	4	0	0	0	0
Tomas	14	.1089	.4679	36.7	0	0	0	1	13	0	0	0	1	0	0	12	0	0	0	0	0	0	0	0	0	1	0	0	0
tomato	45	.4139	4.1430	46.2	8	9	5	2	7	3	10	1	12	1	0	0	5	0	6	1	0	0	14	0	2	2	0	2	0
tomatoes	49	.7514	7.4518	48.7	14	4	5	8	7	5	5	1	5	8	0	2	5	8	0	10	0	0	3	0	4	1	1	2	0
tomb	28	.6719	3.8282	45.8	0	2	1	9	3	5	6	2	1	0	0	1	3	7	0	0	2	2	0	0	2	3	6	1	0
Tomb	2	.2408	.1204	30.8	0	0	0	1	0	1	0	0	0	0	0	0	0	1	0	0	0	0	0	0	0	1	0	0	0
Tombaugh	3	.2437	.2277	33.6	0	1	2	0	0	0	0	0	2	0	0	0	0	0	0	1	0	0	0	0	0	0	0	0	0
Tombeau	2	.0000	.0290	24.6	0	0	0	1	1	0	0	0	0	0	0	0	0	0	0	0	0	0	0	0	0	2	0	0	0
tombo	2	.0000	.0914	29.6	0	2	0	0	0	0	0	0	2	0	0	0	0	0	0	0	0	0	0	0	0	0	0	0	0
tombos	4	.0000	.1827	32.6	0	4	0	0	0	0	0	0	4	0	0	0	0	0	0	0	0	0	0	0	0	0	0	0	0
tomboy	9	.5640	1.1186	40.5	0	1	2	3	2	0	1	0	5	0	0	1	0	0	0	0	0	0	0	0	1	1	0	1	0
tombs	29	.4199	2.6426	44.2	3	3	2	8	3	6	4	0	2	0	0	1	1	10	0	0	0	5	0	0	1	1	8	0	0
tombstone	3	.3394	.2451	33.9	0	0	1	1	1	0	0	0	1	0	0	1	0	0	0	0	0	0	0	0	1	0	0	0	0
tomcat	5	.2025	.3254	35.1	0	3	2	0	0	0	0	0	3	0	0	2	0	0	0	0	0	0	0	0	0	0	0	0	0
tomfoolery	2	.2440	.1132	30.5	0	0	0	0	1	0	1	0	0	0	0	1	0	0	0	0	0	0	0	0	0	0	0	1	0
Tomi	4	.0000	.1827	32.6	0	0	0	4	0	0	0	0	4	0	0	0	0	0	0	0	0	0	0	0	0	0	0	0	0
Tomi's	4	.0000	.1827	32.6	0	0	0	4	0	0	0	0	4	0	0	0	0	0	0	0	0	0	0	0	0	0	0	0	0
Tomiyasu	2	.0000	.0389	25.9	0	0	0	0	0	2	0	0	0	0	0	0	0	2	0	0	0	0	0	0	0	0	0	0	0
Tomlinson	2	.0000	.0290	24.6	0	2	0	0	0	0	0	0	0	0	0	0	0	0	0	0	0	0	0	0	0	2	0	0	0
Tommie	2	.0000	.0243	23.9	0	0	0	0	2	0	0	0	0	0	0	0	0	0	0	0	0	0	0	0	0	0	0	2	0
Tommy	256	.7281	38.374	55.8	143	68	0	20	10	14	1	0	98	1	2	28	12	0	0	0	9	0	3	0	34	56	0	13	0
Tommy's	26	.5881	3.2251	45.1	22	1	0	0	2	1	0	0	6	2	0	5	9	0	0	0	0	0	0	0	1	1	0	2	0
Tomocomo	3	.0000	.0434	26.4	0	3	0	0	0	0	0	0	0	0	0	0	0	0	0	0	0	0	0	0	0	3	0	0	0
Tomohiko	3	.0000	.1370	31.4	3	0	0	0	0	0	0	0	3	0	0	0	0	0	0	0	0	0	0	0	0	0	0	0	0
tomorrow	362	.8326	60.825	57.8	83	85	34	51	58	32	19	0	155	22	9	33	1	14	17	8	4	0	2	3	50	32	1	11	0
tomorrow's	17	.6683	2.3436	43.7	2	1	1	1	6	3	2	1	4	2	1	0	0	0	0	2	0	0	0	1	4	2	1	0	0
Tomos	5	.0000	.2284	33.6	0	5	0	0	0	0	0	0	5	0	0	0	0	0	0	0	0	0	0	0	0	0	0	0	0
Tompkins	2	.1733	.1149	30.6	0	0	1	0	0	0	1	0	1	1	0	0	0	0	0	0	0	0	0	0	0	0	0	0	0
Tomson	6	.0000	.2741	34.4	0	0	6	0	0	0	0	0	6	0	0	0	0	0	0	0	0	0	0	0	0	0	0	0	0
Tomusho	2	.0000	.0243	23.9	0	0	0	0	0	0	2	0	0	0	0	0	0	0	0	0	0	0	0	0	0	0	0	2	0
ton	43	.6577	5.9028	47.7	1	8	5	7	9	9	4	0	13	0	2	0	11	3	2	4	0	0	0	0	0	2	6	0	0
tonal	99	.0161	1.1038	40.4	23	21	19	25	1	9	1	0	0	0	0	0	0	0	0	0	98	0	0	0	0	0	1	0	0
tonality	11	.0000	.0889	29.5	0	0	1	2	3	3	1	1	0	0	0	0	0	0	0	0	11	0	0	0	0	0	0	0	0
tone	484	.5487	54.621	57.4	50	67	45	40	107	112	60	3	35	18	28	28	0	1	0	9	301	4	6	10	16	13	6	9	0
tone-color	2	.0000	.0162	22.1	0	2	0	0	0	0	0	0	0	0	0	0	0	0	0	0	2	0	0	0	0	0	0	0	0
tone-row	4	.0000	.0323	25.1	0	0	0	1	0	3	0	0	0	0	0	0	0	0	0	0	4	0	0	0	0	0	0	0	0
tones	275	.3545	20.742	53.2	18	55	56	41	58	37	10	0	8	1	0	2	0	0	0	1	226	17	2	5	5	4	2	2	0

4N toe's
7A toehold
6A toeholds
7H toenail
8D Toes
3A toeses
7N toff
6N toffee
9B toga
8R togged

7P Togoland
5P toheroa
XR Tohopekaliga
3Q toilet-trained
7R toilets
XB toity
6A Toji
6A Toji's
7R Toklat
6R Tokyo-to-Osaka

8D Tolan
9J Told
7A tolerably
9Q tolerates
7B Tolgo
3R Tolland
8B tollhouse
8A Tolliver
7Q tollways
5A Tolman's

6N toluache
3A Toluca
5A Tolvin
8N tom-cat
6N tom-noddy
6A Tomasson
XR Tomato
7A tomato-and-lettuce
6P tomato-faced
4A tombo's

9L tomboyish
3A tomboys
4R tombstones
4A tomcat'
7R Tommie's
7R Tommonsville
7D tommy
3D TOMMY
6A tommygun
5A tommyknockers

8B Tommys
8P tomtoms
8J tonalities
6F Tonalpohualli
7G tonare
7M Tone
3J tone-the
7D toneless
7D tonelessly
4G tonelle

Word Type	F	D	U	SFI	3 Gr 3	4 Gr 4	5 Gr 5	6 Gr 6	7 Gr 7	8 Gr 8	9 Gr 9	X UnGr	A Read	B Eng & Gr	C Comp	D Lit	E Math	F Soc Stud	G Spell	H Sci	J Music	K Art	L Home Ec	M Shop	N Lib F	P Lib NF	Q Lib Ref	R Mag	S Rel
Tonga	4	.0000	.1827	32.6	0	0	0	4	0	0	0	0	4	0	0	0	0	0	0	0	0	0	0	0	0	0	0	0	0
Tongass	2	.0000	.0389	25.9	0	0	2	0	0	0	0	0	0	0	0	0	0	2	0	0	0	0	0	0	0	0	0	0	0
tongs	12	.5253	1.3678	41.4	4	3	0	1	2	1	1	0	4	0	0	0	0	0	0	3	3	0	1	1	0	0	0	0	0
tongue	281	.8823	49.362	56.9	48	41	22	42	63	22	17	26	58	18	4	31	0	3	6	50	9	2	1	8	50	14	13	13	1
Tongue	3	.2435	.2274	33.6	0	0	0	0	2	1	0	0	2	0	0	0	0	1	0	0	0	0	0	0	0	0	0	0	0
tongue-and-groove	2	.0000	.0050	17.0	0	0	0	0	0	2	0	0	0	0	0	0	0	0	0	0	0	0	0	2	0	0	0	0	0
tongue-lashing	2	.0000	.0290	24.6	0	2	0	0	0	0	0	0	0	0	0	0	0	0	0	0	0	0	0	0	0	2	0	0	0
tongue's	2	.0000	.0215	23.3	0	0	0	0	0	0	2	0	0	0	0	2	0	0	0	0	0	0	0	0	0	0	0	0	0
tongued	2	.2411	.1091	30.4	0	0	0	0	1	1	0	0	0	0	0	1	0	0	0	0	1	0	0	0	0	0	0	0	0
tongues	48	.7448	7.2391	48.6	5	10	3	4	11	5	9	1	8	4	0	9	0	2	3	3	5	0	0	0	2	5	7	0	0
tonguing	4	.0759	.1243	30.9	0	0	0	1	2	1	0	0	1	0	0	0	0	0	0	0	3	0	0	0	0	0	0	0	0
Toni's	2	.0000	.0243	23.9	0	0	0	0	0	0	0	2	0	0	0	0	0	0	0	0	0	0	0	0	0	0	0	2	0
tonic	26	.1310	1.0124	40.1	0	0	7	14	1	1	3	0	4	0	0	0	0	3	0	0	19	0	0	0	0	0	0	0	0
Tonic	2	.0000	.0914	29.6	0	0	0	0	0	2	0	0	2	0	0	0	0	0	0	0	0	0	0	0	0	0	0	0	0
tonics	2	.1787	.1174	30.7	0	0	0	1	1	0	0	0	1	0	0	0	0	0	0	0	0	0	0	0	1	0	0	0	0
tonight	218	.7390	33.208	55.2	37	52	14	28	31	27	28	1	99	9	4	30	0	7	2	2	8	0	0	0	30	23	0	4	0
Tonight	2	.0000	.0162	22.1	0	0	0	0	0	0	2	0	0	0	0	0	0	0	0	0	2	0	0	0	0	0	0	0	0
tonight's	7	.2115	.3607	35.6	0	1	3	0	2	0	0	1	1	0	3	0	0	0	0	0	0	0	0	0	1	0	0	0	0
tonights	2	.0000	.0219	23.4	0	0	0	0	0	1	1	0	0	2	0	0	0	0	0	0	0	0	0	0	0	0	0	2	0
tonnage	2	.0000	.0299	24.8	0	0	0	2	0	0	0	0	0	0	0	0	2	0	0	0	0	0	0	0	0	0	0	0	0
tonneau	2	.1814	.1187	30.7	0	0	1	1	0	0	0	0	1	0	0	0	0	0	0	0	0	0	0	0	0	0	0	1	0
tons	157	.7955	25.165	54.0	13	21	18	23	41	16	22	3	26	1	1	1	15	19	0	20	2	0	0	4	3	17	27	21	0
tonsils	2	.1787	.1174	30.7	0	2	0	0	0	0	0	0	1	0	0	0	0	0	0	0	0	0	0	0	1	0	0	0	0
Tonty	6	.0000	.1167	30.7	0	0	6	0	0	0	0	0	0	0	0	0	0	6	0	0	0	0	0	0	0	0	0	0	0
Tony	166	.6070	22.076	53.4	51	58	6	25	14	6	5	1	113	2	1	0	8	0	5	0	0	0	0	0	25	3	0	9	0
Tony's	18	.3575	1.7250	42.4	5	8	0	3	1	1	0	0	15	0	0	0	0	0	1	0	0	0	0	0	2	0	0	0	0
too	5071	.9623	963.45	69.8	1241	1005	536	623	806	434	329	97	1609	219	58	282	43	433	83	574	115	35	86	35	438	613	145	300	3
Too	3	.2332	.1690	32.3	0	0	1	0	2	0	0	0	0	0	0	0	0	0	0	0	0	0	0	0	0	2	0	1	0
Too-Too	2	.0000	.0234	23.7	0	2	0	0	0	0	0	0	0	0	0	0	0	0	0	0	0	0	0	0	2	0	0	0	0
toodum	12	.0000	.0970	29.9	0	0	0	0	12	0	0	0	0	0	0	0	0	0	0	0	12	0	0	0	0	0	0	0	0
took	2490	.8891	442.22	66.5	532	490	276	321	422	270	136	43	971	62	15	189	74	241	24	76	37	5	1	3	294	242	85	167	4
tool	184	.4340	16.901	52.3	11	14	8	18	46	36	45	6	16	6	1	5	6	5	6	19	1	6	1	73	0	9	15	15	0
Tool	5	.3726	.4014	36.0	0	1	1	0	1	0	2	0	0	1	0	0	0	0	0	0	0	0	0	0	0	0	2	2	0
tooled	4	.3080	.2543	34.1	0	1	0	0	3	0	0	0	0	0	0	1	0	0	0	0	0	1	0	2	0	0	0	0	0
toolholder	5	.0000	.0126	21.0	0	0	0	0	0	0	5	0	0	0	0	0	0	0	0	0	0	0	0	5	0	0	0	0	0
tooling	4	.0935	.0899	29.5	1	0	0	0	3	0	0	0	0	0	0	0	0	0	0	0	0	0	0	3	0	0	1	0	0
toolmaking	2	.0000	.0209	23.2	0	0	0	0	2	0	0	0	0	0	0	0	0	0	0	0	0	0	0	0	0	0	2	0	0
toolrest	2	.0000	.0243	23.9	0	0	0	0	2	0	0	0	0	0	0	0	0	0	0	0	0	0	0	0	0	0	0	2	0
tools	379	.7076	54.450	57.4	46	40	35	49	111	35	54	9	44	8	7	7	17	77	0	39	3	16	4	70	6	26	37	17	1
Tools	3	.0000	.0076	18.8	0	0	0	0	2	1	0	0	0	0	0	0	0	0	0	0	0	0	0	3	0	0	0	0	0
Toombs	3	.2435	.2274	33.6	0	0	0	0	2	1	0	0	2	0	0	0	0	1	0	0	0	0	0	0	0	0	0	0	0
toot	15	.4442	1.5975	42.0	5	5	2	0	3	0	0	0	10	1	0	0	0	0	0	0	0	0	0	0	0	1	0	3	0
tooted	8	.4764	.8926	39.5	1	2	1	1	1	1	1	0	5	0	0	0	0	1	0	0	0	0	0	0	0	1	0	1	0
tooters	2	.0000	.0914	29.6	0	0	0	0	2	0	0	0	2	0	0	0	0	0	0	0	0	0	0	0	0	0	0	0	0
tooth	91	.7720	14.160	51.5	26	8	17	4	26	5	5	0	7	4	0	5	0	0	10	36	1	0	2	1	6	14	2	3	0
toothache	5	.4730	.5355	37.3	0	0	0	2	2	1	0	0	2	1	0	0	0	0	0	1	0	0	0	0	0	0	0	1	0
Toothaker	4	.0000	.0469	26.7	0	0	4	0	0	0	0	0	0	0	0	0	0	0	0	0	0	0	0	0	4	0	0	0	0
toothbrush	7	.3813	.6823	38.3	5	0	0	1	1	0	0	0	5	0	0	0	0	0	0	0	0	0	0	0	0	1	0	1	0
toothbrushes	4	.4574	.4121	36.2	2	0	1	1	0	0	0	0	1	0	0	0	0	1	0	1	0	0	0	0	0	0	0	1	0
toothed	6	.3343	.4412	36.4	4	0	0	0	1	0	1	0	0	0	1	0	0	0	0	0	0	0	0	0	0	4	1	0	0
toothpaste	18	.4541	1.8183	42.6	2	1	9	2	1	0	0	3	3	0	0	0	1	0	0	9	0	0	0	0	4	0	0	1	0
toothpick	22	.5103	2.4528	43.9	10	0	1	3	3	2	2	1	5	1	0	0	0	0	0	11	0	0	2	0	0	2	0	1	0
toothpicks	22	.3378	1.6908	42.3	1	12	0	8	0	0	1	0	2	1	0	0	5	0	0	6	0	5	0	0	0	3	0	0	0
tooting	3	.0397	.0716	28.5	1	1	0	0	1	0	0	0	1	0	2	0	0	0	0	0	0	0	0	0	0	0	0	0	0
tootle	3	.1852	.1342	31.3	2	0	1	0	0	0	0	0	0	0	0	0	0	0	0	0	2	0	0	0	0	1	0	0	0
Tootles	9	.0000	.4111	36.1	0	0	0	9	0	0	0	0	9	0	0	0	0	0	0	0	0	0	0	0	0	0	0	0	0
toots	4	.1497	.2092	33.2	2	2	0	0	0	0	0	0	2	0	0	0	0	0	2	0	0	0	0	0	0	0	0	0	0
Toots	3	.0000	.0352	25.5	0	0	0	0	0	3	0	0	0	0	0	0	0	0	0	0	0	0	0	0	3	0	0	0	0
Toozle	2	.0000	.0914	29.6	2	0	0	0	0	0	0	0	2	0	0	0	0	0	0	0	0	0	0	0	0	0	0	0	0
top	1741	.9222	318.46	65.0	429	308	213	174	267	176	135	39	468	57	18	71	116	119	52	248	35	17	77	68	86	144	49	116	0
Top	20	.4474	1.9367	42.9	1	7	6	1	4	0	0	1	3	0	0	0	0	0	0	0	7	0	0	0	0	4	1	5	0
top-grade	3	.1277	.1363	31.3	1	0	0	0	2	0	0	0	1	0	0	0	0	0	0	0	0	0	0	0	0	0	0	2	0
top-heavy	3	.2181	.1541	31.9	0	1	0	0	1	1	0	0	0	0	0	0	0	0	0	0	0	0	0	0	1	0	2	0	0
top-rated	2	.0000	.0243	23.9	0	0	0	1	0	0	1	0	0	0	0	0	0	0	0	0	0	0	0	0	0	0	0	2	0
top-stitch	2	.0000	.0064	18.1	0	0	0	0	0	1	1	0	0	0	0	0	0	0	0	0	0	0	2	0	0	0	0	0	0
topaz	2	.2331	.1157	30.6	0	0	0	0	1	0	0	1	0	0	0	0	0	0	0	1	0	0	0	0	1	0	0	0	0
topcoat	2	.1605	.0742	28.7	0	0	0	0	1	1	0	0	0	1	1	0	0	0	0	0	0	0	0	0	0	0	0	0	0
Topeka	3	.1639	.1674	32.2	0	2	1	0	0	0	0	0	1	0	0	0	0	2	0	0	0	0	0	0	0	0	0	0	0
topic	370	.3822	30.507	54.8	7	35	52	30	106	62	77	1	25	212	75	2	8	6	20	11	1	0	0	0	0	3	3	4	0
Topic	2	.2300	.1140	30.6	0	0	0	0	0	0	2	0	0	1	0	0	0	0	0	1	0	0	0	0	0	0	0	0	0
topical	5	.2418	.2811	34.5	0	2	0	0	2	0	1	0	0	0	0	0	0	0	0	0	0	0	0	0	0	0	2	3	0
topics	103	.5447	11.753	50.7	2	15	22	14	25	14	10	1	14	55	9	0	4	2	0	5	3	1	0	0	0	1	6	3	0
Topics	2	.2412	.1141	30.6	0	1	0	0	1	0	0	0	0	1	0	0	0	0	0	0	0	0	0	0	0	1	0	0	0
topmast	2	.0000	.0914	29.6	0	0	0	2	0	0	0	0	2	0	0	0	0	0	0	0	0	0	0	0	0	0	0	0	0
topmost	9	.5024	.9989	40.0	1	0	1	3	3	0	1	0	3	0	1	0	0	2	0	1	0	0	0	0	1	0	0	1	0
topographic	9	.3552	.7017	38.5	0	3	0	0	0	4	2	0	0	0	0	0	0	0	0	3	0	0	0	1	0	0	5	0	0
topographical	2	.2446	.1123	30.5	1	0	0	0	0	0	1	0	0	1	0	0	0	0	0	0	0	0	0	0	0	0	1	0	0
topography	11	.3533	.8629	39.4	0	2	1	0	2	1	3	2	0	0	0	0	0	2	0	2	0	0	0	0	0	0	6	1	0
topological	9	.0000	.1347	31.3	0	0	0	0	0	9	0	0	0	0	0	0	9	0	0	0	0	0	0	0	0	0	0	0	0
topologically	4	.1711	.1729	32.4	0	3	0	0	0	1	0	0	0	0	0	0	1	0	0	0	0	0	0	0	0	0	3	0	0
topologists	2	.2391	.1133	30.5	0	1	0	0	0	1	0	0	0	0	0	0	1	0	0	0	0	0	0	0	0	0	1	0	0
topology	35	.0982	1.1397	40.6	0	2	0	0	0	33	0	0	0	0	0	0	33	0	0	0	0	0	0	0	0	0	2	0	0
topped	25	.5046	2.7408	44.4	0	0	3	5	7	5	4	1	7	0	0	2	0	4	0	0	0	0	4	0	2	0	0	6	0
topper	3	.3189	.2058	33.1	0	0	0	0	0	1	1	1	0	0	0	1	0	0	0	0	0	0	1	0	0	0	0	1	0
topping	3	.3390	.2450	33.9	1	0	0	0	2	0	0	0	1	0	0	0	0	0	0	0	0	0	0	0	0	0	1	1	0
topple	9	.5644	1.0627	40.3	3	0	0	0	1	3	2	0	1	0	1	1	0	2	0	0	0	0	0	0	1	1	0	2	0
toppled	10	.5576	1.1981	40.8	1	4	0	1	2	2	0	0	3	0	1	0	0	1	0	1	0	0	0	0	1	2	0	1	0
toppling	3	.2357	.2199	33.4	1	0	0	2	0	0	0	0	2	0	0	0	0	0	0	0	0	0	0	0	0	1	0	0	0
tops	164	.9153	29.766	54.7	39	35	18	21	23	11	12	5	30	2	5	5	3	20	5	28	7	4	4	1	11	12	14	13	0
TOPS	5	.0000	.0608	27.8	0	5	0	0	0	0	0	0	0	0	0	0	0	0	0	0	0	0	0	0	0	0	0	5	0
topsail	2	.2417	.1091	30.4	0	0	0	0	1	0	1	0	0	0	0	0	0	0	0	0	1	0	0	0	0	0	1	0	0
topside	7	.1726	.3988	36.0	0	3	0	4	0	0	0	0	3	0	0	0	0	0	0	0	0	0	0	0	0	4	0	0	0

7A Tongelow
6H TONGUE
7R tongue-defying
XH tongue-inflamation
4N tongue-tied
6J tongue-twister
6R tongue-twisting
9Q tongue-wagging
7Q tongueless
5A tonic-good
3A Tonio
8R Tonkin
9J Tonkurst
3A tonnages
5A tonne
7D Tonquas
7A tonsil
7R tonsillectomy
9H tonsillitis
XR Tonto
8N tony
6P TOO
8N too-bold
8F too-complicated
3A too-large
7A too-often
8A too-soon
6R Tooele
4Q Took
9M tool-
9M tool-and-die
9M tool-steel
4A toolbox
6G toolechest
7R toolkit
9F toolmaker
9D toolroom
3P TOOLS
3A toolshed
6A toom
4P tooter
7R tooth-rimmed
5A toothaches
5H toothbrushing
9R toothless
7R toothpastes
6D tootingest
4P tootled
9D top-hat
6N top-hats
9R top-name
4A top-notch
6J top-o
3P top-of-the-order
5F top-quality
9D top-rating
5J top-sail
7F top-secret
4P top-shaped
8K top-side
9L top-stitched
8L top-stitching
7R top-water
7F topclass
5A tope
7P topflight
5N topgallant
7Q topgrade
7H topheavy
4Q topical-plan
6A topknot
8R topless
XR topline
9A topnotch
8H Topographic
4Q TOPOGRAPHY
7L Topping
4J topses

Word Type	F	D	U	SFI	3 Gr 3	4 Gr 4	5 Gr 5	6 Gr 6	7 Gr 7	8 Gr 8	9 Gr 9	X UnGr	A Read	B Eng & Gr	C Comp	D Lit	E Math	F Soc Stud	G Spell	H Sci	J Music	K Art	L Home Ec	M Shop	N Lib F	P Lib NF	Q Lib Ref	R Mag	S Rel
topsoil	14	.4592	1.3994	41.5	2	0	3	1	3	1	1	3	0	0	0	0	0	4	0	6	0	0	0	0	0	3	0	1	0
topsy-turvy	5	.4685	.5252	37.2	1	2	0	0	1	1	0	0	2	0	0	0	0	0	1	0	0	0	0	0	0	0	1	1	0
Tor	9	.0000	.1750	32.4	0	9	0	0	0	0	0	0	0	0	0	0	0	9	0	0	0	0	0	0	0	0	0	0	0
Torad	15	.0000	.6852	38.4	15	0	0	0	0	0	0	0	15	0	0	0	0	0	0	0	0	0	0	0	0	0	0	0	0
Torad's	2	.0000	.0914	29.6	2	0	0	0	0	0	0	0	2	0	0	0	0	0	0	0	0	0	0	0	0	0	0	0	0
Torah	5	.0000	.0404	26.1	0	0	0	0	0	0	5	0	0	0	0	0	0	0	0	0	5	0	0	0	0	0	0	0	0
torch	28	.5551	3.4094	45.3	3	4	2	3	7	6	3	0	15	1	1	1	0	1	0	1	2	0	0	4	2	0	0	0	0
torchbearer	2	.0000	.0215	23.3	0	0	0	0	0	0	2	0	0	0	0	2	0	0	0	0	0	0	0	0	0	0	0	0	0
torches	24	.5861	3.0086	44.8	4	1	2	6	9	0	2	0	9	0	0	7	0	1	0	0	1	0	0	0	2	2	0	2	0
torchlight	2	.1494	.1045	30.2	0	0	1	0	0	1	0	0	1	0	0	0	0	0	0	0	1	0	0	0	0	0	0	0	0
tore	76	.7493	11.646	50.7	5	18	14	13	13	3	9	1	28	6	0	5	0	1	0	0	5	1	0	0	16	5	6	3	0
toreador	5	.0000	.0404	26.1	0	0	0	0	1	4	0	0	0	0	0	0	0	0	0	0	5	0	0	0	0	0	0	0	0
Toreador	3	.0000	.0243	23.8	1	0	0	0	2	0	0	0	0	0	0	0	0	0	0	0	3	0	0	0	0	0	0	0	0
Tories	6	.4302	.5748	37.6	0	1	1	0	0	4	0	0	1	0	0	0	0	2	0	0	0	0	0	0	2	0	1	0	0
torment	8	.5111	.8642	39.4	0	0	1	1	3	0	3	0	1	0	1	1	0	0	0	0	0	0	0	0	1	3	1	0	0
tormented	10	.4279	.9356	39.7	0	1	1	1	2	0	5	0	1	0	0	1	0	0	0	0	0	0	0	0	1	6	1	0	0
tormenting	3	.3847	.2494	34.0	0	0	0	0	1	1	1	0	0	0	0	0	0	0	0	0	0	0	0	0	1	1	1	0	0
torments	3	.3380	.2439	33.9	0	0	0	1	1	1	0	0	1	1	0	1	0	0	0	0	0	0	0	0	0	0	0	0	0
torn	147	.8837	25.907	54.1	30	25	12	22	26	12	18	2	42	10	5	11	1	15	4	11	1	3	0	3	14	16	4	7	0
tornado	48	.5898	6.0476	47.8	2	1	8	11	2	7	14	3	13	4	0	1	0	1	2	22	0	0	0	0	0	1	0	4	0
tornado's	3	.0000	.0591	27.7	0	0	0	0	0	0	3	0	0	0	0	0	0	0	0	3	0	0	0	0	0	0	0	0	0
tornadoes	16	.5019	1.7307	42.4	1	1	1	4	0	0	7	2	1	0	0	0	0	1	0	9	0	0	0	0	0	2	1	2	0
Toronto	6	.2955	.3942	36.0	0	1	2	0	1	1	1	0	0	1	0	0	0	0	0	0	0	0	0	0	0	0	4	1	0
torpedo	8	.4625	.8334	39.2	0	0	0	2	5	1	0	0	3	0	0	1	0	0	0	0	0	0	0	0	0	2	2	0	0
torpedoes	7	.3232	.5507	37.4	0	0	0	2	4	0	0	1	2	0	0	0	0	0	0	0	0	0	0	0	0	2	0	3	0
torque	5	.0000	.0608	27.8	0	0	0	0	5	0	0	0	0	0	0	0	0	0	0	0	0	0	0	0	0	0	0	5	0
torques	2	.2427	.1159	30.6	0	0	0	0	1	1	0	0	0	0	0	0	1	0	0	0	0	0	0	0	0	0	0	1	0
Torrance	2	.2351	.1166	30.7	0	0	2	0	0	0	0	0	0	0	0	0	0	1	0	0	0	0	0	0	0	0	0	1	0
torrent	19	.6650	2.6002	44.2	1	1	0	7	7	2	0	1	4	2	0	5	0	0	0	0	1	0	0	0	1	1	2	3	0
torrential	3	.3553	.2608	34.2	1	0	0	0	0	1	1	0	1	0	0	0	0	1	0	0	0	0	0	0	0	1	0	0	0
torrents	14	.5234	1.6022	42.0	2	0	1	2	6	0	1	2	4	0	0	0	0	4	0	1	0	0	0	0	2	0	0	3	0
Torres	15	.3496	1.3168	41.2	8	0	0	0	0	5	2	0	8	0	0	5	0	0	0	0	0	0	0	0	0	0	2	0	0
Torrey	4	.0000	.0486	26.9	0	0	0	0	4	0	0	0	0	0	0	0	0	0	0	0	0	0	0	0	0	0	0	4	0
torrid	3	.3776	.2493	34.0	0	0	0	0	1	0	2	0	0	1	0	0	0	0	0	1	0	0	0	0	0	0	0	1	0
Torrington	3	.2279	.2143	33.3	0	0	0	2	1	0	0	0	2	0	0	0	0	0	0	0	0	0	0	0	0	0	0	1	0
torsion	7	.2205	.3670	35.6	0	0	0	0	7	0	0	0	0	0	0	0	0	0	0	0	0	0	0	0	0	0	2	5	0
Torstein	17	.2505	1.0401	40.2	0	0	0	0	2	5	10	0	2	0	0	10	0	0	0	0	0	0	0	0	0	5	0	0	0
tortilla	3	.3832	.2448	33.9	0	1	0	0	1	1	0	0	0	0	0	1	0	0	1	0	0	0	0	0	1	0	0	0	0
tortillas	8	.5935	.9927	40.0	2	2	0	2	0	2	0	0	1	0	0	1	0	3	0	0	1	0	0	0	1	0	0	1	0
tortoise	17	.4222	1.7005	42.3	13	0	1	0	2	1	0	0	9	5	0	0	1	0	0	0	0	0	0	0	0	0	2	0	0
Tortoise	3	.0000	.0328	25.2	0	0	3	0	0	0	0	0	0	3	0	0	0	0	0	0	0	0	0	0	0	0	0	0	0
tortoise-shell	3	.3874	.2487	34.0	0	0	0	0	2	1	0	0	0	1	0	0	0	0	0	0	0	0	0	0	1	0	1	0	0
tortoises	6	.3257	.4333	36.4	2	0	0	0	4	0	0	0	0	2	0	0	0	0	0	1	0	0	0	0	0	0	3	0	0
tortuous	3	.2120	.1548	31.9	0	0	1	0	1	0	1	0	0	0	0	0	0	0	0	0	0	0	0	0	2	1	0	0	0
torture	16	.5622	1.9151	42.8	0	1	1	2	5	2	3	2	4	0	0	3	0	1	0	0	0	0	0	0	4	3	0	1	0
tortured	14	.5218	1.5824	42.0	1	2	0	2	4	2	2	1	4	0	0	0	0	2	0	0	1	1	0	0	0	1	0	5	0
tortures	3	.3418	.2483	33.9	0	0	0	1	0	1	0	1	1	1	0	0	0	0	0	0	0	0	0	0	0	1	0	0	0
torturing	2	.1717	.1142	30.6	0	0	0	0	0	2	0	0	1	0	0	1	0	0	0	0	0	0	0	0	0	0	0	0	0
Toru	13	.1573	.8803	39.4	0	13	0	0	0	0	0	0	12	0	0	0	0	1	0	0	0	0	0	0	0	0	0	0	0
Torwal	11	.0000	.1180	30.7	0	0	6	5	0	0	0	0	0	0	0	11	0	0	0	0	0	0	0	0	0	0	0	0	0
Tory	14	.3860	1.3645	41.3	0	0	0	4	5	3	0	2	9	0	0	0	0	3	0	0	0	0	0	0	2	0	0	0	0
Toslow	2	.0000	.0162	22.1	0	0	0	2	0	0	0	0	0	0	0	0	0	0	0	0	2	0	0	0	0	0	0	0	0
toss	58	.7546	8.9946	49.5	11	5	5	10	12	14	0	1	25	1	0	1	10	2	0	6	2	0	2	0	1	2	0	6	0
tossed	141	.8557	24.247	53.8	24	32	15	22	19	24	5	0	60	4	3	13	5	8	0	1	8	1	2	0	10	20	2	4	0
tosses	18	.6166	2.3459	43.7	4	2	3	3	2	2	2	0	6	0	0	1	4	0	0	1	3	0	0	0	0	2	0	1	0
tossing	47	.7791	7.4669	48.7	4	15	5	6	8	5	3	1	19	3	1	6	1	0	0	4	1	0	0	0	4	6	1	1	0
tot	2	.1717	.1142	30.6	0	0	0	0	2	0	0	0	1	0	0	1	0	0	0	0	0	0	0	0	0	0	0	0	0
total	531	.7324	78.636	59.0	51	59	73	62	119	67	82	18	21	5	3	3	255	56	5	32	2	1	7	11	3	30	40	57	0
TOTAL	2	.0000	.0914	29.6	0	2	0	0	0	0	0	0	2	0	0	0	0	0	0	0	0	0	0	0	0	0	0	0	0
totaled	7	.4379	.6559	38.2	0	0	1	1	0	1	4	0	0	0	0	0	0	1	0	0	0	0	0	0	0	2	1	3	0
totaling	8	.3450	.5900	37.7	0	1	0	0	3	0	3	1	0	0	0	0	0	0	0	0	0	0	2	0	0	0	4	2	0
totalitarian	4	.2285	.2258	33.5	0	0	0	0	0	2	2	0	0	0	0	0	0	2	0	0	0	0	0	0	0	0	2	0	0
totality	2	.0000	.0209	23.2	0	0	0	0	1	0	1	0	0	0	0	0	0	0	0	0	0	0	0	0	0	0	2	0	0
totally	32	.6482	4.2579	46.3	0	0	3	3	13	5	5	3	3	1	0	5	0	2	0	3	1	0	0	0	0	3	3	11	0
totals	10	.3616	.8215	39.1	1	0	3	1	3	0	0	2	1	0	0	0	4	1	0	0	0	0	0	0	0	0	0	4	0
tote	7	.5292	.7626	38.8	0	0	0	1	4	1	1	0	0	0	0	0	0	0	0	0	1	0	1	0	2	1	0	2	0
toted	2	.1787	.1174	30.7	0	0	0	0	1	1	0	0	1	0	0	0	0	0	0	0	0	0	0	0	1	0	0	0	0
totem	11	.3718	.9622	39.8	0	0	2	4	5	0	0	0	4	0	0	1	0	2	2	0	0	2	0	0	0	0	0	0	0
totes	3	.1983	.1396	31.4	0	2	0	0	0	1	0	0	0	0	0	0	0	0	0	0	2	0	0	0	0	0	0	1	0
toting	3	.3399	.2456	33.9	1	0	0	0	2	0	0	0	1	0	0	1	0	0	0	0	0	0	0	0	0	0	0	1	0
Toto	9	.2394	.7075	38.5	8	0	1	0	0	0	0	0	8	0	0	0	0	0	0	0	1	0	0	0	0	0	0	0	0
tottered	2	.2446	.1142	30.6	0	0	0	0	2	0	0	0	0	0	0	0	0	0	0	0	0	0	0	0	1	0	0	1	0
tottering	5	.4122	.4599	36.6	1	0	0	1	2	1	0	0	1	0	0	2	0	0	0	0	0	0	0	0	1	1	0	0	0
totting	3	.2261	.2131	33.3	0	0	0	2	1	0	0	0	2	0	0	0	0	0	0	0	0	0	0	0	1	0	0	0	0
touch	432	.8573	73.923	58.7	74	72	36	56	83	41	58	12	76	22	29	31	7	21	3	93	11	10	10	11	35	32	12	29	0
Touch	2	.1733	.1149	30.6	1	0	0	1	0	0	0	0	1	1	0	0	0	0	0	0	0	0	0	0	0	0	0	0	0
Touch-and-Tell	3	.0000	.0434	26.4	3	0	0	0	0	0	0	0	0	0	0	0	0	0	0	0	0	0	0	0	0	3	0	0	0
touchdown	14	.5944	1.7359	42.4	0	0	3	2	2	2	5	0	2	2	0	0	1	0	0	2	1	0	0	0	1	0	0	5	0
Touchdown	2	.0000	.0243	23.9	0	0	0	1	1	0	0	0	0	0	0	0	0	0	0	0	0	0	0	0	0	0	0	2	0
touchdowns	3	.2300	.1627	32.1	0	0	0	1	2	0	0	0	0	1	0	0	0	0	0	0	0	0	0	0	0	0	0	2	0
touched	198	.7996	32.085	55.1	31	31	19	27	40	22	23	5	71	3	5	28	1	10	0	14	1	2	0	1	35	16	3	8	0
touches	102	.8199	16.795	52.3	16	15	11	21	19	8	10	2	17	1	3	7	2	14	1	26	5	0	0	5	2	5	5	9	0
touching	90	.8603	15.435	51.9	9	13	10	8	23	11	12	4	12	2	5	8	2	2	1	21	1	1	2	1	9	12	5	6	0
touchy	4	.4851	.4029	36.1	0	0	1	0	1	2	0	0	0	1	0	1	0	0	1	0	0	0	0	0	0	0	0	1	0
tough	173	.8599	29.782	54.7	22	12	22	23	51	24	15	4	49	6	0	9	0	13	5	19	2	0	1	4	9	25	11	20	0
tough-looking	2	.1733	.1149	30.6	0	0	0	0	1	0	1	0	1	1	0	0	0	0	0	0	0	0	0	0	0	0	0	0	0
toughened	2	.1717	.1142	30.6	0	0	1	0	0	1	0	0	1	0	0	1	0	0	0	0	0	0	0	0	0	0	0	0	0
tougher	13	.6666	1.7941	42.5	2	2	3	1	4	1	0	0	3	2	0	1	0	2	0	0	0	0	0	0	1	2	0	2	0
toughest	8	.5692	.9453	39.8	0	2	3	0	1	1	1	0	1	0	1	0	0	0	0	0	1	0	0	0	1	1	1	2	0
toughness	14	.2864	.8516	39.3	0	1	2	1	1	0	9	0	0	0	0	0	0	1	0	0	0	1	0	8	0	1	2	1	0
Toulon	2	.2446	.1122	30.5	1	0	0	0	0	1	0	0	0	0	0	1	0	0	0	0	0	0	0	0	0	0	1	0	0
Toulouse	5	.2904	.3732	35.7	1	0	0	0	0	0	3	1	1	0	0	0	0	3	0	1	0	0	0	0	0	0	0	0	0
Toulouse-Lautrec	2	.0000	.0037	15.7	0	1	0	0	0	1	0	0	0	0	0	0	0	0	0	0	0	2	0	0	0	0	0	0	0
tour	51	.6240	6.6043	48.2	2	7	4	7	9	10	10	2	7	2	0	1	1	11	0	0	3	0	0	0	1	5	1	19	0
toured	10	.5608	1.1521	40.6	0	1	2	0	4	2	0	1	0	0	1	1	0	1	0	0	2	0	0	0	0	2	0	3	0

6A topsides
9L topstitching
3P Topsy
5G tor
6Q Torbjorn
5Q Torch
9D torchbearers
6A torchlights
5G tord
8J toreadors
8N tormentin'
5N tormentors
4K torn-paper
3Q torn-up
7R Toronto's
9R torpedoed
7F torpid
8R torpor
7R TorqueFlites
8R Torre
3A Torreses'
8A Tors
9Q torso
XJ torsos
7A Torstein's
7D torturer
4A Toru's
5D Torwal's
6A Tory-lovers
8J Tosca
8P tosh
8E Toss
5R toss-up
7Q tossup
5R Totem
7N totems
XR totted
7P totter'd
5A totters
8F tou-fu
7R toucans
7P touch'd
7P touchable
8A touchin'
6A touchiness
3A touchstone
8R tough-guy
XD tough-minded
7D tough-talking
6N toughening
8B toune
XR Tourer

Word Type	F	D	U	SFI	3 Gr 3	4 Gr 4	5 Gr 5	6 Gr 6	7 Gr 7	8 Gr 8	9 Gr 9	X UnGr	A Read	B Eng & Gr	C Comp	D Lit	E Math	F Soc Stud	G Spell	H Sci	J Music	K Art	L Home Ec	M Shop	N Lib F	P Lib NF	Q Lib Ref	R Mag	S Rel
touring	8	.4347	.7942	39.0	0	1	2	2	1	0	1	1	3	0	0	0	0	0	0	0	1	0	0	0	0	1	0	3	0
tourism	5	.4552	.4847	36.9	0	0	1	2	2	0	0	0	0	0	0	0	0	1	0	0	0	0	0	0	0	1	1	2	0
tourist	39	.7767	6.1103	47.9	5	3	12	4	5	2	6	2	6	2	1	2	0	7	0	0	0	0	0	1	2	6	5	7	0
tourists	67	.6879	9.5284	49.8	15	10	15	13	7	2	3	2	15	4	1	2	0	31	0	0	0	1	0	0	0	2	6	5	0
tourmaline	2	.0000	.0394	26.0	0	0	0	0	0	0	0	2	0	0	0	0	0	0	0	2	0	0	0	0	0	0	0	0	0
tournament	24	.5266	2.8179	44.5	0	2	7	6	5	1	2	1	11	1	0	0	0	7	1	0	0	0	0	0	0	0	0	4	0
tournaments	6	.3454	.5085	37.1	0	1	1	1	1	1	0	1	2	0	0	0	0	2	0	0	0	0	0	0	0	0	0	2	0
tourniquet	2	.0000	.0394	26.0	0	0	0	0	0	0	2	0	0	0	0	0	0	0	0	2	0	0	0	0	0	0	0	0	0
tours	7	.4304	.6531	38.1	0	0	2	2	0	1	2	0	1	0	0	0	0	0	0	0	3	0	0	0	0	1	1	1	0
tousled	3	.3450	.2505	34.0	2	1	0	0	0	0	0	0	1	0	0	0	0	0	0	0	0	0	0	0	1	1	0	0	0
Toutle	4	.0000	.0486	26.9	0	0	0	0	4	0	0	0	0	0	0	0	0	0	0	0	0	0	0	0	0	0	0	4	0
toves	7	.2446	.3875	35.9	0	0	1	6	0	0	0	0	0	6	0	0	0	0	0	0	0	1	0	0	0	0	0	0	0
tow	33	.6489	4.5708	46.6	1	6	0	8	16	1	1	0	19	0	0	1	1	1	1	0	0	0	0	1	0	1	1	7	0
Towanda	2	.1948	.1250	31.0	0	1	0	1	0	0	0	0	1	0	0	0	0	0	0	0	0	0	0	0	0	1	0	0	0
toward	1690	.9244	310.08	64.9	270	322	210	207	343	176	114	48	565	55	20	125	10	148	11	167	29	6	29	22	141	192	56	114	0
towards	103	.6247	13.378	51.3	5	19	12	11	37	11	8	0	23	0	0	15	0	2	1	1	4	0	1	2	46	2	3	3	0
towboats	3	.0000	.0583	27.7	0	0	3	0	0	0	0	0	0	0	0	0	0	3	0	0	0	0	0	0	0	0	0	0	0
towed	18	.6603	2.4999	44.0	0	2	2	4	7	2	1	0	8	0	0	0	0	1	1	1	3	0	0	0	1	0	1	2	0
towel	48	.8033	7.7713	48.9	12	16	4	8	4	3	0	1	9	0	1	1	0	3	1	15	1	1	1	0	8	3	0	4	0
toweling	4	.0683	.0702	28.5	0	2	0	0	2	0	0	0	0	0	0	0	0	0	0	0	0	3	0	0	0	0	0	1	0
towels	47	.7480	7.1487	48.5	14	10	6	2	5	3	3	4	9	1	0	2	2	0	2	14	0	0	2	0	8	1	1	5	0
tower	170	.9040	30.639	54.9	30	28	21	35	23	19	8	6	74	8	1	6	5	18	1	2	6	2	2	6	9	13	6	11	0
Tower	30	.6526	4.1048	46.1	1	4	5	14	3	1	0	2	11	0	0	0	0	3	0	0	0	1	0	0	5	2	4	4	0
towered	23	.5876	2.8427	44.5	1	3	1	2	7	4	4	1	6	1	3	2	0	0	0	1	0	0	0	0	2	2	3	3	0
towering	57	.7370	8.5921	49.3	4	6	11	10	13	9	4	0	13	2	0	1	0	18	0	4	1	0	0	0	3	4	5	6	0
towers	44	.7263	6.5519	48.2	8	6	4	9	5	4	7	1	14	1	2	1	0	6	0	3	1	3	0	1	0	1	7	4	0
Towers	2	.2152	.1357	31.3	1	0	0	0	0	1	0	0	1	0	0	0	0	1	0	0	0	0	0	0	0	0	0	0	0
towing	10	.1541	.4360	36.4	0	2	1	0	6	0	0	1	1	0	0	0	0	0	0	0	0	0	0	0	0	1	0	8	0
town	1219	.9054	219.74	63.4	284	219	123	137	219	131	69	37	432	44	19	92	16	199	12	15	49	3	1	2	97	98	42	97	1
Town	58	.7889	9.2193	49.6	16	11	6	8	9	7	1	0	9	5	1	6	3	16	0	0	7	0	0	0	3	2	3	3	0
town-O	2	.0000	.0162	22.1	2	0	0	0	0	0	0	0	0	0	0	0	0	0	0	0	2	0	0	0	0	0	0	0	0
town's	13	.6511	1.7544	42.4	1	1	4	0	4	3	0	0	3	0	0	2	0	2	0	0	1	0	1	0	2	2	0	0	0
Town's	4	.2348	.2372	33.8	2	0	0	1	0	0	1	0	0	0	0	0	0	3	0	0	0	0	0	0	0	0	1	0	0
Towne	2	.0000	.0219	23.4	0	2	0	0	0	0	0	0	0	2	0	0	0	0	0	0	0	0	0	0	0	0	0	0	0
towns	337	.7288	50.044	57.0	60	59	65	55	48	24	24	2	37	7	0	9	5	165	5	8	3	2	0	2	3	42	30	19	0
Townsend	2	.2441	.1127	30.5	0	0	0	0	1	1	0	0	0	0	0	0	0	0	0	0	0	0	0	0	1	0	1	0	0
townsfolk	3	.2227	.1589	32.0	2	0	0	0	1	0	0	0	0	0	0	0	0	0	0	0	0	0	0	0	2	0	0	1	0
Townshend	2	.1497	.1046	30.2	0	1	1	0	0	0	0	0	1	0	0	0	0	0	1	0	0	0	0	0	0	0	0	0	0
township	6	.4845	.6172	37.9	0	0	1	0	3	2	0	0	0	0	0	1	0	2	0	0	0	0	0	0	0	2	1	0	0
Township	2	.2351	.1166	30.7	0	0	0	0	0	1	1	0	0	0	0	0	0	1	0	0	0	0	0	0	0	0	0	1	0
townsman	3	.2143	.1568	32.0	0	0	0	2	1	0	0	0	0	0	0	0	0	0	0	0	0	0	0	0	0	1	0	2	0
townsmen	2	.0000	.0389	25.9	0	0	0	0	2	0	0	0	0	0	0	0	0	2	0	0	0	0	0	0	0	0	0	0	0
townspeople	23	.7221	3.4052	45.3	3	2	2	5	5	3	1	2	7	1	0	3	0	2	0	0	3	0	0	0	3	1	2	1	0
townswomen	2	.0000	.0215	23.3	0	0	0	0	0	0	2	0	0	0	0	2	0	0	0	0	0	0	0	0	0	0	0	0	0
towpath	3	.3779	.2436	33.9	1	0	1	0	1	0	0	0	0	1	0	0	0	0	0	0	1	0	0	0	0	1	0	0	0
towrope	2	.0000	.0914	29.6	0	0	0	2	0	0	0	0	2	0	0	0	0	0	0	0	0	0	0	0	0	0	0	0	0
tows	2	.1814	.1187	30.7	1	0	0	0	0	0	0	1	1	0	0	0	0	0	0	0	0	0	0	0	0	0	0	1	0
toxic	6	.2278	.3385	35.3	0	1	0	0	3	0	2	0	0	0	0	0	0	0	0	3	0	0	0	0	0	0	3	0	0
toxin	2	.2278	.1128	30.5	0	0	0	0	1	1	0	0	0	0	0	0	0	0	0	1	0	0	0	0	0	0	1	0	0
toxins	4	.2353	.2382	33.8	0	0	0	0	1	0	0	3	0	0	0	0	0	0	0	3	0	0	0	0	0	0	1	0	0
toy	146	.8080	23.834	53.8	63	23	20	22	10	4	3	1	39	8	0	2	18	5	10	41	6	0	1	0	1	5	5	5	0
Toy	2	.0000	.0234	23.7	0	0	2	0	0	0	0	0	0	0	0	0	0	0	0	0	0	0	0	0	2	0	0	0	0
toying	2	.1698	.1133	30.5	0	0	0	1	0	0	1	0	1	0	0	0	0	0	0	0	0	0	0	0	0	0	1	0	0
toys	96	.8331	16.059	52.1	25	22	11	15	8	9	3	3	27	9	3	2	8	8	1	8	2	2	9	1	0	5	2	9	0
Toys	5	.2336	.2953	34.7	1	4	0	0	0	0	0	0	0	0	0	0	0	4	0	0	1	0	0	0	0	0	0	0	0
tr	14	.1052	.4269	36.3	3	3	4	2	1	1	0	0	1	0	0	0	0	0	12	0	0	0	0	0	0	0	1	0	0
tra	3	.0000	.0243	23.8	0	0	0	0	0	3	0	0	0	0	0	0	0	0	0	0	3	0	0	0	0	0	0	0	0
tra-la	2	.0000	.0914	29.6	1	1	0	0	0	0	0	0	2	0	0	0	0	0	0	0	0	0	0	0	0	0	0	0	0
tra-la-la	10	.0000	.4568	36.6	3	7	0	0	0	0	0	0	10	0	0	0	0	0	0	0	0	0	0	0	0	0	0	0	0
trace	151	.9112	27.274	54.4	20	20	16	17	40	20	11	7	18	4	1	8	19	8	3	36	10	2	1	6	9	11	9	6	0
traced	48	.7997	7.6979	48.9	2	6	2	7	13	9	6	3	5	3	0	1	2	1	2	10	2	0	1	4	3	5	6	3	0
tracer	6	.2383	.3631	35.6	0	2	2	2	0	0	0	0	0	0	0	0	0	0	0	4	0	0	0	0	0	2	0	0	0
tracers	3	.2445	.1818	32.6	0	1	0	0	0	1	1	0	0	0	0	0	0	0	0	2	0	0	0	0	0	0	1	0	0
tracery	3	.2599	.1710	32.3	0	1	0	0	0	0	2	0	0	0	0	0	0	0	0	0	0	1	0	0	1	0	1	0	0
traces	41	.7188	5.9727	47.8	3	2	7	5	13	7	4	0	4	1	0	6	0	0	1	6	0	1	0	0	3	5	11	3	0
Tracey	11	.0000	.1337	31.3	0	0	11	0	0	0	0	0	0	0	0	0	0	0	0	0	0	0	0	0	0	0	0	11	0
trachea	14	.2678	.9236	39.7	0	0	0	0	0	2	12	0	0	0	0	0	0	0	1	12	0	0	0	0	0	0	1	0	0
tracheae	3	.1813	.1402	31.5	0	0	0	0	2	0	1	0	0	0	0	0	0	0	0	1	0	0	0	0	0	0	2	0	0
Trachodon	5	.0000	.0724	28.6	3	0	2	0	0	0	0	0	0	0	0	0	0	0	0	0	0	0	0	0	0	5	0	0	0
tracing	30	.4770	2.9483	44.7	1	0	1	4	8	3	12	1	1	2	2	0	1	0	0	5	0	0	10	7	0	1	1	0	0
track	312	.8951	55.742	57.5	36	51	33	48	88	37	16	3	127	14	4	16	18	9	4	18	5	1	0	1	26	27	10	32	0
Track	8	.0000	.3655	35.6	0	7	0	0	1	0	0	0	8	0	0	0	0	0	0	0	0	0	0	0	0	0	0	0	0
tracked	23	.6347	3.1220	44.9	2	2	7	2	10	0	0	0	12	1	0	3	0	0	0	2	0	0	0	0	1	1	0	3	0
trackers	9	.1143	.2890	34.6	0	0	0	1	8	0	0	0	0	0	0	8	0	0	0	0	0	0	0	0	0	0	0	1	0
tracking	9	.5111	.9900	40.0	0	1	1	2	1	3	1	0	2	1	0	0	0	0	1	2	0	1	0	0	0	0	0	2	0
trackless	5	.4350	.4659	36.7	0	0	3	0	2	0	0	0	0	0	0	0	0	1	0	1	1	0	0	0	0	0	2	0	0
tracks	217	.8044	35.377	55.5	52	62	17	32	33	11	9	1	80	8	3	21	1	22	0	2	3	1	0	0	15	43	5	13	0
tract	24	.4894	2.4949	44.0	0	0	0	1	5	4	9	5	1	0	0	0	0	2	1	6	0	0	0	0	0	0	9	5	0
traction	4	.2090	.2014	33.0	0	0	0	0	1	3	0	0	0	0	0	0	0	0	0	0	0	0	0	0	0	0	1	3	0
Traction	2	.0000	.0243	23.9	0	0	0	0	2	0	0	0	0	0	0	0	0	0	0	0	0	0	0	0	0	0	0	2	0
tractor	47	.8135	7.7411	48.9	14	3	12	10	5	1	1	1	18	2	1	0	0	9	3	2	0	0	0	1	4	2	2	3	0
tractors	32	.5477	3.7503	45.7	6	10	5	6	4	1	0	0	5	1	0	0	3	17	1	0	0	0	0	0	0	0	4	1	0
tracts	18	.6409	2.3897	43.8	1	2	0	1	3	6	2	3	2	1	0	0	0	1	0	7	0	0	0	0	1	1	3	2	0
tractus	3	.0000	.0243	23.9	0	2	0	1	0	0	0	0	0	0	0	0	0	0	3	0	0	0	0	0	0	0	0	0	0
Tracy	11	.2070	.8193	39.1	10	0	0	0	0	1	0	0	10	0	0	0	0	0	0	0	0	0	0	0	0	0	0	1	0
trade	479	.7340	71.707	58.6	59	58	110	70	68	83	30	1	75	7	0	1	12	223	9	1	9	1	4	4	11	50	59	13	0
Trade	11	.4232	1.0111	40.0	2	1	2	0	3	0	3	0	1	0	0	0	0	3	0	0	0	0	2	0	0	1	4	0	0
trade-mark	3	.2357	.2199	33.4	2	0	1	0	0	0	0	0	2	0	0	0	0	0	0	0	0	0	0	0	0	1	0	0	0
traded	61	.7377	9.2119	49.6	15	23	9	5	3	5	1	0	15	1	0	1	4	19	2	1	0	0	0	0	2	10	3	3	0
trademark	15	.4185	1.3468	41.3	0	8	0	1	2	2	2	0	1	0	0	1	0	0	2	1	1	0	0	0	0	0	9	0	0
trademarks	6	.4516	.5645	37.5	0	3	0	0	1	1	1	0	0	1	0	0	0	0	1	0	1	0	0	0	0	0	3	0	0
trader	47	.6402	6.3134	48.0	0	28	6	5	3	2	3	0	13	0	0	3	0	14	0	0	1	0	0	0	3	9	4	0	0
Trader	2	.0000	.0914	29.6	0	2	0	0	0	0	0	0	2	0	0	0	0	0	0	0	0	0	0	0	0	0	0	0	0
trader's	2	.2446	.1142	30.6	0	1	0	0	0	0	0	1	0	0	0	0	0	0	0	0	0	0	0	0	1	0	0	1	0
traders	90	.5322	10.261	50.1	10	11	16	13	18	22	0	0	9	2	0	3	0	59	0	0	3	0	0	0	1	6	4	3	0

5P Tourist
9D tourist-class
5P tourist's-eye
7P tourougou
7Q ToursPoitiers
5F Toussaint
7R tout
8F Toutant
XR touted
8N tow-colored
3A towboat
4A towel-horse
9Q towers'
7N Towler's
4A towline
7R Townes
7A townlot
7P townships
4P townward
9B Towser's
7P towship
7Q toxicity
9D toy-size
7A toyed
6J Toyland
7R Toyota
7E TPU
3A tra-la-la-
4J tra-la-la-la
3A tra-lee-lee
8Q traceable
5R Tracey's
7Q tracheids
7A Trachis
5P Trachodons
7M tracings
5A track-laying
7R tracking-camera
7B Tracks
4R tractor-type
6A tractorbuses
8P Tracy's
7J trade-name
7Q trade-unions
4A tradegoods
4Q Trademark
4Q TRADEMARK
8F traders'
3A Traders'

Word Type	F	D	U	SFI	3 Gr 3	4 Gr 4	5 Gr 5	6 Gr 6	7 Gr 7	8 Gr 8	9 Gr 9	X UnGr	A Read	B Eng & Gr	C Comp	D Lit	E Math	F Soc Stud	G Spell	H Sci	J Music	K Art	L Home Ec	M Shop	N Lib F	P Lib NF	Q Lib Ref	R Mag	S Rel
trades	19	.5765	2.3309	43.7	2	2	1	1	3	9	1	0	4	0	0	2	2	8	0	0	0	0	0	1	0	2	0	0	0
Trades	2	.2437	.1129	30.5	1	0	0	0	0	0	1	0	0	0	0	0	0	0	0	0	0	0	0	0	0	0	1	1	0
tradesman	2	.2446	.1125	30.5	0	0	0	0	0	1	1	0	0	1	0	1	0	0	0	0	0	0	0	0	0	0	0	0	0
tradesmen	8	.4823	.8246	39.2	0	0	2	1	1	1	2	1	1	2	0	0	0	1	0	0	0	1	0	0	0	2	1	0	0
trading	159	.5950	19.912	53.0	23	17	43	18	26	23	5	4	20	2	0	3	2	91	1	0	2	0	0	0	5	14	14	5	0
Trading	5	.1118	.2195	33.4	5	0	0	0	0	0	0	0	1	0	0	0	0	4	0	0	0	0	0	0	0	0	0	0	0
tradition	66	.7216	9.6149	49.8	7	1	4	6	16	14	13	5	4	2	1	3	0	7	0	0	8	1	0	0	0	9	17	14	0
traditional	90	.7153	12.993	51.1	3	3	11	10	19	18	24	2	6	2	1	2	0	13	0	0	17	6	0	3	0	7	18	15	0
traditionally	21	.5761	2.4768	43.9	1	0	3	3	8	3	3	0	0	0	0	0	0	2	0	0	3	0	2	0	0	2	6	6	0
traditions	35	.5967	4.3259	46.4	1	0	6	2	8	16	2	0	1	0	0	0	0	14	0	1	2	0	1	0	0	6	9	1	0
traducers	2	.2152	.1357	31.3	0	0	0	0	0	2	0	0	1	0	0	0	0	1	0	0	0	0	0	0	0	0	0	0	0
Traeger	2	.0000	.0290	24.6	0	0	0	0	0	0	2	0	0	0	0	0	0	0	0	0	0	0	0	0	0	2	0	0	0
Trafalgar	3	.2197	.2090	33.2	0	0	1	0	1	0	1	0	2	0	0	0	0	0	0	0	0	0	0	0	0	0	1	0	0
traffic	242	.8701	42.097	56.2	39	28	17	30	58	37	32	1	61	11	2	6	11	58	6	27	4	0	0	1	7	9	13	26	0
Traffic	2	.2351	.1166	30.7	0	0	0	0	0	1	1	0	0	0	0	0	0	1	0	0	0	0	0	0	0	0	0	1	0
traffic-choked	2	.2440	.1132	30.5	0	0	0	1	0	0	1	0	0	0	0	1	0	0	0	0	0	0	0	0	0	0	0	1	0
tragedies	5	.4587	.5207	37.2	0	1	0	0	1	3	0	0	2	0	0	0	0	1	0	0	1	0	0	0	0	0	1	0	0
tragedy	30	.7185	4.3770	46.4	1	2	4	2	9	5	7	0	4	0	0	5	0	3	2	1	3	0	0	0	0	3	4	5	0
tragic	29	.6813	4.0998	46.1	1	1	4	5	7	8	3	0	10	1	0	3	0	2	0	0	4	0	0	0	1	1	1	6	0
tragically	5	.5241	.5599	37.5	0	0	0	0	2	2	1	0	1	0	0	1	0	1	0	0	1	0	0	0	0	0	1	0	0
trahere	3	.0000	.0243	23.9	0	0	0	1	2	0	0	0	0	0	0	0	0	0	3	0	0	0	0	0	0	0	0	0	0
trail	317	.7864	50.818	57.1	38	47	72	52	69	27	5	7	138	8	11	30	2	27	1	6	4	2	0	0	41	30	2	15	0
Trail	26	.5963	3.2354	45.1	4	3	14	3	0	0	1	1	3	0	2	0	0	10	1	0	2	0	0	0	0	4	0	4	0
trailed	23	.6140	2.9891	44.8	1	4	5	2	9	1	0	1	8	1	0	1	0	1	0	0	0	0	0	0	7	3	1	1	0
trailer	38	.6377	5.0769	47.1	16	3	6	0	7	4	2	0	12	5	0	2	0	3	1	0	0	0	0	0	3	0	1	11	0
trailers	10	.4295	.9663	39.9	4	0	1	1	4	0	0	0	2	0	0	0	4	2	0	0	0	0	0	0	0	0	0	2	0
trailing	34	.7621	5.2950	47.2	0	8	4	7	11	4	0	0	12	1	1	2	0	1	0	5	0	0	0	0	4	4	1	3	0
trails	83	.6468	11.142	50.5	11	6	26	11	22	4	0	3	15	0	6	4	0	29	2	1	0	0	0	0	1	13	6	6	0
Trails	2	.2401	.1133	30.5	0	0	1	0	0	0	0	1	0	0	0	0	0	0	0	0	0	0	0	0	0	1	1	0	0
Trailside	2	.0000	.0914	29.6	0	2	0	0	0	0	0	0	2	0	0	0	0	0	0	0	0	0	0	0	0	0	0	0	0
train	556	.8816	97.924	59.9	173	97	81	50	74	37	36	8	188	23	14	41	26	79	15	18	18	1	0	0	22	51	23	37	0
Train	12	.4681	1.1807	40.7	2	5	0	1	2	2	0	0	0	5	0	0	0	2	0	0	3	0	0	0	0	1	0	1	0
train's	2	.1843	.0808	29.1	1	0	0	0	0	0	1	0	0	0	1	0	0	0	0	0	1	0	0	0	0	0	0	0	0
trained	174	.8631	30.099	54.8	23	30	21	34	29	20	12	5	57	7	1	5	0	29	3	13	2	0	2	0	10	20	13	12	0
trainer	18	.5099	1.9985	43.0	4	4	1	3	3	1	2	0	5	0	0	1	0	0	0	0	0	0	0	0	4	6	0	2	0
trainers	8	.5439	.9082	39.6	2	2	1	0	2	0	1	0	1	0	0	0	0	0	0	0	1	1	0	0	1	1	1	2	0
training	225	.8077	36.512	55.6	20	19	31	20	68	30	33	4	35	7	1	6	1	33	0	13	3	0	3	3	10	37	49	24	0
Training	10	.5270	1.1267	40.5	4	0	0	0	3	1	2	0	2	2	0	0	0	0	0	0	0	0	0	0	1	3	0	2	0
trainman	3	.2223	.2106	33.2	3	0	0	0	0	0	0	0	2	1	0	0	0	0	0	0	0	0	0	0	0	0	0	0	0
trainmen	4	.4461	.3986	36.0	2	0	1	0	0	0	1	0	1	1	0	0	0	1	0	0	0	0	0	0	0	0	1	0	0
trains	188	.7509	28.695	54.6	65	27	26	18	26	17	5	4	28	8	1	6	1	79	4	6	2	0	0	0	5	24	8	16	0
trait	26	.6454	3.4579	45.4	2	0	1	14	4	4	1	0	2	2	0	1	1	0	0	13	2	0	2	0	0	0	1	2	0
traitor	12	.3873	1.1653	40.7	0	0	0	3	5	1	3	0	8	0	0	2	0	0	0	0	0	0	0	0	0	0	0	2	0
traitorous	2	.1497	.1046	30.2	0	0	0	0	2	0	0	0	1	0	0	0	0	0	1	0	0	0	0	0	0	0	0	0	0
traitors	4	.2420	.3089	34.9	0	1	0	0	2	0	1	0	3	0	0	0	0	1	0	0	0	0	0	0	0	0	0	0	0
Traitors	3	.0000	.0365	25.6	0	0	0	0	0	0	3	0	0	0	0	0	0	0	0	0	0	0	0	0	0	0	0	3	0
traits	30	.6628	4.0459	46.1	1	0	3	2	15	3	6	0	1	4	0	5	0	0	0	8	1	0	3	0	0	1	5	2	0
trajectory	8	.4695	.8109	39.1	3	0	0	0	2	2	0	1	1	0	0	0	0	0	2	1	0	0	0	0	0	3	0	1	0
Trammell	2	.0000	.0215	23.3	0	0	0	0	2	0	0	0	0	0	0	2	0	0	0	0	0	0	0	0	0	0	0	0	0
tramp	40	.5837	5.1543	47.1	24	1	3	5	6	1	0	0	26	3	0	2	0	0	1	0	0	0	0	0	2	6	0	0	0
tramped	13	.6319	1.7115	42.3	1	2	2	3	2	2	1	0	3	1	0	3	0	1	0	0	0	0	0	0	2	2	0	1	0
tramping	13	.4775	1.3726	41.4	1	2	1	4	2	2	0	1	4	0	0	4	0	1	0	0	0	0	0	0	3	0	0	1	0
trample	7	.5746	.8403	39.2	1	1	0	3	2	0	0	0	1	0	0	2	0	1	0	0	1	0	0	0	0	0	1	1	0
trampled	15	.5862	1.9012	42.8	0	4	1	3	7	0	0	0	7	1	0	0	0	1	0	0	0	0	0	0	3	0	2	1	0
trampling	6	.4156	.5693	37.6	1	0	0	0	2	1	1	1	2	0	1	0	0	1	0	0	1	0	0	0	0	1	0	0	0
tramps	4	.2186	.2141	33.3	0	0	0	0	3	1	0	0	0	0	0	1	0	0	0	0	0	0	0	0	0	3	0	0	0
Tran	4	.2281	.2337	33.7	0	0	0	0	3	1	0	0	0	0	0	0	0	3	0	0	0	0	0	0	0	0	0	1	0
trance	8	.4578	.8443	39.3	1	0	0	1	6	0	0	0	4	0	0	0	0	0	0	0	0	0	0	0	1	1	2	0	0
tranquil	9	.5870	1.1110	40.5	0	3	0	1	2	3	0	0	2	2	0	0	0	1	0	0	1	0	0	0	2	0	0	1	0
tranquility	2	.0000	.0215	23.3	0	0	0	0	0	0	2	0	0	0	0	2	0	0	0	0	0	0	0	0	0	0	0	0	0
tranquilizers	3	.2427	.1822	32.6	0	0	0	0	1	2	0	0	0	0	0	0	0	0	0	2	0	0	0	0	0	0	0	1	0
trans	9	.5022	.9401	39.7	0	1	0	0	2	1	3	2	0	3	0	0	0	0	1	1	0	0	0	0	0	0	3	1	0
Trans-Siberian	2	.0000	.0389	25.9	0	0	0	2	0	0	0	0	0	0	0	0	0	2	0	0	0	0	0	0	0	0	0	0	0
transact	2	.0000	.0290	24.6	0	0	1	0	0	0	1	0	0	0	0	0	0	0	0	0	0	0	0	0	0	2	0	0	0
transaction	2	.2139	.1057	30.2	0	0	0	1	0	1	0	0	0	0	0	0	0	1	1	0	0	0	0	0	0	0	0	0	0
transactions	3	.0000	.0314	25.0	0	0	1	0	1	1	0	0	0	0	0	0	0	0	0	0	0	0	0	0	0	0	0	0	0
transatlantic	2	.1170	.0651	28.1	0	0	0	1	0	1	0	0	0	0	1	0	0	1	0	0	0	0	0	0	0	0	3	0	0
Transatlantic	2	.0000	.0234	23.7	0	0	0	0	2	0	0	0	0	0	0	0	0	0	0	0	0	0	0	0	2	0	0	0	0
transcend	2	.0000	.0243	23.9	0	0	0	0	0	0	0	2	0	0	0	0	0	0	0	0	0	0	0	0	0	0	0	2	0
Transcendentalism	2	.2401	.1133	30.5	0	0	1	0	0	1	0	0	0	0	0	0	0	0	0	0	0	0	0	0	0	1	1	0	0
transcontinental	7	.3252	.5689	37.6	0	2	1	1	0	3	0	0	2	1	0	0	0	4	0	0	0	0	0	0	0	0	0	0	0
transcribe	2	.0000	.0209	23.2	0	0	0	0	2	0	0	0	0	0	0	0	0	0	0	0	0	0	0	0	0	0	2	0	0
transcribed	3	.0995	.1144	30.6	0	0	0	0	0	2	1	0	1	0	0	0	0	0	0	0	2	0	0	0	0	0	0	0	0
transcribing	2	.2446	.1123	30.5	0	0	0	0	2	0	0	0	0	1	0	0	0	0	0	0	0	0	0	0	0	0	1	0	0
transfer	61	.6411	7.9900	49.0	1	3	8	2	18	8	17	4	2	0	1	0	0	3	0	22	2	0	4	9	2	4	8	4	0
transferred	56	.7838	8.8235	49.5	4	1	7	12	10	11	7	4	4	1	0	1	0	6	1	19	2	2	1	3	1	1	9	5	0
transferring	7	.4106	.5999	37.8	0	1	1	1	0	0	2	2	0	0	0	0	0	0	0	0	1	0	0	2	1	0	1	2	0
transfers	5	.0000	.0986	29.9	1	0	2	1	1	0	0	0	0	0	0	0	0	0	0	5	0	0	0	0	0	0	0	0	0
transfixed	2	.0000	.0914	29.6	0	0	0	0	2	0	0	0	2	0	0	0	0	0	0	0	0	0	0	0	0	0	0	0	0
transform	40	.4325	3.7098	45.7	0	1	5	11	3	11	5	4	2	25	0	0	7	1	0	1	1	0	1	0	0	1	0	1	0
transformation	39	.4268	3.5339	45.5	0	0	7	0	8	13	11	0	0	22	0	0	4	0	0	1	0	0	0	0	0	1	6	5	0
transformations	14	.4028	1.2111	40.8	0	0	0	1	5	7	1	0	0	8	0	0	2	1	0	0	0	0	0	0	0	1	2	0	0
transformed	40	.7709	6.1990	47.9	1	1	4	4	8	14	6	2	3	10	1	1	2	4	0	3	2	0	0	0	2	3	7	2	0
transformer	17	.0737	.3182	35.0	0	1	0	1	0	14	1	0	0	0	0	0	0	0	0	1	0	0	0	14	0	0	1	1	0
transformers	4	.0847	.0846	29.3	0	0	0	0	1	3	0	0	0	0	0	0	0	0	0	0	0	0	0	3	0	0	0	1	0
transforming	12	.5753	1.4307	41.6	0	0	0	1	3	4	4	0	0	0	0	0	4	3	0	1	1	1	0	0	0	1	0	1	0
transforms	7	.3902	.5878	37.7	0	0	1	0	2	3	0	1	0	4	0	0	0	0	0	1	1	0	0	0	0	0	0	1	0
transfusion	3	.1650	.1684	32.3	0	0	0	0	3	0	0	0	1	0	0	0	0	0	0	2	0	0	0	0	0	0	0	0	0
transgression	2	.2446	.1142	30.6	0	0	0	0	2	0	0	0	0	0	0	0	0	0	0	0	0	0	0	0	1	0	0	1	0
transgressions	2	.0000	.0243	23.9	0	0	0	1	1	0	0	0	0	0	0	0	0	0	0	0	0	0	0	0	0	0	0	2	0
transient	3	.1858	.1432	31.6	0	0	0	0	2	1	0	0	0	2	0	0	0	1	0	0	0	0	0	0	0	0	0	0	0
transistor	23	.5784	2.7944	44.5	0	1	1	4	3	12	2	0	2	0	0	0	3	2	1	11	0	0	0	2	0	0	1	1	0
transistors	17	.3783	1.5842	42.0	2	1	0	6	1	6	0	0	8	0	0	0	0	0	0	6	0	0	0	0	0	0	3	0	0
transit	3	.3781	.2548	34.1	0	0	0	0	0	2	1	0	0	0	0	0	0	1	0	1	0	0	0	0	0	0	0	1	0
Transit	3	.2427	.1822	32.6	0	0	1	0	2	0	0	0	0	0	0	0	0	0	0	2	0	0	0	0	0	0	0	1	0
transition	14	.5599	1.6243	42.1	1	0	0	2	6	4	1	0	0	0	0	0	0	1	0	3	2	0	0	0	0	1	2	5	0

9F tradition-shattering
7Q traditor
7Q traditors
7R traffic-crash
8J traffic's
9D traffickers
7Q trafficking
9Q Tragicall
5F TRAIL
3J trail-O
9D trailer's
6A Trained
7G trainees
7P trainees'
4N traipsed
7R trajectories
7J tram
5P Tramassene
3A Tramp-Tramp-Tramp
4A tramp's
4A trams
9D tramway
8F Tranquility
XR tranquillity
7N tranquilly
9R Trans
8B trans-
9R trans-Arabian
7Q Trans-Canada
8H trans-Vision
7F Trans-World
8D transacted
7F Transbay
8Q Transcaucasia
7R transcendence
8Q transcendental
5P Transcendentalists
6R transcript
8J transcriptions
6H transducer
7R transducers
7R transected
8D transfigured
7J transfigures
9H transients
9B transire
4Q Transistor

Word Type	F	D	U	SFI	3 Gr 3	4 Gr 4	5 Gr 5	6 Gr 6	7 Gr 7	8 Gr 8	9 Gr 9	X UnGr	A Read	B Eng & Gr	C Comp	D Lit	E Math	F Soc Stud	G Spell	H Sci	J Music	K Art	L Home Ec	M Shop	N Lib F	P Lib NF	Q Lib Ref	R Mag	S Rel
Transition	3	.0000	.0583	27.7	0	0	0	0	3	0	0	0	0	0	0	0	0	3	0	0	0	0	0	0	0	0	0	0	0
transitional	32	.2687	1.8740	42.7	0	0	0	3	5	4	20	0	0	12	13	0	0	2	2	0	0	0	0	0	0	0	0	3	0
transitions	6	.2955	.3942	36.0	0	0	0	1	5	0	0	0	0	1	0	0	0	0	0	0	0	0	0	0	0	0	4	1	0
transitive	34	.0814	.8848	39.5	0	0	2	0	6	11	15	0	0	32	0	0	0	0	0	0	0	0	0	0	0	0	2	0	0
transitively	5	.0000	.0547	27.4	0	0	0	0	3	0	2	0	0	5	0	0	0	0	0	0	0	0	0	0	0	0	0	0	0
transits	3	.0000	.0591	27.7	0	0	0	0	2	0	1	0	0	0	0	0	0	0	0	3	0	0	0	0	0	0	0	0	0
translate	40	.5692	4.7593	46.8	0	3	2	11	9	5	9	1	5	8	0	0	17	0	5	0	2	0	0	0	0	0	1	2	0
translated	38	.7383	5.6495	47.5	0	1	5	6	13	4	6	3	1	9	0	5	5	2	1	2	1	0	0	0	0	6	4	2	0
translating	8	.6723	1.1101	40.5	2	0	0	2	2	1	1	0	2	1	0	1	1	0	1	0	0	0	0	0	1	1	0	0	0
translation	36	.6160	4.5427	46.6	3	3	2	2	16	4	5	1	3	3	0	7	0	2	3	0	7	0	0	0	0	0	10	1	0
translations	13	.6370	1.7017	42.3	0	3	3	1	5	1	0	0	2	2	0	2	0	0	2	0	1	0	0	0	0	1	3	0	0
translator	3	.2233	.1562	31.9	0	0	0	0	2	1	0	0	0	0	0	1	0	0	0	0	0	0	0	0	0	0	2	0	0
translator's	2	.2407	.1138	30.6	0	0	1	0	1	0	0	0	0	0	0	1	0	0	0	0	0	0	0	0	0	1	0	0	0
translators	3	.1169	.1277	31.1	0	0	0	1	0	0	2	0	1	0	0	0	0	0	0	0	0	0	0	0	0	0	2	0	0
translocation	5	.0000	.0523	27.2	0	0	0	0	0	0	0	5	0	0	0	0	0	0	0	0	0	0	0	0	0	0	5	0	0
translocations	2	.0000	.0209	23.2	0	0	0	0	0	0	0	2	0	0	0	0	0	0	0	0	0	0	0	0	0	0	2	0	0
translucent	15	.4529	1.4659	41.7	0	1	0	3	1	4	1	5	0	0	0	0	0	0	1	10	0	0	0	1	0	0	3	0	0
transmission	22	.4232	1.9878	43.0	0	0	0	1	8	8	4	1	1	0	0	0	2	1	0	2	0	0	0	5	0	0	4	7	0
transmissions	4	.0996	.1523	31.8	0	0	0	0	4	0	0	0	1	0	0	0	0	0	0	0	0	0	0	0	0	0	0	3	0
transmit	26	.6150	3.3089	45.2	0	0	2	8	7	6	3	0	1	1	0	1	4	1	0	10	0	0	0	0	0	0	5	3	0
transmits	3	.1650	.1684	32.3	0	0	0	0	0	2	1	0	1	0	0	0	0	0	0	2	0	0	0	0	0	0	0	0	0
transmitted	25	.5459	2.8516	44.6	0	2	1	3	7	7	4	1	2	0	0	0	0	0	0	7	3	0	0	3	0	1	7	2	0
transmitter	39	.5296	4.4019	46.4	1	0	8	11	8	4	5	2	3	0	0	1	0	0	0	24	0	0	0	2	0	1	5	3	0
transmitters	7	.4769	.7602	38.8	0	0	3	1	1	1	0	1	3	0	0	0	0	0	0	2	1	0	0	0	0	1	0	0	0
transmitting	14	.4428	1.3381	41.3	0	0	0	2	4	2	5	1	3	0	0	1	0	0	0	7	0	0	0	0	0	0	4	2	0
transmute	2	.0000	.0914	29.6	0	0	2	0	0	0	0	0	2	0	0	0	0	0	0	0	0	0	0	0	0	0	0	0	0
transmuting	3	.0000	.1370	31.4	0	0	3	0	0	0	0	0	3	0	0	0	0	0	0	0	0	0	0	0	0	0	0	0	0
transoceanic	4	.3286	.3009	34.8	0	0	0	0	1	1	1	1	0	0	0	0	0	1	0	1	0	0	0	0	0	0	0	2	0
transom	3	.2279	.2143	33.3	2	0	0	0	1	0	0	0	2	0	0	0	0	0	0	0	0	0	0	0	0	0	0	1	0
transparency	5	.2227	.2471	33.9	0	0	2	0	3	0	0	0	0	0	0	0	0	0	0	0	0	2	0	0	1	0	2	0	0
transparent	63	.6271	8.1073	49.1	2	7	4	6	12	9	18	5	4	1	2	5	0	0	2	28	0	9	2	4	1	0	3	2	0
transpiration	3	.0000	.0314	25.0	0	0	0	0	3	0	0	0	0	0	0	0	0	0	0	0	0	0	0	0	0	0	3	0	0
transplant	6	.3196	.4245	36.3	0	0	0	0	1	1	1	3	0	1	0	0	0	0	0	0	0	0	0	0	0	0	1	4	0
transplanted	14	.5141	1.5040	41.8	2	0	2	3	3	2	0	2	0	0	0	0	0	3	0	1	2	0	0	0	0	0	4	4	0
transplanting	3	.3764	.2483	33.9	0	0	0	0	1	1	0	1	0	0	0	0	0	0	0	1	0	0	0	0	0	0	1	1	0
transplants	2	.2346	.1166	30.7	0	0	0	0	0	0	0	2	0	0	0	0	0	0	0	1	0	0	0	0	0	0	0	1	0
transpolar	2	.2152	.1357	31.3	0	0	0	0	1	0	1	0	1	0	0	0	0	1	0	0	0	0	0	0	0	0	0	0	0
transport	44	.6895	6.2411	48.0	2	4	5	7	16	3	7	0	9	2	0	0	1	10	0	1	0	0	0	1	3	5	11	1	0
transportation	216	.6888	30.428	54.8	13	20	58	44	36	26	17	2	13	1	1	2	2	113	4	10	0	2	0	4	1	11	41	11	0
transported	33	.6629	4.5240	46.6	0	4	4	5	9	4	7	0	5	0	0	1	0	10	0	5	0	0	0	1	1	4	6	0	0
transporting	12	.5897	1.4993	41.8	2	1	1	2	3	1	2	0	2	0	0	0	0	4	0	3	0	0	0	0	1	1	1	0	0
transports	10	.5493	1.1492	40.6	0	0	0	2	4	2	2	0	0	1	0	0	0	0	0	4	0	0	0	0	1	2	0	2	0
transpose	4	.1770	.1679	32.3	0	0	0	3	0	0	1	0	0	0	0	1	0	0	0	0	3	0	0	0	0	0	0	0	0
transposed	3	.3762	.2496	34.0	0	0	0	0	2	0	0	1	0	0	0	0	0	0	0	1	0	0	0	0	0	1	1	0	0
transposing	2	.0000	.0162	22.1	0	0	0	0	1	1	0	0	0	0	0	0	0	0	0	0	2	0	0	0	0	0	0	0	0
Transvaal	4	.3617	.3220	35.1	0	0	2	0	1	1	0	0	0	0	0	0	0	0	0	1	0	0	0	0	0	2	1	0	0
transversal	8	.0000	.1197	30.8	0	0	0	0	6	1	1	0	0	0	0	0	8	0	0	0	0	0	0	0	0	0	0	0	0
transverse	7	.1048	.2062	33.1	0	0	0	0	0	0	4	3	0	0	0	0	0	0	0	3	0	0	0	4	0	0	0	0	0
Transylvania	2	.2433	.1158	30.6	0	0	1	1	0	0	0	0	0	0	0	0	0	0	0	0	0	0	0	0	0	1	0	1	0
trap	152	.7264	22.708	53.6	24	35	27	26	20	9	6	5	53	2	6	7	0	17	2	7	1	0	0	0	29	9	8	10	1
trap-door	5	.3805	.4235	36.3	2	0	1	2	0	0	0	0	0	0	0	0	0	0	0	2	0	0	0	0	1	2	0	0	0
trap-trap	2	.0000	.0234	23.7	2	0	0	0	0	0	0	0	0	0	0	0	0	0	0	0	0	0	0	0	2	0	0	0	0
trapdoor	5	.2110	.3346	35.2	0	2	0	2	1	0	0	0	3	0	0	0	0	0	0	0	0	0	0	0	0	0	0	2	0
trapdoors	2	.2278	.1128	30.5	0	0	1	0	0	1	0	0	0	0	0	0	0	0	0	1	0	0	0	0	0	0	1	0	0
trapeze	7	.3623	.6333	38.0	2	2	0	0	3	0	0	0	4	0	1	0	0	0	0	0	0	0	0	0	0	1	0	1	0
trapezoid	11	.0000	.1647	32.2	0	0	2	0	0	7	2	0	0	0	0	0	11	0	0	0	0	0	0	0	0	0	0	0	0
trapezoids	3	.0000	.0449	26.5	0	0	0	0	0	3	0	0	0	0	0	0	3	0	0	0	0	0	0	0	0	0	0	0	0
trapped	82	.6646	11.385	50.6	11	13	14	7	11	6	16	4	24	1	0	1	0	6	1	24	1	0	0	0	2	2	2	18	0
trapper	27	.5702	3.3981	45.3	2	3	15	2	3	0	0	2	14	0	0	1	0	7	0	2	0	0	0	0	0	2	0	1	0
trapper's	2	.1814	.1187	30.7	0	0	0	2	0	0	0	0	1	0	0	0	0	0	0	0	0	0	0	0	0	0	0	1	0
trappers	46	.6629	6.3316	48.0	2	4	13	9	7	9	1	1	9	0	0	2	0	20	0	1	2	0	0	0	1	4	3	4	0
trapping	43	.8094	7.0513	48.5	2	7	11	7	9	3	3	1	15	0	0	3	1	7	1	6	1	0	0	0	2	2	3	2	0
trappings	6	.5570	.7172	38.6	0	1	0	1	1	1	2	0	2	0	0	1	0	0	0	0	0	0	0	0	1	0	1	1	0
traps	53	.6922	7.5922	48.8	8	10	13	5	16	0	1	0	16	0	0	1	0	9	1	1	0	0	0	0	8	5	8	4	0
trash	20	.7420	3.0276	44.8	5	3	0	4	4	2	1	1	5	0	0	3	0	3	1	2	2	0	0	0	0	1	1	2	0
trauma	2	.0000	.0243	23.9	0	0	0	0	1	1	0	0	0	0	0	0	0	0	0	0	0	0	0	0	0	0	0	2	0
travel	814	.9108	147.12	61.7	162	140	126	126	115	77	58	10	108	24	2	7	82	176	20	171	13	4	5	6	6	79	56	54	1
Travel	4	.4808	.4056	36.1	1	1	1	0	0	0	1	0	0	1	0	1	0	1	0	0	0	0	0	0	0	0	0	1	0
traveled	307	.8574	52.725	57.2	40	75	53	43	54	26	14	2	77	7	2	14	46	59	1	31	17	0	0	1	5	20	14	13	0
traveler	80	.7973	12.943	51.1	7	14	13	10	15	8	5	8	29	8	0	3	1	6	0	6	1	0	1	0	1	11	9	4	0
Traveler	22	.2548	1.8051	42.6	18	0	2	0	0	1	1	0	20	0	0	1	0	1	0	0	0	0	0	0	0	0	0	0	0
traveler's	3	.3465	.2515	34.0	0	1	1	0	0	0	0	1	1	0	0	0	0	0	0	0	0	0	0	0	0	1	0	1	0
Traveler's	2	.0000	.0914	29.6	0	0	2	0	0	0	0	0	2	0	0	0	0	0	0	0	0	0	0	0	0	0	0	0	0
travelers	112	.7785	17.631	52.5	19	19	23	14	19	9	6	3	19	5	3	3	0	33	0	7	3	0	0	0	3	13	12	11	0
Travelers	2	.1641	.0751	28.8	0	0	0	0	0	2	0	0	0	0	1	0	0	0	0	0	0	0	0	0	0	0	1	0	0
travelers'	2	.2152	.1357	31.3	0	0	0	0	1	1	0	0	1	0	0	0	0	1	0	0	0	0	0	0	0	0	0	0	0
traveling	249	.9003	44.626	56.5	40	39	36	51	36	20	23	4	65	7	0	13	24	38	2	37	10	1	1	1	6	17	8	19	0
travelled	8	.5260	.8702	39.4	0	0	3	1	1	2	0	1	0	0	0	2	1	0	0	0	2	0	0	0	0	1	0	2	0
traveller	2	.1717	.1142	30.6	0	0	0	1	0	0	1	0	1	0	0	1	0	0	0	0	0	0	0	0	0	0	0	0	0
Traveller	3	.2279	.2143	33.3	0	0	0	0	0	2	1	0	2	0	0	0	0	0	0	0	0	0	0	0	0	0	0	1	0
travellers	7	.2191	.3912	35.9	0	0	0	1	6	0	0	0	1	0	0	1	0	0	0	0	0	0	0	0	5	0	0	0	0
travelling	4	.1959	.1920	32.8	0	1	0	0	3	0	0	0	0	0	0	0	0	0	0	0	0	0	0	0	3	0	0	1	0
travels	206	.6957	29.370	54.7	28	29	23	47	29	30	16	4	17	4	0	2	39	17	2	90	5	0	0	0	3	11	8	8	0
Travels	4	.4520	.4002	36.0	0	0	1	1	1	1	0	0	1	1	0	1	0	0	0	0	0	0	0	0	0	1	0	0	0
Travers	3	.3814	.2537	34.0	1	1	0	0	0	0	0	1	0	0	0	0	1	1	0	0	0	0	0	0	0	0	0	1	0
traverse	3	.2926	.1905	32.8	0	0	1	0	0	0	2	0	0	0	0	1	0	0	0	0	0	0	0	1	0	0	0	1	0
Traverse	4	.0996	.1523	31.8	3	0	0	1	0	0	0	0	1	0	0	0	0	0	0	0	0	0	0	0	0	0	0	3	0
traversed	10	.6320	1.2986	41.1	0	0	1	0	5	2	1	1	1	0	0	1	0	0	0	1	0	0	0	1	2	2	1	1	0
Traviata	3	.1852	.1342	31.3	0	0	1	1	0	1	0	0	0	0	0	0	0	0	0	0	2	0	0	0	0	1	0	0	0
Travis	15	.4588	1.6040	42.1	0	7	2	0	1	5	0	0	8	0	0	0	2	0	0	0	0	0	0	0	1	4	0	0	0
travois	4	.0000	.1827	32.6	4	0	0	0	0	0	0	0	4	0	0	0	0	0	0	0	0	0	0	0	0	0	0	0	0
trawlers	7	.1817	.3553	35.5	0	0	0	7	0	0	0	0	0	0	0	0	0	6	0	0	0	0	0	0	0	0	0	1	0
trawls	2	.0000	.0209	23.2	0	0	0	0	2	0	0	0	0	0	0	0	0	0	0	0	0	0	0	0	0	0	2	0	0
tray	63	.7451	9.5453	49.8	13	11	5	7	16	0	11	0	15	4	0	5	6	2	1	7	0	0	8	1	5	4	2	3	0
Tray	3	.0000	.0434	26.4	0	3	0	0	0	0	0	0	0	0	0	0	0	0	0	0	0	0	0	0	0	3	0	0	0
trays	19	.6279	2.5006	44.0	2	3	3	2	4	0	5	0	6	1	0	1	0	4	0	1	0	1	3	1	0	0	0	1	0

7B Transitive
4Q Translation
XQ translocated
3A translucency
4N transmuted
9R transpacific
7Q transpire
XH transplantable

XH transplantation
9Q transplantations
XR Transport
3P Transportation
7R Transportes
6J transposition
9Q transshipment
9Q transuranium

9H transversely
6N Trap
5A trap's
7D Trapeze
7P trapezer
9E Trapezoids
4A traplike
8F trapline

8A Trapper
6A trappin'
9P Trappist
XR traprock
3J Trara
7G trashy
8Q traumas
8R traumatic

XR traumatized
8N Trav's
XR travail
7P travail's
6A travel-worn
7R Travelall
6J Traveled
XR Travelers'

8G Travelstead's
7R traversing
9R travesty
6F trawl
5A trawler
8R Traynor
6G trck
7Q treacheries

Word Type	F	D	U	SFI	3 Gr 3	4 Gr 4	5 Gr 5	6 Gr 6	7 Gr 7	8 Gr 8	9 Gr 9	X UnGr	A Read	B Eng & Gr	C Comp	D Lit	E Math	F Soc Stud	G Spell	H Sci	J Music	K Art	L Home Ec	M Shop	N Lib F	P Lib NF	Q Lib Ref	R Mag	S Rel
treacherous	27	.6925	3.8433	45.8	0	2	2	8	7	4	3	1	6	2	0	3	0	3	1	1	0	0	0	0	3	1	0	7	0
treachery	6	.2426	.3643	35.6	0	0	0	1	4	0	1	0	1	0	0	1	0	0	0	0	0	0	0	0	4	0	0	0	0
tread	15	.4973	1.6055	42.1	1	3	1	3	3	2	1	1	3	0	0	4	0	0	0	0	0	0	0	0	4	1	0	3	0
treading	8	.5179	.8675	39.4	1	1	0	0	1	2	3	0	1	0	1	2	0	0	0	0	0	1	0	0	0	2	1	0	0
treadmill	3	.3769	.2484	34.0	0	1	0	0	1	0	1	0	0	0	0	0	0	1	0	0	0	0	0	0	0	0	1	1	0
treads	5	.4137	.4607	36.6	0	0	1	1	1	0	2	0	1	1	0	2	0	0	0	0	0	0	0	0	0	1	0	0	0
treason	11	.4497	1.1210	40.5	0	0	4	0	3	2	2	0	4	0	0	0	0	1	0	0	0	0	0	0	0	1	4	1	0
treasure	109	.8307	18.306	52.6	22	17	16	26	13	9	1	5	49	5	0	6	0	13	2	1	3	1	0	0	8	7	4	10	0
Treasure	19	.5558	2.2958	43.6	6	4	3	0	6	0	0	0	8	5	0	0	0	1	0	0	0	0	0	0	1	0	2	2	0
treasured	12	.5829	1.4926	41.7	3	1	2	2	1	1	0	2	4	2	0	0	0	1	0	0	1	0	0	0	0	1	0	3	0
treasurer	17	.4298	1.5909	42.0	2	7	0	2	1	3	2	0	1	1	0	0	0	5	0	0	0	0	0	0	0	0	2	8	0
treasures	37	.6911	5.3217	47.3	5	3	13	5	7	2	2	0	14	1	0	4	0	9	0	0	0	1	0	0	2	0	4	2	0
treasuries	2	.0000	.0389	25.9	0	0	0	0	1	0	1	0	0	0	0	0	0	2	0	0	0	0	0	0	0	0	0	0	0
treasury	18	.5180	2.0007	43.0	2	0	5	2	2	2	4	1	3	1	0	0	0	5	0	0	0	0	0	0	0	2	6	1	0
Treasury	24	.4892	2.5166	44.0	12	0	1	0	0	5	6	0	2	0	0	1	0	4	0	0	1	0	0	0	0	12	0	4	0
treat	113	.8503	19.235	52.8	12	23	20	9	29	9	9	2	29	14	0	5	1	4	2	9	7	0	3	0	8	11	11	9	0
Treat	2	.1972	.1262	31.0	0	1	1	0	0	0	0	0	1	0	0	0	1	0	0	0	0	0	0	0	0	0	0	0	0
Treat's	2	.0000	.0914	29.6	0	2	0	0	0	0	0	0	2	0	0	0	0	0	0	0	0	0	0	0	0	0	0	0	0
treated	132	.8830	23.227	53.7	12	11	16	25	23	24	16	5	31	6	1	3	1	22	0	15	7	2	5	5	2	12	14	6	0
treaters	2	.0000	.0050	17.0	0	0	0	0	0	0	2	0	0	0	0	0	0	0	0	0	0	0	0	2	0	0	0	0	0
treaties	25	.4629	2.4892	44.0	2	0	5	0	6	8	4	0	1	0	0	1	0	10	0	0	0	0	0	0	0	3	9	1	0
treating	29	.4153	2.6338	44.2	1	3	6	0	3	5	11	0	4	2	0	0	0	2	0	5	0	0	0	8	1	1	3	3	0
treatise	5	.0743	.1541	31.9	0	0	1	0	1	2	1	0	1	0	0	0	0	0	0	0	0	0	0	0	0	0	4	0	0
treatment	130	.7876	20.630	53.1	0	10	23	13	18	22	38	6	25	3	0	3	0	6	1	24	4	7	6	7	6	7	22	9	0
treatments	8	.4464	.7859	39.0	0	1	0	2	2	1	2	0	1	0	0	0	0	0	0	4	0	0	0	1	0	1	1	0	0
treats	16	.6722	2.2195	43.5	2	5	3	4	1	1	0	0	4	1	0	1	2	0	0	1	3	0	0	0	0	0	2	2	0
treaty	92	.5267	10.323	50.1	4	6	18	7	19	28	10	0	10	0	0	2	0	37	1	1	0	0	0	0	0	6	27	8	0
Treaty	27	.4425	2.5503	44.1	1	0	9	0	6	9	2	0	0	0	0	1	0	9	0	0	0	1	0	0	0	2	14	0	0
treble	6	.1151	.1843	32.7	0	0	2	1	2	0	1	0	0	0	0	0	0	0	0	0	5	0	0	0	0	1	0	0	0
trebles	3	.2124	.1442	31.6	3	0	0	0	0	0	0	0	0	2	1	0	0	0	0	0	0	0	0	0	0	0	0	0	0
tred	2	.1620	.0760	28.8	0	0	0	0	1	0	1	0	0	0	0	0	0	0	0	0	0	0	0	1	0	0	0	1	0
tree	1421	.9218	260.35	64.2	380	292	143	237	191	101	54	23	568	62	11	63	42	82	20	176	53	21	0	11	80	126	43	63	0
Tree	33	.5838	4.1372	46.2	4	8	5	3	7	3	2	1	14	1	0	2	3	0	1	1	9	0	0	0	1	1	0	0	0
tree-lined	3	.3795	.2506	34.0	0	1	0	1	1	0	0	0	0	0	0	0	0	1	0	0	0	0	0	0	1	0	0	1	0
tree-tops	3	.0000	.0352	25.5	0	2	0	1	0	0	0	0	0	0	0	0	0	0	0	0	0	0	0	0	3	0	0	0	0
tree's	6	.4194	.5795	37.6	1	1	1	1	2	0	0	0	2	0	0	0	0	0	0	1	0	0	0	0	0	1	2	0	0
treed	2	.2442	.1134	30.5	0	0	0	1	0	1	0	0	0	1	0	0	0	0	0	0	0	0	0	0	0	0	0	1	0
treeless	19	.4579	1.8536	42.7	2	0	4	3	4	4	1	1	0	1	3	2	0	9	0	1	0	0	0	0	0	0	3	0	0
trees	1645	.9114	297.87	64.7	431	335	190	254	227	117	48	43	424	48	19	84	61	295	14	170	28	48	0	9	89	175	94	86	1
Trees	7	.3441	.5345	37.3	0	1	0	3	1	0	2	0	0	0	0	3	0	0	0	3	0	1	0	0	0	0	0	0	0
treetop	10	.5306	1.1420	40.6	2	3	2	0	2	0	0	1	3	1	1	0	0	0	0	0	0	0	0	0	0	1	1	3	0
treetops	33	.5147	3.7498	45.7	9	7	3	3	7	2	1	1	14	1	5	1	0	3	0	2	1	0	0	0	0	1	3	2	0
trek	4	.3791	.3246	35.1	0	0	2	1	1	0	0	0	0	0	0	0	0	0	0	0	1	0	0	0	0	0	1	2	0
trekked	5	.5599	.5798	37.6	0	1	0	0	3	1	0	0	0	0	0	1	0	1	0	0	0	0	0	0	0	1	1	1	0
trekkers	2	.0000	.0914	29.6	0	0	0	0	0	1	1	0	2	0	0	0	0	0	0	0	0	0	0	0	0	0	0	0	0
treks	2	.2285	.1129	30.5	0	0	0	0	2	0	0	0	0	0	0	0	0	1	0	0	0	0	0	0	0	0	1	0	0
Trelawney	2	.0000	.0234	23.7	0	0	0	0	2	0	0	0	0	0	0	0	0	0	0	0	0	0	0	0	2	0	0	0	0
trellis	5	.2342	.3071	34.9	5	0	0	0	0	0	0	0	1	0	0	0	0	0	0	1	0	0	0	0	3	0	0	0	0
Tremain	4	.1787	.2347	33.7	0	0	0	0	0	4	0	0	2	0	0	0	0	0	0	0	0	0	0	0	2	0	0	0	0
tremble	24	.6324	3.1874	45.0	4	5	3	4	3	2	2	1	8	1	1	1	0	0	0	1	1	0	0	0	7	4	0	0	0
trembled	40	.5770	4.9691	47.0	5	8	4	5	9	7	1	1	17	0	3	6	0	0	0	0	0	0	0	0	7	5	1	1	0
trembles	4	.2995	.2902	34.6	0	0	0	0	3	1	0	0	1	1	0	2	0	0	0	0	0	0	0	0	0	0	0	0	0
trembling	58	.5761	7.1825	48.6	1	16	4	10	16	8	2	1	23	0	1	11	0	0	0	0	0	0	0	0	15	4	0	4	0
tremblingly	2	.1787	.1174	30.7	0	0	1	0	0	1	0	0	1	0	0	0	0	0	0	0	0	0	0	0	1	0	0	0	0
tremendous	125	.9094	22.554	53.5	7	8	15	18	38	23	8	8	21	7	1	6	0	7	2	27	6	2	1	1	7	9	15	13	0
tremendously	19	.6336	2.4938	44.0	0	1	0	5	8	3	0	2	2	0	0	2	0	4	0	5	3	0	0	0	1	0	0	2	0
tremolo	2	.0000	.0162	22.1	0	0	0	0	0	1	1	0	0	0	0	0	0	0	0	0	2	0	0	0	0	0	0	0	0
tremor	2	.1787	.1174	30.7	0	0	1	1	0	0	0	0	1	0	0	0	0	0	0	0	0	0	0	0	1	0	0	0	0
tremors	3	.3452	.2543	34.1	0	0	0	1	0	0	1	1	1	0	0	0	0	0	0	1	0	0	0	0	0	0	0	1	0
tremulous	5	.3472	.3831	35.8	0	1	1	0	2	1	0	0	0	0	0	2	0	1	0	0	0	0	0	0	2	0	0	0	0
trench	17	.6771	2.3598	43.7	0	2	1	3	4	3	2	2	3	0	1	1	1	0	0	1	0	0	0	0	4	1	2	3	0
Trench	5	.2253	.2867	34.6	0	0	0	4	0	0	1	0	0	0	0	0	3	0	0	2	0	0	0	0	0	0	0	0	0
trencher	2	.0000	.0215	23.3	0	0	0	0	0	0	2	0	0	0	0	2	0	0	0	0	0	0	0	0	0	0	0	0	0
trenches	19	.4824	1.9751	43.0	0	3	0	4	5	1	6	0	1	0	0	0	0	1	0	9	0	0	0	0	0	2	5	1	0
trend	27	.6913	3.7732	45.8	0	1	3	1	8	9	5	0	2	0	2	0	1	4	0	0	1	1	1	3	0	0	8	4	0
trends	14	.5245	1.5442	41.9	0	1	0	1	1	6	2	3	1	0	0	0	0	2	0	1	2	0	0	0	0	0	3	5	0
Trent	4	.1873	.1827	32.6	0	1	2	0	0	0	0	1	0	0	0	0	0	0	0	0	0	0	0	0	0	0	3	1	0
Trenton	16	.4230	1.5167	41.8	1	1	0	1	8	5	0	0	3	0	0	0	0	4	0	0	0	0	0	0	7	1	0	1	0
Trepak	2	.0000	.0162	22.1	1	0	0	1	0	0	0	0	0	0	0	0	0	0	0	0	2	0	0	0	0	0	0	0	0
tres	3	.2223	.2106	33.2	0	0	0	0	1	2	0	0	2	1	0	0	0	0	0	0	0	0	0	0	0	0	0	0	0
trespass	2	.0299	.0221	23.4	1	0	0	0	0	0	1	0	0	0	0	0	0	0	0	0	0	0	0	0	0	0	1	0	1
trespasser	2	.1551	.0728	28.6	1	0	0	0	0	1	0	0	0	0	1	0	0	0	0	0	0	0	0	0	1	0	0	0	0
tress	2	.0000	.0914	29.6	1	0	0	1	0	0	0	0	2	0	0	0	0	0	0	0	0	0	0	0	0	0	0	0	0
tresses	3	.0000	.1370	31.4	1	0	0	2	0	0	0	0	3	0	0	0	0	0	0	0	0	0	0	0	0	0	0	0	0
trestle	4	.3192	.3100	34.9	2	0	0	0	1	0	0	1	1	0	0	0	0	0	0	0	0	0	0	0	0	2	0	1	0
tri	2	.1497	.1046	30.2	1	0	0	1	0	0	0	0	1	0	0	0	0	0	1	0	0	0	0	0	0	0	0	0	0
tri-level	2	.0000	.0037	15.7	0	0	0	0	0	2	0	0	0	0	0	0	0	0	0	0	0	2	0	0	0	0	0	0	0
triad	6	.0947	.1661	32.2	0	5	0	0	1	0	0	0	0	0	0	0	0	0	0	1	5	0	0	0	0	0	0	0	0
triads	7	.1925	.3387	35.3	0	3	0	0	3	1	0	0	0	0	0	0	0	0	0	3	4	0	0	0	0	0	0	0	0
trial	130	.7949	20.843	53.2	2	4	17	10	38	34	25	0	26	1	0	11	2	32	6	12	0	0	6	7	4	4	9	10	0
Trial	32	.1483	1.1842	40.7	11	13	3	4	0	1	0	0	0	0	0	0	0	0	26	0	0	0	0	0	0	5	0	1	0
trials	25	.7247	3.7181	45.7	2	3	3	1	4	6	4	2	6	0	0	1	1	7	0	2	0	0	0	0	1	2	2	3	0
triangle	440	.3397	33.747	55.3	24	26	39	70	33	122	122	4	8	0	0	4	376	2	0	7	12	0	1	7	6	12	5	0	0
Triangle	3	.1993	.1435	31.6	0	0	0	1	1	0	1	0	0	0	0	0	2	0	0	0	0	0	0	1	0	0	0	0	0
triangles	193	.3418	14.808	51.7	12	4	8	31	18	83	37	0	1	0	0	0	175	1	0	0	4	2	2	3	0	3	0	2	0
Triangles	2	.0000	.0299	24.8	0	0	0	0	0	0	2	0	0	0	0	0	2	0	0	0	0	0	0	0	0	0	0	0	0
triangular	77	.4173	6.9828	48.4	7	7	21	10	10	19	2	1	1	1	0	0	57	2	0	1	0	0	0	1	2	7	5	0	0
triangulation	2	.0000	.0050	17.0	0	0	0	0	2	0	0	0	0	0	0	0	0	0	0	0	0	0	0	2	0	0	0	0	0
tribal	33	.6767	4.5627	46.6	1	7	6	9	5	4	1	0	1	0	1	1	0	16	0	0	2	0	0	0	2	5	2	3	0
tribe	169	.8296	28.246	54.5	21	42	17	36	31	17	4	1	55	3	0	14	2	27	1	2	6	2	0	0	13	21	11	12	0
Tribe	2	.1814	.1187	30.7	0	1	0	0	1	0	0	0	1	0	0	0	0	0	0	0	0	0	0	0	0	0	0	1	0
tribes	192	.7327	28.664	54.6	36	37	23	34	41	14	6	1	31	4	0	2	0	74	9	0	12	2	0	0	1	23	23	11	0
Tribes	4	.3748	.3275	35.2	1	0	0	0	2	1	0	0	0	0	0	0	2	0	0	0	1	0	0	0	0	1	0	0	0
tribesman	5	.4552	.4847	36.9	0	2	0	1	2	0	0	0	0	0	0	0	0	1	0	0	0	0	0	0	0	1	1	2	0
tribesmen	22	.6379	2.8691	44.6	1	4	3	1	9	2	2	0	0	0	1	1	1	6	0	0	0	0	0	0	0	5	4	4	0

7R treacherously
6A treaded
7P treadle
9Q treasonable
5Q Treaties
8Q Treatises
4P Tredo
7A tree-box
3N tree-branch
5F tree-covered
6H tree-cutting
XR tree-dwelling
3J tree-e-e-e-t
3B tree-e-e-et
6N tree-ferns
6F tree-filled
4A tree-killing
3P tree-nesting
3F tree-shaded
4R tree-swinging
7A tree-trunk
9D tree-trunks
4A treehouse
3P TREES
9Q trefoil
7R treftadaeth
6J treh-pahk
5A trembly
5A tremendous-sized
9H tremens
7N trenchered
5P trenching
8R trend-jumping
7R Trendley
XR Trent's
5Q TrentinoAlto
6J trepak
8H trepanning
9Q trephination
9Q trephined
8C trespassers
3S trespasses
5A Trespassing
XR Tressider
9Q Trevithick
7M Tri-M-Ite
9Q trial-and-error
7P Trials
3Q triangular-shaped
7Q Triassic
5A tribe's
5N tribes-people
XB tribespeople

Word Type	F	D	U	SFI	3 Gr 3	4 Gr 4	5 Gr 5	6 Gr 6	7 Gr 7	8 Gr 8	9 Gr 9	X UnGr	A Read	B Eng & Gr	C Comp	D Lit	E Math	F Soc Stud	G Spell	H Sci	J Music	K Art	L Home Ec	M Shop	N Lib F	P Lib NF	Q Lib Ref	R Mag	S Rel
tribulation	5	.1446	.1801	32.6	0	1	1	1	1	0	1	0	0	0	0	0	0	0	0	0	4	0	0	0	0	0	0	1	0
tribulations	2	.2437	.1129	30.5	1	0	0	0	1	0	0	0	0	0	0	0	0	0	0	0	0	0	0	0	0	0	1	1	0
tribunal	5	.3742	.4184	36.2	0	0	0	1	2	0	1	1	0	0	0	0	0	3	0	0	0	0	0	0	0	0	1	1	0
Tribune	8	.3387	.6580	38.2	0	0	1	0	4	0	3	0	3	0	0	2	0	0	0	0	0	0	0	0	0	0	3	0	0
tributaries	25	.4481	2.4204	43.8	1	2	5	4	11	0	1	1	0	0	0	0	0	14	0	0	0	0	0	0	2	0	5	4	0
tributary	14	.3707	1.1632	40.7	0	2	3	1	7	1	0	0	0	0	0	0	0	9	2	0	0	0	0	0	0	0	0	3	0
tribute	16	.6534	2.1663	43.4	2	1	2	3	4	1	1	2	4	1	1	1	0	1	0	0	0	0	0	0	0	2	3	3	0
trice	3	.2261	.2131	33.3	1	0	0	1	0	1	0	0	2	0	0	0	0	0	0	0	0	0	0	0	1	0	0	0	0
triceps	5	.2213	.2870	34.6	0	0	0	0	0	0	1	4	0	0	0	0	0	0	0	4	0	0	0	0	0	0	1	0	0
triceratops	4	.0000	.0579	27.6	1	3	0	0	0	0	0	0	0	0	0	0	0	0	0	0	0	0	0	0	0	4	0	0	0
Triceratops	8	.0000	.1158	30.6	8	0	0	0	0	0	0	0	0	0	0	0	0	0	0	0	0	0	0	0	0	8	0	0	0
trichina	3	.0945	.0794	29.0	0	0	0	0	1	0	2	0	0	0	0	0	0	0	0	1	0	0	2	0	0	0	0	0	0
trichocysts	2	.0000	.0394	26.0	0	0	0	0	1	0	1	0	0	0	0	0	0	0	0	2	0	0	0	0	0	0	0	0	0
trick	189	.7916	30.435	54.8	67	28	18	21	23	17	11	4	80	6	0	16	6	2	4	2	2	1	2	0	38	16	2	12	0
Trick	2	.1972	.1262	31.0	1	0	1	0	0	0	0	0	1	0	0	0	1	0	0	0	0	0	0	0	0	0	0	0	0
tricked	12	.6633	1.6734	42.2	2	2	2	1	1	1	1	2	5	0	0	1	1	1	0	0	0	0	0	0	1	1	0	2	0
trickery	10	.4661	1.0726	40.3	1	0	1	2	5	0	1	0	5	1	0	1	0	0	0	0	0	0	0	0	0	3	0	0	0
trickle	16	.6548	2.1827	43.4	0	3	3	3	2	3	1	1	4	2	0	1	0	5	0	0	0	0	0	0	1	0	1	2	0
trickled	14	.6659	1.9568	42.9	4	3	2	2	3	0	0	0	6	1	0	1	0	0	0	0	0	0	0	0	1	3	1	1	0
trickles	3	.1934	.1471	31.7	0	1	0	0	2	0	0	0	0	0	0	0	0	1	0	1	0	1	0	0	0	0	0	0	0
trickling	11	.6192	1.4181	41.5	1	2	1	2	0	4	0	1	2	1	0	0	0	1	0	1	1	0	0	0	3	0	0	2	0
trickly	2	.1948	.1250	31.0	1	0	1	0	0	0	0	0	1	0	0	0	0	0	0	0	0	0	0	0	0	1	0	0	0
tricks	139	.8374	23.460	53.7	46	21	19	23	18	2	7	3	58	4	3	9	1	2	7	5	6	0	1	0	17	15	1	10	0
trickster	2	.2427	.1152	30.6	1	0	0	0	1	0	0	0	0	0	0	0	0	0	0	0	0	0	0	0	1	1	0	0	0
tricksters	2	.2407	.1138	30.6	0	0	1	0	0	1	0	0	0	0	0	1	0	0	0	0	0	0	0	0	0	1	0	0	0
tricky	32	.6191	4.1119	46.1	6	9	3	2	8	2	1	1	7	4	0	1	1	0	10	0	0	0	1	0	1	2	0	5	0
Tricky	2	.0000	.0914	29.6	2	0	0	0	0	0	0	0	2	0	0	0	0	0	0	0	0	0	0	0	0	0	0	0	0
tricycle	10	.4146	.8824	39.5	8	0	1	0	0	1	0	0	0	0	0	0	2	0	0	0	0	0	1	0	6	0	0	1	0
tricycles	6	.2360	.3419	35.3	5	0	1	0	0	0	0	0	0	0	0	0	4	0	0	0	0	0	0	0	2	0	0	0	0
trident	3	.1187	.1291	31.1	1	0	0	0	0	1	1	0	1	0	0	2	0	0	0	0	0	0	0	0	0	0	0	0	0
tried	1077	.9057	194.35	62.9	232	214	141	128	190	88	75	9	430	27	7	80	19	94	12	45	18	12	2	1	110	105	30	83	2
tries	123	.8646	21.292	53.3	29	17	11	15	22	15	13	1	37	9	1	7	2	8	2	25	1	0	4	0	6	3	7	11	0
Trieste	7	.3588	.6287	38.0	1	0	3	0	3	0	0	0	3	0	0	0	0	0	0	3	0	0	0	0	0	1	0	0	0
trifle	20	.6224	2.6073	44.2	1	1	3	3	5	3	3	1	6	0	0	3	0	0	0	0	0	1	0	0	5	1	2	2	0
trifles	4	.4525	.3990	36.0	0	0	0	1	1	1	0	1	1	1	0	1	0	0	0	0	0	0	0	0	1	0	0	0	0
trifling	6	.3128	.4118	36.1	0	0	0	0	5	0	0	1	0	0	2	0	0	0	0	1	0	0	0	0	1	1	0	1	0
trigger	21	.5714	2.5154	44.0	1	5	4	0	5	5	1	0	3	0	0	3	0	1	0	4	0	0	0	3	1	4	1	1	0
triggered	9	.4774	.8967	39.5	0	2	0	1	3	1	2	0	0	1	0	0	0	1	0	0	0	1	0	0	0	0	3	3	0
triggerfish	2	.0000	.0209	23.2	0	0	0	0	2	0	0	0	0	0	0	0	0	0	0	0	0	0	0	0	0	0	2	0	0
triggers	2	.2278	.1128	30.5	0	0	0	0	2	0	0	0	0	0	0	0	0	0	0	1	0	0	0	0	0	0	1	0	0
trigon	2	.0000	.0209	23.2	0	0	0	0	0	2	0	0	0	0	0	0	0	0	0	0	0	0	0	0	0	0	2	0	0
trigonometry	4	.3134	.2876	34.6	0	0	2	0	0	0	1	1	0	0	0	0	0	1	0	1	0	0	0	0	0	0	2	0	0
trill	2	.2407	.1090	30.4	0	1	1	0	0	0	0	0	0	1	0	0	0	0	0	0	1	0	0	0	0	0	0	0	0
trilled	2	.2443	.1130	30.5	0	1	0	0	1	0	0	0	0	0	0	1	0	0	0	0	0	0	0	0	1	0	0	0	0
trillion	18	.4440	1.7455	42.4	0	0	1	4	7	6	0	0	0	0	0	1	3	0	0	12	0	0	0	0	0	0	1	1	0
trillions	5	.2424	.2988	34.8	0	0	0	0	1	0	2	2	0	0	0	0	0	0	0	3	0	0	0	0	0	0	2	0	0
trilobite	3	.1813	.1402	31.5	0	0	0	0	2	1	0	0	0	0	0	0	0	0	0	1	0	0	0	0	0	0	2	0	0
trilobites	9	.3377	.6991	38.4	2	0	1	0	2	3	1	0	0	0	0	0	0	0	0	6	0	0	0	0	0	1	2	0	0
trim	74	.6028	9.2573	49.7	8	12	8	5	22	6	13	0	16	1	1	2	0	3	1	0	2	0	17	7	2	13	2	7	0
trimmed	33	.7300	4.9549	47.0	5	9	2	5	5	1	4	2	13	0	0	4	0	1	0	1	0	0	1	2	3	3	3	2	0
trimmer	4	.1483	.1455	31.6	0	2	0	0	2	0	0	0	0	0	0	0	0	0	0	0	0	0	0	2	0	2	0	0	0
trimmers	2	.0000	.0290	24.6	0	2	0	0	0	0	0	0	0	0	0	0	0	0	0	0	0	0	0	0	0	2	0	0	0
trimming	13	.2239	.6540	38.2	0	2	1	0	4	0	5	1	0	0	0	0	2	0	0	0	0	0	7	0	0	2	0	2	0
trimmings	12	.1650	.4771	36.8	0	0	0	1	2	3	6	0	1	1	0	1	0	0	0	0	0	0	8	0	0	0	0	1	0
trims	2	.2421	.0995	30.0	0	0	0	0	1	0	1	0	0	0	0	0	0	0	0	0	0	0	1	1	0	0	0	0	0
Trina	3	.0000	.0352	25.5	0	0	0	0	0	3	0	0	0	0	0	0	0	0	0	0	0	0	0	0	3	0	0	0	0
Trinidad	8	.5336	.9338	39.7	1	3	4	0	0	0	0	0	3	0	0	0	0	0	0	1	1	0	0	0	0	1	0	2	0
Trinity	7	.1462	.2577	34.1	0	1	1	0	2	1	2	0	0	0	0	0	0	0	0	0	1	0	0	0	0	1	3	1	1
trinket	5	.4661	.5245	37.2	2	0	1	1	1	0	0	0	2	0	0	1	0	0	0	0	1	0	0	0	0	1	0	0	0
Trinket	9	.0000	.1055	30.2	0	0	0	9	0	0	0	0	0	0	0	0	0	0	0	0	0	0	0	0	9	0	0	0	0
Trinket's	7	.0000	.0821	29.1	0	0	0	7	0	0	0	0	0	0	0	0	0	0	0	0	0	0	0	0	7	0	0	0	0
trinkets	11	.3796	.9495	39.8	1	3	1	0	2	2	1	1	1	0	0	0	0	4	0	0	0	0	0	0	0	5	0	1	0
trio	16	.4283	1.5388	41.9	0	2	6	2	3	3	0	0	5	1	0	0	0	0	0	0	6	0	0	0	1	0	0	3	0
Trio	3	.0000	.0243	23.8	0	2	1	0	0	0	0	0	0	0	0	0	0	0	0	0	3	0	0	0	0	0	0	0	0
triode	2	.2278	.1128	30.5	0	0	0	0	0	0	2	0	0	0	0	0	0	0	0	1	0	0	0	0	0	0	1	0	0
Triomphe	3	.2043	.1486	31.7	0	1	1	0	1	0	0	0	0	0	0	0	0	0	0	0	0	0	0	0	0	1	2	0	0
trioxide	2	.0000	.0394	26.0	0	0	0	0	0	0	2	0	0	0	0	0	0	0	0	2	0	0	0	0	0	0	0	0	0
trip	693	.9143	125.89	61.0	163	155	100	72	94	53	39	17	196	36	7	20	93	110	20	50	9	3	5	1	12	57	14	60	0
tripe	2	.1948	.1250	31.0	1	0	0	0	1	0	0	0	1	0	0	0	0	0	0	0	0	0	0	0	0	1	0	0	0
triphosphate	2	.2278	.1128	30.5	0	0	0	0	1	0	1	0	0	0	0	0	0	0	0	1	0	0	0	0	0	0	1	0	0
triphylite	2	.0000	.0394	26.0	0	0	0	0	0	0	0	2	0	0	0	0	0	0	0	2	0	0	0	0	0	0	0	0	0
triple	23	.5609	2.6937	44.3	0	3	2	0	5	5	8	0	2	0	0	0	7	1	0	4	3	0	0	3	0	0	1	2	0
Triple	3	.3870	.2492	34.0	0	0	0	2	1	0	0	0	0	0	0	0	0	0	0	0	0	0	0	0	1	0	1	1	0
tripled	7	.4795	.7108	38.5	0	2	0	2	1	0	2	0	0	0	0	0	2	0	0	2	1	0	0	0	0	0	2	0	0
triples	10	.0000	.1497	31.8	0	0	1	0	0	0	9	0	0	0	0	0	10	0	0	0	0	0	0	0	0	0	0	0	0
triplet	3	.0000	.0243	23.8	0	0	1	0	0	2	0	0	0	0	0	0	0	0	0	0	3	0	0	0	0	0	0	0	0
triplets	5	.3008	.3283	35.2	1	0	0	2	1	0	0	1	0	1	0	0	0	0	0	0	3	0	0	0	1	0	0	0	0
tripod	12	.3268	.9634	39.8	0	0	9	0	2	0	1	0	4	0	1	0	0	0	0	0	0	0	0	0	0	7	0	0	0
Tripoli	5	.3812	.4221	36.3	0	1	0	2	0	1	1	0	0	0	0	0	0	3	0	0	1	0	0	0	0	0	1	0	0
tripped	34	.6328	4.5945	46.6	11	7	2	3	4	2	5	0	18	4	0	6	0	0	0	0	0	0	0	1	2	2	0	1	0
tripping	15	.6777	2.0964	43.2	0	2	2	1	6	1	3	0	4	2	0	3	0	0	0	1	0	0	1	0	1	0	1	2	0
trips	152	.8854	26.809	54.3	36	27	21	16	28	14	3	7	32	7	3	6	22	17	0	16	1	2	1	0	4	18	8	15	0
Triptych	2	.0000	.0162	22.1	0	0	1	0	1	0	0	0	0	0	0	0	0	0	0	0	2	0	0	0	0	0	0	0	0
Tristram	3	.1119	.0792	29.0	0	0	1	0	0	2	0	0	0	0	2	0	0	0	0	0	0	0	0	0	0	0	1	0	0
triumph	62	.7313	9.2817	49.7	5	5	8	8	16	9	8	3	17	4	0	13	0	7	0	3	2	0	0	0	3	9	2	2	0
triumphal	4	.4741	.3983	36.0	0	1	0	0	0	1	1	1	0	0	0	1	0	1	0	0	1	0	0	0	0	0	1	0	0
triumphant	28	.5702	3.3749	45.3	1	2	5	5	10	2	2	1	7	0	0	6	0	0	0	1	6	0	0	0	5	2	0	1	0
triumphantly	22	.5575	2.6425	44.2	1	0	6	6	8	0	1	0	8	2	0	5	0	0	0	0	0	0	0	0	5	1	1	0	0
triumphed	4	.4829	.4095	36.1	0	0	1	0	2	1	0	0	0	0	0	0	0	1	0	0	0	0	0	0	1	1	0	1	0
triumphs	10	.4454	.9701	39.9	0	0	1	0	3	4	2	0	1	0	0	1	0	3	0	0	0	0	0	0	0	1	4	0	0
triumvirate	3	.1277	.1363	31.3	0	0	0	0	2	1	0	0	1	0	0	0	0	0	0	0	0	0	0	0	0	0	0	2	0
trivial	5	.4543	.4843	36.9	0	0	0	0	3	0	2	0	0	1	0	0	0	0	0	1	0	0	0	0	0	1	0	2	0
Trixie	8	.0000	.3655	35.6	0	0	0	0	0	8	0	0	8	0	0	0	0	0	0	0	0	0	0	0	0	0	0	0	0
trod	14	.4712	1.4872	41.7	1	0	3	4	4	0	2	0	6	0	0	5	0	0	0	0	1	0	0	0	0	1	1	0	0
trodden	3	.0000	.0067	18.3	0	0	1	0	0	0	2	0	0	0	3	0	0	0	0	0	0	0	0	0	0	0	0	0	0

5Q Tribunal
7R tribunals
6A Tribute
6R tributes
9L trichinosis
7R trick-or-treat
3R trick-or-treating
3N trick-riding
4N trick's
8J tricking
8D Tricksters
XJ tricolor
9L tricot
8L tricots
6R tridacna
8Q Tridacna
7N tridacnae
5Q tridymite
7D trifled
4A Trigger
7R triggering
6G trigraph
3N trike
8H trillionth
4N Trim
7Q Trimble
9D Trimble-toe
5R Trinidadian
6Q trinitrotoluene
5P trinity
8J trios
6N Tripheath
9H triple-F
3Q triple-moated
7P triple-threat
6R triplethreat
8H tripods
3A Tripolitania
6B tripp
9H trisodium
7Q Tristan
8J Triste
8D trite
7R Tritheim
6H tritium
8Q triton
8R triumvirs
9B Trivet
8K trivialities
8A Trix
7N Trixie's
XH troglodyte

Word Type	F	D	U	SFI	3 Gr 3	4 Gr 4	5 Gr 5	6 Gr 6	7 Gr 7	8 Gr 8	9 Gr 9	X UnGr	A Read	B Eng & Gr	C Comp	D Lit	E Math	F Soc Stud	G Spell	H Sci	J Music	K Art	L Home Ec	M Shop	N Lib F	P Lib NF	Q Lib Ref	R Mag	S Rel
Trois-Freres	3	.0000	.0434	26.4	0	0	0	0	0	0	0	3	0	0	0	0	0	0	0	0	0	0	0	0	0	3	0	0	0
Trojan	14	.5117	1.6210	42.1	0	0	1	2	2	8	0	1	8	0	0	0	0	1	1	0	0	0	0	0	0	0	3	1	0
Trojans	18	.2071	1.1917	40.8	0	0	1	13	3	1	0	0	11	7	0	0	0	0	0	0	0	0	0	0	0	0	0	0	0
troll	9	.4794	.9898	40.0	6	1	0	0	2	0	0	0	5	0	0	0	0	0	0	0	1	0	0	0	1	0	0	2	0
trolley	9	.4499	.8717	39.4	1	0	1	0	2	3	2	0	1	2	0	4	0	1	0	0	1	0	0	0	0	0	0	0	0
trolling	5	.3111	.3857	35.9	0	0	3	0	2	0	0	0	1	0	0	0	0	3	0	0	0	0	0	0	0	0	0	1	0
trolls	13	.0705	.3826	35.8	4	9	0	0	0	0	0	0	3	0	0	0	0	0	0	0	10	0	0	0	0	0	0	0	0
trombone	19	.0465	.3266	35.1	1	5	1	2	2	8	0	0	0	0	0	0	1	0	0	0	18	0	0	0	0	0	0	0	0
trombones	11	.0911	.2799	34.5	0	3	1	1	2	3	1	0	0	0	0	0	0	0	0	0	10	0	0	0	0	0	1	0	0
tromped	2	.2443	.1130	30.5	0	0	2	0	0	0	0	0	0	0	0	1	0	0	0	0	0	0	0	0	1	0	0	0	0
troop	35	.4815	3.5888	45.5	6	2	7	2	6	8	4	0	4	3	7	2	6	2	0	1	0	0	0	0	0	5	0	5	0
Troop	6	.2782	.3977	36.0	1	1	2	1	1	0	0	0	1	0	1	0	0	0	0	0	0	0	0	0	0	0	0	4	0
trooped	10	.5412	1.1751	40.7	1	2	1	2	3	1	0	0	4	0	1	0	0	0	0	0	1	0	0	0	2	1	0	1	0
trooper	4	.4538	.4020	36.0	0	0	1	1	2	0	0	0	1	0	0	1	0	0	0	0	0	0	0	0	0	1	0	1	0
troopers	8	.4703	.8584	39.3	0	1	3	0	4	0	0	0	4	2	0	0	0	0	0	0	1	0	0	0	0	0	0	1	0
trooping	5	.4789	.5381	37.3	1	2	0	2	0	0	0	0	2	0	0	0	0	0	0	0	0	0	0	0	1	1	0	1	0
troops	187	.6508	25.036	54.0	6	11	28	13	31	69	23	6	13	4	0	9	1	72	0	0	1	0	0	0	7	21	28	31	0
trophies	5	.4817	.5058	37.0	0	0	0	1	2	2	0	0	0	1	0	1	0	0	0	0	0	0	0	0	0	2	0	1	0
trophy	8	.5338	.9141	39.6	0	3	0	1	2	1	0	1	2	1	0	1	0	0	0	0	0	0	0	0	2	0	0	2	0
Trophy	3	.1277	.1363	31.3	0	0	0	1	2	0	0	0	1	0	0	0	0	0	0	0	0	0	0	0	0	0	0	2	0
tropic	6	.5440	.7057	38.5	1	0	0	2	2	0	1	0	2	0	0	0	0	1	1	0	0	0	0	0	1	0	1	0	0
Tropic	21	.3085	1.5437	41.9	0	6	7	5	3	0	0	0	0	0	0	0	0	15	0	4	0	0	0	0	0	0	2	0	0
tropical	176	.7327	26.235	54.2	9	37	18	32	52	10	13	5	21	1	1	3	1	51	1	30	1	2	1	0	2	13	43	5	0
Tropical	8	.2426	.4880	36.9	0	0	3	4	1	0	0	0	0	0	0	0	0	5	0	0	0	0	0	0	0	3	0	0	0
tropics	51	.5483	5.9149	47.7	2	4	7	7	21	4	6	0	3	0	0	0	0	17	0	13	0	0	0	0	1	3	12	2	0
Tropics	3	.0000	.0583	27.7	0	0	2	1	0	0	0	0	0	0	0	0	0	3	0	0	0	0	0	0	0	0	0	0	0
tropism	2	.0000	.0394	26.0	0	0	0	2	0	0	0	0	0	0	0	0	0	0	0	2	0	0	0	0	0	0	0	0	0
troposphere	6	.2445	.3637	35.6	0	1	1	0	4	0	0	0	0	0	0	0	0	0	0	4	0	0	0	0	0	0	2	0	0
trot	27	.5912	3.4062	45.3	8	5	3	2	5	4	0	0	10	3	1	5	0	0	0	0	0	0	0	0	1	7	0	0	0
trots	6	.1358	.2190	33.4	0	1	0	0	5	0	0	0	0	0	0	5	0	0	0	0	0	0	0	0	0	1	0	0	0
trotted	48	.6151	6.2698	48.0	8	10	5	6	14	3	2	0	19	1	1	8	0	0	0	0	0	0	0	0	9	9	0	1	0
trotter	5	.2422	.3874	35.9	3	2	0	0	0	0	0	0	4	0	0	0	0	0	0	0	0	0	0	0	0	1	0	0	0
Trotter	3	.0000	.0583	27.7	0	0	0	0	0	3	0	0	0	0	0	0	0	3	0	0	0	0	0	0	0	0	0	0	0
trotters	2	.0000	.0290	24.6	0	2	0	0	0	0	0	0	0	0	0	0	0	0	0	0	0	0	0	0	0	2	0	0	0
trotting	21	.3770	1.7941	42.5	3	4	1	6	5	0	1	1	4	0	0	5	0	0	0	0	0	0	0	0	10	2	0	0	0
troubadors	2	.2152	.1357	31.3	0	1	0	0	0	1	0	0	1	0	0	0	0	1	0	0	0	0	0	0	0	0	0	0	0
troubadour	3	.0995	.1144	30.6	0	2	0	1	0	0	0	0	1	0	0	0	0	0	0	0	2	0	0	0	0	0	0	0	0
troubadours	5	.1446	.1801	32.6	0	2	0	1	1	1	0	0	0	0	0	0	0	0	0	0	4	0	0	0	0	0	0	1	0
trouble	695	.8839	122.82	60.9	102	133	87	68	147	84	62	12	280	38	3	62	14	56	18	23	10	1	8	0	62	45	14	61	0
Trouble	8	.0409	.1627	32.1	2	6	0	0	0	0	0	0	1	0	0	0	0	0	7	0	0	0	0	0	0	0	0	0	0
troubled	57	.8169	9.4054	49.7	11	3	5	5	12	11	7	3	19	1	2	5	0	10	0	4	1	0	1	0	5	3	2	4	0
troublemakers	2	.1814	.1187	30.7	0	1	0	1	0	0	0	0	1	0	0	0	0	0	0	0	0	0	0	0	0	0	0	1	0
troubles	76	.6302	10.045	50.0	6	10	9	7	24	10	8	2	23	2	0	8	0	9	3	2	2	0	1	0	4	2	8	11	1
troublesome	42	.7180	6.0976	47.9	1	1	7	4	8	11	9	1	5	2	0	3	0	1	15	3	3	1	1	0	3	1	1	3	0
troubling	5	.3842	.4760	36.8	1	1	0	0	1	0	2	0	3	0	0	1	0	0	0	0	0	0	0	0	0	0	0	1	0
trough	23	.6085	2.9358	44.7	3	6	0	6	7	0	0	1	5	3	0	0	0	2	0	2	0	0	0	0	5	1	0	5	0
Trough	6	.0000	.0628	28.0	0	0	0	6	0	0	0	0	0	0	0	0	0	0	0	0	0	0	0	0	0	0	6	0	0
troughs	7	.5222	.7804	38.9	1	0	1	3	0	2	0	0	1	0	0	1	0	2	0	0	0	0	0	0	0	0	1	2	0
troupe	9	.5378	1.0459	40.2	0	1	2	2	1	1	1	1	3	0	0	0	0	0	0	0	1	0	0	0	0	1	2	2	0
trouping	2	.0000	.0290	24.6	0	2	0	0	0	0	0	0	0	0	0	0	0	0	0	0	0	0	0	0	0	2	0	0	0
trouser	3	.2772	.2004	33.0	0	0	0	1	1	1	0	0	1	0	1	0	0	0	0	0	0	0	1	0	0	0	0	0	0
trousers	60	.7366	9.0934	49.6	11	19	3	8	7	4	4	4	24	4	0	6	0	3	0	1	0	0	2	0	7	10	1	2	0
trout	53	.6451	7.2146	48.6	7	4	3	16	15	6	0	2	21	2	0	3	1	7	0	0	0	0	0	0	1	2	2	14	0
Trout	3	.0000	.0243	23.8	0	0	0	3	0	0	0	0	0	0	0	0	0	0	0	0	3	0	0	0	0	0	0	0	0
Trovatore	2	.0000	.0162	22.1	0	0	0	0	1	1	0	0	0	0	0	0	0	0	0	0	2	0	0	0	0	0	0	0	0
trowel	4	.1717	.2284	33.6	0	0	0	0	2	0	0	2	2	0	0	2	0	0	0	0	0	0	0	0	0	0	0	0	0
troweled	2	.0000	.0243	23.9	0	0	0	0	1	0	0	1	0	0	0	0	0	0	0	0	0	0	0	0	0	0	0	2	0
Troy	36	.5631	4.3887	46.4	0	0	6	13	10	4	2	1	15	10	0	0	0	3	0	0	0	2	0	0	0	1	3	2	0
Troy's	2	.1717	.1142	30.6	0	0	0	0	0	1	1	0	1	0	0	1	0	0	0	0	0	0	0	0	0	0	0	0	0
truancy	2	.0000	.0215	23.3	0	0	0	0	0	0	2	0	0	0	0	2	0	0	0	0	0	0	0	0	0	0	0	0	0
truant	7	.3817	.6819	38.3	0	1	0	0	1	4	1	0	5	0	0	1	0	0	0	0	0	0	0	0	0	1	0	0	0
Trubar	2	.0000	.0209	23.2	0	0	0	0	0	2	0	0	0	0	0	0	0	0	0	0	0	0	0	0	0	0	2	0	0
truce	8	.4186	.7387	38.7	0	0	1	2	4	0	1	0	1	0	0	0	0	1	0	0	0	0	0	0	4	1	0	1	0
truck	410	.9009	73.649	58.7	153	42	63	46	50	18	36	2	156	13	4	25	15	57	2	33	2	3	2	5	37	18	2	36	0
Truck	9	.2102	.6719	38.3	0	8	1	0	0	0	0	0	8	0	0	0	0	0	0	0	0	0	0	0	0	1	0	0	0
truck-farming	2	.0000	.0389	25.9	0	0	0	0	2	0	0	0	0	0	0	0	0	2	0	0	0	0	0	0	0	0	0	0	0
truck's	2	.2446	.1142	30.6	0	0	1	0	1	0	0	0	0	0	0	0	0	0	0	0	0	0	0	0	1	0	0	1	0
trucked	6	.3635	.4910	36.9	1	0	3	2	0	0	0	0	0	0	0	0	0	4	0	0	1	0	0	0	0	0	0	1	0
trucker	2	.1814	.1187	30.7	1	0	0	0	0	0	1	0	1	0	0	0	0	0	0	0	0	0	0	0	0	0	0	1	0
trucking	8	.3952	.7138	38.5	2	0	0	1	1	0	3	1	2	0	0	0	0	0	0	0	0	0	0	1	0	0	1	4	0
Trucking	2	.0000	.0243	23.9	0	0	0	0	0	0	2	0	0	0	0	0	0	0	0	0	0	0	0	0	0	0	0	2	0
truckload	2	.2337	.1157	30.6	0	0	2	0	0	0	0	0	0	0	0	0	0	1	0	0	0	0	0	0	1	0	0	0	0
truckloads	5	.4783	.5121	37.1	1	0	1	0	2	1	0	0	0	0	0	0	0	2	0	1	0	0	0	0	1	0	0	1	0
trucks	209	.8083	34.083	55.3	71	25	40	22	25	14	10	2	50	3	9	1	10	73	6	7	1	3	0	5	7	4	13	17	0
Trudeau	2	.0000	.0243	23.9	0	0	0	0	0	0	2	0	0	0	0	0	0	0	0	0	0	0	0	0	0	0	0	2	0
trudge	4	.2708	.2760	34.4	0	0	1	0	2	0	1	0	1	0	0	2	0	1	0	0	0	0	0	0	0	0	0	0	0
trudged	32	.5710	3.8886	45.9	5	8	2	5	5	5	2	0	10	1	4	5	0	2	0	0	1	0	0	0	4	4	0	1	0
trudging	9	.5101	1.0033	40.0	2	1	2	0	1	2	1	0	3	0	1	2	0	1	0	0	0	0	0	0	1	1	0	0	0
Trudy	25	.1942	1.4086	41.5	0	16	8	0	0	1	0	0	8	1	0	0	0	0	0	0	0	0	0	0	16	0	0	0	0
Trudy's	2	.1787	.1174	30.7	0	1	1	0	0	0	0	0	1	0	0	0	0	0	0	0	0	0	0	0	1	0	0	0	0
true	1696	.8397	285.01	64.5	258	288	172	221	315	197	195	50	269	41	7	68	719	89	24	123	66	5	17	36	40	62	66	63	1
True	61	.2297	3.3420	45.2	1	1	1	2	55	0	1	0	3	1	0	52	0	1	0	0	1	0	1	0	0	1	0	1	0
true-to-life	2	.1717	.1142	30.6	0	0	0	0	1	0	1	0	1	0	0	1	0	0	0	0	0	0	0	0	0	0	0	0	0
truer	4	.4530	.4014	36.0	0	0	0	1	1	1	0	1	1	0	0	0	0	0	0	0	0	0	0	0	0	1	1	0	0
truest	6	.5203	.6617	38.2	0	0	0	0	3	1	1	1	1	0	0	1	0	0	0	0	1	0	0	0	1	0	0	2	0
Trui	10	.0000	.4568	36.6	0	0	0	10	0	0	0	0	10	0	0	0	0	0	0	0	0	0	0	0	0	0	0	0	0
Trujillo	4	.2348	.2372	33.8	0	0	1	0	3	0	0	0	0	0	0	0	0	3	0	0	0	0	0	0	0	0	1	0	0
trulio	7	.1726	.3988	36.0	4	0	3	0	0	0	0	0	3	0	0	0	0	0	0	0	0	0	0	0	0	4	0	0	0
truly	146	.6373	19.258	52.8	12	25	14	13	32	21	23	6	26	9	2	12	1	20	2	8	11	2	2	1	14	14	9	10	3
Truly	2	.1948	.1250	31.0	1	0	1	0	0	0	0	0	1	0	0	0	0	0	0	0	0	0	0	0	0	1	0	0	0
Truman	16	.3046	1.1526	40.6	0	1	0	0	1	10	4	0	0	0	0	0	0	12	0	0	0	0	0	0	0	0	1	3	0
Truman's	4	.0000	.0778	28.9	0	0	0	0	0	4	0	0	0	0	0	0	0	4	0	0	0	0	0	0	0	0	0	0	0
trumpet	77	.3206	5.4854	47.4	10	19	6	10	12	17	2	1	6	2	0	2	0	3	0	2	56	1	0	0	1	2	1	1	0
Trumpet	5	.2183	.2661	34.3	1	4	0	0	0	0	0	0	0	0	0	0	0	0	0	0	1	0	0	0	0	4	0	0	0

3A Troll
4P Trolley
9B trolleys
8D trompin
8D trompin'
7R tromping
6R troop's
5P Trooper
7R Tropicbird
6H tropisms
6H tropistic
5H tropopause
6J troppo
5A Trot
7P troth
8R trotline
7R Trotsky
7R Trotsky's
4P Trotting
4P trotting-horse
3A TROUBLE
7A trouble-maker
7A trouble-makers
7F trouble-shooter
8G trouble-some
5R troubleshooter
8M troubleshooting
3A Troublesome
7R trough's
XR Trouille
9D trounce
7R Troupe
8D trousers'
5N trousies
8G trousseau
XJ trouvere
7H Trowbridge
7R Troxel
4Q troy
5Q Troyon
8Q trs
5Q Truce
6F Trucial
3P truck-garden
5P truck-mounted
9R truck-trailers
7R truckbed
4F truckers
7R truckmen
5B Trucks
7A Trudeau's
5A true-hearted
5B truely
4N truffle
4N truffles
7M truing
8F truism
XJ truix
3P trulli
4Q truly-spaced
9D trumped-up

Word Type	F	D	U	SFI	3 Gr 3	4 Gr 4	5 Gr 5	6 Gr 6	7 Gr 7	8 Gr 8	9 Gr 9	X UnGr	A Read	B Eng & Gr	C Comp	D Lit	E Math	F Soc Stud	G Spell	H Sci	J Music	K Art	L Home Ec	M Shop	N Lib F	P Lib NF	Q Lib Ref	R Mag	S Rel
trumpeted	4	.4525	.4044	36.1	1	0	1	1	0	1	0	0	1	0	0	0	0	1	0	0	0	0	0	0	1	0	0	1	0
trumpeter	5	.4460	.4740	36.8	0	0	2	1	0	0	0	2	0	0	0	0	0	0	0	1	0	0	0	0	1	0	2	1	0
trumpeters	4	.2387	.2178	33.4	2	0	0	0	0	0	2	0	0	0	0	0	0	0	0	0	2	0	0	0	2	0	0	0	0
trumpeting	7	.2326	.5117	37.1	0	3	1	1	0	2	0	0	5	0	0	2	0	0	0	0	0	0	0	0	0	0	0	0	0
trumpets	40	.3930	3.3369	45.2	2	5	4	4	10	10	5	0	1	2	0	3	0	2	0	0	26	0	0	0	1	1	2	1	1
trundle	10	.3080	.8058	39.1	1	5	3	1	0	0	0	0	5	0	0	0	0	0	0	0	0	0	0	0	4	1	0	0	0
trundling	3	.1250	.1342	31.3	1	1	0	0	1	0	0	0	1	0	0	0	0	0	0	0	0	0	0	0	2	0	0	0	0
trunk	186	.7861	29.720	54.7	38	50	10	28	40	13	4	3	66	6	0	16	6	8	1	21	2	7	0	0	22	18	4	9	0
trunkless	2	.0000	.0219	23.4	0	0	0	2	0	0	0	0	0	2	0	0	0	0	0	0	0	0	0	0	0	0	0	0	0
trunks	79	.7746	12.405	50.9	18	19	3	10	18	5	4	2	18	0	0	7	1	8	0	12	1	2	0	0	7	11	10	2	0
truss	13	.0265	.1112	30.5	1	0	0	0	0	0	12	0	0	0	0	0	0	0	0	0	0	0	0	12	0	1	0	0	0
trussed	6	.3810	.5114	37.1	0	0	1	1	2	2	0	0	1	0	0	3	0	0	0	0	0	0	0	0	0	0	1	1	0
trusses	9	.0674	.1627	32.1	2	0	0	0	0	0	7	0	0	0	0	0	0	0	0	0	0	0	0	7	0	2	0	0	0
trust	103	.8116	16.923	52.3	10	20	7	13	21	16	13	3	40	2	2	11	0	10	1	2	2	0	0	0	10	7	7	9	0
Trust	3	.0000	.0314	25.0	0	0	2	0	1	0	0	0	0	0	0	0	0	0	0	0	0	0	0	0	0	0	3	0	0
trusted	43	.4547	4.4176	46.5	2	6	8	4	11	8	3	1	15	3	0	2	0	6	0	1	2	0	0	0	3	5	3	2	1
trustees	10	.5990	1.2270	40.9	2	0	0	0	1	4	1	2	0	2	0	0	0	1	0	0	0	0	0	0	2	1	2	2	0
Trusteeship	4	.1325	.1944	32.9	0	0	0	1	0	1	2	0	1	0	0	0	0	3	0	0	0	0	0	0	0	0	0	0	0
trustful	2	.1717	.1142	30.6	0	0	0	1	1	0	0	0	1	0	0	1	0	0	0	0	0	0	0	0	0	0	0	0	0
trusting	13	.5327	1.5284	41.8	0	3	3	1	3	3	0	0	6	0	0	1	0	0	0	0	0	0	0	0	3	1	0	2	0
trusts	3	.2437	.2277	33.6	1	1	0	1	0	0	0	0	2	0	0	0	0	0	0	1	0	0	0	0	0	0	0	0	0
trustworthy	8	.5710	.9444	39.8	0	0	0	1	3	2	2	0	0	1	1	1	0	1	0	2	0	0	0	0	1	1	0	0	0
trusty	4	.3635	.3138	35.0	0	0	0	1	1	0	2	0	0	1	0	2	0	0	0	0	0	0	0	0	1	0	0	0	0
truth	215	.8526	36.691	55.6	14	17	19	27	47	58	27	6	56	10	3	35	14	15	2	5	1	1	3	0	18	22	11	18	1
Truth	5	.3780	.4114	36.1	2	1	0	0	0	1	0	1	0	1	0	0	0	0	0	0	0	0	0	0	0	2	0	2	0
truthful	9	.5349	1.0608	40.3	2	0	3	0	0	3	1	0	4	1	0	2	0	1	0	0	0	0	0	0	0	0	0	1	0
truthfully	8	.5013	.8703	39.4	1	1	0	1	0	2	2	1	2	0	1	1	0	1	0	0	0	0	0	0	0	2	0	1	0
truths	12	.6015	1.5421	41.9	0	2	0	3	3	3	0	1	5	0	0	2	0	1	0	0	1	0	0	0	0	0	2	1	0
try	1958	.9146	355.31	65.5	370	391	260	242	322	208	136	29	473	150	13	73	141	115	160	247	178	73	40	12	84	108	18	72	1
Trygve	2	.0000	.0389	25.9	0	0	0	0	0	1	1	0	0	0	0	0	0	2	0	0	0	0	0	0	0	0	0	0	0
tryin'	4	.3030	.2949	34.7	1	1	0	0	1	0	1	0	1	0	0	0	0	0	0	0	0	0	0	0	2	0	0	1	0
trying	751	.8902	133.52	61.3	126	148	95	89	141	82	50	20	294	27	1	54	11	59	9	45	9	7	8	2	77	61	11	76	0
tryout	6	.3876	.5836	37.7	1	3	0	0	2	0	0	0	4	0	0	0	0	0	0	0	0	0	0	0	1	0	0	1	0
tryouts	9	.2441	.6912	38.4	2	3	2	2	0	0	0	0	7	0	0	0	0	0	0	0	0	0	0	0	2	0	0	0	0
TS	2	.0000	.0299	24.8	0	0	0	0	2	0	0	0	0	0	0	0	2	0	0	0	0	0	0	0	0	0	0	0	0
Tsar	7	.3133	.4751	36.8	0	0	0	3	2	1	1	0	0	0	0	2	0	0	0	0	4	0	0	0	0	0	1	0	0
tsars	2	.0000	.0389	25.9	0	0	0	2	0	0	0	0	0	0	0	0	0	2	0	0	0	0	0	0	0	0	0	0	0
Tse-tung	3	.3769	.2484	34.0	0	0	2	0	0	1	0	0	0	0	0	0	0	1	0	0	0	0	0	0	0	0	1	1	0
tsetse	4	.0000	.0778	28.9	0	0	0	1	2	0	1	0	0	0	0	0	0	4	0	0	0	0	0	0	0	0	0	0	0
tsu-croo	2	.0000	.0162	22.1	2	0	0	0	0	0	0	0	0	0	0	0	0	0	0	0	2	0	0	0	0	0	0	0	0
Tsu-croo	3	.0000	.0243	23.8	3	0	0	0	0	0	0	0	0	0	0	0	0	0	0	0	3	0	0	0	0	0	0	0	0
tsub	2	.0000	.0389	25.9	0	0	0	0	0	2	0	0	0	0	0	0	0	2	0	0	0	0	0	0	0	0	0	0	0
tsunami	2	.0000	.0394	26.0	0	0	2	0	0	0	0	0	0	0	0	0	0	0	0	2	0	0	0	0	0	0	0	0	0
tt	4	.1757	.1672	32.2	1	0	1	0	2	0	0	0	0	1	0	0	0	0	3	0	0	0	0	0	0	0	0	0	0
tu	2	.1733	.1149	30.6	0	0	0	0	1	1	0	0	1	1	0	0	0	0	0	0	0	0	0	0	0	0	0	0	0
Tu	2	.0000	.0914	29.6	0	2	0	0	0	0	0	0	2	0	0	0	0	0	0	0	0	0	0	0	0	0	0	0	0
TU	4	.0000	.0599	27.8	0	0	1	1	0	2	0	0	0	0	0	0	4	0	0	0	0	0	0	0	0	0	0	0	0
tu-re-lu-re-lu	2	.0000	.0162	22.1	0	2	0	0	0	0	0	0	0	0	0	0	0	0	0	0	2	0	0	0	0	0	0	0	0
tu-whit	2	.0000	.0219	23.4	0	0	0	2	0	0	0	0	0	2	0	0	0	0	0	0	0	0	0	0	0	0	0	0	0
tu-who	2	.0000	.0219	23.4	0	0	0	2	0	0	0	0	0	2	0	0	0	0	0	0	0	0	0	0	0	0	0	0	0
Tuamotu	2	.1948	.1250	31.0	0	0	0	0	1	1	0	0	1	0	0	0	0	0	0	0	0	0	0	0	0	1	0	0	0
Tuan	10	.0000	.1448	31.6	10	0	0	0	0	0	0	0	0	0	0	0	0	0	0	0	0	0	0	0	0	10	0	0	0
Tuan's	2	.0000	.0290	24.6	2	0	0	0	0	0	0	0	0	0	0	0	0	0	0	0	0	0	0	0	0	2	0	0	0
tuatara	11	.0705	.2680	34.3	0	0	0	0	11	0	0	0	0	0	0	0	0	0	0	1	0	0	0	0	0	0	10	0	0
tuataras	2	.0000	.0209	23.2	0	0	0	0	2	0	0	0	0	0	0	0	0	0	0	0	0	0	0	0	0	0	2	0	0
tub	75	.6671	10.589	50.2	9	20	13	8	5	14	2	4	38	1	0	7	0	0	0	14	1	0	0	0	4	1	1	8	0
tuba	17	.1835	.7203	38.6	3	1	1	2	5	5	0	0	0	0	0	0	0	0	0	0	16	1	0	0	0	0	0	0	0
tube	504	.6511	68.094	58.3	42	57	76	40	90	100	67	32	58	0	2	6	7	6	2	327	25	2	2	5	7	3	25	27	0
tube's	2	.0000	.0243	23.9	0	0	0	0	2	0	0	0	0	0	0	0	0	0	0	0	0	0	0	0	0	0	0	2	0
tubelike	2	.2278	.1128	30.5	0	0	2	0	0	0	0	0	0	0	0	0	0	0	0	1	0	0	0	0	0	0	1	0	0
tuber	3	.1320	.1599	32.0	0	2	0	0	0	0	1	0	2	0	0	0	0	0	0	0	0	0	1	0	0	0	0	0	0
tuberculosis	12	.4295	1.1175	40.5	1	1	2	2	0	4	2	0	0	0	0	0	0	1	0	4	0	0	0	0	0	3	4	0	0
Tuberculosis	2	.2278	.1128	30.5	0	0	0	0	0	2	0	0	0	0	0	0	0	0	0	1	0	0	0	0	0	0	1	0	0
tubers	5	.4267	.4793	36.8	0	1	0	1	2	0	0	1	1	0	0	0	0	0	0	1	0	0	0	0	0	2	1	0	0
tubes	177	.6649	24.341	53.9	22	34	11	31	44	19	13	3	22	2	0	1	0	5	0	103	2	2	0	3	8	3	15	11	0
tubing	34	.6381	4.4215	46.5	2	4	4	2	13	1	7	1	0	0	0	1	0	0	0	12	3	0	3	2	0	0	4	9	0
Tubman	9	.2058	.4892	36.9	7	0	0	0	2	0	0	0	1	0	0	1	0	0	0	0	0	0	0	0	0	7	0	0	0
tubs	6	.3539	.5373	37.3	0	2	2	1	0	0	0	1	3	0	0	0	0	0	0	1	0	0	0	0	0	2	0	0	0
tubular	11	.5188	1.1972	40.8	2	0	1	0	2	3	2	1	1	0	0	0	0	0	0	2	0	0	1	1	0	1	5	0	0
tubules	7	.0000	.0733	28.6	0	0	0	0	0	0	7	0	0	0	0	0	0	0	0	0	0	0	0	0	0	0	7	0	0
tuck	13	.3996	1.1536	40.6	2	3	1	1	2	2	2	0	3	0	0	1	0	0	0	0	1	0	4	0	2	2	0	0	0
Tuck	6	.0000	.0869	29.4	0	6	0	0	0	0	0	0	0	0	0	0	0	0	0	0	0	0	0	0	0	6	0	0	0
Tuckahoe	2	.0000	.0914	29.6	0	0	0	2	0	0	0	0	2	0	0	0	0	0	0	0	0	0	0	0	0	0	0	0	0
tucked	56	.7477	8.5916	49.3	9	9	8	7	13	7	2	1	23	2	1	4	0	0	0	3	0	0	2	0	11	3	1	6	0
Tucker	32	.2646	2.3483	43.7	9	14	0	3	0	1	1	4	18	0	0	0	0	2	0	0	1	7	0	0	0	0	0	4	0
Tucker's	7	.0627	.1492	31.7	6	0	0	0	0	0	0	1	1	0	0	0	0	0	0	0	0	5	0	0	0	0	0	1	0
Tuckers	8	.0000	.3655	35.6	7	0	0	0	0	1	0	0	8	0	0	0	0	0	0	0	0	0	0	0	0	0	0	0	0
Tuckers'	2	.0000	.0914	29.6	2	0	0	0	0	0	0	0	2	0	0	0	0	0	0	0	0	0	0	0	0	0	0	0	0
tucking	8	.3267	.6370	38.0	0	1	0	1	5	0	1	0	3	0	0	4	0	0	0	0	0	0	1	0	0	0	0	0	0
tucks	8	.2007	.4180	36.2	1	1	0	1	1	0	4	0	2	0	0	0	0	0	0	0	0	0	4	0	1	0	0	1	0
Tucson	3	.3012	.1987	33.0	0	1	0	1	1	0	0	0	0	0	0	0	1	0	0	0	0	0	1	0	0	0	0	1	0
Tudor	3	.1397	.0937	29.7	0	0	0	0	3	0	0	0	0	0	0	0	0	0	0	0	1	0	0	2	0	0	0	0	0
Tuesday	73	.7528	11.109	50.5	15	14	12	8	7	7	9	1	10	11	3	3	22	5	3	2	6	0	0	0	2	1	0	5	0
Tuesdays	2	.0000	.0299	24.8	1	0	0	1	0	0	0	0	0	0	0	0	2	0	0	0	0	0	0	0	0	0	0	0	0
tuft	8	.3417	.6875	38.4	1	1	0	1	3	1	1	0	4	0	0	0	0	0	0	0	0	0	0	0	3	0	1	0	0
tufts	12	.6112	1.5570	41.9	4	1	0	2	2	2	0	1	4	0	0	1	0	0	0	3	0	0	0	0	1	0	2	1	0
Tufts	2	.0000	.0243	23.9	0	0	0	0	0	1	1	0	0	0	0	0	0	0	0	0	0	0	0	0	0	0	0	2	0
tug	35	.6320	4.7919	46.8	6	13	2	4	5	4	0	1	22	2	0	0	0	3	0	3	0	0	0	0	2	2	0	1	0
tugboat	8	.3743	.7423	38.7	0	6	2	0	0	0	0	0	4	0	0	0	0	2	0	0	0	0	0	0	0	0	0	2	0
tugboats	7	.5549	.8088	39.1	4	2	1	0	0	0	0	0	0	1	0	0	0	3	0	0	1	0	0	0	0	1	1	0	0
tugged	36	.6009	4.7385	46.8	13	7	2	6	3	2	3	0	23	0	0	3	0	1	0	0	0	0	0	0	1	5	1	2	0
tugging	15	.6489	2.0346	43.1	1	6	1	2	3	1	1	0	5	0	0	2	0	0	0	2	0	1	1	0	1	2	0	1	0
tugs	22	.6856	3.1700	45.0	7	7	2	5	1	0	0	0	11	1	0	1	0	1	0	2	2	0	0	0	0	3	0	1	0
Tuhan	5	.0000	.2284	33.6	0	0	0	0	5	0	0	0	5	0	0	0	0	0	0	0	0	0	0	0	0	0	0	0	0

5Q Trumpeter
7Q trumpetings
7R truncate
9M truncated
4N truncheon
6R truncularіopsis
7N trundled
3G Trunk
6Q trunk-like
4P trunkmaker
5F Truro
8F Trustee
4A trustfully
7Q Truth-in-Lending
7A truthfulness
XE Try
4H TRY
6H trypanosome
6H trys
8B ts
6H Ts
4A Tsao
7F tsar
8Q tsar's
4R Tsar's
7D Tsarevna
5P Tse-tung's
7F Tsing
5Q Tsinghua
4A Tsong
8E TSP
5Q Tsung-jen
6J Tsur
6H TT
6A Tuaregs
7Q tuataras'
9D Tubal
4H tube-like
7Q tube-shaped
8H tubeful
9P tuberculars
7N tuberculated
6A tuberculin-tested
XR tubful
3N tubfuls
8H tubule
5G tuch
9L tuck-in
6D tucker
4P tuckered
7Q tuco-tuco
7Q tucunare
4R tudor
9R Tudors
3E Tues
6R Tuesday-night
3B Tuesday's
8Q tufa
6A Tuffy
5P tufted
9D tug-of-war
9K Tugendhut
4J Tuileries

Word Type	F	D	U	SFI	3 Gr 3	4 Gr 4	5 Gr 5	6 Gr 6	7 Gr 7	8 Gr 8	9 Gr 9	X UnGr	A Read	B Eng & Gr	C Comp	D Lit	E Math	F Soc Stud	G Spell	H Sci	J Music	K Art	L Home Ec	M Shop	N Lib F	P Lib NF	Q Lib Ref	R Mag	S Rel
tuition	2	.1698	.1133	30.5	1	0	0	1	0	0	0	0	1	0	0	0	0	0	0	0	0	0	0	0	0	0	1	0	0
tuk	3	.3427	.2477	33.9	0	1	0	0	2	0	0	0	1	0	0	0	0	0	0	0	0	0	0	0	1	0	0	1	0
tukels	3	.0000	.0583	27.7	0	0	0	0	3	0	0	0	0	0	0	0	0	3	0	0	0	0	0	0	0	0	0	0	0
Tula	3	.0000	.0583	27.7	0	0	0	3	0	0	0	0	0	0	0	0	0	3	0	0	0	0	0	0	0	0	0	0	0
Tulagi	2	.0000	.0290	24.6	0	0	0	0	2	0	0	0	0	0	0	0	0	0	0	0	0	0	0	0	0	2	0	0	0
tule	2	.0000	.0389	25.9	0	2	0	0	0	0	0	0	0	0	0	0	0	2	0	0	0	0	0	0	0	0	0	0	0
tulip	20	.6447	2.7273	44.4	8	5	1	1	0	3	2	0	9	0	1	0	1	1	3	2	0	0	0	0	0	0	2	1	0
Tulip	4	.2399	.3011	34.8	2	0	0	1	0	0	1	0	3	1	0	0	0	0	0	0	0	0	0	0	0	0	0	0	0
tulip-shaped	2	.0000	.0234	23.7	0	2	0	0	0	0	0	0	0	0	0	0	0	0	0	0	0	0	0	0	2	0	0	0	0
tulips	15	.5105	1.6632	42.2	6	4	2	0	2	0	1	0	4	1	2	0	0	4	0	0	0	0	0	0	0	1	2	1	0
Tuliyani	5	.0000	.0972	29.9	0	0	0	0	0	5	0	0	0	0	0	0	0	5	0	0	0	0	0	0	0	0	0	0	0
Tully	3	.0000	.1370	31.4	0	0	0	3	0	0	0	0	3	0	0	0	0	0	0	0	0	0	0	0	0	0	0	0	0
Tulsa	5	.3757	.4211	36.2	0	0	0	0	4	0	0	1	0	0	0	0	2	2	0	0	0	0	0	0	0	1	0	0	0
tum	2	.2446	.1142	30.6	0	0	1	0	0	0	0	1	0	0	0	0	0	0	0	0	0	0	0	0	1	0	0	1	0
tum-ti-tum	2	.0000	.0215	23.3	0	0	0	0	0	2	0	0	0	0	0	2	0	0	0	0	0	0	0	0	0	0	0	0	0
tumble	25	.7250	3.7063	45.7	3	4	5	4	4	2	2	1	6	1	0	3	0	5	0	1	4	0	0	0	1	1	2	1	0
tumbled	37	.6965	5.3664	47.3	8	5	7	8	5	2	2	0	16	1	1	3	0	2	0	0	0	0	0	0	5	5	0	4	0
tumbledown	3	.2223	.2106	33.2	2	0	0	0	1	0	0	0	2	1	0	0	0	0	0	0	0	0	0	0	0	0	0	0	0
tumbler	5	.4684	.4982	37.0	2	0	1	1	1	0	0	0	0	0	0	1	0	0	0	1	0	0	0	0	0	2	0	1	0
tumblers	5	.4013	.4531	36.6	0	1	0	1	3	0	0	0	1	0	0	2	0	1	0	0	0	0	0	0	1	0	0	0	0
tumbles	4	.4521	.3985	36.0	1	1	2	0	0	0	0	0	1	1	0	0	0	0	0	0	0	0	0	0	1	0	1	0	0
tumbling	40	.7195	5.9086	47.7	4	6	8	8	5	3	4	2	12	2	1	8	0	4	0	0	0	0	0	0	2	5	1	5	0
tumbrils	2	.0000	.0215	23.3	0	0	0	0	0	0	2	0	0	0	0	2	0	0	0	0	0	0	0	0	0	0	0	0	0
Tumi	2	.0000	.0914	29.6	2	0	0	0	0	0	0	0	2	0	0	0	0	0	0	0	0	0	0	0	0	0	0	0	0
tummies	2	.1787	.1174	30.7	0	1	0	0	0	0	0	1	1	0	0	0	0	0	0	0	0	0	0	0	1	0	0	0	0
tummy	3	.2175	.1545	31.9	0	0	0	0	2	0	0	1	0	0	0	2	0	0	0	0	0	0	0	0	0	0	0	1	0
tumor	32	.1750	1.5170	41.8	0	0	2	0	0	0	24	6	0	0	0	0	0	0	0	8	0	0	0	0	0	24	0	0	0
tumors	5	.3564	.3984	36.0	0	0	0	0	0	1	2	2	0	0	0	0	0	0	0	2	0	0	0	0	0	1	2	0	0
tumpline	4	.2420	.3089	34.9	3	0	0	1	0	0	0	0	3	0	0	0	0	1	0	0	0	0	0	0	0	0	0	0	0
tumult	10	.4157	.9381	39.7	0	0	1	2	3	1	3	0	3	1	0	0	0	0	0	0	3	0	0	0	3	0	0	0	0
tumultuous	5	.2579	.3658	35.6	0	0	1	1	3	0	0	0	3	0	1	0	0	0	0	0	0	0	0	0	0	0	0	1	0
tuna	26	.6972	3.6813	45.7	3	8	2	4	3	1	5	0	0	3	0	1	1	7	0	6	0	0	2	0	3	1	0	2	0
tundra	38	.5684	4.5412	46.6	0	9	7	9	4	2	6	1	3	0	0	0	0	18	1	1	0	0	0	0	5	0	5	5	0
Tundra	3	.1852	.1342	31.3	1	0	0	2	0	0	0	0	0	0	0	0	0	0	0	0	2	0	0	0	0	1	0	0	0
tundras	3	.2425	.1816	32.6	0	0	1	1	0	0	0	1	0	0	0	0	0	2	0	0	0	0	0	0	0	0	0	1	0
tune	309	.3370	23.338	53.7	67	88	55	35	34	16	13	1	42	12	1	12	0	3	3	4	207	0	1	0	7	11	0	6	0
Tune	5	.0619	.1340	31.3	2	0	3	0	0	0	0	0	1	0	0	0	0	0	0	0	4	0	0	0	0	0	0	0	0
tune-up	2	.0000	.0243	23.9	0	0	0	0	2	0	0	0	0	0	0	0	0	0	0	0	0	0	0	0	0	0	0	2	0
tuned	65	.2968	4.3100	46.3	10	15	13	5	17	3	2	0	5	0	1	2	1	0	0	1	51	0	0	1	1	0	0	2	0
tuned-in	2	.0000	.0299	24.8	0	0	2	0	0	0	0	0	0	0	0	0	2	0	0	0	0	0	0	0	0	0	0	0	0
tuneful	5	.2177	.2519	34.0	0	0	0	1	2	1	0	1	0	0	0	0	0	0	0	0	3	0	0	0	0	0	0	2	0
tuneless	2	.2375	.1088	30.4	0	0	0	0	2	0	0	0	0	0	0	0	0	0	0	0	1	0	0	0	0	0	0	1	0
tuner	7	.2320	.3693	35.7	0	1	0	0	1	5	0	0	0	0	0	0	0	0	0	0	5	0	0	0	0	1	1	0	0
tuners	4	.1770	.1679	32.3	0	0	0	0	0	3	1	0	0	0	0	1	0	0	0	0	3	0	0	0	0	0	0	0	0
tunes	79	.1976	3.8356	45.8	13	14	22	9	10	6	3	2	7	0	0	1	0	0	0	1	61	0	0	0	3	2	0	4	0
Tunes	2	.2411	.1091	30.4	1	0	0	0	1	0	0	0	0	0	0	1	0	0	0	0	1	0	0	0	0	0	0	0	0
tung	2	.2305	.1080	30.3	1	0	0	0	0	1	0	0	0	0	0	0	0	0	1	0	0	0	0	0	0	1	0	0	0
Tungom	3	.0000	.1370	31.4	0	0	0	3	0	0	0	0	3	0	0	0	0	0	0	0	0	0	0	0	0	0	0	0	0
tungsten	12	.5633	1.4064	41.5	0	0	1	2	2	5	2	0	0	0	0	0	1	2	0	4	0	0	0	1	0	0	3	1	0
tunic	4	.3381	.3009	34.8	0	0	0	0	1	1	2	0	0	0	0	2	0	1	0	0	0	0	0	0	0	0	0	1	0
tuning	42	.5065	4.5708	46.6	5	6	1	6	10	8	2	4	4	1	0	1	0	0	0	24	8	0	0	0	0	1	1	2	0
Tunis	4	.4478	.4002	36.0	1	1	0	1	1	0	0	0	1	0	0	0	0	1	0	0	0	0	0	0	1	0	1	0	0
Tunisia	11	.2184	.5972	37.8	1	5	0	3	2	0	0	0	0	0	0	0	0	5	0	0	0	0	0	0	0	0	6	0	0
Tunisian	2	.0000	.0209	23.2	0	2	0	0	0	0	0	0	0	0	0	0	0	0	0	0	0	0	0	0	0	0	2	0	0
tunnel	105	.7779	16.739	52.2	27	19	12	14	19	3	3	8	52	0	1	3	0	2	1	11	3	0	0	0	5	11	4	12	0
Tunnel	2	.2375	.1088	30.4	0	0	1	0	0	0	0	1	0	0	0	0	0	0	0	0	1	0	0	0	0	0	0	1	0
tunneling	2	.1698	.1133	30.5	1	0	0	0	1	0	0	0	1	0	0	0	0	0	0	0	0	0	0	0	0	0	1	0	0
tunnels	65	.7597	10.064	50.0	18	14	8	12	5	0	4	4	16	0	0	1	0	11	0	14	0	0	1	1	1	7	4	9	0
Tuolumne	7	.2428	.3968	36.0	0	1	5	0	0	0	1	0	0	1	0	0	0	0	0	1	0	0	0	0	0	0	5	0	0
turban	12	.3119	.9110	39.6	1	4	0	2	5	0	0	0	2	0	0	0	0	6	0	0	0	0	0	0	4	0	0	0	0
turbans	7	.5696	.8349	39.2	1	1	2	0	1	1	1	0	1	0	0	1	0	1	1	0	0	0	0	0	0	1	2	0	0
turbidity	5	.0000	.0986	29.9	0	0	0	0	0	0	5	0	0	0	0	0	0	0	0	5	0	0	0	0	0	0	0	0	0
turbine	44	.4302	4.1161	46.1	0	15	2	4	10	1	11	1	0	0	0	0	0	3	0	21	0	0	0	0	0	0	12	8	0
turbines	20	.4323	1.8687	42.7	0	7	2	3	5	0	3	0	0	0	0	0	0	2	0	7	0	0	0	0	0	0	7	4	0
turbojet	2	.0000	.0394	26.0	0	0	0	0	0	0	2	0	0	0	0	0	0	0	0	2	0	0	0	0	0	0	0	0	0
turbulence	8	.3014	.5511	37.4	0	0	0	0	8	0	0	0	0	0	0	0	0	0	0	2	0	0	0	0	0	0	1	5	0
turbulent	9	.6678	1.2189	40.9	0	0	2	1	2	2	2	0	0	0	0	1	0	1	0	0	1	0	0	0	1	2	1	2	0
ture	2	.0000	.0162	22.1	0	1	0	1	0	0	0	0	0	0	0	0	0	0	2	0	0	0	0	0	0	0	0	0	0
tureen	2	.1948	.1250	31.0	0	1	1	0	0	0	0	0	1	0	0	0	0	0	0	0	0	0	0	0	0	1	0	0	0
turf	24	.5191	2.8756	44.6	4	0	5	8	6	0	1	0	18	1	0	0	0	0	0	0	1	0	0	0	2	0	0	2	0
Turf	3	.2309	.1631	32.1	0	0	0	0	1	0	0	2	0	0	0	1	0	0	0	0	0	0	0	0	0	0	0	2	0
turgid	2	.2437	.1129	30.5	0	0	0	0	1	0	1	0	0	0	0	0	0	0	0	0	0	0	0	0	0	0	1	1	0
turgor	4	.0000	.0419	26.2	0	0	0	0	4	0	0	0	0	0	0	0	0	0	0	0	0	0	0	0	0	0	4	0	0
Turi	3	.0000	.1370	31.4	0	3	0	0	0	0	0	0	3	0	0	0	0	0	0	0	0	0	0	0	0	0	0	0	0
Turin	8	.3692	.6635	38.2	3	0	1	2	1	0	1	0	0	0	0	0	0	4	0	0	0	0	0	0	0	3	1	0	0
Turk	13	.6483	1.7442	42.4	0	2	4	0	0	4	1	2	3	1	1	1	0	1	0	0	2	0	0	0	0	2	0	2	0
turkey	127	.7940	20.385	53.1	68	22	5	6	17	4	5	0	39	8	1	2	1	1	8	0	1	0	3	0	22	9	11	21	0
Turkey	81	.6117	10.391	50.2	7	3	9	6	49	5	2	0	11	3	0	2	0	48	1	0	2	0	0	1	1	8	4	0	0
turkey-cock's	2	.0000	.0215	23.3	0	0	0	0	0	2	0	0	0	0	0	2	0	0	0	0	0	0	0	0	0	0	0	0	0
turkey's	3	.3465	.2515	34.0	1	1	0	0	1	0	0	0	1	0	0	0	0	0	0	0	0	0	0	0	0	1	0	1	0
Turkey's	11	.1284	.4597	36.6	0	0	1	0	10	0	0	0	0	0	0	0	0	10	0	0	0	0	0	0	0	1	0	0	0
turkeys	68	.6184	8.7219	49.4	30	7	5	11	10	3	0	2	10	1	0	2	0	7	1	0	0	0	0	0	25	8	7	7	0
Turkish	63	.6494	8.5380	49.3	0	15	16	1	21	5	2	3	15	1	0	0	0	19	1	0	1	0	0	0	1	15	6	4	0
Turks	40	.5024	4.2722	46.3	0	0	7	0	19	9	1	4	0	2	0	0	0	25	0	1	0	3	0	0	0	5	3	1	0
turmeric	3	.0000	.0365	25.6	0	0	0	0	0	0	0	3	0	0	0	0	0	0	0	0	0	0	0	0	0	0	0	3	0
turmoil	13	.5364	1.4958	41.7	0	1	0	2	5	3	2	0	3	0	0	1	0	2	0	0	0	1	0	0	0	4	0	2	0
turn	1577	.9346	291.76	64.7	322	245	173	164	332	168	147	26	392	72	14	80	23	120	143	195	49	16	64	41	74	128	74	92	0
Turn	3	.3131	.2349	33.7	1	1	0	1	0	0	0	0	1	0	0	0	0	1	0	0	1	0	0	0	0	0	0	0	0
Turnbuckle	2	.0000	.0234	23.7	2	0	0	0	0	0	0	0	0	0	0	0	0	0	0	0	0	0	0	0	2	0	0	0	0
turncoat	3	.3852	.2500	34.0	1	0	0	0	1	0	0	1	0	0	0	1	0	0	0	0	0	0	0	0	0	1	0	1	0
turned	1785	.8891	317.30	65.0	312	354	173	206	378	206	121	35	791	48	11	147	5	117	4	69	27	5	3	19	226	151	49	111	2
turner	7	.4735	.7233	38.6	1	3	0	0	0	3	0	0	2	1	1	0	0	0	0	0	0	0	1	0	0	2	0	0	0
Turner	52	.7063	7.7332	48.9	6	16	9	10	5	5	1	0	33	1	0	0	1	5	0	0	4	1	0	0	1	3	1	2	0

6A Tukahoe
7F tukel
5P Tukulor
7H tularemia
4A tules
5K tulgey
8G tulle
8G Tulle
6A Tully's
8Q Tului
6J Tum
3A tumble-down
XR tumble-dry
4A tumbling-down
3D tumbly-looking
4N Tummy-ache
3J tummy-aches
5K Tumtum
7N tun
7A tun-a-tun-a-tunin'
XR Tuna
3N tuna-fish
7R tunable
8R tuneup
XP Tung-pin
8Q Tungusic
9H tunicates
8R Tuning
7Q tunnel-like
9B tunneled
6R Tunney
8Q Tupi
6A tuppenny-ha'penny
6J Tura
XQ turbaned
8Q turbid
4Q turbine-driven
7R turbo
3F Turbo
7R turbocharger
7R Turbocharger
XR turbocharging
7Q turbogenerators
4Q turboprop
7M turbopumps
7N turbots
7R Turbulence
5P Turfan
4A Turis
4P turk-
7R turke-lepathy
3P Turkestan
8D turkey-cock
7N turkey-pear
8Q Turkic-speaking
7Q turkie
7Q turkies
XR Turku
5N turn-button
9D turn-off
8L turn-under
9D turn'd
3A turn't
7R turnaround
3N Turnbuckle's
9R turndown
5N turned-down

Word Type	F	D	U	SFI	3 Gr 3	4 Gr 4	5 Gr 5	6 Gr 6	7 Gr 7	8 Gr 8	9 Gr 9	X UnGr	A Read	B Eng & Gr	C Comp	D Lit	E Math	F Soc Stud	G Spell	H Sci	J Music	K Art	L Home Ec	M Shop	N Lib F	P Lib NF	Q Lib Ref	R Mag	S Rel
Turner's	6	.3105	.4694	36.7	1	1	0	2	2	0	0	0	2	0	0	0	0	1	0	0	0	0	0	0	0	0	3	0	0
turnin'	2	.1787	.1174	30.7	0	0	0	0	2	0	0	0	1	0	0	0	0	0	0	0	0	0	0	0	1	0	0	0	0
turning	397	.8981	70.999	58.5	47	58	38	62	102	42	41	7	125	15	3	38	3	22	1	47	6	3	9	14	40	31	12	28	0
turning-point	2	.2401	.1133	30.5	0	0	0	0	0	0	2	0	0	0	0	0	0	0	0	0	0	0	0	0	0	1	1	0	0
turnip	16	.5646	1.9883	43.0	7	3	2	0	2	1	1	0	9	0	0	1	0	2	0	0	0	1	1	0	2	0	0	0	0
Turnip-seed	4	.0000	.1827	32.6	4	0	0	0	0	0	0	0	4	0	0	0	0	0	0	0	0	0	0	0	0	0	0	0	0
turnips	53	.6078	6.9368	48.4	29	5	3	11	2	1	2	0	25	1	0	1	0	9	0	1	0	0	1	0	12	3	0	0	0
Turnips	2	.0000	.0914	29.6	1	0	0	1	0	0	0	0	2	0	0	0	0	0	0	0	0	0	0	0	0	0	0	0	0
turnout	2	.0000	.0914	29.6	1	0	0	0	1	0	0	0	2	0	0	0	0	0	0	0	0	0	0	0	0	0	0	0	0
Turnout	2	.0000	.0243	23.9	2	0	0	0	0	0	0	0	2	0	0	0	0	0	0	0	0	0	0	0	0	0	0	0	0
turnover	5	.4500	.5011	37.0	1	0	1	0	0	2	1	0	1	0	0	0	0	2	0	0	0	0	0	0	0	0	1	1	0
turnpike	8	.3948	.7419	38.7	0	0	2	1	5	0	0	0	3	0	0	0	0	0	0	1	0	0	0	0	0	0	3	1	0
turnpikes	2	.2418	.1091	30.4	1	0	1	0	0	0	0	0	1	0	0	0	0	0	1	0	0	0	0	0	0	0	1	0	0
turns	440	.9171	80.010	59.0	94	71	46	50	80	54	31	14	88	15	12	27	8	26	8	79	31	4	3	15	24	42	17	41	0
turntable	2	.2287	.1077	30.3	0	0	0	0	0	2	0	0	0	0	0	0	1	0	0	0	0	0	0	0	0	0	0	0	0
turnvereins	2	.0000	.0209	23.2	0	0	2	0	0	0	0	0	0	0	0	0	0	0	0	0	0	0	0	0	0	2	0	0	0
turpentine	30	.3741	2.4010	43.8	2	1	18	1	0	5	3	0	0	0	0	0	0	2	0	2	0	0	0	6	1	2	17	0	0
Turpin	2	.0000	.0209	23.2	0	0	2	0	0	0	0	0	0	0	0	0	0	0	0	0	0	0	0	0	0	2	0	0	0
turquoise	9	.2288	.6098	37.9	5	1	0	2	1	0	0	0	5	0	0	0	0	1	0	0	0	2	0	0	0	1	0	0	0
turquoises	5	.0000	.2284	33.6	5	0	0	0	0	0	0	0	5	0	0	0	0	0	0	0	0	0	0	0	0	0	0	0	0
turret	11	.4233	1.0712	40.3	4	0	3	2	1	1	0	0	4	0	0	0	0	0	0	0	0	0	0	0	4	2	0	1	0
turreted	2	.2437	.1129	30.5	0	0	1	0	0	1	0	0	0	0	0	0	0	0	0	0	0	0	0	0	0	0	1	1	0
turrets	2	.2446	.1142	30.6	1	0	0	0	1	0	0	0	0	0	0	0	0	0	0	0	0	0	0	0	1	0	0	1	0
turrible	3	.0000	.1370	31.4	0	0	3	0	0	0	0	0	3	0	0	0	0	0	0	0	0	0	0	0	0	0	0	0	0
turtle	104	.8512	17.704	52.5	39	14	16	8	23	0	0	4	21	7	3	2	6	0	1	21	6	1	1	0	3	16	14	2	0
Turtle	58	.3623	5.2244	47.2	15	6	24	13	0	0	0	0	31	22	0	2	0	0	0	0	0	0	0	0	2	1	0	0	0
turtle's	7	.4299	.6948	38.4	2	1	0	3	1	0	0	0	3	0	0	0	0	1	0	1	1	0	0	0	1	0	0	0	0
turtles	95	.6027	12.116	50.8	33	22	2	4	33	0	1	0	27	1	0	1	4	3	0	13	1	0	0	0	2	16	27	0	0
Tuscan	4	.3790	.3299	35.2	1	0	1	1	1	0	0	0	0	0	0	0	0	0	0	0	0	0	0	0	2	1	1	0	0
Tuscany	10	.4257	.9018	39.6	1	0	1	0	3	5	0	0	0	0	0	0	0	0	1	0	0	0	0	0	2	5	2	0	0
Tuscarawas	12	.0000	.1288	31.1	0	0	0	0	12	0	0	0	0	0	0	12	0	0	0	0	0	0	0	0	0	0	0	0	0
Tuscumbia	8	.3552	.6905	38.4	0	1	3	0	0	2	0	2	3	0	0	0	0	0	0	0	0	0	0	0	3	0	2	0	0
Tushi	15	.0000	.2917	34.6	0	0	0	0	0	15	0	0	0	0	0	0	15	0	0	0	0	0	0	0	0	0	0	0	0
tusk	5	.3627	.4135	36.2	0	0	0	2	0	1	1	1	1	0	0	1	0	0	0	1	0	1	0	0	1	0	0	0	0
Tuskegee	7	.2134	.3732	35.7	0	0	1	0	4	1	1	0	0	0	0	4	0	3	0	0	0	0	0	0	0	0	0	0	0
tusker	2	.0000	.0914	29.6	0	0	0	2	0	0	0	0	2	0	0	0	0	0	0	0	0	0	0	0	0	0	0	0	0
tuskers	2	.0000	.0243	23.9	0	0	0	0	2	0	0	0	0	0	0	0	0	0	0	0	0	0	0	0	0	2	0	0	0
tusks	38	.7206	5.7089	47.6	2	8	6	5	12	2	3	0	20	2	0	3	1	4	0	2	0	0	0	0	3	1	0	3	0
tussles	2	.0000	.0215	24.1	0	0	0	0	0	0	2	0	0	0	0	2	0	0	0	0	0	0	0	0	0	0	0	0	0
tut	5	.2342	.2727	34.4	0	2	0	0	1	0	1	1	0	0	0	0	0	3	0	0	0	0	0	0	2	0	0	0	0
Tut-ankh-amon	2	.0000	.0914	29.6	0	0	0	2	0	0	0	0	2	0	0	0	0	0	0	0	0	0	0	0	0	0	0	0	0
Tutei	2	.0000	.0914	29.6	0	0	0	2	0	0	0	0	2	0	0	0	0	0	0	0	0	0	0	0	0	0	0	0	0
tutelage	2	.0000	.0243	23.9	0	0	0	0	1	0	0	1	0	0	0	0	0	0	0	0	0	0	0	0	0	0	2	0	0
Tutok	4	.0000	.0469	26.7	0	0	0	4	0	0	0	0	0	0	0	0	0	0	0	0	0	0	0	0	4	0	0	0	0
tutor	16	.5135	1.8033	42.6	0	8	2	2	4	0	0	0	5	0	0	0	0	2	0	0	0	0	0	0	1	5	0	3	0
tutors	2	.0000	.0243	23.9	0	0	0	0	2	0	0	0	0	0	0	0	0	0	0	0	0	0	0	0	0	2	0	0	0
Tutu	3	.0000	.1370	31.4	3	0	0	0	0	0	0	0	3	0	0	0	0	0	0	0	0	0	0	0	0	0	0	0	0
Tutu's	2	.0000	.0914	29.6	2	0	0	0	0	0	0	0	2	0	0	0	0	0	0	0	0	0	0	0	0	0	0	0	0
tuxedos	2	.2433	.1158	30.6	0	0	0	1	1	0	0	0	0	0	0	0	0	0	0	0	0	0	0	0	1	0	0	1	0
TV	198	.7214	29.146	54.6	51	30	20	34	29	15	17	2	38	16	0	7	19	19	3	11	2	0	4	1	4	1	1	72	0
TVA	18	.1903	.9466	39.8	1	0	14	0	1	1	1	0	0	0	0	0	0	16	0	0	0	0	0	0	0	0	1	0	0
TVS	4	.0000	.0599	27.8	0	0	4	0	0	0	0	0	0	0	0	0	4	0	0	0	0	0	0	0	0	0	0	0	0
tw	4	.1497	.2092	33.2	0	2	0	1	0	1	0	0	2	0	0	0	0	2	0	0	0	0	0	0	0	0	0	0	0
Twaddle	3	.0000	.0365	25.6	0	0	0	3	0	0	0	0	0	0	0	0	0	0	0	0	0	0	0	0	0	0	3	0	0
twain	7	.2375	.5193	37.2	0	1	0	0	0	5	0	1	5	0	0	0	0	0	0	0	0	0	0	0	0	0	2	0	0
Twain	27	.5455	3.3229	45.2	0	3	15	0	3	4	0	2	18	1	1	0	0	1	0	2	0	0	0	0	0	0	4	0	0
Twain's	6	.2223	.4212	36.2	0	0	1	0	2	1	2	0	4	2	0	0	0	0	0	0	0	0	0	0	0	0	0	0	0
twang	8	.4503	.8109	39.1	1	1	2	1	1	3	0	0	3	0	1	0	0	0	0	1	0	0	0	0	0	0	1	0	0
twanged	2	.2443	.1130	30.5	1	0	0	0	0	1	0	0	0	0	0	1	0	0	0	0	0	0	0	0	0	0	1	0	0
twanging	3	.3780	.2436	33.9	0	0	0	0	2	1	0	0	0	0	0	1	0	0	0	0	1	0	0	0	0	0	1	0	0
twangy	2	.0000	.0162	22.1	0	0	0	0	2	0	0	0	0	0	0	0	0	0	0	2	0	0	0	0	0	0	0	0	0
tweed	6	.0879	.1748	32.4	0	0	0	1	2	3	0	0	1	0	0	0	0	1	0	0	4	0	0	0	0	0	0	0	0
tweeds	2	.2152	.1357	31.3	0	0	0	0	2	0	0	0	1	0	0	0	0	0	0	0	0	0	0	1	0	0	0	0	0
Tweedums	2	.0000	.0219	23.4	0	2	0	0	0	0	0	0	0	0	0	0	0	0	0	0	0	0	0	0	2	0	0	0	0
Tweedy	2	.0000	.0914	29.6	0	0	0	2	0	0	0	0	2	0	0	0	0	0	0	0	0	0	0	0	0	0	0	0	0
tweezers	2	.1674	.0805	29.1	0	0	0	0	0	1	0	1	0	0	0	0	0	0	0	0	0	1	0	0	1	0	0	0	0
twelfth	25	.7543	3.8017	45.8	2	3	6	6	2	1	4	1	3	2	0	0	1	2	3	1	4	1	0	0	0	2	4	0	0
Twelfth	3	.0000	.0352	25.5	0	0	0	3	0	0	0	0	0	0	0	0	0	0	0	0	0	0	0	0	3	0	0	0	0
Twelfth-night	3	.0000	.0243	23.8	0	1	0	2	0	0	0	0	0	0	0	0	0	0	0	0	0	0	0	0	3	0	0	0	0
twelfths	4	.0000	.0599	27.8	0	1	3	0	0	0	0	0	0	0	0	0	4	0	0	0	0	0	0	0	0	0	0	0	0
twelve	339	.9340	62.709	58.0	50	66	40	42	77	38	15	11	90	15	4	25	24	27	15	27	23	1	2	2	32	35	3	14	0
Twelve	4	.3071	.2967	34.7	1	1	0	0	0	1	0	0	1	0	0	1	0	0	0	0	2	0	0	0	0	0	0	0	0
twelve-clock	2	.0000	.0299	24.8	0	0	2	0	0	0	0	0	0	0	0	2	0	0	0	0	0	0	0	0	0	0	0	0	0
twelve-inch	4	.3526	.3008	34.8	1	0	0	0	2	1	0	0	0	0	0	0	0	0	0	0	1	1	0	0	0	1	0	1	0
twelve-tone	11	.0000	.0889	29.5	0	0	0	3	0	8	0	0	0	0	0	0	0	0	0	0	11	0	0	0	0	0	0	0	0
twelve-year-old	6	.4741	.6415	38.1	0	2	2	2	0	0	0	0	2	0	0	0	0	2	0	0	0	0	0	0	0	1	0	1	0
twenties	11	.4826	1.1116	40.5	1	0	0	0	5	1	4	0	0	0	0	2	1	2	0	0	4	0	0	0	1	0	0	0	0
twentieth	61	.7016	8.6916	49.4	3	1	6	9	17	19	3	3	9	2	0	0	0	4	5	4	21	2	0	3	2	3	4	2	0
Twentieth	7	.4215	.6585	38.2	0	2	1	0	1	3	0	0	0	1	0	0	0	0	0	0	0	0	0	0	3	0	1	0	0
twentieth-century	11	.5345	1.2068	40.8	0	0	2	0	3	4	2	0	0	1	0	0	0	1	0	0	5	0	0	1	0	1	1	1	0
twenty	387	.8755	67.751	58.3	55	55	43	57	81	50	21	25	124	19	7	36	15	50	9	34	6	0	1	0	29	36	5	16	0
Twenty	4	.4851	.4027	36.1	1	1	0	1	0	0	0	1	1	0	0	0	0	2	0	0	1	0	0	0	0	0	0	0	0
twenty-eight	21	.7445	3.2001	45.1	2	2	2	4	9	0	2	0	7	3	0	2	1	0	1	2	1	0	0	0	3	0	1	0	0
twenty-eighth	2	.2351	.1166	30.7	0	0	0	0	1	1	0	0	0	0	0	0	0	0	0	0	0	0	0	0	1	0	1	0	0
twenty-fifth	8	.4277	.8013	39.0	4	1	0	1	1	1	0	0	4	0	0	0	0	1	0	0	0	0	0	0	1	0	2	0	0
twenty-fifths	2	.0000	.0299	24.8	0	0	0	0	2	0	0	0	0	0	0	2	0	0	0	0	0	0	0	0	0	0	0	0	0
twenty-first	5	.4688	.4931	36.9	2	0	1	1	0	0	1	0	1	0	0	1	0	0	0	0	0	0	0	0	1	0	2	0	0
twenty-five	110	.8862	19.445	52.9	20	12	12	20	23	14	5	4	30	7	1	7	6	17	3	12	2	0	0	0	6	10	3	6	0
twenty-fives	2	.0000	.0299	24.8	0	1	0	0	1	0	0	0	0	0	0	2	0	0	0	0	0	0	0	0	0	0	0	0	0
twenty-foot	4	.3813	.3772	35.8	0	1	2	1	0	0	0	0	2	0	0	0	1	0	0	0	0	0	0	0	1	0	0	0	0
twenty-four	66	.8927	11.716	50.7	9	12	5	10	10	10	7	3	14	6	1	4	0	4	4	9	4	0	3	1	6	7	1	2	0
twenty-four-hour	5	.2443	.3861	35.9	0	0	0	4	0	1	0	0	1	0	0	0	0	0	0	0	0	0	0	0	0	4	0	0	0
twenty-fourth	2	.2152	.1357	31.3	0	0	0	0	2	0	0	0	1	0	0	0	0	0	0	0	0	0	0	0	1	0	0	0	0
Twenty-fourth	2	.0000	.0243	23.9	0	0	0	0	0	0	0	2	0	0	0	0	0	0	0	0	0	0	0	0	0	0	0	2	0

5Q Turners	7D Turns	6H Turubian	5Q Tuxtla	XB twelfth-century	7E twentieths
4A Turners'	4H turnsignal	7N tushes	8D TV-ese	6J twelve-bar	7J Twenty-Four
5F turnest	7Q turnstone	8F Tushi's	6R TV-watching	9R twelve-hour	7G Twenty-Third
3P turneth	5Q Turnverein	5D tusky	8B TWA	4P twelve-inch-wide	5H twenty-degree
9D Turnham	5Q Turpin's	5A tussle	7N TWAIN	3A twelve-pint	7A twenty-eight-inch
7R turnings	6A turtle-doves	XH tussock	4P Twang-g-g	8A twelve-thirty	7A twenty-eight-year-old
4N turnip-brain	9Q turtle-shaped	7D tussocky	7Q tweaked	9D twelvemonth	XR Twenty-fifth
9D turnkey	4P Turtle's	6A tut-tut	7A tweedle-dee	3J twen-ty	8F Twenty-first
3P turnoff	5J turtledoves	8A Tutankhamen	6A Tweedy's	3J twen-ty-three	4A twenty-five-cent
8J Turnover	9R turtleneck	6A tutored	3P Tweet	3J twent-ty-one	5E twenty-fourths
7D Turnpike	6A turtles'	7B tuxedo	9C tweeter	8F Twenties	6A twenty-gun

Word Type	F	D	U	SFI	3 Gr 3	4 Gr 4	5 Gr 5	6 Gr 6	7 Gr 7	8 Gr 8	9 Gr 9	X UnGr	A Read	B Eng & Gr	C Comp	D Lit	E Math	F Soc Stud	G Spell	H Sci	J Music	K Art	L Home Ec	M Shop	N Lib F	P Lib NF	Q Lib Ref	R Mag	S Rel
twenty-nine	18	.6952	2.5812	44.1	2	3	1	4	4	1	1	2	5	2	0	0	4	0	1	2	2	0	0	0	0	1	0	1	0
twenty-one	43	.7241	6.3598	48.0	7	9	4	5	10	5	1	2	8	4	0	5	3	6	1	3	0	0	0	0	0	10	0	3	0
twenty-second	4	.2420	.3089	34.9	1	0	0	2	0	1	0	0	3	0	0	0	0	1	0	0	0	0	0	0	0	0	0	0	0
twenty-seven	16	.6686	2.1979	43.4	3	2	0	6	2	2	0	1	2	0	0	1	4	1	0	1	0	0	0	0	2	3	2	0	0
twenty-seventh	4	.2991	.2943	34.7	3	0	1	0	0	0	0	0	1	0	0	0	0	0	0	0	0	0	0	0	0	1	0	2	0
twenty-six	34	.7454	5.1422	47.1	6	3	5	7	5	5	1	2	6	3	0	2	3	2	7	5	2	0	0	0	1	2	0	1	0
twenty-six-inch	2	.0000	.0914	29.6	0	0	0	0	2	0	0	0	2	0	0	0	0	0	0	0	0	0	0	0	0	0	0	0	0
twenty-sixth	6	.3530	.5299	37.2	2	0	0	2	1	1	0	0	3	0	0	0	0	0	0	0	0	0	0	0	0	1	0	2	0
Twenty-third	5	.2446	.3866	35.9	1	0	0	0	1	3	0	0	4	1	0	0	0	0	0	0	0	0	0	0	0	0	0	0	0
twenty-three	23	.6740	3.1839	45.0	4	2	3	2	6	2	1	3	4	3	0	2	7	1	2	0	1	0	0	0	0	0	0	3	0
twenty-two	29	.7288	4.3564	46.4	3	4	2	7	8	4	1	0	11	1	0	3	1	3	0	1	0	0	0	0	3	3	3	0	0
twenty-year	2	.2139	.1057	30.2	0	0	0	0	1	0	1	0	0	0	0	0	0	1	1	0	0	0	0	0	0	0	0	0	0
twenty-year-old	3	.3418	.2483	33.9	0	0	0	1	1	0	0	1	1	1	0	0	0	0	0	0	0	0	0	0	0	1	0	0	0
twi	2	.0000	.0162	22.1	0	0	2	0	0	0	0	0	0	0	0	0	0	0	2	0	0	0	0	0	0	0	0	0	0
twice	400	.9239	73.199	58.6	55	62	52	54	55	46	67	9	75	22	6	23	74	22	14	31	19	0	13	10	21	28	14	28	0
Twickerham	7	.0000	.0821	29.1	0	0	0	7	0	0	0	0	0	0	0	0	0	0	0	0	0	0	0	0	7	0	0	0	0
Twickerham's	2	.0000	.0234	23.7	0	0	0	2	0	0	0	0	0	0	0	0	0	0	0	0	0	0	0	0	2	0	0	0	0
twiddling	2	.1387	.0689	28.4	0	0	0	1	1	0	0	0	0	0	1	0	0	0	0	0	0	0	0	0	0	1	0	0	0
twig	31	.6913	4.4475	46.5	10	6	5	2	6	1	1	0	9	1	0	1	0	1	0	11	1	0	0	0	3	2	0	2	0
Twig	6	.0000	.2741	34.4	0	6	0	0	0	0	0	0	6	0	0	0	0	0	0	0	0	0	0	0	0	0	0	0	0
twigs	67	.8065	10.909	50.4	17	13	11	9	14	2	1	0	16	1	1	6	0	8	0	15	0	1	0	0	3	9	5	2	0
twilight	42	.6300	5.5032	47.4	3	7	3	7	14	3	5	0	11	2	5	6	0	2	0	0	3	0	0	0	6	2	2	3	0
Twilight	2	.0000	.0162	22.1	1	0	0	1	0	0	0	0	0	0	0	0	0	0	0	0	2	0	0	0	0	0	0	0	0
twilight's	3	.2058	.1429	31.5	0	0	0	0	2	1	0	0	0	1	0	0	0	0	0	0	2	0	0	0	0	0	0	0	0
twill	3	.0000	.0097	19.8	0	0	0	0	0	2	1	0	0	0	0	0	0	0	0	0	0	0	3	0	0	0	0	0	0
twin	64	.8465	10.821	50.3	5	10	7	10	7	8	10	7	7	1	0	2	8	6	6	15	2	0	2	0	2	4	5	4	0
Twin	5	.3842	.4760	36.8	0	1	1	2	0	0	0	1	3	0	0	1	0	0	0	0	0	0	0	0	0	0	0	1	0
twin-engine	2	.2437	.1129	30.5	0	0	1	1	0	0	0	0	0	0	0	0	0	0	0	0	0	0	0	0	0	0	1	1	0
twin's	2	.0000	.0394	26.0	0	0	0	0	0	0	2	0	0	0	0	0	0	0	0	2	0	0	0	0	0	0	0	0	0
twine	19	.5473	2.2861	43.6	6	0	2	0	10	0	0	1	8	0	0	0	0	0	0	7	1	1	0	0	0	0	1	1	0
twined	2	.1698	.1133	30.5	1	0	0	0	0	1	0	0	1	0	0	0	0	0	0	0	0	0	0	0	0	0	1	0	0
twinge	2	.2440	.1132	30.5	0	0	0	0	1	0	0	1	0	0	0	1	0	0	0	0	0	0	0	0	0	0	0	1	0
twining	3	.3346	.2478	33.9	0	0	0	1	1	0	0	1	1	0	0	0	0	0	0	1	0	0	0	0	0	0	1	0	0
Twink	4	.0000	.0469	26.7	0	0	0	0	4	0	0	0	0	0	0	0	0	0	0	0	0	0	0	0	4	0	0	0	0
twinkle	37	.7128	5.4581	47.4	10	10	7	5	1	2	2	0	14	3	0	3	1	0	0	4	1	0	0	0	2	8	0	1	0
Twinkle	4	.0000	.0323	25.1	4	0	0	0	0	0	0	0	0	0	0	0	0	0	0	0	4	0	0	0	0	0	0	0	0
twinkled	16	.5552	1.9669	42.9	5	5	0	2	2	0	1	1	9	0	0	2	0	0	0	0	0	0	0	0	1	2	0	2	0
twinkling	29	.7291	4.3430	46.4	2	5	5	8	5	0	2	2	9	0	1	2	0	1	0	6	2	0	0	0	3	4	0	1	0
twinning	5	.0000	.0986	29.9	0	0	0	0	0	0	0	5	0	0	0	0	0	0	0	5	0	0	0	0	0	0	0	0	0
twins	67	.7909	10.763	50.3	21	22	4	0	4	1	7	8	22	4	0	3	0	9	0	9	0	0	1	0	6	6	1	6	0
Twins	11	.2746	.7136	38.5	0	0	4	1	6	0	0	0	1	0	0	0	0	0	0	0	0	0	0	0	4	0	0	6	0
twirl	6	.4667	.6287	38.0	0	1	1	0	0	4	0	0	2	0	0	0	0	0	1	2	1	0	0	0	0	0	0	0	0
twirled	10	.5595	1.1658	40.7	2	5	0	1	2	0	0	0	1	0	0	3	0	0	0	0	0	0	0	0	2	1	1	2	0
twirler	2	.0000	.0243	23.9	0	0	0	0	2	0	0	0	0	0	0	0	0	0	0	0	0	0	0	0	0	0	0	2	0
twirling	6	.5520	.7154	38.5	0	1	0	1	4	0	0	0	2	0	0	1	0	1	0	0	0	0	0	0	0	0	1	1	0
twirls	4	.3454	.2963	34.7	0	2	0	1	1	0	0	0	0	1	0	1	0	0	0	0	2	0	0	0	0	0	0	0	0
twist	81	.7172	11.845	50.7	16	4	12	12	15	13	7	2	20	3	1	4	0	2	2	8	1	9	2	7	6	5	5	6	0
Twist	6	.2983	.4464	36.5	0	0	0	2	1	2	1	0	2	3	0	1	0	0	0	0	0	0	0	0	0	0	0	0	0
twisted	111	.7851	17.622	52.5	17	11	10	15	26	18	11	3	33	1	1	14	1	4	2	5	0	6	7	6	12	6	1	12	0
twister	6	.3833	.5764	37.6	0	4	2	0	0	0	0	0	4	1	0	0	0	0	0	0	1	0	0	0	0	0	0	0	0
Twister	10	.0000	.1215	30.8	0	9	0	0	0	0	0	1	0	0	0	0	0	0	0	0	0	0	0	0	0	0	0	10	0
twisters	2	.2440	.1132	30.5	1	1	0	0	0	0	0	0	0	0	0	1	0	0	0	0	0	0	0	0	0	0	0	1	0
twisting	60	.7486	9.0567	49.6	4	8	7	6	15	13	6	1	9	0	1	7	0	4	0	5	2	4	6	6	6	3	3	4	0
Twistletree	14	.0000	.6396	38.1	0	0	14	0	0	0	0	0	14	0	0	0	0	0	0	0	0	0	0	0	0	0	0	0	0
twists	18	.5694	2.1146	43.3	3	5	2	1	5	2	0	0	2	0	1	0	0	0	0	2	1	2	0	4	0	3	1	2	0
twitch	6	.4858	.6625	38.2	1	0	2	0	1	0	2	0	3	0	0	1	0	0	0	0	0	0	0	0	0	1	0	1	0
twitched	11	.5073	1.2486	41.0	4	0	2	0	3	0	1	1	5	0	0	1	0	0	0	1	0	0	0	0	3	1	0	0	0
twitches	2	.1698	.1133	30.5	0	0	2	0	0	0	0	0	1	0	0	0	0	0	0	0	0	0	0	0	0	0	1	0	0
twitching	11	.4567	1.1483	40.6	2	1	0	1	6	0	1	0	5	0	0	0	0	0	0	0	0	0	0	0	3	0	2	1	0
twitter	2	.2305	.1080	30.3	1	0	0	0	0	1	0	0	0	0	0	0	0	0	1	0	0	0	0	0	0	1	0	0	0
twittered	7	.3801	.6607	38.2	2	3	0	1	1	0	0	0	4	0	0	1	0	0	0	0	0	0	0	0	0	2	0	0	0
twittering	6	.3241	.4939	36.9	1	0	2	3	0	0	0	0	3	0	0	0	0	0	0	0	2	0	0	0	0	0	0	1	0
two	10085	.9407	1875.7	72.7	1762	1591	1261	1302	1776	1283	912	198	1959	704	121	365	1582	626	1051	902	591	72	94	145	410	593	384	486	0
Two	46	.8164	7.5874	48.8	23	5	1	2	9	2	2	2	18	4	1	0	1	1	1	2	6	0	0	1	5	1	2	3	0
TWO	13	.0882	.3538	35.5	0	0	0	0	1	12	0	0	0	0	0	12	0	0	0	0	0	0	0	0	0	0	0	1	0
two-	11	.5434	1.2227	40.9	3	1	1	0	2	1	1	2	0	0	0	0	0	0	2	0	1	0	0	1	0	0	4	3	0
two-bit	2	.2152	.1357	31.3	0	0	0	0	1	0	1	0	1	0	0	0	0	1	0	0	0	0	0	0	0	0	0	0	0
two-color	2	.0000	.0209	23.2	0	0	0	0	0	0	2	0	0	0	0	0	0	0	0	0	0	0	0	0	0	0	2	0	0
two-cylinder	2	.1483	.0728	28.6	0	0	0	0	1	0	0	1	0	0	0	0	0	0	0	0	0	0	0	1	0	1	0	0	0
two-digit	5	.0000	.0748	28.7	2	0	0	0	0	3	0	0	0	0	0	0	5	0	0	0	0	0	0	0	0	0	0	0	0
two-dimensional	3	.0000	.0449	26.5	0	0	0	0	3	0	0	0	0	0	0	0	3	0	0	0	0	0	0	0	0	0	0	0	0
two-dot	3	.2060	.1430	31.6	1	0	0	0	2	0	0	0	0	1	0	0	0	0	2	0	0	0	0	0	0	0	0	0	0
two-fifths	2	.0000	.0299	24.8	0	0	0	2	0	0	0	0	0	0	0	0	2	0	0	0	0	0	0	0	0	0	0	0	0
two-fold	3	.3263	.2368	33.7	0	0	0	0	1	1	1	0	1	0	0	0	0	0	0	0	1	0	0	0	0	0	0	1	0
two-foot	3	.3847	.2496	34.0	0	0	0	1	1	0	1	0	0	0	0	0	0	0	0	0	0	0	0	0	0	1	1	1	0
two-hand	2	.1948	.1250	31.0	0	0	1	0	1	0	0	0	1	0	0	0	0	0	0	0	0	0	0	0	0	1	0	0	0
two-headed	7	.4818	.7190	38.6	1	2	2	0	0	1	1	0	1	1	0	3	0	0	0	0	1	0	0	0	1	0	0	0	0
two-hour	2	.0000	.0243	23.9	0	0	1	0	1	0	0	0	0	0	0	0	0	0	0	0	0	0	0	0	0	0	0	2	0
two-hundred	2	.1814	.1187	30.7	0	1	0	0	1	0	0	0	1	0	0	0	0	0	0	0	0	0	0	0	0	0	0	1	0
two-hundred-pound	2	.2407	.1138	30.6	0	0	0	0	2	0	0	0	0	0	0	1	0	0	0	0	0	0	0	0	0	1	0	0	0
two-lane	2	.1703	.0781	28.9	0	0	0	1	0	1	0	0	0	1	0	0	0	0	0	0	0	0	0	1	0	0	0	0	0
two-leafed	3	.0000	.1370	31.4	3	0	0	0	0	0	0	0	3	0	0	0	0	0	0	0	0	0	0	0	0	0	0	0	0
two-legged	7	.2926	.4905	36.9	0	4	0	0	3	0	0	0	1	0	0	0	0	0	0	0	0	0	0	0	0	4	2	0	0
two-letter	20	.0337	.3619	35.6	6	1	3	10	0	0	0	0	2	0	0	0	0	0	18	0	0	0	0	0	0	0	0	0	0
two-man	2	.1814	.1187	30.7	1	0	0	0	1	0	0	0	1	0	0	0	0	0	0	0	0	0	0	0	0	0	0	1	0
two-measure	4	.0000	.0323	25.1	0	0	2	1	0	1	0	0	0	0	0	0	0	0	0	0	4	0	0	0	0	0	0	0	0
two-month-old	2	.2440	.1132	30.5	0	0	0	0	1	0	1	0	0	0	0	1	0	0	0	0	0	0	0	0	0	0	0	1	0
two-part	24	.1956	1.0843	40.4	5	5	5	0	7	2	0	0	0	1	0	0	0	0	2	0	20	0	0	0	0	0	0	1	0
two-party	2	.0000	.0914	29.6	0	0	0	0	2	0	0	0	2	0	0	0	0	0	0	0	0	0	0	0	0	0	0	0	0
two-piece	2	.2421	.0995	30.0	0	0	0	0	0	0	2	0	0	0	0	0	0	0	0	0	0	0	1	1	0	0	0	0	0
two-place	2	.0000	.0299	24.8	0	0	0	0	0	0	2	0	0	0	0	0	2	0	0	0	0	0	0	0	0	0	0	0	0

4P twenty-mile
4A twenty-minute
5A twenty-mule
7R Twenty-one
8D twenty-one-gun
3J twenty-penny
7R twenty-pound
6J Twenty-second
7A Twenty-six
XR twenty-story
7N twenty-thirty
9D twenty-vun
7D twentyseven-mile
7Q twice-a-day
5R twice-daily
6R twice-vanquished
4A twiddled
6A twig-and-grass
4A Twig's
5A Twiggs
8L twill-weave
4A twinkly
XH twinned
7R Twins'
4N twirly-whirly
3P TWIST
5Q Twisted
4A twisty
3R twisty-turny
3A twit
6A Twitchell
5A Twitchell's
6A twitterings
9B Two-Gun
3A two-M
7J Two-Part
3A Two-Toed
7N two-acre
5R two-against-one
XR two-and-a-half
5P two-and-a-half-century
9Q two-and-a-quarter-million
7R two-barrel
6A two-bladed
XR two-block
8A two-by-four
7A two-by-fours
9B two-car
6Q two-carat
8M two-coil
4N two-colored
9L two-crust
9E two-day
7P two-engined
6R two-escudo
3P two-faced
5A two-family
6N two-flat
3P two-foot-long
7P two-footed
7A two-forty-five
7R two-fours
7N two-guinea
7N two-handed
7A two-handled
4P two-horse
7F two-house
5A two-hundred-inch
4P two-hundred-yard
4P two-inch-thick
6A two-l
8F two-master
3P two-mile
8F two-million
XR two-million-square-mile
9B two-minute
3J two-months
6E two-ninths
7A two-on-two
7A two-ounce
XH two-plus-two-make-four
8L two-ply

Word Type	F	D	U	SFI	3 Gr 3	4 Gr 4	5 Gr 5	6 Gr 6	7 Gr 7	8 Gr 8	9 Gr 9	X UnGr	A Read	B Eng & Gr	C Comp	D Lit	E Math	F Soc Stud	G Spell	H Sci	J Music	K Art	L Home Ec	M Shop	N Lib F	P Lib NF	Q Lib Ref	R Mag	S Rel
two-point	4	.0000	.0074	18.7	0	0	3	0	1	0	0	0	0	0	0	0	0	0	0	0	0	4	0	0	0	0	0	0	0
two-pound	5	.4407	.4881	36.9	0	0	0	0	2	2	0	1	1	0	0	1	2	0	0	0	0	0	0	0	0	0	0	1	0
two-sided	4	.1494	.1609	32.1	0	3	0	0	1	0	0	0	0	0	0	0	0	0	0	1	0	0	0	0	0	0	3	0	0
two-stage	2	.1972	.1262	31.0	1	1	0	0	0	0	0	0	1	0	0	0	1	0	0	0	0	0	0	0	0	0	0	0	0
two-stepping	2	.0000	.0914	29.6	0	0	2	0	0	0	0	0	2	0	0	0	0	0	0	0	0	0	0	0	0	0	0	0	0
two-storied	3	.3450	.2505	34.0	0	2	0	0	0	1	0	0	1	0	0	0	0	0	0	0	0	0	0	0	1	1	0	0	0
two-story	10	.5365	1.1664	40.7	3	2	0	3	0	1	1	0	3	0	0	0	0	2	0	0	0	0	0	0	0	3	1	1	0
two-syllable	65	.1175	2.2742	43.6	11	14	10	18	5	3	4	0	9	4	0	0	0	0	52	0	0	0	0	0	0	0	0	0	0
two-term	2	.2351	.1166	30.7	0	0	0	0	0	2	0	0	0	0	0	0	0	1	0	0	0	0	0	0	0	0	0	1	0
two-thirds	38	.7169	5.5261	47.4	3	2	4	7	15	5	2	0	3	2	0	0	1	11	0	1	0	0	3	1	1	4	8	3	0
two-thirty	2	.0000	.0215	23.3	0	0	0	0	0	0	2	0	0	0	0	2	0	0	0	0	0	0	0	0	0	0	0	0	0
two-toed	2	.2160	.1362	31.3	1	0	0	0	0	0	1	0	1	0	0	0	0	0	0	1	0	0	0	0	0	0	0	0	0
two-ton	3	.3768	.2437	33.9	0	1	1	0	1	0	0	0	0	0	0	0	0	0	0	0	1	0	0	0	0	1	0	1	0
two-way	17	.4436	1.7885	42.5	1	0	1	1	11	1	2	0	10	0	0	0	1	3	0	0	0	0	2	0	0	1	0	0	0
two-week	9	.5334	.9903	40.0	1	2	0	1	3	1	0	1	0	0	0	3	0	0	0	0	0	0	1	0	1	2	0	2	0
two-wheeled	9	.5391	1.0425	40.2	2	3	0	2	2	0	0	0	2	0	0	1	0	2	0	0	0	0	0	0	2	2	0	0	0
two-winged	2	.2160	.1362	31.3	0	1	0	1	0	0	0	0	1	0	0	0	0	0	0	1	0	0	0	0	0	0	0	0	0
two-word	9	.3066	.6108	37.9	3	0	2	1	0	0	3	0	0	5	0	0	0	0	3	1	0	0	0	0	0	0	0	0	0
two-year	6	.3350	.4461	36.5	0	0	3	0	0	2	1	0	0	0	0	0	0	1	0	0	0	0	0	0	0	0	2	3	0
two-year-old	6	.4309	.5706	37.6	1	2	1	0	1	0	1	0	1	1	0	0	0	0	0	0	0	0	0	0	0	2	0	2	0
two-year-olds	3	.2292	.1615	32.1	0	0	1	2	0	0	0	0	0	0	0	1	0	0	0	0	0	0	0	0	2	0	0	0	0
two's	2	.1494	.1045	30.2	1	0	0	0	0	1	0	0	1	0	0	0	0	0	0	0	1	0	0	0	0	0	0	0	0
twofold	3	.3395	.2468	33.9	0	0	0	1	1	1	0	0	1	0	0	0	0	0	0	0	0	0	0	0	0	1	1	0	0
twopence	2	.2443	.1130	30.5	0	1	0	0	1	0	0	0	0	0	0	1	0	0	0	0	0	0	0	0	1	0	0	0	0
twos	32	.4185	2.9034	44.6	6	8	9	1	2	1	1	4	1	0	0	0	19	1	0	1	7	0	0	0	0	2	0	1	0
ty	4	.0000	.0325	25.1	0	1	2	0	1	0	0	0	0	0	0	0	0	0	4	0	0	0	0	0	0	0	0	0	0
Tybalt	8	.0000	.0859	29.3	0	0	0	0	0	0	8	0	0	0	0	8	0	0	0	0	0	0	0	0	0	0	0	0	0
Tycho	9	.1241	.3747	35.7	0	1	0	0	2	0	0	6	0	0	0	0	0	1	0	8	0	0	0	0	0	0	0	0	0
tying	22	.6423	2.9489	44.7	3	4	4	7	3	1	0	0	6	1	0	1	0	1	1	3	0	1	0	0	7	1	0	0	0
Tyler	4	.3767	.3699	35.7	0	1	0	0	1	0	1	1	2	0	0	0	1	0	0	0	0	0	0	0	0	0	0	1	0
Tylerton	2	.0000	.0243	23.9	0	0	2	0	0	0	0	0	0	0	0	0	0	0	0	0	0	0	0	0	0	0	0	2	0
Tynan	2	.0000	.0243	23.9	0	0	0	0	0	0	0	2	0	0	0	0	0	0	0	0	0	0	0	0	0	0	0	2	0
Tyndale	2	.0000	.0162	22.1	0	0	0	0	2	0	0	0	0	0	0	0	0	0	2	0	0	0	0	0	0	0	0	0	0
type	599	.7147	86.453	59.4	16	34	56	66	128	113	168	18	48	46	3	15	21	49	21	82	45	7	30	102	3	25	77	25	0
Type	12	.1373	.4431	36.5	0	0	0	0	0	1	9	2	0	10	0	0	0	0	0	0	0	0	0	0	0	2	0	0	0
typed	9	.5336	.9887	40.0	0	0	2	0	5	0	2	0	0	2	0	1	3	0	2	0	0	0	0	1	0	0	0	0	0
types	334	.7412	49.883	57.0	3	17	37	23	85	65	86	18	21	14	7	7	11	40	1	65	19	0	23	41	2	17	41	25	0
typesetting	2	.1738	.0790	29.0	0	1	0	0	0	0	1	0	0	0	0	0	0	0	0	0	0	0	0	1	0	0	1	0	0
typewrite	2	.0000	.0219	23.4	0	0	0	0	1	0	1	0	0	2	0	0	0	0	0	0	0	0	0	0	0	0	0	0	0
typewriter	43	.7979	6.8986	48.4	1	3	9	7	13	3	4	3	8	4	2	2	1	0	0	4	3	0	0	2	1	7	5	4	0
typewriters	9	.3319	.6751	38.3	2	0	5	1	1	0	0	0	0	0	0	0	0	4	0	0	0	0	0	0	0	0	4	1	0
typewritten	7	.3194	.4882	36.9	1	0	0	0	4	0	2	0	0	5	0	0	0	0	0	0	0	0	0	1	0	1	0	0	0
typhoid	9	.3209	.6748	38.3	0	2	0	0	1	4	1	1	0	0	0	0	0	0	1	7	0	0	0	0	1	0	0	0	0
Typhon	2	.0000	.0209	23.2	0	0	0	2	0	0	0	0	0	0	0	0	0	0	0	0	0	0	0	0	0	0	2	0	0
typhoon	2	.1249	.0685	28.4	0	0	0	0	1	1	0	0	0	0	0	0	0	0	0	1	0	0	0	1	0	0	0	0	0
typhoons	3	.3385	.2445	33.9	1	1	0	0	1	0	0	0	1	0	0	0	0	0	0	0	0	0	0	0	1	0	1	0	0
typhus	2	.0000	.0394	26.0	0	0	0	0	1	1	0	0	0	0	0	0	0	0	0	2	0	0	0	0	0	0	0	0	0
typical	154	.8646	26.447	54.2	5	5	13	27	49	25	25	5	7	8	5	6	2	16	7	22	19	1	2	9	2	9	23	16	0
typically	16	.5995	1.9999	43.0	0	0	3	2	2	4	4	1	2	0	0	0	0	2	0	3	3	0	0	0	0	1	1	4	0
typifies	4	.1952	.1875	32.7	0	0	0	0	2	0	2	0	0	1	0	0	0	0	0	0	0	0	0	0	0	0	3	0	0
typify	3	.3134	.2351	33.7	0	0	1	1	0	0	1	0	1	0	0	0	0	1	1	0	0	0	0	0	0	0	0	0	0
typing	13	.5478	1.4939	41.7	2	0	0	0	4	1	5	1	1	5	0	0	1	2	0	1	0	0	0	0	0	0	1	2	0
typist	2	.2278	.1128	30.5	0	0	1	1	0	0	0	0	0	0	0	0	0	0	0	1	0	0	0	0	0	0	1	0	0
typists	2	.2285	.1129	30.5	0	0	0	0	1	1	0	0	0	0	0	0	0	1	0	0	0	0	0	0	0	0	1	0	0
tyrannical	2	.2446	.1123	30.5	0	0	0	0	1	0	1	0	0	1	0	0	0	0	0	0	0	0	0	0	0	0	1	0	0
tyrannosaurus	2	.0000	.0290	24.6	0	2	0	0	0	0	0	0	0	0	0	0	0	0	0	0	0	0	0	0	0	2	0	0	0
Tyrannosaurus	9	.2286	.4859	36.9	7	0	0	0	0	0	2	0	0	0	2	0	0	0	0	0	0	0	0	0	0	7	0	0	0
tyranny	12	.6321	1.5824	42.0	2	1	2	1	2	4	0	0	3	1	0	0	0	1	0	0	2	0	0	0	0	3	1	1	0
tyrant	12	.5978	1.5355	41.9	4	0	0	1	1	3	3	0	5	0	0	2	0	1	0	0	1	0	0	0	0	1	2	0	0
Tyrant	5	.3343	.3773	35.8	3	0	0	0	0	2	0	0	0	0	0	0	0	1	0	0	0	0	0	0	0	3	1	0	0
tyrant's	2	.0000	.0219	23.4	0	0	0	0	2	0	0	0	0	2	0	0	0	0	0	0	0	0	0	0	0	0	0	0	0
tyrants	4	.3828	.3305	35.2	0	1	0	1	1	1	0	0	0	1	0	0	0	0	1	0	0	0	0	0	0	2	0	0	0
Tyrants	3	.0000	.0434	26.4	3	0	0	0	0	0	0	0	0	0	0	0	0	0	0	0	0	0	0	0	0	3	0	0	0
tyre	2	.1497	.1046	30.2	0	1	0	0	1	0	0	0	1	0	0	0	0	0	1	0	0	0	0	0	0	0	0	0	0
Tyre	6	.4416	.5686	37.5	1	1	1	1	2	0	0	0	0	0	0	0	0	0	0	1	0	0	0	0	0	3	1	1	0
Tyrol	12	.1188	.3887	35.9	0	0	11	1	0	0	0	0	0	0	0	0	0	0	0	0	1	0	0	0	0	0	11	0	0
Tyrrhenian	3	.1823	.1405	31.5	1	0	0	1	0	1	0	0	0	0	0	0	0	1	0	0	0	0	0	0	0	0	2	0	0
Tzena	2	.0000	.0162	22.1	0	0	0	0	2	0	0	0	0	0	0	0	0	0	0	0	2	0	0	0	0	0	0	0	0
u	215	.2154	11.137	50.5	37	38	46	47	23	18	5	1	19	10	2	0	9	0	169	4	0	0	0	0	1	1	0	0	0
U	124	.6824	17.252	52.4	14	18	10	9	20	21	27	5	6	2	1	0	14	33	1	3	1	0	1	2	0	5	6	49	0
U**	327	.6039	41.012	56.1	26	44	58	38	46	24	78	13	35	3	0	5	11	54	1	13	0	0	3	0	1	17	55	129	0
U-boats	3	.0000	.0314	25.0	0	3	0	0	0	0	0	0	0	0	0	0	0	0	0	0	0	0	0	0	0	0	3	0	0
U-shaped	3	.3764	.2483	33.9	0	0	0	2	0	0	0	1	0	0	0	0	0	0	0	1	0	0	0	0	0	0	1	1	0
u's	7	.2959	.4556	36.6	1	1	1	2	1	0	1	0	0	2	0	0	0	0	4	0	0	0	0	0	0	1	0	0	0
UAR	12	.0000	.1458	31.6	0	0	0	12	0	0	0	0	0	0	0	0	0	0	0	0	0	0	0	0	0	0	0	12	0
Ubangi	2	.0000	.0389	25.9	0	0	0	0	2	0	0	0	0	0	0	0	0	2	0	0	0	0	0	0	0	0	0	0	0
Ubaru	10	.0000	.1945	32.9	0	0	0	10	0	0	0	0	0	0	0	0	0	10	0	0	0	0	0	0	0	0	0	0	0
Ubaru's	3	.0000	.0583	27.7	0	0	0	3	0	0	0	0	0	0	0	0	0	3	0	0	0	0	0	0	0	0	0	0	0
ubiquitous	6	.4901	.6354	38.0	0	0	1	0	2	0	2	1	1	0	0	0	0	0	0	1	0	0	0	0	0	1	2	1	0
UCLA	8	.1444	.3087	34.9	0	0	0	0	3	2	2	1	0	0	0	0	0	0	0	0	0	0	0	0	0	0	1	7	0
UCLA'S	3	.2321	.1635	32.1	0	0	0	0	0	1	1	1	0	0	0	0	0	0	0	0	0	0	0	0	0	0	1	2	0
udder	3	.0000	.1370	31.4	0	0	0	0	3	0	0	0	3	0	0	0	0	0	0	0	0	0	0	0	0	0	0	0	0
UFO	8	.0554	.2106	33.2	0	0	0	0	8	0	0	0	1	0	0	0	0	0	0	0	0	0	0	0	0	0	0	7	0
UFO'S	5	.1496	.2557	34.1	0	0	0	2	3	0	0	0	2	0	0	0	0	0	0	0	0	0	0	0	0	0	0	3	0
Uganda	7	.1825	.3539	35.5	0	5	0	2	0	0	0	0	1	0	0	0	0	1	0	0	0	0	0	0	0	0	0	5	0
ugh	7	.3938	.6124	37.9	1	4	0	0	0	0	1	1	1	0	0	2	0	0	0	0	0	0	0	0	3	1	0	0	0
ugliest	2	.0000	.0914	29.6	1	0	0	0	1	0	0	0	2	0	0	0	0	0	0	0	0	0	0	0	0	0	0	0	0
uglify	2	.0000	.0219	23.4	0	0	2	0	0	0	0	0	0	2	0	0	0	0	0	0	0	0	0	0	0	0	0	0	0
ugliness	5	.3827	.4267	36.3	0	1	1	2	0	1	0	0	1	0	0	1	0	0	0	0	0	1	0	0	1	0	0	1	0
ugly	126	.8102	20.699	53.2	51	21	12	11	15	10	4	2	57	5	1	10	0	2	4	1	12	3	0	0	8	14	1	8	0

7P two-pointer
9F two-price
3Q two-pronged
8R two-room
8D two-score
8B two-seated
9R Two-shoes
7R two-speed
7R two-stemmed
3A two-step
6H two-strand
6R two-strike
7J two-stringed
8L two-strip
6G two-syllables
4N two-thousand
5A two-thousand-pound
7D two-three
6R two-time
3Q two-to-five
3A two-toned
XR two-unit
3G two-vowel
9L two-wall
3N two-wheeler
3N two-wheelers
7H two-wings
5R twosomes
XH Twyman
3P Ty
9D Tybalt's
8F tycoon
7J Tycoon
8F Tydings
8F Tydings-McDuffe
7D tyke
9E Tyler's
5Q Tylor
9D Tyndal's
5Q type-wheel
9Q typecasting
5Q Types
7J Typewriter
9Q typewriterlike
9B typewriting
6P typitoon
8F typographers
9M typography
4G Tyr
3A tyrannosaur
XP tyrannous
XH tyro
9N Tyrolean
5Q Tyrolese
7P Tyrus
XR Tywardreath
6F Tze
5P Tzu
8R U-Haul
4Q U-boat
8M u-shape
4A u-2
9H U-235
9H U-238
7R Ubatuba
6J Ubdugs
XR ubiquituos
7P ubiquity
7F Ucayali
3B uck
8R UCLA-Cal
7J ud
8F Udine
5Q Udolpho
7G ue
5Q Ueno
3A UF
9F Ufa
5K uffish
4R Uganda's
4R Ugandan
4R Ugandans
9R Uggams
8R Ughelli
4A ughr-r-r
4A ughr-r-r-
8A uglier
5B uglification
5B Uglification
5B uglifying

Word Type	F	D	U	SFI	3 Gr 3	4 Gr 4	5 Gr 5	6 Gr 6	7 Gr 7	8 Gr 8	9 Gr 9	X UnGr	A Read	B Eng & Gr	C Comp	D Lit	E Math	F Soc Stud	G Spell	H Sci	J Music	K Art	L Home Ec	M Shop	N Lib F	P Lib NF	Q Lib Ref	R Mag	S Rel
Ugly	13	.0490	.2966	34.7	11	0	0	2	0	0	0	0	2	0	0	0	0	0	0	0	11	0	0	0	0	0	0	0	0
uh	15	.6450	2.0317	43.1	1	2	1	3	1	4	3	0	6	1	0	2	0	0	1	0	0	0	0	0	3	1	0	0	0
uh-huh	11	.4287	1.0773	40.3	3	3	2	2	0	0	1	0	4	2	0	0	0	0	0	0	0	0	0	0	4	0	0	1	0
uh-uh	3	.2223	.2106	33.2	0	2	0	0	0	0	1	0	2	1	0	0	0	0	0	0	0	0	0	0	0	0	0	0	0
uh-uh-	2	.0000	.0914	29.6	0	2	0	0	0	0	0	0	2	0	0	0	0	0	0	0	0	0	0	0	0	0	0	0	0
uhf	2	.0000	.0209	23.2	0	0	0	0	2	0	0	0	0	0	0	0	0	0	0	0	0	0	0	0	0	0	2	0	0
Ujima	3	.0000	.0583	27.7	0	3	0	0	0	0	0	0	0	0	0	0	0	3	0	0	0	0	0	0	0	0	0	0	0
Ukraine	9	.4015	.8115	39.1	0	1	1	2	0	0	5	0	1	0	0	0	0	5	0	0	2	0	0	0	0	0	1	0	0
Ukrainian	3	.1169	.1277	31.1	0	0	1	0	0	2	0	0	1	0	0	0	0	0	0	0	0	0	0	0	0	0	2	0	0
Ukrainians	2	.2285	.1129	30.5	0	0	1	0	1	0	0	0	0	0	0	0	0	1	0	0	0	0	0	0	0	0	1	0	0
ukulele	8	.1764	.3587	35.5	0	1	3	1	2	1	0	0	0	0	0	0	0	3	0	0	5	0	0	0	0	0	0	0	0
ukuleles	3	.0000	.0583	27.7	0	0	3	0	0	0	0	0	0	0	0	0	0	3	0	0	0	0	0	0	0	0	0	0	0
Ulape	4	.0000	.0469	26.7	0	0	0	4	0	0	0	0	0	0	0	0	0	0	0	0	0	0	0	0	4	0	0	0	0
ulcer	5	.0000	.0523	27.2	0	0	0	0	0	0	5	0	0	0	0	0	0	0	0	0	0	0	0	0	0	0	5	0	0
ulcers	5	.0000	.0523	27.2	0	0	0	0	0	0	5	0	0	0	0	0	0	0	0	0	0	0	0	0	0	0	5	0	0
Uldas	2	.0000	.0914	29.6	0	2	0	0	0	0	0	0	2	0	0	0	0	0	0	0	0	0	0	0	0	0	0	0	0
Ulfius	3	.0000	.1370	31.4	0	0	0	3	0	0	0	0	3	0	0	0	0	0	0	0	0	0	0	0	0	0	0	0	0
Ulm	3	.3759	.2498	34.0	0	0	1	1	0	1	0	0	0	0	0	0	1	0	0	1	0	0	0	0	0	0	1	0	0
Ulrich	5	.0000	.0537	27.3	0	0	0	0	0	0	5	0	0	0	0	5	0	0	0	0	0	0	0	0	0	0	0	0	0
Ulster	4	.2107	.2095	33.2	0	0	3	0	0	0	0	1	0	0	0	0	0	0	0	0	0	0	0	0	0	3	0	1	0
ultimate	28	.6438	3.6890	45.7	0	0	1	1	13	6	7	0	1	0	0	2	0	3	0	4	0	0	0	1	0	3	5	9	0
ultimately	20	.4739	2.0042	43.0	0	0	1	1	8	4	5	1	1	0	0	0	0	2	0	0	0	0	1	0	0	1	9	6	0
ultimatum	7	.2022	.3746	35.7	0	0	1	0	2	1	3	0	1	0	0	0	0	0	0	0	0	0	0	0	0	1	0	5	0
ultra	2	.2346	.1166	30.7	0	0	0	0	0	1	0	1	0	0	0	0	0	0	0	1	0	0	0	0	0	0	0	1	0
ultraviolet	52	.2961	3.6671	45.6	0	0	4	12	4	4	5	23	0	0	0	0	0	0	0	39	0	0	0	0	0	1	11	1	0
Uluasat	3	.0000	.1370	31.4	0	0	3	0	0	0	0	0	3	0	0	0	0	0	0	0	0	0	0	0	0	0	0	0	0
Ulysses	67	.4955	7.4499	48.7	1	0	26	7	16	16	0	1	30	0	0	7	0	4	0	1	0	0	0	0	22	1	2	0	0
Ulysses'	5	.3138	.3532	35.5	0	0	4	1	0	0	0	0	0	0	0	1	0	1	0	0	0	0	0	0	3	0	0	0	0
um	9	.3262	.7371	38.7	2	0	1	3	3	0	0	0	4	0	0	0	0	0	1	0	0	0	0	0	4	0	0	0	0
umbilical	3	.3764	.2483	33.9	0	0	0	1	1	0	0	1	0	0	0	0	0	0	0	1	0	0	0	0	0	0	1	1	0
umbra	2	.0000	.0162	22.1	0	1	0	0	1	0	0	0	0	0	0	0	0	0	2	0	0	0	0	0	0	0	0	0	0
umbrage	2	.0000	.0243	23.9	0	0	0	0	1	1	0	0	0	0	0	0	0	0	0	0	0	0	0	0	0	0	0	2	0
umbrageous	2	.0000	.0162	22.1	0	0	0	0	2	0	0	0	0	0	0	0	0	0	2	0	0	0	0	0	0	0	0	0	0
umbrella	51	.6832	7.1703	48.6	15	5	7	16	8	0	0	0	12	2	1	13	0	0	7	7	0	0	0	0	5	3	0	1	0
umbrellas	28	.6748	3.9723	46.0	8	4	3	10	1	2	0	0	12	0	0	4	1	4	0	4	1	0	0	0	0	1	0	1	0
umped	2	.0000	.0914	29.6	2	0	0	0	0	0	0	0	2	0	0	0	0	0	0	0	0	0	0	0	0	0	0	0	0
umpire	25	.6303	3.3189	45.2	4	6	4	2	8	0	1	0	10	0	1	2	0	0	6	0	0	0	0	0	3	1	1	1	0
umpires	3	.2279	.2143	33.3	0	1	1	0	1	0	0	0	2	0	0	0	0	0	0	0	0	0	0	0	0	0	0	1	0
Umtakati	2	.0000	.0914	29.6	0	0	0	2	0	0	0	0	2	0	0	0	0	0	0	0	0	0	0	0	0	0	0	0	0
Umtakati's	2	.0000	.0914	29.6	0	0	0	2	0	0	0	0	2	0	0	0	0	0	0	0	0	0	0	0	0	0	0	0	0
un	34	.3824	2.8684	44.6	4	2	7	14	6	1	0	0	6	3	1	0	0	0	21	0	2	0	0	0	1	0	0	0	0
UN	31	.4031	2.8845	44.6	0	0	0	7	7	15	2	0	6	2	0	0	0	20	0	0	0	0	0	0	0	0	2	1	0
un-	2	.1497	.1046	30.2	0	0	1	1	0	0	0	0	1	0	0	0	0	0	1	0	0	0	0	0	0	0	0	0	0
Una	6	.0000	.2741	34.4	0	6	0	0	0	0	0	0	6	0	0	0	0	0	0	0	0	0	0	0	0	0	0	0	0
unabated	3	.2279	.2143	33.3	1	0	0	0	1	0	1	0	2	0	0	0	0	0	0	0	0	0	0	0	0	0	0	1	0
unable	114	.8801	20.003	53.0	11	10	10	16	30	17	20	0	28	8	0	5	3	10	6	13	1	1	5	0	9	9	12	4	0
unabridged	8	.3095	.5751	37.6	0	0	0	0	3	3	2	0	1	5	0	0	0	0	1	1	0	0	0	0	0	0	0	0	0
unaccented	52	.0602	1.0141	40.1	0	12	16	12	10	2	0	0	0	1	0	0	0	0	50	0	1	0	0	0	0	0	0	0	0
unaccompanied	4	.0000	.0323	25.1	0	1	1	1	0	1	0	0	0	0	0	0	0	0	0	0	4	0	0	0	0	0	0	0	0
unaccountable	3	.2078	.1429	31.5	0	1	0	0	1	1	0	0	0	0	1	0	0	0	0	0	0	0	0	0	2	0	0	0	0
unaccountably	4	.4560	.4041	36.1	1	1	0	0	0	0	1	1	1	0	0	0	0	0	0	0	0	0	0	0	1	1	0	1	0
unaccustomed	4	.3600	.3120	34.9	0	0	0	0	1	0	3	0	0	0	0	2	0	0	0	0	0	0	0	0	1	0	0	1	0
unaffected	7	.4397	.6620	38.2	0	1	0	1	2	2	1	0	1	0	0	2	0	0	0	0	0	1	0	0	0	0	2	1	0
unafraid	8	.0000	.3655	35.6	0	3	2	2	1	0	0	0	8	0	0	0	0	0	0	0	0	0	0	0	0	0	0	0	0
unaided	5	.2213	.2870	34.6	0	0	2	0	1	0	2	0	0	0	0	0	0	0	0	4	0	0	0	0	0	0	1	0	0
unalienable	3	.1639	.1674	32.2	0	0	0	0	1	2	0	0	1	0	0	0	0	2	0	0	0	0	0	0	0	0	0	0	0
unanimous	7	.4499	.7119	38.5	1	0	0	2	0	2	2	0	2	0	0	0	0	2	0	0	0	0	0	0	0	1	0	2	0
unanimously	5	.3468	.3830	35.8	0	0	2	0	0	1	0	2	0	0	0	0	0	1	0	0	0	0	0	0	0	0	2	2	0
unanswered	8	.4278	.7646	38.8	0	0	0	3	0	2	3	0	1	0	1	0	1	2	0	3	0	0	0	0	0	0	0	0	0
unappeased	2	.2441	.1127	30.5	1	0	0	0	1	0	0	0	0	0	0	0	0	0	0	0	0	0	0	0	1	0	1	0	0
unappetizing	2	.1812	.0838	29.2	0	0	0	0	1	0	0	1	0	0	0	0	0	0	0	0	0	0	1	0	0	0	0	1	0
unarmed	11	.5682	1.3202	41.2	0	2	1	0	5	0	3	0	2	0	0	3	0	2	0	0	0	0	0	0	1	1	0	2	0
unashamed	2	.2417	.1091	30.4	0	0	0	0	0	1	1	0	0	0	0	0	0	0	0	0	1	0	0	0	0	0	1	0	0
unassuming	3	.1548	.1479	31.7	0	0	0	0	0	2	1	0	1	0	0	0	0	1	0	0	0	1	0	0	0	0	0	0	0
unattached	4	.1368	.1613	32.1	0	0	0	0	1	2	1	0	1	0	2	0	0	0	0	0	0	0	0	0	0	0	0	1	0
unattainable	2	.2346	.1166	30.7	0	0	0	0	2	0	0	0	0	0	0	0	0	0	0	1	0	0	0	0	0	0	0	1	0
unattractive	2	.0000	.0243	23.9	0	1	0	0	1	0	0	0	0	0	0	0	0	0	0	0	0	0	0	0	0	0	0	2	0
unavoidable	5	.4669	.4888	36.9	0	0	0	0	2	2	1	0	0	2	0	1	0	0	0	0	0	0	0	0	1	0	0	1	0
unaware	22	.7530	3.3568	45.3	0	2	4	3	6	5	2	0	4	2	0	2	0	1	0	1	1	0	0	0	4	4	2	1	0
unawares	2	.0665	.0708	28.5	0	1	0	0	0	0	1	0	1	0	1	0	0	0	0	0	0	0	0	0	0	0	0	0	0
unbalanced	8	.2145	.4146	36.2	0	0	1	0	5	2	0	0	0	0	0	0	0	0	0	4	0	0	0	3	0	0	0	1	0
unbearable	8	.4078	.7551	38.8	1	1	1	2	3	0	0	0	3	0	1	0	0	0	0	0	0	0	0	0	0	2	0	2	0
unbearably	5	.3689	.4527	36.6	0	2	2	0	0	1	0	0	2	0	0	0	0	0	0	2	0	0	0	0	0	0	0	1	0
unbeaten	4	.2446	.2283	33.6	0	0	0	1	1	2	0	0	0	0	0	0	0	0	0	0	0	0	0	0	2	0	0	2	0
unbelief	2	.1494	.1045	30.2	0	0	0	2	0	0	0	0	1	0	0	0	0	0	0	0	1	0	0	0	0	0	0	0	0
unbelievable	25	.8399	4.2006	46.2	1	4	7	1	5	5	2	0	5	3	0	1	1	1	1	1	2	0	0	1	3	3	2	1	0
unbelievably	2	.1523	.0721	28.6	0	0	0	0	2	0	0	0	0	0	1	0	0	0	0	0	0	0	0	0	0	0	0	1	0
unbelieving	6	.2411	.4668	36.7	0	0	3	1	1	1	0	0	5	0	0	0	0	0	0	0	0	0	0	0	0	0	0	1	0
unbelievingly	5	.2445	.3875	35.9	2	1	1	1	0	0	0	0	4	0	0	0	0	0	0	0	0	0	0	0	0	0	0	1	0
unbending	2	.2405	.1205	30.8	0	0	0	0	1	0	0	1	0	0	0	0	0	0	0	1	0	0	0	0	0	1	0	0	0
unbleached	2	.2160	.1362	31.3	0	0	0	1	1	0	0	0	1	0	0	0	0	0	0	1	0	0	0	0	0	0	0	0	0
unborn	12	.5047	1.3127	41.2	2	0	0	3	3	1	1	2	2	0	0	1	0	0	0	5	0	0	0	0	0	0	1	3	0
unbosomings	2	.0000	.0290	24.6	0	0	0	0	0	2	0	0	0	0	0	0	0	0	0	0	0	0	0	0	0	2	0	0	0
unbranded	3	.2187	.1555	31.9	0	0	0	0	0	0	2	1	0	2	0	0	0	0	0	0	0	0	0	0	0	0	0	1	0
unbreakable	5	.2294	.3479	35.4	2	0	0	3	0	0	0	0	3	0	1	0	0	0	0	1	0	0	0	0	0	0	0	0	0
unbridled	2	.2442	.1134	30.5	0	0	0	0	1	0	0	1	0	1	0	0	0	0	0	0	0	0	0	0	0	0	0	1	0
unbroken	29	.6535	3.9055	45.9	3	2	2	5	5	5	7	0	5	0	3	4	0	5	0	2	0	0	0	1	3	2	4	0	0
unbuckled	2	.0000	.0234	23.7	0	0	0	0	1	1	0	0	0	0	0	0	0	0	0	0	0	0	0	0	2	0	0	0	0
unburied	2	.1948	.1250	31.0	0	0	0	1	0	1	0	0	1	0	0	0	0	0	0	0	0	0	0	0	0	1	0	0	0

7N ugly-tempered
4A uh-uh-Listen
3G ui
5P Uighur
7R Uigur
7R Uigurs
4G uilla
7P UK
9F Ukraine's
8J Ukrania
8G ul
7R UL-approved
7P ulama
6R Ulbricht
6R Ulbricht's
7H Ulett
8Q Ulixes
5N ullen
XH ulna
5D ulster
8Q Ultimos
9D Ultimus
XR Ultra-Facial
7R ultra-efficient
7Q ultra-high
XH ultra-thin
XR ultra-violet
8H ultrahigh-frequency
7R ultrapurity
9H ultrasonic
8Q Ulyanovsk
7A um-hum
7Q umbilicus
7Q Umbria
4R Umiak
8F Umiki
8Q Umjetnost
3A umm
3A ummm
3G ump
7D umph
4A umpire-in-chief
9D umpteenth
6A umtente
8F UMW
9G unA2ed**
9R un-American-boy
6G un-known
3J una
9R unabashed
5A Unabridged
9C unaccepting
9D unacquainted
4N unadventurous
9B unalterable
7J unaltered
9F Unam
7N unappeasable
9Q unarguably
9R unarticulated
5E unary
7A unashamedly
9Q unassailable
9C unattended
7R unavailable
7N unavailing
7A unavenged
7N unawed
8H unbalance
6A unbar
6A unbarred
7A unbeatable
7D unbecoming
9D unbecomingly
9D unbeliever
9Q unbend
9M unbent
9J unbidden
7A unbind
7N unblemished
8P unblindfolded
3A unblinking
6B unblown
8P unbolt
8P unbolted
8F unbounded
9Q unbridged
4A unbuckle
6R unbuckles
9D unbuilt
4A unburnable

Word Type	F	D	U	SFI	3 Gr 3	4 Gr 4	5 Gr 5	6 Gr 6	7 Gr 7	8 Gr 8	9 Gr 9	X UnGr	A Read	B Eng & Gr	C Comp	D Lit	E Math	F Soc Stud	G Spell	H Sci	J Music	K Art	L Home Ec	M Shop	N Lib F	P Lib NF	Q Lib Ref	R Mag	S Rel
unburned	3	.2427	.1822	32.6	0	0	0	0	0	2	1	0	0	0	0	0	0	0	0	2	0	0	0	0	0	0	0	1	0
unbuttoned	5	.4526	.4790	36.8	0	1	0	0	1	2	1	0	0	0	0	2	1	0	0	0	0	0	0	0	1	1	0	0	0
uncanny	4	.4530	.4014	36.0	0	1	0	0	2	0	0	1	1	0	0	0	0	0	0	0	0	0	0	0	0	1	1	1	0
Uncas	10	.0828	.2773	34.4	0	0	0	0	9	1	0	0	0	0	0	0	0	1	0	0	0	0	0	0	9	0	0	0	0
unceasing	4	.4484	.4050	36.1	0	0	0	1	0	1	1	1	1	0	0	0	0	1	0	1	0	0	0	0	0	0	1	0	0
uncertain	39	.7667	6.0733	47.8	4	4	3	6	8	9	5	0	11	5	0	3	1	3	1	0	1	0	0	0	3	1	2	8	0
uncertainly	20	.6022	2.5541	44.1	1	3	4	3	7	1	1	0	7	2	0	2	0	0	0	0	0	0	0	0	6	1	1	1	0
uncertainty	10	.7175	1.4474	41.6	0	0	1	0	5	3	0	1	0	1	0	1	0	1	0	2	0	0	1	0	1	1	1	1	0
unchained	2	.1717	.1142	30.6	0	0	1	0	1	0	0	0	1	0	0	1	0	0	0	0	0	0	1	0	0	0	0	1	0
unchallenged	4	.3534	.3078	34.9	1	0	0	0	0	0	1	2	0	1	0	0	0	0	0	0	0	0	0	0	0	1	2	0	0
unchanged	26	.7509	3.9273	45.9	1	1	3	4	7	4	4	2	0	1	1	1	5	3	0	5	1	0	0	0	1	1	6	1	0
unchanging	6	.3267	.4635	36.7	0	2	2	1	0	1	0	0	1	0	0	0	0	1	0	1	0	0	0	0	0	0	3	0	0
uncharged	4	.2278	.2257	33.5	0	0	0	0	1	2	0	1	0	0	0	0	0	0	0	2	0	0	0	0	0	0	2	0	0
uncharted	6	.5035	.6303	38.0	1	0	1	1	1	2	0	0	0	0	0	0	0	1	0	0	2	0	0	0	1	1	0	1	0
unchecked	3	.3870	.2492	34.0	0	1	0	0	1	0	1	0	0	0	0	0	0	0	0	0	0	0	0	0	1	0	1	1	0
uncivilized	3	.2212	.2099	33.2	0	0	1	0	2	0	0	0	2	0	0	1	0	0	0	0	0	0	0	0	0	0	0	0	0
uncle	196	.8115	32.117	55.1	50	51	20	16	24	16	18	1	68	24	5	28	5	5	9	1	1	0	2	1	22	22	1	2	0
Uncle	567	.7208	84.645	59.3	186	119	67	69	70	40	15	1	254	23	1	57	1	29	7	0	14	0	1	0	98	69	0	13	0
uncle's	18	.6321	2.4194	43.8	4	4	1	3	1	3	2	0	9	1	1	3	0	0	1	0	0	0	0	0	2	0	1	0	0
unclean	3	.2196	.1554	31.9	1	0	0	0	1	0	1	0	0	0	0	2	0	0	0	0	0	0	0	0	1	0	0	0	0
unclear	4	.3578	.3091	34.9	0	0	0	0	0	2	2	0	0	1	1	0	0	0	0	1	0	0	0	0	0	0	1	0	0
uncles	14	.2204	.8213	39.1	5	2	1	1	1	1	2	1	3	0	0	0	0	2	0	1	1	0	0	0	0	1	2	3	1
uncluttered	2	.1926	.0867	29.4	0	0	0	0	0	0	2	0	0	0	0	0	0	0	0	0	0	0	1	0	0	0	1	0	0
uncoiled	2	.2300	.1140	30.6	0	1	0	0	0	0	1	0	0	1	0	0	0	0	0	1	0	0	0	0	0	0	0	0	0
uncoiling	2	.1814	.1187	30.7	0	0	0	1	1	0	0	0	1	0	0	0	0	0	0	0	0	0	0	0	0	0	0	1	0
uncombed	3	.0000	.0097	19.8	0	0	0	0	0	3	0	0	0	0	0	0	0	0	0	0	0	0	3	0	0	0	0	0	0
uncomfortable	50	.7166	7.4046	48.7	4	11	8	4	10	6	6	1	19	4	0	6	0	3	0	6	0	0	3	0	2	5	0	2	0
uncomfortably	11	.4827	1.1701	40.7	0	0	3	2	2	1	2	1	3	0	0	0	0	3	0	0	0	1	0	0	2	0	0	2	0
uncommitted	2	.0000	.0243	23.9	0	0	0	0	2	0	0	0	0	0	0	0	0	0	0	0	0	0	0	0	0	0	0	2	0
uncommon	17	.6694	2.3275	43.7	0	0	0	6	3	1	6	1	2	2	0	4	0	2	0	0	1	0	0	0	0	2	3	1	0
uncommonly	2	.1717	.1142	30.6	1	0	0	0	1	0	0	0	1	0	0	1	0	0	0	0	0	0	0	0	0	0	0	0	0
uncompleted	3	.3877	.2482	33.9	0	0	0	0	1	1	1	0	0	1	0	1	0	0	0	0	0	0	0	0	0	0	1	0	0
uncomplicated	3	.3263	.2368	33.7	0	0	0	1	1	0	1	0	1	0	0	0	0	0	0	0	1	0	0	0	0	0	0	1	0
uncomprehending	3	.1832	.1417	31.5	0	0	0	0	1	1	0	1	0	0	0	2	0	0	0	1	0	0	0	0	0	0	0	0	0
uncompromising	6	.4484	.6010	37.8	0	0	0	1	3	1	1	0	2	0	0	1	0	0	0	0	1	0	0	0	0	0	2	0	0
unconcern	5	.5375	.5712	37.6	0	0	0	0	2	1	2	0	1	0	0	1	0	0	0	0	0	0	0	0	1	1	1	0	0
unconcerned	6	.4853	.6619	38.2	0	0	0	2	3	0	0	1	3	0	0	0	0	0	0	0	0	0	0	0	0	1	1	1	0
unconcernedly	2	.2407	.1138	30.6	0	0	0	0	1	1	0	0	0	0	0	1	0	0	0	0	0	0	0	0	0	1	0	0	0
unconquered	3	.2260	.1580	32.0	0	0	0	0	0	2	1	0	0	0	0	2	0	0	0	0	0	0	0	0	0	0	1	0	0
unconscious	25	.6882	3.5258	45.5	0	0	3	0	12	6	3	1	4	3	0	2	0	0	0	5	0	0	0	0	5	1	3	2	0
unconsciously	9	.5597	1.0544	40.2	0	0	0	0	5	2	2	0	1	2	0	0	1	0	0	1	0	0	0	0	2	0	2	0	0
unconsciousness	6	.4683	.5962	37.8	0	0	2	0	2	2	0	0	0	0	0	1	0	0	0	2	0	0	0	0	1	0	2	0	0
unconstitutional	7	.3696	.5775	37.6	0	0	1	0	2	3	1	0	0	0	0	1	0	4	0	0	0	0	0	0	0	0	2	0	0
uncontrollable	2	.1698	.1133	30.5	0	0	0	0	2	0	0	0	1	0	0	0	0	0	0	0	0	0	0	0	0	0	1	0	0
uncontrollably	2	.1717	.1142	30.6	0	0	0	0	2	0	0	0	1	0	0	1	0	0	0	0	0	0	0	0	0	0	0	0	0
uncontrolled	6	.3499	.4688	36.7	0	0	0	1	3	1	1	0	0	0	0	1	0	0	0	2	0	0	0	0	0	0	0	3	0
unconventional	5	.3586	.3883	35.9	0	0	0	0	2	2	1	0	0	1	0	0	0	0	0	0	2	0	0	0	0	2	0	0	0
uncooked	8	.1790	.3335	35.2	0	0	0	1	2	0	5	0	0	0	0	0	0	1	1	1	0	0	5	0	0	0	0	0	0
uncorseted	2	.2407	.1138	30.6	0	0	1	0	0	0	1	0	0	0	0	1	0	0	0	0	0	0	0	0	0	1	0	0	0
uncounted	3	.1813	.1402	31.5	0	0	0	0	3	0	0	0	0	0	0	0	0	0	0	1	0	0	0	0	0	0	2	0	0
uncouth	2	.1698	.1133	30.5	0	0	1	1	0	0	0	0	1	0	0	0	0	0	0	0	0	0	0	0	0	0	1	0	0
uncover	11	.6265	1.4711	41.7	2	3	2	1	2	0	1	0	5	0	0	0	0	0	1	2	0	0	0	0	0	1	1	1	0
uncovered	40	.7010	5.7504	47.6	6	8	4	4	11	0	6	1	10	2	0	2	0	1	0	6	1	3	4	0	3	4	2	2	0
uncovering	4	.4732	.3988	36.0	0	1	0	1	0	1	0	1	0	1	0	0	0	0	1	1	0	0	0	0	0	0	0	1	0
uncovers	3	.2197	.2090	33.2	0	1	0	0	1	1	0	0	2	0	0	0	0	0	0	0	0	0	0	0	0	0	1	0	0
uncurled	3	.2261	.2131	33.3	1	2	0	0	0	0	0	0	2	0	0	0	0	0	0	0	0	0	0	0	1	0	0	0	0
uncut	3	.3030	.1994	33.0	1	0	0	0	2	0	0	0	0	0	0	0	0	0	0	0	0	0	1	0	0	1	0	1	0
und	2	.0000	.0162	22.1	0	0	2	0	0	0	0	0	0	0	0	0	0	0	0	0	2	0	0	0	0	0	0	0	0
undamaged	7	.3817	.6819	38.3	0	0	1	3	0	3	0	0	5	0	0	1	0	0	0	0	0	0	0	0	0	1	0	0	0
undaunted	5	.4503	.5015	37.0	0	0	1	1	0	3	0	0	1	0	0	1	0	2	0	0	0	0	0	0	0	0	0	1	0
undecided	8	.5430	.9441	39.8	1	1	1	1	2	1	1	0	3	0	0	1	0	0	0	0	0	0	0	0	2	1	0	1	0
undecorated	3	.1783	.1304	31.2	0	3	0	0	0	0	0	0	0	0	0	0	0	0	0	0	0	1	0	0	0	2	0	0	0
undefeated	2	.2446	.1142	30.6	0	0	0	0	0	0	2	0	0	0	0	0	0	0	0	0	0	0	0	0	1	0	0	1	0
undeniable	5	.4594	.4873	36.9	0	0	0	0	1	2	1	1	0	1	0	0	0	1	0	0	0	0	0	0	1	0	0	2	0
undeniably	7	.5470	.7881	39.0	0	1	0	0	2	2	1	1	0	1	0	1	0	0	0	0	0	0	0	0	1	0	2	2	0
undependable	2	.2306	.1140	30.6	0	0	0	0	1	0	1	0	0	1	0	0	0	1	0	0	0	0	0	0	0	0	0	0	0
under	2987	.9739	573.45	67.6	636	408	322	348	601	345	255	72	896	130	24	153	75	285	167	292	62	14	66	22	185	227	197	191	1
Under	5	.4597	.4842	36.9	0	1	0	1	3	0	0	0	0	2	0	0	0	0	0	0	0	0	0	0	1	1	0	1	0
UNDER	3	.0000	.1370	31.4	0	0	0	3	0	0	0	0	3	0	0	0	0	0	0	0	0	0	0	0	0	0	0	0	0
Under-Housemaid	2	.0000	.0914	29.6	0	0	0	2	0	0	0	0	2	0	0	0	0	0	0	0	0	0	0	0	0	0	0	0	0
underachieving	2	.0000	.0243	23.9	0	0	0	0	2	0	0	0	0	0	0	0	0	0	0	0	0	0	0	0	0	0	0	2	0
underarm	8	.0000	.0258	24.1	0	0	0	0	2	3	3	0	0	0	0	0	0	0	0	0	0	0	8	0	0	0	0	0	0
underbrush	17	.5648	2.0267	43.1	4	3	4	0	2	2	1	1	3	0	2	0	0	3	0	1	0	0	0	0	1	3	1	3	0
underclothes	5	.2991	.3437	35.4	0	0	1	2	0	0	2	0	1	0	0	1	0	0	1	0	0	0	2	0	0	0	0	0	0
undercoat	16	.0221	.1208	30.8	1	0	0	0	0	9	6	0	0	0	0	0	0	0	0	0	0	0	0	15	0	1	0	0	0
undercollar	2	.0000	.0064	18.1	0	0	0	0	0	2	0	0	0	0	0	0	0	0	0	0	0	0	2	0	0	0	0	0	0
undercover	4	.1760	.1902	32.8	0	0	0	0	3	0	1	0	0	0	0	0	0	1	0	0	0	0	0	0	0	3	0	0	0
undercuff	2	.0000	.0064	18.1	0	0	0	0	0	2	0	0	0	0	0	0	0	0	0	0	0	0	2	0	0	0	0	0	0
undercurrent	3	.3772	.2437	33.9	0	0	2	0	0	0	1	0	0	0	0	0	0	0	0	0	1	0	0	0	1	1	0	0	0
undercurve	4	.1018	.0933	29.7	0	3	0	1	0	0	0	0	0	0	3	0	0	0	1	0	0	0	0	0	0	0	0	0	0
undercut	6	.4345	.5505	37.4	0	0	0	0	4	0	1	1	0	0	0	0	0	0	0	1	0	1	0	0	2	0	1	1	0
underdeveloped	16	.4752	1.6038	42.1	0	1	7	0	4	2	1	1	0	0	0	0	0	2	1	2	0	0	0	0	0	1	8	2	0
underdog	3	.2357	.2199	33.4	0	0	2	0	1	0	0	0	2	0	0	0	0	0	0	0	0	0	0	0	0	1	0	0	0
underestimated	2	.2446	.1142	30.6	0	0	0	0	1	1	0	0	0	0	0	0	0	0	0	0	0	0	0	0	1	0	0	1	0
underfold	2	.0000	.0064	18.1	0	0	0	0	0	2	0	0	0	0	0	0	0	0	0	0	0	0	2	0	0	0	0	0	0
underfoot	7	.4975	.7559	38.8	0	2	1	0	2	1	1	0	2	0	1	0	0	0	0	0	0	0	0	0	1	1	1	1	0
undergo	26	.6870	3.6514	45.6	0	1	1	7	6	5	4	2	2	1	0	0	0	1	0	11	0	0	1	1	0	2	4	3	0
undergoes	8	.2017	.4337	36.4	0	2	0	1	2	1	1	1	0	0	0	0	0	0	0	7	1	0	0	0	0	0	0	0	0
undergoing	11	.5844	1.3302	41.2	0	1	1	1	2	0	6	0	0	0	0	1	0	1	0	3	0	0	0	0	0	1	2	3	0
undergone	10	.6046	1.2542	41.0	0	0	0	3	5	0	2	0	1	1	0	0	0	1	0	2	1	0	0	0	0	0	3	1	0
undergraduate	7	.4524	.6873	38.4	1	0	1	0	2	1	2	0	1	0	0	0	1	0	0	0	0	0	0	0	0	1	3	1	0

9L unbuttered
4P unbutton
5A uncalled-for
7N uncarpeted
7N uncasing
9D unceasingly
9R uncelebrated
8F uncertainties
9D unchangeable
4A Uncheedah
7B uncials
3P uncircumcised
6A unclaimed
7N unclassified
3D UNCLE
4N Uncle's
5A uncleared
6R unclenched
7D unclimbed
7Q uncoil
9H uncombined
9D uncomplaining
9B uncomplimentary
9L uncompromisingly
8Q unconciousness
4Q unconditional
9Q unconditioned
7Q unconfirmed
9H unconformities
9B unconnected
6R Unconquered
9H unconsolidated
7R uncoordinated
5B uncorked
7N uncorrupted
7Q uncountable
9B uncountables
4R uncoupled
8A uncourteously
4A uncourtly
6G uncrushed
5P uncultivable
6G unda
7R undammed
5P undefended
7A undefined
7A undeleterious
7P undelivered
4A undelstand
4A undelstands
7R under-achiever
3H under-and-over
4N under-brush
7H under-cooked
6F under-developed
7R under-equipped
XP under-inspector
5Q under-represented
7L under-stitching
7D Under-the-Hill
XR under-16s
7R underachievement
7R underachievers
7R underarms
3A underbelly
7Q underbody
7R underclass
9L underclothing
4R undercroft
9A underdogs
4N underdone
7Q underestimate
8B underestimating
7N underfed
8L underfolds
8L undergarments
9R undergrad
7R Undergraduate

Word Type	F	D	U	SFI	3 Gr 3	4 Gr 4	5 Gr 5	6 Gr 6	7 Gr 7	8 Gr 8	9 Gr 9	X UnGr	A Read	B Eng & Gr	C Comp	D Lit	E Math	F Soc Stud	G Spell	H Sci	J Music	K Art	L Home Ec	M Shop	N Lib F	P Lib NF	Q Lib Ref	R Mag	S Rel
underground	115	.7477	17.553	52.4	28	15	16	13	19	16	7	1	29	2	0	6	1	17	3	19	0	0	0	0	1	7	18	12	0
Underground	5	.2242	.2842	34.5	3	0	0	0	0	0	2	0	0	0	0	0	0	2	0	0	0	0	0	0	0	3	0	0	0
undergrowth	21	.5573	2.4604	43.9	1	4	1	2	10	1	1	1	4	0	0	3	0	1	0	0	0	2	0	0	5	0	4	2	0
underhand	4	.2191	.2297	33.6	0	3	0	0	1	0	0	0	0	0	0	0	0	0	0	3	0	0	0	0	0	1	0	0	0
underhanded	2	.1551	.0728	28.6	0	0	0	1	0	0	1	0	0	0	1	0	0	0	0	0	0	0	0	0	1	0	0	0	0
underlap	2	.0000	.0064	18.1	0	0	0	0	1	1	0	0	0	0	0	0	0	0	0	0	0	0	2	0	0	0	0	0	0
underlie	5	.3325	.3637	35.6	1	0	0	0	1	1	2	0	0	3	0	0	0	0	0	0	0	0	0	0	0	0	1	1	0
underlies	5	.4672	.4883	36.9	1	0	0	1	2	1	0	0	0	2	0	0	0	0	0	0	1	0	0	0	0	1	1	0	0
underline	416	.3558	33.004	55.2	59	84	84	77	69	19	23	1	68	69	16	0	4	1	255	0	1	0	0	0	0	1	0	1	0
underlined	136	.4425	13.502	51.3	31	33	14	6	27	13	12	0	47	38	1	0	3	0	44	1	1	0	0	0	0	0	0	1	0
underlining	21	.4641	2.1215	43.3	3	2	1	1	6	4	3	1	5	10	0	0	0	0	4	0	0	0	0	1	0	0	0	1	0
underlying	31	.6006	3.8452	45.8	0	0	1	9	6	5	10	0	3	12	0	0	0	0	0	5	5	1	0	0	0	1	3	1	0
undermanned	2	.1948	.1250	31.0	0	0	0	0	1	0	1	0	1	0	0	0	0	0	0	0	0	0	0	0	0	1	0	0	0
undermine	3	.3847	.2496	34.0	0	0	2	0	1	0	0	0	0	0	0	0	0	0	0	0	0	0	0	0	0	1	1	1	0
undermined	3	.3776	.2489	34.0	1	0	0	0	1	1	0	0	0	0	0	1	0	1	0	0	0	0	0	0	0	0	0	1	0
undermining	2	.1641	.0751	28.8	0	0	0	0	1	1	0	0	0	0	1	0	0	0	0	0	0	0	0	0	0	0	1	0	0
underneath	112	.8972	19.981	53.0	28	19	12	10	17	12	11	3	25	1	1	11	1	2	1	19	8	2	2	1	9	18	6	5	0
undernourished	5	.4133	.4663	36.7	0	0	0	0	4	0	1	0	1	0	0	0	0	1	0	1	0	0	1	0	0	1	0	0	0
underpass	2	.0000	.0299	24.8	0	0	0	2	0	0	0	0	0	0	0	0	2	0	0	0	0	0	0	0	0	0	0	0	0
underpinning	2	.2401	.1133	30.5	1	0	0	0	0	1	0	0	0	0	0	0	0	0	0	0	0	0	0	0	0	1	1	0	0
underpowered	2	.2433	.1158	30.6	0	1	0	0	0	0	1	0	0	0	0	0	0	0	0	0	0	0	0	0	0	1	0	1	0
underpress	2	.0000	.0064	18.1	0	0	0	0	0	0	2	0	0	0	0	0	0	0	0	0	0	0	2	0	0	0	0	0	0
underpressing	3	.0000	.0097	19.8	0	0	0	0	0	0	3	0	0	0	0	0	0	0	0	0	0	0	3	0	0	0	0	0	0
underrate	2	.2437	.1129	30.5	0	0	0	0	2	0	0	0	0	0	0	0	0	0	0	0	0	0	0	0	0	0	1	1	0
underrated	2	.2437	.1129	30.5	0	0	0	0	1	1	0	0	0	0	0	0	0	0	0	0	0	0	0	0	0	0	1	1	0
underscored	4	.2408	.2182	33.4	0	0	0	1	0	3	0	0	0	2	0	0	0	0	2	0	0	0	0	0	0	0	0	0	0
undersea	31	.5252	3.5369	45.5	3	10	4	4	8	0	2	0	10	0	0	0	0	0	1	6	0	3	0	0	1	0	7	3	0
Undersecretary	2	.0000	.0914	29.6	0	0	2	0	0	0	0	0	2	0	0	0	0	0	0	0	0	0	0	0	0	0	0	0	0
undershirt	3	.1409	.1472	31.7	0	0	0	1	0	0	2	0	1	0	0	0	0	0	0	0	0	0	0	0	0	2	0	0	0
undershirts	2	.1787	.1174	30.7	0	0	0	1	1	0	0	0	1	0	0	0	0	0	0	0	0	0	0	0	1	0	0	0	0
underside	34	.5051	3.7788	45.8	11	5	3	3	9	0	2	1	11	0	0	1	0	0	0	9	0	0	5	0	1	6	1	0	0
undersized	2	.1497	.1046	30.2	0	0	0	0	1	1	0	0	1	0	0	0	0	0	1	0	0	0	0	0	0	0	0	0	0
understand	1026	.9124	185.94	62.7	112	162	149	110	237	148	98	10	291	101	14	86	75	91	20	97	36	14	22	22	47	57	28	20	5
understandable	12	.6195	1.5497	41.9	0	0	2	2	3	1	3	1	2	0	0	1	0	2	0	1	0	0	0	0	0	2	3	1	0
understandably	5	.4507	.4777	36.8	0	0	0	1	2	1	1	0	0	0	0	2	0	1	0	0	0	0	0	0	0	0	1	1	0
understanding	289	.9240	52.875	57.2	6	19	33	21	82	59	52	17	48	31	5	18	11	33	5	37	14	2	12	8	5	8	28	24	0
understandingly	3	.2212	.2099	33.2	0	1	0	0	1	0	1	0	2	0	0	1	0	0	0	0	0	0	0	0	0	0	0	0	0
understandings	13	.3596	1.1015	40.4	0	1	9	1	1	1	0	0	2	1	0	0	0	9	0	0	1	0	0	0	0	0	0	0	0
understands	41	.4510	4.0615	46.1	5	7	6	4	10	1	6	2	8	11	0	6	0	2	0	4	1	0	0	0	1	4	2	1	1
understatement	3	.2175	.1545	31.9	0	0	0	0	1	1	1	0	0	0	0	2	0	0	0	0	0	0	0	0	0	0	0	1	0
understitch	2	.0000	.0064	18.1	0	0	0	0	1	0	1	0	0	0	0	0	0	0	0	0	0	0	2	0	0	0	0	0	0
understood	183	.8813	32.176	55.1	20	22	30	23	37	20	26	5	51	13	3	15	10	12	0	19	4	0	0	5	14	14	15	8	0
undersurface	3	.2427	.1822	32.6	0	0	1	1	0	0	0	1	0	0	0	0	0	0	0	2	0	0	0	0	0	0	0	1	0
undertake	9	.4923	.9423	39.7	2	0	0	1	3	1	1	1	1	2	0	3	0	0	0	0	0	0	0	0	0	2	0	1	0
undertaken	22	.5500	2.5543	44.1	1	2	2	2	9	2	4	0	3	0	0	1	0	3	0	2	0	0	0	0	1	2	9	1	0
undertaker	3	.2266	.1614	32.1	0	0	0	2	1	0	0	0	0	0	0	0	0	0	0	0	0	0	0	0	1	0	0	2	0
undertakes	3	.2347	.1695	32.3	1	0	0	0	2	0	0	0	0	0	0	0	0	0	0	0	0	0	0	0	1	2	0	0	0
undertaking	12	.5958	1.5299	41.8	0	1	1	1	5	1	2	1	4	0	0	0	0	1	0	3	0	0	0	0	0	1	2	1	0
undertakings	8	.5390	.8919	39.5	0	0	1	1	3	2	1	0	0	1	0	0	0	1	0	1	0	0	1	0	1	0	3	0	0
undertone	4	.2872	.2840	34.5	0	0	0	0	2	1	0	1	1	0	0	2	0	0	0	0	0	0	0	0	0	1	0	0	0
undertook	11	.5790	1.3450	41.3	0	0	2	1	3	4	1	0	2	0	0	1	0	3	0	0	0	0	0	0	0	1	1	3	0
undertow	2	.1733	.1149	30.6	0	0	0	1	0	0	1	0	1	1	0	0	0	0	0	0	0	0	0	0	0	0	0	0	0
underwater	106	.7470	16.226	52.1	11	26	8	26	21	8	3	3	37	2	4	4	0	3	1	19	0	1	0	0	0	7	8	20	0
Underwater	2	.0000	.0914	29.6	0	2	0	0	0	0	0	0	2	0	0	0	0	0	0	0	0	0	0	0	0	0	0	0	0
underway	12	.4720	1.2432	40.9	0	1	0	3	4	3	0	1	3	0	0	0	0	1	0	0	1	0	0	0	0	0	2	5	0
underwear	23	.5244	2.6725	44.3	1	5	6	1	3	5	1	1	11	0	0	0	0	0	0	0	0	0	2	0	5	3	0	2	0
underweight	12	.1696	.5279	37.2	0	0	0	2	2	4	4	0	0	0	0	0	0	0	0	7	0	0	5	0	0	0	0	0	0
underwent	9	.6334	1.1716	40.7	0	1	0	2	1	2	3	0	1	1	0	1	0	1	1	0	0	0	0	0	0	0	2	2	0
Underwood	2	.0000	.0215	23.3	0	0	0	0	0	0	2	0	0	0	0	2	0	0	0	0	0	0	0	0	0	0	0	0	0
underworld	12	.4889	1.2928	41.1	0	1	5	2	1	3	0	0	4	0	0	2	0	1	0	0	1	0	0	0	0	0	4	0	0
underwriting	2	.1698	.1133	30.5	0	0	1	0	0	1	0	0	1	0	0	0	0	0	0	0	0	0	0	0	0	0	1	0	0
undeserved	3	.3870	.2492	34.0	0	0	0	0	3	0	0	0	0	0	0	0	0	0	0	0	0	0	0	0	1	0	1	1	0
undesirable	13	.4820	1.3048	41.2	0	0	0	0	4	5	2	2	0	2	1	0	0	2	0	2	0	0	4	0	0	1	0	1	0
undetected	6	.4471	.6021	37.8	1	0	0	2	1	0	2	0	2	2	0	0	0	0	0	0	0	0	0	0	1	0	1	0	0
undeveloped	7	.2399	.4129	36.2	1	0	2	3	0	1	0	0	0	0	0	0	0	4	0	0	0	0	0	0	0	0	3	0	0
undid	8	.3425	.5971	37.8	1	1	0	1	1	2	2	0	0	1	0	4	0	0	0	0	0	0	0	0	3	0	0	0	0
undigested	7	.1941	.3707	35.7	0	0	2	0	1	3	1	0	0	0	0	0	0	0	0	6	0	0	0	0	0	0	1	0	0
undignified	3	.2197	.2090	33.2	1	0	0	0	0	0	2	0	2	0	0	0	0	0	0	0	0	0	0	0	0	0	1	0	0
undiluted	2	.1812	.0838	29.2	0	0	0	0	1	0	1	0	0	0	0	0	0	0	0	0	0	0	1	0	0	0	0	1	0
undisciplined	2	.1787	.1174	30.7	0	1	0	1	0	0	0	0	1	0	0	0	0	0	0	0	0	0	0	0	1	0	0	0	0
undiscovered	5	.3689	.4527	36.6	0	0	0	0	2	2	0	1	2	0	0	0	0	0	0	2	0	0	0	0	0	0	0	1	0
undiscriminating	2	.2433	.1158	30.6	0	0	0	0	2	0	0	0	0	0	0	0	0	0	0	0	0	0	0	0	0	1	0	1	0
undisguised	2	.1717	.1142	30.6	0	0	0	0	1	1	0	0	1	0	0	1	0	0	0	0	0	0	0	0	0	0	0	0	0
undisputed	2	.2401	.1133	30.5	1	0	1	0	0	0	0	0	0	0	0	0	0	0	0	0	0	0	0	0	0	1	1	0	0
undissolved	2	.2346	.1166	30.7	0	0	0	0	2	0	0	0	0	0	0	0	0	0	0	1	0	0	0	0	0	0	0	1	0
undistinguished	2	.2297	.1135	30.6	0	0	0	0	0	2	0	0	0	0	0	1	0	1	0	0	0	0	0	0	0	0	0	0	0
undisturbed	21	.6843	2.9489	44.7	0	1	3	3	6	2	3	3	4	0	0	0	1	0	0	3	1	0	2	0	1	3	2	4	0
undo	16	.3309	1.2252	40.9	4	0	2	0	4	1	2	3	1	0	0	0	11	0	0	2	0	0	0	0	1	1	0	0	0
undoes	11	.0000	.1647	32.2	3	5	0	0	2	0	1	0	0	0	0	0	11	0	0	0	0	0	0	0	0	0	0	0	0
undoing	9	.5474	1.0343	40.1	1	0	1	0	4	2	0	1	1	0	0	3	2	0	0	0	0	0	0	0	1	1	0	1	0
undone	13	.6268	1.6725	42.2	0	2	1	1	7	0	2	0	1	0	0	2	2	0	0	0	0	0	0	1	2	3	0	2	0
undoubted	3	.1900	.1470	31.7	0	1	0	1	0	0	1	0	0	0	0	0	0	0	0	1	0	0	0	0	2	0	0	0	0
undoubtedly	57	.8046	9.1810	49.6	1	3	3	5	25	6	9	5	6	4	4	1	1	2	2	5	5	0	0	1	5	6	9	6	0
undreamed	4	.4751	.4057	36.1	0	0	0	0	0	2	1	1	0	0	0	0	0	1	0	1	0	0	0	0	1	0	1	0	0
undress	7	.5645	.8570	39.3	1	1	1	0	0	3	1	0	3	1	0	1	0	0	0	0	0	0	0	0	1	1	0	0	0
undressed	9	.5937	1.1258	40.5	0	4	1	1	1	0	0	2	2	0	0	1	0	0	0	1	0	0	0	0	2	2	0	1	0
undressing	2	.0000	.0215	23.3	1	0	0	0	1	0	0	0	0	0	0	2	0	0	0	0	0	0	0	0	0	0	0	0	0
undue	5	.3684	.3867	35.9	0	0	0	0	1	1	3	0	0	0	0	0	0	0	0	1	0	0	2	1	0	0	1	0	0
unduly	8	.5675	.9907	40.0	1	0	0	1	2	1	3	0	4	0	0	1	0	0	0	0	0	0	0	0	1	0	1	1	0
unearthed	12	.5539	1.4349	41.6	2	2	2	1	2	1	2	0	4	0	0	0	0	1	0	1	0	1	0	0	1	2	0	2	0
unearthly	4	.4411	.3879	35.9	0	0	0	0	2	2	0	0	1	0	0	0	0	0	1	0	1	0	0	0	1	0	0	0	0
uneasily	23	.5462	2.7788	44.4	3	4	2	3	7	2	2	0	12	0	0	3	0	1	0	0	0	0	0	0	5	1	1	0	0
uneasiness	9	.5974	1.1456	40.6	0	0	1	0	3	3	1	1	3	1	0	1	0	1	0	1	0	0	0	0	2	0	0	0	0
uneasy	37	.6330	4.9485	46.9	5	2	5	10	9	4	2	0	15	1	1	3	0	1	0	0	0	0	0	0	9	1	0	6	0

3P undergraduates
6F undergrond
7D underhang
7D underlay
7H underlines
5N underlip
6B underpads
9Q underpaid
6A underpants
4A underpart
9Q underpasses
9R underpin
6A underpinnings
5R underprivileged
7H underproduction
7R underscore
7F underscores
7D underscoring
7R Undersea
9F Undersecretary-Generals
3A undersides
8F undersigned
8M undersize
3J undersong
3A underst-
7R understaffed
8N understandin'
8N Understanding
7L UNDERSTANDING
7R understated
9R understates
6R undertaker's
7Q undertakers
9D undervalued
6N underwaist
3P Underwing
7D Underworld
9R underwrite
4Q underwriters
8F underwritten
9D undeserving
7Q undesirables
8R undeterred
6J undimmed
6J Undimmed
7N Undine
9D undistinguishable
7L undivided
9D undramatic
4R undreamed-of
8F undreamed-of-products
8H undulant
9F undulating
7A undulations
4A undust
XH undying
9E unearned
6N unease

Word Type	F	D	U	SFI	3 Gr 3	4 Gr 4	5 Gr 5	6 Gr 6	7 Gr 7	8 Gr 8	9 Gr 9	X UnGr	A Read	B Eng & Gr	C Comp	D Lit	E Math	F Soc Stud	G Spell	H Sci	J Music	K Art	L Home Ec	M Shop	N Lib F	P Lib NF	Q Lib Ref	R Mag	S Rel
uneatable	2	.2407	.1138	30.6	0	0	0	0	1	0	1	0	0	0	0	1	0	0	0	0	0	0	0	0	0	1	0	0	0
uneaten	3	.2433	.1822	32.6	0	1	0	0	1	0	0	1	0	0	0	0	0	0	0	2	0	0	0	0	1	0	0	0	0
uneducated	12	.5469	1.3925	41.4	0	0	2	2	1	2	5	0	2	4	0	1	0	3	0	0	0	0	0	0	0	0	1	1	0
unemotional	2	.2441	.1127	30.5	0	0	1	0	0	0	1	0	0	0	0	0	0	0	0	0	0	0	0	0	1	0	1	0	0
unemotionally	2	.2331	.1157	30.6	0	0	0	0	0	1	0	1	0	0	0	0	0	0	0	1	0	0	0	0	1	0	0	0	0
unemployed	11	.3778	.9366	39.7	0	0	0	0	2	7	2	0	0	0	0	0	0	8	0	0	0	0	0	0	0	1	1	1	0
unemployment	18	.5202	1.9743	43.0	3	1	0	0	5	0	9	0	1	0	0	1	0	4	0	0	0	0	0	0	0	2	3	7	0
unencumbered	2	.1698	.1133	30.5	0	0	0	0	2	0	0	0	1	0	0	0	0	0	0	0	0	0	0	0	0	0	1	0	0
unending	12	.6983	1.7077	42.3	0	1	4	1	2	2	1	1	1	0	0	1	2	3	0	0	1	0	0	0	0	1	1	2	0
unendingly	2	.0000	.0299	24.8	0	0	0	0	0	0	2	0	0	0	0	0	2	0	0	0	0	0	0	0	0	0	0	0	0
unenthusiastic	2	.2351	.1166	30.7	0	0	0	0	0	1	1	0	0	0	0	0	0	1	0	0	0	0	0	0	0	0	0	1	0
unequal	22	.7351	3.2740	45.2	1	3	0	1	6	6	4	1	1	1	0	0	4	4	1	5	3	0	0	0	0	1	1	1	0
unequaled	3	.2222	.1558	31.9	0	0	0	1	0	2	0	0	0	1	0	0	0	0	0	0	0	0	0	0	0	0	2	0	0
unerringly	4	.3745	.3228	35.1	0	0	0	0	3	0	1	0	0	0	0	1	0	0	0	0	0	0	0	0	0	0	1	2	0
uneven	34	.6747	4.6963	46.7	1	7	7	5	5	4	2	3	5	2	1	1	0	3	0	6	11	1	0	0	2	0	0	2	0
unevenly	6	.4021	.5491	37.4	1	1	1	1	1	0	1	0	1	0	0	0	0	1	0	2	0	0	0	0	0	0	2	0	0
unevenness	2	.0000	.0389	25.9	0	0	0	0	0	0	2	0	0	0	0	0	0	2	0	0	0	0	0	0	0	0	2	0	0
unexcitable	2	.0000	.0914	29.6	2	0	0	0	0	0	0	0	2	0	0	0	0	0	0	0	0	0	0	0	0	0	0	0	0
unexcited	2	.2139	.1057	30.2	0	0	1	0	0	1	0	0	0	0	0	0	0	1	1	0	0	0	0	0	0	0	0	0	0
unexpected	81	.7823	12.763	51.1	13	6	4	12	18	12	12	4	17	8	6	8	0	1	13	6	0	2	3	0	4	4	2	7	0
unexpectedly	20	.5434	2.3610	43.7	0	4	1	6	3	2	1	3	8	1	2	3	0	0	0	1	0	0	0	0	1	0	0	4	0
unexpectedness	2	.2387	.1089	30.4	0	0	0	0	1	0	1	0	0	0	0	0	0	0	0	0	1	0	0	0	1	0	0	0	0
unexplained	8	.1984	.4429	36.5	1	0	0	0	2	1	4	0	2	0	0	0	0	0	0	1	0	0	0	0	0	0	5	0	0
unexplored	15	.5813	1.8357	42.6	0	2	4	2	5	1	1	0	2	0	0	0	0	5	0	2	1	0	0	0	0	0	3	2	0
unexposed	3	.2442	.1820	32.6	0	0	0	0	0	0	3	0	0	1	0	0	0	0	0	2	0	0	0	0	0	0	0	0	0
unfair	32	.3936	2.8288	44.5	3	4	7	6	5	4	2	1	5	4	0	1	0	7	0	0	0	0	0	0	4	1	4	5	1
unfamiliar	50	.7499	7.6010	48.8	1	2	7	8	12	14	6	0	12	12	2	3	0	2	7	0	5	0	0	1	0	3	2	1	0
unfasten	2	.1812	.0838	29.2	0	0	0	0	1	0	1	0	0	0	0	0	0	0	0	0	0	0	1	0	0	0	0	1	0
unfastened	9	.3379	.7145	38.5	5	2	0	1	1	0	0	0	2	0	0	0	0	0	0	0	0	0	0	0	5	1	0	1	0
unfathomable	2	.2401	.1133	30.5	0	0	1	0	1	0	0	0	0	0	0	0	0	0	0	0	0	0	0	0	0	1	1	0	0
unfavorable	5	.4582	.4818	36.8	0	0	0	0	1	1	1	2	0	0	0	1	0	0	0	0	0	0	0	0	0	1	2	1	0
unfavorably	3	.3815	.2534	34.0	1	0	0	1	0	1	0	0	0	0	0	0	0	1	0	0	0	0	0	0	0	1	0	1	0
unfeeling	3	.2374	.1625	32.1	0	0	0	0	2	0	1	0	0	0	0	2	0	0	0	0	1	0	0	0	0	0	0	0	0
unfettered	2	.0000	.0162	22.1	0	0	0	0	0	1	0	1	0	0	0	0	0	0	0	0	2	0	0	0	0	0	0	0	0
unfinished	21	.5699	2.5078	44.0	3	3	3	0	6	4	1	1	3	2	0	2	0	6	0	0	0	0	0	3	2	0	1	2	0
unfit	9	.5287	1.0335	40.1	1	1	0	1	3	3	0	0	2	0	0	0	0	3	0	1	0	0	0	0	0	2	1	0	0
unflattering	2	.1948	.1250	31.0	1	0	1	0	0	0	0	0	1	0	0	0	0	0	0	0	0	0	0	0	0	1	0	0	0
unfold	11	.6757	1.5054	41.8	1	0	2	0	1	2	3	2	0	0	1	2	1	1	0	2	0	0	1	0	0	1	1	1	0
unfolded	20	.5851	2.4604	43.9	1	4	2	2	2	4	3	2	5	1	0	0	2	2	0	0	0	0	2	3	1	3	1	0	0
unfolding	7	.5322	.7845	38.9	1	0	1	0	1	3	1	0	1	0	1	0	1	0	0	1	0	0	1	0	1	1	0	0	0
unfolds	5	.4809	.5110	37.1	0	0	1	0	1	1	0	2	0	0	0	0	0	0	0	2	1	0	0	0	0	1	0	1	0
unforeseen	2	.2331	.1157	30.6	0	0	0	1	0	0	0	1	0	0	0	0	0	0	0	1	0	0	0	0	1	0	0	0	0
unforgettable	6	.5496	.7097	38.5	1	0	0	1	3	1	0	0	2	1	0	0	0	0	0	0	1	0	0	0	0	1	0	1	0
unforgiving	2	.1787	.1174	30.7	0	0	0	1	1	0	0	0	1	0	0	0	0	0	0	0	0	0	0	0	1	0	0	0	0
unformed	3	.2143	.1568	32.0	1	0	0	0	0	0	1	1	0	0	0	0	0	0	0	0	0	0	0	0	0	1	0	2	0
unforseen	2	.2337	.1157	30.6	0	1	0	0	0	0	1	0	0	0	0	0	0	1	0	0	0	0	0	0	1	0	0	0	0
unfortunate	32	.6712	4.4182	46.5	3	2	3	8	9	2	4	1	6	1	0	2	0	2	1	1	0	0	0	0	11	2	2	4	0
unfortunately	66	.8084	10.734	50.3	4	3	5	11	24	9	7	3	12	3	2	2	1	14	0	5	0	0	2	0	2	6	8	9	0
unfriendliness	2	.0000	.0219	23.4	0	0	0	0	0	0	2	0	0	2	0	0	0	0	0	0	0	0	0	0	0	0	0	0	0
unfriendly	25	.6899	3.6017	45.6	3	3	7	2	8	2	0	0	10	2	0	1	0	7	1	0	0	0	0	0	1	2	1	0	0
unfurled	2	.2303	.1079	30.3	1	0	0	1	0	0	0	0	0	0	0	0	0	0	0	0	1	0	0	0	0	1	0	0	0
unfurling	2	.2427	.1152	30.6	0	0	1	1	0	0	0	0	0	0	0	0	0	0	0	0	0	0	0	0	1	1	0	0	0
ungainly	10	.4810	1.1144	40.5	0	0	1	2	2	2	2	1	6	0	0	1	0	0	0	0	0	0	0	0	0	2	0	1	0
ungrammatical	11	.0392	.2337	33.7	0	0	1	1	2	2	5	0	1	10	0	0	0	0	0	0	0	0	0	0	0	0	0	0	0
ungrateful	2	.2407	.1138	30.6	0	0	0	0	0	1	1	0	0	0	0	1	0	0	0	0	0	0	0	0	0	1	0	0	0
unguarded	8	.3489	.7525	38.8	0	1	2	3	1	0	0	1	6	0	0	0	0	1	0	1	0	0	0	0	0	0	0	0	0
ungulate	2	.0000	.0209	23.2	0	0	0	0	2	0	0	0	0	0	0	0	0	0	0	0	0	0	0	0	0	0	2	0	0
unhampered	2	.2331	.1157	30.6	0	0	0	1	0	0	0	1	0	0	0	0	0	0	0	1	0	0	0	0	1	0	0	0	0
unhappily	12	.7005	1.7278	42.4	0	2	0	3	4	2	1	0	3	1	0	1	0	1	1	1	0	0	0	0	2	0	0	2	0
unhappiness	8	.5014	.8777	39.4	0	0	2	2	1	3	0	0	3	0	0	1	0	0	2	0	0	0	1	0	0	0	0	1	0
unhappy	144	.8988	25.820	54.1	31	29	14	16	30	14	8	2	61	8	3	12	1	9	3	6	4	1	2	0	13	10	3	8	0
unharmed	7	.4848	.7693	38.9	0	0	3	0	2	1	0	1	3	0	0	0	0	0	0	2	0	0	0	0	1	0	1	0	0
unhatched	5	.4664	.4951	36.9	0	2	1	2	0	0	0	0	0	0	0	0	0	0	0	1	1	0	0	0	0	2	0	1	0
unhealthy	8	.5919	.9719	39.9	1	0	0	0	4	2	1	0	0	0	0	1	0	1	1	1	0	0	0	1	1	2	0	0	0
unheard	13	.6088	1.6817	42.3	0	1	3	1	3	2	3	0	5	0	0	1	0	0	0	0	1	0	0	0	0	2	1	3	0
unheard-of	3	.2279	.2143	33.3	0	1	1	1	0	0	0	0	2	0	0	0	0	0	0	0	0	0	0	0	0	0	0	1	0
unheated	2	.2446	.1257	31.0	0	0	1	0	0	1	0	0	0	0	0	0	0	1	0	1	0	0	0	0	0	0	0	0	0
unheeded	6	.5193	.6609	38.2	0	0	0	1	1	2	2	0	1	1	0	1	0	0	0	0	0	0	0	0	2	0	1	0	0
unhesitatingly	2	.2433	.1158	30.6	0	0	0	0	0	1	1	0	0	0	0	0	0	0	0	0	0	0	0	0	0	1	0	1	0
unhinged	2	.1814	.1187	30.7	0	0	1	0	1	0	0	0	1	0	0	0	0	0	0	0	0	0	0	0	0	0	0	1	0
unhitch	3	.2279	.2143	33.3	1	0	1	1	0	0	0	0	2	0	0	0	0	0	0	0	0	0	0	0	0	0	0	1	0
unhitched	4	.2974	.2886	34.6	1	0	1	0	1	1	0	0	1	0	1	1	0	1	0	0	0	0	0	0	0	0	0	0	0
unhitching	2	.2408	.1204	30.8	0	1	1	0	0	0	0	0	0	0	0	0	0	1	0	0	0	0	0	0	0	1	0	0	0
unhooked	4	.3713	.3634	35.6	1	0	0	0	1	0	2	0	2	0	0	1	0	0	0	0	0	0	0	0	1	0	0	0	0
unhuman	2	.2443	.1130	30.5	0	0	0	0	2	0	0	0	0	0	0	1	0	0	0	0	0	0	0	0	1	0	0	0	0
unhurt	7	.4754	.7760	38.9	1	2	1	0	1	1	1	0	4	0	0	1	0	1	0	1	0	0	0	0	0	0	0	0	0
unicameral	2	.2401	.1133	30.5	0	0	1	0	0	1	0	0	0	0	0	0	0	0	0	0	0	0	0	0	0	1	1	0	0
UNICEF	2	.0000	.0243	23.9	0	2	0	0	0	0	0	0	0	0	0	0	0	0	0	0	0	0	0	0	0	0	0	2	0
unicellular	3	.1813	.1402	31.5	0	0	0	2	0	0	0	1	0	0	0	0	0	0	0	1	0	0	0	0	0	0	2	0	0
unicorn	5	.2445	.3864	35.9	0	4	0	0	1	0	0	0	4	0	0	1	0	0	0	0	0	0	0	0	0	0	0	0	0
Unicorn	3	.2196	.1554	31.9	0	0	1	0	2	0	0	0	0	0	0	2	0	0	0	0	0	0	0	0	1	0	0	0	0
unidentified	4	.4499	.4023	36.0	0	0	1	0	2	0	0	1	1	1	0	0	0	0	0	1	0	0	0	0	0	0	0	1	0
unification	2	.2401	.1133	30.5	1	0	1	0	0	0	0	0	0	0	0	0	0	0	0	0	0	0	0	0	0	1	1	0	0
unified	20	.4582	1.9170	42.8	2	0	3	1	11	2	1	0	0	0	5	0	0	5	0	0	1	1	0	0	0	3	5	0	0
unifiers	3	.0000	.0583	27.7	0	0	0	0	0	3	0	0	0	0	0	0	0	3	0	0	0	0	0	0	0	0	0	0	0
uniform	111	.8055	17.996	52.6	18	19	12	13	20	11	14	4	28	12	8	1	2	2	2	8	2	0	4	2	16	7	8	9	0
uniformed	4	.4530	.4014	36.0	0	2	1	0	0	1	0	0	1	0	0	0	0	0	0	0	0	0	0	0	0	1	1	1	0
uniformity	9	.5267	1.0152	40.1	0	0	0	0	3	2	3	1	2	0	1	1	0	0	0	2	0	0	0	0	0	0	2	1	0
uniformly	15	.4897	1.5478	41.9	0	0	1	2	3	7	2	0	0	0	0	0	6	1	0	2	0	0	1	0	0	0	5	0	0
uniforms	36	.6786	5.0577	47.0	3	3	5	2	6	12	2	3	10	7	0	0	0	7	1	0	3	0	0	0	3	1	0	4	0
unify	4	.4814	.4082	36.1	0	0	0	0	2	1	1	0	0	1	0	0	1	1	0	0	0	0	0	0	0	0	0	1	0
unifying	4	.3856	.3384	35.3	0	0	0	0	0	1	3	0	0	0	0	0	0	2	0	0	1	0	0	0	0	0	1	0	0

9D uneconomic
8B uneconomical
7N unembellished
8A unendurable
9D unenlightened
7D unenterprising
7D unentertaining
XQ unequalled
7N unequally
7Q unequivocally
XR unethical
9P uneventful
8F unexpanding
4N unexpected-
9B unexpressed
7Q unfailing
8B unfailingly
6H unfairly
7Q unfathomed
XR unfeasible
8D unfeathered
7A unfed
6F unfenced
9L unfermented
9H unfertilized
8L unflavored
9P unflinching
8K unflinchingly
6A unflurried
7D unfoldment
7D unforded
7Q unforgivably
9F unfortified
9F unfreezes
9P unfrosted
6R unfroze
5P unfruitful
7D unfunny
7Q unfused
9D ungenerous
7A ungiving
5F unglaciated
4Q unglazed
4N ungovernable
7P ungraciously
7B ungrammatically
7D ungratefulness
9L ungreased
9Q ungripping
XR unguent
8A unguents
6Q ungulates
9D unhallowed
4N unhappier
3A unhappiest
3A Unhappy
6A unharness
6A unharnessing
9D unheedy
9Q unhelped
7Q unhindered
3A unhook
7R unhurried
6G uni
7Q unicorns
4A unicorns'
9B unicycle
7R unicycles
6A Unidentified
5F Unidos
8F Unification
9M Unified
8C Uniform
7A uniform-like
8Q unilateral

Word Type	F	D	U	SFI	3 Gr 3	4 Gr 4	5 Gr 5	6 Gr 6	7 Gr 7	8 Gr 8	9 Gr 9	X UnGr	A Read	B Eng & Gr	C Comp	D Lit	E Math	F Soc Stud	G Spell	H Sci	J Music	K Art	L Home Ec	M Shop	N Lib F	P Lib NF	Q Lib Ref	R Mag	S Rel
unilaterally	7	.3863	.5950	37.7	0	3	1	0	0	3	0	0	0	0	0	0	0	3	0	0	0	0	0	0	0	0	2	2	0
unimaginable	4	.3422	.3030	34.8	0	0	0	0	2	2	0	0	0	0	0	2	0	0	0	1	0	0	0	0	0	0	1	0	0
unimaginative	3	.2524	.1934	32.9	0	0	0	0	1	1	1	0	1	0	0	1	0	0	0	0	0	0	1	0	0	0	0	0	0
unimpaired	3	.3847	.2496	34.0	0	0	1	0	1	0	1	0	0	0	0	0	0	0	0	0	0	0	0	0	0	1	1	1	0
unimportance	2	.1378	.0662	28.2	0	0	0	0	0	1	0	1	0	0	0	0	0	0	0	0	0	1	0	0	0	0	0	1	0
unimportant	14	.5691	1.6702	42.2	0	0	0	3	5	2	3	1	2	2	2	0	0	3	0	2	0	0	1	0	1	0	0	1	0
uninflated	2	.0000	.0394	26.0	0	0	0	0	2	0	0	0	0	0	0	0	0	0	0	2	0	0	0	0	0	0	0	0	0
uninformed	6	.4703	.6066	37.8	0	0	2	0	0	0	3	1	0	0	0	0	0	1	0	2	0	0	0	0	0	2	1	0	0
uninhabitable	4	.1975	.2179	33.4	0	0	0	1	0	3	0	0	0	0	0	0	0	3	0	1	0	0	0	0	0	0	0	0	0
uninhabited	7	.6190	.9109	39.6	0	2	0	1	1	2	0	1	2	1	0	0	0	1	0	0	0	0	0	0	1	0	1	1	0
uninhibited	4	.3711	.3648	35.6	0	0	1	0	2	0	1	0	2	0	0	0	0	0	0	0	0	0	0	0	0	1	1	0	0
unintelligible	2	.1948	.1250	31.0	0	0	2	0	0	0	0	0	1	0	0	0	0	0	0	0	0	0	0	0	0	1	0	0	0
unintentionally	4	.3679	.3346	35.2	0	0	0	0	2	1	1	0	1	0	0	1	0	0	0	0	0	0	1	0	0	0	0	1	0
uninterested	3	.3431	.2528	34.0	0	0	0	0	2	1	0	0	1	0	0	0	0	1	0	0	0	0	0	0	1	0	0	0	0
uninteresting	8	.4632	.8502	39.3	0	3	1	1	2	1	0	0	4	0	0	2	1	0	1	0	0	0	0	0	0	0	0	0	0
uninterrupted	4	.4707	.3979	36.0	0	0	1	0	1	0	1	1	0	0	0	0	0	0	1	1	0	0	0	0	0	1	1	0	0
uninvited	3	.3665	.2411	33.8	0	0	1	1	1	0	0	0	0	0	0	0	0	0	1	1	0	0	0	0	1	0	0	0	0
uninviting	2	.0000	.0209	23.2	1	1	0	0	0	0	0	0	0	0	0	0	0	0	0	0	0	0	0	0	0	0	2	0	0
union	104	.6935	14.695	51.7	3	4	29	8	19	26	14	1	6	0	1	0	26	28	1	2	4	0	0	0	1	4	19	12	0
Union	291	.6209	37.660	55.8	17	17	56	49	52	56	40	4	35	7	0	3	0	135	0	3	3	0	0	0	7	29	41	28	0
Union's	4	.2352	.2332	33.7	0	0	0	1	1	1	1	0	0	0	0	0	0	2	0	0	0	0	0	0	0	0	0	2	0
unionism	2	.2351	.1166	30.7	0	0	0	0	0	1	1	0	0	0	0	0	0	1	0	0	0	0	0	0	0	0	0	1	0
unions	84	.4680	8.3737	49.2	4	1	17	3	10	26	23	0	1	0	0	0	4	26	0	0	0	0	0	0	0	3	26	24	0
unique	132	.8059	21.252	53.3	6	2	8	8	48	27	22	11	8	2	1	3	15	3	2	8	18	5	1	2	0	10	27	27	0
uniquely	3	.2689	.1805	32.6	0	0	0	0	0	2	0	1	0	0	1	0	0	0	0	1	1	0	0	0	0	0	0	0	0
uniqueness	6	.4149	.5541	37.4	0	0	1	0	0	3	2	0	1	0	0	0	2	0	0	0	0	0	0	0	0	1	2	0	0
unison	28	.2755	1.7405	42.4	1	2	3	3	13	0	6	0	1	4	0	0	1	0	0	2	19	0	0	0	0	0	0	1	0
unit	838	.6664	113.41	60.5	82	56	107	69	224	200	87	13	37	16	8	11	267	28	305	50	13	2	12	18	0	10	31	30	0
Unit	219	.3886	18.243	52.6	44	44	32	26	42	19	10	2	12	0	0	0	4	11	155	15	0	1	3	13	1	2	0	2	0
unit-letter	2	.0000	.0209	23.2	0	2	0	0	0	0	0	0	0	0	0	0	0	0	0	0	0	0	0	0	0	0	2	0	0
unit-wholes	2	.0000	.0299	24.8	0	0	2	0	0	0	0	0	0	0	0	0	2	0	0	0	0	0	0	0	0	0	0	0	0
Unitarian	3	.2233	.1562	31.9	0	0	0	0	0	3	0	0	0	0	0	1	0	0	0	0	0	0	0	0	0	0	2	0	0
Unitas	9	.0000	.1094	30.4	0	0	0	6	0	3	0	0	0	0	0	0	0	0	0	0	0	0	0	0	0	0	0	9	0
unite	29	.7028	4.1373	46.2	6	0	1	3	4	10	4	1	1	0	0	1	0	8	0	2	3	1	0	0	0	6	3	4	0
united	65	.7768	10.184	50.1	6	3	6	9	18	18	4	1	6	1	1	1	0	25	0	4	2	0	0	1	4	7	9	4	0
United	137	.6700	19.029	52.8	8	9	23	24	39	13	20	1	26	1	2	3	1	64	1	3	0	0	0	0	1	9	11	15	0
UnitedNations	3	.1639	.1674	32.2	0	0	0	0	1	2	0	0	1	0	0	0	0	2	0	0	0	0	0	0	0	0	0	0	0
UnitedStates	1836	.7299	273.10	64.4	197	291	371	209	262	305	179	22	224	36	5	10	48	827	15	127	72	1	8	5	7	100	282	69	0
UnitedStates'	8	.4085	.7275	38.6	0	2	1	0	3	0	1	1	0	0	0	0	1	5	0	1	0	0	0	0	0	0	0	1	0
unites	5	.4043	.4349	36.4	0	1	0	0	2	1	1	0	0	0	0	1	0	0	0	2	0	0	0	1	0	0	1	0	0
UnitesStates	2	.2152	.1357	31.3	0	0	0	2	0	0	0	0	1	0	0	0	0	1	0	0	0	0	0	0	0	0	0	0	0
uniting	8	.5168	.8864	39.5	2	0	2	1	1	2	0	0	1	0	0	0	0	2	1	2	0	0	0	0	0	0	2	0	0
units	483	.6759	66.444	58.2	25	59	62	31	101	95	100	10	10	11	2	0	271	25	39	50	7	0	8	14	0	5	26	15	0
Units	63	.0142	.6906	38.4	4	12	14	11	16	6	0	0	0	0	0	0	0	1	62	0	0	0	0	0	0	0	0	0	0
units'	6	.0000	.0898	29.5	0	0	0	0	1	0	5	0	0	0	0	0	6	0	0	0	0	0	0	0	0	0	0	0	0
unity	64	.6222	8.1599	49.1	6	5	2	5	22	10	10	4	7	2	11	0	0	8	2	1	11	1	0	1	0	3	9	8	0
Unity	6	.2401	.3399	35.3	0	3	3	0	0	0	0	0	0	0	0	0	0	0	0	0	0	0	0	0	0	3	3	0	0
UNIVAC	2	.0000	.0914	29.6	0	0	0	2	0	0	0	0	2	0	0	0	0	0	0	0	0	0	0	0	0	0	0	0	0
universal	55	.7829	8.6122	49.4	0	6	4	3	9	14	17	2	1	0	1	6	10	2	0	7	7	1	0	3	0	1	11	5	0
Universal	2	.0000	.0389	25.9	0	0	0	0	0	1	1	0	0	0	0	0	0	2	0	0	0	0	0	0	0	0	0	0	0
universally	11	.6691	1.4950	41.7	0	0	1	0	2	5	3	0	1	1	1	0	2	0	1	0	0	0	0	1	0	1	2	1	0
universe	191	.7291	28.247	54.5	14	24	21	29	39	25	26	13	8	5	3	11	13	9	1	89	0	0	1	1	0	11	33	6	0
Universe	6	.5597	.7004	38.5	2	1	0	1	1	1	0	0	0	1	0	0	0	1	0	2	0	0	0	0	1	0	1	0	0
universes	2	.0000	.0394	26.0	0	0	1	0	0	0	0	1	0	0	0	0	0	0	0	2	0	0	0	0	0	0	0	0	0
universities	55	.6446	7.2522	48.6	7	1	6	3	19	7	10	2	2	1	0	1	1	14	0	1	1	0	0	2	0	4	17	11	0
Universities	8	.1220	.2668	34.3	0	0	4	0	2	0	2	0	0	0	0	0	0	0	0	0	0	0	0	0	0	0	7	1	0
university	87	.6554	11.664	50.7	6	7	5	15	20	14	15	5	6	4	0	1	5	13	1	1	1	0	0	0	2	6	23	24	0
University	195	.5938	24.007	53.8	4	7	32	23	59	36	21	13	18	1	0	4	3	16	1	15	5	0	1	0	0	8	63	60	0
unjust	14	.4093	1.2666	41.0	0	0	0	4	5	2	3	0	1	0	1	5	0	7	0	0	0	0	0	0	0	0	0	0	0
unjustified	2	.2351	.1166	30.7	0	0	0	0	0	1	0	1	0	0	0	0	0	1	0	0	0	0	0	0	0	0	0	1	0
unjustly	3	.2332	.1690	32.3	0	0	0	2	0	0	0	1	0	0	0	0	0	0	0	0	0	0	0	0	0	2	0	1	0
Unkar	2	.0000	.0243	23.9	0	0	0	2	0	0	0	0	0	0	0	0	0	0	0	0	0	0	0	0	0	0	0	2	0
unkind	19	.7189	2.8241	44.5	4	2	0	3	6	3	1	0	8	2	0	1	0	1	2	1	0	0	1	0	1	2	0	0	0
unkindly	5	.4688	.5254	37.2	1	1	1	1	0	0	1	0	2	0	0	1	0	0	1	0	0	0	0	0	1	0	0	0	0
unkindness	2	.1497	.1046	30.2	0	1	0	1	0	0	0	0	1	0	0	0	0	0	1	0	0	0	0	0	0	0	0	0	0
unknowing	3	.3674	.2406	33.8	0	0	1	0	1	1	0	0	0	0	0	0	0	1	0	0	1	0	0	0	0	0	1	0	0
unknowingly	3	.2236	.1570	32.0	0	0	0	0	3	0	0	0	0	1	0	2	0	0	0	0	0	0	0	0	0	0	0	0	0
unknown	171	.9244	31.314	55.0	12	11	24	18	46	33	18	9	31	7	0	16	7	23	6	19	6	1	1	3	10	12	19	10	0
Unknown	9	.2321	.4905	36.9	0	1	1	3	0	0	1	3	0	0	0	0	0	0	0	0	0	0	0	0	0	0	3	6	0
unkum	4	.0000	.0323	25.1	4	0	0	0	0	0	0	0	0	0	0	0	0	0	0	0	4	0	0	0	0	0	0	0	0
unladylike	2	.1787	.1174	30.7	0	0	0	1	0	1	0	0	1	0	0	0	0	0	0	0	0	0	0	0	1	0	0	0	0
unlatched	3	.3873	.2495	34.0	0	0	0	1	0	2	0	0	0	0	0	1	0	0	0	0	0	0	0	0	1	0	0	1	0
unlawful	3	.3709	.2499	34.0	0	0	0	0	1	1	1	0	0	0	0	0	0	1	0	1	0	0	0	0	0	0	1	0	0
unlawfully	2	.0000	.0209	23.2	0	1	1	0	0	0	0	0	0	0	0	0	0	0	0	0	0	0	0	0	0	0	2	0	0
unlearned	3	.0000	.0591	27.7	0	0	0	3	0	0	0	0	0	0	0	0	0	0	0	3	0	0	0	0	0	0	0	0	0
unleash	2	.1698	.1133	30.5	0	0	1	0	0	0	1	0	1	0	0	0	0	0	0	0	0	0	0	0	0	0	1	0	0
unless	401	.9205	73.143	58.6	50	35	36	47	77	63	82	11	77	39	10	25	12	34	16	58	10	2	22	4	21	28	12	31	0
unlighted	5	.3300	.4080	36.1	1	0	0	0	3	0	1	0	2	0	0	2	0	0	0	0	0	0	0	0	0	0	0	1	0
unlike	161	.9209	29.355	54.7	10	11	19	20	35	36	25	5	20	8	3	6	10	16	6	30	11	4	2	2	2	5	21	15	0
unlikely	32	.7516	4.8527	46.9	1	1	5	4	13	1	5	2	2	2	0	2	0	5	1	3	0	0	0	0	2	4	4	7	0
unlimited	23	.5785	2.7727	44.4	1	0	1	6	4	8	3	0	1	3	0	0	9	2	0	4	0	0	0	0	0	0	3	1	0
unload	25	.6619	3.4304	45.4	2	6	7	6	1	0	3	0	4	0	1	0	1	11	1	2	0	0	0	0	1	3	0	1	0
unloaded	19	.5667	2.3278	43.7	5	3	3	2	5	1	0	0	6	0	0	1	0	8	0	0	1	0	0	0	1	2	0	0	0
unloading	21	.7096	3.0512	44.8	4	4	4	3	4	0	2	0	4	0	0	1	0	5	0	0	1	0	0	0	3	3	2	2	0
unlock	12	.5276	1.4302	41.6	5	1	1	3	1	1	0	0	7	0	0	1	0	1	0	1	0	0	0	0	0	0	0	2	0
unlocked	10	.4838	1.0755	40.3	0	3	1	1	1	3	1	0	4	1	1	1	0	0	0	0	0	0	0	0	3	0	0	0	0
unlocks	2	.1814	.1187	30.7	0	1	0	0	0	0	0	1	1	0	0	0	0	0	0	0	0	0	0	0	0	0	0	1	0
unloosed	3	.0000	.1370	31.4	0	0	0	3	0	0	0	0	3	0	0	0	0	0	0	0	0	0	0	0	0	0	0	0	0
unloved	2	.0000	.0394	26.0	0	0	0	0	2	0	0	0	0	0	0	0	0	0	0	2	0	0	0	0	0	0	0	0	0
unlucky	17	.7030	2.4523	43.9	0	0	5	6	3	1	2	0	4	0	1	2	1	4	2	0	1	0	0	0	1	1	0	0	0
unmade	2	.2408	.1204	30.8	0	0	0	1	0	1	0	0	0	0	0	0	0	1	0	0	0	0	0	0	0	1	0	0	0
unmanageable	2	.1787	.1174	30.7	0	0	1	0	0	1	0	0	1	0	0	0	0	0	0	0	0	0	0	0	1	0	0	0	0
unmanned	13	.6194	1.6729	42.2	0	1	0	5	4	1	2	0	1	0	0	1	0	1	0	5	0	0	0	0	0	2	1	2	0
unmannerly	3	.1727	.1578	32.0	0	0	0	2	0	1	0	0	1	0	1	0	0	0	0	1	0	0	0	0	0	0	0	0	0
unmarked	6	.4776	.6111	37.9	0	1	2	0	1	2	0	0	0	1	0	0	0	3	0	0	0	0	0	0	0	0	1	1	0

3P unillumined
7Q unimagined
XR unimposing
8D unimpressed
7Q unimprovable
6P unimproved
7H uninitiated
7D uninjured
4G uninked
7J uninspired
9Q unintelligibility
8C unintentional
8R uninvolved
9R unionists
4Q Unionists
8E unit-of-measure
4E unit-region
8F Unitarians
6R Unitas'
4F UNITEDSTATES
5P UnitedKingdom
8C UnitedStages
5A UnitedStares
7E Univac
9C UNIVERSITY
7P university-trained
7R University's
3P unkempt
6G unkindliness
4R unkinks
6H unknow
7R unknowns
8F Unknowns
9P unlaced
7B unlaid
7P unlamented
5R unlatch
8F unlearn
9N unleashed
7D unleashes
5Q unleavened
3A unlessing
9D unlessoned
9Q Unlicensed
9D unlifelike
6B unlifted
7R unlimbered
9B unlined
8A unlived
5A unlocking
6A unloose
XR unloving
4A unluckily
8F unmake

Word Type	F	D	U	SFI	3 Gr 3	4 Gr 4	5 Gr 5	6 Gr 6	7 Gr 7	8 Gr 8	9 Gr 9	X UnGr	A Read	B Eng & Gr	C Comp	D Lit	E Math	F Soc Stud	G Spell	H Sci	J Music	K Art	L Home Ec	M Shop	N Lib F	P Lib NF	Q Lib Ref	R Mag	S Rel
unmarried	7	.3182	.5740	37.6	0	2	1	2	0	2	0	0	3	0	0	0	0	1	0	0	0	0	0	0	0	3	0	0	0
unmerciful	2	.1948	.1250	31.0	1	0	1	0	0	0	0	0	1	0	0	0	0	0	0	0	0	0	0	0	0	1	0	0	0
unmercifully	3	.3801	.2525	34.0	1	0	1	1	0	0	0	0	0	0	0	0	0	0	0	1	0	0	0	0	1	1	0	0	0
unmindful	2	.0000	.0215	23.3	0	0	0	0	2	0	0	0	0	0	0	2	0	0	0	0	0	0	0	0	0	0	0	0	0
unmistakable	14	.6119	1.8151	42.6	2	2	2	1	4	2	1	0	5	0	0	2	0	0	0	0	0	0	0	0	2	3	1	1	0
unmistakably	7	.6202	.9140	39.6	2	0	2	0	2	0	1	0	2	0	0	1	0	0	0	1	0	0	0	0	1	1	0	1	0
unmoved	2	.0000	.0914	29.6	0	0	0	0	2	0	0	0	2	0	0	0	0	0	0	0	0	0	0	0	0	0	0	0	0
unmoving	3	.2261	.2131	33.3	1	0	1	1	0	0	0	0	2	0	0	0	0	0	0	0	0	0	0	0	1	0	0	0	0
unmusical	2	.1843	.0808	29.1	0	0	0	0	0	2	0	0	0	0	1	0	0	0	0	0	1	0	0	0	0	0	0	0	0
unnamed	3	.3234	.2368	33.7	1	0	1	0	0	1	0	0	1	0	0	0	0	0	1	0	0	0	0	0	0	1	0	0	0
unnatural	11	.6410	1.4444	41.6	0	2	2	0	4	1	2	0	1	1	0	2	0	0	0	0	0	0	0	0	2	2	2	1	0
unnecessarily	4	.3111	.2706	34.3	0	0	0	0	4	0	0	0	0	0	1	0	0	0	0	0	0	0	0	0	2	0	0	1	0
unnecessary	34	.7335	5.0044	47.0	0	3	5	4	8	5	9	0	1	6	4	4	1	4	4	1	2	0	2	1	1	3	0	0	0
unnoticed	19	.6875	2.7103	44.3	0	2	3	3	3	6	2	0	7	0	0	3	0	1	0	0	2	0	0	0	1	1	2	2	0
unnumbered	2	.2297	.1135	30.6	0	1	0	0	0	0	1	0	0	0	0	1	0	1	0	0	0	0	0	0	0	0	0	0	0
unobserved	2	.2160	.1362	31.3	0	0	0	1	1	0	0	0	1	0	0	0	0	0	0	1	0	0	0	0	0	0	0	0	0
unobstructed	2	.2405	.1205	30.8	1	0	0	0	1	0	0	0	0	0	0	0	0	0	0	1	0	0	0	0	0	1	0	0	0
unobtrusively	3	.2321	.1635	32.1	0	1	0	0	1	0	0	1	0	0	0	0	0	0	0	0	0	0	0	0	0	0	1	2	0
unoccupied	4	.4854	.4081	36.1	1	0	1	0	1	0	0	1	0	0	0	0	1	0	0	0	0	0	0	0	1	1	1	0	0
unofficial	4	.4570	.4091	36.1	0	0	1	0	2	1	0	0	1	0	0	0	0	1	0	0	0	0	0	0	0	1	0	1	0
unopened	2	.1641	.0751	28.8	0	0	0	0	2	0	0	0	0	0	1	0	0	0	0	0	0	0	0	0	0	0	1	0	0
unpack	8	.5360	.9367	39.7	2	0	0	1	2	3	0	0	3	0	0	1	0	1	0	0	0	0	0	0	2	0	0	1	0
unpacked	5	.4043	.4588	36.6	0	1	1	0	2	0	0	1	1	0	0	0	0	0	0	1	0	0	0	0	2	1	0	0	0
unpacking	2	.1948	.1250	31.0	1	1	0	0	0	0	0	0	1	0	0	0	0	0	0	0	0	0	0	0	0	1	0	0	0
unpaid	6	.4688	.6005	37.8	0	0	0	0	2	2	0	2	0	0	0	0	1	2	0	0	0	0	0	0	1	0	0	2	0
unpainted	11	.5356	1.2822	41.1	1	2	3	1	1	1	2	0	3	0	0	0	0	4	0	0	0	0	0	0	1	2	0	1	0
unpaved	7	.4267	.6640	38.2	2	1	0	1	1	1	0	1	1	0	0	0	0	2	0	0	0	0	0	0	0	2	2	0	0
unpleasant	57	.7199	8.3395	49.2	3	11	6	10	10	11	4	2	9	4	6	5	0	4	1	10	6	0	2	0	3	4	3	0	0
unpleasantly	4	.4570	.4091	36.1	1	1	0	0	2	0	0	0	1	0	0	0	0	1	0	0	0	0	0	0	0	1	0	1	0
unpleasantness	3	.3109	.2027	33.1	0	0	0	1	2	0	0	0	0	0	0	0	0	0	0	0	0	0	1	0	0	1	1	0	0
unpleasing	2	.2407	.1138	30.6	0	0	0	0	0	0	2	0	0	0	0	1	0	0	0	0	0	0	0	0	0	1	0	0	0
unplowed	2	.2285	.1129	30.5	0	0	0	0	1	1	0	0	0	0	0	0	0	1	0	0	0	0	0	0	0	0	1	0	0
unplug	2	.0000	.0914	29.6	2	0	0	0	0	0	0	0	2	0	0	0	0	0	0	0	0	0	0	0	0	0	0	0	0
unpolished	2	.2446	.1122	30.5	0	0	0	0	2	0	0	0	0	0	0	1	0	0	0	0	0	0	0	0	0	0	1	0	0
unpopular	10	.6715	1.3627	41.3	1	0	1	0	2	2	3	1	0	1	0	1	0	2	0	1	0	0	1	0	0	1	2	1	0
unpopularity	2	.1814	.1187	30.7	0	0	0	0	1	1	0	0	1	0	0	0	0	0	0	0	0	0	0	0	0	0	0	1	0
unpopulated	2	.1814	.1187	30.7	0	0	0	1	0	0	0	1	1	0	0	0	0	0	0	0	0	0	0	0	0	0	0	1	0
unprecedented	12	.2545	.7045	38.5	0	0	0	0	6	0	5	1	0	0	0	0	0	0	0	1	0	0	0	0	0	0	8	3	0
unpredictable	8	.5073	.8816	39.5	0	1	1	0	3	2	0	1	2	0	0	0	0	1	0	0	0	0	0	0	0	1	2	2	0
unprepared	4	.4538	.4019	36.0	0	1	0	0	1	2	0	0	1	1	0	0	0	0	0	0	0	0	0	0	1	1	0	0	0
unpretentious	3	.2512	.1929	32.9	0	0	0	1	0	2	0	0	1	1	0	0	0	0	0	0	0	0	1	0	0	0	0	0	0
unprofitable	4	.3782	.3355	35.3	0	0	0	0	3	1	0	0	0	0	0	0	0	2	0	0	1	0	0	0	0	1	0	0	0
unpromising	2	.2351	.1166	30.7	0	0	0	0	0	1	0	1	0	0	0	0	0	1	0	0	0	0	0	0	0	0	0	1	0
unprotected	8	.4915	.8560	39.3	0	1	0	2	3	2	0	0	2	0	0	1	0	0	0	2	1	1	0	0	0	0	0	1	0
unpublished	2	.1948	.1250	31.0	0	0	0	0	1	1	0	0	1	0	0	0	0	0	0	0	0	0	0	0	0	1	0	0	0
unpunctuated	2	.1362	.0684	28.3	0	0	0	0	0	1	1	0	0	0	1	0	1	0	0	0	0	0	0	0	0	0	0	0	0
unpunished	2	.2408	.1204	30.8	0	0	0	0	0	1	1	0	0	0	0	0	0	1	0	0	0	0	0	0	0	1	0	0	0
unqualified	2	.2407	.1138	30.6	0	0	1	0	1	0	0	0	0	0	0	1	0	0	0	0	0	0	0	0	0	1	0	0	0
unquestionably	10	.5222	1.0923	40.4	0	0	0	0	7	0	2	1	1	0	0	1	0	0	0	0	2	0	0	0	1	0	4	1	0
unquestioned	3	.3847	.2494	34.0	0	0	1	1	1	0	0	0	0	0	0	0	0	0	0	0	0	0	0	0	1	1	1	0	0
Unraed	2	.0000	.0209	23.2	0	0	2	0	0	0	0	0	0	0	0	0	0	0	0	0	0	0	0	0	0	0	2	0	0
unravel	5	.3683	.4536	36.6	1	0	4	0	0	0	0	0	2	0	0	0	0	0	0	2	0	0	0	0	0	1	0	0	0
unraveled	3	.0000	.0322	25.1	0	0	0	0	0	1	2	0	0	0	0	3	0	0	0	0	0	0	0	0	0	0	0	0	0
unreal	5	.3472	.3719	35.7	0	0	0	0	1	1	3	0	0	0	0	3	0	0	0	0	0	0	1	0	1	0	0	0	0
unrealistic	4	.2090	.2014	33.0	0	0	0	0	1	1	2	0	0	0	0	0	0	0	0	0	0	0	0	0	0	0	1	3	0
unreasonable	15	.5719	1.8197	42.6	0	0	0	1	2	5	5	2	4	3	0	4	0	2	0	0	0	0	1	0	0	0	0	1	0
unreasonably	2	.2443	.1130	30.5	0	0	1	0	1	0	0	0	0	0	0	1	0	0	0	0	0	0	0	0	1	0	0	0	0
unrecognizable	2	.0000	.0209	23.2	0	0	0	0	2	0	0	0	0	0	0	0	0	0	0	0	0	0	0	0	0	0	2	0	0
unrelated	13	.5684	1.5132	41.8	1	0	2	0	6	2	2	0	0	1	0	0	0	1	1	0	3	0	0	0	0	1	5	1	0
unreliable	7	.5605	.8561	39.3	1	1	0	0	1	2	1	1	3	0	0	0	0	1	0	0	0	0	0	0	0	1	1	1	0
unremitting	3	.3764	.2483	33.9	0	0	0	0	3	0	0	0	0	0	0	0	0	0	0	1	0	0	0	0	0	0	1	1	0
unremittingly	2	.2440	.1132	30.5	0	0	0	0	1	0	1	0	0	0	0	1	0	0	0	0	0	0	0	0	0	0	0	1	0
unresponsive	4	.4518	.3982	36.0	0	0	0	1	2	1	0	0	1	0	0	1	0	0	0	0	0	0	0	0	1	0	1	0	0
unrest	13	.5546	1.5176	41.8	0	1	1	1	6	3	1	0	1	0	0	0	0	5	0	0	0	0	0	0	1	1	2	3	0
unrestrained	2	.2441	.1127	30.5	0	0	0	0	1	0	1	0	0	0	0	0	0	0	0	0	0	0	0	0	1	0	1	0	0
unrestricted	3	.2300	.1627	32.1	0	0	0	0	2	0	1	0	0	1	0	0	0	0	0	0	0	0	0	0	0	0	0	2	0
unripe	2	.2160	.1362	31.3	0	2	0	0	0	0	0	0	1	0	0	0	0	0	0	1	0	0	0	0	0	0	0	0	0
unripened	2	.0000	.0064	18.1	0	0	0	0	2	0	0	0	0	0	0	0	0	0	0	0	0	0	2	0	0	0	0	0	0
unroll	3	.3383	.2498	34.0	2	0	0	0	0	0	1	0	1	1	0	0	0	1	0	0	0	0	0	0	0	0	0	0	0
unrolled	10	.5778	1.2166	40.9	0	4	3	0	2	1	0	0	2	2	0	2	0	1	0	0	0	0	0	0	2	1	0	0	0
unruffled	6	.3521	.4792	36.8	0	1	1	3	1	0	0	0	1	0	1	0	0	0	0	0	0	0	0	0	0	1	0	3	0
unruly	4	.3689	.3191	35.0	0	0	0	1	3	0	0	0	0	0	0	0	0	0	0	0	0	0	0	0	2	0	1	1	0
uns	5	.0000	.0586	27.7	1	0	4	0	0	0	0	0	0	0	0	0	0	0	0	0	0	0	0	0	5	0	0	0	0
unsaddle	3	.3431	.2528	34.0	0	2	0	0	1	0	0	0	1	0	0	0	0	1	0	0	0	0	0	0	1	0	0	0	0
unsafe	11	.6124	1.4351	41.6	2	2	2	1	2	2	0	0	4	1	0	0	0	2	0	1	0	0	0	0	0	0	1	2	0
Unsafe	3	.0000	.0365	25.6	0	0	0	0	3	0	0	0	0	0	0	0	0	0	0	0	0	0	0	0	0	0	0	3	0
unsalted	2	.1907	.0862	29.4	0	0	0	1	1	0	0	0	0	0	0	1	0	0	0	0	0	0	1	0	0	0	0	0	0
unsanitary	7	.6185	.9147	39.6	0	1	1	1	0	2	2	0	2	0	0	1	0	1	0	1	0	0	0	0	1	1	0	0	0
unsatisfactory	7	.4255	.6166	37.9	0	1	0	1	2	2	1	0	0	0	2	1	0	0	0	0	0	0	1	0	1	0	0	2	0
unsatisfied	2	.2346	.1166	30.7	0	0	0	0	0	0	1	1	0	0	0	0	0	0	0	1	0	0	0	0	0	0	0	1	0
unsaturated	2	.0000	.0209	23.2	0	0	0	2	0	0	0	0	0	0	0	0	0	0	0	0	0	0	0	0	0	0	2	0	0
unscalable	2	.1717	.1142	30.6	0	0	0	0	2	0	0	0	1	0	0	1	0	0	0	0	0	0	0	0	0	0	0	0	0
unscathed	4	.4886	.4071	36.1	0	0	0	0	1	1	2	0	0	0	0	1	0	0	0	0	0	0	0	0	1	0	1	1	0
unschooled	2	.2446	.1122	30.5	0	0	0	0	0	0	2	0	0	0	0	1	0	0	0	0	0	0	0	0	0	0	1	0	0
unscientific	4	.3280	.2948	34.7	0	0	0	3	0	0	1	0	0	0	0	0	0	0	0	1	0	0	0	0	0	1	2	0	0
unscramble	22	.1838	.9837	39.9	2	6	7	5	1	0	1	0	1	3	0	0	1	0	17	0	0	0	0	0	0	0	0	0	0
unscrambled	4	.3403	.2934	34.7	1	2	0	0	0	0	1	0	0	1	0	0	0	0	2	0	0	0	0	0	0	0	0	1	0
unscrew	10	.2032	.5164	37.1	0	2	1	2	3	1	0	1	1	0	0	0	0	0	0	4	0	0	0	4	0	0	0	1	0
unscrewed	3	.2208	.1769	32.5	1	1	0	0	1	0	0	0	1	0	0	0	0	0	0	0	0	0	0	1	1	0	0	0	0
unscrupulous	3	.2325	.1651	32.2	0	0	1	0	2	0	0	0	0	0	1	0	0	0	0	1	0	0	0	0	0	1	0	0	0
unsealed	4	.1873	.1827	32.6	0	0	0	0	3	0	1	0	0	0	0	0	0	0	0	0	0	0	0	0	0	0	3	1	0

7N unmasked
5Q unmatched
XH unmated
7H unmeasured
5P unmelodious
XB unmentionables
9R unmilitary
9J unmixed
8D unmolested
7Q Unmoved
4A unmuzzle
4D unnamable
7A unnatchal
9D unnaturally
8E unneeded
9L unnotched
3A unnoticeable
XR unobtrusive
8D unofficially
5Q unorganized
7F unorthodox
8R unpaced
7H unpaired
7Q unpalatable
7A unparalleled
7N unpardonable
7A unpatchable
8A unpatented
5P unpatriotic
7P unpeaceful
7R unpeeled
7D unpeopled
8P unperturbed
3N unpicked
9L unpin
7N unpitying
6R unplanned
7A unplanted
3A unplugged
8F unplundered
7Q unpoliced
9D unpowdered
9D unpracticed
7Q unprecedentedly
9Q unprepossessing
5A unprincipled
9D unprosperous
7N unquenchable
4A unquestionable
8F unquestioning
9D unquestioningly
XQ unquiet
5N unravels
7R unread
9P unreadable
7Q unready
5Q Unready
7P unrealized
9A unreally
6N unreasoning
3N unreconciled
7A unreeled
7B unrehearsed
5A unrelenting
5P unreliably
7Q unrevealing
4B unrhymed
7F unrivaled
3J unrolls
9J unromantic
7Q unruined
7B unruled
3A unrumpled
3Q unsaddled
7A unsaid
9Q unsavoury
5P unscalped
4B unscrambling
4P unscratched
7M unscrewing
5P unscrupulously
7H unseasonable

Word Type	F	D	U	SFI	3 Gr 3	4 Gr 4	5 Gr 5	6 Gr 6	7 Gr 7	8 Gr 8	9 Gr 9	X UnGr	A Read	B Eng & Gr	C Comp	D Lit	E Math	F Soc Stud	G Spell	H Sci	J Music	K Art	L Home Ec	M Shop	N Lib F	P Lib NF	Q Lib Ref	R Mag	S Rel
unseasonably	3	.2227	.1589	32.0	0	2	0	0	1	0	0	0	0	0	0	0	0	0	0	0	0	0	0	0	2	0	0	1	0
unseen	42	.6822	5.9005	47.7	3	2	7	5	15	2	7	1	10	2	0	8	0	2	0	1	0	0	0	0	4	2	5	8	0
unselfish	6	.3797	.5821	37.6	2	1	0	2	0	1	0	0	4	0	0	0	0	1	0	0	0	0	0	0	0	1	0	0	0
unselfishness	3	.2357	.2199	33.4	0	0	0	1	2	0	0	0	2	0	0	0	0	0	0	0	0	0	0	0	0	1	0	0	0
unsettled	9	.4462	.9219	39.6	3	0	3	0	1	2	0	0	3	0	0	0	0	4	0	0	0	0	0	0	0	1	1	0	0
unshaded	7	.1729	.3207	35.1	0	3	0	0	1	3	0	0	0	0	0	0	6	0	0	0	0	0	0	0	0	0	1	0	0
unshakable	2	.1814	.1187	30.7	0	0	1	0	1	0	0	0	1	0	0	0	0	0	0	0	0	0	0	0	0	0	0	1	0
unshaken	2	.2337	.1157	30.6	0	0	0	0	1	1	0	0	0	0	0	0	0	1	0	0	0	0	0	0	1	0	0	0	0
unsheathed	2	.2446	.1142	30.6	0	0	0	1	0	0	1	0	0	0	0	0	0	0	0	0	0	0	0	0	1	0	0	1	0
unshorn	3	.2212	.2099	33.2	0	0	0	1	1	0	1	0	2	0	0	1	0	0	0	0	0	0	0	0	0	0	0	0	0
unsightly	2	.0000	.0914	29.6	0	0	0	1	0	1	0	0	2	0	0	0	0	0	0	0	0	0	0	0	0	0	0	0	0
unskilled	7	.5203	.7841	38.9	2	0	0	0	2	1	2	0	2	0	0	1	0	1	0	0	1	0	0	1	0	0	1	0	0
unsmiling	2	.1814	.1187	30.7	0	1	1	0	0	0	0	0	1	0	0	0	0	0	0	0	0	0	0	0	0	0	0	1	0
unsold	3	.3418	.2483	33.9	0	0	1	0	0	2	0	0	1	1	0	0	0	0	0	0	0	0	0	0	0	1	0	0	0
unsolved	9	.6435	1.1986	40.8	0	0	1	1	2	1	4	0	1	0	0	0	1	1	1	3	0	0	0	0	0	0	1	1	0
unsophisticated	5	.3157	.3561	35.5	0	0	0	0	1	0	1	3	0	1	0	0	0	0	0	1	0	0	0	0	0	0	0	3	0
unsound	3	.2440	.1815	32.6	0	0	0	0	0	1	2	0	0	1	0	0	0	2	0	0	0	0	0	0	0	0	0	0	0
unspeakable	9	.3105	.6712	38.3	0	1	0	1	2	4	0	1	2	0	0	5	0	0	0	1	0	0	0	0	0	0	0	1	0
unspeakably	3	.2120	.1548	31.9	0	0	0	0	2	1	0	0	0	0	0	0	0	0	0	0	0	0	0	0	2	1	0	0	0
unspecialized	3	.2254	.1785	32.5	0	0	0	0	1	0	1	1	0	0	0	0	0	1	0	2	0	0	0	0	0	0	0	0	0
unspecified	2	.2433	.1158	30.6	0	0	1	0	0	1	0	0	0	0	0	0	0	0	0	0	0	0	0	0	0	1	0	1	0
unspectacular	2	.1378	.0662	28.2	0	0	0	0	0	1	1	0	0	0	0	0	0	0	0	0	0	1	0	0	0	0	0	1	0
unspoiled	5	.4391	.4860	36.9	0	0	3	0	0	0	1	1	1	0	0	0	0	0	0	0	0	0	0	0	0	2	1	1	0
unspoken	5	.3300	.4080	36.1	0	0	1	0	3	1	0	0	2	0	0	2	0	0	0	0	0	0	0	0	0	0	0	1	0
unstable	12	.6468	1.6110	42.1	0	0	1	5	2	1	3	0	2	0	0	1	0	1	0	3	0	0	0	0	0	2	2	1	0
unsteadily	2	.0000	.0215	23.3	0	0	0	0	1	1	0	0	0	0	0	2	0	0	0	0	0	0	0	0	0	0	0	0	0
unsteady	5	.4769	.5345	37.3	0	1	0	0	1	1	2	0	2	0	0	1	0	0	0	0	0	0	0	0	1	0	0	1	0
unstraps	2	.0000	.0914	29.6	0	0	0	2	0	0	0	0	2	0	0	0	0	0	0	0	0	0	0	0	0	0	0	0	0
unstressed	14	.0000	.1136	30.6	0	0	0	0	8	6	0	0	0	0	0	0	0	0	14	0	0	0	0	0	0	0	0	0	0
unsuccessful	24	.7557	3.6776	45.7	0	0	4	2	12	3	2	1	4	0	0	3	1	4	0	1	1	0	0	0	2	5	2	1	0
unsuccessfully	4	.2352	.2332	33.7	0	0	1	0	1	0	1	1	0	0	0	0	0	2	0	0	0	0	0	0	0	0	0	2	0
unsuitable	10	.4050	.9077	39.6	0	0	4	1	4	0	0	1	2	0	2	0	0	1	0	2	0	0	0	0	0	0	2	1	0
unsuited	4	.3782	.3355	35.3	0	0	1	2	0	0	1	0	0	0	0	0	0	2	0	0	1	0	0	0	0	1	0	0	0
unsullied	2	.1787	.1174	30.7	0	0	0	0	1	1	0	0	1	0	0	0	0	0	0	0	0	0	0	0	1	0	0	0	0
unsupported	3	.1937	.1495	31.7	0	0	0	0	2	1	0	0	0	0	0	0	0	1	0	0	0	0	0	0	0	0	0	2	0
unsure	5	.5325	.5641	37.5	1	0	0	0	3	1	0	0	1	1	0	1	0	0	0	0	1	0	0	0	0	0	0	1	0
unsurpassed	4	.2160	.2008	33.0	1	0	0	0	2	1	0	0	0	0	0	0	0	0	0	0	1	0	0	0	0	0	3	0	0
unsuspected	2	.2437	.1129	30.5	0	0	0	0	2	0	0	0	0	0	0	0	0	0	0	0	0	0	0	0	0	0	1	1	0
unsuspecting	2	.2405	.1205	30.8	0	0	1	0	0	0	0	1	0	0	0	0	0	0	0	1	0	0	0	0	0	1	0	0	0
unswerving	3	.3776	.2493	34.0	0	0	0	0	1	1	0	1	0	1	0	0	0	0	0	1	0	0	0	0	0	0	0	1	0
unsympathetic	4	.4495	.4018	36.0	0	0	1	0	2	1	0	0	1	0	0	1	0	1	0	0	0	0	0	0	0	0	0	1	0
unsystematic	2	.2446	.1123	30.5	0	0	0	0	1	0	1	0	0	1	0	0	0	0	0	0	0	0	0	0	0	0	1	0	0
untalented	2	.1494	.1045	30.2	0	0	0	0	1	0	1	0	1	0	0	0	0	0	0	0	1	0	0	0	0	0	0	0	0
untamable	2	.0000	.0234	23.7	0	0	0	0	2	0	0	0	0	0	0	0	0	0	0	0	0	0	0	0	2	0	0	0	0
untamed	6	.5923	.7406	38.7	0	1	3	0	1	1	0	0	1	0	0	0	0	1	1	0	1	0	0	0	1	0	1	0	0
untangle	4	.1787	.2347	33.7	1	2	0	0	1	0	0	0	2	0	0	0	0	0	0	0	0	0	0	0	2	0	0	0	0
untangled	3	.3771	.2489	34.0	1	0	0	0	0	0	2	0	0	0	0	1	0	0	0	1	0	0	0	0	0	0	0	1	0
untapped	4	.3350	.3295	35.2	0	0	0	1	2	0	1	0	1	0	0	0	1	2	0	0	0	0	0	0	0	0	0	0	0
untenable	2	.0000	.0209	23.2	0	0	0	0	1	1	0	0	0	0	0	0	0	0	0	0	0	0	0	0	0	0	2	0	0
untended	2	.0000	.0914	29.6	1	0	0	0	1	0	0	0	2	0	0	0	0	0	0	0	0	0	0	0	0	0	0	0	0
untidy	12	.4893	1.2461	41.0	1	6	0	1	0	3	0	1	1	0	0	0	0	0	0	3	0	0	2	0	4	0	1	1	0
untie	14	.6245	1.8719	42.7	6	3	2	0	2	1	0	0	7	0	0	1	2	0	0	0	1	0	0	0	0	2	0	1	0
untied	27	.6493	3.6748	45.7	7	10	4	2	2	2	0	0	9	0	1	1	0	3	0	1	0	0	0	0	6	5	1	0	0
until	2596	.9201	473.93	66.8	451	381	306	284	499	334	273	68	721	80	29	168	54	242	37	262	89	14	142	62	148	221	154	173	0
untimely	3	.2804	.1831	32.6	1	0	0	0	1	0	1	0	0	0	1	1	0	0	0	0	0	0	0	0	1	0	0	0	0
untiring	2	.1787	.1174	30.7	0	0	0	1	1	0	0	0	1	0	0	0	0	0	0	0	0	0	0	0	1	0	0	0	0
unto	83	.5626	9.6968	49.9	40	5	6	7	6	3	16	0	5	4	0	15	0	0	1	0	11	0	0	0	2	41	3	1	0
untold	10	.6303	1.2843	41.1	0	0	1	1	5	2	1	0	0	1	0	3	0	1	0	0	0	0	0	0	1	1	1	2	0
untouched	22	.6501	2.9932	44.8	0	3	5	2	6	5	1	0	7	1	0	3	1	4	0	0	0	0	0	0	3	0	3	0	0
untrained	11	.6624	1.4924	41.7	0	1	1	1	6	2	0	0	1	0	0	1	0	1	0	2	2	0	0	0	0	1	2	1	0
untrammeled	2	.2401	.1133	30.5	0	0	1	0	0	0	1	0	0	0	0	0	0	0	0	0	0	0	0	0	0	1	1	0	0
untreated	2	.2346	.1166	30.7	0	0	0	0	2	0	0	0	0	0	0	0	0	0	0	1	0	0	0	0	0	0	0	1	0
untried	2	.1717	.1142	30.6	0	1	0	0	0	1	0	0	1	0	0	1	0	0	0	0	0	0	0	0	0	0	0	0	0
untrodden	3	.1187	.1291	31.1	0	0	0	0	2	1	0	0	1	0	0	2	0	0	0	0	0	0	0	0	0	0	0	0	0
untroubled	2	.2407	.1138	30.6	0	0	0	1	0	0	1	0	0	0	0	1	0	0	0	0	0	0	0	0	0	1	0	0	0
untrue	6	.4722	.6113	37.9	0	2	0	0	3	1	0	0	1	1	0	1	0	0	0	1	2	0	0	0	0	0	0	0	0
untrustworthy	2	.2437	.1129	30.5	0	0	0	0	2	0	0	0	0	0	0	0	0	0	0	0	0	0	0	0	0	0	1	1	0
untruths	2	.1698	.1133	30.5	0	1	1	0	0	0	0	0	1	0	0	0	0	0	0	0	0	0	0	0	0	0	1	0	0
unturned	3	.1277	.1363	31.3	1	0	1	0	1	0	0	0	1	0	0	0	0	0	0	0	0	0	0	0	0	0	0	2	0
untutored	3	.3768	.2484	34.0	0	0	0	0	2	0	0	1	0	0	0	1	0	0	0	1	0	0	0	0	1	0	0	0	0
untying	4	.2152	.2136	33.3	1	0	0	0	0	3	0	0	0	0	0	0	3	0	0	0	0	0	0	0	1	0	0	0	0
unused	14	.5505	1.6312	42.1	1	1	2	5	1	3	1	0	2	0	0	0	0	4	0	1	0	0	2	0	2	2	0	1	0
unusual	247	.8623	42.594	56.3	19	50	20	45	50	30	24	9	72	26	2	17	5	13	13	21	17	10	2	0	3	12	12	22	0
Unusual	3	.0000	.1370	31.4	1	0	0	2	0	0	0	0	3	0	0	0	0	0	0	0	0	0	0	0	0	0	0	0	0
unusually	61	.7674	9.5246	49.8	6	12	7	9	7	7	11	2	17	5	0	2	0	3	0	8	1	0	0	0	4	10	3	8	0
unveiled	2	.0000	.0243	23.9	0	0	0	2	0	0	0	0	0	0	0	0	0	0	0	0	0	0	0	0	0	0	0	2	0
unveiling	2	.2160	.1362	31.3	0	0	0	0	1	1	0	0	1	0	0	0	0	0	0	1	0	0	0	0	0	0	0	0	0
unvoiced	12	.1392	.4161	36.2	0	2	3	0	4	1	0	2	0	0	0	0	0	0	10	0	0	0	0	0	0	0	2	0	0
unwanted	9	.5805	1.0908	40.4	0	0	1	1	4	1	1	1	1	0	0	0	0	0	0	2	1	0	0	0	0	1	2	2	0
unwary	2	.0000	.0209	23.2	1	0	0	0	1	0	0	0	0	0	0	0	0	0	0	0	0	0	0	0	0	0	2	0	0
unwashed	4	.3387	.3012	34.8	1	0	0	0	0	1	2	0	0	0	0	2	0	0	0	1	0	0	0	0	1	0	0	0	0
unwelcome	7	.5166	.7853	39.0	1	0	0	1	4	1	0	0	2	0	0	1	0	0	0	1	0	0	0	0	1	0	2	0	0
unwholesome	2	.2443	.1130	30.5	0	0	0	0	2	0	0	0	0	0	0	1	0	0	0	0	0	0	0	0	1	0	0	0	0
unwilling	17	.6532	2.3070	43.6	1	1	2	0	6	5	2	0	4	1	0	3	0	4	0	0	0	0	0	0	2	0	2	1	0
unwillingly	8	.5403	.9389	39.7	1	2	1	1	0	2	1	0	3	2	0	1	0	0	0	0	0	0	0	0	0	1	1	0	0
unwind	8	.4292	.7414	38.7	0	2	0	4	0	0	1	1	0	0	1	0	0	0	0	4	0	0	0	0	2	0	0	1	0
unwinding	6	.4634	.5954	37.7	2	1	0	0	0	1	0	2	0	0	0	0	0	1	0	2	1	0	0	0	0	0	0	2	0
unwinds	2	.0000	.0394	26.0	0	0	0	0	0	0	1	1	0	0	0	0	0	0	0	2	0	0	0	0	0	0	0	0	0
unwinking	2	.1717	.1142	30.6	0	0	1	0	1	0	0	0	1	0	0	1	0	0	0	0	0	0	0	0	0	0	0	0	0
unwise	7	.5397	.8109	39.1	1	1	0	1	1	1	1	1	2	0	0	0	0	0	0	1	0	0	1	0	1	0	1	1	0
unwonted	2	.2446	.1142	30.6	0	0	0	0	1	0	0	1	0	0	0	0	0	0	0	0	0	0	0	0	1	0	0	1	0
unworldly	2	.2152	.1357	31.3	0	0	0	0	1	1	0	0	1	0	0	0	0	1	0	0	0	0	0	0	0	0	0	0	0

6N unseats
7R unseaworthy
9R unsecured
4A unseemly
9K unsegregated
7R Unser
6B unserved
7P unserviceable
9D unshaped
7A unshaven
4A unshed
4Q unshielded
8A unshined
8B unsifted
8B unsinkable
8H unslaked
6B unsmote
4A unsnagged
9D unsolicited
8A unstacking
7J unstaged
5A unstained
8H unsterilized
7D unstick
7J unstinting
4A unstrapped
9H unstratified
6R unstrung
XR unstuck
7D unsubstantial
7A unsubtle
3Q unsuitability
XH unsung
XP unsupercharged
9H unsupervised
5Q unsweetened
8J unsyncopated
7R untainted
7B untaken
7J untaught
4D untellable
8F untested
7A unthreatening
6N unties
8D untill
6N untired
9L untoasted
6F untouchability
4Q untouchables
9D untrespassed
7A untruth
7R untunable
4D untwist
8G untwisted
7R unusable
8A unutterable
7B unvanquished
XR unvarnished
7C unveil'd
6P unvexed
7R unvisited
7D unwadded
8F unwarrantable
8R unwarranted
4R unwatched
5F unwatered
XQ unwatering
7N unweariedly
9H unweathered
7N unweeded
7A unwhitewashed
7M unwieldy
8D unwillingness
7D unwitting
9Q unwittingly
7B unworkable
4R unworried
9D unworthier

Word Type	F	D	U	SFI	3 Gr 3	4 Gr 4	5 Gr 5	6 Gr 6	7 Gr 7	8 Gr 8	9 Gr 9	X UnGr	A Read	B Eng & Gr	C Comp	D Lit	E Math	F Soc Stud	G Spell	H Sci	J Music	K Art	L Home Ec	M Shop	N Lib F	P Lib NF	Q Lib Ref	R Mag	S Rel
unworthy	12	.6749	1.6814	42.3	0	3	2	1	3	2	1	0	4	0	0	1	0	0	0	0	1	0	0	0	2	2	1	1	0
unwound	9	.5242	1.0193	40.1	1	1	2	1	3	1	0	0	3	0	1	0	0	0	0	0	2	0	0	0	1	1	0	1	0
unwrap	2	.2130	.1056	30.2	1	0	0	0	1	0	0	0	0	0	0	0	0	0	1	1	0	0	0	0	0	0	0	0	0
unwrapped	14	.4417	1.4470	41.6	4	2	0	2	2	1	3	0	8	0	2	1	0	0	1	0	0	0	0	0	1	1	0	0	0
unwrapping	2	.1787	.1174	30.7	0	0	1	0	1	0	0	0	1	0	0	0	0	0	0	0	0	0	0	0	1	0	0	0	0
unwritten	3	.3874	.2497	34.0	0	0	0	0	2	0	0	1	0	1	0	0	0	0	0	0	0	0	0	0	1	0	0	1	0
unyielding	2	.1787	.1174	30.7	0	0	0	1	0	1	0	0	1	0	0	0	0	0	0	0	0	0	0	0	1	0	0	0	0
up	12776	.9538	2409.0	73.8	2715	2304	1563	1557	2332	1230	812	263	4393	411	105	950	174	760	169	1341	433	55	105	85	1289	1249	368	878	11
Up	13	.5680	1.5610	41.9	6	0	1	1	2	3	0	0	3	1	0	0	0	0	1	2	4	0	0	0	0	1	0	1	0
UP	8	.3805	.7822	38.9	1	1	0	5	0	0	0	1	6	0	0	1	0	0	0	0	0	0	0	0	0	0	0	1	0
up-and-down	8	.5554	.9683	39.9	1	1	1	0	2	1	1	1	3	0	0	0	1	0	0	2	1	0	0	0	0	1	0	0	0
up-draft	3	.0000	.0591	27.7	0	0	0	3	0	0	0	0	0	0	0	0	0	0	0	3	0	0	0	0	0	0	0	0	0
up-to-date	8	.5262	.8867	39.5	2	0	0	0	4	0	2	0	0	0	0	0	0	3	0	1	0	0	0	0	0	1	2	1	0
up-to-the-minute	2	.2351	.1166	30.7	0	1	0	1	0	0	0	0	0	0	0	0	0	1	0	0	0	0	0	0	0	0	0	1	0
upbeat	7	.0000	.0566	27.5	0	4	3	0	0	0	0	0	0	0	0	0	0	0	0	0	7	0	0	0	0	0	0	0	0
upcoming	2	.2433	.1158	30.6	1	0	0	0	0	0	1	0	0	0	0	0	0	0	0	0	0	0	0	0	0	1	0	1	0
updated	2	.2351	.1166	30.7	0	0	0	0	0	2	0	0	0	0	0	0	0	1	0	0	0	0	0	0	0	0	0	1	0
updates	2	.0000	.0299	24.8	0	0	0	0	0	0	2	0	0	0	0	0	2	0	0	0	0	0	0	0	0	0	0	0	0
updrafts	7	.3864	.6753	38.3	0	0	3	1	2	0	1	0	4	0	0	0	0	0	0	2	0	0	0	0	0	0	0	1	0
upgrade	3	.3801	.2525	34.0	1	0	0	1	0	0	1	0	0	0	0	0	0	0	0	1	0	0	0	0	1	1	0	0	0
Upham	2	.0000	.0215	23.3	0	0	0	0	0	2	0	0	0	0	0	2	0	0	0	0	0	0	0	0	0	0	0	0	0
upheaval	7	.2652	.4470	36.5	1	1	0	1	4	0	0	0	1	0	0	0	0	0	0	0	0	0	0	0	0	0	4	2	0
upheavals	3	.3847	.2496	34.0	1	0	0	0	2	0	0	0	0	0	0	0	0	0	0	0	0	0	0	0	0	1	1	1	0
upheld	6	.4189	.5719	37.6	0	0	1	0	1	3	0	1	1	0	0	0	0	3	0	1	0	0	0	0	0	0	1	0	0
uphill	18	.6899	2.5495	44.1	3	1	2	0	8	3	0	1	3	2	0	1	0	1	0	4	0	0	0	0	2	2	3	0	0
uphold	5	.4113	.4624	36.7	0	0	2	0	2	1	0	0	1	0	0	0	0	1	0	0	0	0	0	0	2	0	1	0	0
upholding	2	.2437	.1129	30.5	0	0	1	0	0	1	0	0	0	0	0	0	0	0	0	0	0	0	0	0	0	0	1	1	0
upholstered	7	.4614	.7358	38.7	0	1	1	0	3	1	0	1	3	0	0	0	0	0	0	0	0	0	0	0	1	1	0	2	0
upholstering	2	.0000	.0050	17.0	0	0	0	0	2	0	0	0	0	0	0	0	0	0	0	0	0	0	0	2	0	0	0	0	0
upholstery	10	.5752	1.2220	40.9	0	0	0	1	6	1	1	1	3	0	0	0	0	1	1	0	0	0	1	0	2	0	0	2	0
upkeep	4	.3863	.3417	35.3	0	0	0	0	1	3	0	0	0	1	0	0	0	2	0	0	0	0	0	0	0	0	0	1	0
upland	12	.4890	1.2831	41.1	0	3	5	1	2	1	0	0	2	0	0	2	0	6	0	0	0	0	0	0	0	1	1	0	0
Upland	7	.1897	.3644	35.6	1	0	6	0	0	0	0	0	0	1	0	0	0	6	0	0	0	0	0	0	0	0	0	0	0
uplands	9	.3729	.7461	38.7	1	2	4	1	0	0	1	0	0	0	0	0	0	4	0	0	0	0	0	0	0	2	3	0	0
Uplands	3	.0000	.0583	27.7	0	0	0	0	0	0	3	0	0	0	0	0	0	3	0	0	0	0	0	0	0	0	0	0	0
uplift	5	.5571	.5811	37.6	1	0	0	0	0	3	1	0	0	0	0	0	0	1	0	1	0	0	0	0	0	1	1	1	0
uplifted	6	.4741	.6395	38.1	0	1	0	1	2	0	2	0	2	0	0	0	0	0	0	2	0	0	0	0	1	0	1	0	0
uplifting	6	.4153	.5483	37.4	0	0	0	2	1	2	1	0	1	0	0	2	0	0	0	0	0	0	0	0	0	0	2	1	0
upon	1574	.9434	293.63	64.7	140	152	137	252	327	279	239	48	393	68	35	198	23	106	10	152	76	9	25	35	150	94	130	67	3
upper	327	.8565	55.808	57.5	35	51	34	38	60	56	43	10	34	11	2	8	14	16	2	86	46	4	22	4	14	15	29	20	0
Upper	22	.3843	1.9200	42.8	1	1	10	4	3	3	0	0	3	0	0	0	0	9	0	0	0	0	0	0	0	0	8	2	0
upper-class	2	.2408	.1204	30.8	0	0	1	0	0	1	0	0	0	0	0	0	0	1	0	0	0	0	0	0	0	1	0	0	0
uppermost	7	.5560	.8399	39.2	1	0	0	1	3	1	1	0	2	0	0	0	0	0	0	2	0	0	0	0	1	1	0	1	0
uppers	2	.2446	.1122	30.5	0	0	0	0	1	1	0	0	0	0	0	1	0	0	0	0	0	0	0	0	0	0	1	0	0
Uppers	2	.0000	.0234	23.7	0	0	2	0	0	0	0	0	0	0	0	0	0	0	0	0	0	0	0	0	2	0	0	0	0
uppity	2	.0000	.0914	29.6	0	0	0	2	0	0	0	0	2	0	0	0	0	0	0	0	0	0	0	0	0	0	0	0	0
upraised	6	.5189	.6681	38.2	0	3	2	1	0	0	0	0	1	1	0	0	0	0	0	1	0	0	0	0	1	2	0	0	0
upright	76	.7360	11.373	50.6	3	6	15	9	19	8	8	8	15	0	2	11	1	1	0	9	2	0	0	0	16	2	10	7	0
uprising	14	.4754	1.4199	41.5	1	0	4	1	3	5	0	0	0	0	0	0	0	6	0	0	0	0	0	0	0	2	3	3	0
Uprising	5	.2078	.2673	34.3	0	0	0	0	0	5	0	0	0	0	0	0	0	4	0	0	0	1	0	0	0	0	0	0	0
uprisings	2	.2285	.1129	30.5	0	0	1	0	0	1	0	0	0	0	0	0	0	1	0	0	0	0	0	0	0	0	1	0	0
upriver	8	.1414	.3921	35.9	0	0	0	6	0	2	0	0	3	0	0	0	0	0	0	0	0	0	0	0	0	0	0	5	0
uproar	18	.6668	2.5131	44.0	0	3	3	5	1	5	1	0	7	1	0	2	0	2	0	0	1	0	0	0	3	2	0	0	0
uproariously	5	.3126	.3746	35.7	2	0	1	0	2	0	0	0	1	0	0	0	0	0	0	0	0	0	0	0	2	2	0	0	0
uprooted	4	.4804	.4052	36.1	0	0	0	0	3	1	0	0	0	1	0	0	0	1	0	0	0	0	0	0	0	0	1	1	0
uprooting	4	.3711	.3648	35.6	2	1	1	0	0	0	0	0	2	0	0	0	0	0	0	0	0	0	0	0	0	1	1	0	0
ups	7	.4800	.6921	38.4	0	0	1	0	3	0	2	1	0	1	0	0	0	0	0	1	0	1	2	0	1	0	1	0	0
Upsalquitch	4	.0000	.1827	32.6	0	0	4	0	0	0	0	0	4	0	0	0	0	0	0	0	0	0	0	0	0	0	0	0	0
upset	108	.7947	17.421	52.4	18	25	15	4	20	18	8	0	42	3	1	9	0	4	0	7	1	0	7	1	14	7	1	11	0
upsets	13	.5135	1.4810	41.7	2	1	2	1	1	3	2	1	6	0	0	1	0	0	0	2	0	0	2	1	0	1	0	0	0
upsetting	13	.5498	1.5138	41.8	0	3	0	1	7	2	0	0	3	0	0	1	0	0	0	1	1	0	0	2	3	1	0	1	0
upside	84	.8045	13.676	51.4	25	12	15	12	8	8	4	0	26	2	0	2	0	2	2	22	8	1	0	0	5	7	4	3	0
upside-down	12	.5128	1.3740	41.4	6	1	1	1	2	0	0	1	5	0	0	0	0	1	0	2	0	0	0	0	0	1	0	3	0
Upson	3	.0000	.0434	26.4	3	0	0	0	0	0	0	0	0	0	0	0	0	0	0	0	0	0	0	0	0	3	0	0	0
upstage	16	.2844	1.0216	40.1	0	0	0	5	1	10	0	0	0	0	0	10	0	0	0	0	0	0	0	0	5	0	0	1	0
upstairs	114	.7049	16.709	52.2	30	25	13	16	15	9	5	1	51	6	2	10	0	5	0	1	1	0	0	0	23	11	0	4	0
upstanding	3	.3431	.2528	34.0	1	0	0	1	0	1	0	0	1	0	0	0	0	1	0	0	0	0	0	0	1	0	0	0	0
upstart	2	.2346	.1166	30.7	0	0	0	0	0	1	0	1	0	0	0	0	0	0	0	1	0	0	0	0	0	0	0	1	0
upstate	3	.3450	.2505	34.0	0	1	1	0	1	0	0	0	1	0	0	0	0	0	0	0	0	0	0	0	1	1	0	0	0
upstream	39	.6036	4.9502	46.9	1	6	3	7	15	3	3	1	8	0	0	3	0	7	0	3	0	0	0	0	0	4	2	12	0
upstretched	4	.1787	.2347	33.7	0	2	0	0	1	0	1	0	2	0	0	0	0	0	0	0	0	0	0	0	2	0	0	0	0
upstroke	3	.3632	.2410	33.8	2	0	0	1	0	0	0	0	0	0	0	0	0	0	1	1	0	0	0	0	0	1	0	0	0
upsurge	2	.2437	.1129	30.5	0	0	0	0	1	0	1	0	0	0	0	0	0	0	0	0	0	0	0	0	0	0	1	1	0
upthrusting	2	.2407	.1138	30.6	0	0	0	1	1	0	0	0	0	0	0	1	0	0	0	0	0	0	0	0	0	1	0	0	0
uptight	2	.0000	.0243	23.9	0	0	1	0	1	0	0	0	0	0	0	0	0	0	0	0	0	0	0	0	0	0	0	2	0
uptown	4	.2424	.3036	34.8	2	0	0	0	1	1	0	0	3	0	0	0	0	0	0	0	0	0	0	0	0	0	0	1	0
upturned	12	.5572	1.4367	41.6	3	2	5	0	1	1	0	0	4	0	0	1	0	0	0	0	0	0	0	0	4	1	1	1	0
upward	184	.8533	31.407	55.0	18	26	21	20	48	21	25	5	37	1	2	12	12	9	2	49	6	7	0	2	7	9	15	14	0
Upward	5	.2447	.2801	34.5	0	0	2	0	3	0	0	0	0	0	0	0	0	0	0	0	2	0	0	0	0	0	0	3	0
upward-moving	2	.0000	.0394	26.0	0	0	0	0	2	0	0	0	0	0	0	0	0	0	0	2	0	0	0	0	0	0	0	0	0
upwards	9	.6057	1.1259	40.5	1	1	1	1	2	1	2	0	1	1	1	1	0	0	0	1	0	0	0	0	0	1	1	2	0
upwelling	7	.0000	.1380	31.4	0	0	0	0	0	0	7	0	0	0	0	0	0	0	0	7	0	0	0	0	0	0	0	0	0
ur	7	.0862	.2391	33.8	2	1	0	1	1	2	0	0	2	0	0	0	0	0	5	0	0	0	0	0	0	0	0	0	0
Ur	2	.0000	.0209	23.2	0	1	0	0	0	0	1	0	0	0	0	0	0	0	0	0	0	0	0	0	0	0	2	0	0
Ural	4	.0000	.0778	28.9	0	0	0	2	0	0	2	0	0	0	0	0	0	4	0	0	0	0	0	0	0	0	0	0	0
Urals	11	.2493	.6929	38.4	0	0	0	1	1	0	9	0	0	0	0	0	0	9	0	1	0	0	0	0	0	0	1	0	0
uraninite	4	.0000	.0789	29.0	0	0	0	0	0	0	0	4	0	0	0	0	0	0	0	4	0	0	0	0	0	0	0	0	0
uranium	140	.5959	17.854	52.5	1	3	38	38	23	20	8	9	41	0	0	0	2	13	3	63	0	0	0	1	0	1	13	3	0
uranium-235	7	.0000	.1380	31.4	0	0	0	7	0	0	0	0	0	0	0	0	0	0	0	7	0	0	0	0	0	0	0	0	0
uranium-238	4	.0000	.0789	29.0	0	0	0	3	0	0	1	0	0	0	0	0	0	0	0	4	0	0	0	0	0	0	0	0	0
Uranus	48	.4296	4.6534	46.7	4	17	13	3	1	8	0	2	10	0	0	1	3	0	0	20	0	0	0	0	0	0	14	0	0
urban	50	.4576	4.9261	46.9	0	1	13	21	5	3	7	0	0	0	0	0	0	26	0	1	0	0	0	0	0	3	11	9	0
Urban	16	.1881	.7335	38.7	1	0	13	0	1	1	0	0	0	0	0	0	0	0	0	0	0	0	0	0	0	1	13	2	0
urban-industrial	2	.0000	.0243	23.9	0	0	0	0	2	0	0	0	0	0	0	0	0	0	0	0	0	0	0	0	0	0	0	2	0

9R unwrinkled
3A unzip
7R Up-Tight
3Q up-and-coming
8D up-and-downstage
6J up-beat
7P up-court
3P up-down
7N up-ended
7R up-front
9P up-river
4Q up-to-dateness
7N upbraid
9D upbraided
5P upbringing
6A upcountry
7R update
9R updating
4P updraw
7R upending
7R upgraded
9R upgrading
7J Upharsin
9Q upholds
9D upholsterers'
4J upon't
7R upped
7H upper-air
4J upper-grade
XR upping
7Q Uppsala
8D upraising
6A uprights
6R uprise
9B uproaring
4P uproot
XH uprushing
9R upshot
9E upside-
9L Upside-Down
9H upslope
XR upstages
7M upstore
9K upsweep
6A upswelling
7R upswept
6A uptailed
7R upthrust
7A uptipped
8R Uptown
6P UPWARD
5A upward-beamed
9H uracil
XH uralitic
XH Uraniborg
XH uranium-bearing
7Q uranium-graphite
6H uranium-234
5Q Uranus'
7G urb
7R urban-crisis
XR urban/suburban
5Q Urban's
8F urbane
8R urbanist

Word Type	F	D	U	SFI	3 Gr 3	4 Gr 4	5 Gr 5	6 Gr 6	7 Gr 7	8 Gr 8	9 Gr 9	X UnGr	A Read	B Eng & Gr	C Comp	D Lit	E Math	F Soc Stud	G Spell	H Sci	J Music	K Art	L Home Ec	M Shop	N Lib F	P Lib NF	Q Lib Ref	R Mag	S Rel
urbanized	7	.1817	.3553	35.5	0	0	0	6	0	0	0	1	0	0	0	0	0	6	0	0	0	0	0	0	0	0	0	1	0
urchin	5	.4755	.5327	37.3	0	0	0	2	1	0	1	1	2	0	0	1	0	0	0	0	0	0	0	0	0	0	1	1	0
urchins	8	.4715	.8569	39.3	0	1	0	5	2	0	0	0	3	1	0	0	0	0	0	3	0	0	0	0	1	0	0	0	0
Urdu	2	.1733	.1149	30.6	1	0	0	0	1	0	0	0	1	1	0	0	0	0	0	0	0	0	0	0	0	0	0	0	0
ure	2	.1497	.1046	30.2	1	0	0	1	0	0	0	0	1	0	0	0	0	0	1	0	0	0	0	0	0	0	0	0	0
urea	3	.2445	.1818	32.6	0	0	0	0	2	0	1	0	0	0	0	0	0	0	0	2	0	0	0	0	0	0	1	0	0
ureters	2	.0000	.0209	23.2	0	0	0	0	0	1	1	0	0	0	0	0	0	0	0	0	0	0	0	0	0	0	2	0	0
Urey	5	.0000	.0523	27.2	0	0	0	0	5	0	0	0	0	0	0	0	0	0	0	0	0	0	0	0	0	0	5	0	0
urge	29	.7199	4.2744	46.3	0	2	4	4	3	5	8	3	8	2	0	6	0	2	0	0	1	0	1	0	0	2	2	5	0
urged	74	.7013	10.723	50.3	4	19	14	7	12	12	5	1	22	1	0	3	0	13	0	1	1	0	0	0	9	14	1	9	0
urgency	4	.4802	.4049	36.1	1	0	0	0	0	1	2	0	0	0	0	1	0	1	0	0	0	0	0	0	0	0	1	1	0
urgent	19	.6889	2.6874	44.3	1	0	3	4	3	4	4	0	4	3	0	0	0	2	0	0	1	0	0	0	2	1	2	4	0
urgently	6	.6042	.7573	38.8	1	0	1	1	0	2	1	0	1	1	0	1	0	1	0	0	0	0	0	0	0	1	0	1	0
urges	7	.6001	.8597	39.3	0	0	1	1	2	0	3	0	0	0	0	1	0	1	1	0	0	0	0	0	1	1	2	0	0
urging	28	.6999	4.0459	46.1	1	5	7	4	5	4	2	0	9	1	0	1	0	2	0	0	1	0	0	0	2	2	3	7	0
Uri	11	.0000	.1290	31.1	0	0	0	11	0	0	0	0	0	0	0	0	0	0	0	0	0	0	0	0	11	0	0	0	0
urinary	4	.0000	.0789	29.0	0	0	0	0	0	4	0	0	0	0	0	0	0	0	0	4	0	0	0	0	0	0	0	0	0
urination	3	.0000	.0314	25.0	0	0	0	0	0	2	1	0	0	0	0	0	0	0	0	0	0	0	0	0	0	0	3	0	0
urine	20	.2329	1.1597	40.6	0	4	1	0	2	7	6	0	1	0	0	0	0	0	0	8	0	0	0	0	0	0	11	0	0
urn	2	.2407	.1138	30.6	0	1	0	0	1	0	0	0	0	0	0	1	0	0	0	0	0	0	0	0	0	1	0	0	0
Uruguay	30	.4192	2.7504	44.4	6	0	2	15	4	1	2	0	0	0	0	0	0	18	0	0	1	0	0	0	0	0	7	4	0
Uruguayans	2	.0000	.0243	23.9	0	0	0	2	0	0	0	0	0	0	0	0	0	0	0	0	0	0	0	0	0	0	0	2	0
ury	2	.0000	.0162	22.1	0	0	0	0	0	2	0	0	0	0	0	0	0	0	2	0	0	0	0	0	0	0	0	0	0
us	3929	.6855	556.03	67.5	568	683	445	491	789	488	359	106	1034	259	53	338	182	408	82	326	137	51	26	12	256	334	98	273	60
Us	2	.2437	.1129	30.5	0	0	1	0	0	0	0	1	0	0	0	0	0	0	0	0	0	0	0	0	0	0	1	1	0
US	21	.3732	1.7109	42.3	0	0	0	0	19	0	2	0	0	0	0	0	0	0	0	1	0	0	0	0	0	10	8	2	0
USA	5	.2962	.3718	35.7	0	0	0	0	4	0	1	0	2	0	0	0	0	0	0	0	0	0	0	1	0	0	2	0	0
usable	12	.4929	1.2714	41.0	1	0	4	0	2	3	2	0	2	0	0	0	0	0	0	3	0	0	2	0	0	1	3	1	0
usage	42	.4814	4.2201	46.3	1	0	3	0	13	10	14	1	0	26	0	2	1	0	2	1	0	0	0	0	1	2	4	3	0
usages	5	.0000	.0547	27.4	0	0	0	0	0	3	2	0	0	5	0	0	0	0	0	0	0	0	0	0	0	0	0	0	0
USC	2	.0000	.0243	23.9	0	0	0	0	1	1	0	0	0	0	0	0	0	0	0	0	0	0	0	0	0	0	0	2	0
USC'S	2	.0000	.0243	23.9	0	0	0	0	1	1	0	0	0	0	0	0	0	0	0	0	0	0	0	0	0	0	0	2	0
USDA	3	.0000	.0365	25.6	0	0	0	0	0	0	0	3	0	0	0	0	0	0	0	0	0	0	0	0	0	0	0	3	0
use	7009	.8753	1219.2	70.9	1210	1134	985	974	1096	818	671	121	701	940	137	77	1500	554	925	703	246	179	225	192	78	211	154	187	0
Use	4	.1529	.1647	32.2	0	0	0	1	2	0	0	1	0	3	0	0	0	0	0	1	0	0	0	0	0	0	0	0	0
used	5607	.8902	991.21	70.0	718	746	785	741	1088	772	666	91	791	682	52	84	546	612	315	576	382	146	194	333	97	278	309	210	0
Used	4	.0000	.1827	32.6	0	0	0	0	0	4	0	0	4	0	0	0	0	0	0	0	0	0	0	0	0	0	0	0	0
used-car	2	.0000	.0243	23.9	0	0	0	0	2	0	0	0	0	0	0	0	0	0	0	0	0	0	0	0	0	0	0	2	0
useful	430	.8838	75.632	58.8	40	69	50	57	91	48	59	16	62	25	5	9	26	61	12	106	2	4	7	22	14	27	37	11	0
usefulness	16	.5996	2.0389	43.1	0	1	0	3	3	5	4	0	5	0	0	0	2	0	0	5	0	0	1	1	0	0	2	0	0
useless	86	.8437	14.607	51.6	9	9	12	17	21	5	11	2	33	7	0	1	0	7	2	9	0	0	1	2	6	6	5	7	0
uselessly	4	.2494	.2817	34.5	0	0	2	1	0	1	0	0	2	0	0	0	0	1	0	0	0	0	1	0	0	0	0	0	0
uselessness	2	.2433	.1158	30.6	0	0	0	1	1	0	0	0	0	0	0	0	0	0	0	0	0	0	0	0	0	1	0	1	0
user	21	.5909	2.5467	44.1	1	6	2	0	8	1	2	1	0	2	0	0	0	0	0	3	2	0	0	0	0	3	6	5	0
users	13	.5356	1.4764	41.7	0	3	0	0	4	3	3	0	2	1	0	0	0	1	1	1	0	0	0	0	0	0	1	6	0
uses	603	.8694	104.35	60.2	95	85	73	81	108	83	58	20	72	66	15	0	70	48	24	118	75	7	5	25	1	23	23	31	0
usher	7	.5763	.8424	39.3	0	1	0	0	2	1	3	0	1	2	0	0	0	1	1	0	0	0	0	0	1	0	1	0	0
ushered	6	.6008	.7565	38.8	0	1	0	0	2	2	1	0	1	0	0	1	0	1	0	1	0	0	0	0	0	1	1	0	0
using	1825	.8473	307.91	64.9	198	240	225	264	324	298	244	32	120	224	26	15	573	100	127	174	135	60	85	40	9	47	35	55	0
Using	2	.2152	.1357	31.3	0	0	1	1	0	0	0	0	1	0	0	0	0	1	0	0	0	0	0	0	0	0	0	0	0
Ussachevsky	2	.0000	.0162	22.1	0	0	0	0	0	2	0	0	0	0	0	0	0	0	0	0	2	0	0	0	0	0	0	0	0
Ussher	4	.1873	.1827	32.6	0	0	0	1	3	0	0	0	0	0	0	0	0	0	0	0	0	0	0	0	0	0	3	1	0
USSR	2	.2285	.1129	30.5	0	0	0	0	1	1	0	0	0	0	0	0	0	1	0	0	0	0	0	0	0	0	1	0	0
usual	313	.9416	58.306	57.7	33	68	25	43	63	41	32	8	85	23	3	21	9	11	23	26	8	1	4	5	33	20	14	27	0
usually	1712	.9069	307.82	64.9	183	217	245	224	330	241	225	47	226	199	19	36	46	208	171	248	106	8	62	53	25	80	161	64	0
usurpations	2	.0000	.0389	25.9	0	0	0	0	0	2	0	0	0	0	0	0	0	2	0	0	0	0	0	0	0	0	0	0	0
usurpers	2	.2437	.1129	30.5	0	0	1	1	0	0	0	0	0	0	0	0	0	0	0	0	0	0	0	C	0	0	1	1	0
ut	4	.0000	.1827	32.6	0	0	0	0	0	4	0	0	4	0	0	0	0	0	0	0	0	0	0	0	0	0	0	0	0
Utah	49	.7095	7.1497	48.5	2	9	11	7	8	5	4	3	10	1	0	0	1	12	1	10	1	0	0	0	0	4	1	8	0
utensil	4	.4814	.4082	36.1	0	0	0	0	2	0	1	1	0	1	0	0	1	1	0	0	0	0	0	0	0	0	0	1	0
utensils	29	.5209	3.1521	45.0	0	2	2	6	5	6	7	1	1	0	1	1	0	6	0	4	0	0	8	0	1	4	2	1	0
uterine	2	.0000	.0394	26.0	0	0	0	0	0	0	2	0	0	0	0	0	0	0	0	2	0	0	0	0	0	0	0	0	0
uterus	15	.1285	.6285	38.0	0	0	0	0	2	0	11	2	0	0	0	0	0	0	0	14	0	0	0	0	0	0	1	0	0
Uther	9	.0000	.4111	36.1	0	0	0	9	0	0	0	0	9	0	0	0	0	0	0	0	0	0	0	0	0	0	0	0	0
utilitarian	2	.0000	.0209	23.2	0	0	2	0	0	0	0	0	0	0	0	0	0	0	0	0	0	0	0	0	0	0	2	0	0
utilitarianism	2	.0000	.0209	23.2	0	0	2	0	0	0	0	0	0	0	0	0	0	0	0	0	0	0	0	0	0	0	2	0	0
Utilitarianism	2	.0000	.0209	23.2	0	0	2	0	0	0	0	0	0	0	0	0	0	0	0	0	0	0	0	0	0	0	2	0	0
utilities	8	.4361	.7508	38.8	1	0	0	0	1	5	1	0	0	0	0	0	0	4	0	0	0	0	0	1	0	1	2	0	0
utility	14	.5556	1.5916	42.0	0	0	1	0	6	2	3	2	0	1	0	0	0	1	0	0	0	0	2	1	0	0	4	5	0
utilization	5	.4086	.4442	36.5	0	0	0	0	2	1	2	0	0	0	0	0	0	2	0	1	0	0	1	0	0	0	1	0	0
utilize	11	.5883	1.3272	41.2	0	0	0	2	6	1	1	1	0	1	0	0	0	1	0	1	0	0	0	1	0	1	3	3	0
utilized	12	.5987	1.4818	41.7	0	1	0	0	6	0	2	3	1	0	0	1	0	1	0	2	0	1	1	0	0	0	4	1	0
utilizes	8	.4080	.6952	38.4	0	0	0	0	4	2	1	1	0	0	0	0	0	0	0	1	3	0	0	0	0	0	1	3	0
utilizing	4	.3817	.3247	35.1	1	0	0	0	0	0	2	1	0	0	0	1	0	0	0	0	0	0	0	1	0	1	0	1	0
Utley	5	.0000	.0586	27.7	0	0	0	0	5	0	0	0	0	0	0	0	0	0	0	0	0	0	0	0	5	0	0	0	0
utmost	24	.7748	3.7549	45.7	0	0	1	5	5	7	5	1	5	1	0	3	0	0	0	2	1	1	1	0	5	2	1	2	0
Utopia	4	.3664	.3180	35.0	0	0	0	0	0	2	2	0	0	0	0	0	1	0	1	0	0	0	0	0	0	0	0	2	0
utopian	2	.2351	.1166	30.7	0	0	0	0	1	1	0	0	0	0	0	0	0	1	1	0	0	0	0	0	0	0	0	0	0
Utrecht	2	.0000	.0389	25.9	2	0	0	0	0	0	0	0	0	0	0	0	0	2	0	0	0	0	0	0	0	0	0	0	0
utter	25	.7546	3.8301	45.8	0	2	4	6	5	2	4	2	6	1	1	3	0	2	1	0	0	0	0	0	4	2	1	4	0
Utter	2	.0000	.0037	15.7	1	0	0	0	1	0	0	0	0	0	0	0	0	0	0	0	0	2	0	0	0	0	0	0	0
utterance	8	.5751	.9584	39.8	0	0	0	1	4	1	1	1	1	0	0	2	0	0	0	0	0	0	0	0	2	1	1	1	0
utterances	4	.3306	.2831	34.5	0	0	0	2	0	0	2	0	0	0	1	0	0	0	0	0	1	0	0	0	0	0	0	2	0
uttered	21	.6617	2.8449	44.5	1	2	2	2	6	1	6	1	3	1	1	6	1	0	1	0	0	0	0	0	5	2	0	1	0
uttering	8	.4846	.8986	39.5	0	2	0	4	1	0	1	0	5	0	0	1	0	0	0	0	0	0	0	0	1	1	0	0	0
utterly	32	.6399	4.2390	46.3	2	5	3	3	8	7	3	1	7	2	1	8	0	0	0	0	0	0	0	0	8	1	1	4	0
UV	3	.0000	.0449	26.5	0	0	2	0	0	0	1	0	0	0	0	0	3	0	0	0	0	0	0	0	0	0	0	0	0
uy	2	.0000	.0162	22.1	0	0	0	0	0	2	0	0	0	0	0	0	0	0	2	0	0	0	0	0	0	0	0	0	0
Uzbek	2	.0000	.0209	23.2	0	0	0	0	0	2	0	0	0	0	0	0	0	0	0	0	0	0	0	0	0	0	2	0	0
Uzlian	2	.0000	.0389	25.9	0	2	0	0	0	0	0	0	0	0	0	0	0	2	0	0	0	0	0	0	0	0	0	0	0
v	126	.4755	12.524	51.0	1	22	31	18	10	16	27	1	1	10	1	1	25	0	61	12	0	0	0	0	0	0	14	1	0
V	167	.6792	22.914	53.6	11	15	53	19	28	23	13	5	2	41	0	1	42	2	1	6	37	1	0	10	1	2	13	8	0
V**	6	.3480	.4603	36.6	0	0	0	0	1	5	0	0	0	0	0	1	0	0	1	0	0	0	0	0	0	4	0	0	0
VCe	13	.0000	.1423	31.5	0	7	6	0	0	0	0	0	0	13	0	0	0	0	0	0	0	0	0	0	0	0	0	0	0

8Q ureteral
8Q urethers
8Q urethra
7Q Urey's
6N uri
7Q uric
8Q Uriel
9Q Urinarum
9Q Urine
8B urne
8R urologist
9Q uroscopy
9Q Urubamba
6R Uruguay's
6R Uruguays's
6R Uruguyan
9R US-dominated
8R USAF
6H USE
7J useable
3H USED
8N used-up
7R user's
XR Users'
7A Uses
5G ush
9E ushering
7A ushers
6A USN
7Q Usnea
7R USOC
7Q usque
7R USS
7B usted
9D usurer
7A usurpation
7N usurped
4G ute
8R UTEP
5Q utilitarians
5P Utility
7N Utley's
8F utopia
8F Utopians
3K Utrillo
8A uts
3A Uttar
7P utter'd
4D uttermost
4A uuuuh
7N uv
5E UVW
5R UWI
9D Uzbekistan
3F V-Bar
8E V-E
8F V-J
9M V-belt
9M V-block
7P V-formation

Word Type	F	D	U	SFI	3 Gr 3	4 Gr 4	5 Gr 5	6 Gr 6	7 Gr 7	8 Gr 8	9 Gr 9	X UnGr	A Read	B Eng & Gr	C Comp	D Lit	E Math	F Soc Stud	G Spell	H Sci	J Music	K Art	L Home Ec	M Shop	N Lib F	P Lib NF	Q Lib Ref	R Mag	S Rel
V-shaped	7	.6178	.9138	39.6	0	2	1	0	3	0	1	0	2	0	0	0	0	1	0	1	0	0	0	0	1	1	1	0	0
V-2	3	.2383	.1815	32.6	0	0	0	1	1	1	0	0	0	0	0	0	0	0	0	2	0	0	0	0	0	1	0	0	0
V-8	8	.3147	.5607	37.5	0	0	0	0	4	0	2	2	0	0	0	0	0	0	0	0	0	0	0	0	0	1	2	5	0
v/cv	4	.0000	.0325	25.1	0	1	0	3	0	0	0	0	0	0	0	0	0	0	4	0	0	0	0	0	0	0	0	0	0
V's	5	.3689	.4527	36.6	0	2	2	0	1	0	0	0	2	0	0	0	0	0	0	2	0	0	0	0	0	0	0	1	0
Va	8	.2768	.5099	37.1	0	0	2	0	1	2	3	0	0	0	0	0	0	2	0	0	0	0	0	0	0	0	5	1	0
vacancy	2	.2388	.1089	30.4	0	0	0	0	1	1	0	0	0	0	0	0	0	0	1	0	0	0	0	0	1	0	0	0	0
vacant	31	.7223	4.5690	46.6	2	8	1	7	3	6	3	1	6	5	0	4	0	1	1	4	0	0	0	0	4	4	0	2	0
vacated	2	.1698	.1133	30.5	0	0	1	0	0	0	1	0	1	0	0	0	0	0	0	0	0	0	0	0	0	0	1	0	0
vacation	132	.8340	22.132	53.5	31	33	13	17	14	14	8	2	39	12	6	2	9	20	10	8	2	0	2	0	9	3	2	8	0
Vacation	2	.2408	.1204	30.8	1	1	0	0	0	0	0	0	0	0	0	0	0	1	0	0	0	0	0	0	0	1	0	0	0
vacationers	6	.3079	.4495	36.5	2	1	2	0	1	0	0	0	1	0	0	0	0	3	0	0	0	0	0	0	0	0	2	0	0
vacations	20	.6195	2.5828	44.1	5	5	3	1	3	0	2	1	2	1	0	1	0	10	1	1	0	0	0	0	0	2	0	2	0
vaccinated	5	.4509	.5024	37.0	0	2	0	0	0	0	2	1	1	1	0	0	0	0	0	2	0	0	0	0	0	0	0	1	0
vaccination	10	.5274	1.1417	40.6	2	3	0	2	1	1	1	0	2	0	0	0	2	0	0	4	0	0	0	0	0	0	1	1	0
vaccine	43	.4145	3.9803	46.0	1	10	5	7	11	3	2	4	1	0	0	0	2	5	0	29	0	0	0	0	0	0	1	5	0
vaccines	16	.2381	1.0027	40.0	0	6	1	5	3	0	0	1	1	0	0	0	0	1	0	13	0	0	0	0	0	0	0	1	0
Vachel	2	.1733	.1149	30.6	0	0	1	0	1	0	0	0	1	1	0	0	0	0	0	0	0	0	0	0	0	0	0	0	0
Vactangi	6	.0000	.0657	28.2	0	0	0	0	0	0	6	0	0	6	0	0	0	0	0	0	0	0	0	0	0	0	0	0	0
vacuole	3	.2445	.1818	32.6	0	0	0	1	2	0	0	0	0	0	0	0	0	0	0	2	0	0	0	0	0	0	1	0	0
vacuoles	7	.0000	.1380	31.4	0	0	0	0	6	0	1	0	0	0	0	0	0	0	0	7	0	0	0	0	0	0	0	0	0
vacuum	92	.8030	14.861	51.7	12	5	6	7	30	21	6	5	15	0	3	3	1	6	1	23	6	0	1	3	1	5	3	21	0
vacuuming	2	.2440	.1132	30.5	1	0	0	0	1	0	0	0	0	0	0	1	0	0	0	0	0	0	0	0	0	0	0	1	0
Vada	3	.0000	.0365	25.6	0	0	0	0	3	0	0	0	0	0	0	0	0	0	0	0	0	0	0	0	0	0	0	3	0
Vader	4	.0000	.1827	32.6	0	0	0	0	4	0	0	0	4	0	0	0	0	0	0	0	0	0	0	0	0	0	0	0	0
Vader's	2	.0000	.0914	29.6	0	0	0	0	2	0	0	0	2	0	0	0	0	0	0	0	0	0	0	0	0	0	0	0	0
vagabond	5	.2824	.3832	35.8	0	0	1	3	0	0	1	0	3	0	1	0	0	0	0	0	1	0	0	0	0	0	0	0	0
vagaries	2	.1948	.1250	31.0	0	0	1	0	0	1	0	0	1	0	0	0	0	0	0	0	0	0	0	0	0	1	0	0	0
vagrant	3	.3399	.2456	33.9	0	0	0	0	0	2	0	1	1	0	0	1	0	0	0	0	0	0	0	0	0	0	0	1	0
vague	30	.7700	4.6494	46.7	0	2	3	1	7	5	7	5	3	4	0	3	1	2	0	1	1	0	0	0	5	3	2	5	0
vaguely	18	.5383	2.0487	43.1	0	1	0	1	7	7	2	0	3	0	2	5	0	2	0	1	0	0	0	0	3	0	0	2	0
vagueness	2	.2303	.1079	30.3	0	0	1	0	0	1	0	0	0	0	0	0	0	0	0	0	1	0	0	0	0	1	0	0	0
vaguest	2	.2446	.1122	30.5	0	0	0	0	1	0	1	0	0	0	0	1	0	0	0	0	0	0	0	0	0	0	1	0	0
vain	53	.8262	8.7998	49.4	2	7	5	5	14	14	4	2	14	1	1	5	1	3	1	1	0	1	0	0	9	7	4	5	0
vainglorious	3	.1910	.1473	31.7	0	1	0	1	0	1	0	0	0	0	0	0	0	1	0	0	0	0	0	0	2	0	0	0	0
vainly	16	.6369	2.0855	43.2	0	0	0	1	5	7	3	0	1	1	0	3	0	1	1	0	0	0	0	0	5	2	0	2	0
Valance	4	.0000	.0429	26.3	0	0	0	0	4	0	0	0	0	0	0	4	0	0	0	0	0	0	0	0	0	0	0	0	0
Valdemar	2	.0000	.0290	24.6	0	0	2	0	0	0	0	0	0	0	0	0	0	0	0	0	0	0	0	0	0	2	0	0	0
Valdez	2	.1948	.1250	31.0	0	2	0	0	0	0	0	0	1	0	0	0	0	0	0	0	0	0	0	0	0	1	0	0	0
Valdivia	5	.2112	.2785	34.4	0	0	0	2	2	0	0	1	0	0	0	0	0	4	0	0	0	0	0	0	0	0	0	1	0
vale	6	.5518	.7101	38.5	0	1	0	2	3	0	0	0	2	1	0	1	0	0	1	0	0	0	0	0	1	0	0	0	0
valedictorian	4	.3740	.3661	35.6	0	0	0	0	3	0	1	0	2	0	0	0	0	0	0	0	0	0	0	0	1	0	0	1	0
valence	2	.0000	.0394	26.0	0	0	0	0	2	0	0	0	0	0	0	0	0	0	0	2	0	0	0	0	0	0	0	0	0
valentine	10	.4858	1.0404	40.2	5	0	0	1	1	3	0	0	2	1	0	3	0	0	1	0	3	0	0	0	0	0	0	0	0
Valentine	19	.4509	1.8020	42.6	3	0	0	0	6	8	2	0	1	2	0	9	0	0	0	0	6	0	1	0	0	0	0	0	0
Valentine's	6	.3094	.4557	36.6	1	0	0	0	2	3	0	0	2	0	0	3	0	0	0	0	1	0	0	0	0	0	0	0	0
valentines	13	.3832	1.2644	41.0	12	0	0	0	0	1	0	0	9	2	0	0	2	0	0	0	0	0	0	0	0	0	0	0	0
Valerian	2	.0000	.0290	24.6	0	0	0	0	0	2	0	0	0	0	0	0	0	0	0	0	0	0	0	0	0	2	0	0	0
Valerie	3	.0000	.0352	25.5	3	0	0	0	0	0	0	0	0	0	0	0	0	0	0	0	0	0	0	0	3	0	0	0	0
Valery	4	.2090	.2014	33.0	0	0	0	0	0	0	2	2	0	0	0	0	0	0	0	0	0	0	0	0	0	0	1	3	0
vales	2	.2446	.1125	30.5	0	1	0	0	0	1	0	0	0	1	0	1	0	0	0	0	0	0	0	0	0	0	0	0	0
valet	3	.3842	.2485	34.0	0	1	0	0	1	0	1	0	0	0	0	1	0	0	0	0	0	0	0	0	0	1	1	0	0
Valhalla	3	.0000	.0243	23.8	0	0	0	3	0	0	0	0	0	0	0	0	0	0	0	0	3	0	0	0	0	0	0	0	0
valiant	12	.5728	1.4492	41.6	0	0	0	2	4	1	4	1	3	1	1	4	0	0	0	0	0	0	0	0	0	1	1	1	0
Valiant	3	.2309	.1631	32.1	0	0	0	0	1	2	0	0	0	0	0	1	0	0	0	0	0	0	0	0	0	0	0	2	0
valiantly	6	.4560	.5800	37.6	0	0	1	0	2	3	0	0	0	0	1	0	0	2	0	0	0	0	0	0	1	1	1	0	0
valid	15	.3838	1.2482	41.0	0	0	0	2	4	4	3	2	0	0	0	0	1	2	0	0	0	0	0	0	0	0	6	6	0
validity	3	.0000	.0314	25.0	0	0	0	0	1	2	0	0	0	0	0	0	0	0	0	0	0	0	0	0	0	0	3	0	0
valises	2	.0000	.0243	23.9	0	0	0	0	2	0	0	0	0	0	0	0	0	0	0	0	0	0	0	0	0	0	0	2	0
Valjean	4	.2393	.3005	34.8	0	0	3	0	0	1	0	0	3	0	0	1	0	0	0	0	0	0	0	0	0	0	0	0	0
Valkyries	3	.0000	.0243	23.8	0	0	0	2	0	1	0	0	0	0	0	0	0	0	0	0	3	0	0	0	0	0	0	0	0
valley	373	.8304	62.456	58.0	71	63	79	46	60	22	23	9	130	10	4	24	1	63	2	26	22	0	0	0	22	29	33	7	0
Valley	255	.6507	34.616	55.4	26	42	44	51	34	25	17	16	52	2	0	5	2	123	0	10	12	0	0	0	5	9	15	20	0
VALLEY	2	.1787	.1174	30.7	2	0	0	0	0	0	0	0	1	0	0	0	0	0	0	0	0	0	0	0	1	0	0	0	0
valley's	3	.3231	.2367	33.7	0	0	1	1	0	0	1	0	1	0	0	0	0	0	0	0	1	0	0	0	0	1	0	0	0
valleys	211	.6916	29.940	54.8	34	23	58	34	32	18	8	4	19	3	2	4	0	109	0	17	3	0	0	2	2	26	18	6	0
Valleys	3	.0000	.0583	27.7	0	0	3	0	0	0	0	0	0	0	0	0	0	3	0	0	0	0	0	0	0	0	0	0	0
Vallodia	2	.0000	.0219	23.4	0	0	0	0	0	0	2	0	0	2	0	0	0	0	0	0	0	0	0	0	0	0	0	0	0
valor	5	.2251	.2966	34.7	0	0	0	0	1	3	1	0	1	0	0	3	0	1	0	0	0	0	0	0	0	0	0	0	0
Valse	4	.2303	.2158	33.3	1	0	0	1	1	1	0	0	0	0	0	0	0	0	0	0	2	0	0	0	0	2	0	0	0
valuable	260	.8491	44.236	56.5	23	20	54	58	45	21	33	6	59	13	2	2	4	79	5	23	0	2	12	2	9	9	28	11	0
valuables	4	.0000	.1827	32.6	0	0	0	0	2	0	2	0	4	0	0	0	0	0	0	0	0	0	0	0	0	0	0	0	0
value	512	.7754	79.862	59.0	28	32	48	55	102	101	131	15	47	15	2	4	242	31	2	22	22	8	27	17	7	13	30	23	0
valued	26	.7061	3.7606	45.8	6	0	5	1	7	4	3	0	6	1	0	1	0	4	0	1	3	1	0	0	0	1	6	2	0
valueless	3	.1187	.1291	31.1	0	0	0	0	2	1	0	0	1	0	0	2	0	0	0	0	0	0	0	0	0	0	0	0	0
values	181	.7739	28.134	54.5	1	4	7	7	28	52	78	4	13	5	1	1	76	12	1	5	22	2	11	6	0	7	8	11	0
valve	40	.4825	4.1814	46.2	6	1	7	3	18	0	3	2	8	1	0	0	0	0	0	8	0	0	0	6	0	1	4	12	0
valves	52	.5889	6.4426	48.1	7	5	5	12	10	8	5	0	8	1	0	1	0	2	0	22	9	0	0	0	0	0	5	4	0
Valya	5	.0000	.2284	33.6	5	0	0	0	0	0	0	0	5	0	0	0	0	0	0	0	0	0	0	0	0	0	0	0	0
vampire	9	.1734	.4008	36.0	0	5	0	2	2	0	0	0	0	0	0	0	0	0	0	0	0	0	0	0	0	2	0	7	0
vampires	5	.2423	.2894	34.6	0	2	0	0	3	0	0	0	0	0	0	0	0	0	0	0	0	0	0	0	0	3	0	2	0
van	35	.6814	4.8678	46.9	14	2	2	4	5	7	1	0	5	1	0	1	0	4	2	0	4	2	0	0	11	2	3	0	0
Van	61	.7091	8.7830	49.4	5	9	4	11	7	15	10	0	7	2	0	12	0	6	0	0	0	3	0	1	8	8	1	13	0
VanBuren	12	.4387	1.1828	40.7	0	0	0	0	4	6	0	2	3	2	0	0	0	3	0	0	0	0	0	0	4	0	0	0	0
VanDaan	14	.2407	.7963	39.0	0	0	0	0	0	7	7	0	0	0	0	7	0	0	0	0	0	0	0	0	0	7	0	0	0
VanDerBeek	2	.0000	.0243	23.9	0	0	0	0	0	0	0	2	0	0	0	0	0	0	0	0	0	0	0	0	0	0	0	2	0
vanGogh	2	.1696	.0749	28.7	0	1	0	0	1	0	0	0	0	0	0	0	0	0	0	0	1	1	0	0	0	0	0	0	0
vanLeeuwenhoek	6	.2437	.4554	36.6	4	0	1	1	0	0	0	0	4	0	0	0	0	0	0	2	0	0	0	0	0	0	0	0	0
VanNess	2	.0000	.0914	29.6	2	0	0	0	0	0	0	0	2	0	0	0	0	0	0	0	0	0	0	0	0	0	0	0	0
VanNuys	2	.1814	.1187	30.7	0	0	0	0	2	0	0	0	1	0	0	0	0	0	0	0	0	0	0	0	0	0	0	1	0
VanTassel	2	.0665	.0708	28.5	0	0	0	0	2	0	0	0	1	0	1	0	0	0	0	0	0	0	0	0	0	0	0	0	0

4P V-i-n-e
9P V-mail
9B V-mid
7L V-neck
4P V-shape
5A v-shaped
3B V-5
8D v'ile
6G v's
7F Vaal
8Q vacancies
5R vacation-camping
3J vacation's
6R vacationed
9F vacationer
7H vacationing
6R vacationists
3H vaccinates
XH vaccinators
7H vacuolar
9H vacuum-cleaned
3N vacuum-cleaner
7R vacuum-controlled
7R vacuum-operated
7H vacuum-packed
7Q vacuum-seal
8M vacuum-tube
9Q vacuums
8J vagabonds
9H vagina
XH vaginal
8J vagrant's
9Q vagus
6F VahRiver
9D vailing
8F vainglory
4Q Vaisyas
8D vait
4J Valabre
5P Valais
7N valance
7A Valedictorian
8R valedictorians
6J Valen
5P Valera
7Q validly
6J valkyries
5P Valladolid
8N Vallejo
9H Valles
6F Valletta
5Q Valley's
6E Valleyhill
7N vally
XB Valois
7F Valor
4R valorous
6F Valparaiso
6P Valses
9F valuation
7R valving
9H valvular
4R vampiro
4R VanBenschoten
7A VanBrunt
7A VanBummel
XR VanCampen's
8P VanDaan's
8Q vanDelft
7D VanDenk
XR VanDerBeek's
8Q VanDorn
6R VanDyke
4K VanGogh
4K VanGogh's
7H vanHelmont
7H vanHelmont's
7H VanLeeuwenhoek
7R vanMaanen's
6A vanRhijn
8D VanRipper
8D VanTassel's

Word Type	F	D	U	SFI	3 Gr 3	4 Gr 4	5 Gr 5	6 Gr 6	7 Gr 7	8 Gr 8	9 Gr 9	X UnGr	A Read	B Eng & Gr	C Comp	D Lit	E Math	F Soc Stud	G Spell	H Sci	J Music	K Art	L Home Ec	M Shop	N Lib F	P Lib NF	Q Lib Ref	R Mag	S Rel
VanWinkle	5	.2601	.3673	35.7	0	0	1	0	3	0	1	0	3	0	1	0	0	0	0	0	0	0	0	0	1	0	0	0	0
Van-Buren	2	.0000	.0209	23.2	0	0	2	0	0	0	0	0	0	0	0	0	0	0	0	0	0	0	0	0	0	0	2	0	0
Van's	2	.0000	.0215	23.3	0	0	0	0	0	0	2	0	0	0	0	2	0	0	0	0	0	0	0	0	0	0	0	0	0
vanadium	4	.3359	.2989	34.8	0	0	1	1	1	0	1	0	0	0	0	0	0	1	0	0	0	0	0	0	0	0	2	1	0
Vancouver	9	.4545	.9326	39.7	0	1	7	0	1	0	0	0	3	0	0	1	0	4	0	0	0	0	0	0	0	0	1	0	0
vandal	3	.0000	.0365	25.6	0	2	0	1	0	0	0	0	0	0	0	0	0	0	0	0	0	0	0	0	0	0	0	3	0
vandalism	7	.0000	.0851	29.3	0	6	0	0	1	0	0	0	0	0	0	0	0	0	0	0	0	0	0	0	0	0	0	7	0
vandals	5	.1398	.1959	32.9	0	3	0	0	0	1	0	1	0	0	0	0	0	1	0	0	0	0	0	0	0	0	0	4	0
vandenBerg	2	.0000	.0389	25.9	0	2	0	0	0	0	0	0	0	0	0	0	0	2	0	0	0	0	0	0	0	0	0	0	0
vanderPoel	2	.0000	.0914	29.6	0	2	0	0	0	0	0	0	2	0	0	0	0	0	0	0	0	0	0	0	0	0	0	0	0
Vandermere	2	.0000	.0914	29.6	2	0	0	0	0	0	0	0	2	0	0	0	0	0	0	0	0	0	0	0	0	0	0	0	0
vane	35	.4748	3.6818	45.7	10	0	6	5	9	5	0	0	6	0	1	0	0	0	0	23	0	0	0	0	2	2	1	0	0
vanes	14	.3429	1.1782	40.7	7	0	0	3	0	1	1	2	4	0	0	0	0	0	0	7	0	0	0	0	0	0	0	3	0
Vang	2	.0000	.0290	24.6	0	0	0	0	2	0	0	0	0	0	0	0	0	0	0	0	0	0	0	0	0	2	0	0	0
vangs	4	.0000	.0419	26.2	0	0	0	0	0	0	4	0	0	0	0	0	0	0	0	0	0	0	0	0	0	0	4	0	0
vanguard	5	.4534	.4712	36.7	0	0	0	0	3	2	0	0	0	0	0	0	0	0	2	0	1	0	0	0	0	0	1	1	0
Vanguard	14	.2234	.7653	38.8	0	11	0	2	0	0	0	1	0	0	0	0	0	0	0	0	1	0	0	0	0	12	0	1	0
vanilla	21	.2354	1.1706	40.7	3	3	0	2	8	0	4	1	3	1	0	0	0	1	0	0	0	0	11	0	0	0	2	3	0
vanish	15	.5734	1.8039	42.6	2	1	0	2	6	1	1	2	3	0	0	1	0	0	1	2	1	2	0	0	0	1	2	2	0
vanished	72	.7168	10.631	50.3	3	7	12	16	17	10	6	1	26	2	1	10	0	2	0	0	1	0	0	0	13	4	2	11	0
vanishes	3	.0000	.0591	27.7	0	3	0	0	0	0	0	0	0	0	0	0	0	0	0	3	0	0	0	0	0	0	0	0	0
vanishing	22	.1741	.9696	39.9	0	2	6	0	11	0	3	0	3	0	0	2	0	1	0	0	0	11	0	0	0	3	2	0	0
vanishing-point	3	.0000	.0434	26.4	0	0	0	0	3	0	0	0	0	0	0	0	0	0	0	0	0	0	0	0	0	3	0	0	0
vanity	13	.6010	1.6489	42.2	0	0	0	0	5	3	5	0	4	0	0	2	0	0	0	0	0	0	1	0	2	3	1	0	0
vanquish	2	.2412	.1091	30.4	0	0	0	0	1	0	1	0	0	0	0	1	0	0	1	0	0	0	0	0	0	0	0	0	0
vanquished	3	.3370	.2430	33.9	1	0	0	1	0	1	0	0	1	0	0	1	0	0	0	0	0	0	0	0	0	0	1	0	0
vans	5	.3906	.4360	36.4	1	0	0	3	1	0	0	0	1	0	0	0	0	0	2	0	0	0	0	0	1	0	0	1	0
vantage	7	.5124	.7463	38.7	0	0	0	0	3	0	3	1	0	0	1	2	0	1	0	1	0	0	0	0	1	0	1	0	0
vapor	209	.5291	23.727	53.8	45	30	15	37	39	22	20	1	18	0	5	0	0	4	2	148	0	0	0	1	6	14	10	1	0
vaporize	2	.1814	.1187	30.7	0	0	0	1	0	0	1	0	1	0	0	0	0	0	0	0	0	0	0	0	0	0	0	1	0
vaporizes	3	.3352	.2077	33.2	0	0	1	0	1	1	0	0	0	0	1	0	0	0	0	0	0	0	0	1	0	0	1	0	0
vapors	16	.5587	1.8807	42.7	0	3	0	4	4	1	2	2	1	0	0	2	0	0	0	7	0	0	0	0	0	2	1	3	0
vapour	2	.0000	.0234	23.7	0	0	0	0	2	0	0	0	0	0	0	0	0	0	0	0	0	0	0	0	2	0	0	0	0
vaqueros	4	.3677	.3659	35.6	0	0	2	0	0	2	0	0	2	0	0	1	0	1	0	0	0	0	0	0	0	0	0	0	0
Vardar	2	.0000	.0389	25.9	0	0	0	0	2	0	0	0	0	0	0	0	0	2	0	0	0	0	0	0	0	0	0	0	0
Varese	6	.0000	.0485	26.9	0	5	0	0	1	0	0	0	0	0	0	0	0	0	0	0	6	0	0	0	0	0	0	0	0
variability	3	.1813	.1402	31.5	0	0	0	0	2	0	1	0	0	0	0	0	0	0	0	1	0	0	0	0	0	0	2	0	0
variable	87	.3880	7.4605	48.7	0	8	19	0	6	18	35	1	1	0	0	0	60	0	0	18	0	0	0	4	0	0	4	0	0
variable-speed	2	.1620	.0760	28.8	0	0	0	0	0	0	1	1	0	0	0	0	0	0	0	0	0	0	0	1	0	0	0	1	0
variables	40	.2460	2.3941	43.8	0	2	4	0	3	16	15	0	0	0	0	0	32	0	0	5	0	0	0	0	0	0	2	1	0
Varian	2	.0000	.0209	23.2	0	0	0	0	0	0	2	0	0	0	0	0	0	0	0	0	0	0	0	0	0	0	2	0	0
variant	11	.3216	.7639	38.8	0	1	0	0	4	2	3	1	0	2	0	0	0	0	7	0	0	0	0	0	0	0	1	1	0
variation	63	.6531	8.3286	49.2	0	8	3	4	26	8	10	4	1	3	1	0	3	0	2	12	27	4	0	2	0	1	4	3	0
variations	87	.7610	13.241	51.2	2	6	9	8	30	15	14	3	5	5	4	0	0	2	1	4	23	4	7	4	0	4	17	7	0
Variations	4	.1789	.1692	32.3	0	0	1	1	2	0	0	0	0	0	0	0	0	0	0	0	3	0	0	0	0	0	1	0	0
varied	105	.8408	17.606	52.5	2	8	7	12	33	20	20	3	12	2	2	6	1	17	1	7	12	5	5	4	1	3	18	9	0
variegated	4	.3679	.3138	35.0	1	0	0	0	1	1	0	1	0	0	1	0	0	0	0	0	0	0	0	0	1	1	1	0	0
varies	78	.8125	12.671	51.0	3	7	9	9	19	13	15	3	3	1	1	1	2	11	1	20	8	0	3	3	1	4	16	3	0
varieties	70	.7740	10.919	50.4	3	3	10	7	29	3	8	7	9	12	0	1	0	4	0	14	0	1	2	2	1	4	16	4	0
variety	399	.8197	65.155	58.1	14	26	45	38	109	63	85	19	13	40	14	8	2	40	4	54	57	19	35	9	2	19	60	23	0
various	620	.8547	105.43	60.2	11	45	73	84	164	113	105	25	45	42	16	9	29	55	18	112	49	21	20	46	11	29	97	21	0
variously	4	.1505	.1615	32.1	0	0	0	0	2	2	0	0	0	0	0	0	0	1	0	0	0	0	0	0	0	0	3	0	0
varmint	12	.4591	1.2059	40.8	0	4	1	0	6	0	1	0	2	0	0	0	0	0	0	1	0	0	0	0	4	4	0	1	0
varmints	5	.3769	.4098	36.1	0	3	0	0	2	0	0	0	0	1	0	0	0	0	0	0	0	0	0	0	2	2	0	0	0
varnish	16	.3167	1.1246	40.5	3	0	2	1	4	2	3	1	1	0	0	0	0	0	0	2	0	0	0	6	1	3	2	1	0
varnished	3	.2986	.1936	32.9	0	0	0	0	1	2	0	0	0	0	0	0	0	0	0	0	1	0	0	1	0	1	0	0	0
varnishes	3	.3847	.2496	34.0	1	0	1	0	0	0	0	1	0	0	0	0	0	0	0	0	0	0	0	0	0	1	1	1	0
varsity	13	.5973	1.6426	42.2	0	0	0	2	4	7	0	0	4	2	0	1	0	0	0	0	0	0	0	0	2	1	0	3	0
varve	2	.0000	.0394	26.0	0	0	0	0	0	0	2	0	0	0	0	0	0	0	0	2	0	0	0	0	0	0	0	0	0
varves	4	.0000	.0789	29.0	0	0	0	0	0	0	4	0	0	0	0	0	0	0	0	4	0	0	0	0	0	0	0	0	0
vary	108	.7790	16.837	52.3	3	3	11	14	36	14	19	8	7	3	4	2	1	9	1	15	9	6	12	8	0	5	19	7	0
Varya	8	.0000	.3655	35.6	0	0	8	0	0	0	0	0	8	0	0	0	0	0	0	0	0	0	0	0	0	0	0	0	0
Varyachka	3	.0000	.1370	31.4	0	0	3	0	0	0	0	0	3	0	0	0	0	0	0	0	0	0	0	0	0	0	0	0	0
varying	56	.7974	8.9231	49.5	1	1	3	1	21	16	12	1	2	2	1	1	0	3	0	14	8	3	3	3	1	1	7	7	0
Vasco	6	.2285	.3387	35.3	0	0	3	1	1	1	0	0	0	0	0	0	0	3	0	0	0	0	0	0	0	0	3	0	0
vase	28	.8354	4.6746	46.7	5	2	4	3	10	3	1	0	4	4	0	3	2	2	1	2	0	1	1	0	3	1	3	1	0
vases	10	.3900	.8872	39.5	5	1	1	1	2	0	0	0	1	0	0	0	4	4	0	0	0	0	0	0	0	1	0	0	0
vassals	2	.2446	.1142	30.6	0	0	0	0	2	0	0	0	0	0	0	0	0	0	0	0	0	0	0	0	1	0	0	1	0
Vassar	5	.1993	.2508	34.0	1	3	0	0	0	0	1	0	0	0	0	1	0	0	0	0	0	0	0	0	0	4	0	0	0
vast	307	.8064	49.719	57.0	14	17	57	60	82	33	24	20	29	6	1	4	1	99	3	28	5	2	1	1	13	29	50	35	0
vastly	12	.4869	1.2226	40.9	0	0	1	1	5	1	3	1	0	0	0	1	0	1	0	1	1	0	0	0	0	0	6	2	0
vastness	16	.6770	2.2160	43.5	0	1	5	1	4	2	3	0	2	0	0	1	0	3	0	0	1	0	0	1	0	3	3	2	0
vat	4	.3721	.3175	35.0	0	0	2	1	0	0	1	0	0	0	0	1	0	0	1	0	0	0	0	0	0	0	2	0	0
Vatican	11	.0789	.3005	34.8	0	0	0	0	2	2	7	0	0	0	0	0	0	1	0	0	0	0	0	0	0	0	0	10	0
Vatne	2	.0000	.0290	24.6	0	0	0	0	2	0	0	0	0	0	0	0	0	0	0	0	0	0	0	0	0	2	0	0	0
vats	7	.4285	.6505	38.1	1	1	0	1	0	0	4	0	0	0	0	0	0	2	0	1	0	0	0	0	1	0	0	3	0
vaudeville	8	.2698	.5040	37.0	0	0	4	0	3	1	0	0	1	0	0	0	0	0	0	0	4	0	0	0	0	0	3	0	0
Vaughan	17	.1524	.6630	38.2	0	0	2	6	7	1	1	0	1	0	0	0	0	0	0	0	14	0	0	0	0	0	1	1	0
vault	16	.6297	2.0999	43.2	0	0	3	6	3	1	2	1	3	0	0	0	5	0	0	2	0	0	0	0	2	1	1	2	0
vaulted	5	.3203	.4009	36.0	0	1	1	0	2	1	0	0	2	0	0	0	0	0	0	0	0	0	0	0	0	1	2	0	0
vaulter	2	.0000	.0394	26.0	0	0	2	0	0	0	0	0	0	0	0	0	0	0	0	2	0	0	0	0	0	0	0	0	0
vaulting	4	.2142	.2512	34.0	0	0	0	0	2	0	2	0	2	0	0	0	0	0	0	0	0	1	0	0	0	0	0	1	0
vaults	2	.2346	.1166	30.7	0	0	0	0	1	0	0	1	0	0	0	0	0	0	0	1	0	0	0	0	0	0	0	1	0
Vb	2	.0000	.0219	23.4	0	0	0	0	0	0	2	0	0	2	0	0	0	0	0	0	0	0	0	0	0	0	0	0	0
VC	2	.0000	.0162	22.1	0	2	0	0	0	0	0	0	0	0	0	0	0	0	2	0	0	0	0	0	0	0	0	0	0
vc/v	2	.0000	.0162	22.1	0	0	0	2	0	0	0	0	0	0	0	0	0	0	2	0	0	0	0	0	0	0	0	0	0
vccv	2	.0000	.0162	22.1	0	0	0	2	0	0	0	0	0	0	0	0	0	0	2	0	0	0	0	0	0	0	0	0	0
vcv	3	.0000	.0243	23.9	0	0	0	3	0	0	0	0	0	0	0	0	0	0	3	0	0	0	0	0	0	0	0	0	0
ve	6	.2373	.3249	35.1	0	1	0	1	0	0	4	0	0	0	0	4	0	0	2	0	0	0	0	0	0	0	0	0	0
veal	21	.4596	2.0364	43.1	2	7	0	0	8	0	4	0	1	10	0	0	0	1	0	1	0	0	4	0	0	2	1	1	0
vector	24	.0000	.3592	35.6	0	0	0	0	0	5	19	0	0	0	0	0	24	0	0	0	0	0	0	0	0	0	0	0	0
vectors	13	.0000	.1946	32.9	0	0	0	0	0	3	10	0	0	0	0	0	13	0	0	0	0	0	0	0	0	0	0	0	0
Vee	14	.0000	.6396	38.1	0	0	0	14	0	0	0	0	14	0	0	0	0	0	0	0	0	0	0	0	0	0	0	0	0
veered	3	.2261	.2131	33.3	1	0	1	0	1	0	0	0	2	0	0	0	0	0	0	0	0	0	0	0	1	0	0	0	0

XR Vance
9R vandalized
4R Vandals
5P VandenVosReynaerde
7R Vander
8Q vanderMeer
5P vanderVeen
3A Vanderpane
8D Vanderpool's
6H Vanek
7F Vaner
5R Vanessa
9Q vang
5P vanish'd
7N vanities
7A Vanity
9R Vanocur
9Q Vanolis
7A vanquishing
XH vapor-laden
9Q vapor-tube
7R vaporfree
7H vaporized
5A vaquero
8J Vardell
5N Varden
3A vari-colored
5Q vari-typers
3P variable-stability
9Q Varian's
8E variance
4Q variants
6G Variety
9M Varityper
6N varlet
7N varlets
6B vary-variation
9K Vasari
6Q vascular
7Q vase-shaped
4K vaseline
7D Vaseline
7H vasopressin
9Q vaster
9D vasty
9R Vatican's
7F Vatter
XR Vaucluse
9R vaulters
9D vaulty
8A vaunted
9D vaunting
9M VAXY
6J Vayr-dee
6B vb
4G VCC
7Q veal-calipee
3F vebetables
8J Vechernitsi
7A Vedder
9Q Vedras
7M vee
XH vee-shaped
6A Vee's

Word Type	F	D	U	SFI	3 Gr 3	4 Gr 4	5 Gr 5	6 Gr 6	7 Gr 7	8 Gr 8	9 Gr 9	X UnGr	A Read	B Eng & Gr	C Comp	D Lit	E Math	F Soc Stud	G Spell	H Sci	J Music	K Art	L Home Ec	M Shop	N Lib F	P Lib NF	Q Lib Ref	R Mag	S Rel
veering	3	.3408	.2477	33.9	0	1	0	1	1	0	0	0	1	0	0	1	0	0	0	0	0	0	0	0	0	1	0	0	0
veers	2	.0000	.0394	26.0	0	0	0	1	1	0	0	0	0	0	0	0	0	0	0	2	0	0	0	0	0	0	0	0	0
Vega	5	.0000	.0986	29.9	0	0	1	0	0	0	0	4	0	0	0	0	0	0	0	5	0	0	0	0	0	0	0	0	0
vegetable	112	.5289	12.631	51.0	26	16	9	14	18	9	17	3	24	3	0	1	0	16	5	12	0	0	26	0	4	4	12	5	0
vegetable-fruit	2	.0000	.0394	26.0	1	0	0	1	0	0	0	0	0	0	0	0	0	0	0	2	0	0	0	0	0	0	0	0	0
vegetables	378	.6001	47.337	56.8	90	54	37	45	60	23	62	7	59	7	0	5	0	105	5	51	3	2	84	0	9	22	19	6	1
Vegetables	4	.4016	.3427	35.3	3	0	0	0	0	0	1	0	0	0	0	0	0	0	0	1	0	0	1	0	1	0	1	0	0
vegetarian	2	.0000	.0209	23.2	0	0	0	0	2	0	0	0	0	0	0	0	0	0	0	0	0	0	0	0	0	0	2	0	0
vegetation	57	.6771	7.8724	49.0	2	8	3	8	18	9	6	3	2	0	0	2	0	16	0	8	0	1	0	1	1	4	18	4	0
vehement	4	.3678	.3187	35.0	0	0	1	0	0	2	1	0	0	0	0	0	0	0	0	0	1	0	0	0	0	1	0	2	0
vehemently	6	.4543	.6109	37.9	0	1	2	0	2	0	1	0	2	0	0	0	0	0	0	0	0	0	0	0	1	0	1	2	0
vehicle	68	.6298	8.7904	49.4	2	7	2	9	24	3	15	6	3	1	0	2	4	1	1	19	0	0	0	7	2	3	5	20	0
vehicles	69	.7532	10.518	50.2	4	5	13	5	24	5	13	0	8	1	0	2	1	7	1	13	0	0	0	2	1	9	10	14	0
veil	14	.6019	1.7610	42.5	3	1	2	1	4	1	2	0	3	0	1	3	0	0	0	0	0	0	0	0	1	4	1	1	0
veiled	8	.4586	.7687	38.9	0	0	0	2	2	2	2	0	0	1	0	3	0	0	0	0	2	0	0	0	0	2	0	0	0
veils	7	.3996	.6215	37.9	0	1	3	0	2	0	1	0	1	0	0	0	0	1	0	1	3	0	0	0	0	0	1	0	0
vein	29	.5136	3.1667	45.0	2	9	4	3	2	2	4	3	0	0	0	0	0	1	1	19	1	0	0	0	0	2	4	1	0
veiner	2	.0000	.0050	17.0	0	0	0	0	0	0	2	0	0	0	0	0	0	0	0	0	0	0	0	2	0	0	0	0	0
veins	79	.6558	10.692	50.3	11	9	5	19	7	13	10	5	6	1	0	7	0	2	3	46	1	1	0	0	2	4	6	0	0
Velasco	8	.0000	.0972	29.9	0	0	0	4	0	0	4	0	0	0	0	0	0	0	0	0	0	0	0	0	0	0	0	8	0
Velasco's	2	.0000	.0243	23.9	0	0	0	2	0	0	0	0	0	0	0	0	0	0	0	0	0	0	0	0	0	0	0	2	0
veld	4	.1505	.1615	32.1	0	0	0	1	3	0	0	0	0	0	0	0	0	1	0	0	0	0	0	0	0	0	3	0	0
veldt	9	.0000	.4111	36.1	0	6	0	1	0	0	2	0	9	0	0	0	0	0	0	0	0	0	0	0	0	0	0	0	0
Veldt	9	.0000	.1055	30.2	0	9	0	0	0	0	0	0	0	0	0	0	0	0	0	0	0	0	0	0	9	0	0	0	0
vellum	3	.0000	.0365	25.6	0	0	0	0	3	0	0	0	0	0	0	0	0	0	0	0	0	0	0	0	0	0	0	3	0
velocities	4	.3823	.3406	35.3	0	0	0	0	1	2	0	1	0	0	0	0	1	0	0	2	0	0	0	0	0	0	1	0	0
velocity	62	.6212	7.9349	49.0	0	0	1	11	12	17	16	5	0	0	0	1	10	0	1	29	0	0	0	1	2	0	11	7	0
velvet	50	.8271	8.3005	49.2	3	7	7	11	9	4	6	3	13	3	1	10	0	2	3	4	1	1	3	0	6	1	1	1	0
Velvet	51	.1569	2.0676	43.2	0	0	0	0	49	2	0	0	0	0	0	1	0	0	0	0	0	1	0	0	49	0	0	0	0
Velvet's	3	.0000	.0352	25.5	0	0	0	0	3	0	0	0	0	0	0	0	0	0	0	0	0	0	0	0	3	0	0	0	0
velveteen	4	.1434	.1650	32.2	1	0	0	0	3	0	0	0	1	1	2	0	0	0	0	0	0	0	0	0	0	0	0	0	0
velvets	2	.1378	.0662	28.2	0	0	0	0	0	1	0	1	0	0	0	0	0	0	0	0	0	1	0	0	0	0	0	1	0
velvety	13	.5527	1.5140	41.8	3	2	1	2	2	1	0	2	2	0	0	3	0	0	0	2	3	0	0	0	1	2	0	0	0
ven	4	.1703	.1638	32.1	0	0	0	0	3	1	0	0	0	0	0	0	0	0	3	0	0	0	0	0	1	0	0	0	0
Vendice	5	.0000	.0724	28.6	0	0	0	0	5	0	0	0	0	0	0	0	0	0	0	0	0	0	0	0	0	5	0	0	0
vendor	3	.2346	.1705	32.3	0	2	0	1	0	0	0	0	0	0	0	0	2	0	0	0	0	0	0	0	0	0	0	1	0
vendors	8	.1260	.2975	34.7	1	1	0	2	2	1	1	0	1	0	0	0	0	1	0	0	6	0	0	0	0	0	0	0	0
veneer	2	.0000	.0290	24.6	0	0	1	0	1	0	0	0	0	0	0	0	0	0	0	0	0	0	0	0	0	2	0	0	0
venerable	6	.4726	.5923	37.7	0	1	0	0	1	1	3	0	0	2	0	1	0	0	0	0	0	0	0	0	2	0	1	0	0
veneration	2	.2441	.1127	30.5	0	0	1	0	1	0	0	0	0	0	0	0	0	0	0	0	0	0	0	0	1	0	1	0	0
Venetia	2	.2401	.1133	30.5	0	0	1	0	1	0	0	0	0	0	0	0	0	0	0	0	0	0	0	0	0	1	1	0	0
Venetian	6	.4194	.5498	37.4	0	1	2	0	1	1	1	0	1	0	0	1	0	0	0	0	1	1	0	0	0	2	0	0	0
Venetians	2	.1247	.0633	28.0	0	0	1	0	0	1	0	0	0	0	0	0	0	0	0	0	0	1	0	0	0	1	0	0	0
Venezuela	27	.3442	2.1459	43.3	1	0	9	9	3	2	2	1	0	0	0	0	0	22	0	0	1	0	0	0	0	2	1	1	0
Venezuelan	5	.0000	.0972	29.9	0	0	0	2	0	1	2	0	0	0	0	0	0	5	0	0	0	0	0	0	0	0	0	0	0
Venezuelans	3	.0000	.0583	27.7	0	0	1	2	0	0	0	0	0	0	0	0	0	3	0	0	0	0	0	0	0	0	0	0	0
vengeance	10	.5759	1.1952	40.8	0	0	3	0	5	1	1	0	1	0	0	2	0	0	0	0	1	0	0	0	3	2	1	0	0
vengeful	2	.1733	.1149	30.6	0	0	0	0	2	0	0	0	1	1	0	0	0	0	0	0	0	0	0	0	0	0	0	0	0
Venice	27	.5920	3.3592	45.3	8	0	3	5	3	7	1	0	4	0	0	1	1	9	0	0	1	0	0	0	0	7	4	0	0
venison	22	.5658	2.6221	44.2	5	6	2	1	7	0	1	0	5	0	0	2	0	0	1	0	5	0	0	0	7	1	1	0	0
Venizelos	2	.0000	.0389	25.9	0	0	0	0	2	0	0	0	0	0	0	0	0	2	0	0	0	0	0	0	0	0	0	0	0
Venny	4	.0000	.0579	27.6	0	4	0	0	0	0	0	0	0	0	0	0	0	0	0	0	0	0	0	0	0	4	0	0	0
venom	5	.3144	.3496	35.4	0	0	0	0	4	0	1	0	0	0	0	0	0	0	1	1	0	0	0	0	0	0	3	0	0
vent	16	.6207	2.0391	43.1	0	0	0	0	8	3	1	4	1	0	0	1	0	0	0	2	0	0	0	1	6	2	2	1	0
vented	2	.1814	.1187	30.7	0	0	0	0	2	0	0	0	1	0	0	0	0	0	0	0	0	0	0	0	0	0	0	1	0
ventilated	5	.4536	.4935	36.9	1	0	0	0	1	2	1	0	1	0	0	1	0	0	0	1	1	0	1	0	0	0	0	0	0
ventilating	2	.1698	.1133	30.5	0	0	1	0	1	0	0	0	1	0	0	0	0	0	0	0	0	0	0	0	0	0	1	0	0
ventilation	10	.3809	.7983	39.0	1	0	3	0	4	2	0	0	0	0	0	1	0	0	0	0	1	0	0	3	0	0	4	1	0
ventilator	5	.0000	.0537	27.3	0	0	0	0	0	0	0	5	0	0	0	5	0	0	0	0	0	0	0	0	0	0	0	0	0
ventricle	4	.0000	.0789	29.0	0	0	1	0	0	3	0	0	0	0	0	0	0	0	0	4	0	0	0	0	0	0	0	0	0
ventricles	5	.0000	.0986	29.9	0	0	1	0	0	4	0	0	0	0	0	0	0	0	0	5	0	0	0	0	0	0	0	0	0
ventriloquist	4	.3875	.3418	35.3	0	1	0	2	1	0	0	0	0	0	0	1	0	0	0	2	0	0	0	0	0	0	1	0	0
ventriloquists	2	.0000	.0394	26.0	0	0	0	2	0	0	0	0	0	0	0	0	0	0	0	2	0	0	0	0	0	0	0	0	0
vents	2	.0000	.0914	29.6	0	0	2	0	0	0	0	0	2	0	0	0	0	0	0	0	0	0	0	0	0	0	0	0	0
Ventura	2	.2152	.1357	31.3	0	1	0	0	1	0	0	0	1	0	0	0	0	1	0	0	0	0	0	0	0	0	0	0	0
venture	50	.7281	7.4167	48.7	0	3	7	10	12	7	8	3	11	1	3	4	0	6	1	0	1	0	0	0	4	2	7	10	0
ventured	31	.7119	4.4811	46.5	1	1	6	4	8	6	5	0	3	4	1	1	0	6	0	0	0	0	0	0	2	4	7	3	0
ventures	8	.4318	.7696	38.9	1	0	0	3	0	0	3	1	2	0	0	2	0	0	0	0	0	0	0	0	0	0	1	3	0
Ventures	4	.0000	.1827	32.6	0	4	0	0	0	0	0	0	4	0	0	0	0	0	0	0	0	0	0	0	0	0	0	0	0
venturesome	4	.4525	.4044	36.1	0	0	0	1	1	1	0	1	1	0	0	0	0	1	0	0	0	0	0	0	1	0	0	1	0
venturing	6	.3987	.5361	37.3	0	0	0	1	4	1	0	0	1	0	0	0	0	0	0	1	0	0	0	0	2	0	2	0	0
Venus	151	.5023	16.286	52.1	24	51	12	11	16	4	33	0	4	6	0	3	8	0	1	104	0	0	0	0	0	13	9	3	0
Venus'	3	.0000	.0591	27.7	1	0	0	0	2	0	0	0	0	0	0	0	0	0	0	3	0	0	0	0	0	0	0	0	0
Venutian	13	.0000	.1423	31.5	0	0	0	0	13	0	0	0	0	13	0	0	0	0	0	0	0	0	0	0	0	0	0	0	0
ver-croo	2	.0000	.0162	22.1	2	0	0	0	0	0	0	0	0	0	0	0	0	0	0	0	2	0	0	0	0	0	0	0	0
Ver-croo	3	.0000	.0243	23.8	3	0	0	0	0	0	0	0	0	0	0	0	0	0	0	0	3	0	0	0	0	0	0	0	0
ver-y	2	.0000	.0243	23.9	2	0	0	0	0	0	0	0	0	0	0	0	0	0	0	0	0	0	0	0	0	0	0	2	0
Vera	7	.2373	.3777	35.8	0	5	0	0	2	0	0	0	0	0	0	0	0	0	0	0	0	0	2	0	0	0	0	5	0
Veraart	2	.0000	.0914	29.6	0	0	0	0	0	0	2	0	2	0	0	0	0	0	0	0	0	0	0	0	0	0	0	0	0
Veracruz	6	.2285	.3387	35.3	0	0	5	0	0	1	0	0	0	0	0	0	0	3	0	0	0	0	0	0	0	0	3	0	0
veranda	9	.5409	1.0707	40.3	0	3	0	1	2	1	1	1	4	0	0	1	0	1	0	0	0	0	0	0	2	0	0	1	0
verandas	4	.3701	.3190	35.0	0	1	0	1	1	1	0	0	0	0	0	0	0	1	0	0	0	0	0	1	0	0	1	1	0
verb	885	.3831	72.236	58.6	46	78	137	119	191	141	172	1	16	623	83	3	1	0	148	0	0	0	0	0	0	0	11	0	0
Verb	5	.0767	.1579	32.0	1	0	1	0	3	0	0	0	1	4	0	0	0	0	0	0	0	0	0	0	0	0	0	0	0
verbal	25	.4967	2.5887	44.1	0	0	0	2	3	9	11	0	0	14	0	0	3	1	3	1	1	0	0	0	0	1	1	0	0
verbals	7	.2995	.4514	36.5	0	0	0	0	0	3	4	0	0	4	2	0	0	0	1	0	0	0	0	0	0	0	0	0	0
verbs	583	.3716	46.424	56.7	32	37	76	129	131	80	98	0	9	396	17	7	2	0	146	0	0	0	0	0	0	0	6	0	0
Verbs	2	.2408	.1091	30.4	0	0	1	0	0	0	1	0	0	1	0	0	0	0	1	0	0	0	0	0	0	0	0	0	0
verdant	2	.2446	.1142	30.6	0	0	0	0	1	0	0	1	0	0	0	0	0	0	0	0	0	0	0	0	1	0	0	1	0
Verde	4	.3397	.3024	34.8	0	0	1	0	0	2	0	1	0	2	0	0	0	1	0	0	0	0	0	0	0	0	0	1	0
Verdi	11	.2528	.7007	38.5	0	0	0	4	3	3	1	0	3	0	0	0	0	0	0	0	6	0	0	0	0	0	2	0	0
Verdi's	2	.2303	.1079	30.3	0	0	1	0	0	1	0	0	0	0	0	0	0	0	0	0	1	0	0	0	0	1	0	0	0
verdict	15	.6601	2.0245	43.1	1	1	5	0	2	2	3	1	2	1	0	2	0	0	1	0	1	0	0	0	5	0	2	1	0
verdicts	2	.0000	.0389	25.9	0	0	0	0	0	2	0	0	0	0	0	0	0	2	0	0	0	0	0	0	0	0	0	0	0

7L Vegetable
7L Vegetable-Fruit
9R vegetable-like
7Q vegetarians
7Q vegetative
XH Vegetative
4A veiltail
9D veinous
7P Velasquez
9B Veleike
4N vell
4A velly
XQ velum
7A velvet-black
3A velvet-eyed
5F velvet-like
7D velvet-lined
7P velvetlike
3N Ven-ge-ance
4K Venard
7P Vendice's
8R vending
7F veneers
5E venetian
9Q Veneto-Illyrian
9F Venezuela's
9D venge
9D Vengeance
8G veni-
8Q venial
8G venier
7Q venom-filled
7Q venomous
4A venomously
6F Venta
9H ventifact
8M ventilate
5Q ventilators
8Q ventricular
XR venture's
7Q venturer
7M venturi
9Q venule
9Q venules
4A Venus's-flytrap
4A Venus's-flytraps
8D Venusian
7B Venutian's
7B Venutian's-eye
8A Vera's
7C verb-adverb
6J verbally
8P verbatim
6R verbena
6G verbum

Word Type	F	D	U	SFI	3 Gr 3	4 Gr 4	5 Gr 5	6 Gr 6	7 Gr 7	8 Gr 8	9 Gr 9	X UnGr	A Read	B Eng & Gr	C Comp	D Lit	E Math	F Soc Stud	G Spell	H Sci	J Music	K Art	L Home Ec	M Shop	N Lib F	P Lib NF	Q Lib Ref	R Mag	S Rel
Verdun	2	.2285	.1129	30.5	0	0	0	0	1	1	0	0	0	0	0	0	0	1	0	0	0	0	0	0	0	0	1	0	0
verdure	3	.3766	.2480	33.9	0	0	0	0	2	1	0	0	0	0	0	0	0	1	0	0	0	0	0	0	1	0	1	0	0
Vere	5	.0000	.0972	29.9	0	0	0	0	0	0	5	0	0	0	0	0	0	5	0	0	0	0	0	0	0	0	0	0	0
verge	4	.2947	.2869	34.6	2	1	0	0	0	1	0	0	1	0	0	0	0	0	0	0	0	0	0	0	1	0	2	0	0
verification	3	.2019	.1477	31.7	0	0	0	0	1	2	0	0	0	0	0	0	1	0	0	0	0	0	0	0	0	0	2	0	0
verified	5	.3461	.3825	35.8	0	1	0	0	2	1	1	0	0	0	0	0	0	0	0	1	0	0	0	0	0	0	2	0	0
verify	9	.3957	.7689	38.9	0	0	0	0	2	4	2	1	0	0	0	0	6	0	0	0	0	1	0	0	0	0	1	1	0
verismo	2	.2303	.1079	30.3	0	0	1	0	0	1	0	0	0	0	0	0	0	0	0	0	1	0	0	0	0	1	0	0	0
veritable	5	.3053	.3370	35.3	0	0	0	0	1	0	3	1	0	0	1	0	0	0	0	1	0	0	0	0	0	0	3	0	0
Verlaine	3	.3782	.2435	33.9	0	0	1	0	1	1	0	0	0	0	0	0	0	0	0	0	1	0	0	0	0	1	1	0	0
Vermeer	5	.2394	.2685	34.3	0	0	0	0	0	4	1	0	0	0	0	0	0	0	0	0	0	1	0	0	0	0	4	0	0
vermiculite	12	.3764	1.0067	40.0	0	0	0	0	2	10	0	0	0	0	0	0	0	0	0	8	0	1	0	0	0	0	3	0	0
vermilion	4	.2427	.2305	33.6	0	2	0	0	2	0	0	0	0	0	0	0	0	0	0	0	0	0	0	0	2	2	0	0	0
Vermilion	4	.1966	.1884	32.8	0	0	0	0	0	3	1	0	0	0	0	1	0	0	0	0	0	0	0	0	0	0	3	0	0
vermin	2	.2446	.1122	30.5	0	0	0	0	2	0	0	0	0	0	0	1	0	0	0	0	0	0	0	0	0	0	1	0	0
Vermont	24	.6521	3.2376	45.1	1	4	5	3	0	7	3	1	4	2	1	0	0	8	1	0	1	0	0	0	0	1	0	6	0
Vermont's	2	.0000	.0389	25.9	0	0	1	0	0	1	0	0	0	0	0	0	0	2	0	0	0	0	0	0	0	0	0	0	0
Vermonters	2	.2433	.1158	30.6	1	0	1	0	0	0	0	0	0	0	0	0	0	0	0	0	0	0	0	0	0	1	0	1	0
vernacular	5	.3726	.4014	36.0	0	0	1	0	2	1	0	1	0	1	0	0	0	0	0	0	0	0	0	0	0	0	2	2	0
vernal	5	.3660	.4140	36.2	0	0	1	0	0	0	0	4	0	0	0	0	0	0	0	3	0	0	0	0	0	1	0	1	0
Vernal	3	.0000	.0314	25.0	0	0	3	0	0	0	0	0	0	0	0	0	0	0	0	0	0	0	0	0	0	0	3	0	0
Verne	16	.5383	1.8992	42.8	0	0	2	3	7	0	3	1	7	3	0	0	1	0	0	3	0	0	0	0	0	0	2	0	0
Verne's	3	.1200	.1302	31.1	0	0	0	2	1	0	0	0	1	2	0	0	0	0	0	0	0	0	0	0	0	0	0	0	0
Vernelle	10	.0000	.4568	36.6	0	0	10	0	0	0	0	0	10	0	0	0	0	0	0	0	0	0	0	0	0	0	0	0	0
Vernon	23	.5087	2.5266	44.0	3	3	4	0	1	10	2	0	2	0	0	0	2	14	0	1	1	0	0	0	0	2	0	1	0
Vernon's	2	.2427	.1159	30.6	0	2	0	0	0	0	0	0	0	0	0	0	1	0	0	0	0	0	0	0	0	0	0	1	0
Verona	6	.2212	.4198	36.2	0	0	0	0	0	4	2	0	4	0	0	2	0	0	0	0	0	0	0	0	0	0	0	0	0
Verplanck	3	.0000	.0365	25.6	0	0	0	0	0	3	0	0	0	0	0	0	0	0	0	0	0	0	0	0	0	0	0	3	0
Verrazano	2	.0000	.0209	23.2	0	0	0	0	0	0	2	0	0	0	0	0	0	0	0	0	0	0	0	0	0	0	2	0	0
Verrazano-Narrows	2	.2391	.1133	30.5	0	0	0	1	0	0	1	0	0	0	0	0	1	0	0	0	0	0	0	0	0	0	1	0	0
Verrazano's	2	.0000	.0209	23.2	0	0	0	0	0	0	2	0	0	0	0	0	0	0	0	0	0	0	0	0	0	0	2	0	0
versa	8	.4575	.7628	38.8	0	0	1	0	4	1	2	0	0	0	0	0	0	0	0	0	1	0	0	1	0	0	2	4	0
Versailles	8	.4667	.7915	39.0	0	1	0	1	1	4	0	1	0	0	0	0	0	3	0	0	0	1	0	0	2	1	1	0	0
versatile	16	.5203	1.7453	42.4	0	0	1	2	6	3	2	2	2	0	0	1	0	0	0	0	1	0	2	0	0	0	6	4	0
versatility	3	.2799	.1829	32.6	0	0	0	0	2	1	0	0	0	0	1	0	0	0	0	0	0	0	0	0	0	0	1	1	0
verse	117	.4213	10.506	50.2	20	21	17	15	10	11	22	1	10	14	1	9	0	0	2	0	71	0	0	0	2	2	5	1	0
versed	3	.3871	.2488	34.0	0	1	0	0	0	2	0	0	0	1	0	0	0	0	0	0	0	0	0	0	0	0	1	1	0
verses	45	.3104	3.1878	45.0	10	10	4	7	4	2	6	2	6	1	0	0	0	1	0	1	29	0	0	0	4	1	1	1	0
Verses	2	.0000	.0914	29.6	1	0	0	0	1	0	0	0	2	0	0	0	0	0	0	0	0	0	0	0	0	0	0	0	0
version	81	.5629	9.3815	49.7	0	5	16	8	20	9	20	3	3	6	0	3	0	2	1	2	30	0	0	0	0	4	14	16	0
Version	14	.3392	1.0221	40.1	0	8	1	0	5	0	0	0	0	0	0	0	0	0	3	0	2	0	0	0	0	0	9	0	0
versions	35	.5139	3.7405	45.7	0	2	4	7	12	4	4	2	2	4	0	3	0	0	0	1	14	0	0	0	0	0	6	5	0
versus	3	.0000	.0434	26.4	2	0	0	0	1	0	0	0	0	0	0	0	0	0	0	0	0	0	0	0	0	3	0	0	0
vertebrae	5	.2968	.3358	35.3	0	0	0	0	3	0	2	0	0	0	0	0	0	0	0	1	0	0	0	0	1	0	3	0	0
vertebral	3	.1813	.1402	31.5	0	0	0	0	2	0	1	0	0	0	0	0	0	0	0	1	0	0	0	0	0	0	2	0	0
Vertebrata	2	.2278	.1128	30.5	0	0	0	0	1	0	1	0	0	0	0	0	0	0	0	1	0	0	0	0	0	0	1	0	0
vertebrate	21	.2227	1.1618	40.7	0	0	1	0	15	0	3	2	0	0	0	0	0	0	0	10	0	0	0	0	0	0	11	0	0
vertebrates	36	.2779	2.3663	43.7	2	2	2	1	23	0	6	0	0	0	0	0	0	0	0	19	0	0	0	0	0	0	16	1	0
vertex	43	.0286	.9263	39.7	0	6	2	6	10	10	9	0	2	0	0	0	41	0	0	0	0	0	0	0	0	0	0	0	0
vertical	234	.5527	26.667	54.3	17	35	30	11	55	18	63	5	4	3	0	0	107	7	3	17	5	16	2	45	0	3	9	13	0
vertically	19	.6212	2.4024	43.8	1	0	3	0	9	0	4	2	0	1	0	0	1	0	0	4	1	0	1	3	0	2	4	2	0
vertices	32	.0638	.8454	39.3	0	3	3	5	5	15	1	0	0	0	0	0	31	0	0	0	0	0	0	0	0	0	1	0	0
vertigo	2	.2437	.1129	30.5	0	0	0	0	1	0	0	1	0	0	0	0	0	0	0	0	0	0	0	0	0	0	1	1	0
verve	3	.3826	.2445	33.9	0	0	0	0	1	1	1	0	0	0	0	0	0	0	0	0	1	0	0	0	0	0	1	1	0
very	5997	.9717	1149.1	70.6	1297	1153	646	833	950	531	460	127	1854	300	56	386	67	578	93	787	183	83	83	76	454	524	204	262	7
Very	3	.2283	.1611	32.1	0	3	0	0	0	0	0	0	0	1	0	0	0	0	0	0	0	0	0	0	2	0	0	0	0
Verygood	6	.0000	.2741	34.4	0	0	6	0	0	0	0	0	6	0	0	0	0	0	0	0	0	0	0	0	0	0	0	0	0
Vesalius	4	.0000	.0789	29.0	0	0	0	0	0	3	1	0	0	0	0	0	0	0	0	4	0	0	0	0	0	0	0	0	0
Vespucius	2	.0000	.0209	23.2	0	0	2	0	0	0	0	0	0	0	0	0	0	0	0	0	0	0	0	0	0	0	2	0	0
vessel	84	.7728	13.254	51.2	0	6	10	26	26	7	7	2	34	0	3	2	0	6	0	8	3	1	0	0	4	2	13	8	0
vessel's	5	.3842	.4760	36.8	0	0	0	2	2	0	1	0	3	0	0	1	0	0	0	0	0	0	0	0	0	0	0	1	0
vessels	163	.6785	22.735	53.6	16	12	33	14	31	30	16	11	14	3	0	4	2	32	0	65	2	0	1	0	3	5	27	5	0
vest	21	.6247	2.7508	44.4	3	3	0	2	7	5	1	0	6	0	0	5	3	1	0	0	1	0	0	0	2	0	0	3	0
vestal	2	.2407	.1138	30.6	0	0	0	0	0	0	1	1	0	0	0	1	0	0	0	0	0	0	0	0	0	1	0	0	0
vested	7	.3375	.5334	37.3	0	0	0	0	2	4	1	0	0	0	0	0	0	3	0	0	0	0	0	0	0	1	3	0	0
vestibule	3	.2357	.2199	33.4	0	0	0	1	0	1	0	1	2	0	0	0	0	0	0	0	0	0	0	0	0	1	0	0	0
vestige	2	.2152	.1357	31.3	0	0	1	1	0	0	0	0	1	0	0	0	0	1	0	0	0	0	0	0	0	0	0	0	0
vestiges	4	.3831	.3409	35.3	1	0	0	0	2	1	0	0	0	0	0	0	0	0	0	2	0	0	0	0	0	1	1	0	0
vestments	3	.1910	.1473	31.7	1	0	0	0	1	1	0	0	0	0	0	0	0	1	0	0	0	0	0	0	2	0	0	0	0
Vestris	2	.0000	.0209	23.2	0	0	0	0	0	2	0	0	0	0	0	0	0	0	0	0	0	0	0	0	0	0	2	0	0
vestry	3	.0000	.0352	25.5	0	3	0	0	0	0	0	0	0	0	0	0	0	0	0	0	0	0	0	0	3	0	0	0	0
Vesuvius	16	.5136	1.8803	42.7	1	0	0	13	2	0	0	0	10	0	0	0	0	1	0	1	0	0	0	0	0	2	2	0	0
vet	4	.0996	.1523	31.8	2	1	0	1	0	0	0	0	1	0	0	0	0	0	0	0	0	0	0	0	0	0	0	3	0
veteran	19	.5359	2.1600	43.3	1	1	1	2	7	6	1	0	3	0	1	1	0	3	0	0	0	0	0	0	0	1	1	9	0
VETERAN	5	.0000	.0537	27.3	0	0	0	0	5	0	0	0	0	0	0	5	0	0	0	0	0	0	0	0	0	0	0	0	0
veterans	22	.4320	2.1269	43.3	0	0	2	0	1	16	2	1	3	0	0	0	0	12	0	0	0	0	0	0	0	1	1	5	0
Veterans'	2	.0000	.0209	23.2	0	2	0	0	0	0	0	0	0	0	0	0	0	0	0	0	0	0	0	0	0	0	2	0	0
veterinarian	4	.3862	.3425	35.3	0	0	0	0	2	1	0	1	0	0	0	0	0	0	0	2	0	0	0	0	1	0	0	1	0
veterinary	3	.3870	.2486	34.0	0	1	0	0	1	0	1	0	0	0	0	1	0	0	0	0	0	0	0	0	0	0	1	1	0
veto	15	.3639	1.2247	40.9	7	0	1	0	2	4	1	0	0	0	0	0	0	6	0	0	0	0	0	0	0	7	2	0	0
vetoed	4	.3831	.3415	35.3	1	0	0	0	0	2	1	0	0	0	0	0	0	2	0	0	0	0	0	0	0	1	0	1	0
vetoes	2	.2408	.1204	30.8	1	0	0	0	0	1	0	0	0	0	0	0	0	1	0	0	0	0	0	0	0	1	0	0	0
vetoing	2	.0000	.0290	24.6	2	0	0	0	0	0	0	0	0	0	0	0	0	0	0	0	0	0	0	0	0	2	0	0	0
vexation	3	.1250	.1342	31.3	0	1	1	0	1	0	0	0	1	0	0	0	0	0	0	0	0	0	0	0	2	0	0	0	0
vexed	5	.1530	.1990	33.0	1	0	0	1	0	1	2	0	0	0	0	4	0	0	0	0	0	0	0	0	0	1	0	0	0
vexing	3	.3766	.2497	34.0	0	0	0	0	0	2	1	0	0	0	0	0	0	1	0	0	0	0	0	0	0	1	1	0	0
vhf	3	.0000	.0314	25.0	0	0	0	0	3	0	0	0	0	0	0	0	0	0	0	0	0	0	0	0	0	0	3	0	0
VI	14	.4741	1.3950	41.4	3	1	2	1	2	1	4	0	0	0	0	0	3	1	0	0	1	0	0	0	0	1	7	1	0
vi-	2	.0000	.0914	29.6	0	0	2	0	0	0	0	0	2	0	0	0	0	0	0	0	0	0	0	0	0	0	0	0	0
via	14	.4510	1.3471	41.3	0	0	3	2	4	0	4	1	0	0	0	0	0	2	0	1	0	0	0	0	0	2	2	7	0
Via	4	.3790	.3299	35.2	0	0	2	0	0	1	1	0	0	0	0	0	0	0	0	0	0	0	0	0	0	2	1	1	0
viable	3	.2321	.1635	32.1	0	0	0	1	1	1	0	0	0	0	0	0	0	0	0	0	0	0	0	0	0	0	1	2	0
viaducts	2	.2405	.1205	30.8	1	0	0	0	0	0	0	1	0	0	0	0	0	0	0	1	0	0	0	0	0	1	0	0	0
vibrant	2	.2437	.1129	30.5	1	0	0	0	1	0	0	0	0	0	0	0	0	0	0	0	0	0	0	0	0	0	1	1	0
vibraphone	2	.0000	.0215	23.3	0	0	0	0	2	0	0	0	0	0	0	2	0	0	0	0	0	0	0	0	0	0	0	0	0
vibrate	84	.5976	10.394	50.2	14	7	4	23	12	20	3	1	1	1	0	1	0	0	3	50	18	2	0	1	0	4	3	0	0

9F Vere's
7R Verey
5P Verga
XR Vergilian
XR verging
5P veriest
9Q verifiable
7R verifying
9R verities
8Q Vermeer's
7D vermillion
9H vermin-proof
5R Vermont-NewYork
7R Vermonter
XR vermouth
9R Verna
9E vernier
9Q versification
9Q versified
4Q Versions
3P versts
7B Versus
9R verte
XN Veruca
5P Verwoerd
7Q very-high-frequency
8Q Vesnin
XP vespers
7N vespertilios
5F Vespucci
5B vestigare
7D vests
7P vet's
9Q vetch
8F Veterans
3Q veterinarians
7B vetter
5R vex
4G VHMF
7E vi
8B viaduct
7P vials
3P Viareggio

Word Type	F	D	U	SFI	3 Gr 3	4 Gr 4	5 Gr 5	6 Gr 6	7 Gr 7	8 Gr 8	9 Gr 9	X UnGr	A Read	B Eng & Gr	C Comp	D Lit	E Math	F Soc Stud	G Spell	H Sci	J Music	K Art	L Home Ec	M Shop	N Lib F	P Lib NF	Q Lib Ref	R Mag	S Rel
vibrated	8	.3719	.6725	38.3	1	1	0	2	4	0	0	0	1	0	0	1	0	0	0	3	3	0	0	0	0	0	0	0	0
vibrates	39	.3200	2.8704	44.6	6	3	4	8	10	6	1	1	0	0	0	0	0	0	0	25	12	0	0	0	0	1	1	0	0
vibrating	73	.4163	6.5879	48.2	7	12	9	9	14	18	2	2	1	0	0	0	0	0	0	35	29	0	0	1	0	2	4	1	0
vibration	61	.5478	6.9365	48.4	5	8	9	4	17	9	4	5	2	1	0	0	0	0	0	19	23	0	0	3	2	2	8	1	0
vibrations	132	.4633	13.186	51.2	17	13	6	41	23	23	4	5	2	0	0	0	0	0	2	85	30	0	0	1	0	5	5	2	0
vibrato	3	.0000	.0243	23.8	0	0	0	0	0	2	1	0	0	0	0	0	0	0	0	0	3	0	0	0	0	0	0	0	0
Vic	59	.2675	4.9058	46.9	0	0	0	4	54	1	0	0	52	0	0	0	0	0	0	0	0	0	0	0	0	1	0	6	0
Vic's	4	.0000	.1827	32.6	0	0	0	0	4	0	0	0	4	0	0	0	0	0	0	0	0	0	0	0	0	0	0	0	0
vicar	2	.1494	.1045	30.2	0	0	0	1	1	0	0	0	1	0	0	0	0	0	0	0	1	0	0	0	0	0	0	0	0
Vicara	2	.0000	.0064	18.1	0	0	0	0	0	0	2	0	0	0	0	0	0	0	0	0	0	0	2	0	0	0	0	0	0
vice	14	.5545	1.6294	42.1	0	0	2	0	6	3	3	0	2	0	0	0	0	2	0	0	1	0	0	1	0	0	3	5	0
Vice	25	.4991	2.6436	44.2	0	1	0	0	8	10	3	3	0	0	0	0	0	10	0	0	0	0	0	0	1	4	2	8	0
Vice-President	20	.1791	.9415	39.7	0	0	15	0	0	5	0	0	1	0	0	0	0	5	0	0	0	0	0	0	0	0	14	0	0
vice-presidency	2	.0000	.0209	23.2	0	0	2	0	0	0	0	0	0	0	0	0	0	0	0	0	0	0	0	0	0	0	2	0	0
vice-president	19	.6610	2.6247	44.2	1	1	7	4	3	1	2	0	7	1	1	0	0	2	3	0	0	0	0	0	0	3	1	1	0
vice-presidential	7	.0000	.0733	28.6	0	0	7	0	0	0	0	0	0	0	0	0	0	0	0	0	0	0	0	0	0	0	7	0	0
viceroy	2	.2285	.1129	30.5	1	0	0	1	0	0	0	0	0	0	0	0	0	1	0	0	0	0	0	0	0	0	1	0	0
Viceroy	6	.2431	.3633	35.6	0	3	2	1	0	0	0	0	0	0	0	0	0	4	0	0	0	0	0	0	2	0	0	0	0
viceroyalties	4	.0000	.0778	28.9	0	0	0	4	0	0	0	0	0	0	0	0	0	4	0	0	0	0	0	0	0	0	0	0	0
Vichy	3	.0000	.0583	27.7	0	0	0	0	0	0	3	0	0	0	0	0	0	3	0	0	0	0	0	0	0	0	0	0	0
vicinity	30	.6827	4.1866	46.2	2	1	2	3	11	6	2	3	3	1	0	2	1	1	0	6	0	0	0	0	1	3	8	4	0
vicious	22	.6200	2.8757	44.6	1	1	2	3	8	5	1	1	7	1	0	2	0	0	0	2	0	0	0	0	4	1	0	5	0
viciously	3	.3370	.2430	33.9	0	0	1	1	1	0	0	0	1	0	0	1	0	0	0	0	0	0	0	0	0	0	1	0	0
viciousness	3	.3722	.2508	34.0	0	0	0	0	0	1	1	1	0	0	0	1	0	1	0	1	0	0	0	0	0	0	0	0	0
Vickie	2	.0000	.0299	24.8	0	2	0	0	0	0	0	0	0	0	0	0	2	0	0	0	0	0	0	0	0	0	0	0	0
Vicksburg	3	.2043	.1486	31.7	1	0	0	0	2	0	0	0	0	0	0	0	0	0	0	0	0	0	0	0	0	1	2	0	0
victim	61	.7563	9.3021	49.7	2	6	6	1	26	13	7	0	6	3	1	6	0	0	2	13	1	0	2	0	0	3	16	8	0
victim's	7	.3778	.5715	37.6	0	0	1	0	2	3	1	0	0	1	0	1	0	0	0	1	0	0	0	0	0	0	4	0	0
victims	37	.6581	4.9757	47.0	1	2	3	4	21	3	2	1	2	2	0	2	0	2	1	5	0	0	0	0	0	5	8	10	0
victor	6	.5494	.7094	38.5	0	1	0	1	2	2	0	0	2	0	0	0	0	0	1	0	0	0	0	0	0	1	1	1	0
Victor	47	.3217	3.2977	45.2	24	1	1	6	11	2	1	1	1	1	0	0	0	1	0	0	29	0	0	0	0	3	11	1	0
Victoria	26	.6572	3.5307	45.5	1	8	4	7	4	2	0	0	4	1	0	0	0	7	1	1	1	0	0	0	0	3	4	5	0
Victorian	9	.5904	1.0820	40.3	0	1	3	1	0	2	2	0	0	0	0	1	0	0	0	0	1	1	0	0	1	1	2	2	0
victories	30	.6342	3.9411	46.0	2	3	6	1	4	6	5	3	3	2	0	1	0	11	0	1	0	0	0	0	0	5	5	2	0
victorious	16	.6022	2.0019	43.0	0	2	1	0	5	3	4	1	2	1	0	0	0	3	1	0	1	0	0	0	0	3	5	0	0
victors	7	.2134	.3732	35.7	0	0	0	0	1	2	4	0	0	0	0	4	0	3	0	0	0	0	0	0	0	0	0	0	0
victory	149	.8278	24.757	53.9	8	12	19	20	25	35	26	4	30	5	1	7	0	36	2	1	7	4	0	0	13	22	9	12	0
Victory	4	.4485	.4009	36.0	0	0	0	0	2	2	0	0	1	0	0	0	0	1	0	0	0	0	0	0	0	0	1	1	0
victuals	3	.3873	.2485	34.0	0	0	0	0	2	0	1	0	0	0	0	1	0	0	0	0	0	0	0	0	1	0	1	0	0
vicuna	2	.1812	.0838	29.2	0	0	0	0	1	1	0	0	0	0	0	0	0	0	0	0	0	0	1	0	0	0	0	1	0
vicunas	4	.1611	.1738	32.4	1	0	0	0	3	0	0	0	0	0	0	0	0	0	0	1	0	0	0	0	0	0	0	3	0
vid	4	.0000	.0325	25.1	0	0	0	0	4	0	0	0	0	0	0	0	0	0	4	0	0	0	0	0	0	0	0	0	0
Vidal	3	.0000	.0365	25.6	0	0	2	0	0	0	0	1	0	0	0	0	0	0	0	0	0	0	0	0	0	0	0	3	0
video	2	.0000	.0050	17.0	0	0	0	0	2	0	0	0	0	0	0	0	0	0	0	0	0	0	0	2	0	0	0	0	0
videotape	2	.0000	.0243	23.9	0	0	0	0	0	0	0	2	0	0	0	0	0	0	0	0	0	0	0	0	0	0	0	2	0
vied	4	.4741	.3984	36.0	0	0	0	0	0	3	0	1	0	1	0	0	0	1	0	0	1	0	0	0	0	0	1	0	0
Vieng	2	.0000	.0290	24.6	0	0	0	0	2	0	0	0	0	0	0	0	0	0	0	0	0	0	0	0	0	2	0	0	0
Vienna	31	.4223	2.8128	44.5	1	1	5	4	8	2	9	1	2	0	0	0	0	3	0	0	11	0	0	0	0	5	10	0	0
Viennese	7	.2899	.4509	36.5	1	0	1	3	1	0	1	0	0	0	0	0	0	0	0	0	4	0	0	0	0	2	0	1	0
Vientiane	2	.0000	.0290	24.6	0	0	0	0	0	0	2	0	0	0	0	0	0	0	0	0	0	0	0	0	0	2	0	0	0
Viet	22	.3560	1.7589	42.5	0	0	1	4	4	2	11	0	0	1	0	0	0	10	0	0	0	0	0	0	0	1	0	10	0
VietNam	2	.0000	.0290	24.6	0	0	0	0	2	0	0	0	0	0	0	0	0	0	0	0	0	0	0	0	0	2	0	0	0
Vietcong	3	.0000	.0365	25.6	0	0	0	0	2	0	1	0	0	0	0	0	0	0	0	0	0	0	0	0	0	0	0	3	0
Vietnam	88	.3042	6.1258	47.9	2	3	9	12	19	21	20	2	0	0	0	0	0	26	0	0	0	0	0	0	0	0	9	53	0
Vietnam's	5	.0000	.0608	27.8	0	0	0	0	0	2	3	0	0	0	0	0	0	0	0	0	0	0	0	0	0	0	0	5	0
Vietnamese	43	.1676	1.8715	42.7	5	0	1	4	16	7	10	0	0	0	0	0	0	3	0	0	0	0	0	0	0	2	1	37	0
view	393	.6406	51.686	57.1	13	35	34	48	89	42	124	8	59	14	9	31	3	43	2	30	0	14	3	84	18	20	27	36	0
View	5	.4613	.4882	36.9	0	0	0	3	0	2	0	0	0	0	0	1	0	1	0	0	0	0	0	0	0	0	1	2	0
viewed	38	.7191	5.5711	47.5	0	2	0	2	14	10	8	2	4	2	1	2	0	8	0	12	1	0	0	0	0	0	5	3	0
viewer	3	.2784	.1822	32.6	0	0	0	0	2	0	1	0	0	0	1	1	0	0	0	0	0	0	0	0	0	0	0	1	0
viewers	14	.2780	.9024	39.6	1	5	0	3	0	0	5	0	0	0	0	0	0	2	0	1	0	0	0	0	0	0	1	10	0
viewing	20	.6030	2.5341	44.0	1	2	2	3	3	3	5	1	5	0	2	0	0	1	0	6	0	0	1	2	0	0	1	2	0
viewpoint	9	.4874	.9632	39.8	0	0	1	1	4	0	1	2	3	0	0	1	0	0	0	0	0	0	0	1	0	0	1	3	0
viewpoints	3	.2435	.2274	33.6	0	1	0	0	1	1	1	0	2	0	0	0	0	1	0	0	0	0	0	0	0	0	0	0	0
views	117	.3607	9.0454	49.6	0	5	6	5	21	16	64	0	6	5	0	6	0	14	0	3	1	3	1	53	0	6	9	10	0
vigil	8	.4150	.7417	38.7	0	1	0	0	5	2	0	0	2	3	0	0	0	0	0	0	2	0	0	0	0	0	0	1	0
vigilance	3	.3766	.2497	34.0	0	0	1	0	0	2	0	0	0	0	0	0	0	1	0	0	0	0	0	0	0	1	1	0	0
vigilant	5	.2800	.3594	35.6	0	0	0	1	3	1	0	0	2	0	1	0	0	0	0	0	0	0	0	0	2	0	0	0	0
vignettes	2	.0000	.0243	23.9	0	0	0	0	1	0	1	0	0	0	0	0	0	0	0	0	0	0	0	0	0	0	0	2	0
Vigo	2	.0000	.0215	23.3	0	0	0	0	0	0	2	0	0	0	0	2	0	0	0	0	0	0	0	0	0	0	0	0	0
vigor	27	.8219	4.4340	46.5	0	1	2	2	7	7	7	1	2	2	0	1	0	5	1	3	3	1	1	0	2	0	3	3	0
vigorous	54	.6963	7.6007	48.8	2	2	9	6	10	17	7	1	4	5	0	1	0	5	2	0	19	2	2	0	1	6	6	1	0
vigorously	24	.7602	3.6998	45.7	1	3	2	0	9	7	2	0	5	0	0	0	0	5	1	1	0	0	1	1	3	1	3	3	0
vigour	2	.2446	.1142	30.6	0	1	0	0	1	0	0	0	0	0	0	0	0	0	0	0	0	0	0	0	1	0	2	1	0
VII	10	.5162	1.0781	40.3	2	0	5	0	1	2	0	0	0	0	0	0	3	0	0	1	0	0	0	0	0	3	3	0	0
VIII	9	.5217	.9791	39.9	2	2	1	1	2	0	1	0	0	0	0	0	2	1	1	0	0	0	0	1	0	2	3	0	0
Viki	2	.0000	.0209	23.2	0	0	0	0	2	0	0	0	0	0	0	0	0	0	0	0	0	0	0	0	0	0	2	0	0
Viking	14	.5017	1.5547	41.9	6	1	0	3	2	1	0	1	5	0	0	0	0	2	0	0	0	0	0	0	1	2	4	0	0
Vikings	35	.6340	4.6545	46.7	12	1	10	7	5	0	0	0	10	5	0	0	0	8	1	0	0	0	0	0	0	1	5	5	0
vile	9	.3972	.7847	38.9	0	0	0	1	2	0	5	1	1	1	0	5	0	0	0	0	0	0	0	0	1	1	0	0	0
vilely	2	.0000	.0215	23.3	0	0	0	0	0	0	2	0	0	0	0	2	0	0	0	0	0	0	0	0	0	2	0	0	0
Vilhjalmur	2	.0000	.0290	24.6	2	0	0	0	0	0	0	0	0	0	0	0	0	0	0	0	0	0	0	0	0	0	0	0	0
villa	5	.4713	.4936	36.9	0	0	1	1	3	0	0	0	0	1	0	0	0	0	1	0	0	0	0	0	0	1	0	2	0
Villa	8	.1357	.2969	34.7	1	0	0	0	6	0	1	0	0	0	0	0	0	0	0	0	0	0	0	0	1	0	0	7	0
Villa-Lobos	3	.0000	.0243	23.8	0	0	0	2	1	0	0	0	0	0	0	0	0	0	0	0	3	0	0	0	0	0	0	0	0
Villa's	4	.0000	.0486	26.9	0	0	0	0	4	0	0	0	0	0	0	0	0	0	0	0	0	0	0	0	0	0	0	4	0
village	744	.7730	117.37	60.7	135	167	80	128	129	47	53	5	265	12	4	72	1	194	10	3	16	0	0	0	46	74	27	20	0
Village	34	.6199	4.4039	46.4	8	2	2	7	3	2	9	1	8	1	0	2	0	1	0	0	4	0	0	0	1	9	0	8	0
villager	13	.4726	1.3786	41.4	2	2	3	4	3	0	1	0	4	0	0	0	0	4	0	0	0	0	0	0	0	3	2	0	0
villagers	63	.6615	8.7557	49.4	9	15	4	19	11	1	4	0	22	5	0	3	0	24	0	1	2	0	0	0	1	3	1	0	0
villages	255	.5613	30.405	54.8	35	63	29	55	41	17	15	0	26	2	0	2	0	168	0	2	5	0	0	0	1	21	18	9	1
villain	37	.7003	5.2747	47.2	0	5	8	5	8	2	9	0	6	5	1	6	0	1	8	1	1	0	0	0	5	3	0	0	0
villains	3	.3465	.2515	34.0	0	0	2	0	0	0	1	0	1	0	0	0	0	0	0	0	0	0	0	0	0	1	0	1	0
villainy	3	.3776	.2489	34.0	0	0	0	0	0	2	1	0	0	0	0	1	0	1	0	0	0	0	0	0	0	0	0	1	0

9Q vibration-free
XH vibrational
5Q Vicar
6A vicar's
8A vicarious
9D vicariously
4P Viccars
8F Vice-President-elect
5Q Vice-Presidents
5R vice-dean
5A vice-presidents

5A vicelike
6F viceroyalty
6F Viceroyalty
6F viceroys
4Q Vichy-French
7Q vicissitudes
8R Vickery
8D Vicky
7R Vico
7R Vico's
6J vict'ry

8A Victim
XH victimized
7A victoria
5R Victoria's
4Q Victorien
7J Victrola
XR Victualers'
6J Vidalitas
6B vide
5B video-computers
5B videre

8Q vie
9A vieille
8Q viejo
9Q Vienna's
9Q Viennis
8Q Vietminh
6Q viewer's
6R Viewers
8Q Views
8Q Vigarini
4F Vigil

8R vigils
9R Vigna
5Q VII'S
6F Viipuri
5Q viking
4N viking-proud
9D Vilas
5P vileness
8D Vilhelm
7R vilified
9D vill

XR VillaGesell
6J Villa-Lopos
3P village's
7R Villager
5A villagers'
6A Villages
6N villainous
8D villainously
7N villanous
7R Villanova
4G villanus

Word Type	F	D	U	SFI	3 Gr 3	4 Gr 4	5 Gr 5	6 Gr 6	7 Gr 7	8 Gr 8	9 Gr 9	X UnGr	A Read	B Eng & Gr	C Comp	D Lit	E Math	F Soc Stud	G Spell	H Sci	J Music	K Art	L Home Ec	M Shop	N Lib F	P Lib NF	Q Lib Ref	R Mag	S Rel
Ville	3	.2181	.1541	31.9	0	0	0	1	2	0	0	0	0	0	0	0	0	0	0	0	0	0	0	0	1	0	2	0	0
villi	2	.0000	.0394	26.0	0	0	1	0	0	1	0	0	0	0	0	0	0	0	0	2	0	0	0	0	0	0	0	0	0
Vimy	3	.2212	.2099	33.2	0	0	0	2	0	1	0	0	2	0	0	1	0	0	0	0	0	0	0	0	0	0	0	0	0
Vimy's	2	.0000	.0914	29.6	0	0	0	2	0	0	0	0	2	0	0	0	0	0	0	0	0	0	0	0	0	0	0	0	0
Vince	2	.0000	.0243	23.9	0	0	0	0	0	2	0	0	0	0	0	0	0	0	0	0	0	0	0	0	0	0	0	2	0
Vincennes	13	.3849	1.1075	40.4	0	5	5	0	0	0	3	0	0	0	0	3	0	5	0	0	0	0	0	0	0	5	0	0	0
Vincent	12	.4134	1.0611	40.3	0	1	0	0	5	3	3	0	1	2	0	2	0	1	0	0	1	3	0	0	0	1	1	0	0
Vinci	2	.2401	.1133	30.5	0	0	0	0	2	0	0	0	0	0	0	0	0	0	0	0	0	0	0	0	0	1	1	0	0
vindictive	2	.2441	.1127	30.5	0	0	0	0	1	1	0	0	0	0	0	0	0	0	0	0	0	0	0	0	1	0	1	0	0
Vindobona	2	.0000	.0209	23.2	0	0	0	0	0	0	2	0	0	0	0	0	0	0	0	0	0	0	0	0	0	0	2	0	0
vine	33	.6614	4.6486	46.7	5	2	9	6	9	1	1	0	20	3	0	1	0	0	0	1	1	1	0	0	0	3	3	0	0
vine-covered	3	.2357	.2199	33.4	0	1	0	1	1	0	0	0	2	0	0	0	0	0	0	0	0	0	0	0	0	1	0	0	0
vinegar	47	.6049	5.9023	47.7	6	7	14	2	8	1	7	2	5	1	1	7	0	0	0	19	0	0	7	0	1	2	3	1	0
vinegars	2	.0000	.0064	18.1	0	0	0	0	0	0	2	0	0	0	0	0	0	0	0	0	0	0	2	0	0	0	0	0	0
vines	66	.8036	10.715	50.3	19	8	8	12	13	4	0	2	17	0	1	2	0	13	1	4	1	1	0	0	9	12	1	4	0
vineyard	6	.5528	.7165	38.6	1	3	0	0	1	0	1	0	2	1	0	1	0	1	0	0	0	0	0	0	0	0	0	1	0
vineyards	28	.5920	3.4905	45.4	3	1	6	7	6	3	1	1	4	1	0	1	0	14	0	0	0	0	0	0	1	2	4	1	0
Vinland	7	.1897	.3644	35.6	3	0	0	1	0	3	0	0	0	1	0	0	0	6	0	0	0	0	0	0	0	0	0	0	0
Vinny	37	.1129	2.2903	43.6	0	0	36	0	0	1	0	0	36	0	0	0	0	0	0	0	0	0	0	0	1	0	0	0	0
vino	4	.1672	.1617	32.1	0	0	3	0	0	0	1	0	0	0	0	0	0	0	0	0	3	0	0	0	0	0	0	1	0
Vinson	2	.0000	.0299	24.8	0	2	0	0	0	0	0	0	0	0	0	0	2	0	0	0	0	0	0	0	0	0	0	0	0
vinyl	3	.2410	.1667	32.2	0	0	0	0	1	1	0	1	0	0	0	0	0	0	1	0	0	0	0	0	0	0	0	2	0
viol	3	.0995	.1144	30.6	0	1	0	0	1	1	0	0	1	0	0	0	0	0	0	0	2	0	0	0	0	0	0	0	0
viola	24	.0857	.5910	37.7	1	6	3	3	6	4	0	1	0	0	0	0	0	0	0	0	22	0	0	0	0	1	0	1	0
viola's	2	.0000	.0162	22.1	0	0	1	0	0	1	0	0	0	0	0	0	0	0	0	0	2	0	0	0	0	0	0	0	0
violas	9	.2085	.4305	36.3	0	2	0	1	3	2	1	0	0	1	0	0	0	0	0	0	7	0	0	0	0	0	1	0	0
violate	9	.5381	1.0230	40.1	0	0	0	0	4	3	1	1	0	0	0	0	0	4	0	2	0	0	0	0	0	1	1	1	0
violated	13	.5760	1.5931	42.0	0	0	2	3	2	2	4	0	3	0	0	0	0	3	0	1	0	0	0	0	0	1	2	3	0
violates	2	.2433	.1158	30.6	1	0	0	0	1	0	0	0	0	0	0	0	0	0	0	0	0	0	0	0	0	1	0	1	0
violating	7	.4118	.6266	38.0	0	0	1	1	1	2	2	0	0	0	0	0	0	2	0	1	0	0	0	0	0	0	3	1	0
violation	9	.5859	1.1033	40.4	0	1	1	0	2	3	2	0	1	0	0	1	0	3	1	0	0	0	0	0	0	1	0	2	0
violations	13	.5080	1.4060	41.5	0	0	1	1	6	1	3	1	1	0	0	0	0	3	0	1	0	0	0	0	0	1	2	5	0
violence	73	.6393	9.5632	49.8	0	5	4	6	27	11	16	4	3	0	0	7	0	11	0	5	2	0	0	0	7	5	5	28	0
violent	80	.7968	12.842	51.1	1	7	8	12	28	12	11	1	15	2	3	6	0	7	0	11	4	0	0	0	5	6	8	13	0
violently	31	.7734	4.8841	46.9	3	0	4	7	11	5	1	0	11	1	0	1	0	2	0	2	2	0	0	0	4	2	3	3	0
violet	58	.5150	6.3801	48.0	8	1	7	11	10	3	3	15	6	0	0	3	0	0	0	29	0	5	0	0	5	0	9	1	0
Violet	35	.0156	.5445	37.4	13	0	21	0	0	0	0	1	1	0	0	0	0	0	0	0	0	0	0	0	34	0	0	0	0
violets	24	.7692	3.7073	45.7	8	7	1	3	2	1	0	2	2	1	1	2	0	0	0	2	1	1	0	0	5	3	4	2	0
violin	106	.3754	8.9768	49.5	17	20	13	17	26	12	1	0	22	1	0	0	0	1	3	7	58	0	0	0	2	8	1	3	0
Violin	6	.1370	.2057	33.1	0	3	0	0	2	0	1	0	0	0	0	1	0	0	0	0	5	0	0	0	0	0	0	0	0
violinist	7	.3245	.5125	37.1	0	0	0	2	5	0	0	0	1	0	0	0	0	0	1	0	4	0	0	0	1	0	0	0	0
violinists	3	.2058	.1429	31.5	0	1	0	0	1	1	0	0	0	1	0	0	0	0	0	0	2	0	0	0	0	0	0	0	0
violins	43	.1267	1.5009	41.8	1	7	11	4	12	6	2	0	3	1	0	0	0	1	0	1	36	0	0	0	0	1	0	0	0
violoncello	4	.1534	.1534	31.9	0	0	0	1	2	1	0	0	0	0	0	0	0	0	0	0	3	0	0	0	0	1	0	0	0
viper	3	.3764	.2483	33.9	0	0	0	0	3	0	0	0	0	0	0	0	0	0	0	1	0	0	0	0	0	0	1	1	0
vipers	4	.3831	.3409	35.3	0	0	0	1	3	0	0	0	0	0	0	0	0	0	0	2	0	0	0	0	0	1	1	0	0
Virgen	2	.0000	.0243	23.9	0	0	0	0	2	0	0	0	0	0	0	0	0	0	0	0	0	0	0	0	0	0	0	2	0
Virgil	11	.4663	1.0749	40.3	0	0	2	2	2	4	0	1	0	0	0	3	0	0	0	1	4	0	0	0	0	2	0	1	0
Virgil's	2	.2407	.1138	30.6	0	0	0	1	0	1	0	0	0	0	0	1	0	0	0	0	0	0	0	0	0	1	0	0	0
virgin	15	.5448	1.6944	42.3	0	1	1	1	3	2	4	3	0	0	0	4	0	3	0	0	0	0	0	0	2	0	2	4	0
Virgin	11	.4899	1.1307	40.5	1	1	1	2	1	0	4	1	1	0	0	0	0	2	0	0	3	2	1	0	0	1	1	0	0
Virginia	224	.7162	32.763	55.2	27	48	52	13	22	45	10	7	29	3	2	4	2	88	3	2	8	0	0	0	2	47	21	13	0
Virginia's	9	.5315	1.0012	40.0	5	0	0	0	0	3	1	0	0	0	0	0	1	3	2	0	0	0	0	0	0	2	0	1	0
Virginian	8	.4357	.7602	38.8	1	0	4	0	0	3	0	0	0	1	0	1	0	5	0	0	0	0	0	0	0	1	0	0	0
Virginians	12	.4688	1.2304	40.9	1	1	0	1	1	6	2	0	1	0	0	0	0	6	0	1	0	0	0	0	0	2	0	2	0
Virginny	3	.2071	.1434	31.6	0	0	2	0	1	0	0	0	0	0	0	1	0	0	0	0	2	0	0	0	0	0	0	0	0
virgins	2	.2440	.1132	30.5	0	0	0	0	1	0	1	0	0	0	0	1	0	0	0	0	0	0	0	0	0	0	0	1	0
Viri	2	.0000	.0234	23.7	0	0	0	2	0	0	0	0	0	0	0	0	0	0	0	0	0	0	0	0	2	0	0	0	0
virile	5	.2183	.2661	34.3	0	0	3	0	1	1	0	0	0	0	0	0	0	0	0	0	1	0	0	0	0	4	0	0	0
virtual	8	.5287	.8869	39.5	0	2	1	0	1	0	3	1	0	0	0	0	0	2	0	1	0	0	0	0	0	1	2	2	0
virtually	56	.5865	6.7460	48.3	1	4	8	2	14	10	13	4	0	0	0	1	0	5	1	3	1	0	1	0	0	9	22	13	0
virtue	18	.6054	2.2378	43.5	0	0	4	0	2	5	7	0	0	1	0	5	0	3	0	1	0	0	0	0	0	4	3	1	0
virtues	17	.6343	2.2300	43.5	0	0	1	3	8	2	1	2	3	0	0	2	0	1	0	0	0	1	0	0	2	2	1	5	0
virtuosity	9	.3751	.7221	38.6	0	1	0	0	1	5	1	1	0	0	0	0	0	0	0	0	3	0	0	0	0	0	2	4	0
virtuoso	5	.2656	.3022	34.8	0	0	0	0	3	0	1	1	0	0	0	0	0	0	0	1	3	0	0	0	0	0	0	1	0
virtuous	8	.5772	.9641	39.8	0	2	1	1	2	1	1	0	1	0	0	1	0	0	0	0	0	0	0	0	1	3	1	1	0
virus	48	.4226	4.5665	46.6	2	4	8	14	15	2	0	3	5	1	0	0	0	3	0	32	0	0	0	0	0	0	5	2	0
viruses	66	.2700	4.4531	46.5	0	5	4	17	38	2	0	0	2	0	0	0	0	4	1	55	0	0	0	0	0	0	4	0	0
vis	7	.2301	.3668	35.6	0	0	0	0	4	3	0	0	0	3	0	0	0	0	4	0	0	0	0	0	0	0	0	0	0
visa	2	.1787	.1174	30.7	0	0	0	0	2	0	0	0	1	0	0	0	0	0	0	0	0	0	0	0	1	0	0	0	0
visage	6	.3380	.4878	36.9	0	0	0	2	2	1	1	0	2	2	0	2	0	0	0	0	0	0	0	0	0	0	0	0	0
Visayan	6	.0000	.0628	28.0	6	0	0	0	0	0	0	0	0	0	0	0	0	0	0	0	0	0	0	0	0	0	6	0	0
viscera	3	.2043	.1486	31.7	0	0	0	0	0	0	3	0	0	0	0	0	0	0	0	0	0	0	0	0	0	1	2	0	0
visceral	5	.1649	.2071	33.2	0	0	0	0	1	2	2	0	0	0	0	0	0	0	0	0	0	0	0	0	0	0	4	1	0
viscose	9	.2415	.5492	37.4	0	0	0	0	0	0	9	0	0	0	0	0	0	0	0	8	0	0	1	0	0	0	0	0	0
viscosity	4	.3864	.3418	35.3	0	0	0	0	1	1	1	1	0	0	0	0	0	0	0	2	0	0	0	0	0	0	1	1	0
Viscount	2	.2441	.1127	30.5	0	0	0	0	1	0	1	0	0	0	0	0	0	0	0	0	0	0	0	0	1	0	1	0	0
viscous	4	.2353	.2382	33.8	0	1	1	0	1	0	1	0	0	0	0	0	0	0	0	3	0	0	0	0	0	0	1	0	0
vise	50	.0802	1.0339	40.1	2	1	0	2	18	20	7	0	1	1	0	1	0	1	0	2	0	0	0	41	0	1	1	1	0
visibility	13	.5888	1.6182	42.1	0	0	1	4	3	2	3	0	3	0	1	0	0	0	0	5	0	0	0	1	0	1	1	1	0
visible	99	.8185	16.261	52.1	0	5	6	18	26	13	16	15	14	4	3	5	1	1	0	36	1	0	2	2	5	4	11	10	0
visibly	9	.5099	.9945	40.0	0	0	2	1	3	2	1	0	2	0	0	1	0	1	0	0	0	0	0	0	0	3	0	2	0
vision	78	.8549	13.300	51.2	6	6	2	13	25	17	6	3	11	3	0	10	0	3	1	14	3	3	1	1	7	6	8	7	0
Vision	2	.2442	.1134	30.5	0	1	0	0	0	0	0	1	0	1	0	0	0	0	0	0	0	0	0	0	0	0	0	1	0
visionary	4	.3359	.2989	34.8	0	0	0	0	1	1	2	0	0	0	0	0	0	1	0	0	0	0	0	0	0	0	2	1	0
visions	12	.6373	1.5911	42.0	0	0	0	0	8	3	1	0	3	0	1	2	0	1	0	0	0	0	0	0	1	2	1	1	0
visit	443	.9249	81.244	59.1	107	96	50	61	58	39	24	8	106	27	6	10	4	98	13	40	7	6	8	2	19	43	16	38	0
Visit	2	.2441	.1127	30.5	0	1	1	0	0	0	0	0	0	0	0	0	0	0	0	0	0	0	0	0	1	0	1	0	0
visited	217	.8530	37.103	55.7	26	41	36	40	35	22	13	4	60	20	3	9	10	48	4	7	5	3	0	0	10	12	7	18	1
visiting	90	.8658	15.584	51.9	13	18	13	5	17	12	8	4	25	1	2	4	1	17	1	4	1	2	2	0	3	10	5	12	0
visitor	116	.7531	17.779	52.5	7	6	28	14	32	7	18	4	33	15	4	13	1	8	0	4	2	0	5	0	3	10	7	10	1
visitor's	3	.3769	.2439	33.9	0	0	1	1	1	0	0	0	0	0	0	0	0	0	1	0	0	0	0	0	0	1	0	1	0
visitors	180	.8229	29.705	54.7	34	34	34	29	19	10	15	5	26	7	2	6	1	54	2	1	2	1	6	0	7	20	11	34	0
Visitors	5	.1101	.1543	31.9	0	0	1	2	0	2	0	0	0	0	0	0	0	1	0	0	4	0	0	0	0	0	0	0	0

3P villas
3N Villekulla
7P Villon's
8D vin
7R Vinapu
6A Vinard
9B Vincent's
7G vincere
9K Vinci's
7N vindicate
7A vindication
7A vindictiveness
8N vine-clad
5A vinegar-soy
8F Vineland
7H vinelike
3N viner
4P Vineyard
9B Vinnie
5A Vinny's
5N Vinolia
XR vintage
8G Vinyl
6P violadagamba
9F violators
7R Violence
6R violet-colored
5N Violet's
7P Violette
9J violin-piano
7J Violins
4J violists
7J violoncellos
7J viols
7H viper's
XB viragoes
8Q viral
7H virazon
6H vireos
9Q VIRGIL
7A Virginia-Carolina
7F Virginia-NorthCarolina
9Q Virgins
7H Virgo
6R virility
7H virology
9D virtue's
8J Virtues
5N virtuously
7Q Virunga
7H virus'
8Q visas
3Q Visayas
3P VISE
8G viser
9Q Vishinsky
7M visibiility
9F Visigoth
7Q Visigoths
XH visitants
9D visitation
9D visitin'
7B Visitor

Word Type	F	D	U	SFI	3 Gr 3	4 Gr 4	5 Gr 5	6 Gr 6	7 Gr 7	8 Gr 8	9 Gr 9	X UnGr	A Read	B Eng & Gr	C Comp	D Lit	E Math	F Soc Stud	G Spell	H Sci	J Music	K Art	L Home Ec	M Shop	N Lib F	P Lib NF	Q Lib Ref	R Mag	S Rel
visitors'	4	.4450	.3917	35.9	0	0	0	2	0	1	1	0	1	1	0	1	0	0	1	0	0	0	0	0	0	0	0	0	0
visits	49	.9367	9.0755	49.6	8	3	8	5	12	9	3	1	8	2	1	2	1	5	2	5	1	1	1	1	5	3	4	7	0
visor	6	.5050	.6476	38.1	2	0	0	1	1	0	2	0	1	0	0	2	0	0	0	0	0	0	0	0	1	1	0	1	0
visors	2	.2446	.1125	30.5	0	0	0	0	0	1	1	0	0	1	0	1	0	0	0	0	0	0	0	0	0	0	0	0	0
Vista	10	.3861	.9596	39.8	6	2	1	0	1	0	0	0	6	0	0	0	0	0	0	0	0	0	0	0	0	2	0	2	0
vistas	6	.3305	.4467	36.5	0	0	2	1	2	1	0	0	0	0	0	0	0	0	0	1	0	0	0	0	0	2	0	3	0
Vistas	2	.0000	.0914	29.6	0	0	2	0	0	0	0	0	2	0	0	0	0	0	0	0	0	0	0	0	0	0	0	0	0
visual	43	.7584	6.5205	48.1	4	0	0	3	12	6	11	7	0	5	0	1	0	1	0	4	4	3	2	2	1	3	7	10	0
visualization	2	.0000	.0209	23.2	0	0	0	0	1	1	0	0	0	0	0	0	0	0	0	0	0	0	0	0	0	0	2	0	0
visualize	17	.6832	2.3428	43.7	0	0	0	2	7	1	6	1	0	1	1	3	2	0	4	3	0	0	0	1	0	0	2	0	0
visualized	2	.0000	.0215	23.3	0	0	0	0	1	1	0	0	0	0	0	2	0	0	0	0	0	0	0	0	0	0	0	0	0
vitae	2	.2440	.1132	30.5	0	0	0	0	0	1	1	0	0	0	0	1	0	0	0	0	0	0	0	0	0	0	0	1	0
vital	65	.7559	9.8961	50.0	4	3	5	5	17	12	14	5	5	2	0	0	0	7	1	8	4	2	3	0	0	6	15	12	0
vitality	19	.6839	2.6293	44.2	1	0	2	1	7	4	2	2	1	3	0	0	0	1	0	1	1	1	2	0	0	2	5	2	0
vitally	5	.0743	.1541	31.9	0	1	1	1	0	0	2	0	1	0	0	0	0	0	0	0	0	0	0	0	0	0	4	0	0
vitamin	92	.2862	6.1559	47.9	0	0	31	3	28	9	21	0	2	1	0	0	0	2	0	56	0	0	27	0	0	0	3	1	0
vitamin-D	2	.0000	.0394	26.0	0	0	0	0	2	0	0	0	0	0	0	0	0	0	0	2	0	0	0	0	0	0	0	0	0
vitamins	117	.3545	9.4679	49.8	7	9	27	5	37	12	19	1	14	1	0	0	0	2	0	56	0	0	30	0	0	0	12	2	0
Vito's	3	.0000	.1370	31.4	0	0	0	0	3	0	0	0	3	0	0	0	0	0	0	0	0	0	0	0	0	0	0	0	0
vittles	2	.0000	.0234	23.7	1	0	0	0	1	0	0	0	0	0	0	0	0	0	0	0	0	0	0	0	2	0	0	0	0
Vittore	4	.0000	.0469	26.7	0	0	0	4	0	0	0	0	0	0	0	0	0	0	0	0	0	0	0	0	4	0	0	0	0
Vittorio	2	.2303	.1079	30.3	0	0	2	0	0	0	0	0	0	0	0	0	0	0	0	0	1	0	0	0	0	1	0	0	0
Vitus	2	.0000	.0389	25.9	0	0	2	0	0	0	0	0	0	0	0	0	0	2	0	0	0	0	0	0	0	0	0	0	0
vivace	2	.0000	.0162	22.1	0	0	1	0	1	0	0	0	0	0	0	0	0	0	0	0	2	0	0	0	0	0	0	0	0
vivacious	4	.3670	.3055	34.8	0	0	0	0	1	2	1	0	0	0	1	2	0	0	0	0	0	0	1	0	0	0	0	0	0
vivacity	2	.1839	.0845	29.3	0	0	0	0	1	0	1	0	0	0	0	0	0	0	0	0	0	0	1	0	1	0	0	0	0
Vivaldi	2	.2417	.1091	30.4	0	1	0	0	0	1	0	0	0	0	0	0	0	0	0	0	1	0	0	0	0	0	1	0	0
vive	2	.0000	.0914	29.6	0	0	2	0	0	0	0	0	2	0	0	0	0	0	0	0	0	0	0	0	0	0	0	0	0
vives	2	.0000	.0914	29.6	0	0	2	0	0	0	0	0	2	0	0	0	0	0	0	0	0	0	0	0	0	0	0	0	0
vivianite	2	.0000	.0394	26.0	0	0	0	0	0	0	0	2	0	0	0	0	0	0	0	2	0	0	0	0	0	0	0	0	0
vivid	67	.6553	9.0275	49.6	0	4	6	12	20	10	15	0	14	21	8	5	0	1	1	1	0	2	1	0	3	4	1	5	0
vividly	16	.6147	2.0756	43.2	1	0	1	6	1	4	3	0	6	1	0	3	0	0	0	0	2	1	0	0	0	1	2	0	0
vividness	3	.3399	.2456	33.9	0	1	0	0	0	1	0	1	1	0	0	1	0	0	0	0	0	0	0	0	0	0	0	1	0
vivo	3	.0000	.1370	31.4	0	0	3	0	0	0	0	0	3	0	0	0	0	0	0	0	0	0	0	0	0	0	0	0	0
vixen	2	.0000	.0914	29.6	0	0	0	2	0	0	0	0	2	0	0	0	0	0	0	0	0	0	0	0	0	0	0	0	0
viz	2	.0000	.0234	23.7	0	0	0	2	0	0	0	0	0	0	0	0	0	0	0	0	0	0	0	0	2	0	0	0	0
vizier	2	.1698	.1133	30.5	0	2	0	0	0	0	0	0	1	0	0	0	0	0	0	0	0	0	0	0	0	0	1	0	0
Vizier	4	.0000	.1827	32.6	0	4	0	0	0	0	0	0	4	0	0	0	0	0	0	0	0	0	0	0	0	0	0	0	0
Vladimir	3	.3131	.2349	33.7	0	0	0	1	0	1	1	0	1	0	0	0	0	1	0	0	1	0	0	0	0	0	0	0	0
Vladivostok	11	.1852	.5422	37.3	0	8	0	2	1	0	0	0	0	0	0	0	0	3	0	0	0	0	0	0	0	8	0	0	0
Vlak	2	.0000	.0914	29.6	0	0	0	0	2	0	0	0	2	0	0	0	0	0	0	0	0	0	0	0	0	0	0	0	0
Vltava	3	.1621	.1254	31.0	0	0	0	1	0	2	0	0	0	0	0	0	0	1	0	0	2	0	0	0	0	0	0	0	0
vocabackularily	2	.0000	.0914	29.6	0	2	0	0	0	0	0	0	2	0	0	0	0	0	0	0	0	0	0	0	0	0	0	0	0
vocabularies	2	.2446	.1123	30.5	0	0	0	0	1	0	1	0	0	1	0	0	0	0	0	0	0	0	0	0	0	0	1	0	0
vocabulary	153	.4784	15.370	51.9	4	15	14	19	52	21	26	2	13	46	6	4	2	0	73	2	1	0	0	0	0	1	4	1	0
Vocabulary	15	.0728	.3729	35.7	0	0	1	0	7	0	7	0	1	0	0	0	0	1	13	0	0	0	0	0	0	0	0	0	0
Vocabulary-building	6	.0000	.0487	26.9	0	2	3	1	0	0	0	0	0	0	0	0	0	0	6	0	0	0	0	0	0	0	0	0	0
vocal	94	.5003	9.8196	49.9	8	0	4	14	15	39	6	8	2	4	1	0	0	1	2	21	45	0	0	0	0	1	10	7	0
vocalists	2	.0000	.0162	22.1	0	0	1	0	0	0	1	0	0	0	0	0	0	0	0	0	2	0	0	0	0	0	0	0	0
vocally	2	.0000	.0243	23.9	0	0	0	2	0	0	0	0	0	0	0	0	0	0	0	0	0	0	0	0	0	0	0	2	0
vocation	10	.4286	.9379	39.7	0	0	1	0	2	5	2	0	2	0	0	0	1	1	3	0	0	0	0	2	0	0	0	1	0
vocational	12	.4742	1.1787	40.7	2	0	1	0	2	1	4	2	0	0	0	0	0	1	3	0	0	0	0	2	0	0	4	2	0
vocations	2	.2427	.1159	30.6	0	0	0	0	0	0	1	1	0	0	0	0	1	0	0	0	0	0	0	0	0	0	0	1	0
vodka	4	.2442	.2268	33.6	0	0	0	0	3	0	1	0	0	2	0	0	0	0	0	0	0	0	0	0	0	0	0	2	0
vogue	2	.0000	.0243	23.9	0	0	0	0	0	1	1	0	0	0	0	0	0	0	0	0	0	0	0	0	0	0	0	2	0
voice	1280	.8106	209.79	63.2	182	198	146	185	295	161	103	10	481	99	23	148	1	39	8	29	129	3	4	0	161	87	9	59	0
Voice	21	.3758	1.8344	42.6	0	0	0	0	15	3	2	1	7	0	0	1	0	0	0	0	9	0	0	0	0	1	0	3	0
VOICE	19	.0000	.2039	33.1	0	0	0	0	10	9	0	0	0	0	0	19	0	0	0	0	0	0	0	0	0	0	0	0	0
voiced	36	.4799	3.6284	45.6	0	1	9	4	10	8	1	3	2	8	0	0	0	3	16	0	0	0	0	0	2	1	3	1	0
voiceless	5	.0000	.0547	27.4	0	0	1	0	0	4	0	0	0	5	0	0	0	0	0	0	0	0	0	0	0	0	0	0	0
voices	301	.7092	43.633	56.4	21	41	44	52	60	50	32	1	74	19	8	26	0	8	5	9	85	0	0	0	21	25	7	14	0
Voices	8	.2426	.6298	38.0	0	0	7	0	0	0	1	0	7	0	0	0	0	0	0	0	1	0	0	0	0	0	0	0	0
void	15	.6901	2.1023	43.2	0	0	2	1	3	9	0	0	0	0	0	0	2	4	0	1	1	0	0	0	1	2	3	1	0
voile	2	.0000	.0064	18.1	0	0	0	0	0	2	0	0	0	0	0	0	0	0	0	0	0	0	2	0	0	0	0	0	0
Voiles	7	.0000	.0566	27.5	0	0	7	0	0	0	0	0	0	0	0	0	0	0	0	0	7	0	0	0	0	0	0	0	0
volatile	7	.3515	.5567	37.5	0	0	0	0	1	5	1	0	0	1	0	0	0	0	0	5	0	0	1	0	0	0	0	0	0
volcanic	68	.5513	7.9327	49.0	3	1	9	8	21	3	23	0	4	0	0	1	0	14	1	29	0	0	0	0	1	4	14	0	0
volcanism	9	.2285	.5268	37.2	0	0	0	0	2	3	4	0	0	0	0	0	0	0	0	7	0	0	0	0	0	0	2	0	0
volcano	98	.7738	15.471	51.9	7	10	31	20	19	6	5	0	32	4	1	5	0	7	2	32	0	1	0	0	0	7	6	1	0
Volcano	2	.2152	.1357	31.3	0	1	0	0	0	1	0	0	1	0	0	0	0	1	0	0	0	0	0	0	0	0	0	0	0
volcanoes	96	.5299	10.937	50.4	3	11	22	22	19	2	16	1	11	0	0	1	0	31	0	34	0	0	0	0	1	4	14	0	0
Volga	9	.3430	.7098	38.5	0	0	0	4	0	3	2	0	0	0	0	0	2	6	0	0	0	0	0	0	0	0	1	0	0
Volkswagen	6	.2451	.3685	35.7	0	0	0	1	3	1	1	0	1	1	0	0	0	0	0	0	0	0	0	0	0	0	0	4	0
volley	4	.3869	.3422	35.3	0	1	0	2	1	0	0	0	0	1	0	0	0	0	0	2	0	0	0	0	1	0	0	0	0
volleyball	5	.3838	.4263	36.3	0	2	1	2	0	0	0	0	0	0	0	0	2	0	0	2	0	0	0	0	0	0	1	0	0
volleyed	3	.2028	.1988	33.0	0	0	0	0	3	0	0	0	2	0	0	0	0	0	0	0	1	0	0	0	0	0	0	0	0
volt	6	.4815	.6044	37.8	0	0	1	0	3	2	0	0	0	0	0	0	2	0	1	1	0	0	0	1	0	0	1	0	0
Volta	17	.4367	1.6509	42.2	0	2	0	1	4	0	1	9	1	0	0	0	0	3	0	10	0	0	0	0	0	2	1	0	0
Volta's	4	.3831	.3409	35.3	0	1	0	0	1	0	0	2	0	0	0	0	0	0	0	2	0	0	0	0	0	1	1	0	0
voltage	56	.1017	1.4128	41.5	0	1	2	0	9	41	2	1	0	0	0	0	1	1	0	6	0	0	0	42	0	0	3	3	0
voltage-sensitive	2	.0000	.0243	23.9	0	0	0	0	2	0	0	0	0	0	0	0	0	0	0	0	0	0	0	0	0	0	0	2	0
voltages	5	.3348	.3596	35.6	0	0	0	0	1	2	2	0	0	0	0	0	0	0	0	0	0	0	0	1	0	0	3	1	0
voltaic	2	.0000	.0394	26.0	0	0	0	0	0	0	0	2	0	0	0	0	0	0	0	2	0	0	0	0	0	0	0	0	0
Voltaire	17	.3438	1.2819	41.1	0	0	1	0	2	3	11	0	0	0	0	0	0	1	0	0	1	0	0	0	0	0	4	11	0
Voltaire's	3	.0000	.0365	25.6	0	0	0	0	0	0	3	0	0	0	0	0	0	0	0	0	0	0	0	0	0	0	0	3	0
voltmeter	2	.0000	.0050	17.0	0	0	0	0	0	2	0	0	0	0	0	0	0	0	0	0	0	0	0	2	0	0	0	0	0
volts	16	.2364	.8639	39.4	0	2	2	2	3	7	0	0	0	0	0	0	2	0	0	4	0	0	0	7	0	0	3	0	0
voluble	3	.3399	.2456	33.9	0	0	0	1	1	0	1	0	1	0	0	1	0	0	0	0	0	0	0	0	0	0	0	1	0
volume	294	.7199	42.897	56.3	12	42	16	17	57	88	60	2	11	21	1	6	121	5	0	70	7	1	2	2	3	1	35	8	0
Volume	7	.3114	.5328	37.3	1	2	0	2	2	0	0	0	2	0	0	0	0	0	0	0	0	0	0	0	0	2	3	0	0
volumes	29	.5911	3.5694	45.5	1	0	6	3	3	12	4	0	4	4	1	0	9	0	0	1	0	0	0	0	0	0	8	2	0
voluminous	2	.1160	.0650	28.1	0	0	0	0	2	0	0	0	0	0	1	0	0	0	0	1	0	0	0	0	0	0	0	0	0
voluntarily	10	.5172	1.1075	40.4	0	0	0	1	5	3	1	0	1	0	0	0	0	3	0	2	0	0	0	0	0	0	2	2	0

7N vista
3A VISTA
8K VISUAL
9Q visualizing
7K visually
8R Vitae
9E Vital
7F vitalizing
9L Vitamin
XP vitamin-a
9L Vitamins
5Q Vitanuova
6J vito
8R Vitosha
9R Vittoria
9R Viva
5A viven
8D vivere
5A vivi
XR Viviane
8F Viviani
5A vivimos
7Q vivipara
7Q viviparity
7Q viviparous
7Q viviparus
5A vivis
8D Vixen
7Q vizcacha
7Q vizcachas
4F Vizcaino
5A viziers
5N vizir
8D vizor
9F VJ
XP Vladislav
5Q Vlaminck
9D Vlassovs
8J Vlast
4A vo-cab-u-lar-y
7G vocalis
7J Vocalise
8R vocalist
9A vocalization
7A vocalize
8R vocals
XR Vodka
7J Voi
8Q voiding
XR voila
9R Voinovich
9B Voistinu
7R Voityck
8Q Voivodina
7J volar
7M volcanic-force
7Q volcanoes
9Q volcanologist
7Q volcanologists
7Q vole
7Q voles
6F Volga's
6F Volgograd
8R Volkswagon
6A Vollard
7R Volpe
8Q vols
8M Voltage
5R volubly
8N Volumes
7H voluminously
9R voluntarism

Word Type	F	D	U	SFI	3 Gr 3	4 Gr 4	5 Gr 5	6 Gr 6	7 Gr 7	8 Gr 8	9 Gr 9	X UnGr	A Read	B Eng & Gr	C Comp	D Lit	E Math	F Soc Stud	G Spell	H Sci	J Music	K Art	L Home Ec	M Shop	N Lib F	P Lib NF	Q Lib Ref	R Mag	S Rel
voluntary	26	.5635	3.0654	44.9	0	0	5	1	6	9	5	0	0	0	0	2	0	2	0	13	0	0	0	0	0	3	4	2	0
volunteer	20	.6142	2.6188	44.2	1	2	4	1	2	8	1	1	8	0	0	0	1	2	0	0	0	0	0	0	1	2	1	5	0
Volunteer	2	.2351	.1166	30.7	0	0	0	0	0	1	0	1	0	0	0	0	0	1	0	0	0	0	0	0	0	0	0	1	0
volunteered	14	.5979	1.7893	42.5	0	2	4	3	4	1	0	0	5	0	0	0	1	2	0	0	0	0	0	0	1	2	0	3	0
volunteering	2	.2351	.1166	30.7	0	0	0	0	1	1	0	0	0	0	0	0	0	1	0	0	0	0	0	0	0	0	0	1	0
volunteers	38	.6531	5.1286	47.1	2	3	7	1	5	13	6	1	5	2	0	1	0	11	0	2	0	0	0	0	0	5	4	8	0
Volusia	2	.0000	.0234	23.7	0	0	0	0	2	0	0	0	0	0	0	0	0	0	0	0	0	0	0	0	2	0	0	0	0
vomit	4	.3865	.3420	35.3	0	0	0	0	1	1	1	1	0	0	0	1	0	0	0	2	0	0	0	0	0	0	0	1	0
vomited	2	.2407	.1138	30.6	1	0	0	0	1	0	0	0	0	0	0	1	0	0	0	0	0	0	0	0	0	1	0	0	0
vomiting	6	.1813	.2803	34.5	1	0	1	0	0	4	0	0	0	0	0	0	0	0	0	2	0	0	0	0	0	0	4	0	0
von	7	.3381	.5099	37.1	0	0	0	1	0	5	1	0	0	0	0	0	0	0	0	0	3	0	0	0	0	0	3	1	0
Von	2	.0000	.0914	29.6	0	0	0	0	0	2	0	0	2	0	0	0	0	0	0	0	0	0	0	0	0	0	0	0	0
vonBaldewein	2	.0000	.0914	29.6	0	0	0	2	0	0	0	0	2	0	0	0	0	0	0	0	0	0	0	0	0	0	0	0	0
vonBraun	2	.0000	.0290	24.6	0	0	0	2	0	0	0	0	0	0	0	0	0	0	0	0	0	0	0	0	0	2	0	0	0
VonBulow	2	.0000	.0162	22.1	0	0	0	0	0	0	2	0	0	0	0	0	0	0	0	0	2	0	0	0	0	0	0	0	0
vonGluck	2	.0000	.0162	22.1	0	0	0	0	0	2	0	0	0	0	0	0	0	0	0	0	2	0	0	0	0	0	0	0	0
vonGradwitz	2	.0000	.0215	23.3	0	0	0	0	0	0	2	0	0	0	0	2	0	0	0	0	0	0	0	0	0	0	0	0	0
vonMeck	3	.0000	.0243	23.8	0	0	0	0	0	0	3	0	0	0	0	0	0	0	0	0	3	0	0	0	0	0	0	0	0
VonOsten	3	.0000	.0322	25.1	0	0	0	0	0	0	3	0	0	0	0	3	0	0	0	0	0	0	0	0	0	0	0	0	0
VonSnitz	2	.0000	.0914	29.6	0	0	0	0	2	0	0	0	2	0	0	0	0	0	0	0	0	0	0	0	0	0	0	0	0
Voorhies	2	.0000	.0162	22.1	0	0	2	0	0	0	0	0	0	0	0	0	0	0	0	0	2	0	0	0	0	0	0	0	0
voracious	5	.3303	.3607	35.6	0	0	0	0	3	0	2	0	0	0	0	0	0	0	1	0	0	0	0	0	0	1	3	0	0
vorpal	2	.0000	.0037	15.7	0	0	2	0	0	0	0	0	0	0	0	0	0	0	0	0	0	2	0	0	0	0	0	0	0
Voskrece	3	.0000	.0328	25.2	0	0	0	0	0	0	3	0	0	3	0	0	0	0	0	0	0	0	0	0	0	0	0	0	0
vot	2	.0000	.0162	22.1	0	0	0	2	0	0	0	0	0	0	0	0	0	0	0	0	2	0	0	0	0	0	0	0	0
vote	196	.6757	27.325	54.4	32	11	19	13	25	65	29	2	31	20	8	0	3	92	1	0	0	0	0	1	5	19	10	6	0
Vote	2	.2427	.1152	30.6	0	1	1	0	0	0	0	0	0	0	0	0	0	0	0	0	0	0	0	0	1	1	0	0	0
voted	60	.6765	8.3131	49.2	7	2	10	0	11	20	7	3	5	4	3	1	3	24	0	0	0	0	0	0	1	3	6	10	0
voter	7	.6240	.8986	39.5	0	0	1	0	3	1	2	0	0	1	0	1	0	2	0	1	0	0	0	0	0	1	0	1	0
voters	57	.6043	7.1453	48.5	2	0	7	2	9	16	21	0	3	3	4	0	1	29	2	0	0	0	0	0	0	2	5	8	0
votes	54	.6397	7.1772	48.6	6	0	4	6	11	21	4	2	8	6	0	0	1	23	2	0	0	0	0	0	0	4	6	4	0
voting	41	.4761	4.2636	46.3	7	2	4	4	5	5	14	0	7	3	5	0	0	17	0	0	0	0	0	0	0	7	2	0	0
Votkinsk	2	.0000	.0162	22.1	0	0	0	0	0	0	2	0	0	0	0	0	0	0	0	0	2	0	0	0	0	0	0	0	0
vouch	2	.2306	.1140	30.6	0	0	0	1	1	0	0	0	0	1	0	0	0	1	0	0	0	0	0	0	0	0	0	0	0
vow	11	.6367	1.4596	41.6	2	1	1	4	1	2	0	0	3	0	0	1	0	1	1	0	2	0	0	0	2	1	0	0	0
vowed	8	.5244	.9015	39.5	1	0	0	0	5	1	0	1	2	0	0	2	0	0	0	0	0	0	0	0	0	1	1	2	0
vowel	1484	.1687	63.465	58.0	374	301	278	282	157	64	24	4	123	170	0	1	1	0	1175	0	12	1	0	0	0	0	1	0	0
vowel-consonant	6	.0000	.0487	26.9	0	1	1	0	4	0	0	0	0	0	0	0	0	0	6	0	0	0	0	0	0	0	0	0	0
vowel-consonant-e	15	.0000	.1217	30.9	0	6	4	5	0	0	0	0	0	0	0	0	0	0	15	0	0	0	0	0	0	0	0	0	0
vowel-consonant-silent	5	.0000	.0406	26.1	1	0	2	1	0	1	0	0	0	0	0	0	0	0	5	0	0	0	0	0	0	0	0	0	0
vowel-consonant-vowel	2	.0000	.0162	22.1	0	1	0	0	1	0	0	0	0	0	0	0	0	0	2	0	0	0	0	0	0	0	0	0	0
vowels	285	.2611	18.134	52.6	65	61	41	75	21	15	5	2	62	35	0	0	1	0	178	0	6	0	0	0	0	0	3	0	0
vows	5	.4788	.5421	37.3	1	0	0	1	2	0	1	0	2	0	0	0	0	1	0	0	0	0	0	0	0	1	0	1	0
voyage	154	.7984	25.001	54.0	6	22	40	37	27	19	3	0	60	4	1	5	0	39	3	3	2	0	0	0	7	13	7	10	0
Voyage	2	.1494	.1045	30.2	0	1	0	0	1	0	0	0	1	0	0	0	0	0	0	0	1	0	0	0	0	0	0	0	0
voyaged	3	.1937	.1495	31.7	0	0	0	1	1	1	0	0	0	0	0	0	0	1	0	0	0	0	0	0	0	0	0	2	0
voyager	2	.1717	.1142	30.6	0	0	1	0	1	0	0	0	1	0	0	1	0	0	0	0	0	0	0	0	0	0	0	0	0
Voyager	4	.0000	.1827	32.6	0	0	4	0	0	0	0	0	4	0	0	0	0	0	0	0	0	0	0	0	0	0	0	0	0
voyagers	6	.4222	.5667	37.5	0	0	1	2	1	1	0	1	1	2	0	0	0	0	0	2	0	0	0	0	0	0	0	1	0
voyages	41	.6371	5.4679	47.4	3	4	13	9	10	2	0	0	9	0	0	0	0	13	0	4	0	0	0	0	2	4	6	3	0
Voyages	2	.0000	.0914	29.6	0	1	0	0	1	0	0	0	2	0	0	0	0	0	0	0	0	0	0	0	0	0	0	0	0
Voyageur	2	.0000	.0162	22.1	0	2	0	0	0	0	0	0	0	0	0	0	0	0	0	0	2	0	0	0	0	0	0	0	0
voyageurs	9	.0368	.1714	32.3	0	0	7	0	2	0	0	0	1	0	0	0	0	0	0	0	8	0	0	0	0	0	0	0	0
voyaging	4	.4529	.3998	36.0	0	1	0	0	3	0	0	0	1	0	0	0	0	0	0	0	0	0	0	0	1	0	1	1	0
VP	8	.0000	.0875	29.4	0	0	0	0	2	1	5	0	0	8	0	0	0	0	0	0	0	0	0	0	0	0	0	0	0
Vran's	2	.0000	.0290	24.6	0	0	0	0	2	0	0	0	0	0	0	0	0	0	0	0	0	0	0	0	0	2	0	0	0
vroom	2	.1814	.1187	30.7	1	0	0	0	0	0	1	0	1	0	0	0	0	0	0	0	0	0	0	0	0	0	0	1	0
vs	3	.2159	.1532	31.9	0	0	1	0	1	0	0	1	0	0	0	0	0	0	0	0	0	0	0	0	0	0	2	1	0
vu	2	.0000	.0243	23.9	0	0	0	0	1	0	0	1	0	0	0	0	0	0	0	0	0	0	0	0	0	0	0	2	0
Vuillard	2	.0000	.0037	15.7	0	0	0	0	2	0	0	0	0	0	0	0	0	0	0	0	0	2	0	0	0	0	0	0	0
Vulcan	15	.5947	1.8931	42.8	0	5	3	0	4	2	1	0	5	3	0	1	0	1	3	1	0	0	0	0	0	0	1	0	0
vulcanism	2	.0000	.0394	26.0	0	0	0	0	0	0	2	0	0	0	0	0	0	0	0	2	0	0	0	0	0	0	0	0	0
Vulcanization	2	.0000	.0209	23.2	0	0	2	0	0	0	0	0	0	0	0	0	0	0	0	0	0	0	0	0	0	0	2	0	0
vulcanized	2	.0000	.0209	23.2	0	0	2	0	0	0	0	0	0	0	0	0	0	0	0	0	0	0	0	0	0	0	2	0	0
vulgar	5	.5324	.5639	37.5	0	0	0	0	2	1	2	0	1	0	0	1	0	0	0	0	1	0	0	0	0	0	1	1	0
vulnerable	6	.0000	.0729	28.6	0	0	0	0	2	1	3	0	0	0	0	0	0	0	0	0	0	0	0	0	0	0	0	6	0
vulture	21	.5536	2.5330	44.0	4	0	4	5	4	2	2	0	9	2	0	4	4	0	0	0	0	0	0	0	0	0	2	0	0
vultures	10	.5052	1.0867	40.4	1	1	0	2	4	2	0	0	2	0	0	1	0	1	0	0	0	0	0	0	0	1	4	1	0
VW	8	.1828	.3714	35.7	0	0	1	1	5	1	0	0	0	0	0	0	2	0	0	0	0	0	0	0	0	0	0	6	0
V7	13	.0000	.1051	30.2	0	6	1	2	3	1	0	0	0	0	0	0	0	0	0	0	13	0	0	0	0	0	0	0	0
w	111	.3665	8.7919	49.4	22	18	18	16	18	9	10	0	4	3	3	2	29	0	68	1	0	0	0	0	0	0	1	0	0
W	101	.7454	15.234	51.8	6	13	10	10	18	21	13	10	14	4	7	0	16	4	0	8	3	0	0	2	1	13	18	11	0
W-a-t-e-r	4	.0000	.0579	27.6	0	4	0	0	0	0	0	0	0	0	0	0	0	0	0	0	0	0	0	0	0	4	0	0	0
w's	5	.1531	.1872	32.7	0	3	1	1	0	0	0	0	0	1	0	0	0	0	4	0	0	0	0	0	0	0	0	0	0
WA	3	.0000	.1370	31.4	3	0	0	0	0	0	0	0	3	0	0	0	0	0	0	0	0	0	0	0	0	0	0	0	0
Wabash	5	.2590	.3349	35.2	0	3	2	0	0	0	0	0	1	0	0	0	0	1	0	0	0	0	0	0	0	3	0	0	0
wabe	5	.2380	.2686	34.3	0	0	1	4	0	0	0	0	0	4	0	0	0	0	0	0	0	1	0	0	0	0	0	0	0
wad	3	.3768	.2484	34.0	0	0	1	0	2	0	0	0	0	0	0	1	0	0	0	1	0	0	0	0	1	0	0	0	0
wadded	4	.2919	.2559	34.1	0	4	0	0	0	0	0	0	0	0	0	0	0	0	0	0	0	1	0	0	2	0	0	1	0
wadded-up	2	.2443	.1130	30.5	0	0	0	0	1	1	0	0	0	0	0	1	0	0	0	0	0	0	0	0	1	0	0	0	0
Waddell	5	.2423	.2894	34.6	2	0	0	1	0	2	0	0	0	0	0	0	0	0	0	0	0	0	0	0	0	3	0	2	0
wadding	2	.1717	.1142	30.6	0	0	0	0	2	0	0	0	1	0	0	1	0	0	0	0	0	0	0	0	0	0	0	0	0
waddle	4	.0000	.1827	32.6	1	1	0	0	2	0	0	0	4	0	0	0	0	0	0	0	0	0	0	0	0	0	0	0	0
waddled	16	.4011	1.5019	41.8	5	7	2	0	1	0	0	1	7	0	3	0	0	0	1	0	0	0	0	0	1	3	0	1	0
waddling	5	.3436	.4206	36.2	2	0	0	0	1	0	1	1	2	0	0	1	0	0	0	0	0	0	0	0	0	0	0	2	0
wade	20	.6217	2.6022	44.2	5	1	6	2	5	1	0	0	5	1	0	4	0	1	0	0	0	0	0	0	0	5	2	2	0
Wade	9	.5482	1.0700	40.3	0	0	3	0	0	3	2	1	3	0	0	1	0	2	0	0	0	0	0	0	2	0	0	1	0
Wade-Davis	2	.0000	.0389	25.9	0	0	0	0	0	2	0	0	0	0	0	0	0	2	0	0	0	0	0	0	0	0	0	0	0
waded	33	.6319	4.3554	46.4	8	7	3	5	6	0	2	2	9	0	0	6	0	0	1	0	0	0	0	0	2	6	2	7	0
wades	5	.4751	.5383	37.3	3	1	1	0	0	0	0	0	2	1	0	0	0	1	0	0	0	0	0	0	0	1	0	0	0

XR Volunteers
7F vonBismarck
XP vonBrauchitsch
6P vonBraun's
9J vonBulow
9J VonBulow's
6J vonEisenstein
8D vonFrankenstein
4Q vonFrisch
9Q vonGoethe
9Q vonGuericke
8F vonHindenburg
8E vonLeibniz
9Q vonLiebig
6R vonReding
8R vonRosen
XH vonSterneck
7J VonTilzer
8J vonWeber
7H vonWeizsacker
7A vonWrangel
8Q vonder
8Q vonderOsten-Sacken
8A vont-elles
5P Vordingborg
6J vordt
7A Vorkle
5H vorticella
6F Vosges
9F voter's
5F Voting
9K votive
9R vouched
7G vowel-consonant-consonant
3G vowel-consonant-final
7G vowel-vowel
4G vowel-y
5A Voyager's
5J voyageurs'
7P Vran
7H Vredefort
4N vrouws
8M vulcanite
8G vulcanize
5Q vulcanizing
9H Vulcanus
5P vulgarities
8D vulgarity
7H Vulpes
4A Vulpian
9D Vultures
5B vv
4G VVC
7R VW-based
7R VW-type
7R VW'S
4E VX
8Q Vyatka
6P vying
8J Vysehrad
4E VZ
8H V2
7R V8
7R V8s
3E W-A-M-R
4P W-A-T-
5A w-a-t-e-r
4P W-a-t-e-r
6N w-w-well
7A w-w-what
3A w
3A wll
7D W'Tassone
7A w'en
7B w'er's
8B w'ile
5A wa-al
4P wa-tho-huck
8P wa-wa
8D wa'n't
5R WAC
7A Wachita
6A Wack
7F Waco
8Q Waddill
3J waddle-dee-dee
4P Waddles

Word Type	F	D	U	SFI	3 Gr 3	4 Gr 4	5 Gr 5	6 Gr 6	7 Gr 7	8 Gr 8	9 Gr 9	X UnGr	A Read	B Eng & Gr	C Comp	D Lit	E Math	F Soc Stud	G Spell	H Sci	J Music	K Art	L Home Ec	M Shop	N Lib F	P Lib NF	Q Lib Ref	R Mag	S Rel
wading	17	.5531	2.0221	43.1	3	5	4	4	1	0	0	0	5	0	0	0	0	0	0	2	0	1	0	0	1	5	0	3	0
Wadsworth	3	.3847	.2448	33.9	0	0	2	0	1	0	0	0	0	0	0	1	0	0	0	0	1	0	0	0	0	0	1	0	0
wafers	3	.2330	.1860	32.7	0	1	0	0	0	1	1	0	1	0	0	0	0	0	0	0	0	0	1	0	0	1	0	0	0
waffle	3	.2524	.1934	32.9	0	1	0	0	0	0	2	0	1	0	0	1	0	0	0	0	0	0	1	0	0	0	0	0	0
waffles	5	.0882	.1084	30.3	0	0	0	0	0	0	5	0	0	1	0	0	0	0	0	0	0	0	4	0	0	0	0	0	0
waft	3	.2321	.1635	32.1	0	0	0	0	1	0	0	2	0	0	0	0	0	0	0	0	0	0	0	0	0	0	1	2	0
wag	4	.3661	.3170	35.0	1	1	0	0	1	0	1	0	0	0	0	0	0	0	1	0	0	0	0	0	2	1	0	0	0
Wag	2	.0000	.0215	23.3	0	2	0	0	0	0	0	0	0	0	0	2	0	0	0	0	0	0	0	0	0	0	0	0	0
Waganupa	2	.0000	.0389	25.9	0	0	0	0	0	2	0	0	0	0	0	0	0	2	0	0	0	0	0	0	0	0	0	0	0
wage	37	.4990	3.8854	45.9	2	1	3	1	2	6	22	0	1	1	0	0	2	6	0	0	0	0	2	0	1	1	1	22	0
waged	8	.4331	.7570	38.8	1	0	0	2	3	1	1	0	0	0	0	0	0	5	0	0	0	0	0	0	0	1	1	1	0
Wageni	3	.0000	.0365	25.6	0	3	0	0	0	0	0	0	0	0	0	0	0	0	0	0	0	0	0	0	0	0	0	3	0
wager	8	.2871	.5403	37.3	0	1	1	0	5	0	1	0	1	0	0	3	0	0	0	0	0	0	0	0	4	0	0	0	0
wagering	8	.0000	.1158	30.6	0	0	0	8	0	0	0	0	0	0	0	0	0	0	0	0	0	0	0	0	0	8	0	0	0
wages	74	.7471	11.178	50.5	8	4	7	7	11	14	23	0	5	3	0	2	9	24	0	1	0	0	4	0	3	9	6	8	0
Wages	3	.0000	.0583	27.7	0	0	0	0	0	3	0	0	0	0	0	0	0	3	0	0	0	0	0	0	0	0	0	0	0
wagged	25	.6050	3.2651	45.1	5	7	4	3	5	1	0	0	13	0	0	0	0	1	1	0	0	0	0	0	5	1	1	3	0
wagging	12	.4340	1.2317	40.9	4	0	4	2	2	0	0	0	7	0	1	1	0	0	0	0	0	0	0	0	3	0	0	0	0
waggish	3	.2309	.1631	32.1	0	0	0	1	1	0	1	0	0	0	0	1	0	0	0	0	0	0	0	0	0	0	0	2	0
waging	5	.3023	.3461	35.4	0	0	0	2	2	1	0	0	0	0	0	0	0	1	0	0	0	0	0	0	0	1	0	3	0
Wagner	23	.2045	1.0977	40.4	0	0	3	2	4	12	2	0	0	0	0	0	0	2	0	0	17	0	0	0	0	0	4	0	0
Wagner's	7	.1253	.2239	33.5	0	0	0	0	1	5	1	0	0	0	0	0	0	0	0	0	6	0	0	0	0	0	1	0	0
Wagnerian	3	.0000	.0243	23.8	0	0	0	0	0	1	2	0	0	0	0	0	0	0	0	0	3	0	0	0	0	0	0	0	0
wagon	356	.8048	58.035	57.6	132	72	65	24	32	17	13	1	127	9	1	30	6	36	6	11	10	0	0	1	59	46	2	12	0
Wagon	12	.3469	.8961	39.5	7	5	0	0	0	0	0	0	0	5	0	0	0	0	0	0	5	0	0	0	0	0	0	2	0
wagoner	2	.1717	.1142	30.6	0	0	0	1	0	0	1	0	1	0	0	1	0	0	0	0	0	0	0	0	0	0	0	0	0
wagonload	5	.4727	.5348	37.3	1	0	2	0	0	2	0	0	2	1	0	0	0	1	0	0	0	0	0	0	1	0	0	0	0
wagons	149	.8097	24.317	53.9	42	33	22	17	19	7	5	4	35	2	4	6	2	30	2	3	5	0	0	0	12	27	6	15	0
Wagons	2	.1814	.1187	30.7	1	0	1	0	0	0	0	0	1	0	0	0	0	0	0	0	0	0	0	0	0	0	0	1	0
wagtails	2	.1698	.1133	30.5	0	0	1	0	1	0	0	0	1	0	0	0	0	0	0	0	0	0	0	0	0	0	1	0	0
wah-ka	2	.0000	.0162	22.1	0	0	0	2	0	0	0	0	0	0	0	0	0	0	0	0	2	0	0	0	0	0	0	0	0
wah-wah	2	.0000	.0914	29.6	0	0	2	0	0	0	0	0	2	0	0	0	0	0	0	0	0	0	0	0	0	0	0	0	0
Wahoo	2	.0000	.0914	29.6	0	0	0	2	0	0	0	0	2	0	0	0	0	0	0	0	0	0	0	0	0	0	0	0	0
Waialeale	4	.2163	.2275	33.6	0	2	2	0	0	0	0	0	0	0	0	0	1	3	0	0	0	0	0	0	0	0	0	0	0
waif	4	.3723	.3645	35.6	0	0	0	0	3	0	0	1	2	1	0	0	0	0	0	0	0	0	0	0	0	0	0	1	0
Waikiki	4	.2281	.2337	33.7	0	0	3	1	0	0	0	0	0	0	0	0	0	3	0	0	0	0	0	0	0	0	0	1	0
wail	17	.6755	2.3733	43.8	2	2	3	2	4	0	3	1	5	4	1	1	0	0	0	1	2	0	0	0	1	1	0	1	0
wailed	25	.5355	2.9884	44.8	6	7	3	3	3	1	2	0	14	0	0	3	0	0	0	0	0	0	0	0	4	1	0	3	0
wailing	21	.6401	2.7836	44.4	2	2	2	3	7	2	3	0	5	1	1	5	0	0	0	0	2	0	0	0	4	0	0	3	0
wails	2	.1494	.1045	30.2	1	0	0	0	1	0	0	0	1	0	0	0	0	0	0	0	1	0	0	0	0	0	0	0	0
Waino	5	.0000	.2284	33.6	0	5	0	0	0	0	0	0	5	0	0	0	0	0	0	0	0	0	0	0	0	0	0	0	0
waist	80	.7482	12.235	50.9	9	16	11	11	23	3	5	2	29	1	0	12	0	0	3	6	1	2	7	0	7	6	1	5	0
waist-deep	2	.2407	.1138	30.6	0	1	0	0	1	0	0	0	0	0	0	1	0	0	0	0	0	0	0	0	0	1	0	0	0
waistband	7	.0223	.0943	29.7	0	0	0	1	2	3	1	0	1	0	0	0	0	0	0	0	0	0	6	0	0	0	0	0	0
waistcoat	8	.4411	.8060	39.1	0	1	0	2	0	3	2	0	3	0	0	2	0	1	0	0	0	0	0	0	2	0	0	0	0
waistcoat-pocket	2	.0000	.0234	23.7	0	0	2	0	0	0	0	0	0	0	0	0	0	0	0	0	0	0	0	0	2	0	0	0	0
waistline	21	.1295	.7032	38.5	1	0	1	1	3	13	2	0	3	0	0	0	0	0	0	0	0	1	17	0	0	0	0	0	0
waists	6	.5064	.6287	38.0	1	1	1	1	1	1	0	0	0	0	0	2	0	1	1	0	0	0	1	0	1	0	0	0	0
wait	656	.8213	109.01	60.4	181	156	67	64	104	39	33	12	275	24	3	55	1	43	14	29	5	0	5	0	83	72	5	42	0
Wait	2	.2375	.1088	30.4	1	0	0	0	1	0	0	0	0	0	0	0	0	0	0	0	1	0	0	0	0	0	0	1	0
wait'll	2	.1948	.1250	31.0	0	1	0	0	0	1	0	0	1	0	0	0	0	0	0	0	0	0	0	0	0	1	0	0	0
waited	335	.7292	50.473	57.0	76	73	39	43	47	27	20	10	149	13	2	26	0	5	2	6	4	0	0	0	56	43	1	28	0
waiter	30	.5930	3.7597	45.8	6	1	3	2	6	6	6	0	8	5	0	8	3	3	0	0	0	0	0	0	0	1	0	2	0
Waiter	2	.0000	.0243	23.9	0	2	0	0	0	0	0	0	0	0	0	0	0	0	0	0	0	0	0	0	0	0	0	2	0
waiter's	2	.0000	.0914	29.6	0	0	1	1	0	0	0	0	2	0	0	0	0	0	0	0	0	0	0	0	0	0	0	0	0
waiters	8	.3955	.7583	38.8	1	4	1	0	2	0	0	0	4	1	1	0	2	0	0	0	0	0	0	0	0	0	0	0	0
waitin'	4	.3713	.3634	35.6	0	0	1	0	2	0	1	0	2	0	0	1	0	0	0	0	0	0	0	0	1	0	0	0	0
waiting	493	.8083	80.824	59.1	104	105	46	48	89	55	38	8	210	32	7	48	2	24	3	9	11	0	1	0	61	43	4	38	0
Waiting	3	.2058	.1429	31.5	0	0	0	3	0	0	0	0	0	1	0	0	0	0	0	0	2	0	0	0	0	0	0	0	0
waitresses	3	.1277	.1363	31.3	0	0	0	0	1	2	0	0	1	0	0	0	0	0	0	0	0	0	0	0	0	0	0	2	0
waits	28	.6180	3.5674	45.5	9	0	2	5	9	1	1	1	3	0	0	6	0	1	0	1	6	0	0	0	1	7	1	2	0
Wajir	4	.0000	.0486	26.9	0	0	0	4	0	0	0	0	0	0	0	0	0	0	0	0	0	0	0	0	0	0	0	4	0
Wak	2	.0000	.0243	23.9	0	0	0	2	0	0	0	0	0	0	0	0	0	0	0	0	0	0	0	0	0	0	0	2	0
wake	113	.8115	18.566	52.7	19	25	13	17	20	10	8	1	43	4	1	11	0	4	0	8	2	1	0	0	10	19	1	9	0
waked	8	.4516	.8177	39.1	3	1	0	2	1	0	1	0	3	0	0	2	0	0	0	0	0	0	0	0	2	1	0	0	0
Wakefield	2	.1698	.1133	30.5	0	0	1	0	0	1	0	0	1	0	0	0	0	0	0	0	0	0	0	0	0	0	1	0	0
waken	4	.3813	.3772	35.8	2	1	0	0	0	1	0	0	2	0	0	0	0	1	0	0	0	0	0	0	0	1	0	0	0
wakened	17	.5899	2.2021	43.4	6	1	2	3	3	2	0	0	10	0	0	1	0	2	0	1	0	0	0	0	2	1	0	0	0
wakens	3	.3833	.2447	33.9	0	1	1	0	0	1	0	0	0	0	0	0	0	0	0	0	1	0	0	0	1	0	1	0	0
wakes	23	.7474	3.4936	45.4	9	1	4	3	3	0	3	0	5	1	1	4	0	0	0	4	2	0	0	0	1	3	1	1	0
waking	29	.6516	3.9402	46.0	5	1	2	5	6	4	4	2	9	0	2	4	0	4	0	0	2	0	0	0	5	2	1	0	0
Waksman	4	.0000	.0789	29.0	0	0	0	1	0	0	3	0	0	0	0	0	0	0	0	4	0	0	0	0	0	0	0	0	0
wal	2	.0000	.0914	29.6	2	0	0	0	0	0	0	0	2	0	0	0	0	0	0	0	0	0	0	0	0	0	0	0	0
Waldeck	4	.2424	.3036	34.8	0	0	0	1	0	3	0	0	3	0	0	0	0	0	0	0	0	0	0	0	0	0	0	1	0
Walden	7	.3325	.5327	37.3	0	0	1	0	2	4	0	0	1	1	0	0	0	0	0	0	0	0	0	0	0	1	4	0	0
Waldo	16	.6492	2.2155	43.5	0	2	1	9	2	2	0	0	9	1	0	0	0	1	0	0	1	0	0	0	0	1	2	1	0
Waldo's	2	.0000	.0914	29.6	0	0	0	2	0	0	0	0	2	0	0	0	0	0	0	0	0	0	0	0	0	0	0	0	0
Waldorf	2	.1972	.1262	31.0	0	0	0	0	1	0	1	0	1	0	0	0	1	0	0	0	0	0	0	0	0	0	0	0	0
Wales	43	.5331	4.8053	46.8	0	2	7	17	14	1	2	0	3	1	0	0	0	4	0	1	5	0	0	0	1	4	2	22	0
walk	831	.9407	154.81	61.9	258	139	95	90	142	49	40	18	288	55	14	45	32	45	22	78	36	6	8	1	58	75	19	49	0
Walk	9	.3901	.8508	39.3	4	1	1	0	0	2	1	0	5	0	0	2	0	0	0	0	0	1	0	0	0	0	0	1	0
walked	1030	.7858	165.39	62.2	282	227	100	89	176	99	51	6	499	51	6	77	18	51	14	6	12	1	0	0	136	109	2	48	0
walker	7	.3485	.5579	37.5	3	2	0	0	1	0	1	0	1	0	0	0	0	0	0	0	0	0	0	0	1	1	0	4	0
Walker	28	.5021	3.1438	45.0	15	2	0	7	1	1	0	2	10	2	0	0	0	12	0	0	0	0	0	0	0	2	0	2	0
walkers	4	.4516	.4046	36.1	0	0	1	0	1	1	1	0	1	0	0	1	0	1	0	0	0	0	0	0	0	1	0	0	0
Walkers	2	.0000	.0219	23.4	0	2	0	0	0	0	0	0	0	2	0	0	0	0	0	0	0	0	0	0	0	0	0	0	0
walkie-talkie	9	.2212	.6853	38.4	6	0	0	1	0	2	0	0	8	0	0	0	0	0	0	0	0	0	0	0	0	0	0	1	0
walking	453	.8727	79.232	59.0	131	93	34	56	74	28	27	10	195	21	5	37	5	15	4	25	26	2	1	0	43	34	8	32	0
Walking	8	.1863	.5546	37.4	7	0	0	0	0	1	0	0	7	0	0	0	0	0	0	0	0	1	0	0	0	0	0	0	0
walking-stick	2	.0000	.0914	29.6	2	0	0	0	0	0	0	0	2	0	0	0	0	0	0	0	0	0	0	0	0	0	0	0	0
walks	140	.8419	23.701	53.7	42	24	11	13	16	15	14	5	51	11	1	12	10	3	1	2	8	3	0	0	3	22	3	10	0
wall	642	.9112	116.20	60.7	106	112	78	105	116	71	39	15	165	9	7	54	27	44	3	94	16	14	10	2	78	50	28	41	0
Wall	22	.7276	3.2945	45.2	9	1	4	1	5	0	2	0	8	1	0	1	0	2	0	1	1	1	0	0	0	3	1	3	0
wall-eyed	2	.2387	.1089	30.4	0	0	0	0	1	1	0	0	0	0	0	0	0	0	0	0	1	0	0	0	1	0	0	0	0

6A wadgetty
5P Wadi
3A wadin'
6F wadis
9D wads
5R WAF
XR wafer-thin
5A waferlike
7J wafted
XR wafting
9D wag's
4N Wagai
8F wage-earning
XR wage-price
5B wagered
8F WAGES
3A waggled
3A waggles
3P waggling
7N wagon-seat
8F wagon-wheel
4A wagon'
7R Wagoneer
7P wagoners
8A wagonloads
7Q wags
6R wah
7P Wahhabi
6J wahka
7R wahoo
5F Waianae
5A wailers
7F Wailing
4A Waino's
5Q wainscoting
3A Wainwright
8D waistcoats
7L waistlines
5P Waitangi
XR Waite
3A Waiter's
4N waiting-woman
9B waitress
5R wakeful
9Q wakefulness
9D wakening
3A Waker
3P Walberg
7N Walbrook
9Q Walcheren
7D Waldhoning
8H Waldoboro
8F Waldorf-Astoria
8L wales
9H WALK
3Q walkie-talkies
9D walkin'
5H walking-day
5H walking-days
5H walking-minutes
9D walking-shoe
XR walkout
6J Walkure
4A walkways
7A wall-eye
7R wall-hung

Word Type	F	D	U	SFI	3 Gr 3	4 Gr 4	5 Gr 5	6 Gr 6	7 Gr 7	8 Gr 8	9 Gr 9	X UnGr	A Read	B Eng & Gr	C Comp	D Lit	E Math	F Soc Stud	G Spell	H Sci	J Music	K Art	L Home Ec	M Shop	N Lib F	P Lib NF	Q Lib Ref	R Mag	S Rel
wall-paper	6	.2236	.3140	35.0	0	0	0	0	0	6	0	0	0	2	0	4	0	0	0	0	0	0	0	0	0	0	0	0	0
Wallace	27	.5499	3.1178	44.9	1	15	0	0	8	3	0	0	2	0	0	4	1	2	0	1	0	0	0	0	1	14	1	1	0
Wallaroo	3	.0000	.0583	27.7	0	3	0	0	0	0	0	0	0	0	0	0	0	3	0	0	0	0	0	0	0	0	0	0	0
wallboard	5	.3740	.3977	36.0	1	0	0	1	2	0	1	0	0	0	0	0	0	0	0	1	2	1	0	0	0	0	1	0	0
walled	12	.5267	1.3763	41.4	2	2	0	4	3	1	0	0	3	0	0	0	0	5	1	0	0	0	0	0	0	2	0	1	0
Wallenstein's	3	.0000	.0314	25.0	0	0	0	0	0	0	3	0	0	0	0	0	0	0	0	0	0	0	0	0	0	0	3	0	0
Wallerawang	2	.0000	.0243	23.9	0	0	0	2	0	0	0	0	0	0	0	0	0	0	0	0	0	0	0	0	0	0	0	2	0
wallet	13	.5170	1.4027	41.5	0	0	1	0	5	1	6	0	1	2	1	6	0	0	0	0	0	0	0	0	2	0	0	1	0
wallets	2	.2440	.1132	30.5	0	0	0	1	1	0	0	0	0	0	0	1	0	0	0	0	0	0	0	0	0	0	0	1	0
wallflower	2	.0000	.0243	23.9	0	0	2	0	0	0	0	0	0	0	0	0	0	0	0	0	0	0	0	0	0	0	0	2	0
Wallie	5	.0000	.2284	33.6	0	0	5	0	0	0	0	0	5	0	0	0	0	0	0	0	0	0	0	0	0	0	0	0	0
Wallingford	2	.1494	.1045	30.2	0	0	0	1	0	1	0	0	1	0	0	0	0	0	0	0	1	0	0	0	0	0	0	0	0
Walloomsac	2	.0000	.0914	29.6	0	0	0	0	2	0	0	0	2	0	0	0	0	0	0	0	0	0	0	0	0	0	0	0	0
Walloon	3	.0000	.1370	31.4	0	0	0	3	0	0	0	0	3	0	0	0	0	0	0	0	0	0	0	0	0	0	0	0	0
Walloons	2	.1698	.1133	30.5	0	0	1	1	0	0	0	0	1	0	0	0	0	0	0	0	0	0	0	0	0	0	1	0	0
wallow	4	.3354	.3295	35.2	0	0	1	0	0	2	1	0	1	0	0	0	0	2	0	0	0	0	0	0	0	1	0	0	0
wallowed	7	.5528	.8437	39.3	2	2	0	0	2	1	0	0	3	1	0	1	0	1	0	0	1	0	0	0	0	0	0	0	0
wallowing	6	.5568	.7182	38.6	0	0	1	2	3	0	0	0	2	1	0	1	0	0	0	0	0	0	0	0	1	1	0	0	0
wallpaper	13	.4875	1.3189	41.2	1	4	4	0	2	2	0	0	1	0	0	0	1	0	0	0	0	3	1	1	3	0	0	3	0
walls	478	.8836	84.214	59.3	60	73	72	86	76	45	52	14	110	16	1	29	7	83	2	83	1	14	8	1	20	29	30	43	1
Wally	2	.0665	.0708	28.5	0	0	0	1	1	0	0	0	1	0	1	0	0	0	0	0	0	0	0	0	0	0	0	0	0
walnut	49	.7575	7.4620	48.7	5	8	3	4	20	6	3	0	3	3	1	0	0	5	0	1	2	2	0	2	3	8	2	17	0
Walnut	4	.3795	.3302	35.2	0	3	0	0	0	1	0	0	0	0	0	1	0	0	0	0	0	0	0	0	1	2	0	0	0
walnuts	11	.4445	1.0702	40.3	0	2	2	3	4	0	0	0	0	0	0	1	0	2	0	6	0	0	0	0	0	2	0	0	0
walrus	21	.6625	2.9822	44.7	8	1	8	1	1	1	0	1	14	0	0	1	0	1	0	1	1	0	0	0	1	1	0	1	0
Walrus	22	.4177	2.0112	43.0	7	0	0	0	15	0	0	0	3	8	0	4	0	0	0	0	0	0	0	0	0	0	0	7	0
walruses	5	.3850	.4834	36.8	3	0	2	0	0	0	0	0	3	0	0	0	0	1	0	0	0	0	0	0	0	1	0	0	0
Walsh	3	.1927	.1491	31.7	0	0	1	0	2	0	0	0	0	0	0	0	0	0	0	1	0	0	0	0	0	0	0	2	0
Walt	27	.5103	3.0167	44.8	0	14	1	0	9	2	1	0	6	0	0	1	0	14	0	0	0	0	0	0	2	1	0	3	0
Walt's	2	.0000	.0234	23.7	0	0	0	0	2	0	0	0	0	0	0	0	0	0	0	0	0	0	0	0	2	0	0	0	0
Walter	107	.7525	16.401	52.1	8	23	11	14	15	14	18	4	28	5	0	16	2	8	0	6	6	0	0	0	1	21	3	11	0
Walter's	9	.4584	.8845	39.5	2	1	1	3	1	1	0	0	1	0	0	1	0	0	0	0	3	0	0	0	0	3	0	1	0
Walters	6	.1757	.2765	34.4	5	0	0	0	1	0	0	0	0	0	0	0	0	0	0	0	0	0	0	0	1	5	0	0	0
Waltham	2	.2152	.1357	31.3	0	0	0	0	0	1	1	0	1	0	0	0	0	1	0	0	0	0	0	0	0	0	0	0	0
Walthers	3	.0000	.1370	31.4	3	0	0	0	0	0	0	0	3	0	0	0	0	0	0	0	0	0	0	0	0	0	0	0	0
Walton	4	.1789	.1692	32.3	0	0	1	0	3	0	0	0	0	0	0	0	0	0	0	0	3	0	0	0	0	0	1	0	0
waltz	29	.4240	2.6530	44.2	5	7	0	8	2	7	0	0	4	2	0	0	0	0	0	0	17	1	0	0	1	3	0	1	0
Waltz	4	.1494	.2089	33.2	2	0	0	2	0	0	0	0	2	0	0	0	0	0	0	0	2	0	0	0	0	0	0	0	0
waltzes	6	.3909	.4983	37.0	1	1	0	2	0	0	2	0	0	1	0	0	0	0	0	0	3	0	0	0	1	1	0	0	0
Waltzes	2	.0000	.0162	22.1	0	1	0	1	0	0	0	0	0	0	0	0	0	0	0	0	2	0	0	0	0	0	0	0	0
waltzing	4	.4445	.3917	35.9	1	1	0	0	0	2	0	0	1	0	0	1	0	0	0	0	1	0	0	0	1	0	0	0	0
Waltzing	2	.0000	.0162	22.1	1	1	0	0	0	0	0	0	0	0	0	0	0	0	0	0	2	0	0	0	0	0	0	0	0
Walz	4	.0000	.1827	32.6	0	0	4	0	0	0	0	0	4	0	0	0	0	0	0	0	0	0	0	0	0	0	0	0	0
wampum	10	.3602	.9577	39.8	8	0	1	0	1	0	0	0	8	0	0	1	0	0	0	0	0	0	0	0	0	1	0	0	0
Wampum	3	.0000	.0434	26.4	0	3	0	0	0	0	0	0	0	0	0	0	0	0	0	0	0	0	0	0	0	3	0	0	0
wan	2	.2446	.1142	30.6	0	0	0	0	2	0	0	0	0	0	0	0	0	0	0	0	0	0	0	0	1	0	0	1	0
Wana	9	.2084	.4993	37.0	0	7	0	0	2	0	0	0	0	0	0	0	0	7	0	0	0	0	0	0	0	2	0	0	0
Wanamaker	4	.0000	.0579	27.6	0	4	0	0	0	0	0	0	0	0	0	0	0	0	0	0	0	0	0	0	0	4	0	0	0
Wanamakers	2	.0000	.0290	24.6	0	2	0	0	0	0	0	0	0	0	0	0	0	0	0	0	0	0	0	0	0	2	0	0	0
wanasi	5	.0000	.0972	29.9	0	0	0	0	0	5	0	0	0	0	0	0	0	5	0	0	0	0	0	0	0	0	0	0	0
wand	12	.4705	1.3042	41.2	3	0	0	7	1	0	1	0	7	0	0	2	0	0	0	0	2	0	0	0	0	0	1	0	0
Wanda	8	.0000	.3655	35.6	0	0	0	0	8	0	0	0	8	0	0	0	0	0	0	0	0	0	0	0	0	0	0	0	0
wander	63	.8175	10.392	50.2	15	9	9	8	10	4	8	0	21	2	1	7	0	8	0	1	3	2	0	0	6	5	2	5	0
wandered	74	.7078	10.835	50.3	7	22	15	7	12	6	3	2	27	0	1	11	0	10	0	0	0	0	0	0	10	7	3	5	0
wanderer	8	.6601	1.0887	40.4	1	3	0	1	1	1	1	0	1	0	0	1	0	1	0	2	0	0	0	0	1	0	1	1	0
wanderers	14	.5824	1.7437	42.4	0	4	0	2	7	0	1	0	4	0	0	0	0	3	0	2	0	0	0	0	0	1	3	1	0
wandering	76	.8067	12.376	50.9	4	12	8	21	16	4	5	6	22	1	2	6	0	9	0	4	6	0	0	0	8	5	5	8	0
wanderings	7	.4166	.6628	38.2	0	1	0	0	3	3	0	0	2	0	1	0	0	1	0	1	0	0	0	0	0	0	2	0	0
wanderlust	2	.2441	.1127	30.5	1	1	0	0	0	0	0	0	0	0	0	0	0	0	0	0	0	0	0	0	1	0	1	0	0
wanders	7	.4495	.6964	38.4	1	1	1	0	4	0	0	0	2	0	0	2	0	0	0	0	1	0	0	0	0	0	2	0	0
wands	2	.2446	.1125	30.5	0	1	0	0	1	0	0	0	0	1	0	1	0	0	0	0	0	0	0	0	0	0	0	0	0
wane	5	.3810	.4789	36.8	0	2	0	1	1	0	0	1	3	0	0	0	0	0	0	1	0	0	0	0	0	0	0	1	0
waned	5	.4465	.4743	36.8	0	0	0	1	1	2	1	0	0	0	0	0	0	1	0	0	0	0	0	0	1	0	2	1	0
Waneko	4	.0000	.1827	32.6	0	0	0	0	4	0	0	0	4	0	0	0	0	0	0	0	0	0	0	0	0	0	0	0	0
wanes	2	.1814	.1187	30.7	0	1	0	0	0	1	0	0	1	0	0	0	0	0	0	0	0	0	0	0	0	0	0	1	0
Wang	33	.3495	2.7964	44.5	11	12	0	0	10	0	0	0	12	0	0	10	0	0	0	0	0	0	0	0	0	11	0	0	0
Wang's	6	.3408	.4953	36.9	2	2	0	0	2	0	0	0	2	0	0	2	0	0	0	0	0	0	0	0	0	2	0	0	0
Wangs	2	.0000	.0215	23.3	0	0	0	0	2	0	0	0	0	0	0	2	0	0	0	0	0	0	0	0	0	0	0	0	0
waning	6	.4126	.5469	37.4	1	1	0	2	1	1	0	0	1	0	1	0	0	1	0	0	0	0	0	0	2	0	0	1	0
wanna	6	.3873	.5826	37.7	0	1	0	0	2	0	2	1	4	0	0	1	0	0	0	0	0	0	0	0	0	0	0	1	0
Wanstead	4	.0000	.0579	27.6	0	4	0	0	0	0	0	0	0	0	0	0	0	0	0	0	0	0	0	0	0	4	0	0	0
want	2655	.9255	487.59	66.9	622	535	276	237	471	291	177	46	895	170	17	193	71	217	64	123	33	55	55	20	278	259	21	177	7
wanta	6	.0000	.0644	28.1	0	0	0	0	0	4	2	0	0	0	0	6	0	0	0	0	0	0	0	0	0	0	0	0	0
wanted	1637	.8349	275.77	64.4	411	346	193	207	220	165	72	23	659	51	7	100	50	232	26	33	21	16	4	1	153	178	15	84	7
wanting	61	.7514	9.3685	49.7	4	16	7	6	11	7	7	3	19	4	0	7	0	8	0	4	2	0	0	0	9	6	1	1	0
wanton	4	.4873	.4082	36.1	0	0	1	0	2	0	1	0	0	0	0	1	0	0	0	0	0	0	0	0	1	1	0	1	0
wantonly	2	.2337	.1157	30.6	0	1	0	0	0	1	0	0	0	0	0	0	0	1	0	0	0	0	0	0	1	0	0	0	0
wants	461	.7107	67.532	58.3	129	98	45	39	52	52	34	12	147	40	6	24	33	45	10	23	9	0	8	0	28	51	2	30	5
war	968	.7222	142.74	61.5	85	116	140	109	127	262	115	14	143	25	2	40	0	376	9	8	7	1	0	1	17	136	89	114	0
War	555	.7054	79.879	59.0	23	53	126	78	90	114	58	13	55	12	2	7	4	215	1	11	32	0	0	1	11	56	109	39	0
war-horse	2	.0000	.0914	29.6	0	0	0	2	0	0	0	0	2	0	0	0	0	0	0	0	0	0	0	0	0	0	0	0	0
war-torn	3	.0000	.0583	27.7	0	1	0	0	0	2	0	0	0	0	0	0	0	3	0	0	0	0	0	0	0	0	0	0	0
war's	7	.4529	.6679	38.2	0	2	0	2	1	2	0	0	0	0	0	0	0	1	0	0	3	0	0	0	1	1	0	1	0
warble	2	.2401	.1133	30.5	0	1	0	0	1	0	0	0	0	0	0	0	0	0	0	0	0	0	0	0	0	1	1	0	0
warbled	3	.2028	.1988	33.0	0	1	0	1	0	0	1	0	2	0	0	0	0	0	0	0	1	0	0	0	0	0	0	0	0
warbler	5	.2424	.2988	34.8	0	0	0	0	2	0	0	3	0	0	0	0	0	0	0	3	0	0	0	0	0	0	2	0	0
warblers	9	.3081	.6501	38.1	2	0	0	1	5	0	0	1	1	0	0	0	0	0	0	2	0	0	0	0	0	1	5	0	0
ward	16	.7184	2.3563	43.7	3	1	0	1	1	1	8	1	4	1	0	1	0	3	1	0	1	0	0	0	0	3	0	2	0
Ward	30	.5680	3.7380	45.7	2	3	13	1	5	2	3	1	15	0	0	5	1	4	0	0	0	0	0	0	0	4	0	1	0
Ward's	7	.5548	.8377	39.2	0	3	2	1	1	0	0	0	2	0	0	1	0	2	0	0	0	0	0	0	1	1	0	0	0
warden	14	.4261	1.3366	41.3	0	3	0	4	0	7	0	0	4	0	0	7	0	0	0	0	0	1	0	0	0	1	0	1	0
WARDEN	16	.0000	.1717	32.3	0	0	0	0	0	16	0	0	0	0	0	16	0	0	0	0	0	0	0	0	0	0	0	0	0
warder	2	.1787	.1174	30.7	0	1	1	0	0	0	0	0	1	0	0	0	0	0	0	0	0	0	0	0	1	0	0	0	0
warders	2	.0000	.0914	29.6	0	0	0	2	0	0	0	0	2	0	0	0	0	0	0	0	0	0	0	0	0	0	0	0	0
wardrobe	39	.1244	1.1526	40.6	0	0	0	4	11	6	18	0	1	0	0	5	0	0	0	0	1	0	30	0	2	0	0	0	0
Wardrobe	2	.1812	.0838	29.2	0	0	0	0	1	0	1	0	0	0	0	0	0	0	0	0	0	0	1	0	0	0	0	1	0

4R Wall-of-Truth
XP wall-paintings
6A wall-sized
7P wall-writing
4D WallaWalla
4P Wallace's
6F walled-in
9Q Wallenstein
8R Wallkill
9D wallop
6R walloped
6R walloping
7D Wallowa
6A wallowings
7D wallows
9R walnut-and-fringed-lamps
5Q Walpole's
3R Walrus's
5N waltzed
5J Wan
8F Wanasi
7A Wanda's
4B wander'd
6B Wanderers
6A wanderin'
8J Wandering
6R wangled
5N wanly
7J Want
9D want-wit
4A Wanted
7N wanter
7D wantin'
7Q wantonness
6B wappish
6B wappishly
3A war-bonnet
4A war-cry
6A war-like
7F war-making
7N war-steed
7B war-trumpet
4N warbonnets
7P Warden
8D warden's

Word Type	F	D	U	SFI	3 Gr 3	4 Gr 4	5 Gr 5	6 Gr 6	7 Gr 7	8 Gr 8	9 Gr 9	X UnGr	A Read	B Eng & Gr	C Comp	D Lit	E Math	F Soc Stud	G Spell	H Sci	J Music	K Art	L Home Ec	M Shop	N Lib F	P Lib NF	Q Lib Ref	R Mag	S Rel
wardrobes	2	.0000	.0064	18.1	0	0	0	0	0	1	1	0	0	0	0	0	0	0	0	0	0	0	2	0	0	0	0	0	0
wardroom	5	.0000	.0537	27.3	0	0	0	0	3	2	0	0	0	0	0	5	0	0	0	0	0	0	0	0	0	0	0	0	0
wards	3	.3346	.2478	33.9	0	0	0	0	0	0	2	1	1	0	0	0	0	0	0	1	0	0	0	0	0	0	1	0	0
ware	9	.3111	.6213	37.9	0	5	0	2	0	1	0	1	0	0	0	0	0	0	0	0	0	0	0	0	0	1	5	3	0
Ware	17	.1718	1.1892	40.8	1	0	0	0	1	15	0	0	16	0	0	0	0	0	0	0	0	0	0	0	0	0	0	1	0
Ware's	2	.0000	.0914	29.6	0	0	0	0	0	2	0	0	2	0	0	0	0	0	0	0	0	0	0	0	0	0	0	0	0
warehouse	27	.6271	3.5804	45.5	0	10	2	5	6	2	2	0	10	1	0	2	1	0	0	0	0	0	0	0	1	9	2	1	0
warehousemen	2	.2446	.1184	30.7	0	0	0	0	0	1	1	0	0	0	0	0	1	0	0	0	0	0	0	0	0	1	0	0	0
warehouses	24	.4706	2.4491	43.9	6	1	0	3	12	1	1	0	1	0	0	1	0	16	0	1	0	0	0	2	0	2	0	1	0
wares	19	.6780	2.6671	44.3	2	1	1	7	7	0	1	0	5	0	0	0	0	5	1	0	3	0	0	0	1	2	1	1	0
warfare	41	.6100	5.1510	47.1	2	1	4	7	12	11	4	0	1	0	0	0	0	15	1	0	0	2	0	0	2	4	11	5	0
warhead	5	.2304	.2767	34.4	0	0	0	2	0	3	0	0	0	0	0	0	0	0	0	0	0	0	0	0	0	2	0	3	0
warheads	2	.0000	.0243	23.9	0	0	0	0	0	2	0	0	0	0	0	0	0	0	0	0	0	0	0	0	0	0	0	2	0
Warhol	2	.0000	.0243	23.9	0	0	0	0	0	0	0	2	0	0	0	0	0	0	0	0	0	0	0	0	0	0	0	2	0
warily	7	.4968	.7551	38.8	0	1	0	2	3	0	1	0	2	0	1	1	0	0	0	0	0	0	0	0	1	1	0	1	0
warlike	17	.5843	2.0969	43.2	5	4	0	4	3	1	0	0	3	1	0	0	0	6	0	0	0	0	0	0	2	2	3	0	0
warlord	3	.0000	.0583	27.7	0	0	0	0	0	3	0	0	0	0	0	0	0	3	0	0	0	0	0	0	0	0	0	0	0
warm	1072	.8781	187.93	62.7	321	193	148	116	148	79	51	16	266	17	9	40	1	123	8	262	15	15	36	2	69	118	49	42	0
warm-blooded	29	.4371	2.7819	44.4	6	4	2	2	10	3	0	2	1	0	0	0	0	0	0	16	0	0	0	0	0	7	4	1	0
warm-hearted	3	.3845	.2500	34.0	0	0	0	0	1	1	0	1	0	0	0	1	1	0	0	0	0	0	0	0	0	0	0	1	0
warm-up	4	.3619	.3167	35.0	1	0	0	2	1	0	0	0	0	0	0	0	0	0	0	0	0	0	0	0	1	1	0	2	0
warmed	45	.7348	6.7243	48.3	8	10	7	7	4	3	5	1	5	0	0	5	0	6	0	14	0	0	1	0	2	5	4	3	0
warmer	135	.7235	19.943	53.0	36	32	13	16	23	5	9	1	14	1	0	2	0	23	1	63	1	1	4	0	3	12	7	3	0
warmest	16	.7015	2.2831	43.6	3	3	0	2	6	1	1	0	1	0	0	2	1	1	0	3	0	0	0	0	1	3	3	1	0
warmhearted	2	.2401	.1133	30.5	1	0	1	0	0	0	0	0	0	0	0	0	0	0	0	0	0	0	0	0	0	1	1	0	0
warming	24	.6822	3.4107	45.3	5	5	1	6	1	5	1	0	8	0	0	2	0	1	0	6	0	0	1	0	0	4	1	1	0
warming-up	2	.2278	.1128	30.5	0	2	0	0	0	0	0	0	0	0	0	0	0	0	0	1	0	0	0	0	0	0	1	0	0
warmly	32	.7000	4.6778	46.7	4	7	3	4	2	11	1	0	15	1	0	3	0	3	0	2	0	0	1	0	4	3	0	0	0
warms	31	.4908	3.2975	45.2	10	4	2	5	6	2	2	0	2	1	0	0	0	3	0	17	0	0	0	0	0	6	2	0	0
warmth	112	.7999	18.080	52.6	15	15	12	19	16	11	20	4	30	3	1	10	0	5	0	16	2	1	12	2	11	12	3	4	0
warn	59	.7577	9.2054	49.6	11	14	8	8	12	2	4	0	28	4	0	4	0	3	1	8	0	0	0	0	2	6	1	2	0
warn't	16	.1728	.7251	38.6	0	0	0	0	14	0	2	0	1	0	0	2	0	0	0	0	0	0	0	0	13	0	0	0	0
warned	101	.7268	15.151	51.8	14	23	11	9	21	8	10	5	41	2	3	6	0	8	0	2	1	0	0	0	15	14	0	9	0
Warner	11	.4432	1.0905	40.4	0	2	1	3	5	0	0	0	3	0	0	0	1	0	0	0	0	0	0	0	0	1	1	5	0
warning	140	.8439	23.744	53.8	13	15	24	12	37	21	13	5	48	4	5	10	0	6	0	15	4	1	1	0	8	12	7	19	0
Warning	4	.3213	.2823	34.5	0	0	0	1	1	0	2	0	0	0	0	0	0	0	0	1	0	0	1	0	0	0	2	0	0
warnings	36	.6530	4.9221	46.9	1	4	4	4	17	4	2	0	10	0	0	2	0	1	0	13	0	0	0	0	3	1	3	3	0
warns	15	.6468	2.0238	43.1	3	1	1	3	2	1	4	0	4	2	0	2	0	1	0	2	0	0	0	0	0	0	1	3	0
warp	13	.3149	.9036	39.6	1	1	0	3	4	4	0	0	2	0	0	0	0	1	0	0	0	4	5	0	0	0	1	0	0
warpath	9	.4711	.9619	39.8	0	2	3	0	4	0	0	0	4	0	0	1	0	0	0	0	0	0	0	0	0	2	2	0	0
Warpath	4	.0000	.0778	28.9	0	4	0	0	0	0	0	0	0	0	0	0	0	4	0	0	0	0	0	0	0	0	0	0	0
warped	7	.3967	.6544	38.2	0	0	2	0	1	2	2	0	3	0	0	0	0	0	0	0	0	0	0	1	1	2	0	0	0
warping	3	.0344	.0680	28.3	2	0	0	0	0	1	0	0	1	0	0	0	0	0	0	0	0	2	0	0	0	0	0	0	0
Warr	2	.0000	.0209	23.2	0	0	0	0	2	0	0	0	0	0	0	0	0	0	0	0	0	0	0	0	0	0	2	0	0
warrant	12	.6720	1.6407	42.2	0	0	0	1	5	2	4	0	1	0	1	1	0	1	0	0	0	0	1	0	2	3	1	1	0
Warren	55	.5621	6.5722	48.2	3	1	11	14	7	11	7	1	12	3	0	0	0	9	0	0	1	0	0	0	20	6	0	4	0
Warren's	4	.3391	.3045	34.8	0	0	0	1	0	1	2	0	0	0	0	0	0	1	0	0	0	0	0	0	2	1	0	0	0
warring	7	.4520	.6624	38.2	0	1	1	1	1	0	2	1	0	1	0	0	0	0	0	0	2	0	0	0	0	0	1	3	0
warrior	58	.7736	9.1849	49.6	8	14	12	7	13	2	1	1	27	1	1	2	0	3	2	0	1	0	0	0	7	9	1	4	0
warrior's	4	.3706	.3628	35.6	0	1	0	0	3	0	0	0	2	0	0	0	0	0	0	0	0	0	0	0	1	0	1	0	0
warriors	82	.7572	12.608	51.0	5	18	7	19	24	5	3	1	16	9	1	6	0	20	1	0	1	0	0	0	6	18	2	2	0
wars	96	.6425	12.732	51.0	9	6	16	16	16	20	12	1	7	1	0	3	0	44	1	0	1	0	0	0	4	11	14	10	0
Wars	15	.5231	1.6482	42.2	0	1	4	4	2	2	2	0	0	1	0	0	0	6	0	0	0	0	0	0	0	2	4	2	0
Warsaw	11	.5358	1.2538	41.0	0	0	0	1	5	2	2	1	2	1	0	0	0	1	0	0	0	0	0	0	0	1	2	4	0
warship	9	.5397	1.0155	40.1	0	1	2	0	3	1	2	0	0	1	0	1	0	4	0	0	0	0	0	0	0	0	2	1	0
warships	13	.5731	1.5905	42.0	0	3	3	1	3	2	1	0	3	0	0	0	1	5	0	0	0	0	0	0	1	1	2	0	0
wart	5	.4213	.4686	36.7	0	2	0	0	1	0	2	0	1	0	0	1	0	0	0	0	0	0	0	0	2	1	0	0	0
wartime	24	.5808	2.9518	44.7	0	0	4	3	6	6	2	3	5	0	0	0	0	6	0	0	0	0	0	0	3	3	1	6	0
warts	4	.2445	.3067	34.9	1	2	0	1	0	0	0	0	3	0	0	0	0	0	0	0	0	0	0	0	0	1	0	0	0
warty	9	.0000	.0966	29.8	0	0	0	0	0	9	0	0	0	0	0	9	0	0	0	0	0	0	0	0	0	0	0	0	0
Warwick	7	.3347	.5099	37.1	0	1	3	0	2	0	1	0	0	2	0	1	0	0	0	0	0	0	0	0	0	0	4	0	0
wary	18	.7316	2.6805	44.3	1	0	1	1	8	2	5	0	4	1	1	1	0	1	1	0	0	0	0	0	4	2	1	2	0
was	40934	.9162	7456.8	78.7	6962	7242	5002	5504	7720	4759	2953	792	15374	1281	326	3272	904	3750	420	1205	1118	227	58	48	4533	4276	1756	2366	20
Was	6	.3593	.5335	37.3	0	1	0	3	2	0	0	0	3	1	0	0	0	0	0	0	0	0	0	0	2	0	0	0	0
WAS	3	.3450	.2505	34.0	0	1	1	1	0	0	0	0	1	0	0	0	0	0	0	0	0	0	0	0	1	1	0	0	0
Wasawa	11	.0000	.5025	37.0	0	0	0	0	11	0	0	0	11	0	0	0	0	0	0	0	0	0	0	0	0	0	0	0	0
wash	252	.9306	46.449	56.7	64	63	14	21	35	26	19	10	64	11	4	20	4	14	8	37	7	6	10	5	17	22	7	16	0
Wash	3	.1169	.1277	31.1	0	0	1	0	2	0	0	0	1	0	0	0	0	0	0	0	0	0	0	0	0	0	2	0	0
washable	8	.0000	.0258	24.1	0	0	0	0	0	5	3	0	0	0	0	0	0	0	0	0	0	0	8	0	0	0	0	0	0
washbasin	3	.2347	.1695	32.3	0	3	0	0	0	0	0	0	0	0	0	0	0	0	0	0	0	0	0	0	1	2	0	0	0
washboard	3	.2435	.2274	33.6	0	2	0	0	0	1	0	0	2	0	0	0	0	1	0	0	0	0	0	0	0	0	0	0	0
washbowl	2	.0000	.0914	29.6	1	1	0	0	0	0	0	0	2	0	0	0	0	0	0	0	0	0	0	0	0	0	0	0	0
Washburn	6	.0000	.2741	34.4	0	0	6	0	0	0	0	0	6	0	0	0	0	0	0	0	0	0	0	0	0	0	0	0	0
washcloth	6	.3537	.4522	36.6	1	0	3	0	0	2	0	0	0	2	0	0	0	0	0	0	0	0	2	0	1	1	0	0	0
washed	230	.8859	40.607	56.1	61	37	28	21	44	29	7	3	61	9	7	13	4	25	3	25	3	4	13	1	25	22	7	8	0
washed-out	2	.1814	.1187	30.7	0	1	0	0	1	0	0	0	1	0	0	0	0	0	0	0	0	0	0	0	0	0	0	1	0
washer	16	.6448	2.0935	43.2	0	0	1	1	3	6	1	4	0	1	0	1	3	0	0	2	0	1	0	2	0	1	1	4	0
washers	9	.2632	.5641	37.5	1	0	0	0	2	0	1	5	1	0	0	0	0	0	0	0	0	0	1	0	0	0	0	7	0
washes	23	.6462	3.0546	44.8	7	3	3	2	5	2	1	0	1	5	0	2	0	1	0	10	0	0	1	0	1	1	1	0	0
washhouse	3	.0000	.0365	25.6	0	0	0	3	0	0	0	0	0	0	0	0	0	0	0	0	0	0	0	0	0	0	0	3	0
washing	152	.8151	24.951	54.0	31	23	15	25	22	24	10	2	43	7	7	8	3	13	1	18	6	0	13	5	8	11	1	8	0
Washington	600	.8066	97.439	59.9	83	76	104	48	112	105	57	15	105	12	7	19	23	173	3	12	18	0	2	0	13	63	57	93	0
Washington-on-the-Brazos	2	.0000	.0290	24.6	0	2	0	0	0	0	0	0	0	0	0	0	0	0	0	0	0	0	0	0	0	2	0	0	0
Washington's	36	.6350	4.7207	46.7	5	3	6	2	4	11	5	0	2	3	0	0	0	16	0	1	2	0	0	0	0	6	3	3	0
washout	2	.0000	.0914	29.6	0	0	2	0	0	0	0	0	2	0	0	0	0	0	0	0	0	0	0	0	0	0	0	0	0
washpan	2	.1787	.1174	30.7	0	0	1	0	1	0	0	0	1	0	0	0	0	0	0	0	0	0	0	0	1	0	0	0	0
washrooms	2	.2405	.1205	30.8	1	0	0	1	0	0	0	0	0	0	0	0	0	0	0	1	0	0	0	0	0	1	0	0	0
washstand	2	.1717	.1142	30.6	0	1	0	0	1	0	0	0	1	0	0	1	0	0	0	0	0	0	0	0	0	0	0	0	0
washtub	6	.4849	.6610	38.2	1	1	0	0	2	2	0	0	3	1	0	1	0	0	0	0	0	0	0	0	0	1	0	0	0
wasn't	742	.7289	111.78	60.5	153	179	79	80	136	49	49	17	335	40	4	86	2	10	0	6	7	1	0	0	102	92	2	55	0
wasp	32	.5083	3.5613	45.5	7	0	2	11	7	0	5	0	9	0	0	1	0	0	5	11	0	0	0	0	0	0	6	0	0
Wasp	14	.2156	.6770	38.3	2	0	0	6	6	0	0	0	0	0	6	6	0	0	0	0	0	0	0	0	0	2	0	0	0
wasp's	2	.0000	.0394	26.0	0	0	0	2	0	0	0	0	0	0	0	0	0	0	0	2	0	0	0	0	0	0	0	0	0
Wasp's	2	.1621	.0746	28.7	0	0	0	1	1	0	0	0	0	0	1	1	0	0	0	0	0	0	0	0	0	0	0	0	0
wasps	15	.4165	1.3875	41.4	4	1	1	1	6	1	1	0	3	1	0	0	0	0	1	1	0	0	0	0	0	1	8	0	0
wass	5	.0000	.0547	27.4	0	0	0	0	0	0	5	0	0	5	0	0	0	0	0	0	0	0	0	0	0	0	0	0	0

8P warehouseman
8A Wares
7R Warfield
8Q Warlock
8F warlord's
7Q warlords
7Q warm-bloodedness
6A warm-water
9H warmblooded
4A warmers
7N warming-pan
XR Warnecke
7N warningly
7A Warnings
5R Warrant
7Q warranted
7R warranty
5P warrens
4Q warrior-ruler
4A Warrior's
6P WARTS
9H Wasatch
9L wash-and-wear
7A wash-gray
7N wash-pot
7R washboards
4A washbowls
8L washcloths
4J washerwomen
3P washing-bowl
8A washing-stand
9N washings
4P Washingtons
7N washpans
3A washroom
7P washstands
3A washtubs
4J waspish
3P Wasps
9B wassa
6J wassail
8K Wassily

Word Type	F	D	U	SFI	3 Gr 3	4 Gr 4	5 Gr 5	6 Gr 6	7 Gr 7	8 Gr 8	9 Gr 9	X UnGr	A Read	B Eng & Gr	C Comp	D Lit	E Math	F Soc Stud	G Spell	H Sci	J Music	K Art	L Home Ec	M Shop	N Lib F	P Lib NF	Q Lib Ref	R Mag	S Rel
wast	2	.2303	.1079	30.3	1	0	0	0	1	0	0	0	0	0	0	0	0	0	0	0	1	0	0	0	0	1	0	0	0
waste	191	.7956	30.653	54.9	16	20	38	30	32	22	30	3	33	7	1	10	0	19	3	69	0	0	10	7	9	5	12	6	0
wastebasket	10	.4732	1.1163	40.5	5	2	0	0	1	1	1	0	7	1	0	0	1	0	1	0	0	0	0	0	0	0	0	0	0
wastebaskets	4	.2417	.3089	34.9	3	0	0	1	0	0	0	0	3	0	0	0	0	0	0	1	0	0	0	0	0	0	0	0	0
wasted	50	.8944	8.8951	49.5	8	3	9	4	15	6	4	1	11	1	1	4	2	9	1	3	2	0	1	2	5	3	1	4	0
wasteful	6	.4505	.5815	37.6	2	1	0	2	1	0	0	0	0	0	0	0	0	1	0	2	0	0	0	0	1	0	2	0	0
wastefulness	2	.1497	.1046	30.2	0	0	0	0	1	1	0	0	1	0	0	0	0	0	1	0	0	0	0	0	0	0	0	0	0
wasteland	13	.6488	1.7520	42.4	1	2	2	3	3	0	1	1	2	1	0	1	0	4	0	2	0	0	0	0	0	1	0	2	0
wastelands	4	.1325	.1944	32.9	0	0	0	1	3	0	0	0	1	0	0	0	0	3	0	0	0	0	0	0	0	0	0	0	0
wastepaper	3	.3429	.2528	34.0	0	1	1	0	0	1	0	0	1	0	0	0	0	0	0	1	0	0	0	0	1	0	0	0	0
wastes	72	.5225	8.0160	49.0	13	7	10	6	17	9	10	0	2	1	0	2	0	4	0	48	0	0	0	1	1	1	11	1	0
wasting	26	.7261	3.8800	45.9	3	5	3	0	6	4	4	1	8	2	1	0	0	4	0	2	0	0	0	0	1	3	1	4	0
wastrel	2	.2433	.1158	30.6	0	0	0	1	1	0	0	0	0	0	0	0	0	0	0	0	0	0	0	0	0	1	0	1	0
Wat	35	.1226	1.3095	41.2	0	30	0	5	0	0	0	0	0	0	0	0	0	5	0	0	0	0	0	0	0	30	0	0	0
Watauga	2	.0000	.0290	24.6	0	0	2	0	0	0	0	0	0	0	0	0	0	0	0	0	0	0	0	0	0	2	0	0	0
watch	969	.9235	177.59	62.5	245	233	96	111	133	74	65	12	319	42	27	60	18	53	60	98	27	9	12	2	65	93	20	64	0
Watch	124	.3230	11.449	50.6	11	111	1	0	0	0	1	0	113	0	0	0	1	0	4	1	0	0	0	0	5	0	0	0	0
watchdog	14	.3361	1.3038	41.2	4	2	3	1	1	3	0	0	12	1	0	0	0	0	0	0	0	0	0	0	1	0	0	0	0
watched	687	.8538	118.01	60.7	175	143	77	78	117	53	33	11	304	26	6	60	11	30	3	26	6	3	2	0	105	59	4	41	1
watcher	19	.4662	1.8832	42.7	0	4	0	1	13	0	1	0	1	2	0	10	0	1	0	2	0	0	0	0	0	0	2	1	0
Watcher	3	.0000	.0583	27.7	0	3	0	0	0	0	0	0	0	0	0	0	0	3	0	0	0	0	0	0	0	0	0	0	0
watchers	21	.6961	3.0134	44.8	2	4	2	2	5	2	2	2	5	2	0	3	0	1	0	5	0	0	0	0	2	2	1	0	0
watches	70	.8926	12.443	50.9	16	22	6	8	4	4	9	1	17	4	0	6	7	11	2	9	2	1	2	0	2	2	1	4	0
watchful	22	.5112	2.4942	44.0	5	2	4	3	5	1	2	0	9	0	0	3	0	2	0	0	0	0	0	0	6	2	0	0	0
watching	443	.8440	75.215	58.8	80	89	51	46	91	44	31	11	168	19	5	52	8	21	3	21	8	2	3	1	56	41	7	26	2
watchman	29	.6616	4.0117	46.0	3	3	5	8	0	2	6	2	11	1	1	8	0	1	1	2	1	0	0	0	0	0	0	3	0
watchmen	4	.2847	.2634	34.2	0	0	0	3	0	0	0	1	0	0	0	0	0	1	0	1	2	0	0	0	0	0	0	0	0
water	7194	.8352	1207.3	70.8	1791	1400	959	889	995	566	440	154	1469	77	50	188	78	757	46	2888	51	78	128	26	185	548	335	290	0
Water	33	.7159	4.8722	46.9	12	2	8	0	4	1	3	3	12	5	0	4	0	3	0	2	3	1	0	0	0	1	0	2	0
WATER	2	.2405	.1205	30.8	2	0	0	0	0	0	0	0	0	0	0	0	0	0	0	1	0	0	0	0	0	1	0	0	0
water-color	6	.0000	.0111	20.5	0	2	0	3	1	0	0	0	0	0	0	0	0	0	0	0	0	6	0	0	0	0	0	0	0
water-covered	2	.2446	.1257	31.0	0	1	0	1	0	0	0	0	0	0	0	0	0	1	0	1	0	0	0	0	0	0	0	0	0
water-drop	4	.2305	.2357	33.7	0	3	0	0	0	0	1	0	0	0	0	0	0	0	0	3	0	0	0	0	1	0	0	0	0
water-dwelling	3	.2445	.1818	32.6	0	0	0	0	1	1	0	1	0	0	0	0	0	0	0	2	0	0	0	0	0	0	1	0	0
water-filled	3	.1650	.1684	32.3	2	0	1	0	0	0	0	0	1	0	0	0	0	0	0	2	0	0	0	0	0	0	0	0	0
water-hole	2	.0000	.0914	29.6	2	0	0	0	0	0	0	0	2	0	0	0	0	0	0	0	0	0	0	0	0	0	0	0	0
water-proofing	2	.2401	.1133	30.5	0	0	1	0	0	0	0	1	0	0	0	0	0	0	0	0	0	0	0	0	0	1	1	0	0
water-repellent	2	.0000	.0064	18.1	0	0	0	0	0	2	0	0	0	0	0	0	0	0	0	0	0	0	2	0	0	0	0	0	0
water-ski	2	.0000	.0219	23.4	0	0	0	0	0	2	0	0	0	2	0	0	0	0	0	0	0	0	0	0	0	0	0	0	0
water-skiing	3	.2054	.1422	31.5	1	0	0	1	0	0	0	1	0	0	1	0	0	0	0	0	0	0	0	0	0	0	0	2	0
water-soaked	3	.2212	.2099	33.2	0	0	0	1	1	1	0	0	2	0	0	1	0	0	0	0	0	0	0	0	0	0	0	0	0
water-tight	4	.3860	.3420	35.3	0	0	2	2	0	0	0	0	0	0	0	0	0	2	0	0	0	0	0	0	1	0	0	1	0
water's	34	.6720	4.7195	46.7	9	10	2	2	10	0	1	0	7	0	0	3	0	3	1	2	0	0	0	0	1	12	2	3	0
Waterbury	2	.2351	.1166	30.7	0	0	0	0	0	0	1	1	0	0	0	0	0	1	0	0	0	0	0	0	0	0	0	1	0
watercolor	8	.3450	.5819	37.6	0	0	1	3	2	2	0	0	0	0	1	2	0	1	0	0	0	3	0	0	1	0	0	0	0
watercolors	2	.1473	.0686	28.4	0	0	0	1	0	1	0	0	0	0	0	1	0	0	0	0	0	1	0	0	0	0	0	0	0
watercourses	2	.2437	.1129	30.5	0	0	0	0	1	1	0	0	0	0	0	0	0	0	0	0	0	0	0	0	0	0	1	1	0
watercress	4	.1075	.1027	30.1	0	0	0	0	4	0	0	0	0	0	0	1	0	0	0	0	0	0	3	0	0	0	0	0	0
watered	36	.7005	5.2038	47.2	13	4	3	2	13	0	1	0	9	2	0	2	0	2	0	9	0	0	0	0	3	6	0	3	0
waterfall	27	.6417	3.6667	45.6	7	9	5	5	0	0	0	1	10	1	0	1	0	6	0	4	0	0	0	0	4	0	1	0	0
waterfalls	36	.4210	3.3890	45.3	3	9	9	3	7	1	4	0	4	1	0	0	0	20	0	1	0	0	0	0	0	0	9	1	0
waterfowl	14	.2828	.9728	39.9	0	3	0	0	10	0	0	1	3	0	0	1	0	0	0	0	0	0	0	0	0	1	0	9	0
waterfront	8	.5381	.9335	39.7	2	2	2	1	1	0	0	0	2	0	0	0	0	2	0	1	0	0	0	0	0	2	1	0	0
watering	25	.5986	3.1525	45.0	2	2	7	6	4	1	1	2	5	6	0	0	0	7	0	2	0	0	0	0	3	0	1	1	0
waterless	5	.3926	.4468	36.5	2	1	0	0	2	0	0	0	1	0	0	0	0	1	0	0	0	0	0	0	0	1	2	0	0
waterline	7	.2273	.5357	37.3	1	0	0	1	4	0	0	1	6	0	0	0	0	0	0	0	0	0	0	0	0	1	0	0	0
Waterloo	8	.3555	.6363	38.0	0	0	1	3	0	0	3	1	0	1	0	0	0	4	0	0	0	0	0	0	0	0	3	0	0
watermelon	29	.6990	4.1805	46.2	5	6	9	1	7	0	1	0	7	5	0	0	2	1	1	8	0	0	0	0	2	2	0	1	0
watermelons	11	.5486	1.3263	41.2	3	3	4	0	1	0	0	0	5	0	1	0	1	1	0	1	0	0	0	0	1	1	0	0	0
waterpower	3	.2444	.1814	32.6	0	1	2	0	0	0	0	0	0	0	0	0	0	2	0	0	0	0	0	0	0	0	1	0	0
waterproof	11	.6029	1.3942	41.4	0	0	2	3	4	2	0	0	2	0	0	1	0	3	0	2	1	0	0	0	0	0	2	0	0
waters	345	.7654	53.589	57.3	48	55	51	52	86	24	20	9	66	4	0	16	2	67	1	52	7	0	0	0	11	39	48	32	0
Waters	17	.4522	1.8472	42.7	12	1	0	3	0	0	1	0	12	1	0	0	0	2	0	0	2	0	0	0	0	0	0	0	0
watershed	11	.4646	1.0945	40.4	0	3	2	1	2	0	0	3	0	2	0	0	0	0	0	5	0	0	0	0	1	0	0	3	0
watersheds	3	.2442	.1820	32.6	0	0	1	1	0	0	0	1	0	1	0	0	0	0	0	2	0	0	0	0	0	0	0	0	0
waterside	3	.2321	.1635	32.1	0	2	0	0	1	0	0	0	0	0	0	0	0	0	0	0	0	0	0	0	0	0	1	2	0
watertight	10	.4715	1.1081	40.4	0	0	2	4	1	2	0	1	6	1	0	0	0	2	0	1	0	0	0	0	0	0	0	0	0
Watertown	4	.1112	.1666	32.2	0	3	0	0	0	1	0	0	1	0	0	0	0	0	0	0	0	0	0	0	0	3	0	0	0
Watertown's	2	.0000	.0290	24.6	0	2	0	0	0	0	0	0	0	0	0	0	0	0	0	0	0	0	0	0	0	2	0	0	0
waterway	34	.5283	3.8214	45.8	2	3	13	8	3	1	1	3	2	0	0	0	0	20	0	0	1	0	0	0	2	1	3	5	0
Waterway	9	.3994	.8169	39.1	2	0	6	0	0	0	0	1	1	0	0	0	0	5	0	0	0	0	0	0	0	2	0	1	0
waterways	23	.6045	2.8754	44.6	2	2	6	5	4	1	1	2	0	0	0	0	0	12	0	1	1	0	0	1	0	2	2	4	0
waterworks	6	.1955	.3185	35.0	0	0	0	1	0	5	0	0	0	0	0	0	0	5	0	0	0	0	0	0	0	0	0	1	0
watery	38	.7821	5.9781	47.8	6	4	3	2	13	4	5	1	5	1	0	6	0	2	1	6	1	1	2	0	3	2	8	0	0
watgurwa	3	.0000	.0583	27.7	0	0	0	0	0	3	0	0	0	0	0	0	0	3	0	0	0	0	0	0	0	0	0	0	0
Watkins	12	.4545	1.3168	41.2	8	0	2	0	0	1	1	0	9	1	0	0	1	0	0	0	0	0	0	0	0	0	0	1	0
Watson	34	.6459	4.5921	46.6	2	2	0	5	8	5	7	5	11	0	2	7	2	0	0	2	0	0	0	0	4	4	0	2	0
Watson's	3	.2699	.1789	32.5	0	0	0	0	1	0	1	1	0	0	1	0	0	0	0	0	0	0	0	0	0	1	1	0	0
Watt	11	.4465	1.1048	40.4	4	0	0	2	1	0	3	1	3	0	0	0	0	1	0	2	0	0	0	0	0	1	4	0	0
Watt's	3	.3350	.2478	33.9	0	0	0	1	2	0	0	0	1	0	0	0	0	1	0	0	0	0	0	0	0	0	1	0	0
wattage	2	.0000	.0050	17.0	0	0	0	0	0	2	0	0	0	0	0	0	0	0	0	0	0	0	0	2	0	0	0	0	0
Watteau	2	.1493	.0692	28.4	0	0	1	0	0	0	1	0	0	0	0	0	0	0	0	0	0	1	0	0	0	0	1	0	0
wattle	3	.2378	.1809	32.6	0	0	0	1	2	0	0	0	0	0	0	0	0	2	0	0	0	0	0	0	0	1	0	0	0
watts	7	.3742	.6008	37.8	0	0	5	1	0	1	0	0	1	0	0	0	0	0	0	4	0	0	0	1	0	0	1	0	0
Watts	2	.2433	.1158	30.6	0	1	0	0	0	0	1	0	0	0	0	0	0	0	0	0	0	0	0	0	0	1	0	1	0
Watusi	2	.0000	.0914	29.6	0	0	0	0	2	0	0	0	2	0	0	0	0	0	0	0	0	0	0	0	0	0	0	0	0
wave	318	.8526	54.263	57.3	42	32	24	46	55	54	33	32	71	7	1	21	0	4	5	101	26	4	2	9	12	12	30	13	0
wave-top	2	.0000	.0914	29.6	0	0	0	0	2	0	0	0	2	0	0	0	0	0	0	0	0	0	0	0	0	0	0	0	0
wave's	3	.1169	.1277	31.1	0	0	1	0	2	0	0	0	1	0	0	0	0	0	0	0	0	0	0	0	0	0	2	0	0

7N wastage
5Q waste-disposal
8H waste-laden
7A wastefully
8N wasteless
4P wat
9D wat'ry
4P Wat's
4A Watanabe-san
6A watch-chain
8D watch's
XR watchcry
5A watchdogs
3A watchfully
6A watchfulness
5C watchmaker
9C watchmaker's
5P watchmakers
5P watchmaking
3A watchman's
3N watchroom
3N watchtower
4Q watchtowers
3G wate
8Q Water-Jug
7P water-base
XR water-borne
3P water-bounded
6N water-carrier
XR water-colored
5P water-cooled
3A water-crazy
7Q water-cutting
8L water-displacement
XH water-disposal
5B water-drip
XH water-dwellers
5P water-fall
4A water-flowers
XH water-free
8A water-front
8H water-kilowatt
8A water-lilies
3A water-loving
3A water-mark
4A water-meadows
5R water-oriented
9F water-power
4Q water-proof
7E water-purifying
7Q water-raising
6R water-rats
6H water-sampling
XH water-saving
7D water-skaters
5R water-softened
9H water-soluble
9P water-sounds
8N water-trough
4N water-voles
7D water-worms
7R waterbug
XR Watercolor
3A Waterfield
8Q Waterford
7R waterfowling
9R Waterfront
3P waterhole
3Q waterholes
XR waterings
5B Waterless
4A Waterman
6N watermark
7A watermarket
6P watermen
4F waterpaints
7Q waterpowered
5A waterproofed
6A waters'
3A Waters'
5B watershed's
7D watersplash
XR watersports
7A waterwalls
3P waterweed
5Q Waterwheel
8F waterworn
5N watery-looking
9R WatkinsGlen
7B watsa
8A Watsons
9B watt
7D Wave
5F wave-swept

Word Type	F	D	U	SFI	3 Gr 3	4 Gr 4	5 Gr 5	6 Gr 6	7 Gr 7	8 Gr 8	9 Gr 9	X UnGr	A Read	B Eng & Gr	C Comp	D Lit	E Math	F Soc Stud	G Spell	H Sci	J Music	K Art	L Home Ec	M Shop	N Lib F	P Lib NF	Q Lib Ref	R Mag	S Rel
waved	173	.7701	27.317	54.4	53	56	12	20	18	9	4	1	84	7	3	6	0	7	2	1	3	0	1	0	29	22	1	7	0
wavefront	5	.0000	.0986	29.9	0	0	0	0	0	0	0	5	0	0	0	0	0	0	0	5	0	0	0	0	0	0	0	0	0
wavelength	21	.4077	1.8993	42.8	0	1	9	2	0	4	0	5	0	0	0	0	1	0	0	15	0	0	0	0	1	0	3	1	0
Wavelength	2	.0000	.0243	23.9	0	0	0	0	0	0	0	2	0	0	0	0	0	0	0	0	0	0	0	0	0	0	0	2	0
wavelengths	22	.3674	1.8328	42.6	0	0	2	1	3	3	6	7	0	0	0	0	1	0	0	16	0	0	0	0	0	0	3	2	0
wavelets	7	.1941	.3707	35.7	0	0	0	0	1	0	0	6	0	0	0	0	0	0	0	6	0	0	0	0	0	0	1	0	0
wavelike	4	.0000	.0789	29.0	0	3	0	0	1	0	0	0	0	0	0	0	0	0	0	4	0	0	0	0	0	0	0	0	0
waver	5	.4724	.5348	37.3	0	0	0	2	2	0	1	0	2	0	0	1	0	0	0	1	0	0	0	0	0	0	0	1	0
wavered	8	.4473	.8251	39.2	1	0	2	1	3	0	1	0	4	1	0	1	0	0	0	0	2	0	0	0	0	0	0	0	0
wavering	12	.5960	1.5008	41.8	0	0	1	3	5	2	1	0	3	1	0	3	0	0	0	0	1	0	0	0	2	0	0	2	0
waves	647	.8148	106.02	60.3	75	77	67	120	114	103	63	28	111	8	4	29	4	30	4	246	74	6	0	6	22	31	49	23	0
waving	89	.8143	14.665	51.7	12	20	15	13	14	8	6	1	36	4	1	4	0	3	0	1	3	1	0	0	15	8	5	8	0
wavy	26	.6899	3.6975	45.7	6	5	1	5	6	1	2	0	6	3	0	1	0	0	0	6	1	0	0	1	2	6	0	0	0
Wawona	25	.0000	1.1421	40.6	0	25	0	0	0	0	0	0	25	0	0	0	0	0	0	0	0	0	0	0	0	0	0	0	0
Wawona's	3	.0000	.1370	31.4	0	3	0	0	0	0	0	0	3	0	0	0	0	0	0	0	0	0	0	0	0	0	0	0	0
wax	127	.5084	13.879	51.4	21	34	8	28	14	15	7	0	31	1	1	2	0	2	2	26	7	27	3	2	3	10	10	0	0
waxed	23	.7204	3.3969	45.3	4	4	3	6	1	1	4	0	7	3	0	1	0	0	0	3	0	1	2	0	2	1	1	2	0
waxen	3	.3873	.2485	34.0	0	0	0	1	0	0	2	0	0	0	0	1	0	0	0	0	0	0	0	0	1	0	1	0	0
waxes	2	.0725	.0732	28.6	0	0	0	1	1	0	0	0	1	0	0	0	0	0	0	0	0	0	0	1	0	0	0	0	0
waxing	3	.2360	.1709	32.3	0	0	2	0	0	1	0	0	0	0	0	0	2	0	0	0	0	0	0	0	1	0	0	0	0
waxwings	2	.2278	.1128	30.5	1	0	0	0	1	0	0	0	0	0	0	0	0	0	0	1	0	0	0	0	0	0	1	0	0
waxy	6	.5359	.6882	38.4	1	0	0	2	1	1	1	0	1	1	0	1	0	0	0	2	0	0	0	0	0	1	0	0	0
way	6612	.9823	1278.9	71.1	1270	1211	829	866	1166	642	510	118	1773	425	49	381	426	556	183	793	238	123	99	46	453	481	209	372	5
Way	87	.5085	9.5113	49.8	28	12	15	6	10	12	2	2	4	4	0	1	1	2	0	62	1	0	0	0	2	3	5	2	0
waybills	3	.0000	.1370	31.4	3	0	0	0	0	0	0	0	3	0	0	0	0	0	0	0	0	0	0	0	0	0	0	0	0
Wayne	14	.6132	1.7875	42.5	0	2	0	0	5	4	1	2	2	1	0	2	0	2	0	1	0	0	0	0	0	2	0	4	0
Wayne's	2	.2442	.1134	30.5	0	0	0	0	0	0	1	1	0	1	0	0	0	0	0	0	0	0	0	0	0	0	0	1	0
ways	1899	.9378	352.05	65.5	370	326	264	280	306	172	151	30	218	182	29	41	183	336	103	343	89	58	38	20	30	86	79	60	4
Ways	4	.1854	.1872	32.7	1	0	0	0	0	0	3	0	0	0	0	0	0	0	0	0	0	0	0	0	0	1	0	3	0
wayside	7	.3813	.6823	38.3	4	2	1	0	0	0	0	0	5	0	0	0	0	0	0	0	0	0	0	0	0	1	0	1	0
wayward	3	.2222	.1558	31.9	0	0	0	0	2	1	0	0	0	1	0	0	0	0	0	0	0	0	0	0	0	0	2	0	0
Wazadzki	5	.0000	.0972	29.9	0	0	0	0	5	0	0	0	0	0	0	0	0	5	0	0	0	0	0	0	0	0	0	0	0
Wazadzki's	3	.0000	.0583	27.7	0	0	0	0	3	0	0	0	0	0	0	0	0	3	0	0	0	0	0	0	0	0	0	0	0
we	16452	.9425	3066.8	74.9	2679	2612	2005	2088	2905	2092	1684	387	3633	1215	162	990	2645	1745	647	1333	448	126	68	49	908	1137	271	1035	40
We	22	.5905	2.6813	44.3	2	2	0	5	0	4	6	3	1	1	0	1	0	5	0	0	6	0	0	0	0	2	1	5	0
we-l-l	2	.1814	.1187	30.7	1	0	1	0	0	0	0	0	1	0	0	0	0	0	0	0	0	0	0	0	0	0	0	1	0
we-we'll	2	.0000	.0215	23.3	0	0	0	0	0	2	0	0	0	0	0	2	0	0	0	0	0	0	0	0	0	0	0	0	0
we'd	153	.6599	21.138	53.3	18	42	14	16	40	8	14	1	57	4	0	19	1	3	0	1	1	0	0	0	19	25	0	23	0
we'll	653	.7585	101.53	60.1	150	179	61	97	87	47	25	7	278	11	1	43	5	23	2	6	39	0	1	3	89	113	0	39	0
we're	423	.7436	64.516	58.1	79	112	39	52	83	28	24	6	158	18	1	36	0	7	3	4	10	0	0	2	50	84	0	50	0
we've	238	.6747	33.482	55.2	40	45	27	32	52	23	14	5	89	8	0	29	2	5	0	1	0	0	0	1	32	33	0	38	0
weak	245	.9044	44.055	56.4	20	29	35	43	65	32	15	6	65	12	3	13	0	14	11	46	23	0	4	2	11	14	14	13	0
weaken	12	.5659	1.4277	41.5	3	1	1	0	2	2	2	1	1	0	0	1	0	2	0	3	0	0	0	0	0	2	3	0	0
weakened	32	.7849	5.0615	47.0	0	3	3	3	8	10	3	2	4	1	1	1	0	6	1	4	0	0	0	0	1	5	4	4	0
weakening	8	.4561	.7783	38.9	0	1	1	0	1	2	1	2	0	0	0	0	0	1	0	1	0	0	0	0	0	1	1	4	0
weakens	7	.5113	.7479	38.7	1	0	0	1	2	1	2	0	0	0	0	0	0	1	1	2	0	0	1	0	0	0	2	0	0
weaker	30	.7133	4.3976	46.4	2	2	7	5	3	1	9	1	8	2	0	5	0	1	0	7	0	0	0	1	0	1	3	2	0
weakest	8	.5234	.8980	39.5	1	1	1	1	0	1	3	0	2	0	0	2	0	0	0	1	1	0	0	1	0	1	0	0	0
weakling	3	.3873	.2495	34.0	0	2	0	0	0	1	0	0	0	0	0	1	0	0	0	0	0	0	0	0	1	0	0	1	0
weakly	20	.6638	2.7741	44.4	3	3	4	3	5	1	1	0	8	2	1	4	0	0	0	0	0	0	0	0	1	1	2	1	0
weakness	35	.8338	5.8145	47.6	0	1	4	8	5	7	8	2	2	2	1	3	0	2	1	2	0	1	1	0	4	3	5	8	0
weaknesses	10	.4994	1.0620	40.3	0	0	0	0	1	3	6	0	1	4	0	0	0	2	0	1	0	0	0	1	0	0	1	0	0
wealth	159	.6979	22.691	53.6	13	9	34	21	29	32	14	7	17	3	0	9	0	57	1	7	5	0	0	0	1	18	27	14	0
wealthier	2	.2401	.1133	30.5	1	0	0	0	1	0	0	0	0	0	0	0	0	0	0	0	0	0	0	0	0	1	1	0	0
wealthiest	2	.2297	.1135	30.6	0	0	0	1	0	1	0	0	0	0	0	1	0	1	0	0	0	0	0	0	0	0	0	0	0
wealthy	70	.6978	9.9908	50.0	6	5	10	10	21	7	11	0	10	1	0	2	0	19	4	0	4	0	0	0	0	13	12	5	0
weaned	3	.2078	.1429	31.5	0	0	0	0	1	1	1	0	0	0	1	0	0	0	0	0	0	0	0	0	2	0	0	0	0
weapon	62	.7551	9.4982	49.8	6	9	17	10	9	6	5	0	12	2	1	4	0	5	1	1	1	0	0	0	5	22	4	4	0
weaponry	2	.2285	.1129	30.5	0	0	0	0	2	0	0	0	0	0	0	0	0	1	0	0	0	0	0	0	0	0	1	0	0
weapons	120	.7319	17.881	52.5	2	8	15	24	34	14	18	5	19	1	0	3	0	32	1	7	2	1	0	2	13	14	15	9	1
wear	510	.8138	83.442	59.2	111	81	56	73	89	41	53	6	112	26	4	23	4	62	12	68	16	2	61	7	35	37	13	28	0
wearable	4	.0000	.0129	21.1	0	0	0	0	0	4	0	0	0	0	0	0	0	0	0	0	0	0	4	0	0	0	0	0	0
wearer	7	.1867	.3232	35.1	0	0	0	1	1	1	3	1	1	1	0	0	0	0	0	0	0	0	4	0	0	0	0	1	0
wearers	2	.2405	.1205	30.8	1	0	0	0	0	1	0	0	0	0	0	0	0	0	0	1	0	0	0	0	0	1	0	0	0
wearied	4	.4556	.4079	36.1	0	0	0	0	2	1	1	0	1	0	0	0	0	1	0	0	0	0	0	0	1	1	0	0	0
wearies	2	.0000	.0215	23.3	0	0	0	0	0	0	2	0	0	0	0	2	0	0	0	0	0	0	0	0	0	0	0	0	0
wearily	25	.6207	3.2155	45.1	4	4	1	4	8	3	1	0	4	2	0	3	0	1	0	0	1	0	0	0	9	3	0	2	0
weariness	11	.4204	1.0553	40.2	0	1	3	2	0	3	1	1	3	0	0	0	0	3	0	0	0	0	0	0	4	0	1	0	0
wearing	239	.8921	42.501	56.3	58	34	26	35	39	29	12	6	74	12	4	15	3	23	2	21	5	0	7	1	26	19	4	23	0
wears	74	.8595	12.744	51.1	19	9	16	8	10	8	2	2	23	7	0	4	0	10	4	6	3	0	1	0	4	7	2	3	0
weary	104	.7740	16.435	52.2	12	9	10	17	23	14	15	4	43	2	4	12	0	11	2	1	4	0	0	0	6	9	1	9	0
weas'ly	5	.0000	.0404	26.1	0	5	0	0	0	0	0	0	0	0	0	0	0	0	0	0	5	0	0	0	0	0	0	0	0
weasel	15	.5319	1.7451	42.4	6	4	0	0	4	1	0	0	6	0	0	0	0	0	0	0	2	0	0	0	0	2	1	4	0
Weasel	6	.2411	.3334	35.2	4	0	1	0	0	0	1	0	0	0	0	0	0	0	0	0	2	0	0	0	0	0	0	4	0
weasels	10	.6205	1.2769	41.1	0	4	1	0	4	1	0	0	1	2	0	1	0	0	0	0	0	0	0	0	1	1	1	3	0
weather	990	.8367	166.34	62.2	169	174	163	138	173	90	68	15	192	25	9	24	8	118	21	380	12	0	6	11	32	58	63	31	0
Weather	35	.4608	3.6022	45.6	0	2	5	7	18	2	1	0	6	0	0	1	0	1	0	24	0	0	0	1	0	0	1	1	0
WEATHER	2	.0000	.0394	26.0	2	0	0	0	0	0	0	0	0	0	0	0	0	0	0	2	0	0	0	0	0	0	0	0	0
weather-beaten	4	.1717	.2284	33.6	0	0	1	1	1	1	0	0	2	0	0	2	0	0	0	0	0	0	0	0	0	0	0	0	0
weather-roughened	2	.2440	.1132	30.5	0	0	0	0	1	0	1	0	0	0	0	1	0	0	0	0	0	0	0	0	0	0	0	1	0
weather's	2	.1497	.1046	30.2	0	1	0	0	1	0	0	0	1	0	0	0	0	0	1	0	0	0	0	0	0	0	0	0	0
weatherbeaten	3	.2347	.1695	32.3	0	0	1	0	2	0	0	0	0	0	0	0	0	0	0	0	0	0	0	0	1	2	0	0	0
Weatherby	4	.0000	.0486	26.9	0	0	0	0	4	0	0	0	0	0	0	0	0	0	0	0	0	0	0	0	0	0	0	4	0
weathercock	4	.0000	.0429	26.3	1	1	0	0	0	0	2	0	0	0	0	4	0	0	0	0	0	0	0	0	0	0	0	0	0
weathercocks	2	.0000	.0215	23.3	0	0	0	0	1	0	1	0	0	0	0	2	0	0	0	0	0	0	0	0	0	0	0	0	0
weathered	22	.7055	3.1463	45.0	2	1	2	3	3	3	6	2	1	1	1	2	0	1	0	6	0	1	0	0	2	0	1	6	0
weathering	27	.3635	2.2354	43.5	0	6	4	3	2	0	10	2	0	0	0	0	0	1	0	20	0	0	0	0	0	1	4	1	0
weatherman	32	.4208	3.0853	44.9	4	1	0	7	19	1	0	0	6	0	0	1	1	1	0	21	0	0	0	0	0	1	1	0	0
weatherman's	3	.0000	.0591	27.7	1	0	0	0	2	0	0	0	0	0	0	0	0	0	0	3	0	0	0	0	0	0	0	0	0
weathermen	9	.2286	.6414	38.1	5	0	0	0	3	1	0	0	5	0	0	0	0	0	0	4	0	0	0	0	0	0	0	0	0
weave	53	.6565	7.2096	48.6	10	7	5	9	11	9	2	0	13	1	0	4	0	11	1	3	0	4	6	0	3	5	2	0	0
weaver	9	.6004	1.1450	40.6	0	4	2	0	2	0	0	1	2	0	0	0	0	3	0	1	0	0	0	0	1	1	0	1	0
Weaver	6	.2342	.4625	36.7	0	5	0	0	1	0	0	0	5	0	0	0	1	0	0	0	0	0	0	0	0	0	0	0	0
Weaver's	3	.0000	.1370	31.4	0	3	0	0	0	0	0	0	3	0	0	0	0	0	0	0	0	0	0	0	0	0	0	0	0

XH wavelet
8Q Waveney
8A waverers
4A Waverly
5R WAVES
4D waves'
3P Wax
3A wax-and-feather
6A wax-covered
4K wax-crayon
5Q wax-lined
3R WAY
3A way-back
4J way-hay
6R way-out
3A waybill
9D wayfarer
8J Wayfaring
9D waylaid
3F Wayman
8R Waynesboro
8A Wayo
6J wayte-pipes
3A WA1-2234
7Q WCC
4N WE
4A we-e-ell
3A we'
3A we'l
8A We're
7N we's
3N WE'VE
8R Weak
7P weak-spirited
8D weaklings
9D weal
8B weapon-like
7N weaponless
9D Wear
XB weard
6A Wearer
9Q wearer's
3P wearing-down
8L wearings
6N weasel-eyed
7A weasles
7F weatern
5H weather-forecasting
7H weather-induced
5H weather-observation
5N weather'll
6A weatherboard
7F weatherboarding
6A Weatherford
6A Weatherford's
3P weatherproof
5D weathers
7D weaver's
7Q weaverbirds

Word Type	F	D	U	SFI	3 Gr 3	4 Gr 4	5 Gr 5	6 Gr 6	7 Gr 7	8 Gr 8	9 Gr 9	X UnGr	A Read	B Eng & Gr	C Comp	D Lit	E Math	F Soc Stud	G Spell	H Sci	J Music	K Art	L Home Ec	M Shop	N Lib F	P Lib NF	Q Lib Ref	R Mag	S Rel
weavers	10	.3670	.8994	39.5	0	0	1	5	4	0	0	0	4	0	0	0	0	4	0	0	0	0	0	0	0	0	2	0	0
Weavers	2	.2152	.1357	31.3	0	0	1	1	0	0	0	0	1	0	0	0	0	1	0	0	0	0	0	0	0	0	0	0	0
weaves	12	.4156	1.0603	40.3	5	0	0	1	2	3	1	0	1	0	0	0	0	1	0	2	2	2	4	0	0	0	0	0	0
weaving	69	.6640	9.4468	49.8	9	13	2	15	18	6	4	2	15	1	0	2	0	9	0	7	1	6	7	0	5	4	10	2	0
web	115	.7165	16.914	52.3	14	21	15	37	19	1	8	0	26	1	0	4	0	0	1	42	1	0	0	3	17	9	3	8	0
Web	2	.0000	.0215	23.3	0	0	2	0	0	0	0	0	0	0	0	2	0	0	0	0	0	0	0	0	0	0	0	0	0
Webb	5	.2857	.3530	35.5	3	1	0	0	0	1	0	0	1	0	0	0	0	0	0	0	0	0	0	0	0	3	0	1	0
webbed	12	.6248	1.6039	42.1	6	0	1	2	1	0	1	1	6	0	0	1	0	0	0	0	0	0	0	0	1	2	1	1	0
webbing	4	.3363	.3286	35.2	2	0	0	1	1	0	0	0	1	0	0	0	0	0	0	2	0	0	0	0	1	0	0	0	0
Weber	22	.2949	1.5104	41.8	1	16	3	0	2	0	0	0	1	0	0	0	0	0	0	0	1	0	0	0	0	16	0	4	0
Webern	2	.0000	.0162	22.1	0	2	0	0	0	0	0	0	0	0	0	0	0	0	0	0	2	0	0	0	0	0	0	0	0
webs	30	.6009	3.7753	45.8	8	2	1	14	3	0	2	0	3	1	0	0	0	1	0	14	0	0	0	1	2	7	0	1	0
Webster	61	.5297	7.2524	48.6	0	29	0	3	25	2	1	1	35	2	0	1	1	1	8	0	0	0	0	0	0	13	0	0	0
Webster's	13	.4765	1.3978	41.5	1	0	0	0	7	2	3	0	6	3	0	2	0	0	2	0	0	0	0	0	0	0	0	0	0
wed	13	.3927	1.1625	40.7	2	0	1	1	7	1	1	0	4	0	0	1	0	0	1	0	6	0	0	0	0	0	0	1	0
wedded	7	.3718	.5765	37.6	1	0	0	3	0	0	2	1	1	0	0	2	0	0	0	0	3	0	0	0	0	0	0	1	0
wedding	109	.6891	15.687	52.0	40	18	2	16	13	5	13	2	50	6	0	15	1	1	0	0	8	0	0	0	7	15	0	6	0
weddings	5	.4523	.4696	36.7	1	0	1	0	1	1	1	0	0	0	0	0	0	0	0	0	1	0	1	0	0	0	1	2	0
wedge	34	.6920	4.8073	46.8	10	4	4	7	7	1	1	0	2	0	0	1	2	2	0	17	0	1	0	2	3	1	1	2	0
wedge-mate	2	.0000	.0243	23.9	0	0	0	0	2	0	0	0	0	0	0	0	0	0	0	0	0	0	0	0	0	0	0	2	0
wedge-shaped	9	.4743	.8946	39.5	1	0	1	1	2	2	0	2	0	0	0	0	0	1	3	2	0	1	0	0	0	0	2	0	0
wedged	13	.4998	1.4330	41.6	1	1	1	2	7	0	1	0	5	0	0	1	0	0	0	1	0	0	0	2	2	1	1	0	0
wedges	18	.4710	1.7969	42.5	9	1	1	0	1	1	5	0	0	0	0	0	0	0	0	10	1	0	4	1	0	1	0	1	0
wedging	2	.2433	.1158	30.6	0	0	0	0	1	0	0	1	0	0	0	0	0	0	0	0	0	0	0	0	0	1	0	1	0
wedlock	3	.3795	.2506	34.0	0	1	0	0	0	1	0	1	0	0	0	0	0	1	0	0	0	0	0	0	1	0	0	1	0
Wednesday	48	.7496	7.3045	48.6	12	17	5	3	2	4	5	0	10	4	2	1	13	4	3	0	3	0	0	0	6	1	0	1	0
Wednesday's	2	.1733	.1149	30.6	1	0	0	0	0	1	0	0	1	1	0	0	0	0	0	0	0	0	0	0	0	0	0	0	0
wee	16	.4489	1.6793	42.3	5	7	2	0	0	0	0	2	9	0	0	1	0	0	0	1	4	0	0	0	0	0	0	1	0
Wee	21	.1405	1.3776	41.4	1	0	20	0	0	0	0	0	20	0	0	0	0	0	0	0	0	0	0	0	0	1	0	0	0
Weeck	2	.1948	.1250	31.0	1	0	1	0	0	0	0	0	1	0	0	0	0	0	0	0	0	0	0	0	0	1	0	0	0
weed	40	.8328	6.6919	48.3	10	3	3	12	3	3	1	5	10	1	1	1	0	3	3	8	1	0	0	0	3	2	3	4	0
weeded	3	.2387	.1708	32.3	2	0	0	0	0	0	1	0	0	0	0	0	0	0	0	0	0	0	0	0	0	2	1	0	0
Weedemris	2	.0000	.0215	23.3	0	0	0	0	0	2	0	0	0	0	0	2	0	0	0	0	0	0	0	0	0	0	0	0	0
weeding	9	.4604	.9891	40.0	3	1	4	1	0	0	0	0	6	0	0	1	0	1	0	1	0	0	0	0	0	0	0	0	0
Weedon	2	.0000	.0234	23.7	0	0	0	0	2	0	0	0	0	0	0	0	0	0	0	0	0	0	0	0	2	0	0	0	0
weeds	105	.5478	12.545	51.0	40	14	15	9	21	1	3	2	40	0	3	6	0	16	0	15	0	3	0	0	6	4	7	3	2
weedy	4	.0665	.1417	31.5	1	0	1	0	2	0	0	0	2	0	2	0	0	0	0	0	0	0	0	0	0	0	0	0	0
week	846	.8815	148.56	61.7	201	121	103	103	104	107	82	25	179	52	6	30	157	46	43	56	18	0	17	1	65	60	6	110	0
Week	17	.6286	2.1767	43.4	4	5	5	0	1	2	0	0	0	2	0	0	0	1	0	0	1	0	0	0	5	2	2	4	0
week-end	2	.1814	.1187	30.7	2	0	0	0	0	0	0	0	1	0	0	0	0	0	0	0	0	0	0	0	0	0	0	1	0
week's	28	.7051	3.9983	46.0	4	5	1	6	5	3	3	1	3	1	2	1	0	2	7	1	0	0	1	0	2	1	1	6	0
weekday	4	.2281	.2337	33.7	2	0	0	0	1	0	1	0	0	0	0	0	0	3	0	0	0	0	0	0	0	0	0	1	0
weekdays	2	.1787	.1174	30.7	0	0	0	0	2	0	0	0	1	0	0	0	0	0	0	0	0	0	0	0	1	0	0	0	0
weekend	46	.6557	6.2103	47.9	7	6	6	5	8	6	6	2	9	3	3	1	2	0	1	1	1	0	1	0	3	1	0	20	0
weekends	11	.3423	.8306	39.2	6	0	0	0	0	2	1	2	0	0	0	0	2	0	0	0	0	0	0	0	3	0	0	6	0
weekly	40	.7142	5.8147	47.6	2	4	4	12	4	2	11	1	6	1	0	1	13	2	4	0	0	0	2	0	2	1	1	7	0
Weekly	6	.3932	.5359	37.3	0	3	0	0	2	1	0	0	1	0	0	0	0	1	0	0	0	0	0	0	0	3	1	0	0
weeks	526	.8814	92.562	59.7	133	80	77	62	66	52	40	16	151	16	3	18	49	51	24	53	3	0	3	0	29	60	11	55	0
Weeks	8	.0000	.3655	35.6	8	0	0	0	0	0	0	0	8	0	0	0	0	0	0	0	0	0	0	0	0	0	0	0	0
weel	2	.0000	.0219	23.4	0	0	2	0	0	0	0	0	0	2	0	0	0	0	0	0	0	0	0	0	0	0	0	0	0
Weel	3	.0000	.0243	23.8	0	0	0	3	0	0	0	0	0	0	0	0	0	0	0	0	3	0	0	0	0	0	0	0	0
weep	36	.6618	4.9335	46.9	6	3	4	4	5	2	12	0	10	1	0	11	0	1	1	0	4	0	0	0	1	3	3	1	0
weeping	35	.6278	4.6137	46.6	1	6	7	4	5	2	9	1	12	2	1	12	0	1	0	0	0	0	1	0	4	0	0	2	0
weeps	3	.2380	.1632	32.1	0	0	0	0	2	1	0	0	0	2	0	0	0	0	0	0	1	0	0	0	0	0	0	0	0
weevil	7	.4730	.7463	38.7	1	2	3	0	1	0	0	0	2	0	0	0	0	2	0	2	0	0	0	0	1	0	0	0	0
weevils	6	.2437	.4554	36.6	0	0	4	0	0	1	0	1	4	0	0	0	0	0	0	2	0	0	0	0	0	0	0	0	0
Weezer	3	.0000	.1370	31.4	0	0	0	0	3	0	0	0	3	0	0	0	0	0	0	0	0	0	0	0	0	0	0	0	0
weft	2	.2316	.0949	29.8	0	0	0	1	1	0	0	0	0	0	0	0	0	0	0	0	0	1	1	0	0	0	0	0	0
Wei	3	.1144	.1506	31.8	2	0	0	0	0	0	1	0	2	0	0	0	0	0	0	0	0	0	0	1	0	0	0	0	0
weigh	199	.7108	28.872	54.6	32	29	34	21	35	24	21	3	21	2	0	3	67	5	7	56	0	0	1	1	1	9	14	12	0
weighed	128	.7475	19.482	52.9	16	20	19	18	29	12	14	0	25	0	1	8	31	6	1	19	1	0	0	0	2	26	4	4	0
weighing	54	.7514	8.2150	49.1	1	3	7	8	17	5	9	4	6	1	2	3	13	3	0	11	0	0	0	0	1	3	6	5	0
Weighing	3	.1879	.1589	32.0	1	0	0	0	1	0	1	0	1	0	0	0	0	0	0	0	0	1	0	0	1	0	0	0	0
weighings	3	.2076	.1618	32.1	0	0	0	0	0	2	1	0	0	0	0	0	2	0	0	1	0	0	0	0	0	0	0	0	0
weighs	168	.6086	21.347	53.3	27	25	22	13	36	25	16	4	21	3	0	0	76	2	0	36	0	0	0	4	2	6	5	13	0
weight	610	.8480	103.37	60.1	56	84	83	103	102	94	69	19	67	7	2	11	105	19	2	220	4	8	15	11	24	41	39	35	0
weighted	16	.6798	2.2333	43.5	0	1	2	3	6	1	2	1	2	0	0	2	0	1	0	6	1	0	0	1	1	1	0	1	0
weightless	9	.4297	.8773	39.4	2	0	2	2	2	1	0	0	2	0	0	0	0	0	0	4	0	0	0	0	0	1	2	0	0
weightlessness	11	.4491	1.0819	40.3	1	0	1	4	4	1	0	0	1	0	0	0	0	0	0	5	0	1	0	0	0	3	0	1	0
weights	53	.6491	7.1089	48.5	5	2	8	15	6	9	7	1	6	0	0	0	14	2	0	18	0	0	1	4	2	3	1	2	0
weighty	4	.3071	.2967	34.7	0	1	0	0	2	0	1	0	1	0	0	1	0	0	0	0	0	0	0	0	2	0	0	0	0
Weill	3	.1983	.1396	31.4	0	0	0	1	1	1	0	0	0	0	0	0	0	0	0	0	2	0	0	0	0	0	0	1	0
weir	2	.1787	.1174	30.7	0	1	0	1	0	0	0	0	1	0	0	0	0	0	0	0	0	0	0	0	1	0	0	0	0
weird	32	.6910	4.5371	46.6	1	2	5	6	11	2	3	2	8	3	3	6	0	0	0	2	0	1	0	0	2	2	2	3	0
Weird	3	.0000	.0352	25.5	0	2	1	0	0	0	0	0	0	0	0	0	0	0	0	0	0	0	0	0	3	0	0	0	0
Weiss	3	.0000	.1370	31.4	0	0	3	0	0	0	0	0	3	0	0	0	0	0	0	0	0	0	0	0	0	0	0	0	0
Weitz	4	.0000	.0486	26.9	0	0	0	0	0	0	0	4	0	0	0	0	0	0	0	0	0	0	0	0	0	0	0	4	0
Welch	2	.0000	.0914	29.6	0	2	0	0	0	0	0	0	2	0	0	0	0	0	0	0	0	0	0	0	0	0	0	0	0
welcome	162	.8071	26.431	54.2	34	27	21	20	25	18	14	3	55	5	3	16	0	18	1	2	5	1	6	0	21	13	2	13	1
Welcome	8	.4874	.9007	39.5	6	1	0	0	1	0	0	0	5	1	0	1	0	0	0	0	0	0	0	0	0	0	0	1	0
welcomed	46	.5471	5.3514	47.3	6	8	5	1	12	9	3	2	10	2	4	5	0	9	1	0	1	0	0	0	1	5	3	4	1
welcomes	6	.0789	.2392	33.8	3	1	1	0	0	0	1	0	3	1	0	0	0	0	0	0	0	0	0	0	0	0	1	0	1
welcoming	11	.4743	1.1994	40.8	1	0	2	4	4	0	0	0	6	0	0	2	0	0	0	0	0	0	0	0	2	0	0	1	0
weld	8	.4611	.7630	38.8	0	0	0	3	2	0	2	1	0	0	0	0	0	0	0	0	0	1	0	2	0	2	1	2	0
weldability	2	.0000	.0050	17.0	0	0	0	0	0	0	2	0	0	0	0	0	0	0	0	0	0	0	0	2	0	0	0	0	0
welded	21	.3809	1.7196	42.4	2	1	0	0	13	3	1	1	0	0	0	0	0	2	0	0	0	0	0	3	1	0	1	14	0
welder	3	.1101	.0802	29.0	0	0	0	0	1	1	1	0	0	0	0	0	0	0	0	0	0	0	0	2	0	0	0	1	0
welding	41	.2695	2.5190	44.0	5	2	1	3	13	11	6	0	0	1	0	0	0	1	0	15	0	0	0	15	0	1	0	8	0
Weldon	2	.0000	.0389	25.9	0	0	1	0	0	1	0	0	0	0	0	0	0	2	0	0	0	0	0	0	0	0	0	0	0
welds	2	.1620	.0760	28.8	0	0	0	0	1	0	1	0	0	0	0	0	0	0	0	0	0	0	0	1	0	0	0	1	0
welfare	66	.7585	10.063	50.0	5	0	6	2	16	23	10	4	1	1	0	4	2	14	1	6	0	0	2	1	1	4	16	13	0
Welfare	8	.4753	.8904	39.5	2	1	0	0	4	0	1	0	5	0	0	0	0	1	0	0	0	0	0	0	0	1	1	0	0
well	4255	.9463	796.53	69.0	685	685	488	569	804	484	432	108	1352	247	36	336	43	361	37	312	155	45	151	33	384	331	165	266	1
Well	5	.5142	.5268	37.2	2	1	0	0	1	0	1	0	0	1	0	0	0	0	0	0	1	0	1	0	1	0	1	0	0
well-adjusted	2	.2437	.1129	30.5	0	0	0	0	1	1	0	0	0	0	0	0	0	0	0	0	0	0	0	0	0	0	1	1	0

XB Weavers'
6A weavin'
5N weavy
3F web-like
7A web-weaving
6A Webb's
8Q Weber's
4J Webern's
3H webfeet
4P Websters
8A weddin
6K Wedding
3B wedding-cake
9D wedding-dress
5D Wedge
7R wedge-mating
4A Wedged
9D weds
6J wee-le-wahl
6A weed-covered
XR weed-free
7H weed-killing
8D Weedemris's
6R week-ends
7R Weems
5N weensy
7P Weenty
8A Weep
9D weep'st
8K Weeping
4N weeping-willows
4A Weeps
8B weet
3A Wei's
5R weigh-in
7R weight-lifter
9F weight-producing
5R weight's
6A weighting
6J Weinberger
9L weiners
8J Weinzierl
XR weirdos
3B Weisgard
5P Weizmann
6H Weizsacker
7N welcomings
9M welders
9D Welikan
6R Welk
6J welkin
3P WELL
7A well-a-day
3Q well-aimed

Word Type	F	D	U	SFI	3 Gr 3	4 Gr 4	5 Gr 5	6 Gr 6	7 Gr 7	8 Gr 8	9 Gr 9	X UnGr	A Read	B Eng & Gr	C Comp	D Lit	E Math	F Soc Stud	G Spell	H Sci	J Music	K Art	L Home Ec	M Shop	N Lib F	P Lib NF	Q Lib Ref	R Mag	S Rel
well-armed	3	.3383	.2498	34.0	0	0	1	0	1	1	0	0	1	1	0	0	0	1	0	0	0	0	0	0	0	0	0	0	0
well-balanced	18	.3703	1.5109	41.8	0	0	1	9	3	4	1	0	1	0	0	0	0	1	0	12	1	0	3	0	0	0	0	0	0
well-behaved	7	.3608	.6347	38.0	0	5	0	2	0	0	0	0	4	0	0	2	0	0	0	0	0	0	0	0	0	0	0	1	0
well-being	22	.5377	2.4889	44.0	0	1	0	2	6	3	7	3	2	0	0	0	0	2	0	6	0	0	4	0	1	1	3	3	0
well-built	3	.1832	.1417	31.5	0	0	0	0	1	0	2	0	0	0	0	2	0	0	0	1	0	0	0	0	0	0	0	0	0
well-chosen	5	.4713	.4972	37.0	1	0	0	0	1	1	2	0	1	1	1	0	0	0	0	0	0	0	1	1	0	0	0	0	0
well-constructed	2	.1523	.0721	28.6	0	0	0	0	0	0	1	1	0	0	1	0	0	0	0	0	0	0	0	0	0	0	0	1	0
well-coordinated	2	.2300	.1140	30.6	0	0	0	1	0	1	0	0	0	1	0	0	0	0	0	1	0	0	0	0	0	0	0	0	0
well-cut	2	.1698	.1133	30.5	0	1	0	1	0	0	0	0	1	0	0	0	0	0	0	0	0	0	0	0	0	0	1	0	0
well-defined	4	.4820	.4132	36.2	0	0	0	0	2	1	1	0	0	0	0	0	1	1	0	1	0	0	0	0	0	0	0	1	0
well-developed	12	.5282	1.3467	41.3	0	0	0	1	7	0	3	1	1	3	0	0	0	1	0	5	0	0	1	0	0	1	0	0	0
well-distributed	2	.2408	.1204	30.8	0	0	1	1	0	0	0	0	0	0	0	0	0	1	0	0	0	0	0	0	0	1	0	0	0
well-drained	3	.2950	.1973	33.0	0	0	0	1	0	0	2	0	0	0	0	0	0	1	0	0	0	0	1	0	0	0	1	0	0
well-dressed	5	.3844	.4760	36.8	1	0	1	1	1	1	0	0	3	1	0	0	0	0	0	0	0	0	0	0	1	0	0	0	0
well-drilled	2	.0000	.0389	25.9	0	0	0	0	1	1	0	0	0	0	0	0	0	2	0	0	0	0	0	0	0	0	0	0	0
well-educated	4	.0000	.0778	28.9	0	1	0	0	0	1	2	0	0	0	0	0	0	4	0	0	0	0	0	0	0	0	0	0	0
well-equipped	2	.2278	.1128	30.5	0	0	1	0	1	0	0	0	0	0	0	0	0	0	0	1	0	0	0	0	0	0	1	0	0
well-filled	2	.2412	.1141	30.6	1	0	0	1	0	0	0	0	0	1	0	0	0	0	0	0	0	0	0	0	0	1	0	0	0
well-fitted	2	.2407	.1138	30.6	1	0	0	0	0	0	1	0	0	0	0	1	0	0	0	0	0	0	0	0	0	1	0	0	0
well-fitting	2	.0000	.0064	18.1	0	0	0	0	0	2	0	0	0	0	0	0	0	0	0	0	0	0	2	0	0	0	0	0	0
well-groomed	3	.2400	.1481	31.7	0	0	0	0	0	2	1	0	0	0	1	0	0	0	0	0	0	0	2	0	0	0	0	0	0
well-intentioned	2	.1814	.1187	30.7	0	1	0	0	0	0	0	1	1	0	0	0	0	0	0	0	0	0	0	0	0	0	0	1	0
well-irrigated	2	.2441	.1127	30.5	1	0	0	0	1	0	0	0	0	0	0	0	0	0	0	0	0	0	0	0	1	0	1	0	0
well-kept	6	.4368	.5767	37.6	0	1	0	0	3	1	1	0	1	0	0	1	0	2	0	0	0	0	0	1	1	0	0	0	0
well-known	90	.7983	14.425	51.6	5	9	14	14	21	15	7	5	13	5	0	6	0	12	5	8	17	3	1	0	2	2	12	4	0
well-loved	2	.0000	.0914	29.6	0	0	1	0	1	0	0	0	2	0	0	0	0	0	0	0	0	0	0	0	0	0	0	0	0
well-made	7	.4108	.6271	38.0	0	0	1	0	1	1	3	1	1	0	0	3	0	0	0	0	0	0	1	0	0	0	0	2	0
well-mannered	3	.1060	.1461	31.6	0	0	0	1	2	0	0	0	2	0	1	0	0	0	0	0	0	0	0	0	0	0	0	0	0
well-meaning	3	.1639	.1674	32.2	0	0	0	0	1	2	0	0	1	0	0	0	0	2	0	0	0	0	0	0	0	0	0	0	0
well-nigh	2	.1717	.1142	30.6	0	1	0	1	0	0	0	0	1	0	0	1	0	0	0	0	0	0	0	0	0	0	0	0	0
well-organized	8	.1687	.3522	35.5	1	0	0	1	2	1	3	0	1	1	4	0	0	1	0	1	0	0	0	0	0	0	0	0	0
well-planned	5	.3050	.3337	35.2	1	0	0	1	1	0	2	0	0	1	0	0	0	1	0	0	0	0	2	0	0	0	0	1	0
well-polished	2	.0000	.0914	29.6	0	0	0	1	0	0	0	1	2	0	0	0	0	0	0	0	0	0	0	0	0	0	0	0	0
well-preserved	2	.0000	.0209	23.2	0	1	0	0	0	0	1	0	0	0	0	0	0	0	0	0	0	0	0	0	0	0	2	0	0
well-pressed	3	.0000	.0097	19.8	0	0	0	0	0	3	0	0	0	0	0	0	0	0	0	0	0	0	3	0	0	0	0	0	0
well-protected	3	.3418	.2483	33.9	0	0	1	0	1	1	0	0	1	1	0	0	0	0	0	0	0	0	0	0	0	1	0	0	0
well-run	2	.2408	.1204	30.8	1	1	0	0	0	0	0	0	0	0	0	0	0	1	0	0	0	0	0	0	0	1	0	0	0
well-seasoned	2	.1787	.1174	30.7	0	0	0	1	0	1	0	0	1	0	0	0	0	0	0	0	0	0	0	0	1	0	0	0	0
well-selected	2	.1648	.0800	29.0	0	0	0	0	0	1	1	0	0	0	0	0	1	0	0	0	0	0	1	0	0	0	0	0	0
well-stocked	2	.0857	.0784	28.9	0	1	0	0	0	0	1	0	1	0	0	0	0	0	0	0	0	0	1	0	0	0	0	0	0
well-suited	2	.0000	.0914	29.6	0	2	0	0	0	0	0	0	2	0	0	0	0	0	0	0	0	0	0	0	0	0	0	0	0
well-to-do	6	.4741	.6415	38.1	0	0	1	1	1	3	0	0	2	0	0	0	0	2	0	0	0	0	0	0	0	1	0	1	0
well-trained	8	.5294	.9245	39.7	0	0	0	3	2	1	2	0	2	0	0	0	0	3	0	1	0	0	0	0	0	1	0	1	0
well-traveled	4	.4568	.4091	36.1	1	1	0	1	1	0	0	0	1	0	0	0	0	0	0	1	0	0	0	0	0	1	0	1	0
well-ventilated	2	.0000	.0394	26.0	0	0	0	0	0	0	2	0	0	0	0	0	0	0	0	2	0	0	0	0	0	0	0	0	0
well-watered	2	.0000	.0389	25.9	0	0	2	0	0	0	0	0	0	0	0	0	0	2	0	0	0	0	0	0	0	0	0	0	0
well-worn	2	.2437	.1129	30.5	0	0	0	0	1	0	1	0	0	0	0	0	0	0	0	0	0	0	0	0	0	0	1	1	0
well-written	3	.1699	.1343	31.3	0	0	2	0	1	0	0	0	0	0	1	0	0	2	0	0	0	0	0	0	0	0	0	0	0
Weller	2	.0000	.0215	23.3	0	0	0	0	0	2	0	0	0	0	0	2	0	0	0	0	0	0	0	0	0	0	0	0	0
Welles	6	.1409	.2943	34.7	0	4	0	0	2	0	0	0	2	0	0	0	0	0	0	0	0	0	0	0	0	4	0	0	0
Wellesley	3	.1823	.1405	31.5	0	0	1	0	0	1	1	0	0	0	0	0	0	1	0	0	0	0	0	0	0	0	2	0	0
welling	3	.3870	.2486	34.0	0	0	0	0	2	1	0	0	0	0	0	1	0	0	0	0	0	0	0	0	0	0	1	1	0
Wellington	68	.0862	3.9431	46.0	0	0	66	1	1	0	0	0	66	0	0	0	0	2	0	0	0	0	0	0	0	0	0	0	0
Wellington's	9	.2292	.6951	38.4	0	0	8	0	0	0	1	0	8	0	0	0	0	0	0	0	0	0	0	0	0	0	1	0	0
wells	78	.4278	7.4644	48.7	11	19	15	10	9	8	5	1	5	0	0	0	1	50	0	14	0	0	0	0	1	0	2	5	0
Wells	16	.6024	2.0032	43.0	4	0	0	0	6	5	1	0	2	1	0	4	0	3	0	0	1	0	0	0	0	1	0	4	0
Wells's	4	.0000	.0486	26.9	0	0	0	0	0	4	0	0	0	0	0	0	0	0	0	0	0	0	0	0	0	0	0	4	0
Welsh	38	.5772	4.5081	46.5	0	2	6	9	15	0	6	0	1	4	0	0	0	1	0	0	8	0	0	0	7	3	1	13	0
Welshman	4	.1854	.1872	32.7	0	0	0	1	1	0	2	0	0	0	0	0	0	0	0	0	0	0	0	0	0	1	0	3	0
welts	2	.0665	.0708	28.5	0	0	0	1	0	0	1	0	1	0	1	0	0	0	0	0	0	0	0	0	0	0	0	0	0
Wemba	3	.0000	.0583	27.7	0	3	0	0	0	0	0	0	0	0	0	0	0	3	0	0	0	0	0	0	0	0	0	0	0
Wemba's	7	.0000	.1361	31.3	0	7	0	0	0	0	0	0	0	0	0	0	0	7	0	0	0	0	0	0	0	0	0	0	0
Wen	2	.0000	.0234	23.7	0	0	0	0	2	0	0	0	0	0	0	0	0	0	0	0	0	0	0	0	2	0	0	0	0
wench	3	.3394	.2451	33.9	0	0	0	0	2	0	1	0	1	0	0	1	0	0	0	0	0	0	0	0	1	0	0	0	0
wend	4	.1789	.1692	32.3	1	0	0	1	0	2	0	0	0	0	0	0	0	0	0	0	3	0	0	0	0	0	1	0	0
Wendell	5	.4682	.4985	37.0	0	2	0	0	0	3	0	0	0	0	0	0	0	1	0	0	0	0	0	0	1	2	0	1	0
Wendy	57	.1279	3.6540	45.6	1	0	0	56	0	0	0	0	55	0	0	0	1	1	0	0	0	0	0	0	0	0	0	0	0
Wendy's	4	.0000	.1827	32.6	0	0	0	4	0	0	0	0	4	0	0	0	0	0	0	0	0	0	0	0	0	0	0	0	0
Weng	2	.0000	.0243	23.9	0	0	0	0	0	0	0	2	0	0	0	0	0	0	0	0	0	0	0	0	0	0	0	2	0
went	4132	.8554	710.87	68.5	1159	772	517	519	590	332	178	65	1812	170	29	371	78	275	29	66	89	10	2	0	583	391	48	174	5
Wentworth	2	.0000	.0914	29.6	0	2	0	0	0	0	0	0	2	0	0	0	0	0	0	0	0	0	0	0	0	0	0	0	0
Wentworth's	2	.0000	.0914	29.6	0	2	0	0	0	0	0	0	2	0	0	0	0	0	0	0	0	0	0	0	0	0	0	0	0
Weorman	5	.0000	.2284	33.6	0	0	5	0	0	0	0	0	5	0	0	0	0	0	0	0	0	0	0	0	0	0	0	0	0
weorth	2	.0000	.0162	22.1	0	0	0	2	0	0	0	0	0	0	0	0	0	0	2	0	0	0	0	0	0	0	0	0	0
wept	49	.6927	7.0397	48.5	4	8	5	8	17	1	5	1	19	4	1	11	0	2	0	0	5	0	0	0	1	3	0	3	0
were	17031	.9503	3200.2	75.1	2967	2781	2239	2313	2919	2263	1203	346	4991	597	108	1101	616	2703	188	978	521	164	51	50	1355	1909	771	916	12
weren't	176	.6987	25.490	54.1	47	32	15	22	31	13	14	2	67	30	0	21	0	3	0	5	1	0	1	0	18	17	0	13	0
Werner	5	.3973	.4497	36.5	0	0	0	0	2	0	3	0	1	0	0	0	0	0	0	1	0	0	0	0	0	0	2	1	0
wert	3	.3847	.2490	34.0	0	0	0	0	2	0	1	0	0	1	0	1	0	0	0	0	0	0	0	0	0	1	0	0	0
Wes	2	.1814	.1187	30.7	0	0	1	1	0	0	0	0	1	0	0	0	0	0	0	0	0	0	0	0	0	0	0	1	0
Wesley	7	.3788	.5911	37.7	0	0	0	4	1	1	1	0	1	0	0	0	0	0	0	0	1	0	0	0	0	0	1	4	0
west	557	.7748	87.333	59.4	90	103	108	61	76	64	40	15	75	11	0	20	14	214	3	54	9	1	1	1	9	57	59	29	0
West	520	.8112	84.981	59.3	64	52	91	79	85	117	20	12	110	12	1	20	8	166	3	8	38	0	3	2	11	40	40	58	0
WestVirginia	19	.6398	2.4929	44.0	3	0	4	0	3	8	0	1	1	1	0	0	0	2	0	2	1	0	0	0	0	3	4	5	0
west-coast	5	.0000	.0972	29.9	0	0	0	1	3	0	1	0	0	0	0	0	0	5	0	0	0	0	0	0	0	0	0	0	0
Westbury	2	.0000	.0215	23.3	0	0	0	0	2	0	0	0	0	0	0	2	0	0	0	0	0	0	0	0	0	0	0	0	0
Westchester	2	.0000	.0243	23.9	0	0	0	0	1	0	1	0	0	0	0	0	0	0	0	0	0	0	0	0	0	0	0	2	0
westerly	8	.4198	.7518	38.8	0	2	0	2	2	0	0	2	1	0	0	0	0	4	0	0	0	0	0	0	0	0	1	2	0

9D well-appareled
8H well-baby
9D well-based
6A well-bred
5P well-brought-up
7N well-coached
8B well-concealed
7R well-conceived
4K well-designed
7R well-done
6C well-earned
9F well-enough
7B well-enunciated
7J well-established
9D well-fashioned
8N well-fed
8F well-fertilized
9D well-flowered
9C well-focused
7A well-formed
7R well-greased
3N well-hidden
6R well-if-you-insist
7H well-informed
5Q well-insulated
7A well-knit
3A well-l-l
6N well-laid
5P well-laid-out
4R well-lighted
7D well-liked
7Q well-marked
8J well-modulated
7D well-named
8L well-nourished
9R well-off
8D well-oiled
7P well-ordered
4A well-placed
7F well-populated
9L well-prepared
7R well-publicized
XJ well-read
XH well-rounded
XQ well-scrubbed
8L well-shaped
XB well-sharpened
9F well-situated
3H well-soaked
8J Well-tempered
6R well-tended
6A well-tilled
8A well-tramped
9D well-trimmed
8D well-turned
7B well-ur
7R well-used
7P well-versed
7A well-wisher
8A well's
7C wellbuilt
6A welled
5N weller
8D Weller's
5F wellkept
4E Wells'
8R Wellses
7H wellspring
7R wellwishers
9R Welsh-speaking
8R welshed
6R Welshmen
5R welt
9R welter
7A welterweight
7G wen
9D wench's
7N wending
5R Went
7J wep-i-ed
8B wer
9D weraday
3P WERE
6P Wernher
8R Wersching
7D Weser
6R Wesleyan
8P Wessel
7Q Wessex
9R WestGerman
5Q WestHartford
7H WestPalmBeach
9F WestPoint
8H west-east
9A west-southwest
7R West's
7R Westerfield
6D westering
9B Westerman

Word Type	F	D	U	SFI	3 Gr 3	4 Gr 4	5 Gr 5	6 Gr 6	7 Gr 7	8 Gr 8	9 Gr 9	X UnGr	A Read	B Eng & Gr	C Comp	D Lit	E Math	F Soc Stud	G Spell	H Sci	J Music	K Art	L Home Ec	M Shop	N Lib F	P Lib NF	Q Lib Ref	R Mag	S Rel
western	344	.7260	50.800	57.1	28	29	80	65	74	34	21	13	25	5	1	8	2	165	1	25	10	1	1	1	3	26	53	17	0
Western	284	.7008	40.800	56.1	8	44	40	34	58	67	24	9	39	6	1	1	4	130	0	5	22	0	1	0	4	20	26	25	0
Western-style	2	.2285	.1129	30.5	0	0	1	1	0	0	0	0	0	0	0	0	0	1	0	0	0	0	0	0	0	0	1	0	0
westerners	2	.2433	.1158	30.6	1	0	0	0	0	0	0	1	0	0	0	0	0	0	0	0	0	0	0	0	0	1	0	1	0
Westerners	4	.3677	.3659	35.6	0	0	1	0	2	0	1	0	2	0	0	1	0	1	0	0	0	0	0	0	0	0	0	0	0
Westernization	2	.0000	.0290	24.6	0	0	2	0	0	0	0	0	0	0	0	0	0	0	0	0	0	0	0	0	0	2	0	0	0
westernmost	2	.2285	.1129	30.5	1	0	0	1	0	0	0	0	0	0	0	0	0	1	0	0	0	0	0	0	0	0	1	0	0
westerns	2	.2376	.1088	30.4	0	1	1	0	0	0	0	0	0	0	0	0	0	0	1	0	0	0	0	0	0	0	0	1	0
Westerns	2	.2440	.1132	30.5	0	0	0	1	1	0	0	0	0	0	0	1	0	0	0	0	0	0	0	0	0	0	0	1	0
Westerville	5	.0000	.0748	28.7	0	0	5	0	0	0	0	0	0	0	0	0	5	0	0	0	0	0	0	0	0	0	0	0	0
Westfield	2	.2297	.1135	30.6	0	0	1	0	0	1	0	0	0	0	0	1	0	1	0	0	0	0	0	0	0	0	0	0	0
Westinghouse	3	.3764	.2483	33.9	0	1	0	0	0	0	2	0	0	0	0	0	0	0	0	1	0	0	0	0	0	0	1	1	0
Westminster	12	.5904	1.4583	41.6	0	2	2	3	1	2	2	0	1	2	0	1	0	1	1	0	3	0	0	0	0	0	3	0	0
Westmoreland	2	.0000	.0243	23.9	0	0	0	0	2	0	0	0	0	0	0	0	0	0	0	0	0	0	0	0	0	0	0	2	0
Weston	3	.3370	.2430	33.9	0	0	2	0	1	0	0	0	1	0	0	1	0	0	0	0	0	0	0	0	0	0	1	0	0
Westport	4	.0000	.1827	32.6	0	0	4	0	0	0	0	0	4	0	0	0	0	0	0	0	0	0	0	0	0	0	0	0	0
Westville	7	.0000	.3198	35.0	0	0	0	0	7	0	0	0	7	0	0	0	0	0	0	0	0	0	0	0	0	0	0	0	0
westward	132	.6531	17.836	52.5	8	15	39	9	24	28	7	2	16	0	0	10	0	57	0	8	3	0	0	0	4	11	19	4	0
Westward	5	.3902	.4356	36.4	0	1	1	1	1	0	0	1	1	0	0	0	0	0	0	0	2	0	0	0	1	0	0	1	0
wet	418	.7793	66.113	58.2	133	88	46	54	42	27	21	7	120	18	5	26	0	33	8	78	7	27	1	1	35	35	13	11	0
wet-and-dry	4	.0000	.0778	28.9	0	0	0	0	0	0	4	0	0	0	0	0	0	4	0	0	0	0	0	0	0	0	0	0	0
wetness	5	.4705	.4940	36.9	0	1	1	0	2	0	0	1	0	0	0	1	0	0	0	0	0	0	0	0	0	1	1	2	0
wetted	2	.2331	.1157	30.6	0	0	1	0	0	0	0	1	0	0	0	0	0	0	0	1	0	0	0	0	1	0	0	0	0
wetter	4	.3741	.3400	35.3	1	0	0	1	1	0	1	0	0	0	0	0	0	1	0	2	0	0	0	0	0	1	0	0	0
wettest	5	.4481	.5010	37.0	0	2	1	0	2	0	0	0	1	0	0	0	1	2	0	0	0	0	0	0	0	0	1	0	0
wetting	7	.4575	.7272	38.6	1	2	1	0	2	1	0	0	3	0	0	1	0	0	0	0	0	0	0	0	1	0	2	0	0
WEU	4	.0000	.0486	26.9	0	0	0	0	0	0	4	0	0	0	0	0	0	0	0	0	0	0	0	0	0	0	0	4	0
Wexler	2	.0000	.0243	23.9	0	0	0	0	0	0	2	0	0	0	0	0	0	0	0	0	0	0	0	0	0	0	0	2	0
Wexler's	3	.0000	.0365	25.6	0	0	0	0	0	0	3	0	0	0	0	0	0	0	0	0	0	0	0	0	0	0	0	3	0
wh	36	.0764	.8543	39.3	8	11	3	6	5	1	2	0	1	1	0	0	1	0	33	0	0	0	0	0	0	0	0	0	0
whack	11	.5487	1.3221	41.2	3	2	2	0	0	1	3	0	5	0	0	1	0	0	0	0	0	0	0	0	2	1	0	2	0
WHACK	3	.0000	.0434	26.4	3	0	0	0	0	0	0	0	0	0	0	0	0	0	0	0	0	0	0	0	0	3	0	0	0
whackers	2	.0000	.0290	24.6	0	2	0	0	0	0	0	0	0	0	0	0	0	0	0	0	0	0	0	0	0	2	0	0	0
whacking	4	.3717	.3640	35.6	1	0	1	1	1	0	0	0	2	0	0	1	0	0	0	0	0	0	0	0	0	0	0	1	0
whacks	2	.0000	.0914	29.6	0	0	0	0	1	1	0	0	2	0	0	0	0	0	0	0	0	0	0	0	0	0	0	0	0
whale	274	.7571	42.850	56.3	61	124	8	32	39	5	5	0	148	2	4	1	13	4	2	28	6	0	0	0	8	45	9	4	0
Whale	9	.3038	.6104	37.9	2	6	1	0	0	0	0	0	0	0	0	0	0	0	0	0	0	0	0	0	6	0	1	2	0
whale-catcher	2	.0000	.0290	24.6	2	0	0	0	0	0	0	0	0	0	0	0	0	0	0	0	0	0	0	0	0	2	0	0	0
whale's	17	.4128	1.7142	42.3	1	7	2	5	2	0	0	0	11	0	0	0	0	0	0	0	0	0	0	0	1	1	4	0	0
Whale's	2	.0000	.0234	23.7	0	2	0	0	0	0	0	0	0	0	0	0	0	0	0	0	0	0	0	0	2	0	0	0	0
whalebone	4	.1855	.2376	33.8	0	1	0	1	1	1	0	0	2	0	0	0	0	1	0	0	0	1	0	0	0	0	0	0	0
Whalen	5	.0000	.0537	27.3	0	0	0	0	5	0	0	0	0	0	0	5	0	0	0	0	0	0	0	0	0	0	0	0	0
whaler	10	.2140	.7532	38.8	0	5	0	4	0	0	0	1	9	0	0	0	0	0	0	0	0	0	0	0	0	0	0	1	0
whalerman	6	.0000	.2741	34.4	0	6	0	0	0	0	0	0	6	0	0	0	0	0	0	0	0	0	0	0	0	0	0	0	0
whalers	6	.0000	.2741	34.4	0	5	0	1	0	0	0	0	6	0	0	0	0	0	0	0	0	0	0	0	0	0	0	0	0
whales	151	.6073	19.614	52.9	61	52	2	8	20	1	2	5	60	3	1	0	1	2	0	16	0	0	0	0	2	49	15	2	0
whaling	38	.5672	4.7986	46.8	5	21	5	3	1	1	2	0	24	0	0	0	0	2	0	3	3	0	0	0	0	5	1	0	0
wham	7	.4521	.6875	38.4	1	1	1	0	0	0	4	0	1	0	0	1	0	0	0	1	0	0	0	0	0	0	3	1	0
whar	2	.0000	.0219	23.4	0	0	0	0	0	2	0	0	0	2	0	0	0	0	0	0	0	0	0	0	0	0	0	0	0
wharf	42	.5822	5.3766	47.3	12	10	6	9	3	2	0	0	26	0	2	0	0	0	0	0	0	0	0	0	3	4	2	5	0
Wharf	5	.2800	.3594	35.6	0	0	1	1	0	3	0	0	2	0	1	0	0	0	0	0	0	0	0	0	2	0	0	0	0
wharves	13	.7518	1.9829	43.0	0	2	5	1	3	1	0	1	2	1	0	1	0	3	0	1	1	0	0	0	0	2	1	1	0
what	17709	.9582	3350.1	75.3	3735	2990	2328	2198	2904	1946	1374	234	4189	1930	153	1185	2702	1259	785	1980	566	181	202	97	845	736	211	662	26
What	52	.4542	5.0898	47.1	37	3	3	0	1	6	1	1	3	3	2	1	37	1	0	0	0	0	0	0	0	1	0	4	0
WHAT	10	.4426	.9805	39.9	6	1	1	0	1	0	1	0	1	0	0	0	0	1	0	6	0	0	1	0	0	0	0	1	0
What-do-you-think	2	.0000	.0290	24.6	0	0	0	2	0	0	0	0	0	0	0	0	0	0	0	0	0	0	0	0	0	2	0	0	0
what-is-it	3	.0939	.1398	31.5	0	0	2	0	0	1	0	0	2	0	0	0	0	0	0	0	0	1	0	0	0	0	0	0	0
what'd	7	.3323	.5338	37.3	0	1	1	0	2	0	3	0	1	0	0	4	0	0	0	0	0	0	0	0	1	1	0	0	0
what'll	12	.4406	1.2126	40.8	3	2	0	1	4	1	1	0	5	0	0	3	0	0	0	0	0	0	0	0	3	1	0	0	0
what're	7	.3621	.6358	38.0	1	2	0	1	1	1	1	0	4	0	0	2	0	0	0	0	0	0	0	0	1	0	0	0	0
what's	482	.7293	72.645	58.6	97	103	44	58	78	42	46	14	218	18	2	69	2	6	3	8	9	0	0	0	54	47	0	46	0
What's	7	.1925	.3439	35.4	6	1	0	0	0	0	0	0	0	0	0	0	6	0	1	0	0	0	0	0	0	0	0	0	0
what's-his-name	2	.2446	.1142	30.6	0	1	0	0	0	0	0	1	0	0	0	0	0	0	0	0	0	0	0	0	1	0	0	1	0
what've	2	.0665	.0708	28.5	0	0	0	0	1	1	0	0	1	0	1	0	0	0	0	0	0	0	0	0	0	0	0	0	0
whatcha	2	.1814	.1187	30.7	0	0	1	0	1	0	0	0	1	0	0	0	0	0	0	0	0	0	0	0	0	0	0	1	0
whate'er	3	.2379	.1705	32.3	0	0	0	0	3	0	0	0	0	0	0	1	0	0	0	0	0	0	0	0	0	2	0	0	0
whatever	306	.9014	54.852	57.4	37	37	46	33	60	46	31	16	84	21	8	23	6	19	10	20	4	0	8	1	25	29	15	33	0
whatsoever	5	.3065	.3626	35.6	0	0	0	0	3	1	0	1	1	2	0	0	0	0	0	0	0	0	0	0	0	0	2	0	0
wheat	342	.7665	53.230	57.3	59	62	70	68	49	23	11	0	56	2	2	7	4	160	4	37	10	2	4	0	4	18	28	4	0
Wheat	2	.2351	.1166	30.7	0	0	0	1	1	0	0	0	0	0	0	0	0	1	0	0	0	0	0	0	0	0	0	1	0
whee	2	.0000	.0234	23.7	1	0	0	1	0	0	0	0	0	0	0	0	0	0	0	0	0	0	0	0	2	0	0	0	0
wheedled	4	.4538	.4020	36.0	2	1	0	0	1	0	0	0	1	0	0	1	0	0	0	0	0	0	0	0	0	1	0	1	0
wheel	418	.8735	72.936	58.6	68	86	43	31	103	51	24	12	117	8	6	22	20	21	5	77	5	0	22	4	45	13	18	35	0
Wheel	4	.4735	.3987	36.0	0	0	1	0	0	1	1	1	0	0	0	1	0	1	0	0	1	0	0	0	0	0	0	1	0
wheel-shaped	2	.0000	.0394	26.0	0	0	0	0	1	0	0	1	0	0	0	0	0	0	0	2	0	0	0	0	0	0	0	0	0
wheel's	2	.1717	.1142	30.6	0	0	2	0	0	0	0	0	1	0	0	1	0	0	0	0	0	0	0	0	0	0	0	0	0
wheelbarrow	21	.6740	2.9709	44.7	8	0	0	7	5	0	0	1	10	0	0	0	0	0	1	1	3	0	0	0	2	1	1	2	0
Wheelbarrow	2	.2387	.1089	30.4	1	0	0	0	1	0	0	0	0	0	0	0	0	0	0	0	1	0	0	0	1	0	0	0	0
wheelbarrows	3	.2425	.1816	32.6	0	0	0	3	0	0	0	0	0	0	0	0	0	2	0	0	0	0	0	0	0	0	0	1	0
wheelbase	2	.0000	.0243	23.9	0	0	0	0	2	0	0	0	0	0	0	0	0	0	0	0	0	0	0	0	0	0	0	2	0
wheelchair	4	.3512	.3114	34.9	0	0	2	1	0	0	1	0	0	0	0	0	0	0	0	1	0	0	0	0	0	0	1	2	0
wheeled	27	.6205	3.6368	45.6	5	3	5	4	4	4	2	0	17	0	0	3	0	2	0	0	0	0	0	0	2	1	1	1	0
Wheeler	8	.2332	.6203	37.9	4	0	2	2	0	0	0	0	7	1	0	0	0	0	0	0	0	0	0	0	0	0	0	0	0
wheeling	15	.4907	1.6733	42.2	0	3	3	1	5	3	0	0	8	0	0	4	0	0	0	0	0	0	0	0	0	1	1	1	0
Wheeling	4	.2152	.2714	34.3	0	0	1	0	2	1	0	0	2	0	0	0	0	2	0	0	0	0	0	0	0	0	0	0	0
wheels	287	.9031	51.601	57.1	77	55	33	25	50	26	18	3	94	5	7	10	19	14	2	35	5	2	0	5	16	29	16	28	0
Wheels	658	.0135	31.365	55.0	1	0	0	0	434	223	0	0	657	1	0	0	0	0	0	0	0	0	0	0	0	0	0	0	0
Wheelwright	4	.0000	.1827	32.6	0	4	0	0	0	0	0	0	4	0	0	0	0	0	0	0	0	0	0	0	0	0	0	0	0
wheeze	2	.2137	.1056	30.2	0	0	1	0	0	0	1	0	0	0	0	0	0	1	0	0	1	0	0	0	0	0	0	0	0
wheezed	4	.4543	.4025	36.0	2	0	1	0	0	0	0	1	1	1	0	0	0	0	0	0	0	0	0	0	0	1	0	1	0
wheezing	8	.3813	.7829	38.9	4	0	1	2	1	0	0	0	6	0	0	1	0	0	0	0	0	0	0	0	1	0	0	0	0
wheezy	2	.2446	.1142	30.6	2	0	0	0	0	0	0	0	0	0	0	0	0	0	0	0	0	0	0	0	1	0	0	1	0
whelks	2	.0000	.0209	23.2	0	0	0	0	0	2	0	0	0	0	0	0	0	0	0	0	0	0	0	0	0	0	2	0	0
whelped	2	.1787	.1174	30.7	0	0	0	0	1	0	1	0	1	0	0	0	0	0	0	0	0	0	0	0	1	0	0	0	0

7R western-Kentucky-style
7F Western-equipped
4F western-style
7R Westerner
9Q Westernized
9R Westinghouse's
6A Westman
5Q westward-
5P westward-flowing
4N Wet
8A wet-blanket
9F wet-dry
9D wether
5B wetly
8B weve
4Q Weymouth
7R WGBH
XH wh-i-s-s-s-t
8B wha
5N whaaah
4A whacked
9R whaddaya
7N whah
5P whaka
5P Whakarewarewa
4P whale-oil
6A whaleboat
4F whaleboats
3P whaled
7D Whaling
4N whang
9R whap
5J wharfs
3E What-Are-My-Rules
8K what-if
9B whatch
7R Whatever
6A whatever's
XR Whatman
6R whatsamatter
3A whe-e-e-e
6F wheat-exporting
8F wheat-flour
6A wheat-gold
6F wheat-producing
9F wheat-raising
5Q wheat-shipping
9F wheatland
8H Wheaton
6R whee-ew
3A wheee
9R wheelchairs
4N wheelhouse
7R wheelie
5R wheelless
7A Wheels'
7A Wheels's
4A Wheelwrights'
3A wheezes
3A whelk
XR whelp
7A whelps

Word Type	F	D	U	SFI	3 Gr 3	4 Gr 4	5 Gr 5	6 Gr 6	7 Gr 7	8 Gr 8	9 Gr 9	X UnGr	A Read	B Eng & Gr	C Comp	D Lit	E Math	F Soc Stud	G Spell	H Sci	J Music	K Art	L Home Ec	M Shop	N Lib F	P Lib NF	Q Lib Ref	R Mag	S Rel
when	15886	.9932	3102.8	74.9	3122	2655	1911	2043	2826	1741	1243	345	4488	945	149	1013	757	1115	625	1798	666	152	286	188	1035	1222	539	898	10
When	20	.4988	2.1126	43.2	3	1	2	4	8	2	0	0	3	0	0	3	0	1	1	0	9	0	0	0	1	0	1	1	0
when's	2	.2443	.1130	30.5	0	0	0	1	1	0	1	0	0	0	0	1	0	0	0	0	0	0	0	0	1	0	0	0	0
whence	14	.5597	1.6708	42.2	0	2	1	3	4	2	2	0	4	1	0	3	0	0	0	0	0	0	0	0	4	1	1	0	0
whene'er	3	.2223	.2106	33.2	0	1	2	0	0	0	0	0	2	1	0	0	0	0	0	0	0	0	0	0	0	0	0	0	0
whenever	277	.9320	51.141	57.1	49	43	32	33	59	33	19	9	71	19	4	14	18	15	7	42	7	0	5	7	20	24	7	17	0
whens	2	.1892	.0858	29.3	0	0	0	0	1	1	0	0	0	1	0	0	0	0	0	0	0	0	1	0	0	0	0	0	0
wherEVer	2	.0000	.0215	23.3	0	0	0	0	0	2	0	0	0	0	0	2	0	0	0	0	0	0	0	0	0	0	0	0	0
where	5611	.9794	1082.4	70.3	1206	977	680	684	993	514	444	113	1426	330	70	363	247	770	106	533	211	40	70	59	394	422	244	325	1
Where	3	.2387	.1708	32.3	2	1	0	0	0	0	0	0	0	0	0	0	0	0	0	0	0	0	0	0	0	2	1	0	0
WHERE	3	.2295	.1558	31.9	0	0	0	2	1	0	0	0	0	0	0	0	0	0	0	0	0	0	1	0	2	0	0	0	0
where'd	8	.2816	.5805	37.6	0	1	2	1	3	1	0	0	3	0	0	4	0	0	0	0	0	0	0	0	1	0	0	0	0
where'er	2	.2412	.1141	30.6	1	0	0	0	1	0	0	0	0	1	0	0	0	0	0	0	0	0	0	0	0	1	0	0	0
where's	72	.5712	8.8845	49.5	16	21	3	5	14	6	7	0	30	4	0	8	0	0	0	0	1	0	0	0	20	8	0	1	0
Where's	7	.0000	.0566	27.5	0	0	0	0	0	7	0	0	0	0	0	0	0	0	0	0	7	0	0	0	0	0	0	0	0
whereabouts	6	.4362	.5932	37.7	0	0	1	2	2	1	0	0	2	0	0	2	1	0	0	0	0	0	0	0	0	0	0	1	0
whereas	55	.7897	8.6932	49.4	2	1	2	3	23	12	10	2	3	4	1	3	2	2	1	11	3	0	4	4	0	3	12	2	0
whereby	7	.6623	.9533	39.8	0	0	1	0	1	0	2	3	1	1	0	1	0	1	0	0	0	0	0	0	1	1	0	1	0
wherefore	5	.3161	.3505	35.4	0	0	0	0	2	1	2	0	0	0	0	3	0	0	0	0	0	0	0	0	1	1	1	0	0
wherein	9	.4553	.8736	39.4	2	0	1	0	1	2	3	0	0	3	0	0	0	2	0	0	0	0	0	0	0	3	1	0	0
whereof	7	.4176	.6256	38.0	1	0	0	0	2	1	3	0	0	2	0	3	0	1	0	0	0	0	0	0	0	1	0	0	0
wheres	2	.0000	.0219	23.4	0	0	0	0	0	2	0	0	0	2	0	0	0	0	0	0	0	0	0	0	0	0	0	0	0
whereupon	15	.6702	2.0550	43.1	0	0	3	1	5	3	1	2	2	3	0	1	0	0	0	1	0	0	0	1	4	1	1	1	0
wherever	170	.9191	30.978	54.9	33	21	15	27	42	17	13	2	37	10	5	14	2	25	2	13	16	2	1	3	13	9	7	11	0
whet	2	.2443	.1130	30.5	0	0	0	0	1	0	1	0	0	0	0	1	0	0	0	0	0	0	0	0	1	0	0	0	0
whether	1060	.9512	199.06	63.0	89	129	115	147	234	162	163	21	159	120	17	43	187	54	53	143	24	9	41	5	41	64	52	47	1
whetted	3	.2437	.2277	33.6	0	0	0	2	1	0	0	0	2	0	0	0	0	0	0	1	0	0	0	0	0	0	0	0	0
whew	13	.4387	1.2703	41.0	2	2	7	1	1	0	0	0	4	0	2	0	0	0	0	0	1	0	0	0	4	0	0	2	0
whey	19	.3472	1.5259	41.8	0	1	5	0	12	0	1	0	1	0	0	1	0	0	0	12	0	0	0	0	5	0	0	0	0
which	14016	.9698	2678.3	74.3	1682	1730	1677	1849	3069	1912	1690	407	1938	1053	129	548	1355	1438	1598	1574	751	149	272	228	453	770	1169	578	13
whichever	20	.5650	2.3359	43.7	1	3	1	1	5	5	4	0	2	3	0	2	4	0	3	0	0	0	4	0	1	0	1	0	0
whicker	2	.2443	.1130	30.5	0	0	0	1	1	0	1	0	0	0	0	1	0	0	0	0	0	0	0	0	1	0	0	0	0
whiff	6	.2406	.3642	35.6	1	1	0	0	2	1	1	0	1	0	0	0	0	0	0	0	0	0	0	0	1	0	0	4	0
whiffled	2	.0000	.0219	23.4	0	0	0	2	0	0	0	0	0	2	0	0	0	0	0	0	0	0	0	0	0	0	0	0	0
Whig	7	.5626	.8592	39.3	0	1	1	0	2	2	0	1	3	0	0	0	0	0	0	0	0	0	0	0	1	1	0	1	0
Whigs	8	.5386	.9406	39.7	0	0	2	1	1	2	0	2	3	1	0	0	0	1	0	0	0	0	0	0	1	0	0	2	0
while	2837	.9641	539.77	67.3	472	466	327	370	563	317	243	79	821	108	28	187	47	204	31	242	185	17	40	39	255	261	152	219	1
While	6	.0526	.1436	31.6	1	0	2	1	1	1	0	0	1	0	0	0	0	0	0	0	5	0	0	0	0	0	0	0	0
whilst	8	.5537	.9281	39.7	0	0	2	0	4	0	1	1	1	1	0	1	0	0	0	0	0	0	0	0	3	1	0	1	0
whim	3	.3769	.2484	34.0	0	0	0	0	3	0	0	0	0	0	0	0	0	1	0	0	0	0	0	0	0	0	1	1	0
whimper	12	.5543	1.4751	41.7	1	3	0	3	2	1	1	1	7	0	0	1	0	0	0	0	0	0	0	0	1	0	1	2	0
whimpered	13	.3174	.9891	40.0	1	4	2	1	3	0	2	0	4	0	3	4	0	0	0	0	0	0	0	0	0	2	0	0	0
whimpering	9	.4619	.9114	39.6	1	0	1	2	5	0	0	0	2	0	0	1	0	0	0	0	0	0	0	0	4	1	0	1	0
whimpers	2	.0000	.0215	23.3	0	0	0	0	0	0	2	0	0	0	0	2	0	0	0	0	0	0	0	0	0	0	0	0	0
whimsical	3	.2300	.1627	32.1	0	0	0	0	0	1	0	2	0	1	0	0	0	0	0	0	0	0	0	0	0	0	0	2	0
whin	2	.1948	.1250	31.0	0	1	0	0	0	1	0	0	1	0	0	0	0	0	0	0	0	0	0	0	0	1	0	0	0
whine	13	.6146	1.7079	42.3	2	0	1	1	7	1	1	0	6	1	0	0	0	0	0	0	0	0	0	0	2	1	1	2	0
whined	7	.4080	.6512	38.1	0	1	2	0	3	1	0	0	2	1	0	0	0	0	0	0	0	0	0	0	3	1	0	0	0
whining	8	.5432	.9442	39.8	1	1	3	1	2	0	0	0	3	0	0	0	0	0	0	0	0	0	0	0	2	1	1	1	0
whinnied	12	.4304	1.1922	40.8	4	0	2	1	4	1	0	0	5	0	0	2	0	0	0	0	0	0	0	0	4	1	0	0	0
whinnies	2	.1787	.1174	30.7	0	0	1	1	0	0	0	0	1	0	0	0	0	0	0	0	0	0	0	0	1	0	0	0	0
whinny	12	.5313	1.4134	41.5	1	4	2	1	3	1	0	0	6	0	0	1	0	0	0	0	1	0	0	0	3	1	0	0	0
whinnying	6	.3875	.5826	37.7	0	2	0	1	2	1	0	0	4	0	0	1	0	0	0	0	0	0	0	0	1	0	0	0	0
whip	104	.7116	15.208	51.8	17	25	6	17	20	12	7	0	32	4	2	9	0	0	1	0	0	0	4	0	21	24	0	7	0
Whip	3	.0000	.1370	31.4	3	0	0	0	0	0	0	0	3	0	0	0	0	0	0	0	0	0	0	0	0	0	0	0	0
whipped	59	.5814	7.2910	48.6	6	13	2	5	19	6	5	3	21	0	2	5	0	1	0	0	0	0	11	0	5	7	2	5	0
whipper-in	4	.0000	.0486	26.9	0	0	0	4	0	0	0	0	0	0	0	0	0	0	0	0	0	0	0	0	0	0	0	4	0
whippet	3	.0000	.1370	31.4	0	0	0	0	3	0	0	0	3	0	0	0	0	0	0	0	0	0	0	0	0	0	0	0	0
whippets	3	.0000	.1370	31.4	0	0	0	0	3	0	0	0	3	0	0	0	0	0	0	0	0	0	0	0	0	0	0	0	0
whipping	17	.6771	2.4010	43.8	0	5	1	4	4	1	2	0	7	0	0	0	0	0	0	1	0	0	1	1	2	2	2	1	0
Whipple	3	.0000	.1370	31.4	0	0	0	0	3	0	0	0	3	0	0	0	0	0	0	0	0	0	0	0	0	0	0	0	0
Whipple's	2	.0000	.0914	29.6	0	0	0	0	2	0	0	0	2	0	0	0	0	0	0	0	0	0	0	0	0	0	0	0	0
whippoorwill	9	.3683	.8693	39.4	1	0	0	1	7	0	0	0	7	0	0	1	0	0	0	0	0	0	0	0	0	1	0	0	0
Whippoorwill	2	.0000	.0290	24.6	2	0	0	0	0	0	0	0	0	0	0	0	0	0	0	0	0	0	0	0	0	2	0	0	0
whippoorwill's	2	.2387	.1089	30.4	0	0	0	0	0	1	0	0	0	0	0	0	0	0	0	0	1	0	0	0	1	0	0	0	0
whippoorwills	3	.3231	.2367	33.7	1	0	0	0	1	0	0	0	1	0	0	0	0	0	0	0	0	0	0	0	0	1	0	0	0
whips	17	.6668	2.3657	43.7	2	2	3	2	5	1	2	0	6	0	1	2	0	1	0	3	0	1	0	0	1	1	1	0	0
whipsee	4	.0000	.0323	25.1	3	0	1	0	0	0	0	0	0	0	0	0	0	0	0	0	4	0	0	0	0	0	0	0	0
whipstitch	2	.0000	.0050	17.0	0	0	0	0	2	0	0	0	0	0	0	0	0	0	0	0	0	0	0	2	0	0	0	0	0
whir	5	.4268	.4797	36.8	2	1	1	1	0	0	0	0	1	1	0	0	0	0	0	1	0	0	0	0	0	2	0	0	0
whirl	26	.7646	4.0555	46.1	2	8	8	1	3	2	1	1	9	1	0	2	0	1	2	2	0	0	0	0	1	3	1	4	0
whirled	63	.6346	8.5556	49.3	7	16	11	6	15	6	2	0	34	1	1	3	0	1	0	1	1	0	0	0	13	8	0	2	0
whirling	44	.8293	7.3554	48.7	3	10	10	7	5	3	4	2	15	0	0	1	1	3	0	6	2	1	0	1	5	5	2	2	0
whirlpool	5	.4730	.5355	37.3	1	0	1	2	1	0	0	0	2	1	0	0	0	0	0	1	0	0	0	0	0	0	0	1	0
whirlpools	4	.3104	.2995	34.8	0	0	1	2	1	0	0	0	1	0	0	0	0	0	0	0	0	0	0	0	0	0	1	2	0
whirls	10	.6022	1.2397	40.9	0	2	2	1	4	0	1	0	1	0	0	2	0	0	0	1	2	0	1	0	0	1	2	0	0
whirlwind	10	.7002	1.4318	41.6	1	0	2	2	2	1	2	0	2	2	0	1	0	0	1	1	1	0	0	0	1	1	0	0	0
whirlybird	4	.0000	.0789	29.0	0	0	0	0	0	0	0	4	0	0	0	0	0	0	0	4	0	0	0	0	0	0	0	0	0
whirr	5	.2446	.3872	35.9	4	0	0	1	0	0	0	0	4	0	0	0	0	0	0	0	0	0	0	0	1	0	0	0	0
whirred	3	.3764	.2475	33.9	0	0	1	0	1	0	1	0	0	1	0	1	0	1	0	0	0	0	0	0	0	0	0	0	0
whirring	10	.6555	1.3663	41.4	0	1	1	5	2	1	0	1	3	0	0	2	0	0	0	1	0	0	0	0	1	1	1	1	0
whisk	12	.5138	1.3326	41.2	1	1	1	5	1	0	0	3	3	0	0	1	0	0	0	0	0	0	0	0	2	2	0	4	0
whisked	8	.3451	.6694	38.3	2	1	3	0	0	1	1	0	3	0	0	2	0	0	0	0	0	0	0	0	3	0	0	0	0
whiskered	2	.0000	.0914	29.6	1	0	1	0	0	0	0	0	2	0	0	0	0	0	0	0	0	0	0	0	0	0	0	0	0
whiskers	62	.6885	8.9153	49.5	23	7	4	0	16	2	10	0	27	9	3	2	0	2	0	9	2	0	0	0	6	1	0	1	0
Whiskers	11	.0000	.5025	37.0	11	0	0	0	0	0	0	0	11	0	0	0	0	0	0	0	0	0	0	0	0	0	0	0	0
Whiskers'	3	.0000	.1370	31.4	3	0	0	0	0	0	0	0	3	0	0	0	0	0	0	0	0	0	0	0	0	0	0	0	0
whiskey	7	.5783	.8479	39.3	0	0	1	0	4	1	1	0	1	0	0	1	0	1	0	0	0	0	0	0	2	1	1	0	0
Whiskey	2	.0000	.0209	23.2	0	0	2	0	0	0	0	0	0	0	0	0	0	0	0	0	0	0	0	0	0	0	2	0	0
whisking	8	.2495	.5129	37.1	0	2	2	1	1	0	2	0	2	0	0	1	0	0	0	0	0	0	0	0	5	0	0	0	0
whisks	3	.2442	.1815	32.6	0	0	1	0	2	0	0	0	0	0	0	1	0	2	0	0	0	0	0	0	0	0	0	0	0
whisky	12	.4965	1.2414	40.9	0	0	0	0	5	1	6	0	0	2	0	6	0	1	0	0	0	0	0	0	1	0	1	1	0
whisky-jack	2	.0000	.0234	23.7	0	0	0	0	2	0	0	0	0	0	0	0	0	0	0	0	0	0	0	0	2	0	0	0	0
whisper	72	.7363	10.866	50.4	19	12	10	6	9	8	6	2	26	4	1	10	0	0	0	2	4	1	0	0	17	2	0	5	0
whispered	258	.6576	35.937	55.6	49	79	33	35	33	17	10	2	133	2	1	30	0	2	2	1	2	0	0	0	43	27	0	15	0

7L WHEN
7N whensoever
7A where'll
8A where've
9N whereat
6N whereon
9D whereto
7N whetstone
9M whetting
XH Whewell
7N which-a-way
4N which'd
8D whichway
5K whiffling
7B whiles
9P whiling
7D whims
7Q whimsey
9R whimsy
7R whines
6N whiniver
6R whinneying
7L whiny
6N whip-lashing
3P whip-poor-will
5A whip-tailed
5N whiplash
4P whiplashing
7L Whipped
9B Whippet
7A whippings
3P Whipsaw
7D Whipsnade
6A whipsnap
9F whipt
7R Whirlaway
7B whirligig
3P Whirligig
7R whirligigs
6A whirly
5B whirrr
3B whirs
3R whis-per
4A whish
8N whishing
4P whisht
4N whisker
4N whisker-like
9R whiskey-brown
5R whiskey-running
8A whisper-like
7B whisperer

whispering-wholesale ALPHABETICAL LIST 518

Word Type	F	D	U	SFI	3 Gr 3	4 Gr 4	5 Gr 5	6 Gr 6	7 Gr 7	8 Gr 8	9 Gr 9	X UnGr	A Read	B Eng & Gr	C Comp	D Lit	E Math	F Soc Stud	G Spell	H Sci	J Music	K Art	L Home Ec	M Shop	N Lib F	P Lib NF	Q Lib Ref	R Mag	S Rel
whispering	39	.6881	5.5280	47.4	10	5	7	2	9	2	3	1	11	2	1	10	0	0	0	0	1	0	0	0	7	3	1	3	0
whispers	19	.6067	2.4580	43.9	7	2	1	1	2	2	3	1	8	3	1	2	0	0	0	0	0	0	0	0	0	3	0	2	0
whist	5	.2542	.3208	35.1	0	0	0	1	3	0	0	1	1	0	0	0	0	0	0	0	0	0	0	0	3	1	0	0	0
whistle	158	.7642	24.737	53.9	36	24	27	28	21	14	8	0	71	11	7	5	0	5	4	10	12	0	0	0	15	14	1	3	0
Whistle	5	.0000	.2284	33.6	0	5	0	0	0	0	0	0	5	0	0	0	0	0	0	0	0	0	0	0	0	0	0	0	0
whistled	52	.6432	7.0733	48.5	10	11	6	10	8	3	4	0	23	1	1	6	0	1	0	0	1	0	0	0	10	9	0	0	0
Whistler	2	.0000	.0215	23.3	0	0	2	0	0	0	0	0	0	0	0	2	0	0	0	0	0	0	0	0	0	0	0	0	0
Whistlers	2	.0000	.0215	23.3	0	0	2	0	0	0	0	0	0	0	0	2	0	0	0	0	0	0	0	0	0	0	0	0	0
whistles	39	.6951	5.5898	47.5	15	7	8	3	1	4	1	0	12	11	1	1	0	2	0	2	5	0	0	0	1	1	1	2	0
whistling	53	.7721	8.3595	49.2	10	7	9	9	10	4	3	1	23	1	1	5	0	1	1	1	4	0	0	0	9	4	1	2	0
whit	2	.2433	.1158	30.6	0	0	1	0	0	0	0	1	0	0	0	0	0	0	0	0	0	0	0	0	0	1	0	1	0
Whitby	3	.2260	.1580	32.0	0	0	0	0	1	2	0	0	0	0	0	2	0	0	0	0	0	0	0	0	0	0	1	0	0
Whitcomb	17	.3375	1.5784	42.0	0	3	0	0	14	0	0	0	14	0	0	0	0	0	0	0	0	0	0	0	0	2	0	1	0
white	2085	.9186	380.21	65.8	422	359	206	257	443	182	167	49	618	57	17	231	46	170	19	202	61	49	45	12	168	195	65	130	0
White	325	.7980	52.351	57.2	40	73	29	12	80	55	22	14	80	12	0	18	6	31	3	4	4	1	2	0	61	43	10	50	0
White-Lipped	2	.0000	.0914	29.6	2	0	0	0	0	0	0	0	2	0	0	0	0	0	0	0	0	0	0	0	0	0	0	0	0
white-circled	2	.1787	.1174	30.7	1	1	0	0	0	0	0	0	1	0	0	0	0	0	0	0	0	0	0	0	1	0	0	0	0
white-clad	4	.2433	.2315	33.6	0	2	0	0	1	0	0	1	0	0	0	0	0	0	0	0	0	0	0	0	0	2	0	2	0
white-faced	3	.3450	.2505	34.0	0	2	0	0	1	0	0	0	1	0	0	0	0	0	0	0	0	0	0	0	1	1	0	0	0
white-footed	2	.0000	.0394	26.0	0	0	0	1	0	1	0	0	0	0	0	0	0	0	0	2	0	0	0	0	0	0	0	0	0
White-footed	5	.0000	.2284	33.6	5	0	0	0	0	0	0	0	5	0	0	0	0	0	0	0	0	0	0	0	0	0	0	0	0
white-haired	9	.4415	.8980	39.5	2	3	3	0	1	0	0	0	2	0	0	0	0	4	0	0	0	0	0	0	1	2	0	0	0
white-headed	2	.1698	.1133	30.5	1	0	0	0	1	0	0	0	1	0	0	0	0	0	0	0	0	0	0	0	0	0	1	0	0
white-hot	11	.3864	.9791	39.9	1	4	1	0	1	0	0	4	1	0	0	0	0	3	0	6	0	0	0	0	0	0	0	1	0
white-lipped	8	.0000	.3655	35.6	8	0	0	0	0	0	0	0	8	0	0	0	0	0	0	0	0	0	0	0	0	0	0	0	0
white-nose	2	.0000	.0914	29.6	2	0	0	0	0	0	0	0	2	0	0	0	0	0	0	0	0	0	0	0	0	0	0	0	0
white-robed	2	.2433	.1158	30.6	0	1	0	0	1	0	0	0	0	0	0	0	0	0	0	0	0	0	0	0	0	1	0	1	0
white-skinned	2	.2297	.1135	30.6	0	0	0	0	1	1	0	0	0	0	0	1	0	1	0	0	0	0	0	0	0	0	0	0	0
white-tailed	8	.1707	.3929	35.9	0	0	0	7	0	0	0	1	0	0	0	0	0	0	0	7	0	0	0	0	0	0	0	1	0
white-topped	2	.0000	.0290	24.6	1	1	0	0	0	0	0	0	0	0	0	0	0	0	0	0	0	0	0	0	0	2	0	0	0
white-upturned	2	.0000	.0215	23.3	0	0	0	0	0	0	2	0	0	0	0	2	0	0	0	0	0	0	0	0	0	0	0	0	0
white-washed	2	.1814	.1187	30.7	1	0	0	1	0	0	0	0	1	0	0	0	0	0	0	0	0	0	0	0	0	0	0	1	0
white-winged	2	.1948	.1250	31.0	0	2	0	0	0	0	0	0	1	0	0	0	0	0	0	0	0	0	0	0	0	1	0	0	0
White's	4	.1814	.2373	33.8	0	0	0	0	0	4	0	0	2	0	0	0	0	0	0	0	0	0	0	0	0	0	0	2	0
whitecaps	4	.4518	.3982	36.0	0	0	1	1	1	0	1	0	1	0	0	1	0	0	0	0	0	0	0	0	1	0	1	0	0
whitecock's	2	.0000	.0215	23.3	0	0	0	0	0	2	0	0	0	0	0	2	0	0	0	0	0	0	0	0	0	0	0	0	0
whited	3	.1187	.1291	31.1	0	0	0	0	2	0	1	0	1	0	0	2	0	0	0	0	0	0	0	0	0	0	0	0	0
Whitehill	5	.0000	.2284	33.6	5	0	0	0	0	0	0	0	5	0	0	0	0	0	0	0	0	0	0	0	0	0	0	0	0
whitely	3	.2223	.2106	33.2	1	0	0	1	1	0	0	0	2	1	0	0	0	0	0	0	0	0	0	0	0	0	0	0	0
whitened	3	.3394	.2451	33.9	0	1	0	1	1	0	0	0	1	0	0	1	0	0	0	0	0	0	0	0	1	0	0	0	0
whiteness	12	.6105	1.5651	41.9	4	3	1	2	0	1	1	0	5	1	0	1	0	0	0	1	0	0	0	0	2	2	0	0	0
whiter	6	.4858	.6625	38.2	3	1	0	0	0	0	1	1	3	0	0	1	0	0	0	0	0	0	0	0	0	1	0	1	0
whites	79	.7081	11.301	50.5	3	3	5	3	27	11	21	6	3	0	0	17	0	17	1	1	0	1	10	1	3	7	7	11	0
Whiteside	6	.0000	.0657	28.2	0	0	0	0	0	0	6	0	0	6	0	0	0	0	0	0	0	0	0	0	0	0	0	0	0
whiteskin	2	.2337	.1157	30.6	0	0	0	0	1	1	0	0	0	0	0	0	0	1	0	0	0	0	0	0	1	0	0	0	0
whitest	2	.0000	.0914	29.6	1	1	0	0	0	0	0	0	2	0	0	0	0	0	0	0	0	0	0	0	0	0	0	0	0
Whitetail	7	.0000	.3198	35.0	7	0	0	0	0	0	0	0	7	0	0	0	0	0	0	0	0	0	0	0	0	0	0	0	0
whitewash	13	.4513	1.4231	41.5	6	1	0	0	5	0	1	0	10	0	0	1	0	0	0	0	0	0	0	0	0	1	1	0	0
whitewashed	9	.3396	.7761	38.9	0	2	0	3	4	0	0	0	5	0	1	0	0	0	0	0	0	0	0	0	3	0	0	0	0
whitewashing	5	.2445	.3864	35.9	1	0	0	0	3	0	1	0	4	0	0	1	0	0	0	0	0	0	0	0	0	0	0	0	0
Whitey	27	.4776	2.6913	44.3	5	0	6	9	0	3	4	0	0	3	0	15	0	0	2	0	0	0	0	0	3	3	0	1	0
Whitfield	11	.0000	.5025	37.0	11	0	0	0	0	0	0	0	11	0	0	0	0	0	0	0	0	0	0	0	0	0	0	0	0
Whitfield's	2	.0000	.0914	29.6	2	0	0	0	0	0	0	0	2	0	0	0	0	0	0	0	0	0	0	0	0	0	0	0	0
whither	12	.5612	1.4596	41.6	1	1	1	5	2	1	1	0	5	0	0	2	0	0	1	0	0	0	0	0	2	2	0	0	0
Whitie	9	.0000	.4111	36.1	9	0	0	0	0	0	0	0	9	0	0	0	0	0	0	0	0	0	0	0	0	0	0	0	0
whiting	3	.2181	.1541	31.9	0	0	0	1	2	0	0	0	0	0	0	0	0	0	0	0	0	0	0	0	1	0	2	0	0
whitish	10	.5728	1.2106	40.8	0	1	3	0	3	1	0	2	2	0	0	0	0	0	0	2	0	0	1	0	1	2	0	2	0
Whitman	10	.3670	.8994	39.5	0	0	2	0	3	5	0	0	4	0	0	0	0	4	0	0	0	0	0	0	0	0	2	0	0
Whitman's	2	.2152	.1357	31.3	0	0	1	0	1	0	0	0	1	0	0	0	0	1	0	0	0	0	0	0	0	0	0	0	0
Whitmore	5	.0000	.0547	27.4	0	0	0	0	0	0	5	0	0	5	0	0	0	0	0	0	0	0	0	0	0	0	0	0	0
Whitney	40	.6304	5.2731	47.2	0	6	9	3	2	5	7	8	9	2	0	9	0	13	0	1	0	1	0	0	0	1	4	0	0
Whitney's	6	.2930	.4402	36.4	0	0	3	1	1	1	0	0	1	0	0	0	0	4	0	0	0	0	0	0	0	0	1	0	0
Whittaker	2	.0000	.0914	29.6	2	0	0	0	0	0	0	0	2	0	0	0	0	0	0	0	0	0	0	0	0	0	0	0	0
Whittier	7	.3854	.6844	38.4	0	0	2	0	1	4	0	0	5	0	0	0	0	0	0	0	0	0	0	0	0	0	1	1	0
Whittier's	2	.0000	.0914	29.6	0	0	1	0	0	1	0	0	2	0	0	0	0	0	0	0	0	0	0	0	0	0	0	0	0
Whittington's	2	.0000	.0914	29.6	0	2	0	0	0	0	0	0	2	0	0	0	0	0	0	0	0	0	0	0	0	0	0	0	0
whittle	5	.5402	.5818	37.6	0	1	0	2	2	0	0	0	1	0	0	0	0	1	0	1	0	0	0	0	1	1	0	0	0
whittled	5	.4033	.4470	36.5	1	1	1	1	0	0	0	1	1	0	1	0	0	0	0	0	0	0	0	0	0	1	1	1	0
whittling	8	.5058	.8614	39.4	0	3	0	2	2	1	0	0	1	0	0	1	0	0	0	1	0	0	0	1	1	3	0	0	0
whiz	20	.5915	2.5596	44.1	6	3	2	4	5	0	0	0	9	0	0	3	1	4	0	0	0	0	0	0	0	1	0	2	0
whiz-z-z	2	.0000	.0162	22.1	2	0	0	0	0	0	0	0	0	0	0	0	0	0	0	0	2	0	0	0	0	0	0	0	0
whizz	3	.2120	.1548	31.9	0	0	0	1	1	0	0	1	0	0	0	0	0	0	0	0	0	0	0	0	2	1	0	0	0
whizzed	11	.5432	1.3297	41.2	2	1	3	2	2	1	0	0	6	0	0	1	0	1	0	0	0	0	0	0	1	0	0	2	0
whizzing	8	.5415	.9274	39.7	3	0	3	1	0	0	1	0	2	1	1	0	0	1	0	1	0	0	0	0	1	0	1	0	0
who	7576	.9116	1371.9	71.4	1099	1049	926	943	1526	1066	738	229	2080	414	80	600	161	1060	126	300	288	67	115	18	505	692	370	669	31
Who	32	.1219	1.0872	40.4	7	10	2	3	4	2	2	2	2	8	0	0	0	1	3	0	2	0	0	0	3	2	0	5	6
who-o	3	.0000	.1370	31.4	0	3	0	0	0	0	0	0	3	0	0	0	0	0	0	0	0	0	0	0	0	0	0	0	0
who'd	12	.2661	.7754	38.9	1	1	3	0	4	0	2	1	2	0	0	7	0	0	0	0	0	0	0	0	3	0	0	0	0
who'll	2	.0000	.0914	29.6	0	1	1	0	0	0	0	0	2	0	0	0	0	0	0	0	0	0	0	0	0	0	0	0	0
who's	81	.7060	11.806	50.7	11	14	13	12	19	3	8	1	29	7	0	4	0	0	5	0	2	0	0	0	9	11	0	14	0
Who's	5	.2407	.2808	34.5	0	0	0	0	1	0	3	1	0	2	0	0	0	0	0	0	0	0	0	0	0	0	0	3	0
whoa	16	.5608	1.9733	43.0	6	4	1	0	3	2	0	0	8	0	0	2	0	2	0	0	0	0	0	0	2	2	0	0	0
whoever	44	.6707	6.1534	47.9	7	7	3	6	8	5	7	1	16	4	0	7	0	1	0	0	0	0	0	0	5	7	1	3	0
whole	1886	.9080	340.01	65.3	297	253	283	259	426	161	170	37	384	46	22	95	571	120	23	90	79	15	21	3	120	138	71	85	3
Whole	3	.3382	.2140	33.3	0	0	1	0	1	1	0	0	0	0	0	1	0	0	0	0	1	0	1	0	0	0	0	0	0
whole-grain	6	.0945	.1587	32.0	0	0	1	0	1	4	0	0	0	0	0	0	0	0	0	2	0	0	4	0	0	0	0	0	0
whole-heartedly	2	.2443	.1130	30.5	0	0	0	1	1	0	0	0	0	0	0	1	0	0	0	0	0	0	0	0	1	0	0	0	0
whole-number	18	.0000	.2694	34.3	0	1	2	3	11	1	0	0	0	0	0	0	18	0	0	0	0	0	0	0	0	0	0	0	0
whole-tone	10	.0786	.2348	33.7	0	0	5	1	0	1	3	0	0	0	0	0	0	0	0	0	9	0	0	0	0	1	0	0	0
whole-wheat	4	.1017	.0991	30.0	1	0	0	0	0	0	3	0	0	0	0	0	0	0	0	0	0	0	3	0	1	0	0	0	0
wholeheartedly	3	.2699	.1789	32.5	0	1	0	1	0	0	1	0	0	0	1	0	0	0	0	0	0	0	0	0	0	1	1	0	0
wholesale	19	.5658	2.2561	43.5	4	4	2	2	4	1	2	0	1	0	0	0	1	10	1	0	0	0	0	0	1	0	3	2	0

XP whisperings
7C whisps
9D whispy
3A whisssh
5A whistle-pig
5N Whistler's
3A WHITE
8R WhiteLake
8A white-aproned
6A white-ash
8D white-blazed
3P white-cap
XR white-capped
6R white-caps
4N white-cat
9D white-clothed
7B white-coated
5P white-collar
3A white-covered
6H white-eyed
8A white-furred
5N white-gloved
6H white-light
4N white-mice
7D white-oak
5F white-owned
3A white-painted
4A white-paneled
6A white-pillared
3A white-potted
6P white-powdered
6N white-ringed
7Q white-rumped
7L white-shirt-tie-jacket
8D white-streaked
7Q white-throated
6A white-waterin'
9L white-wine
3J white-wing
9B Whitebread
4R whitecapped
5P Whitechapel
3F Whitecloud
8D whitecock
5F whiteface
9F whitefish
9R Whitehall
4P Whitehaven
8L whiteheads
8N whiten
3P whitens
8D Whiterside
7P Whites
7A whitewashin'
4F Whitham
7R whitish-blond
5A whitish-yellow
4P Whitsuntide
7R Whitten
6R whitter
5C whittles
6N whittlings
XR WHO
3A who-oo-oo
4A who-who
9D who'd've
9D who'da
8R who've
6B whodunit
4A Whodunit
4A WHOEEE
4A whole-hog
6J whole-tones
9D wholehearted

Word Type	F	D	U	SFI	3 Gr 3	4 Gr 4	5 Gr 5	6 Gr 6	7 Gr 7	8 Gr 8	9 Gr 9	X UnGr	A Read	B Eng & Gr	C Comp	D Lit	E Math	F Soc Stud	G Spell	H Sci	J Music	K Art	L Home Ec	M Shop	N Lib F	P Lib NF	Q Lib Ref	R Mag	S Rel
Wholesale	2	.2297	.1135	30.6	0	1	0	0	1	0	0	0	0	0	0	1	0	1	0	0	0	0	0	0	0	0	0	0	0
wholesalers	3	.2159	.1532	31.9	0	0	1	0	2	0	0	0	0	0	0	0	0	0	0	0	0	0	0	0	0	0	2	1	0
wholesome	15	.5789	1.8133	42.6	0	0	0	1	4	3	6	1	3	0	1	1	0	0	1	2	0	0	3	0	0	0	1	3	0
wholly	39	.7296	5.8196	47.6	0	1	4	1	18	8	6	1	11	0	1	5	0	2	2	4	1	0	0	0	1	0	9	3	0
whom	363	.6886	51.108	57.1	21	36	37	57	101	48	54	9	59	52	12	44	0	35	3	11	13	1	2	0	31	42	24	29	5
whomever	2	.2152	.1357	31.3	0	0	0	1	0	0	1	0	1	0	0	0	0	1	0	0	0	0	0	0	0	0	0	0	0
whoo-hoo-hoo	2	.0000	.0914	29.6	2	0	0	0	0	0	0	0	2	0	0	0	0	0	0	0	0	0	0	0	0	0	0	0	0
whoo-oo-oo	4	.3604	.3539	35.5	3	0	0	1	0	0	0	0	2	1	0	0	0	0	0	0	1	0	0	0	0	0	0	0	0
Whoof	4	.0000	.1827	32.6	0	0	0	0	0	4	0	0	4	0	0	0	0	0	0	0	0	0	0	0	0	0	0	0	0
whooosh	2	.0665	.0708	28.5	0	1	0	0	1	0	0	0	1	0	1	0	0	0	0	0	0	0	0	0	0	0	0	0	0
whoop	19	.4981	2.0449	43.1	3	4	0	1	6	5	0	0	5	0	3	2	0	0	0	0	2	0	0	0	1	5	0	1	0
whoopala	2	.0000	.0290	24.6	2	0	0	0	0	0	0	0	0	0	0	0	0	0	0	0	0	0	0	0	0	2	0	0	0
whooped	8	.2341	.6211	37.9	1	0	2	4	1	0	0	0	7	0	0	1	0	0	0	0	0	0	0	0	0	0	0	0	0
whoopee	4	.1854	.1872	32.7	1	1	1	0	1	0	0	0	0	0	0	0	0	0	0	0	0	0	0	0	0	1	0	3	0
whooping	22	.6939	3.1121	44.9	5	5	4	4	3	1	0	0	2	1	0	1	0	0	0	5	1	0	0	0	1	4	5	2	0
whoops	10	.4790	1.0942	40.4	0	1	2	2	1	3	1	0	5	0	0	0	0	0	0	0	0	0	0	0	1	2	0	2	0
whoosh	6	.4826	.6623	38.2	4	1	1	0	0	0	0	0	3	0	0	0	0	1	0	0	0	0	0	0	1	0	0	1	0
whop	6	.2935	.4466	36.5	1	0	0	0	5	0	0	0	2	0	0	0	0	0	0	0	0	0	0	0	0	1	0	3	0
whopping	3	.3399	.2456	33.9	1	0	0	0	0	1	0	1	1	0	0	1	0	0	0	0	0	0	0	0	0	0	0	1	0
whos	2	.0000	.0219	23.4	0	0	0	0	0	1	1	0	0	2	0	0	0	0	0	0	0	0	0	0	0	0	0	0	0
whose	799	.9198	145.56	61.6	50	68	83	89	206	115	150	38	118	30	9	48	152	47	44	50	27	6	2	2	40	78	76	70	0
whup	2	.0000	.0234	23.7	0	0	2	0	0	0	0	0	0	0	0	0	0	0	0	0	0	0	0	0	2	0	0	0	0
why	4147	.9264	761.70	68.8	847	775	452	505	709	515	291	53	1032	356	36	371	373	457	62	606	105	29	39	23	190	259	42	154	13
Why	8	.2186	.4913	36.9	0	3	0	4	1	0	0	0	3	0	0	0	0	1	0	0	4	0	0	0	0	0	0	0	0
WHY	3	.2132	.1795	32.5	1	0	0	0	1	0	1	0	1	0	0	0	0	1	0	0	0	0	1	0	0	0	0	0	0
why's	2	.1648	.0800	29.0	0	1	0	0	0	0	1	0	0	0	0	0	1	0	0	0	0	0	1	0	0	0	0	0	0
whys	3	.3179	.2054	33.1	0	0	0	0	1	2	0	0	0	1	0	0	0	0	0	0	0	0	1	0	0	0	0	1	0
Wi-jun-jon	3	.0000	.1370	31.4	3	0	0	0	0	0	0	0	3	0	0	0	0	0	0	0	0	0	0	0	0	0	0	0	0
wi'	10	.2320	.5334	37.3	0	0	2	1	0	7	0	0	0	7	0	0	0	0	0	0	3	0	0	0	0	0	0	0	0
Wibberley	2	.0000	.0243	23.9	0	0	0	0	0	0	0	2	0	0	0	0	0	0	0	0	0	0	0	0	0	0	0	2	0
wich	2	.2442	.1134	30.5	0	0	0	1	1	0	0	0	0	1	0	0	0	0	0	0	0	0	0	0	0	0	0	1	0
Wichita	8	.1918	.3863	35.9	0	5	1	0	0	1	0	1	0	6	0	0	0	1	0	1	0	0	0	0	0	0	0	0	0
wick	10	.4447	1.0320	40.1	5	3	1	0	0	0	1	0	4	0	0	0	0	2	0	1	0	0	0	0	0	3	0	0	0
wicked	70	.6818	10.052	50.0	9	19	13	11	8	6	1	3	38	2	0	5	0	1	1	0	2	0	0	0	11	4	0	6	0
wickedly	3	.2223	.2106	33.2	0	0	0	0	1	2	0	0	2	1	0	0	0	0	0	0	0	0	0	0	0	0	0	0	0
wickedness	10	.5493	1.2076	40.8	0	0	3	3	2	0	2	0	5	0	0	2	0	0	0	0	0	0	0	0	1	0	1	1	0
wicker	5	.1848	.2301	33.6	0	0	1	1	0	0	1	2	0	1	0	0	0	0	0	0	0	0	0	0	0	0	0	4	0
wicket	4	.4421	.3922	35.9	1	0	1	0	1	1	0	0	1	0	0	0	0	0	1	0	0	0	0	0	1	1	0	0	0
wicks	3	.3553	.2608	34.2	2	1	0	0	0	0	0	0	1	0	0	0	0	1	0	0	0	0	0	0	0	1	0	0	0
wid	4	.4411	.3879	35.9	0	0	1	1	2	0	0	0	1	0	0	0	0	0	1	0	1	0	0	0	1	0	0	0	0
wide	863	.9428	160.95	62.1	174	130	98	112	160	95	74	20	215	17	10	41	74	128	7	70	29	13	23	23	36	74	52	51	0
Wide	7	.2326	.5117	37.1	0	3	0	1	2	1	0	0	5	0	0	2	0	0	0	0	0	0	0	0	0	0	0	0	0
wide-awake	7	.4817	.7812	38.9	2	2	1	1	0	1	0	0	4	0	0	0	0	0	0	1	0	0	0	0	1	1	0	0	0
wide-brimmed	3	.1187	.1291	31.1	1	1	0	0	1	0	0	0	1	0	0	2	0	0	0	0	0	0	0	0	0	0	0	0	0
wide-eyed	8	.4671	.8577	39.3	1	1	2	2	1	1	0	0	4	0	0	1	0	0	0	0	0	0	0	0	2	1	0	0	0
wide-hand	3	.0000	.0449	26.5	3	0	0	0	0	0	0	0	0	0	0	0	3	0	0	0	0	0	0	0	0	0	0	0	0
wide-mouthed	4	.2576	.2681	34.3	1	0	0	1	2	0	0	0	1	0	0	0	0	0	0	2	0	0	1	0	0	0	0	0	0
wide-open	13	.5336	1.4511	41.6	3	3	3	0	2	2	0	0	1	0	0	2	0	0	0	0	0	1	0	0	3	5	0	1	0
wide-spreading	4	.1787	.2347	33.7	0	1	0	1	1	1	0	0	2	0	0	0	0	0	0	0	0	0	0	0	2	0	0	0	0
widely	153	.8583	26.144	54.2	6	9	17	11	37	31	31	11	12	12	1	3	0	24	6	22	13	1	5	2	0	5	30	17	0
widemouthed	3	.2435	.1694	32.3	0	1	0	0	1	0	0	1	0	0	1	0	0	0	0	1	0	0	0	0	0	0	0	1	0
widen	14	.6747	1.9421	42.9	0	1	0	1	7	4	1	0	3	2	0	2	0	2	0	0	0	0	1	1	0	1	0	2	0
widened	23	.7053	3.3434	45.2	3	4	1	6	6	1	2	0	7	0	0	2	0	2	1	1	0	0	0	0	5	1	1	3	0
widening	12	.5754	1.4713	41.7	0	1	1	2	2	4	2	0	4	1	0	2	0	0	0	1	0	1	0	0	0	0	2	1	0
widens	4	.2437	.2257	33.5	0	0	0	1	0	1	1	1	0	0	0	0	0	0	0	0	0	0	0	0	0	0	2	2	0
wider	83	.7831	13.102	51.2	15	10	7	8	23	10	8	2	16	2	2	1	2	8	0	13	12	3	1	8	2	6	5	2	0
widespread	44	.7026	6.2314	47.9	5	2	2	3	18	4	6	4	0	4	0	1	0	3	1	4	6	1	0	0	0	3	14	7	0
widest	28	.7274	4.1521	46.2	3	3	4	4	9	4	1	0	6	0	0	1	2	6	0	1	0	1	2	1	2	0	6	0	0
widow	54	.7519	8.2545	49.2	5	3	11	11	13	3	7	1	12	0	2	2	1	1	0	9	1	0	0	0	10	5	5	6	0
Widow	9	.4282	.8527	39.3	0	2	0	2	5	0	0	0	2	0	0	3	0	0	0	0	1	0	0	0	3	0	0	0	0
WIDOW	10	.0000	.1073	30.3	0	0	0	0	10	0	0	0	0	0	0	10	0	0	0	0	0	0	0	0	0	0	0	0	0
Widow-Maker	5	.2025	.3254	35.1	0	0	3	0	0	2	0	0	3	0	0	2	0	0	0	0	0	0	0	0	0	0	0	0	0
widow's	6	.3053	.4554	36.6	0	2	0	0	1	3	0	0	2	0	0	1	0	0	0	0	0	0	0	0	3	0	0	0	0
widowed	4	.3813	.3772	35.8	0	0	0	0	3	1	0	0	2	0	0	0	0	1	0	0	0	0	0	0	0	1	0	0	0
widower	2	.2152	.1357	31.3	0	0	0	0	0	2	0	0	1	0	0	0	0	1	0	0	0	0	0	0	0	0	0	0	0
widows	7	.2942	.4628	36.7	0	0	1	3	0	0	3	0	0	1	0	1	0	0	0	0	0	0	0	0	0	0	0	5	0
width	149	.6164	18.731	52.7	9	7	16	15	29	23	41	9	4	2	3	1	59	4	0	11	0	1	17	25	3	3	9	7	0
widths	20	.3028	1.3187	41.2	0	1	2	1	8	2	5	1	0	0	0	0	8	0	0	0	0	0	1	8	0	2	0	1	0
wield	3	.3845	.2448	33.9	0	0	2	0	0	0	1	0	0	1	0	0	0	0	0	0	1	0	0	0	0	0	1	0	0
wielded	4	.4518	.3982	36.0	1	0	0	0	3	0	0	0	1	0	0	1	0	0	0	0	0	0	0	0	1	0	1	0	0
Wielemaker	13	.0000	.5939	37.7	0	0	0	13	0	0	0	0	13	0	0	0	0	0	0	0	0	0	0	0	0	0	0	0	0
wiener	5	.3687	.4014	36.0	0	2	0	0	2	0	0	1	0	0	0	0	0	0	0	0	0	0	0	0	0	2	2	1	0
Wiener	6	.0000	.0898	29.5	0	0	0	0	0	0	6	0	0	0	0	0	6	0	0	0	0	0	0	0	0	0	0	0	0
wieners	4	.1873	.1827	32.6	1	0	0	0	3	0	0	0	0	0	0	0	0	0	0	0	0	0	0	0	0	0	3	1	0
wife	636	.7974	103.03	60.1	123	118	66	90	121	50	60	8	262	23	2	80	9	45	7	1	22	3	1	0	35	81	15	47	3
Wife	21	.5304	2.5261	44.0	8	9	1	1	2	0	0	0	14	2	0	1	0	0	0	0	0	0	0	0	3	0	1	0	0
wife's	27	.5748	3.3087	45.2	5	3	4	3	9	0	3	0	8	0	0	7	0	2	0	0	0	0	0	0	3	4	0	3	0
wig	11	.4726	1.1234	40.5	4	1	0	3	0	0	1	2	2	0	0	1	0	0	0	0	1	0	0	0	5	0	0	2	0
Wigg	8	.0000	.0938	29.7	0	0	8	0	0	0	0	0	0	0	0	0	0	0	0	0	0	0	0	0	8	0	0	0	0
wiggle	18	.6701	2.5049	44.0	10	3	0	3	0	2	0	0	5	2	0	1	0	0	0	4	2	0	0	0	2	2	0	0	0
wiggled	22	.5849	2.8352	44.5	14	4	1	0	2	0	1	0	14	1	0	1	0	0	0	0	0	0	0	0	1	2	0	3	0
wigglers	2	.0000	.0914	29.6	0	0	2	0	0	0	0	0	2	0	0	0	0	0	0	0	0	0	0	0	0	0	0	0	0
wiggles	8	.3245	.6106	37.9	3	1	0	0	3	1	0	0	2	0	0	0	0	0	0	0	4	0	0	0	0	1	1	0	0
Wiggles	3	.0000	.0328	25.2	3	0	0	0	0	0	0	0	0	3	0	0	0	0	0	0	0	0	0	0	0	0	0	0	0
wiggling	9	.3442	.7775	38.9	4	1	1	2	1	0	0	0	4	0	0	0	0	0	0	2	0	0	0	0	3	0	0	1	0
wiggly	3	.2279	.2143	33.3	1	0	0	1	1	0	0	0	2	0	0	0	0	0	0	0	0	0	0	0	0	0	0	0	0
Wiggs	2	.0000	.0219	23.4	0	0	0	0	0	2	0	0	0	2	0	0	0	0	0	0	0	0	0	0	0	0	0	0	0
Wigner	2	.0000	.0209	23.2	0	0	0	0	0	0	2	0	0	0	0	0	0	0	0	0	0	0	0	0	0	0	2	0	0
wigs	5	.3902	.4356	36.4	0	1	2	0	0	2	0	0	1	0	0	0	0	0	0	0	2	0	0	0	1	0	0	1	0
wigwam	12	.2546	.8304	39.2	0	4	2	0	1	1	4	0	5	6	0	0	0	0	0	0	0	0	0	0	0	1	0	0	0
wigwams	10	.6160	1.3101	41.2	4	3	0	1	2	0	0	0	4	0	0	0	0	0	1	1	1	0	0	0	1	2	0	0	0
Wiki	9	.0000	.4111	36.1	9	0	0	0	0	0	0	0	9	0	0	0	0	0	0	0	0	0	0	0	0	0	0	0	0
Wilbur	80	.4535	8.3755	49.2	4	46	3	14	9	2	2	0	39	3	0	3	0	1	0	2	0	0	0	0	30	0	1	1	0
Wilbur's	9	.0489	.2191	33.4	0	8	1	0	0	0	0	0	1	0	0	0	0	0	0	0	0	0	0	0	8	0	0	0	0

8B wholl
7Q wholsome
6J Whom
7L WHOM
8R whomp
7D whoo-haw
3A whoo-hoo
3D whoo-ooo-wooo
4A whooo
3A whooo's
4A whoooo
6H whooper
6H whoopers
3A WHOOSH
9N whopper
7A whoppers
9D whore
9R whores
8Q whorls
7N whur's
3A Whush-h-h
3N why'd
3R wibblety-wobblety
9R WichitaFalls
8A Wickaeldroth
7D wicked-looking
6A wickedest-looking
5N wickie
3A wickiup
XR widdershins
8M wide-angle
7F wide-horned
8J wide-range
7H wide-ranging
7E wide-screen
8J wide-spread
7J widely-spread
5H widemouth
9P Wideners
3F widespreading
8A widgeon
7P widowhood
7L Width
7R wieldable
7H wielding
9D wields
6A Wielemaker's
6A Wielemakers
6J wielewaal
6J Wien
9E Wiener's
8G wienerwurst
9Q Wienne
8Q Wiesbaden
8A Wiese
4A wiggle-wagging
XR wiglet
9B wigwag
9N Wigwam
8R Wilber
XH Wilberforce
7A Wilbrook

Word Type	F	D	U	SFI	3 Gr 3	4 Gr 4	5 Gr 5	6 Gr 6	7 Gr 7	8 Gr 8	9 Gr 9	X UnGr	A Read	B Eng & Gr	C Comp	D Lit	E Math	F Soc Stud	G Spell	H Sci	J Music	K Art	L Home Ec	M Shop	N Lib F	P Lib NF	Q Lib Ref	R Mag	S Rel
Wilco	4	.0000	.1827	32.6	0	0	0	2	2	0	0	0	4	0	0	0	0	0	0	0	0	0	0	0	0	0	0	0	0
Wilcox	3	.1277	.1363	31.3	0	1	0	0	0	0	2	0	1	0	0	0	0	0	0	0	0	0	0	0	0	0	0	2	0
wild	929	.9020	166.85	62.2	170	151	130	166	189	57	43	23	314	29	9	84	2	94	15	49	16	10	3	0	106	88	61	47	2
Wild	44	.4194	4.0636	46.1	0	25	2	2	12	1	0	2	6	1	0	1	0	2	0	2	0	0	0	0	27	2	2	1	0
wild-eyed	2	.1733	.1149	30.6	0	0	0	1	1	0	0	0	1	1	0	0	0	0	0	0	0	0	0	0	0	0	0	0	0
wild-looking	2	.0000	.0914	29.6	0	0	0	1	0	1	0	0	2	0	0	0	0	0	0	0	0	0	0	0	0	0	0	0	0
wildcat	13	.5252	1.5644	41.9	2	6	1	3	1	0	0	0	9	0	0	0	0	1	0	0	0	0	0	0	1	1	0	1	0
wildcats	11	.4441	1.1682	40.7	1	5	2	1	1	1	0	0	7	0	0	0	0	1	0	0	0	0	0	0	0	1	2	0	0
wildebeest	6	.3871	.5823	37.7	0	1	2	2	1	0	0	0	4	0	0	0	0	0	0	0	0	0	0	0	0	0	1	1	0
wildebeests	5	.0000	.0523	27.2	1	0	0	0	4	0	0	0	0	0	0	0	0	0	0	0	0	0	0	0	0	0	5	0	0
wilder	11	.5460	1.2647	41.0	1	2	1	2	3	2	0	0	2	0	0	1	0	1	1	0	4	0	0	0	1	0	0	1	0
Wilder	14	.3169	1.1662	40.7	4	0	0	0	9	1	0	0	8	5	0	1	0	0	0	0	0	0	0	0	0	0	0	0	0
Wilder's	2	.0000	.0219	23.4	2	0	0	0	0	0	0	0	0	2	0	0	0	0	0	0	0	0	0	0	0	0	0	0	0
wilderness	132	.7633	20.453	53.1	7	16	38	18	32	12	0	9	26	0	0	6	0	41	1	2	6	1	0	0	7	15	10	17	0
Wilderness	12	.7028	1.7217	42.4	0	2	3	1	0	3	2	1	2	0	0	1	0	1	0	0	1	0	0	0	2	2	1	2	0
wildest	19	.6962	2.7092	44.3	1	3	0	1	7	3	3	1	4	0	0	5	0	0	1	1	1	0	0	0	2	3	1	1	0
wildfire	3	.1060	.1461	31.6	0	0	1	0	1	0	1	0	2	0	1	0	0	0	0	0	0	0	0	0	0	0	0	0	0
wildflowers	4	.4514	.4045	36.1	1	1	0	0	1	1	0	0	1	0	0	1	0	0	0	1	0	0	0	0	0	1	0	0	0
wildfowl	2	.1717	.1142	30.6	0	0	0	0	0	1	1	0	1	0	0	1	0	0	0	0	0	0	0	0	0	0	0	0	0
Wildhorse	3	.0000	.1370	31.4	3	0	0	0	0	0	0	0	3	0	0	0	0	0	0	0	0	0	0	0	0	0	0	0	0
wildlife	52	.5638	6.1466	47.9	2	0	12	8	18	2	2	8	5	1	0	2	0	6	0	9	0	0	0	0	0	1	16	12	0
Wildlife	13	.3319	.9580	39.8	0	1	4	0	5	0	0	3	0	0	0	0	0	0	0	2	0	0	0	0	0	0	5	6	0
wildly	56	.5837	7.0271	48.5	14	14	7	9	9	0	3	0	23	2	0	3	0	0	0	0	0	0	0	0	16	6	1	5	0
wildness	10	.2755	.6296	38.0	1	0	3	1	5	0	0	0	0	0	0	1	0	0	0	0	0	0	0	0	7	2	0	0	0
wilds	13	.5830	1.6290	42.1	0	2	3	1	2	1	2	2	5	0	0	1	0	1	0	0	1	0	0	0	0	4	1	0	0
wiles	4	.0000	.0429	26.3	0	0	0	0	0	0	4	0	0	0	0	4	0	0	0	0	0	0	0	0	0	0	0	0	0
Wiley	3	.2357	.2199	33.4	0	1	0	2	0	0	0	0	2	0	0	0	0	0	0	0	0	0	0	0	0	1	0	0	0
Wilfred	11	.2327	.7122	38.5	6	0	0	1	3	0	1	0	4	0	0	0	0	1	0	0	0	0	0	0	6	0	0	0	0
wilful	2	.0000	.0215	23.3	0	1	0	0	0	0	1	0	0	0	0	2	0	0	0	0	0	0	0	0	0	0	0	0	0
Wilhelm	11	.4417	1.0673	40.3	0	0	0	1	3	1	3	3	1	0	0	0	1	0	0	6	0	1	0	0	0	0	2	0	0
Wilhelmina	2	.0000	.0290	24.6	0	0	0	0	2	0	0	0	0	0	0	0	0	0	0	0	0	0	0	0	0	2	0	0	0
Wilkes	11	.4344	1.0483	40.2	6	0	2	1	0	1	1	0	1	0	0	1	0	0	0	2	0	0	0	0	0	6	1	0	0
Wilkins	2	.2130	.1056	30.2	0	0	0	0	1	0	1	0	0	0	0	0	0	0	1	1	0	0	0	0	0	0	0	0	0
Wilkinson	2	.0000	.0243	23.9	0	0	0	0	0	0	2	0	0	0	0	0	0	0	0	0	0	0	0	0	0	0	0	2	0
will	12646	.9789	2438.1	73.9	2758	1956	1365	1481	2224	1351	1261	250	3077	939	143	613	955	914	536	1551	589	163	374	282	655	774	309	748	24
Will	38	.6057	4.8457	46.9	3	20	2	2	5	0	4	2	10	0	1	6	3	0	0	0	0	0	0	0	0	14	1	3	0
Willa	4	.2381	.2674	34.3	1	1	0	0	1	1	0	0	2	0	1	0	0	0	0	0	0	0	0	0	1	0	0	0	0
Willamette	2	.2351	.1166	30.7	0	0	1	1	0	0	0	0	0	0	0	0	0	1	0	0	0	0	0	0	0	0	0	1	0
Willard	4	.4777	.4005	36.0	0	0	0	1	1	0	2	0	0	0	0	0	1	0	0	0	1	0	0	0	0	1	1	0	0
willed	4	.2969	.2888	34.6	0	0	0	0	3	0	1	0	1	0	0	2	0	0	0	0	0	0	0	0	1	0	0	0	0
willful	2	.2401	.1133	30.5	0	0	1	0	1	0	0	0	0	0	0	0	0	0	0	0	0	0	0	0	0	1	1	0	0
William	469	.7770	73.666	58.7	49	187	57	24	63	41	43	5	88	16	3	13	1	41	10	19	24	2	0	1	8	178	39	26	0
William's	10	.4661	1.0726	40.3	2	5	1	1	1	0	0	0	5	1	0	1	0	0	0	0	0	0	0	0	0	3	0	0	0
Williams	77	.6871	10.856	50.4	7	11	12	18	15	10	1	3	13	5	0	0	0	19	0	1	11	0	0	0	8	4	3	13	0
Williams'	7	.4003	.5970	37.8	1	1	0	1	2	2	0	0	0	0	0	2	0	1	0	0	3	0	0	0	0	0	0	1	0
Williamsburg	26	.6163	3.2787	45.2	2	6	8	1	3	6	0	0	0	0	0	3	0	4	0	0	4	0	0	0	1	9	4	1	0
Williamson	2	.0000	.0914	29.6	0	1	0	1	0	0	0	0	2	0	0	0	0	0	0	0	0	0	0	0	0	0	0	0	0
Williamsport	3	.0000	.1370	31.4	0	1	2	0	0	0	0	0	3	0	0	0	0	0	0	0	0	0	0	0	0	0	0	0	0
Willie	179	.5084	19.367	52.9	27	112	1	3	21	13	2	0	15	0	0	10	2	20	0	0	3	0	0	0	6	95	0	28	0
Willie's	12	.5100	1.3053	41.2	4	7	0	0	0	1	0	0	1	0	0	0	0	3	0	0	0	0	0	0	2	4	0	2	0
willies	2	.1814	.1187	30.7	1	0	0	0	1	0	0	0	1	0	0	0	0	0	0	0	0	0	0	0	0	0	0	1	0
willing	189	.8112	30.962	54.9	15	26	20	34	40	28	23	3	57	4	0	8	4	32	1	7	6	0	4	1	22	15	8	19	1
willingly	9	.4622	.9679	39.9	2	1	0	2	3	1	0	0	5	0	0	0	0	0	0	1	1	0	0	0	2	0	0	0	0
willingness	16	.6358	2.1192	43.3	2	1	2	1	3	3	4	0	3	0	0	1	0	4	0	1	0	0	0	0	0	2	3	2	0
Willoughby	9	.0000	.1303	31.1	0	9	0	0	0	0	0	0	0	0	0	0	0	0	0	0	0	0	0	0	0	9	0	0	0
willow	46	.7634	7.1694	48.6	7	11	4	10	10	1	3	0	17	0	2	5	0	0	1	6	2	0	0	0	3	3	3	4	0
Willow	13	.3962	1.2163	40.9	6	5	1	0	1	0	0	0	5	1	0	0	0	0	0	0	0	0	0	0	1	6	0	0	0
willow-weed	3	.0000	.0328	25.2	3	0	0	0	0	0	0	0	0	3	0	0	0	0	0	0	0	0	0	0	0	0	0	0	0
Willowby	4	.0000	.0429	26.3	0	0	0	0	4	0	0	0	0	0	0	4	0	0	0	0	0	0	0	0	0	0	0	0	0
Willowonder	3	.0000	.1370	31.4	3	0	0	0	0	0	0	0	3	0	0	0	0	0	0	0	0	0	0	0	0	0	0	0	0
willows	22	.5589	2.7304	44.4	2	6	2	3	9	0	0	0	13	0	0	0	0	0	0	1	0	0	0	0	4	2	1	1	0
wills	8	.5847	.9769	39.9	0	0	2	2	1	2	1	0	1	1	0	1	0	2	0	0	0	0	0	0	1	0	2	0	0
Wills	8	.2487	.4927	36.9	3	0	0	0	0	5	0	0	1	0	0	0	0	0	0	0	0	0	0	0	0	2	0	5	0
Willway	2	.0000	.0914	29.6	0	0	0	2	0	0	0	0	2	0	0	0	0	0	0	0	0	0	0	0	0	0	0	0	0
Willy	25	.5022	2.8672	44.6	11	9	4	0	0	0	0	1	15	0	0	0	0	0	0	0	0	0	0	0	1	1	3	5	0
Wilma	24	.1137	1.0029	40.0	17	0	0	7	0	0	0	0	7	0	0	0	0	0	0	0	0	0	0	0	0	0	0	17	0
Wilmington	6	.1339	.2157	33.3	1	0	4	0	0	1	0	0	0	0	0	0	0	0	0	0	0	0	0	0	0	1	5	0	0
Wilse	11	.2006	.5304	37.2	0	0	0	0	8	3	0	0	0	0	0	8	0	0	0	0	0	0	0	0	3	0	0	0	0
Wilson	195	.7389	29.313	54.7	22	38	48	10	11	52	11	3	31	21	0	11	34	46	1	3	0	0	0	0	23	7	2	16	0
Wilson's	18	.4593	1.8249	42.6	1	4	1	1	1	9	1	0	2	0	0	0	3	10	0	0	0	0	0	0	0	2	1	0	0
Wilsons	6	.3876	.5828	37.7	1	4	0	0	0	0	1	0	4	1	0	0	0	0	0	0	0	0	0	0	1	0	0	0	0
Wilsons'	2	.1787	.1174	30.7	1	1	0	0	0	0	0	0	1	0	0	0	0	0	0	0	0	0	0	0	1	0	0	0	0
wilt	26	.4906	2.6577	44.2	1	1	4	2	2	0	15	1	0	0	0	14	0	2	0	0	4	0	0	0	2	2	1	1	0
Wilt's	2	.0000	.0243	23.9	0	0	0	0	0	2	0	0	0	0	0	0	0	0	0	0	0	0	0	0	0	0	0	2	0
wilted	13	.5397	1.5740	42.0	5	0	2	2	2	1	1	0	8	1	0	2	0	0	0	0	0	0	0	0	1	1	0	0	0
wilting	2	.0000	.0219	23.4	0	0	0	0	1	1	0	0	0	2	0	0	0	0	0	0	0	0	0	0	0	0	0	0	0
Wilting	2	.0000	.0914	29.6	0	0	0	2	0	0	0	0	2	0	0	0	0	0	0	0	0	0	0	0	0	0	0	0	0
Wilton	6	.3846	.5813	37.6	0	0	4	0	0	0	2	0	4	0	0	0	0	0	0	0	0	0	0	0	0	1	1	0	0
wily	7	.4281	.6925	38.4	0	2	0	1	1	2	1	0	3	0	1	1	0	1	0	0	0	0	0	0	1	0	0	0	0
win	340	.8336	57.214	57.6	73	41	36	45	58	61	20	6	144	15	2	25	6	27	8	4	4	0	0	0	35	37	12	21	0
Win	3	.0000	.0365	25.6	0	0	0	2	0	1	0	0	0	0	0	0	0	0	0	0	0	0	0	0	0	0	0	3	0
win'ard	2	.0000	.0914	29.6	0	0	0	2	0	0	0	0	2	0	0	0	0	0	0	0	0	0	0	0	0	0	0	0	0
wince	4	.3717	.3640	35.6	0	1	1	0	0	2	0	0	2	0	0	1	0	0	0	0	0	0	0	0	0	0	0	1	0
winced	8	.5675	.9907	40.0	1	0	1	3	2	1	0	0	4	0	0	1	0	0	0	0	0	0	0	0	1	0	1	1	0
winch	4	.3104	.2995	34.8	0	0	0	0	4	0	0	0	1	0	0	0	0	0	0	0	0	0	0	0	0	0	1	2	0
Winchester	7	.3848	.5778	37.6	0	0	0	0	7	0	0	0	0	0	0	2	0	0	0	0	0	0	0	0	0	0	2	3	0
wind	1336	.9063	240.80	63.8	259	249	165	205	229	119	81	29	391	58	29	114	17	47	12	226	69	10	6	4	123	114	43	73	0
Wind	42	.5763	5.2647	47.2	11	13	8	7	1	1	1	0	21	10	0	0	0	1	0	0	3	0	0	0	4	2	1	0	0
wind-blown	3	.2060	.1500	31.8	1	0	0	0	1	0	1	0	0	0	0	2	0	0	0	0	0	0	0	0	0	1	0	0	0
wind-crust	2	.0000	.0215	23.3	0	0	0	0	0	0	2	0	0	0	0	2	0	0	0	0	0	0	0	0	0	0	0	0	0
wind-swept	4	.2969	.2888	34.6	0	1	0	1	0	0	2	0	1	0	0	2	0	0	0	0	0	0	0	0	1	0	0	0	0
wind-up	2	.1432	.0759	28.8	1	0	0	0	0	0	1	0	0	0	0	0	0	0	0	1	0	0	1	0	0	0	0	0	0
wind's	12	.4677	1.2281	40.9	0	1	2	0	3	6	0	0	3	5	0	1	0	0	0	0	0	0	0	0	1	0	2	0	0
Wind's	6	.1200	.2605	34.2	1	2	3	0	0	0	0	0	2	4	0	0	0	0	0	0	0	0	0	0	0	0	0	0	0

4B wilcuma
5A wild-animal
5N wild-berry
8A wild-fowler
9D wild-goose
3A Wild-life
4A wildcat's
9R Wilde
6F wildernesses
8A wildgeese
XR wildlife-rehabilitation
XR wildlife-wise
7D wildy
7Q Wilfrid
5N wilily
5N Wilkins'
8B Wilks
7R WILL
5A will-o'-the-wisp
5P Willem
5P willfully
5A willfulness
8B Willis
4A Willman's
7A Willowbrook
5B Willows
7A willowwild
7A Willsboro
8R willy-nilly
3A Willy's
6A Wilma's
8Q Wilmarth
XR Wilmer
8F Wilmot
7D Wilse's
8R Wilt
7L wilts
9B Wimbledon
7A wimdmills
9A Wimpy
9H win-at-any-cost
9H win-or-get-fired
7A win'
6R Win's
6A Winant
7P Winchell
5P winches
7D wincing
7Q wind-borne
4H wind-driven
4Q wind-pollinated
7N wind-rustled
7N wind-splitters
7Q wind-streamed
XR wind-tossed
7Q wind-trained
5N wind-twisted
XR wind-whipped

Word Type	F	D	U	SFI	3 Gr 3	4 Gr 4	5 Gr 5	6 Gr 6	7 Gr 7	8 Gr 8	9 Gr 9	X UnGr	A Read	B Eng & Gr	C Comp	D Lit	E Math	F Soc Stud	G Spell	H Sci	J Music	K Art	L Home Ec	M Shop	N Lib F	P Lib NF	Q Lib Ref	R Mag	S Rel
winda	2	.1948	.1250	31.0	1	0	1	0	0	0	0	0	1	0	0	0	0	0	0	0	0	0	0	0	0	1	0	0	0
Windale	6	.0000	.0703	28.5	0	0	0	0	6	0	0	0	0	0	0	0	0	0	0	0	0	0	0	0	6	0	0	0	0
windbag	3	.3134	.2351	33.7	0	0	1	1	0	0	1	0	1	0	0	0	0	1	1	0	0	0	0	0	0	0	0	0	0
windblown	6	.5082	.6542	38.2	0	0	1	0	2	2	1	0	1	0	0	1	0	1	0	0	0	0	0	0	1	0	0	2	0
windbreak	5	.4444	.4784	36.8	0	0	1	0	3	1	0	0	0	0	0	0	0	1	0	1	0	0	0	0	1	0	0	2	0
windbreaks	2	.1033	.0599	27.8	0	0	0	0	0	1	0	1	0	0	0	0	0	0	0	1	0	1	0	0	0	0	0	0	0
winded	7	.3308	.5415	37.3	1	2	0	0	1	1	2	0	2	0	2	1	0	0	0	0	1	0	0	0	0	1	0	0	0
winder	3	.0000	.0097	19.8	0	0	0	0	0	0	3	0	0	0	0	0	0	0	0	0	0	0	3	0	0	0	0	0	0
windfall	3	.3390	.2450	33.9	0	0	0	0	2	0	0	1	1	0	0	0	0	0	0	0	0	0	0	0	0	0	1	1	0
windfalls	5	.2086	.3320	35.2	3	0	0	0	0	0	2	0	3	0	0	0	0	0	0	0	0	0	0	0	2	0	0	0	0
winding	69	.8298	11.540	50.6	9	11	13	12	12	7	4	1	24	2	2	3	0	11	1	4	2	0	1	3	5	9	0	2	0
Winding	7	.3161	.5391	37.3	5	1	0	0	0	0	1	0	2	0	0	0	0	0	0	0	0	0	1	0	0	4	0	0	0
windings	14	.0517	.1941	32.9	0	0	0	1	1	12	0	0	0	0	0	0	0	0	0	0	0	0	0	12	0	0	0	2	0
windlass	19	.5099	2.2184	43.5	0	1	3	13	1	1	0	0	11	1	0	0	0	1	0	5	0	0	0	0	0	0	1	0	0
windless	6	.2440	.4665	36.7	0	1	1	2	1	1	0	0	5	0	0	0	0	0	0	0	1	0	0	0	0	0	0	0	0
windmill	33	.7444	4.9922	47.0	11	5	5	4	1	0	6	1	5	0	0	1	0	7	1	5	0	1	0	0	6	4	2	1	0
Windmill	2	.0000	.0394	26.0	0	0	0	2	0	0	0	0	0	0	0	0	0	0	0	2	0	0	0	0	0	0	0	0	0
windmills	29	.6505	3.9177	45.9	4	5	8	3	4	3	1	1	5	0	2	0	0	10	1	4	0	0	0	0	1	3	2	1	0
window	841	.8987	150.77	61.8	259	149	80	111	109	69	54	10	354	45	18	82	12	30	13	49	16	4	5	8	94	60	13	38	0
Window	3	.2279	.2143	33.3	0	0	0	0	0	2	0	1	2	0	0	0	0	0	0	0	0	0	0	0	0	0	0	1	0
window-dresser	2	.0000	.0215	23.3	0	0	0	0	0	2	0	0	0	0	0	2	0	0	0	0	0	0	0	0	0	0	0	0	0
window-sill	2	.1551	.0728	28.6	0	0	0	1	0	1	0	0	0	0	1	0	0	0	0	0	0	0	0	0	1	0	0	0	0
windowpane	6	.4587	.5858	37.7	4	0	0	0	1	1	0	0	0	1	0	0	0	0	0	1	0	0	0	0	2	2	0	0	0
windowpanes	3	.2435	.2274	33.6	0	1	0	0	1	1	0	0	2	0	0	0	0	1	0	0	0	0	0	0	0	0	0	0	0
windows	315	.9185	57.444	57.6	82	49	33	29	61	33	20	8	98	22	5	27	7	31	0	18	5	3	7	10	24	21	14	23	0
windowsill	7	.5208	.7938	39.0	3	3	1	0	0	0	0	0	2	0	0	0	1	0	0	1	0	0	0	0	2	0	0	1	0
windpipe	8	.2467	.5205	37.2	0	2	0	0	1	4	1	0	1	0	0	0	0	0	0	6	0	0	0	0	0	0	0	1	0
winds	367	.7914	58.726	57.7	54	41	77	74	74	14	18	15	69	13	1	9	1	94	1	72	16	0	0	0	11	27	33	20	0
windshield	20	.6940	2.8609	44.6	5	2	2	3	5	1	2	0	6	4	0	1	0	0	0	0	1	0	0	0	2	2	1	3	0
windshields	3	.2261	.2131	33.3	0	0	1	0	2	0	0	0	2	0	0	0	0	0	0	0	0	0	0	0	1	0	0	0	0
Windsor	5	.5346	.5716	37.6	0	1	0	2	1	1	0	0	1	0	0	0	0	1	0	0	0	0	0	0	1	0	1	1	0
windstorm	6	.4127	.5646	37.5	1	0	1	2	1	1	0	0	2	0	0	1	0	0	2	0	0	0	0	0	0	1	0	0	0
WINDSTORM	3	.0000	.1370	31.4	0	0	0	3	0	0	0	0	3	0	0	0	0	0	0	0	0	0	0	0	0	0	0	0	0
windstorms	2	.1814	.1187	30.7	0	0	0	0	0	1	0	1	1	0	0	0	0	0	0	0	0	0	0	0	0	0	0	1	0
windswept	7	.4251	.6594	38.2	1	2	1	1	1	0	0	1	1	0	0	0	0	2	0	0	0	0	0	0	0	0	2	2	0
windup	4	.1112	.1666	32.2	3	0	1	0	0	0	0	0	1	0	0	0	0	0	0	0	0	0	0	0	0	3	0	0	0
windward	7	.5205	.7839	38.9	0	0	1	1	4	0	1	0	1	0	0	0	0	0	0	3	0	0	0	0	1	1	1	0	0
windy	53	.7998	8.6145	49.4	8	15	11	4	7	5	2	1	22	2	1	6	0	3	1	7	1	0	0	0	5	0	3	2	0
Windy	4	.2399	.3011	34.8	3	0	0	0	1	0	0	0	3	1	0	0	0	0	0	0	0	0	0	0	0	0	0	0	0
wine	108	.7749	16.922	52.3	11	10	7	11	12	17	30	10	22	8	1	19	0	17	2	2	0	2	0	0	1	6	6	22	0
Wine	3	.2143	.1568	32.0	0	0	1	0	1	1	0	0	0	0	0	0	0	0	0	0	0	0	0	0	0	1	0	2	0
wine-making	2	.2285	.1129	30.5	1	0	0	0	0	0	1	0	0	0	0	0	0	1	0	0	0	0	0	0	0	0	1	0	0
wine-shop	4	.0000	.0429	26.3	0	0	0	0	0	0	4	0	0	0	0	4	0	0	0	0	0	0	0	0	0	0	0	0	0
wines	20	.4209	1.8561	42.7	6	0	2	4	2	0	1	5	3	0	0	0	0	2	0	0	0	0	0	0	0	1	7	7	0
Winfield	4	.2680	.2737	34.4	0	1	2	0	0	1	0	0	1	0	0	0	0	1	0	0	0	0	0	0	0	0	2	0	0
Winford	3	.0000	.0352	25.5	0	0	0	0	0	3	0	0	0	0	0	0	0	0	0	0	0	0	0	0	3	0	0	0	0
wing	157	.8168	25.929	54.1	32	34	16	15	38	13	6	3	54	5	0	6	0	1	3	41	4	1	0	1	2	13	13	13	0
Wing	8	.1629	.3718	35.7	3	1	0	0	0	0	4	0	1	0	0	0	0	0	0	1	0	0	0	0	0	0	0	6	0
winged	35	.6610	4.8018	46.8	1	2	1	8	10	6	6	1	11	4	0	5	0	0	0	1	2	2	0	0	0	2	7	1	0
winging	2	.0000	.0914	29.6	0	0	0	2	0	0	0	0	2	0	0	0	0	0	0	0	0	0	0	0	0	0	0	0	0
wingless	3	.1813	.1402	31.5	0	0	0	1	1	0	1	0	0	0	0	0	0	0	0	1	0	0	0	0	0	0	2	0	0
wingmen	2	.0000	.0914	29.6	0	0	0	0	2	0	0	0	2	0	0	0	0	0	0	0	0	0	0	0	0	0	0	0	0
wings	514	.7991	83.270	59.2	170	78	52	74	79	27	21	13	177	11	2	38	1	5	2	86	13	14	0	0	18	87	38	22	0
wingsalum	2	.0000	.0162	22.1	0	2	0	0	0	0	0	0	0	0	0	0	0	0	0	0	2	0	0	0	0	0	0	0	0
wingspread	16	.6124	2.0398	43.1	4	3	0	5	3	1	0	0	2	1	0	0	4	0	0	3	0	0	0	0	0	1	1	4	0
wingtip	3	.1277	.1363	31.3	0	0	0	3	0	0	0	0	1	0	0	0	0	0	0	0	0	0	0	0	0	0	0	2	0
wink	36	.7199	5.4033	47.3	19	5	2	5	2	3	0	0	20	1	1	2	0	2	0	1	2	0	0	0	5	1	0	1	0
winked	37	.5202	4.3043	46.3	15	6	6	2	6	0	2	0	19	1	0	4	0	0	0	0	0	0	0	0	8	5	0	0	0
winking	10	.4512	1.0431	40.2	2	3	0	1	3	1	0	0	5	1	0	0	0	0	0	0	0	0	0	0	3	0	1	0	0
Winkle	8	.1892	.3956	36.0	0	0	0	1	4	3	0	0	1	1	0	6	0	0	0	0	0	0	0	0	0	0	0	0	0
Winkler	3	.2257	.1583	32.0	0	0	0	2	1	0	0	0	0	2	0	1	0	0	0	0	0	0	0	0	0	0	0	0	0
WINKLER	4	.0000	.0429	26.3	0	0	0	0	4	0	0	0	0	0	0	4	0	0	0	0	0	0	0	0	0	0	0	0	0
Winkleville	4	.0000	.0778	28.9	0	4	0	0	0	0	0	0	0	0	0	0	0	4	0	0	0	0	0	0	0	0	0	0	0
winks	3	.2187	.1555	31.9	1	0	0	1	0	0	0	1	0	2	0	0	0	0	0	0	0	0	0	0	0	0	0	1	0
Winn	2	.0000	.0290	24.6	0	0	0	2	0	0	0	0	0	0	0	0	0	0	0	0	0	0	0	0	0	2	0	0	0
winner	63	.7899	10.115	50.0	16	7	5	15	9	2	6	3	24	6	0	3	1	2	2	3	0	0	0	0	4	8	3	7	0
Winner	3	.0000	.0352	25.5	0	0	0	0	0	3	0	0	0	0	0	0	0	0	0	0	0	0	0	0	3	0	0	0	0
winner's	2	.0000	.0914	29.6	1	0	0	1	0	0	0	0	2	0	0	0	0	0	0	0	0	0	0	0	0	0	0	0	0
winners	35	.7685	5.4616	47.4	6	3	2	9	3	4	6	2	10	3	1	1	0	2	0	0	1	0	0	0	4	4	3	6	0
Winnie-the-Pooh	5	.2396	.3805	35.8	3	2	0	0	0	0	0	0	4	0	0	0	0	0	1	0	0	0	0	0	0	0	0	0	0
winning	97	.8705	16.882	52.3	7	8	13	9	19	20	14	7	30	7	2	3	4	7	1	3	2	0	1	0	4	14	8	11	0
winnings	2	.2443	.1130	30.5	0	0	0	0	1	0	1	0	0	0	0	1	0	0	0	0	0	0	0	0	1	0	0	0	0
Winnipeg	2	.2285	.1129	30.5	0	1	0	1	0	0	0	0	0	0	0	0	0	1	0	0	0	0	0	0	0	0	1	0	0
wins	50	.8154	8.2196	49.1	8	8	8	0	6	11	6	3	14	5	0	6	4	5	0	3	2	0	1	0	1	5	0	4	0
Winston	13	.6052	1.6575	42.2	0	1	4	0	0	5	3	0	3	2	0	1	0	4	0	0	0	0	0	0	0	0	1	2	0
Wintapi	7	.0000	.0821	29.1	0	0	0	0	7	0	0	0	0	0	0	0	0	0	0	0	0	0	0	0	7	0	0	0	0
winter	1004	.9151	182.50	62.6	242	187	150	142	145	69	44	25	258	30	8	41	9	202	24	133	24	5	8	1	54	106	50	51	0
Winter	22	.7019	3.2128	45.1	7	4	1	2	4	2	2	0	10	2	0	2	0	1	0	0	2	0	0	0	2	1	0	2	0
winter-broken	3	.1187	.1291	31.1	0	0	0	0	3	0	0	0	1	0	0	2	0	0	0	0	0	0	0	0	0	0	0	0	0
winter's	23	.7066	3.3460	45.2	3	1	3	3	8	4	1	0	7	4	0	0	1	2	0	2	2	1	0	0	2	0	2	0	0
Winterberry's	3	.0000	.1370	31.4	3	0	0	0	0	0	0	0	3	0	0	0	0	0	0	0	0	0	0	0	0	0	0	0	0
winters	84	.5327	9.5880	49.8	7	13	19	21	8	6	10	0	8	0	0	1	0	52	0	8	1	0	1	0	1	1	10	1	0
Winters	26	.1449	1.7263	42.4	15	1	5	3	1	1	0	0	25	1	0	0	0	0	0	0	0	0	0	0	0	0	0	0	0
Winters'	4	.0000	.1827	32.6	4	0	0	0	0	0	0	0	4	0	0	0	0	0	0	0	0	0	0	0	0	0	0	0	0
wintertime	20	.6784	2.8622	44.6	5	5	3	1	2	3	0	1	11	3	0	0	0	1	1	0	1	0	0	0	1	1	0	1	0
Winthrop	2	.0000	.0389	25.9	0	0	2	0	0	0	0	0	0	0	0	0	0	2	0	0	0	0	0	0	0	0	0	0	0
wintry	13	.5733	1.5967	42.0	1	4	1	1	2	4	0	0	5	1	1	0	0	0	0	0	1	0	0	0	2	0	0	3	0
Winwood	2	.0000	.0243	23.9	0	0	0	0	0	2	0	0	0	0	0	0	0	0	0	0	0	0	0	0	0	0	0	2	0
wipe	35	.6770	4.9345	46.9	5	6	5	3	7	3	5	1	13	0	0	3	1	1	0	5	0	0	4	1	0	2	2	3	0
wipe-on	2	.0000	.0290	24.6	0	0	0	0	2	0	0	0	0	0	0	0	0	0	0	0	0	0	0	0	0	2	0	0	0
wiped	79	.7322	11.902	50.8	9	18	10	10	19	4	6	3	29	3	0	6	0	6	0	3	1	0	0	0	14	11	2	4	0
wiper	3	.0000	.0243	23.8	3	0	0	0	0	0	0	0	0	0	0	0	0	0	0	0	3	0	0	0	0	0	0	0	0
wipers	2	.2401	.1133	30.5	2	0	0	0	0	0	0	0	0	0	0	0	0	0	0	0	0	0	0	0	0	1	1	0	0
wipes	4	.3709	.3633	35.6	2	0	0	0	2	0	0	0	2	0	0	0	0	0	0	0	0	0	0	0	0	0	1	1	0

6A windbreaker
7F windbreakers
5P windburned
9L winders
4A Windfield
6A windflowers
4N windiest
4A Windjammer
7Q windlasses
9D windmill's
6A windmills'
8D window-dresser's
6A window-pane
6P window-panes
5A window-sills
8D window's
3A Windows
3N Windowshade
7H windpipes
7B windproofs
9D windpuff-bonnet
3N Windrim
7J Winds
3A Windy's
6N wine-colored
9D wine-flask
XR wine-flavored
8A wine-red
XR wine-tasting
7R winemaker
9R winery
8N Winford's
4G WING
7Q wing-fingers
3P wing-level
7R wing-nuts
9D wing'd
6A wingbeat
7N wingfence
7R wingnuts
4A Wings
6E wingspans
XH wingspreads
6A wingtips
7D Winklers
7D Winkles
6J Winnemucca
8A Winnie
6P winsome
5Q Winston-Salem
9R winter-spring
7B winter-time
6J Winter's
3R Winterbinter
3R Winterbinter's
6N wintscha
7R wiper/washer

Word Type	F	D	U	SFI	3 Gr 3	4 Gr 4	5 Gr 5	6 Gr 6	7 Gr 7	8 Gr 8	9 Gr 9	X UnGr	A Read	B Eng & Gr	C Comp	D Lit	E Math	F Soc Stud	G Spell	H Sci	J Music	K Art	L Home Ec	M Shop	N Lib F	P Lib NF	Q Lib Ref	R Mag	S Rel
wiping	25	.5813	3.1085	44.9	5	4	3	5	4	2	2	0	9	1	0	4	0	0	0	0	0	0	0	0	6	3	0	2	0
wire	560	.6843	78.537	59.0	102	62	108	74	62	89	30	33	95	8	1	13	55	14	4	143	3	37	2	66	19	29	27	44	0
Wire	4	.2621	.2596	34.1	0	0	0	1	1	0	0	2	1	0	0	0	0	0	0	0	0	0	0	1	0	0	0	2	0
wire-drawing	2	.1259	.0687	28.4	0	0	0	0	1	1	0	0	0	0	0	0	0	1	0	0	0	0	0	1	0	0	0	0	0
wired	22	.2217	1.1343	40.5	1	2	1	0	5	10	3	0	2	2	0	1	1	1	0	0	0	0	0	12	0	1	1	1	0
wireless	17	.4910	1.8229	42.6	1	1	3	1	2	0	1	8	2	0	0	1	0	4	0	8	0	0	0	0	0	0	2	0	0
wires	205	.7370	30.750	54.9	44	24	25	32	31	37	11	1	42	2	2	7	8	5	1	50	5	5	0	23	5	22	16	12	0
wiring	12	.2493	.7680	38.9	1	2	1	2	2	4	0	0	3	0	0	0	0	2	0	2	0	0	0	4	0	1	0	0	0
wiry	22	.6766	3.0594	44.9	4	4	2	1	5	2	2	2	4	0	0	1	0	2	0	1	0	1	0	0	5	3	1	4	0
Wis	6	.1708	.2605	34.2	0	0	1	0	3	0	0	2	0	0	0	0	0	0	0	0	0	0	0	0	0	0	1	5	0
Wisconsin	44	.8109	7.1547	48.5	3	7	9	6	7	6	4	2	4	1	0	2	4	9	0	5	1	0	0	1	4	1	6	6	0
wisdom	98	.6834	13.944	51.4	9	19	10	20	15	9	14	2	38	5	2	9	0	9	3	1	1	0	0	0	7	9	8	5	1
Wisdom	3	.2212	.2099	33.2	0	0	0	1	0	2	0	0	2	0	0	1	0	0	0	0	0	0	0	0	0	0	0	0	0
wisdom's	2	.1717	.1142	30.6	0	0	0	0	1	1	0	0	1	0	0	1	0	0	0	0	0	0	0	0	0	0	0	0	0
wise	253	.8320	42.387	56.3	45	31	32	42	41	37	19	6	90	12	2	27	2	26	9	11	8	0	17	0	15	15	4	14	1
Wise	13	.4645	1.3145	41.2	3	2	1	4	1	0	0	2	3	0	0	0	0	1	0	1	3	2	0	0	0	0	1	2	0
wisecrack	2	.0000	.0290	24.6	0	0	0	0	1	0	1	0	0	0	0	0	0	0	0	0	0	0	0	0	0	2	0	0	0
wisecracks	2	.0000	.0215	23.3	0	0	0	0	0	0	2	0	0	0	0	2	0	0	0	0	0	0	0	0	0	0	0	0	0
wisely	41	.6793	5.6732	47.5	2	8	1	4	5	4	17	0	4	1	0	5	0	7	1	3	1	0	7	1	3	3	0	5	0
wiser	21	.6035	2.7287	44.4	6	4	2	0	5	4	0	0	10	0	0	2	0	2	0	0	0	0	0	1	2	4	0	0	0
wisest	20	.4624	2.1973	43.4	3	2	2	10	0	2	0	1	13	1	0	0	0	3	0	0	0	0	0	0	0	3	0	0	0
wish	707	.9000	126.68	61.0	163	132	77	82	101	72	69	11	230	45	14	67	55	48	7	34	26	18	17	1	56	65	6	18	0
Wish	3	.2279	.2143	33.3	2	0	0	0	0	1	0	0	2	0	0	0	0	0	0	0	0	0	0	0	0	0	0	1	0
wishbone	2	.2443	.1130	30.5	0	0	0	1	0	1	0	0	0	0	0	1	0	0	0	0	0	0	0	0	1	0	0	0	0
wished	259	.8165	42.804	56.3	56	57	30	31	41	22	18	4	103	6	1	23	4	28	2	5	5	1	1	0	38	27	5	9	1
wishes	128	.8974	22.859	53.6	21	9	13	18	30	14	20	3	34	9	2	10	3	19	7	8	10	0	2	0	7	8	2	7	0
wishful	7	.4592	.7242	38.6	0	0	1	1	2	2	1	0	2	1	0	0	0	3	0	0	0	0	0	0	0	0	1	0	0
wishing	54	.6535	7.4820	48.7	14	4	7	12	10	1	6	0	28	1	0	4	0	1	0	0	0	0	1	0	12	1	2	4	0
Wishing	11	.0000	.5025	37.0	11	0	0	0	0	0	0	0	11	0	0	0	0	0	0	0	0	0	0	0	0	0	0	0	0
wisht	2	.0000	.0234	23.7	0	0	0	0	2	0	0	0	0	0	0	0	0	0	0	0	0	0	0	0	2	0	0	0	0
Wishtego	4	.0000	.0579	27.6	0	4	0	0	0	0	0	0	0	0	0	0	0	0	0	0	0	0	0	0	0	4	0	0	0
wisp	6	.4481	.6020	37.8	1	1	0	0	3	0	0	1	2	2	0	0	0	0	0	0	1	0	0	0	0	0	0	1	0
wisps	8	.5462	.9323	39.7	0	2	0	1	2	3	0	0	2	0	1	1	0	0	0	1	0	0	0	0	1	1	0	1	0
Wisps	3	.0000	.1370	31.4	0	0	0	3	0	0	0	0	3	0	0	0	0	0	0	0	0	0	0	0	0	0	0	0	0
wisteria	2	.2408	.1204	30.8	0	0	1	0	0	1	0	0	0	0	0	0	0	1	0	0	0	0	0	0	0	1	0	0	0
wistful	5	.3469	.4217	36.2	0	0	0	0	4	1	0	0	2	0	0	0	0	0	0	0	1	0	0	0	0	0	0	2	0
wistfully	14	.5331	1.6527	42.2	2	3	0	5	2	0	2	0	7	1	0	3	0	0	0	0	0	0	0	0	2	0	0	1	0
wistfulness	2	.0000	.0234	23.7	1	0	0	0	1	0	0	0	0	0	0	0	0	0	0	0	0	0	0	0	2	0	0	0	0
wit	32	.7139	4.6731	46.7	0	2	8	1	5	3	10	3	8	1	0	8	0	0	1	1	3	0	0	0	3	4	1	2	0
witch	109	.6948	15.762	52.0	36	35	3	13	17	3	2	0	47	2	1	19	0	2	4	2	2	0	0	0	0	8	1	21	0
Witch	5	.2445	.3864	35.9	0	3	0	0	1	1	0	0	4	0	0	1	0	0	0	0	0	0	0	0	0	0	0	0	0
witch-hazel	2	.0000	.0215	23.3	0	0	0	0	1	1	0	0	0	0	0	2	0	0	0	0	0	0	0	0	0	0	0	0	0
witch's	11	.3976	1.0387	40.2	6	0	0	2	3	0	0	0	5	0	0	4	0	0	0	0	0	0	0	0	1	1	0	0	0
Witch's	3	.1187	.1291	31.1	0	2	0	0	0	1	0	0	1	0	0	2	0	0	0	0	0	0	0	0	0	0	0	0	0
witchcraft	13	.3908	1.1209	40.5	0	0	0	0	5	2	6	0	1	3	0	2	0	0	0	0	0	0	0	0	0	7	0	0	0
witches	29	.5857	3.5482	45.5	12	5	2	0	4	3	3	0	5	5	0	2	0	0	0	0	2	2	0	0	0	11	0	2	0
witches'	2	.2407	.1138	30.6	0	0	0	0	2	0	0	0	0	0	0	1	0	0	0	0	0	0	0	0	0	1	0	0	0
witching	2	.0000	.0914	29.6	0	0	0	0	0	2	0	0	2	0	0	0	0	0	0	0	0	0	0	0	0	0	0	0	0
with	30455	.9904	5933.4	77.7	4826	4387	3629	3944	6141	3592	3119	817	7058	1675	358	1937	1518	2205	1702	2439	1430	475	673	529	2238	2374	1550	2253	41
With	16	.5545	1.8339	42.6	2	1	1	2	0	5	1	4	1	1	0	1	0	0	2	0	4	0	0	0	0	1	0	6	0
with-grain	2	.0000	.0064	18.1	0	0	0	0	0	2	0	0	0	0	0	0	0	0	0	0	0	0	2	0	0	0	0	0	0
withal	8	.2924	.5091	37.1	0	0	0	0	3	0	5	0	0	0	2	5	0	0	0	0	0	0	0	0	1	0	0	0	0
withdraw	22	.6902	3.1099	44.9	3	1	4	0	7	5	2	0	3	0	0	1	0	6	1	0	1	0	0	0	0	4	3	3	0
withdrawal	18	.4538	1.7744	42.5	0	1	2	2	3	4	6	0	2	0	0	0	1	3	0	0	0	0	0	0	0	1	2	9	0
withdrawals	2	.2351	.1166	30.7	0	0	0	0	0	0	2	0	0	0	0	0	0	1	0	0	0	0	0	0	0	0	0	1	0
withdrawing	3	.2940	.1911	32.8	0	0	0	0	0	2	1	0	0	0	0	0	0	0	0	0	0	0	0	1	0	0	1	1	0
withdrawn	12	.5881	1.4765	41.7	1	0	1	1	3	5	1	0	2	0	0	4	1	1	0	1	0	0	0	1	0	1	0	1	0
withdraws	2	.1483	.0728	28.6	0	0	0	0	1	0	1	0	0	0	0	0	0	0	0	0	0	0	0	1	0	1	0	0	0
withdrew	25	.7391	3.7563	45.7	1	0	3	5	5	8	2	1	4	0	0	1	2	5	0	1	1	0	0	0	2	3	5	1	0
wither	6	.4238	.5739	37.6	0	0	1	0	2	2	1	0	2	0	0	1	0	0	2	0	0	0	0	0	0	0	1	0	0
withered	16	.1117	.7420	38.7	2	1	3	3	2	3	1	1	8	1	0	1	0	1	0	0	0	0	0	0	0	0	2	1	2
withering	3	.3815	.2534	34.0	0	1	0	0	1	0	1	0	0	0	0	0	0	1	0	0	0	0	0	0	0	1	0	1	0
withers	7	.1288	.2510	34.0	1	2	1	3	0	0	0	0	0	0	0	0	0	0	0	0	0	0	0	0	6	1	0	0	0
Withers	8	.0000	.3655	35.6	8	0	0	0	0	0	0	0	8	0	0	0	0	0	0	0	0	0	0	0	0	0	0	0	0
withheld	7	.4097	.6400	38.1	1	0	0	0	1	0	5	0	1	0	0	0	3	0	0	0	0	0	0	0	0	1	0	2	0
withhold	7	.4677	.7076	38.5	0	1	0	3	0	1	1	1	1	0	0	0	1	1	0	0	2	0	0	0	0	0	0	2	0
withholding	4	.3606	.3161	35.0	0	0	0	1	1	0	2	0	0	0	0	0	1	0	0	0	0	0	0	0	1	0	0	2	0
within	949	.9290	174.44	62.4	64	92	101	125	252	138	147	30	123	36	19	47	24	106	9	168	39	6	25	15	42	72	124	94	0
without	2392	.9726	458.55	66.6	319	349	289	346	459	276	281	73	580	129	35	149	146	163	100	298	80	17	53	31	164	183	114	150	0
Without	5	.3766	.4670	36.7	0	0	0	1	0	4	0	0	3	0	0	0	0	0	0	0	1	0	0	0	0	0	1	0	0
withstand	20	.5942	2.4437	43.9	0	1	2	3	6	2	4	2	0	0	0	0	0	2	0	4	0	0	0	2	1	3	5	3	0
withstood	3	.2357	.2199	33.4	0	0	1	0	1	1	0	0	2	0	0	0	0	0	0	0	0	0	0	0	0	1	0	0	0
Witje	3	.0000	.1370	31.4	0	0	0	3	0	0	0	0	3	0	0	0	0	0	0	0	0	0	0	0	0	0	0	0	0
witness	36	.8036	5.8273	47.7	4	1	1	7	10	5	7	1	9	2	1	6	0	2	1	1	2	0	0	0	1	2	4	5	0
witnessed	14	.5304	1.5683	42.0	0	0	1	1	4	3	5	0	2	0	2	0	0	3	1	0	0	0	0	0	3	0	1	2	0
witnesses	12	.4913	1.2624	41.0	0	0	0	2	2	4	4	0	1	3	0	0	0	5	2	0	0	0	0	0	0	0	0	1	0
witnessing	4	.3415	.3070	34.9	0	0	1	1	1	0	0	1	0	0	0	0	0	0	0	1	0	0	0	0	0	1	0	2	0
wits	35	.6706	4.9021	46.9	2	3	10	8	6	1	5	0	14	1	1	7	0	0	0	0	0	0	0	0	5	4	1	2	0
witty	4	.4538	.4019	36.0	0	1	0	0	1	1	1	0	1	1	0	0	0	0	0	0	0	0	0	0	1	1	0	0	0
Witwatersrand	2	.2152	.1357	31.3	1	0	0	0	1	0	0	0	1	0	0	0	0	1	0	0	0	0	0	0	0	0	0	0	0
wives	68	.6377	9.1975	49.6	3	11	25	8	8	3	6	4	28	0	0	6	0	14	0	0	0	0	0	0	2	5	2	11	0
Wizard	20	.3900	1.8313	42.6	1	8	0	6	0	0	0	5	8	0	0	0	0	0	0	0	6	0	0	0	0	1	0	5	0
wizened	2	.2446	.1142	30.6	0	0	1	1	0	0	0	0	0	0	0	0	0	0	0	0	0	0	0	0	1	0	0	1	0
Wm	3	.0000	.0314	25.0	0	0	0	0	3	0	0	0	0	0	0	0	0	0	0	0	0	0	0	0	0	0	3	0	0
Wo	19	.0000	.8680	39.4	0	0	12	7	0	0	0	0	19	0	0	0	0	0	0	0	0	0	0	0	0	0	0	0	0
wo'n't	2	.0000	.0234	23.7	0	0	2	0	0	0	0	0	0	0	0	0	0	0	0	0	0	0	0	0	2	0	0	0	0
wobble	2	.0000	.0234	23.7	0	0	1	0	1	0	0	0	0	0	0	0	0	0	0	0	0	0	0	0	2	0	0	0	0
wobble-wobble	2	.0000	.0914	29.6	0	2	0	0	0	0	0	0	2	0	0	0	0	0	0	0	0	0	0	0	0	0	0	0	0
Wobblechin	3	.0000	.0328	25.2	3	0	0	0	0	0	0	0	0	3	0	0	0	0	0	0	0	0	0	0	0	0	0	0	0
wobbled	4	.3718	.3639	35.6	1	3	0	0	0	0	0	0	2	1	0	0	0	0	0	0	0	0	0	0	1	0	0	0	0
wobbling	4	.4501	.4035	36.1	2	0	1	0	1	0	0	0	1	0	0	0	0	0	0	1	0	0	0	0	0	1	1	0	0
wobbly	20	.5969	2.5229	44.0	7	1	0	1	8	0	1	2	6	0	0	6	0	0	0	1	0	0	1	0	1	2	0	3	0
Woburn	5	.0000	.0586	27.7	0	0	5	0	0	0	0	0	0	0	0	0	0	0	0	0	0	0	0	0	5	0	0	0	0
woe	14	.6293	1.8251	42.6	3	0	0	6	2	1	2	0	3	3	0	3	0	0	2	0	1	0	0	0	0	1	0	1	0

6H wire-haired
8H wire-mesh
6A wire-rope
4A wired-up
8Q wirephoto
8H Wiscasset
6R Wisconsin's
6A wisecracked
4A wiseman
4A Wisenick
4N Wisest
6A WISH
8B wish'd
8D wishmaking
4P Wishtego's
3A wisped
7F wispy-haired
3Q wistful-looking
9B wit's
8A witch-and-dragon
8D witchdoctor's
4B witchery
5R WITH
7Q Withdrawal
7Q withered-looking
3A Withers'
3P withersoever
8Q Within
7P withouten
5A withstanding
5R witless
7N Witness
9D witness's
9A Witnesses
7D wits'
5P Wittenberg
7P Wittgenstein
9N witticism
8B wittily
8D Wittmer
5A wiz
5B wizard
7R Wizard-ish
6A wizardly
3P wizardry
3E wk
7B wld
7P Wledig
4F WM
5A Wo's
7Q wobbles
4N wobblety
7J Wodehouse
4G Woden
8D woe-begone
4A woebegone

Word Type	F	D	U	SFI	3 Gr 3	4 Gr 4	5 Gr 5	6 Gr 6	7 Gr 7	8 Gr 8	9 Gr 9	X UnGr	A Read	B Eng & Gr	C Comp	D Lit	E Math	F Soc Stud	G Spell	H Sci	J Music	K Art	L Home Ec	M Shop	N Lib F	P Lib NF	Q Lib Ref	R Mag	S Rel
woeful	9	.1025	.2713	34.3	0	0	1	0	0	0	8	0	0	0	0	8	0	0	0	0	0	0	0	0	0	1	0	0	0
woefully	3	.2227	.1589	32.0	0	0	1	1	0	0	0	1	0	0	0	0	0	0	0	0	0	0	0	0	2	0	0	1	0
Woelfchen	4	.0000	.1827	32.6	0	0	0	4	0	0	0	0	4	0	0	0	0	0	0	0	0	0	0	0	0	0	0	0	0
woes	4	.2872	.2840	34.5	1	0	0	0	1	0	2	0	1	0	0	2	0	0	0	0	0	0	0	0	0	1	0	0	0
wok	3	.0000	.1370	31.4	3	0	0	0	0	0	0	0	3	0	0	0	0	0	0	0	0	0	0	0	0	0	0	0	0
woke	133	.6787	19.015	52.8	47	31	15	9	10	10	11	0	70	1	3	14	0	1	1	3	0	0	0	0	16	19	0	5	0
Wol	22	.0000	1.0050	40.0	0	22	0	0	0	0	0	0	22	0	0	0	0	0	0	0	0	0	0	0	0	0	0	0	0
wolf	139	.8086	22.867	53.6	39	40	17	12	15	10	4	2	71	5	0	9	0	5	6	2	3	2	0	0	8	19	5	4	0
Wolf	40	.5349	4.8292	46.8	22	5	2	0	5	6	0	0	26	3	0	7	0	1	0	0	2	0	0	0	1	0	0	0	0
Wolf's	4	.2278	.2911	34.6	2	1	1	0	0	0	0	0	3	0	0	0	0	0	0	0	1	0	0	0	0	0	0	0	0
Wolfe	11	.0000	.2139	33.3	0	0	1	7	0	1	2	0	0	0	0	0	0	11	0	0	0	0	0	0	0	0	0	0	0
Wolferl	7	.0000	.3198	35.0	0	0	7	0	0	0	0	0	7	0	0	0	0	0	0	0	0	0	0	0	0	0	0	0	0
Wolfgang	13	.3416	1.0047	40.0	1	2	3	1	1	3	1	1	2	0	0	0	0	0	0	1	7	0	0	0	0	0	2	1	0
Wolfhardt	5	.0000	.2284	33.6	0	0	0	5	0	0	0	0	5	0	0	0	0	0	0	0	0	0	0	0	0	0	0	0	0
wolfhound	4	.3018	.2919	34.7	0	1	1	0	0	1	1	0	1	2	0	1	0	0	0	0	0	0	0	0	0	0	0	0	0
Wolly	9	.0000	.0728	28.6	0	6	2	1	0	0	0	0	0	0	0	0	0	0	0	0	9	0	0	0	0	0	0	0	0
Wolsey	3	.0000	.0314	25.0	0	0	3	0	0	0	0	0	0	0	0	0	0	0	0	0	0	0	0	0	0	0	3	0	0
wolverine	7	.0000	.0821	29.1	0	0	0	0	7	0	0	0	0	0	0	0	0	0	0	0	0	0	0	0	7	0	0	0	0
wolves	107	.7419	16.362	52.1	16	39	23	3	15	7	2	2	48	4	3	3	0	5	1	3	0	0	0	0	14	18	6	2	0
woman	750	.8293	125.81	61.0	212	98	75	83	140	69	52	21	355	41	14	78	2	41	12	5	12	3	2	0	67	82	7	29	0
Woman	26	.4598	2.7189	44.3	4	12	0	2	2	4	2	0	12	0	0	1	0	1	0	0	1	3	0	0	7	0	1	0	0
WOMAN	30	.0000	.3219	35.1	0	0	0	0	8	15	7	0	0	0	0	30	0	0	0	0	0	0	0	0	0	0	0	0	0
woman-of-all-women	2	.0000	.0914	29.6	0	0	0	2	0	0	0	0	2	0	0	0	0	0	0	0	0	0	0	0	0	0	0	0	0
woman's	57	.7790	9.0205	49.6	8	7	6	6	16	3	5	6	19	7	0	6	1	1	1	1	2	0	0	0	4	8	1	6	0
Woman's	3	.3394	.2451	33.9	0	2	0	0	1	0	0	0	1	0	0	1	0	0	0	0	0	0	0	0	1	0	0	0	0
womanhood	2	.1948	.1250	31.0	0	0	0	0	1	1	0	0	1	0	0	0	0	0	0	0	0	0	0	0	0	1	0	0	0
womanliness	3	.0000	.1370	31.4	0	0	3	0	0	0	0	0	3	0	0	0	0	0	0	0	0	0	0	0	0	0	0	0	0
womb	4	.2428	.2417	33.8	0	0	0	0	1	0	2	1	0	0	0	0	0	0	0	3	1	0	0	0	0	0	0	0	0
Wombat	3	.0000	.0365	25.6	3	0	0	0	0	0	0	0	0	0	0	0	0	0	0	0	0	0	0	0	0	0	0	3	0
women	592	.8465	100.40	60.0	84	100	93	63	118	61	59	14	132	24	6	45	6	147	4	3	14	1	3	0	36	78	32	61	0
Women	7	.4081	.6334	38.0	1	2	1	0	3	0	0	0	1	0	0	0	0	0	0	0	0	0	0	0	0	2	1	3	0
women's	27	.7369	4.0786	46.1	3	3	5	2	7	3	4	0	9	2	1	0	0	3	0	0	1	0	0	0	1	4	2	4	0
womenfolks	2	.0000	.0234	23.7	0	0	0	0	2	0	0	0	0	0	0	0	0	0	0	0	0	0	0	0	2	0	0	0	0
Womrath	4	.2351	.2111	33.2	0	0	0	3	1	0	0	0	0	0	1	3	0	0	0	0	0	0	0	0	0	0	0	0	0
won	446	.8854	78.735	59.0	52	60	53	76	73	85	35	12	121	36	3	23	15	64	10	4	9	1	0	0	31	57	24	47	1
won't	756	.7733	119.44	60.8	170	197	65	98	127	57	30	12	322	22	3	53	2	16	4	12	24	0	4	1	118	122	2	51	0
wond'ring	2	.2411	.1091	30.4	1	0	0	0	0	0	1	0	0	0	0	1	0	0	0	0	1	0	0	0	0	0	0	0	0
wonder	445	.9268	81.818	59.1	86	83	58	77	63	44	26	8	143	14	1	32	8	42	9	33	18	5	5	2	41	53	10	29	0
wondered	257	.7730	40.790	56.1	55	55	39	29	39	23	10	7	130	8	1	12	2	10	2	22	2	0	1	0	21	35	2	8	1
wonderful	411	.6255	54.718	57.4	106	113	45	51	43	24	18	11	185	13	6	26	0	27	5	13	18	5	2	0	41	42	4	18	6
Wonderful	7	.4767	.7154	38.5	0	2	0	1	0	2	2	0	1	2	0	0	0	0	0	1	2	0	0	0	0	0	1	0	0
wonderfully	24	.7204	3.5478	45.5	3	1	2	3	6	5	2	2	7	0	1	2	0	2	0	1	1	0	0	0	4	3	0	3	0
wonderfulness	2	.0000	.0290	24.6	0	0	2	0	0	0	0	0	0	0	0	0	0	0	0	0	0	0	0	0	0	2	0	0	0
wondering	104	.7170	15.389	51.9	15	24	13	9	18	8	13	4	37	2	1	13	0	7	0	8	0	0	0	0	18	11	0	7	0
wonderingly	8	.3650	.7430	38.7	0	2	1	2	2	1	0	0	5	0	0	0	0	0	0	0	0	0	0	0	2	1	0	0	0
wonderland	3	.2279	.2143	33.3	0	0	0	0	2	1	0	0	2	0	0	0	0	0	0	0	0	0	0	0	0	0	0	1	0
Wonderland	6	.4192	.5370	37.3	0	1	3	0	2	0	0	0	0	3	0	1	0	1	0	0	0	0	0	0	0	0	1	0	0
wonderment	7	.4504	.7019	38.5	0	0	1	2	0	2	1	1	2	0	0	1	0	0	0	0	0	0	0	0	2	0	0	2	0
wonders	90	.8154	14.727	51.7	6	15	11	12	23	7	13	3	15	5	1	1	3	9	2	6	4	0	0	0	6	9	20	9	0
wondrous	22	.6253	2.8662	44.6	0	2	2	5	7	4	0	2	5	0	0	6	0	2	1	0	1	0	0	0	1	1	0	5	0
wondrously	5	.3752	.4067	36.1	0	1	1	0	1	2	0	0	0	0	0	2	0	0	0	0	0	0	0	0	0	2	1	0	0
Wong	7	.0000	.3198	35.0	3	0	0	4	0	0	0	0	7	0	0	0	0	0	0	0	0	0	0	0	0	0	0	0	0
Wonka	15	.0000	.1759	32.5	0	0	0	0	0	0	0	15	0	0	0	0	0	0	0	0	0	0	0	0	15	0	0	0	0
wont	9	.4493	.8704	39.4	0	0	0	1	2	2	4	0	1	1	0	4	0	0	0	0	0	0	0	0	2	1	0	0	0
woo	6	.2515	.3690	35.7	0	0	0	0	1	2	3	0	1	0	0	4	0	0	0	0	1	0	0	0	0	0	0	0	0
wooba	6	.0000	.0729	28.6	6	0	0	0	0	0	0	0	0	0	0	0	0	0	0	0	0	0	0	0	0	0	0	6	0
wood	934	.7566	143.14	61.6	206	165	117	112	171	89	49	25	192	10	6	35	8	81	24	124	53	46	0	100	59	99	48	49	0
Wood	21	.6480	2.8039	44.5	5	0	1	2	8	5	0	0	2	0	0	4	2	6	0	1	1	0	0	0	1	0	0	4	0
wood-boring	2	.1698	.1133	30.5	0	0	0	1	1	0	0	0	1	0	0	0	0	0	0	0	0	0	0	0	0	0	1	0	0
wood-burning	5	.3684	.4519	36.6	0	2	0	0	2	0	0	1	2	0	0	0	0	2	0	0	0	0	0	0	0	0	0	1	0
wood-cutters	2	.0000	.0243	23.9	0	0	0	2	0	0	0	0	0	0	0	0	0	0	0	0	0	0	0	0	0	0	0	2	0
wood-eating	4	.0000	.0789	29.0	0	0	0	4	0	0	0	0	0	0	0	0	0	0	0	4	0	0	0	0	0	0	0	0	0
wood-pile	2	.0000	.0215	23.3	0	0	0	0	0	2	0	0	0	0	0	2	0	0	0	0	0	0	0	0	0	0	0	0	0
wood-winds	3	.0000	.0243	23.8	0	0	0	0	0	3	0	0	0	0	0	0	0	0	0	0	3	0	0	0	0	0	0	0	0
wood-working	2	.2408	.1204	30.8	1	0	0	0	0	1	0	0	0	0	0	0	0	1	0	0	0	0	0	0	0	1	0	0	0
Wood's	4	.0000	.1827	32.6	2	2	0	0	0	0	0	0	4	0	0	0	0	0	0	0	0	0	0	0	0	0	0	0	0
Woodard	3	.0000	.0365	25.6	0	0	0	0	0	0	0	3	0	0	0	0	0	0	0	0	0	0	0	0	0	0	0	3	0
woodblocks	2	.0000	.0162	22.1	0	0	0	0	2	0	0	0	0	0	0	0	0	0	0	0	2	0	0	0	0	0	0	0	0
woodbox	6	.3826	.5166	37.1	2	1	2	0	0	1	0	0	1	0	0	1	0	0	0	0	0	0	0	0	3	1	0	0	0
woodburner	3	.0000	.1370	31.4	0	0	3	0	0	0	0	0	3	0	0	0	0	0	0	0	0	0	0	0	0	0	0	0	0
woodchuck	35	.5953	4.6193	46.6	1	2	21	0	8	0	0	3	26	0	1	2	0	0	0	2	0	0	0	0	2	0	1	1	0
Woodchuck	2	.0000	.0914	29.6	1	0	1	0	0	0	0	0	2	0	0	0	0	0	0	0	0	0	0	0	0	0	0	0	0
woodchuck's	4	.3741	.3712	35.7	1	0	1	0	0	0	0	2	2	0	0	0	0	0	0	1	0	0	0	0	0	0	0	1	0
woodchucks	6	.3489	.5194	37.2	0	0	1	0	4	0	1	0	3	0	1	0	0	0	0	0	0	0	0	0	0	1	0	1	0
woodcocks	2	.2387	.1089	30.4	1	0	0	0	1	0	0	0	0	0	0	0	0	0	0	0	1	0	0	0	1	0	0	0	0
woodcut	3	.0000	.0055	17.4	0	0	0	0	3	0	0	0	0	0	0	0	0	0	0	0	0	3	0	0	0	0	0	0	0
woodcutter	26	.2029	1.9279	42.9	8	7	0	11	0	0	0	0	24	0	0	2	0	0	0	0	0	0	0	0	0	0	0	0	0
Woodcutter	7	.0000	.0751	28.8	7	0	0	0	0	0	0	0	0	0	0	7	0	0	0	0	0	0	0	0	0	0	0	0	0
woodcutter's	4	.0000	.1827	32.6	1	2	0	1	0	0	0	0	4	0	0	0	0	0	0	0	0	0	0	0	0	0	0	0	0
Woodcutter's	3	.0000	.0322	25.1	3	0	0	0	0	0	0	0	0	0	0	3	0	0	0	0	0	0	0	0	0	0	0	0	0
wooded	26	.7208	3.8401	45.8	2	6	6	1	5	3	1	2	6	1	0	2	0	6	0	1	0	0	0	0	1	2	3	4	0
wooden	367	.8964	65.592	58.2	75	103	40	58	38	30	14	9	131	10	7	22	1	50	2	18	16	8	1	4	19	45	14	19	0
Woodhouse	2	.0000	.0914	29.6	0	0	2	0	0	0	0	0	2	0	0	0	0	0	0	0	0	0	0	0	0	0	0	0	0
woodland	33	.7734	5.1595	47.1	2	4	4	6	5	6	3	3	5	5	1	2	0	6	1	6	0	0	0	0	0	2	2	3	0
Woodland	2	.2152	.1357	31.3	1	1	0	0	0	0	0	0	1	0	0	0	0	1	0	0	0	0	0	0	0	0	0	0	0
woodlands	9	.5591	1.1046	40.4	1	3	0	3	1	1	0	0	4	0	0	1	0	2	0	1	0	0	0	0	0	0	1	0	0
Woodlands	4	.1112	.1666	32.2	3	1	0	0	0	0	0	0	1	0	0	0	0	0	0	0	0	0	0	0	0	3	0	0	0
Woodlawn	23	.1612	1.0963	40.4	0	0	4	18	1	0	0	0	5	0	0	1	0	0	0	0	0	0	0	0	17	0	0	0	0
Woodlawns	2	.1787	.1174	30.7	0	0	0	1	1	0	0	0	1	0	0	0	0	0	0	0	0	0	0	0	1	0	0	0	0
Woodman	3	.0000	.0322	25.1	0	0	0	0	0	0	3	0	0	0	0	3	0	0	0	0	0	0	0	0	0	0	0	0	0
Woodmont	13	.1013	.3949	36.0	0	0	0	0	12	0	1	0	0	0	0	1	0	0	0	0	0	0	0	0	12	0	0	0	0
woodpecker	19	.5651	2.3277	43.7	2	2	0	3	10	0	0	2	7	0	0	4	0	1	0	5	1	0	0	0	1	0	0	0	0
Woodpecker	3	.0939	.1398	31.5	0	2	0	0	0	1	0	0	2	0	0	0	0	0	0	0	0	1	0	0	0	0	0	0	0
woodpeckers	11	.3928	.9676	39.9	5	1	0	0	4	0	0	1	1	0	0	0	0	0	0	4	0	0	0	0	0	2	4	0	0

9Q Wohler
8B Woke
7N woked
7N wolf-fashion
XP wolf's
7C Wolfeboro
8Q Wolfenbuttel
7N wolfish
7D wolfishly
7Q wolflike
6Q Wollaston

XR wolverines
9D wolvish
9D wolvish-ravening
7R womanizing
4K womans's
9D WOMEN
7Q Women's
6N womenfolk
4F womeras
5R Wonder
4P wonder-box

5A wonder-wise
7R wonderfool
9D wonderful-looking
5A wonderin'
5F wonderlands
9B Wonderment
6R Wonderous
4Q Wonders
5N wonderwear
8C wonderworld
XN Wonka's

7N wonted
5A woo-woo
3A wood-and-metal
7R wood-based
9D wood-birds
7N wood-boats
8N wood-box
9C wood-carved
4A wood-chopper
4A wood-cutter
5J wood-cutter's

7R wood-grain
7R wood-lover
6P wood-nymph
6R wood-processing
7M wood-products
7A wood-stove
3A wood's
8F woodblock
5Q woodcarvers
3P woodcarving
7R woodchuck-hunting

4A woodcutters
7N wooden-headed
7H woodfrog
6R woodland-covered
5A woodland's
6N Woodlawn's
6D Woodlawns'
XP woodlore
7D woodman
7N Woodmontonian
4P Woodmouse

Word Type	F	D	U	SFI	3 Gr 3	4 Gr 4	5 Gr 5	6 Gr 6	7 Gr 7	8 Gr 8	9 Gr 9	X UnGr	A Read	B Eng & Gr	C Comp	D Lit	E Math	F Soc Stud	G Spell	H Sci	J Music	K Art	L Home Ec	M Shop	N Lib F	P Lib NF	Q Lib Ref	R Mag	S Rel
Woodpeckers	6	.0000	.0703	28.5	0	6	0	0	0	0	0	0	0	0	0	0	0	0	0	0	0	0	0	0	6	0	0	0	0
woodpeckers'	2	.0000	.0394	26.0	2	0	0	0	0	0	0	0	0	0	0	0	0	0	0	2	0	0	0	0	0	0	0	0	0
woodpile	8	.4529	.8226	39.2	0	5	0	0	0	2	0	1	3	1	0	1	0	0	0	0	0	0	0	0	0	3	0	0	0
Woodrow	15	.4178	1.3738	41.4	0	6	2	0	1	4	2	0	0	1	0	0	0	7	0	0	0	0	0	0	0	6	1	0	0
woods	557	.8933	99.194	60.0	145	131	70	44	91	37	19	20	191	28	10	52	2	23	11	41	13	5	1	12	63	76	8	21	0
Woods	40	.6941	5.6735	47.5	3	13	9	7	3	3	1	1	7	3	0	4	0	1	0	1	0	1	0	0	13	2	3	5	0
woodshed	7	.2423	.5283	37.2	3	2	0	0	2	0	0	0	5	0	0	0	0	0	0	0	0	0	0	0	0	2	0	0	0
woodsman	7	.5607	.8563	39.3	2	0	2	1	2	0	0	0	3	0	0	1	0	1	0	0	0	0	0	0	1	1	0	0	0
woodsmen	7	.6199	.9135	39.6	0	2	3	1	1	0	0	0	2	0	0	0	0	1	0	0	0	0	0	0	1	1	1	1	0
Woodstock	5	.0000	.0608	27.8	0	0	0	0	0	3	2	0	0	0	0	0	0	0	0	0	0	0	0	0	0	0	0	5	0
woodsy	5	.0000	.2284	33.6	0	0	5	0	0	0	0	0	5	0	0	0	0	0	0	0	0	0	0	0	0	0	0	0	0
woodwind	32	.0314	.4542	36.6	1	7	4	3	10	6	1	0	0	0	0	0	0	0	0	0	31	0	0	0	0	1	0	0	0
woodwinds	29	.0743	.6448	38.1	1	5	4	0	9	5	5	0	0	0	0	0	0	0	0	0	27	0	0	0	0	0	2	0	0
woodwork	4	.3763	.3344	35.2	0	0	0	1	1	2	0	0	1	0	0	0	0	0	0	0	0	0	1	1	0	0	1	0	0
woodworker	4	.2271	.2140	33.3	0	1	0	0	2	0	1	0	0	0	0	0	0	0	0	0	0	0	0	1	0	3	0	0	0
woodworkers	3	.0986	.0757	28.8	0	0	0	0	1	1	1	0	0	0	0	0	0	0	0	0	0	0	0	2	0	1	0	0	0
woodworking	23	.1375	.7934	39.0	0	3	0	0	14	3	3	0	1	0	0	0	0	1	0	0	0	0	0	14	0	6	0	1	0
woody	24	.5267	2.7403	44.4	4	0	4	5	9	1	1	0	5	0	0	0	0	1	0	12	0	0	1	0	0	0	4	1	0
Woody	14	.3344	1.3003	41.1	0	0	5	0	8	0	1	0	12	1	0	0	0	0	0	0	0	0	0	0	0	0	0	1	0
wooers	6	.1717	.3427	35.3	0	0	0	0	3	0	3	0	3	0	0	3	0	0	0	0	0	0	0	0	0	0	0	0	0
woof	3	.3427	.2477	33.9	2	1	0	0	0	0	0	0	1	0	0	0	0	0	0	0	0	0	0	0	1	0	0	1	0
Woof	2	.0000	.0243	23.9	2	0	0	0	0	0	0	0	0	0	0	0	0	0	0	0	0	0	0	0	0	0	0	2	0
wooing	2	.2297	.1135	30.6	0	0	1	0	0	0	1	0	0	0	0	1	0	1	0	0	0	0	0	0	0	0	0	0	0
wool	255	.6875	35.830	55.5	33	40	38	37	43	29	33	2	28	3	0	7	2	74	6	40	7	1	41	5	6	18	9	8	0
wool-like	2	.2106	.0917	29.6	0	0	0	0	0	1	1	0	0	0	0	0	0	0	1	0	0	0	1	0	0	0	0	0	0
woolen	42	.7146	6.1626	47.9	6	8	7	12	2	4	2	1	11	1	2	2	0	9	0	4	0	0	3	0	6	3	1	0	0
woolens	7	.2750	.4308	36.3	0	0	0	0	1	5	0	1	0	0	0	0	0	2	0	0	0	0	3	0	1	0	0	1	0
woolly	11	.5263	1.2741	41.1	2	4	1	1	3	0	0	0	5	0	0	1	0	0	0	0	1	1	0	0	0	1	0	2	0
Woolly	11	.0000	.5025	37.0	11	0	0	0	0	0	0	0	11	0	0	0	0	0	0	0	0	0	0	0	0	0	0	0	0
Woolworth	21	.0546	.5173	37.1	0	20	0	0	0	1	0	0	0	0	0	0	0	1	0	0	0	0	0	0	0	20	0	0	0
woosh	3	.1621	.1254	31.0	2	0	0	1	0	0	0	0	0	0	0	0	0	1	0	0	2	0	0	0	0	0	0	0	0
Wooster	10	.0000	.4568	36.6	0	0	0	10	0	0	0	0	10	0	0	0	0	0	0	0	0	0	0	0	0	0	0	0	0
Wooster's	3	.0000	.1370	31.4	0	0	0	3	0	0	0	0	3	0	0	0	0	0	0	0	0	0	0	0	0	0	0	0	0
Woozy	4	.0000	.0486	26.9	0	4	0	0	0	0	0	0	0	0	0	0	0	0	0	0	0	0	0	0	0	0	0	4	0
Worcester	3	.2445	.1818	32.6	0	0	1	0	2	0	0	0	0	0	0	0	0	0	0	2	0	0	0	0	0	0	1	0	0
Worcestershire	3	.1274	.0913	29.6	0	0	0	0	0	0	2	1	0	0	0	0	0	0	0	0	0	0	2	0	0	0	0	1	0
word	7532	.5197	829.53	69.2	1854	1276	1158	1084	1040	600	464	56	1518	1281	105	120	120	96	3782	101	82	12	7	3	65	103	63	69	5
Word	272	.1614	10.570	50.2	38	60	86	78	6	3	1	0	3	0	0	2	0	0	266	0	0	0	0	0	0	0	0	0	1
word-arithmetic	3	.0000	.0243	23.9	0	0	0	3	0	0	0	0	0	0	0	0	0	0	3	0	0	0	0	0	0	0	0	0	0
word-group	3	.0000	.0328	25.2	0	0	0	1	2	0	0	0	0	3	0	0	0	0	0	0	0	0	0	0	0	0	0	0	0
word's	2	.0000	.0219	23.4	0	0	1	0	1	0	0	0	0	2	0	0	0	0	0	0	0	0	0	0	0	0	0	0	0
wordbook	3	.0000	.1370	31.4	0	2	1	0	0	0	0	0	3	0	0	0	0	0	0	0	0	0	0	0	0	0	0	0	0
worded	2	.2306	.1140	30.6	0	0	0	1	0	1	0	0	0	1	0	0	0	1	0	0	0	0	0	0	0	0	0	0	0
wording	7	.4037	.6382	38.0	0	0	1	0	3	1	2	0	2	2	1	0	0	0	0	0	0	0	0	0	2	0	0	0	0
wordless	3	.2212	.2099	33.2	0	1	0	1	1	0	0	0	2	0	0	1	0	0	0	0	0	0	0	0	0	0	0	0	0
wordlessly	3	.2212	.2099	33.2	2	0	0	0	0	0	1	0	2	0	0	1	0	0	0	0	0	0	0	0	0	0	0	0	0
words	11215	.4756	1124.1	70.5	2206	2016	1897	1857	1692	928	568	51	1200	1930	183	192	154	93	6680	69	324	35	6	12	96	112	57	67	5
Words	492	.0312	6.9931	48.4	24	143	203	103	8	10	1	0	3	3	0	0	0	0	485	0	0	1	0	0	0	0	0	0	0
Wordsworth	6	.1575	.2401	33.8	0	0	0	0	2	3	1	0	0	1	0	5	0	0	0	0	0	0	0	0	0	0	0	0	0
wordy	3	.2124	.1442	31.6	0	0	0	0	1	2	0	0	0	2	1	0	0	0	0	0	0	0	0	0	0	0	0	0	0
wore	320	.8508	54.588	57.4	78	66	34	32	51	30	24	5	100	14	5	35	0	35	16	1	3	2	2	0	52	22	9	24	0
work	4358	.9716	834.67	69.2	844	715	551	542	711	470	419	106	975	195	36	145	324	661	137	462	149	69	65	149	195	324	230	237	5
Work	5	.3180	.3628	35.6	0	0	0	2	0	1	1	1	0	0	0	0	0	0	0	3	0	0	0	1	0	0	0	1	0
work's	3	.0000	.0322	25.1	0	0	0	0	3	0	0	0	0	0	0	3	0	0	0	0	0	0	0	0	0	0	0	0	0
workable	12	.6710	1.6501	42.2	0	1	1	2	3	3	1	1	2	0	0	0	0	1	0	1	1	0	1	1	0	1	1	3	0
workaday	3	.2060	.1500	31.8	1	1	0	0	0	0	1	0	0	0	0	2	0	0	0	0	0	0	0	0	0	1	0	0	0
workbasket	5	.0000	.0161	22.1	0	0	0	0	0	0	5	0	0	0	0	0	0	0	0	0	0	0	5	0	0	0	0	0	0
workbench	6	.4600	.5826	37.7	3	0	1	1	1	0	0	0	0	0	0	0	1	1	0	0	0	1	0	0	1	1	0	1	0
workbook	3	.1434	.1493	31.7	2	1	0	0	0	0	0	0	1	0	0	0	2	0	0	0	0	0	0	0	0	0	0	0	0
workday	2	.2408	.1204	30.8	1	0	1	0	0	0	0	0	0	0	0	0	0	1	0	0	0	0	0	0	0	1	0	0	0
worked	857	.9615	162.71	62.1	147	132	133	113	165	88	64	15	277	40	6	49	25	128	7	40	32	13	7	6	58	78	32	58	1
worked-out	3	.0000	.0449	26.5	0	0	0	0	0	0	0	3	0	0	0	0	3	0	0	0	0	0	0	0	0	0	0	0	0
worker	118	.8113	19.229	52.8	33	11	12	6	18	17	20	1	13	6	0	2	5	32	2	20	3	0	0	5	3	13	8	6	0
Worker	2	.0000	.0215	23.3	0	0	0	0	0	0	2	0	0	0	0	2	0	0	0	0	0	0	0	0	0	0	0	0	0
worker's	4	.3344	.3261	35.1	0	0	0	0	2	2	0	0	1	0	0	0	0	2	0	0	0	0	0	0	0	0	1	0	0
workers	476	.7572	72.988	58.6	96	38	78	72	68	64	56	4	39	10	2	3	5	241	7	32	10	1	1	13	4	43	41	24	0
Workers	5	.3184	.3581	35.5	0	0	1	0	1	0	3	0	0	0	0	0	0	1	0	0	0	0	0	0	0	0	1	3	0
workers'	4	.2183	.2285	33.6	0	0	1	2	0	1	0	0	0	0	0	0	0	3	0	0	0	0	0	0	0	1	0	0	0
Workers'	2	.0000	.0037	15.7	0	0	0	0	0	0	2	0	0	0	0	0	0	0	0	0	0	2	0	0	0	0	0	0	0
workhorse	3	.1277	.1363	31.3	0	1	0	0	2	0	0	0	1	0	0	0	0	0	0	0	0	0	0	0	0	0	0	2	0
workhouse	3	.0000	.1370	31.4	0	0	0	3	0	0	0	0	3	0	0	0	0	0	0	0	0	0	0	0	0	0	0	0	0
workin'	3	.0995	.1144	30.6	0	2	0	1	0	0	0	0	1	0	0	0	0	0	0	0	2	0	0	0	0	0	0	0	0
working	804	.9104	145.28	61.6	132	109	96	81	186	80	101	19	187	26	5	29	49	82	14	66	14	20	25	48	44	64	42	87	2
Working	11	.4226	.9703	39.9	1	3	0	0	1	6	0	0	0	2	0	0	0	0	4	0	4	0	0	0	1	0	0	0	0
workingmen	4	.3711	.3648	35.6	1	0	1	1	0	0	1	0	2	0	0	0	0	0	0	0	0	0	0	0	0	1	1	0	0
workings	12	.5213	1.3347	41.3	1	0	3	1	2	1	4	0	2	0	0	1	0	1	0	1	0	0	0	0	0	1	5	1	0
workman	17	.3755	1.5682	42.0	1	4	4	3	4	0	1	0	9	0	0	1	0	2	0	1	0	0	0	3	0	1	0	0	0
workmanship	13	.3795	1.0481	40.2	1	0	2	2	7	1	0	0	1	0	0	0	0	1	0	0	0	1	1	6	0	2	0	1	0
workmen	77	.7729	12.087	50.8	9	19	19	12	10	2	5	1	19	4	4	0	0	21	0	6	2	1	0	1	2	13	2	2	0
Workmen	2	.0000	.0215	23.3	0	0	0	0	2	0	0	0	0	0	0	2	0	0	0	0	0	0	0	0	0	0	0	0	0
workmen's	2	.1972	.1262	31.0	0	0	0	1	0	0	1	0	1	0	0	0	1	0	0	0	0	0	0	0	0	0	0	0	0
workout	10	.3764	.9244	39.7	2	1	1	0	3	2	1	0	5	0	0	0	0	0	0	0	0	0	0	0	0	3	0	2	0
workouts	7	.3507	.5432	37.3	0	0	1	0	6	0	0	0	0	0	0	0	0	0	0	0	0	0	0	0	2	4	0	1	0
workpiece	21	.1211	.6004	37.8	0	0	0	0	4	0	17	0	0	0	0	0	0	0	0	0	0	0	0	15	0	3	2	1	0
workroom	6	.4394	.6001	37.8	1	2	0	0	1	0	0	2	2	1	0	0	0	0	0	1	0	0	0	0	0	0	0	2	0
workrooms	2	.1698	.1133	30.5	0	0	1	0	0	0	1	0	1	0	0	0	0	0	0	0	0	0	0	0	0	0	1	0	0
works	485	.9262	88.903	59.5	73	64	83	48	75	69	60	13	68	36	6	7	24	44	5	71	59	8	5	9	6	32	64	40	1
Works	10	.5108	1.0867	40.4	2	1	1	0	2	2	1	1	1	0	0	0	0	3	0	0	1	0	0	0	0	0	2	3	0
workshop	23	.5642	2.7878	44.5	1	2	4	5	5	2	3	1	8	0	0	1	0	3	1	2	0	0	0	3	3	0	2	0	0
workshops	10	.4160	.9116	39.6	1	1	0	3	2	1	2	0	0	0	0	0	0	7	0	0	0	0	0	1	0	0	1	1	0
world	2799	.8817	491.79	66.9	399	374	410	426	541	355	208	86	567	108	42	132	58	609	19	258	117	33	18	8	106	247	291	173	13
World	584	.7242	86.087	59.3	57	41	130	97	109	87	53	10	67	19	1	6	3	208	4	16	23	1	0	1	3	71	108	53	0
world-famous	9	.4315	.8564	39.3	1	0	2	2	3	0	1	0	1	0	0	0	0	4	0	0	0	1	0	0	0	1	0	2	0

4N Woodpeckers'
3P woods-ward
7A woodshore
6A woodsmoke
7A woodswise
7R woodturning
5Q Woodville
6A Woodward's
8K WOODY
7A Woody's
3R Woodyard
5F wooed
4N WOOF
7R woofed
9C woofer
9P woofing
8A woofs
9L wool-Vicara-nylon
9L wool-nylon
4A wool-thick
9F wool-trader
9R Woolf
3A Woolly's
7R woolves
7Q Woolwich
4P Woolworth's
9D woos
9R Wooton
4R woozy
7R WORCESTERSHIRE
5Q word-abusers
7D word-bringer
8P word-elements
7P word-for-word
XB word-game
8G word-maker
8A word-recognition
6J word-rhythms
8G word-structure
XB word-study
8B word-twins
8B wordiness
7G wordmakers
4A work-filled
5P work-force
3A work-horses
6A work-raw
7G work-study
9M work-up
9L workbaskets
3P WORKBENCH
9R Workhorse
6A workhouse'll
8F working-class
3F Workman's
8M workmanlike
4R workmates
7N Workmen's
6A WORKS
XR Workshop
4A worktable
8L worktables
3R WORLD
6R world-champion
8A world-championship
7P world-class
9J world-end
8F world-renowned

Word Type	F	D	U	SFI	3 Gr 3	4 Gr 4	5 Gr 5	6 Gr 6	7 Gr 7	8 Gr 8	9 Gr 9	X UnGr	A Read	B Eng & Gr	C Comp	D Lit	E Math	F Soc Stud	G Spell	H Sci	J Music	K Art	L Home Ec	M Shop	N Lib F	P Lib NF	Q Lib Ref	R Mag	S Rel
world-wide	13	.6781	1.8033	42.6	0	1	4	1	2	2	2	1	1	0	0	0	0	1	0	3	1	0	0	0	1	3	2	1	0
world's	284	.6915	40.389	56.1	20	26	43	47	66	29	43	10	48	7	0	1	17	100	0	8	5	1	0	0	0	19	49	29	0
World's	13	.6541	1.7835	42.5	3	0	3	1	4	2	0	0	5	0	0	0	2	1	0	0	1	0	0	1	0	1	1	1	0
worldly	12	.6239	1.5452	41.9	1	0	0	0	6	3	1	1	2	2	0	0	0	1	0	0	2	1	0	0	2	0	1	1	0
worlds	35	.6305	4.5858	46.6	4	1	4	9	13	1	0	3	6	0	0	0	0	5	0	4	0	2	0	0	1	4	4	9	0
Worlds	6	.2899	.4148	36.2	0	0	0	1	1	1	3	0	1	3	0	0	0	0	0	0	0	0	0	0	0	0	0	2	0
worldwide	11	.4454	1.0442	40.2	0	0	3	1	4	0	3	0	0	0	0	0	0	0	0	2	0	0	0	0	0	2	4	3	0
worm	73	.7564	11.280	50.5	33	6	3	8	13	2	7	1	22	3	0	2	2	5	0	13	0	0	0	0	10	8	6	2	0
Worm	2	.1698	.1133	30.5	1	0	1	0	0	0	0	0	1	0	0	0	0	0	0	0	0	0	0	0	0	0	1	0	0
wormed	2	.0000	.0290	24.6	1	1	0	0	0	0	0	0	0	0	0	0	0	0	0	0	0	0	0	0	0	2	0	0	0
wormlike	6	.3813	.5106	37.1	3	0	0	0	1	1	1	0	0	0	0	0	0	0	0	3	0	0	0	0	0	2	1	0	0
worms	119	.6769	16.737	52.2	37	9	7	12	35	8	10	1	29	3	1	9	0	8	0	45	0	0	0	0	1	14	9	0	0
worn	216	.7874	34.369	55.4	20	37	40	24	37	24	32	2	52	15	1	17	0	19	4	29	4	1	23	0	17	19	8	7	0
worn-down	3	.3676	.2407	33.8	0	1	0	0	2	0	0	0	0	0	0	0	0	1	1	0	0	0	0	0	0	0	1	0	0
worn-out	6	.5553	.7208	38.6	2	1	1	1	0	0	0	1	2	1	0	0	0	1	0	0	0	0	0	0	0	1	0	1	0
worried	176	.7234	26.503	54.2	31	55	26	19	18	22	4	1	94	5	3	10	0	9	1	1	0	0	0	0	16	28	1	8	0
worriedly	2	.1814	.1187	30.7	1	1	0	0	0	0	0	0	1	0	0	0	0	0	0	0	0	0	0	0	0	0	0	1	0
worries	23	.7138	3.3453	45.2	2	3	5	1	7	1	4	0	4	0	0	3	0	2	3	1	0	0	0	0	3	1	3	3	0
worrisome	2	.0000	.0215	23.3	0	0	0	0	0	0	2	0	0	0	0	2	0	0	0	0	0	0	0	0	0	0	0	0	0
worry	214	.7538	33.240	55.2	47	60	14	22	28	26	16	1	107	3	0	15	3	8	4	4	0	0	6	0	20	33	1	10	0
worrying	33	.7602	5.1562	47.1	6	3	2	5	10	3	4	0	16	2	1	3	0	1	0	3	0	0	1	0	3	1	0	2	0
worse	180	.8291	30.051	54.8	26	23	21	24	44	16	23	3	60	11	1	21	0	12	5	3	1	0	3	0	22	18	4	19	0
worsened	4	.3602	.3543	35.5	0	0	0	0	2	1	1	0	2	0	0	0	0	0	1	0	0	0	0	0	1	0	0	0	0
worship	95	.4487	9.2261	49.7	10	13	22	14	8	17	11	0	10	1	0	1	0	34	1	0	22	6	0	0	0	5	9	3	3
worship's	2	.0000	.0215	23.3	0	0	0	0	0	0	2	0	0	0	0	2	0	0	0	0	0	0	0	0	0	0	0	0	0
worshiped	15	.5252	1.7098	42.3	1	1	1	7	2	3	0	0	3	1	0	0	0	8	0	0	0	0	0	0	1	1	1	0	0
worshiper	3	.3270	.2028	33.1	0	0	0	0	1	1	1	0	0	0	0	0	0	0	0	0	0	1	0	1	0	0	1	0	0
worshipers	7	.5002	.7449	38.7	0	1	1	0	4	0	1	0	1	2	0	1	0	0	0	0	0	0	0	0	0	1	2	0	0
worshiping	7	.5150	.7469	38.7	1	0	1	0	1	3	1	0	0	1	0	0	0	1	0	0	2	0	0	0	1	0	2	0	0
worshipped	7	.4524	.6741	38.3	1	0	1	2	1	2	0	0	0	0	0	0	0	3	0	0	1	1	0	0	1	1	0	0	0
worst	108	.8284	17.996	52.6	14	11	15	8	24	11	21	4	33	4	0	13	0	6	4	3	0	1	0	1	15	8	10	10	0
worsted	6	.2257	.3132	35.0	0	0	1	0	1	1	3	0	1	0	1	0	0	0	0	0	0	0	4	0	0	0	0	0	0
worsteds	3	.0953	.0796	29.0	0	0	0	0	1	2	0	0	0	0	0	0	0	1	0	0	0	0	2	0	0	0	0	0	0
wort	2	.1733	.1149	30.6	1	1	0	0	0	0	0	0	1	1	0	0	0	0	0	0	0	0	0	0	0	0	0	0	0
worth	327	.9089	59.069	57.7	63	47	48	37	55	34	34	9	91	11	7	25	62	24	3	15	6	1	3	2	18	22	9	28	0
Worth	7	.4383	.6908	38.4	1	0	2	0	0	0	4	0	2	1	0	1	0	0	0	0	0	0	0	0	0	3	0	0	0
worthless	20	.7559	3.0688	44.9	1	3	5	2	3	2	2	2	4	1	1	0	0	2	1	3	0	0	0	0	3	2	1	2	0
worthwhile	26	.6150	3.2901	45.2	0	5	4	2	7	2	5	1	3	4	2	0	0	4	0	2	0	0	5	1	0	1	0	4	0
worthy	51	.5927	6.2922	48.0	3	3	7	6	14	7	10	1	8	2	0	5	0	3	0	1	4	1	0	1	13	5	1	6	1
Wortman	2	.0000	.0234	23.7	0	0	0	0	0	2	0	0	0	0	0	0	0	0	0	0	0	0	0	0	2	0	0	0	0
wot	5	.4766	.5354	37.3	0	0	1	0	2	1	1	0	2	0	0	1	0	0	0	0	0	0	0	0	1	1	0	0	0
Wou-Chiang	5	.0000	.2284	33.6	0	0	5	0	0	0	0	0	5	0	0	0	0	0	0	0	0	0	0	0	0	0	0	0	0
would	11188	.9685	2137.7	73.3	1809	2043	1335	1545	2054	1298	846	258	3592	622	91	839	609	1042	186	990	198	71	69	62	1038	891	279	600	9
Would	3	.0000	.1370	31.4	0	2	0	0	1	0	0	0	3	0	0	0	0	0	0	0	0	0	0	0	0	0	0	0	0
would-be	14	.5162	1.5318	41.9	0	0	0	0	8	1	3	2	2	1	0	4	0	0	0	0	0	0	0	0	0	1	1	5	0
wouldn't	642	.7059	93.884	59.7	124	160	75	58	131	51	32	11	255	16	2	75	4	9	2	8	1	1	1	0	134	76	3	55	0
wound	161	.8171	26.473	54.2	12	17	22	32	31	29	15	3	44	4	1	25	0	5	7	22	2	1	3	12	15	9	4	7	0
wounded	82	.7030	12.000	50.8	3	15	15	8	22	13	6	0	35	3	0	5	0	13	0	0	0	0	0	0	2	10	8	6	0
wounding	4	.4812	.4077	36.1	0	1	0	1	1	1	0	0	0	0	0	1	0	1	0	0	0	0	0	0	0	1	0	1	0
wounds	47	.5611	5.6572	47.5	1	6	3	7	10	16	2	2	15	2	1	6	0	1	1	7	1	0	2	0	3	4	1	2	1
wove	29	.7517	4.4593	46.5	5	2	8	9	3	0	1	1	10	2	1	2	0	5	0	0	0	0	0	0	2	2	3	2	0
woven	84	.6522	11.259	50.5	10	12	11	12	13	19	7	0	11	0	0	3	1	25	0	5	5	2	16	1	2	6	5	2	0
woven-wire	2	.0000	.0914	29.6	2	0	0	0	0	0	0	0	2	0	0	0	0	0	0	0	0	0	0	0	0	0	0	0	0
wow	27	.6117	3.5418	45.5	9	9	0	5	3	0	1	0	13	0	1	4	1	1	0	0	0	0	0	0	0	2	0	5	0
Wow	2	.0000	.0243	23.9	0	1	0	0	1	0	0	0	0	0	0	0	0	0	0	0	0	0	0	0	0	0	0	2	0
WOW	2	.2433	.1158	30.6	2	0	0	0	0	0	0	0	0	0	0	0	0	0	0	0	0	0	0	0	0	1	0	1	0
wowser	6	.0000	.2741	34.4	5	0	0	1	0	0	0	0	6	0	0	0	0	0	0	0	0	0	0	0	0	0	0	0	0
Wowser	2	.0000	.0215	23.3	0	0	0	0	2	0	0	0	0	0	0	2	0	0	0	0	0	0	0	0	0	0	0	0	0
Wowser's	2	.0000	.0215	23.3	0	0	0	0	2	0	0	0	0	0	0	2	0	0	0	0	0	0	0	0	0	0	0	0	0
Wowunupo	4	.0000	.0778	28.9	0	0	0	0	0	4	0	0	0	0	0	0	0	4	0	0	0	0	0	0	0	0	0	0	0
WPA	2	.0000	.0389	25.9	0	0	0	0	0	2	0	0	0	0	0	0	0	2	0	0	0	0	0	0	0	0	0	0	0
wr	4	.2408	.2182	33.4	3	0	1	0	0	0	0	0	0	2	0	0	0	0	2	0	0	0	0	0	0	0	0	0	0
wracked	2	.2337	.1157	30.6	0	0	0	0	1	1	0	0	0	0	0	0	0	1	0	0	0	0	0	0	1	0	0	0	0
wrangler	6	.3339	.4492	36.5	0	0	2	0	3	0	0	1	0	0	0	3	0	2	0	0	0	0	0	0	0	0	0	1	0
wrap	71	.7930	11.283	50.5	19	26	6	2	3	8	5	2	5	4	0	5	3	3	4	12	0	4	5	1	6	16	2	1	0
wrapped	149	.8704	25.947	54.1	25	26	21	19	25	15	15	3	54	6	2	13	3	7	1	10	3	2	12	2	10	10	6	8	0
wrapper	9	.5034	.9920	40.0	2	2	1	0	3	0	1	0	3	0	0	2	0	1	0	0	0	0	1	0	2	0	0	0	0
wrappers	3	.3773	.2505	34.0	1	1	0	1	0	0	0	0	0	0	0	1	1	1	0	0	0	0	0	0	0	0	0	0	0
wrapping	31	.7417	4.6665	46.7	7	6	3	4	5	2	3	1	6	1	1	0	1	0	0	7	0	1	2	3	2	4	0	3	0
wrappings	8	.4643	.7590	38.8	0	2	1	0	0	1	3	1	0	0	0	1	0	0	0	0	1	1	3	0	1	0	0	1	0
wraps	12	.4651	1.2256	40.9	2	3	2	1	1	0	3	0	3	0	0	2	0	0	0	2	0	0	2	0	0	0	0	3	0
wrasse	2	.0000	.0209	23.2	0	0	0	0	2	0	0	0	0	0	0	0	0	0	0	0	0	0	0	0	0	0	2	0	0
wrath	17	.6344	2.2838	43.6	0	0	0	4	8	5	0	0	7	1	0	3	0	1	0	0	0	0	0	0	1	3	0	1	0
wreath	19	.5391	2.1987	43.4	1	7	1	6	2	1	0	1	6	0	1	1	0	0	0	0	6	0	0	0	0	3	0	2	0
wreathed	2	.2440	.1132	30.5	0	0	0	1	1	0	0	0	0	0	0	1	0	0	0	0	0	0	0	0	0	0	0	1	0
wreaths	8	.4030	.7277	38.6	3	3	0	1	0	0	1	0	2	0	1	0	0	0	0	0	0	0	0	0	3	2	0	0	0
wreck	75	.7042	11.092	50.5	6	36	4	9	8	6	5	1	45	2	1	5	0	2	2	0	0	0	0	0	10	4	0	4	0
wreckage	17	.6813	2.4204	43.8	0	3	4	3	4	1	2	0	7	1	0	2	0	1	0	1	0	0	0	0	0	1	1	3	0
wrecked	28	.7297	4.2425	46.3	1	9	9	2	3	1	2	1	14	1	0	2	0	4	0	1	0	0	0	0	2	1	1	2	0
wreckers	3	.1187	.1291	31.1	1	0	0	0	0	2	0	0	1	0	0	2	0	0	0	0	0	0	0	0	0	0	0	0	0
wreckfish	2	.0000	.0209	23.2	0	0	0	0	2	0	0	0	0	0	0	0	0	0	0	0	0	0	0	0	0	0	2	0	0
wrecking	10	.5513	1.1869	40.7	0	3	0	0	0	2	4	1	3	0	0	3	0	1	0	1	0	0	0	0	1	0	1	0	0
wrecks	6	.5438	.6764	38.3	1	2	0	1	1	0	1	0	0	1	0	1	0	1	0	0	0	0	0	0	1	0	0	2	0
wren	16	.5038	1.8261	42.6	9	2	0	1	0	2	2	0	9	4	0	1	0	0	0	0	0	0	0	0	1	0	1	0	0
Wren	6	.1358	.2190	33.4	1	0	0	0	5	0	0	0	0	0	0	5	0	0	0	0	0	0	0	0	0	1	0	0	0
wrench	24	.3416	1.8277	42.6	5	0	1	2	10	1	5	0	5	1	2	1	0	0	1	0	0	0	0	11	1	1	0	1	0
wrenched	13	.6157	1.7085	42.3	0	2	1	3	4	2	1	0	6	2	0	1	0	0	0	0	0	0	0	0	2	0	1	1	0
wrenches	2	.1387	.0689	28.4	1	0	1	0	0	0	0	0	0	0	1	0	0	0	0	0	0	0	0	0	0	1	0	0	0
wrenching	3	.2283	.1611	32.1	0	1	0	1	0	0	0	1	0	1	0	0	0	0	0	0	0	0	0	0	2	0	0	0	0
wrens	8	.4589	.8346	39.2	5	1	0	1	1	0	0	0	3	0	0	0	0	0	0	2	0	0	0	0	1	0	2	0	0
wrest	4	.4560	.4041	36.1	0	0	1	0	2	1	0	0	1	0	0	0	0	0	0	0	0	0	0	0	1	1	0	1	0
wrested	2	.1733	.1149	30.6	0	0	0	1	0	0	1	0	1	1	0	0	0	0	0	0	0	0	0	0	0	0	0	0	0
wrestle	8	.6648	1.1028	40.4	0	1	0	5	0	2	0	0	2	1	0	1	0	1	0	1	1	0	0	0	1	0	0	0	0
wrestled	15	.6178	1.9702	42.9	4	2	1	2	3	3	0	0	6	0	1	1	0	2	0	0	0	0	0	0	2	2	0	1	0

7Q worlde
XR Worley's
3H Worm-Walk
8D worm-eaten
3Q worm-like
8H worm's
7P wormeaten
5A worming
4J Wormwood
5A wormy
7N worn-toothed
6G worning
3A worried-looking
7D worriment
8B worryin'
9B worser
9Q Worship
6P worshipper
9R worst-polluted
9D worthier
7N Worthing
7A Worthmores
8N Wortman's
6J Wotan
6J Wotan's
8D wott
9A would've
7R woulda
5N wouldst
3P Wound
7Q wound-healing
6H wound-up
4A Wounds
6D Wouser
7D wouye
5R wowed
8F wowi
3A wowser's
3A wowsers
9D WQXR
7Q wrack
6R wracking
5B wraith-like
7A wraithlike
5F Wrangell
8F wrangle
3N Wranglers
5P wrangling
7Q wrasse's
7Q wrasses
9D Wrath
8D wrathfully
8F wrathy
5R wreak
5N wreaked
9B Wreck
5A WRECKS
XR wren's
7D Wren's
4P Wrentham

Word Type	F	D	U	SFI	3 Gr 3	4 Gr 4	5 Gr 5	6 Gr 6	7 Gr 7	8 Gr 8	9 Gr 9	X UnGr
wrestler	11	.2230	.6550	38.2	3	7	0	0	0	0	1	0
wrestlers	3	.1548	.1479	31.7	0	0	0	0	2	1	0	0
wrestles	3	.2321	.1635	32.1	0	0	0	0	1	0	1	1
wrestling	10	.4690	1.0718	40.3	0	1	2	1	2	4	0	0
wretched	21	.5461	2.3950	43.8	2	2	3	2	4	3	4	1
wriggle	4	.4514	.4045	36.1	2	0	0	1	1	0	0	0
wriggled	36	.6040	4.7202	46.7	17	2	4	6	3	1	2	1
wriggles	2	.2278	.1128	30.5	1	0	0	0	1	0	0	0
wriggling	18	.5796	2.2077	43.4	2	3	3	2	4	4	0	0
wriggly	4	.2405	.2474	33.9	2	1	1	0	0	0	0	0
Wright	99	.7599	15.426	51.9	9	35	7	8	20	17	3	0
Wright-Humason	3	.0000	.1370	31.4	0	0	3	0	0	0	0	0
Wright's	5	.4758	.5330	37.3	0	0	0	0	1	4	0	0
Wrights	5	.2326	.3837	35.8	1	1	0	2	1	0	0	0
Wrights'	2	.2446	.1123	30.5	0	0	0	0	0	1	1	0
Wrigley	2	.0000	.0290	24.6	2	0	0	0	0	0	0	0
wring	6	.6041	.7607	38.8	0	1	1	1	1	0	1	1
wringing	9	.6157	1.1736	40.7	1	0	1	4	1	0	1	1
wrinkle	8	.1927	.3915	35.9	1	2	0	0	0	3	1	1
wrinkle-resistant	2	.2106	.0917	29.6	0	0	0	0	0	1	1	0
wrinkled	55	.7910	8.8509	49.5	11	13	3	8	10	5	4	1
wrinkles	25	.4914	2.6101	44.2	4	0	5	0	5	1	8	2
wrinkling	11	.3756	.9608	39.8	1	1	0	0	5	1	3	0
wrist	61	.8362	10.238	50.1	9	9	4	11	11	6	9	2
wrists	17	.6672	2.3372	43.7	1	6	4	1	3	1	1	0
wristwatch	2	.1605	.0742	28.7	0	0	0	1	0	0	1	0
writ	10	.4548	.9788	39.9	2	0	0	0	4	0	4	0
write	9846	.4798	994.25	70.0	2317	1874	1889	1508	1216	617	399	26
Write	3	.0000	.0328	25.2	0	0	1	0	2	0	0	0
writer	279	.4355	26.633	54.3	9	38	29	8	65	60	64	6
writer's	25	.2474	1.4537	41.6	0	1	1	1	5	4	13	0
writers	141	.8078	22.833	53.6	15	12	36	9	21	18	26	4
Writers'	6	.0000	.0869	29.4	0	0	0	0	6	0	0	0
writes	70	.7015	9.9557	50.0	14	10	2	4	14	17	8	1
writhed	6	.3615	.4852	36.9	0	0	0	1	2	2	1	0
writhing	9	.4663	.9526	39.8	0	0	0	2	2	2	3	0
writin'	2	.0000	.0914	29.6	0	2	0	0	0	0	0	0
writing	1131	.7377	168.55	62.3	95	148	146	130	268	164	162	18
Writing	13	.3257	.9128	39.6	1	0	1	2	3	6	0	0
writings	51	.6541	6.8469	48.4	0	0	10	10	3	21	5	2
written	1134	.7700	175.53	62.4	142	163	153	192	187	162	118	17
written-over	2	.0000	.0162	22.1	0	0	0	0	1	1	0	0
Wroclaw	2	.0000	.0389	25.9	0	0	0	2	0	0	0	0
wrong	606	.9125	109.87	60.4	107	103	61	61	112	74	75	13
wrongdoer	2	.1717	.1142	30.6	0	0	0	0	2	0	0	0
wrongdoings	2	.0000	.0914	29.6	0	0	2	0	0	0	0	0
wronged	7	.2856	.5277	37.2	0	0	0	2	1	1	3	0
wrongly	3	.3406	.2461	33.9	0	0	1	0	0	0	1	1
wrongs	7	.5035	.7738	38.9	1	0	0	2	3	1	0	0
wrote	877	.8400	147.08	61.7	178	141	150	106	118	113	55	16
wrought	30	.6876	4.2296	46.3	4	1	2	0	8	4	9	2
wrought-iron	6	.4253	.5363	37.3	0	0	0	1	4	1	0	0
wrung	7	.5626	.8592	39.3	0	2	1	1	2	0	1	0
wry	6	.5577	.7197	38.6	0	0	1	1	1	2	1	0
wryly	3	.3847	.2496	34.0	0	0	0	1	1	0	1	0
Ws	2	.0000	.0243	23.9	0	0	0	0	0	0	0	2
Wubber	2	.0000	.0290	24.6	2	0	0	0	0	0	0	0
Wulbari	6	.0000	.0644	28.1	0	0	0	0	6	0	0	0
WUV	2	.0000	.0299	24.8	0	0	2	0	0	0	0	0
wuz	4	.2065	.1985	33.0	0	0	1	0	3	0	0	0
ww	2	.0000	.0394	26.0	0	0	0	2	0	0	0	0
WW	3	.2371	.1813	32.6	0	0	0	2	0	1	0	0
WXB	6	.0000	.0657	28.2	0	0	0	0	0	0	6	0
WXN	2	.0000	.0914	29.6	0	0	0	0	0	2	0	0
WXY	5	.2414	.3872	35.9	0	1	0	0	0	4	0	0
Wyandottes	2	.0000	.0215	23.3	0	0	0	0	2	0	0	0
Wycherly	3	.0000	.0322	25.1	0	0	0	0	3	0	0	0
Wylie	2	.1378	.0662	28.2	0	0	0	0	0	1	1	0
Wynn	2	.0000	.0243	23.9	0	0	0	0	1	0	1	0
Wyo	2	.0000	.0243	23.9	0	0	0	1	1	0	0	0
Wyoming	59	.6243	7.7220	48.9	8	10	20	5	5	9	0	2
Wyoming's	2	.2337	.1157	30.6	0	1	1	0	0	0	0	0
x	1141	.2928	77.489	58.9	113	97	137	234	119	217	212	12
X	156	.7160	22.758	53.6	17	14	20	18	26	33	27	1
x-axis	7	.0000	.1048	30.2	0	0	0	0	0	0	7	0
x-intercepts	7	.0000	.1048	30.2	0	0	0	0	0	0	7	0
x-ray	2	.2391	.1133	30.5	1	0	0	0	0	0	0	1
X-ray	21	.6043	2.6280	44.2	2	3	1	3	4	2	5	1
X-rays	12	.2607	.7086	38.5	0	0	1	1	4	3	3	0
x-segments	2	.0000	.0299	24.8	0	0	2	0	0	0	0	0
x-y	2	.0000	.0299	24.8	0	0	0	0	0	2	0	0
x/y	4	.0000	.0599	27.8	0	0	4	0	0	0	0	0
x's	4	.0000	.0599	27.8	0	1	2	0	0	1	0	0
X's	2	.0000	.0299	24.8	2	0	0	0	0	0	0	0
xanthate	2	.0000	.0394	26.0	0	0	0	0	0	0	2	0
xenon	3	.0000	.0591	27.7	0	0	0	0	2	1	0	0
Xerxes	11	.4484	1.1963	40.8	1	5	0	0	5	0	0	0
Xerxes'	4	.0000	.1827	32.6	0	4	0	0	0	0	0	0
XI	6	.0000	.0898	29.5	4	1	0	0	1	0	0	0
XII	6	.3337	.4486	36.5	2	0	0	0	1	2	0	1
XIII	3	.1434	.1493	31.7	1	1	0	0	0	1	0	0
Xingo	5	.0000	.2284	33.6	0	0	5	0	0	0	0	0

Word Type	A Read	B Eng & Gr	C Comp	D Lit	E Math	F Soc Stud	G Spell	H Sci	J Music	K Art	L Home Ec	M Shop	N Lib F	P Lib NF	Q Lib Ref	R Mag	S Rel
wrestler	3	0	0	7	0	0	0	0	0	0	0	0	0	0	1	0	0
wrestlers	1	0	0	0	0	1	0	0	0	1	0	0	0	0	0	0	0
wrestles	0	0	0	0	0	0	0	0	0	0	0	0	0	0	1	2	0
wrestling	5	0	0	2	0	0	0	0	0	0	0	0	0	0	2	1	0
wretched	1	2	0	8	0	3	0	1	0	0	0	0	0	3	0	3	0
wriggle	1	0	0	1	0	0	0	1	0	0	0	0	0	1	0	0	0
wriggled	20	2	0	3	0	0	0	3	0	0	0	0	5	3	0	0	0
wriggles	0	0	0	0	0	0	0	1	0	0	0	0	0	0	1	0	0
wriggling	5	1	2	2	0	0	0	2	0	0	0	0	4	0	1	1	0
wriggly	1	0	1	0	0	0	0	0	0	0	0	0	0	2	0	0	0
Wright	42	13	0	3	0	11	1	5	0	2	0	0	1	3	8	10	0
Wright-Humason	3	0	0	0	0	0	0	0	0	0	0	0	0	0	0	0	0
Wright's	2	1	0	0	0	0	0	0	0	0	0	0	0	0	1	1	0
Wrights	4	0	0	0	0	1	0	0	0	0	0	0	0	0	0	0	0
Wrights'	0	1	0	0	0	0	0	0	0	0	0	0	0	0	1	0	0
Wrigley	0	0	0	0	0	0	0	0	0	0	0	0	0	2	0	0	0
wring	1	0	0	1	0	1	0	1	0	0	0	0	0	1	0	1	0
wringing	3	1	0	0	0	1	0	0	0	0	0	0	1	2	0	1	0
wrinkle	1	0	0	0	0	2	0	0	0	0	4	0	0	0	0	1	0
wrinkle-resistant	0	0	0	0	0	0	1	0	0	0	1	0	0	0	0	0	0
wrinkled	23	5	0	7	0	0	1	4	1	1	1	0	4	7	0	1	0
wrinkles	3	1	0	2	0	0	0	5	0	0	6	0	4	1	0	3	0
wrinkling	4	0	0	0	0	0	1	0	0	0	3	0	2	1	0	0	0
wrist	16	1	2	6	5	1	1	10	1	1	2	0	2	2	0	11	0
wrists	3	0	0	2	2	0	0	3	1	1	0	0	0	3	0	2	0
wristwatch	0	1	1	0	0	0	0	0	0	0	0	0	0	0	0	0	0
writ	1	0	0	4	0	0	0	0	0	0	0	0	1	3	0	1	0
write	757	1116	164	71	1922	107	5344	92	90	4	8	3	29	78	19	37	5
Write	0	3	0	0	0	0	0	0	0	0	0	0	0	0	0	0	0
writer	65	79	66	9	1	9	2	3	3	1	0	0	1	16	11	13	0
writer's	4	6	11	1	0	0	1	0	0	0	0	0	0	1	1	0	0
writers	19	29	2	6	0	14	6	1	7	2	0	0	1	25	20	9	0
Writers'	0	0	0	0	0	0	0	0	0	0	0	0	0	6	0	0	0
writes	8	15	6	4	3	1	3	3	11	0	0	0	1	4	1	10	0
writhed	1	0	1	3	0	0	0	0	0	0	0	0	0	0	0	1	0
writhing	4	0	0	2	0	0	0	0	0	0	0	0	2	0	0	1	0
writin'	2	0	0	0	0	0	0	0	0	0	0	0	0	0	0	0	0
writing	174	267	102	46	100	32	197	11	64	14	3	5	16	40	24	36	0
Writing	0	3	0	0	0	0	8	0	0	0	0	0	1	0	1	0	0
writings	5	2	0	3	1	11	1	4	1	0	0	1	1	0	20	1	0
written	134	241	18	28	133	67	173	13	205	3	1	4	15	29	40	30	0
written-over	0	0	0	0	0	0	2	0	0	0	0	0	0	0	0	0	0
Wroclaw	0	0	0	0	0	2	0	0	0	0	0	0	0	0	0	0	0
wrong	195	59	5	42	29	27	19	36	9	2	36	3	57	38	8	40	1
wrongdoer	1	0	0	1	0	0	0	0	0	0	0	0	0	0	0	0	0
wrongdoings	2	0	0	0	0	0	0	0	0	0	0	0	0	0	0	0	0
wronged	3	0	0	3	0	1	0	0	0	0	0	0	0	0	0	0	0
wrongly	1	1	0	0	0	0	0	0	0	0	0	0	0	0	0	1	0
wrongs	2	0	0	0	0	1	0	1	0	0	0	0	0	0	2	1	0
wrote	127	90	10	18	81	72	138	19	123	0	1	0	18	63	70	46	1
wrought	7	2	0	7	0	0	0	0	1	0	0	2	5	2	2	2	0
wrought-iron	0	0	1	0	0	1	0	0	0	0	0	1	0	0	0	3	0
wrung	3	0	0	0	0	1	0	0	0	0	0	0	1	1	0	1	0
wry	2	0	0	1	0	0	0	0	0	0	0	0	1	1	0	1	0
wryly	0	0	0	0	0	0	0	0	0	0	0	0	0	1	1	1	0
Ws	0	0	0	0	0	0	0	0	0	0	0	0	0	0	0	2	0
Wubber	0	0	0	0	0	0	0	0	0	0	0	0	0	2	0	0	0
Wulbari	0	0	0	6	0	0	0	0	0	0	0	0	0	0	0	0	0
WUV	0	0	0	0	2	0	0	0	0	0	0	0	0	0	0	0	0
wuz	0	0	0	0	0	0	0	0	0	0	0	0	3	0	1	0	0
ww	0	0	0	0	0	0	0	2	0	0	0	0	0	0	0	0	0
WW	0	0	0	0	1	0	0	2	0	0	0	0	0	0	0	0	0
WXB	0	6	0	0	0	0	0	0	0	0	0	0	0	0	0	0	0
WXN	2	0	0	0	0	0	0	0	0	0	0	0	0	0	0	0	0
WXY	4	0	0	0	1	0	0	0	0	0	0	0	0	0	0	0	0
Wyandottes	0	0	0	2	0	0	0	0	0	0	0	0	0	0	0	0	0
Wycherly	0	0	0	3	0	0	0	0	0	0	0	0	0	0	0	0	0
Wylie	0	0	0	0	0	0	0	0	0	1	0	0	0	0	0	1	0
Wynn	0	0	0	0	0	0	0	0	0	0	0	0	0	0	0	2	0
Wyo	0	0	0	0	0	0	0	0	0	0	0	0	0	0	0	2	0
Wyoming	11	3	0	0	2	22	0	3	0	0	0	0	0	8	1	9	0
Wyoming's	0	0	0	0	0	1	0	0	0	0	0	0	1	0	0	0	0
x	7	7	1	2	1047	0	24	11	1	1	10	18	0	6	0	6	0
X	22	14	4	0	69	0	4	18	1	0	0	4	2	3	6	9	0
x-axis	0	0	0	0	7	0	0	0	0	0	0	0	0	0	0	0	0
x-intercepts	0	0	0	0	7	0	0	0	0	0	0	0	0	0	0	0	0
x-ray	0	0	0	0	1	0	0	0	0	0	0	0	0	0	1	0	0
X-ray	1	0	1	0	0	1	0	7	0	0	0	0	0	3	4	4	0
X-rays	0	0	0	0	0	0	0	1	0	0	0	1	0	0	10	0	0
x-segments	0	0	0	0	2	0	0	0	0	0	0	0	0	0	0	0	0
x-y	0	0	0	0	2	0	0	0	0	0	0	0	0	0	0	0	0
x/y	0	0	0	0	4	0	0	0	0	0	0	0	0	0	0	0	0
x's	0	0	0	0	4	0	0	0	0	0	0	0	0	0	0	0	0
X's	0	0	0	0	2	0	0	0	0	0	0	0	0	0	0	0	0
xanthate	0	0	0	0	0	0	0	2	0	0	0	0	0	0	0	0	0
xenon	0	0	0	0	0	0	0	3	0	0	0	0	0	0	0	0	0
Xerxes	8	0	0	0	0	1	0	0	0	0	0	0	0	1	0	1	0
Xerxes'	4	0	0	0	0	0	0	0	0	0	0	0	0	0	0	0	0
XI	0	0	0	0	6	0	0	0	0	0	0	0	0	0	0	0	0
XII	0	0	0	1	4	0	0	0	0	0	0	0	0	0	0	1	0
XIII	1	0	0	0	2	0	0	0	0	0	0	0	0	0	0	0	0
Xingo	5	0	0	0	0	0	0	0	0	0	0	0	0	0	0	0	0

4D wrestler's
6H Wrestling
3N wretch
9P wretched-looking
8P wretchedness
3H wriggler
3H wrigglers
6B wright
8F wrights
9B wringer
7Q wrings
5B Wrinkle
9L wrinkle-resistance
8G WRITE
8A write-up
7P write-ups
9R Writer-Director
8A Writer's
9R writers'
5B Writhing
3P writs
7B Written
7P wrong-foot
9D wrong'st
9B wrongdoers
9R wrongdoing
6A wrongfully
6A wrongheaded
9F wrongness
7R wrongos
7B wrtng
6R WSA
7G Wshngtn
3P Wu
XR Wulff
7Q Wulfstan
7A Wunderlich
7A wunk
5G wurgen
7Q wurstmacher's
5Q Wurttemberg
8E WVX
7J WWJ
6E WX
4E WXYZ
9D Wyatt
7D WYCHERLY
6P Wyck
7G Wycliffe
7G Wycliffe's
8J Wykeham
5N Wyle
8K Wylie's
6N Wyman
9B wyoming
5F Wythe
4P Wythes
9Q Wyville
6E WZ
6E W4
9E x-component
8E x-coordinate
XH X-irradiation
8R X-rayed
8H x-rays
3P X-1A
3B X-10
3P X-15
9E x/a
5E xa/b**
7E XBC
5P xenophobia
4N Xenophon
7Q Xenopus
7Q Xenopus'
8G Xeres
9M Xerographic
5A Xingo's

Word Type	F	D	U	SFI	3 Gr 3	4 Gr 4	5 Gr 5	6 Gr 6	7 Gr 7	8 Gr 8	9 Gr 9	X UnGr	A Read	B Eng & Gr	C Comp	D Lit	E Math	F Soc Stud	G Spell	H Sci	J Music	K Art	L Home Ec	M Shop	N Lib F	P Lib NF	Q Lib Ref	R Mag	S Rel
xion	2	.0000	.0162	22.1	0	0	0	0	1	1	0	0	0	0	0	0	0	0	2	0	0	0	0	0	0	0	0	0	0
XIV	11	.6054	1.3695	41.4	2	1	1	0	4	2	0	1	1	1	0	0	1	0	0	0	1	1	0	0	0	2	3	1	0
Xury	2	.0000	.0234	23.7	0	0	0	2	0	0	0	0	0	0	0	0	0	0	0	0	0	0	0	0	2	0	0	0	0
XV	3	.1757	.1298	31.1	2	0	0	0	0	1	0	0	0	0	0	0	2	0	0	0	0	1	0	0	0	0	0	0	0
XVI	11	.2991	.7178	38.6	2	0	0	0	2	3	4	0	0	0	0	0	0	1	0	0	0	3	0	0	0	0	5	2	0
XVIII	2	.0000	.0209	23.2	0	0	0	0	0	0	2	0	0	0	0	0	0	0	0	0	0	0	0	0	0	0	2	0	0
XW	2	.0000	.0299	24.8	0	0	0	2	0	0	0	0	0	0	0	0	2	0	0	0	0	0	0	0	0	0	0	0	0
XX	5	.0000	.0748	28.7	4	0	0	0	1	0	0	0	0	0	0	0	5	0	0	0	0	0	0	0	0	0	0	0	0
XXX	4	.0000	.0599	27.8	1	3	0	0	0	0	0	0	0	0	0	0	4	0	0	0	0	0	0	0	0	0	0	0	0
xy	2	.0000	.0299	24.8	0	0	0	0	0	0	2	0	0	0	0	0	2	0	0	0	0	0	0	0	0	0	0	0	0
XY	16	.0000	.2395	33.8	0	1	3	3	0	8	1	0	0	0	0	0	16	0	0	0	0	0	0	0	0	0	0	0	0
Xylonite	2	.0000	.0209	23.2	0	0	2	0	0	0	0	0	0	0	0	0	0	0	0	0	0	0	0	0	0	0	2	0	0
xylophone	13	.1869	.5762	37.6	5	1	1	2	3	1	0	0	0	0	0	0	0	0	0	1	10	0	0	0	0	0	2	0	0
XYW	2	.0000	.0299	24.8	0	0	0	0	2	0	0	0	0	0	0	0	2	0	0	0	0	0	0	0	0	0	0	0	0
XYZ	2	.0000	.0299	24.8	0	0	0	1	1	0	0	0	0	0	0	0	2	0	0	0	0	0	0	0	0	0	0	0	0
X0537	2	.0000	.0914	29.6	2	0	0	0	0	0	0	0	2	0	0	0	0	0	0	0	0	0	0	0	0	0	0	0	0
x10	2	.0000	.0299	24.8	0	0	0	1	1	0	0	0	0	0	0	0	2	0	0	0	0	0	0	0	0	0	0	0	0
x2	2	.0000	.0299	24.8	0	1	0	0	0	1	0	0	0	0	0	0	2	0	0	0	0	0	0	0	0	0	0	0	0
x3	5	.0000	.0748	28.7	0	1	2	0	1	1	0	0	0	0	0	0	5	0	0	0	0	0	0	0	0	0	0	0	0
x4	3	.0000	.0449	26.5	0	2	1	0	0	0	0	0	0	0	0	0	3	0	0	0	0	0	0	0	0	0	0	0	0
x5	4	.0000	.0599	27.8	0	0	0	4	0	0	0	0	0	0	0	0	4	0	0	0	0	0	0	0	0	0	0	0	0
x6	8	.0000	.1197	30.8	0	3	2	3	0	0	0	0	0	0	0	0	8	0	0	0	0	0	0	0	0	0	0	0	0
x7	6	.0000	.0898	29.5	0	3	2	1	0	0	0	0	0	0	0	0	6	0	0	0	0	0	0	0	0	0	0	0	0
x8	3	.0000	.0449	26.5	0	1	0	2	0	0	0	0	0	0	0	0	3	0	0	0	0	0	0	0	0	0	0	0	0
y	540	.3820	44.952	56.5	78	65	61	67	56	109	100	4	36	30	1	0	184	0	267	0	0	0	0	1	1	2	8	10	0
Y	83	.7021	11.903	50.8	17	5	4	10	12	16	17	2	13	12	2	0	30	2	0	5	0	0	0	3	0	2	4	10	0
Y**	2	.0000	.0234	23.7	0	2	0	0	0	0	0	0	0	0	0	0	0	0	0	0	0	0	0	0	2	0	0	0	0
y-coordinate	2	.0000	.0299	24.8	0	0	0	0	0	1	1	0	0	0	0	0	2	0	0	0	0	0	0	0	0	0	0	0	0
y-segments	2	.0000	.0299	24.8	0	0	2	0	0	0	0	0	0	0	0	0	2	0	0	0	0	0	0	0	0	0	0	0	0
Y-shaped	2	.2160	.1362	31.3	1	0	0	1	0	0	0	0	1	0	0	0	0	0	0	1	0	0	0	0	0	0	0	0	0
Y-tube	3	.0000	.0591	27.7	0	0	3	0	0	0	0	0	0	0	0	0	0	0	0	3	0	0	0	0	0	0	0	0	0
y'all	2	.0000	.0243	23.9	0	0	0	0	1	0	1	0	0	0	0	0	0	0	0	0	0	0	0	0	0	0	0	2	0
y's	3	.2444	.1728	32.4	0	0	2	0	0	1	0	0	0	0	0	0	2	0	1	0	0	0	0	0	0	0	0	0	0
ya	10	.4841	1.0457	40.2	0	2	3	1	4	0	0	0	2	1	0	2	0	0	0	0	0	0	0	0	4	0	0	1	0
ya'	2	.0000	.0215	23.3	0	0	0	0	2	0	0	0	0	0	0	2	0	0	0	0	0	0	0	0	0	0	0	0	0
yacht	16	.5185	1.7234	42.4	0	0	0	3	5	4	2	2	0	2	0	1	0	1	0	0	0	0	0	0	2	0	2	8	0
Yacht	5	.1862	.2313	33.6	0	0	0	2	1	0	0	2	0	0	0	1	0	0	0	0	0	0	0	0	0	0	0	4	0
yachting	3	.3408	.2477	33.9	0	1	0	1	1	0	0	0	1	0	0	1	0	0	0	0	0	0	0	0	0	1	0	0	0
yachts	2	.2437	.1129	30.5	0	0	0	1	0	0	1	0	0	0	0	0	0	0	0	0	0	0	0	0	0	0	1	1	0
Yadin	5	.0000	.0724	28.6	0	0	5	0	0	0	0	0	0	0	0	0	0	0	0	0	0	0	0	0	0	5	0	0	0
Yaga	5	.0000	.0608	27.8	5	0	0	0	0	0	0	0	0	0	0	0	0	0	0	0	0	0	0	0	0	0	0	5	0
Yaga's	2	.0000	.0243	23.9	2	0	0	0	0	0	0	0	0	0	0	0	0	0	0	0	0	0	0	0	0	0	0	2	0
yah	19	.2179	1.0859	40.4	11	2	0	5	0	1	0	0	5	0	0	1	0	0	0	0	12	0	0	0	0	0	0	1	0
Yahad	3	.0000	.1370	31.4	0	0	0	0	3	0	0	0	3	0	0	0	0	0	0	0	0	0	0	0	0	0	0	0	0
Yahi	5	.0000	.0972	29.9	0	0	0	0	0	5	0	0	0	0	0	0	0	5	0	0	0	0	0	0	0	0	0	0	0
yak	2	.2160	.1362	31.3	1	1	0	0	0	0	0	0	1	0	0	0	0	0	0	1	0	0	0	0	0	0	0	0	0
Yale	25	.5865	3.0396	44.8	1	0	1	1	6	3	9	4	2	3	0	0	0	1	0	2	0	0	0	0	2	1	5	9	0
Yalouris	2	.0000	.0209	23.2	0	0	0	0	0	0	2	0	0	0	0	0	0	0	0	0	0	0	0	0	0	0	2	0	0
Yama-King	3	.0000	.0434	26.4	0	0	0	0	0	0	0	3	0	0	0	0	0	0	0	0	0	0	0	0	0	3	0	0	0
Yamasaki	2	.0000	.0389	25.9	0	0	0	0	0	2	0	0	0	0	0	0	0	2	0	0	0	0	0	0	0	0	0	0	0
Yan	13	.0000	.5939	37.7	0	0	0	13	0	0	0	0	13	0	0	0	0	0	0	0	0	0	0	0	0	0	0	0	0
Yancy	8	.0000	.3655	35.6	0	0	8	0	0	0	0	0	8	0	0	0	0	0	0	0	0	0	0	0	0	0	0	0	0
Yancy's	2	.0000	.0914	29.6	0	0	2	0	0	0	0	0	2	0	0	0	0	0	0	0	0	0	0	0	0	0	0	0	0
Yangtze	2	.2152	.1357	31.3	0	1	0	1	0	0	0	0	1	0	0	0	0	1	0	0	0	0	0	0	0	0	0	0	0
yank	4	.3071	.2967	34.7	0	0	3	0	0	1	0	0	1	0	0	1	0	0	0	0	0	0	0	0	2	0	0	0	0
yanked	8	.4631	.8513	39.3	2	0	0	1	2	0	3	0	4	2	0	0	0	0	0	0	0	0	0	0	0	1	1	0	0
Yankee	71	.6363	9.5104	49.8	17	20	8	7	11	6	2	0	24	0	0	1	0	8	0	0	7	0	0	0	6	20	1	4	0
Yankees	58	.4770	6.1661	47.9	11	23	7	6	10	0	1	0	19	1	0	0	1	0	0	0	0	0	0	0	9	24	0	4	0
yanking	2	.1814	.1187	30.7	0	1	0	1	0	0	0	0	1	0	0	0	0	0	0	0	0	0	0	0	0	0	0	1	0
yanks	3	.3399	.2456	33.9	1	0	1	0	0	0	1	0	1	0	0	1	0	0	0	0	0	0	0	0	0	0	0	1	0
Yanks	6	.0000	.0869	29.4	4	0	0	2	0	0	0	0	0	0	0	0	0	0	0	0	0	0	0	0	0	6	0	0	0
Yaol	4	.0000	.0429	26.3	0	0	0	0	0	4	0	0	0	0	0	4	0	0	0	0	0	0	0	0	0	0	0	0	0
Yaol's	2	.0000	.0215	23.3	0	0	0	0	0	2	0	0	0	0	0	2	0	0	0	0	0	0	0	0	0	0	0	0	0
yap	4	.2578	.2593	34.1	0	3	0	1	0	0	0	0	1	0	0	0	0	0	0	0	2	0	0	0	0	1	0	0	0
Yap	2	.0000	.0290	24.6	1	1	0	0	0	0	0	0	0	0	0	0	0	0	0	0	0	0	0	0	0	2	0	0	0
yapped	2	.1787	.1174	30.7	0	1	1	0	0	0	0	0	1	0	0	0	0	0	0	0	0	0	0	0	1	0	0	0	0
yapping	3	.3394	.2451	33.9	0	1	1	0	1	0	0	0	1	0	0	1	0	0	0	0	0	0	0	0	1	0	0	0	0
Yarborough	2	.0000	.0243	23.9	0	0	0	0	2	0	0	0	0	0	0	0	0	0	0	0	0	0	0	0	0	0	0	2	0
yard	459	.8656	79.679	59.0	149	84	47	67	52	36	18	6	185	21	7	16	70	10	7	16	1	4	0	5	61	26	7	23	0
Yard	2	.2446	.1142	30.6	0	0	0	0	2	0	0	0	0	0	0	0	0	0	0	0	0	0	0	0	1	0	0	1	0
yard-boy	4	.0000	.1827	32.6	4	0	0	0	0	0	0	0	4	0	0	0	0	0	0	0	0	0	0	0	0	0	0	0	0
yardage	6	.2427	.3478	35.4	0	0	0	1	5	0	0	0	0	0	0	0	3	0	0	0	0	0	0	0	0	0	0	3	0
yards	360	.8088	58.568	57.7	30	52	66	69	81	24	30	8	66	2	4	19	121	17	6	12	3	1	3	0	17	36	13	40	0
yardstick	19	.4029	1.7732	42.5	10	1	6	0	1	0	1	0	4	0	0	0	4	0	0	10	0	0	0	0	0	0	1	0	0
yardsticks	5	.0000	.0748	28.7	5	0	0	0	0	0	0	0	0	0	0	0	5	0	0	0	0	0	0	0	0	0	0	0	0
Yarmouth	3	.0000	.1370	31.4	0	0	0	0	3	0	0	0	3	0	0	0	0	0	0	0	0	0	0	0	0	0	0	0	0
Yarmouth's	3	.0000	.1370	31.4	0	0	0	0	3	0	0	0	3	0	0	0	0	0	0	0	0	0	0	0	0	0	0	0	0
yarn	86	.5309	9.6437	49.8	22	7	11	9	9	16	12	0	17	1	1	1	1	13	1	7	2	10	23	0	6	1	0	2	0
yarns	63	.2050	3.0162	44.8	4	3	1	4	3	33	14	1	7	1	0	1	0	2	0	0	0	2	44	0	0	2	1	3	0
Yaroslav	4	.0000	.0778	28.9	0	0	0	2	0	0	2	0	0	0	0	0	0	4	0	0	0	0	0	0	0	0	0	0	0
yarrow	3	.2197	.2090	33.2	0	0	0	2	0	0	1	0	2	0	0	0	0	0	0	0	0	0	0	0	0	0	1	0	0
Yaso	2	.2411	.1091	30.4	0	1	0	0	1	0	0	0	0	0	0	1	0	0	0	0	1	0	0	0	0	0	0	0	0
Yasu	23	.0000	1.0507	40.2	23	0	0	0	0	0	0	0	23	0	0	0	0	0	0	0	0	0	0	0	0	0	0	0	0
Yasu's	9	.0000	.4111	36.1	9	0	0	0	0	0	0	0	9	0	0	0	0	0	0	0	0	0	0	0	0	0	0	0	0
Yat-sen	3	.2143	.1568	32.0	0	0	1	1	0	0	1	0	0	0	0	0	0	0	0	0	0	0	0	0	0	1	0	2	0
Yates	2	.1948	.1250	31.0	0	0	0	1	0	0	1	0	1	0	0	0	0	0	0	0	0	0	0	0	0	1	0	0	0
yaw	2	.2433	.1158	30.6	1	0	0	0	1	0	0	0	0	0	0	0	0	0	0	0	0	0	0	0	0	1	0	1	0
yawing	4	.3668	.3131	35.0	1	0	0	1	2	0	0	0	0	0	1	1	0	0	0	0	0	0	0	0	1	1	0	0	0
yawk	2	.0000	.0914	29.6	2	0	0	0	0	0	0	0	2	0	0	0	0	0	0	0	0	0	0	0	0	0	0	0	0
yawl	7	.2331	.4206	36.2	0	5	0	2	0	0	0	0	1	0	0	0	0	0	0	0	0	0	0	0	0	5	0	1	0
yawls	2	.0000	.0914	29.6	0	0	0	2	0	0	0	0	2	0	0	0	0	0	0	0	0	0	0	0	0	0	0	0	0
yawn	14	.6135	1.8150	42.6	4	1	0	4	2	3	0	0	5	1	0	4	0	0	0	0	1	0	0	0	1	1	0	1	0
yawned	28	.6016	3.5802	45.5	3	9	2	5	6	1	1	1	10	1	0	4	0	1	0	0	0	0	0	0	7	2	0	3	0
yawning	14	.4267	1.3769	41.4	1	3	0	6	3	1	0	0	5	0	0	0	0	0	0	3	1	0	0	0	5	0	0	0	0

3A Xiquipilco
3E XIX
6E XL
7E XLV
6E XM
5J Xochipilli
6N xuchal
9Q XVI'S
9Q XVII
3E XXI
9E xy/ab
7H xylem
7J xylophone-like
9E xyz
9E xz
8B X34
6E x9
9L Y-Teens
9E y-axis
9E y-component
3P y-o-o-u-u-p
7N y-o-u-u
5E y-segment
4N y-y-yes
6R y-yeah
9D y-you
7E y-4
9E y/b
6A y'know
3K Yachts
5A Yadon
8Q Yahwism
5A Yakima
8A yaks
XR Yale's
7B yaller
7A yaller-toothy
8F Yalta
XP Yama-Kings
8F Yamaguchi
8F Yamassee
7D yammering
8Q yams
6A Yan's
6J Yang
7P yangba
5A Yank
XR Yankeetown
6A Yann
6A Yann's
8D Yap-yurrr
7R yard-high
7A yardarms
9Q yardmaster
5N yardplays
7F Yarmuk
5A Yarn
5A Yat
6R Yavapai
6R yawed
8A yawnin'
7A yawns
9J yawny
8A yawps
9D yaws

Word Type	F	D	U	SFI	3 Gr 3	4 Gr 4	5 Gr 5	6 Gr 6	7 Gr 7	8 Gr 8	9 Gr 9	X UnGr	A Read	B Eng & Gr	C Comp	D Lit	E Math	F Soc Stud	G Spell	H Sci	J Music	K Art	L Home Ec	M Shop	N Lib F	P Lib NF	Q Lib Ref	R Mag	S Rel
yay	2	.1717	.1142	30.6	0	1	0	0	1	0	0	0	1	0	0	1	0	0	0	0	0	0	0	0	0	0	0	0	0
yd	15	.1270	.5643	37.5	0	0	9	0	0	2	4	0	0	0	0	0	14	0	1	0	0	0	0	0	0	0	0	0	0
ye	109	.6197	14.084	51.5	7	16	19	18	30	9	9	1	26	2	0	16	0	1	1	0	23	0	0	0	12	25	2	1	0
Ye	6	.2303	.3236	35.1	3	0	1	2	0	0	0	0	0	0	0	0	0	0	0	0	3	0	0	0	0	3	0	0	0
ye'd	2	.2443	.1130	30.5	0	0	1	0	0	1	0	0	0	0	0	1	0	0	0	0	0	0	0	0	1	0	0	0	0
ye're	2	.2427	.1152	30.6	0	1	1	0	0	0	0	0	0	0	0	0	0	0	0	0	0	0	0	0	1	1	0	0	0
yea	21	.4857	2.1466	43.3	11	0	0	0	2	6	2	0	1	2	0	4	0	3	0	0	8	0	0	0	0	3	0	0	0
yeah	79	.6112	10.313	50.1	6	6	10	4	32	9	9	3	35	3	0	10	0	1	0	0	0	0	0	0	17	3	1	9	0
year	2277	.9265	417.88	66.2	412	379	261	300	342	206	304	73	385	94	24	84	190	399	59	266	41	1	22	2	63	157	163	324	3
Year	61	.7510	9.4520	49.8	15	6	9	14	5	10	2	0	31	1	0	7	0	4	0	4	4	0	1	0	0	2	2	5	0
year-end	2	.0000	.0243	23.9	0	0	0	0	1	0	1	0	0	0	0	0	0	0	0	0	0	0	0	0	0	0	0	2	0
year-old	4	.3415	.3070	34.9	1	0	0	0	1	0	0	2	0	0	0	0	0	0	0	1	0	0	0	0	0	1	0	2	0
year-round	13	.4517	1.2632	41.0	0	0	5	2	4	0	0	2	0	0	0	0	0	6	0	0	0	0	0	0	0	1	3	3	0
year's	57	.7125	8.2658	49.2	7	3	6	2	10	7	19	3	9	12	3	3	1	3	2	4	1	0	0	0	2	2	0	15	0
Year's	24	.7606	3.7359	45.7	6	3	1	8	2	1	3	0	9	2	0	2	2	4	1	0	0	0	0	0	0	2	1	1	0
yearling	5	.4699	.4937	36.9	0	0	2	0	1	0	1	1	0	1	0	1	0	0	0	0	0	0	0	0	0	1	0	2	0
yearlings	6	.5280	.6741	38.3	1	0	3	0	1	0	0	1	1	0	0	1	0	0	0	0	0	0	0	0	1	2	0	1	0
yearly	39	.7472	5.9058	47.7	1	3	7	3	6	6	12	1	6	6	0	0	10	1	1	3	0	0	1	0	1	1	4	5	0
yearn	4	.3331	.2899	34.6	0	0	0	0	4	0	0	0	0	0	0	0	0	0	0	0	0	0	1	0	0	1	0	2	0
yearned	5	.4770	.5360	37.3	2	1	0	0	0	2	0	0	2	0	0	1	0	0	0	0	0	0	0	0	0	1	0	1	0
yearning	11	.6232	1.4076	41.5	2	0	2	1	3	2	1	0	1	0	0	1	0	1	0	0	2	0	0	0	2	0	2	2	0
years	3966	.9312	731.39	68.6	506	525	601	558	808	496	344	128	762	132	18	163	167	856	62	365	143	16	21	9	112	382	347	409	2
Years	9	.6197	1.1529	40.6	0	4	2	1	0	1	0	1	1	0	0	0	0	1	0	1	1	0	0	0	2	0	2	1	0
years'	10	.5633	1.1866	40.7	0	1	1	1	2	2	2	1	2	0	0	0	0	0	1	1	2	0	0	0	0	0	1	3	0
Years'	4	.2348	.2372	33.8	0	0	0	0	0	1	3	0	0	0	0	0	0	3	0	0	0	0	0	0	0	0	1	0	0
yeast	47	.2812	3.3077	45.2	4	1	7	22	7	2	0	4	4	0	0	0	0	0	1	39	1	0	0	0	0	0	2	0	0
yeasts	14	.0869	.5384	37.3	2	0	1	7	0	0	2	2	2	0	0	0	0	0	0	12	0	0	0	0	0	0	0	0	0
yeh	33	.1477	1.3798	41.4	0	1	4	0	9	18	1	0	4	1	0	27	0	0	0	0	0	0	0	0	1	0	0	0	0
Yehudi	12	.0000	.5482	37.4	0	0	0	12	0	0	0	0	12	0	0	0	0	0	0	0	0	0	0	0	0	0	0	0	0
Yehudi's	2	.0000	.0914	29.6	0	0	0	2	0	0	0	0	2	0	0	0	0	0	0	0	0	0	0	0	0	0	0	0	0
yell	57	.5979	7.3747	48.7	22	15	4	7	5	2	2	0	29	0	0	7	0	2	0	0	0	0	0	0	6	8	0	5	0
yella	7	.0000	.0751	28.8	0	0	0	0	7	0	0	0	0	0	0	7	0	0	0	0	0	0	0	0	0	0	0	0	0
yelled	188	.6387	25.836	54.1	55	43	24	27	20	15	4	0	116	4	1	17	0	5	0	0	0	0	0	0	24	15	0	6	0
yeller	8	.2295	.4292	36.3	0	0	0	0	3	1	4	0	0	0	0	5	0	0	0	0	0	0	0	0	3	0	0	0	0
Yeller	19	.1053	.6221	37.9	0	0	0	0	17	2	0	0	1	0	0	1	0	0	0	0	0	0	0	0	17	0	0	0	0
Yeller's	3	.0000	.0352	25.5	0	0	0	0	3	0	0	0	0	0	0	0	0	0	0	0	0	0	0	0	3	0	0	0	0
yelling	59	.6346	7.9020	49.0	15	13	9	2	9	6	4	1	23	1	1	9	0	1	0	0	0	0	0	0	12	10	0	2	0
yellow	615	.9109	111.34	60.5	152	114	74	73	91	45	35	31	180	22	11	40	23	57	5	82	9	20	12	4	46	43	24	37	0
Yellow	20	.6265	2.5863	44.1	0	11	1	3	3	1	0	1	1	1	0	4	1	8	0	0	0	0	0	0	2	1	0	2	0
Yellow-Dog	4	.0000	.1827	32.6	0	4	0	0	0	0	0	0	4	0	0	0	0	0	0	0	0	0	0	0	0	0	0	0	0
yellow-billed	3	.0000	.0322	25.1	0	0	0	0	3	0	0	0	0	0	0	3	0	0	0	0	0	0	0	0	0	0	0	0	0
yellow-brown	3	.2378	.1809	32.6	1	0	1	1	0	0	0	0	0	0	0	0	0	2	0	0	0	0	0	0	0	1	0	0	0
yellow-eyed	2	.2443	.1130	30.5	0	0	0	0	2	0	0	0	0	0	0	1	0	0	0	0	0	0	0	0	1	0	0	0	0
yellow-fever	4	.0000	.1827	32.6	0	0	4	0	0	0	0	0	4	0	0	0	0	0	0	0	0	0	0	0	0	0	0	0	0
yellow-green	8	.3315	.5980	37.8	5	1	0	0	1	0	1	0	1	0	0	0	0	0	0	3	0	2	2	0	0	0	0	0	0
yellow-orange	2	.2316	.0949	29.8	1	0	0	0	1	0	0	0	0	0	0	0	0	0	0	0	0	1	1	0	0	0	0	0	0
yellow-robed	2	.0000	.0234	23.7	2	0	0	0	0	0	0	0	0	0	0	0	0	0	0	0	0	0	0	0	2	0	0	0	0
yellowing	4	.2958	.2914	34.6	1	0	1	0	1	1	0	0	1	0	0	0	0	0	0	0	0	0	0	0	2	1	0	0	0
yellowish	20	.6510	2.6772	44.3	3	4	4	0	2	2	3	2	1	0	0	1	0	2	0	8	0	0	0	1	2	2	3	0	0
yellowish-white	4	.1335	.1958	32.9	1	0	2	0	0	0	0	1	1	0	0	0	0	0	0	3	0	0	0	0	0	0	0	0	0
yellows	9	.4327	.8391	39.2	2	1	1	3	2	0	0	0	1	1	0	0	0	1	0	1	1	2	0	0	0	0	1	1	0
Yellowstone	40	.5680	4.9339	46.9	0	6	17	0	12	1	4	0	14	3	1	0	0	17	0	3	0	0	0	0	0	0	2	0	0
yells	26	.7075	3.8167	45.8	6	4	1	0	2	9	2	2	11	2	0	3	0	2	0	0	0	0	1	0	3	3	0	1	0
yelp	8	.5250	.9224	39.6	2	1	3	0	0	1	1	0	3	0	0	2	0	0	0	1	0	0	0	0	1	1	0	0	0
yelped	6	.2965	.4401	36.4	0	1	1	0	2	2	0	0	2	0	1	0	0	0	0	0	0	0	0	0	3	0	0	0	0
yelping	9	.5225	1.0007	40.0	1	2	0	1	2	1	2	0	2	0	1	3	0	0	0	0	1	0	0	0	0	1	0	1	0
yelps	2	.2427	.1152	30.6	0	1	0	0	0	1	0	0	0	0	0	0	0	0	0	0	0	0	0	0	1	1	0	0	0
Yemen	13	.2157	.7136	38.5	1	0	8	4	0	0	0	0	1	0	0	0	0	4	0	0	0	0	0	0	0	0	8	0	0
yen	9	.3446	.7900	39.0	4	4	0	1	0	0	0	0	4	0	0	0	1	4	0	0	0	0	0	0	0	0	0	0	0
Yengwe	4	.0000	.0429	26.3	0	0	0	0	4	0	0	0	0	0	0	4	0	0	0	0	0	0	0	0	0	0	0	0	0
Yengwes	2	.0000	.0215	23.3	0	0	0	0	2	0	0	0	0	0	0	2	0	0	0	0	0	0	0	0	0	0	0	0	0
Yenisei	3	.0000	.0583	27.7	0	0	0	0	0	0	3	0	0	0	0	0	0	3	0	0	0	0	0	0	0	0	0	0	0
yeomen	2	.0000	.0209	23.2	0	0	0	0	0	0	2	0	0	0	0	0	0	0	0	0	0	0	0	0	0	0	2	0	0
yep	10	.4649	1.0123	40.1	1	0	0	3	3	1	0	2	2	0	0	4	0	0	0	0	0	0	0	0	2	1	0	1	0
yer	13	.2891	.8440	39.3	0	0	6	1	5	1	0	0	0	0	0	3	0	0	0	0	0	0	0	0	9	0	1	0	0
yerba	11	.0602	.3559	35.5	0	0	0	5	6	0	0	0	1	0	0	0	0	10	0	0	0	0	0	0	0	0	0	0	0
Yerkes	3	.2197	.2090	33.2	0	1	0	1	1	0	0	0	2	0	0	0	0	0	0	0	0	0	0	0	0	0	1	0	0
yes	1317	.8342	221.89	63.5	337	328	146	142	165	110	79	10	594	44	7	153	21	59	10	23	26	3	1	3	195	126	2	48	2
Yes	9	.3850	.7971	39.0	2	0	2	1	0	4	0	0	2	1	0	0	5	0	0	0	0	0	0	0	1	0	0	0	0
YES	3	.3467	.2520	34.0	1	0	0	0	2	0	0	0	1	0	0	0	1	0	0	0	0	0	0	0	0	0	0	1	0
yes-men	2	.0000	.0215	23.3	0	0	0	0	0	2	0	0	0	0	0	2	0	0	0	0	0	0	0	0	0	0	0	0	0
yes-no	3	.0000	.0591	27.7	0	0	0	0	0	3	0	0	0	0	0	0	0	0	0	3	0	0	0	0	0	0	0	0	0
Yes/No	4	.0000	.0438	26.4	0	0	0	0	4	0	0	0	0	4	0	0	0	0	0	0	0	0	0	0	0	0	0	0	0
yes'm	9	.4238	.8552	39.3	0	4	0	0	5	0	0	0	2	0	0	1	0	0	0	0	0	0	0	0	2	4	0	0	0
yessir	2	.0000	.0215	23.3	0	0	2	0	0	0	0	0	0	0	0	2	0	0	0	0	0	0	0	0	0	0	0	0	0
yesterday	257	.7710	40.002	56.0	71	52	16	29	42	26	20	1	54	70	9	14	7	4	41	4	3	0	2	0	17	17	1	13	1
yesterday's	11	.5860	1.3497	41.3	3	0	0	1	1	4	1	1	2	0	0	2	0	0	0	0	0	0	0	0	1	2	1	3	0
yestirday	2	.0000	.0215	23.3	0	0	0	0	0	2	0	0	0	0	0	2	0	0	0	0	0	0	0	0	0	0	0	0	0
yestreen	2	.2446	.1125	30.5	0	0	0	0	1	1	0	0	0	1	0	1	0	0	0	0	0	0	0	0	0	0	0	0	0
yet	1325	.9232	242.56	63.8	175	168	139	189	291	144	177	42	320	48	13	126	18	148	11	152	23	6	10	7	102	128	87	126	0
Yffiniac	4	.0000	.1827	32.6	0	0	0	4	0	0	0	0	4	0	0	0	0	0	0	0	0	0	0	0	0	0	0	0	0
yi	2	.1948	.1250	31.0	0	2	0	0	0	0	0	0	1	0	0	0	0	0	0	0	0	0	0	0	0	1	0	0	0
Yi	2	.0000	.0290	24.6	0	0	0	0	0	2	0	0	0	0	0	0	0	0	0	0	0	0	0	0	0	2	0	0	0
Yiddish	3	.1639	.1674	32.2	0	1	0	0	2	0	0	0	1	0	0	0	0	2	0	0	0	0	0	0	0	0	0	0	0
yield	47	.8270	7.7735	48.9	5	1	6	5	18	4	8	0	4	1	0	2	2	6	1	10	2	0	1	1	3	2	11	1	0
yielded	12	.5668	1.4521	41.6	0	1	1	3	2	2	3	0	3	0	0	1	0	2	0	2	0	1	0	0	0	1	0	2	0
yielding	12	.5455	1.3523	41.3	1	0	1	0	6	1	1	2	0	0	0	0	0	0	0	2	0	0	1	0	2	1	5	1	0
yields	27	.6072	3.3948	45.3	2	2	4	2	7	5	4	1	2	1	1	0	6	7	0	0	0	0	0	0	0	1	8	1	0
Yin	7	.0000	.3198	35.0	0	0	0	7	0	0	0	0	7	0	0	0	0	0	0	0	0	0	0	0	0	0	0	0	0
Yipounou	3	.0000	.0328	25.2	0	0	0	0	3	0	0	0	0	3	0	0	0	0	0	0	0	0	0	0	0	0	0	0	0
Yipounous	2	.0000	.0219	23.4	0	0	0	0	2	0	0	0	0	2	0	0	0	0	0	0	0	0	0	0	0	0	0	0	0
yippee	6	.3501	.5265	37.2	3	3	0	0	0	0	0	0	3	0	0	0	0	0	0	0	0	0	0	0	2	1	0	0	0
Yippee	2	.0000	.0914	29.6	0	2	0	0	0	0	0	0	2	0	0	0	0	0	0	0	0	0	0	0	0	0	0	0	0

6A yayaya
7D yayo
8R YazooCity
5E YCF
3A ye
8A ye'll
5N ye've
3P Yea
8D Yealland
3A year-around
5A yearbook
4Q yearbooks
7Q Yeardley
3P Yearling
5B yearns
9Q Yeats
6D Yedda
5A Yedo
8B yeir
5N yellin'
7D yellow-bellied
7R yellow-belly
3P yellow-crested
7Q yellow-dog
7P yellow-eared
8D yellow-gray
4N yellow-haired
4A yellow-maned
8K yellow-ochre
4D yellow-orangey
3N yellow-painted
4A Yellow-shafted
6A yellow-skinned
7P yellow-white
3J yellow-wing
6A yellowbird
8B yellowed
4A yellower
4A yellowish-red
7Q yellowlegs
8A yellowness
5A Yellowstone's
4F yellowtail
7Q yellowwood
7N Yengeese
7D Yengwe's
5F Yerby
8D yerself
7D yessuh
7N yessum
3A Yesterday
XR yesterdays
7D yesternight
XR yesteryears
7N yestiddy
5A YET
7A yeti
6J yew
6E YH
4A yi-yi-yi
5P Yigael
6A Yin's
4D yip
4A yip-yip-yipping
3A yipe
6A yipee-i-o
5B yipes
7R yipped

Word Type	F	D	U	SFI	3 Gr 3	4 Gr 4	5 Gr 5	6 Gr 6	7 Gr 7	8 Gr 8	9 Gr 9	X UnGr	A Read	B Eng & Gr	C Comp	D Lit	E Math	F Soc Stud	G Spell	H Sci	J Music	K Art	L Home Ec	M Shop	N Lib F	P Lib NF	Q Lib Ref	R Mag	S Rel
yipping	3	.3855	.2503	34.0	0	1	1	1	0	0	0	0	0	1	0	0	0	0	0	0	0	0	0	0	0	1	0	1	0
yit	2	.2427	.1152	30.6	0	1	0	0	1	0	0	0	0	0	0	0	0	0	0	0	0	0	0	0	1	1	0	0	0
Ylis	18	.0000	.8223	39.2	0	0	0	0	0	18	0	0	18	0	0	0	0	0	0	0	0	0	0	0	0	0	0	0	0
YMCA	6	.4845	.6604	38.2	1	2	0	0	1	0	2	0	3	1	0	0	0	0	0	0	0	0	0	0	0	1	1	0	0
yo	19	.3582	1.5013	41.8	12	2	1	0	2	2	0	0	2	2	0	2	0	0	0	1	11	0	0	0	1	0	0	0	0
yo'	3	.1187	.1291	31.1	0	1	0	0	0	0	2	0	1	0	0	2	0	0	0	0	0	0	0	0	0	0	0	0	0
yodel	2	.0000	.0914	29.6	0	0	0	0	0	2	0	0	2	0	0	0	0	0	0	0	0	0	0	0	0	0	0	0	0
yodeling	3	.0000	.0243	23.8	0	2	0	0	0	1	0	0	0	0	0	0	0	0	0	0	3	0	0	0	0	0	0	0	0
Yoder	6	.0000	.2741	34.4	6	0	0	0	0	0	0	0	6	0	0	0	0	0	0	0	0	0	0	0	0	0	0	0	0
Yogi	12	.1873	.8618	39.4	0	0	0	1	0	11	0	0	11	0	0	0	0	0	0	0	0	0	0	0	0	1	0	0	0
yoi	2	.0000	.0162	22.1	0	0	0	0	2	0	0	0	0	0	0	0	0	0	0	0	2	0	0	0	0	0	0	0	0
yoke	14	.7232	2.0583	43.1	1	1	2	2	3	3	2	0	2	0	0	0	0	2	0	1	1	0	1	0	2	2	1	2	0
yoked	2	.1948	.1250	31.0	0	1	0	1	0	0	0	0	1	0	0	0	0	0	0	0	0	0	0	0	0	1	0	0	0
yokes	4	.3344	.3261	35.1	0	1	1	0	2	0	0	0	1	0	0	0	0	2	0	0	0	0	0	0	0	0	1	0	0
Yokohama	7	.1536	.2797	34.5	0	0	1	0	6	0	0	0	0	0	0	0	0	0	0	0	0	0	0	0	6	0	1	0	0
Yolande	3	.0000	.0322	25.1	0	0	0	0	0	0	3	0	0	0	0	3	0	0	0	0	0	0	0	0	0	0	0	0	0
yolk	27	.3916	2.2757	43.6	4	0	2	0	10	0	6	5	0	0	0	0	0	0	0	8	0	0	6	0	0	3	10	0	0
yolks	12	.3564	.9255	39.7	0	0	2	0	3	2	4	1	1	0	0	0	0	0	2	1	0	0	5	0	1	0	1	1	0
Yom	4	.0000	.1827	32.6	0	4	0	0	0	0	0	0	4	0	0	0	0	0	0	0	0	0	0	0	0	0	0	0	0
yon	13	.4555	1.3316	41.2	1	2	2	4	2	0	2	0	5	0	0	3	0	0	0	0	3	0	0	0	2	0	0	0	0
yond	2	.0000	.0215	23.3	0	0	0	0	0	0	2	0	0	0	0	2	0	0	0	0	0	0	0	0	0	0	0	0	0
yonder	30	.5622	3.6267	45.6	2	1	6	6	9	1	5	0	11	1	0	10	0	0	0	0	2	0	0	0	3	2	0	1	0
yoo	5	.2025	.3254	35.1	1	4	0	0	0	0	0	0	3	0	0	2	0	0	0	0	0	0	0	0	0	0	0	0	0
YOOOOOOOOOOOOO	2	.0000	.0914	29.6	0	2	0	0	0	0	0	0	2	0	0	0	0	0	0	0	0	0	0	0	0	0	0	0	0
yore	17	.2195	.9414	39.7	0	0	0	0	3	12	2	0	2	0	0	1	0	0	0	0	0	0	0	0	13	0	0	1	0
York	32	.6162	4.0608	46.1	1	9	7	3	8	3	0	1	1	0	0	3	0	7	0	0	0	0	0	0	2	10	4	5	0
York's	3	.2357	.2199	33.4	0	3	0	0	0	0	0	0	2	0	0	0	0	0	0	0	0	0	0	0	0	1	0	0	0
Yorker	3	.2260	.1580	32.0	0	0	1	0	0	2	0	0	0	0	0	2	0	0	0	0	0	0	0	0	0	0	1	0	0
Yorkers	5	.3660	.4089	36.1	0	1	0	1	0	1	2	0	0	0	0	0	0	2	0	0	0	0	0	0	0	1	0	2	0
Yorkshire	3	.3870	.2492	34.0	0	0	1	1	1	0	0	0	0	0	0	0	0	0	0	0	0	0	0	0	1	0	1	1	0
Yorktown	8	.4173	.7517	38.8	2	0	1	0	1	3	0	1	1	0	0	0	0	4	0	0	0	0	0	0	1	2	0	0	0
Yorty	2	.0000	.0243	23.9	0	0	0	0	0	2	0	0	0	0	0	0	0	0	0	0	0	0	0	0	0	0	0	2	0
Yosemite	14	.4804	1.4092	41.5	1	3	7	0	0	0	3	0	0	2	1	0	0	0	0	3	0	0	0	0	0	0	7	1	0
Yost	2	.2351	.1166	30.7	1	0	0	0	1	0	0	0	0	0	0	0	0	1	0	0	0	0	0	0	0	0	0	1	0
you	50957	.9509	9573.0	79.8	10778	9166	6227	6440	8715	5001	3887	743	11777	5168	815	2956	4075	2591	3575	7632	2532	036	477	403	2546	2647	119	1568	40
You	33	.7431	4.9718	47.0	8	6	4	4	2	4	3	2	6	2	0	1	1	2	5	3	4	0	1	0	0	1	0	7	0
YOU	9	.4315	.8801	39.4	3	1	0	1	1	0	3	0	3	0	0	0	1	1	0	1	1	0	2	0	0	0	0	0	0
you-all	7	.1516	.2774	34.4	3	0	2	1	1	0	0	0	0	0	0	1	0	0	0	0	0	0	0	0	6	0	0	0	0
you'd	241	.7761	38.157	55.8	33	50	28	45	39	30	12	4	101	5	1	29	0	2	3	2	5	0	2	3	40	32	0	16	0
you'll	524	.8621	90.611	59.6	73	105	46	86	126	55	18	15	211	19	1	35	8	8	12	2	17	5	4	7	57	77	2	59	0
you're	844	.7858	134.86	61.3	154	177	71	83	205	93	51	10	329	39	3	108	1	7	18	3	15	1	3	3	111	123	2	78	0
You're	4	.4852	.4027	36.1	0	1	0	0	1	2	0	0	0	0	0	1	0	0	0	0	1	0	0	0	0	0	1	1	0
you's	3	.0000	.0352	25.5	0	0	0	0	3	0	0	0	0	0	0	0	0	0	0	0	0	0	0	0	3	0	0	0	0
you've	317	.7823	50.377	57.0	39	52	37	47	71	49	11	11	114	11	2	42	1	3	15	0	5	0	1	2	46	36	0	39	0
young	1920	.9310	354.26	65.5	269	279	252	288	441	188	153	50	546	60	12	204	9	188	14	173	65	6	27	4	112	225	95	178	2
Young	81	.6820	11.492	50.6	17	8	12	7	11	12	5	9	30	0	0	5	1	8	0	0	8	2	0	0	0	5	2	20	0
YOUNG	11	.1062	.3353	35.3	0	0	0	0	2	8	1	0	0	1	0	10	0	0	0	0	0	0	0	0	0	0	0	0	0
Young's	7	.6208	.9186	39.6	2	1	2	0	0	0	1	1	2	0	0	1	1	1	0	1	0	0	0	0	0	1	0	0	0
younger	171	.8811	30.013	54.8	24	39	22	12	21	25	24	4	39	8	6	17	2	11	1	8	1	1	4	2	8	32	12	19	0
Younger	9	.4413	.8931	39.5	0	1	2	2	0	4	0	0	2	2	0	0	0	4	0	0	0	0	0	0	0	0	1	0	0
youngest	67	.7951	10.793	50.3	12	14	5	7	13	10	4	2	21	1	1	6	0	6	0	4	2	0	0	0	4	12	2	8	0
youngster	23	.7620	3.5475	45.5	2	1	2	4	7	5	1	1	5	2	1	2	0	0	0	1	0	0	1	0	1	4	3	3	0
youngsters	40	.6214	5.1346	47.1	2	4	4	5	12	3	6	4	6	0	2	7	0	0	0	0	0	0	0	0	3	5	4	13	0
Youngtown	2	.0000	.0243	23.9	0	0	0	0	0	0	0	2	0	0	0	0	0	0	0	0	0	0	0	0	0	0	0	2	0
youpi-ya	3	.0000	.0434	26.4	3	0	0	0	0	0	0	0	0	0	0	0	0	0	0	0	0	0	0	0	0	3	0	0	0
your	15311	.9107	2763.5	74.4	2958	2710	2004	1848	2537	1581	1454	219	2260	1882	370	671	1103	630	1616	2918	702	410	839	137	433	810	32	475	23
Your	87	.6823	12.154	50.8	24	21	12	10	11	5	0	4	19	5	0	2	1	1	24	1	14	0	2	0	8	6	1	3	0
your'n	2	.2443	.1130	30.5	0	0	1	0	0	1	0	0	0	0	0	1	0	0	0	0	0	0	0	0	1	0	0	0	0
youre	2	.0000	.0219	23.4	0	0	0	0	0	1	1	0	0	2	0	0	0	0	0	0	0	0	0	0	0	0	0	0	0
yours	170	.8394	28.698	54.6	25	25	27	24	21	25	16	7	60	23	1	21	2	8	3	6	1	3	2	0	14	14	0	12	0
Yours	4	.3406	.3119	34.9	0	2	1	0	0	0	1	0	1	1	1	0	0	0	1	0	0	0	0	0	0	0	0	0	0
yourself	812	.8776	142.14	61.5	110	147	119	77	165	103	75	16	221	70	10	51	11	31	73	127	20	17	53	8	28	54	2	36	0
Yourself	4	.3597	.3542	35.5	2	1	1	0	0	0	0	0	2	0	0	0	0	0	0	0	1	0	0	0	0	0	0	1	0
yourselves	30	.6351	3.9362	46.0	2	1	2	6	7	5	7	0	6	3	0	5	0	1	0	0	0	1	4	0	5	5	0	0	0
Youskevitch	3	.0000	.0314	25.0	0	0	0	0	3	0	0	0	0	0	0	0	0	0	0	0	0	0	0	0	0	0	3	0	0
youth	201	.7564	30.757	54.9	7	4	21	16	39	72	39	3	38	17	1	67	0	9	2	1	5	3	1	0	12	14	9	22	0
Youth	14	.4462	1.3156	41.2	0	1	6	1	5	0	1	0	0	2	0	2	0	2	0	0	0	2	0	0	0	0	0	6	0
youth's	7	.2922	.4688	36.7	0	0	0	0	1	4	2	0	1	0	2	3	0	0	0	0	0	0	0	0	0	0	0	1	0
Youth's	3	.0000	.1370	31.4	0	3	0	0	0	0	0	0	3	0	0	0	0	0	0	0	0	0	0	0	0	0	0	0	0
youthful	16	.7473	2.4138	43.8	0	1	4	3	1	3	4	0	2	1	0	1	0	1	1	0	2	0	1	0	1	4	0	2	0
youths	17	.6352	2.2483	43.5	1	0	1	6	5	0	3	1	4	0	0	3	0	2	0	0	0	0	1	0	1	2	0	4	0
yowl	4	.2399	.3011	34.8	0	2	0	2	0	0	0	0	3	1	0	0	0	0	0	0	0	0	0	0	0	0	0	0	0
yowling	2	.1605	.0742	28.7	0	0	1	0	0	1	0	0	0	1	1	0	0	0	0	0	0	0	0	0	0	0	0	0	0
Ypres	2	.0000	.0209	23.2	0	0	0	0	2	0	0	0	0	0	0	0	0	0	0	0	0	0	0	0	0	0	2	0	0
yr	9	.2980	.6136	37.9	0	0	1	0	8	0	0	0	0	0	0	0	7	0	1	0	0	0	0	0	0	0	1	0	0
Ysabel	3	.0000	.0352	25.5	0	0	0	0	0	3	0	0	0	0	0	0	0	0	0	0	0	0	0	0	3	0	0	0	0
Yssel	3	.0000	.0583	27.7	3	0	0	0	0	0	0	0	0	0	0	0	0	3	0	0	0	0	0	0	0	0	0	0	0
ytterbium	3	.0000	.0314	25.0	0	0	0	0	3	0	0	0	0	0	0	0	0	0	0	0	0	0	0	0	0	0	3	0	0
yttrium	2	.0000	.0209	23.2	0	0	0	0	2	0	0	0	0	0	0	0	0	0	0	0	0	0	0	0	0	0	2	0	0
Yucatan	10	.3315	.7984	39.0	0	1	1	0	7	1	0	0	3	1	0	0	0	1	0	0	0	0	0	0	0	0	5	0	0
yucca	12	.3349	.9306	39.7	3	0	0	8	0	0	1	0	0	0	0	0	0	0	0	8	0	0	0	0	0	3	1	0	0
yugit	2	.0000	.0914	29.6	0	0	2	0	0	0	0	0	2	0	0	0	0	0	0	0	0	0	0	0	0	0	0	0	0
Yugoslav	9	.4313	.8327	39.2	0	0	1	0	1	3	4	0	0	0	0	0	0	2	0	0	0	0	0	0	0	1	2	4	0
Yugoslavia	22	.4644	2.2173	43.5	2	0	1	1	13	3	2	0	1	1	0	0	0	14	0	0	1	0	0	0	0	0	4	1	0
Yugoslavia's	4	.1622	.1743	32.4	0	0	0	0	1	0	3	0	0	0	0	0	0	1	0	0	0	0	0	0	0	0	0	3	0
Yugoslavs	2	.0000	.0389	25.9	0	0	0	0	2	0	0	0	0	0	0	0	0	2	0	0	0	0	0	0	0	0	0	0	0
yuh	13	.1350	.6168	37.9	0	0	0	0	13	0	0	0	5	0	0	8	0	0	0	0	0	0	0	0	0	0	0	0	0
Yukon	8	.5431	.9373	39.7	0	1	3	0	3	0	1	0	2	0	0	1	0	3	0	0	0	0	0	0	1	0	1	0	0
Yule	2	.1948	.1250	31.0	1	0	0	1	0	0	0	0	1	0	0	0	0	0	0	0	0	0	0	0	0	1	0	0	0
Yulecake	2	.0000	.0389	25.9	0	2	0	0	0	0	0	0	0	0	0	0	0	2	0	0	0	0	0	0	0	0	0	0	0
Yuletide	3	.2309	.1631	32.1	0	0	0	0	0	0	1	2	0	0	0	1	0	0	0	0	0	0	0	0	0	0	0	2	0
Yum-Yum	6	.0000	.0485	26.9	0	0	0	0	0	6	0	0	0	0	0	0	0	0	0	0	6	0	0	0	0	0	0	0	0
yummy	3	.0000	.0365	25.6	1	2	0	0	0	0	0	0	0	0	0	0	0	0	0	0	0	0	0	0	0	0	0	3	0
Yuna	3	.0000	.0583	27.7	0	0	0	0	0	3	0	0	0	0	0	0	0	3	0	0	0	0	0	0	0	0	0	0	0

6E YL
6E YM
7N yo-ho-ho
5Q Yo-wipe
7A yo're
4J Yodel
5J yodelling
3A Yoder's
XR yoghurt
5A yogurt
8D yokel
8Q yoking
7A Yolchi
7A Yoldash
4P Yolk
9R Yolles
5Q Yomiuri
6R Yonemori
4A Yong
4P Yonny
4A YOOOOO
4A YOOOOOOOOOOOOOOO
4F Yoruba
4R Yoshimura
7F Yost's
4A you-know-what
4A you-know-where
7A you-u-u
7J Youmans
9R young-voter
3A young'uns
7A younglings
5F Youngmobile
7D youngs
3A Youngs
7D youngster's
7R youngsters'
6A Youngstown
7A younguns
4P younker
3P youpi-yi
3P youpi-youpi-youpi-ya
7B your-you're
7D yourn
7A youse
8B youve
7F Ypsilanti
7F Ypsilanti's
7Q yrs
4N Ysobel
8F Yu
7A yuh've
XR yule-log
5J yuletide
6N yum
3A yum-yum
4F Yuma

Word Type	F	D	U	SFI	3 Gr 3	4 Gr 4	5 Gr 5	6 Gr 6	7 Gr 7	8 Gr 8	9 Gr 9	X UnGr	A Read	B Eng & Gr	C Comp	D Lit	E Math	F Soc Stud	G Spell	H Sci	J Music	K Art	L Home Ec	M Shop	N Lib F	P Lib NF	Q Lib Ref	R Mag	S Rel
Yung	7	.0000	.1013	30.1	7	0	0	0	0	0	0	0	0	0	0	0	0	0	0	0	0	0	0	0	0	7	0	0	0
YWCA	5	.0000	.0523	27.2	0	0	0	0	5	0	0	0	0	0	0	0	0	0	0	0	0	0	0	0	0	0	5	0	0
z	100	.3992	8.5479	49.3	11	20	28	6	16	10	8	1	5	17	2	0	17	0	56	0	0	0	0	0	0	3	0	0	0
Z	30	.4836	3.2542	45.1	16	5	1	1	1	1	5	0	13	5	3	0	7	0	0	0	0	0	0	0	0	0	2	0	0
Z**	3	.0000	.0434	26.4	0	0	0	0	3	0	0	0	0	0	0	0	0	0	0	0	0	0	0	0	0	3	0	0	0
z-axis	2	.0000	.0299	24.8	0	0	0	0	0	0	2	0	0	0	0	0	2	0	0	0	0	0	0	0	0	0	0	0	0
Z/28	2	.0000	.0243	23.9	0	0	0	0	2	0	0	0	0	0	0	0	0	0	0	0	0	0	0	0	0	0	0	2	0
Z's	2	.0000	.0914	29.6	2	0	0	0	0	0	0	0	2	0	0	0	0	0	0	0	0	0	0	0	0	0	0	0	0
Zach	2	.2351	.1166	30.7	0	0	0	0	1	1	0	0	0	0	0	0	0	1	0	0	0	0	0	0	0	0	0	1	0
Zacharias	2	.2278	.1128	30.5	0	0	1	0	0	0	1	0	0	0	0	0	0	0	0	1	0	0	0	0	0	0	1	0	0
Zachary	4	.4712	.3988	36.0	2	0	1	0	0	1	0	0	0	0	0	0	0	1	0	0	1	0	0	0	1	1	0	0	0
Zachiel	2	.0000	.0914	29.6	0	0	0	2	0	0	0	0	2	0	0	0	0	0	0	0	0	0	0	0	0	0	0	0	0
Zack	5	.0000	.2284	33.6	0	2	0	1	0	2	0	0	5	0	0	0	0	0	0	0	0	0	0	0	0	0	0	0	0
Zack's	4	.0000	.1827	32.6	0	0	0	0	0	4	0	0	4	0	0	0	0	0	0	0	0	0	0	0	0	0	0	0	0
zag	2	.0000	.0290	24.6	0	0	0	2	0	0	0	0	0	0	0	0	0	0	0	0	0	0	0	0	0	2	0	0	0
zaggled	3	.0000	.1370	31.4	3	0	0	0	0	0	0	0	3	0	0	0	0	0	0	0	0	0	0	0	0	0	0	0	0
Zagreb	6	.1473	.2287	33.6	0	0	0	0	0	5	1	0	0	0	0	0	0	0	0	0	0	0	0	0	0	0	5	1	0
zags	2	.2346	.1166	30.7	0	0	0	1	0	0	1	0	0	0	0	0	0	0	0	1	0	0	0	0	0	0	0	1	0
Zailman	6	.0000	.2741	34.4	6	0	0	0	0	0	0	0	6	0	0	0	0	0	0	0	0	0	0	0	0	0	0	0	0
Zambezi	3	.3763	.2498	34.0	0	0	0	2	1	0	0	0	0	0	0	0	1	1	0	0	0	0	0	0	0	0	1	0	0
Zambia	3	.1639	.1674	32.2	1	0	0	1	1	0	0	0	1	0	0	0	0	2	0	0	0	0	0	0	0	0	0	0	0
Zamboanga	4	.0000	.0419	26.2	4	0	0	0	0	0	0	0	0	0	0	0	0	0	0	0	0	0	0	0	0	0	4	0	0
Zane	2	.0000	.0219	23.4	0	0	1	0	0	0	1	0	0	2	0	0	0	0	0	0	0	0	0	0	0	0	0	0	0
Zanzibar	3	.3350	.2478	33.9	0	1	0	1	1	0	0	0	1	0	0	0	0	1	0	0	0	0	0	0	0	0	1	0	0
Zapata	6	.0000	.0729	28.6	0	0	0	0	5	0	1	0	0	0	0	0	0	0	0	0	0	0	0	0	0	0	0	6	0
Zapatitos	6	.0000	.0485	26.9	6	0	0	0	0	0	0	0	0	0	0	0	0	0	0	0	6	0	0	0	0	0	0	0	0
Zapotec	2	.2351	.1166	30.7	0	0	0	1	1	0	0	0	0	0	0	0	0	1	0	0	0	0	0	0	0	0	0	1	0
Zarina	2	.0000	.0243	23.9	0	0	0	0	0	0	0	2	0	0	0	0	0	0	0	0	0	0	0	0	0	0	0	2	0
ze	8	.3612	.6240	38.0	0	2	1	0	1	4	0	0	0	3	0	0	0	0	1	0	0	0	0	0	4	0	0	0	0
zeal	10	.6089	1.2588	41.0	1	0	2	0	1	2	3	1	1	1	0	2	0	1	0	0	0	0	0	0	0	1	1	3	0
Zealand	70	.5142	7.6570	48.8	1	14	15	8	21	1	10	0	2	3	0	0	0	38	0	1	0	0	0	0	0	10	12	4	0
Zealand's	9	.3432	.6885	38.4	0	0	4	0	4	0	1	0	0	0	0	0	0	2	0	0	0	0	0	0	0	3	4	0	0
Zealander	2	.2401	.1133	30.5	0	0	1	0	1	0	0	0	0	0	0	0	0	0	0	0	0	0	0	0	0	1	1	0	0
Zealanders	8	.3144	.5716	37.6	0	0	6	0	2	0	0	0	0	0	0	0	0	1	0	0	0	0	0	0	0	5	2	0	0
zebra	25	.4990	2.7602	44.4	4	4	3	1	7	1	2	3	9	0	0	1	0	1	0	6	1	3	0	0	1	0	3	0	0
Zebra	7	.3481	.5270	37.2	0	5	0	0	0	2	0	0	0	0	0	1	0	0	0	0	2	0	0	0	4	0	0	0	0
zebras	30	.6034	3.8705	45.9	6	12	0	4	5	2	1	0	12	0	1	1	0	4	0	1	0	0	0	0	0	4	7	0	0
Zebulon	2	.2285	.1129	30.5	0	0	1	0	1	0	0	0	0	0	0	0	0	1	0	0	0	0	0	0	0	0	1	0	0
Zee	5	.1118	.2195	33.4	3	0	0	1	0	1	0	0	1	0	0	0	0	4	0	0	0	0	0	0	0	0	0	0	0
Zeiss	2	.2407	.1138	30.6	0	0	0	0	2	0	0	0	0	0	0	1	0	0	0	0	0	0	0	0	0	1	0	0	0
Zeke	31	.2204	1.9571	42.9	8	19	0	0	4	0	0	0	11	0	0	1	0	0	0	0	0	0	0	0	0	19	0	0	0
ZEKE	16	.0000	.1717	32.3	0	0	0	0	16	0	0	0	0	0	0	16	0	0	0	0	0	0	0	0	0	0	0	0	0
Zeke's	5	.2422	.3874	35.9	4	1	0	0	0	0	0	0	4	0	0	0	0	0	0	0	0	0	0	0	0	1	0	0	0
Zelda	2	.0000	.0389	25.9	0	0	0	0	0	0	2	0	0	0	0	0	0	2	0	0	0	0	0	0	0	0	0	0	0
Zenas	2	.0000	.0234	23.7	0	2	0	0	0	0	0	0	0	0	0	0	0	0	0	0	0	0	0	0	2	0	0	0	0
Zenger	3	.0000	.0583	27.7	0	0	0	0	0	3	0	0	0	0	0	0	0	3	0	0	0	0	0	0	0	0	0	0	0
zenith	7	.5181	.7800	38.9	0	0	1	0	3	3	0	0	1	0	0	0	0	0	0	3	1	0	0	0	0	1	0	1	0
Zephy	2	.0000	.0234	23.7	0	0	2	0	0	0	0	0	0	0	0	0	0	0	0	0	0	0	0	0	2	0	0	0	0
Zephyr	2	.1814	.1187	30.7	0	0	0	2	0	0	0	0	1	0	0	0	0	0	0	0	0	0	0	0	0	0	0	1	0
Zephyrus	3	.0000	.0434	26.4	0	0	0	3	0	0	0	0	0	0	0	0	0	0	0	0	0	0	0	0	0	3	0	0	0
zero	278	.4823	28.745	54.6	24	28	25	32	57	66	42	4	14	2	0	1	186	5	2	38	0	0	0	8	2	11	3	6	0
Zero-maker	2	.0000	.0234	23.7	0	2	0	0	0	0	0	0	0	0	0	0	0	0	0	0	0	0	0	0	2	0	0	0	0
zeroed	2	.2297	.1135	30.6	0	0	0	0	0	2	0	0	0	0	0	1	0	1	0	0	0	0	0	0	0	0	0	0	0
zeroing	2	.0000	.0243	23.9	0	0	0	0	1	1	0	0	0	0	0	0	0	0	0	0	0	0	0	0	0	0	0	2	0
zeros	42	.2019	2.1799	43.4	2	1	3	6	10	9	10	1	1	0	0	0	37	0	1	0	0	0	0	0	0	1	2	0	0
zest	8	.4590	.7911	39.0	1	0	0	1	1	3	1	1	2	0	0	0	0	0	0	0	1	1	2	0	0	0	2	0	0
Zeus	37	.4978	4.1703	46.2	0	1	1	12	0	16	5	2	20	2	0	11	0	0	1	0	0	0	0	0	0	0	1	2	0
Zeus's	4	.2393	.3005	34.8	0	0	0	0	0	3	1	0	3	0	0	1	0	0	0	0	0	0	0	0	0	0	0	0	0
zh	8	.0409	.1627	32.1	0	0	2	2	1	3	0	0	1	0	0	0	0	0	7	0	0	0	0	0	0	0	0	0	0
zhen**	5	.0000	.0406	26.1	0	0	0	2	2	1	0	0	0	0	0	0	0	0	5	0	0	0	0	0	0	0	0	0	0
zhun	2	.0000	.0162	22.1	0	0	0	0	0	2	0	0	0	0	0	0	0	0	2	0	0	0	0	0	0	0	0	0	0
Zi	11	.0000	.5025	37.0	11	0	0	0	0	0	0	0	11	0	0	0	0	0	0	0	0	0	0	0	0	0	0	0	0
Ziemer	7	.0000	.3198	35.0	0	0	0	7	0	0	0	0	7	0	0	0	0	0	0	0	0	0	0	0	0	0	0	0	0
zig	2	.0000	.0290	24.6	0	0	0	2	0	0	0	0	0	0	0	0	0	0	0	0	0	0	0	0	0	2	0	0	0
zig-zag	3	.2197	.2090	33.2	1	0	1	1	0	0	0	0	2	0	0	0	0	0	0	0	0	0	0	0	0	0	1	0	0
zig-zagging	2	.1892	.0858	29.3	0	0	0	0	0	0	2	0	0	1	0	0	0	0	0	0	0	0	1	0	0	0	0	0	0
ziggled	3	.0000	.1370	31.4	3	0	0	0	0	0	0	0	3	0	0	0	0	0	0	0	0	0	0	0	0	0	0	0	0
zigs	2	.2346	.1166	30.7	0	0	0	1	0	0	1	0	0	0	0	0	0	0	0	1	0	0	0	0	0	0	0	1	0
zigzag	14	.5677	1.6917	42.3	5	2	0	1	4	0	2	0	4	0	0	1	0	0	0	3	2	0	2	0	0	1	1	0	0
Zimmer	7	.0000	.0851	29.3	0	0	0	0	0	0	0	7	0	0	0	0	0	0	0	0	0	0	0	0	0	0	0	7	0
zinc	62	.5194	6.9620	48.4	12	5	11	6	9	6	9	4	12	1	0	0	0	14	0	20	2	0	0	8	0	0	3	2	0
zinc-coated	2	.0000	.0394	26.0	0	0	0	0	2	0	0	0	0	0	0	0	0	0	0	2	0	0	0	0	0	0	0	0	0
zing	2	.0000	.0162	22.1	2	0	0	0	0	0	0	0	0	0	0	0	0	0	0	0	2	0	0	0	0	0	0	0	0
Zink	3	.0000	.0434	26.4	0	0	0	0	0	0	0	3	0	0	0	0	0	0	0	0	0	0	0	0	0	3	0	0	0
Zinnen	10	.0000	.4568	36.6	0	10	0	0	0	0	0	0	10	0	0	0	0	0	0	0	0	0	0	0	0	0	0	0	0
zinnias	3	.2283	.1611	32.1	2	0	0	0	0	0	1	0	0	1	0	0	0	0	0	0	0	0	0	0	2	0	0	0	0
Zion	10	.2815	.6940	38.4	1	4	3	0	2	0	0	0	1	0	0	0	0	4	0	0	0	0	0	0	0	5	0	0	0
zip	15	.2390	.8698	39.4	3	0	10	0	0	0	1	1	1	11	0	0	0	1	0	1	0	0	0	0	0	0	0	1	0
Zip	10	.0000	.1094	30.4	1	2	3	0	4	0	0	0	0	10	0	0	0	0	0	0	0	0	0	0	0	0	0	0	0
ZIP	8	.0000	.0875	29.4	0	2	3	1	2	0	0	0	0	8	0	0	0	0	0	0	0	0	0	0	0	0	0	0	0
Zipp	3	.0000	.1370	31.4	3	0	0	0	0	0	0	0	3	0	0	0	0	0	0	0	0	0	0	0	0	0	0	0	0
zipp	2	.0000	.0914	29.6	2	0	0	0	0	0	0	0	2	0	0	0	0	0	0	0	0	0	0	0	0	0	0	0	0
zipped	5	.3836	.4747	36.8	3	0	0	1	0	1	0	0	3	1	0	1	0	0	0	0	0	0	0	0	0	0	0	0	0
zipper	32	.0793	.7323	38.6	4	0	0	0	19	7	2	0	3	0	0	1	0	0	0	0	0	0	26	0	1	0	1	0	0
zippered	2	.0000	.0290	24.6	2	0	0	0	0	0	0	0	0	0	0	0	0	0	0	0	0	0	0	0	0	2	0	0	0
zippers	3	.1367	.0954	29.8	1	0	0	0	0	1	1	0	0	0	0	1	0	0	0	0	0	0	2	0	0	0	0	0	0
zipping	2	.2440	.1132	30.5	0	0	0	1	1	0	0	0	0	0	0	1	0	0	0	0	0	0	0	0	0	0	0	1	0
zirconium	2	.2160	.1362	31.3	1	0	0	0	1	0	0	0	1	0	0	0	0	0	0	1	0	0	0	0	0	0	0	0	0
Zitu	6	.0000	.2741	34.4	0	0	0	6	0	0	0	0	6	0	0	0	0	0	0	0	0	0	0	0	0	0	0	0	0
Ziwiyeh	6	.0000	.0729	28.6	0	0	0	0	6	0	0	0	0	0	0	0	0	0	0	0	0	0	0	0	0	0	0	6	0
Zn	2	.0000	.0394	26.0	0	0	0	0	0	0	2	0	0	0	0	0	0	0	0	2	0	0	0	0	0	0	0	0	0
Znaeym	2	.0000	.0215	23.3	0	0	0	0	0	0	2	0	0	0	0	2	0	0	0	0	0	0	0	0	0	0	0	0	0
zodiac	7	.3557	.5648	37.5	0	0	0	2	0	0	0	5	0	0	0	0	0	0	1	5	0	0	0	0	0	0	1	0	0

3P Yung's
3A yuo
4N yup
6P Yuri
9Q Yuval
3A Yvonne
7Q YWCA'S
6E YZ
9M Y14
3N z-z-z-z
7J Zaandam
3B zacked
8Q Zafar
6P zagging
7P Zal
4Q Zalamea
9F Zambesi
9F zamindars
7R Zanger's
8D zany
7R Zapata's
3J zapatero
6F Zapotecs
7R zapped
3R Zaxik
5A zealots
7N zealous
9D zealously
5A Zeb
4K zebra's
7N zebus
7P Zekes
7P Zelter
XR Zen
8G Zeno
9Q zeolite
9Q zeolites
8Q Zephaniah
7N zephyr
7P Zero
3P zero-delay
XH zero-displacement
7E zero-point
7G zeroes
7P Zeros
6P Zetes
XR Zetterberg
9D Zeus-bred
8D Zeus'
8G zhen
8Q Zholtovski
6P zigging
9Q ziggurat
4P zigzagging
3K zigzags
3A zim
6A Zimmer's
8F Zimmermann
4P Zing-g-g
4A Zinnen's
3H zinnia
7F Zionism
5P Zionism's
9Q Zionist
7R Zip-Zip-Zip
4B Zip's
5Q Zipporah
XR Zita
7J zither-like
9H ZnSO4
7Q Zoarces

Word Type	F	D	U	SFI	3 Gr 3	4 Gr 4	5 Gr 5	6 Gr 6	7 Gr 7	8 Gr 8	9 Gr 9	X UnGr	A Read	B Eng & Gr	C Comp	D Lit	E Math	F Soc Stud	G Spell	H Sci	J Music	K Art	L Home Ec	M Shop	N Lib F	P Lib NF	Q Lib Ref	R Mag	S Rel
Zodiac	2	.2443	.1130	30.5	0	1	0	0	1	0	0	0	0	0	0	1	0	0	0	0	0	0	0	0	1	0	0	0	0
Zola	2	.0000	.0209	23.2	0	0	2	0	0	0	0	0	0	0	0	0	0	0	0	0	0	0	0	0	0	0	2	0	0
Zoltan	6	.1494	.3134	35.0	0	1	0	1	0	4	0	0	3	0	0	0	0	0	0	0	3	0	0	0	0	0	0	0	0
Zoltan's	3	.0000	.1370	31.4	0	0	0	0	0	3	0	0	3	0	0	0	0	0	0	0	0	0	0	0	0	0	0	0	0
Zomo	7	.0000	.3198	35.0	0	0	0	7	0	0	0	0	7	0	0	0	0	0	0	0	0	0	0	0	0	0	0	0	0
zone	71	.7718	11.065	50.4	3	5	9	4	21	17	10	2	8	1	2	2	2	9	3	23	0	0	0	3	0	2	10	6	0
Zone	16	.5089	1.7504	42.4	0	1	2	2	8	2	1	0	1	1	0	0	0	9	0	2	0	0	0	0	0	0	1	2	0
zones	43	.5786	5.2092	47.2	2	1	2	2	16	12	8	0	3	0	0	0	0	8	0	15	0	0	0	2	0	1	11	3	0
Zonguldak	2	.0000	.0389	25.9	0	0	0	0	2	0	0	0	0	0	0	0	0	2	0	0	0	0	0	0	0	0	0	0	0
zoning	5	.2112	.2785	34.4	0	0	0	0	0	5	0	0	0	0	0	0	0	4	0	0	0	0	0	0	0	0	0	1	0
Zoning	2	.2306	.1140	30.6	0	1	0	0	0	1	0	0	0	1	0	0	0	1	0	0	0	0	0	0	0	0	0	0	0
zoo	139	.8027	22.694	53.6	60	27	16	10	13	8	1	4	66	4	2	12	3	4	7	12	3	5	0	0	2	1	3	15	0
Zoo	12	.4510	1.2146	40.8	3	1	4	0	2	1	1	0	4	0	0	2	0	0	0	0	0	0	0	0	4	0	0	2	0
zoogeographer	2	.0000	.0209	23.2	0	0	0	0	2	0	0	0	0	0	0	0	0	0	0	0	0	0	0	0	0	0	2	0	0
zoogeographers	2	.0000	.0209	23.2	0	0	0	0	2	0	0	0	0	0	0	0	0	0	0	0	0	0	0	0	0	0	2	0	0
zoological	7	.4338	.6417	38.1	0	0	0	1	4	2	0	0	0	0	0	2	0	0	0	0	0	0	0	0	0	1	3	1	0
Zoological	5	.3468	.3830	35.8	0	0	0	1	0	0	3	1	0	0	0	0	0	1	0	0	0	0	0	0	0	0	2	2	0
zoologist	3	.3764	.2483	33.9	0	1	0	0	1	0	0	1	0	0	0	0	0	0	0	1	0	0	0	0	0	0	1	1	0
zoologists	8	.5923	.9918	40.0	0	0	2	0	5	0	1	0	1	0	0	1	0	0	1	3	0	0	0	0	0	1	1	0	0
zoology	5	.3022	.3399	35.3	0	0	0	0	3	0	2	0	0	0	0	1	0	1	0	0	0	0	0	0	0	0	3	0	0
zoom	8	.4744	.8100	39.1	3	0	0	0	0	2	1	2	0	1	0	0	0	0	0	4	1	0	0	0	0	0	0	2	0
Zoom	2	.0000	.0234	23.7	0	2	0	0	0	0	0	0	0	0	0	0	0	0	0	0	0	0	0	0	2	0	0	0	0
ZOOM	4	.0000	.1827	32.6	0	4	0	0	0	0	0	0	4	0	0	0	0	0	0	0	0	0	0	0	0	0	0	0	0
zoomed	3	.2223	.2106	33.2	2	0	1	0	0	0	0	0	2	1	0	0	0	0	0	0	0	0	0	0	0	0	0	0	0
zooms	3	.3771	.2489	34.0	1	0	1	0	1	0	0	0	0	0	0	1	0	0	0	1	0	0	0	0	0	0	0	1	0
zoos	32	.7307	4.8319	46.8	7	4	5	2	10	4	0	0	14	2	0	5	0	3	1	3	0	1	0	0	1	1	1	0	0
zop	6	.0000	.0898	29.5	0	0	6	0	0	0	0	0	0	0	0	0	6	0	0	0	0	0	0	0	0	0	0	0	0
Zorach	2	.0000	.0037	15.7	0	0	0	0	0	2	0	0	0	0	0	0	0	0	0	0	0	2	0	0	0	0	0	0	0
zori	10	.1518	.5300	37.2	0	7	0	3	0	0	0	0	3	0	0	0	0	7	0	0	0	0	0	0	0	0	0	0	0
zorrino	2	.0000	.0914	29.6	2	0	0	0	0	0	0	0	2	0	0	0	0	0	0	0	0	0	0	0	0	0	0	0	0
Zoutenaaie	2	.0000	.0290	24.6	0	0	2	0	0	0	0	0	0	0	0	0	0	0	0	0	0	0	0	0	0	2	0	0	0
zowie	4	.0000	.1827	32.6	3	0	0	0	1	0	0	0	4	0	0	0	0	0	0	0	0	0	0	0	0	0	0	0	0
Zsa	2	.0000	.0243	23.9	0	0	2	0	0	0	0	0	0	0	0	0	0	0	0	0	0	0	0	0	0	0	0	2	0
Zuckerman	23	.1440	1.1432	40.6	0	14	9	0	0	0	0	0	9	0	0	0	0	0	0	0	0	0	0	0	14	0	0	0	0
Zuckerman's	2	.1787	.1174	30.7	0	2	0	0	0	0	0	0	1	0	0	0	0	0	0	0	0	0	0	0	1	0	0	0	0
Zuckermans	3	.1250	.1342	31.3	0	2	1	0	0	0	0	0	1	0	0	0	0	0	0	0	0	0	0	0	2	0	0	0	0
Zuider	4	.0000	.0778	28.9	3	0	0	1	0	0	0	0	0	0	0	0	0	4	0	0	0	0	0	0	0	0	0	0	0
Zulu	2	.1787	.1174	30.7	1	0	0	0	1	0	0	0	1	0	0	0	0	0	0	0	0	0	0	0	1	0	0	0	0
Zululand	2	.0000	.0914	29.6	0	0	0	2	0	0	0	0	2	0	0	0	0	0	0	0	0	0	0	0	0	0	0	0	0
Zulus	2	.1698	.1133	30.5	1	0	0	1	0	0	0	0	1	0	0	0	0	0	0	0	0	0	0	0	0	0	1	0	0
Zuni	2	.2303	.1079	30.3	1	0	0	1	0	0	0	0	0	0	0	0	0	0	0	0	1	0	0	0	0	1	0	0	0
Zuniga	2	.2417	.1091	30.4	0	0	0	0	1	1	0	0	0	0	0	0	0	0	0	0	1	0	0	0	0	0	1	0	0
Zurbaran	4	.0000	.0429	26.3	0	0	0	0	4	0	0	0	0	0	0	4	0	0	0	0	0	0	0	0	0	0	0	0	0
Zurich	10	.3687	.8028	39.0	1	0	4	1	1	1	2	0	0	0	0	0	0	0	0	0	0	0	0	0	0	4	4	2	0
Zurn	2	.0000	.0914	29.6	2	0	0	0	0	0	0	0	2	0	0	0	0	0	0	0	0	0	0	0	0	0	0	0	0
Zurns	5	.0000	.2284	33.6	5	0	0	0	0	0	0	0	5	0	0	0	0	0	0	0	0	0	0	0	0	0	0	0	0
Zust	13	.0000	.1882	32.7	0	13	0	0	0	0	0	0	0	0	0	0	0	0	0	0	0	0	0	0	0	13	0	0	0
ZW	2	.0000	.0299	24.8	0	0	2	0	0	0	0	0	0	0	0	0	2	0	0	0	0	0	0	0	0	0	0	0	0
Zworykin	2	.0000	.0914	29.6	0	0	2	0	0	0	0	0	2	0	0	0	0	0	0	0	0	0	0	0	0	0	0	0	0
zygote	12	.0000	.2366	33.7	0	0	0	0	7	0	5	0	0	0	0	0	0	0	0	12	0	0	0	0	0	0	0	0	0
zygotes	3	.1813	.1402	31.5	0	0	0	0	1	0	0	2	0	0	0	0	0	0	0	1	0	0	0	0	0	0	2	0	0
zz	3	.2379	.1631	32.1	0	1	1	0	1	0	0	0	0	2	0	0	0	0	1	0	0	0	0	0	0	0	0	0	0
zzz-zzz-zzz	2	.0000	.0914	29.6	2	0	0	0	0	0	0	0	2	0	0	0	0	0	0	0	0	0	0	0	0	0	0	0	0
0	768	.2677	48.804	56.9	66	45	113	75	123	149	189	8	1	1	0	0	683	6	6	43	0	0	2	13	0	1	6	6	0
0**	5	.2379	.2813	34.5	0	0	0	0	4	0	1	0	0	0	0	0	4	0	0	0	0	0	0	1	0	0	0	0	0
0-1	3	.0000	.0076	18.8	0	0	0	0	0	0	3	0	0	0	0	0	0	0	0	0	0	0	0	3	0	0	0	0	0
0-2	7	.0000	.0177	22.5	0	0	0	0	0	0	7	0	0	0	0	0	0	0	0	0	0	0	0	7	0	0	0	0	0
0/5	2	.0000	.0299	24.8	0	0	0	0	0	2	0	0	0	0	0	0	2	0	0	0	0	0	0	0	0	0	0	0	0
0's	10	.0000	.1497	31.8	0	0	0	9	0	0	1	0	0	0	0	0	10	0	0	0	0	0	0	0	0	0	0	0	0
00	164	.5233	18.514	52.7	48	19	14	18	19	10	16	20	35	0	1	0	81	2	0	8	0	0	1	0	0	6	2	28	0
000	1711	.7524	260.15	64.2	109	183	242	210	380	329	203	55	111	19	5	24	384	276	9	246	1	0	1	18	2	117	258	240	0
000-a-year	4	.1622	.1743	32.4	0	0	0	0	0	2	2	0	0	0	0	0	0	1	0	0	0	0	0	0	0	0	0	3	0
000-acre	3	.2425	.1816	32.6	0	0	1	0	0	1	1	0	0	0	0	0	0	2	0	0	0	0	0	0	0	0	0	1	0
000-foot	12	.5905	1.4604	41.6	0	1	2	2	5	1	1	0	0	0	0	2	1	0	0	3	0	0	0	0	0	1	3	2	0
000-foot-deep	2	.0000	.0243	23.9	0	0	0	0	0	2	0	0	0	0	0	0	0	0	0	0	0	0	0	0	0	0	0	2	0
000-mile	5	.3860	.4348	36.4	0	0	1	2	2	0	0	0	0	0	0	0	0	2	0	2	0	0	0	0	0	0	0	1	0
000's	4	.0000	.0599	27.8	0	0	4	0	0	0	0	0	0	0	0	0	4	0	0	0	0	0	0	0	0	0	0	0	0
000th	2	.0000	.0394	26.0	0	0	0	0	2	0	0	0	0	0	0	0	0	0	0	2	0	0	0	0	0	0	0	0	0
0000	5	.2380	.2764	34.4	0	0	0	0	2	3	0	0	0	0	0	0	2	1	0	0	0	0	2	0	0	0	0	0	0
00005	2	.0000	.0299	24.8	0	0	0	2	0	0	0	0	0	0	0	0	2	0	0	0	0	0	0	0	0	0	0	0	0
0003	2	.0000	.0299	24.8	0	0	0	2	0	0	0	0	0	0	0	0	2	0	0	0	0	0	0	0	0	0	0	0	0
0008	2	.0000	.0299	24.8	0	0	0	0	0	2	0	0	0	0	0	0	2	0	0	0	0	0	0	0	0	0	0	0	0
001	8	.3314	.5909	37.7	0	0	0	0	4	1	3	0	0	0	0	0	6	0	0	0	0	0	0	1	0	0	0	1	0
003	6	.3343	.4438	36.5	0	1	0	0	1	1	3	0	0	0	0	0	4	0	0	0	0	0	0	1	0	0	0	1	0
006	4	.1135	.1696	32.3	0	0	0	4	0	0	0	0	1	0	0	0	3	0	0	0	0	0	0	0	0	0	0	0	0
008	2	.2391	.1133	30.5	0	0	0	1	0	0	1	0	0	0	0	0	1	0	0	0	0	0	0	0	0	0	1	0	0
01	19	.1828	.9202	39.6	0	0	0	6	5	2	6	0	0	0	0	0	16	0	0	2	0	0	0	0	0	0	0	1	0
01's	4	.0000	.0599	27.8	0	0	0	0	0	0	4	0	0	0	0	0	4	0	0	0	0	0	0	0	0	0	0	0	0
012	3	.2019	.1477	31.7	1	0	1	0	1	0	0	0	0	0	0	0	1	0	0	0	0	0	0	0	0	0	2	0	0
013	3	.2086	.1620	32.1	0	1	2	0	0	0	0	0	0	0	0	0	2	1	0	0	0	0	0	0	0	0	0	0	0
014	2	.2391	.1133	30.5	0	0	1	0	0	0	1	0	0	0	0	0	1	0	0	0	0	0	0	0	0	0	1	0	0
02	6	.3024	.4205	36.2	0	0	0	1	2	2	1	0	0	0	0	0	4	0	0	1	0	0	0	0	0	0	0	1	0
02315	2	.0000	.0299	24.8	0	0	0	0	0	2	0	0	0	0	0	0	2	0	0	0	0	0	0	0	0	0	0	0	0
02351	2	.0000	.0299	24.8	0	0	0	0	0	2	0	0	0	0	0	0	2	0	0	0	0	0	0	0	0	0	0	0	0
024	8	.0645	.2421	33.8	0	0	2	0	0	6	0	0	1	0	0	0	7	0	0	0	0	0	0	0	0	0	0	0	0
025	5	.0694	.0889	29.5	0	0	0	0	2	0	3	0	0	0	0	0	0	0	0	0	0	0	0	4	0	0	0	1	0
028	3	.3660	.2695	34.3	0	1	0	0	1	0	1	0	1	0	0	0	0	1	0	1	0	0	0	0	0	0	0	0	0
03	15	.0000	.2245	33.5	0	1	2	8	1	2	1	0	0	0	0	0	15	0	0	0	0	0	0	0	0	0	0	0	0

7H zonda
5A ZOO
6P zoo-lulu
6P zoo-lulus
XR zoo's
7Q zoogeographic
7Q zoogeographical
7Q zoogeographically
7P Zoology
7N zoophyte
7N zoophytes
7Q zooplankton
5D Zoos
5F Zora
8D Zorab
3B zorkles
7N zostera
4P Zouaves
9R Zozo
3P ZROOOOOMMM
4N Zuckermans'
4P ZuiderZee
6A Zumbro
4D zun-zun-zun
4D zun-zunned
3P Zunis
3B zuppingly
6A zwei
6P Zwickau
5A Zworykin's
XR Zyklon
3A zzz
5A ZZZ
9M 0-1-2
4E 0-1000
4E 0-15
4E 0-250
9M 0-3
9M 0-3-4
9M 0-4
9M 0-4-1
7R 0-60
7E 0/14
4E 0/2
8E 0/5xn
8E 0/8
XH 0%
8E 0xn
5E 0x0
8E 0x5
8E 0x8
8A 00P
7R 000-gauss
7Q 000-mile-per-hour
7H 000-odd
4R 000-pound
7R 000-pound-thrust
9R 000-room
6R 000-seat
7H 000-square-mile
7Q 000-year
9Q 000-year-old
9A 000-000
8H 000-2
8E 000000
8E 000000000000001
8E 000000000000005
8H 0000000000055
7E 00001
8E 000012
8E 00005896
9H 0001
9E 00012
7E 00018
9M 00025
8E 000361
7R 000363
7H 0004
6E 0006
6E 0007
8E 0011
7H 0018
6E 002
6E 004
8E 0045
6R 005
6E 0064
6Q 007
6E 007281
7E 0089
9Q 010
5H 011
8E 016
6E 017
8E 019
6P 020
7Q 02115
9E 023
6E 026
6E 027
8Q 029
7E 032

Word Type	F	D	U	SFI	3 Gr 3	4 Gr 4	5 Gr 5	6 Gr 6	7 Gr 7	8 Gr 8	9 Gr 9	X UnGr	A Read	B Eng & Gr	C Comp	D Lit	E Math	F Soc Stud	G Spell	H Sci	J Music	K Art	L Home Ec	M Shop	N Lib F	P Lib NF	Q Lib Ref	R Mag	S Rel
037	3	.0000	.0449	26.5	0	0	3	0	0	0	0	0	0	0	0	0	3	0	0	0	0	0	0	0	0	0	0	0	0
04	3	.2076	.1618	32.1	0	0	1	1	1	0	0	0	0	0	0	0	2	0	0	1	0	0	0	0	0	0	0	0	0
05	15	.3821	1.2676	41.0	1	1	1	2	1	1	5	3	0	1	0	0	9	0	0	2	0	0	0	0	0	3	0	0	0
050	3	.2159	.1532	31.9	1	0	0	1	1	0	0	0	0	0	0	0	0	0	0	0	0	0	0	0	0	0	0	1	0
051	2	.0000	.0299	24.8	0	0	0	0	2	0	0	0	0	0	0	0	2	0	0	0	0	0	0	0	0	0	2	0	0
06	8	.0000	.1197	30.8	0	0	0	8	0	0	0	0	0	0	0	0	8	0	0	0	0	0	0	0	0	0	0	0	0
063	2	.1972	.1262	31.0	1	0	0	1	0	0	0	0	1	0	0	0	1	0	0	0	0	0	0	0	0	0	0	0	0
065	2	.2427	.1159	30.6	0	0	1	1	0	0	0	0	0	0	0	0	1	0	0	0	0	0	0	0	0	0	0	1	0
07	7	.1473	.2916	34.6	0	0	1	4	2	0	0	0	0	0	0	0	6	0	0	0	0	0	0	0	0	1	0	0	0
08	5	.0000	.0748	28.7	0	0	0	3	1	0	1	0	0	0	0	0	5	0	0	0	0	0	0	0	0	0	0	0	0
09	6	.2076	.3235	35.1	0	0	0	2	3	0	1	0	0	0	0	0	4	0	0	2	0	0	0	0	0	0	0	0	0
090909	2	.0000	.0299	24.8	0	0	0	0	0	0	2	0	0	0	0	0	2	0	0	0	0	0	0	0	0	0	0	0	0
092	2	.2417	.1211	30.8	0	1	0	0	0	0	1	0	0	0	0	0	1	1	0	0	0	0	0	0	0	0	0	0	0
096	2	.0000	.0299	24.8	0	0	0	0	0	2	0	0	0	0	0	0	2	0	0	0	0	0	0	0	0	0	0	0	0
1	3222	.7262	473.35	66.8	386	414	363	491	513	538	455	62	185	136	26	11	1805	113	224	153	109	6	71	54	3	70	112	144	0
1**	4	.4629	.4147	36.2	0	1	1	1	1	0	0	0	1	0	0	0	1	1	0	0	0	0	0	0	0	1	0	0	0
1A	4	.0000	.0599	27.8	1	0	2	0	0	0	1	0	0	0	0	0	4	0	0	0	0	0	0	0	0	0	0	0	0
1B	4	.0000	.0599	27.8	1	0	1	1	0	0	1	0	0	0	0	0	4	0	0	0	0	0	0	0	0	0	0	0	0
1H	2	.0000	.0299	24.8	0	0	0	0	0	2	0	0	0	0	0	0	2	0	0	0	0	0	0	0	0	0	0	0	0
1-A	2	.0000	.0243	23.9	0	0	0	0	2	0	0	0	0	0	0	0	0	0	0	0	0	0	0	0	0	0	0	2	0
1-Star	75	.0000	.6087	37.8	0	19	32	24	0	0	0	0	0	0	0	0	0	0	75	0	0	0	0	0	0	0	0	0	0
1-cent	2	.0000	.0299	24.8	0	0	0	0	2	0	0	0	0	0	0	0	2	0	0	0	0	0	0	0	0	0	0	0	0
1-cup	2	.1648	.0800	29.0	0	1	0	0	0	1	0	0	0	0	0	0	1	0	0	0	0	0	1	0	0	0	0	0	0
1-foot	4	.1776	.1927	32.8	0	2	1	0	1	0	0	0	0	0	0	0	3	0	0	1	0	0	0	0	0	0	0	0	0
1-inch	13	.4629	1.2700	41.0	4	0	2	0	1	0	4	2	0	0	0	0	8	0	0	1	0	0	2	1	0	1	0	0	0
1-pound	2	.1457	.0722	28.6	0	0	0	0	0	1	1	0	0	0	0	0	1	0	0	0	0	0	0	1	0	0	0	0	0
1-to-1	7	.0000	.1048	30.2	0	0	0	0	7	0	0	0	0	0	0	0	7	0	0	0	0	0	0	0	0	0	0	0	0
1-1	16	.3203	1.1760	40.7	1	0	0	0	3	4	8	0	1	0	0	0	5	1	0	5	0	0	0	4	0	0	0	0	0
1-10	14	.3489	1.0645	40.3	0	1	0	1	2	8	2	0	0	9	0	0	4	0	0	0	0	0	0	1	0	0	0	0	0
1-11	3	.0000	.0449	26.5	0	0	0	0	3	0	0	0	0	0	0	0	3	0	0	0	0	0	0	0	0	0	0	0	0
1-12	5	.2003	.2535	34.0	0	1	0	2	0	0	2	0	0	1	0	0	4	0	0	0	0	0	0	0	0	0	0	0	0
1-13	2	.2404	.1142	30.6	0	0	0	0	1	1	0	0	0	1	0	0	1	0	0	0	0	0	0	0	0	0	0	0	0
1-14	2	.1249	.0685	28.4	0	0	0	0	1	0	1	0	0	0	0	0	0	0	0	1	0	0	0	1	0	0	0	0	0
1-2	10	.2629	.6099	37.9	0	0	0	1	2	4	3	0	0	0	0	0	4	0	0	3	0	0	0	3	0	0	0	0	0
1-20	11	.0878	.3033	34.8	0	0	0	0	5	5	1	0	0	10	0	0	1	0	0	0	0	0	0	0	0	0	0	0	0
1-3	7	.3829	.5721	37.6	0	0	0	0	2	3	2	0	0	0	0	1	2	0	1	1	0	0	0	2	0	0	0	0	0
1-3-5	2	.0000	.0162	22.1	0	0	1	1	0	0	0	0	0	0	0	0	0	0	0	0	2	0	0	0	0	0	0	0	0
1-4	15	.4885	1.5460	41.9	0	1	0	3	1	7	3	0	1	2	0	0	7	0	4	0	0	0	0	1	0	0	0	0	0
1-5	20	.3598	1.5426	41.9	0	4	0	6	6	4	0	0	0	1	0	0	6	0	12	0	0	0	0	1	0	0	0	0	0
1-6	9	.4518	.8564	39.3	2	0	0	2	1	4	0	0	0	1	0	0	5	0	2	0	0	0	0	1	0	0	0	0	0
1-7	7	.4348	.6537	38.2	0	1	1	3	1	1	0	0	1	1	0	0	1	0	3	0	0	0	0	1	0	0	0	0	0
1-8	15	.5102	1.5867	42.0	0	1	1	1	6	3	3	0	0	3	0	0	8	0	0	0	1	0	1	2	0	0	0	0	0
1-9	5	.3430	.3960	36.0	0	0	0	0	2	2	1	0	1	2	0	0	0	0	0	1	0	0	0	1	0	0	0	0	0
1/	2	.0000	.0299	24.8	0	0	0	2	0	0	0	0	0	0	0	0	2	0	0	0	0	0	0	0	0	0	0	0	0
1/1	2	.0000	.0299	24.8	0	0	0	0	1	1	0	0	0	0	0	0	2	0	0	0	0	0	0	0	0	0	0	0	0
1/10	56	.0977	1.8415	42.7	0	0	0	30	7	6	12	1	0	0	0	0	52	0	0	3	0	0	0	0	0	0	0	1	0
1/100	25	.1440	1.0557	40.2	0	0	2	16	7	0	0	0	1	0	0	0	22	0	0	1	0	0	0	0	0	0	0	1	0
1/1000	10	.0537	.2762	34.4	0	0	1	7	2	0	0	0	1	0	0	0	9	0	0	0	0	0	0	0	0	0	0	0	0
1/11	3	.0000	.0449	26.5	0	0	0	0	0	0	3	0	0	0	0	0	3	0	0	0	0	0	0	0	0	0	0	0	0
1/12	7	.1729	.3207	35.1	0	0	0	2	2	0	3	0	0	0	0	0	6	0	0	0	0	0	0	0	0	0	1	0	0
1/15	2	.0000	.0299	24.8	0	0	0	0	1	1	0	0	0	0	0	0	2	0	0	0	0	0	0	0	0	0	0	0	0
1/16	23	.2981	1.4405	41.6	0	1	0	0	7	3	12	0	0	0	0	0	5	0	0	0	0	0	6	11	0	0	1	0	0
1/16-inch	2	.0000	.0243	23.9	0	0	0	0	2	0	0	0	0	0	0	0	0	0	0	0	0	0	0	0	0	0	0	2	0
1/2	620	.5145	66.849	58.3	55	59	82	112	88	113	104	7	11	3	0	0	422	12	3	35	0	0	51	42	0	11	7	23	0
1/2-foot	2	.0000	.0299	24.8	0	2	0	0	0	0	0	0	0	0	0	0	2	0	0	0	0	0	0	0	0	0	0	0	0
1/2-in	2	.0000	.0243	23.9	0	0	0	0	1	0	0	1	0	0	0	0	0	0	0	0	0	0	0	0	0	0	0	2	0
1/2-inch	9	.3911	.7429	38.7	1	0	2	0	1	2	3	0	0	0	0	0	4	0	0	0	0	0	3	1	0	0	0	1	0
1/2%	9	.1387	.3589	35.5	0	0	0	2	3	0	3	1	0	0	0	0	8	0	0	0	0	0	0	0	0	0	0	1	0
1/2x	2	.0000	.0299	24.8	0	0	0	0	0	0	2	0	0	0	0	0	2	0	0	0	0	0	0	0	0	0	0	0	0
1/2x1/2	2	.0000	.0299	24.8	0	0	0	0	2	0	0	0	0	0	0	0	2	0	0	0	0	0	0	0	0	0	0	0	0
1/25	8	.2857	.5305	37.2	0	0	0	0	4	0	3	1	0	0	0	0	2	0	0	4	0	0	0	2	0	0	0	0	0
1/3	231	.1552	9.9119	50.0	24	28	42	41	51	17	27	1	0	0	0	0	221	0	0	3	1	0	6	0	0	0	0	0	0
1/3%	3	.0000	.0449	26.5	0	0	0	3	0	0	0	0	0	0	0	0	3	0	0	0	0	0	0	0	0	0	0	0	0
1/3x6	2	.0000	.0299	24.8	0	0	0	0	2	0	0	0	0	0	0	0	2	0	0	0	0	0	0	0	0	0	0	0	0
1/30	4	.1776	.1927	32.8	0	0	1	1	2	0	0	0	0	0	0	0	3	0	0	1	0	0	0	0	0	0	0	0	0
1/32	7	.0687	.1430	31.6	0	0	0	0	2	2	3	0	0	0	0	0	0	0	0	2	0	0	0	5	0	0	0	0	0
1/4	342	.4600	33.232	55.2	23	46	51	58	36	43	79	6	1	0	0	0	231	0	0	15	0	0	50	23	0	3	2	17	0
1/4-	2	.2433	.1158	30.6	0	1	0	0	1	0	0	0	0	0	0	0	0	0	0	0	0	0	0	0	0	1	0	1	0
1/4-foot	2	.0000	.0299	24.8	0	2	0	0	0	0	0	0	0	0	0	0	2	0	0	0	0	0	0	0	0	0	0	0	0
1/4-inch	3	.2143	.1568	32.0	0	1	0	0	2	0	0	0	0	0	0	0	0	0	0	0	0	0	0	0	0	1	0	2	0
1/4%	2	.1972	.1262	31.0	0	0	0	1	1	0	0	0	1	0	0	0	1	0	0	0	0	0	0	0	0	0	0	0	0
1/5	53	.0435	1.2078	40.8	2	4	16	16	4	8	3	0	0	0	0	0	52	0	0	0	0	0	0	0	0	0	1	0	0
1/6	52	.0785	1.5606	41.9	8	5	12	9	2	6	10	0	1	0	0	0	48	0	0	3	0	0	0	0	0	0	0	0	0
1/60	9	.0000	.1347	31.3	0	0	2	6	1	0	0	0	0	0	0	0	9	0	0	0	0	0	0	0	0	0	0	0	0
1/64	3	.0803	.0701	28.5	0	0	0	0	1	2	0	0	0	0	0	0	0	0	0	1	0	0	0	2	0	0	0	0	0
1/7	14	.0000	.2096	33.2	1	2	0	1	5	4	1	0	0	0	0	0	14	0	0	0	0	0	0	0	0	0	0	0	0
1/8	77	.4432	7.2119	48.6	5	5	10	11	11	5	30	0	0	0	0	0	48	0	0	4	0	0	14	7	0	0	0	4	0
1/9	9	.0000	.1347	31.3	2	0	0	0	1	2	4	0	0	0	0	0	9	0	0	0	0	0	0	0	0	0	0	0	0
1%	2	.2413	.1212	30.8	0	0	0	1	0	0	0	1	0	0	0	0	1	0	0	1	0	0	0	0	0	0	0	0	0
1's	5	.0000	.0748	28.7	0	0	0	0	0	0	5	0	0	0	0	0	5	0	0	0	0	0	0	0	0	0	0	0	0
1a	10	.1377	.3961	36.0	0	1	0	5	0	0	2	2	0	1	0	0	9	0	0	0	0	0	0	0	0	0	0	0	0
1b	6	.0000	.0898	29.5	0	1	1	2	0	0	0	2	0	0	0	0	6	0	0	0	0	0	0	0	0	0	0	0	0
1c	4	.2345	.2249	33.5	0	1	0	2	1	0	0	0	0	0	0	0	3	0	1	0	0	0	0	0	0	0	0	0	0
1f	3	.0000	.0449	26.5	0	0	0	3	0	0	0	0	0	0	0	0	3	0	0	0	0	0	0	0	0	0	0	0	0
1st	19	.5974	2.3222	43.7	1	5	2	3	2	2	4	0	0	1	0	0	4	2	0	0	5	0	0	0	1	0	4	2	0
1x	2	.0000	.0299	24.8	0	0	0	0	0	2	0	0	0	0	0	0	2	0	0	0	0	0	0	0	0	0	0	0	0

3Q 035
7Q 039
5F 040
6E 043
7Q 046
7Q 049
6R 052
6F 058
7P 060
7R 06002
6E 0672
4F 069
4E 076
7E 078
3Q 084
5Q 086
6Q 08647
7E 089
7E 095
9M 097
6E 098
5E 1C
5E 1D
9E 1E
8E 1-
9H 1-bead
9H 1-cm3
6E 1-degree
4E 1-digit
3E 1-gallon
7R 1-in
6E 1-meter
8E 1-quart
6H 1-square-foot
8M 1-to
9E 1-unit
3P 1-0
9M 1-1a
9M 1-1b
3A 1-1234
7B 1-15
6E 1-16
8E 1-18
9M 1-1957
5B 1-2-3
4A 1-2-3-4
9M 1-2a
9M 1-2b
9M 1-2c
9E 1-22
3A 1-2234
9M 1-3a
9M 1-3b
9M 1-3c
9M 1-3d
9M 1-3e
9H 1-46
6J 1-77
7E 1/-27
9E 1/a
9E 1/a3**
9E 1/b
6E 1/n
8L 1/0
7M 1/10th
9E 1/12n
9H 1/125
6E 1/13
8E 1/18
XH 1/180th
5E 1/19
8M 1/2-foot-long
7R 1/2-incher
XR 1/2-lb
7R 1/2-mile
8H 1/2-minute
8H 1/2-minutes
7R 1/2-ton
6H 1/2-volt
9M 1/2-13
7R 1/2-20
9E 1/2gt
9E 1/2xy
9E 1/2y
7E 1/20
9E 1/2270
7Q 1/250
9H 1/2500
8E 1/273
5E 1/3-4
8E 1/3r
6E 1/360
8L 1/4-cup
6E 1/4-mile
6E 1/4-ounce
5E 1/4-segment
5P 1/4-ton
9M 1/40
XH 1/50
7R 1/5000
6F 1/600
5H 1/65
7E 1/72
7R 1/8-in
7R 1/8-inch-wide
7E 1cm
9H 1cm3
7G 1d
6E 1e
5Q 1ntil
5E 1x1
6E 1x10

Word Type	F	D	U	SFI	3 Gr 3	4 Gr 4	5 Gr 5	6 Gr 6	7 Gr 7	8 Gr 8	9 Gr 9	X UnGr	A Read	B Eng & Gr	C Comp	D Lit	E Math	F Soc Stud	G Spell	H Sci	J Music	K Art	L Home Ec	M Shop	N Lib F	P Lib NF	Q Lib Ref	R Mag	S Rel
1x6	2	.0000	.0299	24.8	0	0	2	0	0	0	0	0	0	0	0	0	2	0	0	0	0	0	0	0	0	0	0	0	0
1x7	2	.0000	.0299	24.8	0	0	0	0	1	1	0	0	0	0	0	0	2	0	0	0	0	0	0	0	0	0	0	0	0
10	1370	.6217	175.32	62.4	169	142	170	179	289	212	172	37	41	29	17	6	878	59	24	88	7	0	14	10	2	48	62	85	0
10-	6	.4705	.6020	37.8	0	0	0	0	4	0	0	2	0	0	0	0	1	0	0	2	0	0	0	0	0	0	1	2	0
10-centimeter	5	.0000	.0748	28.7	0	2	0	0	2	0	1	0	0	0	0	0	5	0	0	0	0	0	0	0	0	0	0	0	0
10-degree	3	.0000	.0449	26.5	0	0	0	3	0	0	0	0	0	0	0	0	3	0	0	0	0	0	0	0	0	0	0	0	0
10-dollar	2	.0000	.0299	24.8	0	0	0	0	2	0	0	0	0	0	0	0	2	0	0	0	0	0	0	0	0	0	0	0	0
10-foot	2	.0000	.0243	23.9	0	1	1	0	0	0	0	0	0	0	0	0	0	0	0	0	0	0	0	0	0	0	0	2	0
10-pound	2	.0000	.0209	23.2	0	0	0	0	2	0	0	0	0	0	0	0	0	0	0	0	0	0	0	0	0	0	2	0	0
10-year	3	.3829	.2504	34.0	0	0	2	1	0	0	0	0	0	0	0	0	1	0	0	0	0	0	0	0	0	1	1	0	0
10-1	2	.0000	.0050	17.0	0	0	0	0	0	1	1	0	0	0	0	0	0	0	0	0	0	0	0	2	0	0	0	0	0
10-10	2	.0000	.0050	17.0	0	0	0	0	0	0	2	0	0	0	0	0	0	0	0	0	0	0	0	2	0	0	0	0	0
10-11	2	.2351	.1166	30.7	0	1	0	0	0	0	1	0	0	0	0	0	0	1	0	0	0	0	0	0	0	0	0	1	0
10-12	2	.1432	.0759	28.8	0	0	0	0	0	1	1	0	0	0	0	0	0	0	0	1	0	0	1	0	0	0	0	0	0
10-13	5	.2379	.2813	34.5	0	1	0	0	0	3	1	0	0	0	0	0	4	0	0	0	0	0	0	1	0	0	0	0	0
10-15	2	.0000	.0050	17.0	0	0	0	0	0	1	1	0	0	0	0	0	0	0	0	0	0	0	0	2	0	0	0	0	0
10-16	2	.0000	.0050	17.0	0	0	0	0	0	1	1	0	0	0	0	0	0	0	0	0	0	0	0	2	0	0	0	0	0
10-17	2	.0000	.0299	24.8	2	0	0	0	0	0	0	0	0	0	0	0	2	0	0	0	0	0	0	0	0	0	0	0	0
10-17c	2	.0000	.0050	17.0	0	0	0	0	0	0	2	0	0	0	0	0	0	0	0	0	0	0	0	2	0	0	0	0	0
10-18	2	.0000	.0050	17.0	0	0	0	0	0	1	1	0	0	0	0	0	0	0	0	0	0	0	0	2	0	0	0	0	0
10-2	4	.0000	.0101	20.0	0	0	0	0	0	1	3	0	0	0	0	0	0	0	0	0	0	0	0	4	0	0	0	0	0
10-26	2	.2413	.1212	30.8	0	0	0	0	1	0	1	0	0	0	0	0	1	0	0	1	0	0	0	0	0	0	0	0	0
10-3	6	.0803	.1402	31.5	0	0	0	0	0	2	4	0	0	0	0	0	0	0	0	2	0	0	0	4	0	0	0	0	0
10-4	4	.2085	.2127	33.3	0	0	0	0	3	1	0	0	0	0	0	0	0	0	0	3	0	0	0	1	0	0	0	0	0
10-6	2	.0725	.0732	28.6	0	0	0	0	0	2	0	0	1	0	0	0	0	0	0	0	0	0	0	1	0	0	0	0	0
10/10	3	.0000	.0449	26.5	0	0	0	1	2	0	0	0	0	0	0	0	3	0	0	0	0	0	0	0	0	0	0	0	0
10/12	2	.0000	.0299	24.8	0	0	2	0	0	0	0	0	0	0	0	0	2	0	0	0	0	0	0	0	0	0	0	0	0
10/5	2	.0000	.0299	24.8	0	0	1	0	1	0	0	0	0	0	0	0	2	0	0	0	0	0	0	0	0	0	0	0	0
10%	18	.4080	1.5938	42.0	0	0	1	2	5	1	8	1	0	2	0	0	12	0	0	1	0	0	0	0	0	0	2	1	0
10's	6	.0000	.0898	29.5	1	0	3	0	1	1	0	0	0	0	0	0	6	0	0	0	0	0	0	0	0	0	0	0	0
10d	2	.0000	.0050	17.0	0	0	0	0	2	0	0	0	0	0	0	0	0	0	0	0	0	0	0	2	0	0	0	0	0
10n	5	.0000	.0748	28.7	0	0	0	0	1	4	0	0	0	0	0	0	5	0	0	0	0	0	0	0	0	0	0	0	0
10s	2	.2412	.1141	30.6	0	0	0	0	1	1	0	0	0	1	0	0	0	0	0	0	0	0	0	0	0	1	0	0	0
10th	5	.3611	.3965	36.0	0	2	1	1	0	1	0	0	0	0	0	0	2	0	0	0	0	0	0	0	0	1	2	0	0
10x	5	.2253	.2867	34.6	0	0	2	0	2	0	1	0	0	0	0	0	3	0	0	2	0	0	0	0	0	0	0	0	0
100	626	.6915	88.262	59.5	46	64	106	111	146	74	67	12	36	5	1	5	298	58	13	66	3	1	0	12	0	33	46	49	0
100-	3	.3390	.2450	33.9	0	0	0	2	1	0	0	0	1	0	0	0	0	0	0	0	0	0	0	0	0	0	1	1	0
100-foot	4	.3366	.3291	35.2	0	0	0	1	2	0	0	1	1	0	0	0	0	0	0	2	0	0	0	0	0	0	0	1	0
100-foot-long	2	.2437	.1129	30.5	0	0	0	1	1	0	0	0	0	0	0	0	0	0	0	0	0	0	0	0	0	0	1	1	0
100-inch	2	.2346	.1166	30.7	0	0	1	0	1	0	0	0	0	0	0	0	0	0	0	1	0	0	0	0	0	0	0	1	0
100-yard	2	.0000	.0299	24.8	0	0	0	0	0	0	2	0	0	0	0	0	2	0	0	0	0	0	0	0	0	0	0	0	0
100-128	2	.0000	.0162	22.1	0	0	1	1	0	0	0	0	0	0	0	0	0	0	2	0	0	0	0	0	0	0	0	0	0
100/100	5	.0000	.0748	28.7	0	0	0	2	3	0	0	0	0	0	0	0	5	0	0	0	0	0	0	0	0	0	0	0	0
100%	4	.0000	.0599	27.8	0	0	0	0	1	0	3	0	0	0	0	0	4	0	0	0	0	0	0	0	0	0	0	0	0
100's	4	.0000	.0599	27.8	2	0	2	0	0	0	0	0	0	0	0	0	4	0	0	0	0	0	0	0	0	0	0	0	0
1000	117	.5880	14.272	51.5	6	14	19	27	28	10	11	2	3	3	0	0	65	19	10	6	2	0	0	1	0	2	4	2	0
1000's	2	.0000	.0299	24.8	2	0	0	0	0	0	0	0	0	0	0	0	2	0	0	0	0	0	0	0	0	0	0	0	0
1001	2	.2351	.1166	30.7	0	0	0	1	0	0	0	1	0	0	0	0	0	1	0	0	0	0	0	0	0	0	0	1	0
101	37	.6593	5.0912	47.1	2	8	1	4	7	13	2	0	13	2	0	0	6	1	8	1	0	0	0	1	0	2	3	0	0
1016	2	.0000	.0209	23.2	1	0	0	0	0	1	0	0	0	0	0	0	0	0	0	0	0	0	0	0	0	0	2	0	0
102	23	.5024	2.4342	43.9	1	2	3	3	5	7	1	1	2	0	0	1	5	2	10	0	0	0	0	1	0	2	0	0	0
103	32	.7549	4.8681	46.9	0	6	6	1	8	7	1	3	1	0	0	0	7	2	4	9	1	1	0	1	0	4	1	1	0
103rd	3	.2398	.1721	32.4	0	0	0	1	2	0	0	0	0	0	0	0	2	0	0	0	0	0	0	0	0	0	1	0	0
104	28	.5671	3.2381	45.1	1	6	4	3	5	5	3	1	0	0	0	0	3	0	15	2	3	1	0	1	0	1	1	1	0
105	35	.7775	5.4456	47.4	3	1	4	2	11	8	5	1	1	2	1	1	7	1	9	3	1	0	1	1	0	2	0	5	0
1050	3	.2398	.1721	32.4	0	1	1	1	0	0	0	0	0	0	0	0	2	0	0	0	0	0	0	0	0	0	1	0	0
106	26	.6377	3.3610	45.3	6	2	4	1	8	3	2	0	0	2	0	0	3	2	10	0	2	0	0	1	0	3	1	2	0
106-107	3	.0000	.0583	27.7	0	0	0	3	0	0	0	0	0	0	0	0	0	3	0	0	0	0	0	0	0	0	0	0	0
1066	11	.4681	1.0725	40.3	0	0	1	2	1	4	0	3	0	6	0	0	0	0	2	1	0	1	0	0	0	0	1	0	0
107	28	.4690	2.7640	44.4	8	3	3	3	6	3	2	0	1	2	0	0	5	2	14	1	1	0	0	0	0	0	1	1	0
108	28	.5305	3.0698	44.9	7	6	3	2	4	4	2	0	1	0	0	2	5	2	13	0	2	0	2	0	0	0	0	1	0
1089	4	.0000	.0579	27.6	4	0	0	0	0	0	0	0	0	0	0	0	0	0	0	0	0	0	0	0	0	4	0	0	0
109	25	.5770	2.9856	44.8	5	6	0	2	9	1	1	1	3	0	0	1	1	2	12	1	1	0	1	1	0	0	0	2	0
1095	2	.2285	.1129	30.5	0	0	1	0	0	1	0	0	0	0	0	0	0	1	0	0	0	0	0	0	0	0	1	0	0
11	318	.7707	49.324	56.9	33	44	38	33	63	54	44	9	26	9	3	0	119	20	24	20	3	0	2	14	0	21	24	33	0
11**	3	.1639	.1674	32.2	0	1	1	0	0	0	1	0	1	0	0	0	0	2	0	0	0	0	0	0	0	0	0	0	0
11-year-old	3	.1937	.1495	31.7	0	0	0	1	0	2	0	0	0	0	0	0	0	1	0	0	0	0	0	0	0	0	0	2	0
11-20	3	.2371	.1813	32.6	0	1	0	0	0	0	2	0	0	0	0	0	1	0	0	2	0	0	0	0	0	0	0	0	0
11-5	2	.1457	.0722	28.6	0	1	0	0	0	1	0	0	0	0	0	0	1	0	0	0	0	0	0	1	0	0	0	0	0
11-9	2	.0000	.0299	24.8	0	1	1	0	0	0	0	0	0	0	0	0	2	0	0	0	0	0	0	0	0	0	0	0	0
11/16	3	.1993	.1435	31.6	0	0	0	0	1	0	2	0	0	0	0	0	2	0	0	0	0	0	0	1	0	0	0	0	0
11th	7	.4228	.6378	38.0	0	1	0	2	2	1	1	0	0	0	0	0	1	2	0	0	0	0	0	0	0	0	3	1	0
110	73	.4046	6.2506	48.0	6	15	3	5	33	8	3	0	1	0	0	0	6	1	49	4	0	0	2	1	0	1	2	6	0
1100	8	.6670	1.0855	40.4	1	0	1	3	0	2	0	1	0	1	0	0	2	1	0	1	1	0	0	0	0	0	1	1	0
1100's	2	.0000	.0209	23.2	0	0	2	0	0	0	0	0	0	0	0	0	0	0	0	0	0	0	0	0	0	0	2	0	0
111	29	.2363	1.6001	42.0	2	19	0	1	2	2	1	2	1	0	0	0	5	2	20	0	0	0	0	0	0	0	1	0	0
1111	2	.0000	.0299	24.8	0	0	0	0	0	0	2	0	0	0	0	0	2	0	0	0	0	0	0	0	0	0	0	0	0
112	51	.2055	2.4480	43.9	8	5	27	5	4	2	0	0	0	0	0	0	6	0	40	2	1	0	0	0	0	1	0	1	0
112103	2	.0000	.0299	24.8	0	0	0	0	0	2	0	0	0	0	0	0	2	0	0	0	0	0	0	0	0	0	0	0	0
113	11	.5117	1.1603	40.6	4	2	2	0	2	0	1	0	0	0	0	0	2	0	5	0	0	0	1	0	0	1	1	1	0
114	17	.3986	1.5097	41.8	3	4	4	0	3	2	1	0	3	1	0	0	2	2	8	0	0	0	0	0	0	1	0	0	0
1140	2	.2413	.1212	30.8	0	0	0	0	1	0	0	1	0	0	0	0	1	0	0	1	0	0	0	0	0	0	0	0	0

9E 1x3/2x3
8E 1x4
8E 1x9
3A 10K
8E 10-a
5Q 10-bell
9H 10-cm3
7R 10-day
8R 10-foot-wide
9R 10-ft-high**
XH 10-inch
7R 10-inch-diameter
9Q 10-inch-long
7R 10-lane
6R 10-mile
9R 10-million-dollar
7R 10-pound-test
7R 10-speed
4P 10-story
8M 10-story-high
8E 10-yd
4E 10-year-old
8R 10-0
8M 10-14
9M 10-17a
9M 10-17b
9M 10-18b
9H 10-19
9M 10-19a
9H 10-20
7E 10-23
9H 10-25
7E 10-28
7E 10-30
7E 10-31
7E 10-33
7E 10-34
7E 10-35
8M 10-5
6Q 10-8
5E 10/14
6Q 10/24ths
5E 10/4
6E 10/8
8E 10m
8E 10x10
8E 10x16
4H 100X
8R 100-day
7E 100-lb
9E 100-meter
6F 100-mile
7R 100-percent
7R 100-plus
7R 100-thousandths
8M 100/Eout
9E 100/110
8M 100/2
4E 100/300
7P 100s
XR 100th
9H 1000-lb
6A 1000-mile
6A 1000-pound
7P 1000s
5E 1000x1000
8M 100000/200
4B 10010
7Q 10022
XR 10023
7Q 10027
6B 1003
5Q 1008
5R 101-foot
9B 101-117
7Q 101st
3E 1010
8E 101001000100001
8E 10110
8F 102-story
6E 102-99
8E 1020
9Q 1030
9F 1036
9M 1037
7A 104th
5Q 1042
7P 105-millimeter
9M 1053
9M 1054
5E 1056
6F 106-
XR 106-berth
8F 106-ton
7R 106th
7E 1060
8H 1063
8E 1075
5F 108-109
8H 1083
5H 1091
8F 1096
7R 11-foot
7E 11-in
8M 11-1
9R 11-1-2
6E 11-13
9H 11-17
9H 11-18
9H 11-19
8M 11-2
8M 11-3
8M 11-4
9H 11-8
6E 11/10
8E 11/12
9E 11/22
7E 11/40
8E 11%
6R 11's
3E 11a
3E 11b
8L 110-111
8C 110-12
7M 110-4A
7M 110-5
7M 110-6
6H 110/1100
7R 110th
7G 111-127
8E 111111
6E 1112
9F 1113
9Q 1115
7R 1115091
7A 112-113
7R 1120
9F 1125
6G 113-127
6P 1130
9Q 1137
4Q 1138-1193
9M 1141
9M 1142

Word Type	F	D	U	SFI	3 Gr 3	4 Gr 4	5 Gr 5	6 Gr 6	7 Gr 7	8 Gr 8	9 Gr 9	X UnGr	A Read	B Eng & Gr	C Comp	D Lit	E Math	F Soc Stud	G Spell	H Sci	J Music	K Art	L Home Ec	M Shop	N Lib F	P Lib NF	Q Lib Ref	R Mag	S Rel
115	23	.7868	3.6575	45.6	6	4	1	1	7	3	1	0	6	0	0	0	3	2	3	1	1	0	1	1	0	1	2	2	0
1150	4	.2875	.2848	34.5	0	0	0	1	0	0	1	2	1	2	0	0	1	0	0	0	0	0	0	0	0	0	0	0	0
1153	3	.0000	.0076	18.8	0	0	0	0	0	0	3	0	0	0	0	0	0	0	0	0	0	0	0	3	0	0	0	0	0
1154	5	.0770	.0947	29.8	0	0	0	0	1	0	4	0	0	0	0	0	0	0	0	0	0	0	0	4	0	0	1	0	0
1157	2	.0000	.0050	17.0	0	0	0	0	0	0	2	0	0	0	0	0	0	0	0	0	0	0	0	2	0	0	0	0	0
116	12	.5399	1.3255	41.2	4	0	1	2	2	1	2	0	0	0	0	0	1	1	3	0	4	1	0	0	0	0	2	0	0
1163	2	.0000	.0243	23.9	0	0	2	0	0	0	0	0	0	0	0	0	0	0	0	0	0	0	0	0	0	0	0	2	0
117	11	.6472	1.4789	41.7	4	3	1	0	1	0	2	0	2	1	0	0	3	1	1	2	0	0	0	0	0	0	0	1	0
1174	2	.2401	.1133	30.5	1	1	0	0	0	0	0	0	0	0	0	0	0	0	0	0	0	0	0	0	0	1	1	0	0
118	12	.4996	1.2455	41.0	3	0	0	3	4	2	0	0	0	1	0	0	3	1	5	0	1	0	0	0	0	0	1	0	0
118-21	2	.0000	.0219	23.4	0	0	0	2	0	0	0	0	0	2	0	0	0	0	0	0	0	0	0	0	0	0	0	0	0
119	9	.4925	.9596	39.8	2	0	1	1	3	2	0	0	2	0	0	0	0	1	0	0	1	0	0	0	0	0	3	2	0
12	755	.6330	98.238	59.9	119	118	106	102	129	95	63	23	32	5	1	6	457	41	23	45	3	0	10	19	1	20	33	59	0
12-foot	4	.3634	.3173	35.0	0	0	0	0	3	1	0	0	0	0	0	0	1	0	0	0	0	0	0	0	0	0	1	2	0
12-hour	8	.0000	.1197	30.8	0	1	0	0	0	7	0	0	0	0	0	0	8	0	0	0	0	0	0	0	0	0	0	0	0
12-inch	2	.1738	.0790	29.0	0	0	0	0	1	0	1	0	0	0	0	0	0	0	0	0	0	0	0	1	0	0	1	0	0
12-man	2	.2346	.1166	30.7	0	0	0	0	1	0	1	0	0	0	0	0	0	0	0	1	0	0	0	0	0	0	0	1	0
12-mile	3	.2427	.1822	32.6	0	0	0	0	2	0	1	0	0	0	0	0	0	0	0	2	0	0	0	0	0	0	0	1	0
12-year-old	5	.3441	.4209	36.2	0	0	1	1	2	0	1	0	2	0	0	0	0	0	0	0	0	0	0	0	0	0	1	2	0
12-1	3	.2076	.1618	32.1	0	0	0	0	0	0	3	0	0	0	0	0	2	0	0	1	0	0	0	0	0	0	0	0	0
12-12	2	.2421	.0995	30.0	0	0	0	0	0	0	2	0	0	0	0	0	0	0	0	0	0	0	1	1	0	0	0	0	0
12-13	6	.1579	.2847	34.5	0	0	1	0	4	1	0	0	0	0	0	0	0	5	0	1	0	0	0	0	0	0	0	0	0
12-15	3	.2371	.1813	32.6	0	0	0	0	0	1	2	0	0	0	0	0	1	0	0	2	0	0	0	0	0	0	0	0	0
12-17	2	.0000	.0299	24.8	0	0	1	0	0	1	0	0	0	0	0	0	2	0	0	0	0	0	0	0	0	0	0	0	0
12-2	2	.1249	.0685	28.4	0	0	0	0	0	1	1	0	0	0	0	0	0	0	0	1	0	0	0	1	0	0	0	0	0
12-3	5	.2379	.2813	34.5	0	1	1	0	0	1	2	0	0	0	0	0	4	0	0	0	0	0	0	1	0	0	0	0	0
12-4	7	.2146	.3579	35.5	0	0	0	0	0	2	5	0	0	0	0	0	5	0	0	0	0	0	0	2	0	0	0	0	0
12-6	3	.2451	.1726	32.4	0	1	0	0	0	1	1	0	0	0	0	0	1	0	0	1	0	0	0	1	0	0	0	0	0
12-7	4	.1670	.1644	32.2	0	0	1	0	0	2	1	0	0	0	0	0	1	0	0	1	0	0	0	2	0	0	0	0	0
12/16	2	.1457	.0722	28.6	0	0	0	0	0	1	1	0	0	0	0	0	1	0	0	0	0	0	0	1	0	0	0	0	0
12/4	3	.0000	.0449	26.5	0	0	1	2	0	0	0	0	0	0	0	0	3	0	0	0	0	0	0	0	0	0	0	0	0
12/5	4	.0000	.0599	27.8	0	0	4	0	0	0	0	0	0	0	0	0	4	0	0	0	0	0	0	0	0	0	0	0	0
12/7	2	.0000	.0299	24.8	0	0	2	0	0	0	0	0	0	0	0	0	2	0	0	0	0	0	0	0	0	0	0	0	0
12%	5	.3809	.4306	36.3	1	0	0	0	0	1	2	1	1	0	0	0	2	0	0	0	0	0	1	0	0	0	0	1	0
12's	2	.2427	.1159	30.6	1	0	0	0	1	0	0	0	0	0	0	0	1	0	0	0	0	0	0	0	0	0	0	1	0
12th	13	.6874	1.8068	42.6	0	2	1	3	3	4	0	0	0	2	0	1	1	1	0	0	0	0	0	0	2	1	2	3	0
12x	4	.0000	.0599	27.8	0	0	0	0	0	0	4	0	0	0	0	0	4	0	0	0	0	0	0	0	0	0	0	0	0
12y	2	.0000	.0299	24.8	0	0	0	0	0	0	2	0	0	0	0	0	2	0	0	0	0	0	0	0	0	0	0	0	0
120	80	.7563	12.261	50.9	9	15	13	12	17	8	5	1	13	2	0	0	26	3	5	7	3	0	0	1	0	8	3	9	0
120-pound	3	.0000	.0434	26.4	0	0	0	0	0	0	0	3	0	0	0	0	0	0	0	0	0	0	0	0	0	3	0	0	0
1200	14	.6559	1.8717	42.7	1	3	0	1	6	2	1	0	0	1	0	0	3	3	0	1	2	0	0	0	0	0	2	2	0
1200's	5	.0000	.0523	27.2	0	0	5	0	0	0	0	0	0	0	0	0	0	0	0	0	0	0	0	0	0	0	5	0	0
121	15	.4190	1.3571	41.3	6	0	1	2	3	2	1	0	0	0	0	0	4	5	5	0	0	0	0	0	0	0	0	1	0
1215	2	.2139	.1057	30.2	0	0	0	0	0	2	0	0	0	0	0	0	0	1	1	0	0	0	0	0	0	0	0	0	0
122	9	.5487	1.0134	40.1	1	1	2	3	1	0	1	0	0	1	0	0	2	1	3	0	1	0	0	1	0	0	0	0	0
123	21	.4294	1.9435	42.9	4	4	0	4	7	1	1	0	0	1	0	0	13	3	3	0	0	0	0	0	0	0	0	1	0
1230	3	.1823	.1405	31.5	0	0	2	0	0	0	1	0	0	0	0	0	0	1	0	0	0	0	0	0	0	0	2	0	0
1232	2	.0000	.0299	24.8	0	1	0	0	0	1	0	0	0	0	0	0	2	0	0	0	0	0	0	0	0	0	0	0	0
1237	2	.2391	.1133	30.5	0	0	0	0	1	0	1	0	0	0	0	0	1	0	0	0	0	0	0	0	0	0	1	0	0
124	18	.4110	1.6241	42.1	1	5	3	5	2	2	0	0	2	0	0	0	6	1	7	1	0	0	0	0	0	0	0	1	0
1241	3	.0000	.0449	26.5	1	0	0	1	0	1	0	0	0	0	0	0	3	0	0	0	0	0	0	0	0	0	0	0	0
1244	2	.0000	.0209	23.2	0	0	0	0	0	0	2	0	0	0	0	0	0	0	0	0	0	0	0	0	0	0	2	0	0
125	54	.5597	6.2989	48.0	7	3	9	9	9	11	5	1	4	0	0	0	20	3	14	0	1	0	0	0	0	5	2	5	0
125th	2	.0000	.0914	29.6	0	0	0	0	2	0	0	0	2	0	0	0	0	0	0	0	0	0	0	0	0	0	0	0	0
1250	4	.3824	.3323	35.2	0	0	1	0	1	0	1	1	0	1	0	0	2	0	0	0	0	0	0	0	0	0	1	0	0
126	26	.4365	2.3847	43.8	4	11	3	5	2	1	0	0	0	1	0	0	8	1	14	0	1	1	0	0	0	0	0	0	0
1260	4	.2220	.2176	33.4	0	0	1	0	3	0	0	0	0	0	0	0	3	0	0	0	0	0	0	0	0	0	1	0	0
1268	2	.0000	.0299	24.8	0	0	1	0	0	1	0	0	0	0	0	0	2	0	0	0	0	0	0	0	0	0	0	0	0
127	21	.3200	1.4641	41.7	1	8	3	5	2	1	1	0	0	0	0	0	3	1	14	0	1	0	0	0	0	1	1	0	0
128	39	.6120	4.9214	46.9	6	4	5	10	4	5	4	1	2	0	0	1	15	6	8	3	1	0	0	2	0	1	0	0	0
128-129	3	.0000	.0583	27.7	0	0	0	3	0	0	0	0	0	0	0	0	0	3	0	0	0	0	0	0	0	0	0	0	0
128-29	2	.0000	.0219	23.4	0	0	0	2	0	0	0	0	0	2	0	0	0	0	0	0	0	0	0	0	0	0	0	0	0
129	20	.4304	1.8069	42.6	1	2	6	8	2	0	1	0	0	0	0	0	3	2	12	0	1	0	0	1	0	0	1	0	0
1296	2	.0000	.0389	25.9	0	0	0	1	0	0	1	0	0	0	0	0	0	2	0	0	0	0	0	0	0	0	0	0	0
13	278	.7647	42.729	56.3	38	37	46	34	46	28	42	7	11	2	1	2	125	17	25	7	5	2	3	3	2	14	22	37	0
13-1	2	.2346	.1166	30.7	0	0	0	0	1	0	1	0	0	0	0	0	0	0	0	1	0	0	0	0	0	0	0	1	0
13-10a	2	.0000	.0050	17.0	0	0	0	0	0	0	2	0	0	0	0	0	0	0	0	0	0	0	0	2	0	0	0	0	0
13-16	4	.0000	.0599	27.8	0	0	0	0	4	0	0	0	0	0	0	0	4	0	0	0	0	0	0	0	0	0	0	0	0
13-17	8	.1967	.3779	35.8	1	0	1	1	4	0	1	0	0	0	0	0	3	0	5	0	0	0	0	0	0	0	0	0	0
13-19	2	.0000	.0299	24.8	0	0	0	0	1	0	1	0	0	0	0	0	2	0	0	0	0	0	0	0	0	0	0	0	0
13-2	2	.2413	.1212	30.8	0	0	0	0	0	0	2	0	0	0	0	0	1	0	0	1	0	0	0	0	0	0	0	0	0
13-22	2	.0000	.0299	24.8	0	0	0	0	1	1	0	0	0	0	0	0	2	0	0	0	0	0	0	0	0	0	0	0	0
13-3	2	.2413	.1212	30.8	0	0	0	0	0	0	2	0	0	0	0	0	1	0	0	1	0	0	0	0	0	0	0	0	0
13-4	2	.0000	.0394	26.0	0	0	0	0	0	0	2	0	0	0	0	0	0	0	0	2	0	0	0	0	0	0	0	0	0
13-8	3	.2264	.1679	32.2	1	1	1	0	0	0	0	0	0	0	0	0	2	0	0	0	0	0	0	0	0	1	0	0	0
13/16	3	.0000	.0449	26.5	0	0	1	0	0	1	1	0	0	0	0	0	3	0	0	0	0	0	0	0	0	0	0	0	0
13%	2	.1648	.0800	29.0	0	0	0	0	0	0	2	0	0	0	0	0	1	0	0	0	0	0	1	0	0	0	0	0	0
13's	2	.2427	.1159	30.6	1	0	0	0	1	0	0	0	0	0	0	0	1	0	0	0	0	0	0	0	0	0	0	1	0
13th	13	.4930	1.3447	41.3	0	0	2	2	3	2	4	0	0	0	0	0	0	2	0	0	0	0	0	0	1	2	5	3	0
13y	2	.0000	.0299	24.8	0	0	0	0	0	0	2	0	0	0	0	0	2	0	0	0	0	0	0	0	0	0	0	0	0
130	32	.7510	4.8587	46.9	4	4	9	5	3	1	5	1	3	2	0	0	8	5	0	2	1	0	0	1	0	2	3	5	0
130-foot	2	.2442	.1134	30.5	0	0	0	1	0	0	1	0	0	1	0	0	0	0	0	0	0	0	0	0	0	0	0	1	0
1300	5	.3188	.3999	36.0	1	2	0	0	2	0	0	0	2	0	0	0	1	0	0	0	0	0	0	0	0	0	2	0	0
1301	4	.0000	.0486	26.9	0	0	0	1	3	0	0	0	0	0	0	0	0	0	0	0	0	0	0	0	0	0	0	4	0
1302	2	.0000	.0389	25.9	0	0	0	0	0	0	2	0	0	0	0	0	0	2	0	0	0	0	0	0	0	0	0	0	0

9M 1143
9M 1145
6E 1147
9M 1156
9M 1158
9M 1159
7R 116-pound
4Q 1164
9M 1166-1168
4Q 1171
6J 1176
6F 118-119
7B 118-132
7F 1180
5Q 1181-1226
4Q 1187
8H 119-125
4Q 1191
4Q 1192
3A 12K
4R 12-
8J 12-bar
5E 12-clock
XR 12-foot-tall
8E 12-ft
7R 12-gauge
6R 12-horse
7Q 12-member
7Q 12-month
4P 12-ounce
7R 12-port
5F 12-year
6R 12-0
9M 12-10
9M 12-11
9H 12-14
9H 12-16
7Q 12-23
8M 12-5
9M 12-9
7R 12/0
6E 12/100
6E 12/15
8E 12/2
7E 12/3
6E 12s
7P 120-yard
7R 1205
6F 1206
7B 121-123
9J 121b
9E 1210
8E 121212
7E 1216
6B 122-23
5Q 1220
9Q 1221
6F 1224
9F 1227
7R 1228
5Q 123-acre
6E 123/1000
8E 123x4
8E 123x400
8E 12345678910111213
8Q 1235
9Q 1238
7G 124-126
6R 124th
9F 1240
7E 1247
XB 1249
7E 1253
5Q 1264
5Q 1265-1321
5P 1269
9B 127-
9H 127-151
8F 1271
6F 1275
9M 1279
8B 1280
6R 1282
7R 129-HR
4F 129-131
5E 1292
9F 1294
8F 1295
9M 13NC
7R 13-
5E 13-n
8H 13-volume
4R 13-year-olds
9M 13-10b
9M 13-11a
7E 13-14
7E 13-15
7E 13-18
7E 13-20
9E 13-20a
9E 13-20b
7E 13-21
7E 13-23
9H 13-25B
6E 13-7
9M 13-9
7E 13/6
9F 13th-century
5A 130-pound
5F 130-134
6B 130-31
8J 1300-1500
5Q 1300's
7R 1300cc
5Q 1304-1374
9F 1309

Word Type	F	D	U	SFI	3 Gr 3	4 Gr 4	5 Gr 5	6 Gr 6	7 Gr 7	8 Gr 8	9 Gr 9	X UnGr	A Read	B Eng & Gr	C Comp	D Lit	E Math	F Soc Stud	G Spell	H Sci	J Music	K Art	L Home Ec	M Shop	N Lib F	P Lib NF	Q Lib Ref	R Mag	S Rel
131	13	.4516	1.2568	41.0	0	3	4	1	0	1	4	0	0	1	0	0	3	6	0	0	0	0	0	2	0	0	1	0	0
132	15	.3642	1.2161	40.8	5	1	1	0	3	1	3	1	1	0	0	0	8	1	0	1	0	0	0	3	0	0	0	1	0
132-134	2	.0000	.0389	25.9	0	0	2	0	0	0	0	0	0	0	0	0	0	2	0	0	0	0	0	0	0	0	0	0	0
133	7	.4696	.6990	38.4	0	0	3	1	1	0	1	1	0	0	0	0	0	2	0	1	0	0	0	1	0	1	0	2	0
1333	3	.0000	.0365	25.6	0	0	0	0	3	0	0	0	0	0	0	0	0	0	0	0	0	0	0	0	0	0	0	3	0
134	11	.3180	.7996	39.0	3	2	1	0	3	1	0	1	0	1	0	0	8	1	0	0	0	0	0	0	0	1	0	0	0
1340	2	.0000	.0162	22.1	0	2	0	0	0	0	0	0	0	0	0	0	0	0	0	0	2	0	0	0	0	0	0	0	0
135	22	.3873	1.8839	42.8	5	0	5	2	4	2	2	2	1	1	0	0	16	0	0	0	0	0	0	1	0	3	0	0	0
136	12	.6208	1.5409	41.9	1	4	3	2	0	0	2	0	1	1	0	0	3	3	0	0	2	0	0	0	0	1	0	1	0
137	6	.4651	.6256	38.0	1	1	0	1	2	1	0	0	2	1	0	0	2	0	0	0	0	0	0	0	0	0	0	1	0
138	13	.5093	1.4013	41.5	5	1	0	4	1	1	1	0	1	4	0	0	5	0	0	1	1	0	0	0	0	0	0	1	0
139	6	.3271	.4728	36.7	0	2	1	1	2	0	0	0	2	2	0	0	0	0	0	0	2	0	0	0	0	0	0	0	0
139-41	3	.0000	.0328	25.2	0	0	0	3	0	0	0	0	0	3	0	0	0	0	0	0	0	0	0	0	0	0	0	0	0
14	305	.7216	44.633	56.5	56	45	34	39	50	34	34	13	22	5	1	3	144	23	23	21	1	0	3	4	0	9	22	24	0
14-	2	.0000	.0243	23.9	0	0	0	0	0	0	0	2	0	0	0	0	0	0	0	0	0	0	0	0	0	0	0	2	0
14-year-old	2	.0000	.0243	23.9	0	0	0	1	0	0	0	1	0	0	0	0	0	0	0	0	0	0	0	0	0	0	0	2	0
14-1	2	.0000	.0394	26.0	0	0	0	0	0	0	2	0	0	0	0	0	0	0	0	2	0	0	0	0	0	0	0	0	0
14-10B	2	.0000	.0394	26.0	0	0	0	0	0	0	2	0	0	0	0	0	0	0	0	2	0	0	0	0	0	0	0	0	0
14-15	6	.4189	.5719	37.6	0	2	0	0	1	1	1	1	1	0	0	0	0	3	0	1	0	0	0	0	0	0	1	0	0
14-16-17	2	.0000	.0064	18.1	0	0	0	0	0	0	2	0	0	0	0	0	0	0	0	0	0	0	2	0	0	0	0	0	0
14-18	2	.2413	.1212	30.8	0	0	0	0	0	1	1	0	0	0	0	0	1	0	0	1	0	0	0	0	0	0	0	0	0
14-2	2	.1249	.0685	28.4	0	0	0	0	0	1	1	0	0	0	0	0	0	0	0	1	0	0	0	1	0	0	0	0	0
14-20	2	.0000	.0299	24.8	0	0	0	0	0	0	2	0	0	0	0	0	2	0	0	0	0	0	0	0	0	0	0	0	0
14-20a	2	.0000	.0299	24.8	0	0	0	0	0	0	2	0	0	0	0	0	2	0	0	0	0	0	0	0	0	0	0	0	0
14-20b	2	.0000	.0299	24.8	0	0	0	0	0	0	2	0	0	0	0	0	2	0	0	0	0	0	0	0	0	0	0	0	0
14-21	3	.0000	.0449	26.5	0	0	0	0	0	1	2	0	0	0	0	0	3	0	0	0	0	0	0	0	0	0	0	0	0
14-4	4	.2857	.2653	34.2	0	0	0	0	0	2	2	0	0	0	0	0	1	0	0	2	0	0	0	1	0	0	0	0	0
14-5	6	.2371	.3626	35.6	0	0	0	2	0	2	2	0	0	0	0	0	2	0	0	4	0	0	0	0	0	0	0	0	0
14-6	2	.0000	.0394	26.0	0	0	0	0	0	1	1	0	0	0	0	0	0	0	0	2	0	0	0	0	0	0	0	0	0
14/16	5	.0000	.0748	28.7	0	0	0	0	5	0	0	0	0	0	0	0	5	0	0	0	0	0	0	0	0	0	0	0	0
14th	18	.6170	2.2600	43.5	0	2	1	0	4	5	5	1	0	3	0	1	0	1	0	0	0	1	0	0	2	2	7	1	0
140	21	.7410	3.1307	45.0	4	2	5	1	3	1	5	0	0	2	0	0	6	3	0	2	1	1	1	0	0	1	3	1	0
140-hp	2	.0000	.0243	23.9	0	0	0	0	2	0	0	0	0	0	0	0	0	0	0	0	0	0	0	0	0	0	0	2	0
140-141	2	.2446	.1257	31.0	1	0	0	1	0	0	0	0	0	0	0	0	0	1	0	1	0	0	0	0	0	0	0	0	0
1400	8	.4737	.8269	39.2	0	1	0	1	3	1	2	0	2	0	0	0	1	0	2	1	0	1	0	0	0	0	0	1	0
1400's	3	.1823	.1405	31.5	0	0	2	0	0	0	1	0	0	0	0	0	0	1	0	0	0	0	0	0	0	0	2	0	0
141	8	.4535	.7798	38.9	0	2	0	0	3	1	2	0	0	0	0	0	2	2	0	2	0	1	0	0	0	0	0	1	0
1415	2	.0000	.0219	23.4	0	0	0	0	1	0	0	1	0	2	0	0	0	0	0	0	0	0	0	0	0	0	0	0	0
1416	3	.2966	.1928	32.9	0	0	0	1	1	1	0	0	0	0	0	0	1	0	1	0	0	0	0	1	0	0	0	0	0
142	5	.4475	.4638	36.7	0	2	0	0	2	0	1	0	0	0	0	0	2	0	0	0	1	0	1	1	0	0	0	0	0
1425	4	.0000	.0599	27.8	4	0	0	0	0	0	0	0	0	0	0	0	4	0	0	0	0	0	0	0	0	0	0	0	0
1428	2	.2412	.1141	30.6	0	0	1	0	0	0	0	1	0	1	0	0	0	0	0	0	0	0	0	0	0	1	0	0	0
143	15	.6915	2.1299	43.3	3	0	0	3	2	2	3	2	3	0	0	0	3	2	0	1	2	0	0	1	0	1	1	1	0
1435	4	.0000	.0599	27.8	4	0	0	0	0	0	0	0	0	0	0	0	4	0	0	0	0	0	0	0	0	0	0	0	0
144	17	.3663	1.3762	41.4	3	3	5	1	1	2	2	0	0	0	0	0	13	1	1	0	1	0	0	0	0	0	1	0	0
1448	2	.1703	.0781	28.9	0	0	0	1	0	0	1	0	0	1	0	0	0	0	0	0	0	0	0	1	0	0	0	0	0
145	7	.3938	.5834	37.7	0	0	0	0	4	1	2	0	0	0	0	0	2	0	1	0	0	0	2	0	0	0	0	2	0
1450	5	.4538	.4783	36.8	0	0	1	1	1	2	0	0	0	1	0	0	0	1	1	0	0	0	0	0	0	0	2	0	0
1452-1519	2	.2404	.0978	29.9	0	0	0	0	0	0	2	0	0	0	0	0	0	0	0	0	0	1	0	1	0	0	0	0	0
1453	3	.3766	.2497	34.0	0	0	2	0	1	0	0	0	0	0	0	0	0	1	0	0	0	0	0	0	0	1	1	0	0
1456	2	.2446	.1257	31.0	0	0	0	1	0	0	0	1	0	0	0	0	0	1	0	1	0	0	0	0	0	0	0	0	0
146	17	.6726	2.3227	43.7	1	0	4	3	5	2	2	0	0	1	0	0	3	7	2	0	1	1	0	1	0	0	1	0	0
147	6	.5269	.6705	38.3	1	1	1	1	1	1	0	0	1	0	0	0	2	0	1	0	1	0	0	0	0	0	0	1	0
1470	2	.0000	.0914	29.6	0	0	0	2	0	0	0	0	2	0	0	0	0	0	0	0	0	0	0	0	0	0	0	0	0
1472	3	.2398	.1721	32.4	0	0	1	0	0	1	1	0	0	0	0	0	2	0	0	0	0	0	0	0	0	0	1	0	0
1476	5	.3351	.3675	35.7	0	0	2	0	2	1	0	0	0	2	0	0	0	1	2	0	0	0	0	0	0	0	0	0	0
148	9	.5839	1.0889	40.4	2	1	0	0	2	1	3	0	1	1	0	0	3	0	1	1	0	0	1	1	0	0	0	0	0
1483	2	.0000	.0209	23.2	0	0	2	0	0	0	0	0	0	0	0	0	0	0	0	0	0	0	0	0	0	0	2	0	0
1488	3	.2444	.1814	32.6	0	0	2	0	0	1	0	0	0	0	0	0	0	2	0	0	0	0	0	0	0	0	1	0	0
1490	3	.2369	.2208	33.4	2	0	0	1	0	0	0	0	2	0	0	0	1	0	0	0	0	0	0	0	0	0	0	0	0
1492	25	.5400	2.8996	44.6	3	2	7	3	6	4	0	0	4	1	0	0	2	12	0	0	0	0	0	0	0	4	2	0	0
1493	2	.2351	.1166	30.7	1	0	1	0	0	0	0	0	0	0	0	0	0	1	0	0	0	0	0	0	0	0	0	1	0
1496	2	.0000	.0389	25.9	0	0	1	0	1	0	0	0	0	0	0	0	0	2	0	0	0	0	0	0	0	0	0	0	0
1497	2	.2285	.1129	30.5	0	0	2	0	0	0	0	0	0	0	0	0	0	1	0	0	0	0	0	0	0	0	1	0	0
15	555	.7216	81.171	59.1	78	61	69	77	103	73	78	16	30	7	3	1	280	29	24	50	2	1	7	8	1	28	25	59	0
15-minute	2	.1432	.0759	28.8	0	0	0	0	1	1	0	0	0	0	0	0	0	0	0	1	0	0	1	0	0	0	0	0	0
15-year-old	5	.0824	.1675	32.2	0	0	0	1	1	1	1	1	1	0	0	0	0	0	0	0	0	0	0	0	0	0	0	4	0
15-10	2	.0000	.0050	17.0	0	0	0	0	1	0	1	0	0	0	0	0	0	0	0	0	0	0	0	2	0	0	0	0	0
15-12	4	.0000	.0101	20.0	0	0	0	0	0	0	4	0	0	0	0	0	0	0	0	0	0	0	0	4	0	0	0	0	0
15-19	3	.1101	.0802	29.0	0	0	0	0	0	2	1	0	0	0	0	0	0	0	0	0	0	0	0	2	0	0	0	1	0
15-20	2	.1620	.0760	28.8	0	0	0	0	0	1	0	1	0	0	0	0	0	0	0	0	0	0	0	1	0	0	0	1	0
15-7	4	.2253	.2138	33.3	0	2	1	0	1	0	0	0	0	0	0	0	3	0	0	0	0	0	0	1	0	0	0	0	0
15-8	4	.2253	.2138	33.3	0	1	1	1	1	0	0	0	0	0	0	0	3	0	0	0	0	0	0	1	0	0	0	0	0
15/14	2	.0000	.0299	24.8	0	0	2	0	0	0	0	0	0	0	0	0	2	0	0	0	0	0	0	0	0	0	0	0	0
15/16	3	.0000	.0449	26.5	0	0	1	0	1	1	0	0	0	0	0	0	3	0	0	0	0	0	0	0	0	0	0	0	0
15/17	4	.0000	.0599	27.8	0	0	4	0	0	0	0	0	0	0	0	0	4	0	0	0	0	0	0	0	0	0	0	0	0
15/2	2	.0000	.0299	24.8	0	0	0	0	1	1	0	0	0	0	0	0	2	0	0	0	0	0	0	0	0	0	0	0	0
15/20	2	.0000	.0299	24.8	0	0	0	0	1	1	0	0	0	0	0	0	2	0	0	0	0	0	0	0	0	0	0	0	0
15/3	2	.0000	.0299	24.8	0	0	0	2	0	0	0	0	0	0	0	0	2	0	0	0	0	0	0	0	0	0	0	0	0
15%	4	.0000	.0599	27.8	0	0	0	0	0	0	4	0	0	0	0	0	4	0	0	0	0	0	0	0	0	0	0	0	0
15th	18	.4209	1.6298	42.1	1	2	2	0	2	7	4	0	0	0	0	0	1	5	1	0	0	0	0	0	0	2	9	0	0
150	116	.8286	19.227	52.8	5	14	13	9	29	22	20	4	10	4	1	1	22	19	0	13	2	0	1	3	0	12	15	13	0
1500	28	.6988	3.9828	46.0	1	2	4	5	12	2	1	1	3	5	0	0	4	3	4	1	0	0	0	0	0	2	4	2	0
1500-pound	2	.0000	.0914	29.6	1	1	0	0	0	0	0	0	2	0	0	0	0	0	0	0	0	0	0	0	0	0	0	0	0

5F 131-133
8H 131-210
9B 1314
8J 1320
6N 1334
7E 1345
XB 1349-1830
7F 1350
5P 1354
6J 136-157
8Q 1360's
8Q 1361
XB 1362
5P 1363
5P 1368
8Q 1369
5P 1376
9F 1377
7M 138-foot
5P 1381
5P 1386
6E 1387/100

5P 1389
4R 1390
5E 1392
9M 1397
5Q 1398
5Q 1399
3A 14K
6Q 14-carat
7M 14-day
8F 14-hour
7R 14-pound-rated
9F 14-to-17-year-old
9H 14-10
9H 14-10A
9H 14-10C
9E 14-22
9H 14-24
9H 14-25
9H 14-26
8M 14-3
9H 14-7
9H 14-8

6Q 14/24ths
9E 14%
3E 14's
6A 14s
XR 14th-century
6E 14xr
4R 140-horsepower
XJ 1400-1600
5P 1405
5P 1412
9H 1413
5P 1413-1421
7Q 142-foot
8R 142-foot-tall
7R 142-ton
7F 142-143
7Q 1420's
5Q 1421
5P 1421-1451
6G 1430
7Q 1430's
5P 1433

8E 144-48-48-48
7B 1440
8F 1442
6B 1444
5Q 1446
7A 145th
3A 1452
5Q 1457
5B 146-47
5Q 1460
5Q 14621
5Q 1465
5Q 1468
8Q 1471
5Q 1478
5B 148-49
5Q 1485
5B 149
6Q 1490-1540
5Q 1491-1547
9M 1494
8Q 1495

5Q 1497-98
7F 1498
7D 1499
6C
15
6R 15-foot-long
XR 15-foot-tall
7R 15-inch
7R 15-mile
6E 15-pound
7Q 15-square-yard
XR 15-year-olds
9D 15-16
8M 15-21
9E 15-22
7E 15-24
8M 15-3
XR 15-30
8M 15-4
7E 15-56
7E 15-57
6E 15-6

7M 15-9
7E 15/
9E 15/10
5E 15/21
7E 15/22
4E 15/30
9E 15/4
5E 15/5
5E 15/6
7E 15a
7E 15b
5E 15q
6A 15years
7R 150-grain
5A 150-mile
7Q 150-pound
7Q 150-ton
8J 150-year
7R 150-170
8E 150%

Word Type	F	D	U	SFI	3 Gr 3	4 Gr 4	5 Gr 5	6 Gr 6	7 Gr 7	8 Gr 8	9 Gr 9	X UnGr	A Read	B Eng & Gr	C Comp	D Lit	E Math	F Soc Stud	G Spell	H Sci	J Music	K Art	L Home Ec	M Shop	N Lib F	P Lib NF	Q Lib Ref	R Mag	S Rel
1500's	7	.2408	.4210	36.2	0	0	4	3	0	0	0	0	0	0	0	0	0	5	0	0	0	0	0	0	0	0	2	0	0
1500s	3	.0000	.1370	31.4	0	3	0	0	0	0	0	0	3	0	0	0	0	0	0	0	0	0	0	0	0	0	0	0	0
1506	3	.3350	.2478	33.9	0	0	2	0	1	0	0	0	1	0	0	0	0	1	0	0	0	0	0	0	0	0	1	0	0
151	6	.3967	.5205	37.2	2	2	0	0	0	2	0	0	0	0	0	0	3	1	0	1	0	0	1	0	0	0	0	0	0
1510	4	.3857	.3385	35.3	0	1	2	1	0	0	0	0	0	0	0	0	0	2	1	0	0	0	0	0	0	0	1	0	0
1511	3	.2043	.1486	31.7	0	0	0	0	2	1	0	0	0	0	0	0	0	0	0	0	0	0	0	0	0	1	2	0	0
1512	3	.2264	.1679	32.2	0	0	2	0	0	1	0	0	0	0	0	0	2	0	0	0	0	0	0	0	0	1	0	0	0
1513	4	.3464	.3040	34.8	0	0	4	0	0	0	0	0	0	0	0	0	0	1	1	0	0	0	0	0	0	0	2	0	0
1516	2	.2446	.1123	30.5	1	0	0	0	0	0	0	1	0	1	0	0	0	0	0	0	0	0	0	0	0	0	1	0	0
1517	3	.0000	.0314	25.0	0	0	1	0	1	1	0	0	0	0	0	0	0	0	0	0	0	0	0	0	0	0	3	0	0
1519	5	.3054	.3916	35.9	2	1	2	0	0	0	0	0	2	0	0	0	0	1	0	0	0	0	0	0	0	0	2	0	0
152	6	.4428	.5681	37.5	1	1	0	2	0	2	0	0	0	0	0	0	2	2	0	0	0	0	1	0	0	0	1	0	0
1520	2	.2285	.1129	30.5	1	0	0	0	0	1	0	0	0	0	0	0	0	1	0	0	0	0	0	0	0	0	1	0	0
1521	3	.1823	.1405	31.5	1	0	2	0	0	0	0	0	0	0	0	0	0	1	0	0	0	0	0	0	0	0	2	0	0
1522	5	.4419	.4983	37.0	0	1	2	1	0	0	1	0	1	0	0	0	0	2	0	1	0	0	0	0	0	0	1	0	0
1523	4	.1112	.1666	32.2	0	1	2	0	1	0	0	0	1	0	0	0	0	0	0	0	0	0	0	0	0	3	0	0	0
1524	2	.0000	.0209	23.2	0	0	0	0	2	0	0	0	0	0	0	0	0	0	0	0	0	0	0	0	0	0	2	0	0
1529	2	.0000	.0209	23.2	0	0	2	0	0	0	0	0	0	0	0	0	0	0	0	0	0	0	0	0	0	0	2	0	0
153	9	.5297	1.0144	40.1	3	3	1	0	1	1	0	0	1	0	0	0	4	1	0	1	1	0	0	0	0	0	0	1	0
1533	2	.2285	.1129	30.5	0	0	1	1	0	0	0	0	0	0	0	0	0	1	0	0	0	0	0	0	0	0	1	0	0
1534	3	.2444	.1814	32.6	0	0	3	0	0	0	0	0	0	0	0	0	0	2	0	0	0	0	0	0	0	0	1	0	0
1537	2	.0000	.0389	25.9	0	0	1	1	0	0	0	0	0	0	0	0	0	2	0	0	0	0	0	0	0	0	0	0	0
1539	3	.2444	.1814	32.6	0	0	2	0	1	0	0	0	0	0	0	0	0	2	0	0	0	0	0	0	0	0	1	0	0
154	11	.4244	1.0259	40.1	1	5	0	2	0	3	0	0	1	0	0	0	6	2	0	0	0	1	0	0	0	0	0	1	0
1540	3	.3769	.2484	34.0	0	0	1	1	1	0	0	0	0	0	0	0	0	1	0	0	0	0	0	0	0	0	1	1	0
1541	2	.2408	.1204	30.8	1	0	0	1	0	0	0	0	0	0	0	0	0	1	0	0	0	0	0	0	0	1	0	0	0
1542	2	.2285	.1129	30.5	0	0	2	0	0	0	0	0	0	0	0	0	0	1	0	0	0	0	0	0	0	0	1	0	0
1543	3	.2254	.1785	32.5	0	0	0	1	0	0	2	0	0	0	0	0	0	1	0	2	0	0	0	0	0	0	0	0	0
1546	2	.2278	.1128	30.5	0	0	0	0	1	0	0	1	0	0	0	0	0	0	0	1	0	0	0	0	0	0	1	0	0
1547	4	.3634	.3173	35.0	0	0	1	0	3	0	0	0	0	0	0	0	1	0	0	0	0	0	0	0	0	0	1	2	0
155	9	.4063	.8170	39.1	0	1	2	1	3	1	1	0	1	0	0	0	4	0	0	2	0	0	0	0	0	0	2	0	0
1550	2	.2278	.1128	30.5	0	0	1	0	0	0	0	1	0	0	0	0	0	0	0	1	0	0	0	0	0	0	1	0	0
1551	2	.2351	.1166	30.7	0	0	0	1	1	0	0	0	0	0	0	0	0	1	0	0	0	0	0	0	0	0	0	1	0
156	11	.3631	.8977	39.5	3	3	0	0	1	3	1	0	1	0	0	0	7	0	0	0	2	0	0	0	0	0	1	0	0
156-157	2	.0000	.0064	18.1	0	0	0	0	0	0	2	0	0	0	0	0	0	0	0	0	0	0	2	0	0	0	0	0	0
1560	2	.0000	.0209	23.2	0	1	0	0	0	1	0	0	0	0	0	0	0	0	0	0	0	0	0	0	0	0	2	0	0
1563	2	.2405	.1205	30.8	0	0	1	0	0	0	0	1	0	0	0	0	0	0	0	1	0	0	0	0	0	1	0	0	0
1564	2	.2401	.1133	30.5	1	0	0	0	1	0	0	0	0	0	0	0	0	0	0	0	0	0	0	0	0	1	1	0	0
1565	3	.1823	.1405	31.5	2	0	1	0	0	0	0	0	0	0	0	0	0	1	0	0	0	0	0	0	0	0	2	0	0
1567-1643	3	.2088	.1442	31.6	0	1	0	0	0	2	0	0	0	0	0	0	0	0	0	0	2	0	0	0	0	0	1	0	0
157	5	.3872	.4352	36.4	2	0	0	1	0	2	0	0	1	0	0	0	2	0	0	0	0	0	1	0	0	0	1	0	0
1571	2	.2446	.1123	30.5	1	0	0	0	0	0	0	1	0	1	0	0	0	0	0	0	0	0	0	0	0	0	1	0	0
158	9	.4506	.9084	39.6	2	3	2	2	0	0	0	0	2	0	0	0	3	3	0	0	1	0	0	0	0	0	0	0	0
158-59	2	.0000	.0219	23.4	0	1	1	0	0	0	0	0	0	2	0	0	0	0	0	0	0	0	0	0	0	0	0	0	0
1580's	2	.2442	.1134	30.5	0	0	0	1	0	0	0	1	0	1	0	0	0	0	0	0	0	0	0	0	0	0	0	1	0
1582	3	.1813	.1402	31.5	0	1	0	0	0	0	2	0	0	0	0	0	0	0	0	1	0	0	0	0	0	0	2	0	0
1583	3	.2364	.1615	32.1	0	0	1	0	0	1	1	0	0	0	0	0	0	0	1	0	0	0	0	0	0	0	2	0	0
1587	3	.3395	.2468	33.9	0	2	0	0	0	0	1	0	1	0	0	0	0	0	0	0	0	0	0	0	0	1	1	0	0
1588	2	.2412	.1141	30.6	0	1	0	0	0	0	0	1	0	1	0	0	0	0	0	0	0	0	0	0	0	1	0	0	0
159	12	.3097	.8589	39.3	2	1	4	0	0	2	3	0	0	0	0	0	8	3	0	0	1	0	0	0	0	0	0	0	0
1590	5	.4288	.4818	36.8	0	3	1	0	0	1	0	0	1	0	0	0	2	0	0	1	0	0	0	0	0	0	1	0	0
1596	3	.2264	.1679	32.2	0	1	0	0	2	0	0	0	0	0	0	0	2	0	0	0	0	0	0	0	0	1	0	0	0
1597	2	.2446	.1184	30.7	0	0	0	1	1	0	0	0	0	0	0	0	1	0	0	0	0	0	0	0	0	1	0	0	0
1598	2	.2437	.1129	30.5	1	0	0	0	0	0	0	1	0	0	0	0	0	0	0	0	0	0	0	0	0	0	1	1	0
16	293	.7036	41.797	56.2	54	36	39	42	49	41	29	3	12	2	1	1	144	13	30	18	5	0	2	8	0	9	25	23	0
16-ounce	3	.0000	.0449	26.5	1	1	0	0	0	1	0	0	0	0	0	0	3	0	0	0	0	0	0	0	0	0	0	0	0
16-year-old	2	.2152	.1357	31.3	1	0	1	0	0	0	0	0	1	0	0	0	0	1	0	0	0	0	0	0	0	0	0	0	0
16-13a	2	.0000	.0050	17.0	0	0	0	0	0	0	2	0	0	0	0	0	0	0	0	0	0	0	0	2	0	0	0	0	0
16-19	2	.0000	.0299	24.8	0	0	0	0	1	1	0	0	0	0	0	0	2	0	0	0	0	0	0	0	0	0	0	0	0
16-3	2	.1249	.0685	28.4	0	0	0	0	1	0	1	0	0	0	0	0	0	0	0	1	0	0	0	1	0	0	0	0	0
16-4	3	.0000	.0076	18.8	0	0	0	0	2	0	1	0	0	0	0	0	0	0	0	0	0	0	0	3	0	0	0	0	0
16/20	2	.0000	.0299	24.8	0	0	2	0	0	0	0	0	0	0	0	0	2	0	0	0	0	0	0	0	0	0	0	0	0
16th	30	.3615	2.3588	43.7	3	1	2	2	10	5	7	0	0	0	0	0	1	2	0	1	0	0	0	0	3	1	20	2	0
160	34	.7310	5.0153	47.0	4	1	4	6	5	9	3	2	0	1	0	0	12	6	0	3	1	0	1	1	0	3	5	1	0
1600	25	.5769	2.9667	44.7	1	0	2	3	8	7	2	2	1	4	0	0	0	1	3	3	8	0	0	0	0	1	4	0	0
1600's	9	.4093	.8403	39.2	1	2	3	1	2	0	0	0	1	0	0	0	0	4	0	3	0	0	0	0	0	1	0	0	0
1603	5	.4767	.5121	37.1	0	0	4	0	0	1	0	0	0	0	0	0	0	2	0	1	0	0	0	0	0	1	1	0	0
1604	3	.3766	.2497	34.0	0	0	1	1	0	0	1	0	0	0	0	0	0	1	0	0	0	0	0	0	0	1	1	0	0
1606	2	.0000	.0389	25.9	0	0	0	0	0	2	0	0	0	0	0	0	0	2	0	0	0	0	0	0	0	0	0	0	0
1607	13	.5191	1.4109	41.5	0	3	3	3	1	3	0	0	0	0	0	0	1	5	3	0	1	0	0	0	0	0	3	0	0
1608	3	.0000	.0583	27.7	0	0	3	0	0	0	0	0	0	0	0	0	0	3	0	0	0	0	0	0	0	0	0	0	0
1609	10	.5413	1.1443	40.6	1	0	2	0	2	5	0	0	1	1	0	0	1	3	0	0	0	0	0	0	0	1	3	0	0
161	7	.3492	.5336	37.3	1	1	1	0	2	1	1	0	0	1	0	0	3	1	0	0	0	0	2	0	0	0	0	0	0
1610	5	.5228	.5608	37.5	0	2	0	1	1	1	0	0	1	0	0	0	1	1	1	0	0	0	0	0	0	0	1	0	0
1611	4	.3602	.3110	34.9	0	2	1	0	1	0	0	0	0	0	0	0	0	0	1	0	0	0	0	0	0	1	2	0	0
1612	2	.2418	.1091	30.4	0	0	1	0	1	0	0	0	0	0	0	0	0	0	1	0	0	0	0	0	0	0	1	0	0
1614	5	.3367	.3770	35.8	0	1	2	1	0	1	0	0	0	0	0	0	0	2	2	0	0	0	0	0	0	1	0	0	0
1617	2	.0000	.0299	24.8	0	0	0	0	0	2	0	0	0	0	0	0	2	0	0	0	0	0	0	0	0	0	0	0	0
1618	2	.2139	.1057	30.2	0	0	1	0	0	1	0	0	0	0	0	0	0	1	1	0	0	0	0	0	0	0	0	0	0
1619	9	.2278	.5242	37.2	0	0	2	0	3	3	1	0	0	0	0	0	0	7	0	0	0	0	0	0	0	0	2	0	0
162	8	.5577	.9441	39.8	0	0	3	1	2	1	0	1	1	0	0	0	3	1	0	1	0	0	0	0	0	0	1	1	0
1620	12	.4032	1.0625	40.3	1	2	5	0	1	3	0	0	1	0	0	0	1	4	5	0	1	0	0	0	0	0	0	0	0
1621	8	.4758	.8206	39.1	0	0	3	1	1	2	1	0	1	0	0	0	0	2	0	0	1	0	0	0	0	1	3	0	0
1622	2	.2285	.1129	30.5	0	0	0	0	1	1	0	0	0	0	0	0	0	1	0	0	0	0	0	0	0	0	1	0	0
1624	5	.3151	.3500	35.4	0	0	2	0	0	3	0	0	0	0	0	0	0	1	1	0	0	0	0	0	0	0	3	0	0
1625	4	.0904	.1412	31.5	1	0	0	0	0	3	0	0	1	0	0	0	0	0	0	0	0	0	0	0	0	0	3	0	0
1629	3	.3827	.2446	33.9	0	0	1	0	0	0	1	1	0	0	0	0	0	0	1	0	0	0	0	0	0	0	1	1	0
163	2	.1814	.1187	30.7	0	0	0	0	1	0	0	1	1	0	0	0	0	0	0	0	0	0	0	0	0	0	0	1	0
1630	5	.3676	.4527	36.6	1	0	1	0	3	0	0	0	2	0	0	0	0	2	0	0	0	0	0	0	0	1	0	0	0
1631	4	.2160	.2008	33.0	1	0	1	0	0	0	2	0	0	0	0	0	0	0	0	0	1	0	0	0	0	0	3	0	0
1632	3	.3762	.2479	33.9	0	0	0	1	0	1	0	1	0	0	0	0	0	0	0	1	0	0	0	0	1	0	1	0	0
1632-1687	2	.2417	.1091	30.4	0	0	0	0	0	2	0	0	0	0	0	0	0	0	0	0	1	0	0	0	0	0	1	0	0

6F 1502
4J 1507
5Q 1509
6P 1509-1547
9R 151-mile-long
5Q 1512-1548
5E 1514
8H 1514-1564
7K 1515
5Q 1519-1559
5Q 1519-21
7M 152-8
8E 152/160
6E 15228
3Q 1526-27
7Q 1527
7M 153-1
7M 153-2
7M 153-3
7M 153-4
9Q 1530
7G 1535
5Q 1536
7M 154-1
7M 154-2
7R 1545
7J 1555-1612
8J 1556
7R 1557
8Q 1560-1609
5Q 1561
5F 1562
5Q 1568-1644
7Q 1569-1589
4Q 1570
8E 1571-1630
6J 1575
XH 1576
8H 1578-1657
7Q 1584
3Q 1589
9Q 1593
6A 1596781
7E 1597/250
7R 16-in
6P 16-inch
8Q 16-mm
9F 16-year
7M 16-1
9M 16-13b
9M 16-13c
9M 16-13d
7R 16-17
7M 16-2
7M 16-5
8H 16-7
5E 16-9
5E 16/3
8E 16/40
7E 16/6
9E 16%
9E 16rs
7E 16x3
7R 160-hp
7E 160-lb
5F 160-164
8E 160-8
7R 1600cc
7Q 1609-1610
8E 161-165
7F 1613
4P 1616
5Q 1618-1648
8G 1628
8H 1628-1694
7H 1631-1687

Word Type	F	D	U	SFI	3 Gr 3	4 Gr 4	5 Gr 5	6 Gr 6	7 Gr 7	8 Gr 8	9 Gr 9	X UnGr	A Read	B Eng & Gr	C Comp	D Lit	E Math	F Soc Stud	G Spell	H Sci	J Music	K Art	L Home Ec	M Shop	N Lib F	P Lib NF	Q Lib Ref	R Mag	S Rel
1633	2	.2285	.1129	30.5	0	0	1	0	0	1	0	0	0	0	0	0	0	1	0	0	0	0	0	0	0	0	1	0	0
1639	3	.3627	.2409	33.8	0	0	1	1	0	1	0	0	0	0	0	0	1	1	0	0	1	0	0	0	0	0	0	0	0
164	5	.4509	.5024	37.0	1	0	2	0	1	0	0	1	1	1	0	0	0	0	0	2	0	0	0	0	0	0	0	1	0
1640	2	.0000	.0389	25.9	0	0	0	0	1	1	0	0	0	0	0	0	0	2	0	0	0	0	0	0	0	0	0	0	0
1641	3	.3763	.2498	34.0	0	1	0	1	0	1	0	0	0	0	0	0	1	1	0	0	0	0	0	0	0	0	1	0	0
1642	4	.3802	.3314	35.2	0	1	0	0	2	1	0	0	0	0	0	0	2	0	0	0	0	0	0	0	0	0	1	1	0
1642-1727	2	.0000	.0394	26.0	0	0	0	1	0	1	0	0	0	0	0	0	0	0	0	2	0	0	0	0	0	0	0	0	0
1643	2	.2417	.1091	30.4	0	0	1	0	1	0	0	0	0	0	0	0	0	0	0	0	1	0	0	0	0	0	1	0	0
1644	3	.0000	.0314	25.0	0	0	1	0	1	0	1	0	0	0	0	0	0	0	0	0	0	0	0	0	0	0	3	0	0
1646-1716	2	.0000	.0299	24.8	0	0	0	0	0	2	0	0	0	0	0	0	2	0	0	0	0	0	0	0	0	0	0	0	0
1649	2	.2285	.1129	30.5	0	0	0	0	0	2	0	0	0	0	0	0	0	1	0	0	0	0	0	0	0	0	1	0	0
165	11	.4626	1.0999	40.4	2	2	1	1	2	3	0	0	1	4	0	0	3	0	0	2	0	0	0	0	0	0	0	1	0
1650	8	.3685	.6487	38.1	1	3	1	0	2	0	1	0	0	0	0	0	0	1	0	1	0	0	0	0	0	2	4	0	0
1652	2	.0000	.0389	25.9	0	0	0	0	2	0	0	0	0	0	0	0	0	2	0	0	0	0	0	0	0	0	0	0	0
1653	2	.1698	.1133	30.5	1	0	0	0	0	1	0	0	1	0	0	0	0	0	0	0	0	0	0	0	0	0	1	0	0
1659	3	.2208	.1563	31.9	0	0	0	1	2	0	0	0	0	2	0	0	0	0	0	0	0	0	0	0	1	0	0	0	0
166	11	.5737	1.3198	41.2	2	1	2	1	1	3	0	1	1	2	0	0	3	2	0	0	0	0	0	0	0	1	2	0	0
1660	2	.0000	.0209	23.2	0	0	0	0	0	2	0	0	0	0	0	0	0	0	0	0	0	0	0	0	0	0	2	0	0
1661	2	.2418	.1091	30.4	0	0	0	0	0	2	0	0	0	0	0	0	0	0	1	0	0	0	0	0	0	0	1	0	0
1662	3	.3769	.2484	34.0	0	1	2	0	0	0	0	0	0	0	0	0	0	1	0	0	0	0	0	0	0	0	1	1	0
1663	2	.0000	.0209	23.2	0	0	0	0	0	1	1	0	0	0	0	0	0	0	0	0	0	0	0	0	0	0	2	0	0
1664	5	.4871	.5122	37.1	0	0	4	0	0	1	0	0	0	0	0	0	0	2	1	0	1	0	0	0	0	0	1	0	0
1666	5	.2035	.2560	34.1	0	0	0	1	0	1	3	0	0	0	0	0	4	0	0	0	0	0	0	0	0	0	1	0	0
167	7	.5400	.7930	39.0	1	1	1	1	0	1	1	1	0	1	0	0	1	1	0	2	0	0	0	0	0	0	0	2	0
1670	2	.2128	.1055	30.2	0	1	0	1	0	0	0	0	0	0	0	0	0	0	0	1	1	0	0	0	0	0	0	0	0
1671	2	.2427	.1159	30.6	0	1	0	0	0	1	0	0	0	0	0	0	1	0	0	0	0	0	0	0	0	0	0	1	0
1674	3	.3759	.2498	34.0	0	0	0	1	1	1	0	0	0	0	0	0	1	0	0	1	0	0	0	0	0	0	1	0	0
1675	4	.3352	.2986	34.8	0	1	1	1	0	1	0	0	0	0	0	0	0	0	0	1	0	0	0	0	0	0	2	1	0
1677	2	.0000	.0394	26.0	0	0	0	2	0	0	0	0	0	0	0	0	0	0	0	2	0	0	0	0	0	0	0	0	0
1678	3	.3709	.2499	34.0	0	0	2	1	0	0	0	0	0	0	0	0	0	1	0	1	0	0	0	0	0	0	1	0	0
168	11	.4266	1.0180	40.1	1	1	5	0	2	1	1	0	0	1	0	0	6	3	0	0	1	0	0	0	0	0	0	0	0
1682	2	.0000	.0209	23.2	0	0	0	0	1	1	0	0	0	0	0	0	0	0	0	0	0	0	0	0	0	0	2	0	0
1685-1750	2	.0000	.0162	22.1	0	0	1	0	1	0	0	0	0	0	0	0	0	0	0	0	2	0	0	0	0	0	0	0	0
1688	6	.4622	.5908	37.7	0	0	0	0	1	5	0	0	0	1	0	0	0	2	0	0	0	0	0	0	0	1	2	0	0
1689	3	.2398	.1721	32.4	0	1	0	0	0	1	1	0	0	0	0	0	2	0	0	0	0	0	0	0	0	0	1	0	0
169	11	.5248	1.1993	40.8	0	2	0	0	3	0	6	0	0	1	0	0	5	0	0	0	2	0	0	0	0	0	1	2	0
1691	3	.0000	.0583	27.7	0	0	1	0	0	2	0	0	0	0	0	0	0	3	0	0	0	0	0	0	0	0	0	0	0
1693	2	.0000	.0389	25.9	0	0	0	0	2	0	0	0	0	0	0	0	0	2	0	0	0	0	0	0	0	0	0	0	0
1699	2	.2137	.1056	30.2	0	0	1	0	1	0	0	0	0	0	0	0	0	1	0	0	1	0	0	0	0	0	0	0	0
17	246	.7119	35.546	55.5	31	42	36	38	39	33	23	4	15	4	1	1	112	20	26	22	3	0	0	5	1	7	13	16	0
17-year-old	4	.1854	.1872	32.7	0	0	0	4	0	0	0	0	0	0	0	0	0	0	0	0	0	0	0	0	0	1	0	3	0
17-2	2	.0000	.0050	17.0	0	0	0	0	0	0	2	0	0	0	0	0	0	0	0	0	0	0	0	2	0	0	0	0	0
17-3	2	.0000	.0050	17.0	0	0	0	0	0	0	2	0	0	0	0	0	0	0	0	0	0	0	0	2	0	0	0	0	0
17n	2	.0000	.0299	24.8	0	0	2	0	0	0	0	0	0	0	0	0	2	0	0	0	0	0	0	0	0	0	0	0	0
17th	27	.5342	2.9924	44.8	0	2	2	0	13	5	5	0	0	0	0	0	0	3	0	4	0	1	0	1	0	2	15	1	0
17th-century	3	.3827	.2446	33.9	0	0	0	1	0	1	1	0	0	0	0	0	0	0	1	0	0	0	0	0	0	0	1	1	0
170	20	.6834	2.8001	44.5	1	1	2	3	6	3	3	1	2	0	0	0	3	7	0	1	1	0	0	1	0	1	3	1	0
1700	10	.5464	1.1324	40.5	1	2	1	3	0	3	0	0	0	1	0	0	1	2	1	0	0	0	0	0	0	1	4	0	0
1700's	33	.6235	4.2351	46.3	4	1	18	4	2	3	1	0	2	1	0	0	0	10	2	1	5	0	0	0	0	2	9	1	0
1704	3	.3783	.2509	34.0	0	0	0	0	1	1	0	1	0	1	0	0	0	1	0	0	0	0	0	0	0	1	0	0	0
1706	7	.4800	.7835	38.9	0	5	1	0	0	0	1	0	4	0	0	0	1	1	0	1	0	0	0	0	0	0	0	0	0
171	8	.6006	1.0033	40.0	1	1	1	1	2	1	1	0	1	1	0	0	2	2	0	0	0	0	0	0	0	0	1	1	0
1710	3	.2088	.1442	31.6	0	0	2	0	0	1	0	0	0	0	0	0	0	0	0	0	2	0	0	0	0	0	1	0	0
1713	2	.0000	.0389	25.9	0	0	0	0	1	1	0	0	0	0	0	0	0	2	0	0	0	0	0	0	0	0	0	0	0
1714	4	.3584	.3227	35.1	2	0	0	0	2	0	0	0	0	0	0	0	2	1	0	0	0	0	0	0	0	1	0	0	0
1714-1787	2	.0000	.0162	22.1	0	0	0	0	0	2	0	0	0	0	0	0	0	0	0	0	2	0	0	0	0	0	0	0	0
1715	3	.2441	.1719	32.4	0	0	1	1	1	0	0	0	0	0	0	0	0	0	0	0	1	0	0	0	0	2	0	0	0
1717	2	.0000	.0290	24.6	0	0	0	0	2	0	0	0	0	0	0	0	0	0	0	0	0	0	0	0	0	2	0	0	0
1718	3	.3766	.2497	34.0	0	1	0	0	1	1	0	0	0	0	0	0	0	1	0	0	0	0	0	0	0	1	1	0	0
172	7	.1926	.3568	35.5	0	0	1	3	1	2	0	0	0	0	0	0	5	2	0	0	0	0	0	0	0	0	0	0	0
1720	2	.2407	.1090	30.4	0	0	0	0	1	1	0	0	0	1	0	0	0	0	0	0	1	0	0	0	0	0	0	0	0
1722	2	.1698	.1133	30.5	0	0	1	0	1	0	0	0	1	0	0	0	0	0	0	0	0	0	0	0	0	0	1	0	0
1724	2	.2418	.1091	30.4	0	0	0	0	2	0	0	0	0	0	0	0	0	0	1	0	0	0	0	0	0	0	1	0	0
1725	3	.3847	.2496	34.0	0	1	1	0	1	0	0	0	0	0	0	0	0	0	0	0	0	0	0	0	0	1	1	1	0
1728	2	.0000	.0299	24.8	0	0	1	0	0	1	0	0	0	0	0	0	2	0	0	0	0	0	0	0	0	0	0	0	0
173	5	.4830	.5074	37.1	1	1	0	1	0	1	1	0	0	1	0	0	2	0	0	0	0	0	0	0	0	0	1	1	0
1730	5	.3832	.4743	36.8	0	0	0	0	4	1	0	0	3	1	0	0	0	0	0	0	0	0	0	0	0	0	1	0	0
1731	2	.2417	.1091	30.4	0	0	2	0	0	0	0	0	0	0	0	0	0	0	0	0	1	0	0	0	0	0	1	0	0
1732	4	.4335	.3907	35.9	1	1	1	0	1	0	0	0	1	0	0	0	1	1	0	0	1	0	0	0	0	0	0	0	0
1733	4	.2285	.2258	33.5	0	0	0	0	1	2	1	0	0	0	0	0	0	2	0	0	0	0	0	0	0	0	2	0	0
1735	2	.2137	.1056	30.2	0	0	0	0	1	1	0	0	0	0	0	0	0	1	0	0	1	0	0	0	0	0	0	0	0
1736	2	.1733	.1149	30.6	0	0	1	0	1	0	0	0	1	1	0	0	0	0	0	0	0	0	0	0	0	0	0	0	0
1738	3	.1823	.1405	31.5	0	1	0	0	0	2	0	0	0	0	0	0	0	1	0	0	0	0	0	0	0	0	2	0	0
174	6	.3390	.4683	36.7	0	0	0	3	0	1	2	0	0	0	0	0	3	1	0	2	0	0	0	0	0	0	0	0	0
1740	4	.1505	.1615	32.1	0	0	1	0	0	2	1	0	0	0	0	0	0	1	0	0	0	0	0	0	0	0	3	0	0
1742	5	.2675	.3146	35.0	0	0	2	0	0	2	1	0	0	0	0	0	0	1	0	1	0	0	0	0	0	0	3	0	0
1743	5	.4499	.5003	37.0	0	0	1	1	1	2	0	0	1	1	0	0	0	2	0	0	0	0	0	0	0	0	1	0	0
1745	4	.4800	.4067	36.1	0	1	0	1	0	1	1	0	0	0	0	0	1	1	0	0	0	0	0	0	1	0	1	0	0
1748	3	.2444	.1814	32.6	0	0	1	0	0	0	2	0	0	0	0	0	0	2	0	0	0	0	0	0	0	0	1	0	0
1749	4	.2680	.2737	34.4	0	0	2	1	1	0	0	0	1	0	0	0	0	1	0	0	0	0	0	0	0	0	2	0	0
175	13	.4780	1.3524	41.3	4	1	3	1	3	1	0	0	2	1	0	0	7	1	0	0	0	0	0	0	0	1	1	0	0
1750	8	.4093	.7047	38.5	0	2	1	1	0	3	1	0	0	0	0	0	0	2	0	1	3	0	0	0	0	0	2	0	0
1750's	2	.0000	.0219	23.4	0	0	0	0	0	0	1	1	0	2	0	0	0	0	0	0	0	0	0	0	0	0	0	0	0
1752	2	.2346	.1166	30.7	0	0	0	1	0	0	0	1	0	0	0	0	0	0	0	1	0	0	0	0	0	0	0	1	0
1753	3	.2479	.1736	32.4	0	0	0	0	2	1	0	0	0	0	0	0	0	1	0	0	0	0	0	1	0	1	0	0	0
1754	5	.2205	.2855	34.6	0	0	1	0	0	3	1	0	0	0	0	0	0	4	0	0	0	0	0	0	0	0	1	0	0
1755	8	.3428	.6031	37.8	0	3	0	1	2	1	1	0	0	4	0	0	0	0	0	0	0	0	0	0	0	3	1	0	0

5Q 1634-1693
5F 1635
5F 1636
8Q 1636-1705
7Q 1638
8Q 1643-1715
9F 1647
5H 1650-1665
7R 1650s
4Q 1653-1713
8Q 1655-1729
XH 1656
4Q 1656-1742
8Q 1657
4J 1658-1695
3B 166-67
5H 1660's
9Q 1665
8Q 1667
6A 1668
8Q 1669
7P 1672-1707
7Q 1676
8H 1679
6R 168-9
5E 1680
5F 1681
9F 1683
4Q 1683-1764
4Q 1684
9K 1684-1721
3P 1685
7J 1685-1759
5Q 1686
8H 1687
8Q 1688-1752
9P 1692
9R 1694
7Q 1697
5Q 1697-1763
7Q 1698
8Q 1698-1739
9K 1699-1779
6R 17-
7A 17-B
4R 17-foot-long
XR 17-incher
XR 17-pound
9F 17-year
9M 17-1
XR 17-18
9M 17-4
9M 17-5
9H 17-6
9M 17-7
6E 17-8
4E 17/3
9E 17%
9E 17y
5Q 170-foot
6E 170-173
8F 1700s
5P 1701-1808
9K 1703-1770
5Q 1706-1739
8Q 1706-1790
7P 1708
7J 1709
XB 1711
4Q 1717-57
5Q 1719
6R 172-foot
7B 172-181
5A 1720's
7A 1723
8Q 1724-1806
7E 1726
8Q 1726-1751
7H 1726-1796
5Q 1727
8Q 1727-1753
8Q 1727-1810
7Q 1729
8Q 1729-1808
8Q 1731-1810
8J 1732-1809
7H 1733-1804
5A 1734
8Q 1736-1801
6A 174-175
8Q 1740-1782
5J 1741
8Q 1741-1787
4Q 1742-86
5Q 1743-1793
7H 1743-1794
5Q 1745-1829
5E 1746
5Q 1747-1748
9K 1748-1825
XR 175-mile
8R 175th
7H 1750-1817
9Q 1751
4Q 1755-1806
9Q 1755-1824
4Q 1755-1828

Word Type	F	D	U	SFI	3 Gr 3	4 Gr 4	5 Gr 5	6 Gr 6	7 Gr 7	8 Gr 8	9 Gr 9	X UnGr	A Read	B Eng & Gr	C Comp	D Lit	E Math	F Soc Stud	G Spell	H Sci	J Music	K Art	L Home Ec	M Shop	N Lib F	P Lib NF	Q Lib Ref	R Mag	S Rel
1756	4	.3782	.3355	35.3	0	1	1	0	0	0	2	0	0	0	0	0	0	2	0	0	1	0	0	0	0	1	0	0	0
1757	5	.2441	.3058	34.9	0	2	0	0	0	1	2	0	0	0	0	0	0	3	0	0	0	0	0	0	0	2	0	0	0
1758	2	.0000	.0290	24.6	0	2	0	0	0	0	0	0	0	0	0	0	0	0	0	0	0	0	0	0	0	2	0	0	0
1759	9	.5186	1.0128	40.1	0	0	1	3	1	2	1	1	2	0	0	0	0	3	0	1	1	0	0	0	0	0	2	0	0
176	10	.3605	.8111	39.1	1	4	1	1	1	1	1	0	0	0	0	0	5	4	1	0	0	0	0	0	0	0	0	0	0
176-177	2	.0000	.0389	25.9	0	0	0	1	1	0	0	0	0	0	0	0	0	2	0	0	0	0	0	0	0	0	0	0	0
176-77	2	.0000	.0219	23.4	2	0	0	0	0	0	0	0	0	2	0	0	0	0	0	0	0	0	0	0	0	0	0	0	0
1760	6	.3079	.4495	36.5	0	0	1	0	1	3	1	0	1	0	0	0	0	3	0	0	0	0	0	0	0	0	2	0	0
1761	4	.3465	.3040	34.8	0	0	1	0	0	3	0	0	0	0	0	0	0	1	0	0	1	0	0	0	0	0	2	0	0
1762	2	.2433	.1158	30.6	0	0	0	0	1	0	1	0	0	0	0	0	0	0	0	0	0	0	0	0	0	1	0	1	0
1763	8	.5449	.9108	39.6	0	1	2	0	0	3	2	0	0	0	0	0	0	4	1	0	1	0	0	0	0	1	1	0	0
1764	4	.2680	.2737	34.4	0	0	2	0	1	0	1	0	1	0	0	0	0	1	0	0	0	0	0	0	0	0	2	0	0
1765	4	.3829	.3404	35.3	0	0	1	0	1	1	1	0	0	0	0	0	0	2	0	0	0	0	0	0	0	1	1	0	0
1766	2	.0000	.0209	23.2	0	0	1	1	0	0	0	0	0	0	0	0	0	0	0	0	0	0	0	0	0	0	2	0	0
1768	4	.2386	.2998	34.8	0	0	2	0	2	0	0	0	3	0	0	0	0	0	0	0	0	0	0	0	0	0	1	0	0
1769	9	.4154	.8582	39.3	0	3	1	1	2	1	1	0	2	0	0	0	0	5	0	0	0	0	0	0	0	0	1	1	0
177	5	.0000	.0972	29.9	0	0	0	5	0	0	0	0	0	0	0	0	0	5	0	0	0	0	0	0	0	0	0	0	0
1770	11	.5474	1.2581	41.0	0	0	1	1	5	1	2	1	1	0	0	1	0	0	0	2	3	0	0	0	0	0	2	2	0
1772	2	.2285	.1129	30.5	0	0	0	1	0	0	1	0	0	0	0	0	0	1	0	0	0	0	0	0	0	0	1	0	0
1773	3	.0000	.1370	31.4	0	0	2	0	1	0	0	0	3	0	0	0	0	0	0	0	0	0	0	0	0	0	0	0	0
1774	8	.5177	.9021	39.6	1	0	3	0	2	1	1	0	2	0	0	0	0	1	0	2	0	0	0	0	1	0	2	0	0
1775	25	.5795	3.1158	44.9	2	4	7	0	6	5	1	0	8	0	0	0	1	9	0	1	1	0	0	0	0	1	4	0	0
1776	24	.4123	2.2025	43.4	1	6	6	0	2	7	2	0	1	0	0	0	1	15	0	1	0	0	0	0	0	1	5	0	0
1777	22	.4547	2.1548	43.3	0	4	2	0	3	13	0	0	0	0	0	0	3	12	0	0	2	0	0	0	0	0	5	0	0
1778	6	.4135	.5580	37.5	0	1	2	0	1	2	0	0	1	0	0	0	0	2	0	0	0	0	0	0	0	1	2	0	0
1779	10	.6931	1.4215	41.5	0	0	4	1	2	1	2	0	2	0	0	1	0	1	0	1	1	0	0	0	1	0	2	1	0
178	10	.5479	1.1492	40.6	3	2	3	0	1	1	0	0	1	3	0	0	2	1	0	0	0	0	0	0	1	0	2	0	0
178-79	2	.0000	.0219	23.4	0	2	0	0	0	0	0	0	0	2	0	0	0	0	0	0	0	0	0	0	0	0	0	0	0
1780	5	.4713	.5334	37.3	0	0	1	1	1	1	0	1	2	0	0	0	0	1	0	0	0	0	0	0	1	0	1	0	0
1781	14	.4388	1.3455	41.3	0	1	3	0	1	7	0	2	1	0	0	0	0	5	0	2	0	0	0	0	1	0	5	0	0
1782	6	.3263	.5043	37.0	0	0	2	0	2	2	0	0	3	0	0	0	0	1	0	0	0	0	0	0	0	0	2	0	0
1783	12	.4327	1.1548	40.6	0	2	3	0	1	6	0	0	1	0	0	0	0	7	0	1	0	0	0	0	0	1	2	0	0
1784	7	.3870	.6746	38.3	0	0	2	2	2	1	0	0	4	0	0	0	0	2	0	0	0	0	0	0	0	0	1	0	0
1785	6	.3723	.5618	37.5	0	1	0	0	3	1	1	0	3	0	0	0	0	2	0	1	0	0	0	0	0	0	0	0	0
1786	6	.3485	.5152	37.1	0	1	2	0	0	3	0	0	2	0	0	0	0	3	0	0	0	0	0	0	0	0	1	0	0
1787	10	.3368	.7697	38.9	1	0	2	0	0	7	0	0	0	0	0	0	0	6	0	0	0	0	0	0	0	1	3	0	0
1788	10	.5642	1.1699	40.7	0	2	2	2	2	1	1	0	0	0	0	0	0	3	0	0	1	0	0	0	0	2	2	2	0
1789	31	.5716	3.6999	45.7	5	2	3	2	2	12	4	1	1	0	0	0	1	14	0	1	0	1	0	0	0	4	8	1	0
179	3	.2264	.1679	32.2	1	1	0	0	0	0	1	0	0	0	0	0	2	0	0	0	0	0	0	0	0	1	0	0	0
1790	10	.5633	1.1878	40.7	0	2	2	0	4	2	0	0	2	0	0	1	0	1	1	0	0	0	0	0	0	0	3	2	0
1791	4	.3359	.2989	34.8	0	0	1	1	1	0	1	0	0	0	0	0	0	1	0	0	0	0	0	0	0	0	2	1	0
1792	8	.3488	.6098	37.9	1	2	3	0	1	0	1	0	0	0	0	0	0	1	0	0	1	0	0	0	0	1	5	0	0
1793	16	.4195	1.4634	41.7	1	1	8	0	2	1	3	0	1	0	0	0	0	3	0	1	0	0	0	0	0	2	8	1	0
1794	5	.1963	.2330	33.7	0	0	3	1	1	0	0	0	0	0	0	0	0	0	0	0	1	0	0	0	0	0	4	0	0
1795	7	.2926	.4664	36.7	0	1	1	1	1	0	3	0	0	0	0	0	0	1	0	0	0	0	0	0	0	2	4	0	0
1796	4	.3359	.2989	34.8	0	0	2	0	1	1	0	0	0	0	0	0	0	1	0	0	0	0	0	0	0	0	2	1	0
1797	5	.4208	.4637	36.7	0	1	3	0	1	0	0	0	1	0	0	0	0	0	0	0	1	0	0	0	0	0	2	1	0
1798	5	.3568	.3984	36.0	0	0	2	0	1	2	0	0	0	0	0	0	0	2	0	0	0	0	0	0	0	1	2	0	0
1799	8	.6156	1.0395	40.2	0	2	1	1	1	2	0	1	2	1	0	0	1	2	0	1	0	0	0	0	0	0	1	0	0
18	371	.6532	49.708	57.0	80	46	67	51	42	57	20	8	24	3	0	2	194	17	19	29	2	0	1	8	0	11	26	35	0
18-foot	2	.2346	.1166	30.7	0	1	0	1	0	0	0	0	0	0	0	0	0	0	0	1	0	0	0	0	0	0	0	1	0
18-6	2	.1249	.0685	28.4	0	0	0	0	0	1	1	0	0	0	0	0	0	0	0	1	0	0	0	1	0	0	0	0	0
18/24	4	.0000	.0599	27.8	0	0	0	0	0	0	4	0	0	0	0	0	4	0	0	0	0	0	0	0	0	0	0	0	0
18%	3	.2346	.1705	32.3	0	0	0	0	0	1	1	1	0	0	0	0	2	0	0	0	0	0	0	0	0	0	0	1	0
18th	36	.5273	3.9531	46.0	0	3	9	2	10	7	5	0	0	0	0	0	1	3	0	3	0	1	0	0	0	10	16	2	0
180	73	.4990	7.8004	48.9	1	5	6	13	17	15	13	3	5	0	0	0	42	8	0	9	0	0	0	1	0	0	5	3	0
180-degree	2	.2391	.1133	30.5	0	0	1	0	1	0	0	0	0	0	0	0	1	0	0	0	0	0	0	0	0	0	1	0	0
180th	3	.2371	.1813	32.6	0	0	0	0	1	2	0	0	0	0	0	0	1	0	0	2	0	0	0	0	0	0	0	0	0
1800	30	.6296	3.9032	45.9	2	2	9	4	5	4	4	0	1	0	0	0	1	11	2	6	0	0	0	0	0	3	5	1	0
1800's	37	.5869	4.5133	46.5	1	3	19	2	3	9	0	0	3	2	0	0	0	13	0	1	4	2	0	0	0	0	11	1	0
1800s	4	.3360	.3283	35.2	0	1	0	1	0	2	0	0	1	0	0	0	0	2	0	0	0	0	0	0	0	0	0	1	0
1801	8	.5285	.9087	39.6	1	1	0	1	1	3	0	1	1	0	0	0	0	2	0	2	0	0	0	0	0	2	0	1	0
1802	5	.3304	.3608	35.6	1	0	2	0	0	1	1	0	0	0	0	0	0	0	0	0	1	0	0	0	0	1	3	0	0
18028	2	.0000	.0299	24.8	0	0	0	0	0	2	0	0	0	0	0	0	2	0	0	0	0	0	0	0	0	0	0	0	0
1803	13	.4924	1.3733	41.4	0	1	4	2	1	4	1	0	1	0	0	0	0	7	1	0	2	0	0	0	0	0	2	0	0
18032	2	.0000	.0299	24.8	0	0	0	0	0	2	0	0	0	0	0	0	2	0	0	0	0	0	0	0	0	0	0	0	0
1804	8	.2490	.5404	37.3	0	1	3	1	2	1	0	0	3	0	0	0	0	1	0	0	0	0	0	0	0	0	4	0	0
1805	7	.3123	.5115	37.1	0	0	2	1	2	2	0	0	1	0	0	0	0	1	0	0	0	0	0	0	0	0	4	1	0
1806	6	.2589	.4107	36.1	0	1	1	0	3	1	0	0	2	0	0	0	0	1	0	0	0	0	0	0	0	0	3	0	0
1807	11	.5640	1.3638	41.3	1	1	1	0	5	1	1	1	5	0	0	0	0	2	0	2	0	0	0	0	0	1	1	0	0
18076	2	.0000	.0299	24.8	0	0	0	0	0	2	0	0	0	0	0	0	2	0	0	0	0	0	0	0	0	0	0	0	0
1808	10	.4929	1.0506	40.2	0	1	5	0	0	1	2	1	1	0	0	0	0	0	0	2	2	0	0	0	0	2	3	0	0
1809	10	.6016	1.2425	40.9	3	1	2	1	1	1	1	0	1	2	0	1	1	0	0	0	0	0	0	0	0	1	3	1	0
181	9	.4881	.9284	39.7	1	0	0	2	4	1	1	0	0	0	0	0	3	3	0	1	0	1	0	1	0	0	0	0	0
1810	5	.3472	.3871	35.9	1	1	2	0	0	1	0	0	0	0	0	0	2	1	0	0	0	0	0	0	0	0	2	0	0
1811	8	.2182	.4452	36.5	1	0	1	4	0	2	0	0	0	0	0	0	0	3	0	0	0	0	0	0	0	5	0	0	0
1812	23	.7171	3.3604	45.3	0	7	3	3	2	5	3	0	3	1	1	0	1	6	0	1	1	0	0	0	0	4	4	1	0
1813	5	.2007	.3235	35.1	0	0	3	1	0	1	0	0	3	0	0	0	0	0	0	0	0	0	0	0	0	0	2	0	0
1813-1901	2	.0000	.0162	22.1	0	0	0	0	1	1	0	0	0	0	0	0	0	0	0	0	2	0	0	0	0	0	0	0	0
1814	20	.5897	2.4848	44.0	1	2	1	4	2	6	4	0	4	0	0	0	0	3	0	2	1	0	0	0	0	3	6	1	0
1815	12	.5910	1.4811	41.7	0	1	1	3	1	0	4	2	2	2	1	0	0	2	0	1	1	0	0	0	0	0	3	0	0
1816	7	.4895	.7401	38.7	1	0	3	1	1	0	1	0	1	0	0	0	0	1	0	0	0	0	0	0	1	3	1	0	0
1817	7	.1471	.3550	35.5	1	1	2	0	0	3	0	0	3	0	0	0	0	0	0	0	0	0	0	0	0	0	4	0	0
1818	7	.4527	.6733	38.3	2	1	0	1	2	1	0	0	0	0	0	2	0	1	0	0	1	0	0	0	0	3	0	0	0
1819	14	.6590	1.9172	42.8	0	3	2	2	5	1	1	0	3	0	0	2	2	3	0	1	0	0	0	0	0	2	1	0	0
182	9	.5074	.9522	39.8	0	3	1	0	3	0	2	0	0	0	0	0	4	2	0	0	1	1	0	1	0	0	0	0	0
1820	12	.5625	1.4065	41.5	1	1	0	2	1	6	1	0	0	0	0	0	0	5	0	1	1	0	0	0	0	1	3	1	0
1820's	3	.1639	.1674	32.2	0	0	0	1	0	2	0	0	1	0	0	0	0	2	0	0	0	0	0	0	0	0	0	0	0
1821	20	.4176	1.8563	42.7	1	0	7	0	4	7	1	0	2	0	0	0	0	8	0	1	0	0	0	0	0	2	7	0	0
1822	11	.5400	1.2911	41.1	1	2	2	1	1	1	1	2	3	0	0	0	0	2	0	2	0	0	0	0	0	3	1	0	0
1823	5	.5599	.5799	37.6	0	2	0	1	0	2	0	0	0	1	0	0	0	0	0	1	0	0	0	0	0	1	1	1	0

8Q 1758-1840
5P 1759-1788
5Q 1760-1767
8Q 1760-1842
5Q 1760's
7H 1769-1832
7H 1769-1839
5A 177-year-old
5Q 1773-1836
7A 1775-1776
7A 1775-76
7Q 1777-78
XH 1778-
9K 1780-1867
7G 1782-1852
5Q 1783-1842
9Q 1785-
8J 1786-1826
4Q 1787-90
4Q 1790-93
8F 1790's
9K 1791-1824
4P 1793-1794
9Q 1793-95
9K 1796-1875
5J 1797-1828
9K 1798-1863
5Q 1799-1850
3A 18K
7E 18-in
7Q 18-inch
XR 18-inch-long
9R 18-mile-long
7Q 18-year-old
9H 18-14
9H 18-15
7Q 18-20
4G 18-25
8M 18-4
8M 18-5
8H 18-7
4E 18-9
8E 18/12
8E 18b
6R 180-million-year-old
8A 180-odd
5Q 1800-1860
8Q 1803-1869
8Q 1804-1864
5Q 1804-1876
4Q 1804-85
5P 1805-1806
7Q 1805-1872
5Q 1806-1873
8Q 1807-1869
7Q 1807-1882
8A 1807-1892
7J 1809-1847
7Q 1809-1880
8J 1810-1849
6P 1810-1856
7Q 1810-1861
7P 1810-51
5Q 1811-1872
8J 1811-1886
9K 1812-1867
5Q 1813-1890
7H 1813-1895
7P 1814-15
9K 1814-1874
9Q 1814-24
7J 1815-1892
9J 1817-1823
5Q 1817-1849
8Q 1817-1862
5Q 1818-1894
3A 182-183
7Q 1820-1878
5Q 1821-1867
5Q 1821-1880
8H 1822-1884
9Q 1823-1902

Word Type	F	D	U	SFI	3 Gr 3	4 Gr 4	5 Gr 5	6 Gr 6	7 Gr 7	8 Gr 8	9 Gr 9	X UnGr	A Read	B Eng & Gr	C Comp	D Lit	E Math	F Soc Stud	G Spell	H Sci	J Music	K Art	L Home Ec	M Shop	N Lib F	P Lib NF	Q Lib Ref	R Mag	S Rel
1824	7	.4389	.6967	38.4	0	0	1	3	0	3	0	0	2	0	0	0	0	2	0	0	0	0	0	0	0	1	2	0	0
1825	12	.4959	1.2657	41.0	2	3	3	0	2	1	1	0	1	0	0	0	0	3	0	0	1	0	0	0	0	1	5	1	0
1826	3	.2815	.1861	32.7	0	1	1	0	0	1	0	0	0	1	0	0	0	0	0	0	0	0	0	1	0	1	0	0	0
1827	7	.4841	.7206	38.6	0	4	1	0	0	2	0	0	0	0	0	0	0	3	0	0	1	0	0	0	0	2	1	0	0
1828	7	.4557	.6859	38.4	1	2	0	1	0	2	1	0	0	0	0	0	0	2	0	1	0	0	0	0	0	2	2	0	0
1829	14	.5542	1.6092	42.1	0	2	5	2	3	0	1	1	0	0	0	0	1	2	0	1	2	0	0	0	0	4	4	0	0
183	13	.5409	1.4692	41.7	5	1	0	3	1	0	3	0	1	2	0	0	7	0	0	0	0	0	1	1	0	0	0	1	0
1830	17	.5019	1.8007	42.6	1	1	6	2	5	2	0	0	1	0	0	0	0	3	2	0	0	0	0	0	0	3	7	1	0
1830's	5	.4727	.5348	37.3	0	0	0	2	0	2	1	0	2	1	0	0	0	1	0	0	0	0	0	0	1	0	0	0	0
1830s	4	.3829	.3404	35.3	0	0	1	0	1	2	0	0	0	0	0	0	0	2	0	0	0	0	0	0	0	1	1	0	0
1831	12	.5860	1.4745	41.7	0	2	2	4	3	1	0	0	2	0	0	0	0	0	0	2	1	0	0	0	0	2	3	2	0
1832	13	.5119	1.4228	41.5	1	2	4	1	1	2	2	0	2	0	0	0	0	2	0	0	2	0	0	0	0	4	3	0	0
1833	5	.4684	.4982	37.0	2	0	0	0	2	0	0	1	0	0	0	0	0	0	0	1	0	0	0	0	0	2	1	1	0
1834	6	.4135	.5580	37.5	0	1	2	0	1	2	0	0	1	0	0	0	0	2	0	0	0	0	0	0	0	1	2	0	0
1835	13	.5772	1.5998	42.0	2	1	3	1	2	2	1	1	4	1	0	0	0	0	0	1	1	0	0	0	0	3	3	0	0
1836	10	.5117	1.0973	40.4	0	3	1	1	1	3	0	1	2	0	0	0	0	0	0	1	1	0	0	0	0	1	4	1	0
1837	9	.4782	.9267	39.7	1	0	0	4	1	2	0	1	1	0	0	0	0	0	0	2	0	0	0	0	0	1	3	2	0
1838	6	.4785	.6269	38.0	1	1	1	1	1	1	0	0	1	0	0	0	0	1	0	1	0	0	0	0	0	1	2	0	0
1839	14	.5108	1.5229	41.8	0	0	3	5	3	3	0	0	2	1	0	0	0	0	0	1	1	0	0	0	0	4	5	0	0
184	10	.5821	1.1981	40.8	1	0	3	2	1	2	1	0	0	1	0	0	3	2	0	0	0	0	1	1	0	2	0	0	0
1840	8	.6720	1.1097	40.5	0	0	1	4	0	2	0	1	2	1	0	0	1	0	0	0	1	0	0	0	0	1	1	1	0
1840's	9	.3855	.7930	39.0	0	0	2	1	0	6	0	0	1	0	0	0	0	6	0	0	1	0	0	0	0	0	1	0	0
1840s	6	.2062	.3286	35.2	0	0	0	0	1	4	1	0	0	0	0	0	0	5	0	0	0	0	0	0	0	0	1	0	0
1841	9	.4098	.7988	39.0	0	0	2	1	1	4	1	0	0	0	0	1	0	3	0	0	0	0	0	0	0	1	4	0	0
1842	7	.3028	.5012	37.0	1	1	4	1	0	0	0	0	1	0	0	0	0	1	0	0	0	0	0	0	0	1	4	0	0
1843	2	.2401	.1133	30.5	0	0	1	1	0	0	0	0	0	0	0	0	0	0	0	0	0	0	0	0	0	1	1	0	0
1844	4	.4530	.4014	36.0	0	1	1	1	1	0	0	0	1	0	0	0	0	0	0	0	0	0	0	0	0	1	1	1	0
1845	14	.4154	1.2954	41.1	1	1	3	1	1	5	2	0	2	0	0	0	0	3	0	1	0	0	0	0	0	2	6	0	0
1846	13	.4895	1.3930	41.4	0	2	2	2	0	7	0	0	3	0	0	0	0	4	0	0	1	0	0	0	0	1	4	0	0
1847	17	.6084	2.1599	43.3	0	2	3	3	2	6	1	0	3	0	0	1	2	3	0	0	1	0	0	0	0	2	5	0	0
1848	19	.4891	2.0108	43.0	0	2	5	0	5	6	0	1	3	0	0	0	1	5	0	0	0	0	0	0	0	1	7	2	0
1849	21	.4707	2.1371	43.3	0	2	6	1	2	9	1	0	2	0	0	0	0	7	0	1	1	0	0	0	0	2	8	0	0
185	19	.5437	2.1812	43.4	0	3	2	1	9	2	2	0	2	2	0	0	10	2	0	0	0	0	0	1	0	1	0	1	0
1850	35	.6861	5.0033	47.0	3	0	8	2	10	12	0	0	12	1	0	0	1	13	1	0	1	0	0	1	0	2	3	0	0
1850's	7	.5088	.7628	38.8	0	1	1	1	1	3	0	0	1	0	0	0	0	2	0	0	1	0	0	0	0	1	2	0	0
1850s	3	.2444	.1814	32.6	0	0	0	0	1	2	0	0	0	0	0	0	0	2	0	0	0	0	0	0	0	0	1	0	0
1851	11	.3980	1.0044	40.0	0	0	1	1	3	5	0	1	3	0	0	1	0	1	0	1	0	0	0	0	0	0	5	0	0
1852	9	.3815	.7699	38.9	0	2	1	0	3	2	1	0	1	0	0	0	0	3	0	0	1	0	0	0	0	0	4	0	0
1853	7	.3563	.5630	37.5	0	0	1	1	1	3	1	0	0	0	0	0	0	4	0	0	0	0	0	0	0	1	2	0	0
1854	15	.3156	1.1530	40.6	0	0	4	1	3	6	1	0	3	0	0	0	0	7	0	0	0	0	0	0	0	0	5	0	0
1855	12	.5256	1.3730	41.4	1	0	2	4	2	3	0	0	4	0	0	1	0	1	0	0	0	0	0	0	0	1	4	1	0
1856	12	.3845	1.0415	40.2	0	0	1	1	2	4	2	2	2	0	0	0	0	2	0	0	0	0	0	0	0	0	5	3	0
1857	10	.2898	.7072	38.5	0	0	3	0	0	7	0	0	1	0	0	0	0	6	0	0	0	0	0	0	0	0	3	0	0
1858	13	.3497	1.0424	40.2	1	2	0	1	2	6	1	0	1	0	0	0	0	6	0	0	0	0	0	0	0	1	5	0	0
1859	20	.5446	2.2472	43.5	1	2	4	2	4	3	4	0	0	0	1	0	0	3	0	0	3	0	0	0	0	3	9	1	0
186	31	.6396	4.0883	46.1	6	4	2	5	5	8	1	0	2	1	0	0	13	1	0	9	0	0	1	1	0	0	2	1	0
1860	31	.6108	3.9712	46.0	5	5	10	2	4	4	1	0	6	0	0	0	0	9	0	0	1	0	0	0	1	6	6	2	0
1860's	10	.5271	1.1400	40.6	0	0	2	3	2	3	0	0	2	0	0	0	0	4	0	0	0	0	0	0	1	2	1	0	0
1861	41	.6056	5.1967	47.2	2	9	7	2	11	10	0	0	7	1	0	1	1	11	0	0	0	0	0	0	1	5	12	2	0
1862	21	.2480	1.2584	41.0	0	4	7	0	0	8	2	0	2	1	0	0	0	2	0	0	0	0	0	0	0	1	15	0	0
1863	12	.4865	1.2468	41.0	1	1	2	0	3	3	2	0	1	1	0	0	0	3	0	0	0	0	0	0	0	1	5	1	0
1864	12	.5130	1.2897	41.1	0	1	1	2	2	6	0	0	0	0	0	0	1	3	0	0	0	0	0	0	1	1	5	1	0
1865	31	.4974	3.3144	45.2	0	4	6	2	2	13	4	0	3	0	0	0	2	12	0	1	0	0	0	0	0	2	10	1	0
1865-1900	2	.0000	.0389	25.9	0	0	0	0	0	2	0	0	0	0	0	0	0	2	0	0	0	0	0	0	0	0	0	0	0
1866	15	.5688	1.7632	42.5	0	2	0	0	5	5	2	1	0	0	0	0	0	4	0	0	1	0	0	0	2	1	5	2	0
1867	18	.3884	1.6146	42.1	1	1	6	2	3	2	2	1	4	0	0	0	0	7	0	0	0	0	0	0	0	0	6	1	0
1868	13	.4660	1.3165	41.2	0	1	2	1	3	2	3	1	2	0	0	0	0	2	0	0	0	0	0	0	0	2	5	2	0
1869	21	.4830	2.1893	43.4	1	4	4	3	1	3	4	1	3	0	0	0	0	4	0	0	0	0	0	0	0	2	6	6	0
187	7	.4994	.7305	38.6	0	3	1	1	1	0	1	0	0	3	0	0	0	1	0	0	1	0	0	0	0	1	0	1	0
1870	28	.5385	3.1737	45.0	3	2	8	3	3	7	2	0	3	1	0	0	1	4	1	1	1	0	0	0	0	3	13	0	0
1870's	15	.5272	1.6838	42.3	0	1	3	7	1	2	1	0	2	0	0	0	0	4	0	0	2	0	0	0	0	4	3	0	0
1871	15	.2021	.7456	38.7	0	0	2	1	3	5	4	0	0	0	0	0	0	3	0	0	0	0	0	0	0	1	11	0	0
1872	13	.7018	1.8546	42.7	1	1	3	4	1	2	1	0	1	0	0	0	2	1	0	1	1	0	0	0	1	2	3	1	0
1873	12	.3867	1.0306	40.1	0	0	4	1	2	4	1	0	1	0	0	0	0	3	0	0	0	0	0	0	0	1	6	1	0
1874	7	.3355	.5082	37.1	0	1	1	0	1	1	3	0	0	0	0	0	0	0	0	0	2	0	0	0	0	0	4	1	0
1875	11	.5606	1.2701	41.0	0	2	0	1	0	2	5	1	0	1	0	0	3	0	0	0	1	0	0	0	0	1	4	1	0
1876	20	.5683	2.3679	43.7	0	2	4	1	2	8	2	1	1	1	0	1	0	7	0	0	1	0	0	0	0	1	7	1	0
1877	18	.4844	1.8985	42.8	0	0	1	1	5	9	2	0	3	0	0	0	0	7	0	1	3	0	0	0	0	0	4	0	0
1878	9	.4914	.9602	39.8	0	1	3	2	1	1	1	0	2	0	0	0	0	1	0	0	1	0	0	0	0	2	3	0	0
1878-1942	2	.2417	.1091	30.4	0	1	0	0	0	1	0	0	0	0	0	0	0	0	0	0	1	0	0	0	0	0	1	0	0
1879	13	.3279	.9534	39.8	0	2	2	1	1	4	3	0	0	0	0	0	4	1	0	1	0	0	0	0	0	0	7	0	0
188	3	.3202	.2063	33.1	1	0	1	0	0	0	1	0	0	0	0	0	0	0	0	0	0	0	1	0	0	0	1	1	0
1880	18	.5499	2.0547	43.1	0	0	3	1	2	8	2	2	0	0	0	0	0	5	0	2	2	0	0	1	0	1	7	0	0
1880's	15	.5582	1.7850	42.5	0	2	5	2	1	5	0	0	3	0	0	0	0	5	0	1	2	0	0	0	0	1	3	0	0
1880s	3	.3769	.2484	34.0	0	0	0	0	1	1	1	0	0	0	0	0	0	1	0	0	0	0	0	0	0	0	1	1	0
1881	15	.4345	1.4322	41.6	0	4	2	0	5	4	0	0	2	0	0	0	2	2	0	1	0	0	0	0	0	1	7	0	0
1882	13	.5976	1.6208	42.1	0	0	2	4	1	3	3	0	2	0	0	0	1	2	0	0	1	0	0	0	0	1	4	2	0
1883	10	.3604	.8257	39.2	0	4	3	0	1	2	0	0	2	1	0	0	0	0	0	0	0	0	0	0	0	2	5	0	0
1884	9	.3554	.7319	38.6	0	2	2	1	1	3	0	0	1	0	0	0	0	3	0	0	0	0	0	0	0	1	4	0	0
1885	11	.4605	1.1131	40.5	0	3	2	0	0	4	1	1	2	0	0	0	0	3	0	0	0	0	0	0	0	1	4	1	0
1886	14	.5453	1.6481	42.2	2	1	3	0	6	2	0	0	4	0	0	0	0	3	0	1	1	0	0	0	0	1	4	0	0
1887	16	.4655	1.6083	42.1	1	0	5	1	4	3	1	1	3	1	0	1	0	0	0	0	2	0	0	0	0	0	8	1	0
1888	15	.6025	1.8869	42.8	0	2	2	1	4	4	1	1	2	1	0	0	0	4	0	1	1	0	0	0	0	2	4	0	0
1889	10	.3903	.8890	39.5	1	2	2	2	2	0	1	0	2	0	0	0	0	1	0	0	0	0	0	0	0	4	3	0	0
189	6	.4531	.5800	37.6	0	1	1	0	1	1	1	1	0	2	0	0	2	0	0	1	0	0	0	0	0	0	0	1	0
1890	22	.6778	3.0428	44.8	0	0	4	2	7	8	1	0	2	0	0	1	0	3	1	1	2	0	0	0	0	4	6	2	0
1890's	6	.2773	.4266	36.3	0	0	0	2	0	4	0	0	1	0	0	0	0	4	0	0	0	0	0	0	0	1	0	0	0
1890s	2	.2285	.1129	30.5	0	0	0	0	1	1	0	0	0	0	0	0	0	1	0	0	0	0	0	0	0	0	1	0	0
1891	9	.3828	.7650	38.8	0	3	1	0	0	3	2	0	1	0	0	0	0	2	0	0	2	0	0	0	0	0	4	0	0
1892	19	.6067	2.4032	43.8	0	2	6	0	4	6	1	0	3	0	0	0	1	4	0	1	4	0	0	0	0	1	4	1	0

8J 1824-1884
4Q 1824-81
8Q 1826-1827
8E 1826-1866
9Q 1827-75
8Q 1828-1829
5Q 1829-1896
9F 1830-1848
4A 1830-1900
7Q 1830-1914
7Q 1831-1849
5Q 1832-1887
7Q 1833-1884
5Q 1833-1896
7J 1833-1897
8H 1834-1907
9Q 1834-82
8Q 1836-1882
8Q 1836-1907
5Q 1837-1920
5Q 1837-38
7J 1838-1875
4F 184-185
5Q 1840-1902
9K 1840-1917
5P 1840-1922
8Q 1841-1915
5Q 1841-1922
5Q 1844-1896
5Q 1846-1923
8Q 1846-1924
8Q 1848-1923
8F 1850-1871
8Q 1851-1929
4Q 1852-54
8Q 1853-1856
7J 1853-1890
5Q 1854-1891
8J 1854-1932
4Q 1855-1925
6A 1856-1857
5Q 1856-1925
9Q 1856-1940
9Q 1857-1911
8J 1858-1924
7R 1858-60
5Q 1859-1927
8F 1860-1910
5Q 1861-1865
8A 1861-1929
9K 1861-1944
7P 1861-63
7Q 1861-71
8J 1862-1918
8J 1864-1949
7Q 1864-70
8Q 1868-1869
7J 1870-1948
8F 1870s
7P 1871-72
5Q 1872-1926
7R 18736
7B 1874-1926
8J 1874-1951
8J 1874-1954
5Q 1874-1960
6P 1875-1937
9E 1875/10000
7D 1876-1941
5Q 1878-1950
8Q 1879-1939
5Q 1879-1955
8Q 1880-1881
9K 1881-1919
8J 1882-
8H 1882-83
9Q 1884-1939
5Q 1884-1960
5Q 1886-1961
5Q 1887-
9Q 1887-1949
8Q 1888-1891
7P 1890-1948
7A 1891-1892
5Q 1891-1895

Word Type	F	D	U	SFI	3 Gr 3	4 Gr 4	5 Gr 5	6 Gr 6	7 Gr 7	8 Gr 8	9 Gr 9	X UnGr	A Read	B Eng & Gr	C Comp	D Lit	E Math	F Soc Stud	G Spell	H Sci	J Music	K Art	L Home Ec	M Shop	N Lib F	P Lib NF	Q Lib Ref	R Mag	S Rel
1893	11	.5339	1.2120	40.8	1	1	2	0	3	3	1	0	0	0	0	0	1	2	0	0	4	0	0	1	0	1	2	0	0
1894	7	.4072	.6365	38.0	0	0	0	0	3	4	0	0	1	0	0	1	0	3	0	0	0	1	0	0	0	0	0	1	0
1894-1895	2	.0000	.0389	25.9	0	0	0	0	0	2	0	0	0	0	0	0	0	2	0	0	0	0	0	0	0	0	0	0	0
1895	12	.6391	1.5919	42.0	0	0	3	0	2	1	3	3	2	0	0	0	0	1	0	2	1	0	0	0	0	3	2	1	0
1896	13	.6757	1.8045	42.6	1	1	3	0	2	3	2	1	2	0	0	1	0	1	0	2	1	0	0	0	0	2	3	1	0
1896-	2	.0000	.0209	23.2	0	0	1	0	0	0	1	0	0	0	0	0	0	0	0	0	0	0	0	0	0	0	2	0	0
1897	7	.3116	.5109	37.1	0	2	1	1	1	2	0	0	1	0	0	0	0	0	0	1	0	0	0	0	0	0	4	1	0
1898	23	.4792	2.3834	43.8	2	1	4	4	2	8	2	0	1	0	0	0	1	14	0	0	0	0	0	0	0	2	3	2	0
1899	6	.3613	.4864	36.9	0	0	0	0	0	2	0	4	0	0	0	0	0	0	0	3	0	0	0	0	0	1	2	0	0
19	134	.7837	21.082	53.2	13	12	17	16	27	31	11	7	9	4	1	1	49	14	12	3	2	1	0	3	0	3	15	17	0
19-year-old	2	.1814	.1187	30.7	0	0	1	0	1	0	0	0	1	0	0	0	0	0	0	0	0	0	0	0	0	0	0	1	0
19-1	5	.0488	.0763	28.8	0	0	0	0	0	3	2	0	0	0	0	0	0	0	0	1	0	0	0	4	0	0	0	0	0
19-12	2	.0000	.0394	26.0	0	0	0	0	0	0	2	0	0	0	0	0	0	0	0	2	0	0	0	0	0	0	0	0	0
19-14	2	.2160	.1362	31.3	0	0	0	0	0	1	1	0	1	0	0	0	0	0	0	1	0	0	0	0	0	0	0	0	0
19-20-21	2	.0000	.0162	22.1	0	0	1	1	0	0	0	0	0	0	0	0	0	0	2	0	0	0	0	0	0	0	0	0	0
19-23	5	.0000	.0406	26.1	0	1	2	0	2	0	0	0	0	0	0	0	0	0	5	0	0	0	0	0	0	0	0	0	0
19-35	2	.0000	.0162	22.1	0	0	0	0	2	0	0	0	0	0	0	0	0	0	2	0	0	0	0	0	0	0	0	0	0
19th	68	.5027	7.1731	48.6	1	5	12	4	15	8	19	4	0	0	0	0	1	10	0	5	1	0	0	0	0	13	29	9	0
190	15	.4688	1.5191	41.8	3	1	2	1	2	0	6	0	1	2	0	0	8	1	0	2	0	0	0	0	0	0	0	1	0
1900	67	.7063	9.7159	49.9	0	7	12	8	10	19	6	5	13	1	0	0	3	21	2	5	3	0	0	0	0	5	12	2	0
1900's	28	.5800	3.3578	45.3	2	1	16	2	3	4	0	0	0	1	0	1	0	13	0	1	6	1	0	0	0	0	5	0	0
1900s	3	.3635	.2410	33.8	0	0	0	1	1	0	1	0	0	0	0	0	0	1	0	0	1	0	0	0	0	1	0	0	0
1901	15	.4689	1.5266	41.8	1	2	2	1	2	4	1	2	2	0	0	0	0	3	0	0	0	0	0	0	0	4	5	1	0
1902	27	.5880	3.3029	45.2	0	1	2	2	2	10	3	7	2	0	0	0	1	7	0	0	1	0	0	0	0	5	7	4	0
1903	19	.5686	2.2858	43.6	0	5	1	3	3	2	3	2	4	2	0	0	0	1	0	2	0	0	0	0	0	1	6	3	0
1904	13	.6681	1.8016	42.6	0	2	1	2	1	4	0	3	3	0	0	0	0	2	0	2	1	0	0	0	0	2	2	1	0
1904-	2	.2417	.1091	30.4	0	0	0	0	1	1	0	0	0	0	0	0	0	0	0	0	1	0	0	0	0	0	1	0	0
1905	19	.5328	2.1620	43.3	1	1	6	2	1	6	2	0	4	0	0	0	1	1	0	1	2	0	0	0	0	3	7	0	0
1906	17	.5752	2.0243	43.1	2	0	0	2	4	6	3	0	1	0	0	1	0	1	0	2	1	1	0	0	0	3	7	0	0
1907	11	.4063	.9719	39.9	0	2	3	2	1	3	0	0	1	0	0	0	0	0	0	0	1	0	0	0	0	2	6	1	0
1908	22	.4499	2.1647	43.4	1	5	2	3	3	6	1	1	3	0	0	1	0	3	0	0	0	0	0	0	0	9	6	0	0
1909	14	.4410	1.3602	41.3	2	2	1	3	2	3	1	0	3	0	0	1	0	1	0	0	1	0	0	0	0	1	7	0	0
191	3	.1858	.1432	31.6	2	1	0	0	0	0	0	0	0	2	0	0	0	1	0	0	0	0	0	0	0	0	0	0	0
1910	31	.7150	4.5222	46.6	2	4	4	4	6	7	2	2	3	1	0	0	2	9	0	5	1	0	0	0	0	4	4	2	0
1911	23	.5757	2.7857	44.4	0	2	6	4	2	5	3	1	4	0	0	0	0	5	0	0	3	0	0	0	0	2	6	3	0
1912	23	.5496	2.6377	44.2	0	2	5	1	7	5	3	0	1	0	0	0	0	4	0	1	1	0	0	0	0	4	8	4	0
1913	28	.5017	3.0303	44.8	4	1	5	2	4	9	3	0	5	0	0	0	0	7	0	0	3	0	0	0	0	4	9	0	0
1914	33	.6714	4.5463	46.6	3	2	5	6	5	6	2	4	3	0	0	0	1	12	1	1	2	0	0	0	0	3	5	5	0
1915	12	.5195	1.3519	41.3	0	0	0	4	1	5	2	0	3	0	0	0	0	2	0	1	0	0	0	0	0	1	4	1	0
1916	13	.3502	1.0171	40.1	1	0	2	1	1	6	2	0	1	0	0	0	0	2	0	0	1	0	0	0	0	0	8	1	0
1917	28	.4711	2.8541	44.6	0	1	5	1	7	10	4	0	2	1	0	0	0	13	0	1	0	0	0	0	0	0	8	3	0
1918	33	.6586	4.4754	46.5	1	2	1	6	4	16	3	0	3	1	0	1	0	16	0	0	1	0	0	1	0	2	5	3	0
1919	20	.5547	2.3657	43.7	1	1	3	0	3	7	5	0	3	0	0	0	2	8	0	1	0	0	0	0	0	3	3	0	0
192	5	.2003	.2535	34.0	1	1	1	0	2	0	0	0	0	1	0	0	4	0	0	0	0	0	0	0	0	0	0	0	0
1920	31	.5736	3.7480	45.7	0	3	10	2	4	9	2	1	4	0	0	0	2	11	0	2	2	0	0	0	0	2	8	0	0
1920's	32	.4957	3.4102	45.3	0	0	8	2	3	18	1	0	1	2	0	0	1	22	0	1	2	0	0	0	0	1	2	0	0
1920s	9	.3613	.7113	38.5	0	0	2	1	3	0	3	0	0	0	0	0	0	0	0	1	0	0	0	0	0	2	5	1	0
1921	15	.5152	1.6653	42.2	0	1	3	4	2	1	4	0	3	0	0	0	0	3	0	0	0	0	0	0	0	2	4	3	0
1922	25	.5347	2.8624	44.6	2	1	7	2	4	5	4	0	5	0	0	0	2	5	0	1	1	0	0	0	0	2	9	0	0
1923	8	.3304	.6314	38.0	0	0	3	1	2	1	1	0	2	0	0	0	0	1	0	0	0	0	0	0	0	1	4	0	0
1924	16	.5369	1.8190	42.6	1	3	4	2	2	3	1	0	1	0	0	0	1	5	0	2	0	0	0	0	0	3	4	0	0
1925	27	.7221	3.9665	46.0	0	1	7	1	9	6	3	0	4	0	0	1	3	2	0	2	1	1	0	0	0	5	6	2	0
1926	19	.6616	2.5997	44.1	0	2	3	3	3	5	2	1	4	0	0	0	3	1	0	1	1	0	0	0	0	2	4	3	0
1927	21	.6230	2.7041	44.3	2	0	4	4	3	8	0	0	2	2	0	1	0	5	0	0	0	0	0	0	0	3	5	3	0
1928	20	.6332	2.6050	44.2	1	0	8	1	5	4	1	0	1	0	0	2	2	4	0	1	0	0	0	0	0	4	5	1	0
1929	30	.6165	3.8259	45.8	2	0	5	5	4	8	5	1	2	0	0	0	3	4	0	4	0	0	0	0	0	5	7	5	0
193	6	.4832	.6173	37.9	0	0	1	2	1	0	2	0	0	1	0	0	2	2	0	0	0	0	0	0	0	0	0	1	0
1930	25	.6871	3.5772	45.5	2	1	5	3	5	9	0	0	9	0	0	1	1	2	0	3	0	0	0	0	0	3	4	2	0
1930's	22	.6534	2.9396	44.7	0	1	4	3	7	6	1	0	1	0	1	0	0	6	0	2	4	0	0	0	0	2	4	2	0
1930s	4	.4803	.4071	36.1	0	0	1	0	3	0	0	0	0	0	0	0	0	0	0	1	0	0	0	0	0	1	1	1	0
1931	23	.7059	3.3219	45.2	1	4	2	3	2	7	2	2	3	0	0	0	2	5	0	3	1	0	0	0	0	4	2	3	0
1932	21	.6231	2.7350	44.4	2	2	0	0	8	6	2	1	4	0	0	0	0	6	0	1	1	0	0	0	0	2	4	3	0
1933	19	.5199	2.0830	43.2	2	0	3	1	2	6	2	3	0	0	0	0	0	7	0	2	0	0	0	0	0	3	5	2	0
1934	14	.5651	1.6461	42.2	1	0	3	0	2	3	1	4	1	0	0	1	0	1	0	0	1	0	0	0	0	5	4	1	0
1935	19	.4971	2.0539	43.1	2	1	4	1	5	3	1	2	4	0	0	0	1	3	0	2	0	0	0	0	0	0	7	2	0
1936	20	.4206	1.8888	42.8	0	1	3	3	6	3	3	1	3	0	0	0	0	9	0	1	0	0	0	0	0	0	6	1	0
1937	22	.4723	2.1896	43.4	0	2	6	1	4	3	5	1	0	0	0	3	0	4	0	0	0	0	0	0	0	2	10	3	0
1938	13	.5940	1.6210	42.1	0	0	1	1	6	4	1	0	2	0	0	0	0	2	0	3	1	0	0	0	0	0	2	3	0
1939	30	.6043	3.7368	45.7	4	1	2	6	5	6	5	1	1	0	0	1	4	6	0	0	1	0	0	0	0	4	10	3	0
194	7	.4509	.6693	38.3	0	0	0	1	3	1	2	0	0	0	0	1	4	0	0	0	1	0	0	0	0	0	1	0	0
1940	39	.6339	5.1112	47.1	3	2	6	4	9	6	9	0	5	1	0	2	2	5	1	4	0	0	0	0	0	4	14	1	0
1940's	8	.4614	.8078	39.1	0	1	1	0	1	2	3	0	2	0	0	0	0	0	0	1	1	0	0	1	0	0	3	0	0
1940s	4	.3134	.2876	34.6	0	0	0	0	3	0	1	0	0	0	0	0	0	1	0	1	0	0	0	0	0	0	2	0	0
1941	32	.5102	3.4591	45.4	1	4	4	7	8	7	0	1	1	1	0	0	0	13	0	1	0	0	0	0	0	1	8	7	0
1942	34	.4232	3.1942	45.0	1	7	5	2	9	7	2	1	6	0	0	0	0	4	0	1	0	0	0	0	0	5	16	2	0
1943	18	.6789	2.4924	44.0	0	3	3	4	1	4	3	0	1	1	0	0	1	3	0	2	1	0	0	0	0	2	5	2	0
1944	27	.5117	2.9281	44.7	2	1	8	2	1	10	2	1	2	0	0	0	1	3	0	4	0	0	0	0	0	2	11	4	0
1945	63	.5773	7.7316	48.9	3	1	12	12	10	19	6	0	11	0	0	0	1	31	0	3	1	0	0	0	0	5	7	4	0
1946	31	.4020	2.8033	44.5	2	2	2	5	3	10	7	0	3	0	0	1	0	16	0	2	0	0	0	0	0	0	9	0	0
1947	30	.3913	2.6050	44.2	0	3	5	1	9	7	4	1	3	0	0	0	0	7	0	0	1	0	0	0	0	2	16	1	0
1948	39	.6684	5.3522	47.3	3	1	5	7	8	7	7	1	5	2	1	0	2	11	0	0	3	0	0	0	0	3	11	1	0
1949	19	.5873	2.3056	43.6	2	0	6	3	1	5	2	0	0	2	0	0	1	6	0	0	0	0	0	0	0	2	4	4	0
195	8	.5019	.8672	39.4	0	1	1	3	1	0	2	0	1	0	0	0	1	4	0	0	1	0	0	0	0	0	1	0	0
1950	30	.6393	3.9850	46.0	1	2	4	3	9	8	3	0	6	0	1	0	5	5	0	0	0	0	0	0	0	2	7	4	0
1950's	8	.4112	.7301	38.6	0	0	1	1	0	3	1	2	1	0	0	0	0	2	0	0	0	0	0	0	0	0	2	3	0
1950s	7	.3695	.5617	37.5	0	0	2	1	3	0	1	0	0	0	0	0	0	0	0	0	0	0	0	0	0	2	3	2	0
1951	29	.6687	3.9788	46.0	1	1	0	5	6	10	6	0	4	0	1	0	2	3	0	3	3	0	0	0	0	3	9	1	0
1951-52	2	.2160	.1362	31.3	0	0	0	0	0	1	1	0	1	0	0	0	0	0	0	1	0	0	0	0	0	0	0	0	0
1952	28	.7042	4.0319	46.1	2	3	2	3	7	5	5	1	4	1	1	0	0	8	0	2	1	0	0	0	0	2	4	5	0
1953	29	.6872	4.0675	46.1	0	2	4	6	7	5	4	1	2	3	0	0	5	2	0	4	0	0	0	0	0	6	3	4	0
1954	40	.6385	5.2625	47.2	2	3	7	5	9	8	4	2	3	1	0	0	1	12	0	2	2	0	0	0	0	3	10	6	0
1955	35	.6718	4.8458	46.9	3	1	2	6	11	9	2	1	6	0	0	0	5	5	0	2	1	0	0	0	0	4	7	5	0
1956	41	.6359	5.3933	47.3	3	1	8	5	8	8	7	1	5	1	0	0	2	10	0	0	1	0	0	0	0	7	9	6	0
1957	47	.6776	6.5120	48.1	2	1	5	10	9	8	7	5	4	0	0	3	3	5	0	3	1	0	0	0	0	13	5	10	0

5Q 1892-
7H 1893-
4B 18938
9E 1894-1964
5Q 1895-1967
8Q 1896-1898
7Q 1897-
8J 1898-1937
7P 1899-1902
3B 19-
3R 19-EA-7
9B 19–
7R 19-foot-wide
9H 19-15
8M 19-2
7D 19-21
7E 19-22
6E 19-24
7Q 19-26
8E 19-27
8M 19-3
8E 19/20
5E 19/24
5Q 19th-
4Q 19th-century
4B 19013
6P 1902-03
8R 1904-1967
5Q 1906-
7P 1906-09
5Q 1908-
4F 1909-13
8H 191-million
9Q 1910s
7F 1912-1913
5Q 1913-
3P 1913-1918
5Q 1915-1941
8F 1917-18
6E 192/100
5E 1920-1929
7Q 1922-24
8A 1926-1927
5Q 1927-1961
5Q 1929-
8E 193-213
7R 1931385
8H 1932-33
6H 1933-45
8Q 1936-1938
5P 1936-1939
8Q 1938-1943
5P 1939-1940
5F 1939-45
9Q 1940-54
8H 1941-42
7R 19468
9H 1953-1965
6R 1954-56
9A 1955-56

					3	4	5	6	7	8	9	X	A	B	C	D	E	F	G	H	J	K	L	M	N	P	Q	R	S
Word Type	F	D	U	SFI	Gr 3	Gr 4	Gr 5	Gr 6	Gr 7	Gr 8	Gr 9	UnGr	Read	Eng & Gr	Comp	Lit	Math	Soc Stud	Spell	Sci	Music	Art	Home Ec	Shop	Lib F	Lib NF	Lib Ref	Mag	Rel
1957-1958	3	.1434	.1493	31.7	0	0	0	1	2	0	0	0	1	0	0	0	2	0	0	0	0	0	0	0	0	0	0	0	0
1958	54	.7468	8.1673	49.1	3	2	8	7	10	10	10	4	6	0	0	2	1	9	0	7	3	0	0	1	0	9	10	6	0
1959	38	.6209	4.8783	46.9	3	2	9	2	9	9	2	2	3	1	0	0	1	10	0	0	1	0	0	0	0	7	7	8	0
196	10	.4260	.9351	39.7	0	1	1	2	4	1	1	0	1	0	0	0	6	0	0	1	0	0	1	0	0	0	0	1	0
1960	87	.7193	12.660	51.0	8	12	12	9	14	25	5	2	2	1	2	0	15	21	1	6	0	0	0	2	0	4	22	11	0
1960's	7	.3766	.5921	37.7	0	1	3	2	0	0	1	0	0	0	0	0	0	3	0	2	0	0	0	0	0	0	2	0	0
1960s	8	.3131	.5594	37.5	0	0	0	0	4	3	1	0	0	0	0	0	0	1	0	0	0	0	0	0	0	0	4	3	0
1961	51	.6141	6.4685	48.1	2	5	4	8	16	9	5	2	2	0	0	1	5	14	0	2	0	0	0	0	0	7	12	8	0
1962	62	.6393	8.1623	49.1	2	11	8	9	10	9	12	1	4	1	0	0	17	7	0	7	0	0	0	0	0	6	11	9	0
1963	50	.6511	6.6970	48.3	2	3	7	8	11	6	13	0	5	0	1	1	3	11	0	1	0	0	0	0	0	5	8	15	0
1964	35	.6813	4.8829	46.9	2	2	8	5	9	4	3	2	4	1	0	2	3	5	0	2	0	0	0	0	0	4	4	10	0
1965	39	.5649	4.6571	46.7	1	2	6	7	11	4	7	1	6	2	0	0	3	8	0	1	0	0	0	0	0	3	1	15	0
1965-66	2	.0000	.0243	23.9	0	0	0	1	1	0	0	0	0	0	0	0	0	0	0	0	0	0	0	0	0	0	0	2	0
1966	34	.4888	3.5328	45.5	0	4	5	5	11	4	4	1	3	0	1	0	1	3	0	1	0	0	0	0	0	0	8	17	0
1967	75	.4507	7.2351	48.6	1	11	5	13	22	7	12	4	2	4	0	0	4	14	0	1	0	0	0	0	0	0	10	40	0
1968	71	.3126	4.9890	47.0	0	2	6	9	33	6	11	4	1	0	0	1	3	4	0	0	0	0	0	0	0	0	12	50	0
1969	28	.2141	1.4447	41.6	1	1	1	5	9	1	8	2	0	0	0	0	0	1	0	0	0	0	0	0	0	0	5	22	0
197	9	.4960	.9434	39.7	2	0	2	0	5	0	0	0	0	2	0	0	4	1	0	1	0	0	0	0	0	0	1	0	0
1970	29	.3649	2.3538	43.7	2	4	0	1	4	4	12	2	1	0	0	0	2	5	0	1	0	0	0	0	0	0	2	18	0
1970's	3	.3781	.2548	34.1	0	1	1	0	0	0	1	0	0	0	0	0	0	1	0	1	0	0	0	0	0	0	0	1	0
1971	8	.3103	.5819	37.6	1	0	0	1	3	0	3	0	1	0	0	0	0	1	0	0	0	0	0	0	0	0	1	5	0
1972	5	.2129	.2689	34.3	0	2	0	0	1	1	1	0	0	0	0	0	0	0	0	2	0	0	0	0	0	0	0	3	0
1973	2	.0000	.0243	23.9	0	0	0	0	0	0	1	1	0	0	0	0	0	0	0	0	0	0	0	0	0	0	0	2	0
1975	6	.3693	.5062	37.0	0	0	1	0	2	1	2	0	0	0	0	0	0	3	0	2	0	0	0	0	0	1	0	0	0
1976	3	.2440	.1815	32.6	0	0	2	0	0	0	1	0	0	1	0	0	0	2	0	0	0	0	0	0	0	0	0	0	0
1979	4	.0000	.0486	26.9	0	0	0	0	0	0	4	0	0	0	0	0	0	0	0	0	0	0	0	0	0	0	0	4	0
198	18	.4631	1.7706	42.5	0	1	1	2	10	0	3	1	0	0	0	0	12	1	0	2	0	1	2	0	0	0	0	0	0
1984	2	.0000	.0243	23.9	0	0	0	0	0	1	1	0	0	0	0	0	0	0	0	0	0	0	0	0	0	0	0	2	0
1985	2	.1814	.1187	30.7	0	1	0	0	0	0	1	0	1	0	0	0	0	0	0	0	0	0	0	0	0	0	0	1	0
1986	3	.0000	.0591	27.7	0	2	0	0	0	0	0	1	0	0	0	0	0	0	0	3	0	0	0	0	0	0	0	0	0
199	3	.3776	.2510	34.0	0	0	2	0	0	0	1	0	0	1	0	0	1	0	0	1	0	0	0	0	0	0	0	0	0
199/200	2	.0000	.0299	24.8	0	2	0	0	0	0	0	0	0	0	0	0	2	0	0	0	0	0	0	0	0	0	0	0	0
1990	7	.2727	.4310	36.3	0	0	0	1	0	6	0	0	0	1	0	5	0	0	0	0	0	0	0	0	0	0	0	1	0
1999	2	.2417	.1211	30.8	0	0	0	1	0	1	0	0	0	0	0	0	1	1	0	0	0	0	0	0	0	0	0	0	0
2	3030	.6405	397.90	66.0	407	326	374	520	427	521	386	69	113	110	5	7	1941	91	193	168	71	8	42	42	1	69	82	87	0
2A	3	.2346	.1705	32.3	1	0	1	0	0	0	1	0	0	0	0	0	2	0	0	0	0	0	0	0	0	0	0	1	0
2B	2	.0000	.0299	24.8	0	0	1	0	0	1	0	0	0	0	0	0	2	0	0	0	0	0	0	0	0	0	0	0	0
2T	2	.0000	.0299	24.8	0	0	0	0	0	2	0	0	0	0	0	0	2	0	0	0	0	0	0	0	0	0	0	0	0
2X2L	3	.0000	.1370	31.4	0	0	0	0	3	0	0	0	3	0	0	0	0	0	0	0	0	0	0	0	0	0	0	0	0
2-	5	.3040	.3256	35.1	0	0	2	0	0	2	1	0	0	0	0	0	1	0	1	0	0	0	0	2	0	0	1	0	0
2-Star	115	.0000	.9333	39.7	0	23	62	30	0	0	0	0	0	0	0	0	0	0	115	0	0	0	0	0	0	0	0	0	0
2-digit	32	.0000	.4790	36.8	5	13	1	1	2	10	0	0	0	0	0	0	32	0	0	0	0	0	0	0	0	0	0	0	0
2-finger-width	2	.0000	.0299	24.8	0	2	0	0	0	0	0	0	0	0	0	0	2	0	0	0	0	0	0	0	0	0	0	0	0
2-foot	2	.1457	.0722	28.6	0	0	0	0	1	1	0	0	0	0	0	0	1	0	0	0	0	0	0	1	0	0	0	0	0
2-inch	15	.4946	1.5515	41.9	1	4	0	0	5	3	1	1	0	0	0	0	9	0	0	1	0	0	1	2	0	0	1	1	0
2-place	6	.0000	.0898	29.5	6	0	0	0	0	0	0	0	0	0	0	0	6	0	0	0	0	0	0	0	0	0	0	0	0
2-1	7	.1741	.3194	35.0	3	0	1	0	2	0	1	0	1	0	0	0	0	0	0	0	0	0	0	3	0	3	0	0	0
2-10	2	.1934	.0846	29.3	0	0	1	0	0	0	1	0	0	0	0	0	0	0	1	0	0	0	0	1	0	0	0	0	0
2-11	2	.0000	.0299	24.8	0	0	0	0	0	0	2	0	0	0	0	0	2	0	0	0	0	0	0	0	0	0	0	0	0
2-12	3	.0000	.0449	26.5	0	0	0	0	0	0	3	0	0	0	0	0	3	0	0	0	0	0	0	0	0	0	0	0	0
2-15	5	.1092	.1537	31.9	0	0	4	0	0	0	1	0	0	0	0	0	0	0	0	1	4	0	0	0	0	0	0	0	0
2-2	5	.0613	.0833	29.2	0	0	0	1	3	1	0	0	0	0	0	0	0	0	0	0	0	0	0	4	0	1	0	0	0
2-3	8	.2315	.4055	36.1	0	0	0	1	3	1	2	1	0	0	1	0	0	1	0	1	0	0	0	5	0	0	0	0	0
2-4	5	.3234	.3461	35.4	1	0	0	0	1	3	0	0	0	0	0	0	1	0	3	0	0	0	0	1	0	0	0	0	0
2-5	6	.2724	.4128	36.2	0	0	0	4	1	0	1	0	1	0	0	0	0	4	0	0	0	0	0	1	0	0	0	0	0
2-6	2	.2413	.1212	30.8	0	0	0	0	0	0	2	0	0	0	0	0	1	0	0	1	0	0	0	0	0	0	0	0	0
2-8	2	.2413	.1212	30.8	0	0	1	0	0	0	1	0	0	0	0	0	1	0	0	1	0	0	0	0	0	0	0	0	0
2/0	2	.2421	.0995	30.0	0	0	0	0	0	1	1	0	0	0	0	0	0	0	0	0	0	0	1	1	0	0	0	0	0
2/10	3	.0000	.0449	26.5	0	0	3	0	0	0	0	0	0	0	0	0	3	0	0	0	0	0	0	0	0	0	0	0	0
2/12	2	.0000	.0299	24.8	0	0	1	0	1	0	0	0	0	0	0	0	2	0	0	0	0	0	0	0	0	0	0	0	0
2/15	2	.0000	.0299	24.8	0	0	0	0	2	0	0	0	0	0	0	0	2	0	0	0	0	0	0	0	0	0	0	0	0
2/2	7	.0000	.1048	30.2	2	1	0	2	0	1	1	0	0	0	0	0	7	0	0	0	0	0	0	0	0	0	0	0	0
2/3	139	.1139	4.9344	46.9	6	21	40	31	14	18	9	0	0	0	0	0	135	0	0	1	0	0	2	0	0	0	1	0	0
2/3x3/4	3	.0000	.0449	26.5	0	0	1	0	0	2	0	0	0	0	0	0	3	0	0	0	0	0	0	0	0	0	0	0	0
2/3x4/5	2	.0000	.0299	24.8	0	0	2	0	0	0	0	0	0	0	0	0	2	0	0	0	0	0	0	0	0	0	0	0	0
2/3x6	2	.0000	.0299	24.8	0	0	0	0	2	0	0	0	0	0	0	0	2	0	0	0	0	0	0	0	0	0	0	0	0
2/4	55	.2678	3.4065	45.3	14	13	9	9	6	3	1	0	0	0	0	0	36	0	0	0	18	0	0	0	0	1	0	0	0
2/5	53	.0435	1.2078	40.8	6	5	16	12	8	5	1	0	0	0	0	0	52	0	0	0	0	0	0	0	0	0	1	0	0
2/6	14	.0000	.2096	33.2	0	7	1	3	1	0	2	0	0	0	0	0	14	0	0	0	0	0	0	0	0	0	0	0	0
2/7	4	.0000	.0599	27.8	0	1	0	0	0	3	0	0	0	0	0	0	4	0	0	0	0	0	0	0	0	0	0	0	0
2/8	10	.2203	.5389	37.3	1	2	0	7	0	0	0	0	0	0	0	0	8	0	0	0	2	0	0	0	0	0	0	0	0
2/9	5	.0000	.0748	28.7	0	1	1	1	2	0	0	0	0	0	0	0	5	0	0	0	0	0	0	0	0	0	0	0	0
2%	6	.3419	.4515	36.5	0	0	0	0	4	1	1	0	0	0	0	0	2	0	0	0	0	0	0	0	0	0	3	1	0
2'	2	.0000	.0299	24.8	0	0	0	2	0	0	0	0	0	0	0	0	2	0	0	0	0	0	0	0	0	0	0	0	0
2's	13	.2092	.6847	38.4	7	0	1	0	1	3	1	0	0	1	0	0	11	0	0	0	0	0	0	0	0	1	0	0	0
2a	8	.1807	.3766	35.8	0	0	0	0	5	1	2	0	0	0	0	0	7	0	1	0	0	0	0	0	0	0	0	0	0
2ab	6	.0000	.0898	29.5	0	0	0	0	0	6	0	0	0	0	0	0	6	0	0	0	0	0	0	0	0	0	0	0	0
2b	18	.3095	1.2540	41.0	0	0	1	1	5	8	2	1	0	0	0	0	12	0	5	0	0	0	0	0	0	0	1	0	0
2d	3	.1205	.0847	29.3	0	0	0	0	2	0	1	0	0	0	0	0	0	0	0	0	0	0	0	2	0	0	1	0	0
2n	2	.0000	.0299	24.8	0	0	0	0	0	1	1	0	0	0	0	0	2	0	0	0	0	0	0	0	0	0	0	0	0
2nd	19	.5831	2.2987	43.6	2	3	2	3	1	4	4	0	1	1	0	0	6	4	0	0	4	0	0	0	0	0	1	2	0
2s	8	.2129	.4245	36.3	0	0	0	0	0	0	6	2	0	0	0	0	6	0	0	0	0	0	0	0	0	0	0	2	0
2x	24	.0499	.5813	37.6	0	0	1	2	1	8	12	0	0	0	0	0	23	0	0	1	0	0	0	0	0	0	0	0	0
2x-segment	2	.0000	.0299	24.8	0	0	2	0	0	0	0	0	0	0	0	0	2	0	0	0	0	0	0	0	0	0	0	0	0
2x1	3	.0000	.0449	26.5	0	0	0	1	2	0	0	0	0	0	0	0	3	0	0	0	0	0	0	0	0	0	0	0	0
2x1/7	2	.0000	.0299	24.8	0	0	0	0	2	0	0	0	0	0	0	0	2	0	0	0	0	0	0	0	0	0	0	0	0
2x10	2	.0000	.0299	24.8	0	0	0	2	0	0	0	0	0	0	0	0	2	0	0	0	0	0	0	0	0	0	0	0	0
2x2x2x2x2	2	.0000	.0299	24.8	0	0	0	0	0	2	0	0	0	0	0	0	2	0	0	0	0	0	0	0	0	0	0	0	0
2x6	3	.0000	.0449	26.5	0	0	2	1	0	0	0	0	0	0	0	0	3	0	0	0	0	0	0	0	0	0	0	0	0
2x7	2	.0000	.0299	24.8	0	0	0	0	0	2	0	0	0	0	0	0	2	0	0	0	0	0	0	0	0	0	0	0	0
2x8	2	.0000	.0299	24.8	0	0	0	2	0	0	0	0	0	0	0	0	2	0	0	0	0	0	0	0	0	0	0	0	0
2y	9	.0000	.1347	31.3	0	0	0	0	0	0	9	0	0	0	0	0	9	0	0	0	0	0	0	0	0	0	0	0	0

5H 1957-58
5H 1957-8
6F 1958-59
6F 1959-1965
5P 1960-1961
5P 1962-1963
6A 1966-mile
7R 1967-1968
6R 1968-69
7R 1969s
6A 197-198
XR 1970-71
7E 1974
9R 1978
XQ 198-199
7Q 1980
6R 1980's
7F 1980s
8H 199-201
6A 1990's
5E 2(5/5)-segment
7R 2GC
XR 2F
9H 2H
9H 2He4
6Q 2H2O
5Q 2O
4E 2-finger
7R 2-in
3E 2-letter
XP 2-liter
8R 2-megaton
6E 2-meter
5E 2-mile
6R 2-million-pound
4R 2-pound
7R 2-qt
4R 2-story
4P 2-0
9H 2-1E
9H 2-14
9M 2-16
5J 2-27
9B 2-3-3
7M 2-49
7M 2-50
9H 2-60
9H 2-61
9H 2-7
8M 2-9
8E 2/a
7E 2/1
7E 2/1x1/7
9E 2/1000
8E 2/20
8E 2/3x3/2
5E 2/36
8E 2/5x7/3
8E 2/7x4
7E 2a-c
9E 2ay
8E 2c
6P 2g
7E 2l
7E 2lw
9E 2m
7E 2r
7E 2w
4E 2x10x3x10
6E 2x100
5H 2x120
5E 2x2
8E 2x2x2x2x2x2x2x2x2
5E 2x4/4
XH 2x46
7E 2x61
5E 2x90
9E 2y/y

Word Type	F	D	U	SFI	3 Gr 3	4 Gr 4	5 Gr 5	6 Gr 6	7 Gr 7	8 Gr 8	9 Gr 9	X UnGr	A Read	B Eng & Gr	C Comp	D Lit	E Math	F Soc Stud	G Spell	H Sci	J Music	K Art	L Home Ec	M Shop	N Lib F	P Lib NF	Q Lib Ref	R Mag	S Rel
20	561	.7701	86.906	59.4	70	53	91	83	113	64	71	16	26	9	2	3	240	31	17	67	8	1	19	5	1	28	48	56	0
20-foot	2	.1814	.1187	30.7	0	0	1	0	0	0	0	1	1	0	0	0	0	0	0	0	0	0	0	0	0	0	0	1	0
20-liter	3	.0000	.0591	27.7	0	0	0	0	0	0	3	0	0	0	0	0	0	0	0	3	0	0	0	0	0	0	0	0	0
20-minute	2	.0000	.0243	23.9	0	0	0	0	0	1	1	0	0	0	0	0	0	0	0	0	0	0	0	0	0	0	0	2	0
20-word	2	.0000	.0299	24.8	0	0	0	2	0	0	0	0	0	0	0	0	2	0	0	0	0	0	0	0	0	0	0	0	0
20-year	2	.2351	.1166	30.7	0	0	0	0	0	1	1	0	0	0	0	0	0	1	0	0	0	0	0	0	0	0	0	1	0
20-year-old	3	.0000	.0365	25.6	0	0	0	1	2	0	0	0	0	0	0	0	0	0	0	0	0	0	0	0	0	0	0	3	0
20-19	3	.0000	.0076	18.8	0	0	0	0	0	0	3	0	0	0	0	0	0	0	0	0	0	0	0	3	0	0	0	0	0
20-2	2	.0000	.0050	17.0	0	0	0	0	0	0	2	0	0	0	0	0	0	0	0	0	0	0	0	2	0	0	0	0	0
20-21	2	.2137	.1056	30.2	0	0	1	1	0	0	0	0	0	0	0	0	0	1	0	0	1	0	0	0	0	0	0	0	0
20-3	2	.0000	.0050	17.0	0	0	0	0	0	0	2	0	0	0	0	0	0	0	0	0	0	0	0	2	0	0	0	0	0
20/80	2	.0000	.0243	23.9	0	0	0	0	2	0	0	0	0	0	0	0	0	0	0	0	0	0	0	0	0	0	0	2	0
20/80's	2	.0000	.0243	23.9	0	0	0	0	2	0	0	0	0	0	0	0	0	0	0	0	0	0	0	0	0	0	0	2	0
20%	14	.1611	.6143	37.9	0	0	0	2	4	1	6	1	0	0	0	0	12	0	0	0	0	0	0	0	0	0	0	2	0
20th	39	.5601	4.5313	46.6	1	0	7	8	14	2	7	0	0	0	0	1	1	8	0	1	0	0	0	0	1	10	13	4	0
20th-century	6	.3198	.4151	36.2	0	0	2	0	1	0	2	1	0	0	0	0	0	0	0	0	0	1	0	0	0	0	4	1	0
200	271	.7473	40.957	56.1	22	19	40	38	73	34	32	13	19	3	0	0	62	50	0	29	2	0	2	5	1	19	38	41	0
200-inch	6	.3769	.5075	37.1	0	1	0	0	4	1	0	0	0	0	0	0	2	0	0	3	0	0	0	0	0	0	0	1	0
200-meter	2	.0000	.0914	29.6	0	0	0	2	0	0	0	0	2	0	0	0	0	0	0	0	0	0	0	0	0	0	0	0	0
200-mile	4	.3740	.3226	35.1	0	0	1	1	0	0	2	0	0	1	0	0	0	0	0	0	0	0	0	0	0	0	1	2	0
200-201	2	.2306	.1140	30.6	0	0	0	1	1	0	0	0	0	1	0	0	0	1	0	0	0	0	0	0	0	0	0	0	0
2000	48	.6720	6.5993	48.2	1	5	2	12	12	2	7	7	3	0	0	0	13	8	0	4	0	1	0	0	0	4	8	7	0
2002	8	.0000	.0972	29.9	0	0	0	0	0	0	0	8	0	0	0	0	0	0	0	0	0	0	0	0	0	0	0	8	0
2003	2	.0000	.0299	24.8	0	0	1	0	0	1	0	0	0	0	0	0	2	0	0	0	0	0	0	0	0	0	0	0	0
201	6	.3849	.5006	37.0	0	2	2	0	1	0	1	0	0	2	0	0	2	0	0	0	0	0	0	0	0	0	0	2	0
202	4	.3630	.3240	35.1	1	0	1	0	0	1	0	1	0	1	0	0	2	0	0	1	0	0	0	0	0	0	0	0	0
2020	2	.0000	.0243	23.9	0	0	0	2	0	0	0	0	0	0	0	0	0	0	0	0	0	0	0	0	0	0	0	2	0
203	7	.3931	.6029	37.8	0	2	1	0	2	1	1	0	0	0	0	0	4	1	0	1	0	0	1	0	0	0	0	0	0
204	8	.3452	.6189	37.9	0	1	0	5	0	0	2	0	0	0	0	0	5	2	0	0	0	0	0	1	0	0	0	0	0
204-205	3	.0000	.0583	27.7	0	0	0	3	0	0	0	0	0	0	0	0	0	3	0	0	0	0	0	0	0	0	0	0	0
205	13	.3342	.9536	39.8	0	0	1	5	4	0	3	0	0	1	0	0	4	3	0	0	0	0	0	4	0	0	1	0	0
2050	2	.0000	.0914	29.6	0	2	0	0	0	0	0	0	2	0	0	0	0	0	0	0	0	0	0	0	0	0	0	0	0
206	17	.5084	1.8351	42.6	0	0	9	3	4	0	1	0	1	1	0	0	10	2	0	1	0	0	0	1	0	0	1	0	0
207	5	.4630	.4824	36.8	0	0	1	1	1	0	2	0	0	1	0	0	1	1	0	0	0	0	1	1	0	0	0	0	0
208	5	.3053	.3464	35.4	1	0	1	2	0	0	1	0	0	0	0	0	3	1	0	0	0	0	0	1	0	0	0	0	0
209	2	.2152	.1357	31.3	1	0	1	0	0	0	0	0	1	0	0	0	0	1	0	0	0	0	0	0	0	0	0	0	0
21	183	.7608	28.042	54.5	23	26	21	31	33	20	23	6	10	9	0	1	83	13	11	12	2	1	1	4	1	7	10	18	0
21-year-old	2	.0000	.0243	23.9	0	0	0	1	0	1	0	0	0	0	0	0	0	0	0	0	0	0	0	0	0	0	0	2	0
21-1	2	.1432	.0759	28.8	0	0	0	0	0	1	1	0	0	0	0	0	0	0	0	1	0	0	1	0	0	0	0	0	0
21/28	6	.0000	.0898	29.5	0	0	6	0	0	0	0	0	0	0	0	0	6	0	0	0	0	0	0	0	0	0	0	0	0
21st	6	.4586	.5797	37.6	0	0	0	2	1	1	2	0	0	0	0	0	1	0	0	0	0	0	0	0	1	0	2	2	0
210	13	.2780	.8479	39.3	0	0	2	4	4	0	3	0	0	0	0	0	9	1	0	0	0	0	0	0	0	0	0	3	0
2100	3	.0000	.0449	26.5	0	0	2	0	0	0	1	0	0	0	0	0	3	0	0	0	0	0	0	0	0	0	0	0	0
211	2	.2437	.1129	30.5	0	0	0	0	0	0	2	0	0	0	0	0	0	0	0	0	0	0	0	0	0	0	1	1	0
212	14	.5030	1.5087	41.8	2	2	2	2	4	1	1	0	1	0	0	0	2	0	0	6	0	0	0	0	0	0	2	3	0
213	10	.4567	.9888	40.0	2	0	1	4	2	0	1	0	0	0	0	0	4	3	0	2	0	0	0	0	0	0	1	0	0
214	6	.4547	.6195	37.9	2	0	1	1	1	0	1	0	2	0	0	0	2	1	0	0	0	0	0	0	0	0	0	1	0
214-215	2	.1442	.0761	28.8	0	0	0	1	0	0	1	0	0	0	0	0	0	1	0	0	0	0	1	0	0	0	0	0	0
215	8	.3919	.6872	38.4	1	1	1	1	1	0	3	0	0	0	0	0	5	1	0	0	0	0	0	0	0	0	1	1	0
216	4	.2009	.2054	33.1	0	1	0	1	1	0	0	1	0	0	0	0	3	0	0	0	0	0	0	0	0	1	0	0	0
216-217	4	.0000	.0438	26.4	0	0	0	4	0	0	0	0	0	4	0	0	0	0	0	0	0	0	0	0	0	0	0	0	0
2160	2	.0000	.0299	24.8	1	1	0	0	0	0	0	0	0	0	0	0	2	0	0	0	0	0	0	0	0	0	0	0	0
217	4	.2404	.2283	33.6	0	1	2	0	1	0	0	0	0	2	0	0	2	0	0	0	0	0	0	0	0	0	0	0	0
218	6	.2121	.3120	34.9	0	1	0	1	3	1	0	0	0	0	0	0	2	0	0	0	0	0	0	0	0	0	0	4	0
219	5	.4095	.4349	36.4	0	1	0	1	0	0	3	0	0	0	0	0	2	0	0	0	0	0	0	1	0	0	1	1	0
22	131	.8319	21.759	53.4	13	13	18	18	29	19	20	1	8	2	1	0	46	9	5	10	1	2	2	2	2	10	11	20	0
22-year-old	2	.0000	.0243	23.9	0	0	0	0	1	1	0	0	0	0	0	0	0	0	0	0	0	0	0	0	0	0	0	2	0
22-13	2	.0000	.0394	26.0	0	0	0	0	0	0	2	0	0	0	0	0	0	0	0	2	0	0	0	0	0	0	0	0	0
22/5	2	.0000	.0299	24.8	0	0	0	0	0	2	0	0	0	0	0	0	2	0	0	0	0	0	0	0	0	0	0	0	0
22/7	6	.0000	.0898	29.5	0	0	0	0	0	6	0	0	0	0	0	0	6	0	0	0	0	0	0	0	0	0	0	0	0
22%	2	.0000	.0299	24.8	0	0	0	1	0	0	1	0	0	0	0	0	2	0	0	0	0	0	0	0	0	0	0	0	0
220	15	.5964	1.8551	42.7	2	3	0	2	2	2	4	0	1	2	0	0	7	1	0	0	0	0	0	0	1	1	1	1	0
2200	5	.3284	.3627	35.6	0	0	0	0	3	1	1	0	0	0	0	0	3	0	0	0	0	0	0	1	0	0	0	1	0
221	15	.4222	1.3743	41.4	0	2	8	0	4	0	1	0	0	1	0	0	10	1	0	1	0	0	0	0	0	1	1	0	0
222	9	.5977	1.1133	40.5	1	1	0	4	0	1	2	0	0	1	0	1	3	2	0	1	0	0	0	0	0	1	0	0	0
223	9	.4307	.8464	39.3	2	1	4	1	0	1	0	0	0	1	0	0	4	3	0	1	0	0	0	0	0	0	0	0	0
224	4	.2391	.2266	33.6	1	2	0	0	1	0	0	0	0	0	0	0	2	0	0	0	0	0	0	0	0	0	2	0	0
225	14	.5523	1.6262	42.1	1	1	1	2	3	3	3	0	1	0	0	0	5	2	0	2	0	0	1	0	0	0	0	3	0
226	5	.4031	.4307	36.3	1	2	0	0	0	1	1	0	0	1	0	0	1	0	0	1	0	1	0	0	0	0	1	0	0
227	6	.2471	.3406	35.3	0	1	0	1	1	2	1	0	0	0	0	0	2	0	0	1	0	2	0	0	0	0	0	1	0
228	5	.2928	.3562	35.5	1	0	0	2	0	1	1	0	1	0	0	0	2	1	0	0	0	1	0	0	0	0	0	0	0
229	3	.2551	.1690	32.3	0	0	1	1	0	0	1	0	0	1	0	0	0	0	0	0	0	1	0	0	0	0	0	1	0
23	153	.7274	22.527	53.5	18	23	24	26	21	19	14	8	8	2	0	0	70	15	12	11	4	1	0	2	1	5	11	11	0
23-year-old	3	.3370	.2430	33.9	0	0	0	0	1	0	2	0	1	0	0	1	0	0	0	0	0	0	0	0	0	0	1	0	0
23rd	2	.0000	.0389	25.9	0	0	0	0	0	2	0	0	0	0	0	0	0	2	0	0	0	0	0	0	0	0	0	0	0
230	12	.6215	1.5204	41.8	2	0	2	0	4	2	2	0	0	2	0	0	3	2	0	0	0	1	0	1	0	0	1	2	0
231	3	.0000	.0449	26.5	1	1	0	0	0	1	0	0	0	0	0	0	3	0	0	0	0	0	0	0	0	0	0	0	0
232	12	.5435	1.3603	41.3	1	1	0	1	3	3	3	0	1	2	0	0	4	0	0	1	1	0	2	0	0	0	1	0	0
233	5	.3835	.4006	36.0	0	1	0	2	1	1	0	0	0	3	0	0	0	0	0	0	0	0	1	1	0	0	0	0	0
234	2	.2391	.1133	30.5	0	0	0	0	1	0	1	0	0	0	0	0	1	0	0	0	0	0	0	0	0	0	1	0	0
2342	2	.0000	.0299	24.8	0	0	2	0	0	0	0	0	0	0	0	0	2	0	0	0	0	0	0	0	0	0	0	0	0
235	13	.5419	1.4744	41.7	0	3	3	0	0	2	4	1	1	4	0	0	4	1	0	0	0	0	1	0	0	0	0	2	0
236	7	.4303	.6528	38.1	0	1	1	3	1	0	1	0	0	1	0	0	1	4	0	0	0	0	1	0	0	0	0	0	0
236-237	2	.0000	.0389	25.9	2	0	0	0	0	0	0	0	0	0	0	0	0	2	0	0	0	0	0	0	0	0	0	0	0
237	11	.5275	1.2567	41.0	1	2	2	3	1	2	0	0	2	0	0	0	3	3	0	2	0	0	0	0	0	0	0	1	0
238	7	.4520	.6850	38.4	1	1	2	1	1	1	0	0	0	0	0	0	1	4	0	0	0	0	0	0	0	0	1	1	0

7R 20-in-wheel-size**
9R 20-inch
6R 20-knot
5E 20-mph
4A 20-pound
XR 20-second
3R 20-story
8R 20-0
9M 20-1
9H 20-12
9H 20-13
9H 20-13A
9H 20-13B
9H 20-14
9M 20-18
9R 20-200
7R 20-29
7A 20-30
5E 20/10
5R 20/20
5F 20's
7M 20d
6P 20g
8B 20s
4E 20x30
5E 20x8
9H 200B
7R 200-foot
6F 200-mile-wide
7Q 200-pound
7R 200-thousandths
8M 200/1000
8M 200/2
5F 200th
6A 2000-foot
XR 20006
5Q 20014
4A 2011
6R 2015
9M 204-207
6R 206th
6E 2062
8E 2073
4E 2080
6H 21-centimeter
6P 21-game
5A 21-mile-wide
6E 21-27
9H 21-9
6E 21/100
7E 21/3
9E 21x
5Q 210-acre
9B 212-13
8B 2137
7E 21430
8E 215x5
8E 215x500
5E 2153
6E 2158
5B 216-17
7R 2168
5B 218-19
5B 218-219
6E 2181
9H 22He4
7D 22-caliber
7R 22-foot-long
3P 22-game
6R 22-story
8H 22-18
XH 22-23
5G 22-23-24
9R 22-24
9H 22-4
9M 22-7a
9M 22-7b
9M 22-8
8E 22/24
5E 22/4
7E 22kg
7H 22nd
7R 220-grain
7E 220-yard
7E 2200/n
9L 221-222
7A 2222222222222
7R 223-foot-span
9B 225-226
6B 225-26
9E 2255
8E 2290
7R 23-geared
7R 23-inch
9Q 23-karat
8E 23-10
8E 23-11
7C 23-24
9E 23-34
8E 23-5
8E 23-6
8E 23-7
8E 23-8
8E 23-9
7N 23d
6F 230-foot
9H 2300
8E 2304
7E 231458
7A 2315
4E 2345
5E 2347
7R 236-foot
6B 237-38

Word Type	F	D	U	SFI	3 Gr 3	4 Gr 4	5 Gr 5	6 Gr 6	7 Gr 7	8 Gr 8	9 Gr 9	X UnGr	A Read	B Eng & Gr	C Comp	D Lit	E Math	F Soc Stud	G Spell	H Sci	J Music	K Art	L Home Ec	M Shop	N Lib F	P Lib NF	Q Lib Ref	R Mag	S Rel
239	3	.2371	.1813	32.6	0	2	0	1	0	0	0	0	0	0	0	0	1	0	0	2	0	0	0	0	0	0	0	0	0
24	334	.6548	44.828	56.5	48	52	49	60	52	38	29	6	17	2	0	1	191	16	6	34	6	1	2	10	1	10	15	22	0
24K	2	.0000	.0914	29.6	2	0	0	0	0	0	0	0	2	0	0	0	0	0	0	0	0	0	0	0	0	0	0	0	0
24-hour	10	.4580	.9915	40.0	0	6	0	2	0	2	0	0	0	0	0	0	1	3	0	3	0	0	0	0	0	0	0	3	0
24-year-old	2	.0000	.0243	23.9	0	0	0	0	0	2	0	0	0	0	0	0	0	0	0	0	0	0	0	0	0	0	0	2	0
24-10	2	.2346	.1166	30.7	0	0	0	0	1	0	1	0	0	0	0	0	0	0	0	1	0	0	0	0	0	0	0	1	0
24-25	3	.3674	.2406	33.8	0	0	0	1	1	0	1	0	0	0	0	0	0	1	0	0	1	0	0	0	0	0	1	0	0
24th	5	.3687	.4014	36.0	0	1	0	2	0	0	2	0	0	0	0	0	0	0	0	0	0	0	0	0	0	2	2	1	0
240	23	.5864	2.8249	44.5	2	7	2	3	4	3	1	1	2	1	0	0	9	3	0	3	0	0	0	0	0	3	0	2	0
240-241	2	.0000	.0389	25.9	0	0	0	2	0	0	0	0	0	0	0	0	0	2	0	0	0	0	0	0	0	0	0	0	0
2400	7	.4913	.7435	38.7	0	2	1	1	2	1	0	0	1	1	0	0	3	1	0	0	0	0	0	0	0	0	0	1	0
241	4	.3475	.3182	35.0	0	1	0	2	0	0	1	0	0	0	0	0	2	1	0	1	0	0	0	0	0	0	0	0	0
242	4	.3822	.3783	35.8	1	0	1	2	0	0	0	0	2	0	0	0	1	0	0	1	0	0	0	0	0	0	0	0	0
243	5	.1926	.2474	33.9	2	1	1	0	1	0	0	0	0	0	0	0	4	0	0	0	0	0	0	0	0	0	0	1	0
244	4	.2253	.2138	33.3	0	0	0	2	0	1	1	0	0	0	0	0	3	0	0	0	0	0	0	1	0	0	0	0	0
245	6	.3460	.4572	36.6	1	0	2	0	0	1	1	1	0	0	0	0	4	0	0	0	0	0	1	0	0	0	0	1	0
246	8	.4090	.7071	38.5	3	1	0	1	0	1	2	0	0	1	0	0	5	1	0	0	0	0	1	0	0	0	0	0	0
246-247	2	.0000	.0389	25.9	0	0	0	2	0	0	0	0	0	0	0	0	0	2	0	0	0	0	0	0	0	0	0	0	0
247	6	.3799	.5095	37.1	0	1	3	0	0	0	2	0	0	1	0	0	2	3	0	0	0	0	0	0	0	0	0	0	0
248	11	.3967	1.0051	40.0	1	5	2	1	2	0	0	0	2	0	0	0	5	2	0	2	0	0	0	0	0	0	0	0	0
249	8	.4703	.7955	39.0	0	2	2	1	2	0	1	0	0	0	0	0	2	2	0	0	2	0	0	0	0	0	2	0	0
25	389	.7565	59.348	57.7	34	51	43	58	88	48	58	9	26	6	1	0	197	20	14	24	3	2	13	1	1	21	24	35	1
25-foot	2	.2408	.1204	30.8	0	1	0	0	0	0	1	0	0	0	0	0	0	1	0	0	0	0	0	0	0	1	0	0	0
25-thousandths	2	.0000	.0243	23.9	0	0	0	0	2	0	0	0	0	0	0	0	0	0	0	0	0	0	0	0	0	0	0	2	0
25-12	2	.0000	.0050	17.0	0	0	0	0	0	1	1	0	0	0	0	0	0	0	0	0	0	0	0	2	0	0	0	0	0
25-29	2	.0000	.0162	22.1	0	0	0	0	2	0	0	0	0	0	0	0	0	0	2	0	0	0	0	0	0	0	0	0	0
25%	19	.3442	1.4610	41.6	0	0	0	7	3	3	6	0	0	0	0	0	15	1	0	0	0	0	1	0	0	0	2	0	0
25th	4	.3578	.3224	35.1	0	0	1	0	0	2	0	1	0	0	0	0	2	0	0	1	0	0	0	0	0	1	0	0	0
250	61	.8009	9.7697	49.9	3	8	6	6	24	5	8	1	1	4	1	0	8	4	0	10	0	1	1	1	0	4	12	14	0
2500	13	.5778	1.5809	42.0	1	1	1	2	5	1	1	1	1	1	0	0	0	4	0	4	0	0	0	0	0	0	1	2	0
252	9	.4992	.9521	39.8	0	4	2	2	0	1	0	0	0	3	0	0	1	3	0	1	0	0	0	0	0	0	0	1	0
253	7	.5089	.7735	38.9	0	6	0	1	0	0	0	0	1	1	0	0	1	3	0	1	0	0	0	0	0	0	0	0	0
254	2	.2427	.1159	30.6	1	0	0	1	0	0	0	0	0	0	0	0	1	0	0	0	0	0	0	0	0	0	0	1	0
255	4	.3396	.3008	34.8	0	0	1	0	0	1	2	0	0	1	0	0	0	1	0	0	0	0	0	0	0	0	2	0	0
256	6	.4860	.6182	37.9	0	0	2	0	2	2	0	0	0	0	0	0	2	0	0	2	1	0	0	0	0	0	1	0	0
257	5	.3371	.3808	35.8	0	2	0	3	0	0	0	0	0	0	0	0	3	1	0	0	0	0	0	0	0	0	1	0	0
258	4	.3623	.3240	35.1	0	2	0	1	1	0	0	0	0	0	0	0	2	1	0	0	0	0	0	0	0	0	0	1	0
259	8	.4947	.8283	39.2	2	0	1	2	1	1	1	0	0	3	0	0	2	0	0	1	0	0	1	0	0	1	0	0	0
26	105	.7709	16.252	52.1	9	15	17	15	25	17	5	2	4	4	1	2	42	9	10	2	2	2	0	0	1	4	12	10	0
26-year-old	2	.1814	.1187	30.7	0	0	0	0	1	0	1	0	1	0	0	0	0	0	0	0	0	0	0	0	0	0	0	1	0
26-10	2	.0000	.0394	26.0	0	0	0	0	0	0	2	0	0	0	0	0	0	0	0	2	0	0	0	0	0	0	0	0	0
26-12	2	.0000	.0394	26.0	0	0	0	0	0	0	2	0	0	0	0	0	0	0	0	2	0	0	0	0	0	0	0	0	0
26-6	2	.1249	.0685	28.4	0	0	0	0	0	0	2	0	0	0	0	0	0	0	0	1	0	0	0	1	0	0	0	0	0
26th	2	.2437	.1129	30.5	0	0	0	1	0	0	1	0	0	0	0	0	0	0	0	0	0	0	0	0	0	0	1	1	0
260	18	.6403	2.3523	43.7	1	2	6	0	2	2	5	0	0	1	0	0	7	3	0	0	1	0	1	0	0	0	2	3	0
2600	6	.4505	.5767	37.6	0	0	0	1	1	0	4	0	0	0	0	0	2	0	0	1	0	0	0	0	0	0	2	1	0
261	4	.3180	.2916	34.6	0	1	1	1	1	0	0	0	0	2	0	0	0	1	0	1	0	0	0	0	0	0	0	0	0
262	7	.4587	.6980	38.4	0	1	1	1	1	1	2	0	1	0	0	0	3	1	0	0	0	0	1	0	0	0	1	0	0
263	7	.4861	.7297	38.6	2	0	0	2	2	0	0	1	0	0	0	0	2	2	0	2	0	0	0	0	0	0	1	0	0
264	7	.3007	.4838	36.8	0	0	2	3	1	1	0	0	0	1	0	0	5	0	0	0	0	0	0	0	0	1	0	0	0
265	10	.3379	.7630	38.8	0	0	3	1	3	2	1	0	0	0	0	1	7	1	0	0	0	0	0	0	0	1	0	0	0
267	8	.4647	.8090	39.1	0	0	1	2	4	0	1	0	1	1	0	0	4	1	0	0	0	0	0	0	0	0	1	0	0
268	10	.2264	.5516	37.4	0	0	6	0	1	1	2	0	0	0	0	0	9	0	0	0	0	0	1	0	0	0	0	0	0
268-269	2	.0000	.0389	25.9	0	0	2	0	0	0	0	0	0	0	0	0	0	2	0	0	0	0	0	0	0	0	0	0	0
2689	2	.0000	.0299	24.8	0	0	2	0	0	0	0	0	0	0	0	0	2	0	0	0	0	0	0	0	0	0	0	0	0
269	7	.4622	.6790	38.3	0	2	1	0	1	2	1	0	0	2	0	0	3	0	0	0	0	0	1	0	0	0	1	0	0
27	138	.6551	18.534	52.7	20	17	22	15	25	22	15	2	9	4	2	0	76	6	4	6	1	0	0	1	0	8	9	12	0
27-year-old	3	.0000	.0365	25.6	0	0	0	0	2	1	0	0	0	0	0	0	0	0	0	0	0	0	0	0	0	0	0	3	0
27-1	2	.0000	.0050	17.0	0	0	0	0	2	0	0	0	0	0	0	0	0	0	0	0	0	0	0	2	0	0	0	0	0
27-10	2	.0000	.0050	17.0	0	0	0	0	2	0	0	0	0	0	0	0	0	0	0	0	0	0	0	2	0	0	0	0	0
27-12	3	.0000	.0076	18.8	0	0	0	0	3	0	0	0	0	0	0	0	0	0	0	0	0	0	0	3	0	0	0	0	0
27-13	3	.0000	.0076	18.8	0	0	0	0	3	0	0	0	0	0	0	0	0	0	0	0	0	0	0	3	0	0	0	0	0
27-14	2	.0000	.0050	17.0	0	0	0	0	2	0	0	0	0	0	0	0	0	0	0	0	0	0	0	2	0	0	0	0	0
27-15	3	.0000	.0076	18.8	0	0	0	0	3	0	0	0	0	0	0	0	0	0	0	0	0	0	0	3	0	0	0	0	0
27-16	3	.0000	.0076	18.8	0	0	0	0	3	0	0	0	0	0	0	0	0	0	0	0	0	0	0	3	0	0	0	0	0
27-8	3	.0000	.0076	18.8	0	0	0	0	3	0	0	0	0	0	0	0	0	0	0	0	0	0	0	3	0	0	0	0	0
270	7	.4213	.6378	38.0	2	1	2	0	1	0	1	0	0	1	0	0	4	1	0	0	0	0	0	0	0	0	1	0	0
2700	4	.4484	.4050	36.1	0	2	0	1	1	0	0	0	1	0	0	0	0	1	0	1	0	0	0	0	0	0	1	0	0
271	5	.3489	.3894	35.9	1	2	1	0	1	0	0	0	0	2	0	0	2	0	0	1	0	0	0	0	0	0	0	0	0
272	8	.5148	.8663	39.4	0	0	1	1	2	2	2	0	0	0	0	0	1	2	0	2	0	0	1	0	0	0	2	0	0
273	5	.1127	.2213	33.4	1	0	2	0	0	2	0	0	1	0	0	0	0	0	0	4	0	0	0	0	0	0	0	0	0
274	2	.1442	.0761	28.8	0	0	0	1	1	0	0	0	0	0	0	0	0	1	0	0	0	0	1	0	0	0	0	0	0
275	10	.5430	1.1180	40.5	1	1	1	2	2	1	2	0	0	1	0	0	1	1	0	0	0	0	2	0	0	1	2	2	0
276	3	.3660	.2695	34.3	0	1	0	1	1	0	0	0	1	0	0	0	0	1	0	1	0	0	0	0	0	0	0	0	0
277	8	.3849	.7035	38.5	0	1	2	1	1	2	1	0	1	0	0	0	1	4	0	1	0	1	0	0	0	0	0	0	0
278	4	.2863	.2552	34.1	1	0	0	0	2	0	1	0	0	0	0	0	2	0	0	0	0	1	0	0	0	0	1	0	0
279	5	.2770	.3490	35.4	0	0	3	1	0	0	1	0	1	0	0	0	0	2	0	1	0	1	0	0	0	0	0	0	0
2796	7	.0000	.0766	28.8	0	1	6	0	0	0	0	0	0	7	0	0	0	0	0	0	0	0	0	0	0	0	0	0	0
28	147	.6406	19.316	52.9	26	18	20	24	29	9	15	6	5	3	0	2	78	2	4	14	3	0	1	0	1	10	8	16	0
28-year-old	3	.2143	.1568	32.0	1	0	0	0	2	0	0	0	0	0	0	0	0	0	0	0	0	0	0	0	0	1	0	2	0
28-1	2	.0000	.0050	17.0	0	0	0	0	2	0	0	0	0	0	0	0	0	0	0	0	0	0	0	2	0	0	0	0	0
28-7	2	.0000	.0243	23.9	0	0	0	0	1	0	1	0	0	0	0	0	0	0	0	0	0	0	0	0	0	0	0	2	0
28th	4	.0759	.1243	30.9	0	0	1	0	3	0	0	0	1	0	0	0	0	0	0	0	3	0	0	0	0	0	0	0	0
280	13	.4815	1.3560	41.3	3	2	1	4	1	2	0	0	2	0	1	0	7	1	0	0	0	0	0	0	0	1	1	0	0
281	4	.2932	.2861	34.6	0	0	0	2	1	1	0	0	1	0	0	0	0	0	0	0	0	0	0	0	0	0	2	1	0

5Q 24-by-6-inch
6E 24-day
3P 24-game
XP 24-h
7E 24-hr
7R 24-page
8A 24-pound
9H 24-1
9H 24-11
9H 24-2
8R 24-23
7R 24-6
7R 240-250
5P 240mm
5E 2418
5E 2419
5B 243-244
7E 2448
4A 246-253
7E 248/8
7E 248/8x1/100
6E 2486
3P 248763
XP 25AB
XP 25B
XP 25C
XR 25-by-25-foot
6A 25-centime
7R 25-mile
9E 25-pound
7Q 25-pounder
9R 25-year
8R 25-year-old
8M 25-10
8M 25-11
8M 25-13
8M 25-14
8E 25-147
8M 25-15
8M 25-16
9E 25-26
9B 25-36
7P 25-4
7E 25/
6E 25/n
6E 25/100
5E 25/3
5E 25/6
7R 250-inch-wall
7H 250-mile-high
9Q 250-million-pound
5P 250-odd
6R 250-square-mile
7F 2500-1500
5E 2500's
5B 251
4B 253-254
6B 253-54
6E 253/1000
7E 2532
8E 2536
4E 2544
4B 256-57
6E 2586
5A 26-foot
7R 26-in
8B 26-inchers
9H 26-1
9H 26-11
9H 26-13
4J 26-29
9M 26-3a
9M 26-3b
9M 26-3c
9M 26-3d
5E 26/3
6F 260-day
5E 2610
5F 262-264
5F 262-267
9B 264-267
4E 2640
4E 2645
6G 2650
4F 266
6F 266-267
6B 267-68
6E 2675
6B 268-69
5E 2688
7M 27-11
9H 27-19
8E 27-29
9E 27-30
4G 27-34
7M 27-4
7M 27-6
7M 27-7
7M 27-9
8Q 274-237B
5F 274-275
6R 274-5
6B 275-76
9E 2753
4E 2763
5E 2764
6B 277-78
6H 2786
9H 28-day
6A 28-pound
7M 28-2
5G 28-29-30
7M 28-3
7M 28-4
7E 28/12
5E 28/15
9E 28%
7R 2800

Word Type	F	D	U	SFI	3 Gr 3	4 Gr 4	5 Gr 5	6 Gr 6	7 Gr 7	8 Gr 8	9 Gr 9	X UnGr	A Read	B Eng & Gr	C Comp	D Lit	E Math	F Soc Stud	G Spell	H Sci	J Music	K Art	L Home Ec	M Shop	N Lib F	P Lib NF	Q Lib Ref	R Mag	S Rel
281-83	2	.0000	.0219	23.4	0	0	0	2	0	0	0	0	0	2	0	0	0	0	0	0	0	0	0	0	0	0	0	0	0
282	10	.4867	1.0525	40.2	1	4	3	0	0	2	0	0	1	1	0	0	4	3	0	0	0	0	0	0	0	0	0	1	0
283	5	.3832	.4257	36.3	1	0	2	1	0	0	1	0	0	1	0	0	2	2	0	0	0	0	0	0	0	0	0	0	0
284	3	.1993	.1435	31.6	0	0	0	1	0	1	1	0	0	0	0	0	2	0	0	0	0	0	0	0	0	0	0	0	0
285	4	.1786	.1933	32.9	1	0	1	0	1	1	0	0	0	0	0	0	3	1	0	0	0	0	0	1	0	0	0	0	0
286	3	.3418	.2486	34.0	0	0	2	0	0	0	0	1	1	1	0	0	1	0	0	0	0	0	0	0	0	0	0	0	0
287	3	.2378	.1809	32.6	0	0	0	0	1	0	1	1	0	0	0	0	0	2	0	0	0	0	0	0	0	1	0	0	0
288	9	.4852	.9442	39.8	3	0	0	1	1	4	0	0	2	3	0	0	2	0	0	0	0	0	0	1	0	0	1	0	0
289	7	.3646	.5589	37.5	1	2	1	0	0	2	0	1	0	4	0	0	1	1	0	0	0	0	0	0	0	0	0	0	0
29	115	.6505	15.373	51.9	14	21	20	11	15	13	18	3	7	3	1	0	60	9	6	14	0	0	0	1	0	5	6	3	0
29x43	2	.0000	.0299	24.8	0	1	0	0	0	1	0	0	0	0	0	0	2	0	0	0	0	0	0	0	0	0	0	0	0
290	8	.4948	.8535	39.3	2	0	0	2	2	0	2	0	1	0	0	0	3	0	0	1	0	0	0	0	0	2	1	0	0
291	4	.4502	.4038	36.1	0	1	0	0	2	0	1	0	1	0	0	0	1	0	0	1	0	0	0	0	0	0	1	0	0
293	3	.1858	.1432	31.6	0	2	0	1	0	0	0	0	0	2	0	0	0	1	0	0	0	0	0	0	0	0	0	0	0
294	4	.2364	.2226	33.5	0	1	1	0	1	1	0	0	0	0	0	0	3	0	0	0	0	0	1	0	0	0	0	0	0
295	4	.3534	.3078	34.9	1	1	0	0	0	1	0	1	0	1	0	0	0	0	0	0	0	0	0	0	0	1	2	0	0
296	2	.0000	.0299	24.8	0	0	1	0	0	1	0	0	0	0	0	0	2	0	0	0	0	0	0	0	0	0	0	0	0
297	7	.3646	.5589	37.5	0	0	0	3	0	4	0	0	0	4	0	0	1	1	0	0	0	0	0	0	0	0	0	1	0
298	8	.3436	.6410	38.1	0	1	1	2	1	3	0	0	2	1	0	0	3	0	0	0	0	0	2	0	0	0	0	0	0
299	2	.0000	.0064	18.1	0	0	0	0	0	2	0	0	0	0	0	0	0	0	0	0	0	0	2	0	0	0	0	0	0
3	2638	.5721	313.54	65.0	400	354	381	352	398	361	334	58	72	66	9	8	1885	72	101	104	73	2	26	33	3	53	68	63	0
3A	2	.0000	.0243	23.9	2	0	0	0	0	0	0	0	0	0	0	0	0	0	0	0	0	0	0	0	0	0	0	2	0
3D	5	.0000	.0092	19.7	0	5	0	0	0	0	0	0	0	0	0	0	0	0	0	0	0	5	0	0	0	0	0	0	0
3Li61H2	2	.0000	.0394	26.0	0	0	0	0	0	0	2	0	0	0	0	0	0	0	0	2	0	0	0	0	0	0	0	0	0
3N	2	.0000	.0299	24.8	0	0	0	0	0	0	2	0	0	0	0	0	2	0	0	0	0	0	0	0	0	0	0	0	0
3-	4	.3230	.2767	34.4	0	0	2	0	0	1	1	0	0	0	0	0	1	0	2	0	0	0	0	1	0	0	0	0	0
3-D	5	.2288	.2760	34.4	0	0	0	0	2	2	0	1	0	0	0	0	2	0	0	0	0	0	0	0	0	0	0	3	0
3-Star	129	.0000	1.0469	40.2	0	41	51	37	0	0	0	0	0	0	0	0	0	0	129	0	0	0	0	0	0	0	0	0	0
3-digit	17	.0000	.2545	34.1	1	7	2	1	1	5	0	0	0	0	0	0	17	0	0	0	0	0	0	0	0	0	0	0	0
3-inch	7	.2446	.4063	36.1	0	4	0	0	2	1	0	0	0	0	0	0	6	0	0	0	0	0	0	1	0	0	0	0	0
3-liter	2	.0000	.0290	24.6	0	0	0	0	0	0	0	2	0	0	0	0	0	0	0	0	0	0	0	0	0	2	0	0	0
3-region	4	.0000	.0599	27.8	0	0	4	0	0	0	0	0	0	0	0	0	4	0	0	0	0	0	0	0	0	0	0	0	0
3-segment	2	.0000	.0299	24.8	0	0	2	0	0	0	0	0	0	0	0	0	2	0	0	0	0	0	0	0	0	0	0	0	0
3-step	6	.0000	.0898	29.5	3	2	1	0	0	0	0	0	0	0	0	0	6	0	0	0	0	0	0	0	0	0	0	0	0
3-0	2	.2433	.1158	30.6	0	1	0	1	0	0	0	0	0	0	0	0	0	0	0	0	0	0	0	0	0	1	0	1	0
3-1	4	.1457	.1444	31.6	0	0	0	0	1	2	1	0	0	0	0	0	2	0	0	0	0	0	0	2	0	0	0	0	0
3-2	3	.2735	.1828	32.6	0	0	0	1	0	2	0	0	0	0	0	0	1	0	0	0	0	0	0	1	0	0	0	1	0
3-3	3	.2966	.1928	32.9	0	0	0	0	0	1	2	0	0	0	0	0	1	0	1	0	0	0	0	1	0	0	0	0	0
3-4	4	.3171	.2598	34.1	0	0	0	0	0	3	1	0	0	0	1	0	0	0	1	0	0	0	0	2	0	0	0	0	0
3-5	2	.2413	.1212	30.8	0	0	0	0	1	1	0	0	0	0	0	0	1	0	0	1	0	0	0	0	0	0	0	0	0
3-6	2	.0000	.0299	24.8	0	0	0	0	1	1	0	0	0	0	0	0	2	0	0	0	0	0	0	0	0	0	0	0	0
3/c	3	.0000	.0449	26.5	0	0	0	0	3	0	0	0	0	0	0	0	3	0	0	0	0	0	0	0	0	0	0	0	0
3/0	2	.2421	.0995	30.0	0	0	0	0	0	2	0	0	0	0	0	0	0	0	0	0	0	0	1	1	0	0	0	0	0
3/1	3	.0000	.0449	26.5	0	0	0	1	0	1	1	0	0	0	0	0	3	0	0	0	0	0	0	0	0	0	0	0	0
3/10	14	.0000	.2096	33.2	0	0	5	1	7	1	0	0	0	0	0	0	14	0	0	0	0	0	0	0	0	0	0	0	0
3/11	7	.0000	.1048	30.2	0	0	0	0	6	1	0	0	0	0	0	0	7	0	0	0	0	0	0	0	0	0	0	0	0
3/12	13	.0000	.1946	32.9	0	5	6	2	0	0	0	0	0	0	0	0	13	0	0	0	0	0	0	0	0	0	0	0	0
3/16	10	.1633	.3980	36.0	0	0	1	0	1	1	6	1	0	0	0	0	4	0	0	1	0	0	0	5	0	0	0	0	0
3/2	30	.0000	.4491	36.5	0	5	5	8	3	7	2	0	0	0	0	0	30	0	0	0	0	0	0	0	0	0	0	0	0
3/3	19	.0000	.2844	34.5	3	1	11	4	0	0	0	0	0	0	0	0	19	0	0	0	0	0	0	0	0	0	0	0	0
3/4	257	.3652	20.740	53.2	6	24	52	77	40	31	26	1	0	0	0	0	215	1	0	5	23	0	2	5	0	1	1	4	0
3/4-inch	4	.2351	.2146	33.3	0	0	0	0	3	1	0	0	0	0	0	0	0	0	0	0	0	0	0	1	0	0	0	3	0
3/40	2	.0000	.0299	24.8	0	0	0	0	2	0	0	0	0	0	0	0	2	0	0	0	0	0	0	0	0	0	0	0	0
3/5	43	.0000	.6436	38.1	5	6	10	8	4	4	6	0	0	0	0	0	43	0	0	0	0	0	0	0	0	0	0	0	0
3/6	26	.0000	.3892	35.9	5	8	7	1	2	1	2	0	0	0	0	0	26	0	0	0	0	0	0	0	0	0	0	0	0
3/7	4	.0000	.0599	27.8	0	2	0	1	0	1	0	0	0	0	0	0	4	0	0	0	0	0	0	0	0	0	0	0	0
3/8	55	.4714	5.4690	47.4	1	9	12	4	8	8	12	1	0	0	0	0	42	0	0	0	3	0	3	4	0	0	1	2	0
3/9	5	.0000	.0748	28.7	0	3	2	0	0	0	0	0	0	0	0	0	5	0	0	0	0	0	0	0	0	0	0	0	0
3%	12	.3114	.8563	39.3	0	0	0	5	4	0	1	2	0	0	0	0	9	0	0	1	0	0	0	0	0	0	1	1	0
3's	8	.0000	.1197	30.8	8	0	0	0	0	0	0	0	0	0	0	0	8	0	0	0	0	0	0	0	0	0	0	0	0
3a	8	.0000	.1197	30.8	0	0	1	0	0	0	7	0	0	0	0	0	8	0	0	0	0	0	0	0	0	0	0	0	0
3c	2	.2289	.1077	30.3	0	0	0	0	1	0	1	0	0	0	0	0	1	0	1	0	0	0	0	0	0	0	0	0	0
3g	2	.0000	.0290	24.6	0	0	0	2	0	0	0	0	0	0	0	0	0	0	0	0	0	0	0	0	0	2	0	0	0
3n	2	.0000	.0299	24.8	0	0	0	0	0	2	0	0	0	0	0	0	2	0	0	0	0	0	0	0	0	0	0	0	0
3rd	12	.4411	1.1259	40.5	1	1	1	3	0	1	4	1	0	0	0	0	5	1	0	0	4	0	0	0	0	1	0	1	0
3s	2	.0000	.0243	23.9	0	0	0	0	0	0	0	2	0	0	0	0	0	0	0	0	0	0	0	0	0	0	0	2	0
3t	4	.0000	.0599	27.8	0	0	0	0	0	4	0	0	0	0	0	0	4	0	0	0	0	0	0	0	0	0	0	0	0
3x	15	.0000	.2245	33.5	0	1	0	0	0	4	10	0	0	0	0	0	15	0	0	0	0	0	0	0	0	0	0	0	0
3x10	2	.0000	.0299	24.8	0	1	0	1	0	0	0	0	0	0	0	0	2	0	0	0	0	0	0	0	0	0	0	0	0
3x2	3	.0000	.0449	26.5	2	0	0	0	0	1	0	0	0	0	0	0	3	0	0	0	0	0	0	0	0	0	0	0	0
3x4	2	.0000	.0299	24.8	0	1	1	0	0	0	0	0	0	0	0	0	2	0	0	0	0	0	0	0	0	0	0	0	0
3x5	3	.0000	.0449	26.5	0	0	0	1	1	1	0	0	0	0	0	0	3	0	0	0	0	0	0	0	0	0	0	0	0
3x7	3	.0000	.0449	26.5	0	2	0	1	0	0	0	0	0	0	0	0	3	0	0	0	0	0	0	0	0	0	0	0	0
3y	3	.0000	.0449	26.5	0	0	3	0	0	0	0	0	0	0	0	0	3	0	0	0	0	0	0	0	0	0	0	0	0
30	531	.7537	80.753	59.1	64	57	77	64	93	79	77	20	36	8	3	2	221	39	11	42	3	0	10	9	1	21	57	68	0
30-foot	2	.2417	.1211	30.8	0	1	0	0	0	1	0	0	0	0	0	0	1	1	0	0	0	0	0	0	0	0	0	0	0
30-odd	2	.2401	.1133	30.5	0	0	1	0	1	0	0	0	0	0	0	0	0	0	0	0	0	0	0	0	0	1	1	0	0
30-year	4	.3704	.3264	35.1	0	0	2	0	0	1	1	0	0	0	0	0	1	0	0	0	0	0	0	0	0	2	0	1	0
30-10	2	.0000	.0243	23.9	0	0	0	0	0	0	2	0	0	0	0	0	0	0	0	0	0	0	0	0	0	0	0	2	0
30-31	2	.2417	.1211	30.8	0	0	0	0	0	2	0	0	0	0	0	0	1	1	0	0	0	0	0	0	0	0	0	0	0
30-60	9	.2328	.4960	37.0	0	0	0	0	1	7	1	0	0	0	0	0	7	0	0	0	0	0	0	2	0	0	0	0	0
30-8	2	.0000	.0243	23.9	0	0	0	0	0	0	2	0	0	0	0	0	0	0	0	0	0	0	0	0	0	0	0	2	0
30%	2	.2413	.1212	30.8	0	0	1	0	0	0	1	0	0	0	0	0	1	0	0	1	0	0	0	0	0	0	0	0	0
30a	3	.2371	.1813	32.6	0	0	0	0	0	1	0	2	0	0	0	0	1	0	0	2	0	0	0	0	0	0	0	0	0
30b	2	.2413	.1212	30.8	0	0	0	0	0	1	0	1	0	0	0	0	1	0	0	1	0	0	0	0	0	0	0	0	0
30c	2	.0000	.0394	26.0	0	0	0	0	0	0	0	2	0	0	0	0	0	0	0	2	0	0	0	0	0	0	0	0	0

9L 282-283
7E 28333
6F 284-285
4E 2847
3H 287-308
8B 288-297
7R 29-inch-diameter
7M 29-1
9M 29-10C
9M 29-12
9M 29-13
9H 29-17
9H 29-3
9C 29-30
9H 29-4
9H 29-5
9L 29-6
5R 29th
6E 2900
7R 2917
8F 292
6F 292-293
6A 294-295
3H 296-99
6E 2965
5E 3(5/5)-segment
9E 3B
6E 3C
7H 3C295
8R 3M
4E 3R4
XR 3Ty
7A 3-all
4E 3-cent
6E 3-dot
7R 3-hp
9L 3-inch-deep
7Q 3-man
7Q 3-manned
9R 3-mile
3E 3-place
7Q 3-to-4-year
4P 3-toed
7Q 3-way
7E 3-year
8A 3-1-2
9M 3-11
8E 3-12
9Q 3-13
9E 3-15
9H 3-16
5Q 3-17
9H 3-20
7H 3-22
7A 3-59
9H 3-7
9H 3-8
8E 3/
7E 3/100
8E 3/2x2/3
7E 3/20
5E 3/3-regions
5E 3/3-segments
XR 3/4-in
XR 3/4-inch-long
5E 3/48
7E 3/5x2/7
5E 3/8-1/4
5E 3/8-1/8
9E 3b
6K 3d
9Q 3d-century
8E 3f
9H 3g/cm3
7E 3in
6E 3xr
9E 3xy
6E 3x0
4E 3x14
6E 3x2/3x2x2
6E 3x2x1/3x2x2
5E 3x3
XP 3x3x3x3
7E 3x41
5E 3x42
8E 3x4672
7E 3x62
8E 3x8
3F 30-day
9F 30-hour
6R 30-manpower
7F 30-million-dollar
8M 30-or
8R 30-piece
7M 30-story
8F 30-ton
7R 30-yard
8M 30-1
9R 30-11
8H 30-16
8M 30-2
8M 30-3
8M 30-4
3F 30-40
8M 30-5
8M 30-6
8M 30-7
7R 30/06
4Q 30's
XH 30d

Word Type	F	D	U	SFI	3 Gr 3	4 Gr 4	5 Gr 5	6 Gr 6	7 Gr 7	8 Gr 8	9 Gr 9	X UnGr	A Read	B Eng & Gr	C Comp	D Lit	E Math	F Soc Stud	G Spell	H Sci	J Music	K Art	L Home Ec	M Shop	N Lib F	P Lib NF	Q Lib Ref	R Mag	S Rel
30th	5	.2542	.3208	35.1	0	0	0	2	1	1	0	1	1	0	0	0	0	0	0	0	0	0	0	0	3	1	0	0	0
30x40	2	.0000	.0299	24.8	0	1	0	0	0	1	0	0	0	0	0	0	2	0	0	0	0	0	0	0	0	0	0	0	0
300	194	.8195	31.886	55.0	15	18	26	33	55	22	23	2	24	7	0	2	41	31	3	21	0	0	3	4	1	15	21	21	0
300-foot	2	.2440	.1132	30.5	0	0	0	0	2	0	0	0	0	0	0	1	0	0	0	0	0	0	0	0	0	0	0	1	0
300x70	2	.0000	.0299	24.8	0	1	0	0	0	1	0	0	0	0	0	0	2	0	0	0	0	0	0	0	0	0	0	0	0
3000	27	.7023	3.8561	45.9	0	3	2	5	10	2	2	3	3	1	0	0	6	2	1	2	0	1	0	1	0	0	8	2	0
3001	2	.0000	.0299	24.8	0	0	0	0	0	0	2	0	0	0	0	0	2	0	0	0	0	0	0	0	0	0	0	0	0
301	3	.3667	.2414	33.8	0	0	1	1	0	0	0	1	0	0	0	0	0	1	1	0	0	0	0	0	0	0	0	1	0
302	4	.3498	.3059	34.9	0	0	1	0	2	0	0	1	0	0	0	0	0	0	0	0	0	0	0	0	0	1	2	1	0
303	4	.3796	.3313	35.2	1	0	0	0	2	0	1	0	0	1	0	0	2	0	0	0	0	0	0	0	0	0	0	1	0
304	4	.3632	.3239	35.1	1	0	0	1	0	1	1	0	0	0	0	1	2	0	0	1	0	0	0	0	0	0	0	0	0
304th	2	.0000	.0215	23.3	0	0	0	0	0	2	0	0	0	0	0	2	0	0	0	0	0	0	0	0	0	0	0	0	0
305	7	.1926	.3568	35.5	2	0	0	2	0	1	2	0	0	0	0	0	5	2	0	0	0	0	0	0	0	0	0	0	0
307	2	.2417	.1211	30.8	0	0	0	1	0	0	1	0	0	0	0	0	1	1	0	0	0	0	0	0	0	0	0	0	0
308	6	.2384	.3434	35.4	0	0	0	0	1	5	0	0	0	2	0	0	4	0	0	0	0	0	0	0	0	0	0	0	0
308-unit	3	.0000	.0449	26.5	0	0	0	0	0	3	0	0	0	0	0	0	3	0	0	0	0	0	0	0	0	0	0	0	0
309	2	.2404	.1142	30.6	1	0	0	0	0	1	0	0	0	1	0	0	1	0	0	0	0	0	0	0	0	0	0	0	0
31	84	.7526	12.727	51.0	13	8	7	11	10	15	15	5	3	6	1	0	31	4	9	9	2	0	0	2	0	4	1	12	0
31st	2	.1814	.1187	30.7	0	0	0	1	1	0	0	0	1	0	0	0	0	0	0	0	0	0	0	0	0	0	0	1	0
310	10	.5637	1.1654	40.7	1	1	1	0	4	1	1	1	0	1	0	0	4	1	0	0	0	0	1	0	0	1	0	2	0
311	4	.4791	.4056	36.1	0	0	0	0	2	2	0	0	0	1	0	0	1	1	0	0	0	0	0	0	0	0	1	0	0
312	10	.4473	.9741	39.9	1	2	2	1	3	0	1	0	1	0	1	0	5	2	0	0	0	0	0	0	0	0	1	0	0
312x67	2	.0000	.0299	24.8	0	1	0	0	0	1	0	0	0	0	0	0	2	0	0	0	0	0	0	0	0	0	0	0	0
313	13	.3754	1.0978	40.4	0	4	1	1	7	0	0	0	2	2	0	7	0	1	0	0	0	0	0	0	0	1	0	0	0
314	4	.0000	.0599	27.8	0	0	0	2	1	0	1	0	0	0	0	0	4	0	0	0	0	0	0	0	0	0	0	0	0
315	8	.5356	.8903	39.5	0	1	1	2	1	2	0	1	0	2	0	0	3	0	0	0	0	0	0	0	0	1	1	1	0
316	4	.0000	.0778	28.9	0	0	1	1	1	1	0	0	0	0	0	0	0	4	0	0	0	0	0	0	0	0	0	0	0
3168	4	.0000	.0599	27.8	0	0	4	0	0	0	0	0	0	0	0	0	4	0	0	0	0	0	0	0	0	0	0	0	0
317	9	.5487	1.0315	40.1	2	1	3	2	1	0	0	0	0	0	0	0	3	2	0	0	0	0	0	0	0	2	1	1	0
318	5	.3331	.3780	35.8	0	4	0	1	0	0	0	0	0	0	0	0	3	1	0	0	0	0	0	0	1	0	0	0	0
319	8	.3115	.5642	37.5	0	0	0	4	4	0	0	0	0	4	0	0	3	1	0	0	0	0	0	0	0	0	0	0	0
32	143	.5797	17.219	52.4	16	27	17	18	28	27	9	1	5	0	1	0	90	6	3	12	1	0	0	5	0	3	7	10	0
320	18	.6320	2.3539	43.7	0	2	5	6	1	4	0	0	2	0	0	0	7	4	0	1	0	0	1	1	0	0	1	1	0
321	8	.4744	.8013	39.0	0	0	3	4	1	0	0	0	0	1	0	0	3	0	0	0	0	0	0	0	0	2	2	0	0
322	3	.3709	.2499	34.0	0	0	1	0	0	2	0	0	0	0	0	0	0	1	0	1	0	0	0	0	0	0	1	0	0
322-324	2	.0000	.0219	23.4	0	0	0	0	2	0	0	0	0	2	0	0	0	0	0	0	0	0	0	0	0	0	0	0	0
323	4	.2335	.2373	33.8	0	0	0	3	0	0	0	1	0	1	0	0	0	0	0	3	0	0	0	0	0	0	0	0	0
324	6	.0000	.0898	29.5	0	2	3	1	0	0	0	0	0	0	0	0	6	0	0	0	0	0	0	0	0	0	0	0	0
325	17	.5729	2.0276	43.1	4	2	0	2	3	2	4	0	1	1	0	0	8	0	0	2	0	0	1	0	0	0	1	3	0
326	8	.3105	.5652	37.5	0	0	5	1	0	1	1	0	0	0	0	0	6	1	0	0	0	0	0	1	0	0	0	0	0
3268	2	.0000	.0299	24.8	0	0	1	0	0	1	0	0	0	0	0	0	2	0	0	0	0	0	0	0	0	0	0	0	0
327	5	.1549	.2195	33.4	1	2	0	1	0	0	1	0	0	0	0	0	4	0	0	1	0	0	0	0	0	0	0	0	0
328	5	.2108	.2501	34.0	0	0	2	0	1	0	2	0	0	0	0	0	2	1	0	0	0	0	0	2	0	0	0	0	0
329	3	.2735	.1828	32.6	0	0	1	0	2	0	0	0	0	0	0	0	1	0	0	0	0	0	0	1	0	0	0	1	0
33	99	.6595	13.339	51.3	7	12	9	20	28	15	6	2	1	3	0	0	48	7	6	17	2	2	0	0	0	1	3	9	0
33-12	2	.0000	.0394	26.0	0	0	0	0	0	0	2	0	0	0	0	0	0	0	0	2	0	0	0	0	0	0	0	0	0
33-4B	2	.0000	.0050	17.0	0	0	0	0	0	0	2	0	0	0	0	0	0	0	0	0	0	0	0	2	0	0	0	0	0
33/47	5	.0000	.0748	28.7	0	0	0	0	5	0	0	0	0	0	0	0	5	0	0	0	0	0	0	0	0	0	0	0	0
330	6	.3876	.5219	37.2	1	2	0	0	1	1	1	0	1	0	0	0	3	0	0	0	0	0	1	0	0	0	0	1	0
331	3	.3815	.2534	34.0	0	0	0	3	0	0	0	0	0	0	0	0	0	1	0	0	0	0	0	0	0	1	0	1	0
332	2	.2306	.1140	30.6	0	0	0	0	1	0	0	1	0	1	0	0	0	1	0	0	0	0	0	0	0	0	0	0	0
332nd	6	.2212	.4538	36.6	0	0	0	5	0	1	0	0	5	0	0	0	0	1	0	0	0	0	0	0	0	0	0	0	0
333	9	.2321	.5049	37.0	0	0	0	0	2	2	5	0	0	0	0	0	8	0	0	0	0	0	1	0	0	0	0	0	0
3333	3	.0000	.0449	26.5	0	0	0	0	3	0	0	0	0	0	0	0	3	0	0	0	0	0	0	0	0	0	0	0	0
334-335	2	.0000	.0389	25.9	0	0	0	2	0	0	0	0	0	0	0	0	0	2	0	0	0	0	0	0	0	0	0	0	0
335	2	.2351	.1166	30.7	0	0	0	1	1	0	0	0	0	0	0	0	0	1	0	0	0	0	0	0	0	0	0	1	0
336	18	.2479	1.0755	40.3	3	1	0	13	0	0	0	1	0	1	0	0	14	0	0	0	0	0	0	0	0	3	0	0	0
337	2	.2427	.1159	30.6	0	0	1	0	0	1	0	0	0	0	0	0	1	0	0	0	0	0	0	0	0	0	0	1	0
338	3	.3814	.2537	34.0	0	0	1	1	1	0	0	0	0	0	0	0	1	1	0	0	0	0	0	0	0	0	0	1	0
339	2	.2417	.1211	30.8	0	0	0	1	0	0	1	0	0	0	0	0	1	1	0	0	0	0	0	0	0	0	0	0	0
34	86	.6658	11.686	50.7	18	13	13	10	11	9	9	3	3	1	1	0	48	3	6	7	3	0	0	1	0	3	4	6	0
340	13	.4414	1.2341	40.9	1	0	4	1	6	1	0	0	0	1	0	0	6	3	0	0	0	0	0	0	0	0	3	0	0
342	9	.3026	.6325	38.0	0	0	3	4	1	1	0	0	0	1	0	0	6	2	0	0	0	0	0	0	0	0	0	0	0
343	4	.3314	.2889	34.6	0	0	0	1	0	0	3	0	0	0	0	0	1	0	0	0	0	0	1	0	0	0	0	2	0
344	6	.0000	.0898	29.5	0	0	4	0	0	2	0	0	0	0	0	0	6	0	0	0	0	0	0	0	0	0	0	0	0
345	4	.3119	.2759	34.4	1	0	0	0	1	1	1	0	0	0	0	0	2	0	0	0	0	0	0	1	0	0	0	1	0
346	5	.0000	.0748	28.7	0	0	2	0	1	2	0	0	0	0	0	0	5	0	0	0	0	0	0	0	0	0	0	0	0
347	7	.2446	.4292	36.3	4	0	0	2	0	1	0	0	0	0	0	0	3	4	0	0	0	0	0	0	0	0	0	0	0
348	3	.2914	.1949	32.9	0	0	0	0	1	1	0	1	0	0	0	0	1	0	0	0	0	0	1	0	0	1	0	0	0
3482	2	.0000	.0299	24.8	0	0	0	1	0	1	0	0	0	0	0	0	2	0	0	0	0	0	0	0	0	0	0	0	0
349	5	.2374	.2760	34.4	0	0	1	0	0	3	1	0	0	0	0	0	2	0	0	1	0	0	2	0	0	0	0	0	0
35	167	.7518	25.282	54.0	17	25	29	20	33	16	23	4	6	2	3	1	89	12	7	5	0	1	5	3	2	8	9	14	0
35-mm	2	.0000	.0209	23.2	0	0	0	0	0	2	0	0	0	0	0	0	0	0	0	0	0	0	0	0	0	0	2	0	0
35%	2	.0000	.0299	24.8	0	0	0	0	1	1	0	0	0	0	0	0	2	0	0	0	0	0	0	0	0	0	0	0	0
350	57	.4515	5.4533	47.4	3	7	6	6	17	8	9	1	2	1	0	0	4	11	0	3	0	0	16	0	0	5	12	3	0
3500	6	.3569	.5238	37.2	2	0	3	0	0	1	0	0	2	0	0	0	2	2	0	0	0	0	0	0	0	0	0	0	0
351	3	.2458	.1728	32.4	0	0	1	0	1	0	1	0	0	0	0	0	1	1	0	0	0	0	0	1	0	0	0	0	0
352	4	.3870	.3289	35.2	0	0	2	0	0	1	1	0	0	0	0	0	1	1	0	0	0	0	1	1	0	0	0	0	0
356	7	.3653	.5885	37.7	3	0	0	0	3	0	1	0	1	0	0	0	4	1	0	0	0	0	0	0	0	0	1	0	0
357	2	.2417	.1211	30.8	0	1	0	0	0	1	0	0	0	0	0	0	1	1	0	0	0	0	0	0	0	0	0	0	0
358	2	.1812	.0838	29.2	0	0	0	0	0	2	0	0	0	0	0	0	0	0	0	0	0	0	1	0	0	0	0	1	0
36	152	.6010	18.810	52.7	24	33	27	18	21	16	9	4	2	2	0	0	106	7	3	4	2	2	3	7	0	1	5	8	0
360	17	.6831	2.3553	43.7	0	1	5	2	2	6	0	1	0	2	0	0	2	4	0	2	0	0	1	1	0	1	4	0	0
3600	8	.4455	.7673	38.8	1	0	0	2	2	1	2	0	0	1	0	0	4	0	0	2	0	0	0	0	0	0	1	0	0

5E 30x42
5E 30x60
5E 30x70
7Q 300-
XR 300-kilowatt
7E 300-lb
6R 300-mile
9H 300-mile-an-hour
4R 300-pound
8A 300-square-foot
9Q 300-ton
6R 300-year-old
9C 300-500
7F 300's
7R 300th
9M 3000-kg
6E 3018
6P 302-mile
5F 304-305
9M 30418
9M 30418a
3P 306
5Q 306-337
6B 309-23
6E 3096
7M 31-1a
7M 31-1b
7R 31-24
6E 31-28
5G 31-32-33
7G 31-35
8E 31-69
7E 31/2
8E 31b
8E 31c
7E 31x1/100
6E 310-foot
7E 3106
7B 311-312
8E 317x8
8E 317x800
7E 3174
6F 318-319
8J 32-measure
9Q 32-year-old
9C 32-33
8E 32-38
9R 32nd
9M 32nds
8M 320-288
4F 320-321
8H 3200
9E 3212
7F 324-330
7E 3256
8Q 326B
7R 326-mile
7B 326-332
8E 32653x1/104
7Q 327BC
6E 3274
XR 32741
7E 329-mile
7H 33-billion-electron-volt
7Q 33-foot
9H 33-11
9H 33-13
8E 33-34
7E 33/100
8E 33/36
9R 33rd
9E 330/100
7E 3300
7E 331/3
7F 332-333
9L 334
8E 336-page
8H 3370
3H 34-37
5E 34/36
8E 34%
6R 34th
8E 34x2
8E 34x200
7R 340-cu-in**
6R 340-41
4E 3400
3E 341
9E 343x
7Q 344-foot
7R 3447
4E 3469
8E 3475
4E 3489
6R 35-foot
7R 35-lb
XR 35-mile
7R 35-year-old
8M 35-10
8M 35-11
9E 35-38
7R 35-39
9E 35-40
9E 35-44
8M 35-6
8M 35-7
8M 35-8
8M 35-9
8E 35/2
7R 35/65
9H 350/5
5F 354
XH 355
7H 355-foot
3P 3560th
3P 3561st
7R 36-in
5P 36-inch
9M 36-line
XP 36-liter
8F 36-year-old
9H 36-7
9H 36-8
6E 36/100
8E 36/80
7R 360-degree

Word Type	F	D	U	SFI	3 Gr 3	4 Gr 4	5 Gr 5	6 Gr 6	7 Gr 7	8 Gr 8	9 Gr 9	X UnGr	A Read	B Eng & Gr	C Comp	D Lit	E Math	F Soc Stud	G Spell	H Sci	J Music	K Art	L Home Ec	M Shop	N Lib F	P Lib NF	Q Lib Ref	R Mag	S Rel
361	2	.2421	.0995	30.0	0	0	0	0	1	0	1	0	0	0	0	0	0	0	0	0	0	0	1	1	0	0	0	0	0
362	9	.4527	.8588	39.3	0	0	0	0	3	1	5	0	0	0	0	0	6	0	0	0	0	0	1	1	0	0	1	0	0
363	6	.3236	.4374	36.4	0	0	0	1	0	0	5	0	0	0	0	0	4	1	0	0	0	0	1	0	0	0	0	0	0
364	4	.3214	.3122	34.9	1	1	0	1	0	0	1	0	1	0	0	0	2	0	0	0	0	0	0	0	0	0	0	1	0
364-365	4	.0000	.0778	28.9	0	0	0	4	0	0	0	0	0	0	0	0	0	4	0	0	0	0	0	0	0	0	0	0	0
365	27	.4752	2.7532	44.4	4	7	7	1	1	0	7	0	1	0	0	0	12	2	0	8	0	0	3	0	0	0	1	0	0
365-day	3	.3848	.2601	34.2	0	0	0	0	2	0	1	0	0	0	0	0	1	1	0	1	0	0	0	0	0	0	0	0	0
366	2	.2417	.1211	30.8	0	1	0	0	0	1	0	0	0	0	0	0	1	1	0	0	0	0	0	0	0	0	0	0	0
3666	2	.2417	.1211	30.8	0	0	0	1	0	1	0	0	0	0	0	0	1	1	0	0	0	0	0	0	0	0	0	0	0
367	7	.5518	.7959	39.0	0	2	0	1	1	2	1	0	0	1	0	0	2	0	0	0	1	0	0	0	0	0	2	1	0
368	5	.2443	.2905	34.6	1	1	1	0	0	0	2	0	0	2	0	0	3	0	0	0	0	0	0	0	0	0	0	0	0
368-369	2	.0000	.0389	25.9	0	0	0	2	0	0	0	0	0	0	0	0	0	2	0	0	0	0	0	0	0	0	0	0	0
369	2	.1442	.0761	28.8	0	0	0	0	0	1	1	0	0	0	0	0	0	1	0	0	0	0	1	0	0	0	0	0	0
37	64	.7284	9.4246	49.7	12	5	10	6	16	4	9	2	2	2	0	1	28	2	0	9	1	2	0	2	1	7	2	5	0
37mm	2	.0000	.0290	24.6	0	0	2	0	0	0	0	0	0	0	0	0	0	0	0	0	0	0	0	0	0	2	0	0	0
37th	3	.2321	.1635	32.1	0	0	0	0	1	0	2	0	0	0	0	0	0	0	0	0	0	0	0	0	0	0	1	2	0
370	2	.2351	.1166	30.7	0	0	1	0	0	0	0	1	0	0	0	0	0	1	0	0	0	0	0	0	0	0	0	1	0
371	6	.4441	.5722	37.6	0	0	0	1	2	2	1	0	0	1	0	0	3	1	0	0	0	0	0	0	0	0	0	1	0
372	2	.2351	.1166	30.7	0	0	0	1	0	0	1	0	0	0	0	0	0	1	0	0	0	0	0	0	0	0	0	1	0
373	3	.2254	.1785	32.5	0	0	1	0	0	2	0	0	0	0	0	0	0	1	0	2	0	0	0	0	0	0	0	0	0
375	17	.4908	1.7553	42.4	1	5	1	2	4	2	1	1	0	0	0	0	7	1	0	0	0	0	2	0	0	5	0	2	0
376	3	.0000	.0449	26.5	0	1	0	0	0	0	2	0	0	0	0	0	3	0	0	0	0	0	0	0	0	0	0	0	0
378	4	.2220	.2176	33.4	0	0	0	2	1	0	1	0	0	0	0	0	3	0	0	0	0	0	0	0	0	0	1	0	0
379	2	.0000	.0299	24.8	0	1	0	0	1	0	0	0	0	0	0	0	2	0	0	0	0	0	0	0	0	0	0	0	0
38	72	.6475	9.5396	49.8	6	11	7	7	20	10	5	6	1	0	0	6	38	8	2	4	3	0	0	1	0	4	1	4	0
380	6	.4639	.5966	37.8	0	0	1	2	1	1	1	0	0	0	0	0	1	2	0	0	0	0	0	0	0	1	0	2	0
381	5	.0000	.0972	29.9	0	0	0	4	0	1	0	0	0	0	0	0	0	5	0	0	0	0	0	0	0	0	0	0	0
382	4	.3050	.3060	34.9	1	0	1	1	1	0	0	0	1	0	0	0	2	0	0	1	0	0	0	0	0	0	0	0	0
383	4	.3831	.3415	35.3	0	0	0	2	2	0	0	0	0	0	0	0	0	2	0	0	0	0	0	0	0	1	0	1	0
384	2	.2391	.1133	30.5	0	0	0	1	1	0	0	0	0	0	0	0	1	0	0	0	0	0	0	0	0	0	1	0	0
386	10	.3905	.8515	39.3	0	3	3	0	2	1	1	0	0	0	0	0	7	1	0	0	0	0	1	0	0	0	1	0	0
387	2	.0000	.0299	24.8	0	1	0	1	0	0	0	0	0	0	0	0	2	0	0	0	0	0	0	0	0	0	0	0	0
389	2	.0000	.0389	25.9	0	0	0	2	0	0	0	0	0	0	0	0	0	2	0	0	0	0	0	0	0	0	0	0	0
39	69	.4720	6.9646	48.4	13	18	6	8	12	5	5	2	2	0	0	0	47	2	2	4	1	0	0	0	1	2	3	5	0
39th	2	.1698	.1133	30.5	0	0	1	1	0	0	0	0	1	0	0	0	0	0	0	0	0	0	0	0	0	0	1	0	0
391	3	.2440	.1815	32.6	0	1	0	2	0	0	0	0	0	1	0	0	0	2	0	0	0	0	0	0	0	0	0	0	0
392	5	.1560	.2202	33.4	1	0	0	1	0	1	2	0	0	0	0	0	4	1	0	0	0	0	0	0	0	0	0	0	0
393	2	.0000	.0389	25.9	0	0	0	1	1	0	0	0	0	0	0	0	0	2	0	0	0	0	0	0	0	0	0	0	0
394	4	.3623	.3240	35.1	0	1	0	2	1	0	0	0	0	0	0	0	2	1	0	0	0	0	0	0	0	0	0	1	0
395	2	.2285	.1129	30.5	0	0	0	2	0	0	0	0	0	0	0	0	0	1	0	0	0	0	0	0	0	0	1	0	0
396	6	.5483	.6856	38.4	2	0	2	0	0	2	0	0	0	1	0	0	1	1	0	0	0	0	0	0	0	2	0	1	0
397	10	.3731	.8200	39.1	4	2	0	0	0	3	1	0	0	1	0	0	7	0	0	0	0	0	0	0	0	0	1	1	0
398	6	.5216	.6640	38.2	1	0	1	1	0	1	2	0	1	0	0	0	1	0	0	0	0	0	1	0	1	1	0	1	0
3982	2	.0000	.0299	24.8	0	0	2	0	0	0	0	0	0	0	0	0	2	0	0	0	0	0	0	0	0	0	0	0	0
399	10	.4274	.9374	39.7	1	0	6	0	1	0	1	1	1	0	0	0	6	0	0	1	0	0	1	0	1	0	0	0	0
4	2059	.5503	236.56	63.7	354	285	283	289	309	264	228	47	49	42	1	13	1473	51	87	88	46	1	24	18	2	52	46	66	0
4A	2	.1972	.1262	31.0	1	0	0	0	0	1	0	0	1	0	0	0	1	0	0	0	0	0	0	0	0	0	0	0	0
4A's	4	.0000	.1827	32.6	4	0	0	0	0	0	0	0	4	0	0	0	0	0	0	0	0	0	0	0	0	0	0	0	0
4C	2	.0000	.0243	23.9	2	0	0	0	0	0	0	0	0	0	0	0	0	0	0	0	0	0	0	0	0	0	0	2	0
4-H	12	.5824	1.4335	41.6	1	2	2	2	1	0	2	2	0	1	0	0	0	3	1	1	2	0	2	0	0	0	0	2	0
4-consonant-silent	2	.0000	.0162	22.1	0	0	0	2	0	0	0	0	0	0	0	0	0	0	2	0	0	0	0	0	0	0	0	0	0
4-digit	18	.0000	.2694	34.3	1	8	2	3	1	3	0	0	0	0	0	0	18	0	0	0	0	0	0	0	0	0	0	0	0
4-h	2	.2408	.1204	30.8	0	0	0	0	0	0	1	1	0	0	0	0	0	1	0	0	0	0	0	0	0	1	0	0	0
4-inch	2	.2278	.1128	30.5	0	0	1	0	0	1	0	0	0	0	0	0	0	0	0	1	0	0	0	0	0	0	1	0	0
4-step	5	.0000	.0748	28.7	3	1	0	1	0	0	0	0	0	0	0	0	5	0	0	0	0	0	0	0	0	0	0	0	0
4-0098	2	.0000	.0215	23.3	0	0	0	0	0	2	0	0	0	0	0	2	0	0	0	0	0	0	0	0	0	0	0	0	0
4-1	4	.2253	.2138	33.3	0	0	0	0	0	3	1	0	0	0	0	0	3	0	0	0	0	0	0	1	0	0	0	0	0
4-1-5	2	.0000	.0914	29.6	0	0	0	0	0	2	0	0	2	0	0	0	0	0	0	0	0	0	0	0	0	0	0	0	0
4-13	2	.0000	.0050	17.0	0	0	0	0	0	0	2	0	0	0	0	0	0	0	0	0	0	0	0	2	0	0	0	0	0
4-14	2	.0000	.0050	17.0	0	0	0	0	0	0	2	0	0	0	0	0	0	0	0	0	0	0	0	2	0	0	0	0	0
4-5	4	.0000	.0778	28.9	0	0	0	2	2	0	0	0	0	0	0	0	0	4	0	0	0	0	0	0	0	0	0	0	0
4-5-6	2	.0000	.0162	22.1	0	0	1	1	0	0	0	0	0	0	0	0	0	0	2	0	0	0	0	0	0	0	0	0	0
4-6	2	.2398	.1138	30.6	0	1	0	0	1	0	0	0	0	0	0	1	1	0	0	0	0	0	0	0	0	0	0	0	0
4-9	3	.2076	.1618	32.1	0	0	0	0	1	0	1	1	0	0	0	0	2	0	0	1	0	0	0	0	0	0	0	0	0
4/c	4	.0000	.0599	27.8	0	0	0	0	4	0	0	0	0	0	0	0	4	0	0	0	0	0	0	0	0	0	0	0	0
4/1	5	.0000	.0748	28.7	0	0	0	5	0	0	0	0	0	0	0	0	5	0	0	0	0	0	0	0	0	0	0	0	0
4/10	14	.1240	.5331	37.3	1	2	7	1	1	2	0	0	0	0	0	0	12	0	0	2	0	0	0	0	0	0	0	0	0
4/100	3	.0000	.0449	26.5	0	0	0	1	2	0	0	0	0	0	0	0	3	0	0	0	0	0	0	0	0	0	0	0	0
4/11	2	.0000	.0299	24.8	0	0	0	0	2	0	0	0	0	0	0	0	2	0	0	0	0	0	0	0	0	0	0	0	0
4/12	3	.0000	.0449	26.5	0	1	2	0	0	0	0	0	0	0	0	0	3	0	0	0	0	0	0	0	0	0	0	0	0
4/15	6	.0000	.0898	29.5	0	0	1	4	1	0	0	0	0	0	0	0	6	0	0	0	0	0	0	0	0	0	0	0	0
4/16	2	.0000	.0299	24.8	0	0	0	0	1	0	1	0	0	0	0	0	2	0	0	0	0	0	0	0	0	0	0	0	0
4/2	6	.0000	.0898	29.5	1	1	0	2	1	1	0	0	0	0	0	0	6	0	0	0	0	0	0	0	0	0	0	0	0
4/24	3	.0000	.0449	26.5	0	2	0	0	1	0	0	0	0	0	0	0	3	0	0	0	0	0	0	0	0	0	0	0	0
4/3	11	.0000	.1647	32.2	0	3	2	2	3	1	0	0	0	0	0	0	11	0	0	0	0	0	0	0	0	0	0	0	0
4/4	29	.2645	1.7553	42.4	1	6	8	8	2	2	2	0	0	0	0	0	14	0	0	0	14	0	0	0	0	1	0	0	0
4/5	25	.0000	.3742	35.7	0	5	4	7	5	3	1	0	0	0	0	0	25	0	0	0	0	0	0	0	0	0	0	0	0
4/6	10	.0000	.1497	31.8	1	3	5	0	0	1	0	0	0	0	0	0	10	0	0	0	0	0	0	0	0	0	0	0	0
4/7	3	.0000	.0449	26.5	0	1	0	0	2	0	0	0	0	0	0	0	3	0	0	0	0	0	0	0	0	0	0	0	0
4/8	12	.0000	.1796	32.5	0	8	1	0	2	1	0	0	0	0	0	0	12	0	0	0	0	0	0	0	0	0	0	0	0
4/9	6	.0000	.0898	29.5	0	1	1	1	0	3	0	0	0	0	0	0	6	0	0	0	0	0	0	0	0	0	0	0	0
4%	10	.3952	.8639	39.4	0	0	0	4	1	0	4	1	0	0	0	0	6	0	0	1	0	0	0	0	0	0	1	2	0
4's	9	.0000	.1347	31.3	7	1	0	0	0	0	1	0	0	0	0	0	9	0	0	0	0	0	0	0	0	0	0	0	0
4a	2	.2289	.1077	30.3	0	0	0	0	1	0	1	0	0	0	0	0	1	0	1	0	0	0	0	0	0	0	0	0	0
4s	2	.0000	.0243	23.9	0	0	0	0	0	0	0	2	0	0	0	0	0	0	0	0	0	0	0	0	0	0	0	2	0
4th	15	.4281	1.3802	41.4	0	1	1	4	5	0	3	1	0	0	0	1	7	1	0	1	0	0	0	0	0	0	5	0	0
4x	5	.0000	.0748	28.7	0	0	0	1	0	1	3	0	0	0	0	0	5	0	0	0	0	0	0	0	0	0	0	0	0
4xn	2	.0000	.0299	24.8	0	0	0	2	0	0	0	0	0	0	0	0	2	0	0	0	0	0	0	0	0	0	0	0	0

7E 3600/3937
6F 362-
7M 362-foot
6F 362-363
7R 363-foot-high
7Q 365th
5F 3651/4
3E 3654
4E 3672
5E 3682
7Q 37-foot
7P 37-millimeter
8R 37-yard
9Q 37-year-old
8E 37-38
7B 37-39
9E 37-40
8R 37-9
6F 370-371
6F 370-373
XR 3700
5E 374
6F 374-375
5Q 375-800
8E 3750000
7A 3764
3A 377
6E 3778
8R 38-caliber
7R 38-year-old
6F 380-381
7P 381/4
6E 3827
6E 385
6F 386-387
5E 3875
7E 388
7R 39A
7P 39-inch
7P 39-18
7P 39-19
7P 39-20
8E 39-42
6E 39-50
8E 39-58
4E 39-6
4E 39-7
9H 39-9
4E 390
7R 390-cubic
8R 390-foot
8E 3900
3E 3925
7E 3937
9E 394-395
XR 395-foot
6F 396-398
6R 396-7
9E 3967
6R 398-400
7B 398-99
8E 398x54
5E 3986
7B 399-400
7H 4-b
5E 4-day
5E 4-pound
8L 4-strips**
9M 4-12
9M 4-15
7Q 4-20
7H 4-21
8H 4-23
8H 4-24
8M 4-28
8M 4-29
3P 4-3
8M 4-30
8M 4-31
8M 4-32
8M 4-60
8M 4-61
8M 4-62
8M 4-63
8E 4-7
8M 4-93
8M 4-94
8M 4-95
8M 4-96
8M 4-97
7E 4/
8L 4/0
6E 4/1/1
8E 4/17
5E 4/5-1
7E 4a-f
3E 4c
7E 4e
7E 4x1
7E 4x10

Word Type	F	D	U	SFI	3 Gr 3	4 Gr 4	5 Gr 5	6 Gr 6	7 Gr 7	8 Gr 8	9 Gr 9	X UnGr	A Read	B Eng & Gr	C Comp	D Lit	E Math	F Soc Stud	G Spell	H Sci	J Music	K Art	L Home Ec	M Shop	N Lib F	P Lib NF	Q Lib Ref	R Mag	S Rel
4x3	8	.0000	.1197	30.8	0	0	4	0	0	4	0	0	0	0	0	0	8	0	0	0	0	0	0	0	0	0	0	0	0
4x36	4	.0000	.0599	27.8	0	0	4	0	0	0	0	0	0	0	0	0	4	0	0	0	0	0	0	0	0	0	0	0	0
4x4	2	.0000	.0299	24.8	0	0	1	0	0	1	0	0	0	0	0	0	2	0	0	0	0	0	0	0	0	0	0	0	0
4x5	2	.0000	.0299	24.8	0	0	0	0	1	1	0	0	0	0	0	0	2	0	0	0	0	0	0	0	0	0	0	0	0
4x6	2	.0000	.0299	24.8	0	0	2	0	0	0	0	0	0	0	0	0	2	0	0	0	0	0	0	0	0	0	0	0	0
4y	4	.0000	.0599	27.8	0	0	2	0	0	0	2	0	0	0	0	0	4	0	0	0	0	0	0	0	0	0	0	0	0
40	318	.6994	45.222	56.6	33	39	60	47	60	40	30	9	16	3	0	2	155	15	3	32	3	2	2	5	0	13	30	37	0
40-mile-per-hour	2	.0000	.0299	24.8	0	0	2	0	0	0	0	0	0	0	0	0	2	0	0	0	0	0	0	0	0	0	0	0	0
40-millimeter	2	.0000	.0290	24.6	0	0	0	0	2	0	0	0	0	0	0	0	0	0	0	0	0	0	0	0	0	2	0	0	0
40-story	2	.2285	.1129	30.5	0	0	0	1	0	0	1	0	0	0	0	0	0	1	0	0	0	0	0	0	0	0	1	0	0
40%	9	.3445	.6961	38.4	0	0	0	2	1	0	5	1	0	0	0	0	6	0	0	2	0	0	1	0	0	0	0	0	0
40's	2	.2285	.1129	30.5	0	1	0	0	0	0	1	0	0	0	0	0	0	1	0	0	0	0	0	0	0	0	1	0	0
40x36	2	.0000	.0299	24.8	0	0	2	0	0	0	0	0	0	0	0	0	2	0	0	0	0	0	0	0	0	0	0	0	0
400	188	.7673	29.039	54.6	19	13	22	37	41	24	27	5	12	3	0	0	54	18	3	19	1	1	5	2	0	8	35	27	0
400-foot	2	.2278	.1128	30.5	0	0	0	0	1	1	0	0	0	0	0	0	0	0	0	1	0	0	0	0	0	0	1	0	0
400's	2	.2285	.1129	30.5	0	0	1	0	1	0	0	0	0	0	0	0	0	1	0	0	0	0	0	0	0	0	1	0	0
4000	11	.5251	1.2636	41.0	3	0	0	2	4	0	1	1	3	0	0	0	3	3	0	1	0	0	0	0	0	0	1	0	0
4004	3	.2159	.1532	31.9	0	0	0	1	2	0	0	0	0	0	0	0	0	0	0	0	0	0	0	0	0	0	2	1	0
401	7	.2465	.4377	36.4	0	0	7	0	0	0	0	0	1	0	0	0	5	0	0	0	0	0	0	0	0	0	1	0	0
402	3	.3780	.2511	34.0	0	0	2	0	0	0	1	0	0	1	0	0	1	1	0	0	0	0	0	0	0	0	0	0	0
403	2	.2427	.1159	30.6	1	0	0	1	0	0	0	0	0	0	0	0	1	0	0	0	0	0	0	0	0	0	0	1	0
405	3	.2228	.1655	32.2	0	0	2	0	0	0	1	0	0	0	0	0	1	0	0	0	0	0	0	0	0	2	0	0	0
406	3	.2277	.1555	31.9	0	0	0	0	2	1	0	0	0	0	0	0	0	0	0	0	0	0	1	0	0	0	0	2	0
407	6	.3033	.4102	36.1	0	0	0	1	0	1	3	1	0	0	0	0	2	1	0	1	0	0	2	0	0	0	0	0	0
408	2	.0000	.0064	18.1	0	0	0	0	0	1	1	0	0	0	0	0	0	0	0	0	0	0	2	0	0	0	0	0	0
409	5	.2802	.3152	35.0	1	0	1	0	0	0	3	0	0	0	0	0	1	1	0	0	0	0	2	0	0	1	0	0	0
41	39	.7260	5.7295	47.6	3	3	9	1	8	8	6	1	3	2	0	0	15	4	0	0	4	1	0	1	0	1	4	4	0
41b	2	.0000	.0299	24.8	0	0	0	0	0	2	0	0	0	0	0	0	2	0	0	0	0	0	0	0	0	0	0	0	0
410	4	.0718	.0837	29.2	0	0	0	0	0	0	4	0	0	0	0	0	0	0	0	1	0	0	3	0	0	0	0	0	0
411	6	.2069	.2907	34.6	0	0	1	0	1	0	4	0	0	0	0	0	0	2	0	0	0	0	3	0	0	0	1	0	0
412	2	.2417	.1211	30.8	0	0	0	0	1	1	0	0	0	0	0	0	1	1	0	0	0	0	0	0	0	0	0	0	0
413	3	.2630	.1786	32.5	0	0	1	0	2	0	0	0	0	0	0	0	1	0	0	0	0	0	0	1	0	1	0	0	0
415	4	.3708	.3650	35.6	1	0	0	2	1	0	0	0	2	0	0	0	1	0	0	0	0	0	0	0	0	0	1	0	0
416	2	.2433	.1158	30.6	1	0	0	0	0	1	0	0	0	0	0	0	0	0	0	0	0	0	0	0	0	1	0	1	0
417	4	.3214	.3122	34.9	1	0	0	1	0	2	0	0	1	0	0	0	2	0	0	0	0	0	0	0	0	0	0	1	0
4179	2	.0000	.0299	24.8	0	0	0	2	0	0	0	0	0	0	0	0	2	0	0	0	0	0	0	0	0	0	0	0	0
418	3	.0000	.0449	26.5	0	2	0	0	0	1	0	0	0	0	0	0	3	0	0	0	0	0	0	0	0	0	0	0	0
42	96	.5550	11.117	50.5	13	13	14	26	14	4	10	2	3	2	0	0	68	4	1	2	1	3	0	1	1	3	3	4	0
42-line	2	.1738	.0790	29.0	0	0	1	0	0	0	1	0	0	0	0	0	0	0	0	0	0	0	0	1	0	0	1	0	0
42nd	3	.1200	.1302	31.1	0	0	0	2	0	1	0	0	1	2	0	0	0	0	0	0	0	0	0	0	0	0	0	0	0
420	7	.3294	.5290	37.2	0	1	3	1	0	2	0	0	0	0	0	0	4	2	0	0	0	0	0	0	0	1	0	0	0
4200	4	.3475	.3182	35.0	0	0	0	2	1	0	1	0	0	0	0	0	2	1	0	1	0	0	0	0	0	0	0	0	0
421	2	.0000	.0299	24.8	0	0	2	0	0	0	0	0	0	0	0	0	2	0	0	0	0	0	0	0	0	0	0	0	0
422	4	.3701	.3190	35.0	0	1	0	1	0	1	1	0	0	0	0	0	0	1	0	0	0	0	0	1	0	0	1	1	0
425	18	.2608	1.0567	40.2	0	2	1	1	8	1	5	0	1	0	0	0	2	0	0	1	0	0	9	0	0	0	2	3	0
426	6	.4399	.5583	37.5	1	1	0	0	2	2	0	0	0	0	0	0	3	0	0	0	0	0	1	0	0	0	1	1	0
427	9	.1049	.3102	34.9	0	1	7	0	0	0	1	0	0	0	0	0	8	1	0	0	0	0	0	0	0	0	0	0	0
428	5	.4538	.4838	36.8	1	0	1	1	1	1	0	0	0	0	0	0	1	0	0	1	0	0	0	0	0	0	1	2	0
429	5	.3954	.4289	36.3	0	0	0	1	2	1	1	0	0	0	0	0	0	1	0	1	0	0	1	0	0	0	0	2	0
4297	2	.0000	.0299	24.8	0	0	1	0	0	1	0	0	0	0	0	0	2	0	0	0	0	0	0	0	0	0	0	0	0
43	59	.5440	6.7243	48.3	15	11	6	7	6	2	8	4	3	4	0	0	38	0	1	3	2	0	0	1	0	0	3	4	0
43x20	2	.0000	.0299	24.8	0	2	0	0	0	0	0	0	0	0	0	0	2	0	0	0	0	0	0	0	0	0	0	0	0
430	5	.4346	.4667	36.7	1	0	2	0	1	0	0	1	0	0	0	0	1	0	0	1	0	0	0	0	0	1	2	0	0
4300	2	.0000	.0394	26.0	0	1	0	0	0	0	0	1	0	0	0	0	0	0	0	2	0	0	0	0	0	0	0	0	0
431	2	.1812	.0838	29.2	0	0	0	1	0	1	0	0	0	0	0	0	0	0	0	0	0	0	1	0	0	0	0	1	0
432	9	.5224	1.0049	40.0	1	4	1	1	0	1	1	0	1	0	0	0	4	1	0	1	0	0	0	0	0	1	1	0	0
4326	2	.0000	.0299	24.8	0	0	0	0	2	0	0	0	0	0	0	0	2	0	0	0	0	0	0	0	0	0	0	0	0
435	5	.4833	.5473	37.4	1	2	1	1	0	0	0	0	2	0	0	0	1	1	0	0	0	0	0	0	0	1	0	0	0
43542	2	.0000	.0299	24.8	0	0	0	0	0	2	0	0	0	0	0	0	2	0	0	0	0	0	0	0	0	0	0	0	0
4356	2	.0000	.0299	24.8	0	0	0	2	0	0	0	0	0	0	0	0	2	0	0	0	0	0	0	0	0	0	0	0	0
436	4	.3639	.3241	35.1	0	1	0	1	2	0	0	0	0	0	0	0	2	1	0	0	0	0	0	0	0	0	1	0	0
438	5	.4157	.4350	36.4	0	0	0	0	1	2	2	0	0	0	0	0	2	0	0	0	0	1	1	0	0	0	1	0	0
439	2	.1926	.0867	29.4	0	0	0	0	1	1	0	0	0	0	0	0	0	0	0	0	0	0	1	0	0	0	1	0	0
44	39	.7121	5.6194	47.5	9	5	2	7	7	3	2	4	1	0	0	1	11	4	3	3	1	2	0	0	0	5	1	7	0
440	10	.4168	.8817	39.5	0	1	1	0	3	4	1	0	0	0	0	0	2	0	0	0	5	0	0	0	0	1	1	1	0
442	2	.0000	.0299	24.8	1	0	1	0	0	0	0	0	0	0	0	0	2	0	0	0	0	0	0	0	0	0	0	0	0
445	2	.2417	.1211	30.8	0	1	0	1	0	0	0	0	0	0	0	0	1	1	0	0	0	0	0	0	0	0	0	0	0
448	2	.1839	.0845	29.3	1	0	0	0	0	1	0	0	0	0	0	0	0	0	0	0	0	0	1	0	1	0	0	0	0
449	4	.3660	.3157	35.0	1	1	0	1	0	1	0	0	0	2	0	0	0	0	0	0	0	0	0	0	1	0	1	0	0
45	169	.6428	22.326	53.5	10	34	20	21	36	29	17	2	16	0	0	1	93	6	0	6	2	2	5	13	1	6	7	11	0
45-degree	7	.0517	.0971	29.9	0	0	0	0	2	3	1	1	0	0	0	0	0	0	0	0	0	0	0	6	0	0	0	1	0
45-minute	2	.0000	.0243	23.9	0	0	0	0	1	0	0	1	0	0	0	0	0	0	0	0	0	0	0	0	0	0	0	2	0
45%	2	.0000	.0064	18.1	0	0	0	0	0	0	2	0	0	0	0	0	0	0	0	0	0	0	2	0	0	0	0	0	0
450	32	.8243	5.2709	47.2	2	3	3	6	9	3	6	0	2	2	0	0	7	6	2	1	0	0	1	1	2	2	3	3	0
4500	3	.3454	.2542	34.1	0	0	1	1	1	0	0	0	1	0	0	0	0	1	0	0	0	0	0	0	0	0	0	1	0
451	7	.5716	.8380	39.2	1	0	0	0	2	2	1	1	1	0	0	1	0	0	0	1	0	0	0	0	1	0	2	1	0
452	10	.4500	.9728	39.9	1	0	1	1	6	1	0	0	1	0	0	0	6	0	0	0	0	0	1	0	1	0	1	0	0
453	4	.4525	.4044	36.1	1	0	0	1	1	1	0	0	1	0	0	0	0	1	0	0	0	0	0	0	1	0	0	1	0
454	7	.2465	.4377	36.4	2	0	0	0	0	1	4	0	1	0	0	0	5	0	0	0	0	0	0	0	0	0	1	0	0
455	5	.1584	.1834	32.6	0	0	0	1	1	3	0	0	0	0	0	0	1	0	0	0	0	0	0	3	0	0	1	0	0
456	7	.1611	.3071	34.9	0	3	0	1	3	0	0	0	0	0	0	0	6	0	0	0	0	0	0	0	0	0	0	1	0
457	7	.2845	.4667	36.7	3	1	0	0	1	1	1	0	0	1	0	0	5	1	0	0	0	0	0	0	0	0	0	0	0
458	4	.3824	.3323	35.2	0	1	0	0	2	0	1	0	0	1	0	0	2	0	0	0	0	0	0	0	0	0	1	0	0
459	2	.2413	.1212	30.8	0	0	1	0	1	0	0	0	0	0	0	0	1	0	0	1	0	0	0	0	0	0	0	0	0
46	49	.8403	8.2109	49.1	4	5	8	4	8	3	9	8	1	1	1	2	13	5	1	11	2	1	0	0	1	3	3	4	0
460	13	.5133	1.4161	41.5	0	1	4	5	0	3	0	0	0	0	0	0	5	2	0	4	0	0	0	0	0	0	1	1	0
461	2	.1926	.0867	29.4	0	0	1	0	0	1	0	0	0	0	0	0	0	0	0	0	0	0	1	0	0	0	1	0	0
462	5	.2207	.2647	34.2	2	2	1	0	0	0	0	0	0	0	0	0	2	0	0	0	0	0	0	0	0	0	3	0	0
463	4	.2364	.2226	33.5	0	1	0	2	0	1	0	0	0	0	0	0	3	0	0	0	0	0	1	0	0	0	0	0	0
464	3	.1434	.1493	31.7	0	2	0	1	0	0	0	0	1	0	0	0	2	0	0	0	0	0	0	0	0	0	0	0	0

5E 4x30
XH 4x46
5E 4x9
5E 4x90
8F 40-acre
6R 40-foot
7H 40-foot-long
XP 40-h
7R 40-horsepower
5P 40-mph
9H 40-1
8J 40-41
7R 40-44
7E 40/30
7M 40d
5P 40mm
5E 40x23
5E 40x60
8H 400-
9Q 400-horsepower
6A 400-meter
7R 400-plus-hp
7B 400-year
3F 400-year-old
9B 402-403
5F 404
4E 4097
4E 41-4
4E 41-5
8E 41a
8E 41d
8E 41e
8E 41f
8E 410-431
5F 411-413
7M 414
6E 4173
7P 42-inch
3Q 42-mile
3P 42-ounce
7R 42-year-old
8E 42-56
9R 42%
6E 42's
8E 4224
4E 4235
7E 424
8F 426-27
4B 426-3587
7R 427-cubic-inch
6A 4280
4E 4286
7R 429's
8A 43-million-dollar
9H 43-1
8E 43-46
7H 43x
4E 43x2
8Q 434-493
6A 437892
8R 44-13
8E 44/7
7R 440-inch
7R 440-to
7P 440-yard
9F 441
XR 4411
4R 444
8L 446
5E 4478
9H 45B
XP 45-h
XR 45-year-old
8M 45-1
8M 45-2B
8M 45-5
9R 45s
7E 454545
3P 45623
6R 458-9
7H 459
8R 46-14
7M 46-2
7M 46-3
7P 461/2
7Q 46219
8E 4623
4E 4628

Word Type	F	D	U	SFI	3 Gr 3	4 Gr 4	5 Gr 5	6 Gr 6	7 Gr 7	8 Gr 8	9 Gr 9	X UnGr	A Read	B Eng & Gr	C Comp	D Lit	E Math	F Soc Stud	G Spell	H Sci	J Music	K Art	L Home Ec	M Shop	N Lib F	P Lib NF	Q Lib Ref	R Mag	S Rel
465	8	.1572	.3447	35.4	0	1	1	1	2	3	0	0	0	1	0	0	7	0	0	0	0	0	0	0	0	0	0	0	0
467	3	.2159	.1533	31.9	0	0	1	0	0	2	0	0	0	0	0	0	2	0	0	0	0	0	1	0	0	0	0	0	0
4672	3	.0000	.0449	26.5	0	0	0	0	0	3	0	0	0	0	0	0	3	0	0	0	0	0	0	0	0	0	0	0	0
468	7	.4213	.6378	38.0	1	1	1	1	0	2	1	0	0	1	0	0	4	1	0	0	0	0	0	0	0	0	1	0	0
469	2	.0000	.0299	24.8	2	0	0	0	0	0	0	0	0	0	0	0	2	0	0	0	0	0	0	0	0	0	0	0	0
47	56	.4471	5.3436	47.3	12	9	1	6	14	7	7	0	0	0	0	0	42	0	1	2	4	0	3	0	1	0	0	3	0
47-4	2	.1249	.0685	28.4	0	0	0	0	0	0	2	0	0	0	0	0	0	0	0	1	0	0	0	1	0	0	0	0	0
471	5	.1156	.1467	31.7	0	1	0	1	0	0	3	0	0	0	0	0	2	0	0	0	0	0	0	3	0	0	0	0	0
472	5	.2379	.2813	34.5	0	0	0	4	0	0	1	0	0	0	0	0	4	0	0	0	0	0	0	1	0	0	0	0	0
474	4	.2421	.1990	33.0	0	0	0	0	0	2	2	0	0	0	0	0	0	0	0	0	0	0	2	2	0	0	0	0	0
475	5	.4046	.4276	36.3	1	0	1	0	1	1	1	0	0	0	0	0	1	0	0	0	0	0	0	1	0	0	2	1	0
476	2	.2437	.1129	30.5	1	0	0	0	0	1	0	0	0	0	0	0	0	0	0	0	0	0	0	0	0	0	1	1	0
477	2	.2391	.1133	30.5	0	0	0	0	0	1	1	0	0	0	0	0	1	0	0	0	0	0	0	0	0	0	1	0	0
48	103	.4906	10.776	50.3	13	28	11	14	15	14	4	4	5	2	0	0	74	4	2	5	1	2	0	0	0	3	2	3	0
48-1	3	.0000	.0076	18.8	0	0	0	0	3	0	0	0	0	0	0	0	0	0	0	0	0	0	0	3	0	0	0	0	0
48-2	2	.0000	.0050	17.0	0	0	0	0	2	0	0	0	0	0	0	0	0	0	0	0	0	0	0	2	0	0	0	0	0
480	13	.5236	1.4235	41.5	0	1	3	0	6	1	1	1	0	0	0	0	4	2	0	2	0	0	0	2	0	1	1	1	0
481	4	.2391	.2266	33.6	0	1	0	1	1	0	1	0	0	0	0	0	2	0	0	0	0	0	0	0	0	0	2	0	0
482	3	.0000	.0449	26.5	0	0	0	0	1	0	2	0	0	0	0	0	3	0	0	0	0	0	0	0	0	0	0	0	0
483	2	.2391	.1133	30.5	1	0	0	0	0	1	0	0	0	0	0	0	1	0	0	0	0	0	0	0	0	0	1	0	0
4840	3	.0000	.0449	26.5	1	0	0	1	0	0	1	0	0	0	0	0	3	0	0	0	0	0	0	0	0	0	0	0	0
485	9	.3308	.7556	38.8	0	4	2	0	1	0	2	0	4	0	0	0	4	0	0	0	0	0	0	0	0	0	0	1	0
486	2	.1972	.1262	31.0	0	2	0	0	0	0	0	0	1	0	0	0	1	0	0	0	0	0	0	0	0	0	0	0	0
487	4	.1786	.1933	32.9	0	2	0	0	0	0	2	0	0	0	0	0	3	1	0	0	0	0	0	0	0	0	0	0	0
488	6	.0000	.0898	29.5	0	0	0	6	0	0	0	0	0	0	0	0	6	0	0	0	0	0	0	0	0	0	0	0	0
49	60	.5815	7.2170	48.6	10	9	11	10	5	11	2	2	1	0	0	0	37	3	4	2	1	2	0	0	0	2	4	4	0
49ers	3	.0000	.0365	25.6	0	0	0	1	0	2	0	0	0	0	0	0	0	0	0	0	0	0	0	0	0	0	0	3	0
49th	3	.0000	.0583	27.7	0	0	3	0	0	0	0	0	0	0	0	0	0	3	0	0	0	0	0	0	0	0	0	0	0
49x6	2	.0000	.0299	24.8	0	0	1	0	0	1	0	0	0	0	0	0	2	0	0	0	0	0	0	0	0	0	0	0	0
490	5	.5357	.5741	37.6	0	1	2	2	0	0	0	0	1	0	0	0	1	1	0	0	0	0	0	0	0	0	1	1	0
492	6	.3349	.4497	36.5	0	0	0	0	1	5	0	0	0	0	0	0	4	0	0	0	0	0	0	0	0	0	1	1	0
493	2	.1926	.0867	29.4	0	0	0	0	0	2	0	0	0	0	0	0	0	0	0	0	0	0	1	0	0	0	1	0	0
495	4	.2163	.2275	33.6	0	0	2	0	0	2	0	0	0	0	0	0	1	3	0	0	0	0	0	0	0	0	0	0	0
496	5	.3371	.3808	35.8	0	0	2	1	1	0	1	0	0	0	0	0	3	1	0	0	0	0	0	0	0	0	1	0	0
498	4	.1972	.2524	34.0	0	0	2	0	2	0	0	0	2	0	0	0	2	0	0	0	0	0	0	0	0	0	0	0	0
5	1804	.5228	198.31	63.0	264	222	209	285	290	246	254	34	42	21	3	2	1321	34	56	86	49	0	11	22	1	41	51	64	0
5(5/5)-segment	3	.0000	.0449	26.5	0	0	3	0	0	0	0	0	0	0	0	0	3	0	0	0	0	0	0	0	0	0	0	0	0
5B	3	.1277	.1363	31.3	2	0	0	0	1	0	0	0	1	0	0	0	0	0	0	0	0	0	0	0	0	0	0	2	0
5-cent	12	.0853	.3695	35.7	1	4	0	0	5	2	0	0	0	0	0	0	11	1	0	0	0	0	0	0	0	0	0	0	0
5-inch	4	.2191	.2297	33.6	0	2	1	1	0	0	0	0	0	0	0	0	0	0	0	3	0	0	0	0	0	1	0	0	0
5-region	3	.0000	.0449	26.5	0	0	3	0	0	0	0	0	0	0	0	0	3	0	0	0	0	0	0	0	0	0	0	0	0
5-segment	2	.0000	.0299	24.8	0	0	2	0	0	0	0	0	0	0	0	0	2	0	0	0	0	0	0	0	0	0	0	0	0
5-step	6	.0000	.0898	29.5	3	0	1	2	0	0	0	0	0	0	0	0	6	0	0	0	0	0	0	0	0	0	0	0	0
5-12	3	.0000	.0449	26.5	0	0	0	0	0	3	0	0	0	0	0	0	3	0	0	0	0	0	0	0	0	0	0	0	0
5-18	2	.2413	.1212	30.8	0	0	0	1	0	0	1	0	0	0	0	0	1	0	0	1	0	0	0	0	0	0	0	0	0
5-2	3	.2371	.1813	32.6	1	0	0	0	0	0	0	2	0	0	0	0	1	0	0	2	0	0	0	0	0	0	0	0	0
5-20	2	.0000	.0394	26.0	0	0	0	0	1	0	1	0	0	0	0	0	0	0	0	2	0	0	0	0	0	0	0	0	0
5-3	2	.0000	.0299	24.8	0	0	0	0	1	1	0	0	0	0	0	0	2	0	0	0	0	0	0	0	0	0	0	0	0
5-6	3	.2254	.1785	32.5	0	0	0	0	0	1	0	2	0	0	0	0	0	1	0	2	0	0	0	0	0	0	0	0	0
5-7	4	.2253	.2138	33.3	0	0	0	1	0	2	1	0	0	0	0	0	3	0	0	0	0	0	0	1	0	0	0	0	0
5/1	3	.0000	.0449	26.5	0	0	0	2	0	1	0	0	0	0	0	0	3	0	0	0	0	0	0	0	0	0	0	0	0
5/10	12	.0000	.1796	32.5	0	1	6	0	2	1	2	0	0	0	0	0	12	0	0	0	0	0	0	0	0	0	0	0	0
5/11	2	.0000	.0299	24.8	0	0	0	0	2	0	0	0	0	0	0	0	2	0	0	0	0	0	0	0	0	0	0	0	0
5/12	11	.0000	.1647	32.2	0	2	5	1	3	0	0	0	0	0	0	0	11	0	0	0	0	0	0	0	0	0	0	0	0
5/15	5	.0000	.0748	28.7	0	1	2	0	0	0	2	0	0	0	0	0	5	0	0	0	0	0	0	0	0	0	0	0	0
5/16	3	.0965	.0750	28.7	0	0	1	0	0	0	2	0	0	0	0	0	1	0	0	0	0	0	0	2	0	0	0	0	0
5/2	17	.1753	.7843	38.9	0	3	8	3	0	2	1	0	0	0	0	0	15	0	2	0	0	0	0	0	0	0	0	0	0
5/25	2	.0000	.0299	24.8	0	0	0	2	0	0	0	0	0	0	0	0	2	0	0	0	0	0	0	0	0	0	0	0	0
5/3	14	.0000	.2096	33.2	0	3	6	3	2	0	0	0	0	0	0	0	14	0	0	0	0	0	0	0	0	0	0	0	0
5/4	14	.1328	.5410	37.3	0	6	2	5	0	1	0	0	0	0	0	0	13	0	0	0	1	0	0	0	0	0	0	0	0
5/5	14	.0000	.2096	33.2	2	1	7	3	1	0	0	0	0	0	0	0	14	0	0	0	0	0	0	0	0	0	0	0	0
5/6	46	.0000	.6885	38.4	0	4	16	14	7	0	5	0	0	0	0	0	46	0	0	0	0	0	0	0	0	0	0	0	0
5/7	9	.0000	.1347	31.3	0	1	6	2	0	0	0	0	0	0	0	0	9	0	0	0	0	0	0	0	0	0	0	0	0
5/8	47	.2816	3.0333	44.8	0	3	8	7	15	11	3	0	0	0	0	0	36	0	0	1	0	0	9	0	0	1	0	0	0
5/8-inch	3	.0000	.0365	25.6	0	0	0	0	3	0	0	0	0	0	0	0	0	0	0	0	0	0	0	0	0	0	0	3	0
5/9	4	.0000	.0599	27.8	0	2	0	0	0	1	1	0	0	0	0	0	4	0	0	0	0	0	0	0	0	0	0	0	0
5%	19	.2999	1.3167	41.2	0	0	0	3	5	2	8	1	0	0	0	0	15	0	0	1	0	0	0	0	0	1	1	1	0
5's	16	.2489	.9624	39.8	8	1	1	0	1	1	4	0	0	1	0	0	13	1	0	0	0	0	0	0	0	1	0	0	0
5th	21	.4163	1.8699	42.7	1	2	3	4	4	0	6	1	0	0	0	0	6	2	1	0	1	0	0	0	0	0	11	0	0
5x	10	.0965	.3291	35.2	0	0	4	0	1	0	5	0	0	0	0	0	9	0	0	1	0	0	0	0	0	0	0	0	0
5x3	3	.0000	.0449	26.5	0	0	2	0	0	1	0	0	0	0	0	0	3	0	0	0	0	0	0	0	0	0	0	0	0
5x5x5	2	.0000	.0299	24.8	0	0	0	0	0	2	0	0	0	0	0	0	2	0	0	0	0	0	0	0	0	0	0	0	0
5y	6	.0000	.0898	29.5	0	0	0	0	0	0	6	0	0	0	0	0	6	0	0	0	0	0	0	0	0	0	0	0	0
50	431	.7323	64.013	58.1	64	54	57	53	79	45	51	28	37	5	4	1	166	37	6	46	1	0	3	2	1	20	37	65	0
50-foot	4	.1622	.1743	32.4	0	1	0	0	1	0	0	2	0	0	0	0	0	1	0	0	0	0	0	0	0	0	0	3	0
50-yard	2	.2427	.1159	30.6	0	0	1	0	0	0	0	1	0	0	0	0	1	0	0	0	0	0	0	0	0	0	0	1	0
50-1	2	.0000	.0050	17.0	0	0	0	0	2	0	0	0	0	0	0	0	0	0	0	0	0	0	0	2	0	0	0	0	0
50%	8	.3401	.6058	37.8	0	0	0	1	1	2	3	1	0	0	0	0	5	0	0	0	0	0	0	0	0	0	2	1	0
50's	2	.1972	.1262	31.0	0	0	1	0	0	1	0	0	1	0	0	0	1	0	0	0	0	0	0	0	0	0	0	0	0
50th	5	.3544	.3958	36.0	0	1	1	1	0	2	0	0	0	0	0	0	2	1	0	0	0	0	0	0	0	0	0	2	0
500	256	.7655	39.543	56.0	12	19	39	27	89	27	28	15	24	5	0	1	57	32	0	21	1	2	0	4	1	29	32	47	0
500-KR	5	.0000	.0608	27.8	0	0	0	0	5	0	0	0	0	0	0	0	0	0	0	0	0	0	0	0	0	0	0	5	0
500-Mile	2	.0000	.0290	24.6	0	0	0	0	0	0	0	2	0	0	0	0	0	0	0	0	0	0	0	0	0	2	0	0	0
500-mile	7	.6184	.9146	39.6	1	0	0	1	2	0	2	1	2	0	0	0	0	1	0	1	0	0	0	0	0	1	1	1	0
500-pound	3	.1937	.1495	31.7	0	1	1	0	1	0	0	0	0	0	0	0	0	1	0	0	0	0	0	0	0	0	0	2	0
500/125	2	.0000	.0299	24.8	0	0	0	2	0	0	0	0	0	0	0	0	2	0	0	0	0	0	0	0	0	0	0	0	0

6E 4652
7Q 466
5E 4692
9Q 47-fold
6R 47-12
9H 47-5
9M 47th
9E 4700
XR 4711
9M 473
5E 4760
7Q 478
4E 479
7M 48-3
7M 48-4
4F 48-49
7M 48-5
9L 48-52
7M 48-6

7M 48-7
9R 48%
7R 4831
XR 484
7H 484-425
5E 4872
3P 48765
4B 48823
4B 48824
6E 489
9E 489-490
5J 49'ers
7R 49er
7P 491
7P 491/4
3P 497
5Q 499
5E 5(5/5)-region
8H 5H

8E 5-
7E 5-day
8D 5-eyed
6A 5-foot-11
7R 5-lug
7Q 5-mile-long
9E 5-y
6E 5-year
8A 5-0-4
9M 5-1
7E 5-10
XR 5-10-10
XR 5-10-5
6R 5-11
9H 5-19
4A 5-2-3
9H 5-21
8M 5-28
8M 5-29

7R 5-3-1
9M 5-3a
9M 5-3b
9M 5-3c
8M 5-30
8M 5-31
8M 5-32
8M 5-33
8M 5-35
4F 5-4-3-2-1-0
9E 5-5
9H 5-9
8A 5-9970
9E 5/13
7E 5/16-inch-thick
4E 5/20
8E 5/22
8E 5/27
7M 5/32

8M 5/34
5E 5/5-segment
5E 5/6-1/2
5E 5/6-1/3
6E 5/7x3/8
3E 5a
9H 5cm3
7P 5d
7E 5in
4Q 5th-century
8E 5x0
4E 5x2x3
4E 5x4
4E 5x6x8
6E 5x7
4E 5x8
5E 5x9
8E 50-
7R 50-cent

8E 50-ft
7R 50-horse
9Q 50-man
9R 50-mile
5E 50-mph
XR 50-page
7Q 50-pounders
6E 50-word
5E 50-16
8E 50/100
5E 50/3
8M 50/50
5E 50x9
7A 500-foot
9H 500-lb
7F 500-year-old
3B 500-1-500

Word Type	F	D	U	SFI	3 Gr 3	4 Gr 4	5 Gr 5	6 Gr 6	7 Gr 7	8 Gr 8	9 Gr 9	X UnGr	A Read	B Eng & Gr	C Comp	D Lit	E Math	F Soc Stud	G Spell	H Sci	J Music	K Art	L Home Ec	M Shop	N Lib F	P Lib NF	Q Lib Ref	R Mag	S Rel
500's	2	.2285	.1129	30.5	0	0	1	0	1	0	0	0	0	0	0	0	0	1	0	0	0	0	0	0	0	0	1	0	0
5000	23	.6510	3.1040	44.9	2	3	2	6	7	2	1	0	4	0	0	0	8	3	0	2	0	0	0	1	0	1	2	2	0
501	3	.2076	.1618	32.1	0	0	1	0	0	1	1	0	0	0	0	0	2	0	0	1	0	0	0	0	0	0	0	0	0
502	4	.4505	.4039	36.1	1	0	2	0	1	0	0	0	1	0	0	0	1	1	0	0	0	0	0	0	0	0	1	0	0
503	2	.2391	.1133	30.5	0	0	1	1	0	0	0	0	0	0	0	0	1	0	0	0	0	0	0	0	0	0	1	0	0
504	3	.0000	.0449	26.5	0	0	1	0	2	0	0	0	0	0	0	0	3	0	0	0	0	0	0	0	0	0	0	0	0
506	3	.1937	.1495	31.7	0	0	1	0	1	1	0	0	0	0	0	0	0	1	0	0	0	0	0	0	0	0	0	2	0
507	2	.0000	.0299	24.8	0	0	1	0	0	0	1	0	0	0	0	0	2	0	0	0	0	0	0	0	0	0	0	0	0
508	2	.2446	.1184	30.7	0	0	0	0	0	1	0	1	0	0	0	0	1	0	0	0	0	0	0	0	0	1	0	0	0
51	35	.6880	4.8877	46.9	6	4	4	3	9	4	4	1	0	1	1	0	15	3	1	3	1	0	0	0	0	3	1	6	0
510	2	.2391	.1133	30.5	0	0	0	0	1	1	0	0	0	0	0	0	1	0	0	0	0	0	0	0	0	0	1	0	0
512	9	.2314	.5437	37.4	0	0	1	2	1	5	0	0	1	0	0	0	6	0	0	2	0	0	0	0	0	0	0	0	0
513	4	.1786	.1933	32.9	0	1	2	0	1	0	0	0	0	0	0	0	3	1	0	0	0	0	0	0	0	0	0	0	0
515	4	.0000	.0599	27.8	0	3	0	1	0	0	0	0	0	0	0	0	4	0	0	0	0	0	0	0	0	0	0	0	0
52	62	.6653	8.4400	49.3	7	8	15	6	9	8	7	2	4	1	1	0	34	3	1	5	3	2	0	0	0	2	1	5	0
520	3	.0000	.0314	25.0	0	0	1	0	2	0	0	0	0	0	0	0	0	0	0	0	0	0	0	0	0	0	3	0	0
5200	2	.2427	.1159	30.6	0	0	0	0	2	0	0	0	0	0	0	0	1	0	0	0	0	0	0	0	0	0	0	1	0
523	7	.1887	.3283	35.2	0	0	1	1	3	2	0	0	0	5	0	0	2	0	0	0	0	0	0	0	0	0	0	0	0
5230	2	.0000	.0162	22.1	0	0	0	0	2	0	0	0	0	0	0	0	0	0	2	0	0	0	0	0	0	0	0	0	0
524	4	.4071	.3450	35.4	0	0	1	0	1	1	1	0	0	0	0	0	1	0	0	0	0	0	1	0	1	0	0	1	0
525	7	.5861	.8478	39.3	2	1	2	0	0	0	1	1	0	1	0	0	1	1	0	1	0	0	0	0	0	1	2	0	0
528	3	.2019	.1477	31.7	0	0	2	0	1	0	0	0	0	0	0	0	1	0	0	0	0	0	0	0	0	0	2	0	0
5280	11	.0000	.1647	32.2	2	2	0	1	0	6	0	0	0	0	0	0	11	0	0	0	0	0	0	0	0	0	0	0	0
53	44	.5532	5.0666	47.0	8	2	9	3	4	10	6	2	1	3	0	0	28	0	0	1	1	1	0	0	0	2	4	3	0
530	2	.2427	.1159	30.6	0	0	0	0	0	0	1	1	0	0	0	0	1	0	0	0	0	0	0	0	0	0	0	1	0
531	3	.2398	.1721	32.4	0	0	0	0	1	2	0	0	0	0	0	0	2	0	0	0	0	0	0	0	0	0	1	0	0
534	2	.2391	.1133	30.5	0	0	0	1	0	1	0	0	0	0	0	0	1	0	0	0	0	0	0	0	0	0	1	0	0
535	3	.3553	.2608	34.2	1	0	0	1	0	1	0	0	1	0	0	0	0	1	0	0	0	0	0	0	0	1	0	0	0
536	2	.0000	.0299	24.8	0	0	2	0	0	0	0	0	0	0	0	0	2	0	0	0	0	0	0	0	0	0	0	0	0
537	6	.1386	.2447	33.9	0	2	4	0	0	0	0	0	0	0	0	0	5	1	0	0	0	0	0	0	0	0	0	0	0
54	52	.5444	5.9103	47.7	5	5	9	11	9	7	6	0	1	1	0	0	35	4	3	0	1	1	0	0	0	1	3	2	0
54x398	2	.0000	.0299	24.8	0	0	0	0	0	2	0	0	0	0	0	0	2	0	0	0	0	0	0	0	0	0	0	0	0
540	7	.3971	.6030	37.8	1	1	2	0	1	0	2	0	0	0	0	0	4	1	0	0	0	0	0	1	0	0	0	1	0
543	2	.2391	.1133	30.5	0	1	0	0	0	1	0	0	0	0	0	0	1	0	0	0	0	0	0	0	0	0	1	0	0
546	2	.2427	.1159	30.6	0	1	0	0	0	1	0	0	0	0	0	0	1	0	0	0	0	0	0	0	0	0	0	1	0
547	5	.0000	.0748	28.7	1	0	2	0	0	1	1	0	0	0	0	0	5	0	0	0	0	0	0	0	0	0	0	0	0
549	6	.3662	.4751	36.8	0	3	1	0	2	0	0	0	0	0	0	0	3	0	0	0	0	0	0	1	0	0	2	0	0
55	48	.7451	7.2070	48.6	7	7	6	7	5	11	5	0	1	3	0	0	14	5	4	5	3	0	0	0	0	4	3	6	0
55-pound	2	.0000	.0394	26.0	0	2	0	0	0	0	0	0	0	0	0	0	0	0	0	2	0	0	0	0	0	0	0	0	0
55%	3	.1125	.0853	29.3	0	0	0	0	0	0	3	0	0	0	0	0	1	0	0	0	0	0	2	0	0	0	0	0	0
550	7	.5007	.7490	38.7	0	3	0	0	2	0	1	1	1	0	0	0	2	0	0	1	0	0	0	1	0	0	1	1	0
5500	2	.2427	.1159	30.6	0	1	0	0	1	0	0	0	0	0	0	0	1	0	0	0	0	0	0	0	0	0	0	1	0
551	2	.0725	.0732	28.6	0	1	0	0	1	0	0	0	1	0	0	0	0	0	0	0	0	0	0	1	0	0	0	0	0
553	2	.2413	.1212	30.8	1	0	0	0	0	0	1	0	0	0	0	0	1	0	0	1	0	0	0	0	0	0	0	0	0
558	2	.2351	.1166	30.7	0	0	0	0	1	1	0	0	0	0	0	0	0	1	0	0	0	0	0	0	0	0	0	1	0
559	5	.2414	.3872	35.9	0	0	4	0	1	0	0	0	4	0	0	0	1	0	0	0	0	0	0	0	0	0	0	0	0
56	86	.5754	10.335	50.1	11	21	13	11	9	8	10	3	5	0	0	1	52	11	2	5	2	0	1	1	1	0	0	5	0
56A	2	.0000	.0914	29.6	0	0	0	2	0	0	0	0	2	0	0	0	0	0	0	0	0	0	0	0	0	0	0	0	0
56-unit	3	.0000	.0449	26.5	0	0	0	0	0	3	0	0	0	0	0	0	3	0	0	0	0	0	0	0	0	0	0	0	0
56-57	2	.1170	.0651	28.1	0	0	0	1	0	1	0	0	0	0	1	0	0	1	0	0	0	0	0	0	0	0	0	0	0
560	3	.2121	.1560	31.9	0	0	0	1	1	0	1	0	0	0	0	0	1	0	0	0	0	0	0	0	0	0	0	2	0
562	2	.2427	.1159	30.6	0	1	0	1	0	0	0	0	0	0	0	0	1	0	0	0	0	0	0	0	0	0	0	1	0
563	2	.2446	.1184	30.7	0	0	1	1	0	0	0	0	0	0	0	0	1	0	0	0	0	0	0	0	0	1	0	0	0
566	2	.0000	.0243	23.9	0	0	0	1	1	0	0	0	0	0	0	0	0	0	0	0	0	0	0	0	0	0	0	2	0
57	36	.4560	3.5142	45.5	4	9	10	2	3	2	6	0	0	0	0	0	22	5	0	1	3	0	0	0	0	0	1	4	0
570	2	.0000	.0389	25.9	0	0	0	0	1	0	1	0	0	0	0	0	0	2	0	0	0	0	0	0	0	0	0	0	0
5700	5	.3317	.3770	35.8	0	0	0	0	2	3	0	0	0	0	0	0	3	1	0	0	0	0	0	0	0	0	0	1	0
571	2	.2391	.1133	30.5	0	0	0	1	1	0	0	0	0	0	0	0	1	0	0	0	0	0	0	0	0	0	1	0	0
575	7	.2784	.4598	36.6	1	0	3	1	0	1	1	0	0	0	0	0	5	1	0	0	0	0	0	0	0	0	0	1	0
578	5	.1560	.2202	33.4	0	0	1	3	0	1	0	0	0	0	0	0	4	1	0	0	0	0	0	0	0	0	0	0	0
58	29	.6252	3.7072	45.7	4	7	5	2	6	3	2	0	0	3	0	0	15	2	2	0	0	1	0	0	0	1	3	2	0
580	2	.0000	.0299	24.8	0	0	2	0	0	0	0	0	0	0	0	0	2	0	0	0	0	0	0	0	0	0	0	0	0
581	3	.2019	.1477	31.7	0	0	0	2	0	1	0	0	0	0	0	0	1	0	0	0	0	0	0	0	0	0	2	0	0
584	2	.2278	.1128	30.5	0	0	0	1	0	0	1	0	0	0	0	0	0	0	0	1	0	0	0	0	0	0	1	0	0
585	2	.0000	.0209	23.2	1	0	0	0	1	0	0	0	0	0	0	0	0	0	0	0	0	0	0	0	0	0	2	0	0
586	2	.2446	.1184	30.7	0	0	1	0	1	0	0	0	0	0	0	0	1	0	0	0	0	0	0	0	0	1	0	0	0
589	3	.0000	.0449	26.5	0	3	0	0	0	0	0	0	0	0	0	0	3	0	0	0	0	0	0	0	0	0	0	0	0
59	38	.5854	4.6247	46.7	4	7	7	2	5	8	4	1	2	2	0	0	21	4	1	1	2	0	0	0	0	1	1	3	0
590	2	.1972	.1262	31.0	0	0	2	0	0	0	0	0	1	0	0	0	1	0	0	0	0	0	0	0	0	0	0	0	0
593	2	.2417	.1211	30.8	0	0	0	0	1	1	0	0	0	0	0	0	1	1	0	0	0	0	0	0	0	0	0	0	0
597	5	.1519	.1991	33.0	0	1	1	1	2	0	0	0	0	4	0	0	1	0	0	0	0	0	0	0	0	0	0	0	0
6	1371	.5793	164.85	62.2	266	194	188	176	188	183	147	29	40	17	1	7	997	36	31	53	38	1	10	18	1	23	39	58	1
6-cent	3	.2346	.1705	32.3	1	0	0	0	2	0	0	0	0	0	0	0	2	0	0	0	0	0	0	0	0	0	0	1	0
6-foot	2	.0000	.0299	24.8	2	0	0	0	0	0	0	0	0	0	0	0	2	0	0	0	0	0	0	0	0	0	0	0	0
6-inch	4	.3121	.2850	34.5	0	0	0	0	1	1	1	1	0	0	0	0	1	0	0	2	0	0	1	0	0	0	0	0	0
6-pound	2	.0000	.0299	24.8	0	0	1	0	0	1	0	0	0	0	0	0	2	0	0	0	0	0	0	0	0	0	0	0	0
6-1	3	.1785	.1397	31.5	0	0	0	0	0	2	1	0	0	0	0	0	0	0	0	2	0	0	0	1	0	0	0	0	0
6-10	2	.0000	.0050	17.0	0	0	0	0	0	2	0	0	0	0	0	0	0	0	0	0	0	0	0	2	0	0	0	0	0
6-2	6	.4003	.5250	37.2	1	0	0	0	1	3	0	1	0	0	0	0	0	0	0	3	0	0	0	1	0	1	0	1	0
6-3	4	.1249	.1371	31.4	0	0	0	0	0	3	1	0	0	0	0	0	0	0	0	2	0	0	0	2	0	0	0	0	0
6-32	2	.0000	.0050	17.0	0	0	0	0	0	2	0	0	0	0	0	0	0	0	0	0	0	0	0	2	0	0	0	0	0
6-4	2	.1620	.0760	28.8	0	0	0	0	1	1	0	0	0	0	0	0	0	0	0	0	0	0	0	1	0	0	0	1	0
6-5	2	.1972	.1262	31.0	0	0	0	1	1	0	0	0	1	0	0	0	1	0	0	0	0	0	0	0	0	0	0	0	0

5P 500th
5E 500x7
5A 5000-mile-a-minute
5P 505
7E 51/2%
7E 51/4
5Q 511
6R 514-15
4E 516
6R 517
7H 52-foot
7R 52-year-old
4E 52-18
4E 52-34
9R 52%
7B 520-529
9H 521
8E 526
3E 5263
7Q 529
8E 53-38
8B 532
5P 533
8B 533-35
4E 5372
7Q 538
5Q 539
5E 5398/60
8M 54-2
8E 54-26
8K 54-55
7K 54-59
7A 54th
3P 54376
7R 545-f
6E 5459
7M 548
7H 55-foot
4H 55-57
6R 55-7
4G 55th
6R 550-ton
7M 552
7M 553-557
7Q 554
3P 555
4E 556
9H 558-559
7M 558-568
7H 56-day
XR 56-degree
5B 56-49
5N 56a
8E 56x7
8E 56x700
7R 560-to
5E 5600
6A 561
5E 565
7E 567
6E 568
5E 5689
9E 569
8R 57-year-old
9R 57%
5E 57x10
5E 57x100
7R 5700-5800
5A 5710
7E 57142857
7E 573
5Q 574
8E 576x4
8E 576x400
4E 5763
5E 5764
5E 577
7M 58-11
7M 58-12
7M 58-13
7M 58-14
7M 58-15
7M 58-16
7M 58-17
7M 58-18
7M 58-19
7M 58-20
9M 58-6
9M 58-7
9M 58-8
6F 5800
4E 582
3E 583
5E 587
6R 59-21
7F 59th
6E 592
7A 594
5Q 594-foot
7R 594-inch
6R 595
7M 596
6A 596781
6A 596782
4A 5988
XR 6A
7P 6U6139
9M 6-
XR 6-acre
7R 6-cylinder
6E 6-digit
4P 6-foot-tall
8R 6-foot-8-inch
7E 6-hr
7R 6-in
7R 6-in-swing**
9F 6-member
7M 6-million
7E 6-ounce
XH 6-petaled
7H 6-ton
6H 6-volt
9F 6-year
8M 6-11
8M 6-11a
8M 6-11b
8M 6-11c
8M 6-11d
7E 6-12
7M 6-22
7M 6-23
7M 6-24

Word Type	F	D	U	SFI	3 Gr 3	4 Gr 4	5 Gr 5	6 Gr 6	7 Gr 7	8 Gr 8	9 Gr 9	X UnGr	A Read	B Eng & Gr	C Comp	D Lit	E Math	F Soc Stud	G Spell	H Sci	J Music	K Art	L Home Ec	M Shop	N Lib F	P Lib NF	Q Lib Ref	R Mag	S Rel
6-7	2	.1738	.0790	29.0	0	0	1	0	0	1	0	0	0	0	0	0	0	0	0	0	0	0	0	1	0	0	1	0	0
6-8	11	.4474	1.0331	40.1	0	0	0	2	3	6	0	0	0	0	0	0	4	0	0	1	3	0	0	2	0	0	1	0	0
6-9	3	.0803	.0701	28.5	0	0	0	0	0	2	1	0	0	0	0	0	0	0	0	1	0	0	0	2	0	0	0	0	0
6/	5	.2379	.2813	34.5	0	0	0	3	0	1	1	0	0	0	0	0	4	0	0	0	0	0	0	1	0	0	0	0	0
6/0	2	.1457	.0722	28.6	0	0	0	0	1	1	0	0	0	0	0	0	1	0	0	0	0	0	0	1	0	0	0	0	0
6/10	11	.0000	.1647	32.2	0	0	8	0	3	0	0	0	0	0	0	0	11	0	0	0	0	0	0	0	0	0	0	0	0
6/100	4	.0000	.0599	27.8	0	0	0	2	2	0	0	0	0	0	0	0	4	0	0	0	0	0	0	0	0	0	0	0	0
6/12	6	.2434	.3455	35.4	0	1	1	3	0	1	0	0	0	0	0	0	5	0	0	0	0	0	0	1	0	0	0	0	0
6/15	5	.0000	.0748	28.7	0	0	0	0	5	0	0	0	0	0	0	0	5	0	0	0	0	0	0	0	0	0	0	0	0
6/16	2	.0000	.0299	24.8	0	0	0	0	0	0	2	0	0	0	0	0	2	0	0	0	0	0	0	0	0	0	0	0	0
6/3	7	.0000	.1048	30.2	2	1	2	0	0	2	0	0	0	0	0	0	7	0	0	0	0	0	0	0	0	0	0	0	0
6/5	4	.0000	.0599	27.8	0	0	4	0	0	0	0	0	0	0	0	0	4	0	0	0	0	0	0	0	0	0	0	0	0
6/6	7	.0000	.1048	30.2	1	0	0	6	0	0	0	0	0	0	0	0	7	0	0	0	0	0	0	0	0	0	0	0	0
6/7	3	.0000	.0449	26.5	0	3	0	0	0	0	0	0	0	0	0	0	3	0	0	0	0	0	0	0	0	0	0	0	0
6/8	19	.1336	.6558	38.2	1	4	11	2	1	0	0	0	0	0	0	0	4	0	0	0	15	0	0	0	0	0	0	0	0
6/9	3	.0000	.0449	26.5	0	0	0	1	0	2	0	0	0	0	0	0	3	0	0	0	0	0	0	0	0	0	0	0	0
6%	11	.1950	.5468	37.4	0	1	0	3	3	2	2	0	0	0	0	0	9	0	0	0	0	0	0	0	0	0	2	0	0
6th	12	.3844	.9959	40.0	0	0	2	4	4	1	1	0	0	0	0	0	6	0	0	0	3	0	0	0	0	0	3	0	0
6x	7	.0000	.1048	30.2	0	0	2	0	0	0	5	0	0	0	0	0	7	0	0	0	0	0	0	0	0	0	0	0	0
6x10	2	.0000	.0299	24.8	0	0	0	1	1	0	0	0	0	0	0	0	2	0	0	0	0	0	0	0	0	0	0	0	0
6x7	3	.0000	.0449	26.5	0	3	0	0	0	0	0	0	0	0	0	0	3	0	0	0	0	0	0	0	0	0	0	0	0
6x8	2	.0000	.0299	24.8	0	1	1	0	0	0	0	0	0	0	0	0	2	0	0	0	0	0	0	0	0	0	0	0	0
6y	2	.0000	.0299	24.8	0	0	2	0	0	0	0	0	0	0	0	0	2	0	0	0	0	0	0	0	0	0	0	0	0
60	238	.7215	34.777	55.4	27	35	21	29	45	41	31	9	11	4	0	0	105	22	5	19	3	0	3	8	1	12	26	19	0
60-degree	3	.1785	.1397	31.5	0	0	0	0	0	1	0	2	0	0	0	0	0	0	0	2	0	0	0	1	0	0	0	0	0
60-inch	2	.2437	.1129	30.5	0	0	0	0	1	0	1	0	0	0	0	0	0	0	0	0	0	0	0	0	0	0	1	1	0
60-pound	5	.2442	.3066	34.9	0	0	0	3	0	0	0	2	0	0	0	0	0	0	0	3	0	0	0	0	0	2	0	0	0
60-61	2	.2128	.1055	30.2	0	1	1	0	0	0	0	0	0	0	0	0	0	0	0	1	1	0	0	0	0	0	0	0	0
60%	3	.2757	.1896	32.8	0	0	0	0	1	0	1	1	0	0	0	0	0	0	0	1	0	0	1	0	0	1	0	0	0
60th	4	.1325	.1944	32.9	0	0	1	1	1	0	1	0	1	0	0	0	0	3	0	0	0	0	0	0	0	0	0	0	0
600	97	.7395	14.543	51.6	14	5	18	15	21	7	13	4	10	1	0	0	21	10	3	16	0	0	0	3	0	7	15	11	0
600-yard	2	.0000	.0299	24.8	0	0	2	0	0	0	0	0	0	0	0	0	2	0	0	0	0	0	0	0	0	0	0	0	0
600's	2	.2446	.1123	30.5	0	0	1	0	1	0	0	0	0	1	0	0	0	0	0	0	0	0	0	0	0	0	1	0	0
6000	11	.4937	1.1754	40.7	2	1	0	2	3	2	0	1	1	0	0	0	4	3	0	2	0	0	0	0	0	0	1	0	0
601	2	.2401	.1133	30.5	0	0	0	0	1	0	0	1	0	0	0	0	0	0	0	0	0	0	0	0	0	1	1	0	0
603	3	.2346	.1705	32.3	0	0	0	2	0	0	1	0	0	0	0	0	2	0	0	0	0	0	0	0	0	0	0	1	0
604	3	.0000	.0449	26.5	3	0	0	0	0	0	0	0	0	0	0	0	3	0	0	0	0	0	0	0	0	0	0	0	0
606	3	.2398	.1721	32.4	0	0	0	0	1	0	2	0	0	0	0	0	2	0	0	0	0	0	0	0	0	0	1	0	0
609	2	.0000	.0299	24.8	0	0	0	1	0	1	0	0	0	0	0	0	2	0	0	0	0	0	0	0	0	0	0	0	0
61	17	.6181	2.1502	43.3	2	4	0	3	1	3	2	2	0	0	0	1	7	1	0	1	2	1	0	0	0	1	0	3	0
610	3	.2444	.1814	32.6	0	0	2	0	1	0	0	0	0	0	0	0	0	2	0	0	0	0	0	0	0	0	1	0	0
612	3	.0000	.0449	26.5	0	0	0	1	2	0	0	0	0	0	0	0	3	0	0	0	0	0	0	0	0	0	0	0	0
615	3	.3862	.2532	34.0	0	0	0	0	2	0	0	1	0	0	0	0	1	0	0	0	0	0	0	0	0	1	0	1	0
619	2	.0000	.0209	23.2	1	0	0	0	0	1	0	0	0	0	0	0	0	0	0	0	0	0	0	0	0	0	2	0	0
62	38	.7331	5.6217	47.5	0	1	9	3	7	11	4	3	1	1	0	0	17	5	1	1	3	1	0	1	0	3	3	1	0
620	3	.3759	.2498	34.0	0	0	1	0	0	0	2	0	0	0	0	0	1	0	0	1	0	0	0	0	0	0	1	0	0
624	3	.0000	.0449	26.5	0	0	1	2	0	0	0	0	0	0	0	0	3	0	0	0	0	0	0	0	0	0	0	0	0
625	6	.1617	.2655	34.2	1	0	0	2	2	0	1	0	0	0	0	0	5	0	0	0	0	0	0	0	0	1	0	0	0
627	3	.0000	.0449	26.5	1	0	0	2	0	0	0	0	0	0	0	0	3	0	0	0	0	0	0	0	0	0	0	0	0
628	2	.2413	.1212	30.8	0	0	0	1	0	0	1	0	0	0	0	0	1	0	0	1	0	0	0	0	0	0	0	0	0
6289	2	.0000	.0299	24.8	0	0	1	0	0	1	0	0	0	0	0	0	2	0	0	0	0	0	0	0	0	0	0	0	0
63	54	.3224	3.9757	46.0	11	12	3	8	9	7	1	3	1	1	1	0	46	1	0	1	1	0	0	0	0	0	0	2	0
630	6	.4338	.5495	37.4	0	0	2	0	3	0	1	0	0	0	0	0	2	0	0	0	0	0	0	1	0	0	1	2	0
632	4	.1786	.1933	32.9	0	1	0	0	1	1	1	0	0	0	0	0	3	1	0	0	0	0	0	0	0	0	0	0	0
6325	2	.0000	.0299	24.8	0	0	0	0	2	0	0	0	0	0	0	0	2	0	0	0	0	0	0	0	0	0	0	0	0
634	2	.2442	.1134	30.5	0	0	0	1	0	0	0	1	0	1	0	0	0	0	0	0	0	0	0	0	0	0	0	1	0
6340	2	.0000	.0299	24.8	0	0	0	0	2	0	0	0	0	0	0	0	2	0	0	0	0	0	0	0	0	0	0	0	0
638	8	.1117	.2829	34.5	7	0	0	0	0	1	0	0	0	0	0	0	0	1	0	0	0	0	0	0	0	7	0	0	0
64	57	.5201	6.2040	47.9	4	6	10	9	9	7	12	0	0	0	1	0	39	2	4	1	1	0	0	0	0	1	5	3	0
64-65	2	.0000	.0219	23.4	0	0	0	2	0	0	0	0	0	2	0	0	0	0	0	0	0	0	0	0	0	0	0	0	0
640	8	.1930	.3947	36.0	0	1	0	3	0	1	3	0	1	0	0	0	4	0	0	0	0	0	0	3	0	0	0	0	0
6425	2	.0000	.0299	24.8	0	0	0	0	2	0	0	0	0	0	0	0	2	0	0	0	0	0	0	0	0	0	0	0	0
643	2	.0000	.0299	24.8	2	0	0	0	0	0	0	0	0	0	0	0	2	0	0	0	0	0	0	0	0	0	0	0	0
647	3	.1865	.1650	32.2	0	0	1	0	0	1	1	0	1	0	0	0	0	1	0	0	0	0	0	1	0	0	0	0	0
649	2	.0000	.0299	24.8	0	0	0	2	0	0	0	0	0	0	0	0	2	0	0	0	0	0	0	0	0	0	0	0	0
65	96	.6131	12.257	50.9	16	7	11	12	15	18	15	2	11	2	0	2	42	7	1	12	0	0	0	0	0	2	4	13	0
65%	2	.2391	.1133	30.5	0	0	0	0	0	0	2	0	0	0	0	0	1	0	0	0	0	0	0	0	0	0	1	0	0
650	15	.5621	1.7508	42.4	1	1	4	0	6	0	0	3	0	1	0	0	3	2	0	1	0	0	0	0	0	4	4	0	0
656	3	.0965	.0750	28.7	0	1	0	0	0	0	2	0	0	0	0	0	1	0	0	0	0	0	0	2	0	0	0	0	0
659	2	.0000	.0050	17.0	0	0	0	0	0	0	2	0	0	0	0	0	0	0	0	0	0	0	0	2	0	0	0	0	0
6598	2	.0000	.0299	24.8	0	0	1	0	0	1	0	0	0	0	0	0	2	0	0	0	0	0	0	0	0	0	0	0	0
66	28	.7226	4.0889	46.1	2	7	4	2	7	4	1	1	1	1	0	0	6	2	4	5	0	0	0	1	2	0	5	1	0
660	5	.2203	.2797	34.5	1	0	0	0	1	0	3	0	1	1	0	0	0	1	0	0	0	0	0	2	0	0	0	0	0
661	5	.1307	.1561	31.9	0	0	0	1	1	0	3	0	0	0	0	0	0	0	0	0	0	0	0	3	0	0	0	2	0
662	2	.0000	.0050	17.0	0	0	0	0	0	0	2	0	0	0	0	0	0	0	0	0	0	0	0	2	0	0	0	0	0
663	3	.0000	.0076	18.8	0	0	0	0	0	0	3	0	0	0	0	0	0	0	0	0	0	0	0	3	0	0	0	0	0
666	4	.2253	.2138	33.3	0	0	0	0	1	0	3	0	0	0	0	0	3	0	0	0	0	0	0	1	0	0	0	0	0
668	2	.0000	.0299	24.8	0	0	1	0	0	1	0	0	0	0	0	0	2	0	0	0	0	0	0	0	0	0	0	0	0
67	34	.4890	3.5243	45.5	4	4	4	5	5	4	8	0	1	0	0	0	21	1	0	3	0	0	0	3	1	0	2	2	0
67-year-old	2	.2433	.1158	30.6	1	0	0	0	0	1	0	0	0	0	0	0	0	0	0	0	0	0	0	0	0	1	0	1	0
670	4	.4629	.4147	36.2	0	0	2	1	1	0	0	0	1	0	0	0	1	1	0	0	0	0	0	0	0	1	0	0	0
671	2	.2413	.1212	30.8	0	0	1	0	0	1	0	0	0	0	0	0	1	0	0	1	0	0	0	0	0	0	0	0	0
673	3	.2346	.1705	32.3	0	0	1	2	0	0	0	0	0	0	0	0	2	0	0	0	0	0	0	0	0	0	0	1	0
674	4	.0000	.0599	27.8	0	0	0	2	0	2	0	0	0	0	0	0	4	0	0	0	0	0	0	0	0	0	0	0	0
6743	2	.0000	.0299	24.8	0	0	2	0	0	0	0	0	0	0	0	0	2	0	0	0	0	0	0	0	0	0	0	0	0
675	7	.4060	.6334	38.0	0	2	2	1	2	0	0	0	1	0	0	0	3	0	0	0	0	0	0	0	0	1	2	0	0
68	37	.6828	5.1392	47.1	4	3	6	4	7	6	6	1	1	1	0	0	18	1	2	4	1	0	0	1	0	3	3	2	0

8M 6-6
6E 6/14
8E 6/20
9M 6/32
3E 6's
6G 6a
6E 6d
7E 6e
6E 6in
8E 6ths
5E 6xn
5E 6x2
5E 6x3
4E 6x39
4E 6x40
7R 60-Hz
5Q 60-day
7R 60-foot
7R 60-m
7R 60-mile
9R 60-to-64
7R 60-70
7E 60/100
5E 60x80
9H 600-foot
6R 600-foot-high
9Q 600-odd
8H 600-1200
9E 600-300
6R 600-601
6F 6000-acre
8E 602
6E 605
3B 60636
4E 6072
8E 6076
6G 6080
8M 61-10
8M 61-11
8M 61-12
8M 61-13
8M 61-14
8M 61-9
5R 61183
5Q 612-foot
7E 6197
7A 62-60
9R 62%
5Q 620-foot
6E 623
6E 62341
8F 626
7E 6261
6R 63-28
9L 63%
6R 630-31
4F 631
7R 637
7H 6377
8R 639
5E 640-foot
8E 641
9D 644-ton
XR 645
5E 646
5E 6474
9R 653908
6P 654
6E 6566
5Q 657
9M 658
8R 66-yard
6R 66-0
7M 66-1B
7M 66-2
7M 66-3
7M 66-4
5B 66-67
6J 66-68
6E 66/1000
9M 6600
9M 664
9M 665
9E 66666
7M 67-1
7M 67-2A
7M 67-3
7M 67-4
7M 67-5
7M 67-6
7M 67-7
XH 6700
7D 6700-foot**
6E 672
8Q 6720
7E 676
5E 677
9E 678
4E 6783
3E 679
8R 68-yards
6R 68-year-old
7M 68-1
7E 68/38
9E 68%

Word Type	F	D	U	SFI	3 Gr 3	4 Gr 4	5 Gr 5	6 Gr 6	7 Gr 7	8 Gr 8	9 Gr 9	X UnGr	A Read	B Eng & Gr	C Comp	D Lit	E Math	F Soc Stud	G Spell	H Sci	J Music	K Art	L Home Ec	M Shop	N Lib F	P Lib NF	Q Lib Ref	R Mag	S Rel
680	3	.3763	.2498	34.0	1	0	0	0	0	1	1	0	0	0	0	0	1	1	0	0	0	0	0	0	0	0	1	0	0
681	3	.3841	.2496	34.0	0	0	1	0	2	0	0	0	0	0	0	0	1	0	0	0	0	0	0	0	0	0	1	1	0
683	4	.1786	.1933	32.9	0	1	1	1	0	0	1	0	0	0	0	0	3	1	0	0	0	0	0	0	0	0	0	0	0
684	3	.3763	.2498	34.0	1	0	1	0	0	1	0	0	0	0	0	0	1	1	0	0	0	0	0	0	0	0	1	0	0
685	4	.2220	.2176	33.4	0	0	0	0	0	0	4	0	0	0	0	0	3	0	0	0	0	0	0	0	0	0	1	0	0
686	2	.0000	.0299	24.8	0	1	0	0	0	1	0	0	0	0	0	0	2	0	0	0	0	0	0	0	0	0	0	0	0
687	5	.0000	.0748	28.7	0	1	1	1	0	2	0	0	0	0	0	0	5	0	0	0	0	0	0	0	0	0	0	0	0
69	32	.5356	3.5814	45.5	9	6	5	1	4	2	2	3	1	0	0	0	21	0	2	0	1	0	0	1	0	2	3	1	0
692	3	.0000	.0449	26.5	0	0	3	0	0	0	0	0	0	0	0	0	3	0	0	0	0	0	0	0	0	0	0	0	0
6925	2	.0000	.0299	24.8	0	0	1	0	0	1	0	0	0	0	0	0	2	0	0	0	0	0	0	0	0	0	0	0	0
693	5	.1792	.2371	33.7	2	0	2	0	0	1	0	0	0	0	0	0	4	0	0	0	0	0	0	0	0	1	0	0	0
698	2	.0000	.0299	24.8	0	0	1	0	0	1	0	0	0	0	0	0	2	0	0	0	0	0	0	0	0	0	0	0	0
7	950	.5718	113.06	60.5	159	134	132	99	160	128	122	16	36	15	2	2	665	38	32	40	15	2	5	14	3	13	29	39	0
7-cent	3	.0000	.0449	26.5	0	0	0	0	2	1	0	0	0	0	0	0	3	0	0	0	0	0	0	0	0	0	0	0	0
7-clock	4	.0000	.0599	27.8	0	0	1	3	0	0	0	0	0	0	0	0	4	0	0	0	0	0	0	0	0	0	0	0	0
7-gram	2	.0000	.0394	26.0	0	0	0	0	0	0	0	2	0	0	0	0	0	0	0	2	0	0	0	0	0	0	0	0	0
7-1	2	.0000	.0394	26.0	0	0	0	0	0	1	1	0	0	0	0	0	0	0	0	2	0	0	0	0	0	0	0	0	0
7-10	2	.0000	.0299	24.8	0	0	0	0	2	0	0	0	0	0	0	0	2	0	0	0	0	0	0	0	0	0	0	0	0
7-11	8	.2095	.3879	35.9	1	2	1	1	3	0	0	0	0	0	0	0	1	0	6	0	0	0	0	0	0	0	1	0	0
7-19	2	.0000	.0394	26.0	0	0	0	0	0	0	2	0	0	0	0	0	0	0	0	2	0	0	0	0	0	0	0	0	0
7-20	2	.2413	.1212	30.8	0	0	0	0	1	0	1	0	0	0	0	0	1	0	0	1	0	0	0	0	0	0	0	0	0
7-21	2	.2278	.1128	30.5	0	0	1	0	1	0	0	0	0	0	0	0	0	0	0	1	0	0	0	0	0	0	1	0	0
7-4	2	.0000	.0394	26.0	0	0	0	0	0	0	2	0	0	0	0	0	0	0	0	2	0	0	0	0	0	0	0	0	0
7/c	3	.0000	.0449	26.5	0	0	0	0	3	0	0	0	0	0	0	0	3	0	0	0	0	0	0	0	0	0	0	0	0
7/10	8	.0645	.2421	33.8	0	0	3	4	1	0	0	0	1	0	0	0	7	0	0	0	0	0	0	0	0	0	0	0	0
7/100	3	.0000	.0449	26.5	0	0	0	0	2	0	1	0	0	0	0	0	3	0	0	0	0	0	0	0	0	0	0	0	0
7/11	3	.0000	.0449	26.5	0	0	0	0	2	1	0	0	0	0	0	0	3	0	0	0	0	0	0	0	0	0	0	0	0
7/12	4	.0000	.0599	27.8	0	0	3	0	1	0	0	0	0	0	0	0	4	0	0	0	0	0	0	0	0	0	0	0	0
7/16	4	.0000	.0599	27.8	0	0	1	1	0	0	2	0	0	0	0	0	4	0	0	0	0	0	0	0	0	0	0	0	0
7/2	3	.0000	.0449	26.5	0	0	3	0	0	0	0	0	0	0	0	0	3	0	0	0	0	0	0	0	0	0	0	0	0
7/20	2	.0000	.0299	24.8	0	0	0	0	1	0	1	0	0	0	0	0	2	0	0	0	0	0	0	0	0	0	0	0	0
7/3	6	.0000	.0898	29.5	0	0	1	2	0	0	3	0	0	0	0	0	6	0	0	0	0	0	0	0	0	0	0	0	0
7/4	8	.2347	.4500	36.5	0	1	2	1	1	1	2	0	0	0	0	0	6	0	0	0	2	0	0	0	0	0	0	0	0
7/5	3	.0000	.0449	26.5	0	0	2	0	1	0	0	0	0	0	0	0	3	0	0	0	0	0	0	0	0	0	0	0	0
7/6	5	.0000	.0748	28.7	0	0	3	2	0	0	0	0	0	0	0	0	5	0	0	0	0	0	0	0	0	0	0	0	0
7/7	2	.0000	.0299	24.8	0	1	0	1	0	0	0	0	0	0	0	0	2	0	0	0	0	0	0	0	0	0	0	0	0
7/8	42	.1024	1.3972	41.5	1	5	17	9	8	2	0	0	0	0	0	0	40	0	0	0	2	0	0	0	0	0	0	0	0
7/8-in	2	.0000	.0243	23.9	0	0	0	0	2	0	0	0	0	0	0	0	0	0	0	0	0	0	0	0	0	0	0	2	0
7/9	3	.0000	.0449	26.5	0	0	1	2	0	0	0	0	0	0	0	0	3	0	0	0	0	0	0	0	0	0	0	0	0
7%	7	.4370	.6555	38.2	0	1	0	1	0	1	0	4	0	0	0	0	2	0	0	1	0	0	0	0	0	0	1	3	0
7's	5	.0000	.0748	28.7	1	0	4	0	0	0	0	0	0	0	0	0	5	0	0	0	0	0	0	0	0	0	0	0	0
7th	12	.4605	1.1691	40.7	1	0	1	2	1	2	5	0	0	0	0	0	4	1	0	0	1	0	0	0	0	1	5	0	0
7x9	3	.0000	.0449	26.5	0	2	1	0	0	0	0	0	0	0	0	0	3	0	0	0	0	0	0	0	0	0	0	0	0
70	157	.7212	22.930	53.6	22	27	25	12	31	24	13	3	8	5	0	0	68	11	7	12	0	0	4	2	0	8	17	15	0
700	68	.7486	10.280	50.1	7	8	7	13	15	7	8	3	4	1	0	3	16	7	1	11	0	2	0	0	0	5	11	7	0
7000	7	.4480	.6745	38.3	0	2	0	3	1	0	1	0	0	0	0	0	3	1	0	0	0	0	0	0	0	2	0	1	0
71	26	.5591	3.0318	44.8	2	6	3	8	2	3	2	0	1	0	0	0	13	1	0	3	0	1	1	0	0	0	0	6	0
71-1	2	.0000	.0050	17.0	0	0	0	0	2	0	0	0	0	0	0	0	0	0	0	0	0	0	0	2	0	0	0	0	0
710	2	.2391	.1133	30.5	0	1	0	0	1	0	0	0	0	0	0	0	1	0	0	0	0	0	0	0	0	0	1	0	0
712	2	.0000	.0299	24.8	0	0	1	1	0	0	0	0	0	0	0	0	2	0	0	0	0	0	0	0	0	0	0	0	0
713	3	.2264	.1679	32.2	2	0	1	0	0	0	0	0	0	0	0	0	2	0	0	0	0	0	0	0	0	1	0	0	0
715	2	.0000	.0299	24.8	0	0	1	0	1	0	0	0	0	0	0	0	2	0	0	0	0	0	0	0	0	0	0	0	0
715/45	2	.0000	.0299	24.8	0	0	0	0	2	0	0	0	0	0	0	0	2	0	0	0	0	0	0	0	0	0	0	0	0
72	55	.5429	6.2551	48.0	7	9	9	15	3	6	4	2	1	2	0	0	35	5	1	4	2	0	1	0	0	2	0	2	0
72-73	2	.0000	.0219	23.4	0	0	1	1	0	0	0	0	0	2	0	0	0	0	0	0	0	0	0	0	0	0	0	0	0
720	3	.2346	.1705	32.3	0	2	0	1	0	0	0	0	0	0	0	0	2	0	0	0	0	0	0	0	0	0	0	1	0
721	2	.2391	.1133	30.5	0	1	0	0	1	0	0	0	0	0	0	0	1	0	0	0	0	0	0	0	0	0	1	0	0
724	2	.0000	.0299	24.8	1	0	0	0	1	0	0	0	0	0	0	0	2	0	0	0	0	0	0	0	0	0	0	0	0
726	2	.2437	.1129	30.5	0	0	1	0	1	0	0	0	0	0	0	0	0	0	0	0	0	0	0	0	0	0	1	1	0
729	9	.2433	.5226	37.2	0	1	0	6	0	2	0	0	0	0	1	0	8	0	0	0	0	0	0	0	0	0	0	0	0
73	32	.4996	3.3703	45.3	0	8	2	6	9	5	2	0	1	1	0	0	22	0	3	0	1	1	0	0	0	0	0	3	0
730	6	.2019	.2954	34.7	1	0	0	1	3	1	0	0	0	0	0	0	2	0	0	0	0	0	0	0	0	0	4	0	0
732	3	.3829	.2504	34.0	0	0	1	0	1	0	0	1	0	0	0	0	1	0	0	0	0	0	0	0	0	1	1	0	0
736	4	.2220	.2176	33.4	0	0	3	1	0	0	0	0	0	0	0	0	3	0	0	0	0	0	0	0	0	0	1	0	0
738	3	.2346	.1705	32.3	0	0	2	0	0	1	0	0	0	0	0	0	2	0	0	0	0	0	0	0	0	0	0	1	0
739	3	.1993	.1435	31.6	0	2	0	0	0	0	1	0	0	0	0	0	2	0	0	0	0	0	0	1	0	0	0	0	0
74	29	.6220	3.7081	45.7	0	5	2	5	4	9	3	1	0	1	0	0	13	6	0	2	1	0	0	1	1	0	0	4	0
74-75	7	.0000	.1361	31.3	0	0	0	5	2	0	0	0	0	0	0	0	0	7	0	0	0	0	0	0	0	0	0	0	0
741	2	.2391	.1133	30.5	0	0	0	1	1	0	0	0	0	0	0	0	1	0	0	0	0	0	0	0	0	0	1	0	0
742	2	.2391	.1133	30.5	0	0	0	0	2	0	0	0	0	0	0	0	1	0	0	0	0	0	0	0	0	0	1	0	0
744	2	.1698	.1133	30.5	0	0	0	0	1	1	0	0	1	0	0	0	0	0	0	0	0	0	0	0	0	0	1	0	0
746	2	.0000	.0299	24.8	0	0	0	0	0	0	2	0	0	0	0	0	2	0	0	0	0	0	0	0	0	0	0	0	0
749	3	.0000	.0449	26.5	0	0	3	0	0	0	0	0	0	0	0	0	3	0	0	0	0	0	0	0	0	0	0	0	0
75	141	.5981	17.442	52.4	18	16	20	12	33	22	14	6	6	1	0	0	84	4	1	6	0	0	3	3	0	7	11	15	0
75/100	3	.0000	.0449	26.5	0	0	0	1	2	0	0	0	0	0	0	0	3	0	0	0	0	0	0	0	0	0	0	0	0
75%	12	.1712	.5747	37.6	1	0	1	4	4	1	1	0	1	1	0	0	10	0	0	0	0	0	0	0	0	0	0	0	0
75th	2	.0000	.0299	24.8	0	0	0	0	0	2	0	0	0	0	0	0	2	0	0	0	0	0	0	0	0	0	0	0	0
750	22	.6911	3.0921	44.9	3	0	5	2	7	3	2	0	0	1	0	0	5	4	0	5	0	0	0	1	0	2	3	1	0
752	2	.1523	.0721	28.6	1	0	0	0	0	1	0	0	0	0	1	0	0	0	0	0	0	0	0	0	0	0	0	1	0
753	3	.0000	.0449	26.5	0	0	2	0	1	0	0	0	0	0	0	0	3	0	0	0	0	0	0	0	0	0	0	0	0
755	3	.2444	.1814	32.6	2	0	0	0	0	0	1	0	0	0	0	0	0	2	0	0	0	0	0	0	0	0	1	0	0
756	2	.2417	.1211	30.8	0	0	0	1	0	1	0	0	0	0	0	0	1	1	0	0	0	0	0	0	0	0	0	0	0
758	2	.2351	.1166	30.7	0	0	0	0	1	1	0	0	0	0	0	0	0	1	0	0	0	0	0	0	0	0	0	1	0
76	32	.5741	3.8426	45.8	2	3	6	6	7	4	3	1	3	2	0	0	17	1	2	1	0	0	0	0	0	3	2	1	0
760	2	.1948	.1250	31.0	1	0	1	0	0	0	0	0	1	0	0	0	0	0	0	0	0	0	0	0	0	1	0	0	0
763	2	.0000	.0299	24.8	0	0	0	1	1	0	0	0	0	0	0	0	2	0	0	0	0	0	0	0	0	0	0	0	0

8Q 6853
9E 685487
7Q 687-714
5E 6874
3Q 688
8Q 689
8Q 6891
9E 69%
5Q 69th
8E 691
8E 691x3
8E 691x300
9Q 693-foot
4E 6950
8D 7X-3824
9L 7-
8J 7-D
5R 7-Up
3E 7-centimeter
8R 7-foot
7R 7-inch
XP 7-liter
9R 7-million-dollar
7E 7-year
9M 7-12
9M 7-13
9M 7-14
3E 7-15
4E 7-3
9E 7-7
7E 7/1000
5E 7/12-1/3
5E 7/12-1/4
7E 7/18
5E 7/6-1/3
5E 7/6-5/6
5E 7/8-1/2
5E 7/8-3/8
8E 7c
7E 7ft
9E 7x
8E 7x1
6E 7x10
8E 7x2
5E 7x24
5E 7x30
5E 7x5
5E 7x60
5E 7x8
4E 7x98
6R 70-foot
9E 70-second
7E 70-year
7M 70-1
6R 70-71
7E 70/100
XR 70%
5E 70x50
6E 70x600
5E 70x80
7D 700-foot
7Q 700-square-mile
5P 700-year
7E 700/1000
5Q 700's
7E 70000
8E 702-397
8E 704x6
8E 704x600
9P 705
3E 7052
6R 706-7
7Q 709
5R 71025
6F 711
6E 712/2
5F 718
7H 72-inch
6E 72/8
XR 72nd
5E 72x10
5E 72x100
7E 7200
9E 723
5E 7242
7F 725
8E 7263
8E 7281
7M 73-2
7E 73kg
4E 7305
5F 731
4E 732-page
XB 734
4R 737
6F 74-81
7Q 742-814
7R 743
8E 745
6R 748-9
7R 75-grain
7M 75-1
5P 750-mile
XH 7500
4E 7532
6P 754
8E 75414
5J 76-77
8D 76th
8E 76x3
8E 76x300
6Q 7600
8F 761st
5E 764

Word Type	F	D	U	SFI	3 Gr 3	4 Gr 4	5 Gr 5	6 Gr 6	7 Gr 7	8 Gr 8	9 Gr 9	X UnGr	A Read	B Eng & Gr	C Comp	D Lit	E Math	F Soc Stud	G Spell	H Sci	J Music	K Art	L Home Ec	M Shop	N Lib F	P Lib NF	Q Lib Ref	R Mag	S Rel
768	3	.2019	.1477	31.7	0	0	1	0	2	0	0	0	0	0	0	0	1	0	0	0	0	0	0	0	0	0	2	0	0
77	15	.5964	1.8795	42.7	1	1	3	2	4	4	0	0	3	2	0	0	4	2	0	0	0	1	0	0	0	2	0	1	0
776	3	.3467	.2520	34.0	0	0	0	1	1	0	0	1	1	0	0	0	1	0	0	0	0	0	0	0	0	0	0	1	0
777	2	.1362	.0684	28.3	0	0	0	1	0	1	0	0	0	0	1	0	1	0	0	0	0	0	0	0	0	0	0	0	0
78	45	.3243	3.3319	45.2	4	10	9	8	5	9	0	0	0	0	0	0	35	2	1	4	0	0	0	0	0	1	1	1	0
78's	2	.0000	.0162	22.1	0	0	0	0	0	2	0	0	0	0	0	0	0	0	0	0	2	0	0	0	0	0	0	0	0
780	3	.2254	.1785	32.5	0	0	1	0	1	0	1	0	0	0	0	0	0	1	0	2	0	0	0	0	0	0	0	0	0
781	2	.2285	.1129	30.5	0	1	0	0	1	0	0	0	0	0	0	0	0	1	0	0	0	0	0	0	0	0	1	0	0
782	2	.0000	.0299	24.8	0	1	1	0	0	0	0	0	0	0	0	0	2	0	0	0	0	0	0	0	0	0	0	0	0
785	2	.2391	.1133	30.5	0	0	1	0	0	0	1	0	0	0	0	0	1	0	0	0	0	0	0	0	0	0	1	0	0
786	3	.0000	.0449	26.5	3	0	0	0	0	0	0	0	0	0	0	0	3	0	0	0	0	0	0	0	0	0	0	0	0
7864	2	.0000	.0299	24.8	0	0	1	0	0	1	0	0	0	0	0	0	2	0	0	0	0	0	0	0	0	0	0	0	0
788	2	.2446	.1184	30.7	0	0	0	1	0	0	0	1	0	0	0	0	1	0	0	0	0	0	0	0	0	1	0	0	0
789	3	.2444	.1728	32.4	0	1	0	0	1	1	0	0	0	0	0	0	2	0	0	0	1	0	0	0	0	0	0	0	0
79	25	.5903	3.0600	44.9	4	3	6	1	6	3	1	1	1	0	0	0	12	0	2	3	0	0	0	0	1	3	1	2	0
790	3	.1434	.1493	31.7	0	1	0	0	2	0	0	0	1	0	0	0	2	0	0	0	0	0	0	0	0	0	0	0	0
7920	2	.0000	.0299	24.8	1	1	0	0	0	0	0	0	0	0	0	0	2	0	0	0	0	0	0	0	0	0	0	0	0
793	2	.2391	.1133	30.5	0	0	1	0	0	0	1	0	0	0	0	0	1	0	0	0	0	0	0	0	0	0	1	0	0
8	1092	.5810	131.59	61.2	198	165	155	145	157	128	131	13	33	12	1	5	763	34	29	42	24	1	20	16	1	26	29	56	0
8-cent	6	.0000	.0898	29.5	0	0	0	0	5	1	0	0	0	0	0	0	6	0	0	0	0	0	0	0	0	0	0	0	0
8-county	2	.0000	.0209	23.2	0	0	0	0	2	0	0	0	0	0	0	0	0	0	0	0	0	0	0	0	0	0	2	0	0
8-inch	5	.2628	.2818	34.5	0	0	0	0	1	0	3	1	0	0	0	0	0	0	0	1	0	0	3	1	0	0	0	0	0
8-ounce	3	.2159	.1533	31.9	0	0	2	0	0	0	1	0	0	0	0	0	2	0	0	0	0	0	1	0	0	0	0	0	0
8-year-old	2	.2346	.1166	30.7	0	0	0	1	0	0	0	1	0	0	0	0	0	0	0	1	0	0	0	0	0	0	0	1	0
8-1	3	.2451	.1726	32.4	0	0	0	0	0	2	1	0	0	0	0	0	1	0	0	1	0	0	0	1	0	0	0	0	0
8-10	2	.1620	.0760	28.8	0	0	0	0	0	1	1	0	0	0	0	0	0	0	0	0	0	0	0	1	0	0	0	1	0
8-18	2	.0000	.0394	26.0	0	0	0	0	0	0	2	0	0	0	0	0	0	0	0	2	0	0	0	0	0	0	0	0	0
8-19	2	.2446	.1257	31.0	0	0	1	0	0	0	1	0	0	0	0	0	0	1	0	1	0	0	0	0	0	0	0	0	0
8-2	4	.1457	.1444	31.6	0	1	0	0	0	2	1	0	0	0	0	0	2	0	0	0	0	0	0	2	0	0	0	0	0
8-3	4	.2865	.2625	34.2	0	0	0	0	0	2	2	0	0	0	0	0	2	0	0	1	0	0	0	1	0	0	0	0	0
8-9	4	.3546	.3122	34.9	0	0	1	0	0	1	2	0	0	0	0	0	0	1	0	0	1	0	0	0	0	0	0	2	0
8/10	5	.0000	.0748	28.7	0	0	1	0	4	0	0	0	0	0	0	0	5	0	0	0	0	0	0	0	0	0	0	0	0
8/100	2	.0000	.0299	24.8	0	0	0	1	1	0	0	0	0	0	0	0	2	0	0	0	0	0	0	0	0	0	0	0	0
8/12	7	.0000	.1048	30.2	0	3	2	1	0	1	0	0	0	0	0	0	7	0	0	0	0	0	0	0	0	0	0	0	0
8/15	6	.0000	.0898	29.5	0	0	1	0	5	0	0	0	0	0	0	0	6	0	0	0	0	0	0	0	0	0	0	0	0
8/3	5	.0000	.0748	28.7	0	0	5	0	0	0	0	0	0	0	0	0	5	0	0	0	0	0	0	0	0	0	0	0	0
8/4	9	.0000	.1347	31.3	2	1	1	4	1	0	0	0	0	0	0	0	9	0	0	0	0	0	0	0	0	0	0	0	0
8/8	7	.0000	.1048	30.2	2	0	0	4	1	0	0	0	0	0	0	0	7	0	0	0	0	0	0	0	0	0	0	0	0
8/9	2	.0000	.0299	24.8	0	0	0	1	0	1	0	0	0	0	0	0	2	0	0	0	0	0	0	0	0	0	0	0	0
8%	3	.2398	.1721	32.4	0	0	0	0	1	0	2	0	0	0	0	0	2	0	0	0	0	0	0	0	0	0	1	0	0
8r	2	.0000	.0299	24.8	0	0	0	0	0	0	2	0	0	0	0	0	2	0	0	0	0	0	0	0	0	0	0	0	0
8th	14	.4472	1.3211	41.2	1	1	3	1	1	1	5	1	0	1	0	0	4	0	1	0	0	0	0	0	0	0	7	1	0
8x16	2	.0000	.0299	24.8	0	0	0	0	0	2	0	0	0	0	0	0	2	0	0	0	0	0	0	0	0	0	0	0	0
8x6	2	.0000	.0299	24.8	0	2	0	0	0	0	0	0	0	0	0	0	2	0	0	0	0	0	0	0	0	0	0	0	0
80	167	.6503	22.311	53.5	24	21	23	24	27	27	19	2	10	3	0	1	75	8	6	27	1	0	1	0	0	3	15	17	0
80%	4	.2129	.2122	33.3	0	0	0	3	0	0	0	1	0	0	0	0	3	0	0	0	0	0	0	0	0	0	0	1	0
800	69	.7636	10.637	50.3	6	6	9	6	20	13	7	2	7	1	0	1	9	12	3	7	0	0	0	1	1	5	16	6	0
8000	12	.3447	.9701	39.9	1	2	0	2	4	1	2	0	2	0	0	0	7	1	0	0	0	0	0	0	0	0	0	2	0
803	3	.2435	.2274	33.6	0	0	0	1	2	0	0	0	2	0	0	0	0	1	0	0	0	0	0	0	0	0	0	0	0
809	3	.1823	.1405	31.5	0	1	0	0	1	1	0	0	0	0	0	0	0	1	0	0	0	0	0	0	0	0	2	0	0
81	34	.5607	3.9434	46.0	2	3	3	2	6	9	7	2	0	1	0	0	21	1	4	0	0	1	0	0	0	1	3	2	0
814	2	.1738	.0790	29.0	0	0	0	0	1	0	1	0	0	0	0	0	0	0	0	0	0	0	0	1	0	0	1	0	0
82	19	.5286	2.0966	43.2	3	1	1	4	5	2	3	0	0	0	0	0	4	5	4	0	0	0	0	0	0	0	1	5	0
82-inch	2	.2437	.1129	30.5	0	1	0	0	0	1	0	0	0	0	0	0	0	0	0	0	0	0	0	0	0	0	1	1	0
82x6	2	.0000	.0299	24.8	0	0	0	2	0	0	0	0	0	0	0	0	2	0	0	0	0	0	0	0	0	0	0	0	0
823	5	.0770	.0947	29.8	0	0	0	1	0	0	4	0	0	0	0	0	0	0	0	0	0	0	0	4	0	0	1	0	0
827	2	.2446	.1123	30.5	0	0	0	0	0	1	0	1	0	1	0	0	0	0	0	0	0	0	0	0	0	0	1	0	0
83	23	.4531	2.2428	43.5	2	3	4	4	4	0	6	0	2	1	0	0	12	0	4	0	0	0	0	0	0	0	4	0	0
832	5	.2429	.2911	34.6	0	0	1	1	1	1	1	0	0	0	0	0	3	0	0	0	0	0	0	0	0	0	0	2	0
8356	2	.0000	.0299	24.8	0	0	0	2	0	0	0	0	0	0	0	0	2	0	0	0	0	0	0	0	0	0	0	0	0
838	7	.0000	.1048	30.2	0	0	4	0	3	0	0	0	0	0	0	0	7	0	0	0	0	0	0	0	0	0	0	0	0
84	38	.5368	4.2693	46.3	1	6	9	3	8	7	1	3	1	1	0	0	25	1	1	1	0	0	0	1	0	1	3	3	0
84-unit	4	.0000	.0599	27.8	0	0	0	0	0	4	0	0	0	0	0	0	4	0	0	0	0	0	0	0	0	0	0	0	0
84-28	2	.0000	.0299	24.8	0	1	1	0	0	0	0	0	0	0	0	0	2	0	0	0	0	0	0	0	0	0	0	0	0
840	9	.2684	.5891	37.7	3	0	2	0	1	3	0	0	1	0	0	0	6	0	0	0	0	0	0	0	0	0	2	0	0
843	2	.2391	.1133	30.5	0	0	0	0	1	0	1	0	0	0	0	0	1	0	0	0	0	0	0	0	0	0	1	0	0
846	4	.2129	.2122	33.3	0	1	2	0	0	0	1	0	0	0	0	0	3	0	0	0	0	0	0	0	0	0	0	1	0
847	7	.0000	.1048	30.2	0	0	1	0	5	1	0	0	0	0	0	0	7	0	0	0	0	0	0	0	0	0	0	0	0
848	2	.2417	.1211	30.8	0	1	1	0	0	0	0	0	0	0	0	0	1	1	0	0	0	0	0	0	0	0	0	0	0
85	66	.7040	9.4111	49.7	7	12	8	5	15	7	11	1	1	2	0	1	29	8	5	4	4	0	0	1	0	0	4	7	0
85%	2	.0000	.0299	24.8	0	0	0	0	0	0	2	0	0	0	0	0	2	0	0	0	0	0	0	0	0	0	0	0	0
850	7	.3892	.6344	38.0	0	1	0	1	3	1	1	0	2	0	0	0	0	0	0	1	0	0	0	0	0	1	0	3	0
851	2	.0000	.0209	23.2	0	0	1	0	1	0	0	0	0	0	0	0	0	0	0	0	0	0	0	0	0	0	2	0	0
857	2	.2408	.1204	30.8	1	0	0	0	0	0	0	1	0	0	0	0	0	1	0	0	0	0	0	0	0	1	0	0	0
86	40	.6354	5.1866	47.1	5	4	5	4	11	5	5	1	0	4	0	1	17	6	7	1	1	0	0	2	0	0	1	0	0
860	2	.0000	.0299	24.8	0	1	1	0	0	0	0	0	0	0	0	0	2	0	0	0	0	0	0	0	0	0	0	0	0
8634	2	.0000	.0299	24.8	0	2	0	0	0	0	0	0	0	0	0	0	2	0	0	0	0	0	0	0	0	0	0	0	0
864	6	.3750	.4962	37.0	0	1	1	1	1	1	1	0	0	0	0	0	3	1	0	1	0	0	0	1	0	0	0	0	0
867	3	.0000	.0449	26.5	1	0	1	0	0	1	0	0	0	0	0	0	3	0	0	0	0	0	0	0	0	0	0	0	0
87	36	.7210	5.2844	47.2	5	6	5	3	9	6	1	1	5	2	0	0	12	4	3	1	1	0	0	0	1	1	1	5	0
87%	2	.1648	.0800	29.0	0	0	0	0	0	1	1	0	0	0	0	0	1	0	0	0	0	0	1	0	0	0	0	0	0
870	2	.2427	.1159	30.6	0	0	0	2	0	0	0	0	0	0	0	0	1	0	0	0	0	0	0	0	0	0	0	1	0
873	3	.0000	.0449	26.5	0	0	0	0	0	0	3	0	0	0	0	0	3	0	0	0	0	0	0	0	0	0	0	0	0
88	44	.6379	5.7303	47.6	4	14	4	9	5	6	2	0	0	8	0	0	20	2	3	4	0	0	0	2	0	1	3	1	0

4E 765
7R 766
4E 767
3E 7684
4E 769
7P 77-footers
7Q 771
5E 772
9H 774
5B 78-79
6Q 78%
7R 7800-foot
5F 784
4E 7863
4P 787
4B 787-0304
5E 7888
8F 789-807
XP 791
9M 796
7R 798
3E 8-hour
7R 8-in
8L 8-inch-square
8E 8-pound
8E 8-11
9H 8-12
9H 8-17
8B 8-19's
9H 8-20
9H 8-22
9H 8-23
9H 8-24
9E 8-4
4E 8-5
9H 8-6
9R 8-8
5E 8/18
7E 8/2
7E 8/20
4E 8/24
8E 8/7
6P 8g
4B 8h
5E 8x
5E 8x/3y
5E 8xn
8E 8x0
6E 8x2
8E 8x3
6E 8x30
4E 8x5
4E 8x50
4E 8x51
5E 8x7
8E 8x8x8x8
7P 80-footer
9Q 80-inch
6B 80-81
7E 80th
8H 800-and
7Q 800-mile-thick
8A 800-pound
8J 800-1150
6F 800's
3P 8000-foot
8E 801
9E 804
9R 805546
5Q 806
9Q 808
8R 81-foot
7E 810
7R 810-inch
9M 811
6E 8134
8M 82-degree
4B 82-83
5J 82-89
5E 820
9M 822-824
7E 8253
3Q 826
8G 827-869
7E 829
9H 83-ton
4E 83-6
4E 83-7
6R 830-31
9E 8333
7E 835
4P 836
6R 836-7
5Q 839
8R 84-year-old
4E 84-56
6E 8437
8E 847-568
7M 85Hoover
7R 85-foot
6F 8500-foot
6A 852
5Q 852-foot
4B 85232
6E 8526/10
3E 854
5E 8541
9M 855
8E 856
5E 8561
7E 857/100
9M 858
8F 859
7M 86-1
7M 86-2
8E 86-38
7B 86th
7Q 860-mile
3E 8603
9E 86407600325
7R 869
7E 87-88
8E 8742
4E 875
8E 876
4B 88-89

Word Type	F	D	U	SFI	3 Gr 3	4 Gr 4	5 Gr 5	6 Gr 6	7 Gr 7	8 Gr 8	9 Gr 9	X UnGr	A Read	B Eng & Gr	C Comp	D Lit	E Math	F Soc Stud	G Spell	H Sci	J Music	K Art	L Home Ec	M Shop	N Lib F	P Lib NF	Q Lib Ref	R Mag	S Rel
880	7	.4360	.6513	38.1	2	0	0	1	1	3	0	0	0	0	0	0	3	0	0	1	2	0	0	0	0	0	1	0	0
884	2	.2391	.1133	30.5	1	0	1	0	0	0	0	0	0	0	0	0	1	0	0	0	0	0	0	0	0	0	1	0	0
89	31	.4917	3.2173	45.1	2	7	8	5	6	2	1	0	0	3	0	0	17	3	5	2	0	0	0	0	0	0	1	0	0
891	2	.1972	.1262	31.0	1	1	0	0	0	0	0	0	1	0	0	0	1	0	0	0	0	0	0	0	0	0	0	0	0
895	2	.0000	.0299	24.8	0	0	0	0	0	0	2	0	0	0	0	0	2	0	0	0	0	0	0	0	0	0	0	0	0
896	2	.0000	.0299	24.8	0	0	0	1	0	1	0	0	0	0	0	0	2	0	0	0	0	0	0	0	0	0	0	0	0
897	2	.0000	.0299	24.8	0	0	1	0	0	1	0	0	0	0	0	0	2	0	0	0	0	0	0	0	0	0	0	0	0
899	2	.2391	.1133	30.5	0	0	1	0	0	1	0	0	0	0	0	0	1	0	0	0	0	0	0	0	0	0	1	0	0
9	811	.5463	92.645	59.7	154	151	85	79	140	95	97	10	19	12	6	1	592	32	17	38	11	0	10	9	0	14	21	29	0
9B	2	.0000	.0219	23.4	0	0	0	0	0	0	2	0	0	2	0	0	0	0	0	0	0	0	0	0	0	0	0	0	0
9-inch	8	.0553	.1197	30.8	0	0	0	0	2	0	6	0	0	0	0	0	0	0	0	0	0	0	7	0	0	0	0	1	0
9-10	5	.0000	.0406	26.1	0	0	0	0	0	5	0	0	0	0	0	0	0	0	5	0	0	0	0	0	0	0	0	0	0
9-11	2	.2427	.1159	30.6	0	0	1	0	0	0	1	0	0	0	0	0	1	0	0	0	0	0	0	0	0	0	0	1	0
9-12	3	.2390	.1719	32.4	0	0	0	0	2	1	0	0	0	0	0	1	2	0	0	0	0	0	0	0	0	0	0	0	0
9-16	2	.2289	.1077	30.3	0	1	0	1	0	0	0	0	0	0	0	0	1	0	1	0	0	0	0	0	0	0	0	0	0
9-20	2	.2413	.1212	30.8	0	0	0	1	1	0	0	0	0	0	0	0	1	0	0	1	0	0	0	0	0	0	0	0	0
9-29	2	.1249	.0685	28.4	0	0	0	0	0	1	1	0	0	0	0	0	0	0	0	1	0	0	0	1	0	0	0	0	0
9-30	2	.1249	.0685	28.4	0	0	0	0	0	1	1	0	0	0	0	0	0	0	0	1	0	0	0	1	0	0	0	0	0
9-9	2	.2413	.1212	30.8	0	0	1	0	0	0	1	0	0	0	0	0	1	0	0	1	0	0	0	0	0	0	0	0	0
9/10	10	.0965	.3291	35.2	0	1	4	1	4	0	0	0	0	0	0	0	9	0	0	1	0	0	0	0	0	0	0	0	0
9/12	14	.0000	.2096	33.2	0	5	1	2	3	0	3	0	0	0	0	0	14	0	0	0	0	0	0	0	0	0	0	0	0
9/17	3	.0000	.0449	26.5	0	0	0	0	3	0	0	0	0	0	0	0	3	0	0	0	0	0	0	0	0	0	0	0	0
9/2	3	.0000	.0449	26.5	0	0	1	1	0	1	0	0	0	0	0	0	3	0	0	0	0	0	0	0	0	0	0	0	0
9/4	2	.0000	.0299	24.8	0	0	0	0	2	0	0	0	0	0	0	0	2	0	0	0	0	0	0	0	0	0	0	0	0
9/5	3	.0000	.0449	26.5	0	0	0	0	1	0	2	0	0	0	0	0	3	0	0	0	0	0	0	0	0	0	0	0	0
9/8	2	.2287	.1077	30.3	0	0	0	0	2	0	0	0	0	0	0	0	1	0	0	0	1	0	0	0	0	0	0	0	0
9%	2	.2391	.1133	30.5	0	1	0	0	0	0	1	0	0	0	0	0	1	0	0	0	0	0	0	0	0	0	1	0	0
9's	6	.1851	.2880	34.6	0	0	4	0	2	0	0	0	0	0	0	1	5	0	0	0	0	0	0	0	0	0	0	0	0
9th	9	.6639	1.2121	40.8	0	1	1	0	4	1	2	0	0	1	0	0	3	0	1	0	0	0	0	0	1	1	1	1	0
9x3	2	.0000	.0299	24.8	0	0	2	0	0	0	0	0	0	0	0	0	2	0	0	0	0	0	0	0	0	0	0	0	0
9x8	2	.0000	.0299	24.8	0	2	0	0	0	0	0	0	0	0	0	0	2	0	0	0	0	0	0	0	0	0	0	0	0
90	186	.6439	24.567	53.9	23	23	22	20	38	34	24	2	8	2	0	0	94	21	8	11	0	0	0	8	4	4	13	13	0
90-mile	2	.1948	.1250	31.0	0	0	1	1	0	0	0	0	1	0	0	0	0	0	0	0	0	0	0	0	0	1	0	0	0
90/10	2	.0000	.0243	23.9	0	0	0	0	2	0	0	0	0	0	0	0	0	0	0	0	0	0	0	0	0	0	0	2	0
90%	4	.0000	.0599	27.8	0	0	0	2	1	0	1	0	0	0	0	0	4	0	0	0	0	0	0	0	0	0	0	0	0
900	30	.5909	3.6935	45.7	2	9	3	1	4	6	3	2	3	3	0	0	10	3	0	1	0	0	0	0	0	0	4	6	0
9000	5	.2237	.3494	35.4	1	0	0	0	4	0	0	0	3	0	0	0	2	0	0	0	0	0	0	0	0	0	0	0	0
904	2	.2437	.1129	30.5	0	0	0	0	2	0	0	0	0	0	0	0	0	0	0	0	0	0	0	0	0	0	1	1	0
906	2	.2391	.1133	30.5	0	0	0	0	0	0	2	0	0	0	0	0	1	0	0	0	0	0	0	0	0	0	1	0	0
91	20	.4811	2.0437	43.1	4	1	6	4	2	2	1	0	0	0	0	0	9	4	4	2	0	0	0	0	0	0	1	0	0
91502	2	.0000	.0243	23.9	0	0	0	0	2	0	0	0	0	0	0	0	0	0	0	0	0	0	0	0	0	0	0	2	0
916	2	.1738	.0790	29.0	0	0	0	0	0	1	1	0	0	0	0	0	0	0	0	0	0	0	0	1	0	0	1	0	0
918	3	.1434	.1493	31.7	2	1	0	0	0	0	0	0	1	0	0	0	2	0	0	0	0	0	0	0	0	0	0	0	0
92	38	.5185	4.1458	46.2	1	3	3	1	13	9	7	1	1	2	0	0	26	1	2	2	0	1	0	0	0	0	1	2	0
92U238	2	.0000	.0394	26.0	0	0	0	1	0	0	1	0	0	0	0	0	0	0	0	2	0	0	0	0	0	0	0	0	0
920	4	.3748	.3292	35.2	0	1	0	0	2	0	1	0	0	1	0	0	2	0	0	0	0	0	0	0	0	1	0	0	0
921	3	.2086	.1620	32.1	0	1	0	0	1	0	1	0	0	0	0	0	2	1	0	0	0	0	0	0	0	0	0	0	0
923	2	.2391	.1133	30.5	0	0	0	2	0	0	0	0	0	0	0	0	1	0	0	0	0	0	0	0	0	0	1	0	0
928	2	.0000	.0299	24.8	0	0	1	0	0	1	0	0	0	0	0	0	2	0	0	0	0	0	0	0	0	0	0	0	0
93	34	.7042	4.8558	46.9	3	3	2	4	9	6	6	1	1	3	0	0	9	5	6	7	1	1	0	1	0	0	0	0	0
931	3	.1277	.1363	31.3	0	0	0	0	3	0	0	0	1	0	0	0	0	0	0	0	0	0	0	0	0	0	0	2	0
94	27	.7670	4.1555	46.2	3	4	3	3	5	5	4	0	2	1	0	1	10	1	3	0	2	1	2	1	0	0	1	2	0
943	2	.2351	.1166	30.7	0	0	0	0	1	1	0	0	0	0	0	0	0	1	0	0	0	0	0	0	0	0	0	1	0
946	2	.2391	.1133	30.5	0	0	0	0	2	0	0	0	0	0	0	0	1	0	0	0	0	0	0	0	0	0	1	0	0
95	55	.6464	7.2731	48.6	2	7	13	10	12	6	4	1	1	1	0	0	29	3	1	4	0	1	1	0	0	2	3	9	0
95%	2	.2427	.1159	30.6	0	0	0	0	0	1	1	0	0	0	0	0	1	0	0	0	0	0	0	0	0	0	0	1	0
951	2	.1483	.0728	28.6	0	0	1	0	0	0	1	0	0	0	0	0	0	0	0	0	0	0	0	1	0	1	0	0	0
952	2	.1249	.0685	28.4	0	0	0	0	0	1	1	0	0	0	0	0	0	0	0	1	0	0	0	1	0	0	0	0	0
954	2	.1457	.0722	28.6	0	0	1	0	0	0	1	0	0	0	0	0	1	0	0	0	0	0	0	1	0	0	0	0	0
955	2	.2413	.1212	30.8	0	0	0	0	1	0	0	1	0	0	0	0	1	0	0	1	0	0	0	0	0	0	0	0	0
958	3	.0000	.0449	26.5	0	0	0	3	0	0	0	0	0	0	0	0	3	0	0	0	0	0	0	0	0	0	0	0	0
96	32	.4000	2.7946	44.5	2	7	6	4	8	4	1	0	0	0	0	2	21	4	4	1	0	0	0	0	0	0	0	0	0
960	3	.3759	.2498	34.0	1	0	2	0	0	0	0	0	0	0	0	0	1	0	0	1	0	0	0	0	0	0	1	0	0
964	4	.3233	.3124	34.9	0	0	1	0	1	1	1	0	1	0	0	0	2	0	0	0	0	0	0	0	0	0	1	0	0
966	2	.2446	.1123	30.5	0	0	1	0	0	1	0	0	0	1	0	0	0	0	0	0	0	0	0	0	0	0	1	0	0
968	2	.2401	.1133	30.5	0	0	2	0	0	0	0	0	0	0	0	0	0	0	0	0	0	0	0	0	0	1	1	0	0
97	25	.6277	3.2074	45.1	4	3	3	4	5	4	1	1	0	0	0	0	10	2	3	2	2	0	1	0	0	0	0	5	0
974	2	.0000	.0299	24.8	0	0	0	0	2	0	0	0	0	0	0	0	2	0	0	0	0	0	0	0	0	0	0	0	0
975	2	.0000	.0299	24.8	0	0	0	0	0	0	2	0	0	0	0	0	2	0	0	0	0	0	0	0	0	0	0	0	0
978	3	.0965	.0750	28.7	0	0	1	0	0	0	2	0	0	0	0	0	1	0	0	0	0	0	0	2	0	0	0	0	0
98	57	.5577	6.6682	48.2	7	8	15	10	8	5	3	1	4	2	0	0	32	3	4	4	0	0	0	0	0	3	3	2	0
984	2	.2417	.1211	30.8	1	1	0	0	0	0	0	0	0	0	0	0	1	1	0	0	0	0	0	0	0	0	0	0	0
985	2	.0000	.0299	24.8	0	0	1	0	0	1	0	0	0	0	0	0	2	0	0	0	0	0	0	0	0	0	0	0	0
99	48	.5805	5.7786	47.6	3	6	7	12	12	5	1	2	1	1	0	0	23	1	6	9	1	0	0	0	0	0	3	3	0
99/100	4	.0000	.0599	27.8	0	2	0	2	0	0	0	0	0	0	0	0	4	0	0	0	0	0	0	0	0	0	0	0	0
99%	2	.1972	.1262	31.0	0	0	0	0	1	1	0	0	1	0	0	0	1	0	0	0	0	0	0	0	0	0	0	0	0
99th	4	.2152	.2714	34.3	0	0	0	2	0	2	0	0	2	0	0	0	0	2	0	0	0	0	0	0	0	0	0	0	0
999	9	.1040	.3090	34.9	6	1	1	0	0	0	0	1	0	0	0	0	8	0	0	1	0	0	0	0	0	0	0	0	0
9999	2	.0000	.0299	24.8	1	0	0	0	1	0	0	0	0	0	0	0	2	0	0	0	0	0	0	0	0	0	0	0	0
$	11	.0000	.1647	32.2	3	1	0	0	1	2	0	4	0	0	0	0	11	0	0	0	0	0	0	0	0	0	0	0	0
$0	4	.0000	.0599	27.8	0	0	0	0	0	0	4	0	0	0	0	0	4	0	0	0	0	0	0	0	0	0	0	0	0
$1	101	.1986	5.1156	47.1	20	12	24	8	7	7	17	6	0	2	0	0	85	0	0	0	0	0	0	0	0	0	0	14	0
$10	30	.3439	2.3030	43.6	4	6	3	6	3	2	3	3	0	0	0	0	20	0	0	0	0	0	0	0	0	1	2	7	0
$100	30	.3866	2.5272	44.0	0	0	2	6	11	1	9	1	0	0	0	0	15	0	0	0	0	0	0	0	0	1	3	11	0

9E 88/
3A 88%
4G 88th
4E 8800
9Q 881
7Q 883
4A 886
7F 887
7R 89-yard
8C 89-90
8D 9W-7679
4E 9-
4E 9-cent
4E 9-day
XP 9-liter
3P 9-principle
XR 9-year-old
8E 9-14
7H 9-21
9H 9-28
8M 9-31
8M 9-32
8M 9-33
8M 9-34
4E 9-4
6E 9/1
7E 9/1000
5E 9/16
5E 9/18
4E 9/27
8E 9/30
8E 9/6
9M 9/64
9E 9/80
9E 9a
8E 9x
8E 9x1
5E 9x6
5E 9x9
9H 90Th234
8M 90-degree
5P 90-foot-high
5Q 90-foot-square
7Q 90-footer
8R 90-minute
4E 90-word
6E 90/100
8E 90/120
7Q 90s
4G 90th
7H 900-foot
XH 900-foot-long
5P 900-odd
7A 900's
7R 90006
7E 9003
8F 901
6E 9021
7Q 903
3E 9035
7Q 908
8Q 909
3J 91a
9R 91st
3E 910
XR 912
7R 91324
7E 916/10
8F 917
8E 92-47
6R 92-65
6R 92-72
8Q 92d
8E 92nd
5Q 9200
XR 92262
4Q 925
7R 92502
7M 926
4F 9280
5E 929
3Q 930
9Q 935
4E 937
5E 9376
4F 938
5Q 939
7R 94-inch
7H 940
4B 94127
3E 944
6E 945
4B 947
4A 948
4E 95-cent
4E 950
8E 9500
5E 956
3A 959
6F 96-97
8H 961
5E 962
7E 9628
8Q 965
6E 967
8F 969th
8E 970
8E 971
8E 973
7R 974-foot
9M 976
XR 9760
8D 9762
9M 977
9M 979
4H 98/100
7E 98x10
4E 98x7
7E 980
7R 986
6P 987
8E 99/300
5E 99x99
9E 990
9A 993
9Q 995
7R 995-percent
6Q (C2H4Cl)2S**
9E (a/b)2**
6G (s)incerely
6G (y)ours

Word Type	F	D	U	SFI	3 Gr 3	4 Gr 4	5 Gr 5	6 Gr 6	7 Gr 7	8 Gr 8	9 Gr 9	X UnGr	A Read	B Eng & Gr	C Comp	D Lit	E Math	F Soc Stud	G Spell	H Sci	J Music	K Art	L Home Ec	M Shop	N Lib F	P Lib NF	Q Lib Ref	R Mag	S Rel
$1000	3	.0000	.0449	26.5	0	0	0	0	2	0	1	0	0	0	0	0	3	0	0	0	0	0	0	0	0	0	0	0	0
$105	2	.2427	.1159	30.6	0	0	0	0	0	0	2	0	0	0	0	0	1	0	0	0	0	0	0	0	0	0	0	1	0
$11	6	.3728	.4895	36.9	0	0	0	0	2	3	1	0	0	0	0	0	3	0	0	0	0	0	0	0	0	0	1	2	0
$110	2	.0000	.0299	24.8	0	0	0	2	0	0	0	0	0	0	0	0	2	0	0	0	0	0	0	0	0	0	0	0	0
$12	17	.2693	1.0761	40.3	2	2	3	4	2	1	3	0	0	0	0	0	13	0	0	0	0	0	0	0	0	0	1	3	0
$120	2	.2442	.1134	30.5	0	0	0	0	0	0	2	0	0	1	0	0	0	0	0	0	0	0	0	0	0	0	0	1	0
$125	2	.0000	.0299	24.8	0	0	0	0	1	0	1	0	0	0	0	0	2	0	0	0	0	0	0	0	0	0	0	0	0
$13	7	.3486	.5372	37.3	0	1	1	2	1	1	1	0	0	0	0	0	5	0	0	0	0	0	1	0	0	0	1	0	0
$14	7	.3591	.5546	37.4	0	0	2	3	2	0	0	0	0	0	0	0	4	0	0	0	0	0	0	0	0	0	1	2	0
$15	15	.4426	1.4130	41.5	0	1	0	2	4	0	7	1	0	0	0	0	8	0	0	0	0	0	1	0	0	0	1	5	0
$150	5	.4309	.4535	36.6	0	0	1	0	1	1	2	0	0	0	0	0	1	0	0	0	0	0	1	0	0	0	1	2	0
$1500	2	.2427	.1159	30.6	0	1	0	0	0	0	0	1	0	0	0	0	1	0	0	0	0	0	0	0	0	0	0	1	0
$151	2	.0000	.0299	24.8	0	0	1	0	0	1	0	0	0	0	0	0	2	0	0	0	0	0	0	0	0	0	0	0	0
$16	4	.3483	.3051	34.8	0	0	1	1	0	0	1	1	0	0	0	0	1	0	0	0	0	0	0	0	0	0	2	1	0
$160	2	.2427	.1159	30.6	0	0	0	1	0	0	0	1	0	0	0	0	1	0	0	0	0	0	0	0	0	0	0	1	0
$17	10	.1298	.3829	35.8	2	0	3	3	1	1	0	0	0	0	0	0	9	0	0	0	0	0	0	0	0	0	0	1	0
$175	3	.2346	.1705	32.3	0	0	0	0	1	0	2	0	0	0	0	0	2	0	0	0	0	0	0	0	0	0	0	1	0
$18	11	.4314	1.0188	40.1	2	0	3	2	2	1	1	0	0	0	0	0	6	0	0	0	0	0	0	0	0	2	2	1	0
$180	3	.2187	.1555	31.9	0	0	0	0	2	0	1	0	0	2	0	0	0	0	0	0	0	0	0	0	0	0	0	1	0
$19	3	.2121	.1560	31.9	0	0	0	1	1	0	1	0	0	0	0	0	1	0	0	0	0	0	0	0	0	0	0	2	0
$2	100	.3257	7.5766	48.8	22	14	17	7	10	9	16	5	10	0	0	0	70	0	0	0	0	0	0	0	0	2	5	13	0
$20	16	.4193	1.4854	41.7	1	2	1	4	2	3	3	0	2	0	0	0	9	0	0	0	0	0	0	0	0	1	1	3	0
$200	17	.4231	1.5734	42.0	0	0	1	2	3	5	6	0	2	0	0	1	3	0	0	0	0	0	0	0	0	0	2	9	0
$2000	4	.3767	.3699	35.7	0	0	1	0	2	1	0	0	2	0	0	0	1	0	0	0	0	0	0	0	0	0	0	1	0
$21	2	.2391	.1133	30.5	0	0	0	0	1	0	1	0	0	0	0	0	1	0	0	0	0	0	0	0	0	0	1	0	0
$22	3	.2197	.2090	33.2	0	2	0	0	1	0	0	0	2	0	0	0	0	0	0	0	0	0	0	0	0	0	1	0	0
$23	2	.0000	.0299	24.8	0	0	1	0	0	0	1	0	0	0	0	0	2	0	0	0	0	0	0	0	0	0	0	0	0
$24	3	.0000	.0449	26.5	0	0	0	0	1	0	2	0	0	0	0	0	3	0	0	0	0	0	0	0	0	0	0	0	0
$240	2	.0000	.0243	23.9	0	0	0	0	0	0	2	0	0	0	0	0	0	0	0	0	0	0	0	0	0	0	0	2	0
$25	14	.2957	.9450	39.8	1	0	0	1	1	2	3	6	0	0	0	0	5	0	0	0	0	0	0	0	0	1	0	8	0
$250	8	.3272	.6306	38.0	0	0	1	2	2	0	2	1	2	0	0	0	3	0	0	0	0	0	0	0	0	0	0	3	0
$26	2	.2427	.1159	30.6	0	0	0	0	2	0	0	0	0	0	0	0	1	0	0	0	0	0	0	0	0	0	0	1	0
$27	2	.2391	.1133	30.5	0	0	0	0	2	0	0	0	0	0	0	0	1	0	0	0	0	0	0	0	0	0	1	0	0
$28	2	.2427	.1159	30.6	0	0	0	0	2	0	0	0	0	0	0	0	1	0	0	0	0	0	0	0	0	0	0	1	0
$288	2	.0000	.0299	24.8	0	0	1	0	0	1	0	0	0	0	0	0	2	0	0	0	0	0	0	0	0	0	0	0	0
$3	56	.2214	3.1429	45.0	9	10	13	4	6	7	6	1	3	0	0	0	46	0	0	0	0	0	0	0	0	0	2	5	0
$30	17	.5298	1.9144	42.8	2	0	2	1	3	3	6	0	3	0	0	0	5	0	0	0	0	0	1	0	0	0	3	5	0
$300	8	.5121	.8923	39.5	0	0	0	1	4	0	2	1	2	1	0	0	3	1	0	0	0	0	0	0	0	0	0	1	0
$3000	2	.2427	.1159	30.6	0	0	0	0	2	0	0	0	0	0	0	0	1	0	0	0	0	0	0	0	0	0	0	1	0
$32	3	.0000	.0449	26.5	0	0	2	0	1	0	0	0	0	0	0	0	3	0	0	0	0	0	0	0	0	0	0	0	0
$34	5	.1926	.2474	33.9	0	0	2	0	2	0	1	0	0	0	0	0	4	0	0	0	0	0	0	0	0	0	0	1	0
$35	12	.4613	1.1930	40.8	2	1	1	2	3	1	2	0	1	0	0	0	6	0	0	0	0	0	0	0	0	1	2	2	0
$350	3	.3841	.2496	34.0	0	0	0	0	1	0	1	1	0	0	0	0	1	0	0	0	0	0	0	0	0	0	1	1	0
$36	2	.0000	.0299	24.8	0	0	0	2	0	0	0	0	0	0	0	0	2	0	0	0	0	0	0	0	0	0	0	0	0
$37	2	.0000	.0219	23.4	0	0	0	0	0	0	2	0	0	2	0	0	0	0	0	0	0	0	0	0	0	0	0	0	0
$375	4	.1786	.1933	32.9	1	0	1	1	0	0	1	0	0	0	0	0	3	1	0	0	0	0	0	0	0	0	0	0	0
$38	3	.0000	.0449	26.5	0	0	2	0	0	1	0	0	0	0	0	0	3	0	0	0	0	0	0	0	0	0	0	0	0
$39	3	.0000	.0449	26.5	0	0	2	0	1	0	0	0	0	0	0	0	3	0	0	0	0	0	0	0	0	0	0	0	0
$4	42	.3542	3.3317	45.2	2	4	9	4	6	6	4	7	1	0	0	0	28	2	0	0	0	0	0	0	0	0	3	8	0
$40	11	.3413	.8358	39.2	0	4	0	1	3	0	2	1	0	0	0	0	6	0	0	0	0	0	0	0	0	0	1	4	0
$400	10	.5491	1.2301	40.9	0	0	0	0	4	6	0	0	6	0	0	0	1	1	0	0	0	0	0	0	0	1	0	1	0
$42	3	.2346	.1705	32.3	0	1	0	0	0	0	2	0	0	0	0	0	2	0	0	0	0	0	0	0	0	0	0	1	0
$44	3	.0000	.0449	26.5	0	0	1	2	0	0	0	0	0	0	0	0	3	0	0	0	0	0	0	0	0	0	0	0	0
$45	2	.1972	.1262	31.0	0	0	0	0	1	0	1	0	1	0	0	0	1	0	0	0	0	0	0	0	0	0	0	0	0
$450	5	.2888	.3568	35.5	0	0	1	0	1	0	3	0	1	0	0	0	3	0	0	0	0	0	0	0	0	0	0	1	0
$46	2	.2427	.1159	30.6	0	0	0	1	0	0	1	0	0	0	0	0	1	0	0	0	0	0	0	0	0	0	0	1	0
$49	5	.1602	.2108	33.2	0	0	1	0	1	0	1	2	0	0	0	0	1	0	0	0	0	0	0	0	0	0	0	4	0
$5	62	.4031	5.5268	47.4	9	13	8	4	10	9	6	3	4	1	0	0	42	4	0	0	0	0	0	0	0	2	4	5	0
$50	20	.4519	1.9926	43.0	1	0	2	5	5	2	1	4	4	0	0	0	5	1	0	0	0	0	0	0	0	0	2	8	0
$500	15	.5590	1.7842	42.5	0	1	1	2	3	3	4	1	3	0	0	0	4	2	0	0	0	0	0	0	0	1	1	4	0
$51	3	.2121	.1560	31.9	0	0	1	0	0	0	0	2	0	0	0	0	1	0	0	0	0	0	0	0	0	0	0	2	0
$52	2	.2437	.1129	30.5	0	0	0	0	1	0	0	1	0	0	0	0	0	0	0	0	0	0	0	0	0	0	1	1	0
$55	4	.2427	.2319	33.7	0	0	2	0	2	0	0	0	0	0	0	0	2	0	0	0	0	0	0	0	0	0	0	2	0
$58	2	.2351	.1166	30.7	0	0	0	1	0	0	1	0	0	0	0	0	0	1	0	0	0	0	0	0	0	0	0	1	0
$6	26	.3976	2.2909	43.6	6	5	3	4	1	3	2	2	2	1	0	0	17	0	0	0	0	0	0	0	0	1	1	4	0
$60	7	.2341	.3937	36.0	0	1	3	0	1	0	2	0	0	0	0	0	3	0	0	0	0	0	0	0	0	0	0	4	0
$600	12	.3467	.9486	39.8	1	0	0	2	2	1	6	0	1	0	0	0	5	1	0	0	0	0	0	0	0	0	0	5	0
$64	2	.2427	.1159	30.6	0	0	0	0	1	0	1	0	0	0	0	0	1	0	0	0	0	0	0	0	0	0	0	1	0
$65	2	.0000	.0299	24.8	0	0	2	0	0	0	0	0	0	0	0	0	2	0	0	0	0	0	0	0	0	0	0	0	0
$68	2	.0000	.0299	24.8	0	0	1	0	0	1	0	0	0	0	0	0	2	0	0	0	0	0	0	0	0	0	0	0	0
$7	25	.3756	2.0998	43.2	4	3	9	2	3	1	1	2	1	0	0	0	17	3	0	0	0	0	0	0	0	1	1	2	0
$700	3	.2121	.1560	31.9	0	0	0	0	3	0	0	0	0	0	0	0	1	0	0	0	0	0	0	0	0	0	0	2	0
$72	3	.2398	.1721	32.4	0	0	1	0	1	0	1	0	0	0	0	0	2	0	0	0	0	0	0	0	0	0	1	0	0
$75	9	.3750	.7354	38.7	0	0	1	0	4	1	3	0	0	2	0	0	3	0	0	0	0	0	0	0	0	0	0	4	0
$7500	2	.0000	.0299	24.8	0	0	0	0	0	0	2	0	0	0	0	0	2	0	0	0	0	0	0	0	0	0	0	0	0
$8	25	.3922	2.2008	43.4	3	4	2	3	5	3	3	2	3	0	0	0	15	1	0	0	0	0	0	0	0	0	2	4	0
$80	7	.3126	.4970	37.0	0	4	1	0	1	0	1	0	0	0	0	0	5	0	0	0	0	0	0	0	0	0	1	1	0
$800	3	.3467	.2520	34.0	1	0	0	0	1	0	0	1	1	0	0	0	1	0	0	0	0	0	0	0	0	0	0	1	0
$85	2	.2401	.1133	30.5	0	0	1	0	0	0	1	0	0	0	0	0	0	0	0	0	0	0	0	0	0	1	1	0	0
$9	16	.2675	1.0346	40.1	2	7	2	0	2	2	1	0	1	0	0	0	12	0	0	0	0	0	0	0	0	1	0	2	0
$90	3	.2159	.1533	31.9	0	1	0	0	0	0	2	0	0	0	0	0	2	0	0	0	0	0	1	0	0	0	0	0	0
$91	2	.2391	.1133	30.5	0	0	0	1	1	0	0	0	0	0	0	0	1	0	0	0	0	0	0	0	0	0	1	0	0
$95	2	.2427	.1159	30.6	0	0	0	0	1	0	1	0	0	0	0	0	1	0	0	0	0	0	0	0	0	0	0	1	0
-	209	.3291	15.642	51.9	29	15	56	11	24	27	42	5	7	0	0	0	176	0	17	1	0	0	1	3	1	0	2	1	0
-able	7	.0000	.0568	27.5	0	0	0	0	0	5	2	0	0	0	0	0	0	0	7	0	0	0	0	0	0	0	0	0	0
-al	11	.1439	.3923	35.9	0	0	2	0	3	6	0	0	0	2	0	0	0	0	9	0	0	0	0	0	0	0	0	0	0
-ally	3	.0000	.0243	23.9	0	0	0	0	0	0	3	0	0	0	0	0	0	0	3	0	0	0	0	0	0	0	0	0	0
-an	2	.0000	.0219	23.4	0	0	1	1	0	0	0	0	0	2	0	0	0	0	0	0	0	0	0	0	0	0	0	0	0
-ance	4	.1757	.1672	32.2	0	0	0	1	2	1	0	0	0	1	0	0	0	0	3	0	0	0	0	0	0	0	0	0	0
-ant	9	.1456	.3393	35.3	0	0	0	4	1	0	4	0	0	8	0	0	0	0	1	0	0	0	0	0	0	0	0	0	0

9Q $11-million
5E $112
9R $115
9Q $121
5E $124
9Q $127
7E $128
7R $140
5E $149
7E $154
8E $155
7E $1600
5E $161
7E $1650
9R $170
9E $1800
9E $182
9R $190
6A $215
9E $2250
3E $227
6E $232
9E $235
6E $2365
7R $24-billion
6E $253
7E $2560
9B $260
9R $266
5E $2800
9E $2850
4E $2947
9E $31
7Q $318
9R $320
9E $325
9Q $337
6E $340
7R $341
9E $345
4E $3460
4E $360
6E $378
7Q $383
6R $4-a-pound
9R $400-a-month
6E $4067
6E $420
4E $440
4E $465
5E $47
7Q $475
9R $477
XR $48
7E $515
7Q $525
7Q $540
5E $549
6E $56
8R $567
4E $59
5A $6000
7Q $61
9E $655
7E $66
9A $68-a-week
6E $69
6E $6958
9R $70
7E $7000
4E $720
6E $7265
5E $73
9Q $74
6E $7654
9E $8000
9E $840
7E $8500
4E $855
9R $87
9E $88
5E $89
5P $892
7E $908
9E $96
XR $965
6Q -NO2
8G -age
6B -ain
6B -am

Word Type	F	D	U	SFI	3 Gr 3	4 Gr 4	5 Gr 5	6 Gr 6	7 Gr 7	8 Gr 8	9 Gr 9	X UnGr	A Read	B Eng & Gr	C Comp	D Lit	E Math	F Soc Stud	G Spell	H Sci	J Music	K Art	L Home Ec	M Shop	N Lib F	P Lib NF	Q Lib Ref	R Mag	S Rel
-ar	6	.0000	.0657	28.2	0	0	6	0	0	0	0	0	0	6	0	0	0	0	0	0	0	0	0	0	0	0	0	0	0
-ary	3	.0000	.0243	23.9	0	0	0	0	2	1	0	0	0	0	0	0	0	0	3	0	0	0	0	0	0	0	0	0	0
-ate	12	.1217	.3999	36.0	0	0	1	9	0	1	1	0	0	11	0	0	0	0	1	0	0	0	0	0	0	0	0	0	0
-ation	14	.2410	.7686	38.9	0	0	0	7	2	3	2	0	0	9	0	0	0	0	5	0	0	0	0	0	0	0	0	0	0
-b	7	.0000	.1048	30.2	0	0	0	0	0	0	7	0	0	0	0	0	7	0	0	0	0	0	0	0	0	0	0	0	0
-ceive	2	.0000	.0219	23.4	0	0	0	0	0	2	0	0	0	2	0	0	0	0	0	0	0	0	0	0	0	0	0	0	0
-d	2	.0000	.0219	23.4	0	0	1	0	0	0	1	0	0	2	0	0	0	0	0	0	0	0	0	0	0	0	0	0	0
-ed	22	.2347	1.1730	40.7	0	0	3	0	6	8	5	0	0	10	0	0	0	0	12	0	0	0	0	0	0	0	0	0	0
-el	2	.2408	.1091	30.4	0	0	1	0	1	0	0	0	0	1	0	0	0	0	1	0	0	0	0	0	0	0	0	0	0
-en	9	.2379	.4894	36.9	0	0	3	2	4	0	0	0	0	6	0	0	0	0	3	0	0	0	0	0	0	0	0	0	0
-ence	6	.1358	.2047	33.1	0	0	0	1	4	1	0	0	0	1	0	0	0	0	5	0	0	0	0	0	0	0	0	0	0
-ense	3	.0000	.0243	23.9	0	0	0	0	3	0	0	0	0	0	0	0	0	0	3	0	0	0	0	0	0	0	0	0	0
-ent	9	.2087	.4425	36.5	0	0	0	3	2	0	4	0	0	7	0	0	0	0	2	0	0	0	0	0	0	0	0	0	0
-er	35	.2441	1.9388	42.9	0	0	10	2	5	13	5	0	0	21	0	0	0	0	14	0	0	0	0	0	0	0	0	0	0
-ery	2	.0000	.0162	22.1	0	0	0	0	2	0	0	0	0	0	0	0	0	0	2	0	0	0	0	0	0	0	0	0	0
-es	21	.1898	.9352	39.7	0	0	3	0	6	11	1	0	0	6	0	0	0	0	15	0	0	0	0	0	0	0	0	0	0
-est	13	.2335	.6968	38.4	0	0	0	0	3	5	5	0	0	9	0	0	0	0	4	0	0	0	0	0	0	0	0	0	0
-ful	7	.1898	.3117	34.9	0	0	2	0	3	2	0	0	0	2	0	0	0	0	5	0	0	0	0	0	0	0	0	0	0
-hound	3	.0000	.0328	25.2	0	0	3	0	0	0	0	0	0	3	0	0	0	0	0	0	0	0	0	0	0	0	0	0	0
-ible	9	.1636	.3552	35.5	0	0	0	1	2	4	2	0	0	2	0	0	0	0	7	0	0	0	0	0	0	0	0	0	0
-il	2	.2408	.1091	30.4	0	0	1	0	1	0	0	0	0	1	0	0	0	0	1	0	0	0	0	0	0	0	0	0	0
-ile	2	.2408	.1091	30.4	0	0	1	0	1	0	0	0	0	1	0	0	0	0	1	0	0	0	0	0	0	0	0	0	0
-in	2	.2300	.1140	30.6	0	0	0	2	0	0	0	0	0	1	0	0	0	0	0	1	0	0	0	0	0	0	0	0	0
-ing	51	.2438	2.8226	44.5	0	0	4	0	18	13	16	0	0	31	0	0	0	0	20	0	0	0	0	0	0	0	0	0	0
-ion	20	.2402	1.0952	40.4	0	0	0	13	0	7	0	0	0	13	0	0	0	0	7	0	0	0	0	0	0	0	0	0	0
-ish	2	.0000	.0219	23.4	0	0	2	0	0	0	0	0	0	2	0	0	0	0	0	0	0	0	0	0	0	0	0	0	0
-ist	3	.2060	.1430	31.6	0	0	1	0	1	1	0	0	0	1	0	0	0	0	2	0	0	0	0	0	0	0	0	0	0
-ition	3	.2379	.1631	32.1	0	0	0	2	1	0	0	0	0	2	0	0	0	0	1	0	0	0	0	0	0	0	0	0	0
-ity	5	.0621	.1343	31.3	0	0	0	0	1	4	0	0	1	0	0	0	0	0	4	0	0	0	0	0	0	0	0	0	0
-ive	6	.1358	.2047	33.1	0	0	1	0	0	5	0	0	0	1	0	0	0	0	5	0	0	0	0	0	0	0	0	0	0
-le	4	.1757	.1672	32.2	0	0	1	0	3	0	0	0	0	1	0	0	0	0	3	0	0	0	0	0	0	0	0	0	0
-less	4	.1757	.1672	32.2	0	0	2	1	0	0	1	0	0	1	0	0	0	0	3	0	0	0	0	0	0	0	0	0	0
-ly	21	.2593	1.2686	41.0	0	1	5	0	2	11	2	0	2	8	0	0	0	0	11	0	0	0	0	0	0	0	0	0	0
-ment	2	.1497	.1046	30.2	0	0	1	0	0	1	0	0	1	0	0	0	0	0	1	0	0	0	0	0	0	0	0	0	0
-n	3	.0000	.0449	26.5	0	0	1	0	0	2	0	0	0	0	0	0	3	0	0	0	0	0	0	0	0	0	0	0	0
-ness	7	.2827	.4647	36.7	0	0	0	0	1	2	4	0	1	4	0	0	0	0	2	0	0	0	0	0	0	0	0	0	0
-or	11	.2745	.6978	38.4	0	0	6	0	3	2	0	0	1	6	0	0	0	0	4	0	0	0	0	0	0	0	0	0	0
-ous	2	.2408	.1091	30.4	0	0	1	0	0	1	0	0	0	1	0	0	0	0	1	0	0	0	0	0	0	0	0	0	0
-pose	3	.0000	.0328	25.2	0	0	0	3	0	0	0	0	0	3	0	0	0	0	0	0	0	0	0	0	0	0	0	0	0
-s	23	.2636	1.3527	41.3	0	0	5	0	4	12	2	0	0	9	0	0	1	0	13	0	0	0	0	0	0	0	0	0	0
-ship	4	.1757	.1672	32.2	0	0	0	2	1	1	0	0	0	1	0	0	0	0	3	0	0	0	0	0	0	0	0	0	0
-tion	2	.2446	.1123	30.5	0	0	0	0	1	0	1	0	0	1	0	0	0	0	0	0	0	0	0	0	0	0	1	0	0
-ular	4	.0000	.0438	26.4	0	0	4	0	0	0	0	0	0	4	0	0	0	0	0	0	0	0	0	0	0	0	0	0	0
-um	2	.2408	.1091	30.4	0	0	0	1	1	0	0	0	0	1	0	0	0	0	1	0	0	0	0	0	0	0	0	0	0
-y	8	.1757	.3345	35.2	0	0	1	1	0	6	0	0	0	2	0	0	0	0	6	0	0	0	0	0	0	0	0	0	0
-0	2	.0000	.0299	24.8	0	0	0	0	0	2	0	0	0	0	0	0	2	0	0	0	0	0	0	0	0	0	0	0	0
-1	38	.0000	.5688	37.5	1	0	3	2	3	9	20	0	0	0	0	0	38	0	0	0	0	0	0	0	0	0	0	0	0
-1/	2	.0000	.0219	23.4	0	0	2	0	0	0	0	0	0	2	0	0	0	0	0	0	0	0	0	0	0	0	0	0	0
-1/3	2	.0000	.0299	24.8	0	0	0	0	1	0	1	0	0	0	0	0	2	0	0	0	0	0	0	0	0	0	0	0	0
-10	9	.0000	.1347	31.3	0	0	0	0	0	5	4	0	0	0	0	0	9	0	0	0	0	0	0	0	0	0	0	0	0
-12	3	.0000	.0449	26.5	0	0	0	1	0	2	0	0	0	0	0	0	3	0	0	0	0	0	0	0	0	0	0	0	0
-2	56	.0000	.8382	39.2	0	0	1	5	5	13	32	0	0	0	0	0	56	0	0	0	0	0	0	0	0	0	0	0	0
-2/3	2	.0000	.0299	24.8	0	0	0	0	0	1	1	0	0	0	0	0	2	0	0	0	0	0	0	0	0	0	0	0	0
-2/5	2	.0000	.0299	24.8	0	0	0	0	0	0	2	0	0	0	0	0	2	0	0	0	0	0	0	0	0	0	0	0	0
-2y	2	.0000	.0299	24.8	0	0	0	0	0	0	2	0	0	0	0	0	2	0	0	0	0	0	0	0	0	0	0	0	0
-24g	5	.0000	.0986	29.9	0	0	0	0	0	0	5	0	0	0	0	0	0	0	0	5	0	0	0	0	0	0	0	0	0
-3	29	.0000	.4341	36.4	0	1	0	6	6	10	6	0	0	0	0	0	29	0	0	0	0	0	0	0	0	0	0	0	0
-3/5	2	.0000	.0299	24.8	0	0	0	0	0	2	0	0	0	0	0	0	2	0	0	0	0	0	0	0	0	0	0	0	0
-4	13	.0000	.1946	32.9	0	0	0	0	3	1	9	0	0	0	0	0	13	0	0	0	0	0	0	0	0	0	0	0	0
-40	3	.0000	.0449	26.5	0	0	0	0	0	3	0	0	0	0	0	0	3	0	0	0	0	0	0	0	0	0	0	0	0
-5	34	.0000	.5089	37.1	0	1	1	0	2	6	24	0	0	0	0	0	34	0	0	0	0	0	0	0	0	0	0	0	0
-50	3	.0000	.0449	26.5	0	0	0	0	0	3	0	0	0	0	0	0	3	0	0	0	0	0	0	0	0	0	0	0	0
-6	5	.0000	.0748	28.7	0	0	0	0	0	1	4	0	0	0	0	0	5	0	0	0	0	0	0	0	0	0	0	0	0
-60	3	.0000	.0449	26.5	0	0	0	0	0	1	2	0	0	0	0	0	3	0	0	0	0	0	0	0	0	0	0	0	0
-7	2	.0000	.0299	24.8	0	0	0	0	0	2	0	0	0	0	0	0	2	0	0	0	0	0	0	0	0	0	0	0	0
-78	3	.0000	.0591	27.7	0	0	0	0	0	0	3	0	0	0	0	0	0	0	0	3	0	0	0	0	0	0	0	0	0
-8	4	.0000	.0599	27.8	0	0	0	0	0	3	1	0	0	0	0	0	4	0	0	0	0	0	0	0	0	0	0	0	0
-9	2	.0000	.0299	24.8	0	0	0	0	0	1	1	0	0	0	0	0	2	0	0	0	0	0	0	0	0	0	0	0	0
/	235	.2841	14.816	51.7	43	11	59	42	38	25	17	0	0	144	0	0	8	0	82	0	1	0	0	0	0	0	0	0	0
/a/	32	.2318	1.6874	42.3	7	8	1	2	8	6	0	0	0	14	0	0	0	0	18	0	0	0	0	0	0	0	0	0	0
/a/**	10	.0000	.0812	29.1	0	1	4	1	4	0	0	0	0	0	0	0	0	0	10	0	0	0	0	0	0	0	0	0	0
/ar/	3	.0000	.0243	23.9	0	0	0	0	3	0	0	0	0	0	0	0	0	0	3	0	0	0	0	0	0	0	0	0	0
/au/	11	.0000	.1204	30.8	0	11	0	0	0	0	0	0	0	11	0	0	0	0	0	0	0	0	0	0	0	0	0	0	0
/ay/	2	.0000	.0219	23.4	0	0	0	0	0	2	0	0	0	2	0	0	0	0	0	0	0	0	0	0	0	0	0	0	0
/b/	11	.1906	.5048	37.0	4	3	3	0	0	1	0	0	0	9	0	0	0	0	2	0	0	0	0	0	0	0	0	0	0
/ch/	19	.2004	.8851	39.5	4	7	0	6	0	2	0	0	0	6	0	0	0	0	13	0	0	0	0	0	0	0	0	0	0
/d/	15	.2434	.8268	39.2	4	2	9	0	0	0	0	0	0	8	0	0	0	0	7	0	0	0	0	0	0	0	0	0	0
/e-l/**	18	.1025	.4988	37.0	0	0	5	13	0	0	0	0	0	2	0	0	0	0	16	0	0	0	0	0	0	0	0	0	0
/e-n/**	2	.0000	.0219	23.4	0	0	1	1	0	0	0	0	0	2	0	0	0	0	0	0	0	0	0	0	0	0	0	0	0
/e-r/**	15	.2366	.8054	39.1	0	0	15	0	0	0	0	0	0	7	0	0	0	0	8	0	0	0	0	0	0	0	0	0	0
/e-s/**	2	.0000	.0162	22.1	0	0	0	0	2	0	0	0	0	0	0	0	0	0	2	0	0	0	0	0	0	0	0	0	0
/e/	34	.2432	1.8723	42.7	4	7	8	3	2	10	0	0	0	18	0	0	0	0	16	0	0	0	0	0	0	0	0	0	0
/f/	35	.2439	1.9332	42.9	6	15	0	7	0	7	0	0	0	19	0	0	0	0	16	0	0	0	0	0	0	0	0	0	0
/g/	16	.2185	.8151	39.1	11	0	1	1	2	0	1	0	0	12	0	0	0	0	4	0	0	0	0	0	0	0	0	0	0
/h/	3	.0000	.0243	23.9	0	0	0	0	0	3	0	0	0	0	0	0	0	0	3	0	0	0	0	0	0	0	0	0	0
/i/	26	.2446	1.4414	41.6	9	7	1	3	0	6	0	0	0	15	0	0	0	0	11	0	0	0	0	0	0	0	0	0	0
/i/**	2	.0000	.0162	22.1	0	0	2	0	0	0	0	0	0	0	0	0	0	0	2	0	0	0	0	0	0	0	0	0	0
/id/	2	.0000	.0162	22.1	0	0	0	0	0	2	0	0	0	0	0	0	0	0	2	0	0	0	0	0	0	0	0	0	0
/j/	33	.2149	1.6305	42.1	11	2	0	7	5	7	1	0	0	12	0	0	0	0	21	0	0	0	0	0	0	0	0	0	0
/k/	40	.2408	2.1818	43.4	8	10	2	3	15	2	0	0	0	20	0	0	0	0	20	0	0	0	0	0	0	0	0	0	0

8G -cation
9B -ceous
9B -cious
7G -cur
7G -ella
6B -em
7G -eous
6R -ephyr
7G -fle
5B -fy
9B -geous
5B -gram
6B -ian
5B -ic
6B -im

8D -ious
6B -ium
7G -ol
6B -om
6B -on
7G -onym
7G -onyma
6B -ply
8G -ry
7B -self
7B -selves
5H -shaped**
9B -sion
7B -st
5B -ster

7F -theism
8G -ty
7G -ul
8G -ure
9E -1/2
5Q -1016
5Q -1060
7H -109
5Q -1099
9F -1100
5Q -1276
8E -13
5Q -1300
5Q -1306
XR -14

9H -15
9E -15/-45
9E -15/4
8Q -1654
4Q -1741
5Q -1881
6Q -196
9E -2x
9E -20
7H -200
8E -26
8H -273
7E -29
9E -3/2
8E -3/5xn

9E -3x
8E -30
6E -300
7H -317
8E -35
7H -38
9E -4x
8E -400
8H -459
9E -5/7
4Q -562
8E -600
9E -8/3
XR -80
5Q -858

8G /-fel/**
7G /au/**
8G /aw/**
7G /azh/
8E /d/**
6B /e-m/**
7B /emereker/**
7B /en/**
7G /er/**
8G /et/**
8B /faynd/
8B /hwic/
7B /in/**

Word Type	F	D	U	SFI	3 Gr 3	4 Gr 4	5 Gr 5	6 Gr 6	7 Gr 7	8 Gr 8	9 Gr 9	X UnGr	A Read	B Eng & Gr	C Comp	D Lit	E Math	F Soc Stud	G Spell	H Sci	J Music	K Art	L Home Ec	M Shop	N Lib F	P Lib NF	Q Lib Ref	R Mag	S Rel
/ks/	2	.0000	.0162	22.1	0	0	0	0	0	2	0	0	0	0	0	0	0	0	2	0	0	0	0	0	0	0	0	0	0
/kw/	4	.0000	.0325	25.1	0	0	0	0	0	4	0	0	0	0	0	0	0	0	4	0	0	0	0	0	0	0	0	0	0
/l/	9	.2444	.4981	37.0	0	5	1	0	2	1	0	0	0	5	0	0	0	0	4	0	0	0	0	0	0	0	0	0	0
/m/	3	.2060	.1430	31.6	0	1	1	0	0	1	0	0	0	1	0	0	0	0	2	0	0	0	0	0	0	0	0	0	0
/n/	4	.2185	.2038	33.1	0	1	3	0	0	0	0	0	0	3	0	0	0	0	1	0	0	0	0	0	0	0	0	0	0
/ng/	4	.1757	.1672	32.2	0	0	1	3	0	0	0	0	0	1	0	0	0	0	3	0	0	0	0	0	0	0	0	0	0
/o/	18	.2330	.9536	39.8	0	8	2	2	3	3	0	0	0	8	0	0	0	0	10	0	0	0	0	0	0	0	0	0	0
/oi/	5	.1531	.1872	32.7	0	1	0	4	0	0	0	0	0	1	0	0	0	0	4	0	0	0	0	0	0	0	0	0	0
/oo/	3	.2060	.1430	31.6	0	0	1	0	0	2	0	0	0	1	0	0	0	0	2	0	0	0	0	0	0	0	0	0	0
/or/	2	.0000	.0162	22.1	0	0	0	0	2	0	0	0	0	0	0	0	0	0	2	0	0	0	0	0	0	0	0	0	0
/ou/	7	.0000	.0568	27.5	0	2	0	4	0	1	0	0	0	0	0	0	0	0	7	0	0	0	0	0	0	0	0	0	0
/p/	16	.2185	.8151	39.1	6	4	3	1	0	2	0	0	0	12	0	0	0	0	4	0	0	0	0	0	0	0	0	0	0
/r/	26	.1957	1.2175	40.9	7	0	2	9	4	4	0	0	0	21	0	0	0	0	5	0	0	0	0	0	0	0	0	0	0
/s/	49	.2443	2.7102	44.3	0	26	5	1	11	6	0	0	0	27	0	0	0	0	22	0	0	0	0	0	0	0	0	0	0
/sh/	16	.1757	.6689	38.3	0	3	1	4	2	4	2	0	0	4	0	0	0	0	12	0	0	0	0	0	0	0	0	0	0
/sk/	2	.0000	.0219	23.4	0	0	0	0	2	0	0	0	0	2	0	0	0	0	0	0	0	0	0	0	0	0	0	0	0
/t/	17	.2432	.9362	39.7	7	1	8	0	1	0	0	0	0	9	0	0	0	0	8	0	0	0	0	0	0	0	0	0	0
/th/	5	.1531	.1872	32.7	0	0	1	2	0	2	0	0	0	1	0	0	0	0	4	0	0	0	0	0	0	0	0	0	0
/u/	27	.2423	1.4880	41.7	10	8	1	4	0	4	0	0	0	17	0	0	0	0	10	0	0	0	0	0	0	0	0	0	0
/ut/	2	.0000	.0162	22.1	0	0	0	0	0	2	0	0	0	0	0	0	0	0	2	0	0	0	0	0	0	0	0	0	0
/v/	12	.2446	.6653	38.2	0	4	3	5	0	0	0	0	0	7	0	0	0	0	5	0	0	0	0	0	0	0	0	0	0
/z/	23	.2446	1.2743	41.1	0	8	6	2	6	1	0	0	0	13	0	0	0	0	10	0	0	0	0	0	0	0	0	0	0
/zhen/**	2	.0000	.0162	22.1	0	0	0	0	2	0	0	0	0	0	0	0	0	0	2	0	0	0	0	0	0	0	0	0	0
/10	2	.0000	.0299	24.8	0	2	0	0	0	0	0	0	0	0	0	0	2	0	0	0	0	0	0	0	0	0	0	0	0
/1000	2	.0000	.0299	24.8	0	0	0	0	2	0	0	0	0	0	0	0	2	0	0	0	0	0	0	0	0	0	0	0	0
/12	3	.0000	.0449	26.5	0	2	0	0	0	1	0	0	0	0	0	0	3	0	0	0	0	0	0	0	0	0	0	0	0
/2	7	.0000	.1048	30.2	0	2	0	1	0	4	0	0	0	0	0	0	7	0	0	0	0	0	0	0	0	0	0	0	0
/3	5	.0000	.0748	28.7	0	0	0	1	0	3	1	0	0	0	0	0	5	0	0	0	0	0	0	0	0	0	0	0	0
/4	4	.0000	.0599	27.8	0	3	0	1	0	0	0	0	0	0	0	0	4	0	0	0	0	0	0	0	0	0	0	0	0
/4x	4	.0000	.0599	27.8	0	0	0	0	0	0	4	0	0	0	0	0	4	0	0	0	0	0	0	0	0	0	0	0	0
/5	13	.0000	.1946	32.9	0	4	0	1	0	4	4	0	0	0	0	0	13	0	0	0	0	0	0	0	0	0	0	0	0
/6	2	.0000	.0299	24.8	1	0	0	1	0	0	0	0	0	0	0	0	2	0	0	0	0	0	0	0	0	0	0	0	0
/60	2	.0000	.0299	24.8	0	0	0	0	0	2	0	0	0	0	0	0	2	0	0	0	0	0	0	0	0	0	0	0	0
/7	2	.0000	.0299	24.8	0	0	0	1	0	1	0	0	0	0	0	0	2	0	0	0	0	0	0	0	0	0	0	0	0
/8	5	.0000	.0748	28.7	0	0	0	4	0	0	1	0	0	0	0	0	5	0	0	0	0	0	0	0	0	0	0	0	0
%	11	.0000	.1647	32.2	0	0	0	8	1	1	1	0	0	0	0	0	11	0	0	0	0	0	0	0	0	0	0	0	0
-fourth	2	.0000	.0299	24.8	2	0	0	0	0	0	0	0	0	0	0	0	2	0	0	0	0	0	0	0	0	0	0	0	0
-segments	4	.0000	.0599	27.8	0	0	4	0	0	0	0	0	0	0	0	0	4	0	0	0	0	0	0	0	0	0	0	0	0
n't	2	.0000	.0914	29.6	2	0	0	0	0	0	0	0	2	0	0	0	0	0	0	0	0	0	0	0	0	0	0	0	0
'	41	.5223	4.6260	46.7	12	14	1	9	3	2	0	0	13	6	0	0	0	1	13	0	0	0	0	0	4	0	3	1	0
'Dwina	5	.0000	.0586	27.7	0	0	0	0	5	0	0	0	0	0	0	0	0	0	0	0	0	0	0	0	5	0	0	0	0
'Nineties	2	.0000	.0162	22.1	0	0	0	0	2	0	0	0	0	0	0	0	0	0	0	0	2	0	0	0	0	0	0	0	0
'Stute	4	.0000	.0469	26.7	0	4	0	0	0	0	0	0	0	0	0	0	0	0	0	0	0	0	0	0	4	0	0	0	0
'Vette	4	.0000	.0486	26.9	0	0	0	0	4	0	0	0	0	0	0	0	0	0	0	0	0	0	0	0	0	0	0	4	0
'a	5	.0000	.0537	27.3	0	0	0	0	0	3	2	0	0	0	0	5	0	0	0	0	0	0	0	0	0	0	0	0	0
'a'	15	.0570	.3979	36.0	0	0	0	0	13	2	0	0	2	0	0	0	0	0	0	0	0	0	0	0	13	0	0	0	0
'at	3	.2261	.2131	33.3	2	0	1	0	0	0	0	0	2	0	0	0	0	0	0	0	0	0	0	0	1	0	0	0	0
'board	2	.0000	.0914	29.6	0	2	0	0	0	0	0	0	2	0	0	0	0	0	0	0	0	0	0	0	0	0	0	0	0
'bout	22	.6160	2.9044	44.6	3	1	1	9	5	0	3	0	11	1	0	2	0	0	0	0	1	0	0	0	5	1	0	1	0
'by	2	.1787	.1174	30.7	1	0	0	1	0	0	0	0	1	0	0	0	0	0	0	0	0	0	0	0	1	0	0	0	0
'cause	20	.5876	2.5180	44.0	2	3	2	2	6	0	5	0	8	0	0	1	0	0	0	0	3	0	0	0	3	4	0	1	0
'cept	2	.1494	.1045	30.2	0	0	1	0	1	0	0	0	1	0	0	0	0	0	0	0	1	0	0	0	0	0	0	0	0
'coon	12	.3591	1.1283	40.5	2	0	0	0	10	0	0	0	9	0	0	0	0	0	0	0	2	0	0	0	1	0	0	0	0
'cos	6	.0000	.2741	34.4	1	0	0	5	0	0	0	0	6	0	0	0	0	0	0	0	0	0	0	0	0	0	0	0	0
'course	6	.0688	.1783	32.5	0	0	4	2	0	0	0	0	1	0	0	0	0	0	0	0	0	0	0	0	5	0	0	0	0
'cross	4	.3604	.3538	35.5	0	1	0	2	0	0	1	0	2	0	0	1	0	0	0	0	1	0	0	0	0	0	0	0	0
'deed	4	.1787	.2347	33.7	0	0	0	0	4	0	0	0	2	0	0	0	0	0	0	0	0	0	0	0	2	0	0	0	0
'dwina	2	.0000	.0234	23.7	0	0	0	0	2	0	0	0	0	0	0	0	0	0	0	0	0	0	0	0	2	0	0	0	0
'e	7	.0000	.0821	29.1	0	0	0	6	1	0	0	0	0	0	0	0	0	0	0	0	0	0	0	0	7	0	0	0	0
'e's	4	.0000	.0469	26.7	0	0	0	4	0	0	0	0	0	0	0	0	0	0	0	0	0	0	0	0	4	0	0	0	0
'ee	4	.0000	.0469	26.7	0	0	0	4	0	0	0	0	0	0	0	0	0	0	0	0	0	0	0	0	4	0	0	0	0
'em	162	.5606	19.538	52.9	13	20	24	21	48	17	16	3	58	1	1	28	0	0	0	0	2	0	0	0	53	9	0	10	0
'er	2	.1948	.1250	31.0	1	0	0	0	1	0	0	0	1	0	0	0	0	0	0	0	0	0	0	0	0	1	0	0	0
'forty-nine	2	.0000	.0162	22.1	0	0	0	2	0	0	0	0	0	0	0	0	0	0	0	0	2	0	0	0	0	0	0	0	0
'fraid	2	.1787	.1174	30.7	0	0	0	0	2	0	0	0	1	0	0	0	0	0	0	0	0	0	0	0	1	0	0	0	0
'im	10	.2210	.5232	37.2	0	1	0	6	1	2	0	0	0	0	0	3	0	0	0	0	0	0	0	0	7	0	0	0	0
'is	3	.1250	.1342	31.3	0	0	0	3	0	0	0	0	1	0	0	0	0	0	0	0	0	0	0	0	2	0	0	0	0
'long	3	.3394	.2451	33.9	0	0	0	1	2	0	0	0	1	0	0	1	0	0	0	0	0	0	0	0	1	0	0	0	0
'm	9	.1315	.3231	35.1	0	0	1	0	8	0	0	0	0	0	0	0	0	0	0	0	0	0	0	0	8	0	1	0	0
'member	3	.3873	.2495	34.0	0	2	0	0	0	0	1	0	0	0	0	1	0	0	0	0	0	0	0	0	1	0	0	1	0
'mid	5	.0000	.0404	26.1	0	5	0	0	0	0	0	0	0	0	0	0	0	0	0	0	5	0	0	0	0	0	0	0	0
'mongst	2	.1787	.1174	30.7	0	0	0	0	2	0	0	0	1	0	0	0	0	0	0	0	0	0	0	0	1	0	0	0	0
'n'	7	.2167	.3907	35.9	1	0	0	1	2	2	1	0	1	0	0	0	0	0	0	0	0	0	0	0	1	0	0	5	0
'neath	7	.3436	.6102	37.9	0	1	3	0	1	1	1	0	4	0	0	1	0	0	0	0	2	0	0	0	0	0	0	0	0
'nough	4	.2048	.1975	33.0	0	0	3	0	0	1	0	0	0	0	0	1	0	0	0	0	0	0	0	0	3	0	0	0	0
'orse	2	.0000	.0234	23.7	0	0	0	2	0	0	0	0	0	0	0	0	0	0	0	0	0	0	0	0	2	0	0	0	0
'possum's	2	.0000	.0162	22.1	0	1	1	0	0	0	0	0	0	0	0	0	0	0	0	0	2	0	0	0	0	0	0	0	0
'possums	2	.2346	.1166	30.7	0	0	0	0	0	0	0	2	0	0	0	0	0	0	0	1	0	0	0	0	0	0	0	1	0
'round	21	.4776	2.1545	43.3	2	8	0	3	2	3	2	1	4	1	0	3	0	0	0	0	9	0	0	0	1	2	0	1	0
's	13	.3463	1.1101	40.5	4	4	0	1	0	1	3	0	6	5	0	0	0	0	2	0	0	0	0	0	0	0	0	0	0
's**	5	.0000	.0748	28.7	5	0	0	0	0	0	0	0	0	0	0	0	5	0	0	0	0	0	0	0	0	0	0	0	0
'satiable	2	.0000	.0234	23.7	0	2	0	0	0	0	0	0	0	0	0	0	0	0	0	0	0	0	0	0	2	0	0	0	0
'sclusively	10	.0000	.1172	30.7	0	10	0	0	0	0	0	0	0	0	0	0	0	0	0	0	0	0	0	0	10	0	0	0	0
'scuse	2	.2407	.1138	30.6	0	1	1	0	0	0	0	0	0	0	0	1	0	0	0	0	0	0	0	0	0	1	0	0	0
'specially	2	.1814	.1187	30.7	0	1	0	1	0	0	0	0	1	0	0	0	0	0	0	0	0	0	0	0	0	0	0	1	0
't	4	.0000	.1827	32.6	1	1	0	0	0	2	0	0	4	0	0	0	0	0	0	0	0	0	0	0	0	0	0	0	0

8B /kae/**
8B /kaew/**
8B /kaw/
7B /krom/**
8B /lat/
8B /let/**
8B /leyen/**
8B /leyin/**
8B /redw/**
7G /shel/**
7G /shes/**
8D /ti-tum-tum-tum
7G /tran(t)s-et-lant-ik/**
8G /u
8G /u/**
8G /ud
8G /ul/
5B /van/
5B /vin/**
6B /w/
8B /werd/**
8B /wic/
8B /wrde/**
5B /zh/
9E /1
8E /13
8E /16
9E /16rs
8E /19
9E /2s
8E /2000
8E /36
6E /50
9E /88
7E -line
3E -sixteenth
3A -thirty
3A 'm
3A 's
3A 't
3A acked
3A alk
3A als
3A anded
3A andwich
3A at
3A ches
3A ckers
3A ench
3A ess
3A ggs
3A ing
3A ip
3A ipper
3A irt
9G ity
3A ll
3A ocks
3A rinning
3A rm
3A s
3A sn't
3A ter
3A ud
3A zip
8D 'A
3A 'Em
3P 'Frisco
5N 'T'
6N 'andle
8A 'ave
3A 'bye
5J 'coon's
3N 'dopted
7N 'dout
6N 'e'll
6A 'ed
8A 'ere
XR 'fifties
7B 'fishhook**
XR 'forties
6N 'gain
7N 'kase
7A 'leben
7N 'lection
6A 'longside
7A 'lowed
3J 'most
4N 'nother
4J 'nuff
8A 'op
4A 'peared
7N 'pears
7N 'possum
6A 'prentice
6A 'prentices
5H 'quake
3A 'ray
9F 'rithmetic
9F 'riting
9D 'scape
4N 'sclusivest
3J 'simmon
6R 'skins
9D 'smatter
7A 'spect
7N 'sturb
4N 'stute
7D 't'll

Word Type	F	D	U	SFI	3 Gr 3	4 Gr 4	5 Gr 5	6 Gr 6	7 Gr 7	8 Gr 8	9 Gr 9	X UnGr	A Read	B Eng & Gr	C Comp	D Lit	E Math	F Soc Stud	G Spell	H Sci	J Music	K Art	L Home Ec	M Shop	N Lib F	P Lib NF	Q Lib Ref	R Mag	S Rel
'tain't	2	.0000	.0234	23.7	0	0	0	0	2	0	0	0	0	0	0	0	0	0	0	0	0	0	0	0	2	0	0	0	0
'tend	2	.0000	.0914	29.6	0	0	0	0	2	0	0	0	2	0	0	0	0	0	0	0	0	0	0	0	0	0	0	0	0
'thout	2	.2443	.1130	30.5	0	0	0	0	2	0	0	0	0	0	0	1	0	0	0	0	0	0	0	0	1	0	0	0	0
'til	13	.3253	.9401	39.7	6	0	0	4	3	0	0	0	1	0	0	0	0	0	0	0	7	0	0	0	3	0	0	2	0
'tis	85	.5730	10.221	50.1	7	10	4	24	14	4	21	1	16	1	0	23	0	1	0	0	8	0	0	0	24	10	1	1	0
'twas	32	.5769	3.8951	45.9	4	2	3	10	10	2	1	0	9	7	0	5	0	0	0	0	8	1	0	0	2	0	0	0	0
'twere	2	.0000	.0215	23.3	0	0	0	0	0	0	2	0	0	0	0	2	0	0	0	0	0	0	0	0	0	0	0	0	0
'twill	8	.2014	.4313	36.3	1	2	1	3	1	0	0	0	2	0	0	0	0	0	0	0	5	0	0	0	1	0	0	0	0
'twould	4	.1787	.2347	33.7	0	0	1	1	2	0	0	0	2	0	0	0	0	0	0	0	0	0	0	0	2	0	0	0	0
'um	3	.0000	.0352	25.5	0	0	0	0	3	0	0	0	0	0	0	0	0	0	0	0	0	0	0	0	0	0	0	0	0
'un	5	.2086	.3320	35.2	3	0	0	1	0	1	0	0	3	0	0	0	0	0	0	0	0	0	0	0	2	0	0	0	0
'uns	2	.0000	.0914	29.6	0	0	0	2	0	0	0	0	2	0	0	0	0	0	0	0	0	0	0	0	0	0	0	0	0
'uz	3	.0000	.0352	25.5	0	0	0	0	3	0	0	0	0	0	0	0	0	0	0	0	0	0	0	0	3	0	0	0	0
'way	17	.5418	1.9422	42.9	3	4	0	2	6	2	0	0	3	1	0	2	0	0	0	0	5	0	0	0	3	3	0	0	0
'20s	3	.0000	.0583	27.7	0	0	0	0	0	3	0	0	0	0	0	0	0	3	0	0	0	0	0	0	0	0	0	0	0
'50s	4	.3519	.3117	34.9	0	0	0	0	1	3	0	0	0	0	0	0	0	1	0	0	0	0	0	0	0	0	0	1	0
'60s	2	.0000	.0243	23.9	0	0	0	0	1	0	1	0	0	0	0	0	0	0	0	0	0	0	0	0	0	0	0	2	0
'63	3	.0000	.0365	25.6	0	0	0	0	3	0	0	0	0	0	0	0	0	0	0	0	0	0	0	0	0	0	0	3	0
'64	4	.0000	.0486	26.9	0	0	0	0	4	0	0	0	0	0	0	0	0	0	0	0	0	0	0	0	0	0	0	4	0
'65	5	.0000	.0608	27.8	0	0	0	0	5	0	0	0	0	0	0	0	0	0	0	0	0	0	0	0	0	0	0	5	0
'66	2	.0000	.0243	23.9	0	0	0	0	2	0	0	0	0	0	0	0	0	0	0	0	0	0	0	0	0	0	0	2	0
'67	3	.0000	.0365	25.6	0	0	0	0	3	0	0	0	0	0	0	0	0	0	0	0	0	0	0	0	0	0	0	3	0
'68	8	.0000	.0972	29.9	0	0	0	2	6	0	0	0	0	0	0	0	0	0	0	0	0	0	0	0	0	0	0	8	0
'69	6	.0000	.0729	28.6	0	0	0	0	4	0	2	0	0	0	0	0	0	0	0	0	0	0	0	0	0	0	0	6	0
'70	2	.1814	.1187	30.7	0	0	0	1	1	0	0	0	1	0	0	0	0	0	0	0	0	0	0	0	0	0	0	1	0
'70s	2	.0000	.0243	23.9	0	0	0	0	0	0	2	0	0	0	0	0	0	0	0	0	0	0	0	0	0	0	0	2	0
'71	2	.0000	.0243	23.9	0	0	0	0	2	0	0	0	0	0	0	0	0	0	0	0	0	0	0	0	0	0	0	2	0
'80s	3	.0000	.0583	27.7	0	0	0	0	0	3	0	0	0	0	0	0	0	3	0	0	0	0	0	0	0	0	0	0	0

8N 'taters	5N 'twasn't	7R '22	7R '51	7R '61	7D '98
XR 'thirties	9D 'twixt	7Q '30s	8N '52	7R '62	6A '99
5Q 'till	6N 'uman	8R '40s	3P '56	9F '72	
6A 'tisn't	7P 'zamine	6J '49-ers	7R '60	7A '76	
7N 'twarn't	7P 'zamined	4J '49ers	9F '60's	9D '83	

Special Notes

At first sight, a number of the word types displayed in the Alphabetical List seem quite strange (often they cannot be found in any dictionary) or even erroneous. While the uninterpreted graphic shapes may well be puzzling, considerable effort has been expended to make the word types as free of error as possible. Before this book was printed, 17,000 citations for suspicious-looking types were inspected; about 7,000 of them were traced further to the original sampling texts for complete verification. This error-detection procedure identified approximately 3,700 keystroking errors in the Corpus, all of which were corrected. These corrections were made *in addition to* those performed in the Corpus input-verification procedure described elsewhere in this book. Nevertheless, it cannot be claimed that the word types are completely free of error. The purpose of the notes that follow, therefore, is to assist the reader in discriminating certain classes of "strange" types from possibly erroneous types.

Types Marked With Double Asterisks

Approximately 170 word types are shown with double asterisks in the Alphabetical List. These types were selected to illustrate ways in which certain types are rendered (printed) differently from their rendering in the original sampling texts. There are, in general, three possible reasons for a double asterisk. The first is that a special character needed was not available on the equipment used to input the Corpus (IBM 029 keypunch). The second is that punctuation or other non-alphabetic characters—especially the comma, period, and parenthesis—were stripped from word types to prepare the records from which the lists in this book were generated. The third is that the original type contained more than the maximum of 25 characters (23 plus two positions for capitalization coding). Therefore, in the list that follows, the left-hand column has been prepared to show the type as it appears in the Alphabetical List; the right-hand column shows a close rendering of the type as it appeared in the original sampling text or offers a brief explanation of the original.

A**	*Initial capitalized* A *in an abbreviation from which the periods were stripped.*
A-shaped**	"A"-shaped
AB's**	A.B.'s
AC's**	A.C.'s
AFL**	A.F.L.
All-the-Elephant-there**	All-the-Elephant-there-was
am+n**	a^{m+n}
am**	a^m
an**	a^n
antidisestablishmentari**	antidisestablishmentarianism
autobiographical**	au.to.bi.o.graph.i.cal
A1**	$A^1 \ldots$
a2/b2**	a^2/b^2
a3**	a^3
a3/a3**	a^3/a^3
A3d**	$A^3 \ldots .d$
A4ly**	$A^4 \ldots .ly$
BCS**	B.C.S.
BCS'**	B.C.S.'
Belond-A-P**	Belond-A.-P.
Bi-Coloured-Python-R**	Bi-Coloured-Python-Rock-Snake
BIA's**	B.I.A.'s
brek'fast**	brek'fast
BVD's**	B.V.D.'s
c/**	c/( )
CC's**	C.C.'s
CIO**	C.I.O.
cm3**	cm^3
Co's**	Co.'s
con'tent**	con'tent
content'**	con tent'
cradle**	cra dle
cub-engineer**	"cub"-engineer
C2H2**	C_2H_2
C2H4Br2**	$C_2H_4Br_2$
C2H4Cl2**	$C_2H_4Cl_2$
DT's**	D.T.'s
ed/**	əd/
ed'esen**	ed'ə sən
Ein**	E_{in}
ekskus'**	eks kūs'
ekskuz'**	eks kūz'
Emax**	E_{max}

Eout**	E$_{out}$	prog'ress**	prog'ress
ern**	ərn	progress'**	pro gress'
extraordinary**	ex...tra...or...di...nar...y	proj'ect**	proj'ect
farther**	far ther	project'**	pro ject'
FDR's**	F.D.R.'s	quality**	qúal‖itý
Fight-the-good-fight-of**	Fight-the-good-fight-of-faith	rec'ord**	rec'ord
fish'hook**	fish'hook	record'**	re cord'
for'hed**	fôr'hed	self-A14**	self-A^{14}. . .
for'id**	fôr'id	shen**	shən
ft-long**	ft.-long	silekt'**	si lekt'
funny**	fun ny	sleep'y**	sleep'y
great-great-great-great**	great-great-great-great-grandmothers, great-great-great-great-grandfathers	Small-person-without-an**	Small-person-without-any-manners-who-ought-to-be-spanked
halvoy**	halvøy	supper**	sup per
He-Who-Cries-When-**	He-Who-Cries-When-the-Wasps-Sting-Him	T-minus-2-hours-and-17-**	T-minus-2-hours-and-17-minutes
		tens**	təns
IGFA**	I.G.F.A.	unA2ed**	unA^2. . .ed
ilekt'**	i lekt'		
in'crease**	in'crease	xa/b**	$\times\frac{a}{b}$
Inc's**	Inc.'s		
increase'**	in crease'	zhen**	zhən
infinite-resource-and-s**	infinite-resource-and-sagacity	1/a3**	1/a^3
kar'ver**	kär'vər	10-ft-high**	10-ft.-high
kas**	kās	20-in-wheel-size**	20-in.-wheel-size
kortez'**	kôr tez'	340-cu-in**	340-cu.-in.
Kqq'/r2**	Kqq'/r^2	4-strips**	4″-strips
Lady-who-asks-a-very-man**	Lady-who-asks-a-very-many-questions	6-in-swing**	6-in.-swing
		6700-foot**	6,700-foot
Man-who-does-not-put-hi**	Man-who-does-not-put-his-foot-forward-in-a-hurry	(C2H4Cl)2S**	(C$_2$H$_4$Cl)$_2$S
		(a/b)2**	(a/b)^2
MD's**	M.D.'s	-shaped**	^-shaped
mercy**	mér‖ćy	/-fel/**	/-fəl/
Mex'ico**	Mex'i co	/a/**	/ā/
minute1**	min ute^1	/au/**	/aú/
MIT's**	M.I.T.'s	/aw/**	/aw, o, o/
mo'tel**	mo tel	/d**	( )/d
muv'e**	muv'ē	/e-l/**	/ə-l/
nh/(2p)**	nh/(2π)	/e-m/**	/ə-m/
novel**	nov el	/e-n/**	/ə-n/
Np**	N$_p$	/e-r/**	/ə-r/
Nprimary/Nsecondary**	N$_{primary}$/N$_{secondary}$	/e-s/**	/ə-s/
Ns**	N$_s$**	/emereker/**	/əmerəkər/
OB's**	O.B.'s	/en/**	/ϑen/
OK**	O.K.	/et/**	/ət/
on'ist**	on'ist	/i/**	/ī/
oy**	øy	/in/**	/θin/
per'fect**	per'fect	/kae/**	/kaə/
perad'**	pə rād'	/kaew/**	/kæw/
perfect'**	per fect'	/krom/**	/krõm/
PhD's**	Ph.D.'s	/let/**	/lət/
pres'ent**	pres'ent	/leyen/**	/leyən/
present'**	pre sent'	/leyin/**	/leyiŋ/
pretekt'**	prə tekt'	/redw/**	/rədw/
		/shel/**	/shəl/

560

/shes/**	/shəs/
/tran(t)s-et-lant-ik/**	\tran(t)s-ət-lant-ik\
/u/**	/ŭ/
/vin/**	\vīn\
/werd/**	/wərd/
/wrde/**	/wrdə/
/zhen/**	/zhən/
'fishhook**   'fish,hook

's**   *Several rebuses involving pictures of animals and plants + 's*

Miscellaneous Unusual Types and Apparent Source Errors

The word types listed below were checked against the sampling texts to be sure that they had been correctly keystroked in the Corpus. Brief explanations of their meaning, or reason for occurring in the sampling text, are given in the right-hand column. Apparent errors in the sources themselves, whether in typography or usage, were not "corrected" for input into the Corpus as a matter of policy. They are listed here, to the extent identified in the error-detection procedure, exactly as they appeared in the original sources.

aggg	Exclamation of disgust
Ahyee-aye-ty-fahve	"Phonetic spelling"
anis	Apparent source error
atchitamon	Described as an "Indian" word for "chipmunk"
behinde	Dialectal item
behine	Dialectal item
behint	Dialectal item
bescreened	Shakespeare
billitch	Nonsense word
binning	Nonsense word
blude-reid	Dialectal (Scottish) item
borogoves	Nonsense word
borryed	Dialectal item
brendly	Nonsense word
brillig	Nonsense word
broadies	Slang
brosket	Nonsense word
buffaloe	Archaic spelling
cantcher	"Phonetic spelling"
cantelopes	Apparent source error
cantyoucantyoucant	Run together for emphasis
clicket	Rendering of foreign pronunciation
clob	Nonsense word
clumb	Variant
connesewer	"Phonetic spelling"
connivering	Malapropism
crabba	Old English
crobble	Nonsense word
cryoton	Apparent source error
cumming's	Apparent source error
deef	Dialect
delegently	Apparent source error
dephyr	Nonsense rhyme (meaning "deafer") with "zephyr"
disirregardless	Cited in discussion of "irregardless"
downity	Contrasted with "uppity"
drea(chipmunk)ming	Nonce word (e e cummings)
Earoon	Hypothetical ancestor of Earth and Moon
fing, fings	Used to show that -er in *finger* does not mean "one who *fings*" or "more *fing*"
floofle	Nonsense word
frobish	Nonsense word
froon	Nonsense word
fruitfull	Archaic
frumious	Nonsense word
frumiously	Nonsense word
frums	Nonsense word
fryed	Apparent source error
g-h-o-t-i	Rendering of "fish" in a discussion of conventional spelling
gloobed	Nonsense word
gorbed	Nonsense word
grees	"Phonetic spelling"
greez	"Phonetic spelling"
gribble	Nonsense word
grop	Nonsense word
grumple	Nonsense word
idear	"Phonetic spelling"
incertain	Archaic
ingenius	Apparent source error
ivver	"Phonetic spelling"
jealious	Shakespeare
jing, jings, Jinks	All in "By j . . ."
keads	Dialectal item
kochokochokocho	Japanese (sound of tickling)
land-	Suspended hyphen in "land- and water-saving problems"
lazyness	Apparent source error
leady	Rendering of foreign pronunciation
lemarkable	Rendering of foreign pronunciation
liger	Cross between a lion and a tiger
longjeray	Rendering of a "common mispronunciation"
mananaesque	From "a mañanaesque way of life"
manxome	Nonsense word
mastadons	Apparent source error
mimsy	Nonsense word
mintral	Apparent source error
Moorth	Hypothetical ancestor of Moon and Earth
motch	Nonsense word
nugful	Nonsense word

opalways, opare, opdid, opput, opthe, opthey, opwhere, opyou	Examples of "op" language
ork	Noise made by a penguin
pepperation	Rendering of "slovenly pronunciation"
plasticene	Apparent source error
Plus	From "Johnny Plus from Addition Land . . ."
prepoceros	Nonsense rhyme with "rhinoceros" (meaning "preposterous")
prid'near	"Phonetic spelling" of dialectal item
proudfully	From a child's narrative
prowlishly	Nonce word (of a cat "prowlishly inclined")
quinking	Spoonerism "the thick quinking – er – quick thinking . . ."
sittyated	"Phonetic spelling" of dialectal item
socker	Swedish
someding	"Phonetic spelling" of dialectal item
syle	Old English
tcusk	Apparent source error
tion	Cross between a tiger and a lion
wrongos	Slang

Abbreviations and Numerals

The word records used to generate the tapes from which this book was prepared were subjected at an earlier stage of processing to a program that stripped the word records of most punctuation — notably, commas and periods. In consequence, there are no abbreviations containing periods and no numbers containing commas or decimals in the Alphabetical List (or the Rank List following). Moreover, a derivative effect in subsequent processing was the creation of certain numerical and alphabetical types (such as *000, 05,* and some individual capitalized alphabetic characters) that were in fact *components* of graphic types that originally contained commas and periods (such as *1,000, $5.05,* and *O.K.*). See the list of types followed by double asterisks for more information.

Incorrectly Combined Word Types

Through a misunderstanding of input instructions, certain compound place names (New York, for example) were keystroked as single words (*NewYork*). This error is limited to relatively few binomial place names and other proper noun phrases.

Deliberately Misspelled Words

In general, the words listed here were misspelled in the source texts so that students could correct them. Most of these misspellings come from a few exercises in English & Grammar materials, but there are also some from the Spelling and the Reading materials. This list is not exhaustive and does not include spellings intended to render dialectal speech.

adress	goed	poofreader
amelia	harvard	rachel
american	heres	roger
Andys	hes	romanian
beautifulest	idaho	russian
bedford	ingersoll	sents
begining	Ive	september
bild	james	sheap
bronx	july	shed
browne	kansas	shouldnt
capaciosity	kathy	suspiciousion
Carakters	kentucky	theyd
carelesly	louisiana	theyll
cawtion	mant	theyre
cemetary	massachusetts	thursday
christopher	mispelled	toolechest
columbus	missouri	tripp
conant	monroe	wate
creole	monroe's	weve
dakota	mutch	wheres
dan	nathaniel	wholl
december	obcur	whos
didn	ohio	wich
easter	oregon	worning
england	orleans	wrtng
extention	peabody	Wshngtn
forgott	persia	wyoming
fourty	persian	youve

Guide to the Rank List

Unlike those appearing in other sources, this rank list of the 86,741 word types found in the AHI Corpus is ordered in terms of U and SFI rather than F. U and SFI are statistics that we believe are more indicative of the true ordering of the types in a corpus of infinite size. Since the total frequency (F) of each type is given, it is possible to compare the rankings by F and U.

For reasons of appearance and easy reference, the information for each type is printed *preceding* that type. The following data are given:

1. The value of U (frequency-per-million, adjusted for D).
2. SFI, the Standard Frequency Index.
3. The value of D, the index of dispersion.
4. The total frequency, F.
5. The word type.

See the Guide to the Alphabetical List for further explanation of the statistics.

After every 100 types, a line is printed indicating the rank of the immediately preceding type. Essentially, this is simply a numbering of the types as they appear in order of U. No account is taken of tied ranks.

There are a very few instances in the Rank List in which certain unrenderable characters produced a rectangular black mark or a blank space. In addition, the magnetic-tape record for one word type, *Marian,* contained a distortion that resulted in the rejection of the word type from the list. These imperfections arose from isolated technical problems and were not considered sufficiently important to repair.

U	SFI	D	F	Word Type
73122.8	88.6	.9969	373123	the
28461.6	84.5	.9912	146001	of
26172.1	84.2	.9940	133899	and
24441.7	83.9	.9948	124959	a
23653.2	83.7	.9909	121347	to
19366.2	82.9	.9938	99108	in
11643.2	80.7	.9710	60852	is
9573.0	79.8	.9509	50957	you
9266.4	79.7	.9932	47443	that
9179.4	79.6	.9863	47284	it
8244.6	79.2	.8928	46249	he
7687.0	78.9	.9942	39322	for
7456.8	78.7	.9162	40934	was
7135.8	78.5	.9948	36482	on
6743.4	78.3	.9647	35454	are
6295.5	78.0	.9941	32208	as
5933.4	77.7	.9904	30455	with
5316.2	77.3	.9134	29268	his
5284.8	77.2	.9702	27620	they
4678.3	76.7	.9921	23975	at
4554.0	76.6	.9732	23746	be
4517.4	76.5	.9851	23301	this
4456.2	76.5	.9940	22799	from
4405.2	76.4	.8440	25932	I
4345.8	76.4	.9889	22337	have
3991.8	76.0	.9502	21283	or
3923.8	75.9	.9879	20189	by
3907.7	75.9	.9949	19976	one
3633.8	75.6	.8865	20511	had
3630.8	75.6	.9898	18645	not
3620.2	75.6	.9542	19196	but
3350.1	75.3	.9582	17709	what
3280.2	75.2	.9797	16997	all
3200.2	75.1	.9503	17031	were
3102.8	74.9	.9932	15886	when
3066.8	74.9	.9425	16452	we
2916.6	74.6	.9738	15194	there
2877.8	74.6	.9563	15247	can
2813.9	74.5	.9717	14696	an
2763.6	74.4	.9107	15311	your
2678.3	74.3	.9698	14016	which
2529.8	74.0	.9675	13258	their
2468.9	73.9	.7898	15309	said
2460.7	73.9	.9667	12907	if
2440.2	73.9	.9755	12695	do
2438.1	73.9	.9789	12646	will
2426.4	73.8	.8513	14290	each
2423.0	73.8	.9851	12496	about
2414.3	73.8	.9154	13303	how
2409.0	73.8	.9538	12776	up
2334.8	73.7	.9655	12252	out
2306.6	73.6	.9757	11997	them
2306.5	73.6	.9731	12022	then
2274.6	73.6	.8238	13653	she
2262.6	73.5	.9415	12158	many
2232.8	73.5	.9834	11534	some
2227.1	73.5	.9794	11543	so
2148.6	73.3	.9361	11611	these
2137.7	73.3	.9685	11188	would
2073.4	73.2	.9816	10729	other
2061.9	73.1	.9865	10620	into
2002.9	73.0	.9812	10369	has
1948.8	72.9	.9917	9992	more
1876.6	72.7	.8147	11375	her
1875.7	72.7	.9407	10085	two
1868.2	72.7	.9781	9696	like
1762.3	72.5	.8129	10703	him
1634.3	72.1	.9734	8518	see
1634.3	72.1	.9833	8441	time
1607.4	72.1	.9459	8585	could
1605.9	72.1	.9584	8483	no
1537.9	71.9	.9327	8333	make
1529.6	71.8	.9725	7982	than
1477.9	71.7	.9805	7655	first
1446.6	71.6	.9582	7645	been
1411.3	71.5	.9512	7512	its
1371.9	71.4	.9116	7576	who
1370.5	71.4	.9264	7457	now
1344.1	71.3	.8385	7989	people
1328.3	71.2	.8356	7898	my
1325.7	71.2	.9482	7073	made
1314.2	71.2	.9679	6882	over
1306.6	71.2	.9173	7169	did
1302.2	71.1	.9076	7206	down
1280.4	71.1	.9885	6583	only
1278.9	71.1	.9823	6612	way
1228.5	70.9	.8936	6916	find
1219.3	70.9	.8753	7009	use
1216.8	70.9	.9269	6635	may
1207.3	70.8	.8352	7194	water
1175.6	70.7	.9570	6220	long
1149.9	70.6	.9347	6204	little
1149.1	70.6	.9717	5997	very
1143.2	70.6	.9814	5915	after
1124.1	70.5	.4756	11215	words
1110.4	70.5	.9733	5789	called
1104.6	70.4	.9536	5858	just
1082.4	70.3	.9794	5611	where
1078.2	70.3	.9431	5785	most
1072.1	70.3	.9601	5655	know

THE PRECEDING WORD TYPE OCCUPIES RANK 100

U	SFI	D	F	Word Type
1069.7	70.3	.9485	5700	get
1056.2	70.2	.9862	5442	through
1055.6	70.2	.9039	5862	back
1034.3	70.1	.9746	5386	much
1011.9	70.1	.9732	5275	before
1008.1	70.0	.9453	5388	go
1007.3	70.0	.9542	5343	good
997.29	70.0	.9245	5448	new
994.25	70.0	.4798	9846	write
993.57	70.0	.8607	5777	our
991.21	70.0	.8902	5607	used
983.63	69.9	.7816	6180	me
971.39	69.9	.8865	5486	man
963.45	69.8	.9623	5071	too
960.91	69.8	.9705	5023	any
937.06	69.7	.9432	5019	day
931.59	69.7	.9383	5022	same
914.23	69.6	.9615	4815	right
894.00	69.5	.9124	4933	look
876.31	69.4	.9318	4746	think
875.79	69.4	.9550	4647	also
871.48	69.4	.9514	4632	around
854.00	69.3	.9920	4377	another
853.23	69.3	.8655	4914	came
836.75	69.2	.8981	4676	come
834.67	69.2	.9716	4358	work
830.82	69.2	.9534	4413	three
829.53	69.2	.5197	7532	word
828.95	69.2	.9768	4307	must
814.42	69.1	.9833	4207	because
813.78	69.1	.9334	4408	does
810.56	69.1	.9587	4285	part
806.95	69.1	.9684	4225	even
798.93	69.0	.9540	4240	place
796.53	69.0	.9463	4255	well
795.09	69.0	.9537	4223	such
794.18	69.0	.9614	4184	here
789.08	69.0	.9797	4089	take
761.70	68.8	.9264	4147	why
754.87	68.8	.9367	4070	things
739.09	68.7	.9671	3875	help
738.97	68.7	.9477	3942	put
731.39	68.6	.9312	3966	years
724.97	68.6	.9339	3926	different
712.19	68.5	.9429	3814	away
711.10	68.5	.9197	3892	again
710.92	68.5	.9248	3873	off
710.87	68.5	.8554	4132	went
708.84	68.5	.9153	3894	old
704.34	68.5	.5550	6059	number
686.78	68.4	.8946	3855	great
686.09	68.4	.9321	3715	tell
680.61	68.3	.8292	4067	men
673.26	68.3	.8606	3916	say
662.52	68.2	.9421	3555	small
654.20	68.2	.9772	3398	every
648.07	68.1	.9784	3362	found
647.85	68.1	.9588	3421	still
632.93	68.0	.9660	3324	between
629.90	68.0	.8360	3766	name
628.42	68.0	.9137	3470	should
612.22	67.9	.8046	3748	Mr
612.07	67.9	.9335	3308	home
611.96	67.9	.8792	3476	big
607.43	67.8	.9090	3366	give
585.08	67.7	.7868	3673	air
583.88	67.7	.8923	3293	line
583.67	67.7	.8141	3572	set
575.23	67.6	.9708	3006	own
573.45	67.6	.9739	2987	under
561.18	67.5	.9250	3057	read
560.99	67.5	.9346	3030	last
559.08	67.5	.9008	3115	never
556.03	67.5	.6855	3929	us
554.95	67.4	.9762	2885	left
547.78	67.4	.9352	2961	end
541.10	67.3	.9675	2835	along
539.77	67.3	.9641	2837	while
532.70	67.3	.9551	2824	might
526.21	67.2	.9795	2727	next
525.74	67.2	.5384	4667	sound
521.90	67.2	.7907	3276	below
521.32	67.2	.9012	2900	saw
516.26	67.1	.9448	2761	something
513.42	67.1	.9088	2835	thought
511.92	67.1	.9829	2646	both
510.04	67.1	.9625	2685	few
509.64	67.1	.9774	2647	those
506.70	67.0	.9667	2657	always
506.25	67.0	.7725	3197	looked
503.91	67.0	.9316	2734	show
499.21	67.0	.9050	2777	large
499.15	67.0	.9698	2611	often
498.81	67.0	.9617	2629	together
496.85	67.0	.8412	2924	asked
496.81	67.0	.9249	2705	house
493.93	66.9	.8531	2881	don't
491.79	66.9	.8817	2799	world
487.80	66.9	.8583	2832	going
487.59	66.9	.9255	2655	want

THE PRECEDING WORD TYPE OCCUPIES RANK 200

U	SFI	D	F	Word Type
484.43	66.9	.9423	2599	school
477.62	66.8	.9326	2588	important
473.93	66.8	.9201	2596	until
473.35	66.8	.7262	3222	1
470.54	66.7	.8711	2720	form
467.35	66.7	.8306	2801	food
466.41	66.7	.9388	2509	keep
465.71	66.7	.9094	2575	children
463.34	66.7	.9169	2545	feet
461.77	66.6	.7707	2953	land
459.47	66.6	.9141	2532	side
458.55	66.6	.9726	2392	without
454.92	66.6	.9021	2529	boy
453.74	66.6	.9407	2435	once
450.23	66.5	.8562	2625	animals
449.34	66.5	.8615	2612	life
444.76	66.5	.9520	2363	enough
442.22	66.5	.8891	2490	took
441.78	66.5	.9855	2278	sometimes
440.50	66.4	.9459	2357	four
439.00	66.4	.8832	2487	head
437.70	66.4	.9659	2298	above
433.99	66.4	.9736	2262	kind
433.46	66.4	.8683	2491	began
432.01	66.4	.9390	2324	almost
431.78	66.4	.8919	2431	live
429.67	66.3	.7528	2831	page
428.73	66.3	.8037	2626	got
424.82	66.3	.7807	2690	earth
423.47	66.3	.9384	2281	need
423.22	66.3	.9516	2250	far
422.15	66.3	.9185	2316	hand
420.88	66.2	.9522	2237	high
417.88	66.2	.9265	2277	year
417.67	66.2	.8928	2343	mother
413.06	66.2	.8715	2376	light
410.45	66.1	.8865	2331	parts
406.70	66.1	.8638	2357	country
405.23	66.1	.9059	2245	father
403.53	66.1	.9358	2176	let
402.27	66.0	.8706	2307	night
398.14	66.0	.7361	2680	following
397.90	66.0	.6405	3030	2
394.01	66.0	.7824	2500	picture
392.50	65.9	.9497	2092	being
392.34	65.9	.7560	2581	study
390.80	65.9	.9447	2094	second
389.32	65.9	.8397	2303	eyes
388.58	65.9	.9180	2129	soon
387.76	65.9	.9579	2051	times
386.62	65.9	.8632	2237	story
386.31	65.9	.9004	2155	boys
381.90	65.8	.9472	2041	since
380.21	65.8	.9186	2085	white
379.81	65.8	.9604	2003	days
378.11	65.8	.9377	2036	ever
373.94	65.7	.7825	2372	paper
371.85	65.7	.9495	1980	hard
368.56	65.7	.9378	1985	near
362.78	65.6	.5529	3122	sentence
361.65	65.6	.9580	1911	better
361.60	65.6	.9738	1884	best
361.27	65.6	.9398	1942	across
361.11	65.6	.9505	1924	during
361.02	65.6	.9501	1923	today
360.10	65.6	.9587	1903	others
359.99	65.6	.9527	1914	however
357.97	65.5	.9224	1956	sure
356.14	65.5	.9165	1962	means
355.65	65.5	.8667	2044	knew
355.61	65.5	.8045	2178	it's
355.31	65.5	.9146	1958	try
354.49	65.5	.8716	2028	told
354.26	65.5	.9310	1920	young
353.01	65.5	.8187	2146	miles
352.58	65.5	.8957	1977	sun
352.05	65.5	.9378	1899	ways
343.71	65.4	.9507	1828	thing
340.01	65.3	.9080	1886	whole
339.90	65.3	.7829	2154	hear
338.75	65.3	.8801	1939	example
338.68	65.3	.8464	1988	heard
337.18	65.3	.9476	1801	several
335.64	65.3	.9138	1854	change
329.65	65.2	.8179	2002	answer
324.86	65.1	.9069	1801	room
322.28	65.1	.8922	1812	sea
321.54	65.1	.9242	1755	against
318.46	65.0	.9222	1741	top
317.30	65.0	.8891	1785	turned
313.54	65.0	.5721	2638	3
312.98	65.0	.9458	1674	learn
312.86	65.0	.8211	1904	point
310.95	64.9	.8417	1843	city
310.19	64.9	.7224	2113	play
310.08	64.9	.9244	1690	toward
308.51	64.9	.9006	1725	five
307.91	64.9	.8473	1825	using
307.83	64.9	.8568	1789	himself
307.82	64.9	.9069	1712	usually

THE PRECEDING WORD TYPE OCCUPIES RANK 300

U	SFI	D	F	Word Type
307.57	64.9	.9136	1694	money
305.34	64.8	.9252	1663	seen
304.35	64.8	.7305	2016	didn't
302.74	64.8	.8575	1752	car
302.23	64.8	.8676	1736	morning
300.37	64.8	.9118	1661	given
297.87	64.7	.9114	1645	trees
296.06	64.7	.7854	1848	I'm
295.73	64.7	.8274	1783	body
293.63	64.7	.9434	1574	upon
292.91	64.7	.8239	1768	family
291.86	64.7	.9201	1599	later
291.76	64.7	.9346	1577	turn
291.59	64.6	.9238	1592	move
290.91	64.6	.8962	1629	face
290.25	64.6	.8196	1748	door
289.37	64.6	.8201	1757	cut
288.19	64.6	.9290	1566	done
286.05	64.6	.9204	1570	group
285.01	64.5	.8397	1696	true
284.86	64.5	.9528	1514	half
284.46	64.5	.5210	2611	sentences
282.24	64.5	.9121	1557	red
281.81	64.5	.9410	1513	fish
279.37	64.5	.7261	1886	plants
277.61	64.4	.8427	1645	living
275.77	64.4	.8349	1637	wanted
275.67	64.4	.8892	1556	black
274.50	64.4	.8466	1616	eat
273.37	64.4	.8972	1534	short
273.10	64.4	.7299	1836	UnitedStates
271.96	64.3	.9311	1473	run
271.86	64.3	.8845	1545	kinds
271.65	64.3	.9457	1453	book
271.42	64.3	.8857	1534	gave
267.97	64.3	.8959	1507	order
267.63	64.3	.9567	1416	open
266.87	64.3	.8845	1511	ground
266.85	64.3	.7772	1715	lines
264.37	64.2	.9047	1469	cold
263.96	64.2	.9428	1414	really
263.51	64.2	.8808	1502	table
260.75	64.2	.9254	1423	remember
260.35	64.2	.9218	1421	tree
260.15	64.2	.7524	1711	000
259.30	64.1	.9730	1352	course
258.87	64.1	.9040	1438	front
258.18	64.1	.9313	1401	known
257.99	64.1	.8170	1575	American
256.87	64.1	.8586	1499	space
256.66	64.1	.9249	1398	inside
252.45	64.0	.9172	1387	ago
251.98	64.0	.9011	1408	making
251.76	64.0	.7572	1619	Mrs
250.26	64.0	.8722	1439	early
250.01	64.0	.7590	1604	I'll
249.17	64.0	.9360	1345	learned
248.69	64.0	.9236	1357	brought
248.66	64.0	.9800	1288	close
248.57	64.0	.8746	1420	nothing
248.14	63.9	.9358	1339	though
247.77	63.9	.8774	1409	started
247.56	63.9	.8896	1397	idea
247.24	63.9	.9053	1374	call
247.03	63.9	.9039	1372	lived
246.45	63.9	.9520	1311	makes
246.38	63.9	.8155	1501	became
245.72	63.9	.9302	1331	looking
245.42	63.9	.7371	1654	add
244.10	63.9	.9476	1304	become
243.77	63.9	.8596	1418	grow
242.66	63.9	.7391	1623	draw
242.56	63.8	.9232	1325	yet
241.40	63.8	.8929	1357	hands
240.98	63.8	.8877	1366	less
240.80	63.8	.8982	1347	John
240.80	63.8	.9063	1336	wind
240.19	63.8	.9046	1337	places
240.18	63.8	.8705	1376	behind
239.08	63.8	.9453	1279	cannot
238.16	63.8	.6711	1738	letter
238.06	63.8	.9182	1308	among
236.56	63.7	.5503	2059	4
236.24	63.7	.7643	1535	A
235.23	63.7	.6396	1798	letters
234.30	63.7	.9165	1289	comes
231.75	63.7	.9281	1260	able
231.49	63.6	.8291	1380	dog
229.85	63.6	.7673	1490	shown
229.22	63.6	.9116	1266	mean
228.35	63.6	.7221	1564	English
228.12	63.6	.9789	1183	rest
227.83	63.6	.9318	1235	perhaps
227.26	63.6	.9620	1198	certain
226.91	63.6	.9321	1229	six
226.78	63.6	.8934	1275	feel
226.28	63.5	.9291	1227	fire
224.13	63.5	.9372	1207	ready
222.21	63.5	.9209	1216	green
221.89	63.5	.8342	1317	yes

THE PRECEDING WORD TYPE OCCUPIES RANK 400

U	SFI	D	F	Word Type
221.36	63.5	.8909	1249	built
221.28	63.4	.9390	1192	special
221.26	63.4	.7883	1374	ran
220.07	63.4	.9762	1144	full
219.74	63.4	.9054	1219	town
219.72	63.4	.7558	1445	complete
219.30	63.4	.7096	1489	oh
218.94	63.4	.9245	1196	person
217.70	63.4	.8851	1233	hot
217.41	63.4	.8985	1214	anything
216.70	63.4	.9162	1192	hold
216.18	63.3	.8445	1281	state
216.13	63.3	.5893	1781	list
215.75	63.3	.7576	1387	stood
215.32	63.3	.9132	1187	hundred
213.42	63.3	.9095	1184	shows
212.74	63.3	.8703	1225	ten
211.75	63.3	.9058	1173	fast
211.66	63.3	.7979	1303	seemed
211.37	63.3	.8540	1231	felt
211.04	63.2	.9421	1131	kept
210.59	63.2	.7906	1321	America
210.06	63.2	.8257	1274	notice
210.05	63.2	.8405	1240	can't
210.02	63.2	.9299	1140	strong
209.79	63.2	.8106	1280	voice
209.29	63.2	.9428	1123	probably
209.22	63.2	.9348	1131	needed
209.02	63.2	.8690	1203	birds
208.36	63.2	.7329	1403	area
208.34	63.2	.8148	1263	horse
207.77	63.2	.7991	1283	Indians
207.59	63.2	.6286	1606	sounds
207.51	63.2	.9249	1132	matter
207.37	63.2	.9731	1081	stand
207.12	63.2	.9100	1145	box
206.96	63.2	.9651	1087	start
206.28	63.1	.7860	1286	that's
206.01	63.1	.8533	1211	class
205.90	63.1	.8607	1198	piece
204.96	63.1	.9290	1112	slowly
203.42	63.1	.7887	1281	surface
202.80	63.1	.8659	1170	river
200.75	63.0	.3433	2582	numbers
200.47	63.0	.8578	1174	common
200.11	63.0	.9328	1081	stop
199.87	63.0	.7560	1294	am
199.80	63.0	.8822	1133	talk
199.62	63.0	.9495	1063	quickly
199.06	63.0	.9512	1060	whether
198.46	63.0	.9273	1079	fine
198.31	63.0	.5228	1804	5
196.62	62.9	.9217	1076	round
196.54	62.9	.8339	1171	dark
196.09	62.9	.8901	1107	girls
195.97	62.9	.8888	1109	past
195.83	62.9	.9310	1061	ball
194.91	62.9	.9032	1084	girl
194.35	62.9	.9057	1077	tried
194.34	62.9	.8757	1106	road
193.88	62.9	.8544	1135	questions
193.67	62.9	.9101	1071	blue
192.60	62.8	.6822	1376	meaning
192.48	62.8	.8528	1123	coming

U	SFI	D	F	Word Type
190.82	62.8	.9699	998	instead
190.80	62.8	.9340	1033	either
190.46	62.8	.9136	1049	held
190.35	62.8	.9010	1061	friends
188.67	62.8	.9533	1002	already
187.93	62.7	.8781	1072	warm
187.88	62.7	.9346	1015	taken
187.53	62.7	.8689	1077	gone
186.39	62.7	.9080	1032	finally
186.27	62.7	.8924	1048	summer
185.94	62.7	.9124	1026	understand
185.69	62.7	.8919	1046	moon
185.62	62.7	.8210	1122	animal
185.36	62.7	.8886	1046	mind
185.22	62.7	.9267	1008	outside
184.82	62.7	.8717	1065	power
184.15	62.7	.7662	1180	says
183.61	62.6	.8196	1117	problem
183.00	62.6	.9721	955	longer
182.50	62.6	.9151	1004	winter
182.15	62.6	.8729	1044	Indian
182.05	62.6	.9207	996	deep
181.41	62.6	.8358	1081	mountains
180.93	62.6	.9275	984	heavy
180.75	62.6	.9180	993	carefully
180.44	62.6	.8883	1022	follow
180.38	62.6	.8585	1048	beautiful
180.31	62.6	.9049	1005	beginning
180.20	62.6	.9116	994	moved
180.18	62.6	.9572	953	everyone
179.67	62.5	.9418	964	leave
179.55	62.5	.8960	1005	everything
179.22	62.5	.9284	974	game
179.00	62.5	.8043	1110	system
178.23	62.5	.8788	1016	bring
177.59	62.5	.9235	969	watch

THE PRECEDING WORD TYPE OCCUPIES RANK 500

U	SFI	D	F	Word Type
176.92	62.5	.8386	1051	shall
176.46	62.5	.8927	993	dry
175.88	62.5	.8924	990	hours
175.53	62.4	.7700	1134	written
175.32	62.4	.6217	1370	10
174.51	62.4	.8126	1057	stopped
174.44	62.4	.9290	949	within
174.34	62.4	.9419	935	floor
174.02	62.4	.7911	1075	Bill
173.96	62.4	.8736	995	ice
173.79	62.4	.8432	1021	ship
173.69	62.4	.9095	962	themselves
173.67	62.4	.8970	976	begin
173.52	62.4	.9498	925	fact
173.50	62.4	.9275	945	third
173.43	62.4	.9010	967	quite
173.01	62.4	.9284	940	carry
172.94	62.4	.9402	930	goes
172.60	62.4	.8816	983	distance
172.42	62.4	.9297	937	although
172.23	62.4	.8923	972	added
171.88	62.4	.9365	927	doing
171.60	62.3	.7277	1138	sat
171.02	62.3	.7170	1168	pictures
170.61	62.3	.9271	930	possible
169.95	62.3	.8370	1016	names
169.64	62.3	.8151	1032	heart
169.49	62.3	.9766	881	having
168.55	62.3	.7377	1131	writing
168.40	62.3	.9343	910	real
168.24	62.3	.8866	956	simple
168.09	62.3	.8863	948	snow
168.09	62.3	.9277	913	getting
168.02	62.3	.9004	938	rain
167.94	62.3	.8367	993	suddenly
167.81	62.2	.9499	894	easy
167.40	62.2	.8963	939	leaves
167.03	62.2	.8795	951	lay
166.86	62.2	.7858	1057	size
166.85	62.2	.9020	929	wild
166.34	62.2	.8367	990	weather
166.23	62.2	.8183	1005	Mother
165.75	62.2	.7639	1056	Miss
165.75	62.2	.9182	909	carried
165.67	62.2	.7853	1057	pattern
165.45	62.2	.8436	976	sky
165.39	62.2	.7858	1030	walked
164.85	62.2	.5793	1371	6
164.78	62.2	.8937	926	main
164.77	62.2	.9132	908	someone
164.53	62.2	.9202	902	ones
164.05	62.1	.8349	984	center
163.68	62.1	.8662	946	named
163.40	62.1	.8931	919	field
163.08	62.1	.8949	914	stay
162.97	62.1	.9460	872	itself
162.71	62.1	.9615	857	worked
162.11	62.1	.8654	933	boat
161.52	62.1	.9195	886	building
161.17	62.1	.9068	895	question
160.95	62.1	.9428	863	wide
160.92	62.1	.9066	892	let's
160.77	62.1	.9247	878	least
160.72	62.1	.8818	917	problems
160.47	62.1	.9190	880	followed
160.23	62.0	.8930	902	books
159.67	62.0	.8862	904	tiny
159.37	62.0	.8799	908	hour
158.76	62.0	.7140	1095	B
158.76	62.0	.8692	910	happened
158.32	62.0	.9424	849	foot
157.95	62.0	.7365	1051	plant
157.90	62.0	.9129	871	moving
157.87	62.0	.8942	886	care
157.64	62.0	.9285	857	low
157.53	62.0	.9241	859	else
157.28	62.0	.8776	895	gold
157.18	62.0	.9261	857	build
157.04	62.0	.8601	913	glass
156.61	61.9	.8439	925	rock
155.94	61.9	.9268	848	tall
155.51	61.9	.9290	844	covered
155.44	61.9	.9533	825	alone
155.29	61.9	.8754	886	reached
155.27	61.9	.9112	858	bottom
154.81	61.9	.9407	831	walk
153.20	61.9	.7715	992	forms
153.09	61.8	.9254	835	takes
152.79	61.8	.7363	1024	check
152.63	61.8	.9003	850	reading
152.49	61.8	.9341	824	fall
152.46	61.8	.8988	851	poor
152.42	61.8	.5925	1223	map
152.40	61.8	.6985	1062	scientists
152.34	61.8	.8158	923	friend
152.04	61.8	.7476	1005	c
151.81	61.8	.7199	1041	language
151.64	61.8	.8883	855	job
151.39	61.8	.6637	1115	points
151.38	61.8	.3273	2100	music

THE PRECEDING WORD TYPE OCCUPIES RANK 600

U	SFI	D	F	Word Type
150.84	61.8	.8634	872	buy
150.77	61.8	.8987	841	window
150.57	61.8	.7643	980	mark
150.56	61.8	.7618	978	ideas
150.32	61.8	.7374	1003	heat
150.21	61.8	.8879	847	grew
150.17	61.8	.6358	1148	listen
150.04	61.8	.8271	900	ask
149.78	61.8	.8766	859	changes
149.38	61.7	.9243	817	single
149.08	61.7	.8438	886	French
148.94	61.7	.9266	811	clear
148.80	61.7	.8084	906	Tom
148.77	61.7	.5973	1190	energy
148.56	61.7	.8815	846	week
148.27	61.7	.8321	891	explain
147.76	61.7	.9143	813	passed
147.55	61.7	.9043	820	lost
147.22	61.7	.9253	802	spring
147.12	61.7	.9108	814	travel
147.08	61.7	.8400	877	wrote
146.67	61.7	.6855	1043	cities
146.54	61.7	.8055	900	farm
146.45	61.7	.7691	945	circle
145.74	61.6	.6535	1043	cried
145.56	61.6	.9198	799	whose
145.51	61.6	.7717	940	correct
145.50	61.6	.8623	841	bed
145.28	61.6	.9104	804	working
145.25	61.6	.6747	1056	measure
145.21	61.6	.9183	797	straight
144.46	61.6	.8170	881	base
144.44	61.6	.8599	838	mountain
144.22	61.6	.9142	793	caught
144.02	61.6	.8268	867	hair
143.81	61.6	.8863	812	bird
143.29	61.6	.7632	933	per
143.14	61.6	.7566	934	wood
143.03	61.6	.9004	797	running
142.93	61.6	.6276	1109	color
142.91	61.6	.7603	928	South
142.77	61.5	.9067	795	groups
142.74	61.5	.7222	968	war
142.42	61.5	.8528	837	members
142.25	61.5	.9105	785	fly
142.14	61.5	.8776	812	yourself
142.11	61.5	.9204	777	decided
140.77	61.5	.8940	792	seem
140.61	61.5	.9418	756	thus
140.57	61.5	.8362	836	legs
140.46	61.5	.9212	769	nearly
140.32	61.5	.7156	965	square
140.28	61.5	.8130	859	England
140.16	61.5	.8339	834	moment
139.84	61.5	.7408	926	North
139.72	61.5	.8357	836	teacher
139.55	61.4	.9062	774	happy
138.67	61.4	.9076	770	changed
138.26	61.4	.6447	1044	products
138.18	61.4	.7206	945	C
138.13	61.4	.9420	741	bright
137.90	61.4	.8189	835	sent
137.90	61.4	.9543	732	present
137.57	61.4	.8235	834	plan
136.89	61.4	.9437	734	rather
136.78	61.4	.6998	962	length
136.38	61.3	.9073	756	looks
135.54	61.3	.9093	750	speed
135.34	61.3	.7803	861	machine
135.03	61.3	.8232	817	information
134.95	61.3	.9546	716	except
134.86	61.3	.7763	863	figure
134.86	61.3	.7858	844	you're
134.84	61.3	.8168	819	minutes
134.83	61.3	.8351	805	free
134.73	61.3	.8474	790	fell
134.58	61.3	.8428	797	suppose
134.47	61.3	.9193	739	natural
134.14	61.3	.7859	843	ocean
133.99	61.3	.5846	1095	government
133.81	61.3	.9083	742	lives
133.52	61.3	.8902	751	trying
133.30	61.2	.8557	776	horses
132.99	61.2	.7920	833	The
132.99	61.2	.6507	1002	s
132.97	61.2	.8867	751	baby
132.65	61.2	.9309	719	taking
132.49	61.2	.8705	761	grass
132.29	61.2	.6442	990	plane
132.01	61.2	.8074	814	pieces
131.89	61.2	.7924	827	sides
131.85	61.2	.8485	770	pulled
131.59	61.2	.5810	1092	8
131.53	61.2	.7714	846	inches
131.46	61.2	.8793	748	street
131.38	61.2	.7843	828	George
131.23	61.2	.7213	879	couldn't
130.86	61.2	.9440	701	reason
130.16	61.1	.8713	751	difference
129.98	61.1	.7949	808	tells

THE PRECEDING WORD TYPE OCCUPIES RANK 700

U	SFI	D	F	Word Type
129.76	61.1	.8217	779	maybe
129.69	61.1	.8859	736	larger
129.48	61.1	.8979	726	history
129.21	61.1	.8946	725	mouth
129.21	61.1	.9231	706	middle
128.72	61.1	.8621	749	step
128.71	61.1	.8902	727	thousands
128.59	61.1	.8630	747	steps
128.39	61.1	.8359	762	cars
128.16	61.1	.8810	730	child
127.43	61.1	.8735	728	opened
127.10	61.0	.9219	694	thinking
126.94	61.0	.8957	710	strange
126.89	61.0	.7997	785	eggs
126.68	61.0	.9000	707	wish
126.31	61.0	.6654	921	soil
126.25	61.0	.8956	710	human
125.89	61.0	.9143	693	trip
125.81	61.0	.8293	750	woman
125.64	61.0	.8926	707	eye
125.56	61.0	.7243	849	milk
125.17	61.0	.8595	731	choose
125.12	61.0	.7802	793	north
125.09	61.0	.9487	667	discovered
124.85	61.0	.8937	702	houses
124.75	61.0	.9149	687	seven
124.74	61.0	.8735	717	easily
124.65	61.0	.8713	717	famous
124.57	61.0	.8648	723	pages
123.90	60.9	.9033	689	late
123.71	60.9	.8316	740	rocks
123.22	60.9	.8885	695	flowers
123.18	60.9	.9158	677	pay
122.95	60.9	.8531	717	sleep
122.91	60.9	.7403	817	iron
122.82	60.9	.8839	695	trouble
122.42	60.9	.9030	681	store
122.34	60.9	.8371	725	beside
122.13	60.9	.8344	731	oil
121.84	60.9	.8348	731	modern
121.51	60.8	.9347	656	filled
121.47	60.8	.8749	695	fun
121.28	60.8	.8951	679	catch
121.09	60.8	.8199	734	growing
121.08	60.8	.8596	705	business
120.76	60.8	.6917	853	countries
120.71	60.8	.8671	696	helped
120.52	60.8	.9380	650	gives
120.25	60.8	.9494	641	exactly
120.22	60.8	.7469	779	Jim
119.81	60.8	.7349	790	King
119.71	60.8	.9328	648	reach
119.60	60.8	.8816	679	lot
119.44	60.8	.7733	756	won't
119.24	60.8	.8180	720	answered
119.21	60.8	.9328	646	case
118.97	60.8	.9053	661	speak
118.83	60.7	.7703	766	shape
118.60	60.7	.9193	651	eight
118.56	60.7	.7132	817	edge
118.56	60.7	.9395	638	seems
118.44	60.7	.8888	669	soft
118.19	60.7	.8302	712	interesting
118.01	60.7	.8538	687	watched
117.80	60.7	.8802	673	formed
117.75	60.7	.8347	701	stories
117.37	60.7	.7730	744	village
117.35	60.7	.8176	718	object
117.28	60.7	.8180	713	stars
117.27	60.7	.9250	640	placed
116.47	60.7	.8509	680	Joe
116.36	60.7	.9555	617	age
116.22	60.7	.8761	663	minute
116.20	60.7	.9112	642	wall
116.14	60.6	.6231	900	b
115.98	60.6	.9342	627	meet
115.97	60.6	.8812	662	record
115.79	60.6	.6396	887	copy
115.29	60.6	.8384	684	forest
115.18	60.6	.7435	761	River
115.15	60.6	.8777	658	months
114.95	60.6	.9531	611	especially
114.37	60.6	.8780	651	dogs
113.89	60.6	.8423	679	necessary
113.57	60.6	.8651	659	lower
113.48	60.5	.9011	634	smaller
113.43	60.5	.7144	767	he's
113.41	60.5	.6664	838	unit
113.32	60.5	.8579	662	flat
113.06	60.5	.5718	950	7
112.76	60.5	.8687	651	direction
112.70	60.5	.7871	709	south
112.47	60.5	.6270	882	subject
112.30	60.5	.8266	677	skin
111.78	60.5	.7289	742	wasn't
111.75	60.5	.7453	730	I've
111.67	60.5	.7231	760	Europe
111.54	60.5	.8194	677	NewYork
111.34	60.5	.9109	615	yellow
111.29	60.5	.7459	731	ships

THE PRECEDING WORD TYPE OCCUPIES RANK 800

U	SFI	D	F	Word Type
111.24	60.5	.8846	630	arms
111.06	60.5	.8921	625	party
110.60	60.4	.8499	651	force
110.41	60.4	.8321	663	test
110.23	60.4	.8280	660	bad
110.12	60.4	.7039	766	temperature
110.01	60.4	.7503	724	pair
109.92	60.4	.8557	639	ahead
109.87	60.4	.9125	606	wrong
109.86	60.4	.9231	601	practice
109.77	60.4	.8095	672	sand
109.64	60.4	.8845	620	tail
109.01	60.4	.8213	656	wait
109.01	60.4	.9304	592	difficult
108.84	60.4	.8862	619	general
108.70	60.4	.9065	604	cover
108.68	60.4	.7840	689	areas
108.58	60.4	.8348	651	material
108.53	60.4	.8859	613	talking
108.49	60.4	.8341	645	isn't
108.38	60.3	.9147	597	thousand
108.37	60.3	.8824	615	sign
108.11	60.3	.8021	674	examples
107.75	60.3	.8413	637	guess
107.68	60.3	.8462	638	begins
107.51	60.3	.9162	591	forward
107.34	60.3	.8861	607	huge
107.24	60.3	.8745	616	needs
107.15	60.3	.9058	595	closed
106.96	60.3	.8648	617	ride
106.94	60.3	.6265	825	region
106.58	60.3	.7942	667	largest
106.50	60.3	.7399	708	answers
106.46	60.3	.9180	585	nor
106.42	60.3	.8933	601	period
106.41	60.3	.8999	594	finished
106.38	60.3	.7422	705	blood
106.25	60.3	.9168	584	rich
106.04	60.3	.8520	620	team
106.02	60.3	.8148	647	waves
105.98	60.3	.9225	579	corner
105.90	60.2	.7745	675	Mary
105.85	60.2	.8483	620	cat
105.75	60.2	.7451	701	amount
105.73	60.2	.8637	610	liked
105.63	60.2	.8775	600	garden
105.63	60.2	.8861	598	led
105.45	60.2	.7333	713	note
105.43	60.2	.8547	620	various
105.19	60.2	.8107	638	race
105.18	60.2	.8829	600	developed
105.03	60.2	.8747	600	bit
104.40	60.2	.7574	678	clothes
104.35	60.2	.8694	603	uses
104.25	60.2	.8837	594	result
104.05	60.2	.8029	646	greater
104.03	60.2	.8616	604	fields
103.90	60.2	.7431	688	New
103.87	60.2	.8874	586	brother
103.86	60.2	.7398	695	addition
103.68	60.2	.8804	590	doesn't
103.66	60.2	.7487	683	states
103.45	60.1	.8790	590	dead
103.37	60.1	.8480	610	weight
103.19	60.1	.8422	611	thin
103.17	60.1	.8709	593	stone
103.17	60.1	.8639	595	hit
103.03	60.1	.7974	636	wife
102.23	60.1	.6088	810	played
101.74	60.1	.8146	619	island
101.70	60.1	.8846	575	standing
101.53	60.1	.8013	624	there's
101.53	60.1	.7585	653	we'll
101.42	60.1	.8617	591	opposite
101.37	60.1	.7870	637	born
101.32	60.1	.9197	556	sense
101.11	60.0	.7562	658	cattle
101.08	60.0	.7552	662	million
101.07	60.0	.9219	552	anyone
100.94	60.0	.8171	618	rule
100.93	60.0	.8371	602	science
100.91	60.0	.9195	554	helps
100.86	60.0	.6455	750	farmers
100.45	60.0	.8130	607	afraid
100.40	60.0	.8465	592	women
100.37	60.0	.8607	586	produce
100.34	60.0	.9032	558	pull
100.32	60.0	.6134	771	son
100.31	60.0	.9410	539	meant
99.853	60.0	.9430	535	broken
99.688	60.0	.8973	560	interest
99.402	60.0	.8294	600	ends
99.194	60.0	.8933	557	woods
98.894	60.0	.7642	636	Henry
98.881	60.0	.9059	548	chance
98.522	59.9	.8474	581	homes
98.442	59.9	.9185	540	thick
98.413	59.9	.8696	565	sight
98.344	59.9	.8556	573	pretty
98.238	59.9	.6330	755	12

THE PRECEDING WORD TYPE OCCUPIES RANK 900

U	SFI	D	F	Word Type
97.924	59.9	.8816	556	train
97.804	59.9	.5050	915	sets
97.778	59.9	.8522	573	fresh
97.601	59.9	.9164	536	faster
97.439	59.9	.8066	600	Washington
97.225	59.9	.8994	543	drive
97.007	59.9	.9436	520	lead
96.973	59.9	.9508	516	break
96.863	59.9	.8826	549	sit
96.824	59.9	.8024	598	bought
96.587	59.8	.8500	568	hundreds
96.570	59.8	.8177	587	radio
96.518	59.8	.7668	626	method
96.440	59.8	.8957	541	gets
96.339	59.8	.6628	688	king
96.329	59.8	.8741	555	similar
96.276	59.8	.9107	532	return
96.264	59.8	.8838	545	corn
96.193	59.8	.8958	540	decide
96.016	59.8	.8954	540	position
96.009	59.8	.8586	557	bear
95.992	59.8	.8839	544	hope
95.888	59.8	.2784	1525	song
95.737	59.8	.8110	582	engine
95.482	59.8	.5259	852	missing
95.471	59.8	.7458	633	France
95.003	59.8	.8918	536	board

U	SFI	D	F	Word Type
94.844	59.8	.7503	624	playing
94.840	59.8	.8547	556	control
94.831	59.8	.8977	531	spread
94.771	59.8	.9488	505	knows
94.341	59.7	.8674	543	evening
94.148	59.7	.8429	557	brown
94.052	59.7	.8712	538	picked
94.020	59.7	.9090	521	clean
93.884	59.7	.7059	642	wouldn't
93.670	59.7	.7222	643	section
93.509	59.7	.9011	522	spent
93.375	59.7	.5416	753	Dan
93.291	59.7	.9098	516	ring
93.231	59.7	.8577	544	higher
92.656	59.7	.8987	518	raised
92.645	59.7	.5463	811	9
92.562	59.7	.8814	526	weeks
92.214	59.6	.8567	538	teeth
92.130	59.6	.8623	533	quiet
91.858	59.6	.8983	515	ancient
91.810	59.6	.8570	532	Jack
91.647	59.6	.9185	502	stick
91.597	59.6	.8256	549	afternoon
91.545	59.6	.9184	502	silver
91.432	59.6	.8328	544	nose
91.324	59.6	.7981	572	century
90.902	59.6	.8661	524	saying
90.769	59.6	.9270	495	therefore
90.749	59.6	.8955	508	flying
90.704	59.6	.8554	531	level
90.611	59.6	.8621	524	you'll
90.403	59.6	.8754	518	death
90.312	59.6	.7296	602	hole
89.843	59.5	.7432	594	coast
89.750	59.5	.8407	533	directions
89.728	59.5	.9076	498	cross
89.717	59.5	.9049	499	sharp
89.612	59.5	.8425	529	fight
89.431	59.5	.7433	597	capital
89.237	59.5	.8250	537	Old
89.149	59.5	.9238	487	fill
89.047	59.5	.9381	480	deal
88.985	59.5	.7631	583	patterns
88.903	59.5	.9262	485	works
88.695	59.5	.8984	495	busy
88.693	59.5	.7826	562	pounds
88.673	59.5	.9219	485	beyond
88.629	59.5	.7793	560	seeds
88.611	59.5	.8149	535	Bob
88.610	59.5	.8452	526	produced
88.509	59.5	.9118	489	fingers
88.498	59.5	.9193	485	send
88.262	59.5	.6915	626	100
88.175	59.5	.5673	735	love
88.124	59.5	.7115	612	materials
88.098	59.4	.8848	500	cool
88.023	59.4	.6507	639	laughed
87.930	59.4	.8797	502	cause
87.884	59.4	.9146	484	man's
87.824	59.4	.9383	473	stands
87.815	59.4	.8085	540	feeling
87.627	59.4	.8430	519	facts
87.553	59.4	.8736	501	please
87.552	59.4	.6902	617	meat
87.444	59.4	.7954	539	lady
87.333	59.4	.7748	557	west
87.321	59.4	.8270	523	glad
87.256	59.4	.7204	593	British
87.210	59.4	.8425	519	action
87.184	59.4	.8403	520	divided
87.065	59.4	.9023	486	greatest
87.046	59.4	.8362	520	happens
86.988	59.4	.9125	480	pass
THE PRECEDING WORD TYPE OCCUPIES RANK 1000				
86.906	59.4	.7701	561	20
86.720	59.4	.8894	489	returned
86.651	59.4	.6839	626	adding
86.552	59.4	.8555	505	ears
86.471	59.4	.8399	512	soldiers
86.453	59.4	.7147	599	type
86.237	59.4	.9244	471	attention
86.226	59.4	.7454	558	shouted
86.136	59.4	.7202	583	gas
86.087	59.3	.7242	584	World
85.725	59.3	.9383	462	actually
85.435	59.3	.8549	497	kitchen
85.349	59.3	.9324	463	alike
85.231	59.3	.9373	459	pick
85.211	59.3	.5602	737	scale
84.996	59.3	.8256	517	basic
84.981	59.3	.8112	520	West
84.933	59.3	.6884	602	President
84.645	59.3	.7208	567	Uncle
84.543	59.3	.6504	617	Johnny
84.270	59.3	.9050	468	happen
84.214	59.3	.8836	478	walls
84.198	59.3	.6601	619	Africa
83.979	59.2	.8792	478	showed
83.933	59.2	.8874	474	safe
83.844	59.2	.8331	501	grown
83.630	59.2	.6678	610	cost
83.442	59.2	.8138	510	wear
83.348	59.2	.9197	457	act
83.270	59.2	.7991	514	wings
83.268	59.2	.8050	507	Paul
83.116	59.2	.8052	511	hat
82.924	59.2	.8399	491	arm
82.686	59.2	.5586	685	believe
82.576	59.2	.6830	597	major
82.481	59.2	.8727	475	becomes
82.388	59.2	.9066	457	gray
82.041	59.1	.8977	459	died
81.934	59.1	.8328	491	bones
81.887	59.1	.8438	482	sitting
81.818	59.1	.9268	445	wonder
81.573	59.1	.8497	483	include
81.543	59.1	.9408	438	interested

U	SFI	D	F	Word Type
81.523	59.1	.8411	486	describe
81.479	59.1	.7580	532	electric
81.325	59.1	.8502	477	sold
81.244	59.1	.9249	443	visit
81.171	59.1	.7216	555	15
81.030	59.1	.8748	464	sheep
80.846	59.1	.7365	534	I'd
80.824	59.1	.8083	493	waiting
80.814	59.1	.8759	461	shoes
80.753	59.1	.7537	531	30
80.580	59.1	.8598	469	office
80.478	59.1	.8460	477	contains
80.466	59.1	.7845	510	row
80.443	59.1	.7151	557	contain
80.180	59.0	.6942	568	objects
80.050	59.0	.8728	461	fit
80.043	59.0	.8457	475	students
80.010	59.0	.9171	440	turns
79.955	59.0	.8103	489	clouds
79.943	59.0	.6948	565	equal
79.879	59.0	.7054	555	War
79.862	59.0	.7754	512	value
79.679	59.0	.8656	459	yard
79.634	59.0	.7449	527	Americans
79.587	59.0	.7272	540	beat
79.481	59.0	.6582	590	inch
79.232	59.0	.8727	453	walking
79.146	59.0	.6702	574	sugar
78.946	59.0	.5823	652	key
78.905	59.0	.4227	860	product
78.870	59.0	.7686	504	desert
78.860	59.0	.8428	465	bank
78.755	59.0	.8922	443	farther
78.735	59.0	.8854	446	won
78.636	59.0	.7324	531	total
78.600	59.0	.8461	462	sell
78.537	59.0	.6843	560	wire
78.465	58.9	.8477	461	rose
78.424	58.9	.6879	554	cotton
78.365	58.9	.8041	485	moves
78.176	58.9	.7464	512	spoke
78.156	58.9	.8615	451	rope
78.045	58.9	.8839	444	rules
77.895	58.9	.8891	439	fear
77.811	58.9	.8703	447	shore
77.745	58.9	.8512	458	throughout
77.509	58.9	.8315	467	compare
77.506	58.9	.6144	604	Sam
77.493	58.9	.7998	478	dollars
77.489	58.9	.2928	1141	x
77.487	58.9	.9047	432	studied
77.259	58.9	.7575	507	movement
77.099	58.9	.6114	602	lands
77.077	58.9	.6477	580	exercise
76.910	58.9	.8246	461	tired
76.905	58.9	.7300	515	bread
76.867	58.9	.8484	452	streets
THE PRECEDING WORD TYPE OCCUPIES RANK 1100				
76.839	58.9	.8220	468	process
76.814	58.9	.7728	490	parents
76.710	58.8	.8306	462	nature
76.231	58.8	.9308	414	apart
76.094	58.8	.8728	436	path
76.005	58.8	.9018	424	careful
75.862	58.8	.9360	410	simply
75.836	58.8	.8010	469	Christmas
75.782	58.8	.8941	426	narrow
75.658	58.8	.4443	782	metal
75.633	58.8	.9136	417	nine
75.632	58.8	.8838	430	useful
75.617	58.8	.8467	447	public
75.473	58.8	.7502	495	buildings
75.409	58.8	.9478	403	according
75.297	58.8	.6450	565	steel
75.279	58.8	.7419	497	salt
75.269	58.8	.8963	421	carrying
75.215	58.8	.8440	443	watching
75.192	58.8	.7986	469	speech
75.137	58.8	.7278	509	machines
75.000	58.8	.9170	412	forth
74.960	58.7	.7216	510	nation
74.916	58.7	.6951	524	rivers
74.876	58.7	.8889	424	knowledge
74.867	58.7	.9146	413	appear
74.762	58.7	.6430	561	insects
74.618	58.7	.8435	440	ate
74.550	58.7	.8661	430	dinner
74.255	58.7	.7994	457	hurt
74.245	58.7	.7956	455	Peter
74.199	58.7	.7551	476	jumped
74.099	58.7	.8906	418	spend
74.018	58.7	.7318	497	experiment
73.941	58.7	.7877	469	marks
73.923	58.7	.8573	432	touch
73.860	58.7	.8527	433	drop
73.816	58.7	.8777	421	chair
73.740	58.7	.7941	461	east
73.682	58.7	.8587	427	dropped
73.666	58.7	.7770	469	William
73.658	58.7	.8927	416	separate
73.649	58.7	.9009	410	truck
73.633	58.7	.3241	1014	sing
73.597	58.7	.8013	458	elements
73.368	58.7	.7758	471	column
73.199	58.6	.9239	400	twice
73.188	58.6	.9100	406	particular
73.180	58.6	.3793	839	paragraph
73.143	58.6	.9205	401	unless
73.140	58.6	.9131	403	spot
73.088	58.6	.9163	402	neither
72.997	58.6	.8380	433	met
72.988	58.6	.7572	476	workers
72.972	58.6	.4002	785	Father
72.936	58.6	.8735	418	wheel
72.769	58.6	.8826	413	continued
72.704	58.6	.9004	406	none
72.645	58.6	.7293	482	what's

U	SFI	D	F	Word Type
72.611	58.6	.8357	430	hill
72.540	58.6	.8866	410	hills
72.434	58.6	.9017	404	older
72.256	58.6	.8850	411	television
72.236	58.6	.3831	885	verb
72.218	58.6	.3687	874	solve
72.207	58.6	.7077	499	pressure
72.202	58.6	.7842	457	report
71.976	58.6	.8082	444	roots
71.956	58.6	.8676	414	farmer
71.890	58.6	.8253	435	count
71.762	58.6	.9595	379	giving
71.707	58.6	.7340	479	trade
71.701	58.6	.9422	385	joined
71.644	58.6	.8335	428	chief
71.635	58.6	.8940	403	month
71.604	58.5	.6475	544	F
71.572	58.5	.7415	476	Spanish
71.551	58.5	.8447	425	terms
71.334	58.5	.8307	427	cloth
71.259	58.5	.7449	476	D
71.244	58.5	.8786	406	doctor
71.222	58.5	.8385	423	indeed
70.999	58.5	.8981	397	turning
70.982	58.5	.5561	608	dance
70.792	58.5	.8681	409	church
70.746	58.5	.8858	403	original
70.658	58.5	.8374	422	enjoy
70.640	58.5	.8233	424	climbed
70.635	58.5	.7190	483	string
70.622	58.5	.7206	473	Sea
70.484	58.5	.7848	443	killed
70.345	58.5	.8724	403	sister
70.333	58.5	.8711	406	familiar
70.316	58.5	.8569	409	hardly
70.310	58.5	.8767	401	onto
70.135	58.5	.9295	381	imagine
70.076	58.5	.8495	411	blow
70.047	58.5	.8917	394	quick
69.683	58.4	.7774	445	law
69.461	58.4	.9248	379	lie
THE PRECEDING WORD TYPE OCCUPIES RANK 1200				
69.380	58.4	.7485	460	final
69.320	58.4	.9338	375	rise
69.202	58.4	.8879	391	certainly
69.138	58.4	.7466	450	Billy
69.110	58.4	.8366	410	loud
69.056	58.4	.8585	402	fair
68.985	58.4	.8658	397	pointed
68.894	58.4	.8542	401	pushed
68.852	58.4	.7822	432	herself
68.699	58.4	.9192	377	learning
68.684	58.4	.8673	396	slow
68.680	58.4	.8279	411	noise
68.661	58.4	.9389	370	marked
68.591	58.4	.6616	507	statement
68.420	58.4	.8516	399	hungry
68.268	58.3	.9522	363	join
68.136	58.3	.8718	392	finding
68.094	58.3	.6511	504	tube
68.080	58.3	.7894	425	rode
67.988	58.3	.8874	384	empty
67.979	58.3	.9280	370	received
67.821	58.3	.7530	444	Jane
67.751	58.3	.8755	387	twenty
67.748	58.3	.8530	396	broke
67.725	58.3	.7902	422	nice
67.716	58.3	.8526	399	effect
67.663	58.3	.8632	392	paid
67.657	58.3	.8643	393	motion
67.637	58.3	.7034	465	myself
67.550	58.3	.8005	415	talked
67.534	58.3	.7176	465	divide
67.532	58.3	.7107	461	wants
67.395	58.3	.8331	404	supply
67.307	58.3	.9201	369	laid
67.161	58.3	.5960	536	crops
67.156	58.3	.8035	416	millions
67.101	58.3	.4006	747	cells
66.941	58.3	.7303	445	dear
66.849	58.3	.5145	620	1/2
66.794	58.2	.8534	389	surprise
66.687	58.2	.7331	451	symbols
66.503	58.2	.8483	391	boats
66.501	58.2	.7731	422	gun
66.444	58.2	.6759	483	units
66.378	58.2	.7356	439	replied
66.364	58.2	.8418	394	families
66.284	58.2	.8849	377	entire
66.232	58.2	.7109	456	fruit
66.213	58.2	.8280	396	crowd
66.196	58.2	.8704	379	tied
66.117	58.2	.8162	403	band
66.113	58.2	.7793	418	wet
66.079	58.2	.7756	419	eating
66.001	58.2	.4821	648	colors
65.925	58.2	.7929	411	Great
65.797	58.2	.8436	390	solid
65.724	58.2	.8969	368	besides
65.702	58.2	.6793	470	northern
65.660	58.2	.3964	776	noun
65.634	58.2	.8205	398	star
65.633	58.2	.8847	372	feed
65.592	58.2	.8964	367	wooden
65.527	58.2	.8750	375	sort
65.344	58.2	.8685	376	lights
65.257	58.1	.7868	412	Greek
65.252	58.1	.8198	393	Red
65.247	58.1	.8687	378	develop
65.224	58.1	.7905	409	Dr
65.216	58.1	.8419	385	shoulder
65.155	58.1	.8197	399	variety
65.131	58.1	.8849	370	season
65.057	58.1	.7835	410	news
64.827	58.1	.8059	399	settled
64.806	58.1	.9244	354	share
64.792	58.1	.9219	354	closer

U	SFI	D	F	Word Type
64.792	58.1	.9151	356	jump
64.763	58.1	.9107	359	regular
64.705	58.1	.8479	383	changing
64.645	58.1	.7227	442	represent
64.635	58.1	.8507	380	opening
64.546	58.1	.8381	383	market
64.516	58.1	.7436	423	we're
64.464	58.1	.7806	403	flew
64.363	58.1	.8735	370	finger
64.264	58.1	.8980	360	expect
64.217	58.1	.7290	432	California
64.172	58.1	.7681	412	army
64.140	58.1	.7729	404	cabin
64.120	58.1	.8423	378	camp
64.065	58.1	.7523	420	schools
64.013	58.1	.7323	431	50
63.808	58.0	.8892	359	danger
63.764	58.0	.8919	360	purpose
63.761	58.0	.8181	386	breakfast
63.604	58.0	.7692	412	proper
63.584	58.0	.8067	391	coat
63.544	58.0	.9095	352	signs
63.529	58.0	.9115	351	faces
63.495	58.0	.9225	347	putting
63.465	58.0	.1687	1484	vowel
THE PRECEDING WORD TYPE OCCUPIES RANK 1300				
63.425	58.0	.8391	376	fishing
63.414	58.0	.8769	362	holding
63.407	58.0	.7173	437	express
63.327	58.0	.7831	398	shot
63.301	58.0	.4568	656	instruments
63.130	58.0	.7619	402	angry
63.088	58.0	.6503	469	southern
63.056	58.0	.7886	396	dress
63.031	58.0	.8450	371	bag
62.939	58.0	.8705	361	proud
62.901	58.0	.8392	373	neck
62.879	58.0	.8226	379	breath
62.840	58.0	.6254	461	Mike
62.833	58.0	.8926	354	strength
62.751	58.0	.9126	347	described
62.746	58.0	.8842	357	member
62.709	58.0	.9340	339	twelve
62.708	58.0	.8204	378	mine
62.651	58.0	.8765	358	heads
62.602	58.0	.9329	339	company
62.594	58.0	.6446	473	current
62.523	58.0	.5114	589	phrase
62.456	58.0	.8304	373	valley
62.342	57.9	.9063	347	directly
62.315	57.9	.7498	414	double
62.267	57.9	.7327	414	till
62.228	57.9	.7588	407	differences
62.224	57.9	.8866	353	match
61.984	57.9	.7426	413	average
61.962	57.9	.8378	371	related
61.953	57.9	.8574	360	die
61.927	57.9	.6786	447	figures
61.925	57.9	.6835	442	liquid
61.785	57.9	.8983	346	caused
61.778	57.9	.8146	376	alive
61.715	57.9	.7904	387	bodies
61.697	57.9	.8885	349	games
61.693	57.9	.9251	337	considered
61.268	57.9	.9122	338	stream
61.247	57.9	.8516	361	provide
61.229	57.9	.8842	347	drink
61.089	57.9	.8945	343	starting
61.043	57.9	.8310	367	reasons
60.932	57.8	.8452	361	experience
60.841	57.8	.8610	354	future
60.825	57.8	.8326	362	tomorrow
60.811	57.8	.8362	361	drove
60.805	57.8	.6599	449	population
60.744	57.8	.7589	395	finish
60.672	57.8	.8919	341	station
60.622	57.8	.9064	337	completely
60.573	57.8	.8500	355	arrived
60.413	57.8	.6879	420	shook
60.373	57.8	.8818	344	stage
60.366	57.8	.4359	625	oxygen
60.348	57.8	.4983	575	poem
60.112	57.8	.5569	516	solution
59.903	57.8	.8684	345	branches
59.851	57.8	.8322	359	roads
59.840	57.8	.6694	432	Mexico
59.805	57.8	.8416	356	degrees
59.773	57.8	.6933	419	coal
59.649	57.8	.8190	364	cent
59.472	57.7	.8256	360	conditions
59.397	57.7	.6634	437	electricity
59.348	57.7	.7565	389	25
59.341	57.7	.7418	390	everybody
59.221	57.7	.5035	563	drawing
59.200	57.7	.8247	359	rate
59.164	57.7	.8712	340	dust
59.069	57.7	.9089	327	worth
59.043	57.7	.8578	346	follows
58.966	57.7	.8072	364	scientific
58.937	57.7	.8212	357	exciting
58.933	57.7	.7979	368	community
58.892	57.7	.7814	367	captain
58.869	57.7	.8491	345	bus
58.840	57.7	.8660	340	protect
58.832	57.7	.5969	480	compound
58.775	57.7	.8676	338	brothers
58.726	57.7	.7914	367	winds
58.713	57.7	.8526	344	raise
58.639	57.7	.9127	324	further
58.568	57.7	.8088	360	yards
58.546	57.7	.8456	347	guide
58.531	57.7	.8456	344	quietly
58.531	57.7	.8029	364	discover
58.526	57.7	.7991	364	East
58.523	57.7	.8672	338	plain
58.497	57.7	.5883	485	correctly
58.478	57.7	.6741	413	smiled

U	SFI	D	F	Word Type
58.464	57.7	.9107	323	keeping
58.346	57.7	.8579	340	steam
58.306	57.7	.9416	313	usual
58.298	57.7	.8851	331	showing
58.293	57.7	.7642	374	telling
58.182	57.6	.8957	327	easier
58.179	57.6	.8547	339	seat
58.176	57.6	.8293	351	range
58.107	57.6	.8334	347	appeared
THE PRECEDING WORD TYPE OCCUPIES RANK 1400				
58.060	57.6	.4838	568	root
58.054	57.6	.8418	346	consider
58.035	57.6	.8048	356	wagon
57.956	57.6	.9049	322	baseball
57.891	57.6	.8573	337	rubber
57.863	57.6	.8164	349	surprised
57.856	57.6	.8302	346	hunting
57.855	57.6	.7543	381	symbol
57.713	57.6	.8427	341	seeing
57.707	57.6	.8403	343	Chinese
57.662	57.6	.7332	386	Pacific
57.501	57.6	.8451	341	support
57.498	57.6	.9251	313	leg
57.444	57.6	.9185	315	windows
57.343	57.6	.6970	398	Texas
57.313	57.6	.6509	429	industry
57.301	57.6	.8287	344	mile
57.299	57.6	.7415	380	forests
57.269	57.6	.8964	321	beneath
57.237	57.6	.8594	334	likely
57.214	57.6	.8336	340	win
57.176	57.6	.8182	346	fence
57.151	57.6	.6453	428	maps
57.121	57.6	.6695	412	believed
57.043	57.6	.5901	460	islands
57.016	57.6	.8806	324	noticed
57.012	57.6	.9208	312	runs
56.930	57.6	.8698	329	centuries
56.888	57.6	.7166	393	popular
56.887	57.6	.8285	339	stayed
56.733	57.5	.7112	393	chart
56.693	57.5	.6885	390	Ann
56.673	57.5	.8440	335	master
56.643	57.5	.8916	319	lake
56.627	57.5	.8614	329	falls
56.610	57.5	.6840	407	d
56.528	57.5	.7661	367	sheet
56.501	57.5	.9041	314	explained
56.481	57.5	.5084	534	notes
56.440	57.5	.7504	371	mass
56.431	57.5	.4567	592	art
56.397	57.5	.8057	346	bottle
56.370	57.5	.8705	324	desk
56.322	57.5	.7151	387	colored
56.305	57.5	.8386	333	nest
56.253	57.5	.8820	319	storm
56.236	57.5	.9195	308	everywhere
56.226	57.5	.9319	305	clearly
56.223	57.5	.8085	348	development
56.161	57.5	.9238	307	closely
56.067	57.5	.9095	311	fourth
56.055	57.5	.8239	339	push
56.025	57.5	.6681	407	Earth
55.975	57.5	.8897	315	rolled
55.895	57.5	.8498	328	flight
55.812	57.5	.8466	328	smoke
55.808	57.5	.8565	327	upper
55.758	57.5	.8343	331	remembered
55.742	57.5	.8951	312	track
55.740	57.5	.8632	324	mixed
55.704	57.5	.8910	314	forget
55.695	57.5	.8207	336	bigger
55.688	57.5	.8239	335	nearby
55.677	57.5	.8700	320	plenty
55.663	57.5	.7695	361	based
55.614	57.5	.9327	301	leaving
55.474	57.4	.6750	396	save
55.471	57.4	.8694	320	belong
55.451	57.4	.7353	371	laws
55.441	57.4	.8088	343	structure
55.436	57.4	.7989	346	height
55.406	57.4	.9170	305	suggested
55.347	57.4	.8045	343	German
55.327	57.4	.7886	349	observe
55.325	57.4	.7827	350	located
55.325	57.4	.8339	330	clock
55.274	57.4	.8761	316	giant
55.239	57.4	.6662	392	Captain
55.232	57.4	.7096	378	smell
55.226	57.4	.7449	364	planes
55.178	57.4	.8193	335	railroad
55.169	57.4	.8699	318	knife
55.039	57.4	.8289	331	grows
55.038	57.4	.5031	523	i
55.016	57.4	.8522	324	results
55.008	57.4	.1894	1217	spelling
55.004	57.4	.8680	317	friendly
54.861	57.4	.7729	352	flow
54.855	57.4	.8966	308	plans
54.852	57.4	.9014	306	whatever
54.841	57.4	.7368	362	barn
54.815	57.4	.8289	330	beauty
54.788	57.4	.8475	321	bell
54.718	57.4	.6255	411	wonderful
54.656	57.4	.9196	300	rapidly
54.623	57.4	.7187	364	Little
54.621	57.4	.5487	484	tone
54.620	57.4	.8346	325	agreed
54.588	57.4	.8508	320	wore
54.557	57.4	.5437	482	ending
THE PRECEDING WORD TYPE OCCUPIES RANK 1500				
54.450	57.4	.7076	379	tools
54.429	57.4	.5747	455	pairs
54.419	57.4	.6223	420	goods
54.387	57.4	.8911	306	fifty
54.324	57.3	.6112	429	nearest
54.263	57.3	.8526	318	wave

U	SFI	D	F	Word Type
54.150	57.3	.6261	420	m
54.056	57.3	.8459	319	sweet
54.051	57.3	.8506	316	deer
54.046	57.3	.7753	342	threw
53.929	57.3	.8773	308	dangerous
53.867	57.3	.7670	348	clothing
53.859	57.3	.8868	305	events
53.597	57.3	.8646	310	leader
53.589	57.3	.7654	345	waters
53.524	57.3	.6488	399	Atlantic
53.454	57.3	.7303	357	lunch
53.454	57.3	.8010	331	boxes
53.432	57.3	.8156	324	mud
53.373	57.3	.8537	314	generally
53.356	57.3	.8225	321	hung
53.336	57.3	.7967	331	ear
53.310	57.3	.7656	343	peace
53.294	57.3	.2174	1052	spell
53.273	57.3	.8966	298	golden
53.230	57.3	.7665	342	wheat
53.165	57.3	.7650	344	chapter
53.151	57.3	.9083	295	immediately
53.086	57.2	.8956	297	gathered
52.889	57.2	.9166	291	favorite
52.875	57.2	.9240	289	understanding
52.856	57.2	.9018	294	apple
52.821	57.2	.7657	342	O
52.811	57.2	.9113	292	expected
52.751	57.2	.8477	309	sad
52.738	57.2	.7492	346	plate
52.735	57.2	.6273	411	score
52.729	57.2	.7914	331	smooth
52.725	57.2	.8574	307	traveled
52.711	57.2	.8508	308	beach
52.561	57.2	.8870	298	service
52.554	57.2	.8502	308	cows
52.548	57.2	.8373	312	sail
52.532	57.2	.7642	340	grain
52.466	57.2	.8532	305	driver
52.394	57.2	.7530	344	forces
52.351	57.2	.7980	325	White
52.296	57.2	.9291	284	telephone
52.238	57.2	.5223	473	singing
52.235	57.2	.5016	481	farms
52.222	57.2	.9015	292	instance
52.187	57.2	.9029	290	swim
52.095	57.2	.7119	357	powerful
52.093	57.2	.7045	361	drew
52.082	57.2	.4647	518	foods
52.051	57.2	.7979	325	bar
52.026	57.2	.6655	379	egg
51.916	57.2	.7375	348	Italy
51.840	57.1	.8460	307	cases
51.830	57.1	.8877	293	meeting
51.755	57.1	.6821	365	shop
51.754	57.1	.7631	336	Germany
51.753	57.1	.7833	325	bowl
51.748	57.1	.8365	308	newspaper
51.702	57.1	.6436	386	fat
51.686	57.1	.6406	393	view
51.679	57.1	.7721	327	cry
51.675	57.1	.8239	310	dressed
51.662	57.1	.8555	303	source
51.610	57.1	.8104	314	hurry
51.601	57.1	.9031	287	wheels
51.583	57.1	.5571	447	Latin
51.558	57.1	.7505	335	nobody
51.539	57.1	.8568	300	James
51.530	57.1	.6319	391	details
51.483	57.1	.7612	330	Dad
51.435	57.1	.6987	360	muscles
51.336	57.1	.7676	332	model
51.332	57.1	.5342	451	climate
51.258	57.1	.9237	280	coffee
51.253	57.1	.8550	298	lifted
51.242	57.1	.8179	312	lies
51.141	57.1	.9320	277	whenever
51.108	57.1	.6886	363	whom
51.077	57.1	.3658	626	silent
51.062	57.1	.9085	283	flower
51.040	57.1	.8779	292	broad
50.997	57.1	.9262	278	serious
50.996	57.1	.8719	294	continue
50.969	57.1	.8537	298	airplane
50.884	57.1	.7877	317	supper
50.881	57.1	.7921	320	methods
50.818	57.1	.7864	317	trail
50.807	57.1	.6168	395	atmosphere
50.800	57.1	.7260	344	western
50.733	57.1	.8367	304	persons
50.729	57.1	.8405	301	handle
50.707	57.1	.5241	462	angle
50.699	57.1	.9057	281	throw
50.667	57.0	.9190	278	allowed
THE PRECEDING WORD TYPE OCCUPIES RANK 1600				
50.625	57.0	.8807	288	keeps
50.575	57.0	.7253	344	drawn
50.568	57.0	.7966	315	leading
50.559	57.0	.8233	304	feathers
50.473	57.0	.7292	335	waited
50.417	57.0	.7472	332	China
50.377	57.0	.7823	317	you've
50.344	57.0	.7961	312	funny
50.252	57.0	.3944	586	dictionary
50.244	57.0	.6884	353	scientist
50.223	57.0	.8902	283	taught
50.185	57.0	.8693	288	climb
50.152	57.0	.7685	321	fighting
50.086	57.0	.8926	282	ordinary
50.047	57.0	.8276	303	series
50.044	57.0	.7288	337	towns
49.989	57.0	.8970	280	burning
49.883	57.0	.7412	334	types
49.882	57.0	.8816	284	extra
49.871	57.0	.8555	292	rough
49.835	57.0	.7567	327	Roman
49.719	57.0	.8064	307	vast

U	SFI	D	F	Word Type
49.708	57.0	.6532	371	18
49.654	57.0	.7788	317	serve
49.633	57.0	.8296	297	riding
49.596	57.0	.9037	276	library
49.561	57.0	.8404	294	helping
49.549	57.0	.8384	296	program
49.539	56.9	.8881	279	magic
49.514	56.9	.8789	283	earlier
49.507	56.9	.8949	279	manner
49.463	56.9	.7907	308	softly
49.451	56.9	.6381	376	chemical
49.447	56.9	.8398	292	suit
49.390	56.9	.7372	331	pencil
49.389	56.9	.3243	689	e
49.362	56.9	.8823	281	tongue
49.324	56.9	.7707	318	11
49.250	56.9	.6783	347	loved
49.190	56.9	.8419	291	struck
49.189	56.9	.6080	386	freedom
49.183	56.9	.6892	345	they're
49.117	56.9	.9142	271	remain
49.086	56.9	.6921	345	planets
49.079	56.9	.6350	369	settlers
49.047	56.9	.8595	286	smallest
48.882	56.9	.8053	302	title
48.804	56.9	.2677	768	0
48.782	56.9	.8026	304	plays
48.776	56.9	.8317	291	fellow
48.715	56.9	.4681	479	cents
48.675	56.9	.7977	301	enemy
48.483	56.9	.7570	314	cloud
48.479	56.9	.8778	276	roof
48.437	56.9	.8708	280	student
48.431	56.9	.8379	287	laugh
48.413	56.8	.7194	326	kill
48.329	56.8	.8754	278	including
48.240	56.8	.8961	270	swimming
48.232	56.8	.8533	284	direct
48.179	56.8	.8569	281	pleasant
48.179	56.8	.8689	278	charge
48.110	56.8	.4986	425	Mama
48.104	56.8	.9034	268	lose
48.086	56.8	.8711	278	individual
48.067	56.8	.9095	266	roll
47.993	56.8	.7775	307	listed
47.954	56.8	.7344	322	growth
47.916	56.8	.7214	327	national
47.907	56.8	.8136	293	speaking
47.864	56.8	.6560	355	regions
47.772	56.8	.6639	356	style
47.760	56.8	.6516	356	political
47.572	56.8	.6297	358	he'd
47.526	56.8	.7981	294	ordered
47.510	56.8	.8430	282	prepared
47.460	56.8	.8147	288	daughter
47.455	56.8	.6363	358	plains
47.453	56.8	.9372	256	studying
47.373	56.8	.8437	279	hall
47.359	56.8	.8027	294	education
47.343	56.8	.8363	283	highest
47.343	56.8	.8507	278	May
47.337	56.8	.6001	378	vegetables
47.286	56.7	.8614	274	signal
47.278	56.7	.6256	364	cup
47.277	56.7	.8661	275	indicate
47.264	56.7	.6419	354	Japanese
47.222	56.7	.7628	307	II
47.222	56.7	.4704	487	design
47.098	56.7	.8468	276	secret
46.927	56.7	.6967	326	copper
46.734	56.7	.7686	295	Frank
46.701	56.7	.8669	269	stones
46.522	56.7	.9012	260	blocks
46.513	56.7	.6934	328	block
46.507	56.7	.7654	302	equipment
46.506	56.7	.8931	262	skill
46.462	56.7	.8700	267	lift
46.459	56.7	.8384	275	lying
THE PRECEDING WORD TYPE OCCUPIES RANK 1700				
46.452	56.7	.9431	249	perfect
46.449	56.7	.9306	252	wash
46.430	56.7	.6692	337	nations
46.424	56.7	.3716	583	verbs
46.412	56.7	.8835	263	cow
46.387	56.7	.8369	277	printed
46.325	56.7	.8887	262	agree
46.307	56.7	.7955	288	sunlight
46.295	56.7	.8158	281	smile
46.269	56.7	.8058	287	expression
46.265	56.7	.8167	281	bow
46.251	56.7	.8066	283	shut
46.214	56.6	.8570	269	shining
46.136	56.6	.9251	252	particularly
46.070	56.6	.7454	301	thank
46.069	56.6	.6918	323	planet
45.967	56.6	.5187	419	property
45.860	56.6	.6729	330	brain
45.852	56.6	.8464	270	bridge
45.799	56.6	.7628	293	asleep
45.790	56.6	.8040	283	taste
45.752	56.6	.8373	273	starts
45.751	56.6	.6967	323	European
45.750	56.6	.7837	289	price
45.741	56.6	.7501	302	scene
45.723	56.6	.9142	252	planned
45.687	56.6	.8300	275	St
45.656	56.6	.3790	545	factors
45.581	56.6	.8445	271	includes
45.564	56.6	.7893	285	battle
45.362	56.6	.6678	331	health
45.316	56.6	.8762	258	sleeping
45.299	56.6	.8067	278	fought
45.285	56.6	.8528	264	cave
45.255	56.6	.6375	332	Ben
45.239	56.6	.5907	378	composition
45.222	56.6	.6994	318	40
45.221	56.6	.8752	259	fur

U	SFI	D	F	Word Type
45.092	56.5	.7181	305	pocket
45.072	56.5	.8791	257	prove
45.033	56.5	.8021	278	holes
44.952	56.5	.3820	540	y
44.889	56.5	.9063	249	knowing
44.864	56.5	.8236	270	police
44.838	56.5	.8249	272	social
44.828	56.5	.6548	334	24
44.826	56.5	.5041	413	factories
44.803	56.5	.8000	275	Mark
44.790	56.5	.5555	381	Asia
44.761	56.5	.8362	266	dishes
44.757	56.5	.7820	286	discuss
44.686	56.5	.8874	253	post
44.653	56.5	.9029	249	enter
44.633	56.5	.7216	305	14
44.626	56.5	.9003	249	traveling
44.616	56.5	.9206	244	crossed
44.575	56.5	.3509	572	n
44.569	56.5	.7726	286	local
44.514	56.5	.7801	281	park
44.473	56.5	.7675	282	brave
44.431	56.5	.8354	264	burned
44.391	56.5	.8869	251	stretched
44.388	56.5	.6503	325	ants
44.386	56.5	.8536	259	shoulders
44.338	56.5	.8613	257	escape
44.329	56.5	.8832	252	mostly
44.327	56.5	.4545	454	division
44.321	56.5	.5302	399	measures
44.291	56.5	.6467	330	clay
44.288	56.5	.7678	282	sailed
44.236	56.5	.8491	260	valuable
44.166	56.5	.7971	274	potatoes
44.142	56.4	.9161	243	tip
44.055	56.4	.9044	245	weak
44.017	56.4	.8213	264	lion
43.991	56.4	.8314	264	poles
43.943	56.4	.6819	310	sir
43.906	56.4	.5611	370	Congress
43.865	56.4	.8273	263	lovely
43.859	56.4	.8752	251	eaten
43.849	56.4	.8829	250	ability
43.809	56.4	.8323	263	balance
43.750	56.4	.9114	242	success
43.745	56.4	.8937	246	search
43.676	56.4	.9068	242	sticks
43.668	56.4	.7861	271	crew
43.633	56.4	.7092	301	voices
43.593	56.4	.8203	266	determine
43.559	56.4	.7917	270	excited
43.556	56.4	.6658	322	parallel
43.504	56.4	.7091	303	represents
43.495	56.4	.3867	530	nouns
43.477	56.4	.7838	273	attack
43.467	56.4	.8180	263	hunt
43.450	56.4	.8188	264	bat
43.379	56.4	.8962	244	increase
43.347	56.4	.7457	286	Lake
43.281	56.4	.9068	241	appears
43.052	56.3	.7377	284	apples
43.046	56.3	.8684	248	neighbors
THE PRECEDING WORD TYPE OCCUPIES RANK 1800				
43.007	56.3	.8190	263	activities
42.989	56.3	.8131	261	Lincoln
42.985	56.3	.7129	299	subjects
42.916	56.3	.8288	258	Paris
42.902	56.3	.8514	252	outer
42.897	56.3	.7199	294	volume
42.893	56.3	.5991	334	sick
42.850	56.3	.7571	274	whale
42.829	56.3	.5779	353	earth's
42.817	56.3	.9158	236	successful
42.808	56.3	.8921	241	invented
42.807	56.3	.8993	239	falling
42.804	56.3	.8165	259	wished
42.759	56.3	.8266	257	entered
42.729	56.3	.7647	278	13
42.718	56.3	.8195	259	excitement
42.702	56.3	.7695	275	quarter
42.701	56.3	.8795	243	log
42.644	56.3	.2906	658	songs
42.621	56.3	.8744	244	cake
42.594	56.3	.8623	247	unusual
42.588	56.3	.8373	255	personal
42.571	56.3	.7808	267	gate
42.554	56.3	.6862	299	jar
42.545	56.3	.6937	300	cream
42.501	56.3	.8921	239	wearing
42.497	56.3	.8348	254	London
42.471	56.3	.8183	258	bone
42.420	56.3	.5248	390	phrases
42.387	56.3	.8320	253	wise
42.375	56.3	.8803	241	birthday
42.325	56.3	.8669	244	papers
42.289	56.3	.8225	256	candy
42.268	56.3	.8176	255	o'clock
42.256	56.3	.8464	248	flag
42.147	56.2	.8341	252	strike
42.130	56.2	.8598	245	gently
42.097	56.2	.8701	242	traffic
42.094	56.2	.2056	800	sum
42.050	56.2	.5939	338	Sally
42.045	56.2	.5855	341	minerals
42.017	56.2	.7789	267	streams
41.963	56.2	.8135	253	article
41.918	56.2	.8695	241	hide
41.890	56.2	.9005	234	recognize
41.873	56.2	.8541	246	recent
41.866	56.2	.8745	241	frequently
41.842	56.2	.7264	284	central
41.822	56.2	.8516	245	shell
41.797	56.2	.7036	293	16
41.778	56.2	.8898	236	court
41.763	56.2	.8359	248	driving
41.755	56.2	.8787	239	gradually
41.747	56.2	.8688	241	remained

U	SFI	D	F	Word Type
41.746	56.2	.6675	304	India
41.738	56.2	.8581	244	automobile
41.710	56.2	.8498	245	safety
41.694	56.2	.7527	274	eastern
41.625	56.2	.8095	255	Boston
41.606	56.2	.8028	259	p
41.507	56.2	.7152	279	hurried
41.481	56.2	.4657	419	meanings
41.435	56.2	.8674	240	arranged
41.417	56.2	.8865	234	tie
41.417	56.2	.8205	250	darkness
41.416	56.2	.8927	233	branch
41.389	56.2	.6330	314	Ocean
41.383	56.2	.7855	262	S
41.324	56.2	.8908	233	fifteen
41.315	56.2	.7001	284	hadn't
41.289	56.2	.8653	239	proved
41.252	56.2	.7584	267	pond
41.250	56.2	.9115	228	holds
41.227	56.2	.8047	253	terrible
41.163	56.1	.7918	258	jobs
41.162	56.1	.7630	262	frightened
41.151	56.1	.8651	238	forced
41.133	56.1	.6102	325	Spain
41.100	56.1	.8237	248	shells
41.089	56.1	.6777	298	function
41.070	56.1	.8931	231	impossible
41.059	56.1	.8322	247	slightly
41.013	56.1	.9242	224	somewhat
41.012	56.1	.6039	327	U **
41.005	56.1	.8427	243	steady
40.997	56.1	.5812	321	Papa
40.957	56.1	.7473	271	200
40.940	56.1	.7228	277	rows
40.919	56.1	.7701	260	listened
40.892	56.1	.7531	267	sang
40.866	56.1	.7854	257	Robert
40.800	56.1	.7008	284	Western
40.790	56.1	.7730	257	wondered
40.755	56.1	.7417	271	Canada
40.746	56.1	.8836	231	passing
40.733	56.1	.8183	249	frame
40.656	56.1	.7841	258	element
40.614	56.1	.6836	290	diagram
40.607	56.1	.8859	230	washed
40.597	56.1	.8469	239	aren't
THE PRECEDING WORD TYPE OCCUPIES RANK 1900				
40.584	56.1	.8400	242	character
40.571	56.1	.9219	222	setting
40.567	56.1	.5042	386	instrument
40.538	56.1	.7902	253	message
40.496	56.1	.8261	243	Street
40.483	56.1	.8250	244	club
40.452	56.1	.4056	446	cell
40.437	56.1	.7961	253	records
40.418	56.1	.9179	222	chosen
40.414	56.1	.7378	265	laughing
40.389	56.1	.6915	284	world's
40.364	56.1	.8045	249	pie
40.361	56.1	.8180	247	appearance
40.303	56.1	.6779	287	Aunt
40.274	56.1	.7368	270	repeated
40.248	56.0	.7926	252	causes
40.217	56.0	.8282	243	situation
40.189	56.0	.3252	574	rhythm
40.185	56.0	.7966	250	supplies
40.147	56.0	.8440	238	thoughts
40.088	56.0	.7590	261	lakes
40.078	56.0	.7584	257	stepped
40.059	56.0	.8844	227	loose
40.046	56.0	.9052	223	increased
40.038	56.0	.7994	248	lips
40.034	56.0	.8527	236	exact
40.002	56.0	.7710	257	yesterday
39.972	56.0	.6985	283	E
39.965	56.0	.8525	235	depends
39.922	56.0	.4513	414	angles
39.917	56.0	.8415	237	factory
39.892	56.0	.8399	237	Charles
39.855	56.0	.8262	241	spirit
39.823	56.0	.6645	291	rays
39.757	56.0	.8075	246	avoid
39.716	56.0	.8762	228	provided
39.714	56.0	.7984	247	player
39.705	56.0	.8556	231	surely
39.703	56.0	.6736	282	sorry
39.687	56.0	.5634	339	cutting
39.670	56.0	.7929	246	father's
39.628	56.0	.8579	232	importance
39.627	56.0	.8739	228	progress
39.625	56.0	.4126	437	paint
39.585	56.0	.8228	239	seconds
39.580	56.0	.7719	254	Richard
39.568	56.0	.7544	257	journey
39.543	56.0	.7655	256	500
39.541	56.0	.8958	222	doubt
39.506	56.0	.7374	266	sections
39.496	56.0	.6820	275	Dick
39.453	56.0	.8405	233	lots
39.375	56.0	.6255	305	statements
39.341	55.9	.7479	260	ruler
39.323	55.9	.8571	229	likes
39.317	55.9	.7657	253	dozen
39.312	55.9	.7011	275	served
39.262	55.9	.8715	225	doors
39.209	55.9	.8604	227	basket
39.206	55.9	.9054	217	thinks
39.183	55.9	.7237	267	established
39.091	55.9	.7524	259	quality
39.075	55.9	.8086	237	deck
39.067	55.9	.7911	247	indicated
39.060	55.9	.8632	227	effort
39.044	55.9	.8364	232	dream
39.029	55.9	.8392	232	pipe
38.944	55.9	.9022	217	harder
38.843	55.9	.5482	330	Alaska
38.826	55.9	.8765	221	pulling
38.732	55.9	.8839	220	flies
38.720	55.9	.7446	256	lesson
38.718	55.9	.7967	240	ended
38.709	55.9	.9028	216	calls
38.701	55.9	.7614	251	dancing
38.692	55.9	.2160	779	spelled
38.663	55.9	.7770	248	Italian
38.658	55.9	.8353	229	chickens
38.646	55.9	.7751	246	engines
38.623	55.9	.7255	259	rod
38.575	55.9	.8984	216	football
38.471	55.9	.9297	209	rooms
38.468	55.9	.8000	240	physical
38.430	55.8	.7947	242	identify
38.407	55.8	.8169	232	cage
38.402	55.8	.7676	247	experiments
38.374	55.8	.7281	256	Tommy
38.346	55.8	.8122	234	drops
38.328	55.8	.8366	229	daily
38.314	55.8	.8857	218	included
38.301	55.8	.7035	265	cook
38.286	55.8	.7508	253	containing
38.276	55.8	.8148	234	players
38.266	55.8	.8050	235	sudden
38.238	55.8	.8486	224	disappeared
38.237	55.8	.8083	234	pole
38.224	55.8	.6381	290	particles
38.222	55.8	.8001	236	joy
38.219	55.8	.5210	349	replace
38.203	55.8	.7138	263	foreign
THE PRECEDING WORD TYPE OCCUPIES RANK 2000				
38.157	55.8	.7761	241	you'd
38.144	55.8	.7134	262	fuel
38.127	55.8	.8374	226	realized
38.100	55.8	.8031	236	Chicago
38.091	55.8	.8528	223	card
38.039	55.8	.8606	221	bill
38.022	55.8	.7631	244	bent
37.908	55.8	.7874	237	haven't
37.896	55.8	.9067	210	hidden
37.715	55.8	.4624	374	carbon
37.704	55.8	.8823	214	thirty
37.673	55.8	.5165	337	Japan
37.668	55.8	.8229	229	allow
37.660	55.8	.6209	291	Union
37.657	55.8	.8744	216	greatly
37.645	55.8	.7610	242	rocket
37.645	55.8	.8348	226	term
37.555	55.7	.7900	235	cap
37.552	55.7	.7585	242	sounded
37.482	55.7	.7145	256	listening
37.449	55.7	.8473	221	jet
37.395	55.7	.7987	230	calling
37.383	55.7	.5671	317	thread
37.363	55.7	.8097	227	Brown
37.279	55.7	.8066	231	created
37.257	55.7	.9176	205	merely
37.235	55.7	.7650	242	represented
37.221	55.7	.5965	283	Grandfather
37.172	55.7	.6474	275	butter
37.163	55.7	.8522	218	dried
37.156	55.7	.7547	244	Thomas
37.103	55.7	.8530	217	visited
37.094	55.7	.8628	215	March
37.088	55.7	.7928	231	chest
37.088	55.7	.3349	474	molecules
37.075	55.7	.8072	229	feelings
37.070	55.7	.6830	264	Negro
37.002	55.7	.8295	222	Saturday
36.991	55.7	.9188	203	shade
36.986	55.7	.8379	220	planted
36.954	55.7	.5475	319	continent
36.942	55.7	.8384	219	pink
36.934	55.7	.8217	223	crowded
36.920	55.7	.6721	264	rice
36.858	55.7	.7563	240	Dutch
36.829	55.7	.8628	213	somewhere
36.827	55.7	.8318	219	courage
36.795	55.7	.8090	225	hunters
36.778	55.7	.7920	229	chicken
36.770	55.7	.8588	215	occur
36.711	55.6	.8237	221	shadow
36.691	55.6	.8526	215	truth
36.687	55.6	.9072	204	due
36.673	55.6	.8363	219	native
36.646	55.6	.8558	214	load
36.574	55.6	.8267	221	orange
36.563	55.6	.8918	206	rolling
36.544	55.6	.7019	254	General
36.542	55.6	.8969	205	begun
36.524	55.6	.8286	219	offered
36.512	55.6	.8077	225	training
36.508	55.6	.6522	273	pitch
36.505	55.6	.8911	206	account
36.499	55.6	.8662	211	discovery
36.494	55.6	.8040	225	creatures
36.487	55.6	.8973	204	honor
36.474	55.6	.7300	247	removed
36.468	55.6	.8450	216	passes
36.461	55.6	.7466	241	Sir
36.434	55.6	.6951	255	blank
36.401	55.6	.8109	222	shirt
36.376	55.6	.8767	208	gather
36.375	55.6	.7415	244	suggest
36.371	55.6	.7316	243	ranch
36.302	55.6	.7658	236	required
36.278	55.6	.6147	283	Black
36.276	55.6	.7219	248	prevent
36.192	55.6	.8703	208	tight
36.156	55.6	.6809	257	House
36.119	55.6	.8780	206	queen
36.079	55.6	.8490	212	enjoyed
36.066	55.6	.8403	214	leaf
36.008	55.6	.8886	203	tin
35.988	55.6	.6031	286	meal
35.947	55.6	.7451	240	available
35.947	55.6	.8328	215	rising
35.947	55.6	.8083	220	ought
35.937	55.6	.6576	258	whispered
35.925	55.6	.7638	234	National
35.861	55.6	.8417	212	Louis
35.851	55.5	.8369	213	straw
35.832	55.5	.8981	201	attached
35.830	55.5	.6875	255	wool
35.793	55.5	.8097	216	duck
35.786	55.5	.7907	223	tears
35.748	55.5	.9109	198	separated
35.741	55.5	.8435	211	cats
35.738	55.5	.8950	201	date
35.709	55.5	.7881	225	layers
35.704	55.5	.8753	204	bark
THE PRECEDING WORD TYPE OCCUPIES RANK 2100				
35.696	55.5	.7857	226	college
35.679	55.5	.8860	202	safely
35.670	55.5	.7668	231	furniture
35.663	55.5	.7781	226	leather
35.647	55.5	.9046	198	noon
35.619	55.5	.8623	207	determined
35.596	55.5	.4901	343	exercises
35.558	55.5	.8764	204	entirely
35.546	55.5	.7119	246	17
35.546	55.5	.3434	460	factor
35.507	55.5	.6917	248	silence
35.498	55.5	.8809	203	combined
35.467	55.5	.8335	213	remains
35.443	55.5	.7252	242	standard
35.425	55.5	.6588	256	saved
35.392	55.5	.8397	211	recently
35.377	55.5	.8044	217	tracks
35.373	55.5	.8595	205	hanging
35.316	55.5	.7680	226	City
35.311	55.5	.6665	254	teach
35.302	55.5	.8754	203	involved
35.245	55.5	.8524	206	biggest
35.235	55.5	.8830	200	gentle
35.170	55.5	.7560	230	strip
35.149	55.5	.8953	197	pack
35.142	55.5	.8911	198	bare
35.124	55.5	.8220	213	classroom
35.121	55.5	.7020	247	press
35.100	55.5	.8788	200	sailors
35.084	55.5	.8612	204	chain
35.040	55.4	.8986	196	bits
35.025	55.4	.8271	209	rabbit
35.024	55.4	.8606	204	shaped
34.935	55.4	.8537	204	breathing
34.933	55.4	.8355	209	helpful
34.855	55.4	.8832	198	newspapers
34.835	55.4	.7590	227	pound
34.831	55.4	.8638	202	pure
34.809	55.4	.7521	225	forgot
34.777	55.4	.3516	460	musical
34.777	55.4	.7215	238	60
34.770	55.4	.6510	259	layer
34.761	55.4	.6493	260	substance
34.752	55.4	.8413	207	choice
34.729	55.4	.7683	224	prepare
34.700	55.4	.8875	196	fixed
34.687	55.4	.6174	271	environment
34.676	55.4	.7214	233	Jimmy
34.619	55.4	.8612	202	highly
34.616	55.4	.6507	255	Valley
34.608	55.4	.7434	230	spoken
34.603	55.4	.8242	209	Sunday
34.587	55.4	.6279	265	oceans
34.542	55.4	.6693	250	disease
34.520	55.4	.7799	219	banks
34.518	55.4	.8329	207	depend
34.506	55.4	.8472	203	sailing
34.503	55.4	.9062	192	shorter
34.493	55.4	.7451	226	snake
34.490	55.4	.7241	233	balloon
34.486	55.4	.7384	225	exclaimed
34.447	55.4	.7120	236	cheese
34.424	55.4	.8576	200	forgotten
34.408	55.4	.7159	233	husband
34.384	55.4	.8567	201	partly
34.381	55.4	.4786	332	atoms
34.376	55.4	.7565	222	blew
34.375	55.4	.7796	217	dollar
34.369	55.4	.7874	216	worn
34.358	55.4	.7898	214	shoot
34.353	55.4	.7864	214	slipped
34.346	55.4	.8481	202	medicine
34.286	55.4	.8405	204	measured
34.259	55.3	.6803	246	receive
34.225	55.3	.8023	213	produces
34.210	55.3	.8106	209	frozen
34.179	55.3	.8180	207	throat
34.168	55.3	.8821	194	supposed
34.114	55.3	.8653	197	pool
34.083	55.3	.8083	209	trucks
34.013	55.3	.8857	193	condition
34.013	55.3	.7802	214	cowboy
33.971	55.3	.8099	207	lonely
33.922	55.3	.8971	190	belongs
33.915	55.3	.8719	195	pine
33.900	55.3	.8024	211	consists
33.873	55.3	.7242	230	citizens
33.859	55.3	.8175	206	Smith
33.858	55.3	.8086	209	conversation
33.850	55.3	.8924	191	collection
33.828	55.3	.8580	198	differ
33.805	55.3	.7713	216	circus
33.777	55.3	.8000	209	audience
33.747	55.3	.3397	440	triangle
33.730	55.3	.5733	278	globe
33.730	55.3	.8318	202	mice
33.713	55.3	.7002	230	Big
33.673	55.3	.8393	200	anywhere
33.553	55.3	.7749	212	fog
33.506	55.3	.8473	196	pet
THE PRECEDING WORD TYPE OCCUPIES RANK 2200				
33.497	55.3	.6469	249	odd
33.486	55.2	.8396	200	influence
33.482	55.2	.6747	238	we've
33.444	55.2	.7236	228	African
33.400	55.2	.8115	205	June
33.389	55.2	.7603	216	logs
33.349	55.2	.8619	194	aid
33.346	55.2	.8856	189	pile
33.318	55.2	.8368	199	July
33.240	55.2	.7538	214	worry
33.232	55.2	.4600	342	1/4
33.212	55.2	.6417	245	she's
33.208	55.2	.7390	218	tonight
33.195	55.2	.8405	196	bushes
33.146	55.2	.8153	201	hoped
33.122	55.2	.8043	206	complex
33.105	55.2	.7218	229	construction
33.097	55.2	.7450	216	author
33.051	55.2	.8042	203	Queen
33.033	55.2	.9210	181	task
33.004	55.2	.3558	416	underline
32.990	55.2	.8333	197	Day
32.977	55.2	.7605	215	research
32.966	55.2	.8791	189	basis
32.909	55.2	.7893	208	principal
32.908	55.2	.3961	379	graph
32.899	55.2	.8386	194	elephant
32.879	55.2	.8161	201	improve
32.821	55.2	.6672	240	fruits
32.791	55.2	.9062	182	oldest
32.778	55.2	.7804	207	mouse
32.763	55.2	.7162	224	Virginia
32.743	55.2	.8462	193	arrow
32.725	55.1	.7956	204	stores
32.723	55.1	.8218	199	organized
32.693	55.1	.5881	265	colonies
32.692	55.1	.8935	184	carries
32.659	55.1	.7281	221	evidence
32.652	55.1	.6438	242	Mississippi
32.650	55.1	.8558	191	studies
32.624	55.1	.8598	191	degree
32.622	55.1	.7091	227	production
32.613	55.1	.8178	198	motor
32.601	55.1	.1291	840	numerals
32.601	55.1	.3575	418	piano
32.598	55.1	.8223	196	handed
32.582	55.1	.8288	195	bears
32.574	55.1	.6575	240	pan
32.572	55.1	.6609	240	theory
32.569	55.1	.8636	189	swing
32.533	55.1	.5173	294	painted
32.516	55.1	.7455	213	knees
32.513	55.1	.7648	209	mirror
32.500	55.1	.7565	210	pony
32.498	55.1	.8797	185	dirt
32.494	55.1	.8493	191	miss
32.484	55.1	.5917	266	thee
32.474	55.1	.4579	333	o
32.431	55.1	.8226	196	route
32.426	55.1	.8962	182	slide
32.400	55.1	.7870	204	couple
32.332	55.1	.6781	235	N
32.325	55.1	.7886	202	mother's
32.309	55.1	.6810	235	create
32.263	55.1	.8790	184	silk
32.245	55.1	.8229	194	burst
32.225	55.1	.8509	189	curious
32.214	55.1	.6209	247	mighty
32.192	55.1	.8500	190	examine
32.181	55.1	.8060	200	combine
32.180	55.1	.6240	251	operation
32.176	55.1	.8813	183	understood
32.165	55.1	.8835	183	realize
32.160	55.1	.8730	185	respect
32.143	55.1	.8851	182	fed
32.118	55.1	.8033	198	owned
32.117	55.1	.8115	196	uncle
32.085	55.1	.7996	198	touched
32.079	55.1	.6915	225	rights
32.066	55.1	.8597	187	concerned
32.062	55.1	.9067	178	covers
32.061	55.1	.8847	182	distant
32.007	55.1	.7921	202	refer
31.983	55.0	.8262	193	lack
31.980	55.0	.4646	320	Betsy
31.977	55.0	.7097	217	anyway
31.921	55.0	.7910	198	babies
31.918	55.0	.7938	199	hearing
31.903	55.0	.8169	194	failed
31.886	55.0	.8195	194	300
31.843	55.0	.4332	343	shapes
31.813	55.0	.6904	223	tea
31.811	55.0	.8118	195	reaches
31.758	55.0	.7697	203	mail
31.757	55.0	.8904	179	stronger
31.749	55.0	.8356	189	poured
31.738	55.0	.7777	200	rushed
31.736	55.0	.5723	269	edges
31.715	55.0	.8319	190	highway
31.709	55.0	.8368	190	periods
THE PRECEDING WORD TYPE OCCUPIES RANK 2300				
31.693	55.0	.7965	199	repeat
31.692	55.0	.6220	232	Andy
31.686	55.0	.8380	189	collect
31.673	55.0	.8449	186	stuck
31.670	55.0	.8118	194	pen
31.665	55.0	.7765	202	pictured
31.626	55.0	.9119	175	excellent
31.610	55.0	.8313	188	blanket
31.606	55.0	.8698	182	aside
31.554	55.0	.8713	181	dig
31.547	55.0	.6742	226	enemies
31.542	55.0	.7542	207	planning
31.496	55.0	.7835	198	pain
31.487	55.0	.6789	228	needle
31.482	55.0	.5816	257	missed
31.481	55.0	.6088	240	nodded
31.470	55.0	.7314	212	connected

U	SFI	D	F	Word Type
31.459	55.0	.7787	199	beans
31.446	55.0	.8464	186	cards
31.407	55.0	.8533	184	upward
31.402	55.0	.9162	173	gain
31.396	55.0	.8495	185	offer
31.365	55.0	.0135	658	Wheels
31.365	55.0	.8265	190	expressed
31.364	55.0	.8107	194	combination
31.336	55.0	.6824	227	spaces
31.314	55.0	.9244	171	unknown
31.283	55.0	.7976	193	luck
31.279	55.0	.7892	197	movements
31.266	55.0	.6112	249	languages
31.255	54.9	.5979	251	brush
31.250	54.9	.9274	170	balls
31.234	54.9	.8286	187	fastened
31.173	54.9	.8113	191	seas
31.164	54.9	.7601	201	Island
31.146	54.9	.8099	192	completed
31.094	54.9	.7312	210	systems
31.054	54.9	.7994	194	features
31.016	54.9	.8598	181	observed
31.007	54.9	.4831	290	Pa
30.994	54.9	.8414	184	Greeks
30.991	54.9	.8037	192	stretch
30.985	54.9	.6860	223	composed
30.978	54.9	.9191	170	wherever
30.962	54.9	.8112	189	willing
30.947	54.9	.8396	184	married
30.941	54.9	.8791	176	fallen
30.911	54.9	.8665	178	landed
30.898	54.9	.7088	214	amounts
30.888	54.9	.7609	202	religious
30.874	54.9	.8560	180	fits
30.799	54.9	.7929	193	sheets
30.797	54.9	.6360	233	orbit
30.781	54.9	.4703	312	review
30.757	54.9	.7564	201	youth
30.754	54.9	.8204	187	bars
30.750	54.9	.7370	205	wires
30.718	54.9	.6423	232	resources
30.711	54.9	.7996	192	designed
30.706	54.9	.6398	233	tax
30.653	54.9	.7956	191	waste
30.639	54.9	.5895	252	Edward
30.639	54.9	.9040	170	tower
30.638	54.9	.8532	179	lamp
30.629	54.9	.7655	198	president
30.621	54.9	.8599	178	comfortable
30.617	54.9	.8494	180	sees
30.593	54.9	.7114	208	tent
30.547	54.8	.7804	194	becoming
30.545	54.8	.6957	213	atomic
30.507	54.8	.3822	370	topic
30.499	54.8	.6827	218	flows
30.490	54.8	.8082	188	locate
30.479	54.8	.6419	224	pleased
30.478	54.8	.6171	238	leaders
30.476	54.8	.6880	215	crop
30.471	54.8	.7922	190	burn
30.452	54.8	.7501	200	outline
30.437	54.8	.8339	182	feels
30.435	54.8	.7916	189	trick
30.428	54.8	.6888	216	transportation
30.422	54.8	.8307	182	bicycle
30.405	54.8	.5613	255	villages
30.400	54.8	.8685	175	thrown
30.396	54.8	.7933	188	buffalo
30.335	54.8	.8538	178	signals
30.319	54.8	.7877	189	pigs
30.273	54.8	.6378	230	aloud
30.253	54.8	.3394	318	Carlos
30.248	54.8	.5727	254	dots
30.200	54.8	.8750	173	spite
30.191	54.8	.5671	254	counting
30.185	54.8	.7309	200	slept
30.104	54.8	.8813	171	landing
30.099	54.8	.8631	174	trained
30.095	54.8	.7928	186	grandfather
30.081	54.8	.8179	182	blowing
30.059	54.8	.8662	175	etc
30.051	54.8	.8291	180	worse
30.044	54.8	.8190	181	boy's
THE PRECEDING WORD TYPE OCCUPIES RANK 2400				
30.039	54.8	.7031	210	Middle
30.030	54.8	.8531	176	accident
30.013	54.8	.8811	171	younger
29.953	54.8	.8675	173	judge
29.940	54.8	.8074	183	stove
29.940	54.8	.6916	211	valleys
29.911	54.8	.7835	189	gasoline
29.897	54.8	.7574	191	castle
29.894	54.8	.6151	229	spider
29.858	54.8	.8353	179	normal
29.792	54.7	.7983	184	steep
29.782	54.7	.8599	173	tough
29.773	54.7	.8363	178	active
29.766	54.7	.9153	164	tops
29.758	54.7	.8637	173	affect
29.732	54.7	.8771	170	bound
29.727	54.7	.8551	174	driven
29.720	54.7	.7861	186	trunk
29.705	54.7	.8229	180	visitors
29.652	54.7	.6981	209	military
29.636	54.7	.8454	176	society
29.626	54.7	.6341	221	stared
29.611	54.7	.8911	167	fairly
29.576	54.7	.7006	207	obtain
29.570	54.7	.6917	208	Mountains
29.512	54.7	.5417	256	reader
29.460	54.7	.8777	169	additional
29.422	54.7	.6646	207	Boy
29.412	54.7	.6442	221	machinery
29.405	54.7	.8730	169	recognized
29.397	54.7	.7926	185	plus
29.393	54.7	.9016	164	hollow
29.373	54.7	.8101	180	explore

U	SFI	D	F	Word Type
29.370	54.7	.6957	206	travels
29.366	54.7	.8599	171	tables
29.364	54.7	.8482	172	bite
29.355	54.7	.9209	161	unlike
29.354	54.7	.7801	184	stairs
29.344	54.7	.8393	174	scattered
29.313	54.7	.7389	195	Wilson
29.299	54.7	.7340	198	percent
29.266	54.7	.8840	166	earn
29.244	54.7	.9278	159	hang
29.236	54.7	.7481	193	State
29.217	54.7	.7401	196	items
29.197	54.7	.7930	184	arrange
29.173	54.6	.9081	162	loss
29.173	54.6	.7869	182	sisters
29.170	54.6	.7676	188	raw
29.146	54.6	.7214	198	TV
29.132	54.6	.8672	168	skins
29.127	54.6	.8182	176	boots
29.110	54.6	.7824	183	Don
29.103	54.6	.8316	174	belt
29.083	54.6	.7107	198	he'll
29.043	54.6	.6875	205	salmon
29.040	54.6	.8467	172	aware
29.039	54.6	.7673	188	400
29.022	54.6	.8774	166	pleasure
28.997	54.6	.7574	189	stored
28.991	54.6	.7828	185	origin
28.949	54.6	.8658	168	perform
28.938	54.6	.8247	174	tank
28.875	54.6	.2458	517	plural
28.872	54.6	.7108	199	weigh
28.848	54.6	.4063	337	adjective
28.841	54.6	.7923	180	gods
28.805	54.6	.7986	179	event
28.804	54.6	.6140	222	Columbus
28.763	54.6	.8056	178	eventually
28.745	54.6	.4823	278	zero
28.729	54.6	.8708	165	bringing
28.724	54.6	.6569	215	remove
28.698	54.6	.8394	170	yours
28.695	54.6	.7509	188	trains
28.690	54.6	.7944	178	neighbor
28.676	54.6	.6833	206	alphabet
28.667	54.6	.8208	174	rises
28.664	54.6	.7327	192	tribes
28.637	54.6	.8711	165	covering
28.624	54.6	.7637	184	stomach
28.618	54.6	.7380	193	select
28.574	54.6	.7524	189	characteristics
28.561	54.6	.8421	169	enormous
28.545	54.6	.5641	243	industrial
28.534	54.6	.6701	206	Australia
28.514	54.6	.4322	303	bells
28.503	54.6	.7662	185	fifth
28.499	54.5	.8301	170	loaded
28.489	54.5	.7363	191	companies
28.459	54.5	.5925	233	poet
28.453	54.5	.8154	174	screen
28.448	54.5	.1518	702	consonant
28.438	54.5	.8601	165	pushing
28.432	54.5	.7802	180	Jones
28.426	54.5	.8911	160	mistake
28.404	54.5	.8553	166	arrows
28.401	54.5	.7787	179	stranger
28.395	54.5	.8449	168	acts
28.393	54.5	.7752	180	thanks
THE PRECEDING WORD TYPE OCCUPIES RANK 2500				
28.388	54.5	.5586	247	specific
28.351	54.5	.8332	169	toes
28.336	54.5	.6261	220	mood
28.315	54.5	.6625	210	negative
28.315	54.5	.8404	169	principles
28.313	54.5	.6642	209	income
28.302	54.5	.8131	174	primitive
28.297	54.5	.8400	168	airplanes
28.293	54.5	.6052	225	false
28.287	54.5	.8354	169	accepted
28.284	54.5	.8860	160	sports
28.280	54.5	.8179	172	September
28.257	54.5	.7739	181	blind
28.256	54.5	.8935	159	accept
28.255	54.5	.6973	201	today's
28.248	54.5	.8776	161	orders
28.247	54.5	.7291	191	universe
28.246	54.5	.8296	169	tribe
28.243	54.5	.8050	173	headed
28.233	54.5	.8190	172	passage
28.205	54.5	.7782	180	obtained
28.200	54.5	.8604	164	surrounded
28.197	54.5	.8935	159	classes
28.185	54.5	.7706	179	somebody
28.163	54.5	.6500	210	compass
28.158	54.5	.6172	221	measuring
28.140	54.5	.3966	315	substances
28.134	54.5	.7739	181	values
28.103	54.5	.9068	156	seldom
28.074	54.5	.5465	247	thou
28.056	54.5	.9007	157	remaining
28.042	54.5	.7608	183	21
28.014	54.5	.8364	166	lucky
28.010	54.5	.7083	192	anybody
27.990	54.5	.8549	164	April
27.974	54.5	.8845	159	naturally
27.957	54.5	.7630	181	automobiles
27.915	54.5	.8008	172	owner
27.912	54.5	.7950	175	grade
27.872	54.5	.8844	158	rings
27.848	54.4	.8907	157	purple
27.834	54.4	.5312	243	seed
27.827	54.4	.7667	176	swam
27.820	54.4	.7832	175	guns
27.801	54.4	.8606	162	rounded
27.798	54.4	.8677	160	rabbits
27.770	54.4	.1520	706	syllables
27.769	54.4	.5807	228	magnet
27.724	54.4	.7884	173	prize

U	SFI	D	F	Word Type
27.637	54.4	.7806	176	T
27.618	54.4	.7330	181	raced
27.614	54.4	.6180	215	colony
27.606	54.4	.8503	162	announced
27.595	54.4	.7373	182	dug
27.584	54.4	.0818	911	numeral
27.548	54.4	.8630	160	compared
27.545	54.4	.7883	174	curve
27.505	54.4	.7889	173	distances
27.495	54.4	.7578	179	Johnson
27.490	54.4	.8821	156	perfectly
27.489	54.4	.7747	173	Man
27.463	54.4	.8106	167	pilot
27.457	54.4	.6707	194	Tim
27.451	54.4	.8336	164	struggle
27.438	54.4	.8039	168	herd
27.432	54.4	.3265	350	Eddie
27.424	54.4	.9244	150	previous
27.418	54.4	.7788	174	Florida
27.409	54.4	.8847	155	pot
27.391	54.4	.7437	182	definition
27.376	54.4	.6819	197	tape
27.375	54.4	.8045	168	porch
27.325	54.4	.6757	196	vote
27.324	54.4	.7910	170	mad
27.317	54.4	.7701	173	waved
27.280	54.4	.7075	189	powder
27.274	54.4	.9112	151	trace
27.260	54.4	.5765	223	Alice
27.233	54.4	.7498	177	gift
27.226	54.3	.7781	172	tightly
27.222	54.3	.6650	201	sizes
27.190	54.3	.7273	185	tests
27.180	54.3	.7257	183	bees
27.166	54.3	.7454	179	happening
27.164	54.3	.8507	159	badly
27.118	54.3	.8791	155	fewer
27.117	54.3	.5954	219	industries
27.072	54.3	.7999	167	nights
27.052	54.3	.8973	152	introduced
27.049	54.3	.8017	168	nails
27.049	54.3	.6473	202	insect
27.029	54.3	.9140	149	halfway
27.024	54.3	.2083	533	syllable
27.024	54.3	.7536	178	principle
26.963	54.3	.8215	164	activity
26.961	54.3	.7053	187	Central
26.959	54.3	.6754	194	temperatures
26.940	54.3	.7997	166	creature
26.940	54.3	.7482	176	Mars
26.927	54.3	.6718	195	dish
THE PRECEDING WORD TYPE OCCUPIES RANK 2600				
26.910	54.3	.3155	350	David
26.887	54.3	.8683	155	handsome
26.875	54.3	.8240	163	mainly
26.862	54.3	.8406	160	teachers
26.859	54.3	.7719	173	pupils
26.855	54.3	.6288	204	breathe
26.820	54.3	.8292	161	swept
26.818	54.3	.7581	173	racing
26.809	54.3	.8854	152	trips
26.793	54.3	.7709	172	firmly
26.781	54.3	.7025	186	Greece
26.775	54.3	.7733	171	hay
26.765	54.3	.8205	162	packed
26.667	54.3	.5527	234	vertical
26.666	54.3	.8364	159	package
26.666	54.3	.7058	184	harbor
26.665	54.3	.7923	167	reports
26.658	54.3	.4127	303	r
26.649	54.3	.7685	172	behavior
26.633	54.3	.4355	279	writer
26.612	54.3	.6971	183	apartment
26.608	54.3	.7852	167	pale
26.588	54.2	.8524	156	destroyed
26.570	54.2	.5083	249	diameter
26.567	54.2	.8017	165	articles
26.553	54.2	.8008	164	settle
26.521	54.2	.8270	161	indicates
26.518	54.2	.9087	147	mentioned
26.518	54.2	.8263	160	collected
26.515	54.2	.8585	155	positions
26.511	54.2	.8767	152	actual
26.503	54.2	.7234	176	worried
26.498	54.2	.8257	159	somehow
26.477	54.2	.7025	184	saddle
26.473	54.2	.8171	161	wound
26.468	54.2	.5680	227	stock
26.462	54.2	.7791	167	officer
26.447	54.2	.8646	154	typical
26.446	54.2	.7824	167	engineer
26.431	54.2	.8071	162	welcome
26.406	54.2	.9046	147	duty
26.391	54.2	.7299	179	dot
26.390	54.2	.5890	210	snakes
26.386	54.2	.8367	156	fix
26.322	54.2	.7922	163	fox
26.317	54.2	.7823	166	refused
26.310	54.2	.6569	193	port
26.295	54.2	.7166	180	bend
26.239	54.2	.4766	262	drawings
26.235	54.2	.7327	176	tropical
26.230	54.2	.7069	181	Gulf
26.201	54.2	.7555	171	stems
26.184	54.2	.8163	159	eager
26.181	54.2	.8211	158	guard
26.144	54.2	.8583	153	widely
26.143	54.2	.7484	171	frog
26.120	54.2	.6559	194	Russia
26.090	54.2	.8498	153	forty
26.069	54.2	.8648	151	flame
26.061	54.2	.7784	164	canoe
26.053	54.2	.8699	150	teams
26.017	54.2	.8084	161	organization
26.009	54.2	.5495	225	atom
25.953	54.1	.8178	158	tide
25.947	54.1	.8704	149	wrapped

U	SFI	D	F	Word Type
25.944	54.1	.7973	161	skills
25.929	54.1	.8168	157	wing
25.913	54.1	.8805	148	gained
25.913	54.1	.6010	206	slaves
25.910	54.1	.5833	212	cooking
25.907	54.1	.8837	147	torn
25.904	54.1	.5739	217	properties
25.903	54.1	.6830	185	horn
25.877	54.1	.7125	175	cowboys
25.864	54.1	.8191	158	effects
25.858	54.1	.8070	159	split
25.853	54.1	.5467	223	Fred
25.849	54.1	.8224	157	former
25.836	54.1	.6387	188	yelled
25.829	54.1	.8533	151	invention
25.820	54.1	.8988	144	unhappy
25.799	54.1	.8591	151	limited
25.791	54.1	.8572	151	movie
25.787	54.1	.7941	162	Rome
25.774	54.1	.6910	180	Prince
25.761	54.1	.9370	139	presented
25.734	54.1	.8703	148	ill
25.715	54.1	.7224	175	Southern
25.683	54.1	.8819	146	shoe
25.665	54.1	.8160	156	puts
25.661	54.1	.8425	152	command
25.659	54.1	.7444	169	Bay
25.641	54.1	.7783	162	managed
25.625	54.1	.8107	157	mental
25.621	54.1	.9468	137	difficulty
25.614	54.1	.7450	167	roar
25.606	54.1	.8770	146	nearer
25.597	54.1	.7790	162	messages
25.589	54.1	.8372	152	adventure
25.584	54.1	.7657	165	Ohio
THE PRECEDING WORD TYPE OCCUPIES RANK 2700				
25.574	54.1	.8744	147	birth
25.564	54.1	.7467	169	circles
25.553	54.1	.8545	149	ducks
25.536	54.1	.7781	162	buried
25.531	54.1	.7693	162	hello
25.514	54.1	.6989	177	declared
25.490	54.1	.6987	176	weren't
25.484	54.1	.6593	188	strips
25.474	54.1	.7794	162	rear
25.470	54.1	.6891	182	performed
25.452	54.1	.8850	144	crack
25.446	54.1	.8289	153	protection
25.443	54.1	.7419	169	brings
25.433	54.1	.6013	199	Maria
25.426	54.1	.7749	163	private
25.423	54.1	.6335	184	goose
25.416	54.1	.7969	157	elephants
25.412	54.1	.7164	175	Russian
25.408	54.0	.6833	183	squares
25.408	54.0	.7592	166	interior
25.401	54.0	.8022	157	chamber
25.373	54.0	.6893	178	jungle
25.370	54.0	.8941	143	replaced
25.345	54.0	.7514	165	belonged
25.310	54.0	.8887	143	dirty
25.300	54.0	.8771	145	noted
25.294	54.0	.7048	178	applied
25.292	54.0	.6659	185	scales
25.282	54.0	.7518	167	35
25.281	54.0	.8433	150	nervous
25.273	54.0	.8619	147	dull
25.269	54.0	.6442	191	brass
25.261	54.0	.9169	139	opportunity
25.221	54.0	.8090	154	hospital
25.213	54.0	.8184	154	occurs
25.212	54.0	.7793	161	sources
25.209	54.0	.7705	162	guests
25.204	54.0	.8363	150	invited
25.179	54.0	.8835	143	seats
25.167	54.0	.8249	152	plastic
25.165	54.0	.7955	157	tons
25.152	54.0	.8524	148	contained
25.111	54.0	.8536	148	definite
25.106	54.0	.3316	335	prime
25.104	54.0	.7062	175	location
25.077	54.0	.8571	146	eleven
25.075	54.0	.8134	154	curved
25.043	54.0	.7970	156	October
25.040	54.0	.7903	155	aboard
25.036	54.0	.6508	187	troops
25.024	54.0	.8107	153	captured
25.022	54.0	.7915	157	spots
25.016	54.0	.8342	149	sink
25.001	54.0	.7984	154	voyage
25.001	54.0	.8269	150	shelf
24.966	54.0	.5925	199	ore
24.951	54.0	.8151	152	washing
24.935	54.0	.7753	159	firm
24.926	54.0	.7435	166	accurate
24.904	54.0	.8695	144	equally
24.901	54.0	.6574	181	Pole
24.880	54.0	.9142	137	crossing
24.877	54.0	.7679	158	Daniel
24.857	54.0	.4515	259	mixture
24.847	54.0	.4879	213	Jeff
24.839	54.0	.7164	170	checked
24.827	53.9	.8499	146	shelter
24.819	53.9	.7996	153	pasture
24.790	53.9	.8844	141	constant
24.788	53.9	.5170	216	soldier
24.760	53.9	.7738	157	shine
24.757	53.9	.8278	149	victory
24.737	53.9	.7642	158	whistle
24.735	53.9	.6861	175	slave
24.735	53.9	.8126	151	breaking
24.729	53.9	.7689	158	dawn
24.726	53.9	.3780	284	farming
24.715	53.9	.7339	166	services
24.707	53.9	.4835	236	equator
24.701	53.9	.6070	198	thy
24.694	53.9	.7288	166	camera

U	SFI	D	F	Word Type
24.685	53.9	.6559	182	opinion
24.684	53.9	.7810	157	characters
24.683	53.9	.8798	141	fully
24.676	53.9	.8456	145	lighted
24.670	53.9	.7819	157	experiences
24.668	53.9	.7807	156	counted
24.661	53.9	.6247	190	pour
24.659	53.9	.7435	164	labor
24.634	53.9	.7655	160	brief
24.627	53.9	.8396	147	properly
24.604	53.9	.8363	146	pointing
24.596	53.9	.7639	158	horns
24.586	53.9	.7358	167	appropriate
24.572	53.9	.8032	152	corners
24.567	53.9	.6439	186	90
24.566	53.9	.9094	136	arrive
24.564	53.9	.4234	257.	gravity
24.540	53.9	.8339	146	fierce
24.535	53.9	.7659	157	bet
THE PRECEDING WORD TYPE OCCUPIES RANK 2800				
24.522	53.9	.7558	161	independent
24.517	53.9	.7956	152	cleared
24.486	53.9	.6476	184	label
24.476	53.9	.8427	145	cast
24.474	53.9	.5775	204	positive
24.463	53.9	.8586	143	occasionally
24.463	53.9	.7985	152	melted
24.451	53.9	.7266	166	peoples
24.410	53.9	.7128	164	crying
24.405	53.9	.8903	138	attempt
24.403	53.9	.7799	154	fires
24.367	53.9	.4637	249	f
24.367	53.9	.8063	151	require
24.361	53.9	.8244	147	sale
24.358	53.9	.8123	150	thumb
24.341	53.9	.6649	177	tubes
24.317	53.9	.8097	149	wagons
24.306	53.9	.7701	157	A**
24.288	53.9	.4084	253	Danny
24.274	53.9	.7988	150	fort
24.272	53.9	.7329	164	film
24.265	53.8	.8264	146	passengers
24.247	53.8	.8557	141	tossed
24.232	53.8	.8880	137	advice
24.223	53.8	.5283	212	arithmetic
24.212	53.8	.7651	156	January
24.192	53.8	.7501	156	donkey
24.189	53.8	.8112	149	discussion
24.163	53.8	.8389	143	shake
24.106	53.8	.8542	141	lessons
24.100	53.8	.8683	139	memory
24.089	53.8	.7333	157	garage
24.070	53.8	.7920	150	glasses
24.035	53.8	.8233	145	pride
24.034	53.8	.7957	150	charged
24.034	53.8	.8798	137	finds
24.018	53.8	.7468	155	policeman
24.007	53.8	.5938	195	University
24.004	53.8	.8208	146	School
24.002	53.8	.7261	159	palace
23.995	53.8	.7836	153	relationship
23.990	53.8	.8000	149	slip
23.965	53.8	.7873	150	Mountain
23.965	53.8	.5741	196	selection
23.941	53.8	.5991	191	satellites
23.927	53.8	.6954	167	NewYorkCity
23.902	53.8	.5891	195	lowest
23.881	53.8	.8181	144	doll
23.851	53.8	.9022	133	satisfied
23.838	53.8	.6357	179	Norway
23.834	53.8	.8080	146	toy
23.834	53.8	.8561	139	hats
23.832	53.8	.7267	162	habits
23.831	53.8	.8232	145	arrangement
23.829	53.8	.4418	236	promised
23.822	53.8	.8697	137	calm
23.795	53.8	.7772	151	Mount
23.760	53.8	.5893	193	Martin
23.752	53.8	.8182	144	rocky
23.747	53.8	.7808	150	neighborhood
23.744	53.8	.8439	140	warning
23.739	53.8	.7648	153	Harry
23.738	53.8	.6745	168	kids
23.738	53.8	.6836	168	cookies
23.736	53.8	.4128	255	metals
23.728	53.8	.8129	144	monkey
23.727	53.8	.5291	209	vapor
23.720	53.8	.7064	161	grabbed
23.711	53.7	.8746	136	deeply
23.709	53.7	.6720	171	currents
23.708	53.7	.7691	151	doctors
23.706	53.7	.8200	145	originally
23.701	53.7	.8419	140	walks
23.701	53.7	.8168	143	happily
23.648	53.7	.8421	140	chairs
23.647	53.7	.8819	134	floating
23.617	53.7	.7539	155	powers
23.606	53.7	.4168	270	adjectives
23.587	53.7	.7405	158	poetry
23.570	53.7	.7978	146	slope
23.540	53.7	.8158	143	bags
23.534	53.7	.3047	328	Star
23.529	53.7	.3889	276	species
23.507	53.7	.6776	171	lengths
23.502	53.7	.8167	143	nuts
23.497	53.7	.8320	141	remarkable
23.491	53.7	.8577	137	August
23.487	53.7	.7249	159	acres
23.460	53.7	.8374	139	tricks
23.458	53.7	.7540	155	essential
23.457	53.7	.8325	141	constantly
23.454	53.7	.6895	167	depth
23.448	53.7	.8474	139	requires
23.444	53.7	.6180	182	mineral
23.440	53.7	.7538	153	canal
23.431	53.7	.7816	147	coach
23.409	53.7	.8370	139	dreams
23.406	53.7	.7291	159	M
23.399	53.7	.8183	143	complicated
23.388	53.7	.7925	146	Lee
THE PRECEDING WORD TYPE OCCUPIES RANK 2900				
23.373	53.7	.2810	279	Casey
23.368	53.7	.6806	164	swung
23.358	53.7	.8334	140	exchange
23.356	53.7	.7548	151	hunter
23.353	53.7	.8698	135	exist
23.349	53.7	.7838	147	reported
23.338	53.7	.3370	309	tune
23.329	53.7	.8593	136	shallow
23.327	53.7	.7840	148	image
23.325	53.7	.6557	172	tobacco
23.279	53.7	.8425	138	stiff
23.277	53.7	.8879	132	increasing
23.251	53.7	.8493	136	precious
23.239	53.7	.8988	130	presents
23.231	53.7	.8024	144	damage
23.227	53.7	.8830	132	treated
23.215	53.7	.7427	153	folks
23.203	53.7	.7947	145	Illinois
23.183	53.7	.7568	152	adult
23.178	53.7	.8438	137	spin
23.164	53.6	.8839	131	shed
23.159	53.6	.7512	152	Philadelphia
23.135	53.6	.8121	140	grandmother
23.131	53.6	.7938	145	customs
23.122	53.6	.5992	185	mathematics
23.086	53.6	.6584	170	heated
23.082	53.6	.7663	146	claws
23.080	53.6	.8753	132	reaching
23.077	53.6	.7438	153	official
23.051	53.6	.8333	138	recall
23.044	53.6	.8198	140	explanation
23.027	53.6	.8857	131	developing
22.990	53.6	.8130	140	mysterious
22.986	53.6	.8620	134	recorded
22.985	53.6	.7869	143	shout
22.981	53.6	.8200	140	practical
22.975	53.6	.7381	153	Pennsylvania
22.970	53.6	.5588	195	t
22.952	53.6	.5898	188	P
22.930	53.6	.7212	157	70
22.914	53.6	.6792	167	V
22.892	53.6	.6313	175	plates
22.871	53.6	.7319	153	officers
22.867	53.6	.8086	139	wolf
22.867	53.6	.8548	134	raising
22.860	53.6	.8270	137	deeper
22.859	53.6	.8974	128	wishes
22.834	53.6	.8448	135	instant
22.833	53.6	.8078	141	writers
22.822	53.6	.7363	151	scared
22.802	53.6	.7609	147	breeze
22.787	53.6	.6534	172	contrast
22.773	53.6	.6765	164	Egypt
22.758	53.6	.7160	156	X
22.757	53.6	.6680	165	mission
22.735	53.6	.7961	140	tales
22.735	53.6	.6785	163	vessels
22.732	53.6	.7262	150	silly
22.724	53.6	.7214	155	border
22.709	53.6	.4461	242	G
22.708	53.6	.7264	152	trap
22.694	53.6	.8027	139	zoo
22.691	53.6	.8837	129	occurred
22.691	53.6	.6979	159	wealth
22.652	53.6	.5396	199	manufacturing
22.645	53.5	.7973	139	Hill
22.645	53.5	.8624	131	fired
22.640	53.5	.7438	149	mill
22.589	53.5	.7275	152	heading
22.586	53.5	.4860	211	Ellen
22.571	53.5	.8385	134	rubbed
22.566	53.5	.8539	132	brick
22.554	53.5	.9094	125	tremendous
22.546	53.5	.4288	243	compounds
22.527	53.5	.7274	153	23
22.522	53.5	.6337	171	chose
22.510	53.5	.6370	172	simplest
22.493	53.5	.8912	127	slight
22.469	53.5	.5341	198	solar
22.452	53.5	.7813	142	grains
22.426	53.5	.8034	139	stated
22.412	53.5	.8172	136	drinking
22.385	53.5	.8280	134	fireplace
22.382	53.5	.8471	132	stops
22.360	53.5	.7434	146	shaking
22.345	53.5	.8756	128	goal
22.342	53.5	.4641	226	rhyme
22.326	53.5	.6428	169	45
22.311	53.5	.6503	167	80
22.307	53.5	.6057	178	facing
22.307	53.5	.7956	139	autumn
22.306	53.5	.8666	129	possibly
22.303	53.5	.8581	130	habit
22.300	53.5	.7981	138	shooting
22.286	53.5	.7714	142	ourselves
22.255	53.5	.7928	140	centers
22.238	53.5	.8376	132	rush
22.229	53.5	.8179	134	soap
22.224	53.5	.8238	134	finest
22.223	53.5	.4915	207	lungs
THE PRECEDING WORD TYPE OCCUPIES RANK 3000				
22.221	53.5	.4724	220	estimate
22.219	53.5	.7883	139	Friday
22.216	53.5	.8658	129	suggests
22.200	53.5	.6212	167	asks
22.190	53.5	.8826	126	lined
22.184	53.5	.8592	129	contest
22.172	53.5	.8625	129	desire
22.162	53.5	.9242	121	tear
22.149	53.5	.8694	127	ladder
22.132	53.5	.8340	132	vacation
22.129	53.4	.8410	132	interests
22.125	53.4	.6832	159	dividing
22.123	53.4	.7398	145	good-by
22.121	53.4	.7962	138	stem
22.104	53.4	.6165	173	railroads
22.090	53.4	.2782	339	equivalent
22.089	53.4	.8157	135	extremely
22.083	53.4	.4782	215	reptiles
22.076	53.4	.6070	166	Tony
22.074	53.4	.7541	145	borrowed
22.067	53.4	.8037	137	extend
22.049	53.4	.8223	133	sunshine
22.021	53.4	.7114	150	fever
22.010	53.4	.7357	147	SanFrancisco
21.988	53.4	.7243	150	imagination
21.970	53.4	.6488	166	background
21.968	53.4	.8111	134	gardens
21.964	53.4	.7142	150	stations
21.955	53.4	.7860	139	earliest
21.948	53.4	.8674	126	foolish
21.928	53.4	.8083	136	effective
21.920	53.4	.8248	132	meanwhile
21.913	53.4	.7091	152	lightly
21.906	53.4	.7745	137	owl
21.896	53.4	.7483	143	beads
21.873	53.4	.7422	142	pig
21.870	53.4	.7324	147	female
21.866	53.4	.8400	130	otherwise
21.857	53.4	.8681	126	mothers
21.837	53.4	.7852	137	fishermen
21.823	53.4	.7607	143	suitable
21.799	53.4	.8250	132	reflected
21.774	53.4	.7701	138	ghost
21.760	53.4	.8325	130	faced
21.759	53.4	.8319	131	22
21.744	53.4	.6851	154	Mexican
21.733	53.4	.8196	132	mounted
21.722	53.4	.6193	170	juice
21.712	53.4	.8475	128	lively
21.693	53.4	.7355	146	device
21.692	53.4	.8279	130	glance
21.684	53.4	.6291	168	description
21.681	53.4	.5448	184	soup
21.674	53.4	.6665	155	Helen
21.673	53.4	.7899	137	devices
21.657	53.4	.5288	186	telescope
21.645	53.4	.7163	148	Park
21.644	53.4	.6917	153	nail
21.601	53.3	.7838	137	responsible
21.596	53.3	.8316	129	hero
21.568	53.3	.7964	134	penny
21.558	53.3	.1637	480	fraction
21.551	53.3	.8328	128	clever
21.543	53.3	.7429	143	chocolate
21.538	53.3	.7358	142	loudly
21.522	53.3	.7871	134	awake
21.517	53.3	.8264	130	flowing
21.510	53.3	.8221	130	code
21.508	53.3	.7914	134	prairie
21.502	53.3	.7834	134	hiding
21.468	53.3	.7628	140	communication
21.458	53.3	.6604	157	deserts
21.449	53.3	.7440	142	masses
21.422	53.3	.5102	197	hydrogen
21.418	53.3	.6562	159	costs
21.417	53.3	.7302	143	Susan
21.399	53.3	.6215	167	formula
21.393	53.3	.5604	181	cardboard
21.387	53.3	.8771	122	stopping
21.347	53.3	.6086	168	weighs
21.344	53.3	.6551	155	asking
21.340	53.3	.8029	132	thrust
21.324	53.3	.7417	142	bands
21.312	53.3	.7870	134	pressed
21.310	53.3	.8838	121	backward
21.302	53.3	.6777	154	lumber
21.292	53.3	.8646	123	tries
21.275	53.3	.6896	151	elected
21.267	53.3	.7167	147	characteristic
21.263	53.3	.7476	141	published
21.252	53.3	.8059	132	unique
21.250	53.3	.7151	143	jacket
21.249	53.3	.7780	136	detail
21.238	53.3	.7430	141	folded
21.218	53.3	.7193	144	explorers
21.216	53.3	.4866	208	project
21.201	53.3	.8275	128	inner
21.200	53.3	.7924	133	heavier
21.194	53.3	.7259	144	largely
21.186	53.3	.8090	130	button
THE PRECEDING WORD TYPE OCCUPIES RANK 3100				
21.181	53.3	.8187	129	expensive
21.179	53.3	.8595	123	tails
21.177	53.3	.8677	122	potato
21.170	53.3	.8157	129	protected
21.154	53.3	.6939	149	medical
21.146	53.3	.6132	164	Jean
21.138	53.3	.6599	153	we'd
21.138	53.3	.7797	134	pulls
21.134	53.2	.7640	135	laughter
21.100	53.2	.7479	138	eats
21.097	53.2	.7084	145	pioneers
21.083	53.2	.4331	224	flour
21.082	53.2	.7837	134	19
21.075	53.2	.7387	139	midnight
21.065	53.2	.6934	148	Army
21.047	53.2	.6970	147	shadows
21.038	53.2	.6265	161	coins
21.032	53.2	.8358	125	float
21.006	53.2	.6651	155	engineers
20.993	53.2	.7969	130	Franklin
20.970	53.2	.6940	149	performance
20.964	53.2	.7770	133	bananas
20.958	53.2	.7924	131	High
20.955	53.2	.8383	125	god
20.948	53.2	.5901	165	candle
20.942	53.2	.7845	133	columns
20.939	53.2	.6837	148	Missouri
20.932	53.2	.6765	148	smiling
20.915	53.2	.7457	140	combinations
20.883	53.2	.8362	125	presence
20.874	53.2	.8500	123	beings
20.869	53.2	.7596	136	November
20.866	53.2	.8082	127	drivers
20.862	53.2	.8252	126	feeding
20.848	53.2	.6946	148	No
20.843	53.2	.7949	130	trial
20.841	53.2	.7296	138	rang
20.836	53.2	.8310	125	calf
20.809	53.2	.7678	135	programs
20.805	53.2	.7488	136	rockets
20.786	53.2	.8865	118	fashion
20.786	53.2	.8349	124	monkeys
20.783	53.2	.8831	118	steadily
20.767	53.2	.8936	117	granted
20.742	53.2	.3545	275	tones
20.740	53.2	.3652	257	3/4
20.734	53.2	.4308	228	My
20.730	53.2	.5857	166	lightning
20.727	53.2	.7397	139	approximately
20.707	53.2	.6882	144	sighed
20.704	53.2	.5047	174	dragon
20.699	53.2	.8102	126	ugly
20.691	53.2	.6417	157	data
20.653	53.1	.4769	198	Ma
20.649	53.1	.7615	133	selling
20.630	53.1	.7876	130	treatment
20.623	53.1	.7325	138	laboratory
20.620	53.1	.8028	128	actions
20.610	53.1	.7705	132	boards
20.573	53.1	.9003	115	examined
20.564	53.1	.7150	140	rifle
20.550	53.1	.6946	146	culture
20.548	53.1	.8032	127	flood
20.542	53.1	.7850	128	Green
20.533	53.1	.7288	136	cart
20.533	53.1	.5700	175	blend
20.531	53.1	.8889	116	sunny
20.525	53.1	.8626	119	beds
20.519	53.1	.6392	155	hammer
20.513	53.1	.7458	135	beam
20.506	53.1	.8905	116	advanced
20.491	53.1	.8801	117	efforts
20.489	53.1	.4997	194	drum
20.489	53.1	.9125	113	ceiling
20.485	53.1	.5748	171	Figure
20.477	53.1	.6867	147	cuts
20.465	53.1	.6795	149	relative
20.456	53.1	.6155	160	crust
20.453	53.1	.7633	132	wilderness
20.445	53.1	.8327	123	selected
20.431	53.1	.5022	187	ain't
20.423	53.1	.8311	122	overhead
20.420	53.1	.7694	131	bases
20.419	53.1	.6114	161	independence
20.413	53.1	.4480	209	electrons
20.411	53.1	.6452	155	operations
20.405	53.1	.7710	131	gay
20.392	53.1	.7550	133	cakes
20.391	53.1	.6660	146	Roosevelt
20.385	53.1	.7940	127	turkey
20.385	53.1	.8424	121	lawn
20.380	53.1	.4645	202	mammals
20.378	53.1	.7452	135	reaction
20.369	53.1	.6502	152	territory
20.358	53.1	.3478	263	k
20.346	53.1	.7195	139	male
20.331	53.1	.7369	136	moisture
20.331	53.1	.6001	164	staff
20.318	53.1	.6022	161	diseases
20.311	53.1	.7899	127	beating
THE PRECEDING WORD TYPE OCCUPIES RANK 3200				
20.303	53.1	.6657	146	ant
20.298	53.1	.5514	170	mines
20.291	53.1	.8971	114	extended
20.289	53.1	.8249	122	adventures
20.278	53.1	.7517	130	goat
20.255	53.1	.8679	117	shared
20.188	53.1	.8609	117	sport
20.156	53.0	.8031	125	claim
20.143	53.0	.6200	157	Mediterranean
20.143	53.0	.7581	132	purposes
20.124	53.0	.7815	127	ladies
20.123	53.0	.8561	118	magazine
20.119	53.0	.8207	121	platform
20.112	53.0	.7972	124	hunted
20.104	53.0	.7865	127	decision
20.092	53.0	.7908	126	apparently
20.086	53.0	.4975	191	electrical
20.069	53.0	.7770	128	picnic
20.058	53.0	.5312	179	religion
20.038	53.0	.6845	141	marry
20.023	53.0	.5691	172	printing
20.022	53.0	.8498	118	pop
20.009	53.0	.5862	159	hey
20.007	53.0	.8722	115	pretend
20.004	53.0	.6911	140	frogs
20.003	53.0	.8801	114	unable
20.003	53.0	.7019	140	brilliant
19.997	53.0	.8063	124	role
19.985	53.0	.8657	116	advantage
19.981	53.0	.8972	112	underneath
19.967	53.0	.7780	127	dam
19.957	53.0	.6694	139	cabbage
19.944	53.0	.8028	123	shiny
19.943	53.0	.7235	135	warmer
19.940	53.0	.7823	127	de
19.939	53.0	.8374	119	Company
19.937	53.0	.8477	117	faint
19.932	53.0	.7692	127	climbing
19.929	53.0	.6044	158	satellite
19.928	53.0	.8616	116	improved
19.926	53.0	.7499	131	kings
19.912	53.0	.5950	159	trading
19.890	53.0	.7675	129	Romans
19.885	53.0	.6343	153	expanded

U	SFI	D	F	Word Type
19.875	53.0	.6126	156	poems
19.858	53.0	.3185	280	folk
19.829	53.0	.8493	117	everyday
19.820	53.0	.7377	131	swift
19.814	53.0	.8364	118	scarcely
19.809	53.0	.7814	126	conclusion
19.804	53.0	.6242	154	blanks
19.796	53.0	.8601	115	gifts
19.793	53.0	.7772	126	enters
19.783	53.0	.7898	122	submarine
19.759	53.0	.6603	145	altitude
19.751	53.0	.7904	123	lock
19.741	53.0	.8850	112	spinning
19.737	53.0	.5564	170	economic
19.736	53.0	.8217	119	jumping
19.734	53.0	.7494	130	ruled
19.720	52.9	.6448	149	Britain
19.672	52.9	.4909	192	apply
19.657	52.9	.8583	115	considerable
19.649	52.9	.8651	114	content
19.646	52.9	.8252	119	directed
19.635	52.9	.7850	124	teaching
19.619	52.9	.8384	116	blankets
19.615	52.9	.8647	114	advance
19.614	52.9	.6073	151	whales
19.597	52.9	.7492	130	commercial
19.594	52.9	.3944	227	g
19.592	52.9	.8028	121	gentleman
19.591	52.9	.6699	139	knocked
19.591	52.9	.8006	122	professional
19.583	52.9	.1492	473	God
19.573	52.9	.8333	117	oak
19.572	52.9	.6760	140	healthy
19.560	52.9	.6773	140	settlement
19.540	52.9	.7415	129	Benjamin
19.539	52.9	.7951	123	comparison
19.538	52.9	.5606	162	'em
19.503	52.9	.7643	126	rare
19.500	52.9	.8099	120	leads
19.492	52.9	.6687	141	bulb
19.482	52.9	.7475	128	weighed
19.465	52.9	.7090	136	commonly
19.445	52.9	.8862	110	twenty-five
19.441	52.9	.3973	214	paragraphs
19.441	52.9	.2904	276	gases
19.425	52.9	.8889	110	practically
19.408	52.9	.8210	118	reference
19.408	52.9	.8161	118	outdoors
19.401	52.9	.0767	673	equation
19.395	52.9	.7819	123	cans
19.386	52.9	.4534	204	accent
19.373	52.9	.8854	110	breaks
19.367	52.9	.5084	179	Willie
19.362	52.9	.6648	143	forming
19.359	52.9	.6718	139	Coast
19.346	52.9	.8195	117	sandy

THE PRECEDING WORD TYPE OCCUPIES RANK 3300

U	SFI	D	F	Word Type
19.331	52.9	.8265	116	delight
19.316	52.9	.6406	147	28
19.300	52.9	.7575	124	digging
19.283	52.9	.8903	109	discussed
19.280	52.9	.7180	132	parties
19.262	52.8	.7911	121	December
19.262	52.8	.3929	226	I
19.259	52.8	.5943	157	construct
19.258	52.8	.6373	146	truly
19.256	52.8	.8049	118	here's
19.242	52.8	.7937	121	striking
19.236	52.8	.7126	131	Massachusetts
19.235	52.8	.8503	113	treat
19.229	52.8	.8113	118	worker
19.227	52.8	.8286	116	150
19.202	52.8	.7214	129	stuff
19.196	52.8	.7003	132	someday
19.191	52.8	.7916	121	portion
19.182	52.8	.8675	111	continues
19.176	52.8	.8530	112	swiftly
19.175	52.8	.8096	118	committee
19.166	52.8	.8374	114	bottles
19.164	52.8	.7484	126	herds
19.163	52.8	.8253	116	surrounding
19.153	52.8	.8405	114	approach
19.153	52.8	.8088	118	occasion
19.151	52.8	.4349	191	promise
19.140	52.8	.7066	132	slopes
19.130	52.8	.8880	108	sixty
19.127	52.8	.4977	179	continents
19.118	52.8	.8400	114	models
19.109	52.8	.5134	175	seasons
19.108	52.8	.7425	125	bedroom
19.100	52.8	.8514	112	hopes
19.097	52.8	.7960	119	palm
19.082	52.8	.6850	131	swallowed
19.079	52.8	.7550	126	primary
19.075	52.8	.7469	125	clues
19.065	52.8	.7459	126	jaws
19.064	52.8	.8966	107	favor
19.063	52.8	.8721	110	prefer
19.054	52.8	.7898	119	dotted
19.044	52.8	.8859	108	returning
19.032	52.8	.6087	148	harm
19.030	52.8	.5863	154	thermometer
19.029	52.8	.6700	137	United
19.017	52.8	.8116	116	storms
19.017	52.8	.8544	111	bush
19.015	52.8	.6787	133	woke
19.013	52.8	.5547	164	measurement
18.990	52.8	.7568	123	marched
18.990	52.8	.7238	129	Irish
18.972	52.8	.6846	135	carriage
18.962	52.8	.5752	157	net
18.954	52.8	.8131	116	comfort
18.953	52.8	.8062	117	pipes
18.932	52.8	.7584	124	item
18.888	52.8	.8595	110	responsibility
18.887	52.8	.7560	124	classmates
18.886	52.8	.7179	126	lad

U	SFI	D	F	Word Type
18.881	52.8	.5996	142	Al
18.875	52.8	.7708	121	ribbon
18.869	52.8	.7446	125	soul
18.859	52.8	.6603	135	roared
18.859	52.8	.8346	113	intended
18.857	52.8	.8559	110	sails
18.850	52.8	.7216	127	shouting
18.849	52.8	.7834	120	numerous
18.847	52.8	.7701	121	bay
18.836	52.8	.7683	121	basketball
18.825	52.7	.7831	119	February
18.811	52.7	.9030	105	attend
18.810	52.7	.6010	152	36
18.808	52.7	.5357	168	fold
18.808	52.7	.8802	107	destroy
18.806	52.7	.8130	115	melting
18.805	52.7	.8147	115	quarters
18.802	52.7	.7470	123	airport
18.798	52.7	.7474	125	relatively
18.795	52.7	.4711	183	Brother
18.793	52.7	.8440	111	surprising
18.783	52.7	.8340	113	receives
18.783	52.7	.6907	133	Department
18.764	52.7	.8243	113	sharply
18.742	52.7	.7399	125	beef
18.734	52.7	.8292	113	describes
18.731	52.7	.6164	149	width
18.729	52.7	.6891	133	muscle
18.729	52.7	.7683	120	coats
18.726	52.7	.7672	121	contact
18.714	52.7	.6174	147	billion
18.705	52.7	.6372	142	communities
18.702	52.7	.8000	116	thirteen
18.693	52.7	.8090	114	pitcher
18.693	52.7	.3963	223	minor
18.691	52.7	.7376	123	statue
18.686	52.7	.8270	113	chiefly
18.630	52.7	.8480	110	moreover
18.610	52.7	.8072	113	baskets
18.566	52.7	.8115	113	wake

THE PRECEDING WORD TYPE OCCUPIES RANK 3400

U	SFI	D	F	Word Type
18.547	52.7	.8420	110	seek
18.540	52.7	.8354	111	damp
18.534	52.7	.6551	138	27
18.531	52.7	.7209	126	shops
18.522	52.7	.7547	121	Switzerland
18.514	52.7	.5233	164	00
18.509	52.7	.6918	132	B**
18.504	52.7	.6445	139	officials
18.496	52.7	.7141	126	louder
18.483	52.7	.8088	114	delicate
18.482	52.7	.7402	122	rats
18.470	52.7	.6364	136	Steve
18.467	52.7	.7022	128	bee
18.465	52.7	.8052	114	coin
18.441	52.7	.7787	117	invisible
18.433	52.7	.7479	120	they'll
18.407	52.6	.8370	109	throwing
18.395	52.6	.8316	110	sending
18.384	52.6	.7234	122	proudly
18.376	52.6	.5535	160	pin
18.373	52.6	.7391	122	rainy
18.372	52.6	.4805	175	mills
18.363	52.6	.8056	112	mate
18.351	52.6	.8117	112	cleaned
18.323	52.6	.7612	117	Arthur
18.321	52.6	.8594	107	rapid
18.306	52.6	.8307	109	treasure
18.304	52.6	.7235	124	blows
18.290	52.6	.5487	160	corresponding
18.287	52.6	.7981	113	sidewalk
18.284	52.6	.8222	111	Elizabeth
18.279	52.6	.5977	147	meals
18.272	52.6	.8384	108	swinging
18.270	52.6	.4878	175	Soviet
18.258	52.6	.7282	123	clue
18.243	52.6	.5333	164	mistakes
18.243	52.6	.3886	219	Unit
18.211	52.6	.7603	119	majority
18.210	52.6	.7234	124	civilization
18.210	52.6	.8332	109	dates
18.208	52.6	.8083	112	hook
18.205	52.6	.7476	119	First
18.204	52.6	.5266	164	magnetic
18.178	52.6	.7232	123	ancestors
18.138	52.6	.7121	124	seized
18.134	52.6	.2611	285	vowels
18.132	52.6	.5157	165	federal
18.129	52.6	.8479	106	crash
18.129	52.6	.8429	108	adds
18.122	52.6	.6236	140	bench
18.121	52.6	.7712	117	provides
18.118	52.6	.8435	107	bucket
18.112	52.6	.5245	157	tickets
18.110	52.6	.7018	127	literature
18.103	52.6	.8444	107	peaceful
18.102	52.6	.7932	113	buttons
18.080	52.6	.7999	112	warmth
18.076	52.6	.6662	127	Mom
18.070	52.6	.7546	119	illustrate
18.067	52.6	.6610	131	Jerry
18.066	52.6	.5758	149	colonists
18.062	52.6	.8211	110	permanent
18.055	52.6	.7683	116	passenger
18.040	52.6	.7020	126	patient
18.040	52.6	.8830	103	serves
18.037	52.6	.7740	114	flash
18.033	52.6	.7941	113	quantities
18.017	52.6	.7729	115	cord
18.016	52.6	.7402	118	Albert
18.007	52.6	.6631	132	stamps
18.006	52.6	.3896	212	strings
17.997	52.6	.8280	108	daylight
17.996	52.6	.8055	111	uniform
17.996	52.6	.8284	108	worst
17.985	52.5	.4157	197	Israel
17.985	52.5	.8675	104	closing

U	SFI	D	F	Word Type
17.964	52.5	.8213	109	grand
17.944	52.5	.7725	115	mild
17.940	52.5	.6850	126	Air
17.938	52.5	.8468	106	entrance
17.935	52.5	.7799	114	America's
17.922	52.5	.5562	154	Christian
17.919	52.5	.7444	117	doorway
17.911	52.5	.8474	106	heavily
17.910	52.5	.7354	118	chin
17.899	52.5	.7811	113	honey
17.898	52.5	.8346	106	peaches
17.891	52.5	.6195	140	acid
17.881	52.5	.7319	120	weapons
17.876	52.5	.7611	117	suggestions
17.871	52.5	.8912	101	reduced
17.864	52.5	.7991	111	longest
17.861	52.5	.6628	131	mechanical
17.855	52.5	.4343	194	tense
17.854	52.5	.5959	140	uranium
17.851	52.5	.5978	143	country's
17.851	52.5	.7579	117	despite
17.851	52.5	.6621	128	lions
17.849	52.5	.6101	138	leaned
17.843	52.5	.7242	119	shone

THE PRECEDING WORD TYPE OCCUPIES RANK 3500

U	SFI	D	F	Word Type
17.836	52.5	.6531	132	westward
17.815	52.5	.7792	113	neat
17.810	52.5	.8275	108	referred
17.810	52.5	.6024	141	Eastern
17.804	52.5	.6070	138	Sue
17.782	52.5	.7856	111	Santa
17.779	52.5	.7531	116	visitor
17.733	52.5	.5194	160	slavery
17.704	52.5	.8512	104	turtle
17.692	52.5	.4424	180	Doctor
17.684	52.5	.7415	116	locked
17.673	52.5	.7685	114	nevertheless
17.660	52.5	.6275	135	moist
17.656	52.5	.8085	108	catching
17.643	52.5	.8037	109	holiday
17.636	52.5	.6961	124	boiling
17.631	52.5	.7785	112	travelers
17.628	52.5	.8322	106	challenge
17.623	52.5	.7265	119	Swiss
17.622	52.5	.7851	111	twisted
17.617	52.5	.6333	136	drill
17.616	52.5	.8255	107	generation
17.615	52.5	.8530	103	bitter
17.610	52.5	.7716	113	altogether
17.606	52.5	.8408	105	varied
17.601	52.5	.7981	109	joke
17.600	52.5	.7302	117	Ralph
17.574	52.4	.7226	120	H
17.567	52.4	.6518	131	dairy
17.566	52.4	.7601	113	feared
17.566	52.4	.7627	112	tiger
17.560	52.4	.8065	108	Hall
17.553	52.4	.7477	115	underground
17.553	52.4	.7209	120	controlled
17.547	52.4	.7801	110	tanks
17.539	52.4	.7570	115	illustrated
17.536	52.4	.8371	105	affected
17.533	52.4	.7093	123	dramatic
17.510	52.4	.8372	104	ripe
17.508	52.4	.4354	194	harmony
17.494	52.4	.8577	102	shortly
17.490	52.4	.7856	110	relief
17.464	52.4	.7288	117	pump
17.461	52.4	.6683	128	sample
17.447	52.4	.7553	114	stable
17.444	52.4	.3137	231	bacteria
17.442	52.4	.5981	141	75
17.423	52.4	.7409	115	insisted
17.421	52.4	.7947	108	upset
17.418	52.4	.7179	117	fool
17.416	52.4	.6083	136	danced
17.414	52.4	.7004	121	rains
17.401	52.4	.7246	116	puzzled
17.387	52.4	.6581	126	Joseph
17.385	52.4	.6524	127	hid
17.378	52.4	.6719	122	Pierre
17.374	52.4	.4824	166	rainfall
17.373	52.4	.5847	143	stroke
17.363	52.4	.7808	109	heels
17.360	52.4	.7103	118	cane
17.352	52.4	.7981	109	impression
17.349	52.4	.7121	116	princess
17.325	52.4	.7219	118	Empire
17.310	52.4	.7385	115	Charlie
17.308	52.4	.6525	128	cups
17.291	52.4	.6263	132	deposits
17.286	52.4	.7927	108	career
17.285	52.4	.6488	125	Navy
17.279	52.4	.5496	151	frames
17.277	52.4	.7964	107	hate
17.274	52.4	.8033	107	demand
17.265	52.4	.5849	138	Senate
17.254	52.4	.7112	119	discoveries
17.252	52.4	.6824	124	U
17.246	52.4	.7801	110	colorful
17.243	52.4	.6075	130	Bear
17.235	52.4	.7086	119	highways
17.222	52.4	.7751	109	races
17.219	52.4	.5797	143	32
17.200	52.4	.2414	292	subtract
17.199	52.4	.5482	150	measurements
17.198	52.4	.8017	107	differently
17.193	52.4	.7090	119	bridges
17.185	52.4	.7992	106	feather
17.180	52.4	.4819	162	forever
17.174	52.3	.8656	99	ropes
17.174	52.3	.3131	251	orchestra
17.141	52.3	.8261	103	picking
17.132	52.3	.8109	105	royal
17.130	52.3	.6173	135	R
17.124	52.3	.8349	102	merchant
17.103	52.3	.7677	109	smart

U	SFI	D	F	Word Type
17.086	52.3	.8836	97	diamond
17.078	52.3	.8956	96	behave
17.066	52.3	.8148	104	lap
17.063	52.3	.7205	115	approached
17.056	52.3	.8170	103	beast
17.052	52.3	.7918	107	attracted
17.038	52.3	.8121	104	Jackson
17.030	52.3	.7837	107	Monday

THE PRECEDING WORD TYPE OCCUPIES RANK 3600

U	SFI	D	F	Word Type
17.028	52.3	.6848	120	fault
17.023	52.3	.6515	125	parade
17.018	52.3	.7117	117	frontier
17.012	52.3	.3239	240	singular
17.007	52.3	.8413	101	remind
17.003	52.3	.4645	174	h
17.003	52.3	.8244	102	brightly
16.998	52.3	.8348	102	producing
16.992	52.3	.7155	116	legend
16.986	52.3	.9212	93	matches
16.985	52.3	.8125	104	clerk
16.972	52.3	.8461	100	monster
16.967	52.3	.1925	337	multiply
16.965	52.3	.8009	105	sweat
16.961	52.3	.4845	162	Constitution
16.933	52.3	.7183	115	Jefferson
16.923	52.3	.8116	103	trust
16.922	52.3	.7749	108	wine
16.921	52.3	.8266	102	sits
16.914	52.3	.7165	115	web
16.901	52.3	.4340	184	tool
16.898	52.3	.7556	111	revolution
16.888	52.3	.7581	110	defense
16.886	52.3	.6531	126	filling
16.883	52.3	.6647	121	mosquitoes
16.882	52.3	.8705	97	winning
16.880	52.3	.5558	143	Pete
16.880	52.3	.8407	100	melt
16.877	52.3	.6592	124	Sun
16.864	52.3	.6902	120	reads
16.863	52.3	.6802	120	Islands
16.856	52.3	.3123	248	predicate
16.848	52.3	.5661	140	thunder
16.837	52.3	.7790	108	vary
16.832	52.3	.6320	128	Lewis
16.832	52.3	.5734	142	expressions
16.820	52.3	.8811	96	concern
16.815	52.3	.6646	124	nuclear
16.813	52.3	.8419	100	movies
16.799	52.3	.8045	103	feast
16.795	52.3	.8199	102	touches
16.788	52.3	.6810	118	leaped
16.752	52.3	.7552	110	structures
16.748	52.2	.7911	105	preparing
16.739	52.2	.7779	105	tunnel
16.737	52.2	.7882	105	numbered
16.737	52.2	.6769	119	worms
16.724	52.2	.5178	142	an'
16.724	52.2	.8079	103	downward
16.721	52.2	.7776	106	searching
16.714	52.2	.7232	113	signed
16.711	52.2	.7158	113	clearing
16.709	52.2	.7049	114	upstairs
16.708	52.2	.7541	109	Betty
16.699	52.2	.7479	111	functions
16.694	52.2	.8002	103	fancy
16.693	52.2	.7490	110	citizen
16.673	52.2	.8362	99	backs
16.654	52.2	.6006	133	cooled
16.653	52.2	.6020	134	print
16.650	52.2	.7318	112	partner
16.641	52.2	.5661	140	Court
16.633	52.2	.6617	122	chemicals
16.631	52.2	.5925	134	aluminum
16.620	52.2	.5519	145	speaker
16.618	52.2	.4725	156	sons
16.602	52.2	.8208	101	J
16.590	52.2	.7568	109	electronic
16.588	52.2	.5027	156	puzzle
16.586	52.2	.7996	103	released
16.583	52.2	.7676	106	hotel
16.583	52.2	.6068	129	Anna
16.579	52.2	.6646	121	mystery
16.573	52.2	.7389	111	adults
16.572	52.2	.7226	113	rolls
16.565	52.2	.7695	107	tend
16.563	52.2	.4981	154	Negroes
16.552	52.2	.8504	97	patch
16.551	52.2	.4389	171	microscope
16.545	52.2	.1346	421	fractions
16.540	52.2	.8912	93	fourteen
16.536	52.2	.3072	244	painting
16.525	52.2	.7162	112	rider
16.525	52.2	.6241	123	Morgan
16.524	52.2	.6714	119	switch
16.524	52.2	.5666	137	they'd
16.521	52.2	.8285	100	relation
16.520	52.2	.7023	115	Fort
16.514	52.2	.6410	125	cycle
16.498	52.2	.7525	108	owners
16.496	52.2	.7210	112	soda
16.495	52.2	.7626	105	alarm
16.492	52.2	.6736	117	staring
16.491	52.2	.8347	99	assume
16.490	52.2	.5805	130	she'd
16.490	52.2	.8289	99	leap
16.476	52.2	.7961	103	conflict
16.475	52.2	.7064	115	sphere
16.462	52.2	.7219	112	harvest
16.453	52.2	.7392	110	authority

THE PRECEDING WORD TYPE OCCUPIES RANK 3700

U	SFI	D	F	Word Type
16.448	52.2	.5951	134	processes
16.444	52.2	.8210	100	adopted
16.439	52.2	.8266	99	lean
16.438	52.2	.4014	181	pennies
16.436	52.2	.8891	93	aim
16.435	52.2	.7740	104	weary
16.432	52.2	.6130	126	Nancy

U	SFI	D	F	Word Type
16.420	52.2	.8258	99	pace
16.410	52.2	.8459	97	custom
16.402	52.1	.5673	138	loop
16.401	52.1	.7525	107	Walter
16.400	52.1	.3851	189	dinosaurs
16.376	52.1	.7369	109	cousin
16.362	52.1	.7419	107	wolves
16.361	52.1	.3082	219	Robin
16.360	52.1	.7854	102	lazy
16.355	52.1	.8315	98	timber
16.347	52.1	.7695	104	sixteen
16.343	52.1	.6727	116	ah
16.343	52.1	.8088	100	pioneer
16.329	52.1	.7205	111	Ireland
16.310	52.1	.8338	98	observation
16.287	52.1	.8472	96	scratch
16.286	52.1	.5023	151	Venus
16.279	52.1	.8260	98	counter
16.261	52.1	.8185	99	visible
16.252	52.1	.7709	105	26
16.243	52.1	.3749	197	circuit
16.226	52.1	.7470	106	underwater
16.225	52.1	.8304	98	depending
16.180	52.1	.7368	106	prince
16.153	52.1	.7179	110	minds
16.147	52.1	.7611	104	attacked
16.134	52.1	.7933	101	council
16.122	52.1	.6846	116	cylinder
16.121	52.1	.8820	92	limit
16.119	52.1	.7122	110	nests
16.091	52.1	.7388	108	qualities
16.086	52.1	.7437	107	estimated
16.085	52.1	.7641	104	Land
16.067	52.1	.8554	94	maple
16.059	52.1	.8331	96	toys
16.057	52.1	.8381	96	obviously
16.046	52.1	.7868	100	ticket
16.038	52.1	.6153	125	Northern
16.027	52.0	.7435	105	bunch
16.020	52.0	.4582	162	entry
16.003	52.0	.6497	120	ease
15.997	52.0	.7687	102	dragged
15.982	52.0	.7856	100	resting
15.967	52.0	.7279	106	sprang
15.964	52.0	.7545	103	disappointed
15.950	52.0	.8307	95	dreamed
15.948	52.0	.5921	122	Dave
15.944	52.0	.6007	129	mix
15.931	52.0	.8312	96	maintain
15.927	52.0	.8348	95	lowered
15.917	52.0	.7132	107	dashed
15.907	52.0	.8525	93	figured
15.905	52.0	.7522	104	earned
15.901	52.0	.3498	210	beats
15.897	52.0	.6158	125	stir
15.889	52.0	.7622	103	succeeded
15.877	52.0	.7147	109	aunt
15.866	52.0	.8960	89	expert
15.861	52.0	.8223	95	eagle
15.861	52.0	.8124	97	ours
15.858	52.0	.7210	108	election
15.857	52.0	.5203	139	rid
15.855	52.0	.7935	99	fitted
15.853	52.0	.7101	109	Arctic
15.853	52.0	.7504	103	silently
15.844	52.0	.7458	104	Colorado
15.843	52.0	.7556	104	magazines
15.839	52.0	.8307	95	grounds
15.837	52.0	.7992	99	sixth
15.829	52.0	.7538	102	creek
15.826	52.0	.5829	131	Egyptian
15.822	52.0	.7183	107	pushes
15.802	52.0	.7237	105	raft
15.792	52.0	.7443	104	acting
15.785	52.0	.8581	92	seriously
15.784	52.0	.7618	102	oranges
15.773	52.0	.7740	101	attract
15.762	52.0	.6948	109	witch
15.750	52.0	.5715	130	march
15.745	52.0	.8340	94	noisy
15.745	52.0	.5917	125	colt
15.744	52.0	.8043	98	associated
15.739	52.0	.6643	112	crawled
15.737	52.0	.8065	96	sailor
15.730	52.0	.8566	92	controls
15.718	52.0	.7183	108	Apollo
15.716	52.0	.8323	94	ribs
15.700	52.0	.5843	128	oven
15.700	52.0	.7815	99	demanded
15.698	52.0	.7633	102	attitude
15.690	52.0	.7706	100	meadow
15.687	52.0	.6891	109	wedding
15.677	52.0	.7518	103	armed

THE PRECEDING WORD TYPE OCCUPIES RANK 3800

U	SFI	D	F	Word Type
15.666	51.9	.6603	112	eagerly
15.652	51.9	.7647	101	Grand
15.646	51.9	.8029	97	matters
15.642	51.9	.3291	209	-
15.630	51.9	.3324	213	artist
15.624	51.9	.7288	105	department
15.618	51.9	.7358	104	berries
15.618	51.9	.7419	104	occupied
15.610	51.9	.6502	114	glanced
15.606	51.9	.8711	90	strongly
15.601	51.9	.8316	93	sword
15.599	51.9	.7687	100	moments
15.591	51.9	.7145	106	drank
15.584	51.9	.8658	90	visiting
15.575	51.9	.7161	105	Chief
15.567	51.9	.4125	171	mold
15.565	51.9	.7123	106	Tom's
15.563	51.9	.8561	91	explored
15.558	51.9	.8521	91	gathering
15.547	51.9	.7668	101	continuous
15.541	51.9	.5648	125	Ned
15.533	51.9	.7776	98	fortune
15.532	51.9	.7791	98	spotted

U	SFI	D	F	Word Type
15.531	51.9	.2835	238	pronunciation
15.531	51.9	.6156	122	fork
15.529	51.9	.6049	123	carved
15.523	51.9	.6632	114	ages
15.522	51.9	.7368	102	queer
15.520	51.9	.6114	118	Ed
15.517	51.9	.8162	94	spare
15.509	51.9	.8398	92	losing
15.496	51.9	.6704	109	sadly
15.483	51.9	.8146	94	cliff
15.480	51.9	.7776	99	L
15.471	51.9	.7738	98	volcano
15.469	51.9	.7407	102	glow
15.469	51.9	.6640	111	cash
15.466	51.9	.7590	100	forehead
15.457	51.9	.7509	102	affairs
15.454	51.9	.8203	94	smoothly
15.439	51.9	.6886	108	slid
15.435	51.9	.8603	90	touching
15.426	51.9	.7599	99	Wright
15.422	51.9	.8698	89	bricks
15.421	51.9	.8101	94	lid
15.418	51.9	.7957	96	afford
15.413	51.9	.5657	133	tap
15.394	51.9	.8192	94	regarded
15.393	51.9	.7814	96	beaver
15.389	51.9	.7170	104	wondering
15.388	51.9	.8284	92	rushing
15.385	51.9	.7793	97	escaped
15.379	51.9	.8168	93	nickel
15.373	51.9	.6505	115	29
15.370	51.9	.4784	153	vocabulary
15.353	51.9	.7906	96	reply
15.353	51.9	.8094	94	capture
15.339	51.9	.7009	106	cargo
15.337	51.9	.7646	99	Council
15.321	51.9	.8043	95	lighter
15.310	51.8	.5255	137	Denmark
15.307	51.8	.7621	100	divisions
15.305	51.8	.7524	99	pockets
15.288	51.8	.8008	94	hoping
15.288	51.8	.4873	151	parentheses
15.278	51.8	.8073	94	sought
15.275	51.8	.7716	98	skeleton
15.267	51.8	.8002	94	Ted
15.253	51.8	.7007	106	governor
15.234	51.8	.7454	101	W
15.228	51.8	.7956	95	sweeping
15.225	51.8	.4500	152	crystals
15.224	51.8	.7881	96	operate
15.218	51.8	.7448	101	extends
15.213	51.8	.5571	130	Bible
15.208	51.8	.7116	104	whip
15.202	51.8	.8349	91	strikes
15.184	51.8	.6058	121	organs
15.182	51.8	.7459	100	admitted
15.181	51.8	.5322	136	ink
15.173	51.8	.8994	85	formal
15.171	51.8	.7764	97	relations
15.170	51.8	.6962	105	moonlight
15.161	51.8	.7780	96	bills
15.156	51.8	.7861	95	cruel
15.155	51.8	.8598	88	springs
15.151	51.8	.7268	101	warned
15.150	51.8	.6262	117	adapted
15.146	51.8	.4725	145	Homer
15.128	51.8	.4940	138	dinosaur
15.121	51.8	.8468	89	kick
15.117	51.8	.8624	88	extreme
15.100	51.8	.8215	91	dad
15.097	51.8	.4204	152	One
15.095	51.8	.7033	104	noises
15.092	51.8	.7417	99	struggled
15.073	51.8	.8514	89	household
15.065	51.8	.8145	92	mention
15.064	51.8	.7736	96	mouths
15.056	51.8	.8582	88	regularly

THE PRECEDING WORD TYPE OCCUPIES RANK 3900

U	SFI	D	F	Word Type
15.050	51.8	.8662	87	delivered
15.049	51.8	.8336	90	newly
15.037	51.8	.7235	102	Kansas
15.035	51.8	.7438	100	shock
15.021	51.8	.5355	135	threads
15.021	51.8	.7350	101	accidents
15.019	51.8	.8977	84	toe
15.019	51.8	.7891	94	Long
15.017	51.8	.6700	105	bike
15.017	51.8	.7630	97	Hudson
15.004	51.8	.7995	93	approaching
15.004	51.8	.8862	85	amazing
15.001	51.8	.8641	87	craft
14.984	51.8	.8086	92	paying
14.980	51.8	.8603	87	permission
14.964	51.8	.5298	134	afterwards
14.964	51.8	.5968	121	international
14.963	51.8	.7895	93	sleepy
14.958	51.7	.5742	128	attractive
14.954	51.7	.7309	101	manufacture
14.954	51.7	.7447	98	hasn't
14.954	51.7	.5130	139	dances
14.953	51.7	.7814	95	overcome
14.944	51.7	.6718	109	astronauts
14.943	51.7	.7338	100	credit
14.939	51.7	.4276	155	Hawaii
14.932	51.7	.3939	168	marbles
14.929	51.7	.7080	104	economy
14.919	51.7	.6864	105	kitten
14.909	51.7	.6765	104	sled
14.907	51.7	.4191	143	Bert
14.895	51.7	.4971	143	pronounced
14.889	51.7	.7683	95	tale
14.884	51.7	.7349	100	prices
14.861	51.7	.8030	92	vacuum
14.858	51.7	.7837	94	release
14.855	51.7	.8850	84	needles
14.850	51.7	.8418	88	blown
14.839	51.7	.6597	108	suits

U	SFI	D	F	Word Type
14.837	51.7	.5737	123	lens
14.828	51.7	.6683	109	pause
14.826	51.7	.7521	96	scratched
14.819	51.7	.6705	107	expedition
14.816	51.7	.2841	235	/
14.808	51.7	.3418	193	triangles
14.797	51.7	.8186	90	stays
14.794	51.7	.8023	92	significant
14.789	51.7	.8440	88	extent
14.788	51.7	.8827	84	seal
14.782	51.7	.7925	93	latest
14.774	51.7	.7215	100	cleaning
14.769	51.7	.7610	95	bath
14.764	51.7	.7642	95	day's
14.762	51.7	.6863	105	ranges
14.761	51.7	.5409	130	tissue
14.758	51.7	.6656	108	site
14.727	51.7	.8154	90	wonders
14.721	51.7	.8194	89	cannon
14.716	51.7	.7772	94	one-half
14.713	51.7	.7096	102	appointed
14.705	51.7	.8297	88	tire
14.696	51.7	.2645	240	notation
14.695	51.7	.6935	104	union
14.694	51.7	.7821	94	refers
14.676	51.7	.7953	92	handling
14.676	51.7	.4234	165	punctuation
14.673	51.7	.7298	98	freezing
14.668	51.7	.7902	92	suffered
14.667	51.7	.7918	92	shelves
14.665	51.7	.8143	89	waving
14.664	51.7	.8170	90	techniques
14.658	51.7	.6688	107	Revolution
14.656	51.7	.4437	156	keys
14.647	51.7	.6360	112	founded
14.642	51.7	.8651	85	rarely
14.630	51.7	.8018	91	latter
14.624	51.7	.7602	94	horseback
14.611	51.6	.2632	238	pronounce
14.610	51.6	.8106	90	defined
14.607	51.6	.8437	86	useless
14.606	51.6	.5444	126	sandwiches
14.598	51.6	.7159	100	skilled
14.581	51.6	.7893	91	delighted
14.579	51.6	.5484	123	glue
14.567	51.6	.7039	102	increases
14.562	51.6	.4618	134	Sarah
14.556	51.6	.5671	123	address
14.552	51.6	.6897	102	grazing
14.549	51.6	.7735	93	knee
14.543	51.6	.7395	97	600
14.539	51.6	.5838	122	errors
14.537	51.6	.8150	89	freely
14.535	51.6	.7189	97	bundle
14.524	51.6	.7573	94	cheeks
14.523	51.6	.6077	114	States
14.519	51.6	.8780	83	seeking
14.516	51.6	.8221	88	solved
14.508	51.6	.7996	89	Road
14.505	51.6	.8543	85	satisfaction
14.497	51.6	.5754	120	nerves

THE PRECEDING WORD TYPE OCCUPIES RANK 4000

U	SFI	D	F	Word Type
14.492	51.6	.7084	100	Clark
14.492	51.6	.5371	128	lever
14.491	51.6	.7915	90	piled
14.490	51.6	.8152	88	rested
14.490	51.6	.7032	99	sack
14.481	51.6	.8054	89	muddy
14.475	51.6	.6853	103	museum
14.475	51.6	.8491	85	exploring
14.472	51.6	.8701	83	acted
14.469	51.6	.8516	85	argument
14.465	51.6	.8371	86	reminded
14.464	51.6	.5927	120	stress
14.464	51.6	.8416	86	capable
14.461	51.6	.8319	87	expand
14.456	51.6	.7761	92	dime
14.453	51.6	.6901	101	freight
14.452	51.6	.8147	88	anxious
14.442	51.6	.6924	101	companions
14.440	51.6	.8169	88	Cape
14.435	51.6	.5315	126	collar
14.434	51.6	.7013	101	Sweden
14.433	51.6	.5415	125	mining
14.433	51.6	.8275	87	survive
14.428	51.6	.8515	85	annual
14.425	51.6	.7983	90	well-known
14.416	51.6	.8354	86	belts
14.410	51.6	.6875	101	Jupiter
14.406	51.6	.7328	97	samples
14.402	51.6	.7860	91	burns
14.381	51.6	.8036	88	squirrel
14.380	51.6	.5486	115	Princess
14.378	51.6	.3007	198	dioxide
14.377	51.6	.7342	97	describing
14.374	51.6	.7904	90	drag
14.372	51.6	.7950	89	cries
14.371	51.6	.8095	88	splendid
14.363	51.6	.7624	93	invite
14.363	51.6	.7335	97	personality
14.357	51.6	.6683	104	shipped
14.349	51.6	.7357	95	mayor
14.346	51.6	.7597	94	contract
14.339	51.6	.7160	98	Kentucky
14.337	51.6	.7922	90	slender
14.329	51.6	.6415	109	fasten
14.325	51.6	.7457	95	flesh
14.322	51.6	.5501	124	assembly
14.313	51.6	.6873	102	colonial
14.309	51.6	.8370	85	nurse
14.307	51.6	.8178	87	cheerful
14.303	51.6	.8045	88	stirred
14.301	51.6	.8416	85	charts
14.280	51.5	.8010	89	existence
14.278	51.5	.7225	98	lists
14.276	51.5	.7586	92	lit
14.272	51.5	.5880	117	1000

U	SFI	D	F	Word Type
14.267	51.5	.8033	88	catches
14.266	51.5	.8596	83	fail
14.262	51.5	.6479	107	Chapter
14.260	51.5	.8964	80	polished
14.258	51.5	.7268	97	influenced
14.251	51.5	.5360	126	tender
14.242	51.5	.8170	86	rides
14.241	51.5	.7480	95	medium
14.239	51.5	.8586	83	peculiar
14.237	51.5	.8188	87	establish
14.235	51.5	.6216	108	dying
14.233	51.5	.5451	123	notebook
14.227	51.5	.7167	96	hated
14.218	51.5	.6231	109	Nations
14.214	51.5	.7930	88	chase
14.208	51.5	.7292	97	emotional
14.192	51.5	.8229	86	historical
14.187	51.5	.6363	106	Mercury
14.183	51.5	.8440	84	tips
14.182	51.5	.8131	87	bold
14.181	51.5	.8195	86	barrel
14.180	51.5	.5251	128	drums
14.176	51.5	.7615	93	illustration
14.176	51.5	.3044	198	Bud
14.175	51.5	.7902	88	kettle
14.170	51.5	.5621	123	horizontal
14.167	51.5	.4350	151	senses
14.160	51.5	.7720	91	tooth
14.157	51.5	.7462	93	target
14.155	51.5	.6859	98	snapped
14.155	51.5	.8351	84	floated
14.154	51.5	.7291	95	fleet
14.146	51.5	.6205	110	bats
14.141	51.5	.6443	107	Federal
14.140	51.5	.7794	89	sooner
14.139	51.5	.7422	93	Club
14.137	51.5	.0272	711	decimal
14.124	51.5	.8146	86	spirits
14.123	51.5	.7846	89	icy
14.123	51.5	.6272	108	inland
14.104	51.5	.3138	206	meter
14.104	51.5	.7968	88	peak
14.091	51.5	.6999	97	merry
14.086	51.5	.4196	157	bass
14.084	51.5	.7756	89	Scott

THE PRECEDING WORD TYPE OCCUPIES RANK 4100

U	SFI	D	F	Word Type
14.084	51.5	.6197	109	ye
14.076	51.5	.7403	92	dive
14.075	51.5	.5472	121	nerve
14.067	51.5	.7327	95	concrete
14.064	51.5	.7057	98	charges
14.063	51.5	.6390	106	League
14.056	51.5	.5530	121	shaded
14.056	51.5	.5695	118	gallons
14.052	51.5	.7305	94	prison
14.041	51.5	.8836	80	generations
14.041	51.5	.7829	88	pets
14.039	51.5	.7293	94	gentlemen
14.037	51.5	.6712	103	procedure
14.035	51.5	.6512	104	geography
14.032	51.5	.7718	90	killing
14.032	51.5	.8535	82	Roger
14.024	51.5	.8154	86	levels
14.023	51.5	.7101	94	parrot
14.022	51.5	.6723	99	screamed
14.022	51.5	.8365	84	playground
14.020	51.5	.6142	108	anger
14.016	51.5	.7792	89	bore
14.012	51.5	.8504	82	rug
14.005	51.5	.7727	89	lasted
13.996	51.5	.6631	99	spear
13.977	51.5	.7404	92	children's
13.976	51.5	.7427	92	shy
13.973	51.5	.7217	94	bubbles
13.971	51.5	.8097	86	possession
13.970	51.5	.6169	106	awful
13.962	51.4	.7149	96	dining
13.956	51.4	.8120	86	sufficient
13.956	51.4	.7397	93	speeds
13.954	51.4	.6578	103	Michigan
13.952	51.4	.7973	86	dock
13.951	51.4	.7993	87	communicate
13.950	51.4	.7170	93	diving
13.949	51.4	.7357	92	footsteps
13.944	51.4	.6834	98	wisdom
13.940	51.4	.6941	97	colder
13.929	51.4	.7705	89	stretches
13.929	51.4	.8354	83	countryside
13.929	51.4	.6169	107	Judy
13.911	51.4	.8090	86	achieved
13.908	51.4	.8098	85	tires
13.903	51.4	.4818	131	spiders
13.897	51.4	.7684	88	cheer
13.894	51.4	.7019	97	titles
13.879	51.4	.5084	127	wax
13.873	51.4	.7261	93	Blue
13.866	51.4	.8450	82	opens
13.860	51.4	.6402	103	Lady
13.856	51.4	.7407	92	parks
13.854	51.4	.7040	95	Judge
13.853	51.4	.3845	160	molecule
13.850	51.4	.2491	170	Ricky
13.845	51.4	.7258	92	shark
13.840	51.4	.6520	103	claimed
13.840	51.4	.4364	149	artists
13.831	51.4	.6557	102	shores
13.830	51.4	.6501	102	hind
13.830	51.4	.8596	81	derived
13.824	51.4	.7272	94	efficient
13.822	51.4	.8331	83	outstanding
13.816	51.4	.6583	102	peaks
13.814	51.4	.8783	79	agent
13.813	51.4	.8516	81	answering
13.811	51.4	.7553	91	standards
13.797	51.4	.6701	99	cone
13.797	51.4	.4933	132	diet
13.794	51.4	.8237	84	relationships

U	SFI	D	F	Word Type
13.792	51.4	.0334	654	equations
13.790	51.4	.7427	91	hides
13.789	51.4	.7157	93	furnace
13.786	51.4	.8054	85	tents
13.771	51.4	.7751	88	severe
13.765	51.4	.7820	87	crown
13.760	51.4	.7019	96	defeated
13.757	51.4	.7045	93	strangers
13.741	51.4	.5087	120	grinned
13.738	51.4	.5989	111	repeating
13.715	51.4	.8843	78	confusion
13.715	51.4	.7175	95	arts
13.712	51.4	.6567	100	bother
13.710	51.4	.8326	82	fond
13.710	51.4	.8400	82	constructed
13.708	51.4	.7284	93	decisions
13.707	51.4	.7657	89	concept
13.695	51.4	.8551	80	chances
13.686	51.4	.7835	87	employed
13.684	51.4	.8589	80	attended
13.683	51.4	.8394	81	rail
13.683	51.4	.5950	110	armies
13.682	51.4	.7405	92	substitute
13.676	51.4	.8045	84	upside
13.661	51.4	.6973	95	hunger
13.655	51.4	.8564	80	difficulties
13.640	51.3	.7737	87	grasses
13.636	51.3	.7339	90	angrily
13.635	51.3	.6582	100	Thanksgiving
THE PRECEDING WORD TYPE OCCUPIES RANK 4200				
13.635	51.3	.7333	90	dare
13.632	51.3	.8309	82	dozens
13.624	51.3	.5040	131	desired
13.623	51.3	.8326	82	closest
13.620	51.3	.7675	87	jelly
13.614	51.3	.4963	127	investigation
13.613	51.3	.7921	85	Jan
13.610	51.3	.5078	126	Brazil
13.606	51.3	.8614	79	fled
13.603	51.3	.7330	91	instructions
13.601	51.3	.8148	83	frost
13.594	51.3	.8647	79	mere
13.592	51.3	.5613	115	marching
13.591	51.3	.8397	81	attempts
13.560	51.3	.7929	85	agreement
13.555	51.3	.7888	85	manager
13.553	51.3	.7163	93	offices
13.539	51.3	.5166	123	Europeans
13.523	51.3	.7572	88	manage
13.518	51.3	.4988	128	Philip
13.518	51.3	.8592	79	encouraged
13.517	51.3	.6761	98	labeled
13.509	51.3	.7182	92	rubbing
13.502	51.3	.4425	136	underlined
13.502	51.3	.7816	86	error
13.501	51.3	.8426	80	floors
13.493	51.3	.8377	80	taller
13.488	51.3	.7128	93	Age
13.488	51.3	.8675	78	lifetime
13.487	51.3	.7948	84	telegraph
13.487	51.3	.5472	117	fossils
13.485	51.3	.6386	102	Canal
13.480	51.3	.7371	89	crept
13.480	51.3	.8168	82	gravel
13.464	51.3	.8804	77	engaged
13.463	51.3	.7330	91	index
13.461	51.3	.7794	85	knock
13.451	51.3	.7216	92	thoroughly
13.448	51.3	.7094	93	baked
13.438	51.3	.7536	88	slice
13.415	51.3	.7206	90	shouldn't
13.414	51.3	.7728	85	coral
13.404	51.3	.8464	79	practiced
13.398	51.3	.7811	85	convinced
13.391	51.3	.8015	83	supplied
13.381	51.3	.6930	93	Colonel
13.379	51.3	.8354	80	proof
13.378	51.3	.7853	84	honest
13.378	51.3	.6247	103	towards
13.376	51.3	.7954	83	pounding
13.370	51.3	.6934	95	pupil
13.341	51.3	.7644	86	pad
13.339	51.3	.6439	100	sales
13.339	51.3	.6595	99	33
13.334	51.2	.5224	120	NewOrleans
13.331	51.2	.8036	83	identified
13.326	51.2	.7332	89	Adams
13.324	51.2	.7924	84	technical
13.320	51.2	.6377	101	axis
13.316	51.2	.8425	79	person's
13.311	51.2	.7308	90	plot
13.309	51.2	.7553	86	hut
13.307	51.2	.7438	87	candles
13.305	51.2	.7339	88	pots
13.300	51.2	.8549	78	vision
13.299	51.2	.7072	93	preceding
13.298	51.2	.8776	76	sorts
13.297	51.2	.8795	76	display
13.294	51.2	.7881	84	host
13.293	51.2	.5061	123	observations
13.293	51.2	.6166	104	taxes
13.292	51.2	.6590	98	balloons
13.289	51.2	.7962	83	cement
13.287	51.2	.6931	92	Eskimos
13.285	51.2	.6839	94	guest
13.282	51.2	.5680	112	manufactured
13.281	51.2	.8341	79	crowds
13.279	51.2	.8183	81	connecting
13.269	51.2	.8296	80	one's
13.254	51.2	.7728	84	vessel
13.253	51.2	.5372	114	hatch
13.241	51.2	.7610	87	variations
13.235	51.2	.7395	87	ashes
13.234	51.2	.1530	306	tens
13.225	51.2	.9113	73	practicing
13.222	51.2	.8116	81	interrupted
13.217	51.2	.7679	85	squirrels
13.217	51.2	.7173	89	beard
13.215	51.2	.4970	124	fertile
13.210	51.2	.7670	85	fame
13.210	51.2	.7802	83	kindly
13.207	51.2	.6598	97	issue
13.204	51.2	.8265	79	peanuts
13.202	51.2	.6762	96	churches
13.200	51.2	.1523	296	Lord
13.198	51.2	.7736	85	individuals
13.191	51.2	.7635	85	elevator
13.187	51.2	.8233	80	causing
13.186	51.2	.4633	132	vibrations
13.186	51.2	.5708	111	pencils
THE PRECEDING WORD TYPE OCCUPIES RANK 4300				
13.178	51.2	.7885	83	rub
13.177	51.2	.5672	110	tides
13.164	51.2	.5861	106	Oregon
13.157	51.2	.8798	75	anchor
13.150	51.2	.8188	80	curtain
13.147	51.2	.4970	127	surfaces
13.144	51.2	.7404	87	seated
13.138	51.2	.6998	90	commander
13.138	51.2	.7419	88	proportion
13.133	51.2	.7724	84	tested
13.125	51.2	.8387	78	fortunately
13.109	51.2	.7844	83	supported
13.107	51.2	.7534	86	sensitive
13.105	51.2	.6877	93	confidence
13.102	51.2	.7831	83	wider
13.100	51.2	.8277	79	blame
13.096	51.2	.8155	80	borrow
13.092	51.2	.8672	76	placing
13.089	51.2	.8136	80	justice
13.086	51.2	.3898	147	Laura
13.078	51.2	.8908	74	distinguish
13.065	51.2	.6653	95	crystal
13.058	51.2	.7983	81	judges
13.053	51.2	.3281	183	theme
13.050	51.2	.9267	71	cherry
13.042	51.2	.7704	84	automatic
13.038	51.2	.7175	89	horizon
13.034	51.2	.7002	90	downstairs
13.028	51.1	.8487	77	reflect
13.023	51.1	.7051	89	goodness
13.022	51.1	.8425	77	restaurant
13.018	51.1	.4716	125	astronomers
13.012	51.1	.5386	115	conductor
13.010	51.1	.7460	85	rat
13.005	51.1	.8185	79	happiness
13.005	51.1	.6390	97	Force
12.998	51.1	.7982	81	sweep
12.993	51.1	.7153	90	traditional
12.992	51.1	.7323	87	D**
12.980	51.1	.6444	97	buying
12.967	51.1	.8952	73	preferred
12.963	51.1	.8545	76	experienced
12.954	51.1	.7354	87	scores
12.951	51.1	.6887	90	champion
12.949	51.1	.3946	147	cooked
12.948	51.1	.6149	100	Ford
12.947	51.1	.6652	94	lamb
12.943	51.1	.7973	80	traveler
12.932	51.1	.6569	95	minister
12.910	51.1	.8918	73	exception
12.907	51.1	.8007	80	grapes.
12.895	51.1	.6596	94	Grant
12.876	51.1	.7389	86	educated
12.864	51.1	.7809	81	cracks
12.852	51.1	.4954	121	governments
12.852	51.1	.7050	90	reduce
12.842	51.1	.7968	80	violent
12.838	51.1	.7829	81	riders
12.837	51.1	.6500	94	flashlight
12.831	51.1	.8233	77	costume
12.827	51.1	.7982	80	contributed
12.826	51.1	.7343	84	Bill's
12.826	51.1	.7984	80	ridges
12.812	51.1	.7061	87	sank
12.802	51.1	.7556	83	delicious
12.801	51.1	.8838	73	concerning
12.794	51.1	.6856	91	battery
12.791	51.1	.5475	110	plateau
12.783	51.1	.3955	146	ray
12.780	51.1	.7330	85	talks
12.779	51.1	.7995	79	ashore
12.764	51.1	.6756	92	shopping
12.763	51.1	.7439	85	heights
12.763	51.1	.7823	81	unexpected
12.761	51.1	.8118	78	mankind
12.753	51.1	.7795	81	neatly
12.749	51.1	.7050	87	pilots
12.746	51.1	.7834	80	lump
12.744	51.1	.8595	74	wears
12.741	51.1	.7248	85	cottage
12.740	51.1	.7780	81	John's
12.733	51.0	.7848	81	obvious
12.732	51.0	.6425	96	wars
12.727	51.0	.7526	84	31
12.727	51.0	.7226	85	Hans
12.712	51.0	.7947	79	alongside
12.709	51.0	.7507	82	knot
12.695	51.0	.6770	92	connect
12.681	51.0	.7448	83	bundles
12.678	51.0	.0603	488	multiplication
12.676	51.0	.7444	83	astronaut
12.671	51.0	.8125	78	varies
12.669	51.0	.6791	91	diagrams
12.666	51.0	.2021	248	consonants
12.663	51.0	.5702	99	Jacob
12.660	51.0	.7193	87	1960
12.648	51.0	.7199	86	packages
12.646	51.0	.5364	113	projects
12.644	51.0	.7794	80	jars
12.639	51.0	.5321	111	Junior
THE PRECEDING WORD TYPE OCCUPIES RANK 4400				
12.638	51.0	.7666	82	grouped
12.631	51.0	.5289	112	vegetable
12.623	51.0	.7214	86	explains
12.623	51.0	.1031	428	suffix
12.619	51.0	.6624	93	doubled
12.608	51.0	.7572	82	warriors
12.602	51.0	.8365	75	dim
12.600	51.0	.7404	83	steal
12.595	51.0	.7675	80	boss
12.591	51.0	.7548	82	defeat
12.583	51.0	.5592	108	grouping
12.579	51.0	.7892	79	skillful
12.579	51.0	.7143	85	Liberty
12.578	51.0	.8233	76	stamp
12.577	51.0	.8104	77	companion
12.573	51.0	.7183	86	conquered
12.567	51.0	.3684	151	nitrogen
12.567	51.0	.7370	84	kite
12.556	51.0	.6812	89	pigeons
12.549	51.0	.7030	86	Pilgrims
12.548	51.0	.7848	79	threatened
12.546	51.0	.7183	85	Linda
12.545	51.0	.5478	105	weeds
12.542	51.0	.7409	83	depths
12.524	51.0	.4755	126	v
12.507	51.0	.7236	84	bull
12.503	51.0	.7971	78	permitted
12.497	51.0	.4664	122	Davy
12.496	51.0	.7676	80	Professor
12.492	51.0	.6703	89	Grandmother
12.485	51.0	.6996	87	puppy
12.483	51.0	.6370	93	servants
12.473	51.0	.7211	83	ax
12.467	51.0	.7463	83	occasions
12.463	51.0	.6587	92	campaign
12.458	51.0	.5977	102	sketch
12.456	51.0	.6162	98	agriculture
12.452	51.0	.6343	94	harmful
12.448	51.0	.7653	80	fathers
12.446	51.0	.7119	85	Duke
12.443	50.9	.8926	70	watches
12.438	50.9	.6316	95	routes
12.437	50.9	.8360	74	geese
12.437	50.9	.8514	73	spreading
12.434	50.9	.7466	81	fellows
12.427	50.9	.6834	89	rulers
12.421	50.9	.8031	77	enable
12.415	50.9	.8419	74	response
12.410	50.9	.7914	77	hen
12.405	50.9	.7746	79	trunks
12.404	50.9	.7647	79	Bell
12.396	50.9	.5871	102	policy
12.396	50.9	.7577	81	repair
12.395	50.9	.8208	75	sunset
12.393	50.9	.9038	69	fastest
12.391	50.9	.6096	97	manners
12.388	50.9	.7272	82	harness
12.382	50.9	.7549	80	clover
12.376	50.9	.8067	76	wandering
12.374	50.9	.7828	78	curiosity
12.373	50.9	.7489	81	moss
12.373	50.9	.8171	75	brushed
12.370	50.9	.8161	75	splash
12.369	50.9	.4083	142	joint
12.363	50.9	.6988	86	Tennessee
12.353	50.9	.8024	76	tennis
12.350	50.9	.7878	78	accurately
12.337	50.9	.7399	82	dresses
12.335	50.9	.8196	75	posts
12.331	50.9	.8346	74	theater
12.323	50.9	.5188	112	LosAngeles
12.321	50.9	.5672	104	density
12.314	50.9	.7470	81	butterflies
12.298	50.9	.8045	76	mule
12.290	50.9	.8581	72	permit
12.289	50.9	.5616	103	Michael
12.274	50.9	.7628	78	pail
12.267	50.9	.8192	75	assumed
12.264	50.9	.7411	82	classified
12.261	50.9	.7627	79	disappear
12.261	50.9	.7563	80	120
12.259	50.9	.7397	82	sequence
12.257	50.9	.6131	96	65
12.256	50.9	.7309	82	ridge
12.254	50.9	.4493	128	baking
12.246	50.9	.6752	89	Egyptians
12.246	50.9	.7788	77	cellar
12.244	50.9	.8618	71	entering
12.238	50.9	.8652	71	meets
12.235	50.9	.7482	80	waist
12.233	50.9	.8225	74	blast
12.233	50.9	.7592	80	increasingly
12.220	50.9	.6278	95	convenient
12.216	50.9	.8051	75	excuse
12.213	50.9	.7921	76	searched
12.210	50.9	.7014	85	ties
12.204	50.9	.8775	70	advantages
12.189	50.9	.7990	76	rank
12.189	50.9	.7493	80	man-made
12.186	50.9	.3117	179	pronoun
THE PRECEDING WORD TYPE OCCUPIES RANK 4500				
12.186	50.9	.7323	82	liberty
12.184	50.9	.5318	107	Simon
12.179	50.9	.9013	68	gum
12.168	50.9	.7436	80	inventions
12.162	50.9	.6393	93	imaginary
12.154	50.8	.6823	87	Your
12.151	50.8	.8091	75	secure
12.142	50.8	.5135	113	frequency
12.137	50.8	.7254	80	helmet
12.133	50.8	.8264	73	costumes
12.133	50.8	.6564	88	lava
12.133	50.8	.7967	75	bang
12.123	50.8	.7799	77	Maine
12.116	50.8	.6027	95	turtles
12.114	50.8	.7210	82	jumps
12.107	50.8	.7570	78	broom
12.101	50.8	.5824	98	cooler
12.096	50.8	.7688	78	inhabitants
12.087	50.8	.7729	77	workmen
12.085	50.8	.7676	77	shepherd
12.084	50.8	.5561	104	solutions
12.081	50.8	.6954	84	smells
12.081	50.8	.7948	75	sliding
12.079	50.8	.7912	75	tasted
12.078	50.8	.4059	137	blade
12.077	50.8	.6993	85	marriage
12.076	50.8	.7506	79	dusty
12.074	50.8	.8525	71	accomplished
12.070	50.8	.6441	90	rods
12.067	50.8	.7731	77	jokes
12.066	50.8	.0439	721	melody
12.065	50.8	.7659	78	echo
12.063	50.8	.8203	73	crushed
12.062	50.8	.7263	80	gear
12.054	50.8	.5939	94	Cook
12.051	50.8	.7583	79	absolute
12.044	50.8	.8631	70	successfully
12.037	50.8	.8502	71	limits
12.035	50.8	.6411	92	circular
12.035	50.8	.6937	84	odor
12.034	50.8	.6808	86	dense
12.033	50.8	.8641	70	fascinating
12.029	50.8	.5078	111	courts
12.029	50.8	.6087	92	kid
12.026	50.8	.8495	71	failure
12.015	50.8	.7859	76	spark
12.014	50.8	.6746	87	purchase
12.006	50.8	.7217	81	saving
12.000	50.8	.7030	82	wounded
11.996	50.8	.8146	73	dolls
11.995	50.8	.2653	143	Bart
11.995	50.8	.6022	97	file
11.993	50.8	.8160	73	define
11.990	50.8	.8613	70	feature
11.979	50.8	.7076	81	flames
11.975	50.8	.5527	99	goats
11.971	50.8	.4137	133	fishes
11.968	50.8	.7614	77	arose
11.965	50.8	.6543	89	Germans
11.964	50.8	.4439	108	Gloria
11.963	50.8	.7731	77	Canadian
11.956	50.8	.8052	74	absorbed
11.954	50.8	.6623	87	cheek
11.952	50.8	.7461	78	Fish
11.946	50.8	.7597	78	grave
11.943	50.8	.6001	94	glaciers
11.942	50.8	.4404	125	magnets
11.937	50.8	.2478	204	alphabetical
11.933	50.8	.6510	88	Rocky
11.930	50.8	.5831	92	Rabbit
11.930	50.8	.6720	85	kicked
11.928	50.8	.5895	96	apron
11.928	50.8	.7976	74	skies
11.924	50.8	.7304	80	canyon
11.922	50.8	.7604	77	butterfly
11.921	50.8	.8418	71	suited
11.914	50.8	.8121	73	paths
11.912	50.8	.8674	69	regard
11.910	50.8	.8803	68	exploration
11.904	50.8	.7337	78	rescue
11.903	50.8	.7021	83	Y
11.902	50.8	.8068	73	Holland
11.902	50.8	.7322	79	wiped
11.901	50.8	.5992	94	Moon
11.900	50.8	.6511	89	county
11.899	50.8	.8504	70	lifting
11.899	50.8	.7784	76	conduct
11.899	50.8	.1562	298	ing
11.895	50.8	.8749	68	eighteen
11.894	50.8	.6189	93	container
11.887	50.8	.8198	72	fearful
11.884	50.7	.8301	71	fairy
11.883	50.7	.7682	76	terror
11.883	50.7	.6221	93	landscape
11.852	50.7	.8347	71	apparent
11.849	50.7	.5527	102	photographs
11.845	50.7	.7172	81	twist
11.845	50.7	.8436	70	lets
11.844	50.7	.6874	85	internal
11.840	50.7	.8112	73	situations
THE PRECEDING WORD TYPE OCCUPIES RANK 4600				
11.839	50.7	.8879	67	drives
11.828	50.7	.7795	75	rim
11.825	50.7	.8036	73	nowhere
11.825	50.7	.7018	83	circumstances
11.821	50.7	.7324	78	drifted
11.817	50.7	.8047	73	investigate
11.815	50.7	.7625	76	chimney
11.811	50.7	.8227	71	customers
11.806	50.7	.7060	81	who's
11.803	50.7	.8055	72	roaring
11.801	50.7	.8351	71	link
11.801	50.7	.7559	76	blossoms
11.795	50.7	.8430	70	absolutely
11.795	50.7	.7696	76	normally
11.792	50.7	.5929	96	drugs
11.790	50.7	.7938	74	quantity
11.786	50.7	.7101	81	endless
11.786	50.7	.7223	79	backed
11.784	50.7	.5991	90	Bobby
11.772	50.7	.6710	85	experts
11.769	50.7	.6990	82	roses
11.766	50.7	.6564	87	Arizona
11.765	50.7	.4495	121	mathematical
11.764	50.7	.4127	127	Netherlands
11.760	50.7	.3286	167	adverb
11.758	50.7	.6540	85	toad
11.755	50.7	.5710	98	latitude
11.753	50.7	.5447	103	topics
11.752	50.7	.0864	501	Fig
11.741	50.7	.8654	68	surroundings
11.740	50.7	.5110	102	Pedro
11.725	50.7	.7953	73	explosion
11.721	50.7	.7996	73	exposed
11.716	50.7	.8927	66	twenty-four

U	SFI	D	F	Word Type
11.711	50.7	.7974	73	invent
11.710	50.7	.6895	83	spacecraft
11.708	50.7	.7643	75	barely
11.705	50.7	.7852	74	Carl
11.703	50.7	.6726	82	Lucy
11.703	50.7	.7657	75	plow
11.701	50.7	.6278	90	markets
11.695	50.7	.4102	118	Hank
11.693	50.7	.7739	74	cracked
11.686	50.7	.6658	86	34
11.681	50.7	.6910	83	Austria
11.668	50.7	.7958	73	child's
11.667	50.7	.5656	99	bacon
11.664	50.7	.6554	87	university
11.660	50.7	.5296	105	photograph
11.658	50.7	.5973	93	Georgia
11.658	50.7	.5833	97	introduction
11.655	50.7	.7520	77	offers
11.652	50.7	.7188	79	fans
11.647	50.7	.8304	70	loses
11.646	50.7	.7493	76	tore
11.646	50.7	.6550	88	strokes
11.644	50.7	.7690	74	sticky
11.630	50.7	.6641	83	Fox
11.625	50.7	.6707	81	divers
11.618	50.7	.8360	69	heavens
11.611	50.6	.7925	72	clocks
11.601	50.6	.8270	70	intelligent
11.597	50.6	.8058	72	distinguished
11.587	50.6	.7853	73	phone
11.583	50.6	.8079	71	drift
11.582	50.6	.8818	66	returns
11.572	50.6	.5928	92	furs
11.566	50.6	.8376	69	caps
11.562	50.6	.7894	73	revealed
11.560	50.6	.6740	84	Napoleon
11.545	50.6	.7664	75	representing
11.542	50.6	.7518	75	Golden
11.541	50.6	.6109	91	Spaniards
11.540	50.6	.8298	69	winding
11.539	50.6	.7982	72	humor
11.537	50.6	.8607	67	nets
11.535	50.6	.7767	73	curled
11.532	50.6	.7230	79	poets
11.530	50.6	.6420	87	Columbia
11.524	50.6	.7425	76	hits
11.518	50.6	.7190	77	parked
11.517	50.6	.8051	71	sights
11.516	50.6	.8387	69	achieve
11.509	50.6	.7279	78	northwest
11.508	50.6	.4889	109	prey
11.502	50.6	.7571	75	Andrew
11.493	50.6	.6539	84	presently
11.492	50.6	.6820	81	Young
11.490	50.6	.7474	75	leaning
11.486	50.6	.7356	76	instantly
11.483	50.6	.7386	76	poison
11.481	50.6	.7803	72	camel
11.478	50.6	.9025	64	checking
11.472	50.6	.6335	86	crazy
11.468	50.6	.6492	84	scrambled
11.467	50.6	.7965	72	comparing
11.464	50.6	.7433	75	stern
11.451	50.6	.4241	130	compositions
11.451	50.6	.8818	65	ribbons
11.449	50.6	.3230	124	Watch
THE PRECEDING WORD TYPE OCCUPIES RANK 4700				
11.449	50.6	.8128	70	daring
11.446	50.6	.6515	85	Connecticut
11.444	50.6	.8055	71	connection
11.440	50.6	.6449	85	hi
11.435	50.6	.8228	69	hired
11.431	50.6	.7731	73	magnificent
11.411	50.6	.7081	79	artificial
11.406	50.6	.8264	69	choosing
11.405	50.6	.7874	71	rent
11.404	50.6	.5715	95	petroleum
11.398	50.6	.7928	71	battles
11.395	50.6	.8002	70	pillow
11.394	50.6	.8353	68	chewing
11.391	50.6	.5202	103	Republic
11.388	50.6	.3213	157	er
11.387	50.6	.6683	84	drama
11.386	50.6	.7275	77	pans
11.385	50.6	.6646	82	trapped
11.379	50.6	.8154	69	faraway
11.378	50.6	.6201	88	sun's
11.377	50.6	.5239	97	begged
11.375	50.6	.6889	80	district
11.373	50.6	.4493	117	Communist
11.373	50.6	.7360	76	upright
11.372	50.6	.6026	92	pressing
11.367	50.6	.7435	74	heroes
11.366	50.6	.7559	74	earthquake
11.365	50.6	.7825	71	slowed
11.361	50.6	.6411	86	matched
11.357	50.6	.3972	130	remainder
11.351	50.6	.6358	85	polar
11.348	50.5	.6745	81	deliver
11.344	50.5	.7105	79	appeal
11.325	50.5	.7385	74	cactus
11.324	50.5	.2628	193	recording
11.324	50.5	.6858	81	civil
11.321	50.5	.4911	107	refrigerator
11.319	50.5	.6266	86	Allen
11.301	50.5	.7081	79	whites
11.299	50.5	.7533	74	greeting
11.298	50.5	.4934	106	GreatBritain
11.297	50.5	.8004	70	canvas
11.294	50.5	.3969	130	sewing
11.293	50.5	.7505	74	shrill
11.283	50.5	.7930	71	wrap
11.281	50.5	.7852	71	Martha
11.280	50.5	.7564	73	worm
11.270	50.5	.7538	74	hobby
11.267	50.5	.8135	69	furthermore
11.266	50.5	.4242	125	rewrite

U	SFI	D	F	Word Type
11.266	50.5	.8225	68	thief
11.264	50.5	.8223	68	Francis
11.260	50.5	.7218	77	impact
11.259	50.5	.6522	84	woven
11.258	50.5	.7567	73	flights
11.257	50.5	.7442	74	letting
11.252	50.5	.7287	76	rainbow
11.252	50.5	.7448	74	throne
11.247	50.5	.7954	70	camping
11.238	50.5	.7937	70	picks
11.238	50.5	.5393	98	Act
11.233	50.5	.7231	75	anxiously
11.227	50.5	.3521	147	designs
11.227	50.5	.7921	70	awakened
11.224	50.5	.7711	71	dog's
11.224	50.5	.8310	67	dropping
11.215	50.5	.8520	66	exists
11.212	50.5	.7351	75	Creek
11.206	50.5	.6920	79	Scotland
11.205	50.5	.8343	67	midst
11.182	50.5	.7138	76	peach
11.178	50.5	.7471	74	wages
11.176	50.5	.5194	102	alcohol
11.174	50.5	.8458	66	people's
11.173	50.5	.7549	73	intelligence
11.168	50.5	.5652	96	paste
11.165	50.5	.3874	133	endings
11.162	50.5	.5987	88	bean
11.161	50.5	.8731	64	dash
11.155	50.5	.7051	77	Marie
11.154	50.5	.6754	81	County
11.152	50.5	.8009	69	abandoned
11.148	50.5	.5861	91	empire
11.147	50.5	.7374	75	benefit
11.145	50.5	.6377	84	spending
11.142	50.5	.6532	82	Royal
11.142	50.5	.6468	83	trails
11.138	50.5	.5969	88	Daddy
11.137	50.5	.2154	215	u
11.135	50.5	.7990	69	grasp
11.135	50.5	.8015	69	afterward
11.134	50.5	.7561	72	lantern
11.117	50.5	.5550	96	42
11.112	50.5	.7318	74	closet
11.111	50.5	.6025	89	Government
11.109	50.5	.7528	73	Tuesday
11.102	50.5	.7872	70	Thursday
11.094	50.5	.6533	82	Far
11.092	50.5	.7042	75	wreck
11.084	50.4	.6299	86	rates
THE PRECEDING WORD TYPE OCCUPIES RANK 4800				
11.079	50.4	.8330	66	handful
11.079	50.4	.5645	95	physics
11.075	50.4	.7253	74	fist
11.068	50.4	.7557	71	jewels
11.065	50.4	.7718	71	zone
11.062	50.4	.6828	79	rugged
11.060	50.4	.7366	73	grab
11.054	50.4	.5592	93	pins
11.054	50.4	.7875	69	flock
11.053	50.4	.5438	96	stirring
11.043	50.4	.7438	73	mainland
11.040	50.4	.7688	71	meetings
11.038	50.4	.7160	75	hop
11.034	50.4	.8165	67	sparkling
11.029	50.4	.3962	127	sings
11.022	50.4	.5377	98	naming
11.016	50.4	.7244	74	pies
11.011	50.4	.6830	78	shots
11.010	50.4	.8090	67	crawl
11.009	50.4	.5948	90	organ
11.008	50.4	.8112	67	gates
11.003	50.4	.7505	72	opinions
10.984	50.4	.7390	72	chased
10.980	50.4	.7625	71	grown-up
10.972	50.4	.6965	76	peered
10.971	50.4	.8924	62	distinct
10.964	50.4	.6543	79	inn
10.962	50.4	.7522	71	farmer's
10.960	50.4	.7829	70	primarily
10.960	50.4	.7673	70	beasts
10.959	50.4	.8555	64	boiled
10.957	50.4	.7416	72	fan
10.955	50.4	.7924	69	III
10.942	50.4	.7029	74	helicopter
10.939	50.4	.7403	73	shipping
10.937	50.4	.5299	96	volcanoes
10.935	50.4	.4290	118	intersection
10.931	50.4	.6243	84	northeast
10.922	50.4	.8826	62	tearing
10.920	50.4	.5230	95	stall
10.919	50.4	.7740	70	varieties
10.919	50.4	.6782	77	rage
10.918	50.4	.6923	76	motors
10.914	50.4	.8081	67	contents
10.912	50.4	.7949	68	crosses
10.912	50.4	.5359	99	precise
10.910	50.4	.8437	64	hose
10.909	50.4	.8065	67	twigs
10.906	50.4	.7408	73	commission
10.905	50.4	.7613	71	stretching
10.890	50.4	.6487	81	dams
10.888	50.4	.7649	70	greeted
10.880	50.4	.3534	132	evil
10.880	50.4	.6683	78	startled
10.870	50.4	.7807	69	skates
10.869	50.4	.7398	73	stages
10.866	50.4	.7363	72	whisper
10.856	50.4	.6871	77	Williams
10.852	50.4	.7839	69	combines
10.852	50.4	.6506	80	loads
10.841	50.4	.7000	76	Civil
10.839	50.4	.7838	68	cared
10.839	50.4	.7851	68	risk
10.836	50.3	.5018	99	mercury
10.836	50.3	.7503	71	restless
10.835	50.3	.7078	74	wandered

U	SFI	D	F	Word Type
10.834	50.3	.6161	86	intervals
10.824	50.3	.8323	65	examination
10.822	50.3	.8174	66	NewJersey
10.821	50.3	.7828	68	dangers
10.821	50.3	.8465	64	twin
10.819	50.3	.6694	79	director
10.816	50.3	.7745	69	defend
10.813	50.3	.5824	91	slant
10.808	50.3	.7158	75	expressing
10.793	50.3	.7951	67	youngest
10.789	50.3	.6797	75	sharks
10.784	50.3	.8562	63	bloom
10.780	50.3	.5796	88	summers
10.776	50.3	.4906	103	48
10.773	50.3	.7645	70	countless
10.767	50.3	.7125	73	socks
10.763	50.3	.7909	67	twins
10.762	50.3	.6398	81	aircraft
10.761	50.3	.7610	70	elsewhere
10.757	50.3	.7897	67	knight
10.751	50.3	.8167	66	emphasis
10.750	50.3	.6706	78	illness
10.748	50.3	.8704	62	awkward
10.745	50.3	.7882	67	jewelry
10.744	50.3	.5620	91	nation's
10.738	50.3	.3576	137	fibers
10.738	50.3	.5896	86	readers
10.734	50.3	.8084	66	unfortunately
10.731	50.3	.7170	74	network
10.726	50.3	.7032	73	paws
10.723	50.3	.3181	116	Marc
10.723	50.3	.7013	74	urged
10.720	50.3	.7236	73	devoted
10.719	50.3	.7523	71	creating
THE PRECEDING WORD TYPE OCCUPIES RANK 4900				
10.719	50.3	.7697	69	attitudes
10.715	50.3	.3738	134	resistance
10.715	50.3	.8036	66	vines
10.713	50.3	.7585	70	shift
10.712	50.3	.5824	83	Jim's
10.707	50.3	.7615	70	consist
10.707	50.3	.7938	67	reasonable
10.706	50.3	.6399	81	Arabs
10.706	50.3	.8297	64	hitting
10.702	50.3	.5081	101	guitar
10.702	50.3	.2226	200	prefix
10.700	50.3	.6973	75	duties
10.699	50.3	.6917	76	accompanied
10.694	50.3	.6498	80	theories
10.692	50.3	.6558	79	veins
10.687	50.3	.8949	60	lamps
10.682	50.3	.5946	85	King's
10.676	50.3	.8647	62	briefly
10.675	50.3	.7420	71	oats
10.665	50.3	.7531	69	swallow
10.662	50.3	.5006	101	rectangular
10.658	50.3	.8063	66	organize
10.653	50.3	.7946	66	flags
10.649	50.3	.7399	70	pirates
10.643	50.3	.7314	71	beaten
10.643	50.3	.8457	63	tasks
10.641	50.3	.7244	73	equipped
10.637	50.3	.7636	69	800
10.633	50.3	.6931	74	hurricane
10.631	50.3	.7800	68	dependent
10.631	50.3	.7168	72	vanished
10.627	50.3	.6914	74	glowing
10.626	50.3	.6373	79	steer
10.618	50.3	.8267	64	collecting
10.618	50.3	.6066	83	dew
10.618	50.3	.8432	63	outward
10.617	50.3	.6707	75	Terry
10.608	50.3	.8431	63	belonging
10.606	50.3	.7332	71	lays
10.602	50.3	.8211	64	injured
10.593	50.3	.6419	81	thickness
10.589	50.2	.6671	75	tub
10.589	50.2	.8003	66	massive
10.587	50.2	.7382	71	existed
10.586	50.2	.8036	65	sticking
10.581	50.2	.7740	67	dreaming
10.580	50.2	.6998	73	clubs
10.571	50.2	.6352	80	settlements
10.570	50.2	.6609	77	pants
10.570	50.2	.1614	272	Word
10.567	50.2	.4993	101	lining
10.567	50.2	.6706	75	steering
10.566	50.2	.6775	74	excitedly
10.563	50.2	.8071	65	olive
10.563	50.2	.7612	68	handkerchief
10.561	50.2	.7622	69	editor
10.561	50.2	.7656	68	genius
10.560	50.2	.5679	87	Juan
10.553	50.2	.7185	72	eastward
10.552	50.2	.7082	73	tenth
10.543	50.2	.4721	104	ounces
10.541	50.2	.6457	77	fisherman
10.538	50.2	.7991	66	necessarily
10.537	50.2	.7396	70	ringing
10.534	50.2	.5945	84	canals
10.530	50.2	.6079	84	output
10.523	50.2	.6487	79	boundary
10.518	50.2	.7532	69	vehicles
10.506	50.2	.4213	117	verse
10.503	50.2	.5138	96	Nile
10.499	50.2	.7165	72	formation
10.497	50.2	.7575	68	legends
10.495	50.2	.7784	67	attempted
10.493	50.2	.7596	68	flowed
10.487	50.2	.7973	66	combining
10.483	50.2	.7598	68	imagined
10.482	50.2	.3521	134	Exercise
10.478	50.2	.7929	65	guards
10.477	50.2	.6860	73	Point
10.477	50.2	.7448	69	limbs
10.470	50.2	.8013	65	offering
10.467	50.2	.6874	73	oxen

U	SFI	D	F	Word Type
10.465	50.2	.6351	79	southward
10.460	50.2	.7778	66	frightening
10.457	50.2	.4008	120	perpendicular
10.450	50.2	.4101	114	coastal
10.448	50.2	.7445	69	confused
10.446	50.2	.7655	67	brakes
10.434	50.2	.8539	61	childhood
10.431	50.2	.6434	76	Emperor
10.426	50.2	.8895	59	scheme
10.420	50.2	.3197	145	paintings
10.416	50.2	.7807	66	scarce
10.415	50.2	.7544	68	remembering
10.409	50.2	.3955	123	skirt
10.407	50.2	.8009	65	joining
10.406	50.2	.1630	260	sung
10.397	50.2	.5835	85	Lakes
10.395	50.2	.7007	72	natives
10.394	50.2	.5976	84	vibrate
THE PRECEDING WORD TYPE OCCUPIES RANK 5000				
10.393	50.2	.7347	70	expansion
10.392	50.2	.8175	63	wander
10.391	50.2	.6117	81	Turkey
10.390	50.2	.7969	64	pounded
10.389	50.2	.7766	66	tallest
10.387	50.2	.7314	70	sacred
10.384	50.2	.5500	91	eighth
10.382	50.2	.6585	77	skull
10.380	50.2	.8016	64	polite
10.350	50.1	.8185	63	alert
10.346	50.1	.7722	66	sells
10.335	50.1	.5754	86	56
10.335	50.1	.8041	64	occupation
10.333	50.1	.7863	65	channel
10.323	50.1	.5267	92	treaty
10.322	50.1	.2611	177	opera
10.321	50.1	.6723	74	gang
10.314	50.1	.4883	97	Grandma
10.313	50.1	.6112	79	yeah
10.308	50.1	.7384	69	halves
10.303	50.1	.7751	66	receiving
10.296	50.1	.5447	84	Oscar
10.286	50.1	.5567	87	relatives
10.285	50.1	.7658	67	evenly
10.285	50.1	.8385	61	enjoying
10.283	50.1	.6585	74	flashed
10.282	50.1	.7579	67	snap
10.280	50.1	.7486	68	700
10.280	50.1	.7072	70	stare
10.279	50.1	.5928	80	smelled
10.275	50.1	.6083	81	boil
10.274	50.1	.7724	65	charming
10.272	50.1	.6949	72	Alexander
10.271	50.1	.7815	65	careless
10.264	50.1	.6271	77	cameras
10.264	50.1	.7252	69	sake
10.263	50.1	.6104	81	leadership
10.261	50.1	.5322	90	traders
10.238	50.1	.8362	61	wrist
10.233	50.1	.6543	74	Governor
10.233	50.1	.5528	87	ranches
10.230	50.1	.7639	66	Three
10.229	50.1	.3629	132	adverbs
10.228	50.1	.8140	63	requirements
10.228	50.1	.8221	62	fountain
10.227	50.1	.8071	63	raises
10.227	50.1	.7303	69	readily
10.224	50.1	.6577	75	shines
10.223	50.1	.6815	73	P **
10.223	50.1	.7909	64	suffering
10.221	50.1	.5730	85	'tis
10.216	50.1	.7400	68	satisfy
10.215	50.1	.7117	71	separates
10.213	50.1	.7569	67	crude
10.206	50.1	.5973	83	expresses
10.205	50.1	.7203	69	shaft
10.191	50.1	.7140	70	reeds
10.190	50.1	.6612	74	Gray
10.190	50.1	.2742	158	multiple
10.187	50.1	.7476	67	detective
10.186	50.1	.7732	65	scored
10.184	50.1	.7768	65	united
10.183	50.1	.7030	72	irregular
10.179	50.1	.2444	170	rectangle
10.178	50.1	.5658	86	agricultural
10.176	50.1	.4723	98	headings
10.173	50.1	.7860	64	comb
10.173	50.1	.8055	63	accounts
10.171	50.1	.7414	67	piles
10.168	50.1	.7280	69	invaded
10.159	50.1	.6366	75	grin
10.159	50.1	.6334	77	poisonous
10.159	50.1	.6724	72	stalk
10.158	50.1	.8640	59	contrary
10.153	50.1	.8040	62	smashed
10.151	50.1	.6106	80	testing
10.151	50.1	.7702	65	knives
10.148	50.1	.7337	67	pit
10.146	50.1	.8653	59	continually
10.139	50.1	.7774	65	involves
10.138	50.1	.7848	64	chains
10.134	50.1	.8418	60	garbage
10.133	50.1	.8290	61	remote
10.127	50.1	.8157	62	abroad
10.121	50.1	.7439	67	hears
10.121	50.1	.5336	89	liquids
10.115	50.0	.7899	63	winner
10.111	50.0	.4263	107	Hemisphere
10.111	50.0	.4691	99	italicized
10.110	50.0	.7352	67	Anne
10.108	50.0	.8030	62	paddle
10.098	50.0	.6620	74	strain
10.096	50.0	.4499	105	heating
10.091	50.0	.7149	69	International
10.088	50.0	.7062	70	Society
10.087	50.0	.7902	63	decorated
10.087	50.0	.7040	69	quit
10.082	50.0	.5878	82	College

U	SFI	D	F	Word Type
10.073	50.0	.8414	60	balanced
10.064	50.0	.7597	65	tunnels

THE PRECEDING WORD TYPE OCCUPIES RANK 5100

U	SFI	D	F	Word Type
10.063	50.0	.7585	66	welfare
10.062	50.0	.8207	61	barren
10.060	50.0	.5985	77	Kate
10.057	50.0	.8395	60	Girl
10.057	50.0	.8529	59	observing
10.056	50.0	.4837	98	equals
10.053	50.0	.7528	66	motions
10.053	50.0	.6934	69	Rock
10.052	50.0	.6818	70	wicked
10.051	50.0	.7172	69	bamboo
10.050	50.0	.8103	62	consisting
10.047	50.0	.6652	73	brake
10.045	50.0	.6302	76	troubles
10.044	50.0	.8227	61	harsh
10.035	50.0	.7447	66	nonsense
10.035	50.0	.7217	69	introduce
10.032	50.0	.6912	69	hurrying
10.032	50.0	.5969	81	Danish
10.031	50.0	.6303	75	Major
10.022	50.0	.7575	65	spun
10.017	50.0	.6291	77	Carol
10.011	50.0	.6396	76	province
10.003	50.0	.8512	59	formerly
9.9908	50.0	.6978	70	wealthy
9.9842	50.0	.6185	78	openings
9.9828	50.0	.6940	71	novel
9.9812	50.0	.0877	319	sums
9.9763	50.0	.6811	71	Saturn
9.9692	50.0	.9142	55	judgment
9.9557	50.0	.7015	70	writes
9.9519	50.0	.7555	65	reputation
9.9451	50.0	.6872	70	ponds
9.9401	50.0	.6195	77	merchants
9.9310	50.0	.6508	73	planting
9.9244	50.0	.6339	75	Kennedy
9.9162	50.0	.7966	62	immediate
9.9119	50.0	.1552	231	1/3
9.9102	50.0	.0839	329	segment
9.9100	50.0	.7542	64	Book
9.9100	50.0	.7299	66	kindness
9.9094	50.0	.3106	140	ft
9.9053	50.0	.4160	109	core
9.9015	50.0	.8416	59	enthusiasm
9.8961	50.0	.7559	65	vital
9.8867	50.0	.2830	145	Jody
9.8854	49.9	.6867	68	hopped
9.8817	49.9	.7647	63	politely
9.8685	49.9	.6956	69	encyclopedia
9.8615	49.9	.6170	77	Service
9.8554	49.9	.3594	119	pollen
9.8516	49.9	.7495	65	assigned
9.8461	49.9	.8317	59	spoil
9.8450	49.9	.7055	67	horse's
9.8416	49.9	.7509	64	camels
9.8405	49.9	.8034	61	automatically
9.8339	49.9	.7765	62	crab
9.8254	49.9	.6215	76	competition
9.8227	49.9	.6437	72	Davis
9.8196	49.9	.5003	94	vocal
9.8145	49.9	.2515	152	germs
9.8128	49.9	.7363	66	borders
9.8111	49.9	.7614	64	opportunities
9.8056	49.9	.8463	58	precisely
9.8026	49.9	.7471	64	fiercely
9.8026	49.9	.7750	62	fright
9.8005	49.9	.5455	87	chorus
9.7951	49.9	.8245	59	damaged
9.7868	49.9	.5965	77	paw
9.7785	49.9	.3419	124	accented
9.7717	49.9	.8438	58	impressed
9.7697	49.9	.8009	61	250
9.7688	49.9	.6863	70	organizations
9.7668	49.9	.6841	69	canoes
9.7642	49.9	.7893	61	mirrors
9.7570	49.9	.6935	67	Donald
9.7494	49.9	.8019	60	downtown
9.7452	49.9	.7167	66	circled
9.7438	49.9	.6653	71	Independence
9.7340	49.9	.7427	64	swamp
9.7303	49.9	.5589	80	Johann
9.7302	49.9	.8398	58	simpler
9.7242	49.9	.5036	91	friction
9.7225	49.9	.6673	71	attacks
9.7223	49.9	.7641	63	sealed
9.7159	49.9	.7063	67	1900
9.7108	49.9	.6934	67	mosquito
9.7093	49.9	.7286	66	preparation
9.7047	49.9	.5630	82	receiver
9.7046	49.9	.5977	78	objective
9.7022	49.9	.7315	64	raccoon
9.6971	49.9	.6762	68	Emily
9.6968	49.9	.5626	83	unto
9.6902	49.9	.7902	61	devised
9.6820	49.9	.8037	60	knots
9.6798	49.9	.6980	68	loaf
9.6733	49.9	.6457	72	scissors
9.6717	49.9	.8322	58	spends
9.6710	49.9	.6351	74	pottery
9.6685	49.9	.5049	90	sandwich
9.6669	49.9	.8123	59	Avenue

THE PRECEDING WORD TYPE OCCUPIES RANK 5200

U	SFI	D	F	Word Type
9.6649	49.9	.7657	62	arrival
9.6637	49.9	.8673	56	considering
9.6630	49.9	.3685	118	Church
9.6571	49.8	.7736	62	proposed
9.6556	49.8	.7575	63	extraordinary
9.6550	49.8	.6716	68	gazed
9.6515	49.8	.6311	74	partners
9.6494	49.8	.8402	57	pumpkin
9.6493	49.8	.7794	61	Joe's
9.6488	49.8	.5744	80	Indies
9.6468	49.8	.7959	60	theirs
9.6437	49.8	.5309	86	yarn
9.6387	49.8	.6614	70	envelope
9.6320	49.8	.5873	78	computer
9.6313	49.8	.4184	106	geometry
9.6290	49.8	.5952	76	okay
9.6269	49.8	.7053	67	Center
9.6210	49.8	.6686	70	aquarium
9.6180	49.8	.7962	60	survey
9.6172	49.8	.7587	63	capacity
9.6154	49.8	.6900	67	homework
9.6149	49.8	.7216	66	tradition
9.6122	49.8	.7120	66	bronze
9.6062	49.8	.5874	78	skirts
9.6048	49.8	.7893	60	armor
9.6005	49.8	.7937	60	hangs
9.5996	49.8	.8097	59	handled
9.5913	49.8	.5931	77	ho
9.5907	49.8	.7934	60	cheap
9.5880	49.8	.5327	84	winters
9.5853	49.8	.7590	63	separately
9.5852	49.8	.7917	60	neighboring
9.5830	49.8	.6085	75	caves
9.5800	49.8	.5338	85	temple
9.5770	49.8	.4481	101	concert
9.5656	49.8	.8030	59	squeezed
9.5632	49.8	.6393	73	violence
9.5587	49.8	.6631	70	Lawrence
9.5586	49.8	.5238	86	priest
9.5564	49.8	.7352	64	dip
9.5559	49.8	.8191	58	keen
9.5514	49.8	.7857	60	owns
9.5475	49.8	.6714	67	robbers
9.5457	49.8	.7656	61	freeze
9.5453	49.8	.7451	63	tray
9.5396	49.8	.6475	72	38
9.5362	49.8	.7743	61	operated
9.5323	49.8	.7666	61	grateful
9.5311	49.8	.6466	72	specialized
9.5284	49.8	.6879	67	tourists
9.5250	49.8	.6645	69	scent
9.5246	49.8	.7674	61	unusually
9.5224	49.8	.1525	257	chords
9.5168	49.8	.7375	64	maximum
9.5168	49.8	.7489	62	striped
9.5139	49.8	.6620	69	ham
9.5113	49.8	.5085	87	Way
9.5104	49.8	.6363	71	Yankee
9.5083	49.8	.5098	87	mountainous
9.5060	49.8	.6952	67	Academy
9.5039	49.8	.5255	85	dissolved
9.5038	49.8	.8431	56	pays
9.4982	49.8	.7551	62	weapon
9.4919	49.8	.7468	63	coarse
9.4830	49.8	.3987	104	Annie
9.4820	49.8	.6899	66	hoofs
9.4772	49.8	.5223	87	musicians
9.4759	49.8	.7024	66	predict
9.4719	49.8	.6302	73	Delaware
9.4712	49.8	.7739	61	hence
9.4679	49.8	.3545	117	vitamins
9.4663	49.8	.6376	72	Erie
9.4564	49.8	.7140	65	historic
9.4520	49.8	.7510	61	Year
9.4514	49.8	.8635	55	continuing
9.4510	49.8	.7377	62	staying
9.4501	49.8	.6930	66	Howard
9.4485	49.8	.7977	59	contributions
9.4468	49.8	.6640	69	weaving
9.4425	49.8	.7154	65	demands
9.4408	49.8	.6380	72	courses
9.4283	49.7	.6393	72	pyramid
9.4271	49.7	.8379	56	beautifully
9.4251	49.7	.8434	56	checks
9.4246	49.7	.7284	64	37
9.4113	49.7	.8120	58	logical
9.4111	49.7	.7040	66	85
9.4080	49.7	.6179	73	attraction
9.4054	49.7	.8169	57	troubled
9.4019	49.7	.4760	93	arc
9.4004	49.7	.1195	303	chord
9.4001	49.7	.8082	58	fantastic
9.3830	49.7	.7402	62	ponies
9.3815	49.7	.5629	81	version
9.3798	49.7	.8191	57	sensible
9.3777	49.7	.7934	58	discouraged
9.3713	49.7	.6929	66	swamps
9.3708	49.7	.8150	57	indoors
9.3689	49.7	.8163	57	thoughtful
9.3685	49.7	.7514	61	wanting

THE PRECEDING WORD TYPE OCCUPIES RANK 5300

U	SFI	D	F	Word Type
9.3650	49.7	.7808	59	seventeen
9.3641	49.7	.6353	71	jungles
9.3640	49.7	.7384	63	developments
9.3569	49.7	.5761	76	brook
9.3556	49.7	.3425	127	dimensions
9.3552	49.7	.7893	59	ideal
9.3540	49.7	.7600	61	operating
9.3509	49.7	.6075	72	paused
9.3352	49.7	.7390	62	cones
9.3304	49.7	.7134	63	ditch
9.3303	49.7	.8847	53	farthest
9.3287	49.7	.7936	58	patience
9.3215	49.7	.7061	65	era
9.3190	49.7	.7868	59	margin
9.3123	49.7	.7796	59	fences
9.3021	49.7	.7563	61	victim
9.3014	49.7	.7331	62	stamped
9.2969	49.7	.7216	63	celebration
9.2952	49.7	.7695	59	banana
9.2887	49.7	.7494	61	boom
9.2887	49.7	.7694	59	hauled
9.2872	49.7	.5609	79	ports
9.2849	49.7	.7068	64	drowned
9.2818	49.7	.7317	61	giants
9.2817	49.7	.7313	62	triumph
9.2814	49.7	.7850	58	tame
9.2762	49.7	.5812	74	admit
9.2738	49.7	.5497	77	Carter
9.2689	49.7	.7801	59	scenes
9.2656	49.7	.7739	59	throws
9.2598	49.7	.8418	55	grease
9.2573	49.7	.6028	74	trim
9.2548	49.7	.8613	54	possibilities
9.2548	49.7	.7735	59	rails
9.2534	49.7	.6776	66	calendar
9.2502	49.7	.7396	61	fate
9.2488	49.7	.8732	53	haul
9.2460	49.7	.4205	104	quotation
9.2371	49.7	.7749	59	assured
9.2342	49.7	.8216	56	recognition
9.2320	49.7	.7682	59	sickness
9.2294	49.7	.8265	56	determines
9.2282	49.7	.6040	70	knights
9.2277	49.7	.6421	70	protective
9.2261	49.7	.4487	95	worship
9.2231	49.6	.4610	92	irrigation
9.2229	49.6	.6698	65	she'll
9.2226	49.6	.6348	68	king's
9.2219	49.6	.6722	67	politics
9.2193	49.6	.7889	58	Town
9.2135	49.6	.7309	61	crocodile
9.2135	49.6	.6257	69	stupid
9.2119	49.6	.7377	61	traded
9.2054	49.6	.3646	112	cube
9.2054	49.6	.7577	59	warn
9.2032	49.6	.6533	68	fiction
9.1975	49.6	.6377	68	wives
9.1949	49.6	.7783	58	smiles
9.1944	49.6	.7058	64	communications
9.1941	49.6	.7196	62	chasing
9.1883	49.6	.7225	63	text
9.1849	49.6	.7736	58	warrior
9.1810	49.6	.8046	57	undoubtedly
9.1807	49.6	.6144	73	reveal
9.1802	49.6	.6653	67	priests
9.1797	49.6	.8023	57	bearing
9.1795	49.6	.7501	60	Cross
9.1770	49.6	.5739	76	Christopher
9.1727	49.6	.8327	55	Fourth
9.1719	49.6	.7577	60	temporary
9.1699	49.6	.4697	90	Louisiana
9.1662	49.6	.7949	57	pouring
9.1632	49.6	.6474	67	pretended
9.1608	49.6	.8298	55	suffer
9.1594	49.6	.7991	57	resemble
9.1585	49.6	.6351	68	muttered
9.1575	49.6	.3944	104	nucleus
9.1572	49.6	.7438	60	shovel
9.1554	49.6	.6985	64	acre
9.1531	49.6	.8373	55	effectively
9.1480	49.6	.8065	56	ragged
9.1458	49.6	.5822	77	styles
9.1443	49.6	.6503	68	launched
9.1382	49.6	.5377	78	capsule
9.1370	49.6	.7964	57	hint
9.1278	49.6	.6324	69	melts
9.1221	49.6	.7697	58	slipping
9.1178	49.6	.6104	70	patted
9.1165	49.6	.4886	88	commerce
9.1150	49.6	.7102	63	cluster
9.1105	49.6	.8774	52	overnight
9.1099	49.6	.7415	60	dipped
9.1081	49.6	.5189	82	belief
9.1033	49.6	.7734	58	prayer
9.1008	49.6	.6966	63	faded
9.0992	49.6	.3206	121	protein
9.0991	49.6	.7070	63	beaches
9.0951	49.6	.8156	55	helpless
9.0936	49.6	.7512	60	images
9.0934	49.6	.7366	60	trousers

THE PRECEDING WORD TYPE OCCUPIES RANK 5400

U	SFI	D	F	Word Type
9.0919	49.6	.6365	69	southwest
9.0890	49.6	.6284	69	lizards
9.0869	49.6	.7330	61	festival
9.0862	49.6	.8023	56	deadly
9.0813	49.6	.7764	57	flashing
9.0789	49.6	.6814	64	Sandy
9.0783	49.6	.6869	64	bird's
9.0782	49.6	.6037	72	spray
9.0765	49.6	.7442	60	pebbles
9.0761	49.6	.4002	98	servant
9.0755	49.6	.6330	68	terribly
9.0755	49.6	.9367	49	visits
9.0721	49.6	.6928	63	roofs
9.0683	49.6	.8392	54	admire
9.0642	49.6	.5254	81	Arab
9.0632	49.6	.6088	72	chemistry
9.0629	49.6	.7900	57	promptly
9.0618	49.6	.6296	68	dared
9.0567	49.6	.7486	60	twisting
9.0546	49.6	.7113	61	ledge
9.0502	49.6	.7109	62	reporter
9.0473	49.6	.8192	55	accustomed
9.0466	49.6	.7988	56	sometime
9.0454	49.6	.3607	117	views
9.0400	49.6	.7818	57	mist
9.0391	49.6	.6751	65	hum
9.0384	49.6	.7266	61	Northwest
9.0374	49.6	.7747	57	foxes
9.0343	49.6	.4141	87	diver
9.0286	49.6	.6491	67	temper
9.0279	49.6	.6690	65	desperate
9.0275	49.6	.6553	67	vivid
9.0272	49.6	.8089	55	flown
9.0260	49.6	.7826	57	bullet
9.0256	49.6	.7895	57	conducted
9.0230	49.6	.6158	71	guides
9.0223	49.6	.5916	69	Admiral
9.0205	49.6	.7790	57	woman's
9.0172	49.6	.6315	69	dissolve
9.0171	49.6	.5853	70	skunk
9.0162	49.6	.5815	74	Rio
9.0156	49.5	.6385	67	plunged
9.0088	49.5	.8036	56	extending
9.0088	49.5	.7173	62	grades
9.0085	49.5	.7415	60	allows
9.0079	49.5	.8024	56	reality
9.0073	49.5	.4831	83	Reed
9.0035	49.5	.8078	55	thirsty
9.0020	49.5	.7062	63	grinding
9.0007	49.5	.7005	63	Samuel
9.0005	49.5	.7458	60	enables
8.9993	49.5	.3984	106	contraction
8.9977	49.5	.8185	55	prominent
8.9971	49.5	.7035	61	coconut
8.9946	49.5	.7546	58	toss
8.9941	49.5	.7805	57	refuse
8.9841	49.5	.7533	59	perfume
8.9811	49.5	.6672	63	Abe
8.9797	49.5	.8116	55	settling
8.9781	49.5	.8441	53	spoiled
8.9768	49.5	.3754	106	violin
8.9727	49.5	.5651	71	Cousin
8.9679	49.5	.8306	54	charm
8.9643	49.5	.6834	64	sponge
8.9638	49.5	.7141	62	tends
8.9624	49.5	.7906	56	plentiful
8.9595	49.5	.2735	105	Jenkins
8.9588	49.5	.7318	60	nobles
8.9555	49.5	.7847	57	creates
8.9550	49.5	.6584	66	carton
8.9534	49.5	.7447	59	builds
8.9498	49.5	.7891	56	marvelous
8.9491	49.5	.6443	67	San
8.9490	49.5	.7391	59	oars
8.9467	49.5	.6417	67	Master
8.9427	49.5	.6507	65	Clara
8.9356	49.5	.7149	61	Table
8.9293	49.5	.5952	72	climates
8.9241	49.5	.7947	56	focus
8.9233	49.5	.8431	53	superior
8.9231	49.5	.7974	56	varying
8.9199	49.5	.7905	56	packing
8.9153	49.5	.6885	62	whiskers
8.9108	49.5	.8216	54	strongest
8.9088	49.5	.7291	60	Bureau
8.8969	49.5	.7020	62	remarked
8.8960	49.5	.7522	58	Spring
8.8957	49.5	.7145	61	fried
8.8951	49.5	.8944	50	wasted
8.8935	49.5	.8297	53	bowls
8.8932	49.5	.7829	56	learns
8.8895	49.5	.7443	58	skim
8.8882	49.5	.4419	89	toads
8.8855	49.5	.7555	58	bomb
8.8845	49.5	.5712	72	where's
8.8835	49.5	.7593	58	application
8.8786	49.5	.7092	61	buses
8.8781	49.5	.6343	66	bowed
8.8780	49.5	.5684	72	Polly
8.8762	49.5	.8710	51	tag

THE PRECEDING WORD TYPE OCCUPIES RANK 5500

U	SFI	D	F	Word Type
8.8749	49.5	.6066	71	seventh
8.8687	49.5	.4051	102	THE
8.8660	49.5	.7205	60	Baltimore
8.8646	49.5	.8195	54	generous
8.8603	49.5	.8574	52	ordinarily
8.8509	49.5	.7910	55	wrinkled
8.8494	49.5	.7709	56	frighten
8.8476	49.5	.8366	53	portions
8.8416	49.5	.7466	58	shoots
8.8407	49.5	.5939	70	Theodore
8.8407	49.5	.5939	70	Theodore
8.8405	49.5	.6883	63	Russians
8.8312	49.5	.8206	54	basically
8.8305	49.5	.6427	67	profit
8.8302	49.5	.3971	103	Century
8.8291	49.5	.4811	85	quart
8.8235	49.5	.7838	56	transferred
8.8219	49.5	.5372	78	lord
8.8189	49.5	.6387	66	pumped
8.8126	49.5	.5057	83	sex
8.8067	49.4	.7040	60	bubble
8.8052	49.4	.7557	57	depended
8.8028	49.4	.6954	62	granite
8.8014	49.4	.8085	54	meadows
8.8007	49.4	.8115	54	barrels
8.7998	49.4	.8262	53	vain
8.7951	49.4	.7325	59	purse
8.7919	49.4	.3665	111	w
8.7904	49.4	.6298	68	vehicle
8.7847	49.4	.8303	53	proceed
8.7830	49.4	.7091	61	Van
8.7825	49.4	.4696	89	ballet
8.7822	49.4	.6513	66	legal
8.7814	49.4	.4818	85	pray
8.7763	49.4	.7508	58	softer
8.7742	49.4	.2371	110	Katie
8.7718	49.4	.7442	58	savage
8.7681	49.4	.7434	58	other's
8.7656	49.4	.6960	61	lane
8.7651	49.4	.6827	63	housing
8.7616	49.4	.7244	59	buffaloes
8.7590	49.4	.7331	59	handles
8.7577	49.4	.6949	61	darker
8.7557	49.4	.6615	63	villagers
8.7451	49.4	.6105	69	boundaries
8.7451	49.4	.7605	57	occasional
8.7430	49.4	.8537	51	carpet
8.7319	49.4	.5979	70	incident
8.7317	49.4	.7922	55	Mary's
8.7294	49.4	.8060	54	performing
8.7291	49.4	.8338	52	spilled
8.7265	49.4	.8228	53	representative
8.7264	49.4	.4415	93	bake
8.7260	49.4	.7429	58	rounds
8.7250	49.4	.7655	56	Death
8.7219	49.4	.6184	68	turkeys
8.7119	49.4	.5091	81	bending
8.7102	49.4	.8730	50	men's
8.7071	49.4	.7307	59	elaborate
8.7042	49.4	.8562	51	framework
8.7042	49.4	.5969	70	radar

U	SFI	D	F	Word Type
8.7039	49.4	.7475	57	pools
8.6995	49.4	.6883	62	Home
8.6988	49.4	.5627	73	o'
8.6985	49.4	.7884	55	emotions
8.6956	49.4	.6999	61	classify
8.6932	49.4	.7897	55	whereas
8.6925	49.4	.7350	57	diamonds
8.6916	49.4	.7016	61	twentieth
8.6900	49.4	.5453	78	repetition
8.6899	49.4	.5831	71	Athens
8.6898	49.4	.6365	66	beams
8.6878	49.4	.8030	54	sturdy
8.6825	49.4	.6282	68	intensity
8.6818	49.4	.6912	61	Fahrenheit
8.6790	49.4	.7594	56	cabins
8.6705	49.4	.8291	52	disturbed
8.6687	49.4	.4200	82	Singer
8.6685	49.4	.8722	50	approaches
8.6682	49.4	.6642	64	entertainment
8.6662	49.4	.5781	69	sheriff
8.6630	49.4	.7737	55	miracle
8.6629	49.4	.7708	55	cherries
8.6629	49.4	.6355	66	southeast
8.6621	49.4	.7669	55	guessed
8.6479	49.4	.6771	61	stew
8.6459	49.4	.6373	66	Ages
8.6424	49.4	.7905	54	radios
8.6412	49.4	.7156	59	mane
8.6374	49.4	.8004	54	determining
8.6302	49.4	.7248	59	candidate
8.6299	49.4	.8838	49	fiery
8.6298	49.4	.7191	59	concentrated
8.6285	49.4	.8115	53	possibility
8.6279	49.4	.8049	53	chores
8.6271	49.4	.6404	65	democracy
8.6239	49.4	.7713	55	roast
8.6236	49.4	.5648	75	contemporary
8.6229	49.4	.8298	52	considerably
8.6224	49.4	.4503	87	rhymes

THE PRECEDING WORD TYPE OCCUPIES RANK 5600

U	SFI	D	F	Word Type
8.6145	49.4	.7998	53	windy
8.6122	49.4	.7829	55	universal
8.6087	49.3	.4899	82	glands
8.6067	49.3	.6974	60	explorer
8.6030	49.3	.4033	96	organisms
8.5968	49.3	.8348	51	tan
8.5958	49.3	.6896	59	crashed
8.5921	49.3	.7370	57	towering
8.5916	49.3	.7477	56	tucked
8.5915	49.3	.7028	59	buds
8.5907	49.3	.7877	54	patches
8.5878	49.3	.7585	56	holidays
8.5875	49.3	.6851	60	Forest
8.5875	49.3	.3971	96	lowlands
8.5808	49.3	.7087	60	architecture
8.5766	49.3	.7088	59	supporting
8.5600	49.3	.6016	67	shame
8.5572	49.3	.7553	56	emergency
8.5556	49.3	.8399	51	roughly
8.5556	49.3	.6346	63	whirled
8.5546	49.3	.3215	118	radius
8.5479	49.3	.3992	100	z
8.5453	49.3	.5196	77	cools
8.5434	49.3	.7182	59	consideration
8.5397	49.3	.6951	59	knelt
8.5380	49.3	.6494	63	Turkish
8.5308	49.3	.6009	67	Number
8.5266	49.3	.8315	51	glimpse
8.5203	49.3	.6576	63	beliefs
8.5188	49.3	.8013	53	furnish
8.5117	49.3	.7721	54	skating
8.5083	49.3	.7456	56	cliffs
8.5062	49.3	.7862	54	detailed
8.5039	49.3	.6530	61	gulls
8.5015	49.3	.7794	54	respond
8.4983	49.3	.6475	64	chalkboard
8.4958	49.3	.5427	72	Joey
8.4896	49.3	.5937	70	secondary
8.4868	49.3	.7028	58	Patrick
8.4851	49.3	.7250	57	draft
8.4789	49.3	.7736	54	seashore
8.4767	49.3	.4569	86	peninsula
8.4686	49.3	.7458	56	parent
8.4604	49.3	.7202	58	tastes
8.4596	49.3	.7152	58	slower
8.4581	49.3	.6776	62	modified
8.4525	49.3	.6923	59	moons
8.4525	49.3	.7883	53	old-fashioned
8.4521	49.3	.5435	71	crocodiles
8.4484	49.3	.4108	94	cubic
8.4472	49.3	.6078	65	Ali
8.4464	49.3	.6212	65	kissed
8.4463	49.3	.6981	59	explaining
8.4400	49.3	.6653	62	52
8.4389	49.3	.6594	63	reverse
8.4380	49.3	.7290	57	divides
8.4361	49.3	.6526	62	huts
8.4343	49.3	.7719	54	operator
8.4337	49.3	.4823	81	batter
8.4326	49.3	.7881	53	quarrel
8.4277	49.3	.6401	64	potential
8.4240	49.3	.7157	57	straightened
8.4212	49.3	.5525	69	Babe
8.4190	49.3	.6553	61	hers
8.4150	49.3	.5963	69	mixing
8.4137	49.2	.7303	57	affects
8.4100	49.2	.7258	56	messenger
8.4097	49.2	.6433	62	clown
8.4090	49.2	.6748	61	so-called
8.4056	49.2	.5017	79	identity
8.4047	49.2	.7136	58	intense
8.4029	49.2	.0796	352	spells
8.4010	49.2	.7556	55	gloves
8.3983	49.2	.7908	53	scout
8.3971	49.2	.7554	55	routine
8.3956	49.2	.8066	52	involving
8.3945	49.2	.6355	62	Senator
8.3930	49.2	.6886	59	outfit
8.3915	49.2	.2972	119	radiation
8.3914	49.2	.7920	53	conscious
8.3899	49.2	.5701	72	proportions
8.3845	49.2	.5548	70	flung
8.3837	49.2	.6727	61	Museum
8.3775	49.2	.7437	55	scarlet
8.3755	49.2	.4535	80	Wilbur
8.3737	49.2	.4680	84	unions
8.3717	49.2	.5863	69	temples
8.3712	49.2	.7466	55	locomotive
8.3707	49.2	.7162	57	procession
8.3699	49.2	.7289	56	noses
8.3694	49.2	.6760	60	Pittsburgh
8.3661	49.2	.8186	51	avoided
8.3658	49.2	.8532	49	fills
8.3611	49.2	.7394	55	slippery
8.3595	49.2	.7721	53	whistling
8.3587	49.2	.7417	56	romantic
8.3569	49.2	.5587	71	insurance
8.3565	49.2	.6088	66	passages
8.3516	49.2	.0565	332	rational
8.3460	49.2	.5943	65	licked

THE PRECEDING WORD TYPE OCCUPIES RANK 5700

U	SFI	D	F	Word Type
8.3455	49.2	.6447	63	Art
8.3450	49.2	.7433	56	foundation
8.3395	49.2	.7199	57	unpleasant
8.3392	49.2	.6526	62	chapters
8.3384	49.2	.7928	52	spears
8.3379	49.2	.6729	59	pearls
8.3356	49.2	.4499	83	grasslands
8.3353	49.2	.8280	50	sunrise
8.3309	49.2	.6024	66	plantation
8.3305	49.2	.7981	52	elbow
8.3298	49.2	.8001	52	previously
8.3290	49.2	.6891	59	peasants
8.3286	49.2	.6531	63	variation
8.3248	49.2	.6424	63	illustrates
8.3247	49.2	.7440	55	ruined
8.3225	49.2	.5628	70	hairs
8.3223	49.2	.7067	58	preserved
8.3223	49.2	.6978	58	raining
8.3216	49.2	.8309	50	easiest
8.3195	49.2	.7170	57	noble
8.3174	49.2	.6913	59	rural
8.3147	49.2	.6267	64	limestone
8.3131	49.2	.6765	60	voted
8.3048	49.2	.7059	57	speeches
8.3031	49.2	.7603	54	scenery
8.3018	49.2	.5891	65	fetch
8.3005	49.2	.8271	50	velvet
8.2995	49.2	.7830	53	pulse
8.2970	49.2	.7344	56	Persian
8.2958	49.2	.5911	67	decay
8.2913	49.2	.5664	69	pastures
8.2893	49.2	.4704	83	thirds
8.2863	49.2	.5484	69	gasped
8.2832	49.2	.6674	61	technology
8.2824	49.2	.7941	52	brand
8.2821	49.2	.8033	51	strangely
8.2816	49.2	.6601	60	streak
8.2800	49.2	.5764	66	Cat
8.2793	49.2	.7330	55	complained
8.2744	49.2	.5294	73	floods
8.2720	49.2	.4314	84	reward
8.2687	49.2	.7550	54	salty
8.2681	49.2	.6039	65	it'll
8.2677	49.2	.4033	89	obey
8.2658	49.2	.7125	57	year's
8.2651	49.2	.7091	56	cheering
8.2600	49.2	.6700	59	courtyard
8.2585	49.2	.7651	53	solemn
8.2563	49.2	.8069	51	favorable
8.2545	49.2	.7519	54	widow
8.2532	49.2	.5909	65	fiddle
8.2514	49.2	.6579	60	professor
8.2510	49.2	.7792	52	perched
8.2502	49.2	.7325	55	carpenter
8.2490	49.2	.8007	51	happier
8.2490	49.2	.7905	52	regardless
8.2485	49.2	.7080	57	blades
8.2478	49.2	.6547	61	skip
8.2444	49.2	.6880	58	stool
8.2435	49.2	.7015	58	creative
8.2431	49.2	.6128	65	hogs
8.2426	49.2	.7477	54	Harold
8.2423	49.2	.6440	62	basin
8.2402	49.2	.6909	58	Douglas
8.2378	49.2	.8249	50	demonstrate
8.2340	49.2	.5785	69	shades
8.2323	49.2	.6883	59	partial
8.2322	49.2	.6909	58	thinner
8.2243	49.2	.1690	182	ed
8.2230	49.2	.5389	72	representatives
8.2203	49.1	.4752	83	complement
8.2196	49.1	.8154	50	wins
8.2188	49.1	.3380	104	Chile
8.2184	49.1	.8129	50	clumsy
8.2162	49.1	.8195	50	joins
8.2150	49.1	.7514	54	weighing
8.2131	49.1	.7229	56	scholars
8.2109	49.1	.8403	49	46
8.2108	49.1	.7664	53	improving
8.2061	49.1	.8216	50	accuracy
8.2024	49.1	.7313	55	rusty
8.2016	49.1	.6005	63	sniffed
8.2012	49.1	.8781	47	frequent
8.2011	49.1	.5294	73	bends
8.1988	49.1	.5399	72	Jewish
8.1961	49.1	.5411	71	assignment
8.1957	49.1	.4815	78	Supreme
8.1935	49.1	.7046	57	possessions
8.1884	49.1	.7421	54	Four
8.1856	49.1	.6859	57	mask
8.1817	49.1	.6008	65	headquarters
8.1783	49.1	.5548	68	guy
8.1773	49.1	.8529	48	interpret
8.1680	49.1	.8076	50	safer
8.1673	49.1	.7468	54	1958
8.1669	49.1	.5896	67	invitation
8.1655	49.1	.8072	50	hooked
8.1623	49.1	.6393	62	1962
8.1599	49.1	.6222	64	unity
8.1581	49.1	.8287	49	seals

THE PRECEDING WORD TYPE OCCUPIES RANK 5800

U	SFI	D	F	Word Type
8.1571	49.1	.6025	64	Kathy
8.1557	49.1	.7803	52	contribution
8.1549	49.1	.5258	74	slices
8.1514	49.1	.5761	63	rally
8.1513	49.1	.6029	63	jerked
8.1498	49.1	.7971	51	clusters
8.1484	49.1	.7201	56	security
8.1444	49.1	.7288	55	palms
8.1434	49.1	.6395	62	lace
8.1416	49.1	.7017	57	marine
8.1405	49.1	.6940	56	snowy
8.1351	49.1	.7271	55	abundance
8.1340	49.1	.6928	58	distributed
8.1256	49.1	.7039	56	coloring
8.1153	49.1	.7456	54	analysis
8.1128	49.1	.7811	51	mound
8.1073	49.1	.6271	63	transparent
8.1045	49.1	.1587	186	AB
8.1038	49.1	.6401	60	hesitated
8.1013	49.1	.4953	75	daytime
8.0962	49.1	.6455	61	preserve
8.0849	49.1	.7523	53	prehistoric
8.0792	49.1	.8019	50	retreat
8.0758	49.1	.7438	54	similarly
8.0750	49.1	.7411	53	Halloween
8.0709	49.1	.6192	63	Peru
8.0686	49.1	.1105	230	segments
8.0675	49.1	.6659	57	diary
8.0650	49.1	.7361	54	masters
8.0633	49.1	.6519	60	marble
8.0623	49.1	.6289	62	conclusions
8.0609	49.1	.7958	50	sweater
8.0580	49.1	.4194	89	engineering
8.0529	49.1	.7853	51	instruction
8.0437	49.1	.7396	54	resulting
8.0428	49.1	.7832	51	enjoyment
8.0414	49.1	.7837	51	folds
8.0372	49.1	.5600	68	SouthCarolina
8.0311	49.0	.0608	300	digits
8.0254	49.0	.6513	60	benefits
8.0246	49.0	.7110	55	brighter
8.0243	49.0	.8569	47	convince
8.0215	49.0	.5323	71	solving
8.0196	49.0	.7817	51	teacher's
8.0185	49.0	.6330	61	Parliament
8.0160	49.0	.5225	72	wastes
8.0131	49.0	.5045	71	Rogers
8.0129	49.0	.8773	46	estate
8.0127	49.0	.7566	52	pitched
8.0071	49.0	.7710	51	chunks
8.0059	49.0	.5277	68	barking
8.0057	49.0	.6906	57	presses
8.0003	49.0	.5211	73	chairman
7.9978	49.0	.6773	58	assembled
7.9956	49.0	.1528	118	Scotty
7.9940	49.0	.5571	70	insert
7.9907	49.0	.4028	90	gallon
7.9900	49.0	.6411	61	transfer
7.9893	49.0	.6875	57	issued
7.9765	49.0	.6992	56	domestic
7.9753	49.0	.3447	92	Buck
7.9753	49.0	.7951	50	precision
7.9751	49.0	.4398	84	canned
7.9723	49.0	.7960	50	providing
7.9717	49.0	.5698	66	Edison
7.9699	49.0	.6844	56	pity
7.9698	49.0	.6372	59	bugs
7.9656	49.0	.8307	48	acquired
7.9646	49.0	.6008	64	Scouts
7.9574	49.0	.7100	54	awoke
7.9574	49.0	.7618	52	reflects
7.9570	49.0	.5987	63	breast
7.9559	49.0	.7834	50	recovered
7.9553	49.0	.7343	53	cloudy
7.9492	49.0	.7263	53	crawling
7.9454	49.0	.5339	70	constitution
7.9430	49.0	.7253	54	laying
7.9416	49.0	.6214	60	Miller
7.9405	49.0	.5878	61	cab
7.9395	49.0	.6694	58	financial
7.9381	49.0	.8001	49	exhausted
7.9349	49.0	.6212	62	velocity
7.9327	49.0	.5513	68	volcanic
7.9315	49.0	.5686	67	approximate
7.9311	49.0	.3873	95	commas
7.9294	49.0	.6479	60	extensive
7.9255	49.0	.7324	53	interpretation
7.9200	49.0	.8142	48	sighted
7.9186	49.0	.6481	58	hush
7.9183	49.0	.7308	53	Margaret
7.9135	49.0	.7106	55	converted
7.9102	49.0	.8196	48	bored
7.9082	49.0	.7495	52	golf
7.9073	49.0	.4610	83	auxiliary
7.9031	49.0	.6028	63	Einstein
7.9021	49.0	.8036	49	succession
7.9020	49.0	.6346	59	yelling
7.8994	49.0	.8044	49	orderly
7.8992	49.0	.4185	90	accompany
7.8987	49.0	.6424	60	matching

THE PRECEDING WORD TYPE OCCUPIES RANK 5900

U	SFI	D	F	Word Type
7.8981	49.0	.3687	93	glory
7.8917	49.0	.7252	53	bride
7.8872	49.0	.3838	92	spoon
7.8820	49.0	.7536	52	arise
7.8811	49.0	.5620	68	marking
7.8725	49.0	.2582	124	faith
7.8724	49.0	.6771	57	vegetation
7.8721	49.0	.4897	71	Grandpa
7.8707	49.0	.4246	87	j
7.8677	49.0	.4576	77	Houston
7.8629	49.0	.5566	68	curves
7.8626	49.0	.3529	104	possessive
7.8572	49.0	.7857	49	crow
7.8569	49.0	.8544	46	feeds
7.8489	48.9	.7495	51	jail
7.8469	48.9	.6083	62	Portuguese
7.8455	48.9	.7510	52	linked
7.8443	48.9	.7687	50	Fair
7.8371	48.9	.7588	51	libraries
7.8369	48.9	.7374	52	brains
7.8355	48.9	.8348	47	advances
7.8323	48.9	.7401	52	ceremony
7.8320	48.9	.5427	66	Jill
7.8304	48.9	.7857	49	swell
7.8284	48.9	.7136	54	amusing
7.8282	48.9	.5069	72	ay
7.8281	48.9	.8350	47	links
7.8265	48.9	.3230	109	chalk
7.8251	48.9	.7535	51	actors
7.8242	48.9	.7914	49	admired
7.8223	48.9	.6018	62	maid
7.8211	48.9	.7280	53	league
7.8164	48.9	.6760	56	computers
7.8164	48.9	.7118	53	hastily
7.8162	48.9	.5009	73	cubes
7.8157	48.9	.7875	49	den
7.8128	48.9	.7108	53	runners
7.8125	48.9	.7452	52	differs
7.8102	48.9	.4915	74	Jews
7.8075	48.9	.6301	60	immigrants
7.8072	48.9	.7588	51	ranks
7.8062	48.9	.6978	54	desperately
7.8046	48.9	.7618	51	span
7.8041	48.9	.7877	49	camps
7.8041	48.9	.7236	53	moral
7.8032	48.9	.8072	48	girl's
7.8005	48.9	.7280	52	bicycles
7.8004	48.9	.4990	73	180
7.7998	48.9	.6713	57	Frederick
7.7995	48.9	.5288	69	Tokyo
7.7983	48.9	.6767	55	growled
7.7952	48.9	.7906	49	occupy
7.7942	48.9	.8071	48	session
7.7926	48.9	.6699	57	array
7.7900	48.9	.6239	59	Ruth
7.7883	48.9	.7491	51	Sound
7.7778	48.9	.8448	46	deepest
7.7757	48.9	.7994	48	ship's
7.7751	48.9	.6237	60	Belgium
7.7747	48.9	.6241	59	Eve
7.7735	48.9	.8270	47	yield
7.7722	48.9	.7330	52	squeeze
7.7713	48.9	.8033	48	towel
7.7599	48.9	.7073	54	naked
7.7595	48.9	.7275	52	patients
7.7572	48.9	.8010	48	dripping
7.7543	48.9	.6181	60	cables
7.7498	48.9	.7011	53	saucer
7.7479	48.9	.6979	55	impressions
7.7464	48.9	.7489	51	stalks
7.7463	48.9	.6567	57	corral
7.7414	48.9	.7697	50	Scout
7.7411	48.9	.8135	47	tractor
7.7408	48.9	.4575	71	robot
7.7406	48.9	.7255	52	deaf
7.7389	48.9	.8015	48	evidently
7.7388	48.9	.6933	55	literally
7.7366	48.9	.6266	60	handwriting
7.7354	48.9	.8839	44	arriving
7.7332	48.9	.7063	52	Turner
7.7329	48.9	.6600	56	Kelly
7.7316	48.9	.5773	63	1945
7.7305	48.9	.7342	52	fragments
7.7280	48.9	.7753	49	inventor
7.7271	48.9	.7217	53	practices
7.7259	48.9	.3563	100	screw
7.7220	48.9	.6243	59	Wyoming
7.7204	48.9	.7179	53	resulted
7.7177	48.9	.7464	51	apparatus
7.7172	48.9	.8214	47	recreation
7.7171	48.9	.5800	64	Joan
7.7169	48.9	.5213	71	hath
7.7167	48.9	.7616	50	succeed
7.7140	48.9	.7222	52	argued
7.7139	48.9	.7989	48	squash
7.7065	48.9	.5422	62	pirate
7.7062	48.9	.7286	52	register
7.7014	48.9	.6921	55	spectacular
7.6987	48.9	.5865	62	flocks
7.6979	48.9	.7997	48	traced

THE PRECEDING WORD TYPE OCCUPIES RANK 6000

U	SFI	D	F	Word Type
7.6968	48.9	.7905	48	steaming
7.6938	48.9	.6327	59	Isles
7.6901	48.9	.6428	59	minimum
7.6876	48.9	.6588	57	Canyon
7.6876	48.9	.7598	50	cork
7.6776	48.9	.7341	51	parking
7.6772	48.9	.5147	70	peas
7.6738	48.9	.5184	68	Amy
7.6684	48.8	.6528	57	customer
7.6672	48.8	.7122	53	maintained
7.6642	48.8	.3461	99	hardest
7.6638	48.8	.8555	45	advertising
7.6602	48.8	.6521	55	Castle
7.6590	48.8	.7023	53	dreadful
7.6570	48.8	.5142	70	Zealand
7.6538	48.8	.7444	50	drugstore
7.6536	48.8	.7397	51	plowed
7.6529	48.8	.4590	75	loves
7.6488	48.8	.2427	117	kingdom
7.6454	48.8	.6982	53	stolen
7.6445	48.8	.5587	62	dived
7.6394	48.8	.6265	58	riches
7.6367	48.8	.7912	48	absence
7.6312	48.8	.7251	52	neutral

U	SFI	D	F	Word Type
7.6277	48.8	.5097	69	nectar
7.6271	48.8	.3978	86	spectrum
7.6241	48.8	.6817	54	robins
7.6233	48.8	.7134	52	fortunate
7.6214	48.8	.6302	57	sigh
7.6197	48.8	.7037	53	Detroit
7.6137	48.8	.6565	57	toast
7.6046	48.8	.3550	86	Teddy
7.6044	48.8	.8009	47	grassy
7.6028	48.8	.7350	50	hens
7.6017	48.8	.6914	54	poverty
7.6010	48.8	.7499	50	unfamiliar
7.6007	48.8	.6963	54	vigorous
7.5982	48.8	.6123	60	drinks
7.5968	48.8	.4128	73	Sandra
7.5955	48.8	.7548	49	firemen
7.5933	48.8	.6146	60	inspired
7.5922	48.8	.5541	67	preceded
7.5922	48.8	.6922	53	traps
7.5917	48.8	.7317	51	smoking
7.5902	48.8	.7692	49	descriptions
7.5874	48.8	.8164	46	Two
7.5820	48.8	.6519	55	farmhouse
7.5810	48.8	.7512	50	installed
7.5780	48.8	.7645	49	dignity
7.5766	48.8	.3257	100	$2
7.5760	48.8	.7064	52	heap
7.5740	48.8	.6584	56	spices
7.5735	48.8	.4174	81	membrane
7.5721	48.8	.8432	45	referring
7.5681	48.8	.6354	57	drying
7.5653	48.8	.6989	53	gauge
7.5645	48.8	.4380	76	guys
7.5628	48.8	.7449	50	assistant
7.5626	48.8	.6038	60	goin'
7.5606	48.8	.4532	69	necklace
7.5597	48.8	.6087	60	Secretary
7.5585	48.8	.6513	55	scare
7.5559	48.8	.7477	50	beginnings
7.5548	48.8	.7735	48	grocery
7.5533	48.8	.4995	71	tissues
7.5520	48.8	.7701	48	buzzing
7.5489	48.8	.4431	77	Cuba
7.5483	48.8	.5611	63	reckon
7.5480	48.8	.7749	48	tackle
7.5431	48.8	.5841	62	shortest
7.5385	48.8	.5738	63	abundant
7.5370	48.8	.5944	60	cure
7.5368	48.8	.5974	60	moth
7.5343	48.8	.4919	72	Ross
7.5342	48.8	.6807	54	mare
7.5335	48.8	.7622	49	rigid
7.5331	48.8	.7210	51	prizes
7.5330	48.8	.6003	60	Foster
7.5327	48.8	.6727	55	supports
7.5296	48.8	.6341	57	northward
7.5288	48.8	.7816	48	demonstrated
7.5265	48.8	.6149	57	ox
7.5263	48.8	.3634	87	Plains
7.5262	48.8	.6309	57	gonna
7.5223	48.8	.6147	57	robin
7.5201	48.8	.7441	50	cousins
7.5199	48.8	.6840	52	Mother's
7.5135	48.8	.8087	46	instinct
7.5094	48.8	.6535	54	thoughtfully
7.5055	48.8	.8543	44	Englishman
7.5014	48.8	.6775	54	fare
7.5007	48.8	.6563	55	Buffalo
7.5005	48.8	.6264	58	hell
7.4983	48.7	.6428	57	fitting
7.4976	48.7	.6631	54	rooster
7.4960	48.7	.7293	51	satisfactory
7.4906	48.7	.7779	48	impressive
7.4866	48.7	.6439	56	ruins
7.4840	48.7	.8125	46	improvement
7.4838	48.7	.6885	52	stole
THE PRECEDING WORD TYPE OCCUPIES RANK 6100				
7.4831	48.7	.6995	52	marsh
7.4830	48.7	.7830	47	strained
7.4826	48.7	.8492	44	deciding
7.4821	48.7	.6648	54	cheerfully
7.4820	48.7	.6535	54	wishing
7.4815	48.7	.6589	56	illustrations
7.4771	48.7	.7168	51	scream
7.4769	48.7	.5591	65	initial
7.4762	48.7	.6916	52	nurses
7.4720	48.7	.7129	51	tangled
7.4669	48.7	.7791	47	tossing
7.4668	48.7	.7326	50	scarf
7.4645	48.7	.6554	54	shivered
7.4644	48.7	.4278	78	wells
7.4620	48.7	.7575	49	walnut
7.4605	48.7	.3880	87	variable
7.4585	48.7	.7182	51	dunes
7.4550	48.7	.6458	55	Olympic
7.4518	48.7	.7514	49	tomatoes
7.4505	48.7	.7465	49	humans
7.4499	48.7	.4955	67	Ulysses
7.4493	48.7	.7073	52	funds
7.4463	48.7	.6532	53	Pat
7.4449	48.7	.7588	48	plainly
7.4449	48.7	.7794	47	seventy
7.4418	48.7	.6291	56	O''
7.4378	48.7	.5186	67	southeastern
7.4345	48.7	.6841	53	plaster
7.4340	48.7	.6823	53	claims
7.4297	48.7	.8004	46	request
7.4272	48.7	.7798	47	fascinated
7.4247	48.7	.7094	51	injury
7.4235	48.7	.7580	48	stout
7.4229	48.7	.7843	47	remark
7.4228	48.7	.7389	49	axes
7.4198	48.7	.7096	51	mantle
7.4167	48.7	.7281	50	venture
7.4140	48.7	.7416	49	chew
7.4123	48.7	.3839	91	clause
7.4106	48.7	.7657	48	Arabian

U	SFI	D	F	Word Type
7.4083	48.7	.3956	87	stanza
7.4046	48.7	.7166	50	uncomfortable
7.4033	48.7	.6455	55	sleeves
7.4004	48.7	.5562	64	devil
7.3999	48.7	.4814	73	geometric
7.3964	48.7	.8825	42	mistaken
7.3959	48.7	.7808	47	determination
7.3906	48.7	.6642	53	reins
7.3894	48.7	.7013	51	decides
7.3854	48.7	.7089	50	gotten
7.3823	48.7	.6458	55	It
7.3809	48.7	.7282	50	Good
7.3809	48.7	.8307	44	sunk
7.3792	48.7	.6723	53	calves
7.3775	48.7	.7708	47	far-off
7.3760	48.7	.6899	52	deserted
7.3751	48.7	.7243	49	curtains
7.3747	48.7	.5979	57	yell
7.3739	48.7	.4567	73	funnel
7.3734	48.7	.8040	46	aspects
7.3717	48.7	.7759	47	remarks
7.3711	48.7	.7735	47	make-believe
7.3681	48.7	.7549	48	emerged
7.3677	48.7	.7041	51	liver
7.3638	48.7	.7633	47	rocking
7.3620	48.7	.4644	73	sodium
7.3586	48.7	.7242	49	rained
7.3581	48.7	.6720	54	distribution
7.3566	48.7	.7069	51	approval
7.3554	48.7	.8293	44	whirling
7.3522	48.7	.8354	44	shifting
7.3470	48.7	.5628	59	Jonathan
7.3435	48.7	.6262	57	Association
7.3392	48.7	.7402	49	conquer
7.3361	48.7	.5974	59	continental
7.3357	48.7	.6769	53	significance
7.3346	48.7	.7489	48	prisoner
7.3344	48.7	.6208	57	Puerto
7.3339	48.7	.5403	65	provinces
7.3287	48.7	.6244	57	listeners
7.3277	48.6	.6832	52	despair
7.3230	48.6	.7364	49	argue
7.3212	48.6	.7163	49	amazed
7.3184	48.6	.6623	53	costly
7.3155	48.6	.6721	53	bounce
7.3133	48.6	.5821	58	barked
7.3131	48.6	.5081	67	billions
7.3131	48.6	.7563	48	civilized
7.3121	48.6	.7687	47	awhile
7.3121	48.6	.8321	44	critical
7.3114	48.6	.6063	58	Mt
7.3092	48.6	.8524	43	draws
7.3091	48.6	.5701	61	schedule
7.3071	48.6	.5024	69	inclined
7.3054	48.6	.6463	55	secretary
7.3045	48.6	.7496	48	Wednesday
7.3035	48.6	.6479	55	isolated
7.2980	48.6	.6602	54	goals
7.2978	48.6	.3911	81	Congo
7.2974	48.6	.6619	54	cooling
THE PRECEDING WORD TYPE OCCUPIES RANK 6200				
7.2971	48.6	.7299	49	hooks
7.2970	48.6	.4532	76	Jo
7.2968	48.6	.6563	55	technique
7.2963	48.6	.5951	58	Sam's
7.2955	48.6	.6310	54	cautiously
7.2937	48.6	.8008	45	policemen
7.2931	48.6	.5139	66	caterpillar
7.2917	48.6	.5265	65	businesses
7.2910	48.6	.5814	59	whipped
7.2903	48.6	.6209	57	chill
7.2862	48.6	.7036	50	clams
7.2848	48.6	.5898	59	elevation
7.2814	48.6	.6721	53	improvements
7.2807	48.6	.7185	50	sheer
7.2804	48.6	.7665	47	handy
7.2802	48.6	.7841	46	patrol
7.2791	48.6	.5422	63	sorrow
7.2764	48.6	.7631	47	flooded
7.2735	48.6	.6863	52	opposed
7.2731	48.6	.6464	55	95
7.2718	48.6	.4179	80	prism
7.2698	48.6	.3397	98	apostrophe
7.2686	48.6	.6982	51	Alabama
7.2686	48.6	.5524	61	context
7.2677	48.6	.7238	49	curiously
7.2612	48.6	.6703	52	Saint
7.2574	48.6	.7984	45	compressed
7.2538	48.6	.7326	49	mechanics
7.2524	48.6	.5297	61	Webster
7.2522	48.6	.6446	55	universities
7.2504	48.6	.7641	47	lone
7.2448	48.6	.7607	47	prayers
7.2433	48.6	.7834	46	identical
7.2414	48.6	.7181	50	copies
7.2405	48.6	.5121	67	electron
7.2391	48.6	.7448	48	tongues
7.2390	48.6	.5881	59	graceful
7.2366	48.6	.7551	47	Harbor
7.2351	48.6	.4507	75	1967
7.2348	48.6	.7145	50	compact
7.2292	48.6	.6380	55	dies
7.2292	48.6	.6358	54	shrugged
7.2286	48.6	.7148	49	Baker
7.2271	48.6	.7112	49	Bob's
7.2232	48.6	.5711	62	descriptive
7.2170	48.6	.5815	60	49
7.2163	48.6	.6644	53	shrubs
7.2146	48.6	.6451	53	trout
7.2137	48.6	.5943	58	friendship
7.2134	48.6	.6351	55	dough
7.2124	48.6	.7225	49	Battle
7.2119	48.6	.4432	77	1/8
7.2096	48.6	.6565	53	weave
7.2094	48.6	.6464	53	stumbled
7.2085	48.6	.6013	55	burro
7.2081	48.6	.7037	51	selecting

U	SFI	D	F	Word Type
7.2071	48.6	.7693	46	sleeps
7.2070	48.6	.7451	48	55
7.2066	48.6	.7542	47	bargain
7.2017	48.6	.7813	46	gap
7.2015	48.6	.7964	45	authors
7.1999	48.6	.2137	129	dimes
7.1997	48.6	.6783	51	mules
7.1994	48.6	.7687	46	displayed
7.1983	48.6	.7750	46	grim
7.1955	48.6	.6995	50	NorthCarolina
7.1930	48.6	.6856	51	patiently
7.1928	48.6	.4485	73	praise
7.1921	48.6	.7332	48	informed
7.1916	48.6	.5604	60	Nevada
7.1892	48.6	.7361	48	farewell
7.1878	48.6	.5010	67	republic
7.1872	48.6	.7504	47	incomplete
7.1825	48.6	.5761	58	trembling
7.1820	48.6	.6520	53	surrender
7.1786	48.6	.3259	96	multiplied
7.1777	48.6	.6236	56	sounding
7.1775	48.6	.7739	46	collects
7.1772	48.6	.6397	54	votes
7.1754	48.6	.5506	63	cabinet
7.1747	48.6	.0751	316	composer
7.1731	48.6	.5027	68	19th
7.1706	48.6	.6364	52	Max
7.1703	48.6	.6832	51	umbrella
7.1694	48.6	.7634	46	willow
7.1687	48.6	.4840	62	Cliff
7.1679	48.6	.7209	48	struggling
7.1622	48.6	.4869	68	plantations
7.1606	48.5	.8110	44	shifted
7.1593	48.5	.7445	47	sideways
7.1580	48.5	.5170	62	thump
7.1555	48.5	.6062	58	moderate
7.1551	48.5	.4478	77	themes
7.1547	48.5	.8109	44	Wisconsin
7.1497	48.5	.7095	49	Utah
7.1487	48.5	.7480	47	towels
7.1483	48.5	.7043	49	astonished
7.1471	48.5	.4228	76	Sahara
7.1455	48.5	.7495	47	knob
7.1453	48.5	.6043	57	voters
THE PRECEDING WORD TYPE OCCUPIES RANK 6300				
7.1420	48.5	.6467	52	moose
7.1416	48.5	.7051	49	lonesome
7.1413	48.5	.7570	47	appreciate
7.1398	48.5	.6465	54	glorious
7.1397	48.5	.8013	44	thirty-five
7.1387	48.5	.5479	63	nineteenth
7.1355	48.5	.6323	53	miserable
7.1351	48.5	.5534	61	lend
7.1333	48.5	.5446	60	Hamilton
7.1327	48.5	.8007	44	silvery
7.1300	48.5	.7031	50	Institute
7.1285	48.5	.5750	60	storage
7.1283	48.5	.5478	63	Q
7.1265	48.5	.7131	49	strands
7.1260	48.5	.8116	44	indicating
7.1192	48.5	.7295	48	mentally
7.1140	48.5	.6989	50	syrup
7.1135	48.5	.6732	52	collections
7.1089	48.5	.6491	53	weights
7.1049	48.5	.7060	49	affair
7.1043	48.5	.7783	45	roam
7.1039	48.5	.6833	50	full-grown
7.1029	48.5	.7422	47	Iowa
7.0981	48.5	.6888	50	batting
7.0951	48.5	.3295	94	Argentina
7.0944	48.5	.6961	50	manufacturers
7.0925	48.5	.6570	51	Karl
7.0921	48.5	.7491	47	evident
7.0915	48.5	.6984	49	popped
7.0912	48.5	.8443	42	athletic
7.0896	48.5	.7773	45	honored
7.0895	48.5	.6331	54	drained
7.0894	48.5	.7863	45	enabled
7.0893	48.5	.6754	51	cultivated
7.0888	48.5	.7429	47	comfortably
7.0882	48.5	.7665	46	exhibit
7.0854	48.5	.6936	50	naval
7.0810	48.5	.7992	44	barns
7.0747	48.5	.4263	76	Communists
7.0733	48.5	.6432	52	whistled
7.0728	48.5	.8184	43	ruin
7.0698	48.5	.7956	44	popcorn
7.0693	48.5	.6624	52	absorb
7.0678	48.5	.6788	50	rack
7.0670	48.5	.7060	49	Nebraska
7.0663	48.5	.5908	56	hatched
7.0656	48.5	.7304	47	echoed
7.0646	48.5	.7716	45	aimed
7.0629	48.5	.5353	62	starch
7.0628	48.5	.6653	52	crime
7.0621	48.5	.8408	42	relaxed
7.0575	48.5	.3163	95	quarts
7.0513	48.5	.8094	43	trapping
7.0491	48.5	.7395	47	resist
7.0484	48.5	.5646	58	Pony
7.0447	48.5	.4066	81	flavor
7.0411	48.5	.6113	54	clung
7.0397	48.5	.6927	49	wept
7.0390	48.5	.7134	49	folding
7.0373	48.5	.7931	44	junior
7.0356	48.5	.7446	46	shouts
7.0336	48.5	.8180	43	lacked
7.0326	48.5	.7852	44	backwards
7.0305	48.5	.7426	47	barrier
7.0299	48.5	.6433	53	Indiana
7.0296	48.5	.8365	42	arrives
7.0273	48.5	.7534	46	graze
7.0271	48.5	.5837	56	wildly
7.0267	48.5	.7925	44	biting
7.0265	48.5	.6873	50	makers
7.0241	48.5	.6573	52	Maryland
7.0236	48.5	.6504	53	aspect

U	SFI	D	F	Word Type
7.0231	48.5	.7340	47	suspended
7.0213	48.5	.2664	111	ratio
7.0161	48.5	.8144	43	encourage
7.0130	48.5	.7285	47	orchard
7.0076	48.5	.8101	43	furnished
7.0065	48.5	.4250	77	joints
7.0038	48.5	.6157	56	tension
6.9986	48.5	.6945	49	bloody
6.9975	48.4	.4502	74	adjust
6.9970	48.4	.1981	144	es
6.9958	48.4	.6547	52	findings
6.9958	48.4	.8546	41	scrape
6.9931	48.4	.0312	492	Words
6.9850	48.4	.7824	44	glittering
6.9828	48.4	.4173	77	triangular
6.9796	48.4	.7179	48	bony
6.9759	48.4	.5290	64	corrected
6.9754	48.4	.6591	50	runner
6.9697	48.4	.7066	48	parlor
6.9695	48.4	.6914	49	sap
6.9663	48.4	.6088	55	grace
6.9653	48.4	.7613	45	punishment
6.9648	48.4	.5160	62	Baby
6.9646	48.4	.4720	69	39
6.9626	48.4	.6272	53	goddess
6.9620	48.4	.5194	62	zinc
6.9605	48.4	.7577	45	signaled
6.9579	48.4	.4829	68	circumference
THE PRECEDING WORD TYPE OCCUPIES RANK 6400				
6.9574	48.4	.6580	51	spreads
6.9571	48.4	.6913	49	lime
6.9547	48.4	.6897	49	Oklahoma
6.9544	48.4	.5949	55	breathed
6.9507	48.4	.7832	44	slides
6.9490	48.4	.7336	47	dealing
6.9454	48.4	.7483	45	puff
6.9451	48.4	.7427	46	strict
6.9412	48.4	.7774	44	spectators
6.9396	48.4	.7759	44	shower
6.9376	48.4	.6549	52	exceptions
6.9368	48.4	.6078	53	turnips
6.9367	48.4	.7715	44	neighbor's
6.9365	48.4	.5478	61	vibration
6.9347	48.4	.8690	40	nineteen
6.9343	48.4	.6382	53	invasion
6.9338	48.4	.4881	67	Catholic
6.9332	48.4	.8455	41	stack
6.9212	48.4	.6558	51	pumps
6.9142	48.4	.7343	46	hotter
6.9106	48.4	.7046	48	threat
6.9089	48.4	.6899	49	pulp
6.9078	48.4	.6212	51	reindeer
6.9063	48.4	.6958	49	humorous
6.9060	48.4	.6047	55	destruction
6.9056	48.4	.7170	47	persuaded
6.9045	48.4	.7697	44	actor
6.9031	48.4	.5525	59	barley
6.8986	48.4	.7979	43	typewriter
6.8980	48.4	.1468	103	Janey
6.8940	48.4	.6938	47	Robinson
6.8932	48.4	.6585	51	savings
6.8847	48.4	.6243	54	pleasing
6.8832	48.4	.6960	49	originated
6.8820	48.4	.8179	42	flattened
6.8810	48.4	.7883	43	lawyer
6.8795	48.4	.7685	44	ripped
6.8793	48.4	.7547	45	pepper
6.8775	48.4	.5049	63	molds
6.8761	48.4	.5631	56	Johnny's
6.8755	48.4	.7741	44	suspect
6.8705	48.4	.6759	49	Florence
6.8668	48.4	.7521	45	prairies
6.8656	48.4	.7230	47	statistics
6.8586	48.4	.5366	60	bolt
6.8547	48.4	.5006	63	commanded
6.8538	48.4	.6749	49	burrow
6.8515	48.4	.7883	43	stripes
6.8509	48.4	.7493	45	hail
6.8484	48.4	.5514	59	drug
6.8482	48.4	.7519	45	sympathy
6.8469	48.4	.6541	51	writings
6.8448	48.4	.6571	49	bumped
6.8430	48.4	.7896	43	coating
6.8423	48.4	.6494	51	cords
6.8404	48.4	.4824	66	reproduce
6.8395	48.4	.5139	63	Julie
6.8382	48.3	.7343	45	buckets
6.8380	48.3	.7250	46	jam
6.8373	48.3	.5705	57	K
6.8357	48.3	.7639	44	circling
6.8355	48.3	.6884	48	reservation
6.8352	48.3	.6997	48	muscular
6.8313	48.3	.5384	59	Bank
6.8292	48.3	.6790	49	bug
6.8240	48.3	.5861	56	Appalachian
6.8192	48.3	.6143	53	Jay
6.8180	48.3	.6075	53	ha
6.8165	48.3	.8031	42	dentist
6.8161	48.3	.6502	51	reactions
6.8150	48.3	.5945	55	celebrated
6.8125	48.3	.7349	45	frowned
6.8117	48.3	.6643	50	followers
6.8117	48.3	.6297	52	Montana
6.8113	48.3	.5919	54	lizard
6.8073	48.3	.5718	55	clapped
6.8037	48.3	.5399	58	Antarctica
6.8036	48.3	.6854	49	facilities
6.8026	48.3	.6259	52	protects
6.8016	48.3	.0459	292	fractional
6.8009	48.3	.7193	46	salesman
6.7971	48.3	.7096	46	shield
6.7964	48.3	.7790	43	cunning
6.7957	48.3	.5251	61	Peninsula
6.7947	48.3	.7582	44	anchored
6.7893	48.3	.6304	51	pitching
6.7860	48.3	.7282	45	lookout
6.7858	48.3	.5893	55	lunar

U	SFI	D	F	Word Type
6.7801	48.3	.8166	41	eighty
6.7767	48.3	.5400	57	maiden
6.7753	48.3	.6032	54	Alps
6.7751	48.3	.4144	75	definitions
6.7739	48.3	.4675	66	cable
6.7726	48.3	.6821	48	rushes
6.7707	48.3	.7073	47	authorities
6.7699	48.3	.6521	51	imitate
6.7695	48.3	.3925	79	listener
6.7671	48.3	.6226	52	barges
6.7641	48.3	.7215	45	awfully
6.7632	48.3	.3691	83	coil
THE PRECEDING WORD TYPE OCCUPIES RANK 6500				
6.7612	48.3	.5783	55	Rose
6.7589	48.3	.7747	43	Main
6.7576	48.3	.7416	44	keeper
6.7565	48.3	.7699	43	blocked
6.7564	48.3	.8194	41	self
6.7463	48.3	.6445	50	Panama
6.7460	48.3	.5865	56	virtually
6.7458	48.3	.8223	41	broadcast
6.7419	48.3	.7831	43	status
6.7404	48.3	.6216	52	hospitals
6.7403	48.3	.5884	56	removing
6.7396	48.3	.7330	45	Building
6.7392	48.3	.6738	48	plug
6.7387	48.3	.7635	43	kicking
6.7373	48.3	.6593	50	develops
6.7352	48.3	.5846	55	payment
6.7344	48.3	.5450	57	Larry
6.7327	48.3	.3551	82	sends
6.7319	48.3	.7775	43	strengthen
6.7303	48.3	.7998	42	arguments
6.7290	48.3	.5964	54	Italians
6.7270	48.3	.7287	45	docks
6.7243	48.3	.7348	45	warmed
6.7243	48.3	.5440	59	43
6.7242	48.3	.6776	47	snail
6.7239	48.3	.7054	46	grip
6.7202	48.3	.6155	51	ashamed
6.7153	48.3	.7909	42	strawberries
6.7094	48.3	.7913	42	hippopotamus
6.7094	48.3	.5874	53	they've
6.7091	48.3	.6238	51	Stone
6.7085	48.3	.8195	41	necessity
6.7079	48.3	.8103	41	campfire
6.7073	48.3	.6667	48	grasshoppers
6.7030	48.3	.5301	59	Jamestown
6.7025	48.3	.7460	44	swings
6.7017	48.3	.6207	52	bury
6.6970	48.3	.6511	50	1963
6.6919	48.3	.8328	40	weed
6.6890	48.3	.6186	52	specimens
6.6865	48.3	.8092	41	odds
6.6834	48.2	.6805	48	survived
6.6798	48.2	.6099	52	spins
6.6794	48.2	.6436	50	disappointment
6.6786	48.2	.7671	43	impulse
6.6784	48.2	.5165	61	grammar
6.6777	48.2	.4655	62	Bruce
6.6728	48.2	.5423	58	Poland
6.6721	48.2	.7147	46	percentage
6.6708	48.2	.4192	74	pork
6.6682	48.2	.5577	57	98
6.6652	48.2	.6076	52	Madame
6.6626	48.2	.7835	42	mount
6.6619	48.2	.5804	55	favored
6.6586	48.2	.6853	47	lip
6.6578	48.2	.6300	51	Arabia
6.6559	48.2	.8091	41	nowadays
6.6539	48.2	.6422	50	businessmen
6.6493	48.2	.2320	124	pronouns
6.6455	48.2	.7737	42	peanut
6.6434	48.2	.3943	77	Philippines
6.6414	48.2	.7584	43	kangaroo
6.6414	48.2	.6011	54	Scandinavian
6.6358	48.2	.2162	133	signature
6.6348	48.2	.7602	43	missile
6.6331	48.2	.7084	45	stuffed
6.6300	48.2	.6809	47	dusk
6.6294	48.2	.6732	48	Graham
6.6286	48.2	.7217	44	scolded
6.6284	48.2	.7408	44	examining
6.6282	48.2	.4210	73	finishing
6.6278	48.2	.7787	42	stepping
6.6270	48.2	.6504	48	ghosts
6.6258	48.2	.4998	64	blends
6.6243	48.2	.7142	45	hillside
6.6241	48.2	.4418	68	orbits
6.6240	48.2	.6247	51	reef
6.6191	48.2	.6331	51	purchased
6.6182	48.2	.1162	184	multiples
6.6176	48.2	.7588	43	soaked
6.6162	48.2	.7278	45	right-hand
6.6150	48.2	.5331	58	mined
6.6083	48.2	.7287	44	blazing
6.6082	48.2	.7972	41	scraped
6.6066	48.2	.5420	58	moths
6.6055	48.2	.7921	41	mast
6.6047	48.2	.5119	61	hive
6.6043	48.2	.5514	53	riddle
6.6043	48.2	.6240	51	tour
6.6032	48.2	.5774	55	fluid
6.6001	48.2	.7648	43	definitely
6.5993	48.2	.6720	48	2000
6.5973	48.2	.7228	45	contribute
6.5924	48.2	.7769	42	repaired
6.5921	48.2	.6715	48	Seattle
6.5917	48.2	.7244	44	carrot
6.5917	48.2	.6996	45	speeding
6.5879	48.2	.4163	73	vibrating
6.5866	48.2	.7213	45	consisted
6.5857	48.2	.4494	67	erosion
THE PRECEDING WORD TYPE OCCUPIES RANK 6600				
6.5796	48.2	.6931	46	carrier
6.5788	48.2	.7366	44	left-hand
6.5750	48.2	.1400	212	fabric
6.5748	48.2	.5780	53	cub
6.5735	48.2	.7266	44	calmly
6.5724	48.2	.7932	41	ignored
6.5722	48.2	.5621	55	Warren
6.5678	48.2	.6203	50	Pop
6.5677	48.2	.7405	43	spy
6.5672	48.2	.7571	43	sensation
6.5665	48.2	.7217	44	molasses
6.5636	48.2	.2419	103	hearts
6.5616	48.2	.7525	43	rattle
6.5615	48.2	.8405	39	encountered
6.5603	48.2	.7503	43	sands
6.5555	48.2	.7102	45	closes
6.5550	48.2	.8012	41	tendency
6.5544	48.2	.7724	42	delay
6.5528	48.2	.6519	49	societies
6.5523	48.2	.5074	61	o'er
6.5519	48.2	.7263	44	towers
6.5495	48.2	.7492	43	debt
6.5473	48.2	.3311	90	comma
6.5471	48.2	.7097	45	innocent
6.5438	48.2	.7131	45	goldfish
6.5435	48.2	.3850	71	lowland
6.5428	48.2	.3973	79	texture
6.5383	48.2	.6140	51	Desert
6.5366	48.2	.8107	40	lasts
6.5351	48.2	.3203	86	speaks
6.5284	48.1	.6484	49	Arkansas
6.5283	48.1	.6266	50	Rockies
6.5280	48.1	.6015	52	musician
6.5205	48.1	.7584	43	visual
6.5202	48.1	.6513	49	creation
6.5186	48.1	.8135	40	entitled
6.5157	48.1	.2474	80	Timothy
6.5155	48.1	.6527	48	ceased
6.5137	48.1	.4670	66	cereal
6.5120	48.1	.6776	47	1957
6.5107	48.1	.6979	45	People
6.5059	48.1	.6361	49	panel
6.5050	48.1	.3931	76	sleeve
6.5040	48.1	.5875	53	minus
6.5023	48.1	.7375	43	haunted
6.5022	48.1	.7264	44	metallic
6.5016	48.1	.7681	42	jaw
6.4987	48.1	.6275	48	hawk
6.4939	48.1	.8339	39	assistance
6.4909	48.1	.7688	42	dominant
6.4892	48.1	.7815	41	bites
6.4874	48.1	.4140	72	fossil
6.4867	48.1	.6350	48	beak
6.4851	48.1	.6560	47	owls
6.4781	48.1	.6166	51	sharing
6.4768	48.1	.7292	44	markings
6.4759	48.1	.3641	78	Rufus
6.4732	48.1	.7167	44	halt
6.4711	48.1	.1117	218	misspelled
6.4707	48.1	.5385	58	static
6.4685	48.1	.6141	51	1961
6.4679	48.1	.5425	54	grinning
6.4654	48.1	.7434	43	observer
6.4636	48.1	.7201	44	guilty
6.4623	48.1	.7084	45	philosophy
6.4620	48.1	.5707	53	fertilizer
6.4607	48.1	.6832	46	NewMexico
6.4581	48.1	.5470	54	hawks
6.4571	48.1	.7574	42	oyster
6.4540	48.1	.4948	58	nylon
6.4523	48.1	.7807	41	buys
6.4474	48.1	.7536	42	peasant
6.4458	48.1	.8446	38	grind
6.4431	48.1	.6421	47	Guard
6.4426	48.1	.5889	52	valves
6.4407	48.1	.6082	51	expenses
6.4396	48.1	.6279	50	Christianity
6.4364	48.1	.7628	42	rely
6.4361	48.1	.8998	36	acquainted
6.4360	48.1	.7330	43	protest
6.4356	48.1	.7126	44	lords
6.4354	48.1	.5296	57	sew
6.4348	48.1	.7280	43	motionless
6.4338	48.1	.8506	38	meaningful
6.4338	48.1	.6644	46	pretending
6.4337	48.1	.6436	49	rests
6.4324	48.1	.7356	43	talent
6.4292	48.1	.8022	40	likewise
6.4274	48.1	.4719	61	Stan
6.4253	48.1	.5099	59	particle
6.4252	48.1	.7454	42	clinging
6.4251	48.1	.6104	50	orchards
6.4228	48.1	.0935	246	composers
6.4205	48.1	.7319	42	cages
6.4179	48.1	.6575	48	excess
6.4128	48.1	.5266	59	desirable
6.4088	48.1	.7369	43	Frenchman
6.4080	48.1	.7407	42	coyotes
6.4070	48.1	.7770	41	crest
6.4043	48.1	.6931	45	denied
THE PRECEDING WORD TYPE OCCUPIES RANK 6700				
6.4043	48.1	.6718	46	echoes
6.4036	48.1	.6964	45	railway
6.4030	48.1	.7040	45	existing
6.3996	48.1	.7326	43	decorations
6.3958	48.1	.8144	39	jagged
6.3949	48.1	.7923	40	stormy
6.3901	48.1	.7435	42	fade
6.3890	48.1	.6881	45	Market
6.3881	48.1	.4876	57	Marco
6.3876	48.1	.6947	44	splashed
6.3861	48.1	.7255	43	kiss
6.3845	48.1	.5859	49	Beach
6.3828	48.1	.6916	45	experimenting
6.3827	48.1	.7434	42	humming
6.3816	48.0	.6415	47	groaned
6.3816	48.0	.6671	46	miners
6.3815	48.0	.5060	58	linen
6.3811	48.0	.6762	46	belly
6.3801	48.0	.5150	58	violet
6.3792	48.0	.7080	44	memories
6.3743	48.0	.6202	48	fighter
6.3722	48.0	.6603	47	leisure
6.3716	48.0	.6619	47	Office
6.3715	48.0	.7088	44	Life
6.3709	48.0	.5588	55	decades
6.3679	48.0	.5973	50	Plymouth
6.3655	48.0	.3766	73	celebrate
6.3647	48.0	.3804	74	holy
6.3646	48.0	.7390	42	greet
6.3613	48.0	.6801	46	immense
6.3612	48.0	.7785	40	juicy
6.3599	48.0	.7003	44	prayed
6.3598	48.0	.7233	43	forbidden
6.3598	48.0	.7241	43	twenty-one
6.3594	48.0	.6519	48	fundamental
6.3587	48.0	.5391	56	imported
6.3569	48.0	.7128	43	bravely
6.3533	48.0	.4789	56	Eric
6.3527	48.0	.7085	43	bait
6.3522	48.0	.6754	45	longed
6.3482	48.0	.5574	53	Herman
6.3473	48.0	.6758	45	secretly
6.3445	48.0	.8270	38	polish
6.3444	48.0	.7295	43	dial
6.3438	48.0	.7502	41	hoop
6.3438	48.0	.4973	59	issues
6.3420	48.0	.5650	53	conservation
6.3335	48.0	.5473	54	Pluto
6.3316	48.0	.6629	46	trappers
6.3309	48.0	.5981	51	Otto
6.3289	48.0	.6675	46	Barbara
6.3271	48.0	.2234	81	Nick
6.3259	48.0	.7414	42	shaken
6.3258	48.0	.6780	46	consult
6.3224	48.0	.7680	41	seventeenth
6.3210	48.0	.5781	53	foil
6.3157	48.0	.8233	38	dumped
6.3143	48.0	.7214	43	navy
6.3134	48.0	.6402	47	trader
6.3132	48.0	.6231	48	grief
6.3118	48.0	.1783	145	sh
6.3113	48.0	.7308	43	sparks
6.3109	48.0	.7642	41	achievements
6.3072	48.0	.8565	37	deals
6.3066	48.0	.8310	38	consequently
6.3050	48.0	.4560	64	dancers
6.3050	48.0	.7669	41	oval
6.3047	48.0	.6522	47	scouts
6.3036	48.0	.7779	40	sore
6.3018	48.0	.6506	47	breed
6.3004	48.0	.5544	54	concepts
6.2997	48.0	.7647	41	ninth
6.2992	48.0	.7515	41	Nature
6.2989	48.0	.5597	54	125
6.2975	48.0	.6548	46	grasshopper
6.2947	48.0	.6945	44	Second
6.2922	48.0	.6346	48	graduated
6.2922	48.0	.5137	57	livestock
6.2922	48.0	.5927	51	worthy
6.2920	48.0	.8024	39	gaining
6.2919	48.0	.6972	44	beets
6.2908	48.0	.5844	50	pistol
6.2899	48.0	.7241	42	glove
6.2898	48.0	.6224	49	addressed
6.2897	48.0	.7020	43	bitterly
6.2896	48.0	.2424	123	seam
6.2873	48.0	.6347	47	Sullivan
6.2861	48.0	.5727	52	expands
6.2806	48.0	.7157	43	burnt
6.2805	48.0	.6791	45	attic
6.2785	48.0	.6294	48	astronomy
6.2767	48.0	.7438	41	cornfield
6.2758	48.0	.6442	48	convenience
6.2729	48.0	.6145	48	jug
6.2698	48.0	.6151	48	trotted
6.2641	48.0	.5003	59	acids
6.2636	48.0	.7270	42	charcoal
6.2629	48.0	.6917	44	prisoners
6.2619	48.0	.5652	53	convention
6.2557	48.0	.6935	45	omitted
THE PRECEDING WORD TYPE OCCUPIES RANK 6800				
6.2551	48.0	.5429	55	72
6.2542	48.0	.7204	43	satisfying
6.2521	48.0	.7307	42	notion
6.2506	48.0	.4046	73	110
6.2504	48.0	.7927	39	comment
6.2466	48.0	.7862	39	shakes
6.2411	48.0	.5324	54	Teacher
6.2411	48.0	.6895	44	transport
6.2370	47.9	.7449	41	seaweed
6.2364	47.9	.8163	38	nursery
6.2334	47.9	.7726	40	seize
6.2322	47.9	.7667	40	lemonade
6.2314	47.9	.7026	44	widespread
6.2297	47.9	.7291	41	basement
6.2293	47.9	.6795	44	lately
6.2265	47.9	.5299	56	Christians
6.2252	47.9	.6901	44	builders
6.2209	47.9	.6869	44	alas
6.2194	47.9	.7164	42	bathroom
6.2192	47.9	.7220	42	humble
6.2191	47.9	.5285	56	System
6.2135	47.9	.6152	47	Anderson
6.2119	47.9	.5319	55	Caribbean
6.2103	47.9	.6557	46	weekend
6.2090	47.9	.5556	53	disk
6.2089	47.9	.5701	52	longitude
6.2045	47.9	.7944	39	comic
6.2040	47.9	.5201	57	64
6.2032	47.9	.7666	40	persuade
6.2029	47.9	.7182	42	shocked
6.2025	47.9	.6971	43	disaster
6.1990	47.9	.7709	40	transformed
6.1987	47.9	.7632	40	carts
6.1968	47.9	.6399	47	halls
6.1962	47.9	.6489	46	Minnesota
6.1961	47.9	.7462	41	gains
6.1918	47.9	.6860	44	locations
6.1915	47.9	.8134	38	deliberately
6.1878	47.9	.5159	57	cocoa
6.1878	47.9	.6188	48	ounce
6.1874	47.9	.6986	43	Madison
6.1868	47.9	.6164	46	Paul's
6.1864	47.9	.6053	47	skimming
6.1863	47.9	.6728	44	Herbert
6.1858	47.9	.3638	78	serving
6.1842	47.9	.7190	42	drawer
6.1832	47.9	.4463	58	catcher
6.1792	47.9	.6387	46	stealing
6.1786	47.9	.5925	50	photo
6.1770	47.9	.6254	47	Country
6.1713	47.9	.6641	44	helpers
6.1711	47.9	.7910	39	losses
6.1669	47.9	.4725	60	solids
6.1661	47.9	.4770	58	Yankees
6.1658	47.9	.7067	42	freezes
6.1638	47.9	.6861	43	lumps
6.1626	47.9	.7146	42	woolen
6.1606	47.9	.5700	51	tilted
6.1599	47.9	.7676	40	association
6.1588	47.9	.8285	37	confident
6.1559	47.9	.2862	92	vitamin
6.1558	47.9	.7847	39	instances
6.1540	47.9	.7076	42	olives
6.1534	47.9	.6707	44	whoever
6.1533	47.9	.7567	40	relax
6.1503	47.9	.5938	50	Czechoslovakia
6.1493	47.9	.6832	44	burden
6.1467	47.9	.2901	97	solo
6.1466	47.9	.5638	52	wildlife
6.1464	47.9	.7304	41	possessed
6.1451	47.9	.7325	41	admiration
6.1404	47.9	.6612	45	protested
6.1394	47.9	.7875	39	present-day
6.1360	47.9	.6912	43	firing
6.1342	47.9	.7288	41	huddled
6.1305	47.9	.7175	42	chips
6.1289	47.9	.4276	59	Hastings
6.1267	47.9	.7249	42	conventional
6.1258	47.9	.3042	88	Vietnam
6.1249	47.9	.7467	40	terrified
6.1248	47.9	.5085	56	Republican
6.1233	47.9	.6376	46	starfish
6.1220	47.9	.6492	45	fins
6.1208	47.9	.7249	41	ridden
6.1168	47.9	.6988	43	conclude
6.1155	47.9	.7142	42	Norwegian
6.1144	47.9	.5903	50	executive
6.1135	47.9	.5967	49	astronomer
6.1134	47.9	.3892	70	radioactive
6.1105	47.9	.6395	45	scratching
6.1103	47.9	.7767	39	tourist
6.1047	47.9	.6280	45	Allan
6.1045	47.9	.7047	42	creeping
6.1008	47.9	.7351	41	beetle
6.1006	47.9	.7180	41	attacking
6.0976	47.9	.7180	42	troublesome
6.0974	47.9	.8166	37	locks
6.0969	47.9	.6959	43	flourished
6.0968	47.9	.5794	51	museums
6.0949	47.8	.6278	46	lambs
THE PRECEDING WORD TYPE OCCUPIES RANK 6900				
6.0931	47.8	.7019	42	clam
6.0931	47.8	.7018	42	lifts
6.0904	47.8	.6770	43	junk
6.0893	47.8	.7661	39	elbows
6.0877	47.8	.1512	163	spellings
6.0832	47.8	.6773	43	amazement
6.0780	47.8	.6532	44	chuckled
6.0758	47.8	.6962	42	cloak
6.0733	47.8	.7667	39	uncertain
6.0728	47.8	.6818	44	distinctive
6.0711	47.8	.7406	40	brother's
6.0709	47.8	.7932	38	strictly
6.0687	47.8	.7424	40	shirts
6.0687	47.8	.6326	46	tapped
6.0685	47.8	.2640	75	Nathan
6.0679	47.8	.6603	45	comparisons
6.0671	47.8	.7708	39	discovering
6.0655	47.8	.6057	49	simplified
6.0629	47.8	.6727	44	pigeon
6.0551	47.8	.6845	43	carnival
6.0520	47.8	.7249	41	suspected
6.0476	47.8	.7036	42	athletes
6.0476	47.8	.7060	42	coals
6.0476	47.8	.5898	48	tornado
6.0466	47.8	.4726	57	Majesty
6.0462	47.8	.6841	43	surprisingly
6.0453	47.8	.6879	42	chiefs
6.0439	47.8	.7309	41	flexible
6.0408	47.8	.6460	45	cigarette
6.0399	47.8	.1095	188	suffixes
6.0346	47.8	.6534	45	skipping
6.0345	47.8	.6343	47	applying
6.0341	47.8	.7133	41	protecting
6.0339	47.8	.7682	39	thereby
6.0297	47.8	.5134	54	Assembly
6.0281	47.8	.6080	48	missionaries
6.0276	47.8	.6147	46	masts
6.0275	47.8	.5807	48	bugle
6.0234	47.8	.4531	59	Frost
6.0187	47.8	.6467	45	react
6.0181	47.8	.7014	41	strap
6.0151	47.8	.6885	43	jury
6.0148	47.8	.4689	59	Andes
6.0085	47.8	.6986	42	mounting
6.0052	47.8	.7218	41	Time
6.0047	47.8	.6771	43	kit
6.0047	47.8	.6593	44	refuge
6.0046	47.8	.7022	41	helper
6.0017	47.8	.8035	37	pines
5.9987	47.8	.7409	39	rocked
5.9961	47.8	.5954	46	helicopters

U	SFI	D	F	Word Type
5.9961	47.8	.7873	38	manufacturer
5.9926	47.8	.4783	59	exports
5.9912	47.8	.6374	44	relay
5.9903	47.8	.7834	38	tended
5.9890	47.8	.7616	39	appreciation
5.9887	47.8	.6921	42	kittens
5.9872	47.8	.5915	46	cheered
5.9854	47.8	.4494	62	paints
5.9844	47.8	.0000	131	Candita
5.9823	47.8	.7438	40	efficiency
5.9820	47.8	.6928	42	smoothed
5.9781	47.8	.7821	38	watery
5.9747	47.8	.6004	47	murmured
5.9729	47.8	.7168	41	axle
5.9727	47.8	.7188	41	traces
5.9721	47.8	.7502	39	balcony
5.9712	47.8	.6397	45	paved
5.9689	47.8	.3944	68	graphs
5.9686	47.8	.4593	62	linking
5.9669	47.8	.6139	45	Parker
5.9666	47.8	.7338	40	caution
5.9657	47.8	.6618	43	beavers
5.9636	47.8	.5982	48	attach
5.9623	47.8	.6328	44	hound
5.9601	47.8	.7086	41	embarrassed
5.9589	47.8	.7422	39	splashing
5.9579	47.8	.7097	41	pursuit
5.9578	47.8	.7229	40	drifting
5.9563	47.7	.5272	51	buggy
5.9556	47.7	.3452	74	Milky
5.9547	47.7	.6386	44	runaway
5.9531	47.7	.5512	51	coasts
5.9518	47.7	.6538	44	curly
5.9495	47.7	.7194	40	luckily
5.9483	47.7	.7238	40	meantime
5.9473	47.7	.6943	41	stillness
5.9455	47.7	.7513	39	spruce
5.9454	47.7	.7603	39	puppet
5.9454	47.7	.6832	42	shattered
5.9436	47.7	.6987	41	jolly
5.9410	47.7	.4932	56	lettuce
5.9382	47.7	.7094	41	gleaming
5.9363	47.7	.6663	42	cricket
5.9361	47.7	.7266	40	consent
5.9341	47.7	.7148	40	secrets
5.9338	47.7	.6442	43	crows
5.9322	47.7	.7737	38	outdoor
5.9312	47.7	.7767	38	arrangements
5.9291	47.7	.6494	45	classic
THE PRECEDING WORD TYPE OCCUPIES RANK 7000				
5.9289	47.7	.6423	45	explanations
5.9286	47.7	.6521	45	acceptable
5.9277	47.7	.6657	43	snails
5.9248	47.7	.6703	42	howling
5.9246	47.7	.6962	42	adjacent
5.9240	47.7	.7041	41	bows
5.9238	47.7	.5797	49	bulletin
5.9225	47.7	.6681	43	rugs
5.9224	47.7	.3856	63	Charlotte
5.9193	47.7	.7303	40	invaders
5.9168	47.7	.4547	59	nut
5.9165	47.7	.7004	41	jammed
5.9153	47.7	.5230	51	lighthouse
5.9149	47.7	.5483	51	tropics
5.9145	47.7	.5205	53	descendants
5.9138	47.7	.6816	42	Southwest
5.9115	47.7	.7455	39	Cleveland
5.9103	47.7	.5444	52	54
5.9102	47.7	.5340	51	aye
5.9086	47.7	.7195	40	tumbling
5.9076	47.7	.8196	36	surround
5.9064	47.7	.7290	40	agencies
5.9061	47.7	.5431	52	Party
5.9059	47.7	.6817	42	beg
5.9058	47.7	.7472	39	yearly
5.9051	47.7	.5174	54	populated
5.9047	47.7	.2896	85	pearl
5.9029	47.7	.6639	43	specially
5.9028	47.7	.6577	43	ton
5.9023	47.7	.6049	47	vinegar
5.9009	47.7	.7257	40	one-third
5.9005	47.7	.6822	42	unseen
5.8990	47.7	.6097	46	Farmer
5.8911	47.7	.8395	35	concentration
5.8909	47.7	.7608	38	frosty
5.8899	47.7	.5741	49	Kingdom
5.8884	47.7	.7113	41	similarities
5.8838	47.7	.7322	39	pedal
5.8800	47.7	.6297	46	heritage
5.8782	47.7	.5868	49	spiritual
5.8775	47.7	.5807	48	nostrils
5.8767	47.7	.7411	39	restored
5.8749	47.7	.7150	40	Lincoln's
5.8744	47.7	.7156	40	loading
5.8737	47.7	.5608	46	pajamas
5.8732	47.7	.6668	43	gestures
5.8725	47.7	.6278	45	restaurants
5.8719	47.7	.8118	36	erect
5.8701	47.7	.6227	46	replacing
5.8687	47.7	.7402	39	amateur
5.8675	47.7	.7288	40	indirect
5.8661	47.7	.5320	49	Mayor
5.8647	47.7	.6262	44	Boone
5.8637	47.7	.7120	40	conscience
5.8620	47.7	.7595	38	Lane
5.8571	47.7	.6911	41	Brooklyn
5.8561	47.7	.7619	38	concluded
5.8561	47.7	.7014	41	distinction
5.8548	47.7	.7025	40	bump
5.8528	47.7	.7006	41	awarded
5.8520	47.7	.6304	45	populations
5.8504	47.7	.7610	38	climbs
5.8504	47.7	.3056	88	prepositional
5.8491	47.7	.7924	37	analyze
5.8489	47.7	.5413	50	Jane's
5.8485	47.7	.6469	44	agents
5.8445	47.7	.4270	64	allowance
5.8391	47.7	.7773	37	slightest
5.8373	47.7	.6177	46	decade
5.8368	47.7	.7799	37	downhill
5.8333	47.7	.8299	35	fir
5.8325	47.7	.5982	46	screaming
5.8316	47.7	.6625	43	drain
5.8297	47.7	.6921	41	horror
5.8290	47.7	.5710	49	Committee
5.8281	47.7	.7324	39	advised
5.8275	47.7	.7206	39	fights
5.8273	47.7	.8036	36	witness
5.8270	47.7	.5017	53	descended
5.8256	47.7	.4448	61	fourths
5.8238	47.7	.6834	42	convert
5.8232	47.7	.7297	39	Bridge
5.8219	47.7	.7596	38	Third
5.8212	47.7	.6072	47	artistic
5.8209	47.6	.6557	43	specimen
5.8196	47.6	.7296	39	wholly
5.8180	47.6	.6227	45	fluffy
5.8180	47.6	.7442	38	sinking
5.8172	47.6	.7226	39	crews
5.8167	47.6	.6878	41	frown
5.8147	47.6	.7142	40	weekly
5.8145	47.6	.8338	35	weakness
5.8135	47.6	.6503	42	gee
5.8126	47.6	.7126	40	sucking
5.8122	47.6	.6983	40	Billy's
5.8122	47.6	.7734	37	grove
5.8077	47.6	.7473	38	bullets
5.8055	47.6	.7105	40	suggestion
5.8046	47.6	.6873	41	backyard
5.8042	47.6	.6797	42	mature
THE PRECEDING WORD TYPE OCCUPIES RANK 7100				
5.8035	47.6	.6522	42	moccasins
5.7965	47.6	.4848	53	Senators
5.7917	47.6	.5554	50	choices
5.7890	47.6	.4443	62	phonograph
5.7874	47.6	.6193	45	Continental
5.7863	47.6	.2707	68	Cadillac
5.7852	47.6	.5164	54	compose
5.7814	47.6	.5989	46	guided
5.7805	47.6	.7676	37	boys'
5.7803	47.6	.7509	38	resembles
5.7801	47.6	.5465	51	cultural
5.7793	47.6	.6994	40	Camp
5.7787	47.6	.7469	38	miniature
5.7786	47.6	.5805	48	99
5.7769	47.6	.6423	42	darted
5.7752	47.6	.6928	41	oral
5.7712	47.6	.7970	36	comparatively
5.7696	47.6	.6203	44	furious
5.7621	47.6	.7512	38	stocks
5.7615	47.6	.6898	40	ankle
5.7600	47.6	.5034	54	punch
5.7599	47.6	.6419	43	richest
5.7589	47.6	.6048	46	binding
5.7588	47.6	.6074	46	Project
5.7587	47.6	.8134	35	fireworks
5.7585	47.6	.7755	37	nicely
5.7572	47.6	.6098	46	ownership
5.7571	47.6	.5391	51	Berlin
5.7532	47.6	.6660	42	Rico
5.7519	47.6	.6878	41	achievement
5.7517	47.6	.6586	42	stockings
5.7504	47.6	.7010	40	uncovered
5.7497	47.6	.7689	37	kills
5.7491	47.6	.6649	42	oath
5.7491	47.6	.7431	38	recalled
5.7479	47.6	.6638	42	Eskimo
5.7479	47.6	.6531	42	galloped
5.7473	47.6	.5832	45	footprints
5.7455	47.6	.3030	87	rhythmic
5.7444	47.6	.6706	42	dedicated
5.7438	47.6	.6836	41	Earl
5.7427	47.6	.5819	47	magnifying
5.7419	47.6	.2590	91	nickels
5.7415	47.6	.6457	42	Officer
5.7414	47.6	.6273	42	harpoon
5.7413	47.6	.6592	41	Sioux
5.7396	47.6	.5509	48	Inca
5.7380	47.6	.6784	41	chatter
5.7373	47.6	.6620	42	reminds
5.7353	47.6	.6971	40	murder
5.7351	47.6	.3768	68	amphibians
5.7327	47.6	.7934	36	involve
5.7311	47.6	.6104	45	laboratories
5.7304	47.6	.6471	42	flapping
5.7303	47.6	.6379	44	88
5.7295	47.6	.7260	39	41
5.7286	47.6	.6340	44	Frenchmen
5.7239	47.6	.6904	40	bounced
5.7238	47.6	.5385	49	Holmes
5.7236	47.6	.6296	44	moon's
5.7229	47.6	.7390	38	ambition
5.7221	47.6	.7345	38	recess
5.7219	47.6	.5837	47	Dear
5.7215	47.6	.6720	41	hearty
5.7215	47.6	.6301	43	schoolhouse
5.7211	47.6	.5502	49	barber
5.7194	47.6	.7420	38	democratic
5.7186	47.6	.3692	68	Portugal
5.7170	47.6	.7533	37	subway
5.7155	47.6	.6802	40	switched
5.7140	47.6	.7366	38	loyal
5.7139	47.6	.7066	39	sponges
5.7104	47.6	.7354	38	refined
5.7090	47.6	.7403	38	clearer
5.7089	47.6	.7206	38	tusks
5.7077	47.6	.6375	43	lawyers
5.7063	47.6	.7665	37	applies
5.7023	47.6	.5655	49	sketches
5.6997	47.6	.4960	54	probability
5.6996	47.6	.6819	40	stooped
5.6903	47.6	.5996	45	Hawaiian
5.6891	47.6	.7067	39	chattering
5.6883	47.5	.7495	37	downstream
5.6883	47.5	.7535	37	snarled
5.6863	47.5	.5948	44	Gary
5.6834	47.5	.7860	36	appearing
5.6829	47.5	.7496	37	boldly
5.6823	47.5	.5689	47	swims
5.6822	47.5	.4297	59	tidal
5.6813	47.5	.7554	37	fatal
5.6813	47.5	.5368	50	legislature
5.6802	47.5	.6876	40	relieved
5.6782	47.5	.6902	40	pebble
5.6769	47.5	.7809	36	completes
5.6755	47.5	.7522	37	fears
5.6746	47.5	.6617	42	experimental
5.6740	47.5	.7464	37	sofa
5.6735	47.5	.6941	40	Woods
5.6733	47.5	.4178	60	sperm
5.6732	47.5	.6793	41	wisely
THE PRECEDING WORD TYPE OCCUPIES RANK 7200				
5.6725	47.5	.8341	34	destroying
5.6721	47.5	.5143	51	Declaration
5.6718	47.5	.5488	49	Revolutionary
5.6664	47.5	.6078	43	rowed
5.6663	47.5	.6913	40	regret
5.6659	47.5	.5027	52	brightness
5.6640	47.5	.6338	43	gigantic
5.6613	47.5	.5080	52	believes
5.6572	47.5	.5611	47	wounds
5.6565	47.5	.7222	38	slippers
5.6556	47.5	.6273	42	poked
5.6530	47.5	.7468	37	eldest
5.6523	47.5	.4225	62	diagonal
5.6519	47.5	.5014	48	Peggy
5.6495	47.5	.7383	38	translated
5.6492	47.5	.4266	60	calcium
5.6490	47.5	.3653	68	plankton
5.6476	47.5	.4802	55	Manhattan
5.6475	47.5	.7571	37	hike
5.6462	47.5	.7760	36	foam
5.6446	47.5	.5265	48	Scrooge
5.6445	47.5	.7835	36	awareness
5.6403	47.5	.7461	37	recover
5.6393	47.5	.6104	44	thicker
5.6387	47.5	.4897	53	molten
5.6359	47.5	.6256	43	Group
5.6353	47.5	.7518	37	modest
5.6345	47.5	.4074	64	Patsy
5.6330	47.5	.6381	43	barriers
5.6324	47.5	.6956	40	slanting
5.6320	47.5	.7086	39	arrested
5.6315	47.5	.2408	102	synonyms
5.6270	47.5	.7053	39	baby's
5.6262	47.5	.8522	33	boot
5.6249	47.5	.2163	106	Beauty
5.6230	47.5	.6546	42	emotion
5.6217	47.5	.7331	38	62
5.6201	47.5	.6904	40	memorize
5.6195	47.5	.6489	41	cradle
5.6194	47.5	.7121	39	44
5.6180	47.5	.7147	38	fry
5.6177	47.5	.7543	37	enlarged
5.6154	47.5	.5418	49	Africans
5.6150	47.5	.7359	37	foggy
5.6142	47.5	.7335	38	altered
5.6142	47.5	.6788	40	slim
5.6122	47.5	.7706	36	maker
5.6076	47.5	.7672	36	cooks
5.6074	47.5	.6891	40	launch
5.5977	47.5	.6729	40	crabs
5.5956	47.5	.6684	40	pier
5.5950	47.5	.3900	64	algae
5.5944	47.5	.2556	93	Romeo
5.5930	47.5	.6078	44	skeletons
5.5923	47.5	.6538	42	influences
5.5918	47.5	.6990	39	laundry
5.5917	47.5	.6761	39	fireman
5.5898	47.5	.6951	39	whistles
5.5885	47.5	.6302	43	colleges
5.5867	47.5	.3862	68	modify
5.5855	47.5	.6050	44	ranchers
5.5842	47.5	.6887	40	cooperation
5.5841	47.5	.4658	55	Hitler
5.5832	47.5	.4414	53	Chris
5.5826	47.5	.6274	43	beetles
5.5808	47.5	.6954	39	paddles
5.5808	47.5	.7284	38	relate
5.5803	47.5	.5254	50	city's
5.5756	47.5	.6118	43	inning
5.5739	47.5	.7615	36	perch
5.5725	47.5	.7009	38	robber
5.5711	47.5	.7191	38	viewed
5.5707	47.5	.6151	44	graduate
5.5706	47.5	.2083	103	heaven
5.5695	47.5	.8415	33	ninety
5.5665	47.5	.6328	43	Scottish
5.5663	47.5	.6506	41	loom
5.5655	47.5	.5924	44	panic
5.5654	47.5	.7320	37	respected
5.5652	47.5	.5486	48	appetite
5.5643	47.5	.7111	38	stray
5.5606	47.5	.8114	34	amusement
5.5595	47.5	.4202	54	Elmer
5.5592	47.5	.5008	52	meats
5.5583	47.4	.4333	58	gills
5.5579	47.4	.6794	39	Hawk
5.5570	47.4	.4960	51	pea
5.5538	47.4	.7322	37	hire
5.5535	47.4	.5352	46	Clyde
5.5534	47.4	.6329	41	colonel
5.5534	47.4	.7393	37	laughs
5.5521	47.4	.6857	40	studio
5.5515	47.4	.7467	36	bowling
5.5495	47.4	.7833	35	impatient
5.5475	47.4	.7582	36	ash
5.5475	47.4	.6780	40	responded
5.5470	47.4	.7847	35	cracking
5.5450	47.4	.7774	35	cares
5.5444	47.4	.3046	76	Amazon
5.5438	47.4	.7574	36	surprises
THE PRECEDING WORD TYPE OCCUPIES RANK 7300				
5.5433	47.4	.7167	38	humid
5.5404	47.4	.7349	37	sleek
5.5362	47.4	.6544	41	perspiration
5.5355	47.4	.6126	44	poetic
5.5336	47.4	.7452	36	crane
5.5302	47.4	.7271	37	sheltered
5.5292	47.4	.5423	48	flowering
5.5292	47.4	.7842	35	heaviest
5.5285	47.4	.7320	37	Field
5.5283	47.4	.7539	36	cling
5.5280	47.4	.6881	39	whispering
5.5268	47.4	.4031	62	$5
5.5261	47.4	.7169	38	two-thirds
5.5229	47.4	.6554	40	driver's
5.5211	47.4	.5623	48	origins
5.5195	47.4	.8040	34	honors
5.5149	47.4	.4045	65	ingredients
5.5136	47.4	.7605	36	sweeps
5.5107	47.4	.6495	41	resolved
5.5102	47.4	.1386	136	replacement
5.5079	47.4	.6723	40	outlines
5.5057	47.4	.5727	43	alley
5.5054	47.4	.6764	39	shivering
5.5044	47.4	.6291	41	author's
5.5032	47.4	.6300	42	twilight
5.5019	47.4	.6986	38	begging
5.5016	47.4	.3266	72	Penny
5.4998	47.4	.6504	41	physically
5.4997	47.4	.3087	71	telescopes
5.4968	47.4	.6895	38	bombs
5.4964	47.4	.5592	47	sprinkle
5.4961	47.4	.6352	41	ferry
5.4951	47.4	.2903	81	proteins
5.4905	47.4	.6911	39	enclosed
5.4904	47.4	.6913	39	Range
5.4903	47.4	.6752	40	Science
5.4902	47.4	.6046	43	rapids
5.4880	47.4	.4727	55	meters
5.4869	47.4	.6432	40	shack
5.4855	47.4	.5859	45	survival
5.4854	47.4	.3206	77	trumpet
5.4849	47.4	.6955	38	suspicious
5.4822	47.4	.5035	49	Antarctic
5.4819	47.4	.7123	38	possess
5.4803	47.4	.6732	40	bond
5.4788	47.4	.4447	50	Hector
5.4778	47.4	.6771	39	rust
5.4741	47.4	.7750	35	newest
5.4710	47.4	.6736	40	conquest
5.4710	47.4	.8026	34	judging
5.4699	47.4	.5754	46	labels
5.4690	47.4	.4714	55	3/8
5.4679	47.4	.6371	41	voyages
5.4666	47.4	.6404	41	lover
5.4664	47.4	.5277	48	latitudes
5.4633	47.4	.6340	41	leaping
5.4618	47.4	.4454	57	administration
5.4616	47.4	.7685	35	winners
5.4609	47.4	.7991	34	quilt
5.4604	47.4	.6312	42	Territory
5.4590	47.4	.5232	50	IV
5.4587	47.4	.7523	36	eliminate
5.4585	47.4	.6534	41	synthetic
5.4581	47.4	.7128	37	twinkle
5.4541	47.4	.6852	39	aged
5.4539	47.4	.6762	39	endure
5.4533	47.4	.4515	57	350
5.4510	47.4	.6395	40	Clarence
5.4490	47.4	.8202	33	birch
5.4480	47.4	.0502	227	subtraction
5.4475	47.4	.6853	38	dumb
5.4473	47.4	.6293	42	oils
5.4464	47.4	.7688	35	calculated
5.4456	47.4	.7775	35	105
5.4454	47.4	.4586	55	fig
5.4450	47.4	.5144	49	migration
5.4426	47.4	.6609	40	levers
5.4420	47.4	.6424	40	blossom
5.4408	47.4	.6995	38	castles
5.4396	47.4	.6144	43	reasoning
5.4395	47.4	.5442	46	Bird
5.4391	47.4	.6539	40	lodge
5.4380	47.4	.6360	40	Ann's
5.4380	47.4	.7270	37	incredible
5.4369	47.4	.7416	36	clump
5.4363	47.4	.5357	47	Dance
5.4352	47.4	.5706	43	taxi
5.4316	47.3	.4890	51	harbors
5.4316	47.3	.7495	36	startling
5.4300	47.3	.4986	47	mat
5.4278	47.3	.6765	39	batteries
5.4272	47.3	.5201	48	ma'am
5.4250	47.3	.7686	35	finer
5.4211	47.3	.7641	35	fished
5.4187	47.3	.7266	37	accomplish
5.4180	47.3	.7738	35	successive
5.4156	47.3	.7621	35	reflection
5.4149	47.3	.7684	35	spine
5.4146	47.3	.6069	42	doughnuts
5.4142	47.3	.4508	57	fiber
THE PRECEDING WORD TYPE OCCUPIES RANK 7400				
5.4141	47.3	.5318	47	patent
5.4140	47.3	.6599	40	best-known
5.4127	47.3	.6626	39	horrible
5.4124	47.3	.3137	77	kernel
5.4107	47.3	.7234	37	concentrate
5.4107	47.3	.7186	36	Hood
5.4092	47.3	.4600	52	onions
5.4075	47.3	.7452	36	distinctly
5.4057	47.3	.3784	66	Stuart
5.4052	47.3	.4875	48	Mama's
5.4033	47.3	.7199	36	wink
5.4030	47.3	.6773	38	sped
5.3981	47.3	.6560	40	opposition
5.3971	47.3	.6385	40	propeller

U	SFI	D	F	Word Type
5.3964	47.3	.7537	35	seventy-five
5.3963	47.3	.6610	39	fairies
5.3954	47.3	.6815	38	Roy
5.3949	47.3	.3723	66	Georgie
5.3933	47.3	.6359	41	1956
5.3931	47.3	.2208	103	nutrients
5.3923	47.3	.5695	45	angel
5.3917	47.3	.6339	42	alternate
5.3900	47.3	.6598	40	educational
5.3857	47.3	.7084	37	odors
5.3854	47.3	.6736	38	swords
5.3837	47.3	.3503	71	abbreviations
5.3823	47.3	.5718	45	productive
5.3816	47.3	.5561	46	textiles
5.3812	47.3	.4132	54	thanked
5.3798	47.3	.5333	46	gypsy
5.3792	47.3	.4688	51	stubborn
5.3790	47.3	.6589	39	canyons
5.3766	47.3	.5952	42	eagles
5.3766	47.3	.5822	42	wharf
5.3762	47.3	.8114	33	apt
5.3761	47.3	.1901	109	multiplying
5.3747	47.3	.7043	37	necks
5.3724	47.3	.4984	49	mushrooms
5.3721	47.3	.6381	41	processing
5.3717	47.3	.6156	41	nervously
5.3716	47.3	.6562	39	obeyed
5.3712	47.3	.5521	46	craftsmen
5.3712	47.3	.7060	37	deposit
5.3700	47.3	.4768	52	carrots
5.3695	47.3	.7098	37	lawns
5.3688	47.3	.6921	37	Lieutenant
5.3681	47.3	.6531	39	stump
5.3680	47.3	.6938	38	powdered
5.3679	47.3	.5975	41	Ray
5.3664	47.3	.6965	37	tumbled
5.3652	47.3	.6913	38	expense
5.3634	47.3	.4318	56	Confederate
5.3625	47.3	.7517	35	hostile
5.3614	47.3	.7161	37	Arabic
5.3589	47.3	.7261	36	myths
5.3587	47.3	.7336	36	leaps
5.3584	47.3	.8108	33	acquire
5.3577	47.3	.5982	43	counts
5.3548	47.3	.6325	41	Morocco
5.3535	47.3	.6518	39	pleaded
5.3524	47.3	.8373	32	insist
5.3522	47.3	.6684	39	1948
5.3514	47.3	.5471	46	welcomed
5.3469	47.3	.5054	48	beloved
5.3436	47.3	.4471	56	47
5.3413	47.3	.6698	39	ranging
5.3408	47.3	.5109	49	meridian
5.3377	47.3	.6201	41	thrilling
5.3307	47.3	.7248	36	organizing
5.3297	47.3	.6131	42	Broadway
5.3257	47.3	.5607	45	Mister
5.3256	47.3	.7260	36	creep
5.3242	47.3	.3942	63	classical
5.3238	47.3	.6064	42	happenings
5.3217	47.3	.6911	37	treasures
5.3215	47.3	.7326	36	absent
5.3212	47.3	.7211	36	flap
5.3209	47.3	.7675	34	ridiculous
5.3206	47.3	.6245	40	anyhow
5.3191	47.3	.5399	45	Newton
5.3191	47.3	.7256	36	rude
5.3161	47.3	.7712	34	chewed
5.3150	47.3	.5592	45	Stanley
5.3149	47.3	.7738	34	one-fourth
5.3141	47.3	.5777	44	circulation
5.3116	47.3	.6401	41	convey
5.3103	47.3	.6027	43	dialogue
5.3100	47.3	.7711	34	Post
5.3073	47.2	.6684	39	History
5.3058	47.2	.5814	44	lemon
5.2983	47.2	.8014	33	courtesy
5.2956	47.2	.5858	44	novels
5.2955	47.2	.6494	39	blackboard
5.2950	47.2	.7621	34	trailing
5.2949	47.2	.5594	45	District
5.2938	47.2	.7075	36	plowing
5.2930	47.2	.8262	32	announce
5.2860	47.2	.5647	45	drilled
5.2850	47.2	.5944	43	medieval
5.2844	47.2	.7210	36	87

THE PRECEDING WORD TYPE OCCUPIES RANK 7500

U	SFI	D	F	Word Type
5.2821	47.2	.7002	37	margins
5.2819	47.2	.6779	38	expeditions
5.2768	47.2	.5978	40	salvage
5.2757	47.2	.7781	34	emphasize
5.2747	47.2	.7003	37	villain
5.2731	47.2	.6304	40	Whitney
5.2709	47.2	.8243	32	450
5.2699	47.2	.7068	37	essentially
5.2695	47.2	.7267	35	nickname
5.2649	47.2	.4069	59	organic
5.2647	47.2	.5763	42	Wind
5.2641	47.2	.7244	36	spiral
5.2625	47.2	.6385	40	1954
5.2622	47.2	.6492	39	bouncing
5.2607	47.2	.6593	39	ammunition
5.2575	47.2	.6479	40	recommended
5.2567	47.2	.5293	43	Shirley
5.2556	47.2	.5757	41	stroked
5.2556	47.2	.6938	36	suitcase
5.2552	47.2	.6769	38	bid
5.2551	47.2	.6732	38	assemble
5.2549	47.2	.6740	38	Jordan
5.2535	47.2	.4389	52	Pasteur
5.2533	47.2	.5480	45	petals
5.2490	47.2	.6782	38	acute
5.2475	47.2	.4449	55	singer
5.2474	47.2	.4099	58	Palestine
5.2469	47.2	.6917	37	desks
5.2456	47.2	.7108	36	promising
5.2442	47.2	.4573	49	reread
5.2426	47.2	.5162	49	recipe
5.2407	47.2	.3391	70	painter
5.2393	47.2	.5780	43	Iceland
5.2367	47.2	.6713	37	tailor
5.2356	47.2	.5879	43	Jenny
5.2341	47.2	.6549	38	glider
5.2338	47.2	.7281	35	brow
5.2332	47.2	.8103	32	outcome
5.2331	47.2	.4403	54	soils
5.2304	47.2	.7349	35	Hills
5.2269	47.2	.0264	265	denominator
5.2264	47.2	.7630	34	associate
5.2246	47.2	.5620	45	posters
5.2244	47.2	.3623	58	Turtle
5.2216	47.2	.6708	37	dragging
5.2212	47.2	.7632	34	confined
5.2146	47.2	.7598	34	astonishing
5.2145	47.2	.6154	41	Class
5.2144	47.2	.4961	48	Silver
5.2132	47.2	.0090	314	quotient
5.2113	47.2	.6797	37	mornings
5.2108	47.2	.7073	36	hips
5.2107	47.2	.7048	36	bursting
5.2093	47.2	.7389	35	desires
5.2092	47.2	.5786	43	zones
5.2079	47.2	.6658	38	encounter
5.2072	47.2	.5680	42	Sammy
5.2070	47.2	.7785	33	pains
5.2062	47.2	.4916	50	adjusted
5.2038	47.2	.7005	36	watered
5.2014	47.2	.7423	34	iceberg
5.1977	47.2	.6110	40	peering
5.1976	47.2	.7143	36	sixteenth
5.1967	47.2	.6056	41	1861
5.1962	47.2	.6031	40	schoolroom
5.1959	47.2	.7188	36	omit
5.1949	47.2	.6843	37	swallows
5.1933	47.2	.5436	44	magician
5.1929	47.2	.7244	35	firewood
5.1929	47.2	.5842	40	ram
5.1910	47.2	.8075	32	destination
5.1896	47.2	.6853	37	phase
5.1885	47.2	.7430	34	Patty
5.1866	47.1	.6354	40	86
5.1850	47.1	.6572	38	listens
5.1843	47.1	.6067	40	shawl
5.1839	47.1	.5991	42	establishment
5.1828	47.1	.6225	40	scraps
5.1827	47.1	.5681	44	La
5.1823	47.1	.6145	39	donkeys
5.1822	47.1	.6787	37	Square
5.1797	47.1	.7505	34	provisions
5.1792	47.1	.6958	36	sadness
5.1790	47.1	.6684	38	benches
5.1717	47.1	.5158	46	grandparents
5.1712	47.1	.6400	39	gaze
5.1690	47.1	.7435	34	Five
5.1670	47.1	.6488	39	literary
5.1669	47.1	.7552	34	reveals
5.1664	47.1	.7657	33	gaily
5.1658	47.1	.6130	41	equality
5.1655	47.1	.5850	41	Galileo
5.1653	47.1	.7444	34	brushing
5.1652	47.1	.4490	54	groove
5.1622	47.1	.2981	75	Bessie
5.1595	47.1	.7734	33	woodland
5.1588	47.1	.5165	47	stake
5.1578	47.1	.5780	43	scrap
5.1562	47.1	.7602	33	worrying
5.1546	47.1	.6310	40	sole

THE PRECEDING WORD TYPE OCCUPIES RANK 7600

U	SFI	D	F	Word Type
5.1545	47.1	.2438	64	Gabby
5.1543	47.1	.5837	40	tramp
5.1527	47.1	.6675	37	couch
5.1510	47.1	.6100	41	warfare
5.1501	47.1	.5970	42	management
5.1498	47.1	.5419	43	jeep
5.1488	47.1	.6521	38	robe
5.1487	47.1	.5719	43	Charley
5.1483	47.1	.7197	35	sacks
5.1474	47.1	.7443	34	evenings
5.1466	47.1	.6115	40	All
5.1430	47.1	.7135	35	snapping
5.1428	47.1	.6626	38	elementary
5.1424	47.1	.7497	34	restore
5.1422	47.1	.7454	34	twenty-six
5.1408	47.1	.7231	35	positively
5.1397	47.1	.7471	34	isolation
5.1396	47.1	.7661	33	Caesar
5.1392	47.1	.6828	37	68
5.1385	47.1	.7238	35	ambitious
5.1372	47.1	.5998	41	fuels
5.1371	47.1	.7649	33	bleeding
5.1350	47.1	.5878	42	terminal
5.1346	47.1	.6214	40	youngsters
5.1334	47.1	.7702	33	athlete
5.1326	47.1	.6944	36	scrub
5.1290	47.1	.4415	51	Gretel
5.1286	47.1	.6531	38	volunteers
5.1260	47.1	.2244	100	rhythms
5.1202	47.1	.6602	37	booming
5.1169	47.1	.4804	48	Spot
5.1167	47.1	.4806	45	Sara
5.1156	47.1	.1986	101	$1
5.1146	47.1	.6861	36	stacked
5.1137	47.1	.5286	45	harvested
5.1135	47.1	.6809	37	roller
5.1124	47.1	.6148	40	Jr
5.1112	47.1	.6339	39	1940
5.1096	47.1	.7442	34	allowing
5.1087	47.1	.6135	40	bulbs
5.1084	47.1	.7067	35	crooked
5.1078	47.1	.6376	39	annually
5.1074	47.1	.7644	33	richer
5.1071	47.1	.6497	38	comrades
5.1020	47.1	.6325	39	channels
5.1019	47.1	.2422	93	morpheme
5.1015	47.1	.6978	35	rag
5.0993	47.1	.7093	35	ginger
5.0980	47.1	.7372	34	china
5.0975	47.1	.7187	35	injuries
5.0966	47.1	.5529	44	plastics
5.0915	47.1	.7263	34	steamboat
5.0912	47.1	.6593	37	101
5.0905	47.1	.7640	33	assist
5.0898	47.1	.4542	52	What
5.0888	47.1	.5350	44	crouched
5.0876	47.1	.6696	37	How
5.0862	47.1	.6361	39	conference
5.0860	47.1	.6336	38	Festival
5.0855	47.1	.4276	50	Chester
5.0832	47.1	.5766	42	atmospheric
5.0825	47.1	.6198	39	swollen
5.0806	47.1	.7466	33	battered
5.0794	47.1	.6040	41	reform
5.0791	47.1	.5971	40	Garden
5.0769	47.1	.6377	38	trailer
5.0766	47.1	.5508	44	festivals
5.0749	47.1	.6890	36	glare
5.0720	47.1	.7033	35	departure
5.0718	47.1	.4978	46	Baba
5.0712	47.1	.6673	37	interfere
5.0712	47.1	.7313	34	Space
5.0705	47.1	.6209	38	Claus
5.0704	47.1	.4971	46	Peters
5.0695	47.0	.6979	35	fists
5.0694	47.0	.2032	107	plurals
5.0687	47.0	.8461	30	outlined
5.0684	47.0	.7602	33	challenged
5.0675	47.0	.6324	38	punished
5.0666	47.0	.5532	44	53
5.0654	47.0	.7076	35	courageous
5.0653	47.0	.4735	49	medicines
5.0649	47.0	.6132	38	Papa's
5.0616	47.0	.4641	48	Chuck
5.0615	47.0	.7849	32	weakened
5.0610	47.0	.6708	37	loops
5.0586	47.0	.2995	72	dressing
5.0584	47.0	.7262	34	exploded
5.0577	47.0	.6786	36	uniforms
5.0568	47.0	.2508	90	tempo
5.0566	47.0	.6488	38	broadcasting
5.0532	47.0	.6565	37	frying
5.0524	47.0	.6418	38	cupboard
5.0520	47.0	.2022	81	Stephen
5.0512	47.0	.6510	37	nap
5.0507	47.0	.7161	34	thieves
5.0489	47.0	.4402	53	stallion
5.0485	47.0	.7788	32	lofty
5.0468	47.0	.6456	38	dislike
5.0451	47.0	.7620	33	eliminated

THE PRECEDING WORD TYPE OCCUPIES RANK 7700

U	SFI	D	F	Word Type
5.0449	47.0	.6116	39	deeds
5.0437	47.0	.7029	35	disappearing
5.0434	47.0	.7238	34	blaze
5.0430	47.0	.6863	36	approved
5.0423	47.0	.6540	37	alarmed
5.0420	47.0	.6490	37	rake
5.0418	47.0	.8084	31	flaps
5.0417	47.0	.6370	37	impatiently
5.0417	47.0	.7221	34	slips
5.0374	47.0	.8058	31	destructive
5.0356	47.0	.7299	34	breathes
5.0350	47.0	.7172	34	alligator
5.0340	47.0	.7163	34	amused
5.0340	47.0	.6262	39	loosely
5.0333	47.0	.6845	35	teasing
5.0331	47.0	.6231	39	prevents
5.0322	47.0	.6050	40	fading
5.0306	47.0	.6811	36	Harris
5.0305	47.0	.6573	37	lovers
5.0278	47.0	.6111	40	hast
5.0233	47.0	.7287	34	dependable
5.0228	47.0	.6636	37	Grace
5.0216	47.0	.5007	46	marker
5.0206	47.0	.5716	42	sidewalks
5.0204	47.0	.7007	35	rustling
5.0200	47.0	.7727	32	plum
5.0177	47.0	.6466	36	fixing
5.0173	47.0	.6445	38	heel
5.0171	47.0	.7733	32	doubtful
5.0156	47.0	.5332	45	Edwards
5.0153	47.0	.7310	34	160
5.0145	47.0	.7086	35	spaced
5.0139	47.0	.7496	33	descent
5.0139	47.0	.6524	37	plump
5.0137	47.0	.4668	50	bonds
5.0136	47.0	.5803	41	Magellan
5.0103	47.0	.6072	40	physician
5.0096	47.0	.7430	33	hog
5.0080	47.0	.5348	44	hotels
5.0077	47.0	.8061	31	affection
5.0047	47.0	.3709	62	crisp
5.0044	47.0	.7335	34	unnecessary
5.0033	47.0	.6861	35	1850
5.0025	47.0	.7538	33	Shakespeare
5.0010	47.0	.7962	31	complain
5.0009	47.0	.7175	34	floats
4.9968	47.0	.7610	32	puppies
4.9934	47.0	.5204	45	Grande
4.9924	47.0	.7499	33	substituted
4.9922	47.0	.7444	33	windmill
4.9890	47.0	.3126	71	1968
4.9887	47.0	.6712	36	amid
4.9873	47.0	.2450	87	Alec
4.9871	47.0	.6786	35	crashing
4.9852	47.0	.7466	33	frantically
4.9852	47.0	.4105	55	pint
4.9848	47.0	.7230	34	perfection
4.9830	47.0	.5730	40	giraffe
4.9815	47.0	.5222	42	duckling
4.9815	47.0	.5631	42	governed
4.9813	47.0	.6512	37	salary
4.9811	47.0	.4120	56	prints
4.9806	47.0	.5541	43	Moscow
4.9805	47.0	.4642	49	accused
4.9802	47.0	.7018	35	conversations
4.9800	47.0	.2778	58	Duncan
4.9792	47.0	.5300	44	Lou
4.9788	47.0	.7172	34	compete
4.9775	47.0	.4957	47	Finland
4.9771	47.0	.7201	34	officially
4.9757	47.0	.6581	37	victims
4.9747	47.0	.7457	33	discussions
4.9718	47.0	.7431	33	You
4.9691	47.0	.5770	40	trembled
4.9685	47.0	.6530	37	inherited
4.9665	47.0	.6639	36	painful
4.9665	47.0	.7442	33	robes
4.9637	47.0	.4115	48	Bradford
4.9622	47.0	.6640	36	mole
4.9614	47.0	.4742	49	calories
4.9614	47.0	.1890	68	Cap
4.9592	47.0	.7197	34	departments
4.9574	47.0	.5589	41	animal's
4.9566	47.0	.6714	36	disappears
4.9552	47.0	.6085	39	brushes
4.9549	47.0	.7300	33	trimmed
4.9548	47.0	.5093	46	policies
4.9536	46.9	.6938	35	foul
4.9502	46.9	.6036	39	upstream
4.9498	46.9	.7894	31	flaming
4.9496	46.9	.6614	36	sloping
4.9485	46.9	.6330	37	uneasy
4.9458	46.9	.6968	35	cylinders
4.9445	46.9	.6798	35	plank
4.9424	46.9	.7575	32	bothered
4.9399	46.9	.7668	32	elegant
4.9396	46.9	.8236	30	separating
4.9387	46.9	.7610	32	bathing
4.9387	46.9	.2094	66	Bitsy
4.9379	46.9	.7123	34	demonstration

THE PRECEDING WORD TYPE OCCUPIES RANK 7800

U	SFI	D	F	Word Type
4.9365	46.9	.6909	34	beggar
4.9348	46.9	.0672	89	Kirby
4.9345	46.9	.6770	35	wipe
4.9344	46.9	.1139	139	2/3
4.9339	46.9	.5680	40	Yellowstone
4.9335	46.9	.6618	36	weep
4.9290	46.9	.7055	34	exchanged
4.9261	46.9	.4576	50	urban
4.9248	46.9	.7070	34	rival
4.9221	46.9	.6530	36	warnings
4.9218	46.9	.6895	35	interpreted
4.9214	46.9	.6120	39	128
4.9174	46.9	.7327	33	overwhelming
4.9170	46.9	.6959	34	seamen
4.9162	46.9	.7259	33	bitten
4.9129	46.9	.8194	30	newer
4.9128	46.9	.3616	58	hypothesis
4.9121	46.9	.7530	32	squeak
4.9113	46.9	.7361	33	deny
4.9095	46.9	.7329	33	attending
4.9093	46.9	.6587	36	Channel
4.9068	46.9	.7790	31	applause
4.9066	46.9	.6740	35	gallop
4.9058	46.9	.2675	59	Vic
4.9052	46.9	.4886	42	Pablo
4.9049	46.9	.7613	32	acceptance
4.9021	46.9	.6706	35	wits
4.9008	46.9	.7211	33	ostrich
4.9007	46.9	.5443	42	curls
4.9004	46.9	.6542	37	Child
4.8986	46.9	.2423	81	chromosomes
4.8976	46.9	.7061	34	navigation
4.8973	46.9	.6596	36	quicker
4.8968	46.9	.8086	30	ignorant
4.8968	46.9	.6792	35	Murphy
4.8912	46.9	.7140	33	crowding
4.8908	46.9	.7799	31	repairs
4.8901	46.9	.7836	31	informal
4.8877	46.9	.6880	35	51
4.8864	46.9	.6477	37	institutions
4.8857	46.9	.6738	35	blacksmith
4.8855	46.9	.6803	35	Harvard
4.8847	46.9	.7479	32	breezes
4.8841	46.9	.7734	31	violently
4.8829	46.9	.6813	35	1964
4.8823	46.9	.5334	43	prosperous
4.8809	46.9	.5683	41	entries
4.8783	46.9	.6209	38	1959
4.8776	46.9	.5582	43	structural
4.8765	46.9	.5950	39	bridle
4.8722	46.9	.7159	33	Water
4.8720	46.9	.5792	40	Penn
4.8712	46.9	.6819	35	govern
4.8706	46.9	.6012	39	auto
4.8699	46.9	.2680	73	highlands
4.8693	46.9	.8101	30	sufficiently
4.8688	46.9	.6474	36	gym
4.8681	46.9	.7549	32	103
4.8680	46.9	.7101	33	driveway
4.8678	46.9	.6814	35	van
4.8643	46.9	.6121	37	raging
4.8641	46.9	.4855	42	Orville
4.8629	46.9	.2671	58	Gunn
4.8629	46.9	.7259	33	summit
4.8598	46.9	.6806	34	sting
4.8590	46.9	.5507	42	phenomenon
4.8589	46.9	.4700	48	magnetism
4.8587	46.9	.7510	32	130
4.8585	46.9	.5453	42	Minister
4.8583	46.9	.7807	31	random
4.8565	46.9	.6899	34	hardships
4.8558	46.9	.7042	34	93
4.8556	46.9	.8099	30	cough
4.8543	46.9	.4495	50	pluck
4.8534	46.9	.6907	34	furiously
4.8532	46.9	.4167	55	clauses
4.8527	46.9	.7516	32	unlikely
4.8517	46.9	.5717	40	homeland

U	SFI	D	F	Word Type
4.8491	46.9	.7588	31	thicket
4.8461	46.9	.6835	35	revolutionary
4.8458	46.9	.6718	35	1955
4.8457	46.9	.6057	38	Will
4.8452	46.9	.6722	35	contests
4.8450	46.9	.7163	33	abruptly
4.8440	46.9	.6216	37	gripped
4.8433	46.9	.6140	38	ferns
4.8418	46.9	.6557	36	Law
4.8402	46.8	.6335	37	expanding
4.8368	46.8	.4665	50	mode
4.8355	46.8	.6370	37	piston
4.8345	46.8	.3466	65	contractions
4.8319	46.8	.7307	32	zoos
4.8294	46.8	.6313	37	retired
4.8292	46.8	.5349	40	Wolf
4.8232	46.8	.7233	33	Agriculture
4.8229	46.8	.1746	68	Nelly
4.8222	46.8	.6699	35	aroused
4.8222	46.8	.7407	32	bunches
4.8213	46.8	.4136	52	pulley
4.8205	46.8	.7094	33	cookie
THE PRECEDING WORD TYPE OCCUPIES RANK 7900				
4.8185	46.8	.5142	44	legislative
4.8170	46.8	.6072	37	caribou
4.8166	46.8	.4976	42	Ivan
4.8146	46.8	.5854	38	slapped
4.8130	46.8	.6473	36	reliable
4.8126	46.8	.5019	45	surgery
4.8123	46.8	.5839	37	Dan's
4.8111	46.8	.7407	32	dimly
4.8079	46.8	.7687	31	neglected
4.8073	46.8	.6920	34	wedge
4.8066	46.8	.0572	197	Freddy
4.8063	46.8	.6661	35	England's
4.8053	46.8	.5331	43	Wales
4.8048	46.8	.7440	32	fatigue
4.8039	46.8	.8244	29	hesitate
4.8036	46.8	.7144	33	lasting
4.8018	46.8	.6610	35	winged
4.8002	46.8	.6300	37	critics
4.7986	46.8	.5672	38	whaling
4.7962	46.8	.6228	37	announcement
4.7946	46.8	.4961	45	poultry
4.7933	46.8	.6183	37	photographic
4.7930	46.8	.5130	44	reproduction
4.7926	46.8	.7039	33	thirst
4.7919	46.8	.6320	35	tug
4.7906	46.8	.5501	40	Antonio
4.7885	46.8	.7648	31	monument
4.7861	46.8	.6555	35	hull
4.7860	46.8	.3921	54	chemists
4.7854	46.8	.5575	39	selections
4.7848	46.8	.6973	33	pits
4.7847	46.8	.6679	35	enterprise
4.7845	46.8	.7228	32	hitched
4.7842	46.8	.4986	45	biscuits
4.7804	46.8	.5591	40	hounds
4.7800	46.8	.5397	42	Peace
4.7795	46.8	.3951	52	rodeo
4.7768	46.8	.4293	48	penguins
4.7757	46.8	.7088	33	awe
4.7736	46.8	.7089	33	exhaust
4.7733	46.8	.5944	39	Part
4.7711	46.8	.6251	36	grunted
4.7681	46.8	.6147	38	infinite
4.7673	46.8	.6385	35	sneeze
4.7672	46.8	.7015	33	curb
4.7637	46.8	.7609	31	delayed
4.7609	46.8	.6463	35	glowed
4.7593	46.8	.6866	34	employ
4.7593	46.8	.5692	40	translate
4.7579	46.8	.3489	62	sauce
4.7570	46.8	.4990	44	tiles
4.7567	46.8	.3499	59	flask
4.7548	46.8	.6000	38	Stream
4.7530	46.8	.5493	41	Justice
4.7525	46.8	.5253	43	elect
4.7509	46.8	.5661	40	classification
4.7496	46.8	.4508	49	Falls
4.7491	46.8	.6895	33	entertain
4.7467	46.8	.7349	32	divine
4.7464	46.8	.5813	39	Rod
4.7459	46.8	.4298	48	knocking
4.7456	46.8	.1749	95	Southeast
4.7440	46.8	.7800	30	plunge
4.7419	46.8	.6769	34	shaggy
4.7417	46.8	.6725	33	ice-cream
4.7393	46.8	.6454	36	movable
4.7390	46.8	.6568	35	enjoys
4.7385	46.8	.6009	36	tugged
4.7358	46.8	.6987	33	collector
4.7350	46.8	.5578	39	Greenland
4.7347	46.8	.7802	30	greatness
4.7342	46.8	.6893	33	oysters
4.7334	46.8	.6181	36	Henry's
4.7319	46.8	.6027	38	elections
4.7302	46.7	.6299	35	oar
4.7244	46.7	.7164	32	butcher
4.7241	46.7	.5309	43	q
4.7212	46.7	.6533	35	textbook
4.7207	46.7	.6350	36	Washington's
4.7206	46.7	.8134	29	advise
4.7202	46.7	.6040	36	wriggled
4.7201	46.7	.7018	33	secured
4.7195	46.7	.6720	34	water's
4.7193	46.7	.3818	57	dictionaries
4.7192	46.7	.6634	34	Taylor
4.7164	46.7	.4814	44	Mexicans
4.7125	46.7	.6933	33	smoked
4.7112	46.7	.6616	34	Palace
4.7089	46.7	.7493	31	thereafter
4.7080	46.7	.5734	39	candidates
4.7070	46.7	.1434	95	Popper
4.7053	46.7	.6497	35	telephones
4.7052	46.7	.7680	30	frail
4.7029	46.7	.5089	44	Albany
4.7028	46.7	.6098	36	Lexington
4.7010	46.7	.4019	55	abbreviation
4.7001	46.7	.6288	35	pouch
4.6987	46.7	.7410	31	cedar
4.6978	46.7	.7706	30	rented
4.6973	46.7	.5547	41	hammering
THE PRECEDING WORD TYPE OCCUPIES RANK 8000				
4.6972	46.7	.6756	34	incidents
4.6971	46.7	.6922	33	aching
4.6964	46.7	.7247	32	imaginative
4.6963	46.7	.6747	34	uneven
4.6950	46.7	.4638	47	magnitude
4.6950	46.7	.7454	31	splendor
4.6946	46.7	.6251	36	license
4.6920	46.7	.6544	35	listing
4.6904	46.7	.7455	31	limp
4.6891	46.7	.6712	34	scalp
4.6848	46.7	.5647	40	breeding
4.6803	46.7	.7964	29	expects
4.6794	46.7	.6924	33	marshes
4.6781	46.7	.3459	61	mi
4.6780	46.7	.5894	37	boiler
4.6778	46.7	.7000	32	warmly
4.6758	46.7	.6782	34	inspection
4.6754	46.7	.6536	35	inspiration
4.6749	46.7	.6895	33	dump
4.6746	46.7	.8354	28	vase
4.6731	46.7	.7139	32	wit
4.6722	46.7	.2127	73	Ramon
4.6694	46.7	.6386	35	puffed
4.6666	46.7	.5453	42	comparative
4.6665	46.7	.7417	31	wrapping
4.6655	46.7	.6180	35	Janet
4.6638	46.7	.5517	40	hemisphere
4.6606	46.7	.6607	34	combat
4.6598	46.7	.4583	47	greens
4.6579	46.7	.6725	34	dominated
4.6575	46.7	.6752	33	fluttered
4.6571	46.7	.5649	39	1965
4.6567	46.7	.6326	35	reared
4.6545	46.7	.6340	35	Vikings
4.6534	46.7	.4296	48	Uranus
4.6528	46.7	.2286	59	Blanche
4.6526	46.7	.6666	34	RhodeIsland
4.6513	46.7	.4403	48	Father's
4.6496	46.7	.7244	32	retain
4.6494	46.7	.6434	34	milking
4.6494	46.7	.7700	30	vague
4.6492	46.7	.7263	31	hurled
4.6486	46.7	.6614	33	vine
4.6465	46.7	.4506	50	contrasting
4.6440	46.7	.7278	31	muffled
4.6436	46.7	.6999	32	cleaner
4.6436	46.7	.5491	40	lenses
4.6433	46.7	.6935	33	attempting
4.6423	46.7	.7996	29	pleasures
4.6417	46.7	.6698	34	Swedish
4.6416	46.7	.6296	35	aw
4.6382	46.7	.6017	37	dye
4.6378	46.7	.7144	32	parcel
4.6374	46.7	.4852	45	physicist
4.6373	46.7	.6602	34	Gold
4.6372	46.7	.3542	57	missions
4.6372	46.7	.6578	34	rifles
4.6346	46.7	.7020	32	limb
4.6344	46.7	.7363	31	profession
4.6339	46.7	.7590	30	misery
4.6336	46.7	.7294	31	click
4.6326	46.7	.3321	52	Devil
4.6325	46.7	.5516	37	macaroni
4.6298	46.7	.5764	37	coconuts
4.6285	46.7	.6945	32	preparations
4.6268	46.7	.5597	38	howled
4.6260	46.7	.5223	41	'
4.6257	46.7	.4491	48	parallels
4.6247	46.7	.5854	38	59
4.6231	46.6	.6911	32	Kitty
4.6223	46.6	.4661	45	President's
4.6222	46.6	.6522	34	raid
4.6219	46.6	.6986	32	silky
4.6219	46.6	.5540	39	slap
4.6215	46.6	.7875	29	drip
4.6215	46.6	.7055	32	lacking
4.6193	46.6	.5953	35	woodchuck
4.6173	46.6	.6028	36	arctic
4.6154	46.6	.7878	29	accordingly
4.6139	46.6	.4845	42	hugged
4.6139	46.6	.7353	31	inevitable
4.6137	46.6	.6278	35	weeping
4.6125	46.6	.7299	31	coated
4.6118	46.6	.6878	33	progressive
4.6117	46.6	.6279	34	Concord
4.6113	46.6	.4890	43	mushroom
4.6109	46.6	.6406	35	smelling
4.6106	46.6	.5418	38	mess
4.6084	46.6	.4387	47	northeastern
4.6065	46.6	.6298	35	jackets
4.6057	46.6	.3831	53	larvae
4.6042	46.6	.6858	33	abilities
4.6013	46.6	.2967	53	Jake
4.6012	46.6	.1784	91	fungi
4.6008	46.6	.1796	93	Cyrus
4.6002	46.6	.5716	39	cultures
4.5998	46.6	.5029	43	dessert
4.5996	46.6	.5086	41	Morse
4.5994	46.6	.5718	39	insulation
4.5968	46.6	.4503	44	thermometers
THE PRECEDING WORD TYPE OCCUPIES RANK 8100				
4.5962	46.6	.5153	42	en
4.5959	46.6	.6397	34	solemnly
4.5956	46.6	.7834	29	mend
4.5945	46.6	.6328	34	tripped
4.5930	46.6	.7276	31	obtaining
4.5921	46.6	.6459	34	Watson
4.5920	46.6	.4471	43	Dawson
4.5917	46.6	.5338	39	Buzz
4.5876	46.6	.6487	34	lick
4.5873	46.6	.5878	38	eighteenth
4.5872	46.6	.6105	35	petition
4.5858	46.6	.6305	35	worlds
4.5825	46.6	.4041	51	oxide
4.5809	46.6	.4511	49	Renaissance
4.5804	46.6	.5296	40	adobe
4.5793	46.6	.2936	54	microbes
4.5785	46.6	.5622	38	Matthew
4.5782	46.6	.5834	38	funeral
4.5777	46.6	.7202	31	stunt
4.5766	46.6	.7582	30	arranging
4.5758	46.6	.6638	33	breathless
4.5758	46.6	.7419	30	shady
4.5757	46.6	.5020	44	adequate
4.5743	46.6	.5974	37	Capitol
4.5738	46.6	.7222	31	gesture
4.5727	46.6	.6122	36	ceremonies
4.5727	46.6	.6874	32	stamping
4.5708	46.6	.6489	33	tow
4.5708	46.6	.5065	42	tuning
4.5690	46.6	.7223	31	vacant
4.5665	46.6	.4226	48	virus
4.5664	46.6	.4970	44	essay
4.5635	46.6	.6612	33	prized
4.5627	46.6	.6767	33	tribal
4.5626	46.6	.5142	40	Lebanon
4.5564	46.6	.6503	34	Hugh
4.5548	46.6	.3363	57	freed
4.5546	46.6	.5904	36	lobsters
4.5546	46.6	.5866	36	slammed
4.5531	46.6	.2335	76	Caddie
4.5531	46.6	.6307	35	teens
4.5529	46.6	.7040	32	commonplace
4.5521	46.6	.6268	35	mats
4.5518	46.6	.5031	43	Hungarian
4.5514	46.6	.6210	35	fighters
4.5512	46.6	.6784	33	appealing
4.5478	46.6	.6462	33	Blake
4.5476	46.6	.6544	33	shiver
4.5463	46.6	.6714	33	1914
4.5462	46.6	.6494	33	doorbell
4.5459	46.6	.4794	42	Po
4.5446	46.6	.4798	44	stocking
4.5434	46.6	.5797	38	extension
4.5427	46.6	.6160	36	translation
4.5425	46.6	.6563	34	repeats
4.5416	46.6	.4529	46	spheres
4.5413	46.6	.5678	38	profits
4.5412	46.6	.6289	35	Amsterdam
4.5412	46.6	.5684	38	tundra
4.5405	46.6	.6559	33	galloping
4.5404	46.6	.4695	44	males
4.5403	46.6	.7359	30	hopeless
4.5399	46.6	.6252	35	SouthDakota
4.5371	46.6	.6910	32	weird
4.5364	46.6	.5930	37	popularity
4.5357	46.6	.7693	29	fro
4.5353	46.6	.6526	33	grizzly
4.5345	46.6	.4111	48	darling
4.5343	46.6	.6135	35	sternly
4.5338	46.6	.3799	56	Anglo-Saxon
4.5334	46.6	.6811	33	subtle
4.5313	46.6	.5601	39	20th
4.5297	46.6	.7491	30	indication
4.5282	46.6	.6394	34	boulders
4.5263	46.6	.4216	49	spinal
4.5257	46.6	.6669	33	chemist
4.5255	46.6	.5532	38	Crusaders
4.5252	46.6	.5683	38	religions
4.5250	46.6	.2990	52	Jason
4.5240	46.6	.6629	33	transported
4.5222	46.6	.7434	30	advancing
4.5222	46.6	.7150	31	1910
4.5200	46.6	.5392	38	Gabriel
4.5197	46.6	.7694	29	surrounds
4.5157	46.5	.5185	42	contour
4.5148	46.5	.6366	34	leopard
4.5141	46.5	.6912	32	respects
4.5137	46.5	.6934	32	deaths
4.5136	46.5	.7626	29	roadside
4.5133	46.5	.5869	37	1800's
4.5113	46.5	.7709	29	nature's
4.5106	46.5	.5906	36	debts
4.5081	46.5	.5772	38	Welsh
4.5078	46.5	.6805	32	owe
4.5076	46.5	.7124	31	judged
4.5075	46.5	.5730	37	lily
4.5057	46.5	.5747	36	haste
4.5050	46.5	.4671	45	Odysseus
4.5041	46.5	.7127	31	intent
4.5023	46.5	.7085	31	bounded
THE PRECEDING WORD TYPE OCCUPIES RANK 8200				
4.5020	46.5	.7055	31	disagree
4.5012	46.5	.5205	40	family's
4.4988	46.5	.6038	36	calculate
4.4987	46.5	.7003	31	furry
4.4977	46.5	.6904	32	passion
4.4950	46.5	.4544	46	pitches
4.4949	46.5	.5970	36	Ridge
4.4948	46.5	.8043	28	conform
4.4929	46.5	.6945	32	enjoyable
4.4920	46.5	.7629	29	tasty
4.4915	46.5	.6441	33	inquired
4.4902	46.5	.4544	45	roamed
4.4862	46.5	.3972	50	delegates
4.4854	46.5	.5422	39	summary
4.4830	46.5	.7563	29	NewHampshire
4.4829	46.5	.5648	37	runway
4.4822	46.5	.6801	32	idle
4.4816	46.5	.8027	28	aids
4.4815	46.5	.6584	33	Alfred
4.4815	46.5	.6274	34	debate
4.4811	46.5	.7119	31	ventured
4.4809	46.5	.7854	28	believing
4.4809	46.5	.7998	28	probable
4.4796	46.5	.6826	32	pear
4.4775	46.5	.6299	34	intend
4.4765	46.5	.7614	29	convincing
4.4763	46.5	.5713	36	Express
4.4754	46.5	.6586	33	1918
4.4753	46.5	.2344	61	Chet
4.4747	46.5	.6294	34	steamer
4.4745	46.5	.4118	49	pints
4.4730	46.5	.1424	115	Nixon
4.4705	46.5	.6281	34	astonishment
4.4694	46.5	.7948	28	strung
4.4685	46.5	.1862	94	Son
4.4660	46.5	.3913	51	export
4.4649	46.5	.2881	66	cardinal
4.4632	46.5	.5630	37	flushed
4.4629	46.5	.6095	35	lest
4.4621	46.5	.7293	30	liking
4.4615	46.5	.6098	34	spaceship
4.4608	46.5	.6745	32	mittens
4.4599	46.5	.7523	29	stroll
4.4593	46.5	.7517	29	wove
4.4588	46.5	.5351	39	slot
4.4586	46.5	.5601	38	pyramids
4.4575	46.5	.2828	66	carbohydrates
4.4566	46.5	.7645	29	persistent
4.4551	46.5	.6477	33	hurriedly
4.4536	46.5	.2530	77	modifiers
4.4531	46.5	.2700	66	viruses
4.4518	46.5	.6377	33	Hope
4.4516	46.5	.6928	31	stiffly
4.4501	46.5	.5843	37	incorrect
4.4480	46.5	.5483	38	Dog
4.4478	46.5	.6873	32	intellectual
4.4475	46.5	.6913	31	twig
4.4464	46.5	.3335	57	loving
4.4458	46.5	.5729	37	dictator
4.4454	46.5	.6427	33	Everest
4.4445	46.5	.6098	35	heats
4.4435	46.5	.5459	38	Highway
4.4422	46.5	.6794	31	coward
4.4396	46.5	.6412	33	toll
4.4368	46.5	.7241	30	settles
4.4366	46.5	.3311	57	polio
4.4362	46.5	.7009	31	document
4.4357	46.5	.6534	33	consequences
4.4345	46.5	.5118	41	Board
4.4342	46.5	.7287	30	devotion
4.4340	46.5	.8219	27	vigor
4.4335	46.5	.4085	44	sub
4.4328	46.5	.8529	26	delivery
4.4293	46.5	.6701	32	forecast
4.4287	46.5	.7520	29	playful
4.4262	46.5	.7289	30	accidentally
4.4253	46.5	.5744	37	Rule
4.4251	46.5	.6835	31	tigers
4.4246	46.5	.7243	30	launching
4.4239	46.5	.6028	35	fury
4.4215	46.5	.7230	30	cigar
4.4215	46.5	.6381	34	tubing
4.4208	46.5	.7782	28	buzz
4.4200	46.5	.5126	40	Gregory
4.4182	46.5	.6712	32	unfortunate
4.4178	46.5	.2910	64	Jerusalem
4.4176	46.5	.4547	43	trusted
4.4174	46.5	.6353	33	pavement
4.4171	46.5	.6402	33	masks
4.4169	46.5	.0341	300	Dictionary
4.4168	46.5	.7009	31	Line
4.4160	46.5	.6501	33	pens
4.4154	46.4	.5026	42	mph
4.4145	46.4	.4468	45	geologists
4.4126	46.4	.4432	46	Harvey
4.4115	46.4	.2952	51	Toby
4.4095	46.4	.3376	55	hilly
4.4069	46.4	.5495	37	ores
4.4067	46.4	.7463	29	birds'
4.4055	46.4	.4617	45	evolved
THE PRECEDING WORD TYPE OCCUPIES RANK 8300				
4.4054	46.4	.7136	30	gingerbread
4.4052	46.4	.6299	34	Section
4.4050	46.4	.6195	33	banging
4.4039	46.4	.6199	34	Village
4.4025	46.4	.7483	29	headlines
4.4023	46.4	.6164	34	dome
4.4021	46.4	.4777	42	Mouse
4.4019	46.4	.5296	39	transmitter
4.4014	46.4	.5099	40	slit
4.4012	46.4	.6403	32	fooled
4.3976	46.4	.7133	30	weaker
4.3958	46.4	.6909	31	declare
4.3957	46.4	.6606	32	hammered
4.3951	46.4	.7477	29	heroic
4.3950	46.4	.6359	34	characterized
4.3941	46.4	.5435	39	pineapple
4.3907	46.4	.7234	30	dealer
4.3895	46.4	.3101	60	textile
4.3887	46.4	.5631	36	Troy
4.3882	46.4	.3502	57	interval
4.3857	46.4	.7407	29	punish
4.3849	46.4	.6385	32	cubs
4.3847	46.4	.6265	33	Ranch
4.3839	46.4	.6972	31	pears
4.3828	46.4	.7008	30	strapped
4.3796	46.4	.5838	36	connects
4.3770	46.4	.7185	30	tragedy
4.3763	46.4	.5678	37	agency
4.3724	46.4	.3029	66	screws
4.3670	46.4	.6417	33	dispute
4.3660	46.4	.6480	32	crickets
4.3657	46.4	.5509	38	operates
4.3651	46.4	.4338	47	rayon
4.3649	46.4	.6050	35	Austrian
4.3646	46.4	.4130	47	fours
4.3641	46.4	.6508	32	booth
4.3620	46.4	.6548	32	hardship
4.3618	46.4	.2451	82	seams
4.3590	46.4	.1090	149	accompaniment
4.3584	46.4	.6278	34	access
4.3570	46.4	.4839	43	elastic

U	SFI	D	F	Word Type
4.3567	46.4	.6850	31	airports
4.3564	46.4	.7288	29	twenty-two
4.3554	46.4	.6319	33	waded
4.3539	46.4	.6180	33	hardware
4.3511	46.4	.1724	94	Shorty
4.3502	46.4	.7267	29	bakery
4.3491	46.4	.7190	30	committees
4.3478	46.4	.3822	51	juices
4,3464	46.4	.2902	63	fats
4.3464	46.4	.4552	43	Idaho
4.3457	46.4	.3649	52	galaxy
4.3439	46.4	.2223	86	symphony
4.3430	46.4	.7291	29	twinkling
4.3426	46.4	.6546	32	rattled
4.3386	46.4	.6279	32	howl
4.3382	46.4	.3962	48	droplets
4.3328	46.4	.6320	32	paddled
4.3324	46.4	.5487	36	guppies
4.3319	46.4	.7699	28	discipline
4.3302	46.4	.7150	30	El
4.3297	46.4	.5779	36	Corps
4.3283	46.4	.5917	35	airline
4.3274	46.4	.7630	28	out-of-doors
4.3260	46.4	.6097	34	reporters
4.3259	46.4	.5967	35	traditions
4.3251	46.4	.6165	34	state's
4.3249	46.4	.7236	29	dread
4.3224	46.4	.5727	36	suspense
4.3221	46.4	.6233	33	rye
4.3200	46.4	.6974	30	killer
4.3192	46.4	.6397	32	harmless
4.3189	46.4	.7014	30	flashes
4.3188	46.4	.5709	35	jack
4.3123	46.3	.7077	30	enthusiastic
4.3103	46.3	.5929	33	bald
4.3100	46.3	.2968	65	tuned
4.3099	46.3	.6785	31	plague
4.3060	46.3	.6408	32	tamed
4.3058	46.3	.7940	27	aims
4.3058	46.3	.6871	30	bedtime
4.3052	46.3	.7046	30	shadowy
4.3044	46.3	.7650	28	removal
4.3043	46.3	.5202	37	winked
4.3026	46.3	.6833	31	Story
4.3000	46.3	.7038	30	gathers
4.2996	46.3	.7274	29	rooted
4.2977	46.3	.4215	44	Eddie's
4.2969	46.3	.7308	29	engage
4.2962	46.3	.7030	30	hopefully
4.2948	46.3	.3634	51	helium
4.2910	46.3	.5726	36	biology
4.2909	46.3	.5976	34	swimmer
4.2897	46.3	.6752	31	manned
4.2895	46.3	.4327	45	digestion
4.2879	46.3	.5896	35	regulations
4.2878	46.3	.7468	28	crushing
4.2861	46.3	.6130	33	feelers
4.2822	46.3	.5733	36	Appalachians
4.2813	46.3	.7842	27	puffs
THE PRECEDING WORD TYPE OCCUPIES RANK 8400				
4.2811	46.3	.6971	30	Fifth
4.2789	46.3	.4781	39	Rosa
4.2748	46.3	.6692	30	puffing
4.2744	46.3	.7199	29	urge
4.2741	46.3	.7267	29	loneliness
4.2737	46.3	.5712	35	pinned
4.2734	46.3	.7495	28	pumping
4.2722	46.3	.5024	40	Turks
4.2719	46.3	.7202	29	housewife
4.2715	46.3	.6449	32	lashed
4.2693	46.3	.5368	38	84
4.2683	46.3	.6955	30	counters
4.2679	46.3	.6749	31	intricate
4.2678	46.3	.5913	33	hoe
4.2657	46.3	.3540	55	enamel
4.2645	46.3	.7264	29	proclaimed
4.2638	46.3	.7018	29	rowboat
4.2636	46.3	.4761	41	voting
4.2623	46.3	.6270	32	Labrador
4.2612	46.3	.7508	28	lame
4.2608	46.3	.5829	35	containers
4.2607	46.3	.6505	32	loan
4.2602	46.3	.5583	34	Manuel
4.2600	46.3	.3861	50	Adam
4.2592	46.3	.5113	39	cancer
4.2592	46.3	.6383	32	departed
4.2588	46.3	.6507	32	Potomac
4.2585	46.3	.5565	37	terrain
4.2579	46.3	.5542	37	lightweight
4.2579	46.3	.6482	32	totally
4.2576	46.3	.5923	34	jets
4.2576	46.3	.4451	44	nesting
4.2574	46.3	.6191	33	Library
4.2573	46.3	.7889	27	confusing
4.2570	46.3	.5270	38	import
4.2553	46.3	.6016	33	Ball
4.2538	46.3	.7083	29	dangling
4.2521	46.3	.7502	28	chop
4.2516	46.3	.5901	34	splits
4.2496	46.3	.7836	27	focused
4.2490	46.3	.2711	71	preposition
4.2488	46.3	.4720	41	Series
4.2473	46.3	.6399	32	brittle
4.2470	46.3	.5516	36	hillsides
4.2435	46.3	.4344	42	snorted
4.2433	46.3	.5554	36	deposited
4.2425	46.3	.7297	28	wrecked
4.2418	46.3	.6638	31	starve
4.2408	46.3	.7138	29	guarded
4.2400	46.3	.6794	30	pinch
4.2390	46.3	.6399	32	utterly
4.2381	46.3	.3470	52	Midwest
4.2378	46.3	.6692	31	stately
4.2372	46.3	.6165	33	Banks
4.2367	46.3	.5281	37	backing
4.2365	46.3	.6842	30	schooner
4.2351	46.3	.6235	33	1700's
4.2349	46.3	.2933	60	Holy
4.2348	46.3	.7188	29	depression
4.2348	46.3	.6622	31	grasped
4.2340	46.3	.7471	28	hiking
4.2337	46.3	.6820	30	railing
4.2329	46.3	.5577	34	motel
4.2326	46.3	.6740	30	homemade
4.2322	46.3	.5431	35	coyote
4.2316	46.3	.5064	40	projection
4.2300	46.3	.6313	32	politicians
4.2296	46.3	.6876	30	wrought
4.2287	46.3	.6819	30	bushels
4.2264	46.3	.0822	173	melodies
4.2257	46.3	.7782	27	anxiety
4.2240	46.3	.5788	35	barge
4.2234	46.3	.3722	51	Administration
4.2234	46.3	.5946	34	surrendered
4.2215	46.3	.7409	28	tidy
4.2214	46.3	.5419	37	infection
4.2213	46.3	.7669	27	apprentice
4.2202	46.3	.6953	30	guidance
4.2201	46.3	.4814	42	usage
4.2197	46.3	.6180	33	chilly
4.2189	46.3	.5121	36	Louise
4.2177	46.3	.6908	29	good-natured
4.2163	46.2	.6404	31	mountainside
4.2158	46.2	.8086	26	mysteries
4.2156	46.2	.6224	32	Horse
4.2153	46.2	.7396	28	earnest
4.2149	46.2	.5385	38	concerns
4.2149	46.2	.6596	31	Jacques
4.2101	46.2	.5663	34	sleds
4.2088	46.2	.6814	30	steak
4.2085	46.2	.3865	48	southwestern
4.2061	46.2	.6893	29	Jack's
4.2059	46.2	.5406	38	imitation
4.2037	46.2	.8024	26	overlooking
4.2012	46.2	.7271	28	thorns
4.2006	46.2	.8399	25	unbelievable
4.1999	46.2	.5135	38	Sierra
4.1970	46.2	.5496	36	crank
4.1964	46.2	.7701	27	challenging
4.1961	46.2	.7615	27	happiest
THE PRECEDING WORD TYPE OCCUPIES RANK 8500				
4.1958	46.2	.3023	63	singers
4.1954	46.2	.5389	37	generator
4.1953	46.2	.6887	29	soundly
4.1948	46.2	.6357	32	Denver
4.1939	46.2	.5977	34	cycles
4.1931	46.2	.7292	28	carriages
4.1919	46.2	.6565	31	loaves
4.1908	46.2	.1977	91	proofread
4.1904	46.2	.6551	31	lieutenant
4.1889	46.2	.6302	32	puzzles
4.1866	46.2	.6827	30	vicinity
4.1822	46.2	.6072	32	dismay
4.1814	46.2	.4825	40	valve
4.1811	46.2	.6746	30	nuisance
4.1805	46.2	.6990	29	watermelon
4.1803	46.2	.7675	27	personally
4.1788	46.2	.7338	28	seemingly
4.1782	46.2	.4237	46	rotation
4.1778	46.2	.4756	38	Alamo
4.1767	46.2	.7307	28	swore
4.1751	46.2	.6409	31	businessman
4.1751	46.2	.6230	32	musket
4.1737	46.2	.5179	39	cathedral
4.1718	46.2	.6168	31	buoy
4.1716	46.2	.7553	27	cozy
4.1708	46.2	.6009	32	overalls
4.1703	46.2	.4978	37	Zeus
4.1696	46.2	.4153	40	Commander
4.1686	46.2	.7328	28	ignore
4.1667	46.2	.5585	35	surf
4.1662	46.2	.5892	34	Asian
4.1662	46.2	.6088	32	Emma
4.1656	46.2	.7308	28	slick
4.1636	46.2	.6959	29	leak
4.1618	46.2	.7108	28	bathtub
4.1606	46.2	.7200	28	graduation
4.1606	46.2	.6815	29	tar
4.1601	46.2	.4466	43	quartz
4.1594	46.2	.6779	30	groves
4.1593	46.2	.5981	34	contrasts
4.1578	46.2	.6472	31	plows
4.1568	46.2	.6564	31	Prize
4.1563	46.2	.7984	26	centered
4.1555	46.2	.7670	27	94
4.1550	46.2	.3945	48	celery
4.1546	46.2	.6534	31	presenting
4.1530	46.2	.6379	31	soaring
4.1523	46.2	.4061	47	Are
4.1521	46.2	.7274	28	widest
4.1498	46.2	.6902	29	explosive
4.1484	46.2	.6627	30	sailboat
4.1477	46.2	.7545	27	prevented
4.1472	46.2	.6369	31	shoved
4.1471	46.2	.6839	30	tack
4.1468	46.2	.6822	30	thorough
4.1464	46.2	.6660	30	nailed
4.1463	46.2	.6978	29	pat
4.1458	46.2	.5185	38	92
4.1440	46.2	.6158	32	logging
4.1433	46.2	.6099	32	scowled
4.1431	46.2	.6856	30	partially
4.1430	46.2	.4139	45	tomato
4.1411	46.2	.6518	30	fingerprints
4.1406	46.2	.6330	32	auditorium
4.1402	46.2	.6016	33	pressures
4.1401	46.2	.7007	29	ivory
4.1394	46.2	.8272	25	luxury
4.1389	46.2	.6989	29	insure
4.1378	46.2	.4644	37	OK
4.1373	46.2	.7028	29	unite
4.1372	46.2	.5838	33	Tree
4.1359	46.2	.7048	29	conceived
4.1355	46.2	.7014	29	Miami
4.1352	46.2	.5452	36	farmland
4.1345	46.2	.6962	29	ski
4.1342	46.2	.7573	27	philosopher
4.1328	46.2	.6990	29	gloomy
4.1304	46.2	.6458	31	slab
4.1300	46.2	.4389	43	northwestern
4.1293	46.2	.6876	29	submarines
4.1288	46.2	.7903	26	noticeable
4.1286	46.2	.6077	33	Night
4.1270	46.2	.6227	32	dove
4.1265	46.2	.4375	40	Hansel
4.1225	46.2	.6052	33	correspondence
4.1224	46.2	.6725	30	theaters
4.1216	46.2	.5983	32	storekeeper
4.1215	46.2	.7103	28	chimneys
4.1214	46.2	.6744	30	apartments
4.1205	46.1	.6702	30	proceeded
4.1202	46.1	.7444	27	throats
4.1181	46.1	.6639	30	dazzling
4.1180	46.1	.5460	36	antennae
4.1161	46.1	.4302	44	turbine
4.1160	46.1	.7257	28	sustained
4.1152	46.1	.7019	29	casual
4.1147	46.1	.5223	37	Jonas
4.1138	46.1	.3035	58	le
4.1128	46.1	.6268	31	suck
4.1127	46.1	.4145	44	impulses
THE PRECEDING WORD TYPE OCCUPIES RANK 8600				
4.1119	46.1	.6191	32	tricky
4.1115	46.1	.7055	28	Pass
4.1111	46.1	.7234	28	oddly
4.1072	46.1	.5916	32	tavern
4.1059	46.1	.5485	36	boring
4.1058	46.1	.4342	41	glacier
4.1056	46.1	.6544	30	leafy
4.1055	46.1	.6450	31	dwellers
4.1052	46.1	.7210	28	prospect
4.1048	46.1	.6526	30	Tower
4.1028	46.1	.8204	25	plums
4.1027	46.1	.1160	136	Chart
4.1024	46.1	.6663	29	mischief
4.0998	46.1	.6813	29	tragic
4.0992	46.1	.6734	29	drown
4.0990	46.1	.5301	36	earthquakes
4.0955	46.1	.6538	30	award
4.0950	46.1	.6624	30	sinks
4.0923	46.1	.6865	29	Boys
4.0915	46.1	.1524	108	jazz
4.0903	46.1	.6004	32	Eagle
4.0896	46.1	.6631	30	reign
4.0889	46.1	.6679	29	soared
4.0889	46.1	.7226	28	66
4.0883	46.1	.6396	31	186
4.0878	46.1	.5962	33	processed
4.0863	46.1	.6700	30	participation
4.0847	46.1	.6483	31	substantial
4.0829	46.1	.4608	40	coastline
4.0822	46.1	.4437	43	reptile
4.0819	46.1	.4769	40	plucked
4.0815	46.1	.6195	32	ruling
4.0815	46.1	.6844	29	shares
4.0786	46.1	.7369	27	women's
4.0770	46.1	.6604	30	prosperity
4.0768	46.1	.3971	46	rounding
4.0767	46.1	.6278	31	grant
4.0756	46.1	.6886	29	profound
4.0729	46.1	.7462	27	energetic
4.0725	46.1	.5563	33	alligators
4.0714	46.1	.7092	28	gleam
4.0703	46.1	.5569	35	teen-agers
4.0700	46.1	.7429	27	recovery
4.0684	46.1	.5641	33	banged
4.0675	46.1	.6872	29	1953
4.0663	46.1	.6532	30	selfish
4.0656	46.1	.7460	27	cease
4.0640	46.1	.6858	29	drunk
4.0636	46.1	.4194	44	Wild
4.0615	46.1	.4510	41	understands
4.0608	46.1	.6162	32	York
4.0604	46.1	.6394	30	grown-ups
4.0598	46.1	.5845	34	architects
4.0593	46.1	.3908	47	posture
4.0584	46.1	.7086	28	rubbish
4.0580	46.1	.4280	44	Philippine
4.0567	46.1	.4511	40	tadpoles
4.0559	46.1	.6822	29	appeals
4.0555	46.1	.7646	26	whirl
4.0502	46.1	.3725	49	speakers
4.0501	46.1	.6130	32	conductors
4.0479	46.1	.4955	37	Neptune
4.0459	46.1	.6628	30	traits
4.0459	46.1	.6999	28	urging
4.0428	46.1	.6836	29	refrigerators
4.0423	46.1	.4403	44	climax
4.0423	46.1	.6046	32	detect
4.0422	46.1	.3994	43	expecting
4.0420	46.1	.6324	30	helplessly
4.0414	46.1	.3587	49	mercy
4.0401	46.1	.5583	34	palaces
4.0395	46.1	.3893	45	Pond
4.0375	46.1	.7038	28	boyhood
4.0374	46.1	.7738	26	gradual
4.0352	46.1	.6256	30	sergeant
4.0339	46.1	.6118	31	loft
4.0331	46.1	.6004	31	tipped
4.0320	46.1	.2564	49	Ella
4.0319	46.1	.7042	28	1952
4.0315	46.1	.4797	37	eh
4.0315	46.1	.4509	43	grooves
4.0299	46.1	.6977	28	skyscrapers
4.0275	46.1	.6551	30	loyalty
4.0265	46.0	.3072	57	protractor
4.0243	46.0	.5772	33	hip
4.0243	46.0	.7386	27	picturesque
4.0241	46.0	.7099	28	over-all
4.0238	46.0	.6071	31	shafts
4.0218	46.0	.7229	27	gale
4.0215	46.0	.6066	32	rotate
4.0207	46.0	.7555	26	loosened
4.0193	46.0	.4768	40	casting
4.0189	46.0	.7298	27	sway
4.0184	46.0	.7026	28	mounds
4.0176	46.0	.5705	33	sewed
4.0175	46.0	.5105	38	indefinite
4.0162	46.0	.5268	36	Kenya
4.0162	46.0	.5718	33	pardon
4.0141	46.0	.7978	25	blunt
4.0138	46.0	.5654	32	Marcus
THE PRECEDING WORD TYPE OCCUPIES RANK 8700				
4.0131	46.0	.6180	31	Oliver
4.0126	46.0	.5941	32	Phil
4.0117	46.0	.6616	29	watchman
4.0113	46.0	.3994	47	Language
4.0098	46.0	.5117	35	Hotel
4.0097	46.0	.6934	28	cheaper
4.0084	46.0	.7069	28	Oriental
4.0076	46.0	.6730	29	Hungary
4.0073	46.0	.7232	27	chests
4.0072	46.0	.3025	57	metric
4.0070	46.0	.5545	34	fin
4.0059	46.0	.7134	28	preliminary
4.0043	46.0	.5524	35	designing
4.0043	46.0	.6077	32	emerge
4.0031	46.0	.5525	34	Democratic
4.0028	46.0	.6260	31	antenna
4.0021	46.0	.0327	225	Bucky
4.0017	46.0	.6534	30	descending
4.0010	46.0	.5787	33	rollers
4.0008	46.0	.7621	26	encouraging
4.0003	46.0	.6084	32	Commission
3.9985	46.0	.7878	25	slowing
3.9983	46.0	.7051	28	week's
3.9978	46.0	.6351	30	stairway
3.9973	46.0	.7283	27	locating
3.9951	46.0	.6474	30	buyer
3.9936	46.0	.7004	28	discarded
3.9932	46.0	.6692	29	myth
3.9929	46.0	.6220	31	infant
3.9918	46.0	.0783	70	Funny
3.9909	46.0	.7500	26	pleasantly
3.9902	46.0	.7210	27	combed
3.9902	46.0	.7641	26	radiant
3.9878	46.0	.6530	30	guarantee
3.9873	46.0	.7533	26	flee
3.9872	46.0	.6952	28	mortar
3.9863	46.0	.6451	29	acorns
3.9850	46.0	.6393	30	1950
3.9844	46.0	.6294	31	completing
3.9844	46.0	.1565	98	prefixes
3.9841	46.0	.7238	27	cat's
3.9835	46.0	.4589	36	Bates
3.9833	46.0	.5563	34	Earth's
3.9828	46.0	.6988	28	1500
3.9825	46.0	.7585	26	faults
3.9820	46.0	.5498	34	cocoon
3.9812	46.0	.6617	29	stoves
3.9806	46.0	.7172	27	Circle
3.9803	46.0	.4145	43	vaccine
3.9799	46.0	.6749	29	permanently
3.9795	46.0	.6506	30	dating
3.9788	46.0	.7224	27	sod
3.9788	46.0	.6687	29	1951
3.9772	46.0	.7126	27	salute
3.9770	46.0	.6753	29	manuscript
3.9761	46.0	.6683	29	coaches
3.9760	46.0	.5086	36	delightful
3.9758	46.0	.6392	30	contented
3.9758	46.0	.5709	33	dissolves
3.9757	46.0	.3224	54	63
3.9738	46.0	.5393	35	migrate
3.9733	46.0	.6229	30	nymphs
3.9723	46.0	.6748	28	umbrellas
3.9712	46.0	.6768	28	hood
3.9712	46.0	.6108	31	1860
3.9696	46.0	.1727	105	stitch
3.9668	46.0	.5202	37	slash
3.9665	46.0	.7221	27	1925
3.9645	46.0	.7832	25	remembers
3.9644	46.0	.6902	28	raindrops
3.9638	46.0	.2752	64	blouse
3.9634	46.0	.6168	31	extinct
3.9626	46.0	.6361	29	explosives
3.9626	46.0	.5038	38	stressed
3.9625	46.0	.4044	46	bulk
3.9617	46.0	.4049	44	annoyed
3.9610	46.0	.7571	26	retained
3.9601	46.0	.5941	32	Persia
3.9593	46.0	.6786	28	glide
3.9576	46.0	.4686	40	rib
3.9574	46.0	.7150	27	roasted
3.9548	46.0	.3425	45	Solomon
3.9541	46.0	.5172	33	Price
3.9535	46.0	.6418	30	assignments
3.9533	46.0	.5804	31	spied
3.9531	46.0	.5273	36	18th
3.9527	46.0	.4293	44	Song
3.9523	46.0	.8221	24	bubbling
3.9499	46.0	.6907	28	reservoir
3.9491	46.0	.6309	29	Peter's
3.9489	46.0	.6181	31	intake
3.9474	46.0	.7044	27	thorn
3.9468	46.0	.3022	55	chlorophyll
3.9461	46.0	.5721	33	pudding
3.9461	46.0	.5515	34	swear
3.9460	46.0	.3140	47	Mack
3.9460	46.0	.7017	27	skyscraper
3.9449	46.0	.7167	27	imprisoned
3.9434	46.0	.5607	34	81
3.9432	46.0	.5794	33	clowns
THE PRECEDING WORD TYPE OCCUPIES RANK 8800				
3.9431	46.0	.0862	68	Wellington
3.9426	46.0	.7478	26	coiled
3.9426	46.0	.3626	49	coordinate
3.9414	46.0	.6428	30	membership

U	SFI	D	F	Word Type
3.9411	46.0	.6342	30	victories
3.9402	46.0	.6516	29	waking
3.9399	46.0	.7422	26	supermarket
3.9394	46.0	.7190	27	personnel
3.9383	46.0	.1937	79	intersect
3.9377	46.0	.5476	33	skate
3.9365	46.0	.5754	33	revolt
3.9362	46.0	.6320	30	Crown
3.9362	46.0	.6351	30	yourselves
3.9358	46.0	.3331	45	Janie
3.9351	45.9	.6201	30	deserve
3.9350	45.9	.6510	29	moan
3.9347	45.9	.6740	28	distress
3.9345	45.9	.0293	191	digit
3.9331	45.9	.7422	26	proves
3.9320	45.9	.5656	33	good-bye
3.9316	45.9	.6444	30	Armstrong
3.9310	45.9	.6430	29	snows
3.9306	45.9	.7484	26	arch
3.9286	45.9	.6610	28	medal
3.9281	45.9	.6053	31	coldest
3.9273	45.9	.7086	27	scatter
3.9273	45.9	.7509	26	unchanged
3.9270	45.9	.7443	26	brisk
3.9268	45.9	.4266	37	Clinton
3.9253	45.9	.7465	26	genuine
3.9252	45.9	.6364	30	identification
3.9249	45.9	.5929	32	privileges
3.9243	45.9	.6367	29	rescued
3.9241	45.9	.6868	28	chariot
3.9238	45.9	.6420	29	stoop
3.9237	45.9	.5043	37	Pan
3.9204	45.9	.2847	62	modifies
3.9186	45.9	.5160	36	reluctantly
3.9183	45.9	.6557	28	merrily
3.9178	45.9	.7322	26	peacefully
3.9177	45.9	.6505	29	windmills
3.9172	45.9	.7760	25	dignified
3.9161	45.9	.7426	26	pads
3.9138	45.9	.6770	28	princes
3.9115	45.9	.7042	27	praised
3.9106	45.9	.6226	30	Norman
3.9090	45.9	.6607	28	awaited
3.9089	45.9	.5582	34	evaluate
3.9087	45.9	.4848	35	Augustus
3.9084	45.9	.3630	48	cavity
3.9066	45.9	.3926	44	mosses
3.9059	45.9	.6423	29	crimson
3.9057	45.9	.6093	31	archaeologists
3.9055	45.9	.6535	29	unbroken
3.9039	45.9	.7449	26	constitute
3.9034	45.9	.6639	28	hamburger
3.9032	45.9	.6296	30	1800
3.9025	45.9	.2951	58	Music
3.9022	45.9	.5570	33	screens
3.9013	45.9	.6028	31	Edmund
3.9002	45.9	.6186	30	mistress
3.8997	45.9	.5389	34	behold
3.8997	45.9	.6314	30	experimentation
3.8995	45.9	.6582	29	lesser
3.8989	45.9	.6151	31	films
3.8980	45.9	.5832	32	grey
3.8967	45.9	.4311	41	respiration
3.8951	45.9	.5769	32	'twas
3.8929	45.9	.8064	24	recognizing
3.8928	45.9	.5317	34	Republicans
3.8925	45.9	.6270	30	hatred
3.8922	45.9	.4966	37	measles
3.8918	45.9	.5373	35	controlling
3.8896	45.9	.7098	27	doctor's
3.8886	45.9	.5710	32	trudged
3.8882	45.9	.7126	27	confuse
3.8862	45.9	.4620	39	Korea
3.8861	45.9	.6787	28	tease
3.8854	45.9	.4990	37	wage
3.8846	45.9	.4057	42	chopped
3.8842	45.9	.6318	30	high-speed
3.8842	45.9	.6084	30	snug
3.8820	45.9	.7077	27	newcomers
3.8800	45.9	.7261	26	wasting
3.8799	45.9	.5859	31	glancing
3.8797	45.9	.6341	29	hairy
3.8794	45.9	.6059	31	sewage
3.8792	45.9	.6689	28	gloom
3.8788	45.9	.4979	35	parachute
3.8785	45.9	.7287	26	pursued
3.8778	45.9	.5353	34	Matt
3.8776	45.9	.6101	31	mechanism
3.8764	45.9	.7072	27	bind
3.8737	45.9	.6367	30	choir
3.8737	45.9	.7228	26	handing
3.8737	45.9	.2193	73	Juliet
3.8725	45.9	.7277	26	stationed
3.8723	45.9	.7341	26	expanse
3.8705	45.9	.6034	30	zebras
3.8701	45.9	.7332	26	foe

THE PRECEDING WORD TYPE OCCUPIES RANK 8900

3.8696	45.9	.6219	30	parades
3.8690	45.9	.6736	28	flourish
3.8676	45.9	.3851	47	Record
3.8666	45.9	.6230	30	George's
3.8647	45.9	.4503	41	Germanic
3.8643	45.9	.6887	27	bright-colored
3.8632	45.9	.6983	27	predicted
3.8625	45.9	.7326	26	someone's
3.8598	45.9	.7664	25	continuously
3.8590	45.9	.5215	35	specialize
3.8587	45.9	.5169	33	Thornton
3.8564	45.9	.6868	27	bin
3.8563	45.9	.5930	31	furnaces
3.8561	45.9	.7023	27	3000
3.8556	45.9	.6883	27	cute
3.8506	45.9	.3050	52	daughters
3.8503	45.9	.6767	28	monthly
3.8498	45.9	.6209	30	prose
3.8484	45.9	.5692	33	stationary
3.8462	45.9	.5693	31	Texans

U	SFI	D	F	Word Type
3.8452	45.8	.6006	31	underlying
3.8449	45.8	.6858	27	bluff
3.8447	45.8	.4448	41	category
3.8436	45.8	.5533	33	Salt
3.8433	45.8	.6925	27	treacherous
3.8432	45.8	.7534	25	hunts
3.8426	45.8	.5741	32	76
3.8401	45.8	.7208	26	wooded
3.8391	45.8	.7979	24	fails
3.8386	45.8	.4172	38	Jerome
3.8386	45.8	.7220	26	tangle
3.8383	45.8	.6742	27	porcupine
3.8381	45.8	.3878	46	Smoky
3.8367	45.8	.6739	28	induced
3.8356	45.8	.1976	79	tunes
3.8355	45.8	.7176	26	scrapbook
3.8351	45.8	.7063	26	thud
3.8350	45.8	.2795	60	synonym
3.8349	45.8	.4043	41	Sultan
3.8348	45.8	.5880	31	perceive
3.8333	45.8	.4641	35	Phoebe
3.8315	45.8	.6525	28	streaks
3.8305	45.8	.7499	25	staggered
3.8301	45.8	.7546	25	utter
3.8297	45.8	.5323	34	nay
3.8283	45.8	.7551	25	admission
3.8282	45.8	.6719	28	tomb
3.8277	45.8	.7188	26	bolted
3.8269	45.8	.6610	28	haze
3.8259	45.8	.6165	30	1929
3.8251	45.8	.5684	32	inhabited
3.8250	45.8	.7264	26	toil
3.8247	45.8	.6420	29	reduction
3.8240	45.8	.7122	26	scoring
3.8239	45.8	.5075	34	snatched
3.8223	45.8	.2889	44	Pooh
3.8217	45.8	.6342	29	compromise
3.8214	45.8	.5283	34	waterway
3.8167	45.8	.7075	26	yells
3.8164	45.8	.4379	39	clapping
3.8147	45.8	.5181	35	buck
3.8133	45.8	.6124	30	Heaven
3.8091	45.8	.6657	28	Family
3.8088	45.8	.7036	26	blinking
3.8087	45.8	.7119	26	squeezing
3.8086	45.8	.5920	31	historians
3.8084	45.8	.6846	27	gracious
3.8079	45.8	.7539	25	reserve
3.8076	45.8	.5838	31	loosen
3.8076	45.8	.2006	77	Luke
3.8063	45.8	.6789	27	Providence
3.8062	45.8	.7419	25	prettiest
3.8044	45.8	.6576	28	greasy
3.8043	45.8	.7146	26	barred
3.8029	45.8	.7162	26	caring
3.8028	45.8	.5546	33	compares
3.8017	45.8	.7543	25	twelfth
3.8016	45.8	.5910	30	carve
3.8015	45.8	.7076	26	hottest
3.8004	45.8	.6361	29	Bull
3.7988	45.8	.6056	30	Times
3.7984	45.8	.7252	26	procedures
3.7981	45.8	.6994	26	schooling
3.7960	45.8	.6585	28	submerged
3.7957	45.8	.7123	26	fragrance
3.7947	45.8	.6795	27	ditches
3.7937	45.8	.5771	31	switches
3.7933	45.8	.5063	33	Monsieur
3.7917	45.8	.7248	26	exit
3.7901	45.8	.5702	32	Orient
3.7897	45.8	.7806	24	Smith's
3.7893	45.8	.6334	29	dolphins
3.7873	45.8	.5822	31	ad
3.7870	45.8	.1642	92	homonyms
3.7869	45.8	.6050	30	encyclopedias
3.7850	45.8	.5364	34	dike
3.7845	45.8	.6657	27	crater
3.7843	45.8	.7193	26	Gilbert
3.7829	45.8	.5342	33	hearth
3.7827	45.8	.6166	29	shrimp

THE PRECEDING WORD TYPE OCCUPIES RANK 9000

3.7788	45.8	.5051	34	underside
3.7785	45.8	.6624	28	penetrate
3.7775	45.8	.6403	29	knit
3.7768	45.8	.7814	24	cleaners
3.7762	45.8	.6868	27	residence
3.7760	45.8	.2460	62	Harriet
3.7756	45.8	.7370	25	appealed
3.7753	45.8	.6009	30	webs
3.7750	45.8	.5250	34	dental
3.7747	45.8	.5625	31	fortunes
3.7732	45.8	.6913	27	trend
3.7728	45.8	.6403	28	pitchers
3.7723	45.8	.4374	35	Bright
3.7718	45.8	.6151	30	comparable
3.7715	45.8	.4447	39	filter
3.7707	45.8	.6753	27	horsemen
3.7679	45.8	.4837	35	panting
3.7657	45.8	.7297	25	gown
3.7635	45.8	.5959	30	dandelion
3.7628	45.8	.6658	27	hopping
3.7615	45.8	.4309	40	carving
3.7607	45.8	.4330	40	Israeli
3.7606	45.8	.7061	26	valued
3.7601	45.8	.7367	25	responsibilities
3.7597	45.8	.5930	30	waiter
3.7593	45.8	.6771	27	notch
3.7577	45.7	.7050	26	strawberry
3.7564	45.7	.4698	34	Glenn
3.7563	45.7	.4052	42	abdomen
3.7563	45.7	.7391	25	withdrew
3.7561	45.7	.6883	26	springtime
3.7560	45.7	.2129	67	organism
3.7559	45.7	.6215	30	simplicity
3.7553	45.7	.4300	40	digestive
3.7552	45.7	.4565	35	Laurie
3.7549	45.7	.7748	24	utmost

U	SFI	D	F	Word Type
3.7542	45.7	.2615	50	Dirk
3.7535	45.7	.7358	25	printer
3.7534	45.7	.5562	32	Geneva
3.7534	45.7	.6921	26	Peak
3.7529	45.7	.7729	24	envy
3.7515	45.7	.5915	30	Murray
3.7503	45.7	.5477	32	tractors
3.7502	45.7	.4822	36	angels
3.7498	45.7	.5147	33	treetops
3.7494	45.7	.5627	31	Room
3.7490	45.7	.4474	38	seaport
3.7489	45.7	.6461	28	helmets
3.7487	45.7	.3792	44	sculptor
3.7480	45.7	.5736	31	1920
3.7477	45.7	.7309	25	spared
3.7475	45.7	.4359	40	quarterback
3.7459	45.7	.6508	28	melancholy
3.7452	45.7	.7374	25	tick
3.7440	45.7	.6270	29	sour
3.7430	45.7	.4187	39	questioned
3.7425	45.7	.6104	30	enriched
3.7424	45.7	.3869	43	iodine
3.7408	45.7	.7359	25	anniversary
3.7405	45.7	.5139	35	versions
3.7393	45.7	.7321	25	insight
3.7393	45.7	.5428	33	mathematician
3.7389	45.7	.6076	29	lobster
3.7380	45.7	.7414	25	storing
3.7380	45.7	.5680	30	Ward
3.7378	45.7	.6874	26	textbooks
3.7370	45.7	.5330	33	contracts
3.7368	45.7	.6043	30	1939
3.7359	45.7	.5382	33	lighting
3.7359	45.7	.7606	24	Year's
3.7348	45.7	.6927	26	skinny
3.7316	45.7	.7264	25	darkened
3.7314	45.7	.2667	58	Beth
3.7312	45.7	.3043	43	boldface
3.7298	45.7	.5607	32	presidential
3.7271	45.7	.4824	36	chlorine
3.7269	45.7	.5617	31	freshman
3.7264	45.7	.7299	25	sill
3.7260	45.7	.5208	33	malaria
3.7248	45.7	.7390	25	reversed
3.7218	45.7	.6223	29	high-school
3.7212	45.7	.5684	30	Porter
3.7207	45.7	.5864	30	countrymen
3.7201	45.7	.6589	27	rowing
3.7196	45.7	.6047	30	inserted
3.7195	45.7	.6912	26	swarmed
3.7183	45.7	.6918	26	paddling
3.7181	45.7	.7247	25	trials
3.7177	45.7	.7341	25	criminal
3.7173	45.7	.6123	28	storyteller
3.7161	45.7	.7406	25	invariably
3.7141	45.7	.5297	32	cargoes
3.7138	45.7	.7681	24	extremes
3.7132	45.7	.7220	25	packs
3.7129	45.7	.5611	30	cheers
3.7127	45.7	.6161	29	foreigners
3.7121	45.7	.5253	33	caterpillars
3.7118	45.7	.4423	38	blessed
3.7116	45.7	.6126	29	landowners
3.7098	45.7	.4325	40	transform

THE PRECEDING WORD TYPE OCCUPIES RANK 9100

3.7094	45.7	.5176	32	terrific
3.7081	45.7	.6074	30	liberal
3.7081	45.7	.6220	29	74
3.7073	45.7	.7692	24	violets
3.7072	45.7	.5959	29	mustn't
3.7072	45.7	.6252	29	58
3.7063	45.7	.7250	25	tumble
3.7042	45.7	.5386	33	maintenance
3.7031	45.7	.6558	27	busily
3.7027	45.7	.3898	43	cartons
3.7023	45.7	.6965	26	talented
3.7006	45.7	.3193	49	sulfur
3.6999	45.7	.4724	37	Eisenhower
3.6999	45.7	.5716	31	1789
3.6998	45.7	.7602	24	vigorously
3.6993	45.7	.6526	28	institution
3.6980	45.7	.6870	26	escapes
3.6979	45.7	.5478	32	forts
3.6975	45.7	.6899	26	wavy
3.6971	45.7	.5898	30	producer
3.6959	45.7	.5841	30	straps
3.6953	45.7	.6538	27	deed
3.6935	45.7	.5909	30	900
3.6927	45.7	.6446	27	cranes
3.6922	45.7	.7239	25	criticism
3.6912	45.7	.5491	31	pal
3.6890	45.7	.6438	28	ultimate
3.6883	45.7	.4344	38	pumpkins
3.6863	45.7	.7222	25	carelessly
3.6860	45.7	.4294	38	crumbs
3.6854	45.7	.5487	30	pup
3.6849	45.7	.4200	40	braces
3.6845	45.7	.5938	30	elder
3.6842	45.7	.4045	40	craters
3.6841	45.7	.4253	39	rotates
3.6840	45.7	.5710	29	Horace
3.6829	45.7	.3030	50	faithful
3.6827	45.7	.7569	24	majestic
3.6819	45.7	.6807	26	screams
3.6818	45.7	.4748	35	vane
3.6813	45.7	.6972	26	tuna
3.6806	45.7	.6682	27	favorites
3.6798	45.7	.7500	24	freshly
3.6797	45.7	.6091	28	Ernest
3.6797	45.7	.7174	25	eyelids
3.6783	45.7	.6588	27	slain
3.6779	45.7	.7569	24	scattering
3.6776	45.7	.7557	24	unsuccessful
3.6772	45.7	.4539	37	digested
3.6771	45.7	.5142	34	madam
3.6768	45.7	.6996	26	reserved
3.6765	45.7	.4945	33	Helen's

U	SFI	D	F	Word Type
3.6748	45.7	.6493	27	untied
3.6739	45.7	.5246	33	offensive
3.6734	45.7	.4035	42	budget
3.6733	45.7	.3011	42	Ferry
3.6724	45.7	.6099	29	thriving
3.6721	45.6	.6560	27	briskly
3.6707	45.6	.5276	33	occupations
3.6706	45.6	.5970	29	scar
3.6691	45.6	.5316	31	Giant
3.6689	45.6	.7407	24	glistening
3.6672	45.6	.7898	23	encouragement
3.6671	45.6	.2961	52	ultraviolet
3.6668	45.6	.5324	33	electronics
3.6667	45.6	.6417	27	waterfall
3.6662	45.6	.7441	24	ladders
3.6651	45.6	.5377	32	slanted
3.6640	45.6	.5982	30	collective
3.6634	45.6	.4278	40	In
3.6629	45.6	.6543	27	peel
3.6603	45.6	.7224	25	erected
3.6594	45.6	.5047	34	catfish
3.6586	45.6	.4324	40	lengthwise
3.6581	45.6	.6023	29	rung
3.6576	45.6	.7048	25	bushy
3.6575	45.6	.7868	23	115
3.6564	45.6	.5655	30	reflecting
3.6547	45.6	.6677	26	guarding
3.6547	45.6	.6738	26	parted
3.6540	45.6	.5825	30	Poles
3.6540	45.6	.1279	57	Wendy
3.6530	45.6	.7466	24	elders
3.6527	45.6	.4156	39	gravitational
3.6524	45.6	.7009	26	clarity
3.6521	45.6	.6182	28	Common
3.6518	45.6	.5582	31	dancer
3.6514	45.6	.6870	26	undergo
3.6512	45.6	.4178	41	Sentence
3.6508	45.6	.4899	35	imports
3.6487	45.6	.5694	29	sparkled
3.6483	45.6	.6872	26	scholar
3.6482	45.6	.6057	28	icebergs
3.6477	45.6	.6838	26	fumes
3.6473	45.6	.2526	61	Moses
3.6467	45.6	.6479	27	baseman
3.6465	45.6	.6697	26	endurance
3.6453	45.6	.6714	26	fluttering
3.6450	45.6	.7525	24	resembled
3.6447	45.6	.6853	26	reasonably

THE PRECEDING WORD TYPE OCCUPIES RANK 9200

3.6442	45.6	.5368	33	advertisements
3.6430	45.6	.6035	28	there'll
3.6421	45.6	.6346	28	corridor
3.6415	45.6	.6103	28	faintly
3.6413	45.6	.6803	26	sighing
3.6407	45.6	.6908	26	strengthened
3.6406	45.6	.7112	25	desolate
3.6395	45.6	.7046	25	thrill
3.6390	45.6	.6686	26	litter
3.6381	45.6	.4411	37	emperor
3.6379	45.6	.4579	37	eaters
3.6368	45.6	.6205	27	wheeled
3.6364	45.6	.7213	25	shorten
3.6334	45.6	.7476	24	relieve
3.6333	45.6	.4556	36	Superior
3.6304	45.6	.4383	38	districts
3.6304	45.6	.7420	24	girls'
3.6297	45.6	.1243	97	simplify
3.6284	45.6	.4799	36	voiced
3.6275	45.6	.3132	52	Benny
3.6274	45.6	.5652	31	radical
3.6273	45.6	.4366	38	fulcrum
3.6267	45.6	.5622	30	yonder
3.6266	45.6	.6100	29	correspond
3.6258	45.6	.6821	26	chambers
3.6249	45.6	.6688	26	builder
3.6238	45.6	.1610	91	la
3.6236	45.6	.6461	27	clutch
3.6207	45.6	.7114	25	registered
3.6182	45.6	.4869	33	Ghost
3.6177	45.6	.4397	35	Randy
3.6169	45.6	.6771	26	longing
3.6158	45.6	.1812	70	respelling
3.6153	45.6	.6633	26	chicks
3.6144	45.6	.4162	39	meteors
3.6136	45.6	.7017	25	sensed
3.6122	45.6	.7445	24	disposal
3.6113	45.6	.5166	33	Industrial
3.6098	45.6	.3813	44	evolution
3.6078	45.6	.6032	29	decorate
3.6073	45.6	.5088	31	sniffing
3.6067	45.6	.5071	34	external
3.6066	45.6	.6231	28	shortage
3.6050	45.6	.6342	27	clatter
3.6035	45.6	.5132	33	Newfoundland
3.6029	45.6	.5997	29	crimes
3.6022	45.6	.4608	35	Weather
3.6017	45.6	.6899	25	unfriendly
3.6013	45.6	.6972	25	mists
3.6009	45.6	.7120	25	guaranteed
3.6003	45.6	.6539	27	supplying
3.5979	45.6	.5597	31	exposure
3.5967	45.6	.4916	31	Glen
3.5963	45.6	.6180	28	solitary
3.5955	45.6	.6220	28	averages
3.5944	45.6	.6013	29	resort
3.5941	45.6	.6808	26	consequence
3.5939	45.6	.1765	80	flute
3.5935	45.6	.5195	30	calico
3.5926	45.6	.6619	26	starved
3.5925	45.6	.6522	26	son's
3.5912	45.6	.6668	26	knitting
3.5908	45.6	.5000	34	lung
3.5907	45.6	.7360	24	consciousness
3.5900	45.6	.6254	27	Edgar
3.5896	45.6	.6336	27	admiring
3.5888	45.5	.4815	35	troop
3.5885	45.5	.5224	33	drilling

U	SFI	D	F	Word Type
3.5874	45.5	.6625	26	concealed
3.5854	45.5	.5229	33	capitalized
3.5844	45.5	.3353	46	promises
3.5831	45.5	.6977	25	spit
3.5814	45.5	.5356	32	69
3.5813	45.5	.4413	37	evaporates
3.5806	45.5	.0585	140	perimeter
3.5804	45.5	.6271	27	warehouse
3.5802	45.5	.6016	28	yawned
3.5793	45.5	.7122	25	kindergarten
3.5772	45.5	.6871	25	1930
3.5766	45.5	.6207	28	reed
3.5763	45.5	.5208	31	Andre
3.5752	45.5	.3798	42	photosynthesis
3.5750	45.5	.6517	27	specialty
3.5750	45.5	.6819	25	threats
3.5748	45.5	.6675	26	else's
3.5734	45.5	.5579	31	Guide
3.5721	45.5	.7044	25	souls
3.5717	45.5	.6337	27	frantic
3.5716	45.5	.6208	28	Memphis
3.5708	45.5	.7311	24	canary
3.5694	45.5	.5911	29	volumes
3.5688	45.5	.4903	31	bishop
3.5676	45.5	.5846	29	accomplishments
3.5674	45.5	.6180	28	waits
3.5656	45.5	.5753	30	Box
3.5649	45.5	.1208	108	th
3.5644	45.5	.6264	27	disgrace
3.5637	45.5	.5127	33	Moore
3.5633	45.5	.4865	34	Stevenson
3.5631	45.5	.6984	25	sneak
THE PRECEDING WORD TYPE OCCUPIES RANK 9300				
3.5630	45.5	.6638	26	contempt
3.5624	45.5	.7361	24	bruised
3.5622	45.5	.7249	24	belongings
3.5619	45.5	.6419	27	efficiently
3.5616	45.5	.6511	27	alternating
3.5613	45.5	.5083	32	wasp
3.5594	45.5	.7162	24	midday
3.5585	45.5	.6534	26	rattlesnakes
3.5578	45.5	.6599	26	mournful
3.5576	45.5	.5176	31	Lion
3.5540	45.5	.6453	27	eraser
3.5537	45.5	.5566	30	dresser
3.5526	45.5	.5279	32	Low
3.5514	45.5	.7210	24	flakes
3.5510	45.5	.5300	31	Keller
3.5504	45.5	.4781	35	Mildred
3.5502	45.5	.5176	32	Khan
3.5491	45.5	.6634	26	Hindu
3.5482	45.5	.4811	35	diaphragm
3.5482	45.5	.5857	29	witches
3.5478	45.5	.7204	24	wonderfully
3.5475	45.5	.7620	23	youngster
3.5473	45.5	.7194	24	digs
3.5460	45.5	.6219	28	economics
3.5449	45.5	.1702	85	percussion
3.5447	45.5	.5910	28	Carroll
3.5445	45.5	.6177	28	ancestor
3.5424	45.5	.6748	25	cavern
3.5421	45.5	.4788	34	Beaver
3.5418	45.5	.6117	27	wow
3.5408	45.5	.6756	26	customary
3.5396	45.5	.6703	26	photography
3.5387	45.5	.3795	40	pours
3.5378	45.5	.6305	27	supreme
3.5370	45.5	.6222	27	apiece
3.5369	45.5	.5252	31	undersea
3.5366	45.5	.4107	39	sandstone
3.5350	45.5	.3914	41	clip
3.5339	45.5	.4268	39	transformation
3.5336	45.5	.5923	28	escaping
3.5330	45.5	.7596	23	sprinkled
3.5329	45.5	.7183	24	bumps
3.5328	45.5	.5384	31	probe
3.5328	45.5	.4888	34	1966
3.5325	45.5	.7216	24	stony
3.5320	45.5	.6197	27	stung
3.5317	45.5	.6462	26	strode
3.5314	45.5	.6029	28	swampy
3.5313	45.5	.5249	31	Babylon
3.5307	45.5	.6572	26	Victoria
3.5294	45.5	.6477	27	stating
3.5293	45.5	.5303	32	flint
3.5273	45.5	.6198	27	rags
3.5260	45.5	.7577	23	cherished
3.5258	45.5	.6882	25	unconscious
3.5253	45.5	.7242	24	scheduled
3.5243	45.5	.4890	34	67
3.5237	45.5	.6672	25	fuss
3.5236	45.5	.5610	30	allies
3.5235	45.5	.4526	36	mammal
3.5232	45.5	.6846	25	Thompson
3.5223	45.5	.5635	29	otter
3.5221	45.5	.4155	40	conjunction
3.5218	45.5	.0534	66	Lindy
3.5212	45.5	.7569	23	blessing
3.5211	45.5	.6671	26	formidable
3.5192	45.5	.3388	44	Plateau
3.5176	45.5	.3207	47	Algeria
3.5175	45.5	.7555	23	boils
3.5174	45.5	.6931	25	hazard
3.5169	45.5	.5910	28	Cooper
3.5162	45.5	.6633	26	opposing
3.5143	45.5	.5842	28	daybreak
3.5142	45.5	.4560	36	57
3.5118	45.5	.6774	25	scampered
3.5118	45.5	.1639	64	Sorrell
3.5109	45.5	.6830	25	intention
3.5109	45.5	.7244	24	swarm
3.5107	45.5	.6408	27	designated
3.5085	45.5	.5391	31	Alan
3.5084	45.5	.7826	22	arguing
3.5083	45.5	.3800	42	italics
3.5052	45.4	.6438	26	needn't
3.5048	45.4	.5457	31	architect
3.5048	45.4	.7405	23	rattlesnake
3.5041	45.4	.5370	30	soybeans
3.5025	45.4	.5073	32	mortal
3.5022	45.4	.7028	24	sundown
3.5020	45.4	.5384	31	foundations
3.5019	45.4	.6713	25	delivering
3.4996	45.4	.6609	26	revolutions
3.4980	45.4	.6078	28	drawers
3.4978	45.4	.7127	24	punched
3.4972	45.4	.7129	24	indirectly
3.4968	45.4	.6851	25	herring
3.4967	45.4	.5103	31	Narrator
3.4950	45.4	.6340	27	regulate
3.4941	45.4	.6423	26	plunging
3.4936	45.4	.7474	23	wakes
3.4923	45.4	.6473	26	crowned
THE PRECEDING WORD TYPE OCCUPIES RANK 9400				
3.4916	45.4	.7044	24	streaked
3.4910	45.4	.5572	30	tile
3.4905	45.4	.5920	28	vineyards
3.4904	45.4	.6138	28	abbreviated
3.4899	45.4	.7008	24	bravery
3.4899	45.4	.3676	40	gin
3.4896	45.4	.7214	24	seasonal
3.4889	45.4	.2919	54	hymn
3.4884	45.4	.4159	35	Sharon
3.4880	45.4	.4583	35	Indonesia
3.4880	45.4	.5067	33	N **
3.4870	45.4	.6888	25	fifteenth
3.4869	45.4	.6168	27	tilt
3.4867	45.4	.7883	22	accepting
3.4865	45.4	.4479	37	Franz
3.4839	45.4	.6344	26	tagged
3.4837	45.4	.5897	29	categories
3.4813	45.4	.6572	26	assuming
3.4805	45.4	.7076	24	everyone's
3.4803	45.4	.4068	39	portrait
3.4802	45.4	.7519	23	kerosene
3.4794	45.4	.7385	23	marvel
3.4792	45.4	.5268	31	Model
3.4785	45.4	.6657	25	aloft
3.4784	45.4	.6152	27	lanes
3.4781	45.4	.7305	23	hurts
3.4778	45.4	.6043	27	shrieked
3.4776	45.4	.6785	25	disguise
3.4748	45.4	.1666	84	salad
3.4745	45.4	.6407	26	revolve
3.4743	45.4	.4111	37	fable
3.4739	45.4	.3989	36	Huck
3.4730	45.4	.7443	23	entertained
3.4717	45.4	.3553	44	arcs
3.4708	45.4	.6057	28	mechanic
3.4704	45.4	.6637	25	commands
3.4700	45.4	.6720	25	seeks
3.4681	45.4	.6717	25	borne
3.4679	45.4	.6723	25	flea
3.4679	45.4	.5758	27	goddesses
3.4679	45.4	.7905	22	overlook
3.4672	45.4	.5930	27	bumping
3.4659	45.4	.5508	30	Sicily
3.4651	45.4	.3754	37	Nautilus
3.4646	45.4	.6274	26	aviation
3.4636	45.4	.6133	26	dragons
3.4633	45.4	.3096	49	Frankie
3.4630	45.4	.7819	22	meaningless
3.4625	45.4	.6978	24	lowering
3.4622	45.4	.0462	146	compute
3.4621	45.4	.6225	27	replaces
3.4618	45.4	.4131	36	swish
3.4615	45.4	.5735	28	dugout
3.4608	45.4	.7737	22	fragrant
3.4591	45.4	.5102	32	1941
3.4588	45.4	.2699	56	Bartholomew
3.4582	45.4	.3598	45	capitals
3.4579	45.4	.6454	26	trait
3.4577	45.4	.5479	28	eyed
3.4569	45.4	.2060	46	Mel
3.4568	45.4	.6108	27	hints
3.4555	45.4	.6715	25	extract
3.4546	45.4	.5088	32	performers
3.4541	45.4	.7015	24	Sacramento
3.4524	45.4	.4943	33	employees
3.4513	45.4	.5662	29	estimates
3.4512	45.4	.6241	27	shortened
3.4509	45.4	.6652	25	brightest
3.4509	45.4	.6557	25	camped
3.4501	45.4	.2924	52	crayons
3.4491	45.4	.6266	26	choking
3.4476	45.4	.5633	28	clipper
3.4475	45.4	.5460	28	Seth
3.4474	45.4	.6426	26	associations
3.4469	45.4	.6199	26	riddles
3.4461	45.4	.6673	25	stirrup
3.4458	45.4	.1245	104	Christ
3.4453	45.4	.6707	25	aided
3.4453	45.4	.4824	32	Sky
3.4446	45.4	.7702	22	forcing
3.4445	45.4	.7062	24	agrees
3.4442	45.4	.5365	30	filament
3.4433	45.4	.7407	23	cooperative
3.4432	45.4	.4163	36	Kit
3.4406	45.4	.6489	25	claw
3.4406	45.4	.7130	23	nod
3.4403	45.4	.5711	29	rebellion
3.4401	45.4	.5422	28	old-time
3.4399	45.4	.7047	24	missionary
3.4397	45.4	.0981	122	ch
3.4395	45.4	.7300	23	grandfather's
3.4380	45.4	.8173	21	fund
3.4376	45.4	.3185	47	cellulose
3.4369	45.4	.4684	34	statues
3.4364	45.4	.6655	25	growl
3.4360	45.4	.6943	24	puzzling
3.4352	45.4	.6612	25	robbed
3.4351	45.4	.6569	25	popping
3.4342	45.4	.7317	23	Memorial
3.4341	45.4	.7265	23	showers
THE PRECEDING WORD TYPE OCCUPIES RANK 9500				
3.4323	45.4	.7356	23	boarded
3.4304	45.4	.6619	25	unload
3.4299	45.4	.6146	27	herbs
3.4296	45.4	.7016	24	struggles
3.4290	45.4	.6210	26	dries
3.4286	45.4	.3601	41	Syria
3.4278	45.4	.6563	25	glaring
3.4276	45.3	.5997	27	growers
3.4275	45.3	.7028	24	hardy
3.4272	45.3	.6205	27	drills
3.4268	45.3	.7358	23	sharpen
3.4265	45.3	.7213	23	horseshoe
3.4262	45.3	.6440	26	assumption
3.4261	45.3	.6640	25	elevators
3.4239	45.3	.5980	28	psychological
3.4236	45.3	.3155	45	thankful
3.4223	45.3	.5081	32	generators
3.4187	45.3	.5646	28	hoarse
3.4169	45.3	.7311	23	pivot
3.4162	45.3	.1479	89	clap
3.4156	45.3	.6936	24	dynamite
3.4155	45.3	.5651	29	elderly
3.4151	45.3	.7316	23	timid
3.4144	45.3	.5172	29	Bunyan
3.4140	45.3	.5538	29	monuments
3.4136	45.3	.7236	23	arrest
3.4133	45.3	.4777	33	comets
3.4132	45.3	.7331	23	bearings
3.4130	45.3	.5442	29	swirling
3.4126	45.3	.7145	23	crippled
3.4116	45.3	.4256	36	biologists
3.4114	45.3	.4980	33	maturity
3.4107	45.3	.6822	24	warming
3.4104	45.3	.6330	26	parents'
3.4103	45.3	.5538	29	Nazi
3.4102	45.3	.4957	32	1920's
3.4094	45.3	.5551	28	torch
3.4088	45.3	.5604	29	shocks
3.4084	45.3	.6158	26	thickly
3.4069	45.3	.5785	27	gleamed
3.4069	45.3	.6443	26	inexpensive
3.4065	45.3	.2678	55	2/4
3.4062	45.3	.5912	27	trot
3.4052	45.3	.6037	27	muzzle
3.4052	45.3	.7221	23	townspeople
3.4028	45.3	.6699	25	executed
3.4022	45.3	.5823	28	confirmed
3.4021	45.3	.5978	27	Pearl
3.4016	45.3	.6575	25	bureau
3.4004	45.3	.6712	25	occurring
3.4004	45.3	.6180	27	overall
3.3994	45.3	.6310	26	Champlain
3.3981	45.3	.5702	27	trapper
3.3973	45.3	.5073	30	scarecrow
3.3969	45.3	.7204	23	waxed
3.3963	45.3	.7236	23	publish
3.3948	45.3	.6072	27	yields
3.3941	45.3	.7043	24	emphasized
3.3933	45.3	.3459	43	nuclei
3.3933	45.3	.6719	24	Rover
3.3919	45.3	.3956	38	Iraq
3.3914	45.3	.6128	27	permits
3.3905	45.3	.6064	27	napkin
3.3890	45.3	.4210	36	waterfalls
3.3889	45.3	.5236	31	securely
3.3876	45.3	.7225	23	privately
3.3862	45.3	.5181	31	payments
3.3840	45.3	.6894	24	Dam
3.3831	45.3	.3961	35	Sheriff
3.3829	45.3	.1702	69	Ethiopia
3.3826	45.3	.6125	26	Brewster
3.3808	45.3	.4695	34	flutes
3.3802	45.3	.7284	23	excessive
3.3799	45.3	.4967	31	detected
3.3774	45.3	.5983	26	quills
3.3774	45.3	.7540	22	Seven
3.3770	45.3	.7501	22	lilies
3.3749	45.3	.5702	28	triumphant
3.3743	45.3	.6446	25	overboard
3.3730	45.3	.7129	23	respectable
3.3721	45.3	.3574	41	fungus
3.3716	45.3	.5439	29	soak
3.3711	45.3	.3975	38	investigations
3.3703	45.3	.4996	32	73
3.3688	45.3	.6217	26	rattling
3.3687	45.3	.7479	22	awaiting
3.3679	45.3	.0000	225	quotients
3.3668	45.3	.6103	27	plywood
3.3655	45.3	.5289	30	Best
3.3647	45.3	.6177	26	ravine
3.3646	45.3	.6866	24	lacks
3.3627	45.3	.4057	33	peacock
3.3611	45.3	.6039	27	earnings
3.3610	45.3	.7130	23	kicks
3.3610	45.3	.6377	26	106
3.3604	45.3	.7171	23	1812
3.3603	45.3	.4470	33	stagecoach
3.3592	45.3	.5920	27	Venice
3.3581	45.3	.6069	26	husky
3.3580	45.3	.5523	29	decrease
THE PRECEDING WORD TYPE OCCUPIES RANK 9600				
3.3578	45.3	.5800	28	1900's
3.3571	45.3	.2251	61	chant
3.3568	45.3	.7530	22	unaware
3.3562	45.3	.6811	24	crumpled
3.3562	45.3	.3306	44	territories
3.3558	45.3	.5701	28	overseas
3.3552	45.3	.5166	31	Atlanta
3.3545	45.3	.7891	21	gymnasium
3.3542	45.3	.4090	37	Rhine
3.3537	45.3	.4690	33	colorless
3.3537	45.3	.6158	26	senior
3.3532	45.3	.6065	27	similarity
3.3531	45.3	.6710	24	racket
3.3530	45.3	.5346	29	partnership
3.3515	45.3	.5322	30	connective
3.3514	45.3	.6443	25	realizing
3.3489	45.2	.6789	24	missiles
3.3485	45.2	.6737	24	piercing
3.3476	45.2	.7020	23	severely
3.3469	45.2	.6307	26	simultaneously
3.3464	45.2	.5589	27	Clay
3.3463	45.2	.6701	24	summertime
3.3460	45.2	.7066	23	winter's
3.3453	45.2	.2951	49	Easter
3.3453	45.2	.6707	24	opponent
3.3453	45.2	.7138	23	worries
3.3441	45.2	.6004	26	constituents
3.3440	45.2	.6674	24	dreaded
3.3434	45.2	.7053	23	widened
3.3429	45.2	.7492	22	resemblance
3.3420	45.2	.2297	61	True
3.3413	45.2	.6532	25	borrowing
3.3403	45.2	.3655	42	hardened
3.3373	45.2	.3762	39	git
3.3371	45.2	.5894	26	ducked
3.3369	45.2	.3930	40	trumpets
3.3357	45.2	.6083	26	biography
3.3357	45.2	.3606	42	onion
3.3353	45.2	.5722	27	clutched
3.3348	45.2	.7090	23	groceries
3.3346	45.2	.5796	27	nightfall
3.3343	45.2	.6292	25	scrubbed
3.3332	45.2	.6964	23	hops
3.3332	45.2	.7048	23	Men
3.3331	45.2	.5533	27	stockade
3.3319	45.2	.3243	45	78
3.3317	45.2	.3542	42	$4
3.3316	45.2	.4264	35	Dewey
3.3301	45.2	.3870	33	cop
3.3299	45.2	.5954	27	Temple
3.3292	45.2	.6316	25	moaned
3.3288	45.2	.4982	32	moods
3.3281	45.2	.6530	25	mutual
3.3271	45.2	.5046	28	greedy
3.3258	45.2	.5000	29	spout
3.3250	45.2	.6687	24	prejudice
3.3246	45.2	.7408	22	high-pitched
3.3246	45.2	.5016	31	Siberia
3.3244	45.2	.5337	29	spaghetti
3.3243	45.2	.7500	22	recognizes
3.3230	45.2	.6089	26	blackness
3.3229	45.2	.5455	27	Twain
3.3219	45.2	.7059	23	1931
3.3211	45.2	.3740	37	dikes
3.3210	45.2	.7078	23	joyful
3.3192	45.2	.5092	31	tighten
3.3189	45.2	.6303	25	umpire
3.3186	45.2	.6670	24	commented
3.3184	45.2	.5801	27	shovels
3.3183	45.2	.5709	27	rudder
3.3182	45.2	.7800	21	guesses
3.3177	45.2	.6260	26	decline
3.3167	45.2	.7494	22	purely
3.3164	45.2	.7012	23	amuse
3.3152	45.2	.6987	23	scooped
3.3144	45.2	.4974	31	1865
3.3126	45.2	.4478	35	performances
3.3125	45.2	.5492	29	Brazilian
3.3120	45.2	.7344	22	instinctively
3.3104	45.2	.5137	29	swan
3.3098	45.2	.6587	24	snowflakes
3.3089	45.2	.6150	26	transmit
3.3087	45.2	.5748	27	wife's
3.3077	45.2	.2812	47	yeast
3.3075	45.2	.5390	29	resource
3.3070	45.2	.1984	72	sculpture
3.3064	45.2	.6477	24	decks
3.3052	45.2	.6306	25	courthouse
3.3042	45.2	.6258	25	master's
3.3039	45.2	.6999	23	summoned
3.3029	45.2	.5880	27	1902
3.3025	45.2	.5999	26	softened
3.3011	45.2	.6399	25	artillery
3.2998	45.2	.7347	22	ignorance
3.2997	45.2	.5058	31	racial
3.2996	45.2	.4205	36	corresponds
3.2989	45.2	.6576	24	streaming
3.2983	45.2	.6456	25	rejected
3.2981	45.2	.4942	31	cultivation
3.2977	45.2	.3217	47	Victor
THE PRECEDING WORD TYPE OCCUPIES RANK 9700				
3.2975	45.2	.6275	25	raged
3.2975	45.2	.4908	31	warms
3.2971	45.2	.5886	26	swayed
3.2966	45.2	.3310	36	Molly
3.2966	45.2	.6618	24	swallowing
3.2965	45.2	.5607	28	cod
3.2956	45.2	.7060	23	assure
3.2950	45.2	.6056	26	Englishmen
3.2945	45.2	.7276	22	Wall
3.2943	45.2	.6634	24	indifferent
3.2941	45.2	.6481	24	homeward
3.2920	45.2	.4890	32	France's
3.2915	45.2	.5715	27	mustache
3.2901	45.2	.6150	26	worthwhile
3.2897	45.2	.7308	22	pane
3.2888	45.2	.2583	40	Alvin
3.2885	45.2	.7270	22	hauling
3.2878	45.2	.6713	24	shingles
3.2870	45.2	.4309	35	committed
3.2869	45.2	.6487	24	Games
3.2863	45.2	.6042	25	joking
3.2863	45.2	.4629	31	Louisa
3.2862	45.2	.5580	28	doughnut
3.2854	45.2	.3315	37	Slim
3.2853	45.2	.5263	29	dolphin
3.2847	45.2	.5262	29	Love
3.2819	45.2	.4786	32	geology
3.2798	45.2	.5151	28	starboard
3.2787	45.2	.6163	26	Williamsburg
3.2765	45.2	.6310	24	shillings
3.2752	45.2	.6649	24	enforce

U	SFI	D	F	Word Type
3.2740	45.2	.7351	22	unequal
3.2739	45.2	.6362	25	copying
3.2738	45.2	.5128	30	offspring
3.2737	45.2	.5367	29	temperate
3.2733	45.1	.5966	26	powered
3.2726	45.1	.5208	30	thimble
3.2707	45.1	.6663	24	conquerors
3.2698	45.1	.6645	24	chooses
3.2695	45.1	.7749	21	thigh
3.2693	45.1	.5141	29	Pecos
3.2677	45.1	.4469	35	blues
3.2673	45.1	.4752	30	Barton
3.2669	45.1	.6951	23	mended
3.2656	45.1	.6582	24	migrating
3.2651	45.1	.6300	24	Nathaniel
3.2651	45.1	.6050	25	wagged
3.2646	45.1	.4885	32	alter
3.2645	45.1	.4373	35	sciences
3.2640	45.1	.3973	33	Kim
3.2639	45.1	.5873	27	Pope
3.2635	45.1	.4902	31	magnesium
3.2632	45.1	.6400	24	scrambling
3.2627	45.1	.5317	29	Democrats
3.2614	45.1	.6405	24	prickly
3.2602	45.1	.6971	23	courteous
3.2593	45.1	.7282	22	carpenters
3.2589	45.1	.2694	47	Arrow
3.2578	45.1	.6663	24	assisted
3.2565	45.1	.6396	25	roles
3.2561	45.1	.6044	26	Cortez
3.2558	45.1	.6619	24	knobs
3.2542	45.1	.4836	30	Z
3.2536	45.1	.6569	24	suspicion
3.2518	45.1	.6837	23	bedding
3.2514	45.1	.5705	26	bade
3.2511	45.1	.6570	24	copied
3.2508	45.1	.5522	27	axe
3.2507	45.1	.6742	23	tighter
3.2495	45.1	.8140	20	attain
3.2488	45.1	.6568	24	mustard
3.2479	45.1	.6722	23	scary
3.2473	45.1	.2127	57	Nigeria
3.2467	45.1	.4601	32	feeder
3.2467	45.1	.5942	26	realm
3.2466	45.1	.7194	22	shrine
3.2437	45.1	.6577	24	cracker
3.2422	45.1	.6054	26	chapel
3.2412	45.1	.4963	30	Rip
3.2405	45.1	.4457	34	fifths
3.2401	45.1	.2874	37	Directions
3.2401	45.1	.6831	23	Gordon
3.2397	45.1	.6353	25	squared
3.2395	45.1	.6555	24	Dame
3.2392	45.1	.5658	26	boxing
3.2386	45.1	.4470	33	planters
3.2381	45.1	.5671	28	104
3.2380	45.1	.4048	37	flats
3.2380	45.1	.4897	31	spoons
3.2376	45.1	.6521	24	Vermont
3.2364	45.1	.7603	21	overlooked
3.2359	45.1	.4831	31	Americas
3.2357	45.1	.6853	23	civilizations
3.2355	45.1	.6919	23	assistants
3.2354	45.1	.5963	26	Trail
3.2351	45.1	.7172	22	drought
3.2340	45.1	.4440	30	Lydia
3.2339	45.1	.6385	24	buckskin
3.2337	45.1	.6103	25	notches
3.2333	45.1	.5384	27	Dean
THE PRECEDING WORD TYPE OCCUPIES RANK 9800				
3.2330	45.1	.6415	24	jeans
3.2322	45.1	.5074	30	audiences
3.2316	45.1	.7301	22	requiring
3.2314	45.1	.3618	36	Sister
3.2300	45.1	.4943	30	colts
3.2291	45.1	.5610	26	arena
3.2286	45.1	.6364	24	jerk
3.2282	45.1	.5615	27	hedge
3.2256	45.1	.6817	23	Nelson
3.2251	45.1	.5881	26	Tommy's
3.2247	45.1	.5782	27	pursue
3.2246	45.1	.2797	47	galaxies
3.2242	45.1	.6711	23	dusted
3.2242	45.1	.5687	26	groan
3.2242	45.1	.6815	23	thrive
3.2227	45.1	.6345	25	exotic
3.2223	45.1	.7218	22	bathe
3.2221	45.1	.6215	25	cigarettes
3.2218	45.1	.2438	40	peddler
3.2215	45.1	.7621	21	advertise
3.2213	45.1	.6232	24	foreman
3.2191	45.1	.5131	29	Quebec
3.2187	45.1	.5145	29	backbone
3.2176	45.1	.4403	32	David's
3.2173	45.1	.4917	31	89
3.2172	45.1	.6359	24	notebooks
3.2161	45.1	.6398	24	airlines
3.2156	45.1	.7170	22	hamburgers
3.2155	45.1	.6207	25	wearily
3.2148	45.1	.6698	23	clutching
3.2146	45.1	.5434	28	observers
3.2132	45.1	.2232	48	Tell
3.2129	45.1	.7005	22	afternoons
3.2128	45.1	.7019	22	Winter
3.2118	45.1	.5260	27	Burns
3.2117	45.1	.6690	23	spill
3.2081	45.1	.6521	24	appointment
3.2081	45.1	.7421	21	starving
3.2080	45.1	.6385	24	Princeton
3.2074	45.1	.6277	25	97
3.2068	45.1	.6077	25	eyebrows
3.2062	45.1	.5455	28	advertisement
3.2040	45.1	.1178	86	abacus
3.2036	45.1	.7365	21	silken
3.2035	45.1	.5919	26	revenge
3.2030	45.1	.4327	34	citrus
3.2024	45.1	.7190	22	monks
3.2016	45.1	.3855	34	Aladdin
3.2008	45.1	.7484	21	cooperate
3.2001	45.1	.7445	21	twenty-eight
3.1993	45.1	.6016	25	choked
3.1988	45.0	.5290	28	Dipper
3.1988	45.0	.4503	33	Moslem
3.1986	45.0	.4008	36	Highlands
3.1981	45.0	.3928	33	Jon
3.1969	45.0	.5143	29	gravely
3.1966	45.0	.6415	24	beer
3.1964	45.0	.5994	25	Marshall
3.1942	45.0	.4232	34	1942
3.1939	45.0	.7544	21	deliberate
3.1936	45.0	.5044	29	stride
3.1925	45.0	.6406	24	captains
3.1920	45.0	.6768	23	starvation
3.1902	45.0	.4561	33	doth
3.1902	45.0	.5476	28	employers
3.1902	45.0	.5314	28	See
3.1894	45.0	.3939	37	meridians
3.1878	45.0	.3104	45	verses
3.1877	45.0	.5680	26	eagerness
3.1874	45.0	.6324	24	tremble
3.1870	45.0	.2402	55	est
3.1855	45.0	.7097	22	Thames
3.1848	45.0	.5287	28	Francois
3.1845	45.0	.4927	30	clips
3.1843	45.0	.1547	47	MG
3.1839	45.0	.6740	23	twenty-three
3.1835	45.0	.5134	29	shading
3.1832	45.0	.5980	25	bobbing
3.1830	45.0	.1441	73	Amos
3.1800	45.0	.4514	32	sampling
3.1789	45.0	.6126	25	shrub
3.1785	45.0	.6124	25	reforms
3.1773	45.0	.6610	23	doves
3.1765	45.0	.4329	31	Belinda
3.1764	45.0	.6402	24	fowl
3.1763	45.0	.5510	26	Agnes
3.1761	45.0	.6413	24	tasting
3.1759	45.0	.6174	25	Russell
3.1749	45.0	.6500	23	screeching
3.1747	45.0	.5258	28	termites
3.1741	45.0	.5567	28	suggesting
3.1737	45.0	.5385	28	1870
3.1734	45.0	.6076	25	objected
3.1725	45.0	.6639	23	adventurous
3.1704	45.0	.6159	25	Interior
3.1703	45.0	.6721	23	photographed
3.1701	45.0	.5527	27	dune
3.1701	45.0	.4550	30	Kay
3.1700	45.0	.6856	22	tugs
3.1697	45.0	.6119	25	Bishop
THE PRECEDING WORD TYPE OCCUPIES RANK 9900				
3.1675	45.0	.5336	28	Belgian
3.1667	45.0	.5136	29	vein
3.1663	45.0	.6431	24	imposed
3.1663	45.0	.5025	29	Karen
3.1660	45.0	.7873	20	abandon
3.1656	45.0	.5678	25	eased
3.1654	45.0	.6183	25	Scandinavia
3.1650	45.0	.7895	20	faithfully
3.1643	45.0	.6621	23	sobbing
3.1625	45.0	.5667	25	deep-sea
3.1618	45.0	.5222	28	Railroad
3.1616	45.0	.6715	23	execution
3.1602	45.0	.6152	25	bulky
3.1596	45.0	.5643	27	consistent
3.1596	45.0	.5446	27	Hebrew
3.1590	45.0	.6592	23	blinded
3.1589	45.0	.3629	40	teaspoon
3.1587	45.0	.6288	24	straws
3.1572	45.0	.4001	34	alloy
3.1571	45.0	.5742	26	harvesting
3.1565	45.0	.6894	22	coffin
3.1563	45.0	.4750	28	flippers
3.1549	45.0	.6098	25	restricted
3.1548	45.0	.6583	23	agony
3.1548	45.0	.6046	25	spurs
3.1545	45.0	.5537	27	Prime
3.1538	45.0	.4549	32	gross
3.1529	45.0	.7343	21	Happy
3.1525	45.0	.5986	25	watering
3.1524	45.0	.6051	24	snout
3.1521	45.0	.5209	29	utensils
3.1512	45.0	.7002	22	owes
3.1501	45.0	.6246	24	pendulum
3.1494	45.0	.6661	23	bays
3.1494	45.0	.6396	24	inward
3.1488	45.0	.6946	22	fortress
3.1485	45.0	.6742	23	maintaining
3.1476	45.0	.5502	27	dwell
3.1476	45.0	.4125	36	finishes
3.1468	45.0	.5883	26	exterior
3.1463	45.0	.7055	22	weathered
3.1460	45.0	.6139	25	adapt
3.1458	45.0	.6298	24	landmarks
3.1452	45.0	.5491	27	Representatives
3.1446	45.0	.3697	38	amino
3.1438	45.0	.5021	28	Walker
3.1429	45.0	.2214	56	$3
3.1419	45.0	.6879	22	threatening
3.1409	45.0	.7400	21	fragile
3.1409	45.0	.1332	67	Pippi
3.1406	45.0	.6279	24	altar
3.1406	45.0	.5537	27	operators
3.1404	45.0	.7415	21	publicly
3.1382	45.0	.6018	25	rattles
3.1380	45.0	.6289	23	lagoon
3.1378	45.0	.6414	23	boxer
3.1375	45.0	.6112	25	sophisticated
3.1373	45.0	.5579	27	algebra
3.1371	45.0	.7776	20	fee
3.1367	45.0	.6718	23	famed
3.1361	45.0	.4660	32	disc
3.1361	45.0	.0823	119	His
3.1358	45.0	.6120	24	cowboy's
3.1354	45.0	.3571	37	Brian
3.1352	45.0	.7767	20	defending
3.1341	45.0	.5688	25	gull
3.1337	45.0	.5932	25	built-in
3.1333	45.0	.7684	20	legendary
3.1317	45.0	.6623	23	crush
3.1315	45.0	.5751	26	Defense
3.1309	45.0	.5659	26	conflicts
3.1307	45.0	.7410	21	140
3.1259	44.9	.6395	24	duplicate
3.1255	44.9	.4981	29	Cairo
3.1247	44.9	.5886	26	intermediate
3.1228	44.9	.6457	23	misfortune
3.1226	44.9	.4588	32	Peking
3.1221	44.9	.6016	24	Bess
3.1220	44.9	.6347	23	tracked
3.1214	44.9	.5597	25	Andy's
3.1207	44.9	.5470	27	ideals
3.1204	44.9	.6832	22	emptied
3.1190	44.9	.6395	23	spikes
3.1186	44.9	.5999	25	arouse
3.1184	44.9	.6226	24	straining
3.1183	44.9	.7784	20	appreciated
3.1178	44.9	.5499	27	Wallace
3.1176	44.9	.6207	24	swimmers
3.1171	44.9	.4466	32	tapping
3.1170	44.9	.5473	27	recalls
3.1168	44.9	.3124	35	braves
3.1158	44.9	.5795	25	1775
3.1156	44.9	.5672	25	Mayflower
3.1143	44.9	.6636	23	philosophers
3.1138	44.9	.7103	21	buzzed
3.1132	44.9	.5517	27	approve
3.1127	44.9	.5474	27	incomes
3.1125	44.9	.4493	32	sac
3.1123	44.9	.6316	23	tickled
3.1121	44.9	.6939	22	whooping
THE PRECEDING WORD TYPE OCCUPIES RANK 10000				
3.1116	44.9	.6295	24	crests
3.1107	44.9	.6018	25	employs
3.1099	44.9	.6902	22	withdraw
3.1098	44.9	.6114	24	cocked
3.1097	44.9	.2913	36	Peg
3.1095	44.9	.4343	32	Cabinet
3.1085	44.9	.5813	25	wiping
3.1051	44.9	.5853	25	Gate
3.1047	44.9	.5659	26	far-away
3.1046	44.9	.5964	25	demanding
3.1042	44.9	.6743	22	cape
3.1040	44.9	.6510	23	5000
3.1034	44.9	.7289	21	adjoining
3.1033	44.9	.5898	25	electrically
3.1032	44.9	.6491	23	hopeful
3.1030	44.9	.5529	27	slang
3.1027	44.9	.4388	30	Hal
3.1026	44.9	.6973	22	accomplishment
3.1020	44.9	.6757	22	slung
3.1014	44.9	.6898	22	noting
3.1013	44.9	.6182	24	stadium
3.1012	44.9	.4980	27	skipper
3.1002	44.9	.5783	25	grumbled
3.1002	44.9	.6181	24	spines
3.0994	44.9	.6727	22	dismal
3.0987	44.9	.6258	24	scope
3.0981	44.9	.6430	23	rebel
3.0981	44.9	.6839	22	savages
3.0971	44.9	.7284	21	clipping
3.0955	44.9	.6624	23	allied
3.0945	44.9	.6802	22	tending
3.0935	44.9	.6797	22	preventing
3.0932	44.9	.6563	23	rancher
3.0921	44.9	.6911	22	750
3.0904	44.9	.1409	63	Nat
3.0903	44.9	.3712	36	Archimedes
3.0890	44.9	.5355	27	speck
3.0882	44.9	.5712	25	breathlessly
3.0871	44.9	.5427	26	giggled
3.0871	44.9	.3996	36	stanzas
3.0860	44.9	.5976	24	boasted
3.0856	44.9	.5212	28	geographic
3.0856	44.9	.6673	22	skunks
3.0853	44.9	.4208	32	weatherman
3.0826	44.9	.6990	22	hammers
3.0824	44.9	.3778	35	Face
3.0819	44.9	.5978	25	reporting
3.0819	44.9	.7087	21	scramble
3.0814	44.9	.4381	32	combustion
3.0791	44.9	.6275	24	eel
3.0786	44.9	.5892	25	radiator
3.0765	44.9	.6508	23	soften
3.0746	44.9	.3389	40	embryo
3.0727	44.9	.6520	23	casts
3.0706	44.9	.3823	37	haiku
3.0702	44.9	.5943	25	founding
3.0699	44.9	.4950	29	crisis
3.0699	44.9	.7625	20	propose
3.0698	44.9	.5305	28	108
3.0695	44.9	.4900	28	Alaskan
3.0688	44.9	.7559	20	worthless
3.0685	44.9	.0000	205	congruent
3.0681	44.9	.5248	28	firms
3.0677	44.9	.5156	28	holder
3.0670	44.9	.6951	21	thundered
3.0664	44.9	.5737	26	eternal
3.0657	44.9	.5816	25	managers
3.0655	44.9	.6248	23	streamed
3.0654	44.9	.5635	26	voluntary
3.0634	44.9	.6786	22	clicking
3.0600	44.9	.5903	25	79
3.0597	44.9	.7056	21	heaped
3.0594	44.9	.6766	22	wiry
3.0592	44.9	.7109	21	checkers
3.0586	44.9	.4847	30	shears
3.0563	44.9	.2542	49	Rules
3.0559	44.9	.6206	23	teased
3.0558	44.9	.5298	28	comedy
3.0546	44.8	.6462	23	washes
3.0536	44.8	.5223	27	rebuilt
3.0524	44.8	.5643	25	Duck
3.0523	44.8	.5634	25	interview
3.0516	44.8	.6718	22	pledge
3.0512	44.8	.7096	21	unloading
3.0509	44.8	.5602	26	compartment
3.0505	44.8	.4893	30	cinnamon
3.0504	44.8	.3838	34	Secret
3.0490	44.8	.3786	35	evaporation
3.0473	44.8	.6240	23	merry-go-round
3.0470	44.8	.5975	24	Monument
3.0465	44.8	.5736	25	painfully
3.0462	44.8	.4261	34	exclamation
3.0462	44.8	.6482	23	inviting
3.0450	44.8	.5913	25	supplement
3.0428	44.8	.6778	22	1890
3.0424	44.8	.6707	22	dainty
3.0418	44.8	.6245	23	swaying
3.0407	44.8	.6429	23	militia
3.0397	44.8	.4805	30	sweaters
3.0396	44.8	.5865	25	Yale
THE PRECEDING WORD TYPE OCCUPIES RANK 10100				
3.0377	44.8	.7141	21	releasing
3.0366	44.8	.6702	22	ripened
3.0359	44.8	.6598	22	absurd
3.0358	44.8	.4877	29	Salem
3.0356	44.8	.5805	25	poorly
3.0354	44.8	.4960	28	Animals
3.0352	44.8	.4719	31	accents
3.0352	44.8	.5783	25	classifications
3.0333	44.8	.6470	23	manual
3.0333	44.8	.2816	47	5/8
3.0332	44.8	.6786	22	obscure
3.0329	44.8	.5808	25	orbiting
3.0318	44.8	.5591	26	71
3.0316	44.8	.5712	25	conviction
3.0315	44.8	.6723	22	slows
3.0310	44.8	.4274	32	cartoons
3.0308	44.8	.6598	22	loveliest
3.0303	44.8	.5017	28	1913
3.0298	44.8	.3033	39	Pocahontas
3.0295	44.8	.6359	23	blamed
3.0295	44.8	.6108	24	eater
3.0289	44.8	.7483	20	discussing
3.0284	44.8	.7033	21	another's
3.0276	44.8	.7044	21	poke
3.0276	44.8	.7420	20	trash
3.0266	44.8	.6582	22	shutters
3.0265	44.8	.4924	26	Midas
3.0264	44.8	.6948	21	banquet
3.0264	44.8	.3925	30	Snake
3.0262	44.8	.5122	28	respectively
3.0260	44.8	.6876	21	captain's
3.0259	44.8	.6672	22	honorable
3.0252	44.8	.5130	28	metropolitan
3.0250	44.8	.3155	44	performer
3.0242	44.8	.3034	42	arteries
3.0233	44.8	.2398	55	poster
3.0218	44.8	.6671	22	lecture
3.0212	44.8	.5594	26	Minor
3.0210	44.8	.5468	26	legislatures
3.0206	44.8	.6455	23	systematic
3.0199	44.8	.5987	24	Show
3.0187	44.8	.6699	22	humanity
3.0173	44.8	.5507	26	collapsed
3.0172	44.8	.6790	21	steered
3.0171	44.8	.5806	24	motioned
3.0167	44.8	.5103	27	Walt
3.0162	44.8	.2050	63	yarns
3.0146	44.8	.5456	26	grimly
3.0144	44.8	.7440	20	shifts
3.0143	44.8	.6621	22	spokes
3.0135	44.8	.7461	20	owing
3.0134	44.8	.6961	21	watchers
3.0133	44.8	.6561	22	quarry
3.0131	44.8	.5385	26	sucked
3.0120	44.8	.6677	22	sleet
3.0119	44.8	.5925	24	newborn
3.0119	44.8	.4907	28	steers
3.0113	44.8	.6086	24	agreements
3.0102	44.8	.6228	23	halted
3.0096	44.8	.7002	21	blooming
3.0086	44.8	.4009	34	Allies
3.0086	44.8	.5861	24	torches
3.0073	44.8	.7473	20	mastered
3.0068	44.8	.6787	21	teapot
3.0057	44.8	.6588	22	cranberries
3.0055	44.8	.7002	21	baggage
3.0047	44.8	.5927	24	bottoms
3.0015	44.8	.6965	21	monarch
3.0011	44.8	.6355	23	physicians
3.0010	44.8	.4730	30	classmate
2.9994	44.8	.6007	23	Pilgrim
2.9989	44.8	.6398	22	mouthful
2.9985	44.8	.5286	27	additions
2.9984	44.8	.6264	23	amounted
2.9984	44.8	.6986	21	laborers
2.9977	44.8	.6254	23	Australian
2.9975	44.8	.7286	20	bounds
2.9949	44.8	.3492	35	aphids
2.9949	44.8	.7002	21	hitherto
2.9940	44.8	.2864	46	cereals
2.9936	44.8	.7375	20	extracted
2.9932	44.8	.6501	22	untouched
2.9925	44.8	.6847	21	planks
2.9924	44.8	.5342	27	17th
2.9914	44.8	.7352	20	consulted
2.9914	44.8	.6487	22	sandals
2.9904	44.8	.7330	20	surge
2.9896	44.8	.4937	28	sock
2.9895	44.8	.6021	24	mansion
2.9894	44.8	.5073	28	disturbances
2.9891	44.8	.6140	23	trailed
2.9884	44.8	.5355	25	wailed
2.9882	44.8	.5698	25	swelled
2.9871	44.8	.6367	23	filed
2.9867	44.8	.6480	22	antelope

U	SFI	D	F	Word Type
2.9866	44.8	.6620	22	proposal
2.9864	44.8	.6999	21	frontiers
2.9856	44.8	.5770	25	109
2.9852	44.7	.7254	20	smash
2.9834	44.7	.5009	27	fables

THE PRECEDING WORD TYPE OCCUPIES RANK 10200

U	SFI	D	F	Word Type
2.9834	44.7	.4103	33	heavenly
2.9831	44.7	.7360	20	school's
2.9829	44.7	.6690	22	spectacle
2.9822	44.7	.6625	21	walrus
2.9817	44.7	.4046	33	citizenship
2.9800	44.7	.6873	21	captive
2.9798	44.7	.0352	196	Test
2.9791	44.7	.4977	29	exposition
2.9789	44.7	.4854	28	Mark's
2.9787	44.7	.3861	34	Small
2.9786	44.7	.6960	21	cosmetics
2.9784	44.7	.6264	23	Ice
2.9780	44.7	.6044	23	Dead
2.9777	44.7	.3802	35	kidneys
2.9772	44.7	.4476	28	Lightning
2.9766	44.7	.5909	23	lady's
2.9763	44.7	.5215	27	consecutive
2.9752	44.7	.5613	25	opponents
2.9724	44.7	.6651	22	indefinitely
2.9709	44.7	.6740	21	wheelbarrow
2.9701	44.7	.6920	21	hoisted
2.9700	44.7	.6001	24	Sherman
2.9693	44.7	.5499	25	anymore
2.9690	44.7	.6867	21	flooding
2.9688	44.7	.6602	22	panels
2.9680	44.7	.7267	20	advertised
2.9674	44.7	.3361	41	ballad
2.9673	44.7	.6898	21	locomotives
2.9668	44.7	.7298	20	ominous
2.9667	44.7	.5769	25	1600
2.9655	44.7	.5801	24	forbidding
2.9649	44.7	.6848	21	flutter
2.9649	44.7	.7255	20	inventing
2.9649	44.7	.6191	23	slipper
2.9642	44.7	.5970	23	fawn
2.9640	44.7	.5188	27	defects
2.9640	44.7	.2011	66	stitches
2.9612	44.7	.6166	23	bustling
2.9601	44.7	.6230	22	telephoned
2.9592	44.7	.6074	23	drifts
2.9588	44.7	.7337	20	resembling
2.9587	44.7	.5269	25	raccoons
2.9575	44.7	.7305	20	charms
2.9573	44.7	.5949	24	governing
2.9566	44.7	.3724	35	disputes
2.9566	44.7	.7345	20	fulfill
2.9566	44.7	.5642	25	quivering
2.9558	44.7	.6896	21	narrower
2.9555	44.7	.5032	25	Bush
2.9550	44.7	.7683	19	crawls
2.9547	44.7	.2258	51	Paraguay
2.9539	44.7	.6378	22	sullen
2.9536	44.7	.6251	22	Revere
2.9529	44.7	.6793	21	roused
2.9518	44.7	.6227	23	calculations
2.9518	44.7	.6638	21	Owl
2.9518	44.7	.5808	24	wartime
2.9517	44.7	.6891	21	strategy
2.9510	44.7	.6327	22	lingered
2.9491	44.7	.6437	22	sip
2.9489	44.7	.6423	22	tying
2.9489	44.7	.6843	21	undisturbed
2.9485	44.7	.4804	28	alloys
2.9483	44.7	.4770	30	tracing
2.9477	44.7	.6100	23	Frances
2.9473	44.7	.5610	25	reception
2.9463	44.7	.5411	26	Corn
2.9454	44.7	.1006	77	Ramona
2.9452	44.7	.6161	23	doubtless
2.9450	44.7	.7250	20	subjected
2.9447	44.7	.7076	20	headlong
2.9445	44.7	.5646	24	cockpit
2.9443	44.7	.5357	24	grins
2.9443	44.7	.6884	21	skillfully
2.9432	44.7	.6870	21	foremost
2.9431	44.7	.6764	21	scorched
2.9407	44.7	.4359	32	ballads
2.9404	44.7	.6856	21	fore
2.9397	44.7	.6796	21	allegiance
2.9396	44.7	.5946	24	forefinger
2.9396	44.7	.6534	22	1930's
2.9390	44.7	.5907	23	nibble
2.9389	44.7	.3769	36	Giants
2.9381	44.7	.5906	24	superiority
2.9372	44.7	.6866	21	hobbies
2.9369	44.7	.6359	22	heed
2.9365	44.7	.7062	20	jewel
2.9361	44.7	.4078	34	conducting
2.9360	44.7	.4157	33	applications
2.9358	44.7	.6085	23	trough
2.9347	44.7	.6691	21	chunk
2.9345	44.7	.4668	29	Colombia
2.9339	44.7	.5208	27	legislation
2.9322	44.7	.4571	30	skillet
2.9316	44.7	.2033	57	Marcy
2.9316	44.7	.4788	28	StLouis
2.9298	44.7	.4804	29	Piper
2.9296	44.7	.5025	27	tightened
2.9295	44.7	.6308	22	noticing
2.9285	44.7	.5403	26	clockwise

THE PRECEDING WORD TYPE OCCUPIES RANK 10300

U	SFI	D	F	Word Type
2.9285	44.7	.1926	55	intestine
2.9281	44.7	.5117	27	1944
2.9277	44.7	.7658	19	spice
2.9275	44.7	.7228	20	necessities
2.9274	44.7	.6740	21	midway
2.9274	44.7	.6435	22	piped
2.9269	44.7	.6222	23	establishing
2.9260	44.7	.6485	22	converting
2.9254	44.7	.5381	26	Isabel
2.9244	44.7	.4506	29	muttering

U	SFI	D	F	Word Type
2.9234	44.7	.4314	31	optical
2.9232	44.7	.3863	34	ions
2.9226	44.7	.5724	24	holly
2.9226	44.7	.5879	24	shaping
2.9217	44.7	.6414	22	assemblies
2.9192	44.7	.4223	32	germ
2.9191	44.7	.7217	20	delicately
2.9191	44.7	.6190	23	penetrating
2.9188	44.7	.7119	20	honestly
2.9187	44.7	.6993	20	drowsy
2.9183	44.7	.4405	29	Becky
2.9178	44.7	.7179	20	prestige
2.9150	44.6	.5320	26	curl
2.9146	44.6	.6747	21	silks
2.9135	44.6	.5562	25	occupies
2.9133	44.6	.7149	20	hard-working
2.9132	44.6	.6238	22	snowstorm
2.9128	44.6	.5689	24	Miles
2.9123	44.6	.4890	26	Sally's
2.9122	44.6	.7156	20	affecting
2.9108	44.6	.4829	28	Iran
2.9085	44.6	.4087	32	Japan's
2.9079	44.6	.5847	23	strangest
2.9074	44.6	.6074	22	fenders
2.9070	44.6	.4611	30	frequencies
2.9068	44.6	.6073	23	dice
2.9061	44.6	.5941	23	ankles
2.9053	44.6	.7090	20	consumed
2.9047	44.6	.3679	30	Ichabod
2.9044	44.6	.6160	22	'bout
2.9043	44.6	.6375	22	Hoover
2.9041	44.6	.6368	22	paces
2.9039	44.6	.6601	21	budge
2.9034	44.6	.4185	32	twos
2.9026	44.6	.6799	21	intimate
2.9024	44.6	.2774	42	barometer
2.9021	44.6	.1712	70	Bach
2.9021	44.6	.7145	20	innumerable
2.9015	44.6	.5744	24	generals
2.9012	44.6	.1993	39	Chad
2.9008	44.6	.3639	32	Henri
2.9008	44.6	.5725	24	slits
2.8996	44.6	.5269	25	Howe
2.8996	44.6	.5400	25	1492
2.8992	44.6	.4090	30	Kenny
2.8983	44.6	.6278	22	climbers
2.8982	44.6	.6079	23	News
2.8975	44.6	.6425	22	fringed
2.8975	44.6	.7070	20	hedges
2.8965	44.6	.5307	26	decoration
2.8960	44.6	.1902	63	hardness
2.8959	44.6	.5575	25	domain
2.8948	44.6	.4701	27	ached
2.8945	44.6	.5625	23	husbands
2.8939	44.6	.5542	24	beamed
2.8939	44.6	.5689	24	Rights
2.8917	44.6	.5491	24	schoolmaster
2.8910	44.6	.4920	26	mattress
2.8896	44.6	.6580	21	forgetting
2.8891	44.6	.5934	24	extensively
2.8877	44.6	.6506	21	ghostly
2.8866	44.6	.6973	20	laden
2.8863	44.6	.6069	22	Hercules
2.8856	44.6	.7051	20	exceedingly
2.8848	44.6	.7132	20	conspicuous
2.8845	44.6	.4031	31	UN
2.8844	44.6	.3936	33	electromagnetic
2.8843	44.6	.5410	25	flickering
2.8836	44.6	.4508	28	chipmunk
2.8815	44.6	.6294	22	disturb
2.8813	44.6	.7017	20	cruelty
2.8809	44.6	.6568	21	poorer
2.8796	44.6	.5966	23	crackling
2.8795	44.6	.2189	53	BC
2.8794	44.6	.7050	20	banded
2.8789	44.6	.4846	27	evergreen
2.8781	44.6	.3875	32	Collins
2.8772	44.6	.6327	22	cultivate
2.8761	44.6	.6644	21	surplus
2.8760	44.6	.5448	25	puppets
2.8760	44.6	.3240	34	Rick
2.8758	44.6	.5182	26	how's
2.8757	44.6	.6200	22	vicious
2.8756	44.6	.5191	24	turf
2.8754	44.6	.6045	23	waterways
2.8752	44.6	.3716	34	Moslems
2.8750	44.6	.6346	22	scenic
2.8748	44.6	.5749	23	grandstand
2.8747	44.6	.6419	21	chopping
2.8747	44.6	.6318	22	profitable

THE PRECEDING WORD TYPE OCCUPIES RANK 10400

U	SFI	D	F	Word Type
2.8738	44.6	.5530	25	Milton
2.8728	44.6	.5958	23	brightened
2.8724	44.6	.6436	22	facial
2.8719	44.6	.2647	43	stopper
2.8707	44.6	.6713	21	attracts
2.8704	44.6	.6562	21	risks
2.8704	44.6	.3200	39	vibrates
2.8692	44.6	.5654	24	Churchill
2.8691	44.6	.6379	22	tribesmen
2.8684	44.6	.3824	34	un
2.8683	44.6	.6578	21	swelling
2.8672	44.6	.5022	25	Willy
2.8671	44.6	.6630	21	eleventh
2.8663	44.6	.3593	36	threes
2.8662	44.6	.6253	22	wondrous
2.8661	44.6	.7053	20	earns
2.8660	44.6	.6782	21	Claude
2.8660	44.6	.6646	21	sermon
2.8652	44.6	.6395	22	limitations
2.8641	44.6	.5544	23	teakettle
2.8640	44.6	.6123	22	miner
2.8638	44.6	.5969	22	blinked
2.8637	44.6	.4641	28	jellyfish
2.8636	44.6	.4647	29	gland
2.8625	44.6	.3687	34	Suez
2.8624	44.6	.5347	25	1922

U	SFI	D	F	Word Type
2.8622	44.6	.4155	31	luncheon
2.8622	44.6	.6784	20	wintertime
2.8619	44.6	.6028	23	naturalist
2.8611	44.6	.7021	20	requirement
2.8609	44.6	.6940	20	windshield
2.8597	44.6	.4902	28	generated
2.8597	44.6	.3685	32	penguin
2.8586	44.6	.4534	27	mumbled
2.8584	44.6	.5966	23	residents
2.8582	44.6	.6910	20	rating
2.8576	44.6	.6661	21	inevitably
2.8571	44.6	.5981	22	championship
2.8562	44.6	.6657	21	dealt
2.8558	44.6	.4307	27	Coach
2.8551	44.6	.3922	29	Crow
2.8543	44.6	.5368	25	Mill
2.8541	44.6	.4711	28	1917
2.8540	44.6	.7493	19	significantly
2.8539	44.6	.6950	20	disliked
2.8538	44.6	.6016	23	comments
2.8529	44.6	.5665	24	phases
2.8525	44.6	.6905	20	gardener
2.8519	44.6	.6164	22	hailed
2.8516	44.6	.5459	25	transmitted
2.8507	44.6	.4655	28	seedlings
2.8501	44.5	.5714	24	splitting
2.8491	44.5	.5724	24	sentimental
2.8463	44.5	.5605	24	Dallas
2.8453	44.5	.5887	22	quail
2.8449	44.5	.6460	21	refusing
2.8449	44.5	.6617	21	uttered
2.8444	44.5	.5481	25	adjusting
2.8440	44.5	.4418	28	Jesse
2.8438	44.5	.3252	31	C **
2.8427	44.5	.5876	23	towered
2.8416	44.5	.7412	19	tedious
2.8415	44.5	.6515	21	Sundays
2.8414	44.5	.6602	21	invading
2.8414	44.5	.5358	25	tags
2.8411	44.5	.6806	20	disgust
2.8406	44.5	.5341	25	kingdoms
2.8405	44.5	.4089	32	coils
2.8400	44.5	.1267	83	pronunciations
2.8396	44.5	.6959	20	rumble
2.8390	44.5	.3405	38	campus
2.8388	44.5	.6921	20	sorted
2.8381	44.5	.2511	50	perspective
2.8376	44.5	.6901	20	gaunt
2.8374	44.5	.6400	21	foothills
2.8369	44.5	.4009	30	papa
2.8367	44.5	.6031	22	milked
2.8363	44.5	.6511	21	pegs
2.8352	44.5	.5849	22	wiggled
2.8349	44.5	.6621	21	reducing
2.8338	44.5	.7313	19	classrooms
2.8334	44.5	.6268	22	refreshments
2.8328	44.5	.3918	32	luminous
2.8327	44.5	.4276	30	hundredth
2.8324	44.5	.4678	28	geographical
2.8318	44.5	.4534	29	marches
2.8313	44.5	.5685	24	doubles
2.8309	44.5	.2307	50	paired
2.8307	44.5	.6807	20	kettles
2.8304	44.5	.5681	24	sober
2.8299	44.5	.5636	24	suburbs
2.8292	44.5	.7301	19	superstition
2.8288	44.5	.5194	26	prevailing
2.8288	44.5	.3936	32	unfair
2.8280	44.5	.3518	36	dart
2.8276	44.5	.6281	22	precautions
2.8271	44.5	.5078	25	amongst
2.8270	44.5	.4772	27	pillows
2.8266	44.5	.6833	20	creaking
2.8266	44.5	.5306	24	Julia

THE PRECEDING WORD TYPE OCCUPIES RANK 10500

U	SFI	D	F	Word Type
2.8258	44.5	.5769	23	mint
2.8256	44.5	.7347	19	sawdust
2.8251	44.5	.3763	34	habitat
2.8250	44.5	.6611	21	detached
2.8249	44.5	.5864	23	240
2.8241	44.5	.7189	19	unkind
2.8239	44.5	.6053	22	hollows
2.8237	44.5	.5001	27	chilled
2.8234	44.5	.6186	22	temporarily
2.8226	44.5	.2438	51	-ing
2.8225	44.5	.6780	20	chipped
2.8224	44.5	.6350	21	eerie
2.8220	44.5	.4341	31	lateral
2.8218	44.5	.4804	25	Crockett
2.8218	44.5	.6018	22	disgusted
2.8214	44.5	.7350	19	bleak
2.8214	44.5	.5542	24	instructed
2.8195	44.5	.7266	19	destined
2.8184	44.5	.7369	19	tempted
2.8179	44.5	.5266	24	tournament
2.8169	44.5	.6249	22	soaking
2.8165	44.5	.6854	20	forks
2.8159	44.5	.4510	29	census
2.8144	44.5	.7149	19	river's
2.8136	44.5	.4849	25	flicked
2.8130	44.5	.5531	23	Ole
2.8129	44.5	.4986	25	sonar
2.8129	44.5	.4887	26	timing
2.8128	44.5	.4223	31	Vienna
2.8121	44.5	.7294	19	gaps
2.8119	44.5	.5050	27	economical
2.8115	44.5	.6172	22	magical
2.8108	44.5	.6825	20	joyous
2.8108	44.5	.7708	18	oiled
2.8105	44.5	.6377	21	creeks
2.8098	44.5	.7194	19	exaggeration
2.8095	44.5	.4762	27	specialists
2.8094	44.5	.6802	20	horny
2.8086	44.5	.5552	23	quiver
2.8068	44.5	.5836	23	canning
2.8066	44.5	.4861	26	telegram
2.8039	44.5	.6480	21	Wood

U	SFI	D	F	Word Type
2.8035	44.5	.6139	22	gong
2.8033	44.5	.4020	31	1946
2.8028	44.5	.6917	20	attained
2.8023	44.5	.6418	21	manger
2.8019	44.5	.5661	24	components
2.8018	44.5	.1055	46	Shadow
2.8006	44.5	.6711	20	harnessed
2.8005	44.5	.6778	20	stubbornly
2.8001	44.5	.6834	20	170
2.7999	44.5	.6515	21	inform
2.7998	44.5	.3436	35	sacrifice
2.7995	44.5	.7669	18	inspected
2.7993	44.5	.5225	25	humidity
2.7990	44.5	.4300	30	Our
2.7984	44.5	.5627	24	spur
2.7974	44.5	.5433	25	Program
2.7973	44.5	.6161	22	disks
2.7964	44.5	.5141	26	interstate
2.7964	44.5	.3495	33	Wang
2.7962	44.5	.5927	22	Horn
2.7960	44.5	.6831	20	airy
2.7957	44.5	.4864	27	minority
2.7956	44.5	.5765	23	froze
2.7955	44.5	.6785	20	Huron
2.7946	44.5	.4000	32	96
2.7944	44.5	.5784	23	transistor
2.7943	44.5	.6815	20	surveying
2.7942	44.5	.3888	30	Sinbad
2.7941	44.5	.4829	28	abstract
2.7938	44.5	.2361	41	Spider
2.7931	44.5	.6528	21	preservation
2.7930	44.5	.6717	20	celebrating
2.7927	44.5	.2404	37	Rikki-tikki
2.7920	44.5	.5974	23	blending
2.7918	44.5	.6619	20	panted
2.7913	44.5	.6615	20	doorstep
2.7896	44.5	.5582	24	handicapped
2.7895	44.5	.6490	21	multitude
2.7893	44.5	.5308	24	squadron
2.7886	44.5	.6113	22	rivals
2.7880	44.5	.6431	21	careers
2.7879	44.5	.4826	27	microphone
2.7878	44.5	.6015	22	complaining
2.7878	44.5	.5642	23	workshop
2.7876	44.5	.6473	21	grid
2.7871	44.5	.6547	21	alternative
2.7857	44.4	.5757	23	1911
2.7855	44.4	.4694	28	rotating
2.7849	44.4	.6006	22	Hayes
2.7846	44.4	.4468	29	fertility
2.7843	44.4	.7128	19	liner
2.7836	44.4	.6401	21	wailing
2.7833	44.4	.5566	23	outlaw
2.7832	44.4	.6040	22	Carson
2.7819	44.4	.4371	29	warm-blooded
2.7817	44.4	.6064	22	crafts
2.7804	44.4	.6102	21	cabbages
2.7802	44.4	.5664	23	reminder

THE PRECEDING WORD TYPE OCCUPIES RANK 10600

U	SFI	D	F	Word Type
2.7789	44.4	.5851	23	declined
2.7788	44.4	.5462	23	uneasily
2.7785	44.4	.5739	23	Aristotle
2.7780	44.4	.6210	21	grownups
2.7780	44.4	.6414	21	rendered
2.7774	44.4	.7153	19	casually
2.7765	44.4	.5614	23	Ernie
2.7764	44.4	.3247	37	exported
2.7762	44.4	.6105	22	Francisco
2.7756	44.4	.7257	19	identifying
2.7755	44.4	.4594	28	dealers
2.7754	44.4	.4396	29	snack
2.7751	44.4	.6219	21	panther
2.7748	44.4	.6001	22	momentum
2.7741	44.4	.6638	20	weakly
2.7731	44.4	.6065	22	episode
2.7727	44.4	.5785	23	unlimited
2.7724	44.4	.5827	23	slabs
2.7719	44.4	.6666	20	clerks
2.7716	44.4	.4374	29	Africa's
2.7716	44.4	.3833	34	re
2.7712	44.4	.4614	27	Coronado
2.7709	44.4	.6095	21	Goose
2.7697	44.4	.6688	20	antlers
2.7693	44.4	.2084	42	Stormalong
2.7688	44.4	.6158	22	horizontally
2.7688	44.4	.6344	21	quarreled
2.7670	44.4	.5512	23	nibbled
2.7663	44.4	.6726	20	enthusiastically
2.7659	44.4	.6973	19	Hopkins
2.7640	44.4	.4690	28	107
2.7626	44.4	.7134	19	paralyzed
2.7616	44.4	.0800	94	decimals
2.7615	44.4	.5763	23	drainage
2.7604	44.4	.5955	22	regained
2.7602	44.4	.4990	25	zebra
2.7600	44.4	.6347	21	fingernails
2.7591	44.4	.7110	19	destroys
2.7581	44.4	.0915	117	garment
2.7574	44.4	.6061	21	bothering
2.7574	44.4	.6639	20	switching
2.7572	44.4	.6345	21	postage
2.7568	44.4	.6508	20	misses
2.7567	44.4	.7056	19	bordering
2.7561	44.4	.4631	28	sites
2.7559	44.4	.5813	23	crucial
2.7541	44.4	.3129	39	Meg
2.7539	44.4	.5312	24	intently
2.7536	44.4	.5480	24	strategic
2.7533	44.4	.5894	22	readings
2.7532	44.4	.4752	27	365
2.7531	44.4	.4676	27	Food
2.7508	44.4	.3945	31	Strait
2.7508	44.4	.6247	21	vest
2.7504	44.4	.4192	30	Uruguay
2.7489	44.4	.6187	21	rosy
2.7484	44.4	.5160	25	phenomena
2.7481	44.4	.6357	21	employment

U	SFI	D	F	Word Type
2.7476	44.4	.6081	21	blazed
2.7476	44.4	.5310	24	examinations
2.7475	44.4	.6364	21	embroidered
2.7465	44.4	.5253	23	earrings
2.7453	44.4	.6936	19	newcomer
2.7453	44.4	.6203	21	reddish
2.7453	44.4	.5892	22	Run
2.7449	44.4	.7062	19	repeatedly
2.7441	44.4	.6228	21	horrid
2.7435	44.4	.6222	21	dismissed
2.7434	44.4	.2231	47	irrigated
2.7431	44.4	.3994	32	body's
2.7417	44.4	.4791	26	Bantu
2.7408	44.4	.5046	25	topped
2.7403	44.4	.4254	28	Iroquois
2.7403	44.4	.5267	24	woody
2.7396	44.4	.4672	27	hump
2.7375	44.4	.5781	23	architectural
2.7370	44.4	.6693	20	medium-sized
2.7365	44.4	.7094	19	staggering
2.7350	44.4	.6231	21	1932
2.7346	44.4	.6545	20	mysteriously
2.7342	44.4	.5885	22	loaned
2.7341	44.4	.5761	23	Normandy
2.7341	44.4	.6582	20	Station
2.7339	44.4	.4154	26	Finn
2.7329	44.4	.5302	24	cured
2.7324	44.4	.6304	21	offense
2.7320	44.4	.4162	31	Bethlehem
2.7318	44.4	.6964	19	outskirts
2.7317	44.4	.6060	21	licking
2.7316	44.4	.5272	24	Curie
2.7315	44.4	.4765	26	spool
2.7309	44.4	.7075	19	honesty
2.7304	44.4	.5589	22	willows
2.7302	44.4	.4235	29	beaks
2.7297	44.4	.5191	25	promote
2.7293	44.4	.6482	20	Dad's
2.7287	44.4	.3688	33	microscopic
2.7287	44.4	.6035	21	wiser
2.7283	44.4	.2806	44	painters
2.7279	44.4	.6252	21	infected
THE PRECEDING WORD TYPE OCCUPIES RANK 10700				
2.7277	44.4	.4409	28	sediment
2.7273	44.4	.6447	20	tulip
2.7265	44.4	.2435	45	neutrons
2.7258	44.4	.6286	21	acquaintance
2.7254	44.4	.5872	22	dashes
2.7247	44.4	.6989	19	occupying
2.7235	44.4	.4904	25	glances
2.7233	44.4	.7075	19	charity
2.7225	44.4	.5070	25	Noah
2.7225	44.3	.6479	20	sighs
2.7224	44.3	.5134	25	tactics
2.7218	44.3	.5709	22	explosions
2.7215	44.3	.4984	26	Protestant
2.7214	44.3	.5258	23	Indians'
2.7206	44.3	.6790	19	drags
2.7205	44.3	.3813	32	environments
2.7200	44.3	.5955	22	sharpened
2.7199	44.3	.5828	22	Susie
2.7191	44.3	.3479	35	thousandths
2.7189	44.3	.4598	26	Woman
2.7171	44.3	.5688	22	smallpox
2.7165	44.3	.6596	20	elm
2.7165	44.3	.6535	20	shabby
2.7163	44.3	.5950	22	ritual
2.7161	44.3	.6066	22	references
2.7158	44.3	.3500	30	sniff
2.7156	44.3	.5367	24	Greenville
2.7139	44.3	.5294	23	scornfully
2.7133	44.3	.6141	21	puddle
2.7122	44.3	.7011	19	favors
2.7115	44.3	.6451	20	padded
2.7106	44.3	.4868	26	Joyce
2.7103	44.3	.6133	21	hub
2.7103	44.3	.6875	19	unnoticed
2.7102	44.3	.2443	49	/s/
2.7093	44.3	.6475	20	mind's
2.7092	44.3	.6962	19	wildest
2.7083	44.3	.6940	19	questioning
2.7081	44.3	.5382	23	make-up
2.7079	44.3	.4488	28	Key
2.7078	44.3	.6977	19	baker
2.7070	44.3	.6614	20	revolving
2.7064	44.3	.0768	92	Exercises
2.7058	44.3	.5958	22	managing
2.7055	44.3	.5129	24	Amendment
2.7044	44.3	.4192	30	On
2.7043	44.3	.4261	29	menu
2.7041	44.3	.3702	29	Miranda
2.7041	44.3	.6230	21	1927
2.7026	44.3	.1945	58	Pattern
2.7024	44.3	.5255	25	overlapping
2.7009	44.3	.5885	21	frowning
2.7003	44.3	.7056	19	grinder
2.7002	44.3	.6876	19	sorting
2.6998	44.3	.5494	23	Sterling
2.6992	44.3	.5364	24	Standard
2.6991	44.3	.6006	21	Friend
2.6990	44.3	.7446	18	deprived
2.6987	44.3	.4445	27	lark
2.6984	44.3	.7313	18	pinched
2.6978	44.3	.5814	21	hash
2.6975	44.3	.6329	20	lion's
2.6974	44.3	.5965	21	bewildered
2.6971	44.3	.5224	24	grating
2.6970	44.3	.5705	23	adhesive
2.6969	44.3	.5474	23	Quaker
2.6967	44.3	.6102	21	queens
2.6958	44.3	.3075	37	genes
2.6952	44.3	.6191	21	brim
2.6945	44.3	.0788	88	Abraham
2.6937	44.3	.5040	25	platinum
2.6937	44.3	.5609	23	triple
2.6935	44.3	.0232	161	Kino
2.6931	44.3	.6923	19	pierced
2.6927	44.3	.5666	22	cruising
2.6922	44.3	.4612	24	Jennifer
2.6913	44.3	.4776	27	Whitey
2.6912	44.3	.6636	20	discharge
2.6902	44.3	.6482	20	thickets
2.6889	44.3	.5819	21	crate
2.6889	44.3	.6870	19	feeble
2.6888	44.3	.1636	67	keyboard
2.6885	44.3	.7334	18	heir
2.6883	44.3	.5900	21	chattered
2.6874	44.3	.6889	19	urgent
2.6863	44.3	.5632	23	joys
2.6862	44.3	.7423	18	demonstrates
2.6843	44.3	.6896	19	gravy
2.6841	44.3	.2552	42	sedimentary
2.6827	44.3	.3721	33	bladder
2.6826	44.3	.5865	22	nymph
2.6818	44.3	.6170	21	super
2.6815	44.3	.5057	25	responses
2.6813	44.3	.5545	22	dwelt
2.6813	44.3	.5905	22	We
2.6810	44.3	.6929	19	promotion
2.6805	44.3	.6313	20	figuring
2.6805	44.3	.7316	18	wary
2.6798	44.3	.6890	19	afloat
2.6798	44.3	.5397	23	breeches
THE PRECEDING WORD TYPE OCCUPIES RANK 10800				
2.6797	44.3	.5655	22	rinse
2.6789	44.3	.3658	29	Locke
2.6786	44.3	.4049	31	Danes
2.6772	44.3	.5478	23	eels
2.6772	44.3	.6510	20	yellowish
2.6768	44.3	.6884	19	prior
2.6765	44.3	.6435	20	qualifications
2.6748	44.3	.5736	22	blond
2.6734	44.3	.7227	18	carpets
2.6725	44.3	.5244	23	underwear
2.6716	44.3	.3663	28	Darling
2.6712	44.3	.5816	22	Richmond
2.6708	44.3	.6824	19	embarrassment
2.6695	44.3	.2427	35	Fats
2.6685	44.3	.4093	30	Italy's
2.6676	44.3	.6381	20	offended
2.6674	44.3	.6510	20	breeds
2.6674	44.3	.6508	20	stripped
2.6671	44.3	.6780	19	wares
2.6670	44.3	.6689	19	shaky
2.6665	44.3	.6510	20	sporting
2.6662	44.3	.5331	23	storehouse
2.6661	44.3	.5943	21	rigging
2.6645	44.3	.5259	24	giraffes
2.6643	44.3	.5349	22	fliers
2.6638	44.3	.5046	24	squatted
2.6634	44.3	.5316	23	hurrah
2.6623	44.3	.6466	20	mingled
2.6620	44.3	.3980	29	Jose
2.6617	44.3	.5970	21	salted
2.6603	44.2	.4786	25	clubhouse
2.6593	44.2	.6752	19	churning
2.6592	44.2	.7278	18	redwood
2.6584	44.2	.2971	37	Atlas
2.6579	44.2	.3041	37	spindle
2.6577	44.2	.4906	26	wilt
2.6574	44.2	.5187	24	chestnut
2.6573	44.2	.6853	19	flax
2.6572	44.2	.6431	20	slate
2.6571	44.2	.4575	27	Kid
2.6569	44.2	.5616	23	accompanying
2.6563	44.2	.6232	20	riverbank
2.6554	44.2	.4750	26	revolves
2.6553	44.2	.5078	24	tadpole
2.6542	44.2	.6008	21	prediction
2.6540	44.2	.6844	19	settings
2.6535	44.2	.4776	26	burrows
2.6531	44.2	.0921	83	subtracted
2.6530	44.2	.4240	29	waltz
2.6528	44.2	.5558	22	handkerchiefs
2.6523	44.2	.5714	22	corporation
2.6517	44.2	.3848	31	eclipse
2.6517	44.2	.6323	20	specks
2.6507	44.2	.6384	20	disturbing
2.6505	44.2	.3994	31	revise
2.6503	44.2	.3903	32	shepherds
2.6487	44.2	.5105	25	mobile
2.6469	44.2	.6778	19	fountains
2.6464	44.2	.7260	18	engagement
2.6463	44.2	.1850	37	Dionisio
2.6458	44.2	.4472	27	females
2.6447	44.2	.4989	24	elk
2.6439	44.2	.4337	25	Timmy
2.6437	44.2	.5986	21	exaggerated
2.6436	44.2	.4396	28	administrative
2.6436	44.2	.4991	25	Vice
2.6434	44.2	.5606	22	rumbling
2.6429	44.2	.5034	24	Havana
2.6429	44.2	.4519	27	republics
2.6427	44.2	.7156	18	ranged
2.6426	44.2	.4199	29	tombs
2.6425	44.2	.5575	22	triumphantly
2.6422	44.2	.6326	20	frenzy
2.6404	44.2	.5337	23	boulder
2.6395	44.2	.5959	21	recite
2.6386	44.2	.5781	22	bearded
2.6385	44.2	.1048	78	ABC
2.6385	44.2	.6169	20	settler
2.6384	44.2	.5374	23	enrolled
2.6382	44.2	.5404	23	drier
2.6380	44.2	.3885	29	friend's
2.6377	44.2	.5327	23	gazing
2.6377	44.2	.5496	23	1912
2.6373	44.2	.5498	23	S**
2.6371	44.2	.7043	18	notices
2.6369	44.2	.7163	18	comical
2.6369	44.2	.3169	35	privilege
2.6367	44.2	.7276	18	token
2.6354	44.2	.6336	20	pneumonia
2.6353	44.2	.5882	21	bushel
2.6350	44.2	.6736	19	await
2.6338	44.2	.4153	29	treating
2.6336	44.2	.6088	21	Artic
2.6336	44.2	.5830	21	bear's
2.6332	44.2	.4836	26	snare
2.6323	44.2	.7235	18	confronted
2.6321	44.2	.5110	24	regiment
2.6316	44.2	.5201	22	Elephant
2.6316	44.2	.7571	17	quill
2.6314	44.2	.6432	20	distribute
THE PRECEDING WORD TYPE OCCUPIES RANK 10900				
2.6306	44.2	.1683	61	Eddy
2.6302	44.2	.6246	20	dwelling
2.6300	44.2	.6743	19	bursts
2.6297	44.2	.6800	19	hesitation
2.6296	44.2	.5699	22	displays
2.6293	44.2	.6839	19	vitality
2.6285	44.2	.5595	23	expressive
2.6280	44.2	.6043	21	X-ray
2.6268	44.2	.1506	61	Example
2.6268	44.2	.5265	23	lids
2.6261	44.2	.5692	22	flannel
2.6257	44.2	.5045	25	connections
2.6256	44.2	.5380	23	ancestry
2.6249	44.2	.6460	19	graveyard
2.6247	44.2	.6610	19	vice-president
2.6244	44.2	.5745	22	celebrations
2.6242	44.2	.6317	20	heaved
2.6242	44.2	.6717	19	stain
2.6240	44.2	.3546	33	Kevin
2.6240	44.2	.7098	18	politician
2.6231	44.2	.6105	21	restrictions
2.6221	44.2	.5658	22	venison
2.6214	44.2	.5043	24	take-off
2.6205	44.2	.6363	20	Ontario
2.6201	44.2	.6267	20	stalked
2.6194	44.2	.5002	25	denote
2.6194	44.2	.5920	21	Six
2.6188	44.2	.5142	24	Butler
2.6188	44.2	.6142	20	volunteer
2.6181	44.2	.6102	21	subsequent
2.6180	44.2	.5839	21	porridge
2.6178	44.2	.6443	20	representation
2.6175	44.2	.6712	19	Fire
2.6142	44.2	.5460	22	Baron
2.6136	44.2	.6600	19	sympathetic
2.6128	44.2	.7053	18	clustered
2.6109	44.2	.5589	22	cuckoo
2.6102	44.2	.6743	19	lemons
2.6101	44.2	.4021	29	polluted
2.6101	44.2	.4914	25	wrinkles
2.6096	44.2	.2981	33	sausages
2.6092	44.2	.5626	22	Emerson
2.6091	44.2	.4432	27	adaptation
2.6086	44.2	.4887	24	butt
2.6085	44.2	.6359	20	destiny
2.6078	44.2	.2937	32	robots
2.6075	44.2	.3850	31	genus
2.6074	44.2	.7025	18	speeded
2.6073	44.2	.6224	20	trifle
2.6072	44.2	.4514	27	photos
2.6069	44.2	.7046	18	regain
2.6067	44.2	.5680	22	ascent
2.6057	44.2	.4107	29	grams
2.6053	44.2	.5408	23	chemically
2.6053	44.2	.3365	28	Loki
2.6050	44.2	.3289	29	Merlin
2.6050	44.2	.6332	20	1928
2.6050	44.2	.3913	30	1947
2.6045	44.2	.2392	45	lb
2.6039	44.2	.0000	57	Ivik
2.6036	44.2	.7026	18	dearly
2.6022	44.2	.6217	20	wade
2.6002	44.2	.6650	19	torrent
2.5997	44.1	.6616	19	1926
2.5996	44.1	.6518	19	Store
2.5995	44.1	.3891	31	coined
2.5987	44.1	.4757	23	Harrisburg
2.5985	44.1	.5537	22	rum
2.5976	44.1	.5099	24	Hollywood
2.5967	44.1	.5245	23	suspension
2.5964	44.1	.5831	21	monsters
2.5961	44.1	.7045	18	picnics
2.5959	44.1	.5811	21	seacoast
2.5955	44.1	.5433	22	doll's
2.5955	44.1	.5146	24	numerical
2.5953	44.1	.5680	22	influential
2.5935	44.1	.4756	25	fern
2.5928	44.1	.6247	20	brace
2.5928	44.1	.6634	19	hazardous
2.5917	44.1	.6610	19	explorations
2.5915	44.1	.4709	26	Catholics
2.5904	44.1	.5953	21	journal
2.5903	44.1	.5532	22	gnawing
2.5901	44.1	.4781	25	offshore
2.5895	44.1	.5692	22	controversy
2.5890	44.1	.6657	19	Charleston
2.5887	44.1	.6134	20	marshy
2.5887	44.1	.3905	29	owed
2.5887	44.1	.4957	25	verbal
2.5886	44.1	.5966	21	Children's
2.5885	44.1	.7037	18	analyzing
2.5881	44.1	.7446	17	ordeal
2.5876	44.1	.5373	22	pails
2.5876	44.1	.4595	26	seaports
2.5872	44.1	.6394	19	strutted
2.5869	44.1	.5695	21	Grandfather's
2.5865	44.1	.4801	25	Burma
2.5863	44.1	.6265	20	Yellow
2.5858	44.1	.5618	21	Bat
2.5852	44.1	.4969	23	braced
THE PRECEDING WORD TYPE OCCUPIES RANK 11000				
2.5849	44.1	.5773	21	grazed
2.5848	44.1	.1101	42	Carver
2.5845	44.1	.4587	24	Carlo
2.5842	44.1	.6943	18	quieter
2.5842	44.1	.6505	19	staircase
2.5840	44.1	.5543	22	bred
2.5838	44.1	.5330	23	densely
2.5836	44.1	.5012	24	charter
2.5829	44.1	.7031	18	cautious
2.5828	44.1	.6954	18	boast
2.5828	44.1	.3747	28	Nana
2.5828	44.1	.6195	20	vacations
2.5821	44.1	.5895	21	Marine
2.5821	44.1	.5860	21	SanDiego
2.5812	44.1	.6952	18	twenty-nine
2.5810	44.1	.4298	27	forested
2.5806	44.1	.6217	20	Grove
2.5784	44.1	.4407	26	packet
2.5774	44.1	.5375	23	considers
2.5772	44.1	.5409	21	Mike's
2.5757	44.1	.6979	18	thirty-seven
2.5752	44.1	.5906	21	Natural
2.5750	44.1	.6503	19	rocker
2.5732	44.1	.6294	19	squealing
2.5731	44.1	.4679	25	delta
2.5716	44.1	.3779	31	Nobel
2.5714	44.1	.6982	18	fashionable
2.5713	44.1	.5045	22	Joy
2.5711	44.1	.1257	78	ly
2.5709	44.1	.5689	21	forefathers
2.5706	44.1	.4520	24	Dennis
2.5694	44.1	.6122	20	bulls
2.5692	44.1	.1368	71	refrain
2.5689	44.1	.7485	17	dipping
2.5689	44.1	.4516	26	Islam
2.5688	44.1	.6499	19	invitations
2.5685	44.1	.3016	35	sacs
2.5684	44.1	.6190	20	sparrows
2.5678	44.1	.2868	38	mathematicians
2.5673	44.1	.7442	17	exceed
2.5670	44.1	.7434	17	survivors
2.5669	44.1	.6382	19	scold
2.5666	44.1	.5962	21	stresses
2.5655	44.1	.6886	18	lengthy
2.5648	44.1	.7388	17	bowing
2.5648	44.1	.7049	18	contracted
2.5636	44.1	.4749	26	optional
2.5635	44.1	.5991	20	fainter
2.5622	44.1	.3458	27	Cloud
2.5622	44.1	.6195	20	gunpowder
2.5619	44.1	.5705	21	propped
2.5614	44.1	.6791	18	soles
2.5614	44.1	.7006	18	stimulate
2.5613	44.1	.6577	19	accumulation
2.5613	44.1	.5287	23	dost
2.5612	44.1	.7030	18	Ring
2.5604	44.1	.7001	18	streamlined
2.5596	44.1	.5915	20	whiz
2.5591	44.1	.4526	27	introduces
2.5588	44.1	.6274	20	daisies
2.5583	44.1	.4099	28	pineapples
2.5577	44.1	.5335	22	blizzard
2.5577	44.1	.7000	18	one-tenth
2.5569	44.1	.5006	24	invested
2.5568	44.1	.3056	39	narrative
2.5564	44.1	.3172	32	nomads
2.5560	44.1	.5095	22	neared
2.5559	44.1	.5390	22	grassland
2.5558	44.1	.3617	32	banjo
2.5543	44.1	.5500	22	undertaken
2.5542	44.1	.6309	19	darting
2.5541	44.1	.6022	20	uncertainly
2.5527	44.1	.5152	23	protests
2.5524	44.1	.4047	28	Basin
2.5523	44.1	.4487	25	Dolittle
2.5517	44.1	.5824	21	chess
2.5515	44.1	.3362	34	motive
2.5515	44.1	.7368	17	neglect
2.5513	44.1	.6370	19	battled
2.5506	44.1	.6960	18	memorable
2.5503	44.1	.4425	27	Treaty
2.5495	44.1	.6899	18	uphill
2.5492	44.1	.0847	71	spores
2.5488	44.1	.3553	31	cock
2.5477	44.1	.6531	19	rein
2.5475	44.1	.0018	297	Spelling
2.5471	44.1	.4970	24	coke
2.5470	44.1	.5560	21	Count
2.5467	44.1	.5909	21	user
2.5465	44.1	.7313	17	carefree
2.5462	44.1	.6408	19	rebuilding
2.5459	44.1	.4825	24	Leonard
2.5459	44.1	.5856	21	sow
2.5450	44.1	.3462	32	hydroelectric
2.5444	44.1	.6216	20	ally
2.5439	44.1	.6822	18	Brown's
2.5436	44.1	.5375	23	Helena
2.5434	44.1	.6005	20	Reverend
2.5422	44.1	.6342	19	plumes
2.5419	44.1	.2622	39	capillaries
THE PRECEDING WORD TYPE OCCUPIES RANK 11100				
2.5414	44.1	.6885	18	pancake
2.5409	44.0	.7930	16	nautical
2.5407	44.0	.6167	20	gears
2.5406	44.0	.1604	56	Fool
2.5401	44.0	.5312	22	catalog
2.5401	44.0	.4425	25	hurricanes
2.5398	44.0	.5441	22	retirement
2.5392	44.0	.6116	20	altitudes
2.5392	44.0	.5522	21	skipped
2.5391	44.0	.6974	18	consistently
2.5378	44.0	.5785	21	founder
2.5375	44.0	.7345	17	barefoot
2.5373	44.0	.0807	117	fabrics
2.5372	44.0	.6250	19	gem
2.5366	44.0	.3213	37	adverbial
2.5366	44.0	.6229	19	mountaintop
2.5363	44.0	.2535	31	Peterson
2.5358	44.0	.4580	25	Doc
2.5356	44.0	.6131	20	superintendent
2.5354	44.0	.5179	23	mow
2.5345	44.0	.6445	19	barks

U	SFI	D	F	Word Type
2.5344	44.0	.6765	18	congratulations
2.5343	44.0	.6429	19	adventurers
2.5341	44.0	.6030	20	viewing
2.5330	44.0	.5536	21	vulture
2.5323	44.0	.6231	20	obstacles
2.5322	44.0	.4211	26	cacao
2.5303	44.0	.5652	21	buckle
2.5299	44.0	.6004	20	marketing
2.5297	44.0	.5958	20	husband's
2.5294	44.0	.6844	18	raiders
2.5292	44.0	.5016	23	Code
2.5292	44.0	.6991	18	substituting
2.5287	44.0	.6873	18	dissatisfied
2.5285	44.0	.5327	22	Jimmy's
2.5284	44.0	.6123	20	compression
2.5281	44.0	.5259	23	mm
2.5280	44.0	.6313	19	forty-five
2.5278	44.0	.5339	22	luster
2.5276	44.0	.6480	19	acceleration
2.5272	44.0	.3866	30	$100
2.5266	44.0	.5087	23	Vernon
2.5261	44.0	.5304	21	Wife
2.5243	44.0	.3294	32	Fairy
2.5234	44.0	.4969	24	converse
2.5229	44.0	.5969	20	wobbly
2.5226	44.0	.3562	31	Piedmont
2.5214	44.0	.5596	22	specified
2.5210	44.0	.3267	32	crackers
2.5203	44.0	.4888	23	Java
2.5202	44.0	.6716	18	interrupt
2.5199	44.0	.4610	25	China's
2.5196	44.0	.5692	21	blackened
2.5192	44.0	.6787	18	poised
2.5190	44.0	.2695	41	welding
2.5181	44.0	.3555	32	sensory
2.5180	44.0	.5876	20	'cause
2.5180	44.0	.3331	31	farmed
2.5178	44.0	.4767	25	Cincinnati
2.5171	44.0	.6468	19	kits
2.5166	44.0	.4892	24	Treasury
2.5156	44.0	.7178	17	announcer
2.5156	44.0	.6042	20	hastened
2.5156	44.0	.4879	25	realistic
2.5154	44.0	.3460	32	geologic
2.5154	44.0	.5714	21	trigger
2.5145	44.0	.4752	25	component
2.5131	44.0	.6668	18	uproar
2.5129	44.0	.5765	21	conserve
2.5125	44.0	.5912	20	busiest
2.5121	44.0	.6643	18	Nicholas
2.5115	44.0	.6398	19	remarkably
2.5112	44.0	.5288	21	hummingbird
2.5103	44.0	.7315	17	inspector
2.5103	44.0	.3861	31	modifying
2.5095	44.0	.3467	31	mouthpiece
2.5091	44.0	.5760	21	logic
2.5083	44.0	.4831	24	involuntary
2.5079	44.0	.3287	34	Custer
2.5078	44.0	.6089	19	doubtfully
2.5078	44.0	.5699	21	unfinished
2.5074	44.0	.6461	19	resentment
2.5073	44.0	.4615	26	headline
2.5070	44.0	.7251	17	Place
2.5059	44.0	.4443	27	overlap
2.5058	44.0	.2051	51	concerts
2.5056	44.0	.4336	26	constellation
2.5053	44.0	.5190	23	revolved
2.5053	44.0	.6798	18	separation
2.5052	44.0	.6722	18	peg
2.5049	44.0	.6701	18	wiggle
2.5048	44.0	.5121	22	sobs
2.5046	44.0	.5561	21	dragonfly
2.5041	44.0	.6821	18	exclusive
2.5040	44.0	.4857	24	antibiotics
2.5040	44.0	.2814	36	bless
2.5028	44.0	.6195	19	stomachs
2.5026	44.0	.3141	36	darts
2.5026	44.0	.6387	19	raids
2.5021	44.0	.6566	18	raincoat

THE PRECEDING WORD TYPE OCCUPIES RANK 11200

U	SFI	D	F	Word Type
2.5021	44.0	.6243	19	soar
2.5019	44.0	.6587	18	din
2.5014	44.0	.6356	19	memorized
2.5012	44.0	.6274	19	directors
2.5012	44.0	.5734	21	initials
2.5010	44.0	.7320	17	receding
2.5006	44.0	.5281	22	Montreal
2.5006	44.0	.6279	19	trays
2.5004	44.0	.0800	104	ou
2.5004	44.0	.5147	23	teenagers
2.4999	44.0	.6603	18	towed
2.4988	44.0	.7290	17	lifeless
2.4982	44.0	.5950	20	Carol's
2.4979	44.0	.6083	20	investment
2.4968	44.0	.5088	23	Quakers
2.4964	44.0	.7212	17	completion
2.4962	44.0	.6349	19	depot
2.4949	44.0	.4894	24	tract
2.4944	44.0	.5591	21	freighters
2.4943	44.0	.6262	19	cider
2.4942	44.0	.5112	22	watchful
2.4941	44.0	.4021	28	silicon
2.4938	44.0	.6336	19	tremendously
2.4936	44.0	.5317	22	edged
2.4934	44.0	.6289	19	gasp
2.4929	44.0	.6398	19	WestVirginia
2.4926	44.0	.4890	25	decorative
2.4924	44.0	.6789	18	1943
2.4914	44.0	.6688	18	fleeing
2.4908	44.0	.6535	18	boughs
2.4900	44.0	.6699	18	tempting
2.4899	44.0	.4015	27	meteor
2.4895	44.0	.6472	18	Chamberlain
2.4892	44.0	.6036	19	horses'
2.4892	44.0	.4629	25	treaties
2.4889	44.0	.6069	19	madly
2.4889	44.0	.5377	22	well-being

U	SFI	D	F	Word Type
2.4888	44.0	.2753	40	recorder
2.4885	44.0	.6396	19	repairing
2.4856	44.0	.6353	19	incredibly
2.4854	44.0	.7670	16	annoying
2.4852	44.0	.4043	27	Dunn
2.4848	44.0	.5897	20	1814
2.4840	44.0	.7232	17	satin
2.4838	44.0	.3233	33	Pakistan
2.4828	43.9	.6840	18	mastery
2.4827	43.9	.6799	18	infinitely
2.4816	43.9	.3745	30	circuits
2.4814	43.9	.6572	18	skaters
2.4809	43.9	.6342	19	supposedly
2.4804	43.9	.4990	24	buttermilk
2.4803	43.9	.5910	20	condemned
2.4803	43.9	.6311	19	shipment
2.4802	43.9	.4397	26	Animal
2.4801	43.9	.6634	18	brand-new
2.4799	43.9	.5329	22	groupings
2.4799	43.9	.2012	53	instrumental
2.4798	43.9	.5683	20	sobbed
2.4796	43.9	.7663	16	chaos
2.4796	43.9	.5460	21	nigh
2.4792	43.9	.6566	18	spat
2.4791	43.9	.6656	18	fantasy
2.4791	43.9	.4231	27	porous
2.4784	43.9	.6114	19	Dark
2.4781	43.9	.5703	21	experimented
2.4780	43.9	.6701	18	steamed
2.4768	43.9	.5761	21	traditionally
2.4767	43.9	.5597	21	strife
2.4764	43.9	.6206	19	Oak
2.4757	43.9	.6583	18	keel
2.4737	43.9	.6612	18	Julius
2.4723	43.9	.6001	19	crates
2.4715	43.9	.5604	21	silverware
2.4711	43.9	.5422	22	blacks
2.4710	43.9	.5938	20	peer
2.4699	43.9	.7008	17	behaved
2.4698	43.9	.4916	24	Edwin
2.4697	43.9	.1522	64	garments
2.4691	43.9	.6084	20	angular
2.4681	43.9	.6634	18	gliding
2.4673	43.9	.6278	19	brilliantly
2.4671	43.9	.6753	18	exclusively
2.4671	43.9	.5840	20	gladly
2.4669	43.9	.3786	29	stimulus
2.4668	43.9	.5040	23	Richard's
2.4663	43.9	.6561	18	lazily
2.4661	43.9	.4052	28	Ike
2.4640	43.9	.4968	23	librarian
2.4639	43.9	.5095	23	composite
2.4635	43.9	.4439	26	Labor
2.4632	43.9	.6695	18	gracefully
2.4631	43.9	.5975	19	glided
2.4619	43.9	.3701	32	adjustment
2.4616	43.9	.6673	18	ingenuity
2.4611	43.9	.6285	19	remedy
2.4605	43.9	.5786	20	projector
2.4604	43.9	.5649	21	targets
2.4604	43.9	.5573	21	undergrowth
2.4604	43.9	.5851	20	unfolded
2.4598	43.9	.5281	22	smog

THE PRECEDING WORD TYPE OCCUPIES RANK 11300

U	SFI	D	F	Word Type
2.4580	43.9	.6067	19	whispers
2.4575	43.9	.5245	22	screwed
2.4574	43.9	.6262	19	socket
2.4571	43.9	.5758	20	hissing
2.4567	43.9	.6448	18	dashing
2.4560	43.9	.3597	31	appliances
2.4554	43.9	.5913	20	brood
2.4552	43.9	.4553	23	eruption
2.4542	43.9	.6145	19	misty
2.4538	43.9	.6967	17	tanned
2.4534	43.9	.4687	24	fertilizers
2.4528	43.9	.5103	22	toothpick
2.4523	43.9	.7030	17	unlucky
2.4521	43.9	.6107	19	battlefield
2.4520	43.9	.2459	34	Coyote
2.4519	43.9	.2570	44	capitalize
2.4510	43.9	.5781	20	knotted
2.4499	43.9	.5319	21	parakeet
2.4491	43.9	.7569	16	devise
2.4491	43.9	.4706	24	warehouses
2.4480	43.9	.2055	51	112
2.4479	43.9	.6222	19	Richards
2.4476	43.9	.1004	66	protoplasm
2.4469	43.9	.3863	28	highland
2.4459	43.9	.6978	17	throng
2.4457	43.9	.6958	17	errands
2.4449	43.9	.5599	20	braid
2.4449	43.9	.3820	29	kernels
2.4446	43.9	.5407	21	chick
2.4445	43.9	.5795	20	patting
2.4445	43.9	.5433	21	rabies
2.4440	43.9	.4246	25	pantry
2.4438	43.9	.3466	32	decreases
2.4437	43.9	.5942	20	withstand
2.4435	43.9	.3381	32	saves
2.4434	43.9	.4590	25	economically
2.4433	43.9	.6652	18	impress
2.4430	43.9	.5769	19	octopus
2.4429	43.9	.2985	36	Phoenix
2.4415	43.9	.3174	32	Cody
2.4409	43.9	.6527	18	collapse
2.4408	43.9	.5838	20	healthful
2.4408	43.9	.7570	16	imagining
2.4399	43.9	.6596	18	balances
2.4398	43.9	.6007	19	Circus
2.4380	43.9	.5622	21	duration
2.4377	43.9	.5176	21	robbery
2.4371	43.9	.4829	24	Education
2.4369	43.9	.5915	20	technological
2.4369	43.9	.5176	21	that'll
2.4368	43.9	.6075	19	foal
2.4368	43.9	.6896	17	shields
2.4349	43.9	.6916	17	numb

U	SFI	D	F	Word Type
2.4345	43.9	.5401	21	maids
2.4342	43.9	.5024	23	102
2.4339	43.9	.7004	17	paradise
2.4338	43.9	.3473	26	Prometheus
2.4336	43.9	.5286	22	historian
2.4336	43.9	.6495	18	leans
2.4331	43.9	.6465	18	spike
2.4323	43.9	.5447	21	thunderstorm
2.4320	43.9	.5899	20	refugees
2.4314	43.9	.6463	18	affectionate
2.4312	43.9	.6496	18	slaughter
2.4297	43.9	.6179	19	radishes
2.4295	43.9	.6438	18	hug
2.4293	43.9	.4770	24	physicists
2.4292	43.9	.5228	22	Daily
2.4290	43.9	.6597	18	grapefruit
2.4285	43.9	.5143	22	semicircle
2.4281	43.9	.4815	23	sunflower
2.4279	43.9	.6564	18	privacy
2.4275	43.9	.6638	18	presidents
2.4274	43.9	.6483	18	flip
2.4273	43.9	.6992	17	brooks
2.4272	43.9	.6538	18	reluctant
2.4271	43.9	.5313	22	excerpts
2.4265	43.8	.4014	24	Conn
2.4259	43.8	.5537	21	large-scale
2.4255	43.8	.6953	17	liners
2.4251	43.8	.6624	18	participate
2.4249	43.8	.6956	17	threaten
2.4243	43.8	.5818	20	accumulated
2.4241	43.8	.5563	21	Byzantine
2.4238	43.8	.5860	20	Milwaukee
2.4232	43.8	.5531	21	equatorial
2.4222	43.8	.5629	21	enclose
2.4220	43.8	.6503	18	obedient
2.4215	43.8	.7453	16	disadvantage
2.4209	43.8	.6676	18	ample
2.4206	43.8	.5516	21	Cub
2.4204	43.8	.4481	25	tributaries
2.4204	43.8	.6813	17	wreckage
2.4202	43.8	.5570	21	stability
2.4201	43.8	.6132	19	fabulous
2.4196	43.8	.2429	31	Boots
2.4194	43.8	.6321	18	uncle's
2.4191	43.8	.4871	22	landlord
2.4191	43.8	.6141	19	mammoth
2.4189	43.8	.6509	18	dwellings

THE PRECEDING WORD TYPE OCCUPIES RANK 11400

U	SFI	D	F	Word Type
2.4184	43.8	.6094	19	guessing
2.4183	43.8	.5693	20	Ken
2.4182	43.8	.6402	18	tiring
2.4179	43.8	.5971	19	rotten
2.4178	43.8	.4022	28	cafeteria
2.4164	43.8	.5699	19	comprehension
2.4164	43.8	.6906	17	healing
2.4164	43.8	.4503	25	Riley
2.4163	43.8	.6438	18	endured
2.4159	43.8	.5244	22	addresses
2.4155	43.8	.5978	19	drooping
2.4152	43.8	.6557	18	ornaments
2.4148	43.8	.4723	22	cheetah
2.4147	43.8	.5864	19	stuffing
2.4144	43.8	.5617	20	snarling
2.4143	43.8	.5447	20	pony's
2.4138	43.8	.7473	16	youthful
2.4136	43.8	.4720	24	ministers
2.4135	43.8	.5223	21	coldly
2.4134	43.8	.5580	20	doghouse
2.4134	43.8	.6869	17	preserves
2.4134	43.8	.4298	24	Skinner
2.4126	43.8	.6043	19	pry
2.4119	43.8	.1892	55	chisel
2.4115	43.8	.3451	29	Carrie
2.4105	43.8	.4361	25	photographer
2.4099	43.8	.6951	17	regarding
2.4098	43.8	.6899	17	looms
2.4092	43.8	.3912	27	oasis
2.4078	43.8	.5380	20	joyfully
2.4076	43.8	.6764	17	forked
2.4065	43.8	.5177	22	Mariner
2.4061	43.8	.6563	18	documents
2.4061	43.8	.5962	19	overland
2.4057	43.8	.3356	29	Dagmar
2.4057	43.8	.3813	28	jealous
2.4056	43.8	.6494	18	starter
2.4051	43.8	.5132	22	counsel
2.4049	43.8	.4910	23	ammonia
2.4048	43.8	.4651	25	crosswise
2.4048	43.8	.3756	25	Gates
2.4042	43.8	.5401	20	blubber
2.4038	43.8	.3590	30	skeletal
2.4037	43.8	.4666	23	alfalfa
2.4037	43.8	.0903	41	Arnie
2.4037	43.8	.6790	17	bumper
2.4032	43.8	.6067	19	1892
2.4027	43.8	.5198	21	storytelling
2.4024	43.8	.6212	19	vertically
2.4021	43.8	.4237	23	Annabelle
2.4012	43.8	.5793	19	purring
2.4011	43.8	.4912	23	estates
2.4010	43.8	.1122	65	Jed
2.4010	43.8	.3741	30	turpentine
2.4010	43.8	.6771	17	whipping
2.4004	43.8	.5426	21	assault
2.4003	43.8	.5283	21	awesome
2.4002	43.8	.6251	18	stair
2.4000	43.8	.5143	22	Fortune
2.3992	43.8	.4969	22	bobbed
2.3983	43.8	.6162	19	outlook
2.3978	43.8	.4481	23	cove
2.3978	43.8	.6891	17	quaint
2.3976	43.8	.5562	20	binoculars
2.3966	43.8	.5683	20	fielder
2.3965	43.8	.4528	25	durable
2.3955	43.8	.4269	25	McCormick
2.3950	43.8	.5461	21	wretched
2.3941	43.8	.2460	40	variables

U	SFI	D	F	Word Type
2.3924	43.8	.5544	20	curling
2.3920	43.8	.6092	19	dreary
2.3909	43.8	.5555	20	caravan
2.3897	43.8	.6409	18	tracts
2.3883	43.8	.6448	18	surgeon
2.3879	43.8	.2766	36	Irving
2.3878	43.8	.3779	24	coop
2.3878	43.8	.6025	19	feat
2.3866	43.8	.5381	21	counties
2.3858	43.8	.6066	19	Health
2.3852	43.8	.6798	17	bumpy
2.3847	43.8	.4365	26	126
2.3836	43.8	.6718	17	rip
2.3834	43.8	.5753	20	perceived
2.3834	43.8	.4792	23	1898
2.3832	43.8	.6614	17	quieted
2.3826	43.8	.6252	18	quest
2.3818	43.8	.5989	19	plots
2.3816	43.8	.6126	18	gait
2.3815	43.8	.6179	18	clad
2.3812	43.8	.6287	18	horseman
2.3810	43.8	.5341	20	Minnie
2.3807	43.8	.4377	25	Lower
2.3801	43.8	.5525	20	cot
2.3799	43.8	.5385	20	hallway
2.3792	43.8	.6446	18	foliage
2.3789	43.8	.5844	19	quickened
2.3763	43.8	.4302	26	purchases
2.3759	43.8	.4365	25	ignition
2.3757	43.8	.5154	22	faculty
2.3755	43.8	.5006	22	predictions

THE PRECEDING WORD TYPE OCCUPIES RANK 11500

U	SFI	D	F	Word Type
2.3753	43.8	.6473	18	auction
2.3749	43.8	.5996	19	probing
2.3744	43.8	.5538	21	lyric
2.3743	43.8	.5779	20	prefers
2.3743	43.8	.6313	18	stinging
2.3741	43.8	.6583	17	Eye
2.3738	43.8	.5171	22	English-speaking
2.3733	43.8	.6755	17	wail
2.3731	43.8	.5466	20	orchids
2.3721	43.8	.5547	20	invade
2.3718	43.8	.6356	18	performs
2.3712	43.7	.5184	22	prescribed
2.3711	43.7	.5864	19	Incas
2.3709	43.7	.6589	17	timed
2.3702	43.7	.5476	20	razor
2.3699	43.7	.6292	18	blasts
2.3697	43.7	.5519	20	heaps
2.3687	43.7	.6055	19	symbolize
2.3680	43.7	.4307	26	fragment
2.3679	43.7	.5683	20	1876
2.3674	43.7	.4592	24	rearrange
2.3669	43.7	.6787	17	richly
2.3668	43.7	.5319	21	Madam
2.3663	43.7	.2779	36	vertebrates
2.3657	43.7	.6668	17	whips
2.3657	43.7	.5547	20	1919
2.3656	43.7	.6755	17	mailed
2.3655	43.7	.4777	22	curving
2.3654	43.7	.5912	19	clambered
2.3654	43.7	.6604	17	fooling
2.3647	43.7	.6311	18	specialist
2.3645	43.7	.5576	20	carriers
2.3638	43.7	.7310	16	darkest
2.3621	43.7	.4945	22	investigating
2.3621	43.7	.7307	16	scoop
2.3616	43.7	.5240	20	saucers
2.3615	43.7	.5798	19	nasty
2.3612	43.7	.6132	18	scars
2.3610	43.7	.0941	74	CD
2.3610	43.7	.5434	20	unexpectedly
2.3605	43.7	.5305	21	taxis
2.3603	43.7	.6056	19	portable
2.3598	43.7	.6771	17	trench
2.3592	43.7	.6320	18	formally
2.3588	43.7	.3615	30	16th
2.3583	43.7	.6658	17	fashioned
2.3582	43.7	.6120	18	stalls
2.3580	43.7	.3166	30	teammate
2.3575	43.7	.6718	17	communicating
2.3575	43.7	.5047	22	Greenwich
2.3571	43.7	.6032	19	Heart
2.3570	43.7	.6739	17	capturing
2.3569	43.7	.7233	16	edible
2.3568	43.7	.5166	21	churn
2.3563	43.7	.7184	16	ward
2.3561	43.7	.4455	22	Oslo
2.3559	43.7	.6610	17	deserved
2.3556	43.7	.5349	20	glared
2.3554	43.7	.5462	20	colleagues
2.3553	43.7	.6831	17	360
2.3549	43.7	.4665	23	lumbering
2.3542	43.7	.6192	18	fanned
2.3541	43.7	.4103	26	Latin-American
2.3541	43.7	.4940	22	playgrounds
2.3539	43.7	.6320	18	320
2.3538	43.7	.3649	29	1970
2.3532	43.7	.2855	35	input
2.3529	43.7	.6255	18	gaping
2.3525	43.7	.6297	18	navigator
2.3523	43.7	.6403	18	260
2.3513	43.7	.3743	29	Mass
2.3509	43.7	.6245	18	grape
2.3499	43.7	.5606	20	enterprises
2.3496	43.7	.7056	16	roaming
2.3493	43.7	.5572	20	greenish
2.3493	43.7	.4942	22	Presidential
2.3491	43.7	.6160	18	crossroads
2.3489	43.7	.5351	21	Research
2.3485	43.7	.6248	18	taut
2.3483	43.7	.2646	32	Tucker
2.3481	43.7	.5963	19	averaging
2.3477	43.7	.7028	16	moaning
2.3476	43.7	.6286	18	intensely
2.3469	43.7	.3438	25	Alligator
2.3464	43.7	.6763	17	employee

U	SFI	D	F	Word Type
2.3462	43.7	.7168	16	fish's
2.3459	43.7	.6166	18	tosses
2.3458	43.7	.5966	19	cheated
2.3455	43.7	.4516	24	symmetry
2.3451	43.7	.5990	19	inherit
2.3448	43.7	.4977	20	Skipper
2.3442	43.7	.3509	26	Nate
2.3440	43.7	.6339	18	Merry
2.3436	43.7	.6683	17	tomorrow's
2.3428	43.7	.6832	17	visualize
2.3426	43.7	.6742	17	regulated
2.3404	43.7	.5238	20	barnyard
2.3404	43.7	.6169	18	inferior
2.3402	43.7	.5942	19	Plan
2.3397	43.7	.4422	24	Naples

THE PRECEDING WORD TYPE OCCUPIES RANK 11600

U	SFI	D	F	Word Type
2.3395	43.7	.5925	19	corruption
2.3394	43.7	.6650	17	glossy
2.3393	43.7	.4790	22	thermal
2.3387	43.7	.4498	22	fudge
2.3381	43.7	.6299	18	cheaply
2.3374	43.7	.5234	20	scolding
2.3372	43.7	.6672	17	wrists
2.3367	43.7	.1570	44	Kilpatrick
2.3364	43.7	.4616	22	gratitude
2.3362	43.7	.6723	17	exceptionally
2.3359	43.7	.5650	20	whichever
2.3354	43.7	.4729	21	roadster
2.3350	43.7	.4631	24	Norse
2.3349	43.7	.2406	31	Aroma
2.3344	43.7	.6735	17	compliment
2.3343	43.7	.6525	17	scanning
2.3334	43.7	.5152	21	chuck
2.3329	43.7	.6702	17	overflow
2.3322	43.7	.4034	24	icebox
2.3309	43.7	.5765	19	trades
2.3294	43.7	.5143	21	fiddler
2.3291	43.7	.5874	19	Prairie
2.3287	43.7	.5958	19	installation
2.3280	43.7	.6214	18	recited
2.3278	43.7	.5667	19	unloaded
2.3277	43.7	.5752	19	gasping
2.3277	43.7	.5651	19	woodpecker
2.3275	43.7	.6694	17	uncommon
2.3274	43.7	.6165	18	lads
2.3271	43.7	.7128	16	stocked
2.3262	43.7	.5731	19	buckles
2.3258	43.7	.4910	22	defenses
2.3254	43.7	.6709	17	ls
2.3251	43.7	.5969	19	notably
2.3248	43.7	.5964	19	investments
2.3246	43.7	.7211	16	maintains
2.3244	43.7	.6130	18	resisted
2.3243	43.7	.2556	39	atlas
2.3242	43.7	.5031	22	Angles
2.3241	43.7	.6032	18	grumbling
2.3232	43.7	.6345	17	screech
2.3231	43.7	.4105	24	bead
2.3230	43.7	.6182	18	blindness
2.3227	43.7	.6726	17	146
2.3223	43.7	.5810	19	occurrence
2.3222	43.7	.5974	19	1st
2.3221	43.7	.6268	18	Nova
2.3218	43.7	.6599	17	celestial
2.3218	43.7	.7017	16	parched
2.3218	43.7	.5105	20	rotor
2.3211	43.7	.1864	43	Carmen
2.3210	43.7	.5633	19	Cumberland
2.3204	43.7	.4281	26	suite
2.3192	43.7	.5627	20	playwright
2.3191	43.7	.2839	27	Granny
2.3178	43.7	.3892	28	dynamic
2.3176	43.7	.6088	18	baths
2.3170	43.6	.5811	18	gems
2.3168	43.6	.5913	18	onward
2.3168	43.6	.6281	18	talents
2.3167	43.6	.5504	20	hemispheres
2.3166	43.6	.5993	18	reasoned
2.3164	43.6	.6296	18	obligation
2.3160	43.6	.7060	16	cushions
2.3159	43.6	.6047	18	monstrous
2.3158	43.6	.5524	20	attractions
2.3158	43.6	.5719	19	reservations
2.3157	43.6	.7032	16	sly
2.3153	43.6	.6178	18	swarms
2.3150	43.6	.6149	18	hemp
2.3144	43.6	.2506	40	Patricia
2.3143	43.6	.4865	21	mush
2.3142	43.6	.6471	17	burrowing
2.3142	43.6	.5805	18	one-room
2.3137	43.6	.7172	16	overwhelmed
2.3133	43.6	.5958	19	relating
2.3128	43.6	.5588	20	illuminated
2.3127	43.6	.6075	18	consented
2.3114	43.6	.5704	19	sheds
2.3112	43.6	.5397	20	decent
2.3109	43.6	.6254	18	immune
2.3104	43.6	.5718	19	cottonwood
2.3094	43.6	.5603	19	Gettysburg
2.3090	43.6	.5761	19	shale
2.3085	43.6	.4567	23	tattered
2.3084	43.6	.3903	23	peccary
2.3081	43.6	.7039	16	sleigh
2.3071	43.6	.3703	25	Blaze
2.3070	43.6	.4613	23	Bears
2.3070	43.6	.6532	17	unwilling
2.3067	43.6	.4120	26	loans
2.3066	43.6	.5685	19	outstretched
2.3064	43.6	.5620	19	coughed
2.3063	43.6	.5712	19	Cotton
2.3060	43.6	.6026	18	sleepily
2.3057	43.6	.6671	17	acknowledged
2.3057	43.6	.5724	19	Caroline
2.3056	43.6	.5873	19	1949
2.3055	43.6	.7577	15	Not
2.3054	43.6	.4943	20	frightful

THE PRECEDING WORD TYPE OCCUPIES RANK 11700

U	SFI	D	F	Word Type
2.3045	43.6	.4418	23	Girls
2.3045	43.6	.6545	17	inclination
2.3037	43.6	.6594	17	memorial
2.3030	43.6	.3439	30	$10
2.3030	43.6	.4796	22	thrilled
2.3027	43.6	.5914	18	monastery
2.3025	43.6	.2526	38	Right
2.3021	43.6	.5515	20	compelled
2.3021	43.6	.5566	20	debris
2.3016	43.6	.3172	31	protons
2.3015	43.6	.3043	26	anteater
2.3000	43.6	.5333	19	Sergeant
2.2991	43.6	.4435	24	regional
2.2987	43.6	.5831	19	2nd
2.2986	43.6	.4742	22	saddled
2.2977	43.6	.6086	18	bustle
2.2974	43.6	.4953	21	peeling
2.2964	43.6	.5618	19	agreeable
2.2963	43.6	.6084	18	nursing
2.2963	43.6	.4968	22	phosphorus
2.2962	43.6	.6359	17	cheery
2.2960	43.6	.7069	16	housewives
2.2958	43.6	.5558	19	Treasure
2.2956	43.6	.5578	19	Base
2.2954	43.6	.3406	30	binary
2.2948	43.6	.5877	19	reduces
2.2946	43.6	.6457	17	Grandmother's
2.2945	43.6	.6153	18	competing
2.2945	43.6	.5906	18	snowing
2.2942	43.6	.5726	19	buyers
2.2942	43.6	.5418	20	focusing
2.2938	43.6	.5953	18	lowly
2.2936	43.6	.4993	22	shalt
2.2931	43.6	.6513	17	publisher
2.2926	43.6	.6625	17	convicted
2.2924	43.6	.4174	22	Jeb
2.2912	43.6	.6522	17	That
2.2909	43.6	.3976	26	$6
2.2904	43.6	.6385	17	roars
2.2903	43.6	.1129	37	Vinny
2.2901	43.6	.4766	22	radioactivity
2.2894	43.6	.5910	18	forgets
2.2890	43.6	.6380	17	somebody's
2.2887	43.6	.4293	23	huh
2.2879	43.6	.6063	18	parchment
2.2878	43.6	.6415	17	resolve
2.2871	43.6	.4913	22	Polish
2.2869	43.6	.4055	23	Jensen
2.2865	43.6	.5838	19	bracelet
2.2861	43.6	.5473	19	twine
2.2860	43.6	.4506	24	signatures
2.2858	43.6	.5686	19	1903
2.2857	43.6	.5088	21	emperors
2.2856	43.6	.4605	22	slums
2.2844	43.6	.6495	17	thinkers
2.2841	43.6	.7033	16	blurred
2.2838	43.6	.6344	17	wrath
2.2837	43.6	.4005	24	mailman
2.2833	43.6	.6038	18	doubted
2.2831	43.6	.6945	16	banner
2.2831	43.6	.6090	18	Saturdays
2.2831	43.6	.7015	16	warmest
2.2828	43.6	.6434	17	purr
2.2823	43.6	.4293	25	tacks
2.2821	43.6	.6530	17	stiffened
2.2803	43.6	.5578	19	terrifying
2.2800	43.6	.4379	24	heredity
2.2797	43.6	.4838	22	speaker's
2.2786	43.6	.5284	20	Irene
2.2786	43.6	.5530	20	mashed
2.2778	43.6	.2970	35	rhyming
2.2774	43.6	.5448	20	entertaining
2.2774	43.6	.4152	25	pollution
2.2767	43.6	.4546	23	spectacles
2.2766	43.6	.6746	16	bandage
2.2757	43.6	.3916	27	yolk
2.2754	43.6	.6472	17	journeys
2.2752	43.6	.5434	20	feudal
2.2751	43.6	.6471	17	obedience
2.2749	43.6	.3720	25	Ben's
2.2742	43.6	.1175	65	two-syllable
2.2739	43.6	.6294	17	nudge
2.2739	43.6	.5585	19	shyly
2.2731	43.6	.4630	23	demonstrations
2.2726	43.6	.7476	15	directing
2.2726	43.6	.5404	20	releases
2.2722	43.6	.6372	17	braided
2.2714	43.6	.6955	16	announces
2.2714	43.6	.6167	18	Biblical
2.2714	43.6	.5751	19	qualified
2.2711	43.6	.6482	17	threshold
2.2698	43.6	.4288	23	observatory
2.2693	43.6	.6877	16	pillars
2.2690	43.6	.7482	15	endlessly
2.2670	43.6	.6076	18	thumbs
2.2667	43.6	.5622	19	preserving
2.2661	43.6	.5716	19	immigrant
2.2661	43.6	.6371	17	exhaustion
2.2658	43.6	.5698	19	three-fourths
2.2630	43.5	.6358	17	fronts

THE PRECEDING WORD TYPE OCCUPIES RANK 11800

U	SFI	D	F	Word Type
2.2625	43.5	.4610	23	Medical
2.2619	43.5	.7041	16	namely
2.2615	43.5	.5851	18	gulped
2.2614	43.5	.2574	37	harp
2.2608	43.5	.6412	17	surveyed
2.2606	43.5	.6519	17	repelled
2.2601	43.5	.3596	29	sandpaper
2.2600	43.5	.6170	18	14th
2.2599	43.5	.5012	21	paraffin
2.2593	43.5	.5339	20	collision
2.2589	43.5	.5493	20	ensure
2.2588	43.5	.6395	17	aft
2.2586	43.5	.7370	15	stab
2.2584	43.5	.3198	33	Baroque
2.2576	43.5	.4992	22	spacing
2.2573	43.5	.2047	43	centimeter
2.2572	43.5	.2516	31	Skip
2.2569	43.5	.5666	19	technicians
2.2566	43.5	.6502	17	shriek
2.2564	43.5	.6529	17	furnishings
2.2564	43.5	.5420	20	shrink
2.2564	43.5	.6956	16	solely
2.2561	43.5	.5658	19	wholesale
2.2555	43.5	.4541	22	Navaho
2.2552	43.5	.3039	31	Morgiana
2.2549	43.5	.5005	21	straighten
2.2531	43.5	.4223	24	Swan
2.2528	43.5	.5903	18	swells
2.2526	43.5	.5836	18	penalty
2.2523	43.5	.6501	17	patriot
2.2518	43.5	.6401	17	obliged
2.2516	43.5	.6868	16	Arnold
2.2514	43.5	.5145	21	excerpt
2.2509	43.5	.6378	17	inventors
2.2507	43.5	.4118	25	gateway
2.2485	43.5	.5838	18	seaman
2.2484	43.5	.5698	19	Arts
2.2483	43.5	.6352	17	youths
2.2480	43.5	.5664	19	finance
2.2472	43.5	.5446	20	1859
2.2442	43.5	.6169	17	comforting
2.2440	43.5	.6545	17	thirteenth
2.2438	43.5	.3892	27	Israelites
2.2438	43.5	.3549	29	Lesson
2.2437	43.5	.5655	19	Free
2.2434	43.5	.5256	20	strains
2.2428	43.5	.4531	23	83
2.2425	43.5	.5984	18	Stars
2.2419	43.5	.5644	18	peeped
2.2419	43.5	.5482	19	reaper
2.2417	43.5	.5380	20	symptoms
2.2414	43.5	.7433	15	richness
2.2412	43.5	.5164	20	feller
2.2409	43.5	.5665	19	narrowed
2.2402	43.5	.6476	17	alien
2.2397	43.5	.4533	21	ouch
2.2397	43.5	.2314	38	Serra
2.2394	43.5	.5379	19	cottages
2.2392	43.5	.5623	19	absorbs
2.2391	43.5	.6652	16	amidst
2.2388	43.5	.3116	25	Taney
2.2386	43.5	.5034	21	serpent
2.2384	43.5	.0000	49	Alonzo
2.2384	43.5	.0000	49	Bearcat
2.2382	43.5	.6673	16	hates
2.2378	43.5	.6054	18	virtue
2.2377	43.5	.1825	44	risen
2.2375	43.5	.6126	17	oatmeal
2.2371	43.5	.4439	23	producers
2.2364	43.5	.3120	32	modifier
2.2363	43.5	.5948	18	killers
2.2362	43.5	.5289	20	quoted
2.2356	43.5	.6607	16	night's
2.2354	43.5	.3635	27	weathering
2.2351	43.5	.1030	66	centimeters
2.2351	43.5	.4683	21	quarreling
2.2349	43.5	.6326	17	Johnson's
2.2346	43.5	.6261	17	nudged
2.2341	43.5	.5957	18	booklet
2.2340	43.5	.5974	18	successor
2.2338	43.5	.6921	16	render
2.2335	43.5	.4712	22	condense
2.2333	43.5	.6798	16	weighted
2.2329	43.5	.4641	21	snow-covered
2.2327	43.5	.6584	16	squad
2.2316	43.5	.5995	18	generate
2.2314	43.5	.4594	21	Bend
2.2312	43.5	.3457	29	jest
2.2301	43.5	.6500	16	sausage
2.2301	43.5	.6409	17	testimony
2.2300	43.5	.6343	17	virtues
2.2287	43.5	.6249	17	dearest
2.2277	43.5	.5637	19	sparrow
2.2273	43.5	.7330	15	satisfactorily
2.2271	43.5	.5640	19	Shakespeare's
2.2258	43.5	.3743	27	Darwin
2.2257	43.5	.5937	18	exhibition
2.2254	43.5	.5862	18	growling
2.2250	43.5	.5200	20	glassy
2.2248	43.5	.6152	17	sprinkling

THE PRECEDING WORD TYPE OCCUPIES RANK 11900

U	SFI	D	F	Word Type
2.2247	43.5	.6274	17	injure
2.2245	43.5	.3715	28	stitched
2.2243	43.5	.4624	21	bales
2.2242	43.5	.6797	16	misunderstanding
2.2240	43.5	.4614	22	daydream
2.2231	43.5	.6321	17	criminals
2.2229	43.5	.5116	21	conveniently
2.2224	43.5	.5026	20	Current
2.2224	43.5	.4666	22	Genghis
2.2217	43.5	.5579	19	Phoenicians
2.2216	43.5	.3307	28	Candy
2.2210	43.5	.5456	19	beech
2.2210	43.5	.5293	20	lettered
2.2206	43.5	.2765	26	Ricky's
2.2201	43.5	.3768	26	cartoon
2.2200	43.5	.6563	16	sunken
2.2195	43.5	.5809	18	Chesapeake
2.2195	43.5	.6722	16	treats
2.2192	43.5	.6713	16	berry
2.2184	43.5	.5099	19	windlass
2.2182	43.5	.3040	25	Hiram
2.2178	43.5	.5279	20	corporations
2.2177	43.5	.5980	18	superb
2.2175	43.5	.5757	18	sprayed
2.2173	43.5	.4644	22	Yugoslavia
2.2171	43.5	.6071	17	fling
2.2171	43.5	.3984	24	peat
2.2169	43.5	.4549	23	offset
2.2168	43.5	.2697	30	glossary
2.2167	43.5	.6687	16	Dorothy
2.2160	43.5	.6770	16	vastness
2.2155	43.5	.6492	16	Waldo
2.2152	43.5	.3911	27	superlative
2.2150	43.5	.5661	18	lance
2.2148	43.5	.4676	21	hibernation
2.2145	43.5	.3651	23	Mabel
2.2143	43.5	.6305	17	Brothers
2.2139	43.5	.4743	22	patriotic
2.2138	43.5	.6682	16	seaward
2.2135	43.5	.4838	21	Fleet
2.2128	43.4	.5801	18	fearless
2.2125	43.4	.6065	17	nicest
2.2099	43.4	.2669	38	collars
2.2099	43.4	.6189	17	lasso
2.2089	43.4	.6681	16	peeled
2.2084	43.4	.5042	20	Magellan's
2.2079	43.4	.3438	29	Reserve
2.2077	43.4	.5796	18	wriggling
2.2060	43.4	.6002	17	Lee's
2.2053	43.4	.6214	17	adventurer
2.2049	43.4	.6649	16	murmur
2.2045	43.4	.5448	19	dagger
2.2037	43.4	.7150	15	illiterate
2.2036	43.4	.5892	18	scorn
2.2033	43.4	.5865	18	McCarthy
2.2025	43.4	.4123	24	1776
2.2021	43.4	.5899	17	wakened
2.2010	43.4	.3751	25	Guinea
2.2008	43.4	.3922	25	$8
2.2003	43.4	.6520	16	rejoiced
2.1992	43.4	.5563	18	Jefferson's
2.1987	43.4	.5391	19	wreath
2.1983	43.4	.6208	17	dinners
2.1980	43.4	.6732	16	cushion
2.1979	43.4	.6686	16	twenty-seven
2.1976	43.4	.5092	19	dwarf
2.1973	43.4	.4624	20	wisest
2.1971	43.4	.6600	16	realizes
2.1969	43.4	.5627	19	damned
2.1966	43.4	.5783	18	Imperial
2.1962	43.4	.4025	25	biological
2.1962	43.4	.6073	17	blasted
2.1961	43.4	.5427	18	foghorn
2.1954	43.4	.4573	22	fuse
2.1949	43.4	.7167	15	exerted
2.1940	43.4	.6161	17	hospitality
2.1938	43.4	.5962	17	breakers
2.1934	43.4	.5916	18	lodging
2.1934	43.4	.6761	16	resign
2.1924	43.4	.4784	20	sloth
2.1923	43.4	.3023	28	Hetty
2.1922	43.4	.4778	21	cruise
2.1922	43.4	.5518	18	nodding
2.1920	43.4	.3842	26	automation
2.1919	43.4	.4573	22	sash
2.1916	43.4	.4929	21	consumer
2.1915	43.4	.6540	16	tackled
2.1912	43.4	.6669	16	gifted
2.1911	43.4	.6704	16	dramatically
2.1909	43.4	.5342	19	harmonica
2.1900	43.4	.4660	22	nasal
2.1899	43.4	.6629	16	rickety
2.1896	43.4	.4723	22	1937
2.1895	43.4	.5374	18	fender
2.1895	43.4	.6584	16	stalking
2.1893	43.4	.4830	21	1869
2.1891	43.4	.4334	23	cold-blooded
2.1876	43.4	.6225	17	reckoned
2.1869	43.4	.6008	17	Race
2.1868	43.4	.4983	21	roadway

THE PRECEDING WORD TYPE OCCUPIES RANK 12000

U	SFI	D	F	Word Type
2.1867	43.4	.2402	28	Tag
2.1857	43.4	.6589	16	Airport
2.1855	43.4	.6162	17	sardines
2.1853	43.4	.6609	16	journeyed
2.1841	43.4	.5743	18	Special
2.1840	43.4	.5794	18	exert
2.1837	43.4	.7054	15	life's
2.1827	43.4	.6548	16	trickle
2.1825	43.4	.3771	22	ducklings
2.1825	43.4	.5592	19	molding
2.1820	43.4	.6557	16	Liverpool
2.1818	43.4	.2408	40	/k/
2.1818	43.4	.6326	17	candies
2.1813	43.4	.5677	18	shudder
2.1812	43.4	.5437	19	185
2.1805	43.4	.6604	16	crowns
2.1805	43.4	.5368	19	regiments
2.1804	43.4	.5270	20	corrections
2.1803	43.4	.6112	17	grasping
2.1799	43.4	.5566	18	raked
2.1799	43.4	.2019	42	zeros
2.1786	43.4	.5331	19	outlet
2.1783	43.4	.6209	17	rumors
2.1781	43.4	.6105	17	despised
2.1778	43.4	.3678	24	bouquets
2.1768	43.4	.5118	20	bough
2.1767	43.4	.6964	15	paced
2.1767	43.4	.6286	17	Week
2.1765	43.4	.1334	55	exponent
2.1758	43.4	.5927	17	homesick
2.1756	43.4	.5952	17	motto
2.1753	43.4	.6144	17	horned
2.1752	43.4	.6629	16	prolonged
2.1750	43.4	.4677	20	redcoats
2.1747	43.4	.6570	16	enchanted
2.1744	43.4	.4026	24	Presidents
2.1741	43.4	.5629	18	staple
2.1739	43.4	.5440	18	honeydew
2.1729	43.4	.5467	19	cavities
2.1725	43.4	.5981	18	emphasizes
2.1724	43.4	.3978	24	Elder
2.1722	43.4	.3658	25	rewarded
2.1720	43.4	.3369	24	Nolan
2.1719	43.4	.6109	17	reefs
2.1705	43.4	.1844	45	tenths
2.1696	43.4	.6987	15	nimble
2.1692	43.4	.0946	69	He
2.1687	43.4	.4866	21	hooves

U	SFI	D	F	Word Type
2.1684	43.4	.5980	17	clipped
2.1680	43.4	.6125	17	luxurious
2.1678	43.4	.5181	19	chuckle
2.1677	43.4	.4699	21	tablecloth
2.1676	43.4	.6259	17	formations
2.1672	43.4	.6576	16	gusts
2.1663	43.4	.6534	16	tribute
2.1653	43.4	.6582	16	Cod
2.1647	43.4	.4499	22	1908
2.1640	43.4	.4577	21	snake's
2.1631	43.4	.5416	19	planter
2.1624	43.3	.5099	20	eroded
2.1620	43.3	.5328	19	1905
2.1613	43.3	.6083	17	crouching
2.1612	43.3	.1975	40	igneous
2.1611	43.3	.4291	23	Cowboy
2.1600	43.3	.5725	18	daydreams
2.1600	43.3	.5359	19	veteran
2.1599	43.3	.6084	17	1847
2.1591	43.3	.5197	19	squid
2.1588	43.3	.6093	17	demon
2.1581	43.3	.6550	16	descend
2.1581	43.3	.5715	18	mellow
2.1569	43.3	.5816	18	functioning
2.1566	43.3	.5498	18	chanting
2.1564	43.3	.5424	19	profile
2.1560	43.3	.5477	19	saws
2.1554	43.3	.6992	15	mite
2.1552	43.3	.5832	18	Eugene
2.1549	43.3	.4915	20	owning
2.1548	43.3	.4547	22	1777
2.1545	43.3	.4776	21	'round
2.1542	43.3	.5060	19	speechless
2.1538	43.3	.7016	15	exquisite
2.1526	43.3	.4550	22	Oil
2.1519	43.3	.6157	17	arches
2.1519	43.3	.4783	20	Out
2.1515	43.3	.1683	44	magma
2.1505	43.3	.4962	21	Colonial
2.1505	43.3	.5772	18	specifically
2.1504	43.3	.5463	18	hermit
2.1504	43.3	.4685	21	Niagara
2.1503	43.3	.1238	57	inverse
2.1502	43.3	.6181	17	61
2.1499	43.3	.1616	52	antonyms
2.1497	43.3	.2855	25	Roland
2.1491	43.3	.5805	18	independently
2.1487	43.3	.4766	21	Aztec
2.1486	43.3	.6519	16	monasteries
2.1482	43.3	.5716	18	patriotism
2.1476	43.3	.5564	18	locker
2.1470	43.3	.6554	16	framed
THE PRECEDING WORD TYPE OCCUPIES RANK 12100				
2.1466	43.3	.4857	21	yea
2.1465	43.3	.4727	20	llamas
2.1462	43.3	.6514	16	submitted
2.1461	43.3	.6417	16	rudely
2.1459	43.3	.3442	27	Venezuela
2.1452	43.3	.5281	18	resolutions
2.1442	43.3	.5399	18	Farm
2.1434	43.3	.6098	17	discourage
2.1432	43.3	.5087	19	awaken
2.1431	43.3	.5064	20	disposition
2.1429	43.3	.4717	20	poisoned
2.1429	43.3	.4849	20	sawmill
2.1429	43.3	.4355	23	tablet
2.1426	43.3	.4992	19	boar
2.1416	43.3	.5813	17	ads
2.1408	43.3	.6409	16	inquisitive
2.1395	43.3	.7009	15	justified
2.1394	43.3	.7038	15	distorted
2.1385	43.3	.6420	16	proposition
2.1383	43.3	.5484	18	motorcycle
2.1373	43.3	.6025	17	polishing
2.1371	43.3	.4707	21	1849
2.1367	43.3	.6326	16	excused
2.1365	43.3	.4762	21	shorts
2.1361	43.3	.6855	15	rusted
2.1356	43.3	.5651	18	relentless
2.1355	43.3	.5939	17	pickles
2.1351	43.3	.4832	19	flares
2.1349	43.3	.4549	22	cheeses
2.1349	43.3	.6062	17	perpetual
2.1344	43.3	.6450	16	expectation
2.1344	43.3	.5085	20	progression
2.1331	43.3	.5860	17	birthdays
2.1323	43.3	.2314	38	Left
2.1320	43.3	.5477	18	barbed
2.1316	43.3	.6392	16	commanding
2.1311	43.3	.2258	28	Luis
2.1310	43.3	.4581	20	Duchess
2.1306	43.3	.6479	16	shocking
2.1301	43.3	.3053	25	braids
2.1299	43.3	.6348	16	car's
2.1299	43.3	.6915	15	143
2.1290	43.3	.4947	20	Europe's
2.1285	43.3	.4225	23	thorax
2.1284	43.3	.4278	23	Nam
2.1275	43.3	.5385	19	Cecil
2.1271	43.3	.6024	17	technically
2.1269	43.3	.4320	22	veterans
2.1267	43.3	.6050	17	assortment
2.1267	43.3	.6405	16	steeple
2.1265	43.3	.6327	16	hummed
2.1255	43.3	.0000	142	numerator
2.1250	43.3	.4030	22	Flying
2.1248	43.3	.5753	18	manuscripts
2.1245	43.3	.6014	17	sulphur
2.1238	43.3	.5934	17	coaxed
2.1238	43.3	.4132	23	fangs
2.1228	43.3	.5515	18	neon
2.1220	43.3	.5050	20	amateurs
2.1220	43.3	.5531	18	shelters
2.1215	43.3	.4641	21	underlining
2.1214	43.3	.3840	24	charging
2.1214	43.3	.2596	37	choral
2.1213	43.3	.5879	17	rig
2.1204	43.3	.2363	39	participle
2.1201	43.3	.5840	17	bogs
2.1197	43.3	.4532	22	Dwight
2.1197	43.3	.5078	20	outbreak
2.1192	43.3	.6358	16	willingness
2.1188	43.3	.6193	16	scan
2.1188	43.3	.6032	17	slots
2.1186	43.3	.6018	17	saint
2.1181	43.3	.6292	16	rustle
2.1180	43.3	.5412	18	feathery
2.1164	43.3	.6552	16	agitated
2.1162	43.3	.5719	18	Saxons
2.1154	43.3	.5059	18	snowshoes
2.1151	43.3	.5062	20	bust
2.1151	43.3	.6132	16	Empress
2.1149	43.3	.6958	15	appetites
2.1148	43.3	.5866	17	slapping
2.1146	43.3	.5694	18	twists
2.1145	43.3	.6302	16	flank
2.1133	43.2	.6652	15	peep
2.1133	43.2	.5941	17	surged
2.1132	43.2	.3537	26	aunts
2.1132	43.2	.5956	17	lurking
2.1131	43.2	.3862	21	Page
2.1131	43.2	.4639	22	relates
2.1126	43.2	.4988	20	When
2.1124	43.2	.6169	16	defendant
2.1120	43.2	.3229	28	scroll
2.1118	43.2	.6341	16	grandchildren
2.1114	43.2	.6492	16	individually
2.1113	43.2	.6878	15	hark
2.1112	43.2	.4111	23	Puritans
2.1103	43.2	.6357	16	rewarding
2.1098	43.2	.3357	26	Column
2.1093	43.2	.7448	14	rob
2.1084	43.2	.6880	15	histories
THE PRECEDING WORD TYPE OCCUPIES RANK 12200				
2.1083	43.2	.3747	25	markers
2.1081	43.2	.4737	21	patents
2.1076	43.2	.5186	19	clasped
2.1069	43.2	.5524	17	AND
2.1067	43.2	.4440	22	Laos
2.1065	43.2	.4566	22	linear
2.1064	43.2	.3585	22	Esther
2.1045	43.2	.6793	15	summer's
2.1042	43.2	.6345	16	plagued
2.1033	43.2	.5879	17	editors
2.1030	43.2	.5707	17	sweets
2.1025	43.2	.4237	22	amendments
2.1023	43.2	.6901	15	void
2.1012	43.2	.4212	22	Rex
2.1008	43.2	.6443	16	recommend
2.1005	43.2	.3812	22	Alex
2.1005	43.2	.5651	18	tapes
2.1000	43.2	.2932	28	penicillin
2.0999	43.2	.5667	18	sector
2.0999	43.2	.6297	16	vault
2.0998	43.2	.3756	25	$7
2.0998	43.2	.6094	17	accidental
2.0993	43.2	.5168	18	Jackson's
2.0991	43.2	.4854	21	inverted
2.0984	43.2	.4197	20	stumps
2.0979	43.2	.5928	17	Indianapolis
2.0978	43.2	.6129	16	ruts
2.0969	43.2	.5843	17	warlike
2.0966	43.2	.5286	19	82
2.0964	43.2	.5961	17	exile
2.0964	43.2	.6777	15	tripping
2.0958	43.2	.6095	16	swirled
2.0935	43.2	.6448	16	washer
2.0933	43.2	.6136	16	defended
2.0932	43.2	.4521	21	sister's
2.0924	43.2	.6380	16	adopt
2.0924	43.2	.5629	18	Napoleon's
2.0920	43.2	.5490	18	aggressive
2.0920	43.2	.3238	27	evaporate
2.0913	43.2	.6297	16	proving
2.0908	43.2	.1877	29	Eyes
2.0908	43.2	.5684	17	roundup
2.0906	43.2	.5098	19	fringe
2.0904	43.2	.3199	23	Dusty
2.0904	43.2	.0837	62	Mafatu
2.0903	43.2	.5846	17	antique
2.0899	43.2	.6877	15	certainty
2.0899	43.2	.6184	16	Naval
2.0895	43.2	.4507	21	lee
2.0894	43.2	.5770	17	doubts
2.0894	43.2	.5911	17	marvels
2.0894	43.2	.5910	17	proceeds
2.0893	43.2	.5924	17	pronouncing
2.0882	43.2	.5720	17	insult
2.0878	43.2	.4913	20	rhinoceros
2.0868	43.2	.4127	24	Own
2.0865	43.2	.6240	16	Lost
2.0862	43.2	.5691	17	Ithaca
2.0855	43.2	.6369	16	vainly
2.0851	43.2	.3725	25	Pueblo
2.0848	43.2	.5376	18	Pete's
2.0848	43.2	.4649	19	Springs
2.0843	43.2	.6148	16	poking
2.0842	43.2	.4988	20	Petersburg
2.0841	43.2	.3219	28	Egypt's
2.0838	43.2	.4178	23	shortstop
2.0837	43.2	.6378	16	Eva
2.0830	43.2	.5199	19	1933
2.0829	43.2	.4620	20	Eli
2.0826	43.2	.6225	16	leash
2.0825	43.2	.5965	17	lowers
2.0824	43.2	.5386	18	math
2.0822	43.2	.6121	16	signaling
2.0819	43.2	.5510	18	manufactures
2.0817	43.2	.6232	16	peril
2.0812	43.2	.2075	28	Ernestine
2.0812	43.2	.5594	17	pods
2.0805	43.2	.5561	18	compounded
2.0794	43.2	.2107	37	refineries
2.0793	43.2	.4942	20	buttered
2.0791	43.2	.3612	25	forecasts
2.0786	43.2	.6367	16	branching
2.0784	43.2	.6335	16	brutal
2.0782	43.2	.5227	18	Marsh
2.0776	43.2	.2806	32	rectangles
2.0776	43.2	.0952	79	schwa
2.0775	43.2	.5962	17	enduring
2.0772	43.2	.6269	16	Highland
2.0765	43.2	.5481	18	hardens
2.0764	43.2	.4768	19	tickle
2.0756	43.2	.6147	16	vividly
2.0753	43.2	.3649	27	allowances
2.0750	43.2	.5197	19	pauses
2.0749	43.2	.4465	20	burner
2.0748	43.2	.4962	20	nobility
2.0724	43.2	.6104	16	rations
2.0721	43.2	.6391	16	persisted
2.0720	43.2	.5819	17	maneuver
2.0713	43.2	.5466	18	lain
2.0701	43.2	.6814	15	mesh
THE PRECEDING WORD TYPE OCCUPIES RANK 12300				
2.0698	43.2	.5838	17	threshing
2.0692	43.2	.5526	18	prisms
2.0688	43.2	.3194	27	Rotterdam
2.0686	43.2	.3231	27	postman
2.0681	43.2	.5988	16	sprout
2.0677	43.2	.2463	36	Midnight
2.0676	43.2	.1569	51	Velvet
2.0672	43.2	.4799	20	dyes
2.0665	43.2	.6592	15	blessings
2.0665	43.2	.2433	27	Sooner
2.0661	43.2	.6380	16	ornament
2.0659	43.2	.6554	15	foes
2.0656	43.2	.5805	17	disposed
2.0636	43.1	.7163	14	bandages
2.0635	43.1	.1203	57	Adlai
2.0632	43.1	.6189	16	haunting
2.0632	43.1	.4978	19	shuddered
2.0631	43.1	.6782	15	possesses
2.0623	43.1	.5047	19	factual
2.0618	43.1	.4470	19	Jackie
2.0614	43.1	.3777	25	ripping
2.0603	43.1	.4817	19	Allegheny
2.0595	43.1	.5430	18	steward
2.0590	43.1	.5928	16	blinding
2.0584	43.1	.1707	44	Beethoven
2.0584	43.1	.6063	16	rehearsal
2.0583	43.1	.7232	14	yoke
2.0582	43.1	.3895	22	Dale
2.0574	43.1	.5153	19	Curtis
2.0572	43.1	.6166	16	frankly
2.0558	43.1	.2212	27	Buster
2.0558	43.1	.6219	16	refusal
2.0550	43.1	.6702	15	whereupon
2.0547	43.1	.5499	18	1880
2.0545	43.1	.6309	16	subdivisions
2.0544	43.1	.5819	17	contributes
2.0539	43.1	.4971	19	1935
2.0532	43.1	.5039	19	Port
2.0531	43.1	.6219	16	parrots
2.0530	43.1	.4784	20	self-government
2.0526	43.1	.4641	21	projected
2.0526	43.1	.5547	17	thundering
2.0524	43.1	.6604	15	docked
2.0518	43.1	.4632	19	Senor
2.0517	43.1	.6569	15	banished
2.0517	43.1	.6269	16	complaint
2.0503	43.1	.3731	24	fission
2.0498	43.1	.6027	16	awards
2.0487	43.1	.6066	16	stumbling
2.0487	43.1	.5383	18	vaguely
2.0483	43.1	.5498	17	dope
2.0483	43.1	.5563	17	snowfall
2.0481	43.1	.3132	29	Inc
2.0480	43.1	.7150	14	berth
2.0480	43.1	.4940	20	script
2.0474	43.1	.4836	20	Athenian
2.0474	43.1	.6035	16	mixes
2.0471	43.1	.6326	16	flexibility
2.0461	43.1	.6067	16	Medicine
2.0456	43.1	.5042	19	lure
2.0454	43.1	.2802	31	ph
2.0454	43.1	.4671	20	refinery
2.0449	43.1	.4981	19	whoop
2.0437	43.1	.4811	20	91
2.0434	43.1	.4790	20	authentic
2.0433	43.1	.4832	19	Side
2.0432	43.1	.6131	16	respectful
2.0431	43.1	.5793	16	Ellis
2.0431	43.1	.5398	18	mob
2.0429	43.1	.5691	17	requests
2.0428	43.1	.6310	16	placement
2.0421	43.1	.4441	21	pests
2.0411	43.1	.4923	18	swooped
2.0410	43.1	.6563	15	employer
2.0410	43.1	.6106	16	feats
2.0404	43.1	.4852	20	conversion
2.0398	43.1	.6124	16	wingspread
2.0394	43.1	.4832	20	Cave
2.0391	43.1	.6207	16	vent
2.0389	43.1	.4840	19	herding
2.0389	43.1	.5996	16	usefulness
2.0386	43.1	.5273	17	pancakes
2.0384	43.1	.4720	20	Down
2.0384	43.1	.5798	17	psychologists
2.0382	43.1	.5824	17	biscuit
2.0379	43.1	.2759	35	lacquer
2.0375	43.1	.5299	18	Security
2.0374	43.1	.6708	15	renewed
2.0373	43.1	.5795	16	hurting
2.0365	43.1	.3265	22	kitty
2.0364	43.1	.4596	21	veal
2.0361	43.1	.5241	18	perception
2.0360	43.1	.3979	23	digest
2.0359	43.1	.5748	17	spacious
2.0357	43.1	.0000	136	addends
2.0353	43.1	.4407	21	Allied
2.0350	43.1	.5068	19	identifies
2.0347	43.1	.6240	16	commissioned
2.0346	43.1	.6489	15	tugging
2.0345	43.1	.5330	17	pelican
THE PRECEDING WORD TYPE OCCUPIES RANK 12400				
2.0334	43.1	.5951	16	tiptoe
2.0326	43.1	.6177	16	notions
2.0319	43.1	.7170	14	sweetness
2.0318	43.1	.6413	15	behaving
2.0317	43.1	.6450	15	uh
2.0311	43.1	.7029	14	cemetery
2.0309	43.1	.3903	24	anatomy
2.0307	43.1	.4469	20	cellophane
2.0304	43.1	.6521	15	stunned
2.0295	43.1	.5693	17	glued
2.0291	43.1	.1906	28	Merle
2.0279	43.1	.3663	26	rpm
2.0276	43.1	.5729	17	325
2.0274	43.1	.5509	17	clumps
2.0274	43.1	.7730	13	imposing
2.0267	43.1	.5648	17	underbrush
2.0264	43.1	.5579	17	gorgeous
2.0264	43.1	.1491	39	Light
2.0250	43.1	.6298	15	ambulance
2.0245	43.1	.6601	15	verdict
2.0243	43.1	.5752	17	1906
2.0238	43.1	.6468	15	warns
2.0226	43.1	.4195	22	projections
2.0221	43.1	.5531	17	wading
2.0216	43.1	.3701	25	install
2.0206	43.1	.5254	18	bison
2.0200	43.1	.3280	26	precipitation
2.0195	43.1	.6471	15	signing
2.0183	43.0	.6116	16	squat
2.0181	43.0	.6542	15	explode
2.0178	43.0	.5723	17	barbarians
2.0178	43.0	.5235	18	Chamber
2.0169	43.0	.7001	14	somber
2.0163	43.0	.2998	28	tariff
2.0160	43.0	.2446	26	Boomer
2.0158	43.0	.5987	16	sprays
2.0148	43.0	.4943	19	complexion
2.0143	43.0	.6576	15	firsthand
2.0138	43.0	.5798	16	boomed
2.0137	43.0	.4277	20	buckwheat
2.0128	43.0	.2034	44	dimension
2.0128	43.0	.6388	15	intentions
2.0125	43.0	.5591	17	maze
2.0123	43.0	.2690	33	anvil
2.0123	43.0	.4301	21	pricked
2.0119	43.0	.5683	17	campaigns
2.0118	43.0	.4620	20	Pharaoh
2.0117	43.0	.6130	16	presentation
2.0116	43.0	.6515	15	bleating
2.0116	43.0	.4648	20	parakeets
2.0112	43.0	.4177	22	Walrus
2.0111	43.0	.5217	18	pills
2.0108	43.0	.6507	15	fringes
2.0108	43.0	.4891	19	1848
2.0106	43.0	.5955	16	superstitions
2.0104	43.0	.4573	20	Explorer
2.0101	43.0	.4026	23	crystalline
2.0100	43.0	.4334	22	Gertrude
2.0099	43.0	.4342	20	Beebe
2.0099	43.0	.6947	14	kidding
2.0094	43.0	.6043	16	differed
2.0092	43.0	.5398	17	fainted
2.0089	43.0	.5988	16	actively
2.0084	43.0	.4140	21	pueblo
2.0079	43.0	.3682	24	Cortes
2.0067	43.0	.5780	17	functional
2.0062	43.0	.4989	19	territorial
2.0044	43.0	.4782	19	greetings
2.0042	43.0	.4739	20	ultimately
2.0041	43.0	.5758	16	tiptoed
2.0036	43.0	.2661	30	teaches
2.0035	43.0	.5808	16	dismounted
2.0032	43.0	.6024	16	Wells
2.0030	43.0	.3280	29	blended
2.0026	43.0	.4269	22	Janus
2.0023	43.0	.6442	15	beforehand
2.0023	43.0	.5769	16	openly
2.0023	43.0	.6431	15	rippling
2.0019	43.0	.6278	15	foolishly
2.0019	43.0	.6022	16	victorious
2.0018	43.0	.4486	20	mates
2.0015	43.0	.6992	14	blasting
2.0012	43.0	.6056	16	lush
2.0009	43.0	.4638	20	groom
2.0007	43.0	.6491	15	exhibited
2.0007	43.0	.5109	18	Fred's
2.0007	43.0	.5180	18	treasury
2.0005	43.0	.4276	20	Rat
2.0005	43.0	.4620	20	spoonful
1.9999	43.0	.5995	16	typically
1.9998	43.0	.6506	15	achieving
1.9998	43.0	.5512	17	lo
1.9992	43.0	.6003	16	penetrated
1.9992	43.0	.5367	17	squinted
1.9990	43.0	.6215	15	poppy
1.9986	43.0	.4290	22	Gutenberg
1.9985	43.0	.5099	18	trainer
1.9983	43.0	.5388	17	thunderous
1.9978	43.0	.5480	17	luggage
1.9975	43.0	.5511	17	silt
THE PRECEDING WORD TYPE OCCUPIES RANK 12500				
1.9974	43.0	.3383	25	hypotheses
1.9974	43.0	.5315	18	kin
1.9972	43.0	.5230	18	decayed
1.9967	43.0	.7090	14	arranges
1.9964	43.0	.6218	15	mink
1.9960	43.0	.4988	19	ceilings
1.9952	43.0	.5148	18	bullfrog
1.9952	43.0	.6394	15	hickory
1.9950	43.0	.4193	21	Iron
1.9949	43.0	.5832	16	thumped
1.9944	43.0	.4590	20	arid

U	SFI	D	F	Word Type
1.9944	43.0	.6086	16	oaks
1.9943	43.0	.4641	20	complexity
1.9943	43.0	.5472	17	forceful
1.9931	43.0	.6052	16	pursuing
1.9927	43.0	.5919	16	gallery
1.9926	43.0	.4519	20	$50
1.9920	43.0	.6027	16	incoming
1.9913	43.0	.5937	16	bordered
1.9911	43.0	.6366	15	oily
1.9910	43.0	.6189	15	sparkle
1.9909	43.0	.4914	19	Hindus
1.9909	43.0	.3059	24	Shane
1.9908	43.0	.6151	15	ranger
1.9905	43.0	.6074	16	pizza
1.9902	43.0	.6380	15	nourishing
1.9901	43.0	.5389	17	delights
1.9899	43.0	.4077	21	thunderstorms
1.9897	43.0	.6542	15	merit
1.9893	43.0	.6376	15	eve
1.9893	43.0	.6970	14	excluded
1.9891	43.0	.6323	15	emblem
1.9891	43.0	.6067	16	monotonous
1.9890	43.0	.6464	15	emotionally
1.9886	43.0	.4843	19	bombing
1.9885	43.0	.4573	20	snacks
1.9884	43.0	.4961	18	fathoms
1.9883	43.0	.5646	16	turnip
1.9878	43.0	.4232	22	transmission
1.9875	43.0	.3416	25	apes
1.9875	43.0	.5581	17	enormously
1.9874	43.0	.5477	17	earnestly
1.9869	43.0	.2737	32	composing
1.9862	43.0	.6337	15	cafe
1.9861	43.0	.5601	17	crook
1.9859	43.0	.5480	17	aqueducts
1.9855	43.0	.5343	18	principally
1.9849	43.0	.5247	18	socially
1.9848	43.0	.4791	19	Evans
1.9843	43.0	.5006	19	incorporated
1.9836	43.0	.4810	19	basins
1.9836	43.0	.5647	17	stimulated
1.9835	43.0	.4101	22	Head
1.9832	43.0	.6358	15	scratches
1.9829	43.0	.7518	13	wharves
1.9826	43.0	.4755	19	stunts
1.9824	43.0	.3116	25	Bering
1.9824	43.0	.4209	21	observes
1.9818	43.0	.6975	14	guitars
1.9805	43.0	.4616	19	skiing
1.9804	43.0	.6847	14	hovering
1.9785	43.0	.6493	15	moderately
1.9783	43.0	.3486	26	merchandise
1.9778	43.0	.5265	17	Sawyer
1.9775	43.0	.6232	15	runways
1.9770	43.0	.5606	17	boating
1.9770	43.0	.6347	15	cucumbers
1.9768	43.0	.6051	16	Ten
1.9764	43.0	.6019	16	overthrown
1.9762	43.0	.4121	19	emeralds
1.9757	43.0	.5317	18	remnants
1.9756	43.0	.6373	15	intensified
1.9751	43.0	.4824	19	trenches
1.9743	43.0	.6019	16	schoolyard
1.9743	43.0	.5923	16	three-year-old
1.9743	43.0	.5202	18	unemployment
1.9742	43.0	.5777	16	leagues
1.9741	43.0	.4419	20	raisins
1.9734	43.0	.6316	15	broader
1.9733	43.0	.5608	16	whoa
1.9730	43.0	.6289	15	tomahawk
1.9729	43.0	.5606	16	bombers
1.9724	42.9	.1126	56	ABCD
1.9724	43.0	.5706	16	scurrying
1.9718	42.9	.5994	16	revived
1.9716	42.9	.6859	14	crashes
1.9712	42.9	.6104	15	sweet-smelling
1.9710	42.9	.4875	18	goggles
1.9706	42.9	.4884	18	sneezed
1.9702	42.9	.6178	15	wrestled
1.9697	42.9	.3965	22	chops
1.9697	42.9	.6374	15	devote
1.9696	42.9	.3819	22	manganese
1.9684	42.9	.1061	59	God's
1.9680	42.9	.6415	15	mackerel
1.9679	42.9	.6882	14	packets
1.9678	42.9	.6281	15	overcoat
1.9669	42.9	.5552	16	twinkled
1.9665	42.9	.5996	16	dialect
1.9662	42.9	.4586	19	Columbus'

THE PRECEDING WORD TYPE OCCUPIES RANK 12600

U	SFI	D	F	Word Type
1.9662	42.9	.4525	20	oxidation
1.9659	42.9	.3104	22	Nell
1.9656	42.9	.5713	16	schoolboy
1.9645	42.9	.6016	16	dictates
1.9644	42.9	.0000	43	frogmen
1.9644	42.9	.0000	43	StGeorge
1.9642	42.9	.4210	19	airmen
1.9641	42.9	.5555	17	nonetheless
1.9639	42.9	.6748	14	clothe
1.9639	42.9	.5213	17	Smiths
1.9638	42.9	.4467	21	Echo
1.9638	42.9	.5499	17	Power
1.9634	42.9	.5914	16	guinea
1.9632	42.9	.3325	26	Boat
1.9628	42.9	.5192	17	snow-capped
1.9624	42.9	.4544	20	duke
1.9624	42.9	.0237	102	remainders
1.9620	42.9	.6041	15	Dayton
1.9618	42.9	.6154	15	departing
1.9617	42.9	.5736	16	Isle
1.9611	42.9	.4255	20	Apache
1.9608	42.9	.4841	19	regulation
1.9607	42.9	.5890	16	formulas
1.9606	42.9	.4154	21	Mission
1.9599	42.9	.3895	24	adjustments
1.9592	42.9	.5901	16	ironically
1.9585	42.9	.1961	39	coordinates
1.9584	42.9	.5919	16	broadcasts
1.9584	42.9	.3665	21	streamers
1.9580	42.9	.6158	15	spies
1.9575	42.9	.6349	15	rendezvous
1.9574	42.9	.5403	16	bunk
1.9572	42.9	.4808	18	lice
1.9571	42.9	.5432	17	imitated
1.9571	42.9	.2204	31	Zeke
1.9569	42.9	.5569	16	squaw
1.9568	42.9	.6659	14	trickled
1.9553	42.9	.5856	16	reserves
1.9553	42.9	.2845	28	Southerners
1.9551	42.9	.4577	20	quotations
1.9550	42.9	.6154	15	murdered
1.9549	42.9	.6350	15	sizable
1.9541	42.9	.6294	15	chanted
1.9534	42.9	.3211	27	Co
1.9530	42.9	.5484	17	leisurely
1.9529	42.9	.4909	19	academic
1.9529	42.9	.6810	14	banker
1.9525	42.9	.6201	15	parting
1.9513	42.9	.6373	15	interference
1.9513	42.9	.6292	15	irresistible
1.9512	42.9	.2903	30	opposites
1.9511	42.9	.5128	17	hilltop
1.9509	42.9	.5963	16	hazards
1.9501	42.9	.5836	16	appearances
1.9490	42.9	.4255	19	Marty
1.9485	42.9	.6623	14	stumble
1.9484	42.9	.6135	15	thrills
1.9483	42.9	.6250	15	epidemic
1.9481	42.9	.2444	24	Bunny
1.9480	42.9	.6769	14	strenuous
1.9479	42.9	.5310	17	skimmed
1.9478	42.9	.6724	14	smack
1.9476	42.9	.3385	21	Lucky
1.9474	42.9	.3340	21	Pieter
1.9472	42.9	.4061	22	knowed
1.9467	42.9	.6693	14	tiresome
1.9463	42.9	.5652	16	sage
1.9460	42.9	.4591	20	discount
1.9458	42.9	.5200	17	hushed
1.9456	42.9	.4854	19	defensive
1.9456	42.9	.0994	59	hundredths
1.9452	42.9	.6302	15	ringed
1.9452	42.9	.5113	17	roping
1.9441	42.9	.6165	15	noblemen
1.9440	42.9	.6198	15	scarves
1.9437	42.9	.5889	16	condensed
1.9435	42.9	.5159	18	steaks
1.9435	42.9	.4294	21	123
1.9429	42.9	.3786	23	electromagnet
1.9423	42.9	.5950	16	soggy
1.9422	42.9	.5418	17	'way
1.9421	42.9	.5872	16	grouse
1.9421	42.9	.6747	14	widen
1.9419	42.9	.5848	16	distinguishing
1.9419	42.9	.5505	16	scrubbing
1.9416	42.9	.3237	28	designer
1.9414	42.9	.4198	21	farmlands
1.9413	42.9	.3729	23	pointer
1.9412	42.9	.6732	14	inadequate
1.9410	42.9	.6255	15	meager
1.9405	42.9	.7368	13	patchwork
1.9404	42.9	.5450	16	half-past
1.9392	42.9	.0268	98	integer
1.9392	42.9	.4487	19	pickers
1.9388	42.9	.2441	35	-er
1.9388	42.9	.4431	20	heave
1.9386	42.9	.6022	15	beheld
1.9383	42.9	.6320	15	hiss
1.9376	42.9	.3862	22	crayfish
1.9374	42.9	.6613	14	calendars

THE PRECEDING WORD TYPE OCCUPIES RANK 12700

U	SFI	D	F	Word Type
1.9368	42.9	.5355	17	blotting
1.9368	42.9	.4564	18	Melbourne
1.9367	42.9	.4474	20	Top
1.9345	42.9	.6122	15	mumps
1.9342	42.9	.5249	17	dozing
1.9332	42.9	.2439	35	/f/
1.9327	42.9	.4108	22	Lorenzo
1.9327	42.9	.3747	20	Theresa
1.9321	42.9	.5446	17	pores
1.9312	42.9	.3431	21	Icarus
1.9312	42.9	.5949	15	schoolbooks
1.9311	42.9	.5768	16	commit
1.9308	42.9	.5761	16	candlelight
1.9293	42.9	.6666	14	failing
1.9287	42.9	.6030	15	terrier
1.9283	42.9	.4550	18	Lt
1.9282	42.9	.4323	20	Honolulu
1.9281	42.9	.3718	21	alchemists
1.9280	42.9	.6184	15	alleys
1.9279	42.9	.2029	26	woodcutter
1.9275	42.8	.7327	13	gossip
1.9273	42.8	.4529	20	cope
1.9272	42.8	.5350	17	aerial
1.9261	42.8	.1353	53	gh
1.9255	42.8	.4523	20	conservative
1.9254	42.8	.4787	19	locust
1.9254	42.8	.6059	15	squeaked
1.9252	42.8	.7207	13	horrified
1.9249	42.8	.5022	18	peppers
1.9245	42.8	.5687	16	fanciful
1.9240	42.8	.5123	17	hanged
1.9235	42.8	.6741	14	fast-moving
1.9235	42.8	.3605	23	Sox
1.9234	42.8	.5491	17	Corporation
1.9232	42.8	.6135	15	badges
1.9230	42.8	.6727	14	broadly
1.9230	42.8	.5633	16	parish
1.9229	42.8	.6666	14	leveled
1.9228	42.8	.4957	18	cavalry
1.9226	42.8	.5767	16	Legion
1.9226	42.8	.6088	15	sailboats
1.9225	42.8	.5139	17	fuzzy
1.9223	42.8	.6294	15	sentiment
1.9218	42.8	.4725	19	glacial
1.9214	42.8	.1738	45	ea
1.9211	42.8	.3610	23	rodents
1.9210	42.8	.3202	21	jade
1.9209	42.8	.5102	18	environmental
1.9204	42.8	.6161	15	throttle
1.9203	42.8	.5584	16	Deer
1.9200	42.8	.3843	22	Upper
1.9194	42.8	.6534	14	investigated
1.9190	42.8	.4264	21	porcelain
1.9187	42.8	.6575	14	superstitious
1.9185	42.8	.5611	16	tiniest
1.9178	42.8	.4688	19	fracture
1.9175	42.8	.2786	28	superhighway
1.9172	42.8	.6590	14	1819
1.9170	42.8	.6061	15	shrank
1.9170	42.8	.4582	20	unified
1.9166	42.8	.3492	24	Ethiopian
1.9165	42.8	.4797	19	edition
1.9165	42.8	.5397	16	headache
1.9154	42.8	.4304	18	Craig
1.9153	42.8	.7248	13	reigned
1.9151	42.8	.4915	17	pampas
1.9151	42.8	.5622	16	torture
1.9150	42.8	.5675	16	maidens
1.9145	42.8	.6755	14	introducing
1.9144	42.8	.5298	17	$30
1.9143	42.8	.5751	16	proceedings
1.9139	42.8	.3864	22	judicial
1.9131	42.8	.2049	38	cutter
1.9130	42.8	.4989	18	California's
1.9130	42.8	.2814	25	Cathy
1.9129	42.8	.6503	14	ridicule
1.9120	42.8	.5411	17	civilian
1.9117	42.8	.5339	17	holdings
1.9113	42.8	.3106	27	hexagon
1.9111	42.8	.4182	21	knitted
1.9108	42.8	.3583	24	milling
1.9105	42.8	.6217	15	clothesline
1.9094	42.8	.5390	17	rated
1.9090	42.8	.6721	14	finely
1.9088	42.8	.5680	16	companionship
1.9086	42.8	.5980	15	coughing
1.9085	42.8	.4610	19	climatic
1.9083	42.8	.5808	16	Oxford
1.9074	42.8	.6093	15	elevated
1.9073	42.8	.5355	17	Morris
1.9065	42.8	.5982	15	mash
1.9065	42.8	.5266	17	Mason
1.9065	42.8	.4917	18	panes
1.9065	42.8	.5756	16	presumably
1.9063	42.8	.7217	13	graciously
1.9059	42.8	.6003	15	Katy
1.9054	42.8	.2854	28	Dodgers
1.9053	42.8	.3768	22	Mac
1.9049	42.8	.7125	13	Olympus
1.9035	42.8	.6088	15	checker

THE PRECEDING WORD TYPE OCCUPIES RANK 12800

U	SFI	D	F	Word Type
1.9035	42.8	.4249	19	nibbling
1.9033	42.8	.4918	18	Danube
1.9029	42.8	.5168	17	Carolina
1.9023	42.8	.6528	14	ignoring
1.9015	42.8	.5081	18	legitimate
1.9012	42.8	.6518	14	mourning
1.9012	42.8	.5117	16	preview
1.9012	42.8	.5862	15	trampled
1.9010	42.8	.5507	16	broth
1.9009	42.8	.5351	16	oncoming
1.9001	42.8	.6126	15	successes
1.8998	42.8	.5023	17	Clerk
1.8993	42.8	.4077	21	wavelength
1.8992	42.8	.5383	16	Verne
1.8990	42.8	.3900	20	Activity
1.8987	42.8	.5753	16	beware
1.8985	42.8	.4844	18	1877
1.8981	42.8	.2594	30	eights
1.8979	42.8	.5683	16	renowned
1.8975	42.8	.4003	20	mustang
1.8969	42.8	.7087	13	drafts
1.8960	42.8	.0149	107	divisible
1.8954	42.8	.6585	14	declaring
1.8949	42.8	.2932	29	instructor
1.8944	42.8	.2254	31	Hale
1.8936	42.8	.6651	14	brooms
1.8933	42.8	.1803	43	phonemes
1.8931	42.8	.5947	15	Vulcan
1.8930	42.8	.6603	14	insane
1.8921	42.8	.6541	14	prospectors
1.8920	42.8	.3886	21	saliva
1.8919	42.8	.5822	15	clawed
1.8918	42.8	.4549	18	footing
1.8917	42.8	.3774	22	Polo
1.8899	42.8	.5888	15	galley
1.8896	42.8	.5912	15	compasses
1.8893	42.8	.3183	25	chloride
1.8893	42.8	.5192	16	Seas
1.8891	42.8	.5759	15	porpoise
1.8888	42.8	.4206	20	1936
1.8882	42.8	.5551	16	locusts
1.8878	42.8	.3148	24	ass
1.8877	42.8	.3148	26	Catherine
1.8876	42.8	.7831	12	assumes
1.8876	42.8	.6092	15	bedrooms
1.8869	42.8	.6025	15	1888
1.8868	42.8	.6618	14	generalizations
1.8867	42.8	.4838	18	north-south
1.8861	42.8	.6072	15	Himalayas
1.8858	42.8	.1365	55	orchestral
1.8857	42.8	.6023	15	resumed
1.8857	42.8	.6541	14	submit
1.8854	42.8	.6462	14	cramped
1.8852	42.8	.6032	15	plumb
1.8850	42.8	.5372	16	duel
1.8845	42.8	.7034	13	confidently
1.8840	42.8	.5646	16	ne'er
1.8839	42.8	.3873	22	135
1.8835	42.7	.5198	17	behaves
1.8832	42.7	.4662	19	watcher
1.8831	42.7	.6066	15	molded
1.8826	42.7	.5880	15	scouting
1.8822	42.7	.4970	18	Mitchell
1.8818	42.7	.5909	15	optimistic
1.8817	42.7	.6074	15	suburb
1.8815	42.7	.4736	17	pinto
1.8814	42.7	.3544	20	boomerang
1.8814	42.7	.4980	17	sayings
1.8811	42.7	.5628	16	consume
1.8809	42.7	.5448	16	aprons
1.8807	42.7	.5587	16	vapors
1.8806	42.7	.5744	16	publication
1.8803	42.7	.5136	16	Vesuvius
1.8799	42.7	.5387	17	Georges
1.8797	42.7	.5415	16	cloths
1.8795	42.7	.5964	15	77
1.8793	42.7	.4870	18	cuttings
1.8791	42.7	.5779	15	Squirrel
1.8790	42.7	.5843	15	draped
1.8790	42.7	.7200	13	stains
1.8783	42.7	.5946	15	betrayed
1.8780	42.7	.3777	21	Tim's
1.8775	42.7	.6630	14	respective
1.8758	42.7	.2815	28	Aires
1.8750	42.7	.5863	15	pelts
1.8749	42.7	.3139	26	saucepan
1.8745	42.7	.5382	16	sneakers
1.8740	42.7	.2687	32	transitional
1.8738	42.7	.5943	15	terraces
1.8736	42.7	.3057	25	stables
1.8734	42.7	.6468	14	Bonnie
1.8724	42.7	.1589	43	improper
1.8723	42.7	.2432	34	/e/
1.8722	42.7	.5590	16	Public
1.8721	42.7	.6335	14	raspberry
1.8719	42.7	.6245	14	untie
1.8717	42.7	.7029	13	disastrous
1.8717	42.7	.7029	13	midsummer
1.8717	42.7	.6559	14	1200
1.8716	42.7	.4370	20	sexual

THE PRECEDING WORD TYPE OCCUPIES RANK 12900

U	SFI	D	F	Word Type
1.8715	42.7	.1676	43	Vietnamese
1.8713	42.7	.7021	13	linger
1.8713	42.7	.4664	19	Maurice
1.8713	42.7	.6536	14	self-confidence
1.8704	42.7	.5041	17	radium
1.8701	42.7	.5238	17	orbital
1.8699	42.7	.5070	17	poplar
1.8699	42.7	.4163	21	5th
1.8687	42.7	.4323	20	turbines
1.8683	42.7	.4123	21	pianist
1.8679	42.7	.2275	32	sediments
1.8676	42.7	.3837	21	Doug
1.8673	42.7	.5908	15	gulf
1.8667	42.7	.6057	15	tablets
1.8665	42.7	.6506	14	bluish
1.8663	42.7	.5846	15	cypress
1.8656	42.7	.3756	23	magnetized
1.8649	42.7	.4534	18	Lisa
1.8647	42.7	.6584	14	dominate
1.8645	42.7	.6478	14	doorways
1.8641	42.7	.3239	23	meteorites
1.8637	42.7	.5201	16	shoving
1.8636	42.7	.5567	16	darken
1.8634	42.7	.2638	32	prepositions
1.8631	42.7	.5224	17	Game
1.8627	42.7	.2725	25	Crowley
1.8626	42.7	.5223	17	fusion
1.8623	42.7	.6417	14	directs
1.8617	42.7	.3947	21	pulleys
1.8615	42.7	.6997	13	betray
1.8612	42.7	.2330	33	intersecting
1.8611	42.7	.4581	19	Pike
1.8610	42.7	.4509	19	sugars
1.8594	42.7	.5768	15	chimpanzee
1.8593	42.7	.3844	20	Sue's
1.8592	42.7	.5846	15	kelp
1.8581	42.7	.6396	14	stale
1.8576	42.7	.6394	14	nourished
1.8572	42.7	.6398	14	fairs
1.8568	42.7	.5111	17	antelopes
1.8567	42.7	.6186	14	petted
1.8566	42.7	.5251	16	gust
1.8566	42.7	.5049	17	Hugo
1.8564	42.7	.5996	15	childish
1.8563	42.7	.5302	17	realism
1.8563	42.7	.4176	20	1821
1.8561	42.7	.4209	20	wines
1.8557	42.7	.4206	19	sakes
1.8556	42.7	.6382	14	conquering
1.8554	42.7	.6326	14	afoot
1.8551	42.7	.5964	15	220
1.8546	42.7	.7018	13	1872
1.8541	42.7	.5976	15	bleached
1.8541	42.7	.6133	14	dollars'
1.8539	42.7	.3836	21	lunches
1.8536	42.7	.4579	19	treeless
1.8532	42.7	.6219	14	farmyard
1.8531	42.7	.6359	14	lent
1.8523	42.7	.6957	13	daydreaming
1.8523	42.7	.4879	17	gallant
1.8520	42.7	.3770	21	earthworms
1.8514	42.7	.3580	21	Burke
1.8513	42.7	.6123	14	soot
1.8510	42.7	.6394	14	menace
1.8504	42.7	.5519	16	self-conscious
1.8501	42.7	.3392	23	baboons
1.8494	42.7	.5216	16	blueberries
1.8493	42.7	.4994	17	slogan
1.8492	42.7	.4491	18	llama
1.8487	42.7	.6313	14	purposely
1.8481	42.7	.6157	14	cautioned
1.8481	42.7	.6413	14	featured
1.8472	42.7	.4522	17	Waters
1.8468	42.7	.5035	17	Social
1.8467	42.7	.6431	14	radish

U	SFI	D	F	Word Type
1.8463	42.7	.5173	17	Milan
1.8462	42.7	.6753	13	chrome
1.8462	42.7	.5385	16	mapped
1.8457	42.7	.3815	22	fluorine
1.8454	42.7	.5139	17	afflicted
1.8453	42.7	.6353	14	mourn
1.8452	42.7	.5444	16	galleries
1.8450	42.7	.5234	17	dandy
1.8448	42.7	.3175	25	snaps
1.8442	42.7	.6022	15	implies
1.8442	42.7	.6010	15	resistant
1.8440	42.7	.5516	15	kennel
1.8437	42.7	.6340	14	golly
1.8436	42.7	.4319	20	Antoine
1.8429	42.7	.4637	17	innkeeper
1.8427	42.7	.6990	13	pieced
1.8426	42.7	.5121	17	Beautiful
1.8423	42.7	.3007	27	nuns
1.8422	42.7	.5161	16	bully
1.8421	42.7	.4440	17	flapped
1.8416	42.7	.6377	14	bulge
1.8415	42.7	.6692	13	shrunk
1.8415	42.7	.0977	56	1/10
1.8412	42.7	.4749	18	patented
1.8410	42.7	.4436	17	Niccolo
THE PRECEDING WORD TYPE OCCUPIES RANK 13000				
1.8406	42.6	.5096	17	Shaw
1.8398	42.6	.5577	15	ferocious
1.8396	42.6	.5023	17	geological
1.8391	42.6	.5455	16	likeness
1.8391	42.6	.6350	14	monk
1.8391	42.6	.4474	17	skis
1.8388	42.6	.5268	16	pleading
1.8381	42.6	.6162	14	commotion
1.8378	42.6	.6415	14	correcting
1.8378	42.6	.6759	13	Sons
1.8373	42.6	.5873	15	exclaim
1.8369	42.6	.6345	14	relied
1.8362	42.6	.5512	16	revelation
1.8361	42.6	.5206	17	consumption
1.8357	42.6	.5813	15	unexplored
1.8351	42.6	.5084	17	206
1.8350	42.6	.7041	13	placid
1.8344	42.6	.3758	21	Voice
1.8341	42.6	.6086	14	awed
1.8341	42.6	.6333	14	middle-aged
1.8340	42.6	.5971	15	restrained
1.8339	42.6	.5545	16	With
1.8336	42.6	.5229	16	captives
1.8332	42.6	.3277	24	thermostat
1.8329	42.6	.5209	16	noisily
1.8328	42.6	.3674	22	wavelengths
1.8326	42.6	.5344	16	foreigner
1.8320	42.6	.3262	20	deerskin
1.8316	42.6	.4720	18	ticks
1.8313	42.6	.1971	25	Fast
1.8313	42.6	.3900	20	Wizard
1.8311	42.6	.6302	14	burial
1.8310	42.6	.6364	14	exceeded
1.8308	42.6	.5088	17	fools
1.8304	42.6	.5762	15	irons
1.8302	42.6	.5878	15	shimmering
1.8297	42.6	.5680	15	flopped
1.8295	42.6	.6759	13	squeal
1.8292	42.6	.3092	25	minstrel
1.8286	42.6	.3721	20	Riggs
1.8283	42.6	.5755	15	burdens
1.8279	42.6	.6843	13	eyesight
1.8277	42.6	.3416	24	wrench
1.8274	42.6	.2896	28	predators
1.8273	42.6	.0000	40	Stutz
1.8271	42.6	.6905	13	preached
1.8261	42.6	.5038	16	wren
1.8256	42.6	.5793	15	Jules
1.8254	42.6	.2639	29	Remember
1.8251	42.6	.6293	14	woe
1.8250	42.6	.4818	18	reflections
1.8249	42.6	.4593	18	Wilson's
1.8246	42.6	.6861	13	bob
1.8244	42.6	.3952	21	bonus
1.8244	42.6	.3272	23	dropper
1.8239	42.6	.5470	16	captivity
1.8238	42.6	.3649	22	asteroids
1.8236	42.6	.5551	15	punching
1.8236	42.6	.4367	20	threaded
1.8235	42.6	.5796	15	infantry
1.8234	42.6	.5788	15	romance
1.8233	42.6	.5484	16	corpse
1.8229	42.6	.4910	17	wireless
1.8227	42.6	.5046	16	Hunt
1.8227	42.6	.5133	17	teeming
1.8226	42.6	.3034	26	larva
1.8223	42.6	.4581	18	to-day
1.8219	42.6	.5819	15	lightest
1.8212	42.6	.3755	23	parsley
1.8212	42.6	.5792	15	supernatural
1.8204	42.6	.5433	16	fresh-water
1.8203	42.6	.4304	17	Paper
1.8199	42.6	.4378	19	sawmills
1.8197	42.6	.5719	15	unreasonable
1.8196	42.6	.2321	32	additive
1.8195	42.6	.5325	16	lab
1.8195	42.6	.5715	15	statesman
1.8193	42.6	.5060	17	savagely
1.8190	42.6	.5369	16	1924
1.8189	42.6	.4880	17	chipmunks
1.8187	42.6	.3640	24	constructions
1.8186	42.6	.5440	15	overturned
1.8185	42.6	.5736	15	pathway
1.8183	42.6	.6019	14	kneeling
1.8183	42.6	.4541	18	toothpaste
1.8180	42.6	.5492	16	prodigious
1.8177	42.6	.6146	14	errand
1.8175	42.6	.4112	20	one-celled
1.8173	42.6	.6783	13	defied
1.8170	42.6	.5100	17	toilet
1.8168	42.6	.5627	15	pondered
1.8166	42.6	.5323	16	rewards
1.8159	42.6	.5214	16	jumper
1.8155	42.6	.3802	21	phosphate
1.8155	42.6	.6347	14	Springfield
1.8151	42.6	.6119	14	unmistakable
1.8150	42.6	.6135	14	yawn
1.8148	42.6	.4919	17	far-reaching
1.8140	42.6	.4761	18	Persians
1.8133	42.6	.5789	15	wholesome
THE PRECEDING WORD TYPE OCCUPIES RANK 13100				
1.8132	42.6	.5543	15	glittered
1.8132	42.6	.4574	18	paralysis
1.8131	42.6	.4305	20	symmetrical
1.8128	42.6	.5299	16	refining
1.8127	42.6	.5257	16	blink
1.8125	42.6	.5510	15	cloudless
1.8117	42.6	.6303	14	forbade
1.8109	42.6	.4035	20	fleets
1.8109	42.6	.6595	13	headlights
1.8108	42.6	.5243	16	mileage
1.8104	42.6	.5247	16	hams
1.8102	42.6	.6293	14	inheritance
1.8102	42.6	.3057	24	parasites
1.8096	42.6	.5248	16	perplexed
1.8087	42.6	.5462	16	hare
1.8085	42.6	.6212	14	receipt
1.8084	42.6	.5327	16	scurried
1.8080	42.6	.4220	20	packaged
1.8073	42.6	.5724	15	Order
1.8069	42.6	.4304	20	129
1.8068	42.6	.6874	13	12th
1.8062	42.6	.2377	34	Romantic
1.8058	42.6	.5702	15	mounts
1.8055	42.6	.6352	14	abrupt
1.8055	42.6	.3473	23	Pyramid
1.8052	42.6	.4213	20	banking
1.8052	42.6	.1830	38	Pontiac
1.8051	42.6	.4726	18	Organization
1.8051	42.6	.2548	22	Traveler
1.8045	42.6	.6757	13	1896
1.8043	42.6	.5563	15	clattering
1.8043	42.6	.5028	17	domination
1.8039	42.6	.5734	15	vanish
1.8035	42.6	.6031	14	onlookers
1.8034	42.6	.5296	16	spiny
1.8033	42.6	.5135	16	tutor
1.8033	42.6	.6781	13	world-wide
1.8029	42.6	.6599	13	Johns
1.8020	42.6	.4509	19	Valentine
1.8016	42.6	.6681	13	1904
1.8015	42.6	.3585	22	neighborhoods
1.8012	42.6	.5520	15	plugged
1.8011	42.6	.6843	13	proclamation
1.8009	42.6	.6798	13	disciplined
1.8007	42.6	.6199	14	disguised
1.8007	42.6	.5019	17	1830
1.7999	42.6	.4459	18	heartbeat
1.7997	42.6	.4526	18	calculating
1.7993	42.6	.6187	14	Raleigh
1.7992	42.6	.3852	21	soluble
1.7985	42.5	.4589	17	chap
1.7979	42.5	.5561	15	blue-green
1.7979	42.5	.4015	20	dis
1.7973	42.5	.4637	17	fiesta
1.7972	42.5	.5095	17	illusion
1.7969	42.5	.4405	17	cinders
1.7969	42.5	.4710	18	wedges
1.7968	42.5	.5742	15	commercials
1.7967	42.5	.1397	48	Agba
1.7965	42.5	.6852	13	ingredient
1.7956	42.5	.6706	13	congress
1.7954	42.5	.6291	14	posed
1.7952	42.5	.5390	15	crossly
1.7950	42.5	.5573	15	morrow
1.7942	42.5	.4332	19	reacts
1.7941	42.5	.5615	15	criticized
1.7941	42.5	.6666	13	tougher
1.7941	42.5	.3770	21	trotting
1.7936	42.5	.7235	12	Dutchman
1.7936	42.5	.5300	16	requested
1.7934	42.5	.5552	15	repay
1.7929	42.5	.5058	16	genie
1.7929	42.5	.5241	16	Marshal
1.7928	42.5	.4805	17	Leo
1.7926	42.5	.5396	15	caboose
1.7922	42.5	.5980	14	peeping
1.7916	42.5	.5439	15	cobra
1.7915	42.5	.4897	16	Daphne
1.7915	42.5	.5380	15	groaning
1.7914	42.5	.5532	15	shove
1.7910	42.5	.5018	17	Journal
1.7909	42.5	.5302	15	Hancock
1.7907	42.5	.5626	15	kissing
1.7903	42.5	.5780	15	justify
1.7903	42.5	.3696	19	Telstar
1.7896	42.5	.4547	18	confess
1.7895	42.5	.6757	13	recognizable
1.7894	42.5	.6026	14	flare
1.7893	42.5	.4906	17	probes
1.7893	42.5	.5979	14	volunteered
1.7889	42.5	.5673	15	avenue
1.7888	42.5	.6103	14	depressed
1.7885	42.5	.4436	17	two-way
1.7881	42.5	.6572	13	foaming
1.7879	42.5	.5017	16	Anne's
1.7878	42.5	.3853	20	splint
1.7875	42.5	.6132	14	Wayne
1.7873	42.5	.5323	15	defiance
1.7873	42.5	.2399	24	plover
1.7872	42.5	.5672	15	pumice
THE PRECEDING WORD TYPE OCCUPIES RANK 13200				
1.7869	42.5	.5441	15	Samson
1.7867	42.5	.6098	14	fatter
1.7867	42.5	.5033	17	Kings
1.7853	42.5	.5140	15	retorted
1.7850	42.5	.5582	15	1880's
1.7849	42.5	.2946	28	Classical
1.7848	42.5	.4303	19	Constantinople
1.7848	42.5	.5702	15	hardwood
1.7847	42.5	.5942	14	hunched
1.7847	42.5	.5256	16	melon
1.7846	42.5	.6205	14	Puget
1.7845	42.5	.6221	14	Bar
1.7844	42.5	.5716	15	enabling
1.7842	42.5	.5590	15	$500
1.7842	42.5	.5492	15	flagpole
1.7841	42.5	.5589	15	frosted
1.7841	42.5	.4480	19	Stanford
1.7835	42.5	.6541	13	World's
1.7833	42.5	.3036	24	Leif
1.7829	42.5	.5017	16	erupted
1.7828	42.5	.5155	16	rafts
1.7827	42.5	.5938	14	tenderly
1.7818	42.5	.6729	13	intolerable
1.7816	42.5	.0000	39	R-80
1.7812	42.5	.6147	14	Gibraltar
1.7812	42.5	.6695	13	spar
1.7810	42.5	.2433	23	quack
1.7805	42.5	.5285	16	embrace
1.7804	42.5	.2185	31	Plain
1.7799	42.5	.5638	15	first-class
1.7798	42.5	.3002	24	drummer
1.7797	42.5	.4318	19	elevations
1.7796	42.5	.1984	38	Debussy
1.7792	42.5	.5975	14	schoolwork
1.7792	42.5	.6160	14	seeming
1.7784	42.5	.6038	14	compassion
1.7784	42.5	.5992	14	grocer
1.7784	42.5	.6141	14	Rhodes
1.7774	42.5	.3401	21	Ryan
1.7771	42.5	.4895	16	baffled
1.7768	42.5	.5196	16	Fleming
1.7767	42.5	.5968	14	billows
1.7766	42.5	.4225	19	lithium
1.7763	42.5	.4473	17	marveled
1.7759	42.5	.5146	16	clinic
1.7757	42.5	.5717	15	frustrated
1.7753	42.5	.4689	16	Cherokee
1.7745	42.5	.7320	12	retire
1.7744	42.5	.4538	18	withdrawal
1.7740	42.5	.5548	15	Corner
1.7737	42.5	.4349	19	terminals
1.7732	42.5	.4029	19	yardstick
1.7731	42.5	.5174	16	sovereign
1.7722	42.5	.5261	16	papyrus
1.7718	42.5	.6510	13	rangers
1.7712	42.5	.6613	13	figs
1.7710	42.5	.5550	15	canopy
1.7709	42.5	.5537	15	disorder
1.7706	42.5	.4631	18	198
1.7704	42.5	.6459	13	solidly
1.7699	42.5	.6141	14	symbolizes
1.7696	42.5	.2428	27	Elsa
1.7689	42.5	.5066	16	cupped
1.7687	42.5	.5018	16	glee
1.7680	42.5	.5552	15	NewEngland
1.7679	42.5	.6124	14	brackets
1.7678	42.5	.5370	16	theatre
1.7675	42.5	.3479	23	pansies
1.7663	42.5	.0000	118	integers
1.7660	42.5	.6634	13	aging
1.7659	42.5	.4448	18	Cathedral
1.7659	42.5	.5505	15	nightly
1.7655	42.5	.6617	13	Last
1.7654	42.5	.5279	16	coasting
1.7651	42.5	.5882	14	rheumatism
1.7645	42.5	.6578	13	laps
1.7642	42.5	.5201	16	brandy
1.7639	42.5	.5376	15	tepees
1.7632	42.5	.4237	18	Mamma
1.7632	42.5	.5688	15	1866
1.7629	42.5	.4522	18	Istanbul
1.7621	42.5	.4389	19	currency
1.7621	42.5	.5300	16	foreground
1.7615	42.5	.5953	14	shrinking
1.7612	42.5	.4671	17	Jerry's
1.7610	42.5	.6019	14	veil
1.7608	42.5	.5198	16	tenants
1.7605	42.5	.2857	25	Ellen's
1.7603	42.5	.6533	13	crumbled
1.7602	42.5	.6058	14	piping
1.7601	42.5	.5824	14	rightly
1.7600	42.5	.5292	16	actress
1.7598	42.5	.4680	18	designers
1.7598	42.5	.6159	14	pp
1.7589	42.5	.3560	22	Viet
1.7588	42.5	.4862	17	Aztecs
1.7587	42.5	.3447	21	Rab
1.7584	42.5	.5758	14	orphan
1.7582	42.5	.5070	16	sprawling
1.7580	42.5	.4249	18	Homer's
THE PRECEDING WORD TYPE OCCUPIES RANK 13300				
1.7578	42.4	.6006	14	impatience
1.7577	42.4	.5885	14	pitcher's
1.7569	42.4	.6022	14	Robert's
1.7567	42.4	.5215	16	risky
1.7567	42.4	.5222	15	Ship
1.7559	42.4	.5413	15	stricken
1.7556	42.4	.5977	14	revealing
1.7555	42.4	.3436	22	guiding
1.7553	42.4	.4908	17	375
1.7553	42.4	.2645	29	4/4
1.7548	42.4	.5487	15	Genoa
1.7545	42.4	.5252	15	loggers
1.7544	42.4	.3756	22	plaintive
1.7544	42.4	.6511	13	town's
1.7542	42.4	.7123	12	emptying
1.7541	42.4	.5346	15	showy
1.7540	42.4	.5880	14	Hospital
1.7539	42.4	.4721	17	east-west
1.7535	42.4	.5616	15	interpretations
1.7533	42.4	.5797	14	fastens
1.7531	42.4	.5933	14	cow's
1.7528	42.4	.3787	21	proportional
1.7525	42.4	.5937	14	jealousy
1.7524	42.4	.3481	22	gaseous
1.7524	42.4	.4818	17	resigned
1.7520	42.4	.6488	13	wasteland
1.7511	42.4	.1850	31	Matthias
1.7508	42.4	.5419	15	hovered
1.7508	42.4	.5621	15	650
1.7504	42.4	.5188	15	nearing
1.7504	42.4	.5089	16	Zone
1.7501	42.4	.5330	15	shave
1.7500	42.4	.2418	31	Sousa
1.7498	42.4	.5191	15	dives
1.7498	42.4	.6003	14	erase
1.7492	42.4	.6431	13	spoils
1.7484	42.4	.5552	15	possum
1.7473	42.4	.5186	16	discrimination
1.7471	42.4	.5877	14	parcels
1.7471	42.4	.4589	18	speculation
1.7464	42.4	.5551	15	shoreline
1.7463	42.4	.3195	23	ameba
1.7462	42.4	.6619	13	insignificant
1.7460	42.4	.5899	14	leaks
1.7460	42.4	.6467	13	mower
1.7457	42.4	.5464	15	fleshy
1.7457	42.4	.4003	17	Nome
1.7456	42.4	.5263	16	avoiding
1.7456	42.4	.2774	23	cadets
1.7455	42.4	.4440	18	trillion
1.7454	42.4	.5387	15	cowardly
1.7453	42.4	.2399	29	adaptations
1.7453	42.4	.5203	16	versatile
1.7451	42.4	.5319	15	weasel
1.7445	42.4	.0617	67	reciprocal
1.7443	42.4	.5066	16	reservoirs
1.7442	42.4	.6483	13	Turk
1.7438	42.4	.4958	17	sequences
1.7437	42.4	.5824	14	wanderers
1.7434	42.4	.5103	16	overseer
1.7431	42.4	.1841	40	recordings
1.7423	42.4	.4059	19	mollusks
1.7421	42.4	.4402	18	opaque
1.7418	42.4	.1840	29	Josh
1.7417	42.4	.3438	22	fertilized
1.7416	42.4	.5432	15	beacon
1.7415	42.4	.3952	20	membranes
1.7410	42.4	.5058	16	forbid
1.7408	42.4	.3953	20	molecular
1.7405	42.4	.2755	28	unison
1.7401	42.4	.6208	13	merciless
1.7399	42.4	.5766	14	thrashed
1.7397	42.4	.4132	19	ban
1.7396	42.4	.4144	19	classifying
1.7395	42.4	.5839	14	swirl
1.7387	42.4	.3683	18	Rob
1.7384	42.4	.6426	13	cellars
1.7383	42.4	.5940	14	diesel
1.7382	42.4	.3534	22	negatives
1.7382	42.4	.4195	19	scraping
1.7377	42.4	.2918	24	Moor
1.7376	42.4	.3647	21	renamed
1.7374	42.4	.5132	15	stewardess
1.7369	42.4	.5920	14	mattered
1.7368	42.4	.6574	13	pagan
1.7367	42.4	.6471	13	rapidity
1.7364	42.4	.4497	16	Round
1.7362	42.4	.5103	16	stakes
1.7359	42.4	.0000	38	Salty
1.7359	42.4	.5944	14	touchdown
1.7358	42.4	.3042	24	jurisdiction
1.7353	42.4	.6441	13	leathery
1.7352	42.4	.3696	21	infections
1.7345	42.4	.5317	15	clippings
1.7344	42.4	.6446	13	grunts
1.7342	42.4	.5861	14	Queen's
1.7340	42.4	.5295	15	rejoicing
1.7338	42.4	.6375	13	sweetest
1.7332	42.4	.4128	19	reactor
1.7324	42.4	.6139	13	dwarfs
THE PRECEDING WORD TYPE OCCUPIES RANK 13400				
1.7310	42.4	.5222	15	grandmother's
1.7308	42.4	.5969	14	commonest
1.7307	42.4	.5220	15	feasting
1.7307	42.4	.5019	16	tornadoes
1.7306	42.4	.5096	16	publishers
1.7305	42.4	.5204	15	Perry
1.7302	42.4	.4995	16	halter
1.7300	42.4	.7162	12	enlarge
1.7299	42.4	.5022	16	Military
1.7296	42.4	.6516	13	diminished
1.7295	42.4	.4509	16	Milt
1.7295	42.4	.5214	16	sketched
1.7289	42.4	.5895	14	bog
1.7286	42.4	.4038	19	radiations
1.7284	42.4	.3462	21	lanky
1.7283	42.4	.5958	14	ostriches
1.7282	42.4	.4509	16	jay
1.7278	42.4	.7005	12	unhappily
1.7271	42.4	.5900	14	everybody's
1.7269	42.4	.5523	15	fastening
1.7265	42.4	.5886	14	squatting
1.7264	42.4	.6010	14	energies
1.7263	42.4	.1449	26	Winters
1.7262	42.4	.5829	14	stubble
1.7259	42.4	.4880	16	rumbled
1.7256	42.4	.5844	14	Roberts
1.7255	42.4	.4638	16	Sherwood
1.7250	42.4	.3575	18	Tony's
1.7248	42.4	.5593	14	mending
1.7247	42.4	.4980	16	mop
1.7247	42.4	.6388	13	obstacle
1.7245	42.4	.0664	83	Review
1.7243	42.4	.4816	16	driftwood
1.7242	42.4	.4924	16	terraced
1.7241	42.4	.6485	13	indignation
1.7235	42.4	.5214	15	sprawled
1.7234	42.4	.5185	16	yacht
1.7232	42.4	.5501	14	bathed

U	SFI	D	F	Word Type
1.7229	42.4	.5839	14	hopelessly
1.7225	42.4	.4789	16	pups
1.7225	42.4	.6154	13	Sonny
1.7220	42.4	.3577	21	Aegean
1.7220	42.4	.5117	16	governmental
1.7217	42.4	.7028	12	Wilderness
1.7216	42.4	.4696	17	softness
1.7214	42.4	.3664	20	reflector
1.7206	42.4	.6419	13	ache
1.7203	42.4	.2960	25	Rockefeller
1.7202	42.4	.6473	13	ardent
1.7197	42.4	.5438	15	aisle
1.7196	42.4	.3809	21	welded
1.7186	42.4	.4629	17	narrator
1.7177	42.3	.5546	14	minded
1.7176	42.3	.4460	18	Fund
1.7175	42.3	.5550	15	demons
1.7173	42.3	.6386	13	stature
1.7172	42.3	.7066	12	derive
1.7167	42.3	.4749	17	Boxer
1.7163	42.3	.5865	14	mutton
1.7163	42.3	.6289	13	scarred
1.7161	42.3	.4694	16	snowed
1.7158	42.3	.6436	13	numbering
1.7152	42.3	.5446	15	fingertips
1.7152	42.3	.5429	15	horizons
1.7149	42.3	.4001	20	skulls
1.7147	42.3	.1311	40	Isaac
1.7147	42.3	.5469	15	nationalism
1.7142	42.3	.4128	17	whale's
1.7137	42.3	.5754	14	prop
1.7132	42.3	.5777	14	sawed
1.7129	42.3	.4100	20	hue
1.7129	42.3	.5199	16	Modern
1.7128	42.3	.5766	14	KansasCity
1.7124	42.3	.6220	13	indignant
1.7122	42.3	.6929	12	comforts
1.7122	42.3	.5463	14	hourglass
1.7121	42.3	.6378	13	conditioning
1.7119	42.3	.5106	16	hoof
1.7117	42.3	.6316	13	manhood
1.7115	42.3	.6319	13	tramped
1.7114	42.3	.5820	14	Archbishop
1.7110	42.3	.4699	16	Hunter
1.7110	42.3	.4377	18	jointed
1.7109	42.3	.3732	21	US
1.7103	42.3	.5197	15	nothin'
1.7101	42.3	.6975	12	mossy
1.7099	42.3	.2613	28	Joel
1.7098	42.3	.3824	18	Perseus
1.7098	42.3	.5252	15	worshiped
1.7097	42.3	.0718	69	ow
1.7090	42.3	.4429	18	biographies
1.7089	42.3	.3075	22	spider's
1.7087	42.3	.4737	17	automated
1.7085	42.3	.6157	13	wrenched
1.7084	42.3	.5780	14	realization
1.7083	42.3	.5440	15	insists
1.7083	42.3	.4558	18	kitchens
1.7079	42.3	.6146	13	whine
1.7077	42.3	.6983	12	unending
1.7070	42.3	.3192	22	oases
THE PRECEDING WORD TYPE OCCUPIES RANK 13500				
1.7063	42.3	.5492	14	drooped
1.7063	42.3	.6271	13	fleece
1.7063	42.3	.4115	20	mallet
1.7061	42.3	.3996	19	pipeline
1.7059	42.3	.3626	19	bikes
1.7057	42.3	.5001	16	chip
1.7057	42.3	.3471	21	comet
1.7057	42.3	.6077	13	overjoyed
1.7054	42.3	.4321	17	denounced
1.7054	42.3	.6397	13	execute
1.7054	42.3	.4825	17	left-handed
1.7052	42.3	.6268	13	felled
1.7052	42.3	.4978	15	snarl
1.7051	42.3	.5060	16	dynasty
1.7037	42.3	.1027	51	dividend
1.7032	42.3	.5747	14	deliveries
1.7032	42.3	.5797	14	promoted
1.7026	42.3	.6095	13	pitiful
1.7025	42.3	.2926	26	tablespoons
1.7024	42.3	.4332	16	bravest
1.7017	42.3	.6370	13	translations
1.7010	42.3	.6132	13	Canary
1.7005	42.3	.4222	17	tortoise
1.6998	42.3	.4306	18	geologist
1.6998	42.3	.1752	24	Kirsten
1.6997	42.3	.6294	13	blush
1.6997	42.3	.6934	12	doubling
1.6996	42.3	.5867	14	cores
1.6986	42.3	.6805	12	excuses
1.6972	42.3	.6121	13	gangplank
1.6970	42.3	.6884	12	thrifty
1.6969	42.3	.4013	19	decaying
1.6968	42.3	.6107	13	canaries
1.6967	42.3	.4995	16	Cambridge
1.6967	42.3	.5689	14	draining
1.6962	42.3	.4700	17	Czech
1.6961	42.3	.5929	13	eighty-seven
1.6958	42.3	.4033	19	Grant's
1.6954	42.3	.5054	15	sob
1.6950	42.3	.5610	14	flick
1.6948	42.3	.6163	13	objection
1.6947	42.3	.1969	37	bolts
1.6944	42.3	.4739	17	De
1.6944	42.3	.5448	15	virgin
1.6937	42.3	.5778	14	Friedrich
1.6929	42.3	.6935	12	displaced
1.6929	42.3	.4972	15	phoned
1.6923	42.3	.4223	16	Frank's
1.6922	42.3	.5914	14	accommodate
1.6921	42.3	.6913	12	cornfields
1.6917	42.3	.5677	14	zigzag
1.6916	42.3	.3760	18	Flip
1.6914	42.3	.3612	21	Cinderella
1.6909	42.3	.1470	41	clamp
1.6909	42.3	.4231	17	Honorable
1.6908	42.3	.3286	23	beverages
1.6908	42.3	.3378	22	toothpicks
1.6906	42.3	.3922	20	Mesopotamia
1.6903	42.3	.0000	37	Kees
1.6903	42.3	.0000	37	mm-mm
1.6900	42.3	.6126	13	abreast
1.6900	42.3	.5422	15	regulates
1.6898	42.3	.3636	21	cleanliness
1.6898	42.3	.6426	13	eliminating
1.6896	42.3	.4007	19	hinge
1.6891	42.3	.3062	24	evaporated
1.6891	42.3	.6032	13	freckles
1.6890	42.3	.4700	17	exhibits
1.6887	42.3	.5854	14	et
1.6886	42.3	.5420	14	swoop
1.6884	42.3	.6249	13	seizing
1.6882	42.3	.5640	14	judgments
1.6880	42.3	.4781	17	linguistic
1.6880	42.3	.4208	18	pedestrian
1.6880	42.3	.6131	13	steamship
1.6877	42.3	.5780	14	madness
1.6876	42.3	.6347	13	confirm
1.6874	42.3	.2318	32	/a/
1.6873	42.3	.6330	13	swarming
1.6872	42.3	.2614	26	cerebrum
1.6868	42.3	.5397	15	Look
1.6867	42.3	.6725	12	grunting
1.6863	42.3	.2632	29	al
1.6860	42.3	.6276	13	patriots
1.6859	42.3	.5790	14	pheasant
1.6850	42.3	.3956	20	modeling
1.6850	42.3	.5966	13	screeched
1.6845	42.3	.6114	13	aiming
1.6841	42.3	.5380	15	conventions
1.6838	42.3	.5272	15	1870's
1.6836	42.3	.5588	14	creaked
1.6835	42.3	.6029	13	sickly
1.6833	42.3	.4035	19	Convention
1.6824	42.3	.6820	12	prejudiced
1.6817	42.3	.6088	13	unheard
1.6816	42.3	.5792	14	sponsored
1.6814	42.3	.5788	14	lightness
1.6814	42.3	.6749	12	unworthy
1.6811	42.3	.5381	14	nominate
1.6810	42.3	.3469	18	Smart
THE PRECEDING WORD TYPE OCCUPIES RANK 13600				
1.6808	42.3	.6017	13	cornered
1.6807	42.3	.5275	15	Rachel
1.6802	42.3	.5741	14	clattered
1.6798	42.3	.6033	13	distrust
1.6798	42.3	.4329	16	poodle
1.6793	42.3	.4489	16	wee
1.6787	42.2	.3747	21	artist's
1.6782	42.2	.0874	61	one-syllable
1.6776	42.2	.4843	15	Open
1.6775	42.2	.4386	18	compressor
1.6764	42.2	.5713	14	amber
1.6764	42.2	.6323	13	semester
1.6763	42.2	.6781	12	friendliness
1.6761	42.2	.6155	13	thirty-two
1.6755	42.2	.5810	14	hammock
1.6749	42.2	.4504	16	bonnet
1.6743	42.2	.6886	12	succeeding
1.6741	42.2	.3504	20	Cochise
1.6739	42.2	.6192	13	shotgun
1.6734	42.2	.6633	12	tricked
1.6733	42.2	.4907	15	wheeling
1.6732	42.2	.1855	37	antonym
1.6729	42.2	.5597	14	hurries
1.6729	42.2	.6194	13	unmanned
1.6728	42.2	.4147	18	Ferdinand
1.6726	42.2	.5814	14	exceeds
1.6725	42.2	.6268	13	undone
1.6717	42.2	.4505	17	illnesses
1.6713	42.2	.3933	19	bounces
1.6710	42.2	.6325	13	removes
1.6708	42.2	.6673	12	risked
1.6708	42.2	.6057	13	swishing
1.6708	42.2	.5597	14	whence
1.6707	42.2	.6321	13	singly
1.6703	42.2	.4189	17	cadmium
1.6702	42.2	.5691	14	unimportant
1.6701	42.2	.5297	15	NewYork's
1.6700	42.2	.6147	13	roped
1.6689	42.2	.5584	14	brine
1.6686	42.2	.2651	20	kayak
1.6681	42.2	.6152	13	discovers
1.6681	42.2	.5380	14	groans
1.6679	42.2	.4789	16	Santo
1.6678	42.2	.6268	13	familiarity
1.6677	42.2	.6382	13	fashions
1.6677	42.2	.5213	15	supermarkets
1.6676	42.2	.6299	13	emerging
1.6672	42.2	.4669	15	billy
1.6671	42.2	.6287	13	damaging
1.6670	42.2	.4974	16	integral
1.6670	42.2	.4348	16	Nebuchadnezzar
1.6670	42.2	.4867	16	provincial
1.6667	42.2	.5204	14	hungrily
1.6667	42.2	.0348	81	Lucinda
1.6653	42.2	.5152	15	1921
1.6651	42.2	.5039	15	kangaroos
1.6648	42.2	.3138	20	hippo
1.6646	42.2	.6674	12	miraculous
1.6638	42.2	.6277	13	Hole
1.6632	42.2	.5105	15	tulips
1.6630	42.2	.6068	13	sorrowful
1.6628	42.2	.5290	14	farmers'
1.6627	42.2	.4567	17	comrade
1.6627	42.2	.6075	13	lied
1.6627	42.2	.5679	14	long-distance
1.6620	42.2	.3487	22	Keep
1.6620	42.2	.4017	19	kites
1.6618	42.2	.6188	13	monarchs
1.6616	42.2	.6728	12	forty-two
1.6610	42.2	.5268	15	eruptions
1.6609	42.2	.5548	14	beggars
1.6609	42.2	.5737	14	delivers
1.6606	42.2	.5395	14	roost
1.6602	42.2	.4883	16	barbs
1.6602	42.2	.5464	14	reminding
1.6600	42.2	.5552	14	Hampton
1.6598	42.2	.6215	13	four-legged
1.6596	42.2	.3667	20	Between
1.6595	42.2	.6580	12	cross-legged
1.6582	42.2	.4508	16	dozed
1.6581	42.2	.6211	13	imprint
1.6580	42.2	.6713	12	handiwork
1.6575	42.2	.5029	15	colds
1.6575	42.2	.6052	13	Winston
1.6566	42.2	.6156	13	Gardens
1.6565	42.2	.5967	13	curse
1.6563	42.2	.4974	16	symbolic
1.6558	42.2	.6722	12	goodly
1.6558	42.2	.6215	13	three-quarters
1.6555	42.2	.6684	12	respectfully
1.6551	42.2	.3871	19	Fanny
1.6551	42.2	.5669	14	global
1.6551	42.2	.5157	15	retreated
1.6549	42.2	.6749	12	choppy
1.6549	42.2	.3580	21	negotiations
1.6546	42.2	.5624	14	dedication
1.6545	42.2	.4108	18	constitutional
1.6545	42.2	.5654	14	participants
1.6544	42.2	.5693	14	attributed
1.6538	42.2	.4949	16	doctrine
THE PRECEDING WORD TYPE OCCUPIES RANK 13700				
1.6534	42.2	.5152	15	airmail
1.6534	42.2	.3234	20	Eliza
1.6531	42.2	.6185	13	Rivers
1.6527	42.2	.5331	14	wistfully
1.6525	42.2	.4829	16	mixtures
1.6522	42.2	.3136	20	Boonesborough
1.6513	42.2	.5564	14	canteen
1.6512	42.2	.1303	39	nonliving
1.6509	42.2	.4367	17	Volta
1.6508	42.2	.5647	14	lends
1.6506	42.2	.5395	14	mummy
1.6505	42.2	.4778	15	miller
1.6504	42.2	.5633	14	combs
1.6502	42.2	.4109	19	conjunctions
1.6501	42.2	.6710	12	workable
1.6500	42.2	.4910	16	Don's
1.6499	42.2	.6025	13	tanning
1.6494	42.2	.4165	18	Tacoma
1.6492	42.2	.2636	25	pronounces
1.6489	42.2	.6010	13	vanity
1.6487	42.2	.4633	16	combing
1.6482	42.2	.3406	21	governors
1.6482	42.2	.4421	17	nomination
1.6482	42.2	.5231	15	Wars
1.6481	42.2	.5453	14	1886
1.6480	42.2	.5994	13	dripped
1.6474	42.2	.5040	15	Franklin's
1.6473	42.2	.4312	17	skated
1.6466	42.2	.4873	15	lariat
1.6464	42.2	.4204	18	Guiana
1.6461	42.2	.5908	13	chore
1.6461	42.2	.5651	14	1934
1.6458	42.2	.2087	28	nephew
1.6457	42.2	.6557	12	depart
1.6451	42.2	.5213	15	alliance
1.6451	42.2	.5274	15	desperation
1.6451	42.2	.6202	13	distinguishes
1.6448	42.2	.5120	15	Patent
1.6447	42.2	.4012	18	Dublin
1.6445	42.2	.4854	16	sifted
1.6443	42.2	.4496	17	segregation
1.6442	42.2	.4385	17	detector
1.6440	42.2	.3487	19	Pa's
1.6428	42.2	.3713	18	Isabella
1.6426	42.2	.5973	13	varsity
1.6422	42.2	.5659	14	Mongolia
1.6420	42.2	.5836	13	mom
1.6418	42.2	.5116	15	grounded
1.6416	42.2	.4637	15	pistols
1.6415	42.2	.4833	15	buttoned
1.6414	42.2	.6110	13	Conference
1.6414	42.2	.6029	13	spirited
1.6409	42.2	.2793	23	Compromise
1.6408	42.2	.5616	14	counterfeit
1.6407	42.2	.6720	12	warrant
1.6405	42.1	.3444	20	Alaska's
1.6400	42.1	.4834	16	Dodge
1.6398	42.1	.5405	14	suction
1.6397	42.1	.3208	23	indented
1.6393	42.1	.5645	14	masterpiece
1.6391	42.1	.4556	17	subsequently
1.6389	42.1	.5575	14	bluebirds
1.6387	42.1	.5192	15	laced
1.6387	42.1	.2070	22	Maggie
1.6383	42.1	.4476	17	inquiry
1.6377	42.1	.5516	14	Andrews
1.6372	42.1	.5207	15	currently
1.6371	42.1	.4381	17	cocoons
1.6370	42.1	.5865	13	hinges
1.6362	42.1	.4500	17	planners
1.6358	42.1	.4620	17	loudness
1.6353	42.1	.5080	15	enemy's
1.6352	42.1	.5322	14	dodged
1.6350	42.1	.3045	23	potassium
1.6350	42.1	.5554	14	sparse
1.6346	42.1	.5975	13	hollowed
1.6345	42.1	.5992	13	flocked
1.6339	42.1	.2966	24	ere
1.6339	42.1	.1884	29	Rosie
1.6338	42.1	.5810	13	arched
1.6338	42.1	.3147	22	precipitate
1.6337	42.1	.5654	14	innovations
1.6330	42.1	.5531	14	athletics
1.6329	42.1	.3600	20	thyroid
1.6327	42.1	.5697	14	reproduced
1.6325	42.1	.5324	14	peck
1.6324	42.1	.7326	11	anew
1.6324	42.1	.5841	13	bouquet
1.6324	42.1	.3200	18	Larkin
1.6322	42.1	.3901	19	More
1.6313	42.1	.5183	15	erasers
1.6312	42.1	.5505	14	unused
1.6310	42.1	.3660	19	Ginger
1.6310	42.1	.5262	15	ingenious
1.6309	42.1	.1488	32	Ribsy
1.6305	42.1	.2149	33	/j/
1.6302	42.1	.2185	32	morphemes
1.6298	42.1	.6510	12	bellows
1.6298	42.1	.4412	17	Buddhist
1.6298	42.1	.4209	18	15th
THE PRECEDING WORD TYPE OCCUPIES RANK 13800				
1.6294	42.1	.5545	14	vice
1.6293	42.1	.5663	14	appliance
1.6291	42.1	.3558	20	Copenhagen
1.6290	42.1	.6123	13	contours
1.6290	42.1	.5830	13	wilds
1.6288	42.1	.6049	13	echoing
1.6288	42.1	.2115	29	Prussia
1.6287	42.1	.6490	12	inspect
1.6279	42.1	.4569	17	incorrectly
1.6278	42.1	.6539	12	knocks
1.6277	42.1	.4389	17	partition
1.6276	42.1	.6032	13	outsiders
1.6273	42.1	.5942	13	critically
1.6272	42.1	.5908	13	anticipation
1.6266	42.1	.3800	19	bauxite
1.6263	42.1	.6035	13	doomed
1.6262	42.1	.5523	14	225
1.6260	42.1	.3577	21	ti
1.6258	42.1	.3920	18	nighttime
1.6252	42.1	.2443	27	Buenos
1.6251	42.1	.5848	13	lobby
1.6250	42.1	.5301	14	hitching
1.6246	42.1	.4940	15	hurray
1.6243	42.1	.5599	14	transition
1.6241	42.1	.4110	18	124
1.6238	42.1	.6533	12	journals
1.6234	42.1	.4420	17	supervision
1.6233	42.1	.5942	13	miracles
1.6227	42.1	.6065	13	perfected
1.6225	42.1	.6515	12	NO
1.6225	42.1	.5426	14	outfits
1.6224	42.1	.5487	14	nightmare
1.6220	42.1	.6442	12	accord
1.6219	42.1	.3601	18	dose
1.6218	42.1	.3742	17	Riding
1.6210	42.1	.5117	14	Trojan
1.6210	42.1	.5940	13	1938
1.6209	42.1	.3502	21	aquatic
1.6208	42.1	.5976	13	1882
1.6206	42.1	.5230	14	mitt
1.6201	42.1	.6655	12	originate
1.6190	42.1	.5881	13	serene
1.6187	42.1	.5317	14	squinting
1.6184	42.1	.3089	22	Bolivia
1.6184	42.1	.5017	15	Nazis
1.6182	42.1	.5888	13	visibility
1.6175	42.1	.2494	26	Brave
1.6174	42.1	.4654	16	Gus
1.6172	42.1	.5249	14	honour
1.6164	42.1	.5933	13	contributing
1.6161	42.1	.6498	12	arises
1.6160	42.1	.4189	18	notable
1.6156	42.1	.4944	15	thumping
1.6155	42.1	.5604	14	termed
1.6147	42.1	.4156	17	Rita
1.6146	42.1	.3884	18	1867
1.6143	42.1	.4997	15	Drake
1.6142	42.1	.4697	16	thousandth
1.6141	42.1	.4844	15	cobbler
1.6141	42.1	.4969	15	diplomacy
1.6137	42.1	.3576	18	FBI
1.6136	42.1	.4687	16	investigators
1.6130	42.1	.5186	14	Mills
1.6130	42.1	.3736	18	Pitt
1.6129	42.1	.5955	13	kisses
1.6128	42.1	.6018	13	Flora
1.6128	42.1	.5176	14	snugly
1.6126	42.1	.3396	22	Phoenician
1.6125	42.1	.4970	15	hopper
1.6123	42.1	.5970	13	flush
1.6121	42.1	.5098	15	Honor
1.6120	42.1	.6417	12	mischievous
1.6117	42.1	.4544	17	amplified
1.6110	42.1	.6468	12	unstable
1.6105	42.1	.5073	15	Foreign
1.6104	42.1	.7157	11	perished
1.6101	42.1	.3263	21	backbones
1.6100	42.1	.2891	23	kinetic
1.6094	42.1	.5880	13	hockey
1.6093	42.1	.3509	17	chute
1.6093	42.1	.5969	13	constructive
1.6093	42.1	.5508	14	northernmost
1.6092	42.1	.5542	14	1829
1.6091	42.1	.7139	11	prowling
1.6090	42.1	.5216	14	relays
1.6087	42.1	.3809	20	bracket
1.6083	42.1	.4420	15	rooting
1.6083	42.1	.4655	16	1887
1.6081	42.1	.6484	12	assurance
1.6076	42.1	.1838	29	Hamlet
1.6073	42.1	.5976	13	mock
1.6072	42.1	.5371	14	si
1.6072	42.1	.4679	16	spanked
1.6070	42.1	.3178	19	Barney
1.6061	42.1	.5775	13	overflowing
1.6055	42.1	.4973	15	tread
1.6040	42.1	.4588	15	Travis
1.6039	42.1	.6248	12	webbed
1.6038	42.1	.4179	17	mister
1.6038	42.1	.4752	16	underdeveloped
THE PRECEDING WORD TYPE OCCUPIES RANK 13900				
1.6036	42.1	.5120	14	titanium

U	SFI	D	F	Word Type
1.6035	42.1	.4812	16	contrasted
1.6030	42.0	.4949	15	spoiling
1.6025	42.0	.6582	12	dictated
1.6022	42.0	.5234	14	torrents
1.6019	42.0	.4240	17	monopoly
1.6018	42.0	.5557	13	drapes
1.6015	42.0	.5380	14	bestowed
1.6015	42.0	.5516	13	Brush
1.6013	42.0	.5125	14	airliner
1.6012	42.0	.5893	13	haircut
1.6010	42.0	.5524	14	disadvantages
1.6010	42.0	.5738	13	muskrats
1.6009	42.0	.4457	15	Col
1.6007	42.0	.4422	17	enrollment
1.6001	42.0	.2363	29	111
1.6000	42.0	.5999	13	flatten
1.5998	42.0	.5772	13	1835
1.5994	42.0	.5045	14	parachutes
1.5991	42.0	.4002	18	co-operation
1.5989	42.0	.0000	35	Henny
1.5986	42.0	.5707	13	brink
1.5985	42.0	.3984	19	Oh
1.5983	42.0	.4749	15	hugging
1.5982	42.0	.6525	12	originality
1.5979	42.0	.4666	16	genetic
1.5976	42.0	.4168	18	Celtic
1.5975	42.0	.4442	15	toot
1.5973	42.0	.5553	14	barbarian
1.5971	42.0	.4456	15	stares
1.5970	42.0	.6408	12	heroine
1.5967	42.0	.5733	13	wintry
1.5965	42.0	.5407	14	furnishes
1.5964	42.0	.5561	13	dusting
1.5958	42.0	.5122	15	Early
1.5957	42.0	.5555	13	barbers
1.5955	42.0	.3459	17	Jeremy
1.5952	42.0	.4298	17	Passage
1.5952	42.0	.5087	14	splintered
1.5948	42.0	.5969	13	student's
1.5946	42.0	.5236	14	Summer
1.5944	42.0	.3978	19	cylindrical
1.5943	42.0	.5800	13	dips
1.5943	42.0	.6375	12	dumping
1.5942	42.0	.5616	14	alternately
1.5941	42.0	.5879	13	beauties
1.5938	42.0	.4080	18	10%
1.5937	42.0	.5942	13	cloves
1.5935	42.0	.6121	12	armadillo
1.5931	42.0	.5760	13	violated
1.5928	42.0	.4761	15	platter
1.5923	42.0	.2443	23	Constance
1.5923	42.0	.4948	15	senator
1.5919	42.0	.6391	12	1895
1.5916	42.0	.5556	14	utility
1.5915	42.0	.4266	16	stubby
1.5914	42.0	.2199	33	shortening
1.5911	42.0	.6373	12	visions
1.5909	42.0	.4298	17	treasurer
1.5907	42.0	.5854	13	staged
1.5905	42.0	.5731	13	warships
1.5904	42.0	.6202	12	buoyancy
1.5902	42.0	.7028	11	straightening
1.5898	42.0	.6096	12	Pierce
1.5898	42.0	.5965	13	Stockholm
1.5886	42.0	.5362	14	sanctuary
1.5883	42.0	.6359	12	stroking
1.5882	42.0	.5339	14	blackberries
1.5878	42.0	.4462	15	Jamie
1.5877	42.0	.6393	12	erased
1.5877	42.0	.5870	13	refuses
1.5875	42.0	.4578	16	Straits
1.5873	42.0	.5331	14	flatboats
1.5872	42.0	.3449	20	modeled
1.5867	42.0	.5102	15	1-8
1.5866	42.0	.4028	18	sequoia
1.5865	42.0	.5502	13	overcame
1.5861	42.0	.5521	13	stormed
1.5856	42.0	.4992	14	elves
1.5854	42.0	.5143	14	serfs
1.5853	42.0	.3015	22	Powell
1.5853	42.0	.2710	24	sliced
1.5852	42.0	.5786	13	Case
1.5851	42.0	.5858	13	subsided
1.5850	42.0	.6491	12	shattering
1.5848	42.0	.5431	14	expelled
1.5848	42.0	.5804	13	hibernating
1.5847	42.0	.6426	12	needing
1.5846	42.0	.5854	13	brooding
1.5845	42.0	.3911	18	Observatory
1.5842	42.0	.3161	22	psychology
1.5842	42.0	.3783	17	transistors
1.5841	42.0	.5070	15	editorial
1.5841	42.0	.3320	18	Encyclopedia
1.5841	42.0	.2722	23	hibernate
1.5839	42.0	.4921	15	Powers
1.5837	42.0	.6438	12	failures
1.5831	42.0	.4843	15	morn
1.5827	42.0	.5818	13	cultivating
1.5826	42.0	.3060	22	kilometers

THE PRECEDING WORD TYPE OCCUPIES RANK 14000

U	SFI	D	F	Word Type
1.5825	42.0	.4513	16	icicles
1.5824	42.0	.5218	14	tortured
1.5824	42.0	.6321	12	tyranny
1.5822	42.0	.5000	15	computed
1.5822	42.0	.6195	12	moat
1.5820	42.0	.3330	17	Eleanor
1.5819	42.0	.2343	28	cuffs
1.5817	42.0	.6418	12	inherent
1.5813	42.0	.4471	15	Andersen
1.5809	42.0	.5778	13	2500
1.5808	42.0	.5406	14	raspberries
1.5806	42.0	.6303	12	agreeing
1.5806	42.0	.2959	18	Fellow
1.5805	42.0	.4591	16	bosom
1.5803	42.0	.5907	13	qualify
1.5799	42.0	.5750	13	filtered
1.5798	42.0	.5872	13	imitating
1.5784	42.0	.3375	17	Whitcomb
1.5783	42.0	.4271	15	black-and-white
1.5782	42.0	.5399	14	harvests
1.5780	42.0	.4640	15	Statue
1.5779	42.0	.4891	15	manor
1.5776	42.0	.5754	13	groped
1.5775	42.0	.6186	12	badge
1.5771	42.0	.5735	13	rewritten
1.5766	42.0	.5807	13	addressing
1.5766	42.0	.4654	15	dazed
1.5764	42.0	.6481	12	dispatch
1.5762	42.0	.5831	13	resolution
1.5759	42.0	.6110	12	hazel
1.5757	42.0	.5323	14	skinned
1.5754	42.0	.5776	13	springing
1.5751	42.0	.5774	13	McKinley
1.5750	42.0	.6340	12	Rainier
1.5746	42.0	.1914	35	soprano
1.5742	42.0	.5389	14	dependence
1.5740	42.0	.5104	14	crusts
1.5740	42.0	.5397	13	meekly
1.5740	42.0	.5397	13	wilted
1.5737	42.0	.6278	12	gnarled
1.5734	42.0	.4231	17	$200
1.5734	42.0	.4016	18	Susan's
1.5733	42.0	.6108	12	earphones
1.5732	42.0	.3898	18	royalty
1.5729	42.0	.5334	14	sensitivity
1.5723	42.0	.3677	19	Pentagon
1.5720	42.0	.6439	12	intelligently
1.5719	42.0	.4832	15	herdsmen
1.5716	42.0	.3260	22	intonation
1.5709	42.0	.5692	13	afire
1.5707	42.0	.4847	15	grubs
1.5707	42.0	.4550	16	Luxembourg
1.5698	42.0	.5258	14	brands
1.5696	42.0	.5959	13	refrigeration
1.5695	42.0	.5413	14	discs
1.5694	42.0	.3178	22	storks
1.5691	42.0	.6081	12	lending
1.5689	42.0	.0880	45	Abby
1.5684	42.0	.4780	15	Charter
1.5683	42.0	.5304	14	witnessed
1.5682	42.0	.3755	17	workman
1.5681	42.0	.4194	17	Czechs
1.5680	42.0	.3794	17	carpenter's
1.5677	42.0	.6458	12	gauze
1.5677	42.0	.2231	28	terminating
1.5673	42.0	.5514	13	flipped
1.5672	42.0	.5604	13	bucking
1.5665	41.9	.4563	16	Abilene
1.5665	41.9	.5318	14	embers
1.5664	41.9	.6049	12	ruffled
1.5660	41.9	.3365	20	irrigate
1.5655	41.9	.5153	14	Reading
1.5655	41.9	.4721	14	Titan
1.5654	41.9	.4613	16	Carpenter
1.5651	41.9	.5405	13	downy
1.5651	41.9	.6321	12	outlying
1.5651	41.9	.6105	12	whiteness
1.5649	41.9	.4196	16	gosh
1.5645	41.9	.5774	13	outnumbered
1.5644	41.9	.6376	12	accordance
1.5644	41.9	.5252	13	wildcat
1.5643	41.9	.6046	12	chirp
1.5642	41.9	.4283	16	Hyde
1.5639	41.9	.5164	14	embarrassing
1.5639	41.9	.1564	23	Link
1.5639	41.9	.1564	23	Squanto
1.5627	41.9	.2698	25	Sidney
1.5625	41.9	.3274	20	Jamaica
1.5624	41.9	.6164	12	clicked
1.5624	41.9	.2896	18	Herr
1.5622	41.9	.6283	12	prevailed
1.5620	41.9	.5623	13	reckless
1.5619	41.9	.3932	18	fluorescent
1.5615	41.9	.6747	11	dreamy
1.5613	41.9	.4772	14	Tiger
1.5612	41.9	.4479	16	photographers
1.5611	41.9	.4370	16	freedoms
1.5610	41.9	.5680	13	Up
1.5607	41.9	.3867	16	Tara
1.5606	41.9	.6334	12	permitting

THE PRECEDING WORD TYPE OCCUPIES RANK 14100

U	SFI	D	F	Word Type
1.5606	41.9	.0785	52	1/6
1.5605	41.9	.6769	11	rippled
1.5602	41.9	.3140	22	situated
1.5597	41.9	.5215	14	dated
1.5594	41.9	.5295	14	bragging
1.5588	41.9	.1880	30	DNA
1.5586	41.9	.5389	13	fireplaces
1.5582	41.9	.5858	13	riot
1.5578	41.9	.6998	11	airfield
1.5570	41.9	.6112	12	tufts
1.5568	41.9	.5360	14	precedes
1.5567	41.9	.5744	13	fruitful
1.5565	41.9	.5839	13	promoting
1.5564	41.9	.5378	14	client
1.5557	41.9	.6139	12	burying
1.5557	41.9	.6228	12	poorest
1.5548	41.9	.4356	15	Dolly
1.5547	41.9	.5017	14	Viking
1.5546	41.9	.4958	14	hitch
1.5544	41.9	.5664	13	pedals
1.5542	41.9	.5273	14	gnaw
1.5538	41.9	.6221	12	scholarship
1.5537	41.9	.6291	12	Cynthia
1.5534	41.9	.4416	16	Li
1.5532	41.9	.5763	13	clergy
1.5532	41.9	.5009	14	NorthDakota
1.5528	41.9	.6365	12	adviser
1.5525	41.9	.3709	19	min
1.5525	41.9	.6857	11	overgrown
1.5524	41.9	.6264	12	reliance
1.5523	41.9	.3344	19	Cogia
1.5523	41.9	.6254	12	endeavor
1.5515	41.9	.4946	15	2-inch
1.5506	41.9	.4158	17	taxation
1.5503	41.9	.5107	14	Phillips
1.5499	41.9	.4915	15	Richardson
1.5497	41.9	.5473	13	Pulitzer
1.5497	41.9	.6195	12	understandable
1.5491	41.9	.2993	22	light-years
1.5491	41.9	.6192	12	platforms
1.5490	41.9	.1980	30	oo
1.5487	41.9	.3415	20	hurdle
1.5487	41.9	.5791	13	plunder
1.5485	41.9	.1959	30	hurdles
1.5484	41.9	.3853	16	boll
1.5483	41.9	.6202	12	fulfilled
1.5479	41.9	.5756	13	bonfire
1.5478	41.9	.4897	15	uniformly
1.5471	41.9	.5683	13	pomp
1.5470	41.9	.5767	13	arising
1.5467	41.9	.4808	15	heartily
1.5467	41.9	.1936	34	tambourine
1.5462	41.9	.6258	12	droop
1.5462	41.9	.5634	13	misleading
1.5461	41.9	.3128	21	gene
1.5460	41.9	.4885	15	1-4
1.5459	41.9	.3681	19	Provinces
1.5455	41.9	.2445	20	Rikki
1.5452	41.9	.6239	12	worldly
1.5450	41.9	.6019	12	gingerly
1.5446	41.9	.5044	14	persecution
1.5442	41.9	.5245	14	trends
1.5438	41.9	.6772	11	beckoned
1.5437	41.9	.3085	21	Tropic
1.5436	41.9	.3502	19	Salk
1.5434	41.9	.5656	13	stained
1.5430	41.9	.4344	17	resin
1.5426	41.9	.3598	20	1-5
1.5424	41.9	.6387	12	selects
1.5421	41.9	.6015	12	truths
1.5420	41.9	.4689	14	goblins
1.5417	41.9	.4495	16	Commerce
1.5417	41.9	.2110	23	Super-Duper
1.5416	41.9	.6818	11	accordion
1.5415	41.9	.4863	15	Moors
1.5413	41.9	.3738	18	Livingston
1.5409	41.9	.6208	12	136
1.5408	41.9	.6050	12	Delta
1.5407	41.9	.6230	12	tangible
1.5405	41.9	.5633	13	innocence
1.5402	41.9	.6338	12	Children
1.5400	41.9	.6064	12	sorrows
1.5399	41.9	.5566	13	cursed
1.5397	41.9	.1300	24	Sharp
1.5395	41.9	.4226	17	files
1.5393	41.9	.4839	15	collisions
1.5393	41.9	.6151	12	fascination
1.5391	41.9	.5784	13	taps
1.5389	41.9	.5598	13	Machine
1.5388	41.9	.4771	14	Paricutin
1.5388	41.9	.4283	16	trio
1.5384	41.9	.6058	12	cleans
1.5384	41.9	.1031	41	Eurasia
1.5383	41.9	.5692	13	armored
1.5383	41.9	.2394	25	Lima
1.5380	41.9	.5469	13	leftover
1.5380	41.9	.4598	15	shoemaker
1.5373	41.9	.6844	11	expose
1.5373	41.9	.4116	17	preacher
1.5371	41.9	.5582	13	annoyance

THE PRECEDING WORD TYPE OCCUPIES RANK 14200

U	SFI	D	F	Word Type
1.5366	41.9	.5193	13	Planet
1.5357	41.9	.6063	12	summon
1.5356	41.9	.5670	13	aristocratic
1.5355	41.9	.5978	12	tyrant
1.5352	41.9	.5715	13	prettier
1.5349	41.9	.6035	12	gulp
1.5347	41.9	.6718	11	entrances
1.5347	41.9	.4445	16	Laboratory
1.5346	41.9	.6200	12	adorned
1.5346	41.9	.6218	12	brows
1.5346	41.9	.5717	13	recreational
1.5342	41.9	.5124	14	annex
1.5340	41.9	.4388	16	slum
1.5338	41.9	.4964	14	Martin's
1.5334	41.9	.4543	16	fret
1.5333	41.9	.5283	14	introductions
1.5332	41.9	.3827	18	carols
1.5331	41.9	.6792	11	quickest
1.5330	41.9	.4754	14	climber
1.5327	41.9	.4721	14	gobbled
1.5318	41.9	.5942	12	blocking
1.5318	41.9	.5162	14	would-be
1.5317	41.9	.6124	12	criticize
1.5317	41.9	.4077	17	Omaha
1.5313	41.9	.3610	19	juvenile
1.5302	41.9	.5976	12	strange-looking
1.5299	41.8	.5958	12	undertaking
1.5295	41.8	.3251	22	pasted
1.5294	41.8	.6163	12	conqueror
1.5294	41.8	.5255	14	publishing
1.5286	41.8	.4553	14	Keith
1.5285	41.8	.5471	13	employing
1.5284	41.8	.6086	12	spectator
1.5284	41.8	.5327	13	trusting
1.5283	41.8	.5324	13	remedies
1.5282	41.8	.5227	13	moccasin
1.5281	41.8	.5596	13	initiative
1.5277	41.8	.5530	13	heirs
1.5274	41.8	.5924	12	red-hot
1.5273	41.8	.4299	16	rammed
1.5273	41.8	.5392	13	thatch
1.5272	41.8	.4165	16	Fisher
1.5270	41.8	.4646	14	donkey's
1.5266	41.8	.4689	15	1901
1.5259	41.8	.3472	19	whey
1.5256	41.8	.3057	21	Disney
1.5256	41.8	.6736	11	frosting
1.5255	41.8	.5241	13	bulldog
1.5254	41.8	.5856	12	Ceres
1.5253	41.8	.5718	13	clan
1.5253	41.8	.6703	11	throbbing
1.5252	41.8	.4348	15	dragonflies
1.5248	41.8	.6055	12	reviewed
1.5245	41.8	.4503	16	diverse
1.5245	41.8	.6819	11	malice
1.5243	41.8	.5354	13	dangerously
1.5238	41.8	.2744	18	rubies
1.5238	41.8	.5979	12	smoky
1.5237	41.8	.6820	11	fireside
1.5235	41.8	.4849	14	secrecy
1.5229	41.8	.5649	13	sender
1.5229	41.8	.5157	13	stepmother
1.5229	41.8	.5108	14	1839
1.5223	41.8	.3658	18	mike
1.5222	41.8	.3128	21	oceanography
1.5220	41.8	.6705	11	seriousness
1.5218	41.8	.4693	15	emitted
1.5214	41.8	.0936	48	AC
1.5214	41.8	.5481	13	escort
1.5213	41.8	.5959	12	churned
1.5204	41.8	.4427	15	boarding
1.5204	41.8	.6680	11	pierce
1.5204	41.8	.2419	27	Robbie
1.5204	41.8	.6215	12	230
1.5202	41.8	.4542	15	howdy
1.5201	41.8	.4519	14	Carey
1.5199	41.8	.5558	13	discontent
1.5191	41.8	.5152	14	Gaza
1.5191	41.8	.4688	15	190
1.5187	41.8	.6145	12	illegal
1.5179	41.8	.5986	12	funniest
1.5179	41.8	.4767	15	People's
1.5176	41.8	.5546	13	unrest
1.5174	41.8	.5912	12	challenges
1.5170	41.8	.1750	32	tumor
1.5169	41.8	.6092	12	saddened
1.5167	41.8	.4230	16	Trenton
1.5160	41.8	.3782	18	senators
1.5157	41.8	.5939	12	leopards
1.5155	41.8	.5309	13	Hamilton's
1.5153	41.8	.6111	12	embroidery
1.5144	41.8	.1532	33	plateaus
1.5141	41.8	.3666	19	cymbals
1.5141	41.8	.2709	25	ion
1.5140	41.8	.5949	12	sunup
1.5140	41.8	.5527	13	velvety
1.5138	41.8	.5498	13	upsetting
1.5136	41.8	.2317	21	antitoxin
1.5132	41.8	.5684	13	unrelated
1.5128	41.8	.5569	13	jingle

THE PRECEDING WORD TYPE OCCUPIES RANK 14300

U	SFI	D	F	Word Type
1.5127	41.8	.4659	15	Do
1.5126	41.8	.5942	12	thronged
1.5125	41.8	.5942	12	prophecy
1.5125	41.8	.5807	12	sadder
1.5119	41.8	.4585	14	Jeanie
1.5118	41.8	.5685	13	secretaries
1.5116	41.8	.5495	13	Siberian
1.5113	41.8	.1551	36	marijuana
1.5112	41.8	.5356	13	outrun
1.5109	41.8	.3703	18	well-balanced
1.5107	41.8	.5511	13	loudest
1.5104	41.8	.2949	22	Weber
1.5101	41.8	.3947	17	negatively
1.5100	41.8	.6165	12	geared
1.5097	41.8	.4500	15	shrieking
1.5097	41.8	.3986	17	114
1.5095	41.8	.3498	16	Ruby
1.5094	41.8	.5554	13	disagreement
1.5087	41.8	.5030	14	212
1.5085	41.8	.2196	26	microorganisms
1.5078	41.8	.3376	17	Gandhi
1.5075	41.8	.0000	33	Brucie
1.5075	41.8	.0000	33	Gertie
1.5075	41.8	.0000	33	Hollis
1.5075	41.8	.0000	33	Hook
1.5061	41.8	.3987	17	attachment
1.5060	41.8	.4797	14	timbers
1.5057	41.8	.5962	12	bristling
1.5055	41.8	.5357	13	clenched
1.5054	41.8	.6757	11	unfold
1.5045	41.8	.4606	14	patched
1.5040	41.8	.5141	14	transplanted
1.5035	41.8	.5986	12	gutter
1.5035	41.8	.3293	18	ten-year-old
1.5033	41.8	.4982	14	collide
1.5033	41.8	.5282	13	ladies'
1.5031	41.8	.5073	14	birthplace
1.5020	41.8	.3354	17	Swift
1.5019	41.8	.4011	16	waddled
1.5017	41.8	.2314	28	Study
1.5015	41.8	.6636	11	prejudices
1.5014	41.8	.6020	12	one-quarter
1.5013	41.8	.6568	11	speedy
1.5013	41.8	.3582	19	yo
1.5011	41.8	.1647	34	Half
1.5009	41.8	.5916	12	illustrating
1.5009	41.8	.1267	43	violins
1.5008	41.8	.4105	17	alphabetically
1.5008	41.8	.5960	12	wavering
1.5005	41.8	.5374	13	shellfish
1.4999	41.8	.4593	14	squirmed
1.4995	41.8	.5995	12	populous
1.4993	41.8	.5897	12	transporting
1.4991	41.8	.3442	16	poodles
1.4990	41.8	.5447	13	surveys
1.4989	41.8	.2454	22	Geiger
1.4983	41.8	.2519	26	Other
1.4981	41.8	.5986	12	refine
1.4978	41.8	.5958	12	fees
1.4977	41.8	.1874	34	ie
1.4977	41.8	.5120	14	nineteenth-century
1.4975	41.8	.5019	14	biologist
1.4966	41.8	.5927	12	freighter
1.4962	41.7	.5870	12	steed
1.4960	41.7	.3176	21	bargaining

U	SFI	D	F	Word Type
1.4959	41.7	.2977	22	repel
1.4958	41.7	.5364	13	turmoil
1.4957	41.7	.5758	12	jams
1.4952	41.7	.4636	15	Director
1.4951	41.7	.5326	13	herder
1.4950	41.7	.6691	11	universally
1.4948	41.7	.4371	16	carp
1.4944	41.7	.5984	12	relaxation
1.4942	41.7	.3475	19	harden
1.4942	41.7	.5938	12	insides
1.4941	41.7	.6012	12	lectures
1.4940	41.7	.3010	22	diameters
1.4940	41.7	.4949	14	somethin'
1.4939	41.7	.5966	12	blueprint
1.4939	41.7	.5478	13	typing
1.4938	41.7	.2286	22	Athena
1.4929	41.7	.3019	23	accessories
1.4928	41.7	.5921	12	prospects
1.4927	41.7	.4050	16	opossum
1.4926	41.7	.5829	12	treasured
1.4924	41.7	.5983	12	smoother
1.4924	41.7	.6624	11	untrained
1.4922	41.7	.2662	25	Sebastian
1.4921	41.7	.4740	14	afar
1.4916	41.7	.4381	14	Myers
1.4911	41.7	.2374	19	Rooster
1.4909	41.7	.6540	11	outset
1.4909	41.7	.5588	12	quota
1.4903	41.7	.4125	17	Etruscans
1.4899	41.7	.6678	11	replies
1.4899	41.7	.2614	24	silica
1.4895	41.7	.5817	12	angered
1.4894	41.7	.6076	12	objections
1.4891	41.7	.5467	13	gums
1.4887	41.7	.5868	12	ambush
THE PRECEDING WORD TYPE OCCUPIES RANK 14400				
1.4884	41.7	.3413	16	landlady
1.4880	41.7	.2423	27	/u/
1.4880	41.7	.4980	14	Cove
1.4879	41.7	.5966	12	blackbirds
1.4878	41.7	.2400	27	punctuate
1.4876	41.7	.5470	13	evidences
1.4873	41.7	.4348	16	Card
1.4873	41.7	.4660	15	ornamental
1.4872	41.7	.4674	15	fortified
1.4872	41.7	.4712	14	trod
1.4868	41.7	.5989	12	breasts
1.4868	41.7	.4067	17	regime
1.4863	41.7	.4907	14	bared
1.4861	41.7	.4451	14	thongs
1.4860	41.7	.1333	23	Bart's
1.4860	41.7	.1333	23	Clipper
1.4860	41.7	.1333	23	Midge
1.4860	41.7	.1333	23	Sequoyah
1.4854	41.7	.4193	16	$20
1.4851	41.7	.4933	14	concessions
1.4851	41.7	.4839	14	sunburn
1.4850	41.7	.4779	14	daddy
1.4848	41.7	.6587	11	governs
1.4847	41.7	.0318	75	Button
1.4847	41.7	.5123	14	representations
1.4841	41.7	.3914	17	Hannah
1.4837	41.7	.5575	12	buckled
1.4834	41.7	.5417	13	splashes
1.4833	41.7	.4612	15	abound
1.4833	41.7	.5838	12	amendment
1.4831	41.7	.5916	12	sprung
1.4829	41.7	.5962	12	compensation
1.4826	41.7	.3500	19	Baltic
1.4826	41.7	.4169	16	blast-off
1.4819	41.7	.3932	17	Sweet
1.4818	41.7	.5987	12	utilized
1.4813	41.7	.6602	11	boon
1.4811	41.7	.5995	12	handicrafts
1.4811	41.7	.5100	13	stacks
1.4811	41.7	.5910	12	1815
1.4810	41.7	.5439	13	resignation
1.4810	41.7	.5135	13	upsets
1.4808	41.7	.5440	13	thine
1.4807	41.7	.4719	14	snip
1.4805	41.7	.5322	13	suppertime
1.4800	41.7	.5421	13	foresight
1.4800	41.7	.5023	14	hamsters
1.4795	41.7	.1222	45	homonym
1.4795	41.7	.3499	17	pest
1.4795	41.7	.4473	14	Rupert
1.4789	41.7	.6472	11	117
1.4788	41.7	.3005	21	Maya
1.4783	41.7	.5482	12	Ark
1.4781	41.7	.3937	17	nozzle
1.4781	41.7	.5197	13	slow-moving
1.4770	41.7	.6003	12	desolation
1.4769	41.7	.6489	11	bloomed
1.4767	41.7	.3702	16	champions
1.4767	41.7	.5064	13	codfish
1.4765	41.7	.5881	12	withdrawn
1.4764	41.7	.5569	12	propellers
1.4764	41.7	.5356	13	users
1.4759	41.7	.5498	13	summed
1.4754	41.7	.4923	14	maples
1.4753	41.7	.1503	22	Sooty
1.4751	41.7	.3791	17	el
1.4751	41.7	.5543	12	whimper
1.4748	41.7	.2735	21	faucet
1.4745	41.7	.5860	12	1831
1.4744	41.7	.5286	13	plumbing
1.4744	41.7	.1835	29	praying
1.4744	41.7	.5419	13	235
1.4743	41.7	.5892	12	decorating
1.4739	41.7	.3455	17	Kon-Tiki
1.4739	41.7	.5804	12	rebuild
1.4737	41.7	.4955	14	graduates
1.4733	41.7	.4579	15	prevention
1.4729	41.7	.4861	14	SaltLakeCity
1.4719	41.7	.5980	12	prompt
1.4716	41.7	.5300	13	shrimps
1.4713	41.7	.5754	12	widening
1.4712	41.7	.5781	12	Flanders
1.4711	41.7	.5015	14	capitol
1.4711	41.7	.6265	11	uncover
1.4708	41.7	.4433	14	boasting
1.4705	41.7	.2439	24	intestines
1.4704	41.7	.5921	12	habitation
1.4703	41.7	.5148	13	bunkhouse
1.4700	41.7	.2661	22	oceanographers
1.4698	41.7	.4652	14	batters
1.4696	41.7	.4319	15	snoring
1.4695	41.7	.2434	25	computations
1.4693	41.7	.2212	21	Nag
1.4692	41.7	.5725	12	eyeglasses
1.4692	41.7	.5817	12	landings
1.4692	41.7	.5409	13	183
1.4690	41.7	.4210	16	Sputnik
1.4684	41.7	.6431	11	holler
1.4683	41.7	.5391	13	eclipses
1.4683	41.7	.5177	13	enraged
THE PRECEDING WORD TYPE OCCUPIES RANK 14500				
1.4676	41.7	.5268	13	Forces
1.4674	41.7	.1089	24	Fez
1.4672	41.7	.3243	16	Orpheus
1.4670	41.7	.3258	19	pupae
1.4669	41.7	.5181	13	jerky
1.4667	41.7	.5935	12	high-quality
1.4666	41.7	.4258	15	bud
1.4665	41.7	.5718	12	convertible
1.4659	41.7	.5270	13	diplomatic
1.4659	41.7	.4041	16	soaks
1.4659	41.7	.4529	15	translucent
1.4656	41.7	.4922	14	pike
1.4654	41.7	.5360	13	implied
1.4651	41.7	.3884	16	paddy
1.4648	41.7	.5886	12	days'
1.4647	41.7	.4285	16	caste
1.4647	41.7	.5223	13	Chase
1.4647	41.7	.5334	13	slack
1.4643	41.7	.4388	14	lass
1.4643	41.7	.3903	16	Mole
1.4642	41.7	.5898	12	critic
1.4641	41.7	.3200	21	127
1.4639	41.7	.5003	14	attorney
1.4638	41.7	.4172	16	costing
1.4634	41.7	.4195	16	1793
1.4629	41.7	.0389	66	associative
1.4628	41.7	.6510	11	educate
1.4627	41.7	.4991	13	Swamp
1.4625	41.7	.5318	13	Babylonian
1.4622	41.6	.5340	13	bleed
1.4622	41.6	.5897	12	proceeding
1.4620	41.6	.5712	12	securing
1.4619	41.6	.6422	11	Bennett
1.4619	41.6	.2725	24	three-dimensional
1.4618	41.6	.0000	32	Alvaro
1.4618	41.6	.4024	16	hatches
1.4616	41.6	.6469	11	carelessness
1.4616	41.6	.4858	14	exits
1.4614	41.6	.4885	14	rebels
1.4610	41.6	.4501	15	M**
1.4610	41.6	.5657	12	peacetime
1.4610	41.6	.3442	19	25%
1.4608	41.6	.5865	12	indications
1.4607	41.6	.5469	12	shoveled
1.4604	41.6	.2836	23	backgrounds
1.4604	41.6	.5905	12	000-foot
1.4603	41.6	.4912	14	emergencies
1.4602	41.6	.3263	19	gravitation
1.4602	41.6	.4152	16	immigration
1.4596	41.6	.6367	11	vow
1.4596	41.6	.5612	12	whither
1.4587	41.6	.5420	12	hummingbirds
1.4587	41.6	.6232	11	rims
1.4584	41.6	.5352	12	beards
1.4584	41.6	.3924	17	carbohydrate
1.4583	41.6	.5904	12	Westminster
1.4575	41.6	.4387	15	hatching
1.4574	41.6	.4414	15	Carnegie
1.4573	41.6	.5774	12	halo
1.4571	41.6	.2903	21	Commonwealth
1.4570	41.6	.5736	12	spurt
1.4569	41.6	.4596	15	personalities
1.4557	41.6	.5605	12	blushed
1.4550	41.6	.3816	17	deficiency
1.4544	41.6	.5560	12	blanketed
1.4544	41.6	.5317	13	humps
1.4539	41.6	.6364	11	affectionately
1.4538	41.6	.5418	13	effectiveness
1.4538	41.6	.5025	13	gratefully
1.4537	41.6	.5735	12	Explorers
1.4537	41.6	.2474	25	writer's
1.4536	41.6	.5154	13	annoy
1.4534	41.6	.4488	15	emery
1.4534	41.6	.4450	15	Sherlock
1.4526	41.6	.6474	11	considerations
1.4525	41.6	.2603	24	Edison's
1.4524	41.6	.4312	16	con
1.4521	41.6	.5327	13	full-time
1.4521	41.6	.5668	12	yielded
1.4520	41.6	.5215	13	devoured
1.4518	41.6	.4353	15	stereo
1.4517	41.6	.2634	24	hymns
1.4514	41.6	.4490	15	dairying
1.4513	41.6	.4841	14	grandeur
1.4511	41.6	.5336	13	wide-open
1.4510	41.6	.6257	11	discomfort
1.4508	41.6	.3776	18	economists
1.4507	41.6	.4635	14	Felix
1.4506	41.6	.4415	15	Buchanan
1.4506	41.6	.5417	12	lanterns
1.4503	41.6	.5845	12	cultured
1.4502	41.6	.5756	12	proprietor
1.4502	41.6	.4762	13	Shop
1.4501	41.6	.4749	13	grub
1.4500	41.6	.5523	12	awakening
1.4499	41.6	.5413	12	Marjorie
1.4497	41.6	.5408	12	gloomily
1.4497	41.6	.3838	15	Tina
1.4496	41.6	.6184	11	slumber
1.4493	41.6	.6405	11	insured
THE PRECEDING WORD TYPE OCCUPIES RANK 14600				
1.4492	41.6	.5728	12	valiant
1.4491	41.6	.6204	11	jumble
1.4489	41.6	.5531	12	medals
1.4484	41.6	.2999	18	Hubert
1.4478	41.6	.1444	29	ogre
1.4477	41.6	.5569	12	carcass
1.4475	41.6	.5781	12	subdued
1.4474	41.6	.5244	13	Scotch
1.4474	41.6	.7175	10	uncertainty
1.4472	41.6	.6346	11	Hell
1.4471	41.6	.6443	11	refreshing
1.4470	41.6	.5629	12	anyone's
1.4470	41.6	.4417	14	unwrapped
1.4467	41.6	.3158	16	Sid
1.4465	41.6	.3441	16	mongoose
1.4463	41.6	.2084	26	Northeast
1.4463	41.6	.4348	15	Rudolph
1.4460	41.6	.6372	11	grotesque
1.4459	41.6	.1520	36	Fern
1.4459	41.6	.3822	17	shipbuilding
1.4456	41.6	.5299	13	Discovery
1.4454	41.6	.6382	11	regularity
1.4451	41.6	.6265	11	distracted
1.4447	41.6	.4115	16	Crusades
1.4447	41.6	.2141	28	1969
1.4444	41.6	.4521	15	millimeters
1.4444	41.6	.6410	11	unnatural
1.4443	41.6	.4879	13	Saskatchewan
1.4442	41.6	.4375	15	everything's
1.4442	41.6	.4014	17	secular
1.4438	41.6	.6212	11	batted
1.4437	41.6	.5652	12	exceptional
1.4437	41.6	.5704	12	hospitable
1.4435	41.6	.5857	12	glows
1.4435	41.6	.5194	13	perches
1.4432	41.6	.6395	11	escorted
1.4431	41.6	.5844	12	symbolized
1.4428	41.6	.0911	46	inequality
1.4427	41.6	.5650	12	courteously
1.4424	41.6	.7139	10	rotting
1.4423	41.6	.6352	11	expectantly
1.4418	41.6	.5024	13	Polar
1.4414	41.6	.2446	26	/i/
1.4412	41.6	.5306	13	mailing
1.4411	41.6	.4073	16	Confederates
1.4407	41.6	.5344	12	Indian's
1.4405	41.6	.2981	23	1/16
1.4403	41.6	.6415	11	dissimilar
1.4402	41.6	.4775	13	Houghton
1.4401	41.6	.5170	13	hereditary
1.4399	41.6	.6317	11	rafters
1.4399	41.6	.6278	11	soccer
1.4398	41.6	.4101	16	Step
1.4397	41.6	.4946	14	bodily
1.4397	41.6	.7077	10	perilous
1.4394	41.6	.6324	11	growls
1.4390	41.6	.5345	12	loomed
1.4390	41.6	.2176	19	Priscilla
1.4385	41.6	.4961	13	heater
1.4385	41.6	.5285	13	mythology
1.4377	41.6	.7077	10	duplicated
1.4376	41.6	.5334	12	teammates
1.4370	41.6	.0000	96	rename
1.4367	41.6	.5572	12	upturned
1.4362	41.6	.5223	13	purifying
1.4358	41.6	.4666	13	comprehend
1.4358	41.6	.3964	17	linoleum
1.4358	41.6	.6335	11	short-lived
1.4354	41.6	.3475	18	Haiti
1.4351	41.6	.5743	12	plastered
1.4351	41.6	.6124	11	unsafe
1.4350	41.6	.4578	13	baron
1.4350	41.6	.4980	13	keg
1.4349	41.6	.5539	12	unearthed
1.4348	41.6	.6193	11	recommendations
1.4346	41.6	.5386	13	reinforced
1.4344	41.6	.4228	15	stooping
1.4342	41.6	.4737	14	plugs
1.4339	41.6	.5428	12	Contents
1.4337	41.6	.3264	19	infrared
1.4336	41.6	.6385	11	shaving
1.4335	41.6	.5824	12	4-H
1.4331	41.6	.5236	13	Near
1.4331	41.6	.6271	11	strive
1.4330	41.6	.4998	13	wedged
1.4322	41.6	.3335	16	Rosy
1.4322	41.6	.4345	15	1881
1.4318	41.6	.7002	10	whirlwind
1.4313	41.6	.2848	22	Filipinos
1.4312	41.6	.6275	11	resorts
1.4311	41.6	.6993	10	Dream
1.4309	41.6	.5841	12	forged
1.4307	41.6	.5394	12	squirt
1.4307	41.6	.5753	12	transforming
1.4304	41.6	.5542	12	thirty-six
1.4302	41.6	.6303	11	searches
1.4302	41.6	.5276	12	unlock
1.4298	41.6	.5188	13	company's
1.4298	41.6	.5398	12	Diamond
1.4298	41.6	.5667	12	politically
THE PRECEDING WORD TYPE OCCUPIES RANK 14700				
1.4298	41.6	.2243	28	quartet
1.4297	41.6	.4806	14	carburetor
1.4295	41.6	.5773	12	seafaring
1.4291	41.6	.4720	14	Copernicus
1.4291	41.6	.3687	17	hybrid
1.4282	41.5	.3782	18	inserting
1.4279	41.5	.4167	15	gotta
1.4277	41.5	.5795	12	animated
1.4277	41.5	.5659	12	weaken
1.4273	41.5	.6151	11	Abbey
1.4262	41.5	.5054	13	lodged
1.4260	41.5	.5684	12	Safety
1.4256	41.5	.2726	24	reader's
1.4249	41.5	.4450	15	motorists
1.4244	41.5	.5046	13	discharged
1.4244	41.5	.5214	13	lash
1.4243	41.5	.6232	11	behalf
1.4240	41.5	.5698	12	Orange
1.4240	41.5	.4786	14	radiate
1.4235	41.5	.5236	13	480
1.4231	41.5	.4513	13	whitewash
1.4228	41.5	.5119	13	1832
1.4226	41.5	.4918	13	frisky
1.4223	41.5	.4948	13	thaw
1.4219	41.5	.5698	12	smoothness
1.4217	41.5	.3462	17	Champion
1.4216	41.5	.5471	12	Ed's
1.4215	41.5	.6931	10	1779
1.4214	41.5	.4639	14	migrations
1.4212	41.5	.4584	13	pals
1.4211	41.5	.4760	14	Flag
1.4209	41.5	.4947	13	firecrackers
1.4208	41.5	.6248	11	balancing
1.4206	41.5	.4270	14	dangled
1.4205	41.5	.2840	20	Crane
1.4201	41.5	.6210	11	big-game
1.4199	41.5	.4754	14	uprising
1.4196	41.5	.5554	12	realities
1.4193	41.5	.6978	10	An
1.4193	41.5	.2428	25	Purdy
1.4189	41.5	.3278	19	Division
1.4188	41.5	.4096	14	Andrea
1.4185	41.5	.6258	11	resent
1.4182	41.5	.4978	13	carvings
1.4181	41.5	.6192	11	trickling
1.4178	41.5	.4926	13	fleas
1.4178	41.5	.5547	12	guardian
1.4177	41.5	.5984	11	Baghdad
1.4177	41.5	.5708	12	Period
1.4175	41.5	.6053	11	stub
1.4171	41.5	.3667	16	cacti
1.4166	41.5	.4146	15	Bulgaria
1.4166	41.5	.5673	12	laurel
1.4164	41.5	.4779	14	monarchy
1.4163	41.5	.2235	27	ether
1.4162	41.5	.0000	31	Kobi
1.4162	41.5	.0000	31	Minnow
1.4161	41.5	.5133	13	460
1.4158	41.5	.2125	23	Tante
1.4152	41.5	.5598	12	Jersey
1.4152	41.5	.0481	60	subtracting
1.4151	41.5	.5545	12	renew
1.4149	41.5	.4278	14	Fulton
1.4147	41.5	.6220	11	commenced
1.4146	41.5	.4591	14	snort
1.4134	41.5	.5313	12	whinny
1.4133	41.5	.5219	13	long-range
1.4130	41.5	.4426	15	$15
1.4129	41.5	.6069	11	eccentric
1.4129	41.5	.3116	19	messengers
1.4128	41.5	.1017	56	voltage
1.4126	41.5	.5596	12	Dickinson
1.4125	41.5	.6002	11	crammed
1.4125	41.5	.6208	11	pearly
1.4124	41.5	.5313	12	mocking
1.4120	41.5	.5356	12	slay
1.4117	41.5	.4685	13	buggies
1.4113	41.5	.4529	14	sportsmen
1.4109	41.5	.5191	13	1607
1.4107	41.5	.4689	14	rosebush
1.4105	41.5	.5683	12	conception
1.4104	41.5	.3955	16	Mohammed
1.4102	41.5	.4030	16	Browns
1.4100	41.5	.5610	12	assign
1.4099	41.5	.4020	15	ripen
1.4098	41.5	.3104	19	steppes
1.4096	41.5	.6312	11	herb
1.4095	41.5	.6227	11	systematically
1.4094	41.5	.4386	15	Ron
1.4093	41.5	.5150	13	pore
1.4092	41.5	.4804	14	Yosemite
1.4090	41.5	.3114	17	Becker
1.4090	41.5	.6214	11	perish
1.4089	41.5	.5678	12	discusses
1.4088	41.5	.5100	13	Babylonians
1.4086	41.5	.1942	25	Trudy
1.4083	41.5	.4142	16	Metropolitan
1.4082	41.5	.4758	14	appointments
1.4081	41.5	.3531	18	Leonardo
1.4080	41.5	.0886	45	Finley
THE PRECEDING WORD TYPE OCCUPIES RANK 14800				
1.4076	41.5	.6232	11	yearning
1.4073	41.5	.1931	30	margarine
1.4071	41.5	.5270	12	blurted
1.4069	41.5	.6086	11	competitive
1.4069	41.5	.5509	12	haunts
1.4065	41.5	.5625	12	1820
1.4064	41.5	.5633	12	tungsten
1.4063	41.5	.5419	12	blistered
1.4063	41.5	.5146	13	Randolph
1.4060	41.5	.5080	13	violations
1.4059	41.5	.4645	14	Britain's
1.4054	41.5	.4416	13	Block
1.4046	41.5	.3342	19	poet's
1.4044	41.5	.6213	11	ideally
1.4042	41.5	.4741	14	labour
1.4027	41.5	.5170	13	wallet
1.4024	41.5	.5135	13	piling
1.4022	41.5	.5609	12	breakdown
1.4019	41.5	.6159	11	ballot
1.4019	41.5	.2053	25	Ecuador
1.4013	41.5	.5093	13	138
1.4012	41.5	.5353	12	sagebrush
1.4011	41.5	.5555	12	strand
1.4010	41.5	.3504	19	harmonies
1.4004	41.5	.5103	13	credited
1.4004	41.5	.5306	12	elephant's
1.4003	41.5	.4573	14	Sydney
1.4001	41.5	.2729	21	carbonate

U	SFI	D	F	Word Type
1.4000	41.5	.5460	12	filthy
1.3999	41.5	.5542	12	hatchet
1.3998	41.5	.5509	12	starlight
1.3996	41.5	.6160	11	spotlight
1.3996	41.5	.5061	13	Survey
1.3994	41.5	.4592	14	topsoil
1.3993	41.5	.6165	11	Exchange
1.3993	41.5	.5115	13	networks
1.3992	41.5	.5137	13	quote
1.3991	41.5	.5497	12	tightening
1.3986	41.5	.5130	13	Nation
1.3984	41.5	.4646	14	locomotion
1.3984	41.5	.4582	14	tankers
1.3983	41.5	.5339	12	rabbit's
1.3981	41.5	.5367	12	surfaced
1.3980	41.5	.4374	13	grabs
1.3978	41.5	.4783	14	portray
1.3978	41.5	.4765	13	Webster's
1.3977	41.5	.6722	10	shilling
1.3973	41.5	.5447	12	diseased
1.3972	41.5	.1024	42	7/8
1.3971	41.5	.2892	20	Knight
1.3960	41.4	.4560	13	autograph
1.3958	41.4	.3300	17	tiller
1.3952	41.4	.3475	17	sweeter
1.3950	41.4	.4959	13	masonry
1.3950	41.4	.5155	13	receivers
1.3950	41.4	.4741	14	VI
1.3948	41.4	.6105	11	foresee
1.3946	41.4	.2101	27	concerto
1.3946	41.4	.6023	11	moment's
1.3942	41.4	.3426	17	gourd
1.3942	41.4	.6029	11	waterproof
1.3941	41.4	.6154	11	Freedom
1.3940	41.4	.6141	11	frayed
1.3940	41.4	.4591	13	Norwegians
1.3930	41.4	.4895	13	1846
1.3927	41.4	.5407	12	greed
1.3927	41.4	.5601	12	periodicals
1.3925	41.4	.4713	14	engineer's
1.3925	41.4	.5469	12	uneducated
1.3923	41.4	.5270	13	patterned
1.3922	41.4	.3802	16	cobalt
1.3920	41.4	.4430	14	immensely
1.3920	41.4	.5174	13	Luther
1.3916	41.4	.3082	20	Mickey
1.3913	41.4	.6045	11	offerings
1.3912	41.4	.4018	15	stimuli
1.3906	41.4	.5997	11	baggy
1.3906	41.4	.5010	13	irritated
1.3903	41.4	.4917	13	Audubon
1.3903	41.4	.4988	13	fibrous
1.3902	41.4	.6237	11	brilliance
1.3902	41.4	.2292	18	Tobias
1.3893	41.4	.6049	11	enrich
1.3893	41.4	.5915	11	Geophysical
1.3892	41.4	.4349	15	designate
1.3892	41.4	.4107	15	teen-age
1.3887	41.4	.5171	12	flinging
1.3878	41.4	.4620	14	Mongols
1.3877	41.4	.3272	18	hither
1.3875	41.4	.4345	14	Boys'
1.3875	41.4	.4165	15	wasps
1.3874	41.4	.3449	18	tenant
1.3872	41.4	.5966	11	sentiments
1.3870	41.4	.4105	15	estimating
1.3868	41.4	.5523	12	drab
1.3861	41.4	.5035	13	epic
1.3859	41.4	.3676	17	converter
1.3858	41.4	.6089	11	bracelets
1.3851	41.4	.2797	22	Ravel
1.3849	41.4	.5333	12	deserves

THE PRECEDING WORD TYPE OCCUPIES RANK 14900

U	SFI	D	F	Word Type
1.3846	41.4	.5320	12	contentedly
1.3846	41.4	.3224	21	darning
1.3845	41.4	.2444	18	Cannon
1.3844	41.4	.4537	13	Edith
1.3843	41.4	.3573	17	Brownsville
1.3843	41.4	.5943	11	tabs
1.3841	41.4	.5844	11	indignantly
1.3841	41.4	.5961	11	retiring
1.3839	41.4	.6145	11	assembling
1.3838	41.4	.4442	14	Chinatown
1.3832	41.4	.3289	15	racetrack
1.3828	41.4	.5003	13	classed
1.3824	41.4	.5060	13	crutch
1.3823	41.4	.2048	28	Garnet
1.3822	41.4	.5128	12	burglar
1.3820	41.4	.5268	12	animals'
1.3819	41.4	.4831	13	hissed
1.3818	41.4	.5046	13	mahogany
1.3817	41.4	.5885	11	Harper
1.3816	41.4	.2861	21	quantum
1.3813	41.4	.2612	24	Thy
1.3808	41.4	.5212	12	ballplayer
1.3808	41.4	.6636	10	profoundly
1.3806	41.4	.6029	11	sheltering
1.3805	41.4	.5967	11	agile
1.3803	41.4	.1934	26	peninsulas
1.3802	41.4	.4281	15	4th
1.3800	41.4	.3606	17	fertilization
1.3799	41.4	.5474	12	manure
1.3799	41.4	.1669	32	Slater
1.3798	41.4	.5540	12	divorce
1.3798	41.4	.1477	33	yeh
1.3797	41.4	.6105	11	loudspeaker
1.3795	41.4	.5521	12	sharper
1.3794	41.4	.5874	11	daintily
1.3794	41.4	.4727	13	Maria's
1.3792	41.4	.5508	12	sterile
1.3790	41.4	.5439	12	brownish
1.3788	41.4	.5461	12	sermons
1.3787	41.4	.5033	13	embedded
1.3786	41.4	.5337	12	barons
1.3786	41.4	.5107	12	chaps
1.3786	41.4	.6139	11	gatherings
1.3786	41.4	.4726	13	villager
1.3784	41.4	.5022	13	Lodge
1.3780	41.4	.4370	15	sieve
1.3778	41.4	.5085	13	competitors
1.3777	41.4	.5518	12	pistons
1.3776	41.4	.5013	13	predecessors
1.3776	41.4	.1405	21	Tanner
1.3776	41.4	.1405	21	Wee
1.3775	41.4	.4897	13	fetched
1.3772	41.4	.6622	10	heart's
1.3769	41.4	.6645	10	hasty
1.3769	41.4	.5886	11	refreshment
1.3769	41.4	.3781	17	Testament
1.3769	41.4	.4267	14	yawning
1.3766	41.4	.4265	14	ladybug
1.3766	41.4	.5022	12	strides
1.3765	41.4	.5857	11	reassuring
1.3764	41.4	.5921	11	straighter
1.3763	41.4	.5267	12	walled
1.3762	41.4	.4214	15	Leroy
1.3762	41.4	.3663	17	144
1.3761	41.4	.5997	11	lumbered
1.3760	41.4	.5197	13	altering
1.3760	41.4	.2727	20	humus
1.3756	41.4	.5871	11	revive
1.3755	41.4	.4610	13	passageway
1.3754	41.4	.5035	12	detergent
1.3751	41.4	.4449	13	fuselage
1.3746	41.4	.4480	14	sensations
1.3745	41.4	.6641	10	hiring
1.3744	41.4	.4481	14	snowman
1.3743	41.4	.4222	15	221
1.3742	41.4	.6633	10	all-important
1.3742	41.4	.5902	11	cartridge
1.3740	41.4	.5128	12	upside-down
1.3738	41.4	.4178	15	Woodrow
1.3736	41.4	.5885	11	cobbled
1.3733	41.4	.4924	13	1803
1.3730	41.4	.6156	11	sincere
1.3730	41.4	.5256	12	1855
1.3726	41.4	.3674	17	gnawed
1.3726	41.4	.6064	11	interfering
1.3726	41.4	.4775	13	tramping
1.3721	41.4	.2569	20	heal
1.3720	41.4	.5266	12	sunlit
1.3718	41.4	.5317	12	saints
1.3715	41.4	.6117	11	needless
1.3715	41.4	.5899	11	sneaking
1.3713	41.4	.4709	14	preference
1.3712	41.4	.6076	11	Carolinas
1.3709	41.4	.4534	14	abolished
1.3706	41.4	.2212	18	Anita
1.3706	41.4	.2212	18	Muir
1.3704	41.4	.2792	22	Row
1.3700	41.4	.4829	13	slam
1.3697	41.4	.5204	12	Cedar
1.3695	41.4	.6054	11	XIV

THE PRECEDING WORD TYPE OCCUPIES RANK 15000

U	SFI	D	F	Word Type
1.3694	41.4	.5882	11	redwoods
1.3693	41.4	.5901	11	knoll
1.3688	41.4	.3297	15	cornmeal
1.3688	41.4	.4987	13	Spaniard
1.3687	41.4	.5119	13	Technology
1.3685	41.4	.4528	14	salamanders
1.3684	41.4	.5627	11	bunks
1.3683	41.4	.4128	15	artery
1.3683	41.4	.5771	11	skidded
1.3681	41.4	.3504	15	lioness
1.3680	41.4	.3141	18	seawater
1.3679	41.4	.5466	12	dealings
1.3678	41.4	.5253	12	tongs
1.3677	41.4	.3587	15	Browning
1.3673	41.4	.3722	17	Robertson
1.3672	41.4	.2914	22	sketching
1.3670	41.4	.4787	13	cowards
1.3670	41.4	.5846	11	overtake
1.3668	41.4	.5815	11	digger
1.3668	41.4	.5585	11	Exeter
1.3667	41.4	.6090	11	evergreens
1.3667	41.4	.5330	12	Snow
1.3663	41.4	.6555	10	whirring
1.3662	41.4	.5572	11	giggle
1.3662	41.4	.4859	13	gladness
1.3662	41.4	.4212	15	To
1.3661	41.4	.6563	10	chanced
1.3653	41.4	.5124	12	sprouted
1.3652	41.4	.3474	15	Lebanese
1.3651	41.4	.5335	12	guilt
1.3648	41.4	.4309	15	chants
1.3646	41.4	.5120	12	emerald
1.3645	41.4	.4347	14	pickup
1.3645	41.3	.3860	14	Tory
1.3642	41.3	.2809	20	Caracas
1.3642	41.3	.2420	17	Katrina
1.3641	41.3	.5969	11	airliners
1.3638	41.3	.5640	11	1807
1.3636	41.3	.4238	14	Harlem
1.3635	41.3	.5011	13	extinction
1.3633	41.3	.5329	12	Owens
1.3632	41.3	.4259	14	housework
1.3627	41.3	.5908	11	croaking
1.3627	41.3	.5823	11	dodge
1.3627	41.3	.6715	10	unpopular
1.3626	41.3	.1582	20	Artie
1.3622	41.3	.3182	18	communism
1.3614	41.3	.5140	12	messy
1.3609	41.3	.5818	11	spurred
1.3608	41.3	.5066	13	dialects
1.3607	41.3	.5619	11	Jacob's
1.3605	41.3	.5049	13	revision
1.3603	41.3	.5435	12	232
1.3602	41.3	.4410	14	1909
1.3596	41.3	.4400	14	spurts
1.3595	41.3	.5846	11	ceremonial
1.3592	41.3	.6552	10	dipper
1.3591	41.3	.6008	11	asters
1.3591	41.3	.5985	11	brotherhood
1.3591	41.3	.5442	12	part-time
1.3590	41.3	.6565	10	homeless
1.3582	41.3	.2567	21	forge
1.3582	41.3	.7478	9	fourteenth
1.3581	41.3	.4575	14	defective
1.3578	41.3	.4933	13	Simpson
1.3573	41.3	.5818	11	Medal
1.3571	41.3	.5716	11	rinsed
1.3571	41.3	.4190	15	121
1.3569	41.3	.3462	15	galleon
1.3568	41.3	.5817	11	Have
1.3568	41.3	.2290	26	hyphen
1.3567	41.3	.5805	11	courtroom
1.3565	41.3	.3896	16	Bohemia
1.3561	41.3	.4602	14	administered
1.3561	41.3	.5502	12	edited
1.3560	41.3	.4815	13	280
1.3551	41.3	.3531	18	shavings
1.3550	41.3	.5301	12	Connie
1.3550	41.3	.3744	16	filings
1.3549	41.3	.4329	14	jot
1.3548	41.3	.5966	11	suffers
1.3544	41.3	.5048	12	bomber
1.3544	41.3	.5242	12	hobbled
1.3542	41.3	.4822	13	tentacles
1.3538	41.3	.4203	15	makeup
1.3537	41.3	.5356	12	terrors
1.3536	41.3	.3989	15	Manager
1.3527	41.3	.2636	23	-s
1.3527	41.3	.4948	13	boatman
1.3524	41.3	.4780	13	175
1.3523	41.3	.5455	12	yielding
1.3522	41.3	.5846	11	creativity
1.3521	41.3	.3007	19	Nasser
1.3519	41.3	.5195	12	1915
1.3518	41.3	.1508	32	Christine
1.3517	41.3	.5358	12	exploit
1.3516	41.3	.5960	11	blotter
1.3511	41.3	.5887	11	applauded
1.3511	41.3	.6588	10	safest
1.3508	41.3	.6547	10	cancel

THE PRECEDING WORD TYPE OCCUPIES RANK 15100

U	SFI	D	F	Word Type
1.3505	41.3	.5220	12	limiting
1.3501	41.3	.2682	23	sharps
1.3500	41.3	.0096	79	subset
1.3497	41.3	.5805	11	immortal
1.3497	41.3	.5860	11	yesterday's
1.3496	41.3	.4518	14	A's
1.3493	41.3	.5594	11	reviewing
1.3491	41.3	.5789	11	Human
1.3491	41.3	.5868	11	month's
1.3488	41.3	.4397	14	ticking
1.3487	41.3	.4942	13	assimilation
1.3485	41.3	.5958	11	deductions
1.3484	41.3	.4810	13	Cuban
1.3479	41.3	.3703	15	Pedro's
1.3476	41.3	.5965	11	cigars
1.3475	41.3	.5794	11	attentively
1.3475	41.3	.5213	12	rightful
1.3472	41.3	.5867	11	dodging
1.3471	41.3	.4510	14	via
1.3469	41.3	.5435	11	inched
1.3468	41.3	.4185	15	trademark
1.3467	41.3	.4506	14	aggression
1.3467	41.3	.5852	11	dizzy
1.3467	41.3	.5282	12	well-developed
1.3466	41.3	.4110	15	plucking
1.3465	41.3	.3763	15	Anchorage
1.3465	41.3	.6505	10	billowing
1.3464	41.3	.5871	11	dingy
1.3464	41.3	.5258	12	light-colored
1.3455	41.3	.5802	11	miraculously
1.3455	41.3	.4971	13	purchasing
1.3455	41.3	.4388	14	1781
1.3452	41.3	.5961	11	pioneering
1.3451	41.3	.6523	10	abide
1.3450	41.3	.5790	11	undertook
1.3448	41.3	.2803	21	deGaulle
1.3447	41.3	.4930	13	13th
1.3445	41.3	.3317	18	spinach
1.3445	41.3	.5914	11	stilts
1.3437	41.3	.5326	12	stocky
1.3434	41.3	.5505	11	defenders
1.3434	41.3	.5391	12	generously
1.3433	41.3	.5320	12	disputed
1.3433	41.3	.5326	12	participated
1.3432	41.3	.2157	25	irrational
1.3431	41.3	.4177	15	crusade
1.3429	41.3	.3241	18	ancestral
1.3429	41.3	.5770	11	pouches
1.3427	41.3	.4792	12	Bing
1.3426	41.3	.3264	18	campers
1.3423	41.3	.5934	11	nationality
1.3423	41.3	.4836	12	shoppers
1.3423	41.3	.4545	13	tinkle
1.3420	41.3	.4660	13	shopkeepers
1.3419	41.3	.5862	11	don
1.3414	41.3	.4772	13	Institution
1.3413	41.3	.5692	11	theft
1.3412	41.3	.6390	10	aches
1.3410	41.3	.4421	13	smugglers
1.3408	41.3	.4825	13	breadth
1.3407	41.3	.4072	15	Guards
1.3406	41.3	.2789	21	Chang
1.3406	41.3	.5219	12	prospered
1.3405	41.3	.5021	13	asset
1.3405	41.3	.6521	10	attendance
1.3404	41.3	.5825	11	Maxwell
1.3401	41.3	.4267	14	cupboards
1.3395	41.3	.5722	11	outpost
1.3395	41.3	.4886	13	thighs
1.3394	41.3	.5254	12	levees
1.3394	41.3	.2073	22	Newton's
1.3393	41.3	.3313	18	Gothic
1.3392	41.3	.6631	10	disagreeable
1.3392	41.3	.4459	14	railways
1.3391	41.3	.5734	11	proven
1.3389	41.3	.5864	11	constituted
1.3389	41.3	.5276	12	rambling
1.3388	41.3	.1871	31	abrasive
1.3388	41.3	.1075	38	computing
1.3385	41.3	.5133	12	postmaster
1.3384	41.3	.5326	12	burnished
1.3384	41.3	.5161	12	leaking
1.3382	41.3	.1742	19	Krishna
1.3381	41.3	.4428	14	transmitting
1.3376	41.3	.6300	10	cures
1.3376	41.3	.6300	10	plume
1.3375	41.3	.6482	10	lessen
1.3375	41.3	.4876	13	Theatre
1.3370	41.3	.5328	12	exploits
1.3370	41.3	.1862	24	globes
1.3370	41.3	.5636	11	nicknamed
1.3369	41.3	.5054	12	Lick
1.3369	41.3	.6260	10	naps
1.3366	41.3	.5524	11	blur
1.3366	41.3	.5612	11	Hard
1.3366	41.3	.4261	14	warden
1.3365	41.3	.5222	12	dentists
1.3364	41.3	.3124	19	seesaw
1.3359	41.3	.4934	13	abbreviate
1.3358	41.3	.5627	11	slaps

THE PRECEDING WORD TYPE OCCUPIES RANK 15200

U	SFI	D	F	Word Type
1.3354	41.3	.3729	14	Gap
1.3350	41.3	.5490	11	narrowly
1.3350	41.3	.6217	10	thickest
1.3348	41.3	.5101	12	booths
1.3348	41.3	.4379	14	Mao
1.3347	41.3	.5213	12	workings
1.3342	41.3	.4921	12	siren
1.3339	41.3	.1220	40	Gen
1.3339	41.3	.4812	12	speedometer
1.3336	41.3	.5785	11	lingering
1.3334	41.2	.5857	11	steals
1.3326	41.2	.5138	12	whisk
1.3324	41.2	.5164	12	landmark
1.3323	41.2	.5676	11	gripping
1.3323	41.2	.5831	11	shallows
1.3320	41.2	.6425	10	racer
1.3316	41.2	.4555	13	yon
1.3314	41.2	.5101	12	almanacs
1.3312	41.2	.5912	11	surest
1.3309	41.2	.4827	13	intensive
1.3309	41.2	.5413	12	pageant
1.3308	41.2	.2203	23	condenses
1.3307	41.2	.3042	15	Concert
1.3304	41.2	.1983	18	Ears
1.3303	41.2	.3780	14	pecking
1.3303	41.2	.4732	12	soldier's
1.3302	41.2	.4513	13	ferryboat
1.3302	41.2	.5844	11	undergoing
1.3298	41.2	.4994	12	mourned
1.3297	41.2	.5432	11	whizzed
1.3295	41.2	.3315	18	Hague
1.3294	41.2	.5257	12	favorably
1.3293	41.2	.0917	44	Jessie
1.3292	41.2	.5771	11	hoods
1.3291	41.2	.5521	11	fencing
1.3289	41.2	.6554	10	earthenware
1.3289	41.2	.5759	11	strewn
1.3287	41.2	.5252	12	Cabin
1.3286	41.2	.5665	11	faltered
1.3284	41.2	.1707	19	Ferris
1.3282	41.2	.2003	27	hostess
1.3278	41.2	.2955	19	isotope
1.3275	41.2	.4257	14	quarrels
1.3272	41.2	.5883	11	utilize
1.3269	41.2	.5853	11	declining
1.3269	41.2	.5540	11	dine
1.3268	41.2	.4370	14	chieftain
1.3268	41.2	.4507	13	saloon
1.3267	41.2	.1620	21	Pepe
1.3266	41.2	.6262	10	headdress
1.3266	41.2	.3172	18	industrialization
1.3265	41.2	.5591	11	brute
1.3265	41.2	.5668	11	flatter
1.3263	41.2	.5486	11	watermelons
1.3257	41.2	.3465	17	Israelis
1.3256	41.2	.4524	14	Progress
1.3255	41.2	.4826	13	ailments
1.3255	41.2	.4523	13	headwaters
1.3255	41.2	.5399	12	116
1.3254	41.2	.5795	11	imply
1.3250	41.2	.4773	13	cholera
1.3250	41.2	.4316	14	teachings
1.3248	41.2	.0000	29	Jorge
1.3244	41.2	.4321	13	haunches
1.3242	41.2	.3405	18	hieroglyphics
1.3229	41.2	.5213	12	crumbling
1.3226	41.2	.3960	14	scythe
1.3225	41.2	.5402	11	caked
1.3225	41.2	.4770	13	ready-made
1.3224	41.2	.4552	14	Go
1.3223	41.2	.4554	13	Montgomery
1.3221	41.2	.5487	11	whack
1.3220	41.2	.5801	11	endowed
1.3218	41.2	.4729	12	stampede
1.3215	41.2	.4905	13	diagonally
1.3215	41.2	.5858	11	focal
1.3214	41.2	.5321	12	statistical
1.3213	41.2	.4060	14	atop
1.3211	41.2	.4472	14	8th
1.3208	41.2	.6405	10	supersonic
1.3203	41.2	.5123	12	mechanically
1.3202	41.2	.5682	11	unarmed
1.3201	41.2	.6475	10	beeswax
1.3201	41.2	.5006	12	Brussels
1.3199	41.2	.5295	12	four-sided
1.3199	41.2	.4726	13	Fun
1.3198	41.2	.5737	11	166
1.3197	41.2	.5372	11	restlessly
1.3197	41.2	.5774	11	seventeenth-century
1.3195	41.2	.1708	27	Pizarro
1.3194	41.2	.4764	13	indicators
1.3194	41.2	.5701	11	pilgrims

U	SFI	D	F	Word Type
1.3190	41.2	.3743	14	cruiser
1.3189	41.2	.4875	13	wallpaper
1.3187	41.2	.3028	20	widths
1.3183	41.2	.5710	11	maternal
1.3182	41.2	.4296	14	commodities
1.3172	41.2	.0000	88	commutative
1.3171	41.2	.5744	11	excellence
1.3168	41.2	.5703	11	detour
THE PRECEDING WORD TYPE OCCUPIES RANK 15300				
1.3168	41.2	.3496	15	Torres
1.3168	41.2	.4545	12	Watkins
1.3167	41.2	.1970	20	broccoli
1.3167	41.2	.2844	19	hyphenated
1.3167	41.2	.2999	19	5%
1.3166	41.2	.4666	13	drains
1.3165	41.2	.4660	13	1868
1.3162	41.2	.5597	11	boxed
1.3158	41.2	.4769	13	interaction
1.3156	41.2	.4462	14	Youth
1.3155	41.2	.2351	23	Barnum
1.3150	41.2	.3504	14	Inn
1.3149	41.2	.3394	16	diphtheria
1.3148	41.2	.1972	29	bassoon
1.3147	41.2	.3957	15	basalt
1.3146	41.2	.0496	83	crayon
1.3146	41.2	.5748	11	exercising
1.3145	41.2	.4918	12	fenced
1.3145	41.2	.5419	11	scorching
1.3145	41.2	.4645	13	Wise
1.3140	41.2	.5230	12	clergyman
1.3138	41.2	.7146	9	pretends
1.3137	41.2	.5523	11	feathered
1.3136	41.2	.5081	12	locates
1.3135	41.2	.0217	136	Jesus
1.3135	41.2	.5216	12	Judy's
1.3132	41.2	.2301	17	Hattie
1.3131	41.2	.5441	11	suspiciously
1.3127	41.2	.5047	12	unborn
1.3123	41.2	.4016	14	mountainsides
1.3121	41.2	.3898	15	bulldozer
1.3120	41.2	.1186	21	Fink
1.3119	41.2	.5062	12	Nellie
1.3119	41.2	.4785	13	This
1.3118	41.2	.5203	12	Hungarians
1.3115	41.2	.5179	12	revolted
1.3113	41.2	.5174	12	Augustine
1.3111	41.2	.3942	15	reflexes
1.3110	41.2	.5431	11	infield
1.3108	41.2	.5408	11	coolness
1.3108	41.2	.1542	37	lathe
1.3107	41.2	.7247	9	Kent
1.3106	41.2	.5777	11	Student
1.3104	41.2	.4552	13	toiled
1.3101	41.2	.6160	10	wigwams
1.3096	41.2	.4649	13	embraced
1.3095	41.2	.1226	35	Wat
1.3092	41.2	.4336	14	electoral
1.3091	41.2	.5702	11	ranching
1.3089	41.2	.3431	15	snorting
1.3085	41.2	.4128	14	bedrock
1.3085	41.2	.4730	12	Glass
1.3081	41.2	.4825	13	Baptist
1.3081	41.2	.4966	12	creak
1.3079	41.2	.3620	15	miserably
1.3077	41.2	.6160	10	thanking
1.3075	41.2	.1963	27	Boyd
1.3072	41.2	.4605	13	honeybees
1.3070	41.2	.6153	10	indifference
1.3069	41.2	.5571	11	cinder
1.3067	41.2	.1274	38	appositive
1.3067	41.2	.5694	11	revolutionized
1.3064	41.2	.4285	14	disappearance
1.3064	41.2	.5643	11	scanned
1.3062	41.2	.5200	12	refugee
1.3061	41.2	.4523	14	seasoning
1.3059	41.2	.4998	12	dribble
1.3059	41.2	.4479	14	printers
1.3058	41.2	.5127	12	displacement
1.3058	41.2	.5061	12	takeoff
1.3055	41.2	.1625	19	Barth
1.3054	41.2	.5579	11	airtight
1.3053	41.2	.5100	12	Willie's
1.3051	41.2	.5193	12	clings
1.3048	41.2	.6272	10	mermaid
1.3048	41.2	.4820	13	undesirable
1.3047	41.2	.4604	13	distilled
1.3046	41.2	.5056	12	detectives
1.3045	41.2	.5746	11	evolve
1.3042	41.2	.4705	12	wand
1.3041	41.2	.3566	16	absorption
1.3041	41.2	.5492	11	chained
1.3038	41.2	.3361	14	watchdog
1.3036	41.2	.5242	12	Outer
1.3035	41.2	.5637	11	shrug
1.3035	41.2	.4302	13	subtopics
1.3034	41.2	.4885	12	pickle
1.3032	41.2	.2713	19	Dick's
1.3031	41.1	.4026	14	subways
1.3029	41.1	.5703	11	heathen
1.3029	41.1	.6395	10	hosts
1.3028	41.1	.5687	11	cornbread
1.3027	41.1	.4458	12	Martian
1.3024	41.1	.6172	10	needy
1.3023	41.1	.4552	12	otters
1.3018	41.1	.4995	12	marrow
1.3014	41.1	.3114	18	Injuns
1.3013	41.1	.2366	20	retina
1.3012	41.1	.4733	12	schooners
1.3010	41.1	.2248	17	Pool
THE PRECEDING WORD TYPE OCCUPIES RANK 15400				
1.3009	41.1	.6325	10	constructing
1.3004	41.1	.6119	10	bucks
1.3003	41.1	.4799	12	Steve's
1.3003	41.1	.3344	14	Woody
1.2995	41.1	.3980	15	pigment
1.2993	41.1	.6177	10	oneself
1.2992	41.1	.4362	14	retail
1.2991	41.1	.4580	13	Divide
1.2988	41.1	.3382	14	diver's
1.2986	41.1	.5604	11	clearance
1.2986	41.1	.6320	10	traversed
1.2979	41.1	.5455	11	charitable
1.2978	41.1	.5636	11	haystack
1.2977	41.1	.4246	14	exploitation
1.2976	41.1	.6393	10	sustain
1.2974	41.1	.2432	17	Huggins
1.2973	41.1	.6091	10	aisles
1.2972	41.1	.5565	11	prosper
1.2971	41.1	.6096	10	appalled
1.2966	41.1	.4677	13	Motors
1.2965	41.1	.4257	14	authorized
1.2965	41.1	.4762	12	posted
1.2964	41.1	.4151	14	Continent
1.2964	41.1	.4358	14	Prague
1.2956	41.1	.3079	19	burlap
1.2954	41.1	.2387	23	Jew
1.2954	41.1	.4154	14	1845
1.2947	41.1	.5748	11	advent
1.2947	41.1	.3299	17	intersections
1.2945	41.1	.2812	20	fer
1.2939	41.1	.6117	10	apprehension
1.2938	41.1	.4418	13	opossums
1.2938	41.1	.4741	12	tallow
1.2937	41.1	.3836	16	improvised
1.2936	41.1	.4629	13	Braille
1.2929	41.1	.3754	15	squeezes
1.2928	41.1	.4009	15	elasticity
1.2928	41.1	.4889	12	underworld
1.2925	41.1	.4938	12	R **
1.2925	41.1	.5735	11	standardized
1.2923	41.1	.4799	12	porthole
1.2923	41.1	.5391	11	stovepipe
1.2921	41.1	.5069	12	monitor
1.2918	41.1	.5610	11	snatch
1.2916	41.1	.6134	10	gleefully
1.2916	41.1	.4583	13	specializes
1.2915	41.1	.5131	12	prophets
1.2913	41.1	.5659	11	sockets
1.2911	41.1	.5400	11	1822
1.2909	41.1	.5620	11	denim
1.2907	41.1	.4603	13	parliament
1.2897	41.1	.5130	12	1864
1.2894	41.1	.5387	11	bellow
1.2886	41.1	.5577	11	contacts
1.2884	41.1	.5492	11	pausing
1.2884	41.1	.5483	11	strolling
1.2879	41.1	.6208	10	deepened
1.2873	41.1	.5640	11	doom
1.2873	41.1	.2754	20	sawing
1.2873	41.1	.4373	14	sweetheart
1.2868	41.1	.5690	11	expectations
1.2867	41.1	.2446	21	cockroaches
1.2863	41.1	.2292	22	Confederation
1.2863	41.1	.6178	10	thwarted
1.2863	41.1	.5424	11	Benedict
1.2862	41.1	.2625	22	Manila
1.2860	41.1	.6052	10	leaked
1.2856	41.1	.6047	10	foothold
1.2855	41.1	.3768	15	pennant
1.2852	41.1	.6024	10	surging
1.2847	41.1	.1635	29	AD
1.2846	41.1	.4543	13	cooky
1.2846	41.1	.4117	14	Roanoke
1.2846	41.1	.5539	11	ruby
1.2845	41.1	.4590	12	firefly
1.2845	41.1	.5381	11	Joseph's
1.2844	41.1	.5483	11	festivities
1.2843	41.1	.1745	31	ei
1.2843	41.1	.6303	10	untold
1.2836	41.1	.5413	11	rooftops
1.2836	41.1	.5447	11	telegrams
1.2834	41.1	.6089	10	hotly
1.2831	41.1	.4890	12	upland
1.2830	41.1	.4754	13	shank
1.2829	41.1	.4491	12	ballroom
1.2827	41.1	.5639	11	appropriately
1.2825	41.1	.4310	13	scented
1.2824	41.1	.5283	11	greedily
1.2824	41.1	.3174	18	Protestants
1.2822	41.1	.5356	11	unpainted
1.2819	41.1	.3438	17	Voltaire
1.2818	41.1	.2068	23	Nels
1.2817	41.1	.5574	11	Allah
1.2811	41.1	.3869	15	Athenians
1.2809	41.1	.4638	12	snuggled
1.2808	41.1	.4183	14	NASA
1.2808	41.1	.4900	12	patron
1.2806	41.1	.5367	11	milkman
1.2803	41.1	.3080	17	Cherokees
1.2803	41.1	.4661	12	inlet
THE PRECEDING WORD TYPE OCCUPIES RANK 15500				
1.2800	41.1	.6239	10	overwhelmingly
1.2795	41.1	.4713	12	cornstalks
1.2795	41.1	.5349	11	squeaky
1.2787	41.1	.6283	10	conditioned
1.2786	41.1	.6270	10	stools
1.2784	41.1	.5390	11	exposing
1.2782	41.1	.4738	12	declaration
1.2778	41.1	.4885	12	huddle
1.2775	41.1	.4201	14	assumptions
1.2775	41.1	.5387	11	conceal
1.2774	41.1	.5633	11	reluctance
1.2773	41.1	.4711	13	associates
1.2771	41.1	.4568	13	poll
1.2769	41.1	.6205	10	weasels
1.2762	41.1	.6069	10	Mail
1.2760	41.1	.5944	10	tempers
1.2758	41.1	.6181	10	exercised
1.2757	41.1	.5333	11	shaved
1.2757	41.1	.5942	10	stirs
1.2756	41.1	.5295	11	smother
1.2752	41.1	.5462	11	partridge
1.2747	41.1	.3637	15	Stamp
1.2746	41.1	.3500	15	speller
1.2745	41.1	.5657	11	adequately
1.2745	41.1	.4573	12	Bean
1.2743	41.1	.2446	23	/z/
1.2741	41.1	.5263	11	woolly
1.2736	41.1	.4203	13	quiz
1.2730	41.0	.3801	15	goodbye
1.2730	41.0	.5077	12	propaganda
1.2727	41.0	.4581	13	parliamentary
1.2720	41.0	.5348	11	corps
1.2719	41.0	.4404	12	Dawn
1.2719	41.0	.5080	12	pregnant
1.2716	41.0	.2818	19	corrosion
1.2715	41.0	.4910	12	feminine
1.2714	41.0	.4506	13	deviations
1.2714	41.0	.4929	12	usable
1.2713	41.0	.3128	18	jig
1.2713	41.0	.2749	19	Manchuria
1.2712	41.0	.4276	14	pasting
1.2708	41.0	.3880	14	sportsmanship
1.2707	41.0	.6159	10	consciously
1.2706	41.0	.5493	11	grandfathers
1.2706	41.0	.2012	22	Missy
1.2704	41.0	.3393	17	i's
1.2704	41.0	.4020	15	nominal
1.2703	41.0	.4387	13	whew
1.2702	41.0	.4803	12	Gemini
1.2701	41.0	.5606	11	1875
1.2700	41.0	.4629	13	1-inch
1.2696	41.0	.5541	11	elimination
1.2696	41.0	.4494	12	Means
1.2692	41.0	.5025	12	breakthrough
1.2691	41.0	.5407	11	gadgets
1.2689	41.0	.5199	11	littlest
1.2688	41.0	.5412	11	nag
1.2688	41.0	.6167	10	precede
1.2687	41.0	.3784	13	Fritz
1.2686	41.0	.2593	21	-ly
1.2686	41.0	.5060	12	shorthand
1.2685	41.0	.6208	10	implications
1.2685	41.0	.4599	12	timidly
1.2683	41.0	.5532	11	corridors
1.2682	41.0	.3724	15	Henderson
1.2679	41.0	.5537	11	ebb
1.2679	41.0	.6121	10	housed
1.2679	41.0	.4908	12	magnified
1.2676	41.0	.3821	15	05
1.2674	41.0	.5540	11	Mistress
1.2671	41.0	.4920	12	interiors
1.2670	41.0	.5051	12	integrated
1.2669	41.0	.5569	11	decisive
1.2669	41.0	.5021	12	heightened
1.2668	41.0	.5441	11	shipwrecked
1.2667	41.0	.3801	15	spectra
1.2667	41.0	.5497	11	teamwork
1.2666	41.0	.1282	33	cm
1.2666	41.0	.4093	14	unjust
1.2657	41.0	.3912	15	Grandma's
1.2657	41.0	.4959	12	1825
1.2650	41.0	.2382	21	Belgians
1.2647	41.0	.3679	16	toasted
1.2647	41.0	.5460	11	wilder
1.2646	41.0	.4105	13	pinata
1.2644	41.0	.2612	21	pro
1.2644	41.0	.3792	14	Tigers
1.2644	41.0	.3832	13	valentines
1.2643	41.0	.5485	11	Irishman
1.2638	41.0	.3237	17	Calif
1.2638	41.0	.5495	11	households
1.2637	41.0	.6176	10	Syrian
1.2636	41.0	.5251	11	4000
1.2635	41.0	.5978	10	Bernard
1.2635	41.0	.5288	11	sombrero
1.2634	41.0	.5076	12	insulated
1.2632	41.0	.4517	13	year-round
1.2630	41.0	.5277	11	strutting
1.2626	41.0	.5079	12	preferably
1.2626	41.0	.3279	16	racers
THE PRECEDING WORD TYPE OCCUPIES RANK 15600				
1.2626	41.0	.5932	10	shuffling
1.2625	41.0	.6101	10	propelled
1.2624	41.0	.6009	10	gadget
1.2624	41.0	.4913	12	witnesses
1.2621	41.0	.3036	18	pope
1.2617	41.0	.4094	14	integration
1.2616	41.0	.5065	12	imprisonment
1.2614	41.0	.1813	27	chromosome
1.2612	41.0	.3724	16	diphthongs
1.2607	41.0	.3470	16	relativity
1.2607	41.0	.1550	24	Tinker
1.2605	41.0	.5983	10	eyeballs
1.2605	41.0	.4914	12	ramp
1.2604	41.0	.5481	11	claiming
1.2603	41.0	.5452	11	nationalities
1.2599	41.0	.3115	18	Abbott
1.2597	41.0	.5932	10	millionaire
1.2596	41.0	.4383	13	mating
1.2591	41.0	.4847	12	Germany's
1.2588	41.0	.6089	10	zeal
1.2587	41.0	.5247	11	Knights
1.2587	41.0	.5247	11	Sudan
1.2586	41.0	.5511	11	correction
1.2585	41.0	.5349	11	glimpses
1.2584	41.0	.6767	9	accounted
1.2584	41.0	.2480	21	1862
1.2583	41.0	.3677	13	Goddard
1.2583	41.0	.5939	10	speculate
1.2581	41.0	.3564	16	Grade
1.2581	41.0	.5474	11	1770
1.2578	41.0	.5498	11	nobleman
1.2575	41.0	.6729	9	hoist
1.2574	41.0	.5441	11	fattening
1.2573	41.0	.1993	26	Brittany
1.2573	41.0	.4862	12	Theater
1.2570	41.0	.1285	30	isotopes
1.2569	41.0	.3123	14	Morgan's
1.2568	41.0	.4516	13	131
1.2567	41.0	.4857	12	banners
1.2567	41.0	.5275	11	237
1.2565	41.0	.5440	11	avenues
1.2561	41.0	.2499	21	publicity
1.2554	41.0	.6153	10	impassable
1.2554	41.0	.3732	15	savanna
1.2551	41.0	.4200	14	stirrups
1.2550	41.0	.4793	12	hot-water
1.2550	41.0	.3246	18	sixth-grade
1.2549	41.0	.4773	12	Conrad
1.2545	41.0	.5133	11	prow
1.2544	41.0	.5319	11	purity
1.2542	41.0	.4606	13	revised
1.2542	41.0	.6046	10	undergone
1.2540	41.0	.5854	10	hunter's
1.2540	41.0	.3095	18	2b
1.2538	41.0	.4893	12	oft
1.2538	41.0	.5358	11	Warsaw
1.2531	41.0	.4434	13	calculation
1.2527	41.0	.4825	12	government's
1.2526	41.0	.3034	19	grammatical
1.2525	41.0	.4943	12	hearings
1.2524	41.0	.6003	10	hoarsely
1.2524	41.0	.6003	10	musty
1.2522	41.0	.3860	13	Peaks
1.2522	41.0	.4619	12	steeply
1.2521	41.0	.3595	13	Melisande
1.2520	41.0	.5264	11	stairways
1.2519	41.0	.4908	12	reckoning
1.2519	41.0	.5201	11	sneered
1.2517	41.0	.5500	11	tipping
1.2509	41.0	.3978	14	Stripes
1.2505	41.0	.4493	12	gorillas
1.2505	41.0	.4576	12	Mohawk
1.2505	41.0	.2558	20	shoo
1.2498	41.0	.6145	10	lavish
1.2496	41.0	.4439	13	Federation
1.2492	41.0	.4884	12	mowing
1.2491	41.0	.4887	12	fingernail
1.2489	41.0	.5267	11	bungalow
1.2489	41.0	.4913	12	localities
1.2486	41.0	.5073	11	twitched
1.2484	41.0	.6055	10	elliptical
1.2483	41.0	.5317	11	Fredericksburg
1.2482	41.0	.3838	15	valid
1.2480	41.0	.6051	10	reunion
1.2477	41.0	.4564	12	strolled
1.2475	41.0	.4325	13	fluids
1.2468	41.0	.4865	12	1863
1.2467	41.0	.3654	14	DiMaggio
1.2465	41.0	.4522	13	graders
1.2465	41.0	.4488	12	Penelope
1.2464	41.0	.6071	10	suet
1.2461	41.0	.4893	12	untidy
1.2458	41.0	.4917	12	Scotia
1.2455	41.0	.4996	12	118
1.2453	41.0	.4902	12	postal
1.2449	41.0	.5637	10	belfry
1.2447	41.0	.3128	17	mutations
1.2445	40.9	.3604	13	Pickett
1.2441	40.9	.5058	11	hard-boiled
1.2440	40.9	.3852	13	scuba
THE PRECEDING WORD TYPE OCCUPIES RANK 15700				
1.2439	40.9	.5400	11	complaints
1.2439	40.9	.5813	10	lilac
1.2438	40.9	.5928	10	tarts
1.2436	40.9	.5496	11	Foundation
1.2436	40.9	.5943	10	leaky
1.2435	40.9	.5343	11	classifies
1.2434	40.9	.5316	11	handmade
1.2434	40.9	.4436	13	linings
1.2432	40.9	.3798	14	scurvy
1.2432	40.9	.4720	12	underway
1.2431	40.9	.5084	11	thirty-three
1.2429	40.9	.5166	11	four-letter
1.2429	40.9	.5841	10	reddish-brown
1.2425	40.9	.6016	10	1809
1.2424	40.9	.2051	19	Bangs
1.2422	40.9	.4509	13	narratives
1.2419	40.9	.5597	10	giggling
1.2419	40.9	.5188	11	smashing
1.2418	40.9	.5796	10	bedside
1.2418	40.9	.3093	17	Bolivar
1.2418	40.9	.3617	13	Downs
1.2417	40.9	.5193	11	one-man
1.2415	40.9	.5181	11	by-product
1.2414	40.9	.5326	11	intellect
1.2414	40.9	.1416	35	operas
1.2414	40.9	.4965	12	whisky
1.2413	40.9	.3450	15	Charlemagne
1.2412	40.9	.5472	11	skit
1.2411	40.9	.4383	13	laser
1.2410	40.9	.4988	12	incidentally
1.2409	40.9	.2194	20	fiords
1.2402	40.9	.5385	11	pledged
1.2400	40.9	.5892	10	thrushes
1.2399	40.9	.3832	14	perfumes
1.2397	40.9	.5205	11	integrity
1.2397	40.9	.6022	10	whirls
1.2396	40.9	.3987	14	seven-year-old
1.2395	40.9	.5208	11	humph
1.2394	40.9	.2607	19	microscopes
1.2393	40.9	.3571	16	baby-sitting
1.2390	40.9	.4464	13	theatrical
1.2389	40.9	.5916	10	exceeding
1.2385	40.9	.4974	12	passionate
1.2384	40.9	.5319	11	panorama
1.2382	40.9	.5179	11	poisoning
1.2379	40.9	.5157	11	dined
1.2375	40.9	.4716	12	safeguard
1.2374	40.9	.4481	13	dorsal
1.2374	40.9	.4837	12	professionals
1.2373	40.9	.5903	10	attendants
1.2372	40.9	.2834	20	rotary
1.2367	40.9	.4832	12	dark-skinned
1.2365	40.9	.5185	11	forelegs
1.2364	40.9	.4851	12	induce
1.2363	40.9	.2945	18	metamorphosis

U	SFI	D	F	Word Type
1.2358	40.9	.4838	12	arrests
1.2355	40.9	.3269	17	lullaby
1.2351	40.9	.6069	10	misunderstood
1.2349	40.9	.1167	37	harpsichord
1.2347	40.9	.4925	12	estuary
1.2347	40.9	.5814	10	obediently
1.2345	40.9	.4725	12	despise
1.2344	40.9	.3748	15	cleanup
1.2341	40.9	.4414	13	340
1.2340	40.9	.0529	68	Haydn
1.2334	40.9	.0000	27	Benjie
1.2334	40.9	.0000	27	Bluey
1.2334	40.9	.0000	27	Cord
1.2334	40.9	.4673	12	decree
1.2333	40.9	.5222	11	editorials
1.2332	40.9	.2865	16	slingshot
1.2327	40.9	.1665	24	collectors
1.2327	40.9	.3920	14	millet
1.2323	40.9	.4727	12	bewildering
1.2320	40.9	.5511	10	brambles
1.2320	40.9	.4354	13	inaugural
1.2317	40.9	.4340	12	wagging
1.2316	40.9	.3660	13	francs
1.2316	40.9	.3413	15	ole
1.2313	40.9	.4264	13	grants
1.2309	40.9	.4808	11	Gift
1.2309	40.9	.4098	13	matted
1.2309	40.9	.4312	13	strayed
1.2304	40.9	.5336	11	clash
1.2304	40.9	.4688	12	Virginians
1.2302	40.9	.5128	11	staffs
1.2301	40.9	.5491	10	$400
1.2301	40.9	.3220	17	cosmic
1.2298	40.9	.5446	11	satire
1.2297	40.9	.5487	10	half-mile
1.2294	40.9	.1527	26	forgive
1.2291	40.9	.6021	10	dictate
1.2289	40.9	.2614	18	cattlemen
1.2289	40.9	.4091	14	dyed
1.2288	40.9	.5901	10	fuses
1.2286	40.9	.1778	23	burros
1.2286	40.9	.5385	11	justly
1.2285	40.9	.1312	29	ovary
1.2284	40.9	.4885	12	tapestry
1.2283	40.9	.5867	10	blinds

THE PRECEDING WORD TYPE OCCUPIES RANK 15800

U	SFI	D	F	Word Type
1.2281	40.9	.5071	11	rigged
1.2281	40.9	.4677	12	wind's
1.2274	40.9	.6564	9	milestone
1.2271	40.9	.3311	15	knuckles
1.2270	40.9	.4806	11	fingered
1.2270	40.9	.5990	10	trustees
1.2269	40.9	.5962	10	analyzed
1.2268	40.9	.4778	11	suitor
1.2266	40.9	.5872	10	slaughtered
1.2265	40.9	.4401	13	Sinai
1.2264	40.9	.5170	11	cocks
1.2264	40.9	.4312	13	Monroe
1.2258	40.9	.6704	9	crumble
1.2258	40.9	.4822	11	Sumner
1.2256	40.9	.4651	12	wraps
1.2255	40.9	.5625	10	thirty-eight
1.2252	40.9	.3309	16	undo
1.2250	40.9	.5479	10	Thumb
1.2247	40.9	.3639	15	veto
1.2245	40.9	.5928	10	ambassador
1.2245	40.9	.4471	12	bellowed
1.2244	40.9	.3951	14	methane
1.2243	40.9	.3322	16	respiratory
1.2240	40.9	.4458	12	Armed
1.2240	40.9	.5472	10	bulged
1.2240	40.9	.3810	14	Confederacy
1.2240	40.9	.3668	15	Neil
1.2240	40.9	.5641	10	progressed
1.2237	40.9	.5616	10	ledges
1.2237	40.9	.5310	11	shark's
1.2236	40.9	.4691	12	oxides
1.2235	40.9	.4818	12	supremacy
1.2234	40.9	.5763	10	idol
1.2234	40.9	.4618	12	Route
1.2232	40.9	.3439	13	honked
1.2231	40.9	.4776	11	dawned
1.2229	40.9	.5058	11	Most
1.2227	40.9	.4180	13	Barry
1.2227	40.9	.3778	14	Hawaii's
1.2227	40.9	.3085	16	orchid
1.2227	40.9	.5434	11	two-
1.2226	40.9	.5398	11	predominantly
1.2226	40.9	.4869	12	vastly
1.2224	40.9	.4893	11	peeked
1.2221	40.9	.5392	11	album
1.2220	40.9	.5752	10	upholstery
1.2218	40.9	.2445	16	Pinkerton
1.2217	40.9	.6071	10	achieves
1.2216	40.9	.4244	12	fumbled
1.2204	40.9	.4000	14	caveman
1.2201	40.9	.4809	11	exchanges
1.2201	40.9	.4787	11	stoutly
1.2200	40.9	.5585	10	squawk
1.2199	40.9	.5246	11	criteria
1.2197	40.9	.4798	12	Asiatic
1.2197	40.9	.4717	12	geyser
1.2195	40.9	.5279	11	ivy
1.2194	40.9	.4548	12	Bremen
1.2189	40.9	.5239	11	ripples
1.2189	40.9	.6678	9	turbulent
1.2184	40.9	.4825	11	skier
1.2182	40.9	.4659	12	Economic
1.2178	40.9	.4440	12	steeper
1.2176	40.9	.4509	12	squaws
1.2175	40.9	.1957	26	/r/
1.2175	40.9	.5550	10	revolver
1.2173	40.9	.5218	11	stringy
1.2172	40.9	.1202	38	clarinet
1.2172	40.9	.3419	14	snowball
1.2170	40.9	.4750	12	mistletoe
1.2169	40.9	.4529	12	catalogue
1.2169	40.9	.5057	11	Fe
1.2169	40.9	.4742	12	gaiety
1.2167	40.9	.2549	19	Centerburg
1.2167	40.9	.5517	10	jugglers
1.2166	40.9	.5778	10	unrolled
1.2163	40.9	.4749	11	hooray
1.2163	40.9	.3962	13	Willow
1.2161	40.8	.5708	10	Evening
1.2161	40.8	.3642	15	132
1.2159	40.8	.5793	10	chink
1.2159	40.8	.4816	11	muskets
1.2158	40.8	.5800	10	doggedly
1.2157	40.8	.5546	10	rascal
1.2154	40.8	.5784	10	dark-haired
1.2152	40.8	.4994	11	eaves
1.2152	40.8	.5670	10	olden
1.2148	40.8	.3645	14	NorthAmerica
1.2146	40.8	.4510	12	Zoo
1.2145	40.8	.4309	13	prohibited
1.2144	40.8	.4803	11	swiftness
1.2138	40.8	.4991	11	Hot
1.2135	40.8	.5760	10	myriad
1.2132	40.8	.5929	10	intrigued
1.2130	40.8	.5522	10	drawbridge
1.2129	40.8	.2603	20	Mayo
1.2128	40.8	.5878	10	indispensable
1.2126	40.8	.4406	12	what'll
1.2125	40.8	.6606	9	chat
1.2124	40.8	.4395	13	glazed
THE PRECEDING WORD TYPE OCCUPIES RANK 15900				
1.2122	40.8	.4717	12	Laredo
1.2121	40.8	.1907	26	harmonic
1.2121	40.8	.6639	9	9th
1.2120	40.8	.5339	11	1893
1.2118	40.8	.4866	11	disobey
1.2117	40.8	.1532	18	decompression
1.2117	40.8	.1532	18	stretcher
1.2115	40.8	.3008	17	diets
1.2111	40.8	.4028	14	transformations
1.2110	40.8	.5346	11	glitter
1.2109	40.8	.5777	10	dials
1.2108	40.8	.4784	11	smacked
1.2108	40.8	.4784	11	squealed
1.2107	40.8	.5706	10	prospective
1.2106	40.8	.6517	9	hemlock
1.2106	40.8	.5728	10	whitish
1.2104	40.8	.4849	12	civic
1.2104	40.8	.6484	9	son-in-law
1.2102	40.8	.5173	11	Louisville
1.2097	40.8	.4338	13	ocean's
1.2094	40.8	.5748	10	inquiring
1.2094	40.8	.5261	11	rotated
1.2089	40.8	.3840	14	Sargent
1.2089	40.8	.5012	11	sloop
1.2085	40.8	.2793	19	greased
1.2084	40.8	.5767	10	inhale
1.2084	40.8	.4627	12	Prince's
1.2082	40.8	.5294	11	banned
1.2082	40.8	.5858	10	captures
1.2082	40.8	.3547	15	Nationalist
1.2081	40.8	.2315	20	Northerners
1.2079	40.8	.2446	20	savannas
1.2078	40.8	.1250	27	Howie
1.2078	40.8	.0435	53	1/5
1.2078	40.8	.0435	53	2/5
1.2077	40.8	.5199	11	impurities
1.2076	40.8	.5028	11	ovens
1.2076	40.8	.5493	10	wickedness
1.2075	40.8	.5564	10	Reynolds
1.2073	40.8	.5533	10	spilling
1.2072	40.8	.4163	12	tarantula
1.2069	40.8	.1692	28	predicates
1.2068	40.8	.5345	11	twentieth-century
1.2066	40.8	.4673	11	apologize
1.2065	40.8	.5240	11	generating
1.2061	40.8	.5638	10	chilling
1.2060	40.8	.4503	12	Flight
1.2059	40.8	.5644	10	dawning
1.2059	40.8	.4591	12	varmint
1.2053	40.8	.5671	10	studded
1.2050	40.8	.3534	15	Goody
1.2049	40.8	.4644	12	Canada's
1.2049	40.8	.4858	12	chili
1.2049	40.8	.5203	11	roommate
1.2048	40.8	.5729	10	Dover
1.2048	40.8	.6478	9	scanty
1.2047	40.8	.4044	12	storeroom
1.2046	40.8	.4571	12	Greater
1.2046	40.8	.6465	9	one-sided
1.2046	40.8	.5675	10	ripening
1.2046	40.8	.5211	11	scoops
1.2044	40.8	.4904	11	horsehair
1.2043	40.8	.4798	11	mussels
1.2042	40.8	.4232	13	strait
1.2039	40.8	.5472	10	straggling
1.2038	40.8	.5182	11	Austin
1.2037	40.8	.2446	20	Lowland
1.2032	40.8	.2909	16	Aaron
1.2032	40.8	.5830	10	acclaim
1.2030	40.8	.5168	11	accumulate
1.2028	40.8	.4368	12	bright-eyed
1.2027	40.8	.5802	10	antics
1.2024	40.8	.4422	13	individuality
1.2022	40.8	.5510	10	Quincy
1.2021	40.8	.5438	10	munching
1.2019	40.8	.6409	9	concentrating
1.2019	40.8	.3235	16	Ponce
1.2017	40.8	.4648	12	diagnosis
1.2016	40.8	.3468	14	Custard
1.2016	40.8	.5832	10	dominates
1.2015	40.8	.5025	11	sagging
1.2011	40.8	.6260	9	crazily
1.2011	40.8	.3585	14	Lafayette
1.2010	40.8	.2071	16	Kangaroo
1.2006	40.8	.5818	10	privileged
1.2005	40.8	.3390	13	Benton
1.1998	40.8	.3388	13	Percival
1.1994	40.8	.5817	10	inhabit
1.1994	40.8	.4743	11	welcoming
1.1993	40.8	.4971	11	bitterness
1.1993	40.8	.5256	11	reverence
1.1993	40.8	.5248	11	169
1.1991	40.8	.5708	10	deepening
1.1991	40.8	.4221	13	episodes
1.1986	40.8	.2333	22	clamps
1.1986	40.8	.5295	11	manipulation
1.1986	40.8	.4243	12	plop
1.1986	40.8	.2964	17	Thailand
1.1986	40.8	.6435	9	unsolved
1.1985	40.8	.3704	15	amplifier
THE PRECEDING WORD TYPE OCCUPIES RANK 16000				
1.1983	40.8	.3988	14	ducts
1.1981	40.8	.3791	14	antiseptic
1.1981	40.8	.5576	10	toppled
1.1981	40.8	.5821	10	184
1.1977	40.8	.3403	13	crowing
1.1977	40.8	.5708	10	delicacy
1.1975	40.8	.4862	11	battering
1.1973	40.8	.4297	12	looming
1.1972	40.8	.5188	11	tubular
1.1970	40.8	.5812	10	Beatrice
1.1969	40.8	.5582	10	eyelashes
1.1968	40.8	.5656	10	remnant
1.1964	40.8	.4759	12	comforted
1.1964	40.8	.1863	23	reflex
1.1963	40.8	.4484	11	Xerxes
1.1962	40.8	.5082	11	flatboat
1.1962	40.8	.4806	11	nicer
1.1959	40.8	.5085	11	congressman
1.1957	40.8	.5698	10	Euclid
1.1954	40.8	.5169	11	resolutely
1.1952	40.8	.5028	11	insulting
1.1952	40.8	.5759	10	vengeance
1.1949	40.8	.5236	11	novelty
1.1941	40.8	.4009	14	Ames
1.1941	40.8	.2504	19	Cambodia
1.1941	40.8	.5060	11	fondly
1.1940	40.8	.2416	18	Grimes
1.1939	40.8	.5800	10	coordinated
1.1937	40.8	.6250	9	importantly
1.1933	40.8	.4739	12	lbs
1.1933	40.8	.5233	11	tapering
1.1930	40.8	.4613	12	$35
1.1929	40.8	.3492	13	Rocket
1.1927	40.8	.5662	10	inhaled
1.1927	40.8	.4725	11	Leopold
1.1926	40.8	.5170	11	bids
1.1923	40.8	.5414	10	punches
1.1922	40.8	.5175	11	donated
1.1922	40.8	.4304	12	whinnied
1.1921	40.8	.4518	12	terns
1.1917	40.8	.2071	18	Trojans
1.1909	40.8	.4015	13	Marines
1.1903	40.8	.4367	12	bareback
1.1903	40.8	.5476	10	camel's
1.1901	40.8	.6457	9	fades
1.1898	40.8	.1749	25	Flower
1.1895	40.8	.4132	13	graphite
1.1892	40.8	.1718	17	Mario
1.1892	40.8	.1718	17	Pancho
1.1892	40.8	.1718	17	Ware
1.1890	40.8	.5027	11	competent
1.1890	40.8	.5177	11	handicaps
1.1889	40.8	.5432	10	barracks
1.1888	40.8	.2916	18	cutters
1.1884	40.7	.6234	9	shuts
1.1883	40.7	.5744	10	heretofore
1.1882	40.7	.5756	10	cemented
1.1878	40.7	.4178	13	Spain's
1.1878	40.7	.5633	10	1790
1.1877	40.7	.0000	26	Epimetheus
1.1877	40.7	.0000	26	Nils
1.1877	40.7	.0000	26	Peasley
1.1877	40.7	.0000	26	Riddler
1.1876	40.7	.4555	12	self-governing
1.1869	40.7	.5513	10	wrecking
1.1866	40.7	.5633	10	years'
1.1861	40.7	.2561	18	Billings
1.1861	40.7	.5619	10	idiot
1.1859	40.7	.5540	10	lotion
1.1851	40.7	.5199	11	bearers
1.1849	40.7	.2193	21	Nantucket
1.1848	40.7	.3181	16	lichens
1.1847	40.7	.5032	11	shingle
1.1847	40.7	.5035	11	Slave
1.1842	40.7	.1483	32	Trial
1.1839	40.7	.5615	10	interpreting
1.1838	40.7	.4317	13	provision
1.1838	40.7	.5616	10	shear
1.1832	40.7	.2840	18	Cubs
1.1832	40.7	.5177	11	prevalent
1.1830	40.7	.5583	10	glimpsed
1.1828	40.7	.5122	11	hysterical
1.1828	40.7	.5049	11	mare's
1.1828	40.7	.4387	12	VanBuren
1.1822	40.7	.4653	11	powdery
1.1822	40.7	.6347	9	sling
1.1819	40.7	.6236	9	eyebrow
1.1816	40.7	.3810	13	grabbing
1.1815	40.7	.5754	10	piers
1.1815	40.7	.4441	12	siege
1.1812	40.7	.4713	11	Don't
1.1812	40.7	.3208	13	Josiah
1.1812	40.7	.5449	10	pried
1.1810	40.7	.5006	11	outright
1.1807	40.7	.3037	17	clothed
1.1807	40.7	.4681	12	Train
1.1806	40.7	.5633	10	bakes
1.1805	40.7	.3761	14	sulfuric
1.1804	40.7	.5565	10	calmed
1.1800	40.7	.5741	10	projecting
THE PRECEDING WORD TYPE OCCUPIES RANK 16100				
1.1799	40.7	.2596	19	punctuated
1.1798	40.7	.5665	10	stupendous
1.1797	40.7	.5108	11	progresses
1.1795	40.7	.4516	12	alight
1.1794	40.7	.4509	11	sinister
1.1793	40.7	.2305	22	Petunia
1.1793	40.7	.5629	10	Saxony
1.1791	40.7	.3866	13	Milk
1.1788	40.7	.2210	23	Linn
1.1787	40.7	.6206	9	batch
1.1787	40.7	.4742	12	vocational
1.1786	40.7	.6222	9	contentment
1.1785	40.7	.5648	10	indoor
1.1783	40.7	.4346	13	garlic
1.1782	40.7	.3429	14	vanes
1.1779	40.7	.3193	15	Caliph
1.1779	40.7	.0362	56	Stevie
1.1776	40.7	.5667	10	concludes
1.1775	40.7	.5084	11	laces
1.1772	40.7	.5395	10	charmed
1.1771	40.7	.4396	12	Crawford
1.1769	40.7	.2831	17	hematite
1.1765	40.7	.5653	10	eighteenth-century
1.1760	40.7	.3203	16	1-1
1.1758	40.7	.3169	16	Oakland
1.1756	40.7	.5358	10	streetcar
1.1755	40.7	.5490	10	overcoming
1.1754	40.7	.5432	10	bosses
1.1754	40.7	.4937	11	6000
1.1751	40.7	.5412	10	trooped
1.1748	40.7	.3804	12	dory
1.1747	40.7	.6331	9	avail
1.1747	40.7	.4780	11	reassured
1.1744	40.7	.3266	16	inert
1.1744	40.7	.4542	12	perspire
1.1743	40.7	.4036	13	Castro
1.1742	40.7	.5623	10	agitation
1.1738	40.7	.4577	12	annexed
1.1737	40.7	.1787	20	Austine
1.1736	40.7	.5410	10	occupants
1.1736	40.7	.4892	11	reformers
1.1736	40.7	.6157	9	wringing
1.1735	40.7	.0442	70	octave
1.1733	40.7	.3076	14	Clement
1.1731	40.7	.3927	14	daffodils
1.1731	40.7	.4451	12	hometown
1.1730	40.7	.2347	22	-ed
1.1728	40.7	.3541	15	Daley
1.1728	40.7	.4182	12	harshly
1.1728	40.7	.4982	11	immigrant
1.1728	40.7	.5570	10	midwestern
1.1727	40.7	.4594	12	Messiah
1.1720	40.7	.6257	9	gowns
1.1716	40.7	.4541	12	near-by
1.1716	40.7	.6334	9	underwent
1.1715	40.7	.5499	10	raking
1.1715	40.7	.5499	10	remembrance
1.1713	40.7	.5050	11	Atomic
1.1712	40.7	.4572	11	homely
1.1711	40.7	.5522	10	aunt's
1.1709	40.7	.5346	10	henceforth
1.1706	40.7	.5697	10	codes
1.1706	40.7	.2354	21	vanilla
1.1705	40.7	.4547	12	G**
1.1705	40.7	.4220	13	Janice
1.1704	40.7	.3686	14	Magic
1.1702	40.7	.4128	13	ethnic
1.1701	40.7	.4159	12	caravans
1.1701	40.7	.4827	11	uncomfortably
1.1699	40.7	.5642	10	1788
1.1697	40.7	.5609	10	dual
1.1695	40.7	.4819	11	labored
1.1694	40.7	.1267	31	Property
1.1692	40.7	.4321	12	readiness
1.1691	40.7	.4634	11	Many
1.1691	40.7	.4605	12	7th
1.1689	40.7	.4076	13	chrysalis
1.1685	40.7	.4392	12	Federalists
1.1685	40.7	.3291	15	infectious
1.1684	40.7	.4843	11	explores
1.1682	40.7	.3655	14	Sierras
1.1682	40.7	.4441	11	wildcats
1.1681	40.7	.5095	11	liberated
1.1679	40.7	.3483	15	Reptiles
1.1678	40.7	.5538	10	indivisible
1.1673	40.7	.5535	10	neighbors'
1.1668	40.7	.5458	10	crag
1.1668	40.7	.5157	11	murky
1.1666	40.7	.5106	11	principal's
1.1665	40.7	.4683	11	duck's
1.1664	40.7	.5365	10	two-story
1.1662	40.7	.3169	14	Wilder
1.1660	40.7	.4288	13	imperative
1.1658	40.7	.5595	10	twirled
1.1656	40.7	.4554	11	Parks
1.1656	40.7	.4953	11	reds
1.1656	40.7	.6146	9	salt-water
1.1656	40.7	.5289	10	squarely
1.1655	40.7	.2011	25	Handel
1.1655	40.7	.2338	21	mew

THE PRECEDING WORD TYPE OCCUPIES RANK 16200

U	SFI	D	F	Word Type
1.1654	40.7	.4397	12	alkali
1.1654	40.7	.5637	10	310
1.1653	40.7	.3873	12	traitor
1.1649	40.7	.5158	11	contemporaries
1.1649	40.7	.2097	23	Maverick
1.1648	40.7	.5104	11	coincidence
1.1648	40.7	.5535	10	poisons
1.1637	40.7	.1303	28	Curly
1.1637	40.7	.2750	19	tablespoon
1.1636	40.7	.3850	12	Knut
1.1632	40.7	.3707	14	tributary
1.1630	40.7	.5482	10	marvelously
1.1627	40.7	.4734	11	apology
1.1625	40.7	.3712	14	prongs
1.1625	40.7	.3927	13	wed
1.1624	40.7	.5268	10	hoot
1.1623	40.7	.4929	11	forerunner
1.1622	40.7	.5396	10	half-dozen

U	SFI	D	F	Word Type
1.1618	40.7	.2227	21	vertebrate
1.1610	40.6	.1913	22	cumulus
1.1610	40.6	.4435	12	sire
1.1609	40.6	.3975	14	screwdriver
1.1606	40.6	.5464	10	ordering
1.1603	40.6	.5476	10	capsules
1.1603	40.6	.2509	18	Theory
1.1603	40.6	.5117	11	113
1.1602	40.6	.6258	9	cleanly
1.1602	40.6	.4935	11	soothing
1.1602	40.6	.5550	10	stifled
1.1599	40.6	.5647	10	ceaseless
1.1599	40.6	.7121	8	disabled
1.1598	40.6	.3733	12	Olympics
1.1598	40.6	.3733	12	Philippe
1.1597	40.6	.2329	20	urine
1.1596	40.6	.4823	11	sneezing
1.1592	40.6	.4963	11	residential
1.1592	40.6	.5405	10	schoolboys
1.1592	40.6	.2610	19	Signor
1.1590	40.6	.5007	11	bamboos
1.1589	40.6	.1019	38	Poppins
1.1588	40.6	.5531	10	reconstruct
1.1588	40.6	.6136	9	seekers
1.1586	40.6	.4813	11	bristles
1.1583	40.6	.5016	11	ills
1.1580	40.6	.3607	14	Lucia
1.1578	40.6	.2855	18	mica
1.1577	40.6	.5514	10	pivoted
1.1576	40.6	.4390	12	Susquehanna
1.1575	40.6	.5496	10	lengthened
1.1574	40.6	.4977	11	periodic
1.1574	40.6	.5496	10	presided
1.1573	40.6	.2308	16	Jumper
1.1572	40.6	.2434	15	Jernegan
1.1567	40.6	.4507	11	butler
1.1564	40.6	.2312	21	clamped
1.1564	40.6	.4957	11	labeling
1.1564	40.6	.3756	13	secession
1.1560	40.6	.3610	12	cask
1.1559	40.6	.6048	9	idly
1.1557	40.6	.4553	12	compulsory
1.1555	40.6	.6075	9	sixty-five
1.1554	40.6	.4703	11	municipal
1.1554	40.6	.3942	13	surviving
1.1553	40.6	.1579	17	Lapps
1.1552	40.6	.5516	10	fitness
1.1548	40.6	.6067	9	banister
1.1548	40.6	.5530	10	freshness
1.1548	40.6	.4327	12	1783
1.1547	40.6	.5407	10	Copper
1.1546	40.6	.6089	9	antennas
1.1541	40.6	.6077	9	Dakota
1.1540	40.6	.3541	13	commissioner
1.1539	40.6	.3473	15	riots
1.1539	40.6	.3579	13	Team
1.1538	40.6	.4782	11	glistened
1.1536	40.6	.3996	13	tuck
1.1535	40.6	.6085	9	Friends
1.1530	40.6	.3156	15	1854
1.1529	40.6	.6197	9	Years
1.1527	40.6	.4345	12	limped
1.1527	40.6	.6033	9	noonday
1.1526	40.6	.0000	77	distributive
1.1526	40.6	.3046	16	Truman
1.1526	40.6	.1244	39	wardrobe
1.1524	40.6	.1864	16	Tee
1.1521	40.6	.5608	10	toured
1.1511	40.6	.1192	32	oi
1.1507	40.6	.5235	10	fur-bearing
1.1507	40.6	.4035	13	priced
1.1506	40.6	.5563	10	affliction
1.1505	40.6	.4309	12	blooded
1.1505	40.6	.5339	10	hedgerows
1.1503	40.6	.5451	10	enforced
1.1501	40.6	.5380	10	fussy
1.1500	40.6	.5516	10	grayish
1.1499	40.6	.5424	10	hives
1.1498	40.6	.6242	9	summarized
1.1495	40.6	.4068	12	chirping
1.1494	40.6	.3797	13	stammered
1.1492	40.6	.5493	10	transports
THE PRECEDING WORD TYPE OCCUPIES RANK 16300				
1.1492	40.6	.5479	10	178
1.1488	40.6	.5132	10	Stop
1.1483	40.6	.4715	11	cyclone
1.1483	40.6	.6018	9	disregarding
1.1483	40.6	.4567	11	twitching
1.1479	40.6	.4658	12	beginner
1.1478	40.6	.0394	52	exponential
1.1471	40.6	.7027	8	gamblers
1.1465	40.6	.5428	10	striding
1.1458	40.6	.4884	11	seeps
1.1456	40.6	.5974	9	uneasiness
1.1453	40.6	.5430	10	conferences
1.1453	40.6	.4417	12	thawed
1.1452	40.6	.3192	14	Bergen
1.1450	40.6	.4089	13	surgical
1.1450	40.6	.6004	9	weaver
1.1448	40.6	.4706	11	orally
1.1447	40.6	.3308	15	deLeon
1.1447	40.6	.4926	11	restraint
1.1443	40.6	.5413	10	1609
1.1440	40.6	.4594	11	repentance
1.1440	40.6	.2186	22	straightedge
1.1438	40.6	.4354	12	dismayed
1.1433	40.6	.5440	10	reviews
1.1433	40.6	.6076	9	schedules
1.1432	40.6	.1440	23	Zuckerman
1.1425	40.6	.4753	11	Giuseppe
1.1425	40.6	.4752	11	resident
1.1421	40.6	.0000	25	Amelia
1.1421	40.6	.0000	25	Bedelia
1.1421	40.6	.0000	25	coupe
1.1421	40.6	.0000	25	Dragon
1.1421	40.6	.0000	25	Wawona
1.1420	40.6	.5306	10	treetop
1.1417	40.6	.5274	10	vaccination
1.1414	40.6	.6144	9	Crusoe
1.1414	40.6	.2230	15	Giles
1.1411	40.6	.5462	10	advocate
1.1410	40.6	.3999	13	resentful
1.1408	40.6	.5332	10	shun
1.1405	40.6	.4894	11	age-old
1.1404	40.6	.4470	12	larynx
1.1402	40.6	.4860	11	crescent
1.1401	40.6	.4076	13	academy
1.1401	40.6	.4525	12	cumulative
1.1400	40.6	.5271	10	1860's
1.1399	40.6	.5957	9	freeing
1.1398	40.6	.6001	9	meandering
1.1397	40.6	.4492	11	outlaws
1.1397	40.6	.0982	35	topology
1.1396	40.6	.4772	11	Norsemen
1.1393	40.6	.6114	9	interfered
1.1390	40.6	.4508	11	Seventh
1.1387	40.6	.4025	13	invasions
1.1385	40.6	.3768	13	shipyards
1.1380	40.6	.5374	10	Like
1.1378	40.6	.5310	10	exploding
1.1373	40.6	.3772	13	rebelled
1.1370	40.6	.3856	13	aborigines
1.1369	40.6	.4150	13	beginners
1.1369	40.6	.5144	10	Herb
1.1369	40.6	.2435	15	Monterrey
1.1368	40.6	.5128	10	navigators
1.1363	40.6	.4388	12	smoothing
1.1362	40.6	.3596	12	Bertie
1.1359	40.6	.3912	13	Coastal
1.1359	40.6	.2513	19	Stephenson
1.1353	40.6	.6025	9	breaths
1.1353	40.6	.3567	14	empires
1.1349	40.5	.3608	12	beehive
1.1349	40.5	.4365	12	colonization
1.1347	40.5	.6002	9	issuing
1.1346	40.5	.6094	9	rousing
1.1345	40.5	.5993	9	dismiss
1.1343	40.5	.2217	22	wired
1.1342	40.5	.6144	9	inhospitable
1.1341	40.5	.1193	37	bias
1.1339	40.5	.5354	10	ramparts
1.1336	40.5	.3283	15	eucalyptus
1.1336	40.5	.3983	13	thyself
1.1329	40.5	.4436	12	murderer
1.1324	40.5	.5464	10	1700
1.1323	40.5	.6195	9	instinctive
1.1316	40.5	.5332	10	parson
1.1314	40.5	.3436	15	controversial
1.1314	40.5	.4458	11	pitchblende
1.1313	40.5	.4430	11	monkey's
1.1312	40.5	.3679	13	pawing
1.1311	40.5	.4525	11	countdown
1.1307	40.5	.4899	11	Virgin
1.1305	40.5	.6094	9	booms
1.1302	40.5	.1138	28	raindrop
1.1300	40.5	.6087	9	distressing
1.1293	40.5	.6080	9	motion-picture
1.1292	40.5	.5381	10	salaries
1.1287	40.5	.4581	11	Drug
1.1286	40.5	.5417	10	sidelines
1.1283	40.5	.3591	12	'coon
1.1281	40.5	.1773	23	Ritchie
1.1279	40.5	.5211	10	icing
THE PRECEDING WORD TYPE OCCUPIES RANK 16400				
1.1274	40.5	.3016	16	parasite
1.1272	40.5	.3570	14	Carr
1.1271	40.5	.3199	15	Colonies
1.1271	40.5	.6109	9	Scots
1.1271	40.5	.4727	11	shipments
1.1267	40.5	.5270	10	Training
1.1266	40.5	.6110	9	Adriatic
1.1266	40.5	.3782	13	starry
1.1265	40.5	.4858	10	Goddess
1.1264	40.5	.6012	9	full-length
1.1262	40.5	.3989	13	Jean's
1.1259	40.5	.6057	9	upwards
1.1259	40.5	.4411	12	3rd
1.1258	40.5	.5937	9	undressed
1.1253	40.5	.4743	11	Jacksonville
1.1251	40.5	.5925	9	initiated
1.1251	40.5	.4189	12	propel
1.1250	40.5	.4191	12	bishops
1.1247	40.5	.4843	10	plaintiff
1.1246	40.5	.3167	16	varnish
1.1244	40.5	.3426	14	garter
1.1243	40.5	.5949	9	Days
1.1242	40.5	.4221	12	delegation
1.1240	40.5	.4312	12	grieved
1.1239	40.5	.4848	11	Almanac
1.1239	40.5	.4313	12	sessions
1.1238	40.5	.4844	10	doorknob
1.1234	40.5	.5903	9	hindered
1.1234	40.5	.4726	11	wig
1.1232	40.5	.3312	14	nightingale
1.1231	40.5	.6081	9	austere
1.1229	40.5	.5941	9	gentleness
1.1228	40.5	.6025	9	easing
1.1225	40.5	.3965	13	tariffs
1.1220	40.5	.5891	9	catastrophe
1.1216	40.5	.4604	11	interpreter
1.1216	40.5	.2438	19	Lo
1.1215	40.5	.5074	10	shoveling
1.1214	40.5	.5345	10	sanitation
1.1212	40.5	.5259	10	communicated
1.1211	40.5	.4410	12	Chapters
1.1210	40.5	.4452	11	Read
1.1210	40.5	.4497	11	treason
1.1209	40.5	.3908	13	witchcraft
1.1208	40.5	.4740	11	appoint
1.1206	40.5	.0578	50	Birdie
1.1203	40.5	.5039	10	overtook
1.1201	40.5	.4803	11	additives
1.1199	40.5	.6011	9	audible
1.1198	40.5	.4373	11	bragged
1.1196	40.5	.4265	12	countenance
1.1193	40.5	.5951	9	striving
1.1191	40.5	.2515	20	ee
1.1186	40.5	.5640	9	tomboy
1.1183	40.5	.5323	10	nomadic
1.1183	40.5	.6074	9	skyline
1.1181	40.5	.4736	10	so's
1.1181	40.5	.3509	14	southernmost
1.1181	40.5	.3586	13	suitors
1.1180	40.5	.5430	10	275
1.1178	40.5	.5147	10	rustled
1.1177	40.5	.5918	9	lashing
1.1175	40.5	.3406	14	short-wave
1.1175	40.5	.4295	12	tuberculosis
1.1174	40.5	.4838	10	candlesticks
1.1174	40.5	.3740	12	latch
1.1173	40.5	.5315	10	islanders
1.1171	40.5	.3815	12	Gomez
1.1165	40.5	.3373	16	mesa
1.1165	40.5	.2639	17	Presidency
1.1163	40.5	.4732	10	wastebasket
1.1162	40.5	.5144	10	termite
1.1161	40.5	.1885	23	Elk
1.1161	40.5	.4019	12	reappeared
1.1160	40.5	.3042	17	bookcase
1.1160	40.5	.2722	18	diversity
1.1157	40.5	.5856	9	overpowering
1.1156	40.5	.5369	10	strove
1.1154	40.5	.4818	10	leapt
1.1153	40.5	.4157	12	there'd
1.1150	40.5	.4710	10	intending
1.1148	40.5	.4860	11	bulging
1.1148	40.5	.5122	10	nothing's
1.1147	40.5	.5270	10	rout
1.1144	40.5	.4810	10	slew
1.1144	40.5	.4810	10	ungainly
1.1143	40.5	.4445	11	bugles
1.1143	40.5	.5970	9	heedless
1.1143	40.5	.3497	14	isthmus
1.1143	40.5	.5869	9	preside
1.1142	40.5	.4164	12	Giovanni
1.1142	40.5	.2457	19	paneling
1.1139	40.5	.5974	9	reigns
1.1137	40.5	.3501	12	flat-topped
1.1137	40.5	.4712	10	Marilyn
1.1135	40.5	.5119	10	pigtails
1.1133	40.5	.5977	9	222
1.1132	40.5	.5097	10	pheasants
1.1131	40.5	.3234	15	Todd
1.1131	40.5	.4605	11	1885
THE PRECEDING WORD TYPE OCCUPIES RANK 16500				
1.1130	40.5	.0181	48	Middletown
1.1130	40.5	.3425	14	terrace
1.1129	40.5	.5577	9	scoffed
1.1129	40.5	.3540	13	thinly
1.1128	40.5	.4351	11	Madrid
1.1126	40.5	.4203	12	sinew
1.1124	40.5	.5114	10	scornful
1.1118	40.5	.4351	12	radiating
1.1117	40.5	.4595	11	apricots
1.1116	40.5	.4826	11	twenties
1.1113	40.5	.3386	14	Herodotus
1.1110	40.5	.5870	9	tranquil
1.1108	40.5	.4197	12	sweeper
1.1106	40.5	.3709	14	misspell
1.1104	40.5	.6013	9	Elements
1.1101	40.5	.3463	13	's
1.1101	40.5	.6723	8	translating
1.1099	40.5	.0603	55	Mozart
1.1099	40.5	.4357	11	nuggets
1.1097	40.5	.4591	11	Malaysia
1.1097	40.5	.6720	8	1840
1.1093	40.5	.3347	15	Lois
1.1092	40.5	.5156	10	open-air
1.1092	40.5	.5226	10	raisin
1.1091	40.4	.3071	16	nitrate
1.1089	40.4	.4838	11	Dove
1.1088	40.4	.3766	12	Hodges
1.1087	40.4	.3589	13	crowed
1.1087	40.4	.3712	13	Puritan
1.1086	40.4	.4537	11	Bronx
1.1085	40.4	.4444	11	forty-eight
1.1083	40.4	.3991	13	locally
1.1081	40.4	.4715	10	watertight
1.1076	40.4	.4677	11	indigo
1.1075	40.4	.3849	13	Vincennes
1.1075	40.4	.5172	10	voluntarily
1.1074	40.4	.5829	9	ignite
1.1074	40.4	.3851	13	Ministers
1.1074	40.4	.5047	10	muskrat
1.1074	40.4	.5265	10	rearranging
1.1072	40.4	.2564	19	gourds
1.1070	40.4	.5782	9	supervise
1.1069	40.4	.6680	8	thirty-one
1.1068	40.4	.6056	9	futile
1.1064	40.4	.4360	12	End
1.1063	40.4	.2925	15	Lionel
1.1056	40.4	.3772	13	Alexandria
1.1055	40.4	.4639	10	ambled
1.1054	40.4	.5592	9	hover
1.1051	40.4	.4637	10	boat's
1.1049	40.4	.5400	10	allotted
1.1048	40.4	.4465	11	Watt
1.1046	40.4	.5057	10	shrilly
1.1046	40.4	.5591	9	woodlands
1.1045	40.4	.4580	11	Colony
1.1044	40.4	.4356	12	ba
1.1043	40.4	.3565	14	convex
1.1042	40.4	.1564	29	ous
1.1038	40.4	.0161	99	tonal
1.1035	40.4	.4455	12	repetitions
1.1033	40.4	.5859	9	violation
1.1028	40.4	.6648	8	wrestle
1.1027	40.4	.3749	13	Sing
1.1023	40.4	.5072	10	asphalt
1.1023	40.4	.5172	10	propulsion
1.1021	40.4	.5321	10	du
1.1021	40.4	.2393	18	solvent
1.1016	40.4	.4136	12	Justin
1.1015	40.4	.5348	10	stark
1.1015	40.4	.3596	13	understandings
1.1012	40.4	.4574	11	broods
1.1011	40.4	.4746	10	red-faced
1.1009	40.4	.5871	9	premium
1.1007	40.4	.5009	10	sheaves
1.1006	40.4	.5145	10	looped
1.1004	40.4	.5305	10	As
1.0999	40.4	.5608	9	grunt
1.0999	40.4	.4626	11	165
1.0995	40.4	.5264	10	Finnish
1.0995	40.4	.4605	11	SanFrancisco's
1.0992	40.4	.3129	15	Attorney
1.0990	40.4	.5263	10	Balkan
1.0989	40.4	.4654	11	papal
1.0987	40.4	.4688	10	Jordan's
1.0985	40.4	.5195	10	illustrious
1.0984	40.4	.5280	10	archaeology
1.0984	40.4	.5121	10	spicy
1.0983	40.4	.2606	17	Hawaiians
1.0982	40.4	.1630	16	Juliana
1.0982	40.4	.5923	9	merge
1.0982	40.4	.3099	16	Nov
1.0981	40.4	.5844	9	offend
1.0981	40.4	.4577	10	sixty-four
1.0980	40.4	.4444	11	herons
1.0980	40.4	.5215	10	pangs
1.0978	40.4	.3754	13	313
1.0977	40.4	.2045	23	Wagner
1.0976	40.4	.5950	9	explicit
1.0976	40.4	.4486	11	quilting
1.0973	40.4	.5279	10	schemes
THE PRECEDING WORD TYPE OCCUPIES RANK 16600				
1.0973	40.4	.5117	10	1836
1.0971	40.4	.5731	9	insulted
1.0966	40.4	.5141	10	endangered
1.0966	40.4	.5580	9	magicians
1.0964	40.4	.3212	15	Chrysler
1.0964	40.4	.0000	24	Colter
1.0964	40.4	.5305	10	Leader
1.0964	40.4	.0000	24	Pakaa
1.0964	40.4	.0000	24	Sweeney
1.0963	40.4	.1612	23	Woodlawn
1.0961	40.4	.1203	31	Nixon's
1.0960	40.4	.5681	9	Some
1.0958	40.4	.3250	12	earmarks
1.0957	40.4	.4722	10	ascended
1.0957	40.4	.5099	10	Joshua
1.0956	40.4	.4232	12	Slavs
1.0955	40.4	.5927	9	committing
1.0954	40.4	.5801	9	Through
1.0953	40.4	.5873	9	eloquent
1.0952	40.4	.2402	20	-ion
1.0952	40.4	.2480	17	ape
1.0950	40.4	.5835	9	elegance
1.0947	40.4	.4694	10	pacing
1.0945	40.4	.4860	10	nursed
1.0945	40.4	.3396	14	salts
1.0945	40.4	.4646	11	watershed
1.0944	40.4	.3492	12	Diego
1.0943	40.4	.4698	10	housekeeper
1.0942	40.4	.4790	10	whoops
1.0939	40.4	.5839	9	flaring
1.0938	40.4	.5248	10	Marquis
1.0937	40.4	.5709	9	continual
1.0936	40.4	.4986	10	blue-white
1.0935	40.4	.6637	8	mid-air
1.0934	40.4	.5775	9	guarantees
1.0933	40.4	.4115	12	choke
1.0931	40.4	.5801	9	porches
1.0931	40.4	.4067	12	Reservation
1.0931	40.4	.5023	10	sagged
1.0931	40.4	.2571	14	Sleepy
1.0928	40.4	.5120	10	momentous
1.0927	40.4	.5071	10	Capital
1.0923	40.4	.5222	10	unquestionably
1.0922	40.4	.3688	13	planet's
1.0919	40.4	.4277	11	Chorus
1.0918	40.4	.3389	14	Problem
1.0916	40.4	.4602	11	enlisted
1.0916	40.4	.5802	9	pension
1.0913	40.4	.4695	10	Remington
1.0911	40.4	.5235	10	marginal
1.0910	40.4	.2445	18	Paleozoic
1.0909	40.4	.4448	11	bounding
1.0908	40.4	.5778	9	kingly
1.0908	40.4	.5805	9	unwanted
1.0906	40.4	.5848	9	improves
1.0906	40.4	.2622	18	theoretical
1.0905	40.4	.4432	11	Warner
1.0900	40.4	.4158	12	Rolfe
1.0898	40.4	.3472	12	redder
1.0895	40.4	.4775	10	playmates
1.0892	40.4	.5021	10	bubbled
1.0892	40.4	.5515	9	easygoing
1.0889	40.4	.5839	9	148
1.0888	40.4	.5745	9	gorges
1.0887	40.4	.6596	8	never-ending
1.0887	40.4	.5178	10	thereof
1.0887	40.4	.6601	8	wanderer
1.0886	40.4	.4603	11	graves
1.0883	40.4	.4999	10	bombardment
1.0883	40.4	.5191	10	forcefully
1.0882	40.4	.4794	10	Pigeon
1.0881	40.4	.2435	19	ironing
1.0880	40.4	.2919	14	Dogs
1.0880	40.4	.4325	11	thatched
1.0879	40.4	.5182	10	revenue
1.0878	40.4	.4903	10	boosted
1.0875	40.4	.4790	10	Rice
1.0872	40.4	.1219	32	Who
1.0869	40.4	.4642	10	long-legged
1.0868	40.4	.4196	12	Kilimanjaro
1.0868	40.4	.4604	11	nutmeg
1.0867	40.4	.5052	10	vultures

U	SFI	D	F	Word Type
1.0867	40.4	.5108	10	Works
1.0863	40.4	.5192	10	Jesuit
1.0859	40.4	.2179	19	yah
1.0858	40.4	.5073	10	enclosing
1.0858	40.4	.4215	12	sanitary
1.0857	40.4	.5741	9	inscription
1.0856	40.4	.3988	12	cheat
1.0856	40.4	.3988	12	oaths
1.0855	40.4	.6670	8	1100
1.0854	40.4	.3715	13	firelight
1.0854	40.4	.4327	12	seasoned
1.0852	40.4	.5531	9	powerfully
1.0852	40.4	.5125	10	slunk
1.0850	40.4	.5528	9	Titus
1.0849	40.4	.5229	10	testify
1.0848	40.4	.2835	17	Donkey
1.0848	40.4	.5031	10	fowls
1.0844	40.4	.2497	17	hormone
THE PRECEDING WORD TYPE OCCUPIES RANK 16700				
1.0843	40.4	.1956	24	two-part
1.0841	40.4	.5136	10	rites
1.0839	40.3	.2401	18	cartilage
1.0838	40.3	.1528	29	nutrition
1.0838	40.3	.3785	11	Quixote
1.0837	40.3	.3781	13	suicide
1.0836	40.3	.5772	9	teller
1.0833	40.3	.5506	9	senseless
1.0830	40.3	.5156	10	bail
1.0825	40.3	.5665	9	racks
1.0825	40.3	.5869	9	standpoint
1.0823	40.3	.5234	10	flared
1.0820	40.3	.2999	16	Chiang
1.0820	40.3	.5904	9	Victorian
1.0819	40.3	.5913	9	reacting
1.0819	40.3	.4491	11	weightlessness
1.0816	40.3	.4138	12	Notre
1.0814	40.3	.4162	12	sparsely
1.0813	40.3	.3414	14	germinate
1.0812	40.3	.5862	9	heron
1.0810	40.3	.3351	12	Huckleberry
1.0804	40.3	.5031	10	pops
1.0802	40.3	.3710	13	milky
1.0797	40.3	.5250	10	graded
1.0796	40.3	.5753	9	admirable
1.0796	40.3	.4574	11	persuasion
1.0793	40.3	.5480	9	forgetful
1.0793	40.3	.4771	10	sue
1.0790	40.3	.3741	12	ruffles
1.0787	40.3	.5092	10	rejection
1.0786	40.3	.4974	10	inscribed
1.0781	40.3	.5162	10	VII
1.0780	40.3	.2361	14	teapots
1.0776	40.3	.4504	11	descendant
1.0776	40.3	.4716	10	scuttled
1.0775	40.3	.5572	9	prancing
1.0774	40.3	.4136	12	rouse
1.0773	40.3	.2712	17	Muslims
1.0773	40.3	.4287	11	uh-huh
1.0771	40.3	.5660	9	homestead
1.0770	40.3	.6662	8	girth
1.0769	40.3	.4233	12	productions
1.0768	40.3	.5094	10	comedies
1.0766	40.3	.5193	10	contention
1.0766	40.3	.3204	15	roan
1.0764	40.3	.4969	10	delays
1.0761	40.3	.2693	17	$12
1.0761	40.3	.5492	9	eighty-five
1.0760	40.3	.3611	13	abdominal
1.0760	40.3	.1105	27	beaker
1.0756	40.3	.5007	10	acorn
1.0755	40.3	.4838	10	unlocked
1.0755	40.3	.2479	18	336
1.0750	40.3	.4280	11	python
1.0749	40.3	.4663	11	Virgil
1.0748	40.3	.5095	10	Euphrates
1.0748	40.3	.4220	11	spokesman
1.0747	40.3	.5011	10	Spanish-American
1.0743	40.3	.5548	9	maneuvering
1.0742	40.3	.3400	14	therapy
1.0739	40.3	.4125	12	liable
1.0738	40.3	.1854	27	lettering
1.0737	40.3	.4995	10	rheumatic
1.0736	40.3	.5066	10	enacted
1.0735	40.3	.5159	10	disturbance
1.0734	40.3	.3177	14	interplanetary
1.0734	40.3	.2433	14	Pamela
1.0728	40.3	.2753	16	LaSalle
1.0728	40.3	.4730	10	moles
1.0727	40.3	.5813	9	Swedes
1.0726	40.3	.4661	10	trickery
1.0726	40.3	.4661	10	William's
1.0725	40.3	.4940	10	essence
1.0725	40.3	.4681	11	1066
1.0722	40.3	.4063	12	admiral
1.0720	40.3	.3559	13	quivered
1.0718	40.3	.4690	10	wrestling
1.0717	40.3	.3706	11	Dancing
1.0717	40.3	.5216	10	omitting
1.0717	40.3	.3629	13	planetary
1.0717	40.3	.5726	9	sidewise
1.0716	40.3	.4988	10	Lions
1.0714	40.3	.2097	16	Pig
1.0714	40.3	.2273	14	rhino
1.0712	40.3	.4233	11	turret
1.0709	40.3	.5083	10	supposing
1.0708	40.3	.3665	13	cone-shaped
1.0708	40.3	.4038	12	navigable
1.0708	40.3	.3066	15	offstage
1.0707	40.3	.5409	9	veranda
1.0702	40.3	.4162	12	Barbary
1.0702	40.3	.5840	9	emphasizing
1.0702	40.3	.4445	11	walnuts
1.0700	40.3	.1822	15	O'Malley
1.0700	40.3	.5482	9	Wade
1.0698	40.3	.5563	9	earthen
1.0697	40.3	.0613	54	syllabic
1.0695	40.3	.4661	10	disbelief
1.0689	40.3	.5753	9	prominence
1.0689	40.3	.4486	11	slogans
THE PRECEDING WORD TYPE OCCUPIES RANK 16800				
1.0687	40.3	.4942	10	imperial
1.0687	40.3	.3738	13	Newcastle
1.0687	40.3	.2560	17	pupa
1.0686	40.3	.3341	12	cougar
1.0682	40.3	.5469	9	Award
1.0680	40.3	.4629	10	Perkins
1.0679	40.3	.5651	9	interestingly
1.0678	40.3	.5639	9	beaters
1.0678	40.3	.3924	12	light-year
1.0676	40.3	.2730	16	Saudi
1.0675	40.3	.4815	10	balconies
1.0675	40.3	.5096	10	Sandburg
1.0675	40.3	.3735	11	skinks
1.0675	40.3	.5053	10	Staff
1.0674	40.3	.3566	14	adieu
1.0674	40.3	.5775	9	small-town
1.0673	40.3	.4417	11	Wilhelm
1.0672	40.3	.2165	14	Jolly
1.0672	40.3	.2165	14	Nightingale
1.0672	40.3	.4941	10	star's
1.0667	40.3	.4017	12	Shepherd
1.0666	40.3	.4943	10	Butte
1.0664	40.3	.2730	16	pinwheel
1.0662	40.3	.3056	15	Ottoman
1.0661	40.3	.4645	10	scampering
1.0656	40.3	.4548	11	hysterically
1.0654	40.3	.5485	9	noiselessly
1.0653	40.3	.3909	12	mealtimes
1.0650	40.3	.3869	11	Falcon
1.0650	40.3	.4566	10	skater
1.0645	40.3	.3489	14	1-10
1.0638	40.3	.5138	10	philosophical
1.0635	40.3	.5126	10	flourishes
1.0631	40.3	.3802	11	scallops
1.0630	40.3	.5680	9	shrewd
1.0628	40.3	.4221	11	haw
1.0627	40.3	.5644	9	topple
1.0625	40.3	.5533	9	healthier
1.0625	40.3	.4032	12	1620
1.0623	40.3	.5449	9	fortnight
1.0621	40.3	.5769	9	hues
1.0620	40.3	.4994	10	weaknesses
1.0619	40.3	.5691	9	scaled
1.0615	40.3	.1648	22	cilia
1.0615	40.3	.4309	11	heaven's
1.0615	40.3	.6263	8	soberly
1.0614	40.3	.5603	9	closeness
1.0613	40.3	.4813	10	nobody's
1.0612	40.3	.3636	11	Laughing
1.0611	40.3	.6260	8	lessened
1.0611	40.3	.4134	12	Vincent
1.0608	40.3	.4453	11	hitter
1.0608	40.3	.3854	11	Maury
1.0608	40.3	.5349	9	truthful
1.0607	40.3	.3752	11	rapped
1.0607	40.3	.3604	13	Salvador
1.0606	40.3	.5052	10	substitutes
1.0603	40.3	.4156	12	weaves
1.0600	40.3	.3047	14	borax
1.0600	40.3	.4477	11	Ceylon
1.0598	40.3	.4969	10	indentured
1.0597	40.3	.4853	10	shuffle
1.0595	40.3	.3866	11	shakily
1.0590	40.2	.2224	19	ellipse
1.0589	40.2	.4609	10	germanium
1.0587	40.2	.4095	11	Moose
1.0581	40.2	.4147	11	Bowman
1.0580	40.2	.4834	10	flicker
1.0580	40.2	.6248	8	tantalizing
1.0579	40.2	.2457	17	niece
1.0574	40.2	.3577	14	reinforce
1.0571	40.2	.5597	9	gunners
1.0570	40.2	.4043	12	Beaumont
1.0567	40.2	.5321	9	makeshift
1.0567	40.2	.0895	38	respellings
1.0567	40.2	.5321	9	tinder
1.0567	40.2	.2608	18	425
1.0566	40.2	.5768	9	publications
1.0562	40.2	.4411	11	screened
1.0559	40.2	.5570	9	capacities
1.0558	40.2	.4789	10	how'd
1.0558	40.2	.6211	8	Joaquin
1.0557	40.2	.1440	25	1/100
1.0554	40.2	.4493	11	botanical
1.0553	40.2	.3820	13	snips
1.0553	40.2	.4204	11	weariness
1.0550	40.2	.2220	18	alcoholic
1.0544	40.2	.5580	9	halts
1.0544	40.2	.4225	11	herders
1.0544	40.2	.5597	9	unconsciously
1.0543	40.2	.4434	11	drone
1.0542	40.2	.5293	9	Police
1.0541	40.2	.6244	8	splendidly
1.0541	40.2	.3842	12	suds
1.0538	40.2	.5084	10	muted
1.0538	40.2	.6377	8	nonstop
1.0535	40.2	.4144	12	Conservatory
1.0530	40.2	.3671	13	generalization
1.0529	40.2	.5062	10	Movement
1.0525	40.2	.4867	10	282
THE PRECEDING WORD TYPE OCCUPIES RANK 16900				
1.0523	40.2	.4002	12	Province
1.0522	40.2	.5566	9	cranberry
1.0521	40.2	.5008	10	hardwoods
1.0520	40.2	.3759	13	browned
1.0519	40.2	.4503	11	circulated
1.0517	40.2	.4706	10	suitcases
1.0515	40.2	.5628	9	tolerant
1.0514	40.2	.5580	9	glides
1.0514	40.2	.5542	9	in-between
1.0509	40.2	.5789	9	harmonious
1.0507	40.2	.0000	23	Hennessey
1.0507	40.2	.4756	10	living-room
1.0507	40.2	.0000	23	Marvello
1.0507	40.2	.0000	23	Ricardo
1.0507	40.2	.0000	23	Yasu
1.0506	40.2	.4929	10	1808
1.0505	40.2	.3899	12	pill
1.0502	40.2	.3659	13	Come
1.0501	40.2	.4372	11	fancied
1.0499	40.2	.3662	12	Mona
1.0498	40.2	.5252	9	sleepers
1.0495	40.2	.4791	10	Luigi
1.0490	40.2	.5354	9	blindly
1.0490	40.2	.4745	10	Brownie
1.0486	40.2	.4332	11	conveyed
1.0483	40.2	.4511	10	exchanging
1.0483	40.2	.4601	11	For
1.0483	40.2	.4344	11	Wilkes
1.0481	40.2	.3795	13	workmanship
1.0478	40.2	.2909	15	breastbone
1.0478	40.2	.0000	70	denominators
1.0473	40.2	.4844	10	consul
1.0473	40.2	.4718	10	plea
1.0469	40.2	.4367	11	converts
1.0469	40.2	.0000	129	3-Star
1.0466	40.2	.5378	9	friends'
1.0464	40.2	.2831	15	plaid
1.0461	40.2	.4988	10	Ronald
1.0459	40.2	.5378	9	troupe
1.0457	40.2	.2359	19	Licks
1.0457	40.2	.4841	10	ya
1.0454	40.2	.5315	9	changeable
1.0454	40.2	.2337	19	closure
1.0454	40.2	.5377	9	Sacred
1.0453	40.2	.4832	10	airfields
1.0451	40.2	.5565	9	sheen
1.0450	40.2	.3425	14	brooch
1.0447	40.2	.5401	9	Congressman
1.0442	40.2	.5361	9	fingertip
1.0442	40.2	.0449	46	Jiya
1.0442	40.2	.4454	11	worldwide
1.0438	40.2	.3518	14	complementary
1.0437	40.2	.4824	10	envelopes
1.0434	40.2	.3496	14	pliers
1.0432	40.2	.5539	9	kneel
1.0432	40.2	.2514	16	plotted
1.0432	40.2	.4337	11	Savannah
1.0431	40.2	.3475	13	explodes
1.0431	40.2	.4512	10	winking
1.0430	40.2	.4831	10	hinder
1.0429	40.2	.4413	11	novelist
1.0425	40.2	.5391	9	two-wheeled
1.0424	40.2	.3497	13	1858
1.0420	40.2	.6172	8	crisscrossed
1.0420	40.2	.4569	10	mountaintops
1.0415	40.2	.4952	10	lavender
1.0415	40.2	.3845	12	1856
1.0414	40.2	.5521	9	pungent
1.0414	40.2	.5508	9	tendencies
1.0413	40.2	.5502	9	surpassed
1.0412	40.2	.5170	9	outsider
1.0411	40.2	.5305	9	sacrificed
1.0410	40.2	.5701	9	petal
1.0409	40.2	.6173	8	anthill
1.0407	40.2	.4524	11	da
1.0405	40.2	.1685	15	Chanticleer
1.0405	40.2	.1685	15	Teddy's
1.0404	40.2	.4858	10	valentine
1.0401	40.2	.6162	8	clears
1.0401	40.2	.2505	17	Torstein
1.0400	40.2	.5591	9	advantageous
1.0400	40.2	.3496	11	Steven
1.0399	40.2	.4557	10	Larsen
1.0397	40.2	.5541	9	passions
1.0396	40.2	.6165	8	rash
1.0395	40.2	.5395	9	Lancaster
1.0395	40.2	.6156	8	1799
1.0394	40.2	.5005	10	chronic
1.0392	40.2	.3252	14	diatoms
1.0390	40.2	.4825	10	pioneered
1.0389	40.2	.3116	15	Mendelssohn
1.0387	40.2	.3197	14	amphibian
1.0387	40.2	.3976	11	witch's
1.0386	40.2	.5295	9	Operation
1.0386	40.2	.3487	11	pallet
1.0385	40.2	.4935	10	flounder
1.0382	40.2	.4912	10	Canterbury
1.0381	40.2	.5363	9	chases
1.0379	40.2	.3396	12	Angel
1.0378	40.2	.4921	10	gorge
THE PRECEDING WORD TYPE OCCUPIES RANK 17000				
1.0378	40.2	.4846	10	relics
1.0377	40.2	.5460	9	hooted
1.0374	40.2	.5505	9	astute
1.0372	40.2	.4954	10	confidential
1.0368	40.2	.3556	12	nods
1.0365	40.2	.5420	9	injustice
1.0365	40.2	.2520	17	suburban
1.0363	40.2	.3640	11	Fiddler
1.0363	40.2	.2904	16	passive
1.0362	40.2	.6293	8	Owen
1.0361	40.2	.5627	9	cite
1.0361	40.2	.3788	12	Monterey
1.0358	40.2	.4844	10	reacted
1.0357	40.2	.4352	11	congressmen
1.0355	40.2	.3427	12	daughter's
1.0352	40.2	.5518	9	implement
1.0352	40.2	.5321	9	lyre
1.0352	40.2	.2030	22	sculptors
1.0348	40.1	.2302	17	paramecium
1.0347	40.1	.2016	19	Region
1.0346	40.1	.2675	16	$9
1.0346	40.1	.3491	13	Hispaniola
1.0346	40.1	.3108	14	roasting
1.0345	40.1	.4333	11	susceptible
1.0343	40.1	.4804	10	ferries
1.0343	40.1	.4940	10	melodious
1.0343	40.1	.5474	9	undoing
1.0342	40.1	.4442	10	Branch
1.0339	40.1	.5487	9	rustic
1.0339	40.1	.0802	50	vise
1.0337	40.1	.5443	9	denying
1.0335	40.1	.5287	9	surveyor
1.0335	40.1	.5287	9	unfit
1.0333	40.1	.5502	9	infinity
1.0332	40.1	.2005	21	shearing
1.0331	40.1	.4474	11	6-8
1.0329	40.1	.4001	11	farmhouses
1.0327	40.1	.4703	10	campfires
1.0323	40.1	.4855	10	Authority
1.0320	40.1	.3849	12	groping
1.0320	40.1	.4439	11	Mme
1.0320	40.1	.4468	11	tensions
1.0320	40.1	.4447	10	wick
1.0319	40.1	.4827	10	pocketbook
1.0316	40.1	.3154	15	complements
1.0315	40.1	.5487	9	317
1.0314	40.1	.4882	10	distraction
1.0312	40.1	.5562	9	one-inch
1.0309	40.1	.4770	10	bombed
1.0308	40.1	.4362	11	drastic
1.0308	40.1	.6151	8	dryly
1.0306	40.1	.3867	12	1873
1.0302	40.1	.4352	11	Carthage
1.0302	40.1	.5277	9	self-respect
1.0302	40.1	.3909	12	spherical
1.0301	40.1	.4933	10	modification
1.0300	40.1	.4108	11	Australia's
1.0300	40.1	.5485	9	Cold
1.0299	40.1	.5383	9	loser
1.0296	40.1	.3095	15	cuff
1.0296	40.1	.2729	15	iris
1.0295	40.1	.5279	9	telltale
1.0293	40.1	.5291	9	Sparta
1.0293	40.1	.4300	11	tanker
1.0285	40.1	.4532	10	guts
1.0282	40.1	.4948	10	decidedly
1.0282	40.1	.4122	11	injected
1.0282	40.1	.4411	10	pa
1.0280	40.1	.5438	9	hourly
1.0280	40.1	.5410	9	prick
1.0279	40.1	.1972	14	Blotto
1.0279	40.1	.1972	14	Lars
1.0275	40.1	.4473	10	projectile
1.0274	40.1	.4746	10	hooking
1.0274	40.1	.3509	11	smarter
1.0273	40.1	.4738	10	bronco
1.0271	40.1	.6134	8	temperament
1.0267	40.1	.3343	14	Lindsay
1.0267	40.1	.5148	9	Poor
1.0267	40.1	.6130	8	pulpit
1.0266	40.1	.5306	9	chugged
1.0265	40.1	.2819	16	Judaism
1.0265	40.1	.5427	9	regretted
1.0264	40.1	.6093	8	disprove
1.0263	40.1	.5222	9	chow
1.0263	40.1	.4201	11	squall
1.0262	40.1	.3896	11	entangled
1.0262	40.1	.4536	10	Guatemala
1.0259	40.1	.4244	11	154
1.0258	40.1	.5335	9	fictional
1.0257	40.1	.5364	9	interruption
1.0256	40.1	.3105	14	inferences
1.0255	40.1	.5391	9	clanging
1.0246	40.1	.2898	13	Bertha
1.0245	40.1	.4571	10	casing
1.0244	40.1	.3980	11	injection
1.0244	40.1	.4387	11	rejoice
1.0243	40.1	.5256	9	Get
1.0241	40.1	.6081	8	rotted
1.0240	40.1	.5440	9	Cemetery
THE PRECEDING WORD TYPE OCCUPIES RANK 17100				
1.0237	40.1	.3806	12	city-states
1.0237	40.1	.6080	8	proclaim
1.0235	40.1	.2136	19	Countries
1.0233	40.1	.6080	8	flier
1.0233	40.1	.2414	17	nutrient
1.0230	40.1	.5029	9	pats
1.0230	40.1	.5381	9	violate
1.0229	40.1	.4684	10	outraged
1.0223	40.1	.5245	9	croak
1.0221	40.1	.4007	11	sunflowers
1.0221	40.1	.3392	14	Version
1.0217	40.1	.5019	9	giggles
1.0216	40.1	.2844	16	upstage
1.0214	40.1	.5239	9	lunged
1.0212	40.1	.5441	9	Emile
1.0212	40.1	.5365	9	majesty
1.0208	40.1	.4047	11	Galileo's
1.0207	40.1	.3704	12	Leiden
1.0206	40.1	.5386	9	Speech
1.0206	40.1	.5239	9	sworn
1.0203	40.1	.3767	11	Cheyenne
1.0203	40.1	.5396	9	complains
1.0203	40.1	.3767	11	Secretariat
1.0200	40.1	.3768	12	soaps
1.0198	40.1	.2541	16	Malcolm
1.0198	40.1	.4700	10	party's
1.0197	40.1	.3212	14	poise
1.0195	40.1	.4649	10	eardrums
1.0194	40.1	.3992	12	Celts
1.0194	40.1	.4296	11	minstrels
1.0193	40.1	.5242	9	unwound
1.0188	40.1	.4314	11	$18
1.0188	40.1	.0950	32	Pullman
1.0188	40.1	.6018	8	rot
1.0187	40.1	.5196	9	Leipzig
1.0187	40.1	.3555	13	seizure
1.0186	40.1	.3891	11	drowning
1.0185	40.1	.5441	9	licensed
1.0184	40.1	.5436	9	marines
1.0184	40.1	.5317	9	swished
1.0184	40.1	.4862	10	threatens
1.0182	40.1	.3584	12	Libya
1.0182	40.1	.4651	10	melons
1.0181	40.1	.4243	11	Ethiopians
1.0180	40.1	.4266	11	168

U	SFI	D	F	Word Type
1.0179	40.1	.5245	9	restrain
1.0178	40.1	.3036	14	dreadfully
1.0177	40.1	.1546	20	dent
1.0176	40.1	.3752	11	it'd
1.0176	40.1	.2999	14	sheriff's
1.0175	40.1	.4362	10	chuckling
1.0175	40.1	.5387	9	Orleans
1.0175	40.1	.2785	17	pose
1.0175	40.1	.2108	21	Thee
1.0173	40.1	.5088	9	eyeing
1.0171	40.1	.3502	13	1916
1.0169	40.1	.4959	10	Kenneth
1.0166	40.1	.4844	10	emerges
1.0165	40.1	.6182	8	peculiarly
1.0163	40.1	.5185	9	grievances
1.0162	40.1	.4484	10	hasten
1.0158	40.1	.4194	11	President-elect
1.0155	40.1	.5452	9	refreshed
1.0155	40.1	.5397	9	warship
1.0154	40.1	.3164	15	media
1.0152	40.1	.3691	12	inorganic
1.0152	40.1	.5267	9	uniformity
1.0151	40.1	.5201	9	morning's
1.0146	40.1	.3034	15	salutation
1.0145	40.1	.1906	14	Arachne
1.0145	40.1	.1906	14	falcon
1.0144	40.1	.5297	9	153
1.0142	40.1	.5397	9	charred
1.0142	40.1	.2592	18	petticoat
1.0141	40.1	.0602	52	unaccented
1.0140	40.1	.3712	12	coverings
1.0134	40.1	.5487	9	122
1.0130	40.1	.4436	10	haymow
1.0130	40.1	.4436	10	heaving
1.0129	40.1	.6018	8	rehearsing
1.0128	40.1	.5170	9	Adam's
1.0128	40.1	.5383	9	intends
1.0128	40.1	.5186	9	1759
1.0127	40.1	.5504	9	aroma
1.0126	40.1	.3210	14	Jess
1.0126	40.1	.5453	9	mastering
1.0125	40.1	.6028	8	anguish
1.0125	40.1	.4185	11	Manchu
1.0124	40.1	.5427	9	Congressional
1.0124	40.1	.1310	26	tonic
1.0123	40.1	.4649	10	yep
1.0122	40.1	.4512	10	sweating
1.0118	40.1	.2395	13	huskies
1.0117	40.1	.5158	9	cleverly
1.0117	40.1	.4529	10	rumor
1.0116	40.0	.0321	55	Otis
1.0114	40.0	.4043	11	distressed
1.0111	40.0	.4232	11	Trade
1.0110	40.0	.6274	8	formality
1.0110	40.0	.3935	11	Magnus

THE PRECEDING WORD TYPE OCCUPIES RANK 17200

U	SFI	D	F	Word Type
1.0110	40.0	.5408	9	pesos
1.0107	40.0	.5215	9	orbited
1.0102	40.0	.4057	11	damages
1.0101	40.0	.4117	10	Straw
1.0097	40.0	.5030	9	attackers
1.0096	40.0	.4176	11	Johnsons
1.0096	40.0	.4729	10	solitude
1.0094	40.0	.4790	9	bandit
1.0094	40.0	.5380	9	highlights
1.0094	40.0	.4789	9	plane's
1.0094	40.0	.4790	9	sheepskin
1.0093	40.0	.6104	8	scrapes
1.0092	40.0	.4876	9	hi-fi
1.0091	40.0	.1879	14	Bozo
1.0091	40.0	.1879	14	Brutus
1.0088	40.0	.1468	20	Odette
1.0085	40.0	.5151	9	quake
1.0084	40.0	.5341	9	secrete
1.0083	40.0	.5321	9	long-term
1.0081	40.0	.4297	10	admiringly
1.0081	40.0	.6018	8	matter-of-fact
1.0080	40.0	.2273	19	colon
1.0079	40.0	.5244	9	peppermint
1.0076	40.0	.4400	10	colleague
1.0075	40.0	.5367	9	daisy
1.0073	40.0	.4631	10	summits
1.0071	40.0	.4837	9	octopuses
1.0070	40.0	.4704	10	teaspoons
1.0069	40.0	.4831	9	fixes
1.0069	40.0	.4665	10	frustration
1.0067	40.0	.5286	9	breaker
1.0067	40.0	.3764	12	vermiculite
1.0065	40.0	.4635	10	inspectors
1.0064	40.0	.4527	10	engine's
1.0062	40.0	.4649	10	encloses
1.0060	40.0	.5312	9	mute
1.0060	40.0	.0279	50	parallelogram
1.0057	40.0	.2510	17	ruffle
1.0055	40.0	.3496	12	that'd
1.0054	40.0	.3618	11	flyway
1.0053	40.0	.3059	12	Emperor's
1.0052	40.0	.4989	9	abuse
1.0051	40.0	.3967	11	248
1.0050	40.0	.0000	22	Chi-Wee
1.0050	40.0	.0000	22	Dilly
1.0050	40.0	.0000	22	Gessler
1.0050	40.0	.0000	22	Haji
1.0050	40.0	.0000	22	Lavendar
1.0050	40.0	.0000	22	Onak
1.0050	40.0	.0000	22	Wol
1.0049	40.0	.5224	9	432
1.0047	40.0	.3416	13	Wolfgang
1.0044	40.0	.3980	11	1851
1.0042	40.0	.4729	10	consulting
1.0042	40.0	.6058	8	impractical
1.0042	40.0	.4733	10	steamers
1.0039	40.0	.5942	8	expertly
1.0033	40.0	.2731	15	Australians
1.0033	40.0	.2393	13	Palos
1.0033	40.0	.5101	9	trudging
1.0033	40.0	.6006	8	171
1.0032	40.0	.4676	10	besieged
1.0029	40.0	.5975	8	Child's
1.0029	40.0	.1137	24	Wilma
1.0028	40.0	.4182	11	Bailey
1.0027	40.0	.2381	16	vaccines
1.0026	40.0	.5074	9	Senior
1.0024	40.0	.5376	9	bruises
1.0024	40.0	.5339	9	contradiction
1.0017	40.0	.4258	11	crises
1.0015	40.0	.4245	11	Folk
1.0014	40.0	.1074	25	Buttons
1.0012	40.0	.3646	11	mustangs
1.0012	40.0	.5315	9	Virginia's
1.0011	40.0	.4334	10	Elliott
1.0007	40.0	.5225	9	yelping
1.0006	40.0	.6094	8	adverse
1.0006	40.0	.4646	10	Kennedy's
1.0003	40.0	.5299	9	gnats
1.0003	40.0	.5155	9	tasteless
1.0002	40.0	.4842	9	somersaults
0.9996	40.0	.5427	9	fresher
0.9995	40.0	.4442	10	boatmen
0.9995	40.0	.5165	9	plotting
0.9993	40.0	.5920	8	repose
0.9992	40.0	.4718	10	rump
0.9992	40.0	.4679	10	spindles
0.9989	40.0	.5920	8	quoting
0.9989	40.0	.5024	9	topmost
0.9987	40.0	.3638	12	surfing
0.9986	40.0	.5917	8	steamy
0.9984	40.0	.3423	13	Normans
0.9979	40.0	.6091	8	captors
0.9977	40.0	.5922	8	scurry
0.9977	40.0	.1647	25	ss
0.9977	40.0	.4339	10	sucks
0.9971	40.0	.3433	12	pleases
0.9969	40.0	.4326	10	sauntered
0.9967	40.0	.4673	9	Debbie
0.9967	40.0	.4365	10	Somalis

THE PRECEDING WORD TYPE OCCUPIES RANK 17300

U	SFI	D	F	Word Type
0.9966	40.0	.4698	9	airways
0.9965	40.0	.4048	10	easel
0.9963	40.0	.4672	9	crossbar
0.9960	40.0	.4352	10	exterminated
0.9960	40.0	.5191	9	stainless
0.9959	40.0	.3844	12	6th
0.9958	40.0	.5288	9	clamor
0.9955	40.0	.5060	9	mornin'
0.9954	40.0	.3569	13	Anglo-Saxons
0.9949	40.0	.5898	8	disasters
0.9947	40.0	.4442	10	Root
0.9945	40.0	.5099	9	visibly
0.9941	40.0	.1948	21	Pier
0.9939	40.0	.5878	8	stead
0.9939	40.0	.5879	8	tidings
0.9938	40.0	.5919	8	junction
0.9935	40.0	.4210	11	teen-ager
0.9933	40.0	.5894	8	excesses
0.9933	40.0	.5925	8	schoolteacher
0.9930	40.0	.3672	12	feldspar
0.9930	40.0	.5923	8	preaching
0.9928	40.0	.5140	9	fireflies
0.9928	40.0	.5008	9	mainsail
0.9927	40.0	.5935	8	tortillas
0.9925	40.0	.3330	13	beta
0.9924	40.0	.5283	9	defines
0.9922	40.0	.3774	11	Sixth
0.9921	40.0	.3968	11	baton
0.9921	40.0	.2071	18	caloric
0.9920	40.0	.5034	9	wrapper
0.9919	40.0	.5329	9	brother-in-law
0.9918	40.0	.5923	8	zoologists
0.9917	40.0	.5144	9	regrets
0.9915	40.0	.4580	10	24-hour
0.9914	40.0	.3401	13	induction
0.9914	40.0	.4649	9	Magna
0.9912	40.0	.5677	8	Almighty
0.9908	40.0	.5938	8	Drive
0.9907	40.0	.5652	8	Daisy
0.9907	40.0	.5675	8	unduly
0.9907	40.0	.5675	8	winced
0.9906	40.0	.5660	8	picket
0.9906	40.0	.5651	8	second-floor
0.9904	40.0	.4003	11	Rebecca
0.9904	40.0	.5851	8	relentlessly
0.9903	40.0	.5662	8	bandanna
0.9903	40.0	.6047	8	gypsies
0.9903	40.0	.5334	9	two-week
0.9902	40.0	.5662	8	snore
0.9901	40.0	.5120	9	parasol
0.9900	40.0	.4605	9	gliders
0.9900	40.0	.5111	9	tracking
0.9898	40.0	.5647	8	suns
0.9898	40.0	.4794	9	troll
0.9897	40.0	.4169	10	liar
0.9896	40.0	.4433	10	puddles
0.9893	40.0	.3478	11	champ
0.9893	40.0	.4707	10	epoch
0.9892	40.0	.5013	9	morsel
0.9891	40.0	.4604	9	weeding
0.9891	40.0	.3174	13	whimpered
0.9890	40.0	.2664	15	cirrus
0.9890	40.0	.3188	13	hammerhead
0.9890	40.0	.2420	13	Nagaina
0.9889	40.0	.3787	12	accelerated
0.9889	40.0	.4987	9	do-it-yourself
0.9888	40.0	.4380	10	bull's
0.9888	40.0	.4567	10	213
0.9887	40.0	.3166	13	Belle
0.9887	40.0	.5336	9	typed
0.9886	39.9	.2268	18	Igor
0.9884	39.9	.5126	9	shielded
0.9882	39.9	.4734	10	historically
0.9880	39.9	.3265	14	Opera
0.9878	39.9	.2110	20	Orchestra
0.9876	39.9	.5044	9	clang
0.9876	39.9	.3653	12	clinics
0.9875	39.9	.4113	11	conifers
0.9874	39.9	.4769	9	buddy
0.9873	39.9	.4263	10	bulletins
0.9873	39.9	.3538	11	homing
0.9873	39.9	.3617	13	shellac
0.9872	39.9	.5108	9	responsive
0.9871	39.9	.5610	8	spades
0.9870	39.9	.4171	11	Ludwig
0.9870	39.9	.4765	9	scrimmage
0.9869	39.9	.5600	8	Hand
0.9867	39.9	.5151	9	pinpoint
0.9866	39.9	.5608	8	flopping
0.9864	39.9	.5605	8	caw
0.9862	39.9	.5222	9	Mormons
0.9861	39.9	.4976	9	lovable
0.9860	39.9	.2181	18	motives
0.9860	39.9	.3438	11	Norton
0.9858	39.9	.5601	8	bewilderment
0.9858	39.9	.6030	8	Heights
0.9858	39.9	.5907	8	imperfect
0.9857	39.9	.5888	8	mortgage
0.9854	39.9	.5608	8	flake
0.9847	39.9	.4793	9	fool's

THE PRECEDING WORD TYPE OCCUPIES RANK 17400

U	SFI	D	F	Word Type
0.9845	39.9	.3109	14	arrowheads
0.9844	39.9	.1420	27	improvise
0.9838	39.9	.4296	10	Canton
0.9838	39.9	.0854	40	dynamics
0.9838	39.9	.4801	9	overhanging
0.9837	39.9	.5106	9	Ranger
0.9837	39.9	.1838	22	unscramble
0.9836	39.9	.5873	8	pecans
0.9835	39.9	.5566	8	horseshoes
0.9835	39.9	.5087	9	nameless
0.9834	39.9	.5876	8	jigsaw
0.9832	39.9	.5094	9	hostility
0.9829	39.9	.4310	10	Manchester
0.9829	39.9	.4241	10	rift
0.9829	39.9	.5915	8	saucy
0.9828	39.9	.0433	60	melodic
0.9828	39.9	.3272	13	sovereignty
0.9822	39.9	.4021	11	conforming
0.9821	39.9	.2622	16	congregation
0.9821	39.9	.5863	8	forty-nine
0.9820	39.9	.2550	15	Map
0.9820	39.9	.4548	10	pueblos
0.9818	39.9	.3754	12	enlightened
0.9816	39.9	.5555	8	blistering
0.9816	39.9	.5201	9	rattler
0.9815	39.9	.3911	10	prowl
0.9814	39.9	.4769	9	Seward
0.9812	39.9	.5042	9	acrobats
0.9806	39.9	.4713	9	championships
0.9806	39.9	.4713	9	grumpy
0.9805	39.9	.4426	10	WHAT
0.9802	39.9	.5098	9	discharges
0.9795	39.9	.5625	8	Fairbanks
0.9793	39.9	.5155	9	adjusts
0.9793	39.9	.3310	13	gram
0.9791	39.9	.5285	9	frivolous
0.9791	39.9	.5217	9	VIII
0.9791	39.9	.3864	11	white-hot
0.9790	39.9	.2211	18	e's
0.9789	39.9	.3642	12	educators
0.9789	39.9	.2480	15	overheard
0.9788	39.9	.2041	22	crease
0.9788	39.9	.4548	10	writ
0.9785	39.9	.5255	9	circumstance
0.9785	39.9	.5643	8	generosity
0.9785	39.9	.5644	8	middle-sized
0.9783	39.9	.5965	8	darkening
0.9783	39.9	.5063	9	discern
0.9783	39.9	.5631	8	great-grandfather
0.9783	39.9	.5061	9	incline
0.9779	39.9	.1750	21	Czar
0.9776	39.9	.4590	10	one-way
0.9774	39.9	.4709	9	dude
0.9771	39.9	.5626	8	Gloucester
0.9771	39.9	.2679	15	swans
0.9770	39.9	.4808	9	Boy's
0.9770	39.9	.5953	8	embracing
0.9770	39.9	.5229	9	simulate
0.9769	39.9	.4201	10	repeal
0.9769	39.9	.5847	8	wills
0.9768	39.9	.5558	8	flaw
0.9768	39.9	.5183	9	realistically
0.9765	39.9	.4028	11	hedgehog
0.9763	39.9	.5052	9	barnacles
0.9761	39.9	.4541	10	Tea
0.9758	39.9	.4350	10	putty
0.9757	39.9	.5193	9	picturing
0.9756	39.9	.5181	9	stationery
0.9753	39.9	.5829	8	administer
0.9753	39.9	.5250	9	bounty
0.9753	39.9	.3204	13	Caspian
0.9752	39.9	.4661	10	inspire
0.9750	39.9	.5229	9	Steel
0.9749	39.9	.4495	10	Charlie's
0.9749	39.9	.5822	8	clashed
0.9748	39.9	.3731	10	Crab
0.9748	39.9	.3377	13	Hansen
0.9745	39.9	.5006	9	joyously
0.9744	39.9	.5024	9	pursuers
0.9741	39.9	.3319	13	Prudence
0.9741	39.9	.3319	13	Pyrenees
0.9741	39.9	.4473	10	312
0.9737	39.9	.4524	10	del
0.9737	39.9	.2145	13	Nessie
0.9736	39.9	.3302	13	Hartford
0.9734	39.9	.4858	9	fearfully
0.9732	39.9	.4679	9	filly
0.9730	39.9	.0000	65	addend
0.9730	39.9	.5236	9	impending
0.9728	39.9	.5967	8	stimulating
0.9728	39.9	.2828	14	waterfowl
0.9728	39.9	.4500	10	452
0.9720	39.9	.3707	10	aardvark
0.9720	39.9	.3707	10	sloped
0.9719	39.9	.5919	8	unhealthy
0.9719	39.9	.4063	11	1907
0.9718	39.9	.5803	8	screening
0.9716	39.9	.3601	12	reel
0.9715	39.9	.4998	9	nipped
0.9712	39.9	.5956	8	rallies

THE PRECEDING WORD TYPE OCCUPIES RANK 17500

U	SFI	D	F	Word Type
0.9711	39.9	.4642	9	Eureka
0.9711	39.9	.3962	11	hares
0.9711	39.9	.3645	11	slashed
0.9710	39.9	.5252	9	Back
0.9710	39.9	.4763	9	bidding
0.9710	39.9	.4381	10	Hollow
0.9708	39.9	.4238	10	attaches
0.9707	39.9	.4879	9	merged
0.9704	39.9	.5054	9	Sand
0.9703	39.9	.4418	10	faulty
0.9703	39.9	.4413	10	thrashing
0.9703	39.9	.4226	11	Working
0.9702	39.9	.5031	9	red-haired
0.9701	39.9	.4295	10	Distinguished
0.9701	39.9	.4454	10	triumphs
0.9701	39.9	.3447	12	8000
0.9700	39.9	.4231	10	hating
0.9700	39.9	.5159	9	stigma
0.9699	39.9	.3757	10	lifeboat
0.9698	39.9	.4661	9	Press
0.9696	39.9	.4702	9	shopkeeper
0.9696	39.9	.1741	22	vanishing
0.9695	39.9	.2436	16	circulatory
0.9694	39.9	.4991	9	battleship
0.9694	39.9	.4956	9	dramas
0.9693	39.9	.2560	17	Berliner
0.9687	39.9	.5909	8	boundless
0.9685	39.9	.3546	12	flavors
0.9683	39.9	.5554	8	up-and-down
0.9682	39.9	.3952	11	naught
0.9680	39.9	.3829	10	Amanda
0.9680	39.9	.5204	9	bastard
0.9679	39.9	.4801	9	secondhand
0.9679	39.9	.4622	9	willingly
0.9676	39.9	.3385	13	Korean
0.9676	39.9	.3928	11	woodpeckers
0.9674	39.9	.5198	9	Evil
0.9674	39.9	.4292	10	gobble
0.9674	39.9	.5791	8	Jasper
0.9674	39.9	.4499	10	skeptical
0.9672	39.9	.2047	13	Storm
0.9671	39.9	.4630	9	momentary
0.9669	39.9	.3313	12	Spitz
0.9667	39.9	.3278	12	drones
0.9666	39.9	.3668	10	Butch
0.9666	39.9	.4409	10	Call
0.9665	39.9	.5091	9	advises
0.9665	39.9	.4473	10	Negev
0.9663	39.9	.4295	10	trailers
0.9659	39.8	.5166	9	focuses
0.9659	39.8	.5893	8	proposes
0.9658	39.8	.4629	10	rebirth
0.9656	39.8	.6800	7	exhibiting
0.9656	39.8	.5073	9	prudent
0.9655	39.8	.2949	14	Fermi
0.9654	39.8	.1004	28	inequalities
0.9652	39.8	.5039	9	massacre
0.9652	39.8	.5052	9	science-fiction
0.9650	39.8	.4942	9	scaly
0.9649	39.8	.3765	10	Patrol
0.9649	39.8	.2705	15	Strong
0.9646	39.8	.5576	8	silenced
0.9646	39.8	.5576	8	sorrowfully
0.9645	39.8	.5610	8	businesslike
0.9642	39.8	.4968	9	bloodshed
0.9642	39.8	.1776	20	sin
0.9641	39.8	.5843	8	incapable
0.9641	39.8	.5772	8	virtuous
0.9640	39.8	.4560	10	assassinated
0.9639	39.8	.2029	13	Aeson
0.9635	39.8	.5861	8	Michel
0.9635	39.8	.3649	10	Nine
0.9634	39.8	.3268	12	tripod
0.9633	39.8	.4927	9	Birthday
0.9632	39.8	.4874	9	viewpoint
0.9628	39.8	.4374	10	ghastly
0.9624	39.8	.2489	16	5's
0.9622	39.8	.5070	9	gullies
0.9622	39.8	.3718	11	totem
0.9620	39.8	.3735	11	bee's
0.9620	39.8	.0349	53	Fogg
0.9620	39.8	.5056	9	programmed
0.9619	39.8	.3696	10	smokestack
0.9619	39.8	.4711	9	warpath
0.9614	39.8	.4854	9	kindling
0.9612	39.8	.2348	17	eighths
0.9610	39.8	.5850	8	compelling
0.9608	39.8	.3756	11	wrinkling
0.9607	39.8	.3753	12	cathedrals
0.9604	39.8	.3805	10	Juan's
0.9603	39.8	.5664	8	feud
0.9603	39.8	.5734	8	masthead
0.9603	39.8	.4389	10	Tales
0.9602	39.8	.4914	9	1878
0.9599	39.8	.4691	9	cleverness
0.9596	39.8	.3861	10	Vista
0.9596	39.8	.4925	9	119
0.9593	39.8	.0000	21	Amed
0.9593	39.8	.0000	21	Chick
0.9593	39.8	.0000	21	Fiat

THE PRECEDING WORD TYPE OCCUPIES RANK 17600

U	SFI	D	F	Word Type
0.9593	39.8	.0000	21	Foxy
0.9593	39.8	.0000	21	Spud
0.9593	39.8	.0000	21	Stuey
0.9593	39.8	.0000	21	Tekana
0.9592	39.8	.4935	9	somersault
0.9590	39.8	.5062	9	relaxing
0.9589	39.8	.3357	13	cues
0.9588	39.8	.4940	9	Hat

U	SFI	D	F	Word Type
0.9587	39.8	.5048	9	residue
0.9586	39.8	.3608	10	Pliny
0.9585	39.8	.4609	9	blackberry
0.9584	39.8	.5751	8	utterance
0.9583	39.8	.5065	9	radiates
0.9581	39.8	.3814	10	hoses
0.9581	39.8	.1557	24	Melvin
0.9580	39.8	.1827	23	Delahanty
0.9580	39.8	.0000	64	divisor
0.9580	39.8	.3854	10	gander
0.9580	39.8	.3319	13	Wildlife
0.9577	39.8	.5549	8	sewers
0.9577	39.8	.3602	10	wampum
0.9567	39.8	.5111	9	defining
0.9567	39.8	.4915	9	reminders
0.9566	39.8	.0439	33	protozoans
0.9564	39.8	.4374	10	lipstick
0.9563	39.8	.4382	10	ambitions
0.9562	39.8	.4536	9	ransom
0.9561	39.8	.4910	9	Enrico
0.9560	39.8	.5479	8	despairing
0.9560	39.8	.5153	9	predominant
0.9559	39.8	.5720	8	prosecution
0.9559	39.8	.5482	8	tightrope
0.9558	39.8	.5699	8	conferred
0.9558	39.8	.2148	14	Suds
0.9557	39.8	.3521	11	Norm
0.9555	39.8	.5479	8	sullenly
0.9553	39.8	.4938	9	Comedy
0.9553	39.8	.4447	10	nervousness
0.9553	39.8	.2973	14	Sale
0.9552	39.8	.5756	8	pitted
0.9551	39.8	.1797	21	anthropologists
0.9551	39.8	.5815	8	gaudy
0.9544	39.8	.3253	11	italic
0.9543	39.8	.4460	10	attentive
0.9543	39.8	.4615	10	Everett
0.9541	39.8	.4084	10	frank
0.9541	39.8	.3610	11	Majesty's
0.9539	39.8	.1626	20	protozoa
0.9538	39.8	.4340	10	forefoot
0.9538	39.8	.3571	12	Mongol
0.9537	39.8	.3358	12	jackals
0.9536	39.8	.2330	18	/o/
0.9536	39.8	.3663	11	Moon's
0.9536	39.8	.3342	13	205
0.9535	39.8	.4501	10	spools
0.9535	39.8	.4451	10	sprightly
0.9534	39.8	.3279	13	1879
0.9533	39.8	.3875	11	hippos
0.9533	39.8	.6623	7	whereby
0.9529	39.8	.2458	15	Crocodile
0.9529	39.8	.2353	16	enzymes
0.9527	39.8	.4642	9	croaked
0.9526	39.8	.6617	7	dummy
0.9526	39.8	.6597	7	resplendent
0.9526	39.8	.4663	9	writhing
0.9525	39.8	.5146	9	caller
0.9525	39.8	.3308	11	Hamelin
0.9522	39.8	.5697	8	feasts
0.9522	39.8	.5074	9	182
0.9521	39.8	.4992	9	252
0.9516	39.8	.5696	8	tarry
0.9515	39.8	.5052	9	AM
0.9514	39.8	.5504	8	massage
0.9514	39.8	.3712	10	sniffles
0.9513	39.8	.3841	10	dreamily
0.9509	39.8	.6607	7	hazy
0.9509	39.8	.4628	9	mailbox
0.9506	39.8	.5706	8	siding
0.9503	39.8	.5838	8	studs
0.9502	39.8	.4485	10	Deep
0.9500	39.8	.3477	12	plaza
0.9500	39.8	.4856	9	restoration
0.9498	39.8	.4677	9	Knox
0.9497	39.8	.5496	8	beckoning
0.9497	39.8	.3859	11	corrugated
0.9497	39.8	.5496	8	gasps
0.9495	39.8	.3836	10	pedestal
0.9495	39.8	.2004	21	recipes
0.9495	39.8	.3796	11	trinkets
0.9493	39.8	.4926	9	hampered
0.9491	39.8	.6578	7	seething
0.9487	39.8	.3543	12	habitats
0.9486	39.8	.3467	12	$600
0.9485	39.8	.2441	15	Berbers
0.9485	39.8	.5474	8	ruff
0.9485	39.8	.5464	8	stowed
0.9482	39.8	.5760	8	tapestries
0.9479	39.8	.2317	17	baleen
0.9479	39.8	.5456	8	smarting
0.9478	39.8	.2801	13	copter
THE PRECEDING WORD TYPE OCCUPIES RANK 17700				
0.9478	39.8	.5455	8	purred
0.9477	39.8	.5626	8	NewYorkState
0.9476	39.8	.5651	8	dire
0.9474	39.8	.4468	9	splinters
0.9469	39.8	.6602	7	medley
0.9469	39.8	.3466	11	sisal
0.9468	39.8	.4299	10	scant
0.9466	39.8	.3619	12	Injun
0.9466	39.8	.1903	18	TVA
0.9463	39.8	.1645	21	Betsy's
0.9463	39.8	.5539	8	evaluation
0.9461	39.8	.2505	17	harmonize
0.9459	39.8	.5643	8	handfuls
0.9458	39.8	.4951	9	Colt
0.9458	39.8	.5635	8	cropping
0.9457	39.8	.2833	15	Friar
0.9454	39.8	.4607	9	spitting
0.9453	39.8	.5692	8	toughest
0.9452	39.8	.4282	10	dusky
0.9452	39.8	.2339	13	husks
0.9452	39.8	.5635	8	painstaking
0.9451	39.8	.5443	8	forty-seven
0.9451	39.8	.5665	8	lecturer
0.9450	39.8	.2957	14	$25
0.9450	39.8	.4024	11	metaphor
0.9450	39.8	.3653	10	rascals
0.9449	39.8	.3694	11	horde
0.9445	39.8	.3542	11	barbecue
0.9444	39.8	.4447	10	bangs
0.9444	39.8	.5447	8	lean-to
0.9444	39.8	.5710	8	trustworthy
0.9442	39.8	.5432	8	whining
0.9442	39.8	.4852	9	288
0.9441	39.8	.2318	13	Pennycuff
0.9441	39.8	.4882	9	straightens
0.9441	39.8	.5430	8	undecided
0.9441	39.8	.5577	8	162
0.9440	39.7	.3817	11	gettin'
0.9440	39.7	.5625	8	reinforcements
0.9439	39.7	.3581	11	Jeff's
0.9439	39.7	.6556	7	rutted
0.9434	39.7	.4960	9	197
0.9431	39.7	.4138	10	Cal
0.9430	39.7	.5635	8	four-fifths
0.9430	39.7	.0000	63	numerators
0.9427	39.7	.5740	8	registers
0.9426	39.7	.6549	7	Shenandoah
0.9425	39.7	.4315	10	taxed
0.9424	39.7	.5427	8	pathetic
0.9423	39.7	.4923	9	undertake
0.9419	39.7	.4120	10	naughty
0.9419	39.7	.5001	9	specialization
0.9418	39.7	.2477	16	Franks
0.9415	39.7	.1791	20	Vice-President
0.9414	39.7	.5616	8	fallow
0.9414	39.7	.2195	17	yore
0.9412	39.7	.5673	8	interchangeable
0.9411	39.7	.4547	10	irritable
0.9410	39.7	.1654	22	Kerry
0.9409	39.7	.5001	9	freshwater
0.9408	39.7	.4200	10	considerate
0.9408	39.7	.4298	10	dormant
0.9406	39.7	.5386	8	shanty
0.9406	39.7	.5386	8	Whigs
0.9405	39.7	.4875	9	responds
0.9402	39.7	.4058	11	clarify
0.9402	39.7	.3630	10	talker
0.9401	39.7	.3253	13	'til
0.9401	39.7	.0749	42	Tchaikovsky
0.9401	39.7	.5022	9	trans
0.9399	39.7	.0852	32	Jethro
0.9399	39.7	.3380	12	Stadium
0.9398	39.7	.4447	10	momentarily
0.9395	39.7	.2458	15	Guam
0.9391	39.7	.4675	9	bearskin
0.9391	39.7	.4675	9	coolly
0.9390	39.7	.1787	16	Annika
0.9389	39.7	.3782	11	Kelvin
0.9389	39.7	.5403	8	unwillingly
0.9387	39.7	.5597	8	supervised
0.9384	39.7	.3382	12	cleft
0.9382	39.7	.5434	8	muggy
0.9381	39.7	.4157	10	tumult
0.9379	39.7	.3312	11	Marley
0.9379	39.7	.4286	10	vocation
0.9377	39.7	.4794	9	cleansing
0.9377	39.7	.4564	9	darkly
0.9377	39.7	.4668	9	littered
0.9376	39.7	.4520	9	catcher's
0.9376	39.7	.5749	8	counselor
0.9375	39.7	.4427	10	Brunswick
0.9375	39.7	.1513	27	subordinate
0.9374	39.7	.1491	25	Bach's
0.9374	39.7	.3847	11	Huguenots
0.9374	39.7	.3895	11	strata
0.9374	39.7	.4274	10	399
0.9373	39.7	.5431	8	Yukon
0.9372	39.7	.5407	8	possessing
0.9371	39.7	.5384	8	slumped
0.9367	39.7	.3510	12	doin'
THE PRECEDING WORD TYPE OCCUPIES RANK 17800				
0.9367	39.7	.4835	9	one-fifth
0.9367	39.7	.5360	8	unpack
0.9366	39.7	.4758	9	hinged
0.9366	39.7	.3778	11	unemployed
0.9363	39.7	.2957	12	gully
0.9363	39.7	.5596	8	Things
0.9362	39.7	.2432	17	/t/
0.9361	39.7	.1937	20	Doodle
0.9360	39.7	.3438	10	cornstalk
0.9357	39.7	.3929	11	revolutionaries
0.9356	39.7	.5618	8	rebellious
0.9356	39.7	.4279	10	tormented
0.9355	39.7	.3878	11	cub's
0.9355	39.7	.5405	8	lima
0.9355	39.7	.3305	13	penetration
0.9352	39.7	.1898	21	-es
0.9352	39.7	.5373	8	bunched
0.9351	39.7	.4260	10	196
0.9348	39.7	.4436	9	Nights
0.9347	39.7	.3800	11	pituitary
0.9347	39.7	.5587	8	tailors
0.9345	39.7	.5417	8	Hiroshima
0.9341	39.7	.4582	9	arsenal
0.9340	39.7	.5360	8	compliments
0.9339	39.7	.1707	19	Edinburgh
0.9339	39.7	.4808	9	shutter
0.9338	39.7	.5332	8	Fathers
0.9338	39.7	.5336	8	tagging
0.9338	39.7	.5336	8	Trinidad
0.9337	39.7	.4293	10	Control
0.9337	39.7	.4459	10	Pine
0.9337	39.7	.2411	12	Ramon's
0.9335	39.7	.5390	8	battlefields
0.9335	39.7	.5381	8	waterfront
0.9333	39.7	.0000	115	2-Star
0.9332	39.7	.4823	9	motels
0.9331	39.7	.4788	9	homespun
0.9331	39.7	.5321	8	inns
0.9330	39.7	.2440	12	Pawnee
0.9326	39.7	.4682	9	contagious
0.9326	39.7	.5584	8	refresh
0.9326	39.7	.4545	9	Vancouver
0.9325	39.7	.4839	9	emigrant
0.9325	39.7	.2383	14	Powhatan
0.9323	39.7	.5462	8	wisps
0.9320	39.7	.3343	12	Capricorn
0.9314	39.7	.5512	8	honoring
0.9310	39.7	.4379	10	subdivision
0.9309	39.7	.3560	12	folder
0.9308	39.7	.4785	9	exhaled
0.9307	39.7	.5356	8	Gray's
0.9306	39.7	.3820	11	casualties
0.9306	39.7	.3349	12	yucca
0.9305	39.7	.5401	8	disagreed
0.9304	39.7	.5649	8	elusive
0.9304	39.7	.2948	13	Lorne
0.9301	39.7	.0646	31	Mammy
0.9299	39.7	.4985	9	texts
0.9292	39.7	.4267	10	legislators
0.9290	39.7	.5544	8	ripple
0.9286	39.7	.4687	9	closets
0.9285	39.7	.5001	9	fellowship
0.9285	39.7	.2748	14	one-word
0.9284	39.7	.4467	9	Drum
0.9284	39.7	.4881	9	181
0.9283	39.7	.2261	12	Jemima
0.9283	39.7	.2261	12	Stormy
0.9281	39.7	.5332	8	dumps
0.9281	39.7	.3511	11	pedestrians
0.9281	39.7	.5537	8	whilst
0.9280	39.7	.4106	10	Gods
0.9278	39.7	.2434	16	skew
0.9277	39.7	.4176	10	contraption
0.9275	39.7	.5554	8	appointing
0.9275	39.7	.5585	8	Drama
0.9274	39.7	.5415	8	whizzing
0.9273	39.7	.5341	8	shoelaces
0.9272	39.7	.4645	9	greyhound
0.9272	39.7	.3154	11	Monkey
0.9271	39.7	.2238	16	Lily
0.9271	39.7	.4014	10	rubs
0.9270	39.7	.5296	8	copperhead
0.9269	39.7	.4578	9	repaid
0.9268	39.7	.2355	12	Else
0.9267	39.7	.5299	8	reap
0.9267	39.7	.4782	9	theoretically
0.9267	39.7	.4782	9	1837
0.9264	39.7	.5380	8	mollusk
0.9263	39.7	.0286	43	vertex
0.9261	39.7	.4519	9	peek
0.9260	39.7	.4182	10	outermost
0.9259	39.7	.5570	8	earthy
0.9256	39.7	.5517	8	exalted
0.9256	39.7	.1444	18	eyepiece
0.9256	39.7	.4183	10	snuff
0.9255	39.7	.4966	9	accepts
0.9255	39.7	.3564	12	yolks
0.9251	39.7	.5603	8	cumbersome
0.9245	39.7	.5294	8	well-trained
0.9244	39.7	.3764	10	Haskell
THE PRECEDING WORD TYPE OCCUPIES RANK 17900				
0.9244	39.7	.3764	10	workout
0.9243	39.7	.0779	29	Duvitch
0.9242	39.7	.4394	10	Morton
0.9239	39.7	.4839	9	craftsmanship
0.9238	39.7	.4172	10	Aden
0.9238	39.7	.2880	13	Electric
0.9237	39.7	.4165	10	emit
0.9237	39.7	.5265	8	gilded
0.9236	39.7	.2678	14	trachea
0.9235	39.7	.5261	8	invalid
0.9233	39.7	.2884	14	SE
0.9231	39.7	.5461	8	evacuated
0.9229	39.7	.4248	10	muffler
0.9225	39.6	.2663	14	hateful
0.9224	39.6	.1806	13	earring
0.9224	39.6	.5250	8	yelp
0.9222	39.6	.5300	8	dispose
0.9222	39.6	.3341	11	Nottingham
0.9221	39.6	.4332	10	Adirondack
0.9221	39.6	.4373	10	locality
0.9219	39.6	.4462	9	unsettled
0.9217	39.6	.3980	10	forwards
0.9217	39.6	.5376	8	pewter
0.9217	39.6	.5510	8	silhouette
0.9216	39.6	.4543	9	astern
0.9215	39.6	.4815	9	rehearsed
0.9213	39.6	.2869	15	accompaniments
0.9207	39.6	.4757	9	sweetly
0.9206	39.6	.1671	19	mucus
0.9206	39.6	.2272	13	Pam
0.9206	39.6	.1671	19	slider
0.9204	39.6	.5496	8	processions
0.9202	39.6	.1828	19	01
0.9201	39.6	.2445	12	Sai
0.9200	39.6	.4374	10	Mercedes
0.9200	39.6	.3685	11	steamships
0.9197	39.6	.5358	8	lurched
0.9197	39.6	.3679	10	Pioneer
0.9195	39.6	.3966	10	Polaris
0.9194	39.6	.4002	11	cabinets
0.9194	39.6	.5541	8	deemed
0.9193	39.6	.2810	15	installment
0.9193	39.6	.5276	8	reject
0.9192	39.6	.3362	12	Masai
0.9190	39.6	.3030	12	Federalist
0.9189	39.6	.1778	19	a's
0.9187	39.6	.2831	14	cupcakes
0.9187	39.6	.5223	8	dimmed
0.9187	39.6	.3111	13	gamma
0.9186	39.6	.6208	7	Young's
0.9182	39.6	.4327	10	glandular
0.9181	39.6	.4276	10	forestry
0.9180	39.6	.5479	8	slowness
0.9178	39.6	.4006	10	devils
0.9177	39.6	.4694	9	murmuring
0.9176	39.6	.5545	8	Harrison
0.9175	39.6	.2323	15	nonmetals
0.9173	39.6	.5352	8	outwitted
0.9171	39.6	.2438	15	centigrade
0.9170	39.6	.2875	15	figurative
0.9170	39.6	.3290	12	flasks
0.9169	39.6	.3471	11	daVinci
0.9169	39.6	.2227	17	Pied
0.9167	39.6	.3631	10	geraniums
0.9167	39.6	.5302	8	Herald
0.9166	39.6	.4172	10	burly
0.9162	39.6	.3856	11	Psalm
0.9162	39.6	.5445	8	springy
0.9160	39.6	.5450	8	attracting
0.9160	39.6	.4187	10	nightgown
0.9160	39.6	.0896	26	solubility
0.9155	39.6	.3489	11	fluff
0.9154	39.6	.4417	9	spattered
0.9152	39.6	.4014	10	Birds
0.9152	39.6	.3477	12	Fine
0.9147	39.6	.4598	9	coastlines
0.9147	39.6	.4507	9	minister's
0.9147	39.6	.5450	8	overran
0.9147	39.6	.6185	7	unsanitary
0.9146	39.6	.3617	10	Flyway
0.9146	39.6	.6184	7	500-mile
0.9144	39.6	.4147	10	abnormal
0.9143	39.6	.4870	9	eminent
0.9142	39.6	.4582	9	blonde
0.9142	39.6	.4541	9	elf
0.9142	39.6	.3754	11	girders
0.9141	39.6	.6230	7	fearing
0.9141	39.6	.5338	8	trophy
0.9140	39.6	.5326	8	loosed
0.9140	39.6	.6202	7	unmistakably
0.9138	39.6	.3167	11	ahoy
0.9138	39.6	.6178	7	V-shaped
0.9137	39.6	.0000	20	Dillinger
0.9137	39.6	.0000	20	Grouch
0.9137	39.6	.0000	20	Hip
0.9137	39.6	.0000	20	Kobo
0.9137	39.6	.0000	20	Lupe
0.9137	39.6	.0000	20	Mellen
0.9137	39.6	.0000	20	Rosalie
0.9137	39.6	.4540	9	shuddering
THE PRECEDING WORD TYPE OCCUPIES RANK 18000				
0.9135	39.6	.6199	7	woodsmen
0.9133	39.6	.4130	10	rejoined
0.9132	39.6	.3151	13	Crete
0.9130	39.6	.5505	8	Anthony
0.9130	39.6	.4866	9	provoked
0.9128	39.6	.3257	13	Writing
0.9127	39.6	.4784	9	Constantine
0.9125	39.6	.5403	8	afforded
0.9125	39.6	.4110	10	hairlike
0.9123	39.6	.5528	8	proofs
0.9121	39.6	.4112	10	high-grade
0.9121	39.6	.5162	8	industrious
0.9119	39.6	.3594	10	avalanche
0.9117	39.6	.6188	7	emptiness
0.9117	39.6	.4754	9	surgeons
0.9116	39.6	.4160	10	workshops
0.9115	39.6	.5497	8	Ruth's
0.9114	39.6	.4195	10	Railway
0.9114	39.6	.4619	9	whimpering
0.9111	39.6	.4264	10	insulating
0.9110	39.6	.3119	12	turban
0.9109	39.6	.3094	13	atlases
0.9109	39.6	.6190	7	uninhabited
0.9108	39.6	.5449	8	1763
0.9107	39.6	.2424	12	Ham
0.9107	39.6	.4362	10	legible
0.9106	39.6	.4197	10	influenza
0.9106	39.6	.6188	7	manifest
0.9105	39.6	.4314	10	folders
0.9104	39.6	.3409	11	IGY
0.9103	39.6	.5445	8	Mohammedan
0.9101	39.6	.4844	9	persist
0.9100	39.6	.5263	8	dilemma
0.9097	39.6	.1086	21	meteorite
0.9095	39.6	.5477	8	accelerate
0.9095	39.6	.5477	8	capabilities
0.9095	39.6	.4109	10	saturated
0.9093	39.6	.5417	8	arrowhead
0.9092	39.6	.2445	15	cytoplasm
0.9092	39.6	.2445	15	reproductive
0.9091	39.6	.1872	15	Sarah's
0.9088	39.6	.3298	12	migrated
0.9088	39.6	.2981	14	Picasso
0.9088	39.6	.5479	8	rap
0.9087	39.6	.3699	11	Bud's
0.9087	39.6	.3127	13	Cupid
0.9087	39.6	.5285	8	1801
0.9085	39.6	.5220	8	potted
0.9084	39.6	.4506	9	158
0.9082	39.6	.4469	9	baseballs
0.9082	39.6	.5439	8	trainers
0.9081	39.6	.5409	8	greets
0.9080	39.6	.4071	10	diversion
0.9078	39.6	.4574	9	alarms
0.9078	39.6	.4756	9	shortages
0.9077	39.6	.4050	10	unsuitable
0.9072	39.6	.5210	8	blizzards
0.9072	39.6	.5317	8	knack
0.9071	39.6	.5277	8	shuffled
0.9070	39.6	.2618	13	squire
0.9069	39.6	.2444	15	Articles
0.9069	39.6	.2444	15	Hooker
0.9067	39.6	.5383	8	disappointments
0.9066	39.6	.4620	9	booster
0.9066	39.6	.4479	9	congratulated
0.9064	39.6	.4348	9	thrusting
0.9061	39.6	.2165	16	plasma
0.9061	39.6	.6185	7	sincerely
0.9059	39.6	.4386	9	lollipop
0.9057	39.6	.4611	9	impure
0.9056	39.6	.3678	11	investors
0.9055	39.6	.4664	9	scoured

U	SFI	D	F	Word Type
0.9054	39.6	.3660	10	black-eyed
0.9053	39.6	.5530	8	intermission
0.9052	39.6	.2615	13	Jody's
0.9052	39.6	.3583	11	manifold
0.9050	39.6	.2434	15	mowed
0.9049	39.6	.5321	8	navigate
0.9048	39.6	.5415	8	derives
0.9047	39.6	.5450	8	air-conditioning
0.9045	39.6	.4354	9	autobiography
0.9045	39.6	.4140	10	thorny
0.9043	39.6	.4884	9	coaster
0.9042	39.6	.2343	15	monoxide
0.9041	39.6	.5510	8	three-year
0.9040	39.6	.4743	9	Construction
0.9040	39.6	.4843	9	fraternity
0.9037	39.6	.3624	10	Mauna
0.9036	39.6	.5472	8	penalties
0.9036	39.6	.3149	13	warp
0.9033	39.6	.5189	8	innermost
0.9033	39.6	.4770	9	jaguar
0.9033	39.6	.3726	11	psychologist
0.9033	39.6	.3925	10	spiked
0.9030	39.6	.5423	8	intercourse
0.9030	39.6	.3133	13	patient's
0.9029	39.6	.5484	8	subscription
0.9028	39.6	.1857	18	fewest
0.9027	39.6	.2278	16	carnivores
0.9027	39.6	.4015	10	drafted
THE PRECEDING WORD TYPE OCCUPIES RANK 18100				
0.9027	39.6	.5381	8	holders
0.9027	39.6	.5366	8	naturalists
0.9026	39.6	.3153	12	Caucasus
0.9026	39.6	.3816	11	simplifying
0.9025	39.6	.5347	8	memorizing
0.9024	39.6	.3569	11	Hopper
0.9024	39.6	.4549	9	rodeos
0.9024	39.6	.2780	14	viewers
0.9022	39.6	.4446	9	mulberry
0.9021	39.6	.4434	9	jogged
0.9021	39.6	.5177	8	1774
0.9019	39.6	.5407	8	gluing
0.9018	39.6	.4257	10	Tuscany
0.9017	39.6	.5220	8	smote
0.9015	39.5	.5244	8	cordially
0.9015	39.5	.5244	8	vowed
0.9012	39.5	.4444	9	Man's
0.9011	39.5	.6110	7	smelt
0.9010	39.5	.4781	9	Belgrade
0.9010	39.5	.4471	9	plumage
0.9010	39.5	.4689	9	thickening
0.9008	39.5	.4878	8	outlining
0.9008	39.5	.3881	10	sewn
0.9007	39.5	.4874	8	Welcome
0.9006	39.5	.4871	8	grandly
0.9006	39.5	.4871	8	hide-and-seek
0.9006	39.5	.4871	8	sipping
0.8999	39.5	.2384	15	ammonium
0.8999	39.5	.4019	10	bluebird
0.8998	39.5	.3885	10	howls
0.8998	39.5	.2004	14	Sire
0.8997	39.5	.4675	9	day-to-day
0.8996	39.5	.3221	12	Bosporus
0.8995	39.5	.1847	15	Ink
0.8994	39.5	.5131	8	moonlit
0.8994	39.5	.3670	10	weavers
0.8994	39.5	.3670	10	Whitman
0.8991	39.5	.5323	8	amusements
0.8991	39.5	.4844	8	peeking
0.8990	39.5	.5492	8	roofing
0.8987	39.5	.4143	10	exuberant
0.8987	39.5	.4846	8	temperamental
0.8987	39.5	.2090	12	tinderbox
0.8986	39.5	.4846	8	uttering
0.8986	39.5	.6240	7	voter
0.8985	39.5	.4646	9	inertia
0.8984	39.5	.2314	14	Rams
0.8983	39.5	.4845	8	peaceable
0.8982	39.5	.5348	8	last-minute
0.8980	39.5	.5234	8	weakest
0.8980	39.5	.4415	9	white-haired
0.8977	39.5	.3631	11	156
0.8975	39.5	.3546	11	Adolf
0.8974	39.5	.4551	9	smelting
0.8973	39.5	.5426	8	freeway
0.8972	39.5	.5175	8	smudge
0.8970	39.5	.4819	9	masterpieces
0.8967	39.5	.4774	9	triggered
0.8965	39.5	.2076	12	Pandora
0.8964	39.5	.4654	9	bristled
0.8963	39.5	.5120	8	grieve
0.8962	39.5	.5203	8	jolt
0.8961	39.5	.3469	12	Wagon
0.8958	39.5	.5379	8	tentative
0.8957	39.5	.4275	10	Bibles
0.8957	39.5	.5294	8	obligations
0.8956	39.5	.4779	9	Score
0.8954	39.5	.3444	11	Red's
0.8953	39.5	.4277	10	Berlioz
0.8953	39.5	.5163	8	innings
0.8948	39.5	.5352	8	nationwide
0.8948	39.5	.2030	18	recorders
0.8947	39.5	.4746	9	couples
0.8946	39.5	.4743	9	wedge-shaped
0.8944	39.5	.2754	15	retrace
0.8943	39.5	.4294	10	Punch
0.8942	39.5	.3422	10	bandits
0.8939	39.5	.1871	18	Evan
0.8938	39.5	.2815	13	reconstruction
0.8937	39.5	.1232	27	ful
0.8937	39.5	.5390	8	supporters
0.8935	39.5	.4013	10	Hickory
0.8933	39.5	.5422	8	Mommy
0.8931	39.5	.4243	9	Miller's
0.8931	39.5	.4413	9	Younger
0.8929	39.5	.3201	10	clucking
0.8929	39.5	.3647	10	Gypsy
0.8927	39.5	.4882	8	ballast
0.8926	39.5	.4764	8	Barnes
0.8926	39.5	.4764	8	Grimm
0.8926	39.5	.4764	8	tooted
0.8925	39.5	.4887	8	chicle
0.8925	39.5	.2305	16	Edward's
0.8923	39.5	.5121	8	$300
0.8923	39.5	.4760	8	snowdrifts
0.8922	39.5	.4409	9	Forge
0.8922	39.5	.2377	15	mentions
0.8919	39.5	.4775	8	banked
0.8919	39.5	.4803	8	Governor's
0.8919	39.5	.5390	8	undertakings
THE PRECEDING WORD TYPE OCCUPIES RANK 18200				
0.8916	39.5	.4773	9	breathtaking
0.8915	39.5	.2522	15	FM
0.8915	39.5	.4725	9	Guy
0.8913	39.5	.0920	25	arthropods
0.8913	39.5	.4758	8	gangster
0.8913	39.5	.3801	10	Heinrich
0.8911	39.5	.3660	10	Centerville
0.8911	39.5	.5132	8	Southerner
0.8910	39.5	.5214	8	burrs
0.8909	39.5	.4756	8	sealskin
0.8908	39.5	.4858	8	Boone's
0.8906	39.5	.4753	8	tailoring
0.8904	39.5	.4753	8	Homestead
0.8904	39.5	.2709	13	monsoon
0.8904	39.5	.4753	8	Welfare
0.8903	39.5	.5356	8	315
0.8901	39.5	.2702	14	starches
0.8897	39.5	.0478	37	Pinocchio
0.8896	39.5	.5338	8	Aiken
0.8894	39.5	.5158	8	furrow
0.8892	39.5	.5069	8	crew's
0.8891	39.5	.5139	8	statesmen
0.8890	39.5	.2986	12	Ted's
0.8890	39.5	.3903	10	1889
0.8887	39.5	.4598	9	apparition
0.8886	39.5	.4645	9	etiquette
0.8886	39.5	.3590	11	Kiev
0.8886	39.5	.1533	17	pastry
0.8883	39.5	.4240	10	four-year
0.8883	39.5	.2028	12	Horner
0.8883	39.5	.0943	33	ng
0.8882	39.5	.5245	8	livelihood
0.8882	39.5	.4354	9	slyly
0.8879	39.5	.4734	9	culprit
0.8878	39.5	.4561	9	astrology
0.8878	39.5	.1795	18	IT
0.8873	39.5	.3307	12	Stewart
0.8872	39.5	.2155	16	Berkeley
0.8872	39.5	.4367	9	scouring
0.8872	39.5	.3900	10	vases
0.8871	39.5	.3418	12	dryers
0.8869	39.5	.5287	8	nears
0.8869	39.5	.5155	8	ten-year
0.8869	39.5	.5287	8	virtual
0.8868	39.5	.4339	9	mattresses
0.8867	39.5	.3418	11	shedding
0.8867	39.5	.5262	8	up-to-date
0.8866	39.5	.4690	9	consistency
0.8866	39.5	.1795	17	eardrum
0.8865	39.5	.6185	7	restoring
0.8864	39.5	.5124	8	disclosed
0.8864	39.5	.5168	8	uniting
0.8863	39.5	.5257	8	spirals
0.8862	39.5	.6060	7	shadowed
0.8861	39.5	.4189	9	deafening
0.8854	39.5	.3591	11	Galen
0.8853	39.5	.2212	17	Dec
0.8851	39.5	.2004	19	/ch/
0.8851	39.5	.2408	15	Eratosthenes
0.8850	39.5	.4789	8	Aleutian
0.8849	39.5	.4564	9	motorcycles
0.8849	39.5	.3419	10	something's
0.8848	39.5	.0814	34	transitive
0.8847	39.5	.5379	8	cue
0.8847	39.5	.4465	9	nonmetallic
0.8847	39.5	.4734	8	Tavern
0.8846	39.5	.2897	13	Basic
0.8845	39.5	.6175	7	restriction
0.8845	39.5	.4584	9	Walter's
0.8844	39.5	.4559	9	synthesis
0.8843	39.5	.4727	8	Burning
0.8841	39.5	.5308	8	arm's
0.8841	39.5	.6009	7	exclude
0.8841	39.5	.3651	11	researchers
0.8839	39.5	.2003	12	Farnsworth
0.8839	39.5	.2003	12	Hare
0.8838	39.5	.5107	8	dreamer
0.8837	39.5	.3153	11	mama
0.8833	39.5	.5305	8	spontaneous
0.8832	39.5	.4596	9	five-year
0.8831	39.5	.5097	8	fugitive
0.8828	39.5	.3139	13	bonding
0.8826	39.5	.3975	9	lemme
0.8826	39.5	.2731	13	porter
0.8826	39.5	.3523	11	swifts
0.8824	39.5	.4146	10	tricycle
0.8822	39.5	.4437	9	brigade
0.8821	39.5	.3912	10	reclaimed
0.8819	39.5	.4545	9	coordination
0.8817	39.5	.4168	10	440
0.8816	39.5	.5358	8	losers
0.8816	39.5	.5074	8	snuffed
0.8816	39.5	.5073	8	unpredictable
0.8814	39.5	.4693	8	peddlers
0.8813	39.5	.3579	11	extraordinarily
0.8810	39.4	.4506	9	acreage
0.8810	39.4	.5370	8	Front
0.8808	39.4	.3552	11	crossword
0.8808	39.4	.4541	9	physiological
0.8806	39.4	.3140	11	firebox
THE PRECEDING WORD TYPE OCCUPIES RANK 18300				
0.8804	39.4	.5175	8	patter
0.8803	39.4	.3902	10	camouflage
0.8803	39.4	.1573	13	Hernandez
0.8803	39.4	.1573	13	Milo
0.8803	39.4	.3778	9	Moffat
0.8803	39.4	.1573	13	Toru
0.8801	39.4	.4315	9	YOU
0.8800	39.4	.4572	9	developmental
0.8799	39.4	.3805	10	niche
0.8797	39.4	.3529	11	Emil
0.8797	39.4	.4260	9	hammocks
0.8795	39.4	.4416	9	gallantly
0.8795	39.4	.1914	19	modes
0.8793	39.4	.4548	9	negligible
0.8788	39.4	.2813	15	fasteners
0.8788	39.4	.4819	8	prune
0.8786	39.4	.2292	16	Argentine
0.8786	39.4	.3770	9	Skeeter
0.8785	39.4	.3840	9	goatskin
0.8784	39.4	.5313	8	Kathy's
0.8782	39.4	.6006	7	gardening
0.8781	39.4	.3608	11	Emmanuel
0.8778	39.4	.3265	12	AE
0.8777	39.4	.6001	7	sorghum
0.8777	39.4	.5014	8	unhappiness
0.8776	39.4	.5243	8	menacing
0.8774	39.4	.1933	17	supplementary
0.8773	39.4	.4297	9	weightless
0.8772	39.4	.3532	11	merriment
0.8772	39.4	.5123	8	mothers'
0.8771	39.4	.5238	8	Ambassador
0.8771	39.4	.4816	8	excite
0.8768	39.4	.3747	9	hoeing
0.8768	39.4	.1294	23	sq
0.8767	39.4	.5070	8	elite
0.8761	39.4	.4943	8	gaped
0.8760	39.4	.3971	10	hordes
0.8759	39.4	.3813	9	sunsets
0.8756	39.4	.3737	9	Davey
0.8756	39.4	.3737	9	plumber
0.8752	39.4	.4489	9	confirmation
0.8752	39.4	.2715	13	fatty
0.8751	39.4	.3506	11	carpentry
0.8749	39.4	.1948	14	Mustard
0.8749	39.4	.5124	8	three-man
0.8747	39.4	.4932	8	prospector
0.8745	39.4	.2687	13	Macedonia
0.8743	39.4	.1506	17	Danny's
0.8741	39.4	.4271	9	thither
0.8740	39.4	.4350	9	earning
0.8740	39.4	.4969	8	pelicans
0.8739	39.4	.4119	9	Mather
0.8737	39.4	.4575	9	dedicate
0.8737	39.4	.5261	8	engulf
0.8737	39.4	.5254	8	scientifically
0.8736	39.4	.4564	9	crowbar
0.8736	39.4	.4553	9	wherein
0.8735	39.4	.3381	11	Capt
0.8732	39.4	.5296	8	manifested
0.8732	39.4	.5061	8	tenement
0.8727	39.4	.5999	7	peacocks
0.8726	39.4	.5937	7	herdsman
0.8725	39.4	.5108	8	engaging
0.8724	39.4	.5289	8	comprise
0.8722	39.4	.1904	15	confessed
0.8722	39.4	.5067	8	sapphire
0.8720	39.4	.3346	11	chromium
0.8719	39.4	.2338	12	Agassiz
0.8717	39.4	.2906	14	alterations
0.8717	39.4	.4499	9	trolley
0.8715	39.4	.5042	8	girdle
0.8714	39.4	.5215	8	administering
0.8712	39.4	.2391	14	Sumter
0.8711	39.4	.4652	9	consuming
0.8711	39.4	.2646	14	Thurber
0.8710	39.4	.3706	9	goblin
0.8707	39.4	.3494	11	detection
0.8707	39.4	.3828	9	Mitty
0.8706	39.4	.5066	8	laborer
0.8706	39.4	.2984	13	portraits
0.8704	39.4	.5014	8	staked
0.8704	39.4	.4493	9	wont
0.8703	39.4	.5013	8	truthfully
0.8702	39.4	.3228	12	guerrillas
0.8702	39.4	.5260	8	travelled
0.8700	39.4	.3552	10	taxpayer
0.8699	39.4	.0549	35	isosceles
0.8699	39.4	.3803	10	Isthmus
0.8699	39.4	.3803	10	Mussolini
0.8698	39.4	.2390	15	zip
0.8697	39.4	.2332	12	geta
0.8697	39.4	.3667	11	gopher
0.8695	39.4	.4459	9	lord's
0.8695	39.4	.4199	9	outfield
0.8694	39.4	.3850	9	Angels
0.8694	39.4	.5074	8	inappropriate
0.8693	39.4	.3683	9	lumberjacks
0.8693	39.4	.5157	8	tapers
0.8693	39.4	.3683	9	whippoorwill
0.8692	39.4	.4362	9	soothe
THE PRECEDING WORD TYPE OCCUPIES RANK 18400				
0.8692	39.4	.4554	9	teen
0.8691	39.4	.3631	11	cult
0.8691	39.4	.5223	8	mystic
0.8691	39.4	.5138	8	perishable
0.8689	39.4	.3053	12	Braddock
0.8689	39.4	.0367	65	hem
0.8689	39.4	.3679	9	licks
0.8687	39.4	.4513	9	area's
0.8685	39.4	.4212	9	puny
0.8684	39.4	.4510	9	battling
0.8682	39.4	.3985	10	sized
0.8682	39.4	.4991	8	subscribe
0.8680	39.4	.5178	8	Agency
0.8680	39.4	.0000	19	DeGree
0.8680	39.4	.0000	19	frogman
0.8680	39.4	.3533	11	porpoises
0.8680	39.4	.0000	19	Standish
0.8680	39.4	.0000	19	Wo
0.8678	39.4	.3176	11	Cyclone
0.8678	39.4	.3804	9	Flyer
0.8678	39.4	.5055	8	strangeness
0.8677	39.4	.4988	8	plied
0.8676	39.4	.4499	9	auditory
0.8676	39.4	.5207	8	pursuits
0.8675	39.4	.5002	8	enveloped
0.8675	39.4	.3616	11	intestinal
0.8675	39.4	.5179	8	treading
0.8672	39.4	.5019	8	195
0.8668	39.4	.2428	13	thru
0.8666	39.4	.5919	7	ravens
0.8665	39.4	.2345	15	geographers
0.8663	39.4	.5917	7	thinker
0.8663	39.4	.5148	8	272
0.8659	39.4	.4445	9	dictatorship
0.8659	39.4	.3652	9	Starkey
0.8655	39.4	.5209	8	buns
0.8654	39.4	.3237	12	fluoride
0.8649	39.4	.5022	8	continuation
0.8649	39.4	.4601	9	shivers
0.8645	39.4	.4552	9	moisten
0.8644	39.4	.4736	8	jabbed
0.8642	39.4	.3697	10	Chicken
0.8642	39.4	.5111	8	torment
0.8641	39.4	.3445	11	hitters
0.8640	39.4	.4959	8	congratulate
0.8640	39.4	.5004	8	flop
0.8640	39.4	.4415	9	foster
0.8640	39.4	.2444	15	sixths
0.8639	39.4	.2231	17	landscapes
0.8639	39.4	.3608	11	shelled
0.8639	39.4	.2364	16	volts
0.8639	39.4	.3952	10	4%
0.8635	39.4	.4379	9	averaged
0.8634	39.4	.4978	8	outlawed
0.8633	39.4	.4469	9	spars
0.8632	39.4	.3914	10	paleontologists
0.8632	39.4	.2749	14	phrasing
0.8629	39.4	.4181	9	Lowell
0.8629	39.4	.3533	11	topography
0.8627	39.4	.4973	8	drive-in
0.8626	39.4	.4970	8	crouch
0.8626	39.4	.4858	8	inexperienced
0.8620	39.4	.4712	8	haughtily
0.8620	39.4	.4102	9	purses
0.8618	39.4	.1873	12	Yogi
0.8617	39.4	.4447	9	horse-drawn
0.8616	39.4	.5072	8	aloof
0.8616	39.4	.2364	16	Johannes
0.8615	39.4	.5636	7	half-way
0.8614	39.4	.4555	9	commissions
0.8614	39.4	.5999	7	deceived
0.8614	39.4	.5890	7	pious
0.8614	39.4	.5058	8	whittling
0.8613	39.4	.5160	8	sprinter
0.8612	39.4	.4695	8	thumps
0.8611	39.4	.2070	13	Lucille
0.8610	39.4	.2213	15	argon
0.8610	39.3	.5134	8	Ph
0.8609	39.3	.3841	9	blower
0.8607	39.3	.3202	12	morality
0.8607	39.3	.4929	8	stripe
0.8606	39.3	.5150	8	intervention
0.8606	39.3	.2129	17	pinning
0.8602	39.3	.2422	14	Buddhism
0.8601	39.3	.4941	8	Andromeda
0.8600	39.3	.4279	9	manly
0.8598	39.3	.3522	11	nominated
0.8598	39.3	.3929	9	quicksilver
0.8597	39.3	.6001	7	urges
0.8595	39.3	.2119	17	OA
0.8594	39.3	.5156	8	blindfolded
0.8594	39.3	.4970	8	domains
0.8594	39.3	.5097	8	ecstasy
0.8594	39.3	.4118	9	lye
0.8592	39.3	.5626	7	Whig
0.8592	39.3	.5626	7	wrung
0.8591	39.3	.4941	8	bullfight
0.8591	39.3	.5897	7	preoccupation
0.8590	39.3	.5624	7	inspecting
0.8589	39.3	.4155	9	coaxing
THE PRECEDING WORD TYPE OCCUPIES RANK 18500				
0.8589	39.3	.1851	19	Indo-European
0.8589	39.3	.3097	12	159
0.8588	39.3	.2345	15	Black's
0.8588	39.3	.4527	9	362
0.8587	39.3	.5891	7	articulate
0.8587	39.3	.5114	8	clearest
0.8587	39.3	.5892	7	hours'
0.8587	39.3	.5891	7	reprinted
0.8586	39.3	.5043	8	asbestos
0.8585	39.3	.2295	16	Elephant's
0.8584	39.3	.5904	7	aiding
0.8584	39.3	.4703	8	troopers
0.8583	39.3	.5651	7	mantelpiece
0.8583	39.3	.4264	9	sinews
0.8583	39.3	.4840	8	Stevens
0.8582	39.3	.4154	9	1769
0.8581	39.3	.5027	8	patrols
0.8581	39.3	.5179	8	seaside
0.8580	39.3	.4811	8	blisters
0.8579	39.3	.5596	7	battleships
0.8579	39.3	.4702	8	recollection
0.8578	39.3	.4511	9	Staten
0.8577	39.3	.4671	8	wide-eyed
0.8575	39.3	.3414	11	broadside
0.8574	39.3	.4905	8	cheating
0.8571	39.3	.2279	12	skiers
0.8570	39.3	.5645	7	mops
0.8570	39.3	.5645	7	undress
0.8569	39.3	.4225	9	lounging
0.8569	39.3	.4715	8	urchins
0.8567	39.3	.4969	8	Business
0.8567	39.3	.5608	7	hovers
0.8567	39.3	.5608	7	record-breaking
0.8566	39.3	.2525	14	involvement
0.8566	39.3	.4713	8	Recovery

U	SFI	D	F	Word Type
0.8565	39.3	.5641	7	clumsily
0.8565	39.3	.3761	10	potent
0.8564	39.3	.4315	9	world-famous
0.8564	39.3	.4518	9	1-6
0.8563	39.3	.5640	7	overtaken
0.8563	39.3	.5607	7	studious
0.8563	39.3	.5607	7	woodsman
0.8563	39.3	.3114	12	3%
0.8562	39.3	.5879	7	speckled
0.8561	39.3	.5605	7	unreliable
0.8560	39.3	.4242	9	Goat
0.8560	39.3	.5859	7	thesis
0.8560	39.3	.4915	8	unprotected
0.8558	39.3	.3891	9	fisherman's
0.8557	39.3	.4936	8	rainbows
0.8555	39.3	.5866	7	implacable
0.8555	39.3	.2437	11	Merchant
0.8555	39.3	.5602	7	merchant's
0.8555	39.3	.2444	11	Paragraph
0.8554	39.3	.3102	11	gardeners
0.8554	39.3	.5045	8	reflective
0.8554	39.3	.3564	9	Rosario
0.8553	39.3	.2432	11	cookbook
0.8553	39.3	.5607	7	hacking
0.8553	39.3	.2432	11	Huffman
0.8553	39.3	.5607	7	knobby
0.8553	39.3	.2432	11	Norris
0.8553	39.3	.5607	7	plead
0.8553	39.3	.2432	11	sports-car
0.8552	39.3	.2573	14	au
0.8552	39.3	.4574	8	lighthouses
0.8552	39.3	.4238	9	yes'm
0.8549	39.3	.3746	10	blushing
0.8547	39.3	.3558	9	Etna
0.8547	39.3	.4925	8	lodges
0.8547	39.3	.3748	9	Myra
0.8547	39.3	.3558	9	refracting
0.8547	39.3	.4989	8	robust
0.8545	39.3	.3015	12	Aleuts
0.8545	39.3	.2969	12	astronomical
0.8545	39.3	.4480	9	Doris
0.8543	39.3	.2665	14	Muslim
0.8543	39.3	.0764	36	wh
0.8542	39.3	.3672	10	Darius
0.8542	39.3	.3732	9	fussing
0.8542	39.3	.3732	9	Pet
0.8541	39.3	.4413	9	investigates
0.8540	39.3	.5861	7	inventory
0.8539	39.3	.5007	8	forearm
0.8538	39.3	.4087	10	filing
0.8538	39.3	.4987	8	Newark
0.8537	39.3	.4658	8	campsite
0.8537	39.3	.4867	8	intact
0.8537	39.3	.5590	7	labors
0.8535	39.3	.5587	7	intercept
0.8535	39.3	.5596	7	mobbed
0.8535	39.3	.5861	7	prostrate
0.8535	39.3	.4948	8	290
0.8534	39.3	.4930	8	silences
0.8532	39.3	.0000	57	polygon
0.8531	39.3	.3228	11	thumbtacks
0.8530	39.3	.5829	7	signify
0.8527	39.3	.3820	10	Astor
0.8527	39.3	.4282	9	Widow
0.8526	39.3	.5590	7	mother-of-pearl
THE PRECEDING WORD TYPE OCCUPIES RANK 18600				
0.8526	39.3	.3851	10	odorless
0.8525	39.3	.4993	8	sneaked
0.8523	39.3	.5918	7	succeeds
0.8522	39.3	.3534	9	Cristobal
0.8521	39.3	.3792	9	bowler
0.8520	39.3	.1942	16	north-seeking
0.8516	39.3	.2864	14	toughness
0.8515	39.3	.3905	10	386
0.8513	39.3	.4631	8	yanked
0.8510	39.3	.5110	8	morals
0.8508	39.3	.3901	9	Walk
0.8507	39.3	.4701	8	conspiracy
0.8507	39.3	.2163	17	diarrhea
0.8506	39.3	.5844	7	imprinted
0.8506	39.3	.5039	8	rollicking
0.8505	39.3	.5819	7	patronage
0.8504	39.3	.4698	8	bottomless
0.8503	39.3	.3913	10	premier
0.8503	39.3	.5036	8	rediscovered
0.8503	39.3	.3351	11	sensing
0.8502	39.3	.4066	9	Fat
0.8502	39.3	.4632	8	uninteresting
0.8501	39.3	.5850	7	lighthearted
0.8501	39.3	.5082	8	Paradise
0.8501	39.3	.2754	12	SantaFe
0.8500	39.3	.4795	8	precaution
0.8498	39.3	.5609	7	Brigade
0.8497	39.3	.3732	10	earths
0.8497	39.3	.2257	16	toaster
0.8496	39.3	.5803	7	speculations
0.8495	39.3	.3781	9	ladle
0.8495	39.3	.2618	14	riboflavin
0.8488	39.3	.4848	8	garages
0.8486	39.3	.5068	8	radial
0.8485	39.3	.5587	7	paleface
0.8483	39.3	.4320	9	sculptured
0.8482	39.3	.2607	13	calorie
0.8482	39.3	.4863	8	Canadians
0.8482	39.3	.4652	8	fifty-two
0.8481	39.3	.1231	20	microbe
0.8479	39.3	.5783	7	whiskey
0.8479	39.3	.2780	13	210
0.8478	39.3	.5788	7	encounters
0.8478	39.3	.4681	8	harmed
0.8478	39.3	.5036	8	scribe
0.8478	39.3	.5861	7	525
0.8477	39.3	.5775	7	broad-shouldered
0.8477	39.3	.4577	8	burr
0.8477	39.3	.4683	8	silversmith
0.8475	39.3	.4725	8	assorted
0.8475	39.3	.4677	8	dried-up
0.8474	39.3	.3695	9	jingling
0.8473	39.3	.4539	8	sarcastic
0.8469	39.3	.4961	8	requesting
0.8465	39.3	.2154	17	stringed
0.8464	39.3	.4853	8	Byrd
0.8464	39.3	.4307	9	223
0.8460	39.3	.3708	10	Amy's
0.8460	39.3	.2489	13	Cindy
0.8460	39.3	.4470	9	dappled
0.8459	39.3	.2319	15	diagonals
0.8459	39.3	.3599	11	specifications
0.8456	39.3	.4715	8	thoroughbred
0.8455	39.3	.3442	10	Bombay
0.8454	39.3	.4552	8	daze
0.8454	39.3	.3683	9	loam
0.8454	39.3	.0638	32	vertices
0.8453	39.3	.3679	9	handsomest
0.8452	39.3	.3414	10	IS
0.8452	39.3	.4992	8	passers-by
0.8451	39.3	.4845	8	aghast
0.8451	39.3	.4845	8	dad's
0.8451	39.3	.0151	46	subsets
0.8450	39.3	.3666	10	geranium
0.8450	39.3	.3449	10	Kalahari
0.8450	39.3	.2133	17	Steps
0.8448	39.3	.5529	7	overpowered
0.8447	39.3	.4189	9	constables
0.8447	39.3	.5764	7	leveling
0.8445	39.3	.4368	9	dislikes
0.8445	39.3	.3189	11	jerking
0.8444	39.3	.5517	7	months'
0.8443	39.3	.3701	9	chopsticks
0.8443	39.3	.4578	8	trance
0.8440	39.3	.4339	9	horsepower
0.8440	39.3	.2891	13	yer
0.8439	39.3	.4590	8	bulges
0.8437	39.3	.3306	11	steamboats
0.8437	39.3	.5528	7	wallowed
0.8436	39.3	.2851	12	Beersheba
0.8434	39.3	.5512	7	delegate
0.8433	39.3	.4839	8	prolific
0.8433	39.3	.4333	9	Telephone
0.8429	39.3	.4894	8	grill
0.8427	39.3	.3119	12	Harlow
0.8427	39.3	.5751	7	skinning
0.8426	39.3	.3589	11	overtones
0.8424	39.3	.5763	7	usher
0.8422	39.3	.2417	15	Rascal
0.8421	39.3	.5011	8	conversely
THE PRECEDING WORD TYPE OCCUPIES RANK 18700				
0.8420	39.3	.3063	11	sanctuaries
0.8419	39.3	.2881	10	Bruno
0.8416	39.3	.5721	7	discretion
0.8416	39.3	.4200	9	scents
0.8414	39.3	.4949	8	applicant
0.8413	39.2	.0974	23	glucose
0.8411	39.2	.4511	8	lovingly
0.8411	39.2	.4511	8	midget
0.8411	39.2	.4811	8	Padua
0.8408	39.2	.5021	8	counterclockwise
0.8407	39.2	.5138	8	fullest
0.8406	39.2	.3365	11	Alberta
0.8406	39.2	.3965	9	drumming
0.8406	39.2	.1096	23	Me
0.8406	39.2	.4543	8	storytellers
0.8405	39.2	.4955	8	prompted
0.8405	39.2	.4955	8	snares
0.8403	39.2	.5746	7	trample
0.8403	39.2	.4093	9	1600's
0.8399	39.2	.5560	7	uppermost
0.8397	39.2	.4217	9	feeders
0.8397	39.2	.3798	9	Tahiti
0.8394	39.2	.2234	11	Jeffrey
0.8391	39.2	.5066	8	conceive
0.8391	39.2	.4991	8	deformed
0.8391	39.2	.4327	9	yellows
0.8390	39.2	.4521	8	JOHN
0.8388	39.2	.5563	7	smeared
0.8387	39.2	.5712	7	horrors
0.8383	39.2	.5718	7	Bus
0.8382	39.2	.0000	56	-2
0.8382	39.2	.4506	8	Dempsey
0.8382	39.2	.5731	7	faintest
0.8381	39.2	.3893	10	attendant
0.8381	39.2	.4923	8	parental
0.8380	39.2	.5539	7	Adams'
0.8380	39.2	.5549	7	ensuing
0.8380	39.2	.5716	7	451
0.8378	39.2	.5487	7	bumblebee
0.8378	39.2	.4850	8	harnesses
0.8378	39.2	.5515	7	professors
0.8377	39.2	.5548	7	Ward's
0.8376	39.2	.4919	8	faiths
0.8376	39.2	.3779	10	federation
0.8376	39.2	.5557	7	recruits
0.8373	39.2	.3310	11	Borneo
0.8373	39.2	.5558	7	curd
0.8373	39.2	.3310	11	Emancipation
0.8372	39.2	.5546	7	constable
0.8372	39.2	.5546	7	decreed
0.8372	39.2	.4386	9	specify
0.8371	39.2	.3938	9	Singing
0.8370	39.2	.5517	7	crackle
0.8368	39.2	.3743	10	boulevards
0.8368	39.2	.4499	8	feasted
0.8368	39.2	.3743	10	postwar
0.8368	39.2	.5555	7	proudest
0.8368	39.2	.4824	8	sealing
0.8368	39.2	.4965	8	sewer
0.8367	39.2	.3983	9	boilers
0.8367	39.2	.4958	8	broiled
0.8366	39.2	.3940	9	playfully
0.8365	39.2	.2937	11	guppy
0.8364	39.2	.1140	20	Haggin
0.8363	39.2	.5060	8	dryer
0.8361	39.2	.2175	14	Hull
0.8359	39.2	.2145	17	Grieg
0.8358	39.2	.3413	11	$40
0.8358	39.2	.5024	8	Ministry
0.8357	39.2	.3816	10	scalps
0.8357	39.2	.5509	7	sprouting
0.8356	39.2	.3410	10	half-hour
0.8355	39.2	.5686	7	diverted
0.8355	39.2	.2434	11	Earnshaw
0.8355	39.2	.2434	11	oarsmen
0.8352	39.2	.5684	7	recommendation
0.8351	39.2	.4251	9	cottonseed
0.8349	39.2	.5696	7	turbans
0.8346	39.2	.5502	7	shreds
0.8346	39.2	.4681	8	skippers
0.8346	39.2	.4589	8	wrens
0.8345	39.2	.4411	9	Be
0.8345	39.2	.2167	11	Canute
0.8345	39.2	.4910	8	clasps
0.8342	39.2	.4334	9	seller
0.8341	39.2	.4748	8	napping
0.8340	39.2	.2922	11	fogs
0.8340	39.2	.5686	7	Horatio
0.8338	39.2	.4898	8	peephole
0.8336	39.2	.4672	8	stranger's
0.8336	39.2	.4582	8	tolls
0.8334	39.2	.4625	8	torpedo
0.8333	39.2	.4377	9	compensate
0.8329	39.2	.3652	10	Marianas
0.8328	39.2	.3817	10	Dobbin
0.8327	39.2	.3615	10	Lights
0.8327	39.2	.4313	9	Yugoslav
0.8325	39.2	.5655	7	fiftieth
0.8324	39.2	.4330	9	Danbury
0.8324	39.2	.2617	14	oblique
THE PRECEDING WORD TYPE OCCUPIES RANK 18800				
0.8322	39.2	.3150	12	linens
0.8322	39.2	.3545	9	Osaka
0.8321	39.2	.3727	10	coloration
0.8321	39.2	.2152	11	Gramp
0.8321	39.2	.2152	11	rampion
0.8319	39.2	.4228	9	reproach
0.8318	39.2	.4301	9	alpha
0.8318	39.2	.4365	9	archaeologist
0.8318	39.2	.2995	12	Maoris
0.8310	39.2	.5514	7	pod
0.8310	39.2	.3248	11	salinity
0.8309	39.2	.4131	9	Thing
0.8308	39.2	.5512	7	disconnected
0.8308	39.2	.5514	7	Thor
0.8307	39.2	.4719	8	devour
0.8307	39.2	.2696	13	Hitler's
0.8306	39.2	.3423	11	weekends
0.8305	39.2	.4857	8	dwindled
0.8304	39.2	.2546	12	wigwam
0.8302	39.2	.4399	9	Gerald
0.8298	39.2	.4738	8	clinical
0.8298	39.2	.3395	10	straits
0.8295	39.2	.3222	12	literal
0.8295	39.2	.3229	11	silkworms
0.8294	39.2	.4614	8	Taylor's
0.8293	39.2	.5618	7	blooms
0.8292	39.2	.3116	11	Doctor's
0.8291	39.2	.5002	8	shrinks
0.8289	39.2	.4259	9	non-Communist
0.8287	39.2	.5489	7	out-of-the-way
0.8286	39.2	.4770	8	diner
0.8285	39.2	.3208	10	Spartans
0.8283	39.2	.4947	8	259
0.8282	39.2	.4181	9	friars
0.8282	39.2	.4935	8	heaters
0.8281	39.2	.4533	8	Munich
0.8277	39.2	.4694	8	livery
0.8276	39.2	.3539	10	Birmingham
0.8276	39.2	.3022	12	infer
0.8275	39.2	.4050	9	bewitched
0.8275	39.2	.1870	14	temptation
0.8274	39.2	.1602	17	Belt
0.8273	39.2	.2348	15	ordinal
0.8273	39.2	.2798	12	Reconstruction
0.8271	39.2	.4295	9	psychiatrists
0.8271	39.2	.4627	8	spaniel
0.8270	39.2	.5609	7	par
0.8269	39.2	.4793	8	bale
0.8269	39.2	.4737	8	1400
0.8268	39.2	.2434	15	/d/
0.8268	39.2	.2853	11	foolishness
0.8268	39.2	.2310	15	groomed
0.8267	39.2	.4761	8	co-operate
0.8266	39.2	.2850	12	Bowl
0.8263	39.2	.4474	8	brag
0.8261	39.2	.3432	10	thoughtless
0.8260	39.2	.4181	9	grenades
0.8260	39.2	.2534	14	lute
0.8259	39.2	.4793	8	lightening
0.8257	39.2	.3604	10	1883
0.8256	39.2	.4067	9	Fork
0.8256	39.2	.4596	8	highwayman
0.8254	39.2	.1656	19	capitalization
0.8254	39.2	.3651	10	Israel's
0.8253	39.2	.4263	9	predecessor
0.8251	39.2	.4837	8	branched
0.8251	39.2	.4777	8	chews
0.8251	39.2	.3856	10	prepares
0.8251	39.2	.4473	8	wavered
0.8249	39.2	.4194	9	disapproval
0.8246	39.2	.3411	11	Mayas
0.8246	39.2	.4066	9	Riverside
0.8246	39.2	.4823	8	tradesmen
0.8245	39.2	.3503	11	anticipated
0.8243	39.2	.0086	64	Juana
0.8242	39.2	.3730	10	homelands
0.8240	39.2	.2440	15	overture
0.8239	39.2	.4897	8	formulated
0.8239	39.2	.4190	9	poker
0.8239	39.2	.3624	10	spokesmen
0.8235	39.2	.1642	12	Addams
0.8235	39.2	.4288	9	installing
0.8235	39.2	.3715	10	introductory
0.8234	39.2	.2395	11	Arthur's
0.8232	39.2	.4535	8	Baseball
0.8231	39.2	.1814	16	griddle
0.8231	39.2	.2094	11	probation
0.8227	39.2	.3066	11	Bushmen
0.8227	39.2	.4825	8	Minneapolis
0.8226	39.2	.4081	9	nosing
0.8226	39.2	.4529	8	woodpile
0.8224	39.2	.1904	17	Denmark's
0.8223	39.2	.3200	12	apostrophes
0.8223	39.2	.0000	18	Arabelle
0.8223	39.2	.0000	18	Chippy
0.8223	39.2	.0000	18	Petros
0.8223	39.2	.0000	18	Skunk
0.8223	39.2	.0000	18	Spunk
0.8223	39.2	.0000	18	Tandy
0.8223	39.2	.0000	18	Ylis
THE PRECEDING WORD TYPE OCCUPIES RANK 18900				
0.8219	39.1	.4630	8	close-up
0.8217	39.1	.4097	9	cafes
0.8217	39.1	.4825	8	Tiber
0.8216	39.1	.1787	14	Bullfinch
0.8216	39.1	.4800	8	livid
0.8215	39.1	.4651	8	overthrow
0.8215	39.1	.3616	10	totals
0.8213	39.1	.2204	14	uncles
0.8212	39.1	.4318	9	avant-garde
0.8212	39.1	.4736	8	straightway
0.8211	39.1	.2175	16	bran
0.8209	39.1	.4207	9	Gonzales
0.8207	39.1	.3617	9	masked
0.8206	39.1	.4758	8	1621
0.8205	39.1	.2562	13	Banner
0.8205	39.1	.2384	11	Hank's
0.8204	39.1	.4061	9	planetarium
0.8204	39.1	.2792	12	sampler
0.8204	39.1	.5624	7	thunders
0.8203	39.1	.4890	8	fittings
0.8203	39.1	.4508	8	Ma'am
0.8202	39.1	.4563	8	clawing
0.8200	39.1	.4521	8	Rene
0.8200	39.1	.3731	10	397
0.8196	39.1	.4552	8	overrun
0.8195	39.1	.5460	7	bawl
0.8195	39.1	.4859	8	dissatisfaction
0.8195	39.1	.4526	8	fumbling
0.8193	39.1	.4830	8	by-products
0.8193	39.1	.2070	11	Russ
0.8193	39.1	.2070	11	Tracy
0.8192	39.1	.5457	7	equaled
0.8192	39.1	.3471	9	gorilla
0.8192	39.1	.3471	9	renters
0.8190	39.1	.5641	7	Chain
0.8184	39.1	.3244	11	Flemish
0.8182	39.1	.4753	8	moustache
0.8181	39.1	.4633	8	jutting
0.8180	39.1	.4045	9	collided
0.8177	39.1	.2208	15	phoebe
0.8177	39.1	.4516	8	waked
0.8176	39.1	.4211	9	three-minute
0.8170	39.1	.4063	9	155
0.8169	39.1	.3994	9	Waterway
0.8167	39.1	.3759	10	regulating
0.8166	39.1	.4752	8	declares
0.8165	39.1	.4673	8	overcast
0.8163	39.1	.5388	7	liberation
0.8161	39.1	.5680	7	inclusion
0.8161	39.1	.5387	7	rents
0.8160	39.1	.4218	9	insect's
0.8160	39.1	.3759	10	NATO
0.8156	39.1	.2379	15	phoneme
0.8155	39.1	.4869	8	incense
0.8154	39.1	.4745	8	feverish
0.8154	39.1	.2898	12	Gobi
0.8154	39.1	.1612	15	Maestro
0.8151	39.1	.2185	16	/g/
0.8151	39.1	.2185	16	/p/
0.8151	39.1	.2435	16	muffin
0.8149	39.1	.3948	9	gape
0.8146	39.1	.3750	10	middle-class
0.8145	39.1	.4752	8	appalling
0.8145	39.1	.2284	13	clicks
0.8144	39.1	.3956	9	experiencing
0.8143	39.1	.1160	19	Berry
0.8143	39.1	.3764	9	Parade
0.8141	39.1	.3288	11	Kaiser
0.8141	39.1	.2152	12	Roosevelt's
0.8137	39.1	.3902	9	claps
0.8135	39.1	.4532	8	stockyards
0.8134	39.1	.3720	10	roughness
0.8133	39.1	.4440	8	boxcars
0.8128	39.1	.3925	10	thicknesses
0.8127	39.1	.3539	10	Crater
0.8127	39.1	.2353	11	Pelias
0.8126	39.1	.3341	11	diffusion
0.8126	39.1	.4837	8	individual's
0.8126	39.1	.1862	17	sectional
0.8125	39.1	.5365	7	Bell's
0.8124	39.1	.4879	8	Conqueror
0.8124	39.1	.1733	14	pyrite
0.8122	39.1	.4740	8	approximated
0.8120	39.1	.3840	9	Rochester
0.8118	39.1	.4432	8	hurtling
0.8117	39.1	.3635	10	Fran
0.8115	39.1	.4290	9	reinforcement
0.8115	39.1	.4015	9	Ukraine
0.8111	39.1	.3605	10	176
0.8110	39.1	.1078	28	rivets
0.8109	39.1	.4867	8	Letters
0.8109	39.1	.4695	8	trajectory
0.8109	39.1	.4503	8	twang
0.8109	39.1	.5397	7	unwise
0.8108	39.1	.3961	9	jackknife
0.8107	39.1	.4694	8	after-school
0.8105	39.1	.3349	11	Julie's
0.8104	39.1	.3947	9	bolls
0.8103	39.1	.4855	8	adjourn

U	SFI	D	F	Word Type
0.8103	39.1	.4751	8	Chilean
THE PRECEDING WORD TYPE OCCUPIES RANK 19000				
0.8102	39.1	.4106	9	superficial
0.8101	39.1	.1813	16	Brandywine
0.8101	39.1	.1813	16	meat-packing
0.8101	39.1	.4484	8	purify
0.8100	39.1	.4030	9	corrupt
0.8100	39.1	.4833	8	downright
0.8100	39.1	.4744	8	zoom
0.8099	39.1	.4749	8	novelists
0.8099	39.1	.4371	8	saddles
0.8099	39.1	.4700	8	stiff-legged
0.8096	39.1	.1126	23	nonfiction
0.8095	39.1	.4843	8	overly
0.8095	39.1	.4085	9	plight
0.8093	39.1	.5393	7	bothers
0.8091	39.1	.3095	11	flukes
0.8091	39.1	.5551	7	thrived
0.8090	39.1	.4168	9	advocated
0.8090	39.1	.2410	14	announcing
0.8090	39.1	.4647	8	267
0.8089	39.1	.4695	8	dialed
0.8089	39.1	.3093	11	insulators
0.8089	39.1	.3992	9	rusting
0.8088	39.1	.5549	7	tugboats
0.8086	39.1	.4559	8	forty-six
0.8086	39.1	.3714	10	globular
0.8085	39.1	.0000	100	autoharp
0.8082	39.1	.0974	30	orchestras
0.8081	39.1	.4673	8	persuading
0.8078	39.1	.5362	7	crags
0.8078	39.1	.5361	7	Tioga
0.8078	39.1	.4614	8	1940's
0.8077	39.1	.3609	9	deerskins
0.8076	39.1	.5373	7	reassuringly
0.8074	39.1	.5369	7	skirted
0.8073	39.1	.5353	7	frigid
0.8067	39.1	.3917	9	DesMoines
0.8061	39.1	.3672	9	alighted
0.8061	39.1	.3672	9	draught
0.8060	39.1	.4411	8	waistcoat
0.8058	39.1	.3080	10	Baldy
0.8058	39.1	.3080	10	trundle
0.8057	39.1	.1128	25	ness
0.8056	39.1	.5590	7	Stevenson's
0.8054	39.1	.2366	15	/e-r/**
0.8053	39.1	.4709	8	fixtures
0.8051	39.1	.4632	8	riverboat
0.8049	39.1	.2928	12	baboon
0.8044	39.1	.5525	7	hoped-for
0.8041	39.1	.3836	9	leader's
0.8041	39.1	.5311	7	lions'
0.8038	39.1	.3467	10	rainwater
0.8037	39.1	.3932	9	clearings
0.8037	39.1	.3932	9	dictators
0.8037	39.1	.3932	9	fatten
0.8037	39.1	.5373	7	merrymaking
0.8036	39.1	.3948	9	Squadron
0.8031	39.0	.4518	8	tern
0.8030	39.0	.3557	10	Picture
0.8028	39.0	.4272	8	Ernst
0.8028	39.0	.3687	10	Zurich
0.8027	39.0	.2410	14	Raven
0.8026	39.0	.4711	8	discontented
0.8026	39.0	.4652	8	jarring
0.8025	39.0	.1905	13	Chouchou
0.8023	39.0	.2736	12	contracting
0.8023	39.0	.2736	12	nitric
0.8020	39.0	.2988	12	Tenzing
0.8019	39.0	.4485	8	Rough
0.8017	39.0	.5319	7	arching
0.8014	39.0	.3314	11	Bradley
0.8013	39.0	.4657	8	inefficient
0.8013	39.0	.4246	9	posing
0.8013	39.0	.4277	8	twenty-fifth
0.8013	39.0	.4744	8	321
0.8012	39.0	.4418	8	mayor's
0.8011	39.0	.5440	7	Azores
0.8011	39.0	.3017	11	Charlestown
0.8006	39.0	.5493	7	amended
0.8006	39.0	.5335	7	folly
0.8004	39.0	.2540	11	Sutter
0.8002	39.0	.5630	7	steeped
0.8001	39.0	.5485	7	GI
0.8001	39.0	.4663	8	lifetimes
0.8000	39.0	.1945	11	Casey's
0.8000	39.0	.1945	11	Gehrig
0.8000	39.0	.5328	7	loot
0.8000	39.0	.4497	8	opener
0.8000	39.0	.4080	9	pulses
0.8000	39.0	.5328	7	scorned
0.7999	39.0	.2881	13	friendships
0.7999	39.0	.4133	9	malnutrition
0.7998	39.0	.3757	10	threading
0.7997	39.0	.5474	7	Aeronautics
0.7996	39.0	.3416	10	Cabot
0.7996	39.0	.1817	15	Galilee
0.7996	39.0	.3180	11	134
0.7995	39.0	.4689	8	Shanghai
0.7994	39.0	.4390	8	dashboard
0.7994	39.0	.3525	10	Georgetown
0.7993	39.0	.4761	8	fervor
THE PRECEDING WORD TYPE OCCUPIES RANK 19100				
0.7992	39.0	.5333	7	cannons
0.7992	39.0	.4745	8	Gun
0.7992	39.0	.4496	8	Marge
0.7988	39.0	.5304	7	basking
0.7988	39.0	.4668	8	occurrences
0.7988	39.0	.5304	7	scoff
0.7988	39.0	.1801	18	th'
0.7988	39.0	.4098	9	1841
0.7984	39.0	.5250	7	flimsy
0.7984	39.0	.3315	10	Yucatan
0.7983	39.0	.3809	10	ventilation
0.7982	39.0	.4629	8	cherish
0.7982	39.0	.4690	8	filth
0.7981	39.0	.4402	8	Rapids

U	SFI	D	F	Word Type
0.7981	39.0	.5269	7	seating
0.7978	39.0	.5452	7	customarily
0.7976	39.0	.4711	8	reconcile
0.7975	39.0	.4225	8	amplifying
0.7975	39.0	.4663	8	Odyssey
0.7971	39.0	.5459	7	survives
0.7971	39.0	.3850	9	Yes
0.7970	39.0	.2369	12	Peary
0.7969	39.0	.4693	8	archaic
0.7967	39.0	.3932	9	Glasgow
0.7963	39.0	.3953	9	excursion
0.7963	39.0	.2407	14	VanDaan
0.7962	39.0	.1920	11	Nick's
0.7961	39.0	.0054	83	Speller
0.7959	39.0	.5518	7	367
0.7957	39.0	.4156	9	Bermuda
0.7956	39.0	.4548	8	Malaya
0.7955	39.0	.4703	8	249
0.7954	39.0	.5362	7	penetrates
0.7953	39.0	.5265	7	mantel
0.7953	39.0	.5420	7	prunes
0.7952	39.0	.2649	13	Creighton
0.7950	39.0	.5227	7	squirming
0.7948	39.0	.5273	7	lament
0.7945	39.0	.5355	7	gentlemanly
0.7943	39.0	.4740	8	blunder
0.7942	39.0	.5251	7	barring
0.7942	39.0	.0731	26	Capulet
0.7942	39.0	.2065	16	Caterpillar
0.7942	39.0	.4347	8	touring
0.7941	39.0	.4363	8	Paz
0.7939	39.0	.4042	9	festive
0.7938	39.0	.5485	7	alignment
0.7938	39.0	.5208	7	windowsill
0.7936	39.0	.3560	10	insulator
0.7936	39.0	.4470	8	spake
0.7934	39.0	.5490	7	thence
0.7934	39.0	.1375	23	woodworking
0.7933	39.0	.0000	53	factorization
0.7932	39.0	.4660	8	long-time
0.7931	39.0	.5403	7	buffer
0.7930	39.0	.3855	9	lumbermen
0.7930	39.0	.5400	7	167
0.7930	39.0	.3855	9	1840's
0.7927	39.0	.4767	8	earthly
0.7926	39.0	.5573	7	adhere
0.7922	39.0	.3861	9	pasteurized
0.7921	39.0	.4610	8	rudeness
0.7918	39.0	.4643	8	impose
0.7917	39.0	.5294	7	Commons
0.7917	39.0	.5294	7	lagoons
0.7916	39.0	.3920	9	Community
0.7915	39.0	.3605	9	aspen
0.7915	39.0	.4667	8	Versailles
0.7914	39.0	.5288	7	abolitionists
0.7914	39.0	.4042	9	demonstrating
0.7914	39.0	.5288	7	handicraft
0.7914	39.0	.3385	9	Mocha
0.7913	39.0	.3626	10	institute
0.7912	39.0	.4596	8	rioting
0.7911	39.0	.2761	11	geysers
0.7911	39.0	.5284	7	self-sufficient
0.7911	39.0	.4590	8	zest
0.7910	39.0	.5438	7	ruthless
0.7903	39.0	.2755	12	mares
0.7902	39.0	.3950	9	bankers
0.7902	39.0	.5384	7	hard-packed
0.7901	39.0	.4654	8	infrequent
0.7900	39.0	.3818	9	Curies
0.7900	39.0	.1026	19	healed
0.7900	39.0	.3446	9	yen
0.7899	39.0	.3891	9	cranked
0.7896	39.0	.3183	10	Nancy's
0.7893	39.0	.4146	9	dictation
0.7892	39.0	.5189	7	elapsed
0.7891	39.0	.2414	14	Thou
0.7889	39.0	.5198	7	diagnose
0.7889	39.0	.3890	9	scratchy
0.7888	39.0	.2682	13	bizarre
0.7886	39.0	.4583	8	irregularly
0.7884	39.0	.2257	13	Faraday
0.7884	39.0	.5204	7	merits
0.7884	39.0	.2260	13	seedling
0.7883	39.0	.4682	8	Olive
0.7883	39.0	.3578	9	Thatcher
0.7883	39.0	.3588	9	name's
THE PRECEDING WORD TYPE OCCUPIES RANK 19200				
0.7881	39.0	.5470	7	undeniably
0.7880	39.0	.3576	10	compartments
0.7879	39.0	.5184	7	delicacies
0.7877	39.0	.4585	8	gauges
0.7876	39.0	.4550	8	adoption
0.7876	39.0	.3791	9	centrifugal
0.7876	39.0	.3791	9	flips
0.7876	39.0	.3725	9	garrison
0.7873	39.0	.4155	9	Lester
0.7871	39.0	.3876	8	aloha
0.7871	39.0	.3207	11	guerrilla
0.7870	39.0	.4284	8	foreseen
0.7870	39.0	.4284	8	itch
0.7867	39.0	.4634	8	misused
0.7867	39.0	.2879	12	Moth
0.7866	39.0	.4674	8	compiled
0.7866	39.0	.5157	7	Excellency
0.7864	39.0	.3979	9	From
0.7864	39.0	.2349	13	pressurized
0.7863	39.0	.5233	7	calms
0.7863	39.0	.5370	7	plagues
0.7862	39.0	.3818	9	cannibals
0.7859	39.0	.4464	8	treatments
0.7858	39.0	.5201	7	flu
0.7858	39.0	.3961	9	Socrates
0.7856	39.0	.3218	11	Alpine
0.7856	39.0	.4624	8	contend
0.7855	39.0	.4614	8	gazelle
0.7853	39.0	.5166	7	unwelcome
0.7852	38.9	.3457	10	deciduous

U	SFI	D	F	Word Type
0.7852	38.9	.3457	10	diffuse
0.7850	38.9	.5365	7	anthropologist
0.7847	38.9	.4279	8	alder
0.7847	38.9	.3972	9	vile
0.7845	38.9	.5322	7	unfolding
0.7843	38.9	.4654	8	chassis
0.7843	38.9	.1414	16	crewmen
0.7843	38.9	.5404	7	footprint
0.7843	38.9	.4879	7	itching
0.7843	38.9	.2639	12	meteorologist
0.7843	38.9	.1753	17	5/2
0.7841	38.9	.3793	9	inauguration
0.7841	38.9	.5203	7	unskilled
0.7840	38.9	.5314	7	thicken
0.7839	38.9	.4890	7	squeaking
0.7839	38.9	.5205	7	windward
0.7838	38.9	.4619	8	full-blooded
0.7838	38.9	.2825	12	Mummy
0.7838	38.9	.5231	7	Nagasaki
0.7836	38.9	.4420	8	forlorn
0.7835	38.9	.4629	8	policeman's
0.7835	38.9	.4800	7	1706
0.7834	38.9	.4874	7	fairness
0.7833	38.9	.4707	8	clear-cut
0.7833	38.9	.3139	9	exaggerations
0.7832	38.9	.4889	7	heather
0.7831	38.9	.1335	16	bathysphere
0.7831	38.9	.4872	7	cluck
0.7830	38.9	.2353	10	Ehre
0.7829	38.9	.4888	7	Jet
0.7829	38.9	.3813	8	wheezing
0.7828	38.9	.3976	9	amazingly
0.7827	38.9	.3810	8	tepee
0.7825	38.9	.5184	7	marriages
0.7824	38.9	.5194	7	glorified
0.7824	38.9	.3808	8	retold
0.7822	38.9	.3805	8	UP
0.7821	38.9	.4825	7	electorate
0.7821	38.9	.4825	7	fenced-in
0.7821	38.9	.1027	21	Kara
0.7820	38.9	.3803	8	Lapland
0.7820	38.9	.5371	7	ridiculed
0.7818	38.9	.3854	9	Russia's
0.7817	38.9	.5124	7	porcupines
0.7814	38.9	.4821	7	foreheads
0.7812	38.9	.4817	7	wide-awake
0.7811	38.9	.3809	8	pelt
0.7811	38.9	.3792	8	scabbard
0.7810	38.9	.5116	7	obeying
0.7808	38.9	.4526	8	Geological
0.7806	38.9	.4519	8	right-handed
0.7804	38.9	.5222	7	troughs
0.7802	38.9	.5314	7	alarming
0.7802	38.9	.4819	7	omen
0.7800	38.9	.5181	7	zenith
0.7799	38.9	.4103	9	Gustav
0.7798	38.9	.4535	8	141
0.7797	38.9	.5478	7	Ancient
0.7796	38.9	.3988	9	denotes
0.7796	38.9	.3838	9	distributor
0.7796	38.9	.1696	16	Mexico's
0.7795	38.9	.3388	10	teaspoonfuls
0.7794	38.9	.3580	10	nationalistic
0.7794	38.9	.1880	15	sulfate
0.7793	38.9	.5379	7	maritime
0.7793	38.9	.3872	8	pokes
0.7791	38.9	.4815	7	smartest
0.7790	38.9	.4540	8	azure
0.7790	38.9	.3872	8	Riders
0.7789	38.9	.4390	8	entertainers
THE PRECEDING WORD TYPE OCCUPIES RANK 19300				
0.7788	38.9	.3598	10	Mart
0.7788	38.9	.3870	8	miner's
0.7788	38.9	.4478	8	storehouses
0.7787	38.9	.4812	7	Hiawatha
0.7787	38.9	.2108	16	operatic
0.7786	38.9	.3383	9	second-hand
0.7785	38.9	.5295	7	docking
0.7784	38.9	.4808	7	tickling
0.7783	38.9	.4561	8	installations
0.7783	38.9	.4561	8	weakening
0.7782	38.9	.1908	17	Lennie
0.7781	38.9	.4807	7	inky
0.7781	38.9	.4807	7	mallards
0.7781	38.9	.4624	8	mortals
0.7781	38.9	.5238	7	sleeper
0.7780	38.9	.3750	9	Brooks
0.7777	38.9	.4458	8	Himalaya
0.7776	38.9	.5300	7	capped
0.7776	38.9	.4859	7	disappoint
0.7775	38.9	.4481	8	memoirs
0.7775	38.9	.5065	7	rougher
0.7775	38.9	.3442	9	wiggling
0.7774	38.9	.5293	7	sincerity
0.7773	38.9	.5178	7	postponed
0.7773	38.9	.3423	10	Prussian
0.7772	38.9	.5239	7	bottled
0.7772	38.9	.3009	10	lawmakers
0.7772	38.9	.4852	7	sarcasm
0.7771	38.9	.3494	9	ol'
0.7768	38.9	.3746	8	Captain's
0.7768	38.9	.4847	7	Never
0.7767	38.9	.4552	8	approves
0.7766	38.9	.0000	17	Electro-Thinker
0.7766	38.9	.5388	7	gal
0.7766	38.9	.0000	17	Hak-Tak
0.7766	38.9	.0000	17	Heracles
0.7766	38.9	.0000	17	Marie-Louise
0.7766	38.9	.0000	17	McGarrity
0.7766	38.9	.0000	17	Miklos
0.7766	38.9	.0000	17	Muggins
0.7766	38.9	.0000	17	OFFICER
0.7766	38.9	.0000	17	Okaro
0.7766	38.9	.0000	17	Preble
0.7766	38.9	.0000	17	Roadmaster
0.7766	38.9	.0000	17	Serafina
0.7762	38.9	.4797	7	devouring

U	SFI	D	F	Word Type
0.7761	38.9	.5170	7	new-born
0.7761	38.9	.4001	9	pregnancy
0.7761	38.9	.3396	9	whitewashed
0.7760	38.9	.3990	9	neutrality
0.7760	38.9	.4754	7	unhurt
0.7759	38.9	.5171	7	Adirondacks
0.7759	38.9	.3384	10	Cork
0.7758	38.9	.4654	8	Standards
0.7757	38.9	.2577	11	erupt
0.7756	38.9	.2258	11	Taft
0.7755	38.9	.4367	8	crisscross
0.7754	38.9	.4069	9	toasters
0.7754	38.9	.2661	12	who'd
0.7753	38.9	.4536	8	advancement
0.7753	38.9	.5229	7	mar
0.7752	38.9	.1756	15	Oersted
0.7749	38.9	.2445	10	Car
0.7748	38.9	.5048	7	Territories
0.7747	38.9	.4817	7	squirrel's
0.7747	38.9	.4223	8	sulkily
0.7746	38.9	.1959	17	ballets
0.7744	38.9	.2414	10	Dot
0.7744	38.9	.4809	7	Noble
0.7742	38.9	.5091	7	founders
0.7740	38.9	.3557	9	Living
0.7739	38.9	.4210	8	handicap
0.7738	38.9	.5035	7	wrongs
0.7737	38.9	.3197	10	Oahu
0.7736	38.9	.4164	8	blueberry
0.7736	38.9	.5197	7	sterling
0.7735	38.9	.5089	7	253
0.7734	38.9	.4553	8	Hawthorne
0.7733	38.9	.5290	7	terminate
0.7732	38.9	.2480	13	Granger
0.7732	38.9	.2446	10	Nan
0.7729	38.9	.3097	10	TNT
0.7726	38.9	.5067	7	emigrated
0.7726	38.9	.4066	9	facility
0.7725	38.9	.3092	12	advisable
0.7725	38.9	.4494	8	moderates
0.7725	38.9	.3875	9	southerners
0.7724	38.9	.4526	8	permissible
0.7723	38.9	.5375	7	tolerated
0.7722	38.9	.5136	7	Hubbard
0.7721	38.9	.4469	8	peers
0.7721	38.9	.5164	7	thaws
0.7720	38.9	.4263	8	Autumn
0.7720	38.9	.2926	12	saxophone
0.7719	38.9	.4264	8	Representative
0.7718	38.9	.3859	9	Griffin
0.7716	38.9	.3841	9	Syracuse
0.7715	38.9	.3372	10	hornblende
0.7713	38.9	.1822	18	tenor
0.7712	38.9	.2023	15	hurdler
THE PRECEDING WORD TYPE OCCUPIES RANK 19400				
0.7711	38.9	.5376	7	Lord's
0.7703	38.9	.4250	8	Airlines
0.7702	38.9	.4083	8	astounded
0.7702	38.9	.3360	10	Centauri
0.7701	38.9	.5165	7	headaches
0.7700	38.9	.4544	8	harassed
0.7700	38.9	.3617	10	narration
0.7699	38.9	.2899	11	dinosaur's
0.7699	38.9	.3193	11	Folks
0.7699	38.9	.3815	9	1852
0.7698	38.9	.3033	10	Cyclops
0.7698	38.9	.2845	12	faggots
0.7697	38.9	.3368	10	Pueblos
0.7697	38.9	.3368	10	1787
0.7696	38.9	.4318	8	ventures
0.7695	38.9	.5170	7	caged
0.7695	38.9	.5302	7	narrowing
0.7693	38.9	.4848	7	unharmed
0.7692	38.9	.4506	8	NewHaven
0.7691	38.9	.3813	9	IN
0.7691	38.9	.1989	12	Snick
0.7690	38.9	.2147	13	Schmidt
0.7689	38.9	.4832	7	crevasses
0.7689	38.9	.3957	9	verify
0.7688	38.9	.4427	8	arrivals
0.7687	38.9	.4848	7	rescuers
0.7687	38.9	.4542	8	sheepishly
0.7687	38.9	.4848	7	springboard
0.7687	38.9	.4586	8	veiled
0.7686	38.9	.2410	14	-ation
0.7686	38.9	.2898	11	Ma's
0.7684	38.9	.4847	7	Ethan
0.7684	38.9	.4529	8	evils
0.7681	38.9	.3462	10	Bo
0.7680	38.9	.2493	12	wiring
0.7679	38.9	.5125	7	sorely
0.7678	38.9	.6230	6	expanses
0.7678	38.9	.4826	7	outburst
0.7678	38.9	.4826	7	tiled
0.7676	38.9	.2554	12	cleavage
0.7676	38.9	.3831	8	Landing
0.7675	38.9	.3944	9	sashes
0.7674	38.8	.2326	10	centavos
0.7674	38.9	.5210	7	contestants
0.7673	38.8	.4512	8	coupled
0.7673	38.8	.4455	8	3600
0.7672	38.8	.5216	7	prowess
0.7672	38.8	.4320	8	rasping
0.7671	38.8	.4399	8	anticipate
0.7671	38.8	.1068	28	flux
0.7670	38.8	.2446	10	carves
0.7665	38.8	.4772	7	signposts
0.7664	38.8	.1241	24	derivative
0.7664	38.8	.5198	7	scoundrel
0.7663	38.8	.5257	7	gamble
0.7662	38.8	.5233	7	pickled
0.7661	38.8	.3930	9	corned
0.7658	38.8	.5337	7	impersonal
0.7657	38.8	.2340	14	Arliss
0.7657	38.8	.1717	11	Fong
0.7656	38.8	.4145	8	blossomed
0.7656	38.8	.3811	8	hoops

U	SFI	D	F	Word Type
0.7655	38.8	.2308	13	invertebrates
0.7654	38.8	.2965	12	chronological
0.7654	38.8	.1975	12	Granddad
0.7653	38.8	.2234	14	Vanguard
0.7650	38.8	.4305	8	invest
0.7650	38.8	.3165	11	modulation
0.7650	38.8	.4567	8	titled
0.7650	38.8	.3828	9	1891
0.7649	38.8	.5103	7	Longfellow
0.7647	38.8	.4181	8	pussy
0.7646	38.8	.4036	8	smoldering
0.7646	38.8	.4278	8	unanswered
0.7642	38.8	.1069	20	neurons
0.7640	38.8	.3692	9	foraging
0.7640	38.8	.5201	7	morale
0.7639	38.8	.3216	11	variant
0.7638	38.8	.2215	10	Argo
0.7638	38.8	.2215	10	goatherd
0.7638	38.8	.6210	6	outgoing
0.7637	38.8	.4767	7	bright-red
0.7630	38.8	.4371	8	circulates
0.7630	38.8	.3704	8	prospecting
0.7630	38.8	.4611	8	weld
0.7630	38.8	.3379	10	265
0.7628	38.8	.4501	8	skeins
0.7628	38.8	.4575	8	versa
0.7628	38.8	.5088	7	1850's
0.7626	38.8	.5292	7	tote
0.7625	38.8	.3529	9	fairest
0.7624	38.8	.4067	8	newsmen
0.7623	38.8	.4014	9	Tiny
0.7622	38.8	.3824	8	hillbilly
0.7622	38.8	.5026	7	oppressed
0.7620	38.8	.2302	13	Brasilia
0.7620	38.8	.3772	9	jib
0.7620	38.8	.3856	8	rubble
0.7620	38.8	.3856	8	Summit
0.7618	38.8	.2244	10	Mechanical
THE PRECEDING WORD TYPE OCCUPIES RANK 19500				
0.7616	38.8	.4500	8	conceivably
0.7616	38.8	.5150	7	embarked
0.7612	38.8	.3436	10	referendum
0.7610	38.8	.2882	12	Alley
0.7610	38.8	.5167	7	contemplate
0.7608	38.8	.5109	7	ancients
0.7607	38.8	.5004	7	repetitive
0.7607	38.8	.6041	6	wring
0.7605	38.8	.2925	11	idiom
0.7605	38.8	.4186	8	Monticello
0.7604	38.8	.2835	11	crustaceans
0.7604	38.8	.5106	7	readying
0.7603	38.8	.4484	8	cradled
0.7603	38.8	.3429	10	ecology
0.7602	38.8	.5064	7	competed
0.7602	38.8	.5253	7	loveliness
0.7602	38.8	.4349	8	perceiving
0.7602	38.8	.4769	7	transmitters
0.7602	38.8	.4357	8	Virginian
0.7601	38.8	.5050	7	paradox
0.7599	38.8	.5061	7	bayonets
0.7598	38.8	.6035	6	foolhardy
0.7598	38.8	.6199	6	inability
0.7598	38.8	.5193	7	oppressive
0.7594	38.8	.3858	9	admits
0.7594	38.8	.4352	8	awkwardly
0.7594	38.8	.2709	12	Bordeaux
0.7594	38.8	.3618	9	Mecca
0.7593	38.8	.5120	7	habitual
0.7593	38.8	.3246	10	soundings
0.7591	38.8	.5092	7	honeycomb
0.7591	38.8	.4849	7	slicing
0.7590	38.8	.4643	8	wrappings
0.7586	38.8	.6052	6	benevolent
0.7586	38.8	.6052	6	interrupting
0.7585	38.8	.4114	8	envied
0.7583	38.8	.3955	8	waiters
0.7581	38.8	.3475	10	erratic
0.7581	38.8	.3758	9	galvanized
0.7581	38.8	.2790	11	roosters
0.7580	38.8	.6046	6	foreboding
0.7580	38.8	.6046	6	headdresses
0.7579	38.8	.5155	7	interchangeably
0.7576	38.8	.5127	7	autobiographical
0.7576	38.8	.6023	6	ruddy
0.7575	38.8	.3336	9	Abner
0.7575	38.8	.3336	9	Annie's
0.7575	38.8	.5082	7	churchyard
0.7575	38.8	.6073	6	jotted
0.7574	38.8	.3751	9	shacks
0.7573	38.8	.3846	9	deJaneiro
0.7573	38.8	.5043	7	receded
0.7573	38.8	.6042	6	urgently
0.7572	38.8	.4236	8	swerved
0.7570	38.8	.3771	8	chum
0.7570	38.8	.3771	8	slicker
0.7570	38.8	.4331	8	waged
0.7569	38.8	.5039	7	beady
0.7569	38.8	.2769	13	gouge
0.7568	38.8	.3889	9	incessant
0.7567	38.8	.6037	6	august
0.7567	38.8	.3391	10	dentist's
0.7566	38.8	.2591	11	Kirk
0.7565	38.8	.5094	7	esteem
0.7565	38.8	.3876	9	explanatory
0.7565	38.8	.6008	6	ushered
0.7561	38.8	.6031	6	netted
0.7561	38.8	.6031	6	oversized
0.7561	38.8	.3788	8	Sounds
0.7560	38.8	.4198	8	impolite
0.7559	38.8	.4775	7	fifty-cent
0.7559	38.8	.4775	7	Jones'
0.7559	38.8	.1336	16	Melissa
0.7559	38.8	.5208	7	misuse
0.7559	38.8	.4975	7	underfoot
0.7558	38.8	.4207	8	advisers
0.7558	38.8	.3779	9	kilometer
0.7558	38.8	.3352	10	Malay

U	SFI	D	F	Word Type
0.7558	38.8	.3002	11	slime
0.7557	38.8	.5197	7	sophomore
0.7556	38.8	.3308	9	485
0.7555	38.8	.0515	46	Him
0.7554	38.8	.6006	6	tireless
0.7553	38.8	.3422	10	attributes
0.7552	38.8	.2013	15	Cole
0.7551	38.8	.4078	8	unbearable
0.7551	38.8	.4968	7	warily
0.7548	38.8	.3332	10	Hatteras
0.7546	38.8	.4412	8	mariners
0.7544	38.8	.3756	8	doings
0.7543	38.8	.5177	7	innate
0.7543	38.8	.2869	12	inventive
0.7542	38.8	.4769	7	enchantment
0.7542	38.8	.4770	7	flickered
0.7540	38.8	.3695	9	colossal
0.7537	38.8	.4039	8	logged
0.7536	38.8	.4416	8	raided
0.7535	38.8	.3407	10	kidney
0.7534	38.8	.3757	9	Norway's
0.7532	38.8	.5219	7	encased
THE PRECEDING WORD TYPE OCCUPIES RANK 19600				
0.7532	38.8	.2140	10	whaler
0.7531	38.8	.3128	10	pantomime
0.7530	38.8	.3237	10	foresters
0.7529	38.8	.2065	15	Saul
0.7528	38.8	.5055	7	boxlike
0.7527	38.8	.2926	9	owl's
0.7527	38.8	.3773	9	Papal
0.7526	38.8	.4295	8	Smokey
0.7525	38.8	.3489	8	unguarded
0.7523	38.8	.1677	17	sovereigns
0.7522	38.8	.5020	7	Mile
0.7519	38.8	.5204	7	discouraging
0.7518	38.8	.4962	7	fiercest
0.7518	38.8	.4122	8	ironed
0.7518	38.8	.4198	8	westerly
0.7517	38.8	.3694	9	chimes
0.7517	38.8	.4173	8	Yorktown
0.7516	38.8	.2906	10	firearms
0.7516	38.8	.4909	7	questionable
0.7515	38.8	.3151	11	castanets
0.7512	38.8	.2415	10	Seller
0.7511	38.8	.4176	8	horribly
0.7511	38.8	.4538	8	outboard
0.7508	38.8	.4361	8	conveyor
0.7508	38.8	.4361	8	utilities
0.7506	38.8	.4286	8	petrified
0.7505	38.8	.4744	7	goody
0.7504	38.8	.3188	11	Charley's
0.7503	38.8	.3679	9	Era
0.7503	38.8	.3058	11	Guild
0.7502	38.8	.3787	8	Glossary
0.7502	38.8	.4161	8	grueling
0.7501	38.8	.5033	7	mightiest
0.7500	38.8	.6013	6	minnows
0.7500	38.8	.6013	6	organizer
0.7500	38.8	.4400	8	sexes
0.7499	38.8	.3120	10	Cap'n
0.7499	38.7	.5138	7	diplomat
0.7499	38.7	.4281	8	immortality
0.7499	38.8	.5026	7	someplace
0.7495	38.7	.6013	6	defiant
0.7495	38.7	.4306	8	isle
0.7495	38.7	.4116	8	tenderness
0.7494	38.7	.3276	9	chandelier
0.7492	38.7	.3832	9	boycott
0.7490	38.7	.5007	7	550
0.7488	38.7	.3998	8	colour
0.7488	38.7	.4927	7	inaccessible
0.7487	38.7	.2407	10	Johnnie
0.7484	38.7	.0000	50	exponents
0.7484	38.7	.4181	8	low-lying
0.7484	38.7	.5024	7	thereupon
0.7483	38.7	.3720	8	Crystal
0.7482	38.7	.1025	27	diphthong
0.7482	38.7	.2233	14	Dixie
0.7479	38.7	.4970	7	illusions
0.7479	38.7	.5113	7	weakens
0.7476	38.7	.0885	27	Guides
0.7474	38.7	.4360	8	contradictions
0.7472	38.7	.2891	10	Denis
0.7470	38.7	.4176	8	threshed
0.7469	38.7	.5150	7	worshiping
0.7466	38.7	.5023	7	impossibility
0.7463	38.7	.5124	7	vantage
0.7463	38.7	.4730	7	weevil
0.7462	38.7	.2130	14	etched
0.7461	38.7	.5962	6	excites
0.7461	38.7	.3729	9	industrialized
0.7461	38.7	.3729	9	uplands
0.7460	38.7	.3669	8	Lamar
0.7458	38.7	.5960	6	ever-changing
0.7457	38.7	.5113	7	asparagus
0.7457	38.7	.4796	7	oilcloth
0.7456	38.7	.4954	7	reliability
0.7456	38.7	.2021	15	1871
0.7455	38.7	.2604	12	boost
0.7454	38.7	.5158	7	bonnets
0.7453	38.7	.3698	8	chloroform
0.7452	38.7	.5019	7	foretell
0.7452	38.7	.3273	10	tanner
0.7449	38.7	.2225	12	teaspoonful
0.7449	38.7	.5002	7	worshipers
0.7447	38.7	.5100	7	pretense
0.7446	38.7	.5978	6	lug
0.7445	38.7	.5084	7	believers
0.7445	38.7	.5905	6	cream-colored
0.7444	38.7	.3380	10	exploited
0.7443	38.7	.3318	10	Gil
0.7443	38.7	.4646	7	hilltops
0.7441	38.7	.3407	10	Blind
0.7440	38.7	.4646	7	Legislature
0.7439	38.7	.4642	7	plodded
0.7439	38.7	.4349	8	splinter
0.7436	38.7	.4642	7	fanning

U	SFI	D	F	Word Type
0.7436	38.7	.3962	8	harnessing
0.7436	38.7	.3962	8	jays
0.7435	38.7	.5075	7	sociology
0.7435	38.7	.3347	10	songbirds
0.7435	38.7	.4913	7	2400
0.7434	38.7	.5134	7	eternally
THE PRECEDING WORD TYPE OCCUPIES RANK 19700				
0.7434	38.7	.5131	7	prevail
0.7434	38.7	.5126	7	profane
0.7433	38.7	.3350	9	Greene
0.7432	38.7	.4081	8	joked
0.7432	38.7	.4362	8	powders
0.7430	38.7	.3650	8	wonderingly
0.7429	38.7	.3911	9	1/2-inch
0.7426	38.7	.4795	7	thoughtfulness
0.7425	38.7	.4355	8	autonomous
0.7425	38.7	.3840	8	spinners
0.7424	38.7	.5064	7	faculties
0.7423	38.7	.3743	8	tugboat
0.7422	38.7	.3079	10	displeased
0.7422	38.7	.3010	11	Peruvian
0.7421	38.7	.4701	7	good-night
0.7421	38.7	.4701	7	Goodman
0.7421	38.7	.4701	7	heeded
0.7421	38.7	.3760	9	refrigerated
0.7420	38.7	.1117	16	withered
0.7419	38.7	.4028	8	Armenian
0.7419	38.7	.3948	8	turnpike
0.7418	38.7	.4114	8	critter
0.7417	38.7	.3793	9	fused
0.7417	38.7	.4150	8	vigil
0.7415	38.7	.1941	14	embryos
0.7414	38.7	.5155	7	forfeit
0.7414	38.7	.4292	8	unwind
0.7412	38.7	.4055	8	sandpipers
0.7410	38.7	.4131	8	StLawrence
0.7408	38.7	.4673	7	hesitantly
0.7408	38.7	.4673	7	regretfully
0.7406	38.7	.4254	8	breach
0.7406	38.7	.4671	7	Clemens
0.7406	38.7	.3791	9	implements
0.7406	38.7	.3317	9	Puss
0.7406	38.7	.5923	6	untamed
0.7405	38.7	.4937	7	bled
0.7404	38.7	.4968	7	bi
0.7401	38.7	.4895	7	1816
0.7400	38.7	.5057	7	ecstatic
0.7400	38.7	.3016	10	latex
0.7399	38.7	.3242	10	tantrums
0.7397	38.7	.4333	8	praises
0.7396	38.7	.3800	9	Damascus
0.7396	38.7	.1689	20	synonymous
0.7395	38.7	.5072	7	retention
0.7394	38.7	.4888	7	housekeeping
0.7394	38.7	.4118	8	negotiate
0.7393	38.7	.4978	7	dilapidated
0.7393	38.7	.4924	7	entrusted
0.7393	38.7	.3831	9	Nashville
0.7393	38.7	.4391	8	routines
0.7392	38.7	.3745	9	essays
0.7392	38.7	.3766	8	headband
0.7388	38.7	.4664	7	moo
0.7387	38.7	.5178	7	expansive
0.7387	38.7	.4186	8	truce
0.7384	38.7	.4387	8	scholarships
0.7374	38.7	.3257	10	concave
0.7371	38.7	.4645	7	steadied
0.7371	38.7	.3262	9	um
0.7369	38.7	.3536	9	grownup
0.7366	38.7	.4626	7	earshot
0.7365	38.7	.4624	7	clanking
0.7365	38.7	.2843	12	discolored
0.7365	38.7	.4191	8	Green's
0.7364	38.7	.3318	10	McClellan
0.7363	38.7	.1931	14	Ababa
0.7363	38.7	.1931	14	Addis
0.7360	38.7	.4349	8	stance
0.7359	38.7	.5000	7	albatrosses
0.7358	38.7	.1409	15	Abigail
0.7358	38.7	.1409	15	Debby
0.7358	38.7	.4614	7	upholstered
0.7355	38.7	.3308	10	Chicago's
0.7354	38.7	.3750	9	$75
0.7354	38.7	.1099	23	evolutionary
0.7351	38.7	.3820	8	apprenticed
0.7351	38.7	.4071	8	dens
0.7351	38.7	.3685	9	theorems
0.7349	38.7	.3598	8	prettily
0.7349	38.7	.3319	10	radicals
0.7347	38.7	.4882	7	plunges
0.7345	38.7	.2255	15	antecedent
0.7344	38.7	.4770	7	overtime
0.7343	38.7	.3501	9	interviews
0.7338	38.7	.2613	11	impeachment
0.7337	38.7	.4868	7	fabricated
0.7336	38.7	.2193	13	chestnuts
0.7336	38.7	.2805	10	Pappy
0.7336	38.7	.2301	14	proofreading
0.7336	38.7	.2806	11	Simon's
0.7335	38.7	.1997	10	Dickie
0.7335	38.7	.1881	16	Urban
0.7333	38.7	.3553	9	doer
0.7333	38.7	.4602	7	one-story
0.7332	38.7	.4738	7	drawl
0.7331	38.7	.3100	10	dame
0.7331	38.7	.3276	10	multiplier
0.7330	38.7	.1655	16	Liza
THE PRECEDING WORD TYPE OCCUPIES RANK 19800				
0.7330	38.7	.3120	10	Toltecs
0.7326	38.6	.4055	8	paralyze
0.7326	38.6	.4055	8	purified
0.7325	38.6	.4057	8	Clark's
0.7325	38.6	.2126	13	south-seeking
0.7323	38.6	.0793	32	zipper
0.7321	38.6	.4846	7	rearranged
0.7319	38.6	.3554	9	1884
0.7317	38.6	.4895	7	embark

U	SFI	D	F	Word Type
0.7317	38.6	.2395	12	Tiros
0.7316	38.6	.4282	8	outing
0.7315	38.6	.3609	9	filmed
0.7313	38.6	.3232	9	a-sailing
0.7313	38.6	.3232	9	Caspar
0.7313	38.6	.4612	7	surrey
0.7313	38.6	.4083	8	suspects
0.7312	38.6	.4050	8	liberties
0.7311	38.6	.3608	9	optics
0.7309	38.6	.0000	16	Chico
0.7309	38.6	.0000	16	Duffy
0.7309	38.6	.0000	16	Francie
0.7309	38.6	.0000	16	Louella
0.7309	38.6	.0000	16	Majda
0.7309	38.6	.0000	16	Meadowlark
0.7309	38.6	.0000	16	Ohiyesa
0.7309	38.6	.2048	10	Priam
0.7309	38.6	.0000	16	Ruffles
0.7309	38.6	.0000	16	Soo-Pung
0.7306	38.6	.4348	8	effected
0.7306	38.6	.4896	7	Her
0.7306	38.6	.4125	8	t's
0.7305	38.6	.4994	7	187
0.7301	38.6	.3797	9	Feb
0.7301	38.6	.4112	8	sects
0.7301	38.6	.4112	8	1950's
0.7299	38.6	.4302	8	particulars
0.7298	38.6	.4635	7	fuzz
0.7297	38.6	.4028	8	Cuzco
0.7297	38.6	.4861	7	263
0.7296	38.6	.4824	7	glories
0.7294	38.6	.4842	7	antagonism
0.7294	38.6	.3662	8	Ticonderoga
0.7293	38.6	.4589	7	squashes
0.7292	38.6	.3593	9	Duquesne
0.7292	38.6	.4781	7	headway
0.7291	38.6	.4090	8	millpond
0.7290	38.6	.4007	8	bonnie
0.7289	38.6	.4661	7	recalling
0.7284	38.6	.4903	7	classics
0.7280	38.6	.3991	8	ale
0.7278	38.6	.4876	7	console
0.7278	38.6	.4871	7	resolute
0.7277	38.6	.3554	9	frontiersmen
0.7277	38.6	.4291	8	standstill
0.7277	38.6	.4030	8	wreaths
0.7276	38.6	.4962	7	devising
0.7276	38.6	.3982	8	sitter
0.7275	38.6	.4534	7	Murphy's
0.7275	38.6	.4520	7	romp
0.7275	38.6	.4085	8	UnitedStates'
0.7272	38.6	.4575	7	wetting
0.7271	38.6	.0665	25	Maureen
0.7270	38.6	.2677	11	molting
0.7270	38.6	.2677	11	sunspots
0.7263	38.6	.4799	7	mutually
0.7260	38.6	.1316	19	Steamboat
0.7258	38.6	.3621	9	boxcar
0.7258	38.6	.3263	10	selective
0.7257	38.6	.4860	7	monotony
0.7255	38.6	.4303	8	conical
0.7254	38.6	.4683	7	brothers'
0.7253	38.6	.4852	7	guttural
0.7252	38.6	.2428	12	amplitude
0.7251	38.6	.3368	10	Chancellor
0.7251	38.6	.1728	16	warn't
0.7250	38.6	.3739	9	roughage
0.7249	38.6	.1823	14	Cancer
0.7248	38.6	.4777	7	pasteurization
0.7247	38.6	.4938	7	obsolete
0.7246	38.6	.3108	11	Impressionism
0.7245	38.6	.4922	7	generates
0.7244	38.6	.4585	7	lubrication
0.7243	38.6	.4594	7	lawful
0.7243	38.6	.4324	8	mosaic
0.7243	38.6	.4162	8	ply
0.7242	38.6	.4770	7	life-giving
0.7242	38.6	.4592	7	wishful
0.7241	38.6	.4589	7	Portland
0.7241	38.6	.2389	13	salvation
0.7241	38.6	.4599	7	slugs
0.7238	38.6	.4832	7	newsboy
0.7237	38.6	.0697	30	NP
0.7234	38.6	.0841	30	derivatives
0.7234	38.6	.4910	7	secures
0.7233	38.6	.4579	7	fraud
0.7233	38.6	.4735	7	turner
0.7229	38.6	.4575	7	campaigning
0.7228	38.6	.5028	7	airs
0.7228	38.6	.4554	7	nick
0.7226	38.6	.5567	6	clasp
THE PRECEDING WORD TYPE OCCUPIES RANK 19900				
0.7226	38.6	.4753	7	overflows
0.7221	38.6	.3751	9	virtuosity
0.7220	38.6	.2763	10	Barrett
0.7220	38.6	.2294	10	Iolcus
0.7219	38.6	.3430	9	gush
0.7219	38.6	.4099	8	roster
0.7218	38.6	.3112	9	Constitutional
0.7218	38.6	.0598	37	symphonic
0.7216	38.6	.4262	8	creases
0.7213	38.6	.4548	7	katydids
0.7209	38.6	.4187	8	recommends
0.7208	38.6	.5553	6	worn-out
0.7207	38.6	.3259	10	Earle
0.7206	38.6	.4841	7	1827
0.7205	38.6	.4914	7	modernized
0.7203	38.6	.1835	17	tuba
0.7202	38.6	.3523	9	addicted
0.7201	38.6	.5580	6	tingling
0.7199	38.6	.4447	7	reeled
0.7197	38.6	.5577	6	cranny
0.7197	38.6	.5577	6	thrice
0.7197	38.6	.5577	6	wry
0.7196	38.6	.3526	8	bonny
0.7195	38.6	.4070	8	humbly
0.7195	38.6	.1736	18	micrometer

U	SFI	D	F	Word Type
0.7195	38.6	.0527	30	respelled
0.7194	38.6	.4878	7	assures
0.7194	38.6	.3505	9	DDT
0.7194	38.6	.5540	6	Engineers
0.7194	38.6	.4530	7	Greenfield
0.7194	38.6	.4893	7	mistakenly
0.7194	38.6	.4530	7	Montcalm
0.7194	38.6	.4530	7	necklaces
0.7193	38.6	.4228	8	profusion
0.7191	38.6	.3270	9	heck
0.7191	38.6	.5573	6	orators
0.7190	38.6	.4818	7	two-headed
0.7187	38.6	.2434	13	se
0.7187	38.6	.4675	7	Stock
0.7186	38.6	.5511	6	air-conditioned
0.7186	38.6	.5536	6	excitable
0.7184	38.6	.3782	8	boastful
0.7184	38.6	.4259	8	forsaken
0.7182	38.6	.5568	6	sedan
0.7182	38.6	.5568	6	wallowing
0.7181	38.6	.5566	6	balsam
0.7179	38.6	.4807	7	shudders
0.7178	38.6	.5530	6	barrage
0.7178	38.6	.3402	10	duplicates
0.7178	38.6	.5538	6	nestled
0.7178	38.6	.5538	6	replying
0.7178	38.6	.2991	11	XVI
0.7177	38.6	.5563	6	deceptive
0.7177	38.6	.5563	6	khaki
0.7177	38.6	.1387	18	ratios
0.7177	38.6	.5526	6	thermos
0.7174	38.6	.4766	7	gazelles
0.7174	38.6	.5562	6	mimicked
0.7173	38.6	.4745	7	landowner
0.7173	38.6	.3535	9	Nez
0.7172	38.6	.5570	6	conceited
0.7172	38.6	.5570	6	trappings
0.7171	38.6	.4040	8	Norfolk
0.7169	38.6	.3028	9	Butter
0.7168	38.6	.4760	7	soothingly
0.7166	38.6	.5497	6	coughs
0.7165	38.6	.2600	10	Dell
0.7165	38.6	.5528	6	vineyard
0.7164	38.6	.5567	6	half-grown
0.7162	38.6	.3184	10	librarians
0.7162	38.6	.3626	9	Political
0.7161	38.5	.1518	17	bisect
0.7161	38.6	.3921	8	driest
0.7159	38.5	.4676	7	arrogant
0.7159	38.5	.2992	10	mirth
0.7159	38.5	.3203	9	Palomar
0.7158	38.5	.5523	6	aimless
0.7158	38.5	.4787	7	drunken
0.7158	38.5	.4787	7	embraces
0.7158	38.5	.4788	7	foodstuffs
0.7158	38.5	.3086	9	Hilo
0.7157	38.5	.0956	27	Petrouchka
0.7157	38.5	.2678	11	soiled
0.7156	38.5	.4730	7	interviewed
0.7155	38.5	.3586	8	stinger
0.7154	38.5	.5520	6	heroism
0.7154	38.5	.5520	6	leaner
0.7154	38.5	.5520	6	twirling
0.7154	38.5	.4767	7	Wonderful
0.7149	38.5	.4197	8	jerks
0.7149	38.5	.4863	7	purification
0.7149	38.5	.4431	7	submerge
0.7148	38.5	.4542	7	cud
0.7148	38.5	.4200	8	emergence
0.7147	38.5	.2353	12	ATP
0.7146	38.5	.4009	8	extensions
0.7146	38.5	.4543	7	humiliating
0.7145	38.5	.3577	8	Here
0.7145	38.5	.3452	9	know-how
0.7145	38.5	.3379	9	unfastened

THE PRECEDING WORD TYPE OCCUPIES RANK 20000

U	SFI	D	F	Word Type
0.7142	38.5	.3202	9	storekeepers
0.7140	38.5	.3453	9	molt
0.7138	38.5	.4675	7	one-sixth
0.7138	38.5	.3952	8	trucking
0.7137	38.5	.3641	9	censorship
0.7136	38.5	.2240	13	DE
0.7136	38.5	.2485	12	oz
0.7136	38.5	.2746	11	Twins
0.7136	38.5	.2157	13	Yemen
0.7135	38.5	.3984	8	Letter
0.7135	38.5	.4114	8	principals
0.7133	38.5	.3471	8	Hart
0.7128	38.5	.4418	7	laboring
0.7128	38.5	.2905	10	six-year-old
0.7127	38.5	.1616	15	Kingston
0.7127	38.5	.1616	15	Mekong
0.7125	38.5	.4261	8	aristocracy
0.7125	38.5	.4444	7	rips
0.7124	38.5	.2408	12	metabolism
0.7123	38.5	.0804	23	replacements
0.7122	38.5	.4159	8	rigors
0.7122	38.5	.2327	11	Wilfred
0.7121	38.5	.4761	7	mango
0.7121	38.5	.4875	7	pupils'
0.7119	38.5	.4499	7	unanimous
0.7116	38.5	.4447	7	Tibet
0.7113	38.5	.3196	9	Lefty
0.7113	38.5	.3613	9	1920s
0.7112	38.5	.1146	18	parasitic
0.7110	38.5	.2320	11	beaming
0.7110	38.5	.4553	7	sag
0.7109	38.5	.4703	7	Alice's
0.7109	38.5	.4633	7	haughty
0.7108	38.5	.3545	8	saluted
0.7108	38.5	.4795	7	tripled
0.7106	38.5	.4529	7	dishonest
0.7103	38.5	.5483	6	blot
0.7102	38.5	.5497	6	clacking
0.7101	38.5	.4919	7	broaden
0.7101	38.5	.5514	6	exertion
0.7101	38.5	.4010	8	succotash
0.7101	38.5	.5518	6	vale
0.7100	38.5	.5512	6	effortless
0.7099	38.5	.5515	6	inquire
0.7098	38.5	.5516	6	self-respecting
0.7098	38.5	.3430	9	Volga
0.7097	38.5	.5514	6	cataract
0.7097	38.5	.5496	6	unforgettable
0.7095	38.5	.5495	6	clank
0.7095	38.5	.2592	11	Dominican
0.7094	38.5	.4104	8	deviation
0.7094	38.5	.4649	7	exclaiming
0.7094	38.5	.5494	6	victor
0.7093	38.5	.3907	8	defiantly
0.7092	38.5	.3530	8	Charles'
0.7092	38.5	.5493	6	odd-looking
0.7091	38.5	.4543	7	Elizabeth's
0.7091	38.5	.3674	9	envious
0.7091	38.5	.4761	7	mansions
0.7091	38.5	.5496	6	outlandish
0.7090	38.5	.3455	9	commissioners
0.7090	38.5	.4731	7	portrayed
0.7089	38.5	.3444	9	burners
0.7088	38.5	.3876	8	repudiated
0.7088	38.5	.3876	8	three-day
0.7086	38.5	.2607	12	X-rays
0.7085	38.5	.3057	9	Cherry
0.7084	38.5	.4207	8	perceptible
0.7082	38.5	.3543	9	motivated
0.7081	38.5	.4656	7	backers
0.7078	38.5	.4562	7	believable
0.7078	38.5	.3257	10	linguists
0.7077	38.5	.4651	7	eminently
0.7076	38.5	.4677	7	withhold
0.7075	38.5	.2394	9	bagpipes
0.7075	38.5	.3836	8	irritating
0.7075	38.5	.4761	7	rooters
0.7075	38.5	.2394	9	Toto
0.7072	38.5	.4118	8	commuting
0.7072	38.5	.4118	8	counterparts
0.7072	38.5	.4118	8	insistence
0.7072	38.5	.2898	10	1857
0.7071	38.5	.4646	7	conflicting
0.7071	38.5	.4090	8	246
0.7070	38.5	.5444	6	money's
0.7069	38.5	.3464	9	lapping
0.7069	38.5	.5432	6	starlit
0.7068	38.5	.1800	10	Bobby's
0.7068	38.5	.2770	11	isometric
0.7067	38.5	.0741	25	MN
0.7067	38.5	.4642	7	schoolchildren
0.7066	38.5	.2940	10	crunching
0.7066	38.5	.3558	8	Lloyd
0.7063	38.5	.3958	8	fussed
0.7063	38.5	.4658	7	jangling
0.7063	38.5	.4346	7	maneuvers
0.7063	38.5	.3958	8	rearing
0.7061	38.5	.5430	6	scribbled
0.7058	38.5	.4589	7	astir
0.7058	38.5	.4804	7	elated

THE PRECEDING WORD TYPE OCCUPIES RANK 20100

U	SFI	D	F	Word Type
0.7057	38.5	.4683	7	conversational
0.7057	38.5	.4418	7	prim
0.7057	38.5	.4683	7	spade
0.7057	38.5	.5440	6	tropic
0.7056	38.5	.2642	11	fain
0.7056	38.5	.5484	6	non
0.7053	38.5	.5437	6	miserly
0.7051	38.5	.4846	7	communal
0.7051	38.5	.3442	9	hereby
0.7050	38.5	.4625	7	alerted
0.7050	38.5	.5437	6	tinkering
0.7048	38.5	.2250	14	ensembles
0.7047	38.5	.4093	8	1750
0.7045	38.5	.3821	8	blacksmiths
0.7045	38.5	.2545	12	unprecedented
0.7044	38.5	.4677	7	affections
0.7043	38.5	.4543	7	good-looking
0.7042	38.5	.4097	8	reversing
0.7042	38.5	.2199	14	Sylvia
0.7041	38.5	.5650	6	inflicted
0.7039	38.5	.5649	6	reorganized
0.7038	38.5	.3088	9	slag
0.7037	38.5	.5649	6	recruited
0.7035	38.5	.3590	8	hyena
0.7035	38.5	.3849	8	277
0.7034	38.5	.2180	13	Sugar
0.7032	38.5	.4071	8	clockwork
0.7032	38.5	.4536	7	flooring
0.7032	38.5	.1295	21	waistline
0.7030	38.5	.4725	7	rallied
0.7029	38.5	.4807	7	pamphlets
0.7027	38.5	.4693	7	productivity
0.7026	38.5	.1824	15	Argentina's
0.7025	38.5	.3097	10	aerospace
0.7025	38.5	.3283	9	breakfasts
0.7025	38.5	.4388	7	chirped
0.7025	38.5	.3283	9	darn
0.7025	38.5	.4782	7	persuasive
0.7024	38.5	.4097	8	duly
0.7023	38.5	.3412	8	cupola
0.7023	38.5	.2880	10	ghettos
0.7022	38.5	.2832	11	Orthodox
0.7020	38.5	.4716	7	Dynasty
0.7019	38.5	.3532	9	prototype
0.7019	38.5	.4504	7	wonderment
0.7017	38.5	.3552	9	lodestone
0.7017	38.5	.4507	7	stacking
0.7017	38.5	.3552	9	topographic
0.7016	38.5	.4440	7	abuses
0.7016	38.5	.4685	7	dislodged
0.7016	38.5	.4423	7	inhabitant
0.7015	38.5	.4639	7	caverns
0.7014	38.5	.4243	8	geometrical
0.7014	38.5	.4224	7	quarrelsome
0.7013	38.5	.2445	12	Deborah
0.7013	38.5	.2574	10	flyways
0.7013	38.5	.2574	10	Jets
0.7011	38.5	.1596	13	Kennie
0.7010	38.5	.5586	6	markedly
0.7009	38.5	.3867	8	best-loved
0.7009	38.5	.3566	9	irony
0.7007	38.5	.5583	6	dangle
0.7007	38.5	.2713	11	Hardy
0.7007	38.5	.4727	7	perceptive
0.7007	38.5	.4727	7	strengths
0.7007	38.5	.2528	11	Verdi
0.7004	38.5	.3466	8	Creator
0.7004	38.5	.4368	7	disappointing
0.7004	38.5	.5597	6	Universe
0.7002	38.5	.4474	7	minks
0.7002	38.5	.4474	7	tins
0.7001	38.5	.5576	6	spans
0.7000	38.5	.4696	7	forage
0.6999	38.5	.4378	7	raincoats
0.6995	38.4	.4688	7	bombarded
0.6991	38.4	.1963	15	Faust
0.6991	38.4	.3377	9	Mesozoic
0.6991	38.4	.3377	9	trilobites
0.6990	38.4	.4696	7	133
0.6989	38.4	.4757	7	fodder
0.6987	38.4	.4786	7	cutouts
0.6986	38.4	.4397	7	crossings
0.6986	38.4	.3043	10	shrines
0.6985	38.4	.3370	9	earthworm
0.6984	38.4	.4507	7	greenhorn
0.6981	38.4	.4652	7	communist
0.6980	38.4	.4587	7	262
0.6978	38.4	.2745	11	-or
0.6976	38.4	.3095	10	all-out
0.6976	38.4	.3095	10	Lyndon
0.6975	38.4	.3959	8	creed
0.6975	38.4	.1547	13	MexicoCity
0.6975	38.4	.3253	10	strengthens
0.6973	38.4	.4640	7	masons
0.6972	38.4	.4748	7	limber
0.6972	38.4	.4450	7	thrower
0.6971	38.4	.4661	7	subdivided
0.6968	38.4	.2335	13	-est
0.6968	38.4	.4240	7	curing
0.6968	38.4	.1568	16	thank-you

THE PRECEDING WORD TYPE OCCUPIES RANK 20200

U	SFI	D	F	Word Type
0.6967	38.4	.4389	7	Navigator
0.6967	38.4	.4389	7	1824
0.6966	38.4	.2810	11	primeval
0.6964	38.4	.1414	17	barter
0.6964	38.4	.4628	7	refill
0.6964	38.4	.2994	10	TO
0.6964	38.4	.4495	7	wanders
0.6963	38.4	.1561	17	confrontation
0.6961	38.4	.3445	9	40%
0.6960	38.4	.3196	8	Marineland
0.6960	38.4	.3534	9	scenting
0.6960	38.4	.2358	13	tenses
0.6958	38.4	.4791	7	enhance
0.6957	38.4	.4085	8	Saints
0.6957	38.4	.2816	11	Semitic
0.6957	38.4	.4629	7	Solon
0.6956	38.4	.3452	9	dressmaker
0.6954	38.4	.2442	9	bunt
0.6954	38.4	.2442	9	kegs
0.6954	38.4	.2442	9	Lazear
0.6952	38.4	.4827	7	downs
0.6952	38.4	.4080	8	utilizes
0.6951	38.4	.2292	9	cheetahs
0.6951	38.4	.2292	9	Essex
0.6951	38.4	.2712	11	LM
0.6951	38.4	.2292	9	Pascual
0.6951	38.4	.2292	9	Wellington's
0.6950	38.4	.4619	7	colonist
0.6950	38.4	.3393	9	excise
0.6948	38.4	.4457	7	comin'
0.6948	38.4	.4299	7	turtle's
0.6946	38.4	.3231	9	Benson
0.6946	38.4	.3488	9	Lola
0.6946	38.4	.4584	7	many-colored
0.6943	38.4	.4446	7	suspicions
0.6942	38.4	.4375	7	Ireland's
0.6940	38.4	.2815	10	Zion
0.6939	38.4	.2378	9	cowhands
0.6938	38.4	.4685	7	impenetrable
0.6937	38.4	.3336	9	Cuba's
0.6936	38.4	.2279	9	Daly
0.6936	38.4	.4621	7	LongIsland
0.6936	38.4	.2735	11	Thomson
0.6935	38.4	.3810	8	flitted
0.6934	38.4	.3107	10	spraying
0.6932	38.4	.4572	7	bygone
0.6932	38.4	.4780	7	suffice
0.6930	38.4	.4285	7	awaits
0.6930	38.4	.4598	7	Gorge
0.6929	38.4	.5614	6	exhibitions
0.6929	38.4	.2493	11	Urals
0.6927	38.4	.4407	7	tacked
0.6925	38.4	.3469	8	Tanganyika
0.6925	38.4	.4559	7	tinted
0.6925	38.4	.4281	7	wily
0.6923	38.4	.4610	7	conducts
0.6923	38.4	.2269	9	Rockne
0.6923	38.4	.2269	9	subheadings
0.6922	38.4	.3198	9	debates
0.6921	38.4	.4800	7	ups
0.6920	38.4	.2838	11	mender
0.6920	38.4	.4635	7	thunderbolt
0.6917	38.4	.4714	7	Insurance
0.6917	38.4	.3401	9	Pericles
0.6917	38.4	.2307	9	salesgirl
0.6915	38.4	.3460	8	Singapore
0.6914	38.4	.4599	7	dependents
0.6914	38.4	.4665	7	Dresden
0.6913	38.4	.0640	34	Helps
0.6913	38.4	.3437	8	Speed
0.6912	38.4	.4680	7	Cavalry
0.6912	38.4	.2441	9	tryouts
0.6911	38.4	.3465	9	Koufax
0.6909	38.4	.3811	8	famished
0.6908	38.4	.4383	7	Worth
0.6906	38.4	.0142	63	Units
0.6905	38.4	.3552	8	Tuscumbia
0.6901	38.4	.3857	8	Osborn
0.6899	38.4	.3461	9	Descartes
0.6898	38.4	.4599	7	economies
0.6897	38.4	.3550	8	neighbours
0.6896	38.4	.4606	7	licorice
0.6896	38.4	.3692	8	milder
0.6895	38.4	.4296	7	playmate
0.6895	38.4	.5594	6	recovering
0.6891	38.4	.4427	7	outs
0.6889	38.4	.4768	7	accessible
0.6888	38.4	.5363	6	lances
0.6888	38.4	.5374	6	recapture
0.6887	38.4	.4361	7	archaeological
0.6887	38.4	.5362	6	Depression
0.6887	38.4	.4533	7	gentry
0.6886	38.4	.5372	6	Bon
0.6886	38.4	.5372	6	furrows
0.6885	38.4	.5361	6	branded
0.6885	38.4	.2839	10	midpoint
0.6885	38.4	.3432	9	Zealand's
0.6885	38.4	.0000	46	5/6
0.6882	38.4	.5370	6	displaying
0.6882	38.4	.4481	7	periodically

THE PRECEDING WORD TYPE OCCUPIES RANK 20300

U	SFI	D	F	Word Type
0.6882	38.4	.5359	6	waxy
0.6881	38.4	.4548	7	artisans
0.6880	38.4	.2430	9	Lon
0.6880	38.4	.2430	9	squawking
0.6880	38.4	.4774	7	surname
0.6878	38.4	.5357	6	avoids
0.6878	38.4	.5357	6	circulate
0.6878	38.4	.2232	9	lady-in-waiting
0.6878	38.4	.2232	9	Lobster
0.6878	38.4	.3428	8	mesquite
0.6878	38.4	.3428	8	SanAntonio
0.6877	38.4	.3676	8	Courage
0.6877	38.4	.1604	14	Monte
0.6876	38.4	.5368	6	rallying
0.6875	38.4	.4378	7	fruitless
0.6875	38.4	.3417	8	tuft
0.6875	38.4	.4521	7	wham
0.6874	38.4	.3817	8	militant
0.6873	38.4	.3407	9	Morning
0.6873	38.4	.4524	7	undergraduate
0.6872	38.4	.5517	6	patrons
0.6872	38.4	.5313	6	ships'
0.6872	38.4	.3919	8	215
0.6871	38.4	.5517	6	notched
0.6871	38.4	.3541	8	Teacher's
0.6869	38.4	.3061	10	deodorant
0.6869	38.4	.5514	6	isles
0.6864	38.4	.3864	8	lousy
0.6863	38.4	.4559	7	mobility
0.6862	38.4	.3406	8	baker's
0.6862	38.4	.4357	7	dryness
0.6862	38.4	.3406	8	grumble
0.6862	38.4	.3414	8	hogan
0.6862	38.4	.0544	31	inflation
0.6862	38.4	.5313	6	sowed
0.6861	38.4	.4531	7	expressways
0.6861	38.4	.2594	11	Star-Spangled
0.6860	38.4	.5303	6	Andean
0.6859	38.4	.5516	6	organizes
0.6859	38.4	.4557	7	1828
0.6858	38.4	.3943	8	decreasing
0.6857	38.4	.2837	9	honking
0.6857	38.4	.4366	7	prophesied
0.6856	38.4	.5558	6	glade
0.6856	38.4	.5483	6	396
0.6854	38.4	.4613	7	Clubs
0.6853	38.4	.2212	9	Amik
0.6853	38.4	.1717	12	Athene
0.6853	38.4	.4208	7	daggers
0.6853	38.4	.2212	9	Ivar
0.6853	38.4	.3729	8	mocked
0.6853	38.4	.2212	9	mousetrap
0.6853	38.4	.2212	9	Ticket
0.6853	38.4	.2212	9	walkie-talkie
0.6852	38.4	.0000	15	Androcles
0.6852	38.4	.0000	15	Bambi
0.6852	38.4	.0000	15	Barbe
0.6852	38.4	.0000	15	Brady
0.6852	38.4	.0000	15	Burr
0.6852	38.4	.0000	15	Chombo
0.6852	38.4	.0000	15	chowder
0.6852	38.4	.0000	15	Crying
0.6852	38.4	.0000	15	Della
0.6852	38.4	.0000	15	Garver
0.6852	38.4	.0000	15	Hodja
0.6852	38.4	.0000	15	Jeanette
0.6852	38.4	.4704	7	journalist
0.6852	38.4	.0000	15	Juanito
0.6852	38.4	.0000	15	Koom
0.6852	38.4	.0000	15	Rafael
0.6852	38.4	.0000	15	Raffy
0.6852	38.4	.3867	7	Rain
0.6852	38.4	.0000	15	Ruzhonka
0.6852	38.4	.3869	7	sunburned
0.6852	38.4	.0000	15	Teeny
0.6852	38.4	.0000	15	Think-and-Do
0.6852	38.4	.0000	15	Torad
0.6850	38.4	.1926	11	Gilson
0.6850	38.4	.4520	7	238
0.6849	38.4	.4384	7	babble
0.6848	38.4	.3858	7	Gabby's
0.6848	38.4	.3858	7	quilts
0.6848	38.4	.3858	7	remorse
0.6848	38.4	.3286	9	shopper
0.6847	38.4	.2889	10	freezer
0.6847	38.4	.4596	7	one-eighth
0.6847	38.4	.2092	13	2's
0.6846	38.4	.3853	7	bad-tempered
0.6846	38.4	.3730	8	fisher

U	SFI	D	F	Word Type
0.6846	38.4	.4730	7	Flat
0.6846	38.4	.3909	8	spills
0.6844	38.4	.3854	7	loon
0.6844	38.4	.3854	7	Whittier
0.6843	38.4	.3381	9	Sardinia
0.6841	38.4	.4357	7	laboriously
0.6838	38.3	.4520	7	fractures
0.6838	38.3	.4194	7	honeysuckle
0.6837	38.3	.3824	8	eventual
0.6837	38.3	.3864	8	interact
0.6836	38.3	.4654	7	handsomely

THE PRECEDING WORD TYPE OCCUPIES RANK 20400

U	SFI	D	F	Word Type
0.6833	38.3	.2928	10	CBS
0.6833	38.3	.5522	6	insofar
0.6833	38.3	.3480	9	rookie
0.6830	38.3	.2437	9	cowbird
0.6830	38.3	.4398	7	exaggerating
0.6826	38.3	.3089	10	crankshaft
0.6825	38.3	.2407	12	Davy's
0.6824	38.3	.3858	7	Hilda
0.6824	38.3	.4496	7	interdependent
0.6823	38.3	.3813	7	keepers
0.6823	38.3	.3815	7	Pleasure
0.6823	38.3	.3813	7	toothbrush
0.6823	38.3	.3813	7	wayside
0.6822	38.3	.4346	7	crafty
0.6821	38.3	.3854	7	Mademoiselle
0.6821	38.3	.1929	14	nominee
0.6820	38.3	.4457	7	coldness
0.6820	38.3	.3817	7	eagle's
0.6819	38.3	.2669	11	carbonated
0.6819	38.3	.4616	7	indigenous
0.6819	38.3	.3817	7	mainmast
0.6819	38.3	.3917	8	offenders
0.6819	38.3	.4515	7	petty
0.6819	38.3	.3817	7	truant
0.6819	38.3	.3817	7	undamaged
0.6817	38.3	.3816	7	falcons
0.6816	38.3	.4587	7	deputy
0.6816	38.3	.4587	7	Executive
0.6816	38.3	.4587	7	masterly
0.6813	38.3	.1672	17	duet
0.6813	38.3	.5515	6	legacy
0.6813	38.3	.3808	7	minnow
0.6813	38.3	.2869	10	overweight
0.6813	38.3	.5427	6	pleasanter
0.6812	38.3	.4461	7	climaxed
0.6812	38.3	.4582	7	collaboration
0.6812	38.3	.4474	7	cranium
0.6809	38.3	.2160	10	stethoscope
0.6807	38.3	.0000	35	Ishi
0.6806	38.3	.3732	8	creeps
0.6806	38.3	.4631	7	sportsman
0.6802	38.3	.3829	7	Langley
0.6802	38.3	.3706	8	Mackinac
0.6802	38.3	.3706	8	specialties
0.6800	38.3	.2342	12	pairing
0.6800	38.3	.3737	8	Sirius
0.6796	38.3	.2025	12	magnetite
0.6796	38.3	.2025	12	protozoan
0.6794	38.3	.4671	7	appease
0.6794	38.3	.2967	9	sorrel
0.6790	38.3	.4622	7	269
0.6787	38.3	.3448	9	Ionian
0.6783	38.3	.5385	6	nurse's
0.6781	38.3	.3115	9	Brenda
0.6781	38.3	.2881	11	ceramics
0.6780	38.3	.0931	21	finite
0.6780	38.3	.3723	8	Ranges
0.6779	38.3	.3065	10	Giraffe
0.6776	38.3	.3017	8	sprint
0.6774	38.3	.2168	14	muffins
0.6773	38.3	.2860	9	Aunty
0.6770	38.3	.2156	14	Wasp
0.6766	38.3	.3744	8	dares
0.6765	38.3	.5399	6	lubricating
0.6764	38.3	.5438	6	wrecks
0.6762	38.3	.5454	6	dwindle
0.6762	38.3	.5454	6	preferring
0.6762	38.3	.5489	6	scuffle
0.6761	38.3	.2007	12	forecasting
0.6761	38.3	.4536	7	inconspicuous
0.6760	38.3	.4262	7	flamingo
0.6760	38.3	.3780	7	Gale
0.6758	38.3	.4464	7	decrees
0.6756	38.3	.4231	7	plundered
0.6756	38.3	.2772	11	polarity
0.6755	38.3	.4365	7	courtyards
0.6754	38.3	.5442	6	Boston's
0.6754	38.3	.4603	7	Daughter
0.6754	38.3	.2996	10	Stalin
0.6753	38.3	.4495	7	liters
0.6753	38.3	.3871	7	Ness
0.6753	38.3	.3864	7	updrafts
0.6752	38.3	.3315	9	filters
0.6752	38.3	.3722	7	Pasadena
0.6751	38.3	.3830	8	Acadia
0.6751	38.3	.3871	7	plovers
0.6751	38.3	.4506	7	preface
0.6751	38.3	.3319	9	typewriters
0.6750	38.3	.4420	7	corals
0.6748	38.3	.3717	7	full-sized
0.6748	38.3	.3717	7	punctures
0.6748	38.3	.3209	9	typhoid
0.6747	38.3	.3212	9	mixer
0.6746	38.3	.4250	7	pulsing
0.6746	38.3	.3870	7	1784
0.6745	38.3	.4480	7	7000
0.6743	38.3	.4090	7	engulfed
0.6741	38.3	.4332	7	presiding
0.6741	38.3	.4524	7	worshipped
0.6741	38.3	.5280	6	yearlings

THE PRECEDING WORD TYPE OCCUPIES RANK 20500

U	SFI	D	F	Word Type
0.6740	38.3	.3716	7	dramatics
0.6740	38.3	.5280	6	intermittent
0.6739	38.3	.4531	7	coincides
0.6739	38.3	.5406	6	incumbent
0.6739	38.3	.5406	6	promoters
0.6738	38.3	.5433	6	all-day
0.6737	38.3	.3715	7	six-foot
0.6734	38.3	.3835	7	anteaters
0.6733	38.3	.4527	7	1818
0.6732	38.3	.4492	7	likenesses
0.6730	38.3	.3469	8	sunglasses
0.6725	38.3	.3719	8	vibrated
0.6724	38.3	.2348	9	caroling
0.6724	38.3	.2348	9	Crossing
0.6724	38.3	.2348	9	Holly
0.6723	38.3	.4547	7	hideous
0.6722	38.3	.1688	12	Blink
0.6719	38.3	.2102	9	Truck
0.6717	38.3	.5433	6	stingy
0.6715	38.3	.4246	7	London's
0.6714	38.3	.2264	12	Numa
0.6714	38.3	.3138	9	spires
0.6713	38.3	.4559	7	Scotland's
0.6712	38.3	.3105	9	unspeakable
0.6710	38.3	.1250	15	Beezus
0.6710	38.3	.3905	8	examines
0.6710	38.3	.4552	7	forebears
0.6708	38.3	.5378	6	browsing
0.6708	38.3	.3630	8	onset
0.6707	38.3	.5210	6	Jan's
0.6706	38.3	.5356	6	tolerance
0.6705	38.3	.5269	6	147
0.6702	38.3	.3614	8	limping
0.6700	38.3	.4489	7	spongy
0.6699	38.3	.4442	7	Just
0.6698	38.3	.4224	7	Appomattox
0.6695	38.3	.3263	8	innocently
0.6695	38.3	.3263	8	swum
0.6694	38.3	.2416	11	Anatolia
0.6694	38.3	.3451	8	dully
0.6694	38.3	.1724	17	Rembrandt
0.6694	38.3	.3451	8	whisked
0.6693	38.3	.4549	7	acknowledge
0.6693	38.3	.3866	8	Brookhaven
0.6693	38.3	.4509	7	194
0.6691	38.3	.4500	7	amplifies
0.6691	38.3	.3208	9	mosque
0.6691	38.3	.3283	8	stomp
0.6691	38.3	.3452	8	Telemachus
0.6690	38.3	.4577	7	ravines
0.6689	38.3	.1757	16	/sh/
0.6689	38.3	.4335	7	noontime
0.6688	38.3	.5191	6	corrals
0.6688	38.3	.5191	6	instituted
0.6688	38.3	.2731	10	Santiago
0.6687	38.3	.1859	11	Persephone
0.6686	38.3	.5188	6	shrieks
0.6685	38.3	.1504	18	Schumann
0.6683	38.2	.3407	8	shined
0.6682	38.2	.3282	8	doubting
0.6682	38.2	.3282	8	storming
0.6681	38.2	.5384	6	concluding
0.6681	38.2	.3753	8	Hopi
0.6681	38.2	.5189	6	upraised
0.6680	38.2	.5189	6	anti-aircraft
0.6680	38.2	.2286	12	BD
0.6680	38.2	.5191	6	chunky
0.6679	38.2	.4540	7	acclaimed
0.6679	38.2	.4529	7	war's
0.6677	38.2	.5185	6	inflated
0.6677	38.2	.2443	11	Portola
0.6677	38.2	.5187	6	prying
0.6676	38.2	.3856	8	inasmuch
0.6676	38.2	.5377	6	objectionable
0.6675	38.2	.3244	9	acquitted
0.6674	38.2	.4055	7	GO
0.6672	38.2	.3081	10	inks
0.6670	38.2	.2977	10	curriculum
0.6669	38.2	.3245	9	Kepler
0.6668	38.2	.3625	8	cobblestones
0.6667	38.2	.3266	9	ascending
0.6666	38.2	.3748	7	fireball
0.6666	38.2	.4878	6	Howard's
0.6664	38.2	.4314	7	pertaining
0.6662	38.2	.3264	8	bathrobe
0.6662	38.2	.3264	8	sassy
0.6660	38.2	.5324	6	spontaneously
0.6659	38.2	.4435	7	administrators
0.6659	38.2	.4435	7	Jesuits
0.6659	38.2	.3703	8	Relations
0.6657	38.2	.4845	6	confiscated
0.6657	38.2	.4845	6	headbands
0.6656	38.2	.4503	7	rewriting
0.6655	38.2	.3715	8	autos
0.6654	38.2	.3400	9	retaining
0.6653	38.2	.2446	12	/v/
0.6651	38.2	.2277	13	Band
0.6651	38.2	.4512	7	eras
0.6650	38.2	.4201	7	dutifully
0.6649	38.2	.3326	9	Browne

THE PRECEDING WORD TYPE OCCUPIES RANK 20600

U	SFI	D	F	Word Type
0.6648	38.2	.5116	6	cheapest
0.6648	38.2	.3028	10	sunfish
0.6646	38.2	.4450	7	destroyers
0.6646	38.2	.3302	8	Tip
0.6645	38.2	.3331	9	assassins
0.6645	38.2	.4834	6	sizzling
0.6644	38.2	.5324	6	arbitrary
0.6644	38.2	.5353	6	Television
0.6643	38.2	.2416	11	nourishment
0.6640	38.2	.5318	6	dogwood
0.6640	38.2	.2086	10	Shep
0.6640	38.2	.4267	7	unpaved
0.6640	38.2	.5216	6	398
0.6639	38.2	.4504	7	Les
0.6637	38.2	.3279	9	Dock
0.6636	38.2	.3774	8	depressions
0.6635	38.2	.3692	8	Turin
0.6632	38.2	.5161	6	governor's
0.6630	38.2	.5161	6	characterize
0.6630	38.2	.5323	6	muster
0.6630	38.2	.1524	17	Vaughan
0.6628	38.2	.3297	9	carrion
0.6628	38.2	.5219	6	resisting
0.6628	38.2	.4166	7	wanderings
0.6628	38.2	.3413	8	Hera
0.6626	38.2	.3128	9	magnification
0.6625	38.2	.2321	12	Betty's
0.6625	38.2	.4859	6	granddaughter
0.6625	38.2	.4858	6	Montclair
0.6625	38.2	.4858	6	twitch
0.6625	38.2	.4858	6	whiter
0.6624	38.2	.4520	7	warring
0.6623	38.2	.4826	6	whoosh
0.6622	38.2	.4868	6	corncob
0.6622	38.2	.4868	6	hour's
0.6621	38.2	.4187	7	grandpa
0.6621	38.2	.4856	6	hurling
0.6620	38.2	.5302	6	bachelor's
0.6620	38.2	.4397	7	unaffected
0.6619	38.2	.4853	6	overflowed
0.6619	38.2	.4853	6	unconcerned
0.6618	38.2	.4866	6	brier
0.6618	38.2	.4312	7	humiliation
0.6618	38.2	.4866	6	relish
0.6617	38.2	.5203	6	truest
0.6616	38.2	.5293	6	moody
0.6615	38.2	.5200	6	snappy
0.6614	38.2	.2071	12	cerebellum
0.6613	38.2	.4862	6	Stokes
0.6610	38.2	.3719	8	armchair
0.6610	38.2	.4862	6	mumble
0.6610	38.2	.4849	6	washtub
0.6609	38.2	.4203	7	greenhouses
0.6609	38.2	.5193	6	peal
0.6609	38.2	.3816	7	tinkling
0.6609	38.2	.5193	6	unheeded
0.6608	38.2	.4862	6	Cats
0.6608	38.2	.4805	6	crow's
0.6608	38.2	.4805	6	Polynesian
0.6607	38.2	.3801	7	twittered
0.6606	38.2	.4812	6	sightseeing
0.6606	38.2	.4802	6	sills
0.6606	38.2	.2369	12	Slade
0.6605	38.2	.4307	7	blob
0.6605	38.2	.4307	7	grudge
0.6604	38.2	.5170	6	muslin
0.6604	38.2	.4859	6	opal
0.6604	38.2	.4809	6	reputations
0.6604	38.2	.4845	6	YMCA
0.6603	38.2	.5303	6	bowstring
0.6603	38.2	.3390	8	curses
0.6603	38.2	.5290	6	defy
0.6603	38.2	.4857	6	disperse
0.6603	38.2	.4201	7	freemen
0.6603	38.2	.4410	7	Ogden
0.6602	38.2	.4858	6	Diana
0.6602	38.2	.4858	6	seaman's
0.6602	38.2	.4858	6	toiling
0.6601	38.2	.4843	6	corresponded
0.6600	38.2	.4808	6	drenched
0.6600	38.2	.5299	6	inseparable
0.6600	38.2	.3878	8	lengthening
0.6600	38.2	.4202	7	recounted
0.6599	38.2	.3383	8	bossy
0.6599	38.2	.5284	6	gall
0.6598	38.2	.4049	7	arbor
0.6598	38.2	.5176	6	Bryant
0.6598	38.2	.5156	6	scraggly
0.6598	38.2	.4805	6	showered
0.6598	38.2	.5158	6	stupidity
0.6598	38.2	.5162	6	sunning
0.6597	38.2	.5282	6	arbitrarily
0.6596	38.2	.2357	9	Annexe
0.6596	38.2	.4856	6	Shelley
0.6595	38.2	.2234	12	metaphors
0.6594	38.2	.4804	6	burrowed
0.6594	38.2	.5153	6	deaden
0.6594	38.2	.3784	7	giddap
0.6594	38.2	.3784	7	knee-deep
0.6594	38.2	.2756	10	Rush

THE PRECEDING WORD TYPE OCCUPIES RANK 20700

U	SFI	D	F	Word Type
0.6594	38.2	.4251	7	windswept
0.6592	38.2	.1396	16	Chip
0.6592	38.2	.4801	6	good-sized
0.6592	38.2	.4801	6	laughable
0.6591	38.2	.5273	6	inflamed
0.6591	38.2	.0238	39	Kino's
0.6591	38.2	.3608	8	limes
0.6590	38.2	.2652	10	alluvial
0.6590	38.2	.4480	7	concentrates
0.6590	38.2	.4798	6	inquiries
0.6590	38.2	.3113	9	literacy
0.6589	38.2	.2831	10	Caleb
0.6589	38.2	.5179	6	hubbub
0.6587	38.2	.2580	11	fisheries
0.6586	38.2	.3548	8	disregard
0.6586	38.2	.3296	9	suspenders
0.6585	38.2	.3227	9	Burger
0.6585	38.2	.4794	6	hindrance
0.6585	38.2	.4794	6	invader
0.6585	38.2	.4215	7	Twentieth
0.6584	38.2	.5160	6	sluggish
0.6584	38.2	.5160	6	streamer
0.6584	38.2	.5160	6	sultry
0.6582	38.2	.3803	8	Delft
0.6581	38.2	.0478	32	Abercrombie
0.6581	38.2	.3347	8	Leaves
0.6580	38.2	.3387	8	Tribune
0.6579	38.2	.1892	13	Anton
0.6579	38.2	.3384	8	coinage
0.6578	38.2	.2508	11	Oysters
0.6574	38.2	.5244	6	exasperating
0.6574	38.2	.5143	6	honourable
0.6574	38.2	.5143	6	manes
0.6574	38.2	.3875	8	repertoire
0.6573	38.2	.5142	6	fervent
0.6572	38.2	.5140	6	calf's
0.6568	38.2	.2339	12	Chairman
0.6567	38.2	.3510	8	decreased
0.6566	38.2	.1235	16	Magnetic
0.6566	38.2	.1235	16	ovum
0.6565	38.2	.4287	7	floundering
0.6562	38.2	.4273	7	stunted
0.6559	38.2	.4379	7	totaled
0.6558	38.2	.1336	19	6/8
0.6556	38.2	.2324	12	campuses
0.6556	38.2	.3174	8	Morrison
0.6555	38.2	.4417	7	collapsing
0.6555	38.2	.4370	7	7%
0.6550	38.2	.2230	11	wrestler
0.6549	38.2	.4152	7	frolic
0.6547	38.2	.5155	6	psalm
0.6546	38.2	.4366	7	financed
0.6546	38.2	.3161	9	Ford's
0.6546	38.2	.3543	8	pep
0.6545	38.2	.5089	6	confine
0.6544	38.2	.5134	6	Short
0.6544	38.2	.3967	7	warped
0.6542	38.2	.4320	7	concentrations
0.6542	38.2	.2934	9	im
0.6542	38.2	.5083	6	nurtured
0.6542	38.2	.5082	6	windblown
0.6540	38.2	.2239	13	trimming
0.6537	38.2	.3744	8	extravagant
0.6537	38.2	.4348	7	1-7
0.6536	38.2	.1637	17	adjustable
0.6536	38.2	.1333	17	sanded
0.6535	38.2	.3318	8	Soldier
0.6535	38.2	.4801	6	sundae
0.6535	38.2	.4797	6	throb
0.6534	38.2	.3679	8	commodity
0.6534	38.2	.2919	10	dey
0.6534	38.2	.5118	6	enmity
0.6534	38.2	.4137	7	noose
0.6533	38.2	.4800	6	pitting
0.6533	38.2	.4118	7	soy
0.6532	38.2	.4285	7	repulsion
0.6531	38.1	.5128	6	spooky
0.6531	38.1	.4304	7	tours
0.6528	38.1	.4356	7	fingering
0.6528	38.1	.3951	7	shoeshine
0.6528	38.1	.4303	7	236
0.6527	38.1	.2348	11	hiked
0.6526	38.1	.2847	10	chantey
0.6526	38.1	.4094	7	lunge
0.6526	38.1	.3589	8	many-celled
0.6525	38.1	.3578	8	four-year-old
0.6525	38.1	.0683	19	inborn
0.6524	38.1	.5082	6	City's
0.6524	38.1	.2304	12	Einstein's
0.6524	38.1	.1981	13	herbivores
0.6524	38.1	.4771	6	possessor
0.6523	38.1	.5080	6	candid
0.6522	38.1	.4116	7	benefited
0.6522	38.1	.5049	6	floodwaters
0.6522	38.1	.4769	6	residences
0.6521	38.1	.4358	7	beneficial
0.6521	38.1	.3765	7	parody
0.6520	38.1	.5050	6	bloc
0.6520	38.1	.5050	6	boulevard
0.6520	38.1	.3065	9	fattened

THE PRECEDING WORD TYPE OCCUPIES RANK 20800

U	SFI	D	F	Word Type
0.6520	38.1	.3838	7	lifelike
0.6520	38.1	.3765	7	pneumatic
0.6519	38.1	.4774	6	sheep's
0.6518	38.1	.4086	7	clink
0.6517	38.1	.5046	6	ranked
0.6516	38.1	.3896	7	compress
0.6516	38.1	.2839	8	poppies
0.6515	38.1	.5066	6	beset
0.6515	38.1	.5102	6	cinch
0.6515	38.1	.5096	6	condemnation
0.6515	38.1	.4099	7	equinox
0.6515	38.1	.5066	6	fiercer
0.6514	38.1	.4111	7	calmness
0.6513	38.1	.4391	7	encompass
0.6513	38.1	.4360	7	880
0.6512	38.1	.3004	10	Lillian
0.6512	38.1	.4080	7	whined
0.6511	38.1	.4136	7	mapping
0.6511	38.1	.3670	8	Sal
0.6511	38.1	.4345	7	stork
0.6510	38.1	.3603	8	oppose
0.6507	38.1	.5051	6	dogged
0.6507	38.1	.2025	10	Fleece
0.6507	38.1	.2025	10	tlot-tlot
0.6506	38.1	.3615	8	maize
0.6505	38.1	.4285	7	vats
0.6504	38.1	.5047	6	cobweb
0.6502	38.1	.4349	7	Maude
0.6502	38.1	.5076	6	Sullivan's
0.6501	38.1	.4100	7	Auguste
0.6501	38.1	.3291	9	poses
0.6501	38.1	.3081	9	warblers
0.6500	38.1	.4349	7	amphibious
0.6500	38.1	.3771	8	stimulates
0.6495	38.1	.1839	15	ai
0.6495	38.1	.4085	7	optimism
0.6495	38.1	.2947	9	playthings
0.6494	38.1	.3606	8	Article
0.6494	38.1	.5081	6	flue
0.6492	38.1	.3728	7	armory
0.6492	38.1	.3728	7	pestle
0.6491	38.1	.3046	9	Hinduism
0.6487	38.1	.3722	7	bargained
0.6487	38.1	.3722	7	gurgle
0.6487	38.1	.4236	7	marred
0.6487	38.1	.3685	8	1650
0.6486	38.1	.2349	11	Ataturk
0.6483	38.1	.5011	6	detested
0.6483	38.1	.3805	8	drastically
0.6481	38.1	.3174	8	mains
0.6479	38.1	.5068	6	buoyant
0.6479	38.1	.4703	6	discouragement

U	SFI	D	F	Word Type
0.6479	38.1	.5068	6	strays
0.6478	38.1	.4190	7	forefeet
0.6477	38.1	.4024	7	numberless
0.6476	38.1	.1173	15	Thorpe
0.6476	38.1	.5050	6	visor
0.6475	38.1	.4044	7	Buff
0.6472	38.1	.3581	8	denser
0.6472	38.1	.4701	6	perils
0.6471	38.1	.4077	7	afore
0.6471	38.1	.4372	7	capita
0.6471	38.1	.3745	8	clouded
0.6471	38.1	.4701	6	sukiyaki
0.6470	38.1	.2076	12	RW
0.6470	38.1	.3940	7	stranded
0.6468	38.1	.2217	11	Rumania
0.6466	38.1	.3698	7	booby
0.6466	38.1	.3698	7	brewing
0.6466	38.1	.3698	7	portage
0.6465	38.1	.1890	9	joey
0.6464	38.1	.5047	6	boldest
0.6463	38.1	.4057	7	rivalries
0.6462	38.1	.0433	34	Donahue
0.6461	38.1	.3929	7	slamming
0.6460	38.1	.2789	8	centaur
0.6459	38.1	.3703	7	petticoats
0.6459	38.1	.5041	6	Roads
0.6459	38.1	.3703	7	sittin'
0.6458	38.1	.3930	7	cowered
0.6457	38.1	.5259	6	irregularities
0.6456	38.1	.3228	9	Byron
0.6456	38.1	.4331	7	mainstream
0.6454	38.1	.2136	11	deposition
0.6454	38.1	.3576	8	tangent
0.6453	38.1	.1880	9	signet
0.6451	38.1	.4223	7	potash
0.6450	38.1	.4157	7	Steward
0.6448	38.1	.4393	7	commend
0.6448	38.1	.0743	29	woodwinds
0.6446	38.1	.3854	7	blue-eyed
0.6446	38.1	.3613	7	Harrodsburg
0.6444	38.1	.2768	10	Siegfried
0.6444	38.1	.4348	7	terminated
0.6441	38.1	.3200	8	protector
0.6439	38.1	.4284	7	Fall
0.6438	38.1	.4293	7	Dry
0.6438	38.1	.5236	6	dulled
0.6438	38.1	.5159	6	nourish
0.6438	38.1	.2425	11	Pie

THE PRECEDING WORD TYPE OCCUPIES RANK 20900

U	SFI	D	F	Word Type
0.6436	38.1	.0000	43	3/5
0.6435	38.1	.3459	8	relayed
0.6434	38.1	.3194	9	Ringling
0.6433	38.1	.3261	8	sprouts
0.6430	38.1	.3474	8	filtration
0.6430	38.1	.4255	7	positioned
0.6426	38.1	.4737	6	anytime
0.6426	38.1	.3666	7	sloshed
0.6426	38.1	.4988	6	stabbed
0.6425	38.1	.4287	7	enriching
0.6424	38.1	.2570	11	inversion
0.6421	38.1	.4703	6	thinnest
0.6420	38.1	.3513	8	Algerian
0.6420	38.1	.3513	8	Mao's
0.6419	38.1	.0867	26	strum
0.6418	38.1	.5195	6	deprive
0.6418	38.1	.3741	8	theology
0.6417	38.1	.4743	6	eyelid
0.6417	38.1	.2926	9	secreted
0.6417	38.1	.4338	7	zoological
0.6416	38.1	.3219	9	candlestick
0.6415	38.1	.4023	7	creepers
0.6415	38.1	.4741	6	twelve-year-old
0.6415	38.1	.4741	6	well-to-do
0.6414	38.1	.2286	9	weathermen
0.6412	38.1	.4965	6	numbness
0.6411	38.1	.4188	7	presume
0.6411	38.1	.4249	7	Rutherford
0.6410	38.1	.4104	7	Kickapoo
0.6410	38.1	.3436	8	298
0.6407	38.1	.2251	11	Pygmies
0.6407	38.1	.4694	6	snowstorms
0.6405	38.1	.3494	8	Swede
0.6404	38.1	.4970	6	stings
0.6403	38.1	.2359	11	autonomic
0.6402	38.1	.3691	7	man-eating
0.6402	38.1	.4746	6	tinfoil
0.6401	38.1	.2364	11	Tierra
0.6400	38.1	.3626	7	Live
0.6400	38.1	.3626	7	redhead
0.6400	38.1	.3626	7	spying
0.6400	38.1	.3626	7	taunted
0.6400	38.1	.4097	7	withheld
0.6399	38.1	.1050	24	abrasives
0.6398	38.1	.4696	6	flowered
0.6398	38.1	.4962	6	gangs
0.6398	38.1	.4731	6	sealskins
0.6397	38.1	.2579	10	downstage
0.6397	38.1	.4741	6	Mine
0.6397	38.1	.4741	6	roomful
0.6396	38.1	.0000	14	Alois
0.6396	38.1	.0000	14	Annette
0.6396	38.1	.0000	14	Benji
0.6396	38.1	.0000	14	Birk
0.6396	38.1	.0000	14	Bowie
0.6396	38.1	.0000	14	Brant
0.6396	38.1	.0000	14	Dibbs
0.6396	38.1	.4743	6	greener
0.6396	38.1	.0000	14	Ivik's
0.6396	38.1	.0000	14	Kirby's
0.6396	38.1	.0000	14	MacSparrow
0.6396	38.1	.0000	14	Manwick
0.6396	38.1	.0000	14	Mariquita
0.6396	38.1	.0000	14	Nicola
0.6396	38.1	.0000	14	Oo
0.6396	38.1	.0000	14	Ookie
0.6396	38.1	.0000	14	Pinkie
0.6396	38.1	.0000	14	quacking
0.6396	38.1	.0000	14	Roxanne
0.6396	38.1	.3608	8	semicolon
0.6396	38.1	.0000	14	Smee
0.6396	38.1	.0000	14	Tad
0.6396	38.1	.0000	14	Twistletree
0.6396	38.1	.0000	14	Vee
0.6395	38.1	.4741	6	brethren
0.6395	38.1	.3787	8	closings
0.6395	38.1	.4958	6	dammed
0.6395	38.1	.2279	9	Houston's
0.6395	38.1	.4741	6	uplifted
0.6394	38.1	.3703	8	NS
0.6392	38.1	.4942	6	anchorage
0.6392	38.1	.2261	9	Feathers
0.6392	38.1	.2261	9	Johanna
0.6392	38.1	.2261	9	Lurvy
0.6392	38.1	.4241	7	precedent
0.6392	38.1	.2261	9	to-morrow
0.6390	38.1	.4121	7	Quarter
0.6389	38.1	.4740	6	blue-black
0.6389	38.1	.4934	6	leggings
0.6388	38.1	.3793	7	Equatorial
0.6388	38.1	.3270	8	hula
0.6387	38.1	.4962	6	archer
0.6387	38.1	.4719	6	inconvenient
0.6387	38.1	.4738	6	shrews
0.6386	38.1	.3994	7	sassafras
0.6383	38.0	.2754	9	State's
0.6382	38.0	.4736	6	Spice
0.6382	38.0	.4037	7	wording
0.6381	38.0	.4682	6	overturn
0.6380	38.0	.2085	12	CO2

THE PRECEDING WORD TYPE OCCUPIES RANK 21000

U	SFI	D	F	Word Type
0.6380	38.0	.3198	9	ecclesiastical
0.6379	38.0	.4256	7	Finance
0.6378	38.0	.3545	8	exultation
0.6378	38.0	.3016	8	gruff
0.6378	38.0	.4228	7	11th
0.6378	38.0	.4213	7	270
0.6378	38.0	.4213	7	468
0.6377	38.0	.4031	7	hustling
0.6377	38.0	.3710	8	observance
0.6375	38.0	.2580	10	Lyon
0.6374	38.0	.1868	14	fallacy
0.6372	38.0	.3953	7	obsidian
0.6371	38.0	.3804	7	taped
0.6370	38.0	.4675	6	greenhouse
0.6370	38.0	.3542	8	locking
0.6370	38.0	.4283	7	professions
0.6370	38.0	.3267	8	tucking
0.6369	38.0	.3223	9	Coffin
0.6368	38.0	.3554	8	leaflets
0.6367	38.0	.3603	7	Barker
0.6367	38.0	.4921	6	mosques
0.6366	38.0	.2096	13	predator
0.6365	38.0	.3622	7	beagle
0.6365	38.0	.1901	13	diacritical
0.6365	38.0	.4128	7	jeweled
0.6365	38.0	.4072	7	1894
0.6364	38.0	.4219	7	expecially
0.6364	38.0	.3689	7	spaceman
0.6363	38.0	.3555	8	Waterloo
0.6360	38.0	.1284	19	List
0.6359	38.0	.3672	7	hen's
0.6359	38.0	.4153	7	lamentations
0.6359	38.0	.3672	7	marsupials
0.6359	38.0	.3672	7	nodules
0.6358	38.0	.3175	9	everlasting
0.6358	38.0	.3621	7	kindest
0.6358	38.0	.2298	10	rainstorm
0.6358	38.0	.3166	9	sharpening
0.6358	38.0	.3621	7	throbbed
0.6358	38.0	.3621	7	what're
0.6354	38.0	.2704	9	tart
0.6354	38.0	.4901	6	ubiquitous
0.6353	38.0	.3462	8	nocturnal
0.6352	38.0	.3683	7	Allegiance
0.6351	38.0	.2382	11	Goliath
0.6349	38.0	.3898	7	dampness
0.6347	38.0	.3608	7	bridal
0.6347	38.0	.3608	7	well-behaved
0.6345	38.0	.3665	7	Benito
0.6345	38.0	.3665	7	Ericson
0.6345	38.0	.3665	7	Fiord
0.6345	38.0	.3665	7	gales
0.6344	38.0	.3892	7	850
0.6343	38.0	.3953	7	backstage
0.6341	38.0	.3128	8	baseball's
0.6340	38.0	.4035	7	Saratoga
0.6338	38.0	.4300	7	revival
0.6337	38.0	.4067	7	enterprising
0.6337	38.0	.2989	8	polyps
0.6336	38.0	.1826	12	grandson
0.6334	38.0	.4081	7	Women
0.6334	38.0	.4060	7	675
0.6333	38.0	.3623	7	crevice
0.6333	38.0	.3623	7	trapeze
0.6332	38.0	.2675	8	Bugs
0.6330	38.0	.3879	7	advisor
0.6330	38.0	.3681	8	polls
0.6329	38.0	.3051	9	timetable
0.6328	38.0	.3067	9	bachelor
0.6328	38.0	.5063	6	interlocked
0.6326	38.0	.3967	7	expectant
0.6326	38.0	.2931	9	Mozambique
0.6325	38.0	.3026	9	342
0.6324	38.0	.2728	9	Stanton
0.6323	38.0	.3945	7	Bunker
0.6322	38.0	.4828	6	apricot
0.6322	38.0	.3455	7	Edam
0.6322	38.0	.2078	12	partitioned
0.6321	38.0	.0844	26	minuet
0.6320	38.0	.4683	6	singled
0.6318	38.0	.3633	7	dark-eyed
0.6318	38.0	.3633	7	oxcarts
0.6316	38.0	.0626	24	hypotenuse
0.6316	38.0	.3086	9	rosin
0.6314	38.0	.3304	8	councils
0.6314	38.0	.3144	9	Socialist
0.6314	38.0	.3304	8	1923
0.6313	38.0	.3475	8	Cooke
0.6310	38.0	.3727	8	partitions
0.6307	38.0	.5060	6	contemptuously
0.6307	38.0	.1282	18	scribes
0.6306	38.0	.3272	8	$250
0.6306	38.0	.3298	8	preyed
0.6305	38.0	.4130	7	H2O
0.6305	38.0	.1787	12	semiarid
0.6304	38.0	.5128	6	Grecian
0.6303	38.0	.3415	8	steeples
0.6303	38.0	.5035	6	uncharted
0.6298	38.0	.2426	8	goodby
0.6298	38.0	.2426	8	Peddler

THE PRECEDING WORD TYPE OCCUPIES RANK 21100

U	SFI	D	F	Word Type
0.6298	38.0	.2426	8	Voices
0.6297	38.0	.2212	9	Sylvie
0.6296	38.0	.2117	13	Peer
0.6296	38.0	.2755	10	wildness
0.6293	38.0	.3270	8	Seneca
0.6290	38.0	.3571	8	Beetle
0.6290	38.0	.4041	7	rider's
0.6287	38.0	.4667	6	megaphone
0.6287	38.0	.0000	42	numeration
0.6287	38.0	.3588	7	Trieste
0.6287	38.0	.4667	6	twirl
0.6287	38.0	.5064	6	waists
0.6286	38.0	.3908	7	badger
0.6286	38.0	.3908	7	lag
0.6286	38.0	.3853	7	silvered
0.6285	38.0	.1285	15	uterus
0.6283	38.0	.3439	8	scum
0.6282	38.0	.3709	8	der
0.6282	38.0	.3145	9	floured
0.6282	38.0	.4093	7	herald
0.6281	38.0	.4072	7	chorused
0.6281	38.0	.4072	7	crunch
0.6281	38.0	.4044	7	freckled
0.6281	38.0	.5055	6	Making
0.6279	38.0	.2729	10	Cretaceous
0.6279	38.0	.3492	7	Pink
0.6279	38.0	.4102	7	sorcerer
0.6278	38.0	.5066	6	essentials
0.6274	38.0	.4061	7	dazzled
0.6274	38.0	.2590	11	flywheel
0.6272	38.0	.4880	6	Sequoia
0.6271	38.0	.4993	6	surpass
0.6271	38.0	.4108	7	well-made
0.6270	38.0	.3579	7	Dakotas
0.6270	38.0	.3579	7	Reed's
0.6270	38.0	.3981	7	Tigris
0.6269	38.0	.4119	7	maturation
0.6269	38.0	.4119	7	thrives
0.6269	38.0	.4785	6	1838
0.6266	38.0	.3412	8	cochlea
0.6266	38.0	.2005	11	Redwood
0.6266	38.0	.4118	7	violating
0.6265	38.0	.3342	8	phosphates
0.6262	38.0	.2844	9	Fields
0.6261	38.0	.4715	6	gashes
0.6260	38.0	.3026	9	assigns
0.6259	38.0	.3548	8	cologne
0.6258	38.0	.3102	9	complexities
0.6257	38.0	.2076	12	secretions
0.6256	38.0	.4076	7	provocative
0.6256	38.0	.4176	7	whereof
0.6256	38.0	.4651	6	137
0.6254	38.0	.4893	6	Laurence
0.6254	38.0	.5026	6	postpone
0.6252	38.0	.4046	7	scowl
0.6249	38.0	.3496	8	motorist
0.6249	38.0	.5093	6	murals
0.6246	38.0	.0533	30	intransitive
0.6245	38.0	.3216	9	audio
0.6244	38.0	.3053	9	migrants
0.6243	38.0	.4620	6	thirty-four
0.6242	38.0	.4255	7	sublime
0.6241	38.0	.1953	13	Abba
0.6240	38.0	.3265	9	flatly
0.6240	38.0	.4623	6	OR
0.6240	38.0	.3612	8	ze
0.6237	38.0	.4206	7	appetizing
0.6237	37.9	.4646	6	brimming
0.6235	37.9	.4207	7	masculine
0.6235	37.9	.4639	6	nought
0.6235	37.9	.3710	7	perseverance
0.6235	37.9	.4640	6	shrewdly
0.6233	37.9	.3157	8	Randall
0.6233	37.9	.4635	6	stringing
0.6230	37.9	.4224	7	coverage
0.6229	37.9	.2732	9	Fairfield
0.6225	37.9	.1275	15	electors
0.6222	37.9	.2351	8	Clarissa
0.6222	37.9	.2351	8	Greenleaf
0.6222	37.9	.2503	11	imitates
0.6222	37.9	.2351	8	kilt
0.6222	37.9	.2351	8	Leonidas
0.6222	37.9	.2351	8	Matilda
0.6221	37.9	.1522	12	Quimby
0.6221	37.9	.1053	19	Yeller
0.6220	37.9	.4658	6	lastly
0.6219	37.9	.4863	6	lurked
0.6217	37.9	.3113	8	Judge's
0.6215	37.9	.2646	10	Ives
0.6215	37.9	.3996	7	veils
0.6213	37.9	.3111	9	Development
0.6213	37.9	.3111	9	ware
0.6211	37.9	.2341	8	blacker
0.6211	37.9	.2341	8	Gwendolyn
0.6211	37.9	.3829	7	ill-fated
0.6211	37.9	.4647	6	outgrown
0.6211	37.9	.2341	8	whooped
0.6209	37.9	.3215	8	meat-eating
0.6208	37.9	.4630	6	Marie's
0.6206	37.9	.2504	10	cauliflower

THE PRECEDING WORD TYPE OCCUPIES RANK 21200

U	SFI	D	F	Word Type
0.6206	37.9	.4917	6	small-scale
0.6203	37.9	.3812	7	barbed-wire
0.6203	37.9	.2332	8	Wheeler
0.6202	37.9	.2620	10	immature
0.6202	37.9	.0467	40	soldering
0.6196	37.9	.3507	8	Frankie's
0.6196	37.9	.3419	8	pus
0.6195	37.9	.4547	6	214
0.6192	37.9	.4049	7	broadened
0.6192	37.9	.4029	7	folklore
0.6191	37.9	.4530	6	fifty-six
0.6191	37.9	.4097	7	misunderstand
0.6189	37.9	.4178	7	Goethe
0.6189	37.9	.3452	8	204
0.6186	37.9	.5013	6	baffle
0.6186	37.9	.3896	7	Florida's
0.6185	37.9	.3508	8	suppressed
0.6183	37.9	.4158	7	eliminates
0.6182	37.9	.4860	6	256
0.6180	37.9	.2175	12	Attucks
0.6174	37.9	.1444	16	module
0.6173	37.9	.4832	6	193
0.6172	37.9	.4845	6	township
0.6171	37.9	.3412	7	chills
0.6170	37.9	.2301	8	bleat
0.6170	37.9	.2301	8	Bridger
0.6170	37.9	.1673	14	connector
0.6170	37.9	.2301	8	d'you
0.6170	37.9	.2648	9	tellers
0.6168	37.9	.1350	13	yuh
0.6167	37.9	.2634	10	Eisenhower's
0.6166	37.9	.4255	7	unsatisfactory
0.6163	37.9	.3941	7	intruders
0.6163	37.9	.4520	6	oblivion
0.6163	37.9	.4520	6	rolled-up
0.6162	37.9	.3351	8	Columbus's
0.6161	37.9	.4826	6	criticizing
0.6161	37.9	.4826	6	long-lasting
0.6161	37.9	.3960	7	nudging
0.6160	37.9	.4780	6	serpents
0.6159	37.9	.3780	7	regards
0.6158	37.9	.3426	8	navigational
0.6158	37.9	.3426	8	outrage
0.6157	37.9	.4206	7	satisfies
0.6156	37.9	.3402	7	insults
0.6156	37.9	.3402	7	landlord's
0.6155	37.9	.4521	6	tapir
0.6154	37.9	.3019	8	Comet
0.6154	37.9	.3957	7	preoccupied
0.6154	37.9	.3957	7	priority
0.6153	37.9	.3483	8	PTA
0.6152	37.9	.2284	8	angrier
0.6152	37.9	.2284	8	gracias
0.6152	37.9	.2284	8	mesas
0.6152	37.9	.2284	8	Sealab
0.6149	37.9	.3486	8	Command
0.6148	37.9	.3545	7	smelters
0.6146	37.9	.3422	8	civilians
0.6144	37.9	.4908	6	routed
0.6143	37.9	.1242	15	Quito
0.6143	37.9	.1611	14	20%
0.6142	37.9	.3553	8	reminiscent
0.6140	37.9	.4819	6	heartbeats
0.6138	37.9	.4816	6	obtains
0.6137	37.9	.1874	12	Ace
0.6136	37.9	.2980	9	yr
0.6135	37.9	.3895	7	Bald
0.6134	37.9	.2445	8	collie
0.6134	37.9	.3481	8	junta
0.6134	37.9	.2445	8	mince
0.6132	37.9	.3149	8	absorbing
0.6132	37.9	.3000	8	semiconductor
0.6131	37.9	.3934	7	hesitating
0.6130	37.9	.4102	7	Hallowe'en
0.6130	37.9	.3356	8	resented
0.6129	37.9	.0924	17	Rontu
0.6129	37.9	.2391	10	Secretary-General
0.6129	37.9	.0924	17	Stan's
0.6128	37.9	.2777	9	Investigation
0.6127	37.9	.4051	7	staples
0.6126	37.9	.2561	10	Montague
0.6125	37.9	.2119	12	bagpipe
0.6125	37.9	.4977	6	lumpy
0.6124	37.9	.3938	7	ugh
0.6122	37.9	.3393	8	Gentlemen
0.6121	37.9	.3774	7	destroyer
0.6120	37.9	.4081	7	inspiring
0.6120	37.9	.3172	9	malt
0.6120	37.9	.2801	9	sheepskins
0.6118	37.9	.4557	6	hunch
0.6118	37.9	.4740	6	pelting
0.6117	37.9	.3415	8	Cyrano
0.6116	37.9	.4782	6	illiteracy
0.6115	37.9	.3204	8	smothered
0.6114	37.9	.2260	11	soups
0.6113	37.9	.3446	7	piglets
0.6113	37.9	.4722	6	untrue
0.6112	37.9	.4790	6	native-born
0.6111	37.9	.1950	12	domesticated
0.6111	37.9	.4776	6	Ho

THE PRECEDING WORD TYPE OCCUPIES RANK 21300

U	SFI	D	F	Word Type
0.6111	37.9	.1843	14	operetta
0.6111	37.9	.4776	6	unmarked
0.6109	37.9	.3800	7	crumbly
0.6109	37.9	.4543	6	vehemently
0.6108	37.9	.4730	6	frightens
0.6108	37.9	.4540	6	hinted
0.6108	37.9	.3066	9	two-word
0.6106	37.9	.3439	7	betting
0.6106	37.9	.3159	9	diction
0.6106	37.9	.3245	8	wiggles
0.6105	37.9	.4005	7	Arlington
0.6104	37.9	.3038	9	Whale
0.6103	37.9	.4187	7	imparted
0.6102	37.9	.3436	7	'neath
0.6102	37.9	.3588	7	cheerily

U	SFI	D	F	Word Type
0.6102	37.9	.3588	7	reformatory
0.6099	37.9	.2629	10	1-2
0.6098	37.9	.2261	10	constituent
0.6098	37.9	.0869	22	ment
0.6098	37.9	.2288	9	turquoise
0.6098	37.9	.3488	8	1792
0.6097	37.9	.4808	6	originating
0.6097	37.9	.4808	6	pessimistic
0.6097	37.9	.4770	6	Platte
0.6094	37.8	.4700	6	serenely
0.6093	37.8	.3443	8	cedars
0.6091	37.8	.3411	8	Le
0.6091	37.8	.1589	13	learnings
0.6090	37.8	.4535	6	rarest
0.6089	37.8	.3813	7	enchanting
0.6088	37.8	.4544	6	manages
0.6087	37.8	.0000	75	1-Star
0.6086	37.8	.2995	8	coveralls
0.6086	37.8	.2995	8	Gas
0.6086	37.8	.4529	6	passport
0.6085	37.8	.4713	6	snowflake
0.6084	37.8	.3024	9	bein'
0.6084	37.8	.2589	11	tapered
0.6083	37.8	.4730	6	Orion
0.6082	37.8	.4933	6	dill
0.6081	37.8	.4784	6	Cascades
0.6081	37.8	.4784	6	metropolis
0.6081	37.8	.3773	7	Prophet
0.6081	37.8	.1409	16	Shelby
0.6077	37.8	.4084	7	commercially
0.6076	37.8	.4108	7	genre
0.6076	37.8	.4746	6	Islamic
0.6075	37.8	.4513	6	notwithstanding
0.6075	37.8	.4513	6	Silas
0.6074	37.8	.2878	9	pi
0.6074	37.8	.4493	6	sputtered
0.6073	37.8	.4510	6	clanged
0.6073	37.8	.4714	6	dictating
0.6073	37.8	.4491	6	fortitude
0.6073	37.8	.4510	6	shrugs
0.6073	37.8	.4725	6	subsistence
0.6072	37.8	.4723	6	atoll
0.6072	37.8	.2424	8	blight
0.6072	37.8	.2424	8	stewardesses
0.6072	37.8	.2424	8	tiger's
0.6071	37.8	.4789	6	Hamburg
0.6070	37.8	.4521	6	drummed
0.6070	37.8	.2553	10	Homo
0.6068	37.8	.4719	6	precinct
0.6067	37.8	.3024	8	brakeman
0.6067	37.8	.3406	8	Frisco
0.6066	37.8	.4764	6	conceded
0.6066	37.8	.4703	6	uninformed
0.6064	37.8	.3397	7	funny-looking
0.6062	37.8	.4693	6	pavements
0.6060	37.8	.2744	9	hoofed
0.6059	37.8	.4799	6	buzzes
0.6059	37.8	.4493	6	Holiday
0.6058	37.8	.4673	6	bedecked
0.6058	37.8	.3401	8	50%
0.6056	37.8	.2417	8	spouting
0.6054	37.8	.3934	7	hominy
0.6054	37.8	.4923	6	resume
0.6052	37.8	.2302	11	longitudinal
0.6051	37.8	.2426	10	cerebral
0.6051	37.8	.2426	10	diffraction
0.6051	37.8	.2426	10	endocrine
0.6051	37.8	.2417	11	hyphens
0.6051	37.8	.2426	10	pulmonary
0.6050	37.8	.2187	8	drawstring
0.6050	37.8	.2187	8	Gunner
0.6050	37.8	.2187	8	lumberjack
0.6047	37.8	.3431	8	bindings
0.6045	37.8	.3894	7	Josef
0.6044	37.8	.3828	7	dun
0.6044	37.8	.4815	6	volt
0.6043	37.8	.3470	8	hollered
0.6042	37.8	.3915	7	tattooed
0.6041	37.8	.4467	6	homecoming
0.6041	37.8	.4467	6	jumpy
0.6040	37.8	.1446	18	Cress
0.6039	37.8	.3356	8	drumhead
0.6037	37.8	.3556	7	cantilever
0.6037	37.8	.2266	11	Lao
0.6036	37.8	.3498	8	adulthood
THE PRECEDING WORD TYPE OCCUPIES RANK 21400				
0.6035	37.8	.2041	11	alchemy
0.6033	37.8	.3809	7	ElPaso
0.6033	37.8	.4473	6	stepladder
0.6032	37.8	.3998	7	entirety
0.6031	37.8	.2862	8	Doubleday
0.6031	37.8	.3428	8	1755
0.6030	37.8	.3971	7	540
0.6029	37.8	.2167	8	Briggs
0.6029	37.8	.3931	7	203
0.6028	37.8	.4715	6	contamination
0.6026	37.8	.4716	6	intellectuals
0.6025	37.8	.4711	6	budding
0.6024	37.8	.3917	7	dank
0.6024	37.8	.3226	9	etching
0.6024	37.8	.3955	7	geometrically
0.6024	37.8	.3917	7	ironic
0.6022	37.8	.2864	9	O'Brien
0.6022	37.8	.2975	9	Pact
0.6021	37.8	.2399	8	Eric's
0.6021	37.8	.2399	8	houseboat
0.6021	37.8	.2399	8	Subject
0.6021	37.8	.4471	6	undetected
0.6020	37.8	.3434	8	antiquity
0.6020	37.8	.4481	6	wisp
0.6020	37.8	.4705	6	10-
0.6018	37.8	.2041	11	narcotics
0.6018	37.8	.4467	6	plaintively
0.6018	37.8	.3286	8	powerhouse
0.6018	37.8	.3596	7	snorkel
0.6017	37.8	.3814	7	knowingly
0.6016	37.8	.3219	8	red-eyed
0.6015	37.8	.3986	7	idols
0.6014	37.8	.4696	6	hanger
0.6014	37.8	.4471	6	props
0.6014	37.8	.4764	6	teamed
0.6013	37.8	.4639	6	Cascade
0.6013	37.8	.4639	6	dissolving
0.6013	37.8	.4697	6	JerseyCity
0.6013	37.8	.4478	6	murderers
0.6013	37.8	.1457	14	skiff
0.6011	37.8	.2393	8	Argus
0.6011	37.8	.2393	8	Ebenezer
0.6011	37.8	.2393	8	Jason's
0.6011	37.8	.2393	8	Swenson
0.6011	37.8	.4846	6	termination
0.6010	37.8	.4484	6	uncompromising
0.6009	37.8	.3278	8	paddock
0.6008	37.8	.3270	8	northerly
0.6008	37.8	.3403	8	null
0.6008	37.8	.3742	7	watts
0.6007	37.8	.3999	7	freshened
0.6005	37.8	.2197	11	Katrin
0.6005	37.8	.4688	6	unpaid
0.6004	37.8	.1211	21	workpiece
0.6002	37.8	.3858	7	Campbell
0.6001	37.8	.4394	6	workroom
0.5999	37.8	.4106	7	transferring
0.5998	37.8	.1341	14	exoskeleton
0.5998	37.8	.4781	6	fuller
0.5998	37.8	.3214	8	seafood
0.5997	37.8	.2386	8	hungrier
0.5995	37.8	.3438	8	journalism
0.5994	37.8	.2838	9	Affairs
0.5992	37.8	.4441	6	fervently
0.5992	37.8	.4441	6	magistrate
0.5991	37.8	.1560	15	beverage
0.5990	37.8	.3352	8	dormitory
0.5990	37.8	.3209	8	Gateway
0.5987	37.8	.4536	6	Company's
0.5986	37.8	.4603	6	fishlike
0.5985	37.8	.4009	7	Primitive
0.5984	37.8	.4763	6	acquiring
0.5983	37.8	.3950	7	shrouded
0.5980	37.8	.3875	7	Calcutta
0.5980	37.8	.3560	8	compel
0.5980	37.8	.4886	6	manipulated
0.5980	37.8	.3315	8	yellow-green
0.5979	37.8	.0000	51	Bumps
0.5979	37.8	.3302	7	inlaid
0.5979	37.8	.2031	11	Sarnoff
0.5979	37.8	.3359	8	socialism
0.5977	37.8	.4433	6	protruded
0.5977	37.8	.0603	38	salads
0.5976	37.8	.2424	10	cortex
0.5976	37.8	.2424	10	herbaceous
0.5976	37.8	.2424	10	neutron
0.5974	37.8	.3023	9	reptilian
0.5973	37.8	.3493	7	Dexter
0.5972	37.8	.3141	8	buff
0.5972	37.8	.4346	6	Dinner
0.5972	37.8	.1014	23	sift
0.5972	37.8	.2184	11	Tunisia
0.5971	37.8	.3421	7	gulping
0.5971	37.8	.1152	17	Sum
0.5971	37.8	.3425	8	undid
0.5970	37.8	.4003	7	Carnival
0.5970	37.8	.4424	6	pacific
0.5970	37.8	.4757	6	proclaims
0.5970	37.8	.4424	6	self-defense
0.5970	37.8	.4003	7	Williams'
THE PRECEDING WORD TYPE OCCUPIES RANK 21500				
0.5969	37.8	.3751	7	buoys
0.5969	37.8	.4590	6	enforces
0.5967	37.8	.4367	6	cobwebs
0.5966	37.8	.4365	6	skyward
0.5966	37.8	.4639	6	380
0.5964	37.8	.3897	7	defender
0.5964	37.8	.3296	7	governess
0.5963	37.8	.3869	7	Mesa
0.5962	37.8	.4683	6	unconsciousness
0.5960	37.8	.2239	10	fads
0.5960	37.8	.4389	6	fantasies
0.5960	37.8	.4389	6	gospel
0.5958	37.8	.2450	10	fiend
0.5957	37.8	.4406	6	ponderous
0.5957	37.8	.4749	6	solves
0.5955	37.7	.4393	6	scuttle
0.5954	37.7	.4634	6	checkups
0.5954	37.7	.4634	6	culmination
0.5954	37.7	.4634	6	unwinding
0.5953	37.7	.1167	15	Bower
0.5953	37.7	.4622	6	empties
0.5953	37.7	.1167	15	Rockport
0.5952	37.7	.4498	6	seacoasts
0.5950	37.7	.2374	11	ceramic
0.5950	37.7	.3889	7	sociable
0.5950	37.7	.3863	7	unilaterally
0.5949	37.7	.4522	6	listless
0.5947	37.7	.0605	26	Phileas
0.5946	37.7	.2395	8	jeeps
0.5946	37.7	.3860	7	profiles
0.5945	37.7	.4380	6	poplars
0.5944	37.7	.4458	6	confided
0.5944	37.7	.4766	6	conveys
0.5941	37.7	.2798	9	Episcopal
0.5941	37.7	.3870	7	pharaohs
0.5940	37.7	.4372	6	Boss
0.5940	37.7	.2230	10	invites
0.5940	37.7	.4604	6	stiffness
0.5939	37.7	.0000	13	Al's
0.5939	37.7	.0000	13	Argonauts
0.5939	37.7	.0000	13	Brockett
0.5939	37.7	.0000	13	Capybara
0.5939	37.7	.0000	13	Chuka
0.5939	37.7	.3353	8	creamy
0.5939	37.7	.0000	13	Crescent
0.5939	37.7	.0000	13	Daedalus
0.5939	37.7	.0000	13	Fdr
0.5939	37.7	.0000	13	Hualachi
0.5939	37.7	.0000	13	Kantchil
0.5939	37.7	.0000	13	Marylou
0.5939	37.7	.0000	13	McGrannery
0.5939	37.7	.0000	13	Milligan
0.5939	37.7	.0000	13	Mols
0.5939	37.7	.4536	6	motorboat
0.5939	37.7	.0000	13	Nibs
0.5939	37.7	.0000	13	oozie
0.5939	37.7	.0000	13	Racky
0.5939	37.7	.0000	13	Sascha
0.5939	37.7	.0000	13	Spotty
0.5939	37.7	.0000	13	Staley
0.5939	37.7	.0000	13	Starfish
0.5939	37.7	.0000	13	Thorfin
0.5939	37.7	.0000	13	Toff
0.5939	37.7	.0000	13	Wielemaker
0.5939	37.7	.0000	13	Yan
0.5937	37.7	.3260	8	eligible
0.5937	37.7	.4659	6	reproducing
0.5936	37.7	.4662	6	comprising
0.5935	37.7	.4600	6	administrator
0.5935	37.7	.4316	6	adversary
0.5935	37.7	.4316	6	breadfruit
0.5933	37.7	.2317	10	Cornwallis
0.5933	37.7	.1814	10	puck
0.5933	37.7	.2418	11	rasp
0.5932	37.7	.4362	6	whereabouts
0.5931	37.7	.3976	7	adapting
0.5931	37.7	.4312	6	dollar's
0.5929	37.7	.3388	8	incongruous
0.5926	37.7	.4699	6	pot-bellied
0.5926	37.7	.4699	6	punishing
0.5924	37.7	.3788	7	northland
0.5923	37.7	.4726	6	venerable
0.5922	37.7	.3842	7	golden-brown
0.5921	37.7	.3766	7	1960's
0.5919	37.7	.2971	8	exaggerate
0.5918	37.7	.2223	11	Jeep
0.5916	37.7	.3611	7	fray
0.5914	37.7	.2621	10	filaments
0.5911	37.7	.4725	6	enhanced
0.5911	37.7	.4626	6	munitions
0.5911	37.7	.4347	6	posterity
0.5911	37.7	.3788	7	Wesley
0.5910	37.7	.0857	24	viola
0.5909	37.7	.4418	6	summarize
0.5909	37.7	.3314	8	001
0.5908	37.7	.4622	6	1688
0.5907	37.7	.2182	11	Bloomington
0.5905	37.7	.2149	12	Bernstein
0.5904	37.7	.3715	7	gazes
0.5903	37.7	.4406	6	ballots
THE PRECEDING WORD TYPE OCCUPIES RANK 21600				
0.5903	37.7	.3736	7	puncture
0.5902	37.7	.4603	6	exhale
0.5902	37.7	.3374	8	kinda
0.5900	37.7	.3450	8	totaling
0.5897	37.7	.3344	8	economist
0.5897	37.7	.4307	6	Ingalls
0.5896	37.7	.4605	6	ooze
0.5895	37.7	.4692	6	liquor
0.5894	37.7	.4408	6	Alessandro
0.5893	37.7	.4676	6	deplorable
0.5891	37.7	.2021	12	anthem
0.5891	37.7	.2684	9	840
0.5890	37.7	.4406	6	bribe
0.5888	37.7	.4598	6	Catholicism
0.5887	37.7	.4649	6	nephews
0.5887	37.7	.2882	8	shouldered
0.5886	37.7	.3921	7	Books
0.5885	37.7	.3450	7	Asa
0.5885	37.7	.4394	6	lingers
0.5885	37.7	.3653	7	356
0.5884	37.7	.3862	7	correspondent
0.5883	37.7	.4312	6	cackling
0.5882	37.7	.4653	6	rehearse
0.5878	37.7	.4293	6	harming
0.5878	37.7	.4292	6	oozed
0.5878	37.7	.4293	6	pleasantest
0.5878	37.7	.3902	7	transforms
0.5877	37.7	.3721	7	asserted
0.5872	37.7	.3301	8	rind
0.5871	37.7	.3047	8	pastime
0.5869	37.7	.1573	11	Maloney
0.5869	37.7	.1787	10	pestering
0.5869	37.7	.4279	6	red-headed
0.5868	37.7	.2699	9	Dodger
0.5868	37.7	.3859	7	nine-year-old
0.5868	37.7	.3617	7	teas
0.5866	37.7	.4533	6	rivalry
0.5865	37.7	.4596	6	Lookout
0.5864	37.7	.4271	6	powerless
0.5863	37.7	.1680	13	median
0.5862	37.7	.3684	7	annals
0.5862	37.7	.0000	50	Arriety
0.5862	37.7	.3306	8	Journey
0.5860	37.7	.3866	7	lusty
0.5858	37.7	.4693	6	complications
0.5858	37.7	.4587	6	windowpane
0.5853	37.7	.1839	11	photoelectric
0.5852	37.7	.1531	17	simile
0.5851	37.7	.2434	10	PT
0.5848	37.7	.4357	6	radiators
0.5847	37.7	.4608	6	contradictory
0.5847	37.7	.4354	6	donor
0.5847	37.7	.5627	5	Laramie
0.5845	37.7	.1990	8	Bunche
0.5845	37.7	.4608	6	chrysanthemums
0.5845	37.7	.1990	8	Grenfell
0.5845	37.7	.1990	8	Kitchen
0.5844	37.7	.3093	8	Bogota
0.5844	37.7	.4347	6	infancy
0.5843	37.7	.2407	10	thickened
0.5841	37.7	.3655	7	frosts
0.5841	37.7	.4567	6	Pope's
0.5840	37.7	.5597	5	cloaks
0.5840	37.7	.3738	7	Fog
0.5840	37.7	.5597	5	opium
0.5840	37.7	.5597	5	respecting
0.5840	37.7	.5597	5	Stonewall
0.5839	37.7	.3185	8	Mercy
0.5837	37.7	.3860	6	fielded
0.5837	37.7	.4250	6	havoc
0.5837	37.7	.3860	6	henhouse
0.5836	37.7	.3876	6	braiding
0.5836	37.7	.4336	6	cupful
0.5836	37.7	.3876	6	lair
0.5836	37.7	.3876	6	tryout
0.5835	37.7	.3800	7	Hundred
0.5835	37.7	.4334	6	Julian
0.5835	37.7	.4247	6	popularly
0.5834	37.7	.2089	8	dragon's
0.5834	37.7	.3938	7	145
0.5833	37.7	.3859	6	fierceness
0.5833	37.7	.3859	6	forenoon
0.5833	37.7	.3859	6	grindstone
0.5833	37.7	.3859	6	itched
0.5833	37.7	.3795	7	rivaled
0.5833	37.7	.3859	6	sipped
0.5832	37.7	.3414	7	spaceships
0.5831	37.7	.5414	5	long-standing
0.5831	37.7	.1029	15	Scooter
0.5830	37.7	.3853	6	ninety-eight
0.5830	37.7	.4382	6	shod
0.5828	37.7	.4138	6	broken-down
0.5828	37.7	.3876	6	jalopy
0.5828	37.7	.4622	6	re-elected
0.5828	37.7	.3876	6	shimmered
0.5828	37.7	.3876	6	Wilsons
0.5827	37.7	.4644	6	ferocity
0.5827	37.7	.4649	6	lithe
0.5827	37.7	.4644	6	naive
0.5826	37.7	.4473	6	doctrines
THE PRECEDING WORD TYPE OCCUPIES RANK 21700				
0.5826	37.7	.4332	6	Iliad
0.5826	37.7	.3873	6	wanna
0.5826	37.7	.3875	6	whinnying
0.5826	37.7	.4600	6	workbench
0.5823	37.7	.3871	6	Basel
0.5823	37.7	.3613	7	conquests
0.5823	37.7	.4330	6	Exposition
0.5823	37.7	.3871	6	ruffians
0.5823	37.7	.3871	6	wildebeest
0.5822	37.7	.3873	6	churns
0.5822	37.7	.3876	6	fairyland
0.5822	37.7	.3852	6	smudged
0.5821	37.6	.3797	6	Coal
0.5821	37.7	.4608	6	favoring
0.5821	37.6	.3797	6	unselfish
0.5819	37.6	.3793	6	bleach
0.5819	37.6	.3793	6	gulps
0.5819	37.6	.3793	6	Shoshone
0.5819	37.6	.3450	8	watercolor
0.5819	37.6	.3103	8	1971
0.5818	37.6	.3850	6	chief's
0.5818	37.6	.5615	5	emigrate
0.5818	37.6	.3850	6	Senecas
0.5818	37.6	.3875	6	stone's
0.5818	37.6	.5402	5	whittle
0.5817	37.6	.3297	8	brownies
0.5817	37.6	.4530	6	preparatory
0.5817	37.6	.4317	6	seaboard
0.5815	37.6	.5612	5	adjourned
0.5815	37.6	.3715	7	Germantown
0.5815	37.6	.3715	7	hardworking
0.5815	37.6	.4505	6	manlike
0.5815	37.6	.4505	6	wasteful
0.5814	37.6	.4524	6	Carter's
0.5813	37.6	.3738	7	conglomerate
0.5813	37.6	.3135	7	sledge
0.5813	37.6	.3846	6	Wilton
0.5813	37.6	.0499	24	2x
0.5811	37.6	.5571	5	uplift
0.5810	37.6	.5608	5	ornate
0.5810	37.6	.3009	8	Rim
0.5809	37.6	.1669	12	bacterium
0.5808	37.6	.4298	6	cyclones
0.5808	37.6	.5605	5	methodically
0.5808	37.6	.2273	11	thiamine
0.5805	37.6	.5605	5	starkly
0.5805	37.6	.2816	8	where'd
0.5803	37.6	.4494	6	dredging
0.5803	37.6	.3807	7	encampment
0.5801	37.6	.5602	5	strongholds
0.5800	37.6	.3790	6	Engineer
0.5800	37.6	.4560	6	valiantly
0.5800	37.6	.4531	6	189
0.5799	37.6	.5595	5	coded
0.5799	37.6	.5599	5	consumes
0.5799	37.6	.2846	9	objectives
0.5799	37.6	.5599	5	1823
0.5798	37.6	.5599	5	citadel
0.5798	37.6	.5599	5	republican
0.5798	37.6	.5599	5	trekked
0.5797	37.6	.3395	7	Domingo
0.5797	37.6	.3240	8	oblong
0.5797	37.6	.3786	6	red-and-white
0.5797	37.6	.4586	6	21st
0.5796	37.6	.3734	7	Play
0.5795	37.6	.5598	5	Chancellorsville
0.5795	37.6	.0000	54	Jem
0.5795	37.6	.4194	6	tree's
0.5794	37.6	.4552	6	acquaintances
0.5793	37.6	.3710	7	mutiny
0.5793	37.6	.4286	6	raiding
0.5793	37.6	.1958	12	sol
0.5793	37.6	.3786	6	taxicabs
0.5790	37.6	.4278	6	ferryboats
0.5790	37.6	.4507	6	Marion
0.5790	37.6	.3216	7	ninety-seven
0.5789	37.6	.4091	6	cluttered
0.5787	37.6	.3079	8	Blaine
0.5787	37.6	.3079	8	debated

U	SFI	D	F	Word Type
0.5787	37.6	.5560	5	grope
0.5787	37.6	.5594	5	indebted
0.5787	37.6	.5605	5	interwoven
0.5787	37.6	.4273	6	Justices
0.5787	37.6	.4273	6	menaced
0.5786	37.6	.2200	11	Hawkins
0.5786	37.6	.4608	6	mankind's
0.5786	37.6	.3675	7	obsession
0.5785	37.6	.3865	7	neighborly
0.5783	37.6	.4338	6	almonds
0.5783	37.6	.2848	8	bedlam
0.5782	37.6	.5555	5	analyses
0.5782	37.6	.1801	11	dark-green
0.5782	37.6	.2355	10	pruning
0.5781	37.6	.5365	5	bathrooms
0.5781	37.6	.4522	6	chaste
0.5780	37.6	.2967	8	cruelly
0.5779	37.6	.4288	6	sizzle
0.5778	37.6	.3848	7	Winchester
0.5777	37.6	.3667	7	relies
0.5776	37.6	.3774	6	taxicab

THE PRECEDING WORD TYPE OCCUPIES RANK 21800

U	SFI	D	F	Word Type
0.5775	37.6	.4323	6	Californians
0.5775	37.6	.4323	6	Elliot
0.5775	37.6	.3696	7	unconstitutional
0.5773	37.6	.3037	8	LatinAmerica
0.5772	37.6	.4319	6	contended
0.5772	37.6	.5389	5	exempt
0.5772	37.6	.5389	5	individualism
0.5771	37.6	.4518	6	accorded
0.5771	37.6	.4518	6	docile
0.5771	37.6	.3770	6	nobly
0.5771	37.6	.1962	12	staccato
0.5770	37.6	.5353	5	bakeries
0.5770	37.6	.4316	6	Facts
0.5770	37.6	.4316	6	marshal
0.5770	37.6	.3627	7	slowest
0.5768	37.6	.1661	12	Montezuma
0.5767	37.6	.3855	7	intricately
0.5767	37.6	.2323	11	squaring
0.5767	37.6	.4368	6	well-kept
0.5767	37.6	.4505	6	2600
0.5766	37.6	.4540	6	Clifford
0.5766	37.6	.2891	8	levy
0.5766	37.6	.3838	6	Noah's
0.5765	37.6	.4500	6	crumple
0.5765	37.6	.5373	5	deriving
0.5765	37.6	.3834	6	Jekyll
0.5765	37.6	.1903	11	manioc
0.5765	37.6	.3718	7	wedded
0.5764	37.6	.3764	6	derrick
0.5764	37.6	.3833	6	twister
0.5763	37.6	.5615	5	mimic
0.5762	37.6	.1869	13	xylophone
0.5761	37.6	.4539	6	pathways
0.5761	37.6	.3759	6	scourge
0.5759	37.6	.3824	6	pacer
0.5759	37.6	.3830	7	stewed
0.5759	37.6	.5401	5	Thousand
0.5757	37.6	.3551	7	Comanche
0.5755	37.6	.1380	14	prophet
0.5755	37.6	.2855	9	Sciences
0.5751	37.6	.5631	5	tinker
0.5751	37.6	.3095	8	unabridged
0.5749	37.6	.4236	6	plodding
0.5749	37.6	.3862	7	softens
0.5748	37.6	.4502	6	brighten
0.5748	37.6	.4302	6	Tories
0.5747	37.6	.3193	8	Future
0.5747	37.6	.1712	12	75%
0.5746	37.6	.5363	5	stomachache
0.5745	37.6	.5363	5	leafless
0.5745	37.6	.3663	7	secretes
0.5744	37.6	.4490	6	orphans
0.5742	37.6	.3306	8	Planets
0.5741	37.6	.5357	5	490
0.5740	37.6	.2213	10	esophagus
0.5740	37.6	.2213	10	Halley's
0.5740	37.6	.2213	10	serum
0.5740	37.6	.3182	7	unmarried
0.5739	37.6	.1230	14	antibodies
0.5739	37.6	.5396	5	reassure
0.5739	37.6	.4238	6	wither
0.5736	37.6	.2253	11	homophones
0.5736	37.6	.3277	7	scuffling
0.5735	37.6	.5392	5	dungeon
0.5735	37.6	.5392	5	inhuman
0.5735	37.6	.5392	5	Paint
0.5734	37.6	.0815	28	gage
0.5734	37.6	.3659	7	sown
0.5733	37.6	.4454	6	disintegrate
0.5733	37.6	.2789	10	taper
0.5732	37.6	.5550	5	majestically
0.5732	37.6	.5554	5	prohibition
0.5732	37.6	.3821	7	sifting
0.5732	37.6	.3772	7	statute
0.5731	37.6	.3716	7	dispatched
0.5731	37.6	.5552	5	sea's
0.5730	37.6	.3650	7	Lindbergh
0.5729	37.6	.5387	5	famine
0.5729	37.6	.2831	9	Gone
0.5729	37.6	.5554	5	Industry
0.5729	37.6	.5554	5	logically
0.5729	37.6	.2831	9	Philistines
0.5729	37.6	.4449	6	resultant
0.5729	37.6	.5387	5	slashing
0.5728	37.6	.5375	5	souvenir
0.5727	37.6	.5559	5	attentions
0.5727	37.6	.5357	5	breezy
0.5727	37.6	.5552	5	counterpart
0.5726	37.6	.3280	7	botanist
0.5726	37.6	.5551	5	capricious
0.5726	37.6	.4518	6	Polynesians
0.5726	37.6	.5354	5	stickers
0.5724	37.6	.3266	7	foreleg
0.5724	37.6	.1878	11	justices
0.5724	37.6	.5384	5	reclining
0.5724	37.6	.5384	5	shingled
0.5723	37.6	.5352	5	plush
0.5722	37.6	.2060	12	adj
0.5722	37.6	.5527	5	partner's
0.5722	37.6	.5531	5	sheath

THE PRECEDING WORD TYPE OCCUPIES RANK 21900

U	SFI	D	F	Word Type
0.5722	37.6	.4441	6	371
0.5721	37.6	.3659	7	setter
0.5721	37.6	.3829	7	1-3
0.5720	37.6	.1717	11	Equator
0.5720	37.6	.2435	10	flavored
0.5720	37.6	.5382	5	hooded
0.5720	37.6	.5534	5	nook
0.5720	37.6	.5382	5	squirm
0.5720	37.6	.4342	6	tempest
0.5719	37.6	.4189	6	upheld
0.5719	37.6	.4189	6	14-15
0.5718	37.6	.2198	10	constellations
0.5718	37.6	.0000	29	pistil
0.5717	37.6	.3643	7	fortifications
0.5716	37.6	.3768	7	pawed
0.5716	37.6	.5389	5	scalding
0.5716	37.6	.5346	5	Windsor
0.5716	37.6	.3144	8	Zealanders
0.5715	37.6	.4456	6	Assistant
0.5715	37.6	.5377	5	cruised
0.5715	37.6	.3778	7	victim's
0.5713	37.6	.4195	6	paled
0.5713	37.6	.2971	8	single-celled
0.5713	37.6	.4195	6	swap
0.5712	37.6	.5386	5	affirmed
0.5712	37.6	.5375	5	purposeful
0.5712	37.6	.5386	5	Saxon
0.5712	37.6	.5375	5	seethed
0.5712	37.6	.5375	5	unconcern
0.5711	37.6	.5334	5	drudgery
0.5711	37.6	.4336	6	humane
0.5711	37.6	.4206	6	mason
0.5711	37.6	.4206	6	Talking
0.5710	37.6	.2292	8	Howell
0.5710	37.6	.5331	5	surges
0.5709	37.6	.4313	6	avert
0.5708	37.6	.3606	7	flaky
0.5707	37.6	.2088	12	alteration
0.5707	37.6	.3415	8	lengthen
0.5707	37.6	.3129	8	Sumatra
0.5706	37.6	.2300	10	cops
0.5706	37.6	.4309	6	two-year-old
0.5705	37.6	.1776	13	Lonnie
0.5705	37.6	.1401	13	mucous
0.5705	37.6	.4297	6	sharp-pointed
0.5704	37.6	.5370	5	anchoring
0.5704	37.6	.3123	8	epidemics
0.5704	37.6	.5370	5	pantaloons
0.5703	37.6	.3836	7	billiard
0.5703	37.6	.5336	5	Flowers
0.5703	37.6	.5336	5	implicit
0.5702	37.6	.5333	5	owner's
0.5702	37.6	.5380	5	snags
0.5699	37.6	.5332	5	britches
0.5699	37.6	.5332	5	Hughes
0.5698	37.6	.5476	5	shippers
0.5697	37.6	.5329	5	bruise
0.5697	37.6	.5329	5	Georg
0.5696	37.6	.3979	6	chalked
0.5696	37.6	.4144	6	charted
0.5695	37.6	.5536	5	Marys
0.5695	37.6	.3269	8	modal
0.5694	37.6	.4549	6	Bells
0.5694	37.6	.5329	5	foresaw
0.5694	37.6	.5474	5	lecturing
0.5693	37.6	.5326	5	chins
0.5693	37.6	.4156	6	trampling
0.5692	37.6	.3731	7	ornamentation
0.5692	37.6	.4470	6	provoking
0.5690	37.6	.4422	6	Archibald
0.5690	37.6	.5475	5	retains
0.5689	37.6	.5473	5	roadways
0.5689	37.5	.3672	7	Silent
0.5689	37.6	.3252	7	transcontinental
0.5688	37.5	.0000	38	-1
0.5688	37.5	.4476	6	bountiful
0.5688	37.5	.4298	6	crackled
0.5687	37.5	.5473	5	dominating
0.5686	37.5	.3585	7	agility
0.5686	37.5	.4416	6	laymen
0.5686	37.5	.4416	6	Tyre
0.5685	37.5	.2387	9	Austria-Hungary
0.5684	37.5	.2243	10	Colombia's
0.5681	37.5	.4428	6	152
0.5679	37.5	.2235	10	follicle
0.5679	37.5	.3766	7	Greg
0.5677	37.5	.2275	8	Agramonte
0.5677	37.5	.2275	8	Philo
0.5677	37.5	.2275	8	rainmakers
0.5675	37.5	.4446	6	cooker
0.5675	37.5	.1957	9	Robin's
0.5672	37.5	.3579	7	influx
0.5672	37.5	.4137	6	suspend
0.5671	37.5	.3040	7	icehouse
0.5671	37.5	.3823	6	pestered
0.5671	37.5	.3806	6	soybean
0.5670	37.5	.2435	10	Selective
0.5667	37.5	.4222	6	voyagers
0.5666	37.5	.3354	7	chimed
0.5666	37.5	.3354	7	noblest

THE PRECEDING WORD TYPE OCCUPIES RANK 22000

U	SFI	D	F	Word Type
0.5666	37.5	.4224	6	thirty-nine
0.5665	37.5	.3356	7	seventy-two
0.5664	37.5	.3675	7	archeologists
0.5664	37.5	.3820	6	blaming
0.5664	37.5	.3822	6	suntan
0.5663	37.5	.3801	6	Costa
0.5663	37.5	.3801	6	crier
0.5663	37.5	.3801	6	eighty-eight
0.5663	37.5	.3669	7	probed
0.5662	37.5	.2225	11	Eileen
0.5660	37.5	.3669	7	capillary
0.5660	37.5	.4426	6	interspersed
0.5660	37.5	.4426	6	scarcity
0.5659	37.5	.1035	15	altimeter
0.5658	37.5	.3485	6	Harpers
0.5656	37.5	.3818	6	able-bodied
0.5656	37.5	.3664	7	facets
0.5656	37.5	.0642	24	Fix
0.5653	37.5	.1391	13	subcontinent
0.5652	37.5	.3816	6	ice-covered
0.5652	37.5	.3105	8	326
0.5651	37.5	.4220	6	perching
0.5650	37.5	.3227	8	stud
0.5649	37.5	.3141	8	hydraulic
0.5649	37.5	.3141	8	oceanic
0.5648	37.5	.4148	6	apparel
0.5648	37.5	.3557	7	zodiac
0.5647	37.5	.4218	6	Arc
0.5647	37.5	.2949	8	soapy
0.5646	37.5	.5306	5	chug
0.5646	37.5	.4409	6	feasible
0.5646	37.5	.0000	39	Finny
0.5646	37.5	.4127	6	windstorm
0.5645	37.5	.4516	6	trademarks
0.5644	37.5	.2379	10	homographs
0.5643	37.5	.2127	10	cradles
0.5643	37.5	.1270	15	yd
0.5642	37.5	.3647	7	desertion
0.5642	37.5	.3567	7	legumes
0.5642	37.5	.3115	8	319
0.5641	37.5	.5305	5	appreciative
0.5641	37.5	.5305	5	arousing
0.5641	37.5	.3645	7	camper
0.5641	37.5	.5325	5	hums
0.5641	37.5	.5325	5	unsure
0.5641	37.5	.2632	9	washers
0.5640	37.5	.0000	29	Metropolis
0.5639	37.5	.5306	5	bargains
0.5639	37.5	.4143	6	bedclothes
0.5639	37.5	.4456	6	Can
0.5639	37.5	.5304	5	flit
0.5639	37.5	.5324	5	imagery
0.5639	37.5	.5304	5	thanksgiving
0.5639	37.5	.5324	5	vulgar
0.5638	37.5	.3259	8	concertos
0.5637	37.5	.4470	6	Donna
0.5636	37.5	.4291	6	catalogs
0.5636	37.5	.5302	5	diffused
0.5636	37.5	.0858	23	ent
0.5636	37.5	.4291	6	lures
0.5635	37.5	.4433	6	designation
0.5634	37.5	.5297	5	excavating
0.5633	37.5	.4419	6	straightforward
0.5633	37.5	.4365	6	strengthening
0.5631	37.5	.3734	6	snowdrift
0.5630	37.5	.3563	7	1853
0.5628	37.5	.3539	7	correlate
0.5628	37.5	.3169	8	cut-out
0.5626	37.5	.4189	6	inject
0.5626	37.5	.1952	12	taconite
0.5625	37.5	.3581	7	dramatized
0.5625	37.5	.4343	6	humanitarian
0.5624	37.5	.4401	6	chiseled
0.5624	37.5	.4234	6	mows
0.5624	37.5	.4492	6	three-
0.5620	37.5	.5251	5	rightfully
0.5619	37.5	.4235	6	necktie
0.5618	37.5	.3723	6	bluffs
0.5618	37.5	.3723	6	1785
0.5617	37.5	.3695	7	1950s
0.5616	37.5	.3238	7	broomstick
0.5615	37.5	.1531	15	etymology
0.5614	37.5	.5247	5	self-control
0.5613	37.5	.4087	6	persimmon
0.5612	37.5	.5244	5	Help
0.5610	37.5	.4274	6	priceless
0.5608	37.5	.2890	8	basketballs
0.5608	37.5	.5243	5	Eight
0.5608	37.5	.3684	7	premiums
0.5608	37.5	.2890	8	sounder
0.5608	37.5	.5228	5	1610
0.5607	37.5	.3147	8	V-8
0.5606	37.5	.5244	5	glorify
0.5604	37.5	.3356	7	pimples
0.5603	37.5	.5244	5	Miguel
0.5602	37.5	.4221	6	Garrett
0.5602	37.5	.2111	10	Jip
0.5602	37.5	.2121	10	kicker
0.5602	37.5	.2111	10	Leopard
0.5601	37.5	.0839	22	carol

THE PRECEDING WORD TYPE OCCUPIES RANK 22100

U	SFI	D	F	Word Type
0.5601	37.5	.4408	6	Mercantile
0.5601	37.5	.5242	5	soars
0.5599	37.5	.5241	5	tragically
0.5596	37.5	.2363	10	ecological
0.5596	37.5	.4255	6	eloquence
0.5595	37.5	.3015	8	repulsive
0.5595	37.5	.1002	17	theorem
0.5594	37.5	.0717	20	equilateral
0.5594	37.5	.3131	8	1960s
0.5590	37.5	.3169	7	catbird
0.5590	37.5	.3126	8	Squire
0.5589	37.5	.2733	9	currencies
0.5589	37.5	.3646	7	289
0.5589	37.5	.3646	7	297
0.5585	37.5	.1983	12	balalaika
0.5585	37.5	.3732	7	continuity
0.5584	37.5	.4206	6	droppings
0.5583	37.5	.3583	7	bumblebees
0.5583	37.5	.4033	6	frostbitten
0.5583	37.5	.2918	8	heavy-duty
0.5583	37.5	.2568	9	indexes
0.5583	37.5	.4377	6	mugs
0.5583	37.5	.4377	6	pastoral
0.5583	37.5	.4399	6	426
0.5582	37.5	.3154	7	grapevine
0.5582	37.5	.3154	7	pun
0.5580	37.5	.4135	6	1778
0.5580	37.5	.4135	6	1834
0.5579	37.5	.2397	10	Fifty
0.5579	37.5	.2302	9	Pavlov
0.5579	37.5	.3485	7	walker
0.5577	37.5	.4382	6	afield
0.5577	37.5	.2487	10	attaching
0.5577	37.5	.3492	7	bullfrogs
0.5577	37.5	.4382	6	ensued
0.5577	37.5	.4228	6	epithets
0.5576	37.5	.2043	11	Elijah
0.5573	37.5	.3117	7	Tabby
0.5569	37.5	.1560	16	forging
0.5568	37.5	.4298	6	B1
0.5567	37.5	.3515	7	volatile
0.5566	37.5	.4369	6	James's
0.5565	37.5	.4364	6	Rhode
0.5564	37.5	.3643	7	ethical
0.5558	37.4	.4207	6	delirious
0.5557	37.4	.4161	6	Patty's
0.5554	37.4	.3665	7	Ambrose
0.5554	37.4	.3134	7	gallows
0.5551	37.4	.4375	6	birch-bark
0.5550	37.4	.4418	6	extras
0.5548	37.4	.1998	11	Oct
0.5546	37.4	.3591	7	$14
0.5546	37.4	.4004	6	begone
0.5546	37.4	.3591	7	conjecture
0.5546	37.4	.1863	8	Walking
0.5544	37.4	.4163	6	princely
0.5543	37.4	.4196	6	Eighth
0.5543	37.4	.3548	7	slimy
0.5542	37.4	.3998	6	fairer
0.5542	37.4	.2368	10	Nero
0.5541	37.4	.2287	9	Alaskans
0.5541	37.4	.1854	11	beseech
0.5541	37.4	.4404	6	Color
0.5541	37.4	.4149	6	uniqueness
0.5540	37.4	.3619	7	Sumerians
0.5538	37.4	.0000	37	lowest-terms
0.5537	37.4	.3500	7	Sheep
0.5535	37.4	.3106	8	chaise
0.5535	37.4	.0524	27	MR
0.5533	37.4	.3452	7	fluctuations
0.5531	37.4	.3579	7	advocates
0.5531	37.4	.3579	7	assets
0.5531	37.4	.3579	7	negotiated
0.5529	37.4	.4391	6	Chronicle
0.5528	37.4	.1093	19	instrumentation
0.5522	37.4	.3975	6	calmer
0.5521	37.4	.4359	6	mingle
0.5520	37.4	.2708	8	Pharaoh's
0.5520	37.4	.2708	8	SanPedro
0.5518	37.4	.4190	6	obeys
0.5516	37.4	.2463	10	Ballet
0.5516	37.4	.2264	10	268
0.5515	37.4	.4180	6	observant
0.5515	37.4	.4180	6	strangled
0.5514	37.4	.3517	7	fifteen-year-old
0.5514	37.4	.4328	6	guiltily
0.5514	37.4	.2443	9	Polk
0.5513	37.4	.2700	8	shaker
0.5512	37.4	.1171	17	Maj
0.5511	37.4	.1850	12	Satan
0.5511	37.4	.3014	8	turbulence
0.5510	37.4	.4347	6	tinsel
0.5508	37.4	.3546	7	overhaul
0.5507	37.4	.3570	7	Deerfield
0.5507	37.4	.1871	9	hartebeest
0.5507	37.4	.3232	7	torpedoes
0.5505	37.4	.4345	6	undercut
0.5504	37.4	.4109	6	eternity
0.5503	37.4	.4391	6	crib
0.5503	37.4	.4293	6	defect

THE PRECEDING WORD TYPE OCCUPIES RANK 22200

U	SFI	D	F	Word Type
0.5502	37.4	.4292	6	backyards
0.5499	37.4	.4103	6	chubby
0.5499	37.4	.4103	6	penned
0.5498	37.4	.3578	7	backboned
0.5498	37.4	.4194	6	Venetian
0.5495	37.4	.2444	9	Aviv
0.5495	37.4	.2445	7	Charta
0.5495	37.4	.2177	8	coaching
0.5495	37.4	.2445	7	Eurydice
0.5495	37.4	.2177	8	Melinda
0.5495	37.4	.2445	7	miller's
0.5495	37.4	.3721	6	queen's
0.5495	37.4	.3721	6	sponsor
0.5495	37.4	.2444	9	Tel
0.5495	37.4	.4338	6	630
0.5494	37.4	.3517	7	congenital
0.5494	37.4	.3718	6	longhorns
0.5494	37.4	.3718	6	slats
0.5494	37.4	.3718	6	ten-foot
0.5493	37.4	.1657	12	Badger
0.5493	37.4	.3716	6	snowballs
0.5492	37.4	.3396	7	scow
0.5492	37.4	.2415	9	viscose
0.5491	37.4	.3517	7	OH
0.5491	37.4	.3517	7	rearrangement
0.5491	37.4	.4021	6	unevenly
0.5488	37.4	.3567	7	Philistine
0.5486	37.4	.4017	6	antimony
0.5484	37.4	.3734	7	divider
0.5483	37.4	.1066	19	ark
0.5483	37.4	.2287	10	cap'n
0.5483	37.4	.3511	7	Thebes
0.5483	37.4	.4153	6	uplifting
0.5482	37.4	.3676	7	alphabetic
0.5482	37.4	.0000	12	Bigfoot
0.5482	37.4	.0000	12	CAP
0.5482	37.4	.0000	12	Dillworth
0.5482	37.4	.0000	12	Drakestail
0.5482	37.4	.0000	12	Ehrhart
0.5482	37.4	.0000	12	Gata
0.5482	37.4	.0000	12	Has-ka
0.5482	37.4	.0000	12	Hippo

U	SFI	D	F	Word Type
0.5482	37.4	.0000	12	Killer
0.5482	37.4	.0000	12	Melindy
0.5482	37.4	.0000	12	Monk
0.5482	37.4	.0000	12	musher
0.5482	37.4	.0000	12	Perrik
0.5482	37.4	.0000	12	Serilda
0.5482	37.4	.0000	12	Snapper
0.5482	37.4	.0000	12	Yehudi
0.5480	37.4	.2276	9	fife
0.5480	37.4	.4124	6	recklessly
0.5480	37.4	.4124	6	sixpence
0.5480	37.4	.3674	6	sundial
0.5479	37.4	.4121	6	crannies
0.5479	37.4	.4121	6	executives
0.5479	37.4	.4121	6	sparked
0.5478	37.4	.3033	8	low-pitched
0.5477	37.4	.3415	7	Rift
0.5477	37.4	.3415	7	southeastward
0.5476	37.4	.2446	10	nutritious
0.5475	37.4	.3786	6	dented
0.5475	37.4	.1729	12	Mantle
0.5475	37.4	.3052	8	Pearson
0.5473	37.4	.4833	5	cornerstone
0.5473	37.4	.4833	5	sixty-eight
0.5473	37.4	.4833	5	435
0.5472	37.4	.3452	7	canes
0.5472	37.4	.2659	8	Raccoon
0.5470	37.4	.3399	7	telecast
0.5469	37.4	.4180	6	Appendix
0.5469	37.4	.3375	7	intrigue
0.5469	37.4	.4126	6	waning
0.5468	37.4	.1950	11	6%
0.5467	37.4	.2402	7	Serapis
0.5467	37.4	.2402	7	Spencer
0.5466	37.4	.3401	7	Federals
0.5466	37.4	.4044	6	handbills
0.5465	37.4	.2988	7	radioed
0.5464	37.4	.3567	7	methinks
0.5462	37.4	.4279	6	dweller
0.5462	37.4	.3368	7	indicator
0.5461	37.4	.2395	7	lifesaving
0.5461	37.4	.2395	7	omens
0.5461	37.4	.2395	7	Petey
0.5461	37.4	.4058	6	scorpions
0.5460	37.4	.1289	13	Saucer
0.5459	37.4	.2297	10	Bragg
0.5457	37.4	.3571	7	coonskin
0.5456	37.4	.2155	8	Blueberry
0.5456	37.4	.2155	8	Grandpa's
0.5456	37.4	.2389	7	Janey's
0.5456	37.4	.2155	8	mutter
0.5456	37.4	.2155	8	Rufe
0.5455	37.4	.2445	9	mutation
0.5455	37.4	.1584	12	overworked
0.5455	37.4	.2445	9	pancreas
0.5453	37.4	.4269	6	downfall
0.5452	37.4	.1277	12	Cale
0.5452	37.4	.3126	8	libretto

THE PRECEDING WORD TYPE OCCUPIES RANK 22300

0.5451	37.4	.3602	7	Abbott's
0.5451	37.4	.4134	6	que
0.5450	37.4	.4267	6	enlarging
0.5448	37.4	.3101	8	illustrative
0.5447	37.4	.2160	8	Jupiter's
0.5447	37.4	.2160	8	Loa
0.5447	37.4	.2160	8	micron
0.5446	37.4	.4299	6	apprenticeship
0.5446	37.4	.2383	9	dandelions
0.5445	37.4	.1034	14	Rapunzel
0.5445	37.4	.0156	35	Violet
0.5444	37.4	.2512	8	Hermes
0.5444	37.4	.3592	7	Roberta
0.5442	37.4	.2444	9	Proclamation
0.5442	37.4	.4781	5	swoops
0.5441	37.4	.2989	7	Mojave
0.5441	37.4	.2989	7	safeguards
0.5439	37.4	.3022	7	Apaches
0.5439	37.4	.3648	7	embarrass
0.5437	37.4	.2366	7	bugler
0.5437	37.4	.2366	7	Cricket
0.5437	37.4	.4291	6	devout
0.5437	37.4	.2366	7	goat's
0.5437	37.4	.2366	7	Parker's
0.5437	37.4	.4311	6	superimposed
0.5437	37.4	.4291	6	Teutonic
0.5437	37.4	.2314	9	512
0.5435	37.4	.3634	7	interminable
0.5435	37.4	.2958	8	Patton
0.5433	37.4	.3527	7	Practice
0.5432	37.3	.1838	10	electrodes
0.5432	37.3	.3507	7	workouts
0.5429	37.3	.3902	6	cucumber
0.5428	37.3	.2152	8	Sanders
0.5426	37.3	.3855	6	outwardly
0.5426	37.3	.3410	7	Periodic
0.5426	37.3	.4284	6	ratings
0.5425	37.3	.2353	7	Dino
0.5425	37.3	.2353	7	Feller
0.5425	37.3	.2353	7	Gant
0.5425	37.3	.4790	5	mailboxes
0.5425	37.3	.2353	7	Paw
0.5425	37.3	.2353	7	sensor
0.5425	37.3	.2353	7	surfers
0.5424	37.3	.3756	6	dumpy
0.5423	37.3	.4080	6	aeronautics
0.5422	37.3	.1852	11	Vladivostok
0.5421	37.3	.2744	8	bulldozers
0.5421	37.3	.4788	5	McKay
0.5421	37.3	.4788	5	racked
0.5421	37.3	.4788	5	vows
0.5420	37.3	.4786	5	abyss
0.5420	37.3	.3415	7	coniferous
0.5420	37.3	.3415	7	lignite
0.5418	37.3	.4315	6	incorporate
0.5417	37.3	.4196	6	equaling
0.5417	37.3	.4196	6	fabled
0.5417	37.3	.4196	6	Petroleum

U	SFI	D	F	Word Type
0.5415	37.3	.3308	7	winded
0.5412	37.3	.4209	6	chauffeur
0.5411	37.3	.2449	9	broadest
0.5411	37.3	.3204	7	Cow
0.5410	37.3	.2999	8	exploiting
0.5410	37.3	.1328	14	5/4
0.5409	37.3	.4115	6	creased
0.5409	37.3	.4776	5	Lighthouse
0.5409	37.3	.4118	6	self-supporting
0.5408	37.3	.2564	10	attractively
0.5404	37.3	.2490	8	1804
0.5403	37.3	.4244	6	incomprehensible
0.5403	37.3	.4050	6	jiffy
0.5403	37.3	.4218	6	sparingly
0.5403	37.3	.2871	8	wager
0.5402	37.3	.3364	7	B2
0.5400	37.3	.4016	6	Bohemian
0.5398	37.3	.3409	7	Ottawa
0.5393	37.3	.4083	6	distinctions
0.5392	37.3	.3922	6	scooter
0.5391	37.3	.3439	7	Mohammedans
0.5391	37.3	.3161	7	Winding
0.5389	37.3	.1990	10	Dred
0.5389	37.3	.2211	8	electrode
0.5389	37.3	.0000	36	endpoint
0.5389	37.3	.2203	10	2/8
0.5388	37.3	.4063	6	scholarly
0.5387	37.3	.3225	8	and/or
0.5387	37.3	.2619	9	Magician
0.5386	37.3	.3657	6	floppy
0.5386	37.3	.3657	6	gaucho
0.5386	37.3	.2444	7	Jenner
0.5386	37.3	.3657	6	Raymond
0.5386	37.3	.2138	10	Taiwan
0.5384	37.3	.0869	14	tendons
0.5384	37.3	.0869	14	yeasts
0.5383	37.3	.2445	7	Booker
0.5383	37.3	.2445	7	clogs
0.5383	37.3	.2616	9	Hawkeye
0.5383	37.3	.4751	5	Jennings
0.5383	37.3	.2445	7	Oldsmobile
0.5383	37.3	.4751	5	ONE

THE PRECEDING WORD TYPE OCCUPIES RANK 22400

0.5383	37.3	.4751	5	pillar
0.5383	37.3	.2445	7	Solomon's
0.5383	37.3	.2445	7	stringent
0.5383	37.3	.4751	5	wades
0.5382	37.3	.4005	6	apprehensive
0.5381	37.3	.4789	5	Cornelius
0.5381	37.3	.3311	7	metamorphic
0.5381	37.3	.3375	7	millimeter
0.5381	37.3	.3311	7	peroxide
0.5381	37.3	.4789	5	pounced
0.5381	37.3	.4789	5	quicksand
0.5381	37.3	.4789	5	schoolgirl
0.5381	37.3	.4789	5	trooping
0.5379	37.3	.2110	8	lacrosse
0.5377	37.3	.4753	5	Angelo
0.5377	37.3	.3545	6	Fighter
0.5377	37.3	.4753	5	offending
0.5377	37.3	.3545	6	paddies
0.5377	37.3	.2912	8	Pirates
0.5376	37.3	.2253	10	encourages
0.5375	37.3	.4740	5	applaud
0.5375	37.3	.4743	5	fifty-five
0.5375	37.3	.4740	5	footwear
0.5374	37.3	.2269	9	fielding
0.5374	37.3	.4039	6	longings
0.5373	37.3	.4222	6	extremity
0.5373	37.3	.3539	6	tubs
0.5372	37.3	.3486	7	$13
0.5372	37.3	.2710	9	di
0.5371	37.3	.3627	6	Associates
0.5371	37.3	.3627	6	disclose
0.5371	37.3	.4707	5	impaired
0.5371	37.3	.4707	5	pasteboard
0.5371	37.3	.3627	6	Prevention
0.5371	37.3	.3697	6	Telegraph
0.5370	37.3	.4201	6	ornamented
0.5370	37.3	.4192	6	Wonderland
0.5368	37.3	.3898	6	purchaser
0.5367	37.3	.3621	6	Clyde's
0.5367	37.3	.3621	6	discreet
0.5367	37.3	.3940	6	faucets
0.5367	37.3	.3621	6	plaque
0.5367	37.3	.4206	6	squeals
0.5366	37.3	.4215	6	earl
0.5365	37.3	.4732	5	adopting
0.5365	37.3	.4732	5	boldness
0.5364	37.3	.3640	6	dragoon
0.5364	37.3	.4730	5	honeybee
0.5364	37.3	.3617	6	panicky
0.5363	37.3	.4253	6	wrought-iron
0.5361	37.3	.3987	6	venturing
0.5360	37.3	.4770	5	disguises
0.5360	37.3	.4770	5	glinted
0.5360	37.3	.4770	5	hopelessness
0.5360	37.3	.4770	5	Olympian
0.5360	37.3	.4770	5	sedate
0.5360	37.3	.4770	5	stalled
0.5360	37.3	.4770	5	yearned
0.5359	37.3	.0685	22	Grey
0.5359	37.3	.3291	7	Henrys
0.5359	37.3	.0685	22	Passepartout
0.5359	37.3	.3932	6	Weekly
0.5357	37.3	.2097	8	bobsled
0.5357	37.3	.2273	7	Mulberry
0.5357	37.3	.2097	8	shan't
0.5357	37.3	.2273	7	waterline
0.5356	37.3	.3298	7	cropland
0.5356	37.3	.4733	5	jeered
0.5356	37.3	.4733	5	newsstand
0.5355	37.3	.4730	5	high-powered
0.5355	37.3	.4730	5	show-off
0.5355	37.3	.4730	5	toothache
0.5355	37.3	.4730	5	whirlpool
0.5354	37.3	.3882	6	flaws

U	SFI	D	F	Word Type
0.5354	37.3	.4766	5	wot
0.5353	37.3	.4763	5	dispensed
0.5353	37.3	.4763	5	hulk
0.5353	37.3	.3677	6	nuzzling
0.5353	37.3	.4763	5	sloshing
0.5352	37.3	.3599	6	fearlessly
0.5352	37.3	.3599	6	flicking
0.5350	37.3	.2465	9	Cornwall
0.5350	37.3	.4727	5	Sisters
0.5349	37.3	.3071	8	Bushman
0.5348	37.3	.3982	6	abused
0.5348	37.3	.3982	6	argues
0.5348	37.3	.4727	5	chatting
0.5348	37.3	.4724	5	footwork
0.5348	37.3	.4727	5	scamper
0.5348	37.3	.4727	5	wagonload
0.5348	37.3	.4724	5	waver
0.5348	37.3	.4727	5	1830's
0.5347	37.3	.4245	6	encircled
0.5346	37.3	.3199	7	coronation
0.5345	37.3	.4769	5	pedaled
0.5345	37.3	.4769	5	piteously
0.5345	37.3	.4769	5	shoemaker's
0.5345	37.3	.3441	7	Trees
0.5345	37.3	.4769	5	unsteady
0.5342	37.3	.3819	6	obscured

THE PRECEDING WORD TYPE OCCUPIES RANK 22500

0.5342	37.3	.4721	5	sandal
0.5342	37.3	.2256	7	stopwatch
0.5342	37.3	.4721	5	surer
0.5341	37.3	.4755	5	moor
0.5341	37.3	.4718	5	outwit
0.5341	37.3	.4718	5	panthers
0.5341	37.3	.4755	5	pelted
0.5341	37.3	.4755	5	thistle
0.5340	37.3	.4715	5	disk-shaped
0.5340	37.3	.4232	6	disregarded
0.5340	37.3	.4715	5	floes
0.5339	37.3	.3598	6	braver
0.5339	37.3	.4764	5	early-morning
0.5339	37.3	.3598	6	fretted
0.5339	37.3	.4764	5	greenery
0.5339	37.3	.3598	6	jeepers
0.5339	37.3	.3598	6	motioning
0.5339	37.3	.4764	5	scaling
0.5339	37.3	.3598	6	stifling
0.5339	37.3	.3598	6	throaty
0.5338	37.3	.3323	7	what'd
0.5336	37.3	.3492	7	161
0.5335	37.3	.4045	6	asunder
0.5335	37.3	.3593	6	Cokes
0.5335	37.3	.3503	7	giddy
0.5335	37.3	.4746	5	hand's
0.5335	37.3	.4762	5	Looking
0.5335	37.3	.3593	6	Was
0.5334	37.3	.4713	5	orator
0.5334	37.3	.3372	7	secretion
0.5334	37.3	.4713	5	shoals
0.5334	37.3	.3375	7	vested
0.5334	37.3	.2320	10	wi'
0.5334	37.3	.4713	5	1780
0.5332	37.3	.4710	5	antarctic
0.5332	37.3	.4761	5	flattering
0.5332	37.3	.4761	5	kennels
0.5331	37.3	.4746	5	eggshell
0.5331	37.3	.4746	5	haunt
0.5331	37.3	.1825	12	indent
0.5331	37.3	.1240	14	4/10
0.5330	37.3	.4758	5	Wright's
0.5328	37.3	.4219	6	constitutes
0.5328	37.3	.3114	7	Volume
0.5327	37.3	.4757	5	comprehended
0.5327	37.3	.4755	5	first-born
0.5327	37.3	.4755	5	fondness
0.5327	37.3	.4755	5	judgement
0.5327	37.3	.4755	5	scantily
0.5327	37.3	.4755	5	serviceable
0.5327	37.3	.4755	5	urchin
0.5327	37.3	.3325	7	Walden
0.5325	37.3	.2239	9	landforms
0.5323	37.3	.3259	7	tilts
0.5323	37.3	.3591	6	metallurgists
0.5323	37.3	.0000	27	stamens
0.5322	37.3	.4031	6	chaparral
0.5322	37.3	.1891	11	rounders
0.5321	37.3	.4134	6	Leningrad
0.5320	37.3	.2889	8	Erik
0.5320	37.3	.4226	6	Hair
0.5320	37.3	.3466	7	physiology
0.5320	37.3	.3960	6	rams
0.5318	37.3	.3511	7	ever-present
0.5318	37.3	.3636	6	scuttling
0.5317	37.3	.3234	7	cited
0.5316	37.3	.1593	12	Alpha
0.5316	37.3	.4695	5	bracing
0.5316	37.3	.4751	5	sneer
0.5315	37.3	.0615	23	Clearwater
0.5315	37.3	.4141	6	sagacity
0.5313	37.3	.4694	5	gallantry
0.5313	37.3	.3564	6	scat
0.5313	37.3	.4694	5	spits
0.5312	37.3	.3629	6	jolted
0.5312	37.3	.3629	6	pilot's
0.5310	37.3	.2862	8	goofy
0.5309	37.3	.3972	6	starred
0.5308	37.2	.3780	6	instincts
0.5307	37.2	.3403	7	anybody's
0.5307	37.2	.1869	11	mealtime
0.5306	37.2	.1104	13	Huckabuck
0.5305	37.2	.2857	8	1/25
0.5304	37.2	.2006	11	Wilse
0.5300	37.2	.1518	10	Boniface
0.5300	37.2	.1518	10	zori
0.5299	37.2	.3246	7	clippers
0.5299	37.2	.3530	6	Peabody
0.5299	37.2	.3530	6	twenty-sixth
0.5297	37.2	.2326	10	needlework

U	SFI	D	F	Word Type
0.5294	37.2	.3990	6	responding
0.5290	37.2	.2312	10	stylus
0.5290	37.2	.3294	7	420
0.5283	37.2	.3966	6	meow
0.5283	37.2	.2423	7	Pierson
0.5283	37.2	.2423	7	Pussy
0.5283	37.2	.2423	7	Simmons
0.5283	37.2	.2423	7	woodshed
0.5282	37.2	.3941	6	leprechaun
0.5281	37.2	.3709	6	sumac

THE PRECEDING WORD TYPE OCCUPIES RANK 22600

0.5280	37.2	.3229	7	cooperatives
0.5279	37.2	.3479	7	inflammatory
0.5279	37.2	.1696	12	underweight
0.5278	37.2	.2938	8	impetus
0.5277	37.2	.2856	7	wronged
0.5276	37.2	.3951	6	Maker
0.5273	37.2	.3318	7	pictorial
0.5270	37.2	.0824	22	Stravinsky
0.5270	37.2	.3481	7	Zebra
0.5269	37.2	.3538	7	attractiveness
0.5269	37.2	.4082	6	immeasurable
0.5269	37.2	.3544	6	runnin'
0.5268	37.2	.2285	9	bromine
0.5268	37.2	.2285	9	Hooke
0.5268	37.2	.3271	7	Rome's
0.5268	37.2	.2285	9	volcanism
0.5268	37.2	.5142	5	Well
0.5265	37.2	.3501	6	delightedly
0.5265	37.2	.3501	6	penknife
0.5265	37.2	.3501	6	snouts
0.5265	37.2	.3501	6	yippee
0.5259	37.2	.3531	6	cleverest
0.5259	37.2	.4091	6	despotism
0.5257	37.2	.2856	8	rhythmically
0.5256	37.2	.3423	7	general's
0.5254	37.2	.4662	5	backwoods
0.5254	37.2	.4665	5	commence
0.5254	37.2	.4662	5	deter
0.5254	37.2	.4687	5	lookin'
0.5254	37.2	.4662	5	newspaperman
0.5254	37.2	.4688	5	unkindly
0.5253	37.2	.4684	5	realist
0.5252	37.2	.4685	5	Anderson's
0.5252	37.2	.4685	5	topsy-turvy
0.5251	37.2	.4686	5	bowman
0.5251	37.2	.4683	5	throngs
0.5250	37.2	.3511	6	exam
0.5250	37.2	.3511	6	hikers
0.5250	37.2	.0191	44	Symphony
0.5250	37.2	.4003	6	6-2
0.5247	37.2	.4662	5	laconic
0.5245	37.2	.4661	5	cutlass
0.5245	37.2	.3548	6	frightfully
0.5245	37.2	.3548	6	hooting
0.5245	37.2	.4661	5	trinket
0.5242	37.2	.3509	6	impressively
0.5242	37.2	.2278	9	Livingstone
0.5242	37.2	.3059	7	lunchtime
0.5242	37.2	.3509	6	McGrath
0.5242	37.2	.3509	6	nightcap
0.5242	37.2	.2278	9	1619
0.5241	37.2	.3431	7	Enemy
0.5241	37.2	.3387	7	Lew
0.5239	37.2	.3414	7	subsidiary
0.5238	37.2	.1181	17	Concerto
0.5238	37.2	.2980	7	oxidized
0.5238	37.2	.3569	6	3500
0.5237	37.2	.3512	6	Historical
0.5236	37.2	.3906	6	Goblin
0.5234	37.2	.2826	8	pecks
0.5232	37.2	.2210	10	'im
0.5232	37.2	.3496	6	cottonwoods
0.5232	37.2	.3496	6	Hyman
0.5230	37.2	.2988	7	Athletics
0.5230	37.2	.4059	6	expended
0.5229	37.2	.4586	5	Frontier
0.5228	37.2	.4101	6	anemia
0.5226	37.2	.2433	9	729
0.5223	37.2	.3873	6	accommodations
0.5223	37.2	.3873	6	devastating
0.5223	37.2	.4597	5	Jones's
0.5223	37.2	.3448	7	Spanish-speaking
0.5222	37.2	.4592	5	sesame
0.5221	37.2	.4087	6	Ladies'
0.5219	37.2	.3876	6	330
0.5216	37.2	.3465	7	jockey
0.5215	37.2	.2438	9	barbershop
0.5213	37.2	.1563	14	harmonizing
0.5212	37.2	.2255	9	Index
0.5211	37.2	.3877	6	bib
0.5209	37.2	.4586	5	disgraceful
0.5208	37.2	.3476	6	adorn
0.5208	37.2	.3476	6	Coronado's
0.5208	37.2	.3506	6	gurgling
0.5208	37.2	.3476	6	teak
0.5207	37.2	.3047	7	Pegasus
0.5207	37.2	.4587	5	robbing
0.5207	37.2	.4587	5	tragedies
0.5205	37.2	.2467	8	windpipe
0.5205	37.2	.3967	6	151
0.5204	37.2	.3918	6	pleasurable
0.5204	37.2	.3946	6	ranking
0.5203	37.2	.3908	6	to-night
0.5201	37.2	.1769	11	garnet
0.5200	37.2	.3423	7	Sphinx
0.5199	37.2	.2782	8	Bristol
0.5199	37.2	.3396	6	flashy
0.5199	37.2	.3396	6	pontoons
0.5199	37.2	.3304	7	roughest
0.5198	37.2	.3852	6	alertness

THE PRECEDING WORD TYPE OCCUPIES RANK 22700

0.5197	37.2	.3444	6	Martha's
0.5197	37.2	.2088	7	sniffs
0.5194	37.2	.3489	6	woodchucks
0.5193	37.2	.2887	7	ma
0.5193	37.2	.2375	7	twain

U	SFI	D	F	Word Type
0.5192	37.2	.4007	6	dullness
0.5192	37.2	.5037	5	dungarees
0.5191	37.2	.0889	17	Putnam
0.5191	37.2	.4614	5	straying
0.5190	37.2	.3894	6	saber
0.5188	37.2	.1255	14	Rudy
0.5186	37.1	.3929	6	nine-tenths
0.5184	37.1	.0970	16	Addition
0.5182	37.1	.2428	9	Planck
0.5180	37.1	.3224	7	sapiens
0.5180	37.1	.2354	9	Switzerland's
0.5178	37.1	.2828	8	eminence
0.5178	37.1	.3427	6	huskily
0.5176	37.1	.3836	6	referee
0.5175	37.1	.4860	5	ascend
0.5175	37.1	.3704	6	bouts
0.5175	37.1	.4860	5	expectancy
0.5175	37.1	.4860	5	tolerate
0.5174	37.1	.3343	7	niggers
0.5173	37.1	.2362	7	Buck's
0.5173	37.1	.2362	7	Donald's
0.5173	37.1	.2362	7	Eb
0.5173	37.1	.4880	5	murderous
0.5173	37.1	.2362	7	ringmaster
0.5173	37.1	.0546	21	Woolworth
0.5172	37.1	.4886	5	Dane
0.5170	37.1	.4858	5	kneels
0.5169	37.1	.4860	5	rabbi
0.5167	37.1	.4882	5	chivalrous
0.5167	37.1	.4882	5	disapprove
0.5167	37.1	.3370	6	kind-hearted
0.5167	37.1	.4882	5	specializing
0.5166	37.1	.3493	6	dome-shaped
0.5166	37.1	.3493	6	Hahn
0.5166	37.1	.3826	6	woodbox
0.5165	37.1	.4856	5	intimately
0.5164	37.1	.3502	6	alphabets
0.5164	37.1	.4858	5	equilibrium
0.5164	37.1	.4858	5	sores
0.5164	37.1	.2032	10	unscrew
0.5163	37.1	.2204	9	Cepheid
0.5163	37.1	.2204	9	Concepts
0.5162	37.1	.3486	6	Bunsen
0.5162	37.1	.3364	6	fawns
0.5162	37.1	.3486	6	lifeguard
0.5162	37.1	.4850	5	payload
0.5160	37.1	.3819	6	maxim
0.5160	37.1	.4854	5	perplexing
0.5159	37.1	.4858	5	dysentery
0.5158	37.1	.4024	6	all-round
0.5158	37.1	.3869	6	fundamentally
0.5155	37.1	.3913	6	combating
0.5153	37.1	.2740	8	inconsistent
0.5152	37.1	.3485	6	Bakers
0.5152	37.1	.3405	6	carabao
0.5152	37.1	.3485	6	1786
0.5151	37.1	.2113	9	Braves
0.5150	37.1	.3400	7	ff
0.5149	37.1	.3969	6	latent
0.5147	37.1	.3477	6	fez
0.5146	37.1	.2909	7	Olsen
0.5146	37.1	.2909	7	Tampa
0.5144	37.1	.0581	20	shortcut
0.5142	37.1	.3791	6	capes
0.5139	37.1	.1673	12	Beagle
0.5139	37.1	.3375	7	dramatization
0.5138	37.1	.4871	5	distort
0.5138	37.1	.1904	10	Gull
0.5138	37.1	.3462	6	philosophies
0.5136	37.1	.4793	5	insecticides
0.5136	37.1	.1594	12	Tomahawk
0.5135	37.1	.1241	13	Bryan
0.5134	37.1	.3249	7	psychiatric
0.5133	37.1	.3324	7	Seminary
0.5132	37.1	.3454	6	communists
0.5132	37.1	.3454	6	pollute
0.5130	37.1	.2334	7	Barrow
0.5130	37.1	.3318	7	patrolled
0.5129	37.1	.4773	5	roomy
0.5129	37.1	.2495	8	whisking
0.5126	37.1	.0575	20	approximation
0.5126	37.1	.3943	6	Assyrians
0.5126	37.1	.4845	5	famines
0.5126	37.1	.1344	12	Finns
0.5126	37.1	.4790	5	roadsides
0.5125	37.1	.4022	6	Report
0.5125	37.1	.3245	7	violinist
0.5122	37.1	.2794	7	heavyweight
0.5122	37.1	.2664	8	season's
0.5122	37.1	.4871	5	1664
0.5121	37.1	.3236	7	crepe
0.5121	37.1	.4767	5	hit-or-miss
0.5121	37.1	.1869	12	participial
0.5121	37.1	.4783	5	truckloads
0.5121	37.1	.4767	5	1603

THE PRECEDING WORD TYPE OCCUPIES RANK 22800

U	SFI	D	F	Word Type
0.5119	37.1	.3626	6	Pilot
0.5117	37.1	.2326	7	Bascom
0.5117	37.1	.2326	7	five-dollar
0.5117	37.1	.2326	7	scamp
0.5117	37.1	.2326	7	seeped
0.5117	37.1	.2326	7	Skinny
0.5117	37.1	.2326	7	trumpeting
0.5117	37.1	.2326	7	Wide
0.5116	37.1	.3745	6	immoral
0.5115	37.1	.3123	7	deceased
0.5115	37.1	.3252	7	equivalents
0.5115	37.1	.3123	7	1805
0.5114	37.1	.3296	7	admirers
0.5114	37.1	.3296	7	Katherine
0.5114	37.1	.2028	10	plant's
0.5114	37.1	.3810	6	trussed
0.5113	37.1	.0000	63	digraph
0.5113	37.1	.4822	5	terramycin
0.5112	37.1	.2360	8	iguana
0.5111	37.1	.3738	6	Geographic
0.5110	37.1	.2087	10	Leon
0.5110	37.1	.4809	5	unfolds
0.5109	37.1	.3227	7	detecting
0.5109	37.1	.3116	7	haven
0.5109	37.1	.4821	5	mysticism
0.5109	37.1	.1777	10	partnerships
0.5109	37.1	.3116	7	1897
0.5107	37.1	.4808	5	Negro's
0.5107	37.1	.1915	11	Thoreau
0.5106	37.1	.3813	6	wormlike
0.5105	37.1	.1487	13	Meredith
0.5105	37.1	.3852	6	playpen
0.5104	37.1	.3730	6	anonymous
0.5104	37.1	.3702	6	lacy
0.5104	37.1	.0912	13	Navahos
0.5104	37.1	.3730	6	shrubbery
0.5103	37.1	.3729	6	taxpayers
0.5101	37.1	.3365	6	birches
0.5101	37.1	.3277	7	differing
0.5100	37.1	.2315	7	camphor
0.5100	37.1	.3399	6	Harvey's
0.5099	37.1	.4077	6	highlight
0.5099	37.1	.3347	7	seagoing
0.5099	37.1	.3193	7	six-thirty
0.5099	37.1	.2768	8	Va
0.5099	37.1	.3381	7	von
0.5099	37.1	.3347	7	Warwick
0.5098	37.1	.3723	6	circuses
0.5098	37.1	.3810	6	Dutchmen
0.5096	37.1	.3781	6	landslides
0.5095	37.1	.1114	16	MAN
0.5095	37.1	.3799	6	247
0.5092	37.1	.1543	11	biceps
0.5092	37.1	.4017	6	cuneiform
0.5092	37.1	.1543	11	quanta
0.5092	37.1	.3400	6	Seine
0.5091	37.1	.3793	6	frigate
0.5091	37.1	.2924	8	withal
0.5090	37.1	.0745	20	Agba's
0.5089	37.1	.0000	34	-5
0.5089	37.1	.3900	6	restful
0.5087	37.1	.1727	12	spatula
0.5086	37.1	.3452	6	Huntington
0.5085	37.1	.3454	6	sparkles
0.5085	37.1	.3454	6	tournaments
0.5083	37.1	.3267	7	Agricultural
0.5083	37.1	.3295	6	hoppers
0.5083	37.1	.3267	7	symptom
0.5082	37.1	.3514	6	rubbers
0.5082	37.1	.3355	7	1874
0.5081	37.1	.3704	6	diplomats
0.5081	37.1	.2439	9	Gabilan
0.5081	37.1	.3704	6	lamented
0.5081	37.1	.4875	5	perforated
0.5078	37.1	.3238	7	smith
0.5077	37.1	.3779	6	freshmen
0.5077	37.1	.3779	6	jointly
0.5075	37.1	.2786	8	incubation
0.5075	37.1	.3769	6	200-inch
0.5074	37.1	.3765	6	floundered
0.5074	37.1	.3765	6	nickering
0.5074	37.1	.3765	6	redness
0.5074	37.1	.3325	7	simulated
0.5074	37.1	.0664	22	SIR
0.5074	37.1	.4830	5	173
0.5073	37.1	.1841	10	lapped
0.5073	37.1	.3425	7	savory
0.5071	37.1	.3288	6	consecrated
0.5070	37.1	.3772	6	imprison
0.5066	37.1	.4854	5	grits
0.5066	37.0	.3281	6	snowplow
0.5064	37.0	.3704	6	cowhide
0.5062	37.0	.4826	5	coons
0.5062	37.0	.3693	6	1975
0.5058	37.0	.1755	10	Brahman
0.5058	37.0	.4817	5	trophies
0.5054	37.0	.2958	7	stint
0.5053	37.0	.4058	6	establishes
0.5052	37.0	.3983	6	Exchequer
0.5051	37.0	.3235	7	Divine

THE PRECEDING WORD TYPE OCCUPIES RANK 22900

U	SFI	D	F	Word Type
0.5050	37.0	.4828	5	abode
0.5050	37.0	.4784	5	cartridges
0.5050	37.0	.3688	6	Devil's
0.5050	37.0	.1920	11	dowels
0.5050	37.0	.3788	6	recipients
0.5049	37.0	.2321	9	333
0.5048	37.0	.1906	11	/b/
0.5048	37.0	.2650	8	forties
0.5048	37.0	.4700	5	Shetland
0.5047	37.0	.4827	5	creams
0.5046	37.0	.3543	6	spluttered
0.5045	37.0	.4510	5	migrates
0.5044	37.0	.0000	47	FATHER
0.5043	37.0	.3380	7	Assyrian
0.5043	37.0	.3263	6	Bluff
0.5043	37.0	.4460	5	carloads
0.5043	37.0	.4815	5	remodeling
0.5043	37.0	.3263	6	1782
0.5041	37.0	.3843	6	advisory
0.5040	37.0	.3948	6	adhered
0.5040	37.0	.2698	8	vaudeville
0.5038	37.0	.3256	6	experimenters
0.5038	37.0	.3256	6	paleontologist
0.5037	37.0	.4505	5	brown-skinned
0.5037	37.0	.4505	5	fascism
0.5037	37.0	.4501	5	round-trip
0.5036	37.0	.3780	6	fractured
0.5032	37.0	.3794	6	disturbs
0.5032	37.0	.2310	7	sandalwood
0.5030	37.0	.2478	8	detergents
0.5030	37.0	.3465	6	flagstaff
0.5030	37.0	.3250	7	swine
0.5029	37.0	.2337	8	Dardanelles
0.5029	37.0	.2337	8	problem-solving
0.5028	37.0	.4459	5	entertainer
0.5028	37.0	.4459	5	Find
0.5027	37.0	.4510	5	cannery
0.5026	37.0	.1894	11	OB
0.5026	37.0	.3829	6	suppers
0.5025	37.0	.0000	11	Alcock
0.5025	37.0	.0000	11	Arnulf
0.5025	37.0	.0000	11	Benn
0.5025	37.0	.0000	11	Beto
0.5025	37.0	.0000	11	Bounce
0.5025	37.0	.0000	11	Dingo
0.5025	37.0	.0000	11	Drat
0.5025	37.0	.0000	11	Florizel
0.5025	37.0	.0000	11	Flyaway
0.5025	37.0	.0000	11	Gabee
0.5025	37.0	.0000	11	gingham
0.5025	37.0	.0000	11	Graylegs
0.5025	37.0	.0000	11	Herdsman
0.5025	37.0	.0000	11	Manaluk
0.5025	37.0	.0000	11	Musky
0.5025	37.0	.0000	11	Odile
0.5025	37.0	.0000	11	Scho
0.5025	37.0	.0000	11	Sibley
0.5025	37.0	.0000	11	Silverspot
0.5025	37.0	.0000	11	Spank
0.5025	37.0	.0000	11	Spink
0.5025	37.0	.0000	11	ta-ump
0.5025	37.0	.0000	11	Tink
0.5025	37.0	.0000	11	Tobe
0.5025	37.0	.0000	11	Wasawa
0.5025	37.0	.0000	11	Whiskers
0.5025	37.0	.0000	11	Whitfield
0.5025	37.0	.0000	11	Wishing
0.5025	37.0	.0000	11	Woolly
0.5025	37.0	.0000	11	Zi
0.5024	37.0	.4509	5	fake
0.5024	37.0	.4932	5	grading
0.5024	37.0	.4509	5	recoil
0.5024	37.0	.4509	5	vaccinated
0.5024	37.0	.4509	5	164
0.5022	37.0	.4490	5	flowerpot
0.5022	37.0	.4490	5	mufflers
0.5021	37.0	.4506	5	mirage
0.5019	37.0	.3702	6	Bruce's
0.5019	37.0	.4506	5	coolest
0.5019	37.0	.3289	6	EARTH
0.5018	37.0	.3928	6	amassed
0.5018	37.0	.4505	5	Bridgeport
0.5018	37.0	.4505	5	cob
0.5017	37.0	.4503	5	crystallize
0.5017	37.0	.1757	12	ity
0.5017	37.0	.1757	12	possessives
0.5015	37.0	.3355	7	allusions
0.5015	37.0	.4503	5	earnestness
0.5015	37.0	.3923	6	perpetually
0.5015	37.0	.4503	5	tailless
0.5015	37.0	.4503	5	undaunted
0.5013	37.0	.1097	17	Mind
0.5012	37.0	.4504	5	pounce
0.5012	37.0	.3940	6	superbly
0.5012	37.0	.3028	7	1842
0.5011	37.0	.4485	5	comics
0.5011	37.0	.4485	5	fostered
0.5011	37.0	.4485	5	Johnston
0.5011	37.0	.4500	5	reborn
0.5011	37.0	.4485	5	streetcars

THE PRECEDING WORD TYPE OCCUPIES RANK 23000

U	SFI	D	F	Word Type
0.5011	37.0	.4500	5	tilled
0.5011	37.0	.4500	5	turnover
0.5010	37.0	.4481	5	wettest
0.5008	37.0	.1754	12	Plum
0.5008	37.0	.2800	8	Scandinavians
0.5007	37.0	.3689	6	scuffed
0.5006	37.0	.4500	5	depositing
0.5006	37.0	.3849	6	201
0.5005	37.0	.3548	6	blundering
0.5004	37.0	.4862	5	facilitate
0.5003	37.0	.3315	6	fainting
0.5003	37.0	.4499	5	1743
0.5002	37.0	.3695	6	benign
0.5002	37.0	.2110	9	Elm
0.5002	37.0	.4699	5	lawnmower
0.5001	37.0	.4498	5	pastured
0.5000	37.0	.3836	6	dampen
0.5000	37.0	.3591	6	malleable
0.4999	37.0	.4638	5	expenditure
0.4999	37.0	.4638	5	jasmine
0.4994	37.0	.1491	12	Dab-Dab
0.4994	37.0	.2697	7	ooh
0.4994	37.0	.3532	6	Shoes
0.4993	37.0	.2084	9	armistice
0.4993	37.0	.3674	6	insistent
0.4993	37.0	.2084	9	Wana
0.4992	37.0	.4428	5	orioles
0.4990	37.0	.3873	6	diminishing
0.4989	37.0	.2386	9	coeducational
0.4989	37.0	.4794	5	coveted
0.4988	37.0	.1025	18	/e-l/**
0.4988	37.0	.4698	5	longingly
0.4988	37.0	.4701	5	mire
0.4987	37.0	.4699	5	fortresses
0.4986	37.0	.4693	5	magistrates
0.4986	37.0	.3912	6	repertory
0.4985	37.0	.4688	5	blue-gray
0.4985	37.0	.4688	5	escarpment
0.4985	37.0	.3776	6	Motor
0.4985	37.0	.4696	5	orange-red
0.4985	37.0	.4682	5	Wendell
0.4984	37.0	.4689	5	capability
0.4984	37.0	.4689	5	sanctioned
0.4984	37.0	.4689	5	Sidon
0.4983	37.0	.3157	7	bat's
0.4983	37.0	.4419	5	sure-footed
0.4983	37.0	.3909	6	waltzes
0.4983	37.0	.4419	5	1522
0.4982	37.0	.3922	6	stiffening
0.4982	37.0	.4684	5	tumbler
0.4982	37.0	.4684	5	1833
0.4981	37.0	.2444	9	/l/
0.4981	37.0	.2444	9	homophone
0.4980	37.0	.2979	7	Folger
0.4980	37.0	.4768	5	notoriously
0.4978	37.0	.3369	6	Fresno
0.4978	37.0	.3365	6	passageways
0.4978	37.0	.3875	6	s'pose
0.4976	37.0	.3654	6	bubbly
0.4974	37.0	.0358	42	Figs
0.4973	37.0	.4755	5	four-wheel
0.4972	37.0	.0978	16	Nurse
0.4972	37.0	.4713	5	well-chosen
0.4971	37.0	.2669	8	modernization
0.4971	37.0	.2669	8	stenographers
0.4970	37.0	.3126	7	$80
0.4969	37.0	.4749	5	loathe
0.4968	37.0	.2588	8	sec
0.4968	37.0	.3769	6	Spacecraft
0.4966	37.0	.3764	6	hydrocarbons
0.4966	37.0	.3162	7	restrict
0.4966	37.0	.2105	9	Super
0.4965	37.0	.3122	7	receipts
0.4963	37.0	.2379	9	ornithology
0.4962	37.0	.4686	5	lawsuit
0.4962	37.0	.3750	6	864
0.4961	37.0	.3692	6	Burgoyne
0.4960	37.0	.3691	6	steppe
0.4960	37.0	.2328	9	30-60
0.4957	37.0	.2274	9	Puzzle
0.4955	37.0	.3644	6	dwarfed
0.4955	37.0	.3427	6	lather
0.4955	37.0	.3350	6	levied
0.4955	37.0	.3427	6	nope
0.4955	37.0	.3427	6	quitting
0.4955	37.0	.3427	6	shaver
0.4954	36.9	.1140	14	multiplicand
0.4954	36.9	.4753	5	op
0.4953	36.9	.3797	6	distortion
0.4953	36.9	.3408	6	inwardly
0.4953	36.9	.3408	6	Koophuis
0.4953	36.9	.3408	6	Wang's
0.4952	36.9	.3712	6	Cook's
0.4952	36.9	.3682	6	luxuries
0.4951	36.9	.4748	5	rapture
0.4951	36.9	.4664	5	unhatched
0.4949	36.9	.0789	19	fauna
0.4949	36.9	.3085	7	Premier
0.4949	36.9	.3085	7	sympathies
0.4946	36.9	.0679	17	Benvolio

THE PRECEDING WORD TYPE OCCUPIES RANK 23100

U	SFI	D	F	Word Type
0.4945	36.9	.4726	5	contemplated
0.4945	36.9	.2414	9	promenade
0.4943	36.9	.4446	5	Fairfax
0.4943	36.9	.3804	6	interchange
0.4943	36.9	.4723	5	sissy
0.4942	36.9	.4436	5	diggers
0.4941	36.9	.4720	5	amenities
0.4941	36.9	.4721	5	boredom
0.4941	36.9	.4720	5	elegantly
0.4941	36.9	.4720	5	nationalist
0.4940	36.9	.4705	5	enviable
0.4940	36.9	.3754	6	larval
0.4940	36.9	.4705	5	planner
0.4940	36.9	.0000	33	polygons
0.4940	36.9	.2364	9	seventh-grade
0.4940	36.9	.4705	5	wetness
0.4939	36.9	.4702	5	commentary
0.4939	36.9	.3697	6	Farmers
0.4939	36.9	.3703	6	Ganges
0.4939	36.9	.4702	5	Magazine
0.4939	36.9	.4702	5	migratory
0.4939	36.9	.3703	6	mobs
0.4939	36.9	.3241	6	twittering
0.4938	36.9	.4716	5	gossamer
0.4937	36.9	.4699	5	flattered
0.4937	36.9	.4699	5	So
0.4937	36.9	.4699	5	yearling
0.4936	36.9	.2407	9	brillig
0.4936	36.9	.3756	6	fugitives
0.4936	36.9	.4713	5	villa
0.4935	36.9	.4536	5	ventilated
0.4934	36.9	.3599	6	archers
0.4934	36.9	.3751	6	cottontail
0.4933	36.9	.4543	5	all's
0.4933	36.9	.4693	5	Numbers
0.4932	36.9	.4691	5	leeway
0.4931	36.9	.1641	11	champagne
0.4931	36.9	.3688	6	growths
0.4931	36.9	.1641	11	lease
0.4931	36.9	.3688	6	pelvis
0.4931	36.9	.4688	5	Principal
0.4931	36.9	.4688	5	twenty-first
0.4930	36.9	.3179	7	Sleep
0.4930	36.9	.3179	7	stepfather
0.4929	36.9	.0000	25	condensation
0.4929	36.9	.3593	6	experimenter
0.4929	36.9	.0000	25	polonium
0.4927	36.9	.2487	8	Wills
0.4924	36.9	.0000	45	determiner
0.4924	36.9	.0000	42	Homily
0.4924	36.9	.3247	7	resemblances
0.4923	36.9	.4738	5	astray
0.4921	36.9	.3648	6	assert
0.4921	36.9	.3785	6	overcoats
0.4918	36.9	.4685	5	complacent
0.4916	36.9	.1526	14	graphic
0.4916	36.9	.3570	6	jumbled
0.4915	36.9	.2867	7	labor-saving
0.4914	36.9	.3527	6	Pikes
0.4913	36.9	.3399	6	downcast
0.4913	36.9	.2186	8	Why
0.4912	36.9	.1415	10	airman
0.4912	36.9	.3243	7	predictable
0.4912	36.9	.3662	6	sentry
0.4911	36.9	.2946	7	Sunrise
0.4910	36.9	.3623	6	gastric
0.4910	36.9	.3623	6	micro-organisms
0.4910	36.9	.3635	6	trucked
0.4907	36.9	.2176	7	Clown

U	SFI	D	F	Word Type
0.4907	36.9	.2668	7	croquet
0.4907	36.9	.3112	6	sharpness
0.4906	36.9	.4712	5	hollering
0.4906	36.9	.4495	5	participating
0.4906	36.9	.3204	6	rink
0.4905	36.9	.2926	7	stag
0.4905	36.9	.2926	7	two-legged
0.4905	36.9	.2321	9	Unknown
0.4904	36.9	.1256	13	curry
0.4904	36.9	.4662	5	patriarch
0.4902	36.9	.3708	6	bread-and-butter
0.4902	36.9	.3394	6	hmmmm
0.4902	36.9	.3394	6	inquiringly
0.4902	36.9	.2439	8	rickets
0.4902	36.9	.3394	6	runt
0.4901	36.9	.4656	5	Badge
0.4900	36.9	.3390	6	passionately
0.4899	36.9	.1647	11	Stegosaurus
0.4899	36.9	.2063	10	suites
0.4896	36.9	.4631	5	Restaurant
0.4895	36.9	.3728	6	$11
0.4895	36.9	.1073	18	beater
0.4894	36.9	.2379	9	-en
0.4893	36.9	.2740	7	antibiotic
0.4893	36.9	.3156	7	coalition
0.4892	36.9	.3077	7	commune
0.4892	36.9	.3814	6	executioner
0.4892	36.9	.3811	6	thirties
0.4892	36.9	.2058	9	Tubman
0.4891	36.9	.3826	6	acoustics
0.4891	36.9	.2047	10	commandments
THE PRECEDING WORD TYPE OCCUPIES RANK 23200				
0.4891	36.9	.4699	5	peculiarities
0.4890	36.9	.2894	7	eight-year-old
0.4890	36.9	.3856	6	simultaneous
0.4889	36.9	.0429	17	anthrax
0.4888	36.9	.4686	5	doze
0.4888	36.9	.2844	7	insights
0.4888	36.9	.2304	8	pranced
0.4888	36.9	.2930	7	quoth
0.4888	36.9	.2844	7	soft-bodied
0.4888	36.9	.4669	5	unavoidable
0.4886	36.9	.2558	8	About
0.4886	36.9	.3473	6	Anders
0.4886	36.9	.3546	6	dimness
0.4885	36.9	.4322	5	Abe's
0.4885	36.9	.2031	9	Joanne
0.4884	36.9	.4689	5	piety
0.4883	36.9	.4403	5	bedspread
0.4883	36.9	.4418	5	coupon
0.4883	36.9	.4418	5	jackrabbit
0.4883	36.9	.4672	5	underlies
0.4882	36.9	.3591	6	decomposition
0.4882	36.9	.4613	5	expired
0.4882	36.9	.3194	7	typewritten
0.4882	36.9	.4613	5	View
0.4881	36.9	.4407	5	fifties
0.4881	36.9	.4407	5	two-pound
0.4880	36.9	.3795	6	cantaloupes
0.4880	36.9	.4626	5	pending
0.4880	36.9	.4625	5	smuggling
0.4880	36.9	.4625	5	stemmed
0.4880	36.9	.2426	8	Tropical
0.4879	36.9	.3710	6	B's
0.4879	36.9	.1427	11	Diving
0.4878	36.9	.3537	6	army's
0.4878	36.9	.4606	5	inaccurate
0.4878	36.9	.3380	6	visage
0.4877	36.9	.4660	5	larder
0.4877	36.9	.4660	5	legion
0.4876	36.9	.0964	17	infinitive
0.4876	36.9	.2762	7	ketch
0.4875	36.9	.4599	5	astonishingly
0.4875	36.9	.4599	5	Barge
0.4875	36.9	.4599	5	disrupted
0.4875	36.9	.4599	5	razor-sharp
0.4875	36.9	.4599	5	rejects
0.4874	36.9	.3234	7	absorbent
0.4874	36.9	.3583	6	addict
0.4873	36.9	.4594	5	undeniable
0.4872	36.9	.4373	5	Carters
0.4872	36.9	.3716	6	Faculty
0.4872	36.9	.4595	5	horrifying
0.4872	36.9	.4663	5	obstructions
0.4872	36.9	.3781	6	resonance
0.4871	36.9	.4592	5	apologies
0.4871	36.9	.1214	12	Manchus
0.4870	36.9	.3577	6	Fabre
0.4870	36.9	.3577	6	H-bomb
0.4869	36.9	.2535	8	mails
0.4869	36.9	.2535	8	Resources
0.4868	36.9	.3852	5	oxcart
0.4868	36.9	.3078	7	sect
0.4867	36.9	.3810	6	gratifying
0.4867	36.9	.3143	6	heart-shaped
0.4867	36.9	.2727	7	Kansas-Nebraska
0.4866	36.9	.3153	6	hoofbeats
0.4866	36.9	.4655	5	instantaneously
0.4866	36.9	.2446	8	sonic
0.4865	36.9	.4652	5	murmurs
0.4864	36.9	.2735	7	boyfriend
0.4864	36.9	.4402	5	dimpled
0.4864	36.9	.4402	5	emancipation
0.4864	36.9	.3613	6	exerts
0.4864	36.9	.3613	6	fossilized
0.4864	36.9	.4405	5	horsemanship
0.4864	36.9	.3613	6	internally
0.4864	36.9	.3613	6	1899
0.4863	36.9	.4395	5	big-eared
0.4863	36.9	.4395	5	idyllic
0.4862	36.9	.4396	5	outcry
0.4861	36.9	.4391	5	Calvin
0.4861	36.9	.4385	5	dispersed
0.4861	36.9	.4385	5	goggling
0.4861	36.9	.4385	5	outdo
0.4861	36.9	.4385	5	spangled
0.4860	36.9	.4391	5	Bavarian
0.4860	36.9	.4391	5	Creeks
0.4860	36.9	.2748	7	priming
0.4860	36.9	.4391	5	unspoiled
0.4859	36.9	.2286	9	Tyrannosaurus
0.4858	36.9	.3612	6	expressly
0.4858	36.9	.3612	6	secede
0.4857	36.9	.4622	5	condemn
0.4857	36.9	.3282	6	nines
0.4856	36.9	.4639	5	intimacy
0.4855	36.9	.4627	5	courageously
0.4854	36.9	.4636	5	didst
0.4853	36.9	.2715	8	gloss
0.4853	36.9	.4419	5	minutes'
0.4853	36.9	.3784	6	receptions
0.4852	36.9	.3567	6	far-flung
THE PRECEDING WORD TYPE OCCUPIES RANK 23300				
0.4852	36.9	.4614	5	headmaster
0.4852	36.9	.3567	6	Michigan's
0.4852	36.9	.3567	6	minorities
0.4852	36.9	.4642	5	mountaineers
0.4852	36.9	.4642	5	sacked
0.4852	36.9	.1915	9	Throne
0.4852	36.9	.3615	6	writhed
0.4849	36.9	.4638	5	attaining
0.4849	36.9	.3456	6	tenements
0.4847	36.9	.4552	5	ironclad
0.4847	36.9	.2736	7	Laura's
0.4847	36.9	.3681	6	Pisa
0.4847	36.9	.4552	5	tourism
0.4847	36.9	.4552	5	tribesman
0.4846	36.9	.3708	6	bearer
0.4846	36.9	.4418	5	Budget
0.4845	36.9	.4613	5	proffered
0.4844	36.9	.2292	9	Achmet
0.4844	36.9	.4547	5	births
0.4844	36.9	.2128	10	Burdick
0.4844	36.9	.2934	7	Gang
0.4844	36.9	.3559	6	petitions
0.4844	36.9	.2292	9	Tiflin
0.4843	36.9	.4543	5	impregnated
0.4843	36.9	.4543	5	trivial
0.4842	36.9	.4597	5	Under
0.4841	36.8	.4616	5	confront
0.4841	36.8	.4605	5	dominions
0.4841	36.8	.4539	5	recruit
0.4840	36.8	.4604	5	graces
0.4840	36.8	.1889	7	Marygold
0.4839	36.8	.4392	5	kingfisher
0.4839	36.8	.2159	9	Rebellion
0.4838	36.8	.4538	5	symbolism
0.4838	36.8	.3007	7	264
0.4838	36.8	.4538	5	428
0.4836	36.8	.4680	5	ineffective
0.4835	36.8	.1952	10	Tin
0.4834	36.8	.3850	5	devious
0.4834	36.8	.3850	5	harrow
0.4834	36.8	.3850	5	Mann
0.4834	36.8	.3850	5	periscope
0.4834	36.8	.3850	5	stagecoaches
0.4834	36.8	.3850	5	teacup
0.4834	36.8	.3850	5	walruses
0.4833	36.8	.3117	6	bleachers
0.4833	36.8	.3585	6	inferiority
0.4833	36.8	.3498	6	meticulous
0.4833	36.8	.3498	6	prehistory
0.4831	36.8	.4612	5	characterizes
0.4831	36.8	.4612	5	radically
0.4829	36.8	.3690	6	barbarous
0.4829	36.8	.3690	6	dewy
0.4829	36.8	.2927	7	diploma
0.4828	36.8	.3838	6	ice-skating
0.4827	36.8	.3530	6	ferment
0.4827	36.8	.4583	5	politeness
0.4825	36.8	.3665	6	celebrates
0.4824	36.8	.1964	10	idioms
0.4824	36.8	.4630	5	207
0.4823	36.8	.4657	5	enlist
0.4823	36.8	.3665	6	sauerkraut
0.4821	36.8	.4587	5	bile
0.4821	36.8	.4587	5	subscribed
0.4819	36.8	.2443	8	Kaskaskia
0.4818	36.8	.4524	5	first-rate
0.4818	36.8	.4561	5	generalized
0.4818	36.8	.2440	8	gill
0.4818	36.8	.2440	8	inflammation
0.4818	36.8	.4369	5	silkworm
0.4818	36.8	.4582	5	unfavorable
0.4818	36.8	.4288	5	1590
0.4817	36.8	.3252	6	astride
0.4817	36.8	.2517	7	heartless
0.4817	36.8	.3626	6	Indonesian
0.4816	36.8	.3526	6	butchered
0.4816	36.8	.4578	5	tier
0.4814	36.8	.0597	22	ARTHUR
0.4814	36.8	.2424	9	discard
0.4811	36.8	.2890	6	awl
0.4810	36.8	.4356	5	leftovers
0.4809	36.8	.4505	5	railings
0.4807	36.8	.4564	5	encompassing
0.4807	36.8	.3616	6	riverboats
0.4805	36.8	.3731	6	comp'ny
0.4804	36.8	.4270	5	bloodthirsty
0.4804	36.8	.3503	6	Lassen
0.4804	36.8	.2658	7	lightship
0.4804	36.8	.4270	5	recruiting
0.4803	36.8	.4272	5	couches
0.4803	36.8	.4272	5	resourceful
0.4800	36.8	.4273	5	meek
0.4798	36.8	.3861	5	bystanders
0.4798	36.8	.3861	5	crewman
0.4798	36.8	.3861	5	eighty-six
0.4797	36.8	.2664	8	Am
0.4797	36.8	.3509	6	Hidalgo
0.4797	36.8	.4268	5	whir
0.4796	36.8	.2583	8	cavalier
0.4794	36.8	.2284	8	discoverer
THE PRECEDING WORD TYPE OCCUPIES RANK 23400				
0.4793	36.8	.4267	5	abundantly
0.4793	36.8	.4267	5	tubers
0.4792	36.8	.3521	6	Athletic
0.4792	36.8	.2053	9	duckbill
0.4792	36.8	.3521	6	floorboards
0.4792	36.8	.3521	6	unruffled
0.4791	36.8	.3814	5	Activities
0.4791	36.8	.3814	5	Cornish
0.4791	36.8	.3814	5	hesitant
0.4791	36.8	.3851	5	Nelson's
0.4791	36.8	.3814	5	picker
0.4790	36.8	.3854	5	Amherst
0.4790	36.8	.3854	5	drowsily
0.4790	36.8	.3854	5	ef
0.4790	36.8	.2486	8	Feast
0.4790	36.8	.3854	5	jeering
0.4790	36.8	.3854	5	lashings
0.4790	36.8	.3854	5	lugged
0.4790	36.8	.3854	5	Meeting
0.4790	36.8	.2585	8	reclamation
0.4790	36.8	.3854	5	roundabout
0.4790	36.8	.4526	5	unbuttoned
0.4790	36.8	.0000	32	2-digit
0.4789	36.8	.3810	5	Chinook
0.4789	36.8	.1564	11	ev'ry
0.4789	36.8	.3810	5	mastodon
0.4789	36.8	.3810	5	wane
0.4788	36.8	.4455	5	conservationists
0.4788	36.8	.4455	5	mastodons
0.4788	36.8	.2322	9	Meat
0.4787	36.8	.4424	5	assists
0.4787	36.8	.0425	23	st
0.4786	36.8	.2361	7	lunchroom
0.4786	36.8	.3492	6	popes
0.4786	36.8	.3492	6	supervises
0.4785	36.8	.4611	5	knuckle
0.4784	36.8	.4444	5	windbreak
0.4783	36.8	.4538	5	1450
0.4782	36.8	.4515	5	lenient
0.4781	36.8	.2454	8	innovation
0.4781	36.8	.0666	14	Sabbath
0.4780	36.8	.4533	5	gondola
0.4780	36.8	.3641	6	mythological
0.4779	36.8	.3803	5	Lizzie
0.4778	36.8	.0429	21	Phantom
0.4777	36.8	.2919	7	Area
0.4777	36.8	.3855	5	bucked
0.4777	36.8	.3855	5	cuddled
0.4777	36.8	.2644	7	Delhi
0.4777	36.8	.3855	5	Durango
0.4777	36.8	.3855	5	lolling
0.4777	36.8	.3855	5	risking
0.4777	36.8	.4507	5	understandably
0.4776	36.8	.0623	18	intersects
0.4774	36.8	.3267	6	Embassy
0.4773	36.8	.3050	7	inanimate
0.4773	36.8	.4499	5	overtaking
0.4772	36.8	.3838	5	kidnaped
0.4772	36.8	.3838	5	mountaineer
0.4771	36.8	.4593	5	satirical
0.4771	36.8	.1650	12	trimmings
0.4770	36.8	.3463	6	clot
0.4770	36.8	.0758	28	textures
0.4769	36.8	.1626	10	bacterial
0.4769	36.8	.1626	10	caries
0.4769	36.8	.1626	10	chloroplasts
0.4769	36.8	.1626	10	distillation
0.4769	36.8	.1626	10	high-power
0.4769	36.8	.1626	10	hormones
0.4769	36.8	.1626	10	medulla
0.4767	36.8	.3833	5	ambrosia
0.4767	36.8	.3833	5	Babe's
0.4767	36.8	.3833	5	beached
0.4767	36.8	.3833	5	common-sense
0.4767	36.8	.3833	5	courier
0.4767	36.8	.3833	5	disrespect
0.4767	36.8	.3833	5	fattest
0.4767	36.8	.3833	5	fetching
0.4767	36.8	.3833	5	jogging
0.4767	36.8	.3833	5	prince's
0.4767	36.8	.3833	5	sizzled
0.4767	36.8	.3833	5	sniffled
0.4767	36.8	.3833	5	spotless
0.4766	36.8	.2123	9	accompanies
0.4766	36.8	.4511	5	Catskills
0.4765	36.8	.2353	8	albumin
0.4765	36.8	.2353	8	diastrophism
0.4765	36.8	.2353	8	Eocene
0.4765	36.8	.2353	8	immunity
0.4764	36.8	.3846	5	boyish
0.4764	36.8	.3846	5	Hear
0.4763	36.8	.4498	5	coupons
0.4763	36.8	.2019	10	frankfurters
0.4762	36.8	.4507	5	intriguing
0.4762	36.8	.4507	5	spatial
0.4760	36.8	.3844	5	blood-red
0.4760	36.8	.1835	10	Gypsies
0.4760	36.8	.4470	5	identifiable
0.4760	36.8	.3844	5	Louie
0.4760	36.8	.4492	5	martial
THE PRECEDING WORD TYPE OCCUPIES RANK 23500				
0.4760	36.8	.3842	5	Nana's
0.4760	36.8	.3416	6	pinwheels
0.4760	36.8	.3842	5	prodded
0.4760	36.8	.3844	5	smithy
0.4760	36.8	.3842	5	taping
0.4760	36.8	.3842	5	troubling
0.4760	36.8	.3842	5	Twin
0.4760	36.8	.3842	5	vessel's
0.4760	36.8	.3844	5	well-dressed
0.4759	36.8	.3826	5	Frozen
0.4759	36.8	.3826	5	lionesses
0.4758	36.8	.1816	11	crotch
0.4758	36.8	.1557	9	giant's
0.4757	36.8	.3449	6	sterilized
0.4756	36.8	.3841	5	bustled
0.4756	36.8	.3841	5	dishwashing
0.4756	36.8	.3841	5	lashes
0.4756	36.8	.3841	5	musing
0.4756	36.8	.3841	5	pigpen
0.4756	36.8	.3841	5	tellin'
0.4755	36.8	.4311	5	alleged
0.4755	36.8	.3779	5	Beirut
0.4755	36.8	.4587	5	handbook
0.4755	36.8	.3779	5	Oaks
0.4755	36.8	.4328	5	Tenth
0.4754	36.8	.4483	5	battlements
0.4754	36.8	.1794	8	chalcopyrite
0.4754	36.8	.2173	9	hippies
0.4754	36.8	.3837	5	Meany
0.4754	36.8	.4483	5	sprawl
0.4753	36.8	.4308	5	Adventures
0.4753	36.8	.3775	5	Antony
0.4753	36.8	.3775	5	chemist's
0.4753	36.8	.3775	5	hamster
0.4753	36.8	.3156	6	Harry's
0.4753	36.8	.2246	9	jesters
0.4752	36.8	.4305	5	exterminate
0.4752	36.8	.4305	5	insolent
0.4752	36.8	.4305	5	stuffy
0.4752	36.8	.3192	7	Swing
0.4751	36.8	.3836	5	deer's
0.4751	36.8	.3836	5	overshoes
0.4751	36.8	.3836	5	Papuan
0.4751	36.8	.3836	5	reappear
0.4751	36.8	.4478	5	system's
0.4751	36.8	.3133	7	Tsar
0.4751	36.8	.3662	6	549
0.4750	36.8	.4319	5	glamour
0.4750	36.8	.3582	6	Marietta
0.4749	36.8	.1820	10	oilmen
0.4747	36.8	.3771	5	convoy
0.4747	36.8	.4296	5	effecting
0.4747	36.8	.3771	5	huff
0.4747	36.8	.4296	5	prowled
0.4747	36.8	.3836	5	zipped
0.4746	36.8	.3767	5	limply
0.4746	36.8	.4459	5	pompous
0.4746	36.8	.1814	8	Sherrill
0.4745	36.8	.2348	8	Alliance
0.4745	36.8	.4293	5	decked
0.4745	36.8	.2163	8	hubs
0.4745	36.8	.2348	8	Perth
0.4745	36.8	.4293	5	repast
0.4745	36.8	.4443	5	san
0.4745	36.8	.4293	5	shyness
0.4744	36.8	.4290	5	cashier's
0.4743	36.8	.1260	13	baptized
0.4743	36.8	.4465	5	inroads
0.4743	36.8	.3832	5	moored
0.4743	36.8	.4465	5	waned
0.4743	36.8	.3832	5	1730
0.4741	36.8	.3688	6	alack
0.4741	36.8	.3416	6	beet
0.4741	36.8	.2345	8	thinned
0.4740	36.8	.2352	9	broil
0.4740	36.8	.3693	6	constricted
0.4740	36.8	.3830	5	grate
0.4740	36.8	.4304	5	sleepless
0.4740	36.8	.4460	5	trumpeter
0.4739	36.8	.3639	6	mildly
0.4739	36.8	.3646	6	Patsy's
0.4738	36.8	.3437	6	Buddhists
0.4737	36.8	.3761	5	braying
0.4737	36.8	.3761	5	hand-to-hand
0.4737	36.8	.4535	5	silo
0.4737	36.8	.3606	6	Stein
0.4736	36.8	.3008	7	axles
0.4735	36.8	.1641	12	baritone
0.4735	36.8	.3757	5	pastries
0.4734	36.8	.0629	16	Brontosaurus
0.4734	36.8	.4311	5	jubilation
0.4733	36.8	.1125	16	diddle
0.4733	36.8	.4347	5	flatcars
0.4733	36.8	.3643	6	Lansing
0.4732	36.8	.0000	24	neuron
0.4732	36.8	.1507	12	Reformation
0.4732	36.7	.1030	16	Spirit
0.4732	36.8	.3105	7	tints
0.4731	36.7	.3773	6	alters
0.4731	36.7	.1197	13	approximations
THE PRECEDING WORD TYPE OCCUPIES RANK 23600				
0.4730	36.7	.3001	7	converge
0.4730	36.7	.3001	7	disorders
0.4730	36.7	.4431	5	grime
0.4730	36.7	.2147	7	gunner
0.4730	36.7	.1615	10	Hellenistic
0.4730	36.7	.4289	5	inveterate
0.4730	36.7	.3560	6	Jennie
0.4730	36.7	.3755	6	prolong
0.4730	36.7	.2820	6	splintering
0.4729	36.7	.0118	77	stitching
0.4729	36.7	.4302	5	tarpaulin
0.4728	36.7	.4538	5	fathom
0.4728	36.7	.2607	7	scrawny
0.4728	36.7	.3271	6	139
0.4727	36.7	.3560	6	composes
0.4727	36.7	.4454	5	culminating
0.4727	36.7	.3596	6	goodies
0.4726	36.7	.3571	6	asserts
0.4726	36.7	.4281	5	grandma
0.4726	36.7	.2664	7	gushed
0.4726	36.7	.4281	5	halting
0.4726	36.7	.4281	5	meanness
0.4726	36.7	.1541	9	Pinals
0.4726	36.7	.4281	5	portal
0.4726	36.7	.4281	5	slouch
0.4721	36.7	.4416	5	surveyors
0.4720	36.7	.4443	5	one-foot
0.4719	36.7	.3587	6	Stay
0.4717	36.7	.3633	6	Bonds
0.4717	36.7	.3638	6	fulfillment
0.4717	36.7	.4426	5	Sicilian
0.4716	36.7	.4243	5	conspirators

U	SFI	D	F	Word Type
0.4716	36.7	.4264	5	resounding
0.4716	36.7	.4243	5	Scilly
0.4716	36.7	.3053	7	softwood
0.4715	36.7	.4241	5	soft-spoken
0.4714	36.7	.4238	5	quick-tempered
0.4713	36.7	.3654	6	dentistry
0.4712	36.7	.1982	10	Alexandra
0.4712	36.7	.2279	9	embossing
0.4712	36.7	.4534	5	vanguard
0.4710	36.7	.4228	5	concede
0.4710	36.7	.4233	5	eight-foot
0.4710	36.7	.4228	5	protruding
0.4710	36.7	.4228	5	ration
0.4709	36.7	.4412	5	multitudes
0.4708	36.7	.1114	16	o's
0.4707	36.7	.4409	5	attrition
0.4707	36.7	.4409	5	prospering
0.4707	36.7	.4409	5	supervisors
0.4705	36.7	.2816	7	amiable
0.4704	36.7	.3627	6	Caldwell
0.4703	36.7	.3583	6	cormorants
0.4703	36.7	.3583	6	thong
0.4702	36.7	.3477	6	lull
0.4700	36.7	.1908	9	Brazil's
0.4697	36.7	.4394	5	magnitudes
0.4696	36.7	.4496	5	adolescent
0.4696	36.7	.3586	6	firecracker
0.4696	36.7	.2924	7	Indus
0.4696	36.7	.0786	20	oratorio
0.4696	36.7	.2924	7	ratified
0.4696	36.7	.4523	5	weddings
0.4695	36.7	.4376	5	excepting
0.4695	36.7	.1787	8	Maypole
0.4694	36.7	.3105	6	Turner's
0.4693	36.7	.4274	5	hoax
0.4692	36.7	.3608	6	Brandenburg
0.4692	36.7	.0846	18	octaves
0.4692	36.7	.3608	6	strikingly
0.4691	36.7	.3504	6	Darkness
0.4688	36.7	.2528	8	approvingly
0.4688	36.7	.2863	7	calculus
0.4688	36.7	.3499	6	uncontrolled
0.4688	36.7	.2922	7	youth's
0.4687	36.7	.4216	5	broken-hearted
0.4687	36.7	.4216	5	hoary
0.4687	36.7	.0756	15	Petit
0.4686	36.7	.4213	5	cravat
0.4686	36.7	.4213	5	flecks
0.4686	36.7	.2768	6	photographing
0.4686	36.7	.4213	5	tethered
0.4686	36.7	.4213	5	wart
0.4685	36.7	.4482	5	superlatives
0.4683	36.7	.3390	6	174
0.4681	36.7	.3555	6	Muriel
0.4681	36.7	.2438	6	pecked
0.4681	36.7	.2438	6	Seeing
0.4680	36.7	.2435	6	Ackley
0.4680	36.7	.2435	6	aha
0.4680	36.7	.2435	6	Conover
0.4680	36.7	.2435	6	droning
0.4680	36.7	.2435	6	ferny
0.4680	36.7	.2435	6	Hades
0.4680	36.7	.2435	6	meatballs
0.4680	36.7	.2435	6	Mint
0.4680	36.7	.2435	6	oaken
0.4679	36.7	.2388	8	Acadians
0.4679	36.7	.4242	5	apprentices
0.4679	36.7	.2432	6	Brer
THE PRECEDING WORD TYPE OCCUPIES RANK 23700				
0.4679	36.7	.2432	6	fleecy
0.4679	36.7	.4354	5	Hero
0.4679	36.7	.2432	6	Hoffman
0.4679	36.7	.2432	6	McIlhenny
0.4679	36.7	.2432	6	Talbot
0.4679	36.7	.1089	14	Tomas
0.4677	36.7	.1103	14	honorary
0.4676	36.7	.1973	10	fullness
0.4674	36.7	.4252	5	droned
0.4674	36.7	.4252	5	Frog
0.4674	36.7	.2281	8	Thant
0.4673	36.7	.2419	6	armour
0.4673	36.7	.2419	6	Dillingham
0.4673	36.7	.2419	6	orphanage
0.4673	36.7	.2419	6	poi
0.4671	36.7	.3765	5	Hen
0.4671	36.7	.3765	5	love's
0.4671	36.7	.3765	5	tattoo
0.4670	36.7	.4352	5	apex
0.4670	36.7	.3753	5	blare
0.4670	36.7	.3766	5	larks
0.4670	36.7	.3766	5	schoolhouses
0.4670	36.7	.3766	5	Without
0.4669	36.7	.2747	6	sickening
0.4668	36.7	.2411	6	afternoon's
0.4668	36.7	.2411	6	dishwasher
0.4668	36.7	.0000	24	Farmington
0.4668	36.7	.4236	5	Literature
0.4668	36.7	.2411	6	Lotion
0.4668	36.7	.2411	6	NOT
0.4668	36.7	.2411	6	plopped
0.4668	36.7	.0000	24	saldu
0.4668	36.7	.2411	6	Thelma
0.4668	36.7	.0000	24	Timer
0.4668	36.7	.2411	6	unbelieving
0.4667	36.7	.4346	5	430
0.4667	36.7	.2845	7	457
0.4665	36.7	.2440	6	councilor
0.4665	36.7	.2440	6	lei
0.4665	36.7	.2440	6	Nannerl
0.4665	36.7	.4218	5	settin'
0.4665	36.7	.2440	6	stampeded
0.4665	36.7	.2440	6	windless
0.4664	36.7	.2537	7	Annapolis
0.4664	36.7	.2926	7	1795
0.4663	36.7	.4133	5	undernourished
0.4662	36.7	.1857	10	grooved
0.4662	36.7	.4234	5	harry
0.4661	36.7	.4223	5	clutter
0.4661	36.7	.4223	5	sledges
0.4660	36.7	.3343	6	naturalized
0.4660	36.7	.4291	5	postcard
0.4659	36.7	.4350	5	trackless
0.4658	36.7	.3720	5	coasted
0.4658	36.7	.3345	6	grower
0.4658	36.7	.3171	6	Highness
0.4657	36.7	.1882	10	Bede
0.4657	36.7	.1323	14	blouses
0.4656	36.7	.4143	5	commuter
0.4656	36.7	.4143	5	disorderly
0.4656	36.7	.4143	5	embodiment
0.4656	36.7	.4143	5	group's
0.4656	36.7	.4143	5	marketplace
0.4656	36.7	.4143	5	Ribbon
0.4656	36.7	.4143	5	ticked
0.4655	36.7	.4140	5	expire
0.4655	36.7	.4140	5	steadfastly
0.4655	36.7	.4224	5	thoroughfare
0.4654	36.7	.4328	5	deep-water
0.4652	36.7	.4137	5	braking
0.4652	36.7	.4137	5	discourages
0.4652	36.7	.4135	5	grisly
0.4652	36.7	.4137	5	interstellar
0.4651	36.7	.4130	5	heifer
0.4649	36.7	.2594	7	bulkhead
0.4649	36.7	.2594	7	casket
0.4649	36.7	.2594	7	emphatically
0.4649	36.7	.3717	6	infants
0.4648	36.7	.4274	5	inch-long
0.4648	36.7	.4190	5	snow-white
0.4648	36.7	.4190	5	someway
0.4647	36.7	.2827	7	-ness
0.4647	36.7	.1597	11	presidency
0.4646	36.7	.3416	6	livin'
0.4646	36.7	.3416	6	prance
0.4644	36.7	.0993	16	Shylock
0.4641	36.7	.4189	5	contemptuous
0.4641	36.7	.1645	11	Jobe
0.4640	36.7	.3747	5	bunny
0.4640	36.7	.3559	6	darned
0.4640	36.7	.0000	31	fives
0.4640	36.7	.0000	31	number-line
0.4639	36.7	.4303	5	Energy
0.4639	36.7	.3163	6	gray-green
0.4639	36.7	.4303	5	heresy
0.4638	36.7	.4433	5	fiddling
0.4638	36.7	.4138	5	Hope's
0.4638	36.7	.4475	5	142
0.4637	36.7	.3306	6	daffodil
0.4637	36.7	.2839	7	doe
THE PRECEDING WORD TYPE OCCUPIES RANK 23800				
0.4637	36.7	.4138	5	knighthood
0.4637	36.7	.3306	6	meteorological
0.4637	36.7	.4138	5	pick-up
0.4637	36.7	.4208	5	reels
0.4637	36.7	.4208	5	1797
0.4636	36.7	.3007	7	firmness
0.4635	36.7	.3267	6	unchanging
0.4634	36.7	.2355	6	begs
0.4634	36.7	.2355	6	Berthe
0.4634	36.7	.2355	6	BIG
0.4634	36.7	.2355	6	Cookies
0.4634	36.7	.2355	6	Fuchs
0.4634	36.7	.4132	5	Kurt
0.4634	36.7	.2355	6	Luck
0.4634	36.7	.4427	5	startlingly
0.4634	36.7	.2355	6	Tarpon
0.4634	36.7	.2355	6	Toad
0.4633	36.7	.1504	10	dominion
0.4633	36.7	.3322	6	makings
0.4632	36.7	.4180	5	rituals
0.4631	36.7	.4174	5	pig's
0.4631	36.7	.4174	5	seclusion
0.4629	36.7	.4161	5	batter's
0.4629	36.7	.4161	5	offenses
0.4628	36.7	.4085	5	delegations
0.4628	36.7	.4085	5	fateful
0.4628	36.7	.4183	5	malady
0.4628	36.7	.4085	5	relevance
0.4628	36.7	.2942	7	widows
0.4627	36.7	.3488	6	inoculations
0.4627	36.7	.3473	6	suffrage
0.4627	36.7	.3588	6	tentatively
0.4626	36.7	.3393	6	padding
0.4625	36.7	.1722	10	crutches
0.4625	36.7	.4178	5	fancier
0.4625	36.7	.0446	16	pipelines
0.4625	36.7	.2342	6	Weaver
0.4624	36.7	.4113	5	uphold
0.4623	36.6	.1940	9	bloodstream
0.4623	36.6	.4110	5	cascade
0.4623	36.6	.4110	5	outbuildings
0.4623	36.6	.4110	5	roundly
0.4622	36.6	.4173	5	all-night
0.4619	36.6	.3385	6	nearness
0.4619	36.6	.4169	5	pygmy
0.4619	36.6	.4169	5	revolutionize
0.4619	36.6	.4169	5	substantially
0.4618	36.6	.4167	5	shrilling
0.4616	36.6	.4401	5	fundamentals
0.4615	36.6	.4091	5	keeper's
0.4615	36.6	.0657	17	renaming
0.4614	36.6	.3549	6	Stetson
0.4613	36.6	.3492	6	red-brown
0.4612	36.6	.4145	5	confinement
0.4612	36.6	.4131	5	sodas
0.4611	36.6	.3625	5	embankment
0.4610	36.6	.3066	7	Debussy's
0.4609	36.6	.3622	5	ford
0.4609	36.6	.1133	18	layout
0.4608	36.6	.3373	6	blest
0.4607	36.6	.4137	5	rendering
0.4607	36.6	.4137	5	treads
0.4606	36.6	.3617	5	Motion
0.4605	36.6	.4321	5	bureaus
0.4603	36.6	.3480	6	maketh
0.4603	36.6	.3098	6	V**
0.4602	36.6	.2808	7	Jonah
0.4602	36.6	.4297	5	mixers
0.4600	36.6	.3542	6	curried
0.4600	36.6	.1951	10	marshmallows
0.4599	36.6	.3089	6	ballplayers
0.4599	36.6	.4122	5	cheerfulness
0.4599	36.6	.4122	5	disdain
0.4599	36.6	.3089	6	domes
0.4599	36.6	.4150	5	editions
0.4599	36.6	.4122	5	flamed
0.4599	36.6	.4122	5	hillock
0.4599	36.6	.4122	5	quaking
0.4599	36.6	.4122	5	semblance
0.4599	36.6	.4122	5	tottering
0.4598	36.6	.3535	6	browse
0.4598	36.6	.2784	7	575
0.4597	36.6	.1284	11	Postmaster
0.4597	36.6	.1284	11	Turkey's
0.4596	36.6	.4372	5	strangle
0.4594	36.6	.4113	5	liveliest
0.4594	36.6	.4113	5	long-suffering
0.4594	36.6	.1792	9	Pampas
0.4594	36.6	.2394	7	penmanship
0.4593	36.6	.3956	5	giver
0.4591	36.6	.4358	5	browns
0.4591	36.6	.3080	6	cutest
0.4591	36.6	.4365	5	populate
0.4588	36.6	.4043	5	unpacked
0.4587	36.6	.4119	5	ascertain
0.4587	36.6	.4119	5	communion
0.4587	36.6	.3493	6	modifications
0.4585	36.6	.4115	5	enclosure
0.4585	36.6	.4236	5	recede
0.4583	36.6	.3419	6	Bern
THE PRECEDING WORD TYPE OCCUPIES RANK 23900				
0.4582	36.6	.3026	7	comprises
0.4581	36.6	.3427	6	billboards
0.4580	36.6	.4326	5	suggestive
0.4579	36.6	.3131	6	high-pressure
0.4579	36.6	.4107	5	lattice
0.4579	36.6	.3131	6	softball
0.4577	36.6	.2118	9	lacing
0.4577	36.6	.3412	6	plant-eating
0.4572	36.6	.3460	6	245
0.4571	36.6	.2977	7	Rameau
0.4570	36.6	.4090	5	electrified
0.4570	36.6	.3228	6	milkweed
0.4569	36.6	.1717	8	Duvitches
0.4568	36.6	.0000	10	Aku
0.4568	36.6	.0000	10	Allerton
0.4568	36.6	.0000	10	Ba-boo
0.4568	36.6	.0000	10	bola
0.4568	36.6	.0000	10	caisson
0.4568	36.6	.0000	10	Catlin
0.4568	36.6	.0000	10	Chiron
0.4568	36.6	.0000	10	crocodile's
0.4568	36.6	.0000	10	Cuhullin
0.4568	36.6	.0000	10	damper
0.4568	36.6	.0000	10	Durkee
0.4568	36.6	.0000	10	Half-Chick
0.4568	36.6	.0000	10	Helper
0.4568	36.6	.0000	10	Housekeeper
0.4568	36.6	.0000	10	Jaguar
0.4568	36.6	.0000	10	Jenks
0.4568	36.6	.0000	10	ki-me-oh
0.4568	36.6	.0000	10	Kriternerk
0.4568	36.6	.0000	10	Mayaguez
0.4568	36.6	.0000	10	McGoogle
0.4568	36.6	.0000	10	Minutemen
0.4568	36.6	.0000	10	Mioshi
0.4568	36.6	.0000	10	Myer
0.4568	36.6	.0000	10	O-me-me
0.4568	36.6	.0000	10	oozies
0.4568	36.6	.0000	10	pandas
0.4568	36.6	.0000	10	Peppi
0.4568	36.6	.0000	10	Possy
0.4568	36.6	.0000	10	Posy
0.4568	36.6	.0000	10	Rolls-Royce
0.4568	36.6	.0000	10	Sacajawea
0.4568	36.6	.0000	10	Shag
0.4568	36.6	.0000	10	Sindre
0.4568	36.6	.0000	10	Singer's
0.4568	36.6	.0000	10	Snooky
0.4568	36.6	.0000	10	squawked
0.4568	36.6	.0000	10	Steinmetz
0.4568	36.6	.0000	10	Thakin
0.4568	36.6	.0000	10	tra-la-la
0.4568	36.6	.0000	10	Trui
0.4568	36.6	.0000	10	Vernelle
0.4568	36.6	.0000	10	Wooster
0.4568	36.6	.0000	10	Zinnen
0.4567	36.6	.2292	9	dissonant
0.4564	36.6	.1511	12	ex
0.4564	36.6	.1812	10	sins
0.4562	36.6	.3121	6	flipping
0.4562	36.6	.3350	6	pulsating
0.4558	36.6	.4047	5	carnations
0.4558	36.6	.1888	9	carolers
0.4557	36.6	.4297	5	conferring
0.4557	36.6	.3094	6	Valentine's
0.4556	36.6	.3212	6	one-hundredth
0.4556	36.6	.2959	7	u's
0.4555	36.6	.3404	6	devoid
0.4554	36.6	.2437	6	beanbag
0.4554	36.6	.2437	6	near-sighted
0.4554	36.6	.2437	6	vanLeeuwenhoek
0.4554	36.6	.2437	6	weevils
0.4554	36.6	.3053	6	widow's
0.4553	36.6	.1259	11	Fairview
0.4548	36.6	.3450	6	canst
0.4548	36.6	.2435	6	honk
0.4548	36.6	.2482	8	Oedipus
0.4548	36.6	.2435	6	shoestring
0.4545	36.6	.3044	6	Peters'
0.4543	36.6	.4326	5	bowels
0.4543	36.6	.4326	5	irritation
0.4543	36.6	.3098	7	kiln
0.4542	36.6	.0314	32	woodwind
0.4540	36.6	.4029	5	booty
0.4539	36.6	.4379	5	aesthetic
0.4538	36.6	.2212	6	Calhoun
0.4538	36.6	.2212	6	Hessians
0.4538	36.6	.2212	6	middy
0.4538	36.6	.2212	6	332nd
0.4536	36.6	.3683	5	immovable
0.4536	36.6	.3683	5	meat-eater
0.4536	36.6	.3683	5	solid-fuel
0.4536	36.6	.3683	5	unravel
0.4535	36.6	.4309	5	$150
0.4535	36.6	.1498	10	Eaton
0.4533	36.6	.2204	6	seeding
0.4532	36.6	.3437	6	Culture
0.4531	36.6	.4013	5	tumblers
0.4530	36.6	.4026	5	Galilei
0.4530	36.6	.2689	7	Had
THE PRECEDING WORD TYPE OCCUPIES RANK 24000				
0.4530	36.6	.3943	5	outrigger
0.4530	36.6	.4374	5	refinements
0.4528	36.6	.3191	6	busses
0.4528	36.6	.1380	12	carbide
0.4527	36.6	.3689	5	erupts
0.4527	36.6	.4035	5	granting
0.4527	36.6	.3676	5	preach
0.4527	36.6	.3672	5	R's
0.4527	36.6	.3676	5	Scott's
0.4527	36.6	.3689	5	unbearably
0.4527	36.6	.3689	5	undiscovered
0.4527	36.6	.3689	5	V's
0.4527	36.6	.3676	5	1630
0.4526	36.6	.4004	5	milled
0.4526	36.6	.4004	5	miners'
0.4524	36.6	.3410	6	oriental
0.4522	36.6	.3687	5	albatross
0.4522	36.6	.3537	6	washcloth
0.4521	36.6	.0900	16	primates
0.4520	36.6	.2756	7	anesthetics
0.4519	36.6	.3684	5	Budapest
0.4519	36.5	.3624	5	hailstones
0.4519	36.6	.3684	5	McCormick's
0.4519	36.6	.3684	5	wood-burning
0.4517	36.5	.3975	5	Janeiro
0.4517	36.5	.3975	5	obligingly
0.4516	36.5	.4303	5	associating
0.4515	36.5	.4003	5	distractions
0.4515	36.5	.3682	5	elaborately
0.4515	36.5	.3682	5	mortally
0.4515	36.5	.3419	6	2%
0.4514	36.5	.2278	8	high-energy
0.4514	36.5	.2278	8	incisors
0.4514	36.5	.4001	5	surmounted
0.4514	36.5	.2995	7	verbals
0.4509	36.5	.3089	6	headman
0.4509	36.5	.2899	7	Viennese
0.4508	36.5	.4244	5	Classic
0.4508	36.5	.2461	7	flagon
0.4508	36.5	.4244	5	midwinter
0.4508	36.5	.3367	6	Rhone
0.4507	36.5	.0000	42	MONAGHAN
0.4506	36.5	.3610	5	cruisers
0.4506	36.5	.3987	5	rawhide
0.4505	36.5	.3676	5	clop
0.4505	36.5	.3421	6	exams
0.4505	36.5	.3421	6	Information
0.4505	36.5	.4020	5	pinching
0.4505	36.5	.2749	7	primitives
0.4505	36.5	.3376	6	sheaf
0.4504	36.5	.3287	6	amperes
0.4504	36.5	.3674	5	needlelike
0.4502	36.5	.4159	5	practicable
0.4501	36.5	.3079	6	egg-shaped
0.4501	36.5	.3079	6	Hutton
0.4501	36.5	.2446	8	karakul
0.4501	36.5	.3079	6	Marconi
0.4500	36.5	.1093	13	coefficient
0.4500	36.5	.3978	5	hauls
0.4500	36.5	.2347	8	7/4
0.4499	36.5	.2991	6	chatted
0.4499	36.5	.2991	6	judges'
0.4497	36.5	.3973	5	dividends
0.4497	36.5	.2626	7	headlight
0.4497	36.5	.3973	5	overlooks
0.4497	36.5	.3973	5	painstakingly
0.4497	36.5	.3349	6	selector
0.4497	36.5	.3973	5	Werner
0.4497	36.5	.3349	6	492
0.4496	36.5	.3954	5	bronzed
0.4496	36.5	.2589	7	Stranger
0.4495	36.5	.4312	5	discord
0.4495	36.5	.3079	6	vacationers
0.4495	36.5	.3079	6	1760
0.4493	36.5	.2586	7	missus
0.4492	36.5	.4222	5	jubilant
0.4492	36.5	.2440	8	perennials
0.4492	36.5	.3339	6	wrangler
0.4491	36.5	.0000	30	factorizations
0.4491	36.5	.0000	30	3/2
0.4488	36.5	.0000	31	Lucretia
0.4486	36.5	.2669	7	concealment
0.4486	36.5	.3337	6	XII
0.4485	36.5	.3356	6	almanac
0.4485	36.5	.2440	7	three-legged
0.4479	36.5	.3343	6	cc
0.4478	36.5	.4071	5	draperies
0.4478	36.5	.3328	6	spinner
0.4477	36.5	.4177	5	diligently
0.4474	36.5	.3327	6	easterly
0.4474	36.5	.3327	6	flora
0.4474	36.5	.1604	11	Kemp
0.4473	36.5	.4038	5	stalwart
0.4472	36.5	.3974	5	slug
0.4470	36.5	.2526	7	Citizens
0.4470	36.5	.3304	6	Internal

U	SFI	D	F	Word Type
0.4470	36.5	.2652	7	upheaval
0.4470	36.5	.4033	5	whittled
0.4468	36.5	.3926	5	adventuring
0.4468	36.5	.3926	5	Clermont

THE PRECEDING WORD TYPE OCCUPIES RANK 24100

U	SFI	D	F	Word Type
0.4468	36.5	.3926	5	Cooperation
0.4468	36.5	.3436	6	curlers
0.4468	36.5	.3926	5	emperor's
0.4468	36.5	.3926	5	gouged
0.4468	36.5	.2829	7	guidelines
0.4468	36.5	.4186	5	hereafter
0.4468	36.5	.3926	5	Meadows
0.4468	36.5	.3436	6	specials
0.4468	36.5	.3926	5	waterless
0.4467	36.5	.3305	6	vistas
0.4466	36.5	.4177	5	Departments
0.4466	36.5	.3334	6	gaff
0.4466	36.5	.4177	5	stifle
0.4466	36.5	.2935	6	whop
0.4464	36.5	.2983	6	Twist
0.4462	36.5	.4023	5	forgiven
0.4461	36.5	.3350	6	freeways
0.4461	36.5	.3350	6	two-year
0.4458	36.5	.2782	6	Chipmunk
0.4458	36.5	.2390	8	Fisheries
0.4457	36.5	.2333	8	Paddy
0.4455	36.5	.3323	6	emigrants
0.4455	36.5	.3343	6	monumental
0.4452	36.5	.3481	6	tangy
0.4452	36.5	.2182	8	1811
0.4451	36.5	.3185	6	hemmed
0.4449	36.5	.3317	6	Brook
0.4449	36.5	.3317	6	magically
0.4448	36.5	.2375	8	CAT
0.4448	36.5	.2526	6	juggling
0.4447	36.5	.4001	5	mentioning
0.4446	36.5	.1968	10	gasket
0.4445	36.5	.4154	5	alabaster
0.4443	36.5	.4025	5	centipede
0.4443	36.5	.1686	10	defeating
0.4443	36.5	.2370	8	Slavic
0.4442	36.5	.3321	6	Hunters
0.4442	36.5	.4086	5	utilization
0.4441	36.5	.3182	6	drummers
0.4438	36.5	.1703	10	Plata
0.4438	36.5	.3343	6	003
0.4436	36.5	.3332	6	sardine
0.4436	36.5	.1963	7	squids
0.4435	36.5	.2771	7	bureaucracy
0.4435	36.5	.3986	5	deft
0.4435	36.5	.2771	7	Gaulle
0.4435	36.5	.2771	7	Malone
0.4434	36.5	.0845	16	Thad
0.4433	36.5	.2203	9	bonded
0.4433	36.5	.1719	9	botanists
0.4433	36.5	.1719	9	epidermis
0.4433	36.5	.1719	9	Koch
0.4433	36.5	.1719	9	Leeuwenhoek
0.4433	36.5	.4022	5	nightgowns
0.4433	36.5	.1719	9	Rumford
0.4432	36.5	.3210	6	mammoths
0.4431	36.5	.1373	12	Type
0.4429	36.5	.2953	6	Notch
0.4429	36.5	.2953	6	precipice
0.4429	36.5	.2953	6	tawny
0.4429	36.5	.1984	8	unexplained
0.4428	36.5	.3346	6	nailing
0.4425	36.5	.2087	9	-ent
0.4425	36.5	.1692	10	galls
0.4425	36.5	.1692	10	refinement
0.4424	36.5	.2809	7	Sentences
0.4423	36.5	.3601	5	blacksmith's
0.4423	36.5	.3601	5	forty-ninth
0.4422	36.5	.2942	6	artificially
0.4422	36.5	.4100	5	blaring
0.4422	36.5	.2942	6	impurity
0.4422	36.5	.2942	6	leeward
0.4422	36.5	.2942	6	searchers
0.4422	36.5	.1953	7	Sinon
0.4420	36.5	.0315	31	Patterns
0.4419	36.5	.0682	16	Pythagorean
0.4418	36.5	.2370	8	Analdas
0.4417	36.5	.2369	6	Dave's
0.4417	36.5	.3261	6	Napier
0.4416	36.4	.1953	7	Ghana
0.4416	36.5	.4163	5	hygiene
0.4416	36.4	.2895	6	ladled
0.4416	36.4	.2895	6	mumbling
0.4415	36.4	.2829	7	forerunners
0.4414	36.4	.2753	7	swordfish
0.4413	36.4	.2932	6	downgrade
0.4412	36.4	.1073	11	Humphrey
0.4412	36.4	.2489	7	Sanderson
0.4412	36.4	.3343	6	toothed
0.4411	36.4	.2423	8	blender
0.4411	36.4	.4280	5	guillotine
0.4411	36.4	.2423	8	permanent-press
0.4411	36.4	.4188	5	predicament
0.4409	36.4	.3947	5	encircle
0.4408	36.4	.4244	5	acquaint
0.4408	36.4	.0392	24	Dill
0.4406	36.4	.3250	6	pecan
0.4406	36.4	.1130	16	primer
0.4405	36.4	.3060	6	Sammy's
0.4404	36.4	.2431	8	godly

THE PRECEDING WORD TYPE OCCUPIES RANK 24200

U	SFI	D	F	Word Type
0.4402	36.4	.2930	6	landlords
0.4402	36.4	.2930	6	Whitney's
0.4401	36.4	.2965	6	yelped
0.4400	36.4	.1939	7	bravo
0.4399	36.4	.3060	6	summarizes
0.4398	36.4	.2810	7	n's
0.4397	36.4	.2357	6	asses
0.4397	36.4	.2357	6	Blackfoot
0.4397	36.4	.2357	6	counterfeiters
0.4397	36.4	.3240	6	IX
0.4397	36.4	.0702	14	Mantell
0.4395	36.4	.4064	5	abounds
0.4395	36.4	.3806	5	dredged
0.4395	36.4	.3806	5	reclaim
0.4394	36.4	.1070	13	Corey
0.4394	36.4	.3915	5	Lame
0.4393	36.4	.1159	13	auger
0.4393	36.4	.2920	6	Fugitive
0.4387	36.4	.3341	6	sophistication
0.4386	36.4	.4063	5	Sandwich
0.4383	36.4	.3939	5	Cat's
0.4383	36.4	.2952	6	dugouts
0.4383	36.4	.2952	6	Speaker
0.4383	36.4	.2952	6	Sweden's
0.4382	36.4	.3936	5	cronies
0.4380	36.4	.1358	12	suh
0.4379	36.4	.2455	7	cameraman
0.4379	36.4	.2896	6	mused
0.4378	36.4	.3226	6	Corinth
0.4378	36.4	.3933	5	They
0.4377	36.4	.2465	7	401
0.4377	36.4	.2465	7	454
0.4376	36.4	.4202	5	dale
0.4374	36.4	.2951	7	monochromatic
0.4374	36.4	.1863	10	swapped
0.4374	36.4	.3236	6	363
0.4372	36.4	.1920	7	crossbow
0.4372	36.4	.1235	15	grooming
0.4372	36.4	.1920	7	hulls
0.4370	36.4	.3361	6	demolished
0.4368	36.4	.3047	6	furthest
0.4368	36.4	.4110	5	survivor
0.4366	36.4	.3207	6	circumscribed
0.4366	36.4	.3375	6	embossed
0.4366	36.4	.2877	6	reddened
0.4364	36.4	.2779	7	Dante
0.4361	36.4	.1610	10	axiom
0.4360	36.4	.1541	10	towing
0.4360	36.4	.3906	5	vans
0.4359	36.4	.0803	17	MAC
0.4359	36.4	.3214	6	neatness
0.4358	36.4	.1975	8	Date
0.4356	36.4	.3902	5	Westward
0.4356	36.4	.3902	5	wigs
0.4355	36.4	.3041	6	bliss
0.4355	36.4	.3041	6	I**
0.4352	36.4	.3909	5	doting
0.4352	36.4	.3872	5	157
0.4351	36.4	.2407	7	kaolin
0.4350	36.4	.3923	5	indulge
0.4350	36.4	.3374	6	Philharmonic
0.4350	36.4	.4157	5	438
0.4349	36.4	.4043	5	unites
0.4349	36.4	.4095	5	219
0.4348	36.4	.3860	5	000-mile
0.4341	36.4	.0000	29	-3
0.4341	36.4	.0000	29	polynomial
0.4338	36.4	.0958	19	planing
0.4338	36.4	.0000	22	spore
0.4337	36.4	.2017	8	undergoes
0.4336	36.4	.2949	6	bland
0.4335	36.4	.3252	6	Commandments
0.4333	36.4	.3829	5	machine-gun
0.4333	36.4	.2014	8	oxidizer
0.4333	36.4	.3257	6	tortoises
0.4331	36.4	.3550	5	Albers
0.4331	36.4	.3546	5	banquets
0.4331	36.4	.3547	5	Brinker
0.4331	36.4	.3547	5	critters
0.4331	36.4	.3547	5	flanks
0.4331	36.4	.3547	5	prophecies
0.4331	36.4	.3550	5	sensibly
0.4331	36.4	.3547	5	squalid
0.4330	36.4	.3722	5	foamy
0.4329	36.4	.3861	5	hopscotch
0.4328	36.4	.3536	5	befall
0.4328	36.4	.3536	5	debating
0.4328	36.4	.3536	5	jingled
0.4328	36.4	.3536	5	market-place
0.4328	36.4	.1963	9	Mustang
0.4328	36.4	.3536	5	pardoned
0.4326	36.4	.3530	5	bayonet
0.4326	36.4	.3530	5	bundled
0.4326	36.4	.2088	9	electronically
0.4326	36.4	.3530	5	Newman
0.4326	36.4	.3530	5	spurted
0.4325	36.4	.2765	6	ailing
0.4325	36.4	.3856	5	Tennyson
0.4324	36.4	.3347	6	contexts
0.4322	36.4	.3888	5	curtained

THE PRECEDING WORD TYPE OCCUPIES RANK 24300

U	SFI	D	F	Word Type
0.4322	36.4	.4087	5	Products
0.4321	36.4	.2194	8	Pascal
0.4319	36.4	.2757	6	cows'
0.4319	36.4	.2757	6	grizzlies
0.4319	36.4	.3767	5	puddings
0.4319	36.4	.2757	6	spacemen
0.4318	36.4	.2818	6	Higgins
0.4315	36.3	.2303	8	fragmentation
0.4315	36.4	.1363	10	ocean-going
0.4313	36.3	.2014	8	'twill
0.4312	36.3	.4073	5	machinist
0.4312	36.3	.3997	5	mechanized
0.4312	36.3	.2793	7	Method
0.4310	36.3	.2727	7	nun
0.4310	36.3	.2727	7	1990
0.4309	36.3	.1231	12	fedayeen
0.4309	36.3	.3541	5	fiddlers
0.4309	36.3	.3875	5	flattery
0.4309	36.3	.3095	6	invert
0.4308	36.3	.2509	8	buttonhole
0.4308	36.3	.2007	8	Lowlands
0.4308	36.3	.3832	5	signified
0.4308	36.3	.2750	7	woolens
0.4307	36.3	.4031	5	226
0.4306	36.3	.3809	5	12%
0.4305	36.3	.2085	9	Theme
0.4305	36.3	.0105	39	tion
0.4305	36.3	.2085	9	violas
0.4303	36.3	.3182	6	Cheops
0.4303	36.3	.1548	11	Michelangelo
0.4303	36.3	.3187	6	quartzite
0.4303	36.3	.1548	11	sculptures
0.4299	36.3	.3819	5	flirting
0.4297	36.3	.2414	7	Carlisle
0.4297	36.3	.4098	5	heyday
0.4295	36.3	.3108	6	oftener
0.4293	36.3	.2635	7	Alameda
0.4293	36.3	.2635	7	Bacon
0.4293	36.3	.2635	7	mortality
0.4293	36.3	.2635	7	registration
0.4292	36.3	.2351	8	headstock
0.4292	36.3	.2295	8	yeller
0.4292	36.3	.2446	7	347
0.4291	36.3	.4086	5	frolics
0.4291	36.3	.2796	6	swineherd
0.4289	36.3	.3954	5	429
0.4286	36.3	.4059	5	aligned
0.4286	36.3	.2279	6	blacked
0.4286	36.3	.2279	6	Brandt
0.4286	36.3	.2279	6	Coke
0.4286	36.3	.2279	6	gobbling
0.4286	36.3	.2279	6	Hoovers
0.4286	36.3	.2279	6	sandhill
0.4286	36.3	.2279	6	steadying
0.4286	36.3	.2279	6	Toby's
0.4279	36.3	.0000	22	Cartier
0.4278	36.3	.3410	5	corncobs
0.4278	36.3	.3995	5	replenish
0.4276	36.3	.2277	8	lore
0.4276	36.3	.3285	6	Records
0.4276	36.3	.4046	5	475
0.4271	36.3	.2446	7	jute
0.4269	36.3	.2241	7	Tilly
0.4269	36.3	.1052	14	tr
0.4268	36.3	.0000	39	auxiliaries
0.4267	36.3	.3302	6	commandment
0.4267	36.3	.3827	5	ugliness
0.4266	36.3	.2773	6	battleground
0.4266	36.3	.2773	6	cobblestone
0.4266	36.3	.2773	6	1890's
0.4263	36.3	.3838	5	volleyball
0.4261	36.3	.2261	6	gatekeeper
0.4261	36.3	.2261	6	hairpins
0.4261	36.3	.2261	6	Perrault
0.4261	36.3	.3818	5	shipwreck
0.4261	36.3	.2261	6	Tall
0.4261	36.3	.2261	6	thar
0.4260	36.3	.1936	9	Chee-Chee
0.4260	36.3	.0905	15	Dotty
0.4260	36.3	.4052	5	informative
0.4259	36.3	.1253	14	chisels
0.4259	36.3	.1601	9	Galaxy
0.4259	36.3	.1601	9	magnifier
0.4257	36.3	.3832	5	283
0.4256	36.3	.3796	5	falsehood
0.4256	36.3	.1628	10	ghetto
0.4256	36.3	.3796	5	mussed
0.4255	36.3	.3206	6	keenly
0.4255	36.3	.2767	6	Sanskrit
0.4252	36.3	.0877	20	basting
0.4252	36.3	.3852	5	exclaims
0.4249	36.3	.3829	5	nitrates
0.4248	36.3	.3736	5	bell-shaped
0.4248	36.3	.4026	5	leaden
0.4247	36.3	.3830	5	Apennines
0.4247	36.3	.3830	5	diggings
0.4247	36.3	.3830	5	Harper's
0.4247	36.3	.3830	5	Negroid
0.4246	36.3	.3380	5	schoolteachers
0.4246	36.3	.3380	5	smelly

THE PRECEDING WORD TYPE OCCUPIES RANK 24400

U	SFI	D	F	Word Type
0.4245	36.3	.2107	8	ploughing
0.4245	36.3	.3734	5	pranks
0.4245	36.3	.3196	6	transplant
0.4245	36.3	.2129	8	2s
0.4244	36.3	.3826	5	cruelest
0.4244	36.3	.3828	5	phantom
0.4243	36.3	.3374	5	convictions
0.4242	36.3	.1697	10	Citronella
0.4242	36.3	.4022	5	ruefully
0.4241	36.3	.2967	6	Sparky
0.4240	36.3	.2416	7	appendages
0.4240	36.3	.2416	7	line-of-sight
0.4240	36.3	.3965	5	thinning
0.4237	36.3	.2977	6	believer
0.4237	36.3	.2977	6	bunting
0.4235	36.3	.1155	12	Lizard
0.4235	36.3	.2978	6	Operations
0.4235	36.3	.3805	5	trap-door
0.4234	36.3	.3921	5	bathes
0.4231	36.3	.3072	6	Highlanders
0.4230	36.3	.3816	5	disintegration
0.4230	36.3	.3816	5	Dmitri
0.4230	36.3	.3816	5	telegraphy
0.4229	36.3	.3175	6	Bug
0.4228	36.3	.3798	5	curbs
0.4228	36.3	.4040	5	permeated
0.4228	36.3	.2373	7	Radical
0.4228	36.3	.4017	5	scrutiny
0.4226	36.3	.0746	13	Hulda
0.4224	36.3	.2412	7	krill
0.4224	36.3	.1591	9	Louisiana's
0.4224	36.3	.2412	7	molars
0.4224	36.3	.2412	7	pharynx
0.4224	36.3	.3206	6	Sports
0.4222	36.3	.3804	5	para
0.4221	36.3	.3812	5	Auld
0.4221	36.3	.3812	5	Chi
0.4221	36.3	.0555	17	oy
0.4221	36.3	.3812	5	Tripoli
0.4219	36.3	.3060	6	Philip's
0.4217	36.3	.2130	8	mug
0.4217	36.3	.3200	6	Promenade
0.4217	36.2	.3469	5	team's
0.4217	36.2	.3469	5	wistful
0.4216	36.2	.3974	5	canceled
0.4216	36.2	.1824	9	OAS
0.4215	36.2	.2430	7	reactors
0.4215	36.2	.3222	6	solace
0.4214	36.2	.3780	5	gullet
0.4214	36.2	.2657	7	subterranean
0.4213	36.2	.3898	5	coincide
0.4213	36.2	.4158	5	ribbed
0.4212	36.2	.2565	7	co-op
0.4212	36.2	.2223	6	Daugherty
0.4212	36.2	.2223	6	motherless
0.4212	36.2	.2223	6	Pantaloon
0.4212	36.2	.2223	6	simpleton
0.4212	36.2	.2223	6	Twain's
0.4211	36.2	.2960	6	brutes
0.4211	36.2	.3757	5	Tulsa
0.4210	36.2	.2941	6	Afraid
0.4210	36.2	.2408	7	Araucanians
0.4210	36.2	.2432	7	Aswan
0.4210	36.2	.3225	6	coordinating
0.4210	36.2	.2408	7	1500's
0.4209	36.2	.3441	5	Deaf
0.4209	36.2	.3441	5	junks
0.4209	36.2	.3441	5	12-year-old
0.4207	36.2	.3943	5	predetermined
0.4207	36.2	.1550	8	Queenie
0.4206	36.2	.2331	7	Alcott
0.4206	36.2	.3436	5	aromatic
0.4206	36.2	.3436	5	bluster
0.4206	36.2	.1172	13	buzzer
0.4206	36.2	.3436	5	thronging
0.4206	36.2	.3436	5	waddling
0.4206	36.2	.2331	7	yawl
0.4205	36.2	.1767	9	Odysseus'
0.4205	36.2	.3024	6	02
0.4204	36.2	.3982	5	bloated
0.4204	36.2	.3775	5	brokers
0.4204	36.2	.3775	5	gulfs
0.4203	36.2	.3432	5	directory
0.4203	36.2	.3432	5	golfer
0.4201	36.2	.3770	5	Douglass
0.4201	36.2	.2626	7	dramatists
0.4201	36.2	.3770	5	Saracens
0.4201	36.2	.3759	5	stoppers
0.4200	36.2	.3779	5	Andros
0.4198	36.2	.2212	6	gestured
0.4198	36.2	.3147	6	inundation
0.4198	36.2	.3974	5	organizational
0.4198	36.2	.2212	6	princesses
0.4198	36.2	.2212	6	Romero
0.4198	36.2	.2212	6	stealthy
0.4198	36.2	.2212	6	Verona
0.4196	36.2	.3451	5	boarder
0.4196	36.2	.3451	5	fleeting
0.4195	36.2	.3749	5	bivalves
0.4195	36.2	.3749	5	conduction

THE PRECEDING WORD TYPE OCCUPIES RANK 24500

U	SFI	D	F	Word Type
0.4195	36.2	.3126	6	depict
0.4195	36.2	.3749	5	interacting
0.4195	36.2	.3749	5	receptacle
0.4194	36.2	.3506	5	electrician
0.4194	36.2	.3414	5	encircling
0.4194	36.2	.3414	5	licenses
0.4194	36.2	.3414	5	smartly
0.4193	36.2	.2366	7	Conservation
0.4193	36.2	.2366	7	psychosis
0.4192	36.2	.2894	6	hayloft
0.4192	36.2	.3159	6	Nemo
0.4192	36.2	.2894	6	papoose
0.4191	36.2	.3791	5	spotty
0.4190	36.2	.3753	5	Surinam
0.4189	36.2	.1983	9	combo
0.4186	36.2	.2185	8	Finch
0.4186	36.2	.3822	5	short-story
0.4185	36.2	.2962	6	Bound
0.4185	36.2	.2179	8	Colchester
0.4184	36.2	.3742	5	exporting
0.4184	36.2	.3742	5	Independent
0.4184	36.2	.3742	5	mestizo
0.4184	36.2	.3742	5	publicized
0.4184	36.2	.3742	5	tribunal
0.4182	36.2	.3097	6	resists
0.4181	36.2	.3416	5	extinguished
0.4181	36.2	.3416	5	plying
0.4181	36.2	.3416	5	Scripture
0.4181	36.2	.3416	5	snakelike
0.4180	36.2	.2197	6	Cup
0.4180	36.2	.3724	5	liquefied
0.4180	36.2	.2991	6	Logan
0.4180	36.2	.2197	6	restlessness
0.4180	36.2	.2007	8	tucks
0.4179	36.2	.3733	5	Hayakawa
0.4178	36.2	.3410	5	bawled
0.4178	36.2	.3410	5	movin'
0.4178	36.2	.3410	5	outran
0.4178	36.2	.3410	5	rummaged
0.4177	36.2	.3014	6	Literary
0.4176	36.2	.2361	7	Cubans
0.4176	36.2	.2361	7	Livestock
0.4176	36.2	.2361	7	Mauritania
0.4175	36.2	.3405	5	crinkled
0.4175	36.2	.2802	6	Dole
0.4175	36.2	.2607	7	Elaine
0.4174	36.2	.2488	7	Caxton
0.4171	36.2	.3666	5	ALL
0.4170	36.2	.3933	5	illuminate
0.4170	36.2	.3473	5	scares
0.4169	36.2	.3717	5	Cause
0.4169	36.2	.3123	6	frontal
0.4167	36.2	.3839	5	home-made
0.4167	36.2	.3468	5	mired
0.4165	36.2	.2634	6	tarnished
0.4165	36.2	.2972	6	tilting
0.4164	36.2	.3834	5	Konrad
0.4162	36.2	.3959	5	prophetic
0.4161	36.2	.1392	12	unvoiced

U	SFI	D	F	Word Type
0.4160	36.2	.3767	5	conspiring
0.4160	36.2	.3767	5	importing
0.4160	36.2	.3767	5	slowdown
0.4158	36.2	.3967	5	deep-set
0.4158	36.2	.3456	5	helm
0.4158	36.2	.3456	5	scrawled
0.4157	36.2	.3375	5	composure
0.4157	36.2	.3691	5	cuticle
0.4157	36.2	.3375	5	humiliated
0.4157	36.2	.3375	5	hustled
0.4157	36.2	.3375	5	indecision
0.4157	36.2	.3691	5	junctions
0.4157	36.2	.3173	6	Menlo
0.4157	36.2	.3691	5	mites
0.4157	36.2	.3691	5	NaCl
0.4157	36.2	.3691	5	solidified
0.4157	36.2	.3691	5	thumbtack
0.4156	36.2	.1502	11	menus
0.4155	36.2	.1998	8	Sultan's
0.4154	36.2	.3753	5	measurable
0.4153	36.2	.2988	6	infernal
0.4152	36.2	.1389	12	Britten
0.4151	36.2	.3343	5	bum
0.4151	36.2	.3343	5	Championship
0.4151	36.2	.3343	5	Denny
0.4151	36.2	.3343	5	guideline
0.4151	36.2	.3343	5	holster
0.4151	36.2	.3343	5	potion
0.4151	36.2	.3343	5	sputter
0.4151	36.2	.3198	6	20th-century
0.4149	36.2	.1564	8	mouse's
0.4149	36.2	.3704	5	reapers
0.4149	36.2	.3704	5	Syrians
0.4148	36.2	.2899	6	Worlds
0.4147	36.2	.4629	4	sameness
0.4147	36.2	.4629	4	1**
0.4147	36.2	.4629	4	670
0.4146	36.2	.3684	5	admitting
0.4146	36.2	.3684	5	annexation
0.4146	36.2	.3684	5	Balkans
0.4146	36.2	.3684	5	contending

THE PRECEDING WORD TYPE OCCUPIES RANK 24600

U	SFI	D	F	Word Type
0.4146	36.2	.3684	5	Javanese
0.4146	36.2	.3684	5	persecuted
0.4146	36.2	.3684	5	proprietors
0.4146	36.2	.2145	8	unbalanced
0.4143	36.2	.3679	5	languid
0.4142	36.2	.1212	9	Kauai
0.4142	36.2	.1212	9	landlocked
0.4142	36.2	.1212	9	Thessaly
0.4141	36.2	.3733	5	balloonist
0.4140	36.2	.3735	5	Door
0.4140	36.2	.3660	5	satellite's
0.4140	36.2	.3660	5	vernal
0.4137	36.2	.2611	6	forester
0.4135	36.2	.3627	5	tusk
0.4134	36.2	.2896	6	swearing
0.4133	36.2	.2395	7	incandescent
0.4133	36.2	.2395	7	photon
0.4133	36.2	.2395	7	scientist's
0.4132	36.2	.3247	6	Chariot
0.4132	36.2	.4820	4	disintegrates
0.4132	36.2	.4820	4	Rouen
0.4132	36.2	.4820	4	well-defined
0.4130	36.2	.2887	6	Hour
0.4129	36.2	.2399	7	co-operative
0.4129	36.2	.2399	7	Deputies
0.4129	36.2	.2399	7	undeveloped
0.4128	36.2	.4818	4	Associate
0.4128	36.2	.3790	5	baited
0.4128	36.2	.4818	4	fifteen-minute
0.4128	36.2	.4818	4	impartial
0.4128	36.2	.4818	4	seashells
0.4128	36.2	.2724	6	2-5
0.4127	36.2	.3651	5	migrant
0.4127	36.2	.3365	5	talons
0.4126	36.2	.3225	6	satins
0.4126	36.2	.2696	6	spattering
0.4125	36.2	.0586	16	dr
0.4123	36.2	.3626	5	fiddles
0.4123	36.2	.4843	4	reopened
0.4121	36.2	.4574	4	Purple
0.4121	36.2	.4574	4	reflectors
0.4121	36.2	.4574	4	simmered
0.4121	36.2	.4574	4	toothbrushes
0.4120	36.1	.3844	5	Dust
0.4118	36.1	.3311	5	mopping
0.4118	36.1	.3786	5	rhetoric
0.4118	36.1	.3374	5	storybook
0.4118	36.1	.1621	10	third-grade
0.4118	36.1	.3128	6	trifling
0.4117	36.1	.3822	5	babe
0.4115	36.1	.4835	4	bagged
0.4115	36.1	.4835	4	milestones
0.4115	36.1	.2590	6	nomad
0.4114	36.1	.1139	13	bimetal
0.4114	36.1	.1099	14	Parthenon
0.4114	36.1	.3780	5	Truth
0.4112	36.1	.3753	5	exiled
0.4112	36.1	.3661	5	imperfections
0.4111	36.1	.0000	9	Appleseed
0.4111	36.1	.0000	9	Bertrand
0.4111	36.1	.0000	9	Bet
0.4111	36.1	.0000	9	Biafu
0.4111	36.1	.0000	9	Bianca
0.4111	36.1	.0000	9	Brok
0.4111	36.1	.0000	9	Chub
0.4111	36.1	.0000	9	Cornflower
0.4111	36.1	.0000	9	councillor
0.4111	36.1	.0000	9	Diablo
0.4111	36.1	.0000	9	Flan
0.4111	36.1	.0000	9	fo'
0.4111	36.1	.0000	9	Garwick
0.4111	36.1	.0000	9	Goosie
0.4111	36.1	.0000	9	Gordy
0.4111	36.1	.0000	9	Hor
0.4111	36.1	.0000	9	jinx
0.4111	36.1	.0000	9	Lofting
0.4111	36.1	.0000	9	Manowar
0.4111	36.1	.0000	9	Marya
0.4111	36.1	.0000	9	Meigs
0.4111	36.1	.0000	9	Milly
0.4111	36.1	.0000	9	Mul
0.4111	36.1	.0000	9	Natua
0.4111	36.1	.0000	9	NC1234
0.4111	36.1	.0000	9	Netta
0.4111	36.1	.0000	9	oogrug
0.4111	36.1	.0000	9	panda
0.4111	36.1	.0000	9	Paulossie
0.4111	36.1	.0000	9	Peanut
0.4111	36.1	.0000	9	Quentin
0.4111	36.1	.3349	5	reddest
0.4111	36.1	.0000	9	righted
0.4111	36.1	.0000	9	Slippy
0.4111	36.1	.0000	9	Snoopy
0.4111	36.1	.0000	9	Speckles
0.4111	36.1	.0000	9	Spiros
0.4111	36.1	.0000	9	Tootles
0.4111	36.1	.0000	9	Uther
0.4111	36.1	.0000	9	veldt
0.4111	36.1	.0000	9	Whitie
0.4111	36.1	.0000	9	Wiki

THE PRECEDING WORD TYPE OCCUPIES RANK 24700

U	SFI	D	F	Word Type
0.4111	36.1	.0000	9	Yasu's
0.4110	36.1	.3706	5	garb
0.4109	36.1	.0513	23	sonata
0.4107	36.1	.3814	5	Christendom
0.4107	36.1	.3814	5	Dante's
0.4107	36.1	.2870	6	intermittently
0.4107	36.1	.2870	6	nausea
0.4107	36.1	.2589	6	1806
0.4105	36.1	.3330	5	deceiving
0.4105	36.1	.3330	5	gavel
0.4105	36.1	.3330	5	snickered
0.4104	36.1	.3047	6	rationale
0.4103	36.1	.3776	5	Delawares
0.4103	36.1	.0976	11	Hannibal
0.4103	36.1	.0976	11	refuges
0.4102	36.1	.2267	7	AF
0.4102	36.1	.3033	6	407
0.4100	36.1	.2827	6	fie
0.4100	36.1	.4784	4	Question
0.4100	36.1	.2827	6	Remus
0.4099	36.1	.3716	5	Faulkner
0.4098	36.1	.3769	5	varmints
0.4097	36.1	.3757	5	convent
0.4097	36.1	.3317	5	Dickson
0.4096	36.1	.4572	4	Meyer
0.4095	36.1	.4829	4	bullying
0.4095	36.1	.4829	4	haircuts
0.4095	36.1	.1843	9	napkins
0.4095	36.1	.4829	4	triumphed
0.4094	36.1	.4826	4	pertinent
0.4093	36.1	.3361	5	dribbled
0.4093	36.1	.3021	6	teenager
0.4091	36.1	.4568	4	airing
0.4091	36.1	.4568	4	ambergris
0.4091	36.1	.4568	4	burned-out
0.4091	36.1	.4570	4	dumplings
0.4091	36.1	.4568	4	sampled
0.4091	36.1	.4777	4	second-largest
0.4091	36.1	.4570	4	teamsters
0.4091	36.1	.4570	4	unofficial
0.4091	36.1	.4570	4	unpleasantly
0.4091	36.1	.4568	4	well-traveled
0.4089	36.1	.3660	5	Manchurian
0.4089	36.1	.3660	5	Yorkers
0.4088	36.1	.3313	5	blankly
0.4088	36.1	.3313	5	bloodshot
0.4088	36.1	.3313	5	eying
0.4088	36.1	.3827	5	furled
0.4088	36.1	.3827	5	glimmer
0.4085	36.1	.3322	5	chimp
0.4085	36.1	.4875	4	derogatory
0.4085	36.1	.2160	6	ionosphere
0.4085	36.1	.4856	4	overloaded
0.4085	36.1	.4767	4	steam-driven
0.4084	36.1	.3120	6	stubs
0.4083	36.1	.4767	4	devastation
0.4083	36.1	.1364	10	radioman
0.4082	36.1	.4817	4	dotting
0.4082	36.1	.4873	4	garret
0.4082	36.1	.4817	4	inept
0.4082	36.1	.4873	4	nigger
0.4082	36.1	.4817	4	outcast
0.4082	36.1	.4817	4	outfitted
0.4082	36.1	.4873	4	Religion
0.4082	36.1	.4817	4	tackling
0.4082	36.1	.4873	4	three-inch
0.4082	36.1	.4814	4	unify
0.4082	36.1	.4814	4	utensil
0.4082	36.1	.4873	4	wanton
0.4081	36.1	.1721	7	cock-a-doodle-doo
0.4081	36.1	.1824	8	coelenterates
0.4081	36.1	.4811	4	elapse
0.4081	36.1	.1824	8	meteorology
0.4081	36.1	.1824	8	neap
0.4081	36.1	.4854	4	unoccupied
0.4080	36.1	.3300	5	hurtled
0.4080	36.1	.3300	5	McLaughlin
0.4080	36.1	.3300	5	unlighted
0.4080	36.1	.3300	5	unspoken
0.4079	36.1	.3569	5	dispersal
0.4079	36.1	.3569	5	interrelationships
0.4079	36.1	.4556	4	long-ago
0.4079	36.1	.4556	4	Malabar
0.4079	36.1	.4556	4	passable
0.4079	36.1	.3569	5	planetoids
0.4079	36.1	.4556	4	spire
0.4079	36.1	.4556	4	wearied
0.4078	36.1	.4870	4	dark-brown
0.4078	36.1	.4870	4	esteemed
0.4078	36.1	.4588	4	gray-haired
0.4078	36.1	.4870	4	intercepted
0.4078	36.1	.4870	4	miseries
0.4078	36.1	.4870	4	sufferings
0.4077	36.1	.4813	4	breakneck
0.4077	36.1	.3760	5	glamorous
0.4077	36.1	.4812	4	wounding
0.4076	36.1	.4809	4	demeanor
0.4076	36.1	.4870	4	divert
0.4076	36.1	.4809	4	fantastically
0.4076	36.1	.4809	4	incision

THE PRECEDING WORD TYPE OCCUPIES RANK 24800

U	SFI	D	F	Word Type
0.4076	36.1	.0360	27	notated
0.4076	36.1	.4870	4	respectability
0.4075	36.1	.4889	4	Easy
0.4075	36.1	.4889	4	jailed
0.4075	36.1	.4889	4	jerkin
0.4075	36.1	.4889	4	limelight
0.4074	36.1	.4870	4	indulged
0.4073	36.1	.3211	5	Buick
0.4073	36.1	.3211	5	Chapel
0.4073	36.1	.3211	5	Peach
0.4073	36.1	.3211	5	pinon
0.4073	36.1	.4887	4	sickened
0.4072	36.1	.1703	9	ab
0.4072	36.1	.4806	4	azaleas
0.4072	36.1	.4806	4	confer
0.4072	36.1	.4806	4	receptive
0.4072	36.1	.4806	4	rental
0.4072	36.1	.4802	4	seventy-six
0.4071	36.1	.4803	4	all-inclusive
0.4071	36.1	.4886	4	bitch
0.4071	36.1	.4800	4	Boyle
0.4071	36.1	.4803	4	counteract
0.4071	36.1	.2152	6	homesteaders
0.4071	36.1	.2152	6	horseless
0.4071	36.1	.4803	4	inhibit
0.4071	36.1	.4886	4	pickerel
0.4071	36.1	.4886	4	unscathed
0.4071	36.1	.4803	4	1930s
0.4070	36.1	.4866	4	congenial
0.4070	36.1	.4866	4	figurehead
0.4070	36.1	.4866	4	grossly
0.4070	36.1	.4866	4	imperceptible
0.4070	36.1	.4764	4	inspects
0.4070	36.1	.4866	4	quarrying
0.4069	36.1	.0278	25	ck
0.4069	36.1	.4866	4	confectionery
0.4069	36.1	.4860	4	discounting
0.4069	36.1	.3204	5	enthusiast
0.4069	36.1	.4866	4	gnat
0.4069	36.1	.4577	4	Henderson's
0.4069	36.1	.4866	4	marshaled
0.4069	36.1	.4866	4	rumps
0.4069	36.1	.3496	5	scooters
0.4069	36.1	.3836	5	subtly
0.4068	36.1	.4887	4	Only
0.4068	36.1	.3326	5	ornery
0.4068	36.1	.4890	4	presumed
0.4068	36.1	.4890	4	putter
0.4067	36.1	.4803	4	intervened
0.4067	36.1	.3752	5	kneaded
0.4067	36.1	.3752	5	retreating
0.4067	36.1	.3752	5	wondrously
0.4067	36.1	.4800	4	1745
0.4066	36.1	.4800	4	outgrow
0.4065	36.1	.3072	6	accelerating
0.4065	36.1	.2444	7	fellers
0.4065	36.1	.2444	7	Maud
0.4065	36.1	.3640	5	palmetto
0.4064	36.1	.4814	4	broad-brimmed
0.4064	36.1	.4814	4	chinked
0.4064	36.1	.3683	5	Meade
0.4064	36.1	.4866	4	obscurity
0.4064	36.1	.4866	4	stubbed
0.4063	36.1	.3554	5	Climate
0.4063	36.1	.3554	5	conserved
0.4063	36.1	.4756	4	eggplant
0.4063	36.1	.4756	4	envelop
0.4063	36.1	.4810	4	nip
0.4063	36.1	.4756	4	nomenclature
0.4063	36.1	.2446	7	radii
0.4063	36.1	.4758	4	roosted
0.4063	36.1	.4500	4	sycamore
0.4063	36.1	.2446	7	3-inch
0.4062	36.1	.3069	5	corduroy
0.4062	36.1	.4799	4	purge
0.4062	36.1	.4799	4	regaining
0.4061	36.1	.3664	5	sinner
0.4060	36.1	.2446	7	estimation
0.4060	36.1	.3668	5	Fountain
0.4060	36.1	.4810	4	Geography
0.4059	36.1	.1464	9	HOW
0.4059	36.1	.3253	5	ignited
0.4059	36.1	.1464	9	molts
0.4059	36.1	.1464	9	stratus
0.4058	36.1	.3750	5	drapery
0.4058	36.1	.3105	6	superhighways
0.4057	36.1	.3278	5	Colo
0.4057	36.1	.4794	4	colonized
0.4057	36.1	.3756	5	Dolphins
0.4057	36.1	.3278	5	southerly
0.4057	36.1	.4751	4	undreamed
0.4056	36.1	.4808	4	infantrymen
0.4056	36.1	.3737	5	steerage
0.4056	36.1	.4808	4	Travel
0.4056	36.1	.4791	4	311
0.4055	36.1	.1804	8	barometers
0.4055	36.1	.2315	8	2-3
0.4054	36.1	.4804	4	animal-like
0.4053	36.1	.4791	4	bidder
0.4053	36.1	.4791	4	deceit

THE PRECEDING WORD TYPE OCCUPIES RANK 24900

U	SFI	D	F	Word Type
0.4053	36.1	.4791	4	Macon
0.4053	36.1	.0797	12	Thunder
0.4052	36.1	.4804	4	aspirations
0.4052	36.1	.4803	4	dab
0.4052	36.1	.4788	4	dispelled
0.4052	36.1	.4804	4	majoring
0.4052	36.1	.4804	4	relying
0.4052	36.1	.4804	4	uprooted
0.4050	36.1	.1813	8	Belem
0.4050	36.1	.4800	4	caviar
0.4050	36.1	.4484	4	charting
0.4050	36.1	.1813	8	city-state
0.4050	36.1	.1813	8	fur-trading
0.4050	36.1	.4800	4	platypus
0.4050	36.1	.4484	4	profitably
0.4050	36.1	.4484	4	unceasing
0.4050	36.1	.4484	4	2700
0.4049	36.1	.4802	4	denounce
0.4049	36.1	.4802	4	drunkenness
0.4049	36.1	.4802	4	inexperience
0.4049	36.1	.4802	4	lender
0.4049	36.1	.4802	4	loyalties
0.4049	36.1	.4802	4	urgency
0.4048	36.1	.4798	4	deficient
0.4048	36.1	.3355	5	Heavens
0.4048	36.1	.3734	5	Kublai
0.4047	36.1	.4802	4	encamped
0.4047	36.1	.4802	4	incurred
0.4047	36.1	.3724	5	substitution
0.4046	36.1	.4516	4	ablaze
0.4046	36.1	.4516	4	Coolidge
0.4046	36.1	.4516	4	gayest
0.4046	36.1	.2446	7	Ninian
0.4046	36.1	.2446	7	Orestes
0.4046	36.1	.4516	4	overwork
0.4046	36.1	.4516	4	ravages
0.4046	36.1	.4516	4	sinful
0.4046	36.1	.4516	4	stragglers
0.4046	36.1	.4516	4	walkers
0.4045	36.1	.4798	4	heaping
0.4045	36.1	.4514	4	inescapable
0.4045	36.1	.4514	4	paler
0.4045	36.1	.4514	4	wildflowers
0.4045	36.1	.4514	4	wriggle
0.4044	36.1	.4525	4	Blossom
0.4044	36.1	.4525	4	casks
0.4044	36.1	.0541	22	counterpoint
0.4044	36.1	.2601	6	fastener
0.4044	36.1	.4522	4	magnifies
0.4044	36.1	.4525	4	Party's
0.4044	36.1	.4525	4	perfumed
0.4044	36.1	.4522	4	thrusts
0.4044	36.1	.4525	4	trumpeted
0.4044	36.1	.4525	4	venturesome
0.4044	36.1	.4525	4	453
0.4043	36.1	.4738	4	habitually
0.4043	36.1	.3652	5	Ostend
0.4043	36.1	.3705	5	Students
0.4042	36.1	.4546	4	five-foot
0.4041	36.1	.0000	27	a/b
0.4041	36.1	.3706	5	Arbor
0.4041	36.1	.4560	4	Brigadier
0.4041	36.1	.0000	27	GCF
0.4041	36.1	.4560	4	hedgerow
0.4041	36.1	.0000	27	Hindu-Arabic
0.4041	36.1	.4560	4	lapse
0.4041	36.1	.0000	27	multiplicative
0.4041	36.1	.0000	27	ones'
0.4041	36.1	.0000	27	parallelograms
0.4041	36.1	.0000	27	primes
0.4041	36.1	.4560	4	raw-boned
0.4041	36.1	.4560	4	unaccountably
0.4041	36.1	.4560	4	wrest
0.4040	36.1	.4799	4	narrows
0.4040	36.1	.4799	4	slander
0.4039	36.1	.4734	4	lichen
0.4039	36.1	.4734	4	spongelike
0.4039	36.1	.4505	4	502
0.4038	36.1	.4502	4	moth's
0.4038	36.1	.4502	4	291
0.4036	36.1	.3750	5	infamous
0.4036	36.1	.3750	5	innards
0.4036	36.1	.3750	5	secluded
0.4036	36.1	.3175	5	sidled
0.4035	36.1	.4501	4	airless
0.4035	36.1	.4504	4	arduous
0.4035	36.1	.4501	4	Glacier
0.4035	36.1	.3751	5	men-at-arms
0.4035	36.1	.4504	4	minted
0.4035	36.1	.4501	4	movers
0.4035	36.1	.4504	4	onslaught
0.4035	36.1	.4501	4	shipboard
0.4035	36.1	.4501	4	starlings
0.4035	36.1	.4501	4	wobbling
0.4034	36.1	.3639	5	distributing
0.4034	36.1	.3636	5	female's
0.4034	36.1	.3639	5	heartland
0.4034	36.1	.3228	5	ja
0.4034	36.1	.3636	5	leached
0.4034	36.1	.3228	5	menagerie

THE PRECEDING WORD TYPE OCCUPIES RANK 25000

U	SFI	D	F	Word Type
0.4034	36.1	.3636	5	reactive
0.4034	36.1	.3639	5	Serbia
0.4034	36.1	.3639	5	Sitka
0.4034	36.1	.3228	5	snatches
0.4032	36.1	.3487	5	Rutgers
0.4032	36.1	.3487	5	sixty-six
0.4031	36.1	.4865	4	spatter
0.4030	36.1	.3577	5	cousin's
0.4029	36.1	.4857	4	garland
0.4029	36.1	.4857	4	listlessly
0.4029	36.1	.4858	4	Palatine
0.4029	36.1	.0621	15	qu
0.4029	36.1	.4851	4	touchy
0.4028	36.1	.4846	4	assent
0.4028	36.1	.3698	5	cache
0.4028	36.1	.2827	6	clogged
0.4028	36.1	.3747	5	disordered
0.4028	36.1	.4846	4	incentive
0.4028	36.1	.3747	5	sentries
0.4027	36.0	.4845	4	acacia
0.4027	36.1	.4851	4	Twenty
0.4027	36.1	.4852	4	You're

U	SFI	D	F	Word Type
0.4026	36.0	.3732	5	externally
0.4026	36.0	.3732	5	grips
0.4025	36.0	.4543	4	jacks
0.4025	36.0	.4543	4	sordid
0.4025	36.0	.4543	4	wheezed
0.4024	36.0	.4502	4	copilot
0.4024	36.0	.4502	4	Fame
0.4024	36.0	.2204	8	Hymn
0.4024	36.0	.4502	4	refuel
0.4023	36.0	.4499	4	inventiveness
0.4023	36.0	.4499	4	slump
0.4023	36.0	.4499	4	unidentified
0.4022	36.0	.3100	5	erasing
0.4022	36.0	.2687	6	Gentleman
0.4021	36.0	.2606	7	coping
0.4021	36.0	.3015	6	finch
0.4021	36.0	.4535	4	Officers
0.4020	36.0	.4535	4	ambling
0.4020	36.0	.4538	4	backstop
0.4020	36.0	.4538	4	brags
0.4020	36.0	.4538	4	clients
0.4020	36.0	.4538	4	corpses
0.4020	36.0	.4538	4	divinity
0.4020	36.0	.4538	4	hundred-yard
0.4020	36.0	.4538	4	jolting
0.4020	36.0	.4535	4	Linda's
0.4020	36.0	.4538	4	ointment
0.4020	36.0	.4538	4	pall
0.4020	36.0	.4538	4	precarious
0.4020	36.0	.4538	4	quirk
0.4020	36.0	.4538	4	rapid-fire
0.4020	36.0	.4538	4	raven
0.4020	36.0	.4538	4	trooper
0.4020	36.0	.4538	4	wheedled
0.4019	36.0	.3734	5	characteristically
0.4019	36.0	.4812	4	conscientious
0.4019	36.0	.4538	4	exasperated
0.4019	36.0	.4815	4	mourners
0.4019	36.0	.2669	6	riveted
0.4019	36.0	.4538	4	unprepared
0.4019	36.0	.4538	4	witty
0.4018	36.0	.4495	4	brigadier
0.4018	36.0	.4495	4	commended
0.4018	36.0	.4820	4	figuratively
0.4018	36.0	.4495	4	fouled
0.4018	36.0	.4820	4	guaranteeing
0.4018	36.0	.4820	4	jack-o'-lantern
0.4018	36.0	.4814	4	masquerade
0.4018	36.0	.4495	4	provoke
0.4018	36.0	.4814	4	quench
0.4018	36.0	.4495	4	steepest
0.4018	36.0	.2679	6	tendrils
0.4018	36.0	.4495	4	unsympathetic
0.4017	36.0	.4492	4	gushes
0.4017	36.0	.4492	4	ominously
0.4016	36.0	.4819	4	augmented
0.4016	36.0	.1222	11	Deck
0.4016	36.0	.4811	4	juniper
0.4016	36.0	.4494	4	loafing
0.4016	36.0	.4820	4	looted
0.4016	36.0	.4819	4	old-world
0.4016	36.0	.4494	4	tarried
0.4015	36.0	.3541	5	bouncy
0.4015	36.0	.4533	4	brooded
0.4015	36.0	.4491	4	feebly
0.4015	36.0	.4533	4	haggard
0.4015	36.0	.4533	4	plod
0.4015	36.0	.4491	4	remotely
0.4015	36.0	.4491	4	spiders'
0.4015	36.0	.4533	4	sunbonnet
0.4014	36.0	.4530	4	abet
0.4014	36.0	.3687	5	adultery
0.4014	36.0	.3417	5	basements
0.4014	36.0	.4530	4	chamois
0.4014	36.0	.4530	4	daredevil
0.4014	36.0	.4530	4	defile
0.4014	36.0	.3687	5	denomination
0.4014	36.0	.3726	5	payrolls

THE PRECEDING WORD TYPE OCCUPIES RANK 25100

U	SFI	D	F	Word Type
0.4014	36.0	.4530	4	peasantry
0.4014	36.0	.3726	5	Sen
0.4014	36.0	.3687	5	socialist
0.4014	36.0	.4530	4	tassel
0.4014	36.0	.3726	5	Tool
0.4014	36.0	.4530	4	truer
0.4014	36.0	.4530	4	uncanny
0.4014	36.0	.4530	4	uniformed
0.4014	36.0	.3726	5	vernacular
0.4014	36.0	.3687	5	wiener
0.4014	36.0	.4530	4	1844
0.4014	36.0	.3687	5	24th
0.4013	36.0	.4861	4	diminutive
0.4012	36.0	.4777	4	follower
0.4012	36.0	.2310	7	igloo
0.4012	36.0	.3701	5	perturbed
0.4011	36.0	.2616	7	crumb
0.4010	36.0	.4487	4	chinks
0.4010	36.0	.4487	4	shin
0.4009	36.0	.4485	4	Adolph
0.4009	36.0	.4485	4	drafty
0.4009	36.0	.4482	4	duplicating
0.4009	36.0	.4485	4	little-known
0.4009	36.0	.4482	4	mainstay
0.4009	36.0	.4482	4	nightmarish
0.4009	36.0	.4485	4	publicize
0.4009	36.0	.4482	4	roughened
0.4009	36.0	.4485	4	rumored
0.4009	36.0	.4485	4	sever
0.4009	36.0	.4485	4	sheared
0.4009	36.0	.4482	4	shoreward
0.4009	36.0	.4485	4	swapping
0.4009	36.0	.4485	4	ten-minute
0.4009	36.0	.3203	5	vaulted
0.4009	36.0	.4485	4	Victory
0.4008	36.0	.1734	9	vampire
0.4007	36.0	.4538	4	hoisting
0.4007	36.0	.4538	4	naw
0.4007	36.0	.4538	4	next-door
0.4007	36.0	.4538	4	ruckus
0.4007	36.0	.4538	4	Somerset
0.4006	36.0	.4839	4	Clair
0.4006	36.0	.3544	5	gossiping
0.4006	36.0	.3544	5	lamenting
0.4006	36.0	.3529	5	packer
0.4006	36.0	.3835	5	233
0.4005	36.0	.1778	8	Hebrews
0.4005	36.0	.4777	4	Willard
0.4004	36.0	.3707	5	flail
0.4004	36.0	.3707	5	ticklish
0.4003	36.0	.1970	8	cockroach
0.4003	36.0	.4535	4	confidentially
0.4003	36.0	.4535	4	curfew
0.4003	36.0	.4535	4	insatiable
0.4003	36.0	.4535	4	shorn
0.4002	36.0	.4520	4	Address
0.4002	36.0	.4520	4	bribed
0.4002	36.0	.2906	6	Figures
0.4002	36.0	.3585	5	regulars
0.4002	36.0	.4478	4	respite
0.4002	36.0	.4478	4	Shannon
0.4002	36.0	.4520	4	Travels
0.4002	36.0	.4478	4	Tunis
0.4001	36.0	.4475	4	contradicted
0.4001	36.0	.4475	4	herrings
0.4001	36.0	.3767	5	renown
0.4001	36.0	.4475	4	self-contained
0.4000	36.0	.2179	8	adv
0.4000	36.0	.3525	5	sellers
0.3999	36.0	.1217	12	-ate
0.3999	36.0	.3188	5	1300
0.3998	36.0	.4529	4	money-making
0.3998	36.0	.4529	4	mystical
0.3998	36.0	.4529	4	scrutinized
0.3998	36.0	.4529	4	voyaging
0.3997	36.0	.2956	6	Jericho
0.3996	36.0	.4514	4	paintbrushes
0.3993	36.0	.4526	4	appropriation
0.3993	36.0	.4470	4	Catskill
0.3993	36.0	.4526	4	inference
0.3993	36.0	.4526	4	leech
0.3993	36.0	.4526	4	Now
0.3993	36.0	.3699	5	pilings
0.3993	36.0	.4466	4	relieving
0.3993	36.0	.4526	4	snoozing
0.3992	36.0	.4510	4	taketh
0.3991	36.0	.2663	6	feudalism
0.3990	36.0	.2059	8	Belinsky
0.3990	36.0	.4525	4	crooning
0.3990	36.0	.3640	5	flattens
0.3990	36.0	.4525	4	grudgingly
0.3990	36.0	.4525	4	interruptions
0.3990	36.0	.4525	4	marshmallow
0.3990	36.0	.4711	4	participant
0.3990	36.0	.4714	4	powwow
0.3990	36.0	.4525	4	reigning
0.3990	36.0	.4730	4	softest
0.3990	36.0	.4525	4	trifles
0.3989	36.0	.3480	5	extracts
0.3989	36.0	.4801	4	subdue

THE PRECEDING WORD TYPE OCCUPIES RANK 25200

U	SFI	D	F	Word Type
0.3988	36.0	.4522	4	apologized
0.3988	36.0	.4712	4	distinguishable
0.3988	36.0	.4522	4	entrails
0.3988	36.0	.4522	4	handshake
0.3988	36.0	.1726	7	realio
0.3988	36.0	.4739	4	tint
0.3988	36.0	.1726	7	topside
0.3988	36.0	.1726	7	trulio
0.3988	36.0	.4732	4	uncovering
0.3988	36.0	.4712	4	Zachary
0.3987	36.0	.1392	10	Pythagoras
0.3987	36.0	.4736	4	signifies
0.3987	36.0	.4735	4	Wheel
0.3986	36.0	.2655	6	eons
0.3986	36.0	.0000	34	Pod
0.3986	36.0	.2655	6	thermodynamics
0.3986	36.0	.4461	4	trainmen
0.3985	36.0	.4519	4	abandoning
0.3985	36.0	.4519	4	Adventure
0.3985	36.0	.4519	4	caldron
0.3985	36.0	.4458	4	doubly
0.3985	36.0	.4519	4	land's
0.3985	36.0	.4458	4	minuscule
0.3985	36.0	.1325	10	pansy
0.3985	36.0	.4521	4	pikes
0.3985	36.0	.4519	4	plaited
0.3985	36.0	.4519	4	premises
0.3985	36.0	.4519	4	Princes
0.3985	36.0	.4713	4	prosecute
0.3985	36.0	.4734	4	Renoir
0.3985	36.0	.4519	4	rumpled
0.3985	36.0	.4713	4	senator's
0.3985	36.0	.4521	4	spurting
0.3985	36.0	.4521	4	tumbles
0.3984	36.0	.3625	5	annum
0.3984	36.0	.3564	5	arisen
0.3984	36.0	.4742	4	bookkeeping
0.3984	36.0	.3568	5	entrenched
0.3984	36.0	.3568	5	Hernando
0.3984	36.0	.4741	4	restrictive
0.3984	36.0	.3564	5	tumors
0.3984	36.0	.4741	4	vied
0.3984	36.0	.3568	5	1798
0.3983	36.0	.4741	4	Jeremiah
0.3983	36.0	.0758	16	MRS
0.3983	36.0	.4712	4	stink
0.3983	36.0	.4741	4	triumphal
0.3982	36.0	.4518	4	clamored
0.3982	36.0	.4518	4	Himalayan
0.3982	36.0	.4708	4	incalculable
0.3982	36.0	.4518	4	reproached
0.3982	36.0	.4711	4	righteousness
0.3982	36.0	.4518	4	unresponsive
0.3982	36.0	.4518	4	whitecaps
0.3982	36.0	.4518	4	wielded
0.3981	36.0	.4737	4	entities
0.3981	36.0	.4737	4	evoke
0.3981	36.0	.4456	4	hamper
0.3981	36.0	.4456	4	honeycombed
0.3981	36.0	.4737	4	matures
0.3981	36.0	.4456	4	thrones
0.3980	36.0	.4452	4	cleansed
0.3980	36.0	.4452	4	flipper
0.3980	36.0	.2031	6	oblige
0.3980	36.0	.1633	10	3/16
0.3979	36.0	.0570	15	'a'
0.3979	36.0	.1940	9	dramatize
0.3979	36.0	.3254	5	regal
0.3979	36.0	.4707	4	uninterrupted
0.3978	36.0	.3496	5	fella
0.3978	36.0	.3496	5	silhouetted
0.3977	36.0	.2028	6	a-blowing
0.3977	36.0	.2028	6	Billings'
0.3977	36.0	.0000	49	Handwriting
0.3977	36.0	.2028	6	Purim
0.3977	36.0	.2782	6	Troop
0.3977	36.0	.3740	5	wallboard
0.3976	36.0	.2997	6	neutrals
0.3976	36.0	.2228	7	Perces
0.3975	36.0	.2409	7	cashier
0.3975	36.0	.4514	4	farsighted
0.3975	36.0	.2435	7	Serbian
0.3974	36.0	.3681	5	Milton's
0.3974	36.0	.3681	5	Seymour
0.3974	36.0	.3642	5	speculating
0.3973	36.0	.3630	5	des
0.3973	36.0	.4632	4	safeguarded
0.3972	36.0	.2103	7	dairies
0.3971	36.0	.3581	5	inactive
0.3970	36.0	.2657	6	drizzle
0.3968	36.0	.2428	7	comprehensive
0.3968	36.0	.2428	7	Tuolumne
0.3966	36.0	.4641	4	best-liked
0.3966	36.0	.4641	4	hilt
0.3965	36.0	.1951	8	Lavoisier
0.3965	36.0	.3611	5	10th
0.3964	36.0	.1748	6	Mustapha
0.3964	36.0	.3102	5	rages
0.3963	36.0	.3676	5	Bartlett
0.3962	36.0	.3744	5	Cohan

THE PRECEDING WORD TYPE OCCUPIES RANK 25300

U	SFI	D	F	Word Type
0.3962	36.0	.2886	6	Nairobi
0.3962	36.0	.2886	6	Radio
0.3961	36.0	.2215	7	Houdini
0.3961	36.0	.2215	7	protesting
0.3961	36.0	.1377	10	1a
0.3960	36.0	.2625	6	player's
0.3960	36.0	.3430	5	1-9
0.3959	36.0	.3713	5	astounding
0.3959	36.0	.2438	7	Cardinal
0.3959	36.0	.2438	7	major-league
0.3959	36.0	.1872	8	Moravian
0.3959	36.0	.3609	5	Schuylkill
0.3959	36.0	.3095	5	silvery-white
0.3958	36.0	.3544	5	50th
0.3956	36.0	.1892	8	Kipling
0.3956	36.0	.2879	6	pathology
0.3956	36.0	.2879	6	psychiatrist
0.3956	36.0	.2879	6	runoff
0.3956	36.0	.3586	5	taxable
0.3956	36.0	.1892	8	Winkle
0.3954	36.0	.3602	5	Emerson's
0.3954	36.0	.3602	5	marries
0.3953	36.0	.2966	6	affiliated
0.3950	36.0	.4710	4	buttercup
0.3950	36.0	.3542	5	Dulles
0.3949	36.0	.1013	13	Beloved
0.3949	36.0	.2293	7	highs
0.3949	36.0	.1013	13	Woodmont
0.3948	36.0	.3667	5	mountain's
0.3948	36.0	.3667	5	plunger
0.3947	36.0	.2632	6	Mighty
0.3947	36.0	.1930	8	640
0.3946	36.0	.3574	5	Roy's
0.3946	36.0	.3656	5	toenails
0.3943	36.0	.3081	5	Kyoto
0.3942	36.0	.2955	6	O'Neill
0.3942	36.0	.2354	7	Shoals
0.3942	36.0	.2955	6	Toronto
0.3942	36.0	.2955	6	transitions
0.3940	36.0	.2267	7	Ararat
0.3940	36.0	.0649	17	Handbook
0.3939	36.0	.0561	21	skips
0.3938	36.0	.2861	6	Commissioner
0.3938	36.0	.2861	6	Today
0.3937	36.0	.2341	7	$60
0.3937	36.0	.2409	7	dogies
0.3937	36.0	.3206	5	meditating
0.3937	36.0	.2409	7	Passion
0.3937	36.0	.3219	5	seaweeds
0.3936	36.0	.2401	7	Butcher
0.3936	36.0	.2401	7	cooped
0.3935	35.9	.3688	5	oleomargarine
0.3933	35.9	.3220	5	Algiers
0.3933	35.9	.3220	5	Commander-in-Chief
0.3933	35.9	.0886	16	steels
0.3931	35.9	.2011	8	LSD
0.3931	35.9	.2011	8	Pork
0.3929	35.9	.1707	8	elongated
0.3929	35.9	.1707	8	white-tailed
0.3927	35.9	.3601	5	Edna
0.3926	35.9	.3608	5	aptly
0.3926	35.9	.3608	5	Government's
0.3925	35.9	.3562	5	communes
0.3925	35.9	.3562	5	debut
0.3925	35.9	.3652	5	domed
0.3925	35.9	.3562	5	Exhibition
0.3925	35.9	.3562	5	geographically
0.3925	35.9	.3562	5	Monza
0.3924	35.9	.3560	5	Snowball
0.3923	35.9	.1439	11	-al
0.3923	35.9	.4398	4	bun
0.3922	35.9	.4421	4	goatee
0.3922	35.9	.4419	4	mocks
0.3922	35.9	.3455	5	novelties
0.3922	35.9	.4419	4	summons
0.3922	35.9	.4421	4	wicket
0.3921	35.9	.1414	8	upriver
0.3920	35.9	.4447	4	lynx
0.3920	35.9	.4419	4	peepers
0.3919	35.9	.4444	4	horrify
0.3919	35.9	.4447	4	rapier
0.3918	35.9	.4442	4	delighting
0.3918	35.9	.4442	4	lowing
0.3918	35.9	.4442	4	piloting
0.3918	35.9	.4442	4	plumper
0.3918	35.9	.4442	4	swaggering
0.3917	35.9	.4445	4	aught
0.3917	35.9	.4443	4	evade
0.3917	35.9	.4445	4	fitfully
0.3917	35.9	.1905	9	homemakers
0.3917	35.9	.4443	4	informally
0.3917	35.9	.4446	4	mmm
0.3917	35.9	.4445	4	mockingbird
0.3917	35.9	.4445	4	radiance
0.3917	35.9	.3596	5	sacking
0.3917	35.9	.4445	4	speedily
0.3917	35.9	.4450	4	visitors'
0.3917	35.9	.4445	4	waltzing
0.3916	35.9	.4441	4	Marguerite
0.3916	35.9	.4445	4	phones

THE PRECEDING WORD TYPE OCCUPIES RANK 25400

U	SFI	D	F	Word Type
0.3916	35.9	.3054	5	1519
0.3915	35.9	.4448	4	Cossack
0.3915	35.9	.4450	4	discus
0.3915	35.9	.4448	4	gayer
0.3915	35.9	.3592	5	groundwork
0.3915	35.9	.4448	4	jovial
0.3915	35.9	.4418	4	Those
0.3915	35.9	.1927	8	wrinkle
0.3914	35.9	.4450	4	banish
0.3914	35.9	.4448	4	Broadcasting
0.3914	35.9	.4448	4	Memory
0.3914	35.9	.4448	4	plundering
0.3913	35.9	.4417	4	fifes
0.3913	35.9	.4417	4	instruct
0.3913	35.9	.4417	4	rowdy
0.3912	35.9	.2191	7	travellers
0.3910	35.9	.4415	4	ensign
0.3910	35.9	.4415	4	misunderstandings
0.3908	35.9	.4408	4	reverses
0.3908	35.9	.4338	4	slosh
0.3907	35.9	.2167	7	'n'
0.3907	35.9	.4339	4	many's
0.3907	35.9	.2425	7	psi
0.3907	35.9	.4335	4	1732
0.3906	35.9	.3599	5	McGregor
0.3906	35.9	.4335	4	night-time
0.3905	35.9	.1430	9	standpipe
0.3904	35.9	.3075	5	bullies
0.3904	35.9	.2916	6	persists
0.3903	35.9	.1112	12	seahorse
0.3902	35.9	.4350	4	landslide
0.3902	35.9	.4350	4	legislator
0.3902	35.9	.4350	4	pastor
0.3900	35.9	.2444	7	ary
0.3900	35.9	.4348	4	low-pressure
0.3900	35.9	.4348	4	reverently
0.3899	35.9	.3607	5	adored
0.3899	35.9	.4344	4	hugs
0.3899	35.9	.4344	4	sandwiched
0.3897	35.9	.4347	4	abalone
0.3897	35.9	.3542	5	differentiate
0.3897	35.9	.3592	5	disciple
0.3897	35.9	.3041	6	Rousseau
0.3896	35.9	.2177	7	madder
0.3895	35.9	.2604	7	quadruple
0.3895	35.9	.3520	5	splotches
0.3894	35.9	.2471	6	Bee
0.3894	35.9	.3489	5	Friendly
0.3894	35.9	.3497	5	piggy
0.3894	35.9	.3638	5	Serge
0.3894	35.9	.3489	5	271
0.3892	35.9	.0000	26	PQ
0.3892	35.9	.0000	26	3/6
0.3891	35.9	.3157	5	accelerator
0.3891	35.9	.3157	5	copperheads
0.3891	35.9	.3426	5	decays
0.3891	35.9	.3157	5	illuminating
0.3891	35.9	.3157	5	Magnesia
0.3891	35.9	.2361	7	rarefied
0.3891	35.9	.1556	12	textured
0.3891	35.9	.3426	5	thick-walled
0.3890	35.9	.4343	4	cavalrymen
0.3889	35.9	.2569	6	catchers
0.3888	35.9	.3152	5	asteroid
0.3888	35.9	.3152	5	Judith
0.3888	35.9	.0814	15	Madge
0.3888	35.9	.1325	8	patio
0.3888	35.9	.3490	5	stalactites
0.3888	35.9	.2885	6	Tech
0.3887	35.9	.4339	4	babies'
0.3887	35.9	.3423	5	Blanc
0.3887	35.9	.4341	4	caved
0.3887	35.9	.4341	4	Pike's
0.3887	35.9	.4341	4	pilgrim
0.3887	35.9	.1188	12	Tyrol
0.3885	35.9	.3628	5	impudent
0.3885	35.9	.4340	4	journeying
0.3885	35.9	.1550	9	Rosebud
0.3884	35.9	.2484	7	borrowings
0.3884	35.9	.4338	4	devoting
0.3884	35.9	.3468	5	enlarges
0.3884	35.9	.4338	4	Grover
0.3884	35.9	.4336	4	hurl
0.3884	35.9	.4336	4	interlocking
0.3883	35.9	.3586	5	unconventional
0.3882	35.9	.2822	6	providence

U	SFI	D	F	Word Type
0.3879	35.9	.2446	7	a'
0.3879	35.9	.4411	4	unearthly
0.3879	35.9	.4411	4	wid
0.3879	35.9	.2095	8	7-11
0.3878	35.9	.3132	5	sprinkler
0.3877	35.9	.2868	6	entity
0.3877	35.9	.1351	10	McCardell
0.3877	35.9	.3148	5	Niger
0.3875	35.9	.2445	5	Alfonso
0.3875	35.9	.2445	5	Alma
0.3875	35.9	.2445	5	amigo
0.3875	35.9	.2446	7	illustrator
0.3875	35.9	.2445	5	loudmouth
0.3875	35.9	.2445	5	McGee
THE PRECEDING WORD TYPE OCCUPIES RANK 25500				
0.3875	35.9	.2445	5	nix
0.3875	35.9	.2445	5	stave
0.3875	35.9	.2445	5	sulking
0.3875	35.9	.2446	7	toves
0.3875	35.9	.2445	5	unbelievingly
0.3874	35.9	.2422	5	busier
0.3874	35.9	.2422	5	fearsome
0.3874	35.9	.2422	5	fine-looking
0.3874	35.9	.2422	5	footman
0.3874	35.9	.2422	5	home-run
0.3874	35.9	.2422	5	irritably
0.3874	35.9	.2422	5	Ned's
0.3874	35.9	.2422	5	oarsman
0.3874	35.9	.2422	5	red-brick
0.3874	35.9	.2422	5	spellbound
0.3874	35.9	.2422	5	trotter
0.3874	35.9	.2422	5	Zeke's
0.3873	35.9	.2210	7	financing
0.3873	35.9	.2093	8	freedom's
0.3873	35.9	.2210	7	Kremlin
0.3873	35.9	.2210	7	leased
0.3872	35.9	.3122	5	caustic
0.3872	35.9	.2446	5	deary
0.3872	35.9	.2446	5	Drummond
0.3872	35.9	.2446	5	fishbone
0.3872	35.9	.2414	5	Ginny
0.3872	35.9	.2446	5	Jake's
0.3872	35.9	.2446	5	jostled
0.3872	35.9	.2446	5	juggler
0.3872	35.9	.2446	5	kinks
0.3872	35.9	.2446	5	nosed
0.3872	35.9	.3122	5	on-the-spot
0.3872	35.9	.3106	5	pillowcase
0.3872	35.9	.2414	5	Rich
0.3872	35.9	.2446	5	scuff
0.3872	35.9	.2446	5	shhh
0.3872	35.9	.2446	5	whirr
0.3872	35.9	.2414	5	WXY
0.3872	35.9	.2414	5	559
0.3871	35.9	.2861	6	Mont
0.3871	35.9	.3472	5	1810
0.3869	35.9	.2202	7	cosmonauts
0.3869	35.9	.0796	13	DC
0.3868	35.9	.3577	5	At
0.3868	35.9	.3577	5	Monitor
0.3868	35.9	.3577	5	mover
0.3867	35.9	.3459	5	calculators
0.3867	35.9	.3684	5	undue
0.3866	35.9	.2446	5	cowhand
0.3866	35.9	.3474	5	Forum
0.3866	35.9	.2446	5	goodness'
0.3866	35.9	.1134	11	mechanisms
0.3866	35.9	.3474	5	Missile
0.3866	35.9	.3474	5	Orinoco
0.3866	35.9	.3623	5	Pieces
0.3866	35.9	.2446	5	sonnets
0.3866	35.9	.3465	5	supplements
0.3866	35.9	.2446	5	terrorized
0.3866	35.9	.2446	5	Twenty-third
0.3864	35.9	.2445	5	artichokes
0.3864	35.9	.2445	5	big-league
0.3864	35.9	.2445	5	blockhouse
0.3864	35.9	.2445	5	catwalk
0.3864	35.9	.2445	5	centaurs
0.3864	35.9	.2445	5	eagles'
0.3864	35.9	.2445	5	hobble
0.3864	35.9	.2445	5	mumbles
0.3864	35.9	.2445	5	Pig's
0.3864	35.9	.2445	5	queerest
0.3864	35.9	.2445	5	Rikki-tikki-tavi
0.3864	35.9	.2445	5	senor
0.3864	35.9	.2445	5	singin'
0.3864	35.9	.2445	5	slumbered
0.3864	35.9	.2445	5	steel-driving
0.3864	35.9	.2445	5	Sunset
0.3864	35.9	.2445	5	swooping
0.3864	35.9	.2445	5	unicorn
0.3864	35.9	.2445	5	whitewashing
0.3864	35.9	.2445	5	Witch
0.3863	35.9	.1918	8	announcements
0.3863	35.9	.3306	5	butterfly's
0.3863	35.9	.3121	5	gruel
0.3863	35.9	.0000	36	MOTHER
0.3863	35.9	.1918	8	Wichita
0.3861	35.9	.2443	5	coax
0.3861	35.9	.2443	5	gadfly
0.3861	35.9	.3467	5	high-altitude
0.3861	35.9	.2443	5	Leto
0.3861	35.9	.2443	5	Odense
0.3861	35.9	.2443	5	portals
0.3861	35.9	.2443	5	renter
0.3861	35.9	.2443	5	Rhoda
0.3861	35.9	.2443	5	twenty-four-hour
0.3860	35.9	.3567	5	presto
0.3859	35.9	.2634	6	Ladder
0.3857	35.9	.3585	5	And
0.3857	35.9	.3111	5	easternmost
0.3857	35.9	.3111	5	surfboard
0.3857	35.9	.3111	5	trolling
0.3854	35.9	.3558	5	Nation's
THE PRECEDING WORD TYPE OCCUPIES RANK 25600				
0.3852	35.9	.3387	5	creations
0.3852	35.9	.1449	10	NBC
0.3851	35.9	.3087	5	maiden's
0.3850	35.9	.2364	7	museum's
0.3849	35.9	.2845	6	fickle
0.3848	35.9	.3082	5	gayly
0.3848	35.9	.3540	5	Grizzly
0.3848	35.9	.0231	22	Sassy
0.3848	35.9	.1637	10	servings
0.3845	35.8	.3574	5	bodyguard
0.3844	35.8	.1543	11	imitations
0.3841	35.8	.3869	4	peaked
0.3841	35.8	.3869	4	sandstorm
0.3841	35.8	.3869	4	syrupy
0.3837	35.8	.2326	5	Alvarez
0.3837	35.8	.2326	5	Augustus'
0.3837	35.8	.2326	5	Fulton's
0.3837	35.8	.2326	5	Lin
0.3837	35.8	.2326	5	McLeod
0.3837	35.8	.2326	5	Togo
0.3837	35.8	.2326	5	Wrights
0.3836	35.8	.3551	5	Performing
0.3834	35.8	.2320	5	hydrant
0.3834	35.8	.2320	5	nested
0.3834	35.8	.2320	5	partisan
0.3834	35.8	.2320	5	queer-looking
0.3834	35.8	.2320	5	searchlight
0.3832	35.8	.2824	5	Rosemary
0.3832	35.8	.2824	5	vagabond
0.3831	35.8	.3472	5	tremulous
0.3830	35.8	.1526	9	chariots
0.3830	35.8	.3468	5	legality
0.3830	35.8	.3468	5	ousted
0.3830	35.8	.3468	5	outbreaks
0.3830	35.8	.3468	5	perennial
0.3830	35.8	.2301	7	Text
0.3830	35.8	.3468	5	unanimously
0.3830	35.8	.3468	5	Zoological
0.3829	35.8	.1298	10	$17
0.3829	35.8	.2181	7	Tatum
0.3828	35.8	.3541	5	grandmothers
0.3828	35.8	.2781	6	interferes
0.3828	35.8	.3049	5	predicting
0.3828	35.8	.3541	5	Shadrach
0.3827	35.8	.3442	5	amplify
0.3826	35.8	.0705	13	trolls
0.3825	35.8	.3461	5	activated
0.3825	35.8	.3048	5	attire
0.3825	35.8	.3461	5	consequent
0.3825	35.8	.3461	5	Mo
0.3825	35.8	.3461	5	verified
0.3823	35.8	.2760	6	Examiner
0.3822	35.8	.2217	6	sugared
0.3820	35.8	.3415	5	Callahan
0.3820	35.8	.1600	6	Fernand
0.3820	35.8	.1600	6	Jar
0.3817	35.8	.2441	7	flavoring
0.3817	35.8	.1643	10	stripping
0.3816	35.8	.3117	5	ballooning
0.3815	35.8	.0567	12	bathyscaphe
0.3814	35.8	.3120	5	Democrat
0.3814	35.8	.2104	7	Harmon
0.3812	35.8	.3036	5	Giza
0.3809	35.8	.3221	5	Apprentice
0.3809	35.8	.3325	5	mercilessly
0.3808	35.8	.3026	5	Lullaby
0.3808	35.8	.1233	9	sacrifices
0.3808	35.8	.3371	5	square-shaped
0.3808	35.8	.3371	5	257
0.3808	35.8	.3371	5	496
0.3807	35.8	.3167	5	guesswork
0.3806	35.8	.0807	14	coolant
0.3806	35.8	.2220	7	Machiavelli
0.3806	35.8	.2220	7	Prix
0.3806	35.8	.3442	5	scarfs
0.3805	35.8	.2396	5	aileron
0.3805	35.8	.2419	7	choreographer
0.3805	35.8	.2881	6	packaging
0.3805	35.8	.2396	5	Winnie-the-Pooh
0.3804	35.8	.2395	5	beeps
0.3804	35.8	.2395	5	Brighty
0.3804	35.8	.2989	6	elektron
0.3804	35.8	.2395	5	Redcoats
0.3804	35.8	.2395	5	Spirits
0.3803	35.8	.2526	7	lighten
0.3800	35.8	.0000	47	pentatonic
0.3792	35.8	.3447	5	cramps
0.3790	35.8	.3475	5	nostalgic
0.3790	35.8	.3475	5	outposts
0.3790	35.8	.2795	6	Perspective
0.3786	35.8	.1972	6	Ken's
0.3783	35.8	.3822	4	242
0.3782	35.8	.2697	6	concession
0.3780	35.8	.3331	5	318
0.3779	35.8	.0565	20	alphabetize
0.3779	35.8	.1967	8	13-17
0.3777	35.8	.2373	7	Vera
0.3775	35.8	.0562	12	Allens
0.3774	35.8	.2451	7	riser
0.3774	35.8	.2258	7	self-sustaining
THE PRECEDING WORD TYPE OCCUPIES RANK 25700				
0.3774	35.8	.2258	7	successors
0.3773	35.8	.3343	5	Dorado
0.3773	35.8	.3812	4	droops
0.3773	35.8	.3812	4	inhaling
0.3773	35.8	.3343	5	Queensland
0.3773	35.8	.3812	4	slowpoke
0.3773	35.8	.3812	4	sunbeams
0.3773	35.8	.3343	5	Tyrant
0.3772	35.8	.3813	4	belching
0.3772	35.8	.3813	4	lifeboats
0.3772	35.8	.3813	4	Overland
0.3772	35.8	.3813	4	ripens
0.3772	35.8	.3813	4	Scarlet
0.3772	35.8	.1071	12	Sham's
0.3772	35.8	.3813	4	twenty-foot
0.3772	35.8	.3813	4	waken
0.3772	35.8	.3813	4	widowed
0.3771	35.8	.3497	5	notify
0.3770	35.8	.3367	5	1614
0.3770	35.8	.3317	5	5700
0.3769	35.8	.2748	6	Carlyle
0.3767	35.8	.3334	5	deities
0.3767	35.8	.3493	5	evidenced
0.3766	35.8	.3359	5	AIR
0.3766	35.8	.0781	15	Latvia
0.3766	35.8	.1807	8	2a
0.3764	35.8	.3141	5	hardheaded
0.3764	35.8	.3141	5	Platt
0.3763	35.8	.1502	9	denoted
0.3758	35.7	.1272	11	Rollo
0.3756	35.7	.0000	35	ATTUCKS
0.3756	35.7	.1515	9	grit
0.3756	35.7	.0000	35	HELENA
0.3756	35.7	.3428	5	insiders
0.3754	35.7	.2926	5	bicarbonate
0.3754	35.7	.1131	14	expenditures
0.3754	35.7	.3444	5	good-tempered
0.3754	35.7	.2926	5	loosens
0.3752	35.7	.3507	5	deftly
0.3752	35.7	.0000	32	Fang
0.3752	35.7	.0000	32	Mi
0.3752	35.7	.3034	6	shrinkage
0.3751	35.7	.2133	7	palindrome
0.3750	35.7	.1948	6	Jam
0.3750	35.7	.1948	6	lookouts
0.3750	35.7	.0365	16	tally
0.3750	35.7	.1948	6	throttles
0.3747	35.7	.1241	9	Tycho
0.3746	35.7	.2022	7	Fuller
0.3746	35.7	.3126	5	highroad
0.3746	35.7	.0000	19	litmus
0.3746	35.7	.1588	7	prone
0.3746	35.7	.3126	5	Ralph's
0.3746	35.7	.3126	5	red-gold
0.3746	35.7	.2022	7	ultimatum
0.3746	35.7	.3126	5	uproariously
0.3745	35.7	.1273	10	Muskrat
0.3744	35.7	.1854	8	Department's
0.3743	35.7	.3810	4	four-hour
0.3742	35.7	.0000	25	one-to-one
0.3742	35.7	.3234	5	penciled
0.3742	35.7	.0000	25	4/5
0.3739	35.7	.2083	7	Mothers
0.3735	35.7	.1843	9	inked
0.3735	35.7	.2284	6	partake
0.3734	35.7	.2280	6	decode
0.3733	35.7	.3286	5	Charlottesville
0.3733	35.7	.1985	7	hack
0.3733	35.7	.1236	10	pact
0.3732	35.7	.2298	7	calibrated
0.3732	35.7	.2904	5	steep-sided
0.3732	35.7	.2904	5	Toulouse
0.3732	35.7	.2134	7	Tuskegee
0.3732	35.7	.2134	7	victors
0.3731	35.7	.2941	6	manufacturer's
0.3729	35.7	.0728	15	Vocabulary
0.3727	35.7	.0606	19	Liszt
0.3724	35.7	.2655	6	Hurons
0.3721	35.7	.1558	8	Buddha
0.3721	35.7	.1558	8	DeSoto
0.3721	35.7	.1558	8	SouthCarolina's
0.3719	35.7	.1542	8	densities
0.3719	35.7	.3472	5	unreal
0.3718	35.7	.2870	6	supple
0.3718	35.7	.2962	5	USA
0.3718	35.7	.1629	8	Wing
0.3717	35.7	.3428	5	prep
0.3714	35.7	.3094	5	Phil's
0.3714	35.7	.1828	8	VW
0.3712	35.7	.2480	6	Associated
0.3712	35.7	.3743	4	beefsteak
0.3712	35.7	.3743	4	disunity
0.3712	35.7	.3741	4	drugstores
0.3712	35.7	.3743	4	fire-breathing
0.3712	35.7	.3743	4	gauchos
0.3712	35.7	.3743	4	Georgia's
0.3712	35.7	.2480	6	H**
0.3712	35.7	.3431	5	jocund
0.3712	35.7	.3743	4	loose-fitting
0.3712	35.7	.3741	4	mater
THE PRECEDING WORD TYPE OCCUPIES RANK 25800				
0.3712	35.7	.3743	4	Pictures
0.3712	35.7	.3741	4	pinnacle
0.3712	35.7	.3743	4	sight-seeing
0.3712	35.7	.3743	4	sloops
0.3712	35.7	.3741	4	woodchuck's
0.3711	35.7	.2655	5	bedraggled
0.3711	35.7	.1178	11	Interstate
0.3711	35.7	.1178	11	Olga
0.3711	35.7	.2620	5	storybooks
0.3710	35.7	.2070	7	Bastille
0.3708	35.7	.1501	9	Burmese
0.3708	35.7	.1501	9	Saigon
0.3707	35.7	.1941	7	fallout
0.3707	35.7	.1941	7	moraines
0.3707	35.7	.1941	7	pellagra
0.3707	35.7	.1941	7	projectors
0.3707	35.7	.1941	7	proton
0.3707	35.7	.1941	7	undigested
0.3707	35.7	.1941	7	wavelets
0.3705	35.7	.0643	13	Polynesia
0.3703	35.7	.3377	5	absently
0.3703	35.7	.2118	7	Argentines
0.3703	35.7	.3377	5	Baboon
0.3703	35.7	.3377	5	Collie
0.3703	35.7	.3377	5	piney
0.3702	35.7	.2643	5	disheveled
0.3700	35.7	.3016	5	estancia
0.3700	35.7	.3016	5	fast-growing
0.3700	35.7	.3011	5	likelihood
0.3700	35.7	.3011	5	myriads
0.3700	35.7	.3016	5	riverbanks
0.3699	35.7	.3767	4	$2000
0.3699	35.7	.3110	5	Eleven
0.3699	35.7	.1560	7	Labadie
0.3699	35.7	.1560	7	ork
0.3699	35.7	.3767	4	Tyler
0.3698	35.7	.3087	5	Raroia
0.3698	35.7	.3087	5	ravenous
0.3697	35.7	.3726	4	bookshelves
0.3697	35.7	.3726	4	chipping
0.3697	35.7	.3726	4	hacked
0.3697	35.7	.3726	4	handsomer
0.3697	35.7	.3726	4	headfirst
0.3697	35.7	.3726	4	sham
0.3697	35.7	.3726	4	slumbering
0.3696	35.7	.3766	4	beleaguered
0.3696	35.7	.3766	4	Brothers'
0.3696	35.7	.3766	4	coloured
0.3696	35.7	.3766	4	customer's
0.3696	35.7	.3766	4	eight-inch
0.3696	35.7	.3766	4	Ferguson
0.3696	35.7	.2673	6	gambling
0.3696	35.7	.3766	4	helter-skelter
0.3696	35.7	.2464	6	Missus
0.3696	35.7	.3766	4	overheated
0.3696	35.7	.3766	4	players'
0.3696	35.7	.3766	4	professor's
0.3695	35.7	.0409	23	alto
0.3695	35.7	.0853	12	5-cent
0.3693	35.7	.2320	7	Caruso
0.3693	35.7	.2320	7	tuner
0.3692	35.7	.3454	5	Geoffrey
0.3691	35.7	.2745	6	percentages
0.3690	35.7	.2515	6	OUT
0.3690	35.7	.2515	6	woo
0.3689	35.7	.2789	6	Camille
0.3689	35.7	.3755	4	empress
0.3687	35.7	.3336	5	contemplating
0.3687	35.7	.2513	6	kinder
0.3687	35.7	.3336	5	repression
0.3686	35.7	.3755	4	bandaged
0.3686	35.7	.3755	4	blindman's
0.3686	35.7	.3755	4	briers
0.3686	35.7	.3755	4	buts
0.3686	35.7	.3755	4	coachman
0.3686	35.7	.3755	4	gruffly
0.3686	35.7	.3755	4	humped
0.3686	35.7	.3755	4	magnolia
0.3686	35.7	.3755	4	misfortunes
0.3686	35.7	.3755	4	nobler
0.3686	35.7	.1922	7	overhauled
0.3686	35.7	.3755	4	passersby
0.3686	35.7	.1151	12	polyphonic
0.3686	35.7	.3755	4	Smiths'
0.3686	35.7	.3755	4	stableboys
0.3685	35.7	.2451	6	needlessly
0.3685	35.7	.2451	6	Volkswagen
0.3683	35.7	.3075	5	browsed
0.3683	35.7	.3307	5	stamina
0.3682	35.7	.3341	5	Chevalier
0.3682	35.7	.1931	7	India's
0.3682	35.7	.1931	7	quarries
0.3682	35.7	.1931	7	Stanley's
0.3681	35.7	.1984	7	Penguins
0.3679	35.7	.3325	5	bub
0.3676	35.7	.2302	6	pickets
0.3675	35.7	.2304	7	interlude
0.3675	35.7	.3351	5	1476
0.3674	35.7	.3392	5	confronts
0.3673	35.7	.2601	5	VanWinkle
THE PRECEDING WORD TYPE OCCUPIES RANK 25900				
0.3672	35.6	.3317	5	mediocre
0.3672	35.6	.3317	5	O'Toole
0.3671	35.6	.2365	5	Loch
0.3671	35.6	.2365	5	microns
0.3671	35.6	.2365	5	rarer
0.3670	35.6	.2205	7	assaults
0.3670	35.6	.2205	7	corporate
0.3670	35.6	.1907	7	digests
0.3670	35.6	.2205	7	setup
0.3670	35.6	.2205	7	torsion
0.3668	35.6	.3688	4	bazaar
0.3668	35.6	.3688	4	crossroad
0.3668	35.6	.2301	7	e/
0.3668	35.6	.3688	4	ewe
0.3668	35.6	.2301	7	vis
0.3667	35.6	.3685	4	toad's
0.3665	35.6	.3114	5	Antoinette
0.3665	35.6	.2299	7	Emmett
0.3664	35.6	.3159	5	bleaching
0.3664	35.6	.3729	4	bluejay
0.3664	35.6	.3729	4	nice-looking
0.3664	35.6	.3085	5	ramshackle
0.3664	35.6	.3729	4	Stories
0.3663	35.6	.2360	5	Feather
0.3663	35.6	.2360	5	Pest
0.3663	35.6	.2360	5	Rica
0.3663	35.6	.2360	5	shipyard
0.3662	35.6	.3087	5	spelt
0.3661	35.6	.3740	4	cudgel
0.3661	35.6	.3740	4	Daddy's
0.3661	35.6	.3740	4	Fatty
0.3661	35.6	.3740	4	gritted
0.3661	35.6	.3740	4	Listen
0.3661	35.6	.3740	4	lunging
0.3661	35.6	.3740	4	piebald
0.3661	35.6	.3740	4	primly
0.3661	35.6	.3740	4	stealthily
0.3661	35.6	.3740	4	valedictorian
0.3660	35.6	.1912	7	Coppermine
0.3659	35.6	.3677	4	accusing
0.3659	35.6	.3677	4	battalion
0.3659	35.6	.3677	4	Coming
0.3659	35.6	.3677	4	denouncing
0.3659	35.6	.3719	4	dialing
0.3659	35.6	.3207	5	liberating
0.3659	35.6	.2443	6	loafers
0.3659	35.6	.3677	4	logger
0.3659	35.6	.3441	5	Monet
0.3659	35.6	.3677	4	newfangled

U	SFI	D	F	Word Type
0.3659	35.6	.3677	4	Primer
0.3659	35.6	.3677	4	vaqueros
0.3659	35.6	.3677	4	Westerners
0.3658	35.6	.2579	5	mooing
0.3658	35.6	.3673	4	thereabouts
0.3658	35.6	.2579	5	tumultuous
0.3657	35.6	.3721	4	cobbler's
0.3657	35.6	.3721	4	gangway
0.3657	35.6	.3721	4	h'm
0.3657	35.6	.3721	4	half-starved
0.3657	35.6	.3721	4	lurching
0.3657	35.6	.1457	9	Macbeth
0.3657	35.6	.3721	4	NOW
0.3657	35.6	.3721	4	reverend
0.3657	35.6	.3721	4	skid
0.3657	35.6	.3721	4	startle
0.3657	35.6	.3721	4	therein
0.3655	35.6	.0000	8	Abbie
0.3655	35.6	.0000	8	Agony
0.3655	35.6	.0000	8	Ama
0.3655	35.6	.0000	8	Arturo
0.3655	35.6	.0000	8	Atti
0.3655	35.6	.0000	8	Barby
0.3655	35.6	.0000	8	Biddie
0.3655	35.6	.0000	8	Brimmer
0.3655	35.6	.0000	8	Busch
0.3655	35.6	.0000	8	Chand
0.3655	35.6	.0000	8	Cliff's
0.3655	35.6	.0000	8	Crawling
0.3655	35.6	.0000	8	Darzee
0.3655	35.6	.0000	8	Driscoll
0.3655	35.6	.0000	8	forklift
0.3655	35.6	.0000	8	Geese
0.3655	35.6	.0000	8	Glorianna
0.3655	35.6	.0000	8	glyph
0.3655	35.6	.0000	8	Greenwood
0.3655	35.6	.0000	8	Gunde
0.3655	35.6	.0000	8	Hiram's
0.3655	35.6	.0000	8	Hofus
0.3655	35.6	.0000	8	Honkebeest
0.3655	35.6	.0000	8	Hylas
0.3655	35.6	.0000	8	Irby
0.3655	35.6	.0000	8	Joaby
0.3655	35.6	.0000	8	Josephine
0.3655	35.6	.0000	8	Joss
0.3655	35.6	.0000	8	Juliska
0.3655	35.6	.0000	8	Ket
0.3655	35.6	.0000	8	Krolugta
0.3655	35.6	.0000	8	Kruesi
0.3655	35.6	.0000	8	Laika
0.3655	35.6	.0000	8	Leona

THE PRECEDING WORD TYPE OCCUPIES RANK 26000

U	SFI	D	F	Word Type
0.3655	35.6	.0000	8	Lucio
0.3655	35.6	.0000	8	Maile
0.3655	35.6	.0000	8	Manuela
0.3655	35.6	.0000	8	Mikey
0.3655	35.6	.0000	8	Nicola's
0.3655	35.6	.0000	8	Peindo
0.3655	35.6	.0000	8	previewing
0.3655	35.6	.0000	8	Princess's
0.3655	35.6	.0000	8	Prissy
0.3655	35.6	.0000	8	Rossi
0.3655	35.6	.0000	8	Sancho
0.3655	35.6	.0000	8	Santy
0.3655	35.6	.0000	8	Sherm
0.3655	35.6	.0000	8	Sjaantje
0.3655	35.6	.0000	8	Ski
0.3655	35.6	.0000	8	Southpaw
0.3655	35.6	.0000	8	spink
0.3655	35.6	.0000	8	Sweetree
0.3655	35.6	.0000	8	Thomis
0.3655	35.6	.0000	8	Track
0.3655	35.6	.0000	8	Trixie
0.3655	35.6	.0000	8	Tuckers
0.3655	35.6	.0000	8	unafraid
0.3655	35.6	.0000	8	Varya
0.3655	35.6	.0000	8	Wanda
0.3655	35.6	.0000	8	Weeks
0.3655	35.6	.0000	8	white-lipped
0.3655	35.6	.0000	8	Withers
0.3655	35.6	.0000	8	Yancy
0.3654	35.6	.3081	5	gable
0.3654	35.6	.3343	5	patterning
0.3654	35.6	.3081	5	shouldering
0.3653	35.6	.3077	5	savagery
0.3652	35.6	.0000	45	Hints
0.3652	35.6	.1147	11	Lance
0.3650	35.6	.3708	4	footballs
0.3650	35.6	.3088	5	repairman
0.3650	35.6	.3275	5	reworked
0.3650	35.6	.3708	4	415
0.3649	35.6	.3285	5	All-American
0.3649	35.6	.3274	5	evaluated
0.3648	35.6	.3711	4	forethought
0.3648	35.6	.3711	4	good-humored
0.3648	35.6	.1475	7	Laurel
0.3648	35.6	.3711	4	shrew
0.3648	35.6	.3711	4	swifter
0.3648	35.6	.3711	4	time-consuming
0.3648	35.6	.3711	4	uninhibited
0.3648	35.6	.3711	4	uprooting
0.3648	35.6	.3711	4	workingmen
0.3647	35.6	.3662	4	buttress
0.3647	35.6	.3662	4	Harding
0.3647	35.6	.3662	4	jenny
0.3647	35.6	.3662	4	lurch
0.3647	35.6	.3662	4	sheathing
0.3646	35.6	.3658	4	handlers
0.3646	35.6	.3658	4	quarantine
0.3646	35.6	.3658	4	refracted
0.3645	35.6	.3723	4	dues
0.3645	35.6	.3723	4	Finn's
0.3645	35.6	.3723	4	frothy
0.3645	35.6	.3723	4	Gail
0.3645	35.6	.3723	4	liveliness
0.3645	35.6	.2811	5	one-hand
0.3645	35.6	.3723	4	rebounded
0.3645	35.6	.3723	4	Sandy's
0.3645	35.6	.3723	4	subscribers
0.3645	35.6	.3723	4	waif
0.3644	35.6	.1897	7	Upland
0.3644	35.6	.1897	7	Vinland
0.3643	35.6	.2427	6	evaporating
0.3643	35.6	.2427	6	menstruation
0.3643	35.6	.2426	6	neighed
0.3643	35.6	.2426	6	Piper's
0.3643	35.6	.2426	6	treachery
0.3642	35.6	.2629	6	Cro-Magnon
0.3642	35.6	.2629	6	Moliere
0.3642	35.6	.2629	6	Monaco
0.3642	35.6	.2406	6	paraded
0.3642	35.6	.2406	6	whiff
0.3640	35.6	.3717	4	dark-blue
0.3640	35.6	.3717	4	Esquire
0.3640	35.6	.3717	4	exasperation
0.3640	35.6	.3717	4	fullback
0.3640	35.6	.3717	4	Granite
0.3640	35.6	.3717	4	Mean
0.3640	35.6	.3717	4	North's
0.3640	35.6	.3717	4	raps
0.3640	35.6	.3717	4	whacking
0.3640	35.6	.3717	4	wince
0.3639	35.6	.3718	4	acrobat
0.3639	35.6	.3718	4	caressing
0.3639	35.6	.3718	4	Dunkirk
0.3639	35.6	.3718	4	nostril
0.3639	35.6	.3718	4	shh
0.3639	35.6	.3291	5	sich
0.3639	35.6	.3718	4	thing's
0.3639	35.6	.3718	4	wobbled
0.3638	35.6	.2061	7	roundness
0.3637	35.6	.2445	6	anemone

THE PRECEDING WORD TYPE OCCUPIES RANK 26100

U	SFI	D	F	Word Type
0.3637	35.6	.2445	6	angstrom
0.3637	35.6	.2445	6	blood-vessel
0.3637	35.6	.3325	5	bull's-eye
0.3637	35.6	.2445	6	excretory
0.3637	35.6	.2445	6	scavengers
0.3637	35.6	.2445	6	troposphere
0.3637	35.6	.3325	5	underlie
0.3636	35.6	.3009	5	gunnery
0.3636	35.6	.3399	5	handbooks
0.3635	35.6	.2252	6	billowy
0.3635	35.6	.2622	6	breakup
0.3635	35.6	.3008	5	Maryville
0.3635	35.6	.2622	6	niches
0.3635	35.6	.0566	14	Tabor
0.3634	35.6	.3713	4	Afric
0.3634	35.6	.3713	4	bedded
0.3634	35.6	.3071	5	Crazy
0.3634	35.6	.3071	5	creaks
0.3634	35.6	.3713	4	flurry
0.3634	35.6	.3713	4	garlands
0.3634	35.6	.3713	4	gentleman's
0.3634	35.6	.3713	4	ill-tempered
0.3634	35.6	.3071	5	limerick
0.3634	35.6	.0000	31	Lullah
0.3634	35.6	.3713	4	maddened
0.3634	35.6	.3713	4	minding
0.3634	35.6	.3713	4	rimmed
0.3634	35.6	.0000	31	Sham
0.3634	35.6	.3071	5	slink
0.3634	35.6	.3713	4	soothed
0.3634	35.6	.3713	4	stateroom
0.3634	35.6	.3713	4	thinkin'
0.3634	35.6	.3713	4	time's
0.3634	35.6	.3713	4	unhooked
0.3634	35.6	.3713	4	waitin'
0.3633	35.6	.3709	4	bramble
0.3633	35.6	.3709	4	devilfish
0.3633	35.6	.3709	4	Franciscans
0.3633	35.6	.3709	4	glint
0.3633	35.6	.3709	4	hairpin
0.3633	35.6	.3709	4	Juarez
0.3633	35.6	.3709	4	matchboxes
0.3633	35.6	.1294	10	Plate
0.3633	35.6	.3709	4	quarter-inch
0.3633	35.6	.3709	4	Rear
0.3633	35.6	.3709	4	roadbed
0.3633	35.6	.2431	6	servitude
0.3633	35.6	.3709	4	Site
0.3633	35.6	.3709	4	sub-zero
0.3633	35.6	.2431	6	Viceroy
0.3633	35.6	.3709	4	wipes
0.3632	35.6	.2425	6	Mexican-American
0.3632	35.6	.2425	6	Nasser's
0.3632	35.6	.2425	6	playwrights
0.3632	35.6	.3283	5	shucks
0.3631	35.6	.2383	6	tracer
0.3630	35.6	.1318	11	RT
0.3629	35.6	.3265	5	Angus
0.3628	35.6	.3706	4	Bad
0.3628	35.6	.3706	4	baleful
0.3628	35.6	.3706	4	carburetors
0.3628	35.6	.2754	5	flyer
0.3628	35.6	.2444	6	Formosa
0.3628	35.6	.2444	6	GreatBritain's
0.3628	35.6	.3186	5	grids
0.3628	35.6	.3706	4	mouthfuls
0.3628	35.6	.3706	4	self-centered
0.3628	35.6	.2444	6	Slidell
0.3628	35.6	.3706	4	warrior's
0.3628	35.6	.3180	5	Work
0.3627	35.6	.3274	5	grandparents'
0.3627	35.6	.3284	5	2200
0.3626	35.6	.3065	5	whatsoever
0.3626	35.6	.2371	6	14-5
0.3624	35.6	.1464	7	Congressmen
0.3624	35.6	.1464	7	Ruhr
0.3624	35.6	.1464	7	run-down
0.3624	35.6	.1464	7	SouthPole
0.3622	35.6	.3702	4	dewdrops
0.3622	35.6	.3702	4	Grass
0.3622	35.6	.3702	4	horsehide
0.3622	35.6	.3702	4	humbug
0.3622	35.6	.3702	4	shooed
0.3620	35.6	.3062	5	denunciation
0.3619	35.6	.0000	25	Otter
0.3619	35.6	.0337	20	two-letter
0.3618	35.6	.3321	5	distract
0.3618	35.6	.2511	6	retarded
0.3618	35.6	.0631	18	Suite
0.3617	35.6	.2378	6	Burgesses
0.3617	35.6	.2378	6	Canberra
0.3617	35.6	.2844	5	monologue
0.3617	35.6	.2378	6	NewWorld
0.3617	35.6	.2378	6	riflemen
0.3616	35.6	.3696	4	bickering
0.3616	35.6	.3696	4	greenish-blue
0.3616	35.6	.3696	4	lifework
0.3616	35.6	.3696	4	mooring
0.3615	35.6	.3306	5	amiably
0.3613	35.6	.3693	4	beeline

THE PRECEDING WORD TYPE OCCUPIES RANK 26200

U	SFI	D	F	Word Type
0.3613	35.6	.2255	6	Dana
0.3613	35.6	.3693	4	grimace
0.3613	35.6	.3693	4	inkling
0.3613	35.6	.3693	4	kindled
0.3613	35.6	.3693	4	loyally
0.3613	35.6	.3693	4	rewrote
0.3612	35.6	.2366	6	Juneau
0.3612	35.6	.2408	6	second-class
0.3612	35.6	.2408	6	Snowy
0.3611	35.6	.2250	7	Hallelujah
0.3611	35.6	.2729	6	inflection
0.3610	35.6	.2168	7	huntin'
0.3608	35.6	.3304	5	collectively
0.3608	35.6	.3304	5	Mallarme
0.3608	35.6	.3304	5	1802
0.3607	35.6	.1506	7	Pepper
0.3607	35.6	.2115	7	tonight's
0.3607	35.6	.3303	5	voracious
0.3600	35.6	.3211	5	potentially
0.3599	35.6	.2135	7	Stout
0.3596	35.6	.3348	5	voltages
0.3595	35.6	.3233	5	adrift
0.3595	35.6	.3233	5	Parson
0.3594	35.6	.2800	5	indomitable
0.3594	35.6	.1285	10	Luzon
0.3594	35.6	.2800	5	vigilant
0.3594	35.6	.2800	5	Wharf
0.3593	35.6	.3338	5	compressive
0.3592	35.6	.0000	24	EF
0.3592	35.6	.0000	24	LCM
0.3592	35.6	.0000	24	vector
0.3590	35.6	.3320	5	placer
0.3589	35.6	.0826	12	polarized
0.3589	35.5	.1387	9	1/2%
0.3588	35.5	.2474	5	dishpan
0.3587	35.5	.1764	8	ukulele
0.3586	35.5	.1351	9	botany
0.3586	35.5	.2228	7	lyrical
0.3585	35.5	.2430	6	Aries
0.3584	35.5	.0990	15	beige
0.3584	35.5	.2429	6	lows
0.3584	35.5	.3241	5	self-help
0.3582	35.5	.1491	7	mermaids
0.3581	35.5	.3184	5	blowers
0.3581	35.5	.3184	5	Bulgarians
0.3581	35.5	.3184	5	D-Day
0.3581	35.5	.3184	5	minimize
0.3581	35.5	.3184	5	negotiation
0.3581	35.5	.3184	5	sabotage
0.3581	35.5	.3184	5	Workers
0.3580	35.5	.3307	5	sensational
0.3580	35.5	.1827	7	smokers
0.3579	35.5	.2146	7	12-4
0.3578	35.5	.3270	5	inadvertently
0.3578	35.5	.3254	5	Tarzan
0.3577	35.5	.2924	5	Bangkok
0.3577	35.5	.3329	5	omission
0.3577	35.5	.3329	5	one-act
0.3576	35.5	.3177	5	fruiting
0.3576	35.5	.3177	5	lotions
0.3576	35.5	.3177	5	Scorpion
0.3570	35.5	.2913	5	coppers
0.3568	35.5	.2888	5	$450
0.3568	35.5	.2267	7	Thurber's
0.3568	35.5	.1926	7	172
0.3568	35.5	.1926	7	305
0.3566	35.5	.0613	18	ance
0.3562	35.5	.2928	5	228
0.3561	35.5	.3157	5	cinema
0.3561	35.5	.3157	5	unsophisticated
0.3560	35.5	.1814	6	counseled
0.3560	35.5	.1814	6	courting
0.3560	35.5	.1814	6	handcuffs
0.3560	35.5	.1814	6	Highways
0.3559	35.5	.0602	11	Asians
0.3559	35.5	.0602	11	yerba
0.3558	35.5	.4352	4	thermoplastic
0.3556	35.5	.2361	6	dilute
0.3553	35.5	.4255	4	spoonfuls
0.3553	35.5	.1817	7	Strip
0.3553	35.5	.3234	5	subdivide
0.3553	35.5	.1817	7	Suzuki
0.3553	35.5	.1817	7	trawlers
0.3553	35.5	.1817	7	urbanized
0.3552	35.5	.1636	9	-ible
0.3552	35.5	.1636	9	ge
0.3552	35.5	.1636	9	homograph
0.3550	35.5	.1471	7	1817
0.3549	35.5	.0000	18	curds
0.3549	35.5	.0000	18	meteorologists
0.3549	35.5	.0000	18	pistils
0.3549	35.5	.0000	18	spectroscope
0.3548	35.5	.3217	5	morsels
0.3545	35.5	.4242	4	affords
0.3545	35.5	.3226	5	Baldwin
0.3545	35.5	.4242	4	flicks
0.3545	35.5	.2661	6	ough
0.3543	35.5	.3599	4	Elf
0.3543	35.5	.3602	4	judge's
0.3543	35.5	.3599	4	mr

THE PRECEDING WORD TYPE OCCUPIES RANK 26300

U	SFI	D	F	Word Type
0.3543	35.5	.3186	5	omits
0.3543	35.5	.3599	4	Swift's
0.3543	35.5	.3602	4	worsened
0.3542	35.5	.3597	4	billed
0.3542	35.5	.3597	4	braved
0.3542	35.5	.3597	4	Bubbles
0.3542	35.5	.3597	4	Cadets
0.3542	35.5	.3597	4	cobbles
0.3542	35.5	.3132	5	pointedly
0.3542	35.5	.2228	7	scrapers
0.3542	35.5	.3597	4	Yourself
0.3541	35.5	.3600	4	Lion's
0.3541	35.5	.2354	6	retell
0.3540	35.5	.2521	6	deposed
0.3540	35.5	.3606	4	phonetic
0.3540	35.5	.2521	6	pilgrimages
0.3540	35.5	.2521	6	quarried
0.3540	35.5	.1513	9	Soap
0.3540	35.5	.3606	4	sub-
0.3540	35.5	.3606	4	tackles
0.3539	35.5	.3606	4	intrude
0.3539	35.5	.3606	4	salutes
0.3539	35.5	.3606	4	sup
0.3539	35.5	.3604	4	swash
0.3539	35.5	.3606	4	Titans
0.3539	35.5	.1825	7	Uganda
0.3539	35.5	.3604	4	whoo-oo-oo
0.3538	35.5	.3604	4	'cross
0.3538	35.5	.3604	4	dejected
0.3538	35.5	.3604	4	exiles
0.3538	35.5	.3604	4	hee
0.3538	35.5	.3604	4	Past
0.3538	35.5	.0882	13	TWO
0.3537	35.5	.3567	4	But
0.3537	35.5	.3124	5	salvaged
0.3537	35.5	.3567	4	square-rigged
0.3537	35.5	.3567	4	tiptoes
0.3536	35.5	.3604	4	handmaidens
0.3535	35.5	.3559	4	Sailor
0.3535	35.5	.3559	4	Strike
0.3534	35.5	.2218	6	printer's
0.3533	35.5	.2684	5	thirteen-year-old
0.3532	35.5	.1757	8	Locomotive
0.3532	35.5	.3138	5	Ulysses'
0.3530	35.5	.2857	5	Webb
0.3529	35.5	.2350	6	Tate
0.3529	35.5	.0352	19	three-syllable
0.3528	35.5	.3181	5	dribbling
0.3528	35.5	.3181	5	jauntily
0.3528	35.5	.4209	4	overpower
0.3528	35.5	.3181	5	Reb
0.3527	35.5	.2680	6	Papers
0.3522	35.5	.1889	7	scalped
0.3522	35.5	.1687	8	well-organized
0.3521	35.5	.1787	6	Benjamin's
0.3521	35.5	.1787	6	Cutter
0.3521	35.5	.1787	6	hamlet
0.3521	35.5	.1787	6	Leblanc
0.3518	35.5	.1239	11	Amen
0.3518	35.5	.2184	6	cutoff
0.3518	35.5	.1010	9	Hanks
0.3518	35.5	.2594	6	mathematically
0.3517	35.5	.2683	6	adolescence
0.3516	35.5	.1325	9	foundry
0.3516	35.5	.1243	9	steadfast
0.3514	35.5	.3163	5	atheist
0.3514	35.5	.2128	7	Durrell
0.3513	35.5	.1361	9	baseboard
0.3513	35.5	.2266	6	boasts
0.3513	35.5	.2266	6	ego
0.3513	35.5	.3056	5	moldy
0.3513	35.5	.3354	5	subordinated
0.3512	35.5	.1493	10	simmer
0.3510	35.5	.3479	4	humorist
0.3510	35.5	.3179	5	Petrarch
0.3509	35.5	.2976	5	dollies
0.3506	35.4	.3470	4	ferried
0.3506	35.4	.3470	4	sneezes
0.3505	35.4	.1332	10	Balder
0.3505	35.4	.3161	5	posse
0.3505	35.4	.3161	5	wherefore
0.3501	35.4	.0440	21	canon
0.3501	35.4	.0000	18	Courts
0.3500	35.4	.3151	5	1624
0.3498	35.4	.2352	6	hostilities
0.3498	35.4	.2352	6	Montevideo
0.3498	35.4	.2352	6	SanJose
0.3497	35.4	.4139	4	detract
0.3497	35.4	.4154	4	narrowest
0.3496	35.4	.0675	15	Neanderthal
0.3496	35.4	.3144	5	venom
0.3494	35.4	.2237	5	9000
0.3493	35.4	.3225	5	firmer
0.3491	35.4	.3143	5	lounge
0.3490	35.4	.1737	8	excavated
0.3490	35.4	.2770	5	279
0.3489	35.4	.1409	9	Oral
0.3487	35.4	.1622	8	Kuwait
0.3486	35.4	.3077	5	Flats
0.3486	35.4	.2379	5	guilds

THE PRECEDING WORD TYPE OCCUPIES RANK 26400

U	SFI	D	F	Word Type
0.3481	35.4	.2804	5	forty-four
0.3479	35.4	.3085	5	ball-point
0.3479	35.4	.2294	5	unbreakable
0.3478	35.4	.3125	5	Month
0.3478	35.4	.3125	5	Steele
0.3478	35.4	.2427	6	yardage
0.3476	35.4	.2307	6	predatory
0.3476	35.4	.2307	6	rigs
0.3475	35.4	.1787	7	HongKong
0.3474	35.4	.2882	5	aide
0.3474	35.4	.0000	24	Beavers
0.3471	35.4	.2218	5	ferryman

U	SFI	D	F	Word Type
0.3471	35.4	.2218	5	jeweler
0.3471	35.4	.2218	5	Kellers
0.3471	35.4	.2357	5	quietness
0.3471	35.4	.2218	5	Toast
0.3470	35.4	.1340	8	loess
0.3470	35.4	.1340	8	Soil
0.3465	35.4	.4098	4	pretzel
0.3464	35.4	.3053	5	208
0.3462	35.4	.3090	5	gumdrops
0.3462	35.4	.2270	6	nominations
0.3461	35.4	.3116	5	anthropological
0.3461	35.4	.3023	5	Dearborn
0.3461	35.4	.3116	5	enforcing
0.3461	35.4	.3023	5	Salmon
0.3461	35.4	.3116	5	spawned
0.3461	35.4	.3116	5	suppression
0.3461	35.4	.3023	5	waging
0.3461	35.4	.3234	5	2-4
0.3460	35.4	.2938	5	cheesecloth
0.3459	35.4	.2664	5	bobcat
0.3459	35.4	.2664	5	fellow's
0.3459	35.4	.2664	5	flattening
0.3457	35.4	.2226	6	a-goin'
0.3457	35.4	.2427	6	Gideon
0.3457	35.4	.2226	6	smokehouse
0.3456	35.4	.1990	7	Na
0.3456	35.4	.2274	6	Thomas's
0.3455	35.4	.2568	6	cadence
0.3455	35.4	.2434	6	6/12
0.3450	35.4	.4071	4	524
0.3448	35.4	.4055	4	cloudiness
0.3448	35.4	.3098	5	Peck
0.3447	35.4	.2901	5	Hi
0.3447	35.4	.1733	6	Mystery
0.3447	35.4	.3005	5	one-piece
0.3447	35.4	.1572	8	465
0.3443	35.4	.0000	23	place-value
0.3443	35.4	.2765	6	shuttle
0.3443	35.4	.0000	23	tens'
0.3442	35.4	.1928	7	DF
0.3441	35.4	.3128	5	foundries
0.3441	35.4	.2398	6	identities
0.3440	35.4	.3849	4	perspiring
0.3439	35.4	.1925	7	What's
0.3437	35.4	.2991	5	underclothes
0.3436	35.4	.2622	6	napped
0.3436	35.4	.2040	7	paraphrase
0.3435	35.4	.2052	7	Clover
0.3434	35.4	.0000	32	CARR
0.3434	35.4	.0000	32	RITCHIE
0.3434	35.4	.2384	6	308
0.3433	35.4	.3053	5	graft
0.3433	35.4	.2249	6	Rusty
0.3433	35.4	.2249	6	slams
0.3429	35.4	.0956	12	Jumbo
0.3428	35.4	.1690	7	anemometer
0.3428	35.4	.1690	7	copepod
0.3428	35.4	.1690	7	thunderhead
0.3427	35.3	.1717	6	caskets
0.3427	35.3	.1717	6	Cochise's
0.3427	35.3	.1717	6	Flicka
0.3427	35.3	.1717	6	grieving
0.3427	35.3	.1717	6	hoo
0.3427	35.3	.1717	6	Louis'
0.3427	35.3	.1717	6	madman
0.3427	35.3	.1717	6	quinine
0.3427	35.3	.1717	6	Saroyan
0.3427	35.3	.1717	6	sweated
0.3427	35.3	.1717	6	three-cornered
0.3427	35.3	.4016	4	Vegetables
0.3427	35.3	.1717	6	wooers
0.3426	35.3	.1581	8	Hab
0.3425	35.3	.3862	4	centipedes
0.3425	35.3	.3094	5	Moore's
0.3425	35.3	.3862	4	veterinarian
0.3424	35.3	.1484	8	carnivorous
0.3422	35.3	.3869	4	volley
0.3421	35.3	.3869	4	Cox
0.3420	35.3	.3860	4	civilize
0.3420	35.3	.3865	4	exhales
0.3420	35.3	.3865	4	sputtering
0.3420	35.3	.3865	4	vomit
0.3420	35.3	.3860	4	water-tight
0.3419	35.3	.2360	6	Alec's
0.3419	35.3	.3827	4	amounting
0.3419	35.3	.3869	4	blackish
0.3419	35.3	.3874	4	blunders
0.3419	35.3	.3869	4	moisture-laden
THE PRECEDING WORD TYPE OCCUPIES RANK 26500				
0.3419	35.3	.2070	7	Private
0.3419	35.3	.2456	6	propelling
0.3419	35.3	.3869	4	stickiness
0.3419	35.3	.2360	6	tricycles
0.3418	35.3	.3864	4	aggregates
0.3418	35.3	.3864	4	bronchial
0.3418	35.3	.3864	4	cardinals
0.3418	35.3	.3864	4	extruded
0.3418	35.3	.3864	4	fatalities
0.3418	35.3	.3874	4	paleontology
0.3418	35.3	.3864	4	ring-necked
0.3418	35.3	.1844	6	tearful
0.3418	35.3	.3864	4	theorized
0.3418	35.3	.3875	4	ventriloquist
0.3418	35.3	.3864	4	viscosity
0.3417	35.3	.2897	5	ceases
0.3417	35.3	.2984	5	dismount
0.3417	35.3	.3863	4	matador
0.3417	35.3	.3863	4	paycheck
0.3417	35.3	.3863	4	real-life
0.3417	35.3	.3867	4	spyglass
0.3417	35.3	.3863	4	upkeep
0.3416	35.3	.4144	4	courtesies
0.3416	35.3	.3863	4	ebony
0.3415	35.3	.3831	4	legally
0.3415	35.3	.3831	4	municipality
0.3415	35.3	.3831	4	outback
0.3415	35.3	.3831	4	plazas
0.3415	35.3	.3831	4	Rugby
0.3415	35.3	.3831	4	silage
0.3415	35.3	.3831	4	vetoed
0.3415	35.3	.3831	4	383
0.3414	35.3	.3832	4	ambassadors
0.3414	35.3	.3832	4	Artillery
0.3414	35.3	.3863	4	atomic-energy
0.3414	35.3	.3874	4	audacious
0.3414	35.3	.3873	4	Babylonia
0.3414	35.3	.3874	4	baptize
0.3414	35.3	.3874	4	consolidated
0.3414	35.3	.3863	4	dictatorships
0.3414	35.3	.3874	4	Euboea
0.3414	35.3	.3832	4	hazelnuts
0.3414	35.3	.2398	6	HI
0.3414	35.3	.3863	4	insuring
0.3414	35.3	.3863	4	irritates
0.3414	35.3	.3805	4	Kosciusko
0.3414	35.3	.3863	4	nationalized
0.3414	35.3	.3863	4	region's
0.3414	35.3	.3863	4	solidarity
0.3414	35.3	.3863	4	Tanzania
0.3413	35.3	.2407	6	dolly
0.3413	35.3	.2407	6	Duff
0.3413	35.3	.2407	6	runaways
0.3412	35.3	.3833	4	binds
0.3412	35.3	.3990	4	down-to-earth
0.3412	35.3	.3833	4	intelligible
0.3412	35.3	.3990	4	manageable
0.3412	35.3	.3990	4	nuclear-powered
0.3410	35.3	.2379	6	Foxx
0.3409	35.3	.3831	4	Corona
0.3409	35.3	.3831	4	expulsion
0.3409	35.3	.3831	4	vestiges
0.3409	35.3	.3831	4	vipers
0.3409	35.3	.3831	4	Volta's
0.3408	35.3	.3831	4	abolish
0.3406	35.3	.2297	6	Shark
0.3406	35.3	.3823	4	stratosphere
0.3406	35.3	.3823	4	velocities
0.3406	35.3	.2471	6	227
0.3405	35.3	.0236	20	Notebook
0.3404	35.3	.3829	4	Acropolis
0.3404	35.3	.3829	4	bask
0.3404	35.3	.3829	4	clashes
0.3404	35.3	.3829	4	Colombian
0.3404	35.3	.3829	4	continent's
0.3404	35.3	.3829	4	Fascist
0.3404	35.3	.3829	4	Hausa
0.3404	35.3	.3829	4	Hemispheres
0.3404	35.3	.3829	4	Minh
0.3404	35.3	.3829	4	paddle-wheel
0.3404	35.3	.3829	4	1765
0.3404	35.3	.3829	4	1830s
0.3403	35.3	.0881	11	duckbills
0.3402	35.3	.1679	7	Johannesburg
0.3402	35.3	.1679	7	Marmara
0.3402	35.3	.2034	7	Reform
0.3400	35.3	.0000	29	Boodles
0.3400	35.3	.1698	6	Dumas
0.3400	35.3	.1698	6	guild
0.3400	35.3	.3741	4	sheaths
0.3400	35.3	.3741	4	wetter
0.3399	35.3	.3022	5	Isaiah
0.3399	35.3	.3022	5	ministry
0.3399	35.3	.2401	6	Unity
0.3399	35.3	.3022	5	zoology
0.3397	35.3	.3145	5	lard
0.3396	35.3	.0690	16	clarinets
0.3394	35.3	.3014	5	cosmos
0.3394	35.3	.3957	4	indigestible
0.3393	35.3	.1456	9	-ant
THE PRECEDING WORD TYPE OCCUPIES RANK 26600				
0.3393	35.3	.2076	6	brindle
0.3392	35.3	.3750	4	bituminous
0.3392	35.3	.3750	4	Oceans
0.3392	35.3	.3750	4	researcher
0.3392	35.3	.3750	4	Signal
0.3391	35.3	.1332	11	Cezanne
0.3390	35.3	.3726	4	Points
0.3390	35.3	.4119	4	resinous
0.3388	35.3	.2766	5	camouflaged
0.3388	35.3	.2766	5	genuinely
0.3388	35.3	.2766	5	gobblers
0.3387	35.3	.3855	4	inversions
0.3387	35.3	.2285	6	Kai-shek
0.3387	35.3	.2218	6	Semites
0.3387	35.3	.1925	7	triads
0.3387	35.3	.2285	6	Vasco
0.3387	35.3	.2285	6	Veracruz
0.3386	35.3	.2437	6	engineered
0.3386	35.3	.3004	5	haphazard
0.3386	35.3	.2437	6	intuition
0.3386	35.3	.2437	6	maneuverability
0.3386	35.3	.2437	6	proponents
0.3386	35.3	.2437	6	scholastic
0.3385	35.3	.2278	6	abscess
0.3385	35.3	.2278	6	boron
0.3385	35.3	.2278	6	ionized
0.3385	35.3	.2278	6	toxic
0.3385	35.3	.3857	4	1510
0.3384	35.3	.3856	4	Clayton
0.3384	35.3	.3856	4	observances
0.3384	35.3	.4050	4	oftentimes
0.3384	35.3	.3856	4	unifying
0.3380	35.3	.3740	4	rundown
0.3379	35.3	.3838	4	butte
0.3379	35.3	.3929	4	starchy
0.3378	35.3	.2753	5	Army's
0.3378	35.3	.2753	5	onstage
0.3376	35.3	.3865	4	mein
0.3376	35.3	.2009	7	neurosis
0.3375	35.3	.3830	4	cancelled
0.3373	35.3	.3739	4	borers
0.3373	35.3	.3739	4	eroding
0.3373	35.3	.3739	4	interprets
0.3373	35.3	.3739	4	Local
0.3370	35.3	.2743	5	dieters
0.3370	35.3	.2743	5	Donovan
0.3370	35.3	.4013	4	nonconductors
0.3370	35.3	.3053	5	publishes
0.3370	35.3	.3053	5	veritable
0.3369	35.3	.3733	4	locals
0.3368	35.3	.4111	4	clean-cut
0.3367	35.3	.1650	6	cottontails
0.3367	35.3	.1088	12	Sec
0.3366	35.3	.1646	8	Seoul
0.3365	35.3	.3730	4	Antilles
0.3365	35.3	.3730	4	Bahamas
0.3365	35.3	.3730	4	dredges
0.3365	35.3	.3730	4	haddock
0.3365	35.3	.3730	4	Nepal
0.3365	35.3	.3730	4	Plant
0.3365	35.3	.3017	5	solidity
0.3360	35.3	.3705	4	qualifies
0.3358	35.3	.1444	9	Sweetheart
0.3358	35.3	.2968	5	vertebrae
0.3355	35.3	.3782	4	Mardi
0.3355	35.3	.3782	4	unprofitable
0.3355	35.3	.3782	4	unsuited
0.3355	35.3	.3782	4	1756
0.3354	35.3	.3695	4	clerk's
0.3354	35.3	.3996	4	manually
0.3353	35.3	.1062	11	YOUNG
0.3352	35.3	.0000	17	phylum
0.3351	35.3	.3689	4	deliberation
0.3351	35.3	.3689	4	postponement
0.3350	35.2	.3686	4	inconvenience
0.3350	35.2	.3686	4	jersey
0.3349	35.2	.2590	5	Leaf
0.3349	35.2	.2590	5	Melville
0.3349	35.2	.2590	5	Wabash
0.3348	35.2	.2956	5	Diaz
0.3348	35.2	.2956	5	idealistic
0.3348	35.2	.2956	5	Municipal
0.3348	35.2	.2956	5	Protection
0.3348	35.2	.2732	5	stilled
0.3348	35.2	.2956	5	Tokyo's
0.3347	35.2	.1639	6	Hong
0.3347	35.2	.1639	6	Kong
0.3347	35.2	.1639	6	open-hearth
0.3346	35.2	.2727	5	basswood
0.3346	35.2	.2110	5	Cochran
0.3346	35.2	.0670	16	ence
0.3346	35.2	.0670	16	fe
0.3346	35.2	.2110	5	inshore
0.3346	35.2	.2110	5	Mate
0.3346	35.2	.3679	4	nagging
0.3346	35.2	.2110	5	nettled
0.3346	35.2	.2110	5	plunked
0.3346	35.2	.2110	5	Rickover
0.3346	35.2	.3679	4	self-confident
0.3346	35.2	.2110	5	trapdoor
THE PRECEDING WORD TYPE OCCUPIES RANK 26700				
0.3346	35.2	.3679	4	unintentionally
0.3345	35.2	.1757	8	-y
0.3344	35.2	.2581	5	dinnertime
0.3344	35.2	.2581	5	five-ton
0.3344	35.2	.1707	7	informs
0.3344	35.2	.3763	4	woodwork
0.3343	35.2	.2445	6	Beauty's
0.3343	35.2	.2948	5	intensively
0.3343	35.2	.2948	5	orthodox
0.3343	35.2	.2948	5	Radiation
0.3343	35.2	.2445	6	Sherry
0.3341	35.2	.1237	8	faceplate
0.3341	35.2	.1859	5	peelings
0.3341	35.2	.0897	15	tailstock
0.3340	35.2	.2849	5	Action
0.3340	35.2	.2811	5	casement
0.3338	35.2	.2718	5	frisking
0.3338	35.2	.2718	5	heh
0.3338	35.2	.2718	5	mamma
0.3337	35.2	.0387	17	Schubert
0.3337	35.2	.3050	5	well-planned
0.3335	35.2	.1790	8	uncooked
0.3334	35.2	.2411	6	Weasel
0.3332	35.2	.0311	34	solder
0.3331	35.2	.0776	13	Decimal
0.3329	35.2	.2412	6	Medium
0.3327	35.2	.0000	31	Atticus
0.3324	35.2	.3641	4	chafing
0.3324	35.2	.2456	6	Gerry
0.3324	35.2	.3641	4	graham
0.3324	35.2	.3641	4	headboard
0.3324	35.2	.3641	4	tidbits
0.3323	35.2	.3824	4	1250
0.3323	35.2	.3824	4	458
0.3322	35.2	.2129	6	bloodhounds
0.3322	35.2	.2129	6	immortals
0.3322	35.2	.2129	6	pew
0.3321	35.2	.2414	6	Hofmann
0.3321	35.2	.2485	6	shredded
0.3320	35.2	.2086	5	'un
0.3320	35.2	.2086	5	befallen
0.3320	35.2	.2086	5	busied
0.3320	35.2	.2086	5	dat
0.3320	35.2	.2086	5	decoy
0.3320	35.2	.2846	5	dyeing
0.3320	35.2	.2086	5	glowered
0.3320	35.2	.2086	5	heem
0.3320	35.2	.2086	5	imploringly
0.3320	35.2	.2086	5	pagoda
0.3320	35.2	.2086	5	Patrolman
0.3320	35.2	.2086	5	Pumpkin
0.3320	35.2	.3844	4	qt
0.3320	35.2	.2086	5	Skinner's
0.3320	35.2	.2086	5	windfalls
0.3316	35.2	.3801	4	lentils
0.3314	35.2	.0695	13	Aldrin
0.3314	35.2	.3802	4	pamphlet
0.3314	35.2	.3802	4	1642
0.3313	35.2	.3796	4	303
0.3312	35.2	.1030	11	Rags
0.3311	35.2	.2401	6	showman
0.3310	35.2	.3816	4	inarticulate
0.3310	35.2	.3785	4	intersected
0.3310	35.2	.3816	4	modestly
0.3310	35.2	.3785	4	Starr
0.3309	35.2	.3813	4	Blackwell
0.3309	35.2	.3813	4	Byzantines
0.3309	35.2	.3813	4	Salisbury
0.3309	35.2	.3838	4	tom-toms
0.3307	35.2	.2071	6	airfoil
0.3307	35.2	.2071	6	amoeba
0.3307	35.2	.2071	6	arthropod
0.3307	35.2	.3832	4	bewitch
0.3307	35.2	.3832	4	Camden
0.3307	35.2	.2071	6	chordates
0.3307	35.2	.2071	6	diffuses
0.3307	35.2	.3809	4	Lear
0.3307	35.2	.1618	9	meringue
0.3307	35.2	.2071	6	multicellular
0.3307	35.2	.2071	6	nucleic
0.3305	35.2	.1342	9	AEC
0.3305	35.2	.3827	4	Butterfly
0.3305	35.2	.3783	4	digestible
0.3305	35.2	.1342	9	reportedly
0.3305	35.2	.3359	4	Roger's
0.3305	35.2	.1294	9	Seville
0.3305	35.2	.3828	4	tyrants
0.3304	35.2	.3362	4	anemones
0.3304	35.2	.3362	4	blossoming
0.3304	35.2	.3362	4	buries
0.3304	35.2	.3362	4	frogs'
0.3304	35.2	.0477	19	ragtime
0.3304	35.2	.3362	4	red-winged
0.3303	35.2	.1422	9	canines
0.3303	35.2	.3799	4	personages
0.3303	35.2	.3799	4	piecing
0.3303	35.2	.3806	4	Reason
0.3302	35.2	.3795	4	coverlet
0.3302	35.2	.3795	4	greatcoat
0.3302	35.2	.3795	4	Walnut
THE PRECEDING WORD TYPE OCCUPIES RANK 26800				
0.3300	35.2	.2391	6	m's
0.3299	35.2	.3790	4	ballistic
0.3299	35.2	.3790	4	Bowen
0.3299	35.2	.3790	4	Cibola
0.3299	35.2	.3790	4	internationally
0.3299	35.2	.3790	4	Shiloh
0.3299	35.2	.3790	4	Suffolk
0.3299	35.2	.3790	4	Sussex
0.3299	35.2	.3790	4	Tuscan
0.3299	35.2	.3790	4	Via
0.3298	35.2	.3786	4	chateau
0.3298	35.2	.3783	4	deity
0.3298	35.2	.3786	4	festering
0.3298	35.2	.2434	6	indenting
0.3298	35.2	.3786	4	massing
0.3298	35.2	.3783	4	southpaw
0.3298	35.2	.3786	4	starched
0.3297	35.2	.3303	4	contaminated
0.3297	35.2	.3779	4	insufficient
0.3297	35.2	.3303	4	seasick
0.3295	35.2	.3354	4	back-breaking
0.3295	35.2	.2445	6	Burnside
0.3295	35.2	.3354	4	confining
0.3295	35.2	.3354	4	fishermen's
0.3295	35.2	.3354	4	Guadalcanal
0.3295	35.2	.3354	4	Hellespont
0.3295	35.2	.3354	4	Monongahela
0.3295	35.2	.3354	4	peaceably
0.3295	35.2	.3354	4	piloted
0.3295	35.2	.3350	4	shipbuilders
0.3295	35.2	.3354	4	stampeding
0.3295	35.2	.3354	4	strategically
0.3295	35.2	.3354	4	Sunshine
0.3295	35.2	.3350	4	untapped
0.3295	35.2	.3354	4	wallow
0.3294	35.2	.3875	4	self-taught
0.3293	35.2	.3771	4	Ad
0.3293	35.2	.3771	4	frolicked
0.3293	35.2	.3771	4	pedigree
0.3293	35.2	.0000	22	regroup
0.3293	35.2	.3771	4	rejecting
0.3293	35.2	.0000	22	sixes
0.3292	35.2	.3799	4	fixture
0.3292	35.2	.3748	4	920
0.3291	35.2	.3799	4	a-running
0.3291	35.2	.3366	4	bypass
0.3291	35.2	.3799	4	Californian
0.3291	35.2	.3366	4	differential
0.3291	35.2	.3366	4	inaudible
0.3291	35.2	.3366	4	overturning
0.3291	35.2	.3366	4	100-foot
0.3291	35.2	.0965	10	5x
0.3291	35.2	.0965	10	9/10
0.3289	35.2	.3870	4	352
0.3288	35.2	.3732	4	C's
0.3288	35.2	.3732	4	Cards
0.3288	35.2	.3013	5	microphones
0.3288	35.2	.3013	5	Praise
0.3287	35.2	.1432	9	grated
0.3286	35.2	.2062	6	Acts
0.3286	35.2	.2062	6	co-operatives
0.3286	35.2	.2062	6	Indochina
0.3286	35.2	.2062	6	pharaoh
0.3286	35.2	.2648	5	restraints
0.3286	35.2	.3686	4	rinsing
0.3286	35.2	.2062	6	Samaria
0.3286	35.2	.3363	4	webbing
0.3286	35.2	.2062	6	1840s
0.3285	35.2	.3288	4	deltas
0.3285	35.2	.3288	4	educating
0.3284	35.2	.2028	6	Neville
0.3283	35.2	.3360	4	accusation
0.3283	35.2	.3360	4	Americans'
0.3283	35.2	.3360	4	church's
0.3283	35.2	.3360	4	Inland
0.3283	35.2	.0804	10	Mafatu's

U	SFI	D	F	Word Type
0.3283	35.2	.0804	10	Mutt
0.3283	35.2	.3360	4	Punta
0.3283	35.2	.3008	5	triplets
0.3283	35.2	.3360	4	1800s
0.3283	35.2	.1887	7	523
0.3281	35.2	.2742	5	Evelyn
0.3279	35.2	.3358	4	Fremont
0.3279	35.2	.3358	4	lawless
0.3278	35.2	.2040	6	injurious
0.3278	35.2	.3884	4	manipulate
0.3277	35.2	.1179	10	coordinator
0.3276	35.2	.1670	7	brickwork
0.3275	35.2	.3748	4	Tribes
0.3274	35.2	.2857	5	dissension
0.3274	35.2	.2857	5	mangrove
0.3274	35.2	.2857	5	resins
0.3273	35.1	.2408	6	ce
0.3272	35.1	.2411	6	Romeo's
0.3271	35.1	.2407	6	Listening
0.3270	35.1	.2045	6	padre
0.3270	35.1	.2321	6	Sloan
0.3270	35.1	.2321	6	spawning
0.3270	35.1	.2321	6	Swahili
0.3270	35.1	.2321	6	televised

THE PRECEDING WORD TYPE OCCUPIES RANK 26900

U	SFI	D	F	Word Type
0.3269	35.1	.3351	4	Ahmed
0.3269	35.1	.3351	4	slither
0.3268	35.1	.2038	5	boathouse
0.3268	35.1	.2038	5	Brink
0.3268	35.1	.2038	5	fox's
0.3268	35.1	.2038	5	igloos
0.3268	35.1	.2988	5	Make
0.3268	35.1	.2849	5	nebulae
0.3268	35.1	.3883	4	sheathed
0.3268	35.1	.2849	5	subsoil
0.3267	35.1	.3348	4	icecaps
0.3267	35.1	.3348	4	microwaves
0.3266	35.1	.3348	4	gutters
0.3266	35.1	.3348	4	Rising
0.3266	35.1	.0465	19	trombone
0.3264	35.1	.2279	5	finder
0.3264	35.1	.3704	4	30-year
0.3263	35.1	.2379	6	dge
0.3261	35.1	.3344	4	alumina
0.3261	35.1	.2222	6	anecdotes
0.3261	35.1	.3344	4	bullfights
0.3261	35.1	.3344	4	Chattanooga
0.3261	35.1	.3344	4	Cradle
0.3261	35.1	.3344	4	equipping
0.3261	35.1	.3344	4	Ordinance
0.3261	35.1	.3344	4	repairmen
0.3261	35.1	.3344	4	serf
0.3261	35.1	.3344	4	sided
0.3261	35.1	.3344	4	tablelands
0.3261	35.1	.3344	4	worker's
0.3261	35.1	.3344	4	yokes
0.3257	35.1	.2031	6	Plato
0.3257	35.1	.2031	6	Shreveport
0.3256	35.1	.3040	5	2-
0.3255	35.1	.0697	11	t'
0.3254	35.1	.2025	5	Brady's
0.3254	35.1	.2025	5	ember
0.3254	35.1	.2025	5	officer's
0.3254	35.1	.2025	5	Ox
0.3254	35.1	.2025	5	tatters
0.3254	35.1	.2025	5	tomcat
0.3254	35.1	.2025	5	Widow-Maker
0.3254	35.1	.2025	5	yoo
0.3253	35.1	.3803	4	one-
0.3252	35.1	.2580	5	administrations
0.3252	35.1	.2580	5	lineup
0.3252	35.1	.2580	5	theatres
0.3252	35.1	.2580	5	therapeutic
0.3251	35.1	.3639	4	graphically
0.3251	35.1	.2343	6	Hey
0.3250	35.1	.1766	7	Communism
0.3250	35.1	.1766	7	compromises
0.3250	35.1	.1766	7	demonstrators
0.3250	35.1	.1766	7	Hesburgh
0.3249	35.1	.2646	5	scalpel
0.3249	35.1	.2373	6	ve
0.3247	35.1	.3817	4	utilizing
0.3246	35.1	.0636	16	dee
0.3246	35.1	.3791	4	trek
0.3243	35.1	.3784	4	salon
0.3243	35.1	.3784	4	tinkers
0.3242	35.1	.3470	4	callers
0.3242	35.1	.3809	4	ovals
0.3241	35.1	.3628	4	exemption
0.3241	35.1	.3639	4	436
0.3240	35.1	.3778	4	comedians
0.3240	35.1	.3778	4	dazzle
0.3240	35.1	.3778	4	edit
0.3240	35.1	.3778	4	gala
0.3240	35.1	.3630	4	202
0.3240	35.1	.3623	4	258
0.3240	35.1	.3623	4	394
0.3239	35.1	.3632	4	304
0.3238	35.1	.3617	4	align
0.3236	35.1	.2303	6	Ye
0.3235	35.1	.2007	5	Farragut
0.3235	35.1	.2076	6	liter
0.3235	35.1	.2076	6	multiplies
0.3235	35.1	.2007	5	pout
0.3235	35.1	.2007	5	prefabricated
0.3235	35.1	.2076	6	09
0.3235	35.1	.2007	5	1813
0.3232	35.1	.2868	5	Heath
0.3232	35.1	.1867	7	wearer
0.3231	35.1	.1315	9	'm
0.3231	35.1	.3778	4	Assisi
0.3231	35.1	.1991	6	doses
0.3231	35.1	.1991	6	jellies
0.3231	35.1	.1991	6	observatories
0.3230	35.1	.2909	5	centerpiece
0.3230	35.1	.2620	5	character's
0.3230	35.1	.2292	6	Cora
0.3230	35.1	.2620	5	glen
0.3230	35.1	.2292	6	Hauser
0.3230	35.1	.2620	5	sawhorse
0.3230	35.1	.2620	5	Sitting
0.3228	35.1	.3757	4	ballerina
0.3228	35.1	.3756	4	celebrity
0.3228	35.1	.3443	4	insecure
0.3228	35.1	.3745	4	lucid

THE PRECEDING WORD TYPE OCCUPIES RANK 27000

U	SFI	D	F	Word Type
0.3228	35.1	.3745	4	persistently
0.3228	35.1	.3745	4	professionally
0.3228	35.1	.3745	4	unerringly
0.3227	35.1	.0952	10	Kenton
0.3227	35.1	.1833	7	lustrous
0.3227	35.1	.3771	4	recesses
0.3227	35.1	.3584	4	1714
0.3226	35.1	.3740	4	armament
0.3226	35.1	.3740	4	Bulgarian
0.3226	35.1	.3740	4	evasion
0.3226	35.1	.3740	4	200-mile
0.3224	35.1	.0939	11	Baxter
0.3224	35.1	.3578	4	25th
0.3223	35.1	.3734	4	loins
0.3223	35.1	.3623	4	mapmakers
0.3223	35.1	.3618	4	resides
0.3223	35.1	.3623	4	temporal
0.3221	35.1	.3609	4	Bello
0.3221	35.1	.3609	4	Foot
0.3221	35.1	.2599	5	Friendship
0.3221	35.1	.3444	4	fulfilling
0.3220	35.1	.3614	4	cattail
0.3220	35.1	.3617	4	hydra
0.3220	35.1	.3617	4	Jura
0.3220	35.1	.3751	4	modern-day
0.3220	35.1	.3614	4	searing
0.3220	35.1	.3617	4	spanning
0.3220	35.1	.3617	4	Transvaal
0.3219	35.1	.3603	4	Anacostia
0.3219	35.1	.3603	4	marshals
0.3219	35.1	.3603	4	moderation
0.3219	35.1	.3603	4	reformer
0.3219	35.1	.3603	4	slaughtering
0.3219	35.1	.0000	30	WOMAN
0.3218	35.1	.3603	4	corkscrew
0.3218	35.1	.1494	8	fluke
0.3218	35.1	.1494	8	fluorescence
0.3218	35.1	.1494	8	lemurs
0.3218	35.1	.1494	8	palladium
0.3216	35.1	.3720	4	burgeoning
0.3216	35.1	.3720	4	irresistibly
0.3216	35.1	.3720	4	notorious
0.3215	35.1	.3743	4	coarser
0.3214	35.1	.3715	4	Dalmatian
0.3213	35.1	.2915	5	impressionist
0.3212	35.1	.3525	4	odd-shaped
0.3211	35.1	.3710	4	Gibson
0.3211	35.1	.3710	4	gusty
0.3211	35.1	.3710	4	quickness
0.3211	35.1	.3710	4	snowshoe
0.3211	35.1	.3710	4	tee
0.3210	35.1	.3727	4	bobcats
0.3210	35.1	.0959	12	moistened
0.3210	35.1	.1981	6	Ones
0.3210	35.1	.3727	4	spasm
0.3208	35.1	.2542	5	barrow
0.3208	35.1	.2542	5	gits
0.3208	35.1	.2542	5	stile
0.3208	35.1	.2542	5	whist
0.3208	35.1	.2542	5	30th
0.3207	35.1	.1965	6	checkup
0.3207	35.1	.1729	7	unshaded
0.3207	35.1	.1729	7	1/12
0.3206	35.1	.3730	4	Cardiff
0.3206	35.1	.3730	4	chugs
0.3206	35.1	.3730	4	gesturing
0.3205	35.1	.3401	4	refilled
0.3205	35.1	.3401	4	salesmen
0.3204	35.1	.3715	4	accursed
0.3204	35.1	.3715	4	snatching
0.3203	35.1	.3793	4	catched
0.3201	35.1	.2063	6	Flaming
0.3201	35.1	.3611	4	three-stage
0.3199	35.0	.2579	5	cantered
0.3199	35.1	.3272	4	g's
0.3199	35.0	.2579	5	mebbe
0.3199	35.0	.2579	5	Scratch
0.3198	35.0	.0000	7	Aari
0.3198	35.0	.0000	7	akua
0.3198	35.0	.0000	7	Archie
0.3198	35.0	.0000	7	Beltsville
0.3198	35.0	.0000	7	Blackfeet
0.3198	35.0	.0000	7	Blanche's
0.3198	35.0	.0000	7	Candita's
0.3198	35.0	.0000	7	Cash
0.3198	35.0	.0000	7	Cassius
0.3198	35.0	.0000	7	Chanuka
0.3198	35.0	.0000	7	Cheerful
0.3198	35.0	.0000	7	Chira's
0.3198	35.0	.0000	7	chiton
0.3198	35.0	.0000	7	Clancy
0.3198	35.0	.0000	7	Cleng
0.3198	35.0	.0000	7	Coppersmith
0.3198	35.0	.0000	7	Courser
0.3198	35.0	.0000	7	crabbits
0.3198	35.0	.0000	7	Deeba
0.3198	35.0	.0000	7	Dellville
0.3198	35.0	.0000	7	Denbooms
0.3198	35.0	.3270	4	dissect
0.3198	35.0	.0000	7	Dona

THE PRECEDING WORD TYPE OCCUPIES RANK 27100

U	SFI	D	F	Word Type
0.3198	35.0	.0000	7	eaglets
0.3198	35.0	.0000	7	Eduardo
0.3198	35.0	.0000	7	Freddie
0.3198	35.0	.0000	7	Fumiko
0.3198	35.0	.0000	7	Funny's
0.3198	35.0	.0000	7	Gamanio
0.3198	35.0	.0000	7	Gawain
0.3198	35.0	.0000	7	Glennie
0.3198	35.0	.0000	7	godmother
0.3198	35.0	.0000	7	Grogan
0.3198	35.0	.0000	7	Helpers
0.3198	35.0	.0000	7	Honey
0.3198	35.0	.0000	7	Huber
0.3198	35.0	.0000	7	huntsman
0.3198	35.0	.0000	7	Ilse
0.3198	35.0	.0000	7	Jacot
0.3198	35.0	.0000	7	Jazbo
0.3198	35.0	.0000	7	jinxed
0.3198	35.0	.0000	7	Joji
0.3198	35.0	.0000	7	jokingly
0.3198	35.0	.0000	7	Joringel
0.3198	35.0	.0000	7	Jurjis
0.3198	35.0	.0000	7	Kasson
0.3198	35.0	.0000	7	Katalin
0.3198	35.0	.0000	7	knothole
0.3198	35.0	.0000	7	Kwaku
0.3198	35.0	.0000	7	lePelican
0.3198	35.0	.0000	7	Lebanons
0.3198	35.0	.0000	7	lop-eared
0.3198	35.0	.0000	7	Maja
0.3198	35.0	.0000	7	Malvo
0.3198	35.0	.0000	7	manhole
0.3198	35.0	.0000	7	matchbox
0.3198	35.0	.0000	7	Mathilde
0.3198	35.0	.0000	7	Meecham
0.3198	35.0	.0000	7	Michelle
0.3198	35.0	.0000	7	Mintzer
0.3198	35.0	.0000	7	Monster
0.3198	35.0	.0000	7	Motel
0.3198	35.0	.0000	7	Oakana
0.3198	35.0	.0000	7	Ondine
0.3198	35.0	.0000	7	Otah
0.3198	35.0	.0000	7	Peregil
0.3198	35.0	.0000	7	Periwinkle
0.3198	35.0	.0000	7	polyp
0.3198	35.0	.0000	7	Ponca
0.3198	35.0	.0000	7	porringer
0.3198	35.0	.0000	7	Portal
0.3198	35.0	.0000	7	Pottleby
0.3198	35.0	.0000	7	Rescue
0.3198	35.0	.0000	7	Rinty
0.3198	35.0	.0000	7	Rodmika
0.3198	35.0	.0000	7	Sacagawea
0.3198	35.0	.0000	7	Seppala
0.3198	35.0	.0000	7	Sharks
0.3198	35.0	.0000	7	Shoie
0.3198	35.0	.0000	7	Shovel
0.3198	35.0	.0000	7	Sissa
0.3198	35.0	.0000	7	Smelly
0.3198	35.0	.0000	7	Speck
0.3198	35.0	.0000	7	steer's
0.3198	35.0	.0000	7	STORYTELLER
0.3198	35.0	.0000	7	Stubbs
0.3198	35.0	.0000	7	Succah
0.3198	35.0	.0000	7	Symi
0.3198	35.0	.0000	7	Toffy
0.3198	35.0	.0000	7	Tolman
0.3198	35.0	.0000	7	Westville
0.3198	35.0	.0000	7	Whitetail
0.3198	35.0	.0000	7	Wolferl
0.3198	35.0	.0000	7	Wong
0.3198	35.0	.0000	7	Yin
0.3198	35.0	.0000	7	Ziemer
0.3198	35.0	.0000	7	Zomo
0.3197	35.0	.1765	8	buffet
0.3197	35.0	.3544	4	sequoias
0.3196	35.0	.1738	7	Rangers
0.3195	35.0	.3271	4	Bengal
0.3195	35.0	.3271	4	goatskins
0.3194	35.0	.3270	4	Glorious
0.3194	35.0	.3270	4	Guayaquil
0.3194	35.0	.3270	4	kookaburra
0.3194	35.0	.3270	4	sheepherders
0.3194	35.0	.1741	7	2-1
0.3193	35.0	.2890	5	seesaws
0.3191	35.0	.3741	4	anguished
0.3191	35.0	.1581	8	hacksaw
0.3191	35.0	.3689	4	Northland
0.3191	35.0	.3689	4	Rider
0.3191	35.0	.3689	4	Steam
0.3191	35.0	.3689	4	unruly
0.3190	35.0	.3701	4	verandas
0.3190	35.0	.3701	4	422
0.3188	35.0	.3683	4	accomplishing
0.3188	35.0	.3683	4	curt
0.3188	35.0	.3683	4	dismissal
0.3188	35.0	.3683	4	dumbfounded
0.3188	35.0	.3683	4	placard
0.3188	35.0	.3683	4	Pygmalion
0.3188	35.0	.3683	4	Saviour

THE PRECEDING WORD TYPE OCCUPIES RANK 27200

U	SFI	D	F	Word Type
0.3187	35.0	.3678	4	Balance
0.3187	35.0	.3678	4	bourgeois
0.3187	35.0	.3678	4	scripts
0.3187	35.0	.3678	4	vehement
0.3185	35.0	.1955	6	appellate
0.3185	35.0	.1955	6	Belleau
0.3185	35.0	.1955	6	Ch'ing
0.3185	35.0	.3678	4	Mammoth
0.3185	35.0	.1955	6	mandate
0.3185	35.0	.1955	6	Nationalists
0.3185	35.0	.3678	4	Sign
0.3185	35.0	.1955	6	tierra
0.3185	35.0	.1955	6	waterworks
0.3184	35.0	.1669	5	inferno
0.3183	35.0	.3726	4	cant
0.3183	35.0	.3727	4	gracefulness
0.3182	35.0	.2557	5	blackout
0.3182	35.0	.2557	5	doorpost
0.3182	35.0	.2557	5	Ida
0.3182	35.0	.1134	10	Margie
0.3182	35.0	.3757	4	practised
0.3182	35.0	.1134	10	Rainsford
0.3182	35.0	.0737	17	transformer
0.3182	35.0	.3475	4	241
0.3182	35.0	.3475	4	4200
0.3180	35.0	.1282	9	Boyer
0.3180	35.0	.3647	4	commencement
0.3180	35.0	.3647	4	cram
0.3180	35.0	.1282	9	Cubbins
0.3180	35.0	.3647	4	fissure
0.3180	35.0	.3647	4	fore-and-aft
0.3180	35.0	.3647	4	Ky
0.3180	35.0	.3647	4	magnet's
0.3180	35.0	.3647	4	Massacre
0.3180	35.0	.3647	4	Okinawa
0.3180	35.0	.3647	4	relevant
0.3180	35.0	.3647	4	retaliated
0.3180	35.0	.3664	4	Utopia
0.3179	35.0	.2227	6	Buzzard
0.3177	35.0	.3641	4	acknowledges
0.3177	35.0	.3641	4	bourbon
0.3177	35.0	.3641	4	contenders
0.3177	35.0	.3641	4	innocent-looking
0.3177	35.0	.2270	6	linguist
0.3177	35.0	.3641	4	oblivious
0.3177	35.0	.3641	4	pivotal
0.3176	35.0	.3675	4	masking
0.3175	35.0	.3637	4	Automobile
0.3175	35.0	.3533	4	grayed
0.3175	35.0	.0831	12	Johnstown
0.3175	35.0	.3637	4	proficiency
0.3175	35.0	.3721	4	spaniels
0.3175	35.0	.3721	4	vat
0.3173	35.0	.1564	8	luve
0.3173	35.0	.3698	4	mispronounced
0.3173	35.0	.3634	4	12-foot
0.3173	35.0	.3634	4	1547
0.3171	35.0	.3689	4	inedible
0.3171	35.0	.3715	4	personalized
0.3170	35.0	.3702	4	curtsy
0.3170	35.0	.3702	4	slurred
0.3170	35.0	.3702	4	solemnity
0.3170	35.0	.3661	4	wag
0.3169	35.0	.2553	5	expedient
0.3169	35.0	.3624	4	hikes
0.3169	35.0	.3624	4	Preston
0.3169	35.0	.3624	4	supervising
0.3168	35.0	.0978	11	Sept
0.3167	35.0	.1694	7	BA
0.3167	35.0	.3619	4	graveled
0.3167	35.0	.2414	6	rebound
0.3167	35.0	.3619	4	toboggan
0.3167	35.0	.3619	4	warm-up
0.3166	35.0	.2128	6	sound-makers
0.3165	35.0	.0383	7	Lot
0.3163	35.0	.3688	4	shaves
0.3161	35.0	.3606	4	withholding
0.3160	35.0	.3439	4	blowtorch
0.3159	35.0	.3314	4	left-over
0.3158	35.0	.3625	4	personage
0.3157	35.0	.3644	4	darkroom
0.3157	35.0	.3671	4	Percy
0.3157	35.0	.3660	4	449
0.3156	35.0	.3447	4	Constant
0.3156	35.0	.3307	4	dark-colored
0.3156	35.0	.3447	4	overriding
0.3156	35.0	.2401	6	Soft
0.3155	35.0	.3619	4	fitful
0.3155	35.0	.0000	16	sepals
0.3155	35.0	.3619	4	swiped
0.3153	35.0	.2530	5	breeders
0.3153	35.0	.2530	5	creosote
0.3153	35.0	.2530	5	liberate
0.3153	35.0	.3614	4	pester
0.3152	35.0	.2802	5	409
0.3150	35.0	.3699	4	alluded
0.3150	35.0	.3675	4	aptitude
0.3150	35.0	.3676	4	consultation
0.3150	35.0	.2133	6	custard
0.3150	35.0	.3676	4	glamor

THE PRECEDING WORD TYPE OCCUPIES RANK 27300

U	SFI	D	F	Word Type
0.3150	35.0	.3676	4	Moorish
0.3150	35.0	.3676	4	motivating
0.3150	35.0	.3676	4	proximity
0.3150	35.0	.3676	4	reconstructed
0.3150	35.0	.0713	9	sulfide
0.3149	35.0	.1929	7	distinctively
0.3149	35.0	.1929	7	Gounod
0.3149	35.0	.1929	7	Gynt
0.3149	35.0	.1929	7	Monteverdi
0.3149	35.0	.1702	7	Mound
0.3149	35.0	.1507	8	serenity
0.3148	35.0	.3605	4	compassionate
0.3148	35.0	.3605	4	pence
0.3147	35.0	.1034	7	bobby
0.3147	35.0	.3641	4	lingo
0.3147	35.0	.3641	4	overwhelm
0.3146	35.0	.2675	5	1742
0.3145	35.0	.1437	7	canneries
0.3145	35.0	.3621	4	consumers
0.3145	35.0	.3648	4	forelock
0.3145	35.0	.3648	4	heralded
0.3145	35.0	.1437	7	Las
0.3143	35.0	.0000	21	computation
0.3143	35.0	.0000	21	quadrilaterals
0.3142	35.0	.2434	6	sirens
0.3141	35.0	.3483	4	rungs
0.3140	35.0	.2236	6	wall-paper
0.3139	35.0	.3584	4	balked
0.3139	35.0	.3584	4	convulsive
0.3139	35.0	.3584	4	futility
0.3139	35.0	.3584	4	laziness
0.3138	35.0	.0880	9	Avery
0.3138	35.0	.3635	4	brutally
0.3138	35.0	.3635	4	cantankerous
0.3138	35.0	.3648	4	mimics
0.3138	35.0	.0880	9	Popper's
0.3138	35.0	.3635	4	trusty
0.3138	35.0	.3679	4	variegated
0.3135	35.0	.3627	4	madrigal

U	SFI	D	F	Word Type
0.3134	35.0	.3393	4	carpeted
0.3134	35.0	.1494	6	quipu
0.3134	35.0	.1494	6	Zoltan
0.3132	35.0	.3613	4	Complete
0.3132	35.0	.3613	4	distracting
0.3132	35.0	.3571	4	Forty
0.3132	35.0	.2257	6	worsted
0.3131	35.0	.3622	4	ado
0.3131	35.0	.3622	4	Digest
0.3131	35.0	.3622	4	humility
0.3131	35.0	.3428	4	robs
0.3131	35.0	.3668	4	yawing
0.3130	35.0	.2217	6	dreamland
0.3130	35.0	.3665	4	excavation
0.3130	35.0	.2217	6	Shakers
0.3130	35.0	.2217	6	Southland
0.3128	35.0	.3663	4	magnificently
0.3126	35.0	.1683	7	five-year-old
0.3126	34.9	.3624	4	limitless
0.3125	34.9	.3229	4	assigning
0.3125	34.9	.0756	10	Rigby
0.3124	34.9	.2467	5	Angela
0.3124	34.9	.2467	5	Courier
0.3124	34.9	.3415	4	emphatic
0.3124	34.9	.2210	6	nutcracker
0.3124	34.9	.3233	4	prescription
0.3124	34.9	.3231	4	reassemble
0.3124	34.9	.3233	4	964
0.3123	34.9	.2392	5	bombings
0.3123	34.9	.2392	5	concocted
0.3123	34.9	.2392	5	Hudson's
0.3123	34.9	.2392	5	Infantry
0.3123	34.9	.2392	5	one-hour
0.3123	34.9	.2392	5	Surfing
0.3122	34.9	.3546	4	Brigham
0.3122	34.9	.3618	4	chronicles
0.3122	34.9	.3546	4	entertainments
0.3122	34.9	.3651	4	novice
0.3122	34.9	.3214	4	364
0.3122	34.9	.3214	4	417
0.3122	34.9	.3546	4	8-9
0.3120	34.9	.3407	4	constructs
0.3120	34.9	.3600	4	unaccustomed
0.3120	34.9	.2121	6	218
0.3119	34.9	.3611	4	adaptable
0.3119	34.9	.3540	4	alluring
0.3119	34.9	.3540	4	analysts
0.3119	34.9	.3540	4	Boulder
0.3119	34.9	.3611	4	coup
0.3119	34.9	.3611	4	covet
0.3119	34.9	.0706	9	Lands
0.3119	34.9	.3611	4	Roses
0.3119	34.9	.3611	4	sanity
0.3119	34.9	.3406	4	Yours
0.3117	34.9	.1898	7	-ful
0.3117	34.9	.3519	4	'50s
0.3117	34.9	.3519	4	acquisition
0.3117	34.9	.3519	4	allegedly
0.3117	34.9	.3519	4	Autobiography
0.3117	34.9	.3519	4	congressional
0.3117	34.9	.3519	4	decimated

THE PRECEDING WORD TYPE OCCUPIES RANK 27400

U	SFI	D	F	Word Type
0.3117	34.9	.3519	4	disability
0.3117	34.9	.3519	4	embittered
0.3117	34.9	.3519	4	expressway
0.3117	34.9	.3519	4	Franciscan
0.3117	34.9	.3519	4	grocers
0.3117	34.9	.3519	4	ponderosa
0.3117	34.9	.3519	4	Porto
0.3117	34.9	.3519	4	skirmishes
0.3117	34.9	.3519	4	Taipei
0.3115	34.9	.3513	4	caving
0.3115	34.9	.3605	4	donations
0.3115	34.9	.3605	4	ethics
0.3115	34.9	.3513	4	fur-lined
0.3115	34.9	.2548	5	lessens
0.3115	34.9	.3513	4	LosAlamos
0.3115	34.9	.3605	4	negotiating
0.3115	34.9	.3513	4	recounts
0.3115	34.9	.3513	4	slugging
0.3114	34.9	.3512	4	conclusive
0.3114	34.9	.3512	4	curator
0.3114	34.9	.3512	4	fissures
0.3114	34.9	.3512	4	Fla
0.3114	34.9	.3512	4	incidence
0.3114	34.9	.3512	4	rationed
0.3114	34.9	.3512	4	sensors
0.3114	34.9	.3512	4	Systems
0.3114	34.9	.3512	4	wheelchair
0.3113	34.9	.3509	4	auctions
0.3113	34.9	.3509	4	compile
0.3112	34.9	.0000	16	Nigerians
0.3112	34.9	.0000	16	Nisei
0.3111	34.9	.3572	4	sweeten
0.3110	34.9	.3503	4	appreciably
0.3110	34.9	.3603	4	Aragon
0.3110	34.9	.3503	4	bibliography
0.3110	34.9	.2187	6	Burbank
0.3110	34.9	.2187	6	derivation
0.3110	34.9	.3603	4	Giacomo
0.3110	34.9	.2187	6	Jocko
0.3110	34.9	.3603	4	supplanted
0.3110	34.9	.3602	4	1611
0.3109	34.9	.2445	5	Lynn
0.3108	34.9	.2196	6	bridled
0.3108	34.9	.2196	6	Freebody
0.3108	34.9	.2196	6	pushmi-pullyu
0.3105	34.9	.2034	6	Beethoven's
0.3105	34.9	.2034	6	light-hearted
0.3105	34.9	.2034	6	strummed
0.3104	34.9	.3210	4	attainment
0.3104	34.9	.3212	4	bets
0.3104	34.9	.3212	4	billowed
0.3104	34.9	.3212	4	cavalcade
0.3104	34.9	.3212	4	Colonel's
0.3104	34.9	.3210	4	Conestoga
0.3104	34.9	.3212	4	damnation
0.3104	34.9	.3215	4	deserters
0.3104	34.9	.3212	4	dogie
0.3104	34.9	.3212	4	door's
0.3104	34.9	.3215	4	flickers
0.3104	34.9	.3212	4	homesteads
0.3104	34.9	.3212	4	Leinster
0.3104	34.9	.3215	4	long-eared
0.3104	34.9	.3212	4	magistrate's
0.3104	34.9	.3215	4	Mansfield
0.3104	34.9	.3215	4	Mecklenburg
0.3104	34.9	.3212	4	Methodist
0.3104	34.9	.3215	4	piracy
0.3104	34.9	.3212	4	Present
0.3104	34.9	.3215	4	Spartan
0.3103	34.9	.3582	4	enigmatic
0.3103	34.9	.3485	4	hospitalization
0.3103	34.9	.3582	4	noteworthy
0.3103	34.9	.3582	4	proclaiming
0.3103	34.9	.3485	4	toddlers
0.3102	34.9	.3688	4	actuality
0.3102	34.9	.3545	4	bins
0.3102	34.9	.3199	4	bonfires
0.3102	34.9	.3199	4	hutch
0.3102	34.9	.3199	4	Nature's
0.3102	34.9	.1049	9	427
0.3101	34.9	.3566	4	devil's
0.3101	34.9	.3733	4	shanks
0.3100	34.9	.3192	4	enroll
0.3100	34.9	.3192	4	foals
0.3100	34.9	.3192	4	Forward
0.3100	34.9	.3192	4	hermetically
0.3100	34.9	.2445	5	kinsman
0.3100	34.9	.3192	4	lifelong
0.3100	34.9	.3192	4	lob
0.3100	34.9	.2445	5	noisiest
0.3100	34.9	.2445	5	puckered
0.3100	34.9	.2445	5	rut
0.3100	34.9	.3192	4	snake-like
0.3100	34.9	.3192	4	tactical
0.3100	34.9	.3192	4	trestle
0.3097	34.9	.2120	6	Lisbeth
0.3097	34.9	.3545	4	Mildred's
0.3097	34.9	.1007	10	Module
0.3096	34.9	.3587	4	toddler
0.3095	34.9	.3553	4	Aesop

THE PRECEDING WORD TYPE OCCUPIES RANK 27500

U	SFI	D	F	Word Type
0.3095	34.9	.3553	4	opportune
0.3094	34.9	.3494	4	detention
0.3094	34.9	.3494	4	remoteness
0.3092	34.9	.3672	4	depicts
0.3092	34.9	.3672	4	stained-glass
0.3091	34.9	.3488	4	deeps
0.3091	34.9	.3488	4	quartered
0.3091	34.9	.3488	4	recourse
0.3091	34.9	.3578	4	unclear
0.3090	34.9	.1040	9	sixteenths
0.3090	34.9	.1040	9	999
0.3089	34.9	.2420	4	Bayonne
0.3089	34.9	.2420	4	Burr's
0.3089	34.9	.2417	4	chirps
0.3089	34.9	.2420	4	competitions
0.3089	34.9	.2420	4	Debs
0.3089	34.9	.2420	4	deliberations
0.3089	34.9	.2417	4	dimples
0.3089	34.9	.2420	4	disobedience
0.3089	34.9	.2420	4	drainpipe
0.3089	34.9	.2417	4	globule
0.3089	34.9	.2420	4	great-grandmother
0.3089	34.9	.2420	4	mediator
0.3089	34.9	.2417	4	Meister
0.3089	34.9	.2420	4	mortars
0.3089	34.9	.2420	4	potter
0.3089	34.9	.2417	4	Slipher
0.3089	34.9	.2420	4	traitors
0.3089	34.9	.2420	4	tumpline
0.3089	34.9	.2420	4	twenty-second
0.3089	34.9	.2417	4	wastebaskets
0.3088	34.9	.1500	6	Constable
0.3087	34.9	.1444	8	minimal
0.3087	34.9	.1444	8	Spock
0.3087	34.9	.1444	8	UCLA
0.3086	34.9	.3477	4	astrologer
0.3085	34.9	.1833	6	cancers
0.3085	34.9	.1833	6	katydid
0.3085	34.9	.1833	6	meat-eaters
0.3085	34.9	.1833	6	outcrops
0.3084	34.9	.2057	6	locus
0.3084	34.9	.1865	7	stimulant
0.3083	34.9	.3530	4	griefs
0.3081	34.9	.3540	4	inhabiting
0.3081	34.9	.3540	4	islets
0.3081	34.9	.2731	5	Kern
0.3081	34.9	.3540	4	oracle
0.3078	34.9	.3534	4	unchallenged
0.3078	34.9	.3534	4	295
0.3077	34.9	.3518	4	boo
0.3077	34.9	.3518	4	Masses
0.3077	34.9	.2351	5	Millard
0.3077	34.9	.3518	4	pallid
0.3077	34.9	.3518	4	payroll
0.3075	34.9	.3454	4	Marcos
0.3073	34.9	.2827	5	durability
0.3073	34.9	.3422	4	lawbreaker
0.3073	34.9	.3422	4	nominally
0.3073	34.9	.3422	4	SanFranciscans
0.3073	34.9	.3422	4	Sinkiang
0.3071	34.9	.2446	4	Dawson's
0.3071	34.9	.2446	4	Jill's
0.3071	34.9	.2446	4	lazier
0.3071	34.9	.2446	4	Maple
0.3071	34.9	.2446	4	MY
0.3071	34.9	.1611	7	perimeters
0.3071	34.9	.3277	4	proverb
0.3071	34.9	.2446	4	Robinson's
0.3071	34.9	.2446	4	seventy-four
0.3071	34.9	.2342	5	trellis
0.3071	34.9	.1611	7	456
0.3070	34.9	.2418	5	contested
0.3070	34.9	.2439	5	humerus
0.3070	34.9	.3504	4	Neal
0.3070	34.9	.2418	5	overlords
0.3070	34.9	.3415	4	sighting
0.3070	34.9	.3415	4	smoothest
0.3070	34.9	.2418	5	subtler
0.3070	34.9	.3415	4	witnessing
0.3070	34.9	.3415	4	year-old
0.3067	34.9	.3409	4	Bonn
0.3067	34.9	.2445	4	Bulltop
0.3067	34.9	.2445	4	Camera
0.3067	34.9	.3409	4	Chevrolet
0.3067	34.9	.2445	4	disheartened
0.3067	34.9	.2445	4	Dismal
0.3067	34.9	.2445	4	duds
0.3067	34.9	.2445	4	forecastle
0.3067	34.9	.2445	4	foxhounds
0.3067	34.9	.2445	4	headstrong
0.3067	34.9	.2445	4	heartbroken
0.3067	34.9	.2445	4	hoofprints
0.3067	34.9	.2445	4	Kennel
0.3067	34.9	.2445	4	misplaced
0.3067	34.9	.2445	4	mutters
0.3067	34.9	.2445	4	neighbour
0.3067	34.9	.2445	4	paraphernalia
0.3067	34.9	.2445	4	Polydeuces
0.3067	34.9	.2445	4	Pratt
0.3067	34.9	.2445	4	ringlets

THE PRECEDING WORD TYPE OCCUPIES RANK 27600

U	SFI	D	F	Word Type
0.3067	34.9	.2445	4	rue
0.3067	34.9	.2445	4	Seventeenth
0.3067	34.9	.2445	4	shepherd's
0.3067	34.9	.2445	4	Simons
0.3067	34.9	.2445	4	sprites
0.3067	34.9	.2445	4	tiredly
0.3067	34.9	.2445	4	warts
0.3066	34.9	.3491	4	beautify
0.3066	34.9	.2442	5	euglena
0.3066	34.9	.2442	5	60-pound
0.3065	34.9	.1875	5	cutworms
0.3065	34.9	.1875	5	searchlights
0.3065	34.9	.2159	6	securities
0.3065	34.9	.1875	5	tarnish
0.3064	34.9	.3402	4	acidity
0.3064	34.9	.3637	4	supplemented
0.3063	34.9	.1245	9	Narcissus
0.3062	34.9	.1822	6	food-processing
0.3062	34.9	.1822	6	Lorraine
0.3062	34.9	.1822	6	Maracaibo
0.3062	34.9	.1822	6	Southeastern
0.3062	34.9	.1822	6	statehood
0.3060	34.9	.1689	7	pointers
0.3060	34.9	.3050	4	382
0.3059	34.9	.3498	4	abdicated
0.3059	34.9	.3498	4	Cities
0.3059	34.9	.3498	4	conservatism
0.3059	34.9	.3498	4	depicted
0.3059	34.9	.3498	4	lucrative
0.3059	34.9	.3498	4	manifestation
0.3059	34.9	.3498	4	pavilion
0.3059	34.9	.3498	4	polled
0.3059	34.9	.3498	4	precipitous
0.3059	34.9	.3498	4	302
0.3058	34.9	.3496	4	bombarding
0.3058	34.9	.2441	5	Bonaparte
0.3058	34.9	.2441	5	colonies'
0.3058	34.9	.2441	5	Succession
0.3058	34.9	.2441	5	1757
0.3055	34.8	.3480	4	Evangeline
0.3055	34.8	.3480	4	hoss
0.3055	34.8	.3670	4	vivacious
0.3054	34.8	.2803	5	applesauce
0.3051	34.8	.3483	4	$16
0.3050	34.8	.1865	5	hippopotamuses
0.3050	34.8	.1865	5	malted
0.3050	34.8	.1865	5	Money
0.3050	34.8	.1865	5	oceangoing
0.3050	34.8	.1865	5	tabi
0.3049	34.8	.3289	4	especial
0.3049	34.8	.3289	4	natures
0.3048	34.8	.1602	7	fathers'
0.3048	34.8	.1070	10	pleural
0.3047	34.8	.3444	4	essayist
0.3047	34.8	.3444	4	generalize
0.3047	34.8	.3444	4	Georgian
0.3047	34.8	.3444	4	lexicon
0.3047	34.8	.3444	4	separator
0.3045	34.8	.1613	7	Lizards
0.3045	34.8	.3391	4	Sultana
0.3045	34.8	.3391	4	Warren's
0.3044	34.8	.2682	5	astonish
0.3044	34.8	.2330	6	cheerless
0.3043	34.8	.3514	4	cents'
0.3043	34.8	.3437	4	imperious
0.3043	34.8	.3279	4	recital
0.3042	34.8	.3384	4	fronds
0.3041	34.8	.3223	4	rejoin
0.3040	34.8	.3465	4	attains
0.3040	34.8	.3464	4	Burgundy
0.3040	34.8	.0000	21	Chanco
0.3040	34.8	.3465	4	Krakow
0.3040	34.8	.3465	4	resigning
0.3040	34.8	.3464	4	1513
0.3040	34.8	.3465	4	1761
0.3039	34.8	.3588	4	edifice
0.3036	34.8	.2424	4	Aerospace
0.3036	34.8	.2424	4	alders
0.3036	34.8	.2424	4	Beau
0.3036	34.8	.2424	4	Bees
0.3036	34.8	.2424	4	bicycling
0.3036	34.8	.2424	4	bunkhouses
0.3036	34.8	.2424	4	chuckles
0.3036	34.8	.2424	4	Cochin
0.3036	34.8	.3266	4	contradict
0.3036	34.8	.2424	4	downed
0.3036	34.8	.1813	5	Dundee
0.3036	34.8	.2424	4	fumed
0.3036	34.8	.2424	4	game's
0.3036	34.8	.2424	4	Hawks
0.3036	34.8	.2424	4	hunches
0.3036	34.8	.2424	4	maned
0.3036	34.8	.2424	4	Massasoit
0.3036	34.8	.2424	4	Mina
0.3036	34.8	.1813	5	MUSIC
0.3036	34.8	.2424	4	Ninth
0.3036	34.8	.2424	4	packsack
0.3036	34.8	.2424	4	quilted
0.3036	34.8	.3266	4	rebuked
0.3036	34.8	.2424	4	Samantha

THE PRECEDING WORD TYPE OCCUPIES RANK 27700

U	SFI	D	F	Word Type
0.3036	34.8	.2424	4	sarcastically
0.3036	34.8	.2424	4	Scotty's
0.3036	34.8	.2424	4	sheepish
0.3036	34.8	.2424	4	steadier
0.3036	34.8	.2424	4	Swanson
0.3036	34.8	.2424	4	thermals
0.3036	34.8	.2424	4	uptown
0.3036	34.8	.2424	4	Waldeck
0.3033	34.8	.3617	4	commendable
0.3033	34.8	.3429	4	Dartmouth
0.3033	34.8	.3024	4	hitches
0.3033	34.8	.3429	4	Pavilion
0.3033	34.8	.3024	4	pretext
0.3033	34.8	.3429	4	prisons
0.3033	34.8	.3024	4	setback
0.3033	34.8	.3024	4	SouthAmerica
0.3033	34.8	.0878	11	1-20
0.3032	34.8	.2444	5	emitting
0.3032	34.8	.2444	5	icebreaker
0.3032	34.8	.2444	5	incisor
0.3031	34.8	.3017	4	Curie's
0.3031	34.8	.3017	4	shooing
0.3030	34.8	.3422	4	unimaginable
0.3028	34.8	.2417	4	afeared
0.3028	34.8	.2417	4	aimlessly
0.3028	34.8	.2417	4	Aroma's
0.3028	34.8	.2417	4	birdhouse
0.3028	34.8	.2417	4	Chincoteague
0.3028	34.8	.2417	4	creaky
0.3028	34.8	.2417	4	dragoons
0.3028	34.8	.2417	4	glumly
0.3028	34.8	.2417	4	gook
0.3028	34.8	.2417	4	grandsons
0.3028	34.8	.2417	4	Horses
0.3028	34.8	.2417	4	hunk
0.3028	34.8	.2417	4	lad's
0.3028	34.8	.2417	4	leashes
0.3028	34.8	.2417	4	milk-white
0.3028	34.8	.2417	4	norther
0.3028	34.8	.2417	4	Oxenthorpe
0.3028	34.8	.2417	4	Penguin
0.3028	34.8	.2417	4	perked
0.3028	34.8	.2417	4	raucous
0.3028	34.8	.2417	4	Reader
0.3028	34.8	.2417	4	Silence
0.3028	34.8	.2417	4	slates
0.3028	34.8	.2417	4	spiky
0.3028	34.8	.2417	4	storerooms
0.3028	34.8	.2417	4	tinkled
0.3027	34.8	.3416	4	thrift
0.3026	34.8	.2445	5	Rumanians
0.3026	34.8	.2445	5	Soviets
0.3024	34.8	.3397	4	public's
0.3024	34.8	.0794	13	Summary
0.3024	34.8	.3397	4	Verde
0.3022	34.8	.1947	6	Been
0.3022	34.8	.2656	5	virtuoso
0.3018	34.8	.2442	5	Loretta
0.3016	34.8	.3231	4	bah
0.3016	34.8	.3445	4	cancels
0.3016	34.8	.3231	4	fidgeted
0.3016	34.8	.3231	4	story's
0.3015	34.8	.3394	4	boardinghouse
0.3015	34.8	.3394	4	endeavoured
0.3015	34.8	.3394	4	half-finished
0.3015	34.8	.3394	4	portly
0.3015	34.8	.3394	4	queue
0.3014	34.8	.3154	4	cutlery
0.3013	34.8	.1585	7	Cary
0.3013	34.8	.3225	4	rigidly
0.3012	34.8	.3387	4	glinting
0.3012	34.8	.3387	4	puffy
0.3012	34.8	.3387	4	sedately
0.3012	34.8	.3387	4	unwashed
0.3011	34.8	.2399	4	Athena's
0.3011	34.8	.2399	4	Caxton's
0.3011	34.8	.2399	4	deceive
0.3011	34.8	.3402	4	decisively
0.3011	34.8	.3402	4	engagements
0.3011	34.8	.2399	4	eyesore
0.3011	34.8	.2399	4	eyewitness
0.3011	34.8	.2399	4	fumble
0.3011	34.8	.2399	4	Jeanne
0.3011	34.8	.3402	4	kindred
0.3011	34.8	.2399	4	leis
0.3011	34.8	.2399	4	Murrow
0.3011	34.8	.2399	4	Pudge
0.3011	34.8	.2399	4	Tulip
0.3011	34.8	.2399	4	Windy
0.3011	34.8	.2399	4	yowl
0.3009	34.8	.3286	4	Delano
0.3009	34.8	.3286	4	destinations
0.3009	34.8	.3381	4	library's
0.3009	34.8	.3457	4	patios
0.3009	34.8	.3286	4	plutonium
0.3009	34.8	.3286	4	recession
0.3009	34.8	.3286	4	transoceanic
0.3009	34.8	.3381	4	tunic
0.3008	34.8	.3396	4	Balboa
0.3008	34.8	.3396	4	Biscay

THE PRECEDING WORD TYPE OCCUPIES RANK 27800

U	SFI	D	F	Word Type
0.3008	34.8	.3395	4	erection
0.3008	34.8	.1046	10	Gallery

U	SFI	D	F	Word Type
0.3008	34.8	.3395	4	invaluable
0.3008	34.8	.3395	4	rupture
0.3008	34.8	.3526	4	twelve-inch
0.3008	34.8	.3396	4	255
0.3006	34.8	.3374	4	deduced
0.3006	34.8	.3374	4	Miracle
0.3005	34.8	.3141	4	Aram
0.3005	34.8	.2393	4	Brag
0.3005	34.8	.2393	4	bullocks
0.3005	34.8	.2393	4	christened
0.3005	34.8	.2393	4	cooper
0.3005	34.8	.3141	4	Crosby
0.3005	34.8	.2393	4	cubits
0.3005	34.8	.3141	4	earmuffs
0.3005	34.8	.3141	4	Fisk
0.3005	34.8	.3141	4	Flood
0.3005	34.8	.2393	4	gangsters
0.3005	34.8	.2393	4	hobbles
0.3005	34.8	.2393	4	kimono
0.3005	34.8	.3141	4	lax
0.3005	34.8	.2393	4	learnin'
0.3005	34.8	.2393	4	loped
0.3005	34.8	.2393	4	mail-order
0.3005	34.8	.2393	4	mewing
0.3005	34.8	.2393	4	Nag's
0.3005	34.8	.2393	4	Ogre
0.3005	34.8	.2393	4	outspread
0.3005	34.8	.2393	4	Pitcairn
0.3005	34.8	.2393	4	pitchforks
0.3005	34.8	.2393	4	Polly's
0.3005	34.8	.2393	4	saddest
0.3005	34.8	.2393	4	sips
0.3005	34.8	.2393	4	snipped
0.3005	34.8	.3141	4	snobbish
0.3005	34.8	.2393	4	SOUND
0.3005	34.8	.3141	4	sponsors
0.3005	34.8	.3141	4	spotting
0.3005	34.8	.2393	4	swerve
0.3005	34.8	.2393	4	Valjean
0.3005	34.8	.0789	11	Vatican
0.3005	34.8	.2393	4	Zeus's
0.3004	34.8	.2050	6	seniors
0.3003	34.8	.2432	5	conjugation
0.3003	34.8	.0000	37	Final
0.3001	34.8	.2865	4	pleated
0.2998	34.8	.2386	4	ambulances
0.2998	34.8	.2386	4	ants'
0.2998	34.8	.2386	4	aviators
0.2998	34.8	.2386	4	chickadees
0.2998	34.8	.2386	4	coffins
0.2998	34.8	.2386	4	crudest
0.2998	34.8	.2386	4	distasteful
0.2998	34.8	.2386	4	falcon's
0.2998	34.8	.2386	4	fraudulent
0.2998	34.8	.2386	4	Gentry
0.2998	34.8	.2386	4	Mermaid
0.2998	34.8	.2386	4	Newbery
0.2998	34.8	.2386	4	Pompeii
0.2998	34.8	.2386	4	scallop
0.2998	34.8	.2386	4	sombreros
0.2998	34.8	.2386	4	Standing
0.2998	34.8	.2386	4	Stanton's
0.2998	34.8	.2386	4	Thermopylae
0.2998	34.8	.2386	4	1768
0.2996	34.8	.3372	4	epoch-making
0.2996	34.8	.3372	4	resided
0.2995	34.8	.3104	4	disarray
0.2995	34.8	.3104	4	documentary
0.2995	34.8	.3104	4	excavations
0.2995	34.8	.3104	4	flamboyant
0.2995	34.8	.3104	4	massed
0.2995	34.8	.3104	4	motorized
0.2995	34.8	.3104	4	Pickering
0.2995	34.8	.3104	4	Plaza
0.2995	34.8	.3104	4	whirlpools
0.2995	34.8	.3104	4	winch
0.2994	34.8	.0000	20	Accuracy
0.2994	34.8	.1397	8	Caddie's
0.2994	34.8	.0000	20	DEF
0.2994	34.8	.2851	4	emblems
0.2994	34.8	.2851	4	helplessness
0.2994	34.8	.0000	20	polynomials
0.2993	34.8	.3366	4	defies
0.2993	34.8	.0829	9	Heidi
0.2993	34.8	.3366	4	imbedded
0.2993	34.8	.0829	9	Jabez
0.2993	34.8	.3366	4	malignant
0.2993	34.8	.0829	9	Manny
0.2993	34.8	.3366	4	Sargasso
0.2993	34.8	.0829	9	Sunny
0.2992	34.8	.3097	4	attuned
0.2992	34.8	.3097	4	gut
0.2992	34.8	.3097	4	nonviolence
0.2992	34.8	.3097	4	Paige
0.2992	34.8	.3097	4	parka
0.2992	34.8	.3097	4	showdown
0.2992	34.8	.3097	4	sluice
0.2992	34.8	.3097	4	smacking

THE PRECEDING WORD TYPE OCCUPIES RANK 27900

U	SFI	D	F	Word Type
0.2992	34.8	.3097	4	sodden
0.2992	34.8	.3097	4	stowing
0.2992	34.8	.3097	4	stunning
0.2990	34.8	.3473	4	Balzac
0.2990	34.8	.3092	4	candidacy
0.2990	34.8	.3092	4	eleven-year-old
0.2990	34.8	.3092	4	insisting
0.2989	34.8	.3359	4	aggressiveness
0.2989	34.8	.3359	4	commanders
0.2989	34.8	.3328	4	deducted
0.2989	34.8	.3359	4	deformity
0.2989	34.8	.3359	4	faction
0.2989	34.8	.3359	4	Manned
0.2989	34.8	.3359	4	manpower
0.2989	34.8	.1937	6	Nippon
0.2989	34.8	.1937	6	re-election
0.2989	34.8	.1937	6	SantaBarbara
0.2989	34.8	.3359	4	vanadium
0.2989	34.8	.3359	4	visionary
0.2989	34.8	.3359	4	1791
0.2989	34.8	.3359	4	1796
0.2988	34.8	.2424	5	accounting
0.2988	34.8	.2424	5	Cambrian
0.2988	34.8	.2424	5	cellular
0.2988	34.8	.2424	5	compresses
0.2988	34.8	.2424	5	cranial
0.2988	34.8	.2424	5	crumbles
0.2988	34.8	.2424	5	dissected
0.2988	34.8	.2424	5	Maxwell's
0.2988	34.8	.2424	5	meiosis
0.2988	34.8	.2424	5	Mid-Ocean
0.2988	34.8	.2424	5	neutralize
0.2988	34.8	.2840	4	Sis
0.2988	34.8	.2424	5	stomata
0.2988	34.8	.2424	5	trillions
0.2988	34.8	.2424	5	warbler
0.2986	34.8	.3352	4	abnormalities
0.2986	34.8	.3123	4	Aladdin's
0.2986	34.8	.3352	4	Bathurst
0.2986	34.8	.3352	4	bronchi
0.2986	34.8	.3123	4	divil
0.2986	34.8	.3352	4	embankments
0.2986	34.8	.3352	4	equalize
0.2986	34.8	.3352	4	initiate
0.2986	34.8	.3352	4	instantaneous
0.2986	34.8	.3352	4	inversely
0.2986	34.8	.3352	4	relaxes
0.2986	34.8	.3123	4	Scheherazade
0.2986	34.8	.3352	4	strontium
0.2986	34.8	.3352	4	1675
0.2985	34.7	.2426	5	Amenhotep
0.2985	34.7	.2426	5	gateways
0.2985	34.7	.2426	5	mestizos
0.2985	34.7	.3499	4	mirrored
0.2985	34.7	.2426	5	Ouachita
0.2985	34.7	.2426	5	proslavery
0.2984	34.7	.2264	5	Chest
0.2983	34.7	.1425	5	Beehive
0.2983	34.7	.1612	8	grinders
0.2982	34.7	.0687	14	organist
0.2981	34.7	.3072	4	degrading
0.2981	34.7	.3072	4	hoard
0.2981	34.7	.3436	4	outlets
0.2981	34.7	.3436	4	slitting
0.2981	34.7	.3072	4	tether
0.2980	34.7	.3501	4	bologna
0.2980	34.7	.3501	4	obligatory
0.2980	34.7	.3497	4	strainer
0.2975	34.7	.2778	5	Mainz
0.2975	34.7	.3573	4	predominance
0.2975	34.7	.1260	8	vendors
0.2974	34.7	.3473	4	comtemporary
0.2974	34.7	.1382	8	Reeves
0.2974	34.7	.3424	4	tempt
0.2973	34.7	.3310	4	faltering
0.2973	34.7	.3310	4	sun-dried
0.2972	34.7	.3468	4	ABC'S
0.2972	34.7	.1440	8	hosiery
0.2971	34.7	.3078	4	hewed
0.2971	34.7	.3078	4	inexplicable
0.2969	34.7	.0318	15	Pee-Wee
0.2969	34.7	.1357	8	Villa
0.2967	34.7	.2800	4	accenting
0.2967	34.7	.3071	4	bawling
0.2967	34.7	.3071	4	blue-and-white
0.2967	34.7	.2691	5	Clarke
0.2967	34.7	.2342	5	Columbine
0.2967	34.7	.2342	5	correlation
0.2967	34.7	.3071	4	craved
0.2967	34.7	.3071	4	froth
0.2967	34.7	.2342	5	Goodwin
0.2967	34.7	.3071	4	grizzled
0.2967	34.7	.3071	4	Hippopotamus
0.2967	34.7	.3071	4	journeymen
0.2967	34.7	.3071	4	pinafore
0.2967	34.7	.3071	4	saddling
0.2967	34.7	.2800	4	sizing
0.2967	34.7	.3071	4	swagger
0.2967	34.7	.3071	4	T-shirt
0.2967	34.7	.3071	4	tensed

THE PRECEDING WORD TYPE OCCUPIES RANK 28000

U	SFI	D	F	Word Type
0.2967	34.7	.3071	4	Twelve
0.2967	34.7	.3071	4	weighty
0.2967	34.7	.3071	4	yank
0.2966	34.7	.2251	5	cursing
0.2966	34.7	.1605	8	interrogative
0.2966	34.7	.1605	8	nominative
0.2966	34.7	.2340	5	streptomycin
0.2966	34.7	.0490	13	Ugly
0.2966	34.7	.2251	5	valor
0.2965	34.7	.3295	4	AN
0.2965	34.7	.3065	4	aperture
0.2965	34.7	.3065	4	fixedly
0.2965	34.7	.3065	4	hah
0.2965	34.7	.3065	4	knowin'
0.2965	34.7	.3135	4	occupant
0.2963	34.7	.3454	4	twirls
0.2961	34.7	.3394	4	engages
0.2960	34.7	.2242	5	deserving
0.2960	34.7	.3463	4	intrusion
0.2957	34.7	.0000	15	convection
0.2956	34.7	.3313	4	disagreements
0.2956	34.7	.3313	4	kapok
0.2956	34.7	.2780	4	roaster
0.2956	34.7	.2780	4	rooftop
0.2956	34.7	.2780	4	schoolmates
0.2956	34.7	.3188	4	sureness
0.2954	34.7	.2019	6	730
0.2953	34.7	.2368	5	acne
0.2953	34.7	.2368	5	hemoglobin
0.2953	34.7	.2336	5	Toys
0.2952	34.7	.3287	4	Covenant
0.2952	34.7	.3287	4	crusaders
0.2952	34.7	.3287	4	dynasties
0.2952	34.7	.3435	4	exemplified
0.2952	34.7	.3287	4	forbids
0.2952	34.7	.3287	4	inaugurated
0.2952	34.7	.3287	4	moors
0.2952	34.7	.3287	4	Portsmouth
0.2952	34.7	.3287	4	sapped
0.2952	34.7	.3287	4	squatter
0.2950	34.7	.3450	4	adept
0.2950	34.7	.3450	4	caffeine
0.2950	34.7	.3446	4	cramp
0.2950	34.7	.2373	5	glassware
0.2950	34.7	.3450	4	obtainable
0.2950	34.7	.3442	4	toasts
0.2949	34.7	.3030	4	brotherly
0.2949	34.7	.3086	4	condescend
0.2949	34.7	.3030	4	favour
0.2949	34.7	.3030	4	ferociously
0.2949	34.7	.3030	4	housecleaning
0.2949	34.7	.3030	4	indifferently
0.2949	34.7	.3030	4	Kate's
0.2949	34.7	.3030	4	lopsided
0.2949	34.7	.3030	4	mortified
0.2949	34.7	.3030	4	snaked
0.2949	34.7	.3030	4	tryin'
0.2948	34.7	.3280	4	airborne
0.2948	34.7	.3280	4	amorphous
0.2948	34.7	.3280	4	barb
0.2948	34.7	.3280	4	Cromwell
0.2948	34.7	.3280	4	fine-grained
0.2948	34.7	.3301	4	judicious
0.2948	34.7	.3280	4	occupational
0.2948	34.7	.3529	4	Scale
0.2948	34.7	.3280	4	unscientific
0.2946	34.7	.3369	4	saver
0.2945	34.7	.3424	4	accompanist
0.2945	34.7	.3396	4	filtering
0.2944	34.7	.2553	5	insanely
0.2943	34.7	.2991	4	clambering
0.2943	34.7	.1409	6	dodgers
0.2943	34.7	.1409	6	Gilbreth
0.2943	34.7	.2991	4	goaded
0.2943	34.7	.1409	6	good-naturedly
0.2943	34.7	.2991	4	Headquarters
0.2943	34.7	.2991	4	Humboldt
0.2943	34.7	.2991	4	insistently
0.2943	34.7	.2991	4	muck
0.2943	34.7	.2991	4	old-timers
0.2943	34.7	.2991	4	tights
0.2943	34.7	.2991	4	twenty-seventh
0.2943	34.7	.1409	6	Welles
0.2942	34.7	.3418	4	recaptured
0.2942	34.7	.3418	4	Russe
0.2941	34.7	.2136	6	crankcase
0.2941	34.7	.3264	4	diamondback
0.2941	34.7	.0164	23	fa
0.2938	34.7	.3075	4	gallops
0.2938	34.7	.3075	4	greenwood
0.2938	34.7	.3075	4	Hail
0.2938	34.7	.3364	4	insecurity
0.2938	34.7	.3075	4	leadeth
0.2938	34.7	.3075	4	Night's
0.2938	34.7	.3364	4	thickens
0.2936	34.7	.2976	4	burdensome
0.2936	34.7	.3408	4	evening's
0.2936	34.7	.3408	4	intensify
0.2936	34.7	.3408	4	music's
0.2934	34.7	.2222	5	anchors

THE PRECEDING WORD TYPE OCCUPIES RANK 28100

U	SFI	D	F	Word Type
0.2934	34.7	.2222	5	deputies
0.2934	34.7	.3403	4	unscrambled
0.2933	34.7	.0619	16	sanding
0.2931	34.7	.3399	4	premiere
0.2928	34.7	.2355	5	courtly
0.2928	34.7	.2213	5	Hippocrates
0.2924	34.7	.0855	12	bassoons
0.2924	34.7	.3060	4	custody
0.2924	34.7	.3060	4	Edition
0.2924	34.7	.3060	4	Frederic
0.2924	34.7	.3060	4	merging
0.2923	34.7	.3026	4	eloquently
0.2923	34.7	.0782	8	internal-combustion
0.2923	34.7	.3256	4	keyed
0.2923	34.7	.0782	8	seismograph
0.2923	34.7	.0782	8	spinnerets
0.2921	34.7	.3057	4	bears'
0.2921	34.7	.3250	4	lukewarm
0.2919	34.7	.3055	4	glimmering
0.2919	34.7	.3018	4	numbed
0.2919	34.7	.3018	4	swivel
0.2919	34.7	.3018	4	wolfhound
0.2918	34.7	.2978	4	revered
0.2917	34.7	.0000	15	Morely
0.2917	34.6	.0000	15	Obet
0.2917	34.6	.0000	15	Purchase
0.2917	34.6	.0000	15	Tushi
0.2916	34.6	.1473	7	rosebushes
0.2916	34.6	.1959	6	scrolls
0.2916	34.6	.1473	7	07
0.2916	34.6	.3180	4	261
0.2914	34.6	.3369	4	banshee
0.2914	34.6	.0398	18	Chopin
0.2914	34.6	.2958	4	dung
0.2914	34.6	.2958	4	Emily's
0.2914	34.6	.2958	4	empty-handed
0.2914	34.6	.2958	4	heartbreaking
0.2914	34.6	.2958	4	hmm
0.2914	34.6	.2958	4	Keeper
0.2914	34.6	.2958	4	nightshirt
0.2914	34.6	.2958	4	nuzzled
0.2914	34.6	.2958	4	yellowing
0.2913	34.6	.2280	4	Apple
0.2913	34.6	.2280	4	getaway
0.2913	34.6	.2280	4	others'
0.2911	34.6	.2278	4	Alexander's
0.2911	34.6	.2278	4	blackbird
0.2911	34.6	.2278	4	dong
0.2911	34.6	.3231	4	illumination
0.2911	34.6	.2278	4	Kidd
0.2911	34.6	.2278	4	marmalade
0.2911	34.6	.2278	4	peacock's
0.2911	34.6	.2278	4	Pledge
0.2911	34.6	.3231	4	reused
0.2911	34.6	.2278	4	slenderer
0.2911	34.6	.2278	4	Soo
0.2911	34.6	.0000	36	timbre
0.2911	34.6	.2278	4	Wolf's
0.2911	34.6	.2429	5	832
0.2910	34.6	.2329	5	three-letter
0.2909	34.6	.3011	4	bower
0.2909	34.6	.3011	4	eluded
0.2909	34.6	.3011	4	enjoined
0.2909	34.6	.3011	4	hair-raising
0.2909	34.6	.3011	4	lieu
0.2909	34.6	.3011	4	pocketed
0.2909	34.6	.3011	4	scepter
0.2909	34.6	.3011	4	squirting
0.2908	34.6	.0914	12	desserts
0.2907	34.6	.2069	6	411
0.2905	34.6	.2443	5	mo
0.2905	34.6	.2443	5	368
0.2903	34.6	.2986	4	macadam
0.2902	34.6	.2995	4	crunched
0.2902	34.6	.2995	4	crusted
0.2902	34.6	.2995	4	homesickness
0.2902	34.6	.2995	4	mournfully
0.2902	34.6	.2995	4	odorous
0.2902	34.6	.2995	4	toadstool
0.2902	34.6	.2995	4	trembles
0.2901	34.6	.3356	4	polishes
0.2899	34.6	.1870	6	foci
0.2899	34.6	.1870	6	man-hours
0.2899	34.6	.3331	4	starters
0.2899	34.6	.3331	4	yearn
0.2898	34.6	.1768	7	tailored
0.2896	34.6	.0574	15	aria
0.2896	34.6	.0775	8	Casas
0.2896	34.6	.0775	8	Ketchikan
0.2896	34.6	.2971	4	Menelaus
0.2896	34.6	.2971	4	misled
0.2895	34.6	.1363	8	Albania
0.2895	34.6	.3334	4	artistry
0.2895	34.6	.0000	20	Esputa
0.2895	34.6	.1363	8	Frankel
0.2895	34.6	.3334	4	Merrimac
0.2895	34.6	.3334	4	popularized
0.2895	34.6	.2557	5	puller
0.2894	34.6	.2423	5	amphitheater
0.2894	34.6	.2988	4	dispassionate

THE PRECEDING WORD TYPE OCCUPIES RANK 28200

U	SFI	D	F	Word Type
0.2894	34.6	.2423	5	dynamometer
0.2894	34.6	.2988	4	Nicolas
0.2894	34.6	.2423	5	Okeechobee
0.2894	34.6	.2423	5	vampires
0.2894	34.6	.2423	5	Waddell
0.2890	34.6	.1143	9	GIRL
0.2890	34.6	.1143	9	Jessica
0.2890	34.6	.1143	9	trackers
0.2889	34.6	.2442	5	palm-clad
0.2889	34.6	.2442	5	stingers
0.2889	34.6	.3314	4	343
0.2888	34.6	.2969	4	ague
0.2888	34.6	.1117	7	buddies
0.2888	34.6	.2969	4	ducats
0.2888	34.6	.2969	4	excelled
0.2888	34.6	.2969	4	flinch
0.2888	34.6	.1117	7	hitchhiking
0.2888	34.6	.2969	4	incessantly
0.2888	34.6	.2969	4	kneeled
0.2888	34.6	.2969	4	mettle
0.2888	34.6	.1457	8	OC
0.2888	34.6	.1457	8	OD
0.2888	34.6	.2969	4	overhung
0.2888	34.6	.1117	7	Patti
0.2888	34.6	.2969	4	Piggy
0.2888	34.6	.2969	4	willed
0.2888	34.6	.2969	4	wind-swept
0.2887	34.6	.2444	5	centrifuge
0.2887	34.6	.2444	5	Cohen
0.2887	34.6	.3318	4	Cooky
0.2887	34.6	.2982	4	Crimean
0.2887	34.6	.2982	4	Jacinto
0.2887	34.6	.2444	5	legions
0.2887	34.6	.3318	4	mailmen
0.2887	34.6	.2444	5	Newport
0.2887	34.6	.2982	4	pincers
0.2887	34.6	.2982	4	sympathized
0.2886	34.6	.2974	4	unhitched
0.2884	34.6	.2088	6	glockenspiel
0.2883	34.6	.2975	4	equestrian
0.2883	34.6	.0500	21	facings
0.2883	34.6	.2975	4	flamingos
0.2883	34.6	.2364	5	FTC
0.2883	34.6	.2975	4	Made
0.2882	34.6	.1131	8	half-gallon
0.2882	34.6	.1083	9	headland
0.2881	34.6	.2954	4	Banana
0.2881	34.6	.2954	4	careering
0.2881	34.6	.2954	4	Elgin
0.2881	34.6	.2954	4	incredulously
0.2881	34.6	.2954	4	Moran
0.2881	34.6	.2954	4	recklessness
0.2881	34.6	.2954	4	stolid
0.2880	34.6	.2351	5	American-made
0.2880	34.6	.1851	6	Joan's
0.2880	34.6	.1851	6	9's
0.2879	34.6	.1253	7	amen
0.2876	34.6	.3134	4	Biafra
0.2876	34.6	.3134	4	fertilize
0.2876	34.6	.3134	4	flavorings
0.2876	34.6	.3134	4	hatcheries
0.2876	34.6	.3134	4	Huns
0.2876	34.6	.3134	4	mucilage
0.2876	34.6	.3134	4	Orientals
0.2876	34.6	.3134	4	theorists
0.2876	34.6	.3134	4	trigonometry

U	SFI	D	F	Word Type
0.2876	34.6	.3134	4	1940s
0.2875	34.6	.2843	4	brew
0.2875	34.6	.2843	4	disdained
0.2875	34.6	.2843	4	forded
0.2875	34.6	.2843	4	four-day
0.2875	34.6	.1324	10	hems
0.2875	34.6	.2843	4	OklahomaCity
0.2875	34.6	.2843	4	Reef
0.2875	34.6	.2843	4	Southwestern
0.2872	34.6	.0526	12	Duckling
0.2871	34.6	.2835	4	congestion
0.2871	34.6	.2835	4	eight-hour
0.2871	34.6	.2835	4	guanacos
0.2871	34.6	.2835	4	inflatable
0.2871	34.6	.2835	4	rampage
0.2871	34.6	.2835	4	ruptured
0.2870	34.6	.2213	5	aorta
0.2870	34.6	.3406	4	Bologna
0.2870	34.6	.2213	5	deflected
0.2870	34.6	.2213	5	Democritus
0.2870	34.6	.2213	5	ecologist
0.2870	34.6	.2213	5	gypsum
0.2870	34.6	.2213	5	invertebrate
0.2870	34.6	.2213	5	life-saving
0.2870	34.6	.2213	5	magnetize
0.2870	34.6	.2213	5	mammary
0.2870	34.6	.2260	5	Mckinley
0.2870	34.6	.2213	5	mesons
0.2870	34.6	.3406	4	oscilloscope
0.2870	34.6	.2213	5	phyla
0.2870	34.6	.2213	5	radiosonde
0.2870	34.6	.2213	5	roundworms
0.2870	34.6	.2213	5	seismic
0.2870	34.6	.2213	5	tapeworms

THE PRECEDING WORD TYPE OCCUPIES RANK 28300

U	SFI	D	F	Word Type
0.2870	34.6	.2213	5	triceps
0.2870	34.6	.2213	5	unaided
0.2869	34.6	.2947	4	droughts
0.2869	34.6	.2947	4	Greeley
0.2869	34.6	.2071	6	Piano
0.2869	34.6	.2278	5	Slow
0.2869	34.6	.2947	4	verge
0.2868	34.6	.1303	8	TIME
0.2867	34.6	.2253	5	Trench
0.2867	34.6	.2253	5	10x
0.2866	34.6	.3284	4	glowworm
0.2865	34.6	.3266	4	perfecting
0.2864	34.6	.0171	22	Know
0.2864	34.6	.0171	22	kw
0.2862	34.6	.1650	7	Lutheran
0.2861	34.6	.2932	4	bridged
0.2861	34.6	.2932	4	decorator
0.2861	34.6	.2932	4	dredge
0.2861	34.6	.2932	4	Mayer
0.2861	34.6	.2060	6	meridiem
0.2861	34.6	.2932	4	Rev
0.2861	34.6	.2932	4	281
0.2859	34.6	.3259	4	Going
0.2859	34.6	.0919	8	Nestor
0.2857	34.6	.1173	10	metalworking
0.2856	34.6	.3267	4	band's
0.2856	34.6	.2891	4	hideout
0.2856	34.6	.3267	4	Joplin
0.2856	34.6	.2918	4	sapphires
0.2856	34.6	.2891	4	Schweitzer
0.2856	34.6	.3267	4	spanned
0.2856	34.6	.2891	4	stratagem
0.2855	34.6	.1564	7	Agnew
0.2855	34.6	.2205	5	Araucanian
0.2855	34.6	.1564	7	Dept
0.2855	34.6	.2205	5	Doctrine
0.2855	34.6	.2205	5	Edmonton
0.2855	34.6	.2205	5	frost-free
0.2855	34.6	.1564	7	III
0.2855	34.6	.2205	5	Kimberley
0.2855	34.6	.2205	5	Mercator
0.2855	34.6	.2205	5	middle-latitude
0.2855	34.6	.2205	5	Paulo
0.2855	34.6	.2205	5	provisional
0.2855	34.6	.2205	5	Sao
0.2855	34.6	.2205	5	1754
0.2852	34.6	.2625	5	cut-off
0.2851	34.5	.1845	6	cantons
0.2851	34.5	.1845	6	Czar's
0.2851	34.5	.2254	5	myrrh
0.2850	34.5	.2260	5	carbons
0.2850	34.5	.2010	5	cheekbones
0.2850	34.5	.2187	5	frog's
0.2850	34.5	.2010	5	sitters
0.2850	34.5	.3121	4	6-inch
0.2848	34.5	.2875	4	Claire
0.2848	34.5	.2875	4	1150
0.2847	34.5	.2904	4	bumbling
0.2847	34.5	.3250	4	D's
0.2847	34.5	.2904	4	jumping-off
0.2847	34.5	.1579	6	12-13
0.2845	34.5	.0848	10	co-ops
0.2844	34.5	.0925	7	forgiveness
0.2844	34.5	.0000	19	3/3
0.2843	34.5	.2190	5	Headman
0.2843	34.5	.2190	5	Hours
0.2843	34.5	.2190	5	Inside
0.2842	34.5	.2242	5	Abbot
0.2842	34.5	.2242	5	abolition
0.2842	34.5	.1126	9	adhesives
0.2842	34.5	.2805	4	flowerpots
0.2842	34.5	.2242	5	Fulani
0.2842	34.5	.2805	4	handler
0.2842	34.5	.0337	14	LaVerne
0.2842	34.5	.2805	4	pant
0.2842	34.5	.2242	5	Underground
0.2841	34.5	.2433	5	birdlike
0.2841	34.5	.2433	5	Mendelssohn's
0.2840	34.5	.2991	4	jugs
0.2840	34.5	.2872	4	nearsighted
0.2840	34.5	.2872	4	reined
0.2840	34.5	.2872	4	undertone
0.2840	34.5	.2872	4	woes
0.2839	34.5	.1093	7	ben
0.2839	34.5	.2235	5	schists
0.2839	34.5	.1093	7	tole
0.2836	34.5	.3290	4	shapers
0.2834	34.5	.2178	5	Arch
0.2834	34.5	.2178	5	Reference
0.2832	34.5	.1544	7	Stephanie
0.2832	34.5	.1826	6	Titanic
0.2831	34.5	.2855	4	absences
0.2831	34.5	.3306	4	cites
0.2831	34.5	.3306	4	utterances
0.2829	34.5	.1117	8	Custis
0.2829	34.5	.3277	4	life-long
0.2829	34.5	.1117	8	638
0.2828	34.5	.2312	5	menacingly
0.2826	34.5	.3219	4	inset
0.2823	34.5	.3184	4	aftermath

THE PRECEDING WORD TYPE OCCUPIES RANK 28400

U	SFI	D	F	Word Type
0.2823	34.5	.0622	17	dividers
0.2823	34.5	.3213	4	Warning
0.2818	34.5	.2144	5	atmospheres
0.2818	34.5	.2847	4	clocked
0.2818	34.5	.2847	4	endow
0.2818	34.5	.2144	5	Epsom
0.2818	34.5	.2847	4	favourable
0.2818	34.5	.2847	4	finches
0.2818	34.5	.2144	5	flashlights
0.2818	34.5	.2847	4	plough
0.2818	34.5	.2847	4	secondly
0.2818	34.5	.2144	5	staghorn
0.2818	34.5	.2628	5	8-inch
0.2817	34.5	.1810	6	Batten
0.2817	34.5	.1537	8	drafting
0.2817	34.5	.2494	4	taffeta
0.2817	34.5	.2494	4	uselessly
0.2816	34.5	.3182	4	boisterous
0.2816	34.5	.3182	4	Pretoria
0.2815	34.5	.2948	4	slinking
0.2814	34.5	.0000	24	Oralee
0.2814	34.5	.1529	7	ospreys
0.2814	34.5	.1529	7	Presley
0.2814	34.5	.1582	6	roasts
0.2813	34.5	.2486	4	slacks
0.2813	34.5	.2379	5	0 **
0.2813	34.5	.2379	5	10-13
0.2813	34.5	.2379	5	12-3
0.2813	34.5	.2379	5	472
0.2813	34.5	.2379	5	6/
0.2812	34.5	.3175	4	predominate
0.2812	34.5	.3175	4	recurring
0.2811	34.5	.2418	5	avid
0.2811	34.5	.2418	5	Liao
0.2811	34.5	.2418	5	lunatic
0.2811	34.5	.3214	4	Manual
0.2811	34.5	.3214	4	moldings
0.2811	34.5	.2418	5	mores
0.2811	34.5	.2418	5	motivation
0.2811	34.5	.2418	5	premise
0.2811	34.5	.2418	5	topical
0.2810	34.5	.1823	6	Axis
0.2810	34.5	.1823	6	chieftains
0.2810	34.5	.1823	6	deSoto
0.2810	34.5	.2092	6	modulated
0.2810	34.5	.1823	6	open-pit
0.2810	34.5	.1823	6	semantics
0.2809	34.5	.3269	4	conditioners
0.2809	34.5	.3269	4	member's
0.2808	34.5	.2407	5	maverick
0.2808	34.5	.2390	5	right-hander
0.2808	34.5	.2407	5	Who's
0.2806	34.5	.3164	4	steely
0.2804	34.5	.2280	5	pattering
0.2803	34.5	.1813	6	aggregate
0.2803	34.5	.1813	6	gametes
0.2803	34.5	.1813	6	mitosis
0.2803	34.5	.1813	6	vomiting
0.2802	34.5	.2387	5	dunno
0.2802	34.5	.2446	5	hemi
0.2801	34.5	.2121	5	biotic
0.2801	34.5	.2121	5	eclipsing
0.2801	34.5	.3232	4	fillets
0.2801	34.5	.3155	4	highness
0.2801	34.5	.2447	5	Ivy
0.2801	34.5	.3155	4	lowness
0.2801	34.5	.2447	5	Sofia
0.2801	34.5	.2447	5	Upward
0.2799	34.5	.0911	11	trombones
0.2797	34.5	.1536	7	Yokohama
0.2797	34.5	.2203	5	660
0.2794	34.5	.1785	6	electromagnets
0.2794	34.5	.2229	5	siesta
0.2786	34.5	.1755	6	coefficients
0.2786	34.5	.1755	6	five-minute
0.2785	34.4	.2112	5	guesser
0.2785	34.4	.2112	5	Kemal
0.2785	34.4	.3130	4	strident
0.2785	34.4	.2112	5	Valdivia
0.2785	34.4	.2112	5	zoning
0.2784	34.4	.2198	5	confederation
0.2776	34.4	.2363	5	Eagles
0.2776	34.4	.2431	5	lugs
0.2776	34.4	.2431	5	tabletop
0.2775	34.4	.3112	4	sixteenth-century
0.2774	34.4	.2721	4	thoroughness
0.2774	34.4	.1516	7	you-all
0.2773	34.4	.0828	10	Uncas
0.2770	34.4	.2442	5	affix
0.2768	34.4	.1660	5	Karen's
0.2767	34.4	.2304	5	Inauguration
0.2767	34.4	.2304	5	majors
0.2767	34.4	.2304	5	warhead
0.2767	34.4	.3230	4	3-
0.2766	34.4	.3056	4	elongation
0.2765	34.4	.1757	6	Walters
0.2764	34.4	.3224	4	adherents
0.2764	34.4	.3135	4	directness
0.2764	34.4	.2380	5	0000
0.2763	34.4	.2440	5	pensive

THE PRECEDING WORD TYPE OCCUPIES RANK 28500

U	SFI	D	F	Word Type
0.2762	34.4	.0537	10	1/1000
0.2761	34.4	.2501	4	correctness
0.2760	34.4	.2708	4	Bedell
0.2760	34.4	.0000	14	cathode
0.2760	34.4	.2708	4	cunningly
0.2760	34.4	.2708	4	footsore
0.2760	34.4	.2708	4	hm
0.2760	34.4	.2708	4	imagines
0.2760	34.4	.2708	4	madmen
0.2760	34.4	.2288	5	Revenue
0.2760	34.4	.2708	4	roving
0.2760	34.4	.2708	4	self-evident
0.2760	34.4	.2708	4	trudge
0.2760	34.4	.2288	5	3-D
0.2760	34.4	.2374	5	349
0.2759	34.4	.1881	6	Enrique
0.2759	34.4	.2522	5	lithograph
0.2759	34.4	.3119	4	345
0.2757	34.4	.1878	6	centre
0.2757	34.4	.1877	5	chapped
0.2757	34.4	.2390	5	excavate
0.2757	34.4	.1877	5	tight-fitting
0.2756	34.4	.1501	7	Celia
0.2756	34.4	.2700	4	incredulity
0.2756	34.4	.0886	11	s's
0.2754	34.4	.2436	5	Ave
0.2754	34.4	.2382	5	cornice
0.2754	34.4	.2382	5	Hassan
0.2754	34.4	.2437	5	humanities
0.2753	34.4	.3189	4	bowsprit
0.2753	34.4	.0772	12	LP
0.2751	34.4	.0000	19	Buffie
0.2751	34.4	.1475	7	contemplative
0.2749	34.4	.3163	4	ellipses
0.2749	34.4	.1038	9	seconded
0.2747	34.4	.2384	5	convivial
0.2747	34.4	.3173	4	Credit
0.2747	34.4	.3173	4	diversified
0.2745	34.4	.1252	8	communicates
0.2745	34.4	.2414	5	Jo's
0.2744	34.4	.2816	4	mightily
0.2743	34.4	.1889	6	constipation
0.2742	34.4	.0724	11	Biddy
0.2741	34.4	.0000	6	'cos
0.2741	34.4	.0000	6	Adair
0.2741	34.4	.0000	6	Alicia
0.2741	34.4	.0000	6	Alkemade
0.2741	34.4	.0000	6	Arabelle's
0.2741	34.4	.0000	6	Axley
0.2741	34.4	.0000	6	b-r-rrm
0.2741	34.4	.0000	6	Benchly
0.2741	34.4	.0000	6	Benedek
0.2741	34.4	.2827	4	beret
0.2741	34.4	.0000	6	Bethenia
0.2741	34.4	.0000	6	Big's
0.2741	34.4	.0000	6	Bonhomme
0.2741	34.4	.0000	6	Bunsuru
0.2741	34.4	.0000	6	burglars
0.2741	34.4	.0000	6	Calhoun's
0.2741	34.4	.0000	6	CC'S**
0.2741	34.4	.0000	6	centavo
0.2741	34.4	.0000	6	Chaffy
0.2741	34.4	.0000	6	Charbonneau
0.2741	34.4	.0000	6	cheep
0.2741	34.4	.0000	6	Chem
0.2741	34.4	.0000	6	Chinese-Americans
0.2741	34.4	.0000	6	Crabapple
0.2741	34.4	.0000	6	cultivator
0.2741	34.4	.0000	6	Cusi
0.2741	34.4	.0000	6	Deanne
0.2741	34.4	.0000	6	Duncan's
0.2741	34.4	.0000	6	Durkee's
0.2741	34.4	.0000	6	Fernanda
0.2741	34.4	.0000	6	Flandin
0.2741	34.4	.0000	6	Flandins
0.2741	34.4	.0000	6	Fritzl
0.2741	34.4	.0000	6	Gompton
0.2741	34.4	.0000	6	Greased
0.2741	34.4	.0000	6	Hatter
0.2741	34.4	.0000	6	Johann's
0.2741	34.4	.0000	6	Kaang
0.2741	34.4	.0000	6	kabunkit
0.2741	34.4	.0000	6	Kanele
0.2741	34.4	.0000	6	Ke-ya
0.2741	34.4	.0000	6	Kidwell
0.2741	34.4	.0000	6	Kul
0.2741	34.4	.0000	6	LaRabida
0.2741	34.4	.0000	6	Laennec
0.2741	34.4	.0000	6	Liesi
0.2741	34.4	.0000	6	Link's
0.2741	34.4	.0000	6	lu
0.2741	34.4	.0000	6	Mallie
0.2741	34.4	.0000	6	Mamita
0.2741	34.4	.0000	6	Manton
0.2741	34.4	.0000	6	Manx
0.2741	34.4	.0000	6	Maryark
0.2741	34.4	.0000	6	Medea
0.2741	34.4	.0000	6	Medio
0.2741	34.4	.0000	6	Minelli
0.2741	34.4	.0000	6	Mitsu

THE PRECEDING WORD TYPE OCCUPIES RANK 28600

U	SFI	D	F	Word Type
0.2741	34.4	.0000	6	Mogo
0.2741	34.4	.0000	6	Myoux
0.2741	34.4	.0000	6	Nelly's
0.2741	34.4	.0000	6	Njoki
0.2741	34.4	.0000	6	O'Linn
0.2741	34.4	.0000	6	Omar
0.2741	34.4	.0000	6	Panza
0.2741	34.4	.0000	6	Peerson
0.2741	34.4	.0000	6	Petrina
0.2741	34.4	.0000	6	Pinzon
0.2741	34.4	.0000	6	PLAP-plap
0.2741	34.4	.0000	6	Pollito
0.2741	34.4	.0000	6	Pound-Sweet
0.2741	34.4	.0000	6	Reacher
0.2741	34.4	.0000	6	Rickey
0.2741	34.4	.0000	6	Rinaldo
0.2741	34.4	.0000	6	Roebling
0.2741	34.4	.0000	6	rogues
0.2741	34.4	.0000	6	Sackman
0.2741	34.4	.0000	6	Schultz
0.2741	34.4	.0000	6	semaphore
0.2741	34.4	.0000	6	Sesame
0.2741	34.4	.0000	6	Shadow's
0.2741	34.4	.0000	6	Slightly
0.2741	34.4	.0000	6	smuggler
0.2741	34.4	.0000	6	Snapper's
0.2741	34.4	.0000	6	Sniggers
0.2741	34.4	.0000	6	Snowshoe
0.2741	34.4	.0000	6	Stickeen
0.2741	34.4	.0000	6	Stina
0.2741	34.4	.0000	6	Strongfort
0.2741	34.4	.0000	6	Tamara
0.2741	34.4	.0000	6	Thoburn
0.2741	34.4	.0000	6	Tick
0.2741	34.4	.0000	6	Timothy's
0.2741	34.4	.0000	6	Tomson
0.2741	34.4	.0000	6	Twig
0.2741	34.4	.0000	6	Una
0.2741	34.4	.0000	6	Verygood
0.2741	34.4	.0000	6	Washburn
0.2741	34.4	.0000	6	whalerman
0.2741	34.4	.0000	6	whalers
0.2741	34.4	.0000	6	wowser
0.2741	34.4	.0000	6	Yoder
0.2741	34.4	.0000	6	Zailman
0.2741	34.4	.0000	6	Zitu
0.2739	34.4	.3123	4	right-angle
0.2738	34.4	.2814	4	Jacqueline
0.2737	34.4	.2680	4	appraisal
0.2737	34.4	.2680	4	globe's
0.2737	34.4	.2680	4	scooping
0.2737	34.4	.2680	4	Seaway
0.2737	34.4	.2680	4	Winfield
0.2737	34.4	.2680	4	1749
0.2737	34.4	.2680	4	1764
0.2736	34.4	.0000	25	graphemes
0.2734	34.4	.1177	8	Lunar
0.2733	34.4	.1634	5	Agamemnon
0.2733	34.4	.1634	5	buffing
0.2733	34.4	.1634	5	craggy
0.2733	34.4	.2672	4	egg-laying
0.2733	34.4	.2672	4	explosively
0.2733	34.4	.1634	5	Herrick
0.2733	34.4	.1634	5	incendiary
0.2733	34.4	.1634	5	Kraler
0.2733	34.4	.2672	4	lethal
0.2733	34.4	.2672	4	millionths
0.2733	34.4	.2672	4	obstruct
0.2733	34.4	.1634	5	Queenie's
0.2733	34.4	.1634	5	Seminoles
0.2733	34.4	.2672	4	silicate
0.2733	34.4	.1634	5	snicker
0.2732	34.4	.2797	4	chortled
0.2732	34.4	.3168	4	grievous
0.2732	34.4	.2797	4	mythical
0.2729	34.4	.3160	4	Siamese
0.2727	34.4	.2342	5	takin'
0.2727	34.4	.2342	5	talkin'
0.2727	34.4	.2342	5	tut
0.2726	34.4	.1277	6	cadet
0.2726	34.4	.2435	5	flotsam
0.2726	34.4	.1277	6	Granny's
0.2726	34.4	.2435	5	intractable
0.2726	34.4	.1277	6	Panther
0.2725	34.4	.3160	4	Stanford's
0.2724	34.4	.2160	4	Godwin
0.2724	34.4	.2160	4	inoculated
0.2724	34.4	.2160	4	sulfides
0.2723	34.4	.0000	14	Roberto
0.2720	34.3	.2327	5	Dow
0.2720	34.3	.2742	4	play-acting
0.2719	34.3	.3192	4	incidental
0.2719	34.3	.3192	4	Parisian
0.2718	34.3	.3141	4	illogical
0.2715	34.3	.2638	4	sightseers
0.2714	34.3	.2152	4	DeWitt
0.2714	34.3	.2454	4	fictitious
0.2714	34.3	.2152	4	Freedoms
0.2714	34.3	.2999	4	geo
0.2714	34.3	.2152	4	Iceland's

THE PRECEDING WORD TYPE OCCUPIES RANK 28700

U	SFI	D	F	Word Type
0.2714	34.3	.2152	4	Koran
0.2714	34.3	.2152	4	scrubby
0.2714	34.3	.2152	4	silversmiths
0.2714	34.3	.2454	4	spangles
0.2714	34.3	.2152	4	Wheeling
0.2714	34.3	.2152	4	99th
0.2713	34.3	.1025	9	woeful
0.2712	34.3	.2332	5	annuals
0.2712	34.3	.2000	5	clothespin
0.2712	34.3	.2734	4	convincingly
0.2712	34.3	.2000	5	corona
0.2711	34.3	.3113	4	showcase
0.2709	34.3	.3160	4	pageantry
0.2706	34.3	.3074	4	butted
0.2706	34.3	.3111	4	unnecessarily
0.2703	34.3	.2390	4	bathtubs
0.2703	34.3	.2316	5	billing
0.2703	34.3	.2316	5	evangelical
0.2703	34.3	.2963	4	everytime
0.2703	34.3	.2316	5	Montenegro
0.2703	34.3	.2316	5	Paleolithic
0.2703	34.3	.2316	5	regulatory
0.2701	34.3	.2324	5	ruining
0.2696	34.3	.2764	4	Thomson's
0.2695	34.3	.1990	5	Abdel
0.2695	34.3	.1990	5	Ch'in
0.2695	34.3	.1990	5	Court's
0.2695	34.3	.3660	3	entrust
0.2695	34.3	.3660	3	estuaries

U	SFI	D	F	Word Type
0.2695	34.3	.1990	5	Evan's
0.2695	34.3	.1990	5	Gamal
0.2695	34.3	.1990	5	leisure-time
0.2695	34.3	.3660	3	neatest
0.2695	34.3	.1990	5	ratification
0.2695	34.3	.1990	5	tanneries
0.2695	34.3	.3660	3	028
0.2695	34.3	.3660	3	276
0.2694	34.3	.0000	18	endpoints
0.2694	34.3	.0000	18	quadrilateral
0.2694	34.3	.0000	18	reciprocals
0.2694	34.3	.0000	18	whole-number
0.2694	34.3	.0000	18	4-digit
0.2693	34.3	.2138	5	Angeles
0.2693	34.3	.2138	5	harassment
0.2693	34.3	.2138	5	Mormon
0.2693	34.3	.2138	5	royalties
0.2692	34.3	.0869	7	cosmetic
0.2692	34.3	.0869	7	mallard
0.2691	34.3	.1018	7	acetylene
0.2691	34.3	.0712	11	Peron
0.2690	34.3	.2251	5	copepods
0.2689	34.3	.2129	5	circulating
0.2689	34.3	.2129	5	exhaustive
0.2689	34.3	.2751	4	Montagues
0.2689	34.3	.2129	5	SST
0.2689	34.3	.2129	5	tendon
0.2689	34.3	.2129	5	1972
0.2687	34.3	.2341	5	Mort
0.2686	34.3	.2744	4	I's
0.2686	34.3	.2744	4	misspelling
0.2686	34.3	.2380	5	slithy
0.2686	34.3	.2380	5	wabe
0.2685	34.3	.2394	5	Braque
0.2685	34.3	.2394	5	Vermeer
0.2684	34.3	.1250	6	Assateague
0.2684	34.3	.1250	6	Clint
0.2684	34.3	.1250	6	Harkness
0.2684	34.3	.1250	6	Karlstead
0.2683	34.3	.2741	4	Ah
0.2683	34.3	.1852	6	brasses
0.2683	34.3	.2741	4	forefront
0.2683	34.3	.1852	6	Ola
0.2682	34.3	.0917	9	Archipelago
0.2682	34.3	.0917	9	Sport
0.2681	34.3	.2576	4	ice-cold
0.2681	34.3	.2576	4	wide-mouthed
0.2680	34.3	.0705	11	tuatara
0.2677	34.3	.1966	5	Northeastern
0.2676	34.3	.2240	5	saddlebags
0.2675	34.3	.3071	4	misconduct
0.2674	34.3	.2381	4	all-fired
0.2674	34.3	.2381	4	first-floor
0.2674	34.3	.2381	4	Willa
0.2673	34.3	.2068	5	casein
0.2673	34.3	.2078	5	Mayan
0.2673	34.3	.2068	5	solidify
0.2673	34.3	.0000	22	Thinkum
0.2673	34.3	.2078	5	Uprising
0.2671	34.3	.0909	9	suicides
0.2671	34.3	.1665	6	three-way
0.2670	34.3	.3060	4	rarity
0.2668	34.3	.0976	10	choruses
0.2668	34.3	.0861	7	fiord
0.2668	34.3	.0976	10	keyboards
0.2668	34.3	.0861	7	NorthPole
0.2668	34.3	.0861	7	tableland
0.2668	34.3	.1220	8	Universities
0.2667	34.3	.1660	6	blueprints
0.2666	34.3	.1825	6	inflected
0.2666	34.3	.3006	4	jealously
THE PRECEDING WORD TYPE OCCUPIES RANK 28800				
0.2665	34.3	.2707	4	fasted
0.2665	34.3	.1240	7	histogram
0.2664	34.3	.2884	4	electricians
0.2663	34.3	.2918	4	acquires
0.2662	34.3	.2358	4	fluted
0.2662	34.3	.2115	5	mullet
0.2662	34.3	.2703	4	Rodeo
0.2662	34.3	.2703	4	spank
0.2662	34.3	.2358	4	strut
0.2661	34.3	.1420	7	Beckett
0.2661	34.3	.1420	7	Circuit
0.2661	34.2	.2968	4	escalators
0.2661	34.3	.2183	5	G's
0.2661	34.3	.2183	5	Moths
0.2661	34.3	.2183	5	Trumpet
0.2661	34.3	.2183	5	virile
0.2660	34.2	.2989	4	Ethel
0.2659	34.2	.0628	13	Ron's
0.2657	34.2	.1467	7	Demetrius
0.2657	34.2	.2226	5	Dooley
0.2657	34.2	.2226	5	Garibaldi
0.2657	34.2	.2226	5	Latins
0.2657	34.2	.2226	5	Napoleonic
0.2657	34.2	.2226	5	Pomerania
0.2657	34.2	.2226	5	theological
0.2656	34.2	.2912	4	jealousies
0.2655	34.2	.1617	6	625
0.2654	34.2	.3020	4	craning
0.2653	34.2	.2857	4	14-4
0.2647	34.2	.2207	5	axioms
0.2647	34.2	.2207	5	equivalence
0.2647	34.2	.2207	5	462
0.2638	34.2	.1422	7	biographical
0.2636	34.2	.0987	9	Minus
0.2634	34.2	.2847	4	watchmen
0.2625	34.2	.2865	4	8-3
0.2621	34.2	.3569	3	five-day
0.2619	34.2	.1226	7	Congolese
0.2619	34.2	.3569	3	fares
0.2619	34.2	.1226	7	Selkirk
0.2617	34.2	.1927	5	Seaboard
0.2615	34.2	.2199	4	quick-drying
0.2615	34.2	.2350	5	tact
0.2611	34.2	.1794	6	Creoles
0.2611	34.2	.1794	6	kinship

U	SFI	D	F	Word Type
0.2611	34.2	.1794	6	layman
0.2609	34.2	.3553	3	agitate
0.2609	34.2	.3553	3	amplifiers
0.2609	34.2	.3553	3	anthracite
0.2609	34.2	.3138	4	bobbins
0.2609	34.2	.3553	3	fierce-looking
0.2609	34.2	.3553	3	jockeying
0.2609	34.2	.3553	3	killdeer
0.2609	34.2	.3553	3	long-horned
0.2609	34.2	.3553	3	mirror's
0.2609	34.2	.3553	3	pitch-dark
0.2609	34.2	.3553	3	succulent
0.2608	34.2	.3553	3	anti-freeze
0.2608	34.2	.3553	3	beadwork
0.2608	34.2	.3553	3	Bond
0.2608	34.2	.3553	3	breakwater
0.2608	34.2	.3553	3	candlemaker
0.2608	34.2	.3553	3	canteens
0.2608	34.2	.3553	3	deserting
0.2608	34.2	.3553	3	eight-thirty
0.2608	34.2	.3553	3	Hickok
0.2608	34.2	.3553	3	Icelandic
0.2608	34.2	.3553	3	Lane's
0.2608	34.2	.3553	3	Laws
0.2608	34.2	.0991	11	mayonnaise
0.2608	34.2	.3553	3	mid-afternoon
0.2608	34.2	.3553	3	moorings
0.2608	34.2	.3553	3	outmoded
0.2608	34.2	.3553	3	perverse
0.2608	34.2	.3553	3	plumber's
0.2608	34.2	.3553	3	rioted
0.2608	34.2	.3553	3	torrential
0.2608	34.2	.3553	3	wicks
0.2608	34.2	.3553	3	535
0.2606	34.2	.0000	18	Mink
0.2605	34.2	.1708	6	Freon
0.2605	34.2	.1708	6	Mich
0.2605	34.2	.1200	6	Steven's
0.2605	34.2	.1708	6	surveillance
0.2605	34.2	.1200	6	Wind's
0.2605	34.2	.1708	6	Wis
0.2601	34.2	.3848	3	radiocarbon
0.2601	34.2	.3848	3	365-day
0.2600	34.1	.2921	4	pith
0.2598	34.1	.3171	4	3-4
0.2597	34.1	.1316	6	Angie
0.2596	34.1	.2621	4	Wire
0.2595	34.1	.1576	6	dowel
0.2594	34.1	.3840	3	Bingham
0.2594	34.1	.3840	3	chicken's
0.2594	34.1	.3840	3	Theodor
0.2593	34.1	.1725	5	all-purpose
0.2593	34.1	.2578	4	minuets
0.2593	34.1	.2578	4	She
0.2593	34.1	.2578	4	singer's
THE PRECEDING WORD TYPE OCCUPIES RANK 28900				
0.2593	34.1	.2578	4	staging
0.2593	34.1	.0859	9	tester
0.2593	34.1	.2578	4	yap
0.2590	34.1	.2052	5	tang
0.2587	34.1	.0000	32	descant
0.2587	34.1	.0000	32	oboe
0.2586	34.1	.2978	4	esthetic
0.2585	34.1	.1688	6	Tinker's
0.2584	34.1	.2055	5	alcove
0.2584	34.1	.2055	5	Galveston
0.2584	34.1	.2353	5	goblets
0.2584	34.1	.2055	5	Runaway
0.2583	34.1	.1187	6	hemlocks
0.2583	34.1	.1187	6	MacGregor
0.2583	34.1	.1187	6	rapping
0.2583	34.1	.0681	9	strumming
0.2582	34.1	.2558	4	descends
0.2580	34.1	.0550	17	gelatin
0.2579	34.1	.0000	22	Conseil
0.2577	34.1	.1462	7	Trinity
0.2576	34.1	.2955	4	smudges
0.2574	34.1	.0683	12	ensemble
0.2574	34.1	.2856	4	entanglements
0.2570	34.1	.3849	3	Colosseum
0.2570	34.1	.1673	6	Elvis
0.2570	34.1	.3849	3	installments
0.2570	34.1	.1673	6	osprey
0.2567	34.1	.2251	5	Cyril
0.2567	34.1	.1314	7	NET
0.2566	34.1	.3528	3	broadcaster
0.2566	34.1	.3528	3	ping
0.2566	34.1	.3064	4	proportioned
0.2566	34.1	.3528	3	ten-dollar
0.2565	34.1	.2240	4	onrushing
0.2563	34.1	.0000	13	collodion
0.2563	34.1	.0000	13	four-o'clock
0.2563	34.1	.0000	13	limewater
0.2563	34.1	.0000	13	ovules
0.2563	34.1	.0000	13	Priestley
0.2562	34.1	.2037	5	blockade
0.2562	34.1	.2037	5	constitutions
0.2562	34.1	.2037	5	copra
0.2562	34.1	.2037	5	Dominion
0.2562	34.1	.2037	5	Kattegat
0.2562	34.1	.2037	5	low-grade
0.2562	34.1	.2037	5	sugarcane
0.2560	34.1	.2035	5	input-output
0.2560	34.1	.2429	5	laminated
0.2560	34.1	.2240	5	spellers
0.2560	34.1	.2035	5	1666
0.2559	34.1	.2919	4	wadded
0.2558	34.1	.2238	5	inflections
0.2558	34.1	.1813	6	oversize
0.2558	34.1	.2238	5	playback
0.2557	34.1	.1496	5	beaver's
0.2557	34.1	.2028	5	booklets
0.2557	34.1	.1496	5	Cathie
0.2557	34.1	.2028	5	cyclotron
0.2557	34.1	.1496	5	editor's
0.2557	34.1	.1496	5	franc
0.2557	34.1	.2028	5	Hertz

U	SFI	D	F	Word Type
0.2557	34.1	.2028	5	heterozygotes
0.2557	34.1	.2028	5	live-bearing
0.2557	34.1	.1496	5	UFO'S
0.2556	34.1	.2223	4	clashing
0.2556	34.1	.1680	6	maxims
0.2556	34.1	.2223	4	Mycenae
0.2555	34.1	.1169	6	Bronze
0.2555	34.1	.1808	6	dimmer
0.2555	34.1	.1169	6	Passover
0.2554	34.1	.1777	5	bloodletting
0.2554	34.1	.1380	7	Dyke
0.2554	34.1	.1380	7	Lenape
0.2552	34.1	.2863	4	278
0.2549	34.1	.2595	4	stay-at-home
0.2548	34.1	.3781	3	Aristarchus
0.2548	34.1	.3781	3	Bryce
0.2548	34.1	.3781	3	deflect
0.2548	34.1	.3781	3	dissection
0.2548	34.1	.3781	3	pondering
0.2548	34.1	.3781	3	transit
0.2548	34.1	.3781	3	1970's
0.2545	34.1	.0000	17	base-ten
0.2545	34.1	.0000	17	push-ups
0.2545	34.1	.0000	17	RS
0.2545	34.1	.0000	17	3-digit
0.2545	34.1	.2582	4	purer
0.2544	34.1	.0759	10	terrestrial
0.2543	34.1	.3452	3	appreciates
0.2543	34.1	.3452	3	charmingly
0.2543	34.1	.3452	3	Conversion
0.2543	34.1	.3452	3	doubters
0.2543	34.1	.3452	3	four-foot
0.2543	34.1	.3452	3	Freud
0.2543	34.1	.3452	3	gorging
0.2543	34.1	.3452	3	gushing
0.2543	34.1	.3452	3	Hayden
0.2543	34.1	.3452	3	high-flying
0.2543	34.1	.3452	3	jiggling
0.2543	34.1	.3452	3	overcrowded
THE PRECEDING WORD TYPE OCCUPIES RANK 29000				
0.2543	34.1	.3452	3	person-to-person
0.2543	34.1	.3452	3	Rudolf
0.2543	34.1	.3452	3	silliness
0.2543	34.1	.3452	3	spurring
0.2543	34.1	.3452	3	succumb
0.2543	34.1	.3452	3	tarantulas
0.2543	34.1	.3452	3	thunderheads
0.2543	34.1	.3080	4	tooled
0.2543	34.1	.3452	3	tremors
0.2542	34.1	.3454	3	Chance
0.2542	34.1	.3454	3	Crockett's
0.2542	34.1	.3454	3	cutaway
0.2542	34.1	.0335	13	Del
0.2542	34.1	.3454	3	don'ts
0.2542	34.1	.3454	3	dukes
0.2542	34.1	.3454	3	ebbing
0.2542	34.1	.3454	3	exaggerates
0.2542	34.1	.3454	3	expensively
0.2542	34.1	.3454	3	grade-school
0.2542	34.1	.3454	3	gymnasiums
0.2542	34.1	.3454	3	impotence
0.2542	34.1	.3454	3	infuriated
0.2542	34.1	.3454	3	isolationism
0.2542	34.1	.3454	3	Lippmann
0.2542	34.1	.3454	3	longtime
0.2542	34.1	.3454	3	Mayor's
0.2542	34.1	.3454	3	Mongolians
0.2542	34.1	.3454	3	mulatto
0.2542	34.1	.3454	3	retake
0.2542	34.1	.3454	3	single-engine
0.2542	34.1	.3454	3	squires
0.2542	34.1	.3454	3	stardom
0.2542	34.1	.3454	3	Stockton
0.2542	34.1	.3454	3	4500
0.2540	34.0	.2571	4	snapshots
0.2539	34.0	.1289	7	full-scale
0.2537	34.0	.3765	3	ground-up
0.2537	34.0	.3814	3	investing
0.2537	34.0	.2761	4	invincible
0.2537	34.0	.3765	3	motley
0.2537	34.0	.3814	3	redheads
0.2537	34.0	.3814	3	Travers
0.2537	34.0	.3814	3	338
0.2536	34.0	.2889	4	ignores
0.2536	34.0	.3811	3	operational
0.2536	34.0	.1660	6	Puddleby
0.2535	34.0	.2003	5	1-12
0.2535	34.0	.2003	5	192
0.2534	34.0	.3811	3	badgers
0.2534	34.0	.3811	3	ballooned
0.2534	34.0	.3815	3	beachhead
0.2534	34.0	.3815	3	Bloody
0.2534	34.0	.3811	3	build-up
0.2534	34.0	.3815	3	burnout
0.2534	34.0	.3815	3	cordial
0.2534	34.0	.3815	3	cuisine
0.2534	34.0	.3811	3	dauntless
0.2534	34.0	.3811	3	deep-seated
0.2534	34.0	.3811	3	Eden
0.2534	34.0	.3815	3	epics
0.2534	34.0	.3815	3	exclusion
0.2534	34.0	.3811	3	fouls
0.2534	34.0	.3815	3	fragmented
0.2534	34.0	.3815	3	fraught
0.2534	34.0	.3811	3	jawbone
0.2534	34.0	.3815	3	Manor
0.2534	34.0	.3815	3	Marxist
0.2534	34.0	.3815	3	million-dollar
0.2534	34.0	.3815	3	motorcade
0.2534	34.0	.3815	3	multicolored
0.2534	34.0	.3815	3	newspapermen
0.2534	34.0	.3815	3	notified
0.2534	34.0	.3811	3	painlessly
0.2534	34.0	.3815	3	prudence
0.2534	34.0	.3815	3	readable
0.2534	34.0	.3811	3	residual
0.2534	34.0	.3811	3	resounds

U	SFI	D	F	Word Type
0.2534	34.0	.3815	3	seabirds
0.2534	34.0	.3815	3	Sonora
0.2534	34.0	.3811	3	sporadic
0.2534	34.0	.3815	3	stewards
0.2534	34.0	.3811	3	subtlety
0.2534	34.0	.3811	3	ten-thousandth
0.2534	34.0	.3815	3	unfavorably
0.2534	34.0	.3815	3	withering
0.2534	34.0	.3815	3	331
0.2533	34.0	.1052	9	acoustical
0.2533	34.0	.1052	9	Bizet
0.2533	34.0	.1052	9	celesta
0.2532	34.0	.1674	5	cooing
0.2532	34.0	.1674	5	cook's
0.2532	34.0	.3862	3	Shaw's
0.2532	34.0	.3862	3	615
0.2531	34.0	.1962	5	cam
0.2531	34.0	.1962	5	sloppy
0.2528	34.0	.3431	3	armloads
0.2528	34.0	.3431	3	Bagdad
0.2528	34.0	.3429	3	Breakfast
0.2528	34.0	.3800	3	compactly
0.2528	34.0	.3431	3	confetti
THE PRECEDING WORD TYPE OCCUPIES RANK 29100				
0.2528	34.0	.3431	3	consolation
0.2528	34.0	.3431	3	Fridays
0.2528	34.0	.3431	3	gash
0.2528	34.0	.3431	3	genii
0.2528	34.0	.3431	3	Granada
0.2528	34.0	.3800	3	half-pint
0.2528	34.0	.3431	3	Hands
0.2528	34.0	.3429	3	hiding-place
0.2528	34.0	.3431	3	housemaids
0.2528	34.0	.3800	3	imaginable
0.2528	34.0	.3429	3	itches
0.2528	34.0	.3429	3	pored
0.2528	34.0	.3431	3	rancher's
0.2528	34.0	.3429	3	shriveled
0.2528	34.0	.3431	3	stevedores
0.2528	34.0	.3431	3	stinking
0.2528	34.0	.3429	3	stupor
0.2528	34.0	.3431	3	terrorizing
0.2528	34.0	.3431	3	thunderstruck
0.2528	34.0	.3431	3	uninterested
0.2528	34.0	.3431	3	unsaddle
0.2528	34.0	.3431	3	upstanding
0.2528	34.0	.3429	3	wastepaper
0.2526	34.0	.3805	3	buffeting
0.2526	34.0	.3805	3	contrive
0.2526	34.0	.3805	3	doorman
0.2526	34.0	.3805	3	endeavors
0.2526	34.0	.3805	3	hungered
0.2526	34.0	.3805	3	perplex
0.2526	34.0	.3805	3	quenched
0.2526	34.0	.3856	3	reams
0.2526	34.0	.3856	3	Simpson's
0.2525	34.0	.3801	3	beechnuts
0.2525	34.0	.3801	3	bungled
0.2525	34.0	.3801	3	inflict
0.2525	34.0	.3801	3	perspectives
0.2525	34.0	.3801	3	unmercifully
0.2525	34.0	.3801	3	upgrade
0.2524	34.0	.1972	4	Greens
0.2524	34.0	.2165	4	ladles
0.2524	34.0	.1194	8	Omega
0.2524	34.0	.1972	4	498
0.2522	34.0	.1468	5	Avondale
0.2522	34.0	.1468	5	Daniel's
0.2522	34.0	.1352	7	Lucie
0.2522	34.0	.2011	5	Ming
0.2522	34.0	.1468	5	parapet
0.2522	34.0	.1468	5	pellets
0.2522	34.0	.1468	5	Penny's
0.2522	34.0	.1468	5	Roadeo
0.2522	34.0	.2011	5	Romulus
0.2522	34.0	.1468	5	Shapiro
0.2522	34.0	.1468	5	shootin'
0.2522	34.0	.1622	5	Shore
0.2521	34.0	.2819	4	delightfully
0.2520	34.0	.3467	3	$800
0.2520	34.0	.3467	3	Chihuahua
0.2520	34.0	.3467	3	fifty-four
0.2520	34.0	.3467	3	mystify
0.2520	34.0	.3467	3	one-dollar
0.2520	34.0	.3467	3	YES
0.2520	34.0	.3467	3	776
0.2519	34.0	.2177	5	Coffee
0.2519	34.0	.2177	5	impassioned
0.2519	34.0	.2177	5	resonant
0.2519	34.0	.2177	5	tuneful
0.2518	34.0	.0203	18	ar
0.2516	34.0	.1618	6	Chemical
0.2516	34.0	.2056	4	shortness
0.2516	34.0	.2512	4	shotguns
0.2516	34.0	.2512	4	skidding
0.2515	34.0	.3465	3	Allison
0.2515	34.0	.3465	3	analyst
0.2515	34.0	.3465	3	animosities
0.2515	34.0	.3465	3	apathy
0.2515	34.0	.3465	3	belted
0.2515	34.0	.3465	3	black-haired
0.2515	34.0	.3465	3	boatloads
0.2515	34.0	.3465	3	breathable
0.2515	34.0	.1361	7	Calvinism
0.2515	34.0	.3465	3	cartwheels
0.2515	34.0	.3465	3	caterwauling
0.2515	34.0	.3465	3	diabolical
0.2515	34.0	.3465	3	diners
0.2515	34.0	.3465	3	dispatches
0.2515	34.0	.3465	3	docility
0.2515	34.0	.3465	3	dreads
0.2515	34.0	.3465	3	emplaced
0.2515	34.0	.3465	3	endeavoring
0.2515	34.0	.3465	3	ethic
0.2515	34.0	.3465	3	exuberance
0.2515	34.0	.3465	3	fingerprint
0.2515	34.0	.3465	3	flushing

U	SFI	D	F	Word Type
0.2515	34.0	.3465	3	Frey
0.2515	34.0	.3465	3	fulltime
0.2515	34.0	.3465	3	Hello
0.2515	34.0	.2446	4	immunization
0.2515	34.0	.3465	3	juggle
0.2515	34.0	.3465	3	long-drawn
0.2515	34.0	.3465	3	madhouse
THE PRECEDING WORD TYPE OCCUPIES RANK 29200				
0.2515	34.0	.3465	3	overdeveloped
0.2515	34.0	.3465	3	paratrooper
0.2515	34.0	.3465	3	roosts
0.2515	34.0	.3465	3	sanction
0.2515	34.0	.3465	3	Services
0.2515	34.0	.3465	3	shunned
0.2515	34.0	.3465	3	sported
0.2515	34.0	.3465	3	tiredness
0.2515	34.0	.3465	3	traveler's
0.2515	34.0	.3465	3	turkey's
0.2515	34.0	.3465	3	villains
0.2514	34.0	.3732	3	Popocatepetl
0.2514	34.0	.3732	3	shortwave
0.2513	34.0	.3863	3	Aid
0.2513	34.0	.3863	3	allegory
0.2513	34.0	.3863	3	bluntly
0.2513	34.0	.3863	3	creepy
0.2513	34.0	.3863	3	downwind
0.2513	34.0	.2942	4	first-aid
0.2513	34.0	.3863	3	fourteen-year-old
0.2513	34.0	.3863	3	frocks
0.2513	34.0	.3863	3	gentlemen's
0.2513	34.0	.1001	8	Hanoi
0.2513	34.0	.1001	8	Kabuki
0.2513	34.0	.3863	3	materialize
0.2513	34.0	.3863	3	proletariat
0.2513	34.0	.3863	3	romances
0.2513	34.0	.3863	3	sponsoring
0.2513	34.0	.3863	3	spunk
0.2513	34.0	.3863	3	Think
0.2512	34.0	.0885	10	choirs
0.2512	34.0	.0885	10	Strauss
0.2512	34.0	.2142	4	sun-warmed
0.2512	34.0	.2142	4	vaulting
0.2511	34.0	.3780	3	misinterpret
0.2511	34.0	.3780	3	402
0.2510	34.0	.1288	7	Beaver's
0.2510	34.0	.1288	7	Dandy
0.2510	34.0	.1288	7	withers
0.2510	34.0	.3776	3	199
0.2509	34.0	.3783	3	Neighbor
0.2509	34.0	.3783	3	Societies
0.2509	34.0	.3783	3	1704
0.2508	34.0	.1993	5	Bessie's
0.2508	34.0	.3722	3	blazes
0.2508	34.0	.1993	5	Coleman
0.2508	34.0	.3722	3	crouches
0.2508	34.0	.3722	3	doughty
0.2508	34.0	.3779	3	hollyhocks
0.2508	34.0	.3722	3	Hurricane
0.2508	34.0	.1993	5	rover
0.2508	34.0	.1993	5	Vassar
0.2508	34.0	.3722	3	viciousness
0.2506	34.0	.3795	3	Allen's
0.2506	34.0	.3795	3	anticipating
0.2506	34.0	.3795	3	dub
0.2506	34.0	.3791	3	eases
0.2506	34.0	.3795	3	forty-one
0.2506	34.0	.3795	3	girded
0.2506	34.0	.3795	3	jeweler's
0.2506	34.0	.3795	3	obsessed
0.2506	34.0	.3795	3	outcroppings
0.2506	34.0	.3791	3	procuring
0.2506	34.0	.3791	3	prosecuted
0.2506	34.0	.3795	3	renounced
0.2506	34.0	.3791	3	Running
0.2506	34.0	.3795	3	speediest
0.2506	34.0	.3795	3	tree-lined
0.2506	34.0	.3795	3	wedlock
0.2505	34.0	.3450	3	alligator's
0.2505	34.0	.3450	3	blackboards
0.2505	34.0	.3450	3	cannon's
0.2505	34.0	.3450	3	caper
0.2505	34.0	.3450	3	cawed
0.2505	34.0	.3450	3	cupping
0.2505	34.0	.3450	3	forgetfulness
0.2505	34.0	.3450	3	guardians
0.2505	34.0	.3450	3	half-heartedly
0.2505	34.0	.3450	3	hornets
0.2505	34.0	.3450	3	huckleberry
0.2505	34.0	.3450	3	impressionable
0.2505	34.0	.3450	3	Mad
0.2505	34.0	.3450	3	midafternoon
0.2505	34.0	.3773	3	namesake
0.2505	34.0	.3450	3	seep
0.2505	34.0	.3773	3	shortsighted
0.2505	34.0	.3450	3	shrugging
0.2505	34.0	.3450	3	siree
0.2505	34.0	.3450	3	slewed
0.2505	34.0	.3450	3	smarted
0.2505	34.0	.3769	3	snail's
0.2505	34.0	.3450	3	tousled
0.2505	34.0	.3450	3	two-storied
0.2505	34.0	.3450	3	upstate
0.2505	34.0	.3450	3	WAS
0.2505	34.0	.3450	3	white-faced
0.2505	34.0	.3773	3	wrappers
0.2504	34.0	.3776	3	annoyances
0.2504	34.0	.3776	3	awe-inspiring
0.2504	34.0	.3776	3	bloodiest
THE PRECEDING WORD TYPE OCCUPIES RANK 29300				
0.2504	34.0	.3776	3	cartload
0.2504	34.0	.3776	3	civilizing
0.2504	34.0	.3776	3	collector's
0.2504	34.0	.3829	3	digital
0.2504	34.0	.3776	3	dishonored
0.2504	34.0	.3776	3	outdid
0.2504	34.0	.3776	3	smooths
0.2504	34.0	.3829	3	10-year
0.2504	34.0	.3829	3	732
0.2503	34.0	.3855	3	allot
0.2503	34.0	.2336	4	conserving
0.2503	34.0	.3772	3	dish-shaped
0.2503	34.0	.3855	3	futhermore
0.2503	34.0	.3849	3	half-inch
0.2503	34.0	.3849	3	Kathleen
0.2503	34.0	.2709	4	Mesopotamians
0.2503	34.0	.2336	4	power-driven
0.2503	34.0	.3772	3	purplish
0.2503	34.0	.3772	3	self-assurance
0.2503	34.0	.3772	3	shockingly
0.2503	34.0	.2709	4	Sumerian
0.2503	34.0	.3855	3	yipping
0.2502	34.0	.2780	4	Beverly
0.2501	34.0	.2108	5	328
0.2500	34.0	.3852	3	aboriginal
0.2500	34.0	.3852	3	accusers
0.2500	34.0	.3852	3	appraised
0.2500	34.0	.1948	4	Benjy
0.2500	34.0	.3852	3	Brownies
0.2500	34.0	.3852	3	buckskins
0.2500	34.0	.3852	3	camellias
0.2500	34.0	.3852	3	chagrin
0.2500	34.0	.1948	4	cloth-covered
0.2500	34.0	.1948	4	commandant
0.2500	34.0	.1948	4	counterfeiter
0.2500	34.0	.1948	4	Crump
0.2500	34.0	.1948	4	cubicle
0.2500	34.0	.3852	3	devoutly
0.2500	34.0	.3848	3	enrolling
0.2500	34.0	.3852	3	fared
0.2500	34.0	.3854	3	five-hundred
0.2500	34.0	.1948	4	five-pound
0.2500	34.0	.1948	4	grounder
0.2500	34.0	.3854	3	herbage
0.2500	34.0	.3852	3	heroically
0.2500	34.0	.3852	3	hocks
0.2500	34.0	.3852	3	injustices
0.2500	34.0	.3854	3	jeers
0.2500	34.0	.3845	3	Joey's
0.2500	34.0	.1948	4	logbook
0.2500	34.0	.3852	3	pageants
0.2500	34.0	.1948	4	Patrick's
0.2500	34.0	.1948	4	playroom
0.2500	34.0	.3852	3	preacher's
0.2500	34.0	.3854	3	prithee
0.2500	34.0	.3852	3	quizzical
0.2500	34.0	.1948	4	Rutledge
0.2500	34.0	.3852	3	satiny
0.2500	34.0	.1948	4	scarcer
0.2500	34.0	.3852	3	scoot
0.2500	34.0	.3854	3	shadowing
0.2500	34.0	.1948	4	sharks'
0.2500	34.0	.1948	4	snorts
0.2500	34.0	.1948	4	step-mother
0.2500	34.0	.3852	3	turncoat
0.2500	34.0	.3845	3	warm-hearted
0.2499	34.0	.3709	3	conforms
0.2499	34.0	.3709	3	emu
0.2499	34.0	.3709	3	encroach
0.2499	34.0	.3709	3	entail
0.2499	34.0	.3709	3	expelling
0.2499	34.0	.3709	3	fluctuating
0.2499	34.0	.3709	3	unlawful
0.2499	34.0	.3709	3	1678
0.2499	34.0	.3709	3	322
0.2498	34.0	.3380	3	all-star
0.2498	34.0	.3383	3	armada
0.2498	34.0	.3380	3	Becky's
0.2498	34.0	.3380	3	Carla
0.2498	34.0	.3380	3	coma
0.2498	34.0	.3763	3	conditional
0.2498	34.0	.3763	3	disciplines
0.2498	34.0	.3380	3	discoverers
0.2498	34.0	.3380	3	harpoons
0.2498	34.0	.3380	3	intentionally
0.2498	34.0	.3380	3	playhouse
0.2498	34.0	.3383	3	roller-skating
0.2498	34.0	.3759	3	Ulm
0.2498	34.0	.3383	3	unroll
0.2498	34.0	.3383	3	well-armed
0.2498	34.0	.3763	3	Zambezi
0.2498	34.0	.3763	3	1641
0.2498	34.0	.3759	3	1674
0.2498	34.0	.3759	3	620
0.2498	34.0	.3763	3	680
0.2498	34.0	.3763	3	684
0.2498	34.0	.3759	3	960
0.2497	34.0	.3766	3	Aberdeen
0.2497	34.0	.3766	3	Advancement
0.2497	34.0	.3766	3	Alban
THE PRECEDING WORD TYPE OCCUPIES RANK 29400				
0.2497	34.0	.3766	3	Alfred's
0.2497	34.0	.3766	3	Antwerp
0.2497	34.0	.1979	5	Bowditch
0.2497	34.0	.3874	3	brews
0.2497	34.0	.3851	3	butcher's
0.2497	34.0	.2389	4	cartwheel
0.2497	34.0	.3766	3	colonialism
0.2497	34.0	.3851	3	Death's
0.2497	34.0	.3851	3	disapprovingly
0.2497	34.0	.3766	3	Donelson
0.2497	34.0	.3766	3	Dordogne
0.2497	34.0	.3766	3	drunkard
0.2497	34.0	.3766	3	Elias
0.2497	34.0	.3851	3	exultant
0.2497	34.0	.3766	3	fashioning
0.2497	34.0	.3851	3	flaxen
0.2497	34.0	.2389	4	flirts
0.2497	34.0	.3874	3	gooey
0.2497	34.0	.3766	3	hires
0.2497	34.0	.3766	3	Huntsville
0.2497	34.0	.3766	3	inefficiency
0.2497	34.0	.3766	3	invoked
0.2497	34.0	.3874	3	irises
0.2497	34.0	.1979	5	Joneses
0.2497	34.0	.3874	3	liege
0.2497	34.0	.3766	3	manmade
0.2497	34.0	.3851	3	misgivings
0.2497	34.0	.3766	3	mistrust
0.2497	34.0	.3766	3	monopolies
0.2497	34.0	.3851	3	nastily
0.2497	34.0	.3766	3	Natal
0.2497	34.0	.3851	3	Ostrich
0.2497	34.0	.2389	4	outgrowth
0.2497	34.0	.3874	3	pampered
0.2497	34.0	.3874	3	pantomiming
0.2497	34.0	.3851	3	pews
0.2497	34.0	.3766	3	plaguing
0.2497	34.0	.3766	3	preachers
0.2497	34.0	.3766	3	prohibiting
0.2497	34.0	.3766	3	ratify
0.2497	34.0	.3874	3	reformed
0.2497	34.0	.3845	3	rescues
0.2497	34.0	.3851	3	ruthlessly
0.2497	34.0	.2389	4	sailor's
0.2497	34.0	.3851	3	saintly
0.2497	34.0	.3874	3	sally
0.2497	34.0	.3766	3	seceded
0.2497	34.0	.3851	3	squabbles
0.2497	34.0	.3851	3	succor
0.2497	34.0	.3874	3	technicolor
0.2497	34.0	.3874	3	unwritten
0.2497	34.0	.3766	3	vexing
0.2497	34.0	.3766	3	vigilance
0.2497	34.0	.3766	3	1453
0.2497	34.0	.3766	3	1604
0.2497	34.0	.3766	3	1718
0.2496	34.0	.3841	3	$350
0.2496	34.0	.3847	3	Alston
0.2496	34.0	.3847	3	assess
0.2496	34.0	.3847	3	Blood
0.2496	34.0	.2385	4	chickadee
0.2496	34.0	.3847	3	cooperated
0.2496	34.0	.3847	3	cosmopolitan
0.2496	34.0	.3841	3	denoting
0.2496	34.0	.3847	3	deployed
0.2496	34.0	.3762	3	discredited
0.2496	34.0	.3847	3	executing
0.2496	34.0	.3762	3	exhausts
0.2496	34.0	.3847	3	federally
0.2496	34.0	.3847	3	formalized
0.2496	34.0	.3762	3	frictional
0.2496	34.0	.3762	3	hour-glass
0.2496	34.0	.3847	3	inserts
0.2496	34.0	.3847	3	instructive
0.2496	34.0	.3847	3	irrelevant
0.2496	34.0	.3762	3	lavas
0.2496	34.0	.3762	3	lessening
0.2496	34.0	.3847	3	Mach
0.2496	34.0	.3762	3	metamorphosed
0.2496	34.0	.3847	3	millennium
0.2496	34.0	.3847	3	ministries
0.2496	34.0	.3762	3	pinhead
0.2496	34.0	.3847	3	progressively
0.2496	34.0	.3762	3	projectiles
0.2496	34.0	.3847	3	promulgated
0.2496	34.0	.3847	3	reorganization
0.2496	34.0	.3847	3	replicas
0.2496	34.0	.3762	3	scarp
0.2496	34.0	.3847	3	Smithsonian
0.2496	34.0	.3762	3	smokeless
0.2496	34.0	.3847	3	sobriquet
0.2496	34.0	.3841	3	spidery
0.2496	34.0	.3847	3	stabilization
0.2496	34.0	.3847	3	stereotyped
0.2496	34.0	.3847	3	strategist
0.2496	34.0	.3847	3	Thirty
0.2496	34.0	.3847	3	Toledo
0.2496	34.0	.3762	3	transposed
0.2496	34.0	.3847	3	two-foot
0.2496	34.0	.3847	3	undermine
THE PRECEDING WORD TYPE OCCUPIES RANK 29500				
0.2496	34.0	.3847	3	unimpaired
0.2496	34.0	.3847	3	upheavals
0.2496	34.0	.3847	3	varnishes
0.2496	34.0	.3847	3	wryly
0.2496	34.0	.3847	3	1725
0.2496	34.0	.3841	3	681
0.2495	34.0	.3873	3	'member
0.2495	34.0	.3873	3	askin'
0.2495	34.0	.3873	3	brandishing
0.2495	34.0	.1953	5	Caliph's
0.2495	34.0	.3873	3	curtsies
0.2495	34.0	.3873	3	finality
0.2495	34.0	.3873	3	haggled
0.2495	34.0	.3873	3	half-breed
0.2495	34.0	.3873	3	haying
0.2495	34.0	.3873	3	javelin
0.2495	34.0	.3873	3	lulled
0.2495	34.0	.3873	3	midwives
0.2495	34.0	.1953	5	semi-circle
0.2495	34.0	.3873	3	Sheridan
0.2495	34.0	.3873	3	stuttered
0.2495	34.0	.3873	3	swiveled
0.2495	34.0	.3873	3	tersely
0.2495	34.0	.3873	3	unlatched
0.2495	34.0	.3873	3	weakling
0.2494	34.0	.3847	3	abdication
0.2494	34.0	.3847	3	betrayal
0.2494	34.0	.1025	9	ci
0.2494	34.0	.3847	3	forcibly
0.2494	34.0	.2694	4	godlike
0.2494	34.0	.3847	3	gummy
0.2494	34.0	.3847	3	lake's
0.2494	34.0	.3847	3	phantoms
0.2494	34.0	.3847	3	rhubarb
0.2494	34.0	.1025	9	sk
0.2494	34.0	.3847	3	spendthrift
0.2494	34.0	.3847	3	tormenting
0.2494	34.0	.3847	3	unquestioned
0.2493	34.0	.3781	3	alma
0.2493	34.0	.3781	3	antiques
0.2493	34.0	.3776	3	assaulted
0.2493	34.0	.3776	3	crimped
0.2493	34.0	.3781	3	disgruntled
0.2493	34.0	.3781	3	full-blown
0.2493	34.0	.3840	3	furnishing
0.2493	34.0	.2380	4	Gregorian
0.2493	34.0	.3781	3	Gutenberg's
0.2493	34.0	.3781	3	Hoover's
0.2493	34.0	.3776	3	launchings
0.2493	34.0	.3781	3	law-abiding
0.2493	34.0	.3781	3	lawlessness
0.2493	34.0	.3776	3	meadowlark
0.2493	34.0	.3781	3	Moby
0.2493	34.0	.3781	3	officals
0.2493	34.0	.1620	5	Pap
0.2493	34.0	.3781	3	quarter-century
0.2493	34.0	.3776	3	shallower
0.2493	34.0	.3781	3	Siam
0.2493	34.0	.3781	3	swirls
0.2493	34.0	.3776	3	torrid
0.2493	34.0	.3776	3	unswerving
0.2492	34.0	.3870	3	aggravating
0.2492	34.0	.3870	3	beaded
0.2492	34.0	.3870	3	Boswell
0.2492	34.0	.3870	3	coffers
0.2492	34.0	.3870	3	commoners
0.2492	34.0	.3870	3	deduction
0.2492	34.0	.3870	3	detriment
0.2492	34.0	.3870	3	heady
0.2492	34.0	.3870	3	rejoining
0.2492	34.0	.3870	3	renewal
0.2492	34.0	.3870	3	skein
0.2492	34.0	.3870	3	splendors
0.2492	34.0	.3870	3	Triple
0.2492	34.0	.3870	3	unchecked
0.2492	34.0	.3870	3	undeserved
0.2492	34.0	.3870	3	Yorkshire
0.2490	34.0	.3872	3	animate
0.2490	34.0	.3847	3	Bub
0.2490	34.0	.3847	3	cringing
0.2490	34.0	.3847	3	exhilarating
0.2490	34.0	.3872	3	free-for-all
0.2490	34.0	.3872	3	Michael's
0.2490	34.0	.3847	3	odious
0.2490	34.0	.3872	3	Peoria
0.2490	34.0	.3847	3	prairie-dog
0.2490	34.0	.3847	3	saddlebag
0.2490	34.0	.3847	3	skewer
0.2490	34.0	.3847	3	slippered
0.2490	34.0	.3847	3	Snyder
0.2490	34.0	.3847	3	wert
0.2489	34.0	.3771	3	absurdly
0.2489	34.0	.3365	3	accumulating
0.2489	34.0	.3875	3	alibi
0.2489	34.0	.3875	3	angers
0.2489	34.0	.3771	3	athlete's
0.2489	34.0	.3369	3	bearable
0.2489	34.0	.3771	3	borderline
0.2489	34.0	.3875	3	busted
0.2489	34.0	.3777	3	demoralized
THE PRECEDING WORD TYPE OCCUPIES RANK 29600				
0.2489	34.0	.3771	3	endowment
0.2489	34.0	.3369	3	enriches
0.2489	34.0	.3776	3	fronting
0.2489	34.0	.3777	3	gristmill
0.2489	34.0	.3369	3	heart-rending
0.2489	34.0	.3369	3	heartsick
0.2489	34.0	.3369	3	impressiveness
0.2489	34.0	.3771	3	inherits
0.2489	34.0	.3771	3	Machines
0.2489	34.0	.3365	3	Makes
0.2489	34.0	.3777	3	mid-day
0.2489	34.0	.3776	3	mislead
0.2489	34.0	.3365	3	moonless
0.2489	34.0	.3771	3	outbursts
0.2489	34.0	.3777	3	perpetuate
0.2489	34.0	.3777	3	philosophically
0.2489	34.0	.3369	3	pigpens
0.2489	34.0	.3776	3	pleas
0.2489	34.0	.3365	3	pounces
0.2489	34.0	.3369	3	preening
0.2489	34.0	.3777	3	profess
0.2489	34.0	.3369	3	restive
0.2489	34.0	.3771	3	retrieving
0.2489	34.0	.3776	3	roundups
0.2489	34.0	.3369	3	scalawags
0.2489	34.0	.3365	3	shell-like
0.2489	34.0	.3776	3	shied
0.2489	34.0	.3369	3	shortcomings
0.2489	34.0	.3365	3	Sims
0.2489	34.0	.3365	3	slipperiness
0.2489	34.0	.3365	3	squirted
0.2489	34.0	.3875	3	sunless
0.2489	34.0	.3776	3	undermined
0.2489	34.0	.3771	3	untangled
0.2489	34.0	.3776	3	villainy
0.2489	34.0	.3771	3	zooms
0.2488	34.0	.3772	3	commencing
0.2488	34.0	.3772	3	crunchy
0.2488	34.0	.3871	3	dogfish
0.2488	34.0	.3871	3	edict
0.2488	34.0	.3871	3	eligibility
0.2488	34.0	.3871	3	mystifying
0.2488	34.0	.3772	3	ninety-nine
0.2488	34.0	.3871	3	recurrent
0.2488	34.0	.3772	3	shoelace
0.2488	34.0	.3871	3	shutdown
0.2488	34.0	.3871	3	spewed
0.2488	34.0	.3871	3	versed
0.2487	34.0	.3874	3	amicable
0.2487	34.0	.3844	3	Canaan
0.2487	34.0	.3874	3	forbear
0.2487	34.0	.3874	3	genial
0.2487	34.0	.3844	3	inflammable
0.2487	34.0	.3844	3	Madeleine
0.2487	34.0	.3844	3	neglecting
0.2487	34.0	.3844	3	Shire

U	SFI	D	F	Word Type
0.2487	34.0	.3844	3	stockholder
0.2487	34.0	.3874	3	tortoise-shell
0.2486	34.0	.3870	3	annihilation
0.2486	34.0	.3870	3	clamorous
0.2486	34.0	.3870	3	covert
0.2486	34.0	.3870	3	dismembered
0.2486	34.0	.3870	3	excessively
0.2486	34.0	.3870	3	flailing
0.2486	34.0	.3870	3	flowery
0.2486	34.0	.3870	3	infused
0.2486	34.0	.3870	3	introspective
0.2486	34.0	.3870	3	magenta
0.2486	34.0	.3870	3	morphine
0.2486	34.0	.3870	3	navel
0.2486	34.0	.3836	3	platoon
0.2486	34.0	.3870	3	prosecutors
0.2486	34.0	.3870	3	pumas
0.2486	34.0	.3870	3	rehabilitate
0.2486	34.0	.3870	3	Religious
0.2486	34.0	.3870	3	revelations
0.2486	34.0	.3418	3	Revere's
0.2486	34.0	.3870	3	sanctity
0.2486	34.0	.3870	3	talkers
0.2486	34.0	.3870	3	veterinary
0.2486	34.0	.3870	3	welling
0.2486	34.0	.3418	3	286
0.2485	34.0	.3873	3	addled
0.2485	34.0	.3873	3	benediction
0.2485	34.0	.3842	3	cast-iron
0.2485	34.0	.3773	3	combatants
0.2485	34.0	.3873	3	commits
0.2485	34.0	.3842	3	feigned
0.2485	34.0	.3773	3	friar
0.2485	34.0	.3842	3	hearsay
0.2485	34.0	.3773	3	hollowing
0.2485	34.0	.3842	3	inscriptions
0.2485	34.0	.3842	3	jackdaws
0.2485	34.0	.3842	3	pilgrimage
0.2485	34.0	.3873	3	propitious
0.2485	34.0	.3873	3	ravage
0.2485	34.0	.3873	3	redoubled
0.2485	34.0	.3773	3	riotous
0.2485	34.0	.3873	3	singularly
0.2485	34.0	.3873	3	spanking

THE PRECEDING WORD TYPE OCCUPIES RANK 29700

U	SFI	D	F	Word Type
0.2485	34.0	.3873	3	Tickets
0.2485	34.0	.3873	3	tomahawks
0.2485	34.0	.3842	3	valet
0.2485	34.0	.3873	3	victuals
0.2485	34.0	.3873	3	waxen
0.2484	34.0	.3769	3	agrarian
0.2484	34.0	.3769	3	Andrei
0.2484	34.0	.3769	3	artifacts
0.2484	34.0	.3769	3	autonomy
0.2484	34.0	.3769	3	belligerent
0.2484	34.0	.3768	3	blindingly
0.2484	34.0	.3835	3	Burt
0.2484	34.0	.3769	3	carpeting
0.2484	34.0	.3769	3	Challenger
0.2484	34.0	.1334	7	clerical
0.2484	34.0	.3769	3	complexes
0.2484	34.0	.3769	3	compliance
0.2484	34.0	.3769	3	cynical
0.2484	34.0	.3769	3	dissenters
0.2484	34.0	.3769	3	emancipated
0.2484	34.0	.3769	3	envoy
0.2484	34.0	.3769	3	geographer
0.2484	34.0	.3769	3	Ginza
0.2484	34.0	.3769	3	hydrographic
0.2484	34.0	.1334	7	Industries
0.2484	34.0	.3769	3	infringe
0.2484	34.0	.3769	3	innocuous
0.2484	34.0	.3769	3	Judean
0.2484	34.0	.3769	3	lipsticks
0.2484	34.0	.3769	3	manifesto
0.2484	34.0	.3769	3	outdated
0.2484	34.0	.3769	3	paradoxically
0.2484	34.0	.3769	3	partisans
0.2484	34.0	.3769	3	pensions
0.2484	34.0	.3769	3	quotes
0.2484	34.0	.3769	3	realms
0.2484	34.0	.3769	3	revoked
0.2484	34.0	.3769	3	scandals
0.2484	34.0	.3769	3	Scotch-Irish
0.2484	34.0	.3769	3	seaworthy
0.2484	34.0	.3769	3	shelling
0.2484	34.0	.3769	3	sloths
0.2484	34.0	.3769	3	stabilize
0.2484	34.0	.3769	3	Stores
0.2484	34.0	.3769	3	streamlining
0.2484	34.0	.3769	3	sympathizers
0.2484	34.0	.3769	3	thoroughgoing
0.2484	34.0	.3769	3	treadmill
0.2484	34.0	.3769	3	Tse-tung
0.2484	34.0	.3768	3	untutored
0.2484	34.0	.3768	3	wad
0.2484	34.0	.3769	3	whim
0.2484	34.0	.3769	3	1540
0.2484	34.0	.3769	3	1662
0.2484	34.0	.3769	3	1880s
0.2483	33.9	.3418	3	blinks
0.2483	33.9	.3764	3	cementing
0.2483	33.9	.2069	5	Choir
0.2483	33.9	.2069	5	Colorado's
0.2483	33.9	.3764	3	conditioner
0.2483	33.9	.3418	3	Dewey's
0.2483	33.9	.3764	3	distorting
0.2483	33.9	.3764	3	emits
0.2483	33.9	.3764	3	entomologist
0.2483	33.9	.3764	3	fertilizing
0.2483	33.9	.3418	3	footstool
0.2483	33.9	.3418	3	foul-smelling
0.2483	33.9	.3764	3	genital
0.2483	33.9	.3764	3	gritty
0.2483	33.9	.3764	3	hot-air
0.2483	33.9	.3764	3	Hume
0.2483	33.9	.3764	3	impelled
0.2483	33.9	.3764	3	inescapably
0.2483	33.9	.3764	3	injects
0.2483	33.9	.3764	3	intrusions
0.2483	33.9	.3764	3	longitudinally
0.2483	33.9	.3764	3	malformations
0.2483	33.9	.3764	3	monotonously
0.2483	33.9	.3764	3	Oceanographic
0.2483	33.9	.3764	3	oddity
0.2483	33.9	.3764	3	pediatrics
0.2483	33.9	.3418	3	pitchfork
0.2483	33.9	.3764	3	push-button
0.2483	33.9	.3764	3	snarls
0.2483	33.9	.3764	3	spectroscopy
0.2483	33.9	.3418	3	tortures
0.2483	33.9	.3764	3	transplanting
0.2483	33.9	.3418	3	twenty-year-old
0.2483	33.9	.3764	3	U-shaped
0.2483	33.9	.3764	3	umbilical
0.2483	33.9	.3764	3	unremitting
0.2483	33.9	.3418	3	unsold
0.2483	33.9	.3764	3	viper
0.2483	33.9	.3418	3	well-protected
0.2483	33.9	.3764	3	Westinghouse
0.2483	33.9	.3764	3	zoologist
0.2482	33.9	.3877	3	chambered
0.2482	33.9	.3877	3	charities
0.2482	33.9	.3877	3	miscellaneous
0.2482	33.9	.3877	3	Scot

THE PRECEDING WORD TYPE OCCUPIES RANK 29800

U	SFI	D	F	Word Type
0.2482	33.9	.3877	3	uncompleted
0.2480	33.9	.3766	3	attested
0.2480	33.9	.3766	3	disorganized
0.2480	33.9	.3766	3	harass
0.2480	33.9	.3766	3	inception
0.2480	33.9	.3766	3	Longstreet
0.2480	33.9	.3766	3	raider
0.2480	33.9	.3766	3	verdure
0.2479	33.9	.3762	3	leguminous
0.2479	33.9	.3762	3	passports
0.2479	33.9	.3407	3	recurrence
0.2479	33.9	.3762	3	strewing
0.2479	33.9	.3762	3	successively
0.2479	33.9	.3407	3	tick-tack-toe
0.2479	33.9	.3762	3	1632
0.2478	33.9	.3346	3	abounding
0.2478	33.9	.3346	3	aragonite
0.2478	33.9	.3346	3	astronautics
0.2478	33.9	.3350	3	bribes
0.2478	33.9	.3350	3	caravels
0.2478	33.9	.3346	3	catapult
0.2478	33.9	.3346	3	chameleons
0.2478	33.9	.3350	3	championed
0.2478	33.9	.3350	3	Deere
0.2478	33.9	.3350	3	Destiny
0.2478	33.9	.3350	3	flesh-eating
0.2478	33.9	.3346	3	floral
0.2478	33.9	.3346	3	fuming
0.2478	33.9	.3350	3	furthering
0.2478	33.9	.3346	3	geophysicists
0.2478	33.9	.3350	3	harvesters
0.2478	33.9	.3350	3	incisive
0.2478	33.9	.3350	3	Kodiak
0.2478	33.9	.3350	3	malarial
0.2478	33.9	.3350	3	Matterhorn
0.2478	33.9	.1599	5	midmorning
0.2478	33.9	.3350	3	millionaires
0.2478	33.9	.3346	3	mimeograph
0.2478	33.9	.3350	3	potters
0.2478	33.9	.3350	3	Pulaski
0.2478	33.9	.3346	3	quirks
0.2478	33.9	.3350	3	replanted
0.2478	33.9	.1599	5	reporter's
0.2478	33.9	.3346	3	rock-hard
0.2478	33.9	.3350	3	rose-colored
0.2478	33.9	.3346	3	salamander
0.2478	33.9	.3350	3	seafarers
0.2478	33.9	.3350	3	slovenly
0.2478	33.9	.3346	3	slumbers
0.2478	33.9	.3346	3	smallish
0.2478	33.9	.3350	3	squalor
0.2478	33.9	.3346	3	strives
0.2478	33.9	.3350	3	summarily
0.2478	33.9	.3350	3	sun-baked
0.2478	33.9	.3346	3	twining
0.2478	33.9	.3346	3	wards
0.2478	33.9	.3350	3	Watt's
0.2478	33.9	.3350	3	Zanzibar
0.2478	33.9	.3350	3	1506
0.2477	33.9	.3427	3	ace
0.2477	33.9	.3427	3	acknowledgment
0.2477	33.9	.3408	3	aflame
0.2477	33.9	.3408	3	bedroll
0.2477	33.9	.3427	3	bon
0.2477	33.9	.3427	3	brightening
0.2477	33.9	.3427	3	canister
0.2477	33.9	.3427	3	contortions
0.2477	33.9	.3408	3	dawdle
0.2477	33.9	.3408	3	despondency
0.2477	33.9	.3408	3	engrossed
0.2477	33.9	.3408	3	evading
0.2477	33.9	.3427	3	gored
0.2477	33.9	.3408	3	gossiped
0.2477	33.9	.3408	3	grubby
0.2477	33.9	.3408	3	heartfelt
0.2477	33.9	.3427	3	Hidden
0.2477	33.9	.3427	3	ho-hum
0.2477	33.9	.3408	3	imps
0.2477	33.9	.3408	3	inclosed
0.2477	33.9	.3427	3	invective
0.2477	33.9	.3427	3	irresponsible
0.2477	33.9	.3427	3	jog
0.2477	33.9	.3427	3	junkyard
0.2477	33.9	.3427	3	lamplight
0.2477	33.9	.3408	3	marksman
0.2477	33.9	.3427	3	marshlands
0.2477	33.9	.3408	3	more'n
0.2477	33.9	.3408	3	mustered
0.2477	33.9	.3427	3	northlands
0.2477	33.9	.3427	3	one-horse
0.2477	33.9	.3427	3	outcropping
0.2477	33.9	.3427	3	perk
0.2477	33.9	.3427	3	preliminaries
0.2477	33.9	.3427	3	quagmire
0.2477	33.9	.3408	3	recollect
0.2477	33.9	.3427	3	resounded
0.2477	33.9	.3408	3	revel
0.2477	33.9	.3408	3	roper
0.2477	33.9	.3408	3	rough-and-ready
0.2477	33.9	.3427	3	Roxbury

THE PRECEDING WORD TYPE OCCUPIES RANK 29900

U	SFI	D	F	Word Type
0.2477	33.9	.3427	3	savor
0.2477	33.9	.3427	3	self-pity
0.2477	33.9	.3427	3	sideline
0.2477	33.9	.3408	3	stomped
0.2477	33.9	.3427	3	throatily
0.2477	33.9	.3427	3	tuk
0.2477	33.9	.3408	3	veering
0.2477	33.9	.3427	3	woof
0.2477	33.9	.3408	3	yachting
0.2475	33.9	.3764	3	Booth
0.2475	33.9	.3764	3	buyer's
0.2475	33.9	.3764	3	colloquial
0.2475	33.9	.3764	3	moans
0.2475	33.9	.3764	3	overdo
0.2475	33.9	.3764	3	sickle
0.2475	33.9	.3764	3	whirred
0.2474	33.9	.1926	5	$34
0.2474	33.9	.1926	5	bulkheads
0.2474	33.9	.2405	4	clothespins
0.2474	33.9	.3759	3	contradicting
0.2474	33.9	.2405	4	eighteen-year-old
0.2474	33.9	.3759	3	elms
0.2474	33.9	.3759	3	faints
0.2474	33.9	.3759	3	icicle
0.2474	33.9	.1926	5	justifies
0.2474	33.9	.2405	4	romped
0.2474	33.9	.1926	5	Sieve
0.2474	33.9	.3759	3	skims
0.2474	33.9	.2405	4	wriggly
0.2474	33.9	.1926	5	243
0.2471	33.9	.3759	3	bakers
0.2471	33.9	.3759	3	barracuda
0.2471	33.9	.3759	3	childless
0.2471	33.9	.3759	3	chronicle
0.2471	33.9	.3759	3	couched
0.2471	33.9	.3759	3	counterattack
0.2471	33.9	.3759	3	disobeying
0.2471	33.9	.3759	3	five-sided
0.2471	33.9	.3759	3	sea-faring
0.2471	33.9	.3759	3	self-sufficiency
0.2471	33.9	.3759	3	smokestacks
0.2471	33.9	.2227	5	transparency
0.2470	33.9	.3754	3	Alexis
0.2470	33.9	.3754	3	corrode
0.2470	33.9	.3394	3	dreamers
0.2470	33.9	.3394	3	Kane
0.2470	33.9	.3754	3	legless
0.2470	33.9	.3394	3	outputs
0.2470	33.9	.3394	3	rationalize
0.2470	33.9	.3394	3	strollers
0.2468	33.9	.3756	3	artillerymen
0.2468	33.9	.3395	3	availability
0.2468	33.9	.3395	3	backbreaking
0.2468	33.9	.3395	3	baffling
0.2468	33.9	.3395	3	bas-relief
0.2468	33.9	.3756	3	bolster
0.2468	33.9	.3395	3	brewery
0.2468	33.9	.0000	23	Buh
0.2468	33.9	.3395	3	colliding
0.2468	33.9	.3395	3	combers
0.2468	33.9	.3756	3	commemorate
0.2468	33.9	.3395	3	conch
0.2468	33.9	.3756	3	consecrate
0.2468	33.9	.3756	3	correspondingly
0.2468	33.9	.3756	3	endanger
0.2468	33.9	.3756	3	facade
0.2468	33.9	.3395	3	gamboling
0.2468	33.9	.3395	3	grief-stricken
0.2468	33.9	.3756	3	heartaches
0.2468	33.9	.3756	3	high-heeled
0.2468	33.9	.3395	3	ideology
0.2468	33.9	.3756	3	influencing
0.2468	33.9	.3395	3	insects'
0.2468	33.9	.3395	3	long-handled
0.2468	33.9	.3395	3	maladies
0.2468	33.9	.0000	23	MAMA
0.2468	33.9	.3395	3	Mobile
0.2468	33.9	.3395	3	NewYorkers
0.2468	33.9	.3395	3	new-fangled
0.2468	33.9	.3395	3	nibbles
0.2468	33.9	.3395	3	omnipresent
0.2468	33.9	.3756	3	ordained
0.2468	33.9	.3756	3	pastors
0.2468	33.9	.3395	3	Regiment
0.2468	33.9	.3395	3	repressed
0.2468	33.9	.3395	3	rudimentary
0.2468	33.9	.3756	3	Salle
0.2468	33.9	.3756	3	smuggled
0.2468	33.9	.3395	3	tenure
0.2468	33.9	.3395	3	tinier
0.2468	33.9	.3395	3	twofold
0.2468	33.9	.3395	3	1587
0.2467	33.9	.3751	3	harms
0.2466	33.9	.2383	4	collies
0.2463	33.9	.0730	11	Blues
0.2463	33.9	.0730	11	Susanna
0.2461	33.9	.3406	3	airstrip
0.2461	33.9	.0000	17	Alf
0.2461	33.9	.3406	3	calloused
0.2461	33.9	.3406	3	Carlos'

THE PRECEDING WORD TYPE OCCUPIES RANK 30000

U	SFI	D	F	Word Type
0.2461	33.9	.3406	3	censure
0.2461	33.9	.3406	3	co-worker
0.2461	33.9	.3406	3	disagreeing
0.2461	33.9	.3406	3	drugged
0.2461	33.9	.3406	3	five-thirty
0.2461	33.9	.3406	3	foreshadow
0.2461	33.9	.3406	3	Kinsale
0.2461	33.9	.0000	17	Mit
0.2461	33.9	.3406	3	munch
0.2461	33.9	.3406	3	Palm
0.2461	33.9	.3406	3	Periodical
0.2461	33.9	.3406	3	Readers'
0.2461	33.9	.3406	3	shrouds
0.2461	33.9	.3406	3	sidetracked
0.2461	33.9	.3406	3	soldiers'
0.2461	33.9	.3406	3	three-mile
0.2461	33.9	.3406	3	wrongly
0.2458	33.9	.2211	5	cartoonists
0.2456	33.9	.3399	3	abating
0.2456	33.9	.3399	3	aglow
0.2456	33.9	.3399	3	appreciatively
0.2456	33.9	.3399	3	babbling
0.2456	33.9	.3399	3	blacktop
0.2456	33.9	.3399	3	brandished
0.2456	33.9	.3399	3	canter
0.2456	33.9	.3399	3	carcasses
0.2456	33.9	.3399	3	chalky
0.2456	33.9	.3399	3	companionable
0.2456	33.9	.3399	3	cornhusk
0.2456	33.9	.3399	3	cowpunching
0.2456	33.9	.3399	3	croon
0.2456	33.9	.3399	3	dismounting
0.2456	33.9	.3399	3	droopy
0.2456	33.9	.3399	3	eatin'
0.2456	33.9	.3399	3	frequented
0.2456	33.9	.3399	3	funerals
0.2456	33.9	.3399	3	Geronimo
0.2456	33.9	.0979	6	Gregor
0.2456	33.9	.3399	3	grimy
0.2456	33.9	.3399	3	harangued
0.2456	33.9	.3399	3	heaviness
0.2456	33.9	.3399	3	hew
0.2456	33.9	.3399	3	householders
0.2456	33.9	.3399	3	informer
0.2456	33.9	.3399	3	K **
0.2456	33.9	.3399	3	keepsake
0.2456	33.9	.3399	3	lugging
0.2456	33.9	.3399	3	luscious
0.2456	33.9	.3399	3	mischievously
0.2456	33.9	.3399	3	musk
0.2456	33.9	.1415	5	O'Grumpity
0.2456	33.9	.3399	3	ploughed
0.2456	33.9	.3399	3	portholes
0.2456	33.9	.3399	3	priest's
0.2456	33.9	.3399	3	sapling
0.2456	33.9	.3399	3	scheming
0.2456	33.9	.1415	5	Somervell
0.2456	33.9	.3399	3	teletypes
0.2456	33.9	.3399	3	thorned
0.2456	33.9	.3399	3	toting
0.2456	33.9	.3399	3	vagrant
0.2456	33.9	.3399	3	vividness
0.2456	33.9	.3399	3	voluble
0.2456	33.9	.3399	3	whopping
0.2456	33.9	.3399	3	yanks
0.2455	33.9	.3400	3	abusing
0.2455	33.9	.3400	3	blushes
0.2455	33.9	.3400	3	caramel
0.2455	33.9	.3400	3	flinching
0.2455	33.9	.2031	4	grays
0.2455	33.9	.3400	3	intrepid
0.2455	33.9	.3400	3	screeches
0.2455	33.9	.3400	3	sillier
0.2455	33.9	.2031	4	six-inch
0.2455	33.9	.2031	4	slugger
0.2455	33.9	.3400	3	stumped
0.2455	33.9	.3400	3	t'other
0.2455	33.9	.2031	4	timeless
0.2453	33.9	.0978	8	Abel
0.2451	33.9	.3394	3	'long
0.2451	33.9	.3394	3	absent-minded
0.2451	33.9	.3394	3	absent-mindedly
0.2451	33.9	.3394	3	acrobatics
0.2451	33.9	.3394	3	almighty
0.2451	33.9	.3394	3	assemblage
0.2451	33.9	.3394	3	bailing
0.2451	33.9	.3394	3	bettered
0.2451	33.9	.3394	3	bishop's
0.2451	33.9	.3394	3	blackening
0.2451	33.9	.3394	3	brawl
0.2451	33.9	.3394	3	crinkles
0.2451	33.9	.3394	3	drowsing
0.2451	33.9	.3394	3	grimness
0.2451	33.9	.3394	3	hain't
0.2451	33.9	.3394	3	half-light
0.2451	33.9	.3394	3	indistinct
0.2451	33.9	.3394	3	lagged
0.2451	33.9	.3394	3	lamed
0.2451	33.9	.3394	3	lamely
0.2451	33.9	.3394	3	lordly

THE PRECEDING WORD TYPE OCCUPIES RANK 30100

U	SFI	D	F	Word Type
0.2451	33.9	.3394	3	Madame's
0.2451	33.9	.3394	3	mate's
0.2451	33.9	.3394	3	methodical
0.2451	33.9	.3394	3	Miz
0.2451	33.9	.3394	3	mustaches
0.2451	33.9	.3394	3	needled
0.2451	33.9	.3394	3	negligent
0.2451	33.9	.3394	3	pa's
0.2451	33.9	.3394	3	pouf
0.2451	33.9	.3394	3	puttin'
0.2451	33.9	.3394	3	rogue
0.2451	33.9	.3394	3	round-up
0.2451	33.9	.3394	3	sayin'
0.2451	33.9	.3394	3	scrabbled
0.2451	33.9	.3394	3	soundlessly
0.2451	33.9	.3394	3	spasms
0.2451	33.9	.3394	3	stench
0.2451	33.9	.3394	3	tangling
0.2451	33.9	.3394	3	tombstone

U	SFI	D	F	Word Type
0.2451	33.9	.3394	3	wench
0.2451	33.9	.3394	3	whitened
0.2451	33.9	.3394	3	Woman's
0.2451	33.9	.3394	3	yapping
0.2450	33.9	.3390	3	ambushed
0.2450	33.9	.3390	3	assisting
0.2450	33.9	.3390	3	balmy
0.2450	33.9	.3390	3	blares
0.2450	33.9	.3390	3	Courthouse
0.2450	33.9	.3390	3	distributes
0.2450	33.9	.3390	3	downriver
0.2450	33.9	.3390	3	envision
0.2450	33.9	.3390	3	fabrication
0.2450	33.9	.3390	3	festoons
0.2450	33.9	.3390	3	financier
0.2450	33.9	.3390	3	four-footed
0.2450	33.9	.3390	3	foyer
0.2450	33.9	.3390	3	French-Canadian
0.2450	33.9	.3390	3	garnered
0.2450	33.9	.2063	5	Goes
0.2450	33.9	.3390	3	goldenrod
0.2450	33.9	.2063	5	hand-clapping
0.2450	33.9	.3390	3	headlands
0.2450	33.9	.3390	3	hoarding
0.2450	33.9	.3390	3	independents
0.2450	33.9	.3390	3	intertwined
0.2450	33.9	.3390	3	Monuments
0.2450	33.9	.3390	3	old-style
0.2450	33.9	.3390	3	plating
0.2450	33.9	.3390	3	ponder
0.2450	33.9	.3390	3	railroading
0.2450	33.9	.2063	5	recitative
0.2450	33.9	.3390	3	riffles
0.2450	33.9	.3390	3	serpentine
0.2450	33.9	.3390	3	stumbles
0.2450	33.9	.3390	3	three-foot
0.2450	33.9	.3390	3	timberland
0.2450	33.9	.3390	3	topping
0.2450	33.9	.3390	3	windfall
0.2450	33.9	.3390	3	100-
0.2449	33.9	.3848	3	Ascension
0.2449	33.9	.3843	3	dis-
0.2449	33.9	.3845	3	Frankfurt
0.2449	33.9	.3845	3	Gerard
0.2449	33.9	.3848	3	lighters
0.2449	33.9	.3845	3	noticeably
0.2448	33.9	.3847	3	Adolphe
0.2448	33.9	.3842	3	Author
0.2448	33.9	.3847	3	beholden
0.2448	33.9	.3845	3	bridging
0.2448	33.9	.3847	3	corporal
0.2448	33.9	.3830	3	Electricity
0.2448	33.9	.3845	3	foregoing
0.2448	33.9	.3842	3	frets
0.2448	33.9	.3845	3	mid-December
0.2448	33.9	.3845	3	Or
0.2448	33.9	.3847	3	sorrowing
0.2448	33.9	.3832	3	tortilla
0.2448	33.9	.3847	3	Wadsworth
0.2448	33.9	.3845	3	wield
0.2447	33.9	.3834	3	cashed
0.2447	33.9	.3831	3	clods
0.2447	33.9	.3815	3	colossus
0.2447	33.9	.3833	3	elaborated
0.2447	33.9	.3831	3	epitaph
0.2447	33.9	.3824	3	fingerprinting
0.2447	33.9	.3833	3	Hanover
0.2447	33.9	.3831	3	lightnings
0.2447	33.9	.3824	3	lingua
0.2447	33.9	.3815	3	litany
0.2447	33.9	.3831	3	loftier
0.2447	33.9	.3815	3	paperback
0.2447	33.9	.3833	3	prickle
0.2447	33.9	.3824	3	replay
0.2447	33.9	.3833	3	repulsed
0.2447	33.9	.3825	3	stagehand
0.2447	33.9	.3833	3	temptations
0.2447	33.9	.3833	3	wakens
0.2447	33.9	.1386	6	537
0.2446	33.9	.3827	3	adaptability
0.2446	33.9	.3824	3	awash

THE PRECEDING WORD TYPE OCCUPIES RANK 30200

U	SFI	D	F	Word Type
0.2446	33.9	.3827	3	bankrupt
0.2446	33.9	.3824	3	beau
0.2446	33.9	.3824	3	brassy
0.2446	33.9	.2045	5	Bucket
0.2446	33.9	.3822	3	Cavaliers
0.2446	33.9	.3822	3	collaborate
0.2446	33.9	.3814	3	communicative
0.2446	33.9	.3824	3	heartbreak
0.2446	33.9	.3824	3	heralding
0.2446	33.9	.3814	3	homage
0.2446	33.9	.3822	3	It's
0.2446	33.9	.3824	3	minimized
0.2446	33.9	.3814	3	nary
0.2446	33.9	.3822	3	Notes
0.2446	33.9	.3824	3	portrayal
0.2446	33.9	.3822	3	proficient
0.2446	33.9	.3824	3	propeller-driven
0.2446	33.9	.3824	3	slated
0.2446	33.9	.3824	3	stanchions
0.2446	33.9	.3824	3	surly
0.2446	33.9	.3827	3	1629
0.2446	33.9	.3827	3	17th-century
0.2445	33.9	.3826	3	analytical
0.2445	33.9	.3385	3	arresting
0.2445	33.9	.3385	3	circlet
0.2445	33.9	.3385	3	consoled
0.2445	33.9	.3385	3	Countess
0.2445	33.9	.3826	3	Croatian
0.2445	33.9	.3826	3	Darby
0.2445	33.9	.3826	3	Give
0.2445	33.9	.3385	3	gophers
0.2445	33.9	.3385	3	grapple
0.2445	33.9	.3385	3	hawthorn
0.2445	33.9	.3385	3	impetuous
0.2445	33.9	.3385	3	Job
0.2445	33.9	.3385	3	jutted
0.2445	33.9	.3826	3	merest
0.2445	33.9	.3826	3	pernicious
0.2445	33.9	.3826	3	portrays
0.2445	33.9	.3385	3	retraced
0.2445	33.9	.3826	3	right-of-way
0.2445	33.9	.3385	3	rime
0.2445	33.9	.3385	3	stanch
0.2445	33.9	.3385	3	straggled
0.2445	33.9	.3826	3	terminology
0.2445	33.9	.3385	3	Terror
0.2445	33.9	.3385	3	typhoons
0.2445	33.9	.3826	3	verve
0.2444	33.9	.2042	5	duc
0.2444	33.9	.2042	5	ick
0.2444	33.9	.2042	5	loath
0.2439	33.9	.3380	3	barricade
0.2439	33.9	.3380	3	begrudged
0.2439	33.9	.3380	3	bridegroom
0.2439	33.9	.3380	3	competitor
0.2439	33.9	.3380	3	confessing
0.2439	33.9	.3380	3	Eastertide
0.2439	33.9	.3769	3	educator
0.2439	33.9	.3769	3	filming
0.2439	33.9	.3380	3	foretells
0.2439	33.9	.3380	3	Gestapo
0.2439	33.9	.3380	3	hisself
0.2439	33.9	.3380	3	madame
0.2439	33.9	.3380	3	matting
0.2439	33.9	.3380	3	Nicky
0.2439	33.9	.3380	3	Phyllis
0.2439	33.9	.3380	3	sound's
0.2439	33.9	.3380	3	threescore
0.2439	33.9	.3380	3	torments
0.2439	33.9	.3769	3	visitor's
0.2438	33.9	.1400	5	anon
0.2438	33.9	.2685	4	bestow
0.2438	33.9	.1400	5	monsieur
0.2437	33.9	.3768	3	adventuresome
0.2437	33.9	.3768	3	ardor
0.2437	33.9	.3772	3	crookedly
0.2437	33.9	.3772	3	dimpling
0.2437	33.9	.3768	3	gamba
0.2437	33.9	.3782	3	grackles
0.2437	33.9	.3768	3	hovels
0.2437	33.9	.3768	3	impart
0.2437	33.9	.3768	3	intoned
0.2437	33.9	.3780	3	Margaret's
0.2437	33.9	.3772	3	masters'
0.2437	33.9	.3772	3	moving-picture
0.2437	33.9	.3772	3	overdone
0.2437	33.9	.3768	3	pretentious
0.2437	33.9	.3768	3	pulsation
0.2437	33.9	.3772	3	toils
0.2437	33.9	.3768	3	two-ton
0.2437	33.9	.3772	3	undercurrent
0.2436	33.9	.3779	3	blindfold
0.2436	33.9	.3853	3	confronting
0.2436	33.9	.3783	3	desiring
0.2436	33.9	.3780	3	Ezekiel
0.2436	33.9	.2040	5	Gay
0.2436	33.9	.3780	3	juke
0.2436	33.9	.3783	3	magnificence
0.2436	33.9	.3780	3	objectively
0.2436	33.9	.3779	3	sonorous

THE PRECEDING WORD TYPE OCCUPIES RANK 30300

U	SFI	D	F	Word Type
0.2436	33.9	.3779	3	sprite
0.2436	33.9	.3779	3	spry
0.2436	33.9	.3779	3	timely
0.2436	33.9	.3779	3	towpath
0.2436	33.9	.3780	3	twanging
0.2435	33.9	.0971	6	almond
0.2435	33.9	.0971	6	Astoria
0.2435	33.9	.3782	3	crested
0.2435	33.9	.3758	3	dix
0.2435	33.9	.3782	3	encompasses
0.2435	33.9	.1901	5	escorts
0.2435	33.9	.0971	6	fiestas
0.2435	33.9	.0971	6	FortWorth
0.2435	33.9	.3782	3	gamut
0.2435	33.9	.1901	5	Haakon
0.2435	33.9	.0971	6	iron-ore
0.2435	33.9	.3849	3	ist
0.2435	33.9	.3782	3	Lincolnshire
0.2435	33.9	.0971	6	Ozark
0.2435	33.9	.3763	3	resolving
0.2435	33.9	.3770	3	rh
0.2435	33.9	.1901	5	sextant
0.2435	33.9	.1901	5	Sol
0.2435	33.9	.3782	3	story-telling
0.2435	33.9	.3782	3	Verlaine
0.2433	33.9	.3374	3	deprecated
0.2433	33.9	.3374	3	insecticide
0.2433	33.9	.3374	3	myrtle
0.2433	33.9	.3374	3	perspicacious
0.2433	33.9	.3374	3	safari
0.2433	33.9	.3374	3	sea-going
0.2433	33.9	.3374	3	senatorial
0.2433	33.9	.3773	3	tempus
0.2432	33.9	.3725	3	Sat
0.2430	33.9	.3370	3	bees'
0.2430	33.9	.3370	3	cicadas
0.2430	33.9	.3370	3	crosser
0.2430	33.9	.3370	3	dabbled
0.2430	33.9	.3370	3	derisively
0.2430	33.9	.3370	3	disgraced
0.2430	33.9	.3370	3	divorced
0.2430	33.9	.3370	3	fennel
0.2430	33.9	.3370	3	gawk
0.2430	33.9	.3370	3	Gunpowder
0.2430	33.9	.3370	3	impeded
0.2430	33.9	.3370	3	lurk
0.2430	33.9	.3829	3	mit
0.2430	33.9	.3370	3	new-found
0.2430	33.9	.3370	3	offender
0.2430	33.9	.3370	3	outlived
0.2430	33.9	.3370	3	splints
0.2430	33.9	.3370	3	tensely
0.2430	33.9	.3370	3	vanquished
0.2430	33.9	.3370	3	viciously
0.2430	33.9	.3370	3	Weston
0.2430	33.9	.3370	3	23-year-old
0.2427	33.9	.3820	3	pianos
0.2421	33.8	.1501	6	Cyprus
0.2421	33.8	.0645	8	regrouped
0.2421	33.8	.0645	8	024
0.2421	33.8	.0645	8	7/10
0.2417	33.8	.2427	4	Pyrex
0.2417	33.8	.2428	4	womb
0.2415	33.8	.1380	5	cobras
0.2415	33.8	.1380	5	oppression
0.2414	33.8	.3667	3	crux
0.2414	33.8	.3667	3	301
0.2412	33.8	.3665	3	Austro-Hungarian
0.2412	33.8	.3669	3	Came
0.2412	33.8	.3665	3	Chiefs
0.2412	33.8	.3637	3	Clydesdale
0.2412	33.8	.3665	3	conglomeration
0.2412	33.8	.3662	3	freshest
0.2412	33.8	.3665	3	gorgeously
0.2412	33.8	.3665	3	launches
0.2412	33.8	.3637	3	piecemeal
0.2412	33.8	.3669	3	poop
0.2412	33.8	.3665	3	renaissance
0.2412	33.8	.3662	3	streamline
0.2411	33.8	.3660	3	hastens
0.2411	33.8	.3765	3	soundproof
0.2411	33.8	.3665	3	uninvited
0.2410	33.8	.3675	3	advertises
0.2410	33.8	.2405	4	corrective
0.2410	33.8	.2405	4	detectors
0.2410	33.8	.2405	4	Eddington
0.2410	33.8	.3635	3	Gras
0.2410	33.8	.3635	3	Harmony
0.2410	33.8	.3635	3	Mall
0.2410	33.8	.3663	3	open-mouthed
0.2410	33.8	.2405	4	orb
0.2410	33.8	.2405	4	self-propelled
0.2410	33.8	.2405	4	semitropical
0.2410	33.8	.3632	3	upstroke
0.2410	33.8	.3635	3	1900s
0.2409	33.8	.3629	3	convulsions
0.2409	33.8	.2425	4	Liliuokalani
0.2409	33.8	.2425	4	Mohammedanism
0.2409	33.8	.3629	3	muddle
0.2409	33.8	.2424	4	tangerines

THE PRECEDING WORD TYPE OCCUPIES RANK 30400

U	SFI	D	F	Word Type
0.2409	33.8	.3627	3	1639
0.2408	33.8	.2197	4	aqualung
0.2408	33.8	.3674	3	cowpuncher
0.2408	33.8	.3668	3	drumbeat
0.2408	33.8	.2408	4	emigration
0.2408	33.8	.2408	4	Employment
0.2408	33.8	.3668	3	enlargement
0.2408	33.8	.3674	3	Garfield
0.2408	33.8	.3674	3	harps
0.2408	33.8	.2408	4	Khan's
0.2408	33.8	.2408	4	Mongolian
0.2408	33.8	.2408	4	Phidias
0.2408	33.8	.2408	4	Stowe
0.2407	33.8	.3668	3	chittering
0.2407	33.8	.3676	3	freezers
0.2407	33.8	.3668	3	keystone
0.2407	33.8	.3676	3	poverty-stricken
0.2407	33.8	.3676	3	terra
0.2407	33.8	.3668	3	toadstools
0.2407	33.8	.3676	3	worn-down
0.2406	33.8	.3674	3	Austrians
0.2406	33.8	.3670	3	deBergerac
0.2406	33.8	.3670	3	Edmond
0.2406	33.8	.3670	3	expel
0.2406	33.8	.3670	3	gen
0.2406	33.8	.3674	3	Henrik
0.2406	33.8	.3674	3	indecisive
0.2406	33.8	.3670	3	puncture-proof
0.2406	33.8	.1101	9	sealer
0.2406	33.8	.3674	3	unknowing
0.2406	33.8	.3674	3	24-25
0.2405	33.8	.3668	3	give-and-take
0.2405	33.8	.3668	3	imposes
0.2405	33.8	.3668	3	interplay
0.2405	33.8	.3668	3	palate
0.2405	33.8	.3668	3	River's
0.2403	33.8	.2132	5	miniatures
0.2401	33.8	.1575	6	Wordsworth
0.2398	33.8	.1361	6	Franco
0.2398	33.8	.1361	6	Fuehrer
0.2398	33.8	.1361	6	Phineas
0.2398	33.8	.1361	6	Rankin
0.2395	33.8	.0000	16	half-lines
0.2395	33.8	.0000	16	nonzero
0.2395	33.8	.0000	16	XY
0.2392	33.8	.0789	6	welcomes
0.2391	33.8	.0862	7	ur
0.2390	33.8	.1143	8	Rite
0.2387	33.8	.2337	4	biographer
0.2387	33.8	.0859	7	Musical
0.2386	33.8	.0956	9	arias
0.2386	33.8	.0956	9	musicals
0.2383	33.8	.1994	5	Knickerbocker
0.2382	33.8	.2353	4	agar
0.2382	33.8	.2353	4	Alluvial
0.2382	33.8	.2353	4	aphid
0.2382	33.8	.2353	4	arsenic
0.2382	33.8	.2353	4	Canis
0.2382	33.8	.2353	4	carnivore
0.2382	33.8	.0460	10	counselors
0.2382	33.8	.2353	4	crystallization
0.2382	33.8	.2353	4	curvature
0.2382	33.8	.2353	4	diurnal
0.2382	33.8	.2353	4	echinoderm
0.2382	33.8	.2353	4	food-chain
0.2382	33.8	.2353	4	Herschel
0.2382	33.8	.2353	4	hydrocarbon
0.2382	33.8	.2353	4	hydrous
0.2382	33.8	.2353	4	krypton
0.2382	33.8	.2353	4	Lawton
0.2382	33.8	.2353	4	micaceous
0.2382	33.8	.2353	4	mole's
0.2382	33.8	.2353	4	near-collision
0.2382	33.8	.2353	4	nitrogen-fixing
0.2382	33.8	.2353	4	non-living
0.2382	33.8	.2353	4	recur
0.2382	33.8	.0460	10	Rican
0.2382	33.8	.2353	4	Shasta
0.2382	33.8	.2353	4	silicates
0.2382	33.8	.2353	4	spiracles
0.2382	33.8	.2353	4	suckers
0.2382	33.8	.2353	4	synchrotron
0.2382	33.8	.2353	4	toxins
0.2382	33.8	.2353	4	viscous
0.2377	33.8	.1213	7	BE
0.2377	33.8	.2344	4	boric
0.2377	33.8	.2344	4	cattails
0.2377	33.8	.2344	4	commoner
0.2377	33.8	.2344	4	pox
0.2376	33.8	.0987	10	interjection
0.2376	33.8	.1855	4	milks
0.2376	33.8	.1855	4	whalebone
0.2373	33.8	.1814	4	amazes
0.2373	33.8	.1814	4	Candle
0.2373	33.8	.2335	4	clots
0.2373	33.8	.1814	4	housemaid
0.2373	33.8	.1814	4	Janie's
0.2373	33.8	.1814	4	Lines
0.2373	33.8	.2335	4	Lister
0.2373	33.8	.1814	4	nah

THE PRECEDING WORD TYPE OCCUPIES RANK 30500

U	SFI	D	F	Word Type
0.2373	33.8	.1814	4	pitifully
0.2373	33.8	.1814	4	poled
0.2373	33.8	.1814	4	president's
0.2373	33.8	.1814	4	Smothers
0.2373	33.8	.1814	4	stretchy
0.2373	33.8	.1814	4	sub's
0.2373	33.8	.1814	4	superiors
0.2373	33.8	.1814	4	sweaty
0.2373	33.8	.1814	4	White's
0.2373	33.8	.2335	4	323
0.2372	33.8	.2348	4	alliances
0.2372	33.8	.2348	4	Apennine
0.2372	33.8	.2348	4	Attica
0.2372	33.8	.2348	4	auk
0.2372	33.8	.2348	4	bartered
0.2372	33.8	.2348	4	Byzantium
0.2372	33.8	.2348	4	chimpanzees
0.2372	33.8	.2348	4	fastest-growing
0.2372	33.8	.2348	4	Flint
0.2372	33.8	.2348	4	meteoroids
0.2372	33.8	.2348	4	outnumber
0.2372	33.8	.2348	4	ponchos
0.2372	33.8	.2348	4	shiploads
0.2372	33.8	.2348	4	South's
0.2372	33.8	.2348	4	Town's
0.2372	33.8	.2348	4	Trujillo
0.2372	33.8	.2348	4	Years'
0.2371	33.7	.1792	5	Tallahassee
0.2371	33.7	.1792	5	693
0.2369	33.7	.3265	3	coach's
0.2369	33.7	.3265	3	martyr
0.2369	33.7	.3265	3	sinker
0.2369	33.7	.3265	3	struts
0.2368	33.7	.3263	3	Automatic
0.2368	33.7	.3263	3	betrothed
0.2368	33.7	.3263	3	defiled
0.2368	33.7	.3263	3	easy-going
0.2368	33.7	.3269	3	eighty-four
0.2368	33.7	.3263	3	fast-flowing
0.2368	33.7	.3234	3	fizz
0.2368	33.7	.3263	3	frankincense
0.2368	33.7	.3263	3	Gabriel's
0.2368	33.7	.1555	6	hv
0.2368	33.7	.3263	3	insignia
0.2368	33.7	.3269	3	janitor
0.2368	33.7	.1555	6	Latvian
0.2368	33.7	.1555	6	linguistics
0.2368	33.7	.3234	3	mitten
0.2368	33.7	.3234	3	overloading
0.2368	33.7	.3263	3	Paloma
0.2368	33.7	.3269	3	plainest
0.2368	33.7	.3269	3	Porter's
0.2368	33.7	.3263	3	reverberating
0.2368	33.7	.3263	3	sentenced
0.2368	33.7	.3263	3	shuttling
0.2368	33.7	.3234	3	sylvan
0.2368	33.7	.3263	3	two-fold
0.2368	33.7	.3263	3	uncomplicated
0.2368	33.7	.3234	3	unnamed
0.2367	33.7	.3231	3	awakens
0.2367	33.7	.3225	3	Brand
0.2367	33.7	.0629	8	caliber
0.2367	33.7	.3231	3	carnivals
0.2367	33.7	.3267	3	confide
0.2367	33.7	.3267	3	cranky
0.2367	33.7	.3267	3	diminish
0.2367	33.7	.3267	3	embellished
0.2367	33.7	.3267	3	fiddler's
0.2367	33.7	.0629	8	hurdling
0.2367	33.7	.3231	3	kettledrum
0.2367	33.7	.3267	3	Ladies
0.2367	33.7	.3267	3	lope
0.2367	33.7	.3267	3	loping
0.2367	33.7	.3231	3	paintbrush
0.2367	33.7	.3267	3	parading
0.2367	33.7	.2338	4	reaping
0.2367	33.7	.3231	3	Reginald
0.2367	33.7	.3267	3	rehearsals
0.2367	33.7	.2338	4	Rotterdam's
0.2367	33.7	.3267	3	shoal
0.2367	33.7	.3267	3	spunky
0.2367	33.7	.3267	3	testament
0.2367	33.7	.3231	3	valley's

U	SFI	D	F	Word Type
0.2367	33.7	.3231	3	whippoorwills
0.2366	33.7	.0000	12	biosphere
0.2366	33.7	.0000	12	bullhead
0.2366	33.7	.0000	12	Calories
0.2366	33.7	.0000	12	terrarium
0.2366	33.7	.0000	12	zygote
0.2365	33.7	.3222	3	Austria's
0.2365	33.7	.3273	3	contractor
0.2365	33.7	.3273	3	escalator
0.2365	33.7	.3273	3	Lilliput
0.2365	33.7	.3273	3	reword
0.2365	33.7	.3273	3	spouts
0.2364	33.7	.3271	3	arouses
0.2364	33.7	.3274	3	fourscore
0.2364	33.7	.3274	3	gridiron
0.2364	33.7	.3274	3	howdah
0.2364	33.7	.3271	3	recitations
THE PRECEDING WORD TYPE OCCUPIES RANK 30600				
0.2364	33.7	.3274	3	robed
0.2364	33.7	.3271	3	sulky
0.2364	33.7	.3274	3	thunderbolts
0.2364	33.7	.3271	3	Tired
0.2363	33.7	.2330	4	Angora
0.2363	33.7	.3272	3	berry's
0.2363	33.7	.3272	3	Birch
0.2363	33.7	.3272	3	blithe
0.2363	33.7	.2330	4	elects
0.2363	33.7	.3272	3	Jove
0.2363	33.7	.3272	3	Lone
0.2363	33.7	.3272	3	moonbeams
0.2363	33.7	.3272	3	morns
0.2363	33.7	.3272	3	Pinto
0.2363	33.7	.3272	3	severing
0.2363	33.7	.2330	4	stockholders
0.2363	33.7	.3272	3	subtitle
0.2363	33.7	.2330	4	surfboarding
0.2363	33.7	.3272	3	swears
0.2362	33.7	.3274	3	Achilles
0.2362	33.7	.3274	3	latter's
0.2361	33.7	.3272	3	bell-like
0.2361	33.7	.3272	3	Breton
0.2361	33.7	.0000	22	DOMIN
0.2361	33.7	.3272	3	Gaucho
0.2361	33.7	.3272	3	numbing
0.2361	33.7	.3272	3	ostentatious
0.2361	33.7	.0000	22	Portia
0.2361	33.7	.3272	3	prays
0.2361	33.7	.3272	3	sculling
0.2361	33.7	.3272	3	switchboard
0.2357	33.7	.2305	4	artesian
0.2357	33.7	.2305	4	pulsate
0.2357	33.7	.2305	4	seventy-nine
0.2357	33.7	.2305	4	water-drop
0.2356	33.7	.1453	6	aides
0.2356	33.7	.1453	6	Cornell
0.2356	33.7	.1453	6	HR
0.2356	33.7	.1453	6	pros
0.2356	33.7	.1453	6	six-day
0.2354	33.7	.1114	8	sc
0.2351	33.7	.3134	3	lassos
0.2351	33.7	.3134	3	typify
0.2351	33.7	.3134	3	windbag
0.2349	33.7	.3131	3	defence
0.2349	33.7	.3131	3	injuring
0.2349	33.7	.3131	3	jostle
0.2349	33.7	.3131	3	low-flying
0.2349	33.7	.3128	3	rocketry
0.2349	33.7	.3128	3	swordsman
0.2349	33.7	.3131	3	Turn
0.2349	33.7	.3131	3	Vladimir
0.2348	33.7	.2287	4	activates
0.2348	33.7	.2287	4	adrenaline
0.2348	33.7	.2287	4	aseptic
0.2348	33.7	.2287	4	collapses
0.2348	33.7	.2287	4	diluted
0.2348	33.7	.2287	4	erratics
0.2348	33.7	.2287	4	faulted
0.2348	33.7	.2287	4	fluoridation
0.2348	33.7	.1112	8	keynote
0.2348	33.7	.2287	4	meteoric
0.2348	33.7	.2287	4	observational
0.2348	33.7	.2287	4	pH
0.2348	33.7	.2287	4	polluting
0.2348	33.7	.2287	4	preventive
0.2348	33.7	.2287	4	saturation
0.2348	33.7	.2287	4	siphon
0.2348	33.7	.2287	4	suture
0.2348	33.7	.2287	4	tenders
0.2348	33.7	.0786	10	whole-tone
0.2347	33.7	.1787	4	'deed
0.2347	33.7	.1787	4	'twould
0.2347	33.7	.1787	4	armful
0.2347	33.7	.1787	4	Barbecue
0.2347	33.7	.1787	4	bellowing
0.2347	33.7	.1787	4	cripple
0.2347	33.7	.3125	3	far-ranging
0.2347	33.7	.1787	4	foretop
0.2347	33.7	.1787	4	He'd
0.2347	33.7	.1787	4	heah
0.2347	33.7	.1787	4	Iki
0.2347	33.7	.1787	4	learnt
0.2347	33.7	.3125	3	mariner
0.2347	33.7	.1787	4	Marley's
0.2347	33.7	.1787	4	petting
0.2347	33.7	.1787	4	pigtail
0.2347	33.7	.3125	3	record-making
0.2347	33.7	.1787	4	reproachfully
0.2347	33.7	.1787	4	roun'
0.2347	33.7	.1787	4	shrilled
0.2347	33.7	.1787	4	Sorrell's
0.2347	33.7	.1787	4	stock-still
0.2347	33.7	.1787	4	terriers
0.2347	33.7	.1787	4	Thornton's
0.2347	33.7	.1787	4	Tremain
0.2347	33.7	.1787	4	untangle
0.2347	33.7	.1787	4	upstretched
0.2347	33.7	.1787	4	wide-spreading
0.2346	33.7	.2298	4	Boulevard
THE PRECEDING WORD TYPE OCCUPIES RANK 30700				
0.2346	33.7	.1508	6	Correct
0.2346	33.7	.2298	4	humpbacked
0.2346	33.7	.2298	4	sea-level
0.2346	33.7	.2298	4	Spotsylvania
0.2344	33.7	.1700	6	Matisse
0.2340	33.7	.0935	8	sphinx
0.2339	33.7	.2218	4	Guggenheim
0.2338	33.7	.1103	7	Borman
0.2338	33.7	.1103	7	Helsinki
0.2337	33.7	.2281	4	agitators
0.2337	33.7	.2281	4	cease-fire
0.2337	33.7	.2281	4	Chileans
0.2337	33.7	.2281	4	czar
0.2337	33.7	.2281	4	devastated
0.2337	33.7	.2281	4	enact
0.2337	33.7	.1205	7	Goodwill
0.2337	33.7	.1205	7	Gustavus
0.2337	33.7	.2281	4	hogans
0.2337	33.7	.2281	4	northerners
0.2337	33.7	.2281	4	poultrymen
0.2337	33.7	.0392	11	Snake-Eye
0.2337	33.7	.2281	4	Somali
0.2337	33.7	.0224	16	three-part
0.2337	33.7	.2281	4	three-sided
0.2337	33.7	.2281	4	Tran
0.2337	33.7	.0392	11	ungrammatical
0.2337	33.7	.2281	4	Waikiki
0.2337	33.7	.2281	4	weekday
0.2334	33.7	.0000	12	Aymara
0.2334	33.7	.0000	12	Kano
0.2332	33.7	.2346	4	backup
0.2332	33.7	.2352	4	Cambodian
0.2332	33.7	.2352	4	Castro's
0.2332	33.7	.2346	4	clapper
0.2332	33.7	.2352	4	Columbia's
0.2332	33.7	.2346	4	Cousteau
0.2332	33.7	.2346	4	cyclamates
0.2332	33.7	.2352	4	Durban
0.2332	33.7	.2346	4	Faraday's
0.2332	33.7	.2352	4	Fidel
0.2332	33.7	.2352	4	four-lane
0.2332	33.7	.2346	4	heroin
0.2332	33.7	.2352	4	Iranian
0.2332	33.7	.2346	4	kneecap
0.2332	33.7	.2352	4	Meir
0.2332	33.7	.2346	4	nonexistent
0.2332	33.7	.2352	4	Policy
0.2332	33.7	.2352	4	Prospect
0.2332	33.7	.2346	4	Sit
0.2332	33.7	.2352	4	snowcapped
0.2332	33.7	.2352	4	superintendents
0.2332	33.7	.2352	4	Union's
0.2332	33.7	.2352	4	unsuccessfully
0.2330	33.7	.3244	3	Falstaff
0.2330	33.7	.3244	3	Pines
0.2330	33.7	.1963	5	1794
0.2329	33.7	.1093	7	Drew
0.2329	33.7	.1443	4	subheads
0.2329	33.7	.1443	4	tableware
0.2328	33.7	.1882	5	childbearing
0.2328	33.7	.1882	5	Judah
0.2328	33.7	.1882	5	landscaping
0.2328	33.7	.1882	5	merger
0.2328	33.7	.1882	5	Millikan
0.2320	33.7	.1493	6	Gordie
0.2320	33.7	.1493	6	Jamison
0.2320	33.7	.1493	6	sergeant-major
0.2319	33.7	.2427	4	$55
0.2319	33.7	.2427	4	Graham's
0.2319	33.7	.2427	4	Mustangs
0.2319	33.7	.2427	4	SAS
0.2316	33.6	.0000	16	Lieve
0.2315	33.6	.2433	4	Bourbons
0.2315	33.6	.2433	4	ineffectual
0.2315	33.6	.2433	4	marshland
0.2315	33.6	.2337	4	Slater's
0.2315	33.6	.2433	4	white-clad
0.2314	33.6	.1419	5	mural
0.2313	33.6	.1862	5	Yacht
0.2307	33.6	.2420	4	convertibles
0.2307	33.6	.1425	6	Myrtle
0.2305	33.6	.2427	4	mongrel
0.2305	33.6	.0386	11	Pud
0.2305	33.6	.2427	4	stallions
0.2305	33.6	.2427	4	vermilion
0.2301	33.6	.1848	5	dissent
0.2301	33.6	.1848	5	Faith
0.2301	33.6	.1848	5	Gene
0.2301	33.6	.1848	5	inconsiderate
0.2301	33.6	.1848	5	Monopoly
0.2301	33.6	.1848	5	subcommittee
0.2301	33.6	.1848	5	wicker
0.2300	33.6	.0915	8	scorpion
0.2298	33.6	.1733	4	chessboard
0.2298	33.6	.0000	21	determiners
0.2298	33.6	.1733	4	imaginations
0.2298	33.6	.1733	4	Log
0.2298	33.6	.0000	21	Mock
0.2298	33.6	.1733	4	na
0.2298	33.6	.1733	4	palomino
THE PRECEDING WORD TYPE OCCUPIES RANK 30800				
0.2298	33.6	.2043	5	rigidity
0.2298	33.6	.1733	4	subtopic
0.2297	33.6	.2191	4	CO
0.2297	33.6	.2097	5	Cream
0.2297	33.6	.2191	4	fetus
0.2297	33.6	.2191	4	flyers
0.2297	33.6	.2191	4	Shepard
0.2297	33.6	.2191	4	underhand
0.2297	33.6	.2191	4	5-inch
0.2294	33.6	.2111	5	gradations
0.2289	33.6	.1854	5	Schiller
0.2287	33.6	.1473	6	alpine
0.2287	33.6	.1473	6	automotive
0.2287	33.6	.2171	4	hangers
0.2287	33.6	.1473	6	piranha
0.2287	33.6	.1473	6	proboscis
0.2287	33.6	.0995	6	staves
0.2287	33.6	.1473	6	Zagreb
0.2286	33.6	.1699	6	rosemary
0.2285	33.6	.2183	4	abolishing
0.2285	33.6	.2183	4	Ashley
0.2285	33.6	.2183	4	Berber
0.2285	33.6	.2183	4	Duluth
0.2285	33.6	.2183	4	Fannin's
0.2285	33.6	.2183	4	Goliad
0.2285	33.6	.2183	4	Islanders
0.2285	33.6	.2183	4	Judiciary
0.2285	33.6	.2183	4	lawmaking
0.2285	33.6	.2183	4	McCarthy's
0.2285	33.6	.2183	4	Nacogdoches
0.2285	33.6	.2183	4	panhandle
0.2285	33.6	.2183	4	Raja
0.2285	33.6	.2183	4	Rhodesia
0.2285	33.6	.2183	4	rulings
0.2285	33.6	.2183	4	Sultans
0.2285	33.6	.2183	4	Tanana
0.2285	33.6	.2183	4	workers'
0.2284	33.6	.0000	5	a-rum-a-tee-tum
0.2284	33.6	.0000	5	aardvarks
0.2284	33.6	.0000	5	afterthought
0.2284	33.6	.1717	4	amulet
0.2284	33.6	.0000	5	Ankeny
0.2284	33.6	.0000	5	Arne
0.2284	33.6	.0000	5	Arnie's
0.2284	33.6	.0000	5	Atri
0.2284	33.6	.0000	5	Balser
0.2284	33.6	.0000	5	Beckie
0.2284	33.6	.0000	5	Belden
0.2284	33.6	.0000	5	Biddlewees
0.2284	33.6	.0000	5	Billiam
0.2284	33.6	.1419	7	blemishes
0.2284	33.6	.0000	5	Bloemfontein
0.2284	33.6	.0000	5	Bo-o-o-n-e
0.2284	33.6	.0000	5	bomberos
0.2284	33.6	.1717	4	bosun's
0.2284	33.6	.0000	5	Calf
0.2284	33.6	.0000	5	cambio
0.2284	33.6	.0000	5	Camelot
0.2284	33.6	.0000	5	carnotite
0.2284	33.6	.0000	5	Chica
0.2284	33.6	.0000	5	Chico's
0.2284	33.6	.0000	5	Childreth
0.2284	33.6	.0000	5	Christophilos
0.2284	33.6	.0000	5	Chuchundra
0.2284	33.6	.0000	5	Codner
0.2284	33.6	.0000	5	Colchians
0.2284	33.6	.0000	5	Coppo
0.2284	33.6	.0000	5	cowherd
0.2284	33.6	.0000	5	Creeper's
0.2284	33.6	.0000	5	Cruelty
0.2284	33.6	.0000	5	Daly's
0.2284	33.6	.0000	5	DDD
0.2284	33.6	.1419	7	dehydrated
0.2284	33.6	.0000	5	Dobarra
0.2284	33.6	.0000	5	Dobson
0.2284	33.6	.0000	5	Doge
0.2284	33.6	.0000	5	double-bit
0.2284	33.6	.1717	4	Duvitches'
0.2284	33.6	.0000	5	Ears'
0.2284	33.6	.0000	5	Eel
0.2284	33.6	.0000	5	Elders
0.2284	33.6	.0000	5	Elspeth
0.2284	33.6	.0000	5	Faggett
0.2284	33.6	.0000	5	Falal
0.2284	33.6	.0000	5	Farnum
0.2284	33.6	.0000	5	Farrington
0.2284	33.6	.0000	5	Farthest-Thrower
0.2284	33.6	.0000	5	Faustino
0.2284	33.6	.0000	5	Ferry's
0.2284	33.6	.0000	5	Flea
0.2284	33.6	.1717	4	flighty
0.2284	33.6	.0000	5	Folgil
0.2284	33.6	.0000	5	Fulke
0.2284	33.6	.0000	5	gam
0.2284	33.6	.0000	5	Gareth
0.2284	33.6	.0000	5	Gasparilla
0.2284	33.6	.0000	5	Gino
0.2284	33.6	.0000	5	goats'
0.2284	33.6	.0000	5	Goober
0.2284	33.6	.0000	5	Grayson's
THE PRECEDING WORD TYPE OCCUPIES RANK 30900				
0.2284	33.6	.0000	5	Grumbie
0.2284	33.6	.0000	5	gyrfalcon
0.2284	33.6	.0000	5	Ha'penny
0.2284	33.6	.0000	5	Halstead
0.2284	33.6	.1717	4	haversack
0.2284	33.6	.0000	5	Hoda
0.2284	33.6	.0000	5	hoed
0.2284	33.6	.0000	5	Hortense
0.2284	33.6	.0000	5	hot-rod
0.2284	33.6	.0000	5	Hunsaker
0.2284	33.6	.0000	5	Hyacinth
0.2284	33.6	.1717	4	interrupts
0.2284	33.6	.0000	5	intruder
0.2284	33.6	.0000	5	Iverson
0.2284	33.6	.0000	5	Jancsi
0.2284	33.6	.0000	5	Jayvees
0.2284	33.6	.0000	5	Joybells
0.2284	33.6	.0000	5	Kerezan
0.2284	33.6	.0000	5	Kilauea
0.2284	33.6	.0000	5	Kioto
0.2284	33.6	.0000	5	Kuma
0.2284	33.6	.0000	5	Kya
0.2284	33.6	.0000	5	Kyrios
0.2284	33.6	.0000	5	Lanes
0.2284	33.6	.0000	5	Lauritz
0.2284	33.6	.0000	5	Lei
0.2284	33.6	.0000	5	Lida
0.2284	33.6	.0000	5	Lightnings
0.2284	33.6	.0000	5	Loki's
0.2284	33.6	.0000	5	Luigia
0.2284	33.6	.0000	5	Lupe's
0.2284	33.6	.0000	5	Magi
0.2284	33.6	.0000	5	Mallory
0.2284	33.6	.0000	5	Malvina
0.2284	33.6	.0000	5	Manaluk's
0.2284	33.6	.0000	5	marathon
0.2284	33.6	.0000	5	McCoul
0.2284	33.6	.0000	5	McVey
0.2284	33.6	.0000	5	Meazles
0.2284	33.6	.0000	5	Mechano
0.2284	33.6	.0000	5	Mikko
0.2284	33.6	.0000	5	Mom's
0.2284	33.6	.0000	5	Mooney
0.2284	33.6	.0000	5	Mortain
0.2284	33.6	.0000	5	Neosho
0.2284	33.6	.0000	5	Nqong
0.2284	33.6	.0000	5	Nyari
0.2284	33.6	.1717	4	oh-oh
0.2284	33.6	.0000	5	Otah's
0.2284	33.6	.0000	5	Owls
0.2284	33.6	.0000	5	Pain-Killer
0.2284	33.6	.1717	4	pained
0.2284	33.6	.0000	5	Patriots
0.2284	33.6	.0000	5	peddler's
0.2284	33.6	.0000	5	Pedrito
0.2284	33.6	.0000	5	Pegleg
0.2284	33.6	.0000	5	phoebes
0.2284	33.6	.0000	5	Ping
0.2284	33.6	.0000	5	Pinkie's
0.2284	33.6	.0000	5	Pirate
0.2284	33.6	.0000	5	Polaski
0.2284	33.6	.0000	5	Porpoise
0.2284	33.6	.0000	5	Poseidon's
0.2284	33.6	.0000	5	Possy's
0.2284	33.6	.0000	5	potlatch
0.2284	33.6	.0000	5	Potts
0.2284	33.6	.0000	5	psst
0.2284	33.6	.0000	5	Quicksilver
0.2284	33.6	.0000	5	Rakumi
0.2284	33.6	.0000	5	Rally
0.2284	33.6	.0000	5	Rank
0.2284	33.6	.0000	5	Readywell
0.2284	33.6	.0000	5	Renaldo's
0.2284	33.6	.0000	5	Renner
0.2284	33.6	.0000	5	Robe
0.2284	33.6	.0000	5	rotors
0.2284	33.6	.0000	5	Rowdy
0.2284	33.6	.0000	5	Rudi
0.2284	33.6	.0000	5	SanJuan
0.2284	33.6	.0000	5	Saunders
0.2284	33.6	.0000	5	Schmeling
0.2284	33.6	.0000	5	sea-gull
0.2284	33.6	.0000	5	Seabold
0.2284	33.6	.0000	5	Singh
0.2284	33.6	.0000	5	smashup
0.2284	33.6	.0000	5	smelter
0.2284	33.6	.0000	5	Sol-leks
0.2284	33.6	.0000	5	Somsak
0.2284	33.6	.1717	4	sooty
0.2284	33.6	.0000	5	Sooty's
0.2284	33.6	.0000	5	Squalus
0.2284	33.6	.0000	5	Steamer
0.2284	33.6	.0000	5	Stormie
0.2284	33.6	.0000	5	Straight
0.2284	33.6	.0000	5	Substance
0.2284	33.6	.0000	5	Sukeforth
0.2284	33.6	.0000	5	Summers
0.2284	33.6	.0000	5	Surtsey
0.2284	33.6	.0000	5	Susy
0.2284	33.6	.0000	5	Svatopluk
THE PRECEDING WORD TYPE OCCUPIES RANK 31000				
0.2284	33.6	.0000	5	svnnch
0.2284	33.6	.0000	5	Sweeney's
0.2284	33.6	.1717	4	sympathize
0.2284	33.6	.1717	4	tap-tapping
0.2284	33.6	.0000	5	Tazieff
0.2284	33.6	.0000	5	Tenley
0.2284	33.6	.0000	5	Theobold
0.2284	33.6	.1717	4	thuds
0.2284	33.6	.0000	5	Thunderbolt
0.2284	33.6	.1717	4	tingled
0.2284	33.6	.0000	5	Tomos
0.2284	33.6	.1717	4	trowel
0.2284	33.6	.0000	5	Tuhan
0.2284	33.6	.0000	5	turquoises
0.2284	33.6	.0000	5	Valya
0.2284	33.6	.0000	5	Waino
0.2284	33.6	.0000	5	Wallie
0.2284	33.6	.1717	4	weather-beaten
0.2284	33.6	.0000	5	Weorman
0.2284	33.6	.0000	5	Whistle
0.2284	33.6	.0000	5	White-footed
0.2284	33.6	.0000	5	Whitehill
0.2284	33.6	.0000	5	Wolfhardt
0.2284	33.6	.0000	5	woodsy
0.2284	33.6	.0000	5	Wou-Chiang
0.2284	33.6	.0000	5	Xingo
0.2284	33.6	.0000	5	Zack
0.2284	33.6	.0000	5	Zurns
0.2283	33.6	.2404	4	Akron
0.2283	33.6	.2446	4	flagged
0.2283	33.6	.2446	4	javelinas
0.2283	33.6	.2446	4	unbeaten
0.2283	33.6	.2404	4	217
0.2282	33.6	.2412	4	akin
0.2282	33.6	.2412	4	settlers'
0.2282	33.6	.2412	4	supervisor
0.2281	33.6	.2306	4	Damon
0.2281	33.6	.1835	6	tensile
0.2280	33.6	.1587	6	pianoforte
0.2279	33.6	.1620	6	micrometers
0.2277	33.6	.2437	3	Aquarium
0.2277	33.6	.2437	3	chocolate-covered
0.2277	33.6	.2437	3	deepen
0.2277	33.6	.2437	3	demolish
0.2277	33.6	.2437	3	fathometer
0.2277	33.6	.2437	3	flops

U	SFI	D	F	Word Type
0.2277	33.6	.2437	3	good-luck
0.2277	33.6	.2437	3	grayish-brown
0.2277	33.6	.2437	3	half-filled
0.2277	33.6	.2437	3	inoculation
0.2277	33.6	.2437	3	juncos
0.2277	33.6	.2437	3	Kahn
0.2277	33.6	.2437	3	Mars'
0.2277	33.6	.2437	3	meanest
0.2277	33.6	.2437	3	phew
0.2277	33.6	.2437	3	prawns
0.2277	33.6	.2437	3	puma
0.2277	33.6	.2437	3	rat-a-tat-tat
0.2277	33.6	.2437	3	rescuing
0.2277	33.6	.2437	3	Rockets
0.2277	33.6	.2437	3	scarecrows
0.2277	33.6	.2437	3	spangle
0.2277	33.6	.2437	3	sprinklers
0.2277	33.6	.1035	7	timer
0.2277	33.6	.2437	3	Tombaugh
0.2277	33.6	.2437	3	trusts
0.2277	33.6	.2437	3	whetted
0.2275	33.6	.2163	4	Waialeale
0.2275	33.6	.2163	4	495
0.2274	33.6	.2435	3	accountable
0.2274	33.6	.2435	3	archery
0.2274	33.6	.2435	3	bad-smelling
0.2274	33.6	.2435	3	Banneker
0.2274	33.6	.2435	3	befriended
0.2274	33.6	.2435	3	bowled
0.2274	33.6	.2435	3	coffeecake
0.2274	33.6	.2435	3	daubed
0.2274	33.6	.2435	3	eider
0.2274	33.6	.2435	3	enlisting
0.2274	33.6	.2435	3	exultantly
0.2274	33.6	.2435	3	footmen
0.2274	33.6	.2435	3	Gramps
0.2274	33.6	.2435	3	Gran
0.2274	33.6	.2435	3	great-great-grandfather
0.2274	33.6	.2435	3	hornet's
0.2274	33.6	.1835	5	knocker
0.2274	33.6	.2435	3	long-lost
0.2274	33.6	.2435	3	NewLondon
0.2274	33.6	.2435	3	opponent's
0.2274	33.6	.2435	3	panned
0.2274	33.6	.2435	3	peddling
0.2274	33.6	.2435	3	Pierre's
0.2274	33.6	.2435	3	Rotary
0.2274	33.6	.2435	3	salting
0.2274	33.6	.2435	3	SanGabriel
0.2274	33.6	.2435	3	Search
0.2274	33.6	.2435	3	second-best
0.2274	33.6	.2435	3	Shan
0.2274	33.6	.2435	3	sheepmen
0.2274	33.6	.2435	3	six-shooter
THE PRECEDING WORD TYPE OCCUPIES RANK 31100				
0.2274	33.6	.2435	3	snowbound
0.2274	33.6	.1396	7	Stegner
0.2274	33.6	.2435	3	suing
0.2274	33.6	.2435	3	swift-moving
0.2274	33.6	.2435	3	thatch-roofed
0.2274	33.6	.2435	3	Today's
0.2274	33.6	.2435	3	Tongue
0.2274	33.6	.2435	3	Toombs
0.2274	33.6	.2435	3	viewpoints
0.2274	33.6	.2435	3	washboard
0.2274	33.6	.2435	3	windowpanes
0.2274	33.6	.2435	3	803
0.2272	33.6	.2657	4	fad
0.2271	33.6	.2010	4	churchmen
0.2271	33.6	.2297	4	Painted
0.2271	33.6	.0958	6	repent
0.2271	33.6	.2010	4	Seal
0.2270	33.6	.0908	8	Delos
0.2270	33.6	.0908	8	Madagascar
0.2270	33.6	.0908	8	Mindanao
0.2268	33.6	.2442	4	anticipates
0.2268	33.6	.2442	4	Carroll's
0.2268	33.6	.2442	4	closed-circuit
0.2268	33.6	.2442	4	Cry
0.2268	33.6	.2442	4	refund
0.2268	33.6	.2442	4	vodka
0.2267	33.6	.1698	4	contrivances
0.2267	33.6	.1698	4	cuckoos
0.2267	33.6	.1698	4	graduating
0.2267	33.6	.1698	4	plausible
0.2267	33.6	.1698	4	Schools
0.2267	33.6	.1698	4	secretary-general
0.2267	33.6	.1698	4	Sonoran
0.2266	33.6	.2401	4	appoints
0.2266	33.6	.2401	4	Centuries
0.2266	33.6	.2401	4	denominations
0.2266	33.6	.2401	4	equable
0.2266	33.6	.2401	4	Missionary
0.2266	33.6	.2391	4	Nebula
0.2266	33.6	.2391	4	osmium
0.2266	33.6	.2391	4	224
0.2266	33.6	.2391	4	481
0.2265	33.6	.1349	4	Alhambra
0.2265	33.6	.1349	4	asthma
0.2265	33.6	.1349	4	deep-throated
0.2265	33.6	.1349	4	lockers
0.2265	33.6	.1349	4	rambled
0.2265	33.6	.1349	4	recompense
0.2265	33.6	.1349	4	riverman
0.2264	33.5	.2440	4	Calypso
0.2264	33.5	.0000	28	cello
0.2264	33.5	.2440	4	exhort
0.2264	33.5	.2440	4	fishy
0.2264	33.5	.2440	4	foray
0.2264	33.5	.2440	4	remotest
0.2264	33.5	.2440	4	saloons
0.2264	33.5	.2440	4	specter
0.2261	33.5	.0900	8	anesthetic
0.2261	33.5	.1820	5	bilingual
0.2261	33.5	.0900	8	Bohr
0.2261	33.5	.1820	5	Canty
0.2261	33.5	.1820	5	Holcomb
0.2261	33.5	.1820	5	Madeline
0.2261	33.5	.0900	8	oviduct
0.2261	33.5	.2640	4	phosphorous
0.2260	33.5	.2443	4	Achmet's
0.2260	33.5	.2443	4	poultice
0.2260	33.5	.2443	4	remuda
0.2258	33.5	.1794	5	alewives
0.2258	33.5	.2285	4	Algerians
0.2258	33.5	.2285	4	aqueduct
0.2258	33.5	.1020	6	Baker's
0.2258	33.5	.2285	4	daGama
0.2258	33.5	.2285	4	establishments
0.2258	33.5	.1794	5	Marcy's
0.2258	33.5	.1794	5	moonshine
0.2258	33.5	.2285	4	Nanking
0.2258	33.5	.2285	4	persecutions
0.2258	33.5	.2285	4	Portugal's
0.2258	33.5	.2285	4	precedents
0.2258	33.5	.2285	4	rain-forest
0.2258	33.5	.2285	4	seaway
0.2258	33.5	.2285	4	totalitarian
0.2258	33.5	.2285	4	1733
0.2257	33.5	.2278	4	acetic
0.2257	33.5	.2437	4	Adrian
0.2257	33.5	.2437	4	affinity
0.2257	33.5	.2437	4	archeological
0.2257	33.5	.2437	4	Arno
0.2257	33.5	.2437	4	Astronomy
0.2257	33.5	.2278	4	Australopithecus
0.2257	33.5	.0256	27	bevel
0.2257	33.5	.2437	4	centralized
0.2257	33.5	.2278	4	coronary
0.2257	33.5	.2437	4	cranks
0.2257	33.5	.2437	4	devotees
0.2257	33.5	.2278	4	digesting
0.2257	33.5	.2278	4	Drosophila
0.2257	33.5	.2437	4	geologically
0.2257	33.5	.2437	4	Gov
THE PRECEDING WORD TYPE OCCUPIES RANK 31200				
0.2257	33.5	.2278	4	hallucinations
0.2257	33.5	.2278	4	Heat
0.2257	33.5	.2437	4	homologous
0.2257	33.5	.2437	4	hyenas
0.2257	33.5	.2278	4	laborious
0.2257	33.5	.2278	4	Lavoisier's
0.2257	33.5	.2437	4	malfunction
0.2257	33.5	.2278	4	metabolic
0.2257	33.5	.2278	4	mimicry
0.2257	33.5	.2437	4	oriented
0.2257	33.5	.2278	4	oval-shaped
0.2257	33.5	.2437	4	PMA
0.2257	33.5	.2437	4	Provencal
0.2257	33.5	.2278	4	receptors
0.2257	33.5	.2278	4	reconstructing
0.2257	33.5	.2437	4	Standby
0.2257	33.5	.2437	4	tetraethyl
0.2257	33.5	.2278	4	uncharged
0.2257	33.5	.2437	4	widens
0.2254	33.5	.0000	21	Coyotito
0.2254	33.5	.0000	21	DYKE
0.2254	33.5	.2441	4	hindquarters
0.2254	33.5	.2441	4	LeHavre
0.2254	33.5	.2441	4	relic
0.2254	33.5	.2441	4	Richardson's
0.2254	33.5	.2441	4	Smollett
0.2253	33.5	.1042	8	Figaro
0.2250	33.5	.2446	4	coudie
0.2249	33.5	.2345	4	1c
0.2247	33.5	.0719	7	Hilltown
0.2246	33.5	.2446	4	Fust
0.2246	33.5	.2446	4	Marlowe
0.2245	33.5	.0000	15	divisibility
0.2245	33.5	.0000	15	factored
0.2245	33.5	.0502	9	Gandhi's
0.2245	33.5	.0000	15	hr
0.2245	33.5	.0000	15	hundreds'
0.2245	33.5	.0000	15	sevens
0.2245	33.5	.0000	15	03
0.2245	33.5	.0000	15	3x
0.2243	33.5	.2446	4	Broom
0.2243	33.5	.2446	4	Caesar's
0.2243	33.5	.2446	4	confines
0.2243	33.5	.2446	4	Corsica
0.2243	33.5	.2446	4	Daw
0.2243	33.5	.1310	5	fourth-grade
0.2243	33.5	.2446	4	Poems
0.2241	33.5	.2243	4	Skills
0.2239	33.5	.1253	7	allegro
0.2239	33.5	.1253	7	Tam
0.2239	33.5	.1253	7	Wagner's
0.2236	33.5	.1935	5	splines
0.2230	33.5	.0851	9	homophonic
0.2230	33.5	.0851	9	oboes
0.2229	33.5	.2333	4	fairy-tale
0.2229	33.5	.2333	4	Reynard
0.2228	33.5	.0000	19	Lina
0.2227	33.5	.1637	6	belting
0.2226	33.5	.2364	4	294
0.2226	33.5	.2364	4	463
0.2225	33.5	.1008	9	homemaker
0.2225	33.5	.1605	6	similes
0.2223	33.5	.0954	5	crosscut
0.2223	33.5	.0283	19	dressings
0.2223	33.5	.2376	4	patties
0.2219	33.5	.2570	4	synthetics
0.2214	33.5	.1801	5	snapshot
0.2213	33.4	.1127	5	carnation
0.2213	33.4	.1127	5	high-tide
0.2213	33.4	.1127	5	sliders
0.2213	33.4	.1127	5	taproot
0.2213	33.4	.1127	5	273
0.2212	33.4	.1475	6	balsa
0.2209	33.4	.1954	5	compulsion
0.2208	33.4	.2369	3	bluejays
0.2208	33.4	.2369	3	five-cent
0.2208	33.4	.2369	3	lampshade
0.2208	33.4	.2369	3	rupees
0.2208	33.4	.2369	3	1490
0.2206	33.4	.2423	4	slippage
0.2206	33.4	.2423	4	spareribs
0.2202	33.4	.1560	5	392
0.2202	33.4	.1560	5	578
0.2199	33.4	.2357	3	Albert's
0.2199	33.4	.2357	3	antagonists
0.2199	33.4	.2357	3	Balaam
0.2199	33.4	.2357	3	Bedloe's
0.2199	33.4	.2357	3	Bender
0.2199	33.4	.2357	3	best-trained
0.2199	33.4	.2357	3	bitterest
0.2199	33.4	.2357	3	Bryn
0.2199	33.4	.2357	3	buffalo's
0.2199	33.4	.2357	3	bumpers
0.2199	33.4	.2357	3	chandeliers
0.2199	33.4	.2357	3	clucked
0.2199	33.4	.2357	3	Cooper's
0.2199	33.4	.2357	3	Craik
0.2199	33.4	.2357	3	cross-stitch
0.2199	33.4	.2357	3	dairymen
0.2199	33.4	.2357	3	dearie
THE PRECEDING WORD TYPE OCCUPIES RANK 31300				
0.2199	33.4	.2357	3	demurely
0.2199	33.4	.2357	3	dizzying
0.2199	33.4	.2357	3	duffel
0.2199	33.4	.0702	7	Elli
0.2199	33.4	.2357	3	Elsa's
0.2199	33.4	.2357	3	exhausting
0.2199	33.4	.2357	3	fishhook
0.2199	33.4	.2357	3	five-gallon
0.2199	33.4	.2357	3	flea-bitten
0.2199	33.4	.2357	3	flexed
0.2199	33.4	.2357	3	foremast
0.2199	33.4	.2357	3	forty-three
0.2199	33.4	.2357	3	Found
0.2199	33.4	.2357	3	gecko
0.2199	33.4	.2357	3	Graves
0.2199	33.4	.2357	3	Gregory's
0.2199	33.4	.2357	3	hair-like
0.2199	33.4	.2357	3	halters
0.2199	33.4	.2357	3	Hawk's
0.2199	33.4	.2357	3	hero's
0.2199	33.4	.2357	3	Inlet
0.2199	33.4	.2357	3	lamb's
0.2199	33.4	.2357	3	line-up
0.2199	33.4	.2357	3	make-believes
0.2199	33.4	.2357	3	man-size
0.2199	33.4	.2357	3	marooned
0.2199	33.4	.2357	3	Mawr
0.2199	33.4	.2357	3	millstones
0.2199	33.4	.2357	3	nightmares
0.2199	33.4	.2357	3	nine-thirty
0.2199	33.4	.2357	3	number-one
0.2199	33.4	.2357	3	Orioles
0.2199	33.4	.2357	3	penniless
0.2199	33.4	.2357	3	persimmons
0.2199	33.4	.2357	3	pontoon
0.2199	33.4	.2357	3	porters
0.2199	33.4	.2357	3	procure
0.2199	33.4	.2357	3	quietest
0.2199	33.4	.2357	3	Rattler
0.2199	33.4	.2357	3	responsibilty
0.2199	33.4	.2357	3	revolvers
0.2199	33.4	.2357	3	Seminole
0.2199	33.4	.2357	3	Sixteenth
0.2199	33.4	.2357	3	smirk
0.2199	33.4	.2357	3	snuffling
0.2199	33.4	.2357	3	snuggle
0.2199	33.4	.2357	3	spyglasses
0.2199	33.4	.2357	3	Striking
0.2199	33.4	.2357	3	stuffs
0.2199	33.4	.2357	3	sub-assemblies
0.2199	33.4	.2357	3	swiftest
0.2199	33.4	.2357	3	third-floor
0.2199	33.4	.2357	3	tidied
0.2199	33.4	.2357	3	tired-looking
0.2199	33.4	.2357	3	toppling
0.2199	33.4	.2357	3	trade-mark
0.2199	33.4	.2357	3	underdog
0.2199	33.4	.2357	3	unselfishness
0.2199	33.4	.2357	3	vestibule
0.2199	33.4	.2357	3	vine-covered
0.2199	33.4	.2357	3	Wiley
0.2199	33.4	.2357	3	withstood
0.2199	33.4	.2357	3	York's
0.2198	33.4	.1781	5	Stella
0.2197	33.4	.1995	4	alkaline
0.2197	33.4	.1995	4	dry-cleaning
0.2197	33.4	.1995	4	headphone
0.2197	33.4	.1995	4	Needham
0.2196	33.4	.1738	5	Gaylord
0.2196	33.4	.1738	5	gelding
0.2196	33.4	.1738	5	Tempest
0.2195	33.4	.1118	5	firehouse
0.2195	33.4	.1118	5	Honshu
0.2195	33.4	.1118	5	kimonos
0.2195	33.4	.1118	5	Speedwell
0.2195	33.4	.1118	5	Trading
0.2195	33.4	.1118	5	Zee
0.2195	33.4	.1549	5	327
0.2194	33.4	.3507	3	Grow
0.2193	33.4	.1786	5	Barbier
0.2193	33.4	.1786	5	Ewell
0.2191	33.4	.0489	9	Wilbur's
0.2190	33.4	.1358	6	trots
0.2190	33.4	.1358	6	Wren
0.2188	33.4	.1190	5	Sleeping
0.2183	33.4	.0000	27	Brahms
0.2183	33.4	.2418	4	farfetched
0.2183	33.4	.0000	27	rondo
0.2182	33.4	.2408	4	bold-faced
0.2182	33.4	.2408	4	gerund
0.2182	33.4	.2408	4	Jutes
0.2182	33.4	.2408	4	onym
0.2182	33.4	.2408	4	participles
0.2182	33.4	.2417	4	re-create
0.2182	33.4	.2408	4	underscored
0.2182	33.4	.2408	4	wr
0.2181	33.4	.1323	7	frankfurter
0.2179	33.4	.1975	4	halibut
0.2179	33.4	.1975	4	uninhabitable
0.2178	33.4	.2387	4	Hermit
THE PRECEDING WORD TYPE OCCUPIES RANK 31400				
0.2178	33.4	.2387	4	trumpeters
0.2177	33.4	.2376	4	avant
0.2177	33.4	.2376	4	Lent
0.2176	33.4	.2220	4	algebraic
0.2176	33.4	.2220	4	cos
0.2176	33.4	.2220	4	Problems
0.2176	33.4	.2220	4	1260
0.2176	33.4	.2220	4	378
0.2176	33.4	.2220	4	685
0.2176	33.4	.2220	4	736
0.2175	33.4	.2375	4	gals
0.2175	33.4	.2375	4	guitarist
0.2172	33.4	.1210	4	Priest
0.2171	33.4	.0000	15	Bolsun
0.2171	33.4	.0000	15	Lokanon
0.2169	33.4	.0000	11	dermis
0.2169	33.4	.0000	11	protists
0.2169	33.4	.0000	11	SCS
0.2168	33.4	.2595	4	directional
0.2167	33.4	.2206	4	Ash
0.2167	33.4	.0252	14	pl
0.2165	33.4	.1751	5	grampa
0.2165	33.4	.1751	5	scapegoat
0.2162	33.3	.1534	5	massacred
0.2162	33.3	.1534	5	rowboats
0.2161	33.3	.2194	4	Sheila
0.2158	33.3	.2303	4	Judas
0.2158	33.3	.2303	4	piper
0.2158	33.3	.2303	4	Ravel's
0.2158	33.3	.2303	4	Valse
0.2157	33.3	.1339	6	chartered
0.2157	33.3	.1339	6	embryonic
0.2157	33.3	.1339	6	interrelated
0.2157	33.3	.1339	6	Wilmington
0.2156	33.3	.1020	7	Fletcher
0.2155	33.3	.1231	6	Companies
0.2155	33.3	.1231	6	lured
0.2155	33.3	.2289	4	sundaes
0.2150	33.3	.2201	4	Eternal
0.2150	33.3	.2201	4	Ibn
0.2150	33.3	.2201	4	Macaulay's
0.2150	33.3	.2201	4	Sorbonne
0.2146	33.3	.0000	20	CALDWELL
0.2146	33.3	.0000	20	Launcelot
0.2146	33.3	.0000	20	Mercutio
0.2146	33.3	.2351	4	Monmouth
0.2146	33.3	.1221	6	Orlando
0.2146	33.3	.2351	4	papermaking
0.2146	33.3	.2351	4	Surface
0.2146	33.3	.2351	4	3/4-inch
0.2145	33.3	.3394	3	Every
0.2145	33.3	.2401	4	phosphor
0.2143	33.3	.2279	3	abbot
0.2143	33.3	.2279	3	Abdul
0.2143	33.3	.2279	3	Advisor
0.2143	33.3	.2279	3	Agent
0.2143	33.3	.2279	3	all-American
0.2143	33.3	.2279	3	assailed
0.2143	33.3	.2279	3	batons
0.2143	33.3	.2279	3	bazaars
0.2143	33.3	.2279	3	belligerently
0.2143	33.3	.2279	3	bien
0.2143	33.3	.2279	3	bowlers
0.2143	33.3	.2279	3	calluses
0.2143	33.3	.2279	3	campgrounds
0.2143	33.3	.1171	7	capstan
0.2143	33.3	.2279	3	champs
0.2143	33.3	.2279	3	co-pilot
0.2143	33.3	.2279	3	coyly
0.2143	33.3	.2279	3	crabapple
0.2143	33.3	.2279	3	curbside
0.2143	33.3	.2279	3	delinquency
0.2143	33.3	.2279	3	Des
0.2143	33.3	.2279	3	desert's
0.2143	33.3	.2279	3	dexterity
0.2143	33.3	.2279	3	dogs'
0.2143	33.3	.2279	3	doused
0.2143	33.3	.2279	3	electing
0.2143	33.3	.2279	3	Eliot
0.2143	33.3	.2279	3	Everybody
0.2143	33.3	.2279	3	fainthearted
0.2143	33.3	.2279	3	feuds
0.2143	33.3	.2279	3	flogging
0.2143	33.3	.2279	3	four-man
0.2143	33.3	.2279	3	fretfully
0.2143	33.3	.2279	3	Geraldine
0.2143	33.3	.2279	3	Giant's
0.2143	33.3	.2279	3	Grocery
0.2143	33.3	.2279	3	handball
0.2143	33.3	.2279	3	happy-go-lucky
0.2143	33.3	.2279	3	headwind
0.2143	33.3	.2279	3	history-making
0.2143	33.3	.2279	3	Holland's
0.2143	33.3	.2279	3	hugely
0.2143	33.3	.2279	3	Invasion
0.2143	33.3	.2279	3	kidnaping
0.2143	33.3	.2279	3	Larry's
0.2143	33.3	.2279	3	Laurie's
0.2143	33.3	.2279	3	Mijbil
0.2143	33.3	.2279	3	mishap
THE PRECEDING WORD TYPE OCCUPIES RANK 31500				
0.2143	33.3	.2279	3	mongooses
0.2143	33.3	.2279	3	muddled
0.2143	33.3	.2279	3	natured
0.2143	33.3	.2279	3	Ocracoke
0.2143	33.3	.2279	3	overpass
0.2143	33.3	.2279	3	Parrot
0.2143	33.3	.2279	3	parrot's
0.2143	33.3	.2279	3	pasty-faced
0.2143	33.3	.2279	3	pirate's

U	SFI	D	F	Word Type
0.2143	33.3	.2279	3	Pop's
0.2143	33.3	.2279	3	poring
0.2143	33.3	.2279	3	portages
0.2143	33.3	.2279	3	Posey
0.2143	33.3	.2279	3	pursed
0.2143	33.3	.2279	3	pushcart
0.2143	33.3	.2279	3	Rand
0.2143	33.3	.2279	3	Rick's
0.2143	33.3	.2279	3	Rockford
0.2143	33.3	.2279	3	rummaging
0.2143	33.3	.2279	3	sass
0.2143	33.3	.2279	3	snored
0.2143	33.3	.2279	3	spiraled
0.2143	33.3	.2279	3	standings
0.2143	33.3	.2279	3	taillight
0.2143	33.3	.2279	3	taillights
0.2143	33.3	.2279	3	Torrington
0.2143	33.3	.2279	3	transom
0.2143	33.3	.2279	3	Traveller
0.2143	33.3	.2279	3	umpires
0.2143	33.3	.2279	3	unabated
0.2143	33.3	.2279	3	unheard-of
0.2143	33.3	.2279	3	unhitch
0.2143	33.3	.2279	3	wiggly
0.2143	33.3	.2279	3	Window
0.2143	33.3	.2279	3	Wish
0.2143	33.3	.2279	3	wonderland
0.2142	33.3	.1712	5	mixed-up
0.2141	33.3	.2186	4	Albrecht
0.2141	33.3	.2186	4	goeth
0.2141	33.3	.3482	3	knead
0.2141	33.3	.2186	4	ramrod
0.2141	33.3	.2186	4	Shawnees
0.2141	33.3	.2186	4	Sibyl
0.2141	33.3	.2186	4	tramps
0.2140	33.3	.3382	3	skilful
0.2140	33.3	.3382	3	Whole
0.2140	33.3	.2271	4	woodworker
0.2139	33.3	.0000	11	Asuncion
0.2139	33.3	.0000	11	Baya
0.2139	33.3	.0000	11	Cabrillo
0.2139	33.3	.0000	11	Wolfe
0.2138	33.3	.2253	4	15-7
0.2138	33.3	.2253	4	15-8
0.2138	33.3	.2253	4	244
0.2138	33.3	.2253	4	4-1
0.2138	33.3	.2253	4	5-7
0.2138	33.3	.2253	4	666
0.2137	33.3	.2517	4	gelatine
0.2136	33.3	.3373	3	admires
0.2136	33.3	.2152	4	untying
0.2134	33.3	.2174	4	bobber
0.2134	33.3	.1314	6	gel
0.2134	33.3	.2174	4	Mack's
0.2134	33.3	.2174	4	Margot
0.2134	33.3	.2174	4	pale-faced
0.2131	33.3	.2261	3	'at
0.2131	33.3	.2261	3	a-coming
0.2131	33.3	.2261	3	Barton's
0.2131	33.3	.2261	3	bayou
0.2131	33.3	.2261	3	betraying
0.2131	33.3	.2261	3	blacken
0.2131	33.3	.2261	3	bloodstained
0.2131	33.3	.2261	3	blundered
0.2131	33.3	.2261	3	clenching
0.2131	33.3	.2261	3	cookhouse
0.2131	33.3	.2261	3	deafness
0.2131	33.3	.2261	3	dears
0.2131	33.3	.2261	3	dooryard
0.2131	33.3	.2261	3	double-quick
0.2131	33.3	.2261	3	dreamt
0.2131	33.3	.2261	3	drouth
0.2131	33.3	.2261	3	duster
0.2131	33.3	.2261	3	essayed
0.2131	33.3	.2261	3	evil-smelling
0.2131	33.3	.2261	3	favourite
0.2131	33.3	.2261	3	fishhead
0.2131	33.3	.2261	3	flailed
0.2131	33.3	.2261	3	friendliest
0.2131	33.3	.2261	3	frisked
0.2131	33.3	.2261	3	Gage
0.2131	33.3	.2261	3	gork
0.2131	33.3	.2261	3	gulls'
0.2131	33.3	.2261	3	heavy-hearted
0.2131	33.3	.2261	3	imploring
0.2131	33.3	.2261	3	low-hanging
0.2131	33.3	.2261	3	m-m-m
0.2131	33.3	.2261	3	meowing
0.2131	33.3	.2261	3	mewed
0.2131	33.3	.2261	3	mittened
0.2131	33.3	.2261	3	mopped

THE PRECEDING WORD TYPE OCCUPIES RANK 31600

U	SFI	D	F	Word Type
0.2131	33.3	.2261	3	noisier
0.2131	33.3	.2261	3	obstinate
0.2131	33.3	.2261	3	orange-colored
0.2131	33.3	.2261	3	Pat's
0.2131	33.3	.2261	3	perplexity
0.2131	33.3	.2261	3	Prescott
0.2131	33.3	.2261	3	Professor's
0.2131	33.3	.2261	3	scooted
0.2131	33.3	.2261	3	scrounging
0.2131	33.3	.2261	3	selfishness
0.2131	33.3	.2261	3	sentinels
0.2131	33.3	.2261	3	single-handed
0.2131	33.3	.2261	3	sixty-nine
0.2131	33.3	.2261	3	skittering
0.2131	33.3	.2261	3	sky's
0.2131	33.3	.2261	3	slaying
0.2131	33.3	.2261	3	squishy
0.2131	33.3	.2261	3	StNicholas
0.2131	33.3	.2261	3	Sukey
0.2131	33.3	.2261	3	sure-enough
0.2131	33.3	.2261	3	tail-feathers
0.2131	33.3	.2261	3	threateningly
0.2131	33.3	.2261	3	totting
0.2131	33.3	.2261	3	trice
0.2131	33.3	.2261	3	uncurled
0.2131	33.3	.2261	3	unmoving
0.2131	33.3	.2261	3	veered
0.2131	33.3	.2261	3	windshields
0.2128	33.3	.1628	5	abortions
0.2128	33.3	.1628	5	cocktail
0.2128	33.3	.1628	5	contends
0.2128	33.3	.1628	5	Kissimmee
0.2127	33.3	.2085	4	barium
0.2127	33.3	.2094	4	lacquered
0.2127	33.3	.2085	4	partway
0.2127	33.3	.2085	4	10-4
0.2123	33.3	.3421	3	binder
0.2122	33.3	.2129	4	derivations
0.2122	33.3	.2129	4	EH
0.2122	33.3	.2129	4	Statistics
0.2122	33.3	.2129	4	80%
0.2122	33.3	.2129	4	846
0.2121	33.3	.1004	7	beheaded
0.2121	33.3	.1697	5	piteous
0.2121	33.3	.2419	4	simmering
0.2120	33.3	.1684	5	Elia
0.2114	33.3	.3319	3	blemish
0.2114	33.3	.1146	7	Brass
0.2114	33.3	.3321	3	credentials
0.2114	33.3	.1146	7	He's
0.2114	33.3	.3321	3	hustle
0.2114	33.3	.3319	3	informality
0.2114	33.3	.1146	7	Shangri-la
0.2114	33.3	.3319	3	suede
0.2112	33.2	.2360	4	Advisory
0.2112	33.2	.0995	7	experimentally
0.2112	33.2	.2248	4	farce
0.2112	33.2	.2248	4	mantles
0.2112	33.2	.2248	4	Ram
0.2111	33.2	.2246	4	Potter
0.2111	33.2	.2431	4	reciting
0.2111	33.2	.2431	4	tinny
0.2111	33.2	.2351	4	Womrath
0.2110	33.2	.0000	18	Gitler
0.2109	33.2	.2130	4	saith
0.2108	33.2	.1602	5	$49
0.2108	33.2	.1602	5	SR
0.2106	33.2	.2313	4	Aunts
0.2106	33.2	.2223	3	Bluebird
0.2106	33.2	.2223	3	bullfighter
0.2106	33.2	.2223	3	catboats
0.2106	33.2	.2223	3	chanty
0.2106	33.2	.2223	3	drenching
0.2106	33.2	.2223	3	Eastman
0.2106	33.2	.2223	3	fidgeting
0.2106	33.2	.2223	3	fortify
0.2106	33.2	.2223	3	goldsmith
0.2106	33.2	.2223	3	Gulch
0.2106	33.2	.2223	3	Hesperides
0.2106	33.2	.2223	3	Husband
0.2106	33.2	.2223	3	jet-propelled
0.2106	33.2	.2223	3	Jonathan's
0.2106	33.2	.2223	3	limericks
0.2106	33.2	.2223	3	lost-and-found
0.2106	33.2	.2223	3	Meadow
0.2106	33.2	.2223	3	Nagel
0.2106	33.2	.2223	3	Pages
0.2106	33.2	.2223	3	Pansy
0.2106	33.2	.0554	8	passer
0.2106	33.2	.2223	3	putt
0.2106	33.2	.2223	3	Sanborn
0.2106	33.2	.2223	3	Sr
0.2106	33.2	.2223	3	subscriber
0.2106	33.2	.2223	3	trainman
0.2106	33.2	.2223	3	tres
0.2106	33.2	.2223	3	tumbledown
0.2106	33.2	.0554	8	UFO
0.2106	33.2	.2223	3	uh-uh
0.2106	33.2	.2223	3	whene'er
0.2106	33.2	.2223	3	whitely

THE PRECEDING WORD TYPE OCCUPIES RANK 31700

U	SFI	D	F	Word Type
0.2106	33.2	.2223	3	wickedly
0.2106	33.2	.2223	3	zoomed
0.2103	33.2	.2296	4	deadline
0.2103	33.2	.2296	4	servicemen
0.2103	33.2	.0803	9	tabular
0.2102	33.2	.0000	26	syncopated
0.2099	33.2	.2212	3	a-stirring
0.2099	33.2	.2212	3	Agamemnon's
0.2099	33.2	.2212	3	bracken
0.2099	33.2	.2212	3	braked
0.2099	33.2	.2212	3	bulwark
0.2099	33.2	.2212	3	Campus
0.2099	33.2	.2212	3	colonel's
0.2099	33.2	.2212	3	complacently
0.2099	33.2	.2212	3	cookstove
0.2099	33.2	.2212	3	couriers
0.2099	33.2	.2212	3	Coyote's
0.2099	33.2	.2212	3	day-time
0.2099	33.2	.2212	3	dumbly
0.2099	33.2	.2212	3	Edith's
0.2099	33.2	.2212	3	Elfland
0.2099	33.2	.2212	3	Elmer's
0.2099	33.2	.2212	3	filly's
0.2099	33.2	.2212	3	gentled
0.2099	33.2	.2212	3	glens
0.2099	33.2	.2212	3	gnaws
0.2099	33.2	.2212	3	goodnight
0.2099	33.2	.2212	3	hag
0.2099	33.2	.2212	3	halfback
0.2099	33.2	.2212	3	hawk's
0.2099	33.2	.2212	3	head-on
0.2099	33.2	.2212	3	heerd
0.2099	33.2	.2212	3	hilarious
0.2099	33.2	.2212	3	ho-ho-ho
0.2099	33.2	.2212	3	hostages
0.2099	33.2	.2212	3	HOUSE
0.2099	33.2	.2212	3	howitzers
0.2099	33.2	.2212	3	jelly-like
0.2099	33.2	.2212	3	ladylike
0.2099	33.2	.2212	3	Lucy's
0.2099	33.2	.2212	3	midair
0.2099	33.2	.2212	3	misjudged
0.2099	33.2	.2212	3	Moab
0.2099	33.2	.2212	3	overhear
0.2099	33.2	.2212	3	padlock
0.2099	33.2	.2212	3	Penfield
0.2099	33.2	.2212	3	Princess'
0.2099	33.2	.2212	3	questioningly
0.2099	33.2	.2212	3	reeling
0.2099	33.2	.2212	3	safekeeping
0.2099	33.2	.2212	3	scowling
0.2099	33.2	.2212	3	sh-h-h
0.2099	33.2	.2212	3	Sheriff's
0.2099	33.2	.2212	3	sightless
0.2099	33.2	.2212	3	sleepiness
0.2099	33.2	.2212	3	somersaulting
0.2099	33.2	.2212	3	sprinted
0.2099	33.2	.2212	3	stuffiness
0.2099	33.2	.2212	3	surrendering
0.2099	33.2	.2212	3	swarthy
0.2099	33.2	.2212	3	taffy
0.2099	33.2	.2212	3	thudded
0.2099	33.2	.2212	3	tight-lipped
0.2099	33.2	.2212	3	timekeeper
0.2099	33.2	.2212	3	uncivilized
0.2099	33.2	.2212	3	understandingly
0.2099	33.2	.2212	3	unshorn
0.2099	33.2	.2212	3	Vimy
0.2099	33.2	.2212	3	water-soaked
0.2099	33.2	.2212	3	Wisdom
0.2099	33.2	.2212	3	wordless
0.2099	33.2	.2212	3	wordlessly
0.2098	33.2	.1668	5	failings
0.2098	33.2	.1668	5	guile
0.2098	33.2	.1668	5	Thomases
0.2096	33.2	.0000	14	divisors
0.2096	33.2	.0000	14	multiplications
0.2096	33.2	.0000	14	1/7
0.2096	33.2	.0000	14	2/6
0.2096	33.2	.0000	14	3/10
0.2096	33.2	.0000	14	5/3
0.2096	33.2	.0000	14	5/5
0.2096	33.2	.0000	14	9/12
0.2095	33.2	.2107	4	abrading
0.2095	33.2	.2107	4	air-cooled
0.2095	33.2	.2107	4	Ashland
0.2095	33.2	.2107	4	booed
0.2095	33.2	.2107	4	Commandant
0.2095	33.2	.2107	4	defeats
0.2095	33.2	.2107	4	determinedly
0.2095	33.2	.2107	4	five-figure
0.2095	33.2	.2107	4	gruesome
0.2095	33.2	.2107	4	humpback
0.2095	33.2	.2107	4	Ocmulgee
0.2095	33.2	.2107	4	sputnik
0.2095	33.2	.2107	4	T-37
0.2095	33.2	.2107	4	thornbush
0.2095	33.2	.2107	4	Ulster
0.2094	33.2	.1677	5	Locke's
0.2092	33.2	.1497	4	bobolink

THE PRECEDING WORD TYPE OCCUPIES RANK 31800

U	SFI	D	F	Word Type
0.2092	33.2	.1497	4	frugal
0.2092	33.2	.1497	4	joe
0.2092	33.2	.1497	4	toots
0.2092	33.2	.1497	4	tw
0.2090	33.2	.2197	3	$22
0.2090	33.2	.2197	3	Allan's
0.2090	33.2	.2197	3	Aluminum
0.2090	33.2	.2197	3	ankle-deep
0.2090	33.2	.2197	3	caretakers
0.2090	33.2	.2197	3	Cloud's
0.2090	33.2	.2197	3	courtship
0.2090	33.2	.2197	3	current's
0.2090	33.2	.2197	3	disintegrated
0.2090	33.2	.2197	3	displeasure
0.2090	33.2	.2197	3	divers'
0.2090	33.2	.2197	3	effigy
0.2090	33.2	.2197	3	endeavored
0.2090	33.2	.2197	3	extrusion
0.2090	33.2	.2197	3	footpath
0.2090	33.2	.2197	3	frolicking
0.2090	33.2	.2197	3	glassed-in
0.2090	33.2	.2197	3	heath
0.2090	33.2	.2197	3	Heine
0.2090	33.2	.2197	3	jester
0.2090	33.2	.2197	3	Lyons
0.2090	33.2	.2197	3	man-of-war
0.2090	33.2	.2197	3	marc
0.2090	33.2	.2197	3	mistreatment
0.2090	33.2	.2197	3	Moll
0.2090	33.2	.2197	3	mostest
0.2090	33.2	.2197	3	noxious
0.2090	33.2	.2197	3	nugget
0.2090	33.2	.2197	3	optimist
0.2090	33.2	.2197	3	plaything
0.2090	33.2	.2197	3	reassurance
0.2090	33.2	.2197	3	replica
0.2090	33.2	.2197	3	sad-looking
0.2090	33.2	.2197	3	self-educated
0.2090	33.2	.2197	3	soft-shelled
0.2090	33.2	.2197	3	straddling
0.2090	33.2	.2197	3	Stuart's
0.2090	33.2	.2197	3	sundials
0.2090	33.2	.2197	3	Teresa
0.2090	33.2	.2197	3	thermo
0.2090	33.2	.2197	3	Trafalgar
0.2090	33.2	.2197	3	uncovers
0.2090	33.2	.2197	3	undignified
0.2090	33.2	.2197	3	yarrow
0.2090	33.2	.2197	3	Yerkes
0.2090	33.2	.2197	3	zig-zag
0.2089	33.2	.1494	4	Burdett
0.2089	33.2	.1494	4	catnip
0.2089	33.2	.1494	4	ding
0.2089	33.2	.1494	4	Forte
0.2089	33.2	.1494	4	Haman
0.2089	33.2	.1494	4	Waltz
0.2088	33.2	.1600	5	spares
0.2087	33.2	.2228	4	growed
0.2087	33.2	.2228	4	Harlequin
0.2087	33.2	.2228	4	pickin'
0.2087	33.2	.2320	4	rouge
0.2087	33.2	.2228	4	Strawberry
0.2085	33.2	.3255	3	preferences
0.2085	33.2	.3255	3	regulator
0.2085	33.2	.3255	3	tartar
0.2081	33.2	.0910	8	Sachs
0.2080	33.2	.3345	3	remedied
0.2079	33.2	.0000	19	adverbials
0.2077	33.2	.3352	3	vaporizes
0.2076	33.2	.1389	6	Boris
0.2076	33.2	.1389	6	impressionism
0.2076	33.2	.1389	6	tambourines
0.2075	33.2	.1493	6	pigments
0.2074	33.2	.2385	4	Delacroix
0.2074	33.2	.2385	4	Grofe
0.2074	33.2	.2385	4	Romanticist
0.2071	33.2	.1649	5	apartheid
0.2071	33.2	.1649	5	arbitration
0.2071	33.2	.1649	5	caraway
0.2071	33.2	.1649	5	Reformed
0.2071	33.2	.1649	5	visceral
0.2068	33.2	.1812	5	Expressionism
0.2068	33.2	.1812	5	mosaics
0.2067	33.2	.0702	10	craftsman
0.2064	33.2	.0457	9	ANNOUNCER
0.2064	33.1	.0457	9	Harve
0.2063	33.1	.3202	3	certified
0.2063	33.1	.3202	3	habit-forming
0.2063	33.1	.3202	3	188
0.2062	33.1	.1998	4	aquariums
0.2062	33.1	.2002	5	gouges
0.2062	33.1	.1048	7	S1
0.2062	33.1	.1048	7	transverse
0.2061	33.1	.3265	3	pare
0.2058	33.1	.3189	3	topper
0.2057	33.1	.1370	6	cadences
0.2057	33.1	.1370	6	Violin
0.2055	33.1	.1075	8	buttonholes
0.2055	33.1	.3298	3	knotty
0.2054	33.1	.3179	3	allspice

THE PRECEDING WORD TYPE OCCUPIES RANK 31900

U	SFI	D	F	Word Type
0.2054	33.1	.2009	4	end-to-end
0.2054	33.1	.2009	4	palindromes
0.2054	33.1	.2009	4	stegosaurus
0.2054	33.1	.2009	4	three-digit
0.2054	33.1	.3179	3	whys
0.2054	33.1	.2009	4	216
0.2047	33.1	.1358	6	-ence
0.2047	33.1	.1358	6	-ive
0.2047	33.1	.2277	4	Ravenna
0.2040	33.1	.2254	4	gimble
0.2040	33.1	.2254	4	gyre
0.2039	33.1	.2188	4	connotation
0.2039	33.1	.0000	19	VOICE
0.2038	33.1	.2185	4	/n/
0.2038	33.1	.2185	4	Nora
0.2036	33.1	.1768	5	launder
0.2034	33.1	.2824	3	pliable
0.2030	33.1	.0449	9	Patagonia
0.2030	33.1	.0449	9	Samarkand
0.2028	33.1	.3270	3	lumberyards
0.2028	33.1	.3270	3	worshiper
0.2027	33.1	.3109	3	applicable
0.2027	33.1	.0797	6	Bronson
0.2027	33.1	.0797	6	Finley's
0.2027	33.1	.3109	3	fulfills
0.2027	33.1	.0000	14	Jed's
0.2027	33.1	.0000	14	Muskrats
0.2027	33.1	.3078	3	Navajo
0.2027	33.1	.0000	14	Protos
0.2027	33.1	.3109	3	unpleasantness
0.2025	33.1	.2176	4	lovers'
0.2025	33.1	.2342	4	toasting
0.2024	33.1	.2195	4	spook
0.2022	33.1	.3096	3	garnished
0.2021	33.1	.0000	25	syncopation
0.2019	33.1	.3132	3	dinnerware
0.2019	33.1	.1160	7	fillings
0.2017	33.0	.3086	3	clammy
0.2017	33.0	.3086	3	clove
0.2017	33.0	.3086	3	Meals
0.2017	33.0	.3086	3	postponing
0.2014	33.0	.2090	4	contraception
0.2014	33.0	.2090	4	Darwin's
0.2014	33.0	.2090	4	Experiments
0.2014	33.0	.2090	4	fact-finding
0.2014	33.0	.2090	4	flanked
0.2014	33.0	.2090	4	formaldehyde
0.2014	33.0	.2090	4	freer
0.2014	33.0	.2090	4	illegally
0.2014	33.0	.2090	4	innovative
0.2014	33.0	.2090	4	interim
0.2014	33.0	.2090	4	licensing
0.2014	33.0	.2090	4	Nikita
0.2014	33.0	.2090	4	phenomenal
0.2014	33.0	.2090	4	Pittsburg
0.2014	33.0	.2090	4	readmission
0.2014	33.0	.2090	4	revenues
0.2014	33.0	.2090	4	sludge
0.2014	33.0	.2090	4	spacecraft's
0.2014	33.0	.2090	4	spawn
0.2014	33.0	.2090	4	subsidized
0.2014	33.0	.2090	4	traction
0.2014	33.0	.2090	4	unrealistic
0.2014	33.0	.2090	4	Valery
0.2010	33.0	.1960	4	calculator
0.2010	33.0	.1960	4	Math
0.2008	33.0	.2160	4	Goethe's
0.2008	33.0	.2160	4	Guido
0.2008	33.0	.2160	4	infest
0.2008	33.0	.2160	4	unsurpassed
0.2008	33.0	.2160	4	1631
0.2007	33.0	.3160	3	cup-shaped
0.2007	33.0	.3160	3	inaccuracy

U	SFI	D	F	Word Type
0.2006	33.0	.2158	4	Frigga
0.2006	33.0	.2158	4	pharmacy
0.2004	33.0	.2772	3	imitators
0.2004	33.0	.2772	3	trouser
0.2003	33.0	.2073	4	cliche
0.2003	33.0	.2073	4	Heck
0.2003	33.0	.2073	4	ingrained
0.2003	33.0	.2073	4	lectern
0.2003	33.0	.2073	4	loopholes
0.2003	33.0	.2073	4	Prof
0.2003	33.0	.2073	4	sandbar
0.2003	33.0	.2073	4	sixteen-year-old
0.2003	33.0	.2073	4	tailgate
0.2002	33.0	.0688	9	phonographs
0.2001	33.0	.2687	3	brunette
0.2001	33.0	.2687	3	scissor
0.2000	33.0	.2685	3	juicier
0.1997	33.0	.3136	3	conveying
0.1996	33.0	.3134	3	exactness
0.1995	33.0	.2059	4	department's
0.1995	33.0	.1143	6	evermore
0.1995	33.0	.2059	4	extinguisher
0.1995	33.0	.2059	4	Gonzalez
0.1995	33.0	.2059	4	lift-off
0.1994	33.0	.3030	3	uncut
0.1993	33.0	.0000	17	Arable
0.1993	33.0	.0000	17	Eelka
THE PRECEDING WORD TYPE OCCUPIES RANK 32000				
0.1993	33.0	.2287	4	keyhole
0.1993	33.0	.0000	17	Spofford
0.1991	33.0	.2060	4	outcomes
0.1991	33.0	.1519	5	597
0.1990	33.0	.2031	3	Brent
0.1990	33.0	.2031	3	Diane
0.1990	33.0	.1530	5	gagged
0.1990	33.0	.2031	3	geographies
0.1990	33.0	.2031	3	linemen
0.1990	33.0	.2031	3	mon
0.1990	33.0	.2031	3	ner
0.1990	33.0	.2031	3	ot
0.1990	33.0	.2031	3	Owl's
0.1990	33.0	.1304	6	Rodgers
0.1990	33.0	.2031	3	shutting
0.1990	33.0	.2031	3	sw
0.1990	33.0	.1530	5	tabor
0.1990	33.0	.1530	5	vexed
0.1990	33.0	.2421	4	474
0.1989	33.0	.0000	19	ethylene
0.1988	33.0	.2028	3	Beasts
0.1988	33.0	.2028	3	chime
0.1988	33.0	.2028	3	Chippewa
0.1988	33.0	.2028	3	Conductor
0.1988	33.0	.2028	3	conductor's
0.1988	33.0	.2028	3	flyin'
0.1988	33.0	.2028	3	frilly
0.1988	33.0	.2028	3	imprints
0.1988	33.0	.2028	3	kayaks
0.1988	33.0	.2028	3	Lucas
0.1988	33.0	.2028	3	meaningfully
0.1988	33.0	.2028	3	new-fallen
0.1988	33.0	.2028	3	overside
0.1988	33.0	.2028	3	Pilgrims'
0.1988	33.0	.2028	3	praising
0.1988	33.0	.2028	3	Spencer's
0.1988	33.0	.2028	3	stow
0.1988	33.0	.2028	3	sun-god
0.1988	33.0	.2028	3	volleyed
0.1988	33.0	.2028	3	warbled
0.1987	33.0	.1133	6	Parsons
0.1987	33.0	.3012	3	Tucson
0.1985	33.0	.2065	4	Conroy
0.1985	33.0	.2065	4	Guillaume
0.1985	33.0	.2065	4	Lisbon
0.1985	33.0	.2065	4	marlin
0.1985	33.0	.0287	12	polka
0.1985	33.0	.2065	4	sedentary
0.1985	33.0	.2065	4	wuz
0.1983	33.0	.3164	3	styling
0.1981	33.0	.3099	3	adhering
0.1980	33.0	.2747	3	clown's
0.1980	33.0	.2153	4	deficiencies
0.1977	33.0	.1349	6	knits
0.1975	33.0	.2048	4	'nough
0.1975	33.0	.2734	3	dampening
0.1975	33.0	.2048	4	jack-knife
0.1975	33.0	.2048	4	mien
0.1975	33.0	.2048	4	Mud
0.1975	33.0	.2048	4	obeisance
0.1975	33.0	.2048	4	pandemonium
0.1975	33.0	.2048	4	Rufus's
0.1973	33.0	.2950	3	machine-made
0.1973	33.0	.2950	3	talcum
0.1973	33.0	.2950	3	well-drained
0.1972	32.9	.0000	10	compressibility
0.1972	32.9	.0000	10	hydroxide
0.1972	32.9	.0000	10	leucocytes
0.1972	32.9	.0000	10	moraine
0.1972	32.9	.0000	10	photosphere
0.1970	32.9	.2942	3	Cereals
0.1970	32.9	.1504	5	Durer
0.1970	32.9	.0000	18	headword
0.1970	32.9	.2942	3	interlock
0.1970	32.9	.2942	3	prescriptions
0.1970	32.9	.2942	3	regulators
0.1970	32.9	.2942	3	thins
0.1967	32.9	.2936	3	Fruit
0.1966	32.9	.2034	4	Beth's
0.1965	32.9	.2011	4	accommodation
0.1965	32.9	.2011	4	Clinic
0.1965	32.9	.0620	7	GE
0.1965	32.9	.2011	4	pampering
0.1965	32.9	.2929	3	reshaped
0.1964	32.9	.1125	6	Dnepr
0.1964	32.9	.1277	6	featuring
0.1964	32.9	.1125	6	Marseille
0.1964	32.9	.1125	6	Parana
0.1964	32.9	.1125	6	Sukarno

U	SFI	D	F	Word Type
0.1963	32.9	.1511	5	periodical
0.1963	32.9	.1511	5	sugary
0.1963	32.9	.1511	5	teemed
0.1960	32.9	.2918	3	DO
0.1959	32.9	.1398	5	Kaiser's
0.1959	32.9	.1398	5	Khrushchev
0.1959	32.9	.1398	5	late-model
0.1959	32.9	.1398	5	Lovell
0.1959	32.9	.1398	5	moon-landing
0.1959	32.9	.1398	5	nostalgia
0.1959	32.9	.1398	5	Peru's
THE PRECEDING WORD TYPE OCCUPIES RANK 32100				
0.1959	32.9	.1398	5	plantings
0.1959	32.9	.1398	5	Reds
0.1959	32.9	.1398	5	studios
0.1959	32.9	.1398	5	vandals
0.1958	32.9	.1335	4	aerials
0.1958	32.9	.1335	4	air-breathing
0.1958	32.9	.1335	4	cinnabar
0.1958	32.9	.1335	4	finders
0.1958	32.9	.1335	4	forecasters
0.1958	32.9	.1335	4	geckos
0.1958	32.9	.1335	4	iguanas
0.1958	32.9	.1335	4	scatters
0.1958	32.9	.1335	4	stagnant
0.1958	32.9	.1335	4	yellowish-white
0.1956	32.9	.1116	6	cardiac
0.1956	32.9	.1116	6	erectus
0.1956	32.9	.2404	4	inking
0.1956	32.9	.1116	6	pacemaker
0.1954	32.9	.1657	5	store's
0.1949	32.9	.2914	3	348
0.1947	32.9	.2887	3	cleanse
0.1946	32.9	.0000	13	-4
0.1946	32.9	.0000	13	/5
0.1946	32.9	.1769	5	Lorenz
0.1946	32.9	.0000	13	Numo
0.1946	32.9	.0000	13	vectors
0.1946	32.9	.0000	13	3/12
0.1945	32.9	.0000	10	Amundsen
0.1945	32.9	.0000	10	Beauregard
0.1945	32.9	.0000	10	Confucius
0.1945	32.9	.0000	10	Hollander
0.1945	32.9	.0000	10	padres
0.1945	32.9	.0000	10	Ubaru
0.1944	32.9	.1325	4	appeasement
0.1944	32.9	.1325	4	Brazos
0.1944	32.9	.1325	4	butchers
0.1944	32.9	.1325	4	coking
0.1944	32.9	.1325	4	condemning
0.1944	32.9	.1325	4	Cruz
0.1944	32.9	.1325	4	Dinwiddie
0.1944	32.9	.1325	4	disunion
0.1944	32.9	.1325	4	Embargo
0.1944	32.9	.2880	3	flabby
0.1944	32.9	.1325	4	hoes
0.1944	32.9	.1325	4	Panhandle
0.1944	32.9	.2880	3	roughed
0.1944	32.9	.1325	4	Trusteeship
0.1944	32.9	.1325	4	wastelands
0.1944	32.9	.1325	4	60th
0.1943	32.9	.1485	5	carat
0.1942	32.9	.0506	8	questioners
0.1942	32.9	.0506	8	Ritchie's
0.1941	32.9	.0517	14	windings
0.1940	32.9	.2540	3	accommodated
0.1940	32.9	.2540	3	basted
0.1940	32.9	.2540	3	Confirmation
0.1940	32.9	.2540	3	felts
0.1940	32.9	.2540	3	light-weight
0.1940	32.9	.2540	3	moderate-sized
0.1940	32.9	.2540	3	seamstress
0.1940	32.9	.2540	3	soya
0.1939	32.9	.2088	4	sweetened
0.1938	32.9	.2867	3	marketed
0.1936	32.9	.2986	3	varnished
0.1935	32.9	.2984	3	downstroke
0.1934	32.9	.2524	3	conceit
0.1934	32.9	.2524	3	taint
0.1934	32.9	.2524	3	Terry's
0.1934	32.9	.2524	3	unimaginative
0.1934	32.9	.2524	3	waffle
0.1933	32.9	.1786	4	$375
0.1933	32.9	.2199	4	machined
0.1933	32.9	.1786	4	285
0.1933	32.9	.1786	4	487
0.1933	32.9	.1786	4	513
0.1933	32.9	.1786	4	632
0.1933	32.9	.1786	4	683
0.1932	32.9	.0000	18	Gratiano
0.1931	32.9	.2017	4	Archaeology
0.1931	32.9	.2017	4	badminton
0.1930	32.9	.3029	3	Deity
0.1929	32.9	.1799	4	minced
0.1929	32.9	.2512	3	unpretentious
0.1928	32.9	.2966	3	1416
0.1928	32.9	.2966	3	3-3
0.1927	32.8	.1776	4	bisectors
0.1927	32.8	.2224	4	Composition
0.1927	32.8	.1776	4	1-foot
0.1927	32.8	.1776	4	1/30
0.1925	32.8	.2065	4	cautions
0.1921	32.8	.0604	7	carter
0.1921	32.8	.0604	7	Christine's
0.1920	32.8	.1999	4	Alva
0.1920	32.8	.1959	4	Coral
0.1920	32.8	.1999	4	mallow
0.1920	32.8	.1999	4	sandbox
0.1920	32.8	.1999	4	Tale
0.1920	32.8	.1959	4	Terrace
0.1920	32.8	.1959	4	travelling
0.1919	32.8	.1370	5	Christopher's
THE PRECEDING WORD TYPE OCCUPIES RANK 32200				
0.1916	32.8	.2003	4	Being
0.1916	32.8	.2003	4	Circe
0.1916	32.8	.2003	4	Coca-Cola
0.1916	32.8	.2003	4	Fabritius

U	SFI	D	F	Word Type
0.1916	32.8	.2003	4	fatherland
0.1916	32.8	.2003	4	slayer
0.1913	32.8	.2946	3	engraved
0.1912	32.8	.2468	3	assuring
0.1912	32.8	.2468	3	iced
0.1912	32.8	.2468	3	snuggling
0.1912	32.8	.2468	3	strictest
0.1912	32.8	.2468	3	talkative
0.1911	32.8	.0496	8	Doolittle
0.1911	32.8	.0496	8	Faneuil
0.1911	32.8	.2940	3	fracturing
0.1911	32.8	.2940	3	high-compression
0.1911	32.8	.2940	3	withdrawing
0.1905	32.8	.2926	3	traverse
0.1903	32.8	.2445	3	Body
0.1903	32.8	.2445	3	chummy
0.1903	32.8	.2445	3	cruises
0.1903	32.8	.2445	3	Direction
0.1903	32.8	.2445	3	eagle-eyed
0.1903	32.8	.2445	3	paring
0.1903	32.8	.2445	3	snagged
0.1902	32.8	.1760	4	capitalist
0.1902	32.8	.1760	4	Savings
0.1902	32.8	.1760	4	undercover
0.1901	32.8	.0762	8	Jazz
0.1900	32.8	.2915	3	deflector
0.1899	32.8	.2765	3	jumpers
0.1899	32.8	.2765	3	spic
0.1897	32.8	.1563	5	Amadeus
0.1897	32.8	.1563	5	Dances
0.1897	32.8	.1563	5	grosso
0.1897	32.8	.1563	5	orchestration
0.1897	32.8	.1563	5	reverent
0.1897	32.8	.1563	5	Stravinsky's
0.1896	32.8	.2757	3	Bread
0.1896	32.8	.1750	4	catsup
0.1896	32.8	.1750	4	Drinker
0.1896	32.8	.2757	3	fevers
0.1896	32.8	.2757	3	helpings
0.1896	32.8	.1750	4	prickles
0.1896	32.8	.2946	3	shimmer
0.1896	32.8	.1750	4	silverfish
0.1896	32.8	.2757	3	60%
0.1895	32.8	.0310	11	Barber
0.1895	32.8	.1971	4	Britches
0.1895	32.8	.1971	4	questioner
0.1893	32.8	.1738	4	pincushion
0.1886	32.8	.0947	5	sixty-three
0.1884	32.8	.1966	4	Pres
0.1884	32.8	.1966	4	thin-walled
0.1884	32.8	.1966	4	Vermilion
0.1883	32.7	.2828	3	silver-white
0.1882	32.7	.0000	13	Antje
0.1882	32.7	.2823	3	counterbalance
0.1882	32.7	.0000	13	Zust
0.1880	32.7	.1934	4	gables
0.1876	32.7	.0000	16	Sylvain
0.1875	32.7	.1952	4	excepted
0.1875	32.7	.1952	4	typifies
0.1872	32.7	.1531	5	/oi/
0.1872	32.7	.1531	5	/th/
0.1872	32.7	.1854	4	Castor
0.1872	32.7	.1854	4	endearing
0.1872	32.7	.1854	4	evangelist
0.1872	32.7	.1854	4	Film
0.1872	32.7	.1854	4	frankness
0.1872	32.7	.1531	5	in-
0.1872	32.7	.1854	4	inspires
0.1872	32.7	.1854	4	intervene
0.1872	32.7	.1531	5	Marcia
0.1872	32.7	.1531	5	o/
0.1872	32.7	.1854	4	precariously
0.1872	32.7	.1854	4	proposals
0.1872	32.7	.1531	5	w's
0.1872	32.7	.1854	4	Ways
0.1872	32.7	.1854	4	Welshman
0.1872	32.7	.1854	4	whoopee
0.1872	32.7	.1854	4	17-year-old
0.1868	32.7	.1528	5	overtone
0.1865	32.7	.2823	3	tabulated
0.1864	32.7	.1919	4	clouts
0.1864	32.7	.1919	4	impassive
0.1864	32.7	.1919	4	Ol'
0.1864	32.7	.1919	4	oughta
0.1864	32.7	.1919	4	pitied
0.1864	32.7	.1919	4	pommel
0.1864	32.7	.1919	4	squashed
0.1864	32.7	.1919	4	stubbornness
0.1863	32.7	.1907	4	Grizzle
0.1863	32.7	.1907	4	Meyers
0.1863	32.7	.1907	4	substandard
0.1861	32.7	.2815	3	1826
0.1860	32.7	.2330	3	candied
0.1860	32.7	.2330	3	Dreams
0.1860	32.7	.2330	3	pucker
0.1860	32.7	.2330	3	schoolmate
THE PRECEDING WORD TYPE OCCUPIES RANK 32300				
0.1860	32.7	.2330	3	wafers
0.1859	32.7	.2870	3	comedian
0.1859	32.7	.0000	23	symphonies
0.1859	32.7	.0234	21	tempera
0.1858	32.7	.2851	3	flagrant
0.1857	32.7	.1828	4	Administration's
0.1857	32.7	.1828	4	Leslie
0.1857	32.7	.1828	4	sectors
0.1854	32.7	.2859	3	enrichment
0.1854	32.7	.2797	3	ream
0.1851	32.7	.2833	3	Carols
0.1850	32.7	.0926	5	Dolphin
0.1850	32.7	.0926	5	Frankfort
0.1850	32.7	.0926	5	Nat's
0.1849	32.7	.1300	6	complexions
0.1848	32.7	.2844	3	brazen
0.1847	32.7	.1892	4	blurting
0.1847	32.7	.1892	4	brochure
0.1847	32.7	.1892	4	pert
0.1847	32.7	.1892	4	petulant

U	SFI	D	F	Word Type
0.1847	32.7	.1892	4	slouching
0.1844	32.7	.1318	5	organizers
0.1843	32.7	.1901	4	abstracted
0.1843	32.7	.1901	4	concentric
0.1843	32.7	.1901	4	hove
0.1843	32.7	.1901	4	impervious
0.1843	32.7	.1901	4	Neolithic
0.1843	32.7	.1151	6	scherzo
0.1843	32.7	.1151	6	treble
0.1841	32.7	.1826	4	Baxters
0.1841	32.7	.1826	4	Bruges
0.1841	32.7	.1826	4	cornucopias
0.1841	32.7	.1826	4	Linden
0.1841	32.7	.1826	4	mought
0.1841	32.7	.1826	4	she-wolf
0.1839	32.6	.1610	5	acetate
0.1839	32.6	.1610	5	basil
0.1836	32.6	.2581	3	cooperating
0.1835	32.6	.2754	3	handlebar
0.1835	32.6	.2754	3	preferable
0.1835	32.6	.2754	3	removable
0.1834	32.6	.1584	5	455
0.1833	32.6	.0886	8	broiling
0.1831	32.6	.2804	3	blackly
0.1831	32.6	.2804	3	deafened
0.1831	32.6	.2804	3	elation
0.1831	32.6	.2804	3	mews
0.1831	32.6	.2804	3	untimely
0.1829	32.6	.2799	3	embody
0.1829	32.6	.2799	3	pelvic
0.1829	32.6	.2799	3	thirty-inch
0.1829	32.6	.2799	3	versatility
0.1828	32.6	.2016	4	hexagonal
0.1828	32.6	.2735	3	3-2
0.1828	32.6	.2735	3	329
0.1827	32.6	.0000	4	't
0.1827	32.6	.0000	4	ae
0.1827	32.6	.0000	4	afikomen
0.1827	32.6	.0000	4	After-Shaving
0.1827	32.6	.0000	4	Agassiz's
0.1827	32.6	.0000	4	Ai
0.1827	32.6	.0000	4	air-mail
0.1827	32.6	.0000	4	alp
0.1827	32.6	.0000	4	alphorn
0.1827	32.6	.0000	4	Alvin's
0.1827	32.6	.0000	4	amigos
0.1827	32.6	.0000	4	angakok
0.1827	32.6	.0000	4	annas
0.1827	32.6	.0000	4	Aphrodite
0.1827	32.6	.0000	4	Arm
0.1827	32.6	.0000	4	Armand
0.1827	32.6	.0000	4	Artist
0.1827	32.6	.0000	4	Atalanta
0.1827	32.6	.0000	4	Aviak
0.1827	32.6	.0000	4	Bakito
0.1827	32.6	.0000	4	Balto
0.1827	32.6	.1873	4	Baptiste
0.1827	32.6	.0000	4	Barnabe
0.1827	32.6	.0000	4	Belindy
0.1827	32.6	.0000	4	Bendy
0.1827	32.6	.0000	4	Better
0.1827	32.6	.0000	4	birdseed
0.1827	32.6	.0000	4	Bixby
0.1827	32.6	.0000	4	Blackbeard
0.1827	32.6	.0000	4	Blanchard
0.1827	32.6	.0000	4	Blandina
0.1827	32.6	.1873	4	Bloomfield
0.1827	32.6	.0000	4	blowhole
0.1827	32.6	.0000	4	Buckingham
0.1827	32.6	.0000	4	Buttercup
0.1827	32.6	.0000	4	cackled
0.1827	32.6	.0000	4	Caddy
0.1827	32.6	.0000	4	Cadillacs
0.1827	32.6	.0000	4	Calchas
0.1827	32.6	.1873	4	Caltech
0.1827	32.6	.1873	4	cascades
0.1827	32.6	.0000	4	Cassim
0.1827	32.6	.0000	4	Catarina
0.1827	32.6	.1873	4	celluloid
0.1827	32.6	.0000	4	Charan
THE PRECEDING WORD TYPE OCCUPIES RANK 32400				
0.1827	32.6	.0000	4	chesten
0.1827	32.6	.0000	4	Chi-Wee's
0.1827	32.6	.0000	4	childer
0.1827	32.6	.0000	4	Chuck's
0.1827	32.6	.0000	4	Cider
0.1827	32.6	.0000	4	Cirque
0.1827	32.6	.0000	4	clicket
0.1827	32.6	.1873	4	Clovis
0.1827	32.6	.0000	4	Cocky
0.1827	32.6	.1873	4	Commercial
0.1827	32.6	.0000	4	Connor-Madison
0.1827	32.6	.1873	4	controversies
0.1827	32.6	.0000	4	corn-husk
0.1827	32.6	.0000	4	Corvisart
0.1827	32.6	.0000	4	Creesy
0.1827	32.6	.0000	4	culvert
0.1827	32.6	.0000	4	Cutie
0.1827	32.6	.0000	4	Dargent
0.1827	32.6	.1873	4	dean
0.1827	32.6	.1873	4	depleted
0.1827	32.6	.0000	4	Derrill
0.1827	32.6	.0000	4	Derry
0.1827	32.6	.0000	4	Diz
0.1827	32.6	.0000	4	Dogood
0.1827	32.6	.0000	4	Donesa
0.1827	32.6	.0000	4	Donsoon
0.1827	32.6	.0000	4	doomsday
0.1827	32.6	.0000	4	Drem
0.1827	32.6	.0000	4	Driss
0.1827	32.6	.0000	4	DTA
0.1827	32.6	.1873	4	Economics
0.1827	32.6	.0000	4	Eielson
0.1827	32.6	.0000	4	electrolyte
0.1827	32.6	.0000	4	Esmeralda
0.1827	32.6	.0000	4	euchh
0.1827	32.6	.1873	4	examiner

U	SFI	D	F	Word Type
0.1827	32.6	.0000	4	Fan-Tan
0.1827	32.6	.0000	4	Fardowners
0.1827	32.6	.0000	4	Farley
0.1827	32.6	.0000	4	Father-Abbot
0.1827	32.6	.0000	4	fireballs
0.1827	32.6	.0000	4	Five-clawed
0.1827	32.6	.0000	4	flensing
0.1827	32.6	.0000	4	foghorns
0.1827	32.6	.0000	4	Folly
0.1827	32.6	.0000	4	fonder
0.1827	32.6	.0000	4	Forestier
0.1827	32.6	.0000	4	fortuneteller
0.1827	32.6	.0000	4	Foxy's
0.1827	32.6	.0000	4	Furloy
0.1827	32.6	.0000	4	gebeta
0.1827	32.6	.0000	4	Gempylus
0.1827	32.6	.0000	4	Gessler's
0.1827	32.6	.0000	4	Gowdy
0.1827	32.6	.0000	4	Grandmarina
0.1827	32.6	.0000	4	Great-Uncle
0.1827	32.6	.0000	4	Grover's
0.1827	32.6	.0000	4	Guelou
0.1827	32.6	.0000	4	Gunn's
0.1827	32.6	.0000	4	gunned
0.1827	32.6	.0000	4	Gyko
0.1827	32.6	.0000	4	Hak-Taks
0.1827	32.6	.0000	4	Hamwi
0.1827	32.6	.0000	4	Hansonville
0.1827	32.6	.0000	4	Heavenly
0.1827	32.6	.0000	4	Hephaestion
0.1827	32.6	.0000	4	Herbert's
0.1827	32.6	.0000	4	hide-out
0.1827	32.6	.0000	4	Highflyer
0.1827	32.6	.0000	4	himation
0.1827	32.6	.0000	4	Honeycutt
0.1827	32.6	.0000	4	hooky
0.1827	32.6	.0000	4	Horizons
0.1827	32.6	.0000	4	horsie
0.1827	32.6	.0000	4	housewreckers
0.1827	32.6	.0000	4	Huber's
0.1827	32.6	.0000	4	hullo
0.1827	32.6	.0000	4	husk
0.1827	32.6	.0000	4	I'
0.1827	32.6	.1873	4	implanted
0.1827	32.6	.1873	4	invisibility
0.1827	32.6	.0000	4	itchy
0.1827	32.6	.0000	4	jai-alai
0.1827	32.6	.0000	4	jarred
0.1827	32.6	.0000	4	Jigori
0.1827	32.6	.0000	4	Jinny
0.1827	32.6	.0000	4	Kenji
0.1827	32.6	.0000	4	Kiehl
0.1827	32.6	.0000	4	Kimo
0.1827	32.6	.0000	4	Kippur
0.1827	32.6	.0000	4	Kobi's
0.1827	32.6	.0000	4	Lajoi
0.1827	32.6	.0000	4	Lakeside
0.1827	32.6	.0000	4	Larkins
0.1827	32.6	.0000	4	Leodegrance
0.1827	32.6	.0000	4	Leona's
0.1827	32.6	.1873	4	limitation
0.1827	32.6	.0000	4	Lindy's
0.1827	32.6	.0000	4	Lizzy
0.1827	32.6	.0000	4	long-nosed
THE PRECEDING WORD TYPE OCCUPIES RANK 32500				
0.1827	32.6	.0000	4	MacLeod
0.1827	32.6	.0000	4	Macauley
0.1827	32.6	.0000	4	Malory
0.1827	32.6	.0000	4	Marc's
0.1827	32.6	.0000	4	Marfa
0.1827	32.6	.0000	4	Margarita
0.1827	32.6	.0000	4	Marsden
0.1827	32.6	.0000	4	meat-hook
0.1827	32.6	.0000	4	meatball
0.1827	32.6	.0000	4	Melindy's
0.1827	32.6	.0000	4	Merle's
0.1827	32.6	.0000	4	Miesje
0.1827	32.6	.0000	4	Moingona
0.1827	32.6	.0000	4	Moneymore
0.1827	32.6	.0000	4	Mor
0.1827	32.6	.0000	4	Morvidd
0.1827	32.6	.0000	4	mushers
0.1827	32.6	.1873	4	nascent
0.1827	32.6	.0000	4	Neeley
0.1827	32.6	.0000	4	Nicolaysen
0.1827	32.6	.0000	4	no'm
0.1827	32.6	.0000	4	Nobody
0.1827	32.6	.0000	4	Nole
0.1827	32.6	.0000	4	Norm's
0.1827	32.6	.0000	4	Olinos
0.1827	32.6	.0000	4	one-legged
0.1827	32.6	.0000	4	opals
0.1827	32.6	.0000	4	Partlet
0.1827	32.6	.0000	4	pato
0.1827	32.6	.0000	4	Peppi's
0.1827	32.6	.0000	4	Pere
0.1827	32.6	.0000	4	Perico
0.1827	32.6	.0000	4	Philosopher's
0.1827	32.6	.0000	4	Phoebe's
0.1827	32.6	.0000	4	Pipp
0.1827	32.6	.0000	4	Polliwog
0.1827	32.6	.0000	4	Pops
0.1827	32.6	.0000	4	pouted
0.1827	32.6	.0000	4	prefab
0.1827	32.6	.0000	4	Prim
0.1827	32.6	.0000	4	Principia
0.1827	32.6	.0000	4	Proserpina
0.1827	32.6	.1873	4	Provence
0.1827	32.6	.0000	4	purdy
0.1827	32.6	.0000	4	Puss-in-Boots
0.1827	32.6	.0000	4	Raman
0.1827	32.6	.0000	4	ramping
0.1827	32.6	.0000	4	Rathbun
0.1827	32.6	.0000	4	ringers
0.1827	32.6	.0000	4	Robinsons
0.1827	32.6	.0000	4	Rodriguez
0.1827	32.6	.0000	4	Rondaro
0.1827	32.6	.0000	4	rubbery
0.1827	32.6	.0000	4	Sabor
0.1827	32.6	.0000	4	Samarai
0.1827	32.6	.0000	4	Sandino
0.1827	32.6	.0000	4	Schleimann
0.1827	32.6	.0000	4	Selma
0.1827	32.6	.0000	4	Sepp
0.1827	32.6	.0000	4	Sequoyah's
0.1827	32.6	.0000	4	Sheba
0.1827	32.6	.0000	4	Shin-n-n-ny
0.1827	32.6	.0000	4	silliest
0.1827	32.6	.0000	4	Simba
0.1827	32.6	.0000	4	Simmons'
0.1827	32.6	.0000	4	Siraj-ed-Din
0.1827	32.6	.0000	4	Slagle
0.1827	32.6	.0000	4	snooze
0.1827	32.6	.0000	4	Softest-Walker
0.1827	32.6	.0000	4	Soperville
0.1827	32.6	.0000	4	souks
0.1827	32.6	.0000	4	Sounder
0.1827	32.6	.0000	4	Stonecrop
0.1827	32.6	.0000	4	Strongest-One
0.1827	32.6	.0000	4	Sun-Dance
0.1827	32.6	.0000	4	Surov's
0.1827	32.6	.0000	4	Suzy
0.1827	32.6	.0000	4	Svatopluk's
0.1827	32.6	.0000	4	Tail
0.1827	32.6	.0000	4	Talore
0.1827	32.6	.0000	4	tar-baby
0.1827	32.6	.0000	4	Terrance
0.1827	32.6	.0000	4	Thankful
0.1827	32.6	.0000	4	Thing-finder
0.1827	32.6	.0000	4	tiddle-iddle
0.1827	32.6	.0000	4	Timbuctoo
0.1827	32.6	.0000	4	Tiziano
0.1827	32.6	.0000	4	tolled
0.1827	32.6	.0000	4	Tom'
0.1827	32.6	.0000	4	tombos
0.1827	32.6	.0000	4	Tomi
0.1827	32.6	.0000	4	Tomi's
0.1827	32.6	.0000	4	Tonga
0.1827	32.6	.0000	4	travois
0.1827	32.6	.1873	4	Trent
0.1827	32.6	.0000	4	Turnip-seed
0.1827	32.6	.1873	4	unsealed
0.1827	32.6	.0000	4	Upsalquitch
0.1827	32.6	.0000	4	Used
0.1827	32.6	.1873	4	Ussher
THE PRECEDING WORD TYPE OCCUPIES RANK 32600				
0.1827	32.6	.0000	4	ut
0.1827	32.6	.0000	4	Vader
0.1827	32.6	.0000	4	valuables
0.1827	32.6	.0000	4	Ventures
0.1827	32.6	.0000	4	Vic's
0.1827	32.6	.0000	4	Vizier
0.1827	32.6	.0000	4	Voyager
0.1827	32.6	.0000	4	waddle
0.1827	32.6	.0000	4	Walz
0.1827	32.6	.0000	4	Waneko
0.1827	32.6	.0000	4	Wendy's
0.1827	32.6	.0000	4	Westport
0.1827	32.6	.0000	4	Wheelwright
0.1827	32.6	.0000	4	Whoof
0.1827	32.6	.1873	4	wieners
0.1827	32.6	.0000	4	Wilco
0.1827	32.6	.0000	4	Winters'
0.1827	32.6	.0000	4	Woelfchen
0.1827	32.6	.0000	4	Wood's
0.1827	32.6	.0000	4	woodcutter's
0.1827	32.6	.0000	4	Xerxes'
0.1827	32.6	.0000	4	yard-boy
0.1827	32.6	.0000	4	Yellow-Dog
0.1827	32.6	.0000	4	yellow-fever
0.1827	32.6	.0000	4	Yffiniac
0.1827	32.6	.0000	4	Yom
0.1827	32.6	.0000	4	Zack's
0.1827	32.6	.0000	4	ZOOM
0.1827	32.6	.0000	4	zowie
0.1827	32.6	.0000	4	4A's
0.1826	32.6	.2793	3	interjections
0.1826	32.6	.1800	4	Newtown
0.1824	32.6	.0000	17	DOCTOR
0.1824	32.6	.0000	17	JIYA
0.1824	32.6	.0000	17	Lorry
0.1824	32.6	.0000	17	Maycomb
0.1824	32.6	.0000	17	NANA
0.1824	32.6	.0000	17	Nerissa
0.1822	32.6	.2427	3	alga
0.1822	32.6	.0706	6	Amish
0.1822	32.6	.2427	3	ascribed
0.1822	32.6	.2427	3	assassin
0.1822	32.6	.2427	3	astigmatic
0.1822	32.6	.2427	3	astrophysicists
0.1822	32.6	.2784	3	beginner's
0.1822	32.6	.2427	3	biochemists
0.1822	32.6	.2427	3	Boothbay
0.1822	32.6	.2784	3	brusque
0.1822	32.6	.2427	3	cajoled
0.1822	32.6	.2433	3	carbolic
0.1822	32.6	.2427	3	clear-air
0.1822	32.6	.2433	3	coarsely
0.1822	32.6	.2427	3	configurations
0.1822	32.6	.0706	6	Cool
0.1822	32.6	.2427	3	culminates
0.1822	32.6	.0706	6	cutthroats
0.1822	32.6	.2427	3	deadening
0.1822	32.6	.2427	3	germinating
0.1822	32.6	.2427	3	grained
0.1822	32.6	.2427	3	hibernated
0.1822	32.6	.2427	3	homozygous
0.1822	32.6	.2427	3	Jeffries
0.1822	32.6	.2427	3	Mental
0.1822	32.6	.2784	3	mishaps
0.1822	32.6	.2427	3	Nimbus
0.1822	32.6	.2433	3	petunias
0.1822	32.6	.2427	3	pock-marked
0.1822	32.6	.2433	3	powering
0.1822	32.6	.2427	3	radiosondes
0.1822	32.6	.2427	3	Ray's
0.1822	32.6	.0706	6	Rosie's
0.1822	32.6	.2427	3	siphons
0.1822	32.6	.2427	3	Storms
0.1822	32.6	.2784	3	thudding
0.1822	32.6	.2427	3	tranquilizers
0.1822	32.6	.2427	3	Transit
0.1822	32.6	.2427	3	unburned
0.1822	32.6	.2427	3	undersurface
0.1822	32.6	.2433	3	uneaten
0.1822	32.6	.2784	3	viewer
0.1822	32.6	.2427	3	12-mile
0.1820	32.6	.2443	3	cookouts
0.1820	32.6	.2443	3	distill
0.1820	32.6	.2443	3	epiglottis
0.1820	32.6	.2443	3	filmy
0.1820	32.6	.2443	3	formless
0.1820	32.6	.2443	3	infantile
0.1820	32.6	.2442	3	intervening
0.1820	32.6	.2442	3	lubricate
0.1820	32.6	.2443	3	moonrise
0.1820	32.6	.2442	3	pepsin
0.1820	32.6	.2443	3	prolongation
0.1820	32.6	.2443	3	prosaic
0.1820	32.6	.2442	3	Rw
0.1820	32.6	.2442	3	sound-wave
0.1820	32.6	.2442	3	unexposed
0.1820	32.6	.2442	3	watersheds
0.1818	32.6	.2445	3	acceptor
0.1818	32.6	.2445	3	adenosine
0.1818	32.6	.0566	7	Albertine
THE PRECEDING WORD TYPE OCCUPIES RANK 32700				
0.1818	32.6	.2445	3	anaerobic
0.1818	32.6	.2445	3	anchovies
0.1818	32.6	.2445	3	basal
0.1818	32.6	.2445	3	beryllium
0.1818	32.6	.2445	3	biologic
0.1818	32.6	.2445	3	bricklayers
0.1818	32.6	.2445	3	clotting
0.1818	32.6	.2445	3	conducive
0.1818	32.6	.2445	3	conserves
0.1818	32.6	.0566	7	Demeter
0.1818	32.6	.0566	7	Diccon
0.1818	32.6	.2445	3	DuPont
0.1818	32.6	.2445	3	duckweed
0.1818	32.6	.2445	3	electric-power
0.1818	32.6	.2445	3	excrete
0.1818	32.6	.2445	3	excretion
0.1818	32.6	.2445	3	funnel-shaped
0.1818	32.6	.2445	3	glaciation
0.1818	32.6	.2445	3	gonads
0.1818	32.6	.2445	3	granular
0.1818	32.6	.2445	3	Guglielmo
0.1818	32.6	.2445	3	halos
0.1818	32.6	.2445	3	heart-lung
0.1818	32.6	.2445	3	heritable
0.1818	32.6	.2445	3	hookworm
0.1818	32.6	.2445	3	Huygens
0.1818	32.6	.2445	3	incompressible
0.1818	32.6	.2445	3	intrinsic
0.1818	32.6	.1982	4	Largo
0.1818	32.6	.2445	3	leaflike
0.1818	32.6	.2445	3	leo
0.1818	32.6	.2445	3	mc2
0.1818	32.6	.2445	3	molar
0.1818	32.6	.0566	7	Momma
0.1818	32.6	.2445	3	monoclinic
0.1818	32.6	.2445	3	mutant
0.1818	32.6	.2445	3	nonconformist
0.1818	32.6	.2445	3	nutshell
0.1818	32.6	.2445	3	observable
0.1818	32.6	.2445	3	pimple
0.1818	32.6	.2445	3	placenta
0.1818	32.6	.2445	3	polymers
0.1818	32.6	.2445	3	Precambrian
0.1818	32.6	.2445	3	preservatives
0.1818	32.6	.2445	3	prismatic
0.1818	32.6	.2445	3	promotes
0.1818	32.6	.2445	3	quadrangle
0.1818	32.6	.2445	3	quantitative
0.1818	32.6	.2445	3	randomly
0.1818	32.6	.2445	3	Refuge
0.1818	32.6	.2445	3	Rochelle
0.1818	32.6	.2445	3	salivary
0.1818	32.6	.2445	3	saprophytes
0.1818	32.6	.2445	3	Schleiden
0.1818	32.6	.2445	3	Schwann
0.1818	32.6	.2445	3	senders
0.1818	32.6	.2445	3	septic
0.1818	32.6	.2445	3	shallow-water
0.1818	32.6	.2445	3	six-sided
0.1818	32.6	.2445	3	staphylococci
0.1818	32.6	.2445	3	synthesize
0.1818	32.6	.2445	3	tenuous
0.1818	32.6	.2445	3	thyroxin
0.1818	32.6	.2445	3	tracers
0.1818	32.6	.2445	3	urea
0.1818	32.6	.2445	3	vacuole
0.1818	32.6	.2445	3	water-dwelling
0.1818	32.6	.2445	3	Worcester
0.1817	32.6	.2679	3	commerical
0.1817	32.6	.2772	3	conjures
0.1816	32.6	.2425	3	anti-American
0.1816	32.6	.2425	3	Ardennes
0.1816	32.6	.2431	3	attends
0.1816	32.6	.2425	3	battalions
0.1816	32.6	.2425	3	Battles
0.1816	32.6	.2425	3	billion-dollar
0.1816	32.6	.2431	3	brides
0.1816	32.6	.2425	3	Broken
0.1816	32.6	.2425	3	chairmen
0.1816	32.6	.2425	3	Churchill's
0.1816	32.6	.2425	3	ColoradoSprings
0.1816	32.6	.2425	3	constitutionally
0.1816	32.6	.2431	3	consuls
0.1816	32.6	.2425	3	Corridor
0.1816	32.6	.2431	3	deceitful
0.1816	32.6	.2425	3	disruption
0.1816	32.6	.2431	3	Durant
0.1816	32.6	.2425	3	expansionist
0.1816	32.6	.2425	3	Flowing
0.1816	32.6	.2425	3	four-room
0.1816	32.6	.1294	5	glassful
0.1816	32.6	.2425	3	Globe
0.1816	32.6	.2425	3	Golda
0.1816	32.6	.2425	3	gravestones
0.1816	32.6	.1294	5	Hillary
0.1816	32.6	.2425	3	imperialism
0.1816	32.6	.2425	3	importers
0.1816	32.6	.2431	3	industrialists
0.1816	32.6	.2425	3	Learn
0.1816	32.6	.2425	3	Los
THE PRECEDING WORD TYPE OCCUPIES RANK 32800				
0.1816	32.6	.2425	3	los
0.1816	32.6	.2425	3	MacLeish
0.1816	32.6	.2425	3	Malta
0.1816	32.6	.2425	3	Marx
0.1816	32.6	.2425	3	megalopolis
0.1816	32.6	.2425	3	Mexican-Americans
0.1816	32.6	.2425	3	mobilized
0.1816	32.6	.2425	3	Monrovia
0.1816	32.6	.2425	3	much-needed
0.1816	32.6	.2431	3	Narragansett
0.1816	32.6	.2425	3	nationalists
0.1816	32.6	.2425	3	prewar
0.1816	32.6	.2425	3	Progressive
0.1816	32.6	.2425	3	rabbis
0.1816	32.6	.2425	3	rebelling
0.1816	32.6	.2425	3	rebellions
0.1816	32.6	.2431	3	resorted
0.1816	32.6	.2425	3	Ricans
0.1816	32.6	.1294	5	Ritter
0.1816	32.6	.2425	3	Roald
0.1816	32.6	.2425	3	Santos
0.1816	32.6	.2425	3	Slope
0.1816	32.6	.2425	3	tilling
0.1816	32.6	.2425	3	tundras
0.1816	32.6	.2425	3	wheelbarrows
0.1816	32.6	.2425	3	000-acre
0.1815	32.6	.2383	3	anemic
0.1815	32.6	.2383	3	Betelgeuse
0.1815	32.6	.2672	3	bookcases
0.1815	32.6	.2672	3	buckling
0.1815	32.6	.2672	3	catalyst
0.1815	32.6	.2440	3	dialogues
0.1815	32.6	.1597	4	endangering
0.1815	32.6	.2442	3	formulate
0.1815	32.6	.2440	3	gasoline-powered
0.1815	32.6	.2383	3	grainy
0.1815	32.6	.2442	3	Hay
0.1815	32.6	.2440	3	Hitchcock
0.1815	32.6	.2383	3	honey-bees
0.1815	32.6	.2442	3	horse-and-buggy
0.1815	32.6	.2440	3	Inaugural
0.1815	32.6	.2440	3	juries
0.1815	32.6	.2383	3	lobed
0.1815	32.6	.2442	3	Narraganset
0.1815	32.6	.1597	4	Pocket
0.1815	32.6	.2383	3	porphyries
0.1815	32.6	.2383	3	squirts
0.1815	32.6	.2383	3	stellar
0.1815	32.6	.2440	3	su
0.1815	32.6	.2383	3	synthesized
0.1815	32.6	.2383	3	Tables
0.1815	32.6	.2440	3	unsound
0.1815	32.6	.2383	3	V-2
0.1815	32.6	.2442	3	whisks
0.1815	32.6	.2440	3	1976
0.1815	32.6	.2440	3	391
0.1814	32.6	.2444	3	arsenals
0.1814	32.6	.2444	3	Asakusa
0.1814	32.6	.2444	3	assaulting
0.1814	32.6	.2444	3	authenticated
0.1814	32.6	.2444	3	Bavaria
0.1814	32.6	.2444	3	Brahmans
0.1814	32.6	.2444	3	Buddha's
0.1814	32.6	.2444	3	Centennial
0.1814	32.6	.2444	3	chancellor
0.1814	32.6	.2444	3	Curtain
0.1814	32.6	.2444	3	dhows
0.1814	32.6	.2444	3	enslaved
0.1814	32.6	.2444	3	flourishing
0.1814	32.6	.2444	3	Guaira
0.1814	32.6	.2444	3	hulling
0.1814	32.6	.2444	3	Hyksos
0.1814	32.6	.2444	3	llanos
0.1814	32.6	.2444	3	McDowell
0.1814	32.6	.2444	3	Michigania
0.1814	32.6	.2444	3	misdemeanors
0.1814	32.6	.2444	3	modernize
0.1814	32.6	.2444	3	monotheism
0.1814	32.6	.2444	3	Orders
0.1814	32.6	.2444	3	Pennines
0.1814	32.6	.2444	3	peonage
0.1814	32.6	.2444	3	Postal
0.1814	32.6	.2444	3	protectorate
0.1814	32.6	.2444	3	pure-blooded
0.1814	32.6	.2444	3	quick-frozen
0.1814	32.6	.2444	3	rainless
0.1814	32.6	.2444	3	raiser
0.1814	32.6	.2444	3	Rappahannock
0.1814	32.6	.2444	3	Redeemer
0.1814	32.6	.2444	3	reforming
0.1814	32.6	.2444	3	sagas
0.1814	32.6	.2444	3	Tagalog
0.1814	32.6	.2444	3	toleration
0.1814	32.6	.2444	3	waterpower
0.1814	32.6	.2444	3	1488
0.1814	32.6	.2444	3	1534
0.1814	32.6	.2444	3	1539
0.1814	32.6	.2444	3	1748
0.1814	32.6	.2444	3	1850s
0.1814	32.6	.2444	3	610

U	SFI	D	F	Word Type
THE PRECEDING WORD TYPE OCCUPIES RANK 32900				
0.1814	32.6	.2444	3	755
0.1813	32.6	.2371	3	binomial
0.1813	32.6	.2045	4	exacting
0.1813	32.6	.2371	3	solver
0.1813	32.6	.2371	3	WW
0.1813	32.6	.2371	3	11-20
0.1813	32.6	.2371	3	12-15
0.1813	32.6	.2371	3	180th
0.1813	32.6	.2371	3	239
0.1813	32.6	.2371	3	30a
0.1813	32.6	.2371	3	5-2
0.1812	32.6	.1989	4	NC
0.1810	32.6	.0337	10	gr
0.1809	32.6	.2378	3	Beecher
0.1809	32.6	.2378	3	Brisbane
0.1809	32.6	.2378	3	Callao
0.1809	32.6	.2378	3	dictatorial
0.1809	32.6	.2378	3	Dreamer
0.1809	32.6	.2378	3	hatreds
0.1809	32.6	.2378	3	judiciary
0.1809	32.6	.2378	3	Lincolns
0.1809	32.6	.2378	3	Loyalists
0.1809	32.6	.2378	3	Medina
0.1809	32.6	.2378	3	nominating
0.1809	32.6	.2378	3	nonwhites
0.1809	32.6	.2378	3	Nordic
0.1809	32.6	.2378	3	oligarchy
0.1809	32.6	.2378	3	one-party
0.1809	32.6	.2378	3	Palma
0.1809	32.6	.2378	3	pasturing
0.1809	32.6	.2378	3	pillaged
0.1809	32.6	.2378	3	Pygmy
0.1809	32.6	.2378	3	Sabine
0.1809	32.6	.2378	3	Sleeper
0.1809	32.6	.2378	3	spearheads
0.1809	32.6	.2378	3	wattle
0.1809	32.6	.2378	3	yellow-brown
0.1809	32.6	.2378	3	287
0.1807	32.6	.2696	3	embodied
0.1806	32.6	.2366	3	Asia's
0.1806	32.6	.2366	3	blonds
0.1806	32.6	.2366	3	Lie
0.1805	32.6	.0336	10	solos
0.1805	32.6	.1449	5	Technique
0.1805	32.6	.2689	3	uniquely
0.1804	32.6	.2332	3	jackhammer
0.1801	32.6	.1446	5	canons
0.1801	32.6	.1446	5	finale
0.1801	32.6	.1446	5	lira
0.1801	32.6	.1446	5	Of
0.1801	32.6	.1446	5	tribulation
0.1801	32.6	.1446	5	troubadours
0.1800	32.6	.2732	3	benefactor
0.1800	32.6	.2286	3	bismuth
0.1800	32.6	.2732	3	Burlington
0.1800	32.6	.2286	3	engravings
0.1797	32.5	.1285	5	administers
0.1797	32.5	.1285	5	Boers
0.1797	32.5	.1285	5	catastrophic
0.1797	32.5	.1285	5	Celebes
0.1797	32.5	.1285	5	colonize
0.1797	32.5	.1285	5	Populist
0.1797	32.5	.1285	5	Ruwenzori
0.1797	32.5	.1285	5	slow-growing
0.1797	32.5	.1285	5	Toleration
0.1796	32.5	.0000	12	AOB
0.1796	32.5	.0000	12	dihedral
0.1796	32.5	.0000	12	GH
0.1796	32.5	.0000	12	Multiplication
0.1796	32.5	.0000	12	Theorem
0.1796	32.5	.0000	12	4/8
0.1796	32.5	.0000	12	5/10
0.1795	32.5	.0742	8	disciples
0.1795	32.5	.1290	6	generic
0.1795	32.5	.2132	3	WHY
0.1793	32.5	.1622	5	Elizabethan
0.1793	32.5	.2269	3	tightness
0.1792	32.5	.2123	3	aired
0.1792	32.5	.2430	3	aureomycin
0.1792	32.5	.2123	3	clarified
0.1792	32.5	.2123	3	FOOD
0.1792	32.5	.2429	3	nova
0.1792	32.5	.2429	3	oriole
0.1792	32.5	.2430	3	robin's
0.1790	32.5	.1275	5	alcohols
0.1790	32.5	.1275	5	anatomical
0.1790	32.5	.1275	5	condor
0.1790	32.5	.1275	5	insidious
0.1790	32.5	.2432	3	inter
0.1790	32.5	.1275	5	ionizing
0.1790	32.5	.2432	3	Judea
0.1790	32.5	.2432	3	Occupation
0.1790	32.5	.2432	3	teachers'
0.1790	32.5	.2432	3	Tokay
0.1789	32.5	.2432	3	baled
0.1789	32.5	.2432	3	Copley
0.1789	32.5	.2699	3	jungly
0.1789	32.5	.2699	3	Watson's
0.1789	32.5	.2699	3	wholeheartedly
0.1788	32.5	.2256	3	motorboats
THE PRECEDING WORD TYPE OCCUPIES RANK 33000				
0.1787	32.5	.2610	3	Angle
0.1787	32.5	.0847	7	Diagram
0.1787	32.5	.0494	14	papier-mache
0.1786	32.5	.1215	6	castings
0.1786	32.5	.2630	3	completeness
0.1786	32.5	.2630	3	413
0.1785	32.5	.2254	3	adapts
0.1785	32.5	.2254	3	Bolivian
0.1785	32.5	.2254	3	brackish
0.1785	32.5	.2254	3	CAN
0.1785	32.5	.2254	3	harvester
0.1785	32.5	.2254	3	lawsuits
0.1785	32.5	.2254	3	mends
0.1785	32.5	.2602	3	pinholes
0.1785	32.5	.2254	3	retard
0.1785	32.5	.2254	3	unspecialized
0.1785	32.5	.2254	3	1543
0.1785	32.5	.2254	3	373
0.1785	32.5	.2254	3	5-6
0.1785	32.5	.2254	3	780
0.1784	32.5	.0841	7	self-tests
0.1783	32.5	.0688	6	'course
0.1783	32.5	.0688	6	Aleut
0.1783	32.5	.0688	6	Ramona's
0.1783	32.5	.0688	6	sitting-room
0.1782	32.5	.1772	4	compounding
0.1782	32.5	.1772	4	conformity
0.1782	32.5	.1772	4	infantryman
0.1782	32.5	.1772	4	pitfalls
0.1782	32.5	.1772	4	punctuating
0.1782	32.5	.1772	4	shifty
0.1780	32.5	.2754	3	soundless
0.1779	32.5	.0839	7	Die
0.1779	32.5	.0000	17	ethyl
0.1779	32.5	.0839	7	harmonics
0.1779	32.5	.1273	5	lawyer's
0.1778	32.5	.2672	3	exorbitant
0.1776	32.5	.2665	3	Cynthia's
0.1776	32.5	.2580	3	detach
0.1776	32.5	.2580	3	Instrument
0.1776	32.5	.1783	4	okra
0.1775	32.5	.2239	3	aeration
0.1775	32.5	.2239	3	Alexandrian
0.1775	32.5	.2239	3	Barbicane
0.1775	32.5	.2239	3	channeled
0.1775	32.5	.2239	3	disrupt
0.1775	32.5	.2239	3	faceless
0.1775	32.5	.2239	3	fines
0.1775	32.5	.2239	3	ice-bound
0.1775	32.5	.2239	3	koala
0.1775	32.5	.2239	3	leaching
0.1775	32.5	.2239	3	northeastward
0.1775	32.5	.2239	3	off-shore
0.1775	32.5	.2239	3	oil-bearing
0.1775	32.5	.2239	3	sandstorms
0.1774	32.5	.0741	7	creamed
0.1774	32.5	.0741	7	drippings
0.1774	32.5	.0000	9	fermentation
0.1774	32.5	.0000	9	galvanometer
0.1774	32.5	.0000	9	long-wave
0.1774	32.5	.0000	9	mercuric
0.1774	32.5	.0000	9	positively-charged
0.1774	32.5	.0000	9	tetanus
0.1773	32.5	.1552	5	Elsie
0.1770	32.5	.1973	4	dexterous
0.1769	32.5	.0295	19	bodice
0.1769	32.5	.2208	3	unscrewed
0.1768	32.5	.1889	4	Joint
0.1766	32.5	.1757	4	corncakes
0.1766	32.5	.1757	4	hadst
0.1766	32.5	.1882	4	opposes
0.1766	32.5	.1757	4	pugilistic
0.1766	32.5	.1757	4	shaven
0.1762	32.5	.0246	21	presser
0.1759	32.5	.2184	3	carvers
0.1759	32.5	.2184	3	engraving
0.1759	32.5	.2184	3	Fin
0.1759	32.5	.2184	3	pinion
0.1759	32.5	.2184	3	plaques
0.1759	32.5	.0000	15	Roop
0.1759	32.5	.2184	3	shooter
0.1759	32.5	.2184	3	thermostats
0.1759	32.5	.0000	15	Wonka
0.1758	32.5	.1220	5	resistors
0.1755	32.4	.1577	4	discharging
0.1753	32.4	.2611	3	semi-circular
0.1752	32.4	.0998	7	draftsmen
0.1751	32.4	.2609	3	complied
0.1751	32.4	.2609	3	pervades
0.1750	32.4	.0000	9	Deal
0.1750	32.4	.0000	9	Hazleton
0.1750	32.4	.0000	9	Hokkaido
0.1750	32.4	.0000	9	Kinshasa
0.1750	32.4	.0000	9	O'Higgins
0.1750	32.4	.0000	9	polder
0.1750	32.4	.0000	9	T'ang
0.1750	32.4	.0000	9	Thrace
0.1750	32.4	.0000	9	Tor
0.1748	32.4	.0879	6	tweed
0.1745	32.4	.1737	4	abdomens
THE PRECEDING WORD TYPE OCCUPIES RANK 33100				
0.1745	32.4	.1737	4	bourgeoisie
0.1745	32.4	.1737	4	Castile
0.1745	32.4	.1737	4	commemorated
0.1745	32.4	.1737	4	conduits
0.1745	32.4	.1737	4	foreseeable
0.1745	32.4	.1737	4	Haarlem
0.1745	32.4	.1737	4	houseflies
0.1745	32.4	.1737	4	Lombardy
0.1745	32.4	.1737	4	long-necked
0.1745	32.4	.1737	4	Magdeburg
0.1745	32.4	.1737	4	Makers
0.1745	32.4	.1737	4	priesthood
0.1745	32.4	.1737	4	quotas
0.1745	32.4	.1737	4	Thoreau's
0.1744	32.4	.0873	6	overhand
0.1743	32.4	.1622	4	activist
0.1743	32.4	.1622	4	Anaheim
0.1743	32.4	.1622	4	Anglo-French
0.1743	32.4	.1622	4	Astronaut
0.1743	32.4	.1622	4	Bucharest
0.1743	32.4	.1622	4	felony
0.1743	32.4	.1622	4	intolerance
0.1743	32.4	.1622	4	liberals
0.1743	32.4	.1622	4	literate
0.1743	32.4	.1622	4	manuals
0.1743	32.4	.1622	4	mystique
0.1743	32.4	.1622	4	protesters
0.1743	32.4	.1622	4	public-relations
0.1743	32.4	.1622	4	racist
0.1743	32.4	.1622	4	Yugoslavia's
0.1743	32.4	.1622	4	000-a-year
0.1743	32.4	.1622	4	50-foot
0.1740	32.4	.0520	12	jointer
0.1738	32.4	.1611	4	adrenalin
0.1738	32.4	.1611	4	hatchery
0.1738	32.4	.1611	4	junkyards
0.1738	32.4	.1611	4	kaleidoscope
0.1738	32.4	.1611	4	microcosm
0.1738	32.4	.1611	4	normality
0.1738	32.4	.1611	4	quarter-mile
0.1738	32.4	.1611	4	sightings
0.1738	32.4	.1611	4	vicunas
0.1737	32.4	.0000	12	Bok
0.1737	32.4	.0000	12	Johnty
0.1737	32.4	.0000	12	Lightoller
0.1737	32.4	.0000	12	Lowe
0.1736	32.4	.2479	3	oozes
0.1736	32.4	.0476	12	scraper
0.1736	32.4	.2537	3	slants
0.1736	32.4	.2479	3	1753
0.1735	32.4	.2638	3	Moonlight
0.1735	32.4	.1926	4	tarragon
0.1734	32.4	.2530	3	coelacanth
0.1734	32.4	.2530	3	hospitalized
0.1734	32.4	.2530	3	retires
0.1729	32.4	.2155	3	flutters
0.1729	32.4	.1711	4	topologically
0.1728	32.4	.2444	3	abc
0.1728	32.4	.2444	3	ac
0.1728	32.4	.2444	3	A2
0.1728	32.4	.2444	3	Fairweather
0.1728	32.4	.2444	3	ii
0.1728	32.4	.1417	4	sleeveless
0.1728	32.4	.2444	3	y's
0.1728	32.4	.2458	3	351
0.1728	32.4	.2444	3	789
0.1727	32.4	.2514	3	fermenting
0.1726	32.4	.2451	3	12-6
0.1726	32.4	.2451	3	8-1
0.1725	32.4	.1907	4	layer-cake
0.1725	32.4	.1409	4	lint
0.1725	32.4	.1409	4	mushy
0.1721	32.4	.2398	3	$72
0.1721	32.4	.2398	3	CH
0.1721	32.4	.2138	3	coal-black
0.1721	32.4	.2138	3	cocker
0.1721	32.4	.2398	3	Gizeh
0.1721	32.4	.2398	3	goliath
0.1721	32.4	.2398	3	interchanged
0.1721	32.4	.2398	3	Publications
0.1721	32.4	.2398	3	103rd
0.1721	32.4	.2398	3	1050
0.1721	32.4	.2398	3	1472
0.1721	32.4	.2398	3	1689
0.1721	32.4	.2398	3	531
0.1721	32.4	.2398	3	606
0.1721	32.4	.2398	3	8%
0.1719	32.4	.2390	3	agates
0.1719	32.4	.2441	3	avast
0.1719	32.4	.2390	3	Closed
0.1719	32.4	.2441	3	Foss
0.1719	32.4	.2441	3	Lamplighter
0.1719	32.4	.2441	3	primus
0.1719	32.4	.2441	3	shakers
0.1719	32.4	.2390	3	surveyors'
0.1719	32.4	.2441	3	1715
0.1719	32.4	.2390	3	9-12
0.1717	32.3	.2384	3	Arlene
0.1717	32.3	.2384	3	brevity
0.1717	32.3	.2384	3	Brillig
THE PRECEDING WORD TYPE OCCUPIES RANK 33200				
0.1717	32.3	.0000	16	DR
0.1717	32.3	.2384	3	pole-vault
0.1717	32.3	.0000	16	Sampson
0.1717	32.3	.2384	3	Smiley
0.1717	32.3	.0000	16	WARDEN
0.1717	32.3	.0000	16	ZEKE
0.1716	32.3	.2124	3	platters
0.1716	32.3	.2124	3	spiced
0.1716	32.3	.2124	3	terrify
0.1714	32.3	.0368	9	voyageurs
0.1712	32.3	.1594	4	arrayed
0.1711	32.3	.0655	6	one-sentence
0.1711	32.3	.0655	6	roadmaster
0.1711	32.3	.1791	4	scans
0.1710	32.3	.2599	3	half-buried
0.1710	32.3	.2599	3	tracery
0.1709	32.3	.2360	3	crocuses
0.1709	32.3	.2360	3	doubloons
0.1709	32.3	.2360	3	waxing
0.1708	32.3	.2387	3	Andover
0.1708	32.3	.2387	3	Augusta
0.1708	32.3	.2387	3	Basque
0.1708	32.3	.2387	3	broad-leaved
0.1708	32.3	.2387	3	canton
0.1708	32.3	.2387	3	Capri
0.1708	32.3	.2387	3	cede
0.1708	32.3	.2387	3	dry-goods
0.1708	32.3	.2387	3	Endeavor
0.1708	32.3	.2387	3	gray-brown
0.1708	32.3	.2387	3	Historic
0.1708	32.3	.2387	3	Leopardi
0.1708	32.3	.2387	3	Maeterlinck
0.1708	32.3	.2387	3	netting
0.1708	32.3	.2387	3	poaching
0.1708	32.3	.2387	3	potentialities
0.1708	32.3	.2387	3	revulsion
0.1708	32.3	.2387	3	skirmish
0.1708	32.3	.2387	3	stemming
0.1708	32.3	.2387	3	Tamerlane
0.1708	32.3	.2387	3	Thayer
0.1708	32.3	.2387	3	weeded
0.1708	32.3	.2387	3	Where
0.1705	32.3	.2346	3	$175
0.1705	32.3	.2346	3	$42
0.1705	32.3	.2379	3	altars
0.1705	32.3	.2379	3	Bengt
0.1705	32.3	.2465	3	clamoring
0.1705	32.3	.2379	3	Custer's
0.1705	32.3	.2379	3	daft
0.1705	32.3	.2379	3	dwelling-place
0.1705	32.3	.2379	3	Furies
0.1705	32.3	.2379	3	Gaelic
0.1705	32.3	.2346	3	galore
0.1705	32.3	.2379	3	gambler
0.1705	32.3	.2346	3	halve
0.1705	32.3	.2465	3	Lady's
0.1705	32.3	.2346	3	monkeys'
0.1705	32.3	.2379	3	negro
0.1705	32.3	.2379	3	NewSalem
0.1705	32.3	.2379	3	Raccoons
0.1705	32.3	.2346	3	refueling
0.1705	32.3	.2379	3	regimentation
0.1705	32.3	.2465	3	reiterated
0.1705	32.3	.2379	3	Rice's
0.1705	32.3	.2346	3	scalene
0.1705	32.3	.2346	3	semicircles
0.1705	32.3	.2379	3	sharp-eyed
0.1705	32.3	.2379	3	spirit's
0.1705	32.3	.2379	3	stealer
0.1705	32.3	.2346	3	three-eighths
0.1705	32.3	.2379	3	three-month
0.1705	32.3	.2346	3	vendor
0.1705	32.3	.2379	3	whate'er
0.1705	32.3	.2379	3	18%
0.1705	32.3	.2346	3	2A
0.1705	32.3	.2346	3	6-cent
0.1705	32.3	.2346	3	603
0.1705	32.3	.2346	3	673
0.1705	32.3	.2346	3	720
0.1705	32.3	.2346	3	738
0.1704	32.3	.1389	5	disconnect
0.1704	32.3	.1853	4	grammatically
0.1704	32.3	.0000	21	sion
0.1703	32.3	.2373	3	Ellie
0.1703	32.3	.2373	3	Harriet's
0.1703	32.3	.2373	3	hit-and-run
0.1701	32.3	.0000	14	Grechko
0.1701	32.3	.2578	3	photographer's
0.1701	32.3	.0000	14	Pompidou
0.1701	32.3	.2578	3	Sarasota
0.1700	32.3	.1315	5	proofreaders
0.1698	32.3	.2138	3	pictographs
0.1697	32.3	.2076	3	baying
0.1697	32.3	.2076	3	deepens
0.1697	32.3	.2076	3	fresh-cut
0.1697	32.3	.2076	3	Spectator
0.1697	32.3	.2076	3	stylish
0.1696	32.3	.1135	4	AT
0.1696	32.3	.2443	3	chock-full
0.1696	32.3	.2443	3	outrageous
THE PRECEDING WORD TYPE OCCUPIES RANK 33300				
0.1696	32.3	.1135	4	Path
0.1696	32.3	.1313	5	Peacock
0.1696	32.3	.1313	5	Preludes
0.1696	32.3	.1313	5	recitatives
0.1696	32.3	.1135	4	retracing
0.1696	32.3	.1135	4	006
0.1695	32.3	.2347	3	brownie
0.1695	32.3	.2347	3	clublike
0.1695	32.3	.2347	3	Crandall
0.1695	32.3	.2347	3	crock
0.1695	32.3	.2347	3	crow's-nest
0.1695	32.3	.2347	3	detachment
0.1695	32.3	.2347	3	Georgie's
0.1695	32.3	.2347	3	Hack
0.1695	32.3	.2563	3	Hound
0.1695	32.3	.2347	3	matey
0.1695	32.3	.2347	3	Messrs
0.1695	32.3	.1135	5	nonferrous
0.1695	32.3	.2347	3	quays
0.1695	32.3	.2347	3	splendour
0.1695	32.3	.2347	3	undertakes
0.1695	32.3	.2347	3	washbasin
0.1695	32.3	.2347	3	weatherbeaten
0.1694	32.3	.2435	3	extravagantly
0.1694	32.3	.2435	3	investigator
0.1694	32.3	.1792	4	libra
0.1694	32.3	.1205	6	lithography
0.1694	32.3	.2435	3	paralleled
0.1694	32.3	.2435	3	smears
0.1694	32.3	.2435	3	Stick
0.1694	32.3	.2435	3	widemouthed
0.1693	32.3	.1937	4	loosening
0.1692	32.3	.1789	4	broadening
0.1692	32.3	.1789	4	designates
0.1692	32.3	.0847	8	full-size
0.1692	32.3	.1789	4	interludes
0.1692	32.3	.1789	4	parodies
0.1692	32.3	.1789	4	pealing
0.1692	32.3	.1789	4	Variations
0.1692	32.3	.1789	4	Walton
0.1692	32.3	.1789	4	wend
0.1690	32.3	.2332	3	antiaircraft
0.1690	32.3	.2332	3	Away
0.1690	32.3	.2332	3	Brooklyn's
0.1690	32.3	.2332	3	bureaucrats
0.1690	32.3	.2332	3	CI
0.1690	32.3	.2332	3	clomp
0.1690	32.3	.2332	3	Decision
0.1690	32.3	.2332	3	duns
0.1690	32.3	.2332	3	Hornsby
0.1690	32.3	.2332	3	jockeys
0.1690	32.3	.2332	3	Larsen's
0.1690	32.3	.2332	3	legacies
0.1690	32.3	.2332	3	lust
0.1690	32.3	.2332	3	Mantle's
0.1690	32.3	.2332	3	meaty
0.1690	32.3	.2332	3	Mercedes-Benz
0.1690	32.3	.2332	3	Mickey's
0.1690	32.3	.2332	3	nonchalant
0.1690	32.3	.2332	3	paneled
0.1690	32.3	.2332	3	Pitman
0.1690	32.3	.2332	3	plies
0.1690	32.3	.2332	3	Pontiac's

U	SFI	D	F	Word Type
0.1690	32.3	.2332	3	Queens
0.1690	32.3	.2332	3	rat's
0.1690	32.3	.2332	3	Reiser
0.1690	32.3	.2332	3	self-righteousness
0.1690	32.3	.2332	3	seventeen-year-old
0.1690	32.3	.2332	3	skittish
0.1690	32.3	.2332	3	Solitary
0.1690	32.3	.2332	3	taboo
0.1690	32.3	.2332	3	Too
0.1690	32.3	.2332	3	unjustly
0.1690	32.3	.2551	3	229
0.1687	32.3	.2051	3	carnage
0.1687	32.3	.2051	3	crack-up
0.1687	32.3	.2051	3	crowning
0.1687	32.3	.2486	3	eye-catching
0.1687	32.3	.2051	3	hindering
0.1687	32.3	.2051	3	irreparable
0.1687	32.3	.2051	3	one-day
0.1687	32.3	.2051	3	piggy-back
0.1687	32.3	.2051	3	pocketknife
0.1687	32.3	.2051	3	pressuring
0.1684	32.3	.1650	3	astronaut's
0.1684	32.3	.1650	3	Aviation
0.1684	32.3	.1650	3	blister
0.1684	32.3	.1650	3	cloudburst
0.1684	32.3	.1650	3	cyclonic
0.1684	32.3	.1650	3	exhaling
0.1684	32.3	.1650	3	eyeball
0.1684	32.3	.1650	3	far-sighted
0.1684	32.3	.1650	3	feeler
0.1684	32.3	.1650	3	forecaster
0.1684	32.3	.1650	3	Heyerdahl
0.1684	32.3	.1650	3	matchsticks
0.1684	32.3	.1650	3	mineralogists
0.1684	32.3	.1650	3	nightshade
0.1684	32.3	.1650	3	paris
0.1684	32.3	.1650	3	pinkish
THE PRECEDING WORD TYPE OCCUPIES RANK 33400				
0.1684	32.3	.1650	3	popgun
0.1684	32.3	.1650	3	silver-colored
0.1684	32.3	.1650	3	tallness
0.1684	32.3	.1650	3	transfusion
0.1684	32.3	.1650	3	transmits
0.1684	32.3	.1650	3	water-filled
0.1679	32.3	.1770	4	calypso
0.1679	32.2	.2264	3	Civilized
0.1679	32.3	.1770	4	lullabies
0.1679	32.2	.2264	3	Starfighter
0.1679	32.3	.1770	4	transpose
0.1679	32.3	.1770	4	tuners
0.1679	32.2	.2264	3	13-8
0.1679	32.2	.2264	3	1512
0.1679	32.2	.2264	3	1596
0.1679	32.2	.2264	3	179
0.1679	32.2	.2264	3	713
0.1676	32.2	.1812	4	browning
0.1676	32.2	.1812	4	loin
0.1675	32.2	.0824	5	Art's
0.1675	32.2	.0824	5	beatings
0.1675	32.2	.0824	5	coed
0.1675	32.2	.0824	5	cross-country
0.1675	32.2	.0824	5	factions
0.1675	32.2	.0824	5	hefty
0.1675	32.2	.0824	5	Heisman
0.1675	32.2	.0824	5	IQ
0.1675	32.2	.0824	5	no-good
0.1675	32.2	.0824	5	Promontory
0.1675	32.2	.0824	5	Reclamation
0.1675	32.2	.0824	5	15-year-old
0.1674	32.2	.1639	3	abounded
0.1674	32.2	.1639	3	Afghanistan
0.1674	32.2	.1639	3	aristocrats
0.1674	32.2	.1639	3	assembly-line
0.1674	32.2	.1639	3	Basra
0.1674	32.2	.1639	3	canvass
0.1674	32.2	.1639	3	Citation
0.1674	32.2	.1639	3	Conscience
0.1674	32.2	.1639	3	good-bys
0.1674	32.2	.1639	3	grapevines
0.1674	32.2	.1639	3	harness-maker
0.1674	32.2	.1639	3	hotheads
0.1674	32.2	.1639	3	LongBeach
0.1674	32.2	.1639	3	manors
0.1674	32.2	.1639	3	Meriwether
0.1674	32.2	.1639	3	once-great
0.1674	32.2	.1639	3	overthrew
0.1674	32.2	.1639	3	packers
0.1674	32.2	.1639	3	Pursuit
0.1674	32.2	.1639	3	reside
0.1674	32.2	.1639	3	Seaside
0.1674	32.2	.1639	3	Seward's
0.1674	32.2	.1639	3	SovietUnion
0.1674	32.2	.1639	3	Topeka
0.1674	32.2	.1639	3	unalienable
0.1674	32.2	.1639	3	UnitedNations
0.1674	32.2	.1639	3	well-meaning
0.1674	32.2	.1639	3	Yiddish
0.1674	32.2	.1639	3	Zambia
0.1674	32.2	.1639	3	11**
0.1674	32.2	.1639	3	1820's
0.1672	32.2	.1757	4	-ance
0.1672	32.2	.1757	4	-le
0.1672	32.2	.1757	4	-less
0.1672	32.2	.1757	4	-ship
0.1672	32.2	.1757	4	/ng/
0.1672	32.2	.1757	4	Adjectives
0.1672	32.2	.1757	4	aleph
0.1672	32.2	.2510	3	childlike
0.1672	32.2	.2292	3	maturing
0.1672	32.2	.2292	3	mowers
0.1672	32.2	.1757	4	Pal
0.1672	32.2	.1757	4	r's
0.1672	32.2	.2292	3	specifying
0.1672	32.2	.1757	4	three-word
0.1672	32.2	.1757	4	tt
0.1669	32.2	.1754	4	slur
0.1668	32.2	.0956	6	prelude
0.1667	32.2	.2411	3	archives
0.1667	32.2	.2411	3	Blake's
0.1667	32.2	.2411	3	Can't
0.1667	32.2	.2411	3	cutback
0.1667	32.2	.2411	3	Drill
0.1667	32.2	.2410	3	err
0.1667	32.2	.2411	3	Finland's
0.1667	32.2	.1462	4	foresail
0.1667	32.2	.2410	3	garde
0.1667	32.2	.2411	3	loaders
0.1667	32.2	.2411	3	Met
0.1667	32.2	.2411	3	RCA
0.1667	32.2	.2411	3	Scene
0.1667	32.2	.2411	3	Soul
0.1667	32.2	.2411	3	teenage
0.1667	32.2	.2410	3	vinyl
0.1666	32.2	.1112	4	brickyard
0.1666	32.2	.1112	4	brontosaurus
0.1666	32.2	.1112	4	Burke's
0.1666	32.2	.1112	4	Carnarvon
0.1666	32.2	.1112	4	conies
THE PRECEDING WORD TYPE OCCUPIES RANK 33500				
0.1666	32.2	.1112	4	Cumberlands
0.1666	32.2	.1112	4	Dinosaurs
0.1666	32.2	.1112	4	Duke's
0.1666	32.2	.1112	4	Girty
0.1666	32.2	.1112	4	goose's
0.1666	32.2	.1112	4	Gracie
0.1666	32.2	.1112	4	oratory
0.1666	32.2	.1112	4	Pond's
0.1666	32.2	.1112	4	purebred
0.1666	32.2	.1112	4	She's
0.1666	32.2	.1112	4	teatime
0.1666	32.2	.1112	4	Watertown
0.1666	32.2	.1112	4	windup
0.1666	32.2	.1112	4	Woodlands
0.1666	32.2	.1112	4	1523
0.1662	32.2	.2478	3	profited
0.1662	32.2	.2478	3	stereotypes
0.1661	32.2	.0947	6	triad
0.1655	32.2	.2401	3	Ainsworth
0.1655	32.2	.1847	4	flatness
0.1655	32.2	.2228	3	Lo's
0.1655	32.2	.2401	3	ME
0.1655	32.2	.2228	3	mints
0.1655	32.2	.2400	3	offence
0.1655	32.2	.2400	3	puppet's
0.1655	32.2	.1439	5	Romanesque
0.1655	32.2	.2228	3	Rosalind
0.1655	32.2	.2228	3	405
0.1653	32.2	.1540	4	Chair
0.1653	32.2	.1540	4	plurality
0.1651	32.2	.2325	3	firmament
0.1651	32.2	.2325	3	long-dead
0.1651	32.2	.2325	3	unscrupulous
0.1650	32.2	.1865	3	coves
0.1650	32.2	.2450	3	matron
0.1650	32.2	.1434	4	velveteen
0.1650	32.2	.1865	3	647
0.1649	32.2	.2444	3	Fiske
0.1648	32.2	.1856	3	annealing
0.1648	32.2	.1856	3	dishwashers
0.1648	32.2	.1856	3	pickling
0.1647	32.2	.0000	11	$
0.1647	32.2	.0000	11	%
0.1647	32.2	.1529	4	departures
0.1647	32.2	.0000	11	L**
0.1647	32.2	.0000	11	nonnegative
0.1647	32.2	.0000	11	pairings
0.1647	32.2	.0000	11	percentile
0.1647	32.2	.0000	11	percents
0.1647	32.2	.0000	11	placeholders
0.1647	32.2	.0000	11	quadratic
0.1647	32.2	.0000	11	regrouping
0.1647	32.2	.1529	4	Roth
0.1647	32.2	.0000	11	Skycrane
0.1647	32.2	.0000	11	superset
0.1647	32.2	.0000	11	trapezoid
0.1647	32.2	.0000	11	undoes
0.1647	32.2	.1529	4	Use
0.1647	32.2	.0000	11	4/3
0.1647	32.2	.0000	11	5/12
0.1647	32.2	.0000	11	5280
0.1647	32.2	.0000	11	6/10
0.1646	32.2	.1724	4	Dietrich
0.1646	32.2	.0598	10	draftsman
0.1644	32.2	.1306	5	coupling
0.1644	32.2	.1670	4	12-7
0.1642	32.2	.1930	3	seamanship
0.1642	32.2	.1930	3	snorkels
0.1642	32.2	.1930	3	snowbanks
0.1641	32.2	.0804	5	Course
0.1641	32.2	.0804	5	Crayne
0.1641	32.2	.0804	5	dining-room
0.1641	32.2	.0804	5	enchantress
0.1641	32.2	.0804	5	fixin'
0.1641	32.2	.0804	5	Freddy's
0.1641	32.2	.0000	15	Insert
0.1641	32.2	.0804	5	leant
0.1641	32.2	.0804	5	Longstocking
0.1641	32.2	.0804	5	mammy
0.1641	32.2	.0000	15	Matrix
0.1641	32.2	.0804	5	Pippi's
0.1641	32.2	.0804	5	pleadingly
0.1640	32.1	.1371	4	glues
0.1640	32.1	.1420	5	letterpress
0.1638	32.1	.0836	8	connotative
0.1638	32.1	.1703	4	ven
0.1635	32.1	.2321	3	Adm
0.1635	32.1	.2321	3	Alamosa
0.1635	32.1	.2321	3	anarchy
0.1635	32.1	.2321	3	B-52
0.1635	32.1	.2321	3	Belknap
0.1635	32.1	.2321	3	beneficiaries
0.1635	32.1	.2321	3	Born
0.1635	32.1	.2321	3	cataloguing
0.1635	32.1	.2321	3	catatonic
0.1635	32.1	.2321	3	chafed
0.1635	32.1	.2321	3	coast-to-coast
0.1635	32.1	.2321	3	college-age
0.1635	32.1	.2321	3	comeback
0.1635	32.1	.2321	3	computer-controlled
THE PRECEDING WORD TYPE OCCUPIES RANK 33600				
0.1635	32.1	.2321	3	concedes
0.1635	32.1	.2321	3	concerted
0.1635	32.1	.2321	3	confirms
0.1635	32.1	.2321	3	deteriorate
0.1635	32.1	.2321	3	Exhibit
0.1635	32.1	.2321	3	feasibility
0.1635	32.1	.2321	3	figurines
0.1635	32.1	.2321	3	fluorides
0.1635	32.1	.2321	3	forays
0.1635	32.1	.2321	3	gearbox
0.1635	32.1	.2321	3	Hammer
0.1635	32.1	.2321	3	headers
0.1635	32.1	.2321	3	implicated
0.1635	32.1	.2321	3	incentives
0.1635	32.1	.2321	3	Ind
0.1635	32.1	.2321	3	innovator
0.1635	32.1	.2321	3	instrumented
0.1635	32.1	.2321	3	intimidated
0.1635	32.1	.2321	3	investigative
0.1635	32.1	.2321	3	issuance
0.1635	32.1	.2321	3	Janis
0.1635	32.1	.2321	3	juxtaposition
0.1635	32.1	.1700	4	ledger
0.1635	32.1	.2321	3	Ljubljana
0.1635	32.1	.2321	3	low-income
0.1635	32.1	.2321	3	Mahatma
0.1635	32.1	.2321	3	Maryland's
0.1635	32.1	.2321	3	Minn
0.1635	32.1	.2321	3	olfactory
0.1635	32.1	.2321	3	one-year
0.1635	32.1	.2321	3	Physical
0.1635	32.1	.2321	3	pinks
0.1635	32.1	.2321	3	platypuses
0.1635	32.1	.2321	3	prestigious
0.1635	32.1	.2321	3	prohibits
0.1635	32.1	.2321	3	psychologically
0.1635	32.1	.2321	3	Rail
0.1635	32.1	.2321	3	rainstorms
0.1635	32.1	.2321	3	reintroduced
0.1635	32.1	.2321	3	repealed
0.1635	32.1	.2321	3	reproductions
0.1635	32.1	.2321	3	resurrection
0.1635	32.1	.2321	3	retailer
0.1635	32.1	.2321	3	self-determination
0.1635	32.1	.2321	3	Slovenia
0.1635	32.1	.2321	3	sowing
0.1635	32.1	.2321	3	specifics
0.1635	32.1	.2321	3	Split
0.1635	32.1	.2321	3	sprockets
0.1635	32.1	.2321	3	stipulated
0.1635	32.1	.2321	3	Strand
0.1635	32.1	.2321	3	superficially
0.1635	32.1	.2321	3	UCLA'S
0.1635	32.1	.2321	3	unobtrusively
0.1635	32.1	.2321	3	viable
0.1635	32.1	.2321	3	waft
0.1635	32.1	.2321	3	waterside
0.1635	32.1	.2321	3	wrestles
0.1635	32.1	.2321	3	37th
0.1634	32.1	.1908	3	Kay's
0.1632	32.1	.1044	5	enamels
0.1632	32.1	.2380	3	enunciate
0.1632	32.1	.2380	3	Please
0.1632	32.1	.2380	3	sty
0.1632	32.1	.2380	3	weeps
0.1631	32.1	.2379	3	-ition
0.1631	32.1	.2309	3	agonizing
0.1631	32.1	.2309	3	butts
0.1631	32.1	.2309	3	chutes
0.1631	32.1	.2379	3	Conquest
0.1631	32.1	.2309	3	Cowboys
0.1631	32.1	.2309	3	Dealer
0.1631	32.1	.2309	3	doublets
0.1631	32.1	.2379	3	eth
0.1631	32.1	.2309	3	front-page
0.1631	32.1	.2309	3	fumbles
0.1631	32.1	.2309	3	gauntlet
0.1631	32.1	.2309	3	Heron
0.1631	32.1	.2309	3	impunity
0.1631	32.1	.2379	3	lanx
0.1631	32.1	.2309	3	likable
0.1631	32.1	.2379	3	nautes
0.1631	32.1	.2309	3	outhouse
0.1631	32.1	.2309	3	Owner
0.1631	32.1	.2309	3	pertains
0.1631	32.1	.2309	3	plummeted
0.1631	32.1	.2309	3	reconciliation
0.1631	32.1	.2309	3	reprisal
0.1631	32.1	.2309	3	roe
0.1631	32.1	.2309	3	smothering
0.1631	32.1	.2309	3	spectacularly
0.1631	32.1	.2309	3	TD
0.1631	32.1	.2309	3	Turf
0.1631	32.1	.2309	3	Valiant
0.1631	32.1	.2309	3	waggish
0.1631	32.1	.2309	3	Yuletide
0.1631	32.1	.2379	3	zz
0.1630	32.1	.1514	4	heaves
0.1630	32.1	.0814	7	niacin
0.1627	32.1	.2300	3	blocker
THE PRECEDING WORD TYPE OCCUPIES RANK 33700				
0.1627	32.1	.2300	3	Buddy
0.1627	32.1	.2300	3	Chapin
0.1627	32.1	.2300	3	cornering
0.1627	32.1	.2300	3	crabapples
0.1627	32.1	.2300	3	crusading
0.1627	32.1	.0409	8	fl
0.1627	32.1	.2300	3	Luce
0.1627	32.1	.2300	3	Merchandise
0.1627	32.1	.2300	3	Miriam
0.1627	32.1	.2300	3	piazza
0.1627	32.1	.2300	3	showplace
0.1627	32.1	.2300	3	subconsciously
0.1627	32.1	.2300	3	Tod
0.1627	32.1	.2300	3	touchdowns
0.1627	32.1	.0409	8	Trouble
0.1627	32.1	.0674	9	trusses
0.1627	32.1	.2300	3	unrestricted
0.1627	32.1	.2300	3	whimsical
0.1627	32.1	.0409	8	zh
0.1625	32.1	.2374	3	Balthasar
0.1625	32.1	.2374	3	Didn't
0.1625	32.1	.2374	3	Fate
0.1625	32.1	.2374	3	prouder
0.1625	32.1	.2374	3	ridin'
0.1625	32.1	.2374	3	stoops
0.1625	32.1	.2374	3	unfeeling
0.1624	32.1	.2386	3	sortie
0.1623	32.1	.0000	20	digraphs
0.1620	32.1	.1675	4	foolers
0.1620	32.1	.2086	3	see-saw
0.1620	32.1	.2086	3	013
0.1620	32.1	.2086	3	921
0.1619	32.1	.2304	3	anal
0.1619	32.1	.2304	3	Benoit
0.1619	32.1	.2304	3	calamity
0.1619	32.1	.2304	3	caress
0.1619	32.1	.2304	3	chronicler
0.1619	32.1	.2304	3	coursed
0.1619	32.1	.2304	3	Cromarty
0.1619	32.1	.2304	3	engrossing
0.1619	32.1	.2304	3	forepaws
0.1619	32.1	.2304	3	goings
0.1619	32.1	.2304	3	hummock
0.1619	32.1	.2304	3	Jethro's
0.1619	32.1	.2304	3	marauding
0.1619	32.1	.2304	3	Mingo
0.1619	32.1	.2304	3	Miracles
0.1619	32.1	.2304	3	sedition
0.1619	32.1	.2304	3	severed
0.1619	32.1	.2304	3	sucker
0.1618	32.1	.2076	3	a-f
0.1618	32.1	.2076	3	ACD
0.1618	32.1	.2076	3	balsa-wood
0.1618	32.1	.2076	3	British-American
0.1618	32.1	.2076	3	Janssen
0.1618	32.1	.2076	3	Reaction
0.1618	32.1	.2076	3	technician
0.1618	32.1	.2076	3	weighings
0.1618	32.1	.2076	3	04
0.1618	32.1	.2076	3	12-1
0.1618	32.1	.2076	3	4-9
0.1618	32.1	.2076	3	501
0.1617	32.1	.1672	4	bongo
0.1617	32.1	.1672	4	lilting
0.1617	32.1	.1672	4	vino
0.1616	32.1	.2365	3	aster
0.1616	32.1	.2365	3	Brotherhood
0.1616	32.1	.2365	3	Demerara
0.1616	32.1	.2365	3	depicting
0.1616	32.1	.2365	3	fandango
0.1616	32.1	.2365	3	foreshadowed
0.1616	32.1	.2365	3	gentler
0.1616	32.1	.2365	3	Gibbons
0.1616	32.1	.2365	3	Lully
0.1616	32.1	.2365	3	Sault
0.1616	32.1	.2365	3	There
0.1615	32.1	.1505	4	antislavery
0.1615	32.1	.2292	3	awry
0.1615	32.1	.1505	4	Baguio
0.1615	32.1	.2292	3	bareheaded
0.1615	32.1	.2292	3	bier
0.1615	32.1	.2292	3	bolder
0.1615	32.1	.2292	3	breech
0.1615	32.1	.1505	4	castes
0.1615	32.1	.2292	3	convulsively
0.1615	32.1	.1505	4	council-manager
0.1615	32.1	.1505	4	Crusade
0.1615	32.1	.2292	3	damps
0.1615	32.1	.1505	4	Djakarta
0.1615	32.1	.1505	4	Fuego
0.1615	32.1	.2292	3	gittin'
0.1615	32.1	.2292	3	grey-green
0.1615	32.1	.2292	3	hatband
0.1615	32.1	.2292	3	hedged
0.1615	32.1	.2292	3	heraldic
0.1615	32.1	.2292	3	Hetty's
0.1615	32.1	.1505	4	jails
0.1615	32.1	.2292	3	Jumbo's
0.1615	32.1	.2292	3	limpid
0.1615	32.1	.2292	3	lordship
THE PRECEDING WORD TYPE OCCUPIES RANK 33800				
0.1615	32.1	.2292	3	McLean
0.1615	32.1	.2292	3	moodily
0.1615	32.1	.1505	4	mortgages
0.1615	32.1	.2292	3	mutilated
0.1615	32.1	.1505	4	Nathanael
0.1615	32.1	.2292	3	oat
0.1615	32.1	.2292	3	patrolman
0.1615	32.1	.2292	3	pug
0.1615	32.1	.2292	3	Rod's
0.1615	32.1	.2292	3	sideboard
0.1615	32.1	.2292	3	skulking
0.1615	32.1	.2292	3	sorta
0.1615	32.1	.2292	3	squalling
0.1615	32.1	.1505	4	subtropical
0.1615	32.1	.2292	3	two-year-olds
0.1615	32.1	.1505	4	variously
0.1615	32.1	.1505	4	veld
0.1615	32.1	.2364	3	1583
0.1615	32.1	.1505	4	1740
0.1614	32.1	.2266	3	admissions
0.1614	32.1	.2266	3	admittedly
0.1614	32.1	.2266	3	angler
0.1614	32.1	.2266	3	clotted
0.1614	32.1	.2266	3	documented
0.1614	32.1	.2266	3	domicile
0.1614	32.1	.2266	3	fibre

U	SFI	D	F	Word Type
0.1614	32.1	.2266	3	goof
0.1614	32.1	.2266	3	grader
0.1614	32.1	.2266	3	hectic
0.1614	32.1	.2266	3	hippie
0.1614	32.1	.2266	3	javelina
0.1614	32.1	.2266	3	Millers
0.1614	32.1	.2266	3	mindless
0.1614	32.1	.2266	3	nubbly
0.1614	32.1	.2266	3	oozing
0.1614	32.1	.2266	3	reveille
0.1614	32.1	.2266	3	salvaging
0.1614	32.1	.2266	3	singlehanded
0.1614	32.1	.1941	3	slivers
0.1614	32.1	.1941	3	Spruce
0.1614	32.1	.2266	3	undertaker
0.1613	32.1	.1368	4	unattached
0.1611	32.1	.1668	4	big-nosed
0.1611	32.1	.2283	3	capsized
0.1611	32.1	.2283	3	Fluff
0.1611	32.1	.2283	3	knotting
0.1611	32.1	.2283	3	overtakes
0.1611	32.1	.2319	3	quickening
0.1611	32.1	.2283	3	rummage
0.1611	32.1	.2283	3	Russo
0.1611	32.1	.2283	3	Sunday-school
0.1611	32.1	.2283	3	Very
0.1611	32.1	.2283	3	wrenching
0.1611	32.1	.2283	3	zinnias
0.1610	32.1	.0000	15	BOY
0.1610	32.1	.0000	15	CHILD
0.1610	32.1	.0000	15	KINO
0.1610	32.1	.0000	15	SNAGGS
0.1609	32.1	.1494	4	Attila
0.1609	32.1	.1494	4	aurora
0.1609	32.1	.1494	4	half-life
0.1609	32.1	.1494	4	hydrofluoric
0.1609	32.1	.1494	4	lawrencium
0.1609	32.1	.1494	4	methyl
0.1609	32.1	.1494	4	Niels
0.1609	32.1	.1494	4	Pre-Cambrian
0.1609	32.1	.1494	4	silicones
0.1609	32.1	.1494	4	two-sided
0.1608	32.1	.1927	3	pastimes
0.1604	32.1	.1101	6	calipers
0.1604	32.1	.0535	8	soldered
0.1600	32.0	.2063	3	Afrikaner
0.1600	32.0	.2063	3	copper-colored
0.1600	32.0	.2063	3	employer's
0.1600	32.0	.2063	3	flagship
0.1600	32.0	.2063	3	giraffe's
0.1600	32.0	.2063	3	Leopoldville
0.1600	32.0	.2063	3	Medellin
0.1600	32.0	.2063	3	modernizing
0.1600	32.0	.2063	3	ox-drawn
0.1600	32.0	.2063	3	Pocahontas'
0.1600	32.0	.2063	3	proverbs
0.1600	32.0	.2063	3	realists
0.1599	32.0	.1320	3	gore
0.1599	32.0	.1648	4	hairline
0.1599	32.0	.1648	4	NOTE
0.1599	32.0	.1320	3	silhouettes
0.1599	32.0	.1320	3	tuber
0.1597	32.0	.2053	3	avenging
0.1597	32.0	.2053	3	cecropia
0.1597	32.0	.2053	3	duck-billed
0.1597	32.0	.2053	3	fingerlike
0.1597	32.0	.2053	3	flea's
0.1597	32.0	.2053	3	ON
0.1597	32.0	.2053	3	peopled
0.1597	32.0	.2053	3	permanence
0.1597	32.0	.2053	3	softwoods
0.1597	32.0	.2053	3	Surgeon
0.1592	32.0	.0000	11	Levi
0.1592	32.0	.0000	11	Prom

THE PRECEDING WORD TYPE OCCUPIES RANK 33900

U	SFI	D	F	Word Type
0.1592	32.0	.0000	11	Susannah
0.1592	32.0	.0000	11	thecodonts
0.1591	32.0	.2147	3	outings
0.1589	32.0	.2227	3	aforementioned
0.1589	32.0	.2227	3	Bears'
0.1589	32.0	.1879	3	befell
0.1589	32.0	.2227	3	blissfully
0.1589	32.0	.2227	3	Bluegrass
0.1589	32.0	.2227	3	capered
0.1589	32.0	.2227	3	chinaberry
0.1589	32.0	.1879	3	congregated
0.1589	32.0	.2227	3	Doggie
0.1589	32.0	.2227	3	festooned
0.1589	32.0	.2227	3	impudence
0.1589	32.0	.2227	3	Jenny's
0.1589	32.0	.2227	3	Knave
0.1589	32.0	.2227	3	Mention
0.1589	32.0	.2227	3	Navigation
0.1589	32.0	.2227	3	Parent
0.1589	32.0	.2227	3	paroxysm
0.1589	32.0	.2227	3	pricking
0.1589	32.0	.2227	3	scoreboard
0.1589	32.0	.2227	3	submission
0.1589	32.0	.2227	3	townsfolk
0.1589	32.0	.2227	3	unseasonably
0.1589	32.0	.1879	3	Weighing
0.1589	32.0	.2227	3	woefully
0.1588	32.0	.2270	3	Britannica
0.1588	32.0	.2270	3	cliches
0.1588	32.0	.2270	3	data-processing
0.1588	32.0	.2270	3	deadlines
0.1588	32.0	.2270	3	Hottentot
0.1588	32.0	.2270	3	McHenry
0.1588	32.0	.2270	3	navigated
0.1588	32.0	.2270	3	Pettigrew
0.1587	32.0	.0799	8	sculptural
0.1587	32.0	.0945	6	whole-grain
0.1585	32.0	.0887	5	dwells
0.1583	32.0	.2257	3	angle-worm
0.1583	32.0	.2257	3	Barn-Owl
0.1583	32.0	.2257	3	bestride
0.1583	32.0	.2257	3	cavalryman

U	SFI	D	F	Word Type
0.1583	32.0	.2257	3	glass-bottomed
0.1583	32.0	.2257	3	Hazel
0.1583	32.0	.2257	3	mix-up
0.1583	32.0	.2257	3	Packard
0.1583	32.0	.2257	3	postcards
0.1583	32.0	.2257	3	Reader's
0.1583	32.0	.2257	3	slop
0.1583	32.0	.2257	3	Winkler
0.1581	32.0	.1738	4	halftone
0.1580	32.0	.2260	3	aide-de-camp
0.1580	32.0	.0000	13	Chevy
0.1580	32.0	.2260	3	discerned
0.1580	32.0	.2260	3	equated
0.1580	32.0	.1735	3	facades
0.1580	32.0	.2260	3	flinty
0.1580	32.0	.2260	3	gurgled
0.1580	32.0	.2260	3	hearthstone
0.1580	32.0	.2260	3	heathens
0.1580	32.0	.0000	13	Hutterites
0.1580	32.0	.2260	3	incandescence
0.1580	32.0	.2260	3	lamentable
0.1580	32.0	.0000	13	Nelsen
0.1580	32.0	.2260	3	Osler
0.1580	32.0	.2260	3	Piedras
0.1580	32.0	.2260	3	shroud
0.1580	32.0	.2260	3	Spence
0.1580	32.0	.2260	3	stealth
0.1580	32.0	.2260	3	Tay
0.1580	32.0	.2260	3	unconquered
0.1580	32.0	.2260	3	Whitby
0.1580	32.0	.2260	3	Yorker
0.1579	32.0	.0767	5	Verb
0.1578	32.0	.1727	3	Diesel
0.1578	32.0	.1727	3	unmannerly
0.1577	32.0	.0000	8	Calorie
0.1577	32.0	.0000	8	Dalton
0.1577	32.0	.0000	8	decompose
0.1577	32.0	.0000	8	Deepstar
0.1577	32.0	.0000	8	echinoderms
0.1577	32.0	.0000	8	electroscope
0.1577	32.0	.0000	8	enzyme
0.1577	32.0	.0000	8	fidelity
0.1577	32.0	.0000	8	hydrochloric
0.1577	32.0	.0000	8	inbred
0.1577	32.0	.0000	8	intrusive
0.1577	32.0	.0000	8	outwash
0.1577	32.0	.0000	8	Roentgen
0.1577	32.0	.0000	8	Roentgen's
0.1570	32.0	.2236	3	badness
0.1570	32.0	.2236	3	bandy
0.1570	32.0	.2236	3	Beulah
0.1570	32.0	.2236	3	bulrushes
0.1570	32.0	.2236	3	Burton
0.1570	32.0	.2236	3	crampons
0.1570	32.0	.2236	3	forget-me-nots
0.1570	32.0	.2236	3	frenzied
0.1570	32.0	.2236	3	gird
0.1570	32.0	.2236	3	gleams

THE PRECEDING WORD TYPE OCCUPIES RANK 34000

U	SFI	D	F	Word Type
0.1570	32.0	.2236	3	jerkily
0.1570	32.0	.2236	3	oration
0.1570	32.0	.2236	3	unknowingly
0.1569	32.0	.2217	3	soupy
0.1568	32.0	.2143	3	agonies
0.1568	32.0	.2143	3	ambivalence
0.1568	32.0	.2143	3	Armada
0.1568	32.0	.2143	3	bigness
0.1568	32.0	.2143	3	buildup
0.1568	32.0	.2143	3	coon
0.1568	32.0	.0857	4	crusty
0.1568	32.0	.2143	3	curbing
0.1568	32.0	.2143	3	Custom
0.1568	32.0	.2143	3	deferred
0.1568	32.0	.2143	3	disillusioned
0.1568	32.0	.2143	3	dogma
0.1568	32.0	.2143	3	Edwardian
0.1568	32.0	.2143	3	fending
0.1568	32.0	.2345	3	fermented
0.1568	32.0	.2143	3	Griffith
0.1568	32.0	.2143	3	hard-bitten
0.1568	32.0	.2143	3	honeymoon
0.1568	32.0	.2143	3	idiotic
0.1568	32.0	.2143	3	inaugurating
0.1568	32.0	.2345	3	insures
0.1568	32.0	.2143	3	Joes
0.1568	32.0	.2143	3	journalistic
0.1568	32.0	.2143	3	landscaped
0.1568	32.0	.2143	3	Launch
0.1568	32.0	.2143	3	lieutenants
0.1568	32.0	.2143	3	linesmen
0.1568	32.0	.2345	3	lubricated
0.1568	32.0	.2143	3	mangoes
0.1568	32.0	.2143	3	Manhattan's
0.1568	32.0	.2143	3	mas
0.1568	32.0	.2143	3	minors
0.1568	32.0	.2143	3	NewJersey's
0.1568	32.0	.2143	3	Nigger
0.1568	32.0	.0857	4	nosebleed
0.1568	32.0	.2143	3	outfielder
0.1568	32.0	.2143	3	painless
0.1568	32.0	.2143	3	populace
0.1568	32.0	.2143	3	portfolio
0.1568	32.0	.2143	3	rapport
0.1568	32.0	.2143	3	ravaged
0.1568	32.0	.2143	3	reconnaissance
0.1568	32.0	.2143	3	retreats
0.1568	32.0	.2143	3	Scientific
0.1568	32.0	.2143	3	separatists
0.1568	32.0	.2143	3	shutouts
0.1568	32.0	.2143	3	Sloppy
0.1568	32.0	.2143	3	Spalding
0.1568	32.0	.2143	3	sparkly
0.1568	32.0	.2143	3	summing
0.1568	32.0	.2143	3	thrall
0.1568	32.0	.2143	3	townsman
0.1568	32.0	.2143	3	unformed
0.1568	32.0	.2143	3	Wine

U	SFI	D	F	Word Type
0.1568	32.0	.2143	3	Yat-sen
0.1568	32.0	.2143	3	1/4-inch
0.1568	32.0	.2143	3	28-year-old
0.1566	31.9	.2335	3	onlooker
0.1564	31.9	.2327	3	angora
0.1564	31.9	.2327	3	chatters
0.1563	31.9	.2208	3	cookery
0.1563	31.9	.2208	3	ducking
0.1563	31.9	.2208	3	gargoyle
0.1563	31.9	.1199	4	hardening
0.1563	31.9	.2208	3	harm's
0.1563	31.9	.2208	3	substitutions
0.1563	31.9	.2208	3	1659
0.1562	31.9	.2233	3	cameramen
0.1562	31.9	.2233	3	constriction
0.1562	31.9	.2233	3	continuance
0.1562	31.9	.2233	3	corollary
0.1562	31.9	.2233	3	diabetes
0.1562	31.9	.0756	5	Hephaestus
0.1562	31.9	.2233	3	impromptu
0.1562	31.9	.2233	3	infidel
0.1562	31.9	.0756	5	Lenore
0.1562	31.9	.2233	3	masque
0.1562	31.9	.2233	3	Places
0.1562	31.9	.0756	5	Socks
0.1562	31.9	.2233	3	stimulation
0.1562	31.9	.2233	3	translator
0.1562	31.9	.2233	3	Unitarian
0.1561	31.9	.1307	5	661
0.1560	31.9	.2121	3	$19
0.1560	31.9	.2121	3	$51
0.1560	31.9	.2121	3	$700
0.1560	31.9	.2121	3	Avon
0.1560	31.9	.2121	3	Elementary
0.1560	31.9	.2121	3	EVA
0.1560	31.9	.2121	3	juniors
0.1560	31.9	.2121	3	king-size
0.1560	31.9	.2121	3	Marvin
0.1560	31.9	.2121	3	Streets
0.1560	31.9	.2121	3	560
0.1558	31.9	.2222	3	Dauphine
0.1558	31.9	.2222	3	discriminate

THE PRECEDING WORD TYPE OCCUPIES RANK 34100

U	SFI	D	F	Word Type
0.1558	31.9	.2222	3	Dort
0.1558	31.9	.2222	3	erroneous
0.1558	31.9	.2222	3	expansions
0.1558	31.9	.2295	3	fretful
0.1558	31.9	.2222	3	intricacies
0.1558	31.9	.2222	3	obstinately
0.1558	31.9	.2222	3	overuse
0.1558	31.9	.2222	3	Piers
0.1558	31.9	.2222	3	unequaled
0.1558	31.9	.2222	3	wayward
0.1558	31.9	.2295	3	WHERE
0.1556	31.9	.0000	8	Frostproof
0.1556	31.9	.0000	8	Iberian
0.1556	31.9	.0000	8	iron-and-steel
0.1556	31.9	.0000	8	Kickapoos
0.1556	31.9	.0000	8	Kuwi
0.1556	31.9	.0000	8	Mij
0.1556	31.9	.0000	8	Pampa
0.1556	31.9	.0000	8	Pinta
0.1555	31.9	.2187	3	$180
0.1555	31.9	.2187	3	American's
0.1555	31.9	.2187	3	Brodie
0.1555	31.9	.2187	3	cartographer
0.1555	31.9	.2187	3	chronologically
0.1555	31.9	.2277	3	Colby
0.1555	31.9	.2187	3	cum
0.1555	31.9	.2187	3	finals
0.1555	31.9	.2187	3	homer
0.1555	31.9	.2187	3	Kelsey
0.1555	31.9	.2187	3	mimeographed
0.1555	31.9	.2187	3	ninth-grade
0.1555	31.9	.2187	3	Oyster
0.1555	31.9	.2277	3	paprika
0.1555	31.9	.2277	3	pushers
0.1555	31.9	.2277	3	researched
0.1555	31.9	.2187	3	sandlot
0.1555	31.9	.2187	3	sidestepped
0.1555	31.9	.2277	3	sirloin
0.1555	31.9	.2187	3	tip-toe
0.1555	31.9	.2187	3	unbranded
0.1555	31.9	.2187	3	winks
0.1555	31.9	.2277	3	406
0.1554	31.9	.2196	3	altercation
0.1554	31.9	.2196	3	bidden
0.1554	31.9	.2196	3	bong
0.1554	31.9	.2196	3	chattel
0.1554	31.9	.2196	3	confession
0.1554	31.9	.2196	3	currying
0.1554	31.9	.2196	3	discourse
0.1554	31.9	.2196	3	doeskin
0.1554	31.9	.2196	3	firelock
0.1554	31.9	.2196	3	fishin'
0.1554	31.9	.2196	3	imaginings
0.1554	31.9	.2196	3	irresponsibility
0.1554	31.9	.2196	3	knapsack
0.1554	31.9	.2196	3	outhouses
0.1554	31.9	.2196	3	purty
0.1554	31.9	.2196	3	remonstrance
0.1554	31.9	.2196	3	Setter
0.1554	31.9	.2196	3	shiftless
0.1554	31.9	.2196	3	somewheres
0.1554	31.9	.2196	3	sufferer
0.1554	31.9	.2196	3	thankfulness
0.1554	31.9	.2196	3	unclean
0.1554	31.9	.2196	3	Unicorn
0.1548	31.9	.2120	3	bellies
0.1548	31.9	.2120	3	Chestnut
0.1548	31.9	.2120	3	concealing
0.1548	31.9	.2120	3	daresay
0.1548	31.9	.2120	3	fishline
0.1548	31.9	.2120	3	half-circle
0.1548	31.9	.2120	3	horseflesh
0.1548	31.9	.2120	3	indenture
0.1548	31.9	.2120	3	lanyard

U	SFI	D	F	Word Type
0.1548	31.9	.2120	3	nickered
0.1548	31.9	.2120	3	palette
0.1548	31.9	.2120	3	pretence
0.1548	31.9	.2120	3	prickly-pear
0.1548	31.9	.2120	3	Rebs
0.1548	31.9	.2120	3	retrieved
0.1548	31.9	.2120	3	ruther
0.1548	31.9	.2120	3	silver-gray
0.1548	31.9	.2120	3	Snowball's
0.1548	31.9	.2120	3	sunned
0.1548	31.9	.2120	3	tortuous
0.1548	31.9	.2120	3	unspeakably
0.1548	31.9	.2120	3	whizz
0.1545	31.9	.2175	3	affronted
0.1545	31.9	.2175	3	Carmichael
0.1545	31.9	.2175	3	catbird's
0.1545	31.9	.2175	3	clinched
0.1545	31.9	.2175	3	discourses
0.1545	31.9	.2175	3	doorjamb
0.1545	31.9	.2175	3	jaunty
0.1545	31.9	.2175	3	modesty
0.1545	31.9	.2175	3	renegade
0.1545	31.9	.2175	3	schooner's
0.1545	31.9	.2175	3	selves
0.1545	31.9	.2175	3	taunt
0.1545	31.9	.2175	3	tummy

THE PRECEDING WORD TYPE OCCUPIES RANK 34200

U	SFI	D	F	Word Type
0.1545	31.9	.2175	3	understatement
0.1543	31.9	.1101	5	durations
0.1543	31.9	.1101	5	Gould
0.1543	31.9	.1101	5	Hammerstein
0.1543	31.9	.1101	5	Visitors
0.1541	31.9	.2181	3	cormorant
0.1541	31.9	.2181	3	disembarked
0.1541	31.9	.2181	3	forsook
0.1541	31.9	.2181	3	Gibbs
0.1541	31.9	.2181	3	Harden
0.1541	31.9	.2181	3	indestructible
0.1541	31.9	.0743	5	Mesabi
0.1541	31.9	.2181	3	meticulously
0.1541	31.9	.2181	3	pectorals
0.1541	31.9	.2181	3	Principles
0.1541	31.9	.0743	5	retainers
0.1541	31.9	.2181	3	riddled
0.1541	31.9	.2181	3	Teeth
0.1541	31.9	.2181	3	top-heavy
0.1541	31.9	.0743	5	treatise
0.1541	31.9	.2181	3	Ville
0.1541	31.9	.0743	5	vitally
0.1541	31.9	.2181	3	whiting
0.1537	31.9	.1092	5	2-15
0.1536	31.9	.0000	19	clef
0.1536	31.9	.0000	19	Nutcracker
0.1536	31.9	.2179	3	pennants
0.1535	31.9	.1735	3	daddy's
0.1535	31.9	.1735	3	lightheartedness
0.1534	31.9	.1649	4	dents
0.1534	31.9	.1534	4	Handel's
0.1534	31.9	.1534	4	impressionistic
0.1534	31.9	.1534	4	Marriage
0.1534	31.9	.1534	4	Marseillaise
0.1534	31.9	.1534	4	soloists
0.1534	31.9	.1534	4	violoncello
0.1533	31.9	.2159	3	$90
0.1533	31.9	.2159	3	467
0.1533	31.9	.2159	3	8-ounce
0.1532	31.9	.2159	3	absorbers
0.1532	31.9	.2159	3	accredited
0.1532	31.9	.2159	3	affiliates
0.1532	31.9	.2159	3	afflicts
0.1532	31.9	.2159	3	autocratic
0.1532	31.9	.2159	3	battery-powered
0.1532	31.9	.2159	3	biochemist
0.1532	31.9	.2159	3	Board's
0.1532	31.9	.2159	3	cartographers
0.1532	31.9	.2159	3	catalogues
0.1532	31.9	.2159	3	censuses
0.1532	31.9	.2159	3	configuration
0.1532	31.9	.2159	3	conjure
0.1532	31.9	.2159	3	defensively
0.1532	31.9	.2159	3	doctorate
0.1532	31.9	.2159	3	ecosystem
0.1532	31.9	.2159	3	emanating
0.1532	31.9	.2159	3	engulfing
0.1532	31.9	.2159	3	esoteric
0.1532	31.9	.2159	3	examiners
0.1532	31.9	.2159	3	Exodus
0.1532	31.9	.2159	3	extremists
0.1532	31.9	.2159	3	Fielding
0.1532	31.9	.2159	3	financially
0.1532	31.9	.2159	3	flair
0.1532	31.9	.2159	3	foregone
0.1532	31.9	.2159	3	Freudian
0.1532	31.9	.2159	3	guillotined
0.1532	31.9	.2159	3	immobility
0.1532	31.9	.2159	3	indicative
0.1532	31.9	.2159	3	inferred
0.1532	31.9	.2159	3	infinitesimal
0.1532	31.9	.2159	3	inherently
0.1532	31.9	.2159	3	latter-day
0.1532	31.9	.2159	3	mailings
0.1532	31.9	.2159	3	misconception
0.1532	31.9	.2159	3	nation-wide
0.1532	31.9	.2159	3	Origin
0.1532	31.9	.2159	3	parole
0.1532	31.9	.2159	3	picaresque
0.1532	31.9	.2159	3	pleurisy
0.1532	31.9	.2159	3	Presbyterian
0.1532	31.9	.2159	3	rearward
0.1532	31.9	.2159	3	resurgent
0.1532	31.9	.2159	3	Rubber
0.1532	31.9	.2159	3	saffron
0.1532	31.9	.2159	3	sempervirens
0.1532	31.9	.2159	3	Serbo-Croatian
0.1532	31.9	.2159	3	Soong
0.1532	31.9	.2159	3	Species
0.1532	31.9	.2159	3	subsist

U	SFI	D	F	Word Type
0.1532	31.9	.2159	3	vs
0.1532	31.9	.2159	3	wholesalers
0.1532	31.9	.2159	3	050
0.1532	31.9	.2159	3	4004
0.1529	31.8	.0760	5	accuse
0.1529	31.8	.2351	3	small-sized
0.1527	31.8	.2107	3	Fear
0.1524	31.8	.0000	13	Lark
0.1523	31.8	.0996	4	backside
0.1523	31.8	.0996	4	blatant

THE PRECEDING WORD TYPE OCCUPIES RANK 34300

U	SFI	D	F	Word Type
0.1523	31.8	.0996	4	ca
0.1523	31.8	.0996	4	Cadet
0.1523	31.8	.0996	4	censors
0.1523	31.8	.0996	4	Christmastime
0.1523	31.8	.0996	4	diagnosed
0.1523	31.8	.0996	4	Establishment
0.1523	31.8	.0996	4	excursions
0.1523	31.8	.0996	4	Fords
0.1523	31.8	.0996	4	foreword
0.1523	31.8	.0996	4	forum
0.1523	31.8	.0996	4	Gallup
0.1523	31.8	.0996	4	island's
0.1523	31.8	.0996	4	jetty
0.1523	31.8	.0996	4	Lilly
0.1523	31.8	.0996	4	lonelier
0.1523	31.8	.0996	4	Lopez
0.1523	31.8	.0996	4	petrels
0.1523	31.8	.0996	4	Philips
0.1523	31.8	.0996	4	puzzlement
0.1523	31.8	.0996	4	Rambler
0.1523	31.8	.0996	4	rationalized
0.1523	31.8	.0996	4	teen-aged
0.1523	31.8	.0996	4	transmissions
0.1523	31.8	.0996	4	Traverse
0.1523	31.8	.0996	4	vet
0.1522	31.8	.1613	4	mottled
0.1521	31.8	.1511	4	decem
0.1521	31.8	.1511	4	Set
0.1519	31.8	.1432	4	ascorbic
0.1519	31.8	.1432	4	interface
0.1519	31.8	.1432	4	Sheet
0.1514	31.8	.2249	3	iv
0.1514	31.8	.2249	3	li
0.1514	31.8	.0986	6	miter
0.1514	31.8	.2249	3	Prayer
0.1512	31.8	.2245	3	anoint
0.1511	31.8	.2074	3	classmate's
0.1511	31.8	.2074	3	dan
0.1511	31.8	.2074	3	familiarize
0.1511	31.8	.2074	3	Henley
0.1511	31.8	.2074	3	kirk
0.1511	31.8	.2074	3	purest
0.1506	31.8	.1144	3	clatters
0.1506	31.8	.1144	3	Wei
0.1505	31.8	.1980	3	cut-up
0.1505	31.8	.1980	3	open-end
0.1504	31.8	.0672	9	cottons
0.1504	31.8	.1970	3	curdle
0.1504	31.8	.1970	3	insertion
0.1504	31.8	.1970	3	kale
0.1504	31.8	.1970	3	overtired
0.1504	31.8	.1970	3	specifies
0.1504	31.8	.1970	3	tablespoonfuls
0.1504	31.8	.1970	3	thiamin
0.1502	31.8	.0000	14	Chumley
0.1502	31.8	.0000	14	Dudley
0.1502	31.8	.0000	14	OLD
0.1501	31.8	.1068	5	Gospel
0.1500	31.8	.2060	3	aloofness
0.1500	31.8	.2060	3	bludgeon
0.1500	31.8	.2060	3	Bruegel
0.1500	31.8	.2060	3	covered-wagon
0.1500	31.8	.2060	3	craned
0.1500	31.8	.2060	3	dabbling
0.1500	31.8	.2060	3	drubbing
0.1500	31.8	.2060	3	e'er
0.1500	31.8	.2060	3	entreating
0.1500	31.8	.2060	3	foal's
0.1500	31.8	.2060	3	grub's
0.1500	31.8	.2060	3	half-naked
0.1500	31.8	.2060	3	Hopalong
0.1500	31.8	.2060	3	lamentation
0.1500	31.8	.2060	3	Paxton
0.1500	31.8	.2060	3	smug
0.1500	31.8	.2060	3	spilt
0.1500	31.8	.2060	3	star-light
0.1500	31.8	.2060	3	stepper
0.1500	31.8	.2060	3	wind-blown
0.1500	31.8	.2060	3	workaday
0.1498	31.8	.1696	4	spooks
0.1497	31.8	.0000	10	algorithm
0.1497	31.8	.0000	10	BAC
0.1497	31.8	.0000	10	bisector
0.1497	31.8	.0000	10	C14
0.1497	31.8	.0000	10	factoring
0.1497	31.8	.0000	10	odometer
0.1497	31.8	.0000	10	triples
0.1497	31.8	.0000	10	O's
0.1497	31.8	.0000	10	4/6
0.1496	31.7	.2297	3	climaxes
0.1495	31.7	.1937	3	affluence
0.1495	31.7	.0974	4	agin
0.1495	31.7	.1937	3	alumni
0.1495	31.7	.0974	4	Andrew's
0.1495	31.7	.1937	3	animism
0.1495	31.7	.1937	3	Arizona's
0.1495	31.7	.1937	3	authoritative
0.1495	31.7	.1937	3	Batista
0.1495	31.7	.1937	3	birthrate
0.1495	31.7	.1937	3	Burma's

THE PRECEDING WORD TYPE OCCUPIES RANK 34400

U	SFI	D	F	Word Type
0.1495	31.7	.0974	4	Burn
0.1495	31.7	.1937	3	checkout
0.1495	31.7	.1937	3	citations
0.1495	31.7	.2227	3	clearness
0.1495	31.7	.2227	3	coal-tar

U	SFI	D	F	Word Type
0.1495	31.7	.1937	3	complacency
0.1495	31.7	.0974	4	Consul
0.1495	31.7	.1937	3	contractors
0.1495	31.7	.1937	3	Crowe
0.1495	31.7	.1937	3	Cultural
0.1495	31.7	.1937	3	Dayan
0.1495	31.7	.1937	3	decision-making
0.1495	31.7	.1937	3	deduct
0.1495	31.7	.1937	3	denunciations
0.1495	31.7	.1937	3	desegregation
0.1495	31.7	.1937	3	East-West
0.1495	31.7	.0974	4	Em
0.1495	31.7	.1937	3	Fu
0.1495	31.7	.0974	4	glisten
0.1495	31.7	.1937	3	Gouverneur
0.1495	31.7	.2227	3	gravure
0.1495	31.7	.0974	4	hesitatingly
0.1495	31.7	.1937	3	jurors
0.1495	31.7	.1937	3	L'Enfant
0.1495	31.7	.1937	3	leasing
0.1495	31.7	.1937	3	Liberian
0.1495	31.7	.2227	3	machine-tool
0.1495	31.7	.1937	3	majorities
0.1495	31.7	.1937	3	Mankind
0.1495	31.7	.1937	3	Marlon
0.1495	31.7	.1937	3	Md
0.1495	31.7	.0974	4	neigh
0.1495	31.7	.1937	3	Peggy's
0.1495	31.7	.0974	4	playin'
0.1495	31.7	.0974	4	pooh
0.1495	31.7	.1937	3	Popular
0.1495	31.7	.2227	3	reciprocating
0.1495	31.7	.1937	3	redemption
0.1495	31.7	.1937	3	SantaCruz
0.1495	31.7	.1937	3	scows
0.1495	31.7	.0974	4	severity
0.1495	31.7	.0974	4	Sisco
0.1495	31.7	.1937	3	sketchy
0.1495	31.7	.0974	4	sunshiny
0.1495	31.7	.1937	3	Thunderbird
0.1495	31.7	.1937	3	Tito
0.1495	31.7	.1937	3	unsupported
0.1495	31.7	.1937	3	voyaged
0.1495	31.7	.1937	3	11-year-old
0.1495	31.7	.1937	3	500-pound
0.1495	31.7	.1937	3	506
0.1493	31.7	.1434	3	aspirin
0.1493	31.7	.1434	3	Fay
0.1493	31.7	.1434	3	Fay's
0.1493	31.7	.1434	3	flatcar
0.1493	31.7	.1434	3	four-digit
0.1493	31.7	.1434	3	Janet's
0.1493	31.7	.1434	3	Karin
0.1493	31.7	.1434	3	Mathematical
0.1493	31.7	.1434	3	sixty-seven
0.1493	31.7	.1434	3	swordtails
0.1493	31.7	.1434	3	workbook
0.1493	31.7	.1434	3	XIII
0.1493	31.7	.1434	3	1957-1958
0.1493	31.7	.1434	3	464
0.1493	31.7	.1434	3	790
0.1493	31.7	.1434	3	918
0.1492	31.7	.0627	7	Tucker's
0.1491	31.7	.1927	3	addiction
0.1491	31.7	.1927	3	albeit
0.1491	31.7	.1927	3	collared
0.1491	31.7	.1927	3	deCristo
0.1491	31.7	.1927	3	denial
0.1491	31.7	.1927	3	Denison
0.1491	31.7	.1927	3	dispel
0.1491	31.7	.2037	3	Elbert
0.1491	31.7	.1927	3	facet
0.1491	31.7	.1927	3	freak
0.1491	31.7	.1927	3	free-form
0.1491	31.7	.1927	3	Harcourt
0.1491	31.7	.1927	3	Indo-Pacific
0.1491	31.7	.1927	3	low-calorie
0.1491	31.7	.2037	3	Meridian
0.1491	31.7	.1927	3	moonship
0.1491	31.7	.1927	3	procaine
0.1491	31.7	.1927	3	readjusting
0.1491	31.7	.1927	3	Sangre
0.1491	31.7	.2037	3	signpost
0.1491	31.7	.1927	3	slimmer
0.1491	31.7	.1927	3	spectrograph
0.1491	31.7	.1927	3	squint
0.1491	31.7	.1927	3	Studies
0.1491	31.7	.1927	3	Walsh
0.1486	31.7	.2043	3	abodes
0.1486	31.7	.2043	3	absolutist
0.1486	31.7	.2043	3	Aurelius
0.1486	31.7	.2043	3	basketry
0.1486	31.7	.2043	3	Bowling
0.1486	31.7	.2043	3	Brest
0.1486	31.7	.2043	3	Conciliation

THE PRECEDING WORD TYPE OCCUPIES RANK 34500

U	SFI	D	F	Word Type
0.1486	31.7	.2043	3	convoying
0.1486	31.7	.2043	3	Councils
0.1486	31.7	.2043	3	democracies
0.1486	31.7	.2043	3	Deuteronomy
0.1486	31.7	.2043	3	Disciples
0.1486	31.7	.2043	3	dominance
0.1486	31.7	.2043	3	ethnological
0.1486	31.7	.2043	3	Fascism
0.1486	31.7	.2043	3	forewings
0.1486	31.7	.2043	3	gneiss
0.1486	31.7	.2043	3	hardiest
0.1486	31.7	.2043	3	Housing
0.1486	31.7	.2043	3	inhibition
0.1486	31.7	.2043	3	institutes
0.1486	31.7	.2043	3	loftiest
0.1486	31.7	.2043	3	Machiavelli's
0.1486	31.7	.2043	3	Monarch
0.1486	31.7	.2043	3	mummies
0.1486	31.7	.2043	3	premieres
0.1486	31.7	.2043	3	Printing
0.1486	31.7	.2043	3	rehabilitation

U	SFI	D	F	Word Type
0.1486	31.7	.2043	3	reputable
0.1486	31.7	.2043	3	students'
0.1486	31.7	.2043	3	supporter
0.1486	31.7	.2043	3	Triomphe
0.1486	31.7	.2043	3	Vicksburg
0.1486	31.7	.2043	3	viscera
0.1486	31.7	.2043	3	1511
0.1483	31.7	.1605	4	exclamatory
0.1481	31.7	.1179	5	surfacing
0.1481	31.7	.2400	3	well-groomed
0.1479	31.7	.1548	3	Rainbow
0.1479	31.7	.1548	3	unassuming
0.1479	31.7	.1548	3	wrestlers
0.1477	31.7	.2019	3	Berne
0.1477	31.7	.2019	3	loci
0.1477	31.7	.2019	3	verification
0.1477	31.7	.2019	3	012
0.1477	31.7	.2019	3	528
0.1477	31.7	.2019	3	581
0.1477	31.7	.2019	3	768
0.1476	31.7	.1539	3	roly-poly
0.1473	31.7	.1910	3	bondage
0.1473	31.7	.1910	3	Copeland
0.1473	31.7	.1910	3	Draco
0.1473	31.7	.1910	3	driveways
0.1473	31.7	.1174	5	Growth
0.1473	31.7	.1910	3	noblemen's
0.1473	31.7	.1910	3	Pounds
0.1473	31.7	.1910	3	prided
0.1473	31.7	.1910	3	smoldered
0.1473	31.7	.1910	3	vainglorious
0.1473	31.7	.1910	3	vestments
0.1472	31.7	.1409	3	BIT
0.1472	31.7	.1409	3	blared
0.1472	31.7	.1409	3	Boreas
0.1472	31.7	.1409	3	brickmaker
0.1472	31.7	.1409	3	Brookville
0.1472	31.7	.1409	3	Buena
0.1472	31.7	.1409	3	Chamberlain's
0.1472	31.7	.1409	3	cockatoos
0.1472	31.7	.1409	3	Cooperstown
0.1472	31.7	.1409	3	Cyrus's
0.1472	31.7	.1409	3	downpour
0.1472	31.7	.1409	3	elephants'
0.1472	31.7	.1409	3	Folger's
0.1472	31.7	.1409	3	formalin
0.1472	31.7	.1409	3	gunfire
0.1472	31.7	.1409	3	half-wild
0.1472	31.7	.1409	3	hiya
0.1472	31.7	.1409	3	homers
0.1472	31.7	.1409	3	Howells
0.1472	31.7	.1409	3	hummingbird's
0.1472	31.7	.1409	3	hundred-pound
0.1472	31.7	.1409	3	Ki
0.1472	31.7	.1409	3	lethargy
0.1472	31.7	.1409	3	Luna
0.1472	31.7	.1409	3	mantelshelf
0.1472	31.7	.1409	3	McCann
0.1472	31.7	.1409	3	Miep
0.1472	31.7	.1409	3	nicknames
0.1472	31.7	.1409	3	reload
0.1472	31.7	.1409	3	safaris
0.1472	31.7	.1409	3	sliver
0.1472	31.7	.1409	3	Spoon
0.1472	31.7	.1409	3	Sportsman's
0.1472	31.7	.1409	3	Summer's
0.1472	31.7	.1409	3	taxiing
0.1472	31.7	.1409	3	Thomas'
0.1472	31.7	.1409	3	undershirt
0.1471	31.7	.1934	3	trickles
0.1470	31.7	.2136	3	caliper
0.1470	31.7	.1900	3	fevered
0.1470	31.7	.1900	3	fifth-grade
0.1470	31.7	.1900	3	Steamship
0.1470	31.7	.2136	3	stonework
0.1470	31.7	.1900	3	undoubted
0.1467	31.7	.1156	5	471
0.1464	31.7	.0725	4	tempered
0.1461	31.6	.1060	3	disconsolate

THE PRECEDING WORD TYPE OCCUPIES RANK 34600

U	SFI	D	F	Word Type
0.1461	31.6	.1060	3	Fisherman's
0.1461	31.6	.1060	3	golfing
0.1461	31.6	.1060	3	husking
0.1461	31.6	.1060	3	Little's
0.1461	31.6	.1060	3	obliging
0.1461	31.6	.1060	3	smashes
0.1461	31.6	.1060	3	storm-swept
0.1461	31.6	.1060	3	well-mannered
0.1461	31.6	.1060	3	wildfire
0.1459	31.6	.2359	3	eyelets
0.1459	31.6	.2359	3	Facing
0.1459	31.6	.2359	3	sieved
0.1458	31.6	.2383	3	lampblack
0.1458	31.6	.0000	12	UAR
0.1455	31.6	.1551	4	aversion
0.1455	31.6	.0000	18	fugue
0.1455	31.6	.0176	18	Savior
0.1455	31.6	.1483	4	trimmer
0.1451	31.6	.2153	3	electricity's
0.1451	31.6	.2153	3	Grammar
0.1451	31.6	.2153	3	impair
0.1448	31.6	.0000	10	furring
0.1448	31.6	.0000	10	Goode
0.1448	31.6	.0000	10	Maori
0.1448	31.6	.0000	10	Psyche
0.1448	31.6	.0000	10	Stengel
0.1448	31.6	.0000	10	Tuan
0.1446	31.6	.2137	3	Bancroft
0.1446	31.6	.2137	3	smite
0.1444	31.6	.0931	4	authors'
0.1444	31.6	.2091	3	bobwhite
0.1444	31.6	.0931	4	Doc's
0.1444	31.6	.0931	4	Ingrid
0.1444	31.6	.0931	4	legibly
0.1444	31.6	.0931	4	Monday's
0.1444	31.6	.1457	4	3-1
0.1444	31.6	.1457	4	8-2

U	SFI	D	F	Word Type
0.1442	31.6	.2088	3	breathy
0.1442	31.6	.2088	3	burlesque
0.1442	31.6	.2088	3	carillon
0.1442	31.6	.2088	3	Chanson
0.1442	31.6	.2088	3	Claudio
0.1442	31.6	.2124	3	concise
0.1442	31.6	.2088	3	descendent
0.1442	31.6	.2088	3	dissonances
0.1442	31.6	.2088	3	Grieg's
0.1442	31.6	.2088	3	harpsichords
0.1442	31.6	.2088	3	heritages
0.1442	31.6	.2088	3	ionization
0.1442	31.6	.2088	3	Orfeo
0.1442	31.6	.2088	3	oscillograph
0.1442	31.6	.2088	3	Palestrina
0.1442	31.6	.2124	3	parenthetical
0.1442	31.6	.2088	3	preludes
0.1442	31.6	.2088	3	rhythmical
0.1442	31.6	.2088	3	Romanticism
0.1442	31.6	.2124	3	trebles
0.1442	31.6	.2124	3	wordy
0.1442	31.6	.2088	3	1567-1643
0.1442	31.6	.2088	3	1710
0.1436	31.6	.2074	3	countess
0.1436	31.6	.0526	6	Forever
0.1436	31.6	.0526	6	half-time
0.1436	31.6	.0526	6	musically
0.1436	31.6	.0526	6	While
0.1435	31.6	.2196	3	accentuate
0.1435	31.6	.1993	3	ASA
0.1435	31.6	.2196	3	compositional
0.1435	31.6	.1993	3	Triangle
0.1435	31.6	.1993	3	11/16
0.1435	31.6	.1993	3	284
0.1435	31.6	.1993	3	739
0.1434	31.6	.2071	3	Acadian
0.1434	31.6	.2071	3	climactic
0.1434	31.6	.2071	3	e'en
0.1434	31.6	.2071	3	Jehovah
0.1434	31.6	.2071	3	jingo
0.1434	31.6	.2071	3	obliquely
0.1434	31.6	.2071	3	shins
0.1434	31.6	.2071	3	Sourwood
0.1434	31.6	.2071	3	sows
0.1434	31.6	.2071	3	Virginny
0.1432	31.6	.1858	3	bitumen
0.1432	31.6	.1858	3	briefcase
0.1432	31.6	.1858	3	classmates'
0.1432	31.6	.1858	3	Crispin
0.1432	31.6	.1858	3	Etiquette
0.1432	31.6	.1858	3	NewYorker
0.1432	31.6	.1858	3	Poetry
0.1432	31.6	.1858	3	solitudes
0.1432	31.6	.1858	3	transient
0.1432	31.6	.1858	3	191
0.1432	31.6	.1858	3	293
0.1430	31.6	.2060	3	-ist
0.1430	31.6	.2060	3	/m/
0.1430	31.6	.2060	3	/oo/
0.1430	31.6	.0919	4	ach
0.1430	31.6	.2060	3	ante
0.1430	31.6	.0919	4	batsman
0.1430	31.6	.0919	4	Bear's

THE PRECEDING WORD TYPE OCCUPIES RANK 34700

U	SFI	D	F	Word Type
0.1430	31.6	.2060	3	cw
0.1430	31.6	.2060	3	hale
0.1430	31.6	.0919	4	J**
0.1430	31.6	.2060	3	lk
0.1430	31.6	.2060	3	noun-verb
0.1430	31.6	.2060	3	pluralize
0.1430	31.6	.0919	4	potbellied
0.1430	31.6	.2060	3	proofreader
0.1430	31.6	.2060	3	Proofreading
0.1430	31.6	.0919	4	talisman
0.1430	31.6	.0919	4	teamster
0.1430	31.6	.2060	3	two-dot
0.1430	31.6	.0687	7	1/32
0.1429	31.5	.2058	3	Baal
0.1429	31.5	.2058	3	ev'rybody
0.1429	31.5	.2078	3	Kathryn
0.1429	31.5	.2078	3	suffocated
0.1429	31.5	.2058	3	tom-tom
0.1429	31.5	.2058	3	twilight's
0.1429	31.5	.2078	3	unaccountable
0.1429	31.5	.2058	3	violinists
0.1429	31.5	.2058	3	Waiting
0.1429	31.5	.2078	3	weaned
0.1428	31.5	.1847	3	devotes
0.1428	31.5	.1847	3	larkspur
0.1428	31.5	.1847	3	magnify
0.1423	31.5	.0996	5	hallowed
0.1423	31.5	.0000	13	juncture
0.1423	31.5	.0000	13	VCe
0.1423	31.5	.0000	13	Venutian
0.1422	31.5	.2054	3	Bentley
0.1422	31.5	.2054	3	chagrined
0.1422	31.5	.2054	3	Land's
0.1422	31.5	.2054	3	outspoken
0.1422	31.5	.2054	3	peerless
0.1422	31.5	.2054	3	round-the-clock
0.1422	31.5	.2054	3	show's
0.1422	31.5	.2054	3	sociologists
0.1422	31.5	.2054	3	water-skiing
0.1420	31.5	.1843	3	Langston
0.1420	31.5	.1843	3	Toba
0.1417	31.5	.1832	3	ascents
0.1417	31.5	.1832	3	beehives
0.1417	31.5	.1832	3	burghers
0.1417	31.5	.1832	3	Cepheus
0.1417	31.5	.1832	3	heals
0.1417	31.5	.1832	3	inquires
0.1417	31.5	.1832	3	spectral
0.1417	31.5	.0665	4	teddy
0.1417	31.5	.1832	3	thoroughfares
0.1417	31.5	.1832	3	uncomprehending
0.1417	31.5	.0665	4	weedy
0.1417	31.5	.1832	3	well-built

U	SFI	D	F	Word Type
0.1412	31.5	.0904	4	apelike
0.1412	31.5	.0904	4	archeologist
0.1412	31.5	.0904	4	cadaver
0.1412	31.5	.0904	4	cicada
0.1412	31.5	.0904	4	electrochemical
0.1412	31.5	.0904	4	iron-bearing
0.1412	31.5	.0904	4	Miner
0.1412	31.5	.0904	4	proliferation
0.1412	31.5	.0904	4	pronghorn
0.1412	31.5	.0904	4	rattlers
0.1412	31.5	.0904	4	rubidium
0.1412	31.5	.0904	4	1625
0.1410	31.5	.1310	4	Meaning
0.1409	31.5	.1032	5	creator
0.1409	31.5	.2012	3	miser
0.1407	31.5	.0000	12	Aouda
0.1407	31.5	.0000	12	Binney
0.1407	31.5	.2009	3	bitty
0.1407	31.5	.2009	3	Burk
0.1407	31.5	.2009	3	clunk
0.1407	31.5	.1307	4	grandiose
0.1407	31.5	.0000	12	Mally
0.1407	31.5	.0000	12	Merrylegs
0.1407	31.5	.0000	12	Misty
0.1407	31.5	.2009	3	schottische
0.1407	31.5	.0000	12	Shora
0.1407	31.5	.0000	12	Teunis
0.1405	31.5	.1823	3	besieging
0.1405	31.5	.1823	3	Bravo
0.1405	31.5	.1823	3	bungalows
0.1405	31.5	.1823	3	charters
0.1405	31.5	.1823	3	Ciudad
0.1405	31.5	.1823	3	colonizing
0.1405	31.5	.1823	3	cults
0.1405	31.5	.1823	3	Defoe
0.1405	31.5	.1823	3	delFuego
0.1405	31.5	.1823	3	flightless
0.1405	31.5	.1823	3	garrisons
0.1405	31.5	.1823	3	imprecise
0.1405	31.5	.1823	3	intensifying
0.1405	31.5	.1823	3	Kannon
0.1405	31.5	.1823	3	lateen
0.1405	31.5	.1823	3	Loire
0.1405	31.5	.1823	3	Malawi
0.1405	31.5	.1823	3	Manassas
0.1405	31.5	.1823	3	millers
0.1405	31.5	.1823	3	Negritos

THE PRECEDING WORD TYPE OCCUPIES RANK 34800

U	SFI	D	F	Word Type
0.1405	31.5	.1823	3	nonwhite
0.1405	31.5	.1823	3	overpopulation
0.1405	31.5	.1823	3	Republics
0.1405	31.5	.1823	3	senate
0.1405	31.5	.1823	3	sewerage
0.1405	31.5	.1823	3	south-central
0.1405	31.5	.1823	3	stoneware
0.1405	31.5	.1823	3	taxing
0.1405	31.5	.1823	3	Tenure
0.1405	31.5	.1823	3	Tyrrhenian
0.1405	31.5	.1823	3	Wellesley
0.1405	31.5	.1823	3	1230
0.1405	31.5	.1823	3	1400's
0.1405	31.5	.1823	3	1521
0.1405	31.5	.1823	3	1565
0.1405	31.5	.1823	3	1738
0.1405	31.5	.1823	3	809
0.1402	31.5	.1813	3	aeronautical
0.1402	31.5	.1813	3	Buffon
0.1402	31.5	.1813	3	conifer
0.1402	31.5	.1813	3	corrosive
0.1402	31.5	.1813	3	cosmology
0.1402	31.5	.1813	3	Erasmus
0.1402	31.5	.1813	3	evolving
0.1402	31.5	.1813	3	food-getting
0.1402	31.5	.1813	3	fraternal
0.1402	31.5	.1813	3	gabbro
0.1402	31.5	.1813	3	ganglia
0.1402	31.5	.1813	3	herbivore
0.1402	31.5	.1813	3	Hermann
0.1402	31.5	.1813	3	incubator
0.1402	31.5	.1813	3	ken
0.1402	31.5	.1813	3	Magnete
0.1402	31.5	.1813	3	midline
0.1402	31.5	.1813	3	nematodes
0.1402	31.5	.1813	3	nitrous
0.1402	31.5	.1813	3	nonconformists
0.1402	31.5	.1813	3	omnivores
0.1402	31.5	.1813	3	overhunting
0.1402	31.5	.1813	3	physiologist
0.1402	31.5	.1813	3	plagioclase
0.1402	31.5	.1813	3	pleura
0.1402	31.5	.1813	3	posterior
0.1402	31.5	.1813	3	reshaping
0.1402	31.5	.1813	3	thorium
0.1402	31.5	.1813	3	titanic
0.1402	31.5	.1813	3	tracheae
0.1402	31.5	.1813	3	trilobite
0.1402	31.5	.1813	3	uncounted
0.1402	31.5	.1813	3	unicellular
0.1402	31.5	.1813	3	variability
0.1402	31.5	.1813	3	vertebral
0.1402	31.5	.1813	3	wingless
0.1402	31.5	.1813	3	zygotes
0.1402	31.5	.0803	6	10-3
0.1402	31.5	.1813	3	1582
0.1398	31.5	.0939	3	Aspen
0.1398	31.5	.1986	3	bonuses
0.1398	31.5	.1986	3	filled-in
0.1398	31.5	.0939	3	Jungle
0.1398	31.5	.0939	3	knotholes
0.1398	31.5	.0939	3	lotus
0.1398	31.5	.1796	3	many-sided
0.1398	31.5	.0939	3	sequins
0.1398	31.5	.1796	3	straddles
0.1398	31.5	.0939	3	what-is-it
0.1398	31.5	.0939	3	Woodpecker
0.1397	31.5	.1785	3	abrasion
0.1397	31.5	.1785	3	four-stroke
0.1397	31.5	.1785	3	liquefy
0.1397	31.5	.1785	3	oxidize
0.1397	31.5	.1785	3	S2
0.1397	31.5	.1785	3	6-1
0.1397	31.5	.1785	3	60-degree
0.1396	31.4	.1983	3	compensator
0.1396	31.4	.1983	3	Farewell
0.1396	31.4	.1983	3	If
0.1396	31.4	.1983	3	jamming
0.1396	31.4	.1983	3	journey's
0.1396	31.4	.1983	3	jubilee
0.1396	31.4	.1983	3	kindle
0.1396	31.4	.1983	3	labelled
0.1396	31.4	.1983	3	Medes
0.1396	31.4	.1983	3	Player
0.1396	31.4	.1983	3	prayerful
0.1396	31.4	.1983	3	reedy
0.1396	31.4	.1983	3	rejoices
0.1396	31.4	.1983	3	revue
0.1396	31.4	.1983	3	Shall
0.1396	31.4	.1983	3	Singers
0.1396	31.4	.1983	3	stylistic
0.1396	31.4	.1983	3	tah
0.1396	31.4	.1983	3	totes
0.1396	31.4	.1983	3	Weill
0.1395	31.4	.0000	13	AUGUST
0.1395	31.4	.0000	13	Calpurnia
0.1395	31.4	.0000	13	FABRY
0.1395	31.4	.0000	13	Nico
0.1392	31.4	.0168	22	rivet
0.1388	31.4	.1927	3	justification

THE PRECEDING WORD TYPE OCCUPIES RANK 34900

U	SFI	D	F	Word Type
0.1385	31.4	.0971	4	legged
0.1383	31.4	.1493	4	Barbizon
0.1383	31.4	.1493	4	Corot
0.1383	31.4	.1493	4	idealized
0.1383	31.4	.1493	4	Rembrandt's
0.1381	31.4	.0821	7	Dacron
0.1380	31.4	.0000	7	ADP
0.1380	31.4	.0000	7	ant's
0.1380	31.4	.0000	7	axon
0.1380	31.4	.0000	7	Bead
0.1380	31.4	.0000	7	Brahe
0.1380	31.4	.0000	7	cm3
0.1380	31.4	.0000	7	corolla
0.1380	31.4	.0000	7	dendrites
0.1380	31.4	.0000	7	dentin
0.1380	31.4	.0000	7	dupp
0.1380	31.4	.0000	7	Felis
0.1380	31.4	.0000	7	flatworms
0.1380	31.4	.0000	7	low-power
0.1380	31.4	.0000	7	lubb
0.1380	31.4	.0000	7	lymph
0.1380	31.4	.0000	7	maltose
0.1380	31.4	.0000	7	Mendel
0.1380	31.4	.0000	7	negatively-charged
0.1380	31.4	.0000	7	Neurospora
0.1380	31.4	.0000	7	overlying
0.1380	31.4	.0000	7	plant-animal
0.1380	31.4	.0000	7	Ptolemaic
0.1380	31.4	.0000	7	Ptolemy
0.1380	31.4	.0000	7	Roux
0.1380	31.4	.0000	7	Sabin
0.1380	31.4	.0000	7	streptococcal
0.1380	31.4	.0000	7	upwelling
0.1380	31.4	.0000	7	uranium-235
0.1380	31.4	.0000	7	vacuoles
0.1376	31.4	.2027	3	Boucher
0.1376	31.4	.2027	3	Cubism
0.1376	31.4	.2027	3	glaze
0.1376	31.4	.2027	3	imperceptibly
0.1376	31.4	.2027	3	Piet
0.1374	31.4	.0000	17	coda
0.1374	31.4	.0000	17	Mozart's
0.1374	31.4	.0000	17	spirituals
0.1371	31.4	.2009	3	Cock
0.1371	31.4	.1249	4	deformation
0.1371	31.4	.1249	4	insoluble
0.1371	31.4	.1249	4	6-3
0.1370	31.4	.0000	3	Aboard
0.1370	31.4	.0000	3	Abou
0.1370	31.4	.0000	3	ABOUT
0.1370	31.4	.0000	3	AC'S**
0.1370	31.4	.0000	3	Aeetes
0.1370	31.4	.0000	3	aeroplane
0.1370	31.4	.0000	3	Agatha
0.1370	31.4	.0000	3	Ah-yo-keh
0.1370	31.4	.0000	3	Alemite
0.1370	31.4	.0000	3	Altdorf
0.1370	31.4	.0000	3	Ambato
0.1370	31.4	.0000	3	Amed's
0.1370	31.4	.0000	3	ami
0.1370	31.4	.0000	3	angakoks
0.1370	31.4	.0000	3	Anteater
0.1370	31.4	.0000	3	Antinous
0.1370	31.4	.0000	3	aren'
0.1370	31.4	.0000	3	Arlee
0.1370	31.4	.0000	3	Armadillo
0.1370	31.4	.0000	3	Arrowhead
0.1370	31.4	.0000	3	Auenbrugger
0.1370	31.4	.0000	3	av
0.1370	31.4	.0000	3	ax-handles
0.1370	31.4	.0000	3	axhead
0.1370	31.4	.0000	3	Babi
0.1370	31.4	.0000	3	Bagasset
0.1370	31.4	.0000	3	Bagby
0.1370	31.4	.0000	3	Bakerville
0.1370	31.4	.0000	3	Bard
0.1370	31.4	.0000	3	Bayard
0.1370	31.4	.0000	3	beastly
0.1370	31.4	.0000	3	Bebrycians
0.1370	31.4	.0000	3	bee-sting
0.1370	31.4	.0000	3	Bert's
0.1370	31.4	.0000	3	best-looking
0.1370	31.4	.0000	3	Bey
0.1370	31.4	.0000	3	Biddie's
0.1370	31.4	.0000	3	Biddlewee
0.1370	31.4	.0000	3	bitterroot
0.1370	31.4	.0000	3	black-and-blue
0.1370	31.4	.0000	3	blotted
0.1370	31.4	.0000	3	boardwalk
0.1370	31.4	.0000	3	boat-in-the-bottle
0.1370	31.4	.0000	3	Bogus
0.1370	31.4	.0000	3	Borre
0.1370	31.4	.0000	3	bowl-like
0.1370	31.4	.0000	3	boxers
0.1370	31.4	.0000	3	Brad
0.1370	31.4	.0000	3	Bradford's
0.1370	31.4	.0000	3	brazenly
0.1370	31.4	.0000	3	breastplate
0.1370	31.4	.0000	3	Bredo
0.1370	31.4	.0000	3	Bredo's

THE PRECEDING WORD TYPE OCCUPIES RANK 35000

U	SFI	D	F	Word Type
0.1370	31.4	.0000	3	Buckle
0.1370	31.4	.0000	3	bulldogger
0.1370	31.4	.0000	3	bulldogs
0.1370	31.4	.0000	3	Bumblebee
0.1370	31.4	.0000	3	Burgess
0.1370	31.4	.0000	3	bushman
0.1370	31.4	.0000	3	bushmen
0.1370	31.4	.0000	3	Bushy
0.1370	31.4	.0000	3	Cantello
0.1370	31.4	.0000	3	CANTELLOS
0.1370	31.4	.0000	3	Caps
0.1370	31.4	.0000	3	Captains
0.1370	31.4	.0000	3	Carvers
0.1370	31.4	.0000	3	Celebration
0.1370	31.4	.0000	3	Chad's
0.1370	31.4	.0000	3	Chalciope
0.1370	31.4	.0000	3	chalking
0.1370	31.4	.0000	3	Chapman
0.1370	31.4	.0000	3	Charcoal
0.1370	31.4	.0000	3	Chinwa
0.1370	31.4	.0000	3	Chippy's
0.1370	31.4	.0000	3	Chira
0.1370	31.4	.0000	3	choosy
0.1370	31.4	.0000	3	christening
0.1370	31.4	.0000	3	Citadel
0.1370	31.4	.0000	3	Clay's
0.1370	31.4	.0000	3	Clutterbuck
0.1370	31.4	.0000	3	coatis
0.1370	31.4	.0000	3	Colchis
0.1370	31.4	.0000	3	colones
0.1370	31.4	.0000	3	Companion
0.1370	31.4	.0000	3	Connor
0.1370	31.4	.0000	3	coppery
0.1370	31.4	.0000	3	Cornelia
0.1370	31.4	.0000	3	Cottage
0.1370	31.4	.0000	3	cougar's
0.1370	31.4	.0000	3	cowbirds
0.1370	31.4	.0000	3	CQ
0.1370	31.4	.0000	3	Craigheads
0.1370	31.4	.0000	3	Cuffe
0.1370	31.4	.0000	3	Czarina
0.1370	31.4	.0000	3	Dacotah
0.1370	31.4	.0000	3	Dairymaid
0.1370	31.4	.0000	3	damsel
0.1370	31.4	.0000	3	Dan'l
0.1370	31.4	.0000	3	day-nursery
0.1370	31.4	.0000	3	Dead-Come-Back-Man
0.1370	31.4	.0000	3	derail
0.1370	31.4	.0000	3	dhoti
0.1370	31.4	.0000	3	Diana-Kate
0.1370	31.4	.0000	3	Dillinger's
0.1370	31.4	.0000	3	disgustedly
0.1370	31.4	.0000	3	dishwater
0.1370	31.4	.0000	3	Dobie
0.1370	31.4	.0000	3	Dolls
0.1370	31.4	.0000	3	Dolls'
0.1370	31.4	.0000	3	doorbells
0.1370	31.4	.0000	3	Dormouse
0.1370	31.4	.0000	3	dressed-up
0.1370	31.4	.0000	3	drumsticks
0.1370	31.4	.0000	3	Duddy
0.1370	31.4	.0000	3	dusters
0.1370	31.4	.0000	3	eaglet
0.1370	31.4	.0000	3	earmark
0.1370	31.4	.0000	3	Earth-born
0.1370	31.4	.0000	3	Effendi
0.1370	31.4	.0000	3	Elkton
0.1370	31.4	.0000	3	ema
0.1370	31.4	.0000	3	Ephialtes
0.1370	31.4	.0000	3	Eris
0.1370	31.4	.0000	3	Eurymachus
0.1370	31.4	.0000	3	eutectic
0.1370	31.4	.0000	3	eyedropper
0.1370	31.4	.0000	3	Fast's
0.1370	31.4	.0000	3	father'll
0.1370	31.4	.0000	3	Fats'
0.1370	31.4	.0000	3	feather-planting
0.1370	31.4	.0000	3	Fertilizer
0.1370	31.4	.0000	3	fire-god
0.1370	31.4	.0000	3	flapjacks
0.1370	31.4	.0000	3	fomites
0.1370	31.4	.0000	3	Footman
0.1370	31.4	.0000	3	Foulis
0.1370	31.4	.0000	3	frogman's
0.1370	31.4	.0000	3	Fuddy
0.1370	31.4	.0000	3	ga-lumping
0.1370	31.4	.0000	3	Gadja
0.1370	31.4	.0000	3	Gardener
0.1370	31.4	.0000	3	Garnerin
0.1370	31.4	.0000	3	Gates's
0.1370	31.4	.0000	3	GEM
0.1370	31.4	.0000	3	Germain-en-Laye
0.1370	31.4	.0000	3	Gian-Carlo
0.1370	31.4	.0000	3	Gloria's
0.1370	31.4	.0000	3	glyphs
0.1370	31.4	.0000	3	Graff
0.1370	31.4	.0000	3	Grantville
0.1370	31.4	.0000	3	grappled
0.1370	31.4	.0000	3	greasewood
0.1370	31.4	.0000	3	GREAT

THE PRECEDING WORD TYPE OCCUPIES RANK 35100

U	SFI	D	F	Word Type
0.1370	31.4	.0000	3	great-uncle
0.1370	31.4	.0000	3	Gruff
0.1370	31.4	.0000	3	Guard's
0.1370	31.4	.0000	3	Guinevere
0.1370	31.4	.0000	3	gunman
0.1370	31.4	.0000	3	Gurt
0.1370	31.4	.0000	3	Hairy
0.1370	31.4	.0000	3	Halliday
0.1370	31.4	.0000	3	hallo
0.1370	31.4	.0000	3	Halloweening
0.1370	31.4	.0000	3	Halmoni
0.1370	31.4	.0000	3	Hand's
0.1370	31.4	.0000	3	harp-strings
0.1370	31.4	.0000	3	Has-ka's
0.1370	31.4	.0000	3	Hattie's
0.1370	31.4	.0000	3	haystacks
0.1370	31.4	.0000	3	he'
0.1370	31.4	.0000	3	Herault
0.1370	31.4	.0000	3	high-councillor
0.1370	31.4	.0000	3	Hilltop
0.1370	31.4	.0000	3	hist
0.1370	31.4	.0000	3	Hook's
0.1370	31.4	.0000	3	Hop
0.1370	31.4	.0000	3	Horace's
0.1370	31.4	.0000	3	horsefly
0.1370	31.4	.0000	3	houn'
0.1370	31.4	.0000	3	Hualachi's
0.1370	31.4	.0000	3	Hump
0.1370	31.4	.0000	3	idiocy
0.1370	31.4	.0000	3	Immortals
0.1370	31.4	.0000	3	infielders
0.1370	31.4	.0000	3	infirmities
0.1370	31.4	.0000	3	Iphias
0.1370	31.4	.0000	3	Irby's
0.1370	31.4	.0000	3	Iva
0.1370	31.4	.0000	3	Ivald
0.1370	31.4	.0000	3	Ivan's
0.1370	31.4	.0000	3	Izak
0.1370	31.4	.0000	3	Jacaranda
0.1370	31.4	.0000	3	Jeanette's
0.1370	31.4	.0000	3	jedges
0.1370	31.4	.0000	3	Jernegan's
0.1370	31.4	.0000	3	Jinny's
0.1370	31.4	.0000	3	Jorinda
0.1370	31.4	.0000	3	jumbo
0.1370	31.4	.0000	3	Junction
0.1370	31.4	.0000	3	Kanana
0.1370	31.4	.0000	3	Kasim
0.1370	31.4	.0000	3	Kearns
0.1370	31.4	.0000	3	keastentroom
0.1370	31.4	.0000	3	Kentuck
0.1370	31.4	.0000	3	Keukenhof
0.1370	31.4	.0000	3	Khaled
0.1370	31.4	.0000	3	kitchen-girl
0.1370	31.4	.0000	3	knobbly
0.1370	31.4	.0000	3	Knockmany
0.1370	31.4	.0000	3	kraal
0.1370	31.4	.0000	3	Krishna's
0.1370	31.4	.0000	3	Krispy-Krackles
0.1370	31.4	.0000	3	Krumm
0.1370	31.4	.0000	3	ladyfingers
0.1370	31.4	.0000	3	Lasky
0.1370	31.4	.0000	3	lassie
0.1370	31.4	.0000	3	Legs
0.1370	31.4	.0000	3	Lidya
0.1370	31.4	.0000	3	loadstone
0.1370	31.4	.0000	3	Lonz
0.1370	31.4	.0000	3	lorikeet
0.1370	31.4	.0000	3	Louise's
0.1370	31.4	.0000	3	Maarman
0.1370	31.4	.0000	3	magician's
0.1370	31.4	.0000	3	Magpie
0.1370	31.4	.0000	3	Malory's
0.1370	31.4	.0000	3	man-carrying
0.1370	31.4	.0000	3	man-of-all-men
0.1370	31.4	.0000	3	Maned
0.1370	31.4	.0000	3	Marco's
0.1370	31.4	.0000	3	Mario's
0.1370	31.4	.0000	3	marionette
0.1370	31.4	.0000	3	Markovna
0.1370	31.4	.0000	3	Marvello's
0.1370	31.4	.0000	3	mateys
0.1370	31.4	.0000	3	Mathew
0.1370	31.4	.0000	3	Matoaka
0.1370	31.4	.0000	3	McLeods
0.1370	31.4	.0000	3	McPhale
0.1370	31.4	.0000	3	Meares
0.1370	31.4	.0000	3	Meeker
0.1370	31.4	.0000	3	Meeling
0.1370	31.4	.0000	3	messmates
0.1370	31.4	.0000	3	metallurgist
0.1370	31.4	.0000	3	metate
0.1370	31.4	.0000	3	Metro
0.1370	31.4	.0000	3	mid-November
0.1370	31.4	.0000	3	Midge's
0.1370	31.4	.0000	3	midstream
0.1370	31.4	.0000	3	Mihailovna
0.1370	31.4	.0000	3	milker
0.1370	31.4	.0000	3	Milo's
0.1370	31.4	.0000	3	Minnow's

THE PRECEDING WORD TYPE OCCUPIES RANK 35200

U	SFI	D	F	Word Type
0.1370	31.4	.0000	3	Minny
0.1370	31.4	.0000	3	Mittens
0.1370	31.4	.0000	3	monkeyshines
0.1370	31.4	.0000	3	mountain-ash
0.1370	31.4	.0000	3	muleback
0.1370	31.4	.0000	3	Naquin
0.1370	31.4	.0000	3	Natua's
0.1370	31.4	.0000	3	Nenana
0.1370	31.4	.0000	3	night-lights
0.1370	31.4	.0000	3	Nole's
0.1370	31.4	.0000	3	Norah
0.1370	31.4	.0000	3	Nordal
0.1370	31.4	.0000	3	Nutmeg
0.1370	31.4	.0000	3	O'Malley's
0.1370	31.4	.0000	3	obi
0.1370	31.4	.0000	3	Obie

U	SFI	D	F	Word Type
0.1370	31.4	.0000	3	Odysseus's
0.1370	31.4	.0000	3	off-off-off
0.1370	31.4	.0000	3	oh-h-h
0.1370	31.4	.0000	3	ook-ook
0.1370	31.4	.0000	3	Orlick
0.1370	31.4	.0000	3	ovenbird
0.1370	31.4	.0000	3	Paddle
0.1370	31.4	.0000	3	pah
0.1370	31.4	.0000	3	paintbox
0.1370	31.4	.0000	3	Palladium
0.1370	31.4	.0000	3	Papapoulos
0.1370	31.4	.0000	3	Papeete
0.1370	31.4	.0000	3	Parkers
0.1370	31.4	.0000	3	Parlormaid
0.1370	31.4	.0000	3	Pastures
0.1370	31.4	.0000	3	Peep
0.1370	31.4	.0000	3	Peg's
0.1370	31.4	.0000	3	Pelion
0.1370	31.4	.0000	3	Pendragon
0.1370	31.4	.0000	3	Perfidy
0.1370	31.4	.0000	3	Perpetual
0.1370	31.4	.0000	3	Persinger
0.1370	31.4	.0000	3	Petersen
0.1370	31.4	.0000	3	Phrixus
0.1370	31.4	.0000	3	pickaxe
0.1370	31.4	.0000	3	pin-striped
0.1370	31.4	.0000	3	Pino
0.1370	31.4	.0000	3	pioneers'
0.1370	31.4	.0000	3	pixies
0.1370	31.4	.0000	3	plainer
0.1370	31.4	.0000	3	planking
0.1370	31.4	.0000	3	PLAP-nothing
0.1370	31.4	.0000	3	plesiosaurus
0.1370	31.4	.0000	3	Pocketful
0.1370	31.4	.0000	3	PONG
0.1370	31.4	.0000	3	postage-stamp
0.1370	31.4	.0000	3	Posy's
0.1370	31.4	.0000	3	powerboat
0.1370	31.4	.0000	3	Preble's
0.1370	31.4	.0000	3	prefabs
0.1370	31.4	.0000	3	Priam's
0.1370	31.4	.0000	3	Priests
0.1370	31.4	.0000	3	Provident
0.1370	31.4	.0000	3	Puffer
0.1370	31.4	.0000	3	punk
0.1370	31.4	.0000	3	puss-in-boots
0.1370	31.4	.0000	3	quick-quick
0.1370	31.4	.0000	3	Racky's
0.1370	31.4	.0000	3	radio-active
0.1370	31.4	.0000	3	ragman
0.1370	31.4	.0000	3	rainmaker
0.1370	31.4	.0000	3	rectory
0.1370	31.4	.0000	3	redskins
0.1370	31.4	.0000	3	Renaldo
0.1370	31.4	.0000	3	Reporter
0.1370	31.4	.0000	3	Ribs
0.1370	31.4	.0000	3	ringer
0.1370	31.4	.0000	3	riverbed
0.1370	31.4	.0000	3	robbers'
0.1370	31.4	.0000	3	Rolls
0.1370	31.4	.0000	3	Romeros
0.1370	31.4	.0000	3	Roncole
0.1370	31.4	.0000	3	Rosa's
0.1370	31.4	.0000	3	Rosamond
0.1370	31.4	.0000	3	Rose-Red
0.1370	31.4	.0000	3	Rosita
0.1370	31.4	.0000	3	Rulers
0.1370	31.4	.0000	3	runned
0.1370	31.4	.0000	3	sailplane
0.1370	31.4	.0000	3	Saint-Moritz
0.1370	31.4	.0000	3	Sascha's
0.1370	31.4	.0000	3	Scaly-Skin
0.1370	31.4	.0000	3	Scurry
0.1370	31.4	.0000	3	seagulls
0.1370	31.4	.0000	3	Seco
0.1370	31.4	.0000	3	Senora
0.1370	31.4	.0000	3	Serafina's
0.1370	31.4	.0000	3	serape
0.1370	31.4	.0000	3	Severn
0.1370	31.4	.0000	3	Sheela
0.1370	31.4	.0000	3	Sherring
0.1370	31.4	.0000	3	shoestrings
0.1370	31.4	.0000	3	Si-Ling-Shi
0.1370	31.4	.0000	3	Silly
THE PRECEDING WORD TYPE OCCUPIES RANK 35300				
0.1370	31.4	.0000	3	Simpleton
0.1370	31.4	.0000	3	Sindbad
0.1370	31.4	.0000	3	Skillbook
0.1370	31.4	.0000	3	Slinger
0.1370	31.4	.0000	3	Slivka
0.1370	31.4	.0000	3	Slue-foot
0.1370	31.4	.0000	3	Smedley
0.1370	31.4	.0000	3	Smiling
0.1370	31.4	.0000	3	sniffling
0.1370	31.4	.0000	3	Snow-White
0.1370	31.4	.0000	3	snuffled
0.1370	31.4	.0000	3	soda-water
0.1370	31.4	.0000	3	song-thrush
0.1370	31.4	.0000	3	Sonny's
0.1370	31.4	.0000	3	speaking-tube
0.1370	31.4	.0000	3	Specials
0.1370	31.4	.0000	3	Speedway
0.1370	31.4	.0000	3	Spot's
0.1370	31.4	.0000	3	Squalus'
0.1370	31.4	.0000	3	Squanto's
0.1370	31.4	.0000	3	Squeaky
0.1370	31.4	.0000	3	StMary's
0.1370	31.4	.0000	3	Stallo
0.1370	31.4	.0000	3	Starry
0.1370	31.4	.0000	3	Stefan
0.1370	31.4	.0000	3	stomping
0.1370	31.4	.0000	3	straddled
0.1370	31.4	.0000	3	Strongfort's
0.1370	31.4	.0000	3	Sudana
0.1370	31.4	.0000	3	SUM
0.1370	31.4	.0000	3	sun-up
0.1370	31.4	.0000	3	Sunflower
0.1370	31.4	.0000	3	Superstition
0.1370	31.4	.0000	3	sward
0.1370	31.4	.0000	3	Ta
0.1370	31.4	.0000	3	tailor-bird
0.1370	31.4	.0000	3	Talbot's
0.1370	31.4	.0000	3	tanbark
0.1370	31.4	.0000	3	Tanta
0.1370	31.4	.0000	3	Tanya
0.1370	31.4	.0000	3	tassels
0.1370	31.4	.0000	3	Teedie
0.1370	31.4	.0000	3	Teichner
0.1370	31.4	.0000	3	Tenerife
0.1370	31.4	.0000	3	Tennis
0.1370	31.4	.0000	3	terror-stricken
0.1370	31.4	.0000	3	Thorarinsson
0.1370	31.4	.0000	3	Tillie
0.1370	31.4	.0000	3	Tomohiko
0.1370	31.4	.0000	3	transmuting
0.1370	31.4	.0000	3	tresses
0.1370	31.4	.0000	3	Tully
0.1370	31.4	.0000	3	Tungom
0.1370	31.4	.0000	3	Turi
0.1370	31.4	.0000	3	turrible
0.1370	31.4	.0000	3	Tutu
0.1370	31.4	.0000	3	two-leafed
0.1370	31.4	.0000	3	udder
0.1370	31.4	.0000	3	Ulfius
0.1370	31.4	.0000	3	Uluasat
0.1370	31.4	.0000	3	UNDER
0.1370	31.4	.0000	3	unloosed
0.1370	31.4	.0000	3	Unusual
0.1370	31.4	.0000	3	Varyachka
0.1370	31.4	.0000	3	Vito's
0.1370	31.4	.0000	3	vivo
0.1370	31.4	.0000	3	WA
0.1370	31.4	.0000	3	Walloon
0.1370	31.4	.0000	3	Walthers
0.1370	31.4	.0000	3	Wawona's
0.1370	31.4	.0000	3	waybills
0.1370	31.4	.0000	3	Weaver's
0.1370	31.4	.0000	3	Weezer
0.1370	31.4	.0000	3	Weiss
0.1370	31.4	.0000	3	Whip
0.1370	31.4	.0000	3	whippet
0.1370	31.4	.0000	3	whippets
0.1370	31.4	.0000	3	Whipple
0.1370	31.4	.0000	3	Whiskers'
0.1370	31.4	.0000	3	who-o
0.1370	31.4	.0000	3	Wi-jun-jon
0.1370	31.4	.0000	3	Wildhorse
0.1370	31.4	.0000	3	Williamsport
0.1370	31.4	.0000	3	Willowonder
0.1370	31.4	.0000	3	WINDSTORM
0.1370	31.4	.0000	3	Winterberry's
0.1370	31.4	.0000	3	Wisps
0.1370	31.4	.0000	3	Witje
0.1370	31.4	.0000	3	wok
0.1370	31.4	.0000	3	womanliness
0.1370	31.4	.0000	3	woodburner
0.1370	31.4	.0000	3	Wooster's
0.1370	31.4	.0000	3	wordbook
0.1370	31.4	.0000	3	workhouse
0.1370	31.4	.0000	3	Would
0.1370	31.4	.0000	3	Wright-Humason
0.1370	31.4	.0000	3	Yahad
0.1370	31.4	.0000	3	Yarmouth
0.1370	31.4	.0000	3	Yarmouth's
0.1370	31.4	.0000	3	Youth's
THE PRECEDING WORD TYPE OCCUPIES RANK 35400				
0.1370	31.4	.0000	3	zaggled
0.1370	31.4	.0000	3	ziggled
0.1370	31.4	.0000	3	Zipp
0.1370	31.4	.0000	3	Zoltan's
0.1370	31.4	.0000	3	1500s
0.1370	31.4	.0000	3	1773
0.1370	31.4	.0000	3	2X2L
0.1365	31.4	.1458	4	Elinor
0.1365	31.4	.0722	5	Rodin
0.1363	31.3	.1277	3	affluent
0.1363	31.3	.1277	3	all-state
0.1363	31.3	.1277	3	astronauts'
0.1363	31.3	.1277	3	black-walnut
0.1363	31.3	.1277	3	Bliss
0.1363	31.3	.1277	3	bluntness
0.1363	31.3	.1277	3	bulldozing
0.1363	31.3	.1277	3	Cale's
0.1363	31.3	.1277	3	catwalks
0.1363	31.3	.1277	3	chums
0.1363	31.3	.1277	3	coached
0.1363	31.3	.1277	3	commuters
0.1363	31.3	.1277	3	Corbin
0.1363	31.3	.1277	3	correspondents
0.1363	31.3	.1277	3	director's
0.1363	31.3	.1277	3	eggshells
0.1363	31.3	.1277	3	ever-increasing
0.1363	31.3	.1277	3	Extension
0.1363	31.3	.1277	3	gamely
0.1363	31.3	.1277	3	grandstands
0.1363	31.3	.1277	3	Horseshoe
0.1363	31.3	.1277	3	impersonality
0.1363	31.3	.1277	3	inflationary
0.1363	31.3	.1277	3	Jenkins'
0.1363	31.3	.1277	3	junipers
0.1363	31.3	.1277	3	lawbreakers
0.1363	31.3	.1277	3	liberalism
0.1363	31.3	.1277	3	Ltd
0.1363	31.3	.1277	3	Maclay
0.1363	31.3	.1277	3	motherhood
0.1363	31.3	.1277	3	nationally
0.1363	31.3	.1277	3	numbly
0.1363	31.3	.1277	3	nutty
0.1363	31.3	.1277	3	Oberlin
0.1363	31.3	.1277	3	pacifist
0.1363	31.3	.1277	3	paper's
0.1363	31.3	.1277	3	Pappas
0.1363	31.3	.1277	3	parkas
0.1363	31.3	.1277	3	Peekskill
0.1363	31.3	.1277	3	pervasive
0.1363	31.3	.1277	3	Pinelli
0.1363	31.3	.1277	3	piqued
0.1363	31.3	.1277	3	pointy
0.1363	31.3	.1277	3	recoveries
0.1363	31.3	.1277	3	reliably
0.1363	31.3	.1277	3	Runner
0.1363	31.3	.1277	3	Sharon's
0.1363	31.3	.1277	3	smidgen
0.1363	31.3	.1277	3	socked
0.1363	31.3	.1277	3	Sportsman
0.1363	31.3	.1277	3	superconductors
0.1363	31.3	.1277	3	tactic
0.1363	31.3	.1277	3	Tex
0.1363	31.3	.1277	3	there're
0.1363	31.3	.1277	3	top-grade
0.1363	31.3	.1277	3	triumvirate
0.1363	31.3	.1277	3	Trophy
0.1363	31.3	.1277	3	unturned
0.1363	31.3	.1277	3	waitresses
0.1363	31.3	.1277	3	Wilcox
0.1363	31.3	.1277	3	wingtip
0.1363	31.3	.1277	3	workhorse
0.1363	31.3	.1277	3	5B
0.1363	31.3	.1277	3	931
0.1362	31.3	.2160	2	Adonis
0.1362	31.3	.2160	2	Around
0.1362	31.3	.2160	2	aspirins
0.1362	31.3	.2160	2	Breslau
0.1362	31.3	.2160	2	bright-yellow
0.1362	31.3	.2160	2	Calder
0.1362	31.3	.2160	2	carbonates
0.1362	31.3	.2160	2	condensing
0.1362	31.3	.2160	2	conductive
0.1362	31.3	.2160	2	corks
0.1362	31.3	.2160	2	crinoline
0.1362	31.3	.2160	2	cure-alls
0.1362	31.3	.2160	2	delirium
0.1362	31.3	.2160	2	devilish
0.1362	31.3	.2160	2	discomforts
0.1362	31.3	.2160	2	dozes
0.1362	31.3	.2160	2	etch
0.1362	31.3	.2160	2	eyestrain
0.1362	31.3	.2160	2	falconry
0.1362	31.3	.2160	2	floodlights
0.1362	31.3	.2160	2	flotation
0.1362	31.3	.2160	2	foretold
0.1362	31.3	.2160	2	fourth-floor
0.1362	31.3	.2160	2	grandparent
0.1362	31.3	.2160	2	Growing
0.1362	31.3	.2160	2	hailstorms
0.1362	31.3	.2160	2	iodide
THE PRECEDING WORD TYPE OCCUPIES RANK 35500				
0.1362	31.3	.2160	2	kitchenware
0.1362	31.3	.2160	2	Leeuwenhoek's
0.1362	31.3	.2160	2	levee
0.1362	31.3	.2160	2	lighter-than-air
0.1362	31.3	.2160	2	nonmetal
0.1362	31.3	.2160	2	northbound
0.1362	31.3	.2160	2	Others
0.1362	31.3	.2160	2	overshadows
0.1362	31.3	.2160	2	Pasteur's
0.1362	31.3	.2160	2	pebbly
0.1362	31.3	.2160	2	perilously
0.1362	31.3	.2160	2	pesky
0.1362	31.3	.2160	2	pioneer's
0.1362	31.3	.2160	2	Pointers
0.1362	31.3	.2160	2	pulpy
0.1362	31.3	.2160	2	refraining
0.1362	31.3	.2160	2	ridding
0.1362	31.3	.2160	2	rocket's
0.1362	31.3	.2160	2	rooster's
0.1362	31.3	.2160	2	Sagittarius
0.1362	31.3	.2160	2	salmon-pink
0.1362	31.3	.2160	2	scientists'
0.1362	31.3	.2160	2	semitransparent
0.1362	31.3	.2160	2	sensibilities
0.1362	31.3	.2160	2	seventy-eight
0.1362	31.3	.2160	2	slow-thinking
0.1362	31.3	.2160	2	smokes
0.1362	31.3	.2160	2	snowdrops
0.1362	31.3	.2160	2	somethings
0.1362	31.3	.2160	2	SOS
0.1362	31.3	.2160	2	sounders
0.1362	31.3	.2160	2	spaded
0.1362	31.3	.2160	2	steel-making
0.1362	31.3	.2160	2	sunspot
0.1362	31.3	.2160	2	sweltering
0.1362	31.3	.2160	2	three-headed
0.1362	31.3	.2160	2	three-toed
0.1362	31.3	.2160	2	toddle
0.1362	31.3	.2160	2	two-toed
0.1362	31.3	.2160	2	two-winged
0.1362	31.3	.2160	2	unbleached
0.1362	31.3	.2160	2	unobserved
0.1362	31.3	.2160	2	unripe
0.1362	31.3	.2160	2	unveiling
0.1362	31.3	.2160	2	Y-shaped
0.1362	31.3	.2160	2	yak
0.1362	31.3	.2160	2	zirconium
0.1362	31.3	.2160	2	19-14
0.1362	31.3	.2160	2	1951-52
0.1361	31.3	.0000	7	Angkor
0.1361	31.3	.0000	7	Angola
0.1361	31.3	.0000	7	Caledonia
0.1361	31.3	.0000	7	Chile's
0.1361	31.3	.0000	7	Dairy
0.1361	31.3	.0000	7	Gatun
0.1361	31.3	.0000	7	Hoff
0.1361	31.3	.0000	7	MacArthur
0.1361	31.3	.0000	7	meseta
0.1361	31.3	.0000	7	Morenci
0.1361	31.3	.0000	7	Nicaragua
0.1361	31.3	.0000	7	Olu
0.1361	31.3	.0000	7	pemmican
0.1361	31.3	.0000	7	Poland's
0.1361	31.3	.0000	7	Slovaks
0.1361	31.3	.0000	7	Tlingit
0.1361	31.3	.0000	7	Wemba's
0.1361	31.3	.0000	7	74-75
0.1357	31.3	.2152	2	Abolitionists
0.1357	31.3	.2152	2	admonished
0.1357	31.3	.2152	2	adornment
0.1357	31.3	.2152	2	adroit
0.1357	31.3	.2152	2	attainable
0.1357	31.3	.2152	2	Bakers'
0.1357	31.3	.2152	2	Beckers
0.1357	31.3	.2152	2	beggar's
0.1357	31.3	.2152	2	belied
0.1357	31.3	.2152	2	bird's-eye
0.1357	31.3	.2152	2	bowstrings
0.1357	31.3	.2152	2	Britons
0.1357	31.3	.2152	2	brocade
0.1357	31.3	.2152	2	Butterfield
0.1357	31.3	.2152	2	canvas-covered
0.1357	31.3	.2152	2	chipper
0.1357	31.3	.2152	2	civics
0.1357	31.3	.2152	2	cockfights
0.1357	31.3	.2152	2	Colored
0.1357	31.3	.2152	2	comply
0.1357	31.3	.2152	2	contemplation
0.1357	31.3	.2152	2	continously
0.1357	31.3	.2152	2	Cornwallis'
0.1357	31.3	.2152	2	CorpusChristi
0.1357	31.3	.2152	2	cotton-growing
0.1357	31.3	.2152	2	councilors
0.1357	31.3	.2152	2	cowshed
0.1357	31.3	.2152	2	daubing
0.1357	31.3	.2152	2	deathbed
0.1357	31.3	.2152	2	debtors'
0.1357	31.3	.2152	2	deprivation
0.1357	31.3	.2152	2	dockworkers
0.1357	31.3	.2152	2	doorsteps
THE PRECEDING WORD TYPE OCCUPIES RANK 35600				
0.1357	31.3	.2152	2	drape
0.1357	31.3	.2152	2	dusts
0.1357	31.3	.2152	2	echos
0.1357	31.3	.2152	2	endorsed
0.1357	31.3	.2152	2	enmities
0.1357	31.3	.2152	2	entitle
0.1357	31.3	.2152	2	esprit
0.1357	31.3	.2152	2	explorers'
0.1357	31.3	.2152	2	fifty-eight
0.1357	31.3	.2152	2	fifty-nine
0.1357	31.3	.2152	2	fifty-one
0.1357	31.3	.2152	2	fishhooks
0.1357	31.3	.2152	2	flagstaffs
0.1357	31.3	.2152	2	Forests
0.1357	31.3	.2152	2	Fortunes
0.1357	31.3	.2152	2	four-tenths
0.1357	31.3	.2152	2	freeman
0.1357	31.3	.2152	2	General's
0.1357	31.3	.2152	2	Godspeed
0.1357	31.3	.2152	2	gossips
0.1357	31.3	.2152	2	Guardian
0.1357	31.3	.2152	2	guilders
0.1357	31.3	.2152	2	half-drowned
0.1357	31.3	.2152	2	half-hidden
0.1357	31.3	.2152	2	harsher
0.1357	31.3	.2152	2	hatchets
0.1357	31.3	.2152	2	healthiest
0.1357	31.3	.2152	2	hotheaded
0.1357	31.3	.2152	2	impel
0.1357	31.3	.2152	2	intern
0.1357	31.3	.2152	2	LaFollette
0.1357	31.3	.2152	2	lifeline
0.1357	31.3	.2152	2	light-blue
0.1357	31.3	.2152	2	Lives
0.1357	31.3	.2152	2	Macy's
0.1357	31.3	.2152	2	magnanimity
0.1357	31.3	.2152	2	mailbags
0.1357	31.3	.2152	2	manoeuvres
0.1357	31.3	.2152	2	Midwesterners
0.1357	31.3	.2152	2	Missouri's
0.1357	31.3	.2152	2	Mono
0.1357	31.3	.2152	2	Moroccan
0.1357	31.3	.2152	2	Natchez
0.1357	31.3	.2152	2	ninety-four
0.1357	31.3	.2152	2	ninety-two
0.1357	31.3	.2152	2	nothingness
0.1357	31.3	.2152	2	Oriole
0.1357	31.3	.2152	2	Osawatomie
0.1357	31.3	.2152	2	Pali
0.1357	31.3	.2152	2	palm-leaf
0.1357	31.3	.2152	2	peace-loving
0.1357	31.3	.2152	2	pell-mell
0.1357	31.3	.2152	2	pledges
0.1357	31.3	.2152	2	preserver
0.1357	31.3	.2152	2	pronouncement
0.1357	31.3	.2152	2	pulpwood
0.1357	31.3	.2152	2	querulous
0.1357	31.3	.2152	2	Rancho
0.1357	31.3	.2152	2	referees
0.1357	31.3	.2152	2	replanting
0.1357	31.3	.2152	2	reposed
0.1357	31.3	.2152	2	roadhouses
0.1357	31.3	.2152	2	ropers
0.1357	31.3	.2152	2	Royale
0.1357	31.3	.2152	2	Salton
0.1357	31.3	.2152	2	self-assertion
0.1357	31.3	.2152	2	severest
0.1357	31.3	.2152	2	sharpest
0.1357	31.3	.2152	2	shipload
0.1357	31.3	.2152	2	showmen
0.1357	31.3	.2152	2	sickles
0.1357	31.3	.2152	2	sidetrack
0.1357	31.3	.2152	2	slaveholding
0.1357	31.3	.2152	2	snowmen
0.1357	31.3	.2152	2	sparing
0.1357	31.3	.2152	2	StJoseph
0.1357	31.3	.2152	2	stone-paved
0.1357	31.3	.2152	2	stuck-up
0.1357	31.3	.2152	2	sun-bleached
0.1357	31.3	.2152	2	surfboards

U	SFI	D	F	Word Type
0.1357	31.3	.2152	2	tactful
0.1357	31.3	.2152	2	Tahoe
0.1357	31.3	.2152	2	tangles
0.1357	31.3	.2152	2	thimbles
0.1357	31.3	.2152	2	Thought
0.1357	31.3	.2152	2	Tinto
0.1357	31.3	.2152	2	Towers
0.1357	31.3	.2152	2	traducers
0.1357	31.3	.2152	2	transpolar
0.1357	31.3	.2152	2	travelers'
0.1357	31.3	.2152	2	troubadors
0.1357	31.3	.2152	2	tweeds
0.1357	31.3	.2152	2	twenty-fourth
0.1357	31.3	.2152	2	two-bit
0.1357	31.3	.2152	2	UnitesStates
0.1357	31.3	.2152	2	unworldly
0.1357	31.3	.2152	2	Using
0.1357	31.3	.2152	2	Ventura
0.1357	31.3	.2152	2	vestige
0.1357	31.3	.2152	2	Volcano
THE PRECEDING WORD TYPE OCCUPIES RANK 35700				
0.1357	31.3	.2152	2	Waltham
0.1357	31.3	.2152	2	Weavers
0.1357	31.3	.2152	2	Whitman's
0.1357	31.3	.2152	2	whomever
0.1357	31.3	.2152	2	widower
0.1357	31.3	.2152	2	Witwatersrand
0.1357	31.3	.2152	2	Woodland
0.1357	31.3	.2152	2	Yangtze
0.1357	31.3	.2152	2	16-year-old
0.1357	31.3	.2152	2	209
0.1347	31.3	.0000	9	-10
0.1347	31.3	.0000	9	counting-number
0.1347	31.3	.0000	9	EFGH
0.1347	31.3	.0000	9	Euler
0.1347	31.3	.0000	9	Leibniz
0.1347	31.3	.0000	9	logarithms
0.1347	31.3	.0000	9	placeholder
0.1347	31.3	.0000	9	PY
0.1347	31.3	.0000	9	Subtraction
0.1347	31.3	.0000	9	subtractions
0.1347	31.3	.0000	9	topological
0.1347	31.3	.0000	9	1/60
0.1347	31.3	.0000	9	1/9
0.1347	31.3	.0000	9	2y
0.1347	31.3	.0000	9	4's
0.1347	31.3	.0000	9	5/7
0.1347	31.3	.0000	9	8/4
0.1344	31.3	.1855	3	dignify
0.1344	31.3	.1855	3	mnemonic
0.1343	31.3	.0621	5	-ity
0.1343	31.3	.0621	5	gl
0.1343	31.3	.0621	5	short-vowel
0.1343	31.3	.1699	3	well-written
0.1342	31.3	.1250	3	'is
0.1342	31.3	.1852	3	anthems
0.1342	31.3	.1250	3	bristle
0.1342	31.3	.1250	3	buccaneers
0.1342	31.3	.1250	3	bumpkin
0.1342	31.3	.1250	3	Charlotte's
0.1342	31.3	.1852	3	clave
0.1342	31.3	.1250	3	cosy
0.1342	31.3	.1250	3	crummy
0.1342	31.3	.1250	3	Dagmar's
0.1342	31.3	.1918	3	darks
0.1342	31.3	.1250	3	derby
0.1342	31.3	.1250	3	drawled
0.1342	31.3	.1250	3	Edmund's
0.1342	31.3	.1250	3	encouragingly
0.1342	31.3	.1250	3	Essays
0.1342	31.3	.1250	3	faked
0.1342	31.3	.1250	3	feelin'
0.1342	31.3	.1250	3	Gracious
0.1342	31.3	.1250	3	grooms
0.1342	31.3	.1250	3	headin'
0.1342	31.3	.1918	3	high-rise
0.1342	31.3	.1250	3	high-spirited
0.1342	31.3	.1250	3	hostler
0.1342	31.3	.1250	3	imp
0.1342	31.3	.1250	3	imperiously
0.1342	31.3	.1250	3	indescribable
0.1342	31.3	.1250	3	Kill
0.1342	31.3	.1250	3	Klickitat
0.1342	31.3	.1250	3	leetle
0.1342	31.3	.1250	3	Lily's
0.1342	31.3	.1250	3	Lords
0.1342	31.3	.1250	3	maddest
0.1342	31.3	.1250	3	makin'
0.1342	31.3	.1852	3	Mer
0.1342	31.3	.1852	3	Minstrels
0.1342	31.3	.1250	3	mistress's
0.1342	31.3	.1918	3	mobiles
0.1342	31.3	.1250	3	motherly
0.1342	31.3	.1250	3	navy-blue
0.1342	31.3	.1250	3	Observer
0.1342	31.3	.1250	3	palmettos
0.1342	31.3	.1250	3	phosphorescent
0.1342	31.3	.1250	3	pickings
0.1342	31.3	.1250	3	presentable
0.1342	31.3	.1852	3	Psalms
0.1342	31.3	.1250	3	punctually
0.1342	31.3	.1250	3	repugnance
0.1342	31.3	.1250	3	Shane's
0.1342	31.3	.1852	3	Sousa's
0.1342	31.3	.1250	3	speared
0.1342	31.3	.1250	3	stabbing
0.1342	31.3	.1250	3	strangling
0.1342	31.3	.1250	3	throwed
0.1342	31.3	.1250	3	Tillamook
0.1342	31.3	.1852	3	tootle
0.1342	31.3	.1852	3	Traviata
0.1342	31.3	.1250	3	trundling
0.1342	31.3	.1852	3	Tundra
0.1342	31.3	.1250	3	vexation
0.1342	31.3	.1250	3	Zuckermans
0.1341	31.3	.1688	3	threadlike
0.1340	31.3	.0619	5	Cajun
0.1340	31.3	.0619	5	Chavez
0.1340	31.3	.0619	5	Farmers'
0.1340	31.3	.0619	5	Hopkinson
0.1340	31.3	.0619	5	Tune
THE PRECEDING WORD TYPE OCCUPIES RANK 35800				
0.1337	31.3	.0000	11	Able
0.1337	31.3	.0000	11	Burd
0.1337	31.3	.0000	11	Cholly
0.1337	31.3	.0000	11	Colts
0.1337	31.3	.0000	11	Fratianno
0.1337	31.3	.0000	11	Hanratty
0.1337	31.3	.0000	11	McDougal
0.1337	31.3	.0000	11	Mosby
0.1337	31.3	.0000	11	Shapley
0.1337	31.3	.0000	11	Tracey
0.1334	31.3	.0493	6	baptism
0.1333	31.2	.1829	3	greek
0.1331	31.2	.1826	3	notating
0.1315	31.2	.0929	6	garnish
0.1313	31.2	.0927	6	Orlon
0.1304	31.2	.1783	3	Haines
0.1304	31.2	.1783	3	Medici
0.1304	31.2	.1783	3	Theseus
0.1304	31.2	.1783	3	undecorated
0.1303	31.1	.0000	9	Allosaurus
0.1303	31.1	.0000	9	Aster
0.1303	31.1	.0000	9	Choate
0.1303	31.1	.0000	9	DeDion
0.1303	31.1	.0000	9	follicles
0.1303	31.1	.0000	9	Inchcape
0.1303	31.1	.0000	9	Jen
0.1303	31.1	.0000	9	Jug
0.1303	31.1	.0000	9	Muong
0.1303	31.1	.0000	9	Rostron
0.1303	31.1	.0000	9	Willoughby
0.1302	31.1	.1200	3	Biography
0.1302	31.1	.1200	3	bookmark
0.1302	31.1	.1200	3	briny
0.1302	31.1	.1200	3	cassowary
0.1302	31.1	.1200	3	Clarice
0.1302	31.1	.1200	3	F's
0.1302	31.1	.1200	3	footbridge
0.1302	31.1	.1200	3	Gazette
0.1302	31.1	.1200	3	Kendall
0.1302	31.1	.1200	3	laughin'
0.1302	31.1	.1200	3	mightn't
0.1302	31.1	.1200	3	rhymed
0.1302	31.1	.1200	3	Robber
0.1302	31.1	.1200	3	Ryrie
0.1302	31.1	.1200	3	stews
0.1302	31.1	.1170	4	Sunnyside
0.1302	31.1	.1200	3	Verne's
0.1302	31.1	.1200	3	42nd
0.1298	31.1	.1757	3	XV
0.1295	31.1	.0099	17	bobbin
0.1294	31.1	.0000	16	timpani
0.1291	31.1	.1187	3	bereft
0.1291	31.1	.1187	3	beseeching
0.1291	31.1	.1187	3	blameless
0.1291	31.1	.1187	3	blustered
0.1291	31.1	.1187	3	calked
0.1291	31.1	.1187	3	cawing
0.1291	31.1	.1187	3	Cimarron
0.1291	31.1	.1187	3	cipher
0.1291	31.1	.1187	3	craziest
0.1291	31.1	.1187	3	d'
0.1291	31.1	.1187	3	disappointedly
0.1291	31.1	.1187	3	dowry
0.1291	31.1	.1187	3	dueling
0.1291	31.1	.1187	3	favoured
0.1291	31.1	.1187	3	Forks
0.1291	31.1	.1187	3	Goldilocks
0.1291	31.1	.1187	3	Hap
0.1291	31.1	.1187	3	hibiscus
0.1291	31.1	.1187	3	hobbling
0.1291	31.1	.1187	3	i'
0.1291	31.1	.1187	3	inkwell
0.1291	31.1	.1187	3	Kingfisher
0.1291	31.1	.1187	3	meneer
0.1291	31.1	.1187	3	meowed
0.1291	31.1	.1187	3	Moffats
0.1291	31.1	.1187	3	patrolling
0.1291	31.1	.1187	3	perplexities
0.1291	31.1	.1187	3	Pinal
0.1291	31.1	.1187	3	playtime
0.1291	31.1	.1187	3	recount
0.1291	31.1	.1187	3	red-white-and-blue
0.1291	31.1	.1187	3	reeked
0.1291	31.1	.1187	3	retort
0.1291	31.1	.1187	3	scribbling
0.1291	31.1	.1187	3	sea-monster
0.1291	31.1	.1187	3	Shawnee
0.1291	31.1	.1187	3	should've
0.1291	31.1	.1187	3	smitten
0.1291	31.1	.1187	3	tardy
0.1291	31.1	.1187	3	taunting
0.1291	31.1	.1187	3	taverns
0.1291	31.1	.1187	3	trident
0.1291	31.1	.1187	3	untrodden
0.1291	31.1	.1187	3	valueless
0.1291	31.1	.1187	3	whited
0.1291	31.1	.1187	3	wide-brimmed
0.1291	31.1	.1187	3	winter-broken
0.1291	31.1	.1187	3	Witch's
0.1291	31.1	.1187	3	wreckers
THE PRECEDING WORD TYPE OCCUPIES RANK 35900				
0.1291	31.1	.1187	3	yo'
0.1290	31.1	.0000	11	Greenbaum
0.1290	31.1	.0000	11	Hikueru
0.1290	31.1	.0000	11	Lapham
0.1290	31.1	.0000	11	Liddy
0.1290	31.1	.0000	11	O'Day
0.1290	31.1	.0000	11	Rubio
0.1290	31.1	.0000	11	Shoestring
0.1290	31.1	.0000	11	Uri
0.1288	31.1	.0000	12	Bassanio
0.1288	31.1	.0000	12	COLONEL
0.1288	31.1	.0000	12	FEATHERTOP
0.1288	31.1	.0000	12	GASCOIGNE
0.1288	31.1	.0000	12	GUIDE
0.1288	31.1	.0000	12	Kitty-Cat
0.1288	31.1	.0000	12	Marthe
0.1288	31.1	.0000	12	Monseigneur
0.1288	31.1	.0000	12	Salerio
0.1288	31.1	.0000	12	Tawik
0.1288	31.1	.0000	12	Tuscarawas
0.1277	31.1	.1169	3	Alexandre
0.1277	31.1	.1169	3	anthropoid
0.1277	31.1	.1169	3	Armistice
0.1277	31.1	.1169	3	Ball's
0.1277	31.1	.1169	3	bombshell
0.1277	31.1	.1169	3	canine
0.1277	31.1	.1169	3	Charlemagne's
0.1277	31.1	.1169	3	Chatham
0.1277	31.1	.1169	3	compels
0.1277	31.1	.1169	3	Danton
0.1277	31.1	.1169	3	Design
0.1277	31.1	.1169	3	dissolution
0.1277	31.1	.1169	3	Effect
0.1277	31.1	.1169	3	endemic
0.1277	31.1	.1169	3	Fisher's
0.1277	31.1	.1169	3	flypaper
0.1277	31.1	.1169	3	full-fledged
0.1277	31.1	.1169	3	Genesis
0.1277	31.1	.1169	3	Grenoble
0.1277	31.1	.1169	3	hapless
0.1277	31.1	.1169	3	immigrated
0.1277	31.1	.1169	3	insensitive
0.1277	31.1	.1169	3	jackal
0.1277	31.1	.1169	3	jewelers
0.1277	31.1	.1169	3	long-lived
0.1277	31.1	.1169	3	mussel
0.1277	31.1	.1169	3	naphtha
0.1277	31.1	.1169	3	preen
0.1277	31.1	.1169	3	propositions
0.1277	31.1	.1169	3	re-entry
0.1277	31.1	.1169	3	reappraisal
0.1277	31.1	.1169	3	rigorous
0.1277	31.1	.1169	3	split-second
0.1277	31.1	.1169	3	Surrey
0.1277	31.1	.1169	3	tenacious
0.1277	31.1	.1169	3	translators
0.1277	31.1	.1169	3	Ukrainian
0.1277	31.1	.1169	3	Wash
0.1277	31.1	.1169	3	wave's
0.1262	31.0	.1972	2	$45
0.1262	31.0	.1972	2	adults'
0.1262	31.0	.1972	2	campground
0.1262	31.0	.1972	2	cogs
0.1262	31.0	.1972	2	ell
0.1262	31.0	.1972	2	FAR
0.1262	31.0	.1972	2	Jennifer's
0.1262	31.0	.1972	2	ketchup
0.1262	31.0	.1972	2	Midwestern
0.1262	31.0	.1972	2	morning-glory
0.1262	31.0	.1972	2	ninety-six
0.1262	31.0	.1972	2	peso
0.1262	31.0	.1972	2	side-by-side
0.1262	31.0	.1972	2	sixty-two
0.1262	31.0	.1972	2	Treat
0.1262	31.0	.1972	2	Trick
0.1262	31.0	.1972	2	two-stage
0.1262	31.0	.1972	2	Waldorf
0.1262	31.0	.1972	2	workmen's
0.1262	31.0	.1972	2	063
0.1262	31.0	.1972	2	1/4%
0.1262	31.0	.1972	2	4A
0.1262	31.0	.1972	2	486
0.1262	31.0	.1972	2	50's
0.1262	31.0	.1972	2	590
0.1262	31.0	.1972	2	6-5
0.1262	31.0	.1972	2	891
0.1262	31.0	.1972	2	99%
0.1258	31.0	.1551	3	calligraphy
0.1257	31.0	.2446	2	Bahama
0.1257	31.0	.2446	2	Civilization
0.1257	31.0	.2446	2	cleavages
0.1257	31.0	.2446	2	clench
0.1257	31.0	.2446	2	clog
0.1257	31.0	.1540	3	coarse-grained
0.1257	31.0	.2446	2	coldblooded
0.1257	31.0	.2446	2	diorama
0.1257	31.0	.2446	2	dissociated
0.1257	31.0	.2446	2	drench
0.1257	31.0	.2446	2	Eggs
0.1257	31.0	.2446	2	equidistant
THE PRECEDING WORD TYPE OCCUPIES RANK 36000				
0.1257	31.0	.2446	2	fish-eating
0.1257	31.0	.2446	2	Floating
0.1257	31.0	.2446	2	food-gatherer
0.1257	31.0	.1540	3	fuzziness
0.1257	31.0	.2446	2	grass-eating
0.1257	31.0	.2446	2	gravels
0.1257	31.0	.2446	2	Heinz
0.1257	31.0	.2446	2	Hipparchus
0.1257	31.0	.2446	2	horsetail
0.1257	31.0	.2446	2	hydroponics
0.1257	31.0	.2446	2	ice-breaking
0.1257	31.0	.2446	2	icebreakers
0.1257	31.0	.2446	2	iridescent
0.1257	31.0	.2446	2	KeyWest
0.1257	31.0	.2446	2	leviathan
0.1257	31.0	.2446	2	lifeblood
0.1257	31.0	.2446	2	MAKE
0.1257	31.0	.2446	2	Merced
0.1257	31.0	.2446	2	moderating
0.1257	31.0	.2446	2	multimillion-dollar
0.1257	31.0	.2446	2	newly-formed
0.1257	31.0	.2446	2	Nicolaus
0.1257	31.0	.2446	2	one-string
0.1257	31.0	.2446	2	pathfinder
0.1257	31.0	.2446	2	pear-shaped
0.1257	31.0	.2446	2	physiographic
0.1257	31.0	.2446	2	plant-like
0.1257	31.0	.2446	2	Platform
0.1257	31.0	.2446	2	portents
0.1257	31.0	.2446	2	protections
0.1257	31.0	.2446	2	reappears
0.1257	31.0	.2446	2	resourcefulness
0.1257	31.0	.2446	2	Safely
0.1257	31.0	.2446	2	Samos
0.1257	31.0	.2446	2	school-age
0.1257	31.0	.2446	2	stainless-steel
0.1257	31.0	.2446	2	subtropics
0.1257	31.0	.2446	2	unheated
0.1257	31.0	.2446	2	water-covered
0.1257	31.0	.2446	2	140-141
0.1257	31.0	.2446	2	1456
0.1257	31.0	.2446	2	8-19
0.1256	31.0	.0000	12	Aug
0.1256	31.0	.0269	15	capacitor
0.1256	31.0	.0000	12	Goodyear
0.1256	31.0	.1624	3	Guernsey
0.1256	31.0	.0000	12	Jutland
0.1254	31.0	.1621	3	Aloha
0.1254	31.0	.1621	3	century's
0.1254	31.0	.1621	3	Forty-Niners
0.1254	31.0	.1621	3	Gilmore
0.1254	31.0	.1621	3	KDKA
0.1254	31.0	.1621	3	Merrill
0.1254	31.0	.1621	3	Vltava
0.1254	31.0	.1621	3	woosh
0.1250	31.0	.1948	2	'er
0.1250	31.0	.1948	2	Account
0.1250	31.0	.1948	2	acrobatic
0.1250	31.0	.1948	2	Alphabet
0.1250	31.0	.1948	2	amalgam
0.1250	31.0	.1948	2	Arnhem
0.1250	31.0	.1948	2	auspicious
0.1250	31.0	.1948	2	back-bedroom
0.1250	31.0	.1948	2	barbarism
0.1250	31.0	.1948	2	begorra
0.1250	31.0	.1948	2	Belinda's
0.1250	31.0	.1948	2	below-zero
0.1250	31.0	.1948	2	benzine
0.1250	31.0	.1948	2	berths
0.1250	31.0	.1948	2	besought
0.1250	31.0	.1948	2	blanketing
0.1250	31.0	.1948	2	bluejay's
0.1250	31.0	.1948	2	Bonanza
0.1250	31.0	.1948	2	brash
0.1250	31.0	.0236	14	breads
0.1250	31.0	.1948	2	Breese
0.1250	31.0	.1948	2	brilliancy
0.1250	31.0	.1948	2	broomsticks
0.1250	31.0	.1948	2	bucketfuls
0.1250	31.0	.1948	2	burp
0.1250	31.0	.1948	2	buzzards
0.1250	31.0	.1948	2	by-line
0.1250	31.0	.1948	2	byre
0.1250	31.0	.1948	2	cabinetmakers
0.1250	31.0	.1948	2	camera's
0.1250	31.0	.1948	2	camp's
0.1250	31.0	.1948	2	caped
0.1250	31.0	.1948	2	cardboard-covered
0.1250	31.0	.1948	2	catapulted
0.1250	31.0	.1948	2	catgut
0.1250	31.0	.1948	2	chalets
0.1250	31.0	.1948	2	checkered
0.1250	31.0	.1948	2	cheeseburgers
0.1250	31.0	.1948	2	Chelsea
0.1250	31.0	.1948	2	Chimney
0.1250	31.0	.1948	2	clipboard
0.1250	31.0	.1948	2	Cloak
0.1250	31.0	.1948	2	clovers
0.1250	31.0	.1948	2	clucks
0.1250	31.0	.1948	2	Cobb
THE PRECEDING WORD TYPE OCCUPIES RANK 36100				
0.1250	31.0	.1948	2	Coffin's
0.1250	31.0	.1948	2	Combs
0.1250	31.0	.1948	2	companion's
0.1250	31.0	.1948	2	compensates
0.1250	31.0	.1948	2	corselet
0.1250	31.0	.1948	2	cotillions
0.1250	31.0	.1948	2	cowlike
0.1250	31.0	.1948	2	depravity
0.1250	31.0	.1948	2	derelict
0.1250	31.0	.1948	2	diligent
0.1250	31.0	.1948	2	dogcarts
0.1250	31.0	.1948	2	doll-like
0.1250	31.0	.1948	2	doorkeeper
0.1250	31.0	.1948	2	dour
0.1250	31.0	.1948	2	ELEPHANT
0.1250	31.0	.1948	2	enamored
0.1250	31.0	.1948	2	endeared
0.1250	31.0	.1948	2	enumerated
0.1250	31.0	.1948	2	Eskimos'
0.1250	31.0	.1948	2	eulogy
0.1250	31.0	.1948	2	evoked
0.1250	31.0	.1948	2	Ewing
0.1250	31.0	.1948	2	ex-slave
0.1250	31.0	.1948	2	Expedition
0.1250	31.0	.1948	2	expedition's
0.1250	31.0	.1948	2	expert's
0.1250	31.0	.1948	2	falsified
0.1250	31.0	.1948	2	fan-shaped
0.1250	31.0	.1948	2	faultless
0.1250	31.0	.1948	2	fielders
0.1250	31.0	.1948	2	fiendish
0.1250	31.0	.1948	2	flat-bottomed
0.1250	31.0	.1948	2	fogbound
0.1250	31.0	.1948	2	footfall
0.1250	31.0	.1948	2	forest-clad
0.1250	31.0	.1948	2	forking
0.1250	31.0	.1948	2	Founding
0.1250	31.0	.1948	2	four-poster
0.1250	31.0	.1948	2	foursquare
0.1250	31.0	.1948	2	fresh-baked
0.1250	31.0	.1948	2	fur-clad
0.1250	31.0	.1948	2	gardener's
0.1250	31.0	.1948	2	glimmered

U	SFI	D	F	Word Type
0.1250	31.0	.1948	2	Goering's
0.1250	31.0	.1948	2	grilled
0.1250	31.0	.1948	2	grillwork
0.1250	31.0	.1948	2	grog
0.1250	31.0	.1948	2	Ground
0.1250	31.0	.1948	2	Grundy
0.1250	31.0	.1948	2	guffawed
0.1250	31.0	.1948	2	half-miler
0.1250	31.0	.1948	2	heavy-footed
0.1250	31.0	.1948	2	heavy-set
0.1250	31.0	.1948	2	Hellas
0.1250	31.0	.1948	2	high-ranking
0.1250	31.0	.1610	3	highest-pitched
0.1250	31.0	.1948	2	highwaymen
0.1250	31.0	.1948	2	honoured
0.1250	31.0	.1948	2	hookers
0.1250	31.0	.1948	2	Horsemen
0.1250	31.0	.1948	2	howitzer
0.1250	31.0	.1948	2	hurlers
0.1250	31.0	.1948	2	Idle
0.1250	31.0	.1948	2	insurrection
0.1250	31.0	.1948	2	janitors
0.1250	31.0	.1948	2	Kelton
0.1250	31.0	.1948	2	Kennedys
0.1250	31.0	.1948	2	kindhearted
0.1250	31.0	.1948	2	kings'
0.1250	31.0	.1948	2	Kon-Tiki's
0.1250	31.0	.1948	2	laddie
0.1250	31.0	.1948	2	ladybird
0.1250	31.0	.1948	2	leadsmen
0.1250	31.0	.1948	2	les
0.1250	31.0	.1948	2	licker
0.1250	31.0	.1948	2	lightens
0.1250	31.0	.1948	2	lover's
0.1250	31.0	.1948	2	maim
0.1250	31.0	.1948	2	Major's
0.1250	31.0	.1948	2	Mantell's
0.1250	31.0	.1948	2	marmot
0.1250	31.0	.1948	2	martyrs
0.1250	31.0	.1948	2	mastiff
0.1250	31.0	.1948	2	mauling
0.1250	31.0	.1948	2	medallion
0.1250	31.0	.1948	2	meowch
0.1250	31.0	.1948	2	Mirrors
0.1250	31.0	.1948	2	miscalculated
0.1250	31.0	.1948	2	misted
0.1250	31.0	.1948	2	Morrissey
0.1250	31.0	.1948	2	mountain-like
0.1250	31.0	.1948	2	mouseholed
0.1250	31.0	.1948	2	moveth
0.1250	31.0	.1948	2	murmurings
0.1250	31.0	.1948	2	nankeen
0.1250	31.0	.1948	2	neckerchief
0.1250	31.0	.1948	2	nerve-shattering
0.1250	31.0	.1948	2	notables
0.1250	31.0	.1948	2	Pensacola
0.1250	31.0	.1948	2	picnickers
THE PRECEDING WORD TYPE OCCUPIES RANK 36200				
0.1250	31.0	.1948	2	pillowed
0.1250	31.0	.1948	2	Pius
0.1250	31.0	.1948	2	Powhatan's
0.1250	31.0	.1948	2	preachy
0.1250	31.0	.1948	2	prodding
0.1250	31.0	.1948	2	quartermaster
0.1250	31.0	.1948	2	rampaging
0.1250	31.0	.1948	2	re-echoed
0.1250	31.0	.1948	2	recedes
0.1250	31.0	.1948	2	recollections
0.1250	31.0	.1948	2	recrossed
0.1250	31.0	.1948	2	rescinded
0.1250	31.0	.1948	2	Riviera
0.1250	31.0	.1948	2	Rogers'
0.1250	31.0	.1948	2	round-faced
0.1250	31.0	.1948	2	sahibs
0.1250	31.0	.1948	2	sandy-haired
0.1250	31.0	.1948	2	satchel
0.1250	31.0	.1948	2	scythes
0.1250	31.0	.1948	2	Seaman
0.1250	31.0	.1948	2	self-controlled
0.1250	31.0	.1948	2	sequel
0.1250	31.0	.1948	2	settler's
0.1250	31.0	.1948	2	seven-thirty
0.1250	31.0	.1948	2	sharp-breaking
0.1250	31.0	.1948	2	shepherdess
0.1250	31.0	.1948	2	shush
0.1250	31.0	.1948	2	sickbed
0.1250	31.0	.1948	2	Skates
0.1250	31.0	.1948	2	smellers
0.1250	31.0	.1948	2	snuffle
0.1250	31.0	.1948	2	sportsmanlike
0.1250	31.0	.1948	2	stockinged
0.1250	31.0	.1948	2	stoutest
0.1250	31.0	.1948	2	Stradivarius
0.1250	31.0	.1948	2	strong-minded
0.1250	31.0	.1948	2	Supper
0.1250	31.0	.1948	2	syndicated
0.1250	31.0	.1948	2	tacking
0.1250	31.0	.1948	2	tall-masted
0.1250	31.0	.1948	2	telegraphed
0.1250	31.0	.1948	2	Terrible
0.1250	31.0	.1948	2	thornlike
0.1250	31.0	.1948	2	thoroughbreds
0.1250	31.0	.1948	2	thousand-dollar
0.1250	31.0	.1948	2	tidbit
0.1250	31.0	.1948	2	Toil
0.1250	31.0	.1948	2	Towanda
0.1250	31.0	.1948	2	trickly
0.1250	31.0	.1948	2	tripe
0.1250	31.0	.1948	2	Truly
0.1250	31.0	.1948	2	Tuamotu
0.1250	31.0	.1948	2	tureen
0.1250	31.0	.1948	2	two-hand
0.1250	31.0	.1948	2	unburied
0.1250	31.0	.1948	2	undermanned
0.1250	31.0	.1948	2	unflattering
0.1250	31.0	.1948	2	unintelligible
0.1250	31.0	.1948	2	unmerciful

U	SFI	D	F	Word Type
0.1250	31.0	.1948	2	unpacking
0.1250	31.0	.1948	2	unpublished
0.1250	31.0	.1948	2	vagaries
0.1250	31.0	.1948	2	Valdez
0.1250	31.0	.1948	2	wait'll
0.1250	31.0	.1948	2	Weeck
0.1250	31.0	.1948	2	whin
0.1250	31.0	.1948	2	white-winged
0.1250	31.0	.1948	2	winda
0.1250	31.0	.1948	2	womanhood
0.1250	31.0	.1948	2	Yates
0.1250	31.0	.1948	2	yi
0.1250	31.0	.1948	2	yoked
0.1250	31.0	.1948	2	Yule
0.1250	31.0	.1948	2	760
0.1250	31.0	.1948	2	90-mile
0.1245	31.0	.0761	4	Challenge
0.1245	31.0	.0761	4	fr
0.1243	30.9	.0759	4	Anthem
0.1243	30.9	.0759	4	cowbells
0.1243	30.9	.0759	4	Follow
0.1243	30.9	.0759	4	gongs
0.1243	30.9	.0759	4	Ride
0.1243	30.9	.0759	4	serenade
0.1243	30.9	.0759	4	tonguing
0.1243	30.9	.0759	4	28th
0.1241	30.9	.1072	5	tines
0.1239	30.9	.1070	5	butterfat
0.1239	30.9	.1070	5	preshrunk
0.1217	30.9	.0000	15	vowel-consonant-e
0.1215	30.8	.0000	10	Abrams
0.1215	30.8	.0000	10	Corvette
0.1215	30.8	.0000	10	grayling
0.1215	30.8	.0000	10	Kerlan
0.1215	30.8	.0000	10	Namath
0.1215	30.8	.0000	10	Packers
0.1215	30.8	.0000	10	Super-Lite
0.1215	30.8	.0000	10	Twister
0.1213	30.8	.0000	15	Album
0.1213	30.8	.0000	15	ron
0.1213	30.8	.0000	15	ta
THE PRECEDING WORD TYPE OCCUPIES RANK 36300				
0.1213	30.8	.0000	15	Tchaikovsky's
0.1212	30.8	.2413	2	BY
0.1212	30.8	.2413	2	consecutively
0.1212	30.8	.2413	2	disintegrations
0.1212	30.8	.2413	2	disregards
0.1212	30.8	.2413	2	halved
0.1212	30.8	.2413	2	kilowatt
0.1212	30.8	.2413	2	lasers
0.1212	30.8	.2413	2	Lunch
0.1212	30.8	.2413	2	one-pint
0.1212	30.8	.2413	2	reconsider
0.1212	30.8	.2413	2	respire
0.1212	30.8	.2413	2	seven-eighths
0.1212	30.8	.2413	2	shuffles
0.1212	30.8	.2413	2	subscript
0.1212	30.8	.2413	2	tabulation
0.1212	30.8	.2413	2	tibia
0.1212	30.8	.2413	2	1%
0.1212	30.8	.2413	2	10-26
0.1212	30.8	.2413	2	1140
0.1212	30.8	.2413	2	13-2
0.1212	30.8	.2413	2	13-3
0.1212	30.8	.2413	2	14-18
0.1212	30.8	.2413	2	2-6
0.1212	30.8	.2413	2	2-8
0.1212	30.8	.2413	2	3-5
0.1212	30.8	.2413	2	30%
0.1212	30.8	.2413	2	30b
0.1212	30.8	.2413	2	459
0.1212	30.8	.2413	2	5-18
0.1212	30.8	.2413	2	553
0.1212	30.8	.2413	2	628
0.1212	30.8	.2413	2	671
0.1212	30.8	.2413	2	7-20
0.1212	30.8	.2413	2	9-20
0.1212	30.8	.2413	2	9-9
0.1212	30.8	.2413	2	955
0.1211	30.8	.2417	2	annexing
0.1211	30.8	.2417	2	assertions
0.1211	30.8	.2417	2	Census
0.1211	30.8	.2417	2	disagrees
0.1211	30.8	.2417	2	donation
0.1211	30.8	.2417	2	eighty-nine
0.1211	30.8	.2417	2	lollipops
0.1211	30.8	.2417	2	reopening
0.1211	30.8	.2417	2	Rushmore
0.1211	30.8	.2417	2	shortcoming
0.1211	30.8	.2417	2	092
0.1211	30.8	.2417	2	1999
0.1211	30.8	.2417	2	30-foot
0.1211	30.8	.2417	2	30-31
0.1211	30.8	.2417	2	307
0.1211	30.8	.2417	2	339
0.1211	30.8	.2417	2	357
0.1211	30.8	.2417	2	366
0.1211	30.8	.2417	2	3666
0.1211	30.8	.2417	2	412
0.1211	30.8	.2417	2	445
0.1211	30.8	.2417	2	593
0.1211	30.8	.2417	2	756
0.1211	30.8	.2417	2	848
0.1211	30.8	.2417	2	984
0.1208	30.8	.0221	16	undercoat
0.1205	30.8	.2405	2	alcoholics
0.1205	30.8	.2405	2	anti-Semitic
0.1205	30.8	.2405	2	assessing
0.1205	30.8	.2405	2	Au
0.1205	30.8	.2405	2	besting
0.1205	30.8	.2405	2	blood-sucking
0.1205	30.8	.2405	2	Calico
0.1205	30.8	.2405	2	constricting
0.1205	30.8	.2405	2	convexity
0.1205	30.8	.2405	2	C12H22O11
0.1205	30.8	.2405	2	Diseases
0.1205	30.8	.2405	2	drinkers

U	SFI	D	F	Word Type
0.1205	30.8	.2405	2	drips
0.1205	30.8	.2405	2	even-tempered
0.1205	30.8	.2405	2	eventful
0.1205	30.8	.2405	2	funnels
0.1205	30.8	.2405	2	germinated
0.1205	30.8	.2405	2	germinates
0.1205	30.8	.2405	2	gestation
0.1205	30.8	.2405	2	gray-white
0.1205	30.8	.2405	2	Grissom
0.1205	30.8	.2405	2	hisses
0.1205	30.8	.2405	2	humbled
0.1205	30.8	.2405	2	indiscriminately
0.1205	30.8	.2405	2	injures
0.1205	30.8	.2405	2	inordinately
0.1205	30.8	.2405	2	kilowatts
0.1205	30.8	.2405	2	lizard-like
0.1205	30.8	.2405	2	logy
0.1205	30.8	.2405	2	mouselike
0.1205	30.8	.2405	2	Nansen
0.1205	30.8	.2405	2	nurseries
0.1205	30.8	.2405	2	on-the-job
0.1205	30.8	.2405	2	paper-thin
0.1205	30.8	.2405	2	parlance
0.1205	30.8	.2405	2	peonies
0.1205	30.8	.2405	2	purposed
THE PRECEDING WORD TYPE OCCUPIES RANK 36400				
0.1205	30.8	.2405	2	quarantined
0.1205	30.8	.2405	2	Redstone
0.1205	30.8	.2405	2	Reich
0.1205	30.8	.2405	2	Rue
0.1205	30.8	.2405	2	scale-like
0.1205	30.8	.2405	2	schoolrooms
0.1205	30.8	.2405	2	sloshes
0.1205	30.8	.2405	2	smacks
0.1205	30.8	.2405	2	spindly
0.1205	30.8	.2405	2	stalagmites
0.1205	30.8	.2405	2	stentor
0.1205	30.8	.2405	2	teletype
0.1205	30.8	.2405	2	testifying
0.1205	30.8	.2405	2	unbending
0.1205	30.8	.2405	2	unobstructed
0.1205	30.8	.2405	2	unsuspecting
0.1205	30.8	.2405	2	viaducts
0.1205	30.8	.2405	2	washrooms
0.1205	30.8	.2405	2	WATER
0.1205	30.8	.2405	2	wearers
0.1205	30.8	.2405	2	1563
0.1204	30.8	.0000	11	/au/
0.1204	30.8	.2408	2	abolitionist
0.1204	30.8	.2408	2	absentee
0.1204	30.8	.2408	2	accusations
0.1204	30.8	.2408	2	Anjou
0.1204	30.8	.2408	2	Ankara
0.1204	30.8	.2408	2	archbishop
0.1204	30.8	.2408	2	Arms
0.1204	30.8	.2408	2	artisan
0.1204	30.8	.2408	2	Ashley's
0.1204	30.8	.2408	2	authorizing
0.1204	30.8	.2408	2	bigotry
0.1204	30.8	.2408	2	bitter-cold
0.1204	30.8	.2408	2	bookseller
0.1204	30.8	.2408	2	borough
0.1204	30.8	.2408	2	Bride
0.1204	30.8	.2408	2	bright-blue
0.1204	30.8	.2408	2	Cadiz
0.1204	30.8	.2408	2	chaff
0.1204	30.8	.2408	2	Chateau
0.1204	30.8	.2408	2	Chicagoan
0.1204	30.8	.2408	2	coffee-producing
0.1204	30.8	.2408	2	cohesion
0.1204	30.8	.2408	2	Congregationalist
0.1204	30.8	.2408	2	crafted
0.1204	30.8	.2408	2	crucified
0.1204	30.8	.2408	2	cuttlefish
0.1204	30.8	.2408	2	decor
0.1204	30.8	.2408	2	degradation
0.1204	30.8	.2408	2	delegated
0.1204	30.8	.2408	2	dirtier
0.1204	30.8	.2408	2	earth-covered
0.1204	30.8	.2408	2	East's
0.1204	30.8	.2408	2	embroidering
0.1204	30.8	.2408	2	empire's
0.1204	30.8	.2408	2	emu's
0.1204	30.8	.2408	2	enormity
0.1204	30.8	.2408	2	entrepreneurs
0.1204	30.8	.2408	2	Eurus
0.1204	30.8	.2408	2	exporters
0.1204	30.8	.2408	2	factory's
0.1204	30.8	.2408	2	farmstead
0.1204	30.8	.2408	2	fifty-seven
0.1204	30.8	.2408	2	Finger
0.1204	30.8	.2408	2	flocking
0.1204	30.8	.2408	2	four-story
0.1204	30.8	.2408	2	fruit-growing
0.1204	30.8	.2408	2	GIS
0.1204	30.8	.2408	2	gladiators
0.1204	30.8	.2408	2	Glendale
0.1204	30.8	.0000	11	Gryphon
0.1204	30.8	.2408	2	Haifa
0.1204	30.8	.2408	2	hailing
0.1204	30.8	.2408	2	Halifax
0.1204	30.8	.2408	2	Hunan
0.1204	30.8	.2408	2	ill-smelling
0.1204	30.8	.2408	2	Illinois's
0.1204	30.8	.2408	2	importation
0.1204	30.8	.2408	2	impulsively
0.1204	30.8	.2408	2	intermarrying
0.1204	30.8	.2408	2	Intracoastal
0.1204	30.8	.2408	2	inviolable
0.1204	30.8	.2408	2	Isabelle
0.1204	30.8	.2408	2	isolating
0.1204	30.8	.2408	2	juggled
0.1204	30.8	.2408	2	justifiably
0.1204	30.8	.2408	2	kangaroo's
0.1204	30.8	.2408	2	keelboats
0.1204	30.8	.2408	2	knight's
0.1204	30.8	.2408	2	lampposts

U	SFI	D	F	Word Type
0.1204	30.8	.2408	2	landholding
0.1204	30.8	.2408	2	Leaning
0.1204	30.8	.2408	2	MacKenzie
0.1204	30.8	.2408	2	moustached
0.1204	30.8	.2408	2	navies
0.1204	30.8	.2408	2	negroes
0.1204	30.8	.2408	2	oppressors
0.1204	30.8	.2408	2	palm-shaded
0.1204	30.8	.2408	2	paradoxes
THE PRECEDING WORD TYPE OCCUPIES RANK 36500				
0.1204	30.8	.2408	2	parasols
0.1204	30.8	.2408	2	parkway
0.1204	30.8	.2408	2	parlors
0.1204	30.8	.2408	2	Partition
0.1204	30.8	.2408	2	Patton's
0.1204	30.8	.2408	2	Plato's
0.1204	30.8	.2408	2	Pompey
0.1204	30.8	.2408	2	postgraduate
0.1204	30.8	.2408	2	presides
0.1204	30.8	.2408	2	Prussians
0.1204	30.8	.2408	2	punishments
0.1204	30.8	.2408	2	re-education
0.1204	30.8	.2408	2	Rebel
0.1204	30.8	.2408	2	rebuffed
0.1204	30.8	.2408	2	redeem
0.1204	30.8	.2408	2	redress
0.1204	30.8	.2408	2	Reno
0.1204	30.8	.2408	2	repacked
0.1204	30.8	.2408	2	revolts
0.1204	30.8	.2408	2	rightness
0.1204	30.8	.2408	2	SanJacinto
0.1204	30.8	.2408	2	Secretaries
0.1204	30.8	.2408	2	Shangri-La
0.1204	30.8	.2408	2	sheep-herding
0.1204	30.8	.2408	2	single-minded
0.1204	30.8	.2408	2	slaughterhouses
0.1204	30.8	.2408	2	Sogne
0.1204	30.8	.2408	2	SouthAmerican
0.1204	30.8	.2408	2	Stalingrad
0.1204	30.8	.2408	2	statuary
0.1204	30.8	.2408	2	surpluses
0.1204	30.8	.2408	2	Tecumseh
0.1204	30.8	.2408	2	Thai
0.1204	30.8	.2408	2	tie-up
0.1204	30.8	.2408	2	tillage
0.1204	30.8	.2408	2	Tomb
0.1204	30.8	.2408	2	unhitching
0.1204	30.8	.2408	2	unmade
0.1204	30.8	.2408	2	unpunished
0.1204	30.8	.2408	2	upper-class
0.1204	30.8	.2408	2	Vacation
0.1204	30.8	.2408	2	vetoes
0.1204	30.8	.2408	2	well-distributed
0.1204	30.8	.2408	2	well-run
0.1204	30.8	.2408	2	wisteria
0.1204	30.8	.2408	2	wood-working
0.1204	30.8	.2408	2	workday
0.1204	30.8	.2408	2	1541
0.1204	30.8	.2408	2	25-foot
0.1204	30.8	.2408	2	4-h
0.1204	30.8	.2408	2	857
0.1197	30.8	.0000	8	c/d
0.1197	30.8	.0000	8	DX
0.1197	30.8	.0000	8	repetend
0.1197	30.8	.0000	8	transversal
0.1197	30.8	.0000	8	x6
0.1197	30.8	.0000	8	06
0.1197	30.8	.0000	8	12-hour
0.1197	30.8	.0000	8	3's
0.1197	30.8	.0000	8	3a
0.1197	30.8	.0000	8	4x3
0.1197	30.8	.0553	8	9-inch
0.1187	30.7	.1814	2	'specially
0.1187	30.7	.1814	2	'70
0.1187	30.7	.1814	2	A-SPREADING
0.1187	30.7	.1814	2	aback
0.1187	30.7	.1814	2	admirably
0.1187	30.7	.1814	2	adorable
0.1187	30.7	.1814	2	advisors
0.1187	30.7	.1814	2	affirmatively
0.1187	30.7	.1814	2	After
0.1187	30.7	.1814	2	air-conditioner
0.1187	30.7	.1814	2	Algernon
0.1187	30.7	.1814	2	alienating
0.1187	30.7	.1814	2	anti
0.1187	30.7	.1814	2	aquanauts
0.1187	30.7	.1814	2	artwork
0.1187	30.7	.1814	2	ashen
0.1187	30.7	.1814	2	assassination
0.1187	30.7	.1814	2	assayed
0.1187	30.7	.1814	2	atomic-powered
0.1187	30.7	.1814	2	Atonement
0.1187	30.7	.1814	2	austerity
0.1187	30.7	.1814	2	Avenger
0.1187	30.7	.1814	2	awning
0.1187	30.7	.1814	2	backer
0.1187	30.7	.1814	2	bandannas
0.1187	30.7	.1814	2	baring
0.1187	30.7	.1814	2	bats'
0.1187	30.7	.1814	2	beacons
0.1187	30.7	.1814	2	beefeaters
0.1187	30.7	.1814	2	befits
0.1187	30.7	.1814	2	Benin
0.1187	30.7	.1814	2	Benning
0.1187	30.7	.1814	2	bill's
0.1187	30.7	.1814	2	Blackbeard's
0.1187	30.7	.1814	2	blandly
0.1187	30.7	.1814	2	bolas
0.1187	30.7	.1814	2	book's
0.1187	30.7	.1814	2	BOOM
THE PRECEDING WORD TYPE OCCUPIES RANK 36600				
0.1187	30.7	.1814	2	Border
0.1187	30.7	.1814	2	boss's
0.1187	30.7	.1814	2	bottlenecks
0.1187	30.7	.1814	2	bounties
0.1187	30.7	.1814	2	braggart
0.1187	30.7	.1814	2	bric-a-brac

U	SFI	D	F	Word Type
0.1187	30.7	.1814	2	Britisher
0.1187	30.7	.1814	2	broach
0.1187	30.7	.1814	2	brusquely
0.1187	30.7	.1814	2	bundling
0.1187	30.7	.1814	2	burdened
0.1187	30.7	.1814	2	business-like
0.1187	30.7	.1814	2	Campfire
0.1187	30.7	.1814	2	carbines
0.1187	30.7	.1814	2	carbon-dioxide
0.1187	30.7	.1814	2	Chandler
0.1187	30.7	.1814	2	Chess
0.1187	30.7	.1814	2	chimps
0.1187	30.7	.1814	2	Chris's
0.1187	30.7	.1814	2	churlish
0.1187	30.7	.1814	2	Clear
0.1187	30.7	.1814	2	Club's
0.1187	30.7	.1814	2	clustering
0.1187	30.7	.1814	2	cocksure
0.1187	30.7	.1814	2	collard
0.1187	30.7	.1814	2	congratulating
0.1187	30.7	.1814	2	consciences
0.1187	30.7	.1814	2	convulsion
0.1187	30.7	.1814	2	copyright
0.1187	30.7	.1814	2	corrupting
0.1187	30.7	.1814	2	crumby
0.1187	30.7	.1814	2	cycling
0.1187	30.7	.1814	2	daunted
0.1187	30.7	.1814	2	dealership
0.1187	30.7	.1814	2	deathless
0.1187	30.7	.1814	2	decoded
0.1187	30.7	.1814	2	deep-diving
0.1187	30.7	.1814	2	dirtiest
0.1187	30.7	.1814	2	discernible
0.1187	30.7	.1814	2	disown
0.1187	30.7	.1814	2	Distance
0.1187	30.7	.1814	2	dockside
0.1187	30.7	.1814	2	Dogwood
0.1187	30.7	.1814	2	doled
0.1187	30.7	.1814	2	Dorchester
0.1187	30.7	.1814	2	dried-out
0.1187	30.7	.1814	2	drivers'
0.1187	30.7	.1814	2	drudge
0.1187	30.7	.1814	2	dudes
0.1187	30.7	.1814	2	dun-colored
0.1187	30.7	.1814	2	effortlessly
0.1187	30.7	.1814	2	ein
0.1187	30.7	.1814	2	electrics
0.1187	30.7	.1814	2	entanglement
0.1187	30.7	.1814	2	entrancing
0.1187	30.7	.1814	2	epitome
0.1187	30.7	.1814	2	Fenwick
0.1187	30.7	.1814	2	fetters
0.1187	30.7	.1814	2	filigree
0.1187	30.7	.1814	2	Fillmore
0.1187	30.7	.1814	2	fishers
0.1187	30.7	.1814	2	Fishery
0.1187	30.7	.1814	2	five-fifteen
0.1187	30.7	.1814	2	fizzled
0.1187	30.7	.1814	2	flannels
0.1187	30.7	.1814	2	Flicker
0.1187	30.7	.1814	2	flier's
0.1187	30.7	.1814	2	flitting
0.1187	30.7	.1814	2	Forbidden
0.1187	30.7	.1814	2	fowling
0.1187	30.7	.1814	2	fretting
0.1187	30.7	.1814	2	frivolity
0.1187	30.7	.1814	2	gigs
0.1187	30.7	.1814	2	gilding
0.1187	30.7	.1814	2	Glamour
0.1187	30.7	.1814	2	glistens
0.1187	30.7	.1814	2	glum
0.1187	30.7	.1814	2	goblet
0.1187	30.7	.1814	2	gold-bearing
0.1187	30.7	.1814	2	great-grandsons
0.1187	30.7	.1814	2	gripes
0.1187	30.7	.1814	2	guardianship
0.1187	30.7	.1814	2	gusting
0.1187	30.7	.1814	2	half-forgotten
0.1187	30.7	.1814	2	hands-off
0.1187	30.7	.1814	2	heatedly
0.1187	30.7	.1814	2	Hedges
0.1187	30.7	.1814	2	Helene
0.1187	30.7	.1814	2	heroes'
0.1187	30.7	.1814	2	hesitates
0.1187	30.7	.1814	2	high-class
0.1187	30.7	.1814	2	high-fashion
0.1187	30.7	.1814	2	high-level
0.1187	30.7	.1814	2	how-to-do-it
0.1187	30.7	.1814	2	how'm
0.1187	30.7	.1814	2	human-interest
0.1187	30.7	.1814	2	idealism
0.1187	30.7	.1814	2	impoverished
0.1187	30.7	.1814	2	indecent
0.1187	30.7	.1814	2	indelicate

THE PRECEDING WORD TYPE OCCUPIES RANK 36700

U	SFI	D	F	Word Type
0.1187	30.7	.1814	2	industrialist
0.1187	30.7	.1814	2	inferiors
0.1187	30.7	.1814	2	initially
0.1187	30.7	.1814	2	initiation
0.1187	30.7	.1814	2	intakes
0.1187	30.7	.1814	2	intolerant
0.1187	30.7	.1814	2	intuitive
0.1187	30.7	.1814	2	irrespective
0.1187	30.7	.1814	2	Jacobson
0.1187	30.7	.1814	2	Jeannie
0.1187	30.7	.1814	2	joke's
0.1187	30.7	.1814	2	joker
0.1187	30.7	.1814	2	jolts
0.1187	30.7	.1814	2	jubilantly
0.1187	30.7	.1814	2	Junior's
0.1187	30.7	.1814	2	kickoff
0.1187	30.7	.1814	2	kidnap
0.1187	30.7	.1814	2	kids'
0.1187	30.7	.1814	2	knockdown
0.1187	30.7	.1814	2	lead-off
0.1187	30.7	.1814	2	leaded
0.1187	30.7	.1814	2	lifesaver
0.1187	30.7	.1814	2	Llewelyn
0.1187	30.7	.1814	2	lobes
0.1187	30.7	.1814	2	loner
0.1187	30.7	.1814	2	Lowry
0.1187	30.7	.1814	2	Majestic
0.1187	30.7	.1814	2	major's
0.1187	30.7	.1814	2	Malcolm's
0.1187	30.7	.1814	2	maneuvered
0.1187	30.7	.1814	2	Marcel
0.1187	30.7	.1814	2	MARCH
0.1187	30.7	.1814	2	matrons
0.1187	30.7	.1814	2	meditation
0.1187	30.7	.1814	2	Mexican's
0.1187	30.7	.1814	2	midseason
0.1187	30.7	.1814	2	mirages
0.1187	30.7	.1814	2	miscalculation
0.1187	30.7	.1814	2	moccasined
0.1187	30.7	.1814	2	moldering
0.1187	30.7	.1814	2	molybdenum
0.1187	30.7	.1814	2	Mounted
0.1187	30.7	.1814	2	mulled
0.1187	30.7	.1814	2	Nashville's
0.1187	30.7	.1814	2	Navy's
0.1187	30.7	.1814	2	niobium
0.1187	30.7	.1814	2	nonpartisan
0.1187	30.7	.1814	2	notching
0.1187	30.7	.1814	2	obliterate
0.1187	30.7	.1814	2	ohhh
0.1187	30.7	.1814	2	ohhhh
0.1187	30.7	.1814	2	openmouthed
0.1187	30.7	.1814	2	oratorical
0.1187	30.7	.1814	2	Orphan
0.1187	30.7	.1814	2	outpouring
0.1187	30.7	.1814	2	overrunning
0.1187	30.7	.1814	2	pack-horse
0.1187	30.7	.1814	2	padlocked
0.1187	30.7	.1814	2	PalmSprings
0.1187	30.7	.1814	2	Paulette
0.1187	30.7	.1814	2	peddles
0.1187	30.7	.1814	2	Peterson's
0.1187	30.7	.1814	2	phlegmatic
0.1187	30.7	.1814	2	phoning
0.1187	30.7	.1814	2	picketed
0.1187	30.7	.1814	2	pigeon-toed
0.1187	30.7	.1814	2	piled-up
0.1187	30.7	.1814	2	pilloried
0.1187	30.7	.1814	2	plods
0.1187	30.7	.1814	2	poncho
0.1187	30.7	.1814	2	potholes
0.1187	30.7	.1814	2	pow
0.1187	30.7	.1814	2	Powder
0.1187	30.7	.1814	2	Prison
0.1187	30.7	.1814	2	programming
0.1187	30.7	.1814	2	proposing
0.1187	30.7	.1814	2	punting
0.1187	30.7	.1814	2	PUSH
0.1187	30.7	.1814	2	rakishly
0.1187	30.7	.1814	2	ram's
0.1187	30.7	.1814	2	Rams'
0.1187	30.7	.1814	2	roosting
0.1187	30.7	.1814	2	Rosemary's
0.1187	30.7	.1814	2	run-of-the-mill
0.1187	30.7	.1814	2	sailplanes
0.1187	30.7	.1814	2	scatterbrained
0.1187	30.7	.1814	2	Scottie
0.1187	30.7	.1814	2	scrapped
0.1187	30.7	.1814	2	searchingly
0.1187	30.7	.1814	2	shameless
0.1187	30.7	.1814	2	shamelessly
0.1187	30.7	.1814	2	shoulder-high
0.1187	30.7	.1814	2	shrouding
0.1187	30.7	.1814	2	sincerest
0.1187	30.7	.1814	2	sit-down
0.1187	30.7	.1814	2	six-story
0.1187	30.7	.1814	2	slashes
0.1187	30.7	.1814	2	slithering
0.1187	30.7	.1814	2	smocks
0.1187	30.7	.1814	2	spaceman's

THE PRECEDING WORD TYPE OCCUPIES RANK 36800

U	SFI	D	F	Word Type
0.1187	30.7	.1814	2	splattered
0.1187	30.7	.1814	2	sportswriters
0.1187	30.7	.1814	2	spouted
0.1187	30.7	.1814	2	sprig
0.1187	30.7	.1814	2	Stacy
0.1187	30.7	.1814	2	staid
0.1187	30.7	.1814	2	stand-up
0.1187	30.7	.1814	2	stoked
0.1187	30.7	.1814	2	stoned
0.1187	30.7	.1814	2	streaking
0.1187	30.7	.1814	2	stripers
0.1187	30.7	.1814	2	Struggling
0.1187	30.7	.1814	2	sturdiest
0.1187	30.7	.1814	2	subterfuge
0.1187	30.7	.1814	2	suicidal
0.1187	30.7	.1814	2	sumptuous
0.1187	30.7	.1814	2	surfer
0.1187	30.7	.1814	2	Tar
0.1187	30.7	.1814	2	tarp
0.1187	30.7	.1814	2	tees
0.1187	30.7	.1814	2	Teletype
0.1187	30.7	.1814	2	ten-yard
0.1187	30.7	.1814	2	tenderhearted
0.1187	30.7	.1814	2	three-pound
0.1187	30.7	.1814	2	Thursdays
0.1187	30.7	.1814	2	Timeless
0.1187	30.7	.1814	2	tingle
0.1187	30.7	.1814	2	tippet
0.1187	30.7	.1814	2	tonneau
0.1187	30.7	.1814	2	tows
0.1187	30.7	.1814	2	trapper's
0.1187	30.7	.1814	2	Tribe
0.1187	30.7	.1814	2	troublemakers
0.1187	30.7	.1814	2	trucker
0.1187	30.7	.1814	2	two-hundred
0.1187	30.7	.1814	2	two-man
0.1187	30.7	.1814	2	uncoiling
0.1187	30.7	.1814	2	unhinged
0.1187	30.7	.1814	2	unlocks
0.1187	30.7	.1814	2	unpopularity
0.1187	30.7	.1814	2	unpopulated
0.1187	30.7	.1814	2	unshakable
0.1187	30.7	.1814	2	unsmiling
0.1187	30.7	.1814	2	VanNuys
0.1187	30.7	.1814	2	vaporize
0.1187	30.7	.1814	2	vented
0.1187	30.7	.1814	2	vroom
0.1187	30.7	.1814	2	Wagons
0.1187	30.7	.1814	2	wanes
0.1187	30.7	.1814	2	washed-out
0.1187	30.7	.1814	2	we-l-l
0.1187	30.7	.1814	2	week-end
0.1187	30.7	.1814	2	well-intentioned
0.1187	30.7	.1814	2	Wes
0.1187	30.7	.1814	2	whatcha
0.1187	30.7	.1814	2	white-washed
0.1187	30.7	.1814	2	willies
0.1187	30.7	.1814	2	windstorms
0.1187	30.7	.1814	2	worriedly
0.1187	30.7	.1814	2	yanking
0.1187	30.7	.1814	2	Zephyr
0.1187	30.7	.1814	2	163
0.1187	30.7	.1814	2	19-year-old
0.1187	30.7	.1814	2	1985
0.1187	30.7	.1814	2	20-foot
0.1187	30.7	.1814	2	26-year-old
0.1187	30.7	.1814	2	31st
0.1184	30.7	.2446	2	accelerates
0.1184	30.7	.2446	2	Bernhard
0.1184	30.7	.2446	2	BX
0.1184	30.7	.2446	2	cubed
0.1184	30.7	.2446	2	deceptively
0.1184	30.7	.2446	2	Erin
0.1184	30.7	.2446	2	Marks
0.1184	30.7	.2446	2	quests
0.1184	30.7	.2446	2	souvenirs
0.1184	30.7	.2446	2	steersman
0.1184	30.7	.2446	2	warehousemen
0.1184	30.7	.2446	2	1597
0.1184	30.7	.2446	2	508
0.1184	30.7	.2446	2	563
0.1184	30.7	.2446	2	586
0.1184	30.7	.2446	2	788
0.1183	30.7	.0000	6	Acrux
0.1183	30.7	.0000	6	aneroid
0.1183	30.7	.0000	6	antiseptics
0.1183	30.7	.0000	6	Arcturus
0.1183	30.7	.0000	6	Azalea
0.1183	30.7	.0000	6	bacilli
0.1183	30.7	.0000	6	beriberi
0.1183	30.7	.0000	6	beryl
0.1183	30.7	.0000	6	body-building
0.1183	30.7	.0000	6	Boyle's
0.1183	30.7	.0000	6	chlorate
0.1183	30.7	.0000	6	corpus
0.1183	30.7	.0000	6	corpuscles
0.1183	30.7	.0000	6	Crucis
0.1183	30.7	.0000	6	Dalton's
0.1183	30.7	.0000	6	Diatryma
0.1183	30.7	.0000	6	drumlin

THE PRECEDING WORD TYPE OCCUPIES RANK 36900

U	SFI	D	F	Word Type
0.1183	30.7	.0000	6	drumlins
0.1183	30.7	.0000	6	electrically-charged
0.1183	30.7	.0000	6	Eohippus
0.1183	30.7	.0000	6	epithelial
0.1183	30.7	.0000	6	FDA
0.1183	30.7	.0000	6	geosynclines
0.1183	30.7	.0000	6	halite
0.1183	30.7	.0000	6	Hubble
0.1183	30.7	.0000	6	lithosphere
0.1183	30.7	.0000	6	luteum
0.1183	30.7	.0000	6	narcotic
0.1183	30.7	.0000	6	ovaries
0.1183	30.7	.0000	6	paralytic
0.1183	30.7	.0000	6	propellants
0.1183	30.7	.0000	6	prothallium
0.1183	30.7	.0000	6	recessive
0.1183	30.7	.0000	6	reproduces
0.1183	30.7	.0000	6	RNA
0.1183	30.7	.0000	6	sealed-in
0.1183	30.7	.0000	6	segmented
0.1183	30.7	.0000	6	subphylum
0.1180	30.7	.0000	11	ADMIRERS
0.1180	30.7	.0000	11	Defarge
0.1180	30.7	.0000	11	GRANDFATHER
0.1180	30.7	.0000	11	Johnie
0.1180	30.7	.0000	11	MARY
0.1180	30.7	.0000	11	McQuiston
0.1180	30.7	.0000	11	OPERATOR
0.1180	30.7	.0000	11	RIGBY
0.1180	30.7	.0000	11	STEELE
0.1180	30.7	.0000	11	Torwal
0.1174	30.7	.1787	2	'by
0.1174	30.7	.1787	2	'fraid
0.1174	30.7	.1787	2	'mongst
0.1174	30.7	.1787	2	aah
0.1174	30.7	.1787	2	absentminded
0.1174	30.7	.1787	2	accusingly
0.1174	30.7	.1787	2	affrighted
0.1174	30.7	.1787	2	aggrieved
0.1174	30.7	.1787	2	alighting
0.1174	30.7	.1787	2	angelfish
0.1174	30.7	.1787	2	annihilated
0.1174	30.7	.1787	2	apologetic
0.1174	30.7	.1787	2	aslant
0.1174	30.7	.1787	2	avariciously
0.1174	30.7	.1787	2	bagful
0.1174	30.7	.1787	2	bated
0.1174	30.7	.1787	2	Beck
0.1174	30.7	.1787	2	bedpost
0.1174	30.7	.1787	2	befitted
0.1174	30.7	.1787	2	biding
0.1174	30.7	.1787	2	bigger'n
0.1174	30.7	.1787	2	bitsy
0.1174	30.7	.1787	2	black-and-silver-striped
0.1174	30.7	.1787	2	bleated
0.1174	30.7	.1787	2	bonbon
0.1174	30.7	.1787	2	botherin'
0.1174	30.7	.1787	2	bravado
0.1174	30.7	.1787	2	breached
0.1174	30.7	.1787	2	bringin'
0.1174	30.7	.1787	2	brownest
0.1174	30.7	.1787	2	cabman
0.1174	30.7	.1787	2	calf-roping
0.1174	30.7	.1787	2	cantle
0.1174	30.7	.1787	2	ceasing
0.1174	30.7	.1787	2	chirpings
0.1174	30.7	.1787	2	Christ's
0.1174	30.7	.1787	2	clumped
0.1174	30.7	.1787	2	confiding
0.1174	30.7	.1787	2	consoling
0.1174	30.7	.1787	2	Consulate
0.1174	30.7	.1787	2	coulda
0.1174	30.7	.1787	2	craze
0.1174	30.7	.1787	2	crimsoned
0.1174	30.7	.1787	2	Cristo
0.1174	30.7	.1787	2	cuffed
0.1174	30.7	.1787	2	Cutter's
0.1174	30.7	.1787	2	d'ye
0.1174	30.7	.1787	2	dander
0.1174	30.7	.1787	2	dasn't
0.1174	30.7	.1787	2	daydreamer
0.1174	30.7	.1787	2	deafeningly
0.1174	30.7	.1787	2	decency
0.1174	30.7	.1787	2	dell
0.1174	30.7	.1787	2	deodorized
0.1174	30.7	.1787	2	Direct
0.1174	30.7	.1787	2	disgusting
0.1174	30.7	.1787	2	disposes
0.1174	30.7	.1787	2	distaste
0.1174	30.7	.1787	2	disused
0.1174	30.7	.1787	2	dollar-sized
0.1174	30.7	.1787	2	dolt
0.1174	30.7	.1787	2	dominoes
0.1174	30.7	.1787	2	down-stream
0.1174	30.7	.1787	2	draggled
0.1174	30.7	.1787	2	drainboard
0.1174	30.7	.1787	2	drat
0.1174	30.7	.1787	2	dreamless
0.1174	30.7	.1787	2	drearily
0.1174	30.7	.1787	2	druther

THE PRECEDING WORD TYPE OCCUPIES RANK 37000

U	SFI	D	F	Word Type
0.1174	30.7	.1787	2	dyin'
0.1174	30.7	.1787	2	Eb's
0.1174	30.7	.1787	2	enfolded
0.1174	30.7	.1787	2	entranced
0.1174	30.7	.1787	2	entreaties
0.1174	30.7	.1787	2	entreaty
0.1174	30.7	.1787	2	fatigued
0.1174	30.7	.1787	2	fielder's
0.1174	30.7	.1787	2	fifty-pound
0.1174	30.7	.1787	2	fish-market
0.1174	30.7	.1787	2	fluffed
0.1174	30.7	.1787	2	flustered
0.1174	30.7	.1787	2	forkful
0.1174	30.7	.1787	2	fortune-teller
0.1174	30.7	.1787	2	foster-father
0.1174	30.7	.1787	2	gag
0.1174	30.7	.1787	2	Gar
0.1174	30.7	.1787	2	gaw
0.1174	30.7	.1787	2	genially
0.1174	30.7	.1787	2	geniuses
0.1174	30.7	.1787	2	Ginger's
0.1174	30.7	.1787	2	good-
0.1174	30.7	.1787	2	good-morning
0.1174	30.7	.1787	2	grandchild
0.1174	30.7	.1787	2	grandpa's
0.1174	30.7	.1787	2	gratification
0.1174	30.7	.1787	2	gravestone
0.1174	30.7	.1787	2	gray-blue
0.1174	30.7	.1787	2	guineas
0.1174	30.7	.1787	2	gusto
0.1174	30.7	.1787	2	hairbrush
0.1174	30.7	.1787	2	half-acre
0.1174	30.7	.1787	2	half-closed
0.1174	30.7	.1787	2	hallways
0.1174	30.7	.1787	2	Hamlet's
0.1174	30.7	.1787	2	harpooner
0.1174	30.7	.1787	2	hm-m
0.1174	30.7	.1787	2	hollers
0.1174	30.7	.1787	2	hump-backed
0.1174	30.7	.1787	2	impartially
0.1174	30.7	.1787	2	inkstand
0.1174	30.7	.1787	2	inmates
0.1174	30.7	.1787	2	It'll
0.1174	30.7	.1787	2	jello
0.1174	30.7	.1787	2	jings
0.1174	30.7	.1787	2	joggled
0.1174	30.7	.1787	2	killin'
0.1174	30.7	.1787	2	late-afternoon
0.1174	30.7	.1787	2	ledgers
0.1174	30.7	.1787	2	lilt
0.1174	30.7	.1787	2	livelier
0.1174	30.7	.1787	2	Lonesome
0.1174	30.7	.1787	2	loup-garou
0.1174	30.7	.1787	2	manfully
0.1174	30.7	.1787	2	mannered
0.1174	30.7	.1787	2	MARK
0.1174	30.7	.1787	2	Mole's
0.1174	30.7	.1787	2	moonfish
0.1174	30.7	.1787	2	moonstones
0.1174	30.7	.1787	2	mutterings
0.1174	30.7	.1787	2	muzzles
0.1174	30.7	.1787	2	mystified
0.1174	30.7	.1787	2	Nance
0.1174	30.7	.1787	2	neighing
0.1174	30.7	.1787	2	nerveless
0.1174	30.7	.1787	2	Norton's
0.1174	30.7	.1787	2	nullified
0.1174	30.7	.1787	2	Odette's
0.1174	30.7	.1787	2	overrated
0.1174	30.7	.1787	2	parley

U	SFI	D	F	Word Type
0.1174	30.7	.1787	2	pellet
0.1174	30.7	.1787	2	Penning
0.1174	30.7	.1787	2	petered
0.1174	30.7	.1787	2	pied
0.1174	30.7	.1787	2	pirating
0.1174	30.7	.1787	2	polo
0.1174	30.7	.1787	2	preened
0.1174	30.7	.1787	2	puppyhood
0.1174	30.7	.1787	2	Quimbys'
0.1174	30.7	.1787	2	quivers
0.1174	30.7	.1787	2	Rab's
0.1174	30.7	.1787	2	rain's
0.1174	30.7	.1787	2	Randall's
0.1174	30.7	.1787	2	rapscallion
0.1174	30.7	.1787	2	rear-vision
0.1174	30.7	.1787	2	reconnoitre
0.1174	30.7	.1787	2	rejoicings
0.1174	30.7	.1787	2	resenting
0.1174	30.7	.1787	2	revelry
0.1174	30.7	.1787	2	riddance
0.1174	30.7	.1787	2	Riddle
0.1174	30.7	.1787	2	roofed
0.1174	30.7	.1787	2	Ross's
0.1174	30.7	.1787	2	scaring
0.1174	30.7	.1787	2	scarring
0.1174	30.7	.1787	2	scones
0.1174	30.7	.1787	2	seein'
0.1174	30.7	.1787	2	shoddy
0.1174	30.7	.1787	2	shoutings
0.1174	30.7	.1787	2	shucked
THE PRECEDING WORD TYPE OCCUPIES RANK 37100				
0.1174	30.7	.1787	2	silvering
0.1174	30.7	.1787	2	skiffs
0.1174	30.7	.1787	2	slackened
0.1174	30.7	.1787	2	sledding
0.1174	30.7	.1787	2	sleepy-looking
0.1174	30.7	.1787	2	slinging
0.1174	30.7	.1787	2	smarty
0.1174	30.7	.1787	2	smithereens
0.1174	30.7	.1787	2	smuggle
0.1174	30.7	.1787	2	snag
0.1174	30.7	.1787	2	soft-boiled
0.1174	30.7	.1787	2	speakin'
0.1174	30.7	.1787	2	spearmint
0.1174	30.7	.1787	2	speculatively
0.1174	30.7	.1787	2	sponging
0.1174	30.7	.1787	2	squarish
0.1174	30.7	.1787	2	squawks
0.1174	30.7	.1787	2	standin'
0.1174	30.7	.1787	2	staunchness
0.1174	30.7	.1787	2	stoking
0.1174	30.7	.1787	2	straggler
0.1174	30.7	.1787	2	stroller
0.1174	30.7	.1787	2	sumacs
0.1174	30.7	.1787	2	sun-browned
0.1174	30.7	.1787	2	Sword
0.1174	30.7	.1787	2	sympathetically
0.1174	30.7	.1787	2	tailcoat
0.1174	30.7	.1787	2	Tanner's
0.1174	30.7	.1787	2	taproom
0.1174	30.7	.1787	2	texas
0.1174	30.7	.1787	2	thats
0.1174	30.7	.1787	2	thieves'
0.1174	30.7	.1787	2	tonics
0.1174	30.7	.1787	2	tonsils
0.1174	30.7	.1787	2	toted
0.1174	30.7	.1787	2	tremblingly
0.1174	30.7	.1787	2	tremor
0.1174	30.7	.1787	2	Trudy's
0.1174	30.7	.1787	2	tummies
0.1174	30.7	.1787	2	turnin'
0.1174	30.7	.1787	2	undershirts
0.1174	30.7	.1787	2	undisciplined
0.1174	30.7	.1787	2	unforgiving
0.1174	30.7	.1787	2	unladylike
0.1174	30.7	.1787	2	unmanageable
0.1174	30.7	.1787	2	unsullied
0.1174	30.7	.1787	2	untiring
0.1174	30.7	.1787	2	unwrapping
0.1174	30.7	.1787	2	unyielding
0.1174	30.7	.1787	2	VALLEY
0.1174	30.7	.1787	2	visa
0.1174	30.7	.1787	2	warder
0.1174	30.7	.1787	2	washpan
0.1174	30.7	.1787	2	weekdays
0.1174	30.7	.1787	2	weir
0.1174	30.7	.1787	2	well-seasoned
0.1174	30.7	.1787	2	whelped
0.1174	30.7	.1787	2	whinnies
0.1174	30.7	.1787	2	white-circled
0.1174	30.7	.1787	2	Wilsons'
0.1174	30.7	.1787	2	Woodlawns
0.1174	30.7	.1787	2	yapped
0.1174	30.7	.1787	2	Zuckerman's
0.1174	30.7	.1787	2	Zulu
0.1172	30.7	.0000	10	'sclusively
0.1172	30.7	.0000	10	Auka
0.1172	30.7	.0000	10	Cadi
0.1172	30.7	.0000	10	deliverance
0.1172	30.7	.0000	10	Dulcey
0.1172	30.7	.0000	10	Hendon
0.1172	30.7	.0000	10	Hertford
0.1172	30.7	.0000	10	Lillybell
0.1172	30.7	.0000	10	Lyte
0.1172	30.7	.0000	10	Obediah
0.1172	30.7	.0000	10	Sentry
0.1172	30.7	.0000	10	Tegumai
0.1172	30.7	.0000	10	thump-thump
0.1167	30.7	.0000	6	Anglo-America
0.1167	30.7	.0000	6	Bernardo
0.1167	30.7	.0000	6	Cali
0.1167	30.7	.0000	6	Carmita
0.1167	30.7	.0000	6	Chou
0.1167	30.7	.0000	6	derricks
0.1167	30.7	.0000	6	Duvall
0.1167	30.7	.0000	6	Englanders
0.1167	30.7	.0000	6	Estancia
0.1167	30.7	.0000	6	Histadrut
0.1167	30.7	.0000	6	Jasim
0.1167	30.7	.0000	6	Jojep
0.1167	30.7	.0000	6	Kamehameha
0.1167	30.7	.0000	6	Longitude
0.1167	30.7	.0000	6	Lundquist
0.1167	30.7	.0000	6	Madre
0.1167	30.7	.0000	6	maguey
0.1167	30.7	.0000	6	Manaus
0.1167	30.7	.0000	6	Nemacolin
0.1167	30.7	.0000	6	Nigerian
0.1167	30.7	.0000	6	oomiak
0.1167	30.7	.0000	6	polders
0.1167	30.7	.0000	6	signers
THE PRECEDING WORD TYPE OCCUPIES RANK 37200				
0.1167	30.7	.0000	6	Silesia
0.1167	30.7	.0000	6	Ta-kuan
0.1167	30.7	.0000	6	tokonoma
0.1167	30.7	.0000	6	Toltec
0.1167	30.7	.0000	6	Tonty
0.1166	30.7	.2351	2	$58
0.1166	30.7	.2346	2	'possums
0.1166	30.7	.2346	2	adulterated
0.1166	30.7	.2346	2	Advanced
0.1166	30.7	.2351	2	advertisers
0.1166	30.7	.2351	2	advising
0.1166	30.7	.2351	2	Afro
0.1166	30.7	.2351	2	air-speed
0.1166	30.7	.2346	2	airship
0.1166	30.7	.2351	2	Albanians
0.1166	30.7	.2351	2	Alonso
0.1166	30.7	.2351	2	angering
0.1166	30.7	.2351	2	antagonize
0.1166	30.7	.2351	2	Arenas
0.1166	30.7	.2351	2	armories
0.1166	30.7	.2351	2	Artesian
0.1166	30.7	.2346	2	between-meal
0.1166	30.7	.2346	2	binaries
0.1166	30.7	.2351	2	blighted
0.1166	30.7	.2346	2	Brace
0.1166	30.7	.2351	2	briefed
0.1166	30.7	.2346	2	Bureau's
0.1166	30.7	.2351	2	butchering
0.1166	30.7	.2351	2	camaraderie
0.1166	30.7	.2351	2	campaigned
0.1166	30.7	.2351	2	cauldrons
0.1166	30.7	.2346	2	Caution
0.1166	30.7	.2351	2	censored
0.1166	30.7	.2351	2	Certificate
0.1166	30.7	.2351	2	Championships
0.1166	30.7	.2351	2	Chisholm
0.1166	30.7	.2351	2	chronometers
0.1166	30.7	.2346	2	churchman
0.1166	30.7	.2351	2	Churchmen
0.1166	30.7	.2346	2	circumnavigation
0.1166	30.7	.2351	2	citizens'
0.1166	30.7	.2346	2	citric
0.1166	30.7	.2351	2	clergymen
0.1166	30.7	.2351	2	Clive
0.1166	30.7	.2351	2	college-trained
0.1166	30.7	.2346	2	concoction
0.1166	30.7	.2351	2	conquistadores
0.1166	30.7	.2351	2	conservatives
0.1166	30.7	.2346	2	controllable
0.1166	30.7	.2351	2	cookers
0.1166	30.7	.2346	2	cortisone
0.1166	30.7	.2346	2	cottonmouth
0.1166	30.7	.2351	2	countered
0.1166	30.7	.2351	2	cowpoke
0.1166	30.7	.2351	2	creditors
0.1166	30.7	.2351	2	crusades
0.1166	30.7	.2351	2	curtailed
0.1166	30.7	.2351	2	Dakar
0.1166	30.7	.2346	2	definitive
0.1166	30.7	.2346	2	dehydration
0.1166	30.7	.2351	2	delved
0.1166	30.7	.2351	2	dependency
0.1166	30.7	.2346	2	desert-like
0.1166	30.7	.2346	2	detonated
0.1166	30.7	.2351	2	developers
0.1166	30.7	.2351	2	disfranchised
0.1166	30.7	.2351	2	disloyalty
0.1166	30.7	.2346	2	disperses
0.1166	30.7	.2351	2	disqualified
0.1166	30.7	.2351	2	dissidents
0.1166	30.7	.2346	2	dissipate
0.1166	30.7	.2351	2	doggone
0.1166	30.7	.2346	2	Drugs
0.1166	30.7	.2346	2	dungeons
0.1166	30.7	.2346	2	earth-moon
0.1166	30.7	.2351	2	endorsing
0.1166	30.7	.2351	2	enjoins
0.1166	30.7	.2346	2	entrapped
0.1166	30.7	.2351	2	espionage
0.1166	30.7	.2351	2	evacuate
0.1166	30.7	.2351	2	evasive
0.1166	30.7	.2351	2	facsimile
0.1166	30.7	.2346	2	falsehoods
0.1166	30.7	.2351	2	federated
0.1166	30.7	.2351	2	filmstrips
0.1166	30.7	.2351	2	first-generation
0.1166	30.7	.2351	2	flaking
0.1166	30.7	.2346	2	flatlands
0.1166	30.7	.2346	2	fluoridated
0.1166	30.7	.2346	2	flywheels
0.1166	30.7	.2346	2	follow-up
0.1166	30.7	.2346	2	Forecast
0.1166	30.7	.2351	2	foreign-owned
0.1166	30.7	.2351	2	Fortas
0.1166	30.7	.2351	2	forthcoming
0.1166	30.7	.2346	2	foursome
0.1166	30.7	.2346	2	genetically
0.1166	30.7	.2346	2	genetics
0.1166	30.7	.2351	2	glass-walled
0.1166	30.7	.2346	2	glycerin
THE PRECEDING WORD TYPE OCCUPIES RANK 37300				
0.1166	30.7	.2351	2	gutted
0.1166	30.7	.2346	2	gyrating
0.1166	30.7	.2351	2	haggling
0.1166	30.7	.2351	2	haphazardly
0.1166	30.7	.2351	2	Heritage
0.1166	30.7	.2351	2	hinterlands
0.1166	30.7	.2351	2	Hollywood's
0.1166	30.7	.2351	2	hulled
0.1166	30.7	.2346	2	humbling
0.1166	30.7	.2346	2	improperly
0.1166	30.7	.2351	2	ineligible
0.1166	30.7	.2351	2	infiltration
0.1166	30.7	.2346	2	inhales
0.1166	30.7	.2351	2	instigated
0.1166	30.7	.2351	2	instructors
0.1166	30.7	.2346	2	invades
0.1166	30.7	.2351	2	ironies
0.1166	30.7	.2346	2	isolate
0.1166	30.7	.2351	2	Junipero
0.1166	30.7	.2351	2	kerosine
0.1166	30.7	.2351	2	knolls
0.1166	30.7	.2351	2	landfall
0.1166	30.7	.2351	2	Latter-day
0.1166	30.7	.2346	2	lefthanded
0.1166	30.7	.2351	2	life-style
0.1166	30.7	.2351	2	lightships
0.1166	30.7	.2351	2	limousine
0.1166	30.7	.2346	2	Linton
0.1166	30.7	.2351	2	long-established
0.1166	30.7	.2346	2	lowermost
0.1166	30.7	.2351	2	mache
0.1166	30.7	.2346	2	malocclusion
0.1166	30.7	.2351	2	managerial
0.1166	30.7	.2351	2	mandatory
0.1166	30.7	.2351	2	Manifesto
0.1166	30.7	.2346	2	mantis
0.1166	30.7	.2346	2	marchers
0.1166	30.7	.2351	2	Mariano
0.1166	30.7	.2351	2	Marquette
0.1166	30.7	.2351	2	McKenna
0.1166	30.7	.2351	2	Merit
0.1166	30.7	.2351	2	midcontinent
0.1166	30.7	.2351	2	Midway
0.1166	30.7	.2351	2	misdemeanor
0.1166	30.7	.2346	2	MOON
0.1166	30.7	.2351	2	Mortgage
0.1166	30.7	.2351	2	Moshe
0.1166	30.7	.2346	2	mothball
0.1166	30.7	.2351	2	moviegoing
0.1166	30.7	.2346	2	muddier
0.1166	30.7	.2346	2	musk-oxen
0.1166	30.7	.2351	2	Nam's
0.1166	30.7	.2346	2	nape
0.1166	30.7	.2351	2	negotiators
0.1166	30.7	.2346	2	neutralizing
0.1166	30.7	.2351	2	Nigeria's
0.1166	30.7	.2351	2	nine-room
0.1166	30.7	.2351	2	nonfarm
0.1166	30.7	.2351	2	Nye
0.1166	30.7	.2346	2	objectors
0.1166	30.7	.2351	2	offends
0.1166	30.7	.2351	2	oil-drilling
0.1166	30.7	.2346	2	oil-filled
0.1166	30.7	.2346	2	openwork
0.1166	30.7	.2351	2	Oroville
0.1166	30.7	.2346	2	overanxious
0.1166	30.7	.2346	2	overhauling
0.1166	30.7	.2346	2	PalmBeach
0.1166	30.7	.2351	2	panicked
0.1166	30.7	.2351	2	papier
0.1166	30.7	.2351	2	Perm
0.1166	30.7	.2346	2	persevered
0.1166	30.7	.2346	2	persuades
0.1166	30.7	.2346	2	pip
0.1166	30.7	.2346	2	Planetarium
0.1166	30.7	.2351	2	politicans
0.1166	30.7	.2351	2	polyglot
0.1166	30.7	.2351	2	powerhouses
0.1166	30.7	.2346	2	probabilities
0.1166	30.7	.2351	2	racism
0.1166	30.7	.2351	2	racists
0.1166	30.7	.2351	2	railroads'
0.1166	30.7	.2351	2	rank-and-file
0.1166	30.7	.2351	2	Recreation
0.1166	30.7	.2346	2	recruitment
0.1166	30.7	.2351	2	regimes
0.1166	30.7	.2346	2	registering
0.1166	30.7	.2346	2	Renfrew
0.1166	30.7	.2351	2	rescind
0.1166	30.7	.2351	2	resentments
0.1166	30.7	.2346	2	retardation
0.1166	30.7	.2346	2	revile
0.1166	30.7	.2351	2	revolting
0.1166	30.7	.2351	2	Romanov
0.1166	30.7	.2351	2	Rusk
0.1166	30.7	.2346	2	salivating
0.1166	30.7	.2346	2	samplings
0.1166	30.7	.2351	2	satires
0.1166	30.7	.2346	2	saucer-shaped
0.1166	30.7	.2346	2	scalds
THE PRECEDING WORD TYPE OCCUPIES RANK 37400				
0.1166	30.7	.2351	2	scrupulous
0.1166	30.7	.2346	2	senile
0.1166	30.7	.2351	2	separatism
0.1166	30.7	.2351	2	shootings
0.1166	30.7	.2346	2	short-range
0.1166	30.7	.2346	2	short-term
0.1166	30.7	.2346	2	sicknesses
0.1166	30.7	.2351	2	Sistine
0.1166	30.7	.2351	2	sit-ins
0.1166	30.7	.2351	2	snakebite
0.1166	30.7	.2346	2	solidifying
0.1166	30.7	.2351	2	songwriters
0.1166	30.7	.2351	2	southwestward
0.1166	30.7	.2351	2	spree
0.1166	30.7	.2351	2	store-bought
0.1166	30.7	.2346	2	suffices
0.1166	30.7	.2351	2	surpassing
0.1166	30.7	.2346	2	susceptibility
0.1166	30.7	.2351	2	sweepers
0.1166	30.7	.2346	2	tankful
0.1166	30.7	.2351	2	Tax
0.1166	30.7	.2351	2	Tehran
0.1166	30.7	.2346	2	telescoping
0.1166	30.7	.2351	2	thin-lipped
0.1166	30.7	.2351	2	THIS
0.1166	30.7	.2346	2	three-strand
0.1166	30.7	.2351	2	thresher
0.1166	30.7	.2351	2	timelessness
0.1166	30.7	.2351	2	Together
0.1166	30.7	.2351	2	Torrance
0.1166	30.7	.2351	2	Township
0.1166	30.7	.2351	2	Traffic
0.1166	30.7	.2346	2	transplants
0.1166	30.7	.2351	2	twenty-eighth
0.1166	30.7	.2351	2	two-term
0.1166	30.7	.2346	2	ultra
0.1166	30.7	.2346	2	unattainable
0.1166	30.7	.2346	2	undissolved
0.1166	30.7	.2351	2	unenthusiastic
0.1166	30.7	.2351	2	unionism
0.1166	30.7	.2351	2	unjustified
0.1166	30.7	.2351	2	unpromising
0.1166	30.7	.2346	2	unsatisfied
0.1166	30.7	.2346	2	untreated
0.1166	30.7	.2351	2	up-to-the-minute
0.1166	30.7	.2351	2	updated
0.1166	30.7	.2346	2	upstart
0.1166	30.7	.2351	2	utopian
0.1166	30.7	.2346	2	vaults
0.1166	30.7	.2351	2	Volunteer
0.1166	30.7	.2351	2	volunteering
0.1166	30.7	.2351	2	Waterbury
0.1166	30.7	.2351	2	Wheat
0.1166	30.7	.2351	2	Willamette
0.1166	30.7	.2351	2	withdrawals
0.1166	30.7	.2351	2	Yost
0.1166	30.7	.2351	2	Zach
0.1166	30.7	.2346	2	zags
0.1166	30.7	.2351	2	Zapotec
0.1166	30.7	.2346	2	zigs
0.1166	30.7	.2351	2	10-11
0.1166	30.7	.2346	2	100-inch
0.1166	30.7	.2351	2	1001
0.1166	30.7	.2346	2	12-man
0.1166	30.7	.2346	2	13-1
0.1166	30.7	.2351	2	1493
0.1166	30.7	.2351	2	1551
0.1166	30.7	.2346	2	1752
0.1166	30.7	.2346	2	18-foot
0.1166	30.7	.2351	2	20-year
0.1166	30.7	.2346	2	24-10
0.1166	30.7	.2351	2	335
0.1166	30.7	.2351	2	370
0.1166	30.7	.2351	2	372
0.1166	30.7	.2351	2	558
0.1166	30.7	.2351	2	758
0.1166	30.7	.2346	2	8-year-old
0.1166	30.7	.2351	2	943
0.1159	30.6	.2427	2	$105
0.1159	30.6	.2427	2	$1500
0.1159	30.6	.2427	2	$160
0.1159	30.6	.2427	2	$26
0.1159	30.6	.2427	2	$28
0.1159	30.6	.2427	2	$3000
0.1159	30.6	.2427	2	$46
0.1159	30.6	.2427	2	$64
0.1159	30.6	.2427	2	$95
0.1159	30.6	.2427	2	allowable
0.1159	30.6	.2427	2	bisected
0.1159	30.6	.2427	2	budgets
0.1159	30.6	.2427	2	Constellation
0.1159	30.6	.2427	2	Discoverer
0.1159	30.6	.2427	2	first-place
0.1159	30.6	.2427	2	Fri
0.1159	30.6	.2427	2	Girls'
0.1159	30.6	.2427	2	golfers
0.1159	30.6	.2427	2	Greatest
0.1159	30.6	.2427	2	inspections
0.1159	30.6	.2427	2	Marlene
0.1159	30.6	.2427	2	megaton
THE PRECEDING WORD TYPE OCCUPIES RANK 37500				
0.1159	30.6	.2427	2	Puzzles
0.1159	30.6	.2427	2	rentals
0.1159	30.6	.2427	2	Sales
0.1159	30.6	.2427	2	TC
0.1159	30.6	.2427	2	technologists
0.1159	30.6	.2427	2	torques
0.1159	30.6	.2427	2	Vernon's
0.1159	30.6	.2427	2	vocations
0.1159	30.6	.2427	2	065
0.1159	30.6	.2427	2	12's
0.1159	30.6	.2427	2	13's
0.1159	30.6	.2427	2	1671
0.1159	30.6	.2427	2	254
0.1159	30.6	.2427	2	337
0.1159	30.6	.2427	2	403
0.1159	30.6	.2427	2	50-yard
0.1159	30.6	.2427	2	5200
0.1159	30.6	.2427	2	530
0.1159	30.6	.2427	2	546
0.1159	30.6	.2427	2	5500
0.1159	30.6	.2427	2	562
0.1159	30.6	.2427	2	870
0.1159	30.6	.2427	2	9-11
0.1159	30.6	.2427	2	95%
0.1158	30.6	.2433	2	accentuated
0.1158	30.6	.2433	2	adamant
0.1158	30.6	.2433	2	agonizingly
0.1158	30.6	.2433	2	Alamein
0.1158	30.6	.2433	2	allegorical
0.1158	30.6	.2433	2	alleviate
0.1158	30.6	.2433	2	alleviated
0.1158	30.6	.2433	2	ambiguous
0.1158	30.6	.2433	2	Auntie

U	SFI	D	F	Word Type
0.1158	30.6	.2433	2	autographed
0.1158	30.6	.2433	2	battler
0.1158	30.6	.2433	2	bedbugs
0.1158	30.6	.2433	2	beep
0.1158	30.6	.2433	2	bikini
0.1158	30.6	.2433	2	blazer
0.1158	30.6	.2433	2	cacophony
0.1158	30.6	.2433	2	capitulate
0.1158	30.6	.2433	2	Cardinals
0.1158	30.6	.2433	2	castaways
0.1158	30.6	.2433	2	catered
0.1158	30.6	.2433	2	cavernous
0.1158	30.6	.2433	2	Centre
0.1158	30.6	.2433	2	certifies
0.1158	30.6	.2433	2	chaplains
0.1158	30.6	.2433	2	charisma
0.1158	30.6	.2433	2	chasms
0.1158	30.6	.2433	2	Childe
0.1158	30.6	.2433	2	clerics
0.1158	30.6	.2433	2	collaborated
0.1158	30.6	.2433	2	communique
0.1158	30.6	.2433	2	cons
0.1158	30.6	.2433	2	consolidate
0.1158	30.6	.2433	2	consolidation
0.1158	30.6	.2433	2	conspire
0.1158	30.6	.2433	2	contacted
0.1158	30.6	.2433	2	counseling
0.1158	30.6	.2433	2	cringe
0.1158	30.6	.2433	2	cubicles
0.1158	30.6	.2433	2	curvy
0.1158	30.6	.2433	2	debutante
0.1158	30.6	.2433	2	defected
0.1158	30.6	.2433	2	dislodge
0.1158	30.6	.2433	2	dismantling
0.1158	30.6	.2433	2	displaces
0.1158	30.6	.2433	2	Dresser
0.1158	30.6	.0000	8	Duckbill
0.1158	30.6	.0000	8	Dumfries
0.1158	30.6	.2433	2	eau
0.1158	30.6	.2433	2	enclaves
0.1158	30.6	.2433	2	entourage
0.1158	30.6	.2433	2	espoused
0.1158	30.6	.2433	2	estranged
0.1158	30.6	.2433	2	euphemisms
0.1158	30.6	.2433	2	faking
0.1158	30.6	.2433	2	ferrying
0.1158	30.6	.2433	2	fiance
0.1158	30.6	.2433	2	Findlay
0.1158	30.6	.2433	2	finer-grained
0.1158	30.6	.2433	2	flip-flops
0.1158	30.6	.2433	2	forthright
0.1158	30.6	.2433	2	fruited
0.1158	30.6	.2433	2	garish
0.1158	30.6	.2433	2	glob
0.1158	30.6	.2433	2	gloriously
0.1158	30.6	.2433	2	gooney
0.1158	30.6	.2433	2	graying
0.1158	30.6	.2433	2	grotto
0.1158	30.6	.2433	2	hard-core
0.1158	30.6	.2433	2	hard-hitting
0.1158	30.6	.2433	2	hardihood
0.1158	30.6	.2433	2	Haven
0.1158	30.6	.2433	2	high-temperature
0.1158	30.6	.2433	2	honest-to-goodness
0.1158	30.6	.2433	2	hookup
0.1158	30.6	.0000	8	Huldah
0.1158	30.6	.2433	2	hypocrisies
THE PRECEDING WORD TYPE OCCUPIES RANK 37600				
0.1158	30.6	.2433	2	impassible
0.1158	30.6	.2433	2	income-tax
0.1158	30.6	.2433	2	indeterminate
0.1158	30.6	.2433	2	infielder
0.1158	30.6	.2433	2	inspirations
0.1158	30.6	.2433	2	justifiable
0.1158	30.6	.2433	2	left-footed
0.1158	30.6	.2433	2	liberally
0.1158	30.6	.2433	2	lightning-fast
0.1158	30.6	.2433	2	loincloths
0.1158	30.6	.2433	2	Longest
0.1158	30.6	.2433	2	Louisa's
0.1158	30.6	.2433	2	Lu
0.1158	30.6	.2433	2	macabre
0.1158	30.6	.2433	2	malnourished
0.1158	30.6	.2433	2	Mamie
0.1158	30.6	.2433	2	Mammals
0.1158	30.6	.2433	2	Manfred
0.1158	30.6	.2433	2	manliness
0.1158	30.6	.0000	8	Manteo
0.1158	30.6	.2433	2	Maris
0.1158	30.6	.2433	2	mechanization
0.1158	30.6	.2433	2	mistress'
0.1158	30.6	.2433	2	monopolistic
0.1158	30.6	.2433	2	murdering
0.1158	30.6	.0000	8	Nantaqua
0.1158	30.6	.2433	2	neater
0.1158	30.6	.2433	2	obsolescence
0.1158	30.6	.2433	2	officialdom
0.1158	30.6	.2433	2	old-timer
0.1158	30.6	.2433	2	Oneida
0.1158	30.6	.2433	2	Oriente
0.1158	30.6	.2433	2	parishioners
0.1158	30.6	.2433	2	passenger-car
0.1158	30.6	.2433	2	passengers'
0.1158	30.6	.2433	2	penchant
0.1158	30.6	.2433	2	Penobscot
0.1158	30.6	.2433	2	pent-up
0.1158	30.6	.2433	2	peppered
0.1158	30.6	.0000	8	Perley
0.1158	30.6	.2433	2	personified
0.1158	30.6	.2433	2	Phoenicia
0.1158	30.6	.2433	2	photogenic
0.1158	30.6	.2433	2	pinprick
0.1158	30.6	.2433	2	Pistol
0.1158	30.6	.2433	2	planter's
0.1158	30.6	.2433	2	Poverty
0.1158	30.6	.2433	2	pre-eminence
0.1158	30.6	.2433	2	Preventive
0.1158	30.6	.2433	2	principality
0.1158	30.6	.2433	2	propagation
0.1158	30.6	.2433	2	propounded
0.1158	30.6	.2433	2	protagonist
0.1158	30.6	.2433	2	puking
0.1158	30.6	.2433	2	quiets
0.1158	30.6	.2433	2	recalcitrant
0.1158	30.6	.2433	2	receiver's
0.1158	30.6	.2433	2	red-coated
0.1158	30.6	.2433	2	redesigned
0.1158	30.6	.2433	2	regattas
0.1158	30.6	.2433	2	remorselessly
0.1158	30.6	.2433	2	renews
0.1158	30.6	.2433	2	restores
0.1158	30.6	.2433	2	retract
0.1158	30.6	.2433	2	retrospect
0.1158	30.6	.2433	2	rhinos
0.1158	30.6	.2433	2	rifleman
0.1158	30.6	.2433	2	Roberts's
0.1158	30.6	.2433	2	roommates
0.1158	30.6	.2433	2	Ruffing
0.1158	30.6	.2433	2	savants
0.1158	30.6	.2433	2	scavenge
0.1158	30.6	.2433	2	scorer
0.1158	30.6	.2433	2	second-place
0.1158	30.6	.2433	2	Senators'
0.1158	30.6	.2433	2	setbacks
0.1158	30.6	.2433	2	seventh-grader
0.1158	30.6	.2433	2	shambles
0.1158	30.6	.2433	2	sieves
0.1158	30.6	.2433	2	skeptic
0.1158	30.6	.2433	2	sleuthing
0.1158	30.6	.2433	2	slicked
0.1158	30.6	.2433	2	sluggers
0.1158	30.6	.2433	2	speedster
0.1158	30.6	.2433	2	stagger
0.1158	30.6	.2433	2	stateside
0.1158	30.6	.2433	2	statistic
0.1158	30.6	.2433	2	stockpile
0.1158	30.6	.2433	2	street-corner
0.1158	30.6	.2433	2	stumblingly
0.1158	30.6	.2433	2	stumpy
0.1158	30.6	.2433	2	sun-flecked
0.1158	30.6	.2433	2	surrealist
0.1158	30.6	.0000	8	Tha
0.1158	30.6	.2433	2	thirty-five-year-old
0.1158	30.6	.2433	2	tight-rope
0.1158	30.6	.0000	8	Tituba
0.1158	30.6	.2433	2	Transylvania
0.1158	30.6	.0000	8	Triceratops
0.1158	30.6	.2433	2	tuxedos
THE PRECEDING WORD TYPE OCCUPIES RANK 37700				
0.1158	30.6	.2433	2	underpowered
0.1158	30.6	.2433	2	undiscriminating
0.1158	30.6	.2433	2	unhesitatingly
0.1158	30.6	.2433	2	unspecified
0.1158	30.6	.2433	2	upcoming
0.1158	30.6	.2433	2	uselessness
0.1158	30.6	.2433	2	Vermonters
0.1158	30.6	.2433	2	violates
0.1158	30.6	.0000	8	wagering
0.1158	30.6	.2433	2	wastrel
0.1158	30.6	.2433	2	Watts
0.1158	30.6	.2433	2	wedging
0.1158	30.6	.2433	2	westerners
0.1158	30.6	.2433	2	whit
0.1158	30.6	.2433	2	white-robed
0.1158	30.6	.2433	2	WOW
0.1158	30.6	.2433	2	yaw
0.1158	30.6	.2433	2	1/4-
0.1158	30.6	.2433	2	1762
0.1158	30.6	.2433	2	3-0
0.1158	30.6	.2433	2	416
0.1158	30.6	.2433	2	67-year-old
0.1157	30.6	.2331	2	amass
0.1157	30.6	.2337	2	avenge
0.1157	30.6	.2331	2	Beginning
0.1157	30.6	.2337	2	breath-taking
0.1157	30.6	.2337	2	brimstone
0.1157	30.6	.2337	2	bullfighting
0.1157	30.6	.2331	2	butternuts
0.1157	30.6	.2337	2	carpetbag
0.1157	30.6	.2331	2	cartilaginous
0.1157	30.6	.2331	2	chameleon
0.1157	30.6	.2337	2	Chingachgook
0.1157	30.6	.2331	2	Christmas-tree
0.1157	30.6	.2337	2	comforters
0.1157	30.6	.2337	2	conjured
0.1157	30.6	.2331	2	cornstarch
0.1157	30.6	.2337	2	cottony
0.1157	30.6	.2331	2	day-by-day
0.1157	30.6	.2337	2	disenchanted
0.1157	30.6	.2337	2	disobedient
0.1157	30.6	.2337	2	dog-headed
0.1157	30.6	.2337	2	donkeys'
0.1157	30.6	.2331	2	doorknobs
0.1157	30.6	.2337	2	Dukes
0.1157	30.6	.2331	2	dummies
0.1157	30.6	.2331	2	Enemies
0.1157	30.6	.2337	2	Eternity
0.1157	30.6	.2337	2	Expansion
0.1157	30.6	.2337	2	flanking
0.1157	30.6	.0562	4	forgave
0.1157	30.6	.2337	2	Friesland
0.1157	30.6	.2331	2	grass-like
0.1157	30.6	.2331	2	groundless
0.1157	30.6	.2337	2	gunny
0.1157	30.6	.2337	2	harshest
0.1157	30.6	.2337	2	Hitchcock's
0.1157	30.6	.2337	2	Holstein
0.1157	30.6	.2337	2	Hooker's
0.1157	30.6	.2337	2	hornets'
0.1157	30.6	.2337	2	implored
0.1157	30.6	.2337	2	inmost
0.1157	30.6	.2337	2	Jacksons'
0.1157	30.6	.2337	2	jeer
0.1157	30.6	.2331	2	loons
0.1157	30.6	.2337	2	lulls
0.1157	30.6	.2337	2	Memories
0.1157	30.6	.2337	2	Messenger
0.1157	30.6	.2331	2	mimosa
0.1157	30.6	.2337	2	molders
0.1157	30.6	.2331	2	obsurity
0.1157	30.6	.2337	2	pervading
0.1157	30.6	.2331	2	picnicking
0.1157	30.6	.2331	2	Pit
0.1157	30.6	.2337	2	plowman
0.1157	30.6	.2337	2	plowshares
0.1157	30.6	.2337	2	pooling
0.1157	30.6	.2331	2	prematurely
0.1157	30.6	.2337	2	rebuff
0.1157	30.6	.2337	2	red-and-white-striped
0.1157	30.6	.2331	2	redden
0.1157	30.6	.2337	2	rustlers
0.1157	30.6	.2331	2	savoring
0.1157	30.6	.2337	2	Serpent
0.1157	30.6	.2337	2	skulked
0.1157	30.6	.2331	2	squeaks
0.1157	30.6	.2331	2	strep
0.1157	30.6	.2337	2	subversive
0.1157	30.6	.2337	2	Thirteen
0.1157	30.6	.2337	2	threshers
0.1157	30.6	.2331	2	timothy
0.1157	30.6	.2337	2	tinge
0.1157	30.6	.2331	2	topaz
0.1157	30.6	.2337	2	truckload
0.1157	30.6	.2331	2	unemotionally
0.1157	30.6	.2331	2	unforeseen
0.1157	30.6	.2337	2	unforseen
0.1157	30.6	.2331	2	unhampered
0.1157	30.6	.2337	2	unshaken
0.1157	30.6	.2337	2	wantonly
THE PRECEDING WORD TYPE OCCUPIES RANK 37800				
0.1157	30.6	.2331	2	wetted
0.1157	30.6	.2337	2	whiteskin
0.1157	30.6	.2337	2	wracked
0.1157	30.6	.2337	2	Wyoming's
0.1155	30.6	.1272	4	Sanforized
0.1154	30.6	.2420	2	Alison
0.1154	30.6	.2420	2	Boyles
0.1154	30.6	.2420	2	Cole's
0.1154	30.6	.2420	2	extracting
0.1154	30.6	.2420	2	Holloways
0.1154	30.6	.2420	2	jack-in-the-box
0.1154	30.6	.2420	2	ninety-five
0.1154	30.6	.2420	2	SEE
0.1154	30.6	.0326	12	sheet-metal
0.1154	30.6	.2420	2	Soda
0.1154	30.6	.2420	2	stretchers
0.1152	30.6	.2427	2	apace
0.1152	30.6	.2427	2	Argyle
0.1152	30.6	.2427	2	banishment
0.1152	30.6	.2427	2	Benny's
0.1152	30.6	.2427	2	blow-holes
0.1152	30.6	.2427	2	bookworm
0.1152	30.6	.2427	2	butchery
0.1152	30.6	.2427	2	cantering
0.1152	30.6	.2427	2	chiefest
0.1152	30.6	.2427	2	chirr
0.1152	30.6	.2427	2	Clerk's
0.1152	30.6	.2427	2	cocky
0.1152	30.6	.2427	2	cog
0.1152	30.6	.2427	2	confidant
0.1152	30.6	.2427	2	congested
0.1152	30.6	.2427	2	conspicuously
0.1152	30.6	.2427	2	copybooks
0.1152	30.6	.2427	2	Creighton's
0.1152	30.6	.2427	2	cross-roads
0.1152	30.6	.2427	2	curbstones
0.1152	30.6	.2427	2	currycomb
0.1152	30.6	.2427	2	cynically
0.1152	30.6	.2427	2	Danger
0.1152	30.6	.2427	2	dignitary
0.1152	30.6	.2427	2	DOG
0.1152	30.6	.2427	2	eleven-thirty
0.1152	30.6	.2427	2	escorting
0.1152	30.6	.2427	2	fibs
0.1152	30.6	.2427	2	fillet
0.1152	30.6	.2427	2	forequarters
0.1152	30.6	.2427	2	four-wheeled
0.1152	30.6	.2427	2	go-to-meeting
0.1152	30.6	.2427	2	gray-headed
0.1152	30.6	.2427	2	Great-aunt
0.1152	30.6	.2427	2	guardhouse
0.1152	30.6	.2427	2	half-asleep
0.1152	30.6	.2427	2	half-hitch
0.1152	30.6	.2427	2	hand-picked
0.1152	30.6	.2427	2	inclinations
0.1152	30.6	.2427	2	jessamine
0.1152	30.6	.2427	2	Jewry
0.1152	30.6	.2427	2	lifebelt
0.1152	30.6	.2427	2	Magnolia
0.1152	30.6	.2427	2	masterful
0.1152	30.6	.2427	2	meanin'
0.1152	30.6	.2427	2	morass
0.1152	30.6	.2427	2	muddied
0.1152	30.6	.2427	2	Mummy's
0.1152	30.6	.2427	2	nags
0.1152	30.6	.2427	2	Neck
0.1152	30.6	.2427	2	oldsters
0.1152	30.6	.2427	2	Otto's
0.1152	30.6	.2427	2	overlaps
0.1152	30.6	.2427	2	pard
0.1152	30.6	.2427	2	raiment
0.1152	30.6	.2427	2	redbud
0.1152	30.6	.2427	2	reflectively
0.1152	30.6	.2427	2	remorseless
0.1152	30.6	.2427	2	resurrected
0.1152	30.6	.2427	2	right-about
0.1152	30.6	.2427	2	Roc
0.1152	30.6	.2427	2	Rube
0.1152	30.6	.2427	2	scholar's
0.1152	30.6	.2427	2	Scotchman
0.1152	30.6	.2427	2	sendeth
0.1152	30.6	.2427	2	sith
0.1152	30.6	.2427	2	snow-topped
0.1152	30.6	.2427	2	snub
0.1152	30.6	.2427	2	strangles
0.1152	30.6	.2427	2	supplication
0.1152	30.6	.2427	2	tensing
0.1152	30.6	.2427	2	testimonial
0.1152	30.6	.2427	2	thereto
0.1152	30.6	.2427	2	thou'st
0.1152	30.6	.2427	2	toddling
0.1152	30.6	.2427	2	trickster
0.1152	30.6	.2427	2	unfurling
0.1152	30.6	.2427	2	Vote
0.1152	30.6	.2427	2	ye're
0.1152	30.6	.2427	2	yelps
0.1152	30.6	.2427	2	yit
0.1149	30.6	.1733	2	affirmative
0.1149	30.6	.1733	2	amaze
0.1149	30.6	.1733	2	Americana
THE PRECEDING WORD TYPE OCCUPIES RANK 37900				
0.1149	30.6	.1733	2	anyways
0.1149	30.6	.1733	2	April's
0.1149	30.6	.1733	2	Arithmetic
0.1149	30.6	.1733	2	artifice
0.1149	30.6	.1733	2	ashcan
0.1149	30.6	.1733	2	ayes
0.1149	30.6	.1733	2	Beanstalk
0.1149	30.6	.1733	2	Benton's
0.1149	30.6	.1733	2	best-
0.1149	30.6	.1733	2	best-dressed
0.1149	30.6	.1733	2	biased
0.1149	30.6	.1733	2	Bicycle
0.1149	30.6	.1733	2	blobs
0.1149	30.6	.1733	2	boars
0.1149	30.6	.1733	2	Brookline
0.1149	30.6	.1733	2	Camel
0.1149	30.6	.1733	2	casements
0.1149	30.6	.1733	2	catboat
0.1149	30.6	.1733	2	chewy
0.1149	30.6	.1733	2	clotheslines
0.1149	30.6	.1733	2	collegiate
0.1149	30.6	.1733	2	Contest
0.1149	30.6	.1733	2	daeg
0.1149	30.6	.1733	2	dakota
0.1149	30.6	.1733	2	dawns
0.1149	30.6	.1733	2	dolphin's
0.1149	30.6	.1733	2	Downing
0.1149	30.6	.1733	2	dva
0.1149	30.6	.1733	2	earthmen
0.1149	30.6	.1733	2	emerald-green
0.1149	30.6	.1733	2	envisioned
0.1149	30.6	.1733	2	Famous
0.1149	30.6	.1733	2	Fiction
0.1149	30.6	.1733	2	Forty-second
0.1149	30.6	.1733	2	four-leaf
0.1149	30.6	.1733	2	Gay's
0.1149	30.6	.1733	2	gladdened
0.1149	30.6	.1733	2	Goody's
0.1149	30.6	.1733	2	Gulliver's
0.1149	30.6	.1733	2	Hal's
0.1149	30.6	.1733	2	hearse
0.1149	30.6	.1733	2	hiccups
0.1149	30.6	.1733	2	ice-skate
0.1149	30.6	.1733	2	Idea
0.1149	30.6	.1733	2	jibes
0.1149	30.6	.1733	2	jiggle
0.1149	30.6	.1733	2	Keokuk
0.1149	30.6	.1733	2	Knute
0.1149	30.6	.1733	2	Leif's
0.1149	30.6	.1733	2	livelong
0.1149	30.6	.1733	2	Loaf
0.1149	30.6	.1733	2	locket
0.1149	30.6	.1733	2	Max's
0.1149	30.6	.1733	2	meted
0.1149	30.6	.1733	2	Millie
0.1149	30.6	.1733	2	mine's
0.1149	30.6	.1733	2	moron
0.1149	30.6	.1733	2	newpapers
0.1149	30.6	.1733	2	nutmegs
0.1149	30.6	.1733	2	odin
0.1149	30.6	.1733	2	openin'
0.1149	30.6	.1733	2	outdoorsman
0.1149	30.6	.1733	2	overdue
0.1149	30.6	.1733	2	pajama
0.1149	30.6	.1733	2	Paragraphs
0.1149	30.6	.1733	2	persuasively
0.1149	30.6	.1733	2	pigskin
0.1149	30.6	.1733	2	poached
0.1149	30.6	.1733	2	pone
0.1149	30.6	.1733	2	Prep
0.1149	30.6	.1733	2	public-address
0.1149	30.6	.1733	2	Pussy-Cat
0.1149	30.6	.1733	2	racquet
0.1149	30.6	.1733	2	rant
0.1149	30.6	.1733	2	rave
0.1149	30.6	.1733	2	redolent
0.1149	30.6	.1733	2	Regina
0.1149	30.6	.1733	2	rumpus
0.1149	30.6	.1733	2	Runnymede
0.1149	30.6	.1733	2	Sail
0.1149	30.6	.1733	2	Saturday's
0.1149	30.6	.1733	2	scandalous
0.1149	30.6	.1733	2	scram
0.1149	30.6	.1733	2	semidarkness
0.1149	30.6	.1733	2	simple-minded
0.1149	30.6	.1733	2	sorcery
0.1149	30.6	.1733	2	souped-up
0.1149	30.6	.1733	2	speedboat
0.1149	30.6	.1733	2	staggers
0.1149	30.6	.1733	2	Stair
0.1149	30.6	.1733	2	starveling
0.1149	30.6	.1733	2	steel-tipped
0.1149	30.6	.1733	2	Strange
0.1149	30.6	.1733	2	Strasbourg
0.1149	30.6	.1733	2	Tompkins
0.1149	30.6	.1733	2	Touch
0.1149	30.6	.1733	2	tough-looking

U	SFI	D	F	Word Type
0.1149	30.6	.1733	2	tu
0.1149	30.6	.1733	2	undertow
0.1149	30.6	.1733	2	Urdu

THE PRECEDING WORD TYPE OCCUPIES RANK 38000

U	SFI	D	F	Word Type
0.1149	30.6	.1733	2	Vachel
0.1149	30.6	.1733	2	vengeful
0.1149	30.6	.1733	2	Wednesday's
0.1149	30.6	.1733	2	wild-eyed
0.1149	30.6	.1733	2	wort
0.1149	30.6	.1733	2	wrested
0.1149	30.6	.1733	2	1736
0.1146	30.6	.0618	7	nutritional
0.1145	30.6	.0997	3	duct
0.1145	30.6	.0997	3	Mae
0.1145	30.6	.0997	3	mis
0.1145	30.6	.0997	3	put-together
0.1145	30.6	.0997	3	Take
0.1144	30.6	.0995	3	alternates
0.1144	30.6	.0995	3	bandstand
0.1144	30.6	.0995	3	Bellini
0.1144	30.6	.0995	3	Bland
0.1144	30.6	.0995	3	clappers
0.1144	30.6	.0995	3	Creation
0.1144	30.6	.0995	3	doggie
0.1144	30.6	.0995	3	expressively
0.1144	30.6	.0995	3	harmonically
0.1144	30.6	.0995	3	hippity
0.1144	30.6	.0995	3	ree
0.1144	30.6	.0995	3	Salzburg
0.1144	30.6	.0995	3	stabs
0.1144	30.6	.0995	3	Stark
0.1144	30.6	.0995	3	Steeple
0.1144	30.6	.0995	3	transcribed
0.1144	30.6	.0995	3	troubadour
0.1144	30.6	.0995	3	viol
0.1144	30.6	.0995	3	workin'
0.1142	30.6	.2446	2	abeyance
0.1142	30.6	.2446	2	abominable
0.1142	30.6	.1717	2	adown
0.1142	30.6	.1717	2	Aesop's
0.1142	30.6	.1717	2	affably
0.1142	30.6	.2446	2	afresh
0.1142	30.6	.2446	2	ails
0.1142	30.6	.1717	2	airily
0.1142	30.6	.2446	2	amiss
0.1142	30.6	.1717	2	amuck
0.1142	30.6	.2446	2	antipathies
0.1142	30.6	.1717	2	Antonio's
0.1142	30.6	.1717	2	applauding
0.1142	30.6	.1717	2	Applegate
0.1142	30.6	.1717	2	appreciating
0.1142	30.6	.1717	2	armchairs
0.1142	30.6	.1717	2	artful
0.1142	30.6	.1717	2	aways
0.1142	30.6	.1717	2	awfulness
0.1142	30.6	.1717	2	babying
0.1142	30.6	.2446	2	Bananas
0.1142	30.6	.2404	2	Barbara's
0.1142	30.6	.1717	2	barefaced
0.1142	30.6	.1717	2	bartering
0.1142	30.6	.1717	2	Basil
0.1142	30.6	.2446	2	Bench
0.1142	30.6	.1717	2	betrothal
0.1142	30.6	.1717	2	blanket's
0.1142	30.6	.1717	2	blazon
0.1142	30.6	.1717	2	blood-soaked
0.1142	30.6	.1717	2	blood-thirsty
0.1142	30.6	.1717	2	bloods
0.1142	30.6	.1717	2	bonjour
0.1142	30.6	.1717	2	booted
0.1142	30.6	.1717	2	braving
0.1142	30.6	.1717	2	Bridges
0.1142	30.6	.1717	2	buckboard
0.1142	30.6	.1717	2	buckbrush
0.1142	30.6	.1717	2	Bulldog
0.1142	30.6	.2446	2	bums
0.1142	30.6	.2446	2	bunions
0.1142	30.6	.2446	2	bunnies
0.1142	30.6	.2446	2	byplay
0.1142	30.6	.1717	2	calabashes
0.1142	30.6	.1717	2	careworn
0.1142	30.6	.2404	2	Carolyn
0.1142	30.6	.1717	2	chestnut-colored
0.1142	30.6	.1717	2	Chinaman
0.1142	30.6	.2446	2	classing
0.1142	30.6	.1717	2	clear-headed
0.1142	30.6	.1717	2	cleave
0.1142	30.6	.1717	2	coiling
0.1142	30.6	.1717	2	columnist
0.1142	30.6	.1717	2	commander's
0.1142	30.6	.2446	2	commutes
0.1142	30.6	.1717	2	companions'
0.1142	30.6	.1717	2	complimenting
0.1142	30.6	.2446	2	confections
0.1142	30.6	.2446	2	connoisseur
0.1142	30.6	.2446	2	contingent
0.1142	30.6	.1717	2	copyreaders
0.1142	30.6	.2446	2	coverts
0.1142	30.6	.1717	2	cowardice
0.1142	30.6	.2446	2	Coy
0.1142	30.6	.2446	2	Crackers
0.1142	30.6	.2446	2	crawly
0.1142	30.6	.1717	2	creamy-white
0.1142	30.6	.2446	2	crooned

THE PRECEDING WORD TYPE OCCUPIES RANK 38100

U	SFI	D	F	Word Type
0.1142	30.6	.1717	2	cuttin'
0.1142	30.6	.1717	2	d'Aulaire
0.1142	30.6	.1717	2	dance-music
0.1142	30.6	.1717	2	dawdling
0.1142	30.6	.1717	2	dearer
0.1142	30.6	.1717	2	decorum
0.1142	30.6	.1717	2	Deepfreeze
0.1142	30.6	.1717	2	Defiance
0.1142	30.6	.1717	2	dejectedly
0.1142	30.6	.1717	2	deliciously
0.1142	30.6	.1717	2	depeopled
0.1142	30.6	.2446	2	desecrated
0.1142	30.6	.2446	2	despondently
0.1142	30.6	.1717	2	devilment
0.1142	30.6	.1717	2	diapers
0.1142	30.6	.1717	2	dimple
0.1142	30.6	.1717	2	disapproved
0.1142	30.6	.1717	2	disclosing
0.1142	30.6	.2446	2	disfigured
0.1142	30.6	.2446	2	disparate
0.1142	30.6	.1717	2	disputing
0.1142	30.6	.1717	2	disrespectful
0.1142	30.6	.2446	2	dolled
0.1142	30.6	.1717	2	Dorothy's
0.1142	30.6	.1717	2	drawback
0.1142	30.6	.1717	2	ducks'
0.1142	30.6	.2446	2	dunk
0.1142	30.6	.1717	2	dutiful
0.1142	30.6	.2446	2	dwindling
0.1142	30.6	.2446	2	Editor
0.1142	30.6	.2404	2	eighth-grade
0.1142	30.6	.2446	2	enquiries
0.1142	30.6	.2446	2	equity
0.1142	30.6	.1717	2	ers
0.1142	30.6	.1717	2	ever'
0.1142	30.6	.1717	2	exacted
0.1142	30.6	.2446	2	excreta
0.1142	30.6	.1717	2	fancies
0.1142	30.6	.1717	2	Farmer's
0.1142	30.6	.1717	2	fatherly
0.1142	30.6	.2446	2	feline
0.1142	30.6	.1717	2	feverishly
0.1142	30.6	.1717	2	fiddled
0.1142	30.6	.1717	2	fightin'
0.1142	30.6	.1717	2	finery
0.1142	30.6	.1717	2	firefighters
0.1142	30.6	.2446	2	Fishes
0.1142	30.6	.1717	2	Flannigans
0.1142	30.6	.1717	2	flatiron
0.1142	30.6	.1717	2	fledglings
0.1142	30.6	.1717	2	florins
0.1142	30.6	.1717	2	foamed
0.1142	30.6	.2446	2	forestall
0.1142	30.6	.2446	2	Forms
0.1142	30.6	.1717	2	frills
0.1142	30.6	.1717	2	frock
0.1142	30.6	.2446	2	frustrations
0.1142	30.6	.2446	2	furtively
0.1142	30.6	.2446	2	galoshes
0.1142	30.6	.1717	2	Gals
0.1142	30.6	.2446	2	gilt
0.1142	30.6	.1717	2	gloating
0.1142	30.6	.2446	2	goggle-eyed
0.1142	30.6	.2446	2	Goldberg
0.1142	30.6	.1717	2	good-for-nothing
0.1142	30.6	.2446	2	gout
0.1142	30.6	.2446	2	gratified
0.1142	30.6	.1717	2	gravelly
0.1142	30.6	.2446	2	groggy
0.1142	30.6	.1717	2	gunwales
0.1142	30.6	.2446	2	hairless
0.1142	30.6	.1717	2	half-afraid
0.1142	30.6	.2446	2	half-dollar
0.1142	30.6	.2446	2	half's
0.1142	30.6	.2446	2	handholds
0.1142	30.6	.1717	2	hangman
0.1142	30.6	.1717	2	Hardware
0.1142	30.6	.1717	2	Havre
0.1142	30.6	.1717	2	hayfield
0.1142	30.6	.1717	2	heartiness
0.1142	30.6	.1717	2	HELP
0.1142	30.6	.2446	2	hi's
0.1142	30.6	.1717	2	honorably
0.1142	30.6	.1717	2	Hood's
0.1142	30.6	.1717	2	hoppity
0.1142	30.6	.1717	2	Horrors
0.1142	30.6	.1717	2	horse-hoofs
0.1142	30.6	.2404	2	housewares
0.1142	30.6	.2446	2	housings
0.1142	30.6	.1717	2	hypnotized
0.1142	30.6	.1717	2	I's
0.1142	30.6	.1717	2	idee
0.1142	30.6	.1717	2	idiots
0.1142	30.6	.1717	2	ignominiously
0.1142	30.6	.2404	2	iii
0.1142	30.6	.1717	2	illumined
0.1142	30.6	.1717	2	immaculate
0.1142	30.6	.1717	2	immured
0.1142	30.6	.1717	2	incongruity
0.1142	30.6	.1717	2	inducement

THE PRECEDING WORD TYPE OCCUPIES RANK 38200

U	SFI	D	F	Word Type
0.1142	30.6	.1717	2	infant's
0.1142	30.6	.2446	2	ingots
0.1142	30.6	.1717	2	Ingri
0.1142	30.6	.1717	2	inn-door
0.1142	30.6	.2446	2	insincerity
0.1142	30.6	.1717	2	instep
0.1142	30.6	.2446	2	insufferable
0.1142	30.6	.2446	2	interminably
0.1142	30.6	.2446	2	intoxicated
0.1142	30.6	.2446	2	ivy-covered
0.1142	30.6	.1717	2	jamcloset
0.1142	30.6	.1717	2	jetted
0.1142	30.6	.1717	2	Kennie's
0.1142	30.6	.2404	2	kickball
0.1142	30.6	.2446	2	kid's
0.1142	30.6	.1717	2	Kruper's
0.1142	30.6	.1717	2	leastways
0.1142	30.6	.1717	2	lectured
0.1142	30.6	.2446	2	Leighton
0.1142	30.6	.1717	2	liftin'
0.1142	30.6	.1717	2	localized
0.1142	30.6	.2404	2	long-playing
0.1142	30.6	.1717	2	lounged
0.1142	30.6	.2446	2	low-growing
0.1142	30.6	.2446	2	Mace
0.1142	30.6	.1717	2	malachite
0.1142	30.6	.2446	2	mania
0.1142	30.6	.1717	2	marriageable
0.1142	30.6	.1717	2	massaging
0.1142	30.6	.1717	2	meddle
0.1142	30.6	.2446	2	menage
0.1142	30.6	.2446	2	Messina
0.1142	30.6	.2446	2	mid-April
0.1142	30.6	.1717	2	misadventure
0.1142	30.6	.1717	2	mislaid
0.1142	30.6	.1717	2	misread
0.1142	30.6	.1717	2	mommy
0.1142	30.6	.1717	2	mouthing
0.1142	30.6	.1717	2	musician's
0.1142	30.6	.2446	2	nagged
0.1142	30.6	.1717	2	newsman
0.1142	30.6	.1717	2	nimbly
0.1142	30.6	.2404	2	NV
0.1142	30.6	.1717	2	obituary
0.1142	30.6	.1717	2	obloquy
0.1142	30.6	.1717	2	oh-h
0.1142	30.6	.1717	2	ordeals
0.1142	30.6	.2446	2	outcries
0.1142	30.6	.2446	2	outdistanced
0.1142	30.6	.2446	2	oxtail
0.1142	30.6	.1717	2	Pablo's
0.1142	30.6	.1717	2	padlocks
0.1142	30.6	.1717	2	Parin
0.1142	30.6	.2446	2	partaking
0.1142	30.6	.2446	2	paving
0.1142	30.6	.1717	2	pawnbroker's
0.1142	30.6	.1717	2	pea-green
0.1142	30.6	.2446	2	Pelly
0.1142	30.6	.2446	2	pendants
0.1142	30.6	.1717	2	pensively
0.1142	30.6	.2446	2	persuasions
0.1142	30.6	.1717	2	petulantly
0.1142	30.6	.2446	2	phonies
0.1142	30.6	.1717	2	pitilessly
0.1142	30.6	.1717	2	Poet
0.1142	30.6	.2446	2	Policeman
0.1142	30.6	.1717	2	postmen
0.1142	30.6	.2446	2	powerlessness
0.1142	30.6	.1717	2	prairie's
0.1142	30.6	.1717	2	princess's
0.1142	30.6	.1717	2	prodigy
0.1142	30.6	.1717	2	promontory
0.1142	30.6	.2446	2	protracted
0.1142	30.6	.1717	2	Put
0.1142	30.6	.1717	2	quirt
0.1142	30.6	.1717	2	rafter
0.1142	30.6	.2446	2	rambles
0.1142	30.6	.1717	2	recitation
0.1142	30.6	.2446	2	reconnoiter
0.1142	30.6	.1717	2	red-coats
0.1142	30.6	.2446	2	reeking
0.1142	30.6	.1717	2	repented
0.1142	30.6	.2446	2	revolutionists
0.1142	30.6	.2446	2	ringtail
0.1142	30.6	.1717	2	Rizk
0.1142	30.6	.1717	2	road's
0.1142	30.6	.1717	2	Robots
0.1142	30.6	.1717	2	Rocks
0.1142	30.6	.1717	2	roebuck
0.1142	30.6	.1717	2	rooked
0.1142	30.6	.2446	2	RPM
0.1142	30.6	.1717	2	ruck
0.1142	30.6	.1717	2	RUFUS
0.1142	30.6	.1717	2	runner's
0.1142	30.6	.1717	2	rustlings
0.1142	30.6	.1717	2	scabbed
0.1142	30.6	.1717	2	scabs
0.1142	30.6	.1717	2	scarfpin
0.1142	30.6	.1717	2	scoffing
0.1142	30.6	.2446	2	scrapbooks

THE PRECEDING WORD TYPE OCCUPIES RANK 38300

U	SFI	D	F	Word Type
0.1142	30.6	.1717	2	scrimped
0.1142	30.6	.1717	2	sea-gull's
0.1142	30.6	.2446	2	second-story
0.1142	30.6	.1717	2	second-team
0.1142	30.6	.2446	2	self-consciousness
0.1142	30.6	.1717	2	serpent's
0.1142	30.6	.1717	2	setters
0.1142	30.6	.2446	2	shamefaced
0.1142	30.6	.2446	2	shapely
0.1142	30.6	.1717	2	shinny
0.1142	30.6	.1717	2	shunted
0.1142	30.6	.2404	2	Signs
0.1142	30.6	.1717	2	sister-in-law
0.1142	30.6	.2404	2	sixth-grader
0.1142	30.6	.1717	2	skitter
0.1142	30.6	.1717	2	skywriter
0.1142	30.6	.2446	2	slush
0.1142	30.6	.1717	2	slushy
0.1142	30.6	.1717	2	snake-bite
0.1142	30.6	.1717	2	sneeringly
0.1142	30.6	.1717	2	snuff-box
0.1142	30.6	.2404	2	somethimes
0.1142	30.6	.1717	2	splayed-out
0.1142	30.6	.1717	2	spluttering
0.1142	30.6	.1717	2	squads
0.1142	30.6	.1717	2	square-jawed
0.1142	30.6	.1717	2	staining
0.1142	30.6	.2404	2	Stamps
0.1142	30.6	.1717	2	stanchest
0.1142	30.6	.1717	2	still-life
0.1142	30.6	.1717	2	stillest
0.1142	30.6	.1717	2	stockades
0.1142	30.6	.2446	2	Stoney
0.1142	30.6	.2446	2	strobe
0.1142	30.6	.2446	2	sugarhouse
0.1142	30.6	.1717	2	sunbaked
0.1142	30.6	.2446	2	suppressing
0.1142	30.6	.2446	2	swamped
0.1142	30.6	.1717	2	sweetmeats
0.1142	30.6	.1717	2	Sylvester
0.1142	30.6	.2446	2	tallied
0.1142	30.6	.1717	2	tankard
0.1142	30.6	.1717	2	taw
0.1142	30.6	.1717	2	taxied
0.1142	30.6	.1717	2	teeny
0.1142	30.6	.1717	2	Telescope
0.1142	30.6	.1717	2	thieving
0.1142	30.6	.1717	2	thinness
0.1142	30.6	.1717	2	thisaway
0.1142	30.6	.1717	2	tolling
0.1142	30.6	.1717	2	torturing
0.1142	30.6	.1717	2	tot
0.1142	30.6	.2446	2	tottered
0.1142	30.6	.1717	2	toughened
0.1142	30.6	.2446	2	trader's
0.1142	30.6	.2446	2	transgression
0.1142	30.6	.1717	2	traveller
0.1142	30.6	.1717	2	Troy's
0.1142	30.6	.2446	2	truck's
0.1142	30.6	.1717	2	true-to-life
0.1142	30.6	.1717	2	trustful
0.1142	30.6	.2446	2	tum
0.1142	30.6	.2446	2	turrets
0.1142	30.6	.1717	2	unchained
0.1142	30.6	.1717	2	uncommonly
0.1142	30.6	.1717	2	uncontrollably
0.1142	30.6	.2446	2	undefeated
0.1142	30.6	.2446	2	underestimated
0.1142	30.6	.1717	2	undisguised
0.1142	30.6	.1717	2	unscalable
0.1142	30.6	.2446	2	unsheathed
0.1142	30.6	.1717	2	untried
0.1142	30.6	.1717	2	unwinking
0.1142	30.6	.2446	2	unwonted
0.1142	30.6	.2446	2	vassals
0.1142	30.6	.2446	2	verdant
0.1142	30.6	.2446	2	vigour
0.1142	30.6	.1717	2	voyager
0.1142	30.6	.1717	2	wadding
0.1142	30.6	.1717	2	wagoner
0.1142	30.6	.2446	2	wan
0.1142	30.6	.1717	2	washstand
0.1142	30.6	.1717	2	well-nigh
0.1142	30.6	.2446	2	what's-his-name
0.1142	30.6	.1717	2	wheel's
0.1142	30.6	.2446	2	wheezy
0.1142	30.6	.1717	2	wildfowl
0.1142	30.6	.1717	2	wisdom's
0.1142	30.6	.2446	2	wizened
0.1142	30.6	.1717	2	wrongdoer
0.1142	30.6	.2446	2	Yard
0.1142	30.6	.1717	2	yay
0.1142	30.6	.2404	2	1-13
0.1142	30.6	.2404	2	309
0.1141	30.6	.2412	2	Ahead
0.1141	30.6	.2412	2	anthology
0.1141	30.6	.2412	2	auld
0.1141	30.6	.2412	2	basketful
0.1141	30.6	.2412	2	Bedford
0.1141	30.6	.2412	2	belay

THE PRECEDING WORD TYPE OCCUPIES RANK 38400

U	SFI	D	F	Word Type
0.1141	30.6	.2412	2	bide
0.1141	30.6	.2412	2	bite-sized
0.1141	30.6	.2412	2	Boats
0.1141	30.6	.2412	2	bores
0.1141	30.6	.2412	2	brochures
0.1141	30.6	.2412	2	bushmaster
0.1141	30.6	.2412	2	cohorts
0.1141	30.6	.2412	2	corrupted
0.1141	30.6	.2412	2	couplets
0.1141	30.6	.2412	2	curlier
0.1141	30.6	.2412	2	deep-drifted
0.1141	30.6	.2412	2	delegates'
0.1141	30.6	.2412	2	expounded
0.1141	30.6	.2412	2	femininity
0.1141	30.6	.2412	2	fictions
0.1141	30.6	.2412	2	Finney
0.1141	30.6	.2412	2	firewater
0.1141	30.6	.2412	2	fleeces
0.1141	30.6	.2412	2	Good-by
0.1141	30.6	.2412	2	great-
0.1141	30.6	.2412	2	griffin
0.1141	30.6	.2412	2	half-moon
0.1141	30.6	.2412	2	intonations
0.1141	30.6	.2412	2	Irishmen
0.1141	30.6	.2412	2	knapsacks
0.1141	30.6	.2412	2	lookout's
0.1141	30.6	.2412	2	McAdam
0.1141	30.6	.2412	2	Moody
0.1141	30.6	.2412	2	mother-in-law
0.1141	30.6	.2412	2	Nightmare
0.1141	30.6	.2412	2	oracular
0.1141	30.6	.2412	2	outfielders
0.1141	30.6	.2412	2	palisade
0.1141	30.6	.2412	2	pantaloon
0.1141	30.6	.2412	2	parlour
0.1141	30.6	.2412	2	parsnips
0.1141	30.6	.2412	2	pater
0.1141	30.6	.2412	2	Payne
0.1141	30.6	.2412	2	recuperate
0.1141	30.6	.2412	2	resents
0.1141	30.6	.2412	2	satirized
0.1141	30.6	.2412	2	Snead
0.1141	30.6	.2412	2	steeds
0.1141	30.6	.2412	2	subjugated
0.1141	30.6	.2412	2	tactfully
0.1141	30.6	.2412	2	toastmaster
0.1141	30.6	.2412	2	Topics
0.1141	30.6	.2412	2	well-filled
0.1141	30.6	.2412	2	where'er
0.1141	30.6	.2412	2	10s
0.1141	30.6	.2412	2	1428
0.1141	30.6	.2412	2	1588
0.1140	30.6	.2300	2	-in
0.1140	30.6	.2306	2	amend
0.1140	30.6	.2300	2	analyzes
0.1140	30.6	.2306	2	armaments
0.1140	30.6	.2306	2	billboard
0.1140	30.6	.2306	2	Bless
0.1140	30.6	.2300	2	boat-shaped
0.1140	30.6	.2306	2	bride's

U	SFI	D	F	Word Type
0.1140	30.6	.2306	2	brutality
0.1140	30.6	.2306	2	cocksureness
0.1140	30.6	.2306	2	Compact
0.1140	30.6	.2306	2	completly
0.1140	30.6	.2300	2	correlated
0.1140	30.6	.2306	2	creole
0.1140	30.6	.2300	2	duller
0.1140	30.6	.2306	2	educations
0.1140	30.6	.2306	2	embalmed
0.1140	30.6	.2306	2	Explorers'
0.1140	30.6	.2306	2	Fenimore
0.1140	30.6	.2306	2	first-hand
0.1140	30.6	.2306	2	foreign-born
0.1140	30.6	.2306	2	Genoese
0.1140	30.6	.2306	2	Hindi
0.1140	30.6	.2306	2	Historians
0.1140	30.6	.2306	2	Hwang
0.1140	30.6	.2300	2	ideographs
0.1140	30.6	.2306	2	imaginatively
0.1140	30.6	.2306	2	Improvement
0.1140	30.6	.2306	2	intoxicating
0.1140	30.6	.2306	2	intruding
0.1140	30.6	.2306	2	invokes
0.1140	30.6	.2300	2	irregularity
0.1140	30.6	.2306	2	irritations
0.1140	30.6	.2306	2	jingles
0.1140	30.6	.2306	2	Kinds
0.1140	30.6	.2306	2	laurels
0.1140	30.6	.2306	2	leather-bound
0.1140	30.6	.2306	2	Lusitania
0.1140	30.6	.2306	2	Lytton
0.1140	30.6	.2306	2	mingling
0.1140	30.6	.2306	2	mockingly
0.1140	30.6	.2306	2	moneys
0.1140	30.6	.2306	2	Name
0.1140	30.6	.2300	2	newscast
0.1140	30.6	.2300	2	overeat
0.1140	30.6	.2300	2	pinhead-sized
0.1140	30.6	.2300	2	recipient
0.1140	30.6	.2306	2	revengeful

THE PRECEDING WORD TYPE OCCUPIES RANK 38500

U	SFI	D	F	Word Type
0.1140	30.6	.2306	2	rite
0.1140	30.6	.2300	2	rosettes
0.1140	30.6	.2300	2	run-off
0.1140	30.6	.2306	2	Scribes
0.1140	30.6	.2306	2	separators
0.1140	30.6	.2306	2	Simms
0.1140	30.6	.2306	2	Sirs
0.1140	30.6	.2300	2	six-
0.1140	30.6	.2306	2	snowplows
0.1140	30.6	.2300	2	sprinkles
0.1140	30.6	.2306	2	stauncher
0.1140	30.6	.2300	2	step-by-step
0.1140	30.6	.2306	2	stopovers
0.1140	30.6	.2306	2	surefooted
0.1140	30.6	.2306	2	Tasmania
0.1140	30.6	.2300	2	Teen-Age
0.1140	30.6	.2306	2	Texan
0.1140	30.6	.2306	2	Then
0.1140	30.6	.2306	2	Tippecanoe
0.1140	30.6	.2300	2	Topic
0.1140	30.6	.2300	2	uncoiled
0.1140	30.6	.2306	2	undependable
0.1140	30.6	.2306	2	vouch
0.1140	30.6	.2300	2	well-coordinated
0.1140	30.6	.2306	2	worded
0.1140	30.6	.2306	2	Zoning
0.1140	30.6	.2306	2	200-201
0.1140	30.6	.2306	2	332
0.1138	30.6	.2407	2	'scuse
0.1138	30.6	.2407	2	abusive
0.1138	30.6	.2407	2	Albemarle
0.1138	30.6	.2398	2	Answer
0.1138	30.6	.2407	2	apple-pie
0.1138	30.6	.2398	2	autobiographies
0.1138	30.6	.2407	2	averted
0.1138	30.6	.2407	2	bandaging
0.1138	30.6	.2398	2	BB
0.1138	30.6	.2407	2	benevolence
0.1138	30.6	.2407	2	beribboned
0.1138	30.6	.2407	2	betcha
0.1138	30.6	.2407	2	bird-lovers
0.1138	30.6	.2407	2	brawn
0.1138	30.6	.2407	2	charnel
0.1138	30.6	.2407	2	coherently
0.1138	30.6	.2407	2	comely
0.1138	30.6	.2407	2	confusions
0.1138	30.6	.2407	2	corncake
0.1138	30.6	.2407	2	cricket's
0.1138	30.6	.2407	2	daringly
0.1138	30.6	.2407	2	dirges
0.1138	30.6	.2407	2	disarming
0.1138	30.6	.2407	2	disdainful
0.1138	30.6	.2407	2	Dolan
0.1138	30.6	.2407	2	Doncaster
0.1138	30.6	.2407	2	dragon-fly
0.1138	30.6	.2407	2	encroachments
0.1138	30.6	.2407	2	excel
0.1138	30.6	.2398	2	forty-foot
0.1138	30.6	.2407	2	Four-Eyes
0.1138	30.6	.2407	2	frill
0.1138	30.6	.2407	2	frilled
0.1138	30.6	.2407	2	frowns
0.1138	30.6	.2407	2	gabble
0.1138	30.6	.2407	2	goest
0.1138	30.6	.2407	2	Granger's
0.1138	30.6	.2407	2	herded
0.1138	30.6	.2407	2	Holmes's
0.1138	30.6	.2407	2	hurtful
0.1138	30.6	.2407	2	idleness
0.1138	30.6	.2407	2	Jimmie
0.1138	30.6	.2407	2	jittery
0.1138	30.6	.2407	2	jowls
0.1138	30.6	.2407	2	Keller's
0.1138	30.6	.2407	2	long-forgotten
0.1138	30.6	.2407	2	low-bid
0.1138	30.6	.2407	2	Magdalene
0.1138	30.6	.2407	2	mangy
0.1138	30.6	.2407	2	mass-produced
0.1138	30.6	.2407	2	miasmas
0.1138	30.6	.2407	2	moped
0.1138	30.6	.2407	2	mould
0.1138	30.6	.2407	2	mountaineer's
0.1138	30.6	.2407	2	mountaineering
0.1138	30.6	.2407	2	murk
0.1138	30.6	.2407	2	Mystic
0.1138	30.6	.2407	2	nerve-racking
0.1138	30.6	.2407	2	newsboy's
0.1138	30.6	.2407	2	Paducah
0.1138	30.6	.2407	2	paling
0.1138	30.6	.2407	2	Perce
0.1138	30.6	.2407	2	Possum
0.1138	30.6	.2407	2	posting
0.1138	30.6	.2407	2	Potter's
0.1138	30.6	.2407	2	primal
0.1138	30.6	.2407	2	Pussick
0.1138	30.6	.2407	2	quaintly
0.1138	30.6	.2407	2	rape
0.1138	30.6	.2407	2	Same
0.1138	30.6	.2407	2	scimitar
0.1138	30.6	.2407	2	scrawl

THE PRECEDING WORD TYPE OCCUPIES RANK 38600

U	SFI	D	F	Word Type
0.1138	30.6	.2407	2	self-importance
0.1138	30.6	.2398	2	seventy-one
0.1138	30.6	.2407	2	shames
0.1138	30.6	.2407	2	sidelong
0.1138	30.6	.2407	2	slavers
0.1138	30.6	.2407	2	spatters
0.1138	30.6	.2398	2	Sporting
0.1138	30.6	.2407	2	Stanoski
0.1138	30.6	.2407	2	swabbed
0.1138	30.6	.2407	2	Takume
0.1138	30.6	.2407	2	tasseled
0.1138	30.6	.2407	2	ten-mile
0.1138	30.6	.2398	2	Tess
0.1138	30.6	.2407	2	thrillers
0.1138	30.6	.2407	2	translator's
0.1138	30.6	.2407	2	tricksters
0.1138	30.6	.2407	2	two-hundred-pound
0.1138	30.6	.2407	2	unconcernedly
0.1138	30.6	.2407	2	uncorseted
0.1138	30.6	.2407	2	uneatable
0.1138	30.6	.2407	2	ungrateful
0.1138	30.6	.2407	2	unpleasing
0.1138	30.6	.2407	2	unqualified
0.1138	30.6	.2407	2	untroubled
0.1138	30.6	.2407	2	upthrusting
0.1138	30.6	.2407	2	urn
0.1138	30.6	.2407	2	vestal
0.1138	30.6	.2407	2	Virgil's
0.1138	30.6	.2407	2	vomited
0.1138	30.6	.2407	2	waist-deep
0.1138	30.6	.2407	2	well-fitted
0.1138	30.6	.2407	2	witches'
0.1138	30.6	.2407	2	Zeiss
0.1138	30.6	.2398	2	4-6
0.1136	30.6	.0000	14	unstressed
0.1135	30.5	.2291	2	angleworm
0.1135	30.6	.2297	2	antidemocratic
0.1135	30.6	.2297	2	antlered
0.1135	30.6	.2297	2	astrolabe
0.1135	30.6	.2297	2	bachelors
0.1135	30.5	.2291	2	belched
0.1135	30.5	.2291	2	bleeds
0.1135	30.6	.2297	2	Bolshoi
0.1135	30.6	.2297	2	Brethren
0.1135	30.6	.2297	2	bridles
0.1135	30.5	.2291	2	broadens
0.1135	30.6	.2297	2	broncho
0.1135	30.6	.2297	2	Cahokia
0.1135	30.5	.2291	2	calming
0.1135	30.6	.2297	2	carload
0.1135	30.5	.2291	2	Cassiopeia
0.1135	30.6	.2297	2	ceaselessly
0.1135	30.6	.2297	2	ceremonious
0.1135	30.5	.2291	2	champing
0.1135	30.5	.2291	2	childbirth
0.1135	30.6	.2297	2	clansmen
0.1135	30.5	.2291	2	co-ordination
0.1135	30.6	.2297	2	comer
0.1135	30.6	.2297	2	condone
0.1135	30.6	.2297	2	convicts
0.1135	30.6	.2297	2	countryfolk
0.1135	30.6	.2297	2	court's
0.1135	30.5	.2291	2	craves
0.1135	30.5	.2291	2	darest
0.1135	30.6	.2297	2	decking
0.1135	30.6	.2297	2	detours
0.1135	30.6	.2297	2	doctoring
0.1135	30.6	.2297	2	endeavour
0.1135	30.6	.2297	2	executions
0.1135	30.6	.2297	2	exulted
0.1135	30.6	.2297	2	Fairfax's
0.1135	30.5	.2291	2	fast-flying
0.1135	30.6	.2297	2	Finch's
0.1135	30.6	.2297	2	flawed
0.1135	30.5	.2291	2	gauged
0.1135	30.6	.2297	2	gettin
0.1135	30.5	.2291	2	gizzard
0.1135	30.5	.2291	2	gobbles
0.1135	30.5	.2291	2	gratify
0.1135	30.6	.2297	2	hallow
0.1135	30.6	.2297	2	hazelnut
0.1135	30.5	.2291	2	healer
0.1135	30.5	.2291	2	hearken
0.1135	30.6	.2297	2	Hebrides
0.1135	30.6	.2297	2	home-making
0.1135	30.5	.2291	2	horseshoe-shaped
0.1135	30.6	.2297	2	Hughes'
0.1135	30.6	.2297	2	Limerick
0.1135	30.6	.2297	2	Loreto
0.1135	30.6	.2297	2	malicious
0.1135	30.6	.2297	2	mayhem
0.1135	30.5	.2291	2	mud-colored
0.1135	30.6	.2297	2	Muse
0.1135	30.6	.2297	2	muse
0.1135	30.6	.2297	2	Nowhere
0.1135	30.6	.2297	2	O'Connor
0.1135	30.6	.2297	2	Palmer
0.1135	30.5	.2291	2	palpable
0.1135	30.5	.2291	2	pigmy
0.1135	30.6	.2297	2	plantain

THE PRECEDING WORD TYPE OCCUPIES RANK 38700

U	SFI	D	F	Word Type
0.1135	30.6	.2297	2	predawn
0.1135	30.6	.2297	2	railed
0.1135	30.5	.2291	2	ravaging
0.1135	30.5	.2291	2	refrained
0.1135	30.6	.2297	2	resolves
0.1135	30.6	.2297	2	sea-hunters
0.1135	30.5	.2291	2	second-growth
0.1135	30.6	.2297	2	sheriffs
0.1135	30.6	.2297	2	signboards
0.1135	30.5	.2291	2	slitted
0.1135	30.6	.2297	2	slouched
0.1135	30.5	.2291	2	steepness
0.1135	30.6	.2297	2	Tashkent
0.1135	30.6	.2297	2	thankless
0.1135	30.6	.2297	2	three-penny
0.1135	30.6	.2297	2	timbered
0.1135	30.6	.2297	2	Tobacco
0.1135	30.6	.2297	2	undistinguished
0.1135	30.6	.2297	2	unnumbered
0.1135	30.6	.2297	2	wealthiest
0.1135	30.6	.2297	2	Westfield
0.1135	30.6	.2297	2	white-skinned
0.1135	30.6	.2297	2	Wholesale
0.1135	30.6	.2297	2	wooing
0.1135	30.6	.2297	2	zeroed
0.1134	30.5	.2442	2	$120
0.1134	30.5	.2442	2	Abrams'
0.1134	30.5	.2442	2	adamantly
0.1134	30.5	.2442	2	agreeably
0.1134	30.5	.2442	2	anciently
0.1134	30.5	.2442	2	assurances
0.1134	30.5	.2442	2	basemen
0.1134	30.5	.2442	2	blowed
0.1134	30.5	.2442	2	Brentwood
0.1134	30.5	.2442	2	Bs
0.1134	30.5	.2442	2	budgeted
0.1134	30.5	.2442	2	Cal's
0.1134	30.5	.2442	2	Cameron
0.1134	30.5	.2442	2	caulking
0.1134	30.5	.2442	2	Clare
0.1134	30.5	.2442	2	cognac
0.1134	30.5	.2442	2	dealers'
0.1134	30.5	.2442	2	Deering's
0.1134	30.5	.2442	2	deleted
0.1134	30.5	.2442	2	desist
0.1134	30.5	.2442	2	deteriorating
0.1134	30.5	.2442	2	evaluations
0.1134	30.5	.2442	2	evangel
0.1134	30.5	.2442	2	facetiously
0.1134	30.5	.2442	2	faroff
0.1134	30.5	.2442	2	fascinates
0.1134	30.5	.2442	2	filthiest
0.1134	30.5	.2442	2	Forster
0.1134	30.5	.2442	2	Fullerton
0.1134	30.5	.2442	2	gags
0.1134	30.5	.2442	2	genteel
0.1134	30.5	.2442	2	gimmicks
0.1134	30.5	.2442	2	gusher
0.1134	30.5	.2442	2	Harley
0.1134	30.5	.2442	2	impeccable
0.1134	30.5	.2442	2	inappropriately
0.1134	30.5	.2442	2	irreverent
0.1134	30.5	.2442	2	jounced
0.1134	30.5	.2442	2	kirtle
0.1134	30.5	.2442	2	Learning
0.1134	30.5	.2442	2	leprechauns
0.1134	30.5	.2442	2	lineman
0.1134	30.5	.2442	2	loco
0.1134	30.5	.2442	2	long-winded
0.1134	30.5	.2442	2	lotta
0.1134	30.5	.2442	2	magazine's
0.1134	30.5	.2442	2	Mater
0.1134	30.5	.2442	2	mid-nineteenth
0.1134	30.5	.2442	2	mistook
0.1134	30.5	.2442	2	mouth-watering
0.1134	30.5	.2442	2	Outline
0.1134	30.5	.2442	2	pal's
0.1134	30.5	.2442	2	parentis
0.1134	30.5	.2442	2	pithy
0.1134	30.5	.2442	2	PM
0.1134	30.5	.2442	2	quits
0.1134	30.5	.2442	2	Redwoods
0.1134	30.5	.2442	2	refunded
0.1134	30.5	.2442	2	regicide
0.1134	30.5	.2442	2	roger
0.1134	30.5	.2442	2	rustles
0.1134	30.5	.2442	2	sanguine
0.1134	30.5	.2442	2	second-string
0.1134	30.5	.2442	2	sifts
0.1134	30.5	.2442	2	Sikes
0.1134	30.5	.2442	2	skimmers
0.1134	30.5	.2442	2	skimped
0.1134	30.5	.2442	2	skits
0.1134	30.5	.2442	2	sleepy-head
0.1134	30.5	.2442	2	stubbled
0.1134	30.5	.2442	2	succinctly
0.1134	30.5	.2442	2	sweepstakes
0.1134	30.5	.2442	2	sweeting
0.1134	30.5	.2442	2	takeoffs
0.1134	30.5	.2442	2	Thinking

THE PRECEDING WORD TYPE OCCUPIES RANK 38800

U	SFI	D	F	Word Type
0.1134	30.5	.2442	2	throbs
0.1134	30.5	.2442	2	thumbed
0.1134	30.5	.2442	2	Title
0.1134	30.5	.2442	2	treed
0.1134	30.5	.2442	2	unbridled
0.1134	30.5	.2442	2	Vision
0.1134	30.5	.2442	2	Wayne's
0.1134	30.5	.2442	2	wich
0.1134	30.5	.2442	2	130-foot
0.1134	30.5	.2442	2	1580's
0.1134	30.5	.2442	2	634
0.1133	30.5	.2391	2	$21
0.1133	30.5	.2391	2	$27
0.1133	30.5	.2401	2	$85
0.1133	30.5	.2391	2	$91
0.1133	30.5	.2401	2	Abbe
0.1133	30.5	.1698	2	Above
0.1133	30.5	.1698	2	accessibility
0.1133	30.5	.2401	2	Adolphus
0.1133	30.5	.2401	2	aftereffects
0.1133	30.5	.2401	2	Algonquian
0.1133	30.5	.1698	2	alternated
0.1133	30.5	.1698	2	Amir
0.1133	30.5	.1698	2	Ana
0.1133	30.5	.1698	2	anomaly
0.1133	30.5	.2401	2	Appian
0.1133	30.5	.1698	2	arenas
0.1133	30.5	.2401	2	aristocrat
0.1133	30.5	.1698	2	Aristotle's
0.1133	30.5	.1698	2	Arkwright's
0.1133	30.5	.1698	2	armadillos
0.1133	30.5	.1698	2	Asgard
0.1133	30.5	.2401	2	australis
0.1133	30.5	.1698	2	ball-shaped
0.1133	30.5	.1698	2	balloting
0.1133	30.5	.1698	2	baneful
0.1133	30.5	.1698	2	beanstalk
0.1133	30.5	.2401	2	Beaufort
0.1133	30.5	.1698	2	bedspreads
0.1133	30.5	.1698	2	Bellerophon
0.1133	30.5	.1698	2	bergamot
0.1133	30.5	.1698	2	bestowing
0.1133	30.5	.1698	2	bicker
0.1133	30.5	.1698	2	bitterns
0.1133	30.5	.1698	2	blames
0.1133	30.5	.2391	2	blastoff
0.1133	30.5	.1698	2	blocs
0.1133	30.5	.1698	2	blurry
0.1133	30.5	.2401	2	Bolero
0.1133	30.5	.1698	2	Bonheur
0.1133	30.5	.1698	2	bossed
0.1133	30.5	.2401	2	Bostonians
0.1133	30.5	.2401	2	burials
0.1133	30.5	.1698	2	caliph
0.1133	30.5	.2401	2	caliphate
0.1133	30.5	.1698	2	Cartwright's
0.1133	30.5	.1698	2	Casa
0.1133	30.5	.1698	2	change-over
0.1133	30.5	.1698	2	chauffeur-driven
0.1133	30.5	.1698	2	check-out
0.1133	30.5	.1698	2	cherishing
0.1133	30.5	.2401	2	Chicagoans
0.1133	30.5	.1698	2	Chihuahuan
0.1133	30.5	.1698	2	chisellike
0.1133	30.5	.2401	2	cliff-top
0.1133	30.5	.1698	2	commute
0.1133	30.5	.2401	2	Concertos
0.1133	30.5	.1698	2	Congregational
0.1133	30.5	.2401	2	Congresses
0.1133	30.5	.2401	2	convict
0.1133	30.5	.2401	2	creeds
0.1133	30.5	.1698	2	Crompton's
0.1133	30.5	.1698	2	crotches
0.1133	30.5	.1698	2	cryolite
0.1133	30.5	.1698	2	Cullen
0.1133	30.5	.2401	2	curiosities
0.1133	30.5	.1698	2	curlews
0.1133	30.5	.1698	2	deParis
0.1133	30.5	.2401	2	debatable
0.1133	30.5	.2401	2	deception
0.1133	30.5	.2401	2	defenseless
0.1133	30.5	.2391	2	designating
0.1133	30.5	.2401	2	detriments
0.1133	30.5	.2401	2	different-looking
0.1133	30.5	.1698	2	Directors
0.1133	30.5	.2391	2	doughnut-shaped
0.1133	30.5	.1698	2	Dragon's
0.1133	30.5	.2401	2	duke's
0.1133	30.5	.1698	2	ear-shattering
0.1133	30.5	.2391	2	Element
0.1133	30.5	.2401	2	elevating
0.1133	30.5	.2401	2	eludes
0.1133	30.5	.2401	2	embassies
0.1133	30.5	.2401	2	enigma
0.1133	30.5	.1698	2	enliven
0.1133	30.5	.2401	2	enlivened
0.1133	30.5	.2391	2	erred
0.1133	30.5	.1698	2	Espana
0.1133	30.5	.2391	2	Ex
0.1133	30.5	.2401	2	excrement

THE PRECEDING WORD TYPE OCCUPIES RANK 38900

U	SFI	D	F	Word Type
0.1133	30.5	.1698	2	exploiters
0.1133	30.5	.1698	2	exquisitely
0.1133	30.5	.1698	2	Fables
0.1133	30.5	.2401	2	facilitated
0.1133	30.5	.1698	2	fakes
0.1133	30.5	.1698	2	falter
0.1133	30.5	.2391	2	farseeing
0.1133	30.5	.1698	2	fastness
0.1133	30.5	.1698	2	fatally
0.1133	30.5	.2401	2	Faure
0.1133	30.5	.2391	2	Fawcett
0.1133	30.5	.1698	2	fend
0.1133	30.5	.2401	2	fezzes
0.1133	30.5	.2401	2	filoplumes
0.1133	30.5	.2401	2	Firth
0.1133	30.5	.1698	2	fish-shaped
0.1133	30.5	.1698	2	flabbergasted
0.1133	30.5	.1698	2	fleet-footed
0.1133	30.5	.1698	2	Flushing
0.1133	30.5	.2401	2	food-gatherers
0.1133	30.5	.1698	2	foolproof
0.1133	30.5	.1698	2	Forty-nine
0.1133	30.5	.1698	2	four-inch

U	SFI	D	F	Word Type
0.1133	30.5	.1698	2	frailties
0.1133	30.5	.1698	2	frescoes
0.1133	30.5	.1698	2	furrowed
0.1133	30.5	.1698	2	Fyn
0.1133	30.5	.2401	2	Gaetano
0.1133	30.5	.2401	2	gannets
0.1133	30.5	.1698	2	Gila
0.1133	30.5	.2401	2	giveth
0.1133	30.5	.2401	2	glades
0.1133	30.5	.1698	2	gluey
0.1133	30.5	.1698	2	gob
0.1133	30.5	.2401	2	Goldoni
0.1133	30.5	.2391	2	Goods
0.1133	30.5	.1698	2	government-owned
0.1133	30.5	.1698	2	Governments
0.1133	30.5	.1698	2	grab-bag
0.1133	30.5	.2401	2	grebes
0.1133	30.5	.2401	2	grounding
0.1133	30.5	.2401	2	guiltless
0.1133	30.5	.1698	2	half-formed
0.1133	30.5	.1698	2	Halley
0.1133	30.5	.1698	2	Hargreaves'
0.1133	30.5	.2401	2	harshness
0.1133	30.5	.1698	2	Heidelberg
0.1133	30.5	.2401	2	hinterland
0.1133	30.5	.1698	2	Hippocratic
0.1133	30.5	.2401	2	honeycombs
0.1133	30.5	.1698	2	humdrum
0.1133	30.5	.1698	2	humors
0.1133	30.5	.2401	2	Humphreys
0.1133	30.5	.1698	2	idealists
0.1133	30.5	.1698	2	immeasurably
0.1133	30.5	.2401	2	impulsive
0.1133	30.5	.2401	2	in-laws
0.1133	30.5	.1698	2	inaccurately
0.1133	30.5	.2401	2	inalienable
0.1133	30.5	.2401	2	incomparable
0.1133	30.5	.2401	2	incompatible
0.1133	30.5	.2401	2	individualistic
0.1133	30.5	.2401	2	inestimable
0.1133	30.5	.2401	2	inexorably
0.1133	30.5	.1698	2	infect
0.1133	30.5	.2401	2	infidelity
0.1133	30.5	.2401	2	injections
0.1133	30.5	.2401	2	insect-eating
0.1133	30.5	.2401	2	instill
0.1133	30.5	.1698	2	insulates
0.1133	30.5	.2401	2	invulnerable
0.1133	30.5	.2401	2	Ipswich
0.1133	30.5	.1698	2	Jacobus
0.1133	30.5	.1698	2	Jeffersonians
0.1133	30.5	.1698	2	jewel-like
0.1133	30.5	.1698	2	jibs
0.1133	30.5	.2401	2	judo
0.1133	30.5	.2401	2	justifying
0.1133	30.5	.2401	2	Kaffirs
0.1133	30.5	.1698	2	karat
0.1133	30.5	.1698	2	Karl's
0.1133	30.5	.2401	2	keen-eyed
0.1133	30.5	.2401	2	Kells
0.1133	30.5	.1698	2	LaFontaine
0.1133	30.5	.1698	2	Laboratories
0.1133	30.5	.2401	2	Lac
0.1133	30.5	.1698	2	lakeside
0.1133	30.5	.1698	2	Lambert
0.1133	30.5	.1698	2	Lamp
0.1133	30.5	.2401	2	Lawrence's
0.1133	30.5	.2401	2	Lawson
0.1133	30.5	.1698	2	leavened
0.1133	30.5	.2401	2	legionaries
0.1133	30.5	.1698	2	Li's
0.1133	30.5	.1698	2	litters
0.1133	30.5	.2401	2	lizardlike
0.1133	30.5	.2401	2	louse
0.1133	30.5	.2401	2	low-voltage
0.1133	30.5	.1698	2	ludicrous
0.1133	30.5	.1698	2	lunatics
THE PRECEDING WORD TYPE OCCUPIES RANK 39000				
0.1133	30.5	.2401	2	lustre
0.1133	30.5	.1698	2	Luther's
0.1133	30.5	.1698	2	Mackintosh
0.1133	30.5	.2401	2	magnanimous
0.1133	30.5	.1698	2	mainspring
0.1133	30.5	.1698	2	meagerly
0.1133	30.5	.1698	2	meddling
0.1133	30.5	.1698	2	Members
0.1133	30.5	.2391	2	Michele
0.1133	30.5	.1698	2	microwave
0.1133	30.5	.1698	2	Misery
0.1133	30.5	.1698	2	Misti
0.1133	30.5	.1698	2	mizzen
0.1133	30.5	.1698	2	mollies
0.1133	30.5	.2391	2	Multiple
0.1133	30.5	.1698	2	multiplicity
0.1133	30.5	.2401	2	narrowness
0.1133	30.5	.1698	2	naturalness
0.1133	30.5	.2401	2	nestlings
0.1133	30.5	.1698	2	NewYorkCity's
0.1133	30.5	.1698	2	Nichols
0.1133	30.5	.1698	2	NorthAtlantic
0.1133	30.5	.2401	2	Nuremberg
0.1133	30.5	.2401	2	obliterated
0.1133	30.5	.2391	2	odder
0.1133	30.5	.2401	2	Offices
0.1133	30.5	.1698	2	offsets
0.1133	30.5	.2391	2	on-off
0.1133	30.5	.2401	2	Organ
0.1133	30.5	.2401	2	Organized
0.1133	30.5	.2401	2	outclassed
0.1133	30.5	.2401	2	ovation
0.1133	30.5	.1698	2	Pan-American
0.1133	30.5	.1698	2	panoramas
0.1133	30.5	.1698	2	papermakers
0.1133	30.5	.2401	2	parentage
0.1133	30.5	.2401	2	payable
0.1133	30.5	.1698	2	Peiping
0.1133	30.5	.1698	2	Pelican
0.1133	30.5	.1698	2	penance
0.1133	30.5	.2401	2	periwinkle
0.1133	30.5	.2391	2	Pharaohs
0.1133	30.5	.1698	2	Physics
0.1133	30.5	.2401	2	pine-forested
0.1133	30.5	.2401	2	Pirandello
0.1133	30.5	.2401	2	plungers
0.1133	30.5	.2391	2	positional
0.1133	30.5	.2401	2	possums
0.1133	30.5	.2401	2	post-war
0.1133	30.5	.2401	2	postmasters
0.1133	30.5	.1698	2	predominating
0.1133	30.5	.1698	2	prescribing
0.1133	30.5	.1698	2	Presidio
0.1133	30.5	.1698	2	preying
0.1133	30.5	.1698	2	preys
0.1133	30.5	.1698	2	principalities
0.1133	30.5	.2401	2	proclamations
0.1133	30.5	.2401	2	procured
0.1133	30.5	.1698	2	progeny
0.1133	30.5	.1698	2	prosecutor
0.1133	30.5	.1698	2	protectively
0.1133	30.5	.2401	2	psittacosis
0.1133	30.5	.1698	2	psychic
0.1133	30.5	.2391	2	Publishing
0.1133	30.5	.2401	2	rainbow-colored
0.1133	30.5	.1698	2	rationally
0.1133	30.5	.1698	2	Ready
0.1133	30.5	.1698	2	reaffirm
0.1133	30.5	.2391	2	rearrangements
0.1133	30.5	.1698	2	red-bearded
0.1133	30.5	.2401	2	redistribution
0.1133	30.5	.2391	2	reductions
0.1133	30.5	.2401	2	regent
0.1133	30.5	.2391	2	Relation
0.1133	30.5	.1698	2	Relativity
0.1133	30.5	.1698	2	reloaded
0.1133	30.5	.2391	2	relocate
0.1133	30.5	.2401	2	repudiation
0.1133	30.5	.1698	2	restricting
0.1133	30.5	.2401	2	revocation
0.1133	30.5	.2401	2	Romney
0.1133	30.5	.2401	2	ruffed
0.1133	30.5	.2391	2	rule-of-thumb
0.1133	30.5	.2401	2	salt-marsh
0.1133	30.5	.1698	2	Sangamon
0.1133	30.5	.2401	2	Sardinian
0.1133	30.5	.2401	2	Sargon
0.1133	30.5	.1698	2	Schenectady
0.1133	30.5	.1698	2	schoolbook
0.1133	30.5	.2401	2	secretariat
0.1133	30.5	.1698	2	self-satisfied
0.1133	30.5	.1698	2	semimetals
0.1133	30.5	.2401	2	shapeless
0.1133	30.5	.2401	2	shawls
0.1133	30.5	.1698	2	Shrewsbury
0.1133	30.5	.2401	2	sideburns
0.1133	30.5	.2401	2	simulator
0.1133	30.5	.2401	2	six-inch-long
0.1133	30.5	.1698	2	skirmishing
0.1133	30.5	.1698	2	skirting
THE PRECEDING WORD TYPE OCCUPIES RANK 39100				
0.1133	30.5	.1698	2	slaving
0.1133	30.5	.2401	2	Slocum
0.1133	30.5	.2401	2	slowworm
0.1133	30.5	.2401	2	Smokies
0.1133	30.5	.1698	2	solders
0.1133	30.5	.2401	2	solicitous
0.1133	30.5	.2401	2	Solomons
0.1133	30.5	.1698	2	sprawls
0.1133	30.5	.2401	2	StAndrews
0.1133	30.5	.1698	2	StElmo's
0.1133	30.5	.2401	2	states'
0.1133	30.5	.2401	2	steadiness
0.1133	30.5	.1698	2	steam-powered
0.1133	30.5	.1698	2	stewardship
0.1133	30.5	.1698	2	stiffen
0.1133	30.5	.1698	2	stipend
0.1133	30.5	.1698	2	stonemason
0.1133	30.5	.2401	2	stupefied
0.1133	30.5	.1698	2	subhead
0.1133	30.5	.1698	2	suddenness
0.1133	30.5	.1698	2	suffocation
0.1133	30.5	.1698	2	superstructure
0.1133	30.5	.2401	2	sustaining
0.1133	30.5	.1698	2	swath
0.1133	30.5	.1698	2	tabletops
0.1133	30.5	.1698	2	tailor-made
0.1133	30.5	.2401	2	telescopic
0.1133	30.5	.2401	2	thenceforth
0.1133	30.5	.2401	2	thereon
0.1133	30.5	.1698	2	thermoscope
0.1133	30.5	.2401	2	thousand-mile
0.1133	30.5	.2401	2	three-wheeled
0.1133	30.5	.2401	2	titular
0.1133	30.5	.2391	2	topologists
0.1133	30.5	.1698	2	toying
0.1133	30.5	.2401	2	Trails
0.1133	30.5	.2401	2	Transcendentalism
0.1133	30.5	.1698	2	tuition
0.1133	30.5	.1698	2	tunneling
0.1133	30.5	.2401	2	turning-point
0.1133	30.5	.1698	2	twined
0.1133	30.5	.1698	2	twitches
0.1133	30.5	.1698	2	uncontrollable
0.1133	30.5	.1698	2	uncouth
0.1133	30.5	.2401	2	underpinning
0.1133	30.5	.1698	2	underwriting
0.1133	30.5	.2401	2	undisputed
0.1133	30.5	.1698	2	unencumbered
0.1133	30.5	.2401	2	unfathomable
0.1133	30.5	.2401	2	unicameral
0.1133	30.5	.2401	2	unification
0.1133	30.5	.1698	2	unleash
0.1133	30.5	.2401	2	untrammeled
0.1133	30.5	.1698	2	untruths
0.1133	30.5	.1698	2	vacated
0.1133	30.5	.2401	2	Venetia
0.1133	30.5	.1698	2	ventilating
0.1133	30.5	.2391	2	Verrazano-Narrows
0.1133	30.5	.2401	2	Vinci
0.1133	30.5	.1698	2	vizier
0.1133	30.5	.1698	2	wagtails
0.1133	30.5	.1698	2	Wakefield
0.1133	30.5	.1698	2	Walloons
0.1133	30.5	.2401	2	warble
0.1133	30.5	.2401	2	warmhearted
0.1133	30.5	.2401	2	water-proofing
0.1133	30.5	.2401	2	wealthier
0.1133	30.5	.1698	2	well-cut
0.1133	30.5	.1698	2	white-headed
0.1133	30.5	.2401	2	willful
0.1133	30.5	.2401	2	wipers
0.1133	30.5	.1698	2	wood-boring
0.1133	30.5	.1698	2	workrooms
0.1133	30.5	.1698	2	Worm
0.1133	30.5	.2391	2	x-ray
0.1133	30.5	.2401	2	Zealander
0.1133	30.5	.1698	2	Zulus
0.1133	30.5	.2391	2	008
0.1133	30.5	.2391	2	014
0.1133	30.5	.2401	2	1174
0.1133	30.5	.2391	2	1237
0.1133	30.5	.2401	2	1564
0.1133	30.5	.1698	2	1653
0.1133	30.5	.1698	2	1722
0.1133	30.5	.2391	2	180-degree
0.1133	30.5	.2401	2	1843
0.1133	30.5	.2391	2	234
0.1133	30.5	.2401	2	30-odd
0.1133	30.5	.2391	2	384
0.1133	30.5	.1698	2	39th
0.1133	30.5	.2391	2	477
0.1133	30.5	.2391	2	483
0.1133	30.5	.2391	2	503
0.1133	30.5	.2391	2	510
0.1133	30.5	.2391	2	534
0.1133	30.5	.2391	2	543
0.1133	30.5	.2391	2	571
0.1133	30.5	.2401	2	601
0.1133	30.5	.2391	2	65%
0.1133	30.5	.2391	2	710
THE PRECEDING WORD TYPE OCCUPIES RANK 39200				
0.1133	30.5	.2391	2	721
0.1133	30.5	.2391	2	741
0.1133	30.5	.2391	2	742
0.1133	30.5	.1698	2	744
0.1133	30.5	.2391	2	785
0.1133	30.5	.2391	2	793
0.1133	30.5	.2391	2	843
0.1133	30.5	.2391	2	884
0.1133	30.5	.2391	2	899
0.1133	30.5	.2391	2	9%
0.1133	30.5	.2391	2	906
0.1133	30.5	.2391	2	923
0.1133	30.5	.2391	2	946
0.1133	30.5	.2401	2	968
0.1132	30.5	.2440	2	abortive
0.1132	30.5	.2440	2	aggravation
0.1132	30.5	.2444	2	alms
0.1132	30.5	.2440	2	antic
0.1132	30.5	.2444	2	approving
0.1132	30.5	.2440	2	arson
0.1132	30.5	.2444	2	Ashur
0.1132	30.5	.2440	2	award-winning
0.1132	30.5	.2440	2	backwater
0.1132	30.5	.2440	2	belly-deep
0.1132	30.5	.2440	2	blanked
0.1132	30.5	.2444	2	bloat
0.1132	30.5	.2440	2	Bottom
0.1132	30.5	.2440	2	Brahma
0.1132	30.5	.2440	2	brushland
0.1132	30.5	.2440	2	brushwood
0.1132	30.5	.2444	2	bullpen
0.1132	30.5	.2440	2	bushed
0.1132	30.5	.2444	2	candy-making
0.1132	30.5	.2440	2	canoeists
0.1132	30.5	.2444	2	Carl's
0.1132	30.5	.2440	2	carted
0.1132	30.5	.2444	2	cheques
0.1132	30.5	.2440	2	chicken-wire
0.1132	30.5	.0000	14	claves
0.1132	30.5	.2444	2	cleverer
0.1132	30.5	.2440	2	close-cropped
0.1132	30.5	.2440	2	cluttering
0.1132	30.5	.2444	2	cohort
0.1132	30.5	.2440	2	commences
0.1132	30.5	.2444	2	complimented
0.1132	30.5	.2440	2	compromising
0.1132	30.5	.2440	2	confessor
0.1132	30.5	.2444	2	congeners
0.1132	30.5	.2444	2	conger
0.1132	30.5	.0000	14	contrapuntal
0.1132	30.5	.0000	14	cornet
0.1132	30.5	.2440	2	Crack
0.1132	30.5	.2444	2	Creative
0.1132	30.5	.2444	2	delaying
0.1132	30.5	.2444	2	delectable
0.1132	30.5	.2440	2	despoiled
0.1132	30.5	.2440	2	dinky
0.1132	30.5	.2444	2	dint
0.1132	30.5	.2440	2	disparagement
0.1132	30.5	.2444	2	ditty
0.1132	30.5	.2440	2	dodges
0.1132	30.5	.2440	2	doleful
0.1132	30.5	.2444	2	donned
0.1132	30.5	.2440	2	Dunbar's
0.1132	30.5	.2440	2	dust-free
0.1132	30.5	.2440	2	Dyer
0.1132	30.5	.2440	2	emissary
0.1132	30.5	.2440	2	energetically
0.1132	30.5	.2440	2	engendered
0.1132	30.5	.2440	2	erupting
0.1132	30.5	.2440	2	exhilarated
0.1132	30.5	.2440	2	fanciest
0.1132	30.5	.2440	2	Farmhouse
0.1132	30.5	.2440	2	Fence
0.1132	30.5	.2440	2	flayed
0.1132	30.5	.2440	2	fledge
0.1132	30.5	.2440	2	fogging
0.1132	30.5	.2440	2	font
0.1132	30.5	.2440	2	frail-looking
0.1132	30.5	.2440	2	French-English
0.1132	30.5	.2440	2	frenziedly
0.1132	30.5	.2440	2	Fuji
0.1132	30.5	.2440	2	fund-raising
0.1132	30.5	.2440	2	gentlefolk
0.1132	30.5	.2440	2	glamorized
0.1132	30.5	.2440	2	glitters
0.1132	30.5	.2440	2	glowering
0.1132	30.5	.2444	2	glub
0.1132	30.5	.2440	2	goading
0.1132	30.5	.2440	2	goldsmiths
0.1132	30.5	.2444	2	gooseberry
0.1132	30.5	.2440	2	half-eaten
0.1132	30.5	.2444	2	half-mast
0.1132	30.5	.2444	2	Halibut
0.1132	30.5	.2440	2	handstand
0.1132	30.5	.0000	14	Haydn's
0.1132	30.5	.2444	2	headstones
0.1132	30.5	.2440	2	healthily
0.1132	30.5	.2440	2	Heaven's
0.1132	30.5	.2440	2	hideaway
THE PRECEDING WORD TYPE OCCUPIES RANK 39300				
0.1132	30.5	.2440	2	hinting
0.1132	30.5	.2440	2	iss
0.1132	30.5	.2440	2	jabbered
0.1132	30.5	.2440	2	jailhouse
0.1132	30.5	.2440	2	Lad
0.1132	30.5	.2440	2	laudable
0.1132	30.5	.2444	2	leadin'
0.1132	30.5	.2444	2	leopard's
0.1132	30.5	.2444	2	lettuces
0.1132	30.5	.2440	2	lisping
0.1132	30.5	.2444	2	longed-for
0.1132	30.5	.2440	2	Longfellow's
0.1132	30.5	.2440	2	luckier
0.1132	30.5	.2440	2	lurid
0.1132	30.5	.2444	2	manicure
0.1132	30.5	.2440	2	maroon
0.1132	30.5	.2440	2	marquee
0.1132	30.5	.2440	2	mart
0.1132	30.5	.2440	2	martyred
0.1132	30.5	.2440	2	maul
0.1132	30.5	.2440	2	memo
0.1132	30.5	.2440	2	mile-long
0.1132	30.5	.2444	2	milliner
0.1132	30.5	.2440	2	mistrusted
0.1132	30.5	.2440	2	morally
0.1132	30.5	.2444	2	mot
0.1132	30.5	.2440	2	motes
0.1132	30.5	.2440	2	musketry
0.1132	30.5	.2444	2	mutt
0.1132	30.5	.2440	2	ne
0.1132	30.5	.2440	2	neighborliness
0.1132	30.5	.2440	2	non-stop
0.1132	30.5	.2444	2	numskull
0.1132	30.5	.2444	2	Oats
0.1132	30.5	.2440	2	obese
0.1132	30.5	.2440	2	off-spring
0.1132	30.5	.2444	2	omnipotent
0.1132	30.5	.2440	2	outcasts
0.1132	30.5	.2440	2	outshone
0.1132	30.5	.2440	2	pain-killer
0.1132	30.5	.2444	2	parent's
0.1132	30.5	.2444	2	pawn
0.1132	30.5	.2440	2	Playhouse
0.1132	30.5	.2440	2	pliant
0.1132	30.5	.2440	2	pomegranate
0.1132	30.5	.2440	2	Portage
0.1132	30.5	.2440	2	possibilites
0.1132	30.5	.2440	2	premature
0.1132	30.5	.2440	2	privy
0.1132	30.5	.2440	2	prodigal
0.1132	30.5	.2440	2	prognosis
0.1132	30.5	.2440	2	public-school
0.1132	30.5	.2440	2	quicken
0.1132	30.5	.2440	2	recounting
0.1132	30.5	.2440	2	regretting
0.1132	30.5	.2440	2	retaliate
0.1132	30.5	.2440	2	reviewers
0.1132	30.5	.2444	2	ribbing
0.1132	30.5	.2440	2	Robbie's
0.1132	30.5	.2440	2	Saddle
0.1132	30.5	.2440	2	Sayre
0.1132	30.5	.2444	2	schoolfellows
0.1132	30.5	.2440	2	scooting
0.1132	30.5	.2440	2	scorning
0.1132	30.5	.2440	2	scuffled
0.1132	30.5	.2440	2	shipshape
0.1132	30.5	.2440	2	shooters
0.1132	30.5	.2440	2	shuttered
0.1132	30.5	.2440	2	sidle
0.1132	30.5	.2444	2	signalled
0.1132	30.5	.2440	2	Sinatra
0.1132	30.5	.2440	2	sleepy-eyed
0.1132	30.5	.2440	2	squandered
0.1132	30.5	.2440	2	square-faced
0.1132	30.5	.2440	2	stags
0.1132	30.5	.2444	2	studiously
0.1132	30.5	.2440	2	Stuyvesant
0.1132	30.5	.2440	2	subjugation
0.1132	30.5	.2440	2	supper-table
0.1132	30.5	.2440	2	taciturn
0.1132	30.5	.2440	2	testified
0.1132	30.5	.2440	2	throwin'
0.1132	30.5	.2444	2	thwarts
0.1132	30.5	.2440	2	tiptoeing
0.1132	30.5	.2440	2	tomfoolery
0.1132	30.5	.2440	2	traffic-choked
0.1132	30.5	.2440	2	twinge

U	SFI	D	F	Word Type
0.1132	30.5	.2440	2	twisters
0.1132	30.5	.2440	2	two-month-old
0.1132	30.5	.2440	2	unremittingly
0.1132	30.5	.2440	2	vacuuming
0.1132	30.5	.2440	2	virgins
0.1132	30.5	.2440	2	vitae
0.1132	30.5	.2440	2	wallets
0.1132	30.5	.2440	2	weather-roughened
0.1132	30.5	.2440	2	Westerns
0.1132	30.5	.2440	2	wreathed
0.1132	30.5	.2440	2	zipping
0.1132	30.5	.2440	2	300-foot
0.1130	30.5	.2443	2	'thout

THE PRECEDING WORD TYPE OCCUPIES RANK 39400

U	SFI	D	F	Word Type
0.1130	30.5	.2443	2	a-wonderin'
0.1130	30.5	.2443	2	admittance
0.1130	30.5	.2443	2	agonized
0.1130	30.5	.2443	2	Airedale
0.1130	30.5	.2443	2	All-State
0.1130	30.5	.2443	2	anywheres
0.1130	30.5	.2443	2	apprehensively
0.1130	30.5	.2443	2	ascertained
0.1130	30.5	.2443	2	bed's
0.1130	30.5	.2443	2	begot
0.1130	30.5	.2443	2	Benbow
0.1130	30.5	.2443	2	benighted
0.1130	30.5	.2443	2	Billie
0.1130	30.5	.2443	2	boar's
0.1130	30.5	.2443	2	can'st
0.1130	30.5	.2443	2	carbine
0.1130	30.5	.2443	2	caressingly
0.1130	30.5	.2443	2	cloakroom
0.1130	30.5	.2443	2	commendation
0.1130	30.5	.2443	2	Coronation
0.1130	30.5	.2443	2	Crocker
0.1130	30.5	.2443	2	cussing
0.1130	30.5	.2443	2	deference
0.1130	30.5	.2443	2	diapered
0.1130	30.5	.2443	2	dictum
0.1130	30.5	.2443	2	diligence
0.1130	30.5	.2443	2	dither
0.1130	30.5	.2443	2	doublet
0.1130	30.5	.2443	2	escapade
0.1130	30.5	.2443	2	Esquimos
0.1130	30.5	.2443	2	Faber's
0.1130	30.5	.2443	2	figgering
0.1130	30.5	.2443	2	Flo
0.1130	30.5	.2443	2	floorboard
0.1130	30.5	.2443	2	fondling
0.1130	30.5	.2443	2	footlights
0.1130	30.5	.2443	2	fortune-telling
0.1130	30.5	.2443	2	Freebody's
0.1130	30.5	.2443	2	Garnet's
0.1130	30.5	.2443	2	gesticulating
0.1130	30.5	.2443	2	gorse
0.1130	30.5	.2443	2	grasshoppers'
0.1130	30.5	.2443	2	green-speckled
0.1130	30.5	.2443	2	groom's
0.1130	30.5	.2443	2	grotesquely
0.1130	30.5	.2443	2	hangin'
0.1130	30.5	.2443	2	headstall
0.1130	30.5	.2443	2	heigh-ho
0.1130	30.5	.2443	2	heinous
0.1130	30.5	.2443	2	heralds
0.1130	30.5	.2443	2	hewing
0.1130	30.5	.2443	2	house's
0.1130	30.5	.2443	2	impish
0.1130	30.5	.2443	2	incrusted
0.1130	30.5	.2443	2	Inspector
0.1130	30.5	.2443	2	interposed
0.1130	30.5	.2443	2	involuntarily
0.1130	30.5	.2443	2	irresolute
0.1130	30.5	.2443	2	jellyfishes
0.1130	30.5	.2443	2	Jumpin'
0.1130	30.5	.2443	2	knave
0.1130	30.5	.2443	2	latigo
0.1130	30.5	.2443	2	lightened
0.1130	30.5	.2443	2	lodger
0.1130	30.5	.2443	2	mangled
0.1130	30.5	.2443	2	Mcgrath
0.1130	30.5	.2443	2	meekness
0.1130	30.5	.2443	2	minute's
0.1130	30.5	.2443	2	mistreated
0.1130	30.5	.2443	2	Mohawks
0.1130	30.5	.2443	2	Mohican
0.1130	30.5	.2443	2	Muffet
0.1130	30.5	.2443	2	musky
0.1130	30.5	.2443	2	must've
0.1130	30.5	.2443	2	nerved
0.1130	30.5	.2443	2	nevermore
0.1130	30.5	.2443	2	Nilsson's
0.1130	30.5	.2443	2	no-oo
0.1130	30.5	.2443	2	Nursery
0.1130	30.5	.2443	2	offen
0.1130	30.5	.2443	2	oiling
0.1130	30.5	.2443	2	papered
0.1130	30.5	.2443	2	pitiable
0.1130	30.5	.2443	2	profanely
0.1130	30.5	.2443	2	quaked
0.1130	30.5	.2443	2	rascally
0.1130	30.5	.2443	2	rashly
0.1130	30.5	.2443	2	ringside
0.1130	30.5	.2443	2	Salinas
0.1130	30.5	.2443	2	she-bear
0.1130	30.5	.2443	2	shellacking
0.1130	30.5	.2443	2	shirt-tail
0.1130	30.5	.2443	2	six-shooters
0.1130	30.5	.2443	2	sledgehammer
0.1130	30.5	.2443	2	sponged
0.1130	30.5	.2443	2	stammering
0.1130	30.5	.2443	2	story-teller
0.1130	30.5	.2443	2	stummick
0.1130	30.5	.2443	2	suspender
0.1130	30.5	.2443	2	tabby

THE PRECEDING WORD TYPE OCCUPIES RANK 39500

U	SFI	D	F	Word Type
0.1130	30.5	.2443	2	teetered
0.1130	30.5	.2443	2	ten-thirty
0.1130	30.5	.2443	2	thereat
0.1130	30.5	.2443	2	thwart
0.1130	30.5	.2443	2	til
0.1130	30.5	.2443	2	to-do
0.1130	30.5	.2443	2	trilled
0.1130	30.5	.2443	2	tromped
0.1130	30.5	.2443	2	twanged
0.1130	30.5	.2443	2	twopence
0.1130	30.5	.2443	2	unhuman
0.1130	30.5	.2443	2	unreasonably
0.1130	30.5	.2443	2	unwholesome
0.1130	30.5	.2443	2	wadded-up
0.1130	30.5	.2443	2	when's
0.1130	30.5	.2443	2	whet
0.1130	30.5	.2443	2	whicker
0.1130	30.5	.2443	2	whole-heartedly
0.1130	30.5	.2443	2	winnings
0.1130	30.5	.2443	2	wishbone
0.1130	30.5	.2443	2	ye'd
0.1130	30.5	.2443	2	yellow-eyed
0.1130	30.5	.2443	2	your'n
0.1130	30.5	.2443	2	Zodiac
0.1129	30.5	.2437	2	$52
0.1129	30.5	.2285	2	abiding
0.1129	30.5	.2285	2	abstain
0.1129	30.5	.2437	2	absurdity
0.1129	30.5	.2285	2	Aconcagua
0.1129	30.5	.2437	2	acquiescence
0.1129	30.5	.2285	2	acquit
0.1129	30.5	.2437	2	acquittal
0.1129	30.5	.2437	2	adaptive
0.1129	30.5	.2285	2	adorning
0.1129	30.5	.2437	2	adversity
0.1129	30.5	.2437	2	afflicting
0.1129	30.5	.2437	2	aficionados
0.1129	30.5	.2285	2	afoul
0.1129	30.5	.2285	2	aggressors
0.1129	30.5	.2437	2	Agreement
0.1129	30.5	.2437	2	Ala
0.1129	30.5	.2285	2	aldermen
0.1129	30.5	.2437	2	alerts
0.1129	30.5	.2437	2	Aleutians
0.1129	30.5	.2285	2	Amharic
0.1129	30.5	.2285	2	anacondas
0.1129	30.5	.2437	2	analogy
0.1129	30.5	.2437	2	Analysis
0.1129	30.5	.2285	2	Andorra
0.1129	30.5	.2437	2	Anglican
0.1129	30.5	.2437	2	Antioch
0.1129	30.5	.2437	2	antisocial
0.1129	30.5	.2437	2	antitrust
0.1129	30.5	.2437	2	anyplace
0.1129	30.5	.2285	2	Aquitaine
0.1129	30.5	.2437	2	archeology
0.1129	30.5	.2437	2	Argonne
0.1129	30.5	.2437	2	Arsenal
0.1129	30.5	.2437	2	art's
0.1129	30.5	.2285	2	Astronauts
0.1129	30.5	.2285	2	Atacama
0.1129	30.5	.2437	2	atolls
0.1129	30.5	.2437	2	atrophy
0.1129	30.5	.2437	2	attachments
0.1129	30.5	.2285	2	attributing
0.1129	30.5	.2285	2	avarice
0.1129	30.5	.2285	2	average-sized
0.1129	30.5	.2437	2	avidly
0.1129	30.5	.2285	2	bailiff
0.1129	30.5	.2437	2	barrister
0.1129	30.5	.2285	2	Basilica
0.1129	30.5	.2285	2	battery-operated
0.1129	30.5	.2285	2	Bethune
0.1129	30.5	.2437	2	biennial
0.1129	30.5	.2437	2	blenders
0.1129	30.5	.2285	2	blockaded
0.1129	30.5	.2285	2	blunted
0.1129	30.5	.2437	2	Bomb
0.1129	30.5	.2285	2	bottleneck
0.1129	30.5	.2437	2	Bourbon
0.1129	30.5	.2285	2	Braxton
0.1129	30.5	.2437	2	breakage
0.1129	30.5	.2285	2	breakwaters
0.1129	30.5	.2285	2	broadleaf
0.1129	30.5	.2437	2	BuenosAires
0.1129	30.5	.2437	2	bunkers
0.1129	30.5	.2285	2	burgesses
0.1129	30.5	.2285	2	Cabot's
0.1129	30.5	.2437	2	Cannes
0.1129	30.5	.2285	2	Carthaginian
0.1129	30.5	.2285	2	Carthaginians
0.1129	30.5	.2285	2	Casablanca
0.1129	30.5	.2437	2	cascading
0.1129	30.5	.2285	2	cassava
0.1129	30.5	.2285	2	castigated
0.1129	30.5	.2437	2	catalogued
0.1129	30.5	.2285	2	cattle-raising
0.1129	30.5	.2437	2	cemeteries
0.1129	30.5	.2437	2	censor
0.1129	30.5	.2285	2	centuries-old

THE PRECEDING WORD TYPE OCCUPIES RANK 39600

U	SFI	D	F	Word Type
0.1129	30.5	.2285	2	certificate
0.1129	30.5	.2285	2	cession
0.1129	30.5	.2437	2	Chattahoochee
0.1129	30.5	.2437	2	chef
0.1129	30.5	.2285	2	Chiang's
0.1129	30.5	.2437	2	civet
0.1129	30.5	.2285	2	Claims
0.1129	30.5	.2437	2	clam's
0.1129	30.5	.2285	2	clearinghouse
0.1129	30.5	.2285	2	climes
0.1129	30.5	.2285	2	co-operatively
0.1129	30.5	.2285	2	cobble-stone
0.1129	30.5	.2437	2	cock's
0.1129	30.5	.2437	2	comically
0.1129	30.5	.2285	2	Commissioners
0.1129	30.5	.2437	2	Complex
0.1129	30.5	.2437	2	compost
0.1129	30.5	.2437	2	Computer
0.1129	30.5	.2437	2	Conditioning
0.1129	30.5	.2437	2	condors
0.1129	30.5	.2437	2	conduit
0.1129	30.5	.2285	2	conquistador
0.1129	30.5	.2437	2	consensus
0.1129	30.5	.2285	2	constrained
0.1129	30.5	.2437	2	consultants
0.1129	30.5	.2437	2	contemporaneous
0.1129	30.5	.2285	2	Coptic
0.1129	30.5	.2437	2	corroded
0.1129	30.5	.2285	2	countries'
0.1129	30.5	.2437	2	cranking
0.1129	30.5	.2437	2	credibility
0.1129	30.5	.2437	2	credits
0.1129	30.5	.2437	2	crevices
0.1129	30.5	.2437	2	crystal's
0.1129	30.5	.2437	2	cumin
0.1129	30.5	.2437	2	curricula
0.1129	30.5	.2437	2	custom-made
0.1129	30.5	.2437	2	cut-and-try
0.1129	30.5	.2437	2	cyclists
0.1129	30.5	.2437	2	cypresses
0.1129	30.5	.2285	2	Dai
0.1129	30.5	.2437	2	dearth
0.1129	30.5	.2285	2	Delaware's
0.1129	30.5	.2437	2	delineated
0.1129	30.5	.2285	2	deport
0.1129	30.5	.2437	2	depreciate
0.1129	30.5	.2437	2	derangement
0.1129	30.5	.2437	2	deservedly
0.1129	30.5	.2437	2	designer's
0.1129	30.5	.2285	2	destitute
0.1129	30.5	.2285	2	deteriorated
0.1129	30.5	.2437	2	deterrent
0.1129	30.5	.2437	2	Dictator
0.1129	30.5	.2437	2	Directory
0.1129	30.5	.2285	2	dishonesty
0.1129	30.5	.2437	2	disparity
0.1129	30.5	.2285	2	disrepair
0.1129	30.5	.2437	2	disruptions
0.1129	30.5	.2437	2	dissident
0.1129	30.5	.2285	2	distilleries
0.1129	30.5	.2437	2	doctoral
0.1129	30.5	.2285	2	doctrinaire
0.1129	30.5	.2437	2	Druids
0.1129	30.5	.2437	2	ecologically
0.1129	30.5	.2437	2	ecologists
0.1129	30.5	.2437	2	edifices
0.1129	30.5	.2285	2	egalite
0.1129	30.5	.2285	2	Eighteenth
0.1129	30.5	.2437	2	Election
0.1129	30.5	.2437	2	electrification
0.1129	30.5	.2285	2	embattled
0.1129	30.5	.2437	2	encyclical
0.1129	30.5	.2285	2	entertains
0.1129	30.5	.2285	2	Ephraim
0.1129	30.5	.2437	2	erosive
0.1129	30.5	.2437	2	Esau
0.1129	30.5	.2437	2	esplanade
0.1129	30.5	.2437	2	Estonia
0.1129	30.5	.2437	2	expend
0.1129	30.5	.2437	2	expressionism
0.1129	30.5	.2437	2	External
0.1129	30.5	.2437	2	extirpation
0.1129	30.5	.2285	2	fabulously
0.1129	30.5	.2437	2	fatherhood
0.1129	30.5	.2285	2	Fermi's
0.1129	30.5	.2437	2	festivity
0.1129	30.5	.2285	2	fiasco
0.1129	30.5	.2285	2	Field's
0.1129	30.5	.2285	2	Fighting
0.1129	30.5	.2285	2	fireproof
0.1129	30.5	.2437	2	five-man
0.1129	30.5	.2285	2	fixatives
0.1129	30.5	.2437	2	flagrantly
0.1129	30.5	.2437	2	flamboyantly
0.1129	30.5	.2437	2	fledgling
0.1129	30.5	.2285	2	food-producing
0.1129	30.5	.2285	2	formidably
0.1129	30.5	.2437	2	formulation
0.1129	30.5	.2437	2	fortification
0.1129	30.5	.2437	2	four-inch-long

THE PRECEDING WORD TYPE OCCUPIES RANK 39700

U	SFI	D	F	Word Type
0.1129	30.5	.2285	2	fraternite
0.1129	30.5	.2285	2	Frederick's
0.1129	30.5	.2285	2	freedom-loving
0.1129	30.5	.2285	2	Fujiyama
0.1129	30.5	.2285	2	futures
0.1129	30.5	.2437	2	futuristic
0.1129	30.5	.2437	2	galactic
0.1129	30.5	.2285	2	galleons
0.1129	30.5	.2285	2	Gama
0.1129	30.5	.2285	2	gatherers
0.1129	30.5	.2285	2	glassmaking
0.1129	30.5	.2437	2	glassy-smooth
0.1129	30.5	.2437	2	gleaned
0.1129	30.5	.2285	2	Goodyear's
0.1129	30.5	.2285	2	graced
0.1129	30.5	.2437	2	gradients
0.1129	30.5	.2285	2	guided-missile
0.1129	30.5	.2285	2	gunboats
0.1129	30.5	.2285	2	Gustave
0.1129	30.5	.2285	2	Haneda
0.1129	30.5	.2437	2	harbored
0.1129	30.5	.2285	2	hard-baked
0.1129	30.5	.2437	2	harelip
0.1129	30.5	.2285	2	harems
0.1129	30.5	.2437	2	Heads
0.1129	30.5	.2437	2	Heber
0.1129	30.5	.2437	2	Hepburn
0.1129	30.5	.2285	2	heroines
0.1129	30.5	.2437	2	high-tension
0.1129	30.5	.2437	2	high-water
0.1129	30.5	.2437	2	hitchhiked
0.1129	30.5	.2437	2	homesteaded
0.1129	30.5	.2285	2	Hub
0.1129	30.5	.2437	2	hysteria
0.1129	30.5	.2285	2	Iguassu
0.1129	30.5	.2285	2	immunities
0.1129	30.5	.2437	2	impeccably
0.1129	30.5	.2437	2	impede
0.1129	30.5	.2437	2	imperfectly
0.1129	30.5	.2437	2	implication
0.1129	30.5	.2437	2	incompetence
0.1129	30.5	.2285	2	incorporates
0.1129	30.5	.2437	2	Indochinese
0.1129	30.5	.2285	2	Indonesians
0.1129	30.5	.2285	2	industriousness
0.1129	30.5	.2285	2	infertile
0.1129	30.5	.2437	2	infiltrated
0.1129	30.5	.2285	2	inflicting
0.1129	30.5	.2437	2	injunction
0.1129	30.5	.2437	2	inoperative
0.1129	30.5	.2437	2	inspirational
0.1129	30.5	.2437	2	Institutes
0.1129	30.5	.2437	2	intangible
0.1129	30.5	.2437	2	interconnected
0.1129	30.5	.2285	2	interned
0.1129	30.5	.2437	2	interstitial
0.1129	30.5	.2437	2	irascible
0.1129	30.5	.2285	2	Irian
0.1129	30.5	.2437	2	irreplaceable
0.1129	30.5	.2437	2	Irvin
0.1129	30.5	.2285	2	jackass
0.1129	30.5	.2285	2	jaguars
0.1129	30.5	.2437	2	jargon
0.1129	30.5	.2437	2	jaw-breaking
0.1129	30.5	.2285	2	Kellogg-Briand
0.1129	30.5	.2437	2	LaGuardia
0.1129	30.5	.2285	2	laborsaving
0.1129	30.5	.2285	2	landholders
0.1129	30.5	.2285	2	landholdings
0.1129	30.5	.2437	2	late-blooming
0.1129	30.5	.2437	2	leases
0.1129	30.5	.2437	2	leftist
0.1129	30.5	.2437	2	legislature's
0.1129	30.5	.2437	2	liability
0.1129	30.5	.2285	2	lianas
0.1129	30.5	.2437	2	Liberation
0.1129	30.5	.2285	2	liberte
0.1129	30.5	.2285	2	limousines
0.1129	30.5	.2285	2	liquors
0.1129	30.5	.2437	2	Lithuania
0.1129	30.5	.2285	2	luxuriously
0.1129	30.5	.2437	2	mace
0.1129	30.5	.2285	2	magnificient
0.1129	30.5	.2437	2	magnum
0.1129	30.5	.2437	2	Mahler
0.1129	30.5	.2285	2	Makassar
0.1129	30.5	.2437	2	malaise
0.1129	30.5	.2437	2	malfunctions
0.1129	30.5	.2437	2	management's
0.1129	30.5	.2285	2	Manitoba
0.1129	30.5	.2285	2	manta
0.1129	30.5	.2285	2	mapmaking
0.1129	30.5	.2437	2	Marble
0.1129	30.5	.2437	2	Material
0.1129	30.5	.2285	2	materially
0.1129	30.5	.2437	2	mayflies
0.1129	30.5	.2437	2	McDonald
0.1129	30.5	.2285	2	melodramatic
0.1129	30.5	.2437	2	memorials
0.1129	30.5	.2437	2	metaphysical

THE PRECEDING WORD TYPE OCCUPIES RANK 39800

U	SFI	D	F	Word Type
0.1129	30.5	.2437	2	Mid-Atlantic
0.1129	30.5	.2437	2	mid-August
0.1129	30.5	.2285	2	mid-latitudes
0.1129	30.5	.2437	2	mid-19th
0.1129	30.5	.2437	2	mid-1950's
0.1129	30.5	.2437	2	mile-wide
0.1129	30.5	.2437	2	Milhous
0.1129	30.5	.2437	2	misconceptions
0.1129	30.5	.2437	2	modernity
0.1129	30.5	.2437	2	monitors
0.1129	30.5	.2285	2	MORE
0.1129	30.5	.2437	2	motivate
0.1129	30.5	.2437	2	multi-colored
0.1129	30.5	.2437	2	near-perfect
0.1129	30.5	.2285	2	nestle
0.1129	30.5	.2285	2	Netherlanders
0.1129	30.5	.2437	2	Nikon
0.1129	30.5	.2437	2	nonconductor
0.1129	30.5	.2437	2	norm
0.1129	30.5	.2437	2	Normal
0.1129	30.5	.2437	2	now-famous
0.1129	30.5	.2437	2	oil-rich
0.1129	30.5	.2285	2	open-minded
0.1129	30.5	.2437	2	open-water
0.1129	30.5	.2437	2	operative
0.1129	30.5	.2437	2	ornithologists
0.1129	30.5	.2285	2	ostensibly
0.1129	30.5	.2285	2	outbound
0.1129	30.5	.2285	2	outnumbering
0.1129	30.5	.2437	2	outstrip
0.1129	30.5	.2285	2	overruled
0.1129	30.5	.2437	2	overt
0.1129	30.5	.2437	2	Painter
0.1129	30.5	.2285	2	Papua
0.1129	30.5	.2285	2	paradoxical
0.1129	30.5	.2437	2	paragon
0.1129	30.5	.2285	2	parishes
0.1129	30.5	.2285	2	pasturage
0.1129	30.5	.2437	2	patrician
0.1129	30.5	.2437	2	pediatrician
0.1129	30.5	.2285	2	perpetrated
0.1129	30.5	.2437	2	pesticides
0.1129	30.5	.2285	2	phlegm
0.1129	30.5	.2437	2	physicist's
0.1129	30.5	.2437	2	picketing
0.1129	30.5	.2437	2	pinpointed
0.1129	30.5	.2437	2	Pitcher
0.1129	30.5	.2437	2	plebeian
0.1129	30.5	.2285	2	plentifully
0.1129	30.5	.2285	2	plumbers

U	SFI	D	F	Word Type
0.1129	30.5	.2285	2	pocketbooks
0.1129	30.5	.2285	2	preeminence
0.1129	30.5	.2437	2	prehensile
0.1129	30.5	.2285	2	Prejudice
0.1129	30.5	.2437	2	prelates
0.1129	30.5	.2437	2	primaeval
0.1129	30.5	.2285	2	profuse
0.1129	30.5	.2437	2	project's
0.1129	30.5	.2285	2	proprietary
0.1129	30.5	.2285	2	Protectorate
0.1129	30.5	.2285	2	province's
0.1129	30.5	.2437	2	pulverized
0.1129	30.5	.2437	2	purists
0.1129	30.5	.2285	2	puritanical
0.1129	30.5	.2437	2	pursuer
0.1129	30.5	.2285	2	pygmies
0.1129	30.5	.2437	2	pyre
0.1129	30.5	.2437	2	questionnaire
0.1129	30.5	.2285	2	rampant
0.1129	30.5	.2437	2	Random
0.1129	30.5	.2285	2	re-established
0.1129	30.5	.2437	2	reappearing
0.1129	30.5	.2285	2	refreshes
0.1129	30.5	.2437	2	refrigerant
0.1129	30.5	.2285	2	regency
0.1129	30.5	.2285	2	remolding
0.1129	30.5	.2285	2	remonstrances
0.1129	30.5	.2285	2	reprisals
0.1129	30.5	.2285	2	reputed
0.1129	30.5	.2285	2	requisite
0.1129	30.5	.2285	2	retailing
0.1129	30.5	.2437	2	Reuther
0.1129	30.5	.2437	2	revert
0.1129	30.5	.2437	2	sabbath
0.1129	30.5	.2285	2	saga
0.1129	30.5	.2437	2	salubrious
0.1129	30.5	.2437	2	science's
0.1129	30.5	.2437	2	Scientist
0.1129	30.5	.2437	2	secretarial
0.1129	30.5	.2437	2	seepage
0.1129	30.5	.2285	2	self-defeating
0.1129	30.5	.2285	2	self-employed
0.1129	30.5	.2437	2	self-imposed
0.1129	30.5	.2437	2	semesters
0.1129	30.5	.2437	2	sexually
0.1129	30.5	.2437	2	Shaftesbury
0.1129	30.5	.2285	2	shambling
0.1129	30.5	.2285	2	Shell
0.1129	30.5	.2437	2	shell-shocked
0.1129	30.5	.2285	2	shopwork

THE PRECEDING WORD TYPE OCCUPIES RANK 39900

U	SFI	D	F	Word Type
0.1129	30.5	.2437	2	sidewhiskers
0.1129	30.5	.2285	2	sieges
0.1129	30.5	.2437	2	SiouxFalls
0.1129	30.5	.2285	2	Skagerrak
0.1129	30.5	.2437	2	smolders
0.1129	30.5	.2437	2	snipe
0.1129	30.5	.2285	2	snow-clad
0.1129	30.5	.2437	2	society's
0.1129	30.5	.2285	2	soldiering
0.1129	30.5	.2285	2	Somme
0.1129	30.5	.2285	2	Sophocles
0.1129	30.5	.2285	2	Soviet-made
0.1129	30.5	.2437	2	specialist's
0.1129	30.5	.2437	2	speculated
0.1129	30.5	.2437	2	speculators
0.1129	30.5	.2437	2	staffed
0.1129	30.5	.2285	2	Stagg
0.1129	30.5	.2437	2	stomach's
0.1129	30.5	.2285	2	stonecutters
0.1129	30.5	.2437	2	stratification
0.1129	30.5	.2437	2	stratum
0.1129	30.5	.2437	2	stupider
0.1129	30.5	.2285	2	subarctic
0.1129	30.5	.2285	2	subconscious
0.1129	30.5	.2437	2	subhuman
0.1129	30.5	.2285	2	Sumer
0.1129	30.5	.2285	2	sun-drenched
0.1129	30.5	.2437	2	supremely
0.1129	30.5	.2285	2	surmise
0.1129	30.5	.2437	2	taboos
0.1129	30.5	.2437	2	Tadzhik
0.1129	30.5	.2285	2	Tariff
0.1129	30.5	.2285	2	Tartar
0.1129	30.5	.2285	2	Tehuantepec
0.1129	30.5	.2437	2	Tenn
0.1129	30.5	.2437	2	terrifies
0.1129	30.5	.2285	2	terrorize
0.1129	30.5	.2285	2	three-fifths
0.1129	30.5	.2437	2	three-speed
0.1129	30.5	.2285	2	Tilden
0.1129	30.5	.2437	2	Tire
0.1129	30.5	.2437	2	Trades
0.1129	30.5	.2285	2	treks
0.1129	30.5	.2437	2	tribulations
0.1129	30.5	.2437	2	turgid
0.1129	30.5	.2437	2	turreted
0.1129	30.5	.2437	2	twin-engine
0.1129	30.5	.2285	2	typists
0.1129	30.5	.2285	2	Ukrainians
0.1129	30.5	.2437	2	underrate
0.1129	30.5	.2437	2	underrated
0.1129	30.5	.2285	2	unplowed
0.1129	30.5	.2437	2	unsuspected
0.1129	30.5	.2437	2	untrustworthy
0.1129	30.5	.2437	2	upholding
0.1129	30.5	.2285	2	uprisings
0.1129	30.5	.2437	2	upsurge
0.1129	30.5	.2437	2	Us
0.1129	30.5	.2285	2	USSR
0.1129	30.5	.2437	2	usurpers
0.1129	30.5	.2285	2	Verdun
0.1129	30.5	.2437	2	vertigo
0.1129	30.5	.2437	2	vibrant
0.1129	30.5	.2285	2	viceroy
0.1129	30.5	.2437	2	watercourses
0.1129	30.5	.2285	2	weaponry
0.1129	30.5	.2437	2	well-adjusted
0.1129	30.5	.2437	2	well-worn
0.1129	30.5	.2285	2	Western-style
0.1129	30.5	.2285	2	westernmost
0.1129	30.5	.2285	2	wine-making
0.1129	30.5	.2285	2	Winnipeg
0.1129	30.5	.2437	2	yachts
0.1129	30.5	.2285	2	Zebulon
0.1129	30.5	.2437	2	100-foot-long
0.1129	30.5	.2285	2	1095
0.1129	30.5	.2285	2	1497
0.1129	30.5	.2285	2	1520
0.1129	30.5	.2285	2	1533
0.1129	30.5	.2285	2	1542
0.1129	30.5	.2437	2	1598
0.1129	30.5	.2285	2	1622
0.1129	30.5	.2285	2	1633
0.1129	30.5	.2285	2	1649
0.1129	30.5	.2285	2	1772
0.1129	30.5	.2285	2	1890s
0.1129	30.5	.2437	2	211
0.1129	30.5	.2437	2	26th
0.1129	30.5	.2285	2	395
0.1129	30.5	.2285	2	40-story
0.1129	30.5	.2285	2	40's
0.1129	30.5	.2285	2	400's
0.1129	30.5	.2437	2	476
0.1129	30.5	.2285	2	500's
0.1129	30.5	.2437	2	60-inch
0.1129	30.5	.2437	2	726
0.1129	30.5	.2285	2	781
0.1129	30.5	.2437	2	82-inch
0.1129	30.5	.2437	2	904
0.1128	30.5	.2278	2	Administrator

THE PRECEDING WORD TYPE OCCUPIES RANK 40000

U	SFI	D	F	Word Type
0.1128	30.5	.2278	2	adrenal
0.1128	30.5	.2278	2	aerodynamics
0.1128	30.5	.2278	2	alloyed
0.1128	30.5	.2278	2	anabolic
0.1128	30.5	.2278	2	anatomist
0.1128	30.5	.2278	2	anatomists
0.1128	30.5	.2278	2	angiosperms
0.1128	30.5	.2278	2	anhydrous
0.1128	30.5	.2278	2	Atheneum
0.1128	30.5	.2278	2	atrium
0.1128	30.5	.2278	2	bacillus
0.1128	30.5	.2278	2	bacteriology
0.1128	30.5	.2278	2	bandlike
0.1128	30.5	.2278	2	bivalve
0.1128	30.5	.2278	2	Bode
0.1128	30.5	.2278	2	Bohr's
0.1128	30.5	.2278	2	borealis
0.1128	30.5	.2278	2	borer
0.1128	30.5	.2278	2	bowl-shaped
0.1128	30.5	.2278	2	brachiopods
0.1128	30.5	.2278	2	bubonic
0.1128	30.5	.2278	2	catabolic
0.1128	30.5	.2278	2	catalysts
0.1128	30.5	.2278	2	cell's
0.1128	30.5	.2278	2	Cenozoic
0.1128	30.5	.2278	2	cohesive
0.1128	30.5	.2278	2	cold-weather
0.1128	30.5	.2278	2	conjectural
0.1128	30.5	.2278	2	constrictors
0.1128	30.5	.2278	2	contributors
0.1128	30.5	.2278	2	C2
0.1128	30.5	.2278	2	dark-gray
0.1128	30.5	.2278	2	deems
0.1128	30.5	.2278	2	degeneration
0.1128	30.5	.2278	2	destructiveness
0.1128	30.5	.2278	2	dilutes
0.1128	30.5	.2278	2	diluting
0.1128	30.5	.2278	2	diorite
0.1128	30.5	.2278	2	diploid
0.1128	30.5	.2278	2	discrepancies
0.1128	30.5	.2278	2	disintegrating
0.1128	30.5	.2278	2	dissections
0.1128	30.5	.2278	2	disulfide
0.1128	30.5	.2278	2	electrolysis
0.1128	30.5	.2278	2	Empires
0.1128	30.5	.2278	2	enforcement
0.1128	30.5	.2278	2	envelops
0.1128	30.5	.2278	2	erodes
0.1128	30.5	.2278	2	excretes
0.1128	30.5	.2278	2	extremities
0.1128	30.5	.2278	2	fertilizes
0.1128	30.5	.2278	2	first-order
0.1128	30.5	.2278	2	fittingly
0.1128	30.5	.2278	2	fluctuation
0.1128	30.5	.2278	2	fort's
0.1128	30.5	.2278	2	Fruits
0.1128	30.5	.2278	2	Galvani
0.1128	30.5	.2278	2	gastropods
0.1128	30.5	.2278	2	geophysicist
0.1128	30.5	.2278	2	glaciated
0.1128	30.5	.2278	2	gravity's
0.1128	30.5	.2278	2	Haber
0.1128	30.5	.2278	2	habitable
0.1128	30.5	.2278	2	heat-producing
0.1128	30.5	.2278	2	hydrated
0.1128	30.5	.2278	2	hydrazine
0.1128	30.5	.2278	2	Hymenoptera
0.1128	30.5	.2278	2	immemorial
0.1128	30.5	.2278	2	immortalized
0.1128	30.5	.2278	2	improbable
0.1128	30.5	.2278	2	insect-eaters
0.1128	30.5	.2278	2	intermingle
0.1128	30.5	.2278	2	intricacy
0.1128	30.5	.2278	2	irrevocably
0.1128	30.5	.2278	2	kryos
0.1128	30.5	.2278	2	ladyslipper
0.1128	30.5	.2278	2	ligaments
0.1128	30.5	.2278	2	linearly
0.1128	30.5	.2278	2	liqueurs
0.1128	30.5	.2278	2	listlessness
0.1128	30.5	.2278	2	lobe
0.1128	30.5	.2278	2	luminosity
0.1128	30.5	.2278	2	magnetizing
0.1128	30.5	.2278	2	manifestations
0.1128	30.5	.2278	2	mantises
0.1128	30.5	.2278	2	mars
0.1128	30.5	.2278	2	mastication
0.1128	30.5	.2278	2	membranous
0.1128	30.5	.2278	2	mid-autumn
0.1128	30.5	.2278	2	mid-ocean
0.1128	30.5	.2278	2	mid-1800's
0.1128	30.5	.2278	2	mineralogically
0.1128	30.5	.2278	2	much-publicized
0.1128	30.5	.2278	2	nebula
0.1128	30.5	.2278	2	nickel-iron
0.1128	30.5	.2278	2	noncircular
0.1128	30.5	.2278	2	nonofficial
0.1128	30.5	.2278	2	nonpoisonous
0.1128	30.5	.2278	2	Occidentals
0.1128	30.5	.2278	2	Oceanography

THE PRECEDING WORD TYPE OCCUPIES RANK 40100

U	SFI	D	F	Word Type
0.1128	30.5	.2278	2	olive-green
0.1128	30.5	.2278	2	overactivity
0.1128	30.5	.2278	2	ozone
0.1128	30.5	.2278	2	permeable
0.1128	30.5	.2278	2	pinches
0.1128	30.5	.2278	2	Pithecanthropus
0.1128	30.5	.2278	2	placental
0.1128	30.5	.2278	2	Planck's
0.1128	30.5	.2278	2	plastids
0.1128	30.5	.2278	2	polymerization
0.1128	30.5	.2278	2	precipitated
0.1128	30.5	.2278	2	predicts
0.1128	30.5	.2278	2	propagating
0.1128	30.5	.2278	2	propels
0.1128	30.5	.2278	2	psychotherapy
0.1128	30.5	.2278	2	retinas
0.1128	30.5	.2278	2	Rhodora
0.1128	30.5	.2278	2	rock's
0.1128	30.5	.2278	2	rodlike
0.1128	30.5	.2278	2	rookeries
0.1128	30.5	.2278	2	rotations
0.1128	30.5	.2278	2	Rutherford's
0.1128	30.5	.2278	2	saline
0.1128	30.5	.2278	2	saprophytic
0.1128	30.5	.2278	2	scotch
0.1128	30.5	.2278	2	Scripps
0.1128	30.5	.2278	2	seafarer
0.1128	30.5	.2278	2	seasonally
0.1128	30.5	.2278	2	shorelines
0.1128	30.5	.2278	2	smasher
0.1128	30.5	.2278	2	solidifies
0.1128	30.5	.2278	2	stereoscopic
0.1128	30.5	.2278	2	Strassmann
0.1128	30.5	.2278	2	structurally
0.1128	30.5	.2278	2	submergence
0.1128	30.5	.2278	2	subside
0.1128	30.5	.2278	2	synapse
0.1128	30.5	.2278	2	then-known
0.1128	30.5	.2278	2	toxin
0.1128	30.5	.2278	2	trapdoors
0.1128	30.5	.2278	2	triggers
0.1128	30.5	.2278	2	triode
0.1128	30.5	.2278	2	triphosphate
0.1128	30.5	.2278	2	tubelike
0.1128	30.5	.2278	2	Tuberculosis
0.1128	30.5	.2278	2	typist
0.1128	30.5	.2278	2	Vertebrata
0.1128	30.5	.2278	2	warming-up
0.1128	30.5	.2278	2	waxwings
0.1128	30.5	.2278	2	well-equipped
0.1128	30.5	.2278	2	wriggles
0.1128	30.5	.2278	2	Zacharias
0.1128	30.5	.2278	2	1546
0.1128	30.5	.2278	2	1550
0.1128	30.5	.2278	2	4-inch
0.1128	30.5	.2278	2	400-foot
0.1128	30.5	.2278	2	584
0.1128	30.5	.2278	2	7-21
0.1127	30.5	.0700	4	adore
0.1127	30.5	.2441	2	afflict
0.1127	30.5	.2441	2	anatomically
0.1127	30.5	.2441	2	annulled
0.1127	30.5	.2441	2	apprehensions
0.1127	30.5	.2441	2	barrenness
0.1127	30.5	.2441	2	beheading
0.1127	30.5	.2441	2	boggy
0.1127	30.5	.2441	2	brainwork
0.1127	30.5	.2441	2	bristly
0.1127	30.5	.2441	2	bronchitis
0.1127	30.5	.2441	2	Brooke
0.1127	30.5	.2441	2	building's
0.1127	30.5	.2441	2	bulbar
0.1127	30.5	.2441	2	buntings
0.1127	30.5	.2441	2	buttery
0.1127	30.5	.2441	2	caudal
0.1127	30.5	.2441	2	cessation
0.1127	30.5	.2441	2	chest-deep
0.1127	30.5	.2441	2	comings
0.1127	30.5	.2441	2	compensated
0.1127	30.5	.2441	2	Corporal
0.1127	30.5	.2441	2	criss-cross
0.1127	30.5	.2441	2	cropped
0.1127	30.5	.2441	2	Crusader
0.1127	30.5	.2441	2	delusion
0.1127	30.5	.2441	2	detaining
0.1127	30.5	.2441	2	dormer
0.1127	30.5	.2441	2	exertions
0.1127	30.5	.2441	2	extant
0.1127	30.5	.2441	2	flints
0.1127	30.5	.2441	2	foothill
0.1127	30.5	.2441	2	fount
0.1127	30.5	.2441	2	halfheartedly
0.1127	30.5	.2441	2	handyman
0.1127	30.5	.2441	2	inboard
0.1127	30.5	.2441	2	indelible
0.1127	30.5	.2441	2	infallibility
0.1127	30.5	.2441	2	iniquity
0.1127	30.5	.2441	2	instructing
0.1127	30.5	.2441	2	intimated
0.1127	30.5	.2441	2	jennet

THE PRECEDING WORD TYPE OCCUPIES RANK 40200

U	SFI	D	F	Word Type
0.1127	30.5	.2441	2	jumbling
0.1127	30.5	.2441	2	lampreys
0.1127	30.5	.2441	2	lat
0.1127	30.5	.2441	2	longleaf
0.1127	30.5	.2441	2	Mackenzie
0.1127	30.5	.2441	2	manometer
0.1127	30.5	.2441	2	midwife
0.1127	30.5	.2441	2	mistaking
0.1127	30.5	.2441	2	mitigate
0.1127	30.5	.2441	2	nacreous
0.1127	30.5	.2441	2	nipping
0.1127	30.5	.2441	2	nondescript
0.1127	30.5	.2441	2	obstruction
0.1127	30.5	.2441	2	paltry
0.1127	30.5	.2441	2	peculiarity
0.1127	30.5	.2441	2	pottage
0.1127	30.5	.2441	2	pre-war
0.1127	30.5	.2441	2	preposterous
0.1127	30.5	.2441	2	primacy
0.1127	30.5	.2441	2	purport
0.1127	30.5	.2441	2	replenished
0.1127	30.5	.2441	2	researching
0.1127	30.5	.2441	2	reverberations
0.1127	30.5	.2441	2	rhododendrons
0.1127	30.5	.2441	2	rounder
0.1127	30.5	.2441	2	sacrosanct
0.1127	30.5	.2441	2	salable
0.1127	30.5	.2441	2	shackles
0.1127	30.5	.2441	2	sharecropper
0.1127	30.5	.2441	2	sic
0.1127	30.5	.2441	2	sociability
0.1127	30.5	.2441	2	spindle-shaped
0.1127	30.5	.2441	2	StVitus's
0.1127	30.5	.2441	2	steam-engine
0.1127	30.5	.2441	2	sunburst
0.1127	30.5	.2441	2	superless
0.1127	30.5	.2441	2	tenacity
0.1127	30.5	.2441	2	Townsend
0.1127	30.5	.2441	2	unappeased
0.1127	30.5	.2441	2	unemotional
0.1127	30.5	.2441	2	unrestrained
0.1127	30.5	.2441	2	veneration
0.1127	30.5	.2441	2	vindictive
0.1127	30.5	.2441	2	Viscount
0.1127	30.5	.2441	2	Visit
0.1127	30.5	.2441	2	wanderlust
0.1127	30.5	.2441	2	well-irrigated
0.1125	30.5	.2446	2	announcers
0.1125	30.5	.0081	17	armature
0.1125	30.5	.2446	2	Awards
0.1125	30.5	.2446	2	beguile
0.1125	30.5	.2446	2	beholding
0.1125	30.5	.2446	2	bifocals
0.1125	30.5	.2446	2	bittern
0.1125	30.5	.2446	2	Bones
0.1125	30.5	.2446	2	buccaneering
0.1125	30.5	.2446	2	coddled
0.1125	30.5	.2446	2	conjuror
0.1125	30.5	.2446	2	deciphered
0.1125	30.5	.2446	2	dishtowel
0.1125	30.5	.2446	2	dog-eared
0.1125	30.5	.2446	2	enow
0.1125	30.5	.2446	2	first-cabin
0.1125	30.5	.2446	2	forsworn
0.1125	30.5	.2446	2	four-clawed
0.1125	30.5	.2446	2	funnier
0.1125	30.5	.2446	2	furtherance
0.1125	30.5	.2446	2	gabled
0.1125	30.5	.2446	2	greenest
0.1125	30.5	.2446	2	gropes
0.1125	30.5	.2446	2	Haircut
0.1125	30.5	.2446	2	Handsome
0.1125	30.5	.2446	2	Harold's
0.1125	30.5	.2446	2	hollerin'
0.1125	30.5	.2446	2	hysterics
0.1125	30.5	.2446	2	Kaatskill
0.1125	30.5	.2446	2	Manley
0.1125	30.5	.2446	2	mayn't
0.1125	30.5	.2446	2	McGinley
0.1125	30.5	.2446	2	nce
0.1125	30.5	.2446	2	noiseless
0.1125	30.5	.2446	2	oarlocks
0.1125	30.5	.2446	2	orations
0.1125	30.5	.2446	2	parson's
0.1125	30.5	.2446	2	peanut-butter
0.1125	30.5	.2446	2	pocket-handkerchief
0.1125	30.5	.2446	2	Purist
0.1125	30.5	.2446	2	quick-witted
0.1125	30.5	.2446	2	Reporting
0.1125	30.5	.2446	2	Roma
0.1125	30.5	.2446	2	sallow
0.1125	30.5	.2446	2	scarecrow's
0.1125	30.5	.2446	2	scruple
0.1125	30.5	.2446	2	Sealed
0.1125	30.5	.2446	2	SF
0.1125	30.5	.2446	2	strenuously
0.1125	30.5	.2446	2	swindle
0.1125	30.5	.2446	2	swordplay
0.1125	30.5	.2446	2	syrups
0.1125	30.5	.2446	2	ta'en

THE PRECEDING WORD TYPE OCCUPIES RANK 40300

U	SFI	D	F	Word Type
0.1125	30.5	.2446	2	Theban
0.1125	30.5	.2446	2	tradesman
0.1125	30.5	.2446	2	vales
0.1125	30.5	.2446	2	visors
0.1125	30.5	.2446	2	wands
0.1125	30.5	.2446	2	yestreen
0.1123	30.5	.2446	2	-tion
0.1123	30.5	.2446	2	above-mentioned
0.1123	30.5	.2446	2	Afghan
0.1123	30.5	.2446	2	alertly
0.1123	30.5	.2446	2	Assyria
0.1123	30.5	.2446	2	authorship
0.1123	30.5	.2446	2	bequeathed

U	SFI	D	F	Word Type
0.1123	30.5	.2446	2	blockading
0.1123	30.5	.2446	2	broad-leafed
0.1123	30.5	.2446	2	bulwarks
0.1123	30.5	.2446	2	Bysshe
0.1123	30.5	.2446	2	Civic
0.1123	30.5	.2446	2	congratulation
0.1123	30.5	.2446	2	crystallized
0.1123	30.5	.2446	2	disputation
0.1123	30.5	.2446	2	emergent
0.1123	30.5	.2446	2	entitles
0.1123	30.5	.2446	2	Firenze
0.1123	30.5	.2446	2	formulating
0.1123	30.5	.2446	2	Gauls
0.1123	30.5	.2446	2	hairbreadth
0.1123	30.5	.2446	2	Halt
0.1123	30.5	.2446	2	indictment
0.1123	30.5	.2446	2	infested
0.1123	30.5	.2446	2	insurgent
0.1123	30.5	.2446	2	interchanging
0.1123	30.5	.2446	2	interjected
0.1123	30.5	.2446	2	intrastate
0.1123	30.5	.2446	2	knobbed
0.1123	30.5	.2446	2	Kurdish
0.1123	30.5	.2446	2	Latham
0.1123	30.5	.2446	2	Leagues
0.1123	30.5	.2446	2	longish
0.1123	30.5	.2446	2	Macedon
0.1123	30.5	.2446	2	magnus
0.1123	30.5	.2446	2	Mandarin
0.1123	30.5	.2446	2	Markland
0.1123	30.5	.2446	2	Mechanics
0.1123	30.5	.2446	2	meshes
0.1123	30.5	.2446	2	moistens
0.1123	30.5	.2446	2	Oz
0.1123	30.5	.2446	2	perpetuity
0.1123	30.5	.2446	2	philanthropies
0.1123	30.5	.2446	2	Pronoun
0.1123	30.5	.2446	2	proviso
0.1123	30.5	.2446	2	provocation
0.1123	30.5	.2446	2	putrid
0.1123	30.5	.2446	2	rugby
0.1123	30.5	.2446	2	self-reliance
0.1123	30.5	.2446	2	Sentinel
0.1123	30.5	.2446	2	softening
0.1123	30.5	.2446	2	stressing
0.1123	30.5	.2446	2	Tenaya
0.1123	30.5	.2446	2	theologian
0.1123	30.5	.2446	2	theologian
0.1123	30.5	.2446	2	Thutmose
0.1123	30.5	.2446	2	ticktacktoe
0.1123	30.5	.2446	2	topographical
0.1123	30.5	.2446	2	transcribing
0.1123	30.5	.2446	2	tyrannical
0.1123	30.5	.2446	2	unsystematic
0.1123	30.5	.2446	2	vocabularies
0.1123	30.5	.2446	2	Wrights'
0.1123	30.5	.2446	2	1516
0.1123	30.5	.2446	2	1571
0.1123	30.5	.2446	2	600's
0.1123	30.5	.2446	2	827
0.1123	30.5	.2446	2	966
0.1122	30.5	.2446	2	abandonment
0.1122	30.5	.2446	2	acclimatization
0.1122	30.5	.2446	2	amalgamated
0.1122	30.5	.2446	2	amethyst
0.1122	30.5	.2446	2	apocryphal
0.1122	30.5	.2446	2	assiduously
0.1122	30.5	.2446	2	berrytime
0.1122	30.5	.2446	2	betimes
0.1122	30.5	.2446	2	blasphemy
0.1122	30.5	.2446	2	Bull's
0.1122	30.5	.2446	2	campaigner
0.1122	30.5	.2446	2	Carel
0.1122	30.5	.2446	2	colorfully
0.1122	30.5	.2446	2	confounds
0.1122	30.5	.2446	2	conscientiously
0.1122	30.5	.2446	2	contradicts
0.1122	30.5	.2446	2	coped
0.1122	30.5	.2446	2	Corners
0.1122	30.5	.2446	2	Council's
0.1122	30.5	.2446	2	deduce
0.1122	30.5	.2446	2	Deliver
0.1122	30.5	.2446	2	detonation
0.1122	30.5	.2446	2	disabling
0.1122	30.5	.2446	2	Ellesmere
0.1122	30.5	.2446	2	encrusted
0.1122	30.5	.2446	2	excruciating

THE PRECEDING WORD TYPE OCCUPIES RANK 40400

U	SFI	D	F	Word Type
0.1122	30.5	.2446	2	exteriors
0.1122	30.5	.2446	2	father-son
0.1122	30.5	.2446	2	featureless
0.1122	30.5	.2446	2	flaccid
0.1122	30.5	.2446	2	forfeiture
0.1122	30.5	.2446	2	grama
0.1122	30.5	.2446	2	grappling
0.1122	30.5	.2446	2	graven
0.1122	30.5	.2446	2	greenbacks
0.1122	30.5	.2446	2	greenish-yellow
0.1122	30.5	.2446	2	Hirsch
0.1122	30.5	.2446	2	Hirsch's
0.1122	30.5	.2446	2	inconstant
0.1122	30.5	.2446	2	insubstantial
0.1122	30.5	.2446	2	INTERNATIONAL
0.1122	30.5	.2446	2	intuitions
0.1122	30.5	.2446	2	Israelite
0.1122	30.5	.2446	2	kelps
0.1122	30.5	.2446	2	Laertes
0.1122	30.5	.2446	2	languor
0.1122	30.5	.2446	2	Love's
0.1122	30.5	.2446	2	Narrows
0.1122	30.5	.2446	2	opportunism
0.1122	30.5	.2446	2	palsy
0.1122	30.5	.2446	2	Port-au-Prince
0.1122	30.5	.2446	2	potentate
0.1122	30.5	.2446	2	resumption
0.1122	30.5	.2446	2	rife
0.1122	30.5	.2446	2	secretive

U	SFI	D	F	Word Type
0.1122	30.5	.2446	2	seizes
0.1122	30.5	.2446	2	semaphores
0.1122	30.5	.2446	2	slews
0.1122	30.5	.2446	2	soured
0.1122	30.5	.2446	2	statuettes
0.1122	30.5	.2446	2	stouter
0.1122	30.5	.2446	2	Studio
0.1122	30.5	.2446	2	suffocating
0.1122	30.5	.2446	2	supposes
0.1122	30.5	.2446	2	suspenseful
0.1122	30.5	.2446	2	tempts
0.1122	30.5	.2446	2	tenfold
0.1122	30.5	.2446	2	tolerable
0.1122	30.5	.2446	2	Toulon
0.1122	30.5	.2446	2	unpolished
0.1122	30.5	.2446	2	unschooled
0.1122	30.5	.2446	2	uppers
0.1122	30.5	.2446	2	vaguest
0.1122	30.5	.2446	2	vermin
0.1121	30.5	.0136	12	hemming
0.1112	30.5	.0265	13	truss
0.1105	30.4	.0908	5	baste
0.1094	30.4	.0000	9	all-time
0.1094	30.4	.0000	9	Berrigan
0.1094	30.4	.0000	9	C-5A
0.1094	30.4	.0000	9	Corvair
0.1094	30.4	.0000	9	Franny
0.1094	30.4	.0000	9	Hee
0.1094	30.4	.0000	9	Honkey
0.1094	30.4	.0000	9	Hutterite
0.1094	30.4	.0000	9	Modcom
0.1094	30.4	.0000	10	Prinz
0.1094	30.4	.0000	10	run-on
0.1094	30.4	.0000	9	Unitas
0.1094	30.4	.0000	10	Zip
0.1091	30.4	.2408	2	-el
0.1091	30.4	.2408	2	-il
0.1091	30.4	.2408	2	-ile
0.1091	30.4	.2408	2	-ous
0.1091	30.4	.2408	2	-um
0.1091	30.4	.2417	2	admirer
0.1091	30.4	.2408	2	ain
0.1091	30.4	.2417	2	andante
0.1091	30.4	.2411	2	antiphony
0.1091	30.4	.2408	2	apostle
0.1091	30.4	.2411	2	applauds
0.1091	30.4	.2412	2	arthritis
0.1091	30.4	.2417	2	articulation
0.1091	30.4	.2417	2	Augustin
0.1091	30.4	.2418	2	aviator
0.1091	30.4	.2411	2	awakes
0.1091	30.4	.2411	2	awaking
0.1091	30.4	.2408	2	baby-sit
0.1091	30.4	.2417	2	balk
0.1091	30.4	.2417	2	ballerinas
0.1091	30.4	.2412	2	Barker's
0.1091	30.4	.2412	2	Bauer
0.1091	30.4	.2411	2	before-mentioned
0.1091	30.4	.2411	2	birthright
0.1091	30.4	.2411	2	bop
0.1091	30.4	.2411	2	broncho's
0.1091	30.4	.2411	2	Butterflies
0.1091	30.4	.2418	2	Calendar
0.1091	30.4	.2417	2	caller's
0.1091	30.4	.2408	2	capitalizing
0.1091	30.4	.2417	2	Capitan
0.1091	30.4	.2411	2	case-hardened
0.1091	30.4	.2411	2	Chichester
0.1091	30.4	.2417	2	classicism
0.1091	30.4	.2418	2	Communication
0.1091	30.4	.2417	2	complication

THE PRECEDING WORD TYPE OCCUPIES RANK 40500

U	SFI	D	F	Word Type
0.1091	30.4	.2417	2	conceals
0.1091	30.4	.2417	2	conceives
0.1091	30.4	.2417	2	conceptions
0.1091	30.4	.2417	2	congregational
0.1091	30.4	.2408	2	conj
0.1091	30.4	.2418	2	conservationist
0.1091	30.4	.2408	2	consonant-y
0.1091	30.4	.2408	2	cosmonaut
0.1091	30.4	.2411	2	crab-shells
0.1091	30.4	.2411	2	Cummings
0.1091	30.4	.2408	2	cwen
0.1091	30.4	.2408	2	dachshund
0.1091	30.4	.2408	2	de-
0.1091	30.4	.2412	2	desperados
0.1091	30.4	.2418	2	dirigible
0.1091	30.4	.2417	2	discloses
0.1091	30.4	.2408	2	distributions
0.1091	30.4	.2408	2	Dolores
0.1091	30.4	.2417	2	Double
0.1091	30.4	.2417	2	Dwarfs
0.1091	30.4	.2412	2	Elder's
0.1091	30.4	.2411	2	elemental
0.1091	30.4	.2411	2	encore
0.1091	30.4	.2411	2	enthralled
0.1091	30.4	.2418	2	envisage
0.1091	30.4	.2417	2	ethereal
0.1091	30.4	.2408	2	etymologies
0.1091	30.4	.2418	2	expels
0.1091	30.4	.2411	2	exulting
0.1091	30.4	.2412	2	faithless
0.1091	30.4	.2411	2	fakirs
0.1091	30.4	.2417	2	Fatherland
0.1091	30.4	.2417	2	Faun
0.1091	30.4	.2412	2	fifteenth-century
0.1091	30.4	.2417	2	florid
0.1091	30.4	.2417	2	folklike
0.1091	30.4	.2417	2	forges
0.1091	30.4	.2418	2	four-
0.1091	30.4	.2412	2	Frankenstein
0.1091	30.4	.2412	2	freckle
0.1091	30.4	.2411	2	ghoul
0.1091	30.4	.2417	2	Gounod's
0.1091	30.4	.2408	2	grammarian
0.1091	30.4	.2408	2	graphein
0.1091	30.4	.2412	2	hackles

U	SFI	D	F	Word Type
0.1091	30.4	.2411	2	hallelujah
0.1091	30.4	.2411	2	hames
0.1091	30.4	.2417	2	harpy
0.1091	30.4	.2411	2	Heard
0.1091	30.4	.2411	2	heart-broken
0.1091	30.4	.2417	2	homo
0.1091	30.4	.2411	2	hovel
0.1091	30.4	.2418	2	IA
0.1091	30.4	.2417	2	Ibsen
0.1091	30.4	.2408	2	ile
0.1091	30.4	.2412	2	in-doors
0.1091	30.4	.2417	2	Innsbruck
0.1091	30.4	.2408	2	int
0.1091	30.4	.2418	2	interchanges
0.1091	30.4	.2417	2	Ira
0.1091	30.4	.2411	2	Jew's
0.1091	30.4	.2411	2	Kiss
0.1091	30.4	.2411	2	Knows
0.1091	30.4	.2417	2	kolo
0.1091	30.4	.2417	2	Lament
0.1091	30.4	.2411	2	laments
0.1091	30.4	.2418	2	Late
0.1091	30.4	.2408	2	lawgiver
0.1091	30.4	.2418	2	layered
0.1091	30.4	.2417	2	Lescaut
0.1091	30.4	.2411	2	MacDonald
0.1091	30.4	.2417	2	manipulating
0.1091	30.4	.2417	2	Manon
0.1091	30.4	.2417	2	matured
0.1091	30.4	.2411	2	meeker
0.1091	30.4	.2411	2	Midsummer
0.1091	30.4	.2418	2	mispronunciations
0.1091	30.4	.2408	2	misspells
0.1091	30.4	.2411	2	Mon
0.1091	30.4	.2408	2	Montagu
0.1091	30.4	.2411	2	Mouse's
0.1091	30.4	.2408	2	nd
0.1091	30.4	.2417	2	Nibelungen
0.1091	30.4	.2411	2	Nocturne
0.1091	30.4	.2417	2	obligated
0.1091	30.4	.2417	2	Ode
0.1091	30.4	.2408	2	one-eyed
0.1091	30.4	.2418	2	oversees
0.1091	30.4	.2408	2	Pack
0.1091	30.4	.2417	2	painter's
0.1091	30.4	.2417	2	Pelleas
0.1091	30.4	.2417	2	pestilence
0.1091	30.4	.2411	2	Piece
0.1091	30.4	.2412	2	pigsty
0.1091	30.4	.2417	2	plexus
0.1091	30.4	.2418	2	Pomeranian
0.1091	30.4	.2411	2	portraying
0.1091	30.4	.2417	2	Pride
0.1091	30.4	.2411	2	primrose
0.1091	30.4	.2408	2	pron

THE PRECEDING WORD TYPE OCCUPIES RANK 40600

U	SFI	D	F	Word Type
0.1091	30.4	.2408	2	pupil's
0.1091	30.4	.2408	2	quire
0.1091	30.4	.2418	2	quixotic
0.1091	30.4	.2411	2	raccoon's
0.1091	30.4	.2411	2	Rachmaninoff
0.1091	30.4	.2418	2	rd
0.1091	30.4	.2411	2	recaptures
0.1091	30.4	.2411	2	reminiscence
0.1091	30.4	.2411	2	reposes
0.1091	30.4	.2412	2	retrieve
0.1091	30.4	.2411	2	riled
0.1091	30.4	.2408	2	rocketed
0.1091	30.4	.2417	2	romanticism
0.1091	30.4	.2418	2	Rostand
0.1091	30.4	.2417	2	rouses
0.1091	30.4	.2417	2	sailing-ship
0.1091	30.4	.2417	2	Salon
0.1091	30.4	.2411	2	Satchmo
0.1091	30.4	.2411	2	Saw
0.1091	30.4	.2411	2	scorns
0.1091	30.4	.2411	2	self-possessed
0.1091	30.4	.2411	2	semi-darkness
0.1091	30.4	.2412	2	Shelley's
0.1091	30.4	.2408	2	sherry
0.1091	30.4	.2408	2	silent-letter
0.1091	30.4	.2412	2	Sneed
0.1091	30.4	.2417	2	Soldiers
0.1091	30.4	.2411	2	Someone
0.1091	30.4	.2412	2	star-shaped
0.1091	30.4	.2411	2	straddle
0.1091	30.4	.2408	2	suey
0.1091	30.4	.2412	2	suspect's
0.1091	30.4	.2408	2	syn-
0.1091	30.4	.2417	2	Synagogue
0.1091	30.4	.2408	2	Synonyms
0.1091	30.4	.2417	2	syrinx
0.1091	30.4	.2411	2	tail's
0.1091	30.4	.2408	2	te
0.1091	30.4	.2417	2	telephony
0.1091	30.4	.2411	2	thought-provoking
0.1091	30.4	.2411	2	tiptop
0.1091	30.4	.2411	2	toilsome
0.1091	30.4	.2411	2	tongued
0.1091	30.4	.2417	2	topsail
0.1091	30.4	.2411	2	Tunes
0.1091	30.4	.2418	2	turnpikes
0.1091	30.4	.2417	2	unashamed
0.1091	30.4	.2412	2	vanquish
0.1091	30.4	.2408	2	Verbs
0.1091	30.4	.2417	2	Vivaldi
0.1091	30.4	.2411	2	wond'ring
0.1091	30.4	.2411	2	Yaso
0.1091	30.4	.2417	2	Zuniga
0.1091	30.4	.2418	2	1612
0.1091	30.4	.2417	2	1632-1687
0.1091	30.4	.2417	2	1643
0.1091	30.4	.2418	2	1661
0.1091	30.4	.2418	2	1724
0.1091	30.4	.2418	2	1731
0.1091	30.4	.2417	2	1878-1942
0.1091	30.4	.2417	2	1904-

U	SFI	D	F	Word Type
0.1090	30.4	.2407	2	assimilated
0.1090	30.4	.2407	2	boo-oo
0.1090	30.4	.2407	2	boo-oo-oom
0.1090	30.4	.2407	2	catchy
0.1090	30.4	.2407	2	cellists
0.1090	30.4	.2407	2	chug-a-chug
0.1090	30.4	.2407	2	colonizers
0.1090	30.4	.2407	2	commentator
0.1090	30.4	.2407	2	consign
0.1090	30.4	.2407	2	Copland's
0.1090	30.4	.2407	2	deckhand
0.1090	30.4	.2407	2	distrusts
0.1090	30.4	.2407	2	harmoniously
0.1090	30.4	.2407	2	heighten
0.1090	30.4	.2407	2	inconceivable
0.1090	30.4	.2407	2	Introduction
0.1090	30.4	.2407	2	laud
0.1090	30.4	.2407	2	Legend
0.1090	30.4	.2407	2	madrigals
0.1090	30.4	.2407	2	melodie
0.1090	30.4	.2407	2	pirates'
0.1090	30.4	.2407	2	progressing
0.1090	30.4	.2407	2	rediscover
0.1090	30.4	.2407	2	rendition
0.1090	30.4	.2407	2	sae
0.1090	30.4	.2407	2	Sociable
0.1090	30.4	.2407	2	stereophonic
0.1090	30.4	.2407	2	thrush
0.1090	30.4	.2407	2	trill
0.1090	30.4	.2407	2	1720
0.1089	30.4	.2387	2	a-laying
0.1089	30.4	.2387	2	bootjack
0.1089	30.4	.2387	2	brokenhearted
0.1089	30.4	.2387	2	brown-eyed
0.1089	30.4	.2387	2	Brunnhilde
0.1089	30.4	.2387	2	crispy
0.1089	30.4	.2388	2	delude
0.1089	30.4	.2387	2	ding-a-ling-a-ling
0.1089	30.4	.2387	2	double-barreled

THE PRECEDING WORD TYPE OCCUPIES RANK 40700

U	SFI	D	F	Word Type
0.1089	30.4	.2387	2	edification
0.1089	30.4	.2387	2	faithfulness
0.1089	30.4	.2387	2	Favorites
0.1089	30.4	.2387	2	fjord
0.1089	30.4	.2387	2	Hanson
0.1089	30.4	.2387	2	Harmonica
0.1089	30.4	.2387	2	impersonating
0.1089	30.4	.2387	2	jewelled
0.1089	30.4	.2388	2	junctures
0.1089	30.4	.2387	2	Marquise
0.1089	30.4	.2387	2	Obadiah
0.1089	30.4	.2388	2	Owen's
0.1089	30.4	.2388	2	paisley
0.1089	30.4	.2387	2	peddle
0.1089	30.4	.2387	2	philosophic
0.1089	30.4	.2387	2	ravishing
0.1089	30.4	.2387	2	Robbins
0.1089	30.4	.2388	2	saluting
0.1089	30.4	.2388	2	self-denial
0.1089	30.4	.2387	2	sinuous
0.1089	30.4	.2388	2	slow-like
0.1089	30.4	.2387	2	soo
0.1089	30.4	.2387	2	Stage
0.1089	30.4	.2388	2	table's
0.1089	30.4	.2387	2	unexpectedness
0.1089	30.4	.2388	2	vacancy
0.1089	30.4	.2387	2	wall-eyed
0.1089	30.4	.2387	2	Wheelbarrow
0.1089	30.4	.2387	2	whippoorwill's
0.1089	30.4	.2387	2	woodcocks
0.1088	30.4	.2375	2	aesthetically
0.1088	30.4	.2375	2	angelic
0.1088	30.4	.2376	2	antebellum
0.1088	30.4	.2376	2	anti-
0.1088	30.4	.2375	2	Antonin
0.1088	30.4	.2376	2	apathetic
0.1088	30.4	.2376	2	articulated
0.1088	30.4	.2375	2	attired
0.1088	30.4	.2375	2	Beast
0.1088	30.4	.2375	2	Becket's
0.1088	30.4	.2376	2	bio
0.1088	30.4	.2375	2	bongos
0.1088	30.4	.2375	2	conga
0.1088	30.4	.2375	2	creditably
0.1088	30.4	.2375	2	crescent-shaped
0.1088	30.4	.2375	2	defying
0.1088	30.4	.2375	2	desecrating
0.1088	30.4	.2376	2	Dickens'
0.1088	30.4	.2375	2	discreetly
0.1088	30.4	.2375	2	Dixon
0.1088	30.4	.2375	2	embellishment
0.1088	30.4	.2376	2	erudite
0.1088	30.4	.2375	2	fleck
0.1088	30.4	.2376	2	Flip's
0.1088	30.4	.2375	2	free-flowing
0.1088	30.4	.2375	2	get-together
0.1088	30.4	.2376	2	GI'S
0.1088	30.4	.2375	2	grouchy
0.1088	30.4	.2375	2	guitarists
0.1088	30.4	.2375	2	handcarts
0.1088	30.4	.2375	2	hanky
0.1088	30.4	.2375	2	high-
0.1088	30.4	.2375	2	Hines
0.1088	30.4	.2376	2	impresses
0.1088	30.4	.2375	2	inexpert
0.1088	30.4	.2375	2	intermingled
0.1088	30.4	.2375	2	Joke
0.1088	30.4	.2376	2	juror
0.1088	30.4	.2376	2	Kellys
0.1088	30.4	.2375	2	Lang
0.1088	30.4	.2376	2	Lessons
0.1088	30.4	.2375	2	merry-go-rounds
0.1088	30.4	.2375	2	mid-October
0.1088	30.4	.2375	2	mingles
0.1088	30.4	.2376	2	mismanagement
0.1088	30.4	.2375	2	Monet's
0.1088	30.4	.2375	2	musette

U	SFI	D	F	Word Type
0.1088	30.4	.2376	2	Myself
0.1088	30.4	.2375	2	nonmaterial
0.1088	30.4	.2375	2	Off
0.1088	30.4	.2375	2	Palestinian
0.1088	30.4	.2375	2	Paso
0.1088	30.4	.2375	2	Phillip
0.1088	30.4	.2376	2	Plexiglas
0.1088	30.4	.2376	2	proofed
0.1088	30.4	.2375	2	prowls
0.1088	30.4	.2375	2	quipus
0.1088	30.4	.2375	2	Recording
0.1088	30.4	.2376	2	rockers
0.1088	30.4	.2376	2	rough-hewn
0.1088	30.4	.2375	2	self-expression
0.1088	30.4	.2375	2	sensuous
0.1088	30.4	.2375	2	Sigmund
0.1088	30.4	.2375	2	slapstick
0.1088	30.4	.2375	2	southland
0.1088	30.4	.2375	2	spliced
0.1088	30.4	.2375	2	Started
0.1088	30.4	.2375	2	Surprise
0.1088	30.4	.2375	2	synopsis
0.1088	30.4	.2375	2	Teller
THE PRECEDING WORD TYPE OCCUPIES RANK 40800				
0.1088	30.4	.2376	2	tom
0.1088	30.4	.2375	2	tuneless
0.1088	30.4	.2375	2	Tunnel
0.1088	30.4	.2375	2	Wait
0.1088	30.4	.2376	2	westerns
0.1084	30.3	.2446	2	aviary
0.1084	30.3	.2446	2	choros
0.1084	30.3	.2446	2	f-p
0.1084	30.3	.2446	2	forte
0.1084	30.3	.2446	2	Kern's
0.1084	30.3	.2446	2	sorrow's
0.1084	30.3	.2446	2	tango
0.1084	30.3	.0882	5	waffles
0.1080	30.3	.2305	2	after-dinner
0.1080	30.3	.2305	2	bye-bye
0.1080	30.3	.2305	2	deface
0.1080	30.3	.2305	2	het
0.1080	30.3	.2305	2	Latin-speaking
0.1080	30.3	.2305	2	Silvia
0.1080	30.3	.2305	2	snobs
0.1080	30.3	.2305	2	taunts
0.1080	30.3	.2305	2	tempestuous
0.1080	30.3	.2305	2	tung
0.1080	30.3	.2305	2	twitter
0.1079	30.3	.2303	2	acquaintanceship
0.1079	30.3	.2303	2	boatman's
0.1079	30.3	.2303	2	boos
0.1079	30.3	.2303	2	Cakewalk
0.1079	30.3	.2303	2	capering
0.1079	30.3	.2303	2	caricature
0.1079	30.3	.2303	2	commemorates
0.1079	30.3	.2303	2	countrymen's
0.1079	30.3	.2303	2	cut-and-dried
0.1079	30.3	.2303	2	deep-rooted
0.1079	30.3	.2303	2	dews
0.1079	30.3	.2303	2	Emanuel
0.1079	30.3	.2303	2	encircles
0.1079	30.3	.2303	2	Etudes
0.1079	30.3	.2303	2	fated
0.1079	30.3	.2303	2	fifty-three
0.1079	30.3	.2303	2	Foley
0.1079	30.3	.2303	2	Foster's
0.1079	30.3	.2303	2	fugues
0.1079	30.3	.2303	2	full-rigged
0.1079	30.3	.2303	2	Gauguin
0.1079	30.3	.2303	2	gib
0.1079	30.3	.2303	2	Golliwog's
0.1079	30.3	.2303	2	good-day
0.1079	30.3	.2303	2	hatter
0.1079	30.3	.2303	2	high-brow
0.1079	30.3	.2303	2	L'Heure
0.1079	30.3	.2303	2	Londonderry
0.1079	30.3	.2303	2	Maiden
0.1079	30.3	.2303	2	metronome
0.1079	30.3	.2303	2	now's
0.1079	30.3	.2303	2	pealed
0.1079	30.3	.2303	2	phrased
0.1079	30.3	.2303	2	pianistic
0.1079	30.3	.2303	2	Picardy
0.1079	30.3	.2303	2	Pimlico
0.1079	30.3	.2303	2	Players
0.1079	30.3	.2303	2	Potatoes
0.1079	30.3	.2303	2	Putnam's
0.1079	30.3	.2303	2	sarabande
0.1079	30.3	.2303	2	Send
0.1079	30.3	.2303	2	smooth-flowing
0.1079	30.3	.2303	2	Starting
0.1079	30.3	.2303	2	swamping
0.1079	30.3	.2303	2	tepid
0.1079	30.3	.2303	2	thorough-bass
0.1079	30.3	.2303	2	Toccata
0.1079	30.3	.2303	2	unfurled
0.1079	30.3	.2303	2	vagueness
0.1079	30.3	.2303	2	Verdi's
0.1079	30.3	.2303	2	verismo
0.1079	30.3	.2303	2	Vittorio
0.1079	30.3	.2303	2	wast
0.1079	30.3	.2303	2	Zuni
0.1077	30.3	.2287	2	A1
0.1077	30.3	.2289	2	bold-face
0.1077	30.3	.2289	2	centum
0.1077	30.3	.2287	2	fay
0.1077	30.3	.2287	2	Janos
0.1077	30.3	.2287	2	Measure
0.1077	30.3	.0516	8	planed
0.1077	30.3	.2287	2	repays
0.1077	30.3	.2289	2	retro
0.1077	30.3	.2287	2	sevenths
0.1077	30.3	.2289	2	thief's
0.1077	30.3	.2287	2	turntable
0.1077	30.3	.2289	2	3c
0.1077	30.3	.2289	2	4a
0.1077	30.3	.2289	2	9-16
0.1077	30.3	.2287	2	9/8
0.1073	30.3	.0000	10	Barricune
0.1073	30.3	.0000	10	Enich
0.1073	30.3	.0000	10	Feathertop
0.1073	30.3	.0000	10	HERMIA
0.1073	30.3	.0000	10	Mateo
0.1073	30.3	.0000	10	Matrena
THE PRECEDING WORD TYPE OCCUPIES RANK 40900				
0.1073	30.3	.0000	10	MEDBOURNE
0.1073	30.3	.0000	10	STEVENSON
0.1073	30.3	.0000	10	WIDOW
0.1063	30.3	.0347	7	sinned
0.1058	30.2	.1587	3	chicory
0.1057	30.2	.2139	2	af
0.1057	30.2	.2139	2	cockpits
0.1057	30.2	.2139	2	convene
0.1057	30.2	.2139	2	Cordoba
0.1057	30.2	.2139	2	French-speaking
0.1057	30.2	.2139	2	Hereford
0.1057	30.2	.2139	2	infirm
0.1057	30.2	.2139	2	Lille
0.1057	30.2	.2139	2	money-lender
0.1057	30.2	.2139	2	Sanford
0.1057	30.2	.2139	2	transaction
0.1057	30.2	.2139	2	twenty-year
0.1057	30.2	.2139	2	unexcited
0.1057	30.2	.2139	2	1215
0.1057	30.2	.2139	2	1618
0.1056	30.2	.2137	2	Anglo-American
0.1056	30.2	.2137	2	approbation
0.1056	30.2	.2137	2	ascendancy
0.1056	30.2	.2137	2	Bennington
0.1056	30.2	.2130	2	borderland
0.1056	30.2	.1584	3	carne
0.1056	30.2	.1584	3	Cheddar
0.1056	30.2	.2137	2	closely-woven
0.1056	30.2	.2130	2	co-operating
0.1056	30.2	.2130	2	earthbound
0.1056	30.2	.2137	2	Even
0.1056	30.2	.2130	2	Faithful
0.1056	30.2	.2137	2	fast-talking
0.1056	30.2	.2137	2	grasps
0.1056	30.2	.2137	2	Grimm's
0.1056	30.2	.2137	2	hollowed-out
0.1056	30.2	.2137	2	homogenized
0.1056	30.2	.2137	2	journeyman
0.1056	30.2	.2137	2	long-existing
0.1056	30.2	.2130	2	Milne
0.1056	30.2	.2130	2	mold's
0.1056	30.2	.2137	2	Montana's
0.1056	30.2	.2137	2	Moravia
0.1056	30.2	.2137	2	Naughty
0.1056	30.2	.2137	2	NewAmsterdam
0.1056	30.2	.2130	2	nuthatch
0.1056	30.2	.2130	2	oversight
0.1056	30.2	.2137	2	Recorder
0.1056	30.2	.2130	2	scour
0.1056	30.2	.2137	2	sky-blue
0.1056	30.2	.2130	2	splatter
0.1056	30.2	.2137	2	threshes
0.1056	30.2	.2130	2	unwrap
0.1056	30.2	.2137	2	wheeze
0.1056	30.2	.2130	2	Wilkins
0.1056	30.2	.2137	2	1699
0.1056	30.2	.2137	2	1735
0.1056	30.2	.2137	2	20-21
0.1055	30.2	.0000	9	Alaric
0.1055	30.2	.2128	2	capers
0.1055	30.2	.0000	9	Derby
0.1055	30.2	.2128	2	driller
0.1055	30.2	.0000	9	Essie
0.1055	30.2	.0000	9	Forrester
0.1055	30.2	.2128	2	gaily-colored
0.1055	30.2	.2128	2	guise
0.1055	30.2	.2128	2	hardtack
0.1055	30.2	.0000	9	Hiller
0.1055	30.2	.0000	9	Magua
0.1055	30.2	.2128	2	mediums
0.1055	30.2	.2128	2	molest
0.1055	30.2	.2128	2	one-two
0.1055	30.2	.2128	2	peeks
0.1055	30.2	.2128	2	predominated
0.1055	30.2	.2128	2	preformed
0.1055	30.2	.2128	2	record-playing
0.1055	30.2	.0000	9	Rugg
0.1055	30.2	.0000	13	sp
0.1055	30.2	.2128	2	spotlights
0.1055	30.2	.2128	2	tightly-stretched
0.1055	30.2	.0000	9	Trinket
0.1055	30.2	.0000	9	Veldt
0.1055	30.2	.2128	2	1670
0.1055	30.2	.2128	2	60-61
0.1051	30.2	.0000	13	composer's
0.1051	30.2	.0000	13	Gershwin
0.1051	30.2	.0000	13	Ko-Ko
0.1051	30.2	.0000	13	maracas
0.1051	30.2	.0000	13	Rhythm
0.1051	30.2	.0000	13	V7
0.1049	30.2	.0465	7	Jesus'
0.1048	30.2	.0000	7	-b
0.1048	30.2	.0000	7	/2
0.1048	30.2	.0000	7	congruence
0.1048	30.2	.0000	7	DB
0.1048	30.2	.0000	7	decimeters
0.1048	30.2	.0000	7	EFG
0.1048	30.2	.0000	7	half-line
0.1048	30.2	.0000	7	inverses
0.1048	30.2	.0000	7	kilograms
THE PRECEDING WORD TYPE OCCUPIES RANK 41000				
0.1048	30.2	.0000	7	PA
0.1048	30.2	.0000	7	pentagon
0.1048	30.2	.0000	7	quartile
0.1048	30.2	.0000	7	RST
0.1048	30.2	.0000	7	subtrahend
0.1048	30.2	.0000	7	x-axis
0.1048	30.2	.0000	7	x-intercepts
0.1048	30.2	.0000	7	1-to-1
0.1048	30.2	.0000	7	2/2
0.1048	30.2	.0000	7	3/11
0.1048	30.2	.0000	7	6/3
0.1048	30.2	.0000	7	6/6
0.1048	30.2	.0000	7	6x
0.1048	30.2	.0000	7	8/12
0.1048	30.2	.0000	7	8/8
0.1048	30.2	.0000	7	838
0.1048	30.2	.0000	7	847
0.1047	30.2	.0000	10	Brig
0.1047	30.2	.0000	10	CSA
0.1047	30.2	.0000	10	gutta-percha
0.1047	30.2	.0000	10	neuroses
0.1046	30.2	.1497	2	-ment
0.1046	30.2	.1497	2	artichoke
0.1046	30.2	.1497	2	Bluebeard
0.1046	30.2	.1497	2	Browns'
0.1046	30.2	.1497	2	Castle's
0.1046	30.2	.1497	2	chortle
0.1046	30.2	.1497	2	chortling
0.1046	30.2	.1497	2	Cone
0.1046	30.2	.1497	2	count-down
0.1046	30.2	.1497	2	cuss
0.1046	30.2	.1497	2	dinghy
0.1046	30.2	.1497	2	ghouls
0.1046	30.2	.1497	2	ire
0.1046	30.2	.1497	2	kyklos
0.1046	30.2	.1497	2	Lilliputians
0.1046	30.2	.1497	2	listings
0.1046	30.2	.1497	2	LOOK
0.1046	30.2	.1497	2	mailman's
0.1046	30.2	.1497	2	mid
0.1046	30.2	.1497	2	motor's
0.1046	30.2	.1497	2	ninetieth
0.1046	30.2	.1497	2	profitless
0.1046	30.2	.1497	2	Proof
0.1046	30.2	.1497	2	pumpernickel
0.1046	30.2	.1497	2	retrorockets
0.1046	30.2	.1497	2	senorita
0.1046	30.2	.1497	2	syllabicated
0.1046	30.2	.1497	2	Tangier
0.1046	30.2	.1497	2	tele
0.1046	30.2	.1497	2	ter
0.1046	30.2	.1497	2	throned
0.1046	30.2	.1497	2	Townshend
0.1046	30.2	.1497	2	traitorous
0.1046	30.2	.1497	2	tri
0.1046	30.2	.1497	2	tyre
0.1046	30.2	.1497	2	un-
0.1046	30.2	.1497	2	undersized
0.1046	30.2	.1497	2	unkindness
0.1046	30.2	.1497	2	ure
0.1046	30.2	.1497	2	wastefulness
0.1046	30.2	.1497	2	weather's
0.1045	30.2	.1494	2	'cept
0.1045	30.2	.1494	2	a-picking
0.1045	30.2	.1494	2	a-swimming
0.1045	30.2	.1494	2	Alden
0.1045	30.2	.1494	2	banjos
0.1045	30.2	.1494	2	barker
0.1045	30.2	.1494	2	Barlow
0.1045	30.2	.1494	2	birdie
0.1045	30.2	.1494	2	bobtail
0.1045	30.2	.1494	2	bookish
0.1045	30.2	.1494	2	bounteous
0.1045	30.2	.1494	2	disuse
0.1045	30.2	.1494	2	Enchanted
0.1045	30.2	.1494	2	exclamations
0.1045	30.2	.1494	2	Exploring
0.1045	30.2	.1494	2	foe's
0.1045	30.2	.1494	2	Gasper
0.1045	30.2	.1494	2	goober
0.1045	30.2	.1494	2	Hallie
0.1045	30.2	.1494	2	Hampshire
0.1045	30.2	.1494	2	Has
0.1045	30.2	.1494	2	haulaway
0.1045	30.2	.1494	2	horror-stricken
0.1045	30.2	.1494	2	indescribably
0.1045	30.2	.1494	2	Jose's
0.1045	30.2	.1494	2	keepin'
0.1045	30.2	.1494	2	Lerner
0.1045	30.2	.1494	2	lightning's
0.1045	30.2	.1494	2	lodgings
0.1045	30.2	.1494	2	lumbers
0.1045	30.2	.1494	2	Married
0.1045	30.2	.1494	2	Mason-Dixon
0.1045	30.2	.1494	2	Mice
0.1045	30.2	.1494	2	mid-March
0.1045	30.2	.1494	2	mightier
0.1045	30.2	.1494	2	Mikado
0.1045	30.2	.1494	2	monotone
0.1045	30.2	.1494	2	Mullins
THE PRECEDING WORD TYPE OCCUPIES RANK 41100				
0.1045	30.2	.1494	2	O's
0.1045	30.2	.1494	2	one-two-three
0.1045	30.2	.1494	2	oppressing
0.1045	30.2	.1494	2	pas
0.1045	30.2	.1494	2	perfuming
0.1045	30.2	.1494	2	poetical
0.1045	30.2	.1494	2	prisoner-of-war
0.1045	30.2	.1494	2	punishable
0.1045	30.2	.1494	2	raves
0.1045	30.2	.1494	2	resound
0.1045	30.2	.1494	2	Roosters
0.1045	30.2	.1494	2	samisen
0.1045	30.2	.1494	2	Sax
0.1045	30.2	.1494	2	shanties
0.1045	30.2	.1494	2	Shoo
0.1045	30.2	.1494	2	sideshows
0.1045	30.2	.1494	2	signer
0.1045	30.2	.1494	2	Sigrid
0.1045	30.2	.1494	2	sirs
0.1045	30.2	.1494	2	stoical
0.1045	30.2	.1494	2	tamp
0.1045	30.2	.1494	2	three's
0.1045	30.2	.1494	2	Tie
0.1045	30.2	.1494	2	Timbuktu
0.1045	30.2	.1494	2	torchlight
0.1045	30.2	.1494	2	two's
0.1045	30.2	.1494	2	unbelief
0.1045	30.2	.1494	2	untalented
0.1045	30.2	.1494	2	vicar
0.1045	30.2	.1494	2	Voyage
0.1045	30.2	.1494	2	wails
0.1045	30.2	.1494	2	Wallingford
0.1038	30.2	.1092	4	lingerie
0.1038	30.2	.1092	4	thyme
0.1027	30.1	.1075	4	watercress
0.1015	30.1	.0177	9	Blouse
0.1013	30.1	.0000	7	bathhouse
0.1013	30.1	.0000	7	Burden
0.1013	30.1	.0000	7	Dandridge
0.1013	30.1	.0000	7	Eggborn
0.1013	30.1	.0000	7	Electra
0.1013	30.1	.0000	7	Harvest
0.1013	30.1	.0000	7	Hoyt
0.1013	30.1	.0000	7	Hurlock
0.1013	30.1	.0000	7	Lyda
0.1013	30.1	.0000	7	Mug
0.1013	30.1	.0000	7	Ostrom
0.1013	30.1	.0000	7	railroaders
0.1013	30.1	.0000	7	rotifer
0.1013	30.1	.0000	7	schist
0.1013	30.1	.0000	7	Sohrab
0.1013	30.1	.0000	7	Stranger's
0.1013	30.1	.0000	7	Yung
0.1003	30.0	.0411	9	subordinating
0.0995	30.0	.2421	2	adheres
0.0995	30.0	.2421	2	back-and-forth
0.0995	30.0	.2440	2	cross-sections
0.0995	30.0	.2421	2	forefingers
0.0995	30.0	.2421	2	gusset
0.0995	30.0	.2440	2	iceman
0.0995	30.0	.2421	2	orderliness
0.0995	30.0	.2421	2	reheat
0.0995	30.0	.2421	2	tinting
0.0995	30.0	.2421	2	trims
0.0995	30.0	.2421	2	two-piece
0.0995	30.0	.2421	2	12-12
0.0995	30.0	.2421	2	2/0
0.0995	30.0	.2421	2	3/0
0.0995	30.0	.2421	2	361
0.0992	30.0	.0659	6	commutator
0.0991	30.0	.1017	4	whole-wheat
0.0988	29.9	.0761	4	Nazareth
0.0986	29.9	.0000	5	-24g
0.0986	29.9	.0000	5	Alpheratz
0.0986	29.9	.0000	5	alum
0.0986	29.9	.0000	5	amphiboles
0.0986	29.9	.0000	5	apogee
0.0986	29.9	.0000	5	auricle
0.0986	29.9	.0000	5	ball-and-socket
0.0986	29.9	.0000	5	Becquerel
0.0986	29.9	.0000	5	Bernoulli's
0.0986	29.9	.0000	5	Bode's
0.0986	29.9	.0000	5	calcite
0.0986	29.9	.0000	5	calyx
0.0986	29.9	.0000	5	Celsius
0.0986	29.9	.0000	5	Chordata
0.0986	29.9	.0000	5	clays
0.0986	29.9	.0000	5	compressible
0.0986	29.9	.0000	5	constants
0.0986	29.9	.0000	5	cornea
0.0986	29.9	.0000	5	Cosmetic
0.0986	29.9	.0000	5	crosswalks
0.0986	29.9	.0000	5	CRUX
0.0986	29.9	.0000	5	ctenophores
0.0986	29.9	.0000	5	decomposed
0.0986	29.9	.0000	5	destructional
0.0986	29.9	.0000	5	driveshaft
0.0986	29.9	.0000	5	droplet
0.0986	29.9	.0000	5	embryology
0.0986	29.9	.0000	5	emitter
THE PRECEDING WORD TYPE OCCUPIES RANK 41200				
0.0986	29.9	.0000	5	exoskeletons
0.0986	29.9	.2431	2	expressiveness
0.0986	29.9	.0000	5	fibrils
0.0986	29.9	.0000	5	hailstone
0.0986	29.9	.0000	5	hypo
0.0986	29.9	.0000	5	JoAnn
0.0986	29.9	.0000	5	Koch's
0.0986	29.9	.0000	5	long-day
0.0986	29.9	.0000	5	luau
0.0986	29.9	.0000	5	mouthparts
0.0986	29.9	.0000	5	notochord
0.0986	29.9	.0000	5	oceanographic
0.0986	29.9	.0000	5	one-hole
0.0986	29.9	.0000	5	paramecia
0.0986	29.9	.0000	5	pegmatite
0.0986	29.9	.0000	5	pegmatites
0.0986	29.9	.0000	5	Penicillium
0.0986	29.9	.0000	5	perigee
0.0986	29.9	.0000	5	Ptolemy's
0.0986	29.9	.0000	5	puffballs
0.0986	29.9	.0000	5	pushups
0.0986	29.9	.0000	5	retouching
0.0986	29.9	.0000	5	stamen
0.0986	29.9	.0000	5	Stonehenge
0.0986	29.9	.0000	5	Sun's
0.0986	29.9	.0000	5	thermonuclear
0.0986	29.9	.0000	5	transfers
0.0986	29.9	.0000	5	turbidity
0.0986	29.9	.0000	5	twinning
0.0986	29.9	.0000	5	Vega
0.0986	29.9	.0000	5	ventricles
0.0986	29.9	.0000	5	wavefront
0.0985	29.9	.0000	9	Adj
0.0985	29.9	.0000	9	conjunctive
0.0985	29.9	.0000	9	nonstandard
0.0985	29.9	.0000	9	single-word
0.0980	29.9	.2388	2	awkwardness
0.0979	29.9	.0197	8	sauces
0.0978	29.9	.2404	2	lower-case
0.0978	29.9	.0994	4	sherbet

U	SFI	D	F	Word Type
0.0978	29.9	.2404	2	1452-1519
0.0975	29.9	.0063	5	Lamb
0.0974	29.9	.0000	12	Linguistic
0.0974	29.9	.0000	12	self-test
0.0972	29.9	.0000	8	'68
0.0972	29.9	.0000	8	abortion
0.0972	29.9	.0000	5	Algeria's
0.0972	29.9	.0000	5	Amharas
0.0972	29.9	.0000	5	Appeals
0.0972	29.9	.0000	5	attorneys
0.0972	29.9	.0000	5	Auckland
0.0972	29.9	.0000	8	Ballard
0.0972	29.9	.0000	5	Banya
0.0972	29.9	.0000	5	BatonRouge
0.0972	29.9	.0000	5	Bindibu
0.0972	29.9	.0000	5	Cabral
0.0972	29.9	.0000	5	Calgary
0.0972	29.9	.0000	5	Cartagena
0.0972	29.9	.0000	5	Cauca
0.0972	29.9	.0000	5	Chichen-Itza
0.0972	29.9	.0000	8	Collier
0.0972	29.9	.0000	5	Dammam
0.0972	29.9	.0000	8	devaluation
0.0972	29.9	.0000	5	Divali
0.0972	29.9	.0000	8	Doane
0.0972	29.9	.0000	5	Elbe
0.0972	29.9	.0000	5	Expeditionary
0.0972	29.9	.0000	5	exporter
0.0972	29.9	.0000	5	forty-niners
0.0972	29.9	.0000	5	Gautama
0.0972	29.9	.0000	8	GM
0.0972	29.9	.0000	5	Guianas
0.0972	29.9	.0000	5	haciendas
0.0972	29.9	.0000	5	Haile
0.0972	29.9	.0000	5	Hollerville
0.0972	29.9	.0000	5	Hottentots
0.0972	29.9	.0000	5	Insull
0.0972	29.9	.0000	5	Jeni
0.0972	29.9	.0000	5	Jezreel
0.0972	29.9	.0000	5	Jimma
0.0972	29.9	.0000	5	Karroo
0.0972	29.9	.0000	5	Kato
0.0972	29.9	.0000	5	Kaweki
0.0972	29.9	.0000	5	Kisangani
0.0972	29.9	.0000	8	Kranz
0.0972	29.9	.0000	5	Lena
0.0972	29.9	.0000	5	Magdalena
0.0972	29.9	.0000	5	Maplewood
0.0972	29.9	.0000	5	Margriet
0.0972	29.9	.0000	8	Muh-koons
0.0972	29.9	.0000	5	Mustafa
0.0972	29.9	.0000	5	Nina
0.0972	29.9	.0000	5	Ohio's
0.0972	29.9	.0000	8	Oppenheimer
0.0972	29.9	.0000	5	ordinances
0.0972	29.9	.0000	5	Polonius
0.0972	29.9	.0000	5	Ribaut
0.0972	29.9	.0000	8	roadrunner
0.0972	29.9	.0000	5	Selassie
0.0972	29.9	.0000	8	Sub
THE PRECEDING WORD TYPE OCCUPIES RANK 41300				
0.0972	29.9	.0000	8	subs
0.0972	29.9	.0000	5	swift-flowing
0.0972	29.9	.0000	5	Tagami
0.0972	29.9	.0000	5	taiga
0.0972	29.9	.0000	5	Tarr
0.0972	29.9	.0000	5	Teotihuacanos
0.0972	29.9	.0000	5	Timawi
0.0972	29.9	.0000	5	Tuliyani
0.0972	29.9	.0000	8	Velasco
0.0972	29.9	.0000	5	Venezuelan
0.0972	29.9	.0000	5	Vere
0.0972	29.9	.0000	5	wanasi
0.0972	29.9	.0000	5	Wazadzki
0.0972	29.9	.0000	5	west-coast
0.0972	29.9	.0000	5	Yahi
0.0972	29.9	.0000	5	177
0.0972	29.9	.0000	8	2002
0.0972	29.9	.0000	5	381
0.0971	29.9	.0517	7	45-degree
0.0970	29.9	.0000	12	Bartok
0.0970	29.9	.0000	12	Clementine
0.0970	29.9	.0000	12	Dixieland
0.0970	29.9	.0000	12	legato
0.0970	29.9	.0000	12	toodum
0.0966	29.8	.0000	9	Ananse
0.0966	29.8	.0000	9	BOTTOM
0.0966	29.8	.0000	9	Cruncher
0.0966	29.8	.0000	9	DAGMAR
0.0966	29.8	.0000	9	EBEN
0.0966	29.8	.0000	9	Fiona
0.0966	29.8	.0000	9	GENTLEMAN
0.0966	29.8	.0000	9	Harriett
0.0966	29.8	.0000	9	Herbie
0.0966	29.8	.0000	9	JENNY
0.0966	29.8	.0000	9	LINDA
0.0966	29.8	.0000	9	MACGREGOR
0.0966	29.8	.0000	9	Manette
0.0966	29.8	.0000	9	McClelland
0.0966	29.8	.0000	9	Pfungst
0.0966	29.8	.0000	9	Poseidon
0.0966	29.8	.0000	9	Ranse
0.0966	29.8	.0000	9	Ricco
0.0966	29.8	.0000	9	Solanio
0.0966	29.8	.0000	9	warty
0.0963	29.8	.1386	3	casings
0.0963	29.8	.1386	3	marjoram
0.0963	29.8	.1386	3	misbehavior
0.0963	29.8	.1386	3	scalloped
0.0963	29.8	.1386	3	sprigs
0.0954	29.8	.1367	3	Different
0.0954	29.8	.1367	3	garters
0.0954	29.8	.1367	3	Sylvia's
0.0954	29.8	.1367	3	zippers
0.0949	29.8	.2316	2	hemline
0.0949	29.8	.2316	2	organdy
0.0949	29.8	.2316	2	weft
0.0949	29.8	.2316	2	yellow-orange
0.0947	29.8	.1352	3	suiting
0.0947	29.8	.0770	5	1154
0.0947	29.8	.0770	5	823
0.0943	29.7	.0404	8	planer
0.0943	29.7	.0223	7	waistband
0.0942	29.7	.0238	13	collage
0.0942	29.7	.0000	9	FHA
0.0942	29.7	.0000	9	photons
0.0942	29.7	.0000	9	Sind
0.0938	29.7	.0000	8	Brackett
0.0938	29.7	.0000	8	Cougar
0.0938	29.7	.0000	8	Dinky
0.0938	29.7	.0000	8	Elna
0.0938	29.7	.0000	8	Lath
0.0938	29.7	.0000	8	Porkey
0.0938	29.7	.0000	8	Proutte
0.0938	29.7	.0000	8	Searcy
0.0938	29.7	.0000	8	Wigg
0.0937	29.7	.1397	3	anvils
0.0937	29.7	.1397	3	Tudor
0.0933	29.7	.0510	7	denotative
0.0933	29.7	.0214	11	sinners
0.0933	29.7	.1018	4	undercurve
0.0925	29.7	.1300	3	plaids
0.0918	29.6	.2109	2	AA
0.0918	29.6	.2109	2	Colors
0.0918	29.6	.2109	2	harmonizes
0.0918	29.6	.2109	2	RIGHT
0.0917	29.6	.2106	2	Camembert
0.0917	29.6	.2106	2	frustrate
0.0917	29.6	.2106	2	Limburger
0.0917	29.6	.2106	2	Patch
0.0917	29.6	.2106	2	Tabasco
0.0917	29.6	.2106	2	wool-like
0.0917	29.6	.2106	2	wrinkle-resistant
0.0914	29.6	.0000	2	n't
0.0914	29.6	.0000	2	'board
0.0914	29.6	.0000	2	'tend
0.0914	29.6	.0000	2	'uns
0.0914	29.6	.0000	2	a-courting
0.0914	29.6	.0000	2	a-rum-a-tee-tum-a-tee-tum
0.0914	29.6	.0000	2	a-sunning
0.0914	29.6	.0000	2	Abby's
THE PRECEDING WORD TYPE OCCUPIES RANK 41400				
0.0914	29.6	.0000	2	Abdulla
0.0914	29.6	.0000	2	Abh
0.0914	29.6	.0000	2	Adamson
0.0914	29.6	.0000	2	adder
0.0914	29.6	.0000	2	Addie
0.0914	29.6	.0000	2	Addio
0.0914	29.6	.0000	2	Adele
0.0914	29.6	.0000	2	Adelina
0.0914	29.6	.0000	2	Admiral's
0.0914	29.6	.0000	2	adventure's
0.0914	29.6	.0000	2	Aea
0.0914	29.6	.0000	2	Aerodrome
0.0914	29.6	.0000	2	Aetes
0.0914	29.6	.0000	2	Agard
0.0914	29.6	.0000	2	ahhh
0.0914	29.6	.0000	2	Air-conditioned
0.0914	29.6	.0000	2	airmanship
0.0914	29.6	.0000	2	Airplane
0.0914	29.6	.0000	2	aleck
0.0914	29.6	.0000	2	Alex'
0.0914	29.6	.0000	2	Alkemade's
0.0914	29.6	.0000	2	allay-oop
0.0914	29.6	.0000	2	Aller
0.0914	29.6	.0000	2	Allerton's
0.0914	29.6	.0000	2	alleyway
0.0914	29.6	.0000	2	Allis
0.0914	29.6	.0000	2	Alonzo's
0.0914	29.6	.0000	2	ambles
0.0914	29.6	.0000	2	Ambulance
0.0914	29.6	.0000	2	Ana's
0.0914	29.6	.0000	2	Anagnos
0.0914	29.6	.0000	2	Andrea's
0.0914	29.6	.0000	2	Annette's
0.0914	29.6	.0000	2	Announcer
0.0914	29.6	.0000	2	Antaeus
0.0914	29.6	.0000	2	anteater's
0.0914	29.6	.0000	2	antechamber
0.0914	29.6	.0000	2	archbishop's
0.0914	29.6	.0000	2	Arikara
0.0914	29.6	.0000	2	armload
0.0914	29.6	.0000	2	aroo-oo-h
0.0914	29.6	.0000	2	arreh
0.0914	29.6	.0000	2	askew
0.0914	29.6	.0000	2	Athamas
0.0914	29.6	.0000	2	Auburn
0.0914	29.6	.0000	2	avenged
0.0914	29.6	.0000	2	awfullest
0.0914	29.6	.0000	2	b
0.0914	29.6	.0000	2	baa
0.0914	29.6	.0000	2	Baba's
0.0914	29.6	.0000	2	Baca
0.0914	29.6	.0000	2	backhand
0.0914	29.6	.0000	2	backslaps
0.0914	29.6	.0000	2	Bairn
0.0914	29.6	.0000	2	Bakersville
0.0914	29.6	.0000	2	Bakery
0.0914	29.6	.0000	2	Balto's
0.0914	29.6	.0000	2	banisters
0.0914	29.6	.0000	2	bareback-riding
0.0914	29.6	.0000	2	barque
0.0914	29.6	.0000	2	Bartholdi
0.0914	29.6	.0000	2	Bataan
0.0914	29.6	.0000	2	battle-ax
0.0914	29.6	.0000	2	Battlefields
0.0914	29.6	.0000	2	bayberry
0.0914	29.6	.0000	2	Beale
0.0914	29.6	.0000	2	Beall
0.0914	29.6	.0000	2	Bearcats
0.0914	29.6	.0000	2	beast's
0.0914	29.6	.0000	2	Becomes
0.0914	29.6	.0000	2	Bedlow
0.0914	29.6	.0000	2	bedsprings
0.0914	29.6	.0000	2	beef-bone
0.0914	29.6	.0000	2	beetle-car
0.0914	29.6	.0000	2	Bellinis
0.0914	29.6	.0000	2	Beraha
0.0914	29.6	.0000	2	Bertillon
0.0914	29.6	.0000	2	best-protected
0.0914	29.6	.0000	2	Bethenia's
0.0914	29.6	.0000	2	betters
0.0914	29.6	.0000	2	Bianca's
0.0914	29.6	.0000	2	billies
0.0914	29.6	.0000	2	biplane
0.0914	29.6	.0000	2	black-top
0.0914	29.6	.0000	2	Blass
0.0914	29.6	.0000	2	Bligh
0.0914	29.6	.0000	2	blimey
0.0914	29.6	.0000	2	bloodhound
0.0914	29.6	.0000	2	Blot
0.0914	29.6	.0000	2	Bluejay
0.0914	29.6	.0000	2	Bluey's
0.0914	29.6	.0000	2	Blumberg
0.0914	29.6	.0000	2	Bo-o-o-o-n-e
0.0914	29.6	.0000	2	bobtailed
0.0914	29.6	.0000	2	Bonatti
0.0914	29.6	.0000	2	Bone
0.0914	29.6	.0000	2	book-learning
0.0914	29.6	.0000	2	boomer
0.0914	29.6	.0000	2	bootblack
0.0914	29.6	.0000	2	Borrowed
THE PRECEDING WORD TYPE OCCUPIES RANK 41500				
0.0914	29.6	.0000	2	Both
0.0914	29.6	.0000	2	bottle-brush
0.0914	29.6	.0000	2	bow-wow-wow
0.0914	29.6	.0000	2	Bowie's
0.0914	29.6	.0000	2	boxing's
0.0914	29.6	.0000	2	Bradburn
0.0914	29.6	.0000	2	braille
0.0914	29.6	.0000	2	Brainard
0.0914	29.6	.0000	2	Brant's
0.0914	29.6	.0000	2	broadcasters
0.0914	29.6	.0000	2	Brom
0.0914	29.6	.0000	2	brontosaur
0.0914	29.6	.0000	2	Brunet
0.0914	29.6	.0000	2	bull-riding
0.0914	29.6	.0000	2	bull-teams
0.0914	29.6	.0000	2	bulldogged
0.0914	29.6	.0000	2	bulldogging
0.0914	29.6	.0000	2	bump
0.0914	29.6	.0000	2	bung
0.0914	29.6	.0000	2	Burgher
0.0914	29.6	.0000	2	Burns's
0.0914	29.6	.0000	2	burro's
0.0914	29.6	.0000	2	Burrowing
0.0914	29.6	.0000	2	Buselapi
0.0914	29.6	.0000	2	BUT
0.0914	29.6	.0000	2	Butler's
0.0914	29.6	.0000	2	Buz
0.0914	29.6	.0000	2	cadets'
0.0914	29.6	.0000	2	Cadore
0.0914	29.6	.0000	2	cairns
0.0914	29.6	.0000	2	caissons
0.0914	29.6	.0000	2	calfskin
0.0914	29.6	.0000	2	Calles
0.0914	29.6	.0000	2	callin'
0.0914	29.6	.0000	2	callus
0.0914	29.6	.0000	2	calmest
0.0914	29.6	.0000	2	calugas
0.0914	29.6	.0000	2	Campers
0.0914	29.6	.0000	2	canapes
0.0914	29.6	.0000	2	Canarsies
0.0914	29.6	.0000	2	Canetto
0.0914	29.6	.0000	2	Cannonball
0.0914	29.6	.0000	2	cannonballs
0.0914	29.6	.0000	2	canoemen
0.0914	29.6	.0000	2	Cantellos
0.0914	29.6	.0000	2	Capes
0.0914	29.6	.0000	2	captions
0.0914	29.6	.0000	2	Capulet's
0.0914	29.6	.0000	2	Carlo's
0.0914	29.6	.0000	2	Carman
0.0914	29.6	.0000	2	Carrington
0.0914	29.6	.0000	2	cart-horses
0.0914	29.6	.0000	2	Carver's
0.0914	29.6	.0000	2	Cathcart
0.0914	29.6	.0000	2	Cavalcades
0.0914	29.6	.0000	2	Centigrade
0.0914	29.6	.0000	2	Cha
0.0914	29.6	.0000	2	chalet
0.0914	29.6	.0000	2	Chanticleer's
0.0914	29.6	.0000	2	Chanuka's
0.0914	29.6	.0000	2	characters'
0.0914	29.6	.0000	2	Charette
0.0914	29.6	.0000	2	Charts
0.0914	29.6	.0000	2	chasm
0.0914	29.6	.0000	2	cheer-cheer
0.0914	29.6	.0000	2	cheer-up
0.0914	29.6	.0000	2	Cheerful's
0.0914	29.6	.0000	2	cheque-book
0.0914	29.6	.0000	2	Chester's
0.0914	29.6	.0000	2	Chet's
0.0914	29.6	.0000	2	Chica's
0.0914	29.6	.0000	2	Chick's
0.0914	29.6	.0000	2	Chickadee
0.0914	29.6	.0000	2	chicken-corn
0.0914	29.6	.0000	2	Chieftain's
0.0914	29.6	.0000	2	Childreth's
0.0914	29.6	.0000	2	chimney-place
0.0914	29.6	.0000	2	Chimp
0.0914	29.6	.0000	2	Ching
0.0914	29.6	.0000	2	Choo
0.0914	29.6	.0000	2	choo
0.0914	29.6	.0000	2	chopped-up
0.0914	29.6	.0000	2	Chris'
0.0914	29.6	.0000	2	cistern
0.0914	29.6	.0000	2	clambake
0.0914	29.6	.0000	2	clangs
0.0914	29.6	.0000	2	Clapping
0.0914	29.6	.0000	2	Clarence's
0.0914	29.6	.0000	2	Clarissa's
0.0914	29.6	.0000	2	Clarkson
0.0914	29.6	.0000	2	Clarksville
0.0914	29.6	.0000	2	Clayte
0.0914	29.6	.0000	2	cleaner-upper
0.0914	29.6	.0000	2	Cleges
0.0914	29.6	.0000	2	Clement's
0.0914	29.6	.0000	2	clickety-clack
0.0914	29.6	.0000	2	Clinton's
0.0914	29.6	.0000	2	clippety-clop
0.0914	29.6	.0000	2	clippity
0.0914	29.6	.0000	2	clong
THE PRECEDING WORD TYPE OCCUPIES RANK 41600				
0.0914	29.6	.0000	2	Clothes
0.0914	29.6	.0000	2	clowns'
0.0914	29.6	.0000	2	club's
0.0914	29.6	.0000	2	clutches
0.0914	29.6	.0000	2	coca-growing
0.0914	29.6	.0000	2	cock-eyed
0.0914	29.6	.0000	2	coco
0.0914	29.6	.0000	2	Colon
0.0914	29.6	.0000	2	Colon's
0.0914	29.6	.0000	2	Colter's
0.0914	29.6	.0000	2	combatant
0.0914	29.6	.0000	2	Connor's
0.0914	29.6	.0000	2	conspirator
0.0914	29.6	.0000	2	copyist
0.0914	29.6	.0000	2	copyists
0.0914	29.6	.0000	2	Cords
0.0914	29.6	.0000	2	Corkonians
0.0914	29.6	.0000	2	Corkscrew
0.0914	29.6	.0000	2	Cornflower's
0.0914	29.6	.0000	2	Cornplanter
0.0914	29.6	.0000	2	cotton-wool
0.0914	29.6	.0000	2	Coulter
0.0914	29.6	.0000	2	Counselor
0.0914	29.6	.0000	2	Counselors
0.0914	29.6	.0000	2	counterfeiting
0.0914	29.6	.0000	2	country-side
0.0914	29.6	.0000	2	Courant
0.0914	29.6	.0000	2	cowbarn
0.0914	29.6	.0000	2	cowherders
0.0914	29.6	.0000	2	cowpox
0.0914	29.6	.0000	2	Crackenberry
0.0914	29.6	.0000	2	Craighead
0.0914	29.6	.0000	2	cre-e-eak
0.0914	29.6	.0000	2	creak-creak
0.0914	29.6	.0000	2	Creep-Along
0.0914	29.6	.0000	2	cremated
0.0914	29.6	.0000	2	Cresta
0.0914	29.6	.0000	2	crocs
0.0914	29.6	.0000	2	Crosetti
0.0914	29.6	.0000	2	crosspieces
0.0914	29.6	.0000	2	Crows
0.0914	29.6	.0000	2	crumpling
0.0914	29.6	.0000	2	Crystal's
0.0914	29.6	.0000	2	crystallographers
0.0914	29.6	.0000	2	cul-de-sac
0.0914	29.6	.0000	2	culpa
0.0914	29.6	.0000	2	cur
0.0914	29.6	.0000	2	curious-looking
0.0914	29.6	.0000	2	Cusi's
0.0914	29.6	.0000	2	cutworm
0.0914	29.6	.0000	2	d'Argons
0.0914	29.6	.0000	2	Dacotahs
0.0914	29.6	.0000	2	Dakin
0.0914	29.6	.0000	2	dangerous-looking
0.0914	29.6	.0000	2	Dare
0.0914	29.6	.0000	2	Darling's
0.0914	29.6	.0000	2	darlings
0.0914	29.6	.0000	2	Davey's
0.0914	29.6	.0000	2	DeGree's
0.0914	29.6	.0000	2	deVincennes
0.0914	29.6	.0000	2	Deane
0.0914	29.6	.0000	2	deep-toned
0.0914	29.6	.0000	2	defrosting
0.0914	29.6	.0000	2	Delicious
0.0914	29.6	.0000	2	demagogues
0.0914	29.6	.0000	2	demerits
0.0914	29.6	.0000	2	Demolition
0.0914	29.6	.0000	2	Denbooms'
0.0914	29.6	.0000	2	denizens
0.0914	29.6	.0000	2	Depot
0.0914	29.6	.0000	2	Detective
0.0914	29.6	.0000	2	Devore's
0.0914	29.6	.0000	2	Diary
0.0914	29.6	.0000	2	Dicksons'
0.0914	29.6	.0000	2	Dictionopolis
0.0914	29.6	.0000	2	diggerfoot
0.0914	29.6	.0000	2	diggin'
0.0914	29.6	.0000	2	Dillworth's
0.0914	29.6	.0000	2	dime-store
0.0914	29.6	.0000	2	dime's
0.0914	29.6	.0000	2	ding-dong-tock
0.0914	29.6	.0000	2	Dining
0.0914	29.6	.0000	2	Dino's
0.0914	29.6	.0000	2	disdainfully
0.0914	29.6	.0000	2	dishonor
0.0914	29.6	.0000	2	Dismael
0.0914	29.6	.0000	2	Disraeli
0.0914	29.6	.0000	2	Distant
0.0914	29.6	.0000	2	do-nothing
0.0914	29.6	.0000	2	Dodo
0.0914	29.6	.0000	2	doffed
0.0914	29.6	.0000	2	dog-train
0.0914	29.6	.0000	2	dogtrot
0.0914	29.6	.0000	2	Donny
0.0914	29.6	.0000	2	Dorset
0.0914	29.6	.0000	2	drawing-room
0.0914	29.6	.0000	2	Drdla's
0.0914	29.6	.0000	2	dream-boat
0.0914	29.6	.0000	2	Dregg's
0.0914	29.6	.0000	2	Driving
THE PRECEDING WORD TYPE OCCUPIES RANK 41700				
0.0914	29.6	.0000	2	duchess
0.0914	29.6	.0000	2	Duffy's
0.0914	29.6	.0000	2	Dumpties

U	SFI	D	F	Word Type
0.0914	29.6	.0000	2	dwarf's
0.0914	29.6	.0000	2	dwellin'
0.0914	29.6	.0000	2	Dyhrenfurth
0.0914	29.6	.0000	2	easels
0.0914	29.6	.0000	2	Eastport
0.0914	29.6	.0000	2	eavesdropping
0.0914	29.6	.0000	2	Ector
0.0914	29.6	.0000	2	Ede
0.0914	29.6	.0000	2	edging
0.0914	29.6	.0000	2	Ehrich
0.0914	29.6	.0000	2	Eielson's
0.0914	29.6	.0000	2	eighteen-pounders
0.0914	29.6	.0000	2	eighty-one
0.0914	29.6	.0000	2	elderberry
0.0914	29.6	.0000	2	Elis
0.0914	29.6	.0000	2	Elizabethtown
0.0914	29.6	.0000	2	Elkhart
0.0914	29.6	.0000	2	Elwell
0.0914	29.6	.0000	2	emigratin'
0.0914	29.6	.0000	2	Emma's
0.0914	29.6	.0000	2	Ena
0.0914	29.6	.0000	2	Endurance
0.0914	29.6	.0000	2	Englewood
0.0914	29.6	.0000	2	Ernestine's
0.0914	29.6	.0000	2	Erymanthus
0.0914	29.6	.0000	2	essed
0.0914	29.6	.0000	2	Eurystheus
0.0914	29.6	.0000	2	Evansville
0.0914	29.6	.0000	2	evilly
0.0914	29.6	.0000	2	eyeshade
0.0914	29.6	.0000	2	FAIR
0.0914	29.6	.0000	2	Fairchild
0.0914	29.6	.0000	2	Faline
0.0914	29.6	.0000	2	Fallen
0.0914	29.6	.0000	2	fanatical
0.0914	29.6	.0000	2	fanbearers
0.0914	29.6	.0000	2	Farley's
0.0914	29.6	.0000	2	Farnsworth's
0.0914	29.6	.0000	2	fastnesses
0.0914	29.6	.0000	2	Fellow's
0.0914	29.6	.0000	2	fidgets
0.0914	29.6	.0000	2	fierce-eyed
0.0914	29.6	.0000	2	Fifty-Mile
0.0914	29.6	.0000	2	filibuster
0.0914	29.6	.0000	2	Finlay
0.0914	29.6	.0000	2	Fire-Boy
0.0914	29.6	.0000	2	fire-crackers
0.0914	29.6	.0000	2	fire-drill
0.0914	29.6	.0000	2	firs
0.0914	29.6	.0000	2	Fish's
0.0914	29.6	.0000	2	fisherwoman
0.0914	29.6	.0000	2	Flash
0.0914	29.6	.0000	2	flecked
0.0914	29.6	.0000	2	Flemings
0.0914	29.6	.0000	2	floor's
0.0914	29.6	.0000	2	Floppy
0.0914	29.6	.0000	2	fluttery
0.0914	29.6	.0000	2	Flyaway's
0.0914	29.6	.0000	2	fo'c's'tle
0.0914	29.6	.0000	2	foreseeing
0.0914	29.6	.0000	2	Fort's
0.0914	29.6	.0000	2	Fortunata
0.0914	29.6	.0000	2	forty-eighth
0.0914	29.6	.0000	2	four-and-twenty
0.0914	29.6	.0000	2	four-thirty
0.0914	29.6	.0000	2	Francoise
0.0914	29.6	.0000	2	free-style
0.0914	29.6	.0000	2	Freylinck
0.0914	29.6	.0000	2	Frisette
0.0914	29.6	.0000	2	Froggie
0.0914	29.6	.0000	2	Frogtown
0.0914	29.6	.0000	2	front-room
0.0914	29.6	.0000	2	Fumiko's
0.0914	29.6	.0000	2	Fuzzy-top
0.0914	29.6	.0000	2	G-Man
0.0914	29.6	.0000	2	gabbling
0.0914	29.6	.0000	2	Gabe
0.0914	29.6	.0000	2	Galt'd
0.0914	29.6	.0000	2	Galts
0.0914	29.6	.0000	2	galvanizing
0.0914	29.6	.0000	2	Gardener's
0.0914	29.6	.0000	2	Gardenia
0.0914	29.6	.0000	2	Garver's
0.0914	29.6	.0000	2	Gentleman's
0.0914	29.6	.0000	2	Gerd
0.0914	29.6	.0000	2	Gian-Carlo's
0.0914	29.6	.0000	2	giddyap
0.0914	29.6	.0000	2	Gingerbread
0.0914	29.6	.0000	2	gladdest
0.0914	29.6	.0000	2	glider's
0.0914	29.6	.0000	2	gloatingly
0.0914	29.6	.0000	2	gluggle-gluggle-gluggle
0.0914	29.6	.0000	2	Gobo
0.0914	29.6	.0000	2	god-spirits
0.0914	29.6	.0000	2	Goddard's
0.0914	29.6	.0000	2	Goering
0.0914	29.6	.0000	2	gold-crowned
				THE PRECEDING WORD TYPE OCCUPIES RANK 41800
0.0914	29.6	.0000	2	Goldie
0.0914	29.6	.0000	2	Goldsmiths'
0.0914	29.6	.0000	2	goose-house
0.0914	29.6	.0000	2	Gordy's
0.0914	29.6	.0000	2	Goto
0.0914	29.6	.0000	2	governorship
0.0914	29.6	.0000	2	Gowdy's
0.0914	29.6	.0000	2	Gozaimasu
0.0914	29.6	.0000	2	Gran'maw
0.0914	29.6	.0000	2	granddad
0.0914	29.6	.0000	2	granddaddy
0.0914	29.6	.0000	2	grapeshot
0.0914	29.6	.0000	2	Grayson
0.0914	29.6	.0000	2	Great-Aunt
0.0914	29.6	.0000	2	Greenlanders
0.0914	29.6	.0000	2	Grenelle
0.0914	29.6	.0000	2	growin'
0.0914	29.6	.0000	2	GrussGott
0.0914	29.6	.0000	2	Gwendolyn's
0.0914	29.6	.0000	2	gyrfalcon's
0.0914	29.6	.0000	2	Ha-ha
0.0914	29.6	.0000	2	Ha-ho
0.0914	29.6	.0000	2	Hackett
0.0914	29.6	.0000	2	hai
0.0914	29.6	.0000	2	Haji's
0.0914	29.6	.0000	2	hala
0.0914	29.6	.0000	2	half-chick
0.0914	29.6	.0000	2	half-submerged
0.0914	29.6	.0000	2	Hallidie
0.0914	29.6	.0000	2	halloo
0.0914	29.6	.0000	2	hammer'll
0.0914	29.6	.0000	2	handbill
0.0914	29.6	.0000	2	hangar
0.0914	29.6	.0000	2	hangars
0.0914	29.6	.0000	2	harboring
0.0914	29.6	.0000	2	hard-earned
0.0914	29.6	.0000	2	hard-won
0.0914	29.6	.0000	2	harpooned
0.0914	29.6	.0000	2	hatchway
0.0914	29.6	.0000	2	Hawke's
0.0914	29.6	.0000	2	hawnk
0.0914	29.6	.0000	2	Hayne
0.0914	29.6	.0000	2	Healthy
0.0914	29.6	.0000	2	heartened
0.0914	29.6	.0000	2	Hector's
0.0914	29.6	.0000	2	heeding
0.0914	29.6	.0000	2	heehaw
0.0914	29.6	.0000	2	Helping
0.0914	29.6	.0000	2	Henny's
0.0914	29.6	.0000	2	Herculaneum
0.0914	29.6	.0000	2	Hernandez's
0.0914	29.6	.0000	2	Herne
0.0914	29.6	.0000	2	hi-ee
0.0914	29.6	.0000	2	Hi-no-yo-o-jin
0.0914	29.6	.0000	2	Higher
0.0914	29.6	.0000	2	Hobbie
0.0914	29.6	.0000	2	Hodja's
0.0914	29.6	.0000	2	Hoevenberg
0.0914	29.6	.0000	2	Hogan
0.0914	29.6	.0000	2	Hollis's
0.0914	29.6	.0000	2	Home-coming
0.0914	29.6	.0000	2	homewards
0.0914	29.6	.0000	2	hon
0.0914	29.6	.0000	2	Horne
0.0914	29.6	.0000	2	hornet
0.0914	29.6	.0000	2	hospitably
0.0914	29.6	.0000	2	Houghton's
0.0914	29.6	.0000	2	house-raising
0.0914	29.6	.0000	2	Houses
0.0914	29.6	.0000	2	how-wow-wow-in-ish-a-shin
0.0914	29.6	.0000	2	Hsi
0.0914	29.6	.0000	2	hum-m-m-m
0.0914	29.6	.0000	2	humour
0.0914	29.6	.0000	2	Humpty
0.0914	29.6	.0000	2	Hundley
0.0914	29.6	.0000	2	husked
0.0914	29.6	.0000	2	Hydarnes
0.0914	29.6	.0000	2	hydrants
0.0914	29.6	.0000	2	hygroscope
0.0914	29.6	.0000	2	ice-locked
0.0914	29.6	.0000	2	Icehouse
0.0914	29.6	.0000	2	ilmenite
0.0914	29.6	.0000	2	imputation
0.0914	29.6	.0000	2	intersectional
0.0914	29.6	.0000	2	Ishan
0.0914	29.6	.0000	2	IT'S
0.0914	29.6	.0000	2	Iverson's
0.0914	29.6	.0000	2	Ivorsens
0.0914	29.6	.0000	2	jab
0.0914	29.6	.0000	2	jabs
0.0914	29.6	.0000	2	James'
0.0914	29.6	.0000	2	Japeth
0.0914	29.6	.0000	2	Jeanie's
0.0914	29.6	.0000	2	Jeb's
0.0914	29.6	.0000	2	Jee-rusalem
0.0914	29.6	.0000	2	jeepney
0.0914	29.6	.0000	2	Jewan
0.0914	29.6	.0000	2	jinni
0.0914	29.6	.0000	2	Jogues
0.0914	29.6	.0000	2	johnnycake
				THE PRECEDING WORD TYPE OCCUPIES RANK 41900
0.0914	29.6	.0000	2	Johnsons'
0.0914	29.6	.0000	2	Jolly's
0.0914	29.6	.0000	2	Jon's
0.0914	29.6	.0000	2	Jonah's
0.0914	29.6	.0000	2	Josefina
0.0914	29.6	.0000	2	Jurjis's
0.0914	29.6	.0000	2	Jutta
0.0914	29.6	.0000	2	Kakapateyuo
0.0914	29.6	.0000	2	Katie's
0.0914	29.6	.0000	2	ke-mo
0.0914	29.6	.0000	2	Keith's
0.0914	29.6	.0000	2	ketches
0.0914	29.6	.0000	2	Khotan
0.0914	29.6	.0000	2	ki-mo
0.0914	29.6	.0000	2	Kiltie
0.0914	29.6	.0000	2	Kind
0.0914	29.6	.0000	2	Kingsland
0.0914	29.6	.0000	2	Kipp
0.0914	29.6	.0000	2	Kirkland
0.0914	29.6	.0000	2	Kirsten's
0.0914	29.6	.0000	2	kitch
0.0914	29.6	.0000	2	Kittery
0.0914	29.6	.0000	2	Kiyoko
0.0914	29.6	.0000	2	klong
0.0914	29.6	.0000	2	knee-high
0.0914	29.6	.0000	2	Kookie
0.0914	29.6	.0000	2	Korth
0.0914	29.6	.0000	2	Kul's
0.0914	29.6	.0000	2	LaBrea
0.0914	29.6	.0000	2	lamppost
0.0914	29.6	.0000	2	Landshort
0.0914	29.6	.0000	2	Langmier
0.0914	29.6	.0000	2	Lantern
0.0914	29.6	.0000	2	Lanterns
0.0914	29.6	.0000	2	Lapp
0.0914	29.6	.0000	2	latched
0.0914	29.6	.0000	2	laughingstock
0.0914	29.6	.0000	2	Laurinchen
0.0914	29.6	.0000	2	Lavendar's
0.0914	29.6	.0000	2	LeClerc
0.0914	29.6	.0000	2	LeClerc's
0.0914	29.6	.0000	2	learn'd
0.0914	29.6	.0000	2	leather-and-rope
0.0914	29.6	.0000	2	Lebarge
0.0914	29.6	.0000	2	left-hander
0.0914	29.6	.0000	2	Lemmons
0.0914	29.6	.0000	2	Len
0.0914	29.6	.0000	2	letup
0.0914	29.6	.0000	2	Liberty's
0.0914	29.6	.0000	2	life-sized
0.0914	29.6	.0000	2	lifeguards
0.0914	29.6	.0000	2	light-brown
0.0914	29.6	.0000	2	lightkeeper
0.0914	29.6	.0000	2	ling-tum
0.0914	29.6	.0000	2	lip-stretching
0.0914	29.6	.0000	2	lite
0.0914	29.6	.0000	2	liverwurst
0.0914	29.6	.0000	2	llamo
0.0914	29.6	.0000	2	lobo
0.0914	29.6	.0000	2	lobsterman
0.0914	29.6	.0000	2	locksmith
0.0914	29.6	.0000	2	Loisel
0.0914	29.6	.0000	2	loiter
0.0914	29.6	.0000	2	longhouses
0.0914	29.6	.0000	2	lookyhere
0.0914	29.6	.0000	2	lovelessness
0.0914	29.6	.0000	2	Low's
0.0914	29.6	.0000	2	Lucifer
0.0914	29.6	.0000	2	Luga
0.0914	29.6	.0000	2	lumberyard
0.0914	29.6	.0000	2	lunchbox
0.0914	29.6	.0000	2	MAin
0.0914	29.6	.0000	2	m-a-r-k
0.0914	29.6	.0000	2	made-to-order
0.0914	29.6	.0000	2	Magee
0.0914	29.6	.0000	2	magnifico
0.0914	29.6	.0000	2	Mainland
0.0914	29.6	.0000	2	Maja's
0.0914	29.6	.0000	2	Mallorys
0.0914	29.6	.0000	2	Mamzell
0.0914	29.6	.0000	2	man-scent
0.0914	29.6	.0000	2	Manuela's
0.0914	29.6	.0000	2	map-making
0.0914	29.6	.0000	2	marge
0.0914	29.6	.0000	2	Marker
0.0914	29.6	.0000	2	Martina
0.0914	29.6	.0000	2	marveling
0.0914	29.6	.0000	2	Marybeth
0.0914	29.6	.0000	2	Massasoit's
0.0914	29.6	.0000	2	Mather's
0.0914	29.6	.0000	2	Matjan
0.0914	29.6	.0000	2	matter-of-factly
0.0914	29.6	.0000	2	mayday
0.0914	29.6	.0000	2	McClung
0.0914	29.6	.0000	2	McGarity
0.0914	29.6	.0000	2	McGoogle's
0.0914	29.6	.0000	2	me-oww
0.0914	29.6	.0000	2	mea
0.0914	29.6	.0000	2	meadowlands
0.0914	29.6	.0000	2	meanly
				THE PRECEDING WORD TYPE OCCUPIES RANK 42000
0.0914	29.6	.0000	2	medal's
0.0914	29.6	.0000	2	medicinal
0.0914	29.6	.0000	2	Medora
0.0914	29.6	.0000	2	mee-ow
0.0914	29.6	.0000	2	Megwa
0.0914	29.6	.0000	2	Mel's
0.0914	29.6	.0000	2	Men's
0.0914	29.6	.0000	2	Mendi
0.0914	29.6	.0000	2	Mendi's
0.0914	29.6	.0000	2	Merlin's
0.0914	29.6	.0000	2	messenger's
0.0914	29.6	.0000	2	Meszar
0.0914	29.6	.0000	2	midshipmen
0.0914	29.6	.0000	2	Milette
0.0914	29.6	.0000	2	milkmaids
0.0914	29.6	.0000	2	Millway
0.0914	29.6	.0000	2	Milly's
0.0914	29.6	.0000	2	MINE
0.0914	29.6	.0000	2	minting
0.0914	29.6	.0000	2	misguided
0.0914	29.6	.0000	2	misshapen
0.0914	29.6	.0000	2	missis
0.0914	29.6	.0000	2	mistiness
0.0914	29.6	.0000	2	Mitsu's
0.0914	29.6	.0000	2	mizzenmast
0.0914	29.6	.0000	2	mohney
0.0914	29.6	.0000	2	moil
0.0914	29.6	.0000	2	Moines
0.0914	29.6	.0000	2	molehills
0.0914	29.6	.0000	2	Molly's
0.0914	29.6	.0000	2	mongoose's
0.0914	29.6	.0000	2	Months
0.0914	29.6	.0000	2	mooed
0.0914	29.6	.0000	2	Moog
0.0914	29.6	.0000	2	Mooneen
0.0914	29.6	.0000	2	mooning
0.0914	29.6	.0000	2	mother'd
0.0914	29.6	.0000	2	motor-driven
0.0914	29.6	.0000	2	Motuan
0.0914	29.6	.0000	2	mouse-catching
0.0914	29.6	.0000	2	Mousey
0.0914	29.6	.0000	2	Mousey's
0.0914	29.6	.0000	2	much-used
0.0914	29.6	.0000	2	mud-rock
0.0914	29.6	.0000	2	Mudville
0.0914	29.6	.0000	2	Mullen's
0.0914	29.6	.0000	2	munched
0.0914	29.6	.0000	2	Myers'
0.0914	29.6	.0000	2	mythologists
0.0914	29.6	.0000	2	namastey
0.0914	29.6	.0000	2	Nannerl's
0.0914	29.6	.0000	2	Nasr-ed-Din
0.0914	29.6	.0000	2	nats
0.0914	29.6	.0000	2	navigating
0.0914	29.6	.0000	2	Nell's
0.0914	29.6	.0000	2	Nemeth
0.0914	29.6	.0000	2	Nephele
0.0914	29.6	.0000	2	Nereus
0.0914	29.6	.0000	2	Netta's
0.0914	29.6	.0000	2	Nevatim
0.0914	29.6	.0000	2	Neverland
0.0914	29.6	.0000	2	Newbold
0.0914	29.6	.0000	2	nibble-nibble
0.0914	29.6	.0000	2	Nicci
0.0914	29.6	.0000	2	Nickels
0.0914	29.6	.0000	2	Nicole
0.0914	29.6	.0000	2	Nils'
0.0914	29.6	.0000	2	nine-fifteen
0.0914	29.6	.0000	2	nip-cat
0.0914	29.6	.0000	2	Nita-san
0.0914	29.6	.0000	2	No-Ears
0.0914	29.6	.0000	2	Norris'
0.0914	29.6	.0000	2	Northman
0.0914	29.6	.0000	2	notetaking
0.0914	29.6	.0000	2	nuisances
0.0914	29.6	.0000	2	nuthin'
0.0914	29.6	.0000	2	Nymphs
0.0914	29.6	.0000	2	obstructionist
0.0914	29.6	.0000	2	Oceaan
0.0914	29.6	.0000	2	Octopus
0.0914	29.6	.0000	2	oddest
0.0914	29.6	.0000	2	Odile's
0.0914	29.6	.0000	2	off-guard
0.0914	29.6	.0000	2	Ogowe
0.0914	29.6	.0000	2	ohayo
0.0914	29.6	.0000	2	oho
0.0914	29.6	.0000	2	Ojibway
0.0914	29.6	.0000	2	Ok
0.0914	29.6	.0000	2	Old-time
0.0914	29.6	.0000	2	Omar's
0.0914	29.6	.0000	2	on-going
0.0914	29.6	.0000	2	one-engine
0.0914	29.6	.0000	2	ook-ook-ook
0.0914	29.6	.0000	2	oom
0.0914	29.6	.0000	2	ooooooh
0.0914	29.6	.0000	2	opinion-forming
0.0914	29.6	.0000	2	Osprey
0.0914	29.6	.0000	2	Otonia
0.0914	29.6	.0000	2	oughtn't
0.0914	29.6	.0000	2	overbearing
				THE PRECEDING WORD TYPE OCCUPIES RANK 42100
0.0914	29.6	.0000	2	owlish
0.0914	29.6	.0000	2	Ozerov
0.0914	29.6	.0000	2	Pablito
0.0914	29.6	.0000	2	Paimpol
0.0914	29.6	.0000	2	pain-filled
0.0914	29.6	.0000	2	Pam's
0.0914	29.6	.0000	2	pamper
0.0914	29.6	.0000	2	panda's
0.0914	29.6	.0000	2	panther's
0.0914	29.6	.0000	2	Panthers
0.0914	29.6	.0000	2	Parry
0.0914	29.6	.0000	2	Pascual's
0.0914	29.6	.0000	2	patients'
0.0914	29.6	.0000	2	Patriot
0.0914	29.6	.0000	2	pattered
0.0914	29.6	.0000	2	Peaches
0.0914	29.6	.0000	2	Peary's
0.0914	29.6	.0000	2	Peccary
0.0914	29.6	.0000	2	Pekinese
0.0914	29.6	.0000	2	penny-winkle
0.0914	29.6	.0000	2	peppercorns
0.0914	29.6	.0000	2	Peralta
0.0914	29.6	.0000	2	Periwinkle's
0.0914	29.6	.0000	2	pet's
0.0914	29.6	.0000	2	Phasis
0.0914	29.6	.0000	2	Pheasant
0.0914	29.6	.0000	2	Philo's
0.0914	29.6	.0000	2	Phipps
0.0914	29.6	.0000	2	Pi-tin-tin
0.0914	29.6	.0000	2	Pick
0.0914	29.6	.0000	2	Picnic
0.0914	29.6	.0000	2	Pidgeon
0.0914	29.6	.0000	2	Pierpont
0.0914	29.6	.0000	2	pilin'
0.0914	29.6	.0000	2	pilothouse
0.0914	29.6	.0000	2	pin-the-tail
0.0914	29.6	.0000	2	Pinch's
0.0914	29.6	.0000	2	Piney
0.0914	29.6	.0000	2	pinto's
0.0914	29.6	.0000	2	Piri
0.0914	29.6	.0000	2	Pitcairn's
0.0914	29.6	.0000	2	pitch-black
0.0914	29.6	.0000	2	Pitch-pine
0.0914	29.6	.0000	2	pitch
0.0914	29.6	.0000	2	pityingly
0.0914	29.6	.0000	2	Placid
0.0914	29.6	.0000	2	platy
0.0914	29.6	.0000	2	PLAY
0.0914	29.6	.0000	2	play-off
0.0914	29.6	.0000	2	play-offs
0.0914	29.6	.0000	2	playfulness
0.0914	29.6	.0000	2	plexiglass
0.0914	29.6	.0000	2	plumed
0.0914	29.6	.0000	2	pocahontas
0.0914	29.6	.0000	2	pokeberry
0.0914	29.6	.0000	2	Polack
0.0914	29.6	.0000	2	polynya
0.0914	29.6	.0000	2	poppycock
0.0914	29.6	.0000	2	Porte
0.0914	29.6	.0000	2	pouncing
0.0914	29.6	.0000	2	PrairieCity
0.0914	29.6	.0000	2	Prean
0.0914	29.6	.0000	2	predisposition
0.0914	29.6	.0000	2	Primus
0.0914	29.6	.0000	2	Provincale
0.0914	29.6	.0000	2	pss
0.0914	29.6	.0000	2	pumpers

U	SFI	D	F	Word Type
0.0914	29.6	.0000	2	Punky
0.0914	29.6	.0000	2	purloin
0.0914	29.6	.0000	2	pussywillows
0.0914	29.6	.0000	2	quacked
0.0914	29.6	.0000	2	quacks
0.0914	29.6	.0000	2	quarter-less
0.0914	29.6	.0000	2	Rabbit's
0.0914	29.6	.0000	2	racecourse
0.0914	29.6	.0000	2	racquets
0.0914	29.6	.0000	2	Radcliffe
0.0914	29.6	.0000	2	raisin'
0.0914	29.6	.0000	2	Ramirez
0.0914	29.6	.0000	2	ranch's
0.0914	29.6	.0000	2	Ranchera
0.0914	29.6	.0000	2	Rangeley
0.0914	29.6	.0000	2	Ranta
0.0914	29.6	.0000	2	Rat's
0.0914	29.6	.0000	2	Ratendon
0.0914	29.6	.0000	2	ratlines
0.0914	29.6	.0000	2	ratted
0.0914	29.6	.0000	2	rattle-trap
0.0914	29.6	.0000	2	re-route
0.0914	29.6	.0000	2	rear-view
0.0914	29.6	.0000	2	Reba
0.0914	29.6	.0000	2	rebounding
0.0914	29.6	.0000	2	recollected
0.0914	29.6	.0000	2	red-and-green
0.0914	29.6	.0000	2	red-rimmed
0.0914	29.6	.0000	2	redskin
0.0914	29.6	.0000	2	referee's
0.0914	29.6	.0000	2	refractor-reflector
0.0914	29.6	.0000	2	Regan
0.0914	29.6	.0000	2	Relais
THE PRECEDING WORD TYPE OCCUPIES RANK 42200				
0.0914	29.6	.0000	2	Relay
0.0914	29.6	.0000	2	relocated
0.0914	29.6	.0000	2	renters'
0.0914	29.6	.0000	2	Reptile
0.0914	29.6	.0000	2	rescuer
0.0914	29.6	.0000	2	reseed
0.0914	29.6	.0000	2	retellings
0.0914	29.6	.0000	2	Revel
0.0914	29.6	.0000	2	Rexy
0.0914	29.6	.0000	2	Rhadan
0.0914	29.6	.0000	2	Rhett
0.0914	29.6	.0000	2	Rhinos
0.0914	29.6	.0000	2	Rikki's
0.0914	29.6	.0000	2	rimrock
0.0914	29.6	.0000	2	Rita's
0.0914	29.6	.0000	2	Rivera
0.0914	29.6	.0000	2	Roadeos
0.0914	29.6	.0000	2	Robot
0.0914	29.6	.0000	2	roc
0.0914	29.6	.0000	2	Rociada
0.0914	29.6	.0000	2	rock-eater
0.0914	29.6	.0000	2	Rockne's
0.0914	29.6	.0000	2	rockweed
0.0914	29.6	.0000	2	Roland's
0.0914	29.6	.0000	2	roller-skate
0.0914	29.6	.0000	2	Rondaros'
0.0914	29.6	.0000	2	roomers
0.0914	29.6	.0000	2	Roosevelts
0.0914	29.6	.0000	2	Rosaline
0.0914	29.6	.0000	2	rosy-faced
0.0914	29.6	.0000	2	roundelay
0.0914	29.6	.0000	2	Rozinante
0.0914	29.6	.0000	2	Ruby-Throat
0.0914	29.6	.0000	2	Rudi's
0.0914	29.6	.0000	2	rum-tum-tiddle-um-tum
0.0914	29.6	.0000	2	rum-tum-tum-tiddle-um
0.0914	29.6	.0000	2	runts
0.0914	29.6	.0000	2	ruse
0.0914	29.6	.0000	2	R300
0.0914	29.6	.0000	2	SOS
0.0914	29.6	.0000	2	sabers
0.0914	29.6	.0000	2	safe-kept
0.0914	29.6	.0000	2	sail-away
0.0914	29.6	.0000	2	sailors'
0.0914	29.6	.0000	2	sainak
0.0914	29.6	.0000	2	SaintLouis
0.0914	29.6	.0000	2	Saint's
0.0914	29.6	.0000	2	salt-makers
0.0914	29.6	.0000	2	saltin'
0.0914	29.6	.0000	2	saltings
0.0914	29.6	.0000	2	Samoset
0.0914	29.6	.0000	2	sand-lot
0.0914	29.6	.0000	2	Sandino's
0.0914	29.6	.0000	2	sawed-off
0.0914	29.6	.0000	2	scare-baby
0.0914	29.6	.0000	2	Schliemann
0.0914	29.6	.0000	2	schoolbag
0.0914	29.6	.0000	2	schoolmaster's
0.0914	29.6	.0000	2	SCORE
0.0914	29.6	.0000	2	Scotts
0.0914	29.6	.0000	2	Screwdrivers'
0.0914	29.6	.0000	2	scrooched
0.0914	29.6	.0000	2	scullion
0.0914	29.6	.0000	2	scupper
0.0914	29.6	.0000	2	seals'
0.0914	29.6	.0000	2	Secession
0.0914	29.6	.0000	2	sectionalism
0.0914	29.6	.0000	2	Seder
0.0914	29.6	.0000	2	seeked
0.0914	29.6	.0000	2	seeping
0.0914	29.6	.0000	2	semicolons
0.0914	29.6	.0000	2	semifinals
0.0914	29.6	.0000	2	senora
0.0914	29.6	.0000	2	Senorita
0.0914	29.6	.0000	2	Sepp's
0.0914	29.6	.0000	2	Sergeant-at-Arms
0.0914	29.6	.0000	2	Sergeant's
0.0914	29.6	.0000	2	Sesamaul
0.0914	29.6	.0000	2	seven-digit
0.0914	29.6	.0000	2	Sewell
0.0914	29.6	.0000	2	Shackleton
0.0914	29.6	.0000	2	shameful
0.0914	29.6	.0000	2	shatter
0.0914	29.6	.0000	2	she'
0.0914	29.6	.0000	2	shelved
0.0914	29.6	.0000	2	Shem
0.0914	29.6	.0000	2	Shin-n-n-n-ny
0.0914	29.6	.0000	2	Shinny
0.0914	29.6	.0000	2	Shoaf
0.0914	29.6	.0000	2	Shoeshine
0.0914	29.6	.0000	2	shopped
0.0914	29.6	.0000	2	Shoshoni
0.0914	29.6	.0000	2	Shot
0.0914	29.6	.0000	2	Shuai
0.0914	29.6	.0000	2	Shubrick
0.0914	29.6	.0000	2	sideheads
0.0914	29.6	.0000	2	Siding
0.0914	29.6	.0000	2	Sikorsky
0.0914	29.6	.0000	2	Sikorsky's
0.0914	29.6	.0000	2	Silverspot's
THE PRECEDING WORD TYPE OCCUPIES RANK 42300				
0.0914	29.6	.0000	2	Silverspray
0.0914	29.6	.0000	2	single-bit
0.0914	29.6	.0000	2	single-footing
0.0914	29.6	.0000	2	Sissa's
0.0914	29.6	.0000	2	six-feet-four
0.0914	29.6	.0000	2	sixtieth
0.0914	29.6	.0000	2	Sjaantje's
0.0914	29.6	.0000	2	skied
0.0914	29.6	.0000	2	Skin
0.0914	29.6	.0000	2	skink
0.0914	29.6	.0000	2	skipper's
0.0914	29.6	.0000	2	Skipper's
0.0914	29.6	.0000	2	Skunk's
0.0914	29.6	.0000	2	slalom
0.0914	29.6	.0000	2	sleepier
0.0914	29.6	.0000	2	sleighbells
0.0914	29.6	.0000	2	Slightly's
0.0914	29.6	.0000	2	slup-slup
0.0914	29.6	.0000	2	Smee's
0.0914	29.6	.0000	2	Smit
0.0914	29.6	.0000	2	Smitty's
0.0914	29.6	.0000	2	smock
0.0914	29.6	.0000	2	smoke's
0.0914	29.6	.0000	2	Snooper
0.0914	29.6	.0000	2	snow's
0.0914	29.6	.0000	2	Snowden
0.0914	29.6	.0000	2	soaped
0.0914	29.6	.0000	2	Solbakken
0.0914	29.6	.0000	2	sonny
0.0914	29.6	.0000	2	Soo-Pung's
0.0914	29.6	.0000	2	sound-pictures
0.0914	29.6	.0000	2	Spaulding
0.0914	29.6	.0000	2	Speck's
0.0914	29.6	.0000	2	Spiridon
0.0914	29.6	.0000	2	squatty
0.0914	29.6	.0000	2	squawkings
0.0914	29.6	.0000	2	stargazer
0.0914	29.6	.0000	2	statesmanship
0.0914	29.6	.0000	2	statures
0.0914	29.6	.0000	2	Stavanger
0.0914	29.6	.0000	2	steelworkers
0.0914	29.6	.0000	2	stick-together
0.0914	29.6	.0000	2	Stickeen's
0.0914	29.6	.0000	2	sticker
0.0914	29.6	.0000	2	stone-deaf
0.0914	29.6	.0000	2	stone-like
0.0914	29.6	.0000	2	stonecutter
0.0914	29.6	.0000	2	Stormy's
0.0914	29.6	.0000	2	Stoutness
0.0914	29.6	.0000	2	stretcher-bearing
0.0914	29.6	.0000	2	stricter
0.0914	29.6	.0000	2	strike-out
0.0914	29.6	.0000	2	Stroop
0.0914	29.6	.0000	2	sugar-cane
0.0914	29.6	.0000	2	sulk
0.0914	29.6	.0000	2	Summerset
0.0914	29.6	.0000	2	sunai
0.0914	29.6	.0000	2	supermen
0.0914	29.6	.0000	2	Sure
0.0914	29.6	.0000	2	Surov
0.0914	29.6	.0000	2	Sutherland
0.0914	29.6	.0000	2	sweet-potato
0.0914	29.6	.0000	2	sweltered
0.0914	29.6	.0000	2	synthesizer
0.0914	29.6	.0000	2	System's
0.0914	29.6	.0000	2	ta-rah-ra-ra-rah
0.0914	29.6	.0000	2	ta-umps
0.0914	29.6	.0000	2	tablecloths
0.0914	29.6	.0000	2	Tag-end
0.0914	29.6	.0000	2	Tainaron
0.0914	29.6	.0000	2	tannery
0.0914	29.6	.0000	2	tattletale
0.0914	29.6	.0000	2	Teeling
0.0914	29.6	.0000	2	Tell's
0.0914	29.6	.0000	2	Telstars
0.0914	29.6	.0000	2	tephra
0.0914	29.6	.0000	2	Texans'
0.0914	29.6	.0000	2	thakin
0.0914	29.6	.0000	2	THAT
0.0914	29.6	.0000	2	THEME
0.0914	29.6	.0000	2	Theo
0.0914	29.6	.0000	2	THEY
0.0914	29.6	.0000	2	thirty-six-inch
0.0914	29.6	.0000	2	thrash
0.0914	29.6	.0000	2	three-decker
0.0914	29.6	.0000	2	three-o'clock
0.0914	29.6	.0000	2	thu'
0.0914	29.6	.0000	2	thundershower
0.0914	29.6	.0000	2	thwap
0.0914	29.6	.0000	2	tick-tick
0.0914	29.6	.0000	2	Tickie
0.0914	29.6	.0000	2	tiki
0.0914	29.6	.0000	2	Tilda
0.0914	29.6	.0000	2	Timing
0.0914	29.6	.0000	2	tinkered
0.0914	29.6	.0000	2	tluth
0.0914	29.6	.0000	2	Tock
0.0914	29.6	.0000	2	Toland
0.0914	29.6	.0000	2	tolerantly
0.0914	29.6	.0000	2	Tolya
THE PRECEDING WORD TYPE OCCUPIES RANK 42400				
0.0914	29.6	.0000	2	tombo
0.0914	29.6	.0000	2	Tonic
0.0914	29.6	.0000	2	tooters
0.0914	29.6	.0000	2	Toozle
0.0914	29.6	.0000	2	topmast
0.0914	29.6	.0000	2	Torad's
0.0914	29.6	.0000	2	TOTAL
0.0914	29.6	.0000	2	towrope
0.0914	29.6	.0000	2	tra-la
0.0914	29.6	.0000	2	Trader
0.0914	29.6	.0000	2	Trailside
0.0914	29.6	.0000	2	transfixed
0.0914	29.6	.0000	2	transmute
0.0914	29.6	.0000	2	Traveler's
0.0914	29.6	.0000	2	Treat's
0.0914	29.6	.0000	2	trekkers
0.0914	29.6	.0000	2	tress
0.0914	29.6	.0000	2	Tricky
0.0914	29.6	.0000	2	Tu
0.0914	29.6	.0000	2	Tuckahoe
0.0914	29.6	.0000	2	Tuckers'
0.0914	29.6	.0000	2	Tumi
0.0914	29.6	.0000	2	Turnips
0.0914	29.6	.0000	2	turnout
0.0914	29.6	.0000	2	tusker
0.0914	29.6	.0000	2	Tut-ankh-amon
0.0914	29.6	.0000	2	Tutei
0.0914	29.6	.0000	2	Tutu's
0.0914	29.6	.0000	2	Tweedy
0.0914	29.6	.0000	2	twenty-six-inch
0.0914	29.6	.0000	2	two-party
0.0914	29.6	.0000	2	two-stepping
0.0914	29.6	.0000	2	ugliest
0.0914	29.6	.0000	2	uh-uh-
0.0914	29.6	.0000	2	Uldas
0.0914	29.6	.0000	2	umped
0.0914	29.6	.0000	2	Umtakati
0.0914	29.6	.0000	2	Umtakati's
0.0914	29.6	.0000	2	Under-Housemaid
0.0914	29.6	.0000	2	Undersecretary
0.0914	29.6	.0000	2	Underwater
0.0914	29.6	.0000	2	unexcitable
0.0914	29.6	.0000	2	UNIVAC
0.0914	29.6	.0000	2	unmoved
0.0914	29.6	.0000	2	unplug
0.0914	29.6	.0000	2	unsightly
0.0914	29.6	.0000	2	unstraps
0.0914	29.6	.0000	2	untended
0.0914	29.6	.0000	2	uppity
0.0914	29.6	.0000	2	Vader's
0.0914	29.6	.0000	2	VanNess
0.0914	29.6	.0000	2	vanderPoel
0.0914	29.6	.0000	2	Vandermere
0.0914	29.6	.0000	2	vents
0.0914	29.6	.0000	2	Veraart
0.0914	29.6	.0000	2	Verses
0.0914	29.6	.0000	2	vi-
0.0914	29.6	.0000	2	Vimy's
0.0914	29.6	.0000	2	Vistas
0.0914	29.6	.0000	2	vive
0.0914	29.6	.0000	2	vives
0.0914	29.6	.0000	2	vixen
0.0914	29.6	.0000	2	Vlak
0.0914	29.6	.0000	2	vocabackularily
0.0914	29.6	.0000	2	Von
0.0914	29.6	.0000	2	vonBaldewein
0.0914	29.6	.0000	2	VonSnitz
0.0914	29.6	.0000	2	Voyages
0.0914	29.6	.0000	2	wah-wah
0.0914	29.6	.0000	2	Wahoo
0.0914	29.6	.0000	2	waiter's
0.0914	29.6	.0000	2	wal
0.0914	29.6	.0000	2	Waldo's
0.0914	29.6	.0000	2	walking-stick
0.0914	29.6	.0000	2	Walloomsac
0.0914	29.6	.0000	2	war-horse
0.0914	29.6	.0000	2	warders
0.0914	29.6	.0000	2	Ware's
0.0914	29.6	.0000	2	washbowl
0.0914	29.6	.0000	2	washout
0.0914	29.6	.0000	2	water-hole
0.0914	29.6	.0000	2	Watusi
0.0914	29.6	.0000	2	wave-top
0.0914	29.6	.0000	2	Welch
0.0914	29.6	.0000	2	well-loved
0.0914	29.6	.0000	2	well-polished
0.0914	29.6	.0000	2	well-suited
0.0914	29.6	.0000	2	Wentworth
0.0914	29.6	.0000	2	Wentworth's
0.0914	29.6	.0000	2	whacks
0.0914	29.6	.0000	2	Whipple's
0.0914	29.6	.0000	2	whiskered
0.0914	29.6	.0000	2	White-Lipped
0.0914	29.6	.0000	2	white-nose
0.0914	29.6	.0000	2	whitest
0.0914	29.6	.0000	2	Whitfield's
0.0914	29.6	.0000	2	Whittaker
0.0914	29.6	.0000	2	Whittier's
0.0914	29.6	.0000	2	Whittington's
0.0914	29.6	.0000	2	who'll
THE PRECEDING WORD TYPE OCCUPIES RANK 42500				
0.0914	29.6	.0000	2	whoo-hoo-hoo
0.0914	29.6	.0000	2	wigglers
0.0914	29.6	.0000	2	wild-looking
0.0914	29.6	.0000	2	Williamson
0.0914	29.6	.0000	2	Willway
0.0914	29.6	.0000	2	Wilting
0.0914	29.6	.0000	2	win'ard
0.0914	29.6	.0000	2	winging
0.0914	29.6	.0000	2	wingmen
0.0914	29.6	.0000	2	winner's
0.0914	29.6	.0000	2	witching
0.0914	29.6	.0000	2	wobble-wobble
0.0914	29.6	.0000	2	woman-of-all-women
0.0914	29.6	.0000	2	Woodchuck
0.0914	29.6	.0000	2	Woodhouse
0.0914	29.6	.0000	2	woven-wire
0.0914	29.6	.0000	2	writin'
0.0914	29.6	.0000	2	wrongdoings
0.0914	29.6	.0000	2	WXN
0.0914	29.6	.0000	2	X0537
0.0914	29.6	.0000	2	Yancy's
0.0914	29.6	.0000	2	yawk
0.0914	29.6	.0000	2	yawls
0.0914	29.6	.0000	2	Yehudi's
0.0914	29.6	.0000	2	Yippee
0.0914	29.6	.0000	2	yodel
0.0914	29.6	.0000	2	YOOOOOOOOOOOOO
0.0914	29.6	.0000	2	yugit
0.0914	29.6	.0000	2	Z's
0.0914	29.6	.0000	2	Zachiel
0.0914	29.6	.0000	2	zipp
0.0914	29.6	.0000	2	zorrino
0.0914	29.6	.0000	2	Zululand
0.0914	29.6	.0000	2	Zurn
0.0914	29.6	.0000	2	Zworykin
0.0914	29.6	.0000	2	zzz-zzz-zzz
0.0914	29.6	.0000	2	125th
0.0914	29.6	.0000	2	1470
0.0914	29.6	.0000	2	1500-pound
0.0914	29.6	.0000	2	200-meter
0.0914	29.6	.0000	2	2050
0.0914	29.6	.0000	2	24K
0.0914	29.6	.0000	2	4-1-5
0.0914	29.6	.0000	2	56A
0.0913	29.6	.1274	3	catchup
0.0913	29.6	.1274	3	doneness
0.0913	29.6	.1274	3	perforation
0.0913	29.6	.1274	3	relishes
0.0913	29.6	.1274	3	Worcestershire
0.0907	29.6	.0454	7	ball-peen
0.0905	29.6	.0145	9	capacitors
0.0899	29.5	.0935	4	jointing
0.0899	29.5	.0935	4	metalwork
0.0899	29.5	.0935	4	tooling
0.0898	29.5	.0000	6	ABD
0.0898	29.5	.0000	6	a2
0.0898	29.5	.0000	6	bc
0.0898	29.5	.0000	6	CA
0.0898	29.5	.0000	6	CAD
0.0898	29.5	.0000	6	collinear
0.0898	29.5	.0000	6	cubit
0.0898	29.5	.0000	6	Examples
0.0898	29.5	.0000	6	Koenigsberg
0.0898	29.5	.0000	6	MNO
0.0898	29.5	.0000	6	non-negative
0.0898	29.5	.0000	6	passenger-miles
0.0898	29.5	.0000	6	PB
0.0898	29.5	.0000	6	popsicles
0.0898	29.5	.0000	6	rhombi
0.0898	29.5	.0000	6	units'
0.0898	29.5	.0000	6	Wiener
0.0898	29.5	.0000	6	XI
0.0898	29.5	.0000	6	x7
0.0898	29.5	.0000	6	zop
0.0898	29.5	.0000	6	1b
0.0898	29.5	.0000	6	10's
0.0898	29.5	.0000	6	2-place
0.0898	29.5	.0000	6	2ab
0.0898	29.5	.0000	6	21/28
0.0898	29.5	.0000	6	22/7
0.0898	29.5	.0000	6	3-step
0.0898	29.5	.0000	6	324
0.0898	29.5	.0000	6	344
0.0898	29.5	.0000	6	4/15
0.0898	29.5	.0000	6	4/2
0.0898	29.5	.0000	6	4/9
0.0898	29.5	.0000	6	488
0.0898	29.5	.0000	6	5-step
0.0898	29.5	.0000	6	5y
0.0898	29.5	.0000	6	7/3
0.0898	29.5	.0000	6	8-cent
0.0898	29.5	.0000	6	8/15
0.0894	29.5	.0368	9	collages
0.0893	29.5	.0000	11	four-syllable
0.0889	29.5	.0000	11	chromatic
0.0889	29.5	.0000	11	Dvorak
0.0889	29.5	.0000	11	Greensleeves
0.0889	29.5	.0000	11	loo
0.0889	29.5	.0000	11	operettas
0.0889	29.5	.0000	11	Prelude
THE PRECEDING WORD TYPE OCCUPIES RANK 42600				
0.0889	29.5	.0694	5	spline
0.0889	29.5	.0000	11	tonality
0.0889	29.5	.0000	11	twelve-tone
0.0889	29.5	.0694	5	025
0.0878	29.4	.1304	3	Pollock
0.0875	29.4	.0000	8	appositives
0.0875	29.4	.0000	8	Besso
0.0875	29.4	.0000	8	Pottapetal
0.0875	29.4	.0000	8	VP
0.0875	29.4	.0000	8	ZIP
0.0871	29.4	.0308	5	nylons
0.0869	29.4	.0000	6	Austerfield
0.0869	29.4	.0000	6	Ban
0.0869	29.4	.0000	6	Berkey
0.0869	29.4	.0000	6	Bethel
0.0869	29.4	.0000	6	cabinetmaking
0.0869	29.4	.0000	6	Elkins
0.0869	29.4	.0000	6	Etty
0.0869	29.4	.0000	6	Isiolo
0.0869	29.4	.0000	6	Listener
0.0869	29.4	.0000	6	Nebeker
0.0869	29.4	.0000	6	Ottomans
0.0869	29.4	.0000	6	P'an
0.0869	29.4	.0000	6	palefaces
0.0869	29.4	.0000	6	Panhard
0.0869	29.4	.0000	6	pickety
0.0869	29.4	.0000	6	Rendova
0.0869	29.4	.0000	6	Rustum
0.0869	29.4	.0000	6	Rustum's
0.0869	29.4	.0000	6	Sendall

U	SFI	D	F	Word Type
0.0869	29.4	.0000	6	Shipman
0.0869	29.4	.0000	6	Soto
0.0869	29.4	.0000	6	Stefansson
0.0869	29.4	.0000	6	tick-birds
0.0869	29.4	.0000	6	Titanic's
0.0869	29.4	.0000	6	Tuck
0.0869	29.4	.0000	6	Writers'
0.0869	29.4	.0000	6	Yanks
0.0868	29.4	.0818	4	brightens
0.0867	29.4	.1926	2	attributable
0.0867	29.4	.1926	2	embarrasses
0.0867	29.4	.1926	2	Families
0.0867	29.4	.1926	2	fostering
0.0867	29.4	.1926	2	Meet
0.0867	29.4	.1926	2	overemphasis
0.0867	29.4	.1926	2	prompts
0.0867	29.4	.1926	2	raffia
0.0867	29.4	.1926	2	reinforcing
0.0867	29.4	.1926	2	retting
0.0867	29.4	.1926	2	shampoos
0.0867	29.4	.1926	2	uncluttered
0.0867	29.4	.1926	2	439
0.0867	29.4	.1926	2	461
0.0867	29.4	.1926	2	493
0.0862	29.4	.1907	2	bridesmaid
0.0862	29.4	.1148	3	confectioners'
0.0862	29.4	.1148	3	giant-sized
0.0862	29.4	.1148	3	lumping
0.0862	29.4	.1907	2	ridiculously
0.0862	29.4	.1907	2	shuttled
0.0862	29.4	.1907	2	singleness
0.0862	29.4	.1907	2	unsalted
0.0861	29.4	.0318	8	oscillator
0.0859	29.3	.0000	8	ADMIRER
0.0859	29.3	.0000	8	ALCHEMIST
0.0859	29.3	.0000	8	Barsad
0.0859	29.3	.0000	8	Baumer
0.0859	29.3	.0000	8	bliggens
0.0859	29.3	.0000	8	GALL
0.0859	29.3	.0000	8	GEORGE
0.0859	29.3	.0000	8	HEIDEGGER
0.0859	29.3	.0000	8	Juana's
0.0859	29.3	.0000	8	PHYSICIAN
0.0859	29.3	.0000	8	Telemachos
0.0859	29.3	.0000	8	Tybalt
0.0858	29.3	.1892	2	accumulates
0.0858	29.3	.0867	4	appendage
0.0858	29.3	.1892	2	centering
0.0858	29.3	.1892	2	fries
0.0858	29.3	.1892	2	hows
0.0858	29.3	.1892	2	overblouse
0.0858	29.3	.1892	2	SC
0.0858	29.3	.1892	2	suitably
0.0858	29.3	.1892	2	whens
0.0858	29.3	.1892	2	zig-zagging
0.0853	29.3	.1125	3	bouillon
0.0853	29.3	.1125	3	55%
0.0851	29.3	.0000	7	Alcindor
0.0851	29.3	.0000	7	Alejandra
0.0851	29.3	.0000	7	bari
0.0851	29.3	.0000	7	Brocklin
0.0851	29.3	.0000	7	Cashman
0.0851	29.3	.0000	7	Chips
0.0851	29.3	.0000	7	coho
0.0851	29.3	.0000	7	commitment
0.0851	29.3	.0000	7	Czechoslovak
0.0851	29.3	.0000	7	Delgado
0.0851	29.3	.0000	7	FID
0.0851	29.3	.0000	7	Haw
0.0851	29.3	.0000	7	Keyes
THE PRECEDING WORD TYPE OCCUPIES RANK 42700				
0.0851	29.3	.0000	7	Laysan
0.0851	29.3	.0000	7	Mays
0.0851	29.3	.0000	7	militants
0.0851	29.3	.0000	7	Mudhen
0.0851	29.3	.0000	7	narwhal
0.0851	29.3	.0000	7	Noland
0.0851	29.3	.0000	7	paisano
0.0851	29.3	.0000	7	pembo
0.0851	29.3	.0000	7	peri
0.0851	29.3	.0000	7	Piddy
0.0851	29.3	.0000	7	rembo-chari
0.0851	29.3	.0000	7	ruchi-pip
0.0851	29.3	.0000	7	Shultz
0.0851	29.3	.0000	7	SNCC
0.0851	29.3	.0000	7	snowmobile
0.0851	29.3	.0000	7	Tarkenton
0.0851	29.3	.0000	7	tembo-no
0.0851	29.3	.0000	7	Tikki
0.0851	29.3	.0000	7	tikki
0.0851	29.3	.0000	7	vandalism
0.0851	29.3	.0000	7	Zimmer
0.0847	29.3	.1937	2	amplification
0.0847	29.3	.1937	2	C-C
0.0847	29.3	.1937	2	diamond-tipped
0.0847	29.3	.1937	2	Lining
0.0847	29.3	.1205	3	overheat
0.0847	29.3	.1205	3	rubberlike
0.0847	29.3	.1205	3	2d
0.0846	29.3	.0847	4	grooving
0.0846	29.3	.1934	2	metal-working
0.0846	29.3	.1934	2	plainness
0.0846	29.3	.0847	4	transformers
0.0846	29.3	.1934	2	2-10
0.0845	29.3	.1839	2	chambray
0.0845	29.3	.1839	2	conversing
0.0845	29.3	.1839	2	fleshed
0.0845	29.3	.1839	2	ice-cube
0.0845	29.3	.1839	2	Joyce's
0.0845	29.3	.1839	2	lapels
0.0845	29.3	.1839	2	millinery
0.0845	29.3	.1839	2	paperweight
0.0845	29.3	.1839	2	pique
0.0845	29.3	.1839	2	proverbial
0.0845	29.3	.1839	2	rinds
0.0845	29.3	.1839	2	shrunken
0.0845	29.3	.1839	2	Sour
0.0845	29.3	.1839	2	spaciousness
0.0845	29.3	.1839	2	vivacity
0.0845	29.3	.1839	2	448
0.0838	29.2	.1812	2	adoring
0.0838	29.2	.1812	2	appetizer
0.0838	29.2	.1812	2	Bel
0.0838	29.2	.1812	2	Choose
0.0838	29.2	.1812	2	crocheted
0.0838	29.2	.1812	2	discarding
0.0838	29.2	.1812	2	dual-purpose
0.0838	29.2	.1812	2	EAT
0.0838	29.2	.1812	2	escarole
0.0838	29.2	.1812	2	exhilaration
0.0838	29.2	.1812	2	gift-wrapping
0.0838	29.2	.1812	2	homey
0.0838	29.2	.1812	2	hop-scotch
0.0838	29.2	.1812	2	itemize
0.0838	29.2	.1812	2	Needs
0.0838	29.2	.1812	2	petite
0.0838	29.2	.1812	2	Pineapple
0.0838	29.2	.1812	2	pinked
0.0838	29.2	.1812	2	polyurethane
0.0838	29.2	.1812	2	preseason
0.0838	29.2	.1812	2	puree
0.0838	29.2	.1812	2	red-orange
0.0838	29.2	.1812	2	rework
0.0838	29.2	.1812	2	sacrificing
0.0838	29.2	.1812	2	sharpens
0.0838	29.2	.1812	2	standard-size
0.0838	29.2	.1812	2	summaries
0.0838	29.2	.1812	2	tenderized
0.0838	29.2	.1812	2	unappetizing
0.0838	29.2	.1812	2	undiluted
0.0838	29.2	.1812	2	unfasten
0.0838	29.2	.1812	2	vicuna
0.0838	29.2	.1812	2	Wardrobe
0.0838	29.2	.1812	2	358
0.0838	29.2	.1812	2	431
0.0837	29.2	.0000	8	Arminius
0.0837	29.2	.0000	8	Cebu
0.0837	29.2	.0000	8	FMCS
0.0837	29.2	.0718	4	knife-edge
0.0837	29.2	.0000	8	Mar
0.0837	29.2	.0000	8	Marat
0.0837	29.2	.0000	8	milligrams
0.0837	29.2	.0000	8	Nantes
0.0837	29.2	.0000	8	Neanderthalers
0.0837	29.2	.0000	8	Picunche
0.0837	29.2	.0000	8	Saladin
0.0837	29.2	.0718	4	410
0.0833	29.2	.0613	5	countersunk
0.0833	29.2	.1174	3	edger
0.0833	29.2	.0613	5	handwheel
0.0833	29.2	.1174	3	serial
THE PRECEDING WORD TYPE OCCUPIES RANK 42800				
0.0833	29.2	.1174	3	striker
0.0833	29.2	.0613	5	2-2
0.0825	29.2	.0847	4	coherent
0.0825	29.2	.0847	4	Floyd
0.0821	29.1	.0000	7	'e
0.0821	29.1	.0000	7	Albe
0.0821	29.1	.0000	7	Ay
0.0821	29.1	.0000	7	Brill
0.0821	29.1	.0000	7	Celyndia
0.0821	29.1	.0000	7	Clavel
0.0821	29.1	.0000	7	Crampfurl
0.0821	29.1	.0000	7	Darnell
0.0821	29.1	.0000	7	Edwina
0.0821	29.1	.0000	7	Eldest
0.0821	29.1	.0000	7	Foran
0.0821	29.1	.0000	7	Genevieve
0.0821	29.1	.0000	7	Heyward
0.0821	29.1	.0000	7	Jella
0.0821	29.1	.0000	7	Jeth
0.0821	29.1	.0000	7	John-go-in-the-Wynd
0.0821	29.1	.0000	7	Leah
0.0821	29.1	.0000	7	Nettie
0.0821	29.1	.0000	7	Pew
0.0821	29.1	.0000	7	Phantom's
0.0821	29.1	.0000	7	PLACE
0.0821	29.1	.0000	7	stallion's
0.0821	29.1	.0000	7	Taffy
0.0821	29.1	.0000	7	Terwilliger
0.0821	29.1	.0000	7	Trinket's
0.0821	29.1	.0000	7	Twickerham
0.0821	29.1	.0000	7	Wintapi
0.0821	29.1	.0000	7	wolverine
0.0819	29.1	.0836	4	declarative
0.0819	29.1	.0836	4	demonstrative
0.0817	29.1	.1187	3	Glory
0.0812	29.1	.0000	10	/a/**
0.0812	29.1	.0000	10	ic
0.0812	29.1	.0000	10	sl
0.0808	29.1	.0000	10	accidentals
0.0808	29.1	.1840	2	Algonquin
0.0808	29.1	.0000	10	basses
0.0808	29.1	.1840	2	beautified
0.0808	29.1	.1843	2	chiming
0.0808	29.1	.1840	2	cursive
0.0808	29.1	.0000	10	Erl-King
0.0808	29.1	.0000	10	Escamillo
0.0808	29.1	.1843	2	feedback
0.0808	29.1	.0000	10	flamenco
0.0808	29.1	.1843	2	halyards
0.0808	29.1	.1843	2	heeled
0.0808	29.1	.1840	2	lumberman
0.0808	29.1	.0000	10	Marching
0.0808	29.1	.1843	2	October's
0.0808	29.1	.0000	10	Overture
0.0808	29.1	.1843	2	restatements
0.0808	29.1	.1843	2	Thompson's
0.0808	29.1	.1843	2	train's
0.0808	29.1	.1843	2	unmusical
0.0806	29.1	.0525	6	Saskia
0.0805	29.1	.1674	2	buttoning
0.0805	29.1	.1674	2	check-up
0.0805	29.1	.1674	2	chronically
0.0805	29.1	.1674	2	Coat
0.0805	29.1	.1674	2	friendless
0.0805	29.1	.1674	2	hard-cooked
0.0805	29.1	.1674	2	hooved
0.0805	29.1	.1674	2	interlaced
0.0805	29.1	.1674	2	Jacket
0.0805	29.1	.1674	2	patty
0.0805	29.1	.1674	2	perforations
0.0805	29.1	.1674	2	predominates
0.0805	29.1	.1674	2	prom
0.0805	29.1	.1674	2	redraw
0.0805	29.1	.1674	2	remodeled
0.0805	29.1	.1674	2	Senegal
0.0805	29.1	.1674	2	styled
0.0805	29.1	.1674	2	thirty-day
0.0805	29.1	.1674	2	tweezers
0.0803	29.0	.0524	3	diaper
0.0803	29.0	.0524	3	dressy
0.0803	29.0	.0524	3	firsts
0.0803	29.0	.0524	3	homelike
0.0803	29.0	.0524	3	noodles
0.0803	29.0	.0524	3	Pima
0.0803	29.0	.0524	3	rancid
0.0802	29.0	.1101	3	coarseness
0.0802	29.0	.1101	3	movable-type
0.0802	29.0	.1101	3	resistor
0.0802	29.0	.1101	3	Rockwell
0.0802	29.0	.1101	3	tempering
0.0802	29.0	.1101	3	tolerances
0.0802	29.0	.1101	3	welder
0.0802	29.0	.1101	3	15-19
0.0800	29.0	.1648	2	cupcake
0.0800	29.0	.1648	2	five-eighths
0.0800	29.0	.1648	2	Measurement
0.0800	29.0	.1648	2	shampoo
0.0800	29.0	.1648	2	well-selected
0.0800	29.0	.1648	2	why's
0.0800	29.0	.1648	2	1-cup
THE PRECEDING WORD TYPE OCCUPIES RANK 42900				
0.0800	29.0	.1648	2	13%
0.0800	29.0	.1648	2	87%
0.0796	29.0	.0412	6	cross-section
0.0796	29.0	.0953	3	ginning
0.0796	29.0	.0412	6	radio-frequency
0.0796	29.0	.0953	3	worsteds
0.0794	29.0	.0751	4	countersink
0.0794	29.0	.0945	3	invisibly
0.0794	29.0	.0945	3	medium-weight
0.0794	29.0	.0254	5	ohms
0.0794	29.0	.0945	3	samplers
0.0794	29.0	.0751	4	slotted
0.0794	29.0	.0945	3	trichina
0.0792	29.0	.1119	3	casualty
0.0792	29.0	.1119	3	Kahan
0.0792	29.0	.1119	3	noisome
0.0792	29.0	.1168	3	stylized
0.0792	29.0	.1119	3	Tristram
0.0790	29.0	.1738	2	alternating-current
0.0790	29.0	.1738	2	B5
0.0790	29.0	.1738	2	cross-sectional
0.0790	29.0	.1738	2	dielectrics
0.0790	29.0	.1738	2	electric-powered
0.0790	29.0	.1738	2	flammable
0.0790	29.0	.1738	2	half-timbered
0.0790	29.0	.1738	2	lubricant
0.0790	29.0	.1738	2	luminescent
0.0790	29.0	.1738	2	oppositely
0.0790	29.0	.1738	2	plated
0.0790	29.0	.1738	2	Provincial
0.0790	29.0	.1738	2	radiated
0.0790	29.0	.1738	2	typesetting
0.0790	29.0	.1738	2	12-inch
0.0790	29.0	.1738	2	42-line
0.0790	29.0	.1738	2	6-7
0.0790	29.0	.1738	2	814
0.0790	29.0	.1738	2	916
0.0789	29.0	.0000	4	accelerators
0.0789	29.0	.0000	4	advancements
0.0789	29.0	.0000	4	amplitudes
0.0789	29.0	.0000	4	anode
0.0789	29.0	.0000	4	Antares
0.0789	29.0	.0000	4	anus
0.0789	29.0	.0000	4	auricles
0.0789	29.0	.0000	4	awakenings
0.0789	29.0	.0000	4	Baade
0.0789	29.0	.0000	4	Baneberry
0.0789	29.0	.0000	4	barnacle
0.0789	29.0	.0000	4	beakers
0.0789	29.0	.0000	4	Berzelius
0.0789	29.0	.0000	4	black-box
0.0789	29.0	.0000	4	bright-line
0.0789	29.0	.0000	4	Capella
0.0789	29.0	.0000	4	Carlotta
0.0789	29.0	.0000	4	Cephei
0.0789	29.0	.0000	4	chitin
0.0789	29.0	.0000	4	combative
0.0789	29.0	.0000	4	commensalism
0.0789	29.0	.0000	4	conformist
0.0789	29.0	.0000	4	constructional
0.0789	29.0	.0000	4	copters
0.0789	29.0	.0000	4	cotidal
0.0789	29.0	.0000	4	cottonmouths
0.0789	29.0	.0000	4	cps
0.0789	29.0	.0000	4	cryogenics
0.0789	29.0	.0000	4	cumulonimbus
0.0789	29.0	.0000	4	cuspids
0.0789	29.0	.0000	4	diatom
0.0789	29.0	.0000	4	erode
0.0789	29.0	.0000	4	Eros
0.0789	29.0	.0000	4	fault-block
0.0789	29.0	.0000	4	faulting
0.0789	29.0	.0000	4	flagellates
0.0789	29.0	.0000	4	food-making
0.0789	29.0	.0000	4	geosyncline
0.0789	29.0	.0000	4	geotropism
0.0789	29.0	.0000	4	germination
0.0789	29.0	.0000	4	Gravitation
0.0789	29.0	.0000	4	Hero's
0.0789	29.0	.0000	4	Humphry
0.0789	29.0	.0000	4	hybrids
0.0789	29.0	.0000	4	hydrosphere
0.0789	29.0	.0000	4	hypersthene
0.0789	29.0	.0000	4	immunological
0.0789	29.0	.0000	4	isobars
0.0789	29.0	.0000	4	jug-o-rum
0.0789	29.0	.0000	4	Klamath
0.0789	29.0	.0000	4	lactose
0.0789	29.0	.0000	4	lemmings
0.0789	29.0	.0000	4	Linnaeus
0.0789	29.0	.0000	4	lit-up
0.0789	29.0	.0000	4	lunologist
0.0789	29.0	.0000	4	mineralogy
0.0789	29.0	.0000	4	monotremes
0.0789	29.0	.0000	4	mutated
0.0789	29.0	.0000	4	nauplius
0.0789	29.0	.0000	4	nonporous
0.0789	29.0	.0000	4	one-seeded
0.0789	29.0	.0000	4	oscillation
0.0789	29.0	.0000	4	Palomar's
THE PRECEDING WORD TYPE OCCUPIES RANK 43000				
0.0789	29.0	.0000	4	parallax
0.0789	29.0	.0000	4	parasite-chain
0.0789	29.0	.0000	4	periwinkles
0.0789	29.0	.0000	4	permanganate
0.0789	29.0	.0000	4	progesterone
0.0789	29.0	.0000	4	puffball
0.0789	29.0	.0000	4	radioisotopes
0.0789	29.0	.0000	4	radiometer
0.0789	29.0	.0000	4	ready-mount
0.0789	29.0	.0000	4	Roll
0.0789	29.0	.0000	4	roundworm
0.0789	29.0	.0000	4	RR
0.0789	29.0	.0000	4	rusts
0.0789	29.0	.0000	4	sedimentation
0.0789	29.0	.0000	4	semidiurnal
0.0789	29.0	.0000	4	shales
0.0789	29.0	.0000	4	skyrocket
0.0789	29.0	.0000	4	slaked
0.0789	29.0	.0000	4	soapless
0.0789	29.0	.0000	4	solute
0.0789	29.0	.0000	4	Spallanzani
0.0789	29.0	.0000	4	Sulzer
0.0789	29.0	.0000	4	swimmerets
0.0789	29.0	.0000	4	tetrachloride
0.0789	29.0	.0000	4	uraninite
0.0789	29.0	.0000	4	uranium-238
0.0789	29.0	.0000	4	urinary
0.0789	29.0	.0000	4	varves
0.0789	29.0	.0000	4	ventricle
0.0789	29.0	.0000	4	Vesalius
0.0789	29.0	.0000	4	Waksman
0.0789	29.0	.0000	4	wavelike
0.0789	29.0	.0000	4	whirlybird
0.0789	29.0	.0000	4	wood-eating
0.0786	29.0	.0778	4	restate
0.0785	28.9	.1718	2	appreciable
0.0785	28.9	.1718	2	aspire
0.0785	28.9	.1718	2	cornices
0.0785	28.9	.1101	3	flirt
0.0785	28.9	.1101	3	Modjeska
0.0784	28.9	.0857	2	adolescents
0.0784	28.9	.0857	2	bulkier
0.0784	28.9	.0857	2	chaotic
0.0784	28.9	.0857	2	cookbooks
0.0784	28.9	.0857	2	day-old
0.0784	28.9	.0857	2	double-knit
0.0784	28.9	.0857	2	Everyone
0.0784	28.9	.0857	2	fun-loving
0.0784	28.9	.0857	2	gloat
0.0784	28.9	.0192	6	Huck's
0.0784	28.9	.0857	2	ices
0.0784	28.9	.0857	2	Important
0.0784	28.9	.0857	2	misbehaves
0.0784	28.9	.0857	2	NEVER
0.0784	28.9	.0857	2	nooks
0.0784	28.9	.0857	2	outstandingly
0.0784	28.9	.0857	2	promptness
0.0784	28.9	.0857	2	punctuality
0.0784	28.9	.0857	2	red-purple
0.0784	28.9	.0857	2	Reuben
0.0784	28.9	.0857	2	sofas
0.0784	28.9	.0857	2	thoughtlessly
0.0784	28.9	.0857	2	well-stocked
0.0781	28.9	.1703	2	crudely
0.0781	28.9	.1703	2	garbage-disposal
0.0781	28.9	.1703	2	NF
0.0781	28.9	.1703	2	nos
0.0781	28.9	.1703	2	originals
0.0781	28.9	.1703	2	Strassburg
0.0781	28.9	.1703	2	two-lane
0.0781	28.9	.1703	2	1448
0.0779	28.9	.1088	3	expository
0.0778	28.9	.0000	4	Adelaide
0.0778	28.9	.0000	4	Alien
0.0778	28.9	.0000	4	Aryans
0.0778	28.9	.0000	4	atole
0.0778	28.9	.0000	4	Balfour
0.0778	28.9	.0000	4	Blaze's
0.0778	28.9	.0000	4	Bogana
0.0778	28.9	.0000	4	Bolivar's
0.0778	28.9	.0000	4	broker
0.0778	28.9	.0000	4	Cabildo
0.0778	28.9	.0000	4	Cantigny
0.0778	28.9	.0000	4	Capetown
0.0778	28.9	.0000	4	Caucasian
0.0778	28.9	.0000	4	causeways
0.0778	28.9	.0000	4	Cobh
0.0778	28.9	.0000	4	colony's
0.0778	28.9	.0000	4	Commodore
0.0778	28.9	.0000	4	Confucianism
0.0778	28.9	.0000	4	Crespi
0.0778	28.9	.0000	4	Danubian
0.0778	28.9	.0000	4	dependencies
0.0778	28.9	.0000	4	dinars

U	SFI	D	F	Word Type
0.0778	28.9	.0000	4	durbar
0.0778	28.9	.0000	4	faller
0.0778	28.9	.0000	4	fellahin
0.0778	28.9	.0000	4	Foch
0.0778	28.9	.0000	4	forest-covered
0.0778	28.9	.0000	4	Fourteenth

THE PRECEDING WORD TYPE OCCUPIES RANK 43100

U	SFI	D	F	Word Type
0.0778	28.9	.0000	4	Fram
0.0778	28.9	.0000	4	Gertrudis
0.0778	28.9	.0000	4	globe-map
0.0778	28.9	.0000	4	Grimsby
0.0778	28.9	.0000	4	Grisdale
0.0778	28.9	.0000	4	Gromyko
0.0778	28.9	.0000	4	Hanno
0.0778	28.9	.0000	4	Howe's
0.0778	28.9	.0000	4	humid-subtropical
0.0778	28.9	.0000	4	impost
0.0778	28.9	.0000	4	irrigating
0.0778	28.9	.0000	4	Ishi's
0.0778	28.9	.0000	4	Izmir
0.0778	28.9	.0000	4	kaoliang
0.0778	28.9	.0000	4	Krogers
0.0778	28.9	.0000	4	landform
0.0778	28.9	.0000	4	landmasses
0.0778	28.9	.0000	4	Liberia
0.0778	28.9	.0000	4	Magyars
0.0778	28.9	.0000	4	Majapa
0.0778	28.9	.0000	4	Managua
0.0778	28.9	.0000	4	mediterranean
0.0778	28.9	.0000	4	Meseta
0.0778	28.9	.0000	4	Mid-East
0.0778	28.9	.0000	4	MillCreekValley
0.0778	28.9	.0000	4	moneyed
0.0778	28.9	.0000	4	monsoons
0.0778	28.9	.0000	4	Monte's
0.0778	28.9	.0000	4	Nast
0.0778	28.9	.0000	4	nationals
0.0778	28.9	.0000	4	naturalization
0.0778	28.9	.0000	4	Naturalization
0.0778	28.9	.0000	4	Netherland
0.0778	28.9	.0000	4	Noriko
0.0778	28.9	.0000	4	Olu's
0.0778	28.9	.0000	4	Pershing
0.0778	28.9	.0000	4	Petrified
0.0778	28.9	.0000	4	pro-slavery
0.0778	28.9	.0000	4	Prussia's
0.0778	28.9	.0000	4	radiotelephone
0.0778	28.9	.0000	4	Rama
0.0778	28.9	.0000	4	Redhorse
0.0778	28.9	.0000	4	Saar
0.0778	28.9	.0000	4	Sedition
0.0778	28.9	.0000	4	Shiro
0.0778	28.9	.0000	4	Slovakia
0.0778	28.9	.0000	4	Sommers
0.0778	28.9	.0000	4	Teotihuacan
0.0778	28.9	.0000	4	Teton
0.0778	28.9	.0000	4	Truman's
0.0778	28.9	.0000	4	tsetse
0.0778	28.9	.0000	4	Ural
0.0778	28.9	.0000	4	viceroyalties
0.0778	28.9	.0000	4	Warpath
0.0778	28.9	.0000	4	well-educated
0.0778	28.9	.0000	4	wet-and-dry
0.0778	28.9	.0000	4	Winkleville
0.0778	28.9	.0000	4	Wowunupo
0.0778	28.9	.0000	4	Yaroslav
0.0778	28.9	.0000	4	Zuider
0.0778	28.9	.0000	4	316
0.0778	28.9	.0000	4	364-365
0.0778	28.9	.0000	4	4-5
0.0772	28.9	.0319	3	overcomes
0.0767	28.8	.1649	2	Stove
0.0767	28.8	.1649	2	TOM
0.0766	28.8	.0000	7	connectives
0.0766	28.8	.0000	7	diagramed
0.0766	28.8	.0000	7	Donahue's
0.0766	28.8	.0000	7	Eliko
0.0766	28.8	.0000	7	Hod
0.0766	28.8	.0000	7	N-V
0.0766	28.8	.0000	7	nominals
0.0766	28.8	.0000	7	sonnet
0.0766	28.8	.0000	7	subordinator
0.0766	28.8	.0000	7	2796
0.0763	28.8	.0488	5	Chap
0.0763	28.8	.0488	5	ductile
0.0763	28.8	.0488	5	19-1
0.0761	28.8	.1442	2	convalescent
0.0761	28.8	.1442	2	craving
0.0761	28.8	.1442	2	Depth
0.0761	28.8	.1442	2	do's
0.0761	28.8	.1442	2	Gorgonzola
0.0761	28.8	.1442	2	low-cost
0.0761	28.8	.1442	2	out-of-bounds
0.0761	28.8	.1442	2	Parmesan
0.0761	28.8	.1442	2	prescribe
0.0761	28.8	.1442	2	reshape
0.0761	28.8	.1442	2	sharkskin
0.0761	28.8	.1442	2	tannic
0.0761	28.8	.1442	2	214-215
0.0761	28.8	.1442	2	274
0.0761	28.8	.1442	2	369
0.0760	28.8	.1620	2	bottoming
0.0760	28.8	.1620	2	buffers
0.0760	28.8	.1620	2	chucked
0.0760	28.8	.1620	2	cross-member
0.0760	28.8	.1620	2	dampened
0.0760	28.8	.1620	2	jettisoned

THE PRECEDING WORD TYPE OCCUPIES RANK 43200

U	SFI	D	F	Word Type
0.0760	28.8	.1620	2	overload
0.0760	28.8	.1620	2	plugging
0.0760	28.8	.1620	2	rebounds
0.0760	28.8	.1620	2	sinkers
0.0760	28.8	.1620	2	stator
0.0760	28.8	.1620	2	tred
0.0760	28.8	.1620	2	variable-speed
0.0760	28.8	.1620	2	welds
0.0760	28.8	.1620	2	15-20
0.0760	28.8	.1620	2	6-4
0.0760	28.8	.1620	2	8-10
0.0759	28.8	.1432	2	Agriculture's
0.0759	28.8	.1432	2	comers
0.0759	28.8	.1432	2	crushes
0.0759	28.8	.1432	2	dangles
0.0759	28.8	.1432	2	disease-producing
0.0759	28.8	.1432	2	fish-liver
0.0759	28.8	.1432	2	Foods
0.0759	28.8	.1432	2	great-grandparents
0.0759	28.8	.1432	2	GROW
0.0759	28.8	.1432	2	hangnails
0.0759	28.8	.1432	2	irritability
0.0759	28.8	.1432	2	OF
0.0759	28.8	.1432	2	palatable
0.0759	28.8	.1432	2	rayons
0.0759	28.8	.1432	2	rewoven
0.0759	28.8	.1042	3	sentinel
0.0759	28.8	.1432	2	wind-up
0.0759	28.8	.1432	2	10-12
0.0759	28.8	.1432	2	15-minute
0.0759	28.8	.1432	2	21-1
0.0757	28.8	.0986	3	annular
0.0757	28.8	.0986	3	patternmaker
0.0757	28.8	.0986	3	woodworkers
0.0751	28.8	.0000	7	Autolycos
0.0751	28.8	.0000	7	Blackbirds
0.0751	28.8	.0000	7	BUSMAN
0.0751	28.8	.1641	2	Cecilia
0.0751	28.8	.0000	7	Chiefmother
0.0751	28.8	.0000	7	DeParma
0.0751	28.8	.1641	2	declines
0.0751	28.8	.0000	7	Ebony
0.0751	28.8	.0000	7	HALLEMEIER
0.0751	28.8	.1641	2	invigorating
0.0751	28.8	.0000	7	Jase
0.0751	28.8	.0000	7	Jinglebob
0.0751	28.8	.0000	7	JOHNNY'S
0.0751	28.8	.0000	7	Marget
0.0751	28.8	.0000	7	MAVERICK
0.0751	28.8	.0000	7	Moreover
0.0751	28.8	.0000	7	PAPA
0.0751	28.8	.1641	2	pathetically
0.0751	28.8	.1641	2	resilient
0.0751	28.8	.1641	2	Spear
0.0751	28.8	.0000	7	Spike
0.0751	28.8	.1641	2	subscriptions
0.0751	28.8	.1641	2	Travelers
0.0751	28.8	.1641	2	undermining
0.0751	28.8	.1641	2	unopened
0.0751	28.8	.0000	7	Woodcutter
0.0751	28.8	.0000	7	yella
0.0750	28.7	.0965	3	ABCDE
0.0750	28.7	.1019	3	Emilio
0.0750	28.7	.1019	3	juveniles
0.0750	28.7	.0965	3	reset
0.0750	28.7	.0965	3	5/16
0.0750	28.7	.0965	3	656
0.0750	28.7	.0965	3	978
0.0749	28.7	.1696	2	Delacroix's
0.0749	28.7	.1696	2	Dukas
0.0749	28.7	.1696	2	Ferde
0.0749	28.7	.1696	2	Impressionist
0.0749	28.7	.1696	2	incorporating
0.0749	28.7	.1696	2	Romanticists
0.0749	28.7	.1696	2	single-line
0.0749	28.7	.1696	2	Sorcerer's
0.0749	28.7	.1696	2	sways
0.0749	28.7	.1696	2	vanGogh
0.0748	28.7	.0000	5	-6
0.0748	28.7	.0000	5	/3
0.0748	28.7	.0000	5	/8
0.0748	28.7	.0000	5	's**
0.0748	28.7	.0000	5	ADC
0.0748	28.7	.0000	5	AOC
0.0748	28.7	.0000	5	arrays
0.0748	28.7	.1693	2	artists'
0.0748	28.7	.0000	5	assessed
0.0748	28.7	.0000	5	Associative
0.0748	28.7	.0000	5	AY
0.0748	28.7	.0000	5	base-five
0.0748	28.7	.0000	5	BOD
0.0748	28.7	.0000	5	broken-line
0.0748	28.7	.0000	5	bx
0.0748	28.7	.0000	5	Commutative
0.0748	28.7	.1693	2	complimentary
0.0748	28.7	.0000	5	congruences
0.0748	28.7	.0000	5	congruency
0.0748	28.7	.0000	5	degree-measure
0.0748	28.7	.0000	5	difference-sum
0.0748	28.7	.0000	5	ED

THE PRECEDING WORD TYPE OCCUPIES RANK 43300

U	SFI	D	F	Word Type
0.0748	28.7	.0000	5	EP
0.0748	28.7	.1693	2	Giotto
0.0748	28.7	.0000	5	graphing
0.0748	28.7	.0000	5	half-plane
0.0748	28.7	.0000	5	half-planes
0.0748	28.7	.0000	5	IJ
0.0748	28.7	.0000	5	JK
0.0748	28.7	.0000	5	Kristy
0.0748	28.7	.0000	5	Left-Distributive
0.0748	28.7	.0000	5	logarithm
0.0748	28.7	.0000	5	markup
0.0748	28.7	.0000	5	Mathematics
0.0748	28.7	.0000	5	MNOP
0.0748	28.7	.0000	5	Monica
0.0748	28.7	.0000	5	n-2
0.0748	28.7	.0000	5	obtuse
0.0748	28.7	.0000	5	Paula
0.0748	28.7	.0000	5	push-up
0.0748	28.7	.0000	5	queen-king
0.0748	28.7	.0000	5	rhombus
0.0748	28.7	.1693	2	Stoics
0.0748	28.7	.0000	5	STUW
0.0748	28.7	.0000	5	two-digit
0.0748	28.7	.0000	5	Westerville
0.0748	28.7	.0000	5	XX
0.0748	28.7	.0000	5	x3
0.0748	28.7	.0000	5	yardsticks
0.0748	28.7	.0000	5	08
0.0748	28.7	.0000	5	1's
0.0748	28.7	.0000	5	10-centimeter
0.0748	28.7	.0000	5	10n
0.0748	28.7	.0000	5	100/100
0.0748	28.7	.0000	5	14/16
0.0748	28.7	.0000	5	2/9
0.0748	28.7	.0000	5	3/9
0.0748	28.7	.0000	5	33/47
0.0748	28.7	.0000	5	346
0.0748	28.7	.0000	5	4-step
0.0748	28.7	.0000	5	4/1
0.0748	28.7	.0000	5	4x
0.0748	28.7	.0000	5	5/15
0.0748	28.7	.0000	5	547
0.0748	28.7	.0000	5	6/15
0.0748	28.7	.0000	5	687
0.0748	28.7	.0000	5	7/6
0.0748	28.7	.0000	5	7's
0.0748	28.7	.0000	5	8/10
0.0748	28.7	.0000	5	8/3
0.0746	28.7	.1621	2	agenda
0.0746	28.7	.1621	2	broken-winged
0.0746	28.7	.1621	2	brown-sounding
0.0746	28.7	.1621	2	by-ways
0.0746	28.7	.1621	2	clinked
0.0746	28.7	.1621	2	contrived
0.0746	28.7	.1621	2	ensilage
0.0746	28.7	.1621	2	fowling-piece
0.0746	28.7	.1621	2	hoots
0.0746	28.7	.1621	2	maker's
0.0746	28.7	.1621	2	molasses-sweet
0.0746	28.7	.1621	2	neat's-foot
0.0746	28.7	.1621	2	pottering
0.0746	28.7	.1621	2	seamed
0.0746	28.7	.1621	2	shaggy-haired
0.0746	28.7	.1621	2	subject's
0.0746	28.7	.1621	2	swart
0.0746	28.7	.1621	2	Wasp's
0.0744	28.7	.0758	4	intensities
0.0744	28.7	.0758	4	Realism
0.0743	28.7	.0437	3	fabricate
0.0743	28.7	.0437	3	honing
0.0743	28.7	.0437	3	testers
0.0742	28.7	.1605	2	Claudia
0.0742	28.7	.1605	2	eddying
0.0742	28.7	.1605	2	letterwriting
0.0742	28.7	.1605	2	loquacious
0.0742	28.7	.1605	2	obsequious
0.0742	28.7	.1605	2	sender's
0.0742	28.7	.1605	2	slurp
0.0742	28.7	.1605	2	smearing
0.0742	28.7	.1605	2	topcoat
0.0742	28.7	.1605	2	wristwatch
0.0742	28.7	.1605	2	yowling
0.0736	28.7	.0290	4	mailbag
0.0733	28.6	.0000	7	Aldrich
0.0733	28.6	.0000	7	alt
0.0733	28.6	.0000	7	crocodilians
0.0733	28.6	.0000	7	cystitis
0.0733	28.6	.0000	7	impeached
0.0733	28.6	.0000	7	Khazars
0.0733	28.6	.0000	7	Latvians
0.0733	28.6	.0609	4	linseed
0.0733	28.6	.0000	7	Macdonald
0.0733	28.6	.0000	7	mayfly
0.0733	28.6	.0000	7	monetary
0.0733	28.6	.0000	7	Penang
0.0733	28.6	.0000	7	Permian
0.0733	28.6	.0000	7	Timur
0.0733	28.6	.0000	7	tubules
0.0733	28.6	.0000	7	vice-presidential
0.0732	28.6	.0725	2	attics

THE PRECEDING WORD TYPE OCCUPIES RANK 43400

U	SFI	D	F	Word Type
0.0732	28.6	.0725	2	framing
0.0732	28.6	.0725	2	one-sixteenth
0.0732	28.6	.0725	2	rectangular-shaped
0.0732	28.6	.0725	2	stapled
0.0732	28.6	.0725	2	timberlands
0.0732	28.6	.0725	2	waxes
0.0732	28.6	.0725	2	10-6
0.0732	28.6	.0725	2	551
0.0730	28.6	.0000	9	br
0.0730	28.6	.0000	9	cr
0.0730	28.6	.0000	9	hw
0.0730	28.6	.0000	9	sound-spellings
0.0730	28.6	.0000	9	tch
0.0729	28.6	.0000	6	'69
0.0729	28.6	.0000	6	activists
0.0729	28.6	.0000	6	agitator
0.0729	28.6	.0000	6	Alioto
0.0729	28.6	.0000	6	AMPI
0.0729	28.6	.0000	6	B&M
0.0729	28.6	.0000	6	BMW
0.0729	28.6	.0000	6	briefing
0.0729	28.6	.0000	6	carb
0.0729	28.6	.0000	6	Carew
0.0729	28.6	.0000	6	DeGaulle
0.0729	28.6	.0000	6	defendants
0.0729	28.6	.0000	6	Erikson
0.0729	28.6	.0000	6	Flossie
0.0729	28.6	.0000	6	fooba
0.0729	28.6	.0000	6	Football
0.0729	28.6	.0000	6	Fouser
0.0729	28.6	.0000	6	Generation
0.0729	28.6	.0000	6	LaPorte
0.0729	28.6	.0000	6	McCovey
0.0729	28.6	.0000	6	Melanie
0.0729	28.6	.0000	6	Model-A
0.0729	28.6	.0000	6	Morrall
0.0729	28.6	.0000	6	Muff
0.0729	28.6	.0000	6	Navaholand
0.0729	28.6	.0000	6	NBA
0.0729	28.6	.0000	6	NFL
0.0729	28.6	.0000	6	nonviolent
0.0729	28.6	.0000	6	option
0.0729	28.6	.0000	6	Poozy
0.0729	28.6	.0000	6	Producers
0.0729	28.6	.0000	6	Sex
0.0729	28.6	.0000	6	Somerville
0.0729	28.6	.0000	6	surtax
0.0729	28.6	.0000	6	Tindell
0.0729	28.6	.0000	6	vulnerable
0.0729	28.6	.0000	6	wooba
0.0729	28.6	.0000	6	Zapata
0.0729	28.6	.0000	6	Ziwiyeh
0.0728	28.6	.0000	9	Ballerina
0.0728	28.6	.0000	9	Banjo
0.0728	28.6	.1551	2	barbels
0.0728	28.6	.1483	2	beading
0.0728	28.6	.1483	2	blocklike
0.0728	28.6	.1551	2	bulks
0.0728	28.6	.1551	2	bystander
0.0728	28.6	.0000	9	C-major
0.0728	28.6	.1483	2	cabinetwork
0.0728	28.6	.0000	9	Chanukah
0.0728	28.6	.1483	2	conveyors
0.0728	28.6	.0000	9	Copland
0.0728	28.6	.0000	9	cornets
0.0728	28.6	.1551	2	disjointed
0.0728	28.6	.1551	2	distraught
0.0728	28.6	.0000	9	Dorian
0.0728	28.6	.1551	2	enquired
0.0728	28.6	.1551	2	equipments
0.0728	28.6	.0000	9	Erlking
0.0728	28.6	.1551	2	faultlessly
0.0728	28.6	.0000	9	fermata
0.0728	28.6	.1483	2	foreshortened
0.0728	28.6	.0000	9	Gesler
0.0728	28.6	.1551	2	jangled
0.0728	28.6	.1551	2	mutineers
0.0728	28.6	.1551	2	obscurely
0.0728	28.6	.1483	2	overlaid
0.0728	28.6	.0000	9	percussive
0.0728	28.6	.1483	2	persons'
0.0728	28.6	.0000	9	piccolo
0.0728	28.6	.1483	2	pie-shaped
0.0728	28.6	.1551	2	pinpoints
0.0728	28.6	.0000	9	Pooh-Bah
0.0728	28.6	.1551	2	prayeth
0.0728	28.6	.0000	9	Refrain
0.0728	28.6	.1551	2	reverberated
0.0728	28.6	.1551	2	rhetorically
0.0728	28.6	.1551	2	Rifle
0.0728	28.6	.0000	9	Saint-Saens
0.0728	28.6	.0000	9	Schuman
0.0728	28.6	.1483	2	Sealacell
0.0728	28.6	.1483	2	surfacer
0.0728	28.6	.1551	2	swaggered
0.0728	28.6	.1551	2	telephoning
0.0728	28.6	.1551	2	trespasser
0.0728	28.6	.1483	2	two-cylinder
0.0728	28.6	.1551	2	underhanded
0.0728	28.6	.1551	2	window-sill

THE PRECEDING WORD TYPE OCCUPIES RANK 43500

U	SFI	D	F	Word Type
0.0728	28.6	.1483	2	withdraws
0.0728	28.6	.0000	9	Wolly
0.0728	28.6	.1483	2	951
0.0727	28.6	.0205	4	synagogue
0.0724	28.6	.0000	5	a-long
0.0724	28.6	.0000	5	Beavers'
0.0724	28.6	.0000	5	Bidwell
0.0724	28.6	.0000	5	bookmakers
0.0724	28.6	.0000	5	bookmaking
0.0724	28.6	.0000	5	Builders
0.0724	28.6	.0000	5	Chaos
0.0724	28.6	.0000	5	Cheboygan
0.0724	28.6	.0000	5	Chieh-hsiu
0.0724	28.6	.0000	5	Chillicothe
0.0724	28.6	.0000	5	Clem
0.0724	28.6	.0000	5	Corey's
0.0724	28.6	.0000	5	cotylosaurs
0.0724	28.6	.0000	5	Deborah's
0.0724	28.6	.0000	5	Dunning
0.0724	28.6	.0000	5	Ehmke
0.0724	28.6	.0000	5	ex-slaves
0.0724	28.6	.0000	5	Fannin
0.0724	28.6	.0000	5	Farmville
0.0724	28.6	.0000	5	grenade
0.0724	28.6	.0000	5	Griscom
0.0724	28.6	.0000	5	Haiphong
0.0724	28.6	.0000	5	Hathorne
0.0724	28.6	.0000	5	Hockley
0.0724	28.6	.0000	5	hurdlers
0.0724	28.6	.0000	5	infeed
0.0724	28.6	.0000	5	Ku
0.0724	28.6	.0000	5	launcher
0.0724	28.6	.0000	5	Lill
0.0724	28.6	.0000	5	McCawley
0.0724	28.6	.0000	5	McNeil
0.0724	28.6	.0000	5	Munda
0.0724	28.6	.0000	5	Mutti
0.0724	28.6	.0000	5	M1
0.0724	28.6	.0000	5	Ohlendorf
0.0724	28.6	.0000	5	Playful
0.0724	28.6	.0000	5	Sa'ud
0.0724	28.6	.0000	5	SAW
0.0724	28.6	.0000	5	Scheme
0.0724	28.6	.0000	5	Schuster
0.0724	28.6	.0000	5	ShiMutale
0.0724	28.6	.0000	5	Slats
0.0724	28.6	.0000	5	Stuck
0.0724	28.6	.0000	5	Swift-goer
0.0724	28.6	.0000	5	Ta-lin
0.0724	28.6	.0000	5	Trachodon
0.0724	28.6	.0000	5	Vendice
0.0724	28.6	.0000	5	Yadin
0.0722	28.6	.1457	2	tabulating
0.0722	28.6	.1457	2	1-pound
0.0722	28.6	.1457	2	11-5
0.0722	28.6	.1457	2	12/16
0.0722	28.6	.1457	2	2-foot

U	SFI	D	F	Word Type
0.0722	28.6	.1457	2	6/0
0.0722	28.6	.1457	2	954
0.0721	28.6	.1523	2	disclosure
0.0721	28.6	.1523	2	fastidious
0.0721	28.6	.1523	2	gold-rush
0.0721	28.6	.1523	2	Headless
0.0721	28.6	.1523	2	Horseman
0.0721	28.6	.1523	2	jousting
0.0721	28.6	.1523	2	moviegoers
0.0721	28.6	.1523	2	narrate
0.0721	28.6	.1523	2	Parking
0.0721	28.6	.1523	2	Pullmans
0.0721	28.6	.1523	2	retriever
0.0721	28.6	.1523	2	rigor
0.0721	28.6	.1523	2	seven-day
0.0721	28.6	.1523	2	seventies
0.0721	28.6	.1523	2	six-foot-long
0.0721	28.6	.1523	2	spearing
0.0721	28.6	.1523	2	straightaway
0.0721	28.6	.1523	2	unbelievably
0.0721	28.6	.1523	2	well-constructed
0.0721	28.6	.1523	2	752
0.0716	28.5	.0397	3	Eileen's
0.0716	28.5	.0397	3	Nokomis
0.0716	28.5	.0397	3	tooting
0.0714	28.5	.0994	3	Alberto
0.0714	28.5	.0994	3	dimensional
0.0714	28.5	.0994	3	Dufy
0.0714	28.5	.0994	3	Honore
0.0714	28.5	.0994	3	Mesopotamian
0.0714	28.5	.0994	3	Millet
0.0714	28.5	.0994	3	Mondrian
0.0714	28.5	.0994	3	Portrait
0.0714	28.5	.0994	3	Rococo
0.0708	28.5	.0665	2	agilely
0.0708	28.5	.0665	2	blockhead
0.0708	28.5	.0665	2	bourne
0.0708	28.5	.0665	2	breezed
0.0708	28.5	.0665	2	buffoons
0.0708	28.5	.0665	2	capsize
0.0708	28.5	.0665	2	cheeky
0.0708	28.5	.0665	2	chugging
0.0708	28.5	.0665	2	Crow's
THE PRECEDING WORD TYPE OCCUPIES RANK 43600				
0.0708	28.5	.0665	2	deluge
0.0708	28.5	.0665	2	enviously
0.0708	28.5	.0665	2	expedite
0.0708	28.5	.0665	2	fairgrounds
0.0708	28.5	.0665	2	glorying
0.0708	28.5	.0665	2	hobo
0.0708	28.5	.0665	2	igniting
0.0708	28.5	.0665	2	merciful
0.0708	28.5	.0665	2	piercingly
0.0708	28.5	.0665	2	regretful
0.0708	28.5	.0665	2	rereading
0.0708	28.5	.0909	3	rex
0.0708	28.5	.0665	2	ropelike
0.0708	28.5	.0665	2	shinnying
0.0708	28.5	.0665	2	solicitude
0.0708	28.5	.0665	2	staysail
0.0708	28.5	.0665	2	Tarrytown
0.0708	28.5	.0665	2	thirty-minute
0.0708	28.5	.0665	2	thrashes
0.0708	28.5	.0665	2	unawares
0.0708	28.5	.0665	2	VanTassel
0.0708	28.5	.0665	2	Wally
0.0708	28.5	.0665	2	welts
0.0708	28.5	.0665	2	what've
0.0708	28.5	.0665	2	whooosh
0.0707	28.5	.0978	3	Chartres
0.0707	28.5	.0978	3	cornhusks
0.0707	28.5	.0978	3	pastels
0.0703	28.5	.0000	6	Bromwell
0.0703	28.5	.0000	6	Bucky's
0.0703	28.5	.0000	6	Bumpo
0.0703	28.5	.0000	6	ca'n't
0.0703	28.5	.0000	6	Carnatic
0.0703	28.5	.0000	6	Cilla
0.0703	28.5	.0000	6	Coppino
0.0703	28.5	.0000	6	deer-lick
0.0703	28.5	.0000	6	Flupp
0.0703	28.5	.0000	6	Forresters
0.0703	28.5	.0000	6	grand-vizir
0.0703	28.5	.0000	6	Grimalkin
0.0703	28.5	.0000	6	horseboys
0.0703	28.5	.0000	6	Idell
0.0703	28.5	.0000	6	Maui
0.0703	28.5	.0000	6	Nanko
0.0703	28.5	.0000	6	Nilsson
0.0703	28.5	.0000	6	Oompa-Loompas
0.0703	28.5	.0000	6	Orlov
0.0703	28.5	.0000	6	Poppers
0.0703	28.5	.0000	6	Ramo
0.0703	28.5	.0000	6	Smoky's
0.0703	28.5	.0000	6	Squealer
0.0703	28.5	.0000	6	Stewy
0.0703	28.5	.0000	6	Stillwater
0.0703	28.5	.0000	6	Stubbins
0.0703	28.5	.0000	6	Templeton
0.0703	28.5	.0000	6	thou'rt
0.0703	28.5	.0000	6	Windale
0.0703	28.5	.0000	6	Woodpeckers
0.0702	28.5	.0966	3	banyan
0.0702	28.5	.0683	4	Botticelli
0.0702	28.5	.0966	3	Still
0.0702	28.5	.0683	4	toweling
0.0701	28.5	.0803	3	globules
0.0701	28.5	.0803	3	high-strength
0.0701	28.5	.0803	3	Leyden
0.0701	28.5	.0803	3	LH
0.0701	28.5	.0803	3	1/64
0.0701	28.5	.0803	3	6-9
0.0696	28.4	.0250	4	Madonna
0.0692	28.4	.1493	2	Aristide
0.0692	28.4	.1493	2	building-up
0.0692	28.4	.1493	2	Daubigny
0.0692	28.4	.1493	2	delineation
0.0692	28.4	.1493	2	disharmonious
0.0692	28.4	.1493	2	Equality
0.0692	28.4	.1493	2	Fontainebleau
0.0692	28.4	.1493	2	Fragonard
0.0692	28.4	.1493	2	Hampstead
0.0692	28.4	.1493	2	Louvre
0.0692	28.4	.1493	2	Marin
0.0692	28.4	.1493	2	nonobjective
0.0692	28.4	.1493	2	Rouault
0.0692	28.4	.1493	2	Watteau
0.0689	28.4	.1387	2	Academic
0.0689	28.4	.1387	2	buttercups
0.0689	28.4	.1387	2	Forbes
0.0689	28.4	.1387	2	hierarchy
0.0689	28.4	.1387	2	landward
0.0689	28.4	.1387	2	Lillian's
0.0689	28.4	.1387	2	overslept
0.0689	28.4	.1387	2	pebbled
0.0689	28.4	.1387	2	precipices
0.0689	28.4	.1387	2	prospector's
0.0689	28.4	.1387	2	recumbent
0.0689	28.4	.1387	2	right-
0.0689	28.4	.1387	2	slaty
0.0689	28.4	.1387	2	twiddling
0.0689	28.4	.1387	2	wrenches
0.0687	28.4	.1259	2	ironwork
0.0687	28.4	.1259	2	kilns
THE PRECEDING WORD TYPE OCCUPIES RANK 43700				
0.0687	28.4	.1259	2	ochre
0.0687	28.4	.1259	2	self-made
0.0687	28.4	.1259	2	stucco
0.0687	28.4	.1259	2	superimpose
0.0687	28.4	.1259	2	wire-drawing
0.0686	28.4	.1473	2	anteroom
0.0686	28.4	.1473	2	buttresses
0.0686	28.4	.1473	2	Cleopatra
0.0686	28.4	.1473	2	hollowness
0.0686	28.4	.1473	2	labyrinths
0.0686	28.4	.1473	2	ping-pong
0.0686	28.4	.1473	2	Roethke
0.0686	28.4	.1473	2	watercolors
0.0685	28.4	.1249	2	ampere
0.0685	28.4	.1249	2	axial
0.0685	28.4	.1249	2	brads
0.0685	28.4	.1249	2	electrolytic
0.0685	28.4	.1249	2	Electrons
0.0685	28.4	.1249	2	fine-tooth
0.0685	28.4	.1249	2	fusible
0.0685	28.4	.1249	2	induces
0.0685	28.4	.1249	2	kinescope
0.0685	28.4	.1249	2	Ohm
0.0685	28.4	.1249	2	orthicon
0.0685	28.4	.1249	2	outer-space
0.0685	28.4	.1249	2	r-f
0.0685	28.4	.1249	2	replaceable
0.0685	28.4	.1249	2	ribbon-shaped
0.0685	28.4	.1249	2	schematic
0.0685	28.4	.1249	2	shortens
0.0685	28.4	.1249	2	single-thickness
0.0685	28.4	.1249	2	standpipes
0.0685	28.4	.1249	2	straight-line
0.0685	28.4	.1249	2	typhoon
0.0685	28.4	.1249	2	1-14
0.0685	28.4	.1249	2	12-2
0.0685	28.4	.1249	2	14-2
0.0685	28.4	.1249	2	16-3
0.0685	28.4	.1249	2	18-6
0.0685	28.4	.1249	2	26-6
0.0685	28.4	.1249	2	47-4
0.0685	28.4	.1249	2	9-29
0.0685	28.4	.1249	2	9-30
0.0685	28.4	.1249	2	952
0.0684	28.3	.1362	2	contraptions
0.0684	28.3	.1362	2	familar
0.0684	28.3	.1362	2	scoutmaster
0.0684	28.3	.1362	2	Stone's
0.0684	28.3	.1362	2	unpunctuated
0.0684	28.3	.1362	2	777
0.0682	28.3	.1458	2	Antelope
0.0682	28.3	.1458	2	beamish
0.0682	28.3	.1458	2	borogoves
0.0682	28.3	.1458	2	gummed
0.0682	28.3	.1458	2	mimsy
0.0682	28.3	.1458	2	mome
0.0682	28.3	.1458	2	Musicians
0.0682	28.3	.1458	2	outgrabe
0.0682	28.3	.1458	2	raths
0.0682	28.3	.1458	2	scudding
0.0682	28.3	.1458	2	sparrow's
0.0680	28.3	.0344	3	teepees
0.0680	28.3	.0344	3	warping
0.0676	28.3	.0580	2	blurring
0.0676	28.3	.0580	2	carpenters'
0.0676	28.3	.0580	2	Dale's
0.0676	28.3	.0902	3	motif
0.0676	28.3	.0580	2	naturalistic
0.0676	28.3	.0580	2	Nicholas'
0.0676	28.3	.0580	2	note-taking
0.0676	28.3	.0580	2	pinatas
0.0676	28.3	.0902	3	primaries
0.0676	28.3	.0580	2	Rumpelstiltskin
0.0676	28.3	.0580	2	sacrilege
0.0676	28.3	.0580	2	sallied
0.0676	28.3	.0580	2	sculptor's
0.0676	28.3	.0580	2	strange-sounding
0.0676	28.3	.0580	2	teepee
0.0669	28.3	.1405	2	Terrific
0.0662	28.2	.1378	2	artifical
0.0662	28.2	.1378	2	Babel
0.0662	28.2	.1378	2	burbled
0.0662	28.2	.1378	2	Cezanne's
0.0662	28.2	.1378	2	conceptual
0.0662	28.2	.1378	2	crisscrossing
0.0662	28.2	.1378	2	dorm
0.0662	28.2	.1378	2	Goya's
0.0662	28.2	.1378	2	nativity
0.0662	28.2	.1378	2	Nike
0.0662	28.2	.1378	2	non-objective
0.0662	28.2	.1378	2	pyramidal
0.0662	28.2	.1378	2	roller-coaster
0.0662	28.2	.1378	2	Spellman
0.0662	28.2	.1378	2	unimportance
0.0662	28.2	.1378	2	unspectacular
0.0662	28.2	.1378	2	velvets
0.0662	28.2	.1378	2	Wylie
0.0660	28.2	.0744	3	rumbles
0.0659	28.2	.0737	3	Experiment
0.0657	28.2	.0000	6	-ar
THE PRECEDING WORD TYPE OCCUPIES RANK 43800				
0.0657	28.2	.0000	6	Adv-m
0.0657	28.2	.0000	6	affixes
0.0657	28.2	.0000	6	Aux
0.0657	28.2	.0000	6	Chancho
0.0657	28.2	.0000	6	Emilia
0.0657	28.2	.0000	6	MC
0.0657	28.2	.0000	6	Nadine
0.0657	28.2	.0000	6	reflexive
0.0657	28.2	.0000	6	Spun
0.0657	28.2	.0000	6	subordination
0.0657	28.2	.0000	6	Vactangi
0.0657	28.2	.0000	6	Whiteside
0.0657	28.2	.0000	6	WXB
0.0651	28.1	.1170	2	burglary
0.0651	28.1	.1170	2	converged
0.0651	28.1	.1170	2	disquieting
0.0651	28.1	.1170	2	impressing
0.0651	28.1	.1170	2	keelboat
0.0651	28.1	.1170	2	safeguarding
0.0651	28.1	.1170	2	transatlantic
0.0651	28.1	.1170	2	56-57
0.0650	28.1	.1160	2	aura
0.0650	28.1	.1160	2	certificates
0.0650	28.1	.1160	2	discards
0.0650	28.1	.1160	2	impersonally
0.0650	28.1	.1160	2	Palisades
0.0650	28.1	.1160	2	screamer
0.0650	28.1	.1160	2	soapsuds
0.0650	28.1	.1160	2	spring's
0.0650	28.1	.1160	2	statistically
0.0650	28.1	.1160	2	voluminous
0.0649	28.1	.0000	8	cl
0.0649	28.1	.0000	8	com
0.0649	28.1	.0000	8	Rulefinder's
0.0649	28.1	.0000	8	Rulescouter's
0.0647	28.1	.0000	8	Amahl
0.0647	28.1	.0000	8	antiphonal
0.0647	28.1	.0000	8	chordal
0.0647	28.1	.0000	8	Comes
0.0647	28.1	.0000	8	derry
0.0647	28.1	.0000	8	doggies
0.0647	28.1	.0000	8	Gottschalk
0.0647	28.1	.0000	8	Graphophone
0.0647	28.1	.0000	8	Loesser
0.0647	28.1	.0000	8	lolly
0.0647	28.1	.0000	8	lyrics
0.0647	28.1	.0000	8	pizzicato
0.0647	28.1	.0000	8	Rossini
0.0644	28.1	.0000	6	Ahmeek
0.0644	28.1	.0000	6	AMAL
0.0644	28.1	.0000	6	apologetically
0.0644	28.1	.0000	6	Diassigue
0.0644	28.1	.0000	6	Didrikson
0.0644	28.1	.0000	6	Ev
0.0644	28.1	.0000	6	Floogle
0.0644	28.1	.0000	6	Gobbo
0.0644	28.1	.0000	6	Gookin
0.0644	28.1	.0000	6	GRAY
0.0644	28.1	.0000	6	Gregorio
0.0644	28.1	.0000	6	Heidegger
0.0644	28.1	.0000	6	Ixtlapan
0.0644	28.1	.0000	6	JODY
0.0644	28.1	.0000	6	KATRIN
0.0644	28.1	.0000	6	Lowdermilk
0.0644	28.1	.0000	6	LYSANDER
0.0644	28.1	.0000	6	Mance
0.0644	28.1	.0000	6	maquis
0.0644	28.1	.0000	6	Mourad
0.0644	28.1	.0000	6	Murdle
0.0644	28.1	.0000	6	night-writing
0.0644	28.1	.0000	20	placket
0.0644	28.1	.0000	6	Skimpy
0.0644	28.1	.0000	6	Son's
0.0644	28.1	.0000	6	Streak
0.0644	28.1	.0000	6	SUDHA
0.0644	28.1	.0000	6	Tildy
0.0644	28.1	.0000	6	TITANIA
0.0644	28.1	.0000	6	wanta
0.0644	28.1	.0000	6	Wulbari
0.0640	28.1	.0801	3	Constable's
0.0640	28.1	.0801	3	Florentine
0.0633	28.0	.1247	2	de'
0.0633	28.0	.1247	2	fluidity
0.0633	28.0	.1247	2	Gioconda
0.0633	28.0	.1247	2	Gogh
0.0633	28.0	.1247	2	pastel
0.0633	28.0	.1247	2	Pieta
0.0633	28.0	.1247	2	pylon
0.0633	28.0	.1247	2	rain-soaked
0.0633	28.0	.1247	2	Venetians
0.0628	28.0	.0000	6	Aarhus
0.0628	28.0	.1223	2	agate
0.0628	28.0	.0000	6	belligerents
0.0628	28.0	.0000	6	calipee
0.0628	28.0	.1223	2	cheerleaders
0.0628	28.0	.0000	6	ethane
0.0628	28.0	.0000	6	glottal
0.0628	28.0	.0000	6	Governors
0.0628	28.0	.0000	6	hawksbill
0.0628	28.0	.0000	6	mammalian
THE PRECEDING WORD TYPE OCCUPIES RANK 43900				
0.0628	28.0	.0000	6	teleosts
0.0628	28.0	.0000	6	Trough
0.0628	28.0	.0000	6	Visayan
0.0619	27.9	.0484	4	cartoonist
0.0608	27.8	.0000	5	'65
0.0608	27.8	.0000	5	AAU
0.0608	27.8	.0000	5	AMC
0.0608	27.8	.0000	5	Amchitka
0.0608	27.8	.0000	5	Another
0.0608	27.8	.0000	5	Apartment
0.0608	27.8	.0000	5	Arrangement
0.0608	27.8	.0000	5	BEDC
0.0608	27.8	.0000	5	birthmark
0.0608	27.8	.0000	5	Bonfiglio
0.0608	27.8	.0000	5	Buffy
0.0608	27.8	.0000	5	bushings
0.0608	27.8	.0000	5	coronet
0.0608	27.8	.0000	5	cutthroat
0.0608	27.8	.0000	5	Dairymen
0.0608	27.8	.0000	5	discoloration
0.0608	27.8	.0000	5	Donnelly
0.0608	27.8	.0000	5	Dowdey
0.0608	27.8	.0000	5	dropout
0.0608	27.8	.0000	5	GMC
0.0608	27.8	.0000	5	goalies
0.0608	27.8	.0000	5	GT
0.0608	27.8	.0000	5	Gumdrop
0.0608	27.8	.0000	5	Henke
0.0608	27.8	.0000	5	Hetrick
0.0608	27.8	.0000	5	Howland
0.0608	27.8	.0000	5	Hull's
0.0608	27.8	.0000	5	Ike's
0.0608	27.8	.0000	5	inbreeding
0.0608	27.8	.0000	5	Kenyatta
0.0608	27.8	.0000	5	Lanciotti
0.0608	27.8	.0000	5	Landry
0.0608	27.8	.0000	5	Likimani
0.0608	27.8	.0000	5	Linen
0.0608	27.8	.0000	5	Mimi
0.0608	27.8	.0000	5	Mortimer
0.0608	27.8	.0000	5	Newsweek
0.0608	27.8	.0000	5	Nipper
0.0608	27.8	.0000	5	Onassis
0.0608	27.8	.0000	5	Persepolis
0.0608	27.8	.0000	5	Peruvians
0.0608	27.8	.0000	5	Quinn
0.0608	27.8	.0000	5	Raiders
0.0608	27.8	.0000	5	Rawlins
0.0608	27.8	.0000	5	sa
0.0608	27.8	.0000	5	Scillies
0.0608	27.8	.0000	5	SDS
0.0608	27.8	.0000	5	sea-run
0.0608	27.8	.0000	5	sex-education
0.0608	27.8	.0000	5	Seybold
0.0608	27.8	.0000	5	Shafter
0.0608	27.8	.0000	5	Shapley's
0.0608	27.8	.0000	5	subcompact
0.0608	27.8	.0000	5	supertrees
0.0608	27.8	.0000	5	TOPS
0.0608	27.8	.0000	5	torque
0.0608	27.8	.0000	5	Vietnam's
0.0608	27.8	.0000	5	Woodstock
0.0608	27.8	.0000	5	Yaga
0.0608	27.8	.0000	5	500-KR
0.0601	27.8	.0652	3	llama's
0.0600	27.8	.0646	3	birdbath
0.0600	27.8	.1042	2	conveyances
0.0600	27.8	.1042	2	creatively
0.0600	27.8	.1042	2	Darrow
0.0600	27.8	.1042	2	Embassies
0.0600	27.8	.0646	3	interweaving
0.0600	27.8	.1042	2	longhorn
0.0600	27.8	.1042	2	mid-fifteenth
0.0600	27.8	.1042	2	minarets
0.0600	27.8	.1042	2	Oaxaca
0.0600	27.8	.1042	2	Puebla
0.0600	27.8	.1042	2	purples
0.0600	27.8	.1042	2	rebozos
0.0600	27.8	.1042	2	Saying
0.0600	27.8	.1042	2	Taxco
0.0600	27.8	.1042	2	Tobey
0.0599	27.8	.0000	4	$0
0.0599	27.8	.0000	4	-8
0.0599	27.8	.0000	4	/4
0.0599	27.8	.0000	4	/4x
0.0599	27.8	.0000	4	-segments
0.0599	27.8	.0000	4	a-d
0.0599	27.8	.0000	4	AR
0.0599	27.8	.0000	4	BAD
0.0599	27.8	.0000	4	base-seven
0.0599	27.8	.0000	4	BF
0.0599	27.8	.0000	4	Bh
0.0599	27.8	.0000	4	birthstone
0.0599	27.8	.0000	4	bisects
0.0599	27.8	.0000	4	b2
0.0599	27.8	.0000	4	carats
0.0599	27.8	.1033	2	cardboards
0.0599	27.8	.1033	2	catastrophes
0.0599	27.8	.0000	4	CB
0.0599	27.8	.0000	4	clockface
THE PRECEDING WORD TYPE OCCUPIES RANK 44000				
0.0599	27.8	.0000	4	concurrent
0.0599	27.8	.0000	4	conversions
0.0599	27.8	.0000	4	cross-product
0.0599	27.8	.0000	4	Danford
0.0599	27.8	.0000	4	decimeter
0.0599	27.8	.0000	4	disjoint
0.0599	27.8	.0000	4	dm
0.0599	27.8	.0000	4	DPF
0.0599	27.8	.1033	2	Ellsworth
0.0599	27.8	.1033	2	encase
0.0599	27.8	.0000	4	EPF
0.0599	27.8	.0000	4	FG
0.0599	27.8	.0000	4	five-clock
0.0599	27.8	.0000	4	Gauss
0.0599	27.8	.0000	4	graphed
0.0599	27.8	.0000	4	half-dollars
0.0599	27.8	.0000	4	Joanne's
0.0599	27.8	.0000	4	KL
0.0599	27.8	.0000	4	LCD
0.0599	27.8	.1033	2	light-and-dark

U	SFI	D	F	Word Type
0.0599	27.8	.0000	4	markdown
0.0599	27.8	.1033	2	Mayans
0.0599	27.8	.0000	4	Midtown
0.0599	27.8	.0000	4	mixed-fraction
0.0599	27.8	.0000	4	monomial
0.0599	27.8	.0000	4	multiplication-addition
0.0599	27.8	.0000	4	Nan's
0.0599	27.8	.0000	4	NL
0.0599	27.8	.0000	4	non-zero
0.0599	27.8	.1033	2	overemphasized
0.0599	27.8	.0000	4	Place-Value
0.0599	27.8	.1033	2	plain-colored
0.0599	27.8	.0000	4	Right-Distributive
0.0599	27.8	.0000	4	scalar
0.0599	27.8	.0000	4	Scored
0.0599	27.8	.0000	4	shortcuts
0.0599	27.8	.0000	4	sit-ups
0.0599	27.8	.0000	4	subtracts
0.0599	27.8	.1033	2	symbolizing
0.0599	27.8	.1033	2	tans
0.0599	27.8	.0000	4	tetrahedron
0.0599	27.8	.0000	4	thousands'
0.0599	27.8	.0000	4	three-place
0.0599	27.8	.0000	4	TU
0.0599	27.8	.0000	4	TVS
0.0599	27.8	.0000	4	twelfths
0.0599	27.8	.1033	2	windbreaks
0.0599	27.8	.0000	4	x/y
0.0599	27.8	.0000	4	x's
0.0599	27.8	.0000	4	XXX
0.0599	27.8	.0000	4	x5
0.0599	27.8	.0000	4	000's
0.0599	27.8	.0000	4	01's
0.0599	27.8	.0000	4	1A
0.0599	27.8	.0000	4	1B
0.0599	27.8	.0000	4	100%
0.0599	27.8	.0000	4	100's
0.0599	27.8	.0000	4	12/5
0.0599	27.8	.0000	4	12x
0.0599	27.8	.0000	4	13-16
0.0599	27.8	.0000	4	1425
0.0599	27.8	.0000	4	1435
0.0599	27.8	.0000	4	15/17
0.0599	27.8	.0000	4	15%
0.0599	27.8	.0000	4	18/24
0.0599	27.8	.0000	4	2/7
0.0599	27.8	.0000	4	3-region
0.0599	27.8	.0000	4	3/7
0.0599	27.8	.0000	4	3t
0.0599	27.8	.0000	4	314
0.0599	27.8	.0000	4	3168
0.0599	27.8	.0000	4	4/c
0.0599	27.8	.0000	4	4x36
0.0599	27.8	.0000	4	4y
0.0599	27.8	.0000	4	5/9
0.0599	27.8	.0000	4	515
0.0599	27.8	.0000	4	6/100
0.0599	27.8	.0000	4	6/5
0.0599	27.8	.0000	4	674
0.0599	27.8	.0000	4	7-clock
0.0599	27.8	.0000	4	7/12
0.0599	27.8	.0000	4	7/16
0.0599	27.8	.0000	4	84-unit
0.0599	27.8	.0000	4	90%
0.0599	27.8	.0000	4	99/100
0.0591	27.7	.0000	3	-78
0.0591	27.7	.0000	3	a-lookin'
0.0591	27.7	.0000	3	acidic
0.0591	27.7	.0000	3	adrenals
0.0591	27.7	.0000	3	advection
0.0591	27.7	.0000	3	afterimage
0.0591	27.7	.0000	3	alanine
0.0591	27.7	.0000	3	Algenib
0.0591	27.7	.0000	3	Alnico
0.0591	27.7	.0000	3	amebas
0.0591	27.7	.0000	3	amphidromic
0.0591	27.7	.0000	3	amylase
0.0591	27.7	.0000	3	anole
0.0591	27.7	.0000	3	anti-matter
0.0591	27.7	.0000	3	ARE
THE PRECEDING WORD TYPE OCCUPIES RANK 44100				
0.0591	27.7	.0000	3	astrologers
0.0591	27.7	.0000	3	Beadle
0.0591	27.7	.0000	3	beechdrops
0.0591	27.7	.0000	3	Beta
0.0591	27.7	.0000	3	blip
0.0591	27.7	.0000	3	brad
0.0591	27.7	.0000	3	Brahe's
0.0591	27.7	.0000	3	broomrape
0.0591	27.7	.0000	3	Buda-Pesth
0.0591	27.7	.0000	3	bullheads
0.0591	27.7	.0000	3	cactuses
0.0591	27.7	.0000	3	Carboniferous
0.0591	27.7	.0000	3	Carothers
0.0591	27.7	.0000	3	Chamberland
0.0591	27.7	.0000	3	chemotherapy
0.0591	27.7	.0000	3	chloroplast
0.0591	27.7	.0000	3	chloroprene
0.0591	27.7	.0000	3	communicable
0.0591	27.7	.0000	3	Copernican
0.0591	27.7	.0000	3	crosswalk
0.0591	27.7	.0000	3	crustal
0.0591	27.7	.0000	3	cutout
0.0591	27.7	.0000	3	Cuvier
0.0591	27.7	.0000	3	declination
0.0591	27.7	.0000	3	deflection
0.0591	27.7	.0000	3	Deneb
0.0591	27.7	.0000	3	diode
0.0591	27.7	.0000	3	ditch-digger
0.0591	27.7	.0000	3	DOES
0.0591	27.7	.0000	3	doldrums
0.0591	27.7	.0000	3	Donnelson
0.0591	27.7	.0000	3	earphone
0.0591	27.7	.0000	3	enstatite
0.0591	27.7	.0000	3	estrus
0.0591	27.7	.0000	3	eustachian
0.0591	27.7	.0000	3	Eustachian
0.0591	27.7	.0000	3	even-numbered
0.0591	27.7	.0000	3	extrusive
0.0591	27.7	.0000	3	Fallopian
0.0591	27.7	.0000	3	Fan
0.0591	27.7	.0000	3	first-magnitude
0.0591	27.7	.0000	3	flagella
0.0591	27.7	.0000	3	flatworm
0.0591	27.7	.0000	3	FLIP
0.0591	27.7	.0000	3	Florey
0.0591	27.7	.0000	3	fluoresce
0.0591	27.7	.0000	3	fructose
0.0591	27.7	.0000	3	Fundy
0.0591	27.7	.0000	3	g/cm3
0.0591	27.7	.0000	3	gametophyte
0.0591	27.7	.0000	3	gemmed
0.0591	27.7	.0000	3	geosynclinal
0.0591	27.7	.0000	3	germ-fighting
0.0591	27.7	.0000	3	glasslike
0.0591	27.7	.0000	3	goal-insight
0.0591	27.7	.0000	3	gooseberries
0.0591	27.7	.0000	3	grass-lands
0.0591	27.7	.0000	3	halfbacks
0.0591	27.7	.0000	3	high-frequency
0.0591	27.7	.0000	3	hognose
0.0591	27.7	.0000	3	hygrometer
0.0591	27.7	.0000	3	H2
0.0591	27.7	.0000	3	insulin
0.0591	27.7	.0000	3	interdependence
0.0591	27.7	.0000	3	interferometer
0.0591	27.7	.0000	3	isoprene
0.0591	27.7	.0000	3	Kon
0.0591	27.7	.0000	3	kwashiorkor
0.0591	27.7	.0000	3	lactic
0.0591	27.7	.0000	3	Lepidoptera
0.0591	27.7	.0000	3	liverworts
0.0591	27.7	.0000	3	lobster's
0.0591	27.7	.0000	3	low-tide
0.0591	27.7	.0000	3	lowest-pitched
0.0591	27.7	.0000	3	lox
0.0591	27.7	.0000	3	magnesia
0.0591	27.7	.0000	3	Malpighi
0.0591	27.7	.0000	3	mass-energy
0.0591	27.7	.0000	3	Meitner
0.0591	27.7	.0000	3	Meteor
0.0591	27.7	.0000	3	millimicrons
0.0591	27.7	.0000	3	millionth
0.0591	27.7	.0000	3	minimum-energy
0.0591	27.7	.0000	3	mitochondria
0.0591	27.7	.0000	3	ml
0.0591	27.7	.0000	3	Mobius
0.0591	27.7	.0000	3	nodal
0.0591	27.7	.0000	3	non-porous
0.0591	27.7	.0000	3	odd-numbered
0.0591	27.7	.0000	3	ophthalmologists
0.0591	27.7	.0000	3	optic
0.0591	27.7	.0000	3	orthoclase
0.0591	27.7	.0000	3	Orthoptera
0.0591	27.7	.0000	3	oviducts
0.0591	27.7	.0000	3	pancreatic
0.0591	27.7	.0000	3	Paramecium
0.0591	27.7	.0000	3	pedalfers
0.0591	27.7	.0000	3	pedipalps
0.0591	27.7	.0000	3	peeper
0.0591	27.7	.0000	3	pellicle
THE PRECEDING WORD TYPE OCCUPIES RANK 44200				
0.0591	27.7	.0000	3	petiole
0.0591	27.7	.0000	3	Petri
0.0591	27.7	.0000	3	phototube
0.0591	27.7	.0000	3	piezo-electric
0.0591	27.7	.0000	3	Pinus
0.0591	27.7	.0000	3	plasmodium
0.0591	27.7	.0000	3	plutonic
0.0591	27.7	.0000	3	prejudging
0.0591	27.7	.0000	3	Priestley's
0.0591	27.7	.0000	3	Priestly
0.0591	27.7	.0000	3	propagated
0.0591	27.7	.0000	3	propellant
0.0591	27.7	.0000	3	propeller's
0.0591	27.7	.0000	3	Prutenicae
0.0591	27.7	.0000	3	ptero
0.0591	27.7	.0000	3	pyrimidine
0.0591	27.7	.0000	3	pyroxenes
0.0591	27.7	.0000	3	pyruvic
0.0591	27.7	.0000	3	ragweed
0.0591	27.7	.0000	3	Redfield
0.0591	27.7	.0000	3	refraction
0.0591	27.7	.0000	3	rhizoids
0.0591	27.7	.0000	3	rose-purple
0.0591	27.7	.0000	3	salol
0.0591	27.7	.0000	3	saltiness
0.0591	27.7	.0000	3	seed-making
0.0591	27.7	.0000	3	set-up
0.0591	27.7	.0000	3	silicious
0.0591	27.7	.0000	3	spinneret
0.0591	27.7	.0000	3	sporophyte
0.0591	27.7	.0000	3	sterilize
0.0591	27.7	.0000	3	stratified
0.0591	27.7	.0000	3	symbiosis
0.0591	27.7	.0000	3	tapeworm
0.0591	27.7	.0000	3	testes
0.0591	27.7	.0000	3	Theobald
0.0591	27.7	.0000	3	thoracic
0.0591	27.7	.0000	3	thymine
0.0591	27.7	.0000	3	Tiki
0.0591	27.7	.0000	3	to-and-fro
0.0591	27.7	.0000	3	tornado's
0.0591	27.7	.0000	3	transits
0.0591	27.7	.0000	3	unlearned
0.0591	27.7	.0000	3	up-draft
0.0591	27.7	.0000	3	vanishes
0.0591	27.7	.0000	3	Venus'
0.0591	27.7	.0000	3	weatherman's
0.0591	27.7	.0000	3	xenon
0.0591	27.7	.0000	3	Y-tube
0.0591	27.7	.0000	3	yes-no
0.0591	27.7	.0000	3	1986
0.0591	27.7	.0000	3	20-liter
0.0586	27.7	.0000	5	'Dwina
0.0586	27.7	.0000	5	Aggy
0.0586	27.7	.0000	5	All-the-Elephant-there**
0.0586	27.7	.0000	5	Argess
0.0586	27.7	.0000	5	badger's
0.0586	27.7	.0000	5	beeches
0.0586	27.7	.0000	5	Brim
0.0586	27.7	.0000	5	Broad
0.0586	27.7	.0000	5	Browdowski
0.0586	27.7	.0000	5	Burdow
0.0586	27.7	.0000	5	Celynida
0.0586	27.7	.0000	5	crucible
0.0586	27.7	.0000	5	Dazzler
0.0586	27.7	.0000	5	eaters-of-men
0.0586	27.7	.0000	5	etci
0.0586	27.7	.0000	5	Gub-Gub
0.0586	27.7	.0000	5	Haggin's
0.0586	27.7	.0000	5	hit's
0.0586	27.7	.0000	5	Hutto
0.0586	27.7	.0000	5	intendant
0.0586	27.7	.0000	5	Kilpatrick's
0.0586	27.7	.0000	5	Lolita
0.0586	27.7	.0000	5	Longridge
0.0586	27.7	.0000	5	Lucinda's
0.0586	27.7	.0000	5	Maimoune
0.0586	27.7	.0000	5	man-animals
0.0586	27.7	.0000	5	Marmot
0.0586	27.7	.0000	5	Moana
0.0586	27.7	.0000	5	Muldoon
0.0586	27.7	.0000	5	Mynderse
0.0586	27.7	.0000	5	Olema
0.0586	27.7	.0000	5	Pretzie
0.0586	27.7	.0000	5	Raider
0.0586	27.7	.0000	5	school-bag
0.0586	27.7	.0000	5	Sees
0.0586	27.7	.0000	5	Spindler
0.0586	27.7	.0000	5	uns
0.0586	27.7	.0000	5	Utley
0.0586	27.7	.0000	5	Woburn
0.0583	27.7	.0000	3	'20s
0.0583	27.7	.0000	3	'80s
0.0583	27.7	.0000	3	Abadan
0.0583	27.7	.0000	3	Achievement
0.0583	27.7	.0000	3	Akiko
0.0583	27.7	.0000	3	Aten
0.0583	27.7	.0000	3	Barten
0.0583	27.7	.0000	3	batboy
0.0583	27.7	.0000	3	Bleeding
THE PRECEDING WORD TYPE OCCUPIES RANK 44300				
0.0583	27.7	.0000	3	blockades
0.0583	27.7	.0000	3	Boniface's
0.0583	27.7	.0000	3	Boxers
0.0583	27.7	.0000	3	chinooks
0.0583	27.7	.0000	3	Colbert
0.0583	27.7	.0000	3	communistic
0.0583	27.7	.0000	3	confederacy
0.0583	27.7	.0000	3	conterminous
0.0583	27.7	.0000	3	Cortes'
0.0583	27.7	.0000	3	Coventry
0.0583	27.7	.0000	3	Covey
0.0583	27.7	.0000	3	cowhides
0.0583	27.7	.0000	3	Crawley
0.0583	27.7	.0000	3	Customs
0.0583	27.7	.0000	3	deChamplain
0.0583	27.7	.0000	3	definitional
0.0583	27.7	.0000	3	delaPlata
0.0583	27.7	.0000	3	dinette
0.0583	27.7	.0000	3	Drift
0.0583	27.7	.0000	3	Elmville
0.0583	27.7	.0000	3	Eritrea
0.0583	27.7	.0000	3	Esmat's
0.0583	27.7	.0000	3	estancias
0.0583	27.7	.0000	3	Estate
0.0583	27.7	.0000	3	Eur-Af-Asia
0.0583	27.7	.0000	3	Fiji
0.0583	27.7	.0000	3	four-footers
0.0583	27.7	.0000	3	Gallas
0.0583	27.7	.0000	3	Grange
0.0583	27.7	.0000	3	Hammarskjold
0.0583	27.7	.0000	3	Hammerfest
0.0583	27.7	.0000	3	haxa
0.0583	27.7	.0000	3	headphones
0.0583	27.7	.0000	3	homeowners
0.0583	27.7	.0000	3	Honduras
0.0583	27.7	.0000	3	humid-continental
0.0583	27.7	.0000	3	Hungary's
0.0583	27.7	.0000	3	hydroelectricity
0.0583	27.7	.0000	3	icecap
0.0583	27.7	.0000	3	ideologies
0.0583	27.7	.0000	3	Iraq's
0.0583	27.7	.0000	3	Kasai
0.0583	27.7	.0000	3	Kokichi
0.0583	27.7	.0000	3	Kyushu
0.0583	27.7	.0000	3	Lachish
0.0583	27.7	.0000	3	Lagos
0.0583	27.7	.0000	3	land-hungry
0.0583	27.7	.0000	3	landmass
0.0583	27.7	.0000	3	lawfully
0.0583	27.7	.0000	3	lobstermen
0.0583	27.7	.0000	3	Lubumbashi
0.0583	27.7	.0000	3	makahiki
0.0583	27.7	.0000	3	Malheur
0.0583	27.7	.0000	3	Malmo
0.0583	27.7	.0000	3	Manygoats
0.0583	27.7	.0000	3	Marne
0.0583	27.7	.0000	3	Matanuska
0.0583	27.7	.0000	3	mayor-council
0.0583	27.7	.0000	3	Mikimoto
0.0583	27.7	.0000	3	mohair
0.0583	27.7	.0000	3	mulattoes
0.0583	27.7	.0000	3	Namese
0.0583	27.7	.0000	3	Nebraska's
0.0583	27.7	.0000	3	north-flowing
0.0583	27.7	.0000	3	Olaf
0.0583	27.7	.0000	3	Oman
0.0583	27.7	.0000	3	overseers
0.0583	27.7	.0000	3	oyez
0.0583	27.7	.0000	3	papacy
0.0583	27.7	.0000	3	Petsamo
0.0583	27.7	.0000	3	Preamble
0.0583	27.7	.0000	3	Proviso
0.0583	27.7	.0000	3	rabbitskin
0.0583	27.7	.0000	3	radiophone
0.0583	27.7	.0000	3	Ras
0.0583	27.7	.0000	3	Recife
0.0583	27.7	.0000	3	Redonda
0.0583	27.7	.0000	3	Samsun
0.0583	27.7	.0000	3	SanFernando
0.0583	27.7	.0000	3	SanLuisObispo
0.0583	27.7	.0000	3	SantaClara
0.0583	27.7	.0000	3	Sayonara
0.0583	27.7	.0000	3	Schuyler
0.0583	27.7	.0000	3	seedbed
0.0583	27.7	.0000	3	Shatt-al-Arab
0.0583	27.7	.0000	3	Shays
0.0583	27.7	.0000	3	shearer
0.0583	27.7	.0000	3	sheepshearers
0.0583	27.7	.0000	3	Sheffield
0.0583	27.7	.0000	3	Shield
0.0583	27.7	.0000	3	shoemakers
0.0583	27.7	.0000	3	Socrates'
0.0583	27.7	.0000	3	Sudanese
0.0583	27.7	.0000	3	Suwa
0.0583	27.7	.0000	3	Tejas
0.0583	27.7	.0000	3	Tenochtitlan
0.0583	27.7	.0000	3	Texian's
0.0583	27.7	.0000	3	Tigreans
0.0583	27.7	.0000	3	towboats
0.0583	27.7	.0000	3	Transition
THE PRECEDING WORD TYPE OCCUPIES RANK 44400				
0.0583	27.7	.0000	3	Tropics
0.0583	27.7	.0000	3	Trotter
0.0583	27.7	.0000	3	tukels
0.0583	27.7	.0000	3	Tula
0.0583	27.7	.0000	3	Ubaru's
0.0583	27.7	.0000	3	Ujima
0.0583	27.7	.0000	3	ukuleles
0.0583	27.7	.0000	3	unifiers
0.0583	27.7	.0000	3	Uplands
0.0583	27.7	.0000	3	Valleys
0.0583	27.7	.0000	3	Venezuelans
0.0583	27.7	.0000	3	Vichy
0.0583	27.7	.0000	3	Wages
0.0583	27.7	.0000	3	Wallaroo
0.0583	27.7	.0000	3	war-torn
0.0583	27.7	.0000	3	warlord
0.0583	27.7	.0000	3	Watcher
0.0583	27.7	.0000	3	watgurwa
0.0583	27.7	.0000	3	Wazadzki's
0.0583	27.7	.0000	3	Wemba
0.0583	27.7	.0000	3	Yenisei
0.0583	27.7	.0000	3	Yssel
0.0583	27.7	.0000	3	Yuna
0.0583	27.7	.0000	3	Zenger
0.0583	27.7	.0000	3	106-107
0.0583	27.7	.0000	3	128-129
0.0583	27.7	.0000	3	1608
0.0583	27.7	.0000	3	1691
0.0583	27.7	.0000	3	204-205
0.0583	27.7	.0000	3	49th
0.0581	27.6	.0000	23	dado
0.0580	27.6	.0000	18	neckline
0.0579	27.6	.0000	4	Aberbrothok
0.0579	27.6	.0000	4	Aeneas
0.0579	27.6	.0000	4	Amberson
0.0579	27.6	.0000	4	Ankylosaurus
0.0579	27.6	.0000	4	Bawtry
0.0579	27.6	.0000	4	blub
0.0579	27.6	.0000	4	cabinetmaker
0.0579	27.6	.0000	4	castor
0.0579	27.6	.0000	4	Chadwick
0.0579	27.6	.0000	4	chaperons
0.0579	27.6	.0000	4	Cliffs
0.0579	27.6	.0000	4	Couperin
0.0579	27.6	.0000	4	Curabel
0.0579	27.6	.0000	4	Cutler
0.0579	27.6	.0000	4	dominie
0.0579	27.6	.0000	4	dumpling
0.0579	27.6	.0000	4	Duttweiler
0.0579	27.6	.0000	4	dyke
0.0579	27.6	.0000	4	Eater
0.0579	27.6	.0000	4	firth
0.0579	27.6	.0000	4	go-between
0.0579	27.6	.0000	4	Hatchet
0.0579	27.6	.0000	4	He'll
0.0579	27.6	.0000	4	Hela
0.0579	27.6	.0000	4	Iguanodon
0.0579	27.6	.0000	4	Kasavubu
0.0579	27.6	.0000	4	ki-yi
0.0579	27.6	.0000	4	Knesset
0.0579	27.6	.0000	4	Let
0.0579	27.6	.0000	4	Lioness
0.0579	27.6	.0000	4	Majors
0.0579	27.6	.0000	4	Margrethe's
0.0579	27.6	.0000	4	Mehitable
0.0579	27.6	.0000	4	Mehmet
0.0579	27.6	.0000	4	middle-distance
0.0579	27.6	.0000	4	Minks
0.0579	27.6	.0000	4	moujik
0.0579	27.6	.0000	4	Nevin
0.0579	27.6	.0000	4	no-hitter
0.0579	27.6	.0000	4	Osburn
0.0579	27.6	.0000	4	pari-mutuel
0.0579	27.6	.0000	4	Peri
0.0579	27.6	.0000	4	Potawatomies
0.0579	27.6	.0000	4	preflight
0.0579	27.6	.0000	4	pussy-cat
0.0579	27.6	.0000	4	re-born
0.0579	27.6	.0000	4	Sa'udi
0.0579	27.6	.0000	4	sans
0.0579	27.6	.0000	4	Songster
0.0579	27.6	.0000	4	Sublette
0.0579	27.6	.0000	4	triceratops
0.0579	27.6	.0000	4	Venny

U	SFI	D	F	Word Type
0.0579	27.6	.0000	4	W-a-t-e-r
0.0579	27.6	.0000	4	Wanamaker
0.0579	27.6	.0000	4	Wanstead
0.0579	27.6	.0000	4	Wishtego
0.0579	27.6	.0000	4	1089
0.0568	27.5	.0000	7	-able
0.0568	27.5	.0000	7	/ou/
0.0568	27.5	.0000	7	bl
0.0568	27.5	.0000	7	ks
0.0568	27.5	.0000	7	ll
0.0568	27.5	.0000	7	long-vowel
0.0568	27.5	.0000	7	Randy's
0.0566	27.5	.0000	7	Bela
0.0566	27.5	.0000	7	cadenza
0.0566	27.5	.0000	7	cellos
0.0566	27.5	.0000	7	chorale
THE PRECEDING WORD TYPE OCCUPIES RANK 44500				
0.0566	27.5	.0000	7	cymbal
0.0566	27.5	.0000	7	D7
0.0566	27.5	.0000	7	four-part
0.0566	27.5	.0000	7	Fugue
0.0566	27.5	.0000	7	gavotte
0.0566	27.5	.0000	7	improvisation
0.0566	27.5	.0000	7	notate
0.0566	27.5	.0000	7	Opus
0.0566	27.5	.0000	7	Purcell
0.0566	27.5	.0000	7	Quartet
0.0566	27.5	.0000	7	quartets
0.0566	27.5	.0000	7	Rubinstein
0.0566	27.5	.0000	7	scale-line
0.0566	27.5	.0000	7	shortnin'
0.0566	27.5	.0000	7	Songs
0.0566	27.5	.0000	7	upbeat
0.0566	27.5	.0000	7	Voiles
0.0566	27.5	.0000	7	Where's
0.0561	27.5	.0589	3	Promised
0.0547	27.4	.0000	5	Adv-f
0.0547	27.4	.0000	5	Adv-p
0.0547	27.4	.0000	5	Boyd's
0.0547	27.4	.0000	5	Carlson
0.0547	27.4	.0000	5	Challico
0.0547	27.4	.0000	5	Cleevendon
0.0547	27.4	.0000	5	Crispian
0.0547	27.4	.0000	5	Danby
0.0547	27.4	.0000	5	diagraming
0.0547	27.4	.0000	5	Ditson
0.0547	27.4	.0000	5	Flores
0.0547	27.4	.0000	5	grapheme
0.0547	27.4	.0000	5	handwritten
0.0547	27.4	.0000	5	infinitives
0.0547	27.4	.0000	5	intensifiers
0.0547	27.4	.0000	5	intransitively
0.0547	27.4	.0000	5	Jacalevna
0.0547	27.4	.0000	5	lang
0.0547	27.4	.0000	5	loanwords
0.0547	27.4	.0000	5	N-V-N
0.0547	27.4	.0000	5	not-words
0.0547	27.4	.0000	5	Spens
0.0547	27.4	.0000	5	transitively
0.0547	27.4	.0000	5	usages
0.0547	27.4	.0000	5	voiceless
0.0547	27.4	.0000	5	wass
0.0547	27.4	.0000	5	Whitmore
0.0537	27.3	.0000	5	'a
0.0537	27.3	.0000	5	ABE
0.0537	27.3	.0000	5	Aigisthos
0.0537	27.3	.0000	5	Barracombie
0.0537	27.3	.0000	5	bird-walkers
0.0537	27.3	.0000	5	Buckles
0.0537	27.3	.0000	5	Bum
0.0537	27.3	.0000	5	colt's
0.0537	27.3	.0000	5	Conestogo
0.0537	27.3	.0000	5	corse
0.0537	27.3	.0000	5	DEMETRIUS
0.0537	27.3	.0000	5	DISSOLVE
0.0537	27.3	.0000	5	entreat
0.0537	27.3	.0000	5	Floogles
0.0537	27.3	.0000	5	Frenchy
0.0537	27.3	.0000	5	Grabow
0.0537	27.3	.0000	5	guv'nor
0.0537	27.3	.0000	5	Havisham
0.0537	27.3	.0000	5	Hermia
0.0537	27.3	.0000	5	JABEZ
0.0537	27.3	.0000	5	Jem's
0.0537	27.3	.0000	5	JOHNNY
0.0537	27.3	.0000	5	Kaseek
0.0537	27.3	.0000	5	linotype
0.0537	27.3	.0000	5	LUKA
0.0537	27.3	.0000	5	MADHAV
0.0537	27.3	.0000	5	mama's
0.0537	27.3	.0000	5	Mamacita
0.0537	27.3	.0000	5	Menelaos
0.0537	27.3	.0000	5	Monaghan
0.0537	27.3	.0000	5	Pennyroyal
0.0537	27.3	.0000	5	POPOV
0.0537	27.3	.0000	5	Sheean
0.0537	27.3	.0000	5	SMITH
0.0537	27.3	.0000	5	Thitpan
0.0537	27.3	.0000	5	Ulrich
0.0537	27.3	.0000	5	ventilator
0.0537	27.3	.0000	5	VETERAN
0.0537	27.3	.0000	5	wardroom
0.0537	27.3	.0000	5	Whalen
0.0523	27.2	.0000	5	Aalborg
0.0523	27.2	.0000	5	anthropology
0.0523	27.2	.0000	5	bionics
0.0523	27.2	.0000	5	Cavendish
0.0523	27.2	.0000	5	Celluloid
0.0523	27.2	.0000	5	Chiapas
0.0523	27.2	.0000	5	Colleges
0.0523	27.2	.0000	5	conquistadors
0.0523	27.2	.0000	5	deferment
0.0523	27.2	.0000	5	Donatists
0.0523	27.2	.0000	5	Edict
0.0523	27.2	.0000	5	Faustus
0.0523	27.2	.0000	5	forelimbs
0.0523	27.2	.0000	5	genera
THE PRECEDING WORD TYPE OCCUPIES RANK 44600				
0.0523	27.2	.0000	5	Gonaives
0.0523	27.2	.0000	5	Greensboro
0.0523	27.2	.0000	5	hartebeests
0.0523	27.2	.0000	5	Herzen
0.0523	27.2	.0000	5	honeypot
0.0523	27.2	.0000	5	matrix
0.0523	27.2	.0000	5	Moros
0.0523	27.2	.0000	5	Negros
0.0523	27.2	.0000	5	Panay
0.0523	27.2	.0000	5	Peron's
0.0523	27.2	.0000	5	Pleistocene
0.0523	27.2	.0000	5	pruned
0.0523	27.2	.0000	5	rodent
0.0523	27.2	.0000	5	Sanctuary
0.0523	27.2	.0000	5	Sapir
0.0523	27.2	.0000	5	Scone
0.0523	27.2	.0000	5	specializations
0.0523	27.2	.0000	5	sprit
0.0523	27.2	.0000	5	translocation
0.0523	27.2	.0000	5	ulcer
0.0523	27.2	.0000	5	ulcers
0.0523	27.2	.0000	5	Urey
0.0523	27.2	.0000	5	wildebeests
0.0523	27.2	.0000	5	YWCA
0.0523	27.2	.0000	5	1200's
0.0487	26.9	.0000	6	ad-
0.0487	26.9	.0000	6	File
0.0487	26.9	.0050	3	frees
0.0487	26.9	.0000	6	Hurdle
0.0487	26.9	.0000	6	ible
0.0487	26.9	.0000	6	ize
0.0487	26.9	.0000	6	Personal
0.0487	26.9	.0000	6	TH
0.0487	26.9	.0000	6	Vocabulary-building
0.0487	26.9	.0000	6	vowel-consonant
0.0486	26.9	.0000	4	'Vette
0.0486	26.9	.0000	4	'64
0.0486	26.9	.0000	4	activism
0.0486	26.9	.0000	4	Adventuress
0.0486	26.9	.0000	4	Afro-American
0.0486	26.9	.0000	4	Against
0.0486	26.9	.0000	4	Albee's
0.0486	26.9	.0000	4	alewife
0.0486	26.9	.0000	4	alienated
0.0486	26.9	.0000	4	alternatives
0.0486	26.9	.0000	4	Avakian
0.0486	26.9	.0000	4	Awful
0.0486	26.9	.0000	4	Bachelors
0.0486	26.9	.0000	4	Bali
0.0486	26.9	.0000	4	Bashar
0.0486	26.9	.0000	4	Batt's
0.0486	26.9	.0000	4	Baugh
0.0486	26.9	.0000	4	best-selling
0.0486	26.9	.0000	4	Birchers
0.0486	26.9	.0000	4	Blatchford
0.0486	26.9	.0000	4	Blatchford's
0.0486	26.9	.0000	4	boobies
0.0486	26.9	.0000	4	Bucher
0.0486	26.9	.0000	4	cannabis
0.0486	26.9	.0000	4	Cartwright
0.0486	26.9	.0000	4	chaplain
0.0486	26.9	.0000	4	Charly
0.0486	26.9	.0000	4	Choice
0.0486	26.9	.0000	4	Cong
0.0486	26.9	.0000	4	Corky
0.0486	26.9	.0000	4	corny
0.0486	26.9	.0000	4	Coronet
0.0486	26.9	.0000	4	Corp
0.0486	26.9	.0000	4	DeGaulle's
0.0486	26.9	.0000	4	Decker
0.0486	26.9	.0000	4	Dumpty
0.0486	26.9	.0000	4	Eads
0.0486	26.9	.0000	4	Elfin
0.0486	26.9	.0000	4	endorsement
0.0486	26.9	.0000	4	erotic
0.0486	26.9	.0000	4	Fallows
0.0486	26.9	.0000	4	frenetic
0.0486	26.9	.0000	4	Frokowski
0.0486	26.9	.0000	4	gobbler
0.0486	26.9	.0000	4	HIGHLIGHTS
0.0486	26.9	.0000	4	Hiro
0.0486	26.9	.0000	4	Hz
0.0486	26.9	.0000	4	Inquiry
0.0486	26.9	.0000	4	investiture
0.0486	26.9	.0000	4	Jesse's
0.0486	26.9	.0000	4	Judson
0.0486	26.9	.0000	4	Koni
0.0486	26.9	.0000	4	Koopman
0.0486	26.9	.0000	4	Liam
0.0486	26.9	.0000	4	Longview
0.0486	26.9	.0000	4	Lump
0.0486	26.9	.0000	4	mahn
0.0486	26.9	.0000	4	Man-God
0.0486	26.9	.0000	4	Mariah
0.0486	26.9	.0000	4	Mazar
0.0486	26.9	.0000	4	megawatts
0.0486	26.9	.0000	4	mellowed
0.0486	26.9	.0000	4	Mets
0.0486	26.9	.0000	4	mid-May
0.0486	26.9	.0000	4	Milrow
THE PRECEDING WORD TYPE OCCUPIES RANK 44700				
0.0486	26.9	.0000	4	Mirror
0.0486	26.9	.0000	4	Mizar
0.0486	26.9	.0000	4	Molinas
0.0486	26.9	.0000	4	Morehead
0.0486	26.9	.0000	4	NCBC
0.0486	26.9	.0000	4	Nooz-hak
0.0486	26.9	.0000	4	n4
0.0486	26.9	.0000	4	origami
0.0486	26.9	.0000	4	Patterson
0.0486	26.9	.0000	4	Pele
0.0486	26.9	.0000	4	Pend
0.0486	26.9	.0000	4	Pomona
0.0486	26.9	.0000	4	psychedelic
0.0486	26.9	.0000	4	Purdue
0.0486	26.9	.0000	4	Purdy's
0.0486	26.9	.0000	4	Quarterback
0.0486	26.9	.0000	4	quarterbacks
0.0486	26.9	.0000	4	rationality
0.0486	26.9	.0000	4	Reagan
0.0486	26.9	.0000	4	rockslides
0.0486	26.9	.0000	4	Rollin
0.0486	26.9	.0000	4	Rugiati
0.0486	26.9	.0000	4	Sanguine
0.0486	26.9	.0000	4	Sassoon
0.0486	26.9	.0000	4	savannah
0.0486	26.9	.0000	4	Shoulders
0.0486	26.9	.0000	4	Soyuz
0.0486	26.9	.0000	4	sportswriter
0.0486	26.9	.0000	4	starring
0.0486	26.9	.0000	4	Suns
0.0486	26.9	.0000	4	Teeter
0.0486	26.9	.0000	4	ten-thousandths
0.0486	26.9	.0000	4	thermistor
0.0486	26.9	.0000	4	Torrey
0.0486	26.9	.0000	4	Toutle
0.0486	26.9	.0000	4	Villa's
0.0486	26.9	.0000	4	Wajir
0.0486	26.9	.0000	4	Weatherby
0.0486	26.9	.0000	4	Weitz
0.0486	26.9	.0000	4	Wells's
0.0486	26.9	.0000	4	WEU
0.0486	26.9	.0000	4	whipper-in
0.0486	26.9	.0000	4	Woozy
0.0486	26.9	.0000	4	1301
0.0486	26.9	.0000	4	1979
0.0485	26.9	.0000	6	Aida
0.0485	26.9	.0000	6	Belshazzar
0.0485	26.9	.0000	6	bimba
0.0485	26.9	.0000	6	Bonkey
0.0485	26.9	.0000	6	Chopin's
0.0485	26.9	.0000	6	Cock-a-doodle-doo
0.0485	26.9	.0000	6	crescendo
0.0485	26.9	.0000	6	Diaghilev
0.0485	26.9	.0000	6	dilly
0.0485	26.9	.0000	6	doo-dah
0.0485	26.9	.0000	6	duple
0.0485	26.9	.0000	6	Fantasia
0.0485	26.9	.0000	6	Finlandia
0.0485	26.9	.0000	6	five-tone
0.0485	26.9	.0000	6	G-major
0.0485	26.9	.0000	6	Gato
0.0485	26.9	.0000	6	HE
0.0485	26.9	.0000	6	Jemmy
0.0485	26.9	.0000	6	Minuet
0.0485	26.9	.0000	6	Mohee
0.0485	26.9	.0000	6	Nanki-Poo
0.0485	26.9	.0000	6	oinka
0.0485	26.9	.0000	6	Pirulero
0.0485	26.9	.0000	6	plainsong
0.0485	26.9	.0000	6	Polka
0.0485	26.9	.0000	6	rah
0.0485	26.9	.0000	6	resonator
0.0485	26.9	.0000	6	Rodolfo
0.0485	26.9	.0000	6	Rye
0.0485	26.9	.0000	6	Save
0.0485	26.9	.0000	6	sonatas
0.0485	26.9	.0000	6	squid-jiggin'
0.0485	26.9	.0000	6	Varese
0.0485	26.9	.0000	6	Yum-Yum
0.0485	26.9	.0000	6	Zapatitos
0.0483	26.8	.0000	15	homemaking
0.0480	26.8	.0379	4	covenant
0.0469	26.7	.0000	4	'Stute
0.0469	26.7	.0000	4	'e's
0.0469	26.7	.0000	4	'ee
0.0469	26.7	.0000	4	Aleda
0.0469	26.7	.0000	4	All-the-Cow-there-was
0.0469	26.7	.0000	4	ASTROGATOR
0.0469	26.7	.0000	4	At-mun-shi
0.0469	26.7	.0000	4	Birtwick
0.0469	26.7	.0000	4	BLACKOUT
0.0469	26.7	.0000	4	Borrowers
0.0469	26.7	.0000	4	brung
0.0469	26.7	.0000	4	cannibal
0.0469	26.7	.0000	4	Chongo
0.0469	26.7	.0000	4	Coachman
0.0469	26.7	.0000	4	CURTAIN
0.0469	26.7	.0000	4	Danhasch
0.0469	26.7	.0000	4	Derwin
0.0469	26.7	.0000	4	Dorsey
THE PRECEDING WORD TYPE OCCUPIES RANK 44800				
0.0469	26.7	.0000	4	Dovey
0.0469	26.7	.0000	4	Driver
0.0469	26.7	.0000	4	Dunnville
0.0469	26.7	.0000	4	Eland
0.0469	26.7	.0000	4	Fang's
0.0469	26.7	.0000	4	Fern's
0.0469	26.7	.0000	4	forepaw
0.0469	26.7	.0000	4	Gagnon
0.0469	26.7	.0000	4	gas-pipe
0.0469	26.7	.0000	4	Greta
0.0469	26.7	.0000	4	Grey's
0.0469	26.7	.0000	4	Helvi
0.0469	26.7	.0000	4	hev
0.0469	26.7	.0000	4	Hullocks
0.0469	26.7	.0000	4	Jaffrey
0.0469	26.7	.0000	4	jus'
0.0469	26.7	.0000	4	Kana
0.0469	26.7	.0000	4	Ko-Ngai
0.0469	26.7	.0000	4	Koodoo
0.0469	26.7	.0000	4	kun
0.0469	26.7	.0000	4	Larkin's
0.0469	26.7	.0000	4	Lavinia
0.0469	26.7	.0000	4	Liddell
0.0469	26.7	.0000	4	Luath
0.0469	26.7	.0000	4	Misses
0.0469	26.7	.0000	4	Nui
0.0469	26.7	.0000	4	Peder
0.0469	26.7	.0000	4	Popsipetels
0.0469	26.7	.0000	4	ranch-hand
0.0469	26.7	.0000	4	Rider's
0.0469	26.7	.0000	4	Rochambeau
0.0469	26.7	.0000	4	Roddenberry
0.0469	26.7	.0000	4	Rofelia
0.0469	26.7	.0000	4	scullery
0.0469	26.7	.0000	4	Seventeen
0.0469	26.7	.0000	4	Tao
0.0469	26.7	.0000	4	Tavana
0.0469	26.7	.0000	4	Tebbits
0.0469	26.7	.0000	4	thermoelement
0.0469	26.7	.0000	4	Tomahawks
0.0469	26.7	.0000	4	Toothaker
0.0469	26.7	.0000	4	Tutok
0.0469	26.7	.0000	4	Twink
0.0469	26.7	.0000	4	Ulape
0.0469	26.7	.0000	4	Vittore
0.0457	26.6	.0000	1	$215
0.0457	26.6	.0000	1	$6000
0.0457	26.6	.0000	1	$68-a-week
0.0457	26.6	.0000	1	-thirty
0.0457	26.6	.0000	1	'm
0.0457	26.6	.0000	1	's
0.0457	26.6	.0000	1	't
0.0457	26.6	.0000	1	acked
0.0457	26.6	.0000	1	alk
0.0457	26.6	.0000	1	als
0.0457	26.6	.0000	1	anded
0.0457	26.6	.0000	1	andwich
0.0457	26.6	.0000	1	at
0.0457	26.6	.0000	1	ches
0.0457	26.6	.0000	1	ckers
0.0457	26.6	.0000	1	ench
0.0457	26.6	.0000	1	ess
0.0457	26.6	.0000	1	ggs
0.0457	26.6	.0000	1	ing
0.0457	26.6	.0000	1	ip
0.0457	26.6	.0000	1	ipper
0.0457	26.6	.0000	1	irt
0.0457	26.6	.0000	1	ll
0.0457	26.6	.0000	1	ocks
0.0457	26.6	.0000	1	rinning
0.0457	26.6	.0000	1	rm
0.0457	26.6	.0000	1	s
0.0457	26.6	.0000	1	sn't
0.0457	26.6	.0000	1	ter
0.0457	26.6	.0000	1	ud
0.0457	26.6	.0000	1	zip
0.0457	26.6	.0000	1	'Em
0.0457	26.6	.0000	1	'ave
0.0457	26.6	.0000	1	'bye
0.0457	26.6	.0000	1	'ed
0.0457	26.6	.0000	1	'ere
0.0457	26.6	.0000	1	'leben
0.0457	26.6	.0000	1	'longside
0.0457	26.6	.0000	1	'lowed
0.0457	26.6	.0000	1	'op
0.0457	26.6	.0000	1	'peared
0.0457	26.6	.0000	1	'prentice
0.0457	26.6	.0000	1	'prentices
0.0457	26.6	.0000	1	'ray
0.0457	26.6	.0000	1	'spect
0.0457	26.6	.0000	1	'tisn't
0.0457	26.6	.0000	1	'76
0.0457	26.6	.0000	1	'99
0.0457	26.6	.0000	1	a-borning
0.0457	26.6	.0000	1	a-buzz
0.0457	26.6	.0000	1	a-callin'
0.0457	26.6	.0000	1	a-choo
0.0457	26.6	.0000	1	a-chunkin'
0.0457	26.6	.0000	1	a-comin'
0.0457	26.6	.0000	1	a-dying
THE PRECEDING WORD TYPE OCCUPIES RANK 44900				
0.0457	26.6	.0000	1	a-flutter
0.0457	26.6	.0000	1	a-glare
0.0457	26.6	.0000	1	a-growing
0.0457	26.6	.0000	1	a-kinda
0.0457	26.6	.0000	1	a-lightly
0.0457	26.6	.0000	1	a-list'nin'
0.0457	26.6	.0000	1	a-prickle
0.0457	26.6	.0000	1	a-scolding
0.0457	26.6	.0000	1	A-shaped**
0.0457	26.6	.0000	1	a-skitin'
0.0457	26.6	.0000	1	A-student
0.0457	26.6	.0000	1	a-stumblin'
0.0457	26.6	.0000	1	a-swellin'
0.0457	26.6	.0000	1	a-tall
0.0457	26.6	.0000	1	a-tchee
0.0457	26.6	.0000	1	a-telling
0.0457	26.6	.0000	1	a-tipsy
0.0457	26.6	.0000	1	a-wanderin'
0.0457	26.6	.0000	1	a-watching
0.0457	26.6	.0000	1	A-1
0.0457	26.6	.0000	1	A-11
0.0457	26.6	.0000	1	a
0.0457	26.6	.0000	1	aaaaaa
0.0457	26.6	.0000	1	aardvark's
0.0457	26.6	.0000	1	abandons
0.0457	26.6	.0000	1	abatement
0.0457	26.6	.0000	1	Abbotts
0.0457	26.6	.0000	1	Abolitionist
0.0457	26.6	.0000	1	Abominable
0.0457	26.6	.0000	1	absolument
0.0457	26.6	.0000	1	Abulbul
0.0457	26.6	.0000	1	abutted
0.0457	26.6	.0000	1	accost
0.0457	26.6	.0000	1	accrue
0.0457	26.6	.0000	1	accuser
0.0457	26.6	.0000	1	accuses
0.0457	26.6	.0000	1	Ace's
0.0457	26.6	.0000	1	acid-loaded
0.0457	26.6	.0000	1	acid-secreting
0.0457	26.6	.0000	1	acme
0.0457	26.6	.0000	1	acre-and-a-half
0.0457	26.6	.0000	1	Active
0.0457	26.6	.0000	1	Acton
0.0457	26.6	.0000	1	actuated
0.0457	26.6	.0000	1	Adams-supported
0.0457	26.6	.0000	1	Adamsale
0.0457	26.6	.0000	1	Adamsons

U	SFI	D	F	Word Type
0.0457	26.6	.0000	1	Addio's
0.0457	26.6	.0000	1	ADF
0.0457	26.6	.0000	1	Adjidaumo
0.0457	26.6	.0000	1	advancin'
0.0457	26.6	.0000	1	adventured
0.0457	26.6	.0000	1	Adventurous
0.0457	26.6	.0000	1	adversary's
0.0457	26.6	.0000	1	Aelder
0.0457	26.6	.0000	1	Aeneas's
0.0457	26.6	.0000	1	aerie
0.0457	26.6	.0000	1	Aero-Medical
0.0457	26.6	.0000	1	Aeson's
0.0457	26.6	.0000	1	Aetes'
0.0457	26.6	.0000	1	affable
0.0457	26.6	.0000	1	affair's
0.0457	26.6	.0000	1	aflutter
0.0457	26.6	.0000	1	after-midnight
0.0457	26.6	.0000	1	aftercabin
0.0457	26.6	.0000	1	afterhatch
0.0457	26.6	.0000	1	Agate
0.0457	26.6	.0000	1	aggregations
0.0457	26.6	.0000	1	aggressions
0.0457	26.6	.0000	1	ahhhhh
0.0457	26.6	.0000	1	ahhhhhh
0.0457	26.6	.0000	1	ahlan-wa-sahlan
0.0457	26.6	.0000	1	aht
0.0457	26.6	.0000	1	ailed
0.0457	26.6	.0000	1	air-blast
0.0457	26.6	.0000	1	air-borne
0.0457	26.6	.0000	1	air-traffic
0.0457	26.6	.0000	1	airhose
0.0457	26.6	.0000	1	airings
0.0457	26.6	.0000	1	airships
0.0457	26.6	.0000	1	airstrips
0.0457	26.6	.0000	1	airwaves
0.0457	26.6	.0000	1	Ak
0.0457	26.6	.0000	1	Akana
0.0457	26.6	.0000	1	Aklavik
0.0457	26.6	.0000	1	Al-ay-ek-sa
0.0457	26.6	.0000	1	alarm-clock
0.0457	26.6	.0000	1	alarm-riders
0.0457	26.6	.0000	1	albinos
0.0457	26.6	.0000	1	Albright
0.0457	26.6	.0000	1	Alcatraz
0.0457	26.6	.0000	1	Alcimide
0.0457	26.6	.0000	1	Aleck's
0.0457	26.6	.0000	1	Aleid
0.0457	26.6	.0000	1	Alexandrova
0.0457	26.6	.0000	1	alfilaria
0.0457	26.6	.0000	1	Alfonso's
0.0457	26.6	.0000	1	Alfredo
0.0457	26.6	.0000	1	alikenesses
0.0457	26.6	.0000	1	Alive
THE PRECEDING WORD TYPE OCCUPIES RANK 45000				
0.0457	26.6	.0000	1	all-around
0.0457	26.6	.0000	1	all-astronaut
0.0457	26.6	.0000	1	all-gifted
0.0457	26.6	.0000	1	Allard
0.0457	26.6	.0000	1	ALLIGATOR
0.0457	26.6	.0000	1	alls
0.0457	26.6	.0000	1	Allston
0.0457	26.6	.0000	1	almond-tree
0.0457	26.6	.0000	1	almost-eleven
0.0457	26.6	.0000	1	almost-forgotten
0.0457	26.6	.0000	1	aloes
0.0457	26.6	.0000	1	Alphonse
0.0457	26.6	.0000	1	alphorns
0.0457	26.6	.0000	1	Alsace
0.0457	26.6	.0000	1	altar's
0.0457	26.6	.0000	1	Alvaro's
0.0457	26.6	.0000	1	ALWAYS
0.0457	26.6	.0000	1	Alyse
0.0457	26.6	.0000	1	Alzate
0.0457	26.6	.0000	1	Amalie
0.0457	26.6	.0000	1	Amanda's
0.0457	26.6	.0000	1	amber-colored
0.0457	26.6	.0000	1	amble
0.0457	26.6	.0000	1	Amboseli
0.0457	26.6	.0000	1	amercy
0.0457	26.6	.0000	1	America'
0.0457	26.6	.0000	1	Amesburg
0.0457	26.6	.0000	1	amicably
0.0457	26.6	.0000	1	Amik's
0.0457	26.6	.0000	1	Amon
0.0457	26.6	.0000	1	Amroo
0.0457	26.6	.0000	1	Amycus
0.0457	26.6	.0000	1	anablep
0.0457	26.6	.0000	1	Anagnos'
0.0457	26.6	.0000	1	anchor's
0.0457	26.6	.0000	1	Andre's
0.0457	26.6	.0000	1	Androcles'
0.0457	26.6	.0000	1	angakok's
0.0457	26.6	.0000	1	angelically
0.0457	26.6	.0000	1	angels'
0.0457	26.6	.0000	1	Angels'
0.0457	26.6	.0000	1	animalports
0.0457	26.6	.0000	1	animals's
0.0457	26.6	.0000	1	Annabelle's
0.0457	26.6	.0000	1	anniversaries
0.0457	26.6	.0000	1	announcer's
0.0457	26.6	.0000	1	anosmics
0.0457	26.6	.0000	1	anser
0.0457	26.6	.0000	1	ant-eating
0.0457	26.6	.0000	1	ant-sniffer
0.0457	26.6	.0000	1	antagonisms
0.0457	26.6	.0000	1	anteating
0.0457	26.6	.0000	1	antediluvian
0.0457	26.6	.0000	1	Antenor
0.0457	26.6	.0000	1	anthills
0.0457	26.6	.0000	1	anti-impeaching
0.0457	26.6	.0000	1	anticontact
0.0457	26.6	.0000	1	antidotes
0.0457	26.6	.0000	1	antigravity
0.0457	26.6	.0000	1	Antin
0.0457	26.6	.0000	1	antiquities
0.0457	26.6	.0000	1	Antone
0.0457	26.6	.0000	1	anythin'
0.0457	26.6	.0000	1	Anza-Borrego
0.0457	26.6	.0000	1	apartment's
0.0457	26.6	.0000	1	apeak
0.0457	26.6	.0000	1	aphids'
0.0457	26.6	.0000	1	Aphrodite's
0.0457	26.6	.0000	1	aplenty
0.0457	26.6	.0000	1	apostates
0.0457	26.6	.0000	1	Appaloosas
0.0457	26.6	.0000	1	appendicitis
0.0457	26.6	.0000	1	appertaining
0.0457	26.6	.0000	1	appetite-satisfying
0.0457	26.6	.0000	1	apple-tart
0.0457	26.6	.0000	1	apprenticing
0.0457	26.6	.0000	1	Apsyrtus
0.0457	26.6	.0000	1	Araby
0.0457	26.6	.0000	1	arbis
0.0457	26.6	.0000	1	arbislach
0.0457	26.6	.0000	1	Archie's
0.0457	26.6	.0000	1	Arcola
0.0457	26.6	.0000	1	Ares
0.0457	26.6	.0000	1	Argentinean
0.0457	26.6	.0000	1	Argonaut
0.0457	26.6	.0000	1	argufying
0.0457	26.6	.0000	1	aright
0.0457	26.6	.0000	1	Arikara's
0.0457	26.6	.0000	1	Aristides
0.0457	26.6	.0000	1	armadillo's
0.0457	26.6	.0000	1	armorer
0.0457	26.6	.0000	1	arrears
0.0457	26.6	.0000	1	arrogating
0.0457	26.6	.0000	1	arroz
0.0457	26.6	.0000	1	ARRS
0.0457	26.6	.0000	1	artfully
0.0457	26.6	.0000	1	articulating
0.0457	26.6	.0000	1	Artie's
0.0457	26.6	.0000	1	artillerists
0.0457	26.6	.0000	1	Artist's
THE PRECEDING WORD TYPE OCCUPIES RANK 45100				
0.0457	26.6	.0000	1	Asaph
0.0457	26.6	.0000	1	asbestoslike
0.0457	26.6	.0000	1	Asbury
0.0457	26.6	.0000	1	ascribes
0.0457	26.6	.0000	1	Ashbellows
0.0457	26.6	.0000	1	asparkle
0.0457	26.6	.0000	1	assail
0.0457	26.6	.0000	1	Assam
0.0457	26.6	.0000	1	Assen
0.0457	26.6	.0000	1	assukiak
0.0457	26.6	.0000	1	astraddle
0.0457	26.6	.0000	1	Atchafalaya
0.0457	26.6	.0000	1	Atchison
0.0457	26.6	.0000	1	Athlete
0.0457	26.6	.0000	1	Atti's
0.0457	26.6	.0000	1	Attic
0.0457	26.6	.0000	1	Atupaluk
0.0457	26.6	.0000	1	Auden
0.0457	26.6	.0000	1	audition
0.0457	26.6	.0000	1	auditoriums
0.0457	26.6	.0000	1	Auenbrugger's
0.0457	26.6	.0000	1	auf
0.0457	26.6	.0000	1	Augeas
0.0457	26.6	.0000	1	Augusto
0.0457	26.6	.0000	1	Aulis
0.0457	26.6	.0000	1	Auslander
0.0457	26.6	.0000	1	autographing
0.0457	26.6	.0000	1	autopsies
0.0457	26.6	.0000	1	avance
0.0457	26.6	.0000	1	aw-w-w-w
0.0457	26.6	.0000	1	awarding
0.0457	26.6	.0000	1	awk
0.0457	26.6	.0000	1	awkward-looking
0.0457	26.6	.0000	1	ax-handle
0.0457	26.6	.0000	1	axheads
0.0457	26.6	.0000	1	axlike
0.0457	26.6	.0000	1	ayoung
0.0457	26.6	.0000	1	Azaz
0.0457	26.6	.0000	1	azurite
0.0457	26.6	.0000	1	b-beads
0.0457	26.6	.0000	1	b-r-r-ring
0.0457	26.6	.0000	1	bll
0.0457	26.6	.0000	1	bts
0.0457	26.6	.0000	1	baa-aa-aa
0.0457	26.6	.0000	1	Babel's
0.0457	26.6	.0000	1	babes
0.0457	26.6	.0000	1	Babis
0.0457	26.6	.0000	1	baby-round
0.0457	26.6	.0000	1	baby-sat
0.0457	26.6	.0000	1	baccy
0.0457	26.6	.0000	1	backache
0.0457	26.6	.0000	1	backboard
0.0457	26.6	.0000	1	backboards
0.0457	26.6	.0000	1	backstroke
0.0457	26.6	.0000	1	backwash
0.0457	26.6	.0000	1	Backyard
0.0457	26.6	.0000	1	bad-mannered
0.0457	26.6	.0000	1	badgered
0.0457	26.6	.0000	1	bag's
0.0457	26.6	.0000	1	Bagby's
0.0457	26.6	.0000	1	Baggott
0.0457	26.6	.0000	1	Baggott's
0.0457	26.6	.0000	1	bailin'
0.0457	26.6	.0000	1	bailiwick
0.0457	26.6	.0000	1	bain't
0.0457	26.6	.0000	1	baked-mud
0.0457	26.6	.0000	1	Balahait
0.0457	26.6	.0000	1	balance-weight
0.0457	26.6	.0000	1	balconied
0.0457	26.6	.0000	1	ball-carrying
0.0457	26.6	.0000	1	Ballaghadereen
0.0457	26.6	.0000	1	Ballarat
0.0457	26.6	.0000	1	balloon-shaped
0.0457	26.6	.0000	1	bally
0.0457	26.6	.0000	1	Balsora
0.0457	26.6	.0000	1	bamboo-matted
0.0457	26.6	.0000	1	Bandit
0.0457	26.6	.0000	1	Bangkok's
0.0457	26.6	.0000	1	bankbook
0.0457	26.6	.0000	1	Banker
0.0457	26.6	.0000	1	banker's
0.0457	26.6	.0000	1	Bannekers
0.0457	26.6	.0000	1	Banquet
0.0457	26.6	.0000	1	Bantam
0.0457	26.6	.0000	1	banter
0.0457	26.6	.0000	1	Bar-K
0.0457	26.6	.0000	1	barb-wire
0.0457	26.6	.0000	1	barba
0.0457	26.6	.0000	1	barbered
0.0457	26.6	.0000	1	bare-sandaled
0.0457	26.6	.0000	1	bargain's
0.0457	26.6	.0000	1	bark-stickers
0.0457	26.6	.0000	1	barkeeper
0.0457	26.6	.0000	1	barlow
0.0457	26.6	.0000	1	Barneses
0.0457	26.6	.0000	1	Barney's
0.0457	26.6	.0000	1	baron's
0.0457	26.6	.0000	1	Baron's
0.0457	26.6	.0000	1	Barpur
0.0457	26.6	.0000	1	Barr
THE PRECEDING WORD TYPE OCCUPIES RANK 45200				
0.0457	26.6	.0000	1	barrel-making
0.0457	26.6	.0000	1	Barrett's
0.0457	26.6	.0000	1	Barretts
0.0457	26.6	.0000	1	barricaded
0.0457	26.6	.0000	1	Barrinish
0.0457	26.6	.0000	1	Bars
0.0457	26.6	.0000	1	Bartholdi's
0.0457	26.6	.0000	1	Bascom's
0.0457	26.6	.0000	1	basest
0.0457	26.6	.0000	1	bashfully
0.0457	26.6	.0000	1	basked
0.0457	26.6	.0000	1	basket's
0.0457	26.6	.0000	1	basques
0.0457	26.6	.0000	1	basta
0.0457	26.6	.0000	1	bathyscaphes
0.0457	26.6	.0000	1	battened
0.0457	26.6	.0000	1	batterings
0.0457	26.6	.0000	1	battle-lit
0.0457	26.6	.0000	1	battle's
0.0457	26.6	.0000	1	battleships'
0.0457	26.6	.0000	1	battlewise
0.0457	26.6	.0000	1	bayous
0.0457	26.6	.0000	1	Beady
0.0457	26.6	.0000	1	Beady-Eyes
0.0457	26.6	.0000	1	beady-eyed
0.0457	26.6	.0000	1	Beale's
0.0457	26.6	.0000	1	BEAN
0.0457	26.6	.0000	1	bean-bag
0.0457	26.6	.0000	1	bean-picker
0.0457	26.6	.0000	1	Bean's
0.0457	26.6	.0000	1	beanburgers
0.0457	26.6	.0000	1	beanings
0.0457	26.6	.0000	1	bear-fighting
0.0457	26.6	.0000	1	bearskins
0.0457	26.6	.0000	1	Beaseley
0.0457	26.6	.0000	1	beauteous
0.0457	26.6	.0000	1	beaver-talk
0.0457	26.6	.0000	1	because-why
0.0457	26.6	.0000	1	bedknob
0.0457	26.6	.0000	1	Bedlam
0.0457	26.6	.0000	1	bedposts
0.0457	26.6	.0000	1	bedroom's
0.0457	26.6	.0000	1	Beechcraft
0.0457	26.6	.0000	1	Beekman
0.0457	26.6	.0000	1	beeped
0.0457	26.6	.0000	1	beetlelike
0.0457	26.6	.0000	1	befriends
0.0457	26.6	.0000	1	begets
0.0457	26.6	.0000	1	beggin'
0.0457	26.6	.0000	1	begonia
0.0457	26.6	.0000	1	behests
0.0457	26.6	.0000	1	Behind
0.0457	26.6	.0000	1	beholder
0.0457	26.6	.0000	1	being-dragged
0.0457	26.6	.0000	1	bejeepers
0.0457	26.6	.0000	1	belches
0.0457	26.6	.0000	1	Believable
0.0457	26.6	.0000	1	believingly
0.0457	26.6	.0000	1	belittle
0.0457	26.6	.0000	1	bell's
0.0457	26.6	.0000	1	belles
0.0457	26.6	.0000	1	Bellows
0.0457	26.6	.0000	1	bellshaped
0.0457	26.6	.0000	1	belly-landing
0.0457	26.6	.0000	1	Belted
0.0457	26.6	.0000	1	bemoaned
0.0457	26.6	.0000	1	Benchly's
0.0457	26.6	.0000	1	Benders
0.0457	26.6	.0000	1	Bendy's
0.0457	26.6	.0000	1	Benedek's
0.0457	26.6	.0000	1	Benito's
0.0457	26.6	.0000	1	Benji's
0.0457	26.6	.0000	1	Benjie's
0.0457	26.6	.0000	1	Bent
0.0457	26.6	.0000	1	Bergen-Belsen
0.0457	26.6	.0000	1	Bergson
0.0457	26.6	.0000	1	Bernice
0.0457	26.6	.0000	1	Berry's
0.0457	26.6	.0000	1	Bertini
0.0457	26.6	.0000	1	Berton
0.0457	26.6	.0000	1	best-beloved
0.0457	26.6	.0000	1	bestest
0.0457	26.6	.0000	1	Beto's
0.0457	26.6	.0000	1	betook
0.0457	26.6	.0000	1	betrayals
0.0457	26.6	.0000	1	better-behaved
0.0457	26.6	.0000	1	better'n
0.0457	26.6	.0000	1	Bettine
0.0457	26.6	.0000	1	Bevis
0.0457	26.6	.0000	1	bevy
0.0457	26.6	.0000	1	bewailing
0.0457	26.6	.0000	1	bewteen
0.0457	26.6	.0000	1	Bey's
0.0457	26.6	.0000	1	Bi
0.0457	26.6	.0000	1	bi-cycle
0.0457	26.6	.0000	1	bi
0.0457	26.6	.0000	1	Biafu's
0.0457	26.6	.0000	1	Bibbs
0.0457	26.6	.0000	1	bibs
0.0457	26.6	.0000	1	Biddlewee's
THE PRECEDING WORD TYPE OCCUPIES RANK 45300				
0.0457	26.6	.0000	1	Biddlewhite
0.0457	26.6	.0000	1	Biddlewhite's
0.0457	26.6	.0000	1	Bifrost
0.0457	26.6	.0000	1	big-eyed
0.0457	26.6	.0000	1	big-leaguers
0.0457	26.6	.0000	1	Bigmouth
0.0457	26.6	.0000	1	Bigsy's
0.0457	26.6	.0000	1	bike's
0.0457	26.6	.0000	1	Bikle
0.0457	26.6	.0000	1	bild
0.0457	26.6	.0000	1	Billy-goat
0.0457	26.6	.0000	1	billy's
0.0457	26.6	.0000	1	biographers
0.0457	26.6	.0000	1	birchbark
0.0457	26.6	.0000	1	bird-banding
0.0457	26.6	.0000	1	birdcage
0.0457	26.6	.0000	1	birdcall
0.0457	26.6	.0000	1	birdcalls
0.0457	26.6	.0000	1	birdland
0.0457	26.6	.0000	1	Birds'
0.0457	26.6	.0000	1	Birora
0.0457	26.6	.0000	1	Bit
0.0457	26.6	.0000	1	bl
0.0457	26.6	.0000	1	black-and-yellow
0.0457	26.6	.0000	1	Black-capped
0.0457	26.6	.0000	1	black-hand
0.0457	26.6	.0000	1	black-looking
0.0457	26.6	.0000	1	black-smudged
0.0457	26.6	.0000	1	black-tipped
0.0457	26.6	.0000	1	Blackfish
0.0457	26.6	.0000	1	blackguard
0.0457	26.6	.0000	1	blackmail
0.0457	26.6	.0000	1	Blacks
0.0457	26.6	.0000	1	Blackwood
0.0457	26.6	.0000	1	Blanca
0.0457	26.6	.0000	1	blaster
0.0457	26.6	.0000	1	Blefuscu
0.0457	26.6	.0000	1	blizzard-swept
0.0457	26.6	.0000	1	blizzard's
0.0457	26.6	.0000	1	blizzardy
0.0457	26.6	.0000	1	block-and-tackle
0.0457	26.6	.0000	1	Block's
0.0457	26.6	.0000	1	blockheaded
0.0457	26.6	.0000	1	blockhouses
0.0457	26.6	.0000	1	bloody-nosed
0.0457	26.6	.0000	1	bloomin'
0.0457	26.6	.0000	1	Bloomingdale
0.0457	26.6	.0000	1	blotch
0.0457	26.6	.0000	1	Blott
0.0457	26.6	.0000	1	Blotto's
0.0457	26.6	.0000	1	blow-down
0.0457	26.6	.0000	1	blow-outs
0.0457	26.6	.0000	1	blowin'
0.0457	26.6	.0000	1	blowy
0.0457	26.6	.0000	1	Blue-Backed
0.0457	26.6	.0000	1	blue-bonneted
0.0457	26.6	.0000	1	blue-checked
0.0457	26.6	.0000	1	blue-gums
0.0457	26.6	.0000	1	blue-jay
0.0457	26.6	.0000	1	blue-wrappered
0.0457	26.6	.0000	1	Bluebird's
0.0457	26.6	.0000	1	bluebottles
0.0457	26.6	.0000	1	blueness
0.0457	26.6	.0000	1	bluffer
0.0457	26.6	.0000	1	bluffers
0.0457	26.6	.0000	1	bluffing
0.0457	26.6	.0000	1	Blumberg's
0.0457	26.6	.0000	1	blustering
0.0457	26.6	.0000	1	bo'sun
0.0457	26.6	.0000	1	board-an'-keep
0.0457	26.6	.0000	1	boarding-house
0.0457	26.6	.0000	1	boaster
0.0457	26.6	.0000	1	boat-steerer
0.0457	26.6	.0000	1	boatload
0.0457	26.6	.0000	1	bob-tail
0.0457	26.6	.0000	1	bobbled
0.0457	26.6	.0000	1	Bobo
0.0457	26.6	.0000	1	boded
0.0457	26.6	.0000	1	bogged
0.0457	26.6	.0000	1	bogle
0.0457	26.6	.0000	1	bogle's
0.0457	26.6	.0000	1	bogus
0.0457	26.6	.0000	1	bois
0.0457	26.6	.0000	1	boisterously
0.0457	26.6	.0000	1	bolognas
0.0457	26.6	.0000	1	bombastic
0.0457	26.6	.0000	1	bombero
0.0457	26.6	.0000	1	Bomberos'
0.0457	26.6	.0000	1	Bonatti's
0.0457	26.6	.0000	1	bone-hard
0.0457	26.6	.0000	1	Bong-tree
0.0457	26.6	.0000	1	Bonham
0.0457	26.6	.0000	1	Bonneville
0.0457	26.6	.0000	1	bonsoir
0.0457	26.6	.0000	1	Bonwit's
0.0457	26.6	.0000	1	boohooing
0.0457	26.6	.0000	1	book-lined
0.0457	26.6	.0000	1	bookkeeper
0.0457	26.6	.0000	1	bookkeepers
0.0457	26.6	.0000	1	bookside
THE PRECEDING WORD TYPE OCCUPIES RANK 45400				
0.0457	26.6	.0000	1	bookstores
0.0457	26.6	.0000	1	boom-boom-boom
0.0457	26.6	.0000	1	boomerangs
0.0457	26.6	.0000	1	Boopfaddle
0.0457	26.6	.0000	1	boreen
0.0457	26.6	.0000	1	bornite
0.0457	26.6	.0000	1	borryed
0.0457	26.6	.0000	1	bossier
0.0457	26.6	.0000	1	BOTH
0.0457	26.6	.0000	1	botheration

U	SFI	D	F	Word Type
0.0457	26.6	.0000	1	Botte
0.0457	26.6	.0000	1	bottle-nosed
0.0457	26.6	.0000	1	Bouncer
0.0457	26.6	.0000	1	bow-legged
0.0457	26.6	.0000	1	bow-wow-ow-ow
0.0457	26.6	.0000	1	bow-wow-ow-ow-ow
0.0457	26.6	.0000	1	bowhead
0.0457	26.6	.0000	1	bowie
0.0457	26.6	.0000	1	bowie-knife
0.0457	26.6	.0000	1	bowin'
0.0457	26.6	.0000	1	Boxing
0.0457	26.6	.0000	1	Boy'll
0.0457	26.6	.0000	1	BR-RAT-TA-TAT-TAT
0.0457	26.6	.0000	1	br-r-r-ring
0.0457	26.6	.0000	1	Brad's
0.0457	26.6	.0000	1	brain's
0.0457	26.6	.0000	1	branch-shaped
0.0457	26.6	.0000	1	branch
0.0457	26.6	.0000	1	branchy
0.0457	26.6	.0000	1	Brand's
0.0457	26.6	.0000	1	brass-buttoned
0.0457	26.6	.0000	1	brave's
0.0457	26.6	.0000	1	brawling
0.0457	26.6	.0000	1	bray
0.0457	26.6	.0000	1	brayed
0.0457	26.6	.0000	1	bread-box
0.0457	26.6	.0000	1	Breadfruit
0.0457	26.6	.0000	1	breadman's
0.0457	26.6	.0000	1	breadwinner
0.0457	26.6	.0000	1	Breakthrough
0.0457	26.6	.0000	1	breasting
0.0457	26.6	.0000	1	breechclout
0.0457	26.6	.0000	1	breed's
0.0457	26.6	.0000	1	breeders'
0.0457	26.6	.0000	1	breeks
0.0457	26.6	.0000	1	breeze-tossed
0.0457	26.6	.0000	1	breezeway
0.0457	26.6	.0000	1	Breukelen
0.0457	26.6	.0000	1	brewer
0.0457	26.6	.0000	1	Brewing
0.0457	26.6	.0000	1	BRIDGE
0.0457	26.6	.0000	1	Bridger's
0.0457	26.6	.0000	1	bright-cheeked
0.0457	26.6	.0000	1	brightly-painted
0.0457	26.6	.0000	1	Brighty's
0.0457	26.6	.0000	1	Brilliant
0.0457	26.6	.0000	1	brindled
0.0457	26.6	.0000	1	brisker
0.0457	26.6	.0000	1	broad-backed
0.0457	26.6	.0000	1	broadax
0.0457	26.6	.0000	1	brocket
0.0457	26.6	.0000	1	brok-
0.0457	26.6	.0000	1	Brok's
0.0457	26.6	.0000	1	broken-up
0.0457	26.6	.0000	1	bronco-busters
0.0457	26.6	.0000	1	broncobusters
0.0457	26.6	.0000	1	BRONX
0.0457	26.6	.0000	1	bronze-topped
0.0457	26.6	.0000	1	brown-haired
0.0457	26.6	.0000	1	brownstone
0.0457	26.6	.0000	1	brrrooom
0.0457	26.6	.0000	1	Brucie's
0.0457	26.6	.0000	1	Brummell
0.0457	26.6	.0000	1	brushwood-fire
0.0457	26.6	.0000	1	Brute
0.0457	26.6	.0000	1	Buck'll
0.0457	26.6	.0000	1	buckboards
0.0457	26.6	.0000	1	buckler
0.0457	26.6	.0000	1	buckoes
0.0457	26.6	.0000	1	budded
0.0457	26.6	.0000	1	buffetings
0.0457	26.6	.0000	1	Bufflao
0.0457	26.6	.0000	1	bugging
0.0457	26.6	.0000	1	buglers
0.0457	26.6	.0000	1	bujeni
0.0457	26.6	.0000	1	bull-voiced
0.0457	26.6	.0000	1	BULL'S-eye
0.0457	26.6	.0000	1	bull's-eyes
0.0457	26.6	.0000	1	Bullfinch's
0.0457	26.6	.0000	1	bullock
0.0457	26.6	.0000	1	bullocks'
0.0457	26.6	.0000	1	bullwhip
0.0457	26.6	.0000	1	bumblings
0.0457	26.6	.0000	1	bummed
0.0457	26.6	.0000	1	Bunch
0.0457	26.6	.0000	1	bundled-up
0.0457	26.6	.0000	1	bunkyojo
0.0457	26.6	.0000	1	bunnykin
0.0457	26.6	.0000	1	bunted
0.0457	26.6	.0000	1	Burica
				THE PRECEDING WORD TYPE OCCUPIES RANK 45500
0.0457	26.6	.0000	1	burned-over
0.0457	26.6	.0000	1	burnishing
0.0457	26.6	.0000	1	Bush's
0.0457	26.6	.0000	1	Bushiya
0.0457	26.6	.0000	1	bushland
0.0457	26.6	.0000	1	bushman's
0.0457	26.6	.0000	1	buster
0.0457	26.6	.0000	1	Buster's
0.0457	26.6	.0000	1	Butch's
0.0457	26.6	.0000	1	BUTTER
0.0457	26.6	.0000	1	Butterfields
0.0457	26.6	.0000	1	butterfish
0.0457	26.6	.0000	1	buttermaking
0.0457	26.6	.0000	1	Byfield
0.0457	26.6	.0000	1	Byoo
0.0457	26.6	.0000	1	Byron's
0.0457	26.6	.0000	1	byway
0.0457	26.6	.0000	1	c-r-onk
0.0457	26.6	.0000	1	cll
0.0457	26.6	.0000	1	crds
0.0457	26.6	.0000	1	c'mon
0.0457	26.6	.0000	1	cabinboy
0.0457	26.6	.0000	1	cable's
0.0457	26.6	.0000	1	Cabots
0.0457	26.6	.0000	1	cackle
0.0457	26.6	.0000	1	cacklings
0.0457	26.6	.0000	1	caddie
0.0457	26.6	.0000	1	caddied
0.0457	26.6	.0000	1	Cages
0.0457	26.6	.0000	1	Cain
0.0457	26.6	.0000	1	cake-baking
0.0457	26.6	.0000	1	calf-like
0.0457	26.6	.0000	1	calomel
0.0457	26.6	.0000	1	calumnies
0.0457	26.6	.0000	1	calving
0.0457	26.6	.0000	1	CAMBIO
0.0457	26.6	.0000	1	camel-thorn
0.0457	26.6	.0000	1	camel's-hair
0.0457	26.6	.0000	1	Camilla
0.0457	26.6	.0000	1	Campers'
0.0457	26.6	.0000	1	camphire
0.0457	26.6	.0000	1	canali
0.0457	26.6	.0000	1	canalman
0.0457	26.6	.0000	1	Canaria
0.0457	26.6	.0000	1	Canaries
0.0457	26.6	.0000	1	canary-coloured
0.0457	26.6	.0000	1	canary-yellow
0.0457	26.6	.0000	1	cancellation
0.0457	26.6	.0000	1	CANDITA
0.0457	26.6	.0000	1	candle-lighted
0.0457	26.6	.0000	1	candleberry
0.0457	26.6	.0000	1	candlelit
0.0457	26.6	.0000	1	cane-seated
0.0457	26.6	.0000	1	canebrake
0.0457	26.6	.0000	1	Cani
0.0457	26.6	.0000	1	canis
0.0457	26.6	.0000	1	cannon-balls
0.0457	26.6	.0000	1	cannon-sized
0.0457	26.6	.0000	1	Cannon's
0.0457	26.6	.0000	1	cannonading
0.0457	26.6	.0000	1	cannoneer
0.0457	26.6	.0000	1	cantonment
0.0457	26.6	.0000	1	Cantor's
0.0457	26.6	.0000	1	Canute's
0.0457	26.6	.0000	1	Cap's
0.0457	26.6	.0000	1	Cape's
0.0457	26.6	.0000	1	captainy
0.0457	26.6	.0000	1	captor
0.0457	26.6	.0000	1	Captured
0.0457	26.6	.0000	1	carabao's
0.0457	26.6	.0000	1	Carakters
0.0457	26.6	.0000	1	caramels
0.0457	26.6	.0000	1	card-house
0.0457	26.6	.0000	1	cardamons
0.0457	26.6	.0000	1	Carefully
0.0457	26.6	.0000	1	carefulness
0.0457	26.6	.0000	1	caretaker
0.0457	26.6	.0000	1	carfare
0.0457	26.6	.0000	1	Carleton
0.0457	26.6	.0000	1	Carlito
0.0457	26.6	.0000	1	Carlton
0.0457	26.6	.0000	1	Carmela
0.0457	26.6	.0000	1	Caroline's
0.0457	26.6	.0000	1	carousel
0.0457	26.6	.0000	1	carpetmaking
0.0457	26.6	.0000	1	Carreno
0.0457	26.6	.0000	1	Carstairs
0.0457	26.6	.0000	1	cart-whip
0.0457	26.6	.0000	1	carting
0.0457	26.6	.0000	1	Cassandra
0.0457	26.6	.0000	1	Cassiterides
0.0457	26.6	.0000	1	cast-off
0.0457	26.6	.0000	1	castle-yard
0.0457	26.6	.0000	1	cat's-claw
0.0457	26.6	.0000	1	cat's-meat-man
0.0457	26.6	.0000	1	Cataline
0.0457	26.6	.0000	1	catalpa
0.0457	26.6	.0000	1	Catfish
0.0457	26.6	.0000	1	Cathy's
0.0457	26.6	.0000	1	catties
				THE PRECEDING WORD TYPE OCCUPIES RANK 45600
0.0457	26.6	.0000	1	cattle's
0.0457	26.6	.0000	1	cattleman
0.0457	26.6	.0000	1	caucus
0.0457	26.6	.0000	1	cauliflowers
0.0457	26.6	.0000	1	cave-like
0.0457	26.6	.0000	1	cavemen
0.0457	26.6	.0000	1	Cavern
0.0457	26.6	.0000	1	Cecco
0.0457	26.6	.0000	1	Cecie
0.0457	26.6	.0000	1	Celine
0.0457	26.6	.0000	1	Cement
0.0457	26.6	.0000	1	cementite
0.0457	26.6	.0000	1	Centaur
0.0457	26.6	.0000	1	centaur's
0.0457	26.6	.0000	1	Ceremonies
0.0457	26.6	.0000	1	cerium
0.0457	26.6	.0000	1	Cessna
0.0457	26.6	.0000	1	chaining
0.0457	26.6	.0000	1	Chaka
0.0457	26.6	.0000	1	chalcocite
0.0457	26.6	.0000	1	Chalk
0.0457	26.6	.0000	1	challengers
0.0457	26.6	.0000	1	chambermaids
0.0457	26.6	.0000	1	champed
0.0457	26.6	.0000	1	chanct
0.0457	26.6	.0000	1	Chand's
0.0457	26.6	.0000	1	chandelled
0.0457	26.6	.0000	1	chandlers
0.0457	26.6	.0000	1	chaparreras
0.0457	26.6	.0000	1	Chaplains
0.0457	26.6	.0000	1	character'll
0.0457	26.6	.0000	1	charlatan
0.0457	26.6	.0000	1	Charlton
0.0457	26.6	.0000	1	Chase's
0.0457	26.6	.0000	1	chaser
0.0457	26.6	.0000	1	chasers
0.0457	26.6	.0000	1	chastising
0.0457	26.6	.0000	1	Chat
0.0457	26.6	.0000	1	chatterin'
0.0457	26.6	.0000	1	Cheat
0.0457	26.6	.0000	1	cheecha
0.0457	26.6	.0000	1	cheep-eep-eep
0.0457	26.6	.0000	1	cheeped
0.0457	26.6	.0000	1	cheeping
0.0457	26.6	.0000	1	cheeriest
0.0457	26.6	.0000	1	cheerleader
0.0457	26.6	.0000	1	Chelmbury
0.0457	26.6	.0000	1	Chelmsford
0.0457	26.6	.0000	1	chemise
0.0457	26.6	.0000	1	Cheney
0.0457	26.6	.0000	1	chestful
0.0457	26.6	.0000	1	chetyre
0.0457	26.6	.0000	1	chewers
0.0457	26.6	.0000	1	Cheyennes'
0.0457	26.6	.0000	1	chicken-from-outer-space
0.0457	26.6	.0000	1	Chickey
0.0457	26.6	.0000	1	chiding
0.0457	26.6	.0000	1	child-face
0.0457	26.6	.0000	1	child-voice
0.0457	26.6	.0000	1	chile
0.0457	26.6	.0000	1	chilliness
0.0457	26.6	.0000	1	chimbley
0.0457	26.6	.0000	1	chimbly
0.0457	26.6	.0000	1	Chimera
0.0457	26.6	.0000	1	chin-ups
0.0457	26.6	.0000	1	china-headed
0.0457	26.6	.0000	1	china-rimmed
0.0457	26.6	.0000	1	Chinee
0.0457	26.6	.0000	1	Ching's
0.0457	26.6	.0000	1	chip-off-the-old-block
0.0457	26.6	.0000	1	Chip's
0.0457	26.6	.0000	1	chipmunk's
0.0457	26.6	.0000	1	Chipmunk's
0.0457	26.6	.0000	1	Chiquita
0.0457	26.6	.0000	1	chirp-chirp-chirp
0.0457	26.6	.0000	1	Chirrup
0.0457	26.6	.0000	1	chirruping
0.0457	26.6	.0000	1	chitons
0.0457	26.6	.0000	1	chitter-chatter
0.0457	26.6	.0000	1	chocks
0.0457	26.6	.0000	1	chocolate-brown
0.0457	26.6	.0000	1	choicest
0.0457	26.6	.0000	1	Choko-Krunch
0.0457	26.6	.0000	1	choo-choo
0.0457	26.6	.0000	1	choos
0.0457	26.6	.0000	1	Chow
0.0457	26.6	.0000	1	Christmasy
0.0457	26.6	.0000	1	Christophilos's
0.0457	26.6	.0000	1	Christowe
0.0457	26.6	.0000	1	chrysocolla
0.0457	26.6	.0000	1	Chucaro
0.0457	26.6	.0000	1	Chucaro's
0.0457	26.6	.0000	1	Chuka's
0.0457	26.6	.0000	1	church-bells
0.0457	26.6	.0000	1	churnin'
0.0457	26.6	.0000	1	Chuto
0.0457	26.6	.0000	1	Cincinnatus
0.0457	26.6	.0000	1	Cinder
0.0457	26.6	.0000	1	Cinderella's
0.0457	26.6	.0000	1	Cinders
				THE PRECEDING WORD TYPE OCCUPIES RANK 45700
0.0457	26.6	.0000	1	cinquefoil
0.0457	26.6	.0000	1	ciphering
0.0457	26.6	.0000	1	circumspection
0.0457	26.6	.0000	1	citation
0.0457	26.6	.0000	1	city-dweller
0.0457	26.6	.0000	1	city-lovers
0.0457	26.6	.0000	1	Civilian
0.0457	26.6	.0000	1	civilised
0.0457	26.6	.0000	1	ckers
0.0457	26.6	.0000	1	cl
0.0457	26.6	.0000	1	clss
0.0457	26.6	.0000	1	clacked
0.0457	26.6	.0000	1	clamber
0.0457	26.6	.0000	1	clamoured
0.0457	26.6	.0000	1	clandestinely
0.0457	26.6	.0000	1	claps'd
0.0457	26.6	.0000	1	Clara's
0.0457	26.6	.0000	1	Claribel
0.0457	26.6	.0000	1	classroom-offices
0.0457	26.6	.0000	1	Claude's
0.0457	26.6	.0000	1	Claus'
0.0457	26.6	.0000	1	Claws
0.0457	26.6	.0000	1	cleanness
0.0457	26.6	.0000	1	clearin'
0.0457	26.6	.0000	1	cleaves
0.0457	26.6	.0000	1	Cliche
0.0457	26.6	.0000	1	click-click-click-CLICK
0.0457	26.6	.0000	1	clickety-click
0.0457	26.6	.0000	1	clifflike
0.0457	26.6	.0000	1	Clifton
0.0457	26.6	.0000	1	Climax
0.0457	26.6	.0000	1	climber's
0.0457	26.6	.0000	1	clinch
0.0457	26.6	.0000	1	clip-clop
0.0457	26.6	.0000	1	Clipper's
0.0457	26.6	.0000	1	clippity-clop
0.0457	26.6	.0000	1	Clooney
0.0457	26.6	.0000	1	cloppity-clop
0.0457	26.6	.0000	1	close-lying
0.0457	26.6	.0000	1	close-mouthed
0.0457	26.6	.0000	1	close-pressing
0.0457	26.6	.0000	1	close-wrapped
0.0457	26.6	.0000	1	closed-in
0.0457	26.6	.0000	1	CLOSER
0.0457	26.6	.0000	1	cloud-like
0.0457	26.6	.0000	1	clouted
0.0457	26.6	.0000	1	clowned
0.0457	26.6	.0000	1	clubbing
0.0457	26.6	.0000	1	clumping
0.0457	26.6	.0000	1	clumsiness
0.0457	26.6	.0000	1	Clymer
0.0457	26.6	.0000	1	co-ed
0.0457	26.6	.0000	1	Co-operative
0.0457	26.6	.0000	1	Coachella
0.0457	26.6	.0000	1	coast-guard
0.0457	26.6	.0000	1	coat-skirts
0.0457	26.6	.0000	1	coati
0.0457	26.6	.0000	1	coatimundi
0.0457	26.6	.0000	1	coating's
0.0457	26.6	.0000	1	Cobbler
0.0457	26.6	.0000	1	Coburg
0.0457	26.6	.0000	1	coca
0.0457	26.6	.0000	1	Cochran's
0.0457	26.6	.0000	1	cockers
0.0457	26.6	.0000	1	cockleburrs
0.0457	26.6	.0000	1	cockney
0.0457	26.6	.0000	1	codger
0.0457	26.6	.0000	1	coffeepot
0.0457	26.6	.0000	1	Cogia's
0.0457	26.6	.0000	1	col
0.0457	26.6	.0000	1	cola-nuts
0.0457	26.6	.0000	1	cold-producing
0.0457	26.6	.0000	1	cold-water
0.0457	26.6	.0000	1	collection-plate
0.0457	26.6	.0000	1	collie's
0.0457	26.6	.0000	1	color-tagged
0.0457	26.6	.0000	1	colossal-osal
0.0457	26.6	.0000	1	columbine
0.0457	26.6	.0000	1	columbines
0.0457	26.6	.0000	1	COME
0.0457	26.6	.0000	1	comedown
0.0457	26.6	.0000	1	comeliness
0.0457	26.6	.0000	1	comfortingly
0.0457	26.6	.0000	1	comic-book
0.0457	26.6	.0000	1	Comiskey
0.0457	26.6	.0000	1	commentators
0.0457	26.6	.0000	1	communings
0.0457	26.6	.0000	1	comparison-contrast
0.0457	26.6	.0000	1	complainingly
0.0457	26.6	.0000	1	Complement
0.0457	26.6	.0000	1	comprehending
0.0457	26.6	.0000	1	comradeship
0.0457	26.6	.0000	1	Con-nor
0.0457	26.6	.0000	1	conciliation
0.0457	26.6	.0000	1	concoct
0.0457	26.6	.0000	1	concurs
0.0457	26.6	.0000	1	concussion
0.0457	26.6	.0000	1	Coney
0.0457	26.6	.0000	1	confoundedly
0.0457	26.6	.0000	1	congregate
				THE PRECEDING WORD TYPE OCCUPIES RANK 45800
0.0457	26.6	.0000	1	conjugating
0.0457	26.6	.0000	1	conjurers
0.0457	26.6	.0000	1	conjuring
0.0457	26.6	.0000	1	conk
0.0457	26.6	.0000	1	Conn's
0.0457	26.6	.0000	1	consome-trate
0.0457	26.6	.0000	1	Conspiracy
0.0457	26.6	.0000	1	conspirator's
0.0457	26.6	.0000	1	constable's
0.0457	26.6	.0000	1	Constables
0.0457	26.6	.0000	1	constance
0.0457	26.6	.0000	1	Constance's
0.0457	26.6	.0000	1	consternation
0.0457	26.6	.0000	1	constituency
0.0457	26.6	.0000	1	consulate
0.0457	26.6	.0000	1	Contact
0.0457	26.6	.0000	1	contaminate
0.0457	26.6	.0000	1	contestant
0.0457	26.6	.0000	1	Continentals'
0.0457	26.6	.0000	1	contra-dance
0.0457	26.6	.0000	1	contradictoriness
0.0457	26.6	.0000	1	contrivance
0.0457	26.6	.0000	1	conventionality
0.0457	26.6	.0000	1	conveyable
0.0457	26.6	.0000	1	conveyer
0.0457	26.6	.0000	1	cook-brother
0.0457	26.6	.0000	1	cooking-stove
0.0457	26.6	.0000	1	Cooks'
0.0457	26.6	.0000	1	cooks'
0.0457	26.6	.0000	1	Coolie
0.0457	26.6	.0000	1	coolies
0.0457	26.6	.0000	1	cooper's
0.0457	26.6	.0000	1	Coopers
0.0457	26.6	.0000	1	copy-reader
0.0457	26.6	.0000	1	copybook
0.0457	26.6	.0000	1	coquettes
0.0457	26.6	.0000	1	coqui
0.0457	26.6	.0000	1	coral-bell
0.0457	26.6	.0000	1	coral-pink
0.0457	26.6	.0000	1	corazon
0.0457	26.6	.0000	1	Cord's
0.0457	26.6	.0000	1	cordage
0.0457	26.6	.0000	1	corn-meal
0.0457	26.6	.0000	1	Cornerstone
0.0457	26.6	.0000	1	cornhill
0.0457	26.6	.0000	1	Corning
0.0457	26.6	.0000	1	cornland
0.0457	26.6	.0000	1	corns
0.0457	26.6	.0000	1	Corvisart's
0.0457	26.6	.0000	1	Cosby's
0.0457	26.6	.0000	1	coterie
0.0457	26.6	.0000	1	Cottontail
0.0457	26.6	.0000	1	count's
0.0457	26.6	.0000	1	Counter-current
0.0457	26.6	.0000	1	countersign
0.0457	26.6	.0000	1	country-bred
0.0457	26.6	.0000	1	coureur
0.0457	26.6	.0000	1	courtier
0.0457	26.6	.0000	1	coverall
0.0457	26.6	.0000	1	coverer
0.0457	26.6	.0000	1	coverin's
0.0457	26.6	.0000	1	cow-quieting
0.0457	26.6	.0000	1	coward's
0.0457	26.6	.0000	1	cowbell
0.0457	26.6	.0000	1	COWBOYS
0.0457	26.6	.0000	1	cowhorse
0.0457	26.6	.0000	1	coyote's
0.0457	26.6	.0000	1	cr-r-rack
0.0457	26.6	.0000	1	cr-r-racking
0.0457	26.6	.0000	1	crckers
0.0457	26.6	.0000	1	cra
0.0457	26.6	.0000	1	craes
0.0457	26.6	.0000	1	crab-eating
0.0457	26.6	.0000	1	Crabapple's

U	SFI	D	F	Word Type
0.0457	26.6	.0000	1	crabmeat
0.0457	26.6	.0000	1	Cracardo
0.0457	26.6	.0000	1	crack-brained
0.0457	26.6	.0000	1	crackbrained
0.0457	26.6	.0000	1	cradle**
0.0457	26.6	.0000	1	cradle-rocker
0.0457	26.6	.0000	1	Cradles
0.0457	26.6	.0000	1	Craft
0.0457	26.6	.0000	1	craftily
0.0457	26.6	.0000	1	craftiness
0.0457	26.6	.0000	1	craggy-horned
0.0457	26.6	.0000	1	Cranberry
0.0457	26.6	.0000	1	CRASH-crash-crash
0.0457	26.6	.0000	1	Crat's
0.0457	26.6	.0000	1	crated
0.0457	26.6	.0000	1	crater-shaped
0.0457	26.6	.0000	1	crating
0.0457	26.6	.0000	1	Cray's
0.0457	26.6	.0000	1	creakings
0.0457	26.6	.0000	1	CREAM
0.0457	26.6	.0000	1	Cream-Sponge
0.0457	26.6	.0000	1	Creamery
0.0457	26.6	.0000	1	creaminal
0.0457	26.6	.0000	1	creature's
0.0457	26.6	.0000	1	credulous
0.0457	26.6	.0000	1	Creesy's

THE PRECEDING WORD TYPE OCCUPIES RANK 45900

U	SFI	D	F	Word Type
0.0457	26.6	.0000	1	crep'
0.0457	26.6	.0000	1	crepe-paper
0.0457	26.6	.0000	1	Cretheus
0.0457	26.6	.0000	1	crevasse
0.0457	26.6	.0000	1	Crew
0.0457	26.6	.0000	1	Crewe
0.0457	26.6	.0000	1	crimson-crossed
0.0457	26.6	.0000	1	cringingly
0.0457	26.6	.0000	1	Crip
0.0457	26.6	.0000	1	crisper
0.0457	26.6	.0000	1	crispest
0.0457	26.6	.0000	1	Crispi's
0.0457	26.6	.0000	1	crittur's
0.0457	26.6	.0000	1	CROAK
0.0457	26.6	.0000	1	croc
0.0457	26.6	.0000	1	crocodilus
0.0457	26.6	.0000	1	Crook
0.0457	26.6	.0000	1	crooked-legged
0.0457	26.6	.0000	1	CROSS-FADE
0.0457	26.6	.0000	1	cross-bred
0.0457	26.6	.0000	1	cross-looking
0.0457	26.6	.0000	1	crosstag
0.0457	26.6	.0000	1	crosstown
0.0457	26.6	.0000	1	crotched
0.0457	26.6	.0000	1	croup
0.0457	26.6	.0000	1	crowbars
0.0457	26.6	.0000	1	crowd-pleasing
0.0457	26.6	.0000	1	crowd's
0.0457	26.6	.0000	1	crows'
0.0457	26.6	.0000	1	crrrack
0.0457	26.6	.0000	1	crucifix
0.0457	26.6	.0000	1	crucifixion
0.0457	26.6	.0000	1	crucifying
0.0457	26.6	.0000	1	Cruiser
0.0457	26.6	.0000	1	crullers
0.0457	26.6	.0000	1	crunch-crunch-crunched
0.0457	26.6	.0000	1	crunchiest
0.0457	26.6	.0000	1	crustily
0.0457	26.6	.0000	1	cryoton
0.0457	26.6	.0000	1	crystallographer
0.0457	26.6	.0000	1	crystallography
0.0457	26.6	.0000	1	Crystals
0.0457	26.6	.0000	1	cubbyhole
0.0457	26.6	.0000	1	Cuckoo
0.0457	26.6	.0000	1	cuddles
0.0457	26.6	.0000	1	cuddly
0.0457	26.6	.0000	1	cuffing
0.0457	26.6	.0000	1	Cuhullin's
0.0457	26.6	.0000	1	Cully
0.0457	26.6	.0000	1	cuplike
0.0457	26.6	.0000	1	cuprite
0.0457	26.6	.0000	1	curdled
0.0457	26.6	.0000	1	currants
0.0457	26.6	.0000	1	Currey
0.0457	26.6	.0000	1	Currier
0.0457	26.6	.0000	1	curveting
0.0457	26.6	.0000	1	cuspidors
0.0457	26.6	.0000	1	customize
0.0457	26.6	.0000	1	cut-cut-a-cut
0.0457	26.6	.0000	1	cut-out-work
0.0457	26.6	.0000	1	cut-steel
0.0457	26.6	.0000	1	cutie
0.0457	26.6	.0000	1	cutter's
0.0457	26.6	.0000	1	d-d-don't
0.0457	26.6	.0000	1	d-e-e-p
0.0457	26.6	.0000	1	D'Artagnan
0.0457	26.6	.0000	1	d'Arthur
0.0457	26.6	.0000	1	d'Entremont
0.0457	26.6	.0000	1	d'reckly
0.0457	26.6	.0000	1	dabble
0.0457	26.6	.0000	1	dabs
0.0457	26.6	.0000	1	dachshunds
0.0457	26.6	.0000	1	daddy'll
0.0457	26.6	.0000	1	dam-building
0.0457	26.6	.0000	1	Damien
0.0457	26.6	.0000	1	Damisa
0.0457	26.6	.0000	1	damsels
0.0457	26.6	.0000	1	dang'rous
0.0457	26.6	.0000	1	DANGER
0.0457	26.6	.0000	1	dangerousness
0.0457	26.6	.0000	1	DANISH
0.0457	26.6	.0000	1	dapple
0.0457	26.6	.0000	1	dapple-gray
0.0457	26.6	.0000	1	dappling
0.0457	26.6	.0000	1	Dar-es-Salaam
0.0457	26.6	.0000	1	Daraprim
0.0457	26.6	.0000	1	dark-red
0.0457	26.6	.0000	1	Dash
0.0457	26.6	.0000	1	dat's
0.0457	26.6	.0000	1	dateless
0.0457	26.6	.0000	1	datelined
0.0457	26.6	.0000	1	daughter-in-law
0.0457	26.6	.0000	1	day-break
0.0457	26.6	.0000	1	day-dreamed
0.0457	26.6	.0000	1	day-in
0.0457	26.6	.0000	1	day-out
0.0457	26.6	.0000	1	daydreamed
0.0457	26.6	.0000	1	Daylight
0.0457	26.6	.0000	1	daylights
0.0457	26.6	.0000	1	Daytime

THE PRECEDING WORD TYPE OCCUPIES RANK 46000

U	SFI	D	F	Word Type
0.0457	26.6	.0000	1	deGrace
0.0457	26.6	.0000	1	deLorge
0.0457	26.6	.0000	1	deLorge's
0.0457	26.6	.0000	1	deTriomphe
0.0457	26.6	.0000	1	DeWitts
0.0457	26.6	.0000	1	dead-letter
0.0457	26.6	.0000	1	dead-right
0.0457	26.6	.0000	1	deadlier
0.0457	26.6	.0000	1	deaf-blind
0.0457	26.6	.0000	1	Dean's
0.0457	26.6	.0000	1	Deanne's
0.0457	26.6	.0000	1	dearskin
0.0457	26.6	.0000	1	DeathValley
0.0457	26.6	.0000	1	death-bed
0.0457	26.6	.0000	1	debauch
0.0457	26.6	.0000	1	debonair
0.0457	26.6	.0000	1	debris-filled
0.0457	26.6	.0000	1	debtors
0.0457	26.6	.0000	1	dedided
0.0457	26.6	.0000	1	dee-dee-dee
0.0457	26.6	.0000	1	Deedee
0.0457	26.6	.0000	1	deeming
0.0457	26.6	.0000	1	deep-blue
0.0457	26.6	.0000	1	deep-freeze
0.0457	26.6	.0000	1	deep-running
0.0457	26.6	.0000	1	deep-rutted
0.0457	26.6	.0000	1	deep-shadowed
0.0457	26.6	.0000	1	deer-meat
0.0457	26.6	.0000	1	Deerford
0.0457	26.6	.0000	1	defamation
0.0457	26.6	.0000	1	deguello
0.0457	26.6	.0000	1	dejection
0.0457	26.6	.0000	1	Dela
0.0457	26.6	.0000	1	delegate's
0.0457	26.6	.0000	1	delicious-tasting
0.0457	26.6	.0000	1	Delivery
0.0457	26.6	.0000	1	demagoguery
0.0457	26.6	.0000	1	Demi-Lune
0.0457	26.6	.0000	1	Demo
0.0457	26.6	.0000	1	democrat
0.0457	26.6	.0000	1	Demoiselle
0.0457	26.6	.0000	1	demolition
0.0457	26.6	.0000	1	Demonstration
0.0457	26.6	.0000	1	Dempsey's
0.0457	26.6	.0000	1	denims
0.0457	26.6	.0000	1	DENMARK
0.0457	26.6	.0000	1	Denny's
0.0457	26.6	.0000	1	dent
0.0457	26.6	.0000	1	deploring
0.0457	26.6	.0000	1	derisive
0.0457	26.6	.0000	1	Derricke
0.0457	26.6	.0000	1	derriere
0.0457	26.6	.0000	1	DesMoines'
0.0457	26.6	.0000	1	desiccated
0.0457	26.6	.0000	1	desolateness
0.0457	26.6	.0000	1	despairers
0.0457	26.6	.0000	1	despairingly
0.0457	26.6	.0000	1	Desperate
0.0457	26.6	.0000	1	detective's
0.0457	26.6	.0000	1	detracted
0.0457	26.6	.0000	1	device's
0.0457	26.6	.0000	1	devises
0.0457	26.6	.0000	1	Devonians
0.0457	26.6	.0000	1	devours
0.0457	26.6	.0000	1	dew-covered
0.0457	26.6	.0000	1	diabetic
0.0457	26.6	.0000	1	Diablo's
0.0457	26.6	.0000	1	Dialing
0.0457	26.6	.0000	1	Diana-Kate's
0.0457	26.6	.0000	1	diatribe
0.0457	26.6	.0000	1	Diavolo
0.0457	26.6	.0000	1	Dicked
0.0457	26.6	.0000	1	dicker
0.0457	26.6	.0000	1	Did
0.0457	26.6	.0000	1	didn
0.0457	26.6	.0000	1	didn'
0.0457	26.6	.0000	1	didos
0.0457	26.6	.0000	1	Diego's
0.0457	26.6	.0000	1	diesel's
0.0457	26.6	.0000	1	dieter
0.0457	26.6	.0000	1	different-colored
0.0457	26.6	.0000	1	Difficult
0.0457	26.6	.0000	1	DIG
0.0457	26.6	.0000	1	Digger
0.0457	26.6	.0000	1	Digger's
0.0457	26.6	.0000	1	dik-dik
0.0457	26.6	.0000	1	dilated
0.0457	26.6	.0000	1	Dillon's
0.0457	26.6	.0000	1	dilly-dallying
0.0457	26.6	.0000	1	ding-dong
0.0457	26.6	.0000	1	Dining's
0.0457	26.6	.0000	1	dinn
0.0457	26.6	.0000	1	dinner's
0.0457	26.6	.0000	1	DINOSAURS
0.0457	26.6	.0000	1	DIONISIO
0.0457	26.6	.0000	1	diplomatically
0.0457	26.6	.0000	1	direful
0.0457	26.6	.0000	1	dirigibles
0.0457	26.6	.0000	1	Dirks
0.0457	26.6	.0000	1	dirt-and-stick

THE PRECEDING WORD TYPE OCCUPIES RANK 46100

U	SFI	D	F	Word Type
0.0457	26.6	.0000	1	dirt-stained
0.0457	26.6	.0000	1	dirty-colored
0.0457	26.6	.0000	1	diry
0.0457	26.6	.0000	1	disappoints
0.0457	26.6	.0000	1	disbelieved
0.0457	26.6	.0000	1	discombobulate
0.0457	26.6	.0000	1	disconcerted
0.0457	26.6	.0000	1	discoursing
0.0457	26.6	.0000	1	disengaged
0.0457	26.6	.0000	1	disfavor
0.0457	26.6	.0000	1	disillusionments
0.0457	26.6	.0000	1	disinfecting
0.0457	26.6	.0000	1	dislocating
0.0457	26.6	.0000	1	Dismael-bek
0.0457	26.6	.0000	1	Dismael's
0.0457	26.6	.0000	1	dismally
0.0457	26.6	.0000	1	dismays
0.0457	26.6	.0000	1	dispirited
0.0457	26.6	.0000	1	dissuading
0.0457	26.6	.0000	1	distance-dialing
0.0457	26.6	.0000	1	distressedly
0.0457	26.6	.0000	1	distressfully
0.0457	26.6	.0000	1	DISTURB
0.0457	26.6	.0000	1	diu
0.0457	26.6	.0000	1	dive-bombs
0.0457	26.6	.0000	1	diyu
0.0457	26.6	.0000	1	dizzily
0.0457	26.6	.0000	1	dizziness
0.0457	26.6	.0000	1	dle
0.0457	26.6	.0000	1	do-it-your-self
0.0457	26.6	.0000	1	do-re-mi
0.0457	26.6	.0000	1	do-re-mi-fa-sol-la
0.0457	26.6	.0000	1	do-re-mi-fa-sol-la-l
0.0457	26.6	.0000	1	Dobie's
0.0457	26.6	.0000	1	docilely
0.0457	26.6	.0000	1	Doctr
0.0457	26.6	.0000	1	Dodgers'
0.0457	26.6	.0000	1	dog-ear
0.0457	26.6	.0000	1	dog-fox
0.0457	26.6	.0000	1	dog-paddle
0.0457	26.6	.0000	1	dog'll
0.0457	26.6	.0000	1	Doge's
0.0457	26.6	.0000	1	dogsled
0.0457	26.6	.0000	1	dogsledders
0.0457	26.6	.0000	1	Dogtooth
0.0457	26.6	.0000	1	doilies
0.0457	26.6	.0000	1	dollhouse
0.0457	26.6	.0000	1	dolly's
0.0457	26.6	.0000	1	Dolphina
0.0457	26.6	.0000	1	don't-care
0.0457	26.6	.0000	1	donate
0.0457	26.6	.0000	1	Doni
0.0457	26.6	.0000	1	Doni's
0.0457	26.6	.0000	1	Dood
0.0457	26.6	.0000	1	Doodleberries
0.0457	26.6	.0000	1	Dorset's
0.0457	26.6	.0000	1	double-decked
0.0457	26.6	.0000	1	double-decker
0.0457	26.6	.0000	1	double-locked
0.0457	26.6	.0000	1	Doug's
0.0457	26.6	.0000	1	DOWN
0.0457	26.6	.0000	1	downdrafts
0.0457	26.6	.0000	1	Downey
0.0457	26.6	.0000	1	downing
0.0457	26.6	.0000	1	downity
0.0457	26.6	.0000	1	downthrust
0.0457	26.6	.0000	1	drssed
0.0457	26.6	.0000	1	drachma
0.0457	26.6	.0000	1	drag-line
0.0457	26.6	.0000	1	dragon-cave
0.0457	26.6	.0000	1	dragon-end
0.0457	26.6	.0000	1	dragonlet
0.0457	26.6	.0000	1	dram-house
0.0457	26.6	.0000	1	draps
0.0457	26.6	.0000	1	drawn-out
0.0457	26.6	.0000	1	Drdla
0.0457	26.6	.0000	1	dreading
0.0457	26.6	.0000	1	dreamful
0.0457	26.6	.0000	1	dreariness
0.0457	26.6	.0000	1	Dreggs'
0.0457	26.6	.0000	1	dregs
0.0457	26.6	.0000	1	drei
0.0457	26.6	.0000	1	Drem's
0.0457	26.6	.0000	1	Dress
0.0457	26.6	.0000	1	dress-ups
0.0457	26.6	.0000	1	dressmakers
0.0457	26.6	.0000	1	drier's
0.0457	26.6	.0000	1	drip-drip
0.0457	26.6	.0000	1	Driss'
0.0457	26.6	.0000	1	drop-the-handkerchief
0.0457	26.6	.0000	1	Drouillard
0.0457	26.6	.0000	1	drum-shaped
0.0457	26.6	.0000	1	dry-tropical
0.0457	26.6	.0000	1	Dryopians
0.0457	26.6	.0000	1	duNation
0.0457	26.6	.0000	1	Dubuque
0.0457	26.6	.0000	1	duelists'
0.0457	26.6	.0000	1	Duivenisse
0.0457	26.6	.0000	1	dulce
0.0457	26.6	.0000	1	dumb-waiter

THE PRECEDING WORD TYPE OCCUPIES RANK 46200

U	SFI	D	F	Word Type
0.0457	26.6	.0000	1	Dumpling
0.0457	26.6	.0000	1	dumpy-looking
0.0457	26.6	.0000	1	dunderheaded
0.0457	26.6	.0000	1	Dungannon
0.0457	26.6	.0000	1	Dupin
0.0457	26.6	.0000	1	During
0.0457	26.6	.0000	1	durn
0.0457	26.6	.0000	1	Durston's
0.0457	26.6	.0000	1	DUST
0.0457	26.6	.0000	1	dustcloths
0.0457	26.6	.0000	1	Dusting
0.0457	26.6	.0000	1	dwarfs'
0.0457	26.6	.0000	1	dwindles
0.0457	26.6	.0000	1	dynamo
0.0457	26.6	.0000	1	e-nor-mous
0.0457	26.6	.0000	1	Eagles'
0.0457	26.6	.0000	1	Ealing
0.0457	26.6	.0000	1	Ear
0.0457	26.6	.0000	1	early-roosting
0.0457	26.6	.0000	1	earnibbling
0.0457	26.6	.0000	1	Earnshaw's
0.0457	26.6	.0000	1	earth-quivering
0.0457	26.6	.0000	1	earthward
0.0457	26.6	.0000	1	easy-like
0.0457	26.6	.0000	1	easy-shooting
0.0457	26.6	.0000	1	easy-to-reach
0.0457	26.6	.0000	1	eaves'
0.0457	26.6	.0000	1	eavesdrop
0.0457	26.6	.0000	1	echo-sounders
0.0457	26.6	.0000	1	Ector's
0.0457	26.6	.0000	1	eddicated
0.0457	26.6	.0000	1	Ede's
0.0457	26.6	.0000	1	Edgewood
0.0457	26.6	.0000	1	Eduardo's
0.0457	26.6	.0000	1	Educator
0.0457	26.6	.0000	1	eee
0.0457	26.6	.0000	1	eee-eee-eee-eee-eee
0.0457	26.6	.0000	1	eeeeyiiii-eeeeeee
0.0457	26.6	.0000	1	eerie-looking
0.0457	26.6	.0000	1	efface
0.0457	26.6	.0000	1	effeminacy
0.0457	26.6	.0000	1	Effie
0.0457	26.6	.0000	1	Effie's
0.0457	26.6	.0000	1	eggburgers
0.0457	26.6	.0000	1	egged
0.0457	26.6	.0000	1	eggplants
0.0457	26.6	.0000	1	eight-and
0.0457	26.6	.0000	1	eight-and-eighty-button
0.0457	26.6	.0000	1	eight-and-one-half-inch
0.0457	26.6	.0000	1	eight-engined
0.0457	26.6	.0000	1	eight-hundred-pound
0.0457	26.6	.0000	1	eight-ounce
0.0457	26.6	.0000	1	eighteen-passenger
0.0457	26.6	.0000	1	eighty-mile
0.0457	26.6	.0000	1	eighty-three
0.0457	26.6	.0000	1	Einar
0.0457	26.6	.0000	1	ejaculated
0.0457	26.6	.0000	1	ElDeguello
0.0457	26.6	.0000	1	Elective
0.0457	26.6	.0000	1	electrically-controlled
0.0457	26.6	.0000	1	electrocute
0.0457	26.6	.0000	1	electrocuted
0.0457	26.6	.0000	1	Elena
0.0457	26.6	.0000	1	elephant-legged
0.0457	26.6	.0000	1	Elevala
0.0457	26.6	.0000	1	elevates
0.0457	26.6	.0000	1	elf's
0.0457	26.6	.0000	1	Ella's
0.0457	26.6	.0000	1	Ellicott's
0.0457	26.6	.0000	1	Ellinor
0.0457	26.6	.0000	1	Elliot's
0.0457	26.6	.0000	1	Elliott's
0.0457	26.6	.0000	1	Elmira
0.0457	26.6	.0000	1	elucidate
0.0457	26.6	.0000	1	Elvington
0.0457	26.6	.0000	1	Elwell's
0.0457	26.6	.0000	1	Elysium
0.0457	26.6	.0000	1	embezzler
0.0457	26.6	.0000	1	embittering
0.0457	26.6	.0000	1	embonpoint
0.0457	26.6	.0000	1	embosomed
0.0457	26.6	.0000	1	embowered
0.0457	26.6	.0000	1	embroiled
0.0457	26.6	.0000	1	eminency
0.0457	26.6	.0000	1	Empress'
0.0457	26.6	.0000	1	emprise
0.0457	26.6	.0000	1	enargite
0.0457	26.6	.0000	1	enchante
0.0457	26.6	.0000	1	encirclement
0.0457	26.6	.0000	1	encode
0.0457	26.6	.0000	1	encroaching
0.0457	26.6	.0000	1	endear
0.0457	26.6	.0000	1	endurable
0.0457	26.6	.0000	1	Enfields
0.0457	26.6	.0000	1	Engine
0.0457	26.6	.0000	1	engine-driven
0.0457	26.6	.0000	1	Enough
0.0457	26.6	.0000	1	Enrico's
0.0457	26.6	.0000	1	Ensuring
0.0457	26.6	.0000	1	entablatures

THE PRECEDING WORD TYPE OCCUPIES RANK 46300

U	SFI	D	F	Word Type
0.0457	26.6	.0000	1	Entangled
0.0457	26.6	.0000	1	entreatings
0.0457	26.6	.0000	1	entryway
0.0457	26.6	.0000	1	Enumclaw
0.0457	26.6	.0000	1	envoys
0.0457	26.6	.0000	1	Epimetheus'
0.0457	26.6	.0000	1	Epiphany
0.0457	26.6	.0000	1	erects
0.0457	26.6	.0000	1	Ernst's
0.0457	26.6	.0000	1	Escalator
0.0457	26.6	.0000	1	Esk
0.0457	26.6	.0000	1	Espy
0.0457	26.6	.0000	1	estanica
0.0457	26.6	.0000	1	Esther's
0.0457	26.6	.0000	1	Estrellita
0.0457	26.6	.0000	1	Estrellita's
0.0457	26.6	.0000	1	Eumaeus
0.0457	26.6	.0000	1	eutectics
0.0457	26.6	.0000	1	Evageline
0.0457	26.6	.0000	1	evaluating
0.0457	26.6	.0000	1	Events
0.0457	26.6	.0000	1	ever'wheres
0.0457	26.6	.0000	1	evermounting
0.0457	26.6	.0000	1	Everson
0.0457	26.6	.0000	1	everythin's
0.0457	26.6	.0000	1	Evian
0.0457	26.6	.0000	1	evil-natured
0.0457	26.6	.0000	1	evil-tasting
0.0457	26.6	.0000	1	evildoers
0.0457	26.6	.0000	1	exaggeratedly
0.0457	26.6	.0000	1	Excalibur
0.0457	26.6	.0000	1	EXCUSE
0.0457	26.6	.0000	1	expounders
0.0457	26.6	.0000	1	expressionless
0.0457	26.6	.0000	1	extolling
0.0457	26.6	.0000	1	extort
0.0457	26.6	.0000	1	Extra

U	SFI	D	F	Word Type
0.0457	26.6	.0000	1	extra-powerful
0.0457	26.6	.0000	1	extra-tall
0.0457	26.6	.0000	1	extractive
0.0457	26.6	.0000	1	extricated
0.0457	26.6	.0000	1	eye-piece
0.0457	26.6	.0000	1	Eyes'
0.0457	26.6	.0000	1	eyewitnesses
0.0457	26.6	.0000	1	f-a-m-i-s-h-e-d
0.0457	26.6	.0000	1	fzz
0.0457	26.6	.0000	1	fa-tee-gay
0.0457	26.6	.0000	1	faddist
0.0457	26.6	.0000	1	fagots
0.0457	26.6	.0000	1	faience
0.0457	26.6	.0000	1	fair-to-middlers
0.0457	26.6	.0000	1	fairhaired
0.0457	26.6	.0000	1	fairy-land
0.0457	26.6	.0000	1	fairy-story
0.0457	26.6	.0000	1	fairy-tales
0.0457	26.6	.0000	1	fairy's
0.0457	26.6	.0000	1	faith's
0.0457	26.6	.0000	1	Falcon's
0.0457	26.6	.0000	1	falconer
0.0457	26.6	.0000	1	Fall-of-the-
0.0457	26.6	.0000	1	Fall-of-the-leaf
0.0457	26.6	.0000	1	falls'
0.0457	26.6	.0000	1	familiar-looking
0.0457	26.6	.0000	1	familiarly
0.0457	26.6	.0000	1	famous-brand
0.0457	26.6	.0000	1	famously
0.0457	26.6	.0000	1	fancy-play
0.0457	26.6	.0000	1	fancying
0.0457	26.6	.0000	1	Fand
0.0457	26.6	.0000	1	Fand's
0.0457	26.6	.0000	1	Fanny's
0.0457	26.6	.0000	1	fare's
0.0457	26.6	.0000	1	farewells
0.0457	26.6	.0000	1	faring
0.0457	26.6	.0000	1	farmhands
0.0457	26.6	.0000	1	farmyards
0.0457	26.6	.0000	1	Farns
0.0457	26.6	.0000	1	Farraguts
0.0457	26.6	.0000	1	farther**
0.0457	26.6	.0000	1	Fascinating
0.0457	26.6	.0000	1	FAST
0.0457	26.6	.0000	1	fast-break
0.0457	26.6	.0000	1	fast-falling
0.0457	26.6	.0000	1	fast-rising
0.0457	26.6	.0000	1	fast-rolling
0.0457	26.6	.0000	1	fastidiously
0.0457	26.6	.0000	1	Father-Sun
0.0457	26.6	.0000	1	fatherless
0.0457	26.6	.0000	1	fatiguee
0.0457	26.6	.0000	1	FCC
0.0457	26.6	.0000	1	feather-shaped
0.0457	26.6	.0000	1	Feather's
0.0457	26.6	.0000	1	featherless
0.0457	26.6	.0000	1	feeling-out
0.0457	26.6	.0000	1	feex
0.0457	26.6	.0000	1	feint
0.0457	26.6	.0000	1	feinting
0.0457	26.6	.0000	1	Felician
0.0457	26.6	.0000	1	Felippe
0.0457	26.6	.0000	1	fellows'
THE PRECEDING WORD TYPE OCCUPIES RANK 46400				
0.0457	26.6	.0000	1	fence-post
0.0457	26.6	.0000	1	fend
0.0457	26.6	.0000	1	fended
0.0457	26.6	.0000	1	ferris
0.0457	26.6	.0000	1	ferroalloy
0.0457	26.6	.0000	1	Fessenden
0.0457	26.6	.0000	1	Fessler
0.0457	26.6	.0000	1	festal
0.0457	26.6	.0000	1	fettered
0.0457	26.6	.0000	1	feverishness
0.0457	26.6	.0000	1	fi
0.0457	26.6	.0000	1	Fichtenhorst
0.0457	26.6	.0000	1	Fiddlers'
0.0457	26.6	.0000	1	fieldglasses
0.0457	26.6	.0000	1	fiendishly
0.0457	26.6	.0000	1	fierce-burning
0.0457	26.6	.0000	1	Fifty-Fifty
0.0457	26.6	.0000	1	fifty-fifty
0.0457	26.6	.0000	1	Fifty-first
0.0457	26.6	.0000	1	fifty-yard
0.0457	26.6	.0000	1	fifty's
0.0457	26.6	.0000	1	fig-eater
0.0457	26.6	.0000	1	FIGHT
0.0457	26.6	.0000	1	filibustering
0.0457	26.6	.0000	1	fin-out
0.0457	26.6	.0000	1	Finder
0.0457	26.6	.0000	1	fine-tasting
0.0457	26.6	.0000	1	finegrained
0.0457	26.6	.0000	1	finger-marks
0.0457	26.6	.0000	1	Finlay's
0.0457	26.6	.0000	1	fire-eaten
0.0457	26.6	.0000	1	fire-eating
0.0457	26.6	.0000	1	firearm
0.0457	26.6	.0000	1	fireboats
0.0457	26.6	.0000	1	fireguard
0.0457	26.6	.0000	1	firepot
0.0457	26.6	.0000	1	firmest
0.0457	26.6	.0000	1	Firpo
0.0457	26.6	.0000	1	First-Aiders
0.0457	26.6	.0000	1	fish-like
0.0457	26.6	.0000	1	fisherfolk
0.0457	26.6	.0000	1	Fishers'
0.0457	26.6	.0000	1	fisherwoman's
0.0457	26.6	.0000	1	fishing-pole's
0.0457	26.6	.0000	1	fishmonger's
0.0457	26.6	.0000	1	fishtailed
0.0457	26.6	.0000	1	fishwheel
0.0457	26.6	.0000	1	fishwheels
0.0457	26.6	.0000	1	fit'n
0.0457	26.6	.0000	1	fitments
0.0457	26.6	.0000	1	five-and-dime
0.0457	26.6	.0000	1	five-part
0.0457	26.6	.0000	1	five-word
0.0457	26.6	.0000	1	fixings
0.0457	26.6	.0000	1	fizzing
0.0457	26.6	.0000	1	Flail
0.0457	26.6	.0000	1	Flamborough
0.0457	26.6	.0000	1	Flan's
0.0457	26.6	.0000	1	flankers
0.0457	26.6	.0000	1	Flannigan
0.0457	26.6	.0000	1	flap-hopping
0.0457	26.6	.0000	1	flapjack
0.0457	26.6	.0000	1	Flapjack
0.0457	26.6	.0000	1	Fleet's
0.0457	26.6	.0000	1	Flier
0.0457	26.6	.0000	1	Flight-Lieutenant
0.0457	26.6	.0000	1	Flinders
0.0457	26.6	.0000	1	flint-headed
0.0457	26.6	.0000	1	flip-flop
0.0457	26.6	.0000	1	flitter
0.0457	26.6	.0000	1	flogged
0.0457	26.6	.0000	1	Flor
0.0457	26.6	.0000	1	florists'
0.0457	26.6	.0000	1	flot
0.0457	26.6	.0000	1	flot's
0.0457	26.6	.0000	1	flots
0.0457	26.6	.0000	1	flouted
0.0457	26.6	.0000	1	flower-peckers
0.0457	26.6	.0000	1	flower-strewn
0.0457	26.6	.0000	1	flower-women
0.0457	26.6	.0000	1	flower's
0.0457	26.6	.0000	1	Flowery
0.0457	26.6	.0000	1	Flt
0.0457	26.6	.0000	1	flunked
0.0457	26.6	.0000	1	flurries
0.0457	26.6	.0000	1	flutist
0.0457	26.6	.0000	1	flutter-kicking
0.0457	26.6	.0000	1	flying-doctor
0.0457	26.6	.0000	1	foam-laced
0.0457	26.6	.0000	1	fog-bound
0.0457	26.6	.0000	1	fog's
0.0457	26.6	.0000	1	Folgil's
0.0457	26.6	.0000	1	folktale
0.0457	26.6	.0000	1	follies
0.0457	26.6	.0000	1	followin'
0.0457	26.6	.0000	1	fondest
0.0457	26.6	.0000	1	foodless
0.0457	26.6	.0000	1	Fooled
0.0457	26.6	.0000	1	foolin'
0.0457	26.6	.0000	1	foot-race
THE PRECEDING WORD TYPE OCCUPIES RANK 46500				
0.0457	26.6	.0000	1	foot-trail
0.0457	26.6	.0000	1	footed
0.0457	26.6	.0000	1	Footmen
0.0457	26.6	.0000	1	footraces
0.0457	26.6	.0000	1	footwalk
0.0457	26.6	.0000	1	fordin'
0.0457	26.6	.0000	1	forearms
0.0457	26.6	.0000	1	forebodings
0.0457	26.6	.0000	1	forecaster's
0.0457	26.6	.0000	1	forecastles
0.0457	26.6	.0000	1	forecloser
0.0457	26.6	.0000	1	Foreseer
0.0457	26.6	.0000	1	forest's
0.0457	26.6	.0000	1	forester's
0.0457	26.6	.0000	1	Forgotten
0.0457	26.6	.0000	1	Forman
0.0457	26.6	.0000	1	Formulae
0.0457	26.6	.0000	1	forsake
0.0457	26.6	.0000	1	Fortain
0.0457	26.6	.0000	1	Fortress
0.0457	26.6	.0000	1	fortresslike
0.0457	26.6	.0000	1	Forty-eighters
0.0457	26.6	.0000	1	Four-Ring
0.0457	26.6	.0000	1	four-stage
0.0457	26.6	.0000	1	four-winged
0.0457	26.6	.0000	1	fourteen-day-old
0.0457	26.6	.0000	1	Fourth-Class
0.0457	26.6	.0000	1	fourth-place
0.0457	26.6	.0000	1	fox-and-geese
0.0457	26.6	.0000	1	fox-bats
0.0457	26.6	.0000	1	foxtrot
0.0457	26.6	.0000	1	foxy
0.0457	26.6	.0000	1	Fra
0.0457	26.6	.0000	1	fracas
0.0457	26.6	.0000	1	fraidy-cat
0.0457	26.6	.0000	1	Fraley
0.0457	26.6	.0000	1	Fraley's
0.0457	26.6	.0000	1	Frame
0.0457	26.6	.0000	1	Francie's
0.0457	26.6	.0000	1	Francois's
0.0457	26.6	.0000	1	Fray
0.0457	26.6	.0000	1	fre
0.0457	26.6	.0000	1	freakish
0.0457	26.6	.0000	1	Fredrick
0.0457	26.6	.0000	1	free-milling
0.0457	26.6	.0000	1	freewheeled
0.0457	26.6	.0000	1	freight-yard
0.0457	26.6	.0000	1	French-Cajun
0.0457	26.6	.0000	1	French-fried
0.0457	26.6	.0000	1	Freneau's
0.0457	26.6	.0000	1	fresh-fallen
0.0457	26.6	.0000	1	fresh-killed
0.0457	26.6	.0000	1	fresh-picked
0.0457	26.6	.0000	1	Freuchen
0.0457	26.6	.0000	1	Friedman
0.0457	26.6	.0000	1	Friedricks
0.0457	26.6	.0000	1	Friend's
0.0457	26.6	.0000	1	friendlier
0.0457	26.6	.0000	1	friendlylike
0.0457	26.6	.0000	1	fringing
0.0457	26.6	.0000	1	Frisette's
0.0457	26.6	.0000	1	frisk
0.0457	26.6	.0000	1	front-porch
0.0457	26.6	.0000	1	frontward
0.0457	26.6	.0000	1	froon
0.0457	26.6	.0000	1	frost-biters
0.0457	26.6	.0000	1	Frow
0.0457	26.6	.0000	1	frow
0.0457	26.6	.0000	1	fruit-picking
0.0457	26.6	.0000	1	fruitcake
0.0457	26.6	.0000	1	fruity
0.0457	26.6	.0000	1	fryer
0.0457	26.6	.0000	1	fu
0.0457	26.6	.0000	1	fueling
0.0457	26.6	.0000	1	Fuerteventura
0.0457	26.6	.0000	1	Fuff
0.0457	26.6	.0000	1	Fulke's
0.0457	26.6	.0000	1	full-flavored
0.0457	26.6	.0000	1	full-throttle
0.0457	26.6	.0000	1	fun-making
0.0457	26.6	.0000	1	funnily
0.0457	26.6	.0000	1	fur-animals
0.0457	26.6	.0000	1	Furlong
0.0457	26.6	.0000	1	furnace-tending
0.0457	26.6	.0000	1	furnace's
0.0457	26.6	.0000	1	furnacelike
0.0457	26.6	.0000	1	furtive
0.0457	26.6	.0000	1	fust
0.0457	26.6	.0000	1	fusty
0.0457	26.6	.0000	1	g-g-got
0.0457	26.6	.0000	1	g-gave
0.0457	26.6	.0000	1	gfts
0.0457	26.6	.0000	1	grl's
0.0457	26.6	.0000	1	gve
0.0457	26.6	.0000	1	g'morning
0.0457	26.6	.0000	1	g'wan
0.0457	26.6	.0000	1	Gabe's
0.0457	26.6	.0000	1	gagman
0.0457	26.6	.0000	1	gainsay
0.0457	26.6	.0000	1	gal-bride
THE PRECEDING WORD TYPE OCCUPIES RANK 46600				
0.0457	26.6	.0000	1	Galena
0.0457	26.6	.0000	1	gallied
0.0457	26.6	.0000	1	game-tracks
0.0457	26.6	.0000	1	Gamper
0.0457	26.6	.0000	1	gangling
0.0457	26.6	.0000	1	gangsters'
0.0457	26.6	.0000	1	Garage
0.0457	26.6	.0000	1	garbage-can
0.0457	26.6	.0000	1	gard
0.0457	26.6	.0000	1	garden-path
0.0457	26.6	.0000	1	garden's
0.0457	26.6	.0000	1	gardenias
0.0457	26.6	.0000	1	Gargantua
0.0457	26.6	.0000	1	Garmisch
0.0457	26.6	.0000	1	Garwick's
0.0457	26.6	.0000	1	Gary's
0.0457	26.6	.0000	1	gas-scorching
0.0457	26.6	.0000	1	Gascon
0.0457	26.6	.0000	1	gasholder
0.0457	26.6	.0000	1	Gaskets
0.0457	26.6	.0000	1	gaslight
0.0457	26.6	.0000	1	gassed
0.0457	26.6	.0000	1	gate-leg
0.0457	26.6	.0000	1	gatekeeper's
0.0457	26.6	.0000	1	Gatwick
0.0457	26.6	.0000	1	gaudiest
0.0457	26.6	.0000	1	Gawain's
0.0457	26.6	.0000	1	gay-colored
0.0457	26.6	.0000	1	gay-coloured
0.0457	26.6	.0000	1	Gazelle
0.0457	26.6	.0000	1	geave
0.0457	26.6	.0000	1	Gedovius
0.0457	26.6	.0000	1	geez
0.0457	26.6	.0000	1	gehts
0.0457	26.6	.0000	1	genista
0.0457	26.6	.0000	1	gentlefolks
0.0457	26.6	.0000	1	gentlest
0.0457	26.6	.0000	1	Georgians
0.0457	26.6	.0000	1	German-born
0.0457	26.6	.0000	1	Gerzah
0.0457	26.6	.0000	1	Gethsemane
0.0457	26.6	.0000	1	ghastlier
0.0457	26.6	.0000	1	ghost-like
0.0457	26.6	.0000	1	ghurush
0.0457	26.6	.0000	1	gibberish
0.0457	26.6	.0000	1	Giedzinski
0.0457	26.6	.0000	1	gift-wraps
0.0457	26.6	.0000	1	gigantic-antic
0.0457	26.6	.0000	1	Gimlet
0.0457	26.6	.0000	1	gimme
0.0457	26.6	.0000	1	ginner
0.0457	26.6	.0000	1	Ginny's
0.0457	26.6	.0000	1	Gino's
0.0457	26.6	.0000	1	Gipson's
0.0457	26.6	.0000	1	girlfriend
0.0457	26.6	.0000	1	girt
0.0457	26.6	.0000	1	girths
0.0457	26.6	.0000	1	Giuseppe's
0.0457	26.6	.0000	1	gla
0.0457	26.6	.0000	1	Gladys
0.0457	26.6	.0000	1	glaringly
0.0457	26.6	.0000	1	glass-stoppered
0.0457	26.6	.0000	1	glazing
0.0457	26.6	.0000	1	gle
0.0457	26.6	.0000	1	glimmerings
0.0457	26.6	.0000	1	glory-singing
0.0457	26.6	.0000	1	Gloucestershire
0.0457	26.6	.0000	1	glub-glub
0.0457	26.6	.0000	1	Glue
0.0457	26.6	.0000	1	Glue-All
0.0457	26.6	.0000	1	glued-on
0.0457	26.6	.0000	1	gnomelike
0.0457	26.6	.0000	1	gnu
0.0457	26.6	.0000	1	gnu-tail
0.0457	26.6	.0000	1	go-o-o
0.0457	26.6	.0000	1	Gobble-uns
0.0457	26.6	.0000	1	Gobble-uns'll
0.0457	26.6	.0000	1	God-blesses
0.0457	26.6	.0000	1	goddess'
0.0457	26.6	.0000	1	godmother's
0.0457	26.6	.0000	1	godsend
0.0457	26.6	.0000	1	goings-on
0.0457	26.6	.0000	1	GOLD
0.0457	26.6	.0000	1	Gold-Digging
0.0457	26.6	.0000	1	gold-eye
0.0457	26.6	.0000	1	gold-flecked
0.0457	26.6	.0000	1	gold-roofed
0.0457	26.6	.0000	1	gold-worked
0.0457	26.6	.0000	1	golden-eyed
0.0457	26.6	.0000	1	Goldens
0.0457	26.6	.0000	1	goldfinch
0.0457	26.6	.0000	1	gollee
0.0457	26.6	.0000	1	Gomera
0.0457	26.6	.0000	1	Gompton's
0.0457	26.6	.0000	1	good-government
0.0457	26.6	.0000	1	good-nights
0.0457	26.6	.0000	1	Goodall
0.0457	26.6	.0000	1	goodhearted
0.0457	26.6	.0000	1	goofed
0.0457	26.6	.0000	1	goon
THE PRECEDING WORD TYPE OCCUPIES RANK 46700				
0.0457	26.6	.0000	1	Gorgons
0.0457	26.6	.0000	1	gossipy
0.0457	26.6	.0000	1	GOT
0.0457	26.6	.0000	1	gougers
0.0457	26.6	.0000	1	gourdful
0.0457	26.6	.0000	1	gowned
0.0457	26.6	.0000	1	gracious'
0.0457	26.6	.0000	1	gradual-like
0.0457	26.6	.0000	1	Graduation
0.0457	26.6	.0000	1	Gradys
0.0457	26.6	.0000	1	grainfields
0.0457	26.6	.0000	1	Gramp's
0.0457	26.6	.0000	1	Grancher
0.0457	26.6	.0000	1	grand-slam
0.0457	26.6	.0000	1	Granddad's
0.0457	26.6	.0000	1	granddaughters
0.0457	26.6	.0000	1	Grandes
0.0457	26.6	.0000	1	grandpas
0.0457	26.6	.0000	1	Grandpere
0.0457	26.6	.0000	1	Grandpop
0.0457	26.6	.0000	1	Grandy
0.0457	26.6	.0000	1	grapeskin
0.0457	26.6	.0000	1	grass-eater
0.0457	26.6	.0000	1	gravest
0.0457	26.6	.0000	1	graveyards
0.0457	26.6	.0000	1	gray-bearded
0.0457	26.6	.0000	1	gray-colored
0.0457	26.6	.0000	1	gray-tin
0.0457	26.6	.0000	1	Graycheek
0.0457	26.6	.0000	1	Graycheek's
0.0457	26.6	.0000	1	grayed-green
0.0457	26.6	.0000	1	grayish-red
0.0457	26.6	.0000	1	GreatUncle
0.0457	26.6	.0000	1	great-coats
0.0457	26.6	.0000	1	great-grandfathers
0.0457	26.6	.0000	1	Great-grandmother
0.0457	26.6	.0000	1	great-granduncle
0.0457	26.6	.0000	1	great-great-grandfathers
0.0457	26.6	.0000	1	great-great-grandparent
0.0457	26.6	.0000	1	great-great-granduncle
0.0457	26.6	.0000	1	Greeks'
0.0457	26.6	.0000	1	green-and-white
0.0457	26.6	.0000	1	green-eyed
0.0457	26.6	.0000	1	green-feathered
0.0457	26.6	.0000	1	green-filtered
0.0457	26.6	.0000	1	green-leaf
0.0457	26.6	.0000	1	Greenland's
0.0457	26.6	.0000	1	Greenleaf'll
0.0457	26.6	.0000	1	greenstone
0.0457	26.6	.0000	1	greensward
0.0457	26.6	.0000	1	Greer
0.0457	26.6	.0000	1	Greetings
0.0457	26.6	.0000	1	Grenfells
0.0457	26.6	.0000	1	Griddle
0.0457	26.6	.0000	1	grille
0.0457	26.6	.0000	1	Gringo
0.0457	26.6	.0000	1	gro-o-o
0.0457	26.6	.0000	1	groceryman
0.0457	26.6	.0000	1	Grosbeaks
0.0457	26.6	.0000	1	grosses
0.0457	26.6	.0000	1	grouching
0.0457	26.6	.0000	1	ground-gainers
0.0457	26.6	.0000	1	grounders
0.0457	26.6	.0000	1	grubbly
0.0457	26.6	.0000	1	grudging
0.0457	26.6	.0000	1	Grune
0.0457	26.6	.0000	1	grunter
0.0457	26.6	.0000	1	gruntingly
0.0457	26.6	.0000	1	gruntings
0.0457	26.6	.0000	1	guanaco
0.0457	26.6	.0000	1	GUARD
0.0457	26.6	.0000	1	Guelou's
0.0457	26.6	.0000	1	guileful
0.0457	26.6	.0000	1	gulf's
0.0457	26.6	.0000	1	gull's
0.0457	26.6	.0000	1	gullibility
0.0457	26.6	.0000	1	gumbo
0.0457	26.6	.0000	1	gun-deck
0.0457	26.6	.0000	1	gun-shot
0.0457	26.6	.0000	1	gunfights
0.0457	26.6	.0000	1	Gungner
0.0457	26.6	.0000	1	Gurley
0.0457	26.6	.0000	1	guttinke
0.0457	26.6	.0000	1	guvs
0.0457	26.6	.0000	1	guzzle
0.0457	26.6	.0000	1	gwine
0.0457	26.6	.0000	1	gym's
0.0457	26.6	.0000	1	h-h-headless
0.0457	26.6	.0000	1	hnd
0.0457	26.6	.0000	1	ha'nted
0.0457	26.6	.0000	1	ha'pence
0.0457	26.6	.0000	1	Ha'penny's
0.0457	26.6	.0000	1	haawwnk
0.0457	26.6	.0000	1	haawwnnkk
0.0457	26.6	.0000	1	habitants
0.0457	26.6	.0000	1	Hadji
0.0457	26.6	.0000	1	hairbrushes
0.0457	26.6	.0000	1	hairdresser
0.0457	26.6	.0000	1	hal-loo
0.0457	26.6	.0000	1	Haleakala
THE PRECEDING WORD TYPE OCCUPIES RANK 46800				

U	SFI	D	F	Word Type
0.0457	26.6	.0000	1	Half-Chick's
0.0457	26.6	.0000	1	half-admiring
0.0457	26.6	.0000	1	half-an-hour
0.0457	26.6	.0000	1	half-black
0.0457	26.6	.0000	1	half-burned
0.0457	26.6	.0000	1	half-choked
0.0457	26.6	.0000	1	half-cropping
0.0457	26.6	.0000	1	half-darkness
0.0457	26.6	.0000	1	half-dead
0.0457	26.6	.0000	1	half-dissolved
0.0457	26.6	.0000	1	half-foot
0.0457	26.6	.0000	1	half-full
0.0457	26.6	.0000	1	half-gay
0.0457	26.6	.0000	1	half-reveal
0.0457	26.6	.0000	1	half-scream
0.0457	26.6	.0000	1	half-serious
0.0457	26.6	.0000	1	half-shut
0.0457	26.6	.0000	1	half-smiled
0.0457	26.6	.0000	1	half-witted
0.0457	26.6	.0000	1	halfhearted
0.0457	26.6	.0000	1	Halfway
0.0457	26.6	.0000	1	Hall-Heroult
0.0457	26.6	.0000	1	Hall's
0.0457	26.6	.0000	1	hallelujah
0.0457	26.6	.0000	1	hallmarked
0.0457	26.6	.0000	1	Halloweens
0.0457	26.6	.0000	1	haltingly
0.0457	26.6	.0000	1	halyard
0.0457	26.6	.0000	1	hamadryad
0.0457	26.6	.0000	1	Hamburger
0.0457	26.6	.0000	1	Hamiltons'
0.0457	26.6	.0000	1	Hampden
0.0457	26.6	.0000	1	Hampton's
0.0457	26.6	.0000	1	Hamwi's
0.0457	26.6	.0000	1	han'
0.0457	26.6	.0000	1	Han's
0.0457	26.6	.0000	1	Hana
0.0457	26.6	.0000	1	hand-clappings
0.0457	26.6	.0000	1	hand-drawn
0.0457	26.6	.0000	1	hand-knitted
0.0457	26.6	.0000	1	hand-lettered
0.0457	26.6	.0000	1	handprints
0.0457	26.6	.0000	1	handsprings
0.0457	26.6	.0000	1	handy-boy
0.0457	26.6	.0000	1	hangar-top
0.0457	26.6	.0000	1	Hansel's
0.0457	26.6	.0000	1	hap'
0.0457	26.6	.0000	1	Happily
0.0457	26.6	.0000	1	Happiness
0.0457	26.6	.0000	1	hard-driven
0.0457	26.6	.0000	1	hard-frozen
0.0457	26.6	.0000	1	hard-hit
0.0457	26.6	.0000	1	hard-to-comprehend
0.0457	26.6	.0000	1	harm-doing
0.0457	26.6	.0000	1	Harmony's
0.0457	26.6	.0000	1	Haroun
0.0457	26.6	.0000	1	Harpoon
0.0457	26.6	.0000	1	harpoon's
0.0457	26.6	.0000	1	harpstrings
0.0457	26.6	.0000	1	Harrington
0.0457	26.6	.0000	1	Haskell's
0.0457	26.6	.0000	1	Haskins
0.0457	26.6	.0000	1	hasn'
0.0457	26.6	.0000	1	Hasn't
0.0457	26.6	.0000	1	HASTA
0.0457	26.6	.0000	1	Hastings'
0.0457	26.6	.0000	1	hatmaker
0.0457	26.6	.0000	1	hatmakers
0.0457	26.6	.0000	1	hatrack
0.0457	26.6	.0000	1	Hats
0.0457	26.6	.0000	1	Hatten
0.0457	26.6	.0000	1	haulin'
0.0457	26.6	.0000	1	hawk-watching
0.0457	26.6	.0000	1	hawked
0.0457	26.6	.0000	1	hawks'
0.0457	26.6	.0000	1	haywire
0.0457	26.6	.0000	1	hazel-tree
0.0457	26.6	.0000	1	He-Who-Cries-When-**
0.0457	26.6	.0000	1	head-end
0.0457	26.6	.0000	1	head-over-heels
0.0457	26.6	.0000	1	headline-diplomacy
0.0457	26.6	.0000	1	Headmaster's
0.0457	26.6	.0000	1	headpiece
0.0457	26.6	.0000	1	headshake
0.0457	26.6	.0000	1	hearkening
0.0457	26.6	.0000	1	heart'll
0.0457	26.6	.0000	1	hearth-fire
0.0457	26.6	.0000	1	heartier
0.0457	26.6	.0000	1	hearties
0.0457	26.6	.0000	1	heartiest
0.0457	26.6	.0000	1	heartwarming
0.0457	26.6	.0000	1	Hearty
0.0457	26.6	.0000	1	Hearty's
0.0457	26.6	.0000	1	hease
0.0457	26.6	.0000	1	heat-measuring
0.0457	26.6	.0000	1	heathenish
0.0457	26.6	.0000	1	heaths
0.0457	26.6	.0000	1	heavenward
0.0457	26.6	.0000	1	heavily-built
0.0457	26.6	.0000	1	Hedge

THE PRECEDING WORD TYPE OCCUPIES RANK 46900

U	SFI	D	F	Word Type
0.0457	26.6	.0000	1	Hedgehog
0.0457	26.6	.0000	1	Hedges'
0.0457	26.6	.0000	1	heelless
0.0457	26.6	.0000	1	heiress
0.0457	26.6	.0000	1	Helfer
0.0457	26.6	.0000	1	Helios
0.0457	26.6	.0000	1	heliport
0.0457	26.6	.0000	1	Helle
0.0457	26.6	.0000	1	helloes
0.0457	26.6	.0000	1	Helped
0.0457	26.6	.0000	1	helpfully
0.0457	26.6	.0000	1	helpfulness
0.0457	26.6	.0000	1	Hemingway
0.0457	26.6	.0000	1	hen-roost
0.0457	26.6	.0000	1	Hennessey's
0.0457	26.6	.0000	1	Henri's
0.0457	26.6	.0000	1	Henriette
0.0457	26.6	.0000	1	Henson
0.0457	26.6	.0000	1	hepaticas
0.0457	26.6	.0000	1	HER
0.0457	26.6	.0000	1	Heraclius
0.0457	26.6	.0000	1	Herb's
0.0457	26.6	.0000	1	herdboy
0.0457	26.6	.0000	1	herewith
0.0457	26.6	.0000	1	Herndon
0.0457	26.6	.0000	1	Hertwig
0.0457	26.6	.0000	1	hesitancy
0.0457	26.6	.0000	1	Hesper
0.0457	26.6	.0000	1	hez
0.0457	26.6	.0000	1	hi-fi's
0.0457	26.6	.0000	1	hiccup
0.0457	26.6	.0000	1	hieroglyph
0.0457	26.6	.0000	1	high-explosive
0.0457	26.6	.0000	1	high-styled
0.0457	26.6	.0000	1	high-top
0.0457	26.6	.0000	1	highscorer's
0.0457	26.6	.0000	1	highwater
0.0457	26.6	.0000	1	hillman
0.0457	26.6	.0000	1	HIM
0.0457	26.6	.0000	1	Hindbad
0.0457	26.6	.0000	1	Hindoo
0.0457	26.6	.0000	1	hindquarter
0.0457	26.6	.0000	1	hinoyojin
0.0457	26.6	.0000	1	hippo's
0.0457	26.6	.0000	1	hippopotomuscle
0.0457	26.6	.0000	1	hippopotomusses
0.0457	26.6	.0000	1	hippopotomust
0.0457	26.6	.0000	1	hippopotomustard
0.0457	26.6	.0000	1	his'n
0.0457	26.6	.0000	1	hive's
0.0457	26.6	.0000	1	hiyup
0.0457	26.6	.0000	1	hmmm
0.0457	26.6	.0000	1	hmmmmm
0.0457	26.6	.0000	1	ho-ho
0.0457	26.6	.0000	1	ho-ho-hoing
0.0457	26.6	.0000	1	ho-ka-he
0.0457	26.6	.0000	1	hobbes
0.0457	26.6	.0000	1	Hobbie's
0.0457	26.6	.0000	1	hobgoblins
0.0457	26.6	.0000	1	hocus-pocus
0.0457	26.6	.0000	1	Hodag
0.0457	26.6	.0000	1	hoein'
0.0457	26.6	.0000	1	hoksila
0.0457	26.6	.0000	1	Hold
0.0457	26.6	.0000	1	Holdfast
0.0457	26.6	.0000	1	hole-in-the-wall
0.0457	26.6	.0000	1	Holidays
0.0457	26.6	.0000	1	hollar
0.0457	26.6	.0000	1	Holmes'
0.0457	26.6	.0000	1	holsters
0.0457	26.6	.0000	1	hombres
0.0457	26.6	.0000	1	Home-Run
0.0457	26.6	.0000	1	home-sick
0.0457	26.6	.0000	1	home's
0.0457	26.6	.0000	1	homebound
0.0457	26.6	.0000	1	homeseekers
0.0457	26.6	.0000	1	Homme
0.0457	26.6	.0000	1	Honest
0.0457	26.6	.0000	1	honey-suckle
0.0457	26.6	.0000	1	honeyed
0.0457	26.6	.0000	1	honker
0.0457	26.6	.0000	1	Honks
0.0457	26.6	.0000	1	honks
0.0457	26.6	.0000	1	hoo-hoo
0.0457	26.6	.0000	1	hoohooed
0.0457	26.6	.0000	1	hoohooing
0.0457	26.6	.0000	1	Hookerville
0.0457	26.6	.0000	1	hookey
0.0457	26.6	.0000	1	hop-skip-and-jump
0.0457	26.6	.0000	1	Hopis
0.0457	26.6	.0000	1	Horiuchi-san
0.0457	26.6	.0000	1	hornbills
0.0457	26.6	.0000	1	Horned
0.0457	26.6	.0000	1	Horner's
0.0457	26.6	.0000	1	horse-hair
0.0457	26.6	.0000	1	Hot-Potato
0.0457	26.6	.0000	1	hot-chick-pea
0.0457	26.6	.0000	1	hot-dog
0.0457	26.6	.0000	1	hot-rods
0.0457	26.6	.0000	1	hounds'

THE PRECEDING WORD TYPE OCCUPIES RANK 47000

U	SFI	D	F	Word Type
0.0457	26.6	.0000	1	hourglasses
0.0457	26.6	.0000	1	house-building
0.0457	26.6	.0000	1	house-flannel
0.0457	26.6	.0000	1	house-moving
0.0457	26.6	.0000	1	house-place
0.0457	26.6	.0000	1	house-work
0.0457	26.6	.0000	1	houseboats
0.0457	26.6	.0000	1	housebreaking
0.0457	26.6	.0000	1	housekeepers
0.0457	26.6	.0000	1	housetop
0.0457	26.6	.0000	1	housetops
0.0457	26.6	.0000	1	how-d'you-do's
0.0457	26.6	.0000	1	howdydo
0.0457	26.6	.0000	1	Howell's
0.0457	26.6	.0000	1	howler
0.0457	26.6	.0000	1	Howler
0.0457	26.6	.0000	1	HOY
0.0457	26.6	.0000	1	hoyee
0.0457	26.6	.0000	1	Hozak
0.0457	26.6	.0000	1	hu-hu
0.0457	26.6	.0000	1	huffing
0.0457	26.6	.0000	1	huffle
0.0457	26.6	.0000	1	hui
0.0457	26.6	.0000	1	hulla
0.0457	26.6	.0000	1	Hulton
0.0457	26.6	.0000	1	Humane
0.0457	26.6	.0000	1	humanized
0.0457	26.6	.0000	1	Humbug
0.0457	26.6	.0000	1	Hummingbird
0.0457	26.6	.0000	1	hummingbirds'
0.0457	26.6	.0000	1	hummocks
0.0457	26.6	.0000	1	hump-back
0.0457	26.6	.0000	1	humpf
0.0457	26.6	.0000	1	Humphrey's
0.0457	26.6	.0000	1	hung-g-g
0.0457	26.6	.0000	1	Hunt's
0.0457	26.6	.0000	1	hunting-dogs
0.0457	26.6	.0000	1	hunting-grounds
0.0457	26.6	.0000	1	huntress
0.0457	26.6	.0000	1	huntsmanship
0.0457	26.6	.0000	1	hurdy-gurdy
0.0457	26.6	.0000	1	hurricane's
0.0457	26.6	.0000	1	hutches
0.0457	26.6	.0000	1	Hyacinth's
0.0457	26.6	.0000	1	hydroplane
0.0457	26.6	.0000	1	Hyman's
0.0457	26.6	.0000	1	hypnotizes
0.0457	26.6	.0000	1	I-I
0.0457	26.6	.0000	1	i
0.0457	26.6	.0000	1	Iagoo
0.0457	26.6	.0000	1	ice-coated
0.0457	26.6	.0000	1	ice-storms
0.0457	26.6	.0000	1	icefall
0.0457	26.6	.0000	1	Icicle
0.0457	26.6	.0000	1	icy-cold
0.0457	26.6	.0000	1	idlers
0.0457	26.6	.0000	1	ies
0.0457	26.6	.0000	1	igg-puh
0.0457	26.6	.0000	1	ill-concealed
0.0457	26.6	.0000	1	ill-gotten
0.0457	26.6	.0000	1	ill-humored
0.0457	26.6	.0000	1	Illegal
0.0457	26.6	.0000	1	immigrate
0.0457	26.6	.0000	1	immunes
0.0457	26.6	.0000	1	impassively
0.0457	26.6	.0000	1	implicitly
0.0457	26.6	.0000	1	important-looking
0.0457	26.6	.0000	1	importanter'n
0.0457	26.6	.0000	1	Impossible
0.0457	26.6	.0000	1	impostors
0.0457	26.6	.0000	1	impotency
0.0457	26.6	.0000	1	inattentiveness
0.0457	26.6	.0000	1	incantations
0.0457	26.6	.0000	1	incautiously
0.0457	26.6	.0000	1	incensed
0.0457	26.6	.0000	1	incompetent
0.0457	26.6	.0000	1	incontinently
0.0457	26.6	.0000	1	incurably
0.0457	26.6	.0000	1	incurring
0.0457	26.6	.0000	1	indebtedness
0.0457	26.6	.0000	1	Indeed
0.0457	26.6	.0000	1	indemnification
0.0457	26.6	.0000	1	Indepentia
0.0457	26.6	.0000	1	Indio
0.0457	26.6	.0000	1	indistinguishable
0.0457	26.6	.0000	1	indulgently
0.0457	26.6	.0000	1	industriously
0.0457	26.6	.0000	1	inertial
0.0457	26.6	.0000	1	inexpensively
0.0457	26.6	.0000	1	infamy
0.0457	26.6	.0000	1	infatuated
0.0457	26.6	.0000	1	Infirmary
0.0457	26.6	.0000	1	information-please
0.0457	26.6	.0000	1	infusing
0.0457	26.6	.0000	1	ingrates
0.0457	26.6	.0000	1	inhibitions
0.0457	26.6	.0000	1	inhibits
0.0457	26.6	.0000	1	Inmate
0.0457	26.6	.0000	1	inn-yard
0.0457	26.6	.0000	1	Innocence

THE PRECEDING WORD TYPE OCCUPIES RANK 47100

U	SFI	D	F	Word Type
0.0457	26.6	.0000	1	insect-size
0.0457	26.6	.0000	1	instant's
0.0457	26.6	.0000	1	instigates
0.0457	26.6	.0000	1	instrumentalist
0.0457	26.6	.0000	1	insurrectionists
0.0457	26.6	.0000	1	intelligibly
0.0457	26.6	.0000	1	intentional
0.0457	26.6	.0000	1	interceptor
0.0457	26.6	.0000	1	interpreters
0.0457	26.6	.0000	1	interracial
0.0457	26.6	.0000	1	interred
0.0457	26.6	.0000	1	interrogation
0.0457	26.6	.0000	1	intimation
0.0457	26.6	.0000	1	intoxication
0.0457	26.6	.0000	1	Inventor
0.0457	26.6	.0000	1	inventors'
0.0457	26.6	.0000	1	inverts
0.0457	26.6	.0000	1	inveteracy
0.0457	26.6	.0000	1	irate
0.0457	26.6	.0000	1	iron-studded
0.0457	26.6	.0000	1	ironhearted
0.0457	26.6	.0000	1	Irons
0.0457	26.6	.0000	1	irrecoverably
0.0457	26.6	.0000	1	Irwin
0.0457	26.6	.0000	1	Isaac's
0.0457	26.6	.0000	1	Ismarus
0.0457	26.6	.0000	1	isolationist
0.0457	26.6	.0000	1	Issippi
0.0457	26.6	.0000	1	it'
0.0457	26.6	.0000	1	itemizing
0.0457	26.6	.0000	1	Ivanova
0.0457	26.6	.0000	1	Ivar's
0.0457	26.6	.0000	1	Ivorsen
0.0457	26.6	.0000	1	j-j-just
0.0457	26.6	.0000	1	jzz
0.0457	26.6	.0000	1	Ja-Nez
0.0457	26.6	.0000	1	Ja's
0.0457	26.6	.0000	1	jabbers
0.0457	26.6	.0000	1	Jack-and-the-beanstalk
0.0457	26.6	.0000	1	jack-o-lantern
0.0457	26.6	.0000	1	jackal's
0.0457	26.6	.0000	1	jackknife's
0.0457	26.6	.0000	1	jackrabbits
0.0457	26.6	.0000	1	jackstones
0.0457	26.6	.0000	1	Jacobins
0.0457	26.6	.0000	1	Jacques's
0.0457	26.6	.0000	1	Jaguars
0.0457	26.6	.0000	1	jailer
0.0457	26.6	.0000	1	jalopies
0.0457	26.6	.0000	1	Jam's
0.0457	26.6	.0000	1	jangle
0.0457	26.6	.0000	1	Jansci
0.0457	26.6	.0000	1	jas
0.0457	26.6	.0000	1	Jataka
0.0457	26.6	.0000	1	Jayvee
0.0457	26.6	.0000	1	Jean-Claude
0.0457	26.6	.0000	1	Jeffrey's
0.0457	26.6	.0000	1	Jehovah's
0.0457	26.6	.0000	1	Jellyfish
0.0457	26.6	.0000	1	Jensen's
0.0457	26.6	.0000	1	Jeremy's
0.0457	26.6	.0000	1	jerkers
0.0457	26.6	.0000	1	Jerome's
0.0457	26.6	.0000	1	jetties
0.0457	26.6	.0000	1	jewel-bright
0.0457	26.6	.0000	1	jing
0.0457	26.6	.0000	1	Jiquipilco
0.0457	26.6	.0000	1	Joaby's
0.0457	26.6	.0000	1	Joao
0.0457	26.6	.0000	1	Jod
0.0457	26.6	.0000	1	Jod's
0.0457	26.6	.0000	1	Johnny-on-the-spot
0.0457	26.6	.0000	1	jointless
0.0457	26.6	.0000	1	joists
0.0457	26.6	.0000	1	jokers
0.0457	26.6	.0000	1	Jolanna
0.0457	26.6	.0000	1	Joppers
0.0457	26.6	.0000	1	Jorge's
0.0457	26.6	.0000	1	Josh's
0.0457	26.6	.0000	1	Josiah's
0.0457	26.6	.0000	1	Joss's
0.0457	26.6	.0000	1	Jotham
0.0457	26.6	.0000	1	jotting
0.0457	26.6	.0000	1	jour
0.0457	26.6	.0000	1	Journal's
0.0457	26.6	.0000	1	journeyings
0.0457	26.6	.0000	1	joviality
0.0457	26.6	.0000	1	Juanito's
0.0457	26.6	.0000	1	juggler's
0.0457	26.6	.0000	1	juiciest
0.0457	26.6	.0000	1	jukebox
0.0457	26.6	.0000	1	Jukes
0.0457	26.6	.0000	1	Juliska's
0.0457	26.6	.0000	1	July's
0.0457	26.6	.0000	1	jungleland
0.0457	26.6	.0000	1	Junk
0.0457	26.6	.0000	1	Jupiter-C
0.0457	26.6	.0000	1	justifications
0.0457	26.6	.0000	1	jut
0.0457	26.6	.0000	1	kaffakalas

THE PRECEDING WORD TYPE OCCUPIES RANK 47200

U	SFI	D	F	Word Type
0.0457	26.6	.0000	1	kaffet
0.0457	26.6	.0000	1	kaffir
0.0457	26.6	.0000	1	Kaiva's
0.0457	26.6	.0000	1	Kaller
0.0457	26.6	.0000	1	Kanana's
0.0457	26.6	.0000	1	Kantchil's
0.0457	26.6	.0000	1	Kapaa
0.0457	26.6	.0000	1	karats
0.0457	26.6	.0000	1	Kasson's
0.0457	26.6	.0000	1	KATIE'D
0.0457	26.6	.0000	1	Katzenellenbogen
0.0457	26.6	.0000	1	keads
0.0457	26.6	.0000	1	keeled
0.0457	26.6	.0000	1	keenest
0.0457	26.6	.0000	1	keenin'
0.0457	26.6	.0000	1	Keeping
0.0457	26.6	.0000	1	Kees'
0.0457	26.6	.0000	1	Kelly's
0.0457	26.6	.0000	1	Kenji's
0.0457	26.6	.0000	1	Kentucky-born
0.0457	26.6	.0000	1	ker-chunking
0.0457	26.6	.0000	1	Kermit
0.0457	26.6	.0000	1	kersplack
0.0457	26.6	.0000	1	kettleful
0.0457	26.6	.0000	1	key's
0.0457	26.6	.0000	1	Khaled's
0.0457	26.6	.0000	1	Khoda-verdikol
0.0457	26.6	.0000	1	Kia-wa-wa
0.0457	26.6	.0000	1	kicked-up
0.0457	26.6	.0000	1	kidnapers
0.0457	26.6	.0000	1	Kidwells
0.0457	26.6	.0000	1	Kiehl's
0.0457	26.6	.0000	1	Kildare
0.0457	26.6	.0000	1	Killy
0.0457	26.6	.0000	1	Kim's
0.0457	26.6	.0000	1	Kimmel
0.0457	26.6	.0000	1	Kimmel's
0.0457	26.6	.0000	1	kind-faced
0.0457	26.6	.0000	1	kindnesses
0.0457	26.6	.0000	1	kinfolks
0.0457	26.6	.0000	1	kingbirds
0.0457	26.6	.0000	1	kingpin
0.0457	26.6	.0000	1	kingship
0.0457	26.6	.0000	1	kink
0.0457	26.6	.0000	1	Kinndli
0.0457	26.6	.0000	1	Kinzua
0.0457	26.6	.0000	1	Kipling's
0.0457	26.6	.0000	1	Kish
0.0457	26.6	.0000	1	kitchen-maid
0.0457	26.6	.0000	1	kitchenette-furnished
0.0457	26.6	.0000	1	Kitt
0.0457	26.6	.0000	1	Kitten's
0.0457	26.6	.0000	1	kitten's
0.0457	26.6	.0000	1	Kitty's
0.0457	26.6	.0000	1	kivvers
0.0457	26.6	.0000	1	klaxons
0.0457	26.6	.0000	1	Kleenex
0.0457	26.6	.0000	1	klompen
0.0457	26.6	.0000	1	kneed
0.0457	26.6	.0000	1	kneepads
0.0457	26.6	.0000	1	knifes
0.0457	26.6	.0000	1	knights'
0.0457	26.6	.0000	1	knockouts
0.0457	26.6	.0000	1	knot-tying

U	SFI	D	F	Word Type
0.0457	26.6	.0000	1	Knots
0.0457	26.6	.0000	1	knottings
0.0457	26.6	.0000	1	know's
0.0457	26.6	.0000	1	knucklers
0.0457	26.6	.0000	1	knuckling
0.0457	26.6	.0000	1	Kobo's
0.0457	26.6	.0000	1	Kochendorfer
0.0457	26.6	.0000	1	komiks
0.0457	26.6	.0000	1	Koponen
0.0457	26.6	.0000	1	Korn
0.0457	26.6	.0000	1	Krasnin
0.0457	26.6	.0000	1	Krisps
0.0457	26.6	.0000	1	Kristen
0.0457	26.6	.0000	1	kroner
0.0457	26.6	.0000	1	Kruger's
0.0457	26.6	.0000	1	Kukupi
0.0457	26.6	.0000	1	Kunming
0.0457	26.6	.0000	1	Kypros
0.0457	26.6	.0000	1	Kyrios's
0.0457	26.6	.0000	1	l-a-u-g-h
0.0457	26.6	.0000	1	l-lady
0.0457	26.6	.0000	1	l'Orient
0.0457	26.6	.0000	1	l'Orient's
0.0457	26.6	.0000	1	LA
0.0457	26.6	.0000	1	LaBahia
0.0457	26.6	.0000	1	LaFontaine's
0.0457	26.6	.0000	1	LaJolla
0.0457	26.6	.0000	1	LaMesa
0.0457	26.6	.0000	1	la-dee-da
0.0457	26.6	.0000	1	laboratory's
0.0457	26.6	.0000	1	Labrador's
0.0457	26.6	.0000	1	Labradors
0.0457	26.6	.0000	1	lackadaisical
0.0457	26.6	.0000	1	Lacour
0.0457	26.6	.0000	1	ladder-rack
0.0457	26.6	.0000	1	ladder's
				THE PRECEDING WORD TYPE OCCUPIES RANK 47300
0.0457	26.6	.0000	1	ladies-in-waiting
0.0457	26.6	.0000	1	ladling
0.0457	26.6	.0000	1	Ladrones
0.0457	26.6	.0000	1	Lady-day
0.0457	26.6	.0000	1	lady-in-wating
0.0457	26.6	.0000	1	lady-size
0.0457	26.6	.0000	1	ladybugs
0.0457	26.6	.0000	1	laise
0.0457	26.6	.0000	1	LakeCity
0.0457	26.6	.0000	1	Lake's
0.0457	26.6	.0000	1	Lakemanu
0.0457	26.6	.0000	1	lama
0.0457	26.6	.0000	1	lamplit
0.0457	26.6	.0000	1	Lana
0.0457	26.6	.0000	1	lanced
0.0457	26.6	.0000	1	land
0.0457	26.6	.0000	1	Landrum
0.0457	26.6	.0000	1	Langford
0.0457	26.6	.0000	1	Langmuir
0.0457	26.6	.0000	1	languished
0.0457	26.6	.0000	1	Lapice
0.0457	26.6	.0000	1	lapis-lazuli
0.0457	26.6	.0000	1	larboard
0.0457	26.6	.0000	1	large-size
0.0457	26.6	.0000	1	large-wheeled
0.0457	26.6	.0000	1	Larraby
0.0457	26.6	.0000	1	Lars'
0.0457	26.6	.0000	1	Lars's
0.0457	26.6	.0000	1	Larsens'
0.0457	26.6	.0000	1	lascar
0.0457	26.6	.0000	1	lassoed
0.0457	26.6	.0000	1	last-forever
0.0457	26.6	.0000	1	lavatories
0.0457	26.6	.0000	1	Lavendars
0.0457	26.6	.0000	1	lavishly
0.0457	26.6	.0000	1	Lawk
0.0457	26.6	.0000	1	laxative
0.0457	26.6	.0000	1	lay-ups
0.0457	26.6	.0000	1	Lazy
0.0457	26.6	.0000	1	lazybones
0.0457	26.6	.0000	1	LeGrand
0.0457	26.6	.0000	1	LeMonde
0.0457	26.6	.0000	1	LeRoy
0.0457	26.6	.0000	1	lead-dog
0.0457	26.6	.0000	1	LEADER
0.0457	26.6	.0000	1	leadsman's
0.0457	26.6	.0000	1	leady
0.0457	26.6	.0000	1	leaf-fringed
0.0457	26.6	.0000	1	leafing
0.0457	26.6	.0000	1	Leaguers
0.0457	26.6	.0000	1	lean-bodied
0.0457	26.6	.0000	1	leapfrog
0.0457	26.6	.0000	1	leather-cheeked
0.0457	26.6	.0000	1	leather-covered
0.0457	26.6	.0000	1	leather-lined
0.0457	26.6	.0000	1	leatherworking
0.0457	26.6	.0000	1	leatle
0.0457	26.6	.0000	1	Leave
0.0457	26.6	.0000	1	leave-taking
0.0457	26.6	.0000	1	lecons
0.0457	26.6	.0000	1	Left-Over
0.0457	26.6	.0000	1	left-behind
0.0457	26.6	.0000	1	lefts
0.0457	26.6	.0000	1	Legislature's
0.0457	26.6	.0000	1	lei-making
0.0457	26.6	.0000	1	Leigh
0.0457	26.6	.0000	1	Leland
0.0457	26.6	.0000	1	Leland's
0.0457	26.6	.0000	1	lemarkable
0.0457	26.6	.0000	1	lemon-meringue
0.0457	26.6	.0000	1	Lenten
0.0457	26.6	.0000	1	lentil
0.0457	26.6	.0000	1	Leominster
0.0457	26.6	.0000	1	leopard-panther
0.0457	26.6	.0000	1	Leopard's
0.0457	26.6	.0000	1	lepers
0.0457	26.6	.0000	1	let's-go-easies
0.0457	26.6	.0000	1	leukemia
0.0457	26.6	.0000	1	Levant
0.0457	26.6	.0000	1	level-headed
0.0457	26.6	.0000	1	Levittown
0.0457	26.6	.0000	1	Lex
0.0457	26.6	.0000	1	liar's
0.0457	26.6	.0000	1	Liberties
0.0457	26.6	.0000	1	lickety-split
0.0457	26.6	.0000	1	Liesi's
0.0457	26.6	.0000	1	life-boats
0.0457	26.6	.0000	1	life-size
0.0457	26.6	.0000	1	lifelines
0.0457	26.6	.0000	1	Liffey
0.0457	26.6	.0000	1	liger
0.0457	26.6	.0000	1	light-foot
0.0457	26.6	.0000	1	light-footed
0.0457	26.6	.0000	1	light-headed
0.0457	26.6	.0000	1	light-heeled
0.0457	26.6	.0000	1	light-purple
0.0457	26.6	.0000	1	light-stand
0.0457	26.6	.0000	1	Light's
0.0457	26.6	.0000	1	lighter-than-aircraft
0.0457	26.6	.0000	1	lightheartedly
				THE PRECEDING WORD TYPE OCCUPIES RANK 47400
0.0457	26.6	.0000	1	lightkeepers
0.0457	26.6	.0000	1	Lijembe's
0.0457	26.6	.0000	1	likings
0.0457	26.6	.0000	1	Lilac
0.0457	26.6	.0000	1	lily-white
0.0457	26.6	.0000	1	Limited
0.0457	26.6	.0000	1	linden
0.0457	26.6	.0000	1	Lindsay's
0.0457	26.6	.0000	1	line-drive
0.0457	26.6	.0000	1	lingonberry
0.0457	26.6	.0000	1	Linian
0.0457	26.6	.0000	1	link's
0.0457	26.6	.0000	1	linnet
0.0457	26.6	.0000	1	linsey
0.0457	26.6	.0000	1	lintel
0.0457	26.6	.0000	1	lion-hearted
0.0457	26.6	.0000	1	Lionel's
0.0457	26.6	.0000	1	Liss
0.0457	26.6	.0000	1	Listening-to-Me-Humming
0.0457	26.6	.0000	1	lit'l
0.0457	26.6	.0000	1	Litefoot
0.0457	26.6	.0000	1	lites
0.0457	26.6	.0000	1	lithographs
0.0457	26.6	.0000	1	LITTLE
0.0457	26.6	.0000	1	littler
0.0457	26.6	.0000	1	Littles
0.0457	26.6	.0000	1	Littleton
0.0457	26.6	.0000	1	lives'
0.0457	26.6	.0000	1	Liza's
0.0457	26.6	.0000	1	Lizabeth
0.0457	26.6	.0000	1	Illama
0.0457	26.6	.0000	1	loa
0.0457	26.6	.0000	1	lobbing
0.0457	26.6	.0000	1	Lode
0.0457	26.6	.0000	1	log-cabin
0.0457	26.6	.0000	1	log's
0.0457	26.6	.0000	1	logger's
0.0457	26.6	.0000	1	logrolling
0.0457	26.6	.0000	1	loike
0.0457	26.6	.0000	1	lollapaloozing
0.0457	26.6	.0000	1	lolled
0.0457	26.6	.0000	1	Loma
0.0457	26.6	.0000	1	lonesome-born
0.0457	26.6	.0000	1	long-boats
0.0457	26.6	.0000	1	long-cherished
0.0457	26.6	.0000	1	long-continued
0.0457	26.6	.0000	1	long-controlled
0.0457	26.6	.0000	1	long-drawn-out
0.0457	26.6	.0000	1	long-expected
0.0457	26.6	.0000	1	long-faced
0.0457	26.6	.0000	1	long-gone
0.0457	26.6	.0000	1	long-unused
0.0457	26.6	.0000	1	longdistance
0.0457	26.6	.0000	1	longdraft
0.0457	26.6	.0000	1	longdrawn
0.0457	26.6	.0000	1	longer-legged
0.0457	26.6	.0000	1	longhouse
0.0457	26.6	.0000	1	looekd
0.0457	26.6	.0000	1	look-out
0.0457	26.6	.0000	1	looker
0.0457	26.6	.0000	1	looking-glass
0.0457	26.6	.0000	1	looky
0.0457	26.6	.0000	1	lopped
0.0457	26.6	.0000	1	loquacity
0.0457	26.6	.0000	1	Lordliness
0.0457	26.6	.0000	1	Loss
0.0457	26.6	.0000	1	lost-plane
0.0457	26.6	.0000	1	losted
0.0457	26.6	.0000	1	Loudspeakers
0.0457	26.6	.0000	1	Loues
0.0457	26.6	.0000	1	Louie's
0.0457	26.6	.0000	1	Louis's
0.0457	26.6	.0000	1	Louisey
0.0457	26.6	.0000	1	Lounge
0.0457	26.6	.0000	1	louring
0.0457	26.6	.0000	1	love-knot
0.0457	26.6	.0000	1	lovin'
0.0457	26.6	.0000	1	loving-kindness
0.0457	26.6	.0000	1	low-bent
0.0457	26.6	.0000	1	low-melting
0.0457	26.6	.0000	1	low-powered
0.0457	26.6	.0000	1	low-spread
0.0457	26.6	.0000	1	Lucius
0.0457	26.6	.0000	1	Luck's
0.0457	26.6	.0000	1	lucre
0.0457	26.6	.0000	1	Luella
0.0457	26.6	.0000	1	Luga's
0.0457	26.6	.0000	1	Luigia's
0.0457	26.6	.0000	1	Lulubelle
0.0457	26.6	.0000	1	lumbago
0.0457	26.6	.0000	1	Lumber
0.0457	26.6	.0000	1	lumberjacket
0.0457	26.6	.0000	1	lun
0.0457	26.6	.0000	1	lunching
0.0457	26.6	.0000	1	luther
0.0457	26.6	.0000	1	Lux'
0.0457	26.6	.0000	1	Lyceum
0.0457	26.6	.0000	1	Lyddy
0.0457	26.6	.0000	1	Lydia's
0.0457	26.6	.0000	1	lynch
				THE PRECEDING WORD TYPE OCCUPIES RANK 47500
0.0457	26.6	.0000	1	lynched
0.0457	26.6	.0000	1	L12B
0.0457	26.6	.0000	1	MArket
0.0457	26.6	.0000	1	m-e-a-t
0.0457	26.6	.0000	1	m-m
0.0457	26.6	.0000	1	m-m-meet
0.0457	26.6	.0000	1	m-merry
0.0457	26.6	.0000	1	m-o-o-n
0.0457	26.6	.0000	1	mlk
0.0457	26.6	.0000	1	Ma'll
0.0457	26.6	.0000	1	ma'm
0.0457	26.6	.0000	1	maa-a-a-a
0.0457	26.6	.0000	1	maa-a-a-a-a
0.0457	26.6	.0000	1	maah
0.0457	26.6	.0000	1	MacDermott
0.0457	26.6	.0000	1	MacDougall
0.0457	26.6	.0000	1	MacPhersons
0.0457	26.6	.0000	1	MacPhersons'
0.0457	26.6	.0000	1	MACHINERY
0.0457	26.6	.0000	1	Macias
0.0457	26.6	.0000	1	mackintosh
0.0457	26.6	.0000	1	MAD
0.0457	26.6	.0000	1	maddening
0.0457	26.6	.0000	1	MADE
0.0457	26.6	.0000	1	made-over
0.0457	26.6	.0000	1	Madison's
0.0457	26.6	.0000	1	madras
0.0457	26.6	.0000	1	Magarac
0.0457	26.6	.0000	1	MAGIQUE
0.0457	26.6	.0000	1	Maitland
0.0457	26.6	.0000	1	makhzan
0.0457	26.6	.0000	1	maleman
0.0457	26.6	.0000	1	mall
0.0457	26.6	.0000	1	Mallet
0.0457	26.6	.0000	1	Mamita's
0.0457	26.6	.0000	1	Mammal
0.0457	26.6	.0000	1	man-destroyer
0.0457	26.6	.0000	1	man-eater
0.0457	26.6	.0000	1	man-shaped
0.0457	26.6	.0000	1	man-to-man
0.0457	26.6	.0000	1	manfish
0.0457	26.6	.0000	1	manhood's
0.0457	26.6	.0000	1	manliest
0.0457	26.6	.0000	1	mannerisms
0.0457	26.6	.0000	1	manning
0.0457	26.6	.0000	1	mans
0.0457	26.6	.0000	1	Manuel's
0.0457	26.6	.0000	1	many-ribbed
0.0457	26.6	.0000	1	many-seeded
0.0457	26.6	.0000	1	many-shaped
0.0457	26.6	.0000	1	map-makers
0.0457	26.6	.0000	1	maravilla
0.0457	26.6	.0000	1	marble-playing
0.0457	26.6	.0000	1	marble-topped
0.0457	26.6	.0000	1	Marfa's
0.0457	26.6	.0000	1	Margarita's
0.0457	26.6	.0000	1	Marge's
0.0457	26.6	.0000	1	Marie-Louise's
0.0457	26.6	.0000	1	mariner's
0.0457	26.6	.0000	1	market's
0.0457	26.6	.0000	1	Markle
0.0457	26.6	.0000	1	Marks's
0.0457	26.6	.0000	1	Marlton's
0.0457	26.6	.0000	1	marozhenoye
0.0457	26.6	.0000	1	marrying
0.0457	26.6	.0000	1	MarsCity
0.0457	26.6	.0000	1	Marshall's
0.0457	26.6	.0000	1	Marshes
0.0457	26.6	.0000	1	marshlander
0.0457	26.6	.0000	1	marshman
0.0457	26.6	.0000	1	Marty's
0.0457	26.6	.0000	1	marygold
0.0457	26.6	.0000	1	masklike
0.0457	26.6	.0000	1	Massac
0.0457	26.6	.0000	1	massaged
0.0457	26.6	.0000	1	masse
0.0457	26.6	.0000	1	master-fiddler
0.0457	26.6	.0000	1	Masterson
0.0457	26.6	.0000	1	Matsuyama
0.0457	26.6	.0000	1	Matthew's
0.0457	26.6	.0000	1	matzoth
0.0457	26.6	.0000	1	Maung
0.0457	26.6	.0000	1	Maury's
0.0457	26.6	.0000	1	Maw
0.0457	26.6	.0000	1	maw
0.0457	26.6	.0000	1	MAY
0.0457	26.6	.0000	1	Mayflowers
0.0457	26.6	.0000	1	McCORMICK
0.0457	26.6	.0000	1	McAllen
0.0457	26.6	.0000	1	McCantry
0.0457	26.6	.0000	1	McCloud
0.0457	26.6	.0000	1	McClung's
0.0457	26.6	.0000	1	McCormick-Manny
0.0457	26.6	.0000	1	McCoy
0.0457	26.6	.0000	1	McGarrity's
0.0457	26.6	.0000	1	McGrannery's
0.0457	26.6	.0000	1	McIvor
0.0457	26.6	.0000	1	McLeod's
0.0457	26.6	.0000	1	McPhales
0.0457	26.6	.0000	1	MDCCLXXVI
				THE PRECEDING WORD TYPE OCCUPIES RANK 47600
0.0457	26.6	.0000	1	mealy
0.0457	26.6	.0000	1	mean-tempered
0.0457	26.6	.0000	1	meanderings
0.0457	26.6	.0000	1	meaner
0.0457	26.6	.0000	1	Meares'
0.0457	26.6	.0000	1	measureless
0.0457	26.6	.0000	1	medallions
0.0457	26.6	.0000	1	medications
0.0457	26.6	.0000	1	medico
0.0457	26.6	.0000	1	medium-done
0.0457	26.6	.0000	1	medium-rare
0.0457	26.6	.0000	1	Medusa
0.0457	26.6	.0000	1	Meecham's
0.0457	26.6	.0000	1	Meeker's
0.0457	26.6	.0000	1	meeting-house
0.0457	26.6	.0000	1	megalopolitan
0.0457	26.6	.0000	1	Megistias
0.0457	26.6	.0000	1	Meharry
0.0457	26.6	.0000	1	Melbourne's
0.0457	26.6	.0000	1	Mellens
0.0457	26.6	.0000	1	melter
0.0457	26.6	.0000	1	Memorandum
0.0457	26.6	.0000	1	Menam
0.0457	26.6	.0000	1	Menches
0.0457	26.6	.0000	1	Menches'
0.0457	26.6	.0000	1	mendicancy
0.0457	26.6	.0000	1	Meneer
0.0457	26.6	.0000	1	menfish
0.0457	26.6	.0000	1	menials
0.0457	26.6	.0000	1	Mennonite
0.0457	26.6	.0000	1	Menuhin
0.0457	26.6	.0000	1	Meriweather
0.0457	26.6	.0000	1	Merki
0.0457	26.6	.0000	1	Merki's
0.0457	26.6	.0000	1	mesdames
0.0457	26.6	.0000	1	meself
0.0457	26.6	.0000	1	mess-attendant
0.0457	26.6	.0000	1	metates
0.0457	26.6	.0000	1	meteorite's
0.0457	26.6	.0000	1	meteoritic
0.0457	26.6	.0000	1	Meter
0.0457	26.6	.0000	1	Mexicans'
0.0457	26.6	.0000	1	mickeys
0.0457	26.6	.0000	1	mid-morning
0.0457	26.6	.0000	1	mid-winter
0.0457	26.6	.0000	1	Middy
0.0457	26.6	.0000	1	midgets
0.0457	26.6	.0000	1	Midlands
0.0457	26.6	.0000	1	midsection
0.0457	26.6	.0000	1	midship
0.0457	26.6	.0000	1	Midshipman
0.0457	26.6	.0000	1	midshipman
0.0457	26.6	.0000	1	midshipman's
0.0457	26.6	.0000	1	midtown
0.0457	26.6	.0000	1	midwatch
0.0457	26.6	.0000	1	might's
0.0457	26.6	.0000	1	might've
0.0457	26.6	.0000	1	Mightiness
0.0457	26.6	.0000	1	mighty-statured
0.0457	26.6	.0000	1	Mikko's
0.0457	26.6	.0000	1	mile-high
0.0457	26.6	.0000	1	milking-stool
0.0457	26.6	.0000	1	milkman's
0.0457	26.6	.0000	1	milkshake
0.0457	26.6	.0000	1	milky-white
0.0457	26.6	.0000	1	Millford
0.0457	26.6	.0000	1	million-miler
0.0457	26.6	.0000	1	million-to-one
0.0457	26.6	.0000	1	millwheel
0.0457	26.6	.0000	1	mincemeat
0.0457	26.6	.0000	1	mindlessness
0.0457	26.6	.0000	1	Miner's
0.0457	26.6	.0000	1	mini-world
0.0457	26.6	.0000	1	Miniken
0.0457	26.6	.0000	1	minions
0.0457	26.6	.0000	1	miniscule
0.0457	26.6	.0000	1	Mintz
0.0457	26.6	.0000	1	Minutes
0.0457	26.6	.0000	1	mio
0.0457	26.6	.0000	1	Mioshi's
0.0457	26.6	.0000	1	miracle-worker
0.0457	26.6	.0000	1	misbehaved
0.0457	26.6	.0000	1	mischief-makers
0.0457	26.6	.0000	1	Misenum
0.0457	26.6	.0000	1	Misfortune
0.0457	26.6	.0000	1	mislay
0.0457	26.6	.0000	1	misrepresents
0.0457	26.6	.0000	1	missile's
0.0457	26.6	.0000	1	Missoula
0.0457	26.6	.0000	1	Missss
0.0457	26.6	.0000	1	Mistah
0.0457	26.6	.0000	1	Mitek
0.0457	26.6	.0000	1	mitts
0.0457	26.6	.0000	1	mix-mux
0.0457	26.6	.0000	1	Mobil
0.0457	26.6	.0000	1	Mocking
0.0457	26.6	.0000	1	modernistic
0.0457	26.6	.0000	1	modifers
0.0457	26.6	.0000	1	Moeder
0.0457	26.6	.0000	1	Moeder's
				THE PRECEDING WORD TYPE OCCUPIES RANK 47700
0.0457	26.6	.0000	1	moidores
0.0457	26.6	.0000	1	moleskin
0.0457	26.6	.0000	1	molly
0.0457	26.6	.0000	1	Molokai
0.0457	26.6	.0000	1	Monarchs
0.0457	26.6	.0000	1	Monarchy
0.0457	26.6	.0000	1	money-back
0.0457	26.6	.0000	1	moneybags
0.0457	26.6	.0000	1	monkey-faced
0.0457	26.6	.0000	1	monkeying
0.0457	26.6	.0000	1	Monsen
0.0457	26.6	.0000	1	Monsen's
0.0457	26.6	.0000	1	Monterrey's
0.0457	26.6	.0000	1	Montignac
0.0457	26.6	.0000	1	monts
0.0457	26.6	.0000	1	Mool
0.0457	26.6	.0000	1	moon-light
0.0457	26.6	.0000	1	moon-washed
0.0457	26.6	.0000	1	moonbus
0.0457	26.6	.0000	1	moonpath
0.0457	26.6	.0000	1	moorish
0.0457	26.6	.0000	1	moos
0.0457	26.6	.0000	1	mope
0.0457	26.6	.0000	1	moppets
0.0457	26.6	.0000	1	moppings
0.0457	26.6	.0000	1	mor
0.0457	26.6	.0000	1	Mor's

U	SFI	D	F	Word Type
0.0457	26.6	.0000	1	moralized
0.0457	26.6	.0000	1	morbid
0.0457	26.6	.0000	1	Morgans'
0.0457	26.6	.0000	1	Morgina
0.0457	26.6	.0000	1	Morrell
0.0457	26.6	.0000	1	Morrell's
0.0457	26.6	.0000	1	Morshead
0.0457	26.6	.0000	1	Morte
0.0457	26.6	.0000	1	Morvidd's
0.0457	26.6	.0000	1	mosquito-bitten
0.0457	26.6	.0000	1	moss-hung
0.0457	26.6	.0000	1	mosta
0.0457	26.6	.0000	1	mother-of-pearl-colored
0.0457	26.6	.0000	1	motorcycling's
0.0457	26.6	.0000	1	motorist's
0.0457	26.6	.0000	1	motormen
0.0457	26.6	.0000	1	Moulay
0.0457	26.6	.0000	1	moulded
0.0457	26.6	.0000	1	mountain-laurel
0.0457	26.6	.0000	1	mountain-lion
0.0457	26.6	.0000	1	mountaineers'
0.0457	26.6	.0000	1	Mourning
0.0457	26.6	.0000	1	mousetraps
0.0457	26.6	.0000	1	movingly
0.0457	26.6	.0000	1	Mowat
0.0457	26.6	.0000	1	Mowgli
0.0457	26.6	.0000	1	much-enduring
0.0457	26.6	.0000	1	mucho
0.0457	26.6	.0000	1	muckrakers
0.0457	26.6	.0000	1	mud-brick
0.0457	26.6	.0000	1	mud-spattered
0.0457	26.6	.0000	1	mud-walled
0.0457	26.6	.0000	1	mudflats
0.0457	26.6	.0000	1	mudhole
0.0457	26.6	.0000	1	muffle
0.0457	26.6	.0000	1	Mufraw
0.0457	26.6	.0000	1	Mugg
0.0457	26.6	.0000	1	Muir's
0.0457	26.6	.0000	1	Muirs
0.0457	26.6	.0000	1	mule-ears
0.0457	26.6	.0000	1	mule's
0.0457	26.6	.0000	1	Mullen
0.0457	26.6	.0000	1	multifaceted
0.0457	26.6	.0000	1	Mulvaney
0.0457	26.6	.0000	1	mum
0.0457	26.6	.0000	1	munition
0.0457	26.6	.0000	1	Munoz
0.0457	26.6	.0000	1	Muscarello
0.0457	26.6	.0000	1	muscle-bound
0.0457	26.6	.0000	1	musculature
0.0457	26.6	.0000	1	Musial
0.0457	26.6	.0000	1	muskrat's
0.0457	26.6	.0000	1	muslin's
0.0457	26.6	.0000	1	mussel-man
0.0457	26.6	.0000	1	mussel-man's
0.0457	26.6	.0000	1	my-uh-children
0.0457	26.6	.0000	1	Myra's
0.0457	26.6	.0000	1	mysel'
0.0457	26.6	.0000	1	mythos
0.0457	26.6	.0000	1	n-n-nothing
0.0457	26.6	.0000	1	n-necklace
0.0457	26.6	.0000	1	n'est-ce
0.0457	26.6	.0000	1	naaw
0.0457	26.6	.0000	1	Nagaina's
0.0457	26.6	.0000	1	Nahum
0.0457	26.6	.0000	1	Nailer
0.0457	26.6	.0000	1	Nailer's
0.0457	26.6	.0000	1	nameplate
0.0457	26.6	.0000	1	Nancy'd
0.0457	26.6	.0000	1	Nanette
0.0457	26.6	.0000	1	Nanook's
0.0457	26.6	.0000	1	narrow-walled
0.0457	26.6	.0000	1	nasally

THE PRECEDING WORD TYPE OCCUPIES RANK 47800

U	SFI	D	F	Word Type
0.0457	26.6	.0000	1	Natalie
0.0457	26.6	.0000	1	natty
0.0457	26.6	.0000	1	natural-wood
0.0457	26.6	.0000	1	Naturalists
0.0457	26.6	.0000	1	Naturalists'
0.0457	26.6	.0000	1	naturellement
0.0457	26.6	.0000	1	Nauplius
0.0457	26.6	.0000	1	Navesink
0.0457	26.6	.0000	1	near-fanatical
0.0457	26.6	.0000	1	Nebri
0.0457	26.6	.0000	1	Necker
0.0457	26.6	.0000	1	nectarines
0.0457	26.6	.0000	1	Nedick's
0.0457	26.6	.0000	1	Need
0.0457	26.6	.0000	1	Needleton
0.0457	26.6	.0000	1	negation
0.0457	26.6	.0000	1	neighbourhood
0.0457	26.6	.0000	1	neighs
0.0457	26.6	.0000	1	nelson
0.0457	26.6	.0000	1	neodymium
0.0457	26.6	.0000	1	nerfing
0.0457	26.6	.0000	1	nerve-wracking
0.0457	26.6	.0000	1	Neteland
0.0457	26.6	.0000	1	nev
0.0457	26.6	.0000	1	never-endin'
0.0457	26.6	.0000	1	never-never
0.0457	26.6	.0000	1	never-satisfied
0.0457	26.6	.0000	1	never-to-be-forgotten
0.0457	26.6	.0000	1	NewGuinea
0.0457	26.6	.0000	1	NewYear
0.0457	26.6	.0000	1	NewYork-Pennsylvania
0.0457	26.6	.0000	1	NewZealand
0.0457	26.6	.0000	1	new-laid
0.0457	26.6	.0000	1	new-made
0.0457	26.6	.0000	1	new-mown
0.0457	26.6	.0000	1	Newberry
0.0457	26.6	.0000	1	Newburgh
0.0457	26.6	.0000	1	newel
0.0457	26.6	.0000	1	newly-built
0.0457	26.6	.0000	1	newly-come
0.0457	26.6	.0000	1	newlyweds
0.0457	26.6	.0000	1	NEWS
0.0457	26.6	.0000	1	newscasters
0.0457	26.6	.0000	1	newsmen's
0.0457	26.6	.0000	1	Nibelungenlied
0.0457	26.6	.0000	1	niceness
0.0457	26.6	.0000	1	nicked
0.0457	26.6	.0000	1	nickel-plated
0.0457	26.6	.0000	1	Nickie
0.0457	26.6	.0000	1	Nicolaysen's
0.0457	26.6	.0000	1	nigger-lovers
0.0457	26.6	.0000	1	night-air
0.0457	26.6	.0000	1	nightie
0.0457	26.6	.0000	1	Niki
0.0457	26.6	.0000	1	nine-and-a-half
0.0457	26.6	.0000	1	nine-going-on-ten
0.0457	26.6	.0000	1	nine-inning
0.0457	26.6	.0000	1	ninety-one
0.0457	26.6	.0000	1	ninety-three
0.0457	26.6	.0000	1	nipa
0.0457	26.6	.0000	1	nippy
0.0457	26.6	.0000	1	Njoki's
0.0457	26.6	.0000	1	no-muscle
0.0457	26.6	.0000	1	no-o-o
0.0457	26.6	.0000	1	no-parking
0.0457	26.6	.0000	1	noise-maker
0.0457	26.6	.0000	1	noise-makers
0.0457	26.6	.0000	1	Nolan's
0.0457	26.6	.0000	1	non-Alaskans
0.0457	26.6	.0000	1	non-existent
0.0457	26.6	.0000	1	nonautomatic
0.0457	26.6	.0000	1	nonconducting
0.0457	26.6	.0000	1	noncotton-growing
0.0457	26.6	.0000	1	none-too-keen
0.0457	26.6	.0000	1	nonfighters
0.0457	26.6	.0000	1	noniron
0.0457	26.6	.0000	1	nonprecious
0.0457	26.6	.0000	1	nonsectional
0.0457	26.6	.0000	1	Noordzee
0.0457	26.6	.0000	1	Nordland
0.0457	26.6	.0000	1	Nordmore
0.0457	26.6	.0000	1	Norman's
0.0457	26.6	.0000	1	Norseman
0.0457	26.6	.0000	1	NorthCarolina's
0.0457	26.6	.0000	1	NorthCarolinian
0.0457	26.6	.0000	1	northers
0.0457	26.6	.0000	1	Norwalk
0.0457	26.6	.0000	1	nosy
0.0457	26.6	.0000	1	not-so-nice
0.0457	26.6	.0000	1	not-too-big
0.0457	26.6	.0000	1	not-too-old
0.0457	26.6	.0000	1	nothin's
0.0457	26.6	.0000	1	NOTHING
0.0457	26.6	.0000	1	nougat
0.0457	26.6	.0000	1	Novac
0.0457	26.6	.0000	1	noways
0.0457	26.6	.0000	1	Noyes
0.0457	26.6	.0000	1	nullah
0.0457	26.6	.0000	1	numerically
0.0457	26.6	.0000	1	nummies

THE PRECEDING WORD TYPE OCCUPIES RANK 47900

U	SFI	D	F	Word Type
0.0457	26.6	.0000	1	Nurses
0.0457	26.6	.0000	1	nut-eater
0.0457	26.6	.0000	1	nutlike
0.0457	26.6	.0000	1	Nyari's
0.0457	26.6	.0000	1	N6A
0.0457	26.6	.0000	1	N91457
0.0457	26.6	.0000	1	O-me-me's
0.0457	26.6	.0000	1	o-o-oh
0.0457	26.6	.0000	1	O'Bannon
0.0457	26.6	.0000	1	O'Keefe
0.0457	26.6	.0000	1	o'erheard
0.0457	26.6	.0000	1	o'fairies
0.0457	26.6	.0000	1	o'nights
0.0457	26.6	.0000	1	OakCity
0.0457	26.6	.0000	1	oak-covered
0.0457	26.6	.0000	1	Oakway
0.0457	26.6	.0000	1	oar-handle
0.0457	26.6	.0000	1	oarlock
0.0457	26.6	.0000	1	oarsman's
0.0457	26.6	.0000	1	Oatmeal
0.0457	26.6	.0000	1	Obedience
0.0457	26.6	.0000	1	Obedient
0.0457	26.6	.0000	1	Objects
0.0457	26.6	.0000	1	obstructed
0.0457	26.6	.0000	1	ocean-bosom
0.0457	26.6	.0000	1	ocotillo
0.0457	26.6	.0000	1	Odenwald
0.0457	26.6	.0000	1	odorant
0.0457	26.6	.0000	1	off-off-off-off
0.0457	26.6	.0000	1	off-the-cuff
0.0457	26.6	.0000	1	off'n
0.0457	26.6	.0000	1	offat
0.0457	26.6	.0000	1	offhandedly
0.0457	26.6	.0000	1	officeholder
0.0457	26.6	.0000	1	Officer's
0.0457	26.6	.0000	1	officers'
0.0457	26.6	.0000	1	Ogburn's
0.0457	26.6	.0000	1	Oglala
0.0457	26.6	.0000	1	ohhhhh
0.0457	26.6	.0000	1	ohhhhhhh
0.0457	26.6	.0000	1	oilskin
0.0457	26.6	.0000	1	Ojibways
0.0457	26.6	.0000	1	okapi
0.0457	26.6	.0000	1	Okaro's
0.0457	26.6	.0000	1	okto
0.0457	26.6	.0000	1	oldtime
0.0457	26.6	.0000	1	Olimpico
0.0457	26.6	.0000	1	Olipai
0.0457	26.6	.0000	1	Olsens
0.0457	26.6	.0000	1	Olson
0.0457	26.6	.0000	1	Olympians
0.0457	26.6	.0000	1	Omi
0.0457	26.6	.0000	1	omnibuses
0.0457	26.6	.0000	1	on-stage
0.0457	26.6	.0000	1	Onak's
0.0457	26.6	.0000	1	onc't
0.0457	26.6	.0000	1	once-a-season
0.0457	26.6	.0000	1	once-fat
0.0457	26.6	.0000	1	once-living
0.0457	26.6	.0000	1	one-fifteen
0.0457	26.6	.0000	1	one-for-the-money
0.0457	26.6	.0000	1	one-fourth-inch
0.0457	26.6	.0000	1	one-goal
0.0457	26.6	.0000	1	one-horned
0.0457	26.6	.0000	1	one-hundred-foot
0.0457	26.6	.0000	1	one-hundred-pound
0.0457	26.6	.0000	1	one-l
0.0457	26.6	.0000	1	one-street
0.0457	26.6	.0000	1	one-wheeled
0.0457	26.6	.0000	1	one-year-old
0.0457	26.6	.0000	1	One's
0.0457	26.6	.0000	1	oneness
0.0457	26.6	.0000	1	oo-oo-oo
0.0457	26.6	.0000	1	ooey
0.0457	26.6	.0000	1	oof
0.0457	26.6	.0000	1	oomp
0.0457	26.6	.0000	1	ooo
0.0457	26.6	.0000	1	ooo-ooo
0.0457	26.6	.0000	1	open-clawed
0.0457	26.6	.0000	1	open-faced
0.0457	26.6	.0000	1	Ophir
0.0457	26.6	.0000	1	opossums'
0.0457	26.6	.0000	1	oppressions
0.0457	26.6	.0000	1	Oquawka
0.0457	26.6	.0000	1	orchestra's
0.0457	26.6	.0000	1	orf
0.0457	26.6	.0000	1	Orson
0.0457	26.6	.0000	1	Orv
0.0457	26.6	.0000	1	Orycteropus
0.0457	26.6	.0000	1	Osceola
0.0457	26.6	.0000	1	ostracism
0.0457	26.6	.0000	1	ostracize
0.0457	26.6	.0000	1	ot-choeck
0.0457	26.6	.0000	1	otherside
0.0457	26.6	.0000	1	Ouri
0.0457	26.6	.0000	1	out-a
0.0457	26.6	.0000	1	out-and-out
0.0457	26.6	.0000	1	out-of-sorts
0.0457	26.6	.0000	1	out-of-the-ordinary
0.0457	26.6	.0000	1	outbluff

THE PRECEDING WORD TYPE OCCUPIES RANK 48000

U	SFI	D	F	Word Type
0.0457	26.6	.0000	1	outcrop
0.0457	26.6	.0000	1	outdone
0.0457	26.6	.0000	1	outdoorsmen
0.0457	26.6	.0000	1	Outfield
0.0457	26.6	.0000	1	outfighting
0.0457	26.6	.0000	1	outflung
0.0457	26.6	.0000	1	outgrin
0.0457	26.6	.0000	1	outholler
0.0457	26.6	.0000	1	outjump
0.0457	26.6	.0000	1	Outlaw
0.0457	26.6	.0000	1	outmatched
0.0457	26.6	.0000	1	outpointing
0.0457	26.6	.0000	1	outride
0.0457	26.6	.0000	1	outriggers
0.0457	26.6	.0000	1	outrope
0.0457	26.6	.0000	1	outshouted
0.0457	26.6	.0000	1	outweighs
0.0457	26.6	.0000	1	outwits
0.0457	26.6	.0000	1	oven's
0.0457	26.6	.0000	1	over-credulous
0.0457	26.6	.0000	1	Overcrowded
0.0457	26.6	.0000	1	overestimated
0.0457	26.6	.0000	1	overflights
0.0457	26.6	.0000	1	overhearing
0.0457	26.6	.0000	1	overlaced
0.0457	26.6	.0000	1	overlapped
0.0457	26.6	.0000	1	overmastered
0.0457	26.6	.0000	1	overmastering
0.0457	26.6	.0000	1	overpowers
0.0457	26.6	.0000	1	overseeing
0.0457	26.6	.0000	1	overshadowed
0.0457	26.6	.0000	1	oversprinkle
0.0457	26.6	.0000	1	overviewing
0.0457	26.6	.0000	1	Owens-Adair
0.0457	26.6	.0000	1	owlets
0.0457	26.6	.0000	1	owners'
0.0457	26.6	.0000	1	ox-carts
0.0457	26.6	.0000	1	oyster-fishermen
0.0457	26.6	.0000	1	oyster-fishing
0.0457	26.6	.0000	1	oyster's
0.0457	26.6	.0000	1	prk
0.0457	26.6	.0000	1	pt
0.0457	26.6	.0000	1	pacemakers
0.0457	26.6	.0000	1	Pacificator
0.0457	26.6	.0000	1	paddlelike
0.0457	26.6	.0000	1	paijaik
0.0457	26.6	.0000	1	pain-crazed
0.0457	26.6	.0000	1	pain-relieving
0.0457	26.6	.0000	1	paint-spotted
0.0457	26.6	.0000	1	paintin'
0.0457	26.6	.0000	1	pale-pink
0.0457	26.6	.0000	1	palely
0.0457	26.6	.0000	1	palpitate
0.0457	26.6	.0000	1	Pamela's
0.0457	26.6	.0000	1	Panchatantra
0.0457	26.6	.0000	1	panic-stricken
0.0457	26.6	.0000	1	panic-struck
0.0457	26.6	.0000	1	panin
0.0457	26.6	.0000	1	pantalettes
0.0457	26.6	.0000	1	papooses
0.0457	26.6	.0000	1	pappy
0.0457	26.6	.0000	1	pappy's
0.0457	26.6	.0000	1	Papua's
0.0457	26.6	.0000	1	Papuans
0.0457	26.6	.0000	1	Paquita
0.0457	26.6	.0000	1	Para
0.0457	26.6	.0000	1	parables
0.0457	26.6	.0000	1	Paraguayan
0.0457	26.6	.0000	1	parchments
0.0457	26.6	.0000	1	Pard
0.0457	26.6	.0000	1	parenthesis
0.0457	26.6	.0000	1	Paricutin's
0.0457	26.6	.0000	1	park-like
0.0457	26.6	.0000	1	park
0.0457	26.6	.0000	1	Parkson
0.0457	26.6	.0000	1	Parl
0.0457	26.6	.0000	1	parleys
0.0457	26.6	.0000	1	paroles
0.0457	26.6	.0000	1	parried
0.0457	26.6	.0000	1	parsimony
0.0457	26.6	.0000	1	parsons
0.0457	26.6	.0000	1	Partidge
0.0457	26.6	.0000	1	Partridge
0.0457	26.6	.0000	1	partridges
0.0457	26.6	.0000	1	paschal
0.0457	26.6	.0000	1	passwords
0.0457	26.6	.0000	1	pasteurize
0.0457	26.6	.0000	1	pat-pats
0.0457	26.6	.0000	1	paternalism
0.0457	26.6	.0000	1	pathological
0.0457	26.6	.0000	1	patina
0.0457	26.6	.0000	1	PATRIOTIC
0.0457	26.6	.0000	1	Patrolmen
0.0457	26.6	.0000	1	patter-patter
0.0457	26.6	.0000	1	Patti's
0.0457	26.6	.0000	1	Paul-Louis-Toussaint
0.0457	26.6	.0000	1	Paulie
0.0457	26.6	.0000	1	Paulossie's
0.0457	26.6	.0000	1	Pavlova
0.0457	26.6	.0000	1	paw-licking

THE PRECEDING WORD TYPE OCCUPIES RANK 48100

U	SFI	D	F	Word Type
0.0457	26.6	.0000	1	pawful
0.0457	26.6	.0000	1	payoffs
0.0457	26.6	.0000	1	Pazians
0.0457	26.6	.0000	1	pea-jacket
0.0457	26.6	.0000	1	peaceful-like
0.0457	26.6	.0000	1	peacock-feather
0.0457	26.6	.0000	1	peanutbutter
0.0457	26.6	.0000	1	pearl-gray
0.0457	26.6	.0000	1	pearl-white
0.0457	26.6	.0000	1	Peasley's
0.0457	26.6	.0000	1	peculiar-looking
0.0457	26.6	.0000	1	peculiarsome
0.0457	26.6	.0000	1	pedagogy
0.0457	26.6	.0000	1	Pedestal
0.0457	26.6	.0000	1	Peel
0.0457	26.6	.0000	1	peep-peeping
0.0457	26.6	.0000	1	peer's
0.0457	26.6	.0000	1	Peerless
0.0457	26.6	.0000	1	Peerson's
0.0457	26.6	.0000	1	peeved
0.0457	26.6	.0000	1	Pegae
0.0457	26.6	.0000	1	pegging
0.0457	26.6	.0000	1	Peindo's
0.0457	26.6	.0000	1	Pell
0.0457	26.6	.0000	1	pendant
0.0457	26.6	.0000	1	pendulous
0.0457	26.6	.0000	1	Pendulous
0.0457	26.6	.0000	1	pendulums
0.0457	26.6	.0000	1	Penhale
0.0457	26.6	.0000	1	pennon
0.0457	26.6	.0000	1	penny's
0.0457	26.6	.0000	1	Pennys
0.0457	26.6	.0000	1	penquin
0.0457	26.6	.0000	1	pentathlon
0.0457	26.6	.0000	1	Pentathlon
0.0457	26.6	.0000	1	pep-talk
0.0457	26.6	.0000	1	pepp
0.0457	26.6	.0000	1	Pepper's
0.0457	26.6	.0000	1	peppery
0.0457	26.6	.0000	1	Peraltas
0.0457	26.6	.0000	1	perdiz
0.0457	26.6	.0000	1	Pere's
0.0457	26.6	.0000	1	Peregil's
0.0457	26.6	.0000	1	peregrine
0.0457	26.6	.0000	1	PERFECT
0.0457	26.6	.0000	1	perfections
0.0457	26.6	.0000	1	perfidious
0.0457	26.6	.0000	1	perfunctorily
0.0457	26.6	.0000	1	periscopes
0.0457	26.6	.0000	1	perjury
0.0457	26.6	.0000	1	perr-rr-fect
0.0457	26.6	.0000	1	Perrik's
0.0457	26.6	.0000	1	persuader
0.0457	26.6	.0000	1	pessimists
0.0457	26.6	.0000	1	Pest's
0.0457	26.6	.0000	1	pesters
0.0457	26.6	.0000	1	pestilential
0.0457	26.6	.0000	1	Petersons
0.0457	26.6	.0000	1	Petrel
0.0457	26.6	.0000	1	PETS
0.0457	26.6	.0000	1	pettier
0.0457	26.6	.0000	1	Pettingill's
0.0457	26.6	.0000	1	Pettingills
0.0457	26.6	.0000	1	Philanthropist
0.0457	26.6	.0000	1	philatelists
0.0457	26.6	.0000	1	Philippi
0.0457	26.6	.0000	1	Phillips'
0.0457	26.6	.0000	1	philoprogenitiveness
0.0457	26.6	.0000	1	phoebes'
0.0457	26.6	.0000	1	Phoebus
0.0457	26.6	.0000	1	Pholus
0.0457	26.6	.0000	1	phonogram
0.0457	26.6	.0000	1	phonograms
0.0457	26.6	.0000	1	phony
0.0457	26.6	.0000	1	Piccaninnies
0.0457	26.6	.0000	1	picked-over
0.0457	26.6	.0000	1	Pickering's
0.0457	26.6	.0000	1	Pico
0.0457	26.6	.0000	1	pictographic
0.0457	26.6	.0000	1	Piermont
0.0457	26.6	.0000	1	Pierson's
0.0457	26.6	.0000	1	pigeon-eggs
0.0457	26.6	.0000	1	Pigeon's
0.0457	26.6	.0000	1	pigeonhole
0.0457	26.6	.0000	1	pigeonholes
0.0457	26.6	.0000	1	pigging
0.0457	26.6	.0000	1	piggish
0.0457	26.6	.0000	1	Piggy-wig
0.0457	26.6	.0000	1	Pigs
0.0457	26.6	.0000	1	pikemen
0.0457	26.6	.0000	1	Pileated

U	SFI	D	F	Word Type
0.0457	26.6	.0000	1	pilfering
0.0457	26.6	.0000	1	pillaging
0.0457	26.6	.0000	1	pillowcases
0.0457	26.6	.0000	1	pin-ups
0.0457	26.6	.0000	1	Pinar
0.0457	26.6	.0000	1	Pinch
0.0457	26.6	.0000	1	pine-covered
0.0457	26.6	.0000	1	pined
0.0457	26.6	.0000	1	Pinetree
THE PRECEDING WORD TYPE OCCUPIES RANK 48200				
0.0457	26.6	.0000	1	piney-woods
0.0457	26.6	.0000	1	Ping's
0.0457	26.6	.0000	1	pinging
0.0457	26.6	.0000	1	pinions
0.0457	26.6	.0000	1	pink-blossomed
0.0457	26.6	.0000	1	pink-cheeked
0.0457	26.6	.0000	1	Pinkerton's
0.0457	26.6	.0000	1	pinned-up
0.0457	26.6	.0000	1	Pino's
0.0457	26.6	.0000	1	Pinzon's
0.0457	26.6	.0000	1	Pipestone
0.0457	26.6	.0000	1	pirates-to-be
0.0457	26.6	.0000	1	Pisgah
0.0457	26.6	.0000	1	pistareens
0.0457	26.6	.0000	1	Pits
0.0457	26.6	.0000	1	Pitter
0.0457	26.6	.0000	1	pityin'
0.0457	26.6	.0000	1	pivot-swing
0.0457	26.6	.0000	1	pla-ty
0.0457	26.6	.0000	1	Placer
0.0457	26.6	.0000	1	plains-dwelling
0.0457	26.6	.0000	1	Plainville
0.0457	26.6	.0000	1	plaiting
0.0457	26.6	.0000	1	plaits
0.0457	26.6	.0000	1	planked
0.0457	26.6	.0000	1	plantin'
0.0457	26.6	.0000	1	plashy
0.0457	26.6	.0000	1	plastering
0.0457	26.6	.0000	1	plasters
0.0457	26.6	.0000	1	plate-glass
0.0457	26.6	.0000	1	platies
0.0457	26.6	.0000	1	platter's
0.0457	26.6	.0000	1	play-actor
0.0457	26.6	.0000	1	Played
0.0457	26.6	.0000	1	Playland
0.0457	26.6	.0000	1	playmaking
0.0457	26.6	.0000	1	Playmate
0.0457	26.6	.0000	1	pleasant-tasting
0.0457	26.6	.0000	1	pleasure-filled
0.0457	26.6	.0000	1	pleasure-seekers
0.0457	26.6	.0000	1	plesent
0.0457	26.6	.0000	1	ploughin'
0.0457	26.6	.0000	1	plump's
0.0457	26.6	.0000	1	Plumtree
0.0457	26.6	.0000	1	plumy
0.0457	26.6	.0000	1	plunk
0.0457	26.6	.0000	1	plunking
0.0457	26.6	.0000	1	plutocratic
0.0457	26.6	.0000	1	poacher
0.0457	26.6	.0000	1	Podarces
0.0457	26.6	.0000	1	Pogo
0.0457	26.6	.0000	1	Poinsett
0.0457	26.6	.0000	1	point-blank
0.0457	26.6	.0000	1	Poirion
0.0457	26.6	.0000	1	poising
0.0457	26.6	.0000	1	poky
0.0457	26.6	.0000	1	Polaskis
0.0457	26.6	.0000	1	pole-and-safety-pin
0.0457	26.6	.0000	1	polestar
0.0457	26.6	.0000	1	POLICE
0.0457	26.6	.0000	1	polio-crippled
0.0457	26.6	.0000	1	polished-looking
0.0457	26.6	.0000	1	politician's
0.0457	26.6	.0000	1	Polizei
0.0457	26.6	.0000	1	polliwogs
0.0457	26.6	.0000	1	pomposity
0.0457	26.6	.0000	1	Ponds
0.0457	26.6	.0000	1	Pontus
0.0457	26.6	.0000	1	pony-face
0.0457	26.6	.0000	1	ponytail
0.0457	26.6	.0000	1	poochie-pies
0.0457	26.6	.0000	1	poodle-sitting
0.0457	26.6	.0000	1	POOF
0.0457	26.6	.0000	1	Pooh's
0.0457	26.6	.0000	1	pool's
0.0457	26.6	.0000	1	Pools
0.0457	26.6	.0000	1	poor-dog
0.0457	26.6	.0000	1	pop-out
0.0457	26.6	.0000	1	pop-up
0.0457	26.6	.0000	1	Poppa
0.0457	26.6	.0000	1	popper
0.0457	26.6	.0000	1	poppers
0.0457	26.6	.0000	1	por
0.0457	26.6	.0000	1	porcupine-quill
0.0457	26.6	.0000	1	porcupine's
0.0457	26.6	.0000	1	porkers
0.0457	26.6	.0000	1	porosus
0.0457	26.6	.0000	1	portcullis
0.0457	26.6	.0000	1	porter's
0.0457	26.6	.0000	1	Possible
0.0457	26.6	.0000	1	post's
0.0457	26.6	.0000	1	potlatches
0.0457	26.6	.0000	1	potting-shed
0.0457	26.6	.0000	1	Pottlebys
0.0457	26.6	.0000	1	Potts'
0.0457	26.6	.0000	1	POUR
0.0457	26.6	.0000	1	pous
0.0457	26.6	.0000	1	poverty-ridden
0.0457	26.6	.0000	1	power-hungry
0.0457	26.6	.0000	1	prce
THE PRECEDING WORD TYPE OCCUPIES RANK 48300				
0.0457	26.6	.0000	1	Pradesh
0.0457	26.6	.0000	1	Praiseworthy
0.0457	26.6	.0000	1	Prancing
0.0457	26.6	.0000	1	pre-Aztec
0.0457	26.6	.0000	1	pre-Olympic
0.0457	26.6	.0000	1	prejudged
0.0457	26.6	.0000	1	premixed
0.0457	26.6	.0000	1	Prentice
0.0457	26.6	.0000	1	prepaid
0.0457	26.6	.0000	1	prepoceros
0.0457	26.6	.0000	1	preponderant
0.0457	26.6	.0000	1	Pres-I-dent
0.0457	26.6	.0000	1	Presser
0.0457	26.6	.0000	1	pretelevision
0.0457	26.6	.0000	1	pretendin'
0.0457	26.6	.0000	1	pretty-please
0.0457	26.6	.0000	1	Preview
0.0457	26.6	.0000	1	previewed
0.0457	26.6	.0000	1	prexie
0.0457	26.6	.0000	1	prid'near
0.0457	26.6	.0000	1	pride's
0.0457	26.6	.0000	1	priestess
0.0457	26.6	.0000	1	priestesses
0.0457	26.6	.0000	1	priestly
0.0457	26.6	.0000	1	primitively
0.0457	26.6	.0000	1	Pringle
0.0457	26.6	.0000	1	Pringle's
0.0457	26.6	.0000	1	Printers
0.0457	26.6	.0000	1	printin'
0.0457	26.6	.0000	1	printing-office
0.0457	26.6	.0000	1	Prioli
0.0457	26.6	.0000	1	prism-fringed
0.0457	26.6	.0000	1	prize-fight
0.0457	26.6	.0000	1	prizefighter
0.0457	26.6	.0000	1	prizemaster
0.0457	26.6	.0000	1	Proclaim
0.0457	26.6	.0000	1	procurator
0.0457	26.6	.0000	1	Procurator
0.0457	26.6	.0000	1	prod
0.0457	26.6	.0000	1	profession's
0.0457	26.6	.0000	1	professorship
0.0457	26.6	.0000	1	Proffessor
0.0457	26.6	.0000	1	proffessor
0.0457	26.6	.0000	1	Promote
0.0457	26.6	.0000	1	prompting
0.0457	26.6	.0000	1	propped-open
0.0457	26.6	.0000	1	Proudfoot
0.0457	26.6	.0000	1	provider
0.0457	26.6	.0000	1	Prowler
0.0457	26.6	.0000	1	prowlishly
0.0457	26.6	.0000	1	Pryce
0.0457	26.6	.0000	1	pssst
0.0457	26.6	.0000	1	publishment
0.0457	26.6	.0000	1	puckery
0.0457	26.6	.0000	1	pudding-face
0.0457	26.6	.0000	1	puddling
0.0457	26.6	.0000	1	puffiness
0.0457	26.6	.0000	1	pummeled
0.0457	26.6	.0000	1	puns
0.0457	26.6	.0000	1	Pupin
0.0457	26.6	.0000	1	Puppets
0.0457	26.6	.0000	1	puppies'
0.0457	26.6	.0000	1	puppy-belly
0.0457	26.6	.0000	1	Purari
0.0457	26.6	.0000	1	PURE
0.0457	26.6	.0000	1	Puritan's
0.0457	26.6	.0000	1	purple-colored
0.0457	26.6	.0000	1	purplish-brown
0.0457	26.6	.0000	1	purposefully
0.0457	26.6	.0000	1	pushin'
0.0457	26.6	.0000	1	puss
0.0457	26.6	.0000	1	puss-in-the-corner
0.0457	26.6	.0000	1	Put-in-Bay
0.0457	26.6	.0000	1	put-out
0.0457	26.6	.0000	1	put-put
0.0457	26.6	.0000	1	Putah
0.0457	26.6	.0000	1	putt-putt-putt
0.0457	26.6	.0000	1	pyatj
0.0457	26.6	.0000	1	pyatnashki
0.0457	26.6	.0000	1	pyjamas
0.0457	26.6	.0000	1	pyrometer
0.0457	26.6	.0000	1	Quail
0.0457	26.6	.0000	1	quails
0.0457	26.6	.0000	1	quaint-looking
0.0457	26.6	.0000	1	quainter
0.0457	26.6	.0000	1	Quarrels
0.0457	26.6	.0000	1	quarter-acre
0.0457	26.6	.0000	1	quarter-turn
0.0457	26.6	.0000	1	quarterdeck
0.0457	26.6	.0000	1	queenlike
0.0457	26.6	.0000	1	quell
0.0457	26.6	.0000	1	Quentin's
0.0457	26.6	.0000	1	quick-action
0.0457	26.6	.0000	1	quick-moving
0.0457	26.6	.0000	1	Quicksilver's
0.0457	26.6	.0000	1	QUIET
0.0457	26.6	.0000	1	quietus
0.0457	26.6	.0000	1	quince
0.0457	26.6	.0000	1	quinking
0.0457	26.6	.0000	1	Quintus
THE PRECEDING WORD TYPE OCCUPIES RANK 48400				
0.0457	26.6	.0000	1	quitter
0.0457	26.6	.0000	1	r-r-rip
0.0457	26.6	.0000	1	r-r-rumbled
0.0457	26.6	.0000	1	R-u-f
0.0457	26.6	.0000	1	r
0.0457	26.6	.0000	1	race-horse
0.0457	26.6	.0000	1	rackets
0.0457	26.6	.0000	1	racking
0.0457	26.6	.0000	1	radiantly
0.0457	26.6	.0000	1	radiogram
0.0457	26.6	.0000	1	radiotelescope
0.0457	26.6	.0000	1	radiotelescopes
0.0457	26.6	.0000	1	Radium
0.0457	26.6	.0000	1	raft's
0.0457	26.6	.0000	1	Rag
0.0457	26.6	.0000	1	ragamuffin
0.0457	26.6	.0000	1	ragged-looking
0.0457	26.6	.0000	1	ragman's
0.0457	26.6	.0000	1	rail-splitter
0.0457	26.6	.0000	1	rain-doors
0.0457	26.6	.0000	1	rain-rutted
0.0457	26.6	.0000	1	rain-wet
0.0457	26.6	.0000	1	rakin'
0.0457	26.6	.0000	1	ramped
0.0457	26.6	.0000	1	ramping-performance
0.0457	26.6	.0000	1	Ran
0.0457	26.6	.0000	1	ranchman
0.0457	26.6	.0000	1	rangeland
0.0457	26.6	.0000	1	rapine
0.0457	26.6	.0000	1	rattletrap
0.0457	26.6	.0000	1	Ratty
0.0457	26.6	.0000	1	ratty
0.0457	26.6	.0000	1	rayed
0.0457	26.6	.0000	1	re-created
0.0457	26.6	.0000	1	re-spon-si-bil-i-ty
0.0457	26.6	.0000	1	readied
0.0457	26.6	.0000	1	readin'
0.0457	26.6	.0000	1	REAL
0.0457	26.6	.0000	1	REAPER
0.0457	26.6	.0000	1	rearview
0.0457	26.6	.0000	1	recheck
0.0457	26.6	.0000	1	rechinked
0.0457	26.6	.0000	1	reclined
0.0457	26.6	.0000	1	recreant
0.0457	26.6	.0000	1	recrossing
0.0457	26.6	.0000	1	Red-Face
0.0457	26.6	.0000	1	Red-Handed
0.0457	26.6	.0000	1	red-and-blue
0.0457	26.6	.0000	1	red-circled
0.0457	26.6	.0000	1	red-handled
0.0457	26.6	.0000	1	red-shirted
0.0457	26.6	.0000	1	red-striped
0.0457	26.6	.0000	1	red-throat
0.0457	26.6	.0000	1	red-topped
0.0457	26.6	.0000	1	red-wheeled
0.0457	26.6	.0000	1	Redbreast
0.0457	26.6	.0000	1	redcap
0.0457	26.6	.0000	1	redeyed
0.0457	26.6	.0000	1	Redheaded
0.0457	26.6	.0000	1	redshanks
0.0457	26.6	.0000	1	reek
0.0457	26.6	.0000	1	refinish
0.0457	26.6	.0000	1	refit
0.0457	26.6	.0000	1	regaling
0.0457	26.6	.0000	1	regenerate
0.0457	26.6	.0000	1	Regional
0.0457	26.6	.0000	1	Regis
0.0457	26.6	.0000	1	regularized
0.0457	26.6	.0000	1	Reilly
0.0457	26.6	.0000	1	Reillys'
0.0457	26.6	.0000	1	reindeer-keeping
0.0457	26.6	.0000	1	reinterpreting
0.0457	26.6	.0000	1	rejoicingly
0.0457	26.6	.0000	1	rejuvenate
0.0457	26.6	.0000	1	reklektion
0.0457	26.6	.0000	1	relent
0.0457	26.6	.0000	1	relented
0.0457	26.6	.0000	1	Reliability
0.0457	26.6	.0000	1	remainer
0.0457	26.6	.0000	1	Remember's
0.0457	26.6	.0000	1	remonstrated
0.0457	26.6	.0000	1	remorsefully
0.0457	26.6	.0000	1	rendezvousing
0.0457	26.6	.0000	1	Renee
0.0457	26.6	.0000	1	renting
0.0457	26.6	.0000	1	rep
0.0457	26.6	.0000	1	replant
0.0457	26.6	.0000	1	repletion
0.0457	26.6	.0000	1	repointed
0.0457	26.6	.0000	1	reprints
0.0457	26.6	.0000	1	reprove
0.0457	26.6	.0000	1	reprovingly
0.0457	26.6	.0000	1	REPTILE
0.0457	26.6	.0000	1	rereads
0.0457	26.6	.0000	1	RESCUE
0.0457	26.6	.0000	1	resentfully
0.0457	26.6	.0000	1	reservers
0.0457	26.6	.0000	1	residing
0.0457	26.6	.0000	1	Resort's
0.0457	26.6	.0000	1	resorting
THE PRECEDING WORD TYPE OCCUPIES RANK 48500				
0.0457	26.6	.0000	1	restart
0.0457	26.6	.0000	1	resting-place
0.0457	26.6	.0000	1	restraining
0.0457	26.6	.0000	1	restringing
0.0457	26.6	.0000	1	retinal
0.0457	26.6	.0000	1	retorts
0.0457	26.6	.0000	1	revelled
0.0457	26.6	.0000	1	reviver
0.0457	26.6	.0000	1	Reyburn
0.0457	26.6	.0000	1	Reynow
0.0457	26.6	.0000	1	Rhett's
0.0457	26.6	.0000	1	Rhetts
0.0457	26.6	.0000	1	Rhetts'
0.0457	26.6	.0000	1	Rhino
0.0457	26.6	.0000	1	Ricardo's
0.0457	26.6	.0000	1	ricebucket
0.0457	26.6	.0000	1	Rickyyyyy
0.0457	26.6	.0000	1	riddle-me-that
0.0457	26.6	.0000	1	riddle-me-this
0.0457	26.6	.0000	1	Riddles
0.0457	26.6	.0000	1	ridge-shaped
0.0457	26.6	.0000	1	ridiculing
0.0457	26.6	.0000	1	ridingest
0.0457	26.6	.0000	1	Ridinghood
0.0457	26.6	.0000	1	Riehls
0.0457	26.6	.0000	1	rifle's
0.0457	26.6	.0000	1	riggings
0.0457	26.6	.0000	1	righteously
0.0457	26.6	.0000	1	righthand
0.0457	26.6	.0000	1	Rinaldos
0.0457	26.6	.0000	1	ring-a-ring
0.0457	26.6	.0000	1	Rinty's
0.0457	26.6	.0000	1	riptide
0.0457	26.6	.0000	1	Rise
0.0457	26.6	.0000	1	river-boat
0.0457	26.6	.0000	1	river-bound
0.0457	26.6	.0000	1	Riveras
0.0457	26.6	.0000	1	Riveras'
0.0457	26.6	.0000	1	rivermen
0.0457	26.6	.0000	1	Rivington
0.0457	26.6	.0000	1	rivulet
0.0457	26.6	.0000	1	rivulets
0.0457	26.6	.0000	1	roadeo
0.0457	26.6	.0000	1	Roadhouse
0.0457	26.6	.0000	1	roadhouse
0.0457	26.6	.0000	1	ROADMASTER
0.0457	26.6	.0000	1	Roadmaster's
0.0457	26.6	.0000	1	Roaring
0.0457	26.6	.0000	1	Robe's
0.0457	26.6	.0000	1	robio
0.0457	26.6	.0000	1	robot's
0.0457	26.6	.0000	1	rock-and-roll
0.0457	26.6	.0000	1	rock-bound
0.0457	26.6	.0000	1	rock-slide
0.0457	26.6	.0000	1	rocker's
0.0457	26.6	.0000	1	rockslide
0.0457	26.6	.0000	1	rodders
0.0457	26.6	.0000	1	rodeo's
0.0457	26.6	.0000	1	Rodmika's
0.0457	26.6	.0000	1	Rodney
0.0457	26.6	.0000	1	Roebling's
0.0457	26.6	.0000	1	roguishly
0.0457	26.6	.0000	1	roll-over
0.0457	26.6	.0000	1	roll-top
0.0457	26.6	.0000	1	Rollick
0.0457	26.6	.0000	1	rollover
0.0457	26.6	.0000	1	Romona
0.0457	26.6	.0000	1	Romsdal
0.0457	26.6	.0000	1	Rondaros
0.0457	26.6	.0000	1	room-sized
0.0457	26.6	.0000	1	Rooms
0.0457	26.6	.0000	1	Roots
0.0457	26.6	.0000	1	rope's
0.0457	26.6	.0000	1	ropewalk
0.0457	26.6	.0000	1	ropingest
0.0457	26.6	.0000	1	rosebeds
0.0457	26.6	.0000	1	Rosella
0.0457	26.6	.0000	1	Roslyn
0.0457	26.6	.0000	1	Rossis
0.0457	26.6	.0000	1	round-topped
0.0457	26.6	.0000	1	rounded-to
0.0457	26.6	.0000	1	Roundeyed
0.0457	26.6	.0000	1	roundish
0.0457	26.6	.0000	1	roundrock
0.0457	26.6	.0000	1	Rourke
0.0457	26.6	.0000	1	roustabouts
0.0457	26.6	.0000	1	Routes
0.0457	26.6	.0000	1	Rovers
0.0457	26.6	.0000	1	royalities
0.0457	26.6	.0000	1	Royce
0.0457	26.6	.0000	1	rubber-soled
0.0457	26.6	.0000	1	ruching
0.0457	26.6	.0000	1	ruckuses
0.0457	26.6	.0000	1	Rudisberg
0.0457	26.6	.0000	1	Rudolph's
0.0457	26.6	.0000	1	rued
0.0457	26.6	.0000	1	ruffling
0.0457	26.6	.0000	1	Ruida
0.0457	26.6	.0000	1	Ruida's
0.0457	26.6	.0000	1	Rum
THE PRECEDING WORD TYPE OCCUPIES RANK 48600				
0.0457	26.6	.0000	1	rumblings
0.0457	26.6	.0000	1	rummages
0.0457	26.6	.0000	1	runabouts
0.0457	26.6	.0000	1	runcible
0.0457	26.6	.0000	1	Runic
0.0457	26.6	.0000	1	Rupert's
0.0457	26.6	.0000	1	Russian-American
0.0457	26.6	.0000	1	rust'y
0.0457	26.6	.0000	1	Rusty's
0.0457	26.6	.0000	1	rutabaga
0.0457	26.6	.0000	1	rutile
0.0457	26.6	.0000	1	Rutile
0.0457	26.6	.0000	1	s-s-s-s-sound
0.0457	26.6	.0000	1	s-s-stand
0.0457	26.6	.0000	1	s-surprise
0.0457	26.6	.0000	1	s-t-r-e-t-c-h-e-d
0.0457	26.6	.0000	1	s-t-r-e-t-c-h-i-n-g
0.0457	26.6	.0000	1	s'matter
0.0457	26.6	.0000	1	s'picious
0.0457	26.6	.0000	1	S's
0.0457	26.6	.0000	1	sab'ring
0.0457	26.6	.0000	1	saber-toothed
0.0457	26.6	.0000	1	sabots
0.0457	26.6	.0000	1	Sabour
0.0457	26.6	.0000	1	sabra
0.0457	26.6	.0000	1	saddle-bow
0.0457	26.6	.0000	1	saddle-bronc
0.0457	26.6	.0000	1	saddlemaker
0.0457	26.6	.0000	1	Safari
0.0457	26.6	.0000	1	SAFE
0.0457	26.6	.0000	1	safe-folded
0.0457	26.6	.0000	1	safety's
0.0457	26.6	.0000	1	sagacious
0.0457	26.6	.0000	1	Sagamon
0.0457	26.6	.0000	1	sagely
0.0457	26.6	.0000	1	sail-aways
0.0457	26.6	.0000	1	sailbag
0.0457	26.6	.0000	1	Sailed
0.0457	26.6	.0000	1	sailmaker
0.0457	26.6	.0000	1	sailplaning
0.0457	26.6	.0000	1	saints-and-dragons
0.0457	26.6	.0000	1	Saki
0.0457	26.6	.0000	1	salarium
0.0457	26.6	.0000	1	salons
0.0457	26.6	.0000	1	salt-clay
0.0457	26.6	.0000	1	salt-pan
0.0457	26.6	.0000	1	salt-pans
0.0457	26.6	.0000	1	saltbush
0.0457	26.6	.0000	1	salvagin'
0.0457	26.6	.0000	1	same's
0.0457	26.6	.0000	1	sampans
0.0457	26.6	.0000	1	sand-colored
0.0457	26.6	.0000	1	sandal-wood
0.0457	26.6	.0000	1	sandbag

U	SFI	D	F	Word Type
0.0457	26.6	.0000	1	sandbank
0.0457	26.6	.0000	1	Sanders'
0.0457	26.6	.0000	1	Sandpiper
0.0457	26.6	.0000	1	sandwichy
0.0457	26.6	.0000	1	sandy-land
0.0457	26.6	.0000	1	sanitarium
0.0457	26.6	.0000	1	Santa's
0.0457	26.6	.0000	1	Sara's
0.0457	26.6	.0000	1	sarcophagus
0.0457	26.6	.0000	1	sarongs
0.0457	26.6	.0000	1	Sarpi
0.0457	26.6	.0000	1	sashayed
0.0457	26.6	.0000	1	Saskatchewan's
0.0457	26.6	.0000	1	satang
0.0457	26.6	.0000	1	sating
0.0457	26.6	.0000	1	satrap
0.0457	26.6	.0000	1	Saucepan
0.0457	26.6	.0000	1	Saunders'
0.0457	26.6	.0000	1	savage-looking
0.0457	26.6	.0000	1	savages'
0.0457	26.6	.0000	1	Saving
0.0457	26.6	.0000	1	savvied
0.0457	26.6	.0000	1	saw-tooth
0.0457	26.6	.0000	1	Sawmills
0.0457	26.6	.0000	1	sayah
0.0457	26.6	.0000	1	Sayor
0.0457	26.6	.0000	1	scarabs
0.0457	26.6	.0000	1	Scarborough
0.0457	26.6	.0000	1	scared-like
0.0457	26.6	.0000	1	SCAT
0.0457	26.6	.0000	1	Scent
0.0457	26.6	.0000	1	Schaefer
0.0457	26.6	.0000	1	schemed
0.0457	26.6	.0000	1	schemers
0.0457	26.6	.0000	1	Schiaparelli
0.0457	26.6	.0000	1	Schleimann's
0.0457	26.6	.0000	1	Scho's
0.0457	26.6	.0000	1	school-houses
0.0457	26.6	.0000	1	schoolday
0.0457	26.6	.0000	1	schoolhalls
0.0457	26.6	.0000	1	schoolmarms'
0.0457	26.6	.0000	1	Schrafft's
0.0457	26.6	.0000	1	Schwartzwalder
0.0457	26.6	.0000	1	scissoring
0.0457	26.6	.0000	1	Scituate
0.0457	26.6	.0000	1	scolds

THE PRECEDING WORD TYPE OCCUPIES RANK 48700

U	SFI	D	F	Word Type
0.0457	26.6	.0000	1	sconces
0.0457	26.6	.0000	1	scornin'
0.0457	26.6	.0000	1	Scotty'll
0.0457	26.6	.0000	1	scourged
0.0457	26.6	.0000	1	scratch-scratch
0.0457	26.6	.0000	1	scrawling
0.0457	26.6	.0000	1	scritch-scratched
0.0457	26.6	.0000	1	scriveners
0.0457	26.6	.0000	1	Scrooge's
0.0457	26.6	.0000	1	scruffy
0.0457	26.6	.0000	1	scuffed-up
0.0457	26.6	.0000	1	Sculpin
0.0457	26.6	.0000	1	Sculpin's
0.0457	26.6	.0000	1	scurvy-ridden
0.0457	26.6	.0000	1	sea-
0.0457	26.6	.0000	1	sea-bird
0.0457	26.6	.0000	1	sea-blue
0.0457	26.6	.0000	1	sea-shell
0.0457	26.6	.0000	1	seacrets
0.0457	26.6	.0000	1	Seafaring
0.0457	26.6	.0000	1	sealers
0.0457	26.6	.0000	1	seaplanes
0.0457	26.6	.0000	1	seasons'
0.0457	26.6	.0000	1	seben
0.0457	26.6	.0000	1	second-base
0.0457	26.6	.0000	1	second-fastest
0.0457	26.6	.0000	1	second-from-the-top
0.0457	26.6	.0000	1	seconds'
0.0457	26.6	.0000	1	secrecy's
0.0457	26.6	.0000	1	sectionalist
0.0457	26.6	.0000	1	seed-filled
0.0457	26.6	.0000	1	seersucker
0.0457	26.6	.0000	1	Segowlee
0.0457	26.6	.0000	1	Seid
0.0457	26.6	.0000	1	Selectman
0.0457	26.6	.0000	1	self-appointed
0.0457	26.6	.0000	1	self-sealing
0.0457	26.6	.0000	1	selfsame
0.0457	26.6	.0000	1	Seller's
0.0457	26.6	.0000	1	Selma's
0.0457	26.6	.0000	1	Selo
0.0457	26.6	.0000	1	semi-precious
0.0457	26.6	.0000	1	semirural
0.0457	26.6	.0000	1	Senatorial
0.0457	26.6	.0000	1	sence
0.0457	26.6	.0000	1	Sensational
0.0457	26.6	.0000	1	sensei
0.0457	26.6	.0000	1	senselessly
0.0457	26.6	.0000	1	sepulchral
0.0457	26.6	.0000	1	Sequoya
0.0457	26.6	.0000	1	Seraphine
0.0457	26.6	.0000	1	Serena
0.0457	26.6	.0000	1	serenading
0.0457	26.6	.0000	1	seringero's
0.0457	26.6	.0000	1	seringueiro's
0.0457	26.6	.0000	1	serving-men
0.0457	26.6	.0000	1	Setting
0.0457	26.6	.0000	1	seven-letter
0.0457	26.6	.0000	1	seventh-graders
0.0457	26.6	.0000	1	seventy-eighth
0.0457	26.6	.0000	1	seventy-ninth
0.0457	26.6	.0000	1	seventy-seven
0.0457	26.6	.0000	1	several-year
0.0457	26.6	.0000	1	Sewell's
0.0457	26.6	.0000	1	sewin'
0.0457	26.6	.0000	1	shadow-flecked
0.0457	26.6	.0000	1	shake-up
0.0457	26.6	.0000	1	Shakur
0.0457	26.6	.0000	1	shamed
0.0457	26.6	.0000	1	shantyboat
0.0457	26.6	.0000	1	sharecrop
0.0457	26.6	.0000	1	Sharks'
0.0457	26.6	.0000	1	Sharp's
0.0457	26.6	.0000	1	sharpener
0.0457	26.6	.0000	1	sharpshooters
0.0457	26.6	.0000	1	Shaving
0.0457	26.6	.0000	1	shaving-lotion
0.0457	26.6	.0000	1	shaynicke
0.0457	26.6	.0000	1	sheep-farmer
0.0457	26.6	.0000	1	sheerest
0.0457	26.6	.0000	1	Shehir
0.0457	26.6	.0000	1	shelf-displays
0.0457	26.6	.0000	1	shellacked
0.0457	26.6	.0000	1	shelly
0.0457	26.6	.0000	1	Shelton
0.0457	26.6	.0000	1	Sheltons
0.0457	26.6	.0000	1	Shepherd's
0.0457	26.6	.0000	1	shepherding
0.0457	26.6	.0000	1	Sheppard
0.0457	26.6	.0000	1	Sheridan's
0.0457	26.6	.0000	1	Sherrills
0.0457	26.6	.0000	1	shhh-shhh
0.0457	26.6	.0000	1	shillelagh
0.0457	26.6	.0000	1	Shin-n-ny
0.0457	26.6	.0000	1	shiniest
0.0457	26.6	.0000	1	shinin'
0.0457	26.6	.0000	1	shininess
0.0457	26.6	.0000	1	ship-to-shore
0.0457	26.6	.0000	1	shirk
0.0457	26.6	.0000	1	shirked

THE PRECEDING WORD TYPE OCCUPIES RANK 48800

U	SFI	D	F	Word Type
0.0457	26.6	.0000	1	Shirl
0.0457	26.6	.0000	1	ShirleyKochendorfer
0.0457	26.6	.0000	1	Shirleys
0.0457	26.6	.0000	1	Shirt
0.0457	26.6	.0000	1	shirtlike
0.0457	26.6	.0000	1	shirtsleeves
0.0457	26.6	.0000	1	shiverin'
0.0457	26.6	.0000	1	shoe-off
0.0457	26.6	.0000	1	shoehorn
0.0457	26.6	.0000	1	shokolad
0.0457	26.6	.0000	1	shoofly
0.0457	26.6	.0000	1	short-
0.0457	26.6	.0000	1	Short-Step
0.0457	26.6	.0000	1	short-handled
0.0457	26.6	.0000	1	shorthose
0.0457	26.6	.0000	1	shotput
0.0457	26.6	.0000	1	shoulder-to-shoulder
0.0457	26.6	.0000	1	shovelfuls
0.0457	26.6	.0000	1	Showers
0.0457	26.6	.0000	1	shriller
0.0457	26.6	.0000	1	shrine-shaped
0.0457	26.6	.0000	1	shu
0.0457	26.6	.0000	1	shunt
0.0457	26.6	.0000	1	shur-r-r
0.0457	26.6	.0000	1	shuttles
0.0457	26.6	.0000	1	shyer
0.0457	26.6	.0000	1	shying
0.0457	26.6	.0000	1	Sibitsky
0.0457	26.6	.0000	1	sick-leave
0.0457	26.6	.0000	1	sickish
0.0457	26.6	.0000	1	Siddy
0.0457	26.6	.0000	1	side-stepped
0.0457	26.6	.0000	1	sideboards
0.0457	26.6	.0000	1	SIDEHEADS
0.0457	26.6	.0000	1	sideslipped
0.0457	26.6	.0000	1	Sidi
0.0457	26.6	.0000	1	siestas
0.0457	26.6	.0000	1	sighings
0.0457	26.6	.0000	1	signless
0.0457	26.6	.0000	1	Sigurdur
0.0457	26.6	.0000	1	Silbernagle
0.0457	26.6	.0000	1	SILENCE
0.0457	26.6	.0000	1	silkier
0.0457	26.6	.0000	1	Sill
0.0457	26.6	.0000	1	sillying
0.0457	26.6	.0000	1	silver-tipped
0.0457	26.6	.0000	1	Silvering
0.0457	26.6	.0000	1	simpleminded
0.0457	26.6	.0000	1	Simpleton's
0.0457	26.6	.0000	1	sinewy
0.0457	26.6	.0000	1	Sing's
0.0457	26.6	.0000	1	singing-birds
0.0457	26.6	.0000	1	SINGLE
0.0457	26.6	.0000	1	singleminded
0.0457	26.6	.0000	1	Sinon's
0.0457	26.6	.0000	1	Sion
0.0457	26.6	.0000	1	sir'd
0.0457	26.6	.0000	1	sired
0.0457	26.6	.0000	1	siren's
0.0457	26.6	.0000	1	sirree
0.0457	26.6	.0000	1	sirupy
0.0457	26.6	.0000	1	sis
0.0457	26.6	.0000	1	Sissy
0.0457	26.6	.0000	1	sister'll
0.0457	26.6	.0000	1	Sisters'
0.0457	26.6	.0000	1	sitch
0.0457	26.6	.0000	1	six-class
0.0457	26.6	.0000	1	six-foot-six
0.0457	26.6	.0000	1	six-hundred-foot
0.0457	26.6	.0000	1	six-page
0.0457	26.6	.0000	1	six-pound
0.0457	26.6	.0000	1	six-room
0.0457	26.6	.0000	1	Sixteen
0.0457	26.6	.0000	1	sixty-first
0.0457	26.6	.0000	1	sixty-five-mile-per-hour
0.0457	26.6	.0000	1	sixty-five's
0.0457	26.6	.0000	1	Sixty-fourth
0.0457	26.6	.0000	1	sixty-one
0.0457	26.6	.0000	1	sizzles
0.0457	26.6	.0000	1	Sjanntje
0.0457	26.6	.0000	1	skrt
0.0457	26.6	.0000	1	skating's
0.0457	26.6	.0000	1	Skavar
0.0457	26.6	.0000	1	Skavinsky
0.0457	26.6	.0000	1	skedaddling
0.0457	26.6	.0000	1	Skidbladner
0.0457	26.6	.0000	1	skin-tight
0.0457	26.6	.0000	1	skip-the-rope
0.0457	26.6	.0000	1	Skip's
0.0457	26.6	.0000	1	skunk's
0.0457	26.6	.0000	1	skurried
0.0457	26.6	.0000	1	sky-lift
0.0457	26.6	.0000	1	sky-travelers
0.0457	26.6	.0000	1	skycraper
0.0457	26.6	.0000	1	skyhigh
0.0457	26.6	.0000	1	skylarking
0.0457	26.6	.0000	1	skyrockets
0.0457	26.6	.0000	1	Skyscraper
0.0457	26.6	.0000	1	skyways
0.0457	26.6	.0000	1	slam-banging

THE PRECEDING WORD TYPE OCCUPIES RANK 48900

U	SFI	D	F	Word Type
0.0457	26.6	.0000	1	slammings
0.0457	26.6	.0000	1	slave-girls
0.0457	26.6	.0000	1	slave's
0.0457	26.6	.0000	1	slays
0.0457	26.6	.0000	1	sled-trains
0.0457	26.6	.0000	1	sleep'y**
0.0457	26.6	.0000	1	sleeping-bunks
0.0457	26.6	.0000	1	sleeved
0.0457	26.6	.0000	1	sleigh-ride
0.0457	26.6	.0000	1	slewin'
0.0457	26.6	.0000	1	slickens
0.0457	26.6	.0000	1	Slim's
0.0457	26.6	.0000	1	sling-shot
0.0457	26.6	.0000	1	slipp
0.0457	26.6	.0000	1	slippy
0.0457	26.6	.0000	1	slob
0.0457	26.6	.0000	1	slobby
0.0457	26.6	.0000	1	slogging
0.0457	26.6	.0000	1	Sloth
0.0457	26.6	.0000	1	slothful
0.0457	26.6	.0000	1	Sloughs
0.0457	26.6	.0000	1	slud
0.0457	26.6	.0000	1	Slugger
0.0457	26.6	.0000	1	sluggishly
0.0457	26.6	.0000	1	slurper
0.0457	26.6	.0000	1	slurping
0.0457	26.6	.0000	1	slushed
0.0457	26.6	.0000	1	smrt
0.0457	26.6	.0000	1	small-club
0.0457	26.6	.0000	1	smarter'n
0.0457	26.6	.0000	1	smartness
0.0457	26.6	.0000	1	smash-up
0.0457	26.6	.0000	1	smatterers
0.0457	26.6	.0000	1	smellin'
0.0457	26.6	.0000	1	Smithy
0.0457	26.6	.0000	1	Smitty
0.0457	26.6	.0000	1	smokehouses
0.0457	26.6	.0000	1	smokelike
0.0457	26.6	.0000	1	smokin'
0.0457	26.6	.0000	1	Smooth
0.0457	26.6	.0000	1	smooth-looking
0.0457	26.6	.0000	1	snagging
0.0457	26.6	.0000	1	snake-charmer
0.0457	26.6	.0000	1	snake-fish
0.0457	26.6	.0000	1	snaky
0.0457	26.6	.0000	1	sneaks
0.0457	26.6	.0000	1	sneers
0.0457	26.6	.0000	1	Snickasee
0.0457	26.6	.0000	1	sniffy
0.0457	26.6	.0000	1	snoofed
0.0457	26.6	.0000	1	Snooky's
0.0457	26.6	.0000	1	snooper
0.0457	26.6	.0000	1	snooping
0.0457	26.6	.0000	1	snoozed
0.0457	26.6	.0000	1	snorin'
0.0457	26.6	.0000	1	snow-flakes
0.0457	26.6	.0000	1	snow-hung
0.0457	26.6	.0000	1	snow-suited
0.0457	26.6	.0000	1	Snowbird
0.0457	26.6	.0000	1	Snowbird's
0.0457	26.6	.0000	1	snowbirds
0.0457	26.6	.0000	1	Snowden's
0.0457	26.6	.0000	1	Snowman
0.0457	26.6	.0000	1	snowslide
0.0457	26.6	.0000	1	snuggles
0.0457	26.6	.0000	1	so-and-so's
0.0457	26.6	.0000	1	soapmaker
0.0457	26.6	.0000	1	soapmaking
0.0457	26.6	.0000	1	Soaring
0.0457	26.6	.0000	1	Sobersides
0.0457	26.6	.0000	1	Sobo
0.0457	26.6	.0000	1	socialized
0.0457	26.6	.0000	1	socker
0.0457	26.6	.0000	1	Socony
0.0457	26.6	.0000	1	sod-covered
0.0457	26.6	.0000	1	sods
0.0457	26.6	.0000	1	sof'
0.0457	26.6	.0000	1	Sofie
0.0457	26.6	.0000	1	soft-drink
0.0457	26.6	.0000	1	soft-feeling
0.0457	26.6	.0000	1	soft-footed
0.0457	26.6	.0000	1	soft-hearted
0.0457	26.6	.0000	1	soft-nosed
0.0457	26.6	.0000	1	soft-soap
0.0457	26.6	.0000	1	softies
0.0457	26.6	.0000	1	Soilers
0.0457	26.6	.0000	1	solaced
0.0457	26.6	.0000	1	solid-looking
0.0457	26.6	.0000	1	som'n
0.0457	26.6	.0000	1	Somebody-or-other
0.0457	26.6	.0000	1	somersaulted
0.0457	26.6	.0000	1	Somethin'
0.0457	26.6	.0000	1	Sonarman
0.0457	26.6	.0000	1	sonars
0.0457	26.6	.0000	1	sonita
0.0457	26.6	.0000	1	sonnet-thing
0.0457	26.6	.0000	1	soot-blackened
0.0457	26.6	.0000	1	soot-smudged
0.0457	26.6	.0000	1	soothes
0.0457	26.6	.0000	1	soothsayer-priest

THE PRECEDING WORD TYPE OCCUPIES RANK 49000

U	SFI	D	F	Word Type
0.0457	26.6	.0000	1	Sorby
0.0457	26.6	.0000	1	Sorcerer-in-Ordinary
0.0457	26.6	.0000	1	sorcerers'
0.0457	26.6	.0000	1	sorghum-molasses
0.0457	26.6	.0000	1	souk
0.0457	26.6	.0000	1	sound-writing
0.0457	26.6	.0000	1	soupbone
0.0457	26.6	.0000	1	Sourdough
0.0457	26.6	.0000	1	sourly
0.0457	26.6	.0000	1	SouthAfrica
0.0457	26.6	.0000	1	SouthDevon
0.0457	26.6	.0000	1	southeasterly
0.0457	26.6	.0000	1	sowbelly
0.0457	26.6	.0000	1	space-ship
0.0457	26.6	.0000	1	spaceboy
0.0457	26.6	.0000	1	spacegirl
0.0457	26.6	.0000	1	Spade
0.0457	26.6	.0000	1	spade-blade
0.0457	26.6	.0000	1	Spadina
0.0457	26.6	.0000	1	spading
0.0457	26.6	.0000	1	spang
0.0457	26.6	.0000	1	spankin'
0.0457	26.6	.0000	1	sparklers
0.0457	26.6	.0000	1	sparred
0.0457	26.6	.0000	1	speargun
0.0457	26.6	.0000	1	spec'
0.0457	26.6	.0000	1	spelldown
0.0457	26.6	.0000	1	spelldowns
0.0457	26.6	.0000	1	SPELLES
0.0457	26.6	.0000	1	spendings
0.0457	26.6	.0000	1	spewing
0.0457	26.6	.0000	1	spheroid
0.0457	26.6	.0000	1	spicy-smelling
0.0457	26.6	.0000	1	spider-webs
0.0457	26.6	.0000	1	spik
0.0457	26.6	.0000	1	spinnin'
0.0457	26.6	.0000	1	spiraling
0.0457	26.6	.0000	1	spiralled
0.0457	26.6	.0000	1	spirit-cliffs
0.0457	26.6	.0000	1	spitefully
0.0457	26.6	.0000	1	Spitfires
0.0457	26.6	.0000	1	spittin'
0.0457	26.6	.0000	1	Spitz-dog
0.0457	26.6	.0000	1	spl
0.0457	26.6	.0000	1	splat
0.0457	26.6	.0000	1	splattering
0.0457	26.6	.0000	1	split-bamboo
0.0457	26.6	.0000	1	sponge-like
0.0457	26.6	.0000	1	spoon-fed
0.0457	26.6	.0000	1	Spot'll
0.0457	26.6	.0000	1	spraining
0.0457	26.6	.0000	1	sprayer
0.0457	26.6	.0000	1	sprightliness
0.0457	26.6	.0000	1	spring-cleaning
0.0457	26.6	.0000	1	spring-well
0.0457	26.6	.0000	1	springless
0.0457	26.6	.0000	1	Springwater
0.0457	26.6	.0000	1	sprints
0.0457	26.6	.0000	1	sproutin'
0.0457	26.6	.0000	1	sprucely
0.0457	26.6	.0000	1	spss
0.0457	26.6	.0000	1	spud
0.0457	26.6	.0000	1	sput-sputs
0.0457	26.6	.0000	1	square-hewn
0.0457	26.6	.0000	1	square-rigger
0.0457	26.6	.0000	1	squaring-off
0.0457	26.6	.0000	1	squatters
0.0457	26.6	.0000	1	ssh
0.0457	26.6	.0000	1	ssssss
0.0457	26.6	.0000	1	StGeorge's
0.0457	26.6	.0000	1	StLucy's
0.0457	26.6	.0000	1	StMark
0.0457	26.6	.0000	1	StMoritz
0.0457	26.6	.0000	1	StPaul's
0.0457	26.6	.0000	1	stnds
0.0457	26.6	.0000	1	stablemen
0.0457	26.6	.0000	1	Stacey
0.0457	26.6	.0000	1	Stadio
0.0457	26.6	.0000	1	stage-manager
0.0457	26.6	.0000	1	stair-step
0.0457	26.6	.0000	1	staking
0.0457	26.6	.0000	1	Staley's
0.0457	26.6	.0000	1	Stall
0.0457	26.6	.0000	1	stan'
0.0457	26.6	.0000	1	Stand-Like-a-Rock
0.0457	26.6	.0000	1	stand-by
0.0457	26.6	.0000	1	standoffish
0.0457	26.6	.0000	1	star-filled
0.0457	26.6	.0000	1	Star's
0.0457	26.6	.0000	1	starburst
0.0457	26.6	.0000	1	Starcher
0.0457	26.6	.0000	1	startingly
0.0457	26.6	.0000	1	Ste-e-even
0.0457	26.6	.0000	1	steaming-hot
0.0457	26.6	.0000	1	steamrollered
0.0457	26.6	.0000	1	steel-like
0.0457	26.6	.0000	1	steelworker
0.0457	26.6	.0000	1	steepened
0.0457	26.6	.0000	1	steepening
0.0457	26.6	.0000	1	steeping

THE PRECEDING WORD TYPE OCCUPIES RANK 49100

U	SFI	D	F	Word Type
0.0457	26.6	.0000	1	steerer
0.0457	26.6	.0000	1	Stefan's
0.0457	26.6	.0000	1	Steinmetz'
0.0457	26.6	.0000	1	stepson
0.0457	26.6	.0000	1	stern-first
0.0457	26.6	.0000	1	sternness
0.0457	26.6	.0000	1	stevedore
0.0457	26.6	.0000	1	stewardess's
0.0457	26.6	.0000	1	sthronshuch
0.0457	26.6	.0000	1	stickball
0.0457	26.6	.0000	1	sticktights
0.0457	26.6	.0000	1	still-breathing
0.0457	26.6	.0000	1	stingray
0.0457	26.6	.0000	1	stoi
0.0457	26.6	.0000	1	stoically
0.0457	26.6	.0000	1	Stollak
0.0457	26.6	.0000	1	stomach-down

U	SFI	D	F	Word Type
0.0457	26.6	.0000	1	stone-blind
0.0457	26.6	.0000	1	stone-tipped
0.0457	26.6	.0000	1	Stonecrop's
0.0457	26.6	.0000	1	stop-and-go
0.0457	26.6	.0000	1	stoplight
0.0457	26.6	.0000	1	store'd
0.0457	26.6	.0000	1	storin'
0.0457	26.6	.0000	1	storm-cloud
0.0457	26.6	.0000	1	storm-tossed
0.0457	26.6	.0000	1	storm's
0.0457	26.6	.0000	1	Storm's
0.0457	26.6	.0000	1	Story-Writing
0.0457	26.6	.0000	1	Stoyan
0.0457	26.6	.0000	1	strafe
0.0457	26.6	.0000	1	straight-ahead
0.0457	26.6	.0000	1	straight-faced
0.0457	26.6	.0000	1	straight-up-and-down
0.0457	26.6	.0000	1	straightness
0.0457	26.6	.0000	1	stramash
0.0457	26.6	.0000	1	strange-acting
0.0457	26.6	.0000	1	Stratton
0.0457	26.6	.0000	1	straw-stuffed
0.0457	26.6	.0000	1	strawcoated
0.0457	26.6	.0000	1	stream's
0.0457	26.6	.0000	1	Streator
0.0457	26.6	.0000	1	Street's
0.0457	26.6	.0000	1	stretcher-bearers
0.0457	26.6	.0000	1	stretchin'
0.0457	26.6	.0000	1	strike-outs
0.0457	26.6	.0000	1	Strikeback
0.0457	26.6	.0000	1	strikers
0.0457	26.6	.0000	1	Stromeyer
0.0457	26.6	.0000	1	strong-armed
0.0457	26.6	.0000	1	strong-looking
0.0457	26.6	.0000	1	strongly-built
0.0457	26.6	.0000	1	strudel
0.0457	26.6	.0000	1	strummin'
0.0457	26.6	.0000	1	struttin'
0.0457	26.6	.0000	1	Stryker
0.0457	26.6	.0000	1	stubbier
0.0457	26.6	.0000	1	stubbly
0.0457	26.6	.0000	1	Stuey's
0.0457	26.6	.0000	1	Stuff
0.0457	26.6	.0000	1	stunting
0.0457	26.6	.0000	1	Sturgis
0.0457	26.6	.0000	1	sub-standard
0.0457	26.6	.0000	1	sub-sub-
0.0457	26.6	.0000	1	sub-sub-sub-contractors
0.0457	26.6	.0000	1	sub-systems
0.0457	26.6	.0000	1	submarine's
0.0457	26.6	.0000	1	subservience
0.0457	26.6	.0000	1	subsiding
0.0457	26.6	.0000	1	subsisted
0.0457	26.6	.0000	1	substantial-looking
0.0457	26.6	.0000	1	substantiating
0.0457	26.6	.0000	1	SUCCESSFULLY
0.0457	26.6	.0000	1	Succos
0.0457	26.6	.0000	1	sugar-water
0.0457	26.6	.0000	1	sulked
0.0457	26.6	.0000	1	summerhouse
0.0457	26.6	.0000	1	sun-blackened
0.0457	26.6	.0000	1	sun-hardened
0.0457	26.6	.0000	1	sun-heat
0.0457	26.6	.0000	1	Sunday-go-to-meeting
0.0457	26.6	.0000	1	sundered
0.0457	26.6	.0000	1	Sunken
0.0457	26.6	.0000	1	sunlamps
0.0457	26.6	.0000	1	sunshine-smelling
0.0457	26.6	.0000	1	sunstroke
0.0457	26.6	.0000	1	sunwarmed
0.0457	26.6	.0000	1	Superbly
0.0457	26.6	.0000	1	superintendence
0.0457	26.6	.0000	1	Superintendent
0.0457	26.6	.0000	1	superjet
0.0457	26.6	.0000	1	supersensitive
0.0457	26.6	.0000	1	supp-
0.0457	26.6	.0000	1	Support
0.0457	26.6	.0000	1	sure's
0.0457	26.6	.0000	1	surfed
0.0457	26.6	.0000	1	surprisin'
0.0457	26.6	.0000	1	Sustaining
0.0457	26.6	.0000	1	suthin'
0.0457	26.6	.0000	1	Sutter's

THE PRECEDING WORD TYPE OCCUPIES RANK 49200

U	SFI	D	F	Word Type
0.0457	26.6	.0000	1	swag
0.0457	26.6	.0000	1	swaller
0.0457	26.6	.0000	1	Swallow
0.0457	26.6	.0000	1	swallow-shadows
0.0457	26.6	.0000	1	swank
0.0457	26.6	.0000	1	Swanson's
0.0457	26.6	.0000	1	Swarthmore
0.0457	26.6	.0000	1	swaths
0.0457	26.6	.0000	1	sweatshirts
0.0457	26.6	.0000	1	Sweep
0.0457	26.6	.0000	1	sweet-talked
0.0457	26.6	.0000	1	sweetie
0.0457	26.6	.0000	1	Sweetree's
0.0457	26.6	.0000	1	swift-footed
0.0457	26.6	.0000	1	Swimming
0.0457	26.6	.0000	1	swimming's
0.0457	26.6	.0000	1	SWOOOOOOOOSH
0.0457	26.6	.0000	1	swoosh
0.0457	26.6	.0000	1	swooshing
0.0457	26.6	.0000	1	swordtail
0.0457	26.6	.0000	1	sylph
0.0457	26.6	.0000	1	Sylvie's
0.0457	26.6	.0000	1	Symi's
0.0457	26.6	.0000	1	Syncom
0.0457	26.6	.0000	1	T-zero
0.0457	26.6	.0000	1	t'ain't
0.0457	26.6	.0000	1	t'ink
0.0457	26.6	.0000	1	Tabby's
0.0457	26.6	.0000	1	Tabitha
0.0457	26.6	.0000	1	tad
0.0457	26.6	.0000	1	Tad's
0.0457	26.6	.0000	1	tadpoles'
0.0457	26.6	.0000	1	Tagoona

U	SFI	D	F	Word Type
0.0457	26.6	.0000	1	tail-end
0.0457	26.6	.0000	1	tailboard
0.0457	26.6	.0000	1	tailorbird
0.0457	26.6	.0000	1	Tailors
0.0457	26.6	.0000	1	tailpipe
0.0457	26.6	.0000	1	tailwind
0.0457	26.6	.0000	1	tainting
0.0457	26.6	.0000	1	taker
0.0457	26.6	.0000	1	talk-talk-talk
0.0457	26.6	.0000	1	talk-talk-talked
0.0457	26.6	.0000	1	talk-talk-talking
0.0457	26.6	.0000	1	talking-to
0.0457	26.6	.0000	1	tall-tale
0.0457	26.6	.0000	1	Tam's
0.0457	26.6	.0000	1	Tamaki
0.0457	26.6	.0000	1	Tamakis
0.0457	26.6	.0000	1	Tamarack
0.0457	26.6	.0000	1	Tamatomo
0.0457	26.6	.0000	1	tamer
0.0457	26.6	.0000	1	tamest
0.0457	26.6	.0000	1	Tane-Matarau
0.0457	26.6	.0000	1	Taney's
0.0457	26.6	.0000	1	Tangiers
0.0457	26.6	.0000	1	tank-house
0.0457	26.6	.0000	1	Tanners
0.0457	26.6	.0000	1	tannin
0.0457	26.6	.0000	1	tantalum
0.0457	26.6	.0000	1	Tappan
0.0457	26.6	.0000	1	Tarascan
0.0457	26.6	.0000	1	Tarascans
0.0457	26.6	.0000	1	Tarbell
0.0457	26.6	.0000	1	tarboosh
0.0457	26.6	.0000	1	tariff-protected
0.0457	26.6	.0000	1	Tarleton
0.0457	26.6	.0000	1	Tarnish's
0.0457	26.6	.0000	1	tarnishes
0.0457	26.6	.0000	1	tartly
0.0457	26.6	.0000	1	taschen
0.0457	26.6	.0000	1	Tasmanian
0.0457	26.6	.0000	1	Tassel
0.0457	26.6	.0000	1	Tassel's
0.0457	26.6	.0000	1	tat-tat
0.0457	26.6	.0000	1	tattle
0.0457	26.6	.0000	1	tattlers
0.0457	26.6	.0000	1	tattooing
0.0457	26.6	.0000	1	taubada
0.0457	26.6	.0000	1	taxi's
0.0457	26.6	.0000	1	taxidermist
0.0457	26.6	.0000	1	taxidermist's
0.0457	26.6	.0000	1	taylor-bird
0.0457	26.6	.0000	1	tea-party
0.0457	26.6	.0000	1	Teaching
0.0457	26.6	.0000	1	teal
0.0457	26.6	.0000	1	teamer
0.0457	26.6	.0000	1	Teams
0.0457	26.6	.0000	1	tear-stained
0.0457	26.6	.0000	1	teaser
0.0457	26.6	.0000	1	tee-hee
0.0457	26.6	.0000	1	Teedie's
0.0457	26.6	.0000	1	Teeny's
0.0457	26.6	.0000	1	teeter
0.0457	26.6	.0000	1	teetering
0.0457	26.6	.0000	1	Teide
0.0457	26.6	.0000	1	Teiglech
0.0457	26.6	.0000	1	Tekana's
0.0457	26.6	.0000	1	tele-
0.0457	26.6	.0000	1	tellurides

THE PRECEDING WORD TYPE OCCUPIES RANK 49300

U	SFI	D	F	Word Type
0.0457	26.6	.0000	1	ten-going-on-eleven
0.0457	26.6	.0000	1	ten-knot
0.0457	26.6	.0000	1	ten-pound
0.0457	26.6	.0000	1	tenderloin
0.0457	26.6	.0000	1	tendin'
0.0457	26.6	.0000	1	Tenedos
0.0457	26.6	.0000	1	tenets
0.0457	26.6	.0000	1	Tennes
0.0457	26.6	.0000	1	Tenney
0.0457	26.6	.0000	1	tent-shaped
0.0457	26.6	.0000	1	Terai
0.0457	26.6	.0000	1	Terrance's
0.0457	26.6	.0000	1	Terranova
0.0457	26.6	.0000	1	Terrapin
0.0457	26.6	.0000	1	terset
0.0457	26.6	.0000	1	terset-huk-fo-o-r
0.0457	26.6	.0000	1	testaments
0.0457	26.6	.0000	1	testily
0.0457	26.6	.0000	1	thnks
0.0457	26.6	.0000	1	Than
0.0457	26.6	.0000	1	than's
0.0457	26.6	.0000	1	Thankful's
0.0457	26.6	.0000	1	that'
0.0457	26.6	.0000	1	thawing
0.0457	26.6	.0000	1	Theebaw
0.0457	26.6	.0000	1	theologian's
0.0457	26.6	.0000	1	theologian's
0.0457	26.6	.0000	1	thereunto
0.0457	26.6	.0000	1	These
0.0457	26.6	.0000	1	Thesiger
0.0457	26.6	.0000	1	Thetis
0.0457	26.6	.0000	1	They're
0.0457	26.6	.0000	1	thick-furred
0.0457	26.6	.0000	1	thick-headedness
0.0457	26.6	.0000	1	thickety
0.0457	26.6	.0000	1	thiefs
0.0457	26.6	.0000	1	thievish
0.0457	26.6	.0000	1	thin-as-a-rake
0.0457	26.6	.0000	1	thin-leafed
0.0457	26.6	.0000	1	third-base
0.0457	26.6	.0000	1	third-rate
0.0457	26.6	.0000	1	thirsting
0.0457	26.6	.0000	1	thirteen-day-old
0.0457	26.6	.0000	1	thirteen-inch
0.0457	26.6	.0000	1	Thirties
0.0457	26.6	.0000	1	thirty-fifth
0.0457	26.6	.0000	1	thirty-five-foot
0.0457	26.6	.0000	1	thirty-footer
0.0457	26.6	.0000	1	this'n

U	SFI	D	F	Word Type
0.0457	26.6	.0000	1	thist
0.0457	26.6	.0000	1	thistledown
0.0457	26.6	.0000	1	Thoedore
0.0457	26.6	.0000	1	tholes
0.0457	26.6	.0000	1	Thomis's
0.0457	26.6	.0000	1	Thor-Able-Star
0.0457	26.6	.0000	1	Thornapple
0.0457	26.6	.0000	1	thornless
0.0457	26.6	.0000	1	Thorveg
0.0457	26.6	.0000	1	thought-out
0.0457	26.6	.0000	1	three-colored
0.0457	26.6	.0000	1	three-foot-square
0.0457	26.6	.0000	1	three-l
0.0457	26.6	.0000	1	three-masted
0.0457	26.6	.0000	1	three-quarter
0.0457	26.6	.0000	1	three-store
0.0457	26.6	.0000	1	three-story
0.0457	26.6	.0000	1	three-ton
0.0457	26.6	.0000	1	three-wheel
0.0457	26.6	.0000	1	threwed
0.0457	26.6	.0000	1	throttled
0.0457	26.6	.0000	1	thru'
0.0457	26.6	.0000	1	Thrust
0.0457	26.6	.0000	1	THUD
0.0457	26.6	.0000	1	thumbprints
0.0457	26.6	.0000	1	thundergust
0.0457	26.6	.0000	1	thundershowers
0.0457	26.6	.0000	1	thwacked
0.0457	26.6	.0000	1	thzt
0.0457	26.6	.0000	1	Tia
0.0457	26.6	.0000	1	Tiby
0.0457	26.6	.0000	1	tick-ets
0.0457	26.6	.0000	1	tick
0.0457	26.6	.0000	1	Tick's
0.0457	26.6	.0000	1	Tide
0.0457	26.6	.0000	1	tidewater
0.0457	26.6	.0000	1	tidying
0.0457	26.6	.0000	1	tiepin
0.0457	26.6	.0000	1	tiger-striped
0.0457	26.6	.0000	1	Tiger's
0.0457	26.6	.0000	1	Tight
0.0457	26.6	.0000	1	Tightness
0.0457	26.6	.0000	1	Timberlake
0.0457	26.6	.0000	1	time-and-a-half
0.0457	26.6	.0000	1	timekeeper's
0.0457	26.6	.0000	1	timepiece
0.0457	26.6	.0000	1	Timmm-berr
0.0457	26.6	.0000	1	tin-bottomed
0.0457	26.6	.0000	1	tinged
0.0457	26.6	.0000	1	Tinsley
0.0457	26.6	.0000	1	tintinnabulation

THE PRECEDING WORD TYPE OCCUPIES RANK 49400

U	SFI	D	F	Word Type
0.0457	26.6	.0000	1	tio
0.0457	26.6	.0000	1	Tio
0.0457	26.6	.0000	1	tipsy-toeing
0.0457	26.6	.0000	1	Tired-Dog
0.0457	26.6	.0000	1	titleholder
0.0457	26.6	.0000	1	tittered
0.0457	26.6	.0000	1	tle
0.0457	26.6	.0000	1	to't
0.0457	26.6	.0000	1	Tobe's
0.0457	26.6	.0000	1	toe-bells
0.0457	26.6	.0000	1	toehold
0.0457	26.6	.0000	1	toeholds
0.0457	26.6	.0000	1	toeses
0.0457	26.6	.0000	1	Toji
0.0457	26.6	.0000	1	Toji's
0.0457	26.6	.0000	1	tolerably
0.0457	26.6	.0000	1	Tolliver
0.0457	26.6	.0000	1	Tolman's
0.0457	26.6	.0000	1	Toluca
0.0457	26.6	.0000	1	Tolvin
0.0457	26.6	.0000	1	Tomasson
0.0457	26.6	.0000	1	tomato-and-lettuce
0.0457	26.6	.0000	1	tombo's
0.0457	26.6	.0000	1	tomboys
0.0457	26.6	.0000	1	tomcat'
0.0457	26.6	.0000	1	tommygun
0.0457	26.6	.0000	1	tommyknockers
0.0457	26.6	.0000	1	Tongelow
0.0457	26.6	.0000	1	tonic-good
0.0457	26.6	.0000	1	Tonio
0.0457	26.6	.0000	1	tonnages
0.0457	26.6	.0000	1	tonne
0.0457	26.6	.0000	1	tonsil
0.0457	26.6	.0000	1	too-large
0.0457	26.6	.0000	1	too-often
0.0457	26.6	.0000	1	too-soon
0.0457	26.6	.0000	1	toolbox
0.0457	26.6	.0000	1	toolshed
0.0457	26.6	.0000	1	toom
0.0457	26.6	.0000	1	toothaches
0.0457	26.6	.0000	1	top-notch
0.0457	26.6	.0000	1	tope
0.0457	26.6	.0000	1	topknot
0.0457	26.6	.0000	1	topnotch
0.0457	26.6	.0000	1	topsides
0.0457	26.6	.0000	1	torchlights
0.0457	26.6	.0000	1	Torreses'
0.0457	26.6	.0000	1	Tors
0.0457	26.6	.0000	1	Torstein's
0.0457	26.6	.0000	1	Toru's
0.0457	26.6	.0000	1	Tory-lovers
0.0457	26.6	.0000	1	totters
0.0457	26.6	.0000	1	touchin'
0.0457	26.6	.0000	1	touchiness
0.0457	26.6	.0000	1	touchstone
0.0457	26.6	.0000	1	towboat
0.0457	26.6	.0000	1	towel-horse
0.0457	26.6	.0000	1	towline
0.0457	26.6	.0000	1	townlot
0.0457	26.6	.0000	1	toyed
0.0457	26.6	.0000	1	tra-la-la-
0.0457	26.6	.0000	1	tra-lee-lee
0.0457	26.6	.0000	1	Trachis
0.0457	26.6	.0000	1	track-laying
0.0457	26.6	.0000	1	tractorbuses

U	SFI	D	F	Word Type
0.0457	26.6	.0000	1	tradegoods
0.0457	26.6	.0000	1	Traders'
0.0457	26.6	.0000	1	Trained
0.0457	26.6	.0000	1	Tramp-Tramp-Tramp
0.0457	26.6	.0000	1	tramp's
0.0457	26.6	.0000	1	trams
0.0457	26.6	.0000	1	translucency
0.0457	26.6	.0000	1	trap's
0.0457	26.6	.0000	1	traplike
0.0457	26.6	.0000	1	Trapper
0.0457	26.6	.0000	1	trappin'
0.0457	26.6	.0000	1	travel-worn
0.0457	26.6	.0000	1	trawler
0.0457	26.6	.0000	1	treaded
0.0457	26.6	.0000	1	tree-box
0.0457	26.6	.0000	1	tree-killing
0.0457	26.6	.0000	1	tree-trunk
0.0457	26.6	.0000	1	treehouse
0.0457	26.6	.0000	1	trembly
0.0457	26.6	.0000	1	tremendous-sized
0.0457	26.6	.0000	1	Trespassing
0.0457	26.6	.0000	1	tribe's
0.0457	26.6	.0000	1	Tribute
0.0457	26.6	.0000	1	Trigger
0.0457	26.6	.0000	1	Tripolitania
0.0457	26.6	.0000	1	Trix
0.0457	26.6	.0000	1	Troll
0.0457	26.6	.0000	1	Trot
0.0457	26.6	.0000	1	TROUBLE
0.0457	26.6	.0000	1	trouble-maker
0.0457	26.6	.0000	1	trouble-makers
0.0457	26.6	.0000	1	Troublesome
0.0457	26.6	.0000	1	Trudeau's
0.0457	26.6	.0000	1	true-hearted
0.0457	26.6	.0000	1	trustfully

THE PRECEDING WORD TYPE OCCUPIES RANK 49500

U	SFI	D	F	Word Type
0.0457	26.6	.0000	1	truthfulness
0.0457	26.6	.0000	1	Tsao
0.0457	26.6	.0000	1	Tsong
0.0457	26.6	.0000	1	Tuaregs
0.0457	26.6	.0000	1	tuberculin-tested
0.0457	26.6	.0000	1	Tuffy
0.0457	26.6	.0000	1	Tukahoe
0.0457	26.6	.0000	1	tules
0.0457	26.6	.0000	1	Tully's
0.0457	26.6	.0000	1	tumble-down
0.0457	26.6	.0000	1	tumbling-down
0.0457	26.6	.0000	1	tun-a-tun-a-tunin'
0.0457	26.6	.0000	1	tuppenny-ha'penny
0.0457	26.6	.0000	1	Turis
0.0457	26.6	.0000	1	turn't
0.0457	26.6	.0000	1	Turners'
0.0457	26.6	.0000	1	turtle-doves
0.0457	26.6	.0000	1	turtles'
0.0457	26.6	.0000	1	tussle
0.0457	26.6	.0000	1	tut-tut
0.0457	26.6	.0000	1	Tutankhamen
0.0457	26.6	.0000	1	tutored
0.0457	26.6	.0000	1	tweedle-dee
0.0457	26.6	.0000	1	Tweedy's
0.0457	26.6	.0000	1	twelve-pint
0.0457	26.6	.0000	1	twelve-thirty
0.0457	26.6	.0000	1	twenty-eight-inch
0.0457	26.6	.0000	1	twenty-eight-year-old
0.0457	26.6	.0000	1	twenty-five-cent
0.0457	26.6	.0000	1	twenty-gun
0.0457	26.6	.0000	1	twenty-minute
0.0457	26.6	.0000	1	twenty-mule
0.0457	26.6	.0000	1	Twenty-six
0.0457	26.6	.0000	1	twiddled
0.0457	26.6	.0000	1	twig-and-grass
0.0457	26.6	.0000	1	Twig's
0.0457	26.6	.0000	1	Twiggs
0.0457	26.6	.0000	1	twinkly
0.0457	26.6	.0000	1	twisty
0.0457	26.6	.0000	1	twit
0.0457	26.6	.0000	1	Twitchell
0.0457	26.6	.0000	1	Twitchell's
0.0457	26.6	.0000	1	twitterings
0.0457	26.6	.0000	1	two-M
0.0457	26.6	.0000	1	Two-Toed
0.0457	26.6	.0000	1	two-bladed
0.0457	26.6	.0000	1	two-by-four
0.0457	26.6	.0000	1	two-by-fours
0.0457	26.6	.0000	1	two-family
0.0457	26.6	.0000	1	two-forty-five
0.0457	26.6	.0000	1	two-handled
0.0457	26.6	.0000	1	two-hundred-inch
0.0457	26.6	.0000	1	two-l
0.0457	26.6	.0000	1	two-on-two
0.0457	26.6	.0000	1	two-ounce
0.0457	26.6	.0000	1	two-step
0.0457	26.6	.0000	1	two-thousand-pound
0.0457	26.6	.0000	1	two-toned
0.0457	26.6	.0000	1	tyrannosaur
0.0457	26.6	.0000	1	u-2
0.0457	26.6	.0000	1	UF
0.0457	26.6	.0000	1	ughr-r-r
0.0457	26.6	.0000	1	ughr-r-r-
0.0457	26.6	.0000	1	uglier
0.0457	26.6	.0000	1	uh-uh-Listen
0.0457	26.6	.0000	1	um-hum
0.0457	26.6	.0000	1	umm
0.0457	26.6	.0000	1	ummm
0.0457	26.6	.0000	1	umpire-in-chief
0.0457	26.6	.0000	1	umtente
0.0457	26.6	.0000	1	Unabridged
0.0457	26.6	.0000	1	unashamedly
0.0457	26.6	.0000	1	unavenged
0.0457	26.6	.0000	1	unbar
0.0457	26.6	.0000	1	unbarred
0.0457	26.6	.0000	1	unbeatable
0.0457	26.6	.0000	1	unbind
0.0457	26.6	.0000	1	unblinking
0.0457	26.6	.0000	1	unbuckle
0.0457	26.6	.0000	1	unburnable
0.0457	26.6	.0000	1	uncalled-for

U	SFI	D	F	Word Type
0.0457	26.6	.0000	1	Uncheedah
0.0457	26.6	.0000	1	unclaimed
0.0457	26.6	.0000	1	uncleared
0.0457	26.6	.0000	1	uncourteously
0.0457	26.6	.0000	1	uncourtly
0.0457	26.6	.0000	1	undefined
0.0457	26.6	.0000	1	undeleterious
0.0457	26.6	.0000	1	undelstand
0.0457	26.6	.0000	1	undelstands
0.0457	26.6	.0000	1	underbelly
0.0457	26.6	.0000	1	underdogs
0.0457	26.6	.0000	1	underpants
0.0457	26.6	.0000	1	underpart
0.0457	26.6	.0000	1	underpinnings
0.0457	26.6	.0000	1	undersides
0.0457	26.6	.0000	1	underst-
0.0457	26.6	.0000	1	undulations
0.0457	26.6	.0000	1	undust
0.0457	26.6	.0000	1	unendurable

THE PRECEDING WORD TYPE OCCUPIES RANK 49600

U	SFI	D	F	Word Type
0.0457	26.6	.0000	1	unfed
0.0457	26.6	.0000	1	unflurried
0.0457	26.6	.0000	1	ungiving
0.0457	26.6	.0000	1	unguents
0.0457	26.6	.0000	1	unhappiest
0.0457	26.6	.0000	1	Unhappy
0.0457	26.6	.0000	1	unharness
0.0457	26.6	.0000	1	unharnessing
0.0457	26.6	.0000	1	unhook
0.0457	26.6	.0000	1	unicorns'
0.0457	26.6	.0000	1	Unidentified
0.0457	26.6	.0000	1	uniform-like
0.0457	26.6	.0000	1	UnitedStares
0.0457	26.6	.0000	1	unlessing
0.0457	26.6	.0000	1	unlived
0.0457	26.6	.0000	1	unlocking
0.0457	26.6	.0000	1	unloose
0.0457	26.6	.0000	1	unluckily
0.0457	26.6	.0000	1	unmuzzle
0.0457	26.6	.0000	1	unnatchal
0.0457	26.6	.0000	1	unnoticeable
0.0457	26.6	.0000	1	unparalleled
0.0457	26.6	.0000	1	unpatchable
0.0457	26.6	.0000	1	unpatented
0.0457	26.6	.0000	1	unplanted
0.0457	26.6	.0000	1	unplugged
0.0457	26.6	.0000	1	unprincipled
0.0457	26.6	.0000	1	unquestionable
0.0457	26.6	.0000	1	unreally
0.0457	26.6	.0000	1	unreeled
0.0457	26.6	.0000	1	unrelenting
0.0457	26.6	.0000	1	unrumpled
0.0457	26.6	.0000	1	unsaid
0.0457	26.6	.0000	1	unseemly
0.0457	26.6	.0000	1	unshaven
0.0457	26.6	.0000	1	unshed
0.0457	26.6	.0000	1	unshined
0.0457	26.6	.0000	1	unsnagged
0.0457	26.6	.0000	1	unstacking
0.0457	26.6	.0000	1	unstained
0.0457	26.6	.0000	1	unstrapped
0.0457	26.6	.0000	1	unsubtle
0.0457	26.6	.0000	1	unthreatening
0.0457	26.6	.0000	1	untruth
0.0457	26.6	.0000	1	unutterable
0.0457	26.6	.0000	1	unwhitewashed
0.0457	26.6	.0000	1	unzip
0.0457	26.6	.0000	1	upcountry
0.0457	26.6	.0000	1	uprights
0.0457	26.6	.0000	1	upswelling
0.0457	26.6	.0000	1	uptailed
0.0457	26.6	.0000	1	uptipped
0.0457	26.6	.0000	1	upward-beamed
0.0457	26.6	.0000	1	Uses
0.0457	26.6	.0000	1	ushers
0.0457	26.6	.0000	1	USN
0.0457	26.6	.0000	1	usurpation
0.0457	26.6	.0000	1	uts
0.0457	26.6	.0000	1	Uttar
0.0457	26.6	.0000	1	uuuuh
0.0457	26.6	.0000	1	v-shaped
0.0457	26.6	.0000	1	Valedictorian
0.0457	26.6	.0000	1	VanBrunt
0.0457	26.6	.0000	1	VanBummel
0.0457	26.6	.0000	1	vanRhijn
0.0457	26.6	.0000	1	Vanderpane
0.0457	26.6	.0000	1	Vanity
0.0457	26.6	.0000	1	vanquishing
0.0457	26.6	.0000	1	vaquero
0.0457	26.6	.0000	1	vari-colored
0.0457	26.6	.0000	1	vaunted
0.0457	26.6	.0000	1	Vedder
0.0457	26.6	.0000	1	Vee's
0.0457	26.6	.0000	1	veiltail
0.0457	26.6	.0000	1	velly
0.0457	26.6	.0000	1	velvet-black
0.0457	26.6	.0000	1	velvet-eyed
0.0457	26.6	.0000	1	venomously
0.0457	26.6	.0000	1	Venus's-flytrap
0.0457	26.6	.0000	1	Venus's-flytraps
0.0457	26.6	.0000	1	Vera's
0.0457	26.6	.0000	1	vicar's
0.0457	26.6	.0000	1	vicarious
0.0457	26.6	.0000	1	vice-presidents
0.0457	26.6	.0000	1	vicelike
0.0457	26.6	.0000	1	Victim
0.0457	26.6	.0000	1	victoria
0.0457	26.6	.0000	1	vieille
0.0457	26.6	.0000	1	villagers'
0.0457	26.6	.0000	1	Villages
0.0457	26.6	.0000	1	Vinard
0.0457	26.6	.0000	1	vindication
0.0457	26.6	.0000	1	vindictiveness
0.0457	26.6	.0000	1	vinegar-soy
0.0457	26.6	.0000	1	Vinny's
0.0457	26.6	.0000	1	Virginia-Carolina
0.0457	26.6	.0000	1	VISTA
0.0457	26.6	.0000	1	viven
0.0457	26.6	.0000	1	vivi
0.0457	26.6	.0000	1	vivimos

THE PRECEDING WORD TYPE OCCUPIES RANK 49700

U	SFI	D	F	Word Type
0.0457	26.6	.0000	1	vivis
0.0457	26.6	.0000	1	viziers
0.0457	26.6	.0000	1	vo-cab-u-lar-y
0.0457	26.6	.0000	1	vocalization
0.0457	26.6	.0000	1	vocalize
0.0457	26.6	.0000	1	Vollard
0.0457	26.6	.0000	1	vonWrangel
0.0457	26.6	.0000	1	vont-elles
0.0457	26.6	.0000	1	Vorkle
0.0457	26.6	.0000	1	Voyager's
0.0457	26.6	.0000	1	Vulpian
0.0457	26.6	.0000	1	w-a-t-e-r
0.0457	26.6	.0000	1	w-w-what
0.0457	26.6	.0000	1	w
0.0457	26.6	.0000	1	wll
0.0457	26.6	.0000	1	w'en
0.0457	26.6	.0000	1	wa-al
0.0457	26.6	.0000	1	Wachita
0.0457	26.6	.0000	1	Wack
0.0457	26.6	.0000	1	wadgetty
0.0457	26.6	.0000	1	wadin'
0.0457	26.6	.0000	1	waferlike
0.0457	26.6	.0000	1	waggled
0.0457	26.6	.0000	1	waggles
0.0457	26.6	.0000	1	wagon'
0.0457	26.6	.0000	1	wagonloads
0.0457	26.6	.0000	1	wailers
0.0457	26.6	.0000	1	Waino's
0.0457	26.6	.0000	1	Wainwright
0.0457	26.6	.0000	1	Waiter's
0.0457	26.6	.0000	1	Waker
0.0457	26.6	.0000	1	walkways
0.0457	26.6	.0000	1	wall-eye
0.0457	26.6	.0000	1	wall-sized
0.0457	26.6	.0000	1	wallowings
0.0457	26.6	.0000	1	Wanda's
0.0457	26.6	.0000	1	wanderin'
0.0457	26.6	.0000	1	Wanted
0.0457	26.6	.0000	1	war-bonnet
0.0457	26.6	.0000	1	war-cry
0.0457	26.6	.0000	1	war-like
0.0457	26.6	.0000	1	Wares
0.0457	26.6	.0000	1	warm-water
0.0457	26.6	.0000	1	warmers
0.0457	26.6	.0000	1	Warnings
0.0457	26.6	.0000	1	Warrior's
0.0457	26.6	.0000	1	wash-gray
0.0457	26.6	.0000	1	washbowls
0.0457	26.6	.0000	1	washing-stand
0.0457	26.6	.0000	1	washroom
0.0457	26.6	.0000	1	washtubs
0.0457	26.6	.0000	1	wastefully
0.0457	26.6	.0000	1	Watanabe-san
0.0457	26.6	.0000	1	watch-chain
0.0457	26.6	.0000	1	watchdogs
0.0457	26.6	.0000	1	watchfully
0.0457	26.6	.0000	1	watchfulness
0.0457	26.6	.0000	1	watchman's
0.0457	26.6	.0000	1	water-crazy
0.0457	26.6	.0000	1	water-flowers
0.0457	26.6	.0000	1	water-front
0.0457	26.6	.0000	1	water-lilies
0.0457	26.6	.0000	1	water-loving
0.0457	26.6	.0000	1	water-mark
0.0457	26.6	.0000	1	water-meadows
0.0457	26.6	.0000	1	Waterfield
0.0457	26.6	.0000	1	Waterman
0.0457	26.6	.0000	1	watermarket
0.0457	26.6	.0000	1	waterproofed
0.0457	26.6	.0000	1	Waters'
0.0457	26.6	.0000	1	waters'
0.0457	26.6	.0000	1	waterwalls
0.0457	26.6	.0000	1	Watsons
0.0457	26.6	.0000	1	waverers
0.0457	26.6	.0000	1	Waverly
0.0457	26.6	.0000	1	wax-and-feather
0.0457	26.6	.0000	1	wax-covered
0.0457	26.6	.0000	1	way-back
0.0457	26.6	.0000	1	waybill
0.0457	26.6	.0000	1	Wayo
0.0457	26.6	.0000	1	WA1-2234
0.0457	26.6	.0000	1	we-e-ell
0.0457	26.6	.0000	1	we'
0.0457	26.6	.0000	1	we'l
0.0457	26.6	.0000	1	We're
0.0457	26.6	.0000	1	Wearer
0.0457	26.6	.0000	1	weasles
0.0457	26.6	.0000	1	weatherboard
0.0457	26.6	.0000	1	Weatherford
0.0457	26.6	.0000	1	Weatherford's
0.0457	26.6	.0000	1	weavin'
0.0457	26.6	.0000	1	web-weaving
0.0457	26.6	.0000	1	Webb's
0.0457	26.6	.0000	1	weddin
0.0457	26.6	.0000	1	Wedged
0.0457	26.6	.0000	1	weed-covered
0.0457	26.6	.0000	1	Weep
0.0457	26.6	.0000	1	Weeps
0.0457	26.6	.0000	1	Wei's
0.0457	26.6	.0000	1	weighting

THE PRECEDING WORD TYPE OCCUPIES RANK 49800

U	SFI	D	F	Word Type
0.0457	26.6	.0000	1	well-a-day
0.0457	26.6	.0000	1	well-bred
0.0457	26.6	.0000	1	well-formed
0.0457	26.6	.0000	1	well-knit
0.0457	26.6	.0000	1	well-l-l
0.0457	26.6	.0000	1	well-placed
0.0457	26.6	.0000	1	well-tilled
0.0457	26.6	.0000	1	well-tramped
0.0457	26.6	.0000	1	well-wisher
0.0457	26.6	.0000	1	well's
0.0457	26.6	.0000	1	welled
0.0457	26.6	.0000	1	welterweight
0.0457	26.6	.0000	1	west-southwest
0.0457	26.6	.0000	1	Westman
0.0457	26.6	.0000	1	wet-blanket
0.0457	26.6	.0000	1	whacked
0.0457	26.6	.0000	1	whaleboat
0.0457	26.6	.0000	1	whatever's
0.0457	26.6	.0000	1	whe-e-e-e
0.0457	26.6	.0000	1	wheat-gold
0.0457	26.6	.0000	1	wheee
0.0457	26.6	.0000	1	Wheels'
0.0457	26.6	.0000	1	Wheels's
0.0457	26.6	.0000	1	Wheelwrights'
0.0457	26.6	.0000	1	wheezes
0.0457	26.6	.0000	1	whelk
0.0457	26.6	.0000	1	whelps
0.0457	26.6	.0000	1	where'll
0.0457	26.6	.0000	1	where've
0.0457	26.6	.0000	1	whip-tailed
0.0457	26.6	.0000	1	whippings
0.0457	26.6	.0000	1	whipsnap
0.0457	26.6	.0000	1	whirly
0.0457	26.6	.0000	1	whish
0.0457	26.6	.0000	1	whisper-like
0.0457	26.6	.0000	1	whissh
0.0457	26.6	.0000	1	whistle-pig
0.0457	26.6	.0000	1	WHITE
0.0457	26.6	.0000	1	white-aproned
0.0457	26.6	.0000	1	white-ash
0.0457	26.6	.0000	1	white-covered
0.0457	26.6	.0000	1	white-furred
0.0457	26.6	.0000	1	white-painted
0.0457	26.6	.0000	1	white-paneled
0.0457	26.6	.0000	1	white-pillared
0.0457	26.6	.0000	1	white-potted
0.0457	26.6	.0000	1	white-waterin'
0.0457	26.6	.0000	1	whitewashin'
0.0457	26.6	.0000	1	whitish-yellow
0.0457	26.6	.0000	1	who-oo-oo
0.0457	26.6	.0000	1	who-who
0.0457	26.6	.0000	1	Whodunit
0.0457	26.6	.0000	1	WHOEEE
0.0457	26.6	.0000	1	whole-hog
0.0457	26.6	.0000	1	whoo-hoo
0.0457	26.6	.0000	1	whooo
0.0457	26.6	.0000	1	whooo's
0.0457	26.6	.0000	1	whoooo
0.0457	26.6	.0000	1	WHOOSH
0.0457	26.6	.0000	1	whoppers
0.0457	26.6	.0000	1	Whush-h-h
0.0457	26.6	.0000	1	Wickaeldroth
0.0457	26.6	.0000	1	wickedest-looking
0.0457	26.6	.0000	1	wickiup
0.0457	26.6	.0000	1	widgeon
0.0457	26.6	.0000	1	Wielemaker's
0.0457	26.6	.0000	1	Wielemakers
0.0457	26.6	.0000	1	Wiese
0.0457	26.6	.0000	1	wiggle-wagging
0.0457	26.6	.0000	1	Wilbrook
0.0457	26.6	.0000	1	wild-animal
0.0457	26.6	.0000	1	wild-fowler
0.0457	26.6	.0000	1	Wild-life
0.0457	26.6	.0000	1	wildcat's
0.0457	26.6	.0000	1	wildgeese
0.0457	26.6	.0000	1	will-o'-the-wisp
0.0457	26.6	.0000	1	willfulness
0.0457	26.6	.0000	1	Willman's
0.0457	26.6	.0000	1	Willowbrook
0.0457	26.6	.0000	1	willowwild
0.0457	26.6	.0000	1	Willsboro
0.0457	26.6	.0000	1	Willy's
0.0457	26.6	.0000	1	Wilma's
0.0457	26.6	.0000	1	wimdmills
0.0457	26.6	.0000	1	Wimpy
0.0457	26.6	.0000	1	win'
0.0457	26.6	.0000	1	Winant
0.0457	26.6	.0000	1	windbreaker
0.0457	26.6	.0000	1	Windfield
0.0457	26.6	.0000	1	windflowers
0.0457	26.6	.0000	1	Windjammer
0.0457	26.6	.0000	1	windmills'
0.0457	26.6	.0000	1	window-pane
0.0457	26.6	.0000	1	window-sills
0.0457	26.6	.0000	1	Windows
0.0457	26.6	.0000	1	Windy's
0.0457	26.6	.0000	1	wine-red
0.0457	26.6	.0000	1	wingbeat
0.0457	26.6	.0000	1	Wings
0.0457	26.6	.0000	1	wingtips

THE PRECEDING WORD TYPE OCCUPIES RANK 49900

U	SFI	D	F	Word Type
0.0457	26.6	.0000	1	Winnie
0.0457	26.6	.0000	1	wire-rope
0.0457	26.6	.0000	1	wired-up
0.0457	26.6	.0000	1	wisecracked
0.0457	26.6	.0000	1	wiseman
0.0457	26.6	.0000	1	Wisenick
0.0457	26.6	.0000	1	WISH
0.0457	26.6	.0000	1	wisped
0.0457	26.6	.0000	1	witch-and-dragon
0.0457	26.6	.0000	1	Withers'
0.0457	26.6	.0000	1	withstanding
0.0457	26.6	.0000	1	Witnesses
0.0457	26.6	.0000	1	wiz
0.0457	26.6	.0000	1	wizardly
0.0457	26.6	.0000	1	Wo's
0.0457	26.6	.0000	1	woebegone
0.0457	26.6	.0000	1	wonder-wise
0.0457	26.6	.0000	1	wonderin'
0.0457	26.6	.0000	1	woo-woo
0.0457	26.6	.0000	1	wood-and-metal
0.0457	26.6	.0000	1	wood-chopper
0.0457	26.6	.0000	1	wood-cutter
0.0457	26.6	.0000	1	wood-stove
0.0457	26.6	.0000	1	wood's
0.0457	26.6	.0000	1	woodcutters
0.0457	26.6	.0000	1	woodland's
0.0457	26.6	.0000	1	woodshore
0.0457	26.6	.0000	1	woodsmoke
0.0457	26.6	.0000	1	woodswise
0.0457	26.6	.0000	1	Woodward's
0.0457	26.6	.0000	1	Woody's
0.0457	26.6	.0000	1	woofs
0.0457	26.6	.0000	1	wool-thick
0.0457	26.6	.0000	1	Woolly's
0.0457	26.6	.0000	1	word-recognition
0.0457	26.6	.0000	1	work-filled
0.0457	26.6	.0000	1	work-horses
0.0457	26.6	.0000	1	work-raw
0.0457	26.6	.0000	1	workhouse'll
0.0457	26.6	.0000	1	WORKS
0.0457	26.6	.0000	1	worktable
0.0457	26.6	.0000	1	world-championship
0.0457	26.6	.0000	1	worming
0.0457	26.6	.0000	1	wormy
0.0457	26.6	.0000	1	worried-looking
0.0457	26.6	.0000	1	Worthmores
0.0457	26.6	.0000	1	would've
0.0457	26.6	.0000	1	Wounds
0.0457	26.6	.0000	1	wowser's
0.0457	26.6	.0000	1	wowsers
0.0457	26.6	.0000	1	wraithlike
0.0457	26.6	.0000	1	WRECKS
0.0457	26.6	.0000	1	write-up
0.0457	26.6	.0000	1	Writer's
0.0457	26.6	.0000	1	wrongfully
0.0457	26.6	.0000	1	wrongheaded
0.0457	26.6	.0000	1	Wunderlich
0.0457	26.6	.0000	1	wunk
0.0457	26.6	.0000	1	Xingo's
0.0457	26.6	.0000	1	Xiquipilco
0.0457	26.6	.0000	1	y'know
0.0457	26.6	.0000	1	Yadon
0.0457	26.6	.0000	1	Yakima
0.0457	26.6	.0000	1	yaks
0.0457	26.6	.0000	1	yaller-toothy
0.0457	26.6	.0000	1	Yan's
0.0457	26.6	.0000	1	Yank
0.0457	26.6	.0000	1	Yann
0.0457	26.6	.0000	1	Yann's
0.0457	26.6	.0000	1	yardarms
0.0457	26.6	.0000	1	Yarn
0.0457	26.6	.0000	1	Yat
0.0457	26.6	.0000	1	yawnin'
0.0457	26.6	.0000	1	yawns
0.0457	26.6	.0000	1	yawps
0.0457	26.6	.0000	1	yayaya
0.0457	26.6	.0000	1	ye
0.0457	26.6	.0000	1	ye'll
0.0457	26.6	.0000	1	year-around
0.0457	26.6	.0000	1	yearbook
0.0457	26.6	.0000	1	Yedo
0.0457	26.6	.0000	1	yellow-maned
0.0457	26.6	.0000	1	Yellow-shafted
0.0457	26.6	.0000	1	yellow-skinned
0.0457	26.6	.0000	1	yellowbird
0.0457	26.6	.0000	1	yellower
0.0457	26.6	.0000	1	yellowish-red
0.0457	26.6	.0000	1	yellowness
0.0457	26.6	.0000	1	Yellowstone's
0.0457	26.6	.0000	1	Yesterday
0.0457	26.6	.0000	1	YET
0.0457	26.6	.0000	1	yeti
0.0457	26.6	.0000	1	yi-yi-yi
0.0457	26.6	.0000	1	Yin's
0.0457	26.6	.0000	1	yip-yip-yipping
0.0457	26.6	.0000	1	yipe
0.0457	26.6	.0000	1	yipee-i-o
0.0457	26.6	.0000	1	yo're
0.0457	26.6	.0000	1	Yoder's
0.0457	26.6	.0000	1	yogurt

THE PRECEDING WORD TYPE OCCUPIES RANK 50000

U	SFI	D	F	Word Type
0.0457	26.6	.0000	1	Yolchi
0.0457	26.6	.0000	1	Yoldash
0.0457	26.6	.0000	1	Yong
0.0457	26.6	.0000	1	YOOOOO
0.0457	26.6	.0000	1	YOOOOOOOOOOOOOOOO
0.0457	26.6	.0000	1	you-know-what
0.0457	26.6	.0000	1	you-know-where
0.0457	26.6	.0000	1	you-u-u
0.0457	26.6	.0000	1	young'uns
0.0457	26.6	.0000	1	younglings
0.0457	26.6	.0000	1	Youngs
0.0457	26.6	.0000	1	Youngstown
0.0457	26.6	.0000	1	younguns
0.0457	26.6	.0000	1	youse
0.0457	26.6	.0000	1	yuh've
0.0457	26.6	.0000	1	yum-yum
0.0457	26.6	.0000	1	yuo
0.0457	26.6	.0000	1	Yvonne
0.0457	26.6	.0000	1	zealots
0.0457	26.6	.0000	1	Zeb
0.0457	26.6	.0000	1	zim
0.0457	26.6	.0000	1	Zimmer's
0.0457	26.6	.0000	1	Zinnen's
0.0457	26.6	.0000	1	ZOO
0.0457	26.6	.0000	1	Zumbro
0.0457	26.6	.0000	1	zwei
0.0457	26.6	.0000	1	Zworykin's
0.0457	26.6	.0000	1	zzz
0.0457	26.6	.0000	1	ZZZ
0.0457	26.6	.0000	1	00P
0.0457	26.6	.0000	1	000-000
0.0457	26.6	.0000	1	1-1234
0.0457	26.6	.0000	1	1-2-3-4
0.0457	26.6	.0000	1	1-2234
0.0457	26.6	.0000	1	10K
0.0457	26.6	.0000	1	1000-mile
0.0457	26.6	.0000	1	1000-pound
0.0457	26.6	.0000	1	104th
0.0457	26.6	.0000	1	112-113
0.0457	26.6	.0000	1	12K
0.0457	26.6	.0000	1	130-pound
0.0457	26.6	.0000	1	14K
0.0457	26.6	.0000	1	14s
0.0457	26.6	.0000	1	145th

U	SFI	D	F	Word Type
0.0457	26.6	.0000	1	1452
0.0457	26.6	.0000	1	15years
0.0457	26.6	.0000	1	150-mile
0.0457	26.6	.0000	1	1596781
0.0457	26.6	.0000	1	1668
0.0457	26.6	.0000	1	17-B
0.0457	26.6	.0000	1	1720's
0.0457	26.6	.0000	1	1723
0.0457	26.6	.0000	1	1734
0.0457	26.6	.0000	1	174-175
0.0457	26.6	.0000	1	177-year-old
0.0457	26.6	.0000	1	1775-1776
0.0457	26.6	.0000	1	1775-76
0.0457	26.6	.0000	1	18K
0.0457	26.6	.0000	1	180-odd
0.0457	26.6	.0000	1	1807-1892
0.0457	26.6	.0000	1	182-183
0.0457	26.6	.0000	1	1830-1900
0.0457	26.6	.0000	1	1856-1857
0.0457	26.6	.0000	1	1861-1929
0.0457	26.6	.0000	1	1891-1892
0.0457	26.6	.0000	1	1926-1927
0.0457	26.6	.0000	1	1955-56
0.0457	26.6	.0000	1	1966-mile
0.0457	26.6	.0000	1	197-198
0.0457	26.6	.0000	1	1990's
0.0457	26.6	.0000	1	20-pound
0.0457	26.6	.0000	1	20-30
0.0457	26.6	.0000	1	2000-foot
0.0457	26.6	.0000	1	2011
0.0457	26.6	.0000	1	21-mile-wide
0.0457	26.6	.0000	1	2222222222222
0.0457	26.6	.0000	1	2315
0.0457	26.6	.0000	1	24-pound
0.0457	26.6	.0000	1	246-253
0.0457	26.6	.0000	1	25-centime
0.0457	26.6	.0000	1	26-foot
0.0457	26.6	.0000	1	28-pound
0.0457	26.6	.0000	1	294-295
0.0457	26.6	.0000	1	3-all
0.0457	26.6	.0000	1	3-1-2
0.0457	26.6	.0000	1	3-59
0.0457	26.6	.0000	1	300-square-foot
0.0457	26.6	.0000	1	3764
0.0457	26.6	.0000	1	377
0.0457	26.6	.0000	1	400-meter
0.0457	26.6	.0000	1	4280
0.0457	26.6	.0000	1	43-million-dollar
0.0457	26.6	.0000	1	437892
0.0457	26.6	.0000	1	5-foot-11
0.0457	26.6	.0000	1	5-0-4
0.0457	26.6	.0000	1	5-2-3
0.0457	26.6	.0000	1	5-9970
0.0457	26.6	.0000	1	500-foot
0.0457	26.6	.0000	1	5000-mile-a-minute
0.0457	26.6	.0000	1	54th

THE PRECEDING WORD TYPE OCCUPIES RANK 50100

U	SFI	D	F	Word Type
0.0457	26.6	.0000	1	561
0.0457	26.6	.0000	1	5710
0.0457	26.6	.0000	1	594
0.0457	26.6	.0000	1	596781
0.0457	26.6	.0000	1	596782
0.0457	26.6	.0000	1	5988
0.0457	26.6	.0000	1	62-60
0.0457	26.6	.0000	1	800-pound
0.0457	26.6	.0000	1	852
0.0457	26.6	.0000	1	88%
0.0457	26.6	.0000	1	886
0.0457	26.6	.0000	1	900's
0.0457	26.6	.0000	1	948
0.0457	26.6	.0000	1	959
0.0457	26.6	.0000	1	993
0.0451	26.5	.0000	14	casserole
0.0451	26.5	.0000	14	seasonings
0.0451	26.5	.0000	14	staystitching
0.0449	26.5	.0000	3	$1000
0.0449	26.5	.0000	3	$24
0.0449	26.5	.0000	3	$32
0.0449	26.5	.0000	3	$38
0.0449	26.5	.0000	3	$39
0.0449	26.5	.0000	3	$44
0.0449	26.5	.0000	3	-n
0.0449	26.5	.0000	3	-12
0.0449	26.5	.0000	3	-40
0.0449	26.5	.0000	3	-50
0.0449	26.5	.0000	3	-60
0.0449	26.5	.0000	3	/12
0.0449	26.5	.0000	3	a/8
0.0449	26.5	.0000	3	ACB
0.0449	26.5	.0000	3	ADHE
0.0449	26.5	.0000	3	AOE
0.0449	26.5	.0000	3	argyrol
0.0449	26.5	.0000	3	a3
0.0449	26.5	.0000	3	b/8
0.0449	26.5	.0000	3	Babbage
0.0449	26.5	.0000	3	babysitting
0.0449	26.5	.0000	3	BAE
0.0449	26.5	.0000	3	c/8
0.0449	26.5	.0000	3	CF
0.0449	26.5	.0000	3	circumferences
0.0449	26.5	.0000	3	COA
0.0449	26.5	.0000	3	coincident
0.0449	26.5	.0000	3	Consolidated
0.0449	26.5	.0000	3	COUNT
0.0449	26.5	.0000	3	DA
0.0449	26.5	.0000	3	degree-measures
0.0449	26.5	.0000	3	dekameters
0.0449	26.5	.0000	3	Developmental
0.0449	26.5	.0000	3	DGP
0.0449	26.5	.0000	3	diametral
0.0449	26.5	.0000	3	dimes'
0.0449	26.5	.0000	3	displacements
0.0449	26.5	.0000	3	dozenal
0.0449	26.5	.0000	3	druggist
0.0449	26.5	.0000	3	EOD
0.0449	26.5	.0000	3	Euclidean
0.0449	26.5	.0000	3	exemptions
0.0449	26.5	.0000	3	Friskies
0.0449	26.5	.0000	3	GHI
0.0449	26.5	.0000	3	gm
0.0449	26.5	.0000	3	Grades
0.0449	26.5	.0000	3	if-then
0.0449	26.5	.0000	3	inclusive
0.0449	26.5	.0000	3	inductive
0.0449	26.5	.0000	3	invariant
0.0449	26.5	.0000	3	IowaCity
0.0449	26.5	.0000	3	JA
0.0449	26.5	.0000	3	JKLM
0.0449	26.5	.0000	3	kg
0.0449	26.5	.0000	3	kilogram
0.0449	26.5	.0000	3	LOM
0.0449	26.5	.0000	3	Marson
0.0449	26.5	.0000	3	May's
0.0449	26.5	.0000	3	medians
0.0449	26.5	.0000	3	Mining
0.0449	26.5	.0000	3	minuend
0.0449	26.5	.0000	3	monomials
0.0449	26.5	.0000	3	n/25
0.0449	26.5	.0000	3	N/9
0.0449	26.5	.0000	3	NAVY
0.0449	26.5	.0000	3	non-Euclidean
0.0449	26.5	.0000	3	Norbert
0.0449	26.5	.0000	3	octagon
0.0449	26.5	.0000	3	OG
0.0449	26.5	.0000	3	palm-width
0.0449	26.5	.0000	3	parabola
0.0449	26.5	.0000	3	PC
0.0449	26.5	.0000	3	pentagonal
0.0449	26.5	.0000	3	PQR
0.0449	26.5	.0000	3	Programmed
0.0449	26.5	.0000	3	quarter's
0.0449	26.5	.0000	3	r/s
0.0449	26.5	.0000	3	Rabdologia
0.0449	26.5	.0000	3	repainted
0.0449	26.5	.0000	3	RP
0.0449	26.5	.0000	3	RV
0.0449	26.5	.0000	3	Squares

THE PRECEDING WORD TYPE OCCUPIES RANK 50200

U	SFI	D	F	Word Type
0.0449	26.5	.0000	3	statistician
0.0449	26.5	.0000	3	Suzanne
0.0449	26.5	.0000	3	T-shaped
0.0449	26.5	.0000	3	ten-thousand
0.0449	26.5	.0000	3	ten-thousands'
0.0449	26.5	.0000	3	tenths'
0.0449	26.5	.0000	3	tetrahedrons
0.0449	26.5	.0000	3	Thompkins
0.0449	26.5	.0000	3	thousandths'
0.0449	26.5	.0000	3	thumb-width
0.0449	26.5	.0000	3	trapezoids
0.0449	26.5	.0000	3	two-dimensional
0.0449	26.5	.0000	3	UV
0.0449	26.5	.0000	3	wide-hand
0.0449	26.5	.0000	3	worked-out
0.0449	26.5	.0000	3	x4
0.0449	26.5	.0000	3	x8
0.0449	26.5	.0000	3	037
0.0449	26.5	.0000	3	1-11
0.0449	26.5	.0000	3	1/11
0.0449	26.5	.0000	3	1/3%
0.0449	26.5	.0000	3	1f
0.0449	26.5	.0000	3	10-degree
0.0449	26.5	.0000	3	10/10
0.0449	26.5	.0000	3	12/4
0.0449	26.5	.0000	3	1241
0.0449	26.5	.0000	3	13/16
0.0449	26.5	.0000	3	14-21
0.0449	26.5	.0000	3	15/16
0.0449	26.5	.0000	3	16-ounce
0.0449	26.5	.0000	3	2-12
0.0449	26.5	.0000	3	2/10
0.0449	26.5	.0000	3	2/3x3/4
0.0449	26.5	.0000	3	2x1
0.0449	26.5	.0000	3	2x6
0.0449	26.5	.0000	3	2100
0.0449	26.5	.0000	3	231
0.0449	26.5	.0000	3	3/c
0.0449	26.5	.0000	3	3/1
0.0449	26.5	.0000	3	3x2
0.0449	26.5	.0000	3	3x5
0.0449	26.5	.0000	3	3x7
0.0449	26.5	.0000	3	3y
0.0449	26.5	.0000	3	308-unit
0.0449	26.5	.0000	3	3333
0.0449	26.5	.0000	3	376
0.0449	26.5	.0000	3	4/100
0.0449	26.5	.0000	3	4/12
0.0449	26.5	.0000	3	4/24
0.0449	26.5	.0000	3	4/7
0.0449	26.5	.0000	3	418
0.0449	26.5	.0000	3	4672
0.0449	26.5	.0000	3	482
0.0449	26.5	.0000	3	4840
0.0449	26.5	.0000	3	5(5/5)-segment
0.0449	26.5	.0000	3	5-region
0.0449	26.5	.0000	3	5-12
0.0449	26.5	.0000	3	5/1
0.0449	26.5	.0000	3	5x3
0.0449	26.5	.0000	3	504
0.0449	26.5	.0000	3	56-unit
0.0449	26.5	.0000	3	589
0.0449	26.5	.0000	3	6/7
0.0449	26.5	.0000	3	6/9
0.0449	26.5	.0000	3	6x7
0.0449	26.5	.0000	3	604
0.0449	26.5	.0000	3	612
0.0449	26.5	.0000	3	624
0.0449	26.5	.0000	3	627
0.0449	26.5	.0000	3	692
0.0449	26.5	.0000	3	7-cent
0.0449	26.5	.0000	3	7/c
0.0449	26.5	.0000	3	7/100
0.0449	26.5	.0000	3	7/11
0.0449	26.5	.0000	3	7/2
0.0449	26.5	.0000	3	7/5
0.0449	26.5	.0000	3	7/9
0.0449	26.5	.0000	3	7x9
0.0449	26.5	.0000	3	749
0.0449	26.5	.0000	3	75/100
0.0449	26.5	.0000	3	753
0.0449	26.5	.0000	3	786
0.0449	26.5	.0000	3	867
0.0449	26.5	.0000	3	873
0.0449	26.5	.0000	3	9/17
0.0449	26.5	.0000	3	9/2
0.0449	26.5	.0000	3	9/5
0.0449	26.5	.0000	3	958
0.0447	26.5	.0366	4	Himself
0.0438	26.4	.0000	4	-ular
0.0438	26.4	.0000	4	Adv-t
0.0438	26.4	.0000	4	alexandrine
0.0438	26.4	.0000	4	Bjarni
0.0438	26.4	.0000	4	ceive
0.0438	26.4	.0000	4	Chalvah
0.0438	26.4	.0000	4	childrens
0.0438	26.4	.0000	4	chronovision
0.0438	26.4	.0000	4	Crispin's
0.0438	26.4	.0000	4	denotation
0.0438	26.4	.0000	4	Gerbertovna

THE PRECEDING WORD TYPE OCCUPIES RANK 50300

U	SFI	D	F	Word Type
0.0438	26.4	.0000	4	guid
0.0438	26.4	.0000	4	Harrow
0.0438	26.4	.0000	4	inflectional
0.0438	26.4	.0000	4	Kepler's
0.0438	26.4	.0000	4	menial
0.0438	26.4	.0000	4	N-lv-adj
0.0438	26.4	.0000	4	N-v-n
0.0438	26.4	.0000	4	n't
0.0438	26.4	.0000	4	Natty
0.0438	26.4	.0000	4	one-paragraph
0.0438	26.4	.0000	4	Proofread
0.0438	26.4	.0000	4	Puzzling
0.0438	26.4	.0000	4	Sennacharib
0.0438	26.4	.0000	4	Seventy
0.0438	26.4	.0000	4	songbook
0.0438	26.4	.0000	4	steamboatman
0.0438	26.4	.0000	4	subordinators
0.0438	26.4	.0000	4	T-do
0.0438	26.4	.0000	4	Yes/No
0.0438	26.4	.0000	4	216-217
0.0434	26.4	.0000	3	abated
0.0434	26.4	.0000	3	abbe's
0.0434	26.4	.0000	3	Aegisthus
0.0434	26.4	.0000	3	AFROTC
0.0434	26.4	.0000	3	Albon
0.0434	26.4	.0000	3	allosaurus
0.0434	26.4	.0000	3	ANIMALS
0.0434	26.4	.0000	3	Aster's
0.0434	26.4	.0000	3	Astrea
0.0434	26.4	.0000	3	Ataturk's
0.0434	26.4	.0000	3	baboons'
0.0434	26.4	.0000	3	baggitaway
0.0434	26.4	.0000	3	bare-knuckle
0.0434	26.4	.0000	3	Battery
0.0434	26.4	.0000	3	Beaujeu
0.0434	26.4	.0000	3	belle
0.0434	26.4	.0000	3	Bemba
0.0434	26.4	.0000	3	Ben-Gurion
0.0434	26.4	.0000	3	Bendigeid
0.0434	26.4	.0000	3	Bettina
0.0434	26.4	.0000	3	blowholes
0.0434	26.4	.0000	3	boroughs
0.0434	26.4	.0000	3	Boula
0.0434	26.4	.0000	3	Boxhall
0.0434	26.4	.0000	3	Breezy
0.0434	26.4	.0000	3	Bronya
0.0434	26.4	.0000	3	bullwhackers
0.0434	26.4	.0000	3	cadres
0.0434	26.4	.0000	3	Cafe
0.0434	26.4	.0000	3	calamus
0.0434	26.4	.0000	3	Carpathia's
0.0434	26.4	.0000	3	Carys
0.0434	26.4	.0000	3	Cayenne
0.0434	26.4	.0000	3	cermets
0.0434	26.4	.0000	3	Chesbro
0.0434	26.4	.0000	3	Chien
0.0434	26.4	.0000	3	chivalry
0.0434	26.4	.0000	3	Chowanoc
0.0434	26.4	.0000	3	chuck-a-luck
0.0434	26.4	.0000	3	Clarks'
0.0434	26.4	.0000	3	Clinch
0.0434	26.4	.0000	3	Clyfton
0.0434	26.4	.0000	3	Cochrane
0.0434	26.4	.0000	3	Comic
0.0434	26.4	.0000	3	Commencement
0.0434	26.4	.0000	3	conservatory
0.0434	26.4	.0000	3	Crawfordsville
0.0434	26.4	.0000	3	Dandridges
0.0434	26.4	.0000	3	demonic
0.0434	26.4	.0000	3	DESERT
0.0434	26.4	.0000	3	Dora
0.0434	26.4	.0000	3	dourness
0.0434	26.4	.0000	3	dukedom
0.0434	26.4	.0000	3	Dumbo
0.0434	26.4	.0000	3	efendi
0.0434	26.4	.0000	3	Ehmke's
0.0434	26.4	.0000	3	Elva
0.0434	26.4	.0000	3	enema
0.0434	26.4	.0000	3	Englishes
0.0434	26.4	.0000	3	Faysal
0.0434	26.4	.0000	3	firebrats
0.0434	26.4	.0000	3	footnotes
0.0434	26.4	.0000	3	Franco-Prussian
0.0434	26.4	.0000	3	Fruitlands
0.0434	26.4	.0000	3	GIs
0.0434	26.4	.0000	3	ga'nzas
0.0434	26.4	.0000	3	Gamble
0.0434	26.4	.0000	3	Gaspard
0.0434	26.4	.0000	3	Glueck
0.0434	26.4	.0000	3	Gosnold
0.0434	26.4	.0000	3	Guntar
0.0434	26.4	.0000	3	Hambletonian
0.0434	26.4	.0000	3	Hawthorne's
0.0434	26.4	.0000	3	hoo-oo
0.0434	26.4	.0000	3	Hoshour
0.0434	26.4	.0000	3	Houei
0.0434	26.4	.0000	3	house-dwellers
0.0434	26.4	.0000	3	hydra's
0.0434	26.4	.0000	3	I-am-blowing
0.0434	26.4	.0000	3	instructor's

THE PRECEDING WORD TYPE OCCUPIES RANK 50400

U	SFI	D	F	Word Type
0.0434	26.4	.0000	3	Iroquoians
0.0434	26.4	.0000	3	Ismay
0.0434	26.4	.0000	3	Italian's
0.0434	26.4	.0000	3	Jencks
0.0434	26.4	.0000	3	Kalmar
0.0434	26.4	.0000	3	Lambu
0.0434	26.4	.0000	3	Lawrenceville
0.0434	26.4	.0000	3	LeMatin
0.0434	26.4	.0000	3	left-overs
0.0434	26.4	.0000	3	Leipsic
0.0434	26.4	.0000	3	Lies
0.0434	26.4	.0000	3	Lussurioso
0.0434	26.4	.0000	3	Lyda's
0.0434	26.4	.0000	3	Manzoni
0.0434	26.4	.0000	3	Margrethe
0.0434	26.4	.0000	3	Mathewson
0.0434	26.4	.0000	3	Matholwch
0.0434	26.4	.0000	3	Mawia
0.0434	26.4	.0000	3	McAlastair
0.0434	26.4	.0000	3	McKinley's
0.0434	26.4	.0000	3	Militia
0.0434	26.4	.0000	3	minutemen
0.0434	26.4	.0000	3	Miranda's
0.0434	26.4	.0000	3	Mors
0.0434	26.4	.0000	3	mutuels
0.0434	26.4	.0000	3	M18
0.0434	26.4	.0000	3	M4
0.0434	26.4	.0000	3	NaMukonda
0.0434	26.4	.0000	3	Osocan
0.0434	26.4	.0000	3	Ottawas
0.0434	26.4	.0000	3	outfeed
0.0434	26.4	.0000	3	Panhards
0.0434	26.4	.0000	3	Parris
0.0434	26.4	.0000	3	Pati
0.0434	26.4	.0000	3	Piato
0.0434	26.4	.0000	3	pieman
0.0434	26.4	.0000	3	plainsmen
0.0434	26.4	.0000	3	planaria
0.0434	26.4	.0000	3	poling
0.0434	26.4	.0000	3	Pollie
0.0434	26.4	.0000	3	Polos
0.0434	26.4	.0000	3	Poplar
0.0434	26.4	.0000	3	porphyry
0.0434	26.4	.0000	3	prick'd
0.0434	26.4	.0000	3	promethea
0.0434	26.4	.0000	3	prometheas
0.0434	26.4	.0000	3	Queensberry
0.0434	26.4	.0000	3	Quonset
0.0434	26.4	.0000	3	Rathmann
0.0434	26.4	.0000	3	Raw-hunt
0.0434	26.4	.0000	3	regatta
0.0434	26.4	.0000	3	Rhiannon
0.0434	26.4	.0000	3	Rit
0.0434	26.4	.0000	3	Roanokes
0.0434	26.4	.0000	3	robins'
0.0434	26.4	.0000	3	Roquerre
0.0434	26.4	.0000	3	Rumley
0.0434	26.4	.0000	3	Sac
0.0434	26.4	.0000	3	Salih
0.0434	26.4	.0000	3	Sammie
0.0434	26.4	.0000	3	Sceaux
0.0434	26.4	.0000	3	Scribner's
0.0434	26.4	.0000	3	Scrooby
0.0434	26.4	.0000	3	semi-automatic
0.0434	26.4	.0000	3	Sendall's
0.0434	26.4	.0000	3	Sepia
0.0434	26.4	.0000	3	sheepfold
0.0434	26.4	.0000	3	sienna
0.0434	26.4	.0000	3	Simenon
0.0434	26.4	.0000	3	sprinters
0.0434	26.4	.0000	3	Spurio
0.0434	26.4	.0000	3	Struthers
0.0434	26.4	.0000	3	thecodont
0.0434	26.4	.0000	3	Theodore's
0.0434	26.4	.0000	3	Theodore's
0.0434	26.4	.0000	3	Tidewater
0.0434	26.4	.0000	3	Timber
0.0434	26.4	.0000	3	Tomocomo
0.0434	26.4	.0000	3	Touch-and-Tell
0.0434	26.4	.0000	3	Tray
0.0434	26.4	.0000	3	Trois-Freres
0.0434	26.4	.0000	3	Tyrants
0.0434	26.4	.0000	3	Upson
0.0434	26.4	.0000	3	vanishing-point
0.0434	26.4	.0000	3	versus
0.0434	26.4	.0000	3	Wampum
0.0434	26.4	.0000	3	WHACK
0.0434	26.4	.0000	3	Yama-King
0.0434	26.4	.0000	3	youpi-ya
0.0434	26.4	.0000	3	Z **
0.0434	26.4	.0000	3	Zephyrus
0.0434	26.4	.0000	3	Zink
0.0434	26.4	.0000	3	120-pound
0.0429	26.3	.0000	4	Andau
0.0429	26.3	.0000	4	Arata
0.0429	26.3	.0000	4	Blade
0.0429	26.3	.0000	4	Buscerck
0.0429	26.3	.0000	4	Capshaw
0.0429	26.3	.0000	4	CARMICHAEL
0.0429	26.3	.0000	4	Carton

THE PRECEDING WORD TYPE OCCUPIES RANK 50500

U	SFI	D	F	Word Type
0.0429	26.3	.0000	4	COBWEB
0.0429	26.3	.0000	4	Doone
0.0429	26.3	.0000	4	ELIZABETH
0.0429	26.3	.0000	4	Ellenwood
0.0429	26.3	.0000	4	Eunice
0.0429	26.3	.0000	4	Eurylochos
0.0429	26.3	.0000	4	Glick

U	SFI	D	F	Word Type
0.0429	26.3	.0000	4	grannies
0.0429	26.3	.0000	4	haybales
0.0429	26.3	.0000	4	Hoffer
0.0429	26.3	.0000	4	hoppity-hop
0.0429	26.3	.0000	4	Houssain
0.0429	26.3	.0000	4	Hub-bub
0.0429	26.3	.0000	4	Inkslinger
0.0429	26.3	.0000	4	Karasik
0.0429	26.3	.0000	4	Lenni
0.0429	26.3	.0000	4	Lestrade
0.0429	26.3	.0000	4	livingroom
0.0429	26.3	.0000	4	Lonnie's
0.0429	26.3	.0000	4	LOVER
0.0429	26.3	.0000	4	Ludlow
0.0429	26.3	.0000	4	Lysander
0.0429	26.3	.0000	4	Manheim
0.0429	26.3	.0000	4	MANSERVANT
0.0429	26.3	.0000	4	Maple-Leaf
0.0429	26.3	.0000	4	Melanthios
0.0429	26.3	.0000	4	Murdle's
0.0429	26.3	.0000	4	Mustardseed
0.0429	26.3	.0000	4	MUSTARDSEED
0.0429	26.3	.0000	4	Nace
0.0429	26.3	.0000	4	NARRATOR
0.0429	26.3	.0000	4	NELS
0.0429	26.3	.0000	4	PEASEBLOSSOM
0.0429	26.3	.0000	4	Phaethon
0.0429	26.3	.0000	4	Pross
0.0429	26.3	.0000	4	Radius
0.0429	26.3	.0000	4	Randal
0.0429	26.3	.0000	4	Robie
0.0429	26.3	.0000	4	Scylla
0.0429	26.3	.0000	4	SECOND
0.0429	26.3	.0000	4	SETSU
0.0429	26.3	.0000	4	Setsu
0.0429	26.3	.0000	4	Sinkfield
0.0429	26.3	.0000	4	Snaggs
0.0429	26.3	.0000	4	Tabor's
0.0429	26.3	.0000	4	Tellson's
0.0429	26.3	.0000	4	THESEUS
0.0429	26.3	.0000	4	Tobby
0.0429	26.3	.0000	4	Valance
0.0429	26.3	.0000	4	weathercock
0.0429	26.3	.0000	4	wiles
0.0429	26.3	.0000	4	Willowby
0.0429	26.3	.0000	4	wine-shop
0.0429	26.3	.0000	4	WINKLER
0.0429	26.3	.0000	4	Yaol
0.0429	26.3	.0000	4	Yengwe
0.0429	26.3	.0000	4	Zurbaran
0.0419	26.2	.0000	4	allantois
0.0419	26.2	.0000	4	Apr
0.0419	26.2	.0000	4	arapaima
0.0419	26.2	.0000	4	avalanches
0.0419	26.2	.0000	4	Barlowe
0.0419	26.2	.0000	4	Basket
0.0419	26.2	.0000	4	Boas
0.0419	26.2	.0000	4	boxwood
0.0419	26.2	.0000	4	carey
0.0419	26.2	.0000	4	chronology
0.0419	26.2	.0000	4	Crawshaw
0.0419	26.2	.0000	4	Davao
0.0419	26.2	.0000	4	diagnostic
0.0419	26.2	.0000	4	Didelphis
0.0419	26.2	.0000	4	Domitian
0.0419	26.2	.0000	4	Dorpat
0.0419	26.2	.0000	4	Dubois
0.0419	26.2	.0000	4	Dusicyon
0.0419	26.2	.0000	4	Economy
0.0419	26.2	.0000	4	eightfold
0.0419	26.2	.0000	4	electromagnetism
0.0419	26.2	.0000	4	emission
0.0419	26.2	.0000	4	empirical
0.0419	26.2	.0000	4	energized
0.0419	26.2	.0000	4	equal-area
0.0419	26.2	.0000	4	Forssmann
0.0419	26.2	.0000	4	Frankish
0.0419	26.2	.0000	4	Gambia
0.0419	26.2	.0000	4	gasolines
0.0419	26.2	.0000	4	Gazetteer-Index
0.0419	26.2	.0000	4	Gell-Mann
0.0419	26.2	.0000	4	handset
0.0419	26.2	.0000	4	human-factors
0.0419	26.2	.0000	4	ichthyosaurs
0.0419	26.2	.0000	4	injunctions
0.0419	26.2	.0000	4	Jocasta
0.0419	26.2	.0000	4	Kherson
0.0419	26.2	.0000	4	Laius
0.0419	26.2	.0000	4	Maritime
0.0419	26.2	.0000	4	Neotropical
0.0419	26.2	.0000	4	nonscientist
0.0419	26.2	.0000	4	north-central
0.0419	26.2	.0000	4	overburden

THE PRECEDING WORD TYPE OCCUPIES RANK 50600

U	SFI	D	F	Word Type
0.0419	26.2	.0000	4	Pantanal
0.0419	26.2	.0000	4	Patagonian
0.0419	26.2	.0000	4	Quezon
0.0419	26.2	.0000	4	ritualistic
0.0419	26.2	.0000	4	saltpeter
0.0419	26.2	.0000	4	sedges
0.0419	26.2	.0000	4	Slovenian
0.0419	26.2	.0000	4	Taft-Hartley
0.0419	26.2	.0000	4	tetrad
0.0419	26.2	.0000	4	THOMSON
0.0419	26.2	.0000	4	thumb-sucking
0.0419	26.2	.0000	4	turgor
0.0419	26.2	.0000	4	vangs
0.0419	26.2	.0000	4	Zamboanga
0.0406	26.1	.0000	5	hieroglyphic
0.0406	26.1	.0000	5	il
0.0406	26.1	.0000	5	nt
0.0406	26.1	.0000	5	pre
0.0406	26.1	.0000	5	Rulemaker's
0.0406	26.1	.0000	5	thr
0.0406	26.1	.0000	5	vowel-consonant-silent
0.0406	26.1	.0000	5	zhen**
0.0406	26.1	.0000	5	19-23
0.0406	26.1	.0000	5	9-10
0.0404	26.1	.0000	5	'mid
0.0404	26.1	.0000	5	Arirang
0.0404	26.1	.0000	5	bamboula
0.0404	26.1	.0000	5	Beckmesser
0.0404	26.1	.0000	5	bela
0.0404	26.1	.0000	5	Bourree
0.0404	26.1	.0000	16	chamfer
0.0404	26.1	.0000	5	chording
0.0404	26.1	.0000	5	contralto
0.0404	26.1	.0000	5	Cowell
0.0404	26.1	.0000	5	Danse
0.0404	26.1	.0000	5	deFalla
0.0404	26.1	.0000	5	downbeat
0.0404	26.1	.0000	5	duma
0.0404	26.1	.0000	5	Eisteddfod
0.0404	26.1	.0000	5	Frere
0.0404	26.1	.0000	5	Hanukkah
0.0404	26.1	.0000	5	harmonization
0.0404	26.1	.0000	5	harmonized
0.0404	26.1	.0000	5	Kodaly
0.0404	26.1	.0000	5	Menotti
0.0404	26.1	.0000	5	Moldau
0.0404	26.1	.0000	5	Moravians
0.0404	26.1	.0000	5	Nowell
0.0404	26.1	.0000	5	oompah
0.0404	26.1	.0000	5	Op
0.0404	26.1	.0000	5	Phonograph
0.0404	26.1	.0000	5	quintet
0.0404	26.1	.0000	16	rabbet
0.0404	26.1	.0000	5	Raggletaggletown
0.0404	26.1	.0000	5	retrograde
0.0404	26.1	.0000	5	Rimsky-Korsakov
0.0404	26.1	.0000	5	Sibelius
0.0404	26.1	.0000	5	Skye
0.0404	26.1	.0000	5	soloist
0.0404	26.1	.0000	5	Sonata
0.0404	26.1	.0000	5	sonata-form
0.0404	26.1	.0000	5	Tainter
0.0404	26.1	.0000	5	timbres
0.0404	26.1	.0000	5	Torah
0.0404	26.1	.0000	5	toreador
0.0404	26.1	.0000	5	weas'ly
0.0394	26.0	.0000	2	adenine
0.0394	26.0	.0000	2	AFFECT
0.0394	26.0	.0000	2	Ag
0.0394	26.0	.0000	2	Agassiz'
0.0394	26.0	.0000	2	ailerons
0.0394	26.0	.0000	2	amoebic
0.0394	26.0	.0000	2	amphibole
0.0394	26.0	.0000	2	Andreas
0.0394	26.0	.0000	2	angle-measuring
0.0394	26.0	.0000	2	anther
0.0394	26.0	.0000	2	anti-particles
0.0394	26.0	.0000	2	antibacterial
0.0394	26.0	.0000	2	antibody
0.0394	26.0	.0000	2	antigen
0.0394	26.0	.0000	2	apatite
0.0394	26.0	.0000	2	apertures
0.0394	26.0	.0000	2	Archeozoic
0.0394	26.0	.0000	2	arginine
0.0394	26.0	.0000	2	arteriosclerosis
0.0394	26.0	.0000	2	asexual
0.0394	26.0	.0000	2	atom's
0.0394	26.0	.0000	2	audio-frequency
0.0394	26.0	.0000	2	Axelrod
0.0394	26.0	.0000	2	axons
0.0394	26.0	.0000	2	Azaleas
0.0394	26.0	.0000	2	B-complex
0.0394	26.0	.0000	2	baking-soda
0.0394	26.0	.0000	2	barometric
0.0394	26.0	.0000	2	batholiths
0.0394	26.0	.0000	2	bee-flower
0.0394	26.0	.0000	2	Beijerinck
0.0394	26.0	.0000	2	Bessel
0.0394	26.0	.0000	2	bicuspids
0.0394	26.0	.0000	2	bilateral

THE PRECEDING WORD TYPE OCCUPIES RANK 50700

U	SFI	D	F	Word Type
0.0394	26.0	.0000	2	biochemical
0.0394	26.0	.0000	2	bite-size
0.0394	26.0	.0000	2	Blizzard
0.0394	26.0	.0000	2	blowout
0.0394	26.0	.0000	2	BOMEX
0.0394	26.0	.0000	2	Borealis
0.0394	26.0	.0000	2	botanically
0.0394	26.0	.0000	2	branchlike
0.0394	26.0	.0000	2	brewers
0.0394	26.0	.0000	2	bricklayer
0.0394	26.0	.0000	2	bromthymol
0.0394	26.0	.0000	2	bronzite
0.0394	26.0	.0000	2	burdock
0.0394	26.0	.0000	2	Ca
0.0394	26.0	.0000	2	CaO
0.0394	26.0	.0000	2	Canaveral
0.0394	26.0	.0000	2	cataloged
0.0394	26.0	.0000	2	cephalothorax
0.0394	26.0	.0000	2	Chandrasekhar
0.0394	26.0	.0000	2	chemosynthetic
0.0394	26.0	.0000	2	chernozems
0.0394	26.0	.0000	2	chlorides
0.0394	26.0	.0000	2	chlorination
0.0394	26.0	.0000	2	ciliated
0.0394	26.0	.0000	2	cloudlike
0.0394	26.0	.0000	2	coatings
0.0394	26.0	.0000	2	cocci
0.0394	26.0	.0000	2	cocktails
0.0394	26.0	.0000	2	coleus
0.0394	26.0	.0000	2	computes
0.0394	26.0	.0000	2	comsumption
0.0394	26.0	.0000	2	concavity
0.0394	26.0	.0000	2	condenser
0.0394	26.0	.0000	2	constancy
0.0394	26.0	.0000	2	constellarium
0.0394	26.0	.0000	2	contractile
0.0394	26.0	.0000	2	converters
0.0394	26.0	.0000	2	coring
0.0394	26.0	.0000	2	cottontail's
0.0394	26.0	.0000	2	cowlick
0.0394	26.0	.0000	2	creeper
0.0394	26.0	.0000	2	cribs
0.0394	26.0	.0000	2	Crick
0.0394	26.0	.0000	2	Crookes
0.0394	26.0	.0000	2	Cruickshank
0.0394	26.0	.0000	2	crustacean
0.0394	26.0	.0000	2	crystal-radio
0.0394	26.0	.0000	2	cud-chewing
0.0394	26.0	.0000	2	cuprammonium
0.0394	26.0	.0000	2	cushioned
0.0394	26.0	.0000	2	Cygnus
0.0394	26.0	.0000	2	cytosine
0.0394	26.0	.0000	2	C3H
0.0394	26.0	.0000	2	daphnias
0.0394	26.0	.0000	2	dark-line
0.0394	26.0	.0000	2	dastardly
0.0394	26.0	.0000	2	deadened
0.0394	26.0	.0000	2	deferent
0.0394	26.0	.0000	2	deflation
0.0394	26.0	.0000	2	deforming
0.0394	26.0	.0000	2	deoxyribose
0.0394	26.0	.0000	2	destinies
0.0394	26.0	.0000	2	diabase
0.0394	26.0	.0000	2	diastase
0.0394	26.0	.0000	2	diatomaceous
0.0394	26.0	.0000	2	diffusing
0.0394	26.0	.0000	2	digester
0.0394	26.0	.0000	2	dihydrogen
0.0394	26.0	.0000	2	Diphda
0.0394	26.0	.0000	2	disease-causing
0.0394	26.0	.0000	2	Dissectograph
0.0394	26.0	.0000	2	distillate
0.0394	26.0	.0000	2	dodder
0.0394	26.0	.0000	2	DON'T
0.0394	26.0	.0000	2	Doppler
0.0394	26.0	.0000	2	dosimeter
0.0394	26.0	.0000	2	downrange
0.0394	26.0	.0000	2	drainpipes
0.0394	26.0	.0000	2	droppers
0.0394	26.0	.0000	2	dry-cell
0.0394	26.0	.0000	2	duckweeds
0.0394	26.0	.0000	2	ductless
0.0394	26.0	.0000	2	dykes
0.0394	26.0	.0000	2	D1
0.0394	26.0	.0000	2	ecologist's
0.0394	26.0	.0000	2	Eddington's
0.0394	26.0	.0000	2	Ehrlich
0.0394	26.0	.0000	2	electric-light
0.0394	26.0	.0000	2	element's
0.0394	26.0	.0000	2	elodea
0.0394	26.0	.0000	2	embryological
0.0394	26.0	.0000	2	endoskeleton
0.0394	26.0	.0000	2	endoskeletons
0.0394	26.0	.0000	2	energizers
0.0394	26.0	.0000	2	energy-producing
0.0394	26.0	.0000	2	Enif
0.0394	26.0	.0000	2	epicycle
0.0394	26.0	.0000	2	epiphytes
0.0394	26.0	.0000	2	equal-sized
0.0394	26.0	.0000	2	equalized

THE PRECEDING WORD TYPE OCCUPIES RANK 50800

U	SFI	D	F	Word Type
0.0394	26.0	.0000	2	Equus
0.0394	26.0	.0000	2	Erosion
0.0394	26.0	.0000	2	erosional
0.0394	26.0	.0000	2	Essa
0.0394	26.0	.0000	2	estrogen
0.0394	26.0	.0000	2	eye-care
0.0394	26.0	.0000	2	faster-moving
0.0394	26.0	.0000	2	FeO
0.0394	26.0	.0000	2	fetal
0.0394	26.0	.0000	2	fibril
0.0394	26.0	.0000	2	filmstrip
0.0394	26.0	.0000	2	fissionable
0.0394	26.0	.0000	2	flagellated
0.0394	26.0	.0000	2	Fleming's
0.0394	26.0	.0000	2	flycatchers
0.0394	26.0	.0000	2	fohn
0.0394	26.0	.0000	2	foodmaking
0.0394	26.0	.0000	2	foot-and-mouth
0.0394	26.0	.0000	2	foraminifers
0.0394	26.0	.0000	2	fossil-hunting
0.0394	26.0	.0000	2	Frisch
0.0394	26.0	.0000	2	Gacrux
0.0394	26.0	.0000	2	galena
0.0394	26.0	.0000	2	gasses
0.0394	26.0	.0000	2	gastrovascular
0.0394	26.0	.0000	2	geneticists
0.0394	26.0	.0000	2	geologist's
0.0394	26.0	.0000	2	glacier's
0.0394	26.0	.0000	2	Golgi
0.0394	26.0	.0000	2	grafted
0.0394	26.0	.0000	2	grasshopper's
0.0394	26.0	.0000	2	great-great-great-great**
0.0394	26.0	.0000	2	Grote
0.0394	26.0	.0000	2	guanine
0.0394	26.0	.0000	2	gulley
0.0394	26.0	.0000	2	gummite
0.0394	26.0	.0000	2	hails
0.0394	26.0	.0000	2	half-ball
0.0394	26.0	.0000	2	half-squat
0.0394	26.0	.0000	2	handrails
0.0394	26.0	.0000	2	Head-Tilt
0.0394	26.0	.0000	2	headgear
0.0394	26.0	.0000	2	high-calorie
0.0394	26.0	.0000	2	homotransplantation
0.0394	26.0	.0000	2	hormone-producing
0.0394	26.0	.0000	2	Humason
0.0394	26.0	.0000	2	Hydra
0.0394	26.0	.0000	2	hydras
0.0394	26.0	.0000	2	hydrate
0.0394	26.0	.0000	2	hydride
0.0394	26.0	.0000	2	Hydrion
0.0394	26.0	.0000	2	hydrogen-1
0.0394	26.0	.0000	2	hydrogen-3
0.0394	26.0	.0000	2	hydrolysis
0.0394	26.0	.0000	2	hydrometer
0.0394	26.0	.0000	2	hygroscopic
0.0394	26.0	.0000	2	hypothalamus
0.0394	26.0	.0000	2	i%
0.0394	26.0	.0000	2	ice-choked
0.0394	26.0	.0000	2	IF
0.0394	26.0	.0000	2	impacted
0.0394	26.0	.0000	2	incinerators
0.0394	26.0	.0000	2	incompletely
0.0394	26.0	.0000	2	infusible
0.0394	26.0	.0000	2	Ingenhousz
0.0394	26.0	.0000	2	interactions
0.0394	26.0	.0000	2	interfaces
0.0394	26.0	.0000	2	interschool
0.0394	26.0	.0000	2	invents
0.0394	26.0	.0000	2	ionize
0.0394	26.0	.0000	2	irradiated
0.0394	26.0	.0000	2	isobar
0.0394	26.0	.0000	2	Iwanovski
0.0394	26.0	.0000	2	Jansky
0.0394	26.0	.0000	2	jaywalking
0.0394	26.0	.0000	2	Jeans
0.0394	26.0	.0000	2	JoAnn's
0.0394	26.0	.0000	2	kernite
0.0394	26.0	.0000	2	Kinetic
0.0394	26.0	.0000	2	kingsnake
0.0394	26.0	.0000	2	kingsnakes
0.0394	26.0	.0000	2	kittens'
0.0394	26.0	.0000	2	Konigsberg
0.0394	26.0	.0000	2	Koons
0.0394	26.0	.0000	2	lactation
0.0394	26.0	.0000	2	laminae
0.0394	26.0	.0000	2	lengthens
0.0394	26.0	.0000	2	light-sensitive
0.0394	26.0	.0000	2	limestones
0.0394	26.0	.0000	2	limonite
0.0394	26.0	.0000	2	Linnaean
0.0394	26.0	.0000	2	Loffler
0.0394	26.0	.0000	2	low-energy
0.0394	26.0	.0000	2	low-frequency
0.0394	26.0	.0000	2	Loyola
0.0394	26.0	.0000	2	lunology
0.0394	26.0	.0000	2	Magnetes
0.0394	26.0	.0000	2	Mammalia
0.0394	26.0	.0000	2	Manson
0.0394	26.0	.0000	2	Marcello

THE PRECEDING WORD TYPE OCCUPIES RANK 50900

U	SFI	D	F	Word Type
0.0394	26.0	.0000	2	Markab
0.0394	26.0	.0000	2	meanders
0.0394	26.0	.0000	2	meltwater
0.0394	26.0	.0000	2	Mendeleyeff
0.0394	26.0	.0000	2	meristematic
0.0394	26.0	.0000	2	message-carrying
0.0394	26.0	.0000	2	metalloids
0.0394	26.0	.0000	2	microbiologists
0.0394	26.0	.0000	2	microorganism
0.0394	26.0	.0000	2	midrib
0.0394	26.0	.0000	2	millibars
0.0394	26.0	.0000	2	milt
0.0394	26.0	.0000	2	mountain-building
0.0394	26.0	.0000	2	Mousetail
0.0394	26.0	.0000	2	multistage
0.0394	26.0	.0000	2	mycelium
0.0394	26.0	.0000	2	N-pole
0.0394	26.0	.0000	2	N-type
0.0394	26.0	.0000	2	Needham's
0.0394	26.0	.0000	2	neutrino
0.0394	26.0	.0000	2	Newcomb
0.0394	26.0	.0000	2	Nicholl
0.0394	26.0	.0000	2	nighthawks
0.0394	26.0	.0000	2	nitrogen-containing
0.0394	26.0	.0000	2	nonskid
0.0394	26.0	.0000	2	nonvascular
0.0394	26.0	.0000	2	nosepiece
0.0394	26.0	.0000	2	notatum
0.0394	26.0	.0000	2	NPN
0.0394	26.0	.0000	2	nucleotide
0.0394	26.0	.0000	2	oceanographer
0.0394	26.0	.0000	2	ocular
0.0394	26.0	.0000	2	odd-toed
0.0394	26.0	.0000	2	ohm
0.0394	26.0	.0000	2	oil-soluble
0.0394	26.0	.0000	2	ointments
0.0394	26.0	.0000	2	olive-jar
0.0394	26.0	.0000	2	Olmsted
0.0394	26.0	.0000	2	one-holed
0.0394	26.0	.0000	2	ophthalmologist
0.0394	26.0	.0000	2	orchard-owners
0.0394	26.0	.0000	2	ornithine
0.0394	26.0	.0000	2	orthodontist
0.0394	26.0	.0000	2	oscillations
0.0394	26.0	.0000	2	overlain
0.0394	26.0	.0000	2	overlies
0.0394	26.0	.0000	2	ovulation
0.0394	26.0	.0000	2	ovule
0.0394	26.0	.0000	2	papillae
0.0394	26.0	.0000	2	parasitism
0.0394	26.0	.0000	2	parasitizes
0.0394	26.0	.0000	2	parasitizing
0.0394	26.0	.0000	2	Pauli
0.0394	26.0	.0000	2	Pelton
0.0394	26.0	.0000	2	Pemaquid
0.0394	26.0	.0000	2	pen-knife
0.0394	26.0	.0000	2	perceiver
0.0394	26.0	.0000	2	Perceiving
0.0394	26.0	.0000	2	perceptions
0.0394	26.0	.0000	2	periosteum
0.0394	26.0	.0000	2	petal-like
0.0394	26.0	.0000	2	petunia
0.0394	26.0	.0000	2	phalanges
0.0394	26.0	.0000	2	phenolphthalein
0.0394	26.0	.0000	2	philosopher-scientists
0.0394	26.0	.0000	2	phosphorescence
0.0394	26.0	.0000	2	phosphors
0.0394	26.0	.0000	2	Piccard
0.0394	26.0	.0000	2	Piezo
0.0394	26.0	.0000	2	Piezo-electric
0.0394	26.0	.0000	2	pinacoid

U	SFI	D	F	Word Type
0.0394	26.0	.0000	2	Pisces
0.0394	26.0	.0000	2	piston-and-cylinder
0.0394	26.0	.0000	2	planetoid
0.0394	26.0	.0000	2	planktonburgers
0.0394	26.0	.0000	2	plastid
0.0394	26.0	.0000	2	PNP
0.0394	26.0	.0000	2	podzols
0.0394	26.0	.0000	2	pollen-carriers
0.0394	26.0	.0000	2	polyhedron
0.0394	26.0	.0000	2	polymer
0.0394	26.0	.0000	2	preventable
0.0394	26.0	.0000	2	prong
0.0394	26.0	.0000	2	Protist
0.0394	26.0	.0000	2	Protozoa
0.0394	26.0	.0000	2	providers
0.0394	26.0	.0000	2	pseudopods
0.0394	26.0	.0000	2	purine
0.0394	26.0	.0000	2	Pushups
0.0394	26.0	.0000	2	pyrosoma
0.0394	26.0	.0000	2	pyroxene
0.0394	26.0	.0000	2	quadrates
0.0394	26.0	.0000	2	quarantines
0.0394	26.0	.0000	2	quasars
0.0394	26.0	.0000	2	radioisotope
0.0394	26.0	.0000	2	rafflesias
0.0394	26.0	.0000	2	ramjet
0.0394	26.0	.0000	2	Rana
0.0394	26.0	.0000	2	ratproof
0.0394	26.0	.0000	2	Reber

THE PRECEDING WORD TYPE OCCUPIES RANK 51000

U	SFI	D	F	Word Type
0.0394	26.0	.0000	2	recombined
0.0394	26.0	.0000	2	rectum
0.0394	26.0	.0000	2	reentrant
0.0394	26.0	.0000	2	reminiscing
0.0394	26.0	.0000	2	Resuscitation
0.0394	26.0	.0000	2	rhizopods
0.0394	26.0	.0000	2	Rhododendrons
0.0394	26.0	.0000	2	ribonucleic
0.0394	26.0	.0000	2	ring-like
0.0394	26.0	.0000	2	Rotation
0.0394	26.0	.0000	2	sabre-toothed
0.0394	26.0	.0000	2	saguaro
0.0394	26.0	.0000	2	sandstones
0.0394	26.0	.0000	2	SATELLITES
0.0394	26.0	.0000	2	scaly-winged
0.0394	26.0	.0000	2	Scheat
0.0394	26.0	.0000	2	Scorpio
0.0394	26.0	.0000	2	scrapings
0.0394	26.0	.0000	2	self-care
0.0394	26.0	.0000	2	Selman
0.0394	26.0	.0000	2	senility
0.0394	26.0	.0000	2	septum
0.0394	26.0	.0000	2	sewage-disposal
0.0394	26.0	.0000	2	sferics
0.0394	26.0	.0000	2	shatters
0.0394	26.0	.0000	2	silts
0.0394	26.0	.0000	2	single-cell
0.0394	26.0	.0000	2	sleets
0.0394	26.0	.0000	2	slower-moving
0.0394	26.0	.0000	2	Soccer
0.0394	26.0	.0000	2	softeners
0.0394	26.0	.0000	2	Solid
0.0394	26.0	.0000	2	solvents
0.0394	26.0	.0000	2	sound-maker
0.0394	26.0	.0000	2	sperms
0.0394	26.0	.0000	2	sphincter
0.0394	26.0	.0000	2	spinel
0.0394	26.0	.0000	2	spirilla
0.0394	26.0	.0000	2	spread-out
0.0394	26.0	.0000	2	Squat
0.0394	26.0	.0000	2	stabilized
0.0394	26.0	.0000	2	stalklike
0.0394	26.0	.0000	2	starling
0.0394	26.0	.0000	2	staurolite
0.0394	26.0	.0000	2	sterilization
0.0394	26.0	.0000	2	straight-winged
0.0394	26.0	.0000	2	submetallic
0.0394	26.0	.0000	2	subparticles
0.0394	26.0	.0000	2	subphyla
0.0394	26.0	.0000	2	substations
0.0394	26.0	.0000	2	sugar-rich
0.0394	26.0	.0000	2	sulfa
0.0394	26.0	.0000	2	sumach
0.0394	26.0	.0000	2	SUN
0.0394	26.0	.0000	2	supercold
0.0394	26.0	.0000	2	superheated
0.0394	26.0	.0000	2	suspensions
0.0394	26.0	.0000	2	sweeteners
0.0394	26.0	.0000	2	swellings
0.0394	26.0	.0000	2	symbiotic
0.0394	26.0	.0000	2	Tabulae
0.0394	26.0	.0000	2	tagboard
0.0394	26.0	.0000	2	THEN
0.0394	26.0	.0000	2	three-cell
0.0394	26.0	.0000	2	three-layer
0.0394	26.0	.0000	2	thrust-to-weight
0.0394	26.0	.0000	2	Thuillier
0.0394	26.0	.0000	2	tourmaline
0.0394	26.0	.0000	2	tourniquet
0.0394	26.0	.0000	2	trichocysts
0.0394	26.0	.0000	2	trioxide
0.0394	26.0	.0000	2	triphylite
0.0394	26.0	.0000	2	tropism
0.0394	26.0	.0000	2	tsunami
0.0394	26.0	.0000	2	turbojet
0.0394	26.0	.0000	2	twin's
0.0394	26.0	.0000	2	typhus
0.0394	26.0	.0000	2	uninflated
0.0394	26.0	.0000	2	universes
0.0394	26.0	.0000	2	unloved
0.0394	26.0	.0000	2	unwinds
0.0394	26.0	.0000	2	upward-moving
0.0394	26.0	.0000	2	uterine
0.0394	26.0	.0000	2	valence
0.0394	26.0	.0000	2	varve
0.0394	26.0	.0000	2	vaulter
0.0394	26.0	.0000	2	veers
0.0394	26.0	.0000	2	vegetable-fruit
0.0394	26.0	.0000	2	ventriloquists
0.0394	26.0	.0000	2	villi
0.0394	26.0	.0000	2	vitamin-D
0.0394	26.0	.0000	2	vivianite
0.0394	26.0	.0000	2	voltaic
0.0394	26.0	.0000	2	vulcanism
0.0394	26.0	.0000	2	wasp's
0.0394	26.0	.0000	2	WEATHER
0.0394	26.0	.0000	2	well-ventilated
0.0394	26.0	.0000	2	wheel-shaped
0.0394	26.0	.0000	2	white-footed
0.0394	26.0	.0000	2	Windmill

THE PRECEDING WORD TYPE OCCUPIES RANK 51100

U	SFI	D	F	Word Type
0.0394	26.0	.0000	2	woodpeckers'
0.0394	26.0	.0000	2	ww
0.0394	26.0	.0000	2	xanthate
0.0394	26.0	.0000	2	zinc-coated
0.0394	26.0	.0000	2	Zn
0.0394	26.0	.0000	2	000th
0.0394	26.0	.0000	2	13-4
0.0394	26.0	.0000	2	14-1
0.0394	26.0	.0000	2	14-10B
0.0394	26.0	.0000	2	14-6
0.0394	26.0	.0000	2	1642-1727
0.0394	26.0	.0000	2	1677
0.0394	26.0	.0000	2	19-12
0.0394	26.0	.0000	2	22-13
0.0394	26.0	.0000	2	26-10
0.0394	26.0	.0000	2	26-12
0.0394	26.0	.0000	2	3Li61H2
0.0394	26.0	.0000	2	30c
0.0394	26.0	.0000	2	33-12
0.0394	26.0	.0000	2	4300
0.0394	26.0	.0000	2	5-20
0.0394	26.0	.0000	2	55-pound
0.0394	26.0	.0000	2	7-gram
0.0394	26.0	.0000	2	7-1
0.0394	26.0	.0000	2	7-19
0.0394	26.0	.0000	2	7-4
0.0394	26.0	.0000	2	8-18
0.0394	26.0	.0000	2	92U238
0.0389	25.9	.0000	2	a-workin'
0.0389	25.9	.0000	2	AAA
0.0389	25.9	.0000	2	abbots
0.0389	25.9	.0000	2	Afars
0.0389	25.9	.0000	2	afterlife
0.0389	25.9	.0000	2	agave
0.0389	25.9	.0000	2	Aiku
0.0389	25.9	.0000	2	all-powerful
0.0389	25.9	.0000	2	all-water
0.0389	25.9	.0000	2	Amarillo
0.0389	25.9	.0000	2	Ambassadors
0.0389	25.9	.0000	2	amending
0.0389	25.9	.0000	2	Amenemhet
0.0389	25.9	.0000	2	Amhara
0.0389	25.9	.0000	2	Anatolian
0.0389	25.9	.0000	2	Ancestors
0.0389	25.9	.0000	2	Antalya
0.0389	25.9	.0000	2	anti-Chinese
0.0389	25.9	.0000	2	anti-slavery
0.0389	25.9	.0000	2	appointee
0.0389	25.9	.0000	2	Aqueduct
0.0389	25.9	.0000	2	Ar-luk
0.0389	25.9	.0000	2	archbishops
0.0389	25.9	.0000	2	Arequipa
0.0389	25.9	.0000	2	assessor
0.0389	25.9	.0000	2	asu
0.0389	25.9	.0000	2	attainder
0.0389	25.9	.0000	2	automobile-assembly
0.0389	25.9	.0000	2	Avignon
0.0389	25.9	.0000	2	Bahrein
0.0389	25.9	.0000	2	Bamboo
0.0389	25.9	.0000	2	bankruptcy
0.0389	25.9	.0000	2	barite
0.0389	25.9	.0000	2	Basins
0.0389	25.9	.0000	2	Battalion
0.0389	25.9	.0000	2	Bautista
0.0389	25.9	.0000	2	beet-sugar
0.0389	25.9	.0000	2	Bismarck
0.0389	25.9	.0000	2	Blessings
0.0389	25.9	.0000	2	blowpipe
0.0389	25.9	.0000	2	Bogana's
0.0389	25.9	.0000	2	bolstered
0.0389	25.9	.0000	2	bondsmen
0.0389	25.9	.0000	2	Bonus
0.0389	25.9	.0000	2	boot-shaped
0.0389	25.9	.0000	2	Boundaries
0.0389	25.9	.0000	2	braseros
0.0389	25.9	.0000	2	briefs
0.0389	25.9	.0000	2	Brugge
0.0389	25.9	.0000	2	Brunei
0.0389	25.9	.0000	2	Buchanan's
0.0389	25.9	.0000	2	Buda
0.0389	25.9	.0000	2	Budd's
0.0389	25.9	.0000	2	Buenaventura
0.0389	25.9	.0000	2	buraku-min
0.0389	25.9	.0000	2	Burger's
0.0389	25.9	.0000	2	businessman's
0.0389	25.9	.0000	2	caliente
0.0389	25.9	.0000	2	Calverts
0.0389	25.9	.0000	2	Cambodians
0.0389	25.9	.0000	2	canalboats
0.0389	25.9	.0000	2	Cantabrian
0.0389	25.9	.0000	2	Cantabrians
0.0389	25.9	.0000	2	Carolines
0.0389	25.9	.0000	2	Catala
0.0389	25.9	.0000	2	Cerro
0.0389	25.9	.0000	2	Chagres
0.0389	25.9	.0000	2	Changing
0.0389	25.9	.0000	2	Chateau-Thierry
0.0389	25.9	.0000	2	Cherrapunji
0.0389	25.9	.0000	2	chinaware
0.0389	25.9	.0000	2	city-dwellers

THE PRECEDING WORD TYPE OCCUPIES RANK 51200

U	SFI	D	F	Word Type
0.0389	25.9	.0000	2	Civics
0.0389	25.9	.0000	2	cliff-dwelling
0.0389	25.9	.0000	2	coal's
0.0389	25.9	.0000	2	coffee-growing
0.0389	25.9	.0000	2	colonists'
0.0389	25.9	.0000	2	containment
0.0389	25.9	.0000	2	convened
0.0389	25.9	.0000	2	Cortinas
0.0389	25.9	.0000	2	cotillion
0.0389	25.9	.0000	2	cotton-picking
0.0389	25.9	.0000	2	cottonseeds
0.0389	25.9	.0000	2	CouncilBluffs
0.0389	25.9	.0000	2	Croats
0.0389	25.9	.0000	2	Crossroads
0.0389	25.9	.0000	2	Cuppere
0.0389	25.9	.0000	2	Dag
0.0389	25.9	.0000	2	Danakils
0.0389	25.9	.0000	2	Danzig
0.0389	25.9	.0000	2	dawana
0.0389	25.9	.0000	2	deForest
0.0389	25.9	.0000	2	deOjeda
0.0389	25.9	.0000	2	dePasco
0.0389	25.9	.0000	2	deckhands
0.0389	25.9	.0000	2	Dessie
0.0389	25.9	.0000	2	director-general
0.0389	25.9	.0000	2	disarmament
0.0389	25.9	.0000	2	disarmed
0.0389	25.9	.0000	2	discussant
0.0389	25.9	.0000	2	dispatcher
0.0389	25.9	.0000	2	disproved
0.0389	25.9	.0000	2	Djibouti
0.0389	25.9	.0000	2	DodgeCity
0.0389	25.9	.0000	2	Doolin
0.0389	25.9	.0000	2	Doolins
0.0389	25.9	.0000	2	double-tracked
0.0389	25.9	.0000	2	Dravidians
0.0389	25.9	.0000	2	druggists
0.0389	25.9	.0000	2	durbars
0.0389	25.9	.0000	2	earls
0.0389	25.9	.0000	2	earners
0.0389	25.9	.0000	2	east-central
0.0389	25.9	.0000	2	empresarios
0.0389	25.9	.0000	2	enlistment
0.0389	25.9	.0000	2	Epirus
0.0389	25.9	.0000	2	epitomized
0.0389	25.9	.0000	2	erebh
0.0389	25.9	.0000	2	Ericsson
0.0389	25.9	.0000	2	Estates-General
0.0389	25.9	.0000	2	Ethiopia's
0.0389	25.9	.0000	2	ethnocentric
0.0389	25.9	.0000	2	Etienne
0.0389	25.9	.0000	2	Eurasian
0.0389	25.9	.0000	2	ewes
0.0389	25.9	.0000	2	excluding
0.0389	25.9	.0000	2	executioners
0.0389	25.9	.0000	2	facto
0.0389	25.9	.0000	2	fanatic
0.0389	25.9	.0000	2	fasting
0.0389	25.9	.0000	2	Fifteenth
0.0389	25.9	.0000	2	FortLaramie
0.0389	25.9	.0000	2	Fourteen
0.0389	25.9	.0000	2	free-soil
0.0389	25.9	.0000	2	Freedmen's
0.0389	25.9	.0000	2	frozen-food
0.0389	25.9	.0000	2	Garvey
0.0389	25.9	.0000	2	gins
0.0389	25.9	.0000	2	Gist
0.0389	25.9	.0000	2	good-tasting
0.0389	25.9	.0000	2	Gota
0.0389	25.9	.0000	2	Gouraud
0.0389	25.9	.0000	2	Grady
0.0389	25.9	.0000	2	graphic-relief
0.0389	25.9	.0000	2	great-grandchildren
0.0389	25.9	.0000	2	Grenville
0.0389	25.9	.0000	2	Guarani
0.0389	25.9	.0000	2	Gullport
0.0389	25.9	.0000	2	half-globes
0.0389	25.9	.0000	2	Hamitic
0.0389	25.9	.0000	2	handbags
0.0389	25.9	.0000	2	handcrafts
0.0389	25.9	.0000	2	Hapsburg
0.0389	25.9	.0000	2	Harald
0.0389	25.9	.0000	2	Harar
0.0389	25.9	.0000	2	hardier
0.0389	25.9	.0000	2	Hawktown
0.0389	25.9	.0000	2	hays
0.0389	25.9	.0000	2	Hemingford
0.0389	25.9	.0000	2	Herzl
0.0389	25.9	.0000	2	hijacked
0.0389	25.9	.0000	2	hijacker
0.0389	25.9	.0000	2	hijackings
0.0389	25.9	.0000	2	Hinduist
0.0389	25.9	.0000	2	Hiromu
0.0389	25.9	.0000	2	hothouses
0.0389	25.9	.0000	2	Huang
0.0389	25.9	.0000	2	Huleh
0.0389	25.9	.0000	2	hydroelectirc
0.0389	25.9	.0000	2	Iberians
0.0389	25.9	.0000	2	Icebox
0.0389	25.9	.0000	2	Ikhnaton

THE PRECEDING WORD TYPE OCCUPIES RANK 51300

U	SFI	D	F	Word Type
0.0389	25.9	.0000	2	indexed
0.0389	25.9	.0000	2	India-Pakistan
0.0389	25.9	.0000	2	industrially
0.0389	25.9	.0000	2	Insull's
0.0389	25.9	.0000	2	intermarried
0.0389	25.9	.0000	2	Intermediate
0.0389	25.9	.0000	2	Iskenderun
0.0389	25.9	.0000	2	Issa
0.0389	25.9	.0000	2	Issas
0.0389	25.9	.0000	2	Jasim's
0.0389	25.9	.0000	2	Jayme
0.0389	25.9	.0000	2	Jerseys
0.0389	25.9	.0000	2	Journeys
0.0389	25.9	.0000	2	Jozef
0.0389	25.9	.0000	2	juju
0.0389	25.9	.0000	2	Kafa
0.0389	25.9	.0000	2	Kaihsienkung
0.0389	25.9	.0000	2	Kalgoorlie
0.0389	25.9	.0000	2	Kaltsuna
0.0389	25.9	.0000	2	Karpur
0.0389	25.9	.0000	2	Kea
0.0389	25.9	.0000	2	kinky
0.0389	25.9	.0000	2	Kroger
0.0389	25.9	.0000	2	Kurds
0.0389	25.9	.0000	2	kuwa
0.0389	25.9	.0000	2	Lachine
0.0389	25.9	.0000	2	LasLomas
0.0389	25.9	.0000	2	Lasuen
0.0389	25.9	.0000	2	Later
0.0389	25.9	.0000	2	LatinAmerican
0.0389	25.9	.0000	2	LatinAmericans
0.0389	25.9	.0000	2	Latitude
0.0389	25.9	.0000	2	latitudinal
0.0389	25.9	.0000	2	Lattimore
0.0389	25.9	.0000	2	law-making
0.0389	25.9	.0000	2	Leander
0.0389	25.9	.0000	2	Leeds
0.0389	25.9	.0000	2	Leidesdorff
0.0389	25.9	.0000	2	Lenin
0.0389	25.9	.0000	2	Libyans
0.0389	25.9	.0000	2	Llanos
0.0389	25.9	.0000	2	lobbyists
0.0389	25.9	.0000	2	Lodge's
0.0389	25.9	.0000	2	Lodz
0.0389	25.9	.0000	2	Lofoten
0.0389	25.9	.0000	2	Lono
0.0389	25.9	.0000	2	loud-speaker
0.0389	25.9	.0000	2	Lourenco
0.0389	25.9	.0000	2	Lovanium
0.0389	25.9	.0000	2	lutfisk
0.0389	25.9	.0000	2	Macedonian
0.0389	25.9	.0000	2	magnesite
0.0389	25.9	.0000	2	Magyar
0.0389	25.9	.0000	2	Malacca
0.0389	25.9	.0000	2	Managua's
0.0389	25.9	.0000	2	manipulator
0.0389	25.9	.0000	2	mapmaker
0.0389	25.9	.0000	2	Marques
0.0389	25.9	.0000	2	Marshalls
0.0389	25.9	.0000	2	McCormicks
0.0389	25.9	.0000	2	McLane
0.0389	25.9	.0000	2	McLane's
0.0389	25.9	.0000	2	meatpacking
0.0389	25.9	.0000	2	mid-1966
0.0389	25.9	.0000	2	midwest
0.0389	25.9	.0000	2	minaret
0.0389	25.9	.0000	2	Minsk
0.0389	25.9	.0000	2	Mixcoatl's
0.0389	25.9	.0000	2	Mixtec
0.0389	25.9	.0000	2	Molali
0.0389	25.9	.0000	2	Mollendo
0.0389	25.9	.0000	2	moss-covered
0.0389	25.9	.0000	2	Mosul
0.0389	25.9	.0000	2	movie-making
0.0389	25.9	.0000	2	Naguib
0.0389	25.9	.0000	2	Nara
0.0389	25.9	.0000	2	Narvik
0.0389	25.9	.0000	2	Natchitoches
0.0389	25.9	.0000	2	Necessity
0.0389	25.9	.0000	2	neckties
0.0389	25.9	.0000	2	NewsTime
0.0389	25.9	.0000	2	Nicaragua's
0.0389	25.9	.0000	2	nickelodeons
0.0389	25.9	.0000	2	Nisei's
0.0389	25.9	.0000	2	Northmen
0.0389	25.9	.0000	2	Northwestern
0.0389	25.9	.0000	2	Noumea
0.0389	25.9	.0000	2	Oath
0.0389	25.9	.0000	2	Ob
0.0389	25.9	.0000	2	Octavian
0.0389	25.9	.0000	2	oil-producing
0.0389	25.9	.0000	2	Olmecs
0.0389	25.9	.0000	2	Olympia
0.0389	25.9	.0000	2	one-hundred
0.0389	25.9	.0000	2	ordain
0.0389	25.9	.0000	2	Orioles'
0.0389	25.9	.0000	2	Ouachitas
0.0389	25.9	.0000	2	out-of-state
0.0389	25.9	.0000	2	Overstreet
0.0389	25.9	.0000	2	Paco

THE PRECEDING WORD TYPE OCCUPIES RANK 51400

U	SFI	D	F	Word Type
0.0389	25.9	.0000	2	Padre
0.0389	25.9	.0000	2	padres'
0.0389	25.9	.0000	2	Panamanians
0.0389	25.9	.0000	2	Paraguayans
0.0389	25.9	.0000	2	Parliamentary
0.0389	25.9	.0000	2	pastureland
0.0389	25.9	.0000	2	patricians
0.0389	25.9	.0000	2	Penn's
0.0389	25.9	.0000	2	Petain
0.0389	25.9	.0000	2	petates
0.0389	25.9	.0000	2	petitioned
0.0389	25.9	.0000	2	Philadelphian
0.0389	25.9	.0000	2	physical-political
0.0389	25.9	.0000	2	picture-map
0.0389	25.9	.0000	2	Piraeus
0.0389	25.9	.0000	2	plantains
0.0389	25.9	.0000	2	plebeians
0.0389	25.9	.0000	2	Poitier
0.0389	25.9	.0000	2	Polo's
0.0389	25.9	.0000	2	PortHuron
0.0389	25.9	.0000	2	Pragmatic
0.0389	25.9	.0000	2	prayer-place
0.0389	25.9	.0000	2	prodigies
0.0389	25.9	.0000	2	Projection
0.0389	25.9	.0000	2	proprietorships
0.0389	25.9	.0000	2	prosecutes
0.0389	25.9	.0000	2	Quechan
0.0389	25.9	.0000	2	rainforest
0.0389	25.9	.0000	2	rainiest
0.0389	25.9	.0000	2	re-entered
0.0389	25.9	.0000	2	readmitted
0.0389	25.9	.0000	2	Real
0.0389	25.9	.0000	2	Reservoir
0.0389	25.9	.0000	2	Ridges

U	SFI	D	F	Word Type
0.0389	25.9	.0000	2	rills
0.0389	25.9	.0000	2	Rimac
0.0389	25.9	.0000	2	Riyadh
0.0389	25.9	.0000	2	Romania
0.0389	25.9	.0000	2	rots
0.0389	25.9	.0000	2	saeters
0.0389	25.9	.0000	2	Safad
0.0389	25.9	.0000	2	Saharan
0.0389	25.9	.0000	2	Salonika
0.0389	25.9	.0000	2	SanFrancisco-Oakland
0.0389	25.9	.0000	2	Sanction
0.0389	25.9	.0000	2	Sanja
0.0389	25.9	.0000	2	scholar-bureaucrats
0.0389	25.9	.0000	2	Scrape
0.0389	25.9	.0000	2	seceding
0.0389	25.9	.0000	2	segregated
0.0389	25.9	.0000	2	self-rule
0.0389	25.9	.0000	2	Serbs
0.0389	25.9	.0000	2	Serpicos
0.0389	25.9	.0000	2	shadoof
0.0389	25.9	.0000	2	shah
0.0389	25.9	.0000	2	Shankillas
0.0389	25.9	.0000	2	Shays'
0.0389	25.9	.0000	2	Shi
0.0389	25.9	.0000	2	Shiro's
0.0389	25.9	.0000	2	short-short
0.0389	25.9	.0000	2	six-sevenths
0.0389	25.9	.0000	2	Slovenes
0.0389	25.9	.0000	2	smelted
0.0389	25.9	.0000	2	Somaliland
0.0389	25.9	.0000	2	Sophia
0.0389	25.9	.0000	2	South-West
0.0389	25.9	.0000	2	south-facing
0.0389	25.9	.0000	2	southerner
0.0389	25.9	.0000	2	SRA
0.0389	25.9	.0000	2	Stampede
0.0389	25.9	.0000	2	Stanet
0.0389	25.9	.0000	2	state-owned
0.0389	25.9	.0000	2	steelmaking
0.0389	25.9	.0000	2	Stettin
0.0389	25.9	.0000	2	Stoke-on-Trent
0.0389	25.9	.0000	2	sub-continent
0.0389	25.9	.0000	2	subversion
0.0389	25.9	.0000	2	superintends
0.0389	25.9	.0000	2	swiss
0.0389	25.9	.0000	2	Sylvis
0.0389	25.9	.0000	2	Syria's
0.0389	25.9	.0000	2	take-over
0.0389	25.9	.0000	2	Tank
0.0389	25.9	.0000	2	Tanura
0.0389	25.9	.0000	2	Taoism
0.0389	25.9	.0000	2	taro
0.0389	25.9	.0000	2	Tartars
0.0389	25.9	.0000	2	Tasman
0.0389	25.9	.0000	2	Tata
0.0389	25.9	.0000	2	teakwood
0.0389	25.9	.0000	2	templada
0.0389	25.9	.0000	2	Thom
0.0389	25.9	.0000	2	three-time
0.0389	25.9	.0000	2	Ti
0.0389	25.9	.0000	2	time-honored
0.0389	25.9	.0000	2	Timor
0.0389	25.9	.0000	2	Tobacconist
0.0389	25.9	.0000	2	Tomiyasu
0.0389	25.9	.0000	2	Tongass
0.0389	25.9	.0000	2	townsmen
THE PRECEDING WORD TYPE OCCUPIES RANK 51500				
0.0389	25.9	.0000	2	Trans-Siberian
0.0389	25.9	.0000	2	treasuries
0.0389	25.9	.0000	2	truck-farming
0.0389	25.9	.0000	2	Trygve
0.0389	25.9	.0000	2	tsars
0.0389	25.9	.0000	2	tsub
0.0389	25.9	.0000	2	tule
0.0389	25.9	.0000	2	Ubangi
0.0389	25.9	.0000	2	unevenness
0.0389	25.9	.0000	2	Universal
0.0389	25.9	.0000	2	usurpations
0.0389	25.9	.0000	2	Utrecht
0.0389	25.9	.0000	2	Uzlian
0.0389	25.9	.0000	2	vandenBerg
0.0389	25.9	.0000	2	Vardar
0.0389	25.9	.0000	2	Venizelos
0.0389	25.9	.0000	2	verdicts
0.0389	25.9	.0000	2	Vermont's
0.0389	25.9	.0000	2	Vitus
0.0389	25.9	.0000	2	Wade-Davis
0.0389	25.9	.0000	2	Waganupa
0.0389	25.9	.0000	2	Weldon
0.0389	25.9	.0000	2	well-drilled
0.0389	25.9	.0000	2	well-watered
0.0389	25.9	.0000	2	Winthrop
0.0389	25.9	.0000	2	WPA
0.0389	25.9	.0000	2	Wroclaw
0.0389	25.9	.0000	2	Yamasaki
0.0389	25.9	.0000	2	Yugoslavs
0.0389	25.9	.0000	2	Yulecake
0.0389	25.9	.0000	2	Zelda
0.0389	25.9	.0000	2	Zonguldak
0.0389	25.9	.0000	2	1296
0.0389	25.9	.0000	2	1302
0.0389	25.9	.0000	2	132-134
0.0389	25.9	.0000	2	1496
0.0389	25.9	.0000	2	1537
0.0389	25.9	.0000	2	1606
0.0389	25.9	.0000	2	1640
0.0389	25.9	.0000	2	1652
0.0389	25.9	.0000	2	1693
0.0389	25.9	.0000	2	1713
0.0389	25.9	.0000	2	176-177
0.0389	25.9	.0000	2	1865-1900
0.0389	25.9	.0000	2	1894-1895
0.0389	25.9	.0000	2	23rd
0.0389	25.9	.0000	2	236-237
0.0389	25.9	.0000	2	240-241
0.0389	25.9	.0000	2	246-247
0.0389	25.9	.0000	2	268-269
0.0389	25.9	.0000	2	334-335
0.0389	25.9	.0000	2	368-369
0.0389	25.9	.0000	2	389
0.0389	25.9	.0000	2	393
0.0389	25.9	.0000	2	570
0.0386	25.9	.0000	12	pleat
0.0365	25.6	.0000	3	'63
0.0365	25.6	.0000	3	'67
0.0365	25.6	.0000	3	academically
0.0365	25.6	.0000	3	ACCION
0.0365	25.6	.0000	3	agnostic
0.0365	25.6	.0000	3	Ahmadabad
0.0365	25.6	.0000	3	Alioto's
0.0365	25.6	.0000	3	All-Star
0.0365	25.6	.0000	3	Alvarado
0.0365	25.6	.0000	3	amphetamines
0.0365	25.6	.0000	3	Amur
0.0365	25.6	.0000	3	Anabaptist
0.0365	25.6	.0000	3	anglers
0.0365	25.6	.0000	3	Any
0.0365	25.6	.0000	3	aphrodisiac
0.0365	25.6	.0000	3	Arabian's
0.0365	25.6	.0000	3	Armageddon
0.0365	25.6	.0000	3	Associations
0.0365	25.6	.0000	3	Ayd
0.0365	25.6	.0000	3	Barnard
0.0365	25.6	.0000	3	bbl
0.0365	25.6	.0000	3	Beatle
0.0365	25.6	.0000	3	Bellrose
0.0365	25.6	.0000	3	Berger
0.0365	25.6	.0000	3	Besterman
0.0365	25.6	.0000	3	Biafran
0.0365	25.6	.0000	3	big-time
0.0365	25.6	.0000	3	birthrates
0.0365	25.6	.0000	3	Blarney
0.0365	25.6	.0000	3	Blow-Up
0.0365	25.6	.0000	3	Bombolini
0.0365	25.6	.0000	3	Bomex
0.0365	25.6	.0000	3	Boom
0.0365	25.6	.0000	3	boosts
0.0365	25.6	.0000	3	Bornstein
0.0365	25.6	.0000	3	borrowers
0.0365	25.6	.0000	3	brainchild
0.0365	25.6	.0000	3	Bucks
0.0365	25.6	.0000	3	Bullet
0.0365	25.6	.0000	3	Bushytail
0.0365	25.6	.0000	3	Buxton
0.0365	25.6	.0000	3	camber
0.0365	25.6	.0000	3	carabinieri
0.0365	25.6	.0000	3	carrousel
THE PRECEDING WORD TYPE OCCUPIES RANK 51600				
0.0365	25.6	.0000	3	Cartoon
0.0365	25.6	.0000	3	celebrities
0.0365	25.6	.0000	3	Cheever
0.0365	25.6	.0000	3	Chips'
0.0365	25.6	.0000	3	Chrysler's
0.0365	25.6	.0000	3	chuck's
0.0365	25.6	.0000	3	civil-rights
0.0365	25.6	.0000	3	Cl-
0.0365	25.6	.0000	3	cloister
0.0365	25.6	.0000	3	cloistered
0.0365	25.6	.0000	3	Closet
0.0365	25.6	.0000	3	Cobra
0.0365	25.6	.0000	3	cohos
0.0365	25.6	.0000	3	commando
0.0365	25.6	.0000	3	competence
0.0365	25.6	.0000	3	con-ver-sa-tion
0.0365	25.6	.0000	3	confrontations
0.0365	25.6	.0000	3	convention's
0.0365	25.6	.0000	3	cool-down
0.0365	25.6	.0000	3	coriander
0.0365	25.6	.0000	3	cross-line
0.0365	25.6	.0000	3	cross-lines
0.0365	25.6	.0000	3	curries
0.0365	25.6	.0000	3	Debre
0.0365	25.6	.0000	3	Delight
0.0365	25.6	.0000	3	Desi
0.0365	25.6	.0000	3	distributors
0.0365	25.6	.0000	3	dropback
0.0365	25.6	.0000	3	DuPont's
0.0365	25.6	.0000	3	dubbed
0.0365	25.6	.0000	3	Eads's
0.0365	25.6	.0000	3	earth-magnet
0.0365	25.6	.0000	3	Emmons
0.0365	25.6	.0000	3	escalation
0.0365	25.6	.0000	3	extinguishing
0.0365	25.6	.0000	3	Ezra
0.0365	25.6	.0000	3	FAA
0.0365	25.6	.0000	3	fanatics
0.0365	25.6	.0000	3	Farms
0.0365	25.6	.0000	3	fined
0.0365	25.6	.0000	3	fingerlings
0.0365	25.6	.0000	3	Forty-first
0.0365	25.6	.0000	3	four-barrel
0.0365	25.6	.0000	3	Frumkin
0.0365	25.6	.0000	3	fuel-and-water
0.0365	25.6	.0000	3	G-2
0.0365	25.6	.0000	3	gamefish
0.0365	25.6	.0000	3	Gaullist
0.0365	25.6	.0000	3	Goldberger
0.0365	25.6	.0000	3	Goury
0.0365	25.6	.0000	3	groovy
0.0365	25.6	.0000	3	Haldeman
0.0365	25.6	.0000	3	Hanae
0.0365	25.6	.0000	3	handgun
0.0365	25.6	.0000	3	handshakes
0.0365	25.6	.0000	3	hard-line
0.0365	25.6	.0000	3	Heathkit
0.0365	25.6	.0000	3	Heinold
0.0365	25.6	.0000	3	hitchhiker
0.0365	25.6	.0000	3	Hutschnecker
0.0365	25.6	.0000	3	hypocrites
0.0365	25.6	.0000	3	Inc's**
0.0365	25.6	.0000	3	indiscriminate
0.0365	25.6	.0000	3	intercom
0.0365	25.6	.0000	3	Interstates
0.0365	25.6	.0000	3	inundated
0.0365	25.6	.0000	3	Iolanda
0.0365	25.6	.0000	3	islands'
0.0365	25.6	.0000	3	Jere
0.0365	25.6	.0000	3	Jomo
0.0365	25.6	.0000	3	journalists
0.0365	25.6	.0000	3	junked
0.0365	25.6	.0000	3	Kampala
0.0365	25.6	.0000	3	Kayapo
0.0365	25.6	.0000	3	Kazan
0.0365	25.6	.0000	3	Kenya's
0.0365	25.6	.0000	3	Kiesinger
0.0365	25.6	.0000	3	Kissinger
0.0365	25.6	.0000	3	Land-Rover
0.0365	25.6	.0000	3	LasVegas
0.0365	25.6	.0000	3	Laugh-In
0.0365	25.6	.0000	3	LBJ
0.0365	25.6	.0000	3	league's
0.0365	25.6	.0000	3	LIFE
0.0365	25.6	.0000	3	Lissa
0.0365	25.6	.0000	3	Lock
0.0365	25.6	.0000	3	long-haired
0.0365	25.6	.0000	3	Lott
0.0365	25.6	.0000	3	M-11
0.0365	25.6	.0000	3	Maltz
0.0365	25.6	.0000	3	Man-God's
0.0365	25.6	.0000	3	Man-Gods'
0.0365	25.6	.0000	3	Maniago
0.0365	25.6	.0000	3	Martinez
0.0365	25.6	.0000	3	McLendon
0.0365	25.6	.0000	3	McNary
0.0365	25.6	.0000	3	Merlyn
0.0365	25.6	.0000	3	Middleville
0.0365	25.6	.0000	3	mighties
0.0365	25.6	.0000	3	mikes
THE PRECEDING WORD TYPE OCCUPIES RANK 51700				
0.0365	25.6	.0000	3	Millerbird
0.0365	25.6	.0000	3	Mitford
0.0365	25.6	.0000	3	moratorium
0.0365	25.6	.0000	3	Mori
0.0365	25.6	.0000	3	MORTIMER
0.0365	25.6	.0000	3	Moynihan
0.0365	25.6	.0000	3	Mzee
0.0365	25.6	.0000	3	Nader
0.0365	25.6	.0000	3	NASCAR
0.0365	25.6	.0000	3	Nascimento
0.0365	25.6	.0000	3	Negoro
0.0365	25.6	.0000	3	neoprene
0.0365	25.6	.0000	3	new-style
0.0365	25.6	.0000	3	newsmagazine
0.0365	25.6	.0000	3	off-farm
0.0365	25.6	.0000	3	Olds
0.0365	25.6	.0000	3	Oppenheimer's
0.0365	25.6	.0000	3	options
0.0365	25.6	.0000	3	Oregon's
0.0365	25.6	.0000	3	ovations
0.0365	25.6	.0000	3	Palmellococcus
0.0365	25.6	.0000	3	Peachtree
0.0365	25.6	.0000	3	Phyl
0.0365	25.6	.0000	3	placate
0.0365	25.6	.0000	3	Pow
0.0365	25.6	.0000	3	Primeval
0.0365	25.6	.0000	3	Pris
0.0365	25.6	.0000	3	Professional
0.0365	25.6	.0000	3	psychiatry
0.0365	25.6	.0000	3	qualifying
0.0365	25.6	.0000	3	query
0.0365	25.6	.0000	3	Raskin
0.0365	25.6	.0000	3	Redskins
0.0365	25.6	.0000	3	reps
0.0365	25.6	.0000	3	restorative
0.0365	25.6	.0000	3	retaliation
0.0365	25.6	.0000	3	reviewer
0.0365	25.6	.0000	3	Rockefellers
0.0365	25.6	.0000	3	rookies
0.0365	25.6	.0000	3	Rosenberg
0.0365	25.6	.0000	3	schizophrenics
0.0365	25.6	.0000	3	second-year
0.0365	25.6	.0000	3	sedans
0.0365	25.6	.0000	3	Seesall
0.0365	25.6	.0000	3	Shea
0.0365	25.6	.0000	3	Shiny-Shack-on-Wheels
0.0365	25.6	.0000	3	Sibiu
0.0365	25.6	.0000	3	SIECUS
0.0365	25.6	.0000	3	Siecus
0.0365	25.6	.0000	3	Simburg
0.0365	25.6	.0000	3	six-cylinder
0.0365	25.6	.0000	3	Skyphone
0.0365	25.6	.0000	3	slow-water
0.0365	25.6	.0000	3	Sonic
0.0365	25.6	.0000	3	Spaceship
0.0365	25.6	.0000	3	sporty
0.0365	25.6	.0000	3	spring-loaded
0.0365	25.6	.0000	3	SST'S
0.0365	25.6	.0000	3	Staubach
0.0365	25.6	.0000	3	Strangler
0.0365	25.6	.0000	3	stylist
0.0365	25.6	.0000	3	subcompacts
0.0365	25.6	.0000	3	sulid
0.0365	25.6	.0000	3	tab
0.0365	25.6	.0000	3	Tet
0.0365	25.6	.0000	3	Thieu
0.0365	25.6	.0000	3	Traitors
0.0365	25.6	.0000	3	turmeric
0.0365	25.6	.0000	3	Twaddle
0.0365	25.6	.0000	3	Unsafe
0.0365	25.6	.0000	3	USDA
0.0365	25.6	.0000	3	Vada
0.0365	25.6	.0000	3	vandal
0.0365	25.6	.0000	3	vellum
0.0365	25.6	.0000	3	Verplanck
0.0365	25.6	.0000	3	Vidal
0.0365	25.6	.0000	3	Vietcong
0.0365	25.6	.0000	3	Voltaire's
0.0365	25.6	.0000	3	Wageni
0.0365	25.6	.0000	3	washhouse
0.0365	25.6	.0000	3	Wexler's
0.0365	25.6	.0000	3	Win
0.0365	25.6	.0000	3	Wombat
0.0365	25.6	.0000	3	Woodard
0.0365	25.6	.0000	3	yummy
0.0365	25.6	.0000	3	1333
0.0365	25.6	.0000	3	20-year-old
0.0365	25.6	.0000	3	27-year-old
0.0365	25.6	.0000	3	49ers
0.0365	25.6	.0000	3	5/8-inch
0.0354	25.5	.0000	11	interfacing
0.0354	25.5	.0000	11	pleats
0.0352	25.5	.0000	3	'um
0.0352	25.5	.0000	3	'uz
0.0352	25.5	.0000	3	a'right
0.0352	25.5	.0000	3	Abercrombie's
0.0352	25.5	.0000	3	acknowledging
0.0352	25.5	.0000	3	Ada
0.0352	25.5	.0000	3	Aernam
0.0352	25.5	.0000	3	aia
THE PRECEDING WORD TYPE OCCUPIES RANK 51800				
0.0352	25.5	.0000	3	Alstyne
0.0352	25.5	.0000	3	ATEOORD
0.0352	25.5	.0000	3	Ath-mun
0.0352	25.5	.0000	3	badmen
0.0352	25.5	.0000	3	bambino
0.0352	25.5	.0000	3	barrier-reef
0.0352	25.5	.0000	3	Bartholomew's
0.0352	25.5	.0000	3	bee-tree
0.0352	25.5	.0000	3	big-mouthed
0.0352	25.5	.0000	3	Brazils
0.0352	25.5	.0000	3	bumming
0.0352	25.5	.0000	3	Burnt
0.0352	25.5	.0000	3	cachalots
0.0352	25.5	.0000	3	Camaralzaman's
0.0352	25.5	.0000	3	Carmelita
0.0352	25.5	.0000	3	Cicero
0.0352	25.5	.0000	3	cocoanuts
0.0352	25.5	.0000	3	coracle
0.0352	25.5	.0000	3	Didd
0.0352	25.5	.0000	3	dirty-little
0.0352	25.5	.0000	3	Dogfish
0.0352	25.5	.0000	3	Dooner
0.0352	25.5	.0000	3	Doubletree
0.0352	25.5	.0000	3	Driver's
0.0352	25.5	.0000	3	Drugstore
0.0352	25.5	.0000	3	ecstatically
0.0352	25.5	.0000	3	Elfred
0.0352	25.5	.0000	3	Filcher
0.0352	25.5	.0000	3	Fire-eater
0.0352	25.5	.0000	3	fitten
0.0352	25.5	.0000	3	gendarmes
0.0352	25.5	.0000	3	Ghalas-at
0.0352	25.5	.0000	3	girl-daughter
0.0352	25.5	.0000	3	Gog
0.0352	25.5	.0000	3	gwyne
0.0352	25.5	.0000	3	Hausers'
0.0352	25.5	.0000	3	Higginson
0.0352	25.5	.0000	3	Homily's
0.0352	25.5	.0000	3	Horican
0.0352	25.5	.0000	3	horseboy
0.0352	25.5	.0000	3	hound's
0.0352	25.5	.0000	3	Howie's
0.0352	25.5	.0000	3	hymnbook
0.0352	25.5	.0000	3	ih
0.0352	25.5	.0000	3	infinite-resource-and-s**
0.0352	25.5	.0000	3	infirmity
0.0352	25.5	.0000	3	Isannah
0.0352	25.5	.0000	3	Jabizri
0.0352	25.5	.0000	3	Karboe
0.0352	25.5	.0000	3	Kiche
0.0352	25.5	.0000	3	Kivi
0.0352	25.5	.0000	3	Kouan-Yu
0.0352	25.5	.0000	3	l-l-lad
0.0352	25.5	.0000	3	Lank
0.0352	25.5	.0000	3	Lark's
0.0352	25.5	.0000	3	Lillybell's
0.0352	25.5	.0000	3	Limpopo
0.0352	25.5	.0000	3	Ma'm
0.0352	25.5	.0000	3	Magog
0.0352	25.5	.0000	3	maser
0.0352	25.5	.0000	3	matchlock
0.0352	25.5	.0000	3	Menotomy
0.0352	25.5	.0000	3	Meredith's
0.0352	25.5	.0000	3	Michot
0.0352	25.5	.0000	3	milk-toast
0.0352	25.5	.0000	3	Mill-wheel
0.0352	25.5	.0000	3	Mis'
0.0352	25.5	.0000	3	mos'
0.0352	25.5	.0000	3	name-tape
0.0352	25.5	.0000	3	nicker
0.0352	25.5	.0000	3	on'y
0.0352	25.5	.0000	3	outen
0.0352	25.5	.0000	3	Patricia's
0.0352	25.5	.0000	3	Payless
0.0352	25.5	.0000	3	perambulator
0.0352	25.5	.0000	3	Persimmon
0.0352	25.5	.0000	3	Pilkington
0.0352	25.5	.0000	3	Pinky
0.0352	25.5	.0000	3	Poore
0.0352	25.5	.0000	3	prayer-books
0.0352	25.5	.0000	3	presentiment
0.0352	25.5	.0000	3	raf'
0.0352	25.5	.0000	3	Reindeer
0.0352	25.5	.0000	3	Reino
0.0352	25.5	.0000	3	Renard
0.0352	25.5	.0000	3	robin's-egg-blue
0.0352	25.5	.0000	3	Ronny
0.0352	25.5	.0000	3	Rosemont
0.0352	25.5	.0000	3	scalplock
0.0352	25.5	.0000	3	scared-cats
0.0352	25.5	.0000	3	Schahriar
0.0352	25.5	.0000	3	Shadrach's
0.0352	25.5	.0000	3	Siders
0.0352	25.5	.0000	3	Sidney's
0.0352	25.5	.0000	3	Slaters
0.0352	25.5	.0000	3	slaughter-house
0.0352	25.5	.0000	3	Snoodie
0.0352	25.5	.0000	3	Stupenfeffer

U	SFI	D	F	Word Type
0.0352	25.5	.0000	3	stupidly
0.0352	25.5	.0000	3	surkus
THE PRECEDING WORD TYPE OCCUPIES RANK 51900				
0.0352	25.5	.0000	3	Sylvanus
0.0352	25.5	.0000	3	Tamenund
0.0352	25.5	.0000	3	Tasky
0.0352	25.5	.0000	3	Telly
0.0352	25.5	.0000	3	Teshumai
0.0352	25.5	.0000	3	Thacia
0.0352	25.5	.0000	3	Thacia's
0.0352	25.5	.0000	3	thou'lt
0.0352	25.5	.0000	3	Toots
0.0352	25.5	.0000	3	tree-tops
0.0352	25.5	.0000	3	Trina
0.0352	25.5	.0000	3	Twelfth
0.0352	25.5	.0000	3	Valerie
0.0352	25.5	.0000	3	Velvet's
0.0352	25.5	.0000	3	vestry
0.0352	25.5	.0000	3	Weird
0.0352	25.5	.0000	3	Winford
0.0352	25.5	.0000	3	Winner
0.0352	25.5	.0000	3	Yeller's
0.0352	25.5	.0000	3	you's
0.0352	25.5	.0000	3	Ysabel
0.0328	25.2	.0000	3	-hound
0.0328	25.2	.0000	3	-pose
0.0328	25.2	.0000	3	american
0.0328	25.2	.0000	3	amiral
0.0328	25.2	.0000	3	beggarly
0.0328	25.2	.0000	3	bodguts
0.0328	25.2	.0000	3	cameo
0.0328	25.2	.0000	3	Cheryll
0.0328	25.2	.0000	3	chessmen
0.0328	25.2	.0000	3	chilblains
0.0328	25.2	.0000	3	Clauses
0.0328	25.2	.0000	3	clincher
0.0328	25.2	.0000	3	Cobras
0.0328	25.2	.0000	3	Compton's
0.0328	25.2	.0000	3	Conquer
0.0328	25.2	.0000	3	deir
0.0328	25.2	.0000	3	delete
0.0328	25.2	.0000	3	Democracy
0.0328	25.2	.0000	3	dormouse
0.0328	25.2	.0000	3	double-space
0.0328	25.2	.0000	3	Drawling
0.0328	25.2	.0000	3	Drawling-master
0.0328	25.2	.0000	3	Eton
0.0328	25.2	.0000	3	feir
0.0328	25.2	.0000	3	felicitations
0.0328	25.2	.0000	3	Feodorovna
0.0328	25.2	.0000	3	forelands
0.0328	25.2	.0000	3	form-class
0.0328	25.2	.0000	3	Frankel's
0.0328	25.2	.0000	3	Freebus
0.0328	25.2	.0000	3	Hale's
0.0328	25.2	.0000	3	Impunity
0.0328	25.2	.0000	3	Keats
0.0328	25.2	.0000	3	knicht
0.0328	25.2	.0000	3	Lacrosse
0.0328	25.2	.0000	3	Lassie
0.0328	25.2	.0000	3	Luba
0.0328	25.2	.0000	3	LV
0.0328	25.2	.0000	3	Marinoff
0.0328	25.2	.0000	3	McDivitt
0.0328	25.2	.0000	3	N-v
0.0328	25.2	.0000	3	natively
0.0328	25.2	.0000	3	Nifty
0.0328	25.2	.0000	3	no-word
0.0328	25.2	.0000	3	nonessential
0.0328	25.2	.0000	3	nonverbal
0.0328	25.2	.0000	3	not-word
0.0328	25.2	.0000	3	NP'S
0.0328	25.2	.0000	3	num
0.0328	25.2	.0000	3	owre
0.0328	25.2	.0000	3	Ozymandias
0.0328	25.2	.0000	3	pentameters
0.0328	25.2	.0000	3	phonemic
0.0328	25.2	.0000	3	Pictured
0.0328	25.2	.0000	3	Polski
0.0328	25.2	.0000	3	post-office
0.0328	25.2	.0000	3	re-
0.0328	25.2	.0000	3	Revise
0.0328	25.2	.0000	3	revising
0.0328	25.2	.0000	3	richt
0.0328	25.2	.0000	3	Rivertown
0.0328	25.2	.0000	3	schip
0.0328	25.2	.0000	3	Schirra
0.0328	25.2	.0000	3	signifying
0.0328	25.2	.0000	3	Smythe
0.0328	25.2	.0000	3	Snipkin
0.0328	25.2	.0000	3	Supply
0.0328	25.2	.0000	3	thair
0.0328	25.2	.0000	3	theres
0.0328	25.2	.0000	3	Tippy
0.0328	25.2	.0000	3	Tocqueville
0.0328	25.2	.0000	3	Tortoise
0.0328	25.2	.0000	3	Voskrece
0.0328	25.2	.0000	3	Wiggles
0.0328	25.2	.0000	3	willow-weed
0.0328	25.2	.0000	3	Wobblechin
0.0328	25.2	.0000	3	word-group
0.0328	25.2	.0000	3	Write
0.0328	25.2	.0000	3	Yipounou
THE PRECEDING WORD TYPE OCCUPIES RANK 52000				
0.0328	25.2	.0000	3	139-41
0.0325	25.1	.0000	4	/kw/
0.0325	25.1	.0000	4	addlegram
0.0325	25.1	.0000	4	adjective-forming
0.0325	25.1	.0000	4	Approaching
0.0325	25.1	.0000	4	Blacky
0.0325	25.1	.0000	4	blend-vowel
0.0325	25.1	.0000	4	Burroughs
0.0325	25.1	.0000	4	Chaucer
0.0325	25.1	.0000	4	ew
0.0325	25.1	.0000	4	five-syllable
0.0325	25.1	.0000	4	ive
0.0325	25.1	.0000	4	Mastery
0.0325	25.1	.0000	4	oa
0.0325	25.1	.0000	4	past-tense
0.0325	25.1	.0000	4	pondo
0.0325	25.1	.0000	4	pos
0.0325	25.1	.0000	4	pr
0.0325	25.1	.0000	4	respell
0.0325	25.1	.0000	4	sanely
0.0325	25.1	.0000	4	singulars
0.0325	25.1	.0000	4	sn
0.0325	25.1	.0000	4	str
0.0325	25.1	.0000	4	ty
0.0325	25.1	.0000	4	v/cv
0.0325	25.1	.0000	4	vid
0.0323	25.1	.0000	4	a-roving
0.0323	25.1	.0000	4	Aeolian
0.0323	25.1	.0000	4	Alleluia
0.0323	25.1	.0000	4	arranger
0.0323	25.1	.0000	4	augmentation
0.0323	25.1	.0000	4	Badinerie
0.0323	25.1	.0000	4	Bamboula
0.0323	25.1	.0000	4	Berliner's
0.0323	25.1	.0000	4	boogie-woogie
0.0323	25.1	.0000	4	Braddledum
0.0323	25.1	.0000	4	cantata
0.0323	25.1	.0000	4	Charlatan
0.0323	25.1	.0000	4	Chaverim
0.0323	25.1	.0000	4	Choral
0.0323	25.1	.0000	4	chromaticism
0.0323	25.1	.0000	4	Clock
0.0323	25.1	.0000	4	Comin'
0.0323	25.1	.0000	4	concertino
0.0323	25.1	.0000	4	contrabassoon
0.0323	25.1	.0000	4	cooed
0.0323	25.1	.0000	4	double-reed
0.0323	25.1	.0000	4	Edvard
0.0323	25.1	.0000	4	Enchanting
0.0323	25.1	.0000	4	extol
0.0323	25.1	.0000	4	feedle
0.0323	25.1	.0000	4	fermatas
0.0323	25.1	.0000	4	Florian's
0.0323	25.1	.0000	4	Flute
0.0323	25.1	.0000	4	Gian
0.0323	25.1	.0000	4	gift-giving
0.0323	25.1	.0000	4	habanera
0.0323	25.1	.0000	4	heel-toe
0.0323	25.1	.0000	4	Hindemith
0.0323	25.1	.0000	4	hoards
0.0323	25.1	.0000	4	Holst
0.0323	25.1	.0000	4	Humperdinck
0.0323	25.1	.0000	4	Il
0.0323	25.1	.0000	4	Ilyitch
0.0323	25.1	.0000	4	improvises
0.0323	25.1	.0000	4	improvising
0.0323	25.1	.0000	4	Infant
0.0323	25.1	.0000	4	Instrumental
0.0323	25.1	.0000	4	Ionisation
0.0323	25.1	.0000	4	Jenny-O
0.0323	25.1	.0000	4	koto
0.0323	25.1	.0000	4	Kum
0.0323	25.1	.0000	4	Lauterbach
0.0323	25.1	.0000	4	MacDowell
0.0323	25.1	.0000	4	Mazurka
0.0323	25.1	.0000	4	Mussorgsky
0.0323	25.1	.0000	4	Pan's
0.0323	25.1	.0000	4	passacaglia
0.0323	25.1	.0000	4	Person's
0.0323	25.1	.0000	4	pianists
0.0323	25.1	.0000	4	plucks
0.0323	25.1	.0000	4	Polina
0.0323	25.1	.0000	4	Polly-wolly-doodle
0.0323	25.1	.0000	4	Porgy
0.0323	25.1	.0000	4	Puccini
0.0323	25.1	.0000	4	rattlin'
0.0323	25.1	.0000	4	recapitulation
0.0323	25.1	.0000	4	recitals
0.0323	25.1	.0000	4	rhapsodies
0.0323	25.1	.0000	4	Rhapsody
0.0323	25.1	.0000	4	Salute
0.0323	25.1	.0000	4	Schubert's
0.0323	25.1	.0000	4	Schuller
0.0323	25.1	.0000	4	Shalom
0.0323	25.1	.0000	4	Showman
0.0323	25.1	.0000	4	sight-singing
0.0323	25.1	.0000	4	skipwise
0.0323	25.1	.0000	4	Smetana
0.0323	25.1	.0000	4	song-like
0.0323	25.1	.0000	4	SPOKEN
THE PRECEDING WORD TYPE OCCUPIES RANK 52100				
0.0323	25.1	.0000	4	stretto
0.0323	25.1	.0000	4	SUNG
0.0323	25.1	.0000	4	Till
0.0323	25.1	.0000	4	Tirilirala
0.0323	25.1	.0000	4	Tog
0.0323	25.1	.0000	4	tone-row
0.0323	25.1	.0000	4	Twinkle
0.0323	25.1	.0000	4	two-measure
0.0323	25.1	.0000	4	unaccompanied
0.0323	25.1	.0000	4	unkum
0.0323	25.1	.0000	4	whipsee
0.0322	25.1	.0000	3	Abram
0.0322	25.1	.0000	3	Amal
0.0322	25.1	.0000	3	Ansel
0.0322	25.1	.0000	3	Apolonia
0.0322	25.1	.0000	3	archy
0.0322	25.1	.0000	3	assemblyman
0.0322	25.1	.0000	3	AVO
0.0322	25.1	.0000	3	bankrout
0.0322	25.1	.0000	3	barber's
0.0322	25.1	.0000	3	Barbier's
0.0322	25.1	.0000	3	basketmaker
0.0322	25.1	.0000	3	Bellario
0.0322	25.1	.0000	3	Between-the-Logs
0.0322	25.1	.0000	3	BILLY
0.0322	25.1	.0000	3	Charybdis
0.0322	25.1	.0000	3	cheater
0.0322	25.1	.0000	3	chooseth
0.0322	25.1	.0000	3	Claesz
0.0322	25.1	.0000	3	CLERK
0.0322	25.1	.0000	3	clout
0.0322	25.1	.0000	3	Cobweb
0.0322	25.1	.0000	3	Coyotito's
0.0322	25.1	.0000	3	Cronk
0.0322	25.1	.0000	3	Cuyloga
0.0322	25.1	.0000	3	Darnay
0.0322	25.1	.0000	3	Daws
0.0322	25.1	.0000	3	deathbox
0.0322	25.1	.0000	3	denies
0.0322	25.1	.0000	3	Diassigue-the-Alligator
0.0322	25.1	.0000	3	Disbeliever
0.0322	25.1	.0000	3	DOCTOR'S
0.0322	25.1	.0000	3	dote
0.0322	25.1	.0000	3	duck-chasing
0.0322	25.1	.0000	3	Elisabeth
0.0322	25.1	.0000	3	Esquimo
0.0322	25.1	.0000	3	Evering
0.0322	25.1	.0000	3	Ewells
0.0322	25.1	.0000	3	Fabry
0.0322	25.1	.0000	3	faire
0.0322	25.1	.0000	3	FIDDLER
0.0322	25.1	.0000	3	fireboat
0.0322	25.1	.0000	3	Francke
0.0322	25.1	.0000	3	Funjo
0.0322	25.1	.0000	3	Gall
0.0322	25.1	.0000	3	GIRL-FRIEND
0.0322	25.1	.0000	3	GOK
0.0322	25.1	.0000	3	Goliath's
0.0322	25.1	.0000	3	Haley
0.0322	25.1	.0000	3	Hans'
0.0322	25.1	.0000	3	Hard-nuts
0.0322	25.1	.0000	3	hastening
0.0322	25.1	.0000	3	Hermia's
0.0322	25.1	.0000	3	Hi-Wah
0.0322	25.1	.0000	3	hiders
0.0322	25.1	.0000	3	Hinch
0.0322	25.1	.0000	3	Hyperion
0.0322	25.1	.0000	3	ifs
0.0322	25.1	.0000	3	is't
0.0322	25.1	.0000	3	jes'
0.0322	25.1	.0000	3	keener
0.0322	25.1	.0000	3	Khosrove
0.0322	25.1	.0000	3	Kyklops
0.0322	25.1	.0000	3	K3
0.0322	25.1	.0000	3	Lafleur
0.0322	25.1	.0000	3	Large
0.0322	25.1	.0000	3	Lass
0.0322	25.1	.0000	3	laughter-silvered
0.0322	25.1	.0000	3	Lawrrrence
0.0322	25.1	.0000	3	Lhevinne
0.0322	25.1	.0000	3	Lollo
0.0322	25.1	.0000	3	m'
0.0322	25.1	.0000	3	Mab
0.0322	25.1	.0000	3	Madge's
0.0322	25.1	.0000	3	mangroves
0.0322	25.1	.0000	3	Margie's
0.0322	25.1	.0000	3	Merriweather
0.0322	25.1	.0000	3	MOTH
0.0322	25.1	.0000	3	musketeers
0.0322	25.1	.0000	3	Nate's
0.0322	25.1	.0000	3	nigger-lover
0.0322	25.1	.0000	3	Nikolai
0.0322	25.1	.0000	3	Noisy
0.0322	25.1	.0000	3	ogre's
0.0322	25.1	.0000	3	Omalia
0.0322	25.1	.0000	3	Parsons'
0.0322	25.1	.0000	3	Peaseblossom
0.0322	25.1	.0000	3	Pentland
0.0322	25.1	.0000	3	Peril
0.0322	25.1	.0000	10	pin-baste
THE PRECEDING WORD TYPE OCCUPIES RANK 52200				
0.0322	25.1	.0000	3	Pip
0.0322	25.1	.0000	3	presumptuous
0.0322	25.1	.0000	3	QUINCE
0.0322	25.1	.0000	3	reg'ment
0.0322	25.1	.0000	3	relapse
0.0322	25.1	.0000	3	Riverbank
0.0322	25.1	.0000	3	roach
0.0322	25.1	.0000	3	Rohde
0.0322	25.1	.0000	3	Samboy
0.0322	25.1	.0000	3	Servant
0.0322	25.1	.0000	3	Servingman
0.0322	25.1	.0000	3	Shawanose
0.0322	25.1	.0000	3	Shikara
0.0322	25.1	.0000	3	Siata
0.0322	25.1	.0000	10	sirup
0.0322	25.1	.0000	3	sleepwalkers
0.0322	25.1	.0000	3	smoke-pall
0.0322	25.1	.0000	3	SODA
0.0322	25.1	.0000	3	sorcerer's
0.0322	25.1	.0000	3	Stryver
0.0322	25.1	.0000	3	Sykes
0.0322	25.1	.0000	3	tacos
0.0322	25.1	.0000	3	tenderfoot
0.0322	25.1	.0000	3	THIRD
0.0322	25.1	.0000	3	unraveled
0.0322	25.1	.0000	3	VonOsten
0.0322	25.1	.0000	3	Woodcutter's
0.0322	25.1	.0000	3	Woodman
0.0322	25.1	.0000	3	work's
0.0322	25.1	.0000	3	Wycherly
0.0322	25.1	.0000	3	yellow-billed
0.0322	25.1	.0000	3	Yolande
0.0314	25.0	.0000	3	abbey
0.0314	25.0	.0000	3	air-supported
0.0314	25.0	.0000	3	Alces
0.0314	25.0	.0000	3	Aldrich's
0.0314	25.0	.0000	3	amniotic
0.0314	25.0	.0000	3	Anasazi
0.0314	25.0	.0000	3	Appam
0.0314	25.0	.0000	3	Archaeopteryx
0.0314	25.0	.0000	3	Argentinian
0.0314	25.0	.0000	3	Armenia
0.0314	25.0	.0000	3	Arminianism
0.0314	25.0	.0000	3	Atlases
0.0314	25.0	.0000	3	Ayr
0.0314	25.0	.0000	3	Babenberg
0.0314	25.0	.0000	3	behavioral
0.0314	25.0	.0000	3	bequests
0.0314	25.0	.0000	3	blastholes
0.0314	25.0	.0000	3	Boleyn
0.0314	25.0	.0000	3	bondholder
0.0314	25.0	.0000	3	breakdowns
0.0314	25.0	.0000	3	calculi
0.0314	25.0	.0000	3	Calderon
0.0314	25.0	.0000	3	Caliphs
0.0314	25.0	.0000	3	callable
0.0314	25.0	.0000	3	Calvin's
0.0314	25.0	.0000	3	cantos
0.0314	25.0	.0000	3	catapults
0.0314	25.0	.0000	3	catheter
0.0314	25.0	.0000	3	chapels
0.0314	25.0	.0000	3	Chibcha
0.0314	25.0	.0000	3	Childeric
0.0314	25.0	.0000	3	chorea
0.0314	25.0	.0000	3	chorion
0.0314	25.0	.0000	3	chromatin
0.0314	25.0	.0000	3	chromosomal
0.0314	25.0	.0000	3	Churches
0.0314	25.0	.0000	3	Combe
0.0314	25.0	.0000	3	commonwealth
0.0314	25.0	.0000	3	confers
0.0314	25.0	.0000	3	conic
0.0314	25.0	.0000	3	Cosway
0.0314	25.0	.0000	3	cretinism
0.0314	25.0	.0000	3	Dart
0.0314	25.0	.0000	3	Dauphin
0.0314	25.0	.0000	3	deSolis
0.0314	25.0	.0000	3	diethyl
0.0314	25.0	.0000	3	differentiated
0.0314	25.0	.0000	3	distilling
0.0314	25.0	.0000	3	Donatello
0.0314	25.0	.0000	3	Dong
0.0314	25.0	.0000	3	Doon
0.0314	25.0	.0000	3	drupe
0.0314	25.0	.0000	3	duodenum
0.0314	25.0	.0000	3	Dwellers
0.0314	25.0	.0000	3	dyad
0.0314	25.0	.0000	3	electroplates
0.0314	25.0	.0000	3	endocrines
0.0314	25.0	.0000	3	Eng
0.0314	25.0	.0000	3	enunciation
0.0314	25.0	.0000	3	epochs
0.0314	25.0	.0000	3	Falkland
0.0314	25.0	.0000	3	Fanfani
0.0314	25.0	.0000	3	fishery
0.0314	25.0	.0000	3	fishes'
0.0314	25.0	.0000	3	Flaubert
0.0314	25.0	.0000	3	fluorspar
0.0314	25.0	.0000	3	frugality
0.0314	25.0	.0000	3	Galen's
THE PRECEDING WORD TYPE OCCUPIES RANK 52300				
0.0314	25.0	.0000	3	Gauchos
0.0314	25.0	.0000	3	Geo
0.0314	25.0	.0000	3	gigas
0.0314	25.0	.0000	3	glomeruli
0.0314	25.0	.0000	3	Gona
0.0314	25.0	.0000	3	gradient
0.0314	25.0	.0000	3	Grenal
0.0314	25.0	.0000	3	Guilford
0.0314	25.0	.0000	3	Hammond
0.0314	25.0	.0000	3	herbarium
0.0314	25.0	.0000	3	herbivorous
0.0314	25.0	.0000	3	homogeneous
0.0314	25.0	.0000	3	Hyatt
0.0314	25.0	.0000	3	imprinting
0.0314	25.0	.0000	3	insectivorous
0.0314	25.0	.0000	3	intellectually
0.0314	25.0	.0000	3	interrelationship
0.0314	25.0	.0000	3	invariants
0.0314	25.0	.0000	3	Ionians
0.0314	25.0	.0000	3	JUDAISM
0.0314	25.0	.0000	3	Jurassic
0.0314	25.0	.0000	3	Kellogg
0.0314	25.0	.0000	3	Kruger
0.0314	25.0	.0000	3	laureates
0.0314	25.0	.0000	3	loggerhead
0.0314	25.0	.0000	3	Lombard
0.0314	25.0	.0000	3	Machu
0.0314	25.0	.0000	3	Marathon
0.0314	25.0	.0000	3	marsupialis
0.0314	25.0	.0000	3	Masbate
0.0314	25.0	.0000	3	Mayapan
0.0314	25.0	.0000	3	Milankovitch
0.0314	25.0	.0000	3	Moho
0.0314	25.0	.0000	3	Mohole
0.0314	25.0	.0000	3	montane
0.0314	25.0	.0000	3	Mussolini's
0.0314	25.0	.0000	3	Newcomen
0.0314	25.0	.0000	3	Newer
0.0314	25.0	.0000	3	NGC
0.0314	25.0	.0000	3	Northumbria
0.0314	25.0	.0000	3	Odin
0.0314	25.0	.0000	3	Older
0.0314	25.0	.0000	3	Ortelius
0.0314	25.0	.0000	3	pacus
0.0314	25.0	.0000	3	pagans
0.0314	25.0	.0000	3	paramount
0.0314	25.0	.0000	3	Pepin
0.0314	25.0	.0000	3	peptic
0.0314	25.0	.0000	3	pericardium
0.0314	25.0	.0000	3	Petar
0.0314	25.0	.0000	3	Picchu
0.0314	25.0	.0000	3	platen
0.0314	25.0	.0000	3	Polybus
0.0314	25.0	.0000	3	postulated
0.0314	25.0	.0000	3	postulates
0.0314	25.0	.0000	3	pre-Christian
0.0314	25.0	.0000	3	predestination
0.0314	25.0	.0000	3	primate
0.0314	25.0	.0000	3	primordial
0.0314	25.0	.0000	3	propulsive
0.0314	25.0	.0000	3	Randers

U	SFI	D	F	Word Type
0.0314	25.0	.0000	3	realskole
0.0314	25.0	.0000	3	Remonstrance
0.0314	25.0	.0000	3	replenishing
0.0314	25.0	.0000	3	reradiate
0.0314	25.0	.0000	3	researches
0.0314	25.0	.0000	3	resuscitation
0.0314	25.0	.0000	3	reversely
0.0314	25.0	.0000	3	Revised
0.0314	25.0	.0000	3	ridley
0.0314	25.0	.0000	3	rotor's
0.0314	25.0	.0000	3	Savoy
0.0314	25.0	.0000	3	Scriptures
0.0314	25.0	.0000	3	semiconductors
0.0314	25.0	.0000	3	sharecroppers
0.0314	25.0	.0000	3	Shiite
0.0314	25.0	.0000	3	sirenians
0.0314	25.0	.0000	3	Stamitz
0.0314	25.0	.0000	3	sultan
0.0314	25.0	.0000	3	superseded
0.0314	25.0	.0000	3	Taung
0.0314	25.0	.0000	3	Technical
0.0314	25.0	.0000	3	tetrapods
0.0314	25.0	.0000	3	thallophytes
0.0314	25.0	.0000	3	transactions
0.0314	25.0	.0000	3	transpiration
0.0314	25.0	.0000	3	Trust
0.0314	25.0	.0000	3	U-boats
0.0314	25.0	.0000	3	urination
0.0314	25.0	.0000	3	validity
0.0314	25.0	.0000	3	Vernal
0.0314	25.0	.0000	3	vhf
0.0314	25.0	.0000	3	Wallenstein's
0.0314	25.0	.0000	3	Wm
0.0314	25.0	.0000	3	Wolsey
0.0314	25.0	.0000	3	Youskevitch
0.0314	25.0	.0000	3	ytterbium
0.0314	25.0	.0000	3	1517
0.0314	25.0	.0000	3	1644
0.0314	25.0	.0000	3	520

THE PRECEDING WORD TYPE OCCUPIES RANK 52400

U	SFI	D	F	Word Type
0.0312	24.9	.0000	14	Auggie
0.0299	24.8	.0000	2	$110
0.0299	24.8	.0000	2	$125
0.0299	24.8	.0000	2	$151
0.0299	24.8	.0000	2	$23
0.0299	24.8	.0000	2	$288
0.0299	24.8	.0000	2	$36
0.0299	24.8	.0000	2	$65
0.0299	24.8	.0000	2	$68
0.0299	24.8	.0000	2	$7500
0.0299	24.8	.0000	2	-0
0.0299	24.8	.0000	2	-1/3
0.0299	24.8	.0000	2	-2/3
0.0299	24.8	.0000	2	-2/5
0.0299	24.8	.0000	2	-2y
0.0299	24.8	.0000	2	-3/5
0.0299	24.8	.0000	2	-7
0.0299	24.8	.0000	2	-9
0.0299	24.8	.0000	2	/10
0.0299	24.8	.0000	2	/1000
0.0299	24.8	.0000	2	/6
0.0299	24.8	.0000	2	/60
0.0299	24.8	.0000	2	/7
0.0299	24.8	.0000	2	-fourth
0.0299	24.8	.0000	2	a/c
0.0299	24.8	.0000	2	a/12
0.0299	24.8	.0000	2	a/6
0.0299	24.8	.0000	2	ABFE
0.0299	24.8	.0000	2	ADB
0.0299	24.8	.0000	2	ADD
0.0299	24.8	.0000	2	Algorithm
0.0299	24.8	.0000	2	Alphonso
0.0299	24.8	.0000	2	AP
0.0299	24.8	.0000	2	asterisks
0.0299	24.8	.0000	2	Avoirdupois
0.0299	24.8	.0000	2	AX
0.0299	24.8	.0000	2	a3/a3**
0.0299	24.8	.0000	2	b/12
0.0299	24.8	.0000	2	b/6
0.0299	24.8	.0000	2	base-
0.0299	24.8	.0000	2	base-six
0.0299	24.8	.0000	2	base-twelve
0.0299	24.8	.0000	2	Bernard's
0.0299	24.8	.0000	2	betweenness
0.0299	24.8	.0000	2	BFGC
0.0299	24.8	.0000	2	bimonthly
0.0299	24.8	.0000	2	Binary
0.0299	24.8	.0000	2	brunettes
0.0299	24.8	.0000	2	Bulldogs
0.0299	24.8	.0000	2	BW
0.0299	24.8	.0000	2	c/12
0.0299	24.8	.0000	2	c/6
0.0299	24.8	.0000	2	capstone
0.0299	24.8	.0000	2	Carole
0.0299	24.8	.0000	2	Cayne's
0.0299	24.8	.0000	2	center-point
0.0299	24.8	.0000	2	CG
0.0299	24.8	.0000	2	circumscribes
0.0299	24.8	.0000	2	clockface-to
0.0299	24.8	.0000	2	COB
0.0299	24.8	.0000	2	conjectured
0.0299	24.8	.0000	2	conjugate
0.0299	24.8	.0000	2	converses
0.0299	24.8	.0000	2	coplanar
0.0299	24.8	.0000	2	corollaries
0.0299	24.8	.0000	2	Coulee
0.0299	24.8	.0000	2	counterexample
0.0299	24.8	.0000	2	Crosstown
0.0299	24.8	.0000	2	Cullinan
0.0299	24.8	.0000	2	CX
0.0299	24.8	.0000	2	cybernetics
0.0299	24.8	.0000	2	c2
0.0299	24.8	.0000	2	DAB
0.0299	24.8	.0000	2	DEC
0.0299	24.8	.0000	2	digit's
0.0299	24.8	.0000	2	discounts
0.0299	24.8	.0000	2	Distributive
0.0299	24.8	.0000	2	down-and-up
0.0299	24.8	.0000	2	Downer
0.0299	24.8	.0000	2	Drawing
0.0299	24.8	.0000	2	EAD
0.0299	24.8	.0000	2	EG
0.0299	24.8	.0000	2	EGH
0.0299	24.8	.0000	2	EGP
0.0299	24.8	.0000	2	encountering
0.0299	24.8	.0000	2	Enid
0.0299	24.8	.0000	2	ERASE
0.0299	24.8	.0000	2	F-104A
0.0299	24.8	.0000	2	factor-product
0.0299	24.8	.0000	2	Fallbrook
0.0299	24.8	.0000	2	FE
0.0299	24.8	.0000	2	FH
0.0299	24.8	.0000	2	fifty-nines
0.0299	24.8	.0000	2	fives'
0.0299	24.8	.0000	2	Foolanian
0.0299	24.8	.0000	2	Freeway
0.0299	24.8	.0000	2	FTA
0.0299	24.8	.0000	2	furlongs
0.0299	24.8	.0000	2	gangplanks
0.0299	24.8	.0000	2	gantry

THE PRECEDING WORD TYPE OCCUPIES RANK 52500

U	SFI	D	F	Word Type
0.0299	24.8	.0000	2	Garry
0.0299	24.8	.0000	2	geometries
0.0299	24.8	.0000	2	GOF
0.0299	24.8	.0000	2	Gottfried
0.0299	24.8	.0000	2	Grayville
0.0299	24.8	.0000	2	half-gallons
0.0299	24.8	.0000	2	Heather
0.0299	24.8	.0000	2	hecto-
0.0299	24.8	.0000	2	hectometer
0.0299	24.8	.0000	2	Hopeville
0.0299	24.8	.0000	2	hundredths'
0.0299	24.8	.0000	2	IJKL
0.0299	24.8	.0000	2	iteration
0.0299	24.8	.0000	2	JKPO
0.0299	24.8	.0000	2	JQ
0.0299	24.8	.0000	2	Katz
0.0299	24.8	.0000	2	kilo
0.0299	24.8	.0000	2	KM
0.0299	24.8	.0000	2	KMN
0.0299	24.8	.0000	2	Kris
0.0299	24.8	.0000	2	lattices
0.0299	24.8	.0000	2	LEM
0.0299	24.8	.0000	2	Levin
0.0299	24.8	.0000	2	liquid-fuel
0.0299	24.8	.0000	2	Lobachevsky
0.0299	24.8	.0000	2	MacGruder
0.0299	24.8	.0000	2	MAH
0.0299	24.8	.0000	2	Marcia's
0.0299	24.8	.0000	2	matchings
0.0299	24.8	.0000	2	MATH
0.0299	24.8	.0000	2	MDXVI
0.0299	24.8	.0000	2	midpoints
0.0299	24.8	.0000	2	Minkowski's
0.0299	24.8	.0000	2	mixed-numeral
0.0299	24.8	.0000	2	MNQ
0.0299	24.8	.0000	2	Moebius
0.0299	24.8	.0000	2	monorail
0.0299	24.8	.0000	2	motor-vehicle
0.0299	24.8	.0000	2	MP
0.0299	24.8	.0000	2	n/4
0.0299	24.8	.0000	2	NewBritain
0.0299	24.8	.0000	2	NMO
0.0299	24.8	.0000	2	NMP
0.0299	24.8	.0000	2	non-metric
0.0299	24.8	.0000	2	non-terminating
0.0299	24.8	.0000	2	noncoplanar
0.0299	24.8	.0000	2	nonparallel
0.0299	24.8	.0000	2	nonprimes
0.0299	24.8	.0000	2	number-naming
0.0299	24.8	.0000	2	OI
0.0299	24.8	.0000	2	one-digit
0.0299	24.8	.0000	2	one-dimensional
0.0299	24.8	.0000	2	pasteurizing
0.0299	24.8	.0000	2	Pattie's
0.0299	24.8	.0000	2	pharmacist
0.0299	24.8	.0000	2	place-values
0.0299	24.8	.0000	2	PQRS
0.0299	24.8	.0000	2	PR
0.0299	24.8	.0000	2	Primes
0.0299	24.8	.0000	2	PRT
0.0299	24.8	.0000	2	prt
0.0299	24.8	.0000	2	Pryor
0.0299	24.8	.0000	2	PSQ
0.0299	24.8	.0000	2	QP
0.0299	24.8	.0000	2	quaternions
0.0299	24.8	.0000	2	Quiz
0.0299	24.8	.0000	2	qx0
0.0299	24.8	.0000	2	Recipe
0.0299	24.8	.0000	2	Recreations
0.0299	24.8	.0000	2	Rectangles
0.0299	24.8	.0000	2	redecorating
0.0299	24.8	.0000	2	rhombuses
0.0299	24.8	.0000	2	ring-toss
0.0299	24.8	.0000	2	Rollins's
0.0299	24.8	.0000	2	RSW
0.0299	24.8	.0000	2	RTV
0.0299	24.8	.0000	2	rubber-sheet
0.0299	24.8	.0000	2	r2
0.0299	24.8	.0000	2	semimonthly
0.0299	24.8	.0000	2	Sidewinder
0.0299	24.8	.0000	2	Sigma
0.0299	24.8	.0000	2	sixth-graders
0.0299	24.8	.0000	2	SP
0.0299	24.8	.0000	2	specially-treated
0.0299	24.8	.0000	2	sportscaster
0.0299	24.8	.0000	2	square-ruled
0.0299	24.8	.0000	2	SSS
0.0299	24.8	.0000	2	ST
0.0299	24.8	.0000	2	STU
0.0299	24.8	.0000	2	suan-pan
0.0299	24.8	.0000	2	SUBTRACT
0.0299	24.8	.0000	2	symmetric
0.0299	24.8	.0000	2	tabulate
0.0299	24.8	.0000	2	Tallyville
0.0299	24.8	.0000	2	Tartaglia
0.0299	24.8	.0000	2	taxpayer's
0.0299	24.8	.0000	2	terminates
0.0299	24.8	.0000	2	THA
0.0299	24.8	.0000	2	Timken
0.0299	24.8	.0000	2	tonnage

THE PRECEDING WORD TYPE OCCUPIES RANK 52600

U	SFI	D	F	Word Type
0.0299	24.8	.0000	2	Triangles
0.0299	24.8	.0000	2	TS
0.0299	24.8	.0000	2	Tuesdays
0.0299	24.8	.0000	2	tuned-in
0.0299	24.8	.0000	2	twelve-clock
0.0299	24.8	.0000	2	twenty-fifths
0.0299	24.8	.0000	2	twenty-fives
0.0299	24.8	.0000	2	two-fifths
0.0299	24.8	.0000	2	two-place
0.0299	24.8	.0000	2	underpass
0.0299	24.8	.0000	2	unendingly
0.0299	24.8	.0000	2	unit-wholes
0.0299	24.8	.0000	2	updates
0.0299	24.8	.0000	2	Vickie
0.0299	24.8	.0000	2	Vinson
0.0299	24.8	.0000	2	WUV
0.0299	24.8	.0000	2	x-segments
0.0299	24.8	.0000	2	x-y
0.0299	24.8	.0000	2	X's
0.0299	24.8	.0000	2	XW
0.0299	24.8	.0000	2	xy
0.0299	24.8	.0000	2	XYW
0.0299	24.8	.0000	2	XYZ
0.0299	24.8	.0000	2	x10
0.0299	24.8	.0000	2	x2
0.0299	24.8	.0000	2	y-coordinate
0.0299	24.8	.0000	2	y-segments
0.0299	24.8	.0000	2	z-axis
0.0299	24.8	.0000	2	ZW
0.0299	24.8	.0000	2	0/5
0.0299	24.8	.0000	2	00005
0.0299	24.8	.0000	2	0003
0.0299	24.8	.0000	2	0008
0.0299	24.8	.0000	2	02315
0.0299	24.8	.0000	2	02351
0.0299	24.8	.0000	2	051
0.0299	24.8	.0000	2	090909
0.0299	24.8	.0000	2	096
0.0299	24.8	.0000	2	1H
0.0299	24.8	.0000	2	1-cent
0.0299	24.8	.0000	2	1/
0.0299	24.8	.0000	2	1/1
0.0299	24.8	.0000	2	1/15
0.0299	24.8	.0000	2	1/2-foot
0.0299	24.8	.0000	2	1/2x
0.0299	24.8	.0000	2	1/2x1/2
0.0299	24.8	.0000	2	1/3x6
0.0299	24.8	.0000	2	1/4-foot
0.0299	24.8	.0000	2	1x
0.0299	24.8	.0000	2	1x6
0.0299	24.8	.0000	2	1x7
0.0299	24.8	.0000	2	10-dollar
0.0299	24.8	.0000	2	10-17
0.0299	24.8	.0000	2	10/12
0.0299	24.8	.0000	2	10/5
0.0299	24.8	.0000	2	100-yard
0.0299	24.8	.0000	2	1000's
0.0299	24.8	.0000	2	11-9
0.0299	24.8	.0000	2	1111
0.0299	24.8	.0000	2	112103
0.0299	24.8	.0000	2	12-17
0.0299	24.8	.0000	2	12/7
0.0299	24.8	.0000	2	12y
0.0299	24.8	.0000	2	1232
0.0299	24.8	.0000	2	1268
0.0299	24.8	.0000	2	13-19
0.0299	24.8	.0000	2	13-22
0.0299	24.8	.0000	2	13y
0.0299	24.8	.0000	2	14-20
0.0299	24.8	.0000	2	14-20a
0.0299	24.8	.0000	2	14-20b
0.0299	24.8	.0000	2	15/14
0.0299	24.8	.0000	2	15/2
0.0299	24.8	.0000	2	15/20
0.0299	24.8	.0000	2	15/3
0.0299	24.8	.0000	2	16-19
0.0299	24.8	.0000	2	16/20
0.0299	24.8	.0000	2	1617
0.0299	24.8	.0000	2	1646-1716
0.0299	24.8	.0000	2	17n
0.0299	24.8	.0000	2	1728
0.0299	24.8	.0000	2	18028
0.0299	24.8	.0000	2	18032
0.0299	24.8	.0000	2	18076
0.0299	24.8	.0000	2	199/200
0.0299	24.8	.0000	2	2B
0.0299	24.8	.0000	2	2T
0.0299	24.8	.0000	2	2-finger-width
0.0299	24.8	.0000	2	2-11
0.0299	24.8	.0000	2	2/12
0.0299	24.8	.0000	2	2/15
0.0299	24.8	.0000	2	2/3x4/5
0.0299	24.8	.0000	2	2/3x6
0.0299	24.8	.0000	2	2'
0.0299	24.8	.0000	2	2n
0.0299	24.8	.0000	2	2x-segment
0.0299	24.8	.0000	2	2x1/7
0.0299	24.8	.0000	2	2x10
0.0299	24.8	.0000	2	2x2x2x2x2
0.0299	24.8	.0000	2	2x7

THE PRECEDING WORD TYPE OCCUPIES RANK 52700

U	SFI	D	F	Word Type
0.0299	24.8	.0000	2	2x8
0.0299	24.8	.0000	2	20-word
0.0299	24.8	.0000	2	2003
0.0299	24.8	.0000	2	2160
0.0299	24.8	.0000	2	22/5
0.0299	24.8	.0000	2	22%
0.0299	24.8	.0000	2	2342
0.0299	24.8	.0000	2	2689
0.0299	24.8	.0000	2	29x43
0.0299	24.8	.0000	2	296
0.0299	24.8	.0000	2	3N
0.0299	24.8	.0000	2	3-segment
0.0299	24.8	.0000	2	3-6
0.0299	24.8	.0000	2	3/40
0.0299	24.8	.0000	2	3n
0.0299	24.8	.0000	2	3x10
0.0299	24.8	.0000	2	3x4
0.0299	24.8	.0000	2	30x40
0.0299	24.8	.0000	2	300x70
0.0299	24.8	.0000	2	3001
0.0299	24.8	.0000	2	312x67
0.0299	24.8	.0000	2	3268
0.0299	24.8	.0000	2	3482
0.0299	24.8	.0000	2	35%
0.0299	24.8	.0000	2	379
0.0299	24.8	.0000	2	387
0.0299	24.8	.0000	2	3982
0.0299	24.8	.0000	2	4/11
0.0299	24.8	.0000	2	4/16
0.0299	24.8	.0000	2	4xn
0.0299	24.8	.0000	2	4x4
0.0299	24.8	.0000	2	4x5
0.0299	24.8	.0000	2	4x6
0.0299	24.8	.0000	2	40-mile-per-hour
0.0299	24.8	.0000	2	40x36
0.0299	24.8	.0000	2	41b
0.0299	24.8	.0000	2	4179
0.0299	24.8	.0000	2	421
0.0299	24.8	.0000	2	4297
0.0299	24.8	.0000	2	43x20
0.0299	24.8	.0000	2	4326
0.0299	24.8	.0000	2	43542
0.0299	24.8	.0000	2	4356
0.0299	24.8	.0000	2	442
0.0299	24.8	.0000	2	469
0.0299	24.8	.0000	2	49x6
0.0299	24.8	.0000	2	5-segment
0.0299	24.8	.0000	2	5-3
0.0299	24.8	.0000	2	5/11
0.0299	24.8	.0000	2	5/25
0.0299	24.8	.0000	2	5x5x5
0.0299	24.8	.0000	2	500/125
0.0299	24.8	.0000	2	507
0.0299	24.8	.0000	2	536
0.0299	24.8	.0000	2	54x398
0.0299	24.8	.0000	2	580
0.0299	24.8	.0000	2	6-foot
0.0299	24.8	.0000	2	6-pound
0.0299	24.8	.0000	2	6/16
0.0299	24.8	.0000	2	6x10
0.0299	24.8	.0000	2	6x8
0.0299	24.8	.0000	2	6y
0.0299	24.8	.0000	2	600-yard
0.0299	24.8	.0000	2	609
0.0299	24.8	.0000	2	6289
0.0299	24.8	.0000	2	6325
0.0299	24.8	.0000	2	6340
0.0299	24.8	.0000	2	6425
0.0299	24.8	.0000	2	643
0.0299	24.8	.0000	2	649
0.0299	24.8	.0000	2	6598
0.0299	24.8	.0000	2	668
0.0299	24.8	.0000	2	6743
0.0299	24.8	.0000	2	686
0.0299	24.8	.0000	2	6925
0.0299	24.8	.0000	2	698
0.0299	24.8	.0000	2	7-10
0.0299	24.8	.0000	2	7/20
0.0299	24.8	.0000	2	7/7
0.0299	24.8	.0000	2	712
0.0299	24.8	.0000	2	715
0.0299	24.8	.0000	2	715/45
0.0299	24.8	.0000	2	724
0.0299	24.8	.0000	2	746
0.0299	24.8	.0000	2	75th
0.0299	24.8	.0000	2	763
0.0299	24.8	.0000	2	782
0.0299	24.8	.0000	2	7864
0.0299	24.8	.0000	2	7920
0.0299	24.8	.0000	2	8/100
0.0299	24.8	.0000	2	8/9
0.0299	24.8	.0000	2	8r
0.0299	24.8	.0000	2	8x16
0.0299	24.8	.0000	2	8x6
0.0299	24.8	.0000	2	82x6
0.0299	24.8	.0000	2	8356
0.0299	24.8	.0000	2	84-28
0.0299	24.8	.0000	2	85%
0.0299	24.8	.0000	2	860
0.0299	24.8	.0000	2	8634

THE PRECEDING WORD TYPE OCCUPIES RANK 52800

U	SFI	D	F	Word Type
0.0299	24.8	.0000	2	895
0.0299	24.8	.0000	2	896
0.0299	24.8	.0000	2	897
0.0299	24.8	.0000	2	9/4
0.0299	24.8	.0000	2	9x3
0.0299	24.8	.0000	2	9x8
0.0299	24.8	.0000	2	928
0.0299	24.8	.0000	2	974
0.0299	24.8	.0000	2	975
0.0299	24.8	.0000	2	985
0.0299	24.8	.0000	2	9999
0.0296	24.7	.0000	16	Illustration
0.0290	24.6	.0000	2	Abbas
0.0290	24.6	.0000	2	ably
0.0290	24.6	.0000	2	Accardi
0.0290	24.6	.0000	2	accustom
0.0290	24.6	.0000	2	acre-feet
0.0290	24.6	.0000	2	adjourns
0.0290	24.6	.0000	2	Adonais
0.0290	24.6	.0000	2	Afrikaners
0.0290	24.6	.0000	2	afterburner
0.0290	24.6	.0000	2	afterburners
0.0290	24.6	.0000	2	Agatha's
0.0290	24.6	.0000	2	Ai-yani

U	SFI	D	F	Word Type
0.0290	24.6	.0000	2	Albion
0.0290	24.6	.0000	2	Algonquians
0.0290	24.6	.0000	2	alludes
0.0290	24.6	.0000	2	Ambitioso
0.0290	24.6	.0000	2	Anansi
0.0290	24.6	.0000	2	Anax
0.0290	24.6	.0000	2	Anhalt-Cothen
0.0290	24.6	.0000	2	Antioquia
0.0290	24.6	.0000	2	antitank
0.0290	24.6	.0000	2	apostolic
0.0290	24.6	.0000	2	Appenzell
0.0290	24.6	.0000	2	Apuane
0.0290	24.6	.0000	2	Arbigland
0.0290	24.6	.0000	2	Archive
0.0290	24.6	.0000	2	ariseth
0.0290	24.6	.0000	9	armhole
0.0290	24.6	.0000	2	armonica
0.0290	24.6	.0000	2	Ashanti
0.0290	24.6	.0000	2	Ashby's
0.0290	24.6	.0000	2	astrocytoma
0.0290	24.6	.0000	2	Atterdag
0.0290	24.6	.0000	2	auspices
0.0290	24.6	.0000	2	Auto-Union
0.0290	24.6	.0000	2	autostrada
0.0290	24.6	.0000	2	Babworth
0.0290	24.6	.0000	2	Bac
0.0290	24.6	.0000	2	BAND
0.0290	24.6	.0000	2	BAR
0.0290	24.6	.0000	2	Baraboo
0.0290	24.6	.0000	2	Barrell
0.0290	24.6	.0000	2	Batouala
0.0290	24.6	.0000	2	Bayezit
0.0290	24.6	.0000	2	beep-beep
0.0290	24.6	.0000	2	Belond
0.0290	24.6	.0000	2	Ben-Gurion's
0.0290	24.6	.0000	2	Bergitta
0.0290	24.6	.0000	2	Bernissart
0.0290	24.6	.0000	2	Berra
0.0290	24.6	.0000	2	Bevens
0.0290	24.6	.0000	2	Bevens'
0.0290	24.6	.0000	2	bickered
0.0290	24.6	.0000	2	Bilsen
0.0290	24.6	.0000	2	Binghamton
0.0290	24.6	.0000	2	Blackie's
0.0290	24.6	.0000	2	Blodeuwedd
0.0290	24.6	.0000	2	Boones
0.0290	24.6	.0000	2	Boran
0.0290	24.6	.0000	2	bowl's
0.0290	24.6	.0000	2	brachiosaurus
0.0290	24.6	.0000	2	Branwen
0.0290	24.6	.0000	2	brickyards
0.0290	24.6	.0000	2	Brodas
0.0290	24.6	.0000	2	Bryan's
0.0290	24.6	.0000	2	Bryans
0.0290	24.6	.0000	2	buckskin-clad
0.0290	24.6	.0000	2	built-ins
0.0290	24.6	.0000	2	Caccini
0.0290	24.6	.0000	2	canary's
0.0290	24.6	.0000	2	Carrara
0.0290	24.6	.0000	2	cashes
0.0290	24.6	.0000	2	Castiza
0.0290	24.6	.0000	2	Caucasoid
0.0290	24.6	.0000	2	Caucasoids
0.0290	24.6	.0000	2	cauldron
0.0290	24.6	.0000	2	Cayuga
0.0290	24.6	.0000	2	centerboards
0.0290	24.6	.0000	2	Ch'en
0.0290	24.6	.0000	2	Chaffray
0.0290	24.6	.0000	2	Chai
0.0290	24.6	.0000	2	Cherith
0.0290	24.6	.0000	2	Chesterton
0.0290	24.6	.0000	2	Chigwell
0.0290	24.6	.0000	2	Chistiansen
0.0290	24.6	.0000	2	Chita
0.0290	24.6	.0000	2	chok'd
0.0290	24.6	.0000	2	Chowanocs
THE PRECEDING WORD TYPE OCCUPIES RANK 52900				
0.0290	24.6	.0000	2	Cinesias
0.0290	24.6	.0000	2	Cleland
0.0290	24.6	.0000	2	clowning
0.0290	24.6	.0000	2	Clytemnestra
0.0290	24.6	.0000	2	Co-hong
0.0290	24.6	.0000	2	coastwatcher
0.0290	24.6	.0000	2	College-in-the-Woods
0.0290	24.6	.0000	2	coming-out
0.0290	24.6	.0000	2	Congo's
0.0290	24.6	.0000	2	Conie
0.0290	24.6	.0000	2	Connally
0.0290	24.6	.0000	2	cooperates
0.0290	24.6	.0000	2	Cormac
0.0290	24.6	.0000	2	Cothen
0.0290	24.6	.0000	2	cradleboard
0.0290	24.6	.0000	2	creepeth
0.0290	24.6	.0000	2	Criger
0.0290	24.6	.0000	2	Croatoan
0.0290	24.6	.0000	2	Crooked
0.0290	24.6	.0000	2	Crump's
0.0290	24.6	.0000	2	debarkation
0.0290	24.6	.0000	2	Description
0.0290	24.6	.0000	2	dinosaurs'
0.0290	24.6	.0000	2	diplodocus
0.0290	24.6	.0000	2	disinfectant
0.0290	24.6	.0000	2	divinities
0.0290	24.6	.0000	2	Dobby
0.0290	24.6	.0000	2	dodger
0.0290	24.6	.0000	2	draughtsman
0.0290	24.6	.0000	2	dribbles
0.0290	24.6	.0000	2	DRILL
0.0290	24.6	.0000	2	droves
0.0290	24.6	.0000	2	Dussel
0.0290	24.6	.0000	2	earthlodge
0.0290	24.6	.0000	2	Easty
0.0290	24.6	.0000	2	Ebbets
0.0290	24.6	.0000	2	Edge
0.0290	24.6	.0000	2	Editor-in-Chief
0.0290	24.6	.0000	2	Egeria
0.0290	24.6	.0000	2	Elco
0.0290	24.6	.0000	2	Ellison
0.0290	24.6	.0000	2	elocution
0.0290	24.6	.0000	2	empire-building
0.0290	24.6	.0000	13	Enoch
0.0290	24.6	.0000	2	Ensign
0.0290	24.6	.0000	2	entrants
0.0290	24.6	.0000	2	Epaminondas
0.0290	24.6	.0000	2	etatism
0.0290	24.6	.0000	2	Etches
0.0290	24.6	.0000	2	Euridice
0.0290	24.6	.0000	2	Everglades
0.0290	24.6	.0000	2	F**
0.0290	24.6	.0000	2	F-106
0.0290	24.6	.0000	2	fagot
0.0290	24.6	.0000	2	fancy-dress
0.0290	24.6	.0000	2	fatalist
0.0290	24.6	.0000	2	Favonius
0.0290	24.6	.0000	2	Ferhat
0.0290	24.6	.0000	2	Fianna
0.0290	24.6	.0000	2	Fierce
0.0290	24.6	.0000	2	fire-eater
0.0290	24.6	.0000	2	fire's
0.0290	24.6	.0000	2	fjords
0.0290	24.6	.0000	2	flameout
0.0290	24.6	.0000	2	flare-out
0.0290	24.6	.0000	2	flintlock
0.0290	24.6	.0000	2	Flower's
0.0290	24.6	.0000	2	Folksong
0.0290	24.6	.0000	2	Foll
0.0290	24.6	.0000	2	follow-my-leader
0.0290	24.6	.0000	2	Fontana
0.0290	24.6	.0000	2	Fool's
0.0290	24.6	.0000	2	footstep
0.0290	24.6	.0000	2	foreshortening
0.0290	24.6	.0000	2	fork's
0.0290	24.6	.0000	2	formalities
0.0290	24.6	.0000	2	four-cent
0.0290	24.6	.0000	2	four-cylinder
0.0290	24.6	.0000	2	free-throw
0.0290	24.6	.0000	2	full-pressure
0.0290	24.6	.0000	2	Furillo
0.0290	24.6	.0000	2	gateposts
0.0290	24.6	.0000	2	gaz'd
0.0290	24.6	.0000	2	Gerson
0.0290	24.6	.0000	2	Gewandhaus
0.0290	24.6	.0000	2	gibs
0.0290	24.6	.0000	2	Gilman
0.0290	24.6	.0000	2	Gilvaethwy
0.0290	24.6	.0000	2	Gionfriddo
0.0290	24.6	.0000	2	Giron
0.0290	24.6	.0000	2	Glarus
0.0290	24.6	.0000	2	godson
0.0290	24.6	.0000	2	Goewin
0.0290	24.6	.0000	2	goslings
0.0290	24.6	.0000	2	grandcolts
0.0290	24.6	.0000	2	great-grandson
0.0290	24.6	.0000	2	Greenie
0.0290	24.6	.0000	2	guidon
0.0290	24.6	.0000	2	Gunboat
0.0290	24.6	.0000	2	Gwydion
THE PRECEDING WORD TYPE OCCUPIES RANK 53000				
0.0290	24.6	.0000	2	Ha
0.0290	24.6	.0000	2	Haaga
0.0290	24.6	.0000	2	Hab's
0.0290	24.6	.0000	2	Hacha
0.0290	24.6	.0000	2	Hambletonian's
0.0290	24.6	.0000	2	HAMMER
0.0290	24.6	.0000	2	hampers
0.0290	24.6	.0000	2	handle-bar
0.0290	24.6	.0000	2	Hapsburgs
0.0290	24.6	.0000	2	hard-pressed
0.0290	24.6	.0000	2	hart
0.0290	24.6	.0000	2	head-shy
0.0290	24.6	.0000	2	heart-breaking
0.0290	24.6	.0000	2	Hendrik
0.0290	24.6	.0000	2	Henrich
0.0290	24.6	.0000	2	hippos'
0.0290	24.6	.0000	2	hoecakes
0.0290	24.6	.0000	2	Holston
0.0290	24.6	.0000	2	hoosband
0.0290	24.6	.0000	2	Hostilius
0.0290	24.6	.0000	2	Humming-bird
0.0290	24.6	.0000	2	Hunger
0.0290	24.6	.0000	2	Hyer
0.0290	24.6	.0000	2	Hyperboreans
0.0290	24.6	.0000	2	hyrax
0.0290	24.6	.0000	2	idling
0.0290	24.6	.0000	2	Iggy
0.0290	24.6	.0000	2	Ignazio
0.0290	24.6	.0000	2	iguanodon
0.0290	24.6	.0000	2	Infanta
0.0290	24.6	.0000	2	installs
0.0290	24.6	.0000	2	IP'S
0.0290	24.6	.0000	2	Janissaries
0.0290	24.6	.0000	2	Jeeps
0.0290	24.6	.0000	2	Jen's
0.0290	24.6	.0000	2	Johnston's
0.0290	24.6	.0000	2	Johnty's
0.0290	24.6	.0000	2	Jorgensen
0.0290	24.6	.0000	2	Juno
0.0290	24.6	.0000	2	Kaata
0.0290	24.6	.0000	2	kapusta
0.0290	24.6	.0000	2	Kemper
0.0290	24.6	.0000	2	Kentons
0.0290	24.6	.0000	2	ker-choo
0.0290	24.6	.0000	2	Kha
0.0290	24.6	.0000	2	Kho
0.0290	24.6	.0000	2	Kiyago
0.0290	24.6	.0000	2	Knives
0.0290	24.6	.0000	2	knoweth
0.0290	24.6	.0000	2	Kula
0.0290	24.6	.0000	2	Kurtis
0.0290	24.6	.0000	2	Kvidal
0.0290	24.6	.0000	2	Lamson
0.0290	24.6	.0000	2	Lavardens
0.0290	24.6	.0000	2	Lazarus
0.0290	24.6	.0000	2	lea
0.0290	24.6	.0000	2	leaf-nosed
0.0290	24.6	.0000	2	Leap
0.0290	24.6	.0000	2	Li'l
0.0290	24.6	.0000	2	lifebelts
0.0290	24.6	.0000	2	lilacs
0.0290	24.6	.0000	2	Llaw
0.0290	24.6	.0000	2	Llew
0.0290	24.6	.0000	2	Locomobile
0.0290	24.6	.0000	2	Lucretia's
0.0290	24.6	.0000	2	Lummox
0.0290	24.6	.0000	2	lump-nosed
0.0290	24.6	.0000	2	Lumumba
0.0290	24.6	.0000	2	lunars
0.0290	24.6	.0000	2	Lussurioso's
0.0290	24.6	.0000	2	Luxembourgers
0.0290	24.6	.0000	2	MacArt
0.0290	24.6	.0000	2	Macroom
0.0290	24.6	.0000	2	Magdalenian
0.0290	24.6	.0000	2	Maglie
0.0290	24.6	.0000	2	Malalo
0.0290	24.6	.0000	2	Manya
0.0290	24.6	.0000	2	Mapai
0.0290	24.6	.0000	2	Marbury
0.0290	24.6	.0000	2	Marti
0.0290	24.6	.0000	2	massa
0.0290	24.6	.0000	2	Massie
0.0290	24.6	.0000	2	Math's
0.0290	24.6	.0000	2	matrimonial
0.0290	24.6	.0000	2	McBrier
0.0290	24.6	.0000	2	McGraw
0.0290	24.6	.0000	2	McGraw's
0.0290	24.6	.0000	2	Medico
0.0290	24.6	.0000	2	meetinghouse
0.0290	24.6	.0000	2	Melanesians
0.0290	24.6	.0000	2	Meo
0.0290	24.6	.0000	2	mercantile
0.0290	24.6	.0000	2	mercenaries
0.0290	24.6	.0000	2	Mestrovich
0.0290	24.6	.0000	2	mightly
0.0290	24.6	.0000	2	miler
0.0290	24.6	.0000	2	Miroirs
0.0290	24.6	.0000	2	Moneybags
0.0290	24.6	.0000	2	Morten
0.0290	24.6	.0000	2	Moses-Poses
THE PRECEDING WORD TYPE OCCUPIES RANK 53100				
0.0290	24.6	.0000	2	Mouvement
0.0290	24.6	.0000	2	mumble-peg
0.0290	24.6	.0000	2	municipalities
0.0290	24.6	.0000	2	Murad
0.0290	24.6	.0000	2	Muscle
0.0290	24.6	.0000	2	Myrrhine
0.0290	24.6	.0000	2	Neapolitans
0.0290	24.6	.0000	2	neck-and-neck
0.0290	24.6	.0000	2	Newbury
0.0290	24.6	.0000	2	Niall
0.0290	24.6	.0000	2	Niall's
0.0290	24.6	.0000	2	Nibel
0.0290	24.6	.0000	2	Niner
0.0290	24.6	.0000	2	No-Hair
0.0290	24.6	.0000	2	no-hitters
0.0290	24.6	.0000	2	nosewheel
0.0290	24.6	.0000	2	Nuit
0.0290	24.6	.0000	2	Nylon
0.0290	24.6	.0000	2	Obed
0.0290	24.6	.0000	2	oddities
0.0290	24.6	.0000	2	Okishgon
0.0290	24.6	.0000	2	onrush
0.0290	24.6	.0000	2	Oo-loo-te-ka
0.0290	24.6	.0000	2	Orbiter
0.0290	24.6	.0000	2	ordinaries
0.0290	24.6	.0000	2	Ormsby
0.0290	24.6	.0000	2	ornitholestes
0.0290	24.6	.0000	2	Ornitholestes
0.0290	24.6	.0000	2	ostracod
0.0290	24.6	.0000	2	Othman's
0.0290	24.6	.0000	2	Pah-Utes
0.0290	24.6	.0000	2	pakehas
0.0290	24.6	.0000	2	panteth
0.0290	24.6	.0000	2	Paramaribo
0.0290	24.6	.0000	2	parsnip
0.0290	24.6	.0000	2	parsonage
0.0290	24.6	.0000	2	parunts
0.0290	24.6	.0000	2	Pauls
0.0290	24.6	.0000	2	Per
0.0290	24.6	.0000	2	Pestalozzi
0.0290	24.6	.0000	2	Petromin
0.0290	24.6	.0000	2	Philleo
0.0290	24.6	.0000	2	piebalds
0.0290	24.6	.0000	2	pillboxes
0.0290	24.6	.0000	2	pimiento
0.0290	24.6	.0000	2	Pirana
0.0290	24.6	.0000	2	plainsman
0.0290	24.6	.0000	2	Plantation
0.0290	24.6	.0000	2	plop-plop
0.0290	24.6	.0000	2	polnena
0.0290	24.6	.0000	2	polyphemus
0.0290	24.6	.0000	2	Pompilius
0.0290	24.6	.0000	2	Pons
0.0290	24.6	.0000	2	Pooneno
0.0290	24.6	.0000	2	postriders
0.0290	24.6	.0000	2	praise-singer's
0.0290	24.6	.0000	2	pricks
0.0290	24.6	.0000	2	prolegs
0.0290	24.6	.0000	2	propwash
0.0290	24.6	.0000	2	Proserpine
0.0290	24.6	.0000	2	Proverbs
0.0290	24.6	.0000	2	Pryderi
0.0290	24.6	.0000	2	PT-59
0.0290	24.6	.0000	2	pugilists
0.0290	24.6	.0000	2	Purser
0.0290	24.6	.0000	2	Pwyll
0.0290	24.6	.0000	2	radial-arm
0.0290	24.6	.0000	2	Ragnhild
0.0290	24.6	.0000	2	raped
0.0290	24.6	.0000	2	re-birth
0.0290	24.6	.0000	2	rear'd
0.0290	24.6	.0000	2	Reeds
0.0290	24.6	.0000	2	Reese
0.0290	24.6	.0000	2	Reynaud
0.0290	24.6	.0000	2	rice-balls
0.0290	24.6	.0000	2	Rinuccini
0.0290	24.6	.0000	2	riverlike
0.0290	24.6	.0000	2	roadsters
0.0290	24.6	.0000	2	robb'st
0.0290	24.6	.0000	2	roundout
0.0290	24.6	.0000	2	salt-camp
0.0290	24.6	.0000	2	salvo
0.0290	24.6	.0000	2	Sanne
0.0290	24.6	.0000	2	Savonarola
0.0290	24.6	.0000	2	scarf-skin
0.0290	24.6	.0000	2	Scouting
0.0290	24.6	.0000	2	scrappy
0.0290	24.6	.0000	9	seamline
0.0290	24.6	.0000	2	self-explanatory
0.0290	24.6	.0000	2	seventeen-thousand-mile
0.0290	24.6	.0000	2	Sextus
0.0290	24.6	.0000	2	shabbiness
0.0290	24.6	.0000	2	Shadwell
0.0290	24.6	.0000	2	shield-shaped
0.0290	24.6	.0000	2	Shipman's
0.0290	24.6	.0000	2	short-legged
0.0290	24.6	.0000	2	Shotton
0.0290	24.6	.0000	2	Sieke
0.0290	24.6	.0000	2	singsong
0.0290	24.6	.0000	2	Sizaire
THE PRECEDING WORD TYPE OCCUPIES RANK 53200				
0.0290	24.6	.0000	2	Skaret
0.0290	24.6	.0000	2	skewbalds
0.0290	24.6	.0000	2	Sokoto
0.0290	24.6	.0000	2	Spartacus
0.0290	24.6	.0000	2	Specht
0.0290	24.6	.0000	2	speedway
0.0290	24.6	.0000	2	spinet
0.0290	24.6	.0000	2	spoonsful
0.0290	24.6	.0000	2	Spreading
0.0290	24.6	.0000	2	Spuhler
0.0290	24.6	.0000	2	squabble
0.0290	24.6	.0000	9	staystitch
0.0290	24.6	.0000	2	stegosaurs
0.0290	24.6	.0000	2	Stevie's
0.0290	24.6	.0000	2	stoneboat
0.0290	24.6	.0000	2	stooges
0.0290	24.6	.0000	2	storekeeper's
0.0290	24.6	.0000	2	Storting
0.0290	24.6	.0000	2	striping
0.0290	24.6	.0000	2	sunnies
0.0290	24.6	.0000	2	swartgevaar
0.0290	24.6	.0000	2	Sweepstakes
0.0290	24.6	.0000	2	Sy
0.0290	24.6	.0000	2	sycamores
0.0290	24.6	.0000	2	Syndicate
0.0290	24.6	.0000	2	T-e-a-c-h-e-r
0.0290	24.6	.0000	2	Talon
0.0290	24.6	.0000	2	Taoist
0.0290	24.6	.0000	2	Task
0.0290	24.6	.0000	2	taters
0.0290	24.6	.0000	2	Tatius
0.0290	24.6	.0000	2	Tear
0.0290	24.6	.0000	2	third-class
0.0290	24.6	.0000	2	tick-bird
0.0290	24.6	.0000	2	Timmie
0.0290	24.6	.0000	2	Ting
0.0290	24.6	.0000	2	Tinnie
0.0290	24.6	.0000	2	Tithers
0.0290	24.6	.0000	2	Todds
0.0290	24.6	.0000	2	Tombeau
0.0290	24.6	.0000	2	Tomlinson
0.0290	24.6	.0000	2	tongue-lashing
0.0290	24.6	.0000	2	Traeger
0.0290	24.6	.0000	2	transact
0.0290	24.6	.0000	2	trimmers
0.0290	24.6	.0000	2	trotters
0.0290	24.6	.0000	2	trouping
0.0290	24.6	.0000	2	Tuan's
0.0290	24.6	.0000	2	Tulagi
0.0290	24.6	.0000	2	tyrannosaurus
0.0290	24.6	.0000	2	unbosomings
0.0290	24.6	.0000	2	Valdemar
0.0290	24.6	.0000	2	Valerian
0.0290	24.6	.0000	2	Vang
0.0290	24.6	.0000	2	Vatne
0.0290	24.6	.0000	2	veneer
0.0290	24.6	.0000	2	vetoing
0.0290	24.6	.0000	2	Vieng
0.0290	24.6	.0000	2	Vientiane
0.0290	24.6	.0000	2	VietNam
0.0290	24.6	.0000	2	Vilhjalmur
0.0290	24.6	.0000	2	vonBraun
0.0290	24.6	.0000	2	Vran's
0.0290	24.6	.0000	2	Wanamakers
0.0290	24.6	.0000	2	Washington-on-the-Brazos
0.0290	24.6	.0000	2	Watauga
0.0290	24.6	.0000	2	Watertown's
0.0290	24.6	.0000	2	Westernization
0.0290	24.6	.0000	2	whackers
0.0290	24.6	.0000	2	whale-catcher
0.0290	24.6	.0000	2	What-do-you-think
0.0290	24.6	.0000	2	Whippoorwill
0.0290	24.6	.0000	2	white-topped
0.0290	24.6	.0000	2	whoopala
0.0290	24.6	.0000	2	Wilhelmina
0.0290	24.6	.0000	2	Winn
0.0290	24.6	.0000	2	wipe-on
0.0290	24.6	.0000	2	wisecrack
0.0290	24.6	.0000	2	wonderfulness
0.0290	24.6	.0000	2	wormed
0.0290	24.6	.0000	2	Wrigley
0.0290	24.6	.0000	2	Wubber
0.0290	24.6	.0000	2	Yap
0.0290	24.6	.0000	2	Yi
0.0290	24.6	.0000	2	zag
0.0290	24.6	.0000	2	zig
0.0290	24.6	.0000	2	zippered
0.0290	24.6	.0000	2	Zoutenaaie

U	SFI	D	F	Word Type
0.0290	24.6	.0000	2	1717
0.0290	24.6	.0000	2	1758
0.0290	24.6	.0000	2	3-liter
0.0290	24.6	.0000	2	3g
0.0290	24.6	.0000	2	37mm
0.0290	24.6	.0000	2	40-millimeter
0.0290	24.6	.0000	2	500-Mile
0.0278	24.4	.0000	11	dielectric
0.0268	24.3	.0000	12	Steinbeck
0.0264	24.2	.0182	2	Abraham's
0.0264	24.2	.0182	2	Blessed
0.0258	24.1	.0000	8	Simple

THE PRECEDING WORD TYPE OCCUPIES RANK 53300

U	SFI	D	F	Word Type
0.0258	24.1	.0000	8	underarm
0.0258	24.1	.0000	8	washable
0.0243	23.9	.0000	2	$240
0.0243	23.9	.0000	3	-ally
0.0243	23.9	.0000	3	-ary
0.0243	23.9	.0000	3	-ense
0.0243	23.9	.0000	3	/ar/
0.0243	23.9	.0000	3	/h/
0.0243	23.9	.0000	2	'60s
0.0243	23.9	.0000	2	'66
0.0243	23.9	.0000	2	'70s
0.0243	23.9	.0000	2	'71
0.0243	23.8	.0000	3	A-B-A
0.0243	23.8	.0000	3	AABB
0.0243	23.8	.0000	3	ABA
0.0243	23.9	.0000	2	ABC-tv
0.0243	23.9	.0000	2	Aberystwyth
0.0243	23.9	.0000	2	ABM
0.0243	23.8	.0000	3	accelerando
0.0243	23.9	.0000	2	accommodating
0.0243	23.9	.0000	2	acreages
0.0243	23.9	.0000	2	activate
0.0243	23.9	.0000	2	actresses
0.0243	23.9	.0000	2	actuation
0.0243	23.9	.0000	2	addicts
0.0243	23.9	.0000	2	adequacy
0.0243	23.9	.0000	2	adjuster
0.0243	23.9	.0000	2	admen
0.0243	23.9	.0000	2	adversaries
0.0243	23.9	.0000	2	advocating
0.0243	23.9	.0000	2	aerated
0.0243	23.9	.0000	2	AFL
0.0243	23.9	.0000	2	AFL-CIO's
0.0243	23.9	.0000	2	AFL-CIO
0.0243	23.9	.0000	2	Albee
0.0243	23.9	.0000	2	albums
0.0243	23.9	.0000	2	allegations
0.0243	23.8	.0000	3	Allegro
0.0243	23.8	.0000	3	altos
0.0243	23.9	.0000	2	alveoli
0.0243	23.8	.0000	3	Amahl's
0.0243	23.9	.0000	2	ambient
0.0243	23.9	.0000	2	ambiguity
0.0243	23.9	.0000	2	AMC'S
0.0243	23.9	.0000	2	AMERICAN
0.0243	23.9	.0000	2	anarchists
0.0243	23.9	.0000	2	Andrews'
0.0243	23.9	.0000	2	animosity
0.0243	23.9	.0000	2	anthologies
0.0243	23.9	.0000	2	anthropomorphism
0.0243	23.9	.0000	2	Anticipations
0.0243	23.8	.0000	3	Antiochus
0.0243	23.9	.0000	2	antiperspirant
0.0243	23.9	.0000	2	antiwar
0.0243	23.9	.0000	2	APBA
0.0243	23.9	.0000	2	apocalyptic
0.0243	23.9	.0000	2	applicants
0.0243	23.9	.0000	3	apprehend
0.0243	23.9	.0000	2	Appropriations
0.0243	23.9	.0000	2	Ara
0.0243	23.9	.0000	2	Arab's
0.0243	23.9	.0000	2	Arcade
0.0243	23.9	.0000	2	Arecibo
0.0243	23.9	.0000	2	Ariz
0.0243	23.9	.0000	2	Armour
0.0243	23.8	.0000	3	Aroon
0.0243	23.9	.0000	2	arrogance
0.0243	23.9	.0000	2	at-home
0.0243	23.9	.0000	2	Athabasca
0.0243	23.9	.0000	2	Atlanta's
0.0243	23.9	.0000	3	Atuk
0.0243	23.9	.0000	2	Auto
0.0243	23.8	.0000	3	Autoharp
0.0243	23.8	.0000	3	B-flat
0.0243	23.8	.0000	3	baby-o
0.0243	23.9	.0000	2	back-pocket
0.0243	23.9	.0000	2	backfield
0.0243	23.9	.0000	2	backpack
0.0243	23.9	.0000	2	backpacks
0.0243	23.9	.0000	2	Bali's
0.0243	23.9	.0000	2	Balinese
0.0243	23.9	.0000	2	Ballinascarthy
0.0243	23.9	.0000	2	Bandana
0.0243	23.9	.0000	2	bandwagon
0.0243	23.9	.0000	2	Bang
0.0243	23.9	.0000	2	Barbados
0.0243	23.9	.0000	2	barbiturates
0.0243	23.9	.0000	2	barman
0.0243	23.9	.0000	2	barriadas
0.0243	23.9	.0000	2	Barske
0.0243	23.9	.0000	2	Basketball
0.0243	23.9	.0000	2	basketball's
0.0243	23.9	.0000	2	Bass
0.0243	23.9	.0000	2	Bay's
0.0243	23.9	.0000	2	Baylor
0.0243	23.9	.0000	2	Bayside
0.0243	23.9	.0000	2	Beatles
0.0243	23.9	.0000	2	Beaubrun
0.0243	23.9	.0000	2	Beban
0.0243	23.9	.0000	2	Beep

THE PRECEDING WORD TYPE OCCUPIES RANK 53400

U	SFI	D	F	Word Type
0.0243	23.9	.0000	2	Behrman
0.0243	23.9	.0000	2	Bendix
0.0243	23.9	.0000	2	Bengtson
0.0243	23.9	.0000	2	benthos
0.0243	23.9	.0000	2	Berri
0.0243	23.9	.0000	2	Besterman's
0.0243	23.9	.0000	2	big-city
0.0243	23.9	.0000	2	bird-aircraft
0.0243	23.9	.0000	2	Bitter
0.0243	23.9	.0000	2	bittersweet
0.0243	23.9	.0000	2	Blades
0.0243	23.9	.0000	2	Blend
0.0243	23.9	.0000	2	Bloom
0.0243	23.8	.0000	3	blue-tail
0.0243	23.9	.0000	2	Blvd
0.0243	23.9	.0000	2	boa
0.0243	23.9	.0000	2	bolt-on
0.0243	23.9	.0000	2	Bombers
0.0243	23.9	.0000	2	boogaloo
0.0243	23.9	.0000	2	booing
0.0243	23.9	.0000	2	boondocks
0.0243	23.9	.0000	2	Boonie-Bike
0.0243	23.9	.0000	2	Borch
0.0243	23.9	.0000	2	bos'n
0.0243	23.9	.0000	2	bos'n's
0.0243	23.9	.0000	2	boycotted
0.0243	23.8	.0000	3	Br'er
0.0243	23.8	.0000	3	Brahms'
0.0243	23.9	.0000	2	brainwashed
0.0243	23.9	.0000	2	Brandle
0.0243	23.9	.0000	2	Brando's
0.0243	23.9	.0000	2	breakaway
0.0243	23.9	.0000	2	Briley
0.0243	23.9	.0000	2	Brodhead
0.0243	23.9	.0000	2	brooder
0.0243	23.9	.0000	2	Bros
0.0243	23.9	.0000	2	Brownell
0.0243	23.9	.0000	2	brush-ins
0.0243	23.9	.0000	2	bucktail
0.0243	23.9	.0000	2	buffs
0.0243	23.9	.0000	2	bugaboo
0.0243	23.9	.0000	2	Burl
0.0243	23.9	.0000	2	bushing
0.0243	23.9	.0000	2	Bye
0.0243	23.9	.0000	2	caddis
0.0243	23.9	.0000	2	Caernarvon
0.0243	23.9	.0000	2	Calculus
0.0243	23.9	.0000	2	campsites
0.0243	23.8	.0000	3	Camptown
0.0243	23.9	.0000	2	camshaft
0.0243	23.9	.0000	2	candor
0.0243	23.9	.0000	2	canisters
0.0243	23.9	.0000	2	Canning
0.0243	23.9	.0000	2	canny
0.0243	23.9	.0000	2	cantaloupe
0.0243	23.8	.0000	3	Cantata
0.0243	23.9	.0000	2	capitulated
0.0243	23.9	.0000	2	caricatured
0.0243	23.9	.0000	2	Carminowe
0.0243	23.9	.0000	2	Carranza
0.0243	23.9	.0000	2	cartopper
0.0243	23.9	.0000	2	Castelli
0.0243	23.9	.0000	2	Catch
0.0243	23.9	.0000	2	catering
0.0243	23.9	.0000	2	Cattle-Fax
0.0243	23.9	.0000	2	cavers
0.0243	23.9	.0000	2	cayenne
0.0243	23.9	.0000	2	centennial
0.0243	23.9	.0000	2	Cepheids
0.0243	23.9	.0000	2	Cesare
0.0243	23.8	.0000	3	chaperone
0.0243	23.9	.0000	2	Chargers
0.0243	23.9	.0000	2	charismatic
0.0243	23.9	.0000	2	Charrasse
0.0243	23.9	.0000	3	Chaucer's
0.0243	23.9	.0000	2	checklists
0.0243	23.9	.0000	2	Chef
0.0243	23.9	.0000	2	cherishes
0.0243	23.9	.0000	2	Chipewyan
0.0243	23.9	.0000	2	Chipping
0.0243	23.9	.0000	2	Chiricahuas
0.0243	23.9	.0000	2	Chitty
0.0243	23.8	.0000	3	choreography
0.0243	23.9	.0000	2	Chung
0.0243	23.9	.0000	3	cial
0.0243	23.9	.0000	2	cinder-block
0.0243	23.9	.0000	2	Clam
0.0243	23.9	.0000	2	clapboard
0.0243	23.9	.0000	2	Clapton
0.0243	23.8	.0000	3	clefs
0.0243	23.9	.0000	2	Cleveland's
0.0243	23.9	.0000	2	clobbered
0.0243	23.9	.0000	2	coeducation
0.0243	23.9	.0000	3	coining
0.0243	23.9	.0000	2	college's
0.0243	23.9	.0000	2	Collegiate
0.0243	23.9	.0000	2	colours
0.0243	23.9	.0000	2	compatriots
0.0243	23.9	.0000	2	compendium
0.0243	23.9	.0000	2	Comptroller

THE PRECEDING WORD TYPE OCCUPIES RANK 53500

U	SFI	D	F	Word Type
0.0243	23.9	.0000	2	computerized
0.0243	23.9	.0000	2	Concannon
0.0243	23.9	.0000	2	Conquistadores
0.0243	23.9	.0000	2	consultant
0.0243	23.9	.0000	2	consultations
0.0243	23.9	.0000	2	consults
0.0243	23.9	.0000	2	contender
0.0243	23.9	.0000	2	convents
0.0243	23.8	.0000	3	Cookie
0.0243	23.9	.0000	2	coonhound
0.0243	23.9	.0000	2	Cooperative
0.0243	23.9	.0000	2	Coordinating
0.0243	23.9	.0000	2	Corcoran
0.0243	23.9	.0000	2	cordless
0.0243	23.9	.0000	2	Cork's
0.0243	23.9	.0000	2	corrects
0.0243	23.9	.0000	2	Cortina
0.0243	23.9	.0000	2	Cory
0.0243	23.9	.0000	2	counter-attack
0.0243	23.8	.0000	3	counter-subject
0.0243	23.8	.0000	3	countermelody
0.0243	23.9	.0000	2	countryman
0.0243	23.9	.0000	2	courted
0.0243	23.9	.0000	2	Coweeman
0.0243	23.8	.0000	3	Creston
0.0243	23.9	.0000	2	Crispus
0.0243	23.9	.0000	2	Croat
0.0243	23.9	.0000	2	Croce
0.0243	23.9	.0000	2	Cross-Florida
0.0243	23.9	.0000	2	crusaded
0.0243	23.9	.0000	2	CSM
0.0243	23.9	.0000	2	curbed
0.0243	23.9	.0000	2	cutability
0.0243	23.9	.0000	2	cutoffs
0.0243	23.9	.0000	2	cwt
0.0243	23.9	.0000	2	cyclamate
0.0243	23.9	.0000	2	cynicism
0.0243	23.9	.0000	3	Cyrillic
0.0243	23.8	.0000	3	C7
0.0243	23.9	.0000	2	d'Ascoli
0.0243	23.9	.0000	2	d'Orleans
0.0243	23.9	.0000	2	Dachau
0.0243	23.8	.0000	3	daddy-o
0.0243	23.9	.0000	2	dais
0.0243	23.9	.0000	2	Darlington
0.0243	23.9	.0000	2	dasher
0.0243	23.9	.0000	2	deGaulle's
0.0243	23.9	.0000	2	dealer's
0.0243	23.9	.0000	2	decentralize
0.0243	23.9	.0000	2	deductible
0.0243	23.9	.0000	2	Defferre's
0.0243	23.9	.0000	2	deja
0.0243	23.9	.0000	2	Delgados
0.0243	23.9	.0000	2	Delicate
0.0243	23.9	.0000	2	deluxe
0.0243	23.9	.0000	2	Demilitarized
0.0243	23.8	.0000	3	descants
0.0243	23.8	.0000	3	descendents
0.0243	23.9	.0000	2	Detroit's
0.0243	23.9	.0000	2	devalued
0.0243	23.9	.0000	2	DiMaggio's
0.0243	23.9	.0000	2	diabetics
0.0243	23.8	.0000	3	Dies
0.0243	23.9	.0000	2	dines
0.0243	23.9	.0000	2	dipstick
0.0243	23.9	.0000	2	disavowed
0.0243	23.9	.0000	2	disciplinary
0.0243	23.9	.0000	2	discotheques
0.0243	23.9	.0000	2	dispositions
0.0243	23.9	.0000	2	Div
0.0243	23.9	.0000	2	DMZ
0.0243	23.8	.0000	3	Donizetti
0.0243	23.9	.0000	2	dons
0.0243	23.9	.0000	2	doolies
0.0243	23.9	.0000	2	Dramatists
0.0243	23.8	.0000	3	dreydl
0.0243	23.9	.0000	2	Drysdale
0.0243	23.9	.0000	2	duMaurier's
0.0243	23.9	.0000	2	Duc
0.0243	23.8	.0000	3	duets
0.0243	23.9	.0000	2	Dunes
0.0243	23.9	.0000	2	earthquake-proof
0.0243	23.9	.0000	2	Easton
0.0243	23.9	.0000	2	ebullience
0.0243	23.9	.0000	2	EDA
0.0243	23.9	.0000	2	editor-in-chief
0.0243	23.8	.0000	3	ee-ri-gi
0.0243	23.9	.0000	2	Ehrlichman
0.0243	23.9	.0000	2	Elochoman
0.0243	23.9	.0000	2	Elysee
0.0243	23.8	.0000	3	emotionalism
0.0243	23.9	.0000	2	Engstrom
0.0243	23.8	.0000	3	Entrance
0.0243	23.9	.0000	2	Erikson's
0.0243	23.8	.0000	3	Eroica
0.0243	23.9	.0000	3	ery
0.0243	23.9	.0000	2	Esperanto
0.0243	23.9	.0000	2	espresso
0.0243	23.8	.0000	3	Etude
0.0243	23.8	.0000	3	Executioner

THE PRECEDING WORD TYPE OCCUPIES RANK 53600

U	SFI	D	F	Word Type
0.0243	23.9	.0000	2	expertise
0.0243	23.9	.0000	2	Expression
0.0243	23.8	.0000	3	extramusical
0.0243	23.9	.0000	3	ey
0.0243	23.9	.0000	2	eyrie
0.0243	23.8	.0000	3	F-major
0.0243	23.9	.0000	2	Fairlane
0.0243	23.9	.0000	2	Falcons
0.0243	23.9	.0000	2	far-out
0.0243	23.9	.0000	2	Farrar
0.0243	23.9	.0000	2	father-and-son
0.0243	23.9	.0000	2	father-in-law
0.0243	23.9	.0000	2	fatigues
0.0243	23.9	.0000	2	Feigen
0.0243	23.8	.0000	3	Feud
0.0243	23.8	.0000	3	Fidelity
0.0243	23.9	.0000	2	film-making
0.0243	23.9	.0000	2	filmmaker
0.0243	23.9	.0000	2	fiscal
0.0243	23.8	.0000	3	Fishers
0.0243	23.9	.0000	2	FITH
0.0243	23.9	.0000	2	Fitz
0.0243	23.9	.0000	2	flanges
0.0243	23.8	.0000	3	flatting
0.0243	23.9	.0000	2	flawless
0.0243	23.9	.0000	2	Fleas
0.0243	23.8	.0000	3	Fledermaus
0.0243	23.9	.0000	2	Florabel
0.0243	23.8	.0000	3	folk-music
0.0243	23.9	.0000	2	folk-rock
0.0243	23.9	.0000	2	Fools
0.0243	23.9	.0000	2	foreign-policy
0.0243	23.9	.0000	2	forgettable
0.0243	23.9	.0000	2	forrard
0.0243	23.8	.0000	3	four-measure
0.0243	23.9	.0000	2	four-speed
0.0243	23.9	.0000	2	four-week
0.0243	23.9	.0000	2	Foyega
0.0243	23.9	.0000	2	fragrances
0.0243	23.9	.0000	2	Frames
0.0243	23.8	.0000	3	Frasquita
0.0243	23.9	.0000	2	Fresca
0.0243	23.9	.0000	2	Fried
0.0243	23.9	.0000	2	front-wheel
0.0243	23.9	.0000	2	frustrating
0.0243	23.9	.0000	2	full-employment
0.0243	23.9	.0000	3	g-h-o-t-i
0.0243	23.9	.0000	2	Gable
0.0243	23.8	.0000	3	Gal
0.0243	23.9	.0000	2	Galapagos
0.0243	23.9	.0000	2	Garagiola
0.0243	23.9	.0000	2	Garcilaso
0.0243	23.9	.0000	2	garrisoned
0.0243	23.9	.0000	2	Gatundu
0.0243	23.9	.0000	2	gawking
0.0243	23.9	.0000	2	GE'S
0.0243	23.8	.0000	3	gee-haw
0.0243	23.8	.0000	3	gents
0.0243	23.9	.0000	2	geodesic
0.0243	23.9	.0000	2	ghost-writing
0.0243	23.8	.0000	3	Gioacchino
0.0243	23.8	.0000	3	Glendy
0.0243	23.8	.0000	3	Glomstulen
0.0243	23.9	.0000	2	glorifies
0.0243	23.9	.0000	2	Glynn
0.0243	23.9	.0000	2	GM'S
0.0243	23.9	.0000	2	go-getter
0.0243	23.8	.0000	3	Godmother
0.0243	23.8	.0000	3	Godounov
0.0243	23.9	.0000	2	going-away
0.0243	23.8	.0000	3	Goldman
0.0243	23.9	.0000	2	Golf
0.0243	23.9	.0000	2	Goofus
0.0243	23.9	.0000	2	gourmet
0.0243	23.9	.0000	2	Gouyave
0.0243	23.9	.0000	2	GP
0.0243	23.9	.0000	2	grad
0.0243	23.9	.0000	2	Grech
0.0243	23.9	.0000	2	Grechko's
0.0243	23.9	.0000	2	greenstick
0.0243	23.9	.0000	2	Grenada
0.0243	23.9	.0000	2	Grimsey's
0.0243	23.9	.0000	2	Grrrr
0.0243	23.8	.0000	3	Gruber
0.0243	23.9	.0000	2	guideway
0.0243	23.9	.0000	2	guru
0.0243	23.9	.0000	2	gymnastics
0.0243	23.9	.0000	2	H/A
0.0243	23.9	.0000	2	Haddock
0.0243	23.9	.0000	2	Haggerty
0.0243	23.9	.0000	2	Hagy
0.0243	23.8	.0000	3	half-note
0.0243	23.9	.0000	2	halftime
0.0243	23.9	.0000	2	Halpern
0.0243	23.9	.0000	2	Hamme
0.0243	23.9	.0000	2	handguns
0.0243	23.9	.0000	2	handloads
0.0243	23.9	.0000	2	harambee
0.0243	23.9	.0000	2	headquartered
0.0243	23.9	.0000	2	Heartbreak

THE PRECEDING WORD TYPE OCCUPIES RANK 53700

U	SFI	D	F	Word Type
0.0243	23.9	.0000	2	Heartland
0.0243	23.8	.0000	3	heav'n
0.0243	23.9	.0000	2	Heinold's
0.0243	23.9	.0000	2	Heiskell
0.0243	23.9	.0000	2	Heller
0.0243	23.9	.0000	2	Henke's
0.0243	23.9	.0000	2	Hepzibah
0.0243	23.9	.0000	2	hexachlorophene
0.0243	23.8	.0000	3	Hi-dee-roon
0.0243	23.9	.0000	2	Hickel
0.0243	23.9	.0000	2	high-performance
0.0243	23.9	.0000	2	high-scoring
0.0243	23.9	.0000	2	Hightower
0.0243	23.8	.0000	3	Himmel
0.0243	23.9	.0000	2	Hinsdale
0.0243	23.9	.0000	2	hitchhikers
0.0243	23.9	.0000	2	Holley
0.0243	23.9	.0000	2	Holleys
0.0243	23.9	.0000	2	holograms
0.0243	23.9	.0000	3	holyday
0.0243	23.9	.0000	2	homesite
0.0243	23.9	.0000	2	homeward-bound
0.0243	23.9	.0000	3	homos
0.0243	23.9	.0000	2	Honda
0.0243	23.9	.0000	2	Honeycreeper
0.0243	23.9	.0000	2	honoraries
0.0243	23.9	.0000	2	hoodlum
0.0243	23.9	.0000	2	hospital's
0.0243	23.9	.0000	2	hot-
0.0243	23.9	.0000	2	Houdini's
0.0243	23.9	.0000	2	Hovercraft
0.0243	23.9	.0000	2	hp
0.0243	23.9	.0000	2	HuntingtonBeach
0.0243	23.9	.0000	2	Husak
0.0243	23.9	.0000	2	hydrology
0.0243	23.9	.0000	2	hydrophones
0.0243	23.9	.0000	3	ia
0.0243	23.9	.0000	3	iceboats
0.0243	23.9	.0000	2	Ickes
0.0243	23.8	.0000	3	idiophones
0.0243	23.9	.0000	2	Illustrated
0.0243	23.9	.0000	2	immersed
0.0243	23.9	.0000	2	immobilized
0.0243	23.9	.0000	2	impossibly
0.0243	23.9	.0000	2	in-depth
0.0243	23.9	.0000	2	inconsequential
0.0243	23.9	.0000	2	indisputable
0.0243	23.9	.0000	2	inducements
0.0243	23.9	.0000	2	indulges
0.0243	23.9	.0000	2	Inns
0.0243	23.9	.0000	2	Instant

U	SFI	D	F	Word Type
0.0243	23.9	.0000	2	instructional
0.0243	23.8	.0000	3	Instruments
0.0243	23.9	.0000	2	interceptions
0.0243	23.9	.0000	2	interpersonal
0.0243	23.9	.0000	2	interviewing
0.0243	23.9	.0000	3	ious
0.0243	23.8	.0000	3	Irae
0.0243	23.9	.0000	2	Israeli-held
0.0243	23.9	.0000	3	ite
0.0243	23.9	.0000	2	Izbushka
0.0243	23.9	.0000	2	jack-o'-lanterns
0.0243	23.9	.0000	2	Jacksons
0.0243	23.9	.0000	2	Jarman
0.0243	23.9	.0000	2	Jeep's
0.0243	23.9	.0000	2	jet-age
0.0243	23.9	.0000	2	Jillson
0.0243	23.9	.0000	2	Joanie
0.0243	23.9	.0000	2	jobless
0.0243	23.9	.0000	2	Jordanian
0.0243	23.9	.0000	2	Josephson
0.0243	23.9	.0000	2	Jurgensen
0.0243	23.9	.0000	2	jurisdictions
0.0243	23.8	.0000	3	kachinas
0.0243	23.9	.0000	2	Kaibab
0.0243	23.9	.0000	2	Kaug
0.0243	23.9	.0000	2	Kazan's
0.0243	23.9	.0000	3	ke
0.0243	23.9	.0000	2	Keas
0.0243	23.8	.0000	3	Keel
0.0243	23.9	.0000	2	Kenyans
0.0243	23.9	.0000	2	Kerr
0.0243	23.9	.0000	2	Khalil
0.0243	23.9	.0000	2	Kiril
0.0243	23.9	.0000	2	Knoop
0.0243	23.9	.0000	2	Know-Nothing
0.0243	23.9	.0000	2	Kobuk
0.0243	23.9	.0000	2	Kook
0.0243	23.9	.0000	2	kooky
0.0243	23.9	.0000	2	Korea's
0.0243	23.9	.0000	2	Kuassi
0.0243	23.9	.0000	2	LaCenter
0.0243	23.9	.0000	2	Lab
0.0243	23.9	.0000	2	Labs
0.0243	23.9	.0000	2	Laird
0.0243	23.9	.0000	2	Lancet
0.0243	23.9	.0000	2	Langanes
0.0243	23.9	.0000	2	Laporte
0.0243	23.9	.0000	2	largemouth
0.0243	23.9	.0000	2	latency

THE PRECEDING WORD TYPE OCCUPIES RANK 53800

U	SFI	D	F	Word Type
0.0243	23.9	.0000	2	Lava
0.0243	23.9	.0000	2	LeMans
0.0243	23.9	.0000	2	leakage
0.0243	23.9	.0000	2	leathered
0.0243	23.9	.0000	2	Lederer
0.0243	23.9	.0000	2	Leeward
0.0243	23.9	.0000	2	Lefevre
0.0243	23.9	.0000	2	left-wing
0.0243	23.9	.0000	2	leggy
0.0243	23.9	.0000	2	lenders
0.0243	23.9	.0000	2	Lennon
0.0243	23.9	.0000	2	levelled
0.0243	23.9	.0000	2	leverage
0.0243	23.9	.0000	2	liberalization
0.0243	23.9	.0000	2	Lichtenstein
0.0243	23.9	.0000	2	life-support
0.0243	23.9	.0000	2	Linen's
0.0243	23.8	.0000	3	Liszt's
0.0243	23.9	.0000	2	litigation
0.0243	23.9	.0000	2	Lizzie's
0.0243	23.9	.0000	2	LNG
0.0243	23.9	.0000	2	Loble
0.0243	23.9	.0000	2	lockings
0.0243	23.9	.0000	2	locos
0.0243	23.9	.0000	2	Lombardi
0.0243	23.9	.0000	2	long-reach
0.0243	23.9	.0000	2	Lovaas
0.0243	23.9	.0000	2	low-branching
0.0243	23.9	.0000	2	Luce's
0.0243	23.9	.0000	2	Luneburg
0.0243	23.9	.0000	2	lunkers
0.0243	23.9	.0000	2	Madero
0.0243	23.9	.0000	2	Madjapahit
0.0243	23.9	.0000	2	Mafia
0.0243	23.9	.0000	2	mag
0.0243	23.9	.0000	2	Magazines'
0.0243	23.9	.0000	2	Magnus's
0.0243	23.9	.0000	2	mam
0.0243	23.9	.0000	2	Man-A-Fre
0.0243	23.9	.0000	2	Man-Gods
0.0243	23.9	.0000	2	Management
0.0243	23.9	.0000	2	manifolds
0.0243	23.9	.0000	2	maple-sugar
0.0243	23.9	.0000	2	Marghuerite
0.0243	23.9	.0000	2	marginally
0.0243	23.9	.0000	2	Marichal
0.0243	23.9	.0000	2	marina
0.0243	23.9	.0000	2	Mariners
0.0243	23.9	.0000	2	Mariners'
0.0243	23.9	.0000	2	Marsh's
0.0243	23.9	.0000	2	Marvel
0.0243	23.9	.0000	2	marvellously
0.0243	23.9	.0000	2	massively
0.0243	23.9	.0000	2	Masters
0.0243	23.8	.0000	3	Mastersingers
0.0243	23.9	.0000	2	Maternite
0.0243	23.9	.0000	2	matoke
0.0243	23.9	.0000	2	Matthiessen
0.0243	23.9	.0000	2	Mau
0.0243	23.9	.0000	2	mausoleum
0.0243	23.9	.0000	2	Maxim
0.0243	23.9	.0000	2	May-June
0.0243	23.8	.0000	3	mazurka
0.0243	23.9	.0000	2	McDaniel
0.0243	23.9	.0000	2	Medano
0.0243	23.9	.0000	2	Median
0.0243	23.9	.0000	2	Mehrer
0.0243	23.9	.0000	2	Melanie's
0.0243	23.9	.0000	2	mellowness
0.0243	23.9	.0000	2	mementos
0.0243	23.9	.0000	2	Metcalf
0.0243	23.9	.0000	2	MGM
0.0243	23.9	.0000	2	mid-July
0.0243	23.9	.0000	2	middlemen
0.0243	23.9	.0000	2	midfield
0.0243	23.9	.0000	2	Mindszenty
0.0243	23.9	.0000	2	minibike
0.0243	23.8	.0000	3	Minstrel
0.0243	23.9	.0000	2	mission's
0.0243	23.8	.0000	3	misspellings
0.0243	23.9	.0000	2	Mixing
0.0243	23.9	.0000	2	mmmm
0.0243	23.8	.0000	3	mn
0.0243	23.9	.0000	2	mobile-home
0.0243	23.9	.0000	2	mod
0.0243	23.9	.0000	2	Model-T
0.0243	23.9	.0000	2	Moldoveanu
0.0243	23.9	.0000	2	Mollet
0.0243	23.8	.0000	3	Molli
0.0243	23.9	.0000	2	monitoring
0.0243	23.9	.0000	2	Monkees
0.0243	23.9	.0000	2	moonlike
0.0243	23.9	.0000	2	Morin
0.0243	23.9	.0000	2	Mothergooseville
0.0243	23.9	.0000	2	motorbike
0.0243	23.9	.0000	2	motoring
0.0243	23.9	.0000	2	Movie-Drome
0.0243	23.9	.0000	2	mpg
0.0243	23.9	.0000	2	Much
0.0243	23.9	.0000	2	mugger

THE PRECEDING WORD TYPE OCCUPIES RANK 53900

U	SFI	D	F	Word Type
0.0243	23.9	.0000	2	Muhler
0.0243	23.9	.0000	2	multimillionaire
0.0243	23.9	.0000	2	Mumford
0.0243	23.9	.0000	2	mundane
0.0243	23.9	.0000	2	Munson
0.0243	23.9	.0000	2	muoi
0.0243	23.9	.0000	2	murex
0.0243	23.8	.0000	3	music-loving
0.0243	23.9	.0000	2	Muskiejump
0.0243	23.8	.0000	3	mutes
0.0243	23.9	.0000	2	Nailles
0.0243	23.9	.0000	2	Namath's
0.0243	23.9	.0000	2	narrates
0.0243	23.9	.0000	2	natal
0.0243	23.9	.0000	2	NATIONAL
0.0243	23.9	.0000	2	Native
0.0243	23.9	.0000	2	nature-writing
0.0243	23.9	.0000	2	NBC-TV
0.0243	23.9	.0000	2	Neb
0.0243	23.9	.0000	2	needlefish
0.0243	23.9	.0000	2	neurotic
0.0243	23.9	.0000	2	newsstands
0.0243	23.8	.0000	3	next-higher
0.0243	23.9	.0000	3	ngk
0.0243	23.9	.0000	2	Nguyen
0.0243	23.9	.0000	2	Nightcrawlers
0.0243	23.8	.0000	3	Nissen
0.0243	23.9	.0000	2	non-verbal
0.0243	23.9	.0000	2	nonadjustable
0.0243	23.8	.0000	3	nonprofessional
0.0243	23.9	.0000	2	Northridge
0.0243	23.9	.0000	2	Novotny
0.0243	23.9	.0000	2	nozzles
0.0243	23.9	.0000	2	nude
0.0243	23.9	.0000	2	nuoc
0.0243	23.9	.0000	2	nuri
0.0243	23.9	.0000	2	O'Neil
0.0243	23.9	.0000	2	O'Rourke
0.0243	23.9	.0000	2	Obregon
0.0243	23.8	.0000	3	obverse
0.0243	23.9	.0000	2	Ocala
0.0243	23.9	.0000	2	Off-Off
0.0243	23.9	.0000	2	oil-level
0.0243	23.9	.0000	2	Okracoke
0.0243	23.9	.0000	2	OldLyme
0.0243	23.9	.0000	2	one-shot
0.0243	23.9	.0000	2	one-thousandth
0.0243	23.9	.0000	2	Opperman's
0.0243	23.9	.0000	2	Oramel
0.0243	23.8	.0000	3	oratorios
0.0243	23.8	.0000	3	orchestrion
0.0243	23.9	.0000	2	Oreille
0.0243	23.8	.0000	3	organum
0.0243	23.9	.0000	2	orthopedist
0.0243	23.9	.0000	2	Orwell
0.0243	23.8	.0000	3	ostinato
0.0243	23.9	.0000	2	ouster
0.0243	23.9	.0000	2	outfitters
0.0243	23.9	.0000	2	Oval
0.0243	23.9	.0000	2	overfalls
0.0243	23.9	.0000	2	oversimplified
0.0243	23.8	.0000	3	overtures
0.0243	23.9	.0000	2	Ozma
0.0243	23.9	.0000	2	Package
0.0243	23.9	.0000	2	Packer
0.0243	23.9	.0000	2	pacts
0.0243	23.9	.0000	2	Padres
0.0243	23.9	.0000	2	Pantycelyn
0.0243	23.9	.0000	2	Parseghian
0.0243	23.9	.0000	2	partakers
0.0243	23.9	.0000	2	passers
0.0243	23.9	.0000	2	Passes
0.0243	23.9	.0000	2	Pasture
0.0243	23.8	.0000	3	patapon
0.0243	23.9	.0000	2	patronyms
0.0243	23.8	.0000	3	Patterning
0.0243	23.9	.0000	2	patty-cakes
0.0243	23.9	.0000	2	Paul-Marc
0.0243	23.9	.0000	2	Payton
0.0243	23.9	.0000	2	Pearce
0.0243	23.8	.0000	3	Peasant
0.0243	23.9	.0000	2	peasants'
0.0243	23.9	.0000	2	Peewee
0.0243	23.9	.0000	2	pegged
0.0243	23.9	.0000	2	Pelz
0.0243	23.9	.0000	2	per-acre
0.0243	23.9	.0000	2	pertained
0.0243	23.8	.0000	3	petit
0.0243	23.9	.0000	2	Petite
0.0243	23.8	.0000	3	Petrouchka's
0.0243	23.9	.0000	2	Petty
0.0243	23.9	.0000	2	Petula
0.0243	23.9	.0000	2	pharmaceutical
0.0243	23.9	.0000	2	Phoenix'
0.0243	23.9	.0000	2	picada
0.0243	23.9	.0000	2	Picasso's
0.0243	23.9	.0000	2	picky
0.0243	23.9	.0000	2	Pinamar
0.0243	23.9	.0000	2	PING
0.0243	23.8	.0000	3	Pish-Tush

THE PRECEDING WORD TYPE OCCUPIES RANK 54000

U	SFI	D	F	Word Type
0.0243	23.8	.0000	3	plainsongs
0.0243	23.9	.0000	2	platitos
0.0243	23.9	.0000	2	Play-Doh
0.0243	23.8	.0000	3	plectra
0.0243	23.9	.0000	2	plentie
0.0243	23.9	.0000	2	pockmarked
0.0243	23.9	.0000	2	Poher
0.0243	23.9	.0000	2	Polanski
0.0243	23.9	.0000	2	Politburo
0.0243	23.9	.0000	2	Poll
0.0243	23.9	.0000	3	pon
0.0243	23.9	.0000	2	Porklet
0.0243	23.9	.0000	2	postured
0.0243	23.9	.0000	2	pre-season
0.0243	23.9	.0000	2	premarital
0.0243	23.9	.0000	2	prenatal
0.0243	23.9	.0000	2	Presents
0.0243	23.9	.0000	2	Presidents'
0.0243	23.9	.0000	2	presidio
0.0243	23.9	.0000	2	presocial
0.0243	23.9	.0000	2	pressured
0.0243	23.9	.0000	2	Preston's
0.0243	23.9	.0000	2	priorities
0.0243	23.9	.0000	2	pro-Soviet
0.0243	23.8	.0000	3	processional
0.0243	23.8	.0000	3	programmatic
0.0243	23.8	.0000	3	Prokofiev
0.0243	23.9	.0000	2	proxemics
0.0243	23.9	.0000	2	Prudhomme
0.0243	23.9	.0000	2	Prune
0.0243	23.9	.0000	2	psychoanalytic
0.0243	23.9	.0000	2	Psychologist
0.0243	23.8	.0000	3	puili
0.0243	23.9	.0000	2	pulpit-voice
0.0243	23.9	.0000	2	pulsar
0.0243	23.9	.0000	2	pulsars
0.0243	23.8	.0000	3	pulsations
0.0243	23.8	.0000	3	Purcell's
0.0243	23.9	.0000	2	Purdue's
0.0243	23.9	.0000	2	PX
0.0243	23.9	.0000	2	Pyrotector
0.0243	23.9	.0000	2	qualifiers
0.0243	23.9	.0000	2	Quiet
0.0243	23.9	.0000	2	Quinn's
0.0243	23.9	.0000	2	quintessence
0.0243	23.8	.0000	3	Races
0.0243	23.9	.0000	2	Racing
0.0243	23.9	.0000	2	Radiant
0.0243	23.9	.0000	2	Rado
0.0243	23.9	.0000	2	Rado's
0.0243	23.9	.0000	2	ramekins
0.0243	23.9	.0000	2	ramifications
0.0243	23.9	.0000	2	rapprochement
0.0243	23.9	.0000	2	Raton
0.0243	23.9	.0000	2	reaffirmed
0.0243	23.9	.0000	2	Red-footed
0.0243	23.9	.0000	2	regionals
0.0243	23.9	.0000	2	Regular
0.0243	23.9	.0000	2	reincarnation
0.0243	23.9	.0000	2	rejoyce
0.0243	23.9	.0000	3	REMEMBER
0.0243	23.9	.0000	2	reminiscences
0.0243	23.9	.0000	2	Rep
0.0243	23.9	.0000	2	repackaged
0.0243	23.9	.0000	2	repressive
0.0243	23.9	.0000	2	repugnant
0.0243	23.9	.0000	2	reunite
0.0243	23.9	.0000	2	rev
0.0243	23.8	.0000	3	Rhody
0.0243	23.9	.0000	2	Rhyne
0.0243	23.9	.0000	2	Rich-ard
0.0243	23.9	.0000	2	Richelieu
0.0243	23.8	.0000	3	Rigoletto
0.0243	23.8	.0000	3	ripieno
0.0243	23.9	.0000	2	risers
0.0243	23.8	.0000	3	ritard
0.0243	23.9	.0000	2	river-barge
0.0243	23.9	.0000	2	roadrunners
0.0243	23.9	.0000	2	Robby
0.0243	23.9	.0000	2	rodding
0.0243	23.9	.0000	2	Roe
0.0243	23.9	.0000	2	Roehr
0.0243	23.9	.0000	2	Roman's
0.0243	23.8	.0000	3	rondeau
0.0243	23.8	.0000	3	Rondo
0.0243	23.9	.0000	2	roped-off
0.0243	23.8	.0000	3	Rossini's
0.0243	23.8	.0000	3	rubato
0.0243	23.8	.0000	3	rumtum
0.0243	23.8	.0000	3	runic
0.0243	23.9	.0000	2	Ruthven
0.0243	23.9	.0000	2	Rysavy's
0.0243	23.9	.0000	2	R10
0.0243	23.9	.0000	2	S-IVB
0.0243	23.9	.0000	2	Salvation
0.0243	23.9	.0000	2	Samoa
0.0243	23.9	.0000	2	Santo's
0.0243	23.9	.0000	2	SAT
0.0243	23.9	.0000	2	Satyagraha
0.0243	23.9	.0000	2	scabbards

THE PRECEDING WORD TYPE OCCUPIES RANK 54100

U	SFI	D	F	Word Type
0.0243	23.9	.0000	2	Scard
0.0243	23.8	.0000	3	Scarlatti
0.0243	23.8	.0000	3	Scherzo
0.0243	23.9	.0000	2	Schett
0.0243	23.9	.0000	2	Scholastic
0.0243	23.8	.0000	3	Schonberg
0.0243	23.8	.0000	3	Schonberg's
0.0243	23.9	.0000	2	Schramm
0.0243	23.9	.0000	2	Schwinn
0.0243	23.9	.0000	3	scort
0.0243	23.9	.0000	3	scrib
0.0243	23.9	.0000	3	scribere
0.0243	23.9	.0000	2	sculpturing
0.0243	23.9	.0000	2	seahorse's
0.0243	23.9	.0000	2	seahorses
0.0243	23.9	.0000	2	Seares
0.0243	23.9	.0000	2	season-long
0.0243	23.8	.0000	3	Seasons
0.0243	23.9	.0000	2	Sejna
0.0243	23.9	.0000	2	semi-desert
0.0243	23.9	.0000	2	seminar
0.0243	23.9	.0000	2	Senate's
0.0243	23.9	.0000	2	Seoul's
0.0243	23.9	.0000	2	Serafine
0.0243	23.9	.0000	2	set-to
0.0243	23.9	.0000	2	sexuality
0.0243	23.9	.0000	2	shad
0.0243	23.9	.0000	2	Shades
0.0243	23.9	.0000	2	Shafter's
0.0243	23.9	.0000	2	Shandon
0.0243	23.8	.0000	3	shantey
0.0243	23.9	.0000	2	sheefish
0.0243	23.9	.0000	2	Shelepin
0.0243	23.9	.0000	2	shifta
0.0243	23.9	.0000	2	Shin
0.0243	23.9	.0000	2	Shiseido
0.0243	23.9	.0000	2	shocker
0.0243	23.9	.0000	2	Shoe
0.0243	23.9	.0000	2	Shoemaker
0.0243	23.9	.0000	2	short-arc
0.0243	23.9	.0000	2	short-cut
0.0243	23.9	.0000	2	Shoulders'
0.0243	23.9	.0000	2	Shula
0.0243	23.8	.0000	3	Shule
0.0243	23.9	.0000	2	Shurcliff
0.0243	23.9	.0000	2	side-looking
0.0243	23.9	.0000	2	sighted-in
0.0243	23.9	.0000	2	Silverplate
0.0243	23.9	.0000	2	singles
0.0243	23.9	.0000	2	six-month
0.0243	23.9	.0000	2	six-ounce
0.0243	23.9	.0000	2	Sizemore
0.0243	23.9	.0000	2	skin's
0.0243	23.9	.0000	2	Skoplje
0.0243	23.9	.0000	2	Skorich
0.0243	23.9	.0000	2	skylights
0.0243	23.9	.0000	2	slackening
0.0243	23.9	.0000	2	slaloms
0.0243	23.9	.0000	2	slimnastics
0.0243	23.9	.0000	2	Sloane
0.0243	23.8	.0000	3	slurs
0.0243	23.9	.0000	3	sm
0.0243	23.9	.0000	2	Smugglers'
0.0243	23.9	.0000	2	Sneem
0.0243	23.9	.0000	2	Snow's
0.0243	23.9	.0000	2	snowmobiler
0.0243	23.9	.0000	2	Soames
0.0243	23.9	.0000	2	SOB'S
0.0243	23.9	.0000	2	sociologist
0.0243	23.9	.0000	2	solstice
0.0243	23.9	.0000	2	sop
0.0243	23.8	.0000	3	sopranos
0.0243	23.9	.0000	2	sound-spelling
0.0243	23.9	.0000	2	Southwark
0.0243	23.9	.0000	2	Sparkler
0.0243	23.9	.0000	2	speleologists
0.0243	23.9	.0000	2	spelunkers
0.0243	23.9	.0000	2	Speyside
0.0243	23.9	.0000	2	Spider's
0.0243	23.9	.0000	2	spillways
0.0243	23.9	.0000	2	splined
0.0243	23.9	.0000	2	spot-welded
0.0243	23.9	.0000	2	sprocket
0.0243	23.9	.0000	2	Stahl
0.0243	23.9	.0000	2	Starfighters
0.0243	23.9	.0000	2	Start
0.0243	23.9	.0000	2	Steelers
0.0243	23.9	.0000	2	steelhead
0.0243	23.9	.0000	2	steeplechase
0.0243	23.9	.0000	2	Steichen
0.0243	23.9	.0000	2	Stephan
0.0243	23.9	.0000	2	Stern
0.0243	23.9	.0000	2	stern-wheeler
0.0243	23.9	.0000	2	Sting
0.0243	23.9	.0000	2	stock-car
0.0243	23.9	.0000	2	Strat-O-Matic
0.0243	23.9	.0000	2	straw-colored
0.0243	23.9	.0000	2	stringer
0.0243	23.8	.0000	3	Strolling
0.0243	23.9	.0000	2	strong-willed

THE PRECEDING WORD TYPE OCCUPIES RANK 54200

U	SFI	D	F	Word Type
0.0243	23.9	.0000	2	Sturgeon
0.0243	23.9	.0000	2	sturgeon
0.0243	23.9	.0000	2	stymied
0.0243	23.9	.0000	2	Submarine
0.0243	23.9	.0000	2	subsidies
0.0243	23.9	.0000	2	subsidize
0.0243	23.9	.0000	2	Suit
0.0243	23.8	.0000	3	Sukkah
0.0243	23.8	.0000	3	Suliram
0.0243	23.9	.0000	2	SunCity
0.0243	23.9	.0000	2	sundry
0.0243	23.9	.0000	2	superconducting
0.0243	23.9	.0000	2	superstar
0.0243	23.9	.0000	2	superstars

U	SFI	D	F	Word Type
0.0243	23.9	.0000	2	Supervisor
0.0243	23.9	.0000	2	suspending
0.0243	23.9	.0000	2	Svoboda
0.0243	23.9	.0000	2	swamplands
0.0243	23.9	.0000	3	syllabication
0.0243	23.9	.0000	2	TV's
0.0243	23.9	.0000	2	tabasco
0.0243	23.9	.0000	2	tacit
0.0243	23.8	.0000	3	taddledum
0.0243	23.9	.0000	2	Tahitian
0.0243	23.9	.0000	2	tailback
0.0243	23.9	.0000	2	takeover
0.0243	23.8	.0000	3	Tallis
0.0243	23.9	.0000	2	taming
0.0243	23.8	.0000	3	Tarriers
0.0243	23.9	.0000	2	tastings
0.0243	23.9	.0000	2	tax-reform
0.0243	23.9	.0000	2	Teal
0.0243	23.9	.0000	2	tear-gas
0.0243	23.9	.0000	2	teleology
0.0243	23.9	.0000	2	terciopelo
0.0243	23.9	.0000	2	terrible-tempered
0.0243	23.9	.0000	2	territoriality
0.0243	23.9	.0000	2	terrorism
0.0243	23.9	.0000	2	terrorists
0.0243	23.9	.0000	2	theocratic
0.0243	23.9	.0000	2	theorist
0.0243	23.9	.0000	2	thermistor's
0.0243	23.9	.0000	2	Thomases'
0.0243	23.9	.0000	2	three-hour
0.0243	23.9	.0000	3	tial
0.0243	23.9	.0000	2	Time's
0.0243	23.9	.0000	2	Tintin
0.0243	23.8	.0000	3	Tirilira
0.0243	23.8	.0000	3	toccata
0.0243	23.9	.0000	2	togetherness
0.0243	23.9	.0000	2	toggle
0.0243	23.9	.0000	2	tokens
0.0243	23.9	.0000	2	Tommie
0.0243	23.9	.0000	2	Tomusho
0.0243	23.9	.0000	2	Toni's
0.0243	23.9	.0000	2	toolrest
0.0243	23.9	.0000	2	top-rated
0.0243	23.8	.0000	3	Toreador
0.0243	23.9	.0000	2	Touchdown
0.0243	23.8	.0000	3	tra
0.0243	23.9	.0000	2	Traction
0.0243	23.9	.0000	3	tractus
0.0243	23.9	.0000	3	trahere
0.0243	23.9	.0000	2	transcend
0.0243	23.9	.0000	2	transgressions
0.0243	23.9	.0000	2	trauma
0.0243	23.8	.0000	3	Trio
0.0243	23.8	.0000	3	triplet
0.0243	23.8	.0000	3	Trout
0.0243	23.9	.0000	2	troweled
0.0243	23.9	.0000	2	Trucking
0.0243	23.9	.0000	2	Trudeau
0.0243	23.8	.0000	3	Tsu-croo
0.0243	23.9	.0000	2	tube's
0.0243	23.9	.0000	2	Tufts
0.0243	23.9	.0000	2	tune-up
0.0243	23.9	.0000	2	Turnout
0.0243	23.9	.0000	2	tuskers
0.0243	23.9	.0000	2	tutelage
0.0243	23.9	.0000	2	tutors
0.0243	23.8	.0000	3	Twelfth-night
0.0243	23.9	.0000	2	Twenty-fourth
0.0243	23.9	.0000	2	twirler
0.0243	23.9	.0000	2	two-hour
0.0243	23.9	.0000	2	Tylerton
0.0243	23.9	.0000	2	Tynan
0.0243	23.9	.0000	2	umbrage
0.0243	23.9	.0000	2	unattractive
0.0243	23.9	.0000	2	uncommitted
0.0243	23.9	.0000	2	underachieving
0.0243	23.9	.0000	2	UNICEF
0.0243	23.9	.0000	2	Unkar
0.0243	23.9	.0000	2	unveiled
0.0243	23.9	.0000	2	uptight
0.0243	23.9	.0000	2	urban-industrial
0.0243	23.9	.0000	2	Uruguayans
0.0243	23.9	.0000	2	USC
0.0243	23.9	.0000	2	USC'S
0.0243	23.9	.0000	2	used-car
0.0243	23.8	.0000	3	Valhalla

THE PRECEDING WORD TYPE OCCUPIES RANK 54300

U	SFI	D	F	Word Type
0.0243	23.9	.0000	2	valises
0.0243	23.8	.0000	3	Valkyries
0.0243	23.9	.0000	2	VanDerBeek
0.0243	23.8	.0000	3	vcv
0.0243	23.9	.0000	2	Velasco's
0.0243	23.8	.0000	3	Ver-croo
0.0243	23.9	.0000	2	ver-y
0.0243	23.8	.0000	3	vibrato
0.0243	23.9	.0000	2	videotape
0.0243	23.9	.0000	2	vignettes
0.0243	23.8	.0000	3	Villa-Lobos
0.0243	23.9	.0000	2	Vince
0.0243	23.9	.0000	2	Virgen
0.0243	23.9	.0000	2	vocally
0.0243	23.9	.0000	2	vogue
0.0243	23.9	.0000	2	voltage-sensitive
0.0243	23.8	.0000	3	vonMeck
0.0243	23.9	.0000	2	vu
0.0243	23.8	.0000	3	Wagnerian
0.0243	23.9	.0000	2	Waiter
0.0243	23.9	.0000	2	Wak
0.0243	23.9	.0000	2	Wallerawang
0.0243	23.9	.0000	2	wallflower
0.0243	23.9	.0000	2	warheads
0.0243	23.9	.0000	2	Warhol
0.0243	23.9	.0000	2	Wavelength
0.0243	23.9	.0000	2	wedge-mate
0.0243	23.8	.0000	3	Weel
0.0243	23.9	.0000	2	Weng
0.0243	23.9	.0000	2	Westchester
0.0243	23.9	.0000	2	Westmoreland
0.0243	23.9	.0000	2	Wexler
0.0243	23.9	.0000	2	wheelbase
0.0243	23.9	.0000	2	Wibberley
0.0243	23.9	.0000	2	Wilkinson
0.0243	23.9	.0000	2	Wilt's
0.0243	23.9	.0000	2	Winwood
0.0243	23.8	.0000	3	wiper
0.0243	23.9	.0000	2	wood-cutters
0.0243	23.8	.0000	3	wood-winds
0.0243	23.9	.0000	2	Woof
0.0243	23.9	.0000	3	word-arithmetic
0.0243	23.9	.0000	2	Wow
0.0243	23.9	.0000	2	Ws
0.0243	23.9	.0000	2	Wynn
0.0243	23.9	.0000	2	Wyo
0.0243	23.9	.0000	2	y'all
0.0243	23.9	.0000	2	Yaga's
0.0243	23.9	.0000	2	Yarborough
0.0243	23.9	.0000	2	year-end
0.0243	23.8	.0000	3	yodeling
0.0243	23.9	.0000	2	Yorty
0.0243	23.9	.0000	2	Youngtown
0.0243	23.9	.0000	2	Z/28
0.0243	23.9	.0000	2	Zarina
0.0243	23.9	.0000	2	zeroing
0.0243	23.9	.0000	2	Zsa
0.0243	23.9	.0000	2	000-foot-deep
0.0243	23.9	.0000	2	1-A
0.0243	23.9	.0000	2	1/16-inch
0.0243	23.9	.0000	2	1/2-in
0.0243	23.9	.0000	2	10-foot
0.0243	23.9	.0000	2	1163
0.0243	23.9	.0000	2	14-
0.0243	23.9	.0000	2	14-year-old
0.0243	23.9	.0000	2	140-hp
0.0243	23.9	.0000	2	1965-66
0.0243	23.9	.0000	2	1973
0.0243	23.9	.0000	2	1984
0.0243	23.9	.0000	2	20-minute
0.0243	23.9	.0000	2	20/80
0.0243	23.9	.0000	2	20/80's
0.0243	23.9	.0000	2	2020
0.0243	23.9	.0000	2	21-year-old
0.0243	23.9	.0000	2	22-year-old
0.0243	23.9	.0000	2	24-year-old
0.0243	23.9	.0000	2	25-thousandths
0.0243	23.9	.0000	2	28-7
0.0243	23.9	.0000	2	3A
0.0243	23.9	.0000	2	3s
0.0243	23.9	.0000	2	30-10
0.0243	23.9	.0000	2	30-8
0.0243	23.9	.0000	2	4C
0.0243	23.9	.0000	2	4s
0.0243	23.9	.0000	2	45-minute
0.0243	23.9	.0000	2	566
0.0243	23.9	.0000	2	7/8-in
0.0243	23.9	.0000	2	90/10
0.0243	23.9	.0000	2	91502
0.0240	23.8	.0000	13	brayer
0.0234	23.7	.0000	2	'dwina
0.0234	23.7	.0000	2	'orse
0.0234	23.7	.0000	2	'satiable
0.0234	23.7	.0000	2	'tain't
0.0234	23.7	.0000	2	acephali
0.0234	23.7	.0000	2	ag'in
0.0234	23.7	.0000	2	air-ship
0.0234	23.7	.0000	2	All-the-Beaver-there-was
0.0234	23.7	.0000	2	All-the-Turtle-there-was
0.0234	23.7	.0000	2	Alligators

THE PRECEDING WORD TYPE OCCUPIES RANK 54400

U	SFI	D	F	Word Type
0.0234	23.7	.0000	2	allus
0.0234	23.7	.0000	2	Amos'
0.0234	23.7	.0000	2	Analdas'
0.0234	23.7	.0000	2	Arables
0.0234	23.7	.0000	2	Arrietty's
0.0234	23.7	.0000	2	assented
0.0234	23.7	.0000	2	At-mun
0.0234	23.7	.0000	2	Ateoord
0.0234	23.7	.0000	2	aue
0.0234	23.7	.0000	2	Austine's
0.0234	23.7	.0000	2	Axe
0.0234	23.7	.0000	2	Azuloy
0.0234	23.7	.0000	2	b'long
0.0234	23.7	.0000	2	back-scratcher
0.0234	23.7	.0000	2	Bag-jagderags
0.0234	23.7	.0000	2	bailey
0.0234	23.7	.0000	2	bar'
0.0234	23.7	.0000	2	Barkham
0.0234	23.7	.0000	2	Bathsheba
0.0234	23.7	.0000	2	beaver-swamp
0.0234	23.7	.0000	2	bedstead
0.0234	23.7	.0000	2	begonias
0.0234	23.7	.0000	2	Belmont
0.0234	23.7	.0000	2	Bergom
0.0234	23.7	.0000	2	Bibby
0.0234	23.7	.0000	2	blotches
0.0234	23.7	.0000	2	blue-ticked
0.0234	23.7	.0000	2	Bluebell
0.0234	23.7	.0000	2	boarders
0.0234	23.7	.0000	2	bobs
0.0234	23.7	.0000	2	bode
0.0234	23.7	.0000	2	Bodger
0.0234	23.7	.0000	2	boiled-sweet
0.0234	23.7	.0000	2	BONG
0.0234	23.7	.0000	2	Boodles'
0.0234	23.7	.0000	2	Bopsulai
0.0234	23.7	.0000	2	Boroughcastle
0.0234	23.7	.0000	2	Boxer's
0.0234	23.7	.0000	2	Bugle
0.0234	23.7	.0000	2	Bumps'
0.0234	23.7	.0000	2	bunching
0.0234	23.7	.0000	2	Burdoo
0.0234	23.7	.0000	2	Button's
0.0234	23.7	.0000	2	buyin'
0.0234	23.7	.0000	2	c-c-come
0.0234	23.7	.0000	2	camomile
0.0234	23.7	.0000	2	Carrie's
0.0234	23.7	.0000	2	carryings
0.0234	23.7	.0000	2	Caschcasch
0.0234	23.7	.0000	2	Cat's-meat-Man
0.0234	23.7	.0000	2	cetacean
0.0234	23.7	.0000	2	chancet
0.0234	23.7	.0000	2	Cherry-Tree
0.0234	23.7	.0000	2	chick-a-la-bye
0.0234	23.7	.0000	2	chopping-block
0.0234	23.7	.0000	2	cocoanut
0.0234	23.7	.0000	2	coffee-pot
0.0234	23.7	.0000	2	Commandment
0.0234	23.7	.0000	2	Comrade
0.0234	23.7	.0000	2	confound
0.0234	23.7	.0000	2	cookin'
0.0234	23.7	.0000	2	Coppinos
0.0234	23.7	.0000	2	cotton-picker
0.0234	23.7	.0000	2	court-room
0.0234	23.7	.0000	2	coxswain
0.0234	23.7	.0000	2	creeturs
0.0234	23.7	.0000	2	crimson-robed
0.0234	23.7	.0000	2	crosslegged
0.0234	23.7	.0000	2	Cucuface
0.0234	23.7	.0000	2	Cuthbert
0.0234	23.7	.0000	2	Cyclone's
0.0234	23.7	.0000	2	Dailey
0.0234	23.7	.0000	2	de-mousing
0.0234	23.7	.0000	2	demijohn
0.0234	23.7	.0000	2	Dennie
0.0234	23.7	.0000	2	Dessert
0.0234	23.7	.0000	2	detained
0.0234	23.7	.0000	2	Dinarzade
0.0234	23.7	.0000	2	Diner
0.0234	23.7	.0000	2	dingblasted
0.0234	23.7	.0000	2	dissipated
0.0234	23.7	.0000	2	diversions
0.0234	23.7	.0000	2	divined
0.0234	23.7	.0000	2	dolefully
0.0234	23.7	.0000	2	Doodle-de-do
0.0234	23.7	.0000	2	Dot-and-Go-One
0.0234	23.7	.0000	2	Dovey's
0.0234	23.7	.0000	2	Eagle's
0.0234	23.7	.0000	2	earwig
0.0234	23.7	.0000	2	Ecrette's
0.0234	23.7	.0000	2	Elka
0.0234	23.7	.0000	2	Elna's
0.0234	23.7	.0000	2	Enders
0.0234	23.7	.0000	2	Endicott
0.0234	23.7	.0000	2	Eulalie
0.0234	23.7	.0000	2	Executors
0.0234	23.7	.0000	2	expiring
0.0234	23.7	.0000	2	Fairy's
0.0234	23.7	.0000	2	Farwell
0.0234	23.7	.0000	2	fast-beating

THE PRECEDING WORD TYPE OCCUPIES RANK 54500

U	SFI	D	F	Word Type
0.0234	23.7	.0000	2	feist
0.0234	23.7	.0000	2	fellahs
0.0234	23.7	.0000	2	fencin'
0.0234	23.7	.0000	2	fergit
0.0234	23.7	.0000	2	ferret
0.0234	23.7	.0000	2	figger
0.0234	23.7	.0000	2	fire-irons
0.0234	23.7	.0000	2	Fishermen
0.0234	23.7	.0000	2	Fishmonger
0.0234	23.7	.0000	2	fix'em
0.0234	23.7	.0000	2	Fleury
0.0234	23.7	.0000	2	fly-away
0.0234	23.7	.0000	2	foaled
0.0234	23.7	.0000	2	foolscap
0.0234	23.7	.0000	2	Foxes
0.0234	23.7	.0000	2	Frosts
0.0234	23.7	.0000	2	furl
0.0234	23.7	.0000	2	Gabilan's
0.0234	23.7	.0000	2	gad
0.0234	23.7	.0000	2	gaiters
0.0234	23.7	.0000	2	Gaylord's
0.0234	23.7	.0000	2	Gedney
0.0234	23.7	.0000	2	gif
0.0234	23.7	.0000	2	gingerale
0.0234	23.7	.0000	2	Given
0.0234	23.7	.0000	2	god's
0.0234	23.7	.0000	2	Godolphin
0.0234	23.7	.0000	2	goggled
0.0234	23.7	.0000	2	grazie
0.0234	23.7	.0000	2	grub-box
0.0234	23.7	.0000	2	gunsmith
0.0234	23.7	.0000	2	half-shaved
0.0234	23.7	.0000	2	halfbreed
0.0234	23.7	.0000	2	hamburg
0.0234	23.7	.0000	2	hankering
0.0234	23.7	.0000	2	hardhead
0.0234	23.7	.0000	2	harness-room
0.0234	23.7	.0000	2	Haroun-al-Raschid
0.0234	23.7	.0000	2	havin'
0.0234	23.7	.0000	2	hedgehogs
0.0234	23.7	.0000	2	heered
0.0234	23.7	.0000	2	Hendon's
0.0234	23.7	.0000	2	Hertford's
0.0234	23.7	.0000	2	holdin'
0.0234	23.7	.0000	2	Horsepepper
0.0234	23.7	.0000	2	Houseman's
0.0234	23.7	.0000	2	hulking
0.0234	23.7	.0000	2	idolized
0.0234	23.7	.0000	2	iffen
0.0234	23.7	.0000	2	indulgence
0.0234	23.7	.0000	2	inkpot
0.0234	23.7	.0000	2	Inman
0.0234	23.7	.0000	2	jamb
0.0234	23.7	.0000	2	John-the-Fletcher
0.0234	23.7	.0000	2	Jolliginki
0.0234	23.7	.0000	2	jollily
0.0234	23.7	.0000	2	jurymen
0.0234	23.7	.0000	2	Kaaren
0.0234	23.7	.0000	2	kedgeree
0.0234	23.7	.0000	2	ki-yi'd
0.0234	23.7	.0000	2	kitchen-floor
0.0234	23.7	.0000	2	la-la-de-da
0.0234	23.7	.0000	2	lady-friend
0.0234	23.7	.0000	2	Lazare
0.0234	23.7	.0000	2	Leading
0.0234	23.7	.0000	2	leavin'
0.0234	23.7	.0000	2	Leeds'
0.0234	23.7	.0000	2	lemon-yellow
0.0234	23.7	.0000	2	lib
0.0234	23.7	.0000	2	Livesey
0.0234	23.7	.0000	2	los'
0.0234	23.7	.0000	2	Lullah's
0.0234	23.7	.0000	2	Lunenberg
0.0234	23.7	.0000	2	Lupy
0.0234	23.7	.0000	2	M'Gonegal
0.0234	23.7	.0000	2	ma'o
0.0234	23.7	.0000	2	Malvolia
0.0234	23.7	.0000	2	Maquas
0.0234	23.7	.0000	2	Marie-Joseph
0.0234	23.7	.0000	2	Marie-Joseph's
0.0234	23.7	.0000	2	Marmee
0.0234	23.7	.0000	2	Marvelous
0.0234	23.7	.0000	2	Mata
0.0234	23.7	.0000	2	Matasaip
0.0234	23.7	.0000	2	match-box
0.0234	23.7	.0000	2	McCarroll
0.0234	23.7	.0000	2	McCrae
0.0234	23.7	.0000	2	mebee
0.0234	23.7	.0000	2	medicine-bag
0.0234	23.7	.0000	2	mid-thwart
0.0234	23.7	.0000	2	mirthless
0.0234	23.7	.0000	2	Mitzi
0.0234	23.7	.0000	2	Mohicans
0.0234	23.7	.0000	2	Monkeys
0.0234	23.7	.0000	2	mourner
0.0234	23.7	.0000	2	mrs
0.0234	23.7	.0000	2	Muldoon's
0.0234	23.7	.0000	2	Mullet
0.0234	23.7	.0000	2	Mulligan
0.0234	23.7	.0000	2	mulsh

THE PRECEDING WORD TYPE OCCUPIES RANK 54600

U	SFI	D	F	Word Type
0.0234	23.7	.0000	2	Nanna
0.0234	23.7	.0000	2	night-shirt
0.0234	23.7	.0000	2	north-east
0.0234	23.7	.0000	2	Nurry
0.0234	23.7	.0000	2	nutting
0.0234	23.7	.0000	2	Oakes
0.0234	23.7	.0000	2	Oceanic
0.0234	23.7	.0000	2	one-thirty
0.0234	23.7	.0000	2	opulent
0.0234	23.7	.0000	2	Oralee's
0.0234	23.7	.0000	2	Orchard
0.0234	23.7	.0000	2	orgy
0.0234	23.7	.0000	2	Paddock
0.0234	23.7	.0000	2	paddocks
0.0234	23.7	.0000	2	Pageant
0.0234	23.7	.0000	2	palanquin
0.0234	23.7	.0000	2	pale-face
0.0234	23.7	.0000	2	Parsley
0.0234	23.7	.0000	2	pathless
0.0234	23.7	.0000	2	Pawn
0.0234	23.7	.0000	2	payah
0.0234	23.7	.0000	2	Pearsons
0.0234	23.7	.0000	2	Peder's
0.0234	23.7	.0000	2	Pee-wee
0.0234	23.7	.0000	2	pencil-sharpening
0.0234	23.7	.0000	2	penguin's
0.0234	23.7	.0000	2	Pennell
0.0234	23.7	.0000	2	perceptibly
0.0234	23.7	.0000	2	periagua
0.0234	23.7	.0000	2	pesetas
0.0234	23.7	.0000	2	Peterkin
0.0234	23.7	.0000	2	Philosophical
0.0234	23.7	.0000	2	pig-nuts
0.0234	23.7	.0000	2	Pilkington's
0.0234	23.7	.0000	2	Pinocchio's
0.0234	23.7	.0000	2	pintadines
0.0234	23.7	.0000	2	Pippilotta
0.0234	23.7	.0000	2	pistol-shot
0.0234	23.7	.0000	2	plateful
0.0234	23.7	.0000	2	pongee
0.0234	23.7	.0000	2	Poppins's
0.0234	23.7	.0000	2	Poppy
0.0234	23.7	.0000	2	Preakness
0.0234	23.7	.0000	2	Pretzie's
0.0234	23.7	.0000	2	Protector
0.0234	23.7	.0000	2	Puddleby-on-the-Marsh
0.0234	23.7	.0000	2	pudgy
0.0234	23.7	.0000	2	Purdys'
0.0234	23.7	.0000	2	Putter
0.0234	23.7	.0000	2	quay
0.0234	23.7	.0000	2	queeck
0.0234	23.7	.0000	2	Queensborough
0.0234	23.7	.0000	2	rabbit-hole
0.0234	23.7	.0000	2	Ramsay
0.0234	23.7	.0000	2	rapscallions
0.0234	23.7	.0000	2	redbirds
0.0234	23.7	.0000	2	reef-passage
0.0234	23.7	.0000	2	remitted
0.0234	23.7	.0000	2	reproaches
0.0234	23.7	.0000	2	retied
0.0234	23.7	.0000	2	righteous
0.0234	23.7	.0000	2	river-wall
0.0234	23.7	.0000	2	Roany
0.0234	23.7	.0000	2	Rosal
0.0234	23.7	.0000	2	rr
0.0234	23.7	.0000	2	Rugg's
0.0234	23.7	.0000	2	sabre
0.0234	23.7	.0000	2	sailing-ships
0.0234	23.7	.0000	2	sand-bank
0.0234	23.7	.0000	2	Sandra's
0.0234	23.7	.0000	2	sandspit
0.0234	23.7	.0000	2	Saucy
0.0234	23.7	.0000	2	savageness
0.0234	23.7	.0000	2	Scales
0.0234	23.7	.0000	2	Schiller's
0.0234	23.7	.0000	2	seegars
0.0234	23.7	.0000	2	seiners
0.0234	23.7	.0000	2	sennit

U	SFI	D	F	Word Type
0.0234	23.7	.0000	2	Shad
0.0234	23.7	.0000	2	Shivery
0.0234	23.7	.0000	2	Shoestring's
0.0234	23.7	.0000	2	shortcake
0.0234	23.7	.0000	2	shorty
0.0234	23.7	.0000	2	Shrimp
0.0234	23.7	.0000	2	Sider
0.0234	23.7	.0000	2	sparin'
0.0234	23.7	.0000	2	speed-limit
0.0234	23.7	.0000	2	spindling
0.0234	23.7	.0000	2	sprigged,
0.0234	23.7	.0000	2	spumes
0.0234	23.7	.0000	2	StMark's
0.0234	23.7	.0000	2	Steiner
0.0234	23.7	.0231	2	Stephen's
0.0234	23.7	.0000	2	stiletto
0.0234	23.7	.0000	2	stripy
0.0234	23.7	.0000	2	studyin'
0.0234	23.7	.0000	2	Super-Duper's
0.0234	23.7	.0000	2	takened
0.0234	23.7	.0000	2	tamanu
0.0234	23.7	.0000	2	Tasky's
THE PRECEDING WORD TYPE OCCUPIES RANK 54700				
0.0234	23.7	.0000	2	team-dogs
0.0234	23.7	.0000	2	testacea
0.0234	23.7	.0000	2	Teunis's
0.0234	23.7	.0000	2	Tewindrow
0.0234	23.7	.0000	2	tight-fisted
0.0234	23.7	.0000	2	Too-Too
0.0234	23.7	.0000	2	Toy
0.0234	23.7	.0000	2	Transatlantic
0.0234	23.7	.0000	2	trap-trap
0.0234	23.7	.0000	2	Trelawney
0.0234	23.7	.0000	2	tulip-shaped
0.0234	23.7	.0000	2	Turnbuckle
0.0234	23.7	.0000	2	Twickerham's
0.0234	23.7	.0000	2	unbuckled
0.0234	23.7	.0000	2	untamable
0.0234	23.7	.0000	2	Uppers
0.0234	23.7	.0000	2	vapour
0.0234	23.7	.0000	2	Viri
0.0234	23.7	.0000	2	vittles
0.0234	23.7	.0000	2	viz
0.0234	23.7	.0000	2	Volusia
0.0234	23.7	.0000	2	waistcoat-pocket
0.0234	23.7	.0000	2	Walt's
0.0234	23.7	.0000	2	Weedon
0.0234	23.7	.0000	2	Wen
0.0234	23.7	.0000	2	Whale's
0.0234	23.7	.0000	2	whee
0.0234	23.7	.0000	2	whisky-jack
0.0234	23.7	.0000	2	whup
0.0234	23.7	.0000	2	wisht
0.0234	23.7	.0000	2	wistfulness
0.0234	23.7	.0000	2	wo'n't
0.0234	23.7	.0000	2	wobble
0.0234	23.7	.0000	2	womenfolks
0.0234	23.7	.0000	2	Wortman
0.0234	23.7	.0000	2	Xury
0.0234	23.7	.0000	2	Y **
0.0234	23.7	.0000	2	yellow-robed
0.0234	23.7	.0000	2	Zenas
0.0234	23.7	.0000	2	Zephy
0.0234	23.7	.0000	2	Zero-maker
0.0234	23.7	.0000	2	Zoom
0.0227	23.6	.0000	9	capacitance
0.0225	23.5	.0000	7	tailor's
0.0225	23.5	.0000	7	take-up
0.0221	23.4	.0299	2	Epistle
0.0221	23.4	.0299	2	savior
0.0221	23.4	.0299	2	trespass
0.0219	23.4	.0000	2	$37
0.0219	23.4	.0000	2	-an
0.0219	23.4	.0000	2	-ceive
0.0219	23.4	.0000	2	-d
0.0219	23.4	.0000	2	-ish
0.0219	23.4	.0000	2	-1/
0.0219	23.4	.0000	2	/ay/
0.0219	23.4	.0000	2	/e-n/**
0.0219	23.4	.0000	2	/sk/
0.0219	23.4	.0000	2	a-bed
0.0219	23.4	.0000	2	ad-dress
0.0219	23.4	.0000	2	ADJ
0.0219	23.4	.0000	2	Adv
0.0219	23.4	.0000	2	advertiser
0.0219	23.4	.0000	2	Agincourt
0.0219	23.4	.0000	2	almirante
0.0219	23.4	.0000	2	amir-al-bahr
0.0219	23.4	.0000	2	and's
0.0219	23.4	.0000	2	anecdote
0.0219	23.4	.0000	2	Angle-land
0.0219	23.4	.0000	2	Anthill
0.0219	23.4	.0000	2	Anthony's
0.0219	23.4	.0000	2	apposition
0.0219	23.4	.0000	2	Artash
0.0219	23.4	.0000	2	Aryan
0.0219	23.4	.0000	2	aux
0.0219	23.4	.0000	2	Bagpipe
0.0219	23.4	.0000	2	benumbed
0.0219	23.4	.0000	2	Bethlehemovich
0.0219	23.4	.0000	2	Bijo
0.0219	23.4	.0000	2	billitch
0.0219	23.4	.0000	2	blude-reid
0.0219	23.4	.0000	2	blunderbuss
0.0219	23.4	.0000	2	Bridget
0.0219	23.4	.0000	2	Brockden
0.0219	23.4	.0000	2	Brook's
0.0219	23.4	.0000	2	browner
0.0219	23.4	.0000	2	Bumppo
0.0219	23.4	.0000	2	c's
0.0219	23.4	.0000	2	Carterville
0.0219	23.4	.0000	2	Centerberg
0.0219	23.4	.0000	2	Cerf
0.0219	23.4	.0000	2	CHAIRMAN
0.0219	23.4	.0000	2	chatterbox
0.0219	23.4	.0000	2	Chauncey
0.0219	23.4	.0000	2	Chef's
0.0219	23.4	.0000	2	choses
0.0219	23.4	.0000	2	Christos
0.0219	23.4	.0000	2	clapt
0.0219	23.4	.0000	2	cleansers
0.0219	23.4	.0000	2	co-ordinate
0.0219	23.4	.0000	2	co-ordinating
THE PRECEDING WORD TYPE OCCUPIES RANK 54800				
0.0219	23.4	.0000	2	Coils
0.0219	23.4	.0000	2	completer
0.0219	23.4	.0000	2	connectors
0.0219	23.4	.0000	2	consonant-shift
0.0219	23.4	.0000	2	conversationalist
0.0219	23.4	.0000	2	coordinators
0.0219	23.4	.0000	2	crustaceous
0.0219	23.4	.0000	2	cucking
0.0219	23.4	.0000	2	Cymbeline
0.0219	23.4	.0000	2	Daniels
0.0219	23.4	.0000	2	deid
0.0219	23.4	.0000	2	Delafield
0.0219	23.4	.0000	2	deleting
0.0219	23.4	.0000	2	deletion
0.0219	23.4	.0000	2	dismantle
0.0219	23.4	.0000	2	double-base
0.0219	23.4	.0000	2	doublechin
0.0219	23.4	.0000	2	Doze
0.0219	23.4	.0000	2	drinkin'
0.0219	23.4	.0000	2	duff
0.0219	23.4	.0000	2	Dunmore
0.0219	23.4	.0000	2	Dzea
0.0219	23.4	.0000	2	easy-to-follow
0.0219	23.4	.0000	2	echoic
0.0219	23.4	.0000	2	eddy
0.0219	23.4	.0000	2	eldern
0.0219	23.4	.0000	2	embroider'd
0.0219	23.4	.0000	2	Emory
0.0219	23.4	.0000	2	english
0.0219	23.4	.0000	2	Englishman's
0.0219	23.4	.0000	2	Essay
0.0219	23.4	.0000	2	expiration
0.0219	23.4	.0000	2	expletives
0.0219	23.4	.0000	2	Fainting
0.0219	23.4	.0000	2	fair-lined
0.0219	23.4	.0000	2	Feodorovna's
0.0219	23.4	.0000	2	Fidele
0.0219	23.4	.0000	2	Findley
0.0219	23.4	.0000	2	fing
0.0219	23.4	.0000	2	fisk
0.0219	23.4	.0000	2	foxhole
0.0219	23.4	.0000	2	Freedman
0.0219	23.4	.0000	2	frontiersman
0.0219	23.4	.0000	2	frontways
0.0219	23.4	.0000	2	frumiously
0.0219	23.4	.0000	2	gawky
0.0219	23.4	.0000	2	Gerbert
0.0219	23.4	.0000	2	gnashings
0.0219	23.4	.0000	2	god-forsaken
0.0219	23.4	.0000	2	good-spell
0.0219	23.4	.0000	2	Goover
0.0219	23.4	.0000	2	Gorman
0.0219	23.4	.0000	2	Grahame
0.0219	23.4	.0000	2	grammarians
0.0219	23.4	.0000	2	grammars
0.0219	23.4	.0000	2	Greentown
0.0219	23.4	.0000	2	Greshkin
0.0219	23.4	.0000	2	grey-
0.0219	23.4	.0000	2	grown-up's
0.0219	23.4	.0000	2	grumple
0.0219	23.4	.0000	2	Gulliver
0.0219	23.4	.0000	2	gum-chewing
0.0219	23.4	.0000	2	half-ounce
0.0219	23.4	.0000	2	Halliburton
0.0219	23.4	.0000	2	Hamlin
0.0219	23.4	.0000	2	Herkimer
0.0219	23.4	.0000	2	Hindustani
0.0219	23.4	.0000	2	Hipshank
0.0219	23.4	.0000	2	Hitty
0.0219	23.4	.0000	2	HO
0.0219	23.4	.0000	2	Illarion
0.0219	23.4	.0000	2	indians
0.0219	23.4	.0000	2	irrigates
0.0219	23.4	.0000	2	Jespersen
0.0219	23.4	.0000	2	Jingle
0.0219	23.4	.0000	2	Karana
0.0219	23.4	.0000	2	Karn
0.0219	23.4	.0000	2	kickshaw
0.0219	23.4	.0000	2	Kinderhook
0.0219	23.4	.0000	2	Lambs
0.0219	23.4	.0000	2	land-crabs
0.0219	23.4	.0000	2	lonesome-looking
0.0219	23.4	.0000	2	lunchman
0.0219	23.4	.0000	2	made-up
0.0219	23.4	.0000	2	mak
0.0219	23.4	.0000	2	Manus
0.0219	23.4	.0000	2	Mare
0.0219	23.4	.0000	2	Masquers
0.0219	23.4	.0000	2	matchmaker
0.0219	23.4	.0000	2	max
0.0219	23.4	.0000	2	Melvil
0.0219	23.4	.0000	2	memorization
0.0219	23.4	.0000	2	Mertons
0.0219	23.4	.0000	2	N-lv-n
0.0219	23.4	.0000	2	N-v-n-n
0.0219	23.4	.0000	2	N-v-ns-n
0.0219	23.4	.0000	2	Nash
0.0219	23.4	.0000	2	newsy
0.0219	23.4	.0000	2	nim
0.0219	23.4	.0000	2	ninth-grader
THE PRECEDING WORD TYPE OCCUPIES RANK 54900				
0.0219	23.4	.0000	2	no-words
0.0219	23.4	.0000	2	noncount
0.0219	23.4	.0000	2	nugful
0.0219	23.4	.0000	2	obj
0.0219	23.4	.0000	2	officious
0.0219	23.4	.0000	2	opwhere
0.0219	23.4	.0000	2	oregon
0.0219	23.4	.0000	2	ORNITHOLOGY
0.0219	23.4	.0000	2	over-used
0.0219	23.4	.0000	2	paragraphing
0.0219	23.4	.0000	2	PATTERN
0.0219	23.4	.0000	2	phonological
0.0219	23.4	.0000	2	Piotr
0.0219	23.4	.0000	2	pipkin
0.0219	23.4	.0000	2	play'd
0.0219	23.4	.0000	2	ponere
0.0219	23.4	.0000	2	pres
0.0219	23.4	.0000	2	present-tense
0.0219	23.4	.0000	2	prestidigitator
0.0219	23.4	.0000	2	programmers
0.0219	23.4	.0000	2	propos'd
0.0219	23.4	.0000	2	prudery
0.0219	23.4	.0000	2	Pyle
0.0219	23.4	.0000	2	Rainsford's
0.0219	23.4	.0000	2	Ravenwood
0.0219	23.4	.0000	2	recline
0.0219	23.4	.0000	2	RLD
0.0219	23.4	.0000	2	Ronkonkoma
0.0219	23.4	.0000	2	rosebud
0.0219	23.4	.0000	2	run-ons
0.0219	23.4	.0000	2	sagu
0.0219	23.4	.0000	2	salem
0.0219	23.4	.0000	2	Sandburg's
0.0219	23.4	.0000	2	Sarowek
0.0219	23.4	.0000	2	satura
0.0219	23.4	.0000	2	Seaography
0.0219	23.4	.0000	2	secare
0.0219	23.4	.0000	2	separable
0.0219	23.4	.0000	2	sexton
0.0219	23.4	.0000	2	shirza
0.0219	23.4	.0000	2	short-order
0.0219	23.4	.0000	2	skirl
0.0219	23.4	.0000	2	Some-one
0.0219	23.4	.0000	2	spacespeak
0.0219	23.4	.0000	2	spak
0.0219	23.4	.0000	2	spatially
0.0219	23.4	.0000	2	Squiles
0.0219	23.4	.0000	2	store-ward
0.0219	23.4	.0000	2	Stretching
0.0219	23.4	.0000	2	strew
0.0219	23.4	.0000	2	strown
0.0219	23.4	.0000	2	Structure
0.0219	23.4	.0000	2	subject-predicate
0.0219	23.4	.0000	2	sweaterandskirt
0.0219	23.4	.0000	2	Swifties
0.0219	23.4	.0000	2	T-cd
0.0219	23.4	.0000	2	T-cdSP
0.0219	23.4	.0000	2	T-wh
0.0219	23.4	.0000	2	tackler
0.0219	23.4	.0000	2	theyre
0.0219	23.4	.0000	2	tho'
0.0219	23.4	.0000	2	Thyrker
0.0219	23.4	.0000	2	tom-tit
0.0219	23.4	.0000	2	tonights
0.0219	23.4	.0000	2	Towne
0.0219	23.4	.0000	2	trunkless
0.0219	23.4	.0000	2	tu-whit
0.0219	23.4	.0000	2	tu-who
0.0219	23.4	.0000	2	Tweedums
0.0219	23.4	.0000	2	typewrite
0.0219	23.4	.0000	2	tyrant's
0.0219	23.4	.0000	2	uglify
0.0219	23.4	.0000	2	unfriendliness
0.0219	23.4	.0000	2	Vallodia
0.0219	23.4	.0000	2	Vb
0.0219	23.4	.0000	2	Walkers
0.0219	23.4	.0000	2	water-ski
0.0219	23.4	.0000	2	weel
0.0219	23.4	.0000	2	whar
0.0219	23.4	.0000	2	wheres
0.0219	23.4	.0000	2	whiffled
0.0219	23.4	.0000	2	whos
0.0219	23.4	.0000	2	Wiggs
0.0219	23.4	.0000	2	Wilder's
0.0219	23.4	.0000	2	wilting
0.0219	23.4	.0000	2	word's
0.0219	23.4	.0000	2	Yipounous
0.0219	23.4	.0000	2	youre
0.0219	23.4	.0000	2	Zane
0.0219	23.4	.0000	2	118-21
0.0219	23.4	.0000	2	128-29
0.0219	23.4	.0000	2	1415
0.0219	23.4	.0000	2	158-59
0.0219	23.4	.0000	2	1750's
0.0219	23.4	.0000	2	176-77
0.0219	23.4	.0000	2	178-79
0.0219	23.4	.0000	2	281-83
0.0219	23.4	.0000	2	322-324
0.0219	23.4	.0000	2	64-65
0.0219	23.4	.0000	2	72-73
THE PRECEDING WORD TYPE OCCUPIES RANK 55000				
0.0219	23.4	.0000	2	9B
0.0215	23.3	.0000	2	'twere
0.0215	23.3	.0000	2	a-dabbling
0.0215	23.3	.0000	2	Abdullah
0.0215	23.3	.0000	2	Agelaos
0.0215	23.3	.0000	2	Aiaian
0.0215	23.3	.0000	2	Alone
0.0215	23.3	.0000	2	Amal's
0.0215	23.3	.0000	2	amphitheatre
0.0215	23.3	.0000	2	amusingly
0.0215	23.3	.0000	2	Ananse's
0.0215	23.3	.0000	2	antagonist
0.0215	23.3	.0000	2	Arata's
0.0215	23.3	.0000	2	Arbuthnot
0.0215	23.3	.0000	2	archy's
0.0215	23.3	.0000	2	Ardeth
0.0215	23.3	.0000	2	Argos
0.0215	23.3	.0000	2	Arrow's
0.0215	23.3	.0000	2	aspens
0.0215	23.3	.0000	2	Atreus
0.0215	23.3	.0000	2	Atticus's
0.0215	23.3	.0000	2	Barefoot
0.0215	23.3	.0000	2	Barnyard
0.0215	23.3	.0000	2	Bat-Poet
0.0215	23.3	.0000	2	Baumer's
0.0215	23.3	.0000	2	Bedells
0.0215	23.3	.0000	2	beeves
0.0215	23.3	.0000	2	beguiled
0.0215	23.3	.0000	2	Belvedere
0.0215	23.3	.0000	2	bescreened
0.0215	23.3	.0000	2	bestrides
0.0215	23.3	.0000	2	bethink
0.0215	23.3	.0000	2	bidders
0.0215	23.3	.0000	2	bird-walker
0.0215	23.3	.0000	2	Boscoe
0.0215	23.3	.0000	2	bosoms
0.0215	23.3	.0000	2	brawls
0.0215	23.3	.0000	2	breakable
0.0215	23.3	.0000	2	briar
0.0215	23.3	.0000	2	bronze-fitted
0.0215	23.3	.0000	2	Buchwald
0.0215	23.3	.0000	2	builded
0.0215	23.3	.0000	2	Bun
0.0215	23.3	.0000	2	Bunyan's
0.0215	23.3	.0000	2	Carlin
0.0215	23.3	.0000	2	Carr's
0.0215	23.3	.0000	2	carriage-door
0.0215	23.3	.0000	2	Celeste
0.0215	23.3	.0000	2	Cerelle
0.0215	23.3	.0000	2	charlotte
0.0215	23.3	.0000	2	chide
0.0215	23.3	.0000	2	chiffarobe
0.0215	23.3	.0000	2	china-store
0.0215	23.3	.0000	2	Chiricahua
0.0215	23.3	.0000	2	cho-co-late
0.0215	23.3	.0000	2	Cholmondeley
0.0215	23.3	.0000	2	cloud-catching's
0.0215	23.3	.0000	2	collards
0.0215	23.3	.0000	2	Com
0.0215	23.3	.0000	2	Competition
0.0215	23.3	.0000	2	conciliating
0.0215	23.3	.0000	2	Corsican
0.0215	23.3	.0000	2	costumbres
0.0215	23.3	.0000	2	couldst
0.0215	23.3	.0000	2	counterman
0.0215	23.3	.0000	2	county's
0.0215	23.3	.0000	2	cradlers
0.0215	23.3	.0000	2	Cratchit
0.0215	23.3	.0000	2	Crest
0.0215	23.3	.0000	2	cricked
0.0215	23.3	.0000	2	Cronks'
0.0215	23.3	.0000	2	Cunningham
0.0215	23.3	.0000	2	cursy
0.0215	23.3	.0000	2	curtly
0.0215	23.3	.0000	2	DALY
0.0215	23.3	.0000	2	damn'
0.0215	23.3	.0000	2	deVilliers
0.0215	23.3	.0000	2	Deadwood
0.0215	23.3	.0000	2	Defarge's
0.0215	23.3	.0000	2	Defarges
0.0215	23.3	.0000	2	derision
0.0215	23.3	.0000	2	derned
0.0215	23.3	.0000	2	detestable
0.0215	23.3	.0000	2	Dill's
0.0215	23.3	.0000	2	Dilworth
0.0215	23.3	.0000	2	dissimulation
0.0215	23.3	.0000	2	distantly
0.0215	23.3	.0000	2	doff
0.0215	23.3	.0000	2	Doria
0.0215	23.3	.0000	2	dram
0.0215	23.3	.0000	2	Dubose
0.0215	23.3	.0000	2	duelist
0.0215	23.3	.0000	2	duelists
0.0215	23.3	.0000	2	Dutchie
0.0215	23.3	.0000	2	Dwamish
0.0215	23.3	.0000	2	EauGalle
0.0215	23.3	.0000	2	eavesdropper
0.0215	23.3	.0000	2	EGEUS
0.0215	23.3	.0000	2	elegy
0.0215	23.3	.0000	2	endgate
THE PRECEDING WORD TYPE OCCUPIES RANK 55100				
0.0215	23.3	.0000	2	entreated
0.0215	23.3	.0000	2	ermine
0.0215	23.3	.0000	2	escapees
0.0215	23.3	.0000	2	Ever
0.0215	23.3	.0000	2	exeunt
0.0215	23.3	.0000	2	Feathertop's
0.0215	23.3	.0000	2	Fee-ona
0.0215	23.3	.0000	2	ferric
0.0215	23.3	.0000	2	fetches
0.0215	23.3	.0000	2	FIRST
0.0215	23.3	.0000	2	fish-tale
0.0215	23.3	.0000	2	Fishye
0.0215	23.3	.0000	2	Fletcher's
0.0215	23.3	.0000	2	flood-circled
0.0215	23.3	.0000	2	footless
0.0215	23.3	.0000	2	fortieth
0.0215	23.3	.0000	2	Framton
0.0215	23.3	.0000	2	frays
0.0215	23.3	.0000	2	free-dom
0.0215	23.3	.0000	2	Frenchy's
0.0215	23.3	.0000	2	FROM
0.0215	23.3	.0000	2	furred
0.0215	23.3	.0000	2	Fuschi
0.0215	23.3	.0000	2	GAFFER
0.0215	23.3	.0000	2	Gambetta
0.0215	23.3	.0000	2	gambol
0.0215	23.3	.0000	2	ganders
0.0215	23.3	.0000	2	gaol
0.0215	23.3	.0000	2	Gath
0.0215	23.3	.0000	2	Gertrud
0.0215	23.3	.0000	2	gloved
0.0215	23.3	.0000	2	gon'
0.0215	23.3	.0000	2	Gone-the-Child
0.0215	23.3	.0000	2	Goodsell
0.0215	23.3	.0000	2	GRANDMOTHER
0.0215	23.3	.0000	2	granny
0.0215	23.3	.0000	2	Grayback
0.0215	23.3	.0000	2	great-hearted
0.0215	23.3	.0000	2	Gretel's
0.0215	23.3	.0000	2	Grieves
0.0215	23.3	.0000	2	Griggs

U	SFI	D	F	Word Type
0.0215	23.3	.0000	2	grimaced
0.0215	23.3	.0000	2	Grummick
0.0215	23.3	.0000	2	Gwai-lin-di
0.0215	23.3	.0000	2	haff
0.0215	23.3	.0000	2	Hahalaba
0.0215	23.3	.0000	2	Harnett
0.0215	23.3	.0000	2	Havisham's
0.0215	23.3	.0000	2	HEADMAN
0.0215	23.3	.0000	2	Heart's
0.0215	23.3	.0000	2	hell-devil
0.0215	23.3	.0000	2	heterodyne
0.0215	23.3	.0000	2	hillfolk
0.0215	23.3	.0000	2	Hippolyta
0.0215	23.3	.0000	2	how're
0.0215	23.3	.0000	2	hundred-year-old
0.0215	23.3	.0000	2	huntsmen
0.0215	23.3	.0000	2	hurricane-proof
0.0215	23.3	.0000	2	idols'
0.0215	23.3	.0000	2	imposition
0.0215	23.3	.0000	2	indios
0.0215	23.3	.0000	2	ipecac
0.0215	23.3	.0000	2	JACK
0.0215	23.3	.0000	2	Jalpa
0.0215	23.3	.0000	2	Jase's
0.0215	23.3	.0000	2	Jest
0.0215	23.3	.0000	2	jests
0.0215	23.3	.0000	2	Jiya's
0.0215	23.3	.0000	2	Johnie's
0.0215	23.3	.0000	2	joshing
0.0215	23.3	.0000	2	kain't
0.0215	23.3	.0000	2	Kass
0.0215	23.3	.0000	2	keer
0.0215	23.3	.0000	2	Kelley
0.0215	23.3	.0000	2	KILLIGREW
0.0215	23.3	.0000	2	Kloo-Teekl
0.0215	23.3	.0000	2	knickers
0.0215	23.3	.0000	2	Kruper
0.0215	23.3	.0000	2	Lacedemon
0.0215	23.3	.0000	2	Lila
0.0215	23.3	.0000	2	liven
0.0215	23.3	.0000	2	looping
0.0215	23.3	.0000	2	LOVERS
0.0215	23.3	.0000	2	Lowy
0.0215	23.3	.0000	2	LUDLOW
0.0215	23.3	.0000	2	Mac's
0.0215	23.3	.0000	2	mackinaw
0.0215	23.3	.0000	2	Magda
0.0215	23.3	.0000	2	Mahoney
0.0215	23.3	.0000	2	MAID
0.0215	23.3	.0000	2	mak'st
0.0215	23.3	.0000	2	mallows
0.0215	23.3	.0000	2	Mandalay
0.0215	23.3	.0000	2	Mantua
0.0215	23.3	.0000	2	Manye
0.0215	23.3	.0000	2	mastadons
0.0215	23.3	.0000	2	Michailovitch
0.0215	23.3	.0000	2	Mide
0.0215	23.3	.0000	2	Millay
0.0215	23.3	.0000	2	MISS
THE PRECEDING WORD TYPE OCCUPIES RANK 55200				
0.0215	23.3	.0000	2	Moller
0.0215	23.3	.0000	2	Montague's
0.0215	23.3	.0000	2	Morgiana's
0.0215	23.3	.0000	2	mud-mixing
0.0215	23.3	.0000	2	Murphys
0.0215	23.3	.0000	2	Muskingum
0.0215	23.3	.0000	2	neck-string
0.0215	23.3	.0000	2	NEIGHBORS
0.0215	23.3	.0000	2	newspaperwoman
0.0215	23.3	.0000	2	nickel's
0.0215	23.3	.0000	2	NINIAN
0.0215	23.3	.0000	2	notary
0.0215	23.3	.0000	2	nu
0.0215	23.3	.0000	2	Nuttel
0.0215	23.3	.0000	2	o'coffee
0.0215	23.3	.0000	2	oak-tree
0.0215	23.3	.0000	2	orderlies
0.0215	23.3	.0000	2	orgies
0.0215	23.3	.0000	2	Oskaloosa
0.0215	23.3	.0000	2	Pallas
0.0215	23.3	.0000	2	Pao
0.0215	23.3	.0000	2	Parnassos
0.0215	23.3	.0000	2	pavane
0.0215	23.3	.0000	2	Peisistratos
0.0215	23.3	.0000	2	Peyton
0.0215	23.3	.0000	2	Phaeacians
0.0215	23.3	.0000	2	pig-headed
0.0215	23.3	.0000	2	pigeon-wing
0.0215	23.3	.0000	2	Pigg
0.0215	23.3	.0000	2	Pignier's
0.0215	23.3	.0000	2	polliwog
0.0215	23.3	.0000	2	popinjay
0.0215	23.3	.0000	2	Porky
0.0215	23.3	.0000	2	Porto-Vecchio
0.0215	23.3	.0000	2	postures
0.0215	23.3	.0000	2	preeminently
0.0215	23.3	.0000	2	pugilist
0.0215	23.3	.0000	2	pugnacious
0.0215	23.3	.0000	2	pulque
0.0215	23.3	.0000	2	queenly
0.0215	23.3	.0000	2	r-r-r-r-rrring
0.0215	23.3	.0000	2	Radley
0.0215	23.3	.0000	2	Rascal's
0.0215	23.3	.0000	2	Rawlings
0.0215	23.3	.0000	2	re-enter
0.0215	23.3	.0000	2	redbird
0.0215	23.3	.0000	2	redoubts
0.0215	23.3	.0000	2	Redskin
0.0215	23.3	.0000	2	reet
0.0215	23.3	.0000	2	refinished
0.0215	23.3	.0000	2	Rennie
0.0215	23.3	.0000	2	reprieve
0.0215	23.3	.0000	2	Rhenish
0.0215	23.3	.0000	2	Ricco's
0.0215	23.3	.0000	2	right-center
0.0215	23.3	.0000	2	roaches
0.0215	23.3	.0000	2	rubbly
0.0215	23.3	.0000	2	Samaritan
0.0215	23.3	.0000	2	Santa-Fe
0.0215	23.3	.0000	2	Sassafras
0.0215	23.3	.0000	2	SCENE
0.0215	23.3	.0000	2	Schulthess
0.0215	23.3	.0000	2	screwing
0.0215	23.3	.0000	2	scrubwoman
0.0215	23.3	.0000	2	sea-shine
0.0215	23.3	.0000	2	sh-h
0.0215	23.3	.0000	2	shaman
0.0215	23.3	.0000	2	shapel
0.0215	23.3	.0000	2	SHEEAN
0.0215	23.3	.0000	2	shekels
0.0215	23.3	.0000	2	Sinkfield's
0.0215	23.3	.0000	2	skirmishers
0.0215	23.3	.0000	2	skywriting
0.0215	23.3	.0000	2	Smiggle
0.0215	23.3	.0000	2	snakefish's
0.0215	23.3	.0000	2	sneering
0.0215	23.3	.0000	2	sniffle
0.0215	23.3	.0000	2	Snipe
0.0215	23.3	.0000	2	solo-dance
0.0215	23.3	.0000	2	sourdough
0.0215	23.3	.0000	2	Spike's
0.0215	23.3	.0000	2	spine-tingling
0.0215	23.3	.0000	2	Stoke
0.0215	23.3	.0000	2	STONE
0.0215	23.3	.0000	2	stoppin'
0.0215	23.3	.0000	2	story-poem
0.0215	23.3	.0000	2	story-poems
0.0215	23.3	.0000	2	strouding
0.0215	23.3	.0000	2	stumblest
0.0215	23.3	.0000	2	subtle-minded
0.0215	23.3	.0000	2	swits
0.0215	23.3	.0000	2	syndicate
0.0215	23.3	.0000	2	taine
0.0215	23.3	.0000	2	tainted
0.0215	23.3	.0000	2	tempter
0.0215	23.3	.0000	2	thefts
0.0215	23.3	.0000	2	Tiresias
0.0215	23.3	.0000	2	tock
0.0215	23.3	.0000	2	tongue's
0.0215	23.3	.0000	2	torchbearer
THE PRECEDING WORD TYPE OCCUPIES RANK 55300				
0.0215	23.3	.0000	2	townswomen
0.0215	23.3	.0000	2	Trammell
0.0215	23.3	.0000	2	tranquility
0.0215	23.3	.0000	2	trencher
0.0215	23.3	.0000	2	truancy
0.0215	23.3	.0000	2	tum-ti-tum
0.0215	23.3	.0000	2	tumbrils
0.0215	23.3	.0000	2	turkey-cock's
0.0215	23.3	.0000	2	tussles
0.0215	23.3	.0000	2	two-thirty
0.0215	23.3	.0000	2	Underwood
0.0215	23.3	.0000	2	undressing
0.0215	23.3	.0000	2	unmindful
0.0215	23.3	.0000	2	unsteadily
0.0215	23.3	.0000	2	Upham
0.0215	23.3	.0000	2	Van's
0.0215	23.3	.0000	2	vibraphone
0.0215	23.3	.0000	2	Vigo
0.0215	23.3	.0000	2	vilely
0.0215	23.3	.0000	2	visualized
0.0215	23.3	.0000	2	vonGradwitz
0.0215	23.3	.0000	2	Wag
0.0215	23.3	.0000	2	Wangs
0.0215	23.3	.0000	2	we-we'll
0.0215	23.3	.0000	2	wearies
0.0215	23.3	.0000	2	weathercocks
0.0215	23.3	.0000	2	Web
0.0215	23.3	.0000	2	Weedemris
0.0215	23.3	.0000	2	Weller
0.0215	23.3	.0000	2	Westbury
0.0215	23.3	.0000	2	wherEVer
0.0215	23.3	.0000	2	whimpers
0.0215	23.3	.0000	2	Whistler
0.0215	23.3	.0000	2	Whistlers
0.0215	23.3	.0000	2	white-upturned
0.0215	23.3	.0000	2	whitecock's
0.0215	23.3	.0000	2	wilful
0.0215	23.3	.0000	2	wind-crust
0.0215	23.3	.0000	2	window-dresser
0.0215	23.3	.0000	2	wisecracks
0.0215	23.3	.0000	2	witch-hazel
0.0215	23.3	.0000	2	wood-pile
0.0215	23.3	.0000	2	Worker
0.0215	23.3	.0000	2	Workmen
0.0215	23.3	.0000	2	worrisome
0.0215	23.3	.0000	2	worship's
0.0215	23.3	.0000	2	Wowser
0.0215	23.3	.0000	2	Wowser's
0.0215	23.3	.0000	2	Wyandottes
0.0215	23.3	.0000	2	ya'
0.0215	23.3	.0000	2	Yaol's
0.0215	23.3	.0000	2	Yengwes
0.0215	23.3	.0000	2	yes-men
0.0215	23.3	.0000	2	yessir
0.0215	23.3	.0000	2	yestirday
0.0215	23.3	.0000	2	yond
0.0215	23.3	.0000	2	Znaeym
0.0215	23.3	.0000	2	304th
0.0215	23.3	.0000	2	4-0098
0.0209	23.2	.0000	2	abaca
0.0209	23.2	.0000	2	Abdulgani
0.0209	23.2	.0000	2	aberrations
0.0209	23.2	.0000	2	Absalom
0.0209	23.2	.0000	2	Abu
0.0209	23.2	.0000	2	Aelfric
0.0209	23.2	.0000	2	Aesir
0.0209	23.2	.0000	2	affiliation
0.0209	23.2	.0000	2	Afrikaans
0.0209	23.2	.0000	2	Agoutis
0.0209	23.2	.0000	2	agreed-on
0.0209	23.2	.0000	2	AGS
0.0209	23.2	.0000	2	Aiguille
0.0209	23.2	.0000	2	Ainus
0.0209	23.2	.0000	2	Alighieri
0.0209	23.2	.0000	2	allay
0.0209	23.2	.0000	2	ALS
0.0209	23.2	.0000	2	Altai
0.0209	23.2	.0000	2	ambushing
0.0209	23.2	.0000	2	Americanists
0.0209	23.2	.0000	2	Amontons
0.0209	23.2	.0000	2	amply
0.0209	23.2	.0000	2	analogies
0.0209	23.2	.0000	2	anaphase
0.0209	23.2	.0000	2	anchorages
0.0209	23.2	.0000	2	Anglicized
0.0209	23.2	.0000	2	antifreeze
0.0209	23.2	.0000	2	Antigone
0.0209	23.2	.0000	2	antiknock
0.0209	23.2	.0000	2	appalls
0.0209	23.2	.0000	2	appropriations
0.0209	23.2	.0000	2	arboreal
0.0209	23.2	.0000	2	Areopagitica
0.0209	23.2	.0000	2	Arminian
0.0209	23.2	.0000	2	Armory
0.0209	23.2	.0000	2	atheists
0.0209	23.2	.0000	2	atonement
0.0209	23.2	.0000	2	Aubrey
0.0209	23.2	.0000	2	Augustinian
0.0209	23.2	.0000	2	australopithecine
0.0209	23.2	.0000	2	australopithecines
THE PRECEDING WORD TYPE OCCUPIES RANK 55400				
0.0209	23.2	.0000	2	baccalaureate
0.0209	23.2	.0000	2	back-seat
0.0209	23.2	.0000	2	ballista
0.0209	23.2	.0000	2	Ballistic
0.0209	23.2	.0000	2	Balmat
0.0209	23.2	.0000	2	Bamberg
0.0209	23.2	.0000	2	Bank's
0.0209	23.2	.0000	2	barbicels
0.0209	23.2	.0000	2	barbules
0.0209	23.2	.0000	2	bards
0.0209	23.2	.0000	2	Bargello
0.0209	23.2	.0000	2	Barlowe's
0.0209	23.2	.0000	2	Barrage
0.0209	23.2	.0000	2	bastnaesite
0.0209	23.2	.0000	2	Bentham
0.0209	23.2	.0000	2	Beowulf
0.0209	23.2	.0000	2	bilaterally
0.0209	23.2	.0000	2	biltong
0.0209	23.2	.0000	2	biochemistry
0.0209	23.2	.0000	2	bioengineers
0.0209	23.2	.0000	2	biophysicist
0.0209	23.2	.0000	2	Boccaccio
0.0209	23.2	.0000	2	Bolingbroke
0.0209	23.2	.0000	2	Bornholm
0.0209	23.2	.0000	2	borrower
0.0209	23.2	.0000	2	bottomlands
0.0209	23.2	.0000	2	boycotts
0.0209	23.2	.0000	2	brainstem
0.0209	23.2	.0000	2	brunt
0.0209	23.2	.0000	2	Bunge
0.0209	23.2	.0000	2	burrowers
0.0209	23.2	.0000	2	Bushnell
0.0209	23.2	.0000	2	buttocks
0.0209	23.2	.0000	2	Caecilian
0.0209	23.2	.0000	2	caimans
0.0209	23.2	.0000	2	calendering
0.0209	23.2	.0000	2	callings
0.0209	23.2	.0000	2	Cameroons
0.0209	23.2	.0000	2	candystick
0.0209	23.2	.0000	2	Canossa
0.0209	23.2	.0000	2	Capetian
0.0209	23.2	.0000	2	Capricornus
0.0209	23.2	.0000	2	Capua
0.0209	23.2	.0000	2	caracal
0.0209	23.2	.0000	2	carapace
0.0209	23.2	.0000	2	cavitation
0.0209	23.2	.0000	2	Cavite
0.0209	23.2	.0000	2	Champagne
0.0209	23.2	.0000	2	Chickamauga
0.0209	23.2	.0000	2	Chronicles
0.0209	23.2	.0000	2	Cichla
0.0209	23.2	.0000	2	circumcision
0.0209	23.2	.0000	2	circumvallation
0.0209	23.2	.0000	2	Cleves
0.0209	23.2	.0000	2	cloaca
0.0209	23.2	.0000	2	co-ordinates
0.0209	23.2	.0000	2	collaborating
0.0209	23.2	.0000	2	conchs
0.0209	23.2	.0000	2	conformal
0.0209	23.2	.0000	2	Conservative
0.0209	23.2	.0000	2	constitutionality
0.0209	23.2	.0000	2	conveniences
0.0209	23.2	.0000	2	copious
0.0209	23.2	.0000	2	Corday
0.0209	23.2	.0000	2	Cordilleran
0.0209	23.2	.0000	2	Coriolis
0.0209	23.2	.0000	2	Cotabato
0.0209	23.2	.0000	2	Counties
0.0209	23.2	.0000	2	cretins
0.0209	23.2	.0000	2	Crimea
0.0209	23.2	.0000	2	crop-share
0.0209	23.2	.0000	2	cummingtonite
0.0209	23.2	.0000	2	Cutchogue
0.0209	23.2	.0000	2	Cyclades
0.0209	23.2	.0000	2	cyclic
0.0209	23.2	.0000	2	C2H4Br2**
0.0209	23.2	.0000	2	d'etat
0.0209	23.2	.0000	2	Dadaism
0.0209	23.2	.0000	2	Dalmatia
0.0209	23.2	.0000	2	Dauberval
0.0209	23.2	.0000	2	Davison
0.0209	23.2	.0000	2	deDanse
0.0209	23.2	.0000	2	deMaguaque
0.0209	23.2	.0000	2	DeStijl
0.0209	23.2	.0000	2	deVega
0.0209	23.2	.0000	2	DeVega's
0.0209	23.2	.0000	2	Decree
0.0209	23.2	.0000	2	deferments
0.0209	23.2	.0000	2	Defoe's
0.0209	23.2	.0000	2	degenerate
0.0209	23.2	.0000	2	Delawareans
0.0209	23.2	.0000	2	Demarcation
0.0209	23.2	.0000	2	Democratic-Republicans
0.0209	23.2	.0000	2	depriving
0.0209	23.2	.0000	2	Devonshire
0.0209	23.2	.0000	2	diadem
0.0209	23.2	.0000	2	Dias
0.0209	23.2	.0000	2	dibromide
0.0209	23.2	.0000	2	Diem
0.0209	23.2	.0000	2	Dinh
THE PRECEDING WORD TYPE OCCUPIES RANK 55500				
0.0209	23.2	.0000	2	Diocletian
0.0209	23.2	.0000	2	Diplomacy
0.0209	23.2	.0000	2	directorates
0.0209	23.2	.0000	2	discrete
0.0209	23.2	.0000	2	disinclination
0.0209	23.2	.0000	2	dispatching
0.0209	23.2	.0000	2	diverge
0.0209	23.2	.0000	2	divergent
0.0209	23.2	.0000	2	diversification
0.0209	23.2	.0000	2	diverticula
0.0209	23.2	.0000	2	Djuanda
0.0209	23.2	.0000	2	Dolce
0.0209	23.2	.0000	2	domesticate
0.0209	23.2	.0000	2	domestication
0.0209	23.2	.0000	2	dominion's
0.0209	23.2	.0000	2	Donatist
0.0209	23.2	.0000	2	Donatus
0.0209	23.2	.0000	2	Doxiadis
0.0209	23.2	.0000	2	Drachenloch
0.0209	23.2	.0000	2	dramatist
0.0209	23.2	.0000	2	drawbridges
0.0209	23.2	.0000	2	drydock
0.0209	23.2	.0000	2	Dubrovnik
0.0209	23.2	.0000	2	dyads
0.0209	23.2	.0000	2	Edinburgh's
0.0209	23.2	.0000	2	Elba
0.0209	23.2	.0000	2	electro-magnetic
0.0209	23.2	.0000	2	embalming
0.0209	23.2	.0000	2	embryo's
0.0209	23.2	.0000	2	empowered
0.0209	23.2	.0000	2	encomienda
0.0209	23.2	.0000	2	enlistments
0.0209	23.2	.0000	2	entomologists
0.0209	23.2	.0000	2	epiphytic
0.0209	23.2	.0000	2	equip
0.0209	23.2	.0000	2	Esbjerg
0.0209	23.2	.0000	2	essences
0.0209	23.2	.0000	2	Etruscan
0.0209	23.2	.0000	2	Evangelical
0.0209	23.2	.0000	2	evangelization
0.0209	23.2	.0000	2	evenly-spaced
0.0209	23.2	.0000	2	everglades
0.0209	23.2	.0000	2	evolutionists
0.0209	23.2	.0000	2	excludes
0.0209	23.2	.0000	2	exudate
0.0209	23.2	.0000	2	eyebars
0.0209	23.2	.0000	2	fattens
0.0209	23.2	.0000	2	faunal
0.0209	23.2	.0000	2	Fed
0.0209	23.2	.0000	2	fibrillation
0.0209	23.2	.0000	2	fistula
0.0209	23.2	.0000	2	Floral
0.0209	23.2	.0000	2	Fluorescence
0.0209	23.2	.0000	2	fluoresces
0.0209	23.2	.0000	2	fly's
0.0209	23.2	.0000	2	forager
0.0209	23.2	.0000	2	free-enterprise
0.0209	23.2	.0000	2	gaff-topsail
0.0209	23.2	.0000	2	Gardel
0.0209	23.2	.0000	2	Gaul
0.0209	23.2	.0000	2	Gaunt
0.0209	23.2	.0000	2	gelatinous
0.0209	23.2	.0000	2	Gentry's
0.0209	23.2	.0000	2	Gilbert's
0.0209	23.2	.0000	2	Giselle
0.0209	23.2	.0000	2	glottis
0.0209	23.2	.0000	2	glycol
0.0209	23.2	.0000	2	Goncalves
0.0209	23.2	.0000	2	googol
0.0209	23.2	.0000	2	Gowrie
0.0209	23.2	.0000	2	Graben
0.0209	23.2	.0000	2	gramophone
0.0209	23.2	.0000	2	granitic
0.0209	23.2	.0000	2	green-turtle
0.0209	23.2	.0000	2	Greenback
0.0209	23.2	.0000	2	Greenway
0.0209	23.2	.0000	2	grosbeaks
0.0209	23.2	.0000	2	guayule
0.0209	23.2	.0000	2	Guericke
0.0209	23.2	.0000	2	guises
0.0209	23.2	.0000	2	Gundulic
0.0209	23.2	.0000	2	gutta
0.0209	23.2	.0000	2	hagfishes
0.0209	23.2	.0000	2	half-lives
0.0209	23.2	.0000	2	Hals
0.0209	23.2	.0000	2	halteres
0.0209	23.2	.0000	2	Hanging
0.0209	23.2	.0000	2	Hedingham
0.0209	23.2	.0000	2	Hegel
0.0209	23.2	.0000	2	hemipenes
0.0209	23.2	.0000	2	heretical
0.0209	23.2	.0000	2	Hetch
0.0209	23.2	.0000	2	Hetchy
0.0209	23.2	.0000	2	heterochromatic
0.0209	23.2	.0000	2	heterozygote
0.0209	23.2	.0000	2	hoarded
0.0209	23.2	.0000	2	holosteans
0.0209	23.2	.0000	2	hominid
0.0209	23.2	.0000	2	Honeywell
0.0209	23.2	.0000	2	Hroudland
THE PRECEDING WORD TYPE OCCUPIES RANK 55600				
0.0209	23.2	.0000	2	Huilliche
0.0209	23.2	.0000	2	Humabom
0.0209	23.2	.0000	2	humanist
0.0209	23.2	.0000	2	Humbert

U	SFI	D	F	Word Type
0.0209	23.2	.0000	2	Hunchback
0.0209	23.2	.0000	2	hundredfold
0.0209	23.2	.0000	2	Huxley
0.0209	23.2	.0000	2	hymenopterans
0.0209	23.2	.0000	2	ice-age
0.0209	23.2	.0000	2	Iguacu
0.0209	23.2	.0000	2	ill-feeling
0.0209	23.2	.0000	2	imagist
0.0209	23.2	.0000	2	imams
0.0209	23.2	.0000	2	impalas
0.0209	23.2	.0000	2	incubate
0.0209	23.2	.0000	2	Inquisition
0.0209	23.2	.0000	2	inter-American
0.0209	23.2	.0000	2	interbreed
0.0209	23.2	.0000	2	interdisciplinary
0.0209	23.2	.0000	2	intergranular
0.0209	23.2	.0000	2	intervenes
0.0209	23.2	.0000	2	intimations
0.0209	23.2	.0000	2	inviable
0.0209	23.2	.0000	2	iridium
0.0209	23.2	.0000	2	Iroquoian
0.0209	23.2	.0000	2	Jagatai
0.0209	23.2	.0000	2	Jahn
0.0209	23.2	.0000	2	jestbooks
0.0209	23.2	.0000	2	Jests
0.0209	23.2	.0000	2	Jos
0.0209	23.2	.0000	2	Jubal
0.0209	23.2	.0000	2	kabuki
0.0209	23.2	.0000	2	Kandahar
0.0209	23.2	.0000	2	Karachi
0.0209	23.2	.0000	2	kauri
0.0209	23.2	.0000	2	khaghan
0.0209	23.2	.0000	2	Khufu
0.0209	23.2	.0000	2	Khufu-onekh
0.0209	23.2	.0000	2	Kirthar
0.0209	23.2	.0000	2	Kitchener
0.0209	23.2	.0000	2	kivas
0.0209	23.2	.0000	2	kiwi
0.0209	23.2	.0000	2	Koelle
0.0209	23.2	.0000	2	Kogler
0.0209	23.2	.0000	2	Kogler's
0.0209	23.2	.0000	2	Kohara
0.0209	23.2	.0000	2	konsepsi
0.0209	23.2	.0000	2	Kronborg
0.0209	23.2	.0000	2	Kuiper
0.0209	23.2	.0000	2	Labor-Management
0.0209	23.2	.0000	2	lac
0.0209	23.2	.0000	2	laminating
0.0209	23.2	.0000	2	Lancastrian
0.0209	23.2	.0000	2	land-dwelling
0.0209	23.2	.0000	2	Langelinie
0.0209	23.2	.0000	2	laryngeal
0.0209	23.2	.0000	2	laureate
0.0209	23.2	.0000	2	Lawless
0.0209	23.2	.0000	2	leavening
0.0209	23.2	.0000	2	leeboard
0.0209	23.2	.0000	2	leeboards
0.0209	23.2	.0000	2	Lemke
0.0209	23.2	.0000	2	lemur
0.0209	23.2	.0000	2	Lenard
0.0209	23.2	.0000	2	libertarian
0.0209	23.2	.0000	2	linkage
0.0209	23.2	.0000	2	lithographic
0.0209	23.2	.0000	2	lithotomy
0.0209	23.2	.0000	2	Livonia
0.0209	23.2	.0000	2	Lloyd's
0.0209	23.2	.0000	2	Lodi
0.0209	23.2	.0000	2	Lope
0.0209	23.2	.0000	2	LOUIS
0.0209	23.2	.0000	2	Lubis
0.0209	23.2	.0000	2	lubricants
0.0209	23.2	.0000	2	luminescence
0.0209	23.2	.0000	2	lumped
0.0209	23.2	.0000	2	lungfishes
0.0209	23.2	.0000	2	Lutheranism
0.0209	23.2	.0000	2	Lyly
0.0209	23.2	.0000	2	magnifications
0.0209	23.2	.0000	2	Mahratta
0.0209	23.2	.0000	2	Mai
0.0209	23.2	.0000	2	male's
0.0209	23.2	.0000	2	mallee
0.0209	23.2	.0000	2	Mannheim
0.0209	23.2	.0000	2	manzanita
0.0209	23.2	.0000	2	Mapuche
0.0209	23.2	.0000	2	Marat's
0.0209	23.2	.0000	2	margraves
0.0209	23.2	.0000	2	marmosas
0.0209	23.2	.0000	2	martins
0.0209	23.2	.0000	2	Masons
0.0209	23.2	.0000	2	Massif
0.0209	23.2	.0000	2	Maudslay
0.0209	23.2	.0000	2	Maximilien
0.0209	23.2	.0000	2	McGill
0.0209	23.2	.0000	2	Mead
0.0209	23.2	.0000	2	mechanistic
0.0209	23.2	.0000	2	Mediation

THE PRECEDING WORD TYPE OCCUPIES RANK 55700

U	SFI	D	F	Word Type
0.0209	23.2	.0000	2	mediators
0.0209	23.2	.0000	2	MEDICO
0.0209	23.2	.0000	2	meditate
0.0209	23.2	.0000	2	mellitus
0.0209	23.2	.0000	2	members'
0.0209	23.2	.0000	2	Merovingians
0.0209	23.2	.0000	2	Meru
0.0209	23.2	.0000	2	metaphase
0.0209	23.2	.0000	2	methanol
0.0209	23.2	.0000	2	Michelmore
0.0209	23.2	.0000	2	microscopists
0.0209	23.2	.0000	2	mid-17th
0.0209	23.2	.0000	2	Migratory
0.0209	23.2	.0000	2	Millais
0.0209	23.2	.0000	2	millennia
0.0209	23.2	.0000	2	Minakami
0.0209	23.2	.0000	2	Mindoro
0.0209	23.2	.0000	2	miniaturist
0.0209	23.2	.0000	2	Mohenjo-Daro
0.0209	23.2	.0000	2	Mohorovicic
0.0209	23.2	.0000	2	molecularly
0.0209	23.2	.0000	2	molehill
0.0209	23.2	.0000	2	Mollweide
0.0209	23.2	.0000	2	monazite
0.0209	23.2	.0000	2	Monge
0.0209	23.2	.0000	2	monkey-eating
0.0209	23.2	.0000	2	Monocacy
0.0209	23.2	.0000	2	Monthly
0.0209	23.2	.0000	2	Moresby
0.0209	23.2	.0000	2	Moro
0.0209	23.2	.0000	2	Mosaic
0.0209	23.2	.0000	2	mosquito's
0.0209	23.2	.0000	2	Mote
0.0209	23.2	.0000	2	Moultrie
0.0209	23.2	.0000	2	myalgia
0.0209	23.2	.0000	2	Mythology
0.0209	23.2	.0000	2	Nasmyth
0.0209	23.2	.0000	2	Nassau
0.0209	23.2	.0000	2	nation-state
0.0209	23.2	.0000	2	Nazaire
0.0209	23.2	.0000	2	Ne'eman
0.0209	23.2	.0000	2	Neanderthaler
0.0209	23.2	.0000	2	nebulium
0.0209	23.2	.0000	2	neurones
0.0209	23.2	.0000	2	NewCastle
0.0209	23.2	.0000	2	Ngo
0.0209	23.2	.0000	2	NH4NO2
0.0209	23.2	.0000	2	Nice
0.0209	23.2	.0000	2	nicotinic
0.0209	23.2	.0000	2	nonprofit
0.0209	23.2	.0000	2	nonsingers
0.0209	23.2	.0000	2	Norris-LaGuardia
0.0209	23.2	.0000	2	north-northwest
0.0209	23.2	.0000	2	Novalis
0.0209	23.2	.0000	2	Noverre
0.0209	23.2	.0000	2	Noverre's
0.0209	23.2	.0000	2	nuovo
0.0209	23.2	.0000	2	nuptial
0.0209	23.2	.0000	2	N2
0.0209	23.2	.0000	2	Odoacer
0.0209	23.2	.0000	2	oestrous
0.0209	23.2	.0000	2	oestrus
0.0209	23.2	.0000	2	Oeuvres
0.0209	23.2	.0000	2	okrug
0.0209	23.2	.0000	2	Oligocene
0.0209	23.2	.0000	2	omnivore
0.0209	23.2	.0000	2	Ont
0.0209	23.2	.0000	2	openpit
0.0209	23.2	.0000	2	optimum
0.0209	23.2	.0000	2	orbicules
0.0209	23.2	.0000	2	Oresund
0.0209	23.2	.0000	2	orifices
0.0209	23.2	.0000	2	oscillating
0.0209	23.2	.0000	2	osmosis
0.0209	23.2	.0000	2	osmotic
0.0209	23.2	.0000	2	Ostade
0.0209	23.2	.0000	2	Osten-Sacken
0.0209	23.2	.0000	2	Otranto
0.0209	23.2	.0000	2	Painting
0.0209	23.2	.0000	2	Palawan
0.0209	23.2	.0000	2	Paleocene
0.0209	23.2	.0000	2	Palms
0.0209	23.2	.0000	2	PaloAlto
0.0209	23.2	.0000	2	Pantelleria
0.0209	23.2	.0000	2	pantomime-ballet
0.0209	23.2	.0000	2	Paracelsus
0.0209	23.2	.0000	2	paramilitary
0.0209	23.2	.0000	2	paraplegia
0.0209	23.2	.0000	2	parietal
0.0209	23.2	.0000	2	parity
0.0209	23.2	.0000	2	Parkesine
0.0209	23.2	.0000	2	Parole
0.0209	23.2	.0000	2	PBP
0.0209	23.2	.0000	2	Peltier
0.0209	23.2	.0000	2	pelvics
0.0209	23.2	.0000	2	peons
0.0209	23.2	.0000	2	pericardial
0.0209	23.2	.0000	2	persistence
0.0209	23.2	.0000	2	PGA
0.0209	23.2	.0000	2	philanthropic

THE PRECEDING WORD TYPE OCCUPIES RANK 55800

U	SFI	D	F	Word Type
0.0209	23.2	.0000	2	phormium
0.0209	23.2	.0000	2	physician's
0.0209	23.2	.0000	2	Physicians
0.0209	23.2	.0000	2	pigmented
0.0209	23.2	.0000	2	pirarucu
0.0209	23.2	.0000	2	pithecoid
0.0209	23.2	.0000	2	placentalike
0.0209	23.2	.0000	2	pollinate
0.0209	23.2	.0000	2	pollinated
0.0209	23.2	.0000	2	Polytechnic
0.0209	23.2	.0000	2	portenos
0.0209	23.2	.0000	2	positives
0.0209	23.2	.0000	2	Potemkin
0.0209	23.2	.0000	2	pre-Columbian
0.0209	23.2	.0000	2	Pre-Raphaelite
0.0209	23.2	.0000	2	predation
0.0209	23.2	.0000	2	premolars
0.0209	23.2	.0000	2	pries
0.0209	23.2	.0000	2	Priority
0.0209	23.2	.0000	2	probabilistic
0.0209	23.2	.0000	2	professorial
0.0209	23.2	.0000	2	profiting
0.0209	23.2	.0000	2	proofsheets
0.0209	23.2	.0000	2	propagate
0.0209	23.2	.0000	2	prophase
0.0209	23.2	.0000	2	prostration
0.0209	23.2	.0000	2	Psychical
0.0209	23.2	.0000	2	psychoses
0.0209	23.2	.0000	2	ptarmigan
0.0209	23.2	.0000	2	pyroxylin
0.0209	23.2	.0000	2	pythons
0.0209	23.2	.0000	2	qualitative
0.0209	23.2	.0000	2	quantitatively
0.0209	23.2	.0000	2	Quantum
0.0209	23.2	.0000	2	questionnaires
0.0209	23.2	.0000	2	Rainey
0.0209	23.2	.0000	2	Rajasthan
0.0209	23.2	.0000	2	Raphael
0.0209	23.2	.0000	2	reabsorbed
0.0209	23.2	.0000	2	recombination
0.0209	23.2	.0000	2	redfish
0.0209	23.2	.0000	2	registrant
0.0209	23.2	.0000	2	reinvaded
0.0209	23.2	.0000	2	Reliance
0.0209	23.2	.0000	2	Rennes
0.0209	23.2	.0000	2	repayment
0.0209	23.2	.0000	2	repelling
0.0209	23.2	.0000	2	Restitution
0.0209	23.2	.0000	2	Rey
0.0209	23.2	.0000	2	rhodium
0.0209	23.2	.0000	2	Riga
0.0209	23.2	.0000	2	Rimbaud
0.0209	23.2	.0000	2	Rockefeller's
0.0209	23.2	.0000	2	Rommel
0.0209	23.2	.0000	2	Roncesvalles
0.0209	23.2	.0000	2	Rosecrans
0.0209	23.2	.0000	2	Rousseau's
0.0209	23.2	.0000	2	Rubens
0.0209	23.2	.0000	2	SALPAC
0.0209	23.2	.0000	2	Samar
0.0209	23.2	.0000	2	SanMartin's
0.0209	23.2	.0000	2	Sangay
0.0209	23.2	.0000	2	sartorius
0.0209	23.2	.0000	2	satiric
0.0209	23.2	.0000	2	Saturn's
0.0209	23.2	.0000	2	Saussure
0.0209	23.2	.0000	2	sayids
0.0209	23.2	.0000	2	Schoeffer
0.0209	23.2	.0000	2	science-oriented
0.0209	23.2	.0000	2	Sedgwick
0.0209	23.2	.0000	2	Seebeck
0.0209	23.2	.0000	2	selenium
0.0209	23.2	.0000	2	Sevastopol
0.0209	23.2	.0000	2	Shanidar
0.0209	23.2	.0000	2	silicone
0.0209	23.2	.0000	2	Silurian
0.0209	23.2	.0000	2	Simbolon
0.0209	23.2	.0000	2	sinusoidal
0.0209	23.2	.0000	2	Sjaelland
0.0209	23.2	.0000	2	skepticism
0.0209	23.2	.0000	2	smorrebrod
0.0209	23.2	.0000	2	snappers
0.0209	23.2	.0000	2	somatotropin
0.0209	23.2	.0000	2	Sometimes
0.0209	23.2	.0000	2	space-time
0.0209	23.2	.0000	2	speciation
0.0209	23.2	.0000	2	spoked
0.0209	23.2	.0000	2	spot-color
0.0209	23.2	.0000	2	springhaas
0.0209	23.2	.0000	2	sprit-end
0.0209	23.2	.0000	2	Squirrel's
0.0209	23.2	.0000	2	StJohn
0.0209	23.2	.0000	2	static-electricity
0.0209	23.2	.0000	2	SteMarie
0.0209	23.2	.0000	2	sternum
0.0209	23.2	.0000	2	stil
0.0209	23.2	.0000	2	still-larger
0.0209	23.2	.0000	2	storages
0.0209	23.2	.0000	2	strategem
0.0209	23.2	.0000	2	stroboscope

THE PRECEDING WORD TYPE OCCUPIES RANK 55900

U	SFI	D	F	Word Type
0.0209	23.2	.0000	2	subduing
0.0209	23.2	.0000	2	subkingdom
0.0209	23.2	.0000	2	subsystems
0.0209	23.2	.0000	2	subterraneous
0.0209	23.2	.0000	2	suppliers
0.0209	23.2	.0000	2	surmises
0.0209	23.2	.0000	2	swallowtails
0.0209	23.2	.0000	2	swat
0.0209	23.2	.0000	2	sweete
0.0209	23.2	.0000	2	synapsed
0.0209	23.2	.0000	2	Szilard
0.0209	23.2	.0000	2	Tamanyan
0.0209	23.2	.0000	2	taxonomic
0.0209	23.2	.0000	2	teardrop
0.0209	23.2	.0000	2	tearing-down
0.0209	23.2	.0000	2	tentacle
0.0209	23.2	.0000	2	Terman
0.0209	23.2	.0000	2	tetrads
0.0209	23.2	.0000	2	tetrapod
0.0209	23.2	.0000	2	Thallophyta
0.0209	23.2	.0000	2	Theodoric
0.0209	23.2	.0000	2	Theodoric
0.0209	23.2	.0000	2	thermoelectric
0.0209	23.2	.0000	2	Thucydides
0.0209	23.2	.0000	2	Toklug-Timur
0.0209	23.2	.0000	2	toolmaking
0.0209	23.2	.0000	2	totality
0.0209	23.2	.0000	2	transcribe
0.0209	23.2	.0000	2	translocations
0.0209	23.2	.0000	2	trawls
0.0209	23.2	.0000	2	triggerfish
0.0209	23.2	.0000	2	trigon
0.0209	23.2	.0000	2	Trubar
0.0209	23.2	.0000	2	tuataras
0.0209	23.2	.0000	2	Tunisian
0.0209	23.2	.0000	2	turnvereins
0.0209	23.2	.0000	2	Turpin
0.0209	23.2	.0000	2	two-color
0.0209	23.2	.0000	2	Typhon
0.0209	23.2	.0000	2	uhf
0.0209	23.2	.0000	2	ungulate
0.0209	23.2	.0000	2	uninviting
0.0209	23.2	.0000	2	unit-letter
0.0209	23.2	.0000	2	unlawfully
0.0209	23.2	.0000	2	Unraed
0.0209	23.2	.0000	2	unrecognizable
0.0209	23.2	.0000	2	unsaturated
0.0209	23.2	.0000	2	untenable
0.0209	23.2	.0000	2	unwary
0.0209	23.2	.0000	2	Ur
0.0209	23.2	.0000	2	ureters
0.0209	23.2	.0000	2	utilitarian
0.0209	23.2	.0000	2	Utilitarianism
0.0209	23.2	.0000	2	utilitarianism
0.0209	23.2	.0000	2	Uzbek
0.0209	23.2	.0000	2	Van-Buren
0.0209	23.2	.0000	2	Varian
0.0209	23.2	.0000	2	vegetarian
0.0209	23.2	.0000	2	Verrazano
0.0209	23.2	.0000	2	Verrazano's
0.0209	23.2	.0000	2	Vespucius
0.0209	23.2	.0000	2	Vestris
0.0209	23.2	.0000	2	Veterans'
0.0209	23.2	.0000	2	vice-presidency
0.0209	23.2	.0000	2	Viki
0.0209	23.2	.0000	2	Vindobona
0.0209	23.2	.0000	2	visualization
0.0209	23.2	.0000	2	Vulcanization
0.0209	23.2	.0000	2	vulcanized
0.0209	23.2	.0000	2	Warr
0.0209	23.2	.0000	2	well-preserved
0.0209	23.2	.0000	2	whelks
0.0209	23.2	.0000	2	Whiskey
0.0209	23.2	.0000	2	Wigner
0.0209	23.2	.0000	2	wrasse
0.0209	23.2	.0000	2	wreckfish
0.0209	23.2	.0000	2	XVIII
0.0209	23.2	.0000	2	Xylonite
0.0209	23.2	.0000	2	Yalouris
0.0209	23.2	.0000	2	yeomen
0.0209	23.2	.0000	2	Ypres
0.0209	23.2	.0000	2	yttrium
0.0209	23.2	.0000	2	Zola
0.0209	23.2	.0000	2	zoogeographer
0.0209	23.2	.0000	2	zoogeographers
0.0209	23.2	.0000	2	10-pound
0.0209	23.2	.0000	2	1016
0.0209	23.2	.0000	2	1100's
0.0209	23.2	.0000	2	1244
0.0209	23.2	.0000	2	1483
0.0209	23.2	.0000	2	1524
0.0209	23.2	.0000	2	1529
0.0209	23.2	.0000	2	1560
0.0209	23.2	.0000	2	1660
0.0209	23.2	.0000	2	1663
0.0209	23.2	.0000	2	1682
0.0209	23.2	.0000	2	1766
0.0209	23.2	.0000	2	1896-
0.0209	23.2	.0000	2	35-mm
0.0209	23.2	.0000	2	585

THE PRECEDING WORD TYPE OCCUPIES RANK 56000

U	SFI	D	F	Word Type
0.0209	23.2	.0000	2	619
0.0209	23.2	.0000	2	8-county
0.0209	23.2	.0000	2	851
0.0208	23.2	.0168	3	parable
0.0207	23.2	.0171	3	psalms
0.0201	23.0	.0000	9	Pidgin
0.0197	22.9	.0000	1	-shaped**
0.0197	22.9	.0000	1	-109
0.0197	22.9	.0000	1	-15
0.0197	22.9	.0000	1	-200
0.0197	22.9	.0000	1	-273
0.0197	22.9	.0000	1	-317
0.0197	22.9	.0000	1	-38
0.0197	22.9	.0000	1	-459
0.0197	22.9	.0000	1	'quake
0.0197	22.9	.0000	1	Abney
0.0197	22.9	.0000	1	abouts
0.0197	22.9	.0000	1	abrade
0.0197	22.9	.0000	1	abscessed
0.0197	22.9	.0000	1	absorbable
0.0197	22.9	.0000	1	absorptions
0.0197	22.9	.0000	1	Acamar
0.0197	22.9	.0000	1	accessory
0.0197	22.9	.0000	1	accumulations
0.0197	22.9	.0000	1	Achernar
0.0197	22.9	.0000	1	acre-by-acre
0.0197	22.9	.0000	1	Actaea
0.0197	22.9	.0000	1	action-reaction
0.0197	22.9	.0000	1	adam's
0.0197	22.9	.0000	1	adaptions
0.0197	22.9	.0000	1	addicting
0.0197	22.9	.0000	1	Additives
0.0197	22.9	.0000	1	adenocarcinoma
0.0197	22.9	.0000	1	adeptly
0.0197	22.9	.0000	1	adiabatic
0.0197	22.9	.0000	1	adjoin
0.0197	22.9	.0000	1	adult's
0.0197	22.9	.0000	1	aerometeorograph
0.0197	22.9	.0000	1	afflictions
0.0197	22.9	.0000	1	afterimages
0.0197	22.9	.0000	1	air-sea
0.0197	22.9	.0000	1	air-vaulted
0.0197	22.9	.0000	1	airlessness
0.0197	22.9	.0000	1	Albireo
0.0197	22.9	.0000	1	Alcohol
0.0197	22.9	.0000	1	alcoholism
0.0197	22.9	.0000	1	alcometer
0.0197	22.9	.0000	1	Alfonsine
0.0197	22.9	.0000	1	Algae
0.0197	22.9	.0000	1	alimentary
0.0197	22.9	.0000	1	all-glass
0.0197	22.9	.0000	1	Almach
0.0197	22.9	.0000	1	Almagest
0.0197	22.9	.0000	1	Almanor
0.0197	22.9	.0000	1	alnico
0.0197	22.9	.0000	1	alot
0.0197	22.9	.0000	1	Alphecca
0.0197	22.9	.0000	1	Altair
0.0197	22.9	.0000	1	altimeters
0.0197	22.9	.0000	1	aluminum-foil
0.0197	22.9	.0000	1	alyssum
0.0197	22.9	.0000	1	amateur's
0.0197	22.9	.0000	1	americanus
0.0197	22.9	.0000	1	ammoniac
0.0197	22.9	.0000	1	Amoeba
0.0197	22.9	.0000	1	amoebas
0.0197	22.9	.0000	1	amphibia
0.0197	22.9	.0000	1	amphibolite

U	SFI	D	F	Word Type
0.0197	22.9	.0000	1	Amphioxus
0.0197	22.9	.0000	1	Amplification
0.0197	22.9	.0000	1	amylose
0.0197	22.9	.0000	1	analytic
0.0197	22.9	.0000	1	anemometers
0.0197	22.9	.0000	1	anesthetized
0.0197	22.9	.0000	1	angel's
0.0197	22.9	.0000	1	animalcule
0.0197	22.9	.0000	1	Animas
0.0197	22.9	.0000	1	annabergite
0.0197	22.9	.0000	1	Anopheles
0.0197	22.9	.0000	1	anterior
0.0197	22.9	.0000	1	antheridia
0.0197	22.9	.0000	1	anti-cyclones
0.0197	22.9	.0000	1	anti-matter-galaxies
0.0197	22.9	.0000	1	anti-universe
0.0197	22.9	.0000	1	anticyclones
0.0197	22.9	.0000	1	antiparticles
0.0197	22.9	.0000	1	antitetanus
0.0197	22.9	.0000	1	Apollonius
0.0197	22.9	.0000	1	appendix
0.0197	22.9	.0000	1	Applicator
0.0197	22.9	.0000	1	aquaculture
0.0197	22.9	.0000	1	aqualungs
0.0197	22.9	.0000	1	aquamarine
0.0197	22.9	.0000	1	aquaria
0.0197	22.9	.0000	1	Aquatic
0.0197	22.9	.0000	1	Aquilegia
0.0197	22.9	.0000	1	arachnid
0.0197	22.9	.0000	1	arachnids
0.0197	22.9	.0000	1	archegonia
0.0197	22.9	.0000	1	archipelago
THE PRECEDING WORD TYPE OCCUPIES RANK 56100				
0.0197	22.9	.0000	1	Ardan
0.0197	22.9	.0000	1	argentum
0.0197	22.9	.0000	1	arrow-like
0.0197	22.9	.0000	1	arsenate
0.0197	22.9	.0000	1	arsenical
0.0197	22.9	.0000	1	artesian-well
0.0197	22.9	.0000	1	ascaris
0.0197	22.9	.0000	1	ascension
0.0197	22.9	.0000	1	assault-and-battery
0.0197	22.9	.0000	1	astrobleme
0.0197	22.9	.0000	1	astronomer's
0.0197	22.9	.0000	1	astronomy's
0.0197	22.9	.0000	1	astrophysics
0.0197	22.9	.0000	1	astutely
0.0197	22.9	.0000	1	ATMOSPHERE
0.0197	22.9	.0000	1	atmospherics
0.0197	22.9	.0000	1	atom-smashing
0.0197	22.9	.0000	1	attest
0.0197	22.9	.0000	1	augite
0.0197	22.9	.0000	1	auks
0.0197	22.9	.0000	1	Australis
0.0197	22.9	.0000	1	autotrophic
0.0197	22.9	.0000	1	avaricious
0.0197	22.9	.0000	1	Aves
0.0197	22.9	.0000	1	Axelrod's
0.0197	22.9	.0000	1	Aycock
0.0197	22.9	.0000	1	B-group
0.0197	22.9	.0000	1	B-vitamin
0.0197	22.9	.0000	1	baa-ing
0.0197	22.9	.0000	1	Baade's
0.0197	22.9	.0000	1	bacillus-swarming
0.0197	22.9	.0000	1	back-boned
0.0197	22.9	.0000	1	backups
0.0197	22.9	.0000	1	Bacteria
0.0197	22.9	.0000	1	bacteriologist
0.0197	22.9	.0000	1	bacteriophages
0.0197	22.9	.0000	1	Badlands
0.0197	22.9	.0000	1	bakterion
0.0197	22.9	.0000	1	balderdash
0.0197	22.9	.0000	1	baling
0.0197	22.9	.0000	1	Ballinger
0.0197	22.9	.0000	1	Banting
0.0197	22.9	.0000	1	Bare
0.0197	22.9	.0000	1	bare-looking
0.0197	22.9	.0000	1	barrelchested
0.0197	22.9	.0000	1	Barringer
0.0197	22.9	.0000	1	basket-makers
0.0197	22.9	.0000	1	batholith
0.0197	22.9	.0000	1	bathy
0.0197	22.9	.0000	1	bathyscaphs
0.0197	22.9	.0000	1	bathyspheres
0.0197	22.9	.0000	1	bathythermographs
0.0197	22.9	.0000	1	Batrachium
0.0197	22.9	.0000	1	bean-shooters
0.0197	22.9	.0000	1	beat-beat-beat
0.0197	22.9	.0000	1	beautifying
0.0197	22.9	.0000	1	behaviors
0.0197	22.9	.0000	1	Behring
0.0197	22.9	.0000	1	below-the-surface
0.0197	22.9	.0000	1	Bemberg
0.0197	22.9	.0000	1	Bernoulli
0.0197	22.9	.0000	1	Berta
0.0197	22.9	.0000	1	betatron
0.0197	22.9	.0000	1	betatrons
0.0197	22.9	.0000	1	Bethe
0.0197	22.9	.0000	1	bettering
0.0197	22.9	.0000	1	between-meals
0.0197	22.9	.0000	1	biblical
0.0197	22.9	.0000	1	bicuspid
0.0197	22.9	.0000	1	bicycle-safety
0.0197	22.9	.0000	1	Billingham
0.0197	22.9	.0000	1	billion-odd
0.0197	22.9	.0000	1	biologist's
0.0197	22.9	.0000	1	bios
0.0197	22.9	.0000	1	Biot
0.0197	22.9	.0000	1	biotin
0.0197	22.9	.0000	1	Birr
0.0197	22.9	.0000	1	black-skinned
0.0197	22.9	.0000	1	blacksmithing
0.0197	22.9	.0000	1	blacktongue
0.0197	22.9	.0000	1	Blast
0.0197	22.9	.0000	1	BLAST
0.0197	22.9	.0000	1	blimplike
0.0197	22.9	.0000	1	block-mounted

U	SFI	D	F	Word Type
0.0197	22.9	.0000	1	blood's
0.0197	22.9	.0000	1	Blue-green
0.0197	22.9	.0000	1	blue-sensitive
0.0197	22.9	.0000	1	Boer
0.0197	22.9	.0000	1	bollworm
0.0197	22.9	.0000	1	Bootes
0.0197	22.9	.0000	1	Boothia
0.0197	22.9	.0000	1	botryoidal
0.0197	22.9	.0000	1	bottling
0.0197	22.9	.0000	1	bowel
0.0197	22.9	.0000	1	bowlegs
0.0197	22.9	.0000	1	Br
0.0197	22.9	.0000	1	brachii
0.0197	22.9	.0000	1	brackish-water
0.0197	22.9	.0000	1	Brah
0.0197	22.9	.0000	1	brain-twisting
THE PRECEDING WORD TYPE OCCUPIES RANK 56200				
0.0197	22.9	.0000	1	bread-cereal
0.0197	22.9	.0000	1	breaking-up
0.0197	22.9	.0000	1	breeder's
0.0197	22.9	.0000	1	brewed
0.0197	22.9	.0000	1	brilliantly-colored
0.0197	22.9	.0000	1	broad-based
0.0197	22.9	.0000	1	bronze-brown
0.0197	22.9	.0000	1	brother-sister
0.0197	22.9	.0000	1	brown-and-white
0.0197	22.9	.0000	1	brr-rr-r-r
0.0197	22.9	.0000	1	Bryophyllum
0.0197	22.9	.0000	1	bryophyte
0.0197	22.9	.0000	1	bryophytes
0.0197	22.9	.0000	1	buccinator
0.0197	22.9	.0000	1	buffed
0.0197	22.9	.0000	1	building-materials
0.0197	22.9	.0000	1	bullfrog's
0.0197	22.9	.0000	1	Burdette
0.0197	22.9	.0000	1	burnable
0.0197	22.9	.0000	1	Burnet
0.0197	22.9	.0000	1	bush-leaguer
0.0197	22.9	.0000	1	buzzers
0.0197	22.9	.0000	1	CaCO3
0.0197	22.9	.0000	1	CaF
0.0197	22.9	.0000	1	CaSO
0.0197	22.9	.0000	1	cablegrams
0.0197	22.9	.0000	1	cafeterias
0.0197	22.9	.0000	1	calcaneus
0.0197	22.9	.0000	1	Caldera
0.0197	22.9	.0000	1	calderas
0.0197	22.9	.0000	1	cambium
0.0197	22.9	.0000	1	can's
0.0197	22.9	.0000	1	Canadian-American
0.0197	22.9	.0000	1	canceling
0.0197	22.9	.0000	1	candytuft
0.0197	22.9	.0000	1	Canidae
0.0197	22.9	.0000	1	cantelopes
0.0197	22.9	.0000	1	Caph
0.0197	22.9	.0000	1	caprice
0.0197	22.9	.0000	1	capsule's
0.0197	22.9	.0000	1	car-hour
0.0197	22.9	.0000	1	carbon-containing
0.0197	22.9	.0000	1	carbonic
0.0197	22.9	.0000	1	carboniferous
0.0197	22.9	.0000	1	Carla's
0.0197	22.9	.0000	1	carmine
0.0197	22.9	.0000	1	carped
0.0197	22.9	.0000	1	cartographic
0.0197	22.9	.0000	1	cashew
0.0197	22.9	.0000	1	cassiterite
0.0197	22.9	.0000	1	catamaran
0.0197	22.9	.0000	1	catbirds
0.0197	22.9	.0000	1	catkins
0.0197	22.9	.0000	1	cauliflower-like
0.0197	22.9	.0000	1	CAUTION
0.0197	22.9	.0000	1	CCL4
0.0197	22.9	.0000	1	cell-wall
0.0197	22.9	.0000	1	celled
0.0197	22.9	.0000	1	cements
0.0197	22.9	.0000	1	cementum
0.0197	22.9	.0000	1	CENTAURUS
0.0197	22.9	.0000	1	Centers
0.0197	22.9	.0000	1	centrally
0.0197	22.9	.0000	1	cerebrospinal
0.0197	22.9	.0000	1	certain-sized
0.0197	22.9	.0000	1	cervix
0.0197	22.9	.0000	1	cesspool
0.0197	22.9	.0000	1	chain-links
0.0197	22.9	.0000	1	chalk-filled
0.0197	22.9	.0000	1	cheeselike
0.0197	22.9	.0000	1	chemical-coated
0.0197	22.9	.0000	1	chiggers
0.0197	22.9	.0000	1	child-guidance
0.0197	22.9	.0000	1	chinook
0.0197	22.9	.0000	1	chitin-like
0.0197	22.9	.0000	1	chlorella
0.0197	22.9	.0000	1	chlorinated
0.0197	22.9	.0000	1	chloro
0.0197	22.9	.0000	1	chloromycetin
0.0197	22.9	.0000	1	chordata
0.0197	22.9	.0000	1	chordate
0.0197	22.9	.0000	1	chromatography
0.0197	22.9	.0000	1	chromosphere
0.0197	22.9	.0000	1	cigarette-smoking
0.0197	22.9	.0000	1	ciliar
0.0197	22.9	.0000	1	Cinderella-like
0.0197	22.9	.0000	1	circuit-closer
0.0197	22.9	.0000	1	cirrostratus
0.0197	22.9	.0000	1	citrulline
0.0197	22.9	.0000	1	clamitans
0.0197	22.9	.0000	1	clamlike
0.0197	22.9	.0000	1	clasping
0.0197	22.9	.0000	1	Claudius
0.0197	22.9	.0000	1	claylike
0.0197	22.9	.0000	1	clematis
0.0197	22.9	.0000	1	click-click
0.0197	22.9	.0000	1	CLIMATE
0.0197	22.9	.0000	1	clinoenstatite
0.0197	22.9	.0000	1	clinohypersthene
0.0197	22.9	.0000	1	clocklike

U	SFI	D	F	Word Type
THE PRECEDING WORD TYPE OCCUPIES RANK 56300				
0.0197	22.9	.0000	1	cloud-cataloguers
0.0197	22.9	.0000	1	cloud-cover
0.0197	22.9	.0000	1	cloudbursts
0.0197	22.9	.0000	1	cloudcap
0.0197	22.9	.0000	1	clover's
0.0197	22.9	.0000	1	club-shaped
0.0197	22.9	.0000	1	cm3**
0.0197	22.9	.0000	1	co-discoverer
0.0197	22.9	.0000	1	co-inventor
0.0197	22.9	.0000	1	Coalsack
0.0197	22.9	.0000	1	coccus
0.0197	22.9	.0000	1	cockroach's
0.0197	22.9	.0000	1	codling
0.0197	22.9	.0000	1	coincided
0.0197	22.9	.0000	1	cola
0.0197	22.9	.0000	1	cold-preventing
0.0197	22.9	.0000	1	cold-wave
0.0197	22.9	.0000	1	collides
0.0197	22.9	.0000	1	columbite
0.0197	22.9	.0000	1	columnar
0.0197	22.9	.0000	1	comb-footed
0.0197	22.9	.0000	1	comet's
0.0197	22.9	.0000	1	Comical
0.0197	22.9	.0000	1	commensal
0.0197	22.9	.0000	1	commensals
0.0197	22.9	.0000	1	community's
0.0197	22.9	.0000	1	comparator
0.0197	22.9	.0000	1	compressibilities
0.0197	22.9	.0000	1	Conant
0.0197	22.9	.0000	1	conchoidal
0.0197	22.9	.0000	1	concoctions
0.0197	22.9	.0000	1	concolor
0.0197	22.9	.0000	1	concretion
0.0197	22.9	.0000	1	cone-bearing
0.0197	22.9	.0000	1	cone-like
0.0197	22.9	.0000	1	confusedly
0.0197	22.9	.0000	1	conks
0.0197	22.9	.0000	1	Conservationist
0.0197	22.9	.0000	1	constrictor
0.0197	22.9	.0000	1	CONSTRUCT
0.0197	22.9	.0000	1	contact-lens
0.0197	22.9	.0000	1	contaminates
0.0197	22.9	.0000	1	contaminating
0.0197	22.9	.0000	1	cooperatively
0.0197	22.9	.0000	1	copepod's
0.0197	22.9	.0000	1	Copernicus'
0.0197	22.9	.0000	1	Coptis
0.0197	22.9	.0000	1	Cordaites
0.0197	22.9	.0000	1	Cordon
0.0197	22.9	.0000	1	corky
0.0197	22.9	.0000	1	corn-grower
0.0197	22.9	.0000	1	cornerstones
0.0197	22.9	.0000	1	coronagraph
0.0197	22.9	.0000	1	corralled
0.0197	22.9	.0000	1	corrosion-resistant
0.0197	22.9	.0000	1	corundum
0.0197	22.9	.0000	1	CORVUS
0.0197	22.9	.0000	1	cots
0.0197	22.9	.0000	1	counter-clockwise
0.0197	22.9	.0000	1	counteracted
0.0197	22.9	.0000	1	counterforce
0.0197	22.9	.0000	1	covalent
0.0197	22.9	.0000	1	cover-up
0.0197	22.9	.0000	1	cowbird's
0.0197	22.9	.0000	1	cowmen
0.0197	22.9	.0000	1	coworker
0.0197	22.9	.0000	1	coworkers
0.0197	22.9	.0000	1	crab's
0.0197	22.9	.0000	1	crackles
0.0197	22.9	.0000	1	cranberry-grower
0.0197	22.9	.0000	1	cranberry-growers
0.0197	22.9	.0000	1	crayfish's
0.0197	22.9	.0000	1	crayfishes
0.0197	22.9	.0000	1	creodonts
0.0197	22.9	.0000	1	crop-damaging
0.0197	22.9	.0000	1	cross-like
0.0197	22.9	.0000	1	cross-stick
0.0197	22.9	.0000	1	Crowfoots
0.0197	22.9	.0000	1	cruciform
0.0197	22.9	.0000	1	Cruickshank's
0.0197	22.9	.0000	1	crystallizations
0.0197	22.9	.0000	1	CS2
0.0197	22.9	.0000	1	Ctenophora
0.0197	22.9	.0000	1	CuSO
0.0197	22.9	.0000	1	cubby-hole
0.0197	22.9	.0000	1	culturing
0.0197	22.9	.0000	1	Curies'
0.0197	22.9	.0000	1	current-carrying
0.0197	22.9	.0000	1	current-detector
0.0197	22.9	.0000	1	cursings
0.0197	22.9	.0000	1	CURVED
0.0197	22.9	.0000	1	cusps
0.0197	22.9	.0000	1	Cycle
0.0197	22.9	.0000	1	C00
0.0197	22.9	.0000	1	C1
0.0197	22.9	.0000	1	C3
0.0197	22.9	.0000	1	C6H1206
0.0197	22.9	.0000	1	d'Ulm
0.0197	22.9	.0000	1	Dak
0.0197	22.9	.0000	1	dankest
THE PRECEDING WORD TYPE OCCUPIES RANK 56400				
0.0197	22.9	.0000	1	daphnia
0.0197	22.9	.0000	1	darker-colored
0.0197	22.9	.0000	1	Data
0.0197	22.9	.0000	1	datoo
0.0197	22.9	.0000	1	dauber
0.0197	22.9	.0000	1	deBlowitz
0.0197	22.9	.0000	1	DeKay
0.0197	22.9	.0000	1	de-modulation
0.0197	22.9	.0000	1	decomposers
0.0197	22.9	.0000	1	deep-focus
0.0197	22.9	.0000	1	deep-pink
0.0197	22.9	.0000	1	deep-sea-diving
0.0197	22.9	.0000	1	deeply-cut
0.0197	22.9	.0000	1	deforms
0.0197	22.9	.0000	1	defroster

U	SFI	D	F	Word Type
0.0197	22.9	.0000	1	degenerates
0.0197	22.9	.0000	1	Delia
0.0197	22.9	.0000	1	demagnetize
0.0197	22.9	.0000	1	deminsion
0.0197	22.9	.0000	1	demounted
0.0197	22.9	.0000	1	denitrifying
0.0197	22.9	.0000	1	denudes
0.0197	22.9	.0000	1	deoxyribonucleic
0.0197	22.9	.0000	1	department-store
0.0197	22.9	.0000	1	deportment
0.0197	22.9	.0000	1	depressant
0.0197	22.9	.0000	1	derGrosse
0.0197	22.9	.0000	1	detaching
0.0197	22.9	.0000	1	deterioration
0.0197	22.9	.0000	1	deuterium
0.0197	22.9	.0000	1	devastatingly
0.0197	22.9	.0000	1	devitalizing
0.0197	22.9	.0000	1	diabolic
0.0197	22.9	.0000	1	diagnosing
0.0197	22.9	.0000	1	diapositives
0.0197	22.9	.0000	1	dicot
0.0197	22.9	.0000	1	dicotyledons
0.0197	22.9	.0000	1	diestrous
0.0197	22.9	.0000	1	diestrus
0.0197	22.9	.0000	1	DIFFERENT
0.0197	22.9	.0000	1	diffracted
0.0197	22.9	.0000	1	dimensionless
0.0197	22.9	.0000	1	diphosphate
0.0197	22.9	.0000	1	dipotassium
0.0197	22.9	.0000	1	disposing
0.0197	22.9	.0000	1	disproportion
0.0197	22.9	.0000	1	disqualifies
0.0197	22.9	.0000	1	disrupts
0.0197	22.9	.0000	1	dissolver
0.0197	22.9	.0000	1	distend
0.0197	22.9	.0000	1	distended
0.0197	22.9	.0000	1	dodecahedrons
0.0197	22.9	.0000	1	dog-sized
0.0197	22.9	.0000	1	dog-walkers
0.0197	22.9	.0000	1	doghouses
0.0197	22.9	.0000	1	doglike
0.0197	22.9	.0000	1	doily
0.0197	22.9	.0000	1	domestica
0.0197	22.9	.0000	1	donor's
0.0197	22.9	.0000	1	donors
0.0197	22.9	.0000	1	Doppler-shifted
0.0197	22.9	.0000	1	dormancy
0.0197	22.9	.0000	1	dot-and-dash
0.0197	22.9	.0000	1	double-headed
0.0197	22.9	.0000	1	double-walled
0.0197	22.9	.0000	1	down-beat
0.0197	22.9	.0000	1	dragonfly-like
0.0197	22.9	.0000	1	drawn-up
0.0197	22.9	.0000	1	driverless
0.0197	22.9	.0000	1	dropsonde
0.0197	22.9	.0000	1	druses
0.0197	22.9	.0000	1	DT'S**
0.0197	22.9	.0000	1	dull-colored
0.0197	22.9	.0000	1	dumfounding
0.0197	22.9	.0000	1	dup
0.0197	22.9	.0000	1	dynamos
0.0197	22.9	.0000	1	Earoon
0.0197	22.9	.0000	1	earth-star
0.0197	22.9	.0000	1	earth-type
0.0197	22.9	.0000	1	earthlight
0.0197	22.9	.0000	1	earthlike
0.0197	22.9	.0000	1	Earthquake
0.0197	22.9	.0000	1	easily-evaporated
0.0197	22.9	.0000	1	ebbed
0.0197	22.9	.0000	1	ectoderm
0.0197	22.9	.0000	1	Edel
0.0197	22.9	.0000	1	edicts
0.0197	22.9	.0000	1	eelgrass
0.0197	22.9	.0000	1	effervescent
0.0197	22.9	.0000	1	eighteen-month
0.0197	22.9	.0000	1	Eighty
0.0197	22.9	.0000	1	Einsteinian
0.0197	22.9	.0000	1	ejecting
0.0197	22.9	.0000	1	electric-current
0.0197	22.9	.0000	1	electrically-driven
0.0197	22.9	.0000	1	electrically-neutral
0.0197	22.9	.0000	1	electrolyzed
0.0197	22.9	.0000	1	electrolyzing
0.0197	22.9	.0000	1	electron-shells
0.0197	22.9	.0000	1	electroplating
THE PRECEDING WORD TYPE OCCUPIES RANK 56500				
0.0197	22.9	.0000	1	element-hunting
0.0197	22.9	.0000	1	elephant-like
0.0197	22.9	.0000	1	Elodea
0.0197	22.9	.0000	1	Elodes
0.0197	22.9	.0000	1	elongations
0.0197	22.9	.0000	1	Embryology
0.0197	22.9	.0000	1	Emission
0.0197	22.9	.0000	1	emissions
0.0197	22.9	.0000	1	emulsifying
0.0197	22.9	.0000	1	encephalitis
0.0197	22.9	.0000	1	Encke
0.0197	22.9	.0000	1	Encke's
0.0197	22.9	.0000	1	encysted
0.0197	22.9	.0000	1	end-member
0.0197	22.9	.0000	1	end-products
0.0197	22.9	.0000	1	endoderm
0.0197	22.9	.0000	1	energy-converting
0.0197	22.9	.0000	1	energy-yielding
0.0197	22.9	.0000	1	enthralling
0.0197	22.9	.0000	1	entrapment
0.0197	22.9	.0000	1	epicenter
0.0197	22.9	.0000	1	epicycles
0.0197	22.9	.0000	1	epidermal
0.0197	22.9	.0000	1	epiphysis
0.0197	22.9	.0000	1	epithelium
0.0197	22.9	.0000	1	Epoch
0.0197	22.9	.0000	1	equalizes
0.0197	22.9	.0000	1	Equinox
0.0197	22.9	.0000	1	equinoxes
0.0197	22.9	.0000	1	equisetums
0.0197	22.9	.0000	1	ergotine

U	SFI	D	F	Word Type
0.0197	22.9	.0000	1	erroneously
0.0197	22.9	.0000	1	esker
0.0197	22.9	.0000	1	estrous
0.0197	22.9	.0000	1	Eta
0.0197	22.9	.0000	1	Etamin
0.0197	22.9	.0000	1	etiolated
0.0197	22.9	.0000	1	Euglena
0.0197	22.9	.0000	1	euglenas
0.0197	22.9	.0000	1	eureka
0.0197	22.9	.0000	1	Eustachean
0.0197	22.9	.0000	1	even-toed
0.0197	22.9	.0000	1	ever-expanding
0.0197	22.9	.0000	1	ever-flowing
0.0197	22.9	.0000	1	everyman's
0.0197	22.9	.0000	1	evolutionarily
0.0197	22.9	.0000	1	exchangers
0.0197	22.9	.0000	1	excreted
0.0197	22.9	.0000	1	excurrent
0.0197	22.9	.0000	1	exo
0.0197	22.9	.0000	1	exosphere
0.0197	22.9	.0000	1	expansible
0.0197	22.9	.0000	1	Experimental
0.0197	22.9	.0000	1	experimentations
0.0197	22.9	.0000	1	external-combustion
0.0197	22.9	.0000	1	extinguishers
0.0197	22.9	.0000	1	extracellular
0.0197	22.9	.0000	1	Extraordinary
0.0197	22.9	.0000	1	extrapolation
0.0197	22.9	.0000	1	extrapolations
0.0197	22.9	.0000	1	eye-blinking
0.0197	22.9	.0000	1	eye-twisting
0.0197	22.9	.0000	1	eyecup
0.0197	22.9	.0000	1	f/7
0.0197	22.9	.0000	1	Fabre's
0.0197	22.9	.0000	1	faintness
0.0197	22.9	.0000	1	fall-winter
0.0197	22.9	.0000	1	familiaris
0.0197	22.9	.0000	1	fanjet
0.0197	22.9	.0000	1	fanshaped
0.0197	22.9	.0000	1	far-distant
0.0197	22.9	.0000	1	far-inks
0.0197	22.9	.0000	1	Faroes
0.0197	22.9	.0000	1	fast-burning
0.0197	22.9	.0000	1	fast-changing
0.0197	22.9	.0000	1	faster-than-sound
0.0197	22.9	.0000	1	fastest-moving
0.0197	22.9	.0000	1	fat-filled
0.0197	22.9	.0000	1	Fauchard
0.0197	22.9	.0000	1	fault-scarp
0.0197	22.9	.0000	1	faunas
0.0197	22.9	.0000	1	feeler-legs
0.0197	22.9	.0000	1	feldspars
0.0197	22.9	.0000	1	Fenner
0.0197	22.9	.0000	1	ferments
0.0197	22.9	.0000	1	fiber-glass
0.0197	22.9	.0000	1	fiberboard
0.0197	22.9	.0000	1	fiberglass
0.0197	22.9	.0000	1	fibro-vascular
0.0197	22.9	.0000	1	fibroplasia
0.0197	22.9	.0000	1	fiery-hot
0.0197	22.9	.0000	1	fifteen-hour
0.0197	22.9	.0000	1	fifty-foot
0.0197	22.9	.0000	1	fifty-thousandth
0.0197	22.9	.0000	1	first-come-first-served
0.0197	22.9	.0000	1	first-quarter
0.0197	22.9	.0000	1	fission-fusion-fission
0.0197	22.9	.0000	1	fissions
0.0197	22.9	.0000	1	five-carbon
0.0197	22.9	.0000	1	five-inch
THE PRECEDING WORD TYPE OCCUPIES RANK 56600				
0.0197	22.9	.0000	1	five-lobed
0.0197	22.9	.0000	1	five-parted
0.0197	22.9	.0000	1	five-penny
0.0197	22.9	.0000	1	Flame
0.0197	22.9	.0000	1	flammability
0.0197	22.9	.0000	1	flash-evaporation
0.0197	22.9	.0000	1	flash-evaporator
0.0197	22.9	.0000	1	flat-bodied
0.0197	22.9	.0000	1	flat-sided
0.0197	22.9	.0000	1	flattened-out
0.0197	22.9	.0000	1	flea-like
0.0197	22.9	.0000	1	Flex
0.0197	22.9	.0000	1	flood-control
0.0197	22.9	.0000	1	floored
0.0197	22.9	.0000	1	floras
0.0197	22.9	.0000	1	florist
0.0197	22.9	.0000	1	florists
0.0197	22.9	.0000	1	fluorite
0.0197	22.9	.0000	1	fluorospar
0.0197	22.9	.0000	1	fog-horn
0.0197	22.9	.0000	1	foibles
0.0197	22.9	.0000	1	folk-inventiveness
0.0197	22.9	.0000	1	folk-shrewdness
0.0197	22.9	.0000	1	follicle-stimulating
0.0197	22.9	.0000	1	Fomalhaut
0.0197	22.9	.0000	1	food-chains
0.0197	22.9	.0000	1	food-makers
0.0197	22.9	.0000	1	food-producer
0.0197	22.9	.0000	1	food-product
0.0197	22.9	.0000	1	food-web
0.0197	22.9	.0000	1	foodmaker
0.0197	22.9	.0000	1	foot-deep
0.0197	22.9	.0000	1	for-uh-min-i-ferz
0.0197	22.9	.0000	1	forceps
0.0197	22.9	.0000	1	Foreland
0.0197	22.9	.0000	1	FortSill
0.0197	22.9	.0000	1	fortnightly
0.0197	22.9	.0000	1	fortuitous
0.0197	22.9	.0000	1	fossil-containing
0.0197	22.9	.0000	1	fouler
0.0197	22.9	.0000	1	four-o'clocks
0.0197	22.9	.0000	1	four-passenger
0.0197	22.9	.0000	1	four-strand
0.0197	22.9	.0000	1	Fourth-of-July
0.0197	22.9	.0000	1	fovea
0.0197	22.9	.0000	1	Fracastoro
0.0197	22.9	.0000	1	Frasch

U	SFI	D	F	Word Type
0.0197	22.9	.0000	1	Fraunhofer
0.0197	22.9	.0000	1	freaks
0.0197	22.9	.0000	1	free-living
0.0197	22.9	.0000	1	free-piston
0.0197	22.9	.0000	1	fresh-looking
0.0197	22.9	.0000	1	freshen
0.0197	22.9	.0000	1	fringe-shift
0.0197	22.9	.0000	1	frond
0.0197	22.9	.0000	1	front-line
0.0197	22.9	.0000	1	fruit-grower
0.0197	22.9	.0000	1	fruit-growers
0.0197	22.9	.0000	1	FSH
0.0197	22.9	.0000	1	full-moon
0.0197	22.9	.0000	1	fulva
0.0197	22.9	.0000	1	funneling
0.0197	22.9	.0000	1	Furnaces
0.0197	22.9	.0000	1	fused-quartz
0.0197	22.9	.0000	1	g/10
0.0197	22.9	.0000	1	galaxy's
0.0197	22.9	.0000	1	gale-force
0.0197	22.9	.0000	1	Galvani's
0.0197	22.9	.0000	1	galvanism
0.0197	22.9	.0000	1	Gamma
0.0197	22.9	.0000	1	GardenCity
0.0197	22.9	.0000	1	Gardiner
0.0197	22.9	.0000	1	gas-filled
0.0197	22.9	.0000	1	gas-water
0.0197	22.9	.0000	1	gastric-juice
0.0197	22.9	.0000	1	gastrocnemius
0.0197	22.9	.0000	1	gauging
0.0197	22.9	.0000	1	gek-ohz
0.0197	22.9	.0000	1	gelatin-like
0.0197	22.9	.0000	1	gene-loci
0.0197	22.9	.0000	1	genetical
0.0197	22.9	.0000	1	Genetics
0.0197	22.9	.0000	1	genitalia
0.0197	22.9	.0000	1	Geologist
0.0197	22.9	.0000	1	Germ
0.0197	22.9	.0000	1	germ-free
0.0197	22.9	.0000	1	germ-killing
0.0197	22.9	.0000	1	germicides
0.0197	22.9	.0000	1	get-up-and-stretch
0.0197	22.9	.0000	1	geyserite
0.0197	22.9	.0000	1	Giordano
0.0197	22.9	.0000	1	glares
0.0197	22.9	.0000	1	glossitis
0.0197	22.9	.0000	1	Glowworm
0.0197	22.9	.0000	1	gluconic
0.0197	22.9	.0000	1	gluelike
0.0197	22.9	.0000	1	gneisses
0.0197	22.9	.0000	1	golds
0.0197	22.9	.0000	1	Goldthread
0.0197	22.9	.0000	1	Goodwin's
THE PRECEDING WORD TYPE OCCUPIES RANK 56700				
0.0197	22.9	.0000	1	gooseneck
0.0197	22.9	.0000	1	Goteborg
0.0197	22.9	.0000	1	grabens
0.0197	22.9	.0000	1	grain-infesting
0.0197	22.9	.0000	1	grass-lined
0.0197	22.9	.0000	1	Gravitational
0.0197	22.9	.0000	1	gravities
0.0197	22.9	.0000	1	grease-spot
0.0197	22.9	.0000	1	Greek-derived
0.0197	22.9	.0000	1	green-black
0.0197	22.9	.0000	1	greenish-white
0.0197	22.9	.0000	1	gremlin
0.0197	22.9	.0000	1	gremlins
0.0197	22.9	.0000	1	griseus
0.0197	22.9	.0000	1	gristlelike
0.0197	22.9	.0000	1	growing-up
0.0197	22.9	.0000	1	growth-stimulating
0.0197	22.9	.0000	1	guinea-pigs
0.0197	22.9	.0000	1	gun-firing
0.0197	22.9	.0000	1	guncotton
0.0197	22.9	.0000	1	Gypsum
0.0197	22.9	.0000	1	gyrates
0.0197	22.9	.0000	1	gyroscopic
0.0197	22.9	.0000	1	H-bombs
0.0197	22.9	.0000	1	Hader
0.0197	22.9	.0000	1	Hahn's
0.0197	22.9	.0000	1	hairy-skinned
0.0197	22.9	.0000	1	half-empty
0.0197	22.9	.0000	1	Hamal
0.0197	22.9	.0000	1	hand-held
0.0197	22.9	.0000	1	hand-sized
0.0197	22.9	.0000	1	handclap
0.0197	22.9	.0000	1	handloom
0.0197	22.9	.0000	1	handwoven
0.0197	22.9	.0000	1	hard-shell
0.0197	22.9	.0000	1	hardpan
0.0197	22.9	.0000	1	Harris'
0.0197	22.9	.0000	1	harrowing
0.0197	22.9	.0000	1	harvestings
0.0197	22.9	.0000	1	hastiness
0.0197	22.9	.0000	1	hatchet-footed
0.0197	22.9	.0000	1	hatchet-shaped
0.0197	22.9	.0000	1	hayfever
0.0197	22.9	.0000	1	headset
0.0197	22.9	.0000	1	healthy-looking
0.0197	22.9	.0000	1	hearers
0.0197	22.9	.0000	1	heat-absorbing
0.0197	22.9	.0000	1	heated-up
0.0197	22.9	.0000	1	HEATER
0.0197	22.9	.0000	1	heatproof
0.0197	22.9	.0000	1	Helens
0.0197	22.9	.0000	1	helical
0.0197	22.9	.0000	1	heliports
0.0197	22.9	.0000	1	Helium
0.0197	22.9	.0000	1	helium-filled
0.0197	22.9	.0000	1	helix
0.0197	22.9	.0000	1	Hellebore
0.0197	22.9	.0000	1	Helleborus
0.0197	22.9	.0000	1	Helpful
0.0197	22.9	.0000	1	Hemisphere's
0.0197	22.9	.0000	1	Heraclides
0.0197	22.9	.0000	1	Heredity
0.0197	22.9	.0000	1	heretic

U	SFI	D	F	Word Type
0.0197	22.9	.0000	1	Hesperornis
0.0197	22.9	.0000	1	heterozygosis
0.0197	22.9	.0000	1	heterozygous
0.0197	22.9	.0000	1	hibernates
0.0197	22.9	.0000	1	high-tides
0.0197	22.9	.0000	1	highbush
0.0197	22.9	.0000	1	higher-grade
0.0197	22.9	.0000	1	Hiroshima-type
0.0197	22.9	.0000	1	hoarfrost
0.0197	22.9	.0000	1	hoists
0.0197	22.9	.0000	1	homecomings
0.0197	22.9	.0000	1	homograft
0.0197	22.9	.0000	1	homografts
0.0197	22.9	.0000	1	homozygotes
0.0197	22.9	.0000	1	honey-bee
0.0197	22.9	.0000	1	Honey-comb
0.0197	22.9	.0000	1	honeylike
0.0197	22.9	.0000	1	Honeysuckle
0.0197	22.9	.0000	1	Hooke's
0.0197	22.9	.0000	1	horoscopes
0.0197	22.9	.0000	1	horseman's
0.0197	22.9	.0000	1	Horwitz's
0.0197	22.9	.0000	1	housecat
0.0197	22.9	.0000	1	HSS
0.0197	22.9	.0000	1	Hula-Hoop
0.0197	22.9	.0000	1	human-directed
0.0197	22.9	.0000	1	hundred-thousandth
0.0197	22.9	.0000	1	hundred-thousandths
0.0197	22.9	.0000	1	hurtles
0.0197	22.9	.0000	1	HUS
0.0197	22.9	.0000	1	Hutton's
0.0197	22.9	.0000	1	hybird
0.0197	22.9	.0000	1	hydrates
0.0197	22.9	.0000	1	hydration
0.0197	22.9	.0000	1	hydrofoil
0.0197	22.9	.0000	1	hydrogen-2
0.0197	22.9	.0000	1	Hydrologic
THE PRECEDING WORD TYPE OCCUPIES RANK 56800				
0.0197	22.9	.0000	1	hydrolyzes
0.0197	22.9	.0000	1	Hyla
0.0197	22.9	.0000	1	hymeno
0.0197	22.9	.0000	1	hypertension
0.0197	22.9	.0000	1	hypnotize
0.0197	22.9	.0000	1	hypnum
0.0197	22.9	.0000	1	hypothetical
0.0197	22.9	.0000	1	H2SO4
0.0197	22.9	.0000	1	Ibex
0.0197	22.9	.0000	1	identifications
0.0197	22.9	.0000	1	Il-16
0.0197	22.9	.0000	1	imbat
0.0197	22.9	.0000	1	immerse
0.0197	22.9	.0000	1	immunized
0.0197	22.9	.0000	1	immunology
0.0197	22.9	.0000	1	implants
0.0197	22.9	.0000	1	inactivation
0.0197	22.9	.0000	1	incinerator
0.0197	22.9	.0000	1	incomparably
0.0197	22.9	.0000	1	inconceivably
0.0197	22.9	.0000	1	inconveniences
0.0197	22.9	.0000	1	incrustation
0.0197	22.9	.0000	1	incurrent
0.0197	22.9	.0000	1	infestations
0.0197	22.9	.0000	1	inflow
0.0197	22.9	.0000	1	infra-red
0.0197	22.9	.0000	1	infusion
0.0197	22.9	.0000	1	inhabits
0.0197	22.9	.0000	1	inhalation
0.0197	22.9	.0000	1	inoculate
0.0197	22.9	.0000	1	insect-pollinated
0.0197	22.9	.0000	1	insect-type
0.0197	22.9	.0000	1	Insecta
0.0197	22.9	.0000	1	insensibility
0.0197	22.9	.0000	1	Inspection
0.0197	22.9	.0000	1	integumentary
0.0197	22.9	.0000	1	interacted
0.0197	22.9	.0000	1	interferometric
0.0197	22.9	.0000	1	intermediate-
0.0197	22.9	.0000	1	intramural
0.0197	22.9	.0000	1	invigorated
0.0197	22.9	.0000	1	ionizes
0.0197	22.9	.0000	1	iron-filing
0.0197	22.9	.0000	1	iron-magnesium
0.0197	22.9	.0000	1	iso
0.0197	22.9	.0000	1	isoprene's
0.0197	22.9	.0000	1	ivory-billed
0.0197	22.9	.0000	1	ivorylike
0.0197	22.9	.0000	1	jack-in-the-pulpit
0.0197	22.9	.0000	1	Jansky's
0.0197	22.9	.0000	1	jet-hours
0.0197	22.9	.0000	1	jet-stream
0.0197	22.9	.0000	1	jewelweed
0.0197	22.9	.0000	1	jig-saw
0.0197	22.9	.0000	1	jiggled
0.0197	22.9	.0000	1	jiggles
0.0197	22.9	.0000	1	Joachimstal
0.0197	22.9	.0000	1	Joly
0.0197	22.9	.0000	1	Jons
0.0197	22.9	.0000	1	Josephus
0.0197	22.9	.0000	1	Judith's
0.0197	22.9	.0000	1	Jump
0.0197	22.9	.0000	1	Jumping
0.0197	22.9	.0000	1	Jurg
0.0197	22.9	.0000	1	kalium
0.0197	22.9	.0000	1	Kalm
0.0197	22.9	.0000	1	Kalmia
0.0197	22.9	.0000	1	kames
0.0197	22.9	.0000	1	kapalilua
0.0197	22.9	.0000	1	Kilborne
0.0197	22.9	.0000	1	kilometerstones
0.0197	22.9	.0000	1	Kissenger
0.0197	22.9	.0000	1	Klaproth
0.0197	22.9	.0000	1	Kleitman
0.0197	22.9	.0000	1	Klien
0.0197	22.9	.0000	1	klunk
0.0197	22.9	.0000	1	knee-jerk
0.0197	22.9	.0000	1	kneecaps
0.0197	22.9	.0000	1	knoblike

U	SFI	D	F	Word Type
0.0197	22.9	.0000	1	knock-knees
0.0197	22.9	.0000	1	Kogan
0.0197	22.9	.0000	1	koh-per-ni-kus
0.0197	22.9	.0000	1	Krause
0.0197	22.9	.0000	1	L-shape
0.0197	22.9	.0000	1	Lambkill
0.0197	22.9	.0000	1	Lamont
0.0197	22.9	.0000	1	lamp's
0.0197	22.9	.0000	1	lamprey
0.0197	22.9	.0000	1	land-
0.0197	22.9	.0000	1	land-life
0.0197	22.9	.0000	1	land-world
0.0197	22.9	.0000	1	large-diameter
0.0197	22.9	.0000	1	large-intestine
0.0197	22.9	.0000	1	larvas
0.0197	22.9	.0000	1	laterites
0.0197	22.9	.0000	1	latrans
0.0197	22.9	.0000	1	Laurels
0.0197	22.9	.0000	1	lava-cinder
0.0197	22.9	.0000	1	lead-blue
0.0197	22.9	.0000	1	lead-206
THE PRECEDING WORD TYPE OCCUPIES RANK 56900				
0.0197	22.9	.0000	1	Leadville
0.0197	22.9	.0000	1	leafy-shoot
0.0197	22.9	.0000	1	leeches
0.0197	22.9	.0000	1	legger
0.0197	22.9	.0000	1	Lenouvel
0.0197	22.9	.0000	1	leonine
0.0197	22.9	.0000	1	lepido
0.0197	22.9	.0000	1	Lepidodendron
0.0197	22.9	.0000	1	Leucippus
0.0197	22.9	.0000	1	Levers
0.0197	22.9	.0000	1	life-bearing
0.0197	22.9	.0000	1	life-sustaining
0.0197	22.9	.0000	1	LIGHT
0.0197	22.9	.0000	1	light-and
0.0197	22.9	.0000	1	light-gathering
0.0197	22.9	.0000	1	light-giving
0.0197	22.9	.0000	1	lighter-than-water
0.0197	22.9	.0000	1	lightship's
0.0197	22.9	.0000	1	Lilliputian
0.0197	22.9	.0000	1	limelike
0.0197	22.9	.0000	1	limy
0.0197	22.9	.0000	1	Linnaeus'
0.0197	22.9	.0000	1	linters
0.0197	22.9	.0000	1	lipids
0.0197	22.9	.0000	1	liqueur
0.0197	22.9	.0000	1	liquid-drop
0.0197	22.9	.0000	1	liquid-in-liquid
0.0197	22.9	.0000	1	liquidlike
0.0197	22.9	.0000	1	liquified
0.0197	22.9	.0000	1	Lise
0.0197	22.9	.0000	1	Litchfield
0.0197	22.9	.0000	1	live-virus
0.0197	22.9	.0000	1	LIVING
0.0197	22.9	.0000	1	logos
0.0197	22.9	.0000	1	long-
0.0197	22.9	.0000	1	long-exposure
0.0197	22.9	.0000	1	long-shafted
0.0197	22.9	.0000	1	long-spurred
0.0197	22.9	.0000	1	look-alike
0.0197	22.9	.0000	1	Lorus
0.0197	22.9	.0000	1	low-boiling-point
0.0197	22.9	.0000	1	low-tides
0.0197	22.9	.0000	1	Lowell's
0.0197	22.9	.0000	1	lower-cost
0.0197	22.9	.0000	1	lub
0.0197	22.9	.0000	1	luminesces
0.0197	22.9	.0000	1	luno
0.0197	22.9	.0000	1	luteinizing
0.0197	22.9	.0000	1	Lw
0.0197	22.9	.0000	1	Lynx
0.0197	22.9	.0000	1	Macmillan
0.0197	22.9	.0000	1	Magellanic
0.0197	22.9	.0000	1	Mainsprings
0.0197	22.9	.0000	1	malformation
0.0197	22.9	.0000	1	maltase
0.0197	22.9	.0000	1	mammal's
0.0197	22.9	.0000	1	manatees
0.0197	22.9	.0000	1	manifests
0.0197	22.9	.0000	1	manipulates
0.0197	22.9	.0000	1	manipulators
0.0197	22.9	.0000	1	Manson's
0.0197	22.9	.0000	1	many-complexioned
0.0197	22.9	.0000	1	many-eyed
0.0197	22.9	.0000	1	Maps
0.0197	22.9	.0000	1	marble's
0.0197	22.9	.0000	1	marblelike
0.0197	22.9	.0000	1	Marconi's
0.0197	22.9	.0000	1	Marfak
0.0197	22.9	.0000	1	Margery
0.0197	22.9	.0000	1	Marmet
0.0197	22.9	.0000	1	Martinus
0.0197	22.9	.0000	1	masticated
0.0197	22.9	.0000	1	matchstick
0.0197	22.9	.0000	1	mated
0.0197	22.9	.0000	1	Mathematike
0.0197	22.9	.0000	1	matings
0.0197	22.9	.0000	1	matter-galaxies
0.0197	22.9	.0000	1	Mazon
0.0197	22.9	.0000	1	meal-times
0.0197	22.9	.0000	1	medium-intensity
0.0197	22.9	.0000	1	megatons
0.0197	22.9	.0000	1	Mendel's
0.0197	22.9	.0000	1	Mendeleyeff's
0.0197	22.9	.0000	1	Mendeleyev
0.0197	22.9	.0000	1	mercurochrome
0.0197	22.9	.0000	1	mercury-lead
0.0197	22.9	.0000	1	mercury-vapor
0.0197	22.9	.0000	1	merry-go
0.0197	22.9	.0000	1	Merry-go-round
0.0197	22.9	.0000	1	merthiolate
0.0197	22.9	.0000	1	Merychippus
0.0197	22.9	.0000	1	Mesohippus
0.0197	22.9	.0000	1	metallic-looking
0.0197	22.9	.0000	1	metamorphose
0.0197	22.9	.0000	1	meteorology's

U	SFI	D	F	Word Type
0.0197	22.9	.0000	1	methylene
0.0197	22.9	.0000	1	Mg0
0.0197	22.9	.0000	1	micas
0.0197	22.9	.0000	1	Michelson
0.0197	22.9	.0000	1	Michelson-Twyman
THE PRECEDING WORD TYPE OCCUPIES RANK 57000				
0.0197	22.9	.0000	1	micro-organism
0.0197	22.9	.0000	1	micro-organsims
0.0197	22.9	.0000	1	Microbes
0.0197	22.9	.0000	1	microbiologist
0.0197	22.9	.0000	1	microcrystalline
0.0197	22.9	.0000	1	microgrooved
0.0197	22.9	.0000	1	microlite
0.0197	22.9	.0000	1	micrometric
0.0197	22.9	.0000	1	microprojector
0.0197	22.9	.0000	1	Microscope
0.0197	22.9	.0000	1	mid-continent
0.0197	22.9	.0000	1	mid-latitude
0.0197	22.9	.0000	1	midblock
0.0197	22.9	.0000	1	middens
0.0197	22.9	.0000	1	middle-ear
0.0197	22.9	.0000	1	millimicron
0.0197	22.9	.0000	1	million-megaton
0.0197	22.9	.0000	1	millipede
0.0197	22.9	.0000	1	millipedes
0.0197	22.9	.0000	1	mimicking
0.0197	22.9	.0000	1	mind-pictures
0.0197	22.9	.0000	1	mineralogical
0.0197	22.9	.0000	1	Minerology
0.0197	22.9	.0000	1	Minkowski
0.0197	22.9	.0000	1	Miocene
0.0197	22.9	.0000	1	Mira
0.0197	22.9	.0000	1	Mirach
0.0197	22.9	.0000	1	MIRROR
0.0197	22.9	.0000	1	Mixer
0.0197	22.9	.0000	1	modulator
0.0197	22.9	.0000	1	mold-like
0.0197	22.9	.0000	1	Molecu
0.0197	22.9	.0000	1	Molecules
0.0197	22.9	.0000	1	molted
0.0197	22.9	.0000	1	molybdate
0.0197	22.9	.0000	1	monitored
0.0197	22.9	.0000	1	monopolize
0.0197	22.9	.0000	1	Montgolfier
0.0197	22.9	.0000	1	moonfull
0.0197	22.9	.0000	1	moonscapes
0.0197	22.9	.0000	1	Moorth
0.0197	22.9	.0000	1	morainal
0.0197	22.9	.0000	1	morganite
0.0197	22.9	.0000	1	mothballs
0.0197	22.9	.0000	1	motifs
0.0197	22.9	.0000	1	Moulton
0.0197	22.9	.0000	1	mountings
0.0197	22.9	.0000	1	Moving
0.0197	22.9	.0000	1	MOVING
0.0197	22.9	.0000	1	mucin
0.0197	22.9	.0000	1	mucopolysaccharide
0.0197	22.9	.0000	1	mugginess
0.0197	22.9	.0000	1	Muller
0.0197	22.9	.0000	1	Mullica
0.0197	22.9	.0000	1	multi-flash
0.0197	22.9	.0000	1	multicelled
0.0197	22.9	.0000	1	multiflora
0.0197	22.9	.0000	1	mumpish
0.0197	22.9	.0000	1	muriatic
0.0197	22.9	.0000	1	Musset
0.0197	22.9	.0000	1	mycological
0.0197	22.9	.0000	1	Myosurus
0.0197	22.9	.0000	1	N's
0.0197	22.9	.0000	1	NaHCO3
0.0197	22.9	.0000	1	NaC1
0.0197	22.9	.0000	1	Naturwissenschaften
0.0197	22.9	.0000	1	neads
0.0197	22.9	.0000	1	near-natural
0.0197	22.9	.0000	1	Necator
0.0197	22.9	.0000	1	necessitating
0.0197	22.9	.0000	1	needle-fine
0.0197	22.9	.0000	1	needle-like
0.0197	22.9	.0000	1	neon-filled
0.0197	22.9	.0000	1	net-veined
0.0197	22.9	.0000	1	neutrinos
0.0197	22.9	.0000	1	Nevadas
0.0197	22.9	.0000	1	NewHampshire's
0.0197	22.9	.0000	1	new-moon
0.0197	22.9	.0000	1	Newtonian
0.0197	22.9	.0000	1	next-inner
0.0197	22.9	.0000	1	next-to-last
0.0197	22.9	.0000	1	nichrome
0.0197	22.9	.0000	1	Nikolaus
0.0197	22.9	.0000	1	nimbostratus
0.0197	22.9	.0000	1	nimbus
0.0197	22.9	.0000	1	nine-month
0.0197	22.9	.0000	1	nipples
0.0197	22.9	.0000	1	nirvana
0.0197	22.9	.0000	1	nitrocellulose
0.0197	22.9	.0000	1	nitrogenous
0.0197	22.9	.0000	1	non-exploding
0.0197	22.9	.0000	1	non-glacial
0.0197	22.9	.0000	1	non-green
0.0197	22.9	.0000	1	non-hunters
0.0197	22.9	.0000	1	non-mutated
0.0197	22.9	.0000	1	non-nutritive
0.0197	22.9	.0000	1	non-permeable
0.0197	22.9	.0000	1	non-smokers
0.0197	22.9	.0000	1	noncharacteristic
0.0197	22.9	.0000	1	nondangerous
THE PRECEDING WORD TYPE OCCUPIES RANK 57100				
0.0197	22.9	.0000	1	nongreen
0.0197	22.9	.0000	1	noniodized
0.0197	22.9	.0000	1	nonluminous
0.0197	22.9	.0000	1	nonmagnetized
0.0197	22.9	.0000	1	nonparasitic
0.0197	22.9	.0000	1	nonperiodic
0.0197	22.9	.0000	1	nonpressurized
0.0197	22.9	.0000	1	nonsmoker
0.0197	22.9	.0000	1	Norddeutscher-Lloyd
0.0197	22.9	.0000	1	Norkay
0.0197	22.9	.0000	1	normal-sized
0.0197	22.9	.0000	1	normals
0.0197	22.9	.0000	1	northeasterly
0.0197	22.9	.0000	1	not-so-dashing
0.0197	22.9	.0000	1	not-too-stylish
0.0197	22.9	.0000	1	not-vaccinated
0.0197	22.9	.0000	1	notebook-size
0.0197	22.9	.0000	1	novas
0.0197	22.9	.0000	1	nuclear-bomb
0.0197	22.9	.0000	1	nucleotides
0.0197	22.9	.0000	1	nut-bearing
0.0197	22.9	.0000	1	N2H4
0.0197	22.9	.0000	1	o-bead
0.0197	22.9	.0000	1	object's
0.0197	22.9	.0000	1	obstinacy
0.0197	22.9	.0000	1	oceans'
0.0197	22.9	.0000	1	octahedrons
0.0197	22.9	.0000	1	OFF
0.0197	22.9	.0000	1	olivine
0.0197	22.9	.0000	1	on-your-own
0.0197	22.9	.0000	1	onca
0.0197	22.9	.0000	1	one-cylinder
0.0197	22.9	.0000	1	one-fourteenth
0.0197	22.9	.0000	1	one-inch-square
0.0197	22.9	.0000	1	one-strand
0.0197	22.9	.0000	1	one-tube
0.0197	22.9	.0000	1	one-twentieth
0.0197	22.9	.0000	1	one-year-olds
0.0197	22.9	.0000	1	opaqueness
0.0197	22.9	.0000	1	open-heart
0.0197	22.9	.0000	1	ophthalmology
0.0197	22.9	.0000	1	opponents'
0.0197	22.9	.0000	1	optick
0.0197	22.9	.0000	1	optik
0.0197	22.9	.0000	1	optimistically
0.0197	22.9	.0000	1	optometrist
0.0197	22.9	.0000	1	optometrists
0.0197	22.9	.0000	1	orange-growers
0.0197	22.9	.0000	1	orange-growing
0.0197	22.9	.0000	1	orb-web
0.0197	22.9	.0000	1	ordinance
0.0197	22.9	.0000	1	ortho
0.0197	22.9	.0000	1	orthodontia
0.0197	22.9	.0000	1	orthorhombic
0.0197	22.9	.0000	1	ossified
0.0197	22.9	.0000	1	out-of-school
0.0197	22.9	.0000	1	outflying
0.0197	22.9	.0000	1	outgrows
0.0197	22.9	.0000	1	outgrowths
0.0197	22.9	.0000	1	ovarian
0.0197	22.9	.0000	1	overbright
0.0197	22.9	.0000	1	overemphasize
0.0197	22.9	.0000	1	overgraze
0.0197	22.9	.0000	1	overgrazed
0.0197	22.9	.0000	1	overlong
0.0197	22.9	.0000	1	overproduction
0.0197	22.9	.0000	1	overruns
0.0197	22.9	.0000	1	overstated
0.0197	22.9	.0000	1	overstretching
0.0197	22.9	.0000	1	OX
0.0197	22.9	.0000	1	oxen's
0.0197	22.9	.0000	1	oxidizers
0.0197	22.9	.0000	1	oxymuriatic
0.0197	22.9	.0000	1	oxytocin
0.0197	22.9	.0000	1	OY
0.0197	22.9	.0000	1	O2
0.0197	22.9	.0000	1	P-type
0.0197	22.9	.0000	1	packing-boxes
0.0197	22.9	.0000	1	packing-cases
0.0197	22.9	.0000	1	pah-ree-koo-teen
0.0197	22.9	.0000	1	palisades
0.0197	22.9	.0000	1	palpi
0.0197	22.9	.0000	1	pan-germ
0.0197	22.9	.0000	1	papilla
0.0197	22.9	.0000	1	parabolic
0.0197	22.9	.0000	1	parabolize
0.0197	22.9	.0000	1	parachutelike
0.0197	22.9	.0000	1	paraffined
0.0197	22.9	.0000	1	parallactic
0.0197	22.9	.0000	1	paralyzes
0.0197	22.9	.0000	1	parameciums
0.0197	22.9	.0000	1	parasitize
0.0197	22.9	.0000	1	parathormone
0.0197	22.9	.0000	1	Parathyroids
0.0197	22.9	.0000	1	parhelic
0.0197	22.9	.0000	1	Parsonstown
0.0197	22.9	.0000	1	particle-wave
0.0197	22.9	.0000	1	parturition
0.0197	22.9	.0000	1	Pasteur-baiters
0.0197	22.9	.0000	1	paternal
THE PRECEDING WORD TYPE OCCUPIES RANK 57200				
0.0197	22.9	.0000	1	pathogens
0.0197	22.9	.0000	1	pathologists
0.0197	22.9	.0000	1	Patriofelis
0.0197	22.9	.0000	1	patters
0.0197	22.9	.0000	1	payloads
0.0197	22.9	.0000	1	PbS
0.0197	22.9	.0000	1	pea-sized
0.0197	22.9	.0000	1	peashooter
0.0197	22.9	.0000	1	pedalfer
0.0197	22.9	.0000	1	pedestrian-vehicle
0.0197	22.9	.0000	1	pediatricians
0.0197	22.9	.0000	1	pedicel
0.0197	22.9	.0000	1	pedocals
0.0197	22.9	.0000	1	pedon
0.0197	22.9	.0000	1	peels
0.0197	22.9	.0000	1	peeper's
0.0197	22.9	.0000	1	peerings
0.0197	22.9	.0000	1	Pelecypoda
0.0197	22.9	.0000	1	pen-sized
0.0197	22.9	.0000	1	pencil-like
0.0197	22.9	.0000	1	pencil-shaped
0.0197	22.9	.0000	1	pencil's
0.0197	22.9	.0000	1	penlights
0.0197	22.9	.0000	1	Pennsylvanian
0.0197	22.9	.0000	1	pentagons
0.0197	22.9	.0000	1	perceives
0.0197	22.9	.0000	1	percolating
0.0197	22.9	.0000	1	peridotite
0.0197	22.9	.0000	1	peristaltic
0.0197	22.9	.0000	1	perspires
0.0197	22.9	.0000	1	pfft
0.0197	22.9	.0000	1	pharmaceuticals
0.0197	22.9	.0000	1	Phenocodus
0.0197	22.9	.0000	1	phenomenally
0.0197	22.9	.0000	1	Phillippine
0.0197	22.9	.0000	1	phloem
0.0197	22.9	.0000	1	phosphoric
0.0197	22.9	.0000	1	photo-sphere
0.0197	22.9	.0000	1	photometer
0.0197	22.9	.0000	1	photometry
0.0197	22.9	.0000	1	photospheric
0.0197	22.9	.0000	1	photosynthetic
0.0197	22.9	.0000	1	phylums
0.0197	22.9	.0000	1	phytoplankton
0.0197	22.9	.0000	1	piezo
0.0197	22.9	.0000	1	Piezo-electricity
0.0197	22.9	.0000	1	piezo-electricity
0.0197	22.9	.0000	1	piezotronics
0.0197	22.9	.0000	1	pigeon-holed
0.0197	22.9	.0000	1	pin's
0.0197	22.9	.0000	1	pinpoint-sharp
0.0197	22.9	.0000	1	pinpricks
0.0197	22.9	.0000	1	pipelike
0.0197	22.9	.0000	1	Piscis
0.0197	22.9	.0000	1	piston-driven
0.0197	22.9	.0000	1	piston-engine
0.0197	22.9	.0000	1	piston-propeller
0.0197	22.9	.0000	1	pitch-like
0.0197	22.9	.0000	1	Pituitary
0.0197	22.9	.0000	1	placentals
0.0197	22.9	.0000	1	Planaria
0.0197	22.9	.0000	1	planetai
0.0197	22.9	.0000	1	planetesimal
0.0197	22.9	.0000	1	plankton-gathering
0.0197	22.9	.0000	1	plankton-rich
0.0197	22.9	.0000	1	plant-eaters
0.0197	22.9	.0000	1	plast
0.0197	22.9	.0000	1	plaster-cracking
0.0197	22.9	.0000	1	plasticene
0.0197	22.9	.0000	1	Plates
0.0197	22.9	.0000	1	platinums
0.0197	22.9	.0000	1	Platyhelminthes
0.0197	22.9	.0000	1	pleistocene
0.0197	22.9	.0000	1	Plicocene
0.0197	22.9	.0000	1	Pliohippus
0.0197	22.9	.0000	1	plopping
0.0197	22.9	.0000	1	Plumier
0.0197	22.9	.0000	1	plyboard
0.0197	22.9	.0000	1	poises
0.0197	22.9	.0000	1	poisonings
0.0197	22.9	.0000	1	polarization
0.0197	22.9	.0000	1	Polaroid
0.0197	22.9	.0000	1	Pole's
0.0197	22.9	.0000	1	polio-causing
0.0197	22.9	.0000	1	polio-fighting
0.0197	22.9	.0000	1	poliomyelitis
0.0197	22.9	.0000	1	pollen-carrier
0.0197	22.9	.0000	1	pollen-carrying
0.0197	22.9	.0000	1	pollywogs
0.0197	22.9	.0000	1	polyestrous
0.0197	22.9	.0000	1	ponente
0.0197	22.9	.0000	1	popguns
0.0197	22.9	.0000	1	poppy-seed
0.0197	22.9	.0000	1	post-hurricane
0.0197	22.9	.0000	1	post-mortem
0.0197	22.9	.0000	1	potable
0.0197	22.9	.0000	1	pouch-bearers
0.0197	22.9	.0000	1	pouched
0.0197	22.9	.0000	1	Pouchet
0.0197	22.9	.0000	1	pouchlike
THE PRECEDING WORD TYPE OCCUPIES RANK 57300				
0.0197	22.9	.0000	1	Pouilly-le-Fort
0.0197	22.9	.0000	1	Poupet
0.0197	22.9	.0000	1	pousse-cafe
0.0197	22.9	.0000	1	precedence
0.0197	22.9	.0000	1	precession
0.0197	22.9	.0000	1	precessional
0.0197	22.9	.0000	1	precipitating
0.0197	22.9	.0000	1	preconceived
0.0197	22.9	.0000	1	precursor
0.0197	22.9	.0000	1	premie
0.0197	22.9	.0000	1	pressure-electricity
0.0197	22.9	.0000	1	Prevailing
0.0197	22.9	.0000	1	problem-questions
0.0197	22.9	.0000	1	Procyon
0.0197	22.9	.0000	1	Profiles
0.0197	22.9	.0000	1	profligate
0.0197	22.9	.0000	1	Proterozoic
0.0197	22.9	.0000	1	prothallia
0.0197	22.9	.0000	1	protist
0.0197	22.9	.0000	1	Protists
0.0197	22.9	.0000	1	protium
0.0197	22.9	.0000	1	protonema
0.0197	22.9	.0000	1	protrudes
0.0197	22.9	.0000	1	Proxima
0.0197	22.9	.0000	1	pseudopregnant
0.0197	22.9	.0000	1	psychrometer
0.0197	22.9	.0000	1	Pt
0.0197	22.9	.0000	1	ptera
0.0197	22.9	.0000	1	pulverulent
0.0197	22.9	.0000	1	punctured
0.0197	22.9	.0000	1	purines
0.0197	22.9	.0000	1	pushpins
0.0197	22.9	.0000	1	Putting
0.0197	22.9	.0000	1	pyrimidines
0.0197	22.9	.0000	1	pyrosomas
0.0197	22.9	.0000	1	P1
0.0197	22.9	.0000	1	Quadrangle
0.0197	22.9	.0000	1	quadrangles
0.0197	22.9	.0000	1	quadrant
0.0197	22.9	.0000	1	quadrate
0.0197	22.9	.0000	1	quart-size
0.0197	22.9	.0000	1	quasi-stellar
0.0197	22.9	.0000	1	queerer
0.0197	22.9	.0000	1	rabbit-proof
0.0197	22.9	.0000	1	radar-equipped
0.0197	22.9	.0000	1	radio-activity
0.0197	22.9	.0000	1	radio-frequencies
0.0197	22.9	.0000	1	radiolarians
0.0197	22.9	.0000	1	radon
0.0197	22.9	.0000	1	rainbow-like
0.0197	22.9	.0000	1	Raindrop
0.0197	22.9	.0000	1	Rance
0.0197	22.9	.0000	1	Rasalague
0.0197	22.9	.0000	1	rawins
0.0197	22.9	.0000	1	rawinsonde
0.0197	22.9	.0000	1	re-converted
0.0197	22.9	.0000	1	re-converts
0.0197	22.9	.0000	1	re-emit
0.0197	22.9	.0000	1	REACT
0.0197	22.9	.0000	1	readjusted
0.0197	22.9	.0000	1	rebranch
0.0197	22.9	.0000	1	Recent
0.0197	22.9	.0000	1	recessivity
0.0197	22.9	.0000	1	recirculated
0.0197	22.9	.0000	1	recombines
0.0197	22.9	.0000	1	recontamination
0.0197	22.9	.0000	1	rectifier
0.0197	22.9	.0000	1	recurved
0.0197	22.9	.0000	1	red-bellied
0.0197	22.9	.0000	1	Redfield's
0.0197	22.9	.0000	1	redistilled
0.0197	22.9	.0000	1	reentrants
0.0197	22.9	.0000	1	refigure
0.0197	22.9	.0000	1	refiner
0.0197	22.9	.0000	1	REFLECTED
0.0197	22.9	.0000	1	REFRACTING
0.0197	22.9	.0000	1	refrigerates
0.0197	22.9	.0000	1	regenerated
0.0197	22.9	.0000	1	regularities
0.0197	22.9	.0000	1	reinfected
0.0197	22.9	.0000	1	Reinfeld
0.0197	22.9	.0000	1	Reinhold
0.0197	22.9	.0000	1	rennin
0.0197	22.9	.0000	1	repairman's
0.0197	22.9	.0000	1	repels
0.0197	22.9	.0000	1	repentant
0.0197	22.9	.0000	1	repenteth
0.0197	22.9	.0000	1	repetitious
0.0197	22.9	.0000	1	replication
0.0197	22.9	.0000	1	repositioned
0.0197	22.9	.0000	1	repositioning
0.0197	22.9	.0000	1	resinosa
0.0197	22.9	.0000	1	respirator
0.0197	22.9	.0000	1	retrolental
0.0197	22.9	.0000	1	revisions
0.0197	22.9	.0000	1	reweaving
0.0197	22.9	.0000	1	Rhodesian
0.0197	22.9	.0000	1	Rhododendron
0.0197	22.9	.0000	1	rhyolite
0.0197	22.9	.0000	1	rhyolitic
THE PRECEDING WORD TYPE OCCUPIES RANK 57400				
0.0197	22.9	.0000	1	ribbon-like
0.0197	22.9	.0000	1	ribose
0.0197	22.9	.0000	1	Riedman
0.0197	22.9	.0000	1	Rigel
0.0197	22.9	.0000	1	righthanded
0.0197	22.9	.0000	1	Ringer-Locke's
0.0197	22.9	.0000	1	ringlike
0.0197	22.9	.0000	1	ringstand
0.0197	22.9	.0000	1	road-builders
0.0197	22.9	.0000	1	roadless
0.0197	22.9	.0000	1	rock-floored
0.0197	22.9	.0000	1	rocket-type
0.0197	22.9	.0000	1	rod-shaped
0.0197	22.9	.0000	1	rod's
0.0197	22.9	.0000	1	roentgen
0.0197	22.9	.0000	1	roofers
0.0197	22.9	.0000	1	rootlike
0.0197	22.9	.0000	1	rosette
0.0197	22.9	.0000	1	Rosse
0.0197	22.9	.0000	1	Rostand's
0.0197	22.9	.0000	1	round-and-round
0.0197	22.9	.0000	1	Roux's
0.0197	22.9	.0000	1	rufus
0.0197	22.9	.0000	1	Ruhle
0.0197	22.9	.0000	1	rumford
0.0197	22.9	.0000	1	S-pole
0.0197	22.9	.0000	1	sabertoothed
0.0197	22.9	.0000	1	sackful
0.0197	22.9	.0000	1	safety-minded
0.0197	22.9	.0000	1	saki
0.0197	22.9	.0000	1	sal
0.0197	22.9	.0000	1	saltation
0.0197	22.9	.0000	1	samara
0.0197	22.9	.0000	1	samaras
0.0197	22.9	.0000	1	same-sized
0.0197	22.9	.0000	1	sandglasses
0.0197	22.9	.0000	1	Saucer's
0.0197	22.9	.0000	1	Savinien
0.0197	22.9	.0000	1	scalelike
0.0197	22.9	.0000	1	scalers
0.0197	22.9	.0000	1	scaly-wings
0.0197	22.9	.0000	1	scaphe
0.0197	22.9	.0000	1	scapula
0.0197	22.9	.0000	1	scarps
0.0197	22.9	.0000	1	scarpside
0.0197	22.9	.0000	1	scavenger
0.0197	22.9	.0000	1	Schatz
0.0197	22.9	.0000	1	Scheelite
0.0197	22.9	.0000	1	Schematisme
0.0197	22.9	.0000	1	school-building
0.0197	22.9	.0000	1	scientific-supply
0.0197	22.9	.0000	1	scientist-occupants
0.0197	22.9	.0000	1	sclera
0.0197	22.9	.0000	1	scrawls
0.0197	22.9	.0000	1	sea-bottom
0.0197	22.9	.0000	1	searcher
0.0197	22.9	.0000	1	searchings
0.0197	22.9	.0000	1	seared

U	SFI	D	F	Word Type
0.0197	22.9	.0000	1	Searles
0.0197	22.9	.0000	1	SEASONS
0.0197	22.9	.0000	1	second-smallest
0.0197	22.9	.0000	1	sectile
0.0197	22.9	.0000	1	Secunderabad
0.0197	22.9	.0000	1	seed-makers
0.0197	22.9	.0000	1	seedling's
0.0197	22.9	.0000	1	seismographs
0.0197	22.9	.0000	1	seismologists
0.0197	22.9	.0000	1	selenite
0.0197	22.9	.0000	1	selenography
0.0197	22.9	.0000	1	self-perpetuating
0.0197	22.9	.0000	1	self-photographs
0.0197	22.9	.0000	1	self-understanding
0.0197	22.9	.0000	1	semi-invalids
0.0197	22.9	.0000	1	semi-molten
0.0197	22.9	.0000	1	semiporous
0.0197	22.9	.0000	1	semirigid
0.0197	22.9	.0000	1	semitropics
0.0197	22.9	.0000	1	Senses
0.0197	22.9	.0000	1	serpent-like
0.0197	22.9	.0000	1	serums
0.0197	22.9	.0000	1	Servetus
0.0197	22.9	.0000	1	seven-month-old
0.0197	22.9	.0000	1	Severe
0.0197	22.9	.0000	1	sews
0.0197	22.9	.0000	1	shallow-
0.0197	22.9	.0000	1	sharply-toothed
0.0197	22.9	.0000	1	Shaula
0.0197	22.9	.0000	1	shear-like
0.0197	22.9	.0000	1	shiny-faced
0.0197	22.9	.0000	1	shipper
0.0197	22.9	.0000	1	shirt-front
0.0197	22.9	.0000	1	shock-softening
0.0197	22.9	.0000	1	short-day
0.0197	22.9	.0000	1	short-horned
0.0197	22.9	.0000	1	short-period
0.0197	22.9	.0000	1	short-tubed
0.0197	22.9	.0000	1	shrimplike
0.0197	22.9	.0000	1	shrubby
0.0197	22.9	.0000	1	sidereal
0.0197	22.9	.0000	1	sideshow
THE PRECEDING WORD TYPE OCCUPIES RANK 57500				
0.0197	22.9	.0000	1	sideward
0.0197	22.9	.0000	1	siliceous
0.0197	22.9	.0000	1	silver-pitchblende
0.0197	22.9	.0000	1	simmers
0.0197	22.9	.0000	1	SIMPLE
0.0197	22.9	.0000	1	simple-looking
0.0197	22.9	.0000	1	single-letter
0.0197	22.9	.0000	1	sinuses
0.0197	22.9	.0000	1	skinlike
0.0197	22.9	.0000	1	sky-mountains
0.0197	22.9	.0000	1	skywards
0.0197	22.9	.0000	1	slake
0.0197	22.9	.0000	1	sleeplike
0.0197	22.9	.0000	1	sloughs
0.0197	22.9	.0000	1	SLOW
0.0197	22.9	.0000	1	Sn
0.0197	22.9	.0000	1	snail-like
0.0197	22.9	.0000	1	snakes'
0.0197	22.9	.0000	1	snapdragon
0.0197	22.9	.0000	1	sniffish
0.0197	22.9	.0000	1	soapflakes
0.0197	22.9	.0000	1	soil-and-land-capability
0.0197	22.9	.0000	1	soil-use
0.0197	22.9	.0000	1	SOLAR
0.0197	22.9	.0000	1	solar-system
0.0197	22.9	.0000	1	solid-in-liquid
0.0197	22.9	.0000	1	solidification
0.0197	22.9	.0000	1	Solstice
0.0197	22.9	.0000	1	solubilities
0.0197	22.9	.0000	1	SONAR
0.0197	22.9	.0000	1	sought-after
0.0197	22.9	.0000	1	Souris
0.0197	22.9	.0000	1	SouthPacific
0.0197	22.9	.0000	1	south-southeast
0.0197	22.9	.0000	1	southcentral
0.0197	22.9	.0000	1	SO4
0.0197	22.9	.0000	1	spacebound
0.0197	22.9	.0000	1	spacelike
0.0197	22.9	.0000	1	sparkling-clear
0.0197	22.9	.0000	1	specially-built
0.0197	22.9	.0000	1	spectrometry
0.0197	22.9	.0000	1	spectroscopes
0.0197	22.9	.0000	1	speedier
0.0197	22.9	.0000	1	spermatozoon
0.0197	22.9	.0000	1	spew
0.0197	22.9	.0000	1	sphere-gas
0.0197	22.9	.0000	1	sphericity
0.0197	22.9	.0000	1	spine-covered
0.0197	22.9	.0000	1	spiny-skinned
0.0197	22.9	.0000	1	spirillum
0.0197	22.9	.0000	1	spleen
0.0197	22.9	.0000	1	splintery
0.0197	22.9	.0000	1	spoilage
0.0197	22.9	.0000	1	sporangia
0.0197	22.9	.0000	1	sporangium
0.0197	22.9	.0000	1	spore-bearing
0.0197	22.9	.0000	1	spring-summer
0.0197	22.9	.0000	1	spumone
0.0197	22.9	.0000	1	squanders
0.0197	22.9	.0000	1	standpoints
0.0197	22.9	.0000	1	stannum
0.0197	22.9	.0000	1	staphylococcus
0.0197	22.9	.0000	1	star-wound
0.0197	22.9	.0000	1	starves
0.0197	22.9	.0000	1	station's
0.0197	22.9	.0000	1	steam-heating
0.0197	22.9	.0000	1	Stehli
0.0197	22.9	.0000	1	Stellaeborg
0.0197	22.9	.0000	1	stemlike
0.0197	22.9	.0000	1	Steno
0.0197	22.9	.0000	1	stereophonically
0.0197	22.9	.0000	1	stereotype
0.0197	22.9	.0000	1	sterilizing
0.0197	22.9	.0000	1	stiffens
0.0197	22.9	.0000	1	stimulants
0.0197	22.9	.0000	1	Stimulated
0.0197	22.9	.0000	1	stoplights
0.0197	22.9	.0000	1	stoppered
0.0197	22.9	.0000	1	storable
0.0197	22.9	.0000	1	storm-ravaged
0.0197	22.9	.0000	1	strain-specific
0.0197	22.9	.0000	1	stratocumulus
0.0197	22.9	.0000	1	stream-deposited
0.0197	22.9	.0000	1	streptococcus
0.0197	22.9	.0000	1	Streptomyces
0.0197	22.9	.0000	1	stretched-out
0.0197	22.9	.0000	1	Stretcher
0.0197	22.9	.0000	1	striated
0.0197	22.9	.0000	1	striations
0.0197	22.9	.0000	1	strike-anywhere
0.0197	22.9	.0000	1	strobus
0.0197	22.9	.0000	1	structured
0.0197	22.9	.0000	1	stubbiness
0.0197	22.9	.0000	1	Stulka
0.0197	22.9	.0000	1	sub-fibrils
0.0197	22.9	.0000	1	sub-microscopic
0.0197	22.9	.0000	1	sub-visible
0.0197	22.9	.0000	1	subconchoidal
0.0197	22.9	.0000	1	subcutaneous
0.0197	22.9	.0000	1	subglacial
THE PRECEDING WORD TYPE OCCUPIES RANK 57600				
0.0197	22.9	.0000	1	sublimes
0.0197	22.9	.0000	1	submerging
0.0197	22.9	.0000	1	submersion
0.0197	22.9	.0000	1	suborder
0.0197	22.9	.0000	1	suborders
0.0197	22.9	.0000	1	Subragmanyan
0.0197	22.9	.0000	1	subscripts
0.0197	22.9	.0000	1	SUBSTANCES
0.0197	22.9	.0000	1	suckled
0.0197	22.9	.0000	1	sufficed
0.0197	22.9	.0000	1	sugar-box
0.0197	22.9	.0000	1	sugar-maple
0.0197	22.9	.0000	1	Sul
0.0197	22.9	.0000	1	sulphuric
0.0197	22.9	.0000	1	Sulzer's
0.0197	22.9	.0000	1	sumachs
0.0197	22.9	.0000	1	summarization
0.0197	22.9	.0000	1	summarizing
0.0197	22.9	.0000	1	super-elastic
0.0197	22.9	.0000	1	super-high
0.0197	22.9	.0000	1	superheating
0.0197	22.9	.0000	1	supervoltage
0.0197	22.9	.0000	1	SURFACE
0.0197	22.9	.0000	1	surgeon-barber
0.0197	22.9	.0000	1	surgically
0.0197	22.9	.0000	1	surmised
0.0197	22.9	.0000	1	surveyor's
0.0197	22.9	.0000	1	sustains
0.0197	22.9	.0000	1	swallow's
0.0197	22.9	.0000	1	swampland
0.0197	22.9	.0000	1	swamplike
0.0197	22.9	.0000	1	swan-neck
0.0197	22.9	.0000	1	syenite
0.0197	22.9	.0000	1	Symbol
0.0197	22.9	.0000	1	symposium
0.0197	22.9	.0000	1	synchrotrons
0.0197	22.9	.0000	1	Syntaxis
0.0197	22.9	.0000	1	synthesizing
0.0197	22.9	.0000	1	synthetically
0.0197	22.9	.0000	1	syphilis
0.0197	22.9	.0000	1	systematize
0.0197	22.9	.0000	1	tachylite
0.0197	22.9	.0000	1	tadpole's
0.0197	22.9	.0000	1	tantalite
0.0197	22.9	.0000	1	tapioca
0.0197	22.9	.0000	1	tapiolite
0.0197	22.9	.0000	1	tapper
0.0197	22.9	.0000	1	taproots
0.0197	22.9	.0000	1	tartrate
0.0197	22.9	.0000	1	technics
0.0197	22.9	.0000	1	TELESCOPE
0.0197	22.9	.0000	1	televise
0.0197	22.9	.0000	1	Telstar's
0.0197	22.9	.0000	1	ten-billionth
0.0197	22.9	.0000	1	ten-cent
0.0197	22.9	.0000	1	ten-division
0.0197	22.9	.0000	1	ten-percent
0.0197	22.9	.0000	1	termites'
0.0197	22.9	.0000	1	terrapins
0.0197	22.9	.0000	1	terraria
0.0197	22.9	.0000	1	test-tube
0.0197	22.9	.0000	1	test-tubeful
0.0197	22.9	.0000	1	testa
0.0197	22.9	.0000	1	testis
0.0197	22.9	.0000	1	thea
0.0197	22.9	.0000	1	thimbleful
0.0197	22.9	.0000	1	THINGS
0.0197	22.9	.0000	1	things-more
0.0197	22.9	.0000	1	thiouracil
0.0197	22.9	.0000	1	third-quarter
0.0197	22.9	.0000	1	thousandfold
0.0197	22.9	.0000	1	thread-like
0.0197	22.9	.0000	1	three-in-one
0.0197	22.9	.0000	1	three-lobed
0.0197	22.9	.0000	1	thrush's
0.0197	22.9	.0000	1	thymus
0.0197	22.9	.0000	1	Thyroid
0.0197	22.9	.0000	1	thyroxine
0.0197	22.9	.0000	1	tide-prediction
0.0197	22.9	.0000	1	Tie-ko
0.0197	22.9	.0000	1	tillites
0.0197	22.9	.0000	1	time-a
0.0197	22.9	.0000	1	tin-can
0.0197	22.9	.0000	1	tipping-bucket
0.0197	22.9	.0000	1	titmouse
0.0197	22.9	.0000	1	toenail
0.0197	22.9	.0000	1	TONGUE
0.0197	22.9	.0000	1	tongue-inflamation
0.0197	22.9	.0000	1	tonsillitis
0.0197	22.9	.0000	1	toothbrushing
0.0197	22.9	.0000	1	topheavy
0.0197	22.9	.0000	1	Topographic
0.0197	22.9	.0000	1	trans-Vision
0.0197	22.9	.0000	1	transducer
0.0197	22.9	.0000	1	transients
0.0197	22.9	.0000	1	transplantable
0.0197	22.9	.0000	1	transplantation
0.0197	22.9	.0000	1	transversely
0.0197	22.9	.0000	1	tree-cutting
0.0197	22.9	.0000	1	tremens
THE PRECEDING WORD TYPE OCCUPIES RANK 57700				
0.0197	22.9	.0000	1	trepanning
0.0197	22.9	.0000	1	trillionth
0.0197	22.9	.0000	1	triple-F
0.0197	22.9	.0000	1	tripods
0.0197	22.9	.0000	1	trisodium
0.0197	22.9	.0000	1	tritium
0.0197	22.9	.0000	1	troglodyte
0.0197	22.9	.0000	1	tropisms
0.0197	22.9	.0000	1	tropistic
0.0197	22.9	.0000	1	tropopause
0.0197	22.9	.0000	1	Trowbridge
0.0197	22.9	.0000	1	TRY
0.0197	22.9	.0000	1	trypanosome
0.0197	22.9	.0000	1	trys
0.0197	22.9	.0000	1	Ts
0.0197	22.9	.0000	1	TT
0.0197	22.9	.0000	1	tube-like
0.0197	22.9	.0000	1	tubeful
0.0197	22.9	.0000	1	tubule
0.0197	22.9	.0000	1	tularemia
0.0197	22.9	.0000	1	tunicates
0.0197	22.9	.0000	1	turnsignal
0.0197	22.9	.0000	1	Turubian
0.0197	22.9	.0000	1	tussock
0.0197	22.9	.0000	1	twenty-degree
0.0197	22.9	.0000	1	twinned
0.0197	22.9	.0000	1	two-plus-two-make-four
0.0197	22.9	.0000	1	two-strand
0.0197	22.9	.0000	1	two-wings
0.0197	22.9	.0000	1	Twyman
0.0197	22.9	.0000	1	tyro
0.0197	22.9	.0000	1	U-235
0.0197	22.9	.0000	1	U-238
0.0197	22.9	.0000	1	Ulett
0.0197	22.9	.0000	1	ulna
0.0197	22.9	.0000	1	ultra-thin
0.0197	22.9	.0000	1	ultrahigh-frequency
0.0197	22.9	.0000	1	ultrasonic
0.0197	22.9	.0000	1	unbalance
0.0197	22.9	.0000	1	uncombined
0.0197	22.9	.0000	1	unconformities
0.0197	22.9	.0000	1	unconsolidated
0.0197	22.9	.0000	1	under-and-over
0.0197	22.9	.0000	1	under-cooked
0.0197	22.9	.0000	1	underlines
0.0197	22.9	.0000	1	underproduction
0.0197	22.9	.0000	1	undulant
0.0197	22.9	.0000	1	undying
0.0197	22.9	.0000	1	unfairly
0.0197	22.9	.0000	1	unfertilized
0.0197	22.9	.0000	1	uninitiated
0.0197	22.9	.0000	1	unknow
0.0197	22.9	.0000	1	unmated
0.0197	22.9	.0000	1	unmeasured
0.0197	22.9	.0000	1	unpaired
0.0197	22.9	.0000	1	unseasonable
0.0197	22.9	.0000	1	unslaked
0.0197	22.9	.0000	1	unsterilized
0.0197	22.9	.0000	1	unstratified
0.0197	22.9	.0000	1	unsung
0.0197	22.9	.0000	1	unsupervised
0.0197	22.9	.0000	1	unweathered
0.0197	22.9	.0000	1	upper-air
0.0197	22.9	.0000	1	uprushing
0.0197	22.9	.0000	1	upslope
0.0197	22.9	.0000	1	uracil
0.0197	22.9	.0000	1	uralitic
0.0197	22.9	.0000	1	Uraniborg
0.0197	22.9	.0000	1	uranium-bearing
0.0197	22.9	.0000	1	uranium-234
0.0197	22.9	.0000	1	USE
0.0197	22.9	.0000	1	USED
0.0197	22.9	.0000	1	vacationing
0.0197	22.9	.0000	1	vaccinates
0.0197	22.9	.0000	1	vaccinators
0.0197	22.9	.0000	1	vacuolar
0.0197	22.9	.0000	1	vacuum-cleaned
0.0197	22.9	.0000	1	vacuum-packed
0.0197	22.9	.0000	1	vagina
0.0197	22.9	.0000	1	vaginal
0.0197	22.9	.0000	1	Valles
0.0197	22.9	.0000	1	valvular
0.0197	22.9	.0000	1	vanHelmont
0.0197	22.9	.0000	1	vanHelmont's
0.0197	22.9	.0000	1	VanLeeuwenhoek
0.0197	22.9	.0000	1	Vanek
0.0197	22.9	.0000	1	vapor-laden
0.0197	22.9	.0000	1	vaporized
0.0197	22.9	.0000	1	vasopressin
0.0197	22.9	.0000	1	vee-shaped
0.0197	22.9	.0000	1	Vegetative
0.0197	22.9	.0000	1	ventifact
0.0197	22.9	.0000	1	vermin-proof
0.0197	22.9	.0000	1	vibrational
0.0197	22.9	.0000	1	victimized
0.0197	22.9	.0000	1	vinelike
0.0197	22.9	.0000	1	viper's
0.0197	22.9	.0000	1	virazon
0.0197	22.9	.0000	1	vireos
0.0197	22.9	.0000	1	Virgo
THE PRECEDING WORD TYPE OCCUPIES RANK 57800				
0.0197	22.9	.0000	1	virology
0.0197	22.9	.0000	1	virus'
0.0197	22.9	.0000	1	visitants
0.0197	22.9	.0000	1	voluminously
0.0197	22.9	.0000	1	vonSterneck
0.0197	22.9	.0000	1	vonWeizsacker
0.0197	22.9	.0000	1	vorticella
0.0197	22.9	.0000	1	Vredefort
0.0197	22.9	.0000	1	Vulcanus
0.0197	22.9	.0000	1	Vulpes
0.0197	22.9	.0000	1	V2
0.0197	22.9	.0000	1	Waldoboro
0.0197	22.9	.0000	1	WALK
0.0197	22.9	.0000	1	walking-day
0.0197	22.9	.0000	1	walking-days
0.0197	22.9	.0000	1	walking-minutes
0.0197	22.9	.0000	1	warmblooded
0.0197	22.9	.0000	1	Wasatch
0.0197	22.9	.0000	1	waste-laden
0.0197	22.9	.0000	1	water-disposal
0.0197	22.9	.0000	1	water-dwellers
0.0197	22.9	.0000	1	water-free
0.0197	22.9	.0000	1	water-kilowatt
0.0197	22.9	.0000	1	water-sampling
0.0197	22.9	.0000	1	water-saving
0.0197	22.9	.0000	1	water-soluble
0.0197	22.9	.0000	1	wavelet
0.0197	22.9	.0000	1	weather-forecasting
0.0197	22.9	.0000	1	weather-induced
0.0197	22.9	.0000	1	weather-observation
0.0197	22.9	.0000	1	webfeet
0.0197	22.9	.0000	1	weed-killing
0.0197	22.9	.0000	1	Weizsacker
0.0197	22.9	.0000	1	well-baby
0.0197	22.9	.0000	1	well-informed
0.0197	22.9	.0000	1	well-rounded
0.0197	22.9	.0000	1	well-soaked
0.0197	22.9	.0000	1	wellspring
0.0197	22.9	.0000	1	WestPalmBeach
0.0197	22.9	.0000	1	west-east
0.0197	22.9	.0000	1	wh-i-s-s-s-t
0.0197	22.9	.0000	1	Wheaton
0.0197	22.9	.0000	1	Whewell
0.0197	22.9	.0000	1	white-eyed
0.0197	22.9	.0000	1	white-light
0.0197	22.9	.0000	1	whooper
0.0197	22.9	.0000	1	whoopers
0.0197	22.9	.0000	1	wide-ranging
0.0197	22.9	.0000	1	widemouth
0.0197	22.9	.0000	1	wielding
0.0197	22.9	.0000	1	Wilberforce
0.0197	22.9	.0000	1	win-at-any-cost
0.0197	22.9	.0000	1	win-or-get-fired
0.0197	22.9	.0000	1	wind-driven
0.0197	22.9	.0000	1	windpipes
0.0197	22.9	.0000	1	wingspreads
0.0197	22.9	.0000	1	wire-haired
0.0197	22.9	.0000	1	wire-mesh
0.0197	22.9	.0000	1	Wiscasset
0.0197	22.9	.0000	1	woodfrog
0.0197	22.9	.0000	1	Worm-Walk
0.0197	22.9	.0000	1	worm's
0.0197	22.9	.0000	1	wound-up
0.0197	22.9	.0000	1	Wrestling
0.0197	22.9	.0000	1	wriggler
0.0197	22.9	.0000	1	wrigglers
0.0197	22.9	.0000	1	X-irradiation
0.0197	22.9	.0000	1	x-rays
0.0197	22.9	.0000	1	xylem
0.0197	22.9	.0000	1	zero-displacement
0.0197	22.9	.0000	1	zinnia
0.0197	22.9	.0000	1	ZnSO4
0.0197	22.9	.0000	1	zonda
0.0197	22.9	.0000	1	0%
0.0197	22.9	.0000	1	000-odd
0.0197	22.9	.0000	1	000-square-mile
0.0197	22.9	.0000	1	000-2
0.0197	22.9	.0000	1	0000000000055
0.0197	22.9	.0000	1	0001
0.0197	22.9	.0000	1	0004
0.0197	22.9	.0000	1	0018
0.0197	22.9	.0000	1	011
0.0197	22.9	.0000	1	1-bead
0.0197	22.9	.0000	1	1-cm3
0.0197	22.9	.0000	1	1-square-foot
0.0197	22.9	.0000	1	1-46
0.0197	22.9	.0000	1	1/125
0.0197	22.9	.0000	1	1/180th
0.0197	22.9	.0000	1	1/2-minute
0.0197	22.9	.0000	1	1/2-minutes
0.0197	22.9	.0000	1	1/2-volt
0.0197	22.9	.0000	1	1/2500
0.0197	22.9	.0000	1	1/50
0.0197	22.9	.0000	1	1/65
0.0197	22.9	.0000	1	1cm3
0.0197	22.9	.0000	1	10-cm3
0.0197	22.9	.0000	1	10-inch
0.0197	22.9	.0000	1	10-19
0.0197	22.9	.0000	1	10-20
0.0197	22.9	.0000	1	10-25
THE PRECEDING WORD TYPE OCCUPIES RANK 57900				
0.0197	22.9	.0000	1	100X
0.0197	22.9	.0000	1	1000-lb
0.0197	22.9	.0000	1	1063
0.0197	22.9	.0000	1	1083
0.0197	22.9	.0000	1	1091
0.0197	22.9	.0000	1	11-17
0.0197	22.9	.0000	1	11-18
0.0197	22.9	.0000	1	11-19
0.0197	22.9	.0000	1	11-8
0.0197	22.9	.0000	1	110/1100
0.0197	22.9	.0000	1	119-125
0.0197	22.9	.0000	1	12-14
0.0197	22.9	.0000	1	12-16
0.0197	22.9	.0000	1	127-151
0.0197	22.9	.0000	1	13-volume
0.0197	22.9	.0000	1	13-25B
0.0197	22.9	.0000	1	131-210
0.0197	22.9	.0000	1	14-10
0.0197	22.9	.0000	1	14-10A
0.0197	22.9	.0000	1	14-10C
0.0197	22.9	.0000	1	14-24

U	SFI	D	F	Word Type
0.0197	22.9	.0000	1	14-25
0.0197	22.9	.0000	1	14-26
0.0197	22.9	.0000	1	14-7
0.0197	22.9	.0000	1	14-8
0.0197	22.9	.0000	1	1413
0.0197	22.9	.0000	1	1514-1564
0.0197	22.9	.0000	1	1576
0.0197	22.9	.0000	1	1578-1657
0.0197	22.9	.0000	1	16-7
0.0197	22.9	.0000	1	1628-1694
0.0197	22.9	.0000	1	1631-1687
0.0197	22.9	.0000	1	1650-1665
0.0197	22.9	.0000	1	1656
0.0197	22.9	.0000	1	1660's
0.0197	22.9	.0000	1	1679
0.0197	22.9	.0000	1	1687
0.0197	22.9	.0000	1	17-6
0.0197	22.9	.0000	1	1726-1796
0.0197	22.9	.0000	1	1733-1804
0.0197	22.9	.0000	1	1743-1794
0.0197	22.9	.0000	1	1750-1817
0.0197	22.9	.0000	1	1769-1832
0.0197	22.9	.0000	1	1769-1839
0.0197	22.9	.0000	1	1778-
0.0197	22.9	.0000	1	18-14
0.0197	22.9	.0000	1	18-15
0.0197	22.9	.0000	1	18-7
0.0197	22.9	.0000	1	1813-1895
0.0197	22.9	.0000	1	1822-1884
0.0197	22.9	.0000	1	1834-1907
0.0197	22.9	.0000	1	1882-83
0.0197	22.9	.0000	1	1893-
0.0197	22.9	.0000	1	19-15
0.0197	22.9	.0000	1	191-million
0.0197	22.9	.0000	1	1932-33
0.0197	22.9	.0000	1	1933-45
0.0197	22.9	.0000	1	1941-42
0.0197	22.9	.0000	1	1953-1965
0.0197	22.9	.0000	1	1957-58
0.0197	22.9	.0000	1	1957-8
0.0197	22.9	.0000	1	199-201
0.0197	22.9	.0000	1	2H
0.0197	22.9	.0000	1	2He4
0.0197	22.9	.0000	1	2-1E
0.0197	22.9	.0000	1	2-14
0.0197	22.9	.0000	1	2-60
0.0197	22.9	.0000	1	2-61
0.0197	22.9	.0000	1	2-7
0.0197	22.9	.0000	1	2x120
0.0197	22.9	.0000	1	2x46
0.0197	22.9	.0000	1	20-12
0.0197	22.9	.0000	1	20-13
0.0197	22.9	.0000	1	20-13A
0.0197	22.9	.0000	1	20-13B
0.0197	22.9	.0000	1	20-14
0.0197	22.9	.0000	1	200B
0.0197	22.9	.0000	1	21-centimeter
0.0197	22.9	.0000	1	21-9
0.0197	22.9	.0000	1	22He4
0.0197	22.9	.0000	1	22-18
0.0197	22.9	.0000	1	22-23
0.0197	22.9	.0000	1	22-4
0.0197	22.9	.0000	1	22nd
0.0197	22.9	.0000	1	2300
0.0197	22.9	.0000	1	24-1
0.0197	22.9	.0000	1	24-11
0.0197	22.9	.0000	1	24-2
0.0197	22.9	.0000	1	250-mile-high
0.0197	22.9	.0000	1	26-1
0.0197	22.9	.0000	1	26-11
0.0197	22.9	.0000	1	26-13
0.0197	22.9	.0000	1	27-19
0.0197	22.9	.0000	1	2786
0.0197	22.9	.0000	1	28-day
0.0197	22.9	.0000	1	287-308
0.0197	22.9	.0000	1	29-17
0.0197	22.9	.0000	1	29-3
0.0197	22.9	.0000	1	29-4
0.0197	22.9	.0000	1	29-5

THE PRECEDING WORD TYPE OCCUPIES RANK 58000

U	SFI	D	F	Word Type
0.0197	22.9	.0000	1	296-99
0.0197	22.9	.0000	1	3C295
0.0197	22.9	.0000	1	3-16
0.0197	22.9	.0000	1	3-20
0.0197	22.9	.0000	1	3-22
0.0197	22.9	.0000	1	3-7
0.0197	22.9	.0000	1	3-8
0.0197	22.9	.0000	1	3g/cm3
0.0197	22.9	.0000	1	30-16
0.0197	22.9	.0000	1	30d
0.0197	22.9	.0000	1	300-mile-an-hour
0.0197	22.9	.0000	1	3200
0.0197	22.9	.0000	1	33-billion-electron-volt
0.0197	22.9	.0000	1	33-11
0.0197	22.9	.0000	1	33-13
0.0197	22.9	.0000	1	3370
0.0197	22.9	.0000	1	34-37
0.0197	22.9	.0000	1	350/5
0.0197	22.9	.0000	1	355
0.0197	22.9	.0000	1	355-foot
0.0197	22.9	.0000	1	36-7
0.0197	22.9	.0000	1	36-8
0.0197	22.9	.0000	1	39-9
0.0197	22.9	.0000	1	4-b
0.0197	22.9	.0000	1	4-21
0.0197	22.9	.0000	1	4-23
0.0197	22.9	.0000	1	4-24
0.0197	22.9	.0000	1	4x46
0.0197	22.9	.0000	1	40-foot-long
0.0197	22.9	.0000	1	40-1
0.0197	22.9	.0000	1	400-
0.0197	22.9	.0000	1	43-1
0.0197	22.9	.0000	1	43x
0.0197	22.9	.0000	1	45B
0.0197	22.9	.0000	1	459
0.0197	22.9	.0000	1	47-5
0.0197	22.9	.0000	1	484-425
0.0197	22.9	.0000	1	5H
0.0197	22.9	.0000	1	5-19
0.0197	22.9	.0000	1	5-21
0.0197	22.9	.0000	1	5-9
0.0197	22.9	.0000	1	5cm3
0.0197	22.9	.0000	1	500-lb
0.0197	22.9	.0000	1	52-foot
0.0197	22.9	.0000	1	521
0.0197	22.9	.0000	1	55-foot
0.0197	22.9	.0000	1	55-57
0.0197	22.9	.0000	1	558-559
0.0197	22.9	.0000	1	56-day
0.0197	22.9	.0000	1	6-petaled
0.0197	22.9	.0000	1	6-ton
0.0197	22.9	.0000	1	6-volt
0.0197	22.9	.0000	1	600-foot
0.0197	22.9	.0000	1	600-1200
0.0197	22.9	.0000	1	6377
0.0197	22.9	.0000	1	6700
0.0197	22.9	.0000	1	72-inch
0.0197	22.9	.0000	1	7500
0.0197	22.9	.0000	1	774
0.0197	22.9	.0000	1	8-12
0.0197	22.9	.0000	1	8-17
0.0197	22.9	.0000	1	8-20
0.0197	22.9	.0000	1	8-22
0.0197	22.9	.0000	1	8-23
0.0197	22.9	.0000	1	8-24
0.0197	22.9	.0000	1	8-6
0.0197	22.9	.0000	1	800-and
0.0197	22.9	.0000	1	83-ton
0.0197	22.9	.0000	1	9-21
0.0197	22.9	.0000	1	9-28
0.0197	22.9	.0000	1	90Th234
0.0197	22.9	.0000	1	900-foot
0.0197	22.9	.0000	1	900-foot-long
0.0197	22.9	.0000	1	940
0.0197	22.9	.0000	1	961
0.0197	22.9	.0000	1	98/100
0.0194	22.9	.0000	1	-theism
0.0194	22.9	.0000	1	-1100
0.0194	22.9	.0000	1	'rithmetic
0.0194	22.9	.0000	1	'riting
0.0194	22.9	.0000	1	'60's
0.0194	22.9	.0000	1	'72
0.0194	22.9	.0000	1	abdicate
0.0194	22.9	.0000	1	Aberdeen-Angus
0.0194	22.9	.0000	1	ablest
0.0194	22.9	.0000	1	abra
0.0194	22.9	.0000	1	abridged
0.0194	22.9	.0000	1	abridging
0.0194	22.9	.0000	1	absolution
0.0194	22.9	.0000	1	Absolved
0.0194	22.9	.0000	1	academies
0.0194	22.9	.0000	1	accession
0.0194	22.9	.0000	1	accountants
0.0194	22.9	.0000	1	Acheson
0.0194	22.9	.0000	1	acidly
0.0194	22.9	.0000	1	acquiesce
0.0194	22.9	.0000	1	acropolis
0.0194	22.9	.0000	1	action-packed
0.0194	22.9	.0000	1	adobes
0.0194	22.9	.0000	1	adulation

THE PRECEDING WORD TYPE OCCUPIES RANK 58100

U	SFI	D	F	Word Type
0.0194	22.9	.0000	1	Adventurers
0.0194	22.9	.0000	1	Advisers
0.0194	22.9	.0000	1	Aeschylus
0.0194	22.9	.0000	1	affiliate
0.0194	22.9	.0000	1	affirmation
0.0194	22.9	.0000	1	affixed
0.0194	22.9	.0000	1	Africanizing
0.0194	22.9	.0000	1	Afrikanders
0.0194	22.9	.0000	1	Afro-Asian
0.0194	22.9	.0000	1	Agana
0.0194	22.9	.0000	1	aggressor
0.0194	22.9	.0000	1	agoing
0.0194	22.9	.0000	1	Agrarians
0.0194	22.9	.0000	1	air-defense
0.0194	22.9	.0000	1	air-filled
0.0194	22.9	.0000	1	air-view
0.0194	22.9	.0000	1	airbrakes
0.0194	22.9	.0000	1	Aix-la-Chapelle
0.0194	22.9	.0000	1	Akh-en-Aten
0.0194	22.9	.0000	1	Aldermanbury
0.0194	22.9	.0000	1	Algonkian
0.0194	22.9	.0000	1	Algonquins
0.0194	22.9	.0000	1	aliens
0.0194	22.9	.0000	1	Alki
0.0194	22.9	.0000	1	all-Ethiopian
0.0194	22.9	.0000	1	all-Negro
0.0194	22.9	.0000	1	all-steel
0.0194	22.9	.0000	1	Allens'
0.0194	22.9	.0000	1	Alliances
0.0194	22.9	.0000	1	allusive
0.0194	22.9	.0000	1	Almaden
0.0194	22.9	.0000	1	almond-shaped
0.0194	22.9	.0000	1	alphabet-makers
0.0194	22.9	.0000	1	Alta
0.0194	22.9	.0000	1	altarpieces
0.0194	22.9	.0000	1	Althing
0.0194	22.9	.0000	1	altiplano
0.0194	22.9	.0000	1	Amazons
0.0194	22.9	.0000	1	Amen-Re
0.0194	22.9	.0000	1	American-born
0.0194	22.9	.0000	1	Americano
0.0194	22.9	.0000	1	Amerigo
0.0194	22.9	.0000	1	Amount
0.0194	22.9	.0000	1	Anastas
0.0194	22.9	.0000	1	Ancestor
0.0194	22.9	.0000	1	Andaman
0.0194	22.9	.0000	1	Angleland
0.0194	22.9	.0000	1	Anglicans
0.0194	22.9	.0000	1	Anguilla
0.0194	22.9	.0000	1	Anne-style
0.0194	22.9	.0000	1	antagonistic
0.0194	22.9	.0000	1	Anti-Atlas
0.0194	22.9	.0000	1	Anti-Nebraska
0.0194	22.9	.0000	1	anti-ballistic
0.0194	22.9	.0000	1	anti-segregation
0.0194	22.9	.0000	1	anti-union
0.0194	22.9	.0000	1	antilynching
0.0194	22.9	.0000	1	antimonopoly
0.0194	22.9	.0000	1	Anzio
0.0194	22.9	.0000	1	AO-wnr
0.0194	22.9	.0000	1	appending
0.0194	22.9	.0000	1	apple-growing
0.0194	22.9	.0000	1	APPLES
0.0194	22.9	.0000	1	appropriated
0.0194	22.9	.0000	1	Ar-luk's
0.0194	22.9	.0000	1	Arabia's
0.0194	22.9	.0000	1	Arabic-speaking
0.0194	22.9	.0000	1	arable
0.0194	22.9	.0000	1	Arakan
0.0194	22.9	.0000	1	Aral
0.0194	22.9	.0000	1	Araucanians'
0.0194	22.9	.0000	1	Archduke
0.0194	22.9	.0000	1	Argentina-Brazil
0.0194	22.9	.0000	1	ARGUMENT
0.0194	22.9	.0000	1	Aristophanes
0.0194	22.9	.0000	1	Arkansas's
0.0194	22.9	.0000	1	armfuls
0.0194	22.9	.0000	1	Armies
0.0194	22.9	.0000	1	arming
0.0194	22.9	.0000	1	armor-covered
0.0194	22.9	.0000	1	armpit
0.0194	22.9	.0000	1	Arnold's
0.0194	22.9	.0000	1	Aroostook
0.0194	22.9	.0000	1	arrowpoint
0.0194	22.9	.0000	1	ascensions
0.0194	22.9	.0000	1	Assembled
0.0194	22.9	.0000	1	Astor's
0.0194	22.9	.0000	1	Atahualpa
0.0194	22.9	.0000	1	Athenians'
0.0194	22.9	.0000	1	Attorney's
0.0194	22.9	.0000	1	attorneys'
0.0194	22.9	.0000	1	August's
0.0194	22.9	.0000	1	Austin's
0.0194	22.9	.0000	1	auto-suggestion
0.0194	22.9	.0000	1	auto-tag
0.0194	22.9	.0000	1	avidity
0.0194	22.9	.0000	1	avocados
0.0194	22.9	.0000	1	avowedly
0.0194	22.9	.0000	1	Awash
0.0194	22.9	.0000	1	awela

THE PRECEDING WORD TYPE OCCUPIES RANK 58200

U	SFI	D	F	Word Type
0.0194	22.9	.0000	1	awnings
0.0194	22.9	.0000	1	axmen
0.0194	22.9	.0000	1	Ayamra
0.0194	22.9	.0000	1	Azimuthal
0.0194	22.9	.0000	1	azimuthal
0.0194	22.9	.0000	1	back-country
0.0194	22.9	.0000	1	backlands
0.0194	22.9	.0000	1	backwoodsmen
0.0194	22.9	.0000	1	baggage-car
0.0194	22.9	.0000	1	bailiffs
0.0194	22.9	.0000	1	baiting
0.0194	22.9	.0000	1	Balkash
0.0194	22.9	.0000	1	Baltimores
0.0194	22.9	.0000	1	banana-shipping
0.0194	22.9	.0000	1	Bancroft's
0.0194	22.9	.0000	1	Bangui
0.0194	22.9	.0000	1	Banias
0.0194	22.9	.0000	1	Baptists
0.0194	22.9	.0000	1	barbaric
0.0194	22.9	.0000	1	Barbarossa
0.0194	22.9	.0000	1	barbershops
0.0194	22.9	.0000	1	Barranquilla
0.0194	22.9	.0000	1	Barrier
0.0194	22.9	.0000	1	Bartolome
0.0194	22.9	.0000	1	Basutoland
0.0194	22.9	.0000	1	battle-field
0.0194	22.9	.0000	1	battlegrounds
0.0194	22.9	.0000	1	Batu
0.0194	22.9	.0000	1	Bauxite
0.0194	22.9	.0000	1	Baya's
0.0194	22.9	.0000	1	Bechuanaland
0.0194	22.9	.0000	1	Bedouin
0.0194	22.9	.0000	1	befit
0.0194	22.9	.0000	1	belch
0.0194	22.9	.0000	1	Belgium's
0.0194	22.9	.0000	1	bellowings
0.0194	22.9	.0000	1	Bemis
0.0194	22.9	.0000	1	Benue
0.0194	22.9	.0000	1	Beria
0.0194	22.9	.0000	1	best-developed
0.0194	22.9	.0000	1	Best's
0.0194	22.9	.0000	1	bestial
0.0194	22.9	.0000	1	Betancourt
0.0194	22.9	.0000	1	better-drained
0.0194	22.9	.0000	1	Bhutan
0.0194	22.9	.0000	1	Big-Foot
0.0194	22.9	.0000	1	big-headed
0.0194	22.9	.0000	1	billeted
0.0194	22.9	.0000	1	billfolds
0.0194	22.9	.0000	1	Biloxi
0.0194	22.9	.0000	1	binge
0.0194	22.9	.0000	1	birthplaces
0.0194	22.9	.0000	1	Bismarck's
0.0194	22.9	.0000	1	Blackburn
0.0194	22.9	.0000	1	blackens
0.0194	22.9	.0000	1	blazers
0.0194	22.9	.0000	1	BLAZERS
0.0194	22.9	.0000	1	Blended
0.0194	22.9	.0000	1	Bliven
0.0194	22.9	.0000	1	bloodily
0.0194	22.9	.0000	1	blueprinted
0.0194	22.9	.0000	1	bluff'd
0.0194	22.9	.0000	1	bobsledding
0.0194	22.9	.0000	1	Bodo
0.0194	22.9	.0000	1	Boeuf
0.0194	22.9	.0000	1	Boise
0.0194	22.9	.0000	1	bongs
0.0194	22.9	.0000	1	book-burning
0.0194	22.9	.0000	1	Booklet
0.0194	22.9	.0000	1	booster's
0.0194	22.9	.0000	1	bora
0.0194	22.9	.0000	1	borderlands
0.0194	22.9	.0000	1	borrower's
0.0194	22.9	.0000	1	Bothnia
0.0194	22.9	.0000	1	bottle-makers
0.0194	22.9	.0000	1	br-r-r
0.0194	22.9	.0000	1	Braddock's
0.0194	22.9	.0000	1	braid-trimmed
0.0194	22.9	.0000	1	brain-
0.0194	22.9	.0000	1	Brando
0.0194	22.9	.0000	1	Brangus
0.0194	22.9	.0000	1	brasero
0.0194	22.9	.0000	1	Brasilia's
0.0194	22.9	.0000	1	Brazilians
0.0194	22.9	.0000	1	brazilwood
0.0194	22.9	.0000	1	Brazzaville
0.0194	22.9	.0000	1	bread-basket
0.0194	22.9	.0000	1	breadbasket
0.0194	22.9	.0000	1	break-through
0.0194	22.9	.0000	1	breech-loading
0.0194	22.9	.0000	1	breweries
0.0194	22.9	.0000	1	brick-lined
0.0194	22.9	.0000	1	bright-green
0.0194	22.9	.0000	1	brightly-dyed
0.0194	22.9	.0000	1	brimless
0.0194	22.9	.0000	1	bristlecone
0.0194	22.9	.0000	1	BRITISH
0.0194	22.9	.0000	1	British-born
0.0194	22.9	.0000	1	brokerage
0.0194	22.9	.0000	1	BROWN

THE PRECEDING WORD TYPE OCCUPIES RANK 58300

U	SFI	D	F	Word Type
0.0194	22.9	.0000	1	Brownshirt
0.0194	22.9	.0000	1	Brownville
0.0194	22.9	.0000	1	brunets
0.0194	22.9	.0000	1	brutalities
0.0194	22.9	.0000	1	Budd
0.0194	22.9	.0000	1	buffalo-skin
0.0194	22.9	.0000	1	Builders-of-America
0.0194	22.9	.0000	1	built-up
0.0194	22.9	.0000	1	Bulbul
0.0194	22.9	.0000	1	bulletproof
0.0194	22.9	.0000	1	burlap-like
0.0194	22.9	.0000	1	Burnside's
0.0194	22.9	.0000	1	Bushki
0.0194	22.9	.0000	1	ButterfieldOverland
0.0194	22.9	.0000	1	By-and-By
0.0194	22.9	.0000	1	byproduct
0.0194	22.9	.0000	1	Byzas
0.0194	22.9	.0000	1	c-4
0.0194	22.9	.0000	1	caballeros
0.0194	22.9	.0000	1	Cabrillo's
0.0194	22.9	.0000	1	cabs
0.0194	22.9	.0000	1	cactus-like
0.0194	22.9	.0000	1	Cairo's
0.0194	22.9	.0000	1	Cajon
0.0194	22.9	.0000	1	Caledonian
0.0194	22.9	.0000	1	calking
0.0194	22.9	.0000	1	Calvinists
0.0194	22.9	.0000	1	Camino
0.0194	22.9	.0000	1	Canarsie
0.0194	22.9	.0000	1	cancelling
0.0194	22.9	.0000	1	Canfield
0.0194	22.9	.0000	1	Canoe
0.0194	22.9	.0000	1	canoeing
0.0194	22.9	.0000	1	Cantonese
0.0194	22.9	.0000	1	canyon-like
0.0194	22.9	.0000	1	Cao
0.0194	22.9	.0000	1	Capon
0.0194	22.9	.0000	1	caption
0.0194	22.9	.0000	1	Captive
0.0194	22.9	.0000	1	Captivity
0.0194	22.9	.0000	1	caravel
0.0194	22.9	.0000	1	Carlsbad
0.0194	22.9	.0000	1	Carpentaria
0.0194	22.9	.0000	1	Carpentier
0.0194	22.9	.0000	1	carpetbaggers
0.0194	22.9	.0000	1	Carrabelle
0.0194	22.9	.0000	1	Carta
0.0194	22.9	.0000	1	Cartier's
0.0194	22.9	.0000	1	cash-starved
0.0194	22.9	.0000	1	caster
0.0194	22.9	.0000	1	castra
0.0194	22.9	.0000	1	Catalogue
0.0194	22.9	.0000	1	catchwords
0.0194	22.9	.0000	1	Cathay
0.0194	22.9	.0000	1	Catlett
0.0194	22.9	.0000	1	cauc
0.0194	22.9	.0000	1	causeway
0.0194	22.9	.0000	1	caved-in
0.0194	22.9	.0000	1	Caverns
0.0194	22.9	.0000	1	cedarwood
0.0194	22.9	.0000	1	census-takers
0.0194	22.9	.0000	1	central-station
0.0194	22.9	.0000	1	centralism
0.0194	22.9	.0000	1	cester
0.0194	22.9	.0000	1	Ch'ien
0.0194	22.9	.0000	1	Ch'ien-lung
0.0194	22.9	.0000	1	Chaco
0.0194	22.9	.0000	1	chain-driven
0.0194	22.9	.0000	1	chain-gang
0.0194	22.9	.0000	1	Chalcidice
0.0194	22.9	.0000	1	Chapelle
0.0194	22.9	.0000	1	Charity
0.0194	22.9	.0000	1	Chelyabinsk
0.0194	22.9	.0000	1	CheminDesDames
0.0194	22.9	.0000	1	Chernigov
0.0194	22.9	.0000	1	chester
0.0194	22.9	.0000	1	Cheviot
0.0194	22.9	.0000	1	chewed-up
0.0194	22.9	.0000	1	chiao-tzu
0.0194	22.9	.0000	1	chicken-raising
0.0194	22.9	.0000	1	Chigago
0.0194	22.9	.0000	1	Chimel
0.0194	22.9	.0000	1	China-Japan
0.0194	22.9	.0000	1	Chinamen
0.0194	22.9	.0000	1	Chinatowns

U	SFI	D	F	Word Type
0.0194	22.9	.0000	1	Chinese-American
0.0194	22.9	.0000	1	chromite
0.0194	22.9	.0000	1	Chu's
0.0194	22.9	.0000	1	Chung-kuo
0.0194	22.9	.0000	1	Chungking
0.0194	22.9	.0000	1	cigarmakers
0.0194	22.9	.0000	1	Circles
0.0194	22.9	.0000	1	City-County
0.0194	22.9	.0000	1	Claggart
0.0194	22.9	.0000	1	clanks
0.0194	22.9	.0000	1	clarifying
0.0194	22.9	.0000	1	clay-brick
0.0194	22.9	.0000	1	Clericis
0.0194	22.9	.0000	1	cleverly-made
0.0194	22.9	.0000	1	clientele

THE PRECEDING WORD TYPE OCCUPIES RANK 58400

U	SFI	D	F	Word Type
0.0194	22.9	.0000	1	clogging
0.0194	22.9	.0000	1	close-set
0.0194	22.9	.0000	1	close-to-shore
0.0194	22.9	.0000	1	clothing-store
0.0194	22.9	.0000	1	Coahuila-Texas
0.0194	22.9	.0000	1	coal-blackened
0.0194	22.9	.0000	1	coal-digging
0.0194	22.9	.0000	1	coal-producing
0.0194	22.9	.0000	1	coaling
0.0194	22.9	.0000	1	coat-of-arms
0.0194	22.9	.0000	1	coatless
0.0194	22.9	.0000	1	cobble-stoned
0.0194	22.9	.0000	1	codfishing
0.0194	22.9	.0000	1	Coffey
0.0194	22.9	.0000	1	cogged
0.0194	22.9	.0000	1	cohesiveness
0.0194	22.9	.0000	1	ColdHarbor
0.0194	22.9	.0000	1	collaborators
0.0194	22.9	.0000	1	Cologne
0.0194	22.9	.0000	1	colonial-style
0.0194	22.9	.0000	1	Colonization
0.0194	22.9	.0000	1	Coloreds
0.0194	22.9	.0000	1	Columbian
0.0194	22.9	.0000	1	Come-outers
0.0194	22.9	.0000	1	commandant-general
0.0194	22.9	.0000	1	commander-in-chief
0.0194	22.9	.0000	1	commingling
0.0194	22.9	.0000	1	committeeman
0.0194	22.9	.0000	1	COMMON
0.0194	22.9	.0000	1	Communist-leaning
0.0194	22.9	.0000	1	Communist-led
0.0194	22.9	.0000	1	compass-rose
0.0194	22.9	.0000	1	competitiveness
0.0194	22.9	.0000	1	compiling
0.0194	22.9	.0000	1	compromised
0.0194	22.9	.0000	1	computors
0.0194	22.9	.0000	1	Concepcion
0.0194	22.9	.0000	1	conclave
0.0194	22.9	.0000	1	condemmed
0.0194	22.9	.0000	1	Confederation's
0.0194	22.9	.0000	1	confounded
0.0194	22.9	.0000	1	Confucian
0.0194	22.9	.0000	1	Congress'
0.0194	22.9	.0000	1	consanguinity
0.0194	22.9	.0000	1	Constantine's
0.0194	22.9	.0000	1	Constantinople's
0.0194	22.9	.0000	1	Constitution's
0.0194	22.9	.0000	1	construed
0.0194	22.9	.0000	1	continentally
0.0194	22.9	.0000	1	Continuing
0.0194	22.9	.0000	1	contrite
0.0194	22.9	.0000	1	conurbation
0.0194	22.9	.0000	1	conurbations
0.0194	22.9	.0000	1	conversation's
0.0194	22.9	.0000	1	conveyance
0.0194	22.9	.0000	1	convoyed
0.0194	22.9	.0000	1	cookstoves
0.0194	22.9	.0000	1	Coosa
0.0194	22.9	.0000	1	copper-skinned
0.0194	22.9	.0000	1	Corbett
0.0194	22.9	.0000	1	Cordier
0.0194	22.9	.0000	1	corporation's
0.0194	22.9	.0000	1	cosmography
0.0194	22.9	.0000	1	costlier
0.0194	22.9	.0000	1	cotton-seed
0.0194	22.9	.0000	1	cottonseed-oil
0.0194	22.9	.0000	1	Coue
0.0194	22.9	.0000	1	cougars
0.0194	22.9	.0000	1	councilmen
0.0194	22.9	.0000	1	countrywomen
0.0194	22.9	.0000	1	couplers
0.0194	22.9	.0000	1	covenants
0.0194	22.9	.0000	1	covets
0.0194	22.9	.0000	1	crackdowns
0.0194	22.9	.0000	1	Crapo
0.0194	22.9	.0000	1	credible
0.0194	22.9	.0000	1	creek-crossings
0.0194	22.9	.0000	1	Croix
0.0194	22.9	.0000	1	crop-lien
0.0194	22.9	.0000	1	cross-stitching
0.0194	22.9	.0000	1	crotchety
0.0194	22.9	.0000	1	crunches
0.0194	22.9	.0000	1	crusader
0.0194	22.9	.0000	1	cul-de-sacs
0.0194	22.9	.0000	1	culinary
0.0194	22.9	.0000	1	cultivates
0.0194	22.9	.0000	1	cure-all
0.0194	22.9	.0000	1	curtail
0.0194	22.9	.0000	1	curtailing
0.0194	22.9	.0000	1	customhouse
0.0194	22.9	.0000	1	Cut
0.0194	22.9	.0000	1	Czechoslovakians
0.0194	22.9	.0000	1	daikon
0.0194	22.9	.0000	1	dairy-farm
0.0194	22.9	.0000	1	dairy-farmland
0.0194	22.9	.0000	1	Damodar
0.0194	22.9	.0000	1	Danish-owned
0.0194	22.9	.0000	1	dartgun
0.0194	22.9	.0000	1	Dashan
0.0194	22.9	.0000	1	daub

THE PRECEDING WORD TYPE OCCUPIES RANK 58500

U	SFI	D	F	Word Type
0.0194	22.9	.0000	1	Dayak
0.0194	22.9	.0000	1	deBelleau
0.0194	22.9	.0000	1	deBrazza
0.0194	22.9	.0000	1	deChamplain's
0.0194	22.9	.0000	1	deLafayette
0.0194	22.9	.0000	1	deLas
0.0194	22.9	.0000	1	deLeon's
0.0194	22.9	.0000	1	deMontcalm
0.0194	22.9	.0000	1	dePortola
0.0194	22.9	.0000	1	deSan
0.0194	22.9	.0000	1	deSoto's
0.0194	22.9	.0000	1	de-salt
0.0194	22.9	.0000	1	deathlike
0.0194	22.9	.0000	1	debasing
0.0194	22.9	.0000	1	debrief
0.0194	22.9	.0000	1	debris-strewn
0.0194	22.9	.0000	1	Decisions
0.0194	22.9	.0000	1	dedicating
0.0194	22.9	.0000	1	deem
0.0194	22.9	.0000	1	deep-lying
0.0194	22.9	.0000	1	deepwater
0.0194	22.9	.0000	1	Deerpath
0.0194	22.9	.0000	1	DEFINITIONAL
0.0194	22.9	.0000	1	defraud
0.0194	22.9	.0000	1	deisel
0.0194	22.9	.0000	1	Delivered
0.0194	22.9	.0000	1	Delmonico's
0.0194	22.9	.0000	1	demi-gods
0.0194	22.9	.0000	1	demilitarized
0.0194	22.9	.0000	1	democrats
0.0194	22.9	.0000	1	Demon
0.0194	22.9	.0000	1	demoralization
0.0194	22.9	.0000	1	denounces
0.0194	22.9	.0000	1	densely-populated
0.0194	22.9	.0000	1	Deposit
0.0194	22.9	.0000	1	Deputy
0.0194	22.9	.0000	1	DesPlaines
0.0194	22.9	.0000	1	dethroned
0.0194	22.9	.0000	1	devastate
0.0194	22.9	.0000	1	diamond-back
0.0194	22.9	.0000	1	Diamonds
0.0194	22.9	.0000	1	Diaz's
0.0194	22.9	.0000	1	dietitian
0.0194	22.9	.0000	1	diffident
0.0194	22.9	.0000	1	Diligence
0.0194	22.9	.0000	1	Dinwiddie's
0.0194	22.9	.0000	1	Diplomatic
0.0194	22.9	.0000	1	disaffection
0.0194	22.9	.0000	1	disavow
0.0194	22.9	.0000	1	disband
0.0194	22.9	.0000	1	discouragements
0.0194	22.9	.0000	1	discouragingly
0.0194	22.9	.0000	1	disfranchising
0.0194	22.9	.0000	1	disheartening
0.0194	22.9	.0000	1	Disneyland
0.0194	22.9	.0000	1	displacing
0.0194	22.9	.0000	1	dispossessed
0.0194	22.9	.0000	1	dissensions
0.0194	22.9	.0000	1	distorts
0.0194	22.9	.0000	1	distressingly
0.0194	22.9	.0000	1	DistrictofColumbia
0.0194	22.9	.0000	1	distrusted
0.0194	22.9	.0000	1	disunite
0.0194	22.9	.0000	1	Dividing
0.0194	22.9	.0000	1	Divisions
0.0194	22.9	.0000	1	do-fu
0.0194	22.9	.0000	1	doddering
0.0194	22.9	.0000	1	dog-sled
0.0194	22.9	.0000	1	Dogger
0.0194	22.9	.0000	1	dogwoods
0.0194	22.9	.0000	1	Dollar
0.0194	22.9	.0000	1	Domestic
0.0194	22.9	.0000	1	Donets
0.0194	22.9	.0000	1	Donnie
0.0194	22.9	.0000	1	Doolins'
0.0194	22.9	.0000	1	dough-mixing
0.0194	22.9	.0000	1	douglas
0.0194	22.9	.0000	1	Douglas'
0.0194	22.9	.0000	1	Douro
0.0194	22.9	.0000	1	douse
0.0194	22.9	.0000	1	Dowager
0.0194	22.9	.0000	1	down-under
0.0194	22.9	.0000	1	dragon-entwined
0.0194	22.9	.0000	1	dragon-ships
0.0194	22.9	.0000	1	Drava
0.0194	22.9	.0000	1	dried-mud
0.0194	22.9	.0000	1	drinker
0.0194	22.9	.0000	1	dropouts
0.0194	22.9	.0000	1	drubbed
0.0194	22.9	.0000	1	dry-farming
0.0194	22.9	.0000	1	dry-weather
0.0194	22.9	.0000	1	drygoods
0.0194	22.9	.0000	1	Dunkers
0.0194	22.9	.0000	1	durra
0.0194	22.9	.0000	1	Duty
0.0194	22.9	.0000	1	Duvall's
0.0194	22.9	.0000	1	dyewood
0.0194	22.9	.0000	1	dynamite-laden
0.0194	22.9	.0000	1	Eagle-scream
0.0194	22.9	.0000	1	ear-piercing

THE PRECEDING WORD TYPE OCCUPIES RANK 58600

U	SFI	D	F	Word Type
0.0194	22.9	.0000	1	earplugs
0.0194	22.9	.0000	1	earthlings
0.0194	22.9	.0000	1	easy-handed
0.0194	22.9	.0000	1	Eaton's
0.0194	22.9	.0000	1	Eban
0.0194	22.9	.0000	1	ebony-black
0.0194	22.9	.0000	1	Ebro
0.0194	22.9	.0000	1	ECAFE
0.0194	22.9	.0000	1	Eckert
0.0194	22.9	.0000	1	editorialized
0.0194	22.9	.0000	1	Ee-say
0.0194	22.9	.0000	1	EEC
0.0194	22.9	.0000	1	egg-marketing
0.0194	22.9	.0000	1	Eiffel
0.0194	22.9	.0000	1	eight-point
0.0194	22.9	.0000	1	eight-room
0.0194	22.9	.0000	1	ejido
0.0194	22.9	.0000	1	Elath
0.0194	22.9	.0000	1	Elburz
0.0194	22.9	.0000	1	electrolytically
0.0194	22.9	.0000	1	elementary-school
0.0194	22.9	.0000	1	Eleven-Cities
0.0194	22.9	.0000	1	eleven-hundred
0.0194	22.9	.0000	1	Emerald
0.0194	22.9	.0000	1	emir
0.0194	22.9	.0000	1	Empire's
0.0194	22.9	.0000	1	emus
0.0194	22.9	.0000	1	Encino
0.0194	22.9	.0000	1	Endeavour
0.0194	22.9	.0000	1	Enforcement
0.0194	22.9	.0000	1	enfranchised
0.0194	22.9	.0000	1	Engels
0.0194	22.9	.0000	1	enroute
0.0194	22.9	.0000	1	episode's
0.0194	22.9	.0000	1	Equidistant
0.0194	22.9	.0000	1	erg
0.0194	22.9	.0000	1	Erich
0.0194	22.9	.0000	1	Ernesto
0.0194	22.9	.0000	1	Esmat
0.0194	22.9	.0000	1	Espanola
0.0194	22.9	.0000	1	essayist-poet
0.0194	22.9	.0000	1	Estados
0.0194	22.9	.0000	1	Estates
0.0194	22.9	.0000	1	EstatesGeneral
0.0194	22.9	.0000	1	Este
0.0194	22.9	.0000	1	Estonians
0.0194	22.9	.0000	1	Euripides
0.0194	22.9	.0000	1	Europa
0.0194	22.9	.0000	1	European-owned
0.0194	22.9	.0000	1	European-style
0.0194	22.9	.0000	1	Europoort
0.0194	22.9	.0000	1	ever-improving
0.0194	22.9	.0000	1	ever-optimistic
0.0194	22.9	.0000	1	ever-widening
0.0194	22.9	.0000	1	evinces
0.0194	22.9	.0000	1	ex-Populist
0.0194	22.9	.0000	1	ex-officers
0.0194	22.9	.0000	1	ex-servicemen
0.0194	22.9	.0000	1	excises
0.0194	22.9	.0000	1	Exclusion
0.0194	22.9	.0000	1	exempting
0.0194	22.9	.0000	1	Exemptions
0.0194	22.9	.0000	1	exiling
0.0194	22.9	.0000	1	exotic-looking
0.0194	22.9	.0000	1	expansively
0.0194	22.9	.0000	1	expediency
0.0194	22.9	.0000	1	expedients
0.0194	22.9	.0000	1	exportation
0.0194	22.9	.0000	1	expostulations
0.0194	22.9	.0000	1	extracurricular
0.0194	22.9	.0000	1	eye-sore
0.0194	22.9	.0000	1	Faiyum
0.0194	22.9	.0000	1	falsity
0.0194	22.9	.0000	1	family-size
0.0194	22.9	.0000	1	fanatically
0.0194	22.9	.0000	1	Fao
0.0194	22.9	.0000	1	farm-holiday
0.0194	22.9	.0000	1	farming-regions
0.0194	22.9	.0000	1	Farmington's
0.0194	22.9	.0000	1	Farther
0.0194	22.9	.0000	1	fascist
0.0194	22.9	.0000	1	FDIC
0.0194	22.9	.0000	1	FDR'S**
0.0194	22.9	.0000	1	fellow-citizens
0.0194	22.9	.0000	1	felonies
0.0194	22.9	.0000	1	Fermis
0.0194	22.9	.0000	1	ferry's
0.0194	22.9	.0000	1	Few
0.0194	22.9	.0000	1	fiery-tempered
0.0194	22.9	.0000	1	fifty-fifth
0.0194	22.9	.0000	1	filling-station
0.0194	22.9	.0000	1	financiers
0.0194	22.9	.0000	1	fine-tipped
0.0194	22.9	.0000	1	finishers
0.0194	22.9	.0000	1	FIRE
0.0194	22.9	.0000	1	fire-insurance
0.0194	22.9	.0000	1	firedrill
0.0194	22.9	.0000	1	firepit
0.0194	22.9	.0000	1	firepits
0.0194	22.9	.0000	1	Fires

THE PRECEDING WORD TYPE OCCUPIES RANK 58700

U	SFI	D	F	Word Type
0.0194	22.9	.0000	1	Fists
0.0194	22.9	.0000	1	FIVE
0.0194	22.9	.0000	1	five-mile
0.0194	22.9	.0000	1	flagship's
0.0194	22.9	.0000	1	flat-soled
0.0194	22.9	.0000	1	Flatbush
0.0194	22.9	.0000	1	flattops
0.0194	22.9	.0000	1	flaxseed
0.0194	22.9	.0000	1	flower-decked
0.0194	22.9	.0000	1	flyleaf
0.0194	22.9	.0000	1	Foch's
0.0194	22.9	.0000	1	foldaway
0.0194	22.9	.0000	1	foot-powered
0.0194	22.9	.0000	1	footmarks
0.0194	22.9	.0000	1	Fordlandia
0.0194	22.9	.0000	1	foreclosure
0.0194	22.9	.0000	1	foredeck
0.0194	22.9	.0000	1	foreign-made
0.0194	22.9	.0000	1	formative
0.0194	22.9	.0000	1	fortful
0.0194	22.9	.0000	1	forty-story
0.0194	22.9	.0000	1	forward-looking
0.0194	22.9	.0000	1	foundered
0.0194	22.9	.0000	1	four-footer
0.0194	22.9	.0000	1	four-hundred-year-old
0.0194	22.9	.0000	1	fox-trot
0.0194	22.9	.0000	1	framers
0.0194	22.9	.0000	1	Franchise
0.0194	22.9	.0000	1	Franco-Ethiopian
0.0194	22.9	.0000	1	Frankfurter
0.0194	22.9	.0000	1	Franklins
0.0194	22.9	.0000	1	Fraunces
0.0194	22.9	.0000	1	freedmen
0.0194	22.9	.0000	1	freeholder
0.0194	22.9	.0000	1	freeholders
0.0194	22.9	.0000	1	Freeman
0.0194	22.9	.0000	1	Freeman's
0.0194	22.9	.0000	1	Freeport
0.0194	22.9	.0000	1	freights
0.0194	22.9	.0000	1	Fremont's
0.0194	22.9	.0000	1	Frenchmen's
0.0194	22.9	.0000	1	fria
0.0194	22.9	.0000	1	friezes
0.0194	22.9	.0000	1	frijoles
0.0194	22.9	.0000	1	Frisbie
0.0194	22.9	.0000	1	frontier-style
0.0194	22.9	.0000	1	fruit-raising
0.0194	22.9	.0000	1	fuel-driven
0.0194	22.9	.0000	1	Fulfillment
0.0194	22.9	.0000	1	fun-food
0.0194	22.9	.0000	1	Func
0.0194	22.9	.0000	1	Functionary
0.0194	22.9	.0000	1	functioned
0.0194	22.9	.0000	1	Fundamental
0.0194	22.9	.0000	1	furfural
0.0194	22.9	.0000	1	Fusiliers
0.0194	22.9	.0000	1	fusing
0.0194	22.9	.0000	1	Gadsden
0.0194	22.9	.0000	1	Gahma
0.0194	22.9	.0000	1	Gaillard
0.0194	22.9	.0000	1	galabias
0.0194	22.9	.0000	1	Galata
0.0194	22.9	.0000	1	Galla
0.0194	22.9	.0000	1	Gallatin
0.0194	22.9	.0000	1	Galvao
0.0194	22.9	.0000	1	Gander
0.0194	22.9	.0000	1	Garonne
0.0194	22.9	.0000	1	gasometers
0.0194	22.9	.0000	1	Gaspar
0.0194	22.9	.0000	1	Gat
0.0194	22.9	.0000	1	Gautama's
0.0194	22.9	.0000	1	Gdynia
0.0194	22.9	.0000	1	gear-cutting
0.0194	22.9	.0000	1	Geographical
0.0194	22.9	.0000	1	Germain
0.0194	22.9	.0000	1	German-American
0.0194	22.9	.0000	1	Ghent
0.0194	22.9	.0000	1	ghost-quiet
0.0194	22.9	.0000	1	gibes
0.0194	22.9	.0000	1	Gilberts
0.0194	22.9	.0000	1	Gilham
0.0194	22.9	.0000	1	ginned
0.0194	22.9	.0000	1	girdling
0.0194	22.9	.0000	1	gloried
0.0194	22.9	.0000	1	goat-raising
0.0194	22.9	.0000	1	Gochiso-sama
0.0194	22.9	.0000	1	God-fearing
0.0194	22.9	.0000	1	Godey's
0.0194	22.9	.0000	1	Goethals
0.0194	22.9	.0000	1	gold-covered
0.0194	22.9	.0000	1	gold-handled
0.0194	22.9	.0000	1	gold-mining
0.0194	22.9	.0000	1	gold-producing
0.0194	22.9	.0000	1	Gompers
0.0194	22.9	.0000	1	Gompers'
0.0194	22.9	.0000	1	Good-bye
0.0194	22.9	.0000	1	Goro
0.0194	22.9	.0000	1	Gotthard
0.0194	22.9	.0000	1	gouging
0.0194	22.9	.0000	1	government-built

THE PRECEDING WORD TYPE OCCUPIES RANK 58800

U	SFI	D	F	Word Type
0.0194	22.9	.0000	1	government-business
0.0194	22.9	.0000	1	government-led
0.0194	22.9	.0000	1	government-operated
0.0194	22.9	.0000	1	grafting
0.0194	22.9	.0000	1	GrandIsland
0.0194	22.9	.0000	1	grantee
0.0194	22.9	.0000	1	gras
0.0194	22.9	.0000	1	grass-covered
0.0194	22.9	.0000	1	Grasslands
0.0194	22.9	.0000	1	Grassmere
0.0194	22.9	.0000	1	gray-clad
0.0194	22.9	.0000	1	Graz
0.0194	22.9	.0000	1	grazes
0.0194	22.9	.0000	1	GREATBRITAIN
0.0194	22.9	.0000	1	Greenfield's
0.0194	22.9	.0000	1	gregory
0.0194	22.9	.0000	1	grievance
0.0194	22.9	.0000	1	gristmills
0.0194	22.9	.0000	1	Groaners
0.0194	22.9	.0000	1	Groton
0.0194	22.9	.0000	1	ground-breaking
0.0194	22.9	.0000	1	ground-hitched
0.0194	22.9	.0000	1	groundnuts
0.0194	22.9	.0000	1	groundskeeper
0.0194	22.9	.0000	1	groundwater
0.0194	22.9	.0000	1	Guadalquivir
0.0194	22.9	.0000	1	Guaranis
0.0194	22.9	.0000	1	guenon
0.0194	22.9	.0000	1	Guerre
0.0194	22.9	.0000	1	GUM
0.0194	22.9	.0000	1	gumwood
0.0194	22.9	.0000	1	gunboat
0.0194	22.9	.0000	1	gunsmiths
0.0194	22.9	.0000	1	Gupta
0.0194	22.9	.0000	1	Haarlem's
0.0194	22.9	.0000	1	hachures
0.0194	22.9	.0000	1	hailstorm
0.0194	22.9	.0000	1	half-barbarian
0.0194	22.9	.0000	1	half-day
0.0194	22.9	.0000	1	half-island
0.0194	22.9	.0000	1	half-sphere
0.0194	22.9	.0000	1	halv
0.0194	22.9	.0000	1	halvoy**
0.0194	22.9	.0000	1	Hamites
0.0194	22.9	.0000	1	Hammurabi
0.0194	22.9	.0000	1	Han
0.0194	22.9	.0000	1	Hancock's
0.0194	22.9	.0000	1	hand-made

U	SFI	D	F	Word Type
0.0194	22.9	.0000	1	hand-talk
0.0194	22.9	.0000	1	hand-woven
0.0194	22.9	.0000	1	handmarks
0.0194	22.9	.0000	1	Hangchow
0.0194	22.9	.0000	1	Happens
0.0194	22.9	.0000	1	Hararge
0.0194	22.9	.0000	1	Harbord
0.0194	22.9	.0000	1	hard-surfaced
0.0194	22.9	.0000	1	harmattan
0.0194	22.9	.0000	1	Harmonious
0.0194	22.9	.0000	1	harried
0.0194	22.9	.0000	1	Harrod
0.0194	22.9	.0000	1	Harvard-Yale
0.0194	22.9	.0000	1	Harvre
0.0194	22.9	.0000	1	hashi
0.0194	22.9	.0000	1	hauntingly
0.0194	22.9	.0000	1	haversacks
0.0194	22.9	.0000	1	Hayes's
0.0194	22.9	.0000	1	Haym
0.0194	22.9	.0000	1	Haymarket
0.0194	22.9	.0000	1	Haynsworth
0.0194	22.9	.0000	1	hayrake
0.0194	22.9	.0000	1	Hazleton's
0.0194	22.9	.0000	1	headhunter
0.0194	22.9	.0000	1	headless
0.0194	22.9	.0000	1	hecklers
0.0194	22.9	.0000	1	Hekla
0.0194	22.9	.0000	1	Helidon
0.0194	22.9	.0000	1	hell-fire
0.0194	22.9	.0000	1	Helsinki's
0.0194	22.9	.0000	1	henceforward
0.0194	22.9	.0000	1	Hendrickson
0.0194	22.9	.0000	1	herders'
0.0194	22.9	.0000	1	hereunto
0.0194	22.9	.0000	1	Hermon
0.0194	22.9	.0000	1	Hernad
0.0194	22.9	.0000	1	Heroism
0.0194	22.9	.0000	1	Hesse
0.0194	22.9	.0000	1	hevea
0.0194	22.9	.0000	1	HEW
0.0194	22.9	.0000	1	hiered
0.0194	22.9	.0000	1	high-back
0.0194	22.9	.0000	1	high-button
0.0194	22.9	.0000	1	high-walled
0.0194	22.9	.0000	1	Highlands-Coastal
0.0194	22.9	.0000	1	Highnesses
0.0194	22.9	.0000	1	highpriced
0.0194	22.9	.0000	1	hijackers
0.0194	22.9	.0000	1	hijacking
0.0194	22.9	.0000	1	hillier
0.0194	22.9	.0000	1	hilliness
0.0194	22.9	.0000	1	hinders
THE PRECEDING WORD TYPE OCCUPIES RANK 58900				
0.0194	22.9	.0000	1	Historian
0.0194	22.9	.0000	1	hodgepodge
0.0194	22.9	.0000	1	Hofuf
0.0194	22.9	.0000	1	hog-slaughtering
0.0194	22.9	.0000	1	Hollander's
0.0194	22.9	.0000	1	holokus
0.0194	22.9	.0000	1	Holstein-Friesian
0.0194	22.9	.0000	1	homebuilder
0.0194	22.9	.0000	1	homesteader
0.0194	22.9	.0000	1	hoodlums
0.0194	22.9	.0000	1	hook-shaped
0.0194	22.9	.0000	1	Hooverville
0.0194	22.9	.0000	1	hoppers'
0.0194	22.9	.0000	1	hornos
0.0194	22.9	.0000	1	Hospitality
0.0194	22.9	.0000	1	hostel
0.0194	22.9	.0000	1	hot-weather
0.0194	22.9	.0000	1	hounded
0.0194	22.9	.0000	1	house-to-house
0.0194	22.9	.0000	1	houseboy
0.0194	22.9	.0000	1	housebroken
0.0194	22.9	.0000	1	housewifes
0.0194	22.9	.0000	1	Hsueh-liang
0.0194	22.9	.0000	1	hubble-bubble
0.0194	22.9	.0000	1	Hubertusburg
0.0194	22.9	.0000	1	Hudson-Mohawk
0.0194	22.9	.0000	1	Huerta
0.0194	22.9	.0000	1	hukilau
0.0194	22.9	.0000	1	hulas
0.0194	22.9	.0000	1	Hurley
0.0194	22.9	.0000	1	Hurston
0.0194	22.9	.0000	1	husbands'
0.0194	22.9	.0000	1	huzzahs
0.0194	22.9	.0000	1	hyacinths
0.0194	22.9	.0000	1	Ibernian
0.0194	22.9	.0000	1	Ibibio
0.0194	22.9	.0000	1	Ibo
0.0194	22.9	.0000	1	ice-clogged
0.0194	22.9	.0000	1	ice-lined
0.0194	22.9	.0000	1	iceboxes
0.0194	22.9	.0000	1	Ictinus
0.0194	22.9	.0000	1	Idaho's
0.0194	22.9	.0000	1	idler
0.0194	22.9	.0000	1	idlest
0.0194	22.9	.0000	1	ikebana
0.0194	22.9	.0000	1	ill-advised
0.0194	22.9	.0000	1	illegality
0.0194	22.9	.0000	1	Illyushin
0.0194	22.9	.0000	1	imperturbable
0.0194	22.9	.0000	1	implemented
0.0194	22.9	.0000	1	imposts
0.0194	22.9	.0000	1	Inca's
0.0194	22.9	.0000	1	incarceration
0.0194	22.9	.0000	1	Income
0.0194	22.9	.0000	1	inconveniencing
0.0194	22.9	.0000	1	Increase
0.0194	22.9	.0000	1	Indian-fighter
0.0194	22.9	.0000	1	indignities
0.0194	22.9	.0000	1	indissolubly
0.0194	22.9	.0000	1	industrialize
0.0194	22.9	.0000	1	ineffectiveness
0.0194	22.9	.0000	1	ingot
0.0194	22.9	.0000	1	inlets
0.0194	22.9	.0000	1	innkeepers
0.0194	22.9	.0000	1	Inouye
0.0194	22.9	.0000	1	insoles
0.0194	22.9	.0000	1	Inspirationists
0.0194	22.9	.0000	1	Institutions
0.0194	22.9	.0000	1	instructs
0.0194	22.9	.0000	1	insurrectionary
0.0194	22.9	.0000	1	insurrections
0.0194	22.9	.0000	1	integrate
0.0194	22.9	.0000	1	intercolonial
0.0194	22.9	.0000	1	Intercourse
0.0194	22.9	.0000	1	Interdependence
0.0194	22.9	.0000	1	intermarriage
0.0194	22.9	.0000	1	intermediate-school
0.0194	22.9	.0000	1	interpositions
0.0194	22.9	.0000	1	Interracial
0.0194	22.9	.0000	1	intimates
0.0194	22.9	.0000	1	intra
0.0194	22.9	.0000	1	Inyo
0.0194	22.9	.0000	1	Iowan
0.0194	22.9	.0000	1	Iquique
0.0194	22.9	.0000	1	Iquitos
0.0194	22.9	.0000	1	Iranians
0.0194	22.9	.0000	1	IRELAND
0.0194	22.9	.0000	1	iron-mining
0.0194	22.9	.0000	1	irreconcilables
0.0194	22.9	.0000	1	irreversible
0.0194	22.9	.0000	1	Irrigate
0.0194	22.9	.0000	1	Ishikari
0.0194	22.9	.0000	1	island-country
0.0194	22.9	.0000	1	island-studded
0.0194	22.9	.0000	1	ISLES
0.0194	22.9	.0000	1	Issei
0.0194	22.9	.0000	1	ISSUES
0.0194	22.9	.0000	1	itadakimasu
0.0194	22.9	.0000	1	Its
0.0194	22.9	.0000	1	Itzcoatl
THE PRECEDING WORD TYPE OCCUPIES RANK 59000				
0.0194	22.9	.0000	1	Ivory
0.0194	22.9	.0000	1	IWW
0.0194	22.9	.0000	1	Ixtaccihuatl
0.0194	22.9	.0000	1	JACL'S
0.0194	22.9	.0000	1	Japanese-Americans
0.0194	22.9	.0000	1	Japanese-held
0.0194	22.9	.0000	1	Japanized
0.0194	22.9	.0000	1	Jeannette
0.0194	22.9	.0000	1	jeopardized
0.0194	22.9	.0000	1	jet-powered
0.0194	22.9	.0000	1	jitney
0.0194	22.9	.0000	1	Jodhpur
0.0194	22.9	.0000	1	joeys
0.0194	22.9	.0000	1	Jojep's
0.0194	22.9	.0000	1	Joliet
0.0194	22.9	.0000	1	Judeans
0.0194	22.9	.0000	1	Jupka
0.0194	22.9	.0000	1	juridical
0.0194	22.9	.0000	1	Jurisdiction
0.0194	22.9	.0000	1	jurists
0.0194	22.9	.0000	1	justiciaries
0.0194	22.9	.0000	1	Juvenile
0.0194	22.9	.0000	1	jyow-dzuh
0.0194	22.9	.0000	1	Kain-tuck
0.0194	22.9	.0000	1	Kaintuck
0.0194	22.9	.0000	1	Kalapana
0.0194	22.9	.0000	1	Kamakura
0.0194	22.9	.0000	1	Kamehameha's
0.0194	22.9	.0000	1	Kan
0.0194	22.9	.0000	1	Kansans
0.0194	22.9	.0000	1	Kanuri
0.0194	22.9	.0000	1	kapa
0.0194	22.9	.0000	1	Kapiolani
0.0194	22.9	.0000	1	Kariba
0.0194	22.9	.0000	1	Kaschau
0.0194	22.9	.0000	1	Kassa
0.0194	22.9	.0000	1	kassalalia
0.0194	22.9	.0000	1	Kato's
0.0194	22.9	.0000	1	Kauai's
0.0194	22.9	.0000	1	Kawata
0.0194	22.9	.0000	1	Kawata's
0.0194	22.9	.0000	1	Kaweki's
0.0194	22.9	.0000	1	Kenai
0.0194	22.9	.0000	1	Kennebec
0.0194	22.9	.0000	1	Khafre
0.0194	22.9	.0000	1	khan's
0.0194	22.9	.0000	1	kidnapped
0.0194	22.9	.0000	1	kidnappers
0.0194	22.9	.0000	1	kidnapping
0.0194	22.9	.0000	1	kidney-shaped
0.0194	22.9	.0000	1	Kievan
0.0194	22.9	.0000	1	kilowatt-hours
0.0194	22.9	.0000	1	kilts
0.0194	22.9	.0000	1	Kings'
0.0194	22.9	.0000	1	Kingston's
0.0194	22.9	.0000	1	Kirkuk
0.0194	22.9	.0000	1	Kiruna
0.0194	22.9	.0000	1	Kiryat
0.0194	22.9	.0000	1	kisser
0.0194	22.9	.0000	1	Kit's
0.0194	22.9	.0000	1	Kitten
0.0194	22.9	.0000	1	Kitts-Nevis-Anguilla
0.0194	22.9	.0000	1	Kiyo
0.0194	22.9	.0000	1	knee-length
0.0194	22.9	.0000	1	knighting
0.0194	22.9	.0000	1	knightly
0.0194	22.9	.0000	1	Knoxville
0.0194	22.9	.0000	1	koala's
0.0194	22.9	.0000	1	koalas
0.0194	22.9	.0000	1	Kopechne
0.0194	22.9	.0000	1	kortez'**
0.0194	22.9	.0000	1	Kosice
0.0194	22.9	.0000	1	Kotoku
0.0194	22.9	.0000	1	Krogers'
0.0194	22.9	.0000	1	Kunari
0.0194	22.9	.0000	1	Kung
0.0194	22.9	.0000	1	Kure
0.0194	22.9	.0000	1	Kuznetsk
0.0194	22.9	.0000	1	Kwai
0.0194	22.9	.0000	1	L'Ouverture
0.0194	22.9	.0000	1	LaChine
0.0194	22.9	.0000	1	LaPlata
0.0194	22.9	.0000	1	labor-degrading
0.0194	22.9	.0000	1	labor's
0.0194	22.9	.0000	1	laconically
0.0194	22.9	.0000	1	Lacq
0.0194	22.9	.0000	1	Laddie
0.0194	22.9	.0000	1	Ladoga
0.0194	22.9	.0000	1	Lafitte
0.0194	22.9	.0000	1	Laicos
0.0194	22.9	.0000	1	laipala
0.0194	22.9	.0000	1	lakeshore
0.0194	22.9	.0000	1	land-form
0.0194	22.9	.0000	1	land-forms
0.0194	22.9	.0000	1	land-holding
0.0194	22.9	.0000	1	land-reform
0.0194	22.9	.0000	1	land-sea
0.0194	22.9	.0000	1	landless
0.0194	22.9	.0000	1	Laotian
0.0194	22.9	.0000	1	lappa
THE PRECEDING WORD TYPE OCCUPIES RANK 59100				
0.0194	22.9	.0000	1	larch
0.0194	22.9	.0000	1	larger-than-life
0.0194	22.9	.0000	1	Latin-America
0.0194	22.9	.0000	1	Lattimore's
0.0194	22.9	.0000	1	Laval
0.0194	22.9	.0000	1	law-maker
0.0194	22.9	.0000	1	LeBourget
0.0194	22.9	.0000	1	Lead
0.0194	22.9	.0000	1	leaderless
0.0194	22.9	.0000	1	leafed
0.0194	22.9	.0000	1	Leakey
0.0194	22.9	.0000	1	Learned
0.0194	22.9	.0000	1	Leary
0.0194	22.9	.0000	1	Leatherstocking
0.0194	22.9	.0000	1	legalistic
0.0194	22.9	.0000	1	legations
0.0194	22.9	.0000	1	Legree
0.0194	22.9	.0000	1	Lemon
0.0194	22.9	.0000	1	lender's
0.0194	22.9	.0000	1	Lenny
0.0194	22.9	.0000	1	Leoni
0.0194	22.9	.0000	1	Leontyne
0.0194	22.9	.0000	1	Lesser
0.0194	22.9	.0000	1	lesser-known
0.0194	22.9	.0000	1	Level
0.0194	22.9	.0000	1	liars
0.0194	22.9	.0000	1	liberator
0.0194	22.9	.0000	1	licentious
0.0194	22.9	.0000	1	life-groupings
0.0194	22.9	.0000	1	Light-Horse
0.0194	22.9	.0000	1	Lighting
0.0194	22.9	.0000	1	Lihue
0.0194	22.9	.0000	1	likely-looking
0.0194	22.9	.0000	1	Linz
0.0194	22.9	.0000	1	lion-like
0.0194	22.9	.0000	1	litchi
0.0194	22.9	.0000	1	litchis
0.0194	22.9	.0000	1	Lithuanians
0.0194	22.9	.0000	1	LittleRock
0.0194	22.9	.0000	1	little-developed
0.0194	22.9	.0000	1	Liu
0.0194	22.9	.0000	1	live-and-let-live
0.0194	22.9	.0000	1	Loess
0.0194	22.9	.0000	1	loincloth
0.0194	22.9	.0000	1	lombard
0.0194	22.9	.0000	1	lomilomi
0.0194	22.9	.0000	1	LongBeach's
0.0194	22.9	.0000	1	long-suspected
0.0194	22.9	.0000	1	Longhorns
0.0194	22.9	.0000	1	Look-It-Up
0.0194	22.9	.0000	1	looting
0.0194	22.9	.0000	1	lords'
0.0194	22.9	.0000	1	Lothaire
0.0194	22.9	.0000	1	LouisXVI
0.0194	22.9	.0000	1	lovelier
0.0194	22.9	.0000	1	low-interest
0.0194	22.9	.0000	1	low-paying
0.0194	22.9	.0000	1	low-quality
0.0194	22.9	.0000	1	Lucerne
0.0194	22.9	.0000	1	Ludendorff
0.0194	22.9	.0000	1	lummux
0.0194	22.9	.0000	1	Lundquists
0.0194	22.9	.0000	1	Lung
0.0194	22.9	.0000	1	Luxemburg
0.0194	22.9	.0000	1	Maas
0.0194	22.9	.0000	1	MacLeish's
0.0194	22.9	.0000	1	Macdonough
0.0194	22.9	.0000	1	Madeira
0.0194	22.9	.0000	1	madwomen
0.0194	22.9	.0000	1	Magistrates'
0.0194	22.9	.0000	1	Magnitogorsk
0.0194	22.9	.0000	1	Mahomet
0.0194	22.9	.0000	1	mainland's
0.0194	22.9	.0000	1	Malo
0.0194	22.9	.0000	1	malos
0.0194	22.9	.0000	1	maltreated
0.0194	22.9	.0000	1	man-hour
0.0194	22.9	.0000	1	man-types
0.0194	22.9	.0000	1	Manchukuo
0.0194	22.9	.0000	1	Mandan
0.0194	22.9	.0000	1	mangels
0.0194	22.9	.0000	1	mangles
0.0194	22.9	.0000	1	Mangrove
0.0194	22.9	.0000	1	Manifest
0.0194	22.9	.0000	1	manorial
0.0194	22.9	.0000	1	manured
0.0194	22.9	.0000	1	many-windowed
0.0194	22.9	.0000	1	Manygoats'
0.0194	22.9	.0000	1	map's
0.0194	22.9	.0000	1	march-ins
0.0194	22.9	.0000	1	Marduk
0.0194	22.9	.0000	1	Marduk's
0.0194	22.9	.0000	1	Margo
0.0194	22.9	.0000	1	Margriet's
0.0194	22.9	.0000	1	Mariposa
0.0194	22.9	.0000	1	Maritsa
0.0194	22.9	.0000	1	marketability
0.0194	22.9	.0000	1	Martians
0.0194	22.9	.0000	1	Martinique
0.0194	22.9	.0000	1	Marylanders
THE PRECEDING WORD TYPE OCCUPIES RANK 59200				
0.0194	22.9	.0000	1	mass-producing
0.0194	22.9	.0000	1	massacres
0.0194	22.9	.0000	1	Matadi
0.0194	22.9	.0000	1	mater's
0.0194	22.9	.0000	1	Matt's
0.0194	22.9	.0000	1	Maturity
0.0194	22.9	.0000	1	mayors
0.0194	22.9	.0000	1	Mazzone
0.0194	22.9	.0000	1	McCarthyism
0.0194	22.9	.0000	1	McCrae's
0.0194	22.9	.0000	1	mechanicks
0.0194	22.9	.0000	1	mechanize
0.0194	22.9	.0000	1	Mechi-Kuwi
0.0194	22.9	.0000	1	Medellin's
0.0194	22.9	.0000	1	medius
0.0194	22.9	.0000	1	Mei
0.0194	22.9	.0000	1	Mekong's
0.0194	22.9	.0000	1	menhaden
0.0194	22.9	.0000	1	mentalities
0.0194	22.9	.0000	1	Mercator's
0.0194	22.9	.0000	1	Merino
0.0194	22.9	.0000	1	merinos
0.0194	22.9	.0000	1	Merinos
0.0194	22.9	.0000	1	merited
0.0194	22.9	.0000	1	metal-detection
0.0194	22.9	.0000	1	metalware
0.0194	22.9	.0000	1	Mex'ico**
0.0194	22.9	.0000	1	Mexican-Spanish
0.0194	22.9	.0000	1	Mexicanos
0.0194	22.9	.0000	1	MiamiBeach
0.0194	22.9	.0000	1	Micmac
0.0194	22.9	.0000	1	Micronesia
0.0194	22.9	.0000	1	mid-Asia
0.0194	22.9	.0000	1	Mid-Continent
0.0194	22.9	.0000	1	mid-January
0.0194	22.9	.0000	1	mid-Pacific
0.0194	22.9	.0000	1	mid-century
0.0194	22.9	.0000	1	mid-eighteenth
0.0194	22.9	.0000	1	mid-1600s
0.0194	22.9	.0000	1	mid-1700s
0.0194	22.9	.0000	1	mid-1850's
0.0194	22.9	.0000	1	Mihiel
0.0194	22.9	.0000	1	Miiko
0.0194	22.9	.0000	1	Mij's
0.0194	22.9	.0000	1	Mikoyan
0.0194	22.9	.0000	1	mildew
0.0194	22.9	.0000	1	militiamen
0.0194	22.9	.0000	1	milkers
0.0194	22.9	.0000	1	milkhouse
0.0194	22.9	.0000	1	Millers'
0.0194	22.9	.0000	1	millowner
0.0194	22.9	.0000	1	Min
0.0194	22.9	.0000	1	mineral-rich
0.0194	22.9	.0000	1	Minoru
0.0194	22.9	.0000	1	mint's
0.0194	22.9	.0000	1	Minuit
0.0194	22.9	.0000	1	Miraflores
0.0194	22.9	.0000	1	misdeeds
0.0194	22.9	.0000	1	Mishima
0.0194	22.9	.0000	1	misjudging
0.0194	22.9	.0000	1	Missionaries
0.0194	22.9	.0000	1	Mississippi's
0.0194	22.9	.0000	1	Mixcoatl
0.0194	22.9	.0000	1	mixing-bowl
0.0194	22.9	.0000	1	Miyoshi
0.0194	22.9	.0000	1	mobilization
0.0194	22.9	.0000	1	Moctezuma
0.0194	22.9	.0000	1	modelled
0.0194	22.9	.0000	1	moderated
0.0194	22.9	.0000	1	Mohammed's
0.0194	22.9	.0000	1	moister
0.0194	22.9	.0000	1	moisture-bearing
0.0194	22.9	.0000	1	Molders'
0.0194	22.9	.0000	1	Mombasa
0.0194	22.9	.0000	1	Monogram
0.0194	22.9	.0000	1	Monomakh
0.0194	22.9	.0000	1	monoplane
0.0194	22.9	.0000	1	Monroe's
0.0194	22.9	.0000	1	Monsoon
0.0194	22.9	.0000	1	Montezuma's
0.0194	22.9	.0000	1	Montgomery's
0.0194	22.9	.0000	1	Montt
0.0194	22.9	.0000	1	moon-shaped
0.0194	22.9	.0000	1	moon-shot
0.0194	22.9	.0000	1	moon-struck
0.0194	22.9	.0000	1	Moreno
0.0194	22.9	.0000	1	Moreno's
0.0194	22.9	.0000	1	Mormonism
0.0194	22.9	.0000	1	Moroccans
0.0194	22.9	.0000	1	Moscow's
0.0194	22.9	.0000	1	Moses'
0.0194	22.9	.0000	1	Mosque
0.0194	22.9	.0000	1	mosquitoes'
0.0194	22.9	.0000	1	motorscooters
0.0194	22.9	.0000	1	movie-maker
0.0194	22.9	.0000	1	mud-daubed
0.0194	22.9	.0000	1	Muggletonians
0.0194	22.9	.0000	1	Mukden
0.0194	22.9	.0000	1	Munroe
0.0194	22.9	.0000	1	Murray-Darling
THE PRECEDING WORD TYPE OCCUPIES RANK 59300				
0.0194	22.9	.0000	1	museum-watgurwa
0.0194	22.9	.0000	1	Mutiny
0.0194	22.9	.0000	1	muzzled
0.0194	22.9	.0000	1	Myna
0.0194	22.9	.0000	1	MyrtleBeach
0.0194	22.9	.0000	1	Nagoya
0.0194	22.9	.0000	1	Nanyang
0.0194	22.9	.0000	1	Narcissa
0.0194	22.9	.0000	1	nation-building
0.0194	22.9	.0000	1	Nationalism
0.0194	22.9	.0000	1	nations'

U	SFI	D	F	Word Type
0.0194	22.9	.0000	1	natural-gas
0.0194	22.9	.0000	1	NE
0.0194	22.9	.0000	1	Neale
0.0194	22.9	.0000	1	near-freezing
0.0194	22.9	.0000	1	near-tragic
0.0194	22.9	.0000	1	Nebuchadrezzar
0.0194	22.9	.0000	1	Neches
0.0194	22.9	.0000	1	Nee-say
0.0194	22.9	.0000	1	Needle
0.0194	22.9	.0000	1	Neisse
0.0194	22.9	.0000	1	Nelsons
0.0194	22.9	.0000	1	neophytes
0.0194	22.9	.0000	1	nephew-caretaker
0.0194	22.9	.0000	1	NewCaledonia
0.0194	22.9	.0000	1	NewEngland's
0.0194	22.9	.0000	1	NewEnglanders
0.0194	22.9	.0000	1	NewNetherland
0.0194	22.9	.0000	1	NewSmyrna
0.0194	22.9	.0000	1	NewSpain
0.0194	22.9	.0000	1	NewYorks
0.0194	22.9	.0000	1	newly-arrived
0.0194	22.9	.0000	1	NewsTime's
0.0194	22.9	.0000	1	NEWSPAPERS
0.0194	22.9	.0000	1	Nicobar
0.0194	22.9	.0000	1	Nicoll
0.0194	22.9	.0000	1	NIGERIA
0.0194	22.9	.0000	1	Niigata
0.0194	22.9	.0000	1	Niihau
0.0194	22.9	.0000	1	Nik
0.0194	22.9	.0000	1	Nik's
0.0194	22.9	.0000	1	Nimitz
0.0194	22.9	.0000	1	Nina's
0.0194	22.9	.0000	1	nine-day
0.0194	22.9	.0000	1	nine-hour
0.0194	22.9	.0000	1	Nineteenth
0.0194	22.9	.0000	1	ninety-eighth
0.0194	22.9	.0000	1	no-smoking
0.0194	22.9	.0000	1	Nob
0.0194	22.9	.0000	1	nobles'
0.0194	22.9	.0000	1	Nomadic
0.0194	22.9	.0000	1	nomads'
0.0194	22.9	.0000	1	nominates
0.0194	22.9	.0000	1	non-British
0.0194	22.9	.0000	1	non-Chinese
0.0194	22.9	.0000	1	non-English
0.0194	22.9	.0000	1	non-Europeans
0.0194	22.9	.0000	1	non-Western
0.0194	22.9	.0000	1	non-demonstrators
0.0194	22.9	.0000	1	non-fiction
0.0194	22.9	.0000	1	non-member
0.0194	22.9	.0000	1	noncombat
0.0194	22.9	.0000	1	north-facing
0.0194	22.9	.0000	1	northerner
0.0194	22.9	.0000	1	northwestward
0.0194	22.9	.0000	1	not-so-smart
0.0194	22.9	.0000	1	not-so-thin
0.0194	22.9	.0000	1	nothing-at-all
0.0194	22.9	.0000	1	Novokuznetsk
0.0194	22.9	.0000	1	Novosibirsk
0.0194	22.9	.0000	1	now-feeble
0.0194	22.9	.0000	1	Nuts
0.0194	22.9	.0000	1	Nuuanu
0.0194	22.9	.0000	1	NW
0.0194	22.9	.0000	1	Nyun
0.0194	22.9	.0000	1	O'Neale
0.0194	22.9	.0000	1	OakPark
0.0194	22.9	.0000	1	oath-taking
0.0194	22.9	.0000	1	Observation
0.0194	22.9	.0000	1	OBSERVER
0.0194	22.9	.0000	1	obstructive
0.0194	22.9	.0000	1	Occupied
0.0194	22.9	.0000	1	offensives
0.0194	22.9	.0000	1	officeholders
0.0194	22.9	.0000	1	officer-training
0.0194	22.9	.0000	1	oil-field
0.0194	22.9	.0000	1	oil-palms
0.0194	22.9	.0000	1	oink
0.0194	22.9	.0000	1	Okhotsk
0.0194	22.9	.0000	1	Olaf's
0.0194	22.9	.0000	1	old-age
0.0194	22.9	.0000	1	Olduvai
0.0194	22.9	.0000	1	olive-skinned
0.0194	22.9	.0000	1	Olmec
0.0194	22.9	.0000	1	once-handsome
0.0194	22.9	.0000	1	once-vast
0.0194	22.9	.0000	1	one-and-a-half-story
0.0194	22.9	.0000	1	one-and-only
0.0194	22.9	.0000	1	Opechancanough
0.0194	22.9	.0000	1	open-row

THE PRECEDING WORD TYPE OCCUPIES RANK 59400

U	SFI	D	F	Word Type
0.0194	22.9	.0000	1	operatives
0.0194	22.9	.0000	1	opihi
0.0194	22.9	.0000	1	Oppressions
0.0194	22.9	.0000	1	Oran
0.0194	22.9	.0000	1	orang-outang
0.0194	22.9	.0000	1	orange-robed
0.0194	22.9	.0000	1	Orator
0.0194	22.9	.0000	1	ordinance-making
0.0194	22.9	.0000	1	Ore
0.0194	22.9	.0000	1	Orizaba
0.0194	22.9	.0000	1	Orkneys
0.0194	22.9	.0000	1	orlon
0.0194	22.9	.0000	1	Ossetians
0.0194	22.9	.0000	1	out-bound
0.0194	22.9	.0000	1	out-produce
0.0194	22.9	.0000	1	outrace
0.0194	22.9	.0000	1	outrages
0.0194	22.9	.0000	1	outranked
0.0194	22.9	.0000	1	outsider's
0.0194	22.9	.0000	1	outswim
0.0194	22.9	.0000	1	over-grazed
0.0194	22.9	.0000	1	over-run
0.0194	22.9	.0000	1	overreached
0.0194	22.9	.0000	1	overrode
0.0194	22.9	.0000	1	overseas-tutored
0.0194	22.9	.0000	1	overstatement
0.0194	22.9	.0000	1	oxhides
0.0194	22.9	.0000	1	oy**
0.0194	22.9	.0000	1	p-47
0.0194	22.9	.0000	1	pagodalike
0.0194	22.9	.0000	1	Paine
0.0194	22.9	.0000	1	Pajarito
0.0194	22.9	.0000	1	Pakistan's
0.0194	22.9	.0000	1	Palenque
0.0194	22.9	.0000	1	paniolos
0.0194	22.9	.0000	1	Paoli
0.0194	22.9	.0000	1	Pape
0.0194	22.9	.0000	1	Paraguay's
0.0194	22.9	.0000	1	paratroopers
0.0194	22.9	.0000	1	parch
0.0194	22.9	.0000	1	pardons
0.0194	22.9	.0000	1	Pares
0.0194	22.9	.0000	1	parklike
0.0194	22.9	.0000	1	Partisan
0.0194	22.9	.0000	1	Pascua
0.0194	22.9	.0000	1	Patents
0.0194	22.9	.0000	1	Paterson's
0.0194	22.9	.0000	1	pathfinders
0.0194	22.9	.0000	1	Patras
0.0194	22.9	.0000	1	patroon
0.0194	22.9	.0000	1	patroons
0.0194	22.9	.0000	1	payed
0.0194	22.9	.0000	1	peace-through-appeasement
0.0194	22.9	.0000	1	peace-time
0.0194	22.9	.0000	1	Peaceful
0.0194	22.9	.0000	1	peacemakers
0.0194	22.9	.0000	1	peak-hatted
0.0194	22.9	.0000	1	PEANUTS
0.0194	22.9	.0000	1	Pechenegs
0.0194	22.9	.0000	1	pedologists
0.0194	22.9	.0000	1	Peloponnesus
0.0194	22.9	.0000	1	peloponnesus
0.0194	22.9	.0000	1	pen-like
0.0194	22.9	.0000	1	Pennine
0.0194	22.9	.0000	1	Pennsylvania's
0.0194	22.9	.0000	1	Pensions
0.0194	22.9	.0000	1	Peoples
0.0194	22.9	.0000	1	peoples's
0.0194	22.9	.0000	1	perdition
0.0194	22.9	.0000	1	Perfectionists
0.0194	22.9	.0000	1	performe
0.0194	22.9	.0000	1	Perisan
0.0194	22.9	.0000	1	permafrost
0.0194	22.9	.0000	1	persevering
0.0194	22.9	.0000	1	pessimism
0.0194	22.9	.0000	1	Petain's
0.0194	22.9	.0000	1	Petitioned
0.0194	22.9	.0000	1	Petitions
0.0194	22.9	.0000	1	pharaoh's
0.0194	22.9	.0000	1	Phi
0.0194	22.9	.0000	1	Philadelphia's
0.0194	22.9	.0000	1	Philosophers
0.0194	22.9	.0000	1	Philosophy
0.0194	22.9	.0000	1	Piao
0.0194	22.9	.0000	1	picture-scroll
0.0194	22.9	.0000	1	piedmont
0.0194	22.9	.0000	1	pillories
0.0194	22.9	.0000	1	Pimwe
0.0194	22.9	.0000	1	Pimwe's
0.0194	22.9	.0000	1	pin-point
0.0194	22.9	.0000	1	Pindus
0.0194	22.9	.0000	1	pinnacles
0.0194	22.9	.0000	1	Pisa's
0.0194	22.9	.0000	1	pitchblack
0.0194	22.9	.0000	1	Pitt's
0.0194	22.9	.0000	1	Pizzaro
0.0194	22.9	.0000	1	plague-ridden
0.0194	22.9	.0000	1	plaintiff's
0.0194	22.9	.0000	1	planter-scalawags
0.0194	22.9	.0000	1	Plassey

THE PRECEDING WORD TYPE OCCUPIES RANK 59500

U	SFI	D	F	Word Type
0.0194	22.9	.0000	1	plateau's
0.0194	22.9	.0000	1	play-soldier
0.0194	22.9	.0000	1	playland
0.0194	22.9	.0000	1	pleasure-seeking
0.0194	22.9	.0000	1	Plums
0.0194	22.9	.0000	1	Poe
0.0194	22.9	.0000	1	Point's
0.0194	22.9	.0000	1	poleward
0.0194	22.9	.0000	1	policing
0.0194	22.9	.0000	1	political-physical
0.0194	22.9	.0000	1	Polk's
0.0194	22.9	.0000	1	Pollard
0.0194	22.9	.0000	1	pollutes
0.0194	22.9	.0000	1	poly-
0.0194	22.9	.0000	1	polytheism
0.0194	22.9	.0000	1	pomegranates
0.0194	22.9	.0000	1	pooled
0.0194	22.9	.0000	1	popinjays
0.0194	22.9	.0000	1	Porcupines
0.0194	22.9	.0000	1	portended
0.0194	22.9	.0000	1	portolani
0.0194	22.9	.0000	1	Post-Reconstruction
0.0194	22.9	.0000	1	Postage
0.0194	22.9	.0000	1	Posterity
0.0194	22.9	.0000	1	Potosi
0.0194	22.9	.0000	1	Potsdam
0.0194	22.9	.0000	1	Pottery
0.0194	22.9	.0000	1	pouchful
0.0194	22.9	.0000	1	Poultry
0.0194	22.9	.0000	1	Powderly
0.0194	22.9	.0000	1	Poznan
0.0194	22.9	.0000	1	practicability
0.0194	22.9	.0000	1	Prado's
0.0194	22.9	.0000	1	Pre-Classic
0.0194	22.9	.0000	1	precipitously
0.0194	22.9	.0000	1	preconquest
0.0194	22.9	.0000	1	premonition
0.0194	22.9	.0000	1	prepayment
0.0194	22.9	.0000	1	preservers
0.0194	22.9	.0000	1	presidios
0.0194	22.9	.0000	1	PRI
0.0194	22.9	.0000	1	Pribilof
0.0194	22.9	.0000	1	priest-architect
0.0194	22.9	.0000	1	Privilege
0.0194	22.9	.0000	1	pro-Communist
0.0194	22.9	.0000	1	pro-Israel
0.0194	22.9	.0000	1	pro-and-con
0.0194	22.9	.0000	1	pro-business
0.0194	22.9	.0000	1	pro-ratification
0.0194	22.9	.0000	1	profit-making
0.0194	22.9	.0000	1	Prohibition
0.0194	22.9	.0000	1	Proletarian
0.0194	22.9	.0000	1	Pronouncing
0.0194	22.9	.0000	1	prospers
0.0194	22.9	.0000	1	prostrated
0.0194	22.9	.0000	1	protectorates
0.0194	22.9	.0000	1	protrude
0.0194	22.9	.0000	1	Provincetown
0.0194	22.9	.0000	1	provincial-minded
0.0194	22.9	.0000	1	Provisional
0.0194	22.9	.0000	1	Prudhoe
0.0194	22.9	.0000	1	Pub
0.0194	22.9	.0000	1	public-spirited
0.0194	22.9	.0000	1	puddlers
0.0194	22.9	.0000	1	PuertoRico
0.0194	22.9	.0000	1	pump's
0.0194	22.9	.0000	1	Pupil
0.0194	22.9	.0000	1	pushcarts
0.0194	22.9	.0000	1	pyramided
0.0194	22.9	.0000	1	Pyramids
0.0194	22.9	.0000	1	pyrites
0.0194	22.9	.0000	1	Qatar
0.0194	22.9	.0000	1	Quadruple
0.0194	22.9	.0000	1	quebracho
0.0194	22.9	.0000	1	Quetzalcoatl
0.0194	22.9	.0000	1	Quito's
0.0194	22.9	.0000	1	racially
0.0194	22.9	.0000	1	radio-telephone
0.0194	22.9	.0000	1	rail-river-rail
0.0194	22.9	.0000	1	rainbearing
0.0194	22.9	.0000	1	rainforests
0.0194	22.9	.0000	1	raisers
0.0194	22.9	.0000	1	rajahs
0.0194	22.9	.0000	1	Ramsey
0.0194	22.9	.0000	1	ranchos
0.0194	22.9	.0000	1	Ransom
0.0194	22.9	.0000	1	ranting
0.0194	22.9	.0000	1	RapidCity
0.0194	22.9	.0000	1	rashness
0.0194	22.9	.0000	1	Raul
0.0194	22.9	.0000	1	raw-fur
0.0194	22.9	.0000	1	re-enslaved
0.0194	22.9	.0000	1	re-equipped
0.0194	22.9	.0000	1	re-examined
0.0194	22.9	.0000	1	readjustment
0.0194	22.9	.0000	1	realignment
0.0194	22.9	.0000	1	reasserting
0.0194	22.9	.0000	1	Rebels
0.0194	22.9	.0000	1	recollecting
0.0194	22.9	.0000	1	reconversion

THE PRECEDING WORD TYPE OCCUPIES RANK 59600

U	SFI	D	F	Word Type
0.0194	22.9	.0000	1	reconvert
0.0194	22.9	.0000	1	reconverted
0.0194	22.9	.0000	1	record-keeping
0.0194	22.9	.0000	1	Recorder's
0.0194	22.9	.0000	1	rectitude
0.0194	22.9	.0000	1	RedCross
0.0194	22.9	.0000	1	red-sleeved
0.0194	22.9	.0000	1	redcoat
0.0194	22.9	.0000	1	redrawn
0.0194	22.9	.0000	1	Redress
0.0194	22.9	.0000	1	reelected
0.0194	22.9	.0000	1	refaced
0.0194	22.9	.0000	1	refines
0.0194	22.9	.0000	1	refrigerating
0.0194	22.9	.0000	1	refutations
0.0194	22.9	.0000	1	Regions
0.0194	22.9	.0000	1	rehire
0.0194	22.9	.0000	1	reiterate
0.0194	22.9	.0000	1	relaying
0.0194	22.9	.0000	1	remover
0.0194	22.9	.0000	1	renounce
0.0194	22.9	.0000	1	reorganize
0.0194	22.9	.0000	1	Repair
0.0194	22.9	.0000	1	repaying
0.0194	22.9	.0000	1	reprehensible
0.0194	22.9	.0000	1	REPUBLIC
0.0194	22.9	.0000	1	republic's
0.0194	22.9	.0000	1	repudiating
0.0194	22.9	.0000	1	resell
0.0194	22.9	.0000	1	resettled
0.0194	22.9	.0000	1	restaurateur
0.0194	22.9	.0000	1	retailers
0.0194	22.9	.0000	1	retards
0.0194	22.9	.0000	1	retrain
0.0194	22.9	.0000	1	retribution
0.0194	22.9	.0000	1	revitalizing
0.0194	22.9	.0000	1	Rhinebeck
0.0194	22.9	.0000	1	rhinoceroses
0.0194	22.9	.0000	1	Rhodesias
0.0194	22.9	.0000	1	Richards's
0.0194	22.9	.0000	1	Rif
0.0194	22.9	.0000	1	Righteous
0.0194	22.9	.0000	1	rigidities
0.0194	22.9	.0000	1	RIO
0.0194	22.9	.0000	1	rioters
0.0194	22.9	.0000	1	risings
0.0194	22.9	.0000	1	roams
0.0194	22.9	.0000	1	Robbery
0.0194	22.9	.0000	1	rock-like
0.0194	22.9	.0000	1	rockcovered
0.0194	22.9	.0000	1	Rodriquez
0.0194	22.9	.0000	1	Rolf
0.0194	22.9	.0000	1	Romulo
0.0194	22.9	.0000	1	rosewood
0.0194	22.9	.0000	1	Rovere
0.0194	22.9	.0000	1	royalists
0.0194	22.9	.0000	1	rum-molasses-slave
0.0194	22.9	.0000	1	Russian-controlled
0.0194	22.9	.0000	1	rust-caked
0.0194	22.9	.0000	1	rutabagas
0.0194	22.9	.0000	1	ruthlessness
0.0194	22.9	.0000	1	Sabah
0.0194	22.9	.0000	1	sabotaged
0.0194	22.9	.0000	1	saboteurs
0.0194	22.9	.0000	1	sadists
0.0194	22.9	.0000	1	safety-glass
0.0194	22.9	.0000	1	Sagres
0.0194	22.9	.0000	1	saint's
0.0194	22.9	.0000	1	Sakhalin
0.0194	22.9	.0000	1	saldu's
0.0194	22.9	.0000	1	salient
0.0194	22.9	.0000	1	salmon-canning
0.0194	22.9	.0000	1	Salonica
0.0194	22.9	.0000	1	salt-mining
0.0194	22.9	.0000	1	saltwater
0.0194	22.9	.0000	1	samurai
0.0194	22.9	.0000	1	SanBernardino
0.0194	22.9	.0000	1	SanBuenaventura
0.0194	22.9	.0000	1	SanJoaquin
0.0194	22.9	.0000	1	SanPedro's
0.0194	22.9	.0000	1	Sanctam
0.0194	22.9	.0000	1	sandbags
0.0194	22.9	.0000	1	SANDWICHES
0.0194	22.9	.0000	1	Sandys
0.0194	22.9	.0000	1	Sanitary
0.0194	22.9	.0000	1	Sansei
0.0194	22.9	.0000	1	SantaAna
0.0194	22.9	.0000	1	Santiago's
0.0194	22.9	.0000	1	sapping
0.0194	22.9	.0000	1	Sarai
0.0194	22.9	.0000	1	sarapes
0.0194	22.9	.0000	1	Sarawak
0.0194	22.9	.0000	1	Sarnoffs
0.0194	22.9	.0000	1	Sava
0.0194	22.9	.0000	1	Savages
0.0194	22.9	.0000	1	scaffold
0.0194	22.9	.0000	1	scandal
0.0194	22.9	.0000	1	scapegoats
0.0194	22.9	.0000	1	scepters
0.0194	22.9	.0000	1	school-board

THE PRECEDING WORD TYPE OCCUPIES RANK 59700

U	SFI	D	F	Word Type
0.0194	22.9	.0000	1	schoolboy's
0.0194	22.9	.0000	1	Scotsmen
0.0194	22.9	.0000	1	Scottsboro
0.0194	22.9	.0000	1	scutage
0.0194	22.9	.0000	1	sea-borne
0.0194	22.9	.0000	1	SEATO
0.0194	22.9	.0000	1	Securities
0.0194	22.9	.0000	1	seed-gathering
0.0194	22.9	.0000	1	seedbeds
0.0194	22.9	.0000	1	segregationist
0.0194	22.9	.0000	1	self-described
0.0194	22.9	.0000	1	self-hypnosis
0.0194	22.9	.0000	1	self-reliant
0.0194	22.9	.0000	1	self-seekers
0.0194	22.9	.0000	1	Selkirk's
0.0194	22.9	.0000	1	semi-arid
0.0194	22.9	.0000	1	Sendai
0.0194	22.9	.0000	1	Sensoji
0.0194	22.9	.0000	1	Separation
0.0194	22.9	.0000	1	Separatists
0.0194	22.9	.0000	1	Sepulchre
0.0194	22.9	.0000	1	Seraglio
0.0194	22.9	.0000	1	Serbia's
0.0194	22.9	.0000	1	Serenity
0.0194	22.9	.0000	1	serfdom
0.0194	22.9	.0000	1	serials
0.0194	22.9	.0000	1	Serpico
0.0194	22.9	.0000	1	Serra's
0.0194	22.9	.0000	1	servant's
0.0194	22.9	.0000	1	Serviceable
0.0194	22.9	.0000	1	Sessue
0.0194	22.9	.0000	1	seven-year
0.0194	22.9	.0000	1	Seventh-Day
0.0194	22.9	.0000	1	severally
0.0194	22.9	.0000	1	severities
0.0194	22.9	.0000	1	Sevres
0.0194	22.9	.0000	1	Sewyne
0.0194	22.9	.0000	1	shadings
0.0194	22.9	.0000	1	shallow-rooted
0.0194	22.9	.0000	1	shallowness
0.0194	22.9	.0000	1	shamma
0.0194	22.9	.0000	1	Shankilla
0.0194	22.9	.0000	1	Shao-ch'i
0.0194	22.9	.0000	1	share-croppers
0.0194	22.9	.0000	1	shareowner
0.0194	22.9	.0000	1	sharp-shooting
0.0194	22.9	.0000	1	shatter-proof
0.0194	22.9	.0000	1	shavers
0.0194	22.9	.0000	1	sheepshearing
0.0194	22.9	.0000	1	sheet-iron
0.0194	22.9	.0000	1	Shikoku
0.0194	22.9	.0000	1	Shima
0.0194	22.9	.0000	1	ship-building
0.0194	22.9	.0000	1	shipbuilder
0.0194	22.9	.0000	1	shipwrights
0.0194	22.9	.0000	1	shopkeeper's
0.0194	22.9	.0000	1	Shorthorn
0.0194	22.9	.0000	1	Shorthorns
0.0194	22.9	.0000	1	showrooms
0.0194	22.9	.0000	1	Shreveport's
0.0194	22.9	.0000	1	shut-off
0.0194	22.9	.0000	1	Siberia's
0.0194	22.9	.0000	1	Sick
0.0194	22.9	.0000	1	sicken
0.0194	22.9	.0000	1	Silk
0.0194	22.9	.0000	1	silk-manufacturing
0.0194	22.9	.0000	1	silt-laden
0.0194	22.9	.0000	1	Simcoe
0.0194	22.9	.0000	1	Simcoe's
0.0194	22.9	.0000	1	simony
0.0194	22.9	.0000	1	Singleton
0.0194	22.9	.0000	1	Sink
0.0194	22.9	.0000	1	Sino-Japanese
0.0194	22.9	.0000	1	six-lane
0.0194	22.9	.0000	1	Six-mile

U	SFI	D	F	Word Type
0.0194	22.9	.0000	1	sixty-one-year
0.0194	22.9	.0000	1	Skagway
0.0194	22.9	.0000	1	skeered
0.0194	22.9	.0000	1	Skokie
0.0194	22.9	.0000	1	slanderers
0.0194	22.9	.0000	1	slap-slapping
0.0194	22.9	.0000	1	slaved
0.0194	22.9	.0000	1	slaveholders
0.0194	22.9	.0000	1	slaveowners
0.0194	22.9	.0000	1	slavery's
0.0194	22.9	.0000	1	slowest-moving
0.0194	22.9	.0000	1	Smaland
0.0194	22.9	.0000	1	small-arms
0.0194	22.9	.0000	1	small-fisted
0.0194	22.9	.0000	1	smoggy
0.0194	22.9	.0000	1	smokehole
0.0194	22.9	.0000	1	smokeholes
0.0194	22.9	.0000	1	Smokes
0.0194	22.9	.0000	1	Smoking
0.0194	22.9	.0000	1	Smyrna
0.0194	22.9	.0000	1	snipers'
0.0194	22.9	.0000	1	Snow-Hut
0.0194	22.9	.0000	1	snow-bound
0.0194	22.9	.0000	1	snowclad
0.0194	22.9	.0000	1	snowcovered
THE PRECEDING WORD TYPE OCCUPIES RANK 59800				
0.0194	22.9	.0000	1	snowless
0.0194	22.9	.0000	1	socialistic
0.0194	22.9	.0000	1	sodbusters
0.0194	22.9	.0000	1	soe
0.0194	22.9	.0000	1	soft-coal
0.0194	22.9	.0000	1	soft-goods
0.0194	22.9	.0000	1	soil-and-climate
0.0194	22.9	.0000	1	soil-forming
0.0194	22.9	.0000	1	Solis
0.0194	22.9	.0000	1	Somalia
0.0194	22.9	.0000	1	song-writer's
0.0194	22.9	.0000	1	Sonoma
0.0194	22.9	.0000	1	Sorrow
0.0194	22.9	.0000	1	sotweed
0.0194	22.9	.0000	1	soundness
0.0194	22.9	.0000	1	SouthCarolinian
0.0194	22.9	.0000	1	spaceflights
0.0194	22.9	.0000	1	Spalding's
0.0194	22.9	.0000	1	Spanish-Indian
0.0194	22.9	.0000	1	spearthrowers
0.0194	22.9	.0000	1	specialities
0.0194	22.9	.0000	1	specie
0.0194	22.9	.0000	1	specters
0.0194	22.9	.0000	1	spender
0.0194	22.9	.0000	1	Spending
0.0194	22.9	.0000	1	sponge-fishing
0.0194	22.9	.0000	1	sportier
0.0194	22.9	.0000	1	sports-minded
0.0194	22.9	.0000	1	spruce-tree
0.0194	22.9	.0000	1	squab
0.0194	22.9	.0000	1	squabbling
0.0194	22.9	.0000	1	squats
0.0194	22.9	.0000	1	Ssuh-chwan
0.0194	22.9	.0000	1	StMary
0.0194	22.9	.0000	1	St-Etienne
0.0194	22.9	.0000	1	stagnation
0.0194	22.9	.0000	1	stand-ins
0.0194	22.9	.0000	1	standard-gauge
0.0194	22.9	.0000	1	Stanleys
0.0194	22.9	.0000	1	state-run
0.0194	22.9	.0000	1	Statute
0.0194	22.9	.0000	1	steel-frame
0.0194	22.9	.0000	1	Stennis
0.0194	22.9	.0000	1	stepped-up
0.0194	22.9	.0000	1	steppingstone
0.0194	22.9	.0000	1	steppingstones
0.0194	22.9	.0000	1	stern-faced
0.0194	22.9	.0000	1	stern-minded
0.0194	22.9	.0000	1	stigmatized
0.0194	22.9	.0000	1	still-dark
0.0194	22.9	.0000	1	stipulation
0.0194	22.9	.0000	1	stockier
0.0194	22.9	.0000	1	stone-age
0.0194	22.9	.0000	1	Stony
0.0194	22.9	.0000	1	strafing
0.0194	22.9	.0000	1	straggle
0.0194	22.9	.0000	1	strangely-carved
0.0194	22.9	.0000	1	strangest-looking
0.0194	22.9	.0000	1	Stratford
0.0194	22.9	.0000	1	streamliners
0.0194	22.9	.0000	1	Strymon
0.0194	22.9	.0000	1	Su
0.0194	22.9	.0000	1	sub-Saharan
0.0194	22.9	.0000	1	subhumid
0.0194	22.9	.0000	1	Submission
0.0194	22.9	.0000	1	subregion
0.0194	22.9	.0000	1	subregions
0.0194	22.9	.0000	1	Subversive
0.0194	22.9	.0000	1	subversives
0.0194	22.9	.0000	1	Sucre
0.0194	22.9	.0000	1	Sudetes
0.0194	22.9	.0000	1	sues
0.0194	22.9	.0000	1	sufferable
0.0194	22.9	.0000	1	sufferage
0.0194	22.9	.0000	1	suffrages
0.0194	22.9	.0000	1	sugar-mill
0.0194	22.9	.0000	1	sugar-plantation
0.0194	22.9	.0000	1	sugar-producing
0.0194	22.9	.0000	1	Sulo
0.0194	22.9	.0000	1	sultans
0.0194	22.9	.0000	1	sun-bathing
0.0194	22.9	.0000	1	Sunda
0.0194	22.9	.0000	1	Sundanese
0.0194	22.9	.0000	1	sunnier
0.0194	22.9	.0000	1	surfboarders
0.0194	22.9	.0000	1	surgeons'
0.0194	22.9	.0000	1	surmount
0.0194	22.9	.0000	1	surpasses
0.0194	22.9	.0000	1	Susitna
0.0194	22.9	.0000	1	suspecting
0.0194	22.9	.0000	1	Suzuki's
0.0194	22.9	.0000	1	Sverdlovsk
0.0194	22.9	.0000	1	SW
0.0194	22.9	.0000	1	Swansea
0.0194	22.9	.0000	1	Swaziland
0.0194	22.9	.0000	1	swept-back
0.0194	22.9	.0000	1	Swordfish
0.0194	22.9	.0000	1	sympathizer
0.0194	22.9	.0000	1	SYSTEM
0.0194	22.9	.0000	1	Szechwan
THE PRECEDING WORD TYPE OCCUPIES RANK 59900				
0.0194	22.9	.0000	1	Tabernacle
0.0194	22.9	.0000	1	tabled
0.0194	22.9	.0000	1	Tabriz
0.0194	22.9	.0000	1	tactless
0.0194	22.9	.0000	1	Tagus
0.0194	22.9	.0000	1	tai
0.0194	22.9	.0000	1	Taka
0.0194	22.9	.0000	1	Taking
0.0194	22.9	.0000	1	Tammany
0.0194	22.9	.0000	1	Tana
0.0194	22.9	.0000	1	tanners
0.0194	22.9	.0000	1	Taoists
0.0194	22.9	.0000	1	Taos
0.0194	22.9	.0000	1	TarponSprings
0.0194	22.9	.0000	1	tartan-kilted
0.0194	22.9	.0000	1	Tatra
0.0194	22.9	.0000	1	Tatras
0.0194	22.9	.0000	1	Taxco's
0.0194	22.9	.0000	1	teaming
0.0194	22.9	.0000	1	Tenneseee-NorthCarolina
0.0194	22.9	.0000	1	Teotihuacano
0.0194	22.9	.0000	1	Terence
0.0194	22.9	.0000	1	terracing
0.0194	22.9	.0000	1	test-drilling
0.0194	22.9	.0000	1	Texian
0.0194	22.9	.0000	1	thatch-roof
0.0194	22.9	.0000	1	Theiler
0.0194	22.9	.0000	1	Their
0.0194	22.9	.0000	1	theoreticians
0.0194	22.9	.0000	1	theorizing
0.0194	22.9	.0000	1	Theresa's
0.0194	22.9	.0000	1	Thierry
0.0194	22.9	.0000	1	thimbleberry
0.0194	22.9	.0000	1	third-largest
0.0194	22.9	.0000	1	third-ranking
0.0194	22.9	.0000	1	Thirteenth
0.0194	22.9	.0000	1	three-and
0.0194	22.9	.0000	1	thresh
0.0194	22.9	.0000	1	throwers
0.0194	22.9	.0000	1	Thye
0.0194	22.9	.0000	1	Tiahuanaco
0.0194	22.9	.0000	1	tickles
0.0194	22.9	.0000	1	Tidelands
0.0194	22.9	.0000	1	tightly-woven
0.0194	22.9	.0000	1	Tigrais
0.0194	22.9	.0000	1	tip-off
0.0194	22.9	.0000	1	tirade
0.0194	22.9	.0000	1	tirades
0.0194	22.9	.0000	1	Tiran
0.0194	22.9	.0000	1	Tito's
0.0194	22.9	.0000	1	tobacco-growing
0.0194	22.9	.0000	1	tobacco-producing
0.0194	22.9	.0000	1	Tonalpohualli
0.0194	22.9	.0000	1	too-complicated
0.0194	22.9	.0000	1	toolmaker
0.0194	22.9	.0000	1	top-quality
0.0194	22.9	.0000	1	top-secret
0.0194	22.9	.0000	1	topclass
0.0194	22.9	.0000	1	torpid
0.0194	22.9	.0000	1	tou-fu
0.0194	22.9	.0000	1	Toussaint
0.0194	22.9	.0000	1	Toutant
0.0194	22.9	.0000	1	traders'
0.0194	22.9	.0000	1	tradition-shattering
0.0194	22.9	.0000	1	TRAIL
0.0194	22.9	.0000	1	Tranquility
0.0194	22.9	.0000	1	Trans-World
0.0194	22.9	.0000	1	Transbay
0.0194	22.9	.0000	1	trapline
0.0194	22.9	.0000	1	trawl
0.0194	22.9	.0000	1	tree-covered
0.0194	22.9	.0000	1	tree-filled
0.0194	22.9	.0000	1	tree-shaded
0.0194	22.9	.0000	1	trouble-shooter
0.0194	22.9	.0000	1	Trucial
0.0194	22.9	.0000	1	truckers
0.0194	22.9	.0000	1	truism
0.0194	22.9	.0000	1	Truro
0.0194	22.9	.0000	1	Trustee
0.0194	22.9	.0000	1	tsar
0.0194	22.9	.0000	1	Tsing
0.0194	22.9	.0000	1	tukel
0.0194	22.9	.0000	1	Turbo
0.0194	22.9	.0000	1	turnest
0.0194	22.9	.0000	1	Tushi's
0.0194	22.9	.0000	1	Twenties
0.0194	22.9	.0000	1	Twenty-first
0.0194	22.9	.0000	1	two-house
0.0194	22.9	.0000	1	two-master
0.0194	22.9	.0000	1	two-million
0.0194	22.9	.0000	1	two-price
0.0194	22.9	.0000	1	tycoon
0.0194	22.9	.0000	1	Tydings
0.0194	22.9	.0000	1	Tydings-McDuffe
0.0194	22.9	.0000	1	typographers
0.0194	22.9	.0000	1	Tze
0.0194	22.9	.0000	1	Ucayali
0.0194	22.9	.0000	1	Udine
0.0194	22.9	.0000	1	Ufa
0.0194	22.9	.0000	1	Ukraine's
THE PRECEDING WORD TYPE OCCUPIES RANK 60000				
0.0194	22.9	.0000	1	Umiki
0.0194	22.9	.0000	1	UMW
0.0194	22.9	.0000	1	Unam
0.0194	22.9	.0000	1	unbounded
0.0194	22.9	.0000	1	uncertainties
0.0194	22.9	.0000	1	under-developed
0.0194	22.9	.0000	1	undergrond
0.0194	22.9	.0000	1	underscores
0.0194	22.9	.0000	1	Undersecretary-Generals
0.0194	22.9	.0000	1	undersigned
0.0194	22.9	.0000	1	underwritten
0.0194	22.9	.0000	1	undreamed-of-products
0.0194	22.9	.0000	1	undulating
0.0194	22.9	.0000	1	unexpanding
0.0194	22.9	.0000	1	unfenced
0.0194	22.9	.0000	1	unfortified
0.0194	22.9	.0000	1	unfreezes
0.0194	22.9	.0000	1	unglaciated
0.0194	22.9	.0000	1	Unidos
0.0194	22.9	.0000	1	Unification
0.0194	22.9	.0000	1	Unitarians
0.0194	22.9	.0000	1	UNITEDSTATES
0.0194	22.9	.0000	1	Unknowns
0.0194	22.9	.0000	1	unlearn
0.0194	22.9	.0000	1	unmake
0.0194	22.9	.0000	1	unorthodox
0.0194	22.9	.0000	1	unplundered
0.0194	22.9	.0000	1	unquestioning
0.0194	22.9	.0000	1	unrivaled
0.0194	22.9	.0000	1	untested
0.0194	22.9	.0000	1	untouchability
0.0194	22.9	.0000	1	unwarrantable
0.0194	22.9	.0000	1	unwatered
0.0194	22.9	.0000	1	urbane
0.0194	22.9	.0000	1	utopia
0.0194	22.9	.0000	1	Utopians
0.0194	22.9	.0000	1	V-Bar
0.0194	22.9	.0000	1	V-J
0.0194	22.9	.0000	1	Vaal
0.0194	22.9	.0000	1	vacationer
0.0194	22.9	.0000	1	VahRiver
0.0194	22.9	.0000	1	vainglory
0.0194	22.9	.0000	1	Valletta
0.0194	22.9	.0000	1	Valor
0.0194	22.9	.0000	1	Valparaiso
0.0194	22.9	.0000	1	valuation
0.0194	22.9	.0000	1	Vaner
0.0194	22.9	.0000	1	Vatter
0.0194	22.9	.0000	1	vebetables
0.0194	22.9	.0000	1	velvet-like
0.0194	22.9	.0000	1	veneers
0.0194	22.9	.0000	1	Venezuela's
0.0194	22.9	.0000	1	Venta
0.0194	22.9	.0000	1	Vere's
0.0194	22.9	.0000	1	Vespucci
0.0194	22.9	.0000	1	Veterans
0.0194	22.9	.0000	1	Vice-President-elect
0.0194	22.9	.0000	1	viceroyalty
0.0194	22.9	.0000	1	Viceroyalty
0.0194	22.9	.0000	1	viceroys
0.0194	22.9	.0000	1	Vigil
0.0194	22.9	.0000	1	Viipuri
0.0194	22.9	.0000	1	Vineland
0.0194	22.9	.0000	1	violators
0.0194	22.9	.0000	1	Virginia-NorthCarolina
0.0194	22.9	.0000	1	Visigoth
0.0194	22.9	.0000	1	vitalizing
0.0194	22.9	.0000	1	Viviani
0.0194	22.9	.0000	1	Vizcaino
0.0194	22.9	.0000	1	VJ
0.0194	22.9	.0000	1	Volga's
0.0194	22.9	.0000	1	Volgograd
0.0194	22.9	.0000	1	vonBismarck
0.0194	22.9	.0000	1	vonHindenburg
0.0194	22.9	.0000	1	Vosges
0.0194	22.9	.0000	1	voter's
0.0194	22.9	.0000	1	Voting
0.0194	22.9	.0000	1	Waco
0.0194	22.9	.0000	1	wadis
0.0194	22.9	.0000	1	wage-earning
0.0194	22.9	.0000	1	WAGES
0.0194	22.9	.0000	1	wagon-wheel
0.0194	22.9	.0000	1	Waianae
0.0194	22.9	.0000	1	Wailing
0.0194	22.9	.0000	1	Waldorf-Astoria
0.0194	22.9	.0000	1	walled-in
0.0194	22.9	.0000	1	Wanasi
0.0194	22.9	.0000	1	war-making
0.0194	22.9	.0000	1	warlord's
0.0194	22.9	.0000	1	water-power
0.0194	22.9	.0000	1	waterpaints
0.0194	22.9	.0000	1	waterworn
0.0194	22.9	.0000	1	wave-swept
0.0194	22.9	.0000	1	Wayman
0.0194	22.9	.0000	1	weatern
0.0194	22.9	.0000	1	weatherboarding
0.0194	22.9	.0000	1	web-like
0.0194	22.9	.0000	1	weight-producing
0.0194	22.9	.0000	1	well-enough
0.0194	22.9	.0000	1	well-fertilized
THE PRECEDING WORD TYPE OCCUPIES RANK 60100				
0.0194	22.9	.0000	1	well-populated
0.0194	22.9	.0000	1	well-situated
0.0194	22.9	.0000	1	wellkept
0.0194	22.9	.0000	1	WestPoint
0.0194	22.9	.0000	1	Western-equipped
0.0194	22.9	.0000	1	western-style
0.0194	22.9	.0000	1	wet-dry
0.0194	22.9	.0000	1	whaleboats
0.0194	22.9	.0000	1	wheat-exporting
0.0194	22.9	.0000	1	wheat-flour
0.0194	22.9	.0000	1	wheat-producing
0.0194	22.9	.0000	1	wheat-raising
0.0194	22.9	.0000	1	wheatland
0.0194	22.9	.0000	1	whipt
0.0194	22.9	.0000	1	white-owned
0.0194	22.9	.0000	1	Whitecloud
0.0194	22.9	.0000	1	whiteface
0.0194	22.9	.0000	1	whitefish
0.0194	22.9	.0000	1	Whitham
0.0194	22.9	.0000	1	wide-horned
0.0194	22.9	.0000	1	widespreading
0.0194	22.9	.0000	1	wildernesses
0.0194	22.9	.0000	1	Wilmot
0.0194	22.9	.0000	1	windbreakers
0.0194	22.9	.0000	1	wispy-haired
0.0194	22.9	.0000	1	WM
0.0194	22.9	.0000	1	womeras
0.0194	22.9	.0000	1	wonderlands
0.0194	22.9	.0000	1	woodblock
0.0194	22.9	.0000	1	wooed
0.0194	22.9	.0000	1	wool-trader
0.0194	22.9	.0000	1	working-class
0.0194	22.9	.0000	1	Workman's
0.0194	22.9	.0000	1	world-renowned
0.0194	22.9	.0000	1	wowi
0.0194	22.9	.0000	1	Wrangell
0.0194	22.9	.0000	1	wrangle
0.0194	22.9	.0000	1	wrathy
0.0194	22.9	.0000	1	wrights
0.0194	22.9	.0000	1	wrongness
0.0194	22.9	.0000	1	Wythe
0.0194	22.9	.0000	1	Yalta
0.0194	22.9	.0000	1	Yamaguchi
0.0194	22.9	.0000	1	Yamassee
0.0194	22.9	.0000	1	Yarmuk
0.0194	22.9	.0000	1	yellowtail
0.0194	22.9	.0000	1	Yerby
0.0194	22.9	.0000	1	Yoruba
0.0194	22.9	.0000	1	Yost's
0.0194	22.9	.0000	1	Youngmobile
0.0194	22.9	.0000	1	Ypsilanti
0.0194	22.9	.0000	1	Ypsilanti's
0.0194	22.9	.0000	1	Yu
0.0194	22.9	.0000	1	Yuma
0.0194	22.9	.0000	1	Zambesi
0.0194	22.9	.0000	1	zamindars
0.0194	22.9	.0000	1	Zapotecs
0.0194	22.9	.0000	1	Zimmermann
0.0194	22.9	.0000	1	Zionism
0.0194	22.9	.0000	1	Zora
0.0194	22.9	.0000	1	040
0.0194	22.9	.0000	1	058
0.0194	22.9	.0000	1	069
0.0194	22.9	.0000	1	1/600
0.0194	22.9	.0000	1	100-mile
0.0194	22.9	.0000	1	102-story
0.0194	22.9	.0000	1	1036
0.0194	22.9	.0000	1	106-
0.0194	22.9	.0000	1	106-ton
0.0194	22.9	.0000	1	108-109
0.0194	22.9	.0000	1	1096
0.0194	22.9	.0000	1	1113
0.0194	22.9	.0000	1	1125
0.0194	22.9	.0000	1	118-119
0.0194	22.9	.0000	1	1180
0.0194	22.9	.0000	1	12-year
0.0194	22.9	.0000	1	1206
0.0194	22.9	.0000	1	1224
0.0194	22.9	.0000	1	1227
0.0194	22.9	.0000	1	1240
0.0194	22.9	.0000	1	1271
0.0194	22.9	.0000	1	1275
0.0194	22.9	.0000	1	129-131
0.0194	22.9	.0000	1	1294
0.0194	22.9	.0000	1	1295
0.0194	22.9	.0000	1	13th-century
0.0194	22.9	.0000	1	130-134
0.0194	22.9	.0000	1	1309
0.0194	22.9	.0000	1	131-133
0.0194	22.9	.0000	1	1350
0.0194	22.9	.0000	1	1377
0.0194	22.9	.0000	1	14-hour
0.0194	22.9	.0000	1	14-to-17-year-old
0.0194	22.9	.0000	1	142-143
0.0194	22.9	.0000	1	1442
0.0194	22.9	.0000	1	1498
0.0194	22.9	.0000	1	1502
0.0194	22.9	.0000	1	1562
0.0194	22.9	.0000	1	16-year
0.0194	22.9	.0000	1	160-164
THE PRECEDING WORD TYPE OCCUPIES RANK 60200				
0.0194	22.9	.0000	1	1613
0.0194	22.9	.0000	1	1635
0.0194	22.9	.0000	1	1636
0.0194	22.9	.0000	1	1647
0.0194	22.9	.0000	1	1681
0.0194	22.9	.0000	1	1683
0.0194	22.9	.0000	1	17-year
0.0194	22.9	.0000	1	1700s
0.0194	22.9	.0000	1	1790's
0.0194	22.9	.0000	1	1830-1848
0.0194	22.9	.0000	1	184-185
0.0194	22.9	.0000	1	1850-1871
0.0194	22.9	.0000	1	1860-1910
0.0194	22.9	.0000	1	1870s
0.0194	22.9	.0000	1	1909-13
0.0194	22.9	.0000	1	1912-1913
0.0194	22.9	.0000	1	1917-18
0.0194	22.9	.0000	1	1939-45
0.0194	22.9	.0000	1	1958-59
0.0194	22.9	.0000	1	1959-1965
0.0194	22.9	.0000	1	1980s
0.0194	22.9	.0000	1	20's
0.0194	22.9	.0000	1	200-mile-wide
0.0194	22.9	.0000	1	200th
0.0194	22.9	.0000	1	230-foot
0.0194	22.9	.0000	1	2500-1500
0.0194	22.9	.0000	1	260-day
0.0194	22.9	.0000	1	262-264
0.0194	22.9	.0000	1	262-267
0.0194	22.9	.0000	1	266
0.0194	22.9	.0000	1	266-267
0.0194	22.9	.0000	1	274-275
0.0194	22.9	.0000	1	284-285
0.0194	22.9	.0000	1	292
0.0194	22.9	.0000	1	292-293
0.0194	22.9	.0000	1	30-day
0.0194	22.9	.0000	1	30-hour
0.0194	22.9	.0000	1	30-million-dollar

U	SFI	D	F	Word Type
0.0194	22.9	.0000	1	30-ton
0.0194	22.9	.0000	1	30-40
0.0194	22.9	.0000	1	300's
0.0194	22.9	.0000	1	304-305
0.0194	22.9	.0000	1	318-319
0.0194	22.9	.0000	1	320-321
0.0194	22.9	.0000	1	324-330
0.0194	22.9	.0000	1	332-333
0.0194	22.9	.0000	1	354
0.0194	22.9	.0000	1	36-year-old
0.0194	22.9	.0000	1	362-
0.0194	22.9	.0000	1	362-363
0.0194	22.9	.0000	1	3651/4
0.0194	22.9	.0000	1	370-371
0.0194	22.9	.0000	1	370-373
0.0194	22.9	.0000	1	374-375
0.0194	22.9	.0000	1	380-381
0.0194	22.9	.0000	1	386-387
0.0194	22.9	.0000	1	396-398
0.0194	22.9	.0000	1	40-acre
0.0194	22.9	.0000	1	400-year-old
0.0194	22.9	.0000	1	404
0.0194	22.9	.0000	1	411-413
0.0194	22.9	.0000	1	426-27
0.0194	22.9	.0000	1	441
0.0194	22.9	.0000	1	48-49
0.0194	22.9	.0000	1	5-4-3-2-1-0
0.0194	22.9	.0000	1	500-year-old
0.0194	22.9	.0000	1	5800
0.0194	22.9	.0000	1	59th
0.0194	22.9	.0000	1	6-member
0.0194	22.9	.0000	1	6-year
0.0194	22.9	.0000	1	6000-acre
0.0194	22.9	.0000	1	626
0.0194	22.9	.0000	1	631
0.0194	22.9	.0000	1	711
0.0194	22.9	.0000	1	718
0.0194	22.9	.0000	1	725
0.0194	22.9	.0000	1	731
0.0194	22.9	.0000	1	74-81
0.0194	22.9	.0000	1	761st
0.0194	22.9	.0000	1	784
0.0194	22.9	.0000	1	789-807
0.0194	22.9	.0000	1	800's
0.0194	22.9	.0000	1	8500-foot
0.0194	22.9	.0000	1	859
0.0194	22.9	.0000	1	887
0.0194	22.9	.0000	1	901
0.0194	22.9	.0000	1	917
0.0194	22.9	.0000	1	9280
0.0194	22.9	.0000	1	938
0.0194	22.9	.0000	1	96-97
0.0194	22.9	.0000	1	969th
0.0193	22.9	.0000	6	directionally
0.0193	22.9	.0000	6	laundering
0.0178	22.5	.0000	8	salutations
0.0177	22.5	.0000	7	Brinell
0.0177	22.5	.0000	7	groover
0.0177	22.5	.0000	7	layouts
0.0177	22.5	.0000	7	sectioning
0.0177	22.5	.0000	7	squareness
0.0177	22.5	.0000	7	tenon
THE PRECEDING WORD TYPE OCCUPIES RANK 60300				
0.0177	22.5	.0000	7	0-2
0.0166	22.2	.0000	9	cut-paper
0.0166	22.2	.0000	9	rubbings
0.0162	22.1	.0000	2	-ery
0.0162	22.1	.0000	2	/e-s/**
0.0162	22.1	.0000	2	/i/**
0.0162	22.1	.0000	2	/id/
0.0162	22.1	.0000	2	/ks/
0.0162	22.1	.0000	2	/or/
0.0162	22.1	.0000	2	/ut/
0.0162	22.1	.0000	2	/zhen/**
0.0162	22.1	.0000	2	'Nineties
0.0162	22.1	.0000	2	'forty-nine
0.0162	22.1	.0000	2	'possum's
0.0162	22.1	.0000	2	A-B-A-C-A
0.0162	22.1	.0000	2	a-courtin'
0.0162	22.1	.0000	2	A-flat
0.0162	22.1	.0000	2	a-giving
0.0162	22.1	.0000	2	a-raking
0.0162	22.1	.0000	2	a-ridin'
0.0162	22.1	.0000	2	a-rovin'
0.0162	22.1	.0000	2	a-singing
0.0162	22.1	.0000	2	AABA
0.0162	22.1	.0000	2	Absolute
0.0162	22.1	.0000	2	Acacia
0.0162	22.1	.0000	2	adagio
0.0162	22.1	.0000	2	afterhold
0.0162	22.1	.0000	2	agootuk
0.0162	22.1	.0000	2	Ahasuerus
0.0162	22.1	.0000	2	Ahrirang
0.0162	22.1	.0000	2	Aids
0.0162	22.1	.0000	2	alla
0.0162	22.1	.0000	2	allemande
0.0162	22.1	.0000	2	alphabetum
0.0162	22.1	.0000	2	alway
0.0162	22.1	.0000	2	ancha
0.0162	22.1	.0000	2	Andalusia
0.0162	22.1	.0000	2	Andante
0.0162	22.1	.0000	2	Andulko
0.0162	22.1	.0000	2	Aragonaise
0.0162	22.1	.0000	2	arahkun
0.0162	22.1	.0000	2	architect's
0.0162	22.1	.0000	2	arco
0.0162	22.1	.0000	2	ation
0.0162	22.1	.0000	2	atonal
0.0162	22.1	.0000	2	Atuk's
0.0162	22.1	.0000	2	avocat
0.0162	22.1	.0000	2	Babbitt
0.0162	22.1	.0000	2	Bachianas
0.0162	22.1	.0000	2	back-to-back
0.0162	22.1	.0000	2	bassoonist
0.0162	22.1	.0000	2	bb
0.0162	22.1	.0000	2	Belshazzar's
0.0162	22.1	.0000	2	Blow
0.0162	22.1	.0000	2	bohte
0.0162	22.1	.0000	2	Bonny
0.0162	22.1	.0000	2	Borodin
0.0162	22.1	.0000	2	bourree
0.0162	22.1	.0000	2	Brasileiras
0.0162	22.1	.0000	2	breve
0.0162	22.1	.0000	2	Builder
0.0162	22.1	.0000	2	bullring
0.0162	22.1	.0000	2	Burroughs'
0.0162	22.1	.0000	2	buskin
0.0162	22.1	.0000	2	bz-z-z
0.0162	22.1	.0000	2	Caipira
0.0162	22.1	.0000	2	Cajuns
0.0162	22.1	.0000	2	calle
0.0162	22.1	.0000	2	camptown
0.0162	22.1	.0000	2	candelabra
0.0162	22.1	.0000	2	candle-lit
0.0162	22.1	.0000	2	cane-break
0.0162	22.1	.0000	2	Cannibal
0.0162	22.1	.0000	2	cappa
0.0162	22.1	.0000	2	Capulets
0.0162	22.1	.0000	2	Carillon
0.0162	22.1	.0000	2	Carry
0.0162	22.1	.0000	2	CEG
0.0162	22.1	.0000	2	cetera
0.0162	22.1	.0000	2	cha
0.0162	22.1	.0000	2	chamber-music
0.0162	22.1	.0000	2	Chant
0.0162	22.1	.0000	2	chevalier
0.0162	22.1	.0000	2	Chianti
0.0162	22.1	.0000	2	Childhood
0.0162	22.1	.0000	2	chun
0.0162	22.1	.0000	2	cious
0.0162	22.1	.0000	2	Classicist
0.0162	22.1	.0000	2	Classmate
0.0162	22.1	.0000	2	clavichord
0.0162	22.1	.0000	2	claymores
0.0162	22.1	.0000	2	clock-work
0.0162	22.1	.0000	2	co
0.0162	22.1	.0000	2	coloristic
0.0162	22.1	.0000	2	com-
0.0162	22.1	.0000	2	combos
0.0162	22.1	.0000	2	concert-band
0.0162	22.1	.0000	2	Concertino
0.0162	22.1	.0000	2	contradance
0.0162	22.1	.0000	2	contradances
THE PRECEDING WORD TYPE OCCUPIES RANK 60400				
0.0162	22.1	.0000	2	Cossacks
0.0162	22.1	.0000	2	counter-rhythms
0.0162	22.1	.0000	2	countersubject
0.0162	22.1	.0000	2	Croakie
0.0162	22.1	.0000	2	D-minor
0.0162	22.1	.0000	2	Dallapiccola
0.0162	22.1	.0000	2	Das
0.0162	22.1	.0000	2	decrescendo
0.0162	22.1	.0000	2	Delilah
0.0162	22.1	.0000	2	Delius
0.0162	22.1	.0000	2	departs
0.0162	22.1	.0000	2	Der
0.0162	22.1	.0000	2	dissonance
0.0162	22.1	.0000	2	Dog's
0.0162	22.1	.0000	2	Domenico
0.0162	22.1	.0000	2	double-vowel
0.0162	22.1	.0000	2	down-right-up
0.0162	22.1	.0000	2	down-up
0.0162	22.1	.0000	2	downstrokes
0.0162	22.1	.0000	2	Drosselmeyer
0.0162	22.1	.0000	2	Ducks
0.0162	22.1	.0000	2	Duet
0.0162	22.1	.0000	2	Dummy
0.0162	22.1	.0000	2	Dun
0.0162	22.1	.0000	2	Dunny
0.0162	22.1	.0000	2	ee-yah
0.0162	22.1	.0000	2	eight-measure
0.0162	22.1	.0000	2	eke
0.0162	22.1	.0000	2	Eldridge
0.0162	22.1	.0000	2	Engelbert
0.0162	22.1	.0000	2	enhances
0.0162	22.1	.0000	2	eous
0.0162	22.1	.0000	2	Erde
0.0162	22.1	.0000	2	Erlking's
0.0162	22.1	.0000	2	etait
0.0162	22.1	.0000	2	Eulenspiegel's
0.0162	22.1	.0000	2	euphonium
0.0162	22.1	.0000	2	evanescent
0.0162	22.1	.0000	2	ex-
0.0162	22.1	.0000	2	excelsis
0.0162	22.1	.0000	2	extens-
0.0162	22.1	.0000	2	Falorie
0.0162	22.1	.0000	2	false-hearted
0.0162	22.1	.0000	2	falsetto
0.0162	22.1	.0000	2	fanfares
0.0162	22.1	.0000	2	feria
0.0162	22.1	.0000	2	figgy
0.0162	22.1	.0000	2	fin'lly
0.0162	22.1	.0000	2	Firebird
0.0162	22.1	.0000	2	first-syllable
0.0162	22.1	.0000	2	five-note
0.0162	22.1	.0000	2	flatt'ring
0.0162	22.1	.0000	2	Flow
0.0162	22.1	.0000	2	Fly
0.0162	22.1	.0000	2	fol
0.0162	22.1	.0000	2	four-line
0.0162	22.1	.0000	2	Foxie
0.0162	22.1	.0000	2	frae
0.0162	22.1	.0000	2	Freedom's
0.0162	22.1	.0000	2	Frideric
0.0162	22.1	.0000	2	Friml
0.0162	22.1	.0000	2	Fugues
0.0162	22.1	.0000	2	FUNDAMENTALS
0.0162	22.1	.0000	2	gamekeeper
0.0162	22.1	.0000	2	gamelan
0.0162	22.1	.0000	2	gard
0.0162	22.1	.0000	2	Gavotte
0.0162	22.1	.0000	2	gi
0.0162	22.1	.0000	2	gid
0.0162	22.1	.0000	2	Ginastera
0.0162	22.1	.0000	2	Glinka's
0.0162	22.1	.0000	2	gloria
0.0162	22.1	.0000	2	Grecians
0.0162	22.1	.0000	2	Greig
0.0162	22.1	.0000	2	grenadiers
0.0162	22.1	.0000	2	guiros
0.0162	22.1	.0000	2	Gustaf's
0.0162	22.1	.0000	2	ha-ja-ha
0.0162	22.1	.0000	2	half-step
0.0162	22.1	.0000	2	han
0.0162	22.1	.0000	2	hard-to-spell
0.0162	22.1	.0000	2	Hary
0.0162	22.1	.0000	2	Hearts
0.0162	22.1	.0000	2	Heav'n
0.0162	22.1	.0000	2	Heave
0.0162	22.1	.0000	2	heaven-rescued
0.0162	22.1	.0000	2	high-arched
0.0162	22.1	.0000	2	hoedown
0.0162	22.1	.0000	2	honours
0.0162	22.1	.0000	2	hopak
0.0162	22.1	.0000	2	humanism
0.0162	22.1	.0000	2	hun
0.0162	22.1	.0000	2	Hundredth
0.0162	22.1	.0000	2	Hurdles
0.0162	22.1	.0000	2	iar
0.0162	22.1	.0000	2	ideograms
0.0162	22.1	.0000	2	ie-ei
0.0162	22.1	.0000	2	ij
0.0162	22.1	.0000	2	Impression
0.0162	22.1	.0000	2	Impressionistic
THE PRECEDING WORD TYPE OCCUPIES RANK 60500				
0.0162	22.1	.0000	2	Improvisation
0.0162	22.1	.0000	2	instrumentalists
0.0162	22.1	.0000	2	intendere
0.0162	22.1	.0000	2	Intermezzo
0.0162	22.1	.0000	2	Interrupted
0.0162	22.1	.0000	2	ir
0.0162	22.1	.0000	2	ish
0.0162	22.1	.0000	2	Jelena
0.0162	22.1	.0000	2	Jig
0.0162	22.1	.0000	2	jiggin'
0.0162	22.1	.0000	2	jongleurs
0.0162	22.1	.0000	2	Juba
0.0162	22.1	.0000	2	juba
0.0162	22.1	.0000	2	Jurisprudence
0.0162	22.1	.0000	2	k's
0.0162	22.1	.0000	2	kettledrums
0.0162	22.1	.0000	2	Khachaturian
0.0162	22.1	.0000	2	ki
0.0162	22.1	.0000	2	Kleine
0.0162	22.1	.0000	2	Kullak
0.0162	22.1	.0000	2	labelling
0.0162	22.1	.0000	2	Ladye
0.0162	22.1	.0000	2	largus
0.0162	22.1	.0000	2	las
0.0162	22.1	.0000	2	lasses
0.0162	22.1	.0000	2	legislate
0.0162	22.1	.0000	2	Lehar
0.0162	22.1	.0000	2	leoht
0.0162	22.1	.0000	2	lesson's
0.0162	22.1	.0000	2	Llangollen
0.0162	22.1	.0000	2	loc
0.0162	22.1	.0000	2	Loesser's
0.0162	22.1	.0000	2	longways
0.0162	22.1	.0000	2	loqu
0.0162	22.1	.0000	2	Lovely
0.0162	22.1	.0000	2	LP'S
0.0162	22.1	.0000	2	lubbers
0.0162	22.1	.0000	2	lutes
0.0162	22.1	.0000	2	lyras
0.0162	22.1	.0000	2	Macabre
0.0162	22.1	.0000	2	Maccabee
0.0162	22.1	.0000	2	major-minor
0.0162	22.1	.0000	2	major-scale
0.0162	22.1	.0000	2	mandolin
0.0162	22.1	.0000	2	marcato
0.0162	22.1	.0000	2	marimba
0.0162	22.1	.0000	2	Master's
0.0162	22.1	.0000	2	melodic-rhythmic
0.0162	22.1	.0000	2	Melody
0.0162	22.1	.0000	2	membranophones
0.0162	22.1	.0000	2	Mene
0.0162	22.1	.0000	2	Meng
0.0162	22.1	.0000	2	menorah
0.0162	22.1	.0000	2	Merry-Go-Round
0.0162	22.1	.0000	2	merrymakers
0.0162	22.1	.0000	2	Meyerbeer
0.0162	22.1	.0000	2	mezzo-soprano
0.0162	22.1	.0000	2	milia
0.0162	22.1	.0000	2	militated
0.0162	22.1	.0000	2	mille
0.0162	22.1	.0000	2	Mlle
0.0162	22.1	.0000	2	Modest
0.0162	22.1	.0000	2	modulate
0.0162	22.1	.0000	2	Modulation
0.0162	22.1	.0000	2	Mohr
0.0162	22.1	.0000	2	mousie
0.0162	22.1	.0000	2	Movements
0.0162	22.1	.0000	2	muktuk
0.0162	22.1	.0000	2	multi-syllabic
0.0162	22.1	.0000	2	Muses
0.0162	22.1	.0000	2	musettes
0.0162	22.1	.0000	2	musicianship
0.0162	22.1	.0000	2	Nacht
0.0162	22.1	.0000	2	nama
0.0162	22.1	.0000	2	Nicolai
0.0162	22.1	.0000	2	Niles
0.0162	22.1	.0000	2	nk
0.0162	22.1	.0000	2	nom
0.0162	22.1	.0000	2	Nouns
0.0162	22.1	.0000	2	nuance
0.0162	22.1	.0000	2	numpire
0.0162	22.1	.0000	2	nursemaids
0.0162	22.1	.0000	2	O'er
0.0162	22.1	.0000	2	ob-
0.0162	22.1	.0000	2	Oe
0.0162	22.1	.0000	2	Offenbach
0.0162	22.1	.0000	2	ohe
0.0162	22.1	.0000	2	Oj
0.0162	22.1	.0000	2	omnibus
0.0162	22.1	.0000	2	one-dot
0.0162	22.1	.0000	2	one-measure
0.0162	22.1	.0000	2	one-vowel
0.0162	22.1	.0000	2	onyma
0.0162	22.1	.0000	2	opera's
0.0162	22.1	.0000	2	orchestrated
0.0162	22.1	.0000	2	organists
0.0162	22.1	.0000	2	Ormin
0.0162	22.1	.0000	2	ory
0.0162	22.1	.0000	2	Othello
0.0162	22.1	.0000	2	p'ison
THE PRECEDING WORD TYPE OCCUPIES RANK 60600				
0.0162	22.1	.0000	2	Palatium
0.0162	22.1	.0000	2	part-singing
0.0162	22.1	.0000	2	partials
0.0162	22.1	.0000	2	Passacaglia
0.0162	22.1	.0000	2	percussions
0.0162	22.1	.0000	2	phonics
0.0162	22.1	.0000	2	Pian'
0.0162	22.1	.0000	2	piano's
0.0162	22.1	.0000	2	pictograms
0.0162	22.1	.0000	2	pipers
0.0162	22.1	.0000	2	Pipes
0.0162	22.1	.0000	2	Piston
0.0162	22.1	.0000	2	pitch-producing
0.0162	22.1	.0000	2	play-parties
0.0162	22.1	.0000	2	play-party
0.0162	22.1	.0000	2	plectrum
0.0162	22.1	.0000	2	poco
0.0162	22.1	.0000	2	poetically
0.0162	22.1	.0000	2	poli
0.0162	22.1	.0000	2	Poulenc's
0.0162	22.1	.0000	2	Pranks
0.0162	22.1	.0000	2	Pretty
0.0162	22.1	.0000	2	progressions
0.0162	22.1	.0000	2	prom'nade
0.0162	22.1	.0000	2	prophesy
0.0162	22.1	.0000	2	pt
0.0162	22.1	.0000	2	puerta
0.0162	22.1	.0000	2	punchers
0.0162	22.1	.0000	2	putz
0.0162	22.1	.0000	2	quarter-tones
0.0162	22.1	.0000	2	Radames
0.0162	22.1	.0000	2	Rain-Mount
0.0162	22.1	.0000	2	Rakoczy
0.0162	22.1	.0000	2	re-dedication
0.0162	22.1	.0000	2	reawakening
0.0162	22.1	.0000	2	rebec
0.0162	22.1	.0000	2	record-makers
0.0162	22.1	.0000	2	Respighi
0.0162	22.1	.0000	2	rhapsody
0.0162	22.1	.0000	2	Rheingold
0.0162	22.1	.0000	2	Rhyme
0.0162	22.1	.0000	2	ri
0.0162	22.1	.0000	2	ringo
0.0162	22.1	.0000	2	Ripple
0.0162	22.1	.0000	2	rocketing
0.0162	22.1	.0000	2	rol
0.0162	22.1	.0000	2	romantic-period
0.0162	22.1	.0000	2	Romberg
0.0162	22.1	.0000	2	Roved
0.0162	22.1	.0000	2	Rover's
0.0162	22.1	.0000	2	Rubinstein's
0.0162	22.1	.0000	2	ruh
0.0162	22.1	.0000	2	runes
0.0162	22.1	.0000	2	Sakura
0.0162	22.1	.0000	2	samba
0.0162	22.1	.0000	2	sane
0.0162	22.1	.0000	2	saxophones
0.0162	22.1	.0000	2	Scenes
0.0162	22.1	.0000	2	Scheherazade's
0.0162	22.1	.0000	2	scr
0.0162	22.1	.0000	2	Scriabin
0.0162	22.1	.0000	2	Sense
0.0162	22.1	.0000	2	Sereni
0.0162	22.1	.0000	2	Sergey
0.0162	22.1	.0000	2	sev'n
0.0162	22.1	.0000	2	shanteyman
0.0162	22.1	.0000	2	shanteys
0.0162	22.1	.0000	2	sharped
0.0162	22.1	.0000	2	She'll
0.0162	22.1	.0000	2	Shostakovitch
0.0162	22.1	.0000	2	shoutin'
0.0162	22.1	.0000	2	showmanship
0.0162	22.1	.0000	2	silver-sweet
0.0162	22.1	.0000	2	Sinda
0.0162	22.1	.0000	2	Skipping
0.0162	22.1	.0000	2	Skoal
0.0162	22.1	.0000	2	sleigh-bells
0.0162	22.1	.0000	2	Smetana's
0.0162	22.1	.0000	2	solidus
0.0162	22.1	.0000	2	solo-chorus
0.0162	22.1	.0000	2	song-writing
0.0162	22.1	.0000	2	song's
0.0162	22.1	.0000	2	Spare
0.0162	22.1	.0000	2	spr
0.0162	22.1	.0000	2	Springtime
0.0162	22.1	.0000	2	squ
0.0162	22.1	.0000	2	squirrels'
0.0162	22.1	.0000	2	step-bend
0.0162	22.1	.0000	2	step-hop
0.0162	22.1	.0000	2	stepwise
0.0162	22.1	.0000	2	String
0.0162	22.1	.0000	2	strums
0.0162	22.1	.0000	2	Sukkot
0.0162	22.1	.0000	2	surnames
0.0162	22.1	.0000	2	sweetheart's
0.0162	22.1	.0000	2	Sweets
0.0162	22.1	.0000	2	SWISH-swish
0.0162	22.1	.0000	2	Syrinx
0.0162	22.1	.0000	2	tambourin
0.0162	22.1	.0000	2	Tannhauser
THE PRECEDING WORD TYPE OCCUPIES RANK 60700				
0.0162	22.1	.0000	2	Tchaikowsky

U	SFI	D	F	Word Type
0.0162	22.1	.0000	2	tempos
0.0162	22.1	.0000	2	tense-forming
0.0162	22.1	.0000	2	terrere
0.0162	22.1	.0000	2	Thine
0.0162	22.1	.0000	2	three-stringed
0.0162	22.1	.0000	2	three-tone
0.0162	22.1	.0000	2	Thro'
0.0162	22.1	.0000	2	tim-ber
0.0162	22.1	.0000	2	Timely
0.0162	22.1	.0000	2	ting
0.0162	22.1	.0000	2	tious
0.0162	22.1	.0000	2	tithery
0.0162	22.1	.0000	2	Titipu
0.0162	22.1	.0000	2	toh
0.0162	22.1	.0000	2	tone-color
0.0162	22.1	.0000	2	Tonight
0.0162	22.1	.0000	2	Toslow
0.0162	22.1	.0000	2	town-O
0.0162	22.1	.0000	2	transposing
0.0162	22.1	.0000	2	tremolo
0.0162	22.1	.0000	2	Trepak
0.0162	22.1	.0000	2	Triptych
0.0162	22.1	.0000	2	Trovatore
0.0162	22.1	.0000	2	tsu-croo
0.0162	22.1	.0000	2	tu-re-lu-re-lu
0.0162	22.1	.0000	2	ture
0.0162	22.1	.0000	2	twangy
0.0162	22.1	.0000	2	twi
0.0162	22.1	.0000	2	Twilight
0.0162	22.1	.0000	2	Tyndale
0.0162	22.1	.0000	2	Tzena
0.0162	22.1	.0000	2	umbra
0.0162	22.1	.0000	2	umbrageous
0.0162	22.1	.0000	2	und
0.0162	22.1	.0000	2	unfettered
0.0162	22.1	.0000	2	ury
0.0162	22.1	.0000	2	Ussachevsky
0.0162	22.1	.0000	2	uy
0.0162	22.1	.0000	2	VC
0.0162	22.1	.0000	2	vc/v
0.0162	22.1	.0000	2	vccv
0.0162	22.1	.0000	2	ver-croo
0.0162	22.1	.0000	2	viola's
0.0162	22.1	.0000	2	vivace
0.0162	22.1	.0000	2	vocalists
0.0162	22.1	.0000	2	VonBulow
0.0162	22.1	.0000	2	vonGluck
0.0162	22.1	.0000	2	Voorhies
0.0162	22.1	.0000	2	vot
0.0162	22.1	.0000	2	Votkinsk
0.0162	22.1	.0000	2	vowel-consonant-vowel
0.0162	22.1	.0000	2	Voyageur
0.0162	22.1	.0000	2	wah-ka
0.0162	22.1	.0000	2	Waltzes
0.0162	22.1	.0000	2	Waltzing
0.0162	22.1	.0000	2	Webern
0.0162	22.1	.0000	2	weorth
0.0162	22.1	.0000	2	whiz-z-z
0.0162	22.1	.0000	2	wingsalum
0.0162	22.1	.0000	2	woodblocks
0.0162	22.1	.0000	2	written-over
0.0162	22.1	.0000	2	xion
0.0162	22.1	.0000	2	yoi
0.0162	22.1	.0000	2	zhun
0.0162	22.1	.0000	2	zing
0.0162	22.1	.0000	2	1-3-5
0.0162	22.1	.0000	2	100-128
0.0162	22.1	.0000	2	1340
0.0162	22.1	.0000	2	1685-1750
0.0162	22.1	.0000	2	1714-1787
0.0162	22.1	.0000	2	1813-1901
0.0162	22.1	.0000	2	19-20-21
0.0162	22.1	.0000	2	19-35
0.0162	22.1	.0000	2	25-29
0.0162	22.1	.0000	2	4-consonant-silent
0.0162	22.1	.0000	2	4-5-6
0.0162	22.1	.0000	2	5230
0.0162	22.1	.0000	2	78's
0.0161	22.1	.0000	5	broiler
0.0161	22.1	.0000	5	chiffon
0.0161	22.1	.0000	5	flavorful
0.0161	22.1	.0000	5	machine-stitch
0.0161	22.1	.0000	5	plackets
0.0161	22.1	.0000	5	workbasket
0.0151	21.8	.0000	6	BHN
0.0151	21.8	.0000	6	compositor
0.0151	21.8	.0000	6	Scleroscope
0.0151	21.8	.0000	6	sensitized
0.0151	21.8	.0000	6	shaper
0.0150	21.8	.0000	1	(a/b)2**
0.0150	21.8	.0000	1	$112
0.0150	21.8	.0000	1	$124
0.0150	21.8	.0000	1	$128
0.0150	21.8	.0000	1	$149
0.0150	21.8	.0000	1	$154
0.0150	21.8	.0000	1	$155
0.0150	21.8	.0000	1	$1600
0.0150	21.8	.0000	1	$161
0.0150	21.8	.0000	1	$1650

THE PRECEDING WORD TYPE OCCUPIES RANK 60800

0.0150	21.8	.0000	1	$1800
0.0150	21.8	.0000	1	$182
0.0150	21.8	.0000	1	$2250
0.0150	21.8	.0000	1	$227
0.0150	21.8	.0000	1	$232
0.0150	21.8	.0000	1	$235
0.0150	21.8	.0000	1	$2365
0.0150	21.8	.0000	1	$253
0.0150	21.8	.0000	1	$2560
0.0150	21.8	.0000	1	$2800
0.0150	21.8	.0000	1	$2850
0.0150	21.8	.0000	1	$2947
0.0150	21.8	.0000	1	$31
0.0150	21.8	.0000	1	$325
0.0150	21.8	.0000	1	$340
0.0150	21.8	.0000	1	$345
0.0150	21.8	.0000	1	$3460

U	SFI	D	F	Word Type
0.0150	21.8	.0000	1	$360
0.0150	21.8	.0000	1	$378
0.0150	21.8	.0000	1	$4067
0.0150	21.8	.0000	1	$420
0.0150	21.8	.0000	1	$440
0.0150	21.8	.0000	1	$465
0.0150	21.8	.0000	1	$47
0.0150	21.8	.0000	1	$515
0.0150	21.8	.0000	1	$549
0.0150	21.8	.0000	1	$56
0.0150	21.8	.0000	1	$59
0.0150	21.8	.0000	1	$655
0.0150	21.8	.0000	1	$66
0.0150	21.8	.0000	1	$69
0.0150	21.8	.0000	1	$6958
0.0150	21.8	.0000	1	$7000
0.0150	21.8	.0000	1	$720
0.0150	21.8	.0000	1	$7265
0.0150	21.8	.0000	1	$73
0.0150	21.8	.0000	1	$7654
0.0150	21.8	.0000	1	$8000
0.0150	21.8	.0000	1	$840
0.0150	21.8	.0000	1	$8500
0.0150	21.8	.0000	1	$855
0.0150	21.8	.0000	1	$88
0.0150	21.8	.0000	1	$89
0.0150	21.8	.0000	1	$908
0.0150	21.8	.0000	1	$96
0.0150	21.8	.0000	1	-1/2
0.0150	21.8	.0000	1	-13
0.0150	21.8	.0000	1	-15/-45
0.0150	21.8	.0000	1	-15/4
0.0150	21.8	.0000	1	-2x
0.0150	21.8	.0000	1	-20
0.0150	21.8	.0000	1	-26
0.0150	21.8	.0000	1	-29
0.0150	21.8	.0000	1	-3/2
0.0150	21.8	.0000	1	-3/5xn
0.0150	21.8	.0000	1	-3x
0.0150	21.8	.0000	1	-30
0.0150	21.8	.0000	1	-300
0.0150	21.8	.0000	1	-35
0.0150	21.8	.0000	1	-4x
0.0150	21.8	.0000	1	-400
0.0150	21.8	.0000	1	-5/7
0.0150	21.8	.0000	1	-600
0.0150	21.8	.0000	1	-8/3
0.0150	21.8	.0000	1	/d**
0.0150	21.8	.0000	1	/1
0.0150	21.8	.0000	1	/13
0.0150	21.8	.0000	1	/16
0.0150	21.8	.0000	1	/16rs
0.0150	21.8	.0000	1	/19
0.0150	21.8	.0000	1	/2s
0.0150	21.8	.0000	1	/2000
0.0150	21.8	.0000	1	/36
0.0150	21.8	.0000	1	/50
0.0150	21.8	.0000	1	/88
0.0150	21.8	.0000	1	-line
0.0150	21.8	.0000	1	-sixteenth
0.0150	21.8	.0000	1	aDC-9
0.0150	21.8	.0000	1	aN
0.0150	21.8	.0000	1	a-b
0.0150	21.8	.0000	1	a-c
0.0150	21.8	.0000	1	a-g
0.0150	21.8	.0000	1	a/n
0.0150	21.8	.0000	1	ab/cd
0.0150	21.8	.0000	1	ABCDA
0.0150	21.8	.0000	1	ABCDEF
0.0150	21.8	.0000	1	ABF
0.0150	21.8	.0000	1	ABP
0.0150	21.8	.0000	1	ABQ
0.0150	21.8	.0000	1	abscissa
0.0150	21.8	.0000	1	abscissas
0.0150	21.8	.0000	1	ac/bc
0.0150	21.8	.0000	1	Aces
0.0150	21.8	.0000	1	ACF
0.0150	21.8	.0000	1	acquaints
0.0150	21.8	.0000	1	Addam's
0.0150	21.8	.0000	1	ADDITION
0.0150	21.8	.0000	1	addition-subtraction
0.0150	21.8	.0000	1	additive-inverse
0.0150	21.8	.0000	1	Adler

THE PRECEDING WORD TYPE OCCUPIES RANK 60900

0.0150	21.8	.0000	1	AEF
0.0150	21.8	.0000	1	AFC
0.0150	21.8	.0000	1	AFT
0.0150	21.8	.0000	1	ah-hah
0.0150	21.8	.0000	1	Airline
0.0150	21.8	.0000	1	airline's
0.0150	21.8	.0000	1	AL
0.0150	21.8	.0000	1	al-Rashid
0.0150	21.8	.0000	1	Alan's
0.0150	21.8	.0000	1	algorism
0.0150	21.8	.0000	1	Alphy
0.0150	21.8	.0000	1	Altoona
0.0150	21.8	.0000	1	am■n**
0.0150	21.8	.0000	1	am**
0.0150	21.8	.0000	1	Amazon's
0.0150	21.8	.0000	1	Ambitious
0.0150	21.8	.0000	1	an**
0.0150	21.8	.0000	1	analogous
0.0150	21.8	.0000	1	Angle-Side-Angle
0.0150	21.8	.0000	1	angle-measure
0.0150	21.8	.0000	1	antelope's
0.0150	21.8	.0000	1	antipodal
0.0150	21.8	.0000	1	AO
0.0150	21.8	.0000	1	AOD
0.0150	21.8	.0000	1	AOG
0.0150	21.8	.0000	1	Apartments
0.0150	21.8	.0000	1	approximating
0.0150	21.8	.0000	1	AREA
0.0150	21.8	.0000	1	AREAS
0.0150	21.8	.0000	1	arithemtic
0.0150	21.8	.0000	1	Arwell
0.0150	21.8	.0000	1	Arwells
0.0150	21.8	.0000	1	ascends

U	SFI	D	F	Word Type
0.0150	21.8	.0000	1	attesting
0.0150	21.8	.0000	1	Avenues
0.0150	21.8	.0000	1	a0
0.0150	21.8	.0000	1	a2/b2**
0.0150	21.8	.0000	1	a3**
0.0150	21.8	.0000	1	bN
0.0150	21.8	.0000	1	b/a
0.0150	21.8	.0000	1	b/c
0.0150	21.8	.0000	1	b/d
0.0150	21.8	.0000	1	Badgers
0.0150	21.8	.0000	1	ballgame
0.0150	21.8	.0000	1	Barbie
0.0150	21.8	.0000	1	barleycorn
0.0150	21.8	.0000	1	barleycorns
0.0150	21.8	.0000	1	basket-ball
0.0150	21.8	.0000	1	BayCity
0.0150	21.8	.0000	1	BCA
0.0150	21.8	.0000	1	BCD
0.0150	21.8	.0000	1	BCGF
0.0150	21.8	.0000	1	BDC
0.0150	21.8	.0000	1	BG
0.0150	21.8	.0000	1	BH
0.0150	21.8	.0000	1	bird-powered
0.0150	21.8	.0000	1	Bisons
0.0150	21.8	.0000	1	BK
0.0150	21.8	.0000	1	Blackton
0.0150	21.8	.0000	1	Blaise
0.0150	21.8	.0000	1	blouse-skirt
0.0150	21.8	.0000	1	Bluejays
0.0150	21.8	.0000	1	BOA
0.0150	21.8	.0000	1	Bolyai
0.0150	21.8	.0000	1	Bona
0.0150	21.8	.0000	1	Bonnard
0.0150	21.8	.0000	1	book-case
0.0150	21.8	.0000	1	bookstore
0.0150	21.8	.0000	1	borrows
0.0150	21.8	.0000	1	box-car
0.0150	21.8	.0000	1	box-cars
0.0150	21.8	.0000	1	BOYS
0.0150	21.8	.0000	1	Brescia
0.0150	21.8	.0000	1	Bret's
0.0150	21.8	.0000	1	BRL
0.0150	21.8	.0000	1	broad-jump
0.0150	21.8	.0000	1	BYC
0.0150	21.8	.0000	1	Byer
0.0150	21.8	.0000	1	c-c
0.0150	21.8	.0000	1	c/**
0.0150	21.8	.0000	1	c/-3
0.0150	21.8	.0000	1	c/a
0.0150	21.8	.0000	1	c/b
0.0150	21.8	.0000	1	CAB
0.0150	21.8	.0000	1	Calculator
0.0150	21.8	.0000	1	called-for
0.0150	21.8	.0000	1	carbon-14
0.0150	21.8	.0000	1	caret
0.0150	21.8	.0000	1	carets
0.0150	21.8	.0000	1	Carson's
0.0150	21.8	.0000	1	catacombs
0.0150	21.8	.0000	1	Catnips
0.0150	21.8	.0000	1	CBD
0.0150	21.8	.0000	1	CE
0.0150	21.8	.0000	1	centi-
0.0150	21.8	.0000	1	CFR
0.0150	21.8	.0000	1	Chefalo
0.0150	21.8	.0000	1	Chihuahuas
0.0150	21.8	.0000	1	circle's
0.0150	21.8	.0000	1	Clarks

THE PRECEDING WORD TYPE OCCUPIES RANK 61000

0.0150	21.8	.0000	1	Clearfield
0.0150	21.8	.0000	1	coin-collection
0.0150	21.8	.0000	1	commutativity
0.0150	21.8	.0000	1	connectivity
0.0150	21.8	.0000	1	Constructions
0.0150	21.8	.0000	1	counting-numbers
0.0150	21.8	.0000	1	CR
0.0150	21.8	.0000	1	cross-cut
0.0150	21.8	.0000	1	crossbones
0.0150	21.8	.0000	1	crosshatched
0.0150	21.8	.0000	1	CS
0.0150	21.8	.0000	1	CTA
0.0150	21.8	.0000	1	cu
0.0150	21.8	.0000	1	currency-breakdown
0.0150	21.8	.0000	1	Curve
0.0150	21.8	.0000	1	CW
0.0150	21.8	.0000	1	CY
0.0150	21.8	.0000	1	d-th
0.0150	21.8	.0000	1	d/c
0.0150	21.8	.0000	1	D'Urfey
0.0150	21.8	.0000	1	DAE
0.0150	21.8	.0000	1	Daisies
0.0150	21.8	.0000	1	Darrell
0.0150	21.8	.0000	1	DART
0.0150	21.8	.0000	1	datum
0.0150	21.8	.0000	1	DBY
0.0150	21.8	.0000	1	DCCLIII
0.0150	21.8	.0000	1	DCG
0.0150	21.8	.0000	1	Debra
0.0150	21.8	.0000	1	deca
0.0150	21.8	.0000	1	deca-
0.0150	21.8	.0000	1	decagon
0.0150	21.8	.0000	1	decathlon
0.0150	21.8	.0000	1	deci-
0.0150	21.8	.0000	1	DEFG
0.0150	21.8	.0000	1	deka-
0.0150	21.8	.0000	1	dekameter
0.0150	21.8	.0000	1	delivery-truck
0.0150	21.8	.0000	1	Density
0.0150	21.8	.0000	1	detaches
0.0150	21.8	.0000	1	DG
0.0150	21.8	.0000	1	dietetics
0.0150	21.8	.0000	1	dietician
0.0150	21.8	.0000	1	dietician's
0.0150	21.8	.0000	1	diez
0.0150	21.8	.0000	1	Differences
0.0150	21.8	.0000	1	different-sized
0.0150	21.8	.0000	1	disproves
0.0150	21.8	.0000	1	divisable

U	SFI	D	F	Word Type
0.0150	21.8	.0000	1	DOA
0.0150	21.8	.0000	1	DOC
0.0150	21.8	.0000	1	dodgeball
0.0150	21.8	.0000	1	DOF
0.0150	21.8	.0000	1	dollar-days
0.0150	21.8	.0000	1	Doubling
0.0150	21.8	.0000	1	doubloon
0.0150	21.8	.0000	1	DPG
0.0150	21.8	.0000	1	duodecimal
0.0150	21.8	.0000	1	dust-speck
0.0150	21.8	.0000	1	DY
0.0150	21.8	.0000	1	E's
0.0150	21.8	.0000	1	Earners
0.0150	21.8	.0000	1	EDC
0.0150	21.8	.0000	1	Eddy's
0.0150	21.8	.0000	1	EFH
0.0150	21.8	.0000	1	EHFG
0.0150	21.8	.0000	1	EHG
0.0150	21.8	.0000	1	eight-cent
0.0150	21.8	.0000	1	eight-tenths
0.0150	21.8	.0000	1	eighteenths
0.0150	21.8	.0000	1	eighth-units
0.0150	21.8	.0000	1	Eilenberg
0.0150	21.8	.0000	1	Elborus
0.0150	21.8	.0000	1	elevens
0.0150	21.8	.0000	1	Elmcourt
0.0150	21.8	.0000	1	employee's
0.0150	21.8	.0000	1	end-of-the-month
0.0150	21.8	.0000	1	end-points
0.0150	21.8	.0000	1	Enyart
0.0150	21.8	.0000	1	EOC
0.0150	21.8	.0000	1	EOF
0.0150	21.8	.0000	1	EOG
0.0150	21.8	.0000	1	EPG
0.0150	21.8	.0000	1	ergs
0.0150	21.8	.0000	1	ES
0.0150	21.8	.0000	1	Euler's
0.0150	21.8	.0000	1	EVEN
0.0150	21.8	.0000	1	ExampleC
0.0150	21.8	.0000	1	Excursion
0.0150	21.8	.0000	1	Exercize
0.0150	21.8	.0000	1	exerting
0.0150	21.8	.0000	1	expanded-numeral
0.0150	21.8	.0000	1	E2
0.0150	21.8	.0000	1	E6
0.0150	21.8	.0000	1	f-h
0.0150	21.8	.0000	1	f/N
0.0150	21.8	.0000	1	FAC
0.0150	21.8	.0000	1	Factor
0.0150	21.8	.0000	1	Family's
0.0150	21.8	.0000	1	FARM

THE PRECEDING WORD TYPE OCCUPIES RANK 61100

0.0150	21.8	.0000	1	farmhand
0.0150	21.8	.0000	1	FB
0.0150	21.8	.0000	1	FBD
0.0150	21.8	.0000	1	FC
0.0150	21.8	.0000	1	FCA
0.0150	21.8	.0000	1	FCT
0.0150	21.8	.0000	1	FD
0.0150	21.8	.0000	1	femur
0.0150	21.8	.0000	1	FGC
0.0150	21.8	.0000	1	FGH
0.0150	21.8	.0000	1	FHG
0.0150	21.8	.0000	1	figure-wheels
0.0150	21.8	.0000	1	Finite
0.0150	21.8	.0000	1	Fiore
0.0150	21.8	.0000	1	first-grade
0.0150	21.8	.0000	1	fishbowl
0.0150	21.8	.0000	1	fishbowls
0.0150	21.8	.0000	1	five-cubed
0.0150	21.8	.0000	1	five-fives
0.0150	21.8	.0000	1	five-month
0.0150	21.8	.0000	1	five-ninths
0.0150	21.8	.0000	1	five-room
0.0150	21.8	.0000	1	five-sevenths
0.0150	21.8	.0000	1	five-squared
0.0150	21.8	.0000	1	five-step
0.0150	21.8	.0000	1	five-tenths
0.0150	21.8	.0000	1	five-thirds
0.0150	21.8	.0000	1	flowerbeds
0.0150	21.8	.0000	1	flyby
0.0150	21.8	.0000	1	FMH
0.0150	21.8	.0000	1	FN
0.0150	21.8	.0000	1	FOB
0.0150	21.8	.0000	1	FOG
0.0150	21.8	.0000	1	Foolania
0.0150	21.8	.0000	1	four-clock
0.0150	21.8	.0000	1	four-eighths
0.0150	21.8	.0000	1	four-mile
0.0150	21.8	.0000	1	four-month
0.0150	21.8	.0000	1	four-place
0.0150	21.8	.0000	1	four-sevenths
0.0150	21.8	.0000	1	FRS
0.0150	21.8	.0000	1	FS
0.0150	21.8	.0000	1	ft-lb
0.0150	21.8	.0000	1	ft-long**
0.0150	21.8	.0000	1	ft/sec
0.0150	21.8	.0000	1	fugit
0.0150	21.8	.0000	1	Furniture
0.0150	21.8	.0000	1	gauge-reading
0.0150	21.8	.0000	1	GEF
0.0150	21.8	.0000	1	Geis
0.0150	21.8	.0000	1	geometer
0.0150	21.8	.0000	1	Geometric
0.0150	21.8	.0000	1	Glen's
0.0150	21.8	.0000	1	GMJ
0.0150	21.8	.0000	1	GOB
0.0150	21.8	.0000	1	GOC
0.0150	21.8	.0000	1	Gold's
0.0150	21.8	.0000	1	green-tinted
0.0150	21.8	.0000	1	Greg's
0.0150	21.8	.0000	1	Gren-ich
0.0150	21.8	.0000	1	HA
0.0150	21.8	.0000	1	half-million
0.0150	21.8	.0000	1	half-ruined
0.0150	21.8	.0000	1	half-spheres
0.0150	21.8	.0000	1	half-unit

U	SFI	D	F	Word Type
0.0150	21.8	.0000	1	half-units
0.0150	21.8	.0000	1	Happyborough
0.0150	21.8	.0000	1	Harbour
0.0150	21.8	.0000	1	Harun
0.0150	21.8	.0000	1	hecto-
0.0150	21.8	.0000	1	heelbones
0.0150	21.8	.0000	1	HEF
0.0150	21.8	.0000	1	Herrick's
0.0150	21.8	.0000	1	high-jump
0.0150	21.8	.0000	1	Hindu-
0.0150	21.8	.0000	1	HJ
0.0150	21.8	.0000	1	Holloway
0.0150	21.8	.0000	1	Hotchkins
0.0150	21.8	.0000	1	HRL
0.0150	21.8	.0000	1	Huff
0.0150	21.8	.0000	1	hundred-millions'
0.0150	21.8	.0000	1	hundred-thousands
0.0150	21.8	.0000	1	hundred's
0.0150	21.8	.0000	1	hundreds-tens-ones
0.0150	21.8	.0000	1	hypothesis/conclusion
0.0150	21.8	.0000	1	Identity
0.0150	21.8	.0000	1	IG
0.0150	21.8	.0000	1	IJK
0.0150	21.8	.0000	1	IJL
0.0150	21.8	.0000	1	impossibilities
0.0150	21.8	.0000	1	Indian-head
0.0150	21.8	.0000	1	inductively
0.0150	21.8	.0000	1	Infinite
0.0150	21.8	.0000	1	initialization
0.0150	21.8	.0000	1	ink-blot
0.0150	21.8	.0000	1	inscribe
0.0150	21.8	.0000	1	interpolation
0.0150	21.8	.0000	1	involution
0.0150	21.8	.0000	1	iota
0.0150	21.8	.0000	1	jackrabbit's
				THE PRECEDING WORD TYPE OCCUPIES RANK 61200
0.0150	21.8	.0000	1	Jamaican
0.0150	21.8	.0000	1	Janes's
0.0150	21.8	.0000	1	Jay's
0.0150	21.8	.0000	1	JB
0.0150	21.8	.0000	1	JD
0.0150	21.8	.0000	1	jelling
0.0150	21.8	.0000	1	jet-plane
0.0150	21.8	.0000	1	JETS
0.0150	21.8	.0000	1	JH
0.0150	21.8	.0000	1	JKL
0.0150	21.8	.0000	1	JO
0.0150	21.8	.0000	1	Kaliningrad
0.0150	21.8	.0000	1	Kathleen's
0.0150	21.8	.0000	1	kgm
0.0150	21.8	.0000	1	Kilmanjaro
0.0150	21.8	.0000	1	kilo-
0.0150	21.8	.0000	1	Kirk's
0.0150	21.8	.0000	1	Klein
0.0150	21.8	.0000	1	Kline
0.0150	21.8	.0000	1	Kline's
0.0150	21.8	.0000	1	KN
0.0150	21.8	.0000	1	knife-axe
0.0150	21.8	.0000	1	Knot
0.0150	21.8	.0000	1	KPM
0.0150	21.8	.0000	1	KPQL
0.0150	21.8	.0000	1	Kraitchik
0.0150	21.8	.0000	1	KRG
0.0150	21.8	.0000	1	Lakeville
0.0150	21.8	.0000	1	last-place
0.0150	21.8	.0000	1	Least
0.0150	21.8	.0000	1	Left-
0.0150	21.8	.0000	1	Leibniz's
0.0150	21.8	.0000	1	Lengths
0.0150	21.8	.0000	1	Leonhard
0.0150	21.8	.0000	1	LF
0.0150	21.8	.0000	1	LG
0.0150	21.8	.0000	1	lh
0.0150	21.8	.0000	1	line-segment
0.0150	21.8	.0000	1	lire
0.0150	21.8	.0000	1	LK
0.0150	21.8	.0000	1	LMN
0.0150	21.8	.0000	1	LNO
0.0150	21.8	.0000	1	logarithmic
0.0150	21.8	.0000	1	longitudes
0.0150	21.8	.0000	1	Longs
0.0150	21.8	.0000	1	LS
0.0150	21.8	.0000	1	Lu-Ann
0.0150	21.8	.0000	1	lw
0.0150	21.8	.0000	1	lwh
0.0150	21.8	.0000	1	LXXV
0.0150	21.8	.0000	1	Lynn's
0.0150	21.8	.0000	1	m/3
0.0150	21.8	.0000	1	MacGruder's
0.0150	21.8	.0000	1	Macy
0.0150	21.8	.0000	1	Maisy
0.0150	21.8	.0000	1	map-to-child
0.0150	21.8	.0000	1	Mapledale
0.0150	21.8	.0000	1	Marla's
0.0150	21.8	.0000	1	Marsha
0.0150	21.8	.0000	1	Marson's
0.0150	21.8	.0000	1	Martins'
0.0150	21.8	.0000	1	Maude's
0.0150	21.8	.0000	1	Mauritian
0.0150	21.8	.0000	1	Maxine
0.0150	21.8	.0000	1	mc
0.0150	21.8	.0000	1	MCVII
0.0150	21.8	.0000	1	MDLXVI
0.0150	21.8	.0000	1	meandered
0.0150	21.8	.0000	1	mega
0.0150	21.8	.0000	1	metrei
0.0150	21.8	.0000	1	microseconds
0.0150	21.8	.0000	1	Midvale
0.0150	21.8	.0000	1	Midville
0.0150	21.8	.0000	1	Milady
0.0150	21.8	.0000	1	milleniums
0.0150	21.8	.0000	1	milli-
0.0150	21.8	.0000	1	milligram
0.0150	21.8	.0000	1	minuends
0.0150	21.8	.0000	1	ML
0.0150	21.8	.0000	1	MMCCCX
0.0150	21.8	.0000	1	Mnq
0.0150	21.8	.0000	1	MO
0.0150	21.8	.0000	1	MON
0.0150	21.8	.0000	1	Mondays
0.0150	21.8	.0000	1	moonweight
0.0150	21.8	.0000	1	MRN
0.0150	21.8	.0000	1	MULTIPLICATION
0.0150	21.8	.0000	1	mystification
0.0150	21.8	.0000	1	N-factorial
0.0150	21.8	.0000	1	n/10
0.0150	21.8	.0000	1	n/100
0.0150	21.8	.0000	1	n/2200
0.0150	21.8	.0000	1	n/48
0.0150	21.8	.0000	1	n/6
0.0150	21.8	.0000	1	n%
0.0150	21.8	.0000	1	Napier's
0.0150	21.8	.0000	1	narrow-hand
0.0150	21.8	.0000	1	near-record
0.0150	21.8	.0000	1	negative/positive/zero
0.0150	21.8	.0000	1	nickels'
				THE PRECEDING WORD TYPE OCCUPIES RANK 61300
0.0150	21.8	.0000	1	Nim
0.0150	21.8	.0000	1	nineteen-year-old
0.0150	21.8	.0000	1	ninths
0.0150	21.8	.0000	1	non-collinear
0.0150	21.8	.0000	1	non-measurement
0.0150	21.8	.0000	1	non-positive
0.0150	21.8	.0000	1	non-repeating
0.0150	21.8	.0000	1	non
0.0150	21.8	.0000	1	nonagon
0.0150	21.8	.0000	1	noncollinear
0.0150	21.8	.0000	1	nonmetric
0.0150	21.8	.0000	1	nonpositive
0.0150	21.8	.0000	1	nonrepeating
0.0150	21.8	.0000	1	nonsquare
0.0150	21.8	.0000	1	nontechnical
0.0150	21.8	.0000	1	nonterminating
0.0150	21.8	.0000	1	NOPQ
0.0150	21.8	.0000	1	nose-to-fingertip
0.0150	21.8	.0000	1	NQL
0.0150	21.8	.0000	1	Nuclear
0.0150	21.8	.0000	1	number-explainer
0.0150	21.8	.0000	1	number-pair
0.0150	21.8	.0000	1	number-ray
0.0150	21.8	.0000	1	numbers-positive
0.0150	21.8	.0000	1	Numeral
0.0150	21.8	.0000	1	numerating
0.0150	21.8	.0000	1	Numo's
0.0150	21.8	.0000	1	nxn
0.0150	21.8	.0000	1	nx0
0.0150	21.8	.0000	1	nx3
0.0150	21.8	.0000	1	nx3/7
0.0150	21.8	.0000	1	nx7
0.0150	21.8	.0000	1	n0n-terminating
0.0150	21.8	.0000	1	O'Boye's
0.0150	21.8	.0000	1	oceanliner
0.0150	21.8	.0000	1	octahedron
0.0150	21.8	.0000	1	octant
0.0150	21.8	.0000	1	ODD
0.0150	21.8	.0000	1	OGIH
0.0150	21.8	.0000	1	OMN
0.0150	21.8	.0000	1	OMP
0.0150	21.8	.0000	1	one-another
0.0150	21.8	.0000	1	one-four
0.0150	21.8	.0000	1	one-handed
0.0150	21.8	.0000	1	one-mile
0.0150	21.8	.0000	1	one-million
0.0150	21.8	.0000	1	one-millions'
0.0150	21.8	.0000	1	one-quart
0.0150	21.8	.0000	1	one-seventh
0.0150	21.8	.0000	1	one-sixtieth
0.0150	21.8	.0000	1	one-thousands'
0.0150	21.8	.0000	1	ones-tens-hundreds
0.0150	21.8	.0000	1	ordinate
0.0150	21.8	.0000	1	overexposed
0.0150	21.8	.0000	1	p%
0.0150	21.8	.0000	1	PAC
0.0150	21.8	.0000	1	parquet
0.0150	21.8	.0000	1	Pascal's
0.0150	21.8	.0000	1	passer-by
0.0150	21.8	.0000	1	PAT
0.0150	21.8	.0000	1	Pattie
0.0150	21.8	.0000	1	Paula's
0.0150	21.8	.0000	1	PBC
0.0150	21.8	.0000	1	pencil-and-paper
0.0150	21.8	.0000	1	pennies'
0.0150	21.8	.0000	1	percentiles
0.0150	21.8	.0000	1	PERIMETER
0.0150	21.8	.0000	1	Perimeter
0.0150	21.8	.0000	1	PERIMETERS
0.0150	21.8	.0000	1	permutation
0.0150	21.8	.0000	1	PF
0.0150	21.8	.0000	1	phramid
0.0150	21.8	.0000	1	pictograph
0.0150	21.8	.0000	1	pin-prick
0.0150	21.8	.0000	1	pizzas
0.0150	21.8	.0000	1	Pleasanttown
0.0150	21.8	.0000	1	Plus
0.0150	21.8	.0000	1	PMO
0.0150	21.8	.0000	1	PNO
0.0150	21.8	.0000	1	PNQ
0.0150	21.8	.0000	1	Polish-American
0.0150	21.8	.0000	1	POLK
0.0150	21.8	.0000	1	polygonal
0.0150	21.8	.0000	1	pong
0.0150	21.8	.0000	1	potentiometer
0.0150	21.8	.0000	1	PQL
0.0150	21.8	.0000	1	PQN
0.0150	21.8	.0000	1	precocious
0.0150	21.8	.0000	1	Preger
0.0150	21.8	.0000	1	printout
0.0150	21.8	.0000	1	Probability
0.0150	21.8	.0000	1	protein-to-carbohydrate
0.0150	21.8	.0000	1	Prudent
0.0150	21.8	.0000	1	Pryor's
0.0150	21.8	.0000	1	PS
0.0150	21.8	.0000	1	QR
0.0150	21.8	.0000	1	QRS
0.0150	21.8	.0000	1	Quadrilaterals
0.0150	21.8	.0000	1	quantifier
0.0150	21.8	.0000	1	quantifiers
				THE PRECEDING WORD TYPE OCCUPIES RANK 61400
0.0150	21.8	.0000	1	quarter-units
0.0150	21.8	.0000	1	quatrilaterals
0.0150	21.8	.0000	1	quickies
0.0150	21.8	.0000	1	r/t
0.0150	21.8	.0000	1	radians
0.0150	21.8	.0000	1	Ranchville
0.0150	21.8	.0000	1	rational-number
0.0150	21.8	.0000	1	rationals
0.0150	21.8	.0000	1	RBC
0.0150	21.8	.0000	1	re-equip
0.0150	21.8	.0000	1	re-name
0.0150	21.8	.0000	1	re-named
0.0150	21.8	.0000	1	rearrangments
0.0150	21.8	.0000	1	recopying
0.0150	21.8	.0000	1	record-player
0.0150	21.8	.0000	1	redefinition
0.0150	21.8	.0000	1	Redtown
0.0150	21.8	.0000	1	refolded
0.0150	21.8	.0000	1	Rent
0.0150	21.8	.0000	1	Reservations
0.0150	21.8	.0000	1	retro-rockets
0.0150	21.8	.0000	1	Reynolds'
0.0150	21.8	.0000	1	Richy
0.0150	21.8	.0000	1	Riemann
0.0150	21.8	.0000	1	ripcord
0.0150	21.8	.0000	1	RIS
0.0150	21.8	.0000	1	RL
0.0150	21.8	.0000	1	Rose's
0.0150	21.8	.0000	1	Rostvold
0.0150	21.8	.0000	1	round-number
0.0150	21.8	.0000	1	RPS
0.0150	21.8	.0000	1	RQ
0.0150	21.8	.0000	1	RSO
0.0150	21.8	.0000	1	RSP
0.0150	21.8	.0000	1	RSTU
0.0150	21.8	.0000	1	rt
0.0150	21.8	.0000	1	RTVX
0.0150	21.8	.0000	1	RU
0.0150	21.8	.0000	1	RUV
0.0150	21.8	.0000	1	R5
0.0150	21.8	.0000	1	s-square
0.0150	21.8	.0000	1	Sandberg
0.0150	21.8	.0000	1	SCHOOL
0.0150	21.8	.0000	1	school-day
0.0150	21.8	.0000	1	scorekeeper
0.0150	21.8	.0000	1	Scoring
0.0150	21.8	.0000	1	screwdrivers
0.0150	21.8	.0000	1	Sections
0.0150	21.8	.0000	1	Segment
0.0150	21.8	.0000	1	Selector
0.0150	21.8	.0000	1	self-service
0.0150	21.8	.0000	1	septagon
0.0150	21.8	.0000	1	seven-ninths
0.0150	21.8	.0000	1	seven-tenths
0.0150	21.8	.0000	1	sharpshooter
0.0150	21.8	.0000	1	shole
0.0150	21.8	.0000	1	Side-Angle-Side
0.0150	21.8	.0000	1	Side-Side-Side
0.0150	21.8	.0000	1	similitude
0.0150	21.8	.0000	1	six-place
0.0150	21.8	.0000	1	sixtieths
0.0150	21.8	.0000	1	skirt-blouse
0.0150	21.8	.0000	1	skydiver
0.0150	21.8	.0000	1	soapcakes
0.0150	21.8	.0000	1	Softball
0.0150	21.8	.0000	1	SOM
0.0150	21.8	.0000	1	speed-skating
0.0150	21.8	.0000	1	spine-tailed
0.0150	21.8	.0000	1	SPT
0.0150	21.8	.0000	1	SPX
0.0150	21.8	.0000	1	Spyglass
0.0150	21.8	.0000	1	SS
0.0150	21.8	.0000	1	Statistical
0.0150	21.8	.0000	1	STK
0.0150	21.8	.0000	1	stutterer
0.0150	21.8	.0000	1	subscribing
0.0150	21.8	.0000	1	subtrahends
0.0150	21.8	.0000	1	subunits
0.0150	21.8	.0000	1	Sums
0.0150	21.8	.0000	1	superscript
0.0150	21.8	.0000	1	supersets
0.0150	21.8	.0000	1	sweater-skirt
0.0150	21.8	.0000	1	sweet-pea
0.0150	21.8	.0000	1	T-bone
0.0150	21.8	.0000	1	t-shaped
0.0150	21.8	.0000	1	T-16
0.0150	21.8	.0000	1	t/r
0.0150	21.8	.0000	1	TA
0.0150	21.8	.0000	1	TAB
0.0150	21.8	.0000	1	Tally
0.0150	21.8	.0000	1	Tammy's
0.0150	21.8	.0000	1	TAP
0.0150	21.8	.0000	1	Tartalea
0.0150	21.8	.0000	1	ten-digit
0.0150	21.8	.0000	1	ten-millions'
0.0150	21.8	.0000	1	ten-thousands
0.0150	21.8	.0000	1	ten-thousandths'
0.0150	21.8	.0000	1	TFC
0.0150	21.8	.0000	1	thermometer's
0.0150	21.8	.0000	1	Thieves
				THE PRECEDING WORD TYPE OCCUPIES RANK 61500
0.0150	21.8	.0000	1	third-graders
0.0150	21.8	.0000	1	thirty-sixes
0.0150	21.8	.0000	1	three-cent
0.0150	21.8	.0000	1	three-tenths
0.0150	21.8	.0000	1	TK
0.0150	21.8	.0000	1	Toss
0.0150	21.8	.0000	1	TPU
0.0150	21.8	.0000	1	Trapezoids
0.0150	21.8	.0000	1	Try
0.0150	21.8	.0000	1	TSP
0.0150	21.8	.0000	1	Tues
0.0150	21.8	.0000	1	twentieths
0.0150	21.8	.0000	1	twenty-fourths
0.0150	21.8	.0000	1	two-day
0.0150	21.8	.0000	1	two-ninths
0.0150	21.8	.0000	1	Tyler's
0.0150	21.8	.0000	1	unary
0.0150	21.8	.0000	1	unearned
0.0150	21.8	.0000	1	unit-of-measure
0.0150	21.8	.0000	1	unit-region
0.0150	21.8	.0000	1	Univac
0.0150	21.8	.0000	1	unneeded
0.0150	21.8	.0000	1	upside-
0.0150	21.8	.0000	1	ushering
0.0150	21.8	.0000	1	UVW
0.0150	21.8	.0000	1	V-E
0.0150	21.8	.0000	1	Valleyhill
0.0150	21.8	.0000	1	variance
0.0150	21.8	.0000	1	venetian
0.0150	21.8	.0000	1	vernier
0.0150	21.8	.0000	1	vi
0.0150	21.8	.0000	1	Vital
0.0150	21.8	.0000	1	vonLeibniz
0.0150	21.8	.0000	1	VX
0.0150	21.8	.0000	1	VZ
0.0150	21.8	.0000	1	W-A-M-R
0.0150	21.8	.0000	1	water-purifying
0.0150	21.8	.0000	1	Wells'
0.0150	21.8	.0000	1	What-Are-My-Rules
0.0150	21.8	.0000	1	wide-screen
0.0150	21.8	.0000	1	Wiener's
0.0150	21.8	.0000	1	wingspans
0.0150	21.8	.0000	1	wk
0.0150	21.8	.0000	1	WVX
0.0150	21.8	.0000	1	WX
0.0150	21.8	.0000	1	WXYZ
0.0150	21.8	.0000	1	WZ
0.0150	21.8	.0000	1	W4
0.0150	21.8	.0000	1	x-component
0.0150	21.8	.0000	1	x-coordinate
0.0150	21.8	.0000	1	x/a
0.0150	21.8	.0000	1	xa/b**
0.0150	21.8	.0000	1	XBC
0.0150	21.8	.0000	1	XIX
0.0150	21.8	.0000	1	XL
0.0150	21.8	.0000	1	XLV
0.0150	21.8	.0000	1	XM
0.0150	21.8	.0000	1	XXI
0.0150	21.8	.0000	1	xy/ab
0.0150	21.8	.0000	1	xyz
0.0150	21.8	.0000	1	xz
0.0150	21.8	.0000	1	x9
0.0150	21.8	.0000	1	y-axis
0.0150	21.8	.0000	1	y-component
0.0150	21.8	.0000	1	y-segment
0.0150	21.8	.0000	1	y-4
0.0150	21.8	.0000	1	y/b
0.0150	21.8	.0000	1	YCF
0.0150	21.8	.0000	1	YH
0.0150	21.8	.0000	1	YL
0.0150	21.8	.0000	1	YM
0.0150	21.8	.0000	1	YZ
0.0150	21.8	.0000	1	zero-point
0.0150	21.8	.0000	1	0-1000
0.0150	21.8	.0000	1	0-15
0.0150	21.8	.0000	1	0-250
0.0150	21.8	.0000	1	0/14
0.0150	21.8	.0000	1	0/2
0.0150	21.8	.0000	1	0/5xn
0.0150	21.8	.0000	1	0/8
0.0150	21.8	.0000	1	0xn
0.0150	21.8	.0000	1	0x0
0.0150	21.8	.0000	1	0x5
0.0150	21.8	.0000	1	0x8
0.0150	21.8	.0000	1	000000
0.0150	21.8	.0000	1	000000000000001
0.0150	21.8	.0000	1	000000000000005
0.0150	21.8	.0000	1	00001
0.0150	21.8	.0000	1	000012
0.0150	21.8	.0000	1	00005896
0.0150	21.8	.0000	1	00012
0.0150	21.8	.0000	1	00018
0.0150	21.8	.0000	1	000361
0.0150	21.8	.0000	1	0006
0.0150	21.8	.0000	1	0007
0.0150	21.8	.0000	1	0011
0.0150	21.8	.0000	1	002
0.0150	21.8	.0000	1	004
0.0150	21.8	.0000	1	0045
0.0150	21.8	.0000	1	0064
				THE PRECEDING WORD TYPE OCCUPIES RANK 61600
0.0150	21.8	.0000	1	007281
0.0150	21.8	.0000	1	0089
0.0150	21.8	.0000	1	016
0.0150	21.8	.0000	1	017
0.0150	21.8	.0000	1	019
0.0150	21.8	.0000	1	023
0.0150	21.8	.0000	1	026
0.0150	21.8	.0000	1	027
0.0150	21.8	.0000	1	032
0.0150	21.8	.0000	1	043
0.0150	21.8	.0000	1	0672
0.0150	21.8	.0000	1	076
0.0150	21.8	.0000	1	078
0.0150	21.8	.0000	1	089
0.0150	21.8	.0000	1	095
0.0150	21.8	.0000	1	098
0.0150	21.8	.0000	1	1
0.0150	21.8	.0000	1	1C
0.0150	21.8	.0000	1	1D
0.0150	21.8	.0000	1	1E
0.0150	21.8	.0000	1	1-
0.0150	21.8	.0000	1	1-degree
0.0150	21.8	.0000	1	1-digit
0.0150	21.8	.0000	1	1-gallon
0.0150	21.8	.0000	1	1-meter
0.0150	21.8	.0000	1	1-quart
0.0150	21.8	.0000	1	1-unit
0.0150	21.8	.0000	1	1-16

U	SFI	D	F	Word Type
0.0150	21.8	.0000	1	1-18
0.0150	21.8	.0000	1	1-22
0.0150	21.8	.0000	1	1/-27
0.0150	21.8	.0000	1	1/a
0.0150	21.8	.0000	1	1/a3**
0.0150	21.8	.0000	1	1/b
0.0150	21.8	.0000	1	1/n
0.0150	21.8	.0000	1	1/12n
0.0150	21.8	.0000	1	1/13
0.0150	21.8	.0000	1	1/18
0.0150	21.8	.0000	1	1/19
0.0150	21.8	.0000	1	1/2gt
0.0150	21.8	.0000	1	1/2xy
0.0150	21.8	.0000	1	1/2y
0.0150	21.8	.0000	1	1/20
0.0150	21.8	.0000	1	1/2270
0.0150	21.8	.0000	1	1/273
0.0150	21.8	.0000	1	1/3-4
0.0150	21.8	.0000	1	1/3r
0.0150	21.8	.0000	1	1/360
0.0150	21.8	.0000	1	1/4-mile
0.0150	21.8	.0000	1	1/4-ounce
0.0150	21.8	.0000	1	1/4-segment
0.0150	21.8	.0000	1	1/72
0.0150	21.8	.0000	1	1cm
0.0150	21.8	.0000	1	1e
0.0150	21.8	.0000	1	1x1
0.0150	21.8	.0000	1	1x10
0.0150	21.8	.0000	1	1x2/3x2
0.0150	21.8	.0000	1	1x3/2x3
0.0150	21.8	.0000	1	1x4
0.0150	21.8	.0000	1	1x9
0.0150	21.8	.0000	1	10-a
0.0150	21.8	.0000	1	10-yd
0.0150	21.8	.0000	1	10-year-old
0.0150	21.8	.0000	1	10-23
0.0150	21.8	.0000	1	10-28
0.0150	21.8	.0000	1	10-30
0.0150	21.8	.0000	1	10-31
0.0150	21.8	.0000	1	10-33
0.0150	21.8	.0000	1	10-34
0.0150	21.8	.0000	1	10-35
0.0150	21.8	.0000	1	10/14
0.0150	21.8	.0000	1	10/4
0.0150	21.8	.0000	1	10/8
0.0150	21.8	.0000	1	10m
0.0150	21.8	.0000	1	10x10
0.0150	21.8	.0000	1	10x16
0.0150	21.8	.0000	1	100-lb
0.0150	21.8	.0000	1	100-meter
0.0150	21.8	.0000	1	100/110
0.0150	21.8	.0000	1	100/300
0.0150	21.8	.0000	1	1000x1000
0.0150	21.8	.0000	1	1010
0.0150	21.8	.0000	1	101001000100001
0.0150	21.8	.0000	1	10110
0.0150	21.8	.0000	1	102-99
0.0150	21.8	.0000	1	1020
0.0150	21.8	.0000	1	1056
0.0150	21.8	.0000	1	1060
0.0150	21.8	.0000	1	1075
0.0150	21.8	.0000	1	11-in
0.0150	21.8	.0000	1	11-13
0.0150	21.8	.0000	1	11/10
0.0150	21.8	.0000	1	11/12
0.0150	21.8	.0000	1	11/22
0.0150	21.8	.0000	1	11/40
0.0150	21.8	.0000	1	11%
0.0150	21.8	.0000	1	11a
0.0150	21.8	.0000	1	11b
0.0150	21.8	.0000	1	111111
0.0150	21.8	.0000	1	1112

THE PRECEDING WORD TYPE OCCUPIES RANK 61700

U	SFI	D	F	Word Type
0.0150	21.8	.0000	1	1147
0.0150	21.8	.0000	1	12-clock
0.0150	21.8	.0000	1	12-ft
0.0150	21.8	.0000	1	12/100
0.0150	21.8	.0000	1	12/15
0.0150	21.8	.0000	1	12/2
0.0150	21.8	.0000	1	12/3
0.0150	21.8	.0000	1	12s
0.0150	21.8	.0000	1	1210
0.0150	21.8	.0000	1	121212
0.0150	21.8	.0000	1	1216
0.0150	21.8	.0000	1	123/1000
0.0150	21.8	.0000	1	123x4
0.0150	21.8	.0000	1	123x400
0.0150	21.8	.0000	1	12345678910111213
0.0150	21.8	.0000	1	1247
0.0150	21.8	.0000	1	1253
0.0150	21.8	.0000	1	1292
0.0150	21.8	.0000	1	13-n
0.0150	21.8	.0000	1	13-14
0.0150	21.8	.0000	1	13-15
0.0150	21.8	.0000	1	13-18
0.0150	21.8	.0000	1	13-20
0.0150	21.8	.0000	1	13-20a
0.0150	21.8	.0000	1	13-20b
0.0150	21.8	.0000	1	13-21
0.0150	21.8	.0000	1	13-23
0.0150	21.8	.0000	1	13-7
0.0150	21.8	.0000	1	13/6
0.0150	21.8	.0000	1	1345
0.0150	21.8	.0000	1	1387/100
0.0150	21.8	.0000	1	1392
0.0150	21.8	.0000	1	14-22
0.0150	21.8	.0000	1	14%
0.0150	21.8	.0000	1	14's
0.0150	21.8	.0000	1	14xr
0.0150	21.8	.0000	1	144-48-48-48
0.0150	21.8	.0000	1	15-pound
0.0150	21.8	.0000	1	15-22
0.0150	21.8	.0000	1	15-24
0.0150	21.8	.0000	1	15-56
0.0150	21.8	.0000	1	15-57
0.0150	21.8	.0000	1	15-6
0.0150	21.8	.0000	1	15/
0.0150	21.8	.0000	1	15/10
0.0150	21.8	.0000	1	15/21
0.0150	21.8	.0000	1	15/22
0.0150	21.8	.0000	1	15/30
0.0150	21.8	.0000	1	15/4
0.0150	21.8	.0000	1	15/5
0.0150	21.8	.0000	1	15/6
0.0150	21.8	.0000	1	15a
0.0150	21.8	.0000	1	15b
0.0150	21.8	.0000	1	15q
0.0150	21.8	.0000	1	150%
0.0150	21.8	.0000	1	1514
0.0150	21.8	.0000	1	152/160
0.0150	21.8	.0000	1	15228
0.0150	21.8	.0000	1	1571-1630
0.0150	21.8	.0000	1	1597/250
0.0150	21.8	.0000	1	16-9
0.0150	21.8	.0000	1	16/3
0.0150	21.8	.0000	1	16/40
0.0150	21.8	.0000	1	16/6
0.0150	21.8	.0000	1	16%
0.0150	21.8	.0000	1	16rs
0.0150	21.8	.0000	1	16x3
0.0150	21.8	.0000	1	160-lb
0.0150	21.8	.0000	1	160-8
0.0150	21.8	.0000	1	161-165
0.0150	21.8	.0000	1	1680
0.0150	21.8	.0000	1	17-8
0.0150	21.8	.0000	1	17/3
0.0150	21.8	.0000	1	17%
0.0150	21.8	.0000	1	17y
0.0150	21.8	.0000	1	170-173
0.0150	21.8	.0000	1	1726
0.0150	21.8	.0000	1	1746
0.0150	21.8	.0000	1	18-in
0.0150	21.8	.0000	1	18-9
0.0150	21.8	.0000	1	18/12
0.0150	21.8	.0000	1	18b
0.0150	21.8	.0000	1	1826-1866
0.0150	21.8	.0000	1	1875/10000
0.0150	21.8	.0000	1	1894-1964
0.0150	21.8	.0000	1	19-22
0.0150	21.8	.0000	1	19-24
0.0150	21.8	.0000	1	19-27
0.0150	21.8	.0000	1	19/20
0.0150	21.8	.0000	1	19/24
0.0150	21.8	.0000	1	192/100
0.0150	21.8	.0000	1	1920-1929
0.0150	21.8	.0000	1	193-213
0.0150	21.8	.0000	1	1974
0.0150	21.8	.0000	1	2(5/5)-segment
0.0150	21.8	.0000	1	2-finger
0.0150	21.8	.0000	1	2-letter
0.0150	21.8	.0000	1	2-meter
0.0150	21.8	.0000	1	2-mile
0.0150	21.8	.0000	1	2/a

THE PRECEDING WORD TYPE OCCUPIES RANK 61800

U	SFI	D	F	Word Type
0.0150	21.8	.0000	1	2/1
0.0150	21.8	.0000	1	2/1x1/7
0.0150	21.8	.0000	1	2/1000
0.0150	21.8	.0000	1	2/20
0.0150	21.8	.0000	1	2/3x3/2
0.0150	21.8	.0000	1	2/36
0.0150	21.8	.0000	1	2/5x7/3
0.0150	21.8	.0000	1	2/7x4
0.0150	21.8	.0000	1	2a-c
0.0150	21.8	.0000	1	2ay
0.0150	21.8	.0000	1	2c
0.0150	21.8	.0000	1	2l
0.0150	21.8	.0000	1	2lw
0.0150	21.8	.0000	1	2m
0.0150	21.8	.0000	1	2r
0.0150	21.8	.0000	1	2w
0.0150	21.8	.0000	1	2x10x3x10
0.0150	21.8	.0000	1	2x100
0.0150	21.8	.0000	1	2x2
0.0150	21.8	.0000	1	2x2x2x2x2x2x2x2x2x2
0.0150	21.8	.0000	1	2x4/4
0.0150	21.8	.0000	1	2x61
0.0150	21.8	.0000	1	2x90
0.0150	21.8	.0000	1	2y/y
0.0150	21.8	.0000	1	20-mph
0.0150	21.8	.0000	1	20/10
0.0150	21.8	.0000	1	20x30
0.0150	21.8	.0000	1	20x8
0.0150	21.8	.0000	1	2062
0.0150	21.8	.0000	1	2073
0.0150	21.8	.0000	1	2080
0.0150	21.8	.0000	1	21-27
0.0150	21.8	.0000	1	21/100
0.0150	21.8	.0000	1	21/3
0.0150	21.8	.0000	1	21x
0.0150	21.8	.0000	1	21430
0.0150	21.8	.0000	1	215x5
0.0150	21.8	.0000	1	215x500
0.0150	21.8	.0000	1	2153
0.0150	21.8	.0000	1	2158
0.0150	21.8	.0000	1	2181
0.0150	21.8	.0000	1	22/24
0.0150	21.8	.0000	1	22/4
0.0150	21.8	.0000	1	22kg
0.0150	21.8	.0000	1	220-yard
0.0150	21.8	.0000	1	2200/n
0.0150	21.8	.0000	1	2255
0.0150	21.8	.0000	1	2290
0.0150	21.8	.0000	1	23-10
0.0150	21.8	.0000	1	23-11
0.0150	21.8	.0000	1	23-34
0.0150	21.8	.0000	1	23-5
0.0150	21.8	.0000	1	23-6
0.0150	21.8	.0000	1	23-7
0.0150	21.8	.0000	1	23-8
0.0150	21.8	.0000	1	23-9
0.0150	21.8	.0000	1	2304
0.0150	21.8	.0000	1	231458
0.0150	21.8	.0000	1	2345
0.0150	21.8	.0000	1	2347
0.0150	21.8	.0000	1	24-day
0.0150	21.8	.0000	1	24-hr
0.0150	21.8	.0000	1	2418
0.0150	21.8	.0000	1	2419
0.0150	21.8	.0000	1	2448
0.0150	21.8	.0000	1	248/8
0.0150	21.8	.0000	1	248/8x1/100
0.0150	21.8	.0000	1	248/8x1/100
0.0150	21.8	.0000	1	2486
0.0150	21.8	.0000	1	25-pound
0.0150	21.8	.0000	1	25-147
0.0150	21.8	.0000	1	25-26
0.0150	21.8	.0000	1	25/
0.0150	21.8	.0000	1	25/n
0.0150	21.8	.0000	1	25/100
0.0150	21.8	.0000	1	25/3
0.0150	21.8	.0000	1	25/6
0.0150	21.8	.0000	1	2500's
0.0150	21.8	.0000	1	253/1000
0.0150	21.8	.0000	1	2532
0.0150	21.8	.0000	1	2536
0.0150	21.8	.0000	1	2544
0.0150	21.8	.0000	1	2586
0.0150	21.8	.0000	1	26/3
0.0150	21.8	.0000	1	2610
0.0150	21.8	.0000	1	2640
0.0150	21.8	.0000	1	2645
0.0150	21.8	.0000	1	2675
0.0150	21.8	.0000	1	2688
0.0150	21.8	.0000	1	27-29
0.0150	21.8	.0000	1	27-30
0.0150	21.8	.0000	1	2753
0.0150	21.8	.0000	1	2763
0.0150	21.8	.0000	1	2764
0.0150	21.8	.0000	1	28/12
0.0150	21.8	.0000	1	28/15
0.0150	21.8	.0000	1	28%
0.0150	21.8	.0000	1	2802
0.0150	21.8	.0000	1	28333
0.0150	21.8	.0000	1	2847

THE PRECEDING WORD TYPE OCCUPIES RANK 61900

U	SFI	D	F	Word Type
0.0150	21.8	.0000	1	2900
0.0150	21.8	.0000	1	2965
0.0150	21.8	.0000	1	3(5/5)-segment
0.0150	21.8	.0000	1	3B
0.0150	21.8	.0000	1	3C
0.0150	21.8	.0000	1	3R4
0.0150	21.8	.0000	1	3-cent
0.0150	21.8	.0000	1	3-dot
0.0150	21.8	.0000	1	3-place
0.0150	21.8	.0000	1	3-year
0.0150	21.8	.0000	1	3-12
0.0150	21.8	.0000	1	3-15
0.0150	21.8	.0000	1	3/
0.0150	21.8	.0000	1	3/100
0.0150	21.8	.0000	1	3/2x2/3
0.0150	21.8	.0000	1	3/20
0.0150	21.8	.0000	1	3/3-regions
0.0150	21.8	.0000	1	3/3-segments
0.0150	21.8	.0000	1	3/48
0.0150	21.8	.0000	1	3/5x2/7
0.0150	21.8	.0000	1	3/8-1/4
0.0150	21.8	.0000	1	3/8-1/8
0.0150	21.8	.0000	1	3b
0.0150	21.8	.0000	1	3f
0.0150	21.8	.0000	1	3in
0.0150	21.8	.0000	1	3xr
0.0150	21.8	.0000	1	3xy
0.0150	21.8	.0000	1	3x0
0.0150	21.8	.0000	1	3x14
0.0150	21.8	.0000	1	3x2/3x2x2
0.0150	21.8	.0000	1	3x2x1/3x2x2
0.0150	21.8	.0000	1	3x3
0.0150	21.8	.0000	1	3x41
0.0150	21.8	.0000	1	3x42
0.0150	21.8	.0000	1	3x4672
0.0150	21.8	.0000	1	3x62
0.0150	21.8	.0000	1	3x8
0.0150	21.8	.0000	1	30x42
0.0150	21.8	.0000	1	30x60
0.0150	21.8	.0000	1	30x70
0.0150	21.8	.0000	1	300-lb
0.0150	21.8	.0000	1	3018
0.0150	21.8	.0000	1	3096
0.0150	21.8	.0000	1	31-28
0.0150	21.8	.0000	1	31-69
0.0150	21.8	.0000	1	31/2
0.0150	21.8	.0000	1	31b
0.0150	21.8	.0000	1	31c
0.0150	21.8	.0000	1	31x1/100
0.0150	21.8	.0000	1	310-foot
0.0150	21.8	.0000	1	3106
0.0150	21.8	.0000	1	317x8
0.0150	21.8	.0000	1	317x800
0.0150	21.8	.0000	1	3174
0.0150	21.8	.0000	1	32-38
0.0150	21.8	.0000	1	3212
0.0150	21.8	.0000	1	3256
0.0150	21.8	.0000	1	32653x1/104
0.0150	21.8	.0000	1	3274
0.0150	21.8	.0000	1	329-mile
0.0150	21.8	.0000	1	33-34
0.0150	21.8	.0000	1	33/100
0.0150	21.8	.0000	1	33/36
0.0150	21.8	.0000	1	330/100
0.0150	21.8	.0000	1	3300
0.0150	21.8	.0000	1	331/3
0.0150	21.8	.0000	1	336-page
0.0150	21.8	.0000	1	34/36
0.0150	21.8	.0000	1	34%
0.0150	21.8	.0000	1	34x2
0.0150	21.8	.0000	1	34x200
0.0150	21.8	.0000	1	3400
0.0150	21.8	.0000	1	341
0.0150	21.8	.0000	1	343x
0.0150	21.8	.0000	1	3469
0.0150	21.8	.0000	1	3475
0.0150	21.8	.0000	1	3489
0.0150	21.8	.0000	1	35-38
0.0150	21.8	.0000	1	35-40
0.0150	21.8	.0000	1	35-44
0.0150	21.8	.0000	1	35/2
0.0150	21.8	.0000	1	36/100
0.0150	21.8	.0000	1	36/80
0.0150	21.8	.0000	1	3600/3937
0.0150	21.8	.0000	1	3654
0.0150	21.8	.0000	1	3672
0.0150	21.8	.0000	1	3682
0.0150	21.8	.0000	1	37-38
0.0150	21.8	.0000	1	37-40
0.0150	21.8	.0000	1	374
0.0150	21.8	.0000	1	3750000
0.0150	21.8	.0000	1	3778
0.0150	21.8	.0000	1	3827
0.0150	21.8	.0000	1	385
0.0150	21.8	.0000	1	3875
0.0150	21.8	.0000	1	388
0.0150	21.8	.0000	1	39-42
0.0150	21.8	.0000	1	39-50
0.0150	21.8	.0000	1	39-58
0.0150	21.8	.0000	1	39-6

THE PRECEDING WORD TYPE OCCUPIES RANK 62000

U	SFI	D	F	Word Type
0.0150	21.8	.0000	1	39-7
0.0150	21.8	.0000	1	390
0.0150	21.8	.0000	1	3900
0.0150	21.8	.0000	1	3925
0.0150	21.8	.0000	1	3937
0.0150	21.8	.0000	1	394-395
0.0150	21.8	.0000	1	3967
0.0150	21.8	.0000	1	398x54
0.0150	21.8	.0000	1	3986
0.0150	21.8	.0000	1	4
0.0150	21.8	.0000	1	4-day
0.0150	21.8	.0000	1	4-pound
0.0150	21.8	.0000	1	4-7
0.0150	21.8	.0000	1	4/
0.0150	21.8	.0000	1	4/1/1
0.0150	21.8	.0000	1	4/17
0.0150	21.8	.0000	1	4/5-1
0.0150	21.8	.0000	1	4a-f
0.0150	21.8	.0000	1	4c
0.0150	21.8	.0000	1	4e
0.0150	21.8	.0000	1	4x1
0.0150	21.8	.0000	1	4x10
0.0150	21.8	.0000	1	4x2
0.0150	21.8	.0000	1	4x30
0.0150	21.8	.0000	1	4x9
0.0150	21.8	.0000	1	4x90
0.0150	21.8	.0000	1	40/30
0.0150	21.8	.0000	1	40x23
0.0150	21.8	.0000	1	40x60
0.0150	21.8	.0000	1	4097
0.0150	21.8	.0000	1	41-4
0.0150	21.8	.0000	1	41-5
0.0150	21.8	.0000	1	41a
0.0150	21.8	.0000	1	41d
0.0150	21.8	.0000	1	41e
0.0150	21.8	.0000	1	41f
0.0150	21.8	.0000	1	410-431
0.0150	21.8	.0000	1	4173
0.0150	21.8	.0000	1	42-56
0.0150	21.8	.0000	1	42's
0.0150	21.8	.0000	1	4224
0.0150	21.8	.0000	1	4235
0.0150	21.8	.0000	1	424
0.0150	21.8	.0000	1	4286
0.0150	21.8	.0000	1	43-46
0.0150	21.8	.0000	1	43x2
0.0150	21.8	.0000	1	44/7
0.0150	21.8	.0000	1	4478
0.0150	21.8	.0000	1	454545
0.0150	21.8	.0000	1	4623
0.0150	21.8	.0000	1	4628
0.0150	21.8	.0000	1	4652
0.0150	21.8	.0000	1	4692
0.0150	21.8	.0000	1	4700
0.0150	21.8	.0000	1	4760
0.0150	21.8	.0000	1	479
0.0150	21.8	.0000	1	4872
0.0150	21.8	.0000	1	489
0.0150	21.8	.0000	1	489-490
0.0150	21.8	.0000	1	5(5/5)-region
0.0150	21.8	.0000	1	5-
0.0150	21.8	.0000	1	5-day
0.0150	21.8	.0000	1	5-y
0.0150	21.8	.0000	1	5-year
0.0150	21.8	.0000	1	5-10
0.0150	21.8	.0000	1	5-5
0.0150	21.8	.0000	1	5/13
0.0150	21.8	.0000	1	5/16-inch-thick
0.0150	21.8	.0000	1	5/20
0.0150	21.8	.0000	1	5/22
0.0150	21.8	.0000	1	5/27
0.0150	21.8	.0000	1	5/5-segment
0.0150	21.8	.0000	1	5/6-1/2
0.0150	21.8	.0000	1	5/6-1/3
0.0150	21.8	.0000	1	5/7x3/8
0.0150	21.8	.0000	1	5a
0.0150	21.8	.0000	1	5in
0.0150	21.8	.0000	1	5x0
0.0150	21.8	.0000	1	5x2x3
0.0150	21.8	.0000	1	5x4
0.0150	21.8	.0000	1	5x6x8
0.0150	21.8	.0000	1	5x7
0.0150	21.8	.0000	1	5x8
0.0150	21.8	.0000	1	5x9
0.0150	21.8	.0000	1	50-
0.0150	21.8	.0000	1	50-ft
0.0150	21.8	.0000	1	50-mph
0.0150	21.8	.0000	1	50-word
0.0150	21.8	.0000	1	50-16
0.0150	21.8	.0000	1	50/100
0.0150	21.8	.0000	1	50/3
0.0150	21.8	.0000	1	50x9

U	SFI	D	F	Word Type
0.0150	21.8	.0000	1	500x7
0.0150	21.8	.0000	1	51/2%
0.0150	21.8	.0000	1	51/4
0.0150	21.8	.0000	1	516
0.0150	21.8	.0000	1	52-18
0.0150	21.8	.0000	1	52-34
0.0150	21.8	.0000	1	526
0.0150	21.8	.0000	1	5263

THE PRECEDING WORD TYPE OCCUPIES RANK 62100

U	SFI	D	F	Word Type
0.0150	21.8	.0000	1	53-38
0.0150	21.8	.0000	1	5372
0.0150	21.8	.0000	1	5398/60
0.0150	21.8	.0000	1	54-26
0.0150	21.8	.0000	1	5459
0.0150	21.8	.0000	1	556
0.0150	21.8	.0000	1	56x7
0.0150	21.8	.0000	1	56x700
0.0150	21.8	.0000	1	5600
0.0150	21.8	.0000	1	565
0.0150	21.8	.0000	1	567
0.0150	21.8	.0000	1	568
0.0150	21.8	.0000	1	5689
0.0150	21.8	.0000	1	569
0.0150	21.8	.0000	1	57x10
0.0150	21.8	.0000	1	57x100
0.0150	21.8	.0000	1	57142857
0.0150	21.8	.0000	1	573
0.0150	21.8	.0000	1	576x4
0.0150	21.8	.0000	1	576x400
0.0150	21.8	.0000	1	5763
0.0150	21.8	.0000	1	5764
0.0150	21.8	.0000	1	577
0.0150	21.8	.0000	1	582
0.0150	21.8	.0000	1	583
0.0150	21.8	.0000	1	587
0.0150	21.8	.0000	1	592
0.0150	21.8	.0000	1	6-digit
0.0150	21.8	.0000	1	6-hr
0.0150	21.8	.0000	1	6-ounce
0.0150	21.8	.0000	1	6-12
0.0150	21.8	.0000	1	6/14
0.0150	21.8	.0000	1	6/20
0.0150	21.8	.0000	1	6's
0.0150	21.8	.0000	1	6d
0.0150	21.8	.0000	1	6e
0.0150	21.8	.0000	1	6in
0.0150	21.8	.0000	1	6ths
0.0150	21.8	.0000	1	6xn
0.0150	21.8	.0000	1	6x2
0.0150	21.8	.0000	1	6x3
0.0150	21.8	.0000	1	6x39
0.0150	21.8	.0000	1	6x40
0.0150	21.8	.0000	1	60/100
0.0150	21.8	.0000	1	60x80
0.0150	21.8	.0000	1	600-300
0.0150	21.8	.0000	1	602
0.0150	21.8	.0000	1	605
0.0150	21.8	.0000	1	6072
0.0150	21.8	.0000	1	6076
0.0150	21.8	.0000	1	6197
0.0150	21.8	.0000	1	623
0.0150	21.8	.0000	1	62341
0.0150	21.8	.0000	1	6261
0.0150	21.8	.0000	1	640-foot
0.0150	21.8	.0000	1	641
0.0150	21.8	.0000	1	646
0.0150	21.8	.0000	1	6474
0.0150	21.8	.0000	1	6566
0.0150	21.8	.0000	1	66/1000
0.0150	21.8	.0000	1	66666
0.0150	21.8	.0000	1	672
0.0150	21.8	.0000	1	676
0.0150	21.8	.0000	1	677
0.0150	21.8	.0000	1	678
0.0150	21.8	.0000	1	6783
0.0150	21.8	.0000	1	679
0.0150	21.8	.0000	1	68/38
0.0150	21.8	.0000	1	68%
0.0150	21.8	.0000	1	685487
0.0150	21.8	.0000	1	6874
0.0150	21.8	.0000	1	69%
0.0150	21.8	.0000	1	691
0.0150	21.8	.0000	1	691x3
0.0150	21.8	.0000	1	691x300
0.0150	21.8	.0000	1	6950
0.0150	21.8	.0000	1	7-centimeter
0.0150	21.8	.0000	1	7-year
0.0150	21.8	.0000	1	7-15
0.0150	21.8	.0000	1	7-3
0.0150	21.8	.0000	1	7-7
0.0150	21.8	.0000	1	7/1000
0.0150	21.8	.0000	1	7/12-1/3
0.0150	21.8	.0000	1	7/12-1/4
0.0150	21.8	.0000	1	7/18
0.0150	21.8	.0000	1	7/6-1/3
0.0150	21.8	.0000	1	7/6-5/6
0.0150	21.8	.0000	1	7/8-1/2
0.0150	21.8	.0000	1	7/8-3/8
0.0150	21.8	.0000	1	7c
0.0150	21.8	.0000	1	7ft
0.0150	21.8	.0000	1	7x
0.0150	21.8	.0000	1	7x1
0.0150	21.8	.0000	1	7x10
0.0150	21.8	.0000	1	7x2
0.0150	21.8	.0000	1	7x24
0.0150	21.8	.0000	1	7x30
0.0150	21.8	.0000	1	7x5
0.0150	21.8	.0000	1	7x60
0.0150	21.8	.0000	1	7x8

THE PRECEDING WORD TYPE OCCUPIES RANK 62200

U	SFI	D	F	Word Type
0.0150	21.8	.0000	1	7x98
0.0150	21.8	.0000	1	70-second
0.0150	21.8	.0000	1	70-year
0.0150	21.8	.0000	1	70/100
0.0150	21.8	.0000	1	70x50
0.0150	21.8	.0000	1	70x600
0.0150	21.8	.0000	1	70x80
0.0150	21.8	.0000	1	700/1000
0.0150	21.8	.0000	1	70000
0.0150	21.8	.0000	1	702-397
0.0150	21.8	.0000	1	704x6
0.0150	21.8	.0000	1	704x600
0.0150	21.8	.0000	1	7052
0.0150	21.8	.0000	1	712/2
0.0150	21.8	.0000	1	72/8
0.0150	21.8	.0000	1	72x10
0.0150	21.8	.0000	1	72x100
0.0150	21.8	.0000	1	7200
0.0150	21.8	.0000	1	723
0.0150	21.8	.0000	1	7242
0.0150	21.8	.0000	1	7263
0.0150	21.8	.0000	1	7281
0.0150	21.8	.0000	1	73kg
0.0150	21.8	.0000	1	7305
0.0150	21.8	.0000	1	732-page
0.0150	21.8	.0000	1	745
0.0150	21.8	.0000	1	7532
0.0150	21.8	.0000	1	75414
0.0150	21.8	.0000	1	76x3
0.0150	21.8	.0000	1	76x300
0.0150	21.8	.0000	1	764
0.0150	21.8	.0000	1	765
0.0150	21.8	.0000	1	767
0.0150	21.8	.0000	1	7684
0.0150	21.8	.0000	1	769
0.0150	21.8	.0000	1	772
0.0150	21.8	.0000	1	7863
0.0150	21.8	.0000	1	7888
0.0150	21.8	.0000	1	8-hour
0.0150	21.8	.0000	1	8-pound
0.0150	21.8	.0000	1	8-11
0.0150	21.8	.0000	1	8-4
0.0150	21.8	.0000	1	8-5
0.0150	21.8	.0000	1	8/18
0.0150	21.8	.0000	1	8/2
0.0150	21.8	.0000	1	8/20
0.0150	21.8	.0000	1	8/24
0.0150	21.8	.0000	1	8/7
0.0150	21.8	.0000	1	8x
0.0150	21.8	.0000	1	8x/3y
0.0150	21.8	.0000	1	8xn
0.0150	21.8	.0000	1	8x0
0.0150	21.8	.0000	1	8x2
0.0150	21.8	.0000	1	8x3
0.0150	21.8	.0000	1	8x30
0.0150	21.8	.0000	1	8x5
0.0150	21.8	.0000	1	8x50
0.0150	21.8	.0000	1	8x51
0.0150	21.8	.0000	1	8x7
0.0150	21.8	.0000	1	8x8x8x8
0.0150	21.8	.0000	1	80th
0.0150	21.8	.0000	1	801
0.0150	21.8	.0000	1	804
0.0150	21.8	.0000	1	810
0.0150	21.8	.0000	1	8134
0.0150	21.8	.0000	1	820
0.0150	21.8	.0000	1	8253
0.0150	21.8	.0000	1	829
0.0150	21.8	.0000	1	83-6
0.0150	21.8	.0000	1	83-7
0.0150	21.8	.0000	1	8333
0.0150	21.8	.0000	1	835
0.0150	21.8	.0000	1	84-56
0.0150	21.8	.0000	1	8437
0.0150	21.8	.0000	1	847-568
0.0150	21.8	.0000	1	8526/10
0.0150	21.8	.0000	1	854
0.0150	21.8	.0000	1	8541
0.0150	21.8	.0000	1	856
0.0150	21.8	.0000	1	8561
0.0150	21.8	.0000	1	857/100
0.0150	21.8	.0000	1	86-38
0.0150	21.8	.0000	1	8603
0.0150	21.8	.0000	1	86407600325
0.0150	21.8	.0000	1	87-88
0.0150	21.8	.0000	1	8742
0.0150	21.8	.0000	1	875
0.0150	21.8	.0000	1	876
0.0150	21.8	.0000	1	88/
0.0150	21.8	.0000	1	8800
0.0150	21.8	.0000	1	9-
0.0150	21.8	.0000	1	9-cent
0.0150	21.8	.0000	1	9-day
0.0150	21.8	.0000	1	9-14
0.0150	21.8	.0000	1	9-4
0.0150	21.8	.0000	1	9/1
0.0150	21.8	.0000	1	9/1000
0.0150	21.8	.0000	1	9/16
0.0150	21.8	.0000	1	9/18
0.0150	21.8	.0000	1	9/27

THE PRECEDING WORD TYPE OCCUPIES RANK 62300

U	SFI	D	F	Word Type
0.0150	21.8	.0000	1	9/30
0.0150	21.8	.0000	1	9/6
0.0150	21.8	.0000	1	9/80
0.0150	21.8	.0000	1	9a
0.0150	21.8	.0000	1	9x
0.0150	21.8	.0000	1	9x1
0.0150	21.8	.0000	1	9x6
0.0150	21.8	.0000	1	9x9
0.0150	21.8	.0000	1	90-word
0.0150	21.8	.0000	1	90/100
0.0150	21.8	.0000	1	90/120
0.0150	21.8	.0000	1	9003
0.0150	21.8	.0000	1	9021
0.0150	21.8	.0000	1	9035
0.0150	21.8	.0000	1	910
0.0150	21.8	.0000	1	916/10
0.0150	21.8	.0000	1	92-47
0.0150	21.8	.0000	1	92nd
0.0150	21.8	.0000	1	929
0.0150	21.8	.0000	1	937
0.0150	21.8	.0000	1	9376
0.0150	21.8	.0000	1	944
0.0150	21.8	.0000	1	945
0.0150	21.8	.0000	1	95-cent
0.0150	21.8	.0000	1	950
0.0150	21.8	.0000	1	9500
0.0150	21.8	.0000	1	956
0.0150	21.8	.0000	1	962
0.0150	21.8	.0000	1	9628
0.0150	21.8	.0000	1	967
0.0150	21.8	.0000	1	970
0.0150	21.8	.0000	1	971
0.0150	21.8	.0000	1	973
0.0150	21.8	.0000	1	98x10
0.0150	21.8	.0000	1	98x7
0.0150	21.8	.0000	1	980
0.0150	21.8	.0000	1	99/300
0.0150	21.8	.0000	1	99x99
0.0150	21.8	.0000	1	990
0.0145	21.6	.0000	1	$892
0.0145	21.6	.0000	1	'Frisco
0.0145	21.6	.0000	1	'zamine
0.0145	21.6	.0000	1	'zamined
0.0145	21.6	.0000	1	'56
0.0145	21.6	.0000	1	A-b-c-d-e-f-g
0.0145	21.6	.0000	1	a-bo-a-ard
0.0145	21.6	.0000	1	a-boar-r-r-rd
0.0145	21.6	.0000	1	a-charging
0.0145	21.6	.0000	1	a-rowing
0.0145	21.6	.0000	1	a-shinin'
0.0145	21.6	.0000	1	a-steering
0.0145	21.6	.0000	1	A/P-22S
0.0145	21.6	.0000	1	AB'S**
0.0145	21.6	.0000	1	abaci
0.0145	21.6	.0000	1	Abako
0.0145	21.6	.0000	1	abattoir
0.0145	21.6	.0000	1	abba
0.0145	21.6	.0000	1	Abd
0.0145	21.6	.0000	1	Abd-el-Kader
0.0145	21.6	.0000	1	Abiah
0.0145	21.6	.0000	1	abrogated
0.0145	21.6	.0000	1	abruptness
0.0145	21.6	.0000	1	Absent
0.0145	21.6	.0000	1	absentmindedly
0.0145	21.6	.0000	1	absolutism
0.0145	21.6	.0000	1	Abyssinian
0.0145	21.6	.0000	1	accentless
0.0145	21.6	.0000	1	acclimatized
0.0145	21.6	.0000	1	acclimatizing
0.0145	21.6	.0000	1	Achelous
0.0145	21.6	.0000	1	actuate
0.0145	21.6	.0000	1	acumen
0.0145	21.6	.0000	1	adazzle
0.0145	21.6	.0000	1	addressee
0.0145	21.6	.0000	1	ADI
0.0145	21.6	.0000	1	adjourning
0.0145	21.6	.0000	1	admirals
0.0145	21.6	.0000	1	admixture
0.0145	21.6	.0000	1	admixtures
0.0145	21.6	.0000	1	adoration
0.0145	21.6	.0000	1	Adriaan
0.0145	21.6	.0000	1	Adrianople
0.0145	21.6	.0000	1	Adventist
0.0145	21.6	.0000	1	adventure-loving
0.0145	21.6	.0000	1	Adventuring
0.0145	21.6	.0000	1	adversely
0.0145	21.6	.0000	1	Advertiser
0.0145	21.6	.0000	1	Advocate
0.0145	21.6	.0000	1	aerobatics
0.0145	21.6	.0000	1	Aerosystems
0.0145	21.6	.0000	1	Afrikaans-speaking
0.0145	21.6	.0000	1	Afrikaner-controlled
0.0145	21.6	.0000	1	Afrikaner's
0.0145	21.6	.0000	1	aftershaft
0.0145	21.6	.0000	1	aftershafts
0.0145	21.6	.0000	1	Agencies
0.0145	21.6	.0000	1	agriculturalists
0.0145	21.6	.0000	1	agronomists
0.0145	21.6	.0000	1	ah-h-h
0.0145	21.6	.0000	1	Ah'm

THE PRECEDING WORD TYPE OCCUPIES RANK 62400

U	SFI	D	F	Word Type
0.0145	21.6	.0000	1	Ahab
0.0145	21.6	.0000	1	ahem
0.0145	21.6	.0000	1	ahhhhhhh
0.0145	21.6	.0000	1	Ahmadu
0.0145	21.6	.0000	1	air-cooling
0.0145	21.6	.0000	1	air-drying
0.0145	21.6	.0000	1	airedale
0.0145	21.6	.0000	1	Airing
0.0145	21.6	.0000	1	airless-spray
0.0145	21.6	.0000	1	AIRPORTS
0.0145	21.6	.0000	1	airspeed
0.0145	21.6	.0000	1	ajar
0.0145	21.6	.0000	1	AKC
0.0145	21.6	.0000	1	Al-Jazair
0.0145	21.6	.0000	1	albino
0.0145	21.6	.0000	1	Albon's
0.0145	21.6	.0000	1	alchemist
0.0145	21.6	.0000	1	Alcott's
0.0145	21.6	.0000	1	Alcotts
0.0145	21.6	.0000	1	Aleck
0.0145	21.6	.0000	1	Algerie
0.0145	21.6	.0000	1	aliases
0.0145	21.6	.0000	1	alienate
0.0145	21.6	.0000	1	all-encompassing
0.0145	21.6	.0000	1	allemandes
0.0145	21.6	.0000	1	Allie
0.0145	21.6	.0000	1	Allisons
0.0145	21.6	.0000	1	allocation
0.0145	21.6	.0000	1	allocations
0.0145	21.6	.0000	1	allosaurs
0.0145	21.6	.0000	1	allures
0.0145	21.6	.0000	1	Almanacs
0.0145	21.6	.0000	1	Alsatians
0.0145	21.6	.0000	1	alternatively
0.0145	21.6	.0000	1	altruism
0.0145	21.6	.0000	1	Alvsborg
0.0145	21.6	.0000	1	Amalfi
0.0145	21.6	.0000	1	ambidextrous
0.0145	21.6	.0000	1	Ambrosiana
0.0145	21.6	.0000	1	ambuscade
0.0145	21.6	.0000	1	AMEBA
0.0145	21.6	.0000	1	ameba's
0.0145	21.6	.0000	1	American-type
0.0145	21.6	.0000	1	Americanism
0.0145	21.6	.0000	1	amidship
0.0145	21.6	.0000	1	amir
0.0145	21.6	.0000	1	Among
0.0145	21.6	.0000	1	amphitheatres
0.0145	21.6	.0000	1	amputate
0.0145	21.6	.0000	1	anachronistic
0.0145	21.6	.0000	1	Anadolu
0.0145	21.6	.0000	1	anatosaurs
0.0145	21.6	.0000	1	anatosaurus
0.0145	21.6	.0000	1	ankylosaurs
0.0145	21.6	.0000	1	ankylosaurus
0.0145	21.6	.0000	1	annexes
0.0145	21.6	.0000	1	annuities
0.0145	21.6	.0000	1	anonymity
0.0145	21.6	.0000	1	answer'd
0.0145	21.6	.0000	1	answerable
0.0145	21.6	.0000	1	ANT
0.0145	21.6	.0000	1	Anti-Slavery
0.0145	21.6	.0000	1	anti-West
0.0145	21.6	.0000	1	anti-church
0.0145	21.6	.0000	1	anti-white
0.0145	21.6	.0000	1	anticapitalist
0.0145	21.6	.0000	1	anticommunist
0.0145	21.6	.0000	1	Antique
0.0145	21.6	.0000	1	anxiety-ridden
0.0145	21.6	.0000	1	anything's
0.0145	21.6	.0000	1	apiary
0.0145	21.6	.0000	1	apostles
0.0145	21.6	.0000	1	apothecary
0.0145	21.6	.0000	1	apothecary's
0.0145	21.6	.0000	1	Appaloosa
0.0145	21.6	.0000	1	appear'd
0.0145	21.6	.0000	1	apple-cheeked
0.0145	21.6	.0000	1	appliqued
0.0145	21.6	.0000	1	appurtenances
0.0145	21.6	.0000	1	Aquilo
0.0145	21.6	.0000	1	Araba
0.0145	21.6	.0000	1	Aramaeans
0.0145	21.6	.0000	1	Araminta
0.0145	21.6	.0000	1	Arcadia
0.0145	21.6	.0000	1	Archimedes'
0.0145	21.6	.0000	1	Archives
0.0145	21.6	.0000	1	Ard
0.0145	21.6	.0000	1	Arendt
0.0145	21.6	.0000	1	Argonautic
0.0145	21.6	.0000	1	aristocracies
0.0145	21.6	.0000	1	Aristophanes'
0.0145	21.6	.0000	1	armor-bearer
0.0145	21.6	.0000	1	armor-piercing
0.0145	21.6	.0000	1	ARMOURED
0.0145	21.6	.0000	1	art-song
0.0145	21.6	.0000	1	articals
0.0145	21.6	.0000	1	Artois
0.0145	21.6	.0000	1	ash-wood
0.0145	21.6	.0000	1	Ashburn
0.0145	21.6	.0000	1	Ashtabula

THE PRECEDING WORD TYPE OCCUPIES RANK 62500

U	SFI	D	F	Word Type
0.0145	21.6	.0000	1	ashy
0.0145	21.6	.0000	1	Asil
0.0145	21.6	.0000	1	Asleep
0.0145	21.6	.0000	1	Asmodeus
0.0145	21.6	.0000	1	assembles
0.0145	21.6	.0000	1	Astors
0.0145	21.6	.0000	1	astroblastoma
0.0145	21.6	.0000	1	Astronautical
0.0145	21.6	.0000	1	asura
0.0145	21.6	.0000	1	Ath
0.0145	21.6	.0000	1	attache
0.0145	21.6	.0000	1	AUGER
0.0145	21.6	.0000	1	Augsbury
0.0145	21.6	.0000	1	Auntie's
0.0145	21.6	.0000	1	Aurelian
0.0145	21.6	.0000	1	aurum
0.0145	21.6	.0000	1	Auster
0.0145	21.6	.0000	1	Auto-Unions
0.0145	21.6	.0000	1	Avernus
0.0145	21.6	.0000	1	Avusrennen
0.0145	21.6	.0000	1	awqaf
0.0145	21.6	.0000	1	axle-deep
0.0145	21.6	.0000	1	Ayin
0.0145	21.6	.0000	1	B-a-b-y
0.0145	21.6	.0000	1	Babworth's
0.0145	21.6	.0000	1	Bachs
0.0145	21.6	.0000	1	BACK
0.0145	21.6	.0000	1	back-yard
0.0145	21.6	.0000	1	backwoodsman
0.0145	21.6	.0000	1	baggage-smashers
0.0145	21.6	.0000	1	Baikal
0.0145	21.6	.0000	1	Baire
0.0145	21.6	.0000	1	Bait
0.0145	21.6	.0000	1	balcony-festooned
0.0145	21.6	.0000	1	BALL
0.0145	21.6	.0000	1	ball-handler
0.0145	21.6	.0000	1	Balle
0.0145	21.6	.0000	1	bam
0.0145	21.6	.0000	1	Bamayassi
0.0145	21.6	.0000	1	Banat
0.0145	21.6	.0000	1	Banda
0.0145	21.6	.0000	1	bandoleers
0.0145	21.6	.0000	1	bangles
0.0145	21.6	.0000	1	barbecues
0.0145	21.6	.0000	1	barbering
0.0145	21.6	.0000	1	Barclay
0.0145	21.6	.0000	1	barefooted
0.0145	21.6	.0000	1	BARGES
0.0145	21.6	.0000	1	bark-covered
0.0145	21.6	.0000	1	Barnato
0.0145	21.6	.0000	1	barrowload
0.0145	21.6	.0000	1	Bas-Ixelles
0.0145	21.6	.0000	1	baseboards
0.0145	21.6	.0000	1	bashful
0.0145	21.6	.0000	1	bashfulness

U	SFI	D	F	Word Type
0.0145	21.6	.0000	1	Basses-Pyrenees
0.0145	21.6	.0000	1	basso
0.0145	21.6	.0000	1	bastions
0.0145	21.6	.0000	1	BAT
0.0145	21.6	.0000	1	bazooka
0.0145	21.6	.0000	1	beachheads
0.0145	21.6	.0000	1	beakfuls
0.0145	21.6	.0000	1	bean-hole
0.0145	21.6	.0000	1	becalmed
0.0145	21.6	.0000	1	beck
0.0145	21.6	.0000	1	bedevil
0.0145	21.6	.0000	1	bedeviled
0.0145	21.6	.0000	1	bee-keeper
0.0145	21.6	.0000	1	beech-tree
0.0145	21.6	.0000	1	Beechland
0.0145	21.6	.0000	1	Beetle's
0.0145	21.6	.0000	1	beggar-priests
0.0145	21.6	.0000	1	beholdeth
0.0145	21.6	.0000	1	behooves
0.0145	21.6	.0000	1	bejabers
0.0145	21.6	.0000	1	Beline
0.0145	21.6	.0000	1	Bellagio
0.0145	21.6	.0000	1	belligerence
0.0145	21.6	.0000	1	Belmore
0.0145	21.6	.0000	1	Belond-AP**
0.0145	21.6	.0000	1	Belond-owned
0.0145	21.6	.0000	1	belowworm
0.0145	21.6	.0000	1	Bembe
0.0145	21.6	.0000	1	Berchtesgaden
0.0145	21.6	.0000	1	berg
0.0145	21.6	.0000	1	berl
0.0145	21.6	.0000	1	Bernadotte
0.0145	21.6	.0000	1	Bernadottes
0.0145	21.6	.0000	1	Bernhard's
0.0145	21.6	.0000	1	Berrys
0.0145	21.6	.0000	1	best-adjusted
0.0145	21.6	.0000	1	betel
0.0145	21.6	.0000	1	Betrand
0.0145	21.6	.0000	1	betrayer
0.0145	21.6	.0000	1	better-educated
0.0145	21.6	.0000	1	better-known
0.0145	21.6	.0000	1	better-quality
0.0145	21.6	.0000	1	better-than-average
0.0145	21.6	.0000	1	Bettys
0.0145	21.6	.0000	1	betwixt

THE PRECEDING WORD TYPE OCCUPIES RANK 62600

U	SFI	D	F	Word Type
0.0145	21.6	.0000	1	Beyoglu
0.0145	21.6	.0000	1	Biagio
0.0145	21.6	.0000	1	bij
0.0145	21.6	.0000	1	billetted
0.0145	21.6	.0000	1	billow
0.0145	21.6	.0000	1	Bills
0.0145	21.6	.0000	1	billygoat
0.0145	21.6	.0000	1	Bilsen's
0.0145	21.6	.0000	1	Binche
0.0145	21.6	.0000	1	bipod
0.0145	21.6	.0000	1	bird-hip
0.0145	21.6	.0000	1	bird-hipped
0.0145	21.6	.0000	1	bison's
0.0145	21.6	.0000	1	bla-bla-bla-bla-bla
0.0145	21.6	.0000	1	blab
0.0145	21.6	.0000	1	black-maned
0.0145	21.6	.0000	1	blackberrying
0.0145	21.6	.0000	1	Blackfoot's
0.0145	21.6	.0000	1	Blackstone
0.0145	21.6	.0000	1	blade-wielding
0.0145	21.6	.0000	1	bladelike
0.0145	21.6	.0000	1	blind-man's
0.0145	21.6	.0000	1	blond-haired
0.0145	21.6	.0000	1	blondes
0.0145	21.6	.0000	1	bloomer
0.0145	21.6	.0000	1	Bloomer
0.0145	21.6	.0000	1	blow-hole
0.0145	21.6	.0000	1	blue-painted
0.0145	21.6	.0000	1	blue-ribbon
0.0145	21.6	.0000	1	Blunt
0.0145	21.6	.0000	1	boastingly
0.0145	21.6	.0000	1	boatlike
0.0145	21.6	.0000	1	bobwhites
0.0145	21.6	.0000	1	Boks'
0.0145	21.6	.0000	1	Bolkestein
0.0145	21.6	.0000	1	Bolsun's
0.0145	21.6	.0000	1	bone-digger
0.0145	21.6	.0000	1	bone-jarring
0.0145	21.6	.0000	1	Bone's
0.0145	21.6	.0000	1	bong-bonged
0.0145	21.6	.0000	1	bonze
0.0145	21.6	.0000	1	book-seller
0.0145	21.6	.0000	1	booklice
0.0145	21.6	.0000	1	bookmakers'
0.0145	21.6	.0000	1	bootshaped
0.0145	21.6	.0000	1	Borgese
0.0145	21.6	.0000	1	Borsalino
0.0145	21.6	.0000	1	boss-giraffe
0.0145	21.6	.0000	1	Botkin's
0.0145	21.6	.0000	1	Bougainville
0.0145	21.6	.0000	1	bow's
0.0145	21.6	.0000	1	bowheads
0.0145	21.6	.0000	1	bowlegged
0.0145	21.6	.0000	1	bowsed
0.0145	21.6	.0000	1	boxer's
0.0145	21.6	.0000	1	boxful
0.0145	21.6	.0000	1	Boycott
0.0145	21.6	.0000	1	BRACE
0.0145	21.6	.0000	1	bradded
0.0145	21.6	.0000	1	brainy
0.0145	21.6	.0000	1	branchlets
0.0145	21.6	.0000	1	Brandel
0.0145	21.6	.0000	1	Branwen's
0.0145	21.6	.0000	1	brashly
0.0145	21.6	.0000	1	brays
0.0145	21.6	.0000	1	breadthwise
0.0145	21.6	.0000	1	Breakfast's
0.0145	21.6	.0000	1	Breckinridge
0.0145	21.6	.0000	1	breeder-trainer-driver
0.0145	21.6	.0000	1	Bresnahan
0.0145	21.6	.0000	1	Brewsters
0.0145	21.6	.0000	1	Briareus
0.0145	21.6	.0000	1	brick's
0.0145	21.6	.0000	1	brickmaking
0.0145	21.6	.0000	1	bridgehead
0.0145	21.6	.0000	1	Bridgman's
0.0145	21.6	.0000	1	brig
0.0145	21.6	.0000	1	brigadier-general
0.0145	21.6	.0000	1	brims
0.0145	21.6	.0000	1	brinded
0.0145	21.6	.0000	1	BRINE
0.0145	21.6	.0000	1	Bristol's
0.0145	21.6	.0000	1	Briton
0.0145	21.6	.0000	1	brittled
0.0145	21.6	.0000	1	BROAD-LEAVED
0.0145	21.6	.0000	1	broad-winged
0.0145	21.6	.0000	1	broidered
0.0145	21.6	.0000	1	bronco-bustin'
0.0145	21.6	.0000	1	Bronson's
0.0145	21.6	.0000	1	Bronto
0.0145	21.6	.0000	1	Brooklyn-born
0.0145	21.6	.0000	1	Brooklynite
0.0145	21.6	.0000	1	broomhandles
0.0145	21.6	.0000	1	broughtest
0.0145	21.6	.0000	1	browbeating
0.0145	21.6	.0000	1	brown-black
0.0145	21.6	.0000	1	brownish-gray
0.0145	21.6	.0000	1	Bruin
0.0145	21.6	.0000	1	bruisers
0.0145	21.6	.0000	1	bruising

THE PRECEDING WORD TYPE OCCUPIES RANK 62700

U	SFI	D	F	Word Type
0.0145	21.6	.0000	1	brushless
0.0145	21.6	.0000	1	Bucketfoot
0.0145	21.6	.0000	1	Bucktown
0.0145	21.6	.0000	1	bucolic
0.0145	21.6	.0000	1	Buffie's
0.0145	21.6	.0000	1	BUGS
0.0145	21.6	.0000	1	Builders'
0.0145	21.6	.0000	1	bull-shouldered
0.0145	21.6	.0000	1	Bulloch
0.0145	21.6	.0000	1	bullwhacker
0.0145	21.6	.0000	1	Bunker's
0.0145	21.6	.0000	1	Bursa
0.0145	21.6	.0000	1	Bushyhead
0.0145	21.6	.0000	1	busting
0.0145	21.6	.0000	1	Butt
0.0145	21.6	.0000	1	butterwoman
0.0145	21.6	.0000	1	buttonless
0.0145	21.6	.0000	1	C-ration
0.0145	21.6	.0000	1	Cabbage
0.0145	21.6	.0000	1	Cairns
0.0145	21.6	.0000	1	Calais
0.0145	21.6	.0000	1	calcified
0.0145	21.6	.0000	1	caldrons
0.0145	21.6	.0000	1	Calloways
0.0145	21.6	.0000	1	calm-spoken
0.0145	21.6	.0000	1	calumny
0.0145	21.6	.0000	1	Camerata
0.0145	21.6	.0000	1	camouflaging
0.0145	21.6	.0000	1	CANAL
0.0145	21.6	.0000	1	candle-light
0.0145	21.6	.0000	1	candle's
0.0145	21.6	.0000	1	candlemaking
0.0145	21.6	.0000	1	Candlemas
0.0145	21.6	.0000	1	Canto
0.0145	21.6	.0000	1	canvas-top
0.0145	21.6	.0000	1	capon
0.0145	21.6	.0000	1	captain-general
0.0145	21.6	.0000	1	carbide-tipped
0.0145	21.6	.0000	1	careening
0.0145	21.6	.0000	1	Cares
0.0145	21.6	.0000	1	CARGO
0.0145	21.6	.0000	1	Carpathia
0.0145	21.6	.0000	1	CARRIAGES
0.0145	21.6	.0000	1	cartel
0.0145	21.6	.0000	1	Cary's
0.0145	21.6	.0000	1	cascaded
0.0145	21.6	.0000	1	casework
0.0145	21.6	.0000	1	Cassadaga
0.0145	21.6	.0000	1	Cassidy
0.0145	21.6	.0000	1	cat-like
0.0145	21.6	.0000	1	Catalans
0.0145	21.6	.0000	1	Catalonia
0.0145	21.6	.0000	1	catching's
0.0145	21.6	.0000	1	Cato
0.0145	21.6	.0000	1	Cattaraugus
0.0145	21.6	.0000	1	Cavalleria
0.0145	21.6	.0000	1	cavelike
0.0145	21.6	.0000	1	caws
0.0145	21.6	.0000	1	cawses
0.0145	21.6	.0000	1	Cecropia
0.0145	21.6	.0000	1	center-field
0.0145	21.6	.0000	1	centerboard
0.0145	21.6	.0000	1	centimeter's
0.0145	21.6	.0000	1	centralize
0.0145	21.6	.0000	1	centred
0.0145	21.6	.0000	1	Cercle
0.0145	21.6	.0000	1	cermet
0.0145	21.6	.0000	1	Cespedes
0.0145	21.6	.0000	1	chaffinches
0.0145	21.6	.0000	1	Chaffray's
0.0145	21.6	.0000	1	Chaim
0.0145	21.6	.0000	1	Chalmers
0.0145	21.6	.0000	1	Chambersburg
0.0145	21.6	.0000	1	Chancellery
0.0145	21.6	.0000	1	chandlery
0.0145	21.6	.0000	1	Chandralehka
0.0145	21.6	.0000	1	chaperoned
0.0145	21.6	.0000	1	Chaplinesque
0.0145	21.6	.0000	1	Charente
0.0145	21.6	.0000	1	chargers
0.0145	21.6	.0000	1	charnel-roof
0.0145	21.6	.0000	1	Charon
0.0145	21.6	.0000	1	Charron
0.0145	21.6	.0000	1	Chautauqua
0.0145	21.6	.0000	1	chawklut
0.0145	21.6	.0000	1	cheats
0.0145	21.6	.0000	1	checkerboard
0.0145	21.6	.0000	1	cheese-butter
0.0145	21.6	.0000	1	chefs
0.0145	21.6	.0000	1	Chekiang
0.0145	21.6	.0000	1	Chemung
0.0145	21.6	.0000	1	Chengchou
0.0145	21.6	.0000	1	cherry-tree
0.0145	21.6	.0000	1	cherubs
0.0145	21.6	.0000	1	chestnut-falls
0.0145	21.6	.0000	1	Chief's
0.0145	21.6	.0000	1	chieftain's
0.0145	21.6	.0000	1	chieftan
0.0145	21.6	.0000	1	childishness
0.0145	21.6	.0000	1	Childs

THE PRECEDING WORD TYPE OCCUPIES RANK 62800

U	SFI	D	F	Word Type
0.0145	21.6	.0000	1	Chimaeras
0.0145	21.6	.0000	1	chimmey
0.0145	21.6	.0000	1	chinquapins
0.0145	21.6	.0000	1	chirpy
0.0145	21.6	.0000	1	chisel-like
0.0145	21.6	.0000	1	chiseling
0.0145	21.6	.0000	1	chitarrone
0.0145	21.6	.0000	1	Chloe
0.0145	21.6	.0000	1	chocolates
0.0145	21.6	.0000	1	chorales
0.0145	21.6	.0000	1	Chowan
0.0145	21.6	.0000	1	Chris'mus
0.0145	21.6	.0000	1	Christianity's
0.0145	21.6	.0000	1	Christiansen
0.0145	21.6	.0000	1	Christy
0.0145	21.6	.0000	1	Chuckawalla
0.0145	21.6	.0000	1	chug-chug
0.0145	21.6	.0000	1	chug-chug-chug
0.0145	21.6	.0000	1	Church-countenanced
0.0145	21.6	.0000	1	church-man
0.0145	21.6	.0000	1	Ciboure
0.0145	21.6	.0000	1	cigar-chewing
0.0145	21.6	.0000	1	cinderman
0.0145	21.6	.0000	1	Cinque
0.0145	21.6	.0000	1	citizen's
0.0145	21.6	.0000	1	city-to-city
0.0145	21.6	.0000	1	clambers
0.0145	21.6	.0000	1	clank'd
0.0145	21.6	.0000	1	clannish
0.0145	21.6	.0000	1	claspers
0.0145	21.6	.0000	1	classless
0.0145	21.6	.0000	1	clavier
0.0145	21.6	.0000	1	CLAW
0.0145	21.6	.0000	1	claybank
0.0145	21.6	.0000	1	claybanks
0.0145	21.6	.0000	1	Claypoole
0.0145	21.6	.0000	1	Click
0.0145	21.6	.0000	1	clickety
0.0145	21.6	.0000	1	climbing's
0.0145	21.6	.0000	1	Cline
0.0145	21.6	.0000	1	clinking
0.0145	21.6	.0000	1	clocking
0.0145	21.6	.0000	1	clop-clop
0.0145	21.6	.0000	1	closed-up
0.0145	21.6	.0000	1	closeup
0.0145	21.6	.0000	1	cloth-wrapped
0.0145	21.6	.0000	1	clothespress
0.0145	21.6	.0000	1	cloud-covered
0.0145	21.6	.0000	1	cloven
0.0145	21.6	.0000	1	cloy
0.0145	21.6	.0000	1	Cloyse
0.0145	21.6	.0000	1	clutch'd
0.0145	21.6	.0000	1	coal-bearing
0.0145	21.6	.0000	1	coal-making
0.0145	21.6	.0000	1	coalbin
0.0145	21.6	.0000	1	coalitions
0.0145	21.6	.0000	1	cobblestoned
0.0145	21.6	.0000	1	cock-crow
0.0145	21.6	.0000	1	Cockers
0.0145	21.6	.0000	1	Cocytus
0.0145	21.6	.0000	1	codliver
0.0145	21.6	.0000	1	coffeegrowers
0.0145	21.6	.0000	1	Colbys
0.0145	21.6	.0000	1	colloquy
0.0145	21.6	.0000	1	Colombians
0.0145	21.6	.0000	1	colonialism's
0.0145	21.6	.0000	1	colonialisms
0.0145	21.6	.0000	1	colonialists'
0.0145	21.6	.0000	1	COLONIES
0.0145	21.6	.0000	1	Coltejer
0.0145	21.6	.0000	1	columned
0.0145	21.6	.0000	1	coma-la
0.0145	21.6	.0000	1	Comanche's
0.0145	21.6	.0000	1	Comanduras
0.0145	21.6	.0000	1	comber
0.0145	21.6	.0000	1	commandant's
0.0145	21.6	.0000	1	Commodus
0.0145	21.6	.0000	1	commons
0.0145	21.6	.0000	1	companionway
0.0145	21.6	.0000	1	compilation
0.0145	21.6	.0000	1	computer-automated
0.0145	21.6	.0000	1	computer-brained
0.0145	21.6	.0000	1	computer-fed
0.0145	21.6	.0000	1	concubines
0.0145	21.6	.0000	1	condemns
0.0145	21.6	.0000	1	condiment
0.0145	21.6	.0000	1	conformation
0.0145	21.6	.0000	1	Congolais
0.0145	21.6	.0000	1	Congos
0.0145	21.6	.0000	1	Connaught
0.0145	21.6	.0000	1	Conqueror's
0.0145	21.6	.0000	1	conscripts
0.0145	21.6	.0000	1	considerateness
0.0145	21.6	.0000	1	Constantin
0.0145	21.6	.0000	1	CONSTITUTION
0.0145	21.6	.0000	1	constitution's
0.0145	21.6	.0000	1	construction-paper
0.0145	21.6	.0000	1	contacting
0.0145	21.6	.0000	1	contagion
0.0145	21.6	.0000	1	Continental's

THE PRECEDING WORD TYPE OCCUPIES RANK 62900

U	SFI	D	F	Word Type
0.0145	21.6	.0000	1	continuo
0.0145	21.6	.0000	1	Convair
0.0145	21.6	.0000	1	convalescence
0.0145	21.6	.0000	1	convulse
0.0145	21.6	.0000	1	Conyers
0.0145	21.6	.0000	1	coo
0.0145	21.6	.0000	1	Cooma
0.0145	21.6	.0000	1	Cooma's
0.0145	21.6	.0000	1	COPEPODS
0.0145	21.6	.0000	1	COPING
0.0145	21.6	.0000	1	cordiality
0.0145	21.6	.0000	1	Corinne
0.0145	21.6	.0000	1	Corix
0.0145	21.6	.0000	1	Coro
0.0145	21.6	.0000	1	corpsmen
0.0145	21.6	.0000	1	corpulent
0.0145	21.6	.0000	1	Corruption
0.0145	21.6	.0000	1	corruptions
0.0145	21.6	.0000	1	Corsair
0.0145	21.6	.0000	1	Corythosaurus
0.0145	21.6	.0000	1	Cossine
0.0145	21.6	.0000	1	costliest
0.0145	21.6	.0000	1	cottagers
0.0145	21.6	.0000	1	cotton-covered
0.0145	21.6	.0000	1	councillors
0.0145	21.6	.0000	1	countenances
0.0145	21.6	.0000	1	Counter
0.0145	21.6	.0000	1	counter-cooperative
0.0145	21.6	.0000	1	countermeasures
0.0145	21.6	.0000	1	countinghouse
0.0145	21.6	.0000	1	country-men
0.0145	21.6	.0000	1	countrysides
0.0145	21.6	.0000	1	couple-color
0.0145	21.6	.0000	1	couplings
0.0145	21.6	.0000	1	courantes
0.0145	21.6	.0000	1	Cowpens
0.0145	21.6	.0000	1	crackpot
0.0145	21.6	.0000	1	cramming
0.0145	21.6	.0000	1	crave
0.0145	21.6	.0000	1	crawl'd
0.0145	21.6	.0000	1	Creamy
0.0145	21.6	.0000	1	creatures'
0.0145	21.6	.0000	1	creditor's
0.0145	21.6	.0000	1	credo
0.0145	21.6	.0000	1	credos
0.0145	21.6	.0000	1	creek's
0.0145	21.6	.0000	1	Cremona
0.0145	21.6	.0000	1	CRICKET
0.0145	21.6	.0000	1	crieth
0.0145	21.6	.0000	1	crinoids
0.0145	21.6	.0000	1	crispy
0.0145	21.6	.0000	1	croaks
0.0145	21.6	.0000	1	Croesus'
0.0145	21.6	.0000	1	crooks
0.0145	21.6	.0000	1	crop-growing
0.0145	21.6	.0000	1	CROSS-CUT
0.0145	21.6	.0000	1	crossbill
0.0145	21.6	.0000	1	crosscurrents
0.0145	21.6	.0000	1	crossing-the-Delaware
0.0145	21.6	.0000	1	crowneth
0.0145	21.6	.0000	1	cubist
0.0145	21.6	.0000	1	Cubs'
0.0145	21.6	.0000	1	cultivable
0.0145	21.6	.0000	1	cultive
0.0145	21.6	.0000	1	CunardLine
0.0145	21.6	.0000	1	curassow
0.0145	21.6	.0000	1	cure's
0.0145	21.6	.0000	1	curled-up
0.0145	21.6	.0000	1	Curlytop
0.0145	21.6	.0000	1	curtsied
0.0145	21.6	.0000	1	Custers
0.0145	21.6	.0000	1	cut-outs
0.0145	21.6	.0000	1	Cuyler
0.0145	21.6	.0000	1	Cypriots
0.0145	21.6	.0000	1	d'Eau
0.0145	21.6	.0000	1	dagger-like
0.0145	21.6	.0000	1	daintiest
0.0145	21.6	.0000	1	daintiness
0.0145	21.6	.0000	1	dairywoman
0.0145	21.6	.0000	1	Daisy's
0.0145	21.6	.0000	1	dallying
0.0145	21.6	.0000	1	damage-control
0.0145	21.6	.0000	1	damnable
0.0145	21.6	.0000	1	damndest
0.0145	21.6	.0000	1	DAN
0.0145	21.6	.0000	1	Daphnis
0.0145	21.6	.0000	1	dark-coated
0.0145	21.6	.0000	1	dark's
0.0145	21.6	.0000	1	Darley
0.0145	21.6	.0000	1	Davis's
0.0145	21.6	.0000	1	davits
0.0145	21.6	.0000	1	Daytona
0.0145	21.6	.0000	1	dazos
0.0145	21.6	.0000	1	deAviles
0.0145	21.6	.0000	1	DeDietrich
0.0145	21.6	.0000	1	deDion
0.0145	21.6	.0000	1	DeFosse
0.0145	21.6	.0000	1	DeLancey
0.0145	21.6	.0000	1	deLibrari
0.0145	21.6	.0000	1	DePottenzuipers

THE PRECEDING WORD TYPE OCCUPIES RANK 63000

U	SFI	D	F	Word Type
0.0145	21.6	.0000	1	deRome
0.0145	21.6	.0000	1	deWaal
0.0145	21.6	.0000	1	dead-ball
0.0145	21.6	.0000	1	dead-pan
0.0145	21.6	.0000	1	deader
0.0145	21.6	.0000	1	deathblow
0.0145	21.6	.0000	1	debutante's
0.0145	21.6	.0000	1	debutantes
0.0145	21.6	.0000	1	debutantes'
0.0145	21.6	.0000	1	debuts
0.0145	21.6	.0000	1	decentralized
0.0145	21.6	.0000	1	deceptions
0.0145	21.6	.0000	1	decorously
0.0145	21.6	.0000	1	Deep-River
0.0145	21.6	.0000	1	deep-fix'd
0.0145	21.6	.0000	1	deflated
0.0145	21.6	.0000	1	dehook
0.0145	21.6	.0000	1	deified

U	SFI	D	F	Word Type
0.0145	21.6	.0000	1	Deledda
0.0145	21.6	.0000	1	Delphi
0.0145	21.6	.0000	1	delphinium
0.0145	21.6	.0000	1	delving
0.0145	21.6	.0000	1	Dembroski
0.0145	21.6	.0000	1	Democratiques
0.0145	21.6	.0000	1	Demosthenes
0.0145	21.6	.0000	1	demotion
0.0145	21.6	.0000	1	Den
0.0145	21.6	.0000	1	denials
0.0145	21.6	.0000	1	Denmark-Norway
0.0145	21.6	.0000	1	denominationally
0.0145	21.6	.0000	1	Depository
0.0145	21.6	.0000	1	dervishes
0.0145	21.6	.0000	1	Deschamps
0.0145	21.6	.0000	1	desolated
0.0145	21.6	.0000	1	despaired
0.0145	21.6	.0000	1	despicable
0.0145	21.6	.0000	1	DiMag
0.0145	21.6	.0000	1	diMonza
0.0145	21.6	.0000	1	diTrevi
0.0145	21.6	.0000	1	diamond-backs
0.0145	21.6	.0000	1	Dickey
0.0145	21.6	.0000	1	didacticism
0.0145	21.6	.0000	1	Died
0.0145	21.6	.0000	1	DienBienPhu
0.0145	21.6	.0000	1	Diesel-electric
0.0145	21.6	.0000	1	differentiates
0.0145	21.6	.0000	1	dignifies
0.0145	21.6	.0000	1	Dilsey
0.0145	21.6	.0000	1	Dilsey's
0.0145	21.6	.0000	1	Dimes
0.0145	21.6	.0000	1	dinin'-table
0.0145	21.6	.0000	1	Dioscuri
0.0145	21.6	.0000	1	Diplocodus
0.0145	21.6	.0000	1	Directive
0.0145	21.6	.0000	1	directive
0.0145	21.6	.0000	1	discerns
0.0145	21.6	.0000	1	Discord
0.0145	21.6	.0000	1	disdainfulness
0.0145	21.6	.0000	1	disembowel
0.0145	21.6	.0000	1	disenfranchised
0.0145	21.6	.0000	1	disengag(ed)
0.0145	21.6	.0000	1	dished
0.0145	21.6	.0000	1	dishfuls
0.0145	21.6	.0000	1	disinterest
0.0145	21.6	.0000	1	disjunctive
0.0145	21.6	.0000	1	dismisses
0.0145	21.6	.0000	1	dismissing
0.0145	21.6	.0000	1	disoriented
0.0145	21.6	.0000	1	dispense
0.0145	21.6	.0000	1	displease
0.0145	21.6	.0000	1	disqualifications
0.0145	21.6	.0000	1	disreputable
0.0145	21.6	.0000	1	Distances
0.0145	21.6	.0000	1	disunited
0.0145	21.6	.0000	1	divised
0.0145	21.6	.0000	1	divisiveness
0.0145	21.6	.0000	1	doctored
0.0145	21.6	.0000	1	Dodger-killer
0.0145	21.6	.0000	1	dog-shopping
0.0145	21.6	.0000	1	Doggett
0.0145	21.6	.0000	1	Doggett's
0.0145	21.6	.0000	1	Dolan's
0.0145	21.6	.0000	1	Dolans
0.0145	21.6	.0000	1	Dominic
0.0145	21.6	.0000	1	don't-give-an-inch
0.0145	21.6	.0000	1	Dooleys
0.0145	21.6	.0000	1	doorstops
0.0145	21.6	.0000	1	Dormitory
0.0145	21.6	.0000	1	Dos
0.0145	21.6	.0000	1	double-crossing
0.0145	21.6	.0000	1	double-header
0.0145	21.6	.0000	1	dovetail-dado
0.0145	21.6	.0000	1	dovetailing
0.0145	21.6	.0000	1	dragons'
0.0145	21.6	.0000	1	DRAW
0.0145	21.6	.0000	1	DRAWN-OUT
0.0145	21.6	.0000	1	DROOP
0.0145	21.6	.0000	1	droshky
0.0145	21.6	.0000	1	dual-hurdling
0.0145	21.6	.0000	1	Duchess'

THE PRECEDING WORD TYPE OCCUPIES RANK 63100

U	SFI	D	F	Word Type
0.0145	21.6	.0000	1	duckbill's
0.0145	21.6	.0000	1	Duckbills
0.0145	21.6	.0000	1	duels
0.0145	21.6	.0000	1	dues-paying
0.0145	21.6	.0000	1	Duesseldorf
0.0145	21.6	.0000	1	dugong
0.0145	21.6	.0000	1	dull-witted
0.0145	21.6	.0000	1	dunny
0.0145	21.6	.0000	1	Durrow
0.0145	21.6	.0000	1	Duryea
0.0145	21.6	.0000	1	dust-collection
0.0145	21.6	.0000	1	dust-covered
0.0145	21.6	.0000	1	dustcloth
0.0145	21.6	.0000	1	dustpans
0.0145	21.6	.0000	1	Dutch-American
0.0145	21.6	.0000	1	Dutti
0.0145	21.6	.0000	1	Dykes
0.0145	21.6	.0000	1	dynastically
0.0145	21.6	.0000	1	Dyved
0.0145	21.6	.0000	1	eagle-like
0.0145	21.6	.0000	1	ear-splitting
0.0145	21.6	.0000	1	eared-seal
0.0145	21.6	.0000	1	eargerly
0.0145	21.6	.0000	1	earmarked
0.0145	21.6	.0000	1	earth-shaking
0.0145	21.6	.0000	1	east-bound
0.0145	21.6	.0000	1	ebullient
0.0145	21.6	.0000	1	eccentrique
0.0145	21.6	.0000	1	Eclipse
0.0145	21.6	.0000	1	eclipsed
0.0145	21.6	.0000	1	ecumenical
0.0145	21.6	.0000	1	Ecumenical
0.0145	21.6	.0000	1	Eddingtons
0.0145	21.6	.0000	1	edge-to-surface
0.0145	21.6	.0000	1	Edirne
0.0145	21.6	.0000	1	Eenty
0.0145	21.6	.0000	1	effigies
0.0145	21.6	.0000	1	effulgence
0.0145	21.6	.0000	1	Egg
0.0145	21.6	.0000	1	Eichmann
0.0145	21.6	.0000	1	eight-cylinder
0.0145	21.6	.0000	1	eight-mule
0.0145	21.6	.0000	1	eight-wheeler
0.0145	21.6	.0000	1	eight-years-olds
0.0145	21.6	.0000	1	eighty-two
0.0145	21.6	.0000	1	Eilat
0.0145	21.6	.0000	1	Einsatzgruppen
0.0145	21.6	.0000	1	Electra's
0.0145	21.6	.0000	1	elf-wife
0.0145	21.6	.0000	1	elfwife
0.0145	21.6	.0000	1	Elimination
0.0145	21.6	.0000	1	elixir
0.0145	21.6	.0000	1	elongating
0.0145	21.6	.0000	1	eloping
0.0145	21.6	.0000	1	Else's
0.0145	21.6	.0000	1	Elston
0.0145	21.6	.0000	1	Elysian
0.0145	21.6	.0000	1	Emancipator
0.0145	21.6	.0000	1	embarkation
0.0145	21.6	.0000	1	embellish
0.0145	21.6	.0000	1	Emersonian
0.0145	21.6	.0000	1	emigrators
0.0145	21.6	.0000	1	emirates
0.0145	21.6	.0000	1	emirs
0.0145	21.6	.0000	1	Emmanuel's
0.0145	21.6	.0000	1	Emmanuele
0.0145	21.6	.0000	1	Emmitsburg
0.0145	21.6	.0000	1	emplacements
0.0145	21.6	.0000	1	emulate
0.0145	21.6	.0000	1	en-jine
0.0145	21.6	.0000	1	enclave
0.0145	21.6	.0000	1	encrease
0.0145	21.6	.0000	1	end-to-edge
0.0145	21.6	.0000	1	end-to-face
0.0145	21.6	.0000	1	enemy-defended
0.0145	21.6	.0000	1	Enfant
0.0145	21.6	.0000	1	Englander
0.0145	21.6	.0000	1	Engraving
0.0145	21.6	.0000	1	enshrine
0.0145	21.6	.0000	1	entails
0.0145	21.6	.0000	1	entitling
0.0145	21.6	.0000	1	Entombment
0.0145	21.6	.0000	1	Envoys
0.0145	21.6	.0000	1	eradicated
0.0145	21.6	.0000	1	erecting
0.0145	21.6	.0000	1	Erisichthon
0.0145	21.6	.0000	1	errest
0.0145	21.6	.0000	1	eruptive
0.0145	21.6	.0000	1	Eryops
0.0145	21.6	.0000	1	espagnole
0.0145	21.6	.0000	1	Espagnole
0.0145	21.6	.0000	1	Esputa's
0.0145	21.6	.0000	1	espy
0.0145	21.6	.0000	1	essayists
0.0145	21.6	.0000	1	Essequibo
0.0145	21.6	.0000	1	esteemeth
0.0145	21.6	.0000	1	esteeming
0.0145	21.6	.0000	1	Estrada
0.0145	21.6	.0000	1	Eterna
0.0145	21.6	.0000	1	Ethelreda

THE PRECEDING WORD TYPE OCCUPIES RANK 63200

U	SFI	D	F	Word Type
0.0145	21.6	.0000	1	Etowah
0.0145	21.6	.0000	1	Etty's
0.0145	21.6	.0000	1	Eucumbene
0.0145	21.6	.0000	1	Eugenie
0.0145	21.6	.0000	1	EUGLENA
0.0145	21.6	.0000	1	EUR
0.0145	21.6	.0000	1	Euxine
0.0145	21.6	.0000	1	evangelize
0.0145	21.6	.0000	1	even-pace
0.0145	21.6	.0000	1	ever-broadening
0.0145	21.6	.0000	1	ever-new
0.0145	21.6	.0000	1	Everetts
0.0145	21.6	.0000	1	EVERGREENS
0.0145	21.6	.0000	1	evil-doing
0.0145	21.6	.0000	1	ewe's
0.0145	21.6	.0000	1	excavators
0.0145	21.6	.0000	1	Exhaust
0.0145	21.6	.0000	1	Exhibits
0.0145	21.6	.0000	1	exodus
0.0145	21.6	.0000	1	expatriates
0.0145	21.6	.0000	1	externalized
0.0145	21.6	.0000	1	extra-good
0.0145	21.6	.0000	1	Extreme
0.0145	21.6	.0000	1	eye-section
0.0145	21.6	.0000	1	Fabricants
0.0145	21.6	.0000	1	Fabricato
0.0145	21.6	.0000	1	FACE
0.0145	21.6	.0000	1	Faces
0.0145	21.6	.0000	1	facetious
0.0145	21.6	.0000	1	FAD
0.0145	21.6	.0000	1	Faeroe
0.0145	21.6	.0000	1	fainteth
0.0145	21.6	.0000	1	fairytale
0.0145	21.6	.0000	1	faithlessness
0.0145	21.6	.0000	1	Falasha
0.0145	21.6	.0000	1	Faluja
0.0145	21.6	.0000	1	fanwise
0.0145	21.6	.0000	1	far-fetched
0.0145	21.6	.0000	1	Far-shooter
0.0145	21.6	.0000	1	Farenholt
0.0145	21.6	.0000	1	Farman
0.0145	21.6	.0000	1	Fartlek
0.0145	21.6	.0000	1	fast-balling
0.0145	21.6	.0000	1	fast-running
0.0145	21.6	.0000	1	fathers-forth
0.0145	21.6	.0000	1	Fatu
0.0145	21.6	.0000	1	favoritism
0.0145	21.6	.0000	1	fearest
0.0145	21.6	.0000	1	federative
0.0145	21.6	.0000	1	feeble-minded
0.0145	21.6	.0000	1	feints
0.0145	21.6	.0000	1	Felicity
0.0145	21.6	.0000	1	fellow-vendors
0.0145	21.6	.0000	1	Fenton
0.0145	21.6	.0000	1	fer-de-lance
0.0145	21.6	.0000	1	fern-clad
0.0145	21.6	.0000	1	ferned
0.0145	21.6	.0000	1	ferrum
0.0145	21.6	.0000	1	fetlocks
0.0145	21.6	.0000	1	field-slave
0.0145	21.6	.0000	1	fieldpiece
0.0145	21.6	.0000	1	Fifteen
0.0145	21.6	.0000	1	figurine
0.0145	21.6	.0000	1	filamental
0.0145	21.6	.0000	1	finches'
0.0145	21.6	.0000	1	fingerbreadth
0.0145	21.6	.0000	1	fingerbreadths
0.0145	21.6	.0000	1	fingerprinted
0.0145	21.6	.0000	1	fire-making
0.0145	21.6	.0000	1	Firefly
0.0145	21.6	.0000	1	fireman's
0.0145	21.6	.0000	1	fireplug
0.0145	21.6	.0000	1	firepower
0.0145	21.6	.0000	1	first-base
0.0145	21.6	.0000	1	first-term
0.0145	21.6	.0000	1	firstborn
0.0145	21.6	.0000	1	fist-flying
0.0145	21.6	.0000	1	Fitch
0.0145	21.6	.0000	1	Fitzpatrick
0.0145	21.6	.0000	1	five-hundred-mile
0.0145	21.6	.0000	1	five-hundred-pound
0.0145	21.6	.0000	1	five-pointed
0.0145	21.6	.0000	1	Fjord
0.0145	21.6	.0000	1	flageolet
0.0145	21.6	.0000	1	Flaherty's
0.0145	21.6	.0000	1	Flapdoodle
0.0145	21.6	.0000	1	flashback
0.0145	21.6	.0000	1	FLEA
0.0145	21.6	.0000	1	flesh-eater
0.0145	21.6	.0000	1	FLIES
0.0145	21.6	.0000	1	floodings
0.0145	21.6	.0000	1	flotilla
0.0145	21.6	.0000	1	fluffed-up
0.0145	21.6	.0000	1	fly-boy
0.0145	21.6	.0000	1	flying-instruction
0.0145	21.6	.0000	1	flying-officer
0.0145	21.6	.0000	1	flying-trapeze
0.0145	21.6	.0000	1	flyweight
0.0145	21.6	.0000	1	fo'c'sle
0.0145	21.6	.0000	1	fob

THE PRECEDING WORD TYPE OCCUPIES RANK 63300

U	SFI	D	F	Word Type
0.0145	21.6	.0000	1	fobs
0.0145	21.6	.0000	1	Fodio
0.0145	21.6	.0000	1	Folded
0.0145	21.6	.0000	1	folia
0.0145	21.6	.0000	1	FOLLICLES
0.0145	21.6	.0000	1	food-laden
0.0145	21.6	.0000	1	foot-stamping
0.0145	21.6	.0000	1	footmaiden
0.0145	21.6	.0000	1	Force's
0.0145	21.6	.0000	1	fore-runner
0.0145	21.6	.0000	1	forestalled
0.0145	21.6	.0000	1	forgiveth
0.0145	21.6	.0000	1	forgottne
0.0145	21.6	.0000	1	format
0.0145	21.6	.0000	1	Forts
0.0145	21.6	.0000	1	forty-five-degree
0.0145	21.6	.0000	1	forward-reaching
0.0145	21.6	.0000	1	forwarded
0.0145	21.6	.0000	1	Fosters
0.0145	21.6	.0000	1	fosters
0.0145	21.6	.0000	1	Foulke
0.0145	21.6	.0000	1	Founder
0.0145	21.6	.0000	1	four-acre
0.0145	21.6	.0000	1	four-and-a-half
0.0145	21.6	.0000	1	four-dimensional
0.0145	21.6	.0000	1	four-horse
0.0145	21.6	.0000	1	foxgloves
0.0145	21.6	.0000	1	Francesca
0.0145	21.6	.0000	1	Franco-Belge
0.0145	21.6	.0000	1	Franco-Belgian
0.0145	21.6	.0000	1	Frau
0.0145	21.6	.0000	1	freeholds
0.0145	21.6	.0000	1	FREIGHTERS
0.0145	21.6	.0000	1	freighting
0.0145	21.6	.0000	1	French-Dutch
0.0145	21.6	.0000	1	French-colonial
0.0145	21.6	.0000	1	Frenchies
0.0145	21.6	.0000	1	fresh-firecoal
0.0145	21.6	.0000	1	Fridtjof
0.0145	21.6	.0000	1	Frisian
0.0145	21.6	.0000	1	frizzle
0.0145	21.6	.0000	1	Frogeye
0.0145	21.6	.0000	1	front-row
0.0145	21.6	.0000	1	front-view
0.0145	21.6	.0000	1	frost-stunted
0.0145	21.6	.0000	1	Frosting
0.0145	21.6	.0000	1	frowningly
0.0145	21.6	.0000	1	FRUIT
0.0145	21.6	.0000	1	fuddled
0.0145	21.6	.0000	1	fudgy
0.0145	21.6	.0000	1	Fukienese
0.0145	21.6	.0000	1	full-colored
0.0145	21.6	.0000	1	fully-grown
0.0145	21.6	.0000	1	Fulsom
0.0145	21.6	.0000	1	Fumblefinger
0.0145	21.6	.0000	1	functionary
0.0145	21.6	.0000	1	Fur
0.0145	21.6	.0000	1	Futurity
0.0145	21.6	.0000	1	G-r-o-u-n-d
0.0145	21.6	.0000	1	Gaels
0.0145	21.6	.0000	1	Gagarin
0.0145	21.6	.0000	1	Gales'
0.0145	21.6	.0000	1	Galleria
0.0145	21.6	.0000	1	Gallipolli
0.0145	21.6	.0000	1	Galway
0.0145	21.6	.0000	1	Gamble's
0.0145	21.6	.0000	1	game-fixing
0.0145	21.6	.0000	1	Gangbusters
0.0145	21.6	.0000	1	gangrenous
0.0145	21.6	.0000	1	garbed
0.0145	21.6	.0000	1	garbled
0.0145	21.6	.0000	1	Garda
0.0145	21.6	.0000	1	Gardiner's
0.0145	21.6	.0000	1	Garibaldi's
0.0145	21.6	.0000	1	garment's
0.0145	21.6	.0000	1	garnets
0.0145	21.6	.0000	1	Garrett's
0.0145	21.6	.0000	1	gashing
0.0145	21.6	.0000	1	gastronomic
0.0145	21.6	.0000	1	GASTROTRICH
0.0145	21.6	.0000	1	gauntly
0.0145	21.6	.0000	1	gavest
0.0145	21.6	.0000	1	gavottes
0.0145	21.6	.0000	1	Gedalge
0.0145	21.6	.0000	1	gendarme
0.0145	21.6	.0000	1	genealogical
0.0145	21.6	.0000	1	Generalissimo
0.0145	21.6	.0000	1	generative
0.0145	21.6	.0000	1	Gennesaret
0.0145	21.6	.0000	1	genocide
0.0145	21.6	.0000	1	gentle-hearted
0.0145	21.6	.0000	1	Geology
0.0145	21.6	.0000	1	Gerbrandy
0.0145	21.6	.0000	1	gerenuk
0.0145	21.6	.0000	1	Gerson's
0.0145	21.6	.0000	1	Gestalt
0.0145	21.6	.0000	1	getters
0.0145	21.6	.0000	1	Gherman
0.0145	21.6	.0000	1	ghostlike
0.0145	21.6	.0000	1	Giants'

THE PRECEDING WORD TYPE OCCUPIES RANK 63400

U	SFI	D	F	Word Type
0.0145	21.6	.0000	1	Gide
0.0145	21.6	.0000	1	gif's
0.0145	21.6	.0000	1	gig
0.0145	21.6	.0000	1	gigues
0.0145	21.6	.0000	1	Gilead
0.0145	21.6	.0000	1	Gilliam
0.0145	21.6	.0000	1	Gilman's
0.0145	21.6	.0000	1	gingerbread-boy
0.0145	21.6	.0000	1	Gingham
0.0145	21.6	.0000	1	Girardot
0.0145	21.6	.0000	1	giveaway
0.0145	21.6	.0000	1	glacier-scored
0.0145	21.6	.0000	1	Gladiators
0.0145	21.6	.0000	1	glider-borne
0.0145	21.6	.0000	1	glio
0.0145	21.6	.0000	1	Gloom
0.0145	21.6	.0000	1	Gloster's
0.0145	21.6	.0000	1	Gloworm
0.0145	21.6	.0000	1	glug
0.0145	21.6	.0000	1	Glug
0.0145	21.6	.0000	1	glutted
0.0145	21.6	.0000	1	gnitten
0.0145	21.6	.0000	1	gnomes
0.0145	21.6	.0000	1	Goal
0.0145	21.6	.0000	1	gobble-uns'll
0.0145	21.6	.0000	1	God-given
0.0145	21.6	.0000	1	Godfrey
0.0145	21.6	.0000	1	gold-colored
0.0145	21.6	.0000	1	gold-town
0.0145	21.6	.0000	1	goldmining
0.0145	21.6	.0000	1	Goode's
0.0145	21.6	.0000	1	Goodhue
0.0145	21.6	.0000	1	goodwill
0.0145	21.6	.0000	1	Goosens
0.0145	21.6	.0000	1	Gordius
0.0145	21.6	.0000	1	Goshen
0.0145	21.6	.0000	1	Goss
0.0145	21.6	.0000	1	Gottlieb
0.0145	21.6	.0000	1	governess'
0.0145	21.6	.0000	1	government-controlled
0.0145	21.6	.0000	1	gradated
0.0145	21.6	.0000	1	gradualism
0.0145	21.6	.0000	1	Grandaddy
0.0145	21.6	.0000	1	grandiosely
0.0145	21.6	.0000	1	Grasshoppers
0.0145	21.6	.0000	1	Gratiana
0.0145	21.6	.0000	1	gray-shingled
0.0145	21.6	.0000	1	gray-silk
0.0145	21.6	.0000	1	graybeards
0.0145	21.6	.0000	1	grayish-white
0.0145	21.6	.0000	1	Grazia
0.0145	21.6	.0000	1	greasy-spoon
0.0145	21.6	.0000	1	great-nephew
0.0145	21.6	.0000	1	great-niece
0.0145	21.6	.0000	1	Grecia
0.0145	21.6	.0000	1	Greco
0.0145	21.6	.0000	1	Greek-speaking
0.0145	21.6	.0000	1	greenish-brown
0.0145	21.6	.0000	1	greenness
0.0145	21.6	.0000	1	Griefs
0.0145	21.6	.0000	1	grievously
0.0145	21.6	.0000	1	Grimari
0.0145	21.6	.0000	1	Grimbert
0.0145	21.6	.0000	1	Griscoms
0.0145	21.6	.0000	1	Grisons
0.0145	21.6	.0000	1	grito
0.0145	21.6	.0000	1	groanings
0.0145	21.6	.0000	1	grot
0.0145	21.6	.0000	1	ground-nesting
0.0145	21.6	.0000	1	ground-roll
0.0145	21.6	.0000	1	Grounds
0.0145	21.6	.0000	1	group-contact
0.0145	21.6	.0000	1	grovelling
0.0145	21.6	.0000	1	Grub
0.0145	21.6	.0000	1	Grumpy
0.0145	21.6	.0000	1	Guantanamo
0.0145	21.6	.0000	1	Guardian's
0.0145	21.6	.0000	1	Guiana's
0.0145	21.6	.0000	1	gun's
0.0145	21.6	.0000	1	gustily
0.0145	21.6	.0000	1	Gwydion's
0.0145	21.6	.0000	1	Gyffe's

U	SFI	D	F	Word Type
0.0145	21.6	.0000	1	Gyffes
0.0145	21.6	.0000	1	Gymnasium
0.0145	21.6	.0000	1	gymnast
0.0145	21.6	.0000	1	gyms
0.0145	21.6	.0000	1	gyrate
0.0145	21.6	.0000	1	ha-yu
0.0145	21.6	.0000	1	habergeon
0.0145	21.6	.0000	1	habituated
0.0145	21.6	.0000	1	Hacha's
0.0145	21.6	.0000	1	Haddonfield
0.0145	21.6	.0000	1	Hadrosaurus
0.0145	21.6	.0000	1	Haiduong
0.0145	21.6	.0000	1	Hainan
0.0145	21.6	.0000	1	Haineses
0.0145	21.6	.0000	1	Haiphong's
0.0145	21.6	.0000	1	hair-ribbon
0.0145	21.6	.0000	1	half-brother
0.0145	21.6	.0000	1	half-dozed
THE PRECEDING WORD TYPE OCCUPIES RANK 63500				
0.0145	21.6	.0000	1	half-sister
0.0145	21.6	.0000	1	half-slouched
0.0145	21.6	.0000	1	half-won
0.0145	21.6	.0000	1	Halket
0.0145	21.6	.0000	1	Hamite
0.0145	21.6	.0000	1	Hamite-Negro
0.0145	21.6	.0000	1	Hammer-Handle
0.0145	21.6	.0000	1	HAND
0.0145	21.6	.0000	1	hand-crafted
0.0145	21.6	.0000	1	hand-washing
0.0145	21.6	.0000	1	hand-writing
0.0145	21.6	.0000	1	handcar
0.0145	21.6	.0000	1	Handicap
0.0145	21.6	.0000	1	Handicraft
0.0145	21.6	.0000	1	handie
0.0145	21.6	.0000	1	handies
0.0145	21.6	.0000	1	Hanseatic
0.0145	21.6	.0000	1	Harbin
0.0145	21.6	.0000	1	hard-riding
0.0145	21.6	.0000	1	hard-to-remember
0.0145	21.6	.0000	1	Harlan
0.0145	21.6	.0000	1	harness-racing
0.0145	21.6	.0000	1	Harpies
0.0145	21.6	.0000	1	harpsichordists
0.0145	21.6	.0000	1	Harroun
0.0145	21.6	.0000	1	Harsimus
0.0145	21.6	.0000	1	Hartnett
0.0145	21.6	.0000	1	Hattiesburg
0.0145	21.6	.0000	1	Hausas
0.0145	21.6	.0000	1	healeth
0.0145	21.6	.0000	1	heardest
0.0145	21.6	.0000	1	heart-stirring
0.0145	21.6	.0000	1	heavier-built
0.0145	21.6	.0000	1	Hecate
0.0145	21.6	.0000	1	heehaws
0.0145	21.6	.0000	1	heehawses
0.0145	21.6	.0000	1	hegemony
0.0145	21.6	.0000	1	Heiman
0.0145	21.6	.0000	1	Helder
0.0145	21.6	.0000	1	helloworm
0.0145	21.6	.0000	1	Hemingway's
0.0145	21.6	.0000	1	hemp-wine
0.0145	21.6	.0000	1	hepatitis
0.0145	21.6	.0000	1	hereabouts
0.0145	21.6	.0000	1	Hershey
0.0145	21.6	.0000	1	Hertfordshire
0.0145	21.6	.0000	1	Herut
0.0145	21.6	.0000	1	Hey-yo
0.0145	21.6	.0000	1	hi-o
0.0145	21.6	.0000	1	Hickerson
0.0145	21.6	.0000	1	Hicks
0.0145	21.6	.0000	1	Hiding
0.0145	21.6	.0000	1	hierarchically
0.0145	21.6	.0000	1	high-bibbed
0.0145	21.6	.0000	1	high-handed
0.0145	21.6	.0000	1	high-placed
0.0145	21.6	.0000	1	high-priced
0.0145	21.6	.0000	1	high-stepping
0.0145	21.6	.0000	1	high-strutting
0.0145	21.6	.0000	1	high-voltage
0.0145	21.6	.0000	1	highball
0.0145	21.6	.0000	1	Highlanders'
0.0145	21.6	.0000	1	highroads
0.0145	21.6	.0000	1	Highsaddle
0.0145	21.6	.0000	1	hill-tops
0.0145	21.6	.0000	1	hillocks
0.0145	21.6	.0000	1	Hillside
0.0145	21.6	.0000	1	hind-quarters
0.0145	21.6	.0000	1	hinging
0.0145	21.6	.0000	1	Hippodrome
0.0145	21.6	.0000	1	Hippolito
0.0145	21.6	.0000	1	Histoires
0.0145	21.6	.0000	1	Hiva
0.0145	21.6	.0000	1	ho-o-o-o-o-o
0.0145	21.6	.0000	1	Hoboken
0.0145	21.6	.0000	1	Hockley's
0.0145	21.6	.0000	1	Hofmeyr
0.0145	21.6	.0000	1	hogsheads
0.0145	21.6	.0000	1	HOLIDAY
0.0145	21.6	.0000	1	holidaymakers
0.0145	21.6	.0000	1	Holsopple
0.0145	21.6	.0000	1	HOLYDAY
0.0145	21.6	.0000	1	Homage
0.0145	21.6	.0000	1	hombria
0.0145	21.6	.0000	1	home-town
0.0145	21.6	.0000	1	hoop-skirts
0.0145	21.6	.0000	1	hop-and-skip
0.0145	21.6	.0000	1	Horn-faced
0.0145	21.6	.0000	1	horn-like
0.0145	21.6	.0000	1	hornlike
0.0145	21.6	.0000	1	horse-pulling
0.0145	21.6	.0000	1	HORSELESS
0.0145	21.6	.0000	1	horsetails
0.0145	21.6	.0000	1	horsewrangler
0.0145	21.6	.0000	1	Hostages
0.0145	21.6	.0000	1	hot-heads
0.0145	21.6	.0000	1	Houk
0.0145	21.6	.0000	1	Houk's
0.0145	21.6	.0000	1	Houtman
0.0145	21.6	.0000	1	Howlett
THE PRECEDING WORD TYPE OCCUPIES RANK 63600				
0.0145	21.6	.0000	1	Hoyt's
0.0145	21.6	.0000	1	HR511
0.0145	21.6	.0000	1	Hsieh
0.0145	21.6	.0000	1	Hsin-hung
0.0145	21.6	.0000	1	Humbolt
0.0145	21.6	.0000	1	humiliations
0.0145	21.6	.0000	1	humorless
0.0145	21.6	.0000	1	Hunter's
0.0145	21.6	.0000	1	Hunts
0.0145	21.6	.0000	1	hurler
0.0145	21.6	.0000	1	Hussar
0.0145	21.6	.0000	1	HYDRA
0.0145	21.6	.0000	1	Hydras
0.0145	21.6	.0000	1	hydraulically
0.0145	21.6	.0000	1	Hyperborean
0.0145	21.6	.0000	1	Iberia
0.0145	21.6	.0000	1	ibn
0.0145	21.6	.0000	1	ice-blocks
0.0145	21.6	.0000	1	ideological
0.0145	21.6	.0000	1	Ides
0.0145	21.6	.0000	1	idolatry
0.0145	21.6	.0000	1	Iguanodons
0.0145	21.6	.0000	1	ill-fitting
0.0145	21.6	.0000	1	ill-health
0.0145	21.6	.0000	1	illusory
0.0145	21.6	.0000	1	Immortal
0.0145	21.6	.0000	1	impairment
0.0145	21.6	.0000	1	imparting
0.0145	21.6	.0000	1	import-export
0.0145	21.6	.0000	1	impudently
0.0145	21.6	.0000	1	in-space
0.0145	21.6	.0000	1	incense-permeated
0.0145	21.6	.0000	1	inclosure
0.0145	21.6	.0000	1	incomprehension
0.0145	21.6	.0000	1	incongruously
0.0145	21.6	.0000	1	increaseth
0.0145	21.6	.0000	1	Independents
0.0145	21.6	.0000	1	Indian-fashion
0.0145	21.6	.0000	1	indite
0.0145	21.6	.0000	1	IndoEuropean
0.0145	21.6	.0000	1	ineffectuality
0.0145	21.6	.0000	1	Inferno
0.0145	21.6	.0000	1	infiltrating
0.0145	21.6	.0000	1	infiltrations
0.0145	21.6	.0000	1	ingratitude
0.0145	21.6	.0000	1	inhumanity
0.0145	21.6	.0000	1	iniquities
0.0145	21.6	.0000	1	INK
0.0145	21.6	.0000	1	ink-slab
0.0145	21.6	.0000	1	inlays
0.0145	21.6	.0000	1	Innerschweiz
0.0145	21.6	.0000	1	Inness
0.0145	21.6	.0000	1	Inness'
0.0145	21.6	.0000	1	inscrutable
0.0145	21.6	.0000	1	insidiously
0.0145	21.6	.0000	1	insignificance
0.0145	21.6	.0000	1	insouciance
0.0145	21.6	.0000	1	institutionalize
0.0145	21.6	.0000	1	insularity
0.0145	21.6	.0000	1	insupportable
0.0145	21.6	.0000	1	interchangeability
0.0145	21.6	.0000	1	interclass
0.0145	21.6	.0000	1	interestedly
0.0145	21.6	.0000	1	interwar
0.0145	21.6	.0000	1	Invisible
0.0145	21.6	.0000	1	IP
0.0145	21.6	.0000	1	Iphigenia
0.0145	21.6	.0000	1	Irgun
0.0145	21.6	.0000	1	Irkutsk
0.0145	21.6	.0000	1	Iroquois'
0.0145	21.6	.0000	1	Irus'
0.0145	21.6	.0000	1	Isengrim
0.0145	21.6	.0000	1	isolationists
0.0145	21.6	.0000	1	Israelis'
0.0145	21.6	.0000	1	Italian-Americans
0.0145	21.6	.0000	1	Italys
0.0145	21.6	.0000	1	ivver
0.0145	21.6	.0000	1	Ixelles
0.0145	21.6	.0000	1	jackdawses
0.0145	21.6	.0000	1	jaded-looking
0.0145	21.6	.0000	1	jam-jams
0.0145	21.6	.0000	1	Jameson
0.0145	21.6	.0000	1	Jamie's
0.0145	21.6	.0000	1	Janissary
0.0145	21.6	.0000	1	Januarius
0.0145	21.6	.0000	1	Jarrott
0.0145	21.6	.0000	1	jauntiness
0.0145	21.6	.0000	1	jawses
0.0145	21.6	.0000	1	Jedidiah
0.0145	21.6	.0000	1	Jenckses
0.0145	21.6	.0000	1	Jerky
0.0145	21.6	.0000	1	jestingly
0.0145	21.6	.0000	1	jet-control
0.0145	21.6	.0000	1	Jeux
0.0145	21.6	.0000	1	Jew-free
0.0145	21.6	.0000	1	jibed
0.0145	21.6	.0000	1	jigs
0.0145	21.6	.0000	1	jihad
0.0145	21.6	.0000	1	jimson
0.0145	21.6	.0000	1	Joany
THE PRECEDING WORD TYPE OCCUPIES RANK 63700				
0.0145	21.6	.0000	1	jokesters
0.0145	21.6	.0000	1	Jopie
0.0145	21.6	.0000	1	Jostedalsbreen
0.0145	21.6	.0000	1	jottings
0.0145	21.6	.0000	1	Joueurs
0.0145	21.6	.0000	1	joyance
0.0145	21.6	.0000	1	Joyeux
0.0145	21.6	.0000	1	Judaea
0.0145	21.6	.0000	1	juggly
0.0145	21.6	.0000	1	jumbies
0.0145	21.6	.0000	1	jungle's
0.0145	21.6	.0000	1	junta's
0.0145	21.6	.0000	1	K'un-lun
0.0145	21.6	.0000	1	Kal
0.0145	21.6	.0000	1	Kal's
0.0145	21.6	.0000	1	Kansu
0.0145	21.6	.0000	1	Katrin's
0.0145	21.6	.0000	1	Katydid
0.0145	21.6	.0000	1	Katydid's
0.0145	21.6	.0000	1	Keefer
0.0145	21.6	.0000	1	Keefer's
0.0145	21.6	.0000	1	Kendallville
0.0145	21.6	.0000	1	Kent's
0.0145	21.6	.0000	1	Kentuckians
0.0145	21.6	.0000	1	Kentucky's
0.0145	21.6	.0000	1	Khalid
0.0145	21.6	.0000	1	khamsin
0.0145	21.6	.0000	1	khomp
0.0145	21.6	.0000	1	Kicva
0.0145	21.6	.0000	1	Kiki
0.0145	21.6	.0000	1	Kilkenny
0.0145	21.6	.0000	1	killer's
0.0145	21.6	.0000	1	kiln-drying
0.0145	21.6	.0000	1	king-sized
0.0145	21.6	.0000	1	Kinnan
0.0145	21.6	.0000	1	kiss'd
0.0145	21.6	.0000	1	Kits
0.0145	21.6	.0000	1	Knapp
0.0145	21.6	.0000	1	knell
0.0145	21.6	.0000	1	knicker
0.0145	21.6	.0000	1	knickerbocker
0.0145	21.6	.0000	1	knickers'
0.0145	21.6	.0000	1	know-alls
0.0145	21.6	.0000	1	knowledgeable
0.0145	21.6	.0000	1	knowns
0.0145	21.6	.0000	1	knowworm
0.0145	21.6	.0000	1	Kobas
0.0145	21.6	.0000	1	Kochersperger
0.0145	21.6	.0000	1	Koeppen
0.0145	21.6	.0000	1	Korson
0.0145	21.6	.0000	1	Koufax's
0.0145	21.6	.0000	1	kouloungoulou
0.0145	21.6	.0000	1	Kourou
0.0145	21.6	.0000	1	Krachi
0.0145	21.6	.0000	1	Kraler's
0.0145	21.6	.0000	1	Ku's
0.0145	21.6	.0000	1	Kubek
0.0145	21.6	.0000	1	Kuei
0.0145	21.6	.0000	1	Kvidal's
0.0145	21.6	.0000	1	ky-yi
0.0145	21.6	.0000	1	l-l-let's
0.0145	21.6	.0000	1	l'Avenir
0.0145	21.6	.0000	1	l'Ecole
0.0145	21.6	.0000	1	l'Espoir
0.0145	21.6	.0000	1	l'Harmonie
0.0145	21.6	.0000	1	Laborites
0.0145	21.6	.0000	1	labyrinth
0.0145	21.6	.0000	1	Lackawanna
0.0145	21.6	.0000	1	ladder-backed
0.0145	21.6	.0000	1	Ladislas
0.0145	21.6	.0000	1	Lafayette's
0.0145	21.6	.0000	1	lake-shore
0.0145	21.6	.0000	1	Lamb's
0.0145	21.6	.0000	1	lamentest
0.0145	21.6	.0000	1	Lamu
0.0145	21.6	.0000	1	land-poor
0.0145	21.6	.0000	1	land-roaming
0.0145	21.6	.0000	1	landscapist
0.0145	21.6	.0000	1	lascivious
0.0145	21.6	.0000	1	late-comers
0.0145	21.6	.0000	1	latifundios
0.0145	21.6	.0000	1	Latium
0.0145	21.6	.0000	1	laugheth
0.0145	21.6	.0000	1	lavatory
0.0145	21.6	.0000	1	Lavine
0.0145	21.6	.0000	1	Law-Courts
0.0145	21.6	.0000	1	Lay
0.0145	21.6	.0000	1	layeth
0.0145	21.6	.0000	1	lazyness
0.0145	21.6	.0000	1	Lazzeri
0.0145	21.6	.0000	1	leadoff
0.0145	21.6	.0000	1	LEAFLETS
0.0145	21.6	.0000	1	League's
0.0145	21.6	.0000	1	lean-tos
0.0145	21.6	.0000	1	Leaping
0.0145	21.6	.0000	1	Leavenworth
0.0145	21.6	.0000	1	lecher
0.0145	21.6	.0000	1	leg-and-rail
0.0145	21.6	.0000	1	legalize
0.0145	21.6	.0000	1	Legends
THE PRECEDING WORD TYPE OCCUPIES RANK 63800				
0.0145	21.6	.0000	1	Legion's
0.0145	21.6	.0000	1	legislated
0.0145	21.6	.0000	1	legitimacy
0.0145	21.6	.0000	1	Leidy
0.0145	21.6	.0000	1	Lenox
0.0145	21.6	.0000	1	leper
0.0145	21.6	.0000	1	leprosy
0.0145	21.6	.0000	1	less-expensive
0.0145	21.6	.0000	1	letter-perfect
0.0145	21.6	.0000	1	Levassor
0.0145	21.6	.0000	1	Levitan
0.0145	21.6	.0000	1	Levite
0.0145	21.6	.0000	1	li'nghas
0.0145	21.6	.0000	1	libera
0.0145	21.6	.0000	1	Libertes
0.0145	21.6	.0000	1	Libra
0.0145	21.6	.0000	1	lickety
0.0145	21.6	.0000	1	Licking
0.0145	21.6	.0000	1	light-edged
0.0145	21.6	.0000	1	light-filled
0.0145	21.6	.0000	1	lightcolored
0.0145	21.6	.0000	1	Lightfoot
0.0145	21.6	.0000	1	likeable
0.0145	21.6	.0000	1	limbering
0.0145	21.6	.0000	1	lineage
0.0145	21.6	.0000	1	Liner
0.0145	21.6	.0000	1	LINERS
0.0145	21.6	.0000	1	LIP
0.0145	21.6	.0000	1	Lipizzans
0.0145	21.6	.0000	1	livable
0.0145	21.6	.0000	1	liveth
0.0145	21.6	.0000	1	Lizza
0.0145	21.6	.0000	1	Llyr
0.0145	21.6	.0000	1	Locust
0.0145	21.6	.0000	1	logbooks
0.0145	21.6	.0000	1	lonelinesses
0.0145	21.6	.0000	1	long-awaited
0.0145	21.6	.0000	1	long-skirted
0.0145	21.6	.0000	1	Long's
0.0145	21.6	.0000	1	longdead
0.0145	21.6	.0000	1	longer-horned
0.0145	21.6	.0000	1	Longnecker
0.0145	21.6	.0000	1	Longueval
0.0145	21.6	.0000	1	lookers
0.0145	21.6	.0000	1	Lopat
0.0145	21.6	.0000	1	Loudoun
0.0145	21.6	.0000	1	lovesome
0.0145	21.6	.0000	1	low-level
0.0145	21.6	.0000	1	lower-class
0.0145	21.6	.0000	1	Lowlanders
0.0145	21.6	.0000	1	luck's
0.0145	21.6	.0000	1	luckless
0.0145	21.6	.0000	1	Luke's
0.0145	21.6	.0000	1	lunar-landing
0.0145	21.6	.0000	1	Lunik
0.0145	21.6	.0000	1	Luxembourgeois
0.0145	21.6	.0000	1	luxuriant
0.0145	21.6	.0000	1	Lydda
0.0145	21.6	.0000	1	Lysistrata's
0.0145	21.6	.0000	1	Lyttle
0.0145	21.6	.0000	1	MacCool
0.0145	21.6	.0000	1	MacKenzie's
0.0145	21.6	.0000	1	Macartney
0.0145	21.6	.0000	1	Macbeth's
0.0145	21.6	.0000	1	Mach-2
0.0145	21.6	.0000	1	Machiavellian
0.0145	21.6	.0000	1	machine-age
0.0145	21.6	.0000	1	Macons
0.0145	21.6	.0000	1	Macsen
0.0145	21.6	.0000	1	madest
0.0145	21.6	.0000	1	Maffeo
0.0145	21.6	.0000	1	Magistrate
0.0145	21.6	.0000	1	maiden-voyage
0.0145	21.6	.0000	1	mail-horse
0.0145	21.6	.0000	1	makest
0.0145	21.6	.0000	1	mambises
0.0145	21.6	.0000	1	mamma's
0.0145	21.6	.0000	1	man-grown
0.0145	21.6	.0000	1	manatee
0.0145	21.6	.0000	1	Manawydan
0.0145	21.6	.0000	1	Mancha
0.0145	21.6	.0000	1	mandamus
0.0145	21.6	.0000	1	Mantis
0.0145	21.6	.0000	1	Mapes
0.0145	21.6	.0000	1	Maran
0.0145	21.6	.0000	1	Marbella
0.0145	21.6	.0000	1	marbled
0.0145	21.6	.0000	1	Margrave
0.0145	21.6	.0000	1	mariner-merchants
0.0145	21.6	.0000	1	marksmen's
0.0145	21.6	.0000	1	marl
0.0145	21.6	.0000	1	Marquesas
0.0145	21.6	.0000	1	marriageble
0.0145	21.6	.0000	1	Marse
0.0145	21.6	.0000	1	Marshmallow
0.0145	21.6	.0000	1	Marspiter
0.0145	21.6	.0000	1	Marteaux
0.0145	21.6	.0000	1	Martini
0.0145	21.6	.0000	1	martyrdom
0.0145	21.6	.0000	1	Marysville
THE PRECEDING WORD TYPE OCCUPIES RANK 63900				
0.0145	21.6	.0000	1	Mascagni
0.0145	21.6	.0000	1	Mascara
0.0145	21.6	.0000	1	Mashed
0.0145	21.6	.0000	1	Mashonaland
0.0145	21.6	.0000	1	Maspiter
0.0145	21.6	.0000	1	mass-produce
0.0145	21.6	.0000	1	Mat
0.0145	21.6	.0000	1	Matachanna
0.0145	21.6	.0000	1	Mathonwy
0.0145	21.6	.0000	1	Matthews
0.0145	21.6	.0000	1	Matthias'
0.0145	21.6	.0000	1	Maurs
0.0145	21.6	.0000	1	Mavis
0.0145	21.6	.0000	1	Mavors
0.0145	21.6	.0000	1	maws
0.0145	21.6	.0000	1	mawses
0.0145	21.6	.0000	1	May-pole
0.0145	21.6	.0000	1	mayest
0.0145	21.6	.0000	1	Maynooth
0.0145	21.6	.0000	1	Mazo's
0.0145	21.6	.0000	1	McBriers
0.0145	21.6	.0000	1	McCann's
0.0145	21.6	.0000	1	McDougald
0.0145	21.6	.0000	1	McElroy
0.0145	21.6	.0000	1	McGhee
0.0145	21.6	.0000	1	McGhee's
0.0145	21.6	.0000	1	McGinnity
0.0145	21.6	.0000	1	McKee
0.0145	21.6	.0000	1	McMullen's
0.0145	21.6	.0000	1	McNeil's
0.0145	21.6	.0000	1	McQuinn
0.0145	21.6	.0000	1	Mcmullen
0.0145	21.6	.0000	1	MD'S**
0.0145	21.6	.0000	1	meadowland
0.0145	21.6	.0000	1	meal-beer
0.0145	21.6	.0000	1	MEASURING
0.0145	21.6	.0000	1	Meath
0.0145	21.6	.0000	1	Meeting-House
0.0145	21.6	.0000	1	Mege
0.0145	21.6	.0000	1	Meherrin
0.0145	21.6	.0000	1	melancholy-minded
0.0145	21.6	.0000	1	melanoma
0.0145	21.6	.0000	1	melodrama
0.0145	21.6	.0000	1	memoir
0.0145	21.6	.0000	1	memorandum

U	SFI	D	F	Word Type
0.0145	21.6	.0000	1	Menendez
0.0145	21.6	.0000	1	Menie
0.0145	21.6	.0000	1	Mentor
0.0145	21.6	.0000	1	mentor
0.0145	21.6	.0000	1	Menuet
0.0145	21.6	.0000	1	mepacrine
0.0145	21.6	.0000	1	mephitic
0.0145	21.6	.0000	1	Mercer's
0.0145	21.6	.0000	1	MERCHANT
0.0145	21.6	.0000	1	mercies
0.0145	21.6	.0000	1	messiah
0.0145	21.6	.0000	1	messin'
0.0145	21.6	.0000	1	metamorphism
0.0145	21.6	.0000	1	methink
0.0145	21.6	.0000	1	mewling
0.0145	21.6	.0000	1	Mi-Careme
0.0145	21.6	.0000	1	miasma
0.0145	21.6	.0000	1	mid-Bosporus
0.0145	21.6	.0000	1	mid-block
0.0145	21.6	.0000	1	mid-court
0.0145	21.6	.0000	1	middle-of-the-road
0.0145	21.6	.0000	1	middle-rail
0.0145	21.6	.0000	1	Middlewest
0.0145	21.6	.0000	1	midland
0.0145	21.6	.0000	1	midships
0.0145	21.6	.0000	1	Miglia
0.0145	21.6	.0000	1	mignonette
0.0145	21.6	.0000	1	mile-and-a-half
0.0145	21.6	.0000	1	milk-and-honey
0.0145	21.6	.0000	1	Millin
0.0145	21.6	.0000	1	Millin's
0.0145	21.6	.0000	1	Millions
0.0145	21.6	.0000	1	milliped
0.0145	21.6	.0000	1	millman
0.0145	21.6	.0000	1	Minahan
0.0145	21.6	.0000	1	mind-picture
0.0145	21.6	.0000	1	Mineral
0.0145	21.6	.0000	1	mineral-bearing
0.0145	21.6	.0000	1	Minty
0.0145	21.6	.0000	1	Minwax
0.0145	21.6	.0000	1	miscall
0.0145	21.6	.0000	1	miscegenation
0.0145	21.6	.0000	1	misinformed
0.0145	21.6	.0000	1	mispelled
0.0145	21.6	.0000	1	mist-filled
0.0145	21.6	.0000	1	Mitchell's
0.0145	21.6	.0000	1	mitered
0.0145	21.6	.0000	1	MITES
0.0145	21.6	.0000	1	mitten-like
0.0145	21.6	.0000	1	MLTD
0.0145	21.6	.0000	1	mockery
0.0145	21.6	.0000	1	modicum
0.0145	21.6	.0000	1	moe
0.0145	21.6	.0000	1	molested
0.0145	21.6	.0000	1	monastic
THE PRECEDING WORD TYPE OCCUPIES RANK 64000				
0.0145	21.6	.0000	1	money-printing
0.0145	21.6	.0000	1	money'
0.0145	21.6	.0000	1	Moneys
0.0145	21.6	.0000	1	mongrels
0.0145	21.6	.0000	1	Monoclonius
0.0145	21.6	.0000	1	monolithic
0.0145	21.6	.0000	1	monologues
0.0145	21.6	.0000	1	moon-god
0.0145	21.6	.0000	1	Moortje
0.0145	21.6	.0000	1	moralists
0.0145	21.6	.0000	1	Morell
0.0145	21.6	.0000	1	Morrison's
0.0145	21.6	.0000	1	Morten's
0.0145	21.6	.0000	1	mortiser
0.0145	21.6	.0000	1	Moscheles
0.0145	21.6	.0000	1	moths'
0.0145	21.6	.0000	1	Motobloc
0.0145	21.6	.0000	1	mottles
0.0145	21.6	.0000	1	moujiks
0.0145	21.6	.0000	1	moundsman
0.0145	21.6	.0000	1	mountain-rocks
0.0145	21.6	.0000	1	mouse-tailed
0.0145	21.6	.0000	1	mpanga
0.0145	21.6	.0000	1	mudholes
0.0145	21.6	.0000	1	mudwalk
0.0145	21.6	.0000	1	Muhlhausen
0.0145	21.6	.0000	1	Muldrow
0.0145	21.6	.0000	1	Mule
0.0145	21.6	.0000	1	multibarreled
0.0145	21.6	.0000	1	multiracialism
0.0145	21.6	.0000	1	Munster
0.0145	21.6	.0000	1	Murdoch
0.0145	21.6	.0000	1	Murray's
0.0145	21.6	.0000	1	Murrumbidgee
0.0145	21.6	.0000	1	murthered
0.0145	21.6	.0000	1	music-drama
0.0145	21.6	.0000	1	Muskrat's
0.0145	21.6	.0000	1	Muskrats'
0.0145	21.6	.0000	1	mustachios
0.0145	21.6	.0000	1	mutants
0.0145	21.6	.0000	1	Mutti's
0.0145	21.6	.0000	1	Mycenaean
0.0145	21.6	.0000	1	mystic-minded
0.0145	21.6	.0000	1	Myths
0.0145	21.6	.0000	1	M19A1
0.0145	21.6	.0000	1	M1917A1
0.0145	21.6	.0000	1	M1919A4
0.0145	21.6	.0000	1	M1919A6
0.0145	21.6	.0000	1	M2
0.0145	21.6	.0000	1	M2's
0.0145	21.6	.0000	1	M20
0.0145	21.6	.0000	1	M3
0.0145	21.6	.0000	1	NaMutale
0.0145	21.6	.0000	1	NaMutale's
0.0145	21.6	.0000	1	NAIL
0.0145	21.6	.0000	1	nail's
0.0145	21.6	.0000	1	nam
0.0145	21.6	.0000	1	nanny-goats
0.0145	21.6	.0000	1	Nantucketer
0.0145	21.6	.0000	1	narrow-minded
0.0145	21.6	.0000	1	nastiness
0.0145	21.6	.0000	1	nationalize
0.0145	21.6	.0000	1	nationhood
0.0145	21.6	.0000	1	naturalism
0.0145	21.6	.0000	1	Naturelles
0.0145	21.6	.0000	1	naughtiness
0.0145	21.6	.0000	1	Nazi-ruled
0.0145	21.6	.0000	1	Nazis'
0.0145	21.6	.0000	1	Nazism
0.0145	21.6	.0000	1	Neapolitan
0.0145	21.6	.0000	1	near-certainty
0.0145	21.6	.0000	1	Nehf
0.0145	21.6	.0000	1	neighings
0.0145	21.6	.0000	1	nest-building
0.0145	21.6	.0000	1	Neua
0.0145	21.6	.0000	1	Neuberger
0.0145	21.6	.0000	1	Neurological
0.0145	21.6	.0000	1	Newburyport
0.0145	21.6	.0000	1	newly-emerged
0.0145	21.6	.0000	1	Newport's
0.0145	21.6	.0000	1	Newsboys'
0.0145	21.6	.0000	1	NF-104A
0.0145	21.6	.0000	1	ni-tro-gen
0.0145	21.6	.0000	1	Niccolo's
0.0145	21.6	.0000	1	niece's
0.0145	21.6	.0000	1	night-and-day
0.0145	21.6	.0000	1	nightflying
0.0145	21.6	.0000	1	Nijmegen
0.0145	21.6	.0000	1	nil
0.0145	21.6	.0000	1	nineties
0.0145	21.6	.0000	1	Nip-nip-nip
0.0145	21.6	.0000	1	nipt
0.0145	21.6	.0000	1	Nishuane
0.0145	21.6	.0000	1	Nocturnes
0.0145	21.6	.0000	1	Noey
0.0145	21.6	.0000	1	Nominating
0.0145	21.6	.0000	1	non-Arab
0.0145	21.6	.0000	1	non-Communists
0.0145	21.6	.0000	1	non-professional
0.0145	21.6	.0000	1	Nonpareil
THE PRECEDING WORD TYPE OCCUPIES RANK 64100				
0.0145	21.6	.0000	1	nonsocialist
0.0145	21.6	.0000	1	noodle-seller
0.0145	21.6	.0000	1	Norden
0.0145	21.6	.0000	1	NorthAmericans
0.0145	21.6	.0000	1	northeast-to-southwest
0.0145	21.6	.0000	1	Nose
0.0145	21.6	.0000	1	nothings
0.0145	21.6	.0000	1	Notus
0.0145	21.6	.0000	1	Novolipki
0.0145	21.6	.0000	1	now-revered
0.0145	21.6	.0000	1	nullify
0.0145	21.6	.0000	1	nunnery
0.0145	21.6	.0000	1	nuptials
0.0145	21.6	.0000	1	Nurburgring
0.0145	21.6	.0000	1	nurse-mare
0.0145	21.6	.0000	1	nursling
0.0145	21.6	.0000	1	Nuru
0.0145	21.6	.0000	1	nut-growing
0.0145	21.6	.0000	1	nutcrackers
0.0145	21.6	.0000	1	Nyantara
0.0145	21.6	.0000	1	O-hi-o
0.0145	21.6	.0000	1	o-oh-oh
0.0145	21.6	.0000	1	O'Connor's
0.0145	21.6	.0000	1	O'Loughlin
0.0145	21.6	.0000	1	O'Neills
0.0145	21.6	.0000	1	o'erspreads
0.0145	21.6	.0000	1	oar-feet
0.0145	21.6	.0000	1	oarsmanship
0.0145	21.6	.0000	1	Obersalzberg
0.0145	21.6	.0000	1	Oblate
0.0145	21.6	.0000	1	obleege
0.0145	21.6	.0000	1	obscene
0.0145	21.6	.0000	1	Obscura
0.0145	21.6	.0000	1	occult
0.0145	21.6	.0000	1	occupiers
0.0145	21.6	.0000	1	ocelli
0.0145	21.6	.0000	1	ochered
0.0145	21.6	.0000	1	odor-message
0.0145	21.6	.0000	1	Oestre
0.0145	21.6	.0000	1	off-color
0.0145	21.6	.0000	1	offal
0.0145	21.6	.0000	1	Offenhauser-powered
0.0145	21.6	.0000	1	official-looking
0.0145	21.6	.0000	1	oft-quoted
0.0145	21.6	.0000	1	oh-oh-oh
0.0145	21.6	.0000	1	OICURMT
0.0145	21.6	.0000	1	ok-a-leek
0.0145	21.6	.0000	1	ok-a-leek-
0.0145	21.6	.0000	1	Ola's
0.0145	21.6	.0000	1	oligarchic
0.0145	21.6	.0000	1	Oluf
0.0145	21.6	.0000	1	Oluf's
0.0145	21.6	.0000	1	Onandaga
0.0145	21.6	.0000	1	One-B
0.0145	21.6	.0000	1	one-cent
0.0145	21.6	.0000	1	one-god
0.0145	21.6	.0000	1	one-hitters
0.0145	21.6	.0000	1	one-hundred-fifty
0.0145	21.6	.0000	1	one-ness
0.0145	21.6	.0000	1	one-run
0.0145	21.6	.0000	1	one-seven
0.0145	21.6	.0000	1	one-stringed
0.0145	21.6	.0000	1	ong
0.0145	21.6	.0000	1	Oo-loo-te-ka's
0.0145	21.6	.0000	1	Ooh
0.0145	21.6	.0000	1	op'd
0.0145	21.6	.0000	1	OPEN
0.0145	21.6	.0000	1	opera-loving
0.0145	21.6	.0000	1	ordnance
0.0145	21.6	.0000	1	Orithyia
0.0145	21.6	.0000	1	ornamenting
0.0145	21.6	.0000	1	Oropeza
0.0145	21.6	.0000	1	OSTRACOD
0.0145	21.6	.0000	1	Othman
0.0145	21.6	.0000	1	Otter's
0.0145	21.6	.0000	1	Otters
0.0145	21.6	.0000	1	Ouia
0.0145	21.6	.0000	1	outclass
0.0145	21.6	.0000	1	OUTER
0.0145	21.6	.0000	1	outfeed-roll
0.0145	21.6	.0000	1	outfoxed
0.0145	21.6	.0000	1	outsail
0.0145	21.6	.0000	1	outsmart
0.0145	21.6	.0000	1	outsmarted
0.0145	21.6	.0000	1	outsoared
0.0145	21.6	.0000	1	over-crowded
0.0145	21.6	.0000	1	overdose
0.0145	21.6	.0000	1	overlordship
0.0145	21.6	.0000	1	overpast
0.0145	21.6	.0000	1	oversee
0.0145	21.6	.0000	1	Oviraptor
0.0145	21.6	.0000	1	own-ness
0.0145	21.6	.0000	1	Owuo
0.0145	21.6	.0000	1	oystermen
0.0145	21.6	.0000	1	PTs
0.0145	21.6	.0000	1	P-u-m-p
0.0145	21.6	.0000	1	Packet
0.0145	21.6	.0000	1	Paddy's
0.0145	21.6	.0000	1	Paestum
0.0145	21.6	.0000	1	pakeha
THE PRECEDING WORD TYPE OCCUPIES RANK 64200				
0.0145	21.6	.0000	1	Palaeolithic
0.0145	21.6	.0000	1	Palaty
0.0145	21.6	.0000	1	pale-lipped
0.0145	21.6	.0000	1	pale-skinned
0.0145	21.6	.0000	1	palefaced
0.0145	21.6	.0000	1	paleontologists'
0.0145	21.6	.0000	1	pales
0.0145	21.6	.0000	1	palindromic
0.0145	21.6	.0000	1	Palomares
0.0145	21.6	.0000	1	PANAMA
0.0145	21.6	.0000	1	Pandit
0.0145	21.6	.0000	1	Pantagraph
0.0145	21.6	.0000	1	pantries
0.0145	21.6	.0000	1	papaws
0.0145	21.6	.0000	1	parakeet's
0.0145	21.6	.0000	1	PARAMECIUM
0.0145	21.6	.0000	1	paratroops
0.0145	21.6	.0000	1	parching
0.0145	21.6	.0000	1	parer
0.0145	21.6	.0000	1	pari-mutuels
0.0145	21.6	.0000	1	Paris-to-Berlin
0.0145	21.6	.0000	1	Paris-to-Bordeaux
0.0145	21.6	.0000	1	Paris-to-Madrid
0.0145	21.6	.0000	1	Paris-to-Toulouse
0.0145	21.6	.0000	1	Parke
0.0145	21.6	.0000	1	Parker-Browne
0.0145	21.6	.0000	1	parochialisms
0.0145	21.6	.0000	1	parodied
0.0145	21.6	.0000	1	parti-colored
0.0145	21.6	.0000	1	pass'd
0.0145	21.6	.0000	1	Passeau
0.0145	21.6	.0000	1	Passenger
0.0145	21.6	.0000	1	passenger-carrying
0.0145	21.6	.0000	1	passeth
0.0145	21.6	.0000	1	passion-winged
0.0145	21.6	.0000	1	pasta
0.0145	21.6	.0000	1	pasturelands
0.0145	21.6	.0000	1	patent-leather
0.0145	21.6	.0000	1	paternalistic
0.0145	21.6	.0000	1	Paterson
0.0145	21.6	.0000	1	path-breaker
0.0145	21.6	.0000	1	pathologist
0.0145	21.6	.0000	1	Patje
0.0145	21.6	.0000	1	patria
0.0145	21.6	.0000	1	Patrice
0.0145	21.6	.0000	1	patronize
0.0145	21.6	.0000	1	Pavan
0.0145	21.6	.0000	1	Pavane
0.0145	21.6	.0000	1	paweth
0.0145	21.6	.0000	1	pawses
0.0145	21.6	.0000	1	pay-shakes-see
0.0145	21.6	.0000	1	peak-load
0.0145	21.6	.0000	1	pearlike
0.0145	21.6	.0000	1	peckety-peck-peck
0.0145	21.6	.0000	1	pedantic
0.0145	21.6	.0000	1	pediment
0.0145	21.6	.0000	1	Pee
0.0145	21.6	.0000	1	PEEN
0.0145	21.6	.0000	1	peg-leg
0.0145	21.6	.0000	1	Pegg
0.0145	21.6	.0000	1	Pekin
0.0145	21.6	.0000	1	Pekingese
0.0145	21.6	.0000	1	peltries
0.0145	21.6	.0000	1	penknives
0.0145	21.6	.0000	1	Pennock
0.0145	21.6	.0000	1	Penns
0.0145	21.6	.0000	1	penny-counting
0.0145	21.6	.0000	1	Per's
0.0145	21.6	.0000	1	Pera
0.0145	21.6	.0000	1	Percheron
0.0145	21.6	.0000	1	performers'
0.0145	21.6	.0000	1	Perished
0.0145	21.6	.0000	1	Perkinses
0.0145	21.6	.0000	1	Perley's
0.0145	21.6	.0000	1	permanency
0.0145	21.6	.0000	1	permeating
0.0145	21.6	.0000	1	perpetual-motion
0.0145	21.6	.0000	1	Personnel
0.0145	21.6	.0000	1	perusing
0.0145	21.6	.0000	1	perverted
0.0145	21.6	.0000	1	Petromin's
0.0145	21.6	.0000	1	Phebe
0.0145	21.6	.0000	1	Philadelphia-born
0.0145	21.6	.0000	1	Philanthropic
0.0145	21.6	.0000	1	Philanthropique
0.0145	21.6	.0000	1	philologist
0.0145	21.6	.0000	1	Phong
0.0145	21.6	.0000	1	photoengraved
0.0145	21.6	.0000	1	pick-up-arm
0.0145	21.6	.0000	1	Pider
0.0145	21.6	.0000	1	pierces
0.0145	21.6	.0000	1	Piety
0.0145	21.6	.0000	1	piglike
0.0145	21.6	.0000	1	Pilate
0.0145	21.6	.0000	1	pileup
0.0145	21.6	.0000	1	pilot-training
0.0145	21.6	.0000	1	pimiento-stuffed
0.0145	21.6	.0000	1	Pinckney
0.0145	21.6	.0000	1	pink-faced
0.0145	21.6	.0000	1	Pinnacle
THE PRECEDING WORD TYPE OCCUPIES RANK 64300				
0.0145	21.6	.0000	1	pintos
0.0145	21.6	.0000	1	pirouette
0.0145	21.6	.0000	1	Pitching
0.0145	21.6	.0000	1	Placerville
0.0145	21.6	.0000	1	Plagues
0.0145	21.6	.0000	1	plaint
0.0145	21.6	.0000	1	PLAN
0.0145	21.6	.0000	1	PLANARIA
0.0145	21.6	.0000	1	planarias
0.0145	21.6	.0000	1	Plank
0.0145	21.6	.0000	1	PLANTS
0.0145	21.6	.0000	1	playroom's
0.0145	21.6	.0000	1	pleasant-looking
0.0145	21.6	.0000	1	pleasure's
0.0145	21.6	.0000	1	plo-y
0.0145	21.6	.0000	1	Plomer
0.0145	21.6	.0000	1	PLOP
0.0145	21.6	.0000	1	Plotsky's
0.0145	21.6	.0000	1	pluck'd
0.0145	21.6	.0000	1	pluckt
0.0145	21.6	.0000	1	poachers
0.0145	21.6	.0000	1	poet-novelist
0.0145	21.6	.0000	1	Pogranichaya
0.0145	21.6	.0000	1	poignancy
0.0145	21.6	.0000	1	Poignees
0.0145	21.6	.0000	1	Polido
0.0145	21.6	.0000	1	political-minded
0.0145	21.6	.0000	1	pompons
0.0145	21.6	.0000	1	Pons'
0.0145	21.6	.0000	1	pontiff
0.0145	21.6	.0000	1	Pontius
0.0145	21.6	.0000	1	pooh-poohed
0.0145	21.6	.0000	1	Poole
0.0145	21.6	.0000	1	POOR
0.0145	21.6	.0000	1	porcelains
0.0145	21.6	.0000	1	porecelain
0.0145	21.6	.0000	1	Porsche
0.0145	21.6	.0000	1	Porsche's
0.0145	21.6	.0000	1	Portolu
0.0145	21.6	.0000	1	Positano
0.0145	21.6	.0000	1	POSITION
0.0145	21.6	.0000	1	positiveness
0.0145	21.6	.0000	1	postdebutantes
0.0145	21.6	.0000	1	postmark
0.0145	21.6	.0000	1	Postmasters
0.0145	21.6	.0000	1	postrider
0.0145	21.6	.0000	1	postrider's
0.0145	21.6	.0000	1	potestas
0.0145	21.6	.0000	1	pow-wow
0.0145	21.6	.0000	1	powder-charged
0.0145	21.6	.0000	1	power-operated
0.0145	21.6	.0000	1	Pozzi
0.0145	21.6	.0000	1	practise
0.0145	21.6	.0000	1	practising
0.0145	21.6	.0000	1	Praetorian
0.0145	21.6	.0000	1	Prairies
0.0145	21.6	.0000	1	praise-singer
0.0145	21.6	.0000	1	praise-singing
0.0145	21.6	.0000	1	Praying
0.0145	21.6	.0000	1	pre-Civil
0.0145	21.6	.0000	1	pre-arranged
0.0145	21.6	.0000	1	pre-race
0.0145	21.6	.0000	1	Prepare
0.0145	21.6	.0000	1	preponderance
0.0145	21.6	.0000	1	preponderantly
0.0145	21.6	.0000	1	prepotency
0.0145	21.6	.0000	1	prerogative
0.0145	21.6	.0000	1	Presiding
0.0145	21.6	.0000	1	press'd
0.0145	21.6	.0000	1	preternatural
0.0145	21.6	.0000	1	prettying
0.0145	21.6	.0000	1	prison-house
0.0145	21.6	.0000	1	privation
0.0145	21.6	.0000	1	Prizes
0.0145	21.6	.0000	1	pro-Ottoman
0.0145	21.6	.0000	1	pro-liberation
0.0145	21.6	.0000	1	problem's
0.0145	21.6	.0000	1	Procession
0.0145	21.6	.0000	1	Proctor
0.0145	21.6	.0000	1	production-type
0.0145	21.6	.0000	1	profaned
0.0145	21.6	.0000	1	professed
0.0145	21.6	.0000	1	professing
0.0145	21.6	.0000	1	profounder
0.0145	21.6	.0000	1	progressivism
0.0145	21.6	.0000	1	Projet
0.0145	21.6	.0000	1	Prom's
0.0145	21.6	.0000	1	Promessi
0.0145	21.6	.0000	1	promiscuity
0.0145	21.6	.0000	1	propagandists
0.0145	21.6	.0000	1	propeller-powered
0.0145	21.6	.0000	1	prosperous-looking
0.0145	21.6	.0000	1	prostitutes
0.0145	21.6	.0000	1	protectors
0.0145	21.6	.0000	1	protoceratops
0.0145	21.6	.0000	1	Protos's
0.0145	21.6	.0000	1	protractors
0.0145	21.6	.0000	1	Provet
0.0145	21.6	.0000	1	provincialism
0.0145	21.6	.0000	1	Proving
THE PRECEDING WORD TYPE OCCUPIES RANK 64400				
0.0145	21.6	.0000	1	provokes
0.0145	21.6	.0000	1	prowler
0.0145	21.6	.0000	1	prows
0.0145	21.6	.0000	1	Prudence's
0.0145	21.6	.0000	1	prune-jack
0.0145	21.6	.0000	1	Pryderi's
0.0145	21.6	.0000	1	pshaws
0.0145	21.6	.0000	1	pshawses

U	SFI	D	F	Word Type
0.0145	21.6	.0000	1	PT-109
0.0145	21.6	.0000	1	PT-114
0.0145	21.6	.0000	1	PT-187
0.0145	21.6	.0000	1	pterosaurs
0.0145	21.6	.0000	1	publicist
0.0145	21.6	.0000	1	puff-puff-puff
0.0145	21.6	.0000	1	pugmarks
0.0145	21.6	.0000	1	Pukekohe
0.0145	21.6	.0000	1	pukka
0.0145	21.6	.0000	1	Pulcinella
0.0145	21.6	.0000	1	pulldown
0.0145	21.6	.0000	1	puller-downers
0.0145	21.6	.0000	1	puncher
0.0145	21.6	.0000	1	punh
0.0145	21.6	.0000	1	punishes
0.0145	21.6	.0000	1	PUPIL'S
0.0145	21.6	.0000	1	purged
0.0145	21.6	.0000	1	pushing-up
0.0145	21.6	.0000	1	PUT
0.0145	21.6	.0000	1	Putnams
0.0145	21.6	.0000	1	putrefying
0.0145	21.6	.0000	1	Pwyll's
0.0145	21.6	.0000	1	pygmoid
0.0145	21.6	.0000	1	Pylades
0.0145	21.6	.0000	1	pyrate
0.0145	21.6	.0000	1	quaintness
0.0145	21.6	.0000	1	Qualla
0.0145	21.6	.0000	1	quarter-
0.0145	21.6	.0000	1	Quartermaster
0.0145	21.6	.0000	1	quelled
0.0145	21.6	.0000	1	Quemados
0.0145	21.6	.0000	1	quick-running
0.0145	21.6	.0000	1	quiet-appearing
0.0145	21.6	.0000	1	quilt-making
0.0145	21.6	.0000	1	Qur'anic
0.0145	21.6	.0000	1	Rabelaisian
0.0145	21.6	.0000	1	radio-shack
0.0145	21.6	.0000	1	Rae
0.0145	21.6	.0000	1	raga
0.0145	21.6	.0000	1	ragas
0.0145	21.6	.0000	1	railhead
0.0145	21.6	.0000	1	Raising
0.0145	21.6	.0000	1	rakers
0.0145	21.6	.0000	1	Raleigh's
0.0145	21.6	.0000	1	Rampart
0.0145	21.6	.0000	1	Randazzo
0.0145	21.6	.0000	1	ranger's
0.0145	21.6	.0000	1	rankling
0.0145	21.6	.0000	1	rapid-firing
0.0145	21.6	.0000	1	Raschi
0.0145	21.6	.0000	1	Raubal
0.0145	21.6	.0000	1	Rawlings'
0.0145	21.6	.0000	1	razors
0.0145	21.6	.0000	1	razzle-dazzler
0.0145	21.6	.0000	1	re-enforcements
0.0145	21.6	.0000	1	re-entering
0.0145	21.6	.0000	1	reaction-control
0.0145	21.6	.0000	1	rear-engined
0.0145	21.6	.0000	1	reaver
0.0145	21.6	.0000	1	rebounder
0.0145	21.6	.0000	1	rebuke
0.0145	21.6	.0000	1	recognizably
0.0145	21.6	.0000	1	Recruiting
0.0145	21.6	.0000	1	recrystallizes
0.0145	21.6	.0000	1	recurred
0.0145	21.6	.0000	1	red-painted
0.0145	21.6	.0000	1	red-winger
0.0145	21.6	.0000	1	redbrick
0.0145	21.6	.0000	1	redeemed
0.0145	21.6	.0000	1	redeemeth
0.0145	21.6	.0000	1	Redhead
0.0145	21.6	.0000	1	redoubtable
0.0145	21.6	.0000	1	redrawing
0.0145	21.6	.0000	1	Reeds'
0.0145	21.6	.0000	1	Reese's
0.0145	21.6	.0000	1	refugee-camp-building
0.0145	21.6	.0000	1	regardeth
0.0145	21.6	.0000	1	regionalist
0.0145	21.6	.0000	1	Register
0.0145	21.6	.0000	1	Reichstag's
0.0145	21.6	.0000	1	reinsmen
0.0145	21.6	.0000	1	reintergrated
0.0145	21.6	.0000	1	Reiser's
0.0145	21.6	.0000	1	rejoiceth
0.0145	21.6	.0000	1	relapses
0.0145	21.6	.0000	1	relief-etched
0.0145	21.6	.0000	1	remittances
0.0145	21.6	.0000	1	Renaissance-style
0.0145	21.6	.0000	1	renders
0.0145	21.6	.0000	1	renovate
0.0145	21.6	.0000	1	renovated
0.0145	21.6	.0000	1	repainting

THE PRECEDING WORD TYPE OCCUPIES RANK 64500

U	SFI	D	F	Word Type
0.0145	21.6	.0000	1	repents
0.0145	21.6	.0000	1	repercussions
0.0145	21.6	.0000	1	rephrasing
0.0145	21.6	.0000	1	representare
0.0145	21.6	.0000	1	repressions
0.0145	21.6	.0000	1	reptile's
0.0145	21.6	.0000	1	republicanism
0.0145	21.6	.0000	1	repulsing
0.0145	21.6	.0000	1	rescrubbing
0.0145	21.6	.0000	1	resettlement
0.0145	21.6	.0000	1	resin-coated
0.0145	21.6	.0000	1	rest-room
0.0145	21.6	.0000	1	resumes
0.0145	21.6	.0000	1	resurgence
0.0145	21.6	.0000	1	retentive
0.0145	21.6	.0000	1	reticular
0.0145	21.6	.0000	1	retransmitted
0.0145	21.6	.0000	1	Reulbach
0.0145	21.6	.0000	1	Revelation
0.0145	21.6	.0000	1	Rex's
0.0145	21.6	.0000	1	Reynaert
0.0145	21.6	.0000	1	Rhapsodie
0.0145	21.6	.0000	1	Rhea
0.0145	21.6	.0000	1	rhino's
0.0145	21.6	.0000	1	Rhodes's
0.0145	21.6	.0000	1	Ri
0.0145	21.6	.0000	1	rib-cage
0.0145	21.6	.0000	1	rice-plants
0.0145	21.6	.0000	1	ricocheted
0.0145	21.6	.0000	1	rifled
0.0145	21.6	.0000	1	right-field
0.0145	21.6	.0000	1	right-footed
0.0145	21.6	.0000	1	Rih
0.0145	21.6	.0000	1	Rin-Tin-Tin
0.0145	21.6	.0000	1	Ringling's
0.0145	21.6	.0000	1	Rios
0.0145	21.6	.0000	1	RIP
0.0145	21.6	.0000	1	Risorgimento
0.0145	21.6	.0000	1	Rit's
0.0145	21.6	.0000	1	ritten
0.0145	21.6	.0000	1	river-bend
0.0145	21.6	.0000	1	Rizzuto
0.0145	21.6	.0000	1	roarer
0.0145	21.6	.0000	1	rockaway
0.0145	21.6	.0000	1	rocket-augmented
0.0145	21.6	.0000	1	Rocking-Horse
0.0145	21.6	.0000	1	rocklike
0.0145	21.6	.0000	1	Rockridge
0.0145	21.6	.0000	1	Rodger
0.0145	21.6	.0000	1	roil
0.0145	21.6	.0000	1	Romans'
0.0145	21.6	.0000	1	romantics
0.0145	21.6	.0000	1	room's
0.0145	21.6	.0000	1	Roquerre's
0.0145	21.6	.0000	1	rosary
0.0145	21.6	.0000	1	rose-moles
0.0145	21.6	.0000	1	ROTIFER
0.0145	21.6	.0000	1	Rotorua
0.0145	21.6	.0000	1	roughhouse
0.0145	21.6	.0000	1	rounder's
0.0145	21.6	.0000	1	Rowe
0.0145	21.6	.0000	1	rug-making
0.0145	21.6	.0000	1	ruler-and-compass
0.0145	21.6	.0000	1	Run-Sheep-Run
0.0145	21.6	.0000	1	run-in
0.0145	21.6	.0000	1	runnings
0.0145	21.6	.0000	1	Russell's
0.0145	21.6	.0000	1	rust-red
0.0145	21.6	.0000	1	Rusticana
0.0145	21.6	.0000	1	Ruysdael
0.0145	21.6	.0000	1	Ryersons
0.0145	21.6	.0000	1	Rysdyk's
0.0145	21.6	.0000	1	sabbatical
0.0145	21.6	.0000	1	Sablons
0.0145	21.6	.0000	1	Sail-Back
0.0145	21.6	.0000	1	Salaga
0.0145	21.6	.0000	1	salesrooms
0.0145	21.6	.0000	1	Salih's
0.0145	21.6	.0000	1	salt-boilers
0.0145	21.6	.0000	1	salt-kettles
0.0145	21.6	.0000	1	salve
0.0145	21.6	.0000	1	Salvemini
0.0145	21.6	.0000	1	Saly
0.0145	21.6	.0000	1	Samuel's
0.0145	21.6	.0000	1	sanctions
0.0145	21.6	.0000	1	sandbanks
0.0145	21.6	.0000	1	Sardauna
0.0145	21.6	.0000	1	sarong-wrapped
0.0145	21.6	.0000	1	satanic
0.0145	21.6	.0000	1	satisfieth
0.0145	21.6	.0000	1	Sauk
0.0145	21.6	.0000	1	Savage
0.0145	21.6	.0000	1	Savonarola's
0.0145	21.6	.0000	1	sawbuck
0.0145	21.6	.0000	1	Saxe-Weimar
0.0145	21.6	.0000	1	say'st
0.0145	21.6	.0000	1	sayen
0.0145	21.6	.0000	1	Scala
0.0145	21.6	.0000	1	scann'd
0.0145	21.6	.0000	1	scantiest

THE PRECEDING WORD TYPE OCCUPIES RANK 64600

U	SFI	D	F	Word Type
0.0145	21.6	.0000	1	scaredy-cats
0.0145	21.6	.0000	1	Scarfoglio
0.0145	21.6	.0000	1	Scheveningen
0.0145	21.6	.0000	1	school-boy
0.0145	21.6	.0000	1	school-master
0.0145	21.6	.0000	1	schoolmasters
0.0145	21.6	.0000	1	schooltime
0.0145	21.6	.0000	1	Schreiner
0.0145	21.6	.0000	1	Schreiner's
0.0145	21.6	.0000	1	scientist-explorer
0.0145	21.6	.0000	1	Scientists
0.0145	21.6	.0000	1	scorneth
0.0145	21.6	.0000	1	Scotsman
0.0145	21.6	.0000	1	scrambles
0.0145	21.6	.0000	1	scramblings
0.0145	21.6	.0000	1	screamingly
0.0145	21.6	.0000	1	screened-in
0.0145	21.6	.0000	1	Scribner
0.0145	21.6	.0000	1	scrouged
0.0145	21.6	.0000	1	Scudder's
0.0145	21.6	.0000	1	Scythian
0.0145	21.6	.0000	1	sea-birds
0.0145	21.6	.0000	1	sea-dyke
0.0145	21.6	.0000	1	Seabird
0.0145	21.6	.0000	1	seal's
0.0145	21.6	.0000	1	Seaport
0.0145	21.6	.0000	1	searcheth
0.0145	21.6	.0000	1	Secondary
0.0145	21.6	.0000	1	sectarian
0.0145	21.6	.0000	1	seduce
0.0145	21.6	.0000	1	seed's
0.0145	21.6	.0000	1	seers
0.0145	21.6	.0000	1	seesawses
0.0145	21.6	.0000	1	seiz'd
0.0145	21.6	.0000	1	Self-Initiated
0.0145	21.6	.0000	1	self-chosen
0.0145	21.6	.0000	1	self-deceiving
0.0145	21.6	.0000	1	self-termed
0.0145	21.6	.0000	1	selflessness
0.0145	21.6	.0000	1	Selim
0.0145	21.6	.0000	1	semi-male
0.0145	21.6	.0000	1	semicircular
0.0145	21.6	.0000	1	semicolonial
0.0145	21.6	.0000	1	semiobscene
0.0145	21.6	.0000	1	Sempre
0.0145	21.6	.0000	1	Senir
0.0145	21.6	.0000	1	sensitively
0.0145	21.6	.0000	1	sensuousness
0.0145	21.6	.0000	1	sentimentales
0.0145	21.6	.0000	1	separatist
0.0145	21.6	.0000	1	SET
0.0145	21.6	.0000	1	seven-and-a-half
0.0145	21.6	.0000	1	seven-story
0.0145	21.6	.0000	1	seventy-foot-long
0.0145	21.6	.0000	1	seventy-ton
0.0145	21.6	.0000	1	sextette
0.0145	21.6	.0000	1	shadowings
0.0145	21.6	.0000	1	shakos
0.0145	21.6	.0000	1	shallop
0.0145	21.6	.0000	1	shamrocks
0.0145	21.6	.0000	1	Shanghainese
0.0145	21.6	.0000	1	shapelessness
0.0145	21.6	.0000	1	shareholders
0.0145	21.6	.0000	1	shareholding
0.0145	21.6	.0000	1	Shari
0.0145	21.6	.0000	1	sharp-spoken
0.0145	21.6	.0000	1	sharp-toed
0.0145	21.6	.0000	1	shearingtime
0.0145	21.6	.0000	1	shelf-fashion
0.0145	21.6	.0000	1	shellbursts
0.0145	21.6	.0000	1	Sherman's
0.0145	21.6	.0000	1	Shibe
0.0145	21.6	.0000	1	shims
0.0145	21.6	.0000	1	shipowner
0.0145	21.6	.0000	1	Shippingport
0.0145	21.6	.0000	1	SHIPS
0.0145	21.6	.0000	1	Ships
0.0145	21.6	.0000	1	shirttail
0.0145	21.6	.0000	1	Shithead
0.0145	21.6	.0000	1	shoe-button
0.0145	21.6	.0000	1	shorthanded
0.0145	21.6	.0000	1	shot-put
0.0145	21.6	.0000	1	Shotton's
0.0145	21.6	.0000	1	shouldest
0.0145	21.6	.0000	1	shoves
0.0145	21.6	.0000	1	show'd
0.0145	21.6	.0000	1	SHRIMPS
0.0145	21.6	.0000	1	shrivel
0.0145	21.6	.0000	1	shure
0.0145	21.6	.0000	1	sidesaddle
0.0145	21.6	.0000	1	sidewinders
0.0145	21.6	.0000	1	sierras
0.0145	21.6	.0000	1	Sighs
0.0145	21.6	.0000	1	Silone
0.0145	21.6	.0000	1	Silverfish
0.0145	21.6	.0000	1	Simonized
0.0145	21.6	.0000	1	Sinbad's
0.0145	21.6	.0000	1	Singakademie
0.0145	21.6	.0000	1	sinister-looking
0.0145	21.6	.0000	1	Sinky

THE PRECEDING WORD TYPE OCCUPIES RANK 64700

U	SFI	D	F	Word Type
0.0145	21.6	.0000	1	Sinnamary
0.0145	21.6	.0000	1	sires
0.0145	21.6	.0000	1	Sirtori
0.0145	21.6	.0000	1	situate
0.0145	21.6	.0000	1	six-eight-wheeler
0.0145	21.6	.0000	1	sixteen-cylinder
0.0145	21.6	.0000	1	sixteen-hundreds
0.0145	21.6	.0000	1	Sizaire-Naudin
0.0145	21.6	.0000	1	Sizaires
0.0145	21.6	.0000	1	sketchbook
0.0145	21.6	.0000	1	Skiko
0.0145	21.6	.0000	1	skillets
0.0145	21.6	.0000	1	skin-made
0.0145	21.6	.0000	1	Sklodovski
0.0145	21.6	.0000	1	Sklodovskis
0.0145	21.6	.0000	1	sky-encircled
0.0145	21.6	.0000	1	Sky-god
0.0145	21.6	.0000	1	SLAM
0.0145	21.6	.0000	1	slave-catcher's
0.0145	21.6	.0000	1	sleuth
0.0145	21.6	.0000	1	sleuths
0.0145	21.6	.0000	1	slickers
0.0145	21.6	.0000	1	slide-hopping
0.0145	21.6	.0000	1	slighted
0.0145	21.6	.0000	1	slit-throat
0.0145	21.6	.0000	1	slow-burning
0.0145	21.6	.0000	1	smartaleck
0.0145	21.6	.0000	1	Smarty
0.0145	21.6	.0000	1	smirch'd
0.0145	21.6	.0000	1	Smoke
0.0145	21.6	.0000	1	smokier
0.0145	21.6	.0000	1	snorers
0.0145	21.6	.0000	1	snores
0.0145	21.6	.0000	1	snow-hidden
0.0145	21.6	.0000	1	snow-wrapped
0.0145	21.6	.0000	1	snuffs
0.0145	21.6	.0000	1	Soaks
0.0145	21.6	.0000	1	soap-box
0.0145	21.6	.0000	1	soarers
0.0145	21.6	.0000	1	Sohrab's
0.0145	21.6	.0000	1	sojourn
0.0145	21.6	.0000	1	Sol's
0.0145	21.6	.0000	1	soldiers-to-be
0.0145	21.6	.0000	1	Solutrean
0.0145	21.6	.0000	1	Solway
0.0145	21.6	.0000	1	Sonatina
0.0145	21.6	.0000	1	SOON
0.0145	21.6	.0000	1	soonest
0.0145	21.6	.0000	1	SOOT
0.0145	21.6	.0000	1	Sorceries
0.0145	21.6	.0000	1	Sorghum
0.0145	21.6	.0000	1	Soria
0.0145	21.6	.0000	1	Sorrel
0.0145	21.6	.0000	1	Sortileges
0.0145	21.6	.0000	1	Soto's
0.0145	21.6	.0000	1	sound-effects
0.0145	21.6	.0000	1	Southside
0.0145	21.6	.0000	1	sovereign's
0.0145	21.6	.0000	1	Soviet-Union
0.0145	21.6	.0000	1	SOW
0.0145	21.6	.0000	1	spa
0.0145	21.6	.0000	1	Spaarndam
0.0145	21.6	.0000	1	SPACE
0.0145	21.6	.0000	1	space-consuming
0.0145	21.6	.0000	1	spacecrafts
0.0145	21.6	.0000	1	Spaniard's
0.0145	21.6	.0000	1	spark-plug
0.0145	21.6	.0000	1	sparkless
0.0145	21.6	.0000	1	sparring
0.0145	21.6	.0000	1	Spartanburg
0.0145	21.6	.0000	1	spats
0.0145	21.6	.0000	1	spear-nosed
0.0145	21.6	.0000	1	special-reaction
0.0145	21.6	.0000	1	spellbinder
0.0145	21.6	.0000	1	spiel
0.0145	21.6	.0000	1	spilikins
0.0145	21.6	.0000	1	spirit-lifting
0.0145	21.6	.0000	1	spirit-men
0.0145	21.6	.0000	1	spiritedly
0.0145	21.6	.0000	1	spiritually
0.0145	21.6	.0000	1	spitz
0.0145	21.6	.0000	1	SPLASH
0.0145	21.6	.0000	1	splashings
0.0145	21.6	.0000	1	spontaneity
0.0145	21.6	.0000	1	spoor
0.0145	21.6	.0000	1	Sposi
0.0145	21.6	.0000	1	Spotswood
0.0145	21.6	.0000	1	sprat
0.0145	21.6	.0000	1	spreadeth
0.0145	21.6	.0000	1	spring-head
0.0145	21.6	.0000	1	springhouse
0.0145	21.6	.0000	1	Springtail
0.0145	21.6	.0000	1	SPRINGTAILS
0.0145	21.6	.0000	1	sprinting
0.0145	21.6	.0000	1	spritten
0.0145	21.6	.0000	1	Spurio's
0.0145	21.6	.0000	1	squabbled
0.0145	21.6	.0000	1	square-bodied
0.0145	21.6	.0000	1	square-riggers
0.0145	21.6	.0000	1	squash-court

THE PRECEDING WORD TYPE OCCUPIES RANK 64800

U	SFI	D	F	Word Type
0.0145	21.6	.0000	1	sssssssssssst
0.0145	21.6	.0000	1	stable-yard
0.0145	21.6	.0000	1	stadholder
0.0145	21.6	.0000	1	stadia
0.0145	21.6	.0000	1	stag's
0.0145	21.6	.0000	1	stampers
0.0145	21.6	.0000	1	Standardbred
0.0145	21.6	.0000	1	stander-uppers
0.0145	21.6	.0000	1	star-bright
0.0145	21.6	.0000	1	stardust
0.0145	21.6	.0000	1	starry-eyed
0.0145	21.6	.0000	1	StateHouse
0.0145	21.6	.0000	1	stationmen
0.0145	21.6	.0000	1	staunched
0.0145	21.6	.0000	1	staunchly
0.0145	21.6	.0000	1	steam-basket
0.0145	21.6	.0000	1	steamcars
0.0145	21.6	.0000	1	Stearns
0.0145	21.6	.0000	1	Steeldust
0.0145	21.6	.0000	1	stem-winding
0.0145	21.6	.0000	1	Stengel's
0.0145	21.6	.0000	1	STENTOR
0.0145	21.6	.0000	1	stepbrothers
0.0145	21.6	.0000	1	Stepchildren
0.0145	21.6	.0000	1	stepmother's
0.0145	21.6	.0000	1	Sternberg
0.0145	21.6	.0000	1	stick-to-it-iveness
0.0145	21.6	.0000	1	stilted
0.0145	21.6	.0000	1	stipple
0.0145	21.6	.0000	1	stomach-ache
0.0145	21.6	.0000	1	stomach-hair
0.0145	21.6	.0000	1	Stoner
0.0145	21.6	.0000	1	stoodest
0.0145	21.6	.0000	1	storage-jar
0.0145	21.6	.0000	1	Storekeeper
0.0145	21.6	.0000	1	storekeeping
0.0145	21.6	.0000	1	Storybook
0.0145	21.6	.0000	1	stows
0.0145	21.6	.0000	1	stranglehold
0.0145	21.6	.0000	1	strangler
0.0145	21.6	.0000	1	strapless
0.0145	21.6	.0000	1	stratifications
0.0145	21.6	.0000	1	Strauses
0.0145	21.6	.0000	1	STRAW
0.0145	21.6	.0000	1	strawses
0.0145	21.6	.0000	1	streetwalkers
0.0145	21.6	.0000	1	Stresa
0.0145	21.6	.0000	1	stretcheth
0.0145	21.6	.0000	1	strikeout
0.0145	21.6	.0000	1	Stringer
0.0145	21.6	.0000	1	STRIPS
0.0145	21.6	.0000	1	strok'd
0.0145	21.6	.0000	1	Strong's
0.0145	21.6	.0000	1	Strongs
0.0145	21.6	.0000	1	Strongs'
0.0145	21.6	.0000	1	Stuarts
0.0145	21.6	.0000	1	Studios
0.0145	21.6	.0000	1	STUPID
0.0145	21.6	.0000	1	Sturzo
0.0145	21.6	.0000	1	Stygian
0.0145	21.6	.0000	1	subatomic
0.0145	21.6	.0000	1	subdues
0.0145	21.6	.0000	1	subjecting
0.0145	21.6	.0000	1	subjectively
0.0145	21.6	.0000	1	Submachine
0.0145	21.6	.0000	1	subservient
0.0145	21.6	.0000	1	subsidy
0.0145	21.6	.0000	1	subtil
0.0145	21.6	.0000	1	successor's
0.0145	21.6	.0000	1	Sudden
0.0145	21.6	.0000	1	suffusions
0.0145	21.6	.0000	1	Sukenik

U	SFI	D	F	Word Type
0.0145	21.6	.0000	1	Sulivan
0.0145	21.6	.0000	1	sulphur-bottom
0.0145	21.6	.0000	1	sulphurous
0.0145	21.6	.0000	1	sultanate
0.0145	21.6	.0000	1	Sum'll
0.0145	21.6	.0000	1	Sum's
0.0145	21.6	.0000	1	Sumbawa
0.0145	21.6	.0000	1	sun-bright
0.0145	21.6	.0000	1	sun-reflecting
0.0145	21.6	.0000	1	sun-worshiping
0.0145	21.6	.0000	1	superhuman
0.0145	21.6	.0000	1	superintendent's
0.0145	21.6	.0000	1	Superman
0.0145	21.6	.0000	1	Supervacuo
0.0145	21.6	.0000	1	suppress
0.0145	21.6	.0000	1	Surgeon's
0.0145	21.6	.0000	1	surges'
0.0145	21.6	.0000	1	surrealists
0.0145	21.6	.0000	1	surrenders
0.0145	21.6	.0000	1	Survive
0.0145	21.6	.0000	1	Susannah's
0.0145	21.6	.0000	1	Susans
0.0145	21.6	.0000	1	Sustagen
0.0145	21.6	.0000	1	sutured
0.0145	21.6	.0000	1	swaddling
0.0145	21.6	.0000	1	swallow-tailed
0.0145	21.6	.0000	1	swallowtail
0.0145	21.6	.0000	1	Swamps

THE PRECEDING WORD TYPE OCCUPIES RANK 64900

U	SFI	D	F	Word Type
0.0145	21.6	.0000	1	Sweden-Finland
0.0145	21.6	.0000	1	sweet-natured
0.0145	21.6	.0000	1	swift-running
0.0145	21.6	.0000	1	swishy-wishy
0.0145	21.6	.0000	1	swisssh
0.0145	21.6	.0000	1	switchboards
0.0145	21.6	.0000	1	switchman
0.0145	21.6	.0000	1	SWOOSH
0.0145	21.6	.0000	1	symbolically
0.0145	21.6	.0000	1	synagogues
0.0145	21.6	.0000	1	T-r-e-l-l-i-s
0.0145	21.6	.0000	1	T-shirts
0.0145	21.6	.0000	1	Ta-lin's
0.0145	21.6	.0000	1	tabernas
0.0145	21.6	.0000	1	table-tennis
0.0145	21.6	.0000	1	Tactical
0.0145	21.6	.0000	1	taillike
0.0145	21.6	.0000	1	takers
0.0145	21.6	.0000	1	talc
0.0145	21.6	.0000	1	tam-o'-shanter
0.0145	21.6	.0000	1	tamandua
0.0145	21.6	.0000	1	tank-like
0.0145	21.6	.0000	1	TANKERS
0.0145	21.6	.0000	1	tao
0.0145	21.6	.0000	1	TARDIGRADE
0.0145	21.6	.0000	1	tardigrade
0.0145	21.6	.0000	1	tares
0.0145	21.6	.0000	1	Tarshish
0.0145	21.6	.0000	1	tautline
0.0145	21.6	.0000	1	taxidermy
0.0145	21.6	.0000	1	taxiway
0.0145	21.6	.0000	1	Tayxas
0.0145	21.6	.0000	1	tcusk
0.0145	21.6	.0000	1	Te-a-o-ga
0.0145	21.6	.0000	1	tea-pots
0.0145	21.6	.0000	1	tear-streaked
0.0145	21.6	.0000	1	Tear's
0.0145	21.6	.0000	1	tempestuously
0.0145	21.6	.0000	1	temptingly
0.0145	21.6	.0000	1	TEN
0.0145	21.6	.0000	1	ten-gallon
0.0145	21.6	.0000	1	ten-ton
0.0145	21.6	.0000	1	ten-volume
0.0145	21.6	.0000	1	tenderer
0.0145	21.6	.0000	1	tenny-runners
0.0145	21.6	.0000	1	tentfolk
0.0145	21.6	.0000	1	termini
0.0145	21.6	.0000	1	tern's
0.0145	21.6	.0000	1	Terre
0.0145	21.6	.0000	1	territory-wide
0.0145	21.6	.0000	1	Teshura
0.0145	21.6	.0000	1	test-pilot
0.0145	21.6	.0000	1	Texel
0.0145	21.6	.0000	1	Teyjat
0.0145	21.6	.0000	1	Thayers
0.0145	21.6	.0000	1	thecondonts
0.0145	21.6	.0000	1	theorbo
0.0145	21.6	.0000	1	there-of
0.0145	21.6	.0000	1	theses
0.0145	21.6	.0000	1	thin-faced
0.0145	21.6	.0000	1	thin-sliced
0.0145	21.6	.0000	1	Thirst
0.0145	21.6	.0000	1	thitten
0.0145	21.6	.0000	1	thorn-covered
0.0145	21.6	.0000	1	Thoroughbred
0.0145	21.6	.0000	1	Thoughts
0.0145	21.6	.0000	1	Three-Horned
0.0145	21.6	.0000	1	three-horn
0.0145	21.6	.0000	1	three-horned
0.0145	21.6	.0000	1	Three-hundred
0.0145	21.6	.0000	1	three-hundred
0.0145	21.6	.0000	1	three-lane
0.0145	21.6	.0000	1	thriller
0.0145	21.6	.0000	1	throatless
0.0145	21.6	.0000	1	THROUGH
0.0145	21.6	.0000	1	throwback
0.0145	21.6	.0000	1	thugs
0.0145	21.6	.0000	1	thunder-cart
0.0145	21.6	.0000	1	thunder-spirits
0.0145	21.6	.0000	1	Thurgau
0.0145	21.6	.0000	1	Tibbs
0.0145	21.6	.0000	1	Tibetans
0.0145	21.6	.0000	1	Tiger-Cat
0.0145	21.6	.0000	1	tight-throated
0.0145	21.6	.0000	1	tights-covered
0.0145	21.6	.0000	1	times'
0.0145	21.6	.0000	1	tinker's
0.0145	21.6	.0000	1	Tinnie's
0.0145	21.6	.0000	1	Tintoretto's
0.0145	21.6	.0000	1	tip-cart
0.0145	21.6	.0000	1	Tishbite
0.0145	21.6	.0000	1	Titian
0.0145	21.6	.0000	1	Titicaca
0.0145	21.6	.0000	1	Titov
0.0145	21.6	.0000	1	TLC
0.0145	21.6	.0000	1	Todd,/
0.0145	21.6	.0000	1	Todd's
0.0145	21.6	.0000	1	Togoland
0.0145	21.6	.0000	1	toheroa
0.0145	21.6	.0000	1	tomato-faced

THE PRECEDING WORD TYPE OCCUPIES RANK 65000

U	SFI	D	F	Word Type
0.0145	21.6	.0000	1	tomtoms
0.0145	21.6	.0000	1	TOO
0.0145	21.6	.0000	1	TOOLS
0.0145	21.6	.0000	1	tooter
0.0145	21.6	.0000	1	tootled
0.0145	21.6	.0000	1	top-of-the-order
0.0145	21.6	.0000	1	top-shaped
0.0145	21.6	.0000	1	topflight
0.0145	21.6	.0000	1	Topsy
0.0145	21.6	.0000	1	tosh
0.0145	21.6	.0000	1	totter'd
0.0145	21.6	.0000	1	touch'd
0.0145	21.6	.0000	1	touchable
0.0145	21.6	.0000	1	Tourist
0.0145	21.6	.0000	1	tourist's-eye
0.0145	21.6	.0000	1	tourougou
0.0145	21.6	.0000	1	townships
0.0145	21.6	.0000	1	townward
0.0145	21.6	.0000	1	towship
0.0145	21.6	.0000	1	Trachodons
0.0145	21.6	.0000	1	Tracy's
0.0145	21.6	.0000	1	trainees'
0.0145	21.6	.0000	1	Tramassene
0.0145	21.6	.0000	1	Transcendentalists
0.0145	21.6	.0000	1	Transportation
0.0145	21.6	.0000	1	trapezer
0.0145	21.6	.0000	1	Trappist
0.0145	21.6	.0000	1	travail's
0.0145	21.6	.0000	1	treadle
0.0145	21.6	.0000	1	Tredo
0.0145	21.6	.0000	1	tree-nesting
0.0145	21.6	.0000	1	TREES
0.0145	21.6	.0000	1	trenching
0.0145	21.6	.0000	1	Trials
0.0145	21.6	.0000	1	trinity
0.0145	21.6	.0000	1	triple-threat
0.0145	21.6	.0000	1	Trolley
0.0145	21.6	.0000	1	Trooper
0.0145	21.6	.0000	1	troth
0.0145	21.6	.0000	1	Trotting
0.0145	21.6	.0000	1	trotting-horse
0.0145	21.6	.0000	1	truck-garden
0.0145	21.6	.0000	1	truck-mounted
0.0145	21.6	.0000	1	trulli
0.0145	21.6	.0000	1	trunkmaker
0.0145	21.6	.0000	1	Tse-tung's
0.0145	21.6	.0000	1	tuberculars
0.0145	21.6	.0000	1	tuckered
0.0145	21.6	.0000	1	tufted
0.0145	21.6	.0000	1	Tukulor
0.0145	21.6	.0000	1	Tung-pin
0.0145	21.6	.0000	1	Turfan
0.0145	21.6	.0000	1	turk-
0.0145	21.6	.0000	1	Turkestan
0.0145	21.6	.0000	1	turneth
0.0145	21.6	.0000	1	turnoff
0.0145	21.6	.0000	1	Turtle's
0.0145	21.6	.0000	1	Twang-g-g
0.0145	21.6	.0000	1	Tweet
0.0145	21.6	.0000	1	twelve-inch-wide
0.0145	21.6	.0000	1	twenty-mile
0.0145	21.6	.0000	1	TWIST
0.0145	21.6	.0000	1	two-and-a-half-century
0.0145	21.6	.0000	1	two-engined
0.0145	21.6	.0000	1	two-faced
0.0145	21.6	.0000	1	two-foot-long
0.0145	21.6	.0000	1	two-footed
0.0145	21.6	.0000	1	two-horse
0.0145	21.6	.0000	1	two-hundred-yard
0.0145	21.6	.0000	1	two-inch-thick
0.0145	21.6	.0000	1	two-mile
0.0145	21.6	.0000	1	two-pointer
0.0145	21.6	.0000	1	Ty
0.0145	21.6	.0000	1	typitoon
0.0145	21.6	.0000	1	tyrannous
0.0145	21.6	.0000	1	Tyrus
0.0145	21.6	.0000	1	Tzu
0.0145	21.6	.0000	1	ubiquity
0.0145	21.6	.0000	1	Uighur
0.0145	21.6	.0000	1	UK
0.0145	21.6	.0000	1	ulama
0.0145	21.6	.0000	1	unblindfolded
0.0145	21.6	.0000	1	unbolt
0.0145	21.6	.0000	1	unbolted
0.0145	21.6	.0000	1	unbutton
0.0145	21.6	.0000	1	uncircumcised
0.0145	21.6	.0000	1	uncultivable
0.0145	21.6	.0000	1	undefended
0.0145	21.6	.0000	1	undelivered
0.0145	21.6	.0000	1	under-inspector
0.0145	21.6	.0000	1	undergraduates
0.0145	21.6	.0000	1	Underwing
0.0145	21.6	.0000	1	uneventful
0.0145	21.6	.0000	1	unflinching
0.0145	21.6	.0000	1	unfrosted
0.0145	21.6	.0000	1	unfruitful
0.0145	21.6	.0000	1	ungraciously
0.0145	21.6	.0000	1	unillumined
0.0145	21.6	.0000	1	unimproved
0.0145	21.6	.0000	1	UnitedKingdom

THE PRECEDING WORD TYPE OCCUPIES RANK 65100

U	SFI	D	F	Word Type
0.0145	21.6	.0000	1	university-trained
0.0145	21.6	.0000	1	unkempt
0.0145	21.6	.0000	1	unlaced
0.0145	21.6	.0000	1	unlamented
0.0145	21.6	.0000	1	unmelodious
0.0145	21.6	.0000	1	unpatriotic
0.0145	21.6	.0000	1	unpeaceful
0.0145	21.6	.0000	1	unperturbed
0.0145	21.6	.0000	1	unreadable
0.0145	21.6	.0000	1	unrealized
0.0145	21.6	.0000	1	unreliably
0.0145	21.6	.0000	1	unscalped
0.0145	21.6	.0000	1	unscratched
0.0145	21.6	.0000	1	unscrupulously
0.0145	21.6	.0000	1	unserviceable
0.0145	21.6	.0000	1	unsupercharged
0.0145	21.6	.0000	1	unvexed
0.0145	21.6	.0000	1	up-court
0.0145	21.6	.0000	1	up-down
0.0145	21.6	.0000	1	up-river
0.0145	21.6	.0000	1	upbringing
0.0145	21.6	.0000	1	updraw
0.0145	21.6	.0000	1	uproot
0.0145	21.6	.0000	1	UPWARD
0.0145	21.6	.0000	1	Utility
0.0145	21.6	.0000	1	utter'd
0.0145	21.6	.0000	1	V-formation
0.0145	21.6	.0000	1	V-i-n-e
0.0145	21.6	.0000	1	V-mail
0.0145	21.6	.0000	1	V-shape
0.0145	21.6	.0000	1	Valais
0.0145	21.6	.0000	1	Valera
0.0145	21.6	.0000	1	Valladolid
0.0145	21.6	.0000	1	Valses
0.0145	21.6	.0000	1	VanDaan's
0.0145	21.6	.0000	1	VandenVosReynaerde
0.0145	21.6	.0000	1	vanderVeen
0.0145	21.6	.0000	1	vanish'd
0.0145	21.6	.0000	1	variable-stability
0.0145	21.6	.0000	1	Velasquez
0.0145	21.6	.0000	1	velvetlike
0.0145	21.6	.0000	1	Vendice's
0.0145	21.6	.0000	1	verbatim
0.0145	21.6	.0000	1	Verga
0.0145	21.6	.0000	1	veriest
0.0145	21.6	.0000	1	versts
0.0145	21.6	.0000	1	Verwoerd
0.0145	21.6	.0000	1	vespers
0.0145	21.6	.0000	1	vet's
0.0145	21.6	.0000	1	vials
0.0145	21.6	.0000	1	Viareggio
0.0145	21.6	.0000	1	Viccars
0.0145	21.6	.0000	1	vileness
0.0145	21.6	.0000	1	village's
0.0145	21.6	.0000	1	villas
0.0145	21.6	.0000	1	Villon's
0.0145	21.6	.0000	1	Vineyard
0.0145	21.6	.0000	1	violadagamba
0.0145	21.6	.0000	1	Violette
0.0145	21.6	.0000	1	VISE
0.0145	21.6	.0000	1	vitamin-a
0.0145	21.6	.0000	1	Vladislav
0.0145	21.6	.0000	1	vonBrauchitsch
0.0145	21.6	.0000	1	vonBraun's
0.0145	21.6	.0000	1	Vordingborg
0.0145	21.6	.0000	1	Vran
0.0145	21.6	.0000	1	vulgarities
0.0145	21.6	.0000	1	vying
0.0145	21.6	.0000	1	W-A-T-
0.0145	21.6	.0000	1	W-a-t-e-r
0.0145	21.6	.0000	1	wa-tho-huck
0.0145	21.6	.0000	1	wa-wa
0.0145	21.6	.0000	1	Waddles
0.0145	21.6	.0000	1	Wadi
0.0145	21.6	.0000	1	waggling
0.0145	21.6	.0000	1	wagoners
0.0145	21.6	.0000	1	Wahhabi
0.0145	21.6	.0000	1	Waitangi
0.0145	21.6	.0000	1	Walberg
0.0145	21.6	.0000	1	wall-paintings
0.0145	21.6	.0000	1	wall-writing
0.0145	21.6	.0000	1	Wallace's
0.0145	21.6	.0000	1	Warden
0.0145	21.6	.0000	1	warehouseman
0.0145	21.6	.0000	1	warrens
0.0145	21.6	.0000	1	WARTS
0.0145	21.6	.0000	1	washing-bowl
0.0145	21.6	.0000	1	Washingtons
0.0145	21.6	.0000	1	washstands
0.0145	21.6	.0000	1	Wasps
0.0145	21.6	.0000	1	wat
0.0145	21.6	.0000	1	Wat's
0.0145	21.6	.0000	1	watchmakers
0.0145	21.6	.0000	1	watchmaking
0.0145	21.6	.0000	1	water-base
0.0145	21.6	.0000	1	water-bounded
0.0145	21.6	.0000	1	water-cooled
0.0145	21.6	.0000	1	water-fall
0.0145	21.6	.0000	1	water-sounds
0.0145	21.6	.0000	1	waterhole

THE PRECEDING WORD TYPE OCCUPIES RANK 65200

U	SFI	D	F	Word Type
0.0145	21.6	.0000	1	watermen
0.0145	21.6	.0000	1	waterweed
0.0145	21.6	.0000	1	Wax
0.0145	21.6	.0000	1	weak-spirited
0.0145	21.6	.0000	1	wearing-down
0.0145	21.6	.0000	1	weatherproof
0.0145	21.6	.0000	1	Websters
0.0145	21.6	.0000	1	Weenty
0.0145	21.6	.0000	1	Weizmann
0.0145	21.6	.0000	1	WELL
0.0145	21.6	.0000	1	well-brought-up
0.0145	21.6	.0000	1	well-laid-out
0.0145	21.6	.0000	1	well-ordered
0.0145	21.6	.0000	1	well-versed
0.0145	21.6	.0000	1	WERE
0.0145	21.6	.0000	1	Wernher
0.0145	21.6	.0000	1	Wessel
0.0145	21.6	.0000	1	westward-flowing
0.0145	21.6	.0000	1	whaka
0.0145	21.6	.0000	1	Whakarewarewa
0.0145	21.6	.0000	1	whale-oil
0.0145	21.6	.0000	1	whaled
0.0145	21.6	.0000	1	whiling
0.0145	21.6	.0000	1	whip-poor-will
0.0145	21.6	.0000	1	whiplashing
0.0145	21.6	.0000	1	Whipsaw
0.0145	21.6	.0000	1	Whirligig
0.0145	21.6	.0000	1	whisht
0.0145	21.6	.0000	1	whisperings
0.0145	21.6	.0000	1	white-cap
0.0145	21.6	.0000	1	white-collar
0.0145	21.6	.0000	1	white-powdered
0.0145	21.6	.0000	1	Whitechapel
0.0145	21.6	.0000	1	Whitehaven
0.0145	21.6	.0000	1	whitens
0.0145	21.6	.0000	1	Whites
0.0145	21.6	.0000	1	Whitsuntide
0.0145	21.6	.0000	1	Wideners
0.0145	21.6	.0000	1	widowhood
0.0145	21.6	.0000	1	Willem
0.0145	21.6	.0000	1	willfully
0.0145	21.6	.0000	1	Winchell
0.0145	21.6	.0000	1	winches
0.0145	21.6	.0000	1	windburned
0.0145	21.6	.0000	1	window-panes
0.0145	21.6	.0000	1	wing-level
0.0145	21.6	.0000	1	winsome
0.0145	21.6	.0000	1	Wishtego's
0.0145	21.6	.0000	1	withersoever
0.0145	21.6	.0000	1	withouten
0.0145	21.6	.0000	1	Wittenberg
0.0145	21.6	.0000	1	Wittgenstein
0.0145	21.6	.0000	1	wizardry
0.0145	21.6	.0000	1	Wledig
0.0145	21.6	.0000	1	wolf's
0.0145	21.6	.0000	1	wonder-box
0.0145	21.6	.0000	1	wood-nymph
0.0145	21.6	.0000	1	woodcarving
0.0145	21.6	.0000	1	woodlore
0.0145	21.6	.0000	1	Woodmouse
0.0145	21.6	.0000	1	woods-ward
0.0145	21.6	.0000	1	woofing
0.0145	21.6	.0000	1	Woolworth's
0.0145	21.6	.0000	1	word-elements
0.0145	21.6	.0000	1	word-for-word
0.0145	21.6	.0000	1	work-force
0.0145	21.6	.0000	1	WORKBENCH
0.0145	21.6	.0000	1	world-class
0.0145	21.6	.0000	1	wormeaten
0.0145	21.6	.0000	1	worshipper
0.0145	21.6	.0000	1	Wound
0.0145	21.6	.0000	1	wrangling
0.0145	21.6	.0000	1	Wrentham
0.0145	21.6	.0000	1	wretched-looking
0.0145	21.6	.0000	1	wretchedness
0.0145	21.6	.0000	1	write-ups
0.0145	21.6	.0000	1	writs
0.0145	21.6	.0000	1	wrong-foot
0.0145	21.6	.0000	1	Wu
0.0145	21.6	.0000	1	Wyck
0.0145	21.6	.0000	1	Wythes
0.0145	21.6	.0000	1	X-1A
0.0145	21.6	.0000	1	X-15
0.0145	21.6	.0000	1	xenophobia
0.0145	21.6	.0000	1	y-o-o-u-u-p
0.0145	21.6	.0000	1	Yama-Kings
0.0145	21.6	.0000	1	yangba
0.0145	21.6	.0000	1	Yea
0.0145	21.6	.0000	1	Yearling
0.0145	21.6	.0000	1	yellow-crested
0.0145	21.6	.0000	1	yellow-eared
0.0145	21.6	.0000	1	yellow-white
0.0145	21.6	.0000	1	Yigael
0.0145	21.6	.0000	1	Yolk
0.0145	21.6	.0000	1	Yonny
0.0145	21.6	.0000	1	younker
0.0145	21.6	.0000	1	youpi-yi
0.0145	21.6	.0000	1	youpi-youpi-youpi-ya
0.0145	21.6	.0000	1	Yung's
0.0145	21.6	.0000	1	Yuri

THE PRECEDING WORD TYPE OCCUPIES RANK 65300

U	SFI	D	F	Word Type
0.0145	21.6	.0000	1	zagging
0.0145	21.6	.0000	1	Zal
0.0145	21.6	.0000	1	Zekes
0.0145	21.6	.0000	1	Zelter
0.0145	21.6	.0000	1	Zero
0.0145	21.6	.0000	1	zero-delay
0.0145	21.6	.0000	1	Zeros
0.0145	21.6	.0000	1	Zetes
0.0145	21.6	.0000	1	zigging
0.0145	21.6	.0000	1	zigzagging
0.0145	21.6	.0000	1	Zing-g-g
0.0145	21.6	.0000	1	Zionism's
0.0145	21.6	.0000	1	zoo-lulu
0.0145	21.6	.0000	1	zoo-lulus
0.0145	21.6	.0000	1	Zoology
0.0145	21.6	.0000	1	Zouaves
0.0145	21.6	.0000	1	ZROOOOOMMM
0.0145	21.6	.0000	1	ZuiderZee
0.0145	21.6	.0000	1	Zunis
0.0145	21.6	.0000	1	Zwickau
0.0145	21.6	.0000	1	020
0.0145	21.6	.0000	1	060
0.0145	21.6	.0000	1	1-0
0.0145	21.6	.0000	1	1/4-ton
0.0145	21.6	.0000	1	10-story
0.0145	21.6	.0000	1	100s
0.0145	21.6	.0000	1	1000s
0.0145	21.6	.0000	1	105-millimeter
0.0145	21.6	.0000	1	1130
0.0145	21.6	.0000	1	12-ounce
0.0145	21.6	.0000	1	120-yard
0.0145	21.6	.0000	1	1269
0.0145	21.6	.0000	1	1354
0.0145	21.6	.0000	1	1363
0.0145	21.6	.0000	1	1368

U	SFI	D	F	Word Type
0.0145	21.6	.0000	1	1376
0.0145	21.6	.0000	1	1381
0.0145	21.6	.0000	1	1386
0.0145	21.6	.0000	1	1389
0.0145	21.6	.0000	1	1405
0.0145	21.6	.0000	1	1412
0.0145	21.6	.0000	1	1413-1421
0.0145	21.6	.0000	1	1421-1451
0.0145	21.6	.0000	1	1433
0.0145	21.6	.0000	1	1509-1547
0.0145	21.6	.0000	1	16-inch
0.0145	21.6	.0000	1	1616
0.0145	21.6	.0000	1	1672-1707
0.0145	21.6	.0000	1	1685
0.0145	21.6	.0000	1	1692
0.0145	21.6	.0000	1	1701-1808
0.0145	21.6	.0000	1	1708
0.0145	21.6	.0000	1	1759-1788
0.0145	21.6	.0000	1	1793-1794
0.0145	21.6	.0000	1	1805-1806
0.0145	21.6	.0000	1	1810-1856
0.0145	21.6	.0000	1	1810-51
0.0145	21.6	.0000	1	1814-15
0.0145	21.6	.0000	1	1840-1922
0.0145	21.6	.0000	1	1861-63
0.0145	21.6	.0000	1	1871-72
0.0145	21.6	.0000	1	1875-1937
0.0145	21.6	.0000	1	1890-1948
0.0145	21.6	.0000	1	1899-1902
0.0145	21.6	.0000	1	1902-03
0.0145	21.6	.0000	1	1906-09
0.0145	21.6	.0000	1	1913-1918
0.0145	21.6	.0000	1	1936-1939
0.0145	21.6	.0000	1	1939-1940
0.0145	21.6	.0000	1	1960-1961
0.0145	21.6	.0000	1	1962-1963
0.0145	21.6	.0000	1	2-liter
0.0145	21.6	.0000	1	2-0
0.0145	21.6	.0000	1	2g
0.0145	21.6	.0000	1	20g
0.0145	21.6	.0000	1	21-game
0.0145	21.6	.0000	1	22-game
0.0145	21.6	.0000	1	24-game
0.0145	21.6	.0000	1	24-h
0.0145	21.6	.0000	1	240mm
0.0145	21.6	.0000	1	248763
0.0145	21.6	.0000	1	25AB
0.0145	21.6	.0000	1	25B
0.0145	21.6	.0000	1	25C
0.0145	21.6	.0000	1	25-4
0.0145	21.6	.0000	1	250-odd
0.0145	21.6	.0000	1	3-toed
0.0145	21.6	.0000	1	3x3x3x3
0.0145	21.6	.0000	1	302-mile
0.0145	21.6	.0000	1	306
0.0145	21.6	.0000	1	3560th
0.0145	21.6	.0000	1	3561st
0.0145	21.6	.0000	1	36-inch
0.0145	21.6	.0000	1	36-liter
0.0145	21.6	.0000	1	37-millimeter
0.0145	21.6	.0000	1	381/4
0.0145	21.6	.0000	1	39-inch
0.0145	21.6	.0000	1	39-18
0.0145	21.6	.0000	1	39-19
0.0145	21.6	.0000	1	39-20

THE PRECEDING WORD TYPE OCCUPIES RANK 65400

U	SFI	D	F	Word Type
0.0145	21.6	.0000	1	4-3
0.0145	21.6	.0000	1	40-h
0.0145	21.6	.0000	1	40-mph
0.0145	21.6	.0000	1	40mm
0.0145	21.6	.0000	1	42-inch
0.0145	21.6	.0000	1	42-ounce
0.0145	21.6	.0000	1	440-yard
0.0145	21.6	.0000	1	45-h
0.0145	21.6	.0000	1	45623
0.0145	21.6	.0000	1	461/2
0.0145	21.6	.0000	1	48765
0.0145	21.6	.0000	1	491
0.0145	21.6	.0000	1	491/4
0.0145	21.6	.0000	1	497
0.0145	21.6	.0000	1	5d
0.0145	21.6	.0000	1	500th
0.0145	21.6	.0000	1	505
0.0145	21.6	.0000	1	533
0.0145	21.6	.0000	1	54376
0.0145	21.6	.0000	1	555
0.0145	21.6	.0000	1	6U6139
0.0145	21.6	.0000	1	6-foot-tall
0.0145	21.6	.0000	1	654
0.0145	21.6	.0000	1	7-liter
0.0145	21.6	.0000	1	700-year
0.0145	21.6	.0000	1	705
0.0145	21.6	.0000	1	750-mile
0.0145	21.6	.0000	1	754
0.0145	21.6	.0000	1	77-footers
0.0145	21.6	.0000	1	787
0.0145	21.6	.0000	1	791
0.0145	21.6	.0000	1	8g
0.0145	21.6	.0000	1	80-footer
0.0145	21.6	.0000	1	8000-foot
0.0145	21.6	.0000	1	836
0.0145	21.6	.0000	1	9-liter
0.0145	21.6	.0000	1	9-principle
0.0145	21.6	.0000	1	90-foot-high
0.0145	21.6	.0000	1	900-odd
0.0145	21.6	.0000	1	987
0.0129	21.1	.0000	4	bastings
0.0129	21.1	.0000	4	Bread-Cereal
0.0129	21.1	.0000	4	creaming
0.0129	21.1	.0000	4	croutons
0.0129	21.1	.0000	4	darner
0.0129	21.1	.0000	4	double-boiler
0.0129	21.1	.0000	4	horse-radish
0.0129	21.1	.0000	4	necklines
0.0129	21.1	.0000	4	one-hot-dish
0.0129	21.1	.0000	4	overstitching
0.0129	21.1	.0000	4	quarter-pound
0.0129	21.1	.0000	4	ready-to-eat
0.0129	21.1	.0000	4	returnable
0.0129	21.1	.0000	4	selvage
0.0129	21.1	.0000	4	selvages
0.0129	21.1	.0000	4	tantrum
0.0129	21.1	.0000	4	wearable
0.0126	21.0	.0000	5	beveled
0.0126	21.0	.0000	5	brittleness
0.0126	21.0	.0000	5	cross-feed
0.0126	21.0	.0000	5	dimensioning
0.0126	21.0	.0000	5	fps
0.0126	21.0	.0000	5	freehand
0.0126	21.0	.0000	5	ga
0.0126	21.0	.0000	5	Hardness
0.0126	21.0	.0000	5	in-feed
0.0126	21.0	.0000	5	kerf
0.0126	21.0	.0000	5	out-feed
0.0126	21.0	.0000	5	riveting
0.0126	21.0	.0000	5	tap-drill
0.0126	21.0	.0000	5	toolholder
0.0122	20.8	.0000	1	$115
0.0122	20.8	.0000	1	$140
0.0122	20.8	.0000	1	$170
0.0122	20.8	.0000	1	$190
0.0122	20.8	.0000	1	$24-billion
0.0122	20.8	.0000	1	$266
0.0122	20.8	.0000	1	$320
0.0122	20.8	.0000	1	$341
0.0122	20.8	.0000	1	$4-a-pound
0.0122	20.8	.0000	1	$400-a-month
0.0122	20.8	.0000	1	$477
0.0122	20.8	.0000	1	$48
0.0122	20.8	.0000	1	$567
0.0122	20.8	.0000	1	$70
0.0122	20.8	.0000	1	$87
0.0122	20.8	.0000	1	$965
0.0122	20.8	.0000	1	-ephyr
0.0122	20.8	.0000	1	-14
0.0122	20.8	.0000	1	-80
0.0122	20.8	.0000	1	'fifties
0.0122	20.8	.0000	1	'forties
0.0122	20.8	.0000	1	'skins
0.0122	20.8	.0000	1	'thirties
0.0122	20.8	.0000	1	'22
0.0122	20.8	.0000	1	'40s
0.0122	20.8	.0000	1	'51
0.0122	20.8	.0000	1	'60
0.0122	20.8	.0000	1	'61
0.0122	20.8	.0000	1	'62

THE PRECEDING WORD TYPE OCCUPIES RANK 65500

U	SFI	D	F	Word Type
0.0122	20.8	.0000	1	A-arms
0.0122	20.8	.0000	1	a-bit-under-$2000
0.0122	20.8	.0000	1	a-building
0.0122	20.8	.0000	1	a-diorable
0.0122	20.8	.0000	1	a-h-h-h
0.0122	20.8	.0000	1	a-plenty
0.0122	20.8	.0000	1	a-wonder
0.0122	20.8	.0000	1	AA/F
0.0122	20.8	.0000	1	abducted
0.0122	20.8	.0000	1	Abernathy
0.0122	20.8	.0000	1	abets
0.0122	20.8	.0000	1	Abington
0.0122	20.8	.0000	1	abortionist
0.0122	20.8	.0000	1	abortionists
0.0122	20.8	.0000	1	about-face
0.0122	20.8	.0000	1	above-water
0.0122	20.8	.0000	1	Abramses
0.0122	20.8	.0000	1	abrazo
0.0122	20.8	.0000	1	Abricot
0.0122	20.8	.0000	1	absorber
0.0122	20.8	.0000	1	Absurd
0.0122	20.8	.0000	1	abutment
0.0122	20.8	.0000	1	academics
0.0122	20.8	.0000	1	accademies
0.0122	20.8	.0000	1	acclimated
0.0122	20.8	.0000	1	Achilles'
0.0122	20.8	.0000	1	achoo
0.0122	20.8	.0000	1	acidulous
0.0122	20.8	.0000	1	acoustic
0.0122	20.8	.0000	1	acquirable
0.0122	20.8	.0000	1	acrid
0.0122	20.8	.0000	1	acrimonious
0.0122	20.8	.0000	1	actors'
0.0122	20.8	.0000	1	actuator
0.0122	20.8	.0000	1	adage
0.0122	20.8	.0000	1	Adamowicz
0.0122	20.8	.0000	1	adapter
0.0122	20.8	.0000	1	adapters
0.0122	20.8	.0000	1	add-oil
0.0122	20.8	.0000	1	addictive
0.0122	20.8	.0000	1	Adenauer
0.0122	20.8	.0000	1	adeptness
0.0122	20.8	.0000	1	adhesive-backed
0.0122	20.8	.0000	1	adipose
0.0122	20.8	.0000	1	adjoins
0.0122	20.8	.0000	1	adjustable-voltage
0.0122	20.8	.0000	1	Administrations
0.0122	20.8	.0000	1	admiral's
0.0122	20.8	.0000	1	admonish
0.0122	20.8	.0000	1	Adolfo
0.0122	20.8	.0000	1	Adolpho
0.0122	20.8	.0000	1	adorns
0.0122	20.8	.0000	1	Adriana
0.0122	20.8	.0000	1	Ads
0.0122	20.8	.0000	1	adulatory
0.0122	20.8	.0000	1	Adventuress's
0.0122	20.8	.0000	1	Adviser
0.0122	20.8	.0000	1	AEC'S
0.0122	20.8	.0000	1	Aedan's
0.0122	20.8	.0000	1	aerodynamic
0.0122	20.8	.0000	1	AFB
0.0122	20.8	.0000	1	aflare
0.0122	20.8	.0000	1	Afro-Americans
0.0122	20.8	.0000	1	afterbath
0.0122	20.8	.0000	1	ag
0.0122	20.8	.0000	1	agency's
0.0122	20.8	.0000	1	agendas
0.0122	20.8	.0000	1	aggg
0.0122	20.8	.0000	1	aggrandisement
0.0122	20.8	.0000	1	Aging
0.0122	20.8	.0000	1	aground
0.0122	20.8	.0000	1	Agua
0.0122	20.8	.0000	1	Ahmadi
0.0122	20.8	.0000	1	Ahnapee
0.0122	20.8	.0000	1	AHRA
0.0122	20.8	.0000	1	Ahyee-aye-ty-fahve
0.0122	20.8	.0000	1	AiResearch
0.0122	20.8	.0000	1	Air-India
0.0122	20.8	.0000	1	Air-Lines
0.0122	20.8	.0000	1	air-driven
0.0122	20.8	.0000	1	air-supply
0.0122	20.8	.0000	1	air-to-ground
0.0122	20.8	.0000	1	air-transport
0.0122	20.8	.0000	1	air-weapon
0.0122	20.8	.0000	1	Aircraft
0.0122	20.8	.0000	1	Airheart
0.0122	20.8	.0000	1	Airhearts
0.0122	20.8	.0000	1	airly
0.0122	20.8	.0000	1	Airmanship
0.0122	20.8	.0000	1	Al-Fatah
0.0122	20.8	.0000	1	al-Shatti
0.0122	20.8	.0000	1	Alamogordo
0.0122	20.8	.0000	1	alarmingly
0.0122	20.8	.0000	1	alaska
0.0122	20.8	.0000	1	Albano
0.0122	20.8	.0000	1	Alcindor's
0.0122	20.8	.0000	1	Alco
0.0122	20.8	.0000	1	Aldolph
0.0122	20.8	.0000	1	Aldrin's
0.0122	20.8	.0000	1	Aleksandr

THE PRECEDING WORD TYPE OCCUPIES RANK 65600

U	SFI	D	F	Word Type
0.0122	20.8	.0000	1	alerting
0.0122	20.8	.0000	1	Alfa
0.0122	20.8	.0000	1	algal
0.0122	20.8	.0000	1	alienation
0.0122	20.8	.0000	1	Alioto-arranged
0.0122	20.8	.0000	1	Alison's
0.0122	20.8	.0000	1	all-European
0.0122	20.8	.0000	1	All-Pro
0.0122	20.8	.0000	1	all-black
0.0122	20.8	.0000	1	all-male
0.0122	20.8	.0000	1	all-new
0.0122	20.8	.0000	1	all-professional
0.0122	20.8	.0000	1	allayed
0.0122	20.8	.0000	1	allegation
0.0122	20.8	.0000	1	allegories
0.0122	20.8	.0000	1	Allendale
0.0122	20.8	.0000	1	Allentown
0.0122	20.8	.0000	1	alleyways
0.0122	20.8	.0000	1	Allyson
0.0122	20.8	.0000	1	almendro
0.0122	20.8	.0000	1	alongshore
0.0122	20.8	.0000	1	Alpert
0.0122	20.8	.0000	1	Alphonzo
0.0122	20.8	.0000	1	Alpo
0.0122	20.8	.0000	1	Alselmo
0.0122	20.8	.0000	1	ALSEP
0.0122	20.8	.0000	1	Alsop
0.0122	20.8	.0000	1	Altamaha
0.0122	20.8	.0000	1	Altamonte
0.0122	20.8	.0000	1	Altgeld
0.0122	20.8	.0000	1	altho'
0.0122	20.8	.0000	1	aluminumized
0.0122	20.8	.0000	1	alveolus
0.0122	20.8	.0000	1	Alvina
0.0122	20.8	.0000	1	Amalgamated
0.0122	20.8	.0000	1	amateur-built
0.0122	20.8	.0000	1	amateurism
0.0122	20.8	.0000	1	ambience
0.0122	20.8	.0000	1	American-controlled
0.0122	20.8	.0000	1	Americanese
0.0122	20.8	.0000	1	AMF
0.0122	20.8	.0000	1	Amman
0.0122	20.8	.0000	1	amoral
0.0122	20.8	.0000	1	amputation
0.0122	20.8	.0000	1	AMT
0.0122	20.8	.0000	1	AN/FSR-2
0.0122	20.8	.0000	1	anachronism
0.0122	20.8	.0000	1	anathema
0.0122	20.8	.0000	1	ancien
0.0122	20.8	.0000	1	Andersons'
0.0122	20.8	.0000	1	angling
0.0122	20.8	.0000	1	animated-live-action
0.0122	20.8	.0000	1	animation
0.0122	20.8	.0000	1	anis
0.0122	20.8	.0000	1	AnnArbor
0.0122	20.8	.0000	1	Ann-Margret
0.0122	20.8	.0000	1	Ann-Margret's
0.0122	20.8	.0000	1	Annahoj
0.0122	20.8	.0000	1	Anne-Marie
0.0122	20.8	.0000	1	annotated
0.0122	20.8	.0000	1	annoys
0.0122	20.8	.0000	1	anodized
0.0122	20.8	.0000	1	ans
0.0122	20.8	.0000	1	ante-bellum
0.0122	20.8	.0000	1	Antenna
0.0122	20.8	.0000	1	anti-Castro
0.0122	20.8	.0000	1	anti-Irish
0.0122	20.8	.0000	1	anti-Know-Nothing
0.0122	20.8	.0000	1	Anti-Locust
0.0122	20.8	.0000	1	anti-U
0.0122	20.8	.0000	1	anti-ballistic-missile
0.0122	20.8	.0000	1	anti-blemish
0.0122	20.8	.0000	1	anti-cavity
0.0122	20.8	.0000	1	anti-doping
0.0122	20.8	.0000	1	anti-inflammants
0.0122	20.8	.0000	1	anti-inflation
0.0122	20.8	.0000	1	anti-inflationary
0.0122	20.8	.0000	1	anti-insomnia
0.0122	20.8	.0000	1	anti-intellectualism
0.0122	20.8	.0000	1	anti-religious
0.0122	20.8	.0000	1	anti-tension
0.0122	20.8	.0000	1	anti-trust
0.0122	20.8	.0000	1	antipollution
0.0122	20.8	.0000	1	antiquarian
0.0122	20.8	.0000	1	antiquated
0.0122	20.8	.0000	1	antique-car
0.0122	20.8	.0000	1	antisubmarine
0.0122	20.8	.0000	1	antisway
0.0122	20.8	.0000	1	antithesis
0.0122	20.8	.0000	1	Anyone
0.0122	20.8	.0000	1	Anything
0.0122	20.8	.0000	1	apartment-sized
0.0122	20.8	.0000	1	aperitifs
0.0122	20.8	.0000	1	Apollo's
0.0122	20.8	.0000	1	Apollos
0.0122	20.8	.0000	1	apologizing
0.0122	20.8	.0000	1	Appalachicola
0.0122	20.8	.0000	1	Appalled
0.0122	20.8	.0000	1	appeased
0.0122	20.8	.0000	1	Appliance

THE PRECEDING WORD TYPE OCCUPIES RANK 65700

U	SFI	D	F	Word Type
0.0122	20.8	.0000	1	appliance's
0.0122	20.8	.0000	1	Appreciation
0.0122	20.8	.0000	1	approximates
0.0122	20.8	.0000	1	APRO
0.0122	20.8	.0000	1	apropos
0.0122	20.8	.0000	1	Aquarian
0.0122	20.8	.0000	1	Aquarius
0.0122	20.8	.0000	1	aquatint
0.0122	20.8	.0000	1	Arab-Israeli
0.0122	20.8	.0000	1	arabesque
0.0122	20.8	.0000	1	Aramco's
0.0122	20.8	.0000	1	Arantes
0.0122	20.8	.0000	1	arbiter
0.0122	20.8	.0000	1	arboretum
0.0122	20.8	.0000	1	arch-Stalinist
0.0122	20.8	.0000	1	Architect
0.0122	20.8	.0000	1	Arctic's
0.0122	20.8	.0000	1	ardderchag
0.0122	20.8	.0000	1	ardently
0.0122	20.8	.0000	1	Arecibo's
0.0122	20.8	.0000	1	Aretha
0.0122	20.8	.0000	1	argumentative
0.0122	20.8	.0000	1	Argyllshire
0.0122	20.8	.0000	1	Armchair
0.0122	20.8	.0000	1	armes
0.0122	20.8	.0000	1	Army-McCarthy
0.0122	20.8	.0000	1	aroma-chemicals
0.0122	20.8	.0000	1	aromatherapy
0.0122	20.8	.0000	1	Arouet
0.0122	20.8	.0000	1	aroun-
0.0122	20.8	.0000	1	around-town
0.0122	20.8	.0000	1	arrogantly
0.0122	20.8	.0000	1	arrow's
0.0122	20.8	.0000	1	Artes
0.0122	20.8	.0000	1	Artful
0.0122	20.8	.0000	1	Artinish
0.0122	20.8	.0000	1	artist-producer
0.0122	20.8	.0000	1	asafoetida
0.0122	20.8	.0000	1	Asan
0.0122	20.8	.0000	1	ascendant
0.0122	20.8	.0000	1	Asclepius
0.0122	20.8	.0000	1	Ase-bun
0.0122	20.8	.0000	1	ash-blond
0.0122	20.8	.0000	1	Ashford
0.0122	20.8	.0000	1	ashtray
0.0122	20.8	.0000	1	assailing
0.0122	20.8	.0000	1	Assassin
0.0122	20.8	.0000	1	assassin-turned-informer
0.0122	20.8	.0000	1	assassinate
0.0122	20.8	.0000	1	assertive
0.0122	20.8	.0000	1	assuredly
0.0122	20.8	.0000	1	asterisk
0.0122	20.8	.0000	1	Astros
0.0122	20.8	.0000	1	AT&T
0.0122	20.8	.0000	1	Atco
0.0122	20.8	.0000	1	Athalie
0.0122	20.8	.0000	1	athwart
0.0122	20.8	.0000	1	Atlantans
0.0122	20.8	.0000	1	Atlantic-salmon
0.0122	20.8	.0000	1	atmospherically
0.0122	20.8	.0000	1	Atoll
0.0122	20.8	.0000	1	atomized
0.0122	20.8	.0000	1	atonality
0.0122	20.8	.0000	1	ATS-3
0.0122	20.8	.0000	1	attests
0.0122	20.8	.0000	1	Attitudes
0.0122	20.8	.0000	1	Attuck's
0.0122	20.8	.0000	1	auburn
0.0122	20.8	.0000	1	auctioneer
0.0122	20.8	.0000	1	audacity
0.0122	20.8	.0000	1	audibles
0.0122	20.8	.0000	1	Audience
0.0122	20.8	.0000	1	auditor
0.0122	20.8	.0000	1	Audrey
0.0122	20.8	.0000	1	Audubon's
0.0122	20.8	.0000	1	Auerswald
0.0122	20.8	.0000	1	Auguste's
0.0122	20.8	.0000	1	Australasia
0.0122	20.8	.0000	1	authentically
0.0122	20.8	.0000	1	author-director
0.0122	20.8	.0000	1	authoritarian
0.0122	20.8	.0000	1	authorization
0.0122	20.8	.0000	1	auto-racing's
0.0122	20.8	.0000	1	autoclavable
0.0122	20.8	.0000	1	autoclaving
0.0122	20.8	.0000	1	autoharps
0.0122	20.8	.0000	1	Automotive
0.0122	20.8	.0000	1	Avakian's
0.0122	20.8	.0000	1	average-size
0.0122	20.8	.0000	1	avocado
0.0122	20.8	.0000	1	Ayala
0.0122	20.8	.0000	1	AYC
0.0122	20.8	.0000	1	Ayllon
0.0122	20.8	.0000	1	Azerbaijan
0.0122	20.8	.0000	1	Azrin
0.0122	20.8	.0000	1	B-52s
0.0122	20.8	.0000	1	B'nai
0.0122	20.8	.0000	1	B'rith
0.0122	20.8	.0000	1	baaing

U	SFI	D	F	Word Type
0.0122	20.8	.0000	1	Babler
				THE PRECEDING WORD TYPE OCCUPIES RANK 65800
0.0122	20.8	.0000	1	Babler's
0.0122	20.8	.0000	1	baby-sitter
0.0122	20.8	.0000	1	babyhood
0.0122	20.8	.0000	1	Bach-rock
0.0122	20.8	.0000	1	Bachelor
0.0122	20.8	.0000	1	back-alley
0.0122	20.8	.0000	1	back-up
0.0122	20.8	.0000	1	backdoor
0.0122	20.8	.0000	1	Background
0.0122	20.8	.0000	1	backlash
0.0122	20.8	.0000	1	backlog
0.0122	20.8	.0000	1	backpackers
0.0122	20.8	.0000	1	Backstairs
0.0122	20.8	.0000	1	backwoodsy
0.0122	20.8	.0000	1	bad-dream
0.0122	20.8	.0000	1	bad-looking
0.0122	20.8	.0000	1	Badminton
0.0122	20.8	.0000	1	bag-dir
0.0122	20.8	.0000	1	Bain
0.0122	20.8	.0000	1	Baines
0.0122	20.8	.0000	1	Bakersfield
0.0122	20.8	.0000	1	balance-vote
0.0122	20.8	.0000	1	Balenciaga
0.0122	20.8	.0000	1	Balkhash
0.0122	20.8	.0000	1	ballclub
0.0122	20.8	.0000	1	baller
0.0122	20.8	.0000	1	ballet-like
0.0122	20.8	.0000	1	balloonists
0.0122	20.8	.0000	1	ballplayer's
0.0122	20.8	.0000	1	Balls
0.0122	20.8	.0000	1	banal
0.0122	20.8	.0000	1	banality
0.0122	20.8	.0000	1	bandied
0.0122	20.8	.0000	1	banding
0.0122	20.8	.0000	1	Bandon
0.0122	20.8	.0000	1	banged-up
0.0122	20.8	.0000	1	Bangor
0.0122	20.8	.0000	1	bank's
0.0122	20.8	.0000	1	banning
0.0122	20.8	.0000	1	banshees
0.0122	20.8	.0000	1	Bara
0.0122	20.8	.0000	1	Barb-arians
0.0122	20.8	.0000	1	BARBECUED
0.0122	20.8	.0000	1	Barbra
0.0122	20.8	.0000	1	Barcelona
0.0122	20.8	.0000	1	bardic
0.0122	20.8	.0000	1	bare-assed
0.0122	20.8	.0000	1	bare-knuckled
0.0122	20.8	.0000	1	Bargaining
0.0122	20.8	.0000	1	barged
0.0122	20.8	.0000	1	Barillet
0.0122	20.8	.0000	1	barley-planting
0.0122	20.8	.0000	1	barman's
0.0122	20.8	.0000	1	barnacle-encrusted
0.0122	20.8	.0000	1	baroque
0.0122	20.8	.0000	1	Barracuda
0.0122	20.8	.0000	1	barrages
0.0122	20.8	.0000	1	barricading
0.0122	20.8	.0000	1	Barrios
0.0122	20.8	.0000	1	bases-loaded
0.0122	20.8	.0000	1	bash
0.0122	20.8	.0000	1	basics
0.0122	20.8	.0000	1	basketweave
0.0122	20.8	.0000	1	Basswood
0.0122	20.8	.0000	1	Bastile
0.0122	20.8	.0000	1	batches
0.0122	20.8	.0000	1	bath's
0.0122	20.8	.0000	1	bathos
0.0122	20.8	.0000	1	Batman
0.0122	20.8	.0000	1	Baton
0.0122	20.8	.0000	1	Battey
0.0122	20.8	.0000	1	Battista
0.0122	20.8	.0000	1	battle-hardened
0.0122	20.8	.0000	1	battlefronts
0.0122	20.8	.0000	1	Batts
0.0122	20.8	.0000	1	bawdiness
0.0122	20.8	.0000	1	bawdy
0.0122	20.8	.0000	1	bay's
0.0122	20.8	.0000	1	Baylor's
0.0122	20.8	.0000	1	BCS**
0.0122	20.8	.0000	1	BCS'**
0.0122	20.8	.0000	1	BD-1
0.0122	20.8	.0000	1	BD-4
0.0122	20.8	.0000	1	BD-4's
0.0122	20.8	.0000	1	be-in
0.0122	20.8	.0000	1	beachfront
0.0122	20.8	.0000	1	beachside
0.0122	20.8	.0000	1	beadyeyed
0.0122	20.8	.0000	1	Beagle's
0.0122	20.8	.0000	1	Beatles'
0.0122	20.8	.0000	1	beaut
0.0122	20.8	.0000	1	beautification
0.0122	20.8	.0000	1	beckons
0.0122	20.8	.0000	1	bed-wetting
0.0122	20.8	.0000	1	bedazzlements
0.0122	20.8	.0000	1	BEDC-presiding
0.0122	20.8	.0000	1	BEDC'S
0.0122	20.8	.0000	1	Bede's
0.0122	20.8	.0000	1	befitting
0.0122	20.8	.0000	1	befuddle
				THE PRECEDING WORD TYPE OCCUPIES RANK 65900
0.0122	20.8	.0000	1	befuddled
0.0122	20.8	.0000	1	begat
0.0122	20.8	.0000	1	beget
0.0122	20.8	.0000	1	begotten
0.0122	20.8	.0000	1	Behavior
0.0122	20.8	.0000	1	behaviorism
0.0122	20.8	.0000	1	behead
0.0122	20.8	.0000	1	behemoths
0.0122	20.8	.0000	1	bejeweled
0.0122	20.8	.0000	1	bell-bottoms
0.0122	20.8	.0000	1	bella
0.0122	20.8	.0000	1	Bellas
0.0122	20.8	.0000	1	bellbottoms
0.0122	20.8	.0000	1	belli
0.0122	20.8	.0000	1	belling
0.0122	20.8	.0000	1	Bellingham
0.0122	20.8	.0000	1	bellwether
0.0122	20.8	.0000	1	Belmondo
0.0122	20.8	.0000	1	Beloit
0.0122	20.8	.0000	1	below-the-front-bumper
0.0122	20.8	.0000	1	Benane
0.0122	20.8	.0000	1	benchtop
0.0122	20.8	.0000	1	bender
0.0122	20.8	.0000	1	benefactors
0.0122	20.8	.0000	1	benefiting
0.0122	20.8	.0000	1	benevolents
0.0122	20.8	.0000	1	Bengals
0.0122	20.8	.0000	1	Bensen
0.0122	20.8	.0000	1	Berkshires
0.0122	20.8	.0000	1	Berliners
0.0122	20.8	.0000	1	Berlitz
0.0122	20.8	.0000	1	Berries
0.0122	20.8	.0000	1	beslime
0.0122	20.8	.0000	1	bespectacled
0.0122	20.8	.0000	1	BEST
0.0122	20.8	.0000	1	best-kept
0.0122	20.8	.0000	1	best-named
0.0122	20.8	.0000	1	best-seller
0.0122	20.8	.0000	1	bested
0.0122	20.8	.0000	1	betrays
0.0122	20.8	.0000	1	Beverage
0.0122	20.8	.0000	1	Beverley
0.0122	20.8	.0000	1	bi-monthly
0.0122	20.8	.0000	1	BIA'S**
0.0122	20.8	.0000	1	Biafra's
0.0122	20.8	.0000	1	Biafrans
0.0122	20.8	.0000	1	Biff
0.0122	20.8	.0000	1	BigSur
0.0122	20.8	.0000	1	big-bass
0.0122	20.8	.0000	1	big-displacement
0.0122	20.8	.0000	1	big-government
0.0122	20.8	.0000	1	big-inch
0.0122	20.8	.0000	1	big-university
0.0122	20.8	.0000	1	bigger-than-ever
0.0122	20.8	.0000	1	biggies
0.0122	20.8	.0000	1	bikemakers
0.0122	20.8	.0000	1	bikini-clad
0.0122	20.8	.0000	1	bilious
0.0122	20.8	.0000	1	billets
0.0122	20.8	.0000	1	Biologists
0.0122	20.8	.0000	1	bipartisan
0.0122	20.8	.0000	1	bird-eating
0.0122	20.8	.0000	1	birdsongs
0.0122	20.8	.0000	1	biretta
0.0122	20.8	.0000	1	birth-control
0.0122	20.8	.0000	1	Biscayne
0.0122	20.8	.0000	1	bisexual
0.0122	20.8	.0000	1	bisque
0.0122	20.8	.0000	1	Bitterroot
0.0122	20.8	.0000	1	biz
0.0122	20.8	.0000	1	black-
0.0122	20.8	.0000	1	black-and-gold
0.0122	20.8	.0000	1	black-elastic
0.0122	20.8	.0000	1	black-fringed
0.0122	20.8	.0000	1	black-gloved
0.0122	20.8	.0000	1	black-green
0.0122	20.8	.0000	1	black-leather
0.0122	20.8	.0000	1	black-tinted
0.0122	20.8	.0000	1	blackballed
0.0122	20.8	.0000	1	Blackfooted
0.0122	20.8	.0000	1	blacktails
0.0122	20.8	.0000	1	blacktopped
0.0122	20.8	.0000	1	blacktopping
0.0122	20.8	.0000	1	blah
0.0122	20.8	.0000	1	Blaiberg
0.0122	20.8	.0000	1	Blanton
0.0122	20.8	.0000	1	blarney
0.0122	20.8	.0000	1	Blarney's
0.0122	20.8	.0000	1	blase
0.0122	20.8	.0000	1	blesses
0.0122	20.8	.0000	1	Blimp
0.0122	20.8	.0000	1	Blindness
0.0122	20.8	.0000	1	blocked-off
0.0122	20.8	.0000	1	blokes
0.0122	20.8	.0000	1	blood-and-guts
0.0122	20.8	.0000	1	BLOODSTOCK
0.0122	20.8	.0000	1	bloody-mindedness
0.0122	20.8	.0000	1	Blossom's
0.0122	20.8	.0000	1	blowdowns
0.0122	20.8	.0000	1	BLS
				THE PRECEDING WORD TYPE OCCUPIES RANK 66000
0.0122	20.8	.0000	1	bludgeoned
0.0122	20.8	.0000	1	blue-and-yellow
0.0122	20.8	.0000	1	blue-collar
0.0122	20.8	.0000	1	Blue-footed
0.0122	20.8	.0000	1	blue-grey
0.0122	20.8	.0000	1	blue-lined
0.0122	20.8	.0000	1	blue-pencil
0.0122	20.8	.0000	1	Bluebirds
0.0122	20.8	.0000	1	Bluefaced
0.0122	20.8	.0000	1	Blueprint
0.0122	20.8	.0000	1	bluffed
0.0122	20.8	.0000	1	Bo's
0.0122	20.8	.0000	1	boated
0.0122	20.8	.0000	1	boaters
0.0122	20.8	.0000	1	boatnook
0.0122	20.8	.0000	1	boatyard
0.0122	20.8	.0000	1	bobby-soxer
0.0122	20.8	.0000	1	Bodrugan
0.0122	20.8	.0000	1	Bodrugan's
0.0122	20.8	.0000	1	body-builder
0.0122	20.8	.0000	1	bodyguards
0.0122	20.8	.0000	1	Boeing
0.0122	20.8	.0000	1	bogeymen
0.0122	20.8	.0000	1	boggles
0.0122	20.8	.0000	1	Bohnson
0.0122	20.8	.0000	1	bollixed
0.0122	20.8	.0000	1	Bolshevik
0.0122	20.8	.0000	1	bolstering
0.0122	20.8	.0000	1	bolsters
0.0122	20.8	.0000	1	bolting
0.0122	20.8	.0000	1	Bompensiero
0.0122	20.8	.0000	1	bonanza
0.0122	20.8	.0000	1	bonbons
0.0122	20.8	.0000	1	bone-rattling
0.0122	20.8	.0000	1	boned
0.0122	20.8	.0000	1	boneless
0.0122	20.8	.0000	1	Bonne
0.0122	20.8	.0000	1	Bonnier
0.0122	20.8	.0000	1	Boobies
0.0122	20.8	.0000	1	booby-bomb
0.0122	20.8	.0000	1	boogie
0.0122	20.8	.0000	1	book-movie
0.0122	20.8	.0000	1	bookmobile
0.0122	20.8	.0000	1	bookshelf
0.0122	20.8	.0000	1	boosting
0.0122	20.8	.0000	1	Boot
0.0122	20.8	.0000	1	boot-sole
0.0122	20.8	.0000	1	border-to-border
0.0122	20.8	.0000	1	Borg-Warner
0.0122	20.8	.0000	1	borning
0.0122	20.8	.0000	1	Bosnia-Herzegovina
0.0122	20.8	.0000	1	botched
0.0122	20.8	.0000	1	bottle-top
0.0122	20.8	.0000	1	Bottom-Fix
0.0122	20.8	.0000	1	boudoirs
0.0122	20.8	.0000	1	bouillabaisse
0.0122	20.8	.0000	1	boulder-paved
0.0122	20.8	.0000	1	Bournemouth
0.0122	20.8	.0000	1	Bouvet
0.0122	20.8	.0000	1	Bouvier
0.0122	20.8	.0000	1	Bowhemia
0.0122	20.8	.0000	1	Bowler
0.0122	20.8	.0000	1	Bowlers
0.0122	20.8	.0000	1	Bowles
0.0122	20.8	.0000	1	bowling's
0.0122	20.8	.0000	1	box's
0.0122	20.8	.0000	1	boxy
0.0122	20.8	.0000	1	BOY'S
0.0122	20.8	.0000	1	Bozeman
0.0122	20.8	.0000	1	bra-less
0.0122	20.8	.0000	1	Bradley's
0.0122	20.8	.0000	1	Brahm's
0.0122	20.8	.0000	1	brain-scratching
0.0122	20.8	.0000	1	brandaris
0.0122	20.8	.0000	1	Braniff
0.0122	20.8	.0000	1	Braniff's
0.0122	20.8	.0000	1	Braquette
0.0122	20.8	.0000	1	Braves'
0.0122	20.8	.0000	1	braze
0.0122	20.8	.0000	1	brazing
0.0122	20.8	.0000	1	breaded
0.0122	20.8	.0000	1	Break
0.0122	20.8	.0000	1	breakeven
0.0122	20.8	.0000	1	breakout
0.0122	20.8	.0000	1	bream
0.0122	20.8	.0000	1	breasted
0.0122	20.8	.0000	1	breather
0.0122	20.8	.0000	1	breathing-grade
0.0122	20.8	.0000	1	Brecht's
0.0122	20.8	.0000	1	breeze-rippled
0.0122	20.8	.0000	1	Brenda's
0.0122	20.8	.0000	1	Brendan
0.0122	20.8	.0000	1	brevet
0.0122	20.8	.0000	1	Brezhnev
0.0122	20.8	.0000	1	briefcases
0.0122	20.8	.0000	1	briefings
0.0122	20.8	.0000	1	brightly-colored
0.0122	20.8	.0000	1	Briley's
0.0122	20.8	.0000	1	British-made
0.0122	20.8	.0000	1	broached
				THE PRECEDING WORD TYPE OCCUPIES RANK 66100
0.0122	20.8	.0000	1	Broadcasters
0.0122	20.8	.0000	1	broadies
0.0122	20.8	.0000	1	brocaded
0.0122	20.8	.0000	1	bronchioles
0.0122	20.8	.0000	1	bronzes
0.0122	20.8	.0000	1	brooders
0.0122	20.8	.0000	1	brook-and-brown
0.0122	20.8	.0000	1	Broudy
0.0122	20.8	.0000	1	Brownell's
0.0122	20.8	.0000	1	Brownmiller
0.0122	20.8	.0000	1	brrr
0.0122	20.8	.0000	1	brush-in
0.0122	20.8	.0000	1	brushed-on
0.0122	20.8	.0000	1	brushy-limbed
0.0122	20.8	.0000	1	brutalized
0.0122	20.8	.0000	1	bruuummpphh
0.0122	20.8	.0000	1	BSU
0.0122	20.8	.0000	1	Bubba
0.0122	20.8	.0000	1	bucket-seat
0.0122	20.8	.0000	1	Buckminster
0.0122	20.8	.0000	1	Bucknum
0.0122	20.8	.0000	1	buckshot
0.0122	20.8	.0000	1	bucktails
0.0122	20.8	.0000	1	Buddah
0.0122	20.8	.0000	1	buddy-bodyguards
0.0122	20.8	.0000	1	budgerigars
0.0122	20.8	.0000	1	budget-battered
0.0122	20.8	.0000	1	budgeting
0.0122	20.8	.0000	1	buffalo-drawn
0.0122	20.8	.0000	1	Buffern
0.0122	20.8	.0000	1	bugaboos
0.0122	20.8	.0000	1	bugaloo
0.0122	20.8	.0000	1	bugged
0.0122	20.8	.0000	1	builder-architect
0.0122	20.8	.0000	1	builder's
0.0122	20.8	.0000	1	building-trade
0.0122	20.8	.0000	1	buildups
0.0122	20.8	.0000	1	Built
0.0122	20.8	.0000	1	Bukich
0.0122	20.8	.0000	1	Bulgarian-Soviet
0.0122	20.8	.0000	1	Bulge
0.0122	20.8	.0000	1	Bulletin
0.0122	20.8	.0000	1	Bulletins
0.0122	20.8	.0000	1	Bullitt
0.0122	20.8	.0000	1	Bulls
0.0122	20.8	.0000	1	bumpity-bump
0.0122	20.8	.0000	1	bureaucracies
0.0122	20.8	.0000	1	bureaucrat's
0.0122	20.8	.0000	1	bureaucratic
0.0122	20.8	.0000	1	burgling
0.0122	20.8	.0000	1	Burkhart
0.0122	20.8	.0000	1	burl
0.0122	20.8	.0000	1	Burma-Shave
0.0122	20.8	.0000	1	Burmans
0.0122	20.8	.0000	1	burn-outs
0.0122	20.8	.0000	1	Burnham
0.0122	20.8	.0000	1	Burros
0.0122	20.8	.0000	1	Burwood
0.0122	20.8	.0000	1	bush-jacket
0.0122	20.8	.0000	1	businessmen's
0.0122	20.8	.0000	1	Buss
0.0122	20.8	.0000	1	Bussell
0.0122	20.8	.0000	1	bussing
0.0122	20.8	.0000	1	butlers
0.0122	20.8	.0000	1	butt-of-jokes
0.0122	20.8	.0000	1	Butterscotch
0.0122	20.8	.0000	1	buttes
0.0122	20.8	.0000	1	Button-Eyes
0.0122	20.8	.0000	1	button-down
0.0122	20.8	.0000	1	Butts
0.0122	20.8	.0000	1	buttstock
0.0122	20.8	.0000	1	BVD'S**
0.0122	20.8	.0000	1	by-your-leave
0.0122	20.8	.0000	1	bypassing
0.0122	20.8	.0000	1	Byrnes
0.0122	20.8	.0000	1	C-141
0.0122	20.8	.0000	1	C-4
0.0122	20.8	.0000	1	C-5A's
0.0122	20.8	.0000	1	c'est
0.0122	20.8	.0000	1	Caaale
0.0122	20.8	.0000	1	caches
0.0122	20.8	.0000	1	Cactus
0.0122	20.8	.0000	1	cage-like
0.0122	20.8	.0000	1	Cager
0.0122	20.8	.0000	1	calamities
0.0122	20.8	.0000	1	Calas
0.0122	20.8	.0000	1	calibration
0.0122	20.8	.0000	1	calisthenics
0.0122	20.8	.0000	1	call-up
0.0122	20.8	.0000	1	Callahan's
0.0122	20.8	.0000	1	Calle
0.0122	20.8	.0000	1	Callender
0.0122	20.8	.0000	1	Calley
0.0122	20.8	.0000	1	Calling
0.0122	20.8	.0000	1	Callville
0.0122	20.8	.0000	1	Caloosahatchee
0.0122	20.8	.0000	1	Calvinist
0.0122	20.8	.0000	1	Camaro
0.0122	20.8	.0000	1	Camaros
0.0122	20.8	.0000	1	Cambay
				THE PRECEDING WORD TYPE OCCUPIES RANK 66200
0.0122	20.8	.0000	1	camel-colored
0.0122	20.8	.0000	1	camelback
0.0122	20.8	.0000	1	camera-like
0.0122	20.8	.0000	1	camp-out
0.0122	20.8	.0000	1	camp-outs
0.0122	20.8	.0000	1	camper's
0.0122	20.8	.0000	1	campesinos
0.0122	20.8	.0000	1	Can-Am
0.0122	20.8	.0000	1	Cana
0.0122	20.8	.0000	1	Canadensis
0.0122	20.8	.0000	1	cancer-causing
0.0122	20.8	.0000	1	cancer-like
0.0122	20.8	.0000	1	CANDIDATES
0.0122	20.8	.0000	1	candidly
0.0122	20.8	.0000	1	candlelighted
0.0122	20.8	.0000	1	candour
0.0122	20.8	.0000	1	Candy's
0.0122	20.8	.0000	1	Cannery
0.0122	20.8	.0000	1	cannons'
0.0122	20.8	.0000	1	canoeloads
0.0122	20.8	.0000	1	cantaloup-size
0.0122	20.8	.0000	1	canted
0.0122	20.8	.0000	1	canvasback
0.0122	20.8	.0000	1	canvases
0.0122	20.8	.0000	1	CapCom
0.0122	20.8	.0000	1	Capability
0.0122	20.8	.0000	1	Capek
0.0122	20.8	.0000	1	capitivity
0.0122	20.8	.0000	1	capitol's
0.0122	20.8	.0000	1	Capitoline
0.0122	20.8	.0000	1	Capone
0.0122	20.8	.0000	1	Captaine
0.0122	20.8	.0000	1	captained
0.0122	20.8	.0000	1	captioned
0.0122	20.8	.0000	1	captious
0.0122	20.8	.0000	1	captivating
0.0122	20.8	.0000	1	car-pool
0.0122	20.8	.0000	1	car-trunk
0.0122	20.8	.0000	1	carabiniere
0.0122	20.8	.0000	1	Carats
0.0122	20.8	.0000	1	carbs
0.0122	20.8	.0000	1	cardamom
0.0122	20.8	.0000	1	cargo-carrying
0.0122	20.8	.0000	1	Carilo
0.0122	20.8	.0000	1	Carlen
0.0122	20.8	.0000	1	Carmelite
0.0122	20.8	.0000	1	carminative
0.0122	20.8	.0000	1	Carpathian
0.0122	20.8	.0000	1	carport
0.0122	20.8	.0000	1	Carriacou
0.0122	20.8	.0000	1	Carriage
0.0122	20.8	.0000	1	Carrick
0.0122	20.8	.0000	1	Carried
0.0122	20.8	.0000	1	Carrousel
0.0122	20.8	.0000	1	carrousels
0.0122	20.8	.0000	1	Cars
0.0122	20.8	.0000	1	cartopper's
0.0122	20.8	.0000	1	cartwheeling
0.0122	20.8	.0000	1	Cashman's
0.0122	20.8	.0000	1	Caslavska
0.0122	20.8	.0000	1	Cassatt
0.0122	20.8	.0000	1	Cassell

U	SFI	D	F	Word Type
0.0122	20.8	.0000	1	cassock
0.0122	20.8	.0000	1	castigates
0.0122	20.8	.0000	1	Castilian
0.0122	20.8	.0000	1	Castillon
0.0122	20.8	.0000	1	castle-like
0.0122	20.8	.0000	1	Castor's
0.0122	20.8	.0000	1	casus
0.0122	20.8	.0000	1	Caswell
0.0122	20.8	.0000	1	CAT-clawed
0.0122	20.8	.0000	1	cataclysm
0.0122	20.8	.0000	1	catafalque
0.0122	20.8	.0000	1	Catamaran
0.0122	20.8	.0000	1	catatonia
0.0122	20.8	.0000	1	cater
0.0122	20.8	.0000	1	caters
0.0122	20.8	.0000	1	cathedral-like
0.0122	20.8	.0000	1	Catherine's
0.0122	20.8	.0000	1	Cathlamet
0.0122	20.8	.0000	1	catnapped
0.0122	20.8	.0000	1	Catoctin
0.0122	20.8	.0000	1	CATS
0.0122	20.8	.0000	1	Cattlemen's
0.0122	20.8	.0000	1	Causes
0.0122	20.8	.0000	1	cautionary
0.0122	20.8	.0000	1	Cavanagh
0.0122	20.8	.0000	1	cavier
0.0122	20.8	.0000	1	cavitate
0.0122	20.8	.0000	1	CCNY
0.0122	20.8	.0000	1	ceasefire
0.0122	20.8	.0000	1	ceded
0.0122	20.8	.0000	1	cello-like
0.0122	20.8	.0000	1	Centauro
0.0122	20.8	.0000	1	centerfield
0.0122	20.8	.0000	1	centerline
0.0122	20.8	.0000	1	ceremoniously
0.0122	20.8	.0000	1	certify
0.0122	20.8	.0000	1	certifying
0.0122	20.8	.0000	1	certitude
THE PRECEDING WORD TYPE OCCUPIES RANK 66300				
0.0122	20.8	.0000	1	cfm
0.0122	20.8	.0000	1	chaco
0.0122	20.8	.0000	1	chain-smokes
0.0122	20.8	.0000	1	chain's
0.0122	20.8	.0000	1	chairmanship
0.0122	20.8	.0000	1	Champaign-Urbana
0.0122	20.8	.0000	1	Champernoune
0.0122	20.8	.0000	1	Champions
0.0122	20.8	.0000	1	channelled
0.0122	20.8	.0000	1	chape
0.0122	20.8	.0000	1	chaperones
0.0122	20.8	.0000	1	chapes
0.0122	20.8	.0000	1	Chaplin
0.0122	20.8	.0000	1	charade
0.0122	20.8	.0000	1	Charger
0.0122	20.8	.0000	1	charitably
0.0122	20.8	.0000	1	Charles's
0.0122	20.8	.0000	1	Charly's
0.0122	20.8	.0000	1	charmer
0.0122	20.8	.0000	1	Charpentier
0.0122	20.8	.0000	1	chastise
0.0122	20.8	.0000	1	Chatelet
0.0122	20.8	.0000	1	chatty
0.0122	20.8	.0000	1	chaw
0.0122	20.8	.0000	1	checkpoints
0.0122	20.8	.0000	1	Cheever's
0.0122	20.8	.0000	1	Chen
0.0122	20.8	.0000	1	Chequamegon
0.0122	20.8	.0000	1	cherry-red
0.0122	20.8	.0000	1	Chevette
0.0122	20.8	.0000	1	Chevy-Ford
0.0122	20.8	.0000	1	Chevys
0.0122	20.8	.0000	1	chic
0.0122	20.8	.0000	1	CHICKEN
0.0122	20.8	.0000	1	Chicken-Hearted
0.0122	20.8	.0000	1	CHIDE
0.0122	20.8	.0000	1	Chigi
0.0122	20.8	.0000	1	child's-eye-view
0.0122	20.8	.0000	1	chilis
0.0122	20.8	.0000	1	chiller
0.0122	20.8	.0000	1	chilly-wonderful
0.0122	20.8	.0000	1	Ching-ling
0.0122	20.8	.0000	1	Chippendale
0.0122	20.8	.0000	1	Chirpie
0.0122	20.8	.0000	1	chit'lins
0.0122	20.8	.0000	1	chomped
0.0122	20.8	.0000	1	choreful
0.0122	20.8	.0000	1	chortles
0.0122	20.8	.0000	1	Christie
0.0122	20.8	.0000	1	Christina
0.0122	20.8	.0000	1	Christmases
0.0122	20.8	.0000	1	Chrome
0.0122	20.8	.0000	1	chromed
0.0122	20.8	.0000	1	Chuar
0.0122	20.8	.0000	1	chucking
0.0122	20.8	.0000	1	Chula
0.0122	20.8	.0000	1	chumming
0.0122	20.8	.0000	1	Chungshan
0.0122	20.8	.0000	1	church-state
0.0122	20.8	.0000	1	chutney
0.0122	20.8	.0000	1	chutneys
0.0122	20.8	.0000	1	CIA
0.0122	20.8	.0000	1	CIE
0.0122	20.8	.0000	1	cilantro
0.0122	20.8	.0000	1	Cinema
0.0122	20.8	.0000	1	cinematically
0.0122	20.8	.0000	1	cinematographer
0.0122	20.8	.0000	1	cinematographers
0.0122	20.8	.0000	1	cinnamon-colored
0.0122	20.8	.0000	1	Cinzano
0.0122	20.8	.0000	1	cir-cum-stan-ces
0.0122	20.8	.0000	1	circ
0.0122	20.8	.0000	1	Circraft
0.0122	20.8	.0000	1	circularizes
0.0122	20.8	.0000	1	Cirey
0.0122	20.8	.0000	1	cirrhosis
0.0122	20.8	.0000	1	citified
0.0122	20.8	.0000	1	citizenry
0.0122	20.8	.0000	1	Citoyen
0.0122	20.8	.0000	1	citronella
0.0122	20.8	.0000	1	city-wide
0.0122	20.8	.0000	1	civil-engineering
0.0122	20.8	.0000	1	clamming
0.0122	20.8	.0000	1	clams'
0.0122	20.8	.0000	1	clamshell-type
0.0122	20.8	.0000	1	clap-and-stomp
0.0122	20.8	.0000	1	Clapton's
0.0122	20.8	.0000	1	Classified
0.0122	20.8	.0000	1	Classroom
0.0122	20.8	.0000	1	clean-shaven
0.0122	20.8	.0000	1	clean-up
0.0122	20.8	.0000	1	cleanups
0.0122	20.8	.0000	1	Clear-Air
0.0122	20.8	.0000	1	cleaver
0.0122	20.8	.0000	1	Cleaver
0.0122	20.8	.0000	1	Clements
0.0122	20.8	.0000	1	Clendenin
0.0122	20.8	.0000	1	clerihews
0.0122	20.8	.0000	1	clicker
0.0122	20.8	.0000	1	cliff's
THE PRECEDING WORD TYPE OCCUPIES RANK 66400				
0.0122	20.8	.0000	1	climb-out
0.0122	20.8	.0000	1	clobber
0.0122	20.8	.0000	1	clodbusters
0.0122	20.8	.0000	1	Cloggers
0.0122	20.8	.0000	1	cloisters
0.0122	20.8	.0000	1	clomped
0.0122	20.8	.0000	1	close-harmony
0.0122	20.8	.0000	1	CLOSED
0.0122	20.8	.0000	1	closed-circut
0.0122	20.8	.0000	1	closeted
0.0122	20.8	.0000	1	Clotheshorse
0.0122	20.8	.0000	1	Cloudcroft
0.0122	20.8	.0000	1	clownish
0.0122	20.8	.0000	1	cloying
0.0122	20.8	.0000	1	clubman's
0.0122	20.8	.0000	1	clutch-pedal
0.0122	20.8	.0000	1	Clutter
0.0122	20.8	.0000	1	Co-Producer
0.0122	20.8	.0000	1	co-authors
0.0122	20.8	.0000	1	co-chairman
0.0122	20.8	.0000	1	co-director
0.0122	20.8	.0000	1	co-founder
0.0122	20.8	.0000	1	Co-op
0.0122	20.8	.0000	1	co-producer
0.0122	20.8	.0000	1	co-producers
0.0122	20.8	.0000	1	co-promoter
0.0122	20.8	.0000	1	co-star
0.0122	20.8	.0000	1	co-stars
0.0122	20.8	.0000	1	Co's**
0.0122	20.8	.0000	1	coalesce
0.0122	20.8	.0000	1	Coalition
0.0122	20.8	.0000	1	coaster-brake
0.0122	20.8	.0000	1	coaxes
0.0122	20.8	.0000	1	cobwebby
0.0122	20.8	.0000	1	cockbirds
0.0122	20.8	.0000	1	Cocke
0.0122	20.8	.0000	1	cockles
0.0122	20.8	.0000	1	coconut-husk
0.0122	20.8	.0000	1	code-named
0.0122	20.8	.0000	1	Coeur
0.0122	20.8	.0000	1	COFFEE-OTHERS
0.0122	20.8	.0000	1	coffeehouse
0.0122	20.8	.0000	1	coffeehouses
0.0122	20.8	.0000	1	Coghlan
0.0122	20.8	.0000	1	Cognac
0.0122	20.8	.0000	1	cohort's
0.0122	20.8	.0000	1	coinciding
0.0122	20.8	.0000	1	cold-war
0.0122	20.8	.0000	1	coleslaw
0.0122	20.8	.0000	1	Colgems
0.0122	20.8	.0000	1	Coliseum
0.0122	20.8	.0000	1	collaborations
0.0122	20.8	.0000	1	collarbone
0.0122	20.8	.0000	1	collard-greens
0.0122	20.8	.0000	1	Collective
0.0122	20.8	.0000	1	collectives
0.0122	20.8	.0000	1	collegian
0.0122	20.8	.0000	1	Collier's
0.0122	20.8	.0000	1	Colliers
0.0122	20.8	.0000	1	colliery
0.0122	20.8	.0000	1	colognes
0.0122	20.8	.0000	1	color-field
0.0122	20.8	.0000	1	color-glutted
0.0122	20.8	.0000	1	color-movie
0.0122	20.8	.0000	1	color-over-black
0.0122	20.8	.0000	1	color-television
0.0122	20.8	.0000	1	Colorado-Kansas
0.0122	20.8	.0000	1	Colton
0.0122	20.8	.0000	1	column-mounted
0.0122	20.8	.0000	1	Combs'
0.0122	20.8	.0000	1	Comden
0.0122	20.8	.0000	1	Comdr
0.0122	20.8	.0000	1	come-hithery
0.0122	20.8	.0000	1	comic-ominous
0.0122	20.8	.0000	1	Commander's
0.0122	20.8	.0000	1	commandos'
0.0122	20.8	.0000	1	commercialized
0.0122	20.8	.0000	1	Commie
0.0122	20.8	.0000	1	commissar
0.0122	20.8	.0000	1	commissars
0.0122	20.8	.0000	1	commissionership
0.0122	20.8	.0000	1	Communications
0.0122	20.8	.0000	1	communicator
0.0122	20.8	.0000	1	communism's
0.0122	20.8	.0000	1	Communist-Socialist
0.0122	20.8	.0000	1	Communist-ruled
0.0122	20.8	.0000	1	Communists'
0.0122	20.8	.0000	1	commuters'
0.0122	20.8	.0000	1	companies'
0.0122	20.8	.0000	1	compartment's
0.0122	20.8	.0000	1	compartmentalized
0.0122	20.8	.0000	1	compatriot
0.0122	20.8	.0000	1	compensating
0.0122	20.8	.0000	1	Competitive
0.0122	20.8	.0000	1	competitor's
0.0122	20.8	.0000	1	complexion-consoling
0.0122	20.8	.0000	1	complicate
0.0122	20.8	.0000	1	compressed-air
0.0122	20.8	.0000	1	compulsively
0.0122	20.8	.0000	1	concentratedly
THE PRECEDING WORD TYPE OCCUPIES RANK 66500				
0.0122	20.8	.0000	1	concern's
0.0122	20.8	.0000	1	conciliatory
0.0122	20.8	.0000	1	condensations
0.0122	20.8	.0000	1	condescension
0.0122	20.8	.0000	1	Condon
0.0122	20.8	.0000	1	condones
0.0122	20.8	.0000	1	CONDUCT
0.0122	20.8	.0000	1	confectioner
0.0122	20.8	.0000	1	confesses
0.0122	20.8	.0000	1	Confession
0.0122	20.8	.0000	1	confessions
0.0122	20.8	.0000	1	Conflict
0.0122	20.8	.0000	1	Congregation
0.0122	20.8	.0000	1	congregations
0.0122	20.8	.0000	1	Conni
0.0122	20.8	.0000	1	Connie's
0.0122	20.8	.0000	1	Conningham
0.0122	20.8	.0000	1	Connolly
0.0122	20.8	.0000	1	connotes
0.0122	20.8	.0000	1	Conny
0.0122	20.8	.0000	1	Conrad's
0.0122	20.8	.0000	1	consecration
0.0122	20.8	.0000	1	conservatives'
0.0122	20.8	.0000	1	Consistent
0.0122	20.8	.0000	1	consortium
0.0122	20.8	.0000	1	constantly-in-view
0.0122	20.8	.0000	1	construction-industry
0.0122	20.8	.0000	1	constructionist
0.0122	20.8	.0000	1	Consulich
0.0122	20.8	.0000	1	consultative
0.0122	20.8	.0000	1	contaminator
0.0122	20.8	.0000	1	contemplatives
0.0122	20.8	.0000	1	Contempt
0.0122	20.8	.0000	1	contemptible
0.0122	20.8	.0000	1	contentions
0.0122	20.8	.0000	1	Contingent
0.0122	20.8	.0000	1	contraceptives
0.0122	20.8	.0000	1	Contramaestre
0.0122	20.8	.0000	1	Contributions
0.0122	20.8	.0000	1	contriving
0.0122	20.8	.0000	1	control-rod
0.0122	20.8	.0000	1	controlled-access
0.0122	20.8	.0000	1	controllers
0.0122	20.8	.0000	1	conundrum
0.0122	20.8	.0000	1	Convent
0.0122	20.8	.0000	1	Converter-Dryer
0.0122	20.8	.0000	1	convinces
0.0122	20.8	.0000	1	convulsing
0.0122	20.8	.0000	1	Conway
0.0122	20.8	.0000	1	Coolant
0.0122	20.8	.0000	1	Coolidge's
0.0122	20.8	.0000	1	cooly
0.0122	20.8	.0000	1	cooperator
0.0122	20.8	.0000	1	cooperators
0.0122	20.8	.0000	1	CoosBay
0.0122	20.8	.0000	1	Copage
0.0122	20.8	.0000	1	copper-red
0.0122	20.8	.0000	1	copter's
0.0122	20.8	.0000	1	copyable
0.0122	20.8	.0000	1	Coralburst
0.0122	20.8	.0000	1	cordwood
0.0122	20.8	.0000	1	CORNBREAD
0.0122	20.8	.0000	1	Cornet
0.0122	20.8	.0000	1	cornflakes
0.0122	20.8	.0000	1	cornstick
0.0122	20.8	.0000	1	Corolla
0.0122	20.8	.0000	1	corps'
0.0122	20.8	.0000	1	corpulency
0.0122	20.8	.0000	1	corralling
0.0122	20.8	.0000	1	Correspondence
0.0122	20.8	.0000	1	Correspondent
0.0122	20.8	.0000	1	Corrington
0.0122	20.8	.0000	1	Corvairs
0.0122	20.8	.0000	1	Corvettes
0.0122	20.8	.0000	1	Cory's
0.0122	20.8	.0000	1	Cosmetics
0.0122	20.8	.0000	1	cost-of-living
0.0122	20.8	.0000	1	cost-push
0.0122	20.8	.0000	1	Couch
0.0122	20.8	.0000	1	council's
0.0122	20.8	.0000	1	Counsel
0.0122	20.8	.0000	1	counter-counter-attack
0.0122	20.8	.0000	1	counter-demonstration
0.0122	20.8	.0000	1	counter-revolutionary
0.0122	20.8	.0000	1	counterbore
0.0122	20.8	.0000	1	countercurrents
0.0122	20.8	.0000	1	counterfeits
0.0122	20.8	.0000	1	Counterpoint
0.0122	20.8	.0000	1	country-and-Western
0.0122	20.8	.0000	1	country-and-western
0.0122	20.8	.0000	1	country-seat
0.0122	20.8	.0000	1	countrywide
0.0122	20.8	.0000	1	couple's
0.0122	20.8	.0000	1	court-ordered
0.0122	20.8	.0000	1	courtside
0.0122	20.8	.0000	1	Coutts's
0.0122	20.8	.0000	1	cove's
0.0122	20.8	.0000	1	Coveleski
0.0122	20.8	.0000	1	Coveralls
0.0122	20.8	.0000	1	cow-calf
THE PRECEDING WORD TYPE OCCUPIES RANK 66600				
0.0122	20.8	.0000	1	Cowboys'
0.0122	20.8	.0000	1	cowering
0.0122	20.8	.0000	1	cowling
0.0122	20.8	.0000	1	Cowlitz
0.0122	20.8	.0000	1	Cowper
0.0122	20.8	.0000	1	Cozad
0.0122	20.8	.0000	1	cozied
0.0122	20.8	.0000	1	crab-apples
0.0122	20.8	.0000	1	crackdown
0.0122	20.8	.0000	1	cracky
0.0122	20.8	.0000	1	craft's
0.0122	20.8	.0000	1	cram-packed
0.0122	20.8	.0000	1	crap
0.0122	20.8	.0000	1	Crashley
0.0122	20.8	.0000	1	cravenly
0.0122	20.8	.0000	1	crawlers
0.0122	20.8	.0000	1	crayon-on-cardboard
0.0122	20.8	.0000	1	creamery
0.0122	20.8	.0000	1	creators
0.0122	20.8	.0000	1	credulity
0.0122	20.8	.0000	1	Cree
0.0122	20.8	.0000	1	Creme
0.0122	20.8	.0000	1	creosoted
0.0122	20.8	.0000	1	crescents
0.0122	20.8	.0000	1	cretonnes
0.0122	20.8	.0000	1	cribbing
0.0122	20.8	.0000	1	crick-cracking
0.0122	20.8	.0000	1	crime-prevention
0.0122	20.8	.0000	1	Crimson
0.0122	20.8	.0000	1	Crises
0.0122	20.8	.0000	1	crisis-filled
0.0122	20.8	.0000	1	crisis-intervention
0.0122	20.8	.0000	1	Critical
0.0122	20.8	.0000	1	Critics
0.0122	20.8	.0000	1	critiques
0.0122	20.8	.0000	1	Croatia
0.0122	20.8	.0000	1	Croatia's
0.0122	20.8	.0000	1	cronyism
0.0122	20.8	.0000	1	Cronyn
0.0122	20.8	.0000	1	Crop-Growers
0.0122	20.8	.0000	1	croplands
0.0122	20.8	.0000	1	cross-checked
0.0122	20.8	.0000	1	cross-pollination
0.0122	20.8	.0000	1	cross-stitched
0.0122	20.8	.0000	1	crossbelts
0.0122	20.8	.0000	1	crosshairs
0.0122	20.8	.0000	1	crosshatch
0.0122	20.8	.0000	1	crosshatchings
0.0122	20.8	.0000	1	crossmember
0.0122	20.8	.0000	1	crossmembers
0.0122	20.8	.0000	1	crosswinds
0.0122	20.8	.0000	1	crow-count
0.0122	20.8	.0000	1	Crucible
0.0122	20.8	.0000	1	cruder
0.0122	20.8	.0000	1	crudity
0.0122	20.8	.0000	1	Cruel
0.0122	20.8	.0000	1	cruiser's
0.0122	20.8	.0000	1	crusade's
0.0122	20.8	.0000	1	crushers
0.0122	20.8	.0000	1	crystal-clear
0.0122	20.8	.0000	1	Cs
0.0122	20.8	.0000	1	Cuauhtemoc
0.0122	20.8	.0000	1	Cues
0.0122	20.8	.0000	1	cul-ti-va-ted
0.0122	20.8	.0000	1	culprits
0.0122	20.8	.0000	1	cultivators
0.0122	20.8	.0000	1	culturally
0.0122	20.8	.0000	1	curacas
0.0122	20.8	.0000	1	curl-consistency
0.0122	20.8	.0000	1	currie
0.0122	20.8	.0000	1	Curry
0.0122	20.8	.0000	1	curtails
0.0122	20.8	.0000	1	curved-blade
0.0122	20.8	.0000	1	cushiony
0.0122	20.8	.0000	1	cussed
0.0122	20.8	.0000	1	cussedness
0.0122	20.8	.0000	1	Customer
0.0122	20.8	.0000	1	cut-over
0.0122	20.8	.0000	1	cuticles
0.0122	20.8	.0000	1	cutlasses
0.0122	20.8	.0000	1	Cuyahoga
0.0122	20.8	.0000	1	cyclamate-based
0.0122	20.8	.0000	1	cyclemakers
0.0122	20.8	.0000	1	cyclists'
0.0122	20.8	.0000	1	Cymru
0.0122	20.8	.0000	1	cystadlevaeth
0.0122	20.8	.0000	1	Czapski
0.0122	20.8	.0000	1	Czapski's
0.0122	20.8	.0000	1	czars
0.0122	20.8	.0000	1	d'Alene
0.0122	20.8	.0000	1	d'Estaing
0.0122	20.8	.0000	1	d'Oreilles
0.0122	20.8	.0000	1	d'Orsay
0.0122	20.8	.0000	1	d'affaires
0.0122	20.8	.0000	1	d'art
0.0122	20.8	.0000	1	dabbed
0.0122	20.8	.0000	1	dabbing
0.0122	20.8	.0000	1	dacha
0.0122	20.8	.0000	1	Dachshund
0.0122	20.8	.0000	1	Daffy
THE PRECEDING WORD TYPE OCCUPIES RANK 66700				
0.0122	20.8	.0000	1	Daffynishion
0.0122	20.8	.0000	1	Dahl
0.0122	20.8	.0000	1	Dall
0.0122	20.8	.0000	1	Dallas'
0.0122	20.8	.0000	1	Dalrymple
0.0122	20.8	.0000	1	dam-builders
0.0122	20.8	.0000	1	dam's
0.0122	20.8	.0000	1	Dame's
0.0122	20.8	.0000	1	damnably
0.0122	20.8	.0000	1	damp-dry
0.0122	20.8	.0000	1	damsite
0.0122	20.8	.0000	1	Danae
0.0122	20.8	.0000	1	Danish-German
0.0122	20.8	.0000	1	Darby's
0.0122	20.8	.0000	1	dark-rimmed
0.0122	20.8	.0000	1	darte
0.0122	20.8	.0000	1	Darwinian
0.0122	20.8	.0000	1	Daryle
0.0122	20.8	.0000	1	dashikis
0.0122	20.8	.0000	1	data-hunting
0.0122	20.8	.0000	1	date-palm
0.0122	20.8	.0000	1	dazzles
0.0122	20.8	.0000	1	DC-7
0.0122	20.8	.0000	1	deCardenas
0.0122	20.8	.0000	1	DeCarlos

U	SFI	D	F	Word Type
0.0122	20.8	.0000	1	DeLeon
0.0122	20.8	.0000	1	DeLorenzo
0.0122	20.8	.0000	1	DeRosa
0.0122	20.8	.0000	1	DeScherer
0.0122	20.8	.0000	1	deSmet
0.0122	20.8	.0000	1	DeWolfe
0.0122	20.8	.0000	1	de-kinkers
0.0122	20.8	.0000	1	de-press-ing
0.0122	20.8	.0000	1	Deacon
0.0122	20.8	.0000	1	Deacon's
0.0122	20.8	.0000	1	deadfall
0.0122	20.8	.0000	1	deafen
0.0122	20.8	.0000	1	Deal's
0.0122	20.8	.0000	1	debaucher
0.0122	20.8	.0000	1	debuting
0.0122	20.8	.0000	1	decapitate
0.0122	20.8	.0000	1	deceives
0.0122	20.8	.0000	1	deceleration
0.0122	20.8	.0000	1	Deception
0.0122	20.8	.0000	1	decoding
0.0122	20.8	.0000	1	decoratively
0.0122	20.8	.0000	1	Decro
0.0122	20.8	.0000	1	deejay
0.0122	20.8	.0000	1	deepseated
0.0122	20.8	.0000	1	Deerfield's
0.0122	20.8	.0000	1	Deering
0.0122	20.8	.0000	1	defaulted
0.0122	20.8	.0000	1	defeatism
0.0122	20.8	.0000	1	defectives
0.0122	20.8	.0000	1	defending-champion
0.0122	20.8	.0000	1	defends
0.0122	20.8	.0000	1	defense's
0.0122	20.8	.0000	1	defenseman's
0.0122	20.8	.0000	1	Defferre
0.0122	20.8	.0000	1	deficit
0.0122	20.8	.0000	1	deflate
0.0122	20.8	.0000	1	deflator
0.0122	20.8	.0000	1	defoliated
0.0122	20.8	.0000	1	deforestation
0.0122	20.8	.0000	1	deftness
0.0122	20.8	.0000	1	defunct
0.0122	20.8	.0000	1	defuzzing
0.0122	20.8	.0000	1	degraded
0.0122	20.8	.0000	1	delNorte
0.0122	20.8	.0000	1	Delco
0.0122	20.8	.0000	1	Delcos
0.0122	20.8	.0000	1	delegently
0.0122	20.8	.0000	1	delinquents
0.0122	20.8	.0000	1	deliriously
0.0122	20.8	.0000	1	deliveryman
0.0122	20.8	.0000	1	Dem
0.0122	20.8	.0000	1	Demers
0.0122	20.8	.0000	1	demise
0.0122	20.8	.0000	1	demonstrator
0.0122	20.8	.0000	1	demoted
0.0122	20.8	.0000	1	denouement
0.0122	20.8	.0000	1	Denson
0.0122	20.8	.0000	1	Dentistry
0.0122	20.8	.0000	1	denuded
0.0122	20.8	.0000	1	Dependence-producing
0.0122	20.8	.0000	1	Dependent
0.0122	20.8	.0000	1	dephyr
0.0122	20.8	.0000	1	Depict
0.0122	20.8	.0000	1	deplore
0.0122	20.8	.0000	1	deploying
0.0122	20.8	.0000	1	deployment
0.0122	20.8	.0000	1	depository
0.0122	20.8	.0000	1	depraved
0.0122	20.8	.0000	1	deranged
0.0122	20.8	.0000	1	DesBartlett
0.0122	20.8	.0000	1	Deschutes
0.0122	20.8	.0000	1	deserter
0.0122	20.8	.0000	1	design-oriented
0.0122	20.8	.0000	1	Desire
0.0122	20.8	.0000	1	Destresed
THE PRECEDING WORD TYPE OCCUPIES RANK 66800				
0.0122	20.8	.0000	1	destructively
0.0122	20.8	.0000	1	detains
0.0122	20.8	.0000	1	detectably
0.0122	20.8	.0000	1	Detective-Inspector
0.0122	20.8	.0000	1	DETOUR
0.0122	20.8	.0000	1	deuteride
0.0122	20.8	.0000	1	Deva
0.0122	20.8	.0000	1	devalue
0.0122	20.8	.0000	1	devaluing
0.0122	20.8	.0000	1	Device
0.0122	20.8	.0000	1	Devido
0.0122	20.8	.0000	1	devil-may-care
0.0122	20.8	.0000	1	devil-worshipers
0.0122	20.8	.0000	1	Devils
0.0122	20.8	.0000	1	deviser
0.0122	20.8	.0000	1	devourers
0.0122	20.8	.0000	1	DFL
0.0122	20.8	.0000	1	diMedici
0.0122	20.8	.0000	1	Diabetics
0.0122	20.8	.0000	1	diathermy
0.0122	20.8	.0000	1	die-hard
0.0122	20.8	.0000	1	diesel-electric
0.0122	20.8	.0000	1	diesels
0.0122	20.8	.0000	1	diet-proof
0.0122	20.8	.0000	1	dieted
0.0122	20.8	.0000	1	dieticians
0.0122	20.8	.0000	1	Dietrich's
0.0122	20.8	.0000	1	differentiations
0.0122	20.8	.0000	1	diking
0.0122	20.8	.0000	1	dilemmas
0.0122	20.8	.0000	1	diminishingly
0.0122	20.8	.0000	1	dinghies
0.0122	20.8	.0000	1	dinner-party
0.0122	20.8	.0000	1	dioceses
0.0122	20.8	.0000	1	Diomeders
0.0122	20.8	.0000	1	Dior's
0.0122	20.8	.0000	1	dip-in-sugar
0.0122	20.8	.0000	1	dippers
0.0122	20.8	.0000	1	directorate
0.0122	20.8	.0000	1	directories
0.0122	20.8	.0000	1	Dirksen's
0.0122	20.8	.0000	1	dirtying
0.0122	20.8	.0000	1	disabilities
0.0122	20.8	.0000	1	disallegiance
0.0122	20.8	.0000	1	disappointingly
0.0122	20.8	.0000	1	disbanded
0.0122	20.8	.0000	1	discolorations
0.0122	20.8	.0000	1	discontinuity
0.0122	20.8	.0000	1	discos
0.0122	20.8	.0000	1	discotheque
0.0122	20.8	.0000	1	disillusionment
0.0122	20.8	.0000	1	disinclined
0.0122	20.8	.0000	1	disinterring
0.0122	20.8	.0000	1	dismaying
0.0122	20.8	.0000	1	disparages
0.0122	20.8	.0000	1	disparaging
0.0122	20.8	.0000	1	dispensation
0.0122	20.8	.0000	1	disqualify
0.0122	20.8	.0000	1	disquisition
0.0122	20.8	.0000	1	dissents
0.0122	20.8	.0000	1	dissertation
0.0122	20.8	.0000	1	distorter
0.0122	20.8	.0000	1	distrusting
0.0122	20.8	.0000	1	disturbingly
0.0122	20.8	.0000	1	diverges
0.0122	20.8	.0000	1	divest
0.0122	20.8	.0000	1	Division's
0.0122	20.8	.0000	1	diwaniyyah
0.0122	20.8	.0000	1	Dizzy
0.0122	20.8	.0000	1	do-it-yourselfers
0.0122	20.8	.0000	1	do-your-own-thing
0.0122	20.8	.0000	1	Doane's
0.0122	20.8	.0000	1	Dobbins
0.0122	20.8	.0000	1	DobbsFerry
0.0122	20.8	.0000	1	doctor-of-divinity
0.0122	20.8	.0000	1	doctors'
0.0122	20.8	.0000	1	dodderer
0.0122	20.8	.0000	1	Dodgem
0.0122	20.8	.0000	1	dogmatically
0.0122	20.8	.0000	1	Doing
0.0122	20.8	.0000	1	Dolittles
0.0122	20.8	.0000	1	dolphin-ologist
0.0122	20.8	.0000	1	Dom
0.0122	20.8	.0000	1	dome-like
0.0122	20.8	.0000	1	domestics
0.0122	20.8	.0000	1	Domres
0.0122	20.8	.0000	1	Domres'
0.0122	20.8	.0000	1	Donnelley
0.0122	20.8	.0000	1	doped
0.0122	20.8	.0000	1	dorados
0.0122	20.8	.0000	1	dormitories
0.0122	20.8	.0000	1	Dorough
0.0122	20.8	.0000	1	dos
0.0122	20.8	.0000	1	Dostoevsky
0.0122	20.8	.0000	1	double-checking
0.0122	20.8	.0000	1	double-cropping
0.0122	20.8	.0000	1	double-dealing
0.0122	20.8	.0000	1	double-deck
0.0122	20.8	.0000	1	double-ended
0.0122	20.8	.0000	1	double-ribbed
THE PRECEDING WORD TYPE OCCUPIES RANK 66900				
0.0122	20.8	.0000	1	double-thick
0.0122	20.8	.0000	1	Doubt
0.0122	20.8	.0000	1	doubtlessly
0.0122	20.8	.0000	1	Doud
0.0122	20.8	.0000	1	doughboy
0.0122	20.8	.0000	1	Dovie
0.0122	20.8	.0000	1	Dowdey's
0.0122	20.8	.0000	1	down-to-pavement
0.0122	20.8	.0000	1	downgraded
0.0122	20.8	.0000	1	dozer
0.0122	20.8	.0000	1	Dracula
0.0122	20.8	.0000	1	draft-card
0.0122	20.8	.0000	1	draftees
0.0122	20.8	.0000	1	drakes
0.0122	20.8	.0000	1	drawbacks
0.0122	20.8	.0000	1	drawnout
0.0122	20.8	.0000	1	dreamboat
0.0122	20.8	.0000	1	dreaming-spired
0.0122	20.8	.0000	1	Dreser
0.0122	20.8	.0000	1	dressmaking
0.0122	20.8	.0000	1	Drew's
0.0122	20.8	.0000	1	drifter
0.0122	20.8	.0000	1	drinkable
0.0122	20.8	.0000	1	drippy
0.0122	20.8	.0000	1	driveshafts
0.0122	20.8	.0000	1	Drivotrainers
0.0122	20.8	.0000	1	drooled
0.0122	20.8	.0000	1	droshkies
0.0122	20.8	.0000	1	Drs
0.0122	20.8	.0000	1	drudging
0.0122	20.8	.0000	1	drug-company
0.0122	20.8	.0000	1	drug-taking
0.0122	20.8	.0000	1	dry-docked
0.0122	20.8	.0000	1	duMaurier
0.0122	20.8	.0000	1	duPerron
0.0122	20.8	.0000	1	dual-four
0.0122	20.8	.0000	1	dual-mode
0.0122	20.8	.0000	1	Duane
0.0122	20.8	.0000	1	Dubcek
0.0122	20.8	.0000	1	dubious
0.0122	20.8	.0000	1	Duchy
0.0122	20.8	.0000	1	duck-shaped
0.0122	20.8	.0000	1	Duck's
0.0122	20.8	.0000	1	Dude
0.0122	20.8	.0000	1	dulcimers
0.0122	20.8	.0000	1	dull-yellow
0.0122	20.8	.0000	1	dulls
0.0122	20.8	.0000	1	dumbest
0.0122	20.8	.0000	1	Dummit
0.0122	20.8	.0000	1	Dunaway
0.0122	20.8	.0000	1	Dunderberg
0.0122	20.8	.0000	1	Dunnellen
0.0122	20.8	.0000	1	dunning
0.0122	20.8	.0000	1	Durrenmatt
0.0122	20.8	.0000	1	dust-caked
0.0122	20.8	.0000	1	dustfree
0.0122	20.8	.0000	1	dustup
0.0122	20.8	.0000	1	DWI
0.0122	20.8	.0000	1	Dworetsky
0.0122	20.8	.0000	1	Dylan
0.0122	20.8	.0000	1	dynamism
0.0122	20.8	.0000	1	dynanometer
0.0122	20.8	.0000	1	Dynastes
0.0122	20.8	.0000	1	e-eich
0.0122	20.8	.0000	1	ear-blasting
0.0122	20.8	.0000	1	earlywarning
0.0122	20.8	.0000	1	earned-run
0.0122	20.8	.0000	1	earth-circling
0.0122	20.8	.0000	1	Earth-circling
0.0122	20.8	.0000	1	earth-orbiting
0.0122	20.8	.0000	1	Earthly
0.0122	20.8	.0000	1	earthworkers
0.0122	20.8	.0000	1	EASEP
0.0122	20.8	.0000	1	EastGrandForks
0.0122	20.8	.0000	1	Eastland's
0.0122	20.8	.0000	1	easy-on-ulcer
0.0122	20.8	.0000	1	easy-to-assemble
0.0122	20.8	.0000	1	Ebsen's
0.0122	20.8	.0000	1	ecclesiasticize
0.0122	20.8	.0000	1	Eckstein
0.0122	20.8	.0000	1	Economists
0.0122	20.8	.0000	1	Eda
0.0122	20.8	.0000	1	Edina
0.0122	20.8	.0000	1	Editorial
0.0122	20.8	.0000	1	Edsel
0.0122	20.8	.0000	1	Edson
0.0122	20.8	.0000	1	educationists
0.0122	20.8	.0000	1	Edwards'
0.0122	20.8	.0000	1	Edwards's
0.0122	20.8	.0000	1	EEEEEEEEEEEEEEEK
0.0122	20.8	.0000	1	EEEEEEEEEEEEEEK
0.0122	20.8	.0000	1	ees
0.0122	20.8	.0000	1	effaced
0.0122	20.8	.0000	1	Effects
0.0122	20.8	.0000	1	Eg
0.0122	20.8	.0000	1	Egalite
0.0122	20.8	.0000	1	egregious
0.0122	20.8	.0000	1	eight-foot-long
0.0122	20.8	.0000	1	eight-hour-day
0.0122	20.8	.0000	1	eight-lane
THE PRECEDING WORD TYPE OCCUPIES RANK 67000				
0.0122	20.8	.0000	1	eight-state
0.0122	20.8	.0000	1	eight-wheel
0.0122	20.8	.0000	1	eight-wheeled
0.0122	20.8	.0000	1	Eight's
0.0122	20.8	.0000	1	eighties
0.0122	20.8	.0000	1	Eighty-ninth
0.0122	20.8	.0000	1	eighty-one-year-old
0.0122	20.8	.0000	1	eighty-some
0.0122	20.8	.0000	1	Eire's
0.0122	20.8	.0000	1	Eisner
0.0122	20.8	.0000	1	ejection-seat
0.0122	20.8	.0000	1	Ejnar
0.0122	20.8	.0000	1	ElSegundo
0.0122	20.8	.0000	1	elan
0.0122	20.8	.0000	1	eland
0.0122	20.8	.0000	1	elapsed-time
0.0122	20.8	.0000	1	elbows-inside-the-knees
0.0122	20.8	.0000	1	electric-drive
0.0122	20.8	.0000	1	electric-motor
0.0122	20.8	.0000	1	Electric's
0.0122	20.8	.0000	1	electrical-resistance
0.0122	20.8	.0000	1	Electro-Motive
0.0122	20.8	.0000	1	electro-optical
0.0122	20.8	.0000	1	electrochemistry
0.0122	20.8	.0000	1	electromotors
0.0122	20.8	.0000	1	electroreceptors
0.0122	20.8	.0000	1	eleven-room
0.0122	20.8	.0000	1	ELF
0.0122	20.8	.0000	1	Elfin's
0.0122	20.8	.0000	1	Elmhurst
0.0122	20.8	.0000	1	Eloy
0.0122	20.8	.0000	1	elude
0.0122	20.8	.0000	1	Elvar
0.0122	20.8	.0000	1	embarking
0.0122	20.8	.0000	1	embarrassingly
0.0122	20.8	.0000	1	emblazoned
0.0122	20.8	.0000	1	EMD
0.0122	20.8	.0000	1	Emeritus
0.0122	20.8	.0000	1	Emery
0.0122	20.8	.0000	1	Emiliano
0.0122	20.8	.0000	1	Emilie
0.0122	20.8	.0000	1	emissaries
0.0122	20.8	.0000	1	Emmerich
0.0122	20.8	.0000	1	Emmons'
0.0122	20.8	.0000	1	empathize
0.0122	20.8	.0000	1	EMPI
0.0122	20.8	.0000	1	EMPI'S
0.0122	20.8	.0000	1	employees'
0.0122	20.8	.0000	1	enamelled
0.0122	20.8	.0000	1	enchanter
0.0122	20.8	.0000	1	energy-filled
0.0122	20.8	.0000	1	enfold
0.0122	20.8	.0000	1	enforcer
0.0122	20.8	.0000	1	engine-mounting
0.0122	20.8	.0000	1	enginewright
0.0122	20.8	.0000	1	English-made
0.0122	20.8	.0000	1	English-trained
0.0122	20.8	.0000	1	English-type
0.0122	20.8	.0000	1	Enjoyable
0.0122	20.8	.0000	1	enmeshed
0.0122	20.8	.0000	1	Enos
0.0122	20.8	.0000	1	enplaned
0.0122	20.8	.0000	1	enquiry
0.0122	20.8	.0000	1	Enriques
0.0122	20.8	.0000	1	ensues
0.0122	20.8	.0000	1	ensured
0.0122	20.8	.0000	1	ensures
0.0122	20.8	.0000	1	Enterprises
0.0122	20.8	.0000	1	enterprize
0.0122	20.8	.0000	1	enthusiasms
0.0122	20.8	.0000	1	enticements
0.0122	20.8	.0000	1	entomological
0.0122	20.8	.0000	1	entrepreneur
0.0122	20.8	.0000	1	entrusting
0.0122	20.8	.0000	1	Enugu
0.0122	20.8	.0000	1	enunciating
0.0122	20.8	.0000	1	Environmental
0.0122	20.8	.0000	1	environs
0.0122	20.8	.0000	1	epaulets
0.0122	20.8	.0000	1	epicurean
0.0122	20.8	.0000	1	Episcopalians
0.0122	20.8	.0000	1	Episcopalians'
0.0122	20.8	.0000	1	episodic
0.0122	20.8	.0000	1	epitomizes
0.0122	20.8	.0000	1	epochal
0.0122	20.8	.0000	1	equalled
0.0122	20.8	.0000	1	ERA
0.0122	20.8	.0000	1	Eradicate
0.0122	20.8	.0000	1	erectly
0.0122	20.8	.0000	1	Erickson
0.0122	20.8	.0000	1	ermine-trimmed
0.0122	20.8	.0000	1	Erofei
0.0122	20.8	.0000	1	erogenous
0.0122	20.8	.0000	1	erosion-control
0.0122	20.8	.0000	1	erotica
0.0122	20.8	.0000	1	Ersabas
0.0122	20.8	.0000	1	ersatz
0.0122	20.8	.0000	1	escalating
0.0122	20.8	.0000	1	eschew
0.0122	20.8	.0000	1	escrow
THE PRECEDING WORD TYPE OCCUPIES RANK 67100				
0.0122	20.8	.0000	1	ESEA
0.0122	20.8	.0000	1	Esposito
0.0122	20.8	.0000	1	esquamulose
0.0122	20.8	.0000	1	ESSA
0.0122	20.8	.0000	1	EST
0.0122	20.8	.0000	1	esthetically
0.0122	20.8	.0000	1	ethologists
0.0122	20.8	.0000	1	ETO
0.0122	20.8	.0000	1	Eufemio
0.0122	20.8	.0000	1	euphemism
0.0122	20.8	.0000	1	euphorically
0.0122	20.8	.0000	1	Eustis
0.0122	20.8	.0000	1	evangelism
0.0122	20.8	.0000	1	evangelistic
0.0122	20.8	.0000	1	Evans'
0.0122	20.8	.0000	1	evaporator
0.0122	20.8	.0000	1	ever-rising
0.0122	20.8	.0000	1	Everybody's
0.0122	20.8	.0000	1	Everything
0.0122	20.8	.0000	1	evocation
0.0122	20.8	.0000	1	evokes
0.0122	20.8	.0000	1	ex-Communists
0.0122	20.8	.0000	1	ex-Presidents
0.0122	20.8	.0000	1	ex-actress
0.0122	20.8	.0000	1	ex-convict
0.0122	20.8	.0000	1	ex-cop
0.0122	20.8	.0000	1	ex-managers
0.0122	20.8	.0000	1	ex-production
0.0122	20.8	.0000	1	ex-publisher's
0.0122	20.8	.0000	1	ex-reformer
0.0122	20.8	.0000	1	exbanker
0.0122	20.8	.0000	1	excels
0.0122	20.8	.0000	1	ExcelsiorSprings
0.0122	20.8	.0000	1	excerpted
0.0122	20.8	.0000	1	Executives
0.0122	20.8	.0000	1	exhalations
0.0122	20.8	.0000	1	exhortation
0.0122	20.8	.0000	1	existential
0.0122	20.8	.0000	1	existentialist
0.0122	20.8	.0000	1	exiting
0.0122	20.8	.0000	1	exonerate
0.0122	20.8	.0000	1	expanding-point
0.0122	20.8	.0000	1	expeditionary
0.0122	20.8	.0000	1	expense-paid
0.0122	20.8	.0000	1	Experience
0.0122	20.8	.0000	1	explayer
0.0122	20.8	.0000	1	Exploration
0.0122	20.8	.0000	1	explosiveness
0.0122	20.8	.0000	1	Expos
0.0122	20.8	.0000	1	exposes
0.0122	20.8	.0000	1	exterminating
0.0122	20.8	.0000	1	extirpated
0.0122	20.8	.0000	1	extra-fresh
0.0122	20.8	.0000	1	extrapolate
0.0122	20.8	.0000	1	extravehicular
0.0122	20.8	.0000	1	extricating
0.0122	20.8	.0000	1	eye-opening
0.0122	20.8	.0000	1	Eyebrow
0.0122	20.8	.0000	1	eyefilling
0.0122	20.8	.0000	1	eyetalian
0.0122	20.8	.0000	1	eyries
0.0122	20.8	.0000	1	Ezra's
0.0122	20.8	.0000	1	F-104
0.0122	20.8	.0000	1	f'r
0.0122	20.8	.0000	1	FA'S
0.0122	20.8	.0000	1	fab
0.0122	20.8	.0000	1	Fabbio
0.0122	20.8	.0000	1	Fabians
0.0122	20.8	.0000	1	Fabians'
0.0122	20.8	.0000	1	facedown
0.0122	20.8	.0000	1	factory-built
0.0122	20.8	.0000	1	Fagaras
0.0122	20.8	.0000	1	Fagin
0.0122	20.8	.0000	1	fair-skinned
0.0122	20.8	.0000	1	fair's
0.0122	20.8	.0000	1	Faith's
0.0122	20.8	.0000	1	Fajen
0.0122	20.8	.0000	1	fall-spawning
0.0122	20.8	.0000	1	fallacious
0.0122	20.8	.0000	1	Falstaffian
0.0122	20.8	.0000	1	Famers
0.0122	20.8	.0000	1	family-life
0.0122	20.8	.0000	1	family-owned
0.0122	20.8	.0000	1	Famine
0.0122	20.8	.0000	1	fanfare
0.0122	20.8	.0000	1	fang
0.0122	20.8	.0000	1	farm-equipment
0.0122	20.8	.0000	1	farm-to-market
0.0122	20.8	.0000	1	farmer-gas

U	SFI	D	F	Word Type
0.0122	20.8	.0000	1	farmer-turned-realtor
0.0122	20.8	.0000	1	fast-flashing
0.0122	20.8	.0000	1	fast-paced
0.0122	20.8	.0000	1	fasts
0.0122	20.8	.0000	1	fat-tailed
0.0122	20.8	.0000	1	fatality
0.0122	20.8	.0000	1	fave
0.0122	20.8	.0000	1	Favell
0.0122	20.8	.0000	1	favor-doing
0.0122	20.8	.0000	1	Favorite
0.0122	20.8	.0000	1	Faye
THE PRECEDING WORD TYPE OCCUPIES RANK 67200				
0.0122	20.8	.0000	1	Fayerweather
0.0122	20.8	.0000	1	Faygo
0.0122	20.8	.0000	1	fealty
0.0122	20.8	.0000	1	fearfuls
0.0122	20.8	.0000	1	Fearsome
0.0122	20.8	.0000	1	fearsomely
0.0122	20.8	.0000	1	feast-or-famine
0.0122	20.8	.0000	1	feather's
0.0122	20.8	.0000	1	featherbed
0.0122	20.8	.0000	1	Feelin'
0.0122	20.8	.0000	1	Feiffer
0.0122	20.8	.0000	1	Feldman
0.0122	20.8	.0000	1	fellas
0.0122	20.8	.0000	1	Fellowship
0.0122	20.8	.0000	1	Felse
0.0122	20.8	.0000	1	femininely
0.0122	20.8	.0000	1	fenugreek
0.0122	20.8	.0000	1	Feodor
0.0122	20.8	.0000	1	Ferber
0.0122	20.8	.0000	1	ferociousness
0.0122	20.8	.0000	1	ferreting
0.0122	20.8	.0000	1	fetuses
0.0122	20.8	.0000	1	feuding
0.0122	20.8	.0000	1	Ffrancis
0.0122	20.8	.0000	1	fibroblasts
0.0122	20.8	.0000	1	fiddleback
0.0122	20.8	.0000	1	field-test
0.0122	20.8	.0000	1	Fielder
0.0122	20.8	.0000	1	fifteen-mile
0.0122	20.8	.0000	1	fifteenth-anniversary
0.0122	20.8	.0000	1	fifth-best
0.0122	20.8	.0000	1	fifth-place
0.0122	20.8	.0000	1	fifth-round
0.0122	20.8	.0000	1	figment
0.0122	20.8	.0000	1	figura
0.0122	20.8	.0000	1	Filbert
0.0122	20.8	.0000	1	file-drawers
0.0122	20.8	.0000	1	filet
0.0122	20.8	.0000	1	Fillet
0.0122	20.8	.0000	1	fillip
0.0122	20.8	.0000	1	Fillmores
0.0122	20.8	.0000	1	filmic
0.0122	20.8	.0000	1	filmmakers
0.0122	20.8	.0000	1	Films
0.0122	20.8	.0000	1	Finalizer
0.0122	20.8	.0000	1	fine-featured
0.0122	20.8	.0000	1	finesse
0.0122	20.8	.0000	1	fingerlings'
0.0122	20.8	.0000	1	Finkbine
0.0122	20.8	.0000	1	Finladn
0.0122	20.8	.0000	1	Finletter
0.0122	20.8	.0000	1	Finnair
0.0122	20.8	.0000	1	fire-detection
0.0122	20.8	.0000	1	fire-extinguishing
0.0122	20.8	.0000	1	Firearms
0.0122	20.8	.0000	1	firefighting
0.0122	20.8	.0000	1	fireflies'
0.0122	20.8	.0000	1	firm's
0.0122	20.8	.0000	1	firmed
0.0122	20.8	.0000	1	Firming
0.0122	20.8	.0000	1	first-down
0.0122	20.8	.0000	1	first-half
0.0122	20.8	.0000	1	first-name
0.0122	20.8	.0000	1	first-sign-of-spring
0.0122	20.8	.0000	1	first-year
0.0122	20.8	.0000	1	Fischbach
0.0122	20.8	.0000	1	Fischer
0.0122	20.8	.0000	1	Fisherman
0.0122	20.8	.0000	1	fitly
0.0122	20.8	.0000	1	Fitzgerald
0.0122	20.8	.0000	1	five-shooter
0.0122	20.8	.0000	1	five-year-olds
0.0122	20.8	.0000	1	fixed-wing
0.0122	20.8	.0000	1	Flagstaff
0.0122	20.8	.0000	1	flak
0.0122	20.8	.0000	1	flame-blue
0.0122	20.8	.0000	1	Flamm
0.0122	20.8	.0000	1	flasher
0.0122	20.8	.0000	1	flat-rate
0.0122	20.8	.0000	1	Flatheads
0.0122	20.8	.0000	1	flecking
0.0122	20.8	.0000	1	fledged
0.0122	20.8	.0000	1	Flemming
0.0122	20.8	.0000	1	Flights
0.0122	20.8	.0000	1	flings
0.0122	20.8	.0000	1	flintlocks
0.0122	20.8	.0000	1	Flit
0.0122	20.8	.0000	1	floodplains
0.0122	20.8	.0000	1	Florentines
0.0122	20.8	.0000	1	Flossie's
0.0122	20.8	.0000	1	fluently
0.0122	20.8	.0000	1	flummadiddle
0.0122	20.8	.0000	1	fluorocarbon
0.0122	20.8	.0000	1	foaling
0.0122	20.8	.0000	1	foam-flecked
0.0122	20.8	.0000	1	foam-padded
0.0122	20.8	.0000	1	Foccart
0.0122	20.8	.0000	1	fogged
0.0122	20.8	.0000	1	fold-back
0.0122	20.8	.0000	1	folk-hero
THE PRECEDING WORD TYPE OCCUPIES RANK 67300				
0.0122	20.8	.0000	1	folktales
0.0122	20.8	.0000	1	folkways
0.0122	20.8	.0000	1	food-bearing
0.0122	20.8	.0000	1	foolery

U	SFI	D	F	Word Type
0.0122	20.8	.0000	1	foot-locker
0.0122	20.8	.0000	1	foot-slogging
0.0122	20.8	.0000	1	footage
0.0122	20.8	.0000	1	football's
0.0122	20.8	.0000	1	footboard
0.0122	20.8	.0000	1	Footsore
0.0122	20.8	.0000	1	forbearance
0.0122	20.8	.0000	1	forced-labor
0.0122	20.8	.0000	1	FORD
0.0122	20.8	.0000	1	Ford-O-Matic
0.0122	20.8	.0000	1	Fords's
0.0122	20.8	.0000	1	forebear
0.0122	20.8	.0000	1	foreboded
0.0122	20.8	.0000	1	foreign-accent
0.0122	20.8	.0000	1	foreign-exchange
0.0122	20.8	.0000	1	foreigner's
0.0122	20.8	.0000	1	forest-ringed
0.0122	20.8	.0000	1	Forgedtrue
0.0122	20.8	.0000	1	fork-tongued
0.0122	20.8	.0000	1	Forked
0.0122	20.8	.0000	1	Formula
0.0122	20.8	.0000	1	FortMyers
0.0122	20.8	.0000	1	FortWorth-Dallas
0.0122	20.8	.0000	1	fortifier
0.0122	20.8	.0000	1	Fortresses
0.0122	20.8	.0000	1	Fortunato
0.0122	20.8	.0000	1	Foundation-funded
0.0122	20.8	.0000	1	Foundations
0.0122	20.8	.0000	1	Founders
0.0122	20.8	.0000	1	four-and-five-letter
0.0122	20.8	.0000	1	four-banger
0.0122	20.8	.0000	1	four-bedroom
0.0122	20.8	.0000	1	four-engine
0.0122	20.8	.0000	1	four-piece
0.0122	20.8	.0000	1	four-power
0.0122	20.8	.0000	1	four-stroker
0.0122	20.8	.0000	1	four-throat
0.0122	20.8	.0000	1	four-wheel-drive
0.0122	20.8	.0000	1	Foursome
0.0122	20.8	.0000	1	fourth-story
0.0122	20.8	.0000	1	Fowler
0.0122	20.8	.0000	1	foxhound
0.0122	20.8	.0000	1	Foyt
0.0122	20.8	.0000	1	Foyt's
0.0122	20.8	.0000	1	framboise
0.0122	20.8	.0000	1	Framing
0.0122	20.8	.0000	1	franca
0.0122	20.8	.0000	1	Francaise
0.0122	20.8	.0000	1	France-Soir
0.0122	20.8	.0000	1	Francesco
0.0122	20.8	.0000	1	franchise
0.0122	20.8	.0000	1	Franco-American
0.0122	20.8	.0000	1	Francois-Marie
0.0122	20.8	.0000	1	frangipani
0.0122	20.8	.0000	1	Franny's
0.0122	20.8	.0000	1	Fraser
0.0122	20.8	.0000	1	fratricidal
0.0122	20.8	.0000	1	fratricide
0.0122	20.8	.0000	1	freaked
0.0122	20.8	.0000	1	freakiest
0.0122	20.8	.0000	1	free-floating
0.0122	20.8	.0000	1	free-flying
0.0122	20.8	.0000	1	free-spoken
0.0122	20.8	.0000	1	free-wheeling
0.0122	20.8	.0000	1	freebooter
0.0122	20.8	.0000	1	Freeborn
0.0122	20.8	.0000	1	freelance
0.0122	20.8	.0000	1	Freestone
0.0122	20.8	.0000	1	freewheeling
0.0122	20.8	.0000	1	freighted
0.0122	20.8	.0000	1	French-made
0.0122	20.8	.0000	1	Fresco
0.0122	20.8	.0000	1	Fria
0.0122	20.8	.0000	1	frictionless
0.0122	20.8	.0000	1	FRIED
0.0122	20.8	.0000	1	Frigatebirds
0.0122	20.8	.0000	1	frizz
0.0122	20.8	.0000	1	front-runner
0.0122	20.8	.0000	1	front-spring
0.0122	20.8	.0000	1	front-yard
0.0122	20.8	.0000	1	frontwheel
0.0122	20.8	.0000	1	frosty-cold
0.0122	20.8	.0000	1	frozen-rubber
0.0122	20.8	.0000	1	fryed
0.0122	20.8	.0000	1	fryers
0.0122	20.8	.0000	1	Ft
0.0122	20.8	.0000	1	fuchsia
0.0122	20.8	.0000	1	fueled
0.0122	20.8	.0000	1	Fulgencio
0.0122	20.8	.0000	1	full-blade
0.0122	20.8	.0000	1	full-bloods
0.0122	20.8	.0000	1	full-course
0.0122	20.8	.0000	1	full-page
0.0122	20.8	.0000	1	full-powered
0.0122	20.8	.0000	1	fully-independent
0.0122	20.8	.0000	1	Fumio
THE PRECEDING WORD TYPE OCCUPIES RANK 67400				
0.0122	20.8	.0000	1	funky
0.0122	20.8	.0000	1	funnel's
0.0122	20.8	.0000	1	furnace-brazed
0.0122	20.8	.0000	1	Fury
0.0122	20.8	.0000	1	fusillade
0.0122	20.8	.0000	1	fustiness
0.0122	20.8	.0000	1	fuzzlike
0.0122	20.8	.0000	1	G-One
0.0122	20.8	.0000	1	gab
0.0122	20.8	.0000	1	Gabon
0.0122	20.8	.0000	1	Gabor
0.0122	20.8	.0000	1	Gabrielson
0.0122	20.8	.0000	1	Gallant
0.0122	20.8	.0000	1	galleass
0.0122	20.8	.0000	1	gallery-theaters
0.0122	20.8	.0000	1	Gallery's
0.0122	20.8	.0000	1	galling
0.0122	20.8	.0000	1	Galloping
0.0122	20.8	.0000	1	gambit
0.0122	20.8	.0000	1	gambles

U	SFI	D	F	Word Type
0.0122	20.8	.0000	1	gamekeepers
0.0122	20.8	.0000	1	Gamelan
0.0122	20.8	.0000	1	Garaci
0.0122	20.8	.0000	1	garble
0.0122	20.8	.0000	1	Garcia
0.0122	20.8	.0000	1	gardened
0.0122	20.8	.0000	1	Gardner
0.0122	20.8	.0000	1	garlic-reeking
0.0122	20.8	.0000	1	Garlits
0.0122	20.8	.0000	1	Garner
0.0122	20.8	.0000	1	gas-burning
0.0122	20.8	.0000	1	gas-escape
0.0122	20.8	.0000	1	gas-power
0.0122	20.8	.0000	1	gas-powered
0.0122	20.8	.0000	1	gas-turbine
0.0122	20.8	.0000	1	gasket-sealed
0.0122	20.8	.0000	1	gasoline-driven
0.0122	20.8	.0000	1	Gasperi
0.0122	20.8	.0000	1	Gaston
0.0122	20.8	.0000	1	gatherum
0.0122	20.8	.0000	1	Gator
0.0122	20.8	.0000	1	Gaulle's
0.0122	20.8	.0000	1	gavels
0.0122	20.8	.0000	1	gearing
0.0122	20.8	.0000	1	Gellis
0.0122	20.8	.0000	1	gels
0.0122	20.8	.0000	1	Geminis
0.0122	20.8	.0000	1	gemmologist
0.0122	20.8	.0000	1	Gemutlichkeit
0.0122	20.8	.0000	1	gen-er-a-tion
0.0122	20.8	.0000	1	genealogies
0.0122	20.8	.0000	1	general-in-chief
0.0122	20.8	.0000	1	generalship
0.0122	20.8	.0000	1	Genesco
0.0122	20.8	.0000	1	Genesee
0.0122	20.8	.0000	1	genitals
0.0122	20.8	.0000	1	gent-ly
0.0122	20.8	.0000	1	gentle-voiced
0.0122	20.8	.0000	1	genuflection
0.0122	20.8	.0000	1	GEOGRAPHIC
0.0122	20.8	.0000	1	Geographic's
0.0122	20.8	.0000	1	geophagy
0.0122	20.8	.0000	1	gerbils
0.0122	20.8	.0000	1	Gerhart
0.0122	20.8	.0000	1	Gesell
0.0122	20.8	.0000	1	Geste
0.0122	20.8	.0000	1	get-away
0.0122	20.8	.0000	1	getup
0.0122	20.8	.0000	1	Ghias
0.0122	20.8	.0000	1	ghosting
0.0122	20.8	.0000	1	Gibsons
0.0122	20.8	.0000	1	Gifford
0.0122	20.8	.0000	1	Gigi
0.0122	20.8	.0000	1	gill-rattling
0.0122	20.8	.0000	1	girl-boy
0.0122	20.8	.0000	1	Girona
0.0122	20.8	.0000	1	Girona's
0.0122	20.8	.0000	1	Giscard
0.0122	20.8	.0000	1	Gish
0.0122	20.8	.0000	1	glad-hearted
0.0122	20.8	.0000	1	Gladewater
0.0122	20.8	.0000	1	glassed
0.0122	20.8	.0000	1	glassing
0.0122	20.8	.0000	1	Glatthorn
0.0122	20.8	.0000	1	glean
0.0122	20.8	.0000	1	Globetrotters
0.0122	20.8	.0000	1	Gloeilampenfabrieken
0.0122	20.8	.0000	1	gloomey
0.0122	20.8	.0000	1	Gloriana
0.0122	20.8	.0000	1	glory-seeking
0.0122	20.8	.0000	1	Glove
0.0122	20.8	.0000	1	Gloves
0.0122	20.8	.0000	1	Gnats
0.0122	20.8	.0000	1	go-go
0.0122	20.8	.0000	1	go-kart
0.0122	20.8	.0000	1	go-round
0.0122	20.8	.0000	1	goalie
0.0122	20.8	.0000	1	goaltenders
0.0122	20.8	.0000	1	gobbler-chasing
0.0122	20.8	.0000	1	Gobel
THE PRECEDING WORD TYPE OCCUPIES RANK 67500				
0.0122	20.8	.0000	1	Godard
0.0122	20.8	.0000	1	goddam
0.0122	20.8	.0000	1	goddamned
0.0122	20.8	.0000	1	gold-laced
0.0122	20.8	.0000	1	gold-plated
0.0122	20.8	.0000	1	gold-tiled
0.0122	20.8	.0000	1	Golddiggers
0.0122	20.8	.0000	1	Goldfarb
0.0122	20.8	.0000	1	Goldwater
0.0122	20.8	.0000	1	golf-bag
0.0122	20.8	.0000	1	golfers'
0.0122	20.8	.0000	1	Gonzaga
0.0122	20.8	.0000	1	good-performing
0.0122	20.8	.0000	1	good-size
0.0122	20.8	.0000	1	good-will
0.0122	20.8	.0000	1	good-working
0.0122	20.8	.0000	1	Goodell
0.0122	20.8	.0000	1	Goodlad
0.0122	20.8	.0000	1	goody-goody
0.0122	20.8	.0000	1	gooneys
0.0122	20.8	.0000	1	goopy
0.0122	20.8	.0000	1	Gore
0.0122	20.8	.0000	1	Gosse
0.0122	20.8	.0000	1	government-run
0.0122	20.8	.0000	1	GOW-choz
0.0122	20.8	.0000	1	Grabber
0.0122	20.8	.0000	1	Graceful
0.0122	20.8	.0000	1	Graceland
0.0122	20.8	.0000	1	graciousness
0.0122	20.8	.0000	1	graffiti
0.0122	20.8	.0000	1	grafts
0.0122	20.8	.0000	1	Graham-style
0.0122	20.8	.0000	1	Grail
0.0122	20.8	.0000	1	grain-devouring
0.0122	20.8	.0000	1	granaries
0.0122	20.8	.0000	1	grandee

U	SFI	D	F	Word Type
0.0122	20.8	.0000	1	grandmas
0.0122	20.8	.0000	1	grape-like
0.0122	20.8	.0000	1	grapeless
0.0122	20.8	.0000	1	Graphic
0.0122	20.8	.0000	1	Graphics
0.0122	20.8	.0000	1	gratia
0.0122	20.8	.0000	1	gratifyingly
0.0122	20.8	.0000	1	gratuitous
0.0122	20.8	.0000	1	gray-black
0.0122	20.8	.0000	1	Grayling
0.0122	20.8	.0000	1	Graysquirrel
0.0122	20.8	.0000	1	greasepaint
0.0122	20.8	.0000	1	greatgrandson
0.0122	20.8	.0000	1	greats
0.0122	20.8	.0000	1	Gredy
0.0122	20.8	.0000	1	green-and-gold
0.0122	20.8	.0000	1	green-and-yellow
0.0122	20.8	.0000	1	Greenberg
0.0122	20.8	.0000	1	Greenbriar
0.0122	20.8	.0000	1	gregaria
0.0122	20.8	.0000	1	Gregg
0.0122	20.8	.0000	1	Grenadian
0.0122	20.8	.0000	1	grief's
0.0122	20.8	.0000	1	Grier
0.0122	20.8	.0000	1	Griese
0.0122	20.8	.0000	1	grieves
0.0122	20.8	.0000	1	Grill
0.0122	20.8	.0000	1	Grimme
0.0122	20.8	.0000	1	Grimsey
0.0122	20.8	.0000	1	gringos
0.0122	20.8	.0000	1	gripe
0.0122	20.8	.0000	1	griping
0.0122	20.8	.0000	1	GROAR
0.0122	20.8	.0000	1	groin
0.0122	20.8	.0000	1	groovier
0.0122	20.8	.0000	1	Groovy
0.0122	20.8	.0000	1	Grospiron
0.0122	20.8	.0000	1	grosser
0.0122	20.8	.0000	1	Grotto
0.0122	20.8	.0000	1	ground-floor
0.0122	20.8	.0000	1	groundskeepers
0.0122	20.8	.0000	1	grower's
0.0122	20.8	.0000	1	Growers
0.0122	20.8	.0000	1	growingly
0.0122	20.8	.0000	1	Grown-up
0.0122	20.8	.0000	1	growth-minded
0.0122	20.8	.0000	1	GRRRRRRRR
0.0122	20.8	.0000	1	grudges
0.0122	20.8	.0000	1	GSNARRRRRRRL
0.0122	20.8	.0000	1	GT-18
0.0122	20.8	.0000	1	guamil
0.0122	20.8	.0000	1	Guanajay
0.0122	20.8	.0000	1	Guernica
0.0122	20.8	.0000	1	Guerrilla
0.0122	20.8	.0000	1	guerrillero
0.0122	20.8	.0000	1	guesstimate
0.0122	20.8	.0000	1	guesthouse
0.0122	20.8	.0000	1	guidebooks
0.0122	20.8	.0000	1	Guitar
0.0122	20.8	.0000	1	guitar-plucking
0.0122	20.8	.0000	1	Guitarist-Composer
0.0122	20.8	.0000	1	Gujarati
0.0122	20.8	.0000	1	gulches
0.0122	20.8	.0000	1	Gump
THE PRECEDING WORD TYPE OCCUPIES RANK 67600				
0.0122	20.8	.0000	1	gun-control
0.0122	20.8	.0000	1	gun-fetishist
0.0122	20.8	.0000	1	gung-ho
0.0122	20.8	.0000	1	gunners'
0.0122	20.8	.0000	1	gurgles
0.0122	20.8	.0000	1	Gustavo
0.0122	20.8	.0000	1	guten
0.0122	20.8	.0000	1	gymnasts
0.0122	20.8	.0000	1	Gyrocopter
0.0122	20.8	.0000	1	H&G
0.0122	20.8	.0000	1	haaa-raaam-bayyy
0.0122	20.8	.0000	1	Hackettstown
0.0122	20.8	.0000	1	Hadl
0.0122	20.8	.0000	1	Hadley
0.0122	20.8	.0000	1	Hague's
0.0122	20.8	.0000	1	hair-oil
0.0122	20.8	.0000	1	hairdos
0.0122	20.8	.0000	1	hairstyling
0.0122	20.8	.0000	1	half-back-option
0.0122	20.8	.0000	1	half-hearted
0.0122	20.8	.0000	1	half-stood
0.0122	20.8	.0000	1	half-told
0.0122	20.8	.0000	1	halfmile
0.0122	20.8	.0000	1	Hallam
0.0122	20.8	.0000	1	Hallmark
0.0122	20.8	.0000	1	hallucinogenic
0.0122	20.8	.0000	1	Halon
0.0122	20.8	.0000	1	hambone
0.0122	20.8	.0000	1	Hammacher-Schlemmer
0.0122	20.8	.0000	1	hammer-thrower
0.0122	20.8	.0000	1	hammerhead's
0.0122	20.8	.0000	1	hammerheads
0.0122	20.8	.0000	1	Hammerin'
0.0122	20.8	.0000	1	hammermill
0.0122	20.8	.0000	1	hampering
0.0122	20.8	.0000	1	hand-cutting
0.0122	20.8	.0000	1	handgun-carrying
0.0122	20.8	.0000	1	handheld
0.0122	20.8	.0000	1	Handicapped
0.0122	20.8	.0000	1	handlebars
0.0122	20.8	.0000	1	handsaw
0.0122	20.8	.0000	1	handstands
0.0122	20.8	.0000	1	hang-ups
0.0122	20.8	.0000	1	hangers-on
0.0122	20.8	.0000	1	Hansbrough-Newlands
0.0122	20.8	.0000	1	Hanslin
0.0122	20.8	.0000	1	Hapgood
0.0122	20.8	.0000	1	HAPPENED
0.0122	20.8	.0000	1	hara-kiri
0.0122	20.8	.0000	1	hard-bodied
0.0122	20.8	.0000	1	hard-driving
0.0122	20.8	.0000	1	hard-rock

U	SFI	D	F	Word Type
0.0122	20.8	.0000	1	hardcover
0.0122	20.8	.0000	1	harem
0.0122	20.8	.0000	1	harmfulness
0.0122	20.8	.0000	1	Harmsworth
0.0122	20.8	.0000	1	harum-scarum
0.0122	20.8	.0000	1	Harvard's
0.0122	20.8	.0000	1	Harvester
0.0122	20.8	.0000	1	Hasanlu
0.0122	20.8	.0000	1	Hasler
0.0122	20.8	.0000	1	Haswell
0.0122	20.8	.0000	1	hate-mongers
0.0122	20.8	.0000	1	Hathorn
0.0122	20.8	.0000	1	hav-a-leena
0.0122	20.8	.0000	1	Havasupai
0.0122	20.8	.0000	1	Haw's
0.0122	20.8	.0000	1	hawk-bill
0.0122	20.8	.0000	1	HAY
0.0122	20.8	.0000	1	head-shop
0.0122	20.8	.0000	1	header
0.0122	20.8	.0000	1	Headlamp
0.0122	20.8	.0000	1	headliner
0.0122	20.8	.0000	1	headmasters
0.0122	20.8	.0000	1	headsets
0.0122	20.8	.0000	1	Hearl
0.0122	20.8	.0000	1	heaven-sent
0.0122	20.8	.0000	1	heavy-handed
0.0122	20.8	.0000	1	heavy-thighed
0.0122	20.8	.0000	1	heavyset
0.0122	20.8	.0000	1	Hedley
0.0122	20.8	.0000	1	heedlessly
0.0122	20.8	.0000	1	hefted
0.0122	20.8	.0000	1	heftier
0.0122	20.8	.0000	1	heightening
0.0122	20.8	.0000	1	Hein
0.0122	20.8	.0000	1	Heiskell's
0.0122	20.8	.0000	1	heliarc
0.0122	20.8	.0000	1	Helicom
0.0122	20.8	.0000	1	helicoptered
0.0122	20.8	.0000	1	HELL
0.0122	20.8	.0000	1	hell-for-leather
0.0122	20.8	.0000	1	hell-raising
0.0122	20.8	.0000	1	Hell's
0.0122	20.8	.0000	1	Hellenes
0.0122	20.8	.0000	1	Hellenic
0.0122	20.8	.0000	1	hellgrammite
0.0122	20.8	.0000	1	helmeted
0.0122	20.8	.0000	1	helmsman
0.0122	20.8	.0000	1	helmsman's
THE PRECEDING WORD TYPE OCCUPIES RANK 67700				
0.0122	20.8	.0000	1	hemis
0.0122	20.8	.0000	1	hemorrhaging
0.0122	20.8	.0000	1	Hempstead
0.0122	20.8	.0000	1	Henrietta
0.0122	20.8	.0000	1	hephyr
0.0122	20.8	.0000	1	Hepzibah's
0.0122	20.8	.0000	1	herculean
0.0122	20.8	.0000	1	hercules
0.0122	20.8	.0000	1	Here's
0.0122	20.8	.0000	1	Hermannstadt
0.0122	20.8	.0000	1	hero-turned-traitor
0.0122	20.8	.0000	1	hero-worship
0.0122	20.8	.0000	1	hero-worshipped
0.0122	20.8	.0000	1	Herring
0.0122	20.8	.0000	1	Hertzsprung
0.0122	20.8	.0000	1	Hesburgh's
0.0122	20.8	.0000	1	Hesikiah
0.0122	20.8	.0000	1	Hessian
0.0122	20.8	.0000	1	Hewitt
0.0122	20.8	.0000	1	Heyman
0.0122	20.8	.0000	1	hgl
0.0122	20.8	.0000	1	hibernations
0.0122	20.8	.0000	1	hiccough
0.0122	20.8	.0000	1	hiccuped
0.0122	20.8	.0000	1	Hicketheier
0.0122	20.8	.0000	1	Hickethier
0.0122	20.8	.0000	1	Hickethier's
0.0122	20.8	.0000	1	hide-outs
0.0122	20.8	.0000	1	hideouts
0.0122	20.8	.0000	1	hierarchies
0.0122	20.8	.0000	1	Higby
0.0122	20.8	.0000	1	high-beam
0.0122	20.8	.0000	1	high-compressions
0.0122	20.8	.0000	1	high-desert
0.0122	20.8	.0000	1	high-fire
0.0122	20.8	.0000	1	high-living
0.0122	20.8	.0000	1	high-octane
0.0122	20.8	.0000	1	high-pressured
0.0122	20.8	.0000	1	high-wheeler
0.0122	20.8	.0000	1	highest-grade
0.0122	20.8	.0000	1	highest-level
0.0122	20.8	.0000	1	highest-powered
0.0122	20.8	.0000	1	highest-ranking
0.0122	20.8	.0000	1	highline
0.0122	20.8	.0000	1	highpoint
0.0122	20.8	.0000	1	highwing
0.0122	20.8	.0000	1	hiker
0.0122	20.8	.0000	1	hin
0.0122	20.8	.0000	1	Hinds
0.0122	20.8	.0000	1	hindsight
0.0122	20.8	.0000	1	Hinduism's
0.0122	20.8	.0000	1	Hine's
0.0122	20.8	.0000	1	Hingham
0.0122	20.8	.0000	1	hins
0.0122	20.8	.0000	1	hippie-esque
0.0122	20.8	.0000	1	hippie-haired
0.0122	20.8	.0000	1	hippocampus
0.0122	20.8	.0000	1	hippy
0.0122	20.8	.0000	1	Hiroshi
0.0122	20.8	.0000	1	Hirshberg's
0.0122	20.8	.0000	1	hirsute
0.0122	20.8	.0000	1	Hispanic
0.0122	20.8	.0000	1	Hispanic-studies
0.0122	20.8	.0000	1	histologist
0.0122	20.8	.0000	1	historiographer
0.0122	20.8	.0000	1	hit-run
0.0122	20.8	.0000	1	hmmmmph
0.0122	20.8	.0000	1	Ho-shu
0.0122	20.8	.0000	1	hoar
0.0122	20.8	.0000	1	hob
0.0122	20.8	.0000	1	Hockey
0.0122	20.8	.0000	1	hockey's
0.0122	20.8	.0000	1	Hodaka
0.0122	20.8	.0000	1	Hodge
0.0122	20.8	.0000	1	Hodson
0.0122	20.8	.0000	1	hoelike
0.0122	20.8	.0000	1	Hoffert
0.0122	20.8	.0000	1	Hoffmann-LaRoche
0.0122	20.8	.0000	1	hog-calling
0.0122	20.8	.0000	1	hogwash
0.0122	20.8	.0000	1	Holbrook
0.0122	20.8	.0000	1	Holden
0.0122	20.8	.0000	1	holdout
0.0122	20.8	.0000	1	holdover
0.0122	20.8	.0000	1	holed
0.0122	20.8	.0000	1	hologram
0.0122	20.8	.0000	1	Holtzman
0.0122	20.8	.0000	1	home-building
0.0122	20.8	.0000	1	home-turf
0.0122	20.8	.0000	1	homebuilts
0.0122	20.8	.0000	1	homicidal
0.0122	20.8	.0000	1	homicide
0.0122	20.8	.0000	1	homosexuals
0.0122	20.8	.0000	1	Hondas
0.0122	20.8	.0000	1	Honker
0.0122	20.8	.0000	1	Honolulu's
0.0122	20.8	.0000	1	honorary-degree
0.0122	20.8	.0000	1	hoodlum-haunted
0.0122	20.8	.0000	1	Hoosiers
0.0122	20.8	.0000	1	hop-up
THE PRECEDING WORD TYPE OCCUPIES RANK 67800				
0.0122	20.8	.0000	1	Hopa
0.0122	20.8	.0000	1	hopefuls
0.0122	20.8	.0000	1	Hopewell
0.0122	20.8	.0000	1	horn-blowing
0.0122	20.8	.0000	1	Horowitz
0.0122	20.8	.0000	1	horse-loving
0.0122	20.8	.0000	1	HORSES
0.0122	20.8	.0000	1	horsey
0.0122	20.8	.0000	1	Hosmer
0.0122	20.8	.0000	1	Hostetler
0.0122	20.8	.0000	1	Hosts
0.0122	20.8	.0000	1	hot-dogs
0.0122	20.8	.0000	1	hot-spot
0.0122	20.8	.0000	1	hotplate
0.0122	20.8	.0000	1	hotspots
0.0122	20.8	.0000	1	Hotz
0.0122	20.8	.0000	1	Hough
0.0122	20.8	.0000	1	Hour-Radio
0.0122	20.8	.0000	1	house-bound
0.0122	20.8	.0000	1	housecats
0.0122	20.8	.0000	1	Howes
0.0122	20.8	.0000	1	Howland's
0.0122	20.8	.0000	1	HRM
0.0122	20.8	.0000	1	ht
0.0122	20.8	.0000	1	hubcaps
0.0122	20.8	.0000	1	Hubert's
0.0122	20.8	.0000	1	hudsonius
0.0122	20.8	.0000	1	hued
0.0122	20.8	.0000	1	huffed
0.0122	20.8	.0000	1	huffs
0.0122	20.8	.0000	1	huffy
0.0122	20.8	.0000	1	hugeness
0.0122	20.8	.0000	1	Hugger
0.0122	20.8	.0000	1	Hulick
0.0122	20.8	.0000	1	hullabaloo
0.0122	20.8	.0000	1	Hulme
0.0122	20.8	.0000	1	Humanae
0.0122	20.8	.0000	1	Humenick
0.0122	20.8	.0000	1	Humphries
0.0122	20.8	.0000	1	hundred-act
0.0122	20.8	.0000	1	Hunedoara
0.0122	20.8	.0000	1	hung-over
0.0122	20.8	.0000	1	hungering
0.0122	20.8	.0000	1	hunker
0.0122	20.8	.0000	1	hunkered
0.0122	20.8	.0000	1	Hunterdon
0.0122	20.8	.0000	1	Huong
0.0122	20.8	.0000	1	Huong's
0.0122	20.8	.0000	1	Hurst/Airheart
0.0122	20.8	.0000	1	hurtle
0.0122	20.8	.0000	1	Hutschnecker's
0.0122	20.8	.0000	1	hyacinth-dotted
0.0122	20.8	.0000	1	hydrides
0.0122	20.8	.0000	1	hydro-generators
0.0122	20.8	.0000	1	hydrologists
0.0122	20.8	.0000	1	Hyena
0.0122	20.8	.0000	1	hypalon
0.0122	20.8	.0000	1	hyped-up
0.0122	20.8	.0000	1	hypochondriacal
0.0122	20.8	.0000	1	hypothesized
0.0122	20.8	.0000	1	I-270
0.0122	20.8	.0000	1	i-5
0.0122	20.8	.0000	1	i-95
0.0122	20.8	.0000	1	I-95
0.0122	20.8	.0000	1	Ia
0.0122	20.8	.0000	1	Ian
0.0122	20.8	.0000	1	IBM
0.0122	20.8	.0000	1	ice-filled
0.0122	20.8	.0000	1	ice-packed
0.0122	20.8	.0000	1	Ich
0.0122	20.8	.0000	1	Identification
0.0122	20.8	.0000	1	identification-card
0.0122	20.8	.0000	1	ideologues
0.0122	20.8	.0000	1	idolaters
0.0122	20.8	.0000	1	idyllically
0.0122	20.8	.0000	1	IGFA**
0.0122	20.8	.0000	1	Ignatius
0.0122	20.8	.0000	1	ignoble
0.0122	20.8	.0000	1	Igor's
0.0122	20.8	.0000	1	Ikarus
0.0122	20.8	.0000	1	Ileana
0.0122	20.8	.0000	1	ilk
0.0122	20.8	.0000	1	ill-trained
0.0122	20.8	.0000	1	Illinois'
0.0122	20.8	.0000	1	illogic
0.0122	20.8	.0000	1	illuminates
0.0122	20.8	.0000	1	illusive
0.0122	20.8	.0000	1	imbalance
0.0122	20.8	.0000	1	imitative
0.0122	20.8	.0000	1	immaculately
0.0122	20.8	.0000	1	imminent
0.0122	20.8	.0000	1	immobile
0.0122	20.8	.0000	1	immorality
0.0122	20.8	.0000	1	impediments
0.0122	20.8	.0000	1	impetuosity
0.0122	20.8	.0000	1	implacably
0.0122	20.8	.0000	1	importations
0.0122	20.8	.0000	1	importuning
0.0122	20.8	.0000	1	impounded
0.0122	20.8	.0000	1	impoundments
THE PRECEDING WORD TYPE OCCUPIES RANK 67900				
0.0122	20.8	.0000	1	improvisational
0.0122	20.8	.0000	1	in-person
0.0122	20.8	.0000	1	in-school
0.0122	20.8	.0000	1	inadequacy
0.0122	20.8	.0000	1	inaugurals
0.0122	20.8	.0000	1	inaugurate
0.0122	20.8	.0000	1	incapacitated
0.0122	20.8	.0000	1	Inch
0.0122	20.8	.0000	1	inching
0.0122	20.8	.0000	1	inchoate
0.0122	20.8	.0000	1	incompetently
0.0122	20.8	.0000	1	incurable
0.0122	20.8	.0000	1	indecipherable
0.0122	20.8	.0000	1	indelicacy
0.0122	20.8	.0000	1	indemnity
0.0122	20.8	.0000	1	Indianapolis-Attucks
0.0122	20.8	.0000	1	Indianhead
0.0122	20.8	.0000	1	indicted
0.0122	20.8	.0000	1	indicts
0.0122	20.8	.0000	1	Indira
0.0122	20.8	.0000	1	indiscernible
0.0122	20.8	.0000	1	indulging
0.0122	20.8	.0000	1	industry's
0.0122	20.8	.0000	1	ineffectively
0.0122	20.8	.0000	1	ineluctably
0.0122	20.8	.0000	1	infatuation
0.0122	20.8	.0000	1	inflatable-type
0.0122	20.8	.0000	1	INFLATION
0.0122	20.8	.0000	1	inflator
0.0122	20.8	.0000	1	inflexible
0.0122	20.8	.0000	1	inflight
0.0122	20.8	.0000	1	informants
0.0122	20.8	.0000	1	infrared-sensing
0.0122	20.8	.0000	1	infringing
0.0122	20.8	.0000	1	Ingenue
0.0122	20.8	.0000	1	Inglis
0.0122	20.8	.0000	1	Initial
0.0122	20.8	.0000	1	inland-waterway
0.0122	20.8	.0000	1	inlay
0.0122	20.8	.0000	1	inner-wall
0.0122	20.8	.0000	1	Innovations
0.0122	20.8	.0000	1	innovators
0.0122	20.8	.0000	1	inpatients
0.0122	20.8	.0000	1	inputs
0.0122	20.8	.0000	1	insensitivity
0.0122	20.8	.0000	1	instant-fit
0.0122	20.8	.0000	1	INSTEAD
0.0122	20.8	.0000	1	instigation
0.0122	20.8	.0000	1	instilled
0.0122	20.8	.0000	1	instilling
0.0122	20.8	.0000	1	Institut
0.0122	20.8	.0000	1	institutional
0.0122	20.8	.0000	1	instrument-lined
0.0122	20.8	.0000	1	insufficiency
0.0122	20.8	.0000	1	insular
0.0122	20.8	.0000	1	intelligentsia
0.0122	20.8	.0000	1	intensive-training
0.0122	20.8	.0000	1	inter-relationship
0.0122	20.8	.0000	1	interacts
0.0122	20.8	.0000	1	intercede
0.0122	20.8	.0000	1	intercity
0.0122	20.8	.0000	1	intercontinental
0.0122	20.8	.0000	1	interest-bearing
0.0122	20.8	.0000	1	Interior's
0.0122	20.8	.0000	1	interlarded
0.0122	20.8	.0000	1	intermediate-size
0.0122	20.8	.0000	1	interregnum
0.0122	20.8	.0000	1	interviewer
0.0122	20.8	.0000	1	INTERVIEWS
0.0122	20.8	.0000	1	intimidation
0.0122	20.8	.0000	1	intones
0.0122	20.8	.0000	1	intoxicates
0.0122	20.8	.0000	1	intranauts
0.0122	20.8	.0000	1	intriguingly
0.0122	20.8	.0000	1	invariable
0.0122	20.8	.0000	1	invincibility
0.0122	20.8	.0000	1	invitational
0.0122	20.8	.0000	1	Involvement
0.0122	20.8	.0000	1	IQS
0.0122	20.8	.0000	1	iron-fisted
0.0122	20.8	.0000	1	ironmasters
0.0122	20.8	.0000	1	Ironworkers
0.0122	20.8	.0000	1	irresistibility
0.0122	20.8	.0000	1	Iselin
0.0122	20.8	.0000	1	Iskenderian
0.0122	20.8	.0000	1	Isky
0.0122	20.8	.0000	1	islet
0.0122	20.8	.0000	1	Isolda
0.0122	20.8	.0000	1	Isolda's
0.0122	20.8	.0000	1	Issues
0.0122	20.8	.0000	1	Italian-style
0.0122	20.8	.0000	1	itinerary
0.0122	20.8	.0000	1	jackboots
0.0122	20.8	.0000	1	jacketed
0.0122	20.8	.0000	1	jacking
0.0122	20.8	.0000	1	jaded
0.0122	20.8	.0000	1	jag
0.0122	20.8	.0000	1	Jailhouse
0.0122	20.8	.0000	1	Jaloux
0.0122	20.8	.0000	1	Jap
THE PRECEDING WORD TYPE OCCUPIES RANK 68000				
0.0122	20.8	.0000	1	jarad
0.0122	20.8	.0000	1	jaundiced
0.0122	20.8	.0000	1	jaunt
0.0122	20.8	.0000	1	Java's
0.0122	20.8	.0000	1	Jawaharlal
0.0122	20.8	.0000	1	Jaycees
0.0122	20.8	.0000	1	Jean-Luc
0.0122	20.8	.0000	1	Jean-Paul
0.0122	20.8	.0000	1	Jean-Pierre
0.0122	20.8	.0000	1	jeep's
0.0122	20.8	.0000	1	Jekyll-to-Hyde
0.0122	20.8	.0000	1	JELLY
0.0122	20.8	.0000	1	Jennie's
0.0122	20.8	.0000	1	jeopardy
0.0122	20.8	.0000	1	JerseyCity's
0.0122	20.8	.0000	1	Jesup
0.0122	20.8	.0000	1	jet-setters
0.0122	20.8	.0000	1	jet's
0.0122	20.8	.0000	1	jetliners
0.0122	20.8	.0000	1	jetting
0.0122	20.8	.0000	1	jettisons
0.0122	20.8	.0000	1	Jewel
0.0122	20.8	.0000	1	jibing
0.0122	20.8	.0000	1	Jillson's
0.0122	20.8	.0000	1	jims
0.0122	20.8	.0000	1	JLIT
0.0122	20.8	.0000	1	jobbers
0.0122	20.8	.0000	1	Jocko's
0.0122	20.8	.0000	1	JOD
0.0122	20.8	.0000	1	jogs
0.0122	20.8	.0000	1	Johhny's
0.0122	20.8	.0000	1	johnboats
0.0122	20.8	.0000	1	Jordanians
0.0122	20.8	.0000	1	Josip
0.0122	20.8	.0000	1	Joxer
0.0122	20.8	.0000	1	JS
0.0122	20.8	.0000	1	JSH
0.0122	20.8	.0000	1	judgeship
0.0122	20.8	.0000	1	juice-making
0.0122	20.8	.0000	1	Julio
0.0122	20.8	.0000	1	jungle-gym
0.0122	20.8	.0000	1	Junius
0.0122	20.8	.0000	1	junk-car
0.0122	20.8	.0000	1	junky
0.0122	20.8	.0000	1	just-plain-fun
0.0122	20.8	.0000	1	jut-jawed
0.0122	20.8	.0000	1	juxtaposed
0.0122	20.8	.0000	1	Kadar
0.0122	20.8	.0000	1	Kahuku
0.0122	20.8	.0000	1	Kalama
0.0122	20.8	.0000	1	Kalamazoo
0.0122	20.8	.0000	1	Kalashnikov
0.0122	20.8	.0000	1	kaleidoscopes
0.0122	20.8	.0000	1	kaleidoscopic
0.0122	20.8	.0000	1	Kalitta
0.0122	20.8	.0000	1	Kalstrom
0.0122	20.8	.0000	1	Kandy
0.0122	20.8	.0000	1	Kans
0.0122	20.8	.0000	1	Kapp
0.0122	20.8	.0000	1	kaput
0.0122	20.8	.0000	1	Karel
0.0122	20.8	.0000	1	kari
0.0122	20.8	.0000	1	Karwat
0.0122	20.8	.0000	1	kat
0.0122	20.8	.0000	1	Katzenberg
0.0122	20.8	.0000	1	Kaug's
0.0122	20.8	.0000	1	Kay-O
0.0122	20.8	.0000	1	Kazakh
0.0122	20.8	.0000	1	Kazakhs
0.0122	20.8	.0000	1	Keach
0.0122	20.8	.0000	1	keels
0.0122	20.8	.0000	1	Keen
0.0122	20.8	.0000	1	Keen's
0.0122	20.8	.0000	1	Kel
0.0122	20.8	.0000	1	Kellogg's
0.0122	20.8	.0000	1	kelpfish
0.0122	20.8	.0000	1	Kelvinator
0.0122	20.8	.0000	1	Kennecott
0.0122	20.8	.0000	1	Kenyan
0.0122	20.8	.0000	1	Keokee
0.0122	20.8	.0000	1	Kepes
0.0122	20.8	.0000	1	kerchiefs
0.0122	20.8	.0000	1	kerplunk
0.0122	20.8	.0000	1	Kerry's
0.0122	20.8	.0000	1	KeyBiscayne
0.0122	20.8	.0000	1	Keynes
0.0122	20.8	.0000	1	Keystone
0.0122	20.8	.0000	1	keyways
0.0122	20.8	.0000	1	Khabarov
0.0122	20.8	.0000	1	Khabarov's
0.0122	20.8	.0000	1	Khalil's
0.0122	20.8	.0000	1	Khan-style
0.0122	20.8	.0000	1	Khartoum
0.0122	20.8	.0000	1	KH3
0.0122	20.8	.0000	1	kickboards
0.0122	20.8	.0000	1	kidded
0.0122	20.8	.0000	1	kidnaper's
0.0122	20.8	.0000	1	kike
0.0122	20.8	.0000	1	Kikuyu
0.0122	20.8	.0000	1	Killan
THE PRECEDING WORD TYPE OCCUPIES RANK 68100				
0.0122	20.8	.0000	1	Killarney
0.0122	20.8	.0000	1	Killdeer
0.0122	20.8	.0000	1	Killebrew
0.0122	20.8	.0000	1	Kilmarth
0.0122	20.8	.0000	1	Kilmer
0.0122	20.8	.0000	1	kindergarteners
0.0122	20.8	.0000	1	kindlier
0.0122	20.8	.0000	1	kindliest
0.0122	20.8	.0000	1	kingcraft
0.0122	20.8	.0000	1	Kingdom's
0.0122	20.8	.0000	1	Kirgiz
0.0122	20.8	.0000	1	Kissinger's
0.0122	20.8	.0000	1	Kiwanis
0.0122	20.8	.0000	1	klepto
0.0122	20.8	.0000	1	Klinger

U	SFI	D	F	Word Type
0.0122	20.8	.0000	1	Kloman
0.0122	20.8	.0000	1	knife-sharp
0.0122	20.8	.0000	1	knock-back
0.0122	20.8	.0000	1	knock-kneed
0.0122	20.8	.0000	1	knockabout
0.0122	20.8	.0000	1	Knopf
0.0122	20.8	.0000	1	Know-Nothings
0.0122	20.8	.0000	1	Knuckler
0.0122	20.8	.0000	1	Kodiak-bear-class
0.0122	20.8	.0000	1	Kogaku
0.0122	20.8	.0000	1	Kohl's
0.0122	20.8	.0000	1	kongoni
0.0122	20.8	.0000	1	Koni-Stahl
0.0122	20.8	.0000	1	kooks
0.0122	20.8	.0000	1	Koolau
0.0122	20.8	.0000	1	Koreans
0.0122	20.8	.0000	1	Korianinen
0.0122	20.8	.0000	1	Korner
0.0122	20.8	.0000	1	Kororareka
0.0122	20.8	.0000	1	Kotzebue
0.0122	20.8	.0000	1	Koy
0.0122	20.8	.0000	1	Kranz's
0.0122	20.8	.0000	1	Kremlin's
0.0122	20.8	.0000	1	kreplach
0.0122	20.8	.0000	1	Krishnas
0.0122	20.8	.0000	1	Kuchel
0.0122	20.8	.0000	1	kudo
0.0122	20.8	.0000	1	Kullyspell
0.0122	20.8	.0000	1	Kundera
0.0122	20.8	.0000	1	Kundera's
0.0122	20.8	.0000	1	Kupperman
0.0122	20.8	.0000	1	Kurdistan
0.0122	20.8	.0000	1	Kutenais
0.0122	20.8	.0000	1	Kuwait's
0.0122	20.8	.0000	1	Kuwaitis
0.0122	20.8	.0000	1	Kwame
0.0122	20.8	.0000	1	Kylmerth
0.0122	20.8	.0000	1	L-e-r-o-y
0.0122	20.8	.0000	1	L-88
0.0122	20.8	.0000	1	l'ile
0.0122	20.8	.0000	1	LaPorte's
0.0122	20.8	.0000	1	LaRoche's
0.0122	20.8	.0000	1	labor-relations
0.0122	20.8	.0000	1	labs
0.0122	20.8	.0000	1	lace-and-carnation
0.0122	20.8	.0000	1	Lackland
0.0122	20.8	.0000	1	lacquer's
0.0122	20.8	.0000	1	lacquerers
0.0122	20.8	.0000	1	lacquering
0.0122	20.8	.0000	1	LagunaBeach
0.0122	20.8	.0000	1	lake-side
0.0122	20.8	.0000	1	Lambeau
0.0122	20.8	.0000	1	Lamonica
0.0122	20.8	.0000	1	Lanciotti's
0.0122	20.8	.0000	1	land-grant
0.0122	20.8	.0000	1	land-locked
0.0122	20.8	.0000	1	land-management
0.0122	20.8	.0000	1	landing-gear
0.0122	20.8	.0000	1	landloving
0.0122	20.8	.0000	1	Landry's
0.0122	20.8	.0000	1	Landsburg
0.0122	20.8	.0000	1	Langer
0.0122	20.8	.0000	1	Langrenus
0.0122	20.8	.0000	1	Langsley
0.0122	20.8	.0000	1	Laocoon
0.0122	20.8	.0000	1	lapses
0.0122	20.8	.0000	1	Lapwai
0.0122	20.8	.0000	1	larcenous
0.0122	20.8	.0000	1	larder's
0.0122	20.8	.0000	1	large-headed
0.0122	20.8	.0000	1	largemouths
0.0122	20.8	.0000	1	largesse
0.0122	20.8	.0000	1	Lascaux
0.0122	20.8	.0000	1	late-November
0.0122	20.8	.0000	1	late-summer
0.0122	20.8	.0000	1	laterally
0.0122	20.8	.0000	1	laude
0.0122	20.8	.0000	1	laugh-filled
0.0122	20.8	.0000	1	launchers
0.0122	20.8	.0000	1	Lavin
0.0122	20.8	.0000	1	Lawson's
0.0122	20.8	.0000	1	laxity
0.0122	20.8	.0000	1	layoff
0.0122	20.8	.0000	1	Lea
0.0122	20.8	.0000	1	lead-in
THE PRECEDING WORD TYPE OCCUPIES RANK 68200				
0.0122	20.8	.0000	1	Leaders
0.0122	20.8	.0000	1	leaflet
0.0122	20.8	.0000	1	Lean
0.0122	20.8	.0000	1	learn-to-sail
0.0122	20.8	.0000	1	leathery-leafed
0.0122	20.8	.0000	1	Leavitt
0.0122	20.8	.0000	1	leek
0.0122	20.8	.0000	1	Leewards
0.0122	20.8	.0000	1	Leewards'
0.0122	20.8	.0000	1	left-arm
0.0122	20.8	.0000	1	left-field
0.0122	20.8	.0000	1	leftists
0.0122	20.8	.0000	1	Leftists
0.0122	20.8	.0000	1	Leftover
0.0122	20.8	.0000	1	legal-size
0.0122	20.8	.0000	1	legally-elected
0.0122	20.8	.0000	1	legitimately
0.0122	20.8	.0000	1	Leighton's
0.0122	20.8	.0000	1	leitmotiv
0.0122	20.8	.0000	1	Lemhi
0.0122	20.8	.0000	1	Lending
0.0122	20.8	.0000	1	Lenor
0.0122	20.8	.0000	1	Lentil
0.0122	20.8	.0000	1	Lentz
0.0122	20.8	.0000	1	Lenya
0.0122	20.8	.0000	1	Leon's
0.0122	20.8	.0000	1	Leonid
0.0122	20.8	.0000	1	leopard-skin
0.0122	20.8	.0000	1	leopardskins
0.0122	20.8	.0000	1	leotard-like
0.0122	20.8	.0000	1	Leprechaun

U	SFI	D	F	Word Type
0.0122	20.8	.0000	1	less-well-known
0.0122	20.8	.0000	1	letterman
0.0122	20.8	.0000	1	level-compensating
0.0122	20.8	.0000	1	lever-action
0.0122	20.8	.0000	1	Levy
0.0122	20.8	.0000	1	Lewellen
0.0122	20.8	.0000	1	liaison
0.0122	20.8	.0000	1	Liaison
0.0122	20.8	.0000	1	liberal-arts
0.0122	20.8	.0000	1	liberalize
0.0122	20.8	.0000	1	Liberals
0.0122	20.8	.0000	1	libertad
0.0122	20.8	.0000	1	Libertyville
0.0122	20.8	.0000	1	license-holders
0.0122	20.8	.0000	1	Licensed
0.0122	20.8	.0000	1	Lichtenstein's
0.0122	20.8	.0000	1	Lief
0.0122	20.8	.0000	1	Lieut
0.0122	20.8	.0000	1	life-and-death
0.0122	20.8	.0000	1	life-span
0.0122	20.8	.0000	1	lifejacketed
0.0122	20.8	.0000	1	liftoff
0.0122	20.8	.0000	1	light-skinned
0.0122	20.8	.0000	1	light-tan
0.0122	20.8	.0000	1	lightbulb
0.0122	20.8	.0000	1	Lightship
0.0122	20.8	.0000	1	Lilienfield
0.0122	20.8	.0000	1	limbic-lobe
0.0122	20.8	.0000	1	lime-green
0.0122	20.8	.0000	1	Limoges
0.0122	20.8	.0000	1	Lincoln-Mercury
0.0122	20.8	.0000	1	Lincoln-Roosevelt
0.0122	20.8	.0000	1	Linear
0.0122	20.8	.0000	1	linebacker
0.0122	20.8	.0000	1	Linemen
0.0122	20.8	.0000	1	Lingo
0.0122	20.8	.0000	1	liniment
0.0122	20.8	.0000	1	Linnea
0.0122	20.8	.0000	1	linseed-oil
0.0122	20.8	.0000	1	Linville
0.0122	20.8	.0000	1	Liquefied
0.0122	20.8	.0000	1	liquid-level
0.0122	20.8	.0000	1	litera-graphic
0.0122	20.8	.0000	1	Litman
0.0122	20.8	.0000	1	Littlefield
0.0122	20.8	.0000	1	liveable
0.0122	20.8	.0000	1	Liz
0.0122	20.8	.0000	1	Llywelyn
0.0122	20.8	.0000	1	LM'S
0.0122	20.8	.0000	1	load-pulling
0.0122	20.8	.0000	1	loanable
0.0122	20.8	.0000	1	lobsterback
0.0122	20.8	.0000	1	locale
0.0122	20.8	.0000	1	Lockheed
0.0122	20.8	.0000	1	Lockheed-Georgia
0.0122	20.8	.0000	1	Lockheed-Georgia's
0.0122	20.8	.0000	1	lockjaw
0.0122	20.8	.0000	1	Lockridge
0.0122	20.8	.0000	1	Lockwood
0.0122	20.8	.0000	1	Loco
0.0122	20.8	.0000	1	lodgepole
0.0122	20.8	.0000	1	Lofchie
0.0122	20.8	.0000	1	Logging
0.0122	20.8	.0000	1	logotype
0.0122	20.8	.0000	1	Loin
0.0122	20.8	.0000	1	Lompoc
0.0122	20.8	.0000	1	Loneliness
0.0122	20.8	.0000	1	Lonely
0.0122	20.8	.0000	1	LongBranch
THE PRECEDING WORD TYPE OCCUPIES RANK 68300				
0.0122	20.8	.0000	1	long-shot
0.0122	20.8	.0000	1	long-simmering
0.0122	20.8	.0000	1	long-sought-after
0.0122	20.8	.0000	1	long-tailed
0.0122	20.8	.0000	1	long-unchallenged
0.0122	20.8	.0000	1	longer-reach
0.0122	20.8	.0000	1	longest-surviving
0.0122	20.8	.0000	1	longs
0.0122	20.8	.0000	1	longshoreman
0.0122	20.8	.0000	1	longshoremen
0.0122	20.8	.0000	1	Look-in
0.0122	20.8	.0000	1	loop-the-loop
0.0122	20.8	.0000	1	loopwind
0.0122	20.8	.0000	1	loose-jointed
0.0122	20.8	.0000	1	loose-tongued
0.0122	20.8	.0000	1	loosing
0.0122	20.8	.0000	1	Lorain
0.0122	20.8	.0000	1	loran
0.0122	20.8	.0000	1	Lorna
0.0122	20.8	.0000	1	lost-time
0.0122	20.8	.0000	1	Lotte
0.0122	20.8	.0000	1	lottery
0.0122	20.8	.0000	1	Lotts
0.0122	20.8	.0000	1	Lotus
0.0122	20.8	.0000	1	loud-and-soft
0.0122	20.8	.0000	1	loudmouthed
0.0122	20.8	.0000	1	Louis-Philippe
0.0122	20.8	.0000	1	Lovat
0.0122	20.8	.0000	1	love-in
0.0122	20.8	.0000	1	loveable
0.0122	20.8	.0000	1	Loved
0.0122	20.8	.0000	1	low-budget
0.0122	20.8	.0000	1	low-cholesterol
0.0122	20.8	.0000	1	low-pitch
0.0122	20.8	.0000	1	low-sodium
0.0122	20.8	.0000	1	loyality
0.0122	20.8	.0000	1	LSU
0.0122	20.8	.0000	1	Lucie-FortMyers
0.0122	20.8	.0000	1	Luckey
0.0122	20.8	.0000	1	luckiest
0.0122	20.8	.0000	1	Ludington
0.0122	20.8	.0000	1	Ludvik
0.0122	20.8	.0000	1	lukewarmly
0.0122	20.8	.0000	1	Lundy
0.0122	20.8	.0000	1	Lundy's
0.0122	20.8	.0000	1	Lycoming
0.0122	20.8	.0000	1	Lydell

U	SFI	D	F	Word Type
0.0122	20.8	.0000	1	Lynch
0.0122	20.8	.0000	1	Lynchburg
0.0122	20.8	.0000	1	Lyonsdale
0.0122	20.8	.0000	1	L4J
0.0122	20.8	.0000	1	L5
0.0122	20.8	.0000	1	M-1
0.0122	20.8	.0000	1	M/T
0.0122	20.8	.0000	1	MacCartans
0.0122	20.8	.0000	1	macaws
0.0122	20.8	.0000	1	Macedonians
0.0122	20.8	.0000	1	macehead
0.0122	20.8	.0000	1	Macgillycuddy's
0.0122	20.8	.0000	1	machine-gun-like
0.0122	20.8	.0000	1	machinelike
0.0122	20.8	.0000	1	Machold
0.0122	20.8	.0000	1	Mackey
0.0122	20.8	.0000	1	Madeiras
0.0122	20.8	.0000	1	Madhukar
0.0122	20.8	.0000	1	Madras
0.0122	20.8	.0000	1	Madsen
0.0122	20.8	.0000	1	Maggie's
0.0122	20.8	.0000	1	magisterially
0.0122	20.8	.0000	1	magpies
0.0122	20.8	.0000	1	Maine-built
0.0122	20.8	.0000	1	Maine's
0.0122	20.8	.0000	1	Maintenance
0.0122	20.8	.0000	1	major-league-stock-car
0.0122	20.8	.0000	1	major-leaguer
0.0122	20.8	.0000	1	Make-up
0.0122	20.8	.0000	1	mako
0.0122	20.8	.0000	1	maktabah
0.0122	20.8	.0000	1	malacologists
0.0122	20.8	.0000	1	maladie
0.0122	20.8	.0000	1	maladroit
0.0122	20.8	.0000	1	male-female
0.0122	20.8	.0000	1	maleness
0.0122	20.8	.0000	1	malevolently
0.0122	20.8	.0000	1	Maligne
0.0122	20.8	.0000	1	Malinovsky
0.0122	20.8	.0000	1	Mallets
0.0122	20.8	.0000	1	Malraux
0.0122	20.8	.0000	1	Malthusian
0.0122	20.8	.0000	1	maltreatment
0.0122	20.8	.0000	1	Mamas
0.0122	20.8	.0000	1	Mamie's
0.0122	20.8	.0000	1	man-powered
0.0122	20.8	.0000	1	management-consultant
0.0122	20.8	.0000	1	manager's
0.0122	20.8	.0000	1	mananaesque
0.0122	20.8	.0000	1	Mandragora
0.0122	20.8	.0000	1	Mangelsen
0.0122	20.8	.0000	1	maniacal
0.0122	20.8	.0000	1	manic
THE PRECEDING WORD TYPE OCCUPIES RANK 68400				
0.0122	20.8	.0000	1	manicured
0.0122	20.8	.0000	1	Manifesto's
0.0122	20.8	.0000	1	Mankind's
0.0122	20.8	.0000	1	manlihood
0.0122	20.8	.0000	1	Mannean
0.0122	20.8	.0000	1	Manners
0.0122	20.8	.0000	1	mannish
0.0122	20.8	.0000	1	manos
0.0122	20.8	.0000	1	Mans
0.0122	20.8	.0000	1	Manteuffel
0.0122	20.8	.0000	1	mantlepiece
0.0122	20.8	.0000	1	Manufacturers
0.0122	20.8	.0000	1	many-layered
0.0122	20.8	.0000	1	Maravich's
0.0122	20.8	.0000	1	Margolis
0.0122	20.8	.0000	1	maribou
0.0122	20.8	.0000	1	Marina
0.0122	20.8	.0000	1	Marinos
0.0122	20.8	.0000	1	Marketing
0.0122	20.8	.0000	1	Markets
0.0122	20.8	.0000	1	Marlik
0.0122	20.8	.0000	1	marmots
0.0122	20.8	.0000	1	Marner
0.0122	20.8	.0000	1	Marriner
0.0122	20.8	.0000	1	marry-go-round
0.0122	20.8	.0000	1	marshalled
0.0122	20.8	.0000	1	Martian's
0.0122	20.8	.0000	1	Marx's
0.0122	20.8	.0000	1	Maryann
0.0122	20.8	.0000	1	Maryann's
0.0122	20.8	.0000	1	mascara
0.0122	20.8	.0000	1	Maserati
0.0122	20.8	.0000	1	Maslowski
0.0122	20.8	.0000	1	Masonic
0.0122	20.8	.0000	1	Masque
0.0122	20.8	.0000	1	masquerading
0.0122	20.8	.0000	1	Massachusetts'
0.0122	20.8	.0000	1	Massachusetts's
0.0122	20.8	.0000	1	Masson
0.0122	20.8	.0000	1	masturbation
0.0122	20.8	.0000	1	mate-selection
0.0122	20.8	.0000	1	Mateos
0.0122	20.8	.0000	1	materialistic
0.0122	20.8	.0000	1	materialized
0.0122	20.8	.0000	1	Matsushita
0.0122	20.8	.0000	1	matzo-ball
0.0122	20.8	.0000	1	Mau-Mau
0.0122	20.8	.0000	1	Mawson
0.0122	20.8	.0000	1	Maxey
0.0122	20.8	.0000	1	maxima
0.0122	20.8	.0000	1	MAYBE
0.0122	20.8	.0000	1	Mayberry
0.0122	20.8	.0000	1	Maynard
0.0122	20.8	.0000	1	Mazatzal
0.0122	20.8	.0000	1	Maze
0.0122	20.8	.0000	1	Maziere
0.0122	20.8	.0000	1	Maziere's
0.0122	20.8	.0000	1	Mazmanian
0.0122	20.8	.0000	1	McAfee
0.0122	20.8	.0000	1	McCaffrey
0.0122	20.8	.0000	1	McCay
0.0122	20.8	.0000	1	McChesney
0.0122	20.8	.0000	1	McCready

U	SFI	D	F	Word Type
0.0122	20.8	.0000	1	McCullough
0.0122	20.8	.0000	1	McDougal's
0.0122	20.8	.0000	1	McEwen
0.0122	20.8	.0000	1	McFarland
0.0122	20.8	.0000	1	McGillicutty
0.0122	20.8	.0000	1	McGraw-Hill
0.0122	20.8	.0000	1	McIlhenney
0.0122	20.8	.0000	1	McLains
0.0122	20.8	.0000	1	McLaren
0.0122	20.8	.0000	1	McLeave
0.0122	20.8	.0000	1	McMahon
0.0122	20.8	.0000	1	McQueen
0.0122	20.8	.0000	1	Meanies
0.0122	20.8	.0000	1	med
0.0122	20.8	.0000	1	Medicare
0.0122	20.8	.0000	1	Medicated
0.0122	20.8	.0000	1	Meehanite
0.0122	20.8	.0000	1	Meer
0.0122	20.8	.0000	1	Meier
0.0122	20.8	.0000	1	Meinhardt
0.0122	20.8	.0000	1	melancholic
0.0122	20.8	.0000	1	melange
0.0122	20.8	.0000	1	Melburn
0.0122	20.8	.0000	1	meld
0.0122	20.8	.0000	1	melodramatically
0.0122	20.8	.0000	1	melodrame
0.0122	20.8	.0000	1	Melon
0.0122	20.8	.0000	1	Melrakkasletta
0.0122	20.8	.0000	1	Member
0.0122	20.8	.0000	1	memento
0.0122	20.8	.0000	1	memorialized
0.0122	20.8	.0000	1	memos
0.0122	20.8	.0000	1	mendacity
0.0122	20.8	.0000	1	mental-hospital
0.0122	20.8	.0000	1	mentality
0.0122	20.8	.0000	1	Mercer
0.0122	20.8	.0000	1	Mercilessly
THE PRECEDING WORD TYPE OCCUPIES RANK 68500				
0.0122	20.8	.0000	1	Merrick
0.0122	20.8	.0000	1	Merrifield
0.0122	20.8	.0000	1	Messer
0.0122	20.8	.0000	1	Messier
0.0122	20.8	.0000	1	Messieurs
0.0122	20.8	.0000	1	metallastic
0.0122	20.8	.0000	1	Metromedia
0.0122	20.8	.0000	1	Meuse-Argonne
0.0122	20.8	.0000	1	Michelle's
0.0122	20.8	.0000	1	mid-September
0.0122	20.8	.0000	1	mid-Winter
0.0122	20.8	.0000	1	mid-channel
0.0122	20.8	.0000	1	mid-country
0.0122	20.8	.0000	1	mid-course
0.0122	20.8	.0000	1	mid-state
0.0122	20.8	.0000	1	mid-1930's
0.0122	20.8	.0000	1	midcourse
0.0122	20.8	.0000	1	middle-career
0.0122	20.8	.0000	1	Middlesex
0.0122	20.8	.0000	1	middleweight
0.0122	20.8	.0000	1	middling
0.0122	20.8	.0000	1	Mideast
0.0122	20.8	.0000	1	midnight-blue
0.0122	20.8	.0000	1	Midwesterner
0.0122	20.8	.0000	1	midyear
0.0122	20.8	.0000	1	Might
0.0122	20.8	.0000	1	mignon
0.0122	20.8	.0000	1	migrant-worker
0.0122	20.8	.0000	1	miked
0.0122	20.8	.0000	1	mild-mannered
0.0122	20.8	.0000	1	mile-and-a-half-long
0.0122	20.8	.0000	1	mile-deep
0.0122	20.8	.0000	1	mile-thick
0.0122	20.8	.0000	1	Milford
0.0122	20.8	.0000	1	milieu
0.0122	20.8	.0000	1	milieus
0.0122	20.8	.0000	1	militancy
0.0122	20.8	.0000	1	militants'
0.0122	20.8	.0000	1	military-industrial
0.0122	20.8	.0000	1	military-rocket
0.0122	20.8	.0000	1	mill's
0.0122	20.8	.0000	1	milliseconds
0.0122	20.8	.0000	1	Millward
0.0122	20.8	.0000	1	Milne's
0.0122	20.8	.0000	1	Mime
0.0122	20.8	.0000	1	Mimi's
0.0122	20.8	.0000	1	mind-set
0.0122	20.8	.0000	1	minefield
0.0122	20.8	.0000	1	mineralogist
0.0122	20.8	.0000	1	minesweeper
0.0122	20.8	.0000	1	Mini-Cooper
0.0122	20.8	.0000	1	mini-golf
0.0122	20.8	.0000	1	mini-kite
0.0122	20.8	.0000	1	mini-loaves
0.0122	20.8	.0000	1	mini-parks
0.0122	20.8	.0000	1	mini-sanctuary
0.0122	20.8	.0000	1	mini-skirt
0.0122	20.8	.0000	1	mini-skirts
0.0122	20.8	.0000	1	Miniatures
0.0122	20.8	.0000	1	Minimals
0.0122	20.8	.0000	1	minirecession
0.0122	20.8	.0000	1	miniskirted
0.0122	20.8	.0000	1	miniskirts
0.0122	20.8	.0000	1	Minkegizis
0.0122	20.8	.0000	1	Minnesotan
0.0122	20.8	.0000	1	Minto
0.0122	20.8	.0000	1	minute-by-minute
0.0122	20.8	.0000	1	minutiae
0.0122	20.8	.0000	1	minx
0.0122	20.8	.0000	1	Miquelle
0.0122	20.8	.0000	1	Misbegotten
0.0122	20.8	.0000	1	misconstrued
0.0122	20.8	.0000	1	misfire
0.0122	20.8	.0000	1	Mishe-Nahma
0.0122	20.8	.0000	1	misinterpretations
0.0122	20.8	.0000	1	mismatches
0.0122	20.8	.0000	1	misquotation
0.0122	20.8	.0000	1	misquoted
0.0122	20.8	.0000	1	misrepresented

U	SFI	D	F	Word Type
0.0122	20.8	.0000	1	misshapened
0.0122	20.8	.0000	1	Missouri-Kansas-Texas
0.0122	20.8	.0000	1	Missy's
0.0122	20.8	.0000	1	MIT
0.0122	20.8	.0000	1	Mitchell-Finch
0.0122	20.8	.0000	1	Mitsubishi
0.0122	20.8	.0000	1	Mitterrand
0.0122	20.8	.0000	1	Mizar's
0.0122	20.8	.0000	1	mobilize
0.0122	20.8	.0000	1	mobsman's
0.0122	20.8	.0000	1	Mod
0.0122	20.8	.0000	1	modacrylic
0.0122	20.8	.0000	1	model-A
0.0122	20.8	.0000	1	Model-As
0.0122	20.8	.0000	1	Modified
0.0122	20.8	.0000	1	Moeller
0.0122	20.8	.0000	1	Mogollon
0.0122	20.8	.0000	1	moistly
0.0122	20.8	.0000	1	moldlike
0.0122	20.8	.0000	1	momento
0.0122	20.8	.0000	1	Monets

THE PRECEDING WORD TYPE OCCUPIES RANK 68600

U	SFI	D	F	Word Type
0.0122	20.8	.0000	1	MONEY
0.0122	20.8	.0000	1	money-bearing
0.0122	20.8	.0000	1	mongeese
0.0122	20.8	.0000	1	Mongolian-Chinese
0.0122	20.8	.0000	1	monkey-like
0.0122	20.8	.0000	1	Monkey's
0.0122	20.8	.0000	1	monofilament
0.0122	20.8	.0000	1	monoliths
0.0122	20.8	.0000	1	monopolized
0.0122	20.8	.0000	1	Montevideo's
0.0122	20.8	.0000	1	Montini
0.0122	20.8	.0000	1	Montreat
0.0122	20.8	.0000	1	Monts-deserts
0.0122	20.8	.0000	1	Monty
0.0122	20.8	.0000	1	MONY'S
0.0122	20.8	.0000	1	moon-magnet
0.0122	20.8	.0000	1	moonquake
0.0122	20.8	.0000	1	moonquakes
0.0122	20.8	.0000	1	moonwalk
0.0122	20.8	.0000	1	moonward
0.0122	20.8	.0000	1	moppy-haired
0.0122	20.8	.0000	1	Moratorium
0.0122	20.8	.0000	1	morbidly
0.0122	20.8	.0000	1	more-conservative
0.0122	20.8	.0000	1	more-elaborate
0.0122	20.8	.0000	1	more-or-less
0.0122	20.8	.0000	1	more-than-liberal
0.0122	20.8	.0000	1	Morelos
0.0122	20.8	.0000	1	Morgen
0.0122	20.8	.0000	1	Morne
0.0122	20.8	.0000	1	morning-staff
0.0122	20.8	.0000	1	Morrill
0.0122	20.8	.0000	1	Morrow
0.0122	20.8	.0000	1	mortis
0.0122	20.8	.0000	1	Mosca
0.0122	20.8	.0000	1	Moth's
0.0122	20.8	.0000	1	mothers-in-law
0.0122	20.8	.0000	1	motivates
0.0122	20.8	.0000	1	motorcars
0.0122	20.8	.0000	1	motorcyclists
0.0122	20.8	.0000	1	Motordrome
0.0122	20.8	.0000	1	MOTORS
0.0122	20.8	.0000	1	mottling
0.0122	20.8	.0000	1	Mougins
0.0122	20.8	.0000	1	MountWashington
0.0122	20.8	.0000	1	Mountaineers
0.0122	20.8	.0000	1	mousery
0.0122	20.8	.0000	1	moustaches
0.0122	20.8	.0000	1	mouthwash
0.0122	20.8	.0000	1	movie-book
0.0122	20.8	.0000	1	movie-dromes
0.0122	20.8	.0000	1	movie-mag
0.0122	20.8	.0000	1	movie-mural
0.0122	20.8	.0000	1	movie's
0.0122	20.8	.0000	1	Movies
0.0122	20.8	.0000	1	Moynahan
0.0122	20.8	.0000	1	much-feared
0.0122	20.8	.0000	1	much-maligned
0.0122	20.8	.0000	1	Muff's
0.0122	20.8	.0000	1	Mugur
0.0122	20.8	.0000	1	Muh-koons'
0.0122	20.8	.0000	1	muh-zay
0.0122	20.8	.0000	1	mule-drawn
0.0122	20.8	.0000	1	muleriders
0.0122	20.8	.0000	1	mulling
0.0122	20.8	.0000	1	multi-lane
0.0122	20.8	.0000	1	multiethnic
0.0122	20.8	.0000	1	multilateral
0.0122	20.8	.0000	1	multiple-stage
0.0122	20.8	.0000	1	multipurpose
0.0122	20.8	.0000	1	Mumy
0.0122	20.8	.0000	1	munch-and-crunch
0.0122	20.8	.0000	1	Munson's
0.0122	20.8	.0000	1	murder-stoppers
0.0122	20.8	.0000	1	Murderers'
0.0122	20.8	.0000	1	murderously
0.0122	20.8	.0000	1	Murex
0.0122	20.8	.0000	1	Muscovy
0.0122	20.8	.0000	1	Musee
0.0122	20.8	.0000	1	muskeg
0.0122	20.8	.0000	1	Muskiejump's
0.0122	20.8	.0000	1	Mutual
0.0122	20.8	.0000	1	muzzle-loader
0.0122	20.8	.0000	1	muzzle-loaders
0.0122	20.8	.0000	1	mynah
0.0122	20.8	.0000	1	myrmidons
0.0122	20.8	.0000	1	mythmaking
0.0122	20.8	.0000	1	NASA's
0.0122	20.8	.0000	1	NY
0.0122	20.8	.0000	1	NYC
0.0122	20.8	.0000	1	N-10Y
0.0122	20.8	.0000	1	NAB
0.0122	20.8	.0000	1	Nabarro
0.0122	20.8	.0000	1	nabbed
0.0122	20.8	.0000	1	Nacionales
0.0122	20.8	.0000	1	Nagafuchi
0.0122	20.8	.0000	1	NAIA
0.0122	20.8	.0000	1	Nailles's
0.0122	20.8	.0000	1	Naismith
0.0122	20.8	.0000	1	naisty

THE PRECEDING WORD TYPE OCCUPIES RANK 68700

U	SFI	D	F	Word Type
0.0122	20.8	.0000	1	naivete
0.0122	20.8	.0000	1	Nakamura's
0.0122	20.8	.0000	1	namecalling
0.0122	20.8	.0000	1	Named
0.0122	20.8	.0000	1	narcissism
0.0122	20.8	.0000	1	narrator's
0.0122	20.8	.0000	1	NASA'S
0.0122	20.8	.0000	1	Naselle
0.0122	20.8	.0000	1	Nasser-oriented
0.0122	20.8	.0000	1	Natick
0.0122	20.8	.0000	1	national-security
0.0122	20.8	.0000	1	nature-watching
0.0122	20.8	.0000	1	Naugahyde
0.0122	20.8	.0000	1	nauseous
0.0122	20.8	.0000	1	Navaholand's
0.0122	20.8	.0000	1	Navarro
0.0122	20.8	.0000	1	navigates
0.0122	20.8	.0000	1	navy-bean
0.0122	20.8	.0000	1	Nazionale
0.0122	20.8	.0000	1	NBC'S
0.0122	20.8	.0000	1	NCAA
0.0122	20.8	.0000	1	NCBC'S
0.0122	20.8	.0000	1	Ne
0.0122	20.8	.0000	1	near-Pentecostal
0.0122	20.8	.0000	1	near-mink
0.0122	20.8	.0000	1	near-stock
0.0122	20.8	.0000	1	Neave
0.0122	20.8	.0000	1	neckbones
0.0122	20.8	.0000	1	necking
0.0122	20.8	.0000	1	needful
0.0122	20.8	.0000	1	needle-bearing
0.0122	20.8	.0000	1	needleful
0.0122	20.8	.0000	1	negotiators'
0.0122	20.8	.0000	1	negritude
0.0122	20.8	.0000	1	Nehru
0.0122	20.8	.0000	1	Neighborhood
0.0122	20.8	.0000	1	neighborhood-size
0.0122	20.8	.0000	1	nemesis
0.0122	20.8	.0000	1	neo-Dada
0.0122	20.8	.0000	1	nerve-jangling
0.0122	20.8	.0000	1	networks'
0.0122	20.8	.0000	1	neutron-activation
0.0122	20.8	.0000	1	NewBethel's
0.0122	20.8	.0000	1	NewSeabury
0.0122	20.8	.0000	1	NewYorkCrusade
0.0122	20.8	.0000	1	new-old
0.0122	20.8	.0000	1	Newfield
0.0122	20.8	.0000	1	newsboys
0.0122	20.8	.0000	1	Newsweek's
0.0122	20.8	.0000	1	NFL'S
0.0122	20.8	.0000	1	Ngamia
0.0122	20.8	.0000	1	ngamia
0.0122	20.8	.0000	1	NHL
0.0122	20.8	.0000	1	NHRA
0.0122	20.8	.0000	1	NiagaraFalls
0.0122	20.8	.0000	1	nick-name
0.0122	20.8	.0000	1	Nickel
0.0122	20.8	.0000	1	Nicks
0.0122	20.8	.0000	1	Nielsen
0.0122	20.8	.0000	1	Niggers
0.0122	20.8	.0000	1	night-flier
0.0122	20.8	.0000	1	night-flying
0.0122	20.8	.0000	1	night-hidden
0.0122	20.8	.0000	1	nightclub
0.0122	20.8	.0000	1	Nihoa
0.0122	20.8	.0000	1	nimble-footed
0.0122	20.8	.0000	1	nimbleness
0.0122	20.8	.0000	1	nimrods
0.0122	20.8	.0000	1	nine-hole
0.0122	20.8	.0000	1	nine-hours
0.0122	20.8	.0000	1	nine-thrity
0.0122	20.8	.0000	1	nine-volt
0.0122	20.8	.0000	1	nineteen-sixties
0.0122	20.8	.0000	1	niobate
0.0122	20.8	.0000	1	Nipper's
0.0122	20.8	.0000	1	Nipsey
0.0122	20.8	.0000	1	nitpickers
0.0122	20.8	.0000	1	Nittany
0.0122	20.8	.0000	1	Nixons
0.0122	20.8	.0000	1	No-Cal
0.0122	20.8	.0000	1	no-ball
0.0122	20.8	.0000	1	no-go
0.0122	20.8	.0000	1	no-hit
0.0122	20.8	.0000	1	no-loss
0.0122	20.8	.0000	1	no-man's
0.0122	20.8	.0000	1	no-man's-land
0.0122	20.8	.0000	1	no-nonsense
0.0122	20.8	.0000	1	nobilis
0.0122	20.8	.0000	1	noddies
0.0122	20.8	.0000	1	noisemakers
0.0122	20.8	.0000	1	non-Alpine
0.0122	20.8	.0000	1	non-Catholic
0.0122	20.8	.0000	1	non-Scouts
0.0122	20.8	.0000	1	non-farm
0.0122	20.8	.0000	1	non-physical
0.0122	20.8	.0000	1	non-profit
0.0122	20.8	.0000	1	non-stock
0.0122	20.8	.0000	1	nonchalance
0.0122	20.8	.0000	1	nonchurched
0.0122	20.8	.0000	1	noncontroversial

THE PRECEDING WORD TYPE OCCUPIES RANK 68800

U	SFI	D	F	Word Type
0.0122	20.8	.0000	1	nondealer
0.0122	20.8	.0000	1	nonflammability
0.0122	20.8	.0000	1	noninterference
0.0122	20.8	.0000	1	noninvolvement
0.0122	20.8	.0000	1	nonnative
0.0122	20.8	.0000	1	nonpolitical
0.0122	20.8	.0000	1	nonrelatives
0.0122	20.8	.0000	1	nonsanctioned
0.0122	20.8	.0000	1	nontoxic
0.0122	20.8	.0000	1	nontoxicity
0.0122	20.8	.0000	1	Nonviolent
0.0122	20.8	.0000	1	noooo
0.0122	20.8	.0000	1	NORAD
0.0122	20.8	.0000	1	Norelco-built
0.0122	20.8	.0000	1	Norelco's
0.0122	20.8	.0000	1	NorthHollywood
0.0122	20.8	.0000	1	north-country
0.0122	20.8	.0000	1	north-to-south
0.0122	20.8	.0000	1	Northcliffe
0.0122	20.8	.0000	1	northerns
0.0122	20.8	.0000	1	northing
0.0122	20.8	.0000	1	northwoods
0.0122	20.8	.0000	1	nosedive
0.0122	20.8	.0000	1	not-fully-seated
0.0122	20.8	.0000	1	not-so-lean
0.0122	20.8	.0000	1	not-yet-born
0.0122	20.8	.0000	1	novel's
0.0122	20.8	.0000	1	Novelist
0.0122	20.8	.0000	1	now-dead
0.0122	20.8	.0000	1	now-expendable
0.0122	20.8	.0000	1	now-forgotten
0.0122	20.8	.0000	1	noys
0.0122	20.8	.0000	1	NPPC
0.0122	20.8	.0000	1	nuclear-electric
0.0122	20.8	.0000	1	nuclear-nonproliferation
0.0122	20.8	.0000	1	Nudge
0.0122	20.8	.0000	1	nudity
0.0122	20.8	.0000	1	nukes
0.0122	20.8	.0000	1	Nuns
0.0122	20.8	.0000	1	nuts-and-bolts
0.0122	20.8	.0000	1	OFallon
0.0122	20.8	.0000	1	000000oooo
0.0122	20.8	.0000	1	O-ring-sealed
0.0122	20.8	.0000	1	O'Boyle
0.0122	20.8	.0000	1	O'Casey
0.0122	20.8	.0000	1	O'Casey's
0.0122	20.8	.0000	1	O'Hare
0.0122	20.8	.0000	1	O'Leary
0.0122	20.8	.0000	1	O'Learys'
0.0122	20.8	.0000	1	O'Neil's
0.0122	20.8	.0000	1	Oakland's
0.0122	20.8	.0000	1	oarmen
0.0122	20.8	.0000	1	OB'S**
0.0122	20.8	.0000	1	Obed's
0.0122	20.8	.0000	1	Ober
0.0122	20.8	.0000	1	objectivity
0.0122	20.8	.0000	1	objets
0.0122	20.8	.0000	1	obliteration
0.0122	20.8	.0000	1	obnoxious
0.0122	20.8	.0000	1	obolinqui
0.0122	20.8	.0000	1	obscenities
0.0122	20.8	.0000	1	obscenity
0.0122	20.8	.0000	1	obstetrician
0.0122	20.8	.0000	1	obstreperous
0.0122	20.8	.0000	1	obtrusive
0.0122	20.8	.0000	1	obviate
0.0122	20.8	.0000	1	Oceanographer
0.0122	20.8	.0000	1	ocelots
0.0122	20.8	.0000	1	Octavio
0.0122	20.8	.0000	1	odd-job
0.0122	20.8	.0000	1	odor-causing
0.0122	20.8	.0000	1	odoriferous
0.0122	20.8	.0000	1	odour
0.0122	20.8	.0000	1	Oedipe
0.0122	20.8	.0000	1	OEM
0.0122	20.8	.0000	1	oenologists
0.0122	20.8	.0000	1	off-balance
0.0122	20.8	.0000	1	off-camera
0.0122	20.8	.0000	1	off-limits
0.0122	20.8	.0000	1	off-season
0.0122	20.8	.0000	1	off-the-farm
0.0122	20.8	.0000	1	off-trail
0.0122	20.8	.0000	1	OFFER
0.0122	20.8	.0000	1	Official
0.0122	20.8	.0000	1	offscreen
0.0122	20.8	.0000	1	Ogle
0.0122	20.8	.0000	1	ohboyohboy
0.0122	20.8	.0000	1	ohmic
0.0122	20.8	.0000	1	oil-base
0.0122	20.8	.0000	1	oil-powered
0.0122	20.8	.0000	1	oil-well
0.0122	20.8	.0000	1	ok
0.0122	20.8	.0000	1	okayed
0.0122	20.8	.0000	1	Oklahoman
0.0122	20.8	.0000	1	Oklawaha
0.0122	20.8	.0000	1	OLDSMOBILE
0.0122	20.8	.0000	1	oldtimer
0.0122	20.8	.0000	1	oleaginous
0.0122	20.8	.0000	1	Ollan
0.0122	20.8	.0000	1	Olsen's

THE PRECEDING WORD TYPE OCCUPIES RANK 68900

U	SFI	D	F	Word Type
0.0122	20.8	.0000	1	On-Heliopolis
0.0122	20.8	.0000	1	on-her-toes
0.0122	20.8	.0000	1	on-the-road
0.0122	20.8	.0000	1	on-the-roader
0.0122	20.8	.0000	1	onboard
0.0122	20.8	.0000	1	once-a-week
0.0122	20.8	.0000	1	once-arrogant
0.0122	20.8	.0000	1	once-big
0.0122	20.8	.0000	1	one-degree
0.0122	20.8	.0000	1	one-for-four
0.0122	20.8	.0000	1	one-hundred-million
0.0122	20.8	.0000	1	one-minute
0.0122	20.8	.0000	1	one-pound
0.0122	20.8	.0000	1	one-sixth-mile
0.0122	20.8	.0000	1	one-thirtieth
0.0122	20.8	.0000	1	one-upmanship
0.0122	20.8	.0000	1	Ongais
0.0122	20.8	.0000	1	ongoing
0.0122	20.8	.0000	1	Onion
0.0122	20.8	.0000	1	Ono
0.0122	20.8	.0000	1	oomph
0.0122	20.8	.0000	1	Open-ended
0.0122	20.8	.0000	1	open-header
0.0122	20.8	.0000	1	open-up
0.0122	20.8	.0000	1	openness
0.0122	20.8	.0000	1	opiate
0.0122	20.8	.0000	1	opiates
0.0122	20.8	.0000	1	Opie
0.0122	20.8	.0000	1	Opossum
0.0122	20.8	.0000	1	Opperman
0.0122	20.8	.0000	1	opposers
0.0122	20.8	.0000	1	oppress
0.0122	20.8	.0000	1	OPPY
0.0122	20.8	.0000	1	Opry
0.0122	20.8	.0000	1	optically
0.0122	20.8	.0000	1	optimological
0.0122	20.8	.0000	1	ORANGE-peel
0.0122	20.8	.0000	1	Ordaz
0.0122	20.8	.0000	1	order's
0.0122	20.8	.0000	1	Oregonians
0.0122	20.8	.0000	1	Oreille's
0.0122	20.8	.0000	1	organ's
0.0122	20.8	.0000	1	Organizations
0.0122	20.8	.0000	1	orgiastic
0.0122	20.8	.0000	1	orientation
0.0122	20.8	.0000	1	Origami
0.0122	20.8	.0000	1	originator
0.0122	20.8	.0000	1	Orinda
0.0122	20.8	.0000	1	Orinda's
0.0122	20.8	.0000	1	Orlu
0.0122	20.8	.0000	1	Orly
0.0122	20.8	.0000	1	Orpington
0.0122	20.8	.0000	1	Orr
0.0122	20.8	.0000	1	orthodoxy
0.0122	20.8	.0000	1	Orwell's
0.0122	20.8	.0000	1	oscillates
0.0122	20.8	.0000	1	Oskar
0.0122	20.8	.0000	1	Osteen
0.0122	20.8	.0000	1	Ostwald
0.0122	20.8	.0000	1	other-wordly
0.0122	20.8	.0000	1	Otsego
0.0122	20.8	.0000	1	otter's
0.0122	20.8	.0000	1	oui
0.0122	20.8	.0000	1	ourself
0.0122	20.8	.0000	1	ousting
0.0122	20.8	.0000	1	out-of-staters
0.0122	20.8	.0000	1	outasight
0.0122	20.8	.0000	1	outfitter
0.0122	20.8	.0000	1	outfitters-guides
0.0122	20.8	.0000	1	outflow
0.0122	20.8	.0000	1	outgo
0.0122	20.8	.0000	1	outpatient
0.0122	20.8	.0000	1	outpoll
0.0122	20.8	.0000	1	outrageously
0.0122	20.8	.0000	1	outraging
0.0122	20.8	.0000	1	outreach
0.0122	20.8	.0000	1	outsize
0.0122	20.8	.0000	1	outspokenly
0.0122	20.8	.0000	1	outta
0.0122	20.8	.0000	1	ouzel
0.0122	20.8	.0000	1	over-anxious
0.0122	20.8	.0000	1	over-long
0.0122	20.8	.0000	1	over-the-counter
0.0122	20.8	.0000	1	over-the-road
0.0122	20.8	.0000	1	overabundant
0.0122	20.8	.0000	1	overblown
0.0122	20.8	.0000	1	Overcome
0.0122	20.8	.0000	1	overdrive
0.0122	20.8	.0000	1	overdriving
0.0122	20.8	.0000	1	overhang
0.0122	20.8	.0000	1	overplayed
0.0122	20.8	.0000	1	overpopulated
0.0122	20.8	.0000	1	overriders
0.0122	20.8	.0000	1	overseer's
0.0122	20.8	.0000	1	overshadow
0.0122	20.8	.0000	1	overtaxing
0.0122	20.8	.0000	1	overweening
0.0122	20.8	.0000	1	owl-like
0.0122	20.8	.0000	1	oxbow
0.0122	20.8	.0000	1	Ozarks

THE PRECEDING WORD TYPE OCCUPIES RANK 69000

U	SFI	D	F	Word Type
0.0122	20.8	.0000	1	PA'S
0.0122	20.8	.0000	1	Paar
0.0122	20.8	.0000	1	Pachacamac
0.0122	20.8	.0000	1	Packing
0.0122	20.8	.0000	1	paddlewheels
0.0122	20.8	.0000	1	Paihia
0.0122	20.8	.0000	1	Paik
0.0122	20.8	.0000	1	Paik's
0.0122	20.8	.0000	1	pain-killers
0.0122	20.8	.0000	1	paint-by-the-number
0.0122	20.8	.0000	1	painterliness
0.0122	20.8	.0000	1	paisano's
0.0122	20.8	.0000	1	Paiute
0.0122	20.8	.0000	1	palatial
0.0122	20.8	.0000	1	Palatka
0.0122	20.8	.0000	1	palazzi
0.0122	20.8	.0000	1	palazzo
0.0122	20.8	.0000	1	pale-faces
0.0122	20.8	.0000	1	Palmellococcus'
0.0122	20.8	.0000	1	Pamir
0.0122	20.8	.0000	1	panaceas
0.0122	20.8	.0000	1	panache
0.0122	20.8	.0000	1	Panasonic
0.0122	20.8	.0000	1	Panic
0.0122	20.8	.0000	1	panjandrum
0.0122	20.8	.0000	1	pants-leg
0.0122	20.8	.0000	1	Papas
0.0122	20.8	.0000	1	paperboard
0.0122	20.8	.0000	1	Pappas'
0.0122	20.8	.0000	1	parachuted
0.0122	20.8	.0000	1	paralleling
0.0122	20.8	.0000	1	paralyzing
0.0122	20.8	.0000	1	Parent-Teacher
0.0122	20.8	.0000	1	Parhart
0.0122	20.8	.0000	1	ParisIsland
0.0122	20.8	.0000	1	Parisians
0.0122	20.8	.0000	1	Parkinson
0.0122	20.8	.0000	1	parodist
0.0122	20.8	.0000	1	Parthenia
0.0122	20.8	.0000	1	participates
0.0122	20.8	.0000	1	participatory
0.0122	20.8	.0000	1	particulates

U	SFI	D	F	Word Type
0.0122	20.8	.0000	1	partified
0.0122	20.8	.0000	1	Pasadella
0.0122	20.8	.0000	1	Paseo
0.0122	20.8	.0000	1	pass-receiving
0.0122	20.8	.0000	1	passbook
0.0122	20.8	.0000	1	passionless
0.0122	20.8	.0000	1	past-due
0.0122	20.8	.0000	1	pastel-hued
0.0122	20.8	.0000	1	Pastore
0.0122	20.8	.0000	1	Pastrengo
0.0122	20.8	.0000	1	patois
0.0122	20.8	.0000	1	patriarchal
0.0122	20.8	.0000	1	patricidal
0.0122	20.8	.0000	1	Paulsen
0.0122	20.8	.0000	1	pauperized
0.0122	20.8	.0000	1	Pavlovich
0.0122	20.8	.0000	1	Pawnees
0.0122	20.8	.0000	1	paychecks
0.0122	20.8	.0000	1	Payload
0.0122	20.8	.0000	1	payload's
0.0122	20.8	.0000	1	Payson
0.0122	20.8	.0000	1	Payson-Pine
0.0122	20.8	.0000	1	Payton's
0.0122	20.8	.0000	1	PBA
0.0122	20.8	.0000	1	pea-vine
0.0122	20.8	.0000	1	peaking
0.0122	20.8	.0000	1	Pear
0.0122	20.8	.0000	1	Pearls
0.0122	20.8	.0000	1	peccaries
0.0122	20.8	.0000	1	pedaling
0.0122	20.8	.0000	1	pedicab
0.0122	20.8	.0000	1	pedicabs
0.0122	20.8	.0000	1	peepin'
0.0122	20.8	.0000	1	Peeples
0.0122	20.8	.0000	1	pelagic
0.0122	20.8	.0000	1	Pelham
0.0122	20.8	.0000	1	Pelvis
0.0122	20.8	.0000	1	Pemetic
0.0122	20.8	.0000	1	pen-pals
0.0122	20.8	.0000	1	peninsula's
0.0122	20.8	.0000	1	Penney
0.0122	20.8	.0000	1	Pennmarva
0.0122	20.8	.0000	1	penstocks
0.0122	20.8	.0000	1	Pentecostal
0.0122	20.8	.0000	1	penthouses
0.0122	20.8	.0000	1	peon
0.0122	20.8	.0000	1	people-eaters
0.0122	20.8	.0000	1	people'd
0.0122	20.8	.0000	1	Pepperland
0.0122	20.8	.0000	1	Peppiatt
0.0122	20.8	.0000	1	per-capita
0.0122	20.8	.0000	1	perceptiveness
0.0122	20.8	.0000	1	percolate
0.0122	20.8	.0000	1	Pergament
0.0122	20.8	.0000	1	Perhaps
0.0122	20.8	.0000	1	Perigron
0.0122	20.8	.0000	1	period-luminosity
0.0122	20.8	.0000	1	periphery

THE PRECEDING WORD TYPE OCCUPIES RANK 69100

U	SFI	D	F	Word Type
0.0122	20.8	.0000	1	permissiveness
0.0122	20.8	.0000	1	permless
0.0122	20.8	.0000	1	permutations
0.0122	20.8	.0000	1	perpetrator
0.0122	20.8	.0000	1	perquisites
0.0122	20.8	.0000	1	Persepolitan
0.0122	20.8	.0000	1	persulphate
0.0122	20.8	.0000	1	Peskay
0.0122	20.8	.0000	1	Pests
0.0122	20.8	.0000	1	pet-food
0.0122	20.8	.0000	1	peters
0.0122	20.8	.0000	1	petitioning
0.0122	20.8	.0000	1	petrel
0.0122	20.8	.0000	1	petrol
0.0122	20.8	.0000	1	Petton
0.0122	20.8	.0000	1	Pfc
0.0122	20.8	.0000	1	phantasmagoric
0.0122	20.8	.0000	1	Phelps
0.0122	20.8	.0000	1	philanderer
0.0122	20.8	.0000	1	philanthropy
0.0122	20.8	.0000	1	Phillies
0.0122	20.8	.0000	1	philosopher-activist
0.0122	20.8	.0000	1	philosophize
0.0122	20.8	.0000	1	phoniness
0.0122	20.8	.0000	1	Photography
0.0122	20.8	.0000	1	photojournalists
0.0122	20.8	.0000	1	phoughsleoti
0.0122	20.8	.0000	1	physical-education
0.0122	20.8	.0000	1	physiography
0.0122	20.8	.0000	1	Physiologist
0.0122	20.8	.0000	1	picaresques
0.0122	20.8	.0000	1	pick-me-up
0.0122	20.8	.0000	1	pickers'
0.0122	20.8	.0000	1	Pickford
0.0122	20.8	.0000	1	pickie
0.0122	20.8	.0000	1	Pickup
0.0122	20.8	.0000	1	pickup-camper
0.0122	20.8	.0000	1	pictoral
0.0122	20.8	.0000	1	picture-book
0.0122	20.8	.0000	1	Pictures'
0.0122	20.8	.0000	1	pie-eating
0.0122	20.8	.0000	1	pigmentation
0.0122	20.8	.0000	1	Pilate-like
0.0122	20.8	.0000	1	pile-driver
0.0122	20.8	.0000	1	Pilots
0.0122	20.8	.0000	1	Pin
0.0122	20.8	.0000	1	pin-oak
0.0122	20.8	.0000	1	Pinchot
0.0122	20.8	.0000	1	pine-lined
0.0122	20.8	.0000	1	pinged
0.0122	20.8	.0000	1	pinheads
0.0122	20.8	.0000	1	pinna
0.0122	20.8	.0000	1	Pinson
0.0122	20.8	.0000	1	pinyons
0.0122	20.8	.0000	1	pipe-rack
0.0122	20.8	.0000	1	pipe-smoking
0.0122	20.8	.0000	1	piquant
0.0122	20.8	.0000	1	piscatorial
0.0122	20.8	.0000	1	Pittsfield
0.0122	20.8	.0000	1	pivots
0.0122	20.8	.0000	1	PL
0.0122	20.8	.0000	1	placards
0.0122	20.8	.0000	1	plagiarism
0.0122	20.8	.0000	1	plagiarize
0.0122	20.8	.0000	1	plagiarizing
0.0122	20.8	.0000	1	Plaid
0.0122	20.8	.0000	1	plainclothesmen
0.0122	20.8	.0000	1	Plaines
0.0122	20.8	.0000	1	plasm
0.0122	20.8	.0000	1	plastic-like
0.0122	20.8	.0000	1	plaudits
0.0122	20.8	.0000	1	Players'
0.0122	20.8	.0000	1	playgoer
0.0122	20.8	.0000	1	playoff
0.0122	20.8	.0000	1	playoffs
0.0122	20.8	.0000	1	playwrighting
0.0122	20.8	.0000	1	pleasantries
0.0122	20.8	.0000	1	plenum
0.0122	20.8	.0000	1	plink-plink
0.0122	20.8	.0000	1	plippty-plop
0.0122	20.8	.0000	1	PLISS
0.0122	20.8	.0000	1	pliz
0.0122	20.8	.0000	1	plotless
0.0122	20.8	.0000	1	ploy
0.0122	20.8	.0000	1	Plug
0.0122	20.8	.0000	1	plugcasting
0.0122	20.8	.0000	1	plumping
0.0122	20.8	.0000	1	plumpish
0.0122	20.8	.0000	1	Plunkett's
0.0122	20.8	.0000	1	plusher
0.0122	20.8	.0000	1	Plutarch
0.0122	20.8	.0000	1	PM'S
0.0122	20.8	.0000	1	Pocatello
0.0122	20.8	.0000	1	pocket-passing
0.0122	20.8	.0000	1	Pocono
0.0122	20.8	.0000	1	poignant
0.0122	20.8	.0000	1	Polacks
0.0122	20.8	.0000	1	polarize
0.0122	20.8	.0000	1	polarizes
0.0122	20.8	.0000	1	pole-vaulting

THE PRECEDING WORD TYPE OCCUPIES RANK 69200

U	SFI	D	F	Word Type
0.0122	20.8	.0000	1	policy-committee
0.0122	20.8	.0000	1	Polident
0.0122	20.8	.0000	1	Polish-Americans
0.0122	20.8	.0000	1	politic
0.0122	20.8	.0000	1	politicking
0.0122	20.8	.0000	1	Pollak
0.0122	20.8	.0000	1	polling
0.0122	20.8	.0000	1	pollsters
0.0122	20.8	.0000	1	pollutants
0.0122	20.8	.0000	1	polyunsaturated
0.0122	20.8	.0000	1	pomes
0.0122	20.8	.0000	1	ponderosas
0.0122	20.8	.0000	1	pontoon-type
0.0122	20.8	.0000	1	pooh-bah
0.0122	20.8	.0000	1	pooped
0.0122	20.8	.0000	1	Popescu
0.0122	20.8	.0000	1	porbeagle
0.0122	20.8	.0000	1	porgy
0.0122	20.8	.0000	1	porker
0.0122	20.8	.0000	1	Porklets
0.0122	20.8	.0000	1	pornography
0.0122	20.8	.0000	1	Porsches
0.0122	20.8	.0000	1	portability
0.0122	20.8	.0000	1	ported
0.0122	20.8	.0000	1	portentous
0.0122	20.8	.0000	1	Portman
0.0122	20.8	.0000	1	portrayals
0.0122	20.8	.0000	1	positioning
0.0122	20.8	.0000	1	possessiveness
0.0122	20.8	.0000	1	possibles
0.0122	20.8	.0000	1	post-fledging
0.0122	20.8	.0000	1	post-season
0.0122	20.8	.0000	1	posterish
0.0122	20.8	.0000	1	postmistress
0.0122	20.8	.0000	1	postpaid
0.0122	20.8	.0000	1	postprandial
0.0122	20.8	.0000	1	Pot
0.0122	20.8	.0000	1	potlicker
0.0122	20.8	.0000	1	Poughkeepsie
0.0122	20.8	.0000	1	powed
0.0122	20.8	.0000	1	Powell's
0.0122	20.8	.0000	1	power-assisted
0.0122	20.8	.0000	1	power-producing
0.0122	20.8	.0000	1	power-train
0.0122	20.8	.0000	1	Powers'
0.0122	20.8	.0000	1	POWS
0.0122	20.8	.0000	1	Powys
0.0122	20.8	.0000	1	practical-minded
0.0122	20.8	.0000	1	practitioners
0.0122	20.8	.0000	1	pragmatist's
0.0122	20.8	.0000	1	Prague's
0.0122	20.8	.0000	1	pre-World
0.0122	20.8	.0000	1	pre-determine
0.0122	20.8	.0000	1	pre-heated
0.0122	20.8	.0000	1	pre-order
0.0122	20.8	.0000	1	precedency
0.0122	20.8	.0000	1	predator-prey
0.0122	20.8	.0000	1	predestined
0.0122	20.8	.0000	1	predicaments
0.0122	20.8	.0000	1	pregame
0.0122	20.8	.0000	1	prejudicing
0.0122	20.8	.0000	1	prelaunch
0.0122	20.8	.0000	1	premed
0.0122	20.8	.0000	1	premeds
0.0122	20.8	.0000	1	Preminger
0.0122	20.8	.0000	1	prepackaged
0.0122	20.8	.0000	1	preparedness
0.0122	20.8	.0000	1	preschool
0.0122	20.8	.0000	1	preschoolers
0.0122	20.8	.0000	1	prescience
0.0122	20.8	.0000	1	Preservation
0.0122	20.8	.0000	1	preservative
0.0122	20.8	.0000	1	Presley's
0.0122	20.8	.0000	1	presupposed
0.0122	20.8	.0000	1	pretechnological
0.0122	20.8	.0000	1	pretender
0.0122	20.8	.0000	1	prettified
0.0122	20.8	.0000	1	price-wage
0.0122	20.8	.0000	1	prideful
0.0122	20.8	.0000	1	Princeton's
0.0122	20.8	.0000	1	Principality
0.0122	20.8	.0000	1	Principals
0.0122	20.8	.0000	1	principals'
0.0122	20.8	.0000	1	prisoners'
0.0122	20.8	.0000	1	prisonlike
0.0122	20.8	.0000	1	pristine
0.0122	20.8	.0000	1	prizewinning
0.0122	20.8	.0000	1	Pro
0.0122	20.8	.0000	1	pro-European
0.0122	20.8	.0000	1	pro-Gaullist
0.0122	20.8	.0000	1	Pro-Quarterback
0.0122	20.8	.0000	1	pro-concentration
0.0122	20.8	.0000	1	processors
0.0122	20.8	.0000	1	proferring
0.0122	20.8	.0000	1	professes
0.0122	20.8	.0000	1	PROFESSORS
0.0122	20.8	.0000	1	proffer
0.0122	20.8	.0000	1	proffering
0.0122	20.8	.0000	1	profundity
0.0122	20.8	.0000	1	program's

THE PRECEDING WORD TYPE OCCUPIES RANK 69300

U	SFI	D	F	Word Type
0.0122	20.8	.0000	1	programed
0.0122	20.8	.0000	1	programmer
0.0122	20.8	.0000	1	Prohibited
0.0122	20.8	.0000	1	proliferate
0.0122	20.8	.0000	1	Promise
0.0122	20.8	.0000	1	promoter
0.0122	20.8	.0000	1	promotional
0.0122	20.8	.0000	1	pronouncements
0.0122	20.8	.0000	1	propjet
0.0122	20.8	.0000	1	proportionally
0.0122	20.8	.0000	1	prosecution-fearing
0.0122	20.8	.0000	1	Prospera
0.0122	20.8	.0000	1	protean
0.0122	20.8	.0000	1	protuberant
0.0122	20.8	.0000	1	Provision
0.0122	20.8	.0000	1	proxemic
0.0122	20.8	.0000	1	pshaw
0.0122	20.8	.0000	1	psyche
0.0122	20.8	.0000	1	psychiatrist's
0.0122	20.8	.0000	1	psyching
0.0122	20.8	.0000	1	psycho-cybernetics
0.0122	20.8	.0000	1	psychoanalysis
0.0122	20.8	.0000	1	psychoanalyst
0.0122	20.8	.0000	1	psychoanalyst's
0.0122	20.8	.0000	1	Psychologists
0.0122	20.8	.0000	1	psychotic
0.0122	20.8	.0000	1	psychotics
0.0122	20.8	.0000	1	PT-76
0.0122	20.8	.0000	1	Ptakovina
0.0122	20.8	.0000	1	puberty
0.0122	20.8	.0000	1	public-maintenance
0.0122	20.8	.0000	1	publicizing
0.0122	20.8	.0000	1	Pucci
0.0122	20.8	.0000	1	Pueblo's
0.0122	20.8	.0000	1	Pugh
0.0122	20.8	.0000	1	pullout
0.0122	20.8	.0000	1	pundits
0.0122	20.8	.0000	1	PURDY'S
0.0122	20.8	.0000	1	pure-bred
0.0122	20.8	.0000	1	Purina
0.0122	20.8	.0000	1	Purina-Taiyo
0.0122	20.8	.0000	1	Puritanical
0.0122	20.8	.0000	1	purpler
0.0122	20.8	.0000	1	purser
0.0122	20.8	.0000	1	purserettes
0.0122	20.8	.0000	1	push/pull
0.0122	20.8	.0000	1	pushbutton
0.0122	20.8	.0000	1	pushrod
0.0122	20.8	.0000	1	putable-in
0.0122	20.8	.0000	1	Putney
0.0122	20.8	.0000	1	puzzlers
0.0122	20.8	.0000	1	Pycope
0.0122	20.8	.0000	1	Pyrrhus
0.0122	20.8	.0000	1	qu'est-ce
0.0122	20.8	.0000	1	quadrennial
0.0122	20.8	.0000	1	Quai
0.0122	20.8	.0000	1	quarter-miling
0.0122	20.8	.0000	1	quarterback's
0.0122	20.8	.0000	1	quarterlies
0.0122	20.8	.0000	1	quartermile
0.0122	20.8	.0000	1	quasi-queasy
0.0122	20.8	.0000	1	quasifederal
0.0122	20.8	.0000	1	Quechuan
0.0122	20.8	.0000	1	queuing
0.0122	20.8	.0000	1	quibble
0.0122	20.8	.0000	1	quick-to-make
0.0122	20.8	.0000	1	quickens
0.0122	20.8	.0000	1	quickie
0.0122	20.8	.0000	1	Quidley
0.0122	20.8	.0000	1	Quintor
0.0122	20.8	.0000	1	Quirinale
0.0122	20.8	.0000	1	Quizword
0.0122	20.8	.0000	1	quotes-within-quotes
0.0122	20.8	.0000	1	Raab
0.0122	20.8	.0000	1	Raccoon's
0.0122	20.8	.0000	1	race-car
0.0122	20.8	.0000	1	racer's
0.0122	20.8	.0000	1	Raceway
0.0122	20.8	.0000	1	racing-power
0.0122	20.8	.0000	1	radar-navigator
0.0122	20.8	.0000	1	radiator-related
0.0122	20.8	.0000	1	radio-telescope
0.0122	20.8	.0000	1	radioing
0.0122	20.8	.0000	1	Radiophysics
0.0122	20.8	.0000	1	radjas
0.0122	20.8	.0000	1	Radman
0.0122	20.8	.0000	1	ragazza
0.0122	20.8	.0000	1	raggedy
0.0122	20.8	.0000	1	ragouts
0.0122	20.8	.0000	1	Rahman
0.0122	20.8	.0000	1	rail-backed
0.0122	20.8	.0000	1	rainbow-hued
0.0122	20.8	.0000	1	rainbow-ribboned
0.0122	20.8	.0000	1	raindrop-shaped
0.0122	20.8	.0000	1	rainsuit
0.0122	20.8	.0000	1	raky
0.0122	20.8	.0000	1	Ralston
0.0122	20.8	.0000	1	rampaged
0.0122	20.8	.0000	1	ramps
0.0122	20.8	.0000	1	rampway

THE PRECEDING WORD TYPE OCCUPIES RANK 69400

U	SFI	D	F	Word Type
0.0122	20.8	.0000	1	rand
0.0122	20.8	.0000	1	rangelands
0.0122	20.8	.0000	1	ranger-naturalists
0.0122	20.8	.0000	1	Rano
0.0122	20.8	.0000	1	ransacked
0.0122	20.8	.0000	1	rantings
0.0122	20.8	.0000	1	rapid's
0.0122	20.8	.0000	1	rapist
0.0122	20.8	.0000	1	Raraku
0.0122	20.8	.0000	1	Rascals
0.0122	20.8	.0000	1	Raskin's
0.0122	20.8	.0000	1	Rasmussen
0.0122	20.8	.0000	1	raspberry-flavored
0.0122	20.8	.0000	1	rat-killing
0.0122	20.8	.0000	1	rats'
0.0122	20.8	.0000	1	Ratterree
0.0122	20.8	.0000	1	Rattle
0.0122	20.8	.0000	1	razed
0.0122	20.8	.0000	1	re-form
0.0122	20.8	.0000	1	re-run
0.0122	20.8	.0000	1	reactor's
0.0122	20.8	.0000	1	Reactors
0.0122	20.8	.0000	1	readmit
0.0122	20.8	.0000	1	ready-to-go
0.0122	20.8	.0000	1	reaffirmation
0.0122	20.8	.0000	1	reaffirms
0.0122	20.8	.0000	1	Reagan's
0.0122	20.8	.0000	1	realtor
0.0122	20.8	.0000	1	reappointed
0.0122	20.8	.0000	1	rear-spring
0.0122	20.8	.0000	1	rearmament
0.0122	20.8	.0000	1	reassessing
0.0122	20.8	.0000	1	reattached
0.0122	20.8	.0000	1	rebelliousness
0.0122	20.8	.0000	1	recalibrating
0.0122	20.8	.0000	1	recapitalize
0.0122	20.8	.0000	1	receptionist
0.0122	20.8	.0000	1	receptor
0.0122	20.8	.0000	1	recharged
0.0122	20.8	.0000	1	rechristened
0.0122	20.8	.0000	1	Recker
0.0122	20.8	.0000	1	reclaimable
0.0122	20.8	.0000	1	reconciled
0.0122	20.8	.0000	1	reconstitute
0.0122	20.8	.0000	1	reconstituted
0.0122	20.8	.0000	1	record-setting
0.0122	20.8	.0000	1	recorder's
0.0122	20.8	.0000	1	recuperation
0.0122	20.8	.0000	1	recuperative
0.0122	20.8	.0000	1	recycling
0.0122	20.8	.0000	1	red-and-gold
0.0122	20.8	.0000	1	red-and-yellow
0.0122	20.8	.0000	1	red-lined
0.0122	20.8	.0000	1	red-roofed
0.0122	20.8	.0000	1	Red-tailed
0.0122	20.8	.0000	1	Redbirds
0.0122	20.8	.0000	1	reddens
0.0122	20.8	.0000	1	reddish-bronze
0.0122	20.8	.0000	1	reddish-purple
0.0122	20.8	.0000	1	Redemptoristine
0.0122	20.8	.0000	1	redevelopment
0.0122	20.8	.0000	1	redirects
0.0122	20.8	.0000	1	redlight
0.0122	20.8	.0000	1	Redmond-Bend
0.0122	20.8	.0000	1	redone
0.0122	20.8	.0000	1	redundant
0.0122	20.8	.0000	1	RedwoodCity
0.0122	20.8	.0000	1	Reeks
0.0122	20.8	.0000	1	reenlistment
0.0122	20.8	.0000	1	reentered
0.0122	20.8	.0000	1	reestablish
0.0122	20.8	.0000	1	reexamination
0.0122	20.8	.0000	1	ref
0.0122	20.8	.0000	1	refectory
0.0122	20.8	.0000	1	reflectance
0.0122	20.8	.0000	1	Reflection
0.0122	20.8	.0000	1	Reforma
0.0122	20.8	.0000	1	reformism
0.0122	20.8	.0000	1	refractive
0.0122	20.8	.0000	1	refresher
0.0122	20.8	.0000	1	refried
0.0122	20.8	.0000	1	refunds
0.0122	20.8	.0000	1	refuted
0.0122	20.8	.0000	1	regeneration
0.0122	20.8	.0000	1	regimented
0.0122	20.8	.0000	1	registrations
0.0122	20.8	.0000	1	regrowth
0.0122	20.8	.0000	1	regurgitated
0.0122	20.8	.0000	1	rehashed
0.0122	20.8	.0000	1	rehashes
0.0122	20.8	.0000	1	reheated
0.0122	20.8	.0000	1	rehired
0.0122	20.8	.0000	1	Reid
0.0122	20.8	.0000	1	reimburse
0.0122	20.8	.0000	1	reinforces
0.0122	20.8	.0000	1	Reinhart
0.0122	20.8	.0000	1	rejetting
0.0122	20.8	.0000	1	rekindle
0.0122	20.8	.0000	1	relaxers
0.0122	20.8	.0000	1	releasible

THE PRECEDING WORD TYPE OCCUPIES RANK 69500

U	SFI	D	F	Word Type
0.0122	20.8	.0000	1	relief's
0.0122	20.8	.0000	1	reliefs
0.0122	20.8	.0000	1	remaking
0.0122	20.8	.0000	1	remanufactured
0.0122	20.8	.0000	1	remarriage

U	SFI	D	F	Word Type
0.0122	20.8	.0000	1	reminisces
0.0122	20.8	.0000	1	remote-controlled
0.0122	20.8	.0000	1	Remy
0.0122	20.8	.0000	1	renewable
0.0122	20.8	.0000	1	renewing
0.0122	20.8	.0000	1	Renoir's
0.0122	20.8	.0000	1	renomination
0.0122	20.8	.0000	1	Renshaw
0.0122	20.8	.0000	1	reorient
0.0122	20.8	.0000	1	repair-cost
0.0122	20.8	.0000	1	repairable
0.0122	20.8	.0000	1	reparations
0.0122	20.8	.0000	1	repatriate
0.0122	20.8	.0000	1	repave
0.0122	20.8	.0000	1	Replay
0.0122	20.8	.0000	1	replaying
0.0122	20.8	.0000	1	replete
0.0122	20.8	.0000	1	report's
0.0122	20.8	.0000	1	Report's
0.0122	20.8	.0000	1	repository
0.0122	20.8	.0000	1	Requiem
0.0122	20.8	.0000	1	rerunning
0.0122	20.8	.0000	1	resenter
0.0122	20.8	.0000	1	resignations
0.0122	20.8	.0000	1	resized
0.0122	20.8	.0000	1	resort-studded
0.0122	20.8	.0000	1	resoundingly
0.0122	20.8	.0000	1	Respect
0.0122	20.8	.0000	1	restaining
0.0122	20.8	.0000	1	restaurant-tearoom
0.0122	20.8	.0000	1	restorer
0.0122	20.8	.0000	1	resubmitted
0.0122	20.8	.0000	1	resurveyed
0.0122	20.8	.0000	1	retails
0.0122	20.8	.0000	1	retaliating
0.0122	20.8	.0000	1	retaliatory
0.0122	20.8	.0000	1	retiree
0.0122	20.8	.0000	1	retirees
0.0122	20.8	.0000	1	retractable
0.0122	20.8	.0000	1	retraction
0.0122	20.8	.0000	1	retrenchment
0.0122	20.8	.0000	1	retrieval
0.0122	20.8	.0000	1	retroactively
0.0122	20.8	.0000	1	Revival
0.0122	20.8	.0000	1	Revivals
0.0122	20.8	.0000	1	revoir
0.0122	20.8	.0000	1	revs
0.0122	20.8	.0000	1	reworking
0.0122	20.8	.0000	1	Reynold
0.0122	20.8	.0000	1	Rhinelanders
0.0122	20.8	.0000	1	Rib
0.0122	20.8	.0000	1	ribbon-tied
0.0122	20.8	.0000	1	RIBS
0.0122	20.8	.0000	1	rich-with-protein
0.0122	20.8	.0000	1	Richter
0.0122	20.8	.0000	1	Rickover's
0.0122	20.8	.0000	1	ridgetop
0.0122	20.8	.0000	1	righthander
0.0122	20.8	.0000	1	righting
0.0122	20.8	.0000	1	rights-of-way
0.0122	20.8	.0000	1	ring-around-a-rosy
0.0122	20.8	.0000	1	ring's
0.0122	20.8	.0000	1	Ringo
0.0122	20.8	.0000	1	rinses
0.0122	20.8	.0000	1	Ripening
0.0122	20.8	.0000	1	riskier
0.0122	20.8	.0000	1	ritualized
0.0122	20.8	.0000	1	Ritz
0.0122	20.8	.0000	1	riverboatmen
0.0122	20.8	.0000	1	road-building
0.0122	20.8	.0000	1	road-racing
0.0122	20.8	.0000	1	road-trips
0.0122	20.8	.0000	1	roadrunner's
0.0122	20.8	.0000	1	Roblee
0.0122	20.8	.0000	1	Rochet
0.0122	20.8	.0000	1	rock-and-brush
0.0122	20.8	.0000	1	rock-group
0.0122	20.8	.0000	1	rock-steady
0.0122	20.8	.0000	1	rocketings
0.0122	20.8	.0000	1	Rocky's
0.0122	20.8	.0000	1	rod-handling
0.0122	20.8	.0000	1	rod-like
0.0122	20.8	.0000	1	Rodehaver
0.0122	20.8	.0000	1	Rodion
0.0122	20.8	.0000	1	roes
0.0122	20.8	.0000	1	Rolfe's
0.0122	20.8	.0000	1	Romani
0.0122	20.8	.0000	1	Rona
0.0122	20.8	.0000	1	Ronnie
0.0122	20.8	.0000	1	Rookie
0.0122	20.8	.0000	1	roomiest
0.0122	20.8	.0000	1	rooming
0.0122	20.8	.0000	1	rootless
0.0122	20.8	.0000	1	ropework
0.0122	20.8	.0000	1	rose-pink
THE PRECEDING WORD TYPE OCCUPIES RANK 69600				
0.0122	20.8	.0000	1	Rosen
0.0122	20.8	.0000	1	Rosenbloom
0.0122	20.8	.0000	1	Rothesay
0.0122	20.8	.0000	1	rotisserie
0.0122	20.8	.0000	1	rotund
0.0122	20.8	.0000	1	Rouge
0.0122	20.8	.0000	1	rough-cut
0.0122	20.8	.0000	1	rough-house
0.0122	20.8	.0000	1	rough-poured
0.0122	20.8	.0000	1	rough-riding
0.0122	20.8	.0000	1	rough-shod
0.0122	20.8	.0000	1	roulade
0.0122	20.8	.0000	1	Roundheads
0.0122	20.8	.0000	1	roustabout
0.0122	20.8	.0000	1	rowan
0.0122	20.8	.0000	1	rowels
0.0122	20.8	.0000	1	Rowland
0.0122	20.8	.0000	1	Royals
0.0122	20.8	.0000	1	Royce's
0.0122	20.8	.0000	1	Royersford
0.0122	20.8	.0000	1	Rozelle
0.0122	20.8	.0000	1	Rs
0.0122	20.8	.0000	1	RS'S
0.0122	20.8	.0000	1	rub-a-dub-dub
0.0122	20.8	.0000	1	rubberized
0.0122	20.8	.0000	1	rubella
0.0122	20.8	.0000	1	Ruby's
0.0122	20.8	.0000	1	Ruger
0.0122	20.8	.0000	1	Rugiati's
0.0122	20.8	.0000	1	ruling-class
0.0122	20.8	.0000	1	Rumania's
0.0122	20.8	.0000	1	rumination
0.0122	20.8	.0000	1	Rumor
0.0122	20.8	.0000	1	rumples
0.0122	20.8	.0000	1	run-it-up-the-flagpole
0.0122	20.8	.0000	1	runner-up
0.0122	20.8	.0000	1	Runners
0.0122	20.8	.0000	1	Rupp
0.0122	20.8	.0000	1	Ruritanian
0.0122	20.8	.0000	1	rusher
0.0122	20.8	.0000	1	Ruspoli
0.0122	20.8	.0000	1	Russias
0.0122	20.8	.0000	1	rusted-out
0.0122	20.8	.0000	1	rustly
0.0122	20.8	.0000	1	Ryland
0.0122	20.8	.0000	1	R9
0.0122	20.8	.0000	1	S&M
0.0122	20.8	.0000	1	S&M's
0.0122	20.8	.0000	1	S-cast
0.0122	20.8	.0000	1	s-s-sir
0.0122	20.8	.0000	1	s-90
0.0122	20.8	.0000	1	saddler
0.0122	20.8	.0000	1	Saf-Guard
0.0122	20.8	.0000	1	Safeguard
0.0122	20.8	.0000	1	Safka
0.0122	20.8	.0000	1	Saguaro
0.0122	20.8	.0000	1	Saidenberg
0.0122	20.8	.0000	1	Saigon's
0.0122	20.8	.0000	1	Sailing
0.0122	20.8	.0000	1	sailmaster
0.0122	20.8	.0000	1	Saint-Jean
0.0122	20.8	.0000	1	Sainte-Marie
0.0122	20.8	.0000	1	sainthood
0.0122	20.8	.0000	1	Sajid
0.0122	20.8	.0000	1	Salada
0.0122	20.8	.0000	1	salaried
0.0122	20.8	.0000	1	sales-order
0.0122	20.8	.0000	1	salesmanship
0.0122	20.8	.0000	1	salinities
0.0122	20.8	.0000	1	Salmon's
0.0122	20.8	.0000	1	salmon's
0.0122	20.8	.0000	1	salmons'
0.0122	20.8	.0000	1	saltbox
0.0122	20.8	.0000	1	SanBernardo
0.0122	20.8	.0000	1	SanLeandro
0.0122	20.8	.0000	1	SanLuis
0.0122	20.8	.0000	1	SanMarino
0.0122	20.8	.0000	1	SanMateo
0.0122	20.8	.0000	1	SanPablo
0.0122	20.8	.0000	1	SanRafael
0.0122	20.8	.0000	1	San-San
0.0122	20.8	.0000	1	sanatorium
0.0122	20.8	.0000	1	sandbars
0.0122	20.8	.0000	1	sandblasted
0.0122	20.8	.0000	1	Sander
0.0122	20.8	.0000	1	Sandoz
0.0122	20.8	.0000	1	sanguinary
0.0122	20.8	.0000	1	Sapirstein
0.0122	20.8	.0000	1	Saragat
0.0122	20.8	.0000	1	Sargent's
0.0122	20.8	.0000	1	sartorial
0.0122	20.8	.0000	1	Sartres
0.0122	20.8	.0000	1	Sassoon's
0.0122	20.8	.0000	1	Satchel
0.0122	20.8	.0000	1	SAUCY
0.0122	20.8	.0000	1	savaged
0.0122	20.8	.0000	1	savored
0.0122	20.8	.0000	1	saw-duty
0.0122	20.8	.0000	1	sawhorses
0.0122	20.8	.0000	1	Saylor
THE PRECEDING WORD TYPE OCCUPIES RANK 69700				
0.0122	20.8	.0000	1	SCAA'S
0.0122	20.8	.0000	1	scab-resistant
0.0122	20.8	.0000	1	scallop-edge
0.0122	20.8	.0000	1	Scards
0.0122	20.8	.0000	1	Scarface
0.0122	20.8	.0000	1	scarlet-red
0.0122	20.8	.0000	1	Scatter
0.0122	20.8	.0000	1	SCCA
0.0122	20.8	.0000	1	scene's
0.0122	20.8	.0000	1	Schaeffer
0.0122	20.8	.0000	1	Schiefer
0.0122	20.8	.0000	1	Schifano
0.0122	20.8	.0000	1	Schistocerca
0.0122	20.8	.0000	1	schizo's
0.0122	20.8	.0000	1	schizophrenic
0.0122	20.8	.0000	1	Schleidt
0.0122	20.8	.0000	1	schlepp
0.0122	20.8	.0000	1	Schneider
0.0122	20.8	.0000	1	school-ager
0.0122	20.8	.0000	1	school-bond
0.0122	20.8	.0000	1	schoolman
0.0122	20.8	.0000	1	Schwartz
0.0122	20.8	.0000	1	Schweizer
0.0122	20.8	.0000	1	scintillating
0.0122	20.8	.0000	1	scoots
0.0122	20.8	.0000	1	scorers'
0.0122	20.8	.0000	1	Scorpion's
0.0122	20.8	.0000	1	Scottsdale
0.0122	20.8	.0000	1	scoured-the
0.0122	20.8	.0000	1	Scout-o-rama
0.0122	20.8	.0000	1	Scoutmaster
0.0122	20.8	.0000	1	scouts'
0.0122	20.8	.0000	1	scrambler
0.0122	20.8	.0000	1	scramblers
0.0122	20.8	.0000	1	screenplay
0.0122	20.8	.0000	1	screenwriter
0.0122	20.8	.0000	1	screwless
0.0122	20.8	.0000	1	scrimmaging
0.0122	20.8	.0000	1	scriptural
0.0122	20.8	.0000	1	scriptwriter
0.0122	20.8	.0000	1	scrummaging
0.0122	20.8	.0000	1	scrupulously
0.0122	20.8	.0000	1	Scudder
0.0122	20.8	.0000	1	sculled
0.0122	20.8	.0000	1	sculpted
0.0122	20.8	.0000	1	scuttlebutt
0.0122	20.8	.0000	1	sea-feeding
0.0122	20.8	.0000	1	Seafair
0.0122	20.8	.0000	1	sealed-off
0.0122	20.8	.0000	1	sealife
0.0122	20.8	.0000	1	seamounts
0.0122	20.8	.0000	1	Sean
0.0122	20.8	.0000	1	Sears
0.0122	20.8	.0000	1	seashell
0.0122	20.8	.0000	1	seat-belt
0.0122	20.8	.0000	1	seater
0.0122	20.8	.0000	1	Seattle's
0.0122	20.8	.0000	1	second-autumn
0.0122	20.8	.0000	1	second-baseman
0.0122	20.8	.0000	1	second-generation
0.0122	20.8	.0000	1	second-rate
0.0122	20.8	.0000	1	sects'
0.0122	20.8	.0000	1	Secular
0.0122	20.8	.0000	1	Secunda
0.0122	20.8	.0000	1	seduced
0.0122	20.8	.0000	1	sedulous
0.0122	20.8	.0000	1	seedless
0.0122	20.8	.0000	1	Seeds
0.0122	20.8	.0000	1	Seemed
0.0122	20.8	.0000	1	Seen
0.0122	20.8	.0000	1	Segal
0.0122	20.8	.0000	1	Seguret
0.0122	20.8	.0000	1	seigneur
0.0122	20.8	.0000	1	seismometers
0.0122	20.8	.0000	1	Sejna's
0.0122	20.8	.0000	1	Selena
0.0122	20.8	.0000	1	self-certainty
0.0122	20.8	.0000	1	self-deception
0.0122	20.8	.0000	1	self-deceptively
0.0122	20.8	.0000	1	self-destruction
0.0122	20.8	.0000	1	self-discipline
0.0122	20.8	.0000	1	self-disqualification
0.0122	20.8	.0000	1	self-doubt
0.0122	20.8	.0000	1	self-hatred
0.0122	20.8	.0000	1	self-loathing
0.0122	20.8	.0000	1	self-portrait
0.0122	20.8	.0000	1	self-preservation
0.0122	20.8	.0000	1	self-serving
0.0122	20.8	.0000	1	self-sorrow
0.0122	20.8	.0000	1	self-tapping
0.0122	20.8	.0000	1	Selkirks
0.0122	20.8	.0000	1	seller's
0.0122	20.8	.0000	1	sellout
0.0122	20.8	.0000	1	semaphoring
0.0122	20.8	.0000	1	semi-autobiography
0.0122	20.8	.0000	1	semi-finals
0.0122	20.8	.0000	1	semi-religious
0.0122	20.8	.0000	1	semi-suicidal
0.0122	20.8	.0000	1	semikit
0.0122	20.8	.0000	1	seminaries
THE PRECEDING WORD TYPE OCCUPIES RANK 69800				
0.0122	20.8	.0000	1	seminars
0.0122	20.8	.0000	1	semipro
0.0122	20.8	.0000	1	send-off
0.0122	20.8	.0000	1	Sensenbrenner
0.0122	20.8	.0000	1	Sensory
0.0122	20.8	.0000	1	sensuously
0.0122	20.8	.0000	1	sentimentalism
0.0122	20.8	.0000	1	septuagenarians
0.0122	20.8	.0000	1	sequential
0.0122	20.8	.0000	1	sequined
0.0122	20.8	.0000	1	Serb
0.0122	20.8	.0000	1	sere
0.0122	20.8	.0000	1	serialized
0.0122	20.8	.0000	1	Seronera
0.0122	20.8	.0000	1	serrated
0.0122	20.8	.0000	1	service/repair
0.0122	20.8	.0000	1	sessile
0.0122	20.8	.0000	1	seven-member
0.0122	20.8	.0000	1	seventy-seven-year-old
0.0122	20.8	.0000	1	sex-in-class
0.0122	20.8	.0000	1	sex-in-school
0.0122	20.8	.0000	1	sex-related
0.0122	20.8	.0000	1	sexy
0.0122	20.8	.0000	1	Seydhisfjordhur
0.0122	20.8	.0000	1	Sgt
0.0122	20.8	.0000	1	shadow-box
0.0122	20.8	.0000	1	Shadows
0.0122	20.8	.0000	1	shag
0.0122	20.8	.0000	1	Shakespeares
0.0122	20.8	.0000	1	shallow-reach
0.0122	20.8	.0000	1	shampooing
0.0122	20.8	.0000	1	Shape
0.0122	20.8	.0000	1	shape-up
0.0122	20.8	.0000	1	sharp-lady-teller
0.0122	20.8	.0000	1	sharpshooter's
0.0122	20.8	.0000	1	shaver's
0.0122	20.8	.0000	1	shearwaters
0.0122	20.8	.0000	1	sheave
0.0122	20.8	.0000	1	Shelbys
0.0122	20.8	.0000	1	shell-bearing
0.0122	20.8	.0000	1	shellings
0.0122	20.8	.0000	1	shelterbelt
0.0122	20.8	.0000	1	Shepley
0.0122	20.8	.0000	1	Sher
0.0122	20.8	.0000	1	sherbert
0.0122	20.8	.0000	1	Shilshole
0.0122	20.8	.0000	1	shimmed
0.0122	20.8	.0000	1	shingly
0.0122	20.8	.0000	1	Shinjuku
0.0122	20.8	.0000	1	Shiprock
0.0122	20.8	.0000	1	Shirahama
0.0122	20.8	.0000	1	Shiroma
0.0122	20.8	.0000	1	shlocks
0.0122	20.8	.0000	1	shock's
0.0122	20.8	.0000	1	shockers
0.0122	20.8	.0000	1	Shoji
0.0122	20.8	.0000	1	Shook
0.0122	20.8	.0000	1	shoot-the-looters
0.0122	20.8	.0000	1	shop-lines
0.0122	20.8	.0000	1	shop-owner
0.0122	20.8	.0000	1	shoplifts
0.0122	20.8	.0000	1	shopping's
0.0122	20.8	.0000	1	shopworn
0.0122	20.8	.0000	1	Shorebirds
0.0122	20.8	.0000	1	shorebirds
0.0122	20.8	.0000	1	ShortHills
0.0122	20.8	.0000	1	short-changed
0.0122	20.8	.0000	1	short-cycle
0.0122	20.8	.0000	1	short-duration
0.0122	20.8	.0000	1	short-needled
0.0122	20.8	.0000	1	shortlived
0.0122	20.8	.0000	1	Shorts
0.0122	20.8	.0000	1	shot-peened
0.0122	20.8	.0000	1	show-biz
0.0122	20.8	.0000	1	Shows
0.0122	20.8	.0000	1	shrapnel
0.0122	20.8	.0000	1	shredders
0.0122	20.8	.0000	1	Shrimpy
0.0122	20.8	.0000	1	Shrimpy's
0.0122	20.8	.0000	1	Shubert
0.0122	20.8	.0000	1	shunners
0.0122	20.8	.0000	1	shut-down
0.0122	20.8	.0000	1	Sibiu's
0.0122	20.8	.0000	1	siblings
0.0122	20.8	.0000	1	sidearm
0.0122	20.8	.0000	1	sidestepping
0.0122	20.8	.0000	1	sidewheel
0.0122	20.8	.0000	1	sightseer
0.0122	20.8	.0000	1	Signals
0.0122	20.8	.0000	1	Sigworth
0.0122	20.8	.0000	1	silk-bound
0.0122	20.8	.0000	1	silos
0.0122	20.8	.0000	1	Silvano
0.0122	20.8	.0000	1	SilverSprings
0.0122	20.8	.0000	1	silver-blue
0.0122	20.8	.0000	1	silver-handled
0.0122	20.8	.0000	1	silver-painted
0.0122	20.8	.0000	1	silver-zinc
0.0122	20.8	.0000	1	Simca
0.0122	20.8	.0000	1	Simcox
THE PRECEDING WORD TYPE OCCUPIES RANK 69900				
0.0122	20.8	.0000	1	simple-lever
0.0122	20.8	.0000	1	Sinclair
0.0122	20.8	.0000	1	single-file
0.0122	20.8	.0000	1	single-four
0.0122	20.8	.0000	1	single-lift
0.0122	20.8	.0000	1	single-overhead-camshaft
0.0122	20.8	.0000	1	single-wing
0.0122	20.8	.0000	1	single-witness
0.0122	20.8	.0000	1	singlehandler
0.0122	20.8	.0000	1	singling
0.0122	20.8	.0000	1	Sino-Soviet
0.0122	20.8	.0000	1	siphoned
0.0122	20.8	.0000	1	sitar
0.0122	20.8	.0000	1	sited
0.0122	20.8	.0000	1	Sites
0.0122	20.8	.0000	1	Six-Pack
0.0122	20.8	.0000	1	six-footer
0.0122	20.8	.0000	1	six-hour
0.0122	20.8	.0000	1	sixteen-year-olds
0.0122	20.8	.0000	1	sixth-inning
0.0122	20.8	.0000	1	sixty-year
0.0122	20.8	.0000	1	sixtyish
0.0122	20.8	.0000	1	skater's
0.0122	20.8	.0000	1	skeptically
0.0122	20.8	.0000	1	skeptics
0.0122	20.8	.0000	1	sketchiest
0.0122	20.8	.0000	1	skewbacks
0.0122	20.8	.0000	1	skin-pampering
0.0122	20.8	.0000	1	Skorpios
0.0122	20.8	.0000	1	Skorzeny
0.0122	20.8	.0000	1	skunked
0.0122	20.8	.0000	1	sky-high
0.0122	20.8	.0000	1	skyball
0.0122	20.8	.0000	1	Skylark
0.0122	20.8	.0000	1	skyrocketed
0.0122	20.8	.0000	1	slack-water
0.0122	20.8	.0000	1	slags
0.0122	20.8	.0000	1	slap-shot
0.0122	20.8	.0000	1	slate-gray
0.0122	20.8	.0000	1	sleeping-bag-bed
0.0122	20.8	.0000	1	sleepwalking
0.0122	20.8	.0000	1	slicks
0.0122	20.8	.0000	1	slim-down
0.0122	20.8	.0000	1	slip-in
0.0122	20.8	.0000	1	slit-eyed
0.0122	20.8	.0000	1	slobs
0.0122	20.8	.0000	1	slouches
0.0122	20.8	.0000	1	slough
0.0122	20.8	.0000	1	Slovenia's
0.0122	20.8	.0000	1	sluiced
0.0122	20.8	.0000	1	smallmouth
0.0122	20.8	.0000	1	smart-alecky
0.0122	20.8	.0000	1	Smear
0.0122	20.8	.0000	1	smog-shrouded
0.0122	20.8	.0000	1	Smoggy
0.0122	20.8	.0000	1	smoke-blackened
0.0122	20.8	.0000	1	Smoked
0.0122	20.8	.0000	1	smoked-pork-rib
0.0122	20.8	.0000	1	smolts
0.0122	20.8	.0000	1	smoothworking
0.0122	20.8	.0000	1	snappily
0.0122	20.8	.0000	1	snapping-back
0.0122	20.8	.0000	1	snazzy
0.0122	20.8	.0000	1	snobbism
0.0122	20.8	.0000	1	Snowdon
0.0122	20.8	.0000	1	soap-bubble
0.0122	20.8	.0000	1	sober-eyed
0.0122	20.8	.0000	1	soccer-style
0.0122	20.8	.0000	1	sociological

U	SFI	D	F	Word Type
0.0122	20.8	.0000	1	sofa-bed
0.0122	20.8	.0000	1	soft-ly
0.0122	20.8	.0000	1	soft-pedaled
0.0122	20.8	.0000	1	softface
0.0122	20.8	.0000	1	Soichi
0.0122	20.8	.0000	1	soldiery
0.0122	20.8	.0000	1	solid-bushed
0.0122	20.8	.0000	1	somebody'd
0.0122	20.8	.0000	1	son-of-a-gun
0.0122	20.8	.0000	1	song-birds
0.0122	20.8	.0000	1	Sooners
0.0122	20.8	.0000	1	soph
0.0122	20.8	.0000	1	Sophocles'
0.0122	20.8	.0000	1	sops
0.0122	20.8	.0000	1	Sopwith
0.0122	20.8	.0000	1	sorrowless
0.0122	20.8	.0000	1	sorties
0.0122	20.8	.0000	1	souffle
0.0122	20.8	.0000	1	souffles
0.0122	20.8	.0000	1	soulmates
0.0122	20.8	.0000	1	sound-deadening
0.0122	20.8	.0000	1	soundtrack
0.0122	20.8	.0000	1	soup's
0.0122	20.8	.0000	1	souqs
0.0122	20.8	.0000	1	SouthVietnam's
0.0122	20.8	.0000	1	south-side
0.0122	20.8	.0000	1	south's
0.0122	20.8	.0000	1	Southwesterners
0.0122	20.8	.0000	1	Southworth
0.0122	20.8	.0000	1	Soviet-American
0.0122	20.8	.0000	1	Soviet-Chinese

THE PRECEDING WORD TYPE OCCUPIES RANK 70000

U	SFI	D	F	Word Type
0.0122	20.8	.0000	1	Soviet-built
0.0122	20.8	.0000	1	space-shot
0.0122	20.8	.0000	1	spacers
0.0122	20.8	.0000	1	spaceship's
0.0122	20.8	.0000	1	spacesuits
0.0122	20.8	.0000	1	Spanish-born
0.0122	20.8	.0000	1	Spanky
0.0122	20.8	.0000	1	Spark
0.0122	20.8	.0000	1	Sparks
0.0122	20.8	.0000	1	Sparky's
0.0122	20.8	.0000	1	spas
0.0122	20.8	.0000	1	spate
0.0122	20.8	.0000	1	spates
0.0122	20.8	.0000	1	Speaks
0.0122	20.8	.0000	1	spear-like
0.0122	20.8	.0000	1	spearheaded
0.0122	20.8	.0000	1	spearlike
0.0122	20.8	.0000	1	special-forces
0.0122	20.8	.0000	1	special-summer
0.0122	20.8	.0000	1	Specialist
0.0122	20.8	.0000	1	specialists'
0.0122	20.8	.0000	1	specification
0.0122	20.8	.0000	1	specificity
0.0122	20.8	.0000	1	specs
0.0122	20.8	.0000	1	spectaculars
0.0122	20.8	.0000	1	spectrographic
0.0122	20.8	.0000	1	speculative
0.0122	20.8	.0000	1	speech-writers
0.0122	20.8	.0000	1	speechwriter
0.0122	20.8	.0000	1	Speeds
0.0122	20.8	.0000	1	Speer
0.0122	20.8	.0000	1	Speleology
0.0122	20.8	.0000	1	spenders
0.0122	20.8	.0000	1	Sperry
0.0122	20.8	.0000	1	spews
0.0122	20.8	.0000	1	spider-webbed
0.0122	20.8	.0000	1	spiffiest
0.0122	20.8	.0000	1	spilleth
0.0122	20.8	.0000	1	Spinney
0.0122	20.8	.0000	1	spinsters
0.0122	20.8	.0000	1	Spire
0.0122	20.8	.0000	1	spirituality
0.0122	20.8	.0000	1	Spivenses
0.0122	20.8	.0000	1	splashy
0.0122	20.8	.0000	1	splinter-proof
0.0122	20.8	.0000	1	split-twig
0.0122	20.8	.0000	1	Splits
0.0122	20.8	.0000	1	splotchy
0.0122	20.8	.0000	1	splurge
0.0122	20.8	.0000	1	Spoiler
0.0122	20.8	.0000	1	spoiler
0.0122	20.8	.0000	1	Sponheim
0.0122	20.8	.0000	1	spoofing
0.0122	20.8	.0000	1	spooked
0.0122	20.8	.0000	1	Sport's
0.0122	20.8	.0000	1	sporters
0.0122	20.8	.0000	1	sporting-goods
0.0122	20.8	.0000	1	sportscasters
0.0122	20.8	.0000	1	Sportvan
0.0122	20.8	.0000	1	spotlighted
0.0122	20.8	.0000	1	spotters
0.0122	20.8	.0000	1	spouse
0.0122	20.8	.0000	1	spraddled
0.0122	20.8	.0000	1	Sprague-Martell
0.0122	20.8	.0000	1	spray-throwing
0.0122	20.8	.0000	1	sprees
0.0122	20.8	.0000	1	spring-board
0.0122	20.8	.0000	1	Springfields
0.0122	20.8	.0000	1	SPRINKEL
0.0122	20.8	.0000	1	sprung-open
0.0122	20.8	.0000	1	Spur-Rowell
0.0122	20.8	.0000	1	Sp4
0.0122	20.8	.0000	1	Squad
0.0122	20.8	.0000	1	squadrons
0.0122	20.8	.0000	1	square-tube
0.0122	20.8	.0000	1	squinchy
0.0122	20.8	.0000	1	squirms
0.0122	20.8	.0000	1	squirreling
0.0122	20.8	.0000	1	SRO
0.0122	20.8	.0000	1	Ssss
0.0122	20.8	.0000	1	Sssssss
0.0122	20.8	.0000	1	ST-148
0.0122	20.8	.0000	1	stabilizer
0.0122	20.8	.0000	1	stadiums
0.0122	20.8	.0000	1	staffers
0.0122	20.8	.0000	1	stage-whispered
0.0122	20.8	.0000	1	stageful
0.0122	20.8	.0000	1	staircased
0.0122	20.8	.0000	1	staircases
0.0122	20.8	.0000	1	Stairs
0.0122	20.8	.0000	1	stalemated
0.0122	20.8	.0000	1	stalemating
0.0122	20.8	.0000	1	Stalinism
0.0122	20.8	.0000	1	STALKING
0.0122	20.8	.0000	1	stanchion
0.0122	20.8	.0000	1	stand-outs
0.0122	20.8	.0000	1	standby
0.0122	20.8	.0000	1	standout
0.0122	20.8	.0000	1	Stanfield
0.0122	20.8	.0000	1	stank

THE PRECEDING WORD TYPE OCCUPIES RANK 70100

U	SFI	D	F	Word Type
0.0122	20.8	.0000	1	stannous
0.0122	20.8	.0000	1	star-detonating
0.0122	20.8	.0000	1	starkers
0.0122	20.8	.0000	1	starlight's
0.0122	20.8	.0000	1	Stars'
0.0122	20.8	.0000	1	Starve
0.0122	20.8	.0000	1	stashed
0.0122	20.8	.0000	1	State-designate
0.0122	20.8	.0000	1	state-police
0.0122	20.8	.0000	1	State-supported
0.0122	20.8	.0000	1	State-wide
0.0122	20.8	.0000	1	statewide
0.0122	20.8	.0000	1	statutes
0.0122	20.8	.0000	1	steak-maker
0.0122	20.8	.0000	1	steel-and-glass
0.0122	20.8	.0000	1	steel-cold
0.0122	20.8	.0000	1	steel-mill
0.0122	20.8	.0000	1	steel-rimmed
0.0122	20.8	.0000	1	steely-eyed
0.0122	20.8	.0000	1	Steering
0.0122	20.8	.0000	1	Stefanich
0.0122	20.8	.0000	1	stepbrother
0.0122	20.8	.0000	1	stepchildren
0.0122	20.8	.0000	1	stepfather's
0.0122	20.8	.0000	1	steppin'
0.0122	20.8	.0000	1	stepsister
0.0122	20.8	.0000	1	Stern's
0.0122	20.8	.0000	1	sterner
0.0122	20.8	.0000	1	StevensPoint
0.0122	20.8	.0000	1	stick-shift
0.0122	20.8	.0000	1	STICKS
0.0122	20.8	.0000	1	stiffer
0.0122	20.8	.0000	1	still-buried
0.0122	20.8	.0000	1	still-plentiful
0.0122	20.8	.0000	1	still-wet
0.0122	20.8	.0000	1	Stilt
0.0122	20.8	.0000	1	Stingray
0.0122	20.8	.0000	1	Stockings
0.0122	20.8	.0000	1	stockmaker
0.0122	20.8	.0000	1	stockmaking
0.0122	20.8	.0000	1	stockpiles
0.0122	20.8	.0000	1	Stokely
0.0122	20.8	.0000	1	Stonebreaker
0.0122	20.8	.0000	1	Stoned
0.0122	20.8	.0000	1	StoneyPoint
0.0122	20.8	.0000	1	Storch
0.0122	20.8	.0000	1	stowaway
0.0122	20.8	.0000	1	straggly
0.0122	20.8	.0000	1	straight-back
0.0122	20.8	.0000	1	Strang
0.0122	20.8	.0000	1	strangulation
0.0122	20.8	.0000	1	strategists
0.0122	20.8	.0000	1	Strates
0.0122	20.8	.0000	1	Strathmore
0.0122	20.8	.0000	1	Strawberries
0.0122	20.8	.0000	1	strawberry-blond
0.0122	20.8	.0000	1	stream-of-consciousness
0.0122	20.8	.0000	1	streamliner
0.0122	20.8	.0000	1	street-type
0.0122	20.8	.0000	1	streetable
0.0122	20.8	.0000	1	Streetcar
0.0122	20.8	.0000	1	Streisand
0.0122	20.8	.0000	1	stridency
0.0122	20.8	.0000	1	stringently
0.0122	20.8	.0000	1	strip-mined
0.0122	20.8	.0000	1	Stroller's
0.0122	20.8	.0000	1	strongbox
0.0122	20.8	.0000	1	Strongside
0.0122	20.8	.0000	1	strontium-rich
0.0122	20.8	.0000	1	Stu
0.0122	20.8	.0000	1	stubble-bearded
0.0122	20.8	.0000	1	student-government
0.0122	20.8	.0000	1	student-oriented
0.0122	20.8	.0000	1	study-time
0.0122	20.8	.0000	1	stuff's
0.0122	20.8	.0000	1	Stuffed
0.0122	20.8	.0000	1	stultifying
0.0122	20.8	.0000	1	Stump
0.0122	20.8	.0000	1	stumpers
0.0122	20.8	.0000	1	sub-2000-rpm
0.0122	20.8	.0000	1	subcategories
0.0122	20.8	.0000	1	Subcommittee
0.0122	20.8	.0000	1	SUBCOMPACTS
0.0122	20.8	.0000	1	subcontracted
0.0122	20.8	.0000	1	subcultures
0.0122	20.8	.0000	1	subjectivity
0.0122	20.8	.0000	1	subjugate
0.0122	20.8	.0000	1	sublimate
0.0122	20.8	.0000	1	sublimely
0.0122	20.8	.0000	1	submits
0.0122	20.8	.0000	1	submitting
0.0122	20.8	.0000	1	subsidiaries
0.0122	20.8	.0000	1	subsisting
0.0122	20.8	.0000	1	Suburban
0.0122	20.8	.0000	1	suburbanites
0.0122	20.8	.0000	1	subvert
0.0122	20.8	.0000	1	succinct
0.0122	20.8	.0000	1	Suede
0.0122	20.8	.0000	1	suffit
0.0122	20.8	.0000	1	sugar-coated

THE PRECEDING WORD TYPE OCCUPIES RANK 70200

U	SFI	D	F	Word Type
0.0122	20.8	.0000	1	sugar-coating
0.0122	20.8	.0000	1	sugarfree
0.0122	20.8	.0000	1	Suisun
0.0122	20.8	.0000	1	sultry-voiced
0.0122	20.8	.0000	1	summa
0.0122	20.8	.0000	1	summer-resident
0.0122	20.8	.0000	1	summerized
0.0122	20.8	.0000	1	sun-bronzed
0.0122	20.8	.0000	1	sun-cooked
0.0122	20.8	.0000	1	sun-heated
0.0122	20.8	.0000	1	sun-javelins
0.0122	20.8	.0000	1	sun-kilned
0.0122	20.8	.0000	1	sun-measurement
0.0122	20.8	.0000	1	sunbathing
0.0122	20.8	.0000	1	Sunizona
0.0122	20.8	.0000	1	sunshield
0.0122	20.8	.0000	1	sunsuit
0.0122	20.8	.0000	1	super-accurate
0.0122	20.8	.0000	1	super-block
0.0122	20.8	.0000	1	super-blocks
0.0122	20.8	.0000	1	super-car
0.0122	20.8	.0000	1	super-cool
0.0122	20.8	.0000	1	super-cultured
0.0122	20.8	.0000	1	super-pitcher
0.0122	20.8	.0000	1	super-rich
0.0122	20.8	.0000	1	super-ruin
0.0122	20.8	.0000	1	super-structure
0.0122	20.8	.0000	1	super-subjectivity
0.0122	20.8	.0000	1	super-systems
0.0122	20.8	.0000	1	supercharged
0.0122	20.8	.0000	1	superduper
0.0122	20.8	.0000	1	superfecund
0.0122	20.8	.0000	1	superfluous
0.0122	20.8	.0000	1	supernova
0.0122	20.8	.0000	1	superpool
0.0122	20.8	.0000	1	superseding
0.0122	20.8	.0000	1	supersonically
0.0122	20.8	.0000	1	supertanker
0.0122	20.8	.0000	1	supertankers
0.0122	20.8	.0000	1	supervened
0.0122	20.8	.0000	1	Supervisory
0.0122	20.8	.0000	1	supine
0.0122	20.8	.0000	1	supplant
0.0122	20.8	.0000	1	supplemental
0.0122	20.8	.0000	1	supportive
0.0122	20.8	.0000	1	surcharge
0.0122	20.8	.0000	1	sure-fingered
0.0122	20.8	.0000	1	surf-swept
0.0122	20.8	.0000	1	surface-feeding
0.0122	20.8	.0000	1	surfers'
0.0122	20.8	.0000	1	surficial
0.0122	20.8	.0000	1	surfmen
0.0122	20.8	.0000	1	surge-driven
0.0122	20.8	.0000	1	surrogate
0.0122	20.8	.0000	1	Suzy's
0.0122	20.8	.0000	1	swallower
0.0122	20.8	.0000	1	swastika
0.0122	20.8	.0000	1	swatches
0.0122	20.8	.0000	1	sweats
0.0122	20.8	.0000	1	sweatshirt
0.0122	20.8	.0000	1	swept-wing
0.0122	20.8	.0000	1	swerving
0.0122	20.8	.0000	1	Swim
0.0122	20.8	.0000	1	swindler
0.0122	20.8	.0000	1	swing-wing
0.0122	20.8	.0000	1	swinger
0.0122	20.8	.0000	1	swingers
0.0122	20.8	.0000	1	switch-over
0.0122	20.8	.0000	1	switchers
0.0122	20.8	.0000	1	Swope
0.0122	20.8	.0000	1	Sycamore
0.0122	20.8	.0000	1	sycophants
0.0122	20.8	.0000	1	Sydney's
0.0122	20.8	.0000	1	syndrome
0.0122	20.8	.0000	1	T-Bird
0.0122	20.8	.0000	1	T-minus-2-hours-and-17-**
0.0122	20.8	.0000	1	T-minus-9-seconds
0.0122	20.8	.0000	1	T-38
0.0122	20.8	.0000	1	Tab
0.0122	20.8	.0000	1	table-desk
0.0122	20.8	.0000	1	tabloid
0.0122	20.8	.0000	1	tach
0.0122	20.8	.0000	1	Tackle
0.0122	20.8	.0000	1	Tahitians
0.0122	20.8	.0000	1	Tahuya
0.0122	20.8	.0000	1	TaiChiChuan
0.0122	20.8	.0000	1	Taipei's
0.0122	20.8	.0000	1	Taiyo
0.0122	20.8	.0000	1	Takano
0.0122	20.8	.0000	1	take-home
0.0122	20.8	.0000	1	takeovers
0.0122	20.8	.0000	1	tamarind
0.0122	20.8	.0000	1	Tamil
0.0122	20.8	.0000	1	tandems
0.0122	20.8	.0000	1	tangentially
0.0122	20.8	.0000	1	tangents
0.0122	20.8	.0000	1	Tanker
0.0122	20.8	.0000	1	tanker's
0.0122	20.8	.0000	1	Tanya's
0.0122	20.8	.0000	1	taperground

THE PRECEDING WORD TYPE OCCUPIES RANK 70300

U	SFI	D	F	Word Type
0.0122	20.8	.0000	1	tapirs
0.0122	20.8	.0000	1	Taps
0.0122	20.8	.0000	1	tar-black
0.0122	20.8	.0000	1	targeting
0.0122	20.8	.0000	1	Tarkenton's
0.0122	20.8	.0000	1	Tarn
0.0122	20.8	.0000	1	tat-tat-tat
0.0122	20.8	.0000	1	tax-cutting
0.0122	20.8	.0000	1	tax-free
0.0122	20.8	.0000	1	taxbreak
0.0122	20.8	.0000	1	Tchikrin
0.0122	20.8	.0000	1	TDC
0.0122	20.8	.0000	1	TDS
0.0122	20.8	.0000	1	Teach
0.0122	20.8	.0000	1	teach-ins
0.0122	20.8	.0000	1	teaching-technology
0.0122	20.8	.0000	1	Teamster
0.0122	20.8	.0000	1	tear-blinded
0.0122	20.8	.0000	1	Tebbetts
0.0122	20.8	.0000	1	technocratic
0.0122	20.8	.0000	1	technocrats
0.0122	20.8	.0000	1	tedium
0.0122	20.8	.0000	1	tee-ers
0.0122	20.8	.0000	1	teems
0.0122	20.8	.0000	1	teenies
0.0122	20.8	.0000	1	Teens
0.0122	20.8	.0000	1	Teh-chuan
0.0122	20.8	.0000	1	teleplay
0.0122	20.8	.0000	1	Television-Allen
0.0122	20.8	.0000	1	television's
0.0122	20.8	.0000	1	tellingly
0.0122	20.8	.0000	1	tempora
0.0122	20.8	.0000	1	ten-day
0.0122	20.8	.0000	1	ten-man
0.0122	20.8	.0000	1	ten-ounce
0.0122	20.8	.0000	1	Tend'r
0.0122	20.8	.0000	1	Tenderloin
0.0122	20.8	.0000	1	tengo
0.0122	20.8	.0000	1	tent-shaded
0.0122	20.8	.0000	1	tentful
0.0122	20.8	.0000	1	Teodoro
0.0122	20.8	.0000	1	teonanctatl
0.0122	20.8	.0000	1	Terns
0.0122	20.8	.0000	1	terrorist
0.0122	20.8	.0000	1	tete-a-tete
0.0122	20.8	.0000	1	textile-mill
0.0122	20.8	.0000	1	tha's
0.0122	20.8	.0000	1	Thad's
0.0122	20.8	.0000	1	thalidomide
0.0122	20.8	.0000	1	thanx
0.0122	20.8	.0000	1	that-this
0.0122	20.8	.0000	1	thatched-roof
0.0122	20.8	.0000	1	theatergoer
0.0122	20.8	.0000	1	theatergoers
0.0122	20.8	.0000	1	theatricality
0.0122	20.8	.0000	1	Theda
0.0122	20.8	.0000	1	thees
0.0122	20.8	.0000	1	Them
0.0122	20.8	.0000	1	therapist
0.0122	20.8	.0000	1	therapists
0.0122	20.8	.0000	1	Thermos
0.0122	20.8	.0000	1	thesaurus
0.0122	20.8	.0000	1	thespian
0.0122	20.8	.0000	1	They've
0.0122	20.8	.0000	1	Thieu's
0.0122	20.8	.0000	1	thighbone
0.0122	20.8	.0000	1	Thinker
0.0122	20.8	.0000	1	third-party
0.0122	20.8	.0000	1	third-world
0.0122	20.8	.0000	1	third-year
0.0122	20.8	.0000	1	thirteen-gun
0.0122	20.8	.0000	1	thirty-ninth
0.0122	20.8	.0000	1	Thorney
0.0122	20.8	.0000	1	three-button
0.0122	20.8	.0000	1	three-by-five-inch
0.0122	20.8	.0000	1	three-cabin
0.0122	20.8	.0000	1	three-deep
0.0122	20.8	.0000	1	three-ounce
0.0122	20.8	.0000	1	three-piece
0.0122	20.8	.0000	1	three-rib
0.0122	20.8	.0000	1	three-step
0.0122	20.8	.0000	1	three-unit
0.0122	20.8	.0000	1	three-weak
0.0122	20.8	.0000	1	three-year-olds
0.0122	20.8	.0000	1	Threepenny
0.0122	20.8	.0000	1	threesome
0.0122	20.8	.0000	1	Thresher
0.0122	20.8	.0000	1	thriftily
0.0122	20.8	.0000	1	thrill-a-minute
0.0122	20.8	.0000	1	throat-tearing
0.0122	20.8	.0000	1	Throop
0.0122	20.8	.0000	1	through-the-water
0.0122	20.8	.0000	1	thrusters
0.0122	20.8	.0000	1	thub-thub-thubbing
0.0122	20.8	.0000	1	thumbs-up
0.0122	20.8	.0000	1	thundercloud
0.0122	20.8	.0000	1	thusly
0.0122	20.8	.0000	1	thwarting
0.0122	20.8	.0000	1	Tibbar
0.0122	20.8	.0000	1	Tic-Tac-Toe

THE PRECEDING WORD TYPE OCCUPIES RANK 70400

U	SFI	D	F	Word Type
0.0122	20.8	.0000	1	ticketed
0.0122	20.8	.0000	1	tideline
0.0122	20.8	.0000	1	tie-ins
0.0122	20.8	.0000	1	tight-clenched
0.0122	20.8	.0000	1	tightens
0.0122	20.8	.0000	1	Tijuana
0.0122	20.8	.0000	1	tilth
0.0122	20.8	.0000	1	time-to-time
0.0122	20.8	.0000	1	Timers'
0.0122	20.8	.0000	1	timetables
0.0122	20.8	.0000	1	tingly
0.0122	20.8	.0000	1	tip-top
0.0122	20.8	.0000	1	tippling
0.0122	20.8	.0000	1	titans
0.0122	20.8	.0000	1	Titusville
0.0122	20.8	.0000	1	Toadstool
0.0122	20.8	.0000	1	togged
0.0122	20.8	.0000	1	Tohopekaliga
0.0122	20.8	.0000	1	toilets
0.0122	20.8	.0000	1	Toklat
0.0122	20.8	.0000	1	Tokyo-to-Osaka
0.0122	20.8	.0000	1	Tolland
0.0122	20.8	.0000	1	Tomato
0.0122	20.8	.0000	1	tombstones
0.0122	20.8	.0000	1	Tommie's
0.0122	20.8	.0000	1	Tommonsville
0.0122	20.8	.0000	1	tongue-defying
0.0122	20.8	.0000	1	tongue-twisting
0.0122	20.8	.0000	1	Tonkin
0.0122	20.8	.0000	1	tonsillectomy
0.0122	20.8	.0000	1	Tonto
0.0122	20.8	.0000	1	Tooele

U	SFI	D	F	Word Type
0.0122	20.8	.0000	1	toolkit
0.0122	20.8	.0000	1	tooth-rimmed
0.0122	20.8	.0000	1	toothless
0.0122	20.8	.0000	1	toothpastes
0.0122	20.8	.0000	1	top-name
0.0122	20.8	.0000	1	top-water
0.0122	20.8	.0000	1	topless
0.0122	20.8	.0000	1	topline
0.0122	20.8	.0000	1	Toronto's
0.0122	20.8	.0000	1	torpedoed
0.0122	20.8	.0000	1	torpor
0.0122	20.8	.0000	1	TorqueFlites
0.0122	20.8	.0000	1	Torre
0.0122	20.8	.0000	1	toss-up
0.0122	20.8	.0000	1	Totem
0.0122	20.8	.0000	1	totted
0.0122	20.8	.0000	1	toucans
0.0122	20.8	.0000	1	tough-guy
0.0122	20.8	.0000	1	Tourer
0.0122	20.8	.0000	1	tout
0.0122	20.8	.0000	1	touted
0.0122	20.8	.0000	1	Townes
0.0122	20.8	.0000	1	Toyota
0.0122	20.8	.0000	1	Tracey's
0.0122	20.8	.0000	1	tracking-camera
0.0122	20.8	.0000	1	tractor-type
0.0122	20.8	.0000	1	traffic-crash
0.0122	20.8	.0000	1	trajectories
0.0122	20.8	.0000	1	tranquillity
0.0122	20.8	.0000	1	Trans
0.0122	20.8	.0000	1	trans-Arabian
0.0122	20.8	.0000	1	transcendence
0.0122	20.8	.0000	1	transcript
0.0122	20.8	.0000	1	transducers
0.0122	20.8	.0000	1	transected
0.0122	20.8	.0000	1	transpacific
0.0122	20.8	.0000	1	Transport
0.0122	20.8	.0000	1	Transportes
0.0122	20.8	.0000	1	traprock
0.0122	20.8	.0000	1	traumatic
0.0122	20.8	.0000	1	traumatized
0.0122	20.8	.0000	1	travail
0.0122	20.8	.0000	1	Travelall
0.0122	20.8	.0000	1	Travelers'
0.0122	20.8	.0000	1	traversing
0.0122	20.8	.0000	1	travesty
0.0122	20.8	.0000	1	Traynor
0.0122	20.8	.0000	1	treacherously
0.0122	20.8	.0000	1	tree-dwelling
0.0122	20.8	.0000	1	tree-swinging
0.0122	20.8	.0000	1	treftadaeth
0.0122	20.8	.0000	1	trend-jumping
0.0122	20.8	.0000	1	Trendley
0.0122	20.8	.0000	1	Trent's
0.0122	20.8	.0000	1	Tressider
0.0122	20.8	.0000	1	tribunals
0.0122	20.8	.0000	1	tributes
0.0122	20.8	.0000	1	trick-or-treat
0.0122	20.8	.0000	1	trick-or-treating
0.0122	20.8	.0000	1	tridacna
0.0122	20.8	.0000	1	triggering
0.0122	20.8	.0000	1	Trinidadian
0.0122	20.8	.0000	1	triplethreat
0.0122	20.8	.0000	1	Tritheim
0.0122	20.8	.0000	1	triumvirs
0.0122	20.8	.0000	1	tromping
0.0122	20.8	.0000	1	troop's
0.0122	20.8	.0000	1	Tropicbird

THE PRECEDING WORD TYPE OCCUPIES RANK 70500

U	SFI	D	F	Word Type
0.0122	20.8	.0000	1	trotline
0.0122	20.8	.0000	1	Trotsky
0.0122	20.8	.0000	1	Trotsky's
0.0122	20.8	.0000	1	troubleshooter
0.0122	20.8	.0000	1	trough's
0.0122	20.8	.0000	1	Trouille
0.0122	20.8	.0000	1	Troupe
0.0122	20.8	.0000	1	Troxel
0.0122	20.8	.0000	1	truck-trailers
0.0122	20.8	.0000	1	truckbed
0.0122	20.8	.0000	1	truckmen
0.0122	20.8	.0000	1	truncate
0.0122	20.8	.0000	1	trunculariopsis
0.0122	20.8	.0000	1	Tsar's
0.0122	20.8	.0000	1	tubful
0.0122	20.8	.0000	1	tudor
0.0122	20.8	.0000	1	Tudors
0.0122	20.8	.0000	1	Tuesday-night
0.0122	20.8	.0000	1	tumble-dry
0.0122	20.8	.0000	1	Tuna
0.0122	20.8	.0000	1	tunable
0.0122	20.8	.0000	1	tuneup
0.0122	20.8	.0000	1	Tuning
0.0122	20.8	.0000	1	Tunney
0.0122	20.8	.0000	1	turbo
0.0122	20.8	.0000	1	Turbocharger
0.0122	20.8	.0000	1	turbocharger
0.0122	20.8	.0000	1	turbocharging
0.0122	20.8	.0000	1	Turbulence
0.0122	20.8	.0000	1	turke-lepathy
0.0122	20.8	.0000	1	Turku
0.0122	20.8	.0000	1	turnaround
0.0122	20.8	.0000	1	turndown
0.0122	20.8	.0000	1	turnings
0.0122	20.8	.0000	1	turtleneck
0.0122	20.8	.0000	1	TV-watching
0.0122	20.8	.0000	1	twelve-hour
0.0122	20.8	.0000	1	Twenty-fifth
0.0122	20.8	.0000	1	Twenty-one
0.0122	20.8	.0000	1	twenty-pound
0.0122	20.8	.0000	1	twenty-story
0.0122	20.8	.0000	1	twice-daily
0.0122	20.8	.0000	1	twice-vanquished
0.0122	20.8	.0000	1	Twins'
0.0122	20.8	.0000	1	twisty-turny
0.0122	20.8	.0000	1	two-against-one
0.0122	20.8	.0000	1	two-and-a-half
0.0122	20.8	.0000	1	two-barrel
0.0122	20.8	.0000	1	two-block
0.0122	20.8	.0000	1	two-escudo
0.0122	20.8	.0000	1	two-fours
0.0122	20.8	.0000	1	two-million-square-mile
0.0122	20.8	.0000	1	two-room
0.0122	20.8	.0000	1	Two-shoes
0.0122	20.8	.0000	1	two-speed
0.0122	20.8	.0000	1	two-stemmed
0.0122	20.8	.0000	1	two-strike
0.0122	20.8	.0000	1	two-time
0.0122	20.8	.0000	1	two-unit
0.0122	20.8	.0000	1	twosomes
0.0122	20.8	.0000	1	Tywardreath
0.0122	20.8	.0000	1	U-Haul
0.0122	20.8	.0000	1	Ubatuba
0.0122	20.8	.0000	1	ubiquituos
0.0122	20.8	.0000	1	UCLA-Cal
0.0122	20.8	.0000	1	Uganda's
0.0122	20.8	.0000	1	Ugandan
0.0122	20.8	.0000	1	Ugandans
0.0122	20.8	.0000	1	Uggams
0.0122	20.8	.0000	1	Ughelli
0.0122	20.8	.0000	1	Uigur
0.0122	20.8	.0000	1	Uigurs
0.0122	20.8	.0000	1	UL-approved
0.0122	20.8	.0000	1	Ulbricht
0.0122	20.8	.0000	1	Ulbricht's
0.0122	20.8	.0000	1	Ultra-Facial
0.0122	20.8	.0000	1	ultra-efficient
0.0122	20.8	.0000	1	ultra-violet
0.0122	20.8	.0000	1	ultrapurity
0.0122	20.8	.0000	1	Umiak
0.0122	20.8	.0000	1	un-American-boy
0.0122	20.8	.0000	1	unabashed
0.0122	20.8	.0000	1	unarticulated
0.0122	20.8	.0000	1	unavailable
0.0122	20.8	.0000	1	unbuckles
0.0122	20.8	.0000	1	uncelebrated
0.0122	20.8	.0000	1	unclenched
0.0122	20.8	.0000	1	Unconquered
0.0122	20.8	.0000	1	uncoordinated
0.0122	20.8	.0000	1	uncoupled
0.0122	20.8	.0000	1	undammed
0.0122	20.8	.0000	1	under-achiever
0.0122	20.8	.0000	1	under-equipped
0.0122	20.8	.0000	1	under-16s
0.0122	20.8	.0000	1	underachievement
0.0122	20.8	.0000	1	underachievers
0.0122	20.8	.0000	1	underarms
0.0122	20.8	.0000	1	underclass
0.0122	20.8	.0000	1	undercroft
0.0122	20.8	.0000	1	undergrad

THE PRECEDING WORD TYPE OCCUPIES RANK 70600

U	SFI	D	F	Word Type
0.0122	20.8	.0000	1	Undergraduate
0.0122	20.8	.0000	1	underpin
0.0122	20.8	.0000	1	underprivileged
0.0122	20.8	.0000	1	underscore
0.0122	20.8	.0000	1	Undersea
0.0122	20.8	.0000	1	understaffed
0.0122	20.8	.0000	1	understated
0.0122	20.8	.0000	1	understates
0.0122	20.8	.0000	1	undertaker's
0.0122	20.8	.0000	1	underwrite
0.0122	20.8	.0000	1	undeterred
0.0122	20.8	.0000	1	undreamed-of
0.0122	20.8	.0000	1	unethical
0.0122	20.8	.0000	1	unfeasible
0.0122	20.8	.0000	1	unfroze
0.0122	20.8	.0000	1	unguent
0.0122	20.8	.0000	1	unhurried
0.0122	20.8	.0000	1	unicycles
0.0122	20.8	.0000	1	unimposing
0.0122	20.8	.0000	1	uninvolved
0.0122	20.8	.0000	1	unionists
0.0122	20.8	.0000	1	Unitas'
0.0122	20.8	.0000	1	University's
0.0122	20.8	.0000	1	unkinks
0.0122	20.8	.0000	1	unknowns
0.0122	20.8	.0000	1	unlatch
0.0122	20.8	.0000	1	unlimbered
0.0122	20.8	.0000	1	unloving
0.0122	20.8	.0000	1	unmilitary
0.0122	20.8	.0000	1	unobtrusive
0.0122	20.8	.0000	1	unpaced
0.0122	20.8	.0000	1	unpeeled
0.0122	20.8	.0000	1	unplanned
0.0122	20.8	.0000	1	unread
0.0122	20.8	.0000	1	unseaworthy
0.0122	20.8	.0000	1	unsecured
0.0122	20.8	.0000	1	Unser
0.0122	20.8	.0000	1	unstrung
0.0122	20.8	.0000	1	unstuck
0.0122	20.8	.0000	1	untainted
0.0122	20.8	.0000	1	untunable
0.0122	20.8	.0000	1	unusable
0.0122	20.8	.0000	1	unvarnished
0.0122	20.8	.0000	1	unvisited
0.0122	20.8	.0000	1	unwarranted
0.0122	20.8	.0000	1	unwatched
0.0122	20.8	.0000	1	unworried
0.0122	20.8	.0000	1	unwrinkled
0.0122	20.8	.0000	1	Up-Tight
0.0122	20.8	.0000	1	up-front
0.0122	20.8	.0000	1	update
0.0122	20.8	.0000	1	updating
0.0122	20.8	.0000	1	upending
0.0122	20.8	.0000	1	upgraded
0.0122	20.8	.0000	1	upgrading
0.0122	20.8	.0000	1	upped
0.0122	20.8	.0000	1	upping
0.0122	20.8	.0000	1	uprise
0.0122	20.8	.0000	1	upshot
0.0122	20.8	.0000	1	upstages
0.0122	20.8	.0000	1	upswept
0.0122	20.8	.0000	1	upthrust
0.0122	20.8	.0000	1	Uptown
0.0122	20.8	.0000	1	urban-crisis
0.0122	20.8	.0000	1	urban/suburban
0.0122	20.8	.0000	1	urbanist
0.0122	20.8	.0000	1	urologist
0.0122	20.8	.0000	1	Uruguay's
0.0122	20.8	.0000	1	Uruguays's
0.0122	20.8	.0000	1	Uruguyan
0.0122	20.8	.0000	1	US-dominated
0.0122	20.8	.0000	1	USAF
0.0122	20.8	.0000	1	user's
0.0122	20.8	.0000	1	Users'
0.0122	20.8	.0000	1	USOC
0.0122	20.8	.0000	1	USS
0.0122	20.8	.0000	1	UTEP
0.0122	20.8	.0000	1	UWI
0.0122	20.8	.0000	1	vacation-camping
0.0122	20.8	.0000	1	vacationed
0.0122	20.8	.0000	1	vacationists
0.0122	20.8	.0000	1	vacuum-controlled
0.0122	20.8	.0000	1	vacuum-operated
0.0122	20.8	.0000	1	valedictorians
0.0122	20.8	.0000	1	valorous
0.0122	20.8	.0000	1	valving
0.0122	20.8	.0000	1	vampiro
0.0122	20.8	.0000	1	VanBenschoten
0.0122	20.8	.0000	1	VanCampen's
0.0122	20.8	.0000	1	VanDerBeek's
0.0122	20.8	.0000	1	VanDyke
0.0122	20.8	.0000	1	vanMaanen's
0.0122	20.8	.0000	1	Vance
0.0122	20.8	.0000	1	vandalized
0.0122	20.8	.0000	1	Vandals
0.0122	20.8	.0000	1	Vander
0.0122	20.8	.0000	1	Vanessa
0.0122	20.8	.0000	1	Vanocur
0.0122	20.8	.0000	1	vaporfree
0.0122	20.8	.0000	1	Vatican's

THE PRECEDING WORD TYPE OCCUPIES RANK 70700

U	SFI	D	F	Word Type
0.0122	20.8	.0000	1	Vaucluse
0.0122	20.8	.0000	1	vaulters
0.0122	20.8	.0000	1	vegetable-like
0.0122	20.8	.0000	1	vending
0.0122	20.8	.0000	1	venture's
0.0122	20.8	.0000	1	verbena
0.0122	20.8	.0000	1	Verey
0.0122	20.8	.0000	1	Vergilian
0.0122	20.8	.0000	1	verging
0.0122	20.8	.0000	1	verifying
0.0122	20.8	.0000	1	verities
0.0122	20.8	.0000	1	Vermont-NewYork
0.0122	20.8	.0000	1	Vermonter
0.0122	20.8	.0000	1	vermouth
0.0122	20.8	.0000	1	Verna
0.0122	20.8	.0000	1	verte
0.0122	20.8	.0000	1	vex
0.0122	20.8	.0000	1	vice-dean
0.0122	20.8	.0000	1	Vickery
0.0122	20.8	.0000	1	Vico
0.0122	20.8	.0000	1	Vico's
0.0122	20.8	.0000	1	Victoria's
0.0122	20.8	.0000	1	Victualers'
0.0122	20.8	.0000	1	Viewers
0.0122	20.8	.0000	1	vigils
0.0122	20.8	.0000	1	Vigna
0.0122	20.8	.0000	1	vilified
0.0122	20.8	.0000	1	VillaGesell
0.0122	20.8	.0000	1	Villager
0.0122	20.8	.0000	1	Villanova
0.0122	20.8	.0000	1	Vinapu
0.0122	20.8	.0000	1	vintage
0.0122	20.8	.0000	1	Violence
0.0122	20.8	.0000	1	violet-colored
0.0122	20.8	.0000	1	virility
0.0122	20.8	.0000	1	Vitae
0.0122	20.8	.0000	1	Vitosha
0.0122	20.8	.0000	1	Vittoria
0.0122	20.8	.0000	1	Viva
0.0122	20.8	.0000	1	Viviane
0.0122	20.8	.0000	1	vocalist
0.0122	20.8	.0000	1	vocals
0.0122	20.8	.0000	1	Vodka
0.0122	20.8	.0000	1	voila
0.0122	20.8	.0000	1	Voinovich
0.0122	20.8	.0000	1	Voityck
0.0122	20.8	.0000	1	Volkswagon
0.0122	20.8	.0000	1	Volpe
0.0122	20.8	.0000	1	volubly
0.0122	20.8	.0000	1	voluntarism
0.0122	20.8	.0000	1	Volunteers
0.0122	20.8	.0000	1	vonReding
0.0122	20.8	.0000	1	vonRosen
0.0122	20.8	.0000	1	vouched
0.0122	20.8	.0000	1	VW-based
0.0122	20.8	.0000	1	VW-type
0.0122	20.8	.0000	1	VW'S
0.0122	20.8	.0000	1	V8
0.0122	20.8	.0000	1	V8s
0.0122	20.8	.0000	1	WAC
0.0122	20.8	.0000	1	WAF
0.0122	20.8	.0000	1	wafer-thin
0.0122	20.8	.0000	1	wafting
0.0122	20.8	.0000	1	wage-price
0.0122	20.8	.0000	1	Wagoneer
0.0122	20.8	.0000	1	wah
0.0122	20.8	.0000	1	wahoo
0.0122	20.8	.0000	1	Waite
0.0122	20.8	.0000	1	wakeful
0.0122	20.8	.0000	1	walkout
0.0122	20.8	.0000	1	wall-hung
0.0122	20.8	.0000	1	Wall-of-Truth
0.0122	20.8	.0000	1	Wallkill
0.0122	20.8	.0000	1	walloped
0.0122	20.8	.0000	1	walloping
0.0122	20.8	.0000	1	walnut-and-fringed-lamps
0.0122	20.8	.0000	1	Walrus's
0.0122	20.8	.0000	1	wangled
0.0122	20.8	.0000	1	Warfield
0.0122	20.8	.0000	1	Warnecke
0.0122	20.8	.0000	1	Warrant
0.0122	20.8	.0000	1	warranty
0.0122	20.8	.0000	1	washboards
0.0122	20.8	.0000	1	watchcry
0.0122	20.8	.0000	1	water-borne
0.0122	20.8	.0000	1	water-colored
0.0122	20.8	.0000	1	water-oriented
0.0122	20.8	.0000	1	water-rats
0.0122	20.8	.0000	1	water-softened
0.0122	20.8	.0000	1	waterbug
0.0122	20.8	.0000	1	Watercolor
0.0122	20.8	.0000	1	waterfowling
0.0122	20.8	.0000	1	Waterfront
0.0122	20.8	.0000	1	waterings
0.0122	20.8	.0000	1	watersports
0.0122	20.8	.0000	1	WatkinsGlen
0.0122	20.8	.0000	1	WAVES
0.0122	20.8	.0000	1	WAY
0.0122	20.8	.0000	1	way-out
0.0122	20.8	.0000	1	Waynesboro

THE PRECEDING WORD TYPE OCCUPIES RANK 70800

U	SFI	D	F	Word Type
0.0122	20.8	.0000	1	Weak
0.0122	20.8	.0000	1	wedge-mating
0.0122	20.8	.0000	1	weed-free
0.0122	20.8	.0000	1	week-ends
0.0122	20.8	.0000	1	Weems
0.0122	20.8	.0000	1	weigh-in
0.0122	20.8	.0000	1	weight-lifter
0.0122	20.8	.0000	1	weight's
0.0122	20.8	.0000	1	weirdos
0.0122	20.8	.0000	1	Welk
0.0122	20.8	.0000	1	well-conceived
0.0122	20.8	.0000	1	well-done
0.0122	20.8	.0000	1	well-greased
0.0122	20.8	.0000	1	well-if-you-insist
0.0122	20.8	.0000	1	well-lighted
0.0122	20.8	.0000	1	well-off
0.0122	20.8	.0000	1	well-publicized
0.0122	20.8	.0000	1	well-tended
0.0122	20.8	.0000	1	well-used
0.0122	20.8	.0000	1	Wellses
0.0122	20.8	.0000	1	wellwishers
0.0122	20.8	.0000	1	Welsh-speaking
0.0122	20.8	.0000	1	welshed
0.0122	20.8	.0000	1	Welshmen
0.0122	20.8	.0000	1	welt
0.0122	20.8	.0000	1	welter
0.0122	20.8	.0000	1	Went
0.0122	20.8	.0000	1	Wersching
0.0122	20.8	.0000	1	Wesleyan
0.0122	20.8	.0000	1	WestGerman
0.0122	20.8	.0000	1	West's
0.0122	20.8	.0000	1	Westerfield
0.0122	20.8	.0000	1	western-Kentucky-style
0.0122	20.8	.0000	1	Westerner
0.0122	20.8	.0000	1	Westinghouse's
0.0122	20.8	.0000	1	WGBH
0.0122	20.8	.0000	1	whaddaya
0.0122	20.8	.0000	1	whap
0.0122	20.8	.0000	1	Whatever
0.0122	20.8	.0000	1	Whatman
0.0122	20.8	.0000	1	whatsamatter
0.0122	20.8	.0000	1	whee-ew
0.0122	20.8	.0000	1	wheelchairs
0.0122	20.8	.0000	1	wheelie
0.0122	20.8	.0000	1	wheelless
0.0122	20.8	.0000	1	whelp
0.0122	20.8	.0000	1	whimsy
0.0122	20.8	.0000	1	whines
0.0122	20.8	.0000	1	whinneying
0.0122	20.8	.0000	1	Whirlaway
0.0122	20.8	.0000	1	whirligigs
0.0122	20.8	.0000	1	whis-per
0.0122	20.8	.0000	1	whiskey-brown
0.0122	20.8	.0000	1	whiskey-running
0.0122	20.8	.0000	1	WhiteLake
0.0122	20.8	.0000	1	white-capped
0.0122	20.8	.0000	1	white-caps
0.0122	20.8	.0000	1	whitecapped
0.0122	20.8	.0000	1	Whitehall
0.0122	20.8	.0000	1	whitish-blond
0.0122	20.8	.0000	1	Whitten
0.0122	20.8	.0000	1	whitter
0.0122	20.8	.0000	1	WHO
0.0122	20.8	.0000	1	who've
0.0122	20.8	.0000	1	whomp
0.0122	20.8	.0000	1	whores
0.0122	20.8	.0000	1	wibblety-wobblety
0.0122	20.8	.0000	1	WichitaFalls
0.0122	20.8	.0000	1	widdershins
0.0122	20.8	.0000	1	wieldable
0.0122	20.8	.0000	1	wiglet
0.0122	20.8	.0000	1	Wilber
0.0122	20.8	.0000	1	Wilde
0.0122	20.8	.0000	1	wildlife-rehabilitation
0.0122	20.8	.0000	1	wildlife-wise
0.0122	20.8	.0000	1	WILL
0.0122	20.8	.0000	1	willy-nilly
0.0122	20.8	.0000	1	Wilmer
0.0122	20.8	.0000	1	Wilt
0.0122	20.8	.0000	1	Win's
0.0122	20.8	.0000	1	wind-tossed
0.0122	20.8	.0000	1	wind-whipped
0.0122	20.8	.0000	1	wine-flavored
0.0122	20.8	.0000	1	wine-tasting
0.0122	20.8	.0000	1	winemaker
0.0122	20.8	.0000	1	winery
0.0122	20.8	.0000	1	wing-nuts
0.0122	20.8	.0000	1	wingnuts
0.0122	20.8	.0000	1	winter-spring
0.0122	20.8	.0000	1	Winterbinter
0.0122	20.8	.0000	1	Winterbinter's
0.0122	20.8	.0000	1	wiper/washer
0.0122	20.8	.0000	1	Wisconsin's
0.0122	20.8	.0000	1	WITH
0.0122	20.8	.0000	1	witless
0.0122	20.8	.0000	1	Wizard-ish

U	SFI	D	F	Word Type
0.0122	20.8	.0000	1	wolverines
0.0122	20.8	.0000	1	womanizing
0.0122	20.8	.0000	1	Wonder
0.0122	20.8	.0000	1	wonderfool

THE PRECEDING WORD TYPE OCCUPIES RANK 70900

U	SFI	D	F	Word Type
0.0122	20.8	.0000	1	Wonderous
0.0122	20.8	.0000	1	wood-based
0.0122	20.8	.0000	1	wood-grain
0.0122	20.8	.0000	1	wood-lover
0.0122	20.8	.0000	1	wood-processing
0.0122	20.8	.0000	1	woodchuck-hunting
0.0122	20.8	.0000	1	woodland-covered
0.0122	20.8	.0000	1	woodturning
0.0122	20.8	.0000	1	Woodyard
0.0122	20.8	.0000	1	woofed
0.0122	20.8	.0000	1	Woolf
0.0122	20.8	.0000	1	woolves
0.0122	20.8	.0000	1	Wooton
0.0122	20.8	.0000	1	woozy
0.0122	20.8	.0000	1	WORCESTERSHIRE
0.0122	20.8	.0000	1	Workhorse
0.0122	20.8	.0000	1	workmates
0.0122	20.8	.0000	1	Workshop
0.0122	20.8	.0000	1	WORLD
0.0122	20.8	.0000	1	world-champion
0.0122	20.8	.0000	1	Worley's
0.0122	20.8	.0000	1	worst-polluted
0.0122	20.8	.0000	1	woulda
0.0122	20.8	.0000	1	wowed
0.0122	20.8	.0000	1	wracking
0.0122	20.8	.0000	1	wreak
0.0122	20.8	.0000	1	wren's
0.0122	20.8	.0000	1	Writer-Director
0.0122	20.8	.0000	1	writers'
0.0122	20.8	.0000	1	wrongdoing
0.0122	20.8	.0000	1	wrongos
0.0122	20.8	.0000	1	WSA
0.0122	20.8	.0000	1	Wulff
0.0122	20.8	.0000	1	X-rayed
0.0122	20.8	.0000	1	y-yeah
0.0122	20.8	.0000	1	Yale's
0.0122	20.8	.0000	1	Yankeetown
0.0122	20.8	.0000	1	yard-high
0.0122	20.8	.0000	1	Yavapai
0.0122	20.8	.0000	1	yawed
0.0122	20.8	.0000	1	YazooCity
0.0122	20.8	.0000	1	yellow-belly
0.0122	20.8	.0000	1	yesterdays
0.0122	20.8	.0000	1	yesteryears
0.0122	20.8	.0000	1	yipped
0.0122	20.8	.0000	1	yoghurt
0.0122	20.8	.0000	1	Yolles
0.0122	20.8	.0000	1	Yonemori
0.0122	20.8	.0000	1	Yoshimura
0.0122	20.8	.0000	1	young-voter
0.0122	20.8	.0000	1	youngsters'
0.0122	20.8	.0000	1	yule-log
0.0122	20.8	.0000	1	Zanger's
0.0122	20.8	.0000	1	Zapata's
0.0122	20.8	.0000	1	zapped
0.0122	20.8	.0000	1	Zaxik
0.0122	20.8	.0000	1	Zen
0.0122	20.8	.0000	1	Zetterberg
0.0122	20.8	.0000	1	Zip-Zip-Zip
0.0122	20.8	.0000	1	Zita
0.0122	20.8	.0000	1	zoo's
0.0122	20.8	.0000	1	Zozo
0.0122	20.8	.0000	1	Zyklon
0.0122	20.8	.0000	1	0-60
0.0122	20.8	.0000	1	000-gauss
0.0122	20.8	.0000	1	000-pound
0.0122	20.8	.0000	1	000-pound-thrust
0.0122	20.8	.0000	1	000-room
0.0122	20.8	.0000	1	000-seat
0.0122	20.8	.0000	1	000363
0.0122	20.8	.0000	1	005
0.0122	20.8	.0000	1	052
0.0122	20.8	.0000	1	06002
0.0122	20.8	.0000	1	1-in
0.0122	20.8	.0000	1	1/2-incher
0.0122	20.8	.0000	1	1/2-lb
0.0122	20.8	.0000	1	1/2-mile
0.0122	20.8	.0000	1	1/2-ton
0.0122	20.8	.0000	1	1/2-20
0.0122	20.8	.0000	1	1/5000
0.0122	20.8	.0000	1	1/8-in
0.0122	20.8	.0000	1	1/8-inch-wide
0.0122	20.8	.0000	1	10-day
0.0122	20.8	.0000	1	10-foot-wide
0.0122	20.8	.0000	1	10-ft-high**
0.0122	20.8	.0000	1	10-inch-diameter
0.0122	20.8	.0000	1	10-lane
0.0122	20.8	.0000	1	10-mile
0.0122	20.8	.0000	1	10-million-dollar
0.0122	20.8	.0000	1	10-pound-test
0.0122	20.8	.0000	1	10-speed
0.0122	20.8	.0000	1	10-0
0.0122	20.8	.0000	1	100-day
0.0122	20.8	.0000	1	100-percent
0.0122	20.8	.0000	1	100-plus
0.0122	20.8	.0000	1	100-thousandths
0.0122	20.8	.0000	1	100th
0.0122	20.8	.0000	1	10023
0.0122	20.8	.0000	1	101-foot
0.0122	20.8	.0000	1	106-berth

THE PRECEDING WORD TYPE OCCUPIES RANK 71000

U	SFI	D	F	Word Type
0.0122	20.8	.0000	1	106th
0.0122	20.8	.0000	1	11-foot
0.0122	20.8	.0000	1	11-1-2
0.0122	20.8	.0000	1	11's
0.0122	20.8	.0000	1	110th
0.0122	20.8	.0000	1	1115091
0.0122	20.8	.0000	1	1120
0.0122	20.8	.0000	1	116-pound
0.0122	20.8	.0000	1	12-
0.0122	20.8	.0000	1	12-foot-tall
0.0122	20.8	.0000	1	12-gauge
0.0122	20.8	.0000	1	12-horse
0.0122	20.8	.0000	1	12-port
0.0122	20.8	.0000	1	12-0
0.0122	20.8	.0000	1	12/0
0.0122	20.8	.0000	1	1205
0.0122	20.8	.0000	1	1228
0.0122	20.8	.0000	1	124th
0.0122	20.8	.0000	1	1282
0.0122	20.8	.0000	1	129-HR
0.0122	20.8	.0000	1	13-
0.0122	20.8	.0000	1	13-year-olds
0.0122	20.8	.0000	1	1300cc
0.0122	20.8	.0000	1	1390
0.0122	20.8	.0000	1	14-pound-rated
0.0122	20.8	.0000	1	14th-century
0.0122	20.8	.0000	1	140-horsepower
0.0122	20.8	.0000	1	142-foot-tall
0.0122	20.8	.0000	1	142-ton
0.0122	20.8	.0000	1	15-foot-long
0.0122	20.8	.0000	1	15-foot-tall
0.0122	20.8	.0000	1	15-inch
0.0122	20.8	.0000	1	15-mile
0.0122	20.8	.0000	1	15-year-olds
0.0122	20.8	.0000	1	15-30
0.0122	20.8	.0000	1	150-grain
0.0122	20.8	.0000	1	150-170
0.0122	20.8	.0000	1	151-mile-long
0.0122	20.8	.0000	1	1545
0.0122	20.8	.0000	1	1557
0.0122	20.8	.0000	1	16-in
0.0122	20.8	.0000	1	16-17
0.0122	20.8	.0000	1	160-hp
0.0122	20.8	.0000	1	1600cc
0.0122	20.8	.0000	1	1650s
0.0122	20.8	.0000	1	168-9
0.0122	20.8	.0000	1	1694
0.0122	20.8	.0000	1	17-
0.0122	20.8	.0000	1	17-foot-long
0.0122	20.8	.0000	1	17-incher
0.0122	20.8	.0000	1	17-pound
0.0122	20.8	.0000	1	17-18
0.0122	20.8	.0000	1	172-foot
0.0122	20.8	.0000	1	175-mile
0.0122	20.8	.0000	1	175th
0.0122	20.8	.0000	1	18-inch-long
0.0122	20.8	.0000	1	18-mile-long
0.0122	20.8	.0000	1	180-million-year-old
0.0122	20.8	.0000	1	1858-60
0.0122	20.8	.0000	1	18736
0.0122	20.8	.0000	1	19-EA-7
0.0122	20.8	.0000	1	19-foot-wide
0.0122	20.8	.0000	1	1904-1967
0.0122	20.8	.0000	1	1931385
0.0122	20.8	.0000	1	19468
0.0122	20.8	.0000	1	1954-56
0.0122	20.8	.0000	1	1967-1968
0.0122	20.8	.0000	1	1968-69
0.0122	20.8	.0000	1	1969s
0.0122	20.8	.0000	1	1970-71
0.0122	20.8	.0000	1	1978
0.0122	20.8	.0000	1	1980's
0.0122	20.8	.0000	1	2GC
0.0122	20.8	.0000	1	2F
0.0122	20.8	.0000	1	2-in
0.0122	20.8	.0000	1	2-megaton
0.0122	20.8	.0000	1	2-million-pound
0.0122	20.8	.0000	1	2-pound
0.0122	20.8	.0000	1	2-qt
0.0122	20.8	.0000	1	2-story
0.0122	20.8	.0000	1	20-in-wheel-size**
0.0122	20.8	.0000	1	20-inch
0.0122	20.8	.0000	1	20-knot
0.0122	20.8	.0000	1	20-second
0.0122	20.8	.0000	1	20-story
0.0122	20.8	.0000	1	20-0
0.0122	20.8	.0000	1	20-200
0.0122	20.8	.0000	1	20-29
0.0122	20.8	.0000	1	20/20
0.0122	20.8	.0000	1	200-foot
0.0122	20.8	.0000	1	200-thousandths
0.0122	20.8	.0000	1	20006
0.0122	20.8	.0000	1	2015
0.0122	20.8	.0000	1	206th
0.0122	20.8	.0000	1	2168
0.0122	20.8	.0000	1	22-foot-long
0.0122	20.8	.0000	1	22-story
0.0122	20.8	.0000	1	22-24
0.0122	20.8	.0000	1	220-grain
0.0122	20.8	.0000	1	223-foot-span

THE PRECEDING WORD TYPE OCCUPIES RANK 71100

U	SFI	D	F	Word Type
0.0122	20.8	.0000	1	23-geared
0.0122	20.8	.0000	1	23-inch
0.0122	20.8	.0000	1	236-foot
0.0122	20.8	.0000	1	24-page
0.0122	20.8	.0000	1	24-23
0.0122	20.8	.0000	1	24-6
0.0122	20.8	.0000	1	240-250
0.0122	20.8	.0000	1	25-by-25-foot
0.0122	20.8	.0000	1	25-mile
0.0122	20.8	.0000	1	25-year
0.0122	20.8	.0000	1	25-year-old
0.0122	20.8	.0000	1	250-inch-wall
0.0122	20.8	.0000	1	250-square-mile
0.0122	20.8	.0000	1	26-in
0.0122	20.8	.0000	1	274-5
0.0122	20.8	.0000	1	2800
0.0122	20.8	.0000	1	29-inch-diameter
0.0122	20.8	.0000	1	29th
0.0122	20.8	.0000	1	2917
0.0122	20.8	.0000	1	3M
0.0122	20.8	.0000	1	3Ty
0.0122	20.8	.0000	1	3-hp
0.0122	20.8	.0000	1	3-mile
0.0122	20.8	.0000	1	3/4-in
0.0122	20.8	.0000	1	3/4-inch-long
0.0122	20.8	.0000	1	30-manpower
0.0122	20.8	.0000	1	30-piece
0.0122	20.8	.0000	1	30-yard
0.0122	20.8	.0000	1	30-11
0.0122	20.8	.0000	1	30/06
0.0122	20.8	.0000	1	300-kilowatt
0.0122	20.8	.0000	1	300-mile
0.0122	20.8	.0000	1	300-pound
0.0122	20.8	.0000	1	300-year-old
0.0122	20.8	.0000	1	300th
0.0122	20.8	.0000	1	31-24
0.0122	20.8	.0000	1	32nd
0.0122	20.8	.0000	1	326-mile
0.0122	20.8	.0000	1	32741
0.0122	20.8	.0000	1	33rd
0.0122	20.8	.0000	1	34th
0.0122	20.8	.0000	1	340-cu-in**
0.0122	20.8	.0000	1	340-41
0.0122	20.8	.0000	1	3447
0.0122	20.8	.0000	1	35-foot
0.0122	20.8	.0000	1	35-lb
0.0122	20.8	.0000	1	35-mile
0.0122	20.8	.0000	1	35-year-old
0.0122	20.8	.0000	1	35-39
0.0122	20.8	.0000	1	35/65
0.0122	20.8	.0000	1	36-in
0.0122	20.8	.0000	1	360-degree
0.0122	20.8	.0000	1	363-foot-high
0.0122	20.8	.0000	1	37-yard
0.0122	20.8	.0000	1	37-9
0.0122	20.8	.0000	1	3700
0.0122	20.8	.0000	1	38-caliber
0.0122	20.8	.0000	1	38-year-old
0.0122	20.8	.0000	1	39A
0.0122	20.8	.0000	1	390-cubic
0.0122	20.8	.0000	1	390-foot
0.0122	20.8	.0000	1	395-foot
0.0122	20.8	.0000	1	396-7
0.0122	20.8	.0000	1	398-400
0.0122	20.8	.0000	1	40-foot
0.0122	20.8	.0000	1	40-horsepower
0.0122	20.8	.0000	1	40-44
0.0122	20.8	.0000	1	400-plus-hp
0.0122	20.8	.0000	1	42-year-old
0.0122	20.8	.0000	1	42%
0.0122	20.8	.0000	1	427-cubic-inch
0.0122	20.8	.0000	1	429's
0.0122	20.8	.0000	1	44-13
0.0122	20.8	.0000	1	440-inch
0.0122	20.8	.0000	1	440-to
0.0122	20.8	.0000	1	4411
0.0122	20.8	.0000	1	444
0.0122	20.8	.0000	1	45-year-old
0.0122	20.8	.0000	1	45s
0.0122	20.8	.0000	1	458-9
0.0122	20.8	.0000	1	46-14
0.0122	20.8	.0000	1	47-12
0.0122	20.8	.0000	1	4711
0.0122	20.8	.0000	1	48%
0.0122	20.8	.0000	1	4831
0.0122	20.8	.0000	1	484
0.0122	20.8	.0000	1	49er
0.0122	20.8	.0000	1	5-lug
0.0122	20.8	.0000	1	5-10-10
0.0122	20.8	.0000	1	5-10-5
0.0122	20.8	.0000	1	5-11
0.0122	20.8	.0000	1	5-3-1
0.0122	20.8	.0000	1	50-cent
0.0122	20.8	.0000	1	50-horse
0.0122	20.8	.0000	1	50-mile
0.0122	20.8	.0000	1	50-page
0.0122	20.8	.0000	1	514-15
0.0122	20.8	.0000	1	517
0.0122	20.8	.0000	1	52-year-old
0.0122	20.8	.0000	1	52%

THE PRECEDING WORD TYPE OCCUPIES RANK 71200

U	SFI	D	F	Word Type
0.0122	20.8	.0000	1	545-f
0.0122	20.8	.0000	1	55-7
0.0122	20.8	.0000	1	550-ton
0.0122	20.8	.0000	1	56-degree
0.0122	20.8	.0000	1	560-to
0.0122	20.8	.0000	1	57-year-old
0.0122	20.8	.0000	1	57%
0.0122	20.8	.0000	1	5700-5800
0.0122	20.8	.0000	1	59-21
0.0122	20.8	.0000	1	594-inch
0.0122	20.8	.0000	1	595
0.0122	20.8	.0000	1	6A
0.0122	20.8	.0000	1	6-acre
0.0122	20.8	.0000	1	6-cylinder
0.0122	20.8	.0000	1	6-foot-8-inch
0.0122	20.8	.0000	1	6-in
0.0122	20.8	.0000	1	6-in-swing**
0.0122	20.8	.0000	1	60-Hz
0.0122	20.8	.0000	1	60-foot
0.0122	20.8	.0000	1	60-m
0.0122	20.8	.0000	1	60-mile
0.0122	20.8	.0000	1	60-to-64
0.0122	20.8	.0000	1	60-70
0.0122	20.8	.0000	1	600-foot-high
0.0122	20.8	.0000	1	600-601
0.0122	20.8	.0000	1	61183
0.0122	20.8	.0000	1	62%
0.0122	20.8	.0000	1	63-28
0.0122	20.8	.0000	1	630-31
0.0122	20.8	.0000	1	637
0.0122	20.8	.0000	1	639
0.0122	20.8	.0000	1	645
0.0122	20.8	.0000	1	653908
0.0122	20.8	.0000	1	66-yard
0.0122	20.8	.0000	1	66-0
0.0122	20.8	.0000	1	68-yards
0.0122	20.8	.0000	1	68-year-old
0.0122	20.8	.0000	1	7-Up
0.0122	20.8	.0000	1	7-foot
0.0122	20.8	.0000	1	7-inch
0.0122	20.8	.0000	1	7-million-dollar
0.0122	20.8	.0000	1	70-foot
0.0122	20.8	.0000	1	70-71
0.0122	20.8	.0000	1	70%
0.0122	20.8	.0000	1	706-7
0.0122	20.8	.0000	1	71025
0.0122	20.8	.0000	1	72nd
0.0122	20.8	.0000	1	737
0.0122	20.8	.0000	1	743
0.0122	20.8	.0000	1	748-9
0.0122	20.8	.0000	1	75-grain
0.0122	20.8	.0000	1	766
0.0122	20.8	.0000	1	7800-foot
0.0122	20.8	.0000	1	798
0.0122	20.8	.0000	1	8-in
0.0122	20.8	.0000	1	8-8
0.0122	20.8	.0000	1	805546
0.0122	20.8	.0000	1	81-foot
0.0122	20.8	.0000	1	810-inch
0.0122	20.8	.0000	1	830-31
0.0122	20.8	.0000	1	836-7
0.0122	20.8	.0000	1	84-year-old
0.0122	20.8	.0000	1	85-foot
0.0122	20.8	.0000	1	869
0.0122	20.8	.0000	1	89-yard
0.0122	20.8	.0000	1	9-year-old
0.0122	20.8	.0000	1	90-minute
0.0122	20.8	.0000	1	90006
0.0122	20.8	.0000	1	91st
0.0122	20.8	.0000	1	912
0.0122	20.8	.0000	1	91324
0.0122	20.8	.0000	1	92-65
0.0122	20.8	.0000	1	92-72
0.0122	20.8	.0000	1	92262
0.0122	20.8	.0000	1	92502
0.0122	20.8	.0000	1	94-inch
0.0122	20.8	.0000	1	974-foot
0.0122	20.8	.0000	1	9760
0.0122	20.8	.0000	1	986
0.0122	20.8	.0000	1	995-percent
0.0117	20.7	.0000	1	'T'
0.0117	20.7	.0000	1	'andle
0.0117	20.7	.0000	1	'dopted
0.0117	20.7	.0000	1	'dout
0.0117	20.7	.0000	1	'e'll
0.0117	20.7	.0000	1	'gain
0.0117	20.7	.0000	1	'kase
0.0117	20.7	.0000	1	'lection
0.0117	20.7	.0000	1	'nother
0.0117	20.7	.0000	1	'pears
0.0117	20.7	.0000	1	'possum
0.0117	20.7	.0000	1	'sclusivest
0.0117	20.7	.0000	1	'sturb
0.0117	20.7	.0000	1	'stute
0.0117	20.7	.0000	1	'taters
0.0117	20.7	.0000	1	'twarn't
0.0117	20.7	.0000	1	'twasn't
0.0117	20.7	.0000	1	'uman
0.0117	20.7	.0000	1	'52
0.0117	20.7	.0000	1	a-a-ah

THE PRECEDING WORD TYPE OCCUPIES RANK 71300

U	SFI	D	F	Word Type
0.0117	20.7	.0000	1	a-barking
0.0117	20.7	.0000	1	a-booming
0.0117	20.7	.0000	1	a-borrowing
0.0117	20.7	.0000	1	a-buyin'
0.0117	20.7	.0000	1	a-doin'
0.0117	20.7	.0000	1	a-doing
0.0117	20.7	.0000	1	a-gittin'
0.0117	20.7	.0000	1	a-going
0.0117	20.7	.0000	1	a-hunting
0.0117	20.7	.0000	1	a-patchin'
0.0117	20.7	.0000	1	a-rubbishing
0.0117	20.7	.0000	1	a-sorrowing
0.0117	20.7	.0000	1	a-tou-tou-tou-tou
0.0117	20.7	.0000	1	a-tremble
0.0117	20.7	.0000	1	a-weaving
0.0117	20.7	.0000	1	abates
0.0117	20.7	.0000	1	abduction
0.0117	20.7	.0000	1	acclamations
0.0117	20.7	.0000	1	aclostones
0.0117	20.7	.0000	1	acquisitiveness
0.0117	20.7	.0000	1	across't
0.0117	20.7	.0000	1	acrost
0.0117	20.7	.0000	1	acuteness
0.0117	20.7	.0000	1	Ada's
0.0117	20.7	.0000	1	Advantages
0.0117	20.7	.0000	1	ADVENTURES
0.0117	20.7	.0000	1	aeroplanes
0.0117	20.7	.0000	1	aeryoplanes
0.0117	20.7	.0000	1	age-worn
0.0117	20.7	.0000	1	aggrandizements
0.0117	20.7	.0000	1	aggreement
0.0117	20.7	.0000	1	aginst
0.0117	20.7	.0000	1	ailin'
0.0117	20.7	.0000	1	airhole
0.0117	20.7	.0000	1	albacore
0.0117	20.7	.0000	1	aldermanic
0.0117	20.7	.0000	1	Alger
0.0117	20.7	.0000	1	All-Stars
0.0117	20.7	.0000	1	Alleghany
0.0117	20.7	.0000	1	Alstyne's
0.0117	20.7	.0000	1	amethysts
0.0117	20.7	.0000	1	Amma
0.0117	20.7	.0000	1	amulets
0.0117	20.7	.0000	1	anableps
0.0117	20.7	.0000	1	anchor-chain
0.0117	20.7	.0000	1	ancient-looking
0.0117	20.7	.0000	1	Andersens
0.0117	20.7	.0000	1	andiron
0.0117	20.7	.0000	1	anonymously
0.0117	20.7	.0000	1	anthropophagy
0.0117	20.7	.0000	1	antipathy
0.0117	20.7	.0000	1	anything-land
0.0117	20.7	.0000	1	aphis
0.0117	20.7	.0000	1	appareled
0.0117	20.7	.0000	1	appellation
0.0117	20.7	.0000	1	appertain
0.0117	20.7	.0000	1	apteronotes
0.0117	20.7	.0000	1	Arable's
0.0117	20.7	.0000	1	arbors

U	SFI	D	F	Word Type
0.0117	20.7	.0000	1	archangel
0.0117	20.7	.0000	1	archway
0.0117	20.7	.0000	1	archways
0.0117	20.7	.0000	1	arf-arf
0.0117	20.7	.0000	1	Argess'
0.0117	20.7	.0000	1	Arliss's
0.0117	20.7	.0000	1	Arnaud's
0.0117	20.7	.0000	1	arrowless
0.0117	20.7	.0000	1	artichoke-boilers
0.0117	20.7	.0000	1	artifices
0.0117	20.7	.0000	1	ash-hopper
0.0117	20.7	.0000	1	ashhopper
0.0117	20.7	.0000	1	aspirant
0.0117	20.7	.0000	1	aspiring
0.0117	20.7	.0000	1	ast
0.0117	20.7	.0000	1	astonishments
0.0117	20.7	.0000	1	at-at-at
0.0117	20.7	.0000	1	austere-looking
0.0117	20.7	.0000	1	autumnal
0.0117	20.7	.0000	1	Azalie
0.0117	20.7	.0000	1	Azuloy's
0.0117	20.7	.0000	1	azurors
0.0117	20.7	.0000	1	b-b-bless
0.0117	20.7	.0000	1	b-b-breed
0.0117	20.7	.0000	1	b-b-bullet
0.0117	20.7	.0000	1	Baby's
0.0117	20.7	.0000	1	back-fired
0.0117	20.7	.0000	1	back-garden
0.0117	20.7	.0000	1	backdrop
0.0117	20.7	.0000	1	bacons
0.0117	20.7	.0000	1	bad-
0.0117	20.7	.0000	1	Badger's
0.0117	20.7	.0000	1	Bahman
0.0117	20.7	.0000	1	bailed
0.0117	20.7	.0000	1	baits
0.0117	20.7	.0000	1	baler
0.0117	20.7	.0000	1	balistae
0.0117	20.7	.0000	1	balking
0.0117	20.7	.0000	1	balled
0.0117	20.7	.0000	1	ballgames
0.0117	20.7	.0000	1	bambinos
THE PRECEDING WORD TYPE OCCUPIES RANK 71400				
0.0117	20.7	.0000	1	band-concert
0.0117	20.7	.0000	1	bandy-legged
0.0117	20.7	.0000	1	bank-notes
0.0117	20.7	.0000	1	Bantu's
0.0117	20.7	.0000	1	barbeque
0.0117	20.7	.0000	1	Baring
0.0117	20.7	.0000	1	barkin'
0.0117	20.7	.0000	1	barley-cakes
0.0117	20.7	.0000	1	barnyards
0.0117	20.7	.0000	1	barrows
0.0117	20.7	.0000	1	baser
0.0117	20.7	.0000	1	Basinghall
0.0117	20.7	.0000	1	batten
0.0117	20.7	.0000	1	battle-scarred
0.0117	20.7	.0000	1	battle-viewing
0.0117	20.7	.0000	1	Batulcar's
0.0117	20.7	.0000	1	Baviaan
0.0117	20.7	.0000	1	bawdkin
0.0117	20.7	.0000	1	bawdricks
0.0117	20.7	.0000	1	Baxter's
0.0117	20.7	.0000	1	bay-head
0.0117	20.7	.0000	1	bayed
0.0117	20.7	.0000	1	bead-rings
0.0117	20.7	.0000	1	beat-up
0.0117	20.7	.0000	1	Beauregarde
0.0117	20.7	.0000	1	beckon
0.0117	20.7	.0000	1	bed-maker
0.0117	20.7	.0000	1	bed-maker's
0.0117	20.7	.0000	1	bed-time
0.0117	20.7	.0000	1	bedewed
0.0117	20.7	.0000	1	bedfellow
0.0117	20.7	.0000	1	bee's-wax
0.0117	20.7	.0000	1	Beef
0.0117	20.7	.0000	1	BEEN
0.0117	20.7	.0000	1	bees'-wax
0.0117	20.7	.0000	1	beetle's
0.0117	20.7	.0000	1	beginnin'
0.0117	20.7	.0000	1	Beginnings
0.0117	20.7	.0000	1	behaviour
0.0117	20.7	.0000	1	behine
0.0117	20.7	.0000	1	beldame
0.0117	20.7	.0000	1	bellerin'
0.0117	20.7	.0000	1	Belmont's
0.0117	20.7	.0000	1	belongin'
0.0117	20.7	.0000	1	ben'
0.0117	20.7	.0000	1	Benamuckee
0.0117	20.7	.0000	1	Benches
0.0117	20.7	.0000	1	bendin'
0.0117	20.7	.0000	1	Benedicite
0.0117	20.7	.0000	1	Beneteau
0.0117	20.7	.0000	1	beruffled
0.0117	20.7	.0000	1	besom
0.0117	20.7	.0000	1	bestrewn
0.0117	20.7	.0000	1	Bi-Coloured-Python-R**
0.0117	20.7	.0000	1	big-deal
0.0117	20.7	.0000	1	big-starred
0.0117	20.7	.0000	1	bight
0.0117	20.7	.0000	1	Billerica
0.0117	20.7	.0000	1	Billingsgate
0.0117	20.7	.0000	1	bilobed
0.0117	20.7	.0000	1	bindweed
0.0117	20.7	.0000	1	bingo
0.0117	20.7	.0000	1	Binney's
0.0117	20.7	.0000	1	bird-like
0.0117	20.7	.0000	1	Birdsong
0.0117	20.7	.0000	1	Biscuits
0.0117	20.7	.0000	1	bitterer
0.0117	20.7	.0000	1	blabber
0.0117	20.7	.0000	1	Black-boy
0.0117	20.7	.0000	1	black-coated
0.0117	20.7	.0000	1	black-dotted
0.0117	20.7	.0000	1	blacker-than-night
0.0117	20.7	.0000	1	blackjack
0.0117	20.7	.0000	1	Blackwell's
0.0117	20.7	.0000	1	blade-bone

U	SFI	D	F	Word Type
0.0117	20.7	.0000	1	Blancas
0.0117	20.7	.0000	1	bleatings
0.0117	20.7	.0000	1	blenched
0.0117	20.7	.0000	1	blessin'
0.0117	20.7	.0000	1	blissful
0.0117	20.7	.0000	1	blithely
0.0117	20.7	.0000	1	block-house
0.0117	20.7	.0000	1	Blockheads
0.0117	20.7	.0000	1	blocky
0.0117	20.7	.0000	1	bloodcurdling
0.0117	20.7	.0000	1	blotchy
0.0117	20.7	.0000	1	bluebells
0.0117	20.7	.0000	1	blueberry-pickers
0.0117	20.7	.0000	1	bluegrass
0.0117	20.7	.0000	1	blusterous
0.0117	20.7	.0000	1	boat-racing
0.0117	20.7	.0000	1	boatswain
0.0117	20.7	.0000	1	Boco
0.0117	20.7	.0000	1	body-coat
0.0117	20.7	.0000	1	Bolshie
0.0117	20.7	.0000	1	boneset
0.0117	20.7	.0000	1	BONGGGG
0.0117	20.7	.0000	1	bonitos
0.0117	20.7	.0000	1	Bonte-Buck
0.0117	20.7	.0000	1	Bood
THE PRECEDING WORD TYPE OCCUPIES RANK 71500				
0.0117	20.7	.0000	1	boodles
0.0117	20.7	.0000	1	book-shelves
0.0117	20.7	.0000	1	Boom's
0.0117	20.7	.0000	1	boot-box
0.0117	20.7	.0000	1	bootlaces
0.0117	20.7	.0000	1	Bopsulai's
0.0117	20.7	.0000	1	bossing
0.0117	20.7	.0000	1	Bourbonnais
0.0117	20.7	.0000	1	bow-and-arrow
0.0117	20.7	.0000	1	bowser-hound
0.0117	20.7	.0000	1	br-r-r-r-r-r
0.0117	20.7	.0000	1	Brackett's
0.0117	20.7	.0000	1	Bradshaw
0.0117	20.7	.0000	1	brain-racking
0.0117	20.7	.0000	1	brainstorms
0.0117	20.7	.0000	1	brainworkers
0.0117	20.7	.0000	1	brass-heeled
0.0117	20.7	.0000	1	Brave's
0.0117	20.7	.0000	1	brazier
0.0117	20.7	.0000	1	bread-and-jam
0.0117	20.7	.0000	1	breakfast's
0.0117	20.7	.0000	1	breakin'
0.0117	20.7	.0000	1	breast-bands
0.0117	20.7	.0000	1	breathings
0.0117	20.7	.0000	1	brier-patches
0.0117	20.7	.0000	1	Brigadier's
0.0117	20.7	.0000	1	Brillon
0.0117	20.7	.0000	1	Bromwell's
0.0117	20.7	.0000	1	bronc
0.0117	20.7	.0000	1	Broom-Cupboard
0.0117	20.7	.0000	1	broom-handle
0.0117	20.7	.0000	1	brown-paper
0.0117	20.7	.0000	1	brownie's
0.0117	20.7	.0000	1	brumal
0.0117	20.7	.0000	1	brute's
0.0117	20.7	.0000	1	buccaneer
0.0117	20.7	.0000	1	buck's
0.0117	20.7	.0000	1	Buckets
0.0117	20.7	.0000	1	Bucklersbury
0.0117	20.7	.0000	1	bud's
0.0117	20.7	.0000	1	budged
0.0117	20.7	.0000	1	budges
0.0117	20.7	.0000	1	bugle-blast
0.0117	20.7	.0000	1	bulgy
0.0117	20.7	.0000	1	bulked
0.0117	20.7	.0000	1	Bullivant
0.0117	20.7	.0000	1	bullyrag
0.0117	20.7	.0000	1	Bulrushers
0.0117	20.7	.0000	1	Bumpo's
0.0117	20.7	.0000	1	Bunsby
0.0117	20.7	.0000	1	Burnach
0.0117	20.7	.0000	1	Bush-Buck
0.0117	20.7	.0000	1	Bushes
0.0117	20.7	.0000	1	Butcher's
0.0117	20.7	.0000	1	Butchers
0.0117	20.7	.0000	1	Butters
0.0117	20.7	.0000	1	buttonhook
0.0117	20.7	.0000	1	c-c-colt
0.0117	20.7	.0000	1	c-come
0.0117	20.7	.0000	1	ca'm
0.0117	20.7	.0000	1	cachalot's
0.0117	20.7	.0000	1	cain't
0.0117	20.7	.0000	1	calcimine
0.0117	20.7	.0000	1	Caliban
0.0117	20.7	.0000	1	CALIFORNIA
0.0117	20.7	.0000	1	calling-like
0.0117	20.7	.0000	1	cam'st
0.0117	20.7	.0000	1	camel-necked
0.0117	20.7	.0000	1	camp-fire
0.0117	20.7	.0000	1	Canadas
0.0117	20.7	.0000	1	Canty's
0.0117	20.7	.0000	1	cantyoucantyoucant
0.0117	20.7	.0000	1	cap-screwer
0.0117	20.7	.0000	1	Capa
0.0117	20.7	.0000	1	Capernaum
0.0117	20.7	.0000	1	capriscus
0.0117	20.7	.0000	1	capting
0.0117	20.7	.0000	1	Carabine
0.0117	20.7	.0000	1	cardigan
0.0117	20.7	.0000	1	Carmelita's
0.0117	20.7	.0000	1	Caroliny
0.0117	20.7	.0000	1	carp-fish
0.0117	20.7	.0000	1	carragheen
0.0117	20.7	.0000	1	Carrol
0.0117	20.7	.0000	1	carry-all
0.0117	20.7	.0000	1	carter's
0.0117	20.7	.0000	1	carthorse
0.0117	20.7	.0000	1	cashmere-sweater
0.0117	20.7	.0000	1	casuarinae
0.0117	20.7	.0000	1	catapulting
0.0117	20.7	.0000	1	catcalls

U	SFI	D	F	Word Type
0.0117	20.7	.0000	1	catch-as-catch-can
0.0117	20.7	.0000	1	caterer
0.0117	20.7	.0000	1	Caterpillar's
0.0117	20.7	.0000	1	cattiness
0.0117	20.7	.0000	1	catty-shaped
0.0117	20.7	.0000	1	cautioning
0.0117	20.7	.0000	1	cave-life
0.0117	20.7	.0000	1	cave-wall
0.0117	20.7	.0000	1	cavily
THE PRECEDING WORD TYPE OCCUPIES RANK 71600				
0.0117	20.7	.0000	1	cavorted
0.0117	20.7	.0000	1	cayuse
0.0117	20.7	.0000	1	ceilinged
0.0117	20.7	.0000	1	celerity
0.0117	20.7	.0000	1	Cellini
0.0117	20.7	.0000	1	Celyndia's
0.0117	20.7	.0000	1	centerboard-case
0.0117	20.7	.0000	1	centronotes
0.0117	20.7	.0000	1	centses
0.0117	20.7	.0000	1	cervical
0.0117	20.7	.0000	1	Cetacean
0.0117	20.7	.0000	1	cetaceous
0.0117	20.7	.0000	1	Ceuta
0.0117	20.7	.0000	1	Ch
0.0117	20.7	.0000	1	chafe
0.0117	20.7	.0000	1	CHAIR
0.0117	20.7	.0000	1	champion's
0.0117	20.7	.0000	1	Chancery
0.0117	20.7	.0000	1	chanst
0.0117	20.7	.0000	1	chatelaine
0.0117	20.7	.0000	1	chats
0.0117	20.7	.0000	1	Cheapside
0.0117	20.7	.0000	1	Chee-Chee's
0.0117	20.7	.0000	1	cheeriness
0.0117	20.7	.0000	1	cheese-making
0.0117	20.7	.0000	1	cherry-trees
0.0117	20.7	.0000	1	Cheshire-Cat
0.0117	20.7	.0000	1	chess-board
0.0117	20.7	.0000	1	chest-level
0.0117	20.7	.0000	1	chestnut-burrs
0.0117	20.7	.0000	1	chestnut's
0.0117	20.7	.0000	1	Chevrolet's
0.0117	20.7	.0000	1	Chevvy
0.0117	20.7	.0000	1	Chickahominy
0.0117	20.7	.0000	1	chillier
0.0117	20.7	.0000	1	chin-up
0.0117	20.7	.0000	1	chirrups
0.0117	20.7	.0000	1	chivvied
0.0117	20.7	.0000	1	chivvying
0.0117	20.7	.0000	1	CHOCOLATE
0.0117	20.7	.0000	1	chop-whiskers
0.0117	20.7	.0000	1	Christmas-time
0.0117	20.7	.0000	1	chrysontera
0.0117	20.7	.0000	1	church-mice
0.0117	20.7	.0000	1	church-tower
0.0117	20.7	.0000	1	Churchyard
0.0117	20.7	.0000	1	cineraria
0.0117	20.7	.0000	1	cinerarias
0.0117	20.7	.0000	1	circuitous
0.0117	20.7	.0000	1	clammed
0.0117	20.7	.0000	1	clapperdogeons
0.0117	20.7	.0000	1	claspknife
0.0117	20.7	.0000	1	Claus's
0.0117	20.7	.0000	1	clean-looking
0.0117	20.7	.0000	1	Clearwater's
0.0117	20.7	.0000	1	clobbering
0.0117	20.7	.0000	1	clodhopper
0.0117	20.7	.0000	1	clomping
0.0117	20.7	.0000	1	close-drawn
0.0117	20.7	.0000	1	CLOSES
0.0117	20.7	.0000	1	clothes-sack
0.0117	20.7	.0000	1	cloud-rack
0.0117	20.7	.0000	1	clown-faces
0.0117	20.7	.0000	1	clubbed
0.0117	20.7	.0000	1	clumb
0.0117	20.7	.0000	1	clumpy
0.0117	20.7	.0000	1	coarsest
0.0117	20.7	.0000	1	coat-room
0.0117	20.7	.0000	1	Coates
0.0117	20.7	.0000	1	cobble
0.0117	20.7	.0000	1	cobra's
0.0117	20.7	.0000	1	cockatoo
0.0117	20.7	.0000	1	cocoa-tree
0.0117	20.7	.0000	1	cocoanut-tree
0.0117	20.7	.0000	1	coffeepot's
0.0117	20.7	.0000	1	cogitations
0.0117	20.7	.0000	1	coiled-up
0.0117	20.7	.0000	1	Colby's
0.0117	20.7	.0000	1	collarless
0.0117	20.7	.0000	1	color-sergeant
0.0117	20.7	.0000	1	Comet's
0.0117	20.7	.0000	1	comf'table
0.0117	20.7	.0000	1	comfortable-looking
0.0117	20.7	.0000	1	commandeth
0.0117	20.7	.0000	1	commenting
0.0117	20.7	.0000	1	commissary-general
0.0117	20.7	.0000	1	commitments
0.0117	20.7	.0000	1	Compagnie-Nationale
0.0117	20.7	.0000	1	company-front
0.0117	20.7	.0000	1	Compared
0.0117	20.7	.0000	1	compassion-inspiring
0.0117	20.7	.0000	1	comprised
0.0117	20.7	.0000	1	condescended
0.0117	20.7	.0000	1	confectioner's
0.0117	20.7	.0000	1	Confectionery
0.0117	20.7	.0000	1	Confessor's
0.0117	20.7	.0000	1	confirming
0.0117	20.7	.0000	1	conflagration
0.0117	20.7	.0000	1	conjuration
0.0117	20.7	.0000	1	conjurer
THE PRECEDING WORD TYPE OCCUPIES RANK 71700				
0.0117	20.7	.0000	1	conking
0.0117	20.7	.0000	1	connivance
0.0117	20.7	.0000	1	connivering
0.0117	20.7	.0000	1	consideringly
0.0117	20.7	.0000	1	consigned
0.0117	20.7	.0000	1	Contrasted

U	SFI	D	F	Word Type
0.0117	20.7	.0000	1	conversed
0.0117	20.7	.0000	1	convolvulus-runners
0.0117	20.7	.0000	1	convulsed
0.0117	20.7	.0000	1	coon's
0.0117	20.7	.0000	1	coops
0.0117	20.7	.0000	1	Copp's
0.0117	20.7	.0000	1	copse
0.0117	20.7	.0000	1	Coquin
0.0117	20.7	.0000	1	corn-cakes
0.0117	20.7	.0000	1	corn-cob
0.0117	20.7	.0000	1	corn-feast
0.0117	20.7	.0000	1	cotton-blond
0.0117	20.7	.0000	1	Cougar's
0.0117	20.7	.0000	1	council-fires
0.0117	20.7	.0000	1	councilman
0.0117	20.7	.0000	1	country-wards
0.0117	20.7	.0000	1	countrybred
0.0117	20.7	.0000	1	coursers
0.0117	20.7	.0000	1	courtiers
0.0117	20.7	.0000	1	covetous
0.0117	20.7	.0000	1	cow-hand
0.0117	20.7	.0000	1	cow-horn
0.0117	20.7	.0000	1	cow-pea
0.0117	20.7	.0000	1	Coward
0.0117	20.7	.0000	1	cowbo-o-oy
0.0117	20.7	.0000	1	cowhorses
0.0117	20.7	.0000	1	cowlicks
0.0117	20.7	.0000	1	cowpeas
0.0117	20.7	.0000	1	Crandalls
0.0117	20.7	.0000	1	Crawfish
0.0117	20.7	.0000	1	crazed
0.0117	20.7	.0000	1	creeped
0.0117	20.7	.0000	1	crestfallen
0.0117	20.7	.0000	1	crick
0.0117	20.7	.0000	1	crimers
0.0117	20.7	.0000	1	crisped
0.0117	20.7	.0000	1	Crocker's
0.0117	20.7	.0000	1	crockery
0.0117	20.7	.0000	1	crookedy
0.0117	20.7	.0000	1	Crookshank
0.0117	20.7	.0000	1	croqueted
0.0117	20.7	.0000	1	croqueting
0.0117	20.7	.0000	1	cross-rib
0.0117	20.7	.0000	1	cross-trees
0.0117	20.7	.0000	1	crowbait
0.0117	20.7	.0000	1	crucibles
0.0117	20.7	.0000	1	crude-looking
0.0117	20.7	.0000	1	crumpets
0.0117	20.7	.0000	1	crumples
0.0117	20.7	.0000	1	crums
0.0117	20.7	.0000	1	Cuby
0.0117	20.7	.0000	1	culverins
0.0117	20.7	.0000	1	cumbered
0.0117	20.7	.0000	1	Cunard
0.0117	20.7	.0000	1	cupboard-stairway
0.0117	20.7	.0000	1	cupfuls
0.0117	20.7	.0000	1	curassavian
0.0117	20.7	.0000	1	Curdy
0.0117	20.7	.0000	1	currant
0.0117	20.7	.0000	1	currant-bunny
0.0117	20.7	.0000	1	curtiosity
0.0117	20.7	.0000	1	curtsey
0.0117	20.7	.0000	1	Cuspid
0.0117	20.7	.0000	1	Cuspidor
0.0117	20.7	.0000	1	custom's
0.0117	20.7	.0000	1	cut-bank
0.0117	20.7	.0000	1	cutbanks
0.0117	20.7	.0000	1	Cuthbert's
0.0117	20.7	.0000	1	cutter-rigged
0.0117	20.7	.0000	1	cutterigsloop
0.0117	20.7	.0000	1	cycle-path
0.0117	20.7	.0000	1	cypher
0.0117	20.7	.0000	1	d-d-d
0.0117	20.7	.0000	1	dace
0.0117	20.7	.0000	1	Dahr
0.0117	20.7	.0000	1	daintier
0.0117	20.7	.0000	1	daisy-chain
0.0117	20.7	.0000	1	DAM
0.0117	20.7	.0000	1	Dana's
0.0117	20.7	.0000	1	dancin'
0.0117	20.7	.0000	1	Dandy's
0.0117	20.7	.0000	1	danged
0.0117	20.7	.0000	1	Darnells
0.0117	20.7	.0000	1	daystar
0.0117	20.7	.0000	1	Dazzler's
0.0117	20.7	.0000	1	deBureford
0.0117	20.7	.0000	1	deMalaga
0.0117	20.7	.0000	1	deMare
0.0117	20.7	.0000	1	deTodoslosSantos
0.0117	20.7	.0000	1	deacons
0.0117	20.7	.0000	1	dead-O
0.0117	20.7	.0000	1	dead-beats
0.0117	20.7	.0000	1	decalcomanias
0.0117	20.7	.0000	1	decamp
THE PRECEDING WORD TYPE OCCUPIES RANK 71800				
0.0117	20.7	.0000	1	Decapods
0.0117	20.7	.0000	1	Deceit
0.0117	20.7	.0000	1	declamatory
0.0117	20.7	.0000	1	declivity
0.0117	20.7	.0000	1	decrepitude
0.0117	20.7	.0000	1	deef
0.0117	20.7	.0000	1	deep-creased
0.0117	20.7	.0000	1	deer-hound
0.0117	20.7	.0000	1	defenceless
0.0117	20.7	.0000	1	Delicatessa
0.0117	20.7	.0000	1	dells
0.0117	20.7	.0000	1	demesne
0.0117	20.7	.0000	1	demolishing
0.0117	20.7	.0000	1	denned
0.0117	20.7	.0000	1	dentuso
0.0117	20.7	.0000	1	deprecatingly
0.0117	20.7	.0000	1	deprecatory
0.0117	20.7	.0000	1	derided
0.0117	20.7	.0000	1	despisable
0.0117	20.7	.0000	1	Dhondaram
0.0117	20.7	.0000	1	dibs
0.0117	20.7	.0000	1	dickey

U	SFI	D	F	Word Type
0.0117	20.7	.0000	1	Difficulty
0.0117	20.7	.0000	1	dignities
0.0117	20.7	.0000	1	dims
0.0117	20.7	.0000	1	ding-dong-ding-dong
0.0117	20.7	.0000	1	Dinky's
0.0117	20.7	.0000	1	dinner-time
0.0117	20.7	.0000	1	Dinsmore
0.0117	20.7	.0000	1	directors'
0.0117	20.7	.0000	1	dirtied
0.0117	20.7	.0000	1	discoloured
0.0117	20.7	.0000	1	discomposed
0.0117	20.7	.0000	1	disencumbered
0.0117	20.7	.0000	1	disfigure
0.0117	20.7	.0000	1	dissipating
0.0117	20.7	.0000	1	distastefully
0.0117	20.7	.0000	1	dive'
0.0117	20.7	.0000	1	diverging
0.0117	20.7	.0000	1	do-gooders
0.0117	20.7	.0000	1	Docia
0.0117	20.7	.0000	1	Dodworth
0.0117	20.7	.0000	1	doffing
0.0117	20.7	.0000	1	dog-days
0.0117	20.7	.0000	1	dog-musher
0.0117	20.7	.0000	1	dogcatcher's
0.0117	20.7	.0000	1	doin's
0.0117	20.7	.0000	1	Donahoe
0.0117	20.7	.0000	1	DOOM
0.0117	20.7	.0000	1	Dorcas
0.0117	20.7	.0000	1	dormice
0.0117	20.7	.0000	1	dosing
0.0117	20.7	.0000	1	dotard
0.0117	20.7	.0000	1	Dotty's
0.0117	20.7	.0000	1	double-barrelled
0.0117	20.7	.0000	1	doubled-up
0.0117	20.7	.0000	1	Doune
0.0117	20.7	.0000	1	Dowgate
0.0117	20.7	.0000	1	down-stairs
0.0117	20.7	.0000	1	Downdale
0.0117	20.7	.0000	1	doxies
0.0117	20.7	.0000	1	Dragon-Seal
0.0117	20.7	.0000	1	dragon's-breath
0.0117	20.7	.0000	1	Dravidian
0.0117	20.7	.0000	1	drawed
0.0117	20.7	.0000	1	drawing-pencils
0.0117	20.7	.0000	1	dress-up
0.0117	20.7	.0000	1	dressing-room
0.0117	20.7	.0000	1	dronings
0.0117	20.7	.0000	1	drooling
0.0117	20.7	.0000	1	drumlike
0.0117	20.7	.0000	1	Drummonds
0.0117	20.7	.0000	1	duc's
0.0117	20.7	.0000	1	ducal
0.0117	20.7	.0000	1	duck-language
0.0117	20.7	.0000	1	Durant's
0.0117	20.7	.0000	1	Durham
0.0117	20.7	.0000	1	dusk-dark
0.0117	20.7	.0000	1	Dygert
0.0117	20.7	.0000	1	E**
0.0117	20.7	.0000	1	eagle-feathers
0.0117	20.7	.0000	1	eaglefeather
0.0117	20.7	.0000	1	earldom
0.0117	20.7	.0000	1	early-closing
0.0117	20.7	.0000	1	Easter's
0.0117	20.7	.0000	1	Easy-to-Read
0.0117	20.7	.0000	1	eavesdroppers
0.0117	20.7	.0000	1	Ecclesiastical
0.0117	20.7	.0000	1	eclat
0.0117	20.7	.0000	1	ecstasies
0.0117	20.7	.0000	1	edgy
0.0117	20.7	.0000	1	Eelka's
0.0117	20.7	.0000	1	Efraim
0.0117	20.7	.0000	1	Efraim's
0.0117	20.7	.0000	1	Eggletina's
0.0117	20.7	.0000	1	ejaculating
0.0117	20.7	.0000	1	Elephants
0.0117	20.7	.0000	1	Eliza's
0.0117	20.7	.0000	1	emperor-holocanthus
0.0117	20.7	.0000	1	emulating

THE PRECEDING WORD TYPE OCCUPIES RANK 71900

U	SFI	D	F	Word Type
0.0117	20.7	.0000	1	en'
0.0117	20.7	.0000	1	enchantments
0.0117	20.7	.0000	1	encompassed
0.0117	20.7	.0000	1	Energetic
0.0117	20.7	.0000	1	Entomological
0.0117	20.7	.0000	1	entymologist
0.0117	20.7	.0000	1	enveloping
0.0117	20.7	.0000	1	Epps'
0.0117	20.7	.0000	1	erector
0.0117	20.7	.0000	1	Ernie's
0.0117	20.7	.0000	1	erosions
0.0117	20.7	.0000	1	erstwhile
0.0117	20.7	.0000	1	Esq
0.0117	20.7	.0000	1	etcetera
0.0117	20.7	.0000	1	eunuchs
0.0117	20.7	.0000	1	evasions
0.0117	20.7	.0000	1	everlastingly
0.0117	20.7	.0000	1	everywheres
0.0117	20.7	.0000	1	excellently
0.0117	20.7	.0000	1	executor
0.0117	20.7	.0000	1	expectin'
0.0117	20.7	.0000	1	expectoration
0.0117	20.7	.0000	1	explorin
0.0117	20.7	.0000	1	expostulated
0.0117	20.7	.0000	1	extra-special
0.0117	20.7	.0000	1	exult
0.0117	20.7	.0000	1	eye-lashes
0.0117	20.7	.0000	1	eye-reach
0.0117	20.7	.0000	1	eyelash
0.0117	20.7	.0000	1	faileth
0.0117	20.7	.0000	1	failin'
0.0117	20.7	.0000	1	fan-tail
0.0117	20.7	.0000	1	fangled
0.0117	20.7	.0000	1	Far-Off
0.0117	20.7	.0000	1	farthings
0.0117	20.7	.0000	1	Farwell's
0.0117	20.7	.0000	1	fas'
0.0117	20.7	.0000	1	fast-a
0.0117	20.7	.0000	1	fastenings
0.0117	20.7	.0000	1	Father'll
0.0117	20.7	.0000	1	fatiguing
0.0117	20.7	.0000	1	Fatso
0.0117	20.7	.0000	1	fatuous
0.0117	20.7	.0000	1	faze
0.0117	20.7	.0000	1	feather-light
0.0117	20.7	.0000	1	feedin'
0.0117	20.7	.0000	1	feedn'
0.0117	20.7	.0000	1	fei
0.0117	20.7	.0000	1	feller'll
0.0117	20.7	.0000	1	fellow-Christians
0.0117	20.7	.0000	1	fellow-rascal
0.0117	20.7	.0000	1	felonious
0.0117	20.7	.0000	1	felt-lined
0.0117	20.7	.0000	1	fencerow
0.0117	20.7	.0000	1	ferine
0.0117	20.7	.0000	1	fern-table
0.0117	20.7	.0000	1	ferry-boat
0.0117	20.7	.0000	1	fervency
0.0117	20.7	.0000	1	festerin'
0.0117	20.7	.0000	1	fettle
0.0117	20.7	.0000	1	fever-trees
0.0117	20.7	.0000	1	fib
0.0117	20.7	.0000	1	ficuses
0.0117	20.7	.0000	1	fidgetin'
0.0117	20.7	.0000	1	fidgety
0.0117	20.7	.0000	1	Fieldmouse's
0.0117	20.7	.0000	1	fight'n
0.0117	20.7	.0000	1	Filial
0.0117	20.7	.0000	1	finest-blooded
0.0117	20.7	.0000	1	finger's
0.0117	20.7	.0000	1	Fishhook
0.0117	20.7	.0000	1	fishing-boat
0.0117	20.7	.0000	1	fishing-sloop
0.0117	20.7	.0000	1	fishless
0.0117	20.7	.0000	1	Fishmonger's
0.0117	20.7	.0000	1	five-and-thirty
0.0117	20.7	.0000	1	fixin
0.0117	20.7	.0000	1	fizzed
0.0117	20.7	.0000	1	fladbrod
0.0117	20.7	.0000	1	flame-jets
0.0117	20.7	.0000	1	flappy
0.0117	20.7	.0000	1	flat-brimmed
0.0117	20.7	.0000	1	flatirons
0.0117	20.7	.0000	1	flatwoods
0.0117	20.7	.0000	1	fleetingly
0.0117	20.7	.0000	1	fleetness
0.0117	20.7	.0000	1	Flexible
0.0117	20.7	.0000	1	flicker's
0.0117	20.7	.0000	1	flinders
0.0117	20.7	.0000	1	flirted
0.0117	20.7	.0000	1	flower-bed
0.0117	20.7	.0000	1	flower-beds
0.0117	20.7	.0000	1	fly-whisk
0.0117	20.7	.0000	1	fo'c's'le
0.0117	20.7	.0000	1	foamite
0.0117	20.7	.0000	1	Fodder-wing
0.0117	20.7	.0000	1	Fogg's
0.0117	20.7	.0000	1	footfalls
0.0117	20.7	.0000	1	forasmuch
0.0117	20.7	.0000	1	forcible

THE PRECEDING WORD TYPE OCCUPIES RANK 72000

U	SFI	D	F	Word Type
0.0117	20.7	.0000	1	fore-quarter
0.0117	20.7	.0000	1	fore-quarters
0.0117	20.7	.0000	1	fore-topsail
0.0117	20.7	.0000	1	forkfuls
0.0117	20.7	.0000	1	forlornly
0.0117	20.7	.0000	1	Forth
0.0117	20.7	.0000	1	Fortnightly
0.0117	20.7	.0000	1	forty-fifth
0.0117	20.7	.0000	1	foun'
0.0117	20.7	.0000	1	fox-hearted
0.0117	20.7	.0000	1	FRANKLIN
0.0117	20.7	.0000	1	freckle-faced
0.0117	20.7	.0000	1	freckled-faced
0.0117	20.7	.0000	1	Freebody'll
0.0117	20.7	.0000	1	french
0.0117	20.7	.0000	1	Frenchers
0.0117	20.7	.0000	1	Fresh
0.0117	20.7	.0000	1	fresh-turned
0.0117	20.7	.0000	1	frigate's
0.0117	20.7	.0000	1	Frisky
0.0117	20.7	.0000	1	frockcoat
0.0117	20.7	.0000	1	frosted-glass
0.0117	20.7	.0000	1	frozen-hearted
0.0117	20.7	.0000	1	frying-pan
0.0117	20.7	.0000	1	fuchsias
0.0117	20.7	.0000	1	full-stretch
0.0117	20.7	.0000	1	Furina
0.0117	20.7	.0000	1	furlong
0.0117	20.7	.0000	1	fusses
0.0117	20.7	.0000	1	G-type
0.0117	20.7	.0000	1	ga-loups
0.0117	20.7	.0000	1	Gabilans
0.0117	20.7	.0000	1	gaggle
0.0117	20.7	.0000	1	galeolaria
0.0117	20.7	.0000	1	Galilean
0.0117	20.7	.0000	1	Galileans
0.0117	20.7	.0000	1	gallberry
0.0117	20.7	.0000	1	gallopin'
0.0117	20.7	.0000	1	gallumph
0.0117	20.7	.0000	1	gambits
0.0117	20.7	.0000	1	Gamut
0.0117	20.7	.0000	1	gang's
0.0117	20.7	.0000	1	garfish
0.0117	20.7	.0000	1	gaspipe
0.0117	20.7	.0000	1	Gassers
0.0117	20.7	.0000	1	gastroscope
0.0117	20.7	.0000	1	gee-pole
0.0117	20.7	.0000	1	Gemma
0.0117	20.7	.0000	1	genie's
0.0117	20.7	.0000	1	genlman's
0.0117	20.7	.0000	1	gentlewoman
0.0117	20.7	.0000	1	Geppetto
0.0117	20.7	.0000	1	Geppetto's
0.0117	20.7	.0000	1	gesticulation
0.0117	20.7	.0000	1	get-up
0.0117	20.7	.0000	1	getchu
0.0117	20.7	.0000	1	Giafar
0.0117	20.7	.0000	1	Giltspur
0.0117	20.7	.0000	1	gimlet
0.0117	20.7	.0000	1	ginseng
0.0117	20.7	.0000	1	girl-daughter's
0.0117	20.7	.0000	1	girlie
0.0117	20.7	.0000	1	girlish
0.0117	20.7	.0000	1	Gitano
0.0117	20.7	.0000	1	Gitano's
0.0117	20.7	.0000	1	givin'
0.0117	20.7	.0000	1	gladsome
0.0117	20.7	.0000	1	globicephali
0.0117	20.7	.0000	1	glutinous
0.0117	20.7	.0000	1	glutton
0.0117	20.7	.0000	1	gnapan
0.0117	20.7	.0000	1	gnawin'
0.0117	20.7	.0000	1	go-o-o-ne
0.0117	20.7	.0000	1	goatsack
0.0117	20.7	.0000	1	Goblin's
0.0117	20.7	.0000	1	goby
0.0117	20.7	.0000	1	Godamighty
0.0117	20.7	.0000	1	goddaughter
0.0117	20.7	.0000	1	going-to-bed
0.0117	20.7	.0000	1	gold-fish
0.0117	20.7	.0000	1	golden-tailed
0.0117	20.7	.0000	1	goldfields
0.0117	20.7	.0000	1	good-payin'
0.0117	20.7	.0000	1	good's
0.0117	20.7	.0000	1	Gooseberry
0.0117	20.7	.0000	1	Gordons
0.0117	20.7	.0000	1	Gossips
0.0117	20.7	.0000	1	Grahamsville
0.0117	20.7	.0000	1	graining
0.0117	20.7	.0000	1	Gran'
0.0117	20.7	.0000	1	grandees
0.0117	20.7	.0000	1	grandsire
0.0117	20.7	.0000	1	grass-patches
0.0117	20.7	.0000	1	gratefulness
0.0117	20.7	.0000	1	gravelled
0.0117	20.7	.0000	1	gray-and
0.0117	20.7	.0000	1	gray-and-white
0.0117	20.7	.0000	1	gray-trunked
0.0117	20.7	.0000	1	grayness
0.0117	20.7	.0000	1	Great-Grandfather

THE PRECEDING WORD TYPE OCCUPIES RANK 72100

U	SFI	D	F	Word Type
0.0117	20.7	.0000	1	Great-grandfather's
0.0117	20.7	.0000	1	great-grandmother's
0.0117	20.7	.0000	1	greedier
0.0117	20.7	.0000	1	Greenbaum's
0.0117	20.7	.0000	1	greenbug
0.0117	20.7	.0000	1	Grennan
0.0117	20.7	.0000	1	Greyhound
0.0117	20.7	.0000	1	greyhounds
0.0117	20.7	.0000	1	greyish-brownish
0.0117	20.7	.0000	1	greyish-yellowish
0.0117	20.7	.0000	1	greyish-yellowish-reddish
0.0117	20.7	.0000	1	Grimeses'
0.0117	20.7	.0000	1	grimmer
0.0117	20.7	.0000	1	grinds
0.0117	20.7	.0000	1	grog-shop
0.0117	20.7	.0000	1	grooms'
0.0117	20.7	.0000	1	grossing
0.0117	20.7	.0000	1	Growers'
0.0117	20.7	.0000	1	Grows
0.0117	20.7	.0000	1	gruesome-looking
0.0117	20.7	.0000	1	guardedly
0.0117	20.7	.0000	1	Guilderland
0.0117	20.7	.0000	1	Guildhall
0.0117	20.7	.0000	1	Guilty
0.0117	20.7	.0000	1	gunner's
0.0117	20.7	.0000	1	gunny-sack
0.0117	20.7	.0000	1	gunshop
0.0117	20.7	.0000	1	Gussie
0.0117	20.7	.0000	1	gymkhana
0.0117	20.7	.0000	1	Gymkhana's
0.0117	20.7	.0000	1	h-h-h-h-h
0.0117	20.7	.0000	1	h'mm
0.0117	20.7	.0000	1	ha'
0.0117	20.7	.0000	1	hadn'
0.0117	20.7	.0000	1	Haggin'll
0.0117	20.7	.0000	1	hair-stiffening
0.0117	20.7	.0000	1	hair's
0.0117	20.7	.0000	1	half-awake
0.0117	20.7	.0000	1	half-blown
0.0117	20.7	.0000	1	half-devoured
0.0117	20.7	.0000	1	half-drunken
0.0117	20.7	.0000	1	half-looking
0.0117	20.7	.0000	1	half-not-looking
0.0117	20.7	.0000	1	half-open
0.0117	20.7	.0000	1	half-opened
0.0117	20.7	.0000	1	half-piece
0.0117	20.7	.0000	1	half-reluctantly
0.0117	20.7	.0000	1	half-rotten
0.0117	20.7	.0000	1	half-savage
0.0117	20.7	.0000	1	half-sob
0.0117	20.7	.0000	1	half-started
0.0117	20.7	.0000	1	half-suspended
0.0117	20.7	.0000	1	half-tamed
0.0117	20.7	.0000	1	half-turned
0.0117	20.7	.0000	1	halfpenny
0.0117	20.7	.0000	1	halfways
0.0117	20.7	.0000	1	hall-oo
0.0117	20.7	.0000	1	Hallek
0.0117	20.7	.0000	1	hand-barrow
0.0117	20.7	.0000	1	hand-forged
0.0117	20.7	.0000	1	hand-painted
0.0117	20.7	.0000	1	hand-pick
0.0117	20.7	.0000	1	handhold
0.0117	20.7	.0000	1	handspike
0.0117	20.7	.0000	1	handspring
0.0117	20.7	.0000	1	hang-dog
0.0117	20.7	.0000	1	Hankinsons
0.0117	20.7	.0000	1	Hansen's
0.0117	20.7	.0000	1	harbour
0.0117	20.7	.0000	1	hard-headed
0.0117	20.7	.0000	1	hard-nosed
0.0117	20.7	.0000	1	Hardens
0.0117	20.7	.0000	1	Harrisville
0.0117	20.7	.0000	1	harrowed
0.0117	20.7	.0000	1	Hartebeest
0.0117	20.7	.0000	1	hasp
0.0117	20.7	.0000	1	hassock
0.0117	20.7	.0000	1	hatboxes
0.0117	20.7	.0000	1	haunch
0.0117	20.7	.0000	1	hawksbills
0.0117	20.7	.0000	1	haws
0.0117	20.7	.0000	1	haycock
0.0117	20.7	.0000	1	He-e-enry
0.0117	20.7	.0000	1	he'p
0.0117	20.7	.0000	1	he'ped
0.0117	20.7	.0000	1	head-down
0.0117	20.7	.0000	1	Headshrinkers
0.0117	20.7	.0000	1	headstalls
0.0117	20.7	.0000	1	hearten
0.0117	20.7	.0000	1	hearth-brush
0.0117	20.7	.0000	1	heatpump
0.0117	20.7	.0000	1	heavy-jowled
0.0117	20.7	.0000	1	heifers
0.0117	20.7	.0000	1	Helderbergs
0.0117	20.7	.0000	1	hell's
0.0117	20.7	.0000	1	Helvetia
0.0117	20.7	.0000	1	Helvetius
0.0117	20.7	.0000	1	Helvi's
0.0117	20.7	.0000	1	Hendreary
0.0117	20.7	.0000	1	hermit's

THE PRECEDING WORD TYPE OCCUPIES RANK 72200

U	SFI	D	F	Word Type
0.0117	20.7	.0000	1	hero-commander
0.0117	20.7	.0000	1	hero-worshiping
0.0117	20.7	.0000	1	Herod
0.0117	20.7	.0000	1	Hezron
0.0117	20.7	.0000	1	hi-yi
0.0117	20.7	.0000	1	hibisci
0.0117	20.7	.0000	1	hiccuping
0.0117	20.7	.0000	1	hid'n
0.0117	20.7	.0000	1	HIDDEN
0.0117	20.7	.0000	1	hide's
0.0117	20.7	.0000	1	hidin'
0.0117	20.7	.0000	1	hifi
0.0117	20.7	.0000	1	high-ceilinged
0.0117	20.7	.0000	1	high-collared
0.0117	20.7	.0000	1	high-crested
0.0117	20.7	.0000	1	high-crowned
0.0117	20.7	.0000	1	high-flyin'
0.0117	20.7	.0000	1	high-held
0.0117	20.7	.0000	1	Highness's
0.0117	20.7	.0000	1	hightail
0.0117	20.7	.0000	1	hightailed
0.0117	20.7	.0000	1	Hiller's
0.0117	20.7	.0000	1	Hin
0.0117	20.7	.0000	1	hind-leg
0.0117	20.7	.0000	1	hindlegs
0.0117	20.7	.0000	1	Hit
0.0117	20.7	.0000	1	hmph
0.0117	20.7	.0000	1	hoarhound
0.0117	20.7	.0000	1	Hobbs
0.0117	20.7	.0000	1	Hogarth
0.0117	20.7	.0000	1	hogged
0.0117	20.7	.0000	1	hoghouse
0.0117	20.7	.0000	1	home-hearths
0.0117	20.7	.0000	1	honeyjar
0.0117	20.7	.0000	1	Honourable
0.0117	20.7	.0000	1	hoof-beats
0.0117	20.7	.0000	1	hook-and-ladders
0.0117	20.7	.0000	1	hookah
0.0117	20.7	.0000	1	Hopping
0.0117	20.7	.0000	1	Hornback
0.0117	20.7	.0000	1	hornpipes
0.0117	20.7	.0000	1	horse-breaker
0.0117	20.7	.0000	1	horse-colt
0.0117	20.7	.0000	1	horse-noises
0.0117	20.7	.0000	1	horse-skin
0.0117	20.7	.0000	1	horsefeathers
0.0117	20.7	.0000	1	horseplay
0.0117	20.7	.0000	1	horsewhipping
0.0117	20.7	.0000	1	horsing
0.0117	20.7	.0000	1	hosses
0.0117	20.7	.0000	1	hot-pot
0.0117	20.7	.0000	1	hound'll
0.0117	20.7	.0000	1	house-dog
0.0117	20.7	.0000	1	house-trailer
0.0117	20.7	.0000	1	houseless
0.0117	20.7	.0000	1	how-do
0.0117	20.7	.0000	1	how-does-it-make
0.0117	20.7	.0000	1	how'll
0.0117	20.7	.0000	1	Huggins'
0.0117	20.7	.0000	1	Hugh's
0.0117	20.7	.0000	1	hulloa
0.0117	20.7	.0000	1	humbler
0.0117	20.7	.0000	1	humbugged
0.0117	20.7	.0000	1	hummin'
0.0117	20.7	.0000	1	hunching
0.0117	20.7	.0000	1	hunger-madness
0.0117	20.7	.0000	1	hunkydory
0.0117	20.7	.0000	1	hunter-build
0.0117	20.7	.0000	1	hunting-knife
0.0117	20.7	.0000	1	hunting-shirt
0.0117	20.7	.0000	1	hurted
0.0117	20.7	.0000	1	hurtfulness
0.0117	20.7	.0000	1	husbanded
0.0117	20.7	.0000	1	Hutchinson's
0.0117	20.7	.0000	1	Huttos
0.0117	20.7	.0000	1	Hwang-tao
0.0117	20.7	.0000	1	hypocritical
0.0117	20.7	.0000	1	ice-edged
0.0117	20.7	.0000	1	ichthyologists
0.0117	20.7	.0000	1	ichthyophthirius
0.0117	20.7	.0000	1	Idell's
0.0117	20.7	.0000	1	ill-informed
0.0117	20.7	.0000	1	ill-looking
0.0117	20.7	.0000	1	ill-paved
0.0117	20.7	.0000	1	ill-temper
0.0117	20.7	.0000	1	illimitable

U	SFI	D	F	Word Type
0.0117	20.7	.0000	1	imperturbability
0.0117	20.7	.0000	1	impotent
0.0117	20.7	.0000	1	incarnation
0.0117	20.7	.0000	1	inch-by-inch
0.0117	20.7	.0000	1	inch-square
0.0117	20.7	.0000	1	incitement
0.0117	20.7	.0000	1	inclement
0.0117	20.7	.0000	1	incommunicable
0.0117	20.7	.0000	1	inexpressible
0.0117	20.7	.0000	1	inflexibility
0.0117	20.7	.0000	1	ingenio
0.0117	20.7	.0000	1	ingenuous
0.0117	20.7	.0000	1	ingratiating
0.0117	20.7	.0000	1	injun
THE PRECEDING WORD TYPE OCCUPIES RANK 72300				
0.0117	20.7	.0000	1	inkbottle
0.0117	20.7	.0000	1	insensible
0.0117	20.7	.0000	1	insolence
0.0117	20.7	.0000	1	instants
0.0117	20.7	.0000	1	insurmountable
0.0117	20.7	.0000	1	intellects
0.0117	20.7	.0000	1	interlacing
0.0117	20.7	.0000	1	inwards
0.0117	20.7	.0000	1	Irishman's
0.0117	20.7	.0000	1	iron-gray
0.0117	20.7	.0000	1	iron-like
0.0117	20.7	.0000	1	ironbound
0.0117	20.7	.0000	1	irreproachable
0.0117	20.7	.0000	1	irresolutely
0.0117	20.7	.0000	1	Ismael
0.0117	20.7	.0000	1	j-j-jumps
0.0117	20.7	.0000	1	jabbing
0.0117	20.7	.0000	1	Jabizri's
0.0117	20.7	.0000	1	Jackson-fork
0.0117	20.7	.0000	1	jailbird
0.0117	20.7	.0000	1	jamboree
0.0117	20.7	.0000	1	Jamin
0.0117	20.7	.0000	1	Jannough's
0.0117	20.7	.0000	1	Janus'
0.0117	20.7	.0000	1	jawin'
0.0117	20.7	.0000	1	jay-birds
0.0117	20.7	.0000	1	jedgin'
0.0117	20.7	.0000	1	Jeff'll
0.0117	20.7	.0000	1	Jehoshaphat
0.0117	20.7	.0000	1	jerkins
0.0117	20.7	.0000	1	jewel-bag
0.0117	20.7	.0000	1	jewellery
0.0117	20.7	.0000	1	jib-boom
0.0117	20.7	.0000	1	jigged
0.0117	20.7	.0000	1	jigging
0.0117	20.7	.0000	1	jillion
0.0117	20.7	.0000	1	jimpson
0.0117	20.7	.0000	1	Jinks
0.0117	20.7	.0000	1	jis'
0.0117	20.7	.0000	1	Jobe's
0.0117	20.7	.0000	1	jockey's
0.0117	20.7	.0000	1	joggling
0.0117	20.7	.0000	1	Jong
0.0117	20.7	.0000	1	Journey's
0.0117	20.7	.0000	1	joy-flames
0.0117	20.7	.0000	1	judgings
0.0117	20.7	.0000	1	Jumpin
0.0117	20.7	.0000	1	jumpsome
0.0117	20.7	.0000	1	jungle-paths
0.0117	20.7	.0000	1	junior-class
0.0117	20.7	.0000	1	Juniper
0.0117	20.7	.0000	1	Jute
0.0117	20.7	.0000	1	Keene
0.0117	20.7	.0000	1	Kenilworth
0.0117	20.7	.0000	1	kennel-dog
0.0117	20.7	.0000	1	kep'
0.0117	20.7	.0000	1	Kernstawk
0.0117	20.7	.0000	1	Kessie
0.0117	20.7	.0000	1	ketched
0.0117	20.7	.0000	1	kettle-holder
0.0117	20.7	.0000	1	Kevin's
0.0117	20.7	.0000	1	ki-yi's
0.0117	20.7	.0000	1	kick'm
0.0117	20.7	.0000	1	kin-folks
0.0117	20.7	.0000	1	Kingsbridge
0.0117	20.7	.0000	1	Kingsworthy
0.0117	20.7	.0000	1	kinked
0.0117	20.7	.0000	1	Kiouni
0.0117	20.7	.0000	1	kite-flying
0.0117	20.7	.0000	1	kited
0.0117	20.7	.0000	1	knaves
0.0117	20.7	.0000	1	knee'd
0.0117	20.7	.0000	1	knifing
0.0117	20.7	.0000	1	Knightrider
0.0117	20.7	.0000	1	knitter
0.0117	20.7	.0000	1	Ko-Nagi
0.0117	20.7	.0000	1	Kolokolo
0.0117	20.7	.0000	1	Kossie
0.0117	20.7	.0000	1	Kreutznaer
0.0117	20.7	.0000	1	L-shaped
0.0117	20.7	.0000	1	LaLongue
0.0117	20.7	.0000	1	labours
0.0117	20.7	.0000	1	labre
0.0117	20.7	.0000	1	labres
0.0117	20.7	.0000	1	lacerations
0.0117	20.7	.0000	1	Lady-who-asks-a-very-man*
0.0117	20.7	.0000	1	laggard
0.0117	20.7	.0000	1	Laguna
0.0117	20.7	.0000	1	lan'
0.0117	20.7	.0000	1	lank
0.0117	20.7	.0000	1	Laphams
0.0117	20.7	.0000	1	las'
0.0117	20.7	.0000	1	lath
0.0117	20.7	.0000	1	laths
0.0117	20.7	.0000	1	Latour
0.0117	20.7	.0000	1	Latrelle
0.0117	20.7	.0000	1	lawn-mower
0.0117	20.7	.0000	1	laws-a-me
0.0117	20.7	.0000	1	lazing
0.0117	20.7	.0000	1	LeRenard
THE PRECEDING WORD TYPE OCCUPIES RANK 72400				
0.0117	20.7	.0000	1	LeSubtil

U	SFI	D	F	Word Type
0.0117	20.7	.0000	1	lead-pencil
0.0117	20.7	.0000	1	lean-bellied
0.0117	20.7	.0000	1	leanness
0.0117	20.7	.0000	1	least-religious
0.0117	20.7	.0000	1	leathers
0.0117	20.7	.0000	1	leave-
0.0117	20.7	.0000	1	leavings
0.0117	20.7	.0000	1	leer
0.0117	20.7	.0000	1	Leeroy's
0.0117	20.7	.0000	1	leftward
0.0117	20.7	.0000	1	leg's
0.0117	20.7	.0000	1	legal-like
0.0117	20.7	.0000	1	legatee
0.0117	20.7	.0000	1	Legions
0.0117	20.7	.0000	1	Lem
0.0117	20.7	.0000	1	Lepine
0.0117	20.7	.0000	1	lepped
0.0117	20.7	.0000	1	Lesseps
0.0117	20.7	.0000	1	Letham
0.0117	20.7	.0000	1	Lianas
0.0117	20.7	.0000	1	Lib
0.0117	20.7	.0000	1	libbing
0.0117	20.7	.0000	1	libs
0.0117	20.7	.0000	1	Liddell's
0.0117	20.7	.0000	1	lieutenant-colonel
0.0117	20.7	.0000	1	Lifebuoy
0.0117	20.7	.0000	1	lightning-rods
0.0117	20.7	.0000	1	lightsome
0.0117	20.7	.0000	1	lightwood
0.0117	20.7	.0000	1	likeliest
0.0117	20.7	.0000	1	lille
0.0117	20.7	.0000	1	lineaments
0.0117	20.7	.0000	1	lingy
0.0117	20.7	.0000	1	lipped
0.0117	20.7	.0000	1	Lisle
0.0117	20.7	.0000	1	lisped
0.0117	20.7	.0000	1	little-girlish
0.0117	20.7	.0000	1	liveried
0.0117	20.7	.0000	1	livers
0.0117	20.7	.0000	1	livery-man
0.0117	20.7	.0000	1	livery-stable-man
0.0117	20.7	.0000	1	lizard's
0.0117	20.7	.0000	1	Lockhart
0.0117	20.7	.0000	1	lockouts
0.0117	20.7	.0000	1	log-books
0.0117	20.7	.0000	1	Lolita's
0.0117	20.7	.0000	1	Londoner
0.0117	20.7	.0000	1	lonesome-like
0.0117	20.7	.0000	1	lonesomest
0.0117	20.7	.0000	1	long-departed
0.0117	20.7	.0000	1	longbladed
0.0117	20.7	.0000	1	longbows
0.0117	20.7	.0000	1	Longings
0.0117	20.7	.0000	1	looka
0.0117	20.7	.0000	1	lookit
0.0117	20.7	.0000	1	loose-kneed
0.0117	20.7	.0000	1	Lordship
0.0117	20.7	.0000	1	Lornes'
0.0117	20.7	.0000	1	louis
0.0117	20.7	.0000	1	louts
0.0117	20.7	.0000	1	love-lornity
0.0117	20.7	.0000	1	Lover
0.0117	20.7	.0000	1	loving-cup
0.0117	20.7	.0000	1	low-skimming
0.0117	20.7	.0000	1	lowed
0.0117	20.7	.0000	1	Loy
0.0117	20.7	.0000	1	lubber
0.0117	20.7	.0000	1	LUCKY
0.0117	20.7	.0000	1	Ludgate
0.0117	20.7	.0000	1	lunch-room
0.0117	20.7	.0000	1	lustily
0.0117	20.7	.0000	1	Lybia
0.0117	20.7	.0000	1	Lyte's
0.0117	20.7	.0000	1	Lytes
0.0117	20.7	.0000	1	Lytes'
0.0117	20.7	.0000	1	m-m-mare
0.0117	20.7	.0000	1	m-m-maybe
0.0117	20.7	.0000	1	m-m-months
0.0117	20.7	.0000	1	Ma'o
0.0117	20.7	.0000	1	ma's
0.0117	20.7	.0000	1	machine-gunning
0.0117	20.7	.0000	1	mackereel
0.0117	20.7	.0000	1	Mackrelmint
0.0117	20.7	.0000	1	Maddox
0.0117	20.7	.0000	1	madreporical
0.0117	20.7	.0000	1	magnates
0.0117	20.7	.0000	1	magnifying-glass
0.0117	20.7	.0000	1	magnolias
0.0117	20.7	.0000	1	maigres
0.0117	20.7	.0000	1	mail-boat
0.0117	20.7	.0000	1	main-sail
0.0117	20.7	.0000	1	main-topsail
0.0117	20.7	.0000	1	mainlander
0.0117	20.7	.0000	1	Mako
0.0117	20.7	.0000	1	malignancy
0.0117	20.7	.0000	1	malingering
0.0117	20.7	.0000	1	Malthace
0.0117	20.7	.0000	1	mammas
0.0117	20.7	.0000	1	Mammoths
THE PRECEDING WORD TYPE OCCUPIES RANK 72500				
0.0117	20.7	.0000	1	mammy's
0.0117	20.7	.0000	1	man-animal
0.0117	20.7	.0000	1	man-fashion
0.0117	20.7	.0000	1	man-hole
0.0117	20.7	.0000	1	Man-who-does-not-put-hi**
0.0117	20.7	.0000	1	maneater
0.0117	20.7	.0000	1	manikin
0.0117	20.7	.0000	1	manoeuvre
0.0117	20.7	.0000	1	mantilla
0.0117	20.7	.0000	1	many-tined
0.0117	20.7	.0000	1	mape
0.0117	20.7	.0000	1	marae
0.0117	20.7	.0000	1	March's
0.0117	20.7	.0000	1	margaritifera
0.0117	20.7	.0000	1	marigold
0.0117	20.7	.0000	1	markin'
0.0117	20.7	.0000	1	marlinspike

U	SFI	D	F	Word Type
0.0117	20.7	.0000	1	MARMALADE
0.0117	20.7	.0000	1	marquis
0.0117	20.7	.0000	1	marshaling
0.0117	20.7	.0000	1	marten
0.0117	20.7	.0000	1	marvelling
0.0117	20.7	.0000	1	masers
0.0117	20.7	.0000	1	massacree
0.0117	20.7	.0000	1	mast-head
0.0117	20.7	.0000	1	masted
0.0117	20.7	.0000	1	masterminded
0.0117	20.7	.0000	1	matlike
0.0117	20.7	.0000	1	matrimony
0.0117	20.7	.0000	1	Matthewson
0.0117	20.7	.0000	1	maunders
0.0117	20.7	.0000	1	mawnin'
0.0117	20.7	.0000	1	McClellan's
0.0117	20.7	.0000	1	McLean's
0.0117	20.7	.0000	1	McLeans
0.0117	20.7	.0000	1	me-e-e
0.0117	20.7	.0000	1	me'll
0.0117	20.7	.0000	1	me's
0.0117	20.7	.0000	1	measly
0.0117	20.7	.0000	1	meat's
0.0117	20.7	.0000	1	Meccano
0.0117	20.7	.0000	1	meddled
0.0117	20.7	.0000	1	meditated
0.0117	20.7	.0000	1	meditatively
0.0117	20.7	.0000	1	meed
0.0117	20.7	.0000	1	meetcha
0.0117	20.7	.0000	1	Meg's
0.0117	20.7	.0000	1	Megara
0.0117	20.7	.0000	1	Melancholy
0.0117	20.7	.0000	1	Meleagrina
0.0117	20.7	.0000	1	Meloche
0.0117	20.7	.0000	1	mendy-bag
0.0117	20.7	.0000	1	Menomonie
0.0117	20.7	.0000	1	merchandises
0.0117	20.7	.0000	1	merriest
0.0117	20.7	.0000	1	merry-makers
0.0117	20.7	.0000	1	Merry's
0.0117	20.7	.0000	1	Mesrour
0.0117	20.7	.0000	1	messed
0.0117	20.7	.0000	1	Messengers
0.0117	20.7	.0000	1	messier
0.0117	20.7	.0000	1	Metallumai
0.0117	20.7	.0000	1	Mi's
0.0117	20.7	.0000	1	micical
0.0117	20.7	.0000	1	mid-stream
0.0117	20.7	.0000	1	Midnight's
0.0117	20.7	.0000	1	midwifery
0.0117	20.7	.0000	1	Miles's
0.0117	20.7	.0000	1	milk-shake
0.0117	20.7	.0000	1	milkgourd
0.0117	20.7	.0000	1	millrace
0.0117	20.7	.0000	1	millstone
0.0117	20.7	.0000	1	mimosas
0.0117	20.7	.0000	1	mindin'
0.0117	20.7	.0000	1	Mingos
0.0117	20.7	.0000	1	Minister's
0.0117	20.7	.0000	1	Minquon
0.0117	20.7	.0000	1	mintral
0.0117	20.7	.0000	1	misbecoming
0.0117	20.7	.0000	1	miscreant
0.0117	20.7	.0000	1	misfits
0.0117	20.7	.0000	1	missin'
0.0117	20.7	.0000	1	missive
0.0117	20.7	.0000	1	Misty's
0.0117	20.7	.0000	1	mittered
0.0117	20.7	.0000	1	mix-ups
0.0117	20.7	.0000	1	mmph
0.0117	20.7	.0000	1	moanings
0.0117	20.7	.0000	1	Mohawks'
0.0117	20.7	.0000	1	molestation
0.0117	20.7	.0000	1	Mollie
0.0117	20.7	.0000	1	molluska
0.0117	20.7	.0000	1	money-box
0.0117	20.7	.0000	1	money-boxes
0.0117	20.7	.0000	1	money-sack
0.0117	20.7	.0000	1	moo-oo-oo
0.0117	20.7	.0000	1	moon-dappled
0.0117	20.7	.0000	1	moon-white
0.0117	20.7	.0000	1	moose-meat
0.0117	20.7	.0000	1	moostrap
THE PRECEDING WORD TYPE OCCUPIES RANK 72600				
0.0117	20.7	.0000	1	mortgaged
0.0117	20.7	.0000	1	morts
0.0117	20.7	.0000	1	Motley
0.0117	20.7	.0000	1	mouldy
0.0117	20.7	.0000	1	mountain-peak
0.0117	20.7	.0000	1	mouse-cry
0.0117	20.7	.0000	1	mown
0.0117	20.7	.0000	1	much-prized
0.0117	20.7	.0000	1	muck-rakin'
0.0117	20.7	.0000	1	mud-cap
0.0117	20.7	.0000	1	mud-roofed
0.0117	20.7	.0000	1	mud-stripes
0.0117	20.7	.0000	1	Mulai
0.0117	20.7	.0000	1	mullein
0.0117	20.7	.0000	1	Mum
0.0117	20.7	.0000	1	mummeries
0.0117	20.7	.0000	1	Mummers'
0.0117	20.7	.0000	1	mummy's
0.0117	20.7	.0000	1	Murrel's
0.0117	20.7	.0000	1	mus'
0.0117	20.7	.0000	1	muscle-building
0.0117	20.7	.0000	1	muscled
0.0117	20.7	.0000	1	MUSH
0.0117	20.7	.0000	1	musket-shot
0.0117	20.7	.0000	1	mussed-up
0.0117	20.7	.0000	1	Mussulman
0.0117	20.7	.0000	1	mutton-bone
0.0117	20.7	.0000	1	muzzle-loadin'
0.0117	20.7	.0000	1	My-Son-Ralph's
0.0117	20.7	.0000	1	Mynheers
0.0117	20.7	.0000	1	Nadie
0.0117	20.7	.0000	1	nailfile
0.0117	20.7	.0000	1	Nannie

U	SFI	D	F	Word Type
0.0117	20.7	.0000	1	Nannies
0.0117	20.7	.0000	1	nappy
0.0117	20.7	.0000	1	natur'
0.0117	20.7	.0000	1	nauseated
0.0117	20.7	.0000	1	neighbouring
0.0117	20.7	.0000	1	neighbourly
0.0117	20.7	.0000	1	nenni
0.0117	20.7	.0000	1	Nepos
0.0117	20.7	.0000	1	Nes
0.0117	20.7	.0000	1	Nettie's
0.0117	20.7	.0000	1	nettles
0.0117	20.7	.0000	1	NewIpswich
0.0117	20.7	.0000	1	Next
0.0117	20.7	.0000	1	next's
0.0117	20.7	.0000	1	Nibley's
0.0117	20.7	.0000	1	nigger-traders
0.0117	20.7	.0000	1	night-goin'
0.0117	20.7	.0000	1	night-watchman
0.0117	20.7	.0000	1	nine-o'clock
0.0117	20.7	.0000	1	Ninety-Mile-Curve
0.0117	20.7	.0000	1	nitwit
0.0117	20.7	.0000	1	no-o-o-o
0.0117	20.7	.0000	1	noblewoman
0.0117	20.7	.0000	1	nobody'd
0.0117	20.7	.0000	1	noggin
0.0117	20.7	.0000	1	Noll's
0.0117	20.7	.0000	1	nonparticipating
0.0117	20.7	.0000	1	nonsensical
0.0117	20.7	.0000	1	noontide
0.0117	20.7	.0000	1	north-bound
0.0117	20.7	.0000	1	northwards
0.0117	20.7	.0000	1	Nortons'
0.0117	20.7	.0000	1	nosey
0.0117	20.7	.0000	1	note-books
0.0117	20.7	.0000	1	nougats
0.0117	20.7	.0000	1	nowheres
0.0117	20.7	.0000	1	nubbins
0.0117	20.7	.0000	1	nuclear-electronic
0.0117	20.7	.0000	1	numnah
0.0117	20.7	.0000	1	Nurmi
0.0117	20.7	.0000	1	Nurmis
0.0117	20.7	.0000	1	nut-brown
0.0117	20.7	.0000	1	nut-errant
0.0117	20.7	.0000	1	nut's
0.0117	20.7	.0000	1	o-r-r-r-h
0.0117	20.7	.0000	1	o-r-r-r-r-h
0.0117	20.7	.0000	1	O'Day's
0.0117	20.7	.0000	1	o'erwrought
0.0117	20.7	.0000	1	oakwood
0.0117	20.7	.0000	1	oar-blade
0.0117	20.7	.0000	1	Obediah's
0.0117	20.7	.0000	1	obsequies
0.0117	20.7	.0000	1	Observers
0.0117	20.7	.0000	1	odontognathes
0.0117	20.7	.0000	1	off-Broadway
0.0117	20.7	.0000	1	Offal
0.0117	20.7	.0000	1	offhand
0.0117	20.7	.0000	1	office-safe
0.0117	20.7	.0000	1	oil-room
0.0117	20.7	.0000	1	OK**
0.0117	20.7	.0000	1	old-country
0.0117	20.7	.0000	1	oleander
0.0117	20.7	.0000	1	olivella
0.0117	20.7	.0000	1	Olney
0.0117	20.7	.0000	1	omnipotence
0.0117	20.7	.0000	1	on-run
0.0117	20.7	.0000	1	oncet
THE PRECEDING WORD TYPE OCCUPIES RANK 72700				
0.0117	20.7	.0000	1	onliest
0.0117	20.7	.0000	1	onwards
0.0117	20.7	.0000	1	oo-oo
0.0117	20.7	.0000	1	oppressiveness
0.0117	20.7	.0000	1	oppressor's
0.0117	20.7	.0000	1	ORANGE
0.0117	20.7	.0000	1	Orchard's
0.0117	20.7	.0000	1	ordainment
0.0117	20.7	.0000	1	organisation
0.0117	20.7	.0000	1	orneriness
0.0117	20.7	.0000	1	Ostand
0.0117	20.7	.0000	1	Otis's
0.0117	20.7	.0000	1	otterlike
0.0117	20.7	.0000	1	ottoman
0.0117	20.7	.0000	1	out-a-condition
0.0117	20.7	.0000	1	out-run
0.0117	20.7	.0000	1	out-stretched
0.0117	20.7	.0000	1	outmaneuver
0.0117	20.7	.0000	1	outwards
0.0117	20.7	.0000	1	outwitting
0.0117	20.7	.0000	1	over-ruling
0.0117	20.7	.0000	1	over-sized
0.0117	20.7	.0000	1	overanxiousness
0.0117	20.7	.0000	1	overbalanced
0.0117	20.7	.0000	1	overflowings
0.0117	20.7	.0000	1	overreach
0.0117	20.7	.0000	1	overstepped
0.0117	20.7	.0000	1	overstrung
0.0117	20.7	.0000	1	ownin'
0.0117	20.7	.0000	1	oxblood
0.0117	20.7	.0000	1	oxygen-hydrogen-carbon
0.0117	20.7	.0000	1	oysterer
0.0117	20.7	.0000	1	Oysterville
0.0117	20.7	.0000	1	Ozell
0.0117	20.7	.0000	1	p-p-performance
0.0117	20.7	.0000	1	p-p-pop
0.0117	20.7	.0000	1	p-paddock
0.0117	20.7	.0000	1	p'r'aps
0.0117	20.7	.0000	1	Pachyderm
0.0117	20.7	.0000	1	pacified
0.0117	20.7	.0000	1	paddle-steamer
0.0117	20.7	.0000	1	paddle-wheels
0.0117	20.7	.0000	1	pagodas
0.0117	20.7	.0000	1	pahua
0.0117	20.7	.0000	1	pailful
0.0117	20.7	.0000	1	Painkiller
0.0117	20.7	.0000	1	paint-can
0.0117	20.7	.0000	1	palanquins
0.0117	20.7	.0000	1	palki-garis

U	SFI	D	F	Word Type
0.0117	20.7	.0000	1	pallets
0.0117	20.7	.0000	1	pallor
0.0117	20.7	.0000	1	palmistry
0.0117	20.7	.0000	1	palter
0.0117	20.7	.0000	1	pandanus
0.0117	20.7	.0000	1	panful
0.0117	20.7	.0000	1	pang
0.0117	20.7	.0000	1	panties
0.0117	20.7	.0000	1	pantouffles
0.0117	20.7	.0000	1	paragons
0.0117	20.7	.0000	1	parboil
0.0117	20.7	.0000	1	parchesi
0.0117	20.7	.0000	1	pardonable
0.0117	20.7	.0000	1	pared
0.0117	20.7	.0000	1	parenchyma
0.0117	20.7	.0000	1	pareu
0.0117	20.7	.0000	1	Parizade
0.0117	20.7	.0000	1	Parkin's
0.0117	20.7	.0000	1	partiality
0.0117	20.7	.0000	1	Passy
0.0117	20.7	.0000	1	patchy-blatchy
0.0117	20.7	.0000	1	patty-pans
0.0117	20.7	.0000	1	Pau
0.0117	20.7	.0000	1	pea-shellers
0.0117	20.7	.0000	1	pearl-oyster
0.0117	20.7	.0000	1	peculiar-shaped
0.0117	20.7	.0000	1	pedestals
0.0117	20.7	.0000	1	Pee-Wee's
0.0117	20.7	.0000	1	peeper-frogs
0.0117	20.7	.0000	1	peerage
0.0117	20.7	.0000	1	penguins'
0.0117	20.7	.0000	1	Pennell's
0.0117	20.7	.0000	1	penning
0.0117	20.7	.0000	1	pent
0.0117	20.7	.0000	1	Pepito
0.0117	20.7	.0000	1	peradventure
0.0117	20.7	.0000	1	perambulating
0.0117	20.7	.0000	1	percenter
0.0117	20.7	.0000	1	Pereire
0.0117	20.7	.0000	1	perishing
0.0117	20.7	.0000	1	Perk
0.0117	20.7	.0000	1	perpendicularity
0.0117	20.7	.0000	1	perpetrators
0.0117	20.7	.0000	1	persecutors
0.0117	20.7	.0000	1	Perviz
0.0117	20.7	.0000	1	petromyzons-pricka
0.0117	20.7	.0000	1	Pew's
0.0117	20.7	.0000	1	Phantom'll
0.0117	20.7	.0000	1	Pharisee
0.0117	20.7	.0000	1	Phelps's
0.0117	20.7	.0000	1	Phewie
THE PRECEDING WORD TYPE OCCUPIES RANK 72800				
0.0117	20.7	.0000	1	Philly
0.0117	20.7	.0000	1	physetera
0.0117	20.7	.0000	1	pickereel
0.0117	20.7	.0000	1	Pickett's
0.0117	20.7	.0000	1	Picketts
0.0117	20.7	.0000	1	Pickhatchet
0.0117	20.7	.0000	1	piecy
0.0117	20.7	.0000	1	Pieface
0.0117	20.7	.0000	1	pigeons's
0.0117	20.7	.0000	1	pigs'
0.0117	20.7	.0000	1	Pilgrim's
0.0117	20.7	.0000	1	pilot-bread
0.0117	20.7	.0000	1	pinchers
0.0117	20.7	.0000	1	pine-needle
0.0117	20.7	.0000	1	Pink-toed
0.0117	20.7	.0000	1	pintadine
0.0117	20.7	.0000	1	pison
0.0117	20.7	.0000	1	piston-rod
0.0117	20.7	.0000	1	pities
0.0117	20.7	.0000	1	pitter-pattering
0.0117	20.7	.0000	1	pivoting
0.0117	20.7	.0000	1	placatingly
0.0117	20.7	.0000	1	placidly
0.0117	20.7	.0000	1	plaice
0.0117	20.7	.0000	1	plait
0.0117	20.7	.0000	1	planty
0.0117	20.7	.0000	1	plowshare
0.0117	20.7	.0000	1	plucky
0.0117	20.7	.0000	1	plum-cake
0.0117	20.7	.0000	1	pluming
0.0117	20.7	.0000	1	pluttifikation
0.0117	20.7	.0000	1	pocket-knife
0.0117	20.7	.0000	1	pocket-money
0.0117	20.7	.0000	1	Pocomoke
0.0117	20.7	.0000	1	pokeberries
0.0117	20.7	.0000	1	Pokes
0.0117	20.7	.0000	1	Polynesia's
0.0117	20.7	.0000	1	Pomfret
0.0117	20.7	.0000	1	pompadour
0.0117	20.7	.0000	1	pony-carts
0.0117	20.7	.0000	1	poor-box
0.0117	20.7	.0000	1	pooty
0.0117	20.7	.0000	1	Popish
0.0117	20.7	.0000	1	pork-chop
0.0117	20.7	.0000	1	Porkey's
0.0117	20.7	.0000	1	porte-cochere
0.0117	20.7	.0000	1	possessors
0.0117	20.7	.0000	1	pot-lid
0.0117	20.7	.0000	1	potato-picking
0.0117	20.7	.0000	1	potencies
0.0117	20.7	.0000	1	potency
0.0117	20.7	.0000	1	potful
0.0117	20.7	.0000	1	potting
0.0117	20.7	.0000	1	pouch-strings
0.0117	20.7	.0000	1	poulticed
0.0117	20.7	.0000	1	Pounds'
0.0117	20.7	.0000	1	Prawns
0.0117	20.7	.0000	1	pre-game
0.0117	20.7	.0000	1	pre-med
0.0117	20.7	.0000	1	Preacher
0.0117	20.7	.0000	1	preamble
0.0117	20.7	.0000	1	predisposed
0.0117	20.7	.0000	1	presuming
0.0117	20.7	.0000	1	prettiness
0.0117	20.7	.0000	1	prised
0.0117	20.7	.0000	1	prison-bars
0.0117	20.7	.0000	1	prolongations
0.0117	20.7	.0000	1	propaty
0.0117	20.7	.0000	1	propension
0.0117	20.7	.0000	1	proteges
0.0117	20.7	.0000	1	protuberances
0.0117	20.7	.0000	1	proudfully
0.0117	20.7	.0000	1	Prouttes
0.0117	20.7	.0000	1	providentially
0.0117	20.7	.0000	1	prowlin'
0.0117	20.7	.0000	1	pullin'
0.0117	20.7	.0000	1	pullulate
0.0117	20.7	.0000	1	Pumpkin's
0.0117	20.7	.0000	1	punkin-heads
0.0117	20.7	.0000	1	punks
0.0117	20.7	.0000	1	Puppy
0.0117	20.7	.0000	1	purple-like
0.0117	20.7	.0000	1	purpleblack
0.0117	20.7	.0000	1	Purvis
0.0117	20.7	.0000	1	push-push-push
0.0117	20.7	.0000	1	pyramid-shaped
0.0117	20.7	.0000	1	Quagga
0.0117	20.7	.0000	1	quakingly
0.0117	20.7	.0000	1	quare
0.0117	20.7	.0000	1	quavery
0.0117	20.7	.0000	1	questing
0.0117	20.7	.0000	1	quicker'n
0.0117	20.7	.0000	1	quid
0.0117	20.7	.0000	1	quietude
0.0117	20.7	.0000	1	Quite
0.0117	20.7	.0000	1	R-R-Roxana
0.0117	20.7	.0000	1	r-r-rising
0.0117	20.7	.0000	1	rabbit-eared
0.0117	20.7	.0000	1	rabbit-skin
0.0117	20.7	.0000	1	rabble
THE PRECEDING WORD TYPE OCCUPIES RANK 72900				
0.0117	20.7	.0000	1	rackety
0.0117	20.7	.0000	1	rag-money
0.0117	20.7	.0000	1	Rags-an'-Bottles
0.0117	20.7	.0000	1	Raider's
0.0117	20.7	.0000	1	Rain-Pipes
0.0117	20.7	.0000	1	rain-butt
0.0117	20.7	.0000	1	rain-washed
0.0117	20.7	.0000	1	ramblings
0.0117	20.7	.0000	1	ramming
0.0117	20.7	.0000	1	Ramo's
0.0117	20.7	.0000	1	rampart
0.0117	20.7	.0000	1	ranch-cup
0.0117	20.7	.0000	1	rancor
0.0117	20.7	.0000	1	Rangoon
0.0117	20.7	.0000	1	rapt
0.0117	20.7	.0000	1	rat-racing
0.0117	20.7	.0000	1	raveled
0.0117	20.7	.0000	1	raving
0.0117	20.7	.0000	1	ray-fish
0.0117	20.7	.0000	1	razzed
0.0117	20.7	.0000	1	re-baited
0.0117	20.7	.0000	1	re-enforced
0.0117	20.7	.0000	1	re-enters
0.0117	20.7	.0000	1	re-union
0.0117	20.7	.0000	1	realising
0.0117	20.7	.0000	1	reasserted
0.0117	20.7	.0000	1	rebelliously
0.0117	20.7	.0000	1	reck'ned
0.0117	20.7	.0000	1	reckonin'
0.0117	20.7	.0000	1	recognised
0.0117	20.7	.0000	1	recommenced
0.0117	20.7	.0000	1	rectilinear
0.0117	20.7	.0000	1	red-beaked
0.0117	20.7	.0000	1	red-bird
0.0117	20.7	.0000	1	red-cheeked
0.0117	20.7	.0000	1	red-flannel
0.0117	20.7	.0000	1	red-head
0.0117	20.7	.0000	1	redheaded
0.0117	20.7	.0000	1	redoubling
0.0117	20.7	.0000	1	reed-fringed
0.0117	20.7	.0000	1	relict
0.0117	20.7	.0000	1	relicts
0.0117	20.7	.0000	1	relinquish
0.0117	20.7	.0000	1	remarking
0.0117	20.7	.0000	1	remission
0.0117	20.7	.0000	1	remoter
0.0117	20.7	.0000	1	remunerations
0.0117	20.7	.0000	1	rending
0.0117	20.7	.0000	1	repine
0.0117	20.7	.0000	1	repinings
0.0117	20.7	.0000	1	report-card
0.0117	20.7	.0000	1	reposeful
0.0117	20.7	.0000	1	reproachful-like
0.0117	20.7	.0000	1	reproaching
0.0117	20.7	.0000	1	reproved
0.0117	20.7	.0000	1	repudiate
0.0117	20.7	.0000	1	requireth
0.0117	20.7	.0000	1	reseeding
0.0117	20.7	.0000	1	residuary
0.0117	20.7	.0000	1	resignedly
0.0117	20.7	.0000	1	Resurrection
0.0117	20.7	.0000	1	retched
0.0117	20.7	.0000	1	retchings
0.0117	20.7	.0000	1	Retriever
0.0117	20.7	.0000	1	riata
0.0117	20.7	.0000	1	ribcage
0.0117	20.7	.0000	1	Ricky-ticky
0.0117	20.7	.0000	1	ridging
0.0117	20.7	.0000	1	rifts
0.0117	20.7	.0000	1	rile
0.0117	20.7	.0000	1	rimed
0.0117	20.7	.0000	1	ringingly
0.0117	20.7	.0000	1	ripped-open
0.0117	20.7	.0000	1	risk's
0.0117	20.7	.0000	1	rivaling
0.0117	20.7	.0000	1	river-front
0.0117	20.7	.0000	1	roadstead
0.0117	20.7	.0000	1	ROBBED
0.0117	20.7	.0000	1	robber-crab
0.0117	20.7	.0000	1	Roberge
0.0117	20.7	.0000	1	Roberge's
0.0117	20.7	.0000	1	Rochambeau's
0.0117	20.7	.0000	1	rock-cod
0.0117	20.7	.0000	1	rock-rabbits
0.0117	20.7	.0000	1	Rocking
0.0117	20.7	.0000	1	rolling-pin
0.0117	20.7	.0000	1	Rontu's
0.0117	20.7	.0000	1	roof-board
0.0117	20.7	.0000	1	rookery
0.0117	20.7	.0000	1	rose-leafy
0.0117	20.7	.0000	1	Rosh
0.0117	20.7	.0000	1	rosily
0.0117	20.7	.0000	1	round-about-ways
0.0117	20.7	.0000	1	round-eyed
0.0117	20.7	.0000	1	round-log
0.0117	20.7	.0000	1	roundheaded
0.0117	20.7	.0000	1	roundtailed
0.0117	20.7	.0000	1	routs
0.0117	20.7	.0000	1	Roxie
0.0117	20.7	.0000	1	rubbage
THE PRECEDING WORD TYPE OCCUPIES RANK 73000				
0.0117	20.7	.0000	1	rubber-neck
0.0117	20.7	.0000	1	rubbery-looking
0.0117	20.7	.0000	1	rubdown
0.0117	20.7	.0000	1	ruffian
0.0117	20.7	.0000	1	Ruffler
0.0117	20.7	.0000	1	Ruffler's
0.0117	20.7	.0000	1	rumours
0.0117	20.7	.0000	1	running-away
0.0117	20.7	.0000	1	runty
0.0117	20.7	.0000	1	russet
0.0117	20.7	.0000	1	rustlin'
0.0117	20.7	.0000	1	S-turn
0.0117	20.7	.0000	1	Saala
0.0117	20.7	.0000	1	Saala's
0.0117	20.7	.0000	1	Sabbath-breaking
0.0117	20.7	.0000	1	sachem
0.0117	20.7	.0000	1	Sacrament
0.0117	20.7	.0000	1	sacrilegious
0.0117	20.7	.0000	1	sadden
0.0117	20.7	.0000	1	saddens
0.0117	20.7	.0000	1	saddle-blanket
0.0117	20.7	.0000	1	sadiron
0.0117	20.7	.0000	1	Saints'
0.0117	20.7	.0000	1	Salamis
0.0117	20.7	.0000	1	salao
0.0117	20.7	.0000	1	Sallie
0.0117	20.7	.0000	1	salt-rising
0.0117	20.7	.0000	1	salvia
0.0117	20.7	.0000	1	sandiest-yellowish
0.0117	20.7	.0000	1	sandy-coloured
0.0117	20.7	.0000	1	sandy-yellow-brownish
0.0117	20.7	.0000	1	sandy-yellowish
0.0117	20.7	.0000	1	sapling-Dante
0.0117	20.7	.0000	1	sardine's
0.0117	20.7	.0000	1	Sarepta
0.0117	20.7	.0000	1	Sassanidae
0.0117	20.7	.0000	1	satiate
0.0117	20.7	.0000	1	satisfactions
0.0117	20.7	.0000	1	saucily
0.0117	20.7	.0000	1	Savile
0.0117	20.7	.0000	1	saw-file
0.0117	20.7	.0000	1	saw-toothed
0.0117	20.7	.0000	1	SAWYER
0.0117	20.7	.0000	1	scalping
0.0117	20.7	.0000	1	scalplocks
0.0117	20.7	.0000	1	scamped
0.0117	20.7	.0000	1	scantling
0.0117	20.7	.0000	1	scarerabbit
0.0117	20.7	.0000	1	scathed
0.0117	20.7	.0000	1	scepticism
0.0117	20.7	.0000	1	Schahzeman
0.0117	20.7	.0000	1	school-time
0.0117	20.7	.0000	1	school-yard
0.0117	20.7	.0000	1	schoolmarm
0.0117	20.7	.0000	1	schoolyards
0.0117	20.7	.0000	1	Scientists'
0.0117	20.7	.0000	1	scimitars
0.0117	20.7	.0000	1	scissored
0.0117	20.7	.0000	1	scombrus
0.0117	20.7	.0000	1	Scoot
0.0117	20.7	.0000	1	scootched
0.0117	20.7	.0000	1	scoundrels
0.0117	20.7	.0000	1	scrabbling
0.0117	20.7	.0000	1	screamin'
0.0117	20.7	.0000	1	screw-driver
0.0117	20.7	.0000	1	scribble
0.0117	20.7	.0000	1	scribblers
0.0117	20.7	.0000	1	scribbles
0.0117	20.7	.0000	1	scribe's
0.0117	20.7	.0000	1	scripture
0.0117	20.7	.0000	1	scroonched
0.0117	20.7	.0000	1	scuffing
0.0117	20.7	.0000	1	scything
0.0117	20.7	.0000	1	sea-mile
0.0117	20.7	.0000	1	sea-salute
0.0117	20.7	.0000	1	sea-song
0.0117	20.7	.0000	1	sea-unicorns
0.0117	20.7	.0000	1	sea-voyages
0.0117	20.7	.0000	1	sea-water
0.0117	20.7	.0000	1	seining
0.0117	20.7	.0000	1	self-consciously
0.0117	20.7	.0000	1	self-sacrificing
0.0117	20.7	.0000	1	Semina's
0.0117	20.7	.0000	1	sepulchre
0.0117	20.7	.0000	1	serge
0.0117	20.7	.0000	1	sergeant's
0.0117	20.7	.0000	1	servants'
0.0117	20.7	.0000	1	servitors
0.0117	20.7	.0000	1	setter's
0.0117	20.7	.0000	1	seven-dollar
0.0117	20.7	.0000	1	seventy-five-cent
0.0117	20.7	.0000	1	sewers'
0.0117	20.7	.0000	1	shackled
0.0117	20.7	.0000	1	shad-bellied
0.0117	20.7	.0000	1	shaggy-lookin'
0.0117	20.7	.0000	1	Shank
0.0117	20.7	.0000	1	sharpenin'
0.0117	20.7	.0000	1	shed's
0.0117	20.7	.0000	1	sheeted
0.0117	20.7	.0000	1	shell-fish
THE PRECEDING WORD TYPE OCCUPIES RANK 73100				
0.0117	20.7	.0000	1	Shep'll
0.0117	20.7	.0000	1	Sherry's
0.0117	20.7	.0000	1	ship-rats
0.0117	20.7	.0000	1	ship-wrecked
0.0117	20.7	.0000	1	shirt-sleeved
0.0117	20.7	.0000	1	shirtwaist
0.0117	20.7	.0000	1	shoe-leather
0.0117	20.7	.0000	1	shoeless
0.0117	20.7	.0000	1	shopping-list
0.0117	20.7	.0000	1	Shora's
0.0117	20.7	.0000	1	short-cropped
0.0117	20.7	.0000	1	Shorty's
0.0117	20.7	.0000	1	shoulder-of-mutton
0.0117	20.7	.0000	1	shovelled
0.0117	20.7	.0000	1	SHOW
0.0117	20.7	.0000	1	showcases
0.0117	20.7	.0000	1	sick-room
0.0117	20.7	.0000	1	side-stepping
0.0117	20.7	.0000	1	side-whiskers
0.0117	20.7	.0000	1	Sieur
0.0117	20.7	.0000	1	signalized
0.0117	20.7	.0000	1	signboard
0.0117	20.7	.0000	1	signor's
0.0117	20.7	.0000	1	Signor's
0.0117	20.7	.0000	1	silencing
0.0117	20.7	.0000	1	Silsbee
0.0117	20.7	.0000	1	Silsbees
0.0117	20.7	.0000	1	sim
0.0117	20.7	.0000	1	Simeon
0.0117	20.7	.0000	1	singing-bird
0.0117	20.7	.0000	1	singsonging
0.0117	20.7	.0000	1	Sinks
0.0117	20.7	.0000	1	sinner's
0.0117	20.7	.0000	1	sinnin'
0.0117	20.7	.0000	1	Sintram
0.0117	20.7	.0000	1	sissies
0.0117	20.7	.0000	1	sissiest
0.0117	20.7	.0000	1	sisterly
0.0117	20.7	.0000	1	sittyated
0.0117	20.7	.0000	1	six-and-twenty
0.0117	20.7	.0000	1	sk'yerd
0.0117	20.7	.0000	1	skim-milk
0.0117	20.7	.0000	1	Skookum
0.0117	20.7	.0000	1	skunk-cabbage
0.0117	20.7	.0000	1	sky-journey
0.0117	20.7	.0000	1	skylight
0.0117	20.7	.0000	1	slacked
0.0117	20.7	.0000	1	slat-backed
0.0117	20.7	.0000	1	slavered
0.0117	20.7	.0000	1	slavishly
0.0117	20.7	.0000	1	sled-dog
0.0117	20.7	.0000	1	sledge-hammer
0.0117	20.7	.0000	1	Slewfoot
0.0117	20.7	.0000	1	slighting
0.0117	20.7	.0000	1	slippery-slidy
0.0117	20.7	.0000	1	slithered
0.0117	20.7	.0000	1	slops
0.0117	20.7	.0000	1	slow-poke
0.0117	20.7	.0000	1	slow-tracked
0.0117	20.7	.0000	1	slow-trailing
0.0117	20.7	.0000	1	slushy-squshy
0.0117	20.7	.0000	1	Small-person-without-an**
0.0117	20.7	.0000	1	smartin'
0.0117	20.7	.0000	1	Smasher
0.0117	20.7	.0000	1	smelliest
0.0117	20.7	.0000	1	smoking-den
0.0117	20.7	.0000	1	smooth-tongued
0.0117	20.7	.0000	1	Smoothfield
0.0117	20.7	.0000	1	smouldering
0.0117	20.7	.0000	1	Snail
0.0117	20.7	.0000	1	snaking
0.0117	20.7	.0000	1	snapdragons
0.0117	20.7	.0000	1	sneakin'
0.0117	20.7	.0000	1	snickering
0.0117	20.7	.0000	1	sniffly
0.0117	20.7	.0000	1	snipping
0.0117	20.7	.0000	1	Snipps
0.0117	20.7	.0000	1	snuffing
0.0117	20.7	.0000	1	soda-pop
0.0117	20.7	.0000	1	sodded
0.0117	20.7	.0000	1	soft-eyed
0.0117	20.7	.0000	1	soft-tanned
0.0117	20.7	.0000	1	soil's
0.0117	20.7	.0000	1	soldiership
0.0117	20.7	.0000	1	Sole
0.0117	20.7	.0000	1	solemnized
0.0117	20.7	.0000	1	somersets
0.0117	20.7	.0000	1	somethin's
0.0117	20.7	.0000	1	Sophia's
0.0117	20.7	.0000	1	sopping
0.0117	20.7	.0000	1	Sorrowing
0.0117	20.7	.0000	1	sorters
0.0117	20.7	.0000	1	SouthSeas
0.0117	20.7	.0000	1	Southampton
0.0117	20.7	.0000	1	southwards
0.0117	20.7	.0000	1	space-sick
0.0117	20.7	.0000	1	spasmodic
0.0117	20.7	.0000	1	speckly
0.0117	20.7	.0000	1	speckly-spickly
0.0117	20.7	.0000	1	Spider-monkey
THE PRECEDING WORD TYPE OCCUPIES RANK 73200				
0.0117	20.7	.0000	1	spider-web
0.0117	20.7	.0000	1	spile
0.0117	20.7	.0000	1	Spinach
0.0117	20.7	.0000	1	Spindlers
0.0117	20.7	.0000	1	spindlin'
0.0117	20.7	.0000	1	spinning-wheel
0.0117	20.7	.0000	1	spit-spot
0.0117	20.7	.0000	1	splendidest
0.0117	20.7	.0000	1	split-rail
0.0117	20.7	.0000	1	spookiest
0.0117	20.7	.0000	1	Spooner
0.0117	20.7	.0000	1	spring-guns

U	SFI	D	F	Word Type
0.0117	20.7	.0000	1	spunkiness
0.0117	20.7	.0000	1	Spur
0.0117	20.7	.0000	1	spurned
0.0117	20.7	.0000	1	Spurs
0.0117	20.7	.0000	1	Spy
0.0117	20.7	.0000	1	spy-glass
0.0117	20.7	.0000	1	squalls
0.0117	20.7	.0000	1	StDenis
0.0117	20.7	.0000	1	StFrancis
0.0117	20.7	.0000	1	stable-men
0.0117	20.7	.0000	1	stableful
0.0117	20.7	.0000	1	stage-scared
0.0117	20.7	.0000	1	stairhead
0.0117	20.7	.0000	1	stake-racing
0.0117	20.7	.0000	1	standeth
0.0117	20.7	.0000	1	stargazing
0.0117	20.7	.0000	1	Starter
0.0117	20.7	.0000	1	stationmaster
0.0117	20.7	.0000	1	stayin'
0.0117	20.7	.0000	1	steadies
0.0117	20.7	.0000	1	steamer's
0.0117	20.7	.0000	1	Stewards'
0.0117	20.7	.0000	1	Stewpot
0.0117	20.7	.0000	1	stick-and-mud
0.0117	20.7	.0000	1	stickin'
0.0117	20.7	.0000	1	stid
0.0117	20.7	.0000	1	stink's
0.0117	20.7	.0000	1	stinks
0.0117	20.7	.0000	1	stoat
0.0117	20.7	.0000	1	stone-topped
0.0117	20.7	.0000	1	Stood
0.0117	20.7	.0000	1	store-room
0.0117	20.7	.0000	1	storks'
0.0117	20.7	.0000	1	story-book
0.0117	20.7	.0000	1	Storyland
0.0117	20.7	.0000	1	straight-away
0.0117	20.7	.0000	1	stratagems
0.0117	20.7	.0000	1	stud's
0.0117	20.7	.0000	1	Stupid
0.0117	20.7	.0000	1	sturdily
0.0117	20.7	.0000	1	stuttering
0.0117	20.7	.0000	1	Subtil
0.0117	20.7	.0000	1	sugar-hogshead
0.0117	20.7	.0000	1	sumfn
0.0117	20.7	.0000	1	summation
0.0117	20.7	.0000	1	sumpin'
0.0117	20.7	.0000	1	sun-colored
0.0117	20.7	.0000	1	sun-kissed
0.0117	20.7	.0000	1	sun-suit
0.0117	20.7	.0000	1	sunbonnets
0.0117	20.7	.0000	1	Sunday-like
0.0117	20.7	.0000	1	surgeon's
0.0117	20.7	.0000	1	surmounting
0.0117	20.7	.0000	1	surmullet
0.0117	20.7	.0000	1	surprising-
0.0117	20.7	.0000	1	surreptitiously
0.0117	20.7	.0000	1	swaps
0.0117	20.7	.0000	1	swathed
0.0117	20.7	.0000	1	swilling
0.0117	20.7	.0000	1	swingy
0.0117	20.7	.0000	1	swop
0.0117	20.7	.0000	1	T-T-T-Twickerham
0.0117	20.7	.0000	1	t-t-triumph
0.0117	20.7	.0000	1	t'eef
0.0117	20.7	.0000	1	tabu
0.0117	20.7	.0000	1	tachometer
0.0117	20.7	.0000	1	Taffimai
0.0117	20.7	.0000	1	taffy-colored
0.0117	20.7	.0000	1	tail-holt
0.0117	20.7	.0000	1	tailed
0.0117	20.7	.0000	1	tall-windowed
0.0117	20.7	.0000	1	tamping
0.0117	20.7	.0000	1	Tankadere
0.0117	20.7	.0000	1	Tankadere's
0.0117	20.7	.0000	1	tanner's
0.0117	20.7	.0000	1	Taocat
0.0117	20.7	.0000	1	tap-dancing
0.0117	20.7	.0000	1	tap-room
0.0117	20.7	.0000	1	tapa
0.0117	20.7	.0000	1	Tapu
0.0117	20.7	.0000	1	tar-paper
0.0117	20.7	.0000	1	tarlaton
0.0117	20.7	.0000	1	Tartary
0.0117	20.7	.0000	1	tauntingly
0.0117	20.7	.0000	1	Teagarden
0.0117	20.7	.0000	1	Tears
0.0117	20.7	.0000	1	teasin'
0.0117	20.7	.0000	1	teats

THE PRECEDING WORD TYPE OCCUPIES RANK 73300

U	SFI	D	F	Word Type
0.0117	20.7	.0000	1	Teavee
0.0117	20.7	.0000	1	teched
0.0117	20.7	.0000	1	teething
0.0117	20.7	.0000	1	Tegumai's
0.0117	20.7	.0000	1	teks
0.0117	20.7	.0000	1	Telemachus'
0.0117	20.7	.0000	1	Telly's
0.0117	20.7	.0000	1	temperaments
0.0117	20.7	.0000	1	Templeton's
0.0117	20.7	.0000	1	tempters
0.0117	20.7	.0000	1	ten-second
0.0117	20.7	.0000	1	ten-week
0.0117	20.7	.0000	1	tenderfeet
0.0117	20.7	.0000	1	tenderfoots
0.0117	20.7	.0000	1	tenpence
0.0117	20.7	.0000	1	tenpenny
0.0117	20.7	.0000	1	tent-like
0.0117	20.7	.0000	1	tent-roof
0.0117	20.7	.0000	1	Terwilliger's
0.0117	20.7	.0000	1	Tessin
0.0117	20.7	.0000	1	tetrarch's
0.0117	20.7	.0000	1	th-th-there
0.0117	20.7	.0000	1	thick-leaved
0.0117	20.7	.0000	1	thick-set
0.0117	20.7	.0000	1	THINK
0.0117	20.7	.0000	1	Thinkalot
0.0117	20.7	.0000	1	Thirty-Ninth
0.0117	20.7	.0000	1	Thirty-Seventh
0.0117	20.7	.0000	1	thirty-thirty
0.0117	20.7	.0000	1	thorn-bush
0.0117	20.7	.0000	1	thorn-tails
0.0117	20.7	.0000	1	thousand-pound
0.0117	20.7	.0000	1	three-base
0.0117	20.7	.0000	1	three-four
0.0117	20.7	.0000	1	three-thousand
0.0117	20.7	.0000	1	threepenny-bit
0.0117	20.7	.0000	1	thrummed
0.0117	20.7	.0000	1	thumb-tacks
0.0117	20.7	.0000	1	Thumpy
0.0117	20.7	.0000	1	thunderation
0.0117	20.7	.0000	1	thundery
0.0117	20.7	.0000	1	ti-ti
0.0117	20.7	.0000	1	Tiberias
0.0117	20.7	.0000	1	Tiberius
0.0117	20.7	.0000	1	ticket-window
0.0117	20.7	.0000	1	tide-water
0.0117	20.7	.0000	1	tide's
0.0117	20.7	.0000	1	Tidy
0.0117	20.7	.0000	1	tiger-eyed
0.0117	20.7	.0000	1	tight-waisted
0.0117	20.7	.0000	1	tightly-wrapped
0.0117	20.7	.0000	1	Timi
0.0117	20.7	.0000	1	tine
0.0117	20.7	.0000	1	Tingou
0.0117	20.7	.0000	1	Tipple
0.0117	20.7	.0000	1	title-deeds
0.0117	20.7	.0000	1	tittle
0.0117	20.7	.0000	1	to-morrow's
0.0117	20.7	.0000	1	to-wit
0.0117	20.7	.0000	1	Tobacconist's
0.0117	20.7	.0000	1	tobacker
0.0117	20.7	.0000	1	tobogganed
0.0117	20.7	.0000	1	toe-tips
0.0117	20.7	.0000	1	toe's
0.0117	20.7	.0000	1	toff
0.0117	20.7	.0000	1	toffee
0.0117	20.7	.0000	1	toluache
0.0117	20.7	.0000	1	tom-cat
0.0117	20.7	.0000	1	tom-noddy
0.0117	20.7	.0000	1	tongue-tied
0.0117	20.7	.0000	1	tony
0.0117	20.7	.0000	1	too-bold
0.0117	20.7	.0000	1	top-hats
0.0117	20.7	.0000	1	topgallant
0.0117	20.7	.0000	1	tormentin'
0.0117	20.7	.0000	1	tormentors
0.0117	20.7	.0000	1	totems
0.0117	20.7	.0000	1	toughening
0.0117	20.7	.0000	1	tow-colored
0.0117	20.7	.0000	1	Towler's
0.0117	20.7	.0000	1	traipsed
0.0117	20.7	.0000	1	tranquilly
0.0117	20.7	.0000	1	transmuted
0.0117	20.7	.0000	1	Trap
0.0117	20.7	.0000	1	Trav's
0.0117	20.7	.0000	1	tree-branch
0.0117	20.7	.0000	1	tree-ferns
0.0117	20.7	.0000	1	trenchered
0.0117	20.7	.0000	1	tribes-people
0.0117	20.7	.0000	1	trick-riding
0.0117	20.7	.0000	1	trick's
0.0117	20.7	.0000	1	tridacnae
0.0117	20.7	.0000	1	trike
0.0117	20.7	.0000	1	Trim
0.0117	20.7	.0000	1	Tripheath
0.0117	20.7	.0000	1	Trixie's
0.0117	20.7	.0000	1	trousies
0.0117	20.7	.0000	1	truffle
0.0117	20.7	.0000	1	truffles
0.0117	20.7	.0000	1	truncheon

THE PRECEDING WORD TYPE OCCUPIES RANK 73400

U	SFI	D	F	Word Type
0.0117	20.7	.0000	1	trundled
0.0117	20.7	.0000	1	tuberculated
0.0117	20.7	.0000	1	tubfuls
0.0117	20.7	.0000	1	Tummy-ache
0.0117	20.7	.0000	1	tun
0.0117	20.7	.0000	1	tuna-fish
0.0117	20.7	.0000	1	turbots
0.0117	20.7	.0000	1	turkey-pear
0.0117	20.7	.0000	1	turn-button
0.0117	20.7	.0000	1	Turnbuckle's
0.0117	20.7	.0000	1	turned-down
0.0117	20.7	.0000	1	turnip-brain
0.0117	20.7	.0000	1	tushes
0.0117	20.7	.0000	1	TWAIN
0.0117	20.7	.0000	1	twenty-thirty
0.0117	20.7	.0000	1	twirly-whirly
0.0117	20.7	.0000	1	two-acre
0.0117	20.7	.0000	1	two-colored
0.0117	20.7	.0000	1	two-flat
0.0117	20.7	.0000	1	two-guinea
0.0117	20.7	.0000	1	two-handed
0.0117	20.7	.0000	1	two-thousand
0.0117	20.7	.0000	1	two-wheeler
0.0117	20.7	.0000	1	two-wheelers
0.0117	20.7	.0000	1	Tyrolean
0.0117	20.7	.0000	1	ugly-tempered
0.0117	20.7	.0000	1	ullen
0.0117	20.7	.0000	1	unadventurous
0.0117	20.7	.0000	1	unappeasable
0.0117	20.7	.0000	1	unavailing
0.0117	20.7	.0000	1	unawed
0.0117	20.7	.0000	1	unblemished
0.0117	20.7	.0000	1	uncarpeted
0.0117	20.7	.0000	1	uncasing
0.0117	20.7	.0000	1	unclassified
0.0117	20.7	.0000	1	Uncle's
0.0117	20.7	.0000	1	uncorrupted
0.0117	20.7	.0000	1	under-brush
0.0117	20.7	.0000	1	underdone
0.0117	20.7	.0000	1	underfed
0.0117	20.7	.0000	1	underlip
0.0117	20.7	.0000	1	understandin'
0.0117	20.7	.0000	1	Understanding
0.0117	20.7	.0000	1	underwaist
0.0117	20.7	.0000	1	Undine
0.0117	20.7	.0000	1	unease
0.0117	20.7	.0000	1	unembellished
0.0117	20.7	.0000	1	unequally
0.0117	20.7	.0000	1	unexpected-
0.0117	20.7	.0000	1	ungovernable
0.0117	20.7	.0000	1	unhappier
0.0117	20.7	.0000	1	unleashed
0.0117	20.7	.0000	1	unmasked
0.0117	20.7	.0000	1	unpardonable
0.0117	20.7	.0000	1	unpicked
0.0117	20.7	.0000	1	unpitying
0.0117	20.7	.0000	1	unquenchable
0.0117	20.7	.0000	1	unravels
0.0117	20.7	.0000	1	unreasoning
0.0117	20.7	.0000	1	unreconciled
0.0117	20.7	.0000	1	unseats
0.0117	20.7	.0000	1	unties
0.0117	20.7	.0000	1	untired
0.0117	20.7	.0000	1	unweariedly
0.0117	20.7	.0000	1	unweeded
0.0117	20.7	.0000	1	up-ended
0.0117	20.7	.0000	1	upbraid
0.0117	20.7	.0000	1	uri
0.0117	20.7	.0000	1	used-up
0.0117	20.7	.0000	1	usurped
0.0117	20.7	.0000	1	Utley's
0.0117	20.7	.0000	1	uv
0.0117	20.7	.0000	1	vacuum-cleaner
0.0117	20.7	.0000	1	valance
0.0117	20.7	.0000	1	Vallejo
0.0117	20.7	.0000	1	vally
0.0117	20.7	.0000	1	vanities
0.0117	20.7	.0000	1	Varden
0.0117	20.7	.0000	1	varlet
0.0117	20.7	.0000	1	varlets
0.0117	20.7	.0000	1	vell
0.0117	20.7	.0000	1	Ven-ge-ance
0.0117	20.7	.0000	1	Veruca
0.0117	20.7	.0000	1	vespertilios
0.0117	20.7	.0000	1	viking-proud
0.0117	20.7	.0000	1	villainous
0.0117	20.7	.0000	1	villanous
0.0117	20.7	.0000	1	Villekulla
0.0117	20.7	.0000	1	vindicate
0.0117	20.7	.0000	1	vine-clad
0.0117	20.7	.0000	1	viner
0.0117	20.7	.0000	1	Vinolia
0.0117	20.7	.0000	1	Violet's
0.0117	20.7	.0000	1	virtuously
0.0117	20.7	.0000	1	vista
0.0117	20.7	.0000	1	vizir
0.0117	20.7	.0000	1	Volumes
0.0117	20.7	.0000	1	vrouws
0.0117	20.7	.0000	1	w-w-well
0.0117	20.7	.0000	1	Wagai

THE PRECEDING WORD TYPE OCCUPIES RANK 73500

U	SFI	D	F	Word Type
0.0117	20.7	.0000	1	wagon-seat
0.0117	20.7	.0000	1	waiting-woman
0.0117	20.7	.0000	1	Walbrook
0.0117	20.7	.0000	1	waltzed
0.0117	20.7	.0000	1	wanly
0.0117	20.7	.0000	1	wanter
0.0117	20.7	.0000	1	war-steed
0.0117	20.7	.0000	1	warbonnets
0.0117	20.7	.0000	1	warming-pan
0.0117	20.7	.0000	1	warningly
0.0117	20.7	.0000	1	wash-pot
0.0117	20.7	.0000	1	washings
0.0117	20.7	.0000	1	washpans
0.0117	20.7	.0000	1	wastage
0.0117	20.7	.0000	1	wasteless
0.0117	20.7	.0000	1	watchroom
0.0117	20.7	.0000	1	watchtower
0.0117	20.7	.0000	1	water-carrier
0.0117	20.7	.0000	1	water-trough
0.0117	20.7	.0000	1	water-voles
0.0117	20.7	.0000	1	watermark
0.0117	20.7	.0000	1	watery-looking
0.0117	20.7	.0000	1	WE
0.0117	20.7	.0000	1	we's
0.0117	20.7	.0000	1	WE'VE
0.0117	20.7	.0000	1	weaponless
0.0117	20.7	.0000	1	weasel-eyed
0.0117	20.7	.0000	1	weather'll
0.0117	20.7	.0000	1	weavy
0.0117	20.7	.0000	1	weensy
0.0117	20.7	.0000	1	weeping-willows
0.0117	20.7	.0000	1	welcomings
0.0117	20.7	.0000	1	well-coached
0.0117	20.7	.0000	1	well-fed
0.0117	20.7	.0000	1	well-hidden
0.0117	20.7	.0000	1	well-laid
0.0117	20.7	.0000	1	weller
0.0117	20.7	.0000	1	wending
0.0117	20.7	.0000	1	Wet
0.0117	20.7	.0000	1	whaaah
0.0117	20.7	.0000	1	whah
0.0117	20.7	.0000	1	whang
0.0117	20.7	.0000	1	wheelhouse
0.0117	20.7	.0000	1	whensoever
0.0117	20.7	.0000	1	whereat
0.0117	20.7	.0000	1	whereon
0.0117	20.7	.0000	1	whetstone
0.0117	20.7	.0000	1	which-a-way
0.0117	20.7	.0000	1	which'd
0.0117	20.7	.0000	1	whiniver
0.0117	20.7	.0000	1	whip-lashing
0.0117	20.7	.0000	1	whiplash
0.0117	20.7	.0000	1	whishing
0.0117	20.7	.0000	1	whisker
0.0117	20.7	.0000	1	whisker-like
0.0117	20.7	.0000	1	Whistler's
0.0117	20.7	.0000	1	white-cat
0.0117	20.7	.0000	1	white-gloved
0.0117	20.7	.0000	1	white-mice
0.0117	20.7	.0000	1	white-ringed
0.0117	20.7	.0000	1	whiten
0.0117	20.7	.0000	1	whittlings
0.0117	20.7	.0000	1	whopper
0.0117	20.7	.0000	1	whur's
0.0117	20.7	.0000	1	why'd
0.0117	20.7	.0000	1	wickie
0.0117	20.7	.0000	1	Wigwam
0.0117	20.7	.0000	1	wild-berry
0.0117	20.7	.0000	1	wilily
0.0117	20.7	.0000	1	Wilkins'
0.0117	20.7	.0000	1	wind-rustled
0.0117	20.7	.0000	1	wind-splitters
0.0117	20.7	.0000	1	wind-twisted
0.0117	20.7	.0000	1	windiest
0.0117	20.7	.0000	1	Windowshade
0.0117	20.7	.0000	1	Windrim
0.0117	20.7	.0000	1	wine-colored
0.0117	20.7	.0000	1	Winford's
0.0117	20.7	.0000	1	wingfence
0.0117	20.7	.0000	1	wintscha
0.0117	20.7	.0000	1	Wisest
0.0117	20.7	.0000	1	Witness
0.0117	20.7	.0000	1	witticism
0.0117	20.7	.0000	1	wobblety
0.0117	20.7	.0000	1	woked
0.0117	20.7	.0000	1	wolf-fashion
0.0117	20.7	.0000	1	wolfish
0.0117	20.7	.0000	1	womenfolk
0.0117	20.7	.0000	1	wonderwear
0.0117	20.7	.0000	1	Wonka's
0.0117	20.7	.0000	1	wonted
0.0117	20.7	.0000	1	wood-boats
0.0117	20.7	.0000	1	wood-box
0.0117	20.7	.0000	1	wooden-headed
0.0117	20.7	.0000	1	Woodlawn's
0.0117	20.7	.0000	1	Woodmontonian
0.0117	20.7	.0000	1	Woodpeckers'
0.0117	20.7	.0000	1	WOOF
0.0117	20.7	.0000	1	Workmen's
0.0117	20.7	.0000	1	worn-toothed

THE PRECEDING WORD TYPE OCCUPIES RANK 73600

U	SFI	D	F	Word Type
0.0117	20.7	.0000	1	Worthing
0.0117	20.7	.0000	1	Wortman's
0.0117	20.7	.0000	1	wouldst
0.0117	20.7	.0000	1	Wranglers
0.0117	20.7	.0000	1	wreaked
0.0117	20.7	.0000	1	wretch
0.0117	20.7	.0000	1	Wyle
0.0117	20.7	.0000	1	Wyman
0.0117	20.7	.0000	1	Xenophon
0.0117	20.7	.0000	1	xuchal
0.0117	20.7	.0000	1	y-o-u-u
0.0117	20.7	.0000	1	y-y-yes
0.0117	20.7	.0000	1	yardplays
0.0117	20.7	.0000	1	ye've
0.0117	20.7	.0000	1	yellin'
0.0117	20.7	.0000	1	yellow-haired
0.0117	20.7	.0000	1	yellow-painted
0.0117	20.7	.0000	1	Yengeese
0.0117	20.7	.0000	1	yessum
0.0117	20.7	.0000	1	yestiddy
0.0117	20.7	.0000	1	yo-ho-ho
0.0117	20.7	.0000	1	Ysobel
0.0117	20.7	.0000	1	yum
0.0117	20.7	.0000	1	yup
0.0117	20.7	.0000	1	z-z-z-z-z
0.0117	20.7	.0000	1	zealous
0.0117	20.7	.0000	1	zebus
0.0117	20.7	.0000	1	zephyr
0.0117	20.7	.0000	1	zoophyte
0.0117	20.7	.0000	1	zoophytes
0.0117	20.7	.0000	1	zostera
0.0117	20.7	.0000	1	Zuckermans'
0.0117	20.7	.0000	1	1334
0.0117	20.7	.0000	1	23d
0.0117	20.7	.0000	1	56a
0.0112	20.5	.0000	5	Bowers
0.0111	20.5	.0000	6	water-color
0.0109	20.4	.0000	1	$260
0.0109	20.4	.0000	1	-ain
0.0109	20.4	.0000	1	-am
0.0109	20.4	.0000	1	-ceous
0.0109	20.4	.0000	1	-cious
0.0109	20.4	.0000	1	-em
0.0109	20.4	.0000	1	-fy
0.0109	20.4	.0000	1	-geous
0.0109	20.4	.0000	1	-gram
0.0109	20.4	.0000	1	-ian
0.0109	20.4	.0000	1	-ic
0.0109	20.4	.0000	1	-im
0.0109	20.4	.0000	1	-ium
0.0109	20.4	.0000	1	-om
0.0109	20.4	.0000	1	-on
0.0109	20.4	.0000	1	-ply
0.0109	20.4	.0000	1	-self
0.0109	20.4	.0000	1	-selves
0.0109	20.4	.0000	1	-sion
0.0109	20.4	.0000	1	-st
0.0109	20.4	.0000	1	-ster
0.0109	20.4	.0000	1	/e-m/**
0.0109	20.4	.0000	1	/emereker/**
0.0109	20.4	.0000	1	/en/**
0.0109	20.4	.0000	1	/faynd/
0.0109	20.4	.0000	1	/hwic/
0.0109	20.4	.0000	1	/in/**
0.0109	20.4	.0000	1	/kae/**
0.0109	20.4	.0000	1	/kaew/**
0.0109	20.4	.0000	1	/kaw/
0.0109	20.4	.0000	1	/krom/**
0.0109	20.4	.0000	1	/lat/
0.0109	20.4	.0000	1	/let/**
0.0109	20.4	.0000	1	/leyen/**
0.0109	20.4	.0000	1	/leyin/**
0.0109	20.4	.0000	1	/redw/**
0.0109	20.4	.0000	1	/van/
0.0109	20.4	.0000	1	/vin/**
0.0109	20.4	.0000	1	/w/

U	SFI	D	F	Word Type
0.0109	20.4	.0000	1	/werd/**
0.0109	20.4	.0000	1	/wic/
0.0109	20.4	.0000	1	/wrde/**
0.0109	20.4	.0000	1	/zh/
0.0109	20.4	.0000	1	'fishhook**
0.0109	20.4	.0000	1	▮
0.0109	20.4	.0000	1	A-OK
0.0109	20.4	.0000	1	a-cooling
0.0109	20.4	.0000	1	a-fishing
0.0109	20.4	.0000	1	a-groaning
0.0109	20.4	.0000	1	a-musing
0.0109	20.4	.0000	1	a-tumble
0.0109	20.4	.0000	1	a-warming
0.0109	20.4	.0000	1	Aberdour
0.0109	20.4	.0000	1	abolish/abolition
0.0109	20.4	.0000	1	abominate
0.0109	20.4	.0000	1	aboone
0.0109	20.4	.0000	1	Abyssinians
0.0109	20.4	.0000	1	acceptably
0.0109	20.4	.0000	1	accident-free
0.0109	20.4	.0000	1	Accidents
0.0109	20.4	.0000	1	acted-upon
0.0109	20.4	.0000	1	Acting
0.0109	20.4	.0000	1	AD-dress

THE PRECEDING WORD TYPE OCCUPIES RANK 73700

U	SFI	D	F	Word Type
0.0109	20.4	.0000	1	adress
0.0109	20.4	.0000	1	Advice
0.0109	20.4	.0000	1	advise/eyes
0.0109	20.4	.0000	1	aerogram
0.0109	20.4	.0000	1	aerosol
0.0109	20.4	.0000	1	Aggie
0.0109	20.4	.0000	1	aggressively
0.0109	20.4	.0000	1	Aileen
0.0109	20.4	.0000	1	air-line
0.0109	20.4	.0000	1	air-raid
0.0109	20.4	.0000	1	alarum
0.0109	20.4	.0000	1	ALBERT
0.0109	20.4	.0000	1	alehouse
0.0109	20.4	.0000	1	Alex's
0.0109	20.4	.0000	1	alimonia
0.0109	20.4	.0000	1	all-dreaded
0.0109	20.4	.0000	1	aller
0.0109	20.4	.0000	1	allotment
0.0109	20.4	.0000	1	allude
0.0109	20.4	.0000	1	allusion
0.0109	20.4	.0000	1	Aloud
0.0109	20.4	.0000	1	alright
0.0109	20.4	.0000	1	Althea
0.0109	20.4	.0000	1	Ambition
0.0109	20.4	.0000	1	amelia
0.0109	20.4	.0000	1	amity
0.0109	20.4	.0000	1	amusin'
0.0109	20.4	.0000	1	and-so
0.0109	20.4	.0000	1	Andys
0.0109	20.4	.0000	1	Anglish
0.0109	20.4	.0000	1	AngloSaxon
0.0109	20.4	.0000	1	Angus'
0.0109	20.4	.0000	1	anno
0.0109	20.4	.0000	1	annoyingly
0.0109	20.4	.0000	1	Answering
0.0109	20.4	.0000	1	Ant
0.0109	20.4	.0000	1	antecedents
0.0109	20.4	.0000	1	anticipate/anticipation
0.0109	20.4	.0000	1	antidisestablishmentari**
0.0109	20.4	.0000	1	antipasto
0.0109	20.4	.0000	1	Antonia
0.0109	20.4	.0000	1	Ants
0.0109	20.4	.0000	1	Apostate
0.0109	20.4	.0000	1	APP
0.0109	20.4	.0000	1	apply-application
0.0109	20.4	.0000	1	Aqua-Lung
0.0109	20.4	.0000	1	arborous
0.0109	20.4	.0000	1	archaeologist's
0.0109	20.4	.0000	1	Arlo's
0.0109	20.4	.0000	1	armbands
0.0109	20.4	.0000	1	arme
0.0109	20.4	.0000	1	ascribe
0.0109	20.4	.0000	1	asinine/asininity
0.0109	20.4	.0000	1	Askew
0.0109	20.4	.0000	1	Askew's
0.0109	20.4	.0000	1	assaying
0.0109	20.4	.0000	1	astron
0.0109	20.4	.0000	1	astronomers'
0.0109	20.4	.0000	1	Attack
0.0109	20.4	.0000	1	Australian's
0.0109	20.4	.0000	1	AUXILIARIES
0.0109	20.4	.0000	1	auxuliaries
0.0109	20.4	.0000	1	aver
0.0109	20.4	.0000	1	B-130
0.0109	20.4	.0000	1	baby-sits
0.0109	20.4	.0000	1	bailer
0.0109	20.4	.0000	1	Balloon
0.0109	20.4	.0000	1	baloney
0.0109	20.4	.0000	1	Balto-Slavic
0.0109	20.4	.0000	1	bang-up
0.0109	20.4	.0000	1	bannanner
0.0109	20.4	.0000	1	bapples
0.0109	20.4	.0000	1	baptist
0.0109	20.4	.0000	1	Barabino
0.0109	20.4	.0000	1	bares
0.0109	20.4	.0000	1	Bartholomovich
0.0109	20.4	.0000	1	Barto
0.0109	20.4	.0000	1	basinet
0.0109	20.4	.0000	1	bassinet
0.0109	20.4	.0000	1	battercakes
0.0109	20.4	.0000	1	Beachcombers
0.0109	20.4	.0000	1	Beacon
0.0109	20.4	.0000	1	beagles
0.0109	20.4	.0000	1	beaklike
0.0109	20.4	.0000	1	beal
0.0109	20.4	.0000	1	Beau-Dur
0.0109	20.4	.0000	1	beautifulest
0.0109	20.4	.0000	1	Bechtelsville
0.0109	20.4	.0000	1	bedford
0.0109	20.4	.0000	1	befooled
0.0109	20.4	.0000	1	Beh-eh
0.0109	20.4	.0000	1	Beh-eh-h'
0.0109	20.4	.0000	1	bell-wether
0.0109	20.4	.0000	1	Belloc's
0.0109	20.4	.0000	1	bellying
0.0109	20.4	.0000	1	Benet's
0.0109	20.4	.0000	1	Bengali
0.0109	20.4	.0000	1	Bergman's
0.0109	20.4	.0000	1	Besso's
0.0109	20.4	.0000	1	best-laid

THE PRECEDING WORD TYPE OCCUPIES RANK 73800

U	SFI	D	F	Word Type
0.0109	20.4	.0000	1	bestraddle
0.0109	20.4	.0000	1	bete
0.0109	20.4	.0000	1	beth
0.0109	20.4	.0000	1	Beth-le-hem
0.0109	20.4	.0000	1	bh
0.0109	20.4	.0000	1	Biggs
0.0109	20.4	.0000	1	bilge
0.0109	20.4	.0000	1	Billys
0.0109	20.4	.0000	1	binning
0.0109	20.4	.0000	1	biography's
0.0109	20.4	.0000	1	bisecting
0.0109	20.4	.0000	1	black-feathered
0.0109	20.4	.0000	1	black-penciled
0.0109	20.4	.0000	1	blackbeard
0.0109	20.4	.0000	1	blackest
0.0109	20.4	.0000	1	blanca
0.0109	20.4	.0000	1	Blear
0.0109	20.4	.0000	1	bleary
0.0109	20.4	.0000	1	Blenheim
0.0109	20.4	.0000	1	blood-curdling
0.0109	20.4	.0000	1	blue-speckled
0.0109	20.4	.0000	1	Bluffs
0.0109	20.4	.0000	1	bo
0.0109	20.4	.0000	1	boc
0.0109	20.4	.0000	1	Bohemians
0.0109	20.4	.0000	1	bombards
0.0109	20.4	.0000	1	book-file
0.0109	20.4	.0000	1	booklovers
0.0109	20.4	.0000	1	bookseller's
0.0109	20.4	.0000	1	Boothe
0.0109	20.4	.0000	1	boppling
0.0109	20.4	.0000	1	Boring
0.0109	20.4	.0000	1	Borough
0.0109	20.4	.0000	1	borrowers'
0.0109	20.4	.0000	1	Bostonian
0.0109	20.4	.0000	1	bot
0.0109	20.4	.0000	1	bouncer
0.0109	20.4	.0000	1	boxtop
0.0109	20.4	.0000	1	boy-oh-boy
0.0109	20.4	.0000	1	Boyds
0.0109	20.4	.0000	1	breakfasted
0.0109	20.4	.0000	1	breastplates
0.0109	20.4	.0000	1	Bree
0.0109	20.4	.0000	1	brendly
0.0109	20.4	.0000	1	bridesmaids
0.0109	20.4	.0000	1	Brief
0.0109	20.4	.0000	1	briefer
0.0109	20.4	.0000	1	bristler
0.0109	20.4	.0000	1	bronx
0.0109	20.4	.0000	1	brosket
0.0109	20.4	.0000	1	brothers-in-law
0.0109	20.4	.0000	1	broths
0.0109	20.4	.0000	1	browne
0.0109	20.4	.0000	1	Brubaker
0.0109	20.4	.0000	1	Bruces
0.0109	20.4	.0000	1	bu
0.0109	20.4	.0000	1	Buckfield
0.0109	20.4	.0000	1	bugling
0.0109	20.4	.0000	1	Build
0.0109	20.4	.0000	1	bulkily
0.0109	20.4	.0000	1	bulletin-board
0.0109	20.4	.0000	1	Bullfrog
0.0109	20.4	.0000	1	bungle
0.0109	20.4	.0000	1	bunked
0.0109	20.4	.0000	1	Burns'
0.0109	20.4	.0000	1	Burnsville
0.0109	20.4	.0000	1	bursted
0.0109	20.4	.0000	1	but-ur
0.0109	20.4	.0000	1	but's
0.0109	20.4	.0000	1	buzzard
0.0109	20.4	.0000	1	C-100
0.0109	20.4	.0000	1	cabin-boy
0.0109	20.4	.0000	1	cah
0.0109	20.4	.0000	1	caique
0.0109	20.4	.0000	1	call'd
0.0109	20.4	.0000	1	Camel's
0.0109	20.4	.0000	1	Canaanite
0.0109	20.4	.0000	1	Canadian's
0.0109	20.4	.0000	1	capaciosity
0.0109	20.4	.0000	1	capacious
0.0109	20.4	.0000	1	capacious/capacity
0.0109	20.4	.0000	1	Carriageway
0.0109	20.4	.0000	1	cart-wheel
0.0109	20.4	.0000	1	casa
0.0109	20.4	.0000	1	Castillo
0.0109	20.4	.0000	1	cat-danger
0.0109	20.4	.0000	1	Cates
0.0109	20.4	.0000	1	cathedra
0.0109	20.4	.0000	1	catlike
0.0109	20.4	.0000	1	caveat
0.0109	20.4	.0000	1	cellar-dwellers
0.0109	20.4	.0000	1	cemetary
0.0109	20.4	.0000	1	centripetal
0.0109	20.4	.0000	1	cestus
0.0109	20.4	.0000	1	chalice
0.0109	20.4	.0000	1	chalkboards
0.0109	20.4	.0000	1	character-sketching
0.0109	20.4	.0000	1	characterization
0.0109	20.4	.0000	1	Charleses
0.0109	20.4	.0000	1	charley

THE PRECEDING WORD TYPE OCCUPIES RANK 73900

U	SFI	D	F	Word Type
0.0109	20.4	.0000	1	Cheers
0.0109	20.4	.0000	1	Chesterfield
0.0109	20.4	.0000	1	chetireh
0.0109	20.4	.0000	1	chewing-gum
0.0109	20.4	.0000	1	chiang
0.0109	20.4	.0000	1	chien
0.0109	20.4	.0000	1	chilblain
0.0109	20.4	.0000	1	chimney-sweepers
0.0109	20.4	.0000	1	Choctaw
0.0109	20.4	.0000	1	chonan
0.0109	20.4	.0000	1	christopher
0.0109	20.4	.0000	1	Chug
0.0109	20.4	.0000	1	Chutney's
0.0109	20.4	.0000	1	circumspect
0.0109	20.4	.0000	1	citron
0.0109	20.4	.0000	1	Ck
0.0109	20.4	.0000	1	classwork
0.0109	20.4	.0000	1	Claudine
0.0109	20.4	.0000	1	climbing-rope
0.0109	20.4	.0000	1	clob
0.0109	20.4	.0000	1	close-trimmed
0.0109	20.4	.0000	1	Closer
0.0109	20.4	.0000	1	closer-fitting
0.0109	20.4	.0000	1	clothers
0.0109	20.4	.0000	1	coccospheres
0.0109	20.4	.0000	1	cocoa-colored
0.0109	20.4	.0000	1	COD
0.0109	20.4	.0000	1	cognate
0.0109	20.4	.0000	1	coherence
0.0109	20.4	.0000	1	cold-bloodedly
0.0109	20.4	.0000	1	colons
0.0109	20.4	.0000	1	color-words
0.0109	20.4	.0000	1	columbus
0.0109	20.4	.0000	1	columnists
0.0109	20.4	.0000	1	Combo
0.0109	20.4	.0000	1	cometh
0.0109	20.4	.0000	1	comforter
0.0109	20.4	.0000	1	comic-strip
0.0109	20.4	.0000	1	commode
0.0109	20.4	.0000	1	comp
0.0109	20.4	.0000	1	compiler
0.0109	20.4	.0000	1	comradeships
0.0109	20.4	.0000	1	con-
0.0109	20.4	.0000	1	conant
0.0109	20.4	.0000	1	concerti
0.0109	20.4	.0000	1	concisely
0.0109	20.4	.0000	1	Conditional
0.0109	20.4	.0000	1	condolence
0.0109	20.4	.0000	1	confute
0.0109	20.4	.0000	1	Conjunctive
0.0109	20.4	.0000	1	conjuncts
0.0109	20.4	.0000	1	Connell
0.0109	20.4	.0000	1	connotations
0.0109	20.4	.0000	1	constructor
0.0109	20.4	.0000	1	consummation
0.0109	20.4	.0000	1	Content
0.0109	20.4	.0000	1	contrac'
0.0109	20.4	.0000	1	conveyancer
0.0109	20.4	.0000	1	Coogan's
0.0109	20.4	.0000	1	coots
0.0109	20.4	.0000	1	Core
0.0109	20.4	.0000	1	cork-heild
0.0109	20.4	.0000	1	corker
0.0109	20.4	.0000	1	cornu
0.0109	20.4	.0000	1	correlative
0.0109	20.4	.0000	1	Cosgrave
0.0109	20.4	.0000	1	Costumes
0.0109	20.4	.0000	1	cote
0.0109	20.4	.0000	1	Cottonwood
0.0109	20.4	.0000	1	counting-out
0.0109	20.4	.0000	1	country-fresh
0.0109	20.4	.0000	1	coupla
0.0109	20.4	.0000	1	Courvoisier
0.0109	20.4	.0000	1	cousine
0.0109	20.4	.0000	1	Crafts
0.0109	20.4	.0000	1	cramponed
0.0109	20.4	.0000	1	creels
0.0109	20.4	.0000	1	Crenshaw's
0.0109	20.4	.0000	1	Crestwood
0.0109	20.4	.0000	1	crickling
0.0109	20.4	.0000	1	Cried
0.0109	20.4	.0000	1	Criticism
0.0109	20.4	.0000	1	croak-croak-croak
0.0109	20.4	.0000	1	crobble
0.0109	20.4	.0000	1	crook's
0.0109	20.4	.0000	1	Crooner
0.0109	20.4	.0000	1	cross-ways
0.0109	20.4	.0000	1	crossbars
0.0109	20.4	.0000	1	cryin'
0.0109	20.4	.0000	1	cub-engineer**
0.0109	20.4	.0000	1	cubby-holes
0.0109	20.4	.0000	1	cuds
0.0109	20.4	.0000	1	cultus
0.0109	20.4	.0000	1	cupples
0.0109	20.4	.0000	1	current-events
0.0109	20.4	.0000	1	cursives
0.0109	20.4	.0000	1	custodians
0.0109	20.4	.0000	1	cutlets
0.0109	20.4	.0000	1	d-o-u-g-h
0.0109	20.4	.0000	1	D-500

THE PRECEDING WORD TYPE OCCUPIES RANK 74000

U	SFI	D	F	Word Type
0.0109	20.4	.0000	1	daeghwamlican
0.0109	20.4	.0000	1	dales
0.0109	20.4	.0000	1	Dalewood
0.0109	20.4	.0000	1	Danaides
0.0109	20.4	.0000	1	Dancer
0.0109	20.4	.0000	1	Dangerous
0.0109	20.4	.0000	1	dangly
0.0109	20.4	.0000	1	Danite
0.0109	20.4	.0000	1	dapper
0.0109	20.4	.0000	1	darr-dit-dit-dit
0.0109	20.4	.0000	1	darr-dit-dit-dit-darr
0.0109	20.4	.0000	1	Darrel
0.0109	20.4	.0000	1	datebook
0.0109	20.4	.0000	1	Daugherty's
0.0109	20.4	.0000	1	dauphin
0.0109	20.4	.0000	1	DAVID
0.0109	20.4	.0000	1	Dawn's
0.0109	20.4	.0000	1	day-dreams
0.0109	20.4	.0000	1	day-long
0.0109	20.4	.0000	1	daydreamitis
0.0109	20.4	.0000	1	deSanMarcos
0.0109	20.4	.0000	1	deadlie
0.0109	20.4	.0000	1	deadwood
0.0109	20.4	.0000	1	debauched
0.0109	20.4	.0000	1	december
0.0109	20.4	.0000	1	declarations
0.0109	20.4	.0000	1	deep-dish
0.0109	20.4	.0000	1	deepfreeze
0.0109	20.4	.0000	1	Deever
0.0109	20.4	.0000	1	Defining
0.0109	20.4	.0000	1	degrade
0.0109	20.4	.0000	1	dehul
0.0109	20.4	.0000	1	deip
0.0109	20.4	.0000	1	deletes
0.0109	20.4	.0000	1	Demonstratives
0.0109	20.4	.0000	1	Denise
0.0109	20.4	.0000	1	dentifrice
0.0109	20.4	.0000	1	Derision
0.0109	20.4	.0000	1	Det
0.0109	20.4	.0000	1	Determiner
0.0109	20.4	.0000	1	detrimental
0.0109	20.4	.0000	1	deus
0.0109	20.4	.0000	1	Deutschland
0.0109	20.4	.0000	1	dh
0.0109	20.4	.0000	1	diagrammed
0.0109	20.4	.0000	1	Diagrams
0.0109	20.4	.0000	1	dialog
0.0109	20.4	.0000	1	Dickens
0.0109	20.4	.0000	1	Dickensian
0.0109	20.4	.0000	1	dict
0.0109	20.4	.0000	1	DID
0.0109	20.4	.0000	1	didn'▮
0.0109	20.4	.0000	1	didnht
0.0109	20.4	.0000	1	Diogenes
0.0109	20.4	.0000	1	Dirck
0.0109	20.4	.0000	1	discontinue
0.0109	20.4	.0000	1	discourteous
0.0109	20.4	.0000	1	dishcloth
0.0109	20.4	.0000	1	Disjunctive
0.0109	20.4	.0000	1	dismantled
0.0109	20.4	.0000	1	distinctiveness
0.0109	20.4	.0000	1	Distraction
0.0109	20.4	.0000	1	dit-darr-darr
0.0109	20.4	.0000	1	Diversion
0.0109	20.4	.0000	1	DLR
0.0109	20.4	.0000	1	Domini
0.0109	20.4	.0000	1	donna
0.0109	20.4	.0000	1	dont
0.0109	20.4	.0000	1	double-check
0.0109	20.4	.0000	1	dove's
0.0109	20.4	.0000	1	Doze's
0.0109	20.4	.0000	1	DP
0.0109	20.4	.0000	1	Dragnet
0.0109	20.4	.0000	1	dramatizing
0.0109	20.4	.0000	1	droopy-headed
0.0109	20.4	.0000	1	drowns
0.0109	20.4	.0000	1	drum's
0.0109	20.4	.0000	1	DS
0.0109	20.4	.0000	1	Dual
0.0109	20.4	.0000	1	duck-shootin'
0.0109	20.4	.0000	1	dud
0.0109	20.4	.0000	1	Dumferling
0.0109	20.4	.0000	1	dunces
0.0109	20.4	.0000	1	Dunmores
0.0109	20.4	.0000	1	dusty-coated
0.0109	20.4	.0000	1	Earthman's
0.0109	20.4	.0000	1	easter
0.0109	20.4	.0000	1	Easterner
0.0109	20.4	.0000	1	educate-education
0.0109	20.4	.0000	1	eeny
0.0109	20.4	.0000	1	eight-century
0.0109	20.4	.0000	1	eight-page
0.0109	20.4	.0000	1	eir
0.0109	20.4	.0000	1	eject
0.0109	20.4	.0000	1	ejection
0.0109	20.4	.0000	1	elaboration
0.0109	20.4	.0000	1	elbowed
0.0109	20.4	.0000	1	electric-eye
0.0109	20.4	.0000	1	ellipsis
0.0109	20.4	.0000	1	Elmwood

THE PRECEDING WORD TYPE OCCUPIES RANK 74100

U	SFI	D	F	Word Type
0.0109	20.4	.0000	1	Elvers
0.0109	20.4	.0000	1	Emilia's
0.0109	20.4	.0000	1	Emmy
0.0109	20.4	.0000	1	emptor
0.0109	20.4	.0000	1	en-1
0.0109	20.4	.0000	1	en-2
0.0109	20.4	.0000	1	encases
0.0109	20.4	.0000	1	engag'd
0.0109	20.4	.0000	1	Enginer
0.0109	20.4	.0000	1	england
0.0109	20.4	.0000	1	English-French
0.0109	20.4	.0000	1	engrosses
0.0109	20.4	.0000	1	Enjoy
0.0109	20.4	.0000	1	enslave
0.0109	20.4	.0000	1	Entertainment
0.0109	20.4	.0000	1	epigrams
0.0109	20.4	.0000	1	equating
0.0109	20.4	.0000	1	erasures
0.0109	20.4	.0000	1	Erna's
0.0109	20.4	.0000	1	ess
0.0109	20.4	.0000	1	establish'd
0.0109	20.4	.0000	1	etymological
0.0109	20.4	.0000	1	Evanston
0.0109	20.4	.0000	1	everyones
0.0109	20.4	.0000	1	Evidence
0.0109	20.4	.0000	1	execute/execution
0.0109	20.4	.0000	1	exorciser
0.0109	20.4	.0000	1	expectedness
0.0109	20.4	.0000	1	Explaining
0.0109	20.4	.0000	1	expletive
0.0109	20.4	.0000	1	exposures
0.0109	20.4	.0000	1	extemporaneous
0.0109	20.4	.0000	1	eye-witnesses
0.0109	20.4	.0000	1	f's
0.0109	20.4	.0000	1	Fabian's
0.0109	20.4	.0000	1	facere
0.0109	20.4	.0000	1	fadom
0.0109	20.4	.0000	1	Faerie
0.0109	20.4	.0000	1	fahg

U	SFI	D	F	Word Type
0.0109	20.4	.0000	1	familys
0.0109	20.4	.0000	1	far-surrounding
0.0109	20.4	.0000	1	fawg
0.0109	20.4	.0000	1	Fear-not
0.0109	20.4	.0000	1	federal-aid
0.0109	20.4	.0000	1	Feeling
0.0109	20.4	.0000	1	feit
0.0109	20.4	.0000	1	ferre
0.0109	20.4	.0000	1	ffe
0.0109	20.4	.0000	1	fifth-
0.0109	20.4	.0000	1	fifth-hand
0.0109	20.4	.0000	1	fiftie
0.0109	20.4	.0000	1	fifty-story
0.0109	20.4	.0000	1	Fight-the-good-fight-of**
0.0109	20.4	.0000	1	figurin'
0.0109	20.4	.0000	1	finalists
0.0109	20.4	.0000	1	fings
0.0109	20.4	.0000	1	finish'd
0.0109	20.4	.0000	1	Finney's
0.0109	20.4	.0000	1	fio
0.0109	20.4	.0000	1	fire-reel
0.0109	20.4	.0000	1	firemen's
0.0109	20.4	.0000	1	first-person
0.0109	20.4	.0000	1	fish-line
0.0109	20.4	.0000	1	fish'hook**
0.0109	20.4	.0000	1	five-haired
0.0109	20.4	.0000	1	five-letter
0.0109	20.4	.0000	1	five-seven-five
0.0109	20.4	.0000	1	fix'd
0.0109	20.4	.0000	1	flabbed
0.0109	20.4	.0000	1	flappers
0.0109	20.4	.0000	1	flitter-twitters
0.0109	20.4	.0000	1	floofle
0.0109	20.4	.0000	1	fluffiest
0.0109	20.4	.0000	1	flushes
0.0109	20.4	.0000	1	foglights
0.0109	20.4	.0000	1	foreclaws
0.0109	20.4	.0000	1	foreland
0.0109	20.4	.0000	1	foresty
0.0109	20.4	.0000	1	forgo
0.0109	20.4	.0000	1	forgott
0.0109	20.4	.0000	1	Form
0.0109	20.4	.0000	1	formidable-looking
0.0109	20.4	.0000	1	Fosdick
0.0109	20.4	.0000	1	foul-shooting
0.0109	20.4	.0000	1	foulard
0.0109	20.4	.0000	1	fourth-
0.0109	20.4	.0000	1	fourty
0.0109	20.4	.0000	1	fragmentary
0.0109	20.4	.0000	1	frangere
0.0109	20.4	.0000	1	Fre
0.0109	20.4	.0000	1	FRED
0.0109	20.4	.0000	1	Freiberg
0.0109	20.4	.0000	1	fretwork
0.0109	20.4	.0000	1	Friday's
0.0109	20.4	.0000	1	frighteningly
0.0109	20.4	.0000	1	frigidaire
0.0109	20.4	.0000	1	frobish
0.0109	20.4	.0000	1	Frost's
0.0109	20.4	.0000	1	frothing
0.0109	20.4	.0000	1	frums

THE PRECEDING WORD TYPE OCCUPIES RANK 74200

U	SFI	D	F	Word Type
0.0109	20.4	.0000	1	Full
0.0109	20.4	.0000	1	furlough
0.0109	20.4	.0000	1	Fust's
0.0109	20.4	.0000	1	Gail's
0.0109	20.4	.0000	1	Galahad
0.0109	20.4	.0000	1	gargled
0.0109	20.4	.0000	1	gargouille
0.0109	20.4	.0000	1	Garth
0.0109	20.4	.0000	1	gas-light
0.0109	20.4	.0000	1	GC
0.0109	20.4	.0000	1	Gene's
0.0109	20.4	.0000	1	Gensfleisch
0.0109	20.4	.0000	1	gentian
0.0109	20.4	.0000	1	Gentile
0.0109	20.4	.0000	1	Geologists
0.0109	20.4	.0000	1	germ-laden
0.0109	20.4	.0000	1	getter
0.0109	20.4	.0000	1	geyserlike
0.0109	20.4	.0000	1	gg
0.0109	20.4	.0000	1	ghost-writer
0.0109	20.4	.0000	1	Glee
0.0109	20.4	.0000	1	gloatin'
0.0109	20.4	.0000	1	gloobed
0.0109	20.4	.0000	1	Glover's
0.0109	20.4	.0000	1	glutteral
0.0109	20.4	.0000	1	goed
0.0109	20.4	.0000	1	Gogio
0.0109	20.4	.0000	1	gonnagetit
0.0109	20.4	.0000	1	gorbed
0.0109	20.4	.0000	1	Gorham
0.0109	20.4	.0000	1	grammaticality
0.0109	20.4	.0000	1	greasiest
0.0109	20.4	.0000	1	great-great
0.0109	20.4	.0000	1	grees
0.0109	20.4	.0000	1	greez
0.0109	20.4	.0000	1	Gremlin
0.0109	20.4	.0000	1	gribble
0.0109	20.4	.0000	1	Grief
0.0109	20.4	.0000	1	grimmest
0.0109	20.4	.0000	1	grop
0.0109	20.4	.0000	1	gryphon
0.0109	20.4	.0000	1	Gryphon's
0.0109	20.4	.0000	1	gryphons
0.0109	20.4	.0000	1	Gubser
0.0109	20.4	.0000	1	Gulls
0.0109	20.4	.0000	1	gunnels
0.0109	20.4	.0000	1	gurgle-gurgle
0.0109	20.4	.0000	1	h'ugh
0.0109	20.4	.0000	1	hahf
0.0109	20.4	.0000	1	Hailstones
0.0109	20.4	.0000	1	half-boots
0.0109	20.4	.0000	1	half-familiar
0.0109	20.4	.0000	1	Halliburton's
0.0109	20.4	.0000	1	hallmark
0.0109	20.4	.0000	1	handbag
0.0109	20.4	.0000	1	hard-surface
0.0109	20.4	.0000	1	hard-to-get
0.0109	20.4	.0000	1	harme
0.0109	20.4	.0000	1	Hartshorne
0.0109	20.4	.0000	1	harvard
0.0109	20.4	.0000	1	Hate-evil
0.0109	20.4	.0000	1	Hathaway's
0.0109	20.4	.0000	1	Haunted
0.0109	20.4	.0000	1	hayrack
0.0109	20.4	.0000	1	Head-in-Air
0.0109	20.4	.0000	1	headwords
0.0109	20.4	.0000	1	hearer
0.0109	20.4	.0000	1	heartful
0.0109	20.4	.0000	1	heavy-bodied
0.0109	20.4	.0000	1	Helluland
0.0109	20.4	.0000	1	heraldry
0.0109	20.4	.0000	1	heres
0.0109	20.4	.0000	1	herisson
0.0109	20.4	.0000	1	Herjolfsson
0.0109	20.4	.0000	1	herns
0.0109	20.4	.0000	1	hero-tales
0.0109	20.4	.0000	1	Heroes
0.0109	20.4	.0000	1	hes
0.0109	20.4	.0000	1	hexameter
0.0109	20.4	.0000	1	hexameters
0.0109	20.4	.0000	1	Hide-and-Go-Seek
0.0109	20.4	.0000	1	high-buttoned
0.0109	20.4	.0000	1	high-diving
0.0109	20.4	.0000	1	Highest
0.0109	20.4	.0000	1	highty-tighty
0.0109	20.4	.0000	1	Hilaire
0.0109	20.4	.0000	1	hir
0.0109	20.4	.0000	1	hlaf
0.0109	20.4	.0000	1	hlafdige
0.0109	20.4	.0000	1	hlafweard
0.0109	20.4	.0000	1	Hobbies
0.0109	20.4	.0000	1	Hobby
0.0109	20.4	.0000	1	hog-nosed
0.0109	20.4	.0000	1	hogger
0.0109	20.4	.0000	1	hogger's
0.0109	20.4	.0000	1	hoiting
0.0109	20.4	.0000	1	hoity
0.0109	20.4	.0000	1	hoity-toity
0.0109	20.4	.0000	1	holdless
0.0109	20.4	.0000	1	homeroom

THE PRECEDING WORD TYPE OCCUPIES RANK 74300

U	SFI	D	F	Word Type
0.0109	20.4	.0000	1	Homework
0.0109	20.4	.0000	1	honor's
0.0109	20.4	.0000	1	Horn-Webler
0.0109	20.4	.0000	1	hospitalium
0.0109	20.4	.0000	1	Housman
0.0109	20.4	.0000	1	hoyden
0.0109	20.4	.0000	1	hummmmm
0.0109	20.4	.0000	1	humpy
0.0109	20.4	.0000	1	Hurry
0.0109	20.4	.0000	1	hurry-scurry
0.0109	20.4	.0000	1	hushes
0.0109	20.4	.0000	1	hypnotism
0.0109	20.4	.0000	1	I-1
0.0109	20.4	.0000	1	icon
0.0109	20.4	.0000	1	idaho
0.0109	20.4	.0000	1	idear
0.0109	20.4	.0000	1	Igel
0.0109	20.4	.0000	1	illegible
0.0109	20.4	.0000	1	immodest
0.0109	20.4	.0000	1	Imogen
0.0109	20.4	.0000	1	imoto
0.0109	20.4	.0000	1	inconclusive
0.0109	20.4	.0000	1	Indefinites
0.0109	20.4	.0000	1	indefinites
0.0109	20.4	.0000	1	indention
0.0109	20.4	.0000	1	indicare
0.0109	20.4	.0000	1	indict
0.0109	20.4	.0000	1	Indo-Iranian
0.0109	20.4	.0000	1	inelegant
0.0109	20.4	.0000	1	infans
0.0109	20.4	.0000	1	infinitesimally
0.0109	20.4	.0000	1	infrequently
0.0109	20.4	.0000	1	ingersoll
0.0109	20.4	.0000	1	insipid
0.0109	20.4	.0000	1	insolently
0.0109	20.4	.0000	1	insurgents
0.0109	20.4	.0000	1	intensifier
0.0109	20.4	.0000	1	intensifies
0.0109	20.4	.0000	1	internship
0.0109	20.4	.0000	1	interrogated
0.0109	20.4	.0000	1	Intransitive
0.0109	20.4	.0000	1	Introductions
0.0109	20.4	.0000	1	invidious
0.0109	20.4	.0000	1	Invitations
0.0109	20.4	.0000	1	IO
0.0109	20.4	.0000	1	ironical
0.0109	20.4	.0000	1	Irvings's
0.0109	20.4	.0000	1	Isabel's
0.0109	20.4	.0000	1	isinglass
0.0109	20.4	.0000	1	its-it's
0.0109	20.4	.0000	1	Ivanitch
0.0109	20.4	.0000	1	Ive
0.0109	20.4	.0000	1	J-La
0.0109	20.4	.0000	1	Jabberwocky
0.0109	20.4	.0000	1	Jacalevna's
0.0109	20.4	.0000	1	Jack-o'-Lantern
0.0109	20.4	.0000	1	Jacobs
0.0109	20.4	.0000	1	jail-breaker
0.0109	20.4	.0000	1	jam-packed
0.0109	20.4	.0000	1	james
0.0109	20.4	.0000	1	Jameses
0.0109	20.4	.0000	1	jaw-wagging
0.0109	20.4	.0000	1	jaybirds
0.0109	20.4	.0000	1	jet-blast
0.0109	20.4	.0000	1	jet-piercer
0.0109	20.4	.0000	1	jinan
0.0109	20.4	.0000	1	jine
0.0109	20.4	.0000	1	jingle-jingle
0.0109	20.4	.0000	1	jingle-jingling
0.0109	20.4	.0000	1	jokebox
0.0109	20.4	.0000	1	Jonesville
0.0109	20.4	.0000	1	Joris
0.0109	20.4	.0000	1	joyless
0.0109	20.4	.0000	1	Judd
0.0109	20.4	.0000	1	juggles
0.0109	20.4	.0000	1	jujitsu
0.0109	20.4	.0000	1	Julia's
0.0109	20.4	.0000	1	july
0.0109	20.4	.0000	1	Junto
0.0109	20.4	.0000	1	k'hinkali
0.0109	20.4	.0000	1	kansas
0.0109	20.4	.0000	1	kathy
0.0109	20.4	.0000	1	keck
0.0109	20.4	.0000	1	kembs
0.0109	20.4	.0000	1	Kendrick
0.0109	20.4	.0000	1	Kenneth's
0.0109	20.4	.0000	1	kentucky
0.0109	20.4	.0000	1	KHCAL
0.0109	20.4	.0000	1	Kidnapped
0.0109	20.4	.0000	1	kiosk
0.0109	20.4	.0000	1	kirtel
0.0109	20.4	.0000	1	kleenex
0.0109	20.4	.0000	1	kne
0.0109	20.4	.0000	1	kneader
0.0109	20.4	.0000	1	kneads
0.0109	20.4	.0000	1	Kneeaz
0.0109	20.4	.0000	1	Knit
0.0109	20.4	.0000	1	Knowles
0.0109	20.4	.0000	1	komatics
0.0109	20.4	.0000	1	Korrect

THE PRECEDING WORD TYPE OCCUPIES RANK 74400

U	SFI	D	F	Word Type
0.0109	20.4	.0000	1	Kraft
0.0109	20.4	.0000	1	Kubie
0.0109	20.4	.0000	1	L-50
0.0109	20.4	.0000	1	L'Engle
0.0109	20.4	.0000	1	l'anglaise
0.0109	20.4	.0000	1	labboard
0.0109	20.4	.0000	1	Ladner
0.0109	20.4	.0000	1	lags
0.0109	20.4	.0000	1	laith
0.0109	20.4	.0000	1	Lambarene
0.0109	20.4	.0000	1	Lamorisse
0.0109	20.4	.0000	1	Lang's
0.0109	20.4	.0000	1	Langland
0.0109	20.4	.0000	1	Langro
0.0109	20.4	.0000	1	Languages
0.0109	20.4	.0000	1	lapsed
0.0109	20.4	.0000	1	Lardner
0.0109	20.4	.0000	1	lateness
0.0109	20.4	.0000	1	Laverne
0.0109	20.4	.0000	1	leakproof
0.0109	20.4	.0000	1	Learn-wisdom
0.0109	20.4	.0000	1	learning-knight
0.0109	20.4	.0000	1	lecherous
0.0109	20.4	.0000	1	left-to-right
0.0109	20.4	.0000	1	leftenant
0.0109	20.4	.0000	1	Leiningen
0.0109	20.4	.0000	1	Lemmon
0.0109	20.4	.0000	1	Lepanto
0.0109	20.4	.0000	1	Lesley
0.0109	20.4	.0000	1	letter-wide
0.0109	20.4	.0000	1	levered
0.0109	20.4	.0000	1	lexicographer
0.0109	20.4	.0000	1	lightning-flash
0.0109	20.4	.0000	1	linguistically
0.0109	20.4	.0000	1	Linking
0.0109	20.4	.0000	1	linking-verb
0.0109	20.4	.0000	1	Linsky
0.0109	20.4	.0000	1	Lion-Hearted
0.0109	20.4	.0000	1	LISA
0.0109	20.4	.0000	1	listener's
0.0109	20.4	.0000	1	listeners'
0.0109	20.4	.0000	1	litigant
0.0109	20.4	.0000	1	litterbugs
0.0109	20.4	.0000	1	little-used
0.0109	20.4	.0000	1	lkd
0.0109	20.4	.0000	1	loamy
0.0109	20.4	.0000	1	loanword
0.0109	20.4	.0000	1	Locklin
0.0109	20.4	.0000	1	logographs
0.0109	20.4	.0000	1	Lois's
0.0109	20.4	.0000	1	long-stemmed
0.0109	20.4	.0000	1	Lonny
0.0109	20.4	.0000	1	Looy
0.0109	20.4	.0000	1	louisiana
0.0109	20.4	.0000	1	lov'd
0.0109	20.4	.0000	1	lovebirds
0.0109	20.4	.0000	1	Luster
0.0109	20.4	.0000	1	Lyman
0.0109	20.4	.0000	1	M-1000
0.0109	20.4	.0000	1	MacAdam
0.0109	20.4	.0000	1	MacMahon
0.0109	20.4	.0000	1	macintosh
0.0109	20.4	.0000	1	Magical
0.0109	20.4	.0000	1	magnetisms
0.0109	20.4	.0000	1	Mailed
0.0109	20.4	.0000	1	mair
0.0109	20.4	.0000	1	majuscule
0.0109	20.4	.0000	1	Make-Believe
0.0109	20.4	.0000	1	Make-believe
0.0109	20.4	.0000	1	maligned
0.0109	20.4	.0000	1	maltreat
0.0109	20.4	.0000	1	Malvern
0.0109	20.4	.0000	1	mandoline
0.0109	20.4	.0000	1	manhoods
0.0109	20.4	.0000	1	Marian's
0.0109	20.4	.0000	1	Marigold
0.0109	20.4	.0000	1	marksmanship
0.0109	20.4	.0000	1	marsh-mist
0.0109	20.4	.0000	1	marshall
0.0109	20.4	.0000	1	masculinity
0.0109	20.4	.0000	1	masqueraded
0.0109	20.4	.0000	1	massachusetts
0.0109	20.4	.0000	1	matko
0.0109	20.4	.0000	1	Maugham
0.0109	20.4	.0000	1	meanw'ile
0.0109	20.4	.0000	1	meeny
0.0109	20.4	.0000	1	mellowest
0.0109	20.4	.0000	1	melvin
0.0109	20.4	.0000	1	Mennonites
0.0109	20.4	.0000	1	mer
0.0109	20.4	.0000	1	mercy**
0.0109	20.4	.0000	1	Merriam
0.0109	20.4	.0000	1	Merryweather
0.0109	20.4	.0000	1	Mesmer
0.0109	20.4	.0000	1	mesmerism
0.0109	20.4	.0000	1	metaphorical
0.0109	20.4	.0000	1	Microteknic
0.0109	20.4	.0000	1	mid-season
0.0109	20.4	.0000	1	mid-sentence
0.0109	20.4	.0000	1	Midland

THE PRECEDING WORD TYPE OCCUPIES RANK 74500

U	SFI	D	F	Word Type
0.0109	20.4	.0000	1	Mifflin
0.0109	20.4	.0000	1	Milano
0.0109	20.4	.0000	1	Millbrook
0.0109	20.4	.0000	1	miny
0.0109	20.4	.0000	1	mirry
0.0109	20.4	.0000	1	Mirzah
0.0109	20.4	.0000	1	misapplied
0.0109	20.4	.0000	1	miscues
0.0109	20.4	.0000	1	misinterpretation
0.0109	20.4	.0000	1	misinterpreted
0.0109	20.4	.0000	1	mislaying
0.0109	20.4	.0000	1	mispronounce
0.0109	20.4	.0000	1	mispronouncing
0.0109	20.4	.0000	1	mispronunciation
0.0109	20.4	.0000	1	misreading
0.0109	20.4	.0000	1	missouri
0.0109	20.4	.0000	1	Missourian
0.0109	20.4	.0000	1	Misspelled
0.0109	20.4	.0000	1	Mitch
0.0109	20.4	.0000	1	mitre
0.0109	20.4	.0000	1	mlle
0.0109	20.4	.0000	1	modals
0.0109	20.4	.0000	1	modifer
0.0109	20.4	.0000	1	modus
0.0109	20.4	.0000	1	moisseron
0.0109	20.4	.0000	1	mom's
0.0109	20.4	.0000	1	monogram
0.0109	20.4	.0000	1	monroe
0.0109	20.4	.0000	1	monroe's
0.0109	20.4	.0000	1	moon-flecked
0.0109	20.4	.0000	1	moone
0.0109	20.4	.0000	1	mopes
0.0109	20.4	.0000	1	moray
0.0109	20.4	.0000	1	morne
0.0109	20.4	.0000	1	motch
0.0109	20.4	.0000	1	mousehole
0.0109	20.4	.0000	1	mouser
0.0109	20.4	.0000	1	mousseron
0.0109	20.4	.0000	1	movability
0.0109	20.4	.0000	1	movables
0.0109	20.4	.0000	1	moveless
0.0109	20.4	.0000	1	movie-goers
0.0109	20.4	.0000	1	moviegoers'
0.0109	20.4	.0000	1	mumbler
0.0109	20.4	.0000	1	Murrays
0.0109	20.4	.0000	1	Murry
0.0109	20.4	.0000	1	mus
0.0109	20.4	.0000	1	muscheron
0.0109	20.4	.0000	1	musculus
0.0109	20.4	.0000	1	mustering-out
0.0109	20.4	.0000	1	mutch
0.0109	20.4	.0000	1	NP's
0.0109	20.4	.0000	1	N-LV-N
0.0109	20.4	.0000	1	N-Lv-N
0.0109	20.4	.0000	1	N-lnv-n
0.0109	20.4	.0000	1	N-v-ns
0.0109	20.4	.0000	1	Nakashi
0.0109	20.4	.0000	1	nakedness
0.0109	20.4	.0000	1	NAME
0.0109	20.4	.0000	1	Napoli
0.0109	20.4	.0000	1	narcissus
0.0109	20.4	.0000	1	Nasturtium
0.0109	20.4	.0000	1	nathaniel
0.0109	20.4	.0000	1	nauseam
0.0109	20.4	.0000	1	negotiator
0.0109	20.4	.0000	1	neisan
0.0109	20.4	.0000	1	neologism
0.0109	20.4	.0000	1	nestling
0.0109	20.4	.0000	1	never-questioned
0.0109	20.4	.0000	1	newsworthy
0.0109	20.4	.0000	1	nifty
0.0109	20.4	.0000	1	nine-line
0.0109	20.4	.0000	1	nipp'd
0.0109	20.4	.0000	1	NJ
0.0109	20.4	.0000	1	noire
0.0109	20.4	.0000	1	non-criminals
0.0109	20.4	.0000	1	nonaction
0.0109	20.4	.0000	1	noncountable
0.0109	20.4	.0000	1	nondefinite
0.0109	20.4	.0000	1	Nonfiction
0.0109	20.4	.0000	1	nonpoetic
0.0109	20.4	.0000	1	nonrestrictive
0.0109	20.4	.0000	1	North-Easter
0.0109	20.4	.0000	1	Noun
0.0109	20.4	.0000	1	noun-signal
0.0109	20.4	.0000	1	noun-verb-noun
0.0109	20.4	.0000	1	Novotny's
0.0109	20.4	.0000	1	NS-V
0.0109	20.4	.0000	1	numismatists
0.0109	20.4	.0000	1	NYU
0.0109	20.4	.0000	1	O'Brian
0.0109	20.4	.0000	1	O'Dell
0.0109	20.4	.0000	1	O'Grumpity's
0.0109	20.4	.0000	1	O'Hara
0.0109	20.4	.0000	1	o'erlooking
0.0109	20.4	.0000	1	oblig'd
0.0109	20.4	.0000	1	obs
0.0109	20.4	.0000	1	obscuring
0.0109	20.4	.0000	1	observ'd
0.0109	20.4	.0000	1	Oceanside

THE PRECEDING WORD TYPE OCCUPIES RANK 74600

U	SFI	D	F	Word Type
0.0109	20.4	.0000	1	ochestvo
0.0109	20.4	.0000	1	off-schedule

U	SFI	D	F	Word Type
0.0109	20.4	.0000	1	Often
0.0109	20.4	.0000	1	oftenest
0.0109	20.4	.0000	1	ohio
0.0109	20.4	.0000	1	okeh
0.0109	20.4	.0000	1	Olive's
0.0109	20.4	.0000	1	Oll
0.0109	20.4	.0000	1	on-the-scene
0.0109	20.4	.0000	1	one-family
0.0109	20.4	.0000	1	onoma
0.0109	20.4	.0000	1	OOPSA
0.0109	20.4	.0000	1	OP
0.0109	20.4	.0000	1	opalways
0.0109	20.4	.0000	1	opare
0.0109	20.4	.0000	1	opdid
0.0109	20.4	.0000	1	opforks
0.0109	20.4	.0000	1	Opinion
0.0109	20.4	.0000	1	opput
0.0109	20.4	.0000	1	opthe
0.0109	20.4	.0000	1	opthey
0.0109	20.4	.0000	1	opyou
0.0109	20.4	.0000	1	Orchid
0.0109	20.4	.0000	1	orleans
0.0109	20.4	.0000	1	otherwhere
0.0109	20.4	.0000	1	out-talked
0.0109	20.4	.0000	1	outfeilders
0.0109	20.4	.0000	1	outlive
0.0109	20.4	.0000	1	outlives
0.0109	20.4	.0000	1	over-generalization
0.0109	20.4	.0000	1	overgoing
0.0109	20.4	.0000	1	overoil
0.0109	20.4	.0000	1	overused
0.0109	20.4	.0000	1	overworking
0.0109	20.4	.0000	1	p's
0.0109	20.4	.0000	1	pacifier
0.0109	20.4	.0000	1	paff
0.0109	20.4	.0000	1	Pal's
0.0109	20.4	.0000	1	palabra
0.0109	20.4	.0000	1	pale-gray
0.0109	20.4	.0000	1	Pantaleone
0.0109	20.4	.0000	1	pantsandshirt
0.0109	20.4	.0000	1	paragraphein
0.0109	20.4	.0000	1	parsing
0.0109	20.4	.0000	1	passerby
0.0109	20.4	.0000	1	password
0.0109	20.4	.0000	1	Patrickovna
0.0109	20.4	.0000	1	peabody
0.0109	20.4	.0000	1	penalized
0.0109	20.4	.0000	1	pencil-drawn
0.0109	20.4	.0000	1	Pennyworth
0.0109	20.4	.0000	1	peony
0.0109	20.4	.0000	1	per-
0.0109	20.4	.0000	1	peridinians
0.0109	20.4	.0000	1	perky
0.0109	20.4	.0000	1	Perrin
0.0109	20.4	.0000	1	persia
0.0109	20.4	.0000	1	persian
0.0109	20.4	.0000	1	personalize
0.0109	20.4	.0000	1	Personification
0.0109	20.4	.0000	1	Persuasion
0.0109	20.4	.0000	1	pessimist
0.0109	20.4	.0000	1	Petrograd
0.0109	20.4	.0000	1	Pets
0.0109	20.4	.0000	1	Ph-i-i-i-t-t
0.0109	20.4	.0000	1	Philad'a
0.0109	20.4	.0000	1	philatelist
0.0109	20.4	.0000	1	Phncn
0.0109	20.4	.0000	1	phonac
0.0109	20.4	.0000	1	Phrase
0.0109	20.4	.0000	1	physic
0.0109	20.4	.0000	1	picnic-supper
0.0109	20.4	.0000	1	picture-drawings
0.0109	20.4	.0000	1	picture-making
0.0109	20.4	.0000	1	piff
0.0109	20.4	.0000	1	Pinkham
0.0109	20.4	.0000	1	Planning
0.0109	20.4	.0000	1	plashless
0.0109	20.4	.0000	1	playd
0.0109	20.4	.0000	1	playwright's
0.0109	20.4	.0000	1	Ploughman
0.0109	20.4	.0000	1	Plural
0.0109	20.4	.0000	1	pn
0.0109	20.4	.0000	1	pocketsful
0.0109	20.4	.0000	1	pollywog
0.0109	20.4	.0000	1	poolroom
0.0109	20.4	.0000	1	Popes
0.0109	20.4	.0000	1	porcine
0.0109	20.4	.0000	1	porcus
0.0109	20.4	.0000	1	pork-chops
0.0109	20.4	.0000	1	porta
0.0109	20.4	.0000	1	Porterfield
0.0109	20.4	.0000	1	portioned
0.0109	20.4	.0000	1	portus
0.0109	20.4	.0000	1	posies
0.0109	20.4	.0000	1	pot's
0.0109	20.4	.0000	1	potpourri
0.0109	20.4	.0000	1	poultry-yard
0.0109	20.4	.0000	1	praiseworthy
0.0109	20.4	.0000	1	pranksters

THE PRECEDING WORD TYPE OCCUPIES RANK 74700

U	SFI	D	F	Word Type
0.0109	20.4	.0000	1	pre-scientific
0.0109	20.4	.0000	1	Predicate
0.0109	20.4	.0000	1	prelate
0.0109	20.4	.0000	1	prepose
0.0109	20.4	.0000	1	preposition-shifting
0.0109	20.4	.0000	1	prettied
0.0109	20.4	.0000	1	pretzels
0.0109	20.4	.0000	1	prima
0.0109	20.4	.0000	1	printshop
0.0109	20.4	.0000	1	prize-winning
0.0109	20.4	.0000	1	profane/profanity
0.0109	20.4	.0000	1	prognosticate
0.0109	20.4	.0000	1	promissory
0.0109	20.4	.0000	1	proofreads
0.0109	20.4	.0000	1	prosecute-prosecution
0.0109	20.4	.0000	1	Prospecting
0.0109	20.4	.0000	1	provocations
0.0109	20.4	.0000	1	provoke-provocation
0.0109	20.4	.0000	1	prudish
0.0109	20.4	.0000	1	public-house
0.0109	20.4	.0000	1	publick
0.0109	20.4	.0000	1	pull-a-button
0.0109	20.4	.0000	1	pullover
0.0109	20.4	.0000	1	punch-marks
0.0109	20.4	.0000	1	punctual
0.0109	20.4	.0000	1	punner
0.0109	20.4	.0000	1	punster
0.0109	20.4	.0000	1	punt
0.0109	20.4	.0000	1	pupil-teacher
0.0109	20.4	.0000	1	puppy's
0.0109	20.4	.0000	1	purist
0.0109	20.4	.0000	1	push-a-button
0.0109	20.4	.0000	1	Python
0.0109	20.4	.0000	1	Quadruped
0.0109	20.4	.0000	1	qualification
0.0109	20.4	.0000	1	quality**
0.0109	20.4	.0000	1	que'que
0.0109	20.4	.0000	1	quelque
0.0109	20.4	.0000	1	quien
0.0109	20.4	.0000	1	Quince
0.0109	20.4	.0000	1	quitted
0.0109	20.4	.0000	1	quizzed
0.0109	20.4	.0000	1	r-adders
0.0109	20.4	.0000	1	r-droppers
0.0109	20.4	.0000	1	r-o-u-g-h
0.0109	20.4	.0000	1	R-339-40
0.0109	20.4	.0000	1	R-340
0.0109	20.4	.0000	1	rachel
0.0109	20.4	.0000	1	Racket
0.0109	20.4	.0000	1	racketeer
0.0109	20.4	.0000	1	Radbourne
0.0109	20.4	.0000	1	radio-sending
0.0109	20.4	.0000	1	raggeder
0.0109	20.4	.0000	1	rakish
0.0109	20.4	.0000	1	Ralphie
0.0109	20.4	.0000	1	ravioli
0.0109	20.4	.0000	1	Rd
0.0109	20.4	.0000	1	reclines
0.0109	20.4	.0000	1	Recorded
0.0109	20.4	.0000	1	Reeling
0.0109	20.4	.0000	1	reformate
0.0109	20.4	.0000	1	reformation
0.0109	20.4	.0000	1	refreshingly
0.0109	20.4	.0000	1	refurnish
0.0109	20.4	.0000	1	regulate/regulation
0.0109	20.4	.0000	1	reindeer-sled
0.0109	20.4	.0000	1	Relative
0.0109	20.4	.0000	1	relive
0.0109	20.4	.0000	1	remember'd
0.0109	20.4	.0000	1	rend
0.0109	20.4	.0000	1	rephrases
0.0109	20.4	.0000	1	Reports
0.0109	20.4	.0000	1	repulsively
0.0109	20.4	.0000	1	restated
0.0109	20.4	.0000	1	restricts
0.0109	20.4	.0000	1	Result
0.0109	20.4	.0000	1	reve
0.0109	20.4	.0000	1	revellers
0.0109	20.4	.0000	1	reworded
0.0109	20.4	.0000	1	Rhonda
0.0109	20.4	.0000	1	Rin
0.0109	20.4	.0000	1	rinks
0.0109	20.4	.0000	1	Rite-Spot
0.0109	20.4	.0000	1	roadblock
0.0109	20.4	.0000	1	roadbuilder
0.0109	20.4	.0000	1	Roberta's
0.0109	20.4	.0000	1	Robyn
0.0109	20.4	.0000	1	rock-beating
0.0109	20.4	.0000	1	rocketeer
0.0109	20.4	.0000	1	romanian
0.0109	20.4	.0000	1	rope-jumping
0.0109	20.4	.0000	1	Roper
0.0109	20.4	.0000	1	Rosetta
0.0109	20.4	.0000	1	Rosi
0.0109	20.4	.0000	1	Roundabout
0.0109	20.4	.0000	1	rum-colored
0.0109	20.4	.0000	1	Rumanian
0.0109	20.4	.0000	1	run-togethers
0.0109	20.4	.0000	1	rune
0.0109	20.4	.0000	1	Runs

THE PRECEDING WORD TYPE OCCUPIES RANK 74800

U	SFI	D	F	Word Type
0.0109	20.4	.0000	1	Rural
0.0109	20.4	.0000	1	russian
0.0109	20.4	.0000	1	Russian-Japanese
0.0109	20.4	.0000	1	Ruthie
0.0109	20.4	.0000	1	s'en
0.0109	20.4	.0000	1	sabe
0.0109	20.4	.0000	1	Sadducism
0.0109	20.4	.0000	1	Sadie
0.0109	20.4	.0000	1	Saffron
0.0109	20.4	.0000	1	sags
0.0109	20.4	.0000	1	salesclerk
0.0109	20.4	.0000	1	sampan
0.0109	20.4	.0000	1	SanNicholas
0.0109	20.4	.0000	1	sapodilla
0.0109	20.4	.0000	1	satira
0.0109	20.4	.0000	1	Saturday-night
0.0109	20.4	.0000	1	saunter
0.0109	20.4	.0000	1	Say
0.0109	20.4	.0000	1	Scamp
0.0109	20.4	.0000	1	scampers
0.0109	20.4	.0000	1	scandalized
0.0109	20.4	.0000	1	Scandinavians'
0.0109	20.4	.0000	1	sceptre
0.0109	20.4	.0000	1	Schoffer
0.0109	20.4	.0000	1	schoone
0.0109	20.4	.0000	1	scoffingly
0.0109	20.4	.0000	1	screwball
0.0109	20.4	.0000	1	scrivener
0.0109	20.4	.0000	1	Scrumptious
0.0109	20.4	.0000	1	scudded
0.0109	20.4	.0000	1	Sea-Wind
0.0109	20.4	.0000	1	sea-fight
0.0109	20.4	.0000	1	sea-lice
0.0109	20.4	.0000	1	sealing-wax
0.0109	20.4	.0000	1	seamews
0.0109	20.4	.0000	1	Season
0.0109	20.4	.0000	1	second-grade
0.0109	20.4	.0000	1	seconding
0.0109	20.4	.0000	1	sect-
0.0109	20.4	.0000	1	sedative
0.0109	20.4	.0000	1	segmental
0.0109	20.4	.0000	1	seon
0.0109	20.4	.0000	1	september
0.0109	20.4	.0000	1	seven-pound
0.0109	20.4	.0000	1	seven-sentence
0.0109	20.4	.0000	1	shabby-looking
0.0109	20.4	.0000	1	shaked
0.0109	20.4	.0000	1	shaws
0.0109	20.4	.0000	1	shedule
0.0109	20.4	.0000	1	Shenton's
0.0109	20.4	.0000	1	shepherd-swains
0.0109	20.4	.0000	1	shes
0.0109	20.4	.0000	1	Shippen
0.0109	20.4	.0000	1	Shona
0.0109	20.4	.0000	1	shoon
0.0109	20.4	.0000	1	shouldnt
0.0109	20.4	.0000	1	sidecar
0.0109	20.4	.0000	1	silvaticus
0.0109	20.4	.0000	1	silver-feathered
0.0109	20.4	.0000	1	Simpkins
0.0109	20.4	.0000	1	Sincerely
0.0109	20.4	.0000	1	Singular
0.0109	20.4	.0000	1	sitteth
0.0109	20.4	.0000	1	skiddoo
0.0109	20.4	.0000	1	skimp
0.0109	20.4	.0000	1	skimpy
0.0109	20.4	.0000	1	slantwise
0.0109	20.4	.0000	1	slat
0.0109	20.4	.0000	1	slippin'
0.0109	20.4	.0000	1	sloucher
0.0109	20.4	.0000	1	slow-up
0.0109	20.4	.0000	1	sluggard
0.0109	20.4	.0000	1	smaller-wheeled
0.0109	20.4	.0000	1	smoke-jumper
0.0109	20.4	.0000	1	sneaky
0.0109	20.4	.0000	1	snick
0.0109	20.4	.0000	1	Snood
0.0109	20.4	.0000	1	snoofing
0.0109	20.4	.0000	1	snoozes
0.0109	20.4	.0000	1	snowfalls
0.0109	20.4	.0000	1	so-o-o-o
0.0109	20.4	.0000	1	soft-and-white
0.0109	20.4	.0000	1	sojourned
0.0109	20.4	.0000	1	Someones
0.0109	20.4	.0000	1	Somnium
0.0109	20.4	.0000	1	Sophie
0.0109	20.4	.0000	1	sophomores
0.0109	20.4	.0000	1	sorcerers
0.0109	20.4	.0000	1	soth
0.0109	20.4	.0000	1	sour-looking
0.0109	20.4	.0000	1	sower
0.0109	20.4	.0000	1	SP-1
0.0109	20.4	.0000	1	SP-2
0.0109	20.4	.0000	1	Spaceman
0.0109	20.4	.0000	1	Spacemen
0.0109	20.4	.0000	1	Spacemen's
0.0109	20.4	.0000	1	spade-work
0.0109	20.4	.0000	1	spadesman
0.0109	20.4	.0000	1	spaker
0.0109	20.4	.0000	1	sparrows'

THE PRECEDING WORD TYPE OCCUPIES RANK 74900

U	SFI	D	F	Word Type
0.0109	20.4	.0000	1	spear-sharp
0.0109	20.4	.0000	1	specific-detail
0.0109	20.4	.0000	1	spell-bound
0.0109	20.4	.0000	1	Spenser
0.0109	20.4	.0000	1	Speyer's
0.0109	20.4	.0000	1	sphinxlike
0.0109	20.4	.0000	1	spinge
0.0109	20.4	.0000	1	spinosus
0.0109	20.4	.0000	1	spintains
0.0109	20.4	.0000	1	spitted
0.0109	20.4	.0000	1	spittoon
0.0109	20.4	.0000	1	splotching
0.0109	20.4	.0000	1	sports-writer's
0.0109	20.4	.0000	1	sportsman's
0.0109	20.4	.0000	1	sprained
0.0109	20.4	.0000	1	Sprayberry
0.0109	20.4	.0000	1	spurn
0.0109	20.4	.0000	1	SSSTT
0.0109	20.4	.0000	1	stabil
0.0109	20.4	.0000	1	stage-plank
0.0109	20.4	.0000	1	stalactite
0.0109	20.4	.0000	1	stalagmite
0.0109	20.4	.0000	1	stapler
0.0109	20.4	.0000	1	starer
0.0109	20.4	.0000	1	starless
0.0109	20.4	.0000	1	stationers
0.0109	20.4	.0000	1	steadiment
0.0109	20.4	.0000	1	steams
0.0109	20.4	.0000	1	steepy
0.0109	20.4	.0000	1	Stefferud
0.0109	20.4	.0000	1	Stella's
0.0109	20.4	.0000	1	stercoris
0.0109	20.4	.0000	1	stig
0.0109	20.4	.0000	1	stig-
0.0109	20.4	.0000	1	stigan
0.0109	20.4	.0000	1	stigrap
0.0109	20.4	.0000	1	stigweard
0.0109	20.4	.0000	1	stinch
0.0109	20.4	.0000	1	storme
0.0109	20.4	.0000	1	story-playing
0.0109	20.4	.0000	1	Strachey
0.0109	20.4	.0000	1	strapping
0.0109	20.4	.0000	1	Strength
0.0109	20.4	.0000	1	stress-shift
0.0109	20.4	.0000	1	stretch'd
0.0109	20.4	.0000	1	strolls
0.0109	20.4	.0000	1	Strovalone
0.0109	20.4	.0000	1	stub-tailed
0.0109	20.4	.0000	1	study-hall
0.0109	20.4	.0000	1	stuffin'
0.0109	20.4	.0000	1	stupidest
0.0109	20.4	.0000	1	Sturbridge
0.0109	20.4	.0000	1	sty-rope
0.0109	20.4	.0000	1	sub-branch
0.0109	20.4	.0000	1	sub-branches
0.0109	20.4	.0000	1	subj
0.0109	20.4	.0000	1	subject-verb
0.0109	20.4	.0000	1	subject-verb-complement
0.0109	20.4	.0000	1	subpoints
0.0109	20.4	.0000	1	substand
0.0109	20.4	.0000	1	sulphur-bottomed
0.0109	20.4	.0000	1	sun-cracked
0.0109	20.4	.0000	1	super-intelligent
0.0109	20.4	.0000	1	Supporting
0.0109	20.4	.0000	1	surf-riding
0.0109	20.4	.0000	1	SUSHES
0.0109	20.4	.0000	1	suspicious/suspicion
0.0109	20.4	.0000	1	suspiciousion
0.0109	20.4	.0000	1	swain
0.0109	20.4	.0000	1	swains
0.0109	20.4	.0000	1	swim-bladder
0.0109	20.4	.0000	1	swinelike
0.0109	20.4	.0000	1	swoons
0.0109	20.4	.0000	1	syle
0.0109	20.4	.0000	1	Symposium
0.0109	20.4	.0000	1	syntax
0.0109	20.4	.0000	1	T-Yes/No
0.0109	20.4	.0000	1	T-formation
0.0109	20.4	.0000	1	T-imp
0.0109	20.4	.0000	1	T-object
0.0109	20.4	.0000	1	T-terminal
0.0109	20.4	.0000	1	tailspin
0.0109	20.4	.0000	1	Taken
0.0109	20.4	.0000	1	Talmud
0.0109	20.4	.0000	1	tamada
0.0109	20.4	.0000	1	tamarisk
0.0109	20.4	.0000	1	tames
0.0109	20.4	.0000	1	Tanganyikan
0.0109	20.4	.0000	1	Tarantula
0.0109	20.4	.0000	1	tearfully
0.0109	20.4	.0000	1	technicalities
0.0109	20.4	.0000	1	teir
0.0109	20.4	.0000	1	teller's
0.0109	20.4	.0000	1	Telling
0.0109	20.4	.0000	1	Tennyson's
0.0109	20.4	.0000	1	Textbook
0.0109	20.4	.0000	1	thame
0.0109	20.4	.0000	1	Thank-you
0.0109	20.4	.0000	1	thank-you-letter
0.0109	20.4	.0000	1	theayter

THE PRECEDING WORD TYPE OCCUPIES RANK 75000

U	SFI	D	F	Word Type
0.0109	20.4	.0000	1	theirself
0.0109	20.4	.0000	1	Theodora
0.0109	20.4	.0000	1	Theodora
0.0109	20.4	.0000	1	Theophilus
0.0109	20.4	.0000	1	there-their
0.0109	20.4	.0000	1	therefrom
0.0109	20.4	.0000	1	they's
0.0109	20.4	.0000	1	theyd
0.0109	20.4	.0000	1	theyll
0.0109	20.4	.0000	1	thincan
0.0109	20.4	.0000	1	third-person
0.0109	20.4	.0000	1	Thirtieth
0.0109	20.4	.0000	1	thish-yer
0.0109	20.4	.0000	1	thocht
0.0109	20.4	.0000	1	thoroughful
0.0109	20.4	.0000	1	Thread
0.0109	20.4	.0000	1	THREE
0.0109	20.4	.0000	1	three-pronged
0.0109	20.4	.0000	1	three-room
0.0109	20.4	.0000	1	ths
0.0109	20.4	.0000	1	thunder-stone
0.0109	20.4	.0000	1	thunderclaps
0.0109	20.4	.0000	1	thundersticks
0.0109	20.4	.0000	1	thursday
0.0109	20.4	.0000	1	Thursday's
0.0109	20.4	.0000	1	Thyangboche
0.0109	20.4	.0000	1	ticker
0.0109	20.4	.0000	1	tie-in
0.0109	20.4	.0000	1	Tigris-Euphrates
0.0109	20.4	.0000	1	Tiles
0.0109	20.4	.0000	1	time-saver
0.0109	20.4	.0000	1	titlts
0.0109	20.4	.0000	1	to-daeg
0.0109	20.4	.0000	1	to-too
0.0109	20.4	.0000	1	tobaccos
0.0109	20.4	.0000	1	toga
0.0109	20.4	.0000	1	toity
0.0109	20.4	.0000	1	Tolgo
0.0109	20.4	.0000	1	tollhouse
0.0109	20.4	.0000	1	Tommys
0.0109	20.4	.0000	1	toune
0.0109	20.4	.0000	1	Towser's
0.0109	20.4	.0000	1	Tracks
0.0109	20.4	.0000	1	trans-
0.0109	20.4	.0000	1	transire
0.0109	20.4	.0000	1	Transitive
0.0109	20.4	.0000	1	tree-e-e-et
0.0109	20.4	.0000	1	tribespeople
0.0109	20.4	.0000	1	tripp
0.0109	20.4	.0000	1	Trivet
0.0109	20.4	.0000	1	trolleys
0.0109	20.4	.0000	1	Trucks
0.0109	20.4	.0000	1	truely
0.0109	20.4	.0000	1	ts
0.0109	20.4	.0000	1	Tuesday's
0.0109	20.4	.0000	1	tunneled
0.0109	20.4	.0000	1	tuxedo
0.0109	20.4	.0000	1	TWA
0.0109	20.4	.0000	1	twelfth-century
0.0109	20.4	.0000	1	Two-Gun
0.0109	20.4	.0000	1	two-car
0.0109	20.4	.0000	1	two-minute
0.0109	20.4	.0000	1	two-seated
0.0109	20.4	.0000	1	typewriting
0.0109	20.4	.0000	1	uck
0.0109	20.4	.0000	1	uglification

U	SFI	D	F	Word Type
0.0109	20.4	.0000	1	Uglification
0.0109	20.4	.0000	1	uglifying
0.0109	20.4	.0000	1	unalterable
0.0109	20.4	.0000	1	unblown
0.0109	20.4	.0000	1	uncials
0.0109	20.4	.0000	1	uncomplimentary
0.0109	20.4	.0000	1	unconnected
0.0109	20.4	.0000	1	uncorked
0.0109	20.4	.0000	1	uncountables
0.0109	20.4	.0000	1	underestimating
0.0109	20.4	.0000	1	underpads
0.0109	20.4	.0000	1	uneconomical
0.0109	20.4	.0000	1	unexpressed
0.0109	20.4	.0000	1	unfailingly
0.0109	20.4	.0000	1	ungrammatically
0.0109	20.4	.0000	1	unicycle
0.0109	20.4	.0000	1	unlaid
0.0109	20.4	.0000	1	unlifted
0.0109	20.4	.0000	1	unlined
0.0109	20.4	.0000	1	unmentionables
0.0109	20.4	.0000	1	unrehearsed
0.0109	20.4	.0000	1	unrhymed
0.0109	20.4	.0000	1	unruled
0.0109	20.4	.0000	1	unscrambling
0.0109	20.4	.0000	1	unserved
0.0109	20.4	.0000	1	unsifted
0.0109	20.4	.0000	1	unsinkable
0.0109	20.4	.0000	1	unsmote
0.0109	20.4	.0000	1	untaken
0.0109	20.4	.0000	1	unvanquished
0.0109	20.4	.0000	1	unworkable
0.0109	20.4	.0000	1	uproaring
0.0109	20.4	.0000	1	urne
0.0109	20.4	.0000	1	usted
THE PRECEDING WORD TYPE OCCUPIES RANK 75100				
0.0109	20.4	.0000	1	V-mid
0.0109	20.4	.0000	1	V-5
0.0109	20.4	.0000	1	Valois
0.0109	20.4	.0000	1	vary-variation
0.0109	20.4	.0000	1	vb
0.0109	20.4	.0000	1	Veleike
0.0109	20.4	.0000	1	Venutian's
0.0109	20.4	.0000	1	Venutian's-eye
0.0109	20.4	.0000	1	Versus
0.0109	20.4	.0000	1	vestigare
0.0109	20.4	.0000	1	vetter
0.0109	20.4	.0000	1	viaduct
0.0109	20.4	.0000	1	vide
0.0109	20.4	.0000	1	video-computers
0.0109	20.4	.0000	1	videre
0.0109	20.4	.0000	1	Vincent's
0.0109	20.4	.0000	1	Vinnie
0.0109	20.4	.0000	1	viragoes
0.0109	20.4	.0000	1	Visitor
0.0109	20.4	.0000	1	Voistinu
0.0109	20.4	.0000	1	vv
0.0109	20.4	.0000	1	w'er's
0.0109	20.4	.0000	1	w'ile
0.0109	20.4	.0000	1	wagered
0.0109	20.4	.0000	1	waitress
0.0109	20.4	.0000	1	wander'd
0.0109	20.4	.0000	1	Wanderers
0.0109	20.4	.0000	1	wappish
0.0109	20.4	.0000	1	wappishly
0.0109	20.4	.0000	1	war-trumpet
0.0109	20.4	.0000	1	wassa
0.0109	20.4	.0000	1	water-drip
0.0109	20.4	.0000	1	Waterless
0.0109	20.4	.0000	1	watershed's
0.0109	20.4	.0000	1	watsa
0.0109	20.4	.0000	1	watt
0.0109	20.4	.0000	1	weapon-like
0.0109	20.4	.0000	1	weard
0.0109	20.4	.0000	1	Weavers'
0.0109	20.4	.0000	1	wedding-cake
0.0109	20.4	.0000	1	weet
0.0109	20.4	.0000	1	Weisgard
0.0109	20.4	.0000	1	well-concealed
0.0109	20.4	.0000	1	well-enunciated
0.0109	20.4	.0000	1	well-sharpened
0.0109	20.4	.0000	1	well-ur
0.0109	20.4	.0000	1	wer
0.0109	20.4	.0000	1	Westerman
0.0109	20.4	.0000	1	wetly
0.0109	20.4	.0000	1	weve
0.0109	20.4	.0000	1	wha
0.0109	20.4	.0000	1	whatch
0.0109	20.4	.0000	1	whiles
0.0109	20.4	.0000	1	Whippet
0.0109	20.4	.0000	1	whirligig
0.0109	20.4	.0000	1	whirrr
0.0109	20.4	.0000	1	whirs
0.0109	20.4	.0000	1	whisperer
0.0109	20.4	.0000	1	white-coated
0.0109	20.4	.0000	1	Whitebread
0.0109	20.4	.0000	1	whodunit
0.0109	20.4	.0000	1	wholl
0.0109	20.4	.0000	1	wigwag
0.0109	20.4	.0000	1	wilcuma
0.0109	20.4	.0000	1	Wilks
0.0109	20.4	.0000	1	Willis
0.0109	20.4	.0000	1	Willows
0.0109	20.4	.0000	1	Wimbledon
0.0109	20.4	.0000	1	windproofs
0.0109	20.4	.0000	1	winter-time
0.0109	20.4	.0000	1	wish'd
0.0109	20.4	.0000	1	wit's
0.0109	20.4	.0000	1	witchery
0.0109	20.4	.0000	1	wittily
0.0109	20.4	.0000	1	wizard
0.0109	20.4	.0000	1	wld
0.0109	20.4	.0000	1	Woke
0.0109	20.4	.0000	1	Wonderment
0.0109	20.4	.0000	1	word-game
0.0109	20.4	.0000	1	word-study
0.0109	20.4	.0000	1	word-twins
0.0109	20.4	.0000	1	wordiness
0.0109	20.4	.0000	1	worryin'
0.0109	20.4	.0000	1	worser
0.0109	20.4	.0000	1	wraith-like
0.0109	20.4	.0000	1	Wreck
0.0109	20.4	.0000	1	wright
0.0109	20.4	.0000	1	wringer
0.0109	20.4	.0000	1	Wrinkle
0.0109	20.4	.0000	1	Writhing
0.0109	20.4	.0000	1	Written
0.0109	20.4	.0000	1	wrongdoers
0.0109	20.4	.0000	1	wrtng
0.0109	20.4	.0000	1	wyoming
0.0109	20.4	.0000	1	X-10
0.0109	20.4	.0000	1	X34
0.0109	20.4	.0000	1	yaller
0.0109	20.4	.0000	1	yearns
0.0109	20.4	.0000	1	yeir
0.0109	20.4	.0000	1	yellowed
THE PRECEDING WORD TYPE OCCUPIES RANK 75200				
0.0109	20.4	.0000	1	yipes
0.0109	20.4	.0000	1	your-you're
0.0109	20.4	.0000	1	youve
0.0109	20.4	.0000	1	zacked
0.0109	20.4	.0000	1	Zip's
0.0109	20.4	.0000	1	zorkles
0.0109	20.4	.0000	1	zuppingly
0.0109	20.4	.0000	1	1-15
0.0109	20.4	.0000	1	1-2-3
0.0109	20.4	.0000	1	10010
0.0109	20.4	.0000	1	1003
0.0109	20.4	.0000	1	101-117
0.0109	20.4	.0000	1	118-132
0.0109	20.4	.0000	1	121-123
0.0109	20.4	.0000	1	122-23
0.0109	20.4	.0000	1	1249
0.0109	20.4	.0000	1	127-
0.0109	20.4	.0000	1	1280
0.0109	20.4	.0000	1	130-31
0.0109	20.4	.0000	1	1314
0.0109	20.4	.0000	1	1349-1830
0.0109	20.4	.0000	1	1362
0.0109	20.4	.0000	1	1440
0.0109	20.4	.0000	1	1444
0.0109	20.4	.0000	1	146-47
0.0109	20.4	.0000	1	148-49
0.0109	20.4	.0000	1	149
0.0109	20.4	.0000	1	166-67
0.0109	20.4	.0000	1	1711
0.0109	20.4	.0000	1	172-181
0.0109	20.4	.0000	1	1874-1926
0.0109	20.4	.0000	1	18938
0.0109	20.4	.0000	1	19-
0.0109	20.4	.0000	1	19–
0.0109	20.4	.0000	1	19013
0.0109	20.4	.0000	1	2-3-3
0.0109	20.4	.0000	1	20s
0.0109	20.4	.0000	1	212-13
0.0109	20.4	.0000	1	2137
0.0109	20.4	.0000	1	216-17
0.0109	20.4	.0000	1	218-19
0.0109	20.4	.0000	1	218-219
0.0109	20.4	.0000	1	225-226
0.0109	20.4	.0000	1	225-26
0.0109	20.4	.0000	1	237-38
0.0109	20.4	.0000	1	243-244
0.0109	20.4	.0000	1	25-36
0.0109	20.4	.0000	1	251
0.0109	20.4	.0000	1	253-254
0.0109	20.4	.0000	1	253-54
0.0109	20.4	.0000	1	256-57
0.0109	20.4	.0000	1	26-inchers
0.0109	20.4	.0000	1	264-267
0.0109	20.4	.0000	1	267-68
0.0109	20.4	.0000	1	268-69
0.0109	20.4	.0000	1	275-76
0.0109	20.4	.0000	1	277-78
0.0109	20.4	.0000	1	288-297
0.0109	20.4	.0000	1	309-23
0.0109	20.4	.0000	1	311-312
0.0109	20.4	.0000	1	326-332
0.0109	20.4	.0000	1	37-39
0.0109	20.4	.0000	1	398-99
0.0109	20.4	.0000	1	399-400
0.0109	20.4	.0000	1	400-year
0.0109	20.4	.0000	1	402-403
0.0109	20.4	.0000	1	426-3587
0.0109	20.4	.0000	1	48823
0.0109	20.4	.0000	1	48824
0.0109	20.4	.0000	1	500-1-500
0.0109	20.4	.0000	1	520-529
0.0109	20.4	.0000	1	532
0.0109	20.4	.0000	1	533-35
0.0109	20.4	.0000	1	56-49
0.0109	20.4	.0000	1	60636
0.0109	20.4	.0000	1	66-67
0.0109	20.4	.0000	1	734
0.0109	20.4	.0000	1	78-79
0.0109	20.4	.0000	1	787-0304
0.0109	20.4	.0000	1	8-19's
0.0109	20.4	.0000	1	8h
0.0109	20.4	.0000	1	80-81
0.0109	20.4	.0000	1	82-83
0.0109	20.4	.0000	1	85232
0.0109	20.4	.0000	1	86th
0.0109	20.4	.0000	1	88-89
0.0109	20.4	.0000	1	94127
0.0109	20.4	.0000	1	947
0.0107	20.3	.0000	1	-ious
0.0107	20.3	.0000	1	/ti-tum-tum-tum
0.0107	20.3	.0000	1	'A
0.0107	20.3	.0000	1	'scape
0.0107	20.3	.0000	1	'smatter
0.0107	20.3	.0000	1	't'll
0.0107	20.3	.0000	1	'twixt
0.0107	20.3	.0000	1	'83
0.0107	20.3	.0000	1	'98
0.0107	20.3	.0000	1	
0.0107	20.3	.0000	1	a-all
0.0107	20.3	.0000	1	a-cap'ring
THE PRECEDING WORD TYPE OCCUPIES RANK 75300				
0.0107	20.3	.0000	1	a-clinking
0.0107	20.3	.0000	1	a-fighting
0.0107	20.3	.0000	1	a-hold
0.0107	20.3	.0000	1	a-ketchin'
0.0107	20.3	.0000	1	a-quiver
0.0107	20.3	.0000	1	a-raiding
0.0107	20.3	.0000	1	a-shining
0.0107	20.3	.0000	1	a-standin'
0.0107	20.3	.0000	1	a-standing
0.0107	20.3	.0000	1	A'astonah
0.0107	20.3	.0000	1	abashed
0.0107	20.3	.0000	1	Abba's
0.0107	20.3	.0000	1	abducting
0.0107	20.3	.0000	1	abed
0.0107	20.3	.0000	1	Abenakis
0.0107	20.3	.0000	1	abetted
0.0107	20.3	.0000	1	abhorred
0.0107	20.3	.0000	1	abhorrence
0.0107	20.3	.0000	1	Abinadab
0.0107	20.3	.0000	1	abject
0.0107	20.3	.0000	1	ablative
0.0107	20.3	.0000	1	aboot
0.0107	20.3	.0000	1	abstractedly
0.0107	20.3	.0000	1	abstraction
0.0107	20.3	.0000	1	absurdities
0.0107	20.3	.0000	1	accomodate
0.0107	20.3	.0000	1	accordin'
0.0107	20.3	.0000	1	accoutered
0.0107	20.3	.0000	1	accouterments
0.0107	20.3	.0000	1	Achaean
0.0107	20.3	.0000	1	Ackley's
0.0107	20.3	.0000	1	actin'
0.0107	20.3	.0000	1	adjective-happy
0.0107	20.3	.0000	1	Advance
0.0107	20.3	.0000	1	adze
0.0107	20.3	.0000	1	afeard
0.0107	20.3	.0000	1	affray
0.0107	20.3	.0000	1	affront
0.0107	20.3	.0000	1	aforesaid
0.0107	20.3	.0000	1	after-effects
0.0107	20.3	.0000	1	afterhours
0.0107	20.3	.0000	1	againe
0.0107	20.3	.0000	1	agape
0.0107	20.3	.0000	1	agleam
0.0107	20.3	.0000	1	ague-fit
0.0107	20.3	.0000	1	Ahmeek's
0.0107	20.3	.0000	1	Ahwelab
0.0107	20.3	.0000	1	Aigisthos'
0.0107	20.3	.0000	1	Alcides
0.0107	20.3	.0000	1	alderman
0.0107	20.3	.0000	1	ale-house
0.0107	20.3	.0000	1	Aleppo
0.0107	20.3	.0000	1	Alexandra's
0.0107	20.3	.0000	1	Aljinavich
0.0107	20.3	.0000	1	all-comprehensive
0.0107	20.3	.0000	1	alternations
0.0107	20.3	.0000	1	AMAL'S
0.0107	20.3	.0000	1	Amalekites
0.0107	20.3	.0000	1	amasses
0.0107	20.3	.0000	1	amazedly
0.0107	20.3	.0000	1	amber-tinted
0.0107	20.3	.0000	1	ambrosial
0.0107	20.3	.0000	1	ambuscadoes
0.0107	20.3	.0000	1	Amphithea
0.0107	20.3	.0000	1	Amphitrite
0.0107	20.3	.0000	1	anchorstone
0.0107	20.3	.0000	1	angel-cake
0.0107	20.3	.0000	1	angelical
0.0107	20.3	.0000	1	angled
0.0107	20.3	.0000	1	Angleworm
0.0107	20.3	.0000	1	anointest
0.0107	20.3	.0000	1	another'n
0.0107	20.3	.0000	1	answerer
0.0107	20.3	.0000	1	apathetically
0.0107	20.3	.0000	1	ape's
0.0107	20.3	.0000	1	APLEY
0.0107	20.3	.0000	1	Appassionata
0.0107	20.3	.0000	1	apple-orchard
0.0107	20.3	.0000	1	appropiate
0.0107	20.3	.0000	1	apricocks
0.0107	20.3	.0000	1	Aprils
0.0107	20.3	.0000	1	aqua
0.0107	20.3	.0000	1	ar-r
0.0107	20.3	.0000	1	Arabians
0.0107	20.3	.0000	1	Arak
0.0107	20.3	.0000	1	Aramco
0.0107	20.3	.0000	1	arbitrating
0.0107	20.3	.0000	1	arc-light
0.0107	20.3	.0000	1	Archuleta
0.0107	20.3	.0000	1	Argives
0.0107	20.3	.0000	1	argosies
0.0107	20.3	.0000	1	Army-type
0.0107	20.3	.0000	1	Arrivederci
0.0107	20.3	.0000	1	ashcake
0.0107	20.3	.0000	1	ashwood
0.0107	20.3	.0000	1	Asiatics
0.0107	20.3	.0000	1	asperity
0.0107	20.3	.0000	1	aspired
0.0107	20.3	.0000	1	asquealing
0.0107	20.3	.0000	1	assailant
THE PRECEDING WORD TYPE OCCUPIES RANK 75400				
0.0107	20.3	.0000	1	assassin's
0.0107	20.3	.0000	1	asymmetrical
0.0107	20.3	.0000	1	asymmetrically
0.0107	20.3	.0000	1	Athens'
0.0107	20.3	.0000	1	atomies
0.0107	20.3	.0000	1	Atreus'
0.0107	20.3	.0000	1	atrocious
0.0107	20.3	.0000	1	attaboy
0.0107	20.3	.0000	1	attendeth
0.0107	20.3	.0000	1	Attorney-at-Law
0.0107	20.3	.0000	1	attorney's
0.0107	20.3	.0000	1	Attucks'
0.0107	20.3	.0000	1	auctioned
0.0107	20.3	.0000	1	audibly
0.0107	20.3	.0000	1	augments
0.0107	20.3	.0000	1	Aunty's
0.0107	20.3	.0000	1	automatons
0.0107	20.3	.0000	1	Autumn's
0.0107	20.3	.0000	1	awe-struck
0.0107	20.3	.0000	1	axle's
0.0107	20.3	.0000	1	B-u-s
0.0107	20.3	.0000	1	b'jiminey
0.0107	20.3	.0000	1	babbled
0.0107	20.3	.0000	1	babby
0.0107	20.3	.0000	1	babied
0.0107	20.3	.0000	1	back-somersault
0.0107	20.3	.0000	1	backward-facing
0.0107	20.3	.0000	1	badman
0.0107	20.3	.0000	1	bagpiper
0.0107	20.3	.0000	1	Bakebe
0.0107	20.3	.0000	1	Balboni
0.0107	20.3	.0000	1	Baleful
0.0107	20.3	.0000	1	ball's
0.0107	20.3	.0000	1	banishing
0.0107	20.3	.0000	1	BANK
0.0107	20.3	.0000	1	Banking-house
0.0107	20.3	.0000	1	banking-house
0.0107	20.3	.0000	1	banknotes
0.0107	20.3	.0000	1	bannerlike
0.0107	20.3	.0000	1	bannister
0.0107	20.3	.0000	1	bantam
0.0107	20.3	.0000	1	baptismal
0.0107	20.3	.0000	1	barbell
0.0107	20.3	.0000	1	barn-door
0.0107	20.3	.0000	1	Barnabas
0.0107	20.3	.0000	1	Barnett
0.0107	20.3	.0000	1	barrel-flash
0.0107	20.3	.0000	1	Barrens
0.0107	20.3	.0000	1	Barricune's
0.0107	20.3	.0000	1	Bartlett's
0.0107	20.3	.0000	1	basketwork
0.0107	20.3	.0000	1	bass-baritone
0.0107	20.3	.0000	1	Bassanio's
0.0107	20.3	.0000	1	batata
0.0107	20.3	.0000	1	battery's
0.0107	20.3	.0000	1	be'st
0.0107	20.3	.0000	1	beadbonny
0.0107	20.3	.0000	1	Beads
0.0107	20.3	.0000	1	bearlike
0.0107	20.3	.0000	1	beatified
0.0107	20.3	.0000	1	beatifying
0.0107	20.3	.0000	1	Beatrice's
0.0107	20.3	.0000	1	bechanced
0.0107	20.3	.0000	1	becometh
0.0107	20.3	.0000	1	bedaubed
0.0107	20.3	.0000	1	bee-taming
0.0107	20.3	.0000	1	before-death
0.0107	20.3	.0000	1	begrudge
0.0107	20.3	.0000	1	beguil'd
0.0107	20.3	.0000	1	beguiling
0.0107	20.3	.0000	1	behinde
0.0107	20.3	.0000	1	behint
0.0107	20.3	.0000	1	Bejance
0.0107	20.3	.0000	1	belated
0.0107	20.3	.0000	1	Bellacoola
0.0107	20.3	.0000	1	Bellario's
0.0107	20.3	.0000	1	bellied
0.0107	20.3	.0000	1	Benedict's
0.0107	20.3	.0000	1	benefice
0.0107	20.3	.0000	1	bent-over
0.0107	20.3	.0000	1	berating
0.0107	20.3	.0000	1	berberris
0.0107	20.3	.0000	1	berhyme
0.0107	20.3	.0000	1	berry-picking
0.0107	20.3	.0000	1	besett
0.0107	20.3	.0000	1	bespattered
0.0107	20.3	.0000	1	besplashed
0.0107	20.3	.0000	1	bespoke
0.0107	20.3	.0000	1	best-regarded
0.0107	20.3	.0000	1	bestir
0.0107	20.3	.0000	1	bestrode
0.0107	20.3	.0000	1	betroth'd
0.0107	20.3	.0000	1	BETSY
0.0107	20.3	.0000	1	Beyond
0.0107	20.3	.0000	1	Bibb
0.0107	20.3	.0000	1	billiards
0.0107	20.3	.0000	1	biogen
0.0107	20.3	.0000	1	bird-waking
0.0107	20.3	.0000	1	bird's-nest
0.0107	20.3	.0000	1	bis-
THE PRECEDING WORD TYPE OCCUPIES RANK 75500				
0.0107	20.3	.0000	1	bit-roller
0.0107	20.3	.0000	1	Bixler
0.0107	20.3	.0000	1	black-footed
0.0107	20.3	.0000	1	Blackbird
0.0107	20.3	.0000	1	blackguards
0.0107	20.3	.0000	1	blackline
0.0107	20.3	.0000	1	blacklisted
0.0107	20.3	.0000	1	blackthorn
0.0107	20.3	.0000	1	bladed
0.0107	20.3	.0000	1	Blaiseville
0.0107	20.3	.0000	1	bleakest
0.0107	20.3	.0000	1	blent
0.0107	20.3	.0000	1	blue-
0.0107	20.3	.0000	1	blue-clothed
0.0107	20.3	.0000	1	blue-prowed
0.0107	20.3	.0000	1	bluecoat
0.0107	20.3	.0000	1	bluer
0.0107	20.3	.0000	1	bluish-white
0.0107	20.3	.0000	1	blunt-nosed
0.0107	20.3	.0000	1	Boar
0.0107	20.3	.0000	1	bob-white
0.0107	20.3	.0000	1	bodde
0.0107	20.3	.0000	1	boddee
0.0107	20.3	.0000	1	bodes
0.0107	20.3	.0000	1	Bogart
0.0107	20.3	.0000	1	bolt-action
0.0107	20.3	.0000	1	Boo
0.0107	20.3	.0000	1	boorish
0.0107	20.3	.0000	1	Borup's

U	SFI	D	F	Word Type
0.0107	20.3	.0000	1	bossin'
0.0107	20.3	.0000	1	bounceful
0.0107	20.3	.0000	1	Bour-the-King
0.0107	20.3	.0000	1	bout
0.0107	20.3	.0000	1	bow-boy's
0.0107	20.3	.0000	1	bowlders
0.0107	20.3	.0000	1	boylike
0.0107	20.3	.0000	1	Brailles
0.0107	20.3	.0000	1	branding
0.0107	20.3	.0000	1	brass-mounted
0.0107	20.3	.0000	1	brass-tack
0.0107	20.3	.0000	1	brat
0.0107	20.3	.0000	1	bravos
0.0107	20.3	.0000	1	breaches
0.0107	20.3	.0000	1	brick-red
0.0107	20.3	.0000	1	Bricktop
0.0107	20.3	.0000	1	bridle-rein
0.0107	20.3	.0000	1	bright-russet
0.0107	20.3	.0000	1	bright-veined
0.0107	20.3	.0000	1	Brightest
0.0107	20.3	.0000	1	broad-browed
0.0107	20.3	.0000	1	broadsword
0.0107	20.3	.0000	1	brogue
0.0107	20.3	.0000	1	brogues
0.0107	20.3	.0000	1	broken-legged
0.0107	20.3	.0000	1	broncobuster
0.0107	20.3	.0000	1	broncos
0.0107	20.3	.0000	1	brook-bottom
0.0107	20.3	.0000	1	BROOKLYN
0.0107	20.3	.0000	1	Browning's
0.0107	20.3	.0000	1	brush-house
0.0107	20.3	.0000	1	brush-scrubbing
0.0107	20.3	.0000	1	brutish
0.0107	20.3	.0000	1	Buchwald's
0.0107	20.3	.0000	1	bulky-looking
0.0107	20.3	.0000	1	bull-pen
0.0107	20.3	.0000	1	bunker
0.0107	20.3	.0000	1	burdening
0.0107	20.3	.0000	1	burgher's
0.0107	20.3	.0000	1	burglaries
0.0107	20.3	.0000	1	burglarizing
0.0107	20.3	.0000	1	burial-ground
0.0107	20.3	.0000	1	burnin'
0.0107	20.3	.0000	1	Burris
0.0107	20.3	.0000	1	buryin'
0.0107	20.3	.0000	1	Busman
0.0107	20.3	.0000	1	busying
0.0107	20.3	.0000	1	butch
0.0107	20.3	.0000	1	butt-shaft
0.0107	20.3	.0000	1	butter's
0.0107	20.3	.0000	1	button-down-the-front
0.0107	20.3	.0000	1	buyers'
0.0107	20.3	.0000	1	buzz-saw
0.0107	20.3	.0000	1	by-and-by
0.0107	20.3	.0000	1	by-street
0.0107	20.3	.0000	1	Byrd's
0.0107	20.3	.0000	1	c-o-c-a-c-o-l-a
0.0107	20.3	.0000	1	cacahuatl
0.0107	20.3	.0000	1	calculatingly
0.0107	20.3	.0000	1	Calpurnia's
0.0107	20.3	.0000	1	camellia
0.0107	20.3	.0000	1	Campo
0.0107	20.3	.0000	1	campstool
0.0107	20.3	.0000	1	Canai
0.0107	20.3	.0000	1	caned
0.0107	20.3	.0000	1	Canukiesung
0.0107	20.3	.0000	1	Capels
0.0107	20.3	.0000	1	capitalists
0.0107	20.3	.0000	1	capsizing
0.0107	20.3	.0000	1	carbarn
0.0107	20.3	.0000	1	careen

THE PRECEDING WORD TYPE OCCUPIES RANK 75600

U	SFI	D	F	Word Type
0.0107	20.3	.0000	1	caressed
0.0107	20.3	.0000	1	Carmon
0.0107	20.3	.0000	1	carr
0.0107	20.3	.0000	1	CARR'S
0.0107	20.3	.0000	1	cartway
0.0107	20.3	.0000	1	carver
0.0107	20.3	.0000	1	cashing
0.0107	20.3	.0000	1	Catawba
0.0107	20.3	.0000	1	Catawbas
0.0107	20.3	.0000	1	cattle-brands
0.0107	20.3	.0000	1	Cautious
0.0107	20.3	.0000	1	cave-mouth
0.0107	20.3	.0000	1	Cayugas
0.0107	20.3	.0000	1	centerstage
0.0107	20.3	.0000	1	cerecloth
0.0107	20.3	.0000	1	chaffed
0.0107	20.3	.0000	1	chainlets
0.0107	20.3	.0000	1	chalks
0.0107	20.3	.0000	1	chamberlain
0.0107	20.3	.0000	1	chanter
0.0107	20.3	.0000	1	chanteys
0.0107	20.3	.0000	1	charger
0.0107	20.3	.0000	1	charger's
0.0107	20.3	.0000	1	CHARLEY
0.0107	20.3	.0000	1	Chatfield
0.0107	20.3	.0000	1	checkmate
0.0107	20.3	.0000	1	chickenheads
0.0107	20.3	.0000	1	Chicky
0.0107	20.3	.0000	1	Chiefly
0.0107	20.3	.0000	1	Chiefmother's
0.0107	20.3	.0000	1	Childsley
0.0107	20.3	.0000	1	Chingokhos
0.0107	20.3	.0000	1	chirred
0.0107	20.3	.0000	1	chittered
0.0107	20.3	.0000	1	chokecherries
0.0107	20.3	.0000	1	choler
0.0107	20.3	.0000	1	choleric
0.0107	20.3	.0000	1	choppin'
0.0107	20.3	.0000	1	chounce
0.0107	20.3	.0000	1	christ'ning
0.0107	20.3	.0000	1	CHRISTINE
0.0107	20.3	.0000	1	chronicled
0.0107	20.3	.0000	1	churchlike
0.0107	20.3	.0000	1	churring
0.0107	20.3	.0000	1	cinched
0.0107	20.3	.0000	1	cinching
0.0107	20.3	.0000	1	cinchona
0.0107	20.3	.0000	1	Clan
0.0107	20.3	.0000	1	Clarences
0.0107	20.3	.0000	1	clean-out
0.0107	20.3	.0000	1	cleaner's
0.0107	20.3	.0000	1	Clears
0.0107	20.3	.0000	1	cleat
0.0107	20.3	.0000	1	cleaving
0.0107	20.3	.0000	1	Cliburn's
0.0107	20.3	.0000	1	clime
0.0107	20.3	.0000	1	clip-clopping
0.0107	20.3	.0000	1	clique
0.0107	20.3	.0000	1	clodhoppers
0.0107	20.3	.0000	1	cloud-shrouded
0.0107	20.3	.0000	1	cloud-wreathed
0.0107	20.3	.0000	1	clouding
0.0107	20.3	.0000	1	clouds'
0.0107	20.3	.0000	1	clubfoot
0.0107	20.3	.0000	1	co-pastors
0.0107	20.3	.0000	1	coachmakers
0.0107	20.3	.0000	1	coasters
0.0107	20.3	.0000	1	coastguardsman
0.0107	20.3	.0000	1	coat-collar
0.0107	20.3	.0000	1	coattails
0.0107	20.3	.0000	1	cobber
0.0107	20.3	.0000	1	cockatrice
0.0107	20.3	.0000	1	cockiness
0.0107	20.3	.0000	1	cold-cream
0.0107	20.3	.0000	1	collandered
0.0107	20.3	.0000	1	collapsible
0.0107	20.3	.0000	1	collectedly
0.0107	20.3	.0000	1	colliers
0.0107	20.3	.0000	1	Collins'
0.0107	20.3	.0000	1	colloquialism
0.0107	20.3	.0000	1	colloquialisms
0.0107	20.3	.0000	1	Colly
0.0107	20.3	.0000	1	coltish
0.0107	20.3	.0000	1	combats
0.0107	20.3	.0000	1	comets'
0.0107	20.3	.0000	1	comfy
0.0107	20.3	.0000	1	compactness
0.0107	20.3	.0000	1	compellingly
0.0107	20.3	.0000	1	composedly
0.0107	20.3	.0000	1	compressing
0.0107	20.3	.0000	1	concord
0.0107	20.3	.0000	1	concourse
0.0107	20.3	.0000	1	condoled
0.0107	20.3	.0000	1	condoling
0.0107	20.3	.0000	1	confabbing
0.0107	20.3	.0000	1	Confessor
0.0107	20.3	.0000	1	Confusion
0.0107	20.3	.0000	1	confusion's
0.0107	20.3	.0000	1	conglomerations
0.0107	20.3	.0000	1	Conklin

THE PRECEDING WORD TYPE OCCUPIES RANK 75700

U	SFI	D	F	Word Type
0.0107	20.3	.0000	1	connesewer
0.0107	20.3	.0000	1	connesewers
0.0107	20.3	.0000	1	constrains
0.0107	20.3	.0000	1	contemplates
0.0107	20.3	.0000	1	contraband
0.0107	20.3	.0000	1	contrition
0.0107	20.3	.0000	1	conwey
0.0107	20.3	.0000	1	coolie
0.0107	20.3	.0000	1	cop's
0.0107	20.3	.0000	1	cop'st
0.0107	20.3	.0000	1	copper-brown
0.0107	20.3	.0000	1	Coppery
0.0107	20.3	.0000	1	copywriter
0.0107	20.3	.0000	1	cornel
0.0107	20.3	.0000	1	coroner's
0.0107	20.3	.0000	1	corpse-hued
0.0107	20.3	.0000	1	corpselike
0.0107	20.3	.0000	1	corroborating
0.0107	20.3	.0000	1	Corwin
0.0107	20.3	.0000	1	costumbre
0.0107	20.3	.0000	1	coteries
0.0107	20.3	.0000	1	could'a
0.0107	20.3	.0000	1	counterbalanced
0.0107	20.3	.0000	1	countervail
0.0107	20.3	.0000	1	Coupvray
0.0107	20.3	.0000	1	court-yard
0.0107	20.3	.0000	1	courtier's
0.0107	20.3	.0000	1	courtiers'
0.0107	20.3	.0000	1	covey
0.0107	20.3	.0000	1	cowboys'
0.0107	20.3	.0000	1	cowpokes
0.0107	20.3	.0000	1	cowslip
0.0107	20.3	.0000	1	Crane's
0.0107	20.3	.0000	1	Cratchits
0.0107	20.3	.0000	1	craven
0.0107	20.3	.0000	1	Crawford's
0.0107	20.3	.0000	1	craziness
0.0107	20.3	.0000	1	crepey
0.0107	20.3	.0000	1	crimpy
0.0107	20.3	.0000	1	criticising
0.0107	20.3	.0000	1	crocodile-tears
0.0107	20.3	.0000	1	Crocodile's
0.0107	20.3	.0000	1	Cronin
0.0107	20.3	.0000	1	Cronk's
0.0107	20.3	.0000	1	Cronks
0.0107	20.3	.0000	1	Cronos
0.0107	20.3	.0000	1	Cronus
0.0107	20.3	.0000	1	cross-examination
0.0107	20.3	.0000	1	cross-fade
0.0107	20.3	.0000	1	cross-graining
0.0107	20.3	.0000	1	cross-street
0.0107	20.3	.0000	1	Crow-bait
0.0107	20.3	.0000	1	CROWD
0.0107	20.3	.0000	1	Croydon
0.0107	20.3	.0000	1	Crumb
0.0107	20.3	.0000	1	crumbed
0.0107	20.3	.0000	1	crushing-shed
0.0107	20.3	.0000	1	crutch/of
0.0107	20.3	.0000	1	Cubby
0.0107	20.3	.0000	1	cuckoo-bird
0.0107	20.3	.0000	1	cuckoo's
0.0107	20.3	.0000	1	cued
0.0107	20.3	.0000	1	culminated
0.0107	20.3	.0000	1	cups'n
0.0107	20.3	.0000	1	curative
0.0107	20.3	.0000	1	cureless
0.0107	20.3	.0000	1	Curly's
0.0107	20.3	.0000	1	currish
0.0107	20.3	.0000	1	cursed'st
0.0107	20.3	.0000	1	curtseys
0.0107	20.3	.0000	1	CUT
0.0107	20.3	.0000	1	cuttings-up
0.0107	20.3	.0000	1	Cuyloga's
0.0107	20.3	.0000	1	Cwm
0.0107	20.3	.0000	1	Cyclamen
0.0107	20.3	.0000	1	cyclamen
0.0107	20.3	.0000	1	Cydonians
0.0107	20.3	.0000	1	Cypress
0.0107	20.3	.0000	1	d-d-do
0.0107	20.3	.0000	1	d'acclimatation
0.0107	20.3	.0000	1	d'escrime
0.0107	20.3	.0000	1	dad'll
0.0107	20.3	.0000	1	Dadda
0.0107	20.3	.0000	1	Daddies
0.0107	20.3	.0000	1	dads
0.0107	20.3	.0000	1	dagger-pointed
0.0107	20.3	.0000	1	dallied
0.0107	20.3	.0000	1	damning
0.0107	20.3	.0000	1	dang
0.0107	20.3	.0000	1	daren't
0.0107	20.3	.0000	1	Daring
0.0107	20.3	.0000	1	Darney
0.0107	20.3	.0000	1	dartles
0.0107	20.3	.0000	1	daunting
0.0107	20.3	.0000	1	DAVY
0.0107	20.3	.0000	1	Daw's
0.0107	20.3	.0000	1	Dawlish
0.0107	20.3	.0000	1	dawnlit
0.0107	20.3	.0000	1	daws
0.0107	20.3	.0000	1	deCassagnac

THE PRECEDING WORD TYPE OCCUPIES RANK 75800

U	SFI	D	F	Word Type
0.0107	20.3	.0000	1	DeWiart
0.0107	20.3	.0000	1	Deas
0.0107	20.3	.0000	1	death-darting
0.0107	20.3	.0000	1	death-marked
0.0107	20.3	.0000	1	decently
0.0107	20.3	.0000	1	decoction
0.0107	20.3	.0000	1	decrepit
0.0107	20.3	.0000	1	deflowered
0.0107	20.3	.0000	1	dehelm
0.0107	20.3	.0000	1	Del's
0.0107	20.3	.0000	1	deliberated
0.0107	20.3	.0000	1	deliberating
0.0107	20.3	.0000	1	delicatessen
0.0107	20.3	.0000	1	deliciousness
0.0107	20.3	.0000	1	demented
0.0107	20.3	.0000	1	Demeter's
0.0107	20.3	.0000	1	demigod
0.0107	20.3	.0000	1	demur
0.0107	20.3	.0000	1	Denunciation
0.0107	20.3	.0000	1	deplorably
0.0107	20.3	.0000	1	dere
0.0107	20.3	.0000	1	desecrator
0.0107	20.3	.0000	1	desisted
0.0107	20.3	.0000	1	desultory
0.0107	20.3	.0000	1	determinations
0.0107	20.3	.0000	1	detonations
0.0107	20.3	.0000	1	detractors
0.0107	20.3	.0000	1	devis'd
0.0107	20.3	.0000	1	Dew
0.0107	20.3	.0000	1	dew-dropping
0.0107	20.3	.0000	1	dew-wet
0.0107	20.3	.0000	1	dewberries
0.0107	20.3	.0000	1	dewberry
0.0107	20.3	.0000	1	diFrancesco
0.0107	20.3	.0000	1	Dialect
0.0107	20.3	.0000	1	Diccon's
0.0107	20.3	.0000	1	dickens
0.0107	20.3	.0000	1	didn'
0.0107	20.3	.0000	1	Dido
0.0107	20.3	.0000	1	dietetic
0.0107	20.3	.0000	1	diffidence
0.0107	20.3	.0000	1	dilate
0.0107	20.3	.0000	1	Dill'll
0.0107	20.3	.0000	1	dingbat
0.0107	20.3	.0000	1	dinged
0.0107	20.3	.0000	1	dining-table
0.0107	20.3	.0000	1	diningroom
0.0107	20.3	.0000	1	dinkum
0.0107	20.3	.0000	1	Diplomats
0.0107	20.3	.0000	1	direst
0.0107	20.3	.0000	1	dirk
0.0107	20.3	.0000	1	dirt-smeared
0.0107	20.3	.0000	1	disagreeably
0.0107	20.3	.0000	1	disarm
0.0107	20.3	.0000	1	disconcerting
0.0107	20.3	.0000	1	discontinued
0.0107	20.3	.0000	1	discords
0.0107	20.3	.0000	1	disengage
0.0107	20.3	.0000	1	disgorged
0.0107	20.3	.0000	1	disinterestedly
0.0107	20.3	.0000	1	disowned
0.0107	20.3	.0000	1	Dispatch
0.0107	20.3	.0000	1	dissatisfy
0.0107	20.3	.0000	1	dissemblers
0.0107	20.3	.0000	1	dissolv'd
0.0107	20.3	.0000	1	distressful
0.0107	20.3	.0000	1	divideth
0.0107	20.3	.0000	1	divinest
0.0107	20.3	.0000	1	DKYE
0.0107	20.3	.0000	1	doc
0.0107	20.3	.0000	1	dogwood-bloom
0.0107	20.3	.0000	1	dole-dark
0.0107	20.3	.0000	1	Dolios
0.0107	20.3	.0000	1	Dolt
0.0107	20.3	.0000	1	dolts
0.0107	20.3	.0000	1	Donnybrook
0.0107	20.3	.0000	1	doon
0.0107	20.3	.0000	1	door-chink
0.0107	20.3	.0000	1	doorstone
0.0107	20.3	.0000	1	Doria's
0.0107	20.3	.0000	1	dosed
0.0107	20.3	.0000	1	dosy-do
0.0107	20.3	.0000	1	double-bladed
0.0107	20.3	.0000	1	doublings
0.0107	20.3	.0000	1	Doughboy
0.0107	20.3	.0000	1	doughtier
0.0107	20.3	.0000	1	DOUGLAS
0.0107	20.3	.0000	1	Dourak
0.0107	20.3	.0000	1	dove-feathered
0.0107	20.3	.0000	1	Dowdy
0.0107	20.3	.0000	1	dowdy
0.0107	20.3	.0000	1	Dowitt's
0.0107	20.3	.0000	1	draggin'
0.0107	20.3	.0000	1	draggle
0.0107	20.3	.0000	1	drakes'
0.0107	20.3	.0000	1	drawing-rooms
0.0107	20.3	.0000	1	drea(chipmunk)ming
0.0107	20.3	.0000	1	dreamlike
0.0107	20.3	.0000	1	dressers
0.0107	20.3	.0000	1	dressing-gown

THE PRECEDING WORD TYPE OCCUPIES RANK 75900

U	SFI	D	F	Word Type
0.0107	20.3	.0000	1	drifters
0.0107	20.3	.0000	1	driftin'
0.0107	20.3	.0000	1	Drinking
0.0107	20.3	.0000	1	driveth
0.0107	20.3	.0000	1	drool
0.0107	20.3	.0000	1	dross
0.0107	20.3	.0000	1	drub
0.0107	20.3	.0000	1	Drummer
0.0107	20.3	.0000	1	Dubose's
0.0107	20.3	.0000	1	ducat
0.0107	20.3	.0000	1	Dud
0.0107	20.3	.0000	1	duded
0.0107	20.3	.0000	1	DUFFY
0.0107	20.3	.0000	1	dugway
0.0107	20.3	.0000	1	dumbshow
0.0107	20.3	.0000	1	Dumpground
0.0107	20.3	.0000	1	dungaree
0.0107	20.3	.0000	1	Dunnoo
0.0107	20.3	.0000	1	dupe
0.0107	20.3	.0000	1	duped
0.0107	20.3	.0000	1	Durrell's
0.0107	20.3	.0000	1	Dusk
0.0107	20.3	.0000	1	dust-colored
0.0107	20.3	.0000	1	Duvitch's
0.0107	20.3	.0000	1	Eadom
0.0107	20.3	.0000	1	early-day
0.0107	20.3	.0000	1	early-risen
0.0107	20.3	.0000	1	earth-treading
0.0107	20.3	.0000	1	earworms
0.0107	20.3	.0000	1	eating-place
0.0107	20.3	.0000	1	Ebony's
0.0107	20.3	.0000	1	Ecole
0.0107	20.3	.0000	1	Eddenburrough
0.0107	20.3	.0000	1	eddied
0.0107	20.3	.0000	1	eewoonuck
0.0107	20.3	.0000	1	effectually
0.0107	20.3	.0000	1	Egeus
0.0107	20.3	.0000	1	egg-layer
0.0107	20.3	.0000	1	Eisenhowers'
0.0107	20.3	.0000	1	Elah
0.0107	20.3	.0000	1	election'd
0.0107	20.3	.0000	1	elephant-trunks
0.0107	20.3	.0000	1	elflocks
0.0107	20.3	.0000	1	Eliab
0.0107	20.3	.0000	1	Elk's
0.0107	20.3	.0000	1	Elouise
0.0107	20.3	.0000	1	embrasure
0.0107	20.3	.0000	1	empathy
0.0107	20.3	.0000	1	enamor'd
0.0107	20.3	.0000	1	Encinal
0.0107	20.3	.0000	1	encumbered
0.0107	20.3	.0000	1	endeth
0.0107	20.3	.0000	1	endureth
0.0107	20.3	.0000	1	engine-power
0.0107	20.3	.0000	1	Englishwoman
0.0107	20.3	.0000	1	Enich's
0.0107	20.3	.0000	1	enlightenment
0.0107	20.3	.0000	1	ennoble
0.0107	20.3	.0000	1	enraptured
0.0107	20.3	.0000	1	enrobe
0.0107	20.3	.0000	1	enslaving
0.0107	20.3	.0000	1	entwined
0.0107	20.3	.0000	1	enumerate
0.0107	20.3	.0000	1	eon
0.0107	20.3	.0000	1	ep
0.0107	20.3	.0000	1	epithet
0.0107	20.3	.0000	1	equably
0.0107	20.3	.0000	1	ermine's
0.0107	20.3	.0000	1	errs
0.0107	20.3	.0000	1	Escrime
0.0107	20.3	.0000	1	escrime
0.0107	20.3	.0000	1	Estella
0.0107	20.3	.0000	1	Estella's
0.0107	20.3	.0000	1	Etukishook
0.0107	20.3	.0000	1	Eumaeos
0.0107	20.3	.0000	1	Eunice's
0.0107	20.3	.0000	1	Euryalos
0.0107	20.3	.0000	1	Eurycleia
0.0107	20.3	.0000	1	Eurymachos
0.0107	20.3	.0000	1	evacuation
0.0107	20.3	.0000	1	Evangeline's
0.0107	20.3	.0000	1	EVERYTHING
0.0107	20.3	.0000	1	evicted
0.0107	20.3	.0000	1	Evremonde
0.0107	20.3	.0000	1	Ex-as-per-at-ing
0.0107	20.3	.0000	1	ex-ballplayer
0.0107	20.3	.0000	1	ex-florist
0.0107	20.3	.0000	1	ex-soldier
0.0107	20.3	.0000	1	exc
0.0107	20.3	.0000	1	excitements
0.0107	20.3	.0000	1	exhalant
0.0107	20.3	.0000	1	exhorting
0.0107	20.3	.0000	1	exit-hole

U	SFI	D	F	Word Type
0.0107	20.3	.0000	1	expounding
0.0107	20.3	.0000	1	extermination
0.0107	20.3	.0000	1	exultingly
0.0107	20.3	.0000	1	Exundas
0.0107	20.3	.0000	1	eyelike
0.0107	20.3	.0000	1	eyes'
0.0107	20.3	.0000	1	eyeshine

THE PRECEDING WORD TYPE OCCUPIES RANK 76000

U	SFI	D	F	Word Type
0.0107	20.3	.0000	1	eyne
0.0107	20.3	.0000	1	F-o-r-
0.0107	20.3	.0000	1	FADE
0.0107	20.3	.0000	1	fair-flowing
0.0107	20.3	.0000	1	fairies'
0.0107	20.3	.0000	1	fairy-lanterns
0.0107	20.3	.0000	1	Fake
0.0107	20.3	.0000	1	fakir
0.0107	20.3	.0000	1	falce
0.0107	20.3	.0000	1	Falconbridge
0.0107	20.3	.0000	1	Falcone's
0.0107	20.3	.0000	1	false-fronted
0.0107	20.3	.0000	1	falsely
0.0107	20.3	.0000	1	falseness
0.0107	20.3	.0000	1	falters
0.0107	20.3	.0000	1	fanaticism
0.0107	20.3	.0000	1	Fanelli
0.0107	20.3	.0000	1	fantasticoes
0.0107	20.3	.0000	1	far-famed
0.0107	20.3	.0000	1	Farjeon
0.0107	20.3	.0000	1	farm-mates
0.0107	20.3	.0000	1	farmboy
0.0107	20.3	.0000	1	farmwork
0.0107	20.3	.0000	1	Farrel
0.0107	20.3	.0000	1	Farrels
0.0107	20.3	.0000	1	farthing
0.0107	20.3	.0000	1	fashionmongers
0.0107	20.3	.0000	1	fatuously
0.0107	20.3	.0000	1	fault-finding
0.0107	20.3	.0000	1	fawn-froth
0.0107	20.3	.0000	1	Fayetteville
0.0107	20.3	.0000	1	feelingly
0.0107	20.3	.0000	1	feign
0.0107	20.3	.0000	1	felicity
0.0107	20.3	.0000	1	fell-frowning
0.0107	20.3	.0000	1	fellowships
0.0107	20.3	.0000	1	fetchin'
0.0107	20.3	.0000	1	fia
0.0107	20.3	.0000	1	fiction-writing
0.0107	20.3	.0000	1	fictionalizes
0.0107	20.3	.0000	1	fierce-hued
0.0107	20.3	.0000	1	fieriest
0.0107	20.3	.0000	1	fifteenth-early
0.0107	20.3	.0000	1	fiftyseven
0.0107	20.3	.0000	1	figgered
0.0107	20.3	.0000	1	fight's
0.0107	20.3	.0000	1	filial
0.0107	20.3	.0000	1	finances
0.0107	20.3	.0000	1	Finches
0.0107	20.3	.0000	1	fire-lock
0.0107	20.3	.0000	1	fire-wand
0.0107	20.3	.0000	1	firesticks
0.0107	20.3	.0000	1	firewrought
0.0107	20.3	.0000	1	firings
0.0107	20.3	.0000	1	fish-bait
0.0107	20.3	.0000	1	fishified
0.0107	20.3	.0000	1	fishknife
0.0107	20.3	.0000	1	fishpond
0.0107	20.3	.0000	1	fishwives
0.0107	20.3	.0000	1	fittest
0.0107	20.3	.0000	1	Fitzgerald's
0.0107	20.3	.0000	1	five-and-twentieth
0.0107	20.3	.0000	1	five-point-nine
0.0107	20.3	.0000	1	Flack
0.0107	20.3	.0000	1	flagman
0.0107	20.3	.0000	1	flailsome
0.0107	20.3	.0000	1	flatfooted
0.0107	20.3	.0000	1	fleeter
0.0107	20.3	.0000	1	Flicka's
0.0107	20.3	.0000	1	flied
0.0107	20.3	.0000	1	flipflops
0.0107	20.3	.0000	1	floodlike
0.0107	20.3	.0000	1	Floogle's
0.0107	20.3	.0000	1	Floogles'
0.0107	20.3	.0000	1	flow'ring
0.0107	20.3	.0000	1	flowers'
0.0107	20.3	.0000	1	flunk
0.0107	20.3	.0000	1	flurried
0.0107	20.3	.0000	1	FLUTE
0.0107	20.3	.0000	1	flutter-butterfly
0.0107	20.3	.0000	1	follow'd
0.0107	20.3	.0000	1	fondled
0.0107	20.3	.0000	1	Fong's
0.0107	20.3	.0000	1	footpaths
0.0107	20.3	.0000	1	foraged
0.0107	20.3	.0000	1	force-break
0.0107	20.3	.0000	1	forceless
0.0107	20.3	.0000	1	fore-legs
0.0107	20.3	.0000	1	fore-paws
0.0107	20.3	.0000	1	forecourt
0.0107	20.3	.0000	1	foreflipper
0.0107	20.3	.0000	1	foreshadowing
0.0107	20.3	.0000	1	foreshadows
0.0107	20.3	.0000	1	forest-roof
0.0107	20.3	.0000	1	Forestville
0.0107	20.3	.0000	1	Forever-Mountain
0.0107	20.3	.0000	1	forgit
0.0107	20.3	.0000	1	formin'
0.0107	20.3	.0000	1	forswear
0.0107	20.3	.0000	1	fortune's

THE PRECEDING WORD TYPE OCCUPIES RANK 76100

U	SFI	D	F	Word Type
0.0107	20.3	.0000	1	forty-odd
0.0107	20.3	.0000	1	four-forty
0.0107	20.3	.0000	1	four-layered
0.0107	20.3	.0000	1	Fourtou
0.0107	20.3	.0000	1	fowerscore
0.0107	20.3	.0000	1	Fox's
0.0107	20.3	.0000	1	Foxfire
0.0107	20.3	.0000	1	frailest
0.0107	20.3	.0000	1	Fraud
0.0107	20.3	.0000	1	frauds
0.0107	20.3	.0000	1	freckle-nosed
0.0107	20.3	.0000	1	Free-Soilers
0.0107	20.3	.0000	1	free-roaming
0.0107	20.3	.0000	1	free-verse
0.0107	20.3	.0000	1	Freemason
0.0107	20.3	.0000	1	freshet
0.0107	20.3	.0000	1	freshets
0.0107	20.3	.0000	1	frighted
0.0107	20.3	.0000	1	frisks
0.0107	20.3	.0000	1	frock-coat
0.0107	20.3	.0000	1	front-parlor
0.0107	20.3	.0000	1	frontline
0.0107	20.3	.0000	1	fruitlessly
0.0107	20.3	.0000	1	fulsome
0.0107	20.3	.0000	1	Fundamentalist
0.0107	20.3	.0000	1	fur-hooded
0.0107	20.3	.0000	1	fur's
0.0107	20.3	.0000	1	furbish
0.0107	20.3	.0000	1	Furness
0.0107	20.3	.0000	1	G-men
0.0107	20.3	.0000	1	G-o-d
0.0107	20.3	.0000	1	g'nite
0.0107	20.3	.0000	1	Gaa-kl
0.0107	20.3	.0000	1	Gabelle
0.0107	20.3	.0000	1	gaited
0.0107	20.3	.0000	1	Galagos
0.0107	20.3	.0000	1	Galagos'
0.0107	20.3	.0000	1	gallipot
0.0107	20.3	.0000	1	Gambetta's
0.0107	20.3	.0000	1	Gambling
0.0107	20.3	.0000	1	gamecocks
0.0107	20.3	.0000	1	Ganawese
0.0107	20.3	.0000	1	garden-chair
0.0107	20.3	.0000	1	GARDENER
0.0107	20.3	.0000	1	Gardner's
0.0107	20.3	.0000	1	Garoghlanian
0.0107	20.3	.0000	1	gas-station
0.0107	20.3	.0000	1	Gascoigne
0.0107	20.3	.0000	1	gashed
0.0107	20.3	.0000	1	gat
0.0107	20.3	.0000	1	gaud
0.0107	20.3	.0000	1	gauntleted
0.0107	20.3	.0000	1	Gauthier
0.0107	20.3	.0000	1	gauzy
0.0107	20.3	.0000	1	Gawd
0.0107	20.3	.0000	1	geh
0.0107	20.3	.0000	1	generaled
0.0107	20.3	.0000	1	generation's
0.0107	20.3	.0000	1	genies
0.0107	20.3	.0000	1	German-English
0.0107	20.3	.0000	1	germane
0.0107	20.3	.0000	1	geste
0.0107	20.3	.0000	1	ghost-footfall
0.0107	20.3	.0000	1	gi'
0.0107	20.3	.0000	1	giant-like
0.0107	20.3	.0000	1	gila
0.0107	20.3	.0000	1	Gilbreths
0.0107	20.3	.0000	1	Giles'
0.0107	20.3	.0000	1	gipsy's
0.0107	20.3	.0000	1	girted
0.0107	20.3	.0000	1	gist
0.0107	20.3	.0000	1	gleek
0.0107	20.3	.0000	1	Glenfield
0.0107	20.3	.0000	1	glent
0.0107	20.3	.0000	1	glisters
0.0107	20.3	.0000	1	glow-worm's
0.0107	20.3	.0000	1	gnashed
0.0107	20.3	.0000	1	go-ahead
0.0107	20.3	.0000	1	go-den
0.0107	20.3	.0000	1	goa
0.0107	20.3	.0000	1	god-den
0.0107	20.3	.0000	1	godfathers
0.0107	20.3	.0000	1	gods'
0.0107	20.3	.0000	1	Gogo
0.0107	20.3	.0000	1	gold-white
0.0107	20.3	.0000	1	golden-haired
0.0107	20.3	.0000	1	golden-throated
0.0107	20.3	.0000	1	Goldfinch
0.0107	20.3	.0000	1	good-morrow
0.0107	20.3	.0000	1	Gookin's
0.0107	20.3	.0000	1	gopher's
0.0107	20.3	.0000	1	gore-blood
0.0107	20.3	.0000	1	gorged
0.0107	20.3	.0000	1	Gorgon
0.0107	20.3	.0000	1	Gorgons'
0.0107	20.3	.0000	1	Gortyn
0.0107	20.3	.0000	1	gossamers
0.0107	20.3	.0000	1	gossipings
0.0107	20.3	.0000	1	got'm
0.0107	20.3	.0000	1	gota

THE PRECEDING WORD TYPE OCCUPIES RANK 76200

U	SFI	D	F	Word Type
0.0107	20.3	.0000	1	Gott
0.0107	20.3	.0000	1	Grace's
0.0107	20.3	.0000	1	grandsir
0.0107	20.3	.0000	1	grass-thatched
0.0107	20.3	.0000	1	Gratiano's
0.0107	20.3	.0000	1	gratis
0.0107	20.3	.0000	1	graved
0.0107	20.3	.0000	1	gray-coated
0.0107	20.3	.0000	1	Grayback's
0.0107	20.3	.0000	1	greasiness
0.0107	20.3	.0000	1	greaves
0.0107	20.3	.0000	1	green-figured
0.0107	20.3	.0000	1	green-plush
0.0107	20.3	.0000	1	green-white
0.0107	20.3	.0000	1	greensilver
0.0107	20.3	.0000	1	Grimesby
0.0107	20.3	.0000	1	grist
0.0107	20.3	.0000	1	grosbeak
0.0107	20.3	.0000	1	grossness
0.0107	20.3	.0000	1	groveled
0.0107	20.3	.0000	1	grubbiness
0.0107	20.3	.0000	1	grubbing
0.0107	20.3	.0000	1	Guaranteed
0.0107	20.3	.0000	1	guff
0.0107	20.3	.0000	1	Guiseppe
0.0107	20.3	.0000	1	gun-club
0.0107	20.3	.0000	1	gunfight
0.0107	20.3	.0000	1	Gunlock
0.0107	20.3	.0000	1	gunning
0.0107	20.3	.0000	1	gunshots
0.0107	20.3	.0000	1	Guthrie
0.0107	20.3	.0000	1	Guthrie's
0.0107	20.3	.0000	1	guy's
0.0107	20.3	.0000	1	hafta
0.0107	20.3	.0000	1	Hah-nee's
0.0107	20.3	.0000	1	haiku-like
0.0107	20.3	.0000	1	hail'd
0.0107	20.3	.0000	1	hair-dye
0.0107	20.3	.0000	1	hair-pulling
0.0107	20.3	.0000	1	hair-tip
0.0107	20.3	.0000	1	half-Indian
0.0107	20.3	.0000	1	half-bald
0.0107	20.3	.0000	1	half-block
0.0107	20.3	.0000	1	half-column
0.0107	20.3	.0000	1	half-crying
0.0107	20.3	.0000	1	half-decks
0.0107	20.3	.0000	1	half-degree
0.0107	20.3	.0000	1	half-grin
0.0107	20.3	.0000	1	half-laughing
0.0107	20.3	.0000	1	half-moons
0.0107	20.3	.0000	1	half-white
0.0107	20.3	.0000	1	half-world
0.0107	20.3	.0000	1	hall's
0.0107	20.3	.0000	1	HALLENMEIER
0.0107	20.3	.0000	1	haltered
0.0107	20.3	.0000	1	hamlets
0.0107	20.3	.0000	1	hand-hold
0.0107	20.3	.0000	1	hand-me-down
0.0107	20.3	.0000	1	handclasps
0.0107	20.3	.0000	1	handfulla
0.0107	20.3	.0000	1	Handley
0.0107	20.3	.0000	1	Handley-Page
0.0107	20.3	.0000	1	hange'd
0.0107	20.3	.0000	1	hangman's
0.0107	20.3	.0000	1	Hanlon
0.0107	20.3	.0000	1	Happened
0.0107	20.3	.0000	1	happenin'
0.0107	20.3	.0000	1	harangue
0.0107	20.3	.0000	1	hard-fated
0.0107	20.3	.0000	1	hard-looking
0.0107	20.3	.0000	1	hard-rutted
0.0107	20.3	.0000	1	hard-tipped
0.0107	20.3	.0000	1	Hargest
0.0107	20.3	.0000	1	harkened
0.0107	20.3	.0000	1	harlots
0.0107	20.3	.0000	1	Harnett's
0.0107	20.3	.0000	1	hateth
0.0107	20.3	.0000	1	hatless
0.0107	20.3	.0000	1	hawking
0.0107	20.3	.0000	1	Hawthorn
0.0107	20.3	.0000	1	hayseed
0.0107	20.3	.0000	1	hazarded
0.0107	20.3	.0000	1	He-Who-Knows-the-Marks
0.0107	20.3	.0000	1	he-men
0.0107	20.3	.0000	1	head-dress
0.0107	20.3	.0000	1	head-high
0.0107	20.3	.0000	1	head's
0.0107	20.3	.0000	1	headsails
0.0107	20.3	.0000	1	healthgiving
0.0107	20.3	.0000	1	healths
0.0107	20.3	.0000	1	hearest
0.0107	20.3	.0000	1	heart-in-throat
0.0107	20.3	.0000	1	heart's-ease
0.0107	20.3	.0000	1	heartening
0.0107	20.3	.0000	1	heathpacks
0.0107	20.3	.0000	1	heavies
0.0107	20.3	.0000	1	Hedin
0.0107	20.3	.0000	1	hee'd
0.0107	20.3	.0000	1	heeling
0.0107	20.3	.0000	1	Heidegger's

THE PRECEDING WORD TYPE OCCUPIES RANK 76300

U	SFI	D	F	Word Type
0.0107	20.3	.0000	1	Heidi's
0.0107	20.3	.0000	1	HELENA'S
0.0107	20.3	.0000	1	Helens's
0.0107	20.3	.0000	1	hell-roosters
0.0107	20.3	.0000	1	HELLO
0.0107	20.3	.0000	1	Hemlock
0.0107	20.3	.0000	1	hemorrhaged
0.0107	20.3	.0000	1	Hemstreet
0.0107	20.3	.0000	1	henpecked
0.0107	20.3	.0000	1	HERALD
0.0107	20.3	.0000	1	herdboys
0.0107	20.3	.0000	1	Herefords
0.0107	20.3	.0000	1	herein
0.0107	20.3	.0000	1	Herman's
0.0107	20.3	.0000	1	HERREN
0.0107	20.3	.0000	1	hie
0.0107	20.3	.0000	1	higgled
0.0107	20.3	.0000	1	high-caste
0.0107	20.3	.0000	1	high-headed
0.0107	20.3	.0000	1	high-toned
0.0107	20.3	.0000	1	High's
0.0107	20.3	.0000	1	highborn
0.0107	20.3	.0000	1	Highwayman
0.0107	20.3	.0000	1	hijjus
0.0107	20.3	.0000	1	hilarity
0.0107	20.3	.0000	1	hildings
0.0107	20.3	.0000	1	hildy
0.0107	20.3	.0000	1	Hillary's
0.0107	20.3	.0000	1	hillfolks
0.0107	20.3	.0000	1	hillfolks'
0.0107	20.3	.0000	1	hind'red
0.0107	20.3	.0000	1	hippity-hop
0.0107	20.3	.0000	1	HIPPOLYTA
0.0107	20.3	.0000	1	hitchpost
0.0107	20.3	.0000	1	hitchrail
0.0107	20.3	.0000	1	Hognose
0.0107	20.3	.0000	1	Holderness
0.0107	20.3	.0000	1	hollowly
0.0107	20.3	.0000	1	holp
0.0107	20.3	.0000	1	hombre
0.0107	20.3	.0000	1	honey-coloured
0.0107	20.3	.0000	1	Honored
0.0107	20.3	.0000	1	hooraw
0.0107	20.3	.0000	1	hooroar
0.0107	20.3	.0000	1	hooroaring
0.0107	20.3	.0000	1	hooroars
0.0107	20.3	.0000	1	Hopalong's
0.0107	20.3	.0000	1	Hor-rid
0.0107	20.3	.0000	1	horray
0.0107	20.3	.0000	1	horticultural
0.0107	20.3	.0000	1	hot-cool-headed
0.0107	20.3	.0000	1	hour-long
0.0107	20.3	.0000	1	housebreaker
0.0107	20.3	.0000	1	housefly
0.0107	20.3	.0000	1	housewife's
0.0107	20.3	.0000	1	hov'ring
0.0107	20.3	.0000	1	how-do-you-do
0.0107	20.3	.0000	1	However
0.0107	20.3	.0000	1	Hug
0.0107	20.3	.0000	1	huge-appearing
0.0107	20.3	.0000	1	Hulla-Baloo's
0.0107	20.3	.0000	1	hum-clack
0.0107	20.3	.0000	1	humanness
0.0107	20.3	.0000	1	humanoids
0.0107	20.3	.0000	1	humble-bees
0.0107	20.3	.0000	1	humbleness
0.0107	20.3	.0000	1	humdinger
0.0107	20.3	.0000	1	humored
0.0107	20.3	.0000	1	Humoresque
0.0107	20.3	.0000	1	hunchbacked
0.0107	20.3	.0000	1	hunks
0.0107	20.3	.0000	1	hunt's-up
0.0107	20.3	.0000	1	hurtig
0.0107	20.3	.0000	1	husband-friend
0.0107	20.3	.0000	1	Hyrcanian
0.0107	20.3	.0000	1	Hyyenaes
0.0107	20.3	.0000	1	I'da
0.0107	20.3	.0000	1	Iardanos
0.0107	20.3	.0000	1	Icarios'
0.0107	20.3	.0000	1	ice-axe
0.0107	20.3	.0000	1	ice-axes
0.0107	20.3	.0000	1	icily
0.0107	20.3	.0000	1	Idiots
0.0107	20.3	.0000	1	idles
0.0107	20.3	.0000	1	illuminations
0.0107	20.3	.0000	1	illumine
0.0107	20.3	.0000	1	Ilsebill
0.0107	20.3	.0000	1	impediment
0.0107	20.3	.0000	1	imperil
0.0107	20.3	.0000	1	implore
0.0107	20.3	.0000	1	importunity
0.0107	20.3	.0000	1	impute
0.0107	20.3	.0000	1	in-and-out
0.0107	20.3	.0000	1	in-under
0.0107	20.3	.0000	1	inaudibly
0.0107	20.3	.0000	1	inaugurates
0.0107	20.3	.0000	1	Incestuous
0.0107	20.3	.0000	1	inclemency
0.0107	20.3	.0000	1	inclines
0.0107	20.3	.0000	1	incoherent

THE PRECEDING WORD TYPE OCCUPIES RANK 76400

U	SFI	D	F	Word Type
0.0107	20.3	.0000	1	incur
0.0107	20.3	.0000	1	indecencies
0.0107	20.3	.0000	1	Indian-sacred
0.0107	20.3	.0000	1	inexecrable
0.0107	20.3	.0000	1	infirmary
0.0107	20.3	.0000	1	infold
0.0107	20.3	.0000	1	infractions
0.0107	20.3	.0000	1	infuse
0.0107	20.3	.0000	1	initial-letter
0.0107	20.3	.0000	1	inkstands
0.0107	20.3	.0000	1	innately
0.0107	20.3	.0000	1	inquisitively
0.0107	20.3	.0000	1	insanity
0.0107	20.3	.0000	1	inscrolled
0.0107	20.3	.0000	1	insculped
0.0107	20.3	.0000	1	inside-out
0.0107	20.3	.0000	1	insomuch
0.0107	20.3	.0000	1	integument
0.0107	20.3	.0000	1	intercession
0.0107	20.3	.0000	1	interlopers
0.0107	20.3	.0000	1	Internationale
0.0107	20.3	.0000	1	interoffice
0.0107	20.3	.0000	1	intrigues
0.0107	20.3	.0000	1	Inversnaid
0.0107	20.3	.0000	1	Issa's
0.0107	20.3	.0000	1	Ithakos
0.0107	20.3	.0000	1	ivied
0.0107	20.3	.0000	1	IXL
0.0107	20.3	.0000	1	J-79
0.0107	20.3	.0000	1	Jabez's
0.0107	20.3	.0000	1	jackdaw
0.0107	20.3	.0000	1	Jacks
0.0107	20.3	.0000	1	jackstraws
0.0107	20.3	.0000	1	Jacobin
0.0107	20.3	.0000	1	jail-house
0.0107	20.3	.0000	1	jailing
0.0107	20.3	.0000	1	Jamshedpur
0.0107	20.3	.0000	1	JANE
0.0107	20.3	.0000	1	jealious
0.0107	20.3	.0000	1	Jerries
0.0107	20.3	.0000	1	JESS
0.0107	20.3	.0000	1	Jesu
0.0107	20.3	.0000	1	jet-black
0.0107	20.3	.0000	1	jew's
0.0107	20.3	.0000	1	jewellers
0.0107	20.3	.0000	1	jibe
0.0107	20.3	.0000	1	jiminey
0.0107	20.3	.0000	1	Jinglebob'd
0.0107	20.3	.0000	1	jinglebobbed
0.0107	20.3	.0000	1	jingly
0.0107	20.3	.0000	1	jinn
0.0107	20.3	.0000	1	Joab
0.0107	20.3	.0000	1	job-stealer
0.0107	20.3	.0000	1	JODY'S
0.0107	20.3	.0000	1	JOE
0.0107	20.3	.0000	1	Joe'd

U	SFI	D	F	Word Type
0.0107	20.3	.0000	1	joggle
0.0107	20.3	.0000	1	johnson
0.0107	20.3	.0000	1	join-stools
0.0107	20.3	.0000	1	joiner
0.0107	20.3	.0000	1	jouncing
0.0107	20.3	.0000	1	ju
0.0107	20.3	.0000	1	Juicy
0.0107	20.3	.0000	1	jukella
0.0107	20.3	.0000	1	Juliets
0.0107	20.3	.0000	1	jumbly
0.0107	20.3	.0000	1	Jury
0.0107	20.3	.0000	1	jury's
0.0107	20.3	.0000	1	justling
0.0107	20.3	.0000	1	KA-chow
0.0107	20.3	.0000	1	kaka
0.0107	20.3	.0000	1	Kanahawas
0.0107	20.3	.0000	1	Kangshung
0.0107	20.3	.0000	1	Karait
0.0107	20.3	.0000	1	Karendouah
0.0107	20.3	.0000	1	Kasimar
0.0107	20.3	.0000	1	Katrinka
0.0107	20.3	.0000	1	Kaye
0.0107	20.3	.0000	1	keenness
0.0107	20.3	.0000	1	keepest
0.0107	20.3	.0000	1	keerful
0.0107	20.3	.0000	1	Keerist
0.0107	20.3	.0000	1	Kewpie
0.0107	20.3	.0000	1	Khoda
0.0107	20.3	.0000	1	kickety
0.0107	20.3	.0000	1	kickin'
0.0107	20.3	.0000	1	Kid's
0.0107	20.3	.0000	1	kiddo
0.0107	20.3	.0000	1	Kilbourne
0.0107	20.3	.0000	1	KING
0.0107	20.3	.0000	1	Kingfisher's
0.0107	20.3	.0000	1	KINO'S
0.0107	20.3	.0000	1	kinsmen
0.0107	20.3	.0000	1	Kittaniny
0.0107	20.3	.0000	1	Kloo-teekl
0.0107	20.3	.0000	1	knifed
0.0107	20.3	.0000	1	knight-errant
0.0107	20.3	.0000	1	kochokochokocho
0.0107	20.3	.0000	1	Kool-Aid
0.0107	20.3	.0000	1	Koppelberg
THE PRECEDING WORD TYPE OCCUPIES RANK 76500				
0.0107	20.3	.0000	1	Koquaeunquas
0.0107	20.3	.0000	1	Korbes
0.0107	20.3	.0000	1	Kortschagins
0.0107	20.3	.0000	1	Koyo
0.0107	20.3	.0000	1	Krieger
0.0107	20.3	.0000	1	Kruif
0.0107	20.3	.0000	1	Kschippihelleu
0.0107	20.3	.0000	1	Kumba
0.0107	20.3	.0000	1	kvas
0.0107	20.3	.0000	1	Kyklops'
0.0107	20.3	.0000	1	lace-curtain-Irish
0.0107	20.3	.0000	1	ladyship
0.0107	20.3	.0000	1	lambaste
0.0107	20.3	.0000	1	lambing
0.0107	20.3	.0000	1	lameness
0.0107	20.3	.0000	1	land-spies
0.0107	20.3	.0000	1	landlubbers
0.0107	20.3	.0000	1	Landscape
0.0107	20.3	.0000	1	languish
0.0107	20.3	.0000	1	languors
0.0107	20.3	.0000	1	lankly
0.0107	20.3	.0000	1	Lansdale
0.0107	20.3	.0000	1	Laodamas
0.0107	20.3	.0000	1	lap-elephant
0.0107	20.3	.0000	1	lapis
0.0107	20.3	.0000	1	large-eyed
0.0107	20.3	.0000	1	large-pattern
0.0107	20.3	.0000	1	larrup
0.0107	20.3	.0000	1	Lasher
0.0107	20.3	.0000	1	latticed
0.0107	20.3	.0000	1	laughing-stock
0.0107	20.3	.0000	1	Laureate
0.0107	20.3	.0000	1	lavender's
0.0107	20.3	.0000	1	lawbooks
0.0107	20.3	.0000	1	lawyers'
0.0107	20.3	.0000	1	layest
0.0107	20.3	.0000	1	lazuli
0.0107	20.3	.0000	1	lazy-pacing
0.0107	20.3	.0000	1	Le-jardin
0.0107	20.3	.0000	1	le's
0.0107	20.3	.0000	1	leadcolour
0.0107	20.3	.0000	1	Leader's
0.0107	20.3	.0000	1	Leadership
0.0107	20.3	.0000	1	leastwise
0.0107	20.3	.0000	1	leathern
0.0107	20.3	.0000	1	leead-er
0.0107	20.3	.0000	1	leers
0.0107	20.3	.0000	1	leg-iron
0.0107	20.3	.0000	1	legerdemain
0.0107	20.3	.0000	1	Lemnos
0.0107	20.3	.0000	1	Lennie's
0.0107	20.3	.0000	1	less'ned
0.0107	20.3	.0000	1	Lestrade's
0.0107	20.3	.0000	1	letter-writing
0.0107	20.3	.0000	1	letter'll
0.0107	20.3	.0000	1	letter's
0.0107	20.3	.0000	1	lever-wise
0.0107	20.3	.0000	1	lewd
0.0107	20.3	.0000	1	libation
0.0107	20.3	.0000	1	Lichas
0.0107	20.3	.0000	1	lickings
0.0107	20.3	.0000	1	Licksians
0.0107	20.3	.0000	1	life-sapping
0.0107	20.3	.0000	1	lifeboat's
0.0107	20.3	.0000	1	lighter-hued
0.0107	20.3	.0000	1	lilac-bush
0.0107	20.3	.0000	1	Limberlock
0.0107	20.3	.0000	1	limbo
0.0107	20.3	.0000	1	lime-filled
0.0107	20.3	.0000	1	linkmen
0.0107	20.3	.0000	1	Linn's
0.0107	20.3	.0000	1	lip-like
0.0107	20.3	.0000	1	live'd
0.0107	20.3	.0000	1	livelihoods
0.0107	20.3	.0000	1	livings
0.0107	20.3	.0000	1	loafed
0.0107	20.3	.0000	1	loafer
0.0107	20.3	.0000	1	loathed
0.0107	20.3	.0000	1	loathing
0.0107	20.3	.0000	1	loathsome
0.0107	20.3	.0000	1	lodgefire
0.0107	20.3	.0000	1	loftily
0.0107	20.3	.0000	1	log-rolling
0.0107	20.3	.0000	1	logged-out
0.0107	20.3	.0000	1	loll
0.0107	20.3	.0000	1	lollipop-hard
0.0107	20.3	.0000	1	loneliest
0.0107	20.3	.0000	1	long-experienced
0.0107	20.3	.0000	1	long-forgotton
0.0107	20.3	.0000	1	long-leggedness
0.0107	20.3	.0000	1	long-neck
0.0107	20.3	.0000	1	look-arounds
0.0107	20.3	.0000	1	look'd
0.0107	20.3	.0000	1	lop
0.0107	20.3	.0000	1	lorded
0.0107	20.3	.0000	1	lording
0.0107	20.3	.0000	1	Lorne's
0.0107	20.3	.0000	1	Lorry's
0.0107	20.3	.0000	1	lott'ry
0.0107	20.3	.0000	1	love-devouring
THE PRECEDING WORD TYPE OCCUPIES RANK 76600				
0.0107	20.3	.0000	1	love-lord
0.0107	20.3	.0000	1	love-news
0.0107	20.3	.0000	1	low-beamed
0.0107	20.3	.0000	1	low'r
0.0107	20.3	.0000	1	lucent
0.0107	20.3	.0000	1	Lucille's
0.0107	20.3	.0000	1	ludicrously
0.0107	20.3	.0000	1	Ludlow's
0.0107	20.3	.0000	1	luff
0.0107	20.3	.0000	1	Lug
0.0107	20.3	.0000	1	lunkhead
0.0107	20.3	.0000	1	lunkheads
0.0107	20.3	.0000	1	lurker
0.0107	20.3	.0000	1	lyin'
0.0107	20.3	.0000	1	lymph-lined
0.0107	20.3	.0000	1	lymphatic
0.0107	20.3	.0000	1	Ma-ry
0.0107	20.3	.0000	1	MacMillan's
0.0107	20.3	.0000	1	mach
0.0107	20.3	.0000	1	machine-like
0.0107	20.3	.0000	1	Madhav
0.0107	20.3	.0000	1	Madhav's
0.0107	20.3	.0000	1	madwoman
0.0107	20.3	.0000	1	Maestro's
0.0107	20.3	.0000	1	maggots
0.0107	20.3	.0000	1	magic-makers
0.0107	20.3	.0000	1	magics
0.0107	20.3	.0000	1	maidenhair
0.0107	20.3	.0000	1	maidenheads
0.0107	20.3	.0000	1	mail-opener
0.0107	20.3	.0000	1	maimed
0.0107	20.3	.0000	1	Maimie
0.0107	20.3	.0000	1	Maitre
0.0107	20.3	.0000	1	malacca
0.0107	20.3	.0000	1	mallets
0.0107	20.3	.0000	1	malmsey
0.0107	20.3	.0000	1	Maloney's
0.0107	20.3	.0000	1	mamas
0.0107	20.3	.0000	1	Manette's
0.0107	20.3	.0000	1	Mannering
0.0107	20.3	.0000	1	manuring
0.0107	20.3	.0000	1	marchin'
0.0107	20.3	.0000	1	Marcum
0.0107	20.3	.0000	1	Marget's
0.0107	20.3	.0000	1	Marlow
0.0107	20.3	.0000	1	Marquis's
0.0107	20.3	.0000	1	marriage-day
0.0107	20.3	.0000	1	marshal's
0.0107	20.3	.0000	1	Marta
0.0107	20.3	.0000	1	Marthe's
0.0107	20.3	.0000	1	MARTIN
0.0107	20.3	.0000	1	Mask
0.0107	20.3	.0000	1	masquerades
0.0107	20.3	.0000	1	Massey
0.0107	20.3	.0000	1	Mastodonic
0.0107	20.3	.0000	1	match'd
0.0107	20.3	.0000	1	Mathiesen
0.0107	20.3	.0000	1	Matrena's
0.0107	20.3	.0000	1	Mattie
0.0107	20.3	.0000	1	Maudie
0.0107	20.3	.0000	1	mauled
0.0107	20.3	.0000	1	mauve
0.0107	20.3	.0000	1	Maycomb's
0.0107	20.3	.0000	1	Mayella's
0.0107	20.3	.0000	1	mayst
0.0107	20.3	.0000	1	McConnellsburg
0.0107	20.3	.0000	1	McGurn
0.0107	20.3	.0000	1	McKenney
0.0107	20.3	.0000	1	McKenneys
0.0107	20.3	.0000	1	Meachachtinny
0.0107	20.3	.0000	1	mean-souled
0.0107	20.3	.0000	1	measuredly
0.0107	20.3	.0000	1	Mechelit
0.0107	20.3	.0000	1	meetest
0.0107	20.3	.0000	1	Mekness
0.0107	20.3	.0000	1	melee
0.0107	20.3	.0000	1	Melora
0.0107	20.3	.0000	1	Memedhakemo
0.0107	20.3	.0000	1	memorably
0.0107	20.3	.0000	1	memory's
0.0107	20.3	.0000	1	MEN
0.0107	20.3	.0000	1	menagerie-keepers
0.0107	20.3	.0000	1	Mendota
0.0107	20.3	.0000	1	Mengue
0.0107	20.3	.0000	1	mercenary
0.0107	20.3	.0000	1	merchantmen
0.0107	20.3	.0000	1	Mercyless
0.0107	20.3	.0000	1	merrier
0.0107	20.3	.0000	1	Merriweather's
0.0107	20.3	.0000	1	messes
0.0107	20.3	.0000	1	mete
0.0107	20.3	.0000	1	Metro-Goldwyn
0.0107	20.3	.0000	1	MG'S
0.0107	20.3	.0000	1	mid-leap
0.0107	20.3	.0000	1	MIKE
0.0107	20.3	.0000	1	mildewed
0.0107	20.3	.0000	1	milkmen
0.0107	20.3	.0000	1	milkwhite
0.0107	20.3	.0000	1	Millay's
0.0107	20.3	.0000	1	milldam
THE PRECEDING WORD TYPE OCCUPIES RANK 76700				
0.0107	20.3	.0000	1	milliner's
0.0107	20.3	.0000	1	million-dot
0.0107	20.3	.0000	1	Minas
0.0107	20.3	.0000	1	mincing
0.0107	20.3	.0000	1	Mingoes
0.0107	20.3	.0000	1	minim
0.0107	20.3	.0000	1	minor-league
0.0107	20.3	.0000	1	minxes
0.0107	20.3	.0000	1	misconstrue
0.0107	20.3	.0000	1	misgave
0.0107	20.3	.0000	1	misgives
0.0107	20.3	.0000	1	mislike
0.0107	20.3	.0000	1	misrepresentation
0.0107	20.3	.0000	1	mission-house
0.0107	20.3	.0000	1	mistreat
0.0107	20.3	.0000	1	mmmmm-hmmmm
0.0107	20.3	.0000	1	Moffats'
0.0107	20.3	.0000	1	Molting
0.0107	20.3	.0000	1	MONAGAN
0.0107	20.3	.0000	1	MONAHAN
0.0107	20.3	.0000	1	Mongrels
0.0107	20.3	.0000	1	monkey-puzzle
0.0107	20.3	.0000	1	Monsieur's
0.0107	20.3	.0000	1	montage
0.0107	20.3	.0000	1	Montala
0.0107	20.3	.0000	1	Montferrat
0.0107	20.3	.0000	1	Mood
0.0107	20.3	.0000	1	moonlighting
0.0107	20.3	.0000	1	moonshines
0.0107	20.3	.0000	1	moping
0.0107	20.3	.0000	1	Moreover's
0.0107	20.3	.0000	1	morose
0.0107	20.3	.0000	1	morrah
0.0107	20.3	.0000	1	mortal's
0.0107	20.3	.0000	1	mortared
0.0107	20.3	.0000	1	mortify
0.0107	20.3	.0000	1	moss-greened
0.0107	20.3	.0000	1	Mosten's
0.0107	20.3	.0000	1	Mourad's
0.0107	20.3	.0000	1	mouse-haired
0.0107	20.3	.0000	1	mousers
0.0107	20.3	.0000	1	mousie-men
0.0107	20.3	.0000	1	Mouth
0.0107	20.3	.0000	1	mouthed
0.0107	20.3	.0000	1	movers'-talk
0.0107	20.3	.0000	1	moving-slow
0.0107	20.3	.0000	1	Mrunas
0.0107	20.3	.0000	1	much-nourishing
0.0107	20.3	.0000	1	mudbank
0.0107	20.3	.0000	1	mukluks
0.0107	20.3	.0000	1	mulberries
0.0107	20.3	.0000	1	muleteers
0.0107	20.3	.0000	1	mundo
0.0107	20.3	.0000	1	muscle-shredding
0.0107	20.3	.0000	1	Muscovite
0.0107	20.3	.0000	1	Muscovites
0.0107	20.3	.0000	1	mushiness
0.0107	20.3	.0000	1	Musician
0.0107	20.3	.0000	1	musings
0.0107	20.3	.0000	1	mustang-running
0.0107	20.3	.0000	1	mutely
0.0107	20.3	.0000	1	mutilations
0.0107	20.3	.0000	1	Mynheer
0.0107	20.3	.0000	1	myopic
0.0107	20.3	.0000	1	n-no
0.0107	20.3	.0000	1	Nahar
0.0107	20.3	.0000	1	nailed-down
0.0107	20.3	.0000	1	naively
0.0107	20.3	.0000	1	Nanticokes
0.0107	20.3	.0000	1	nastiest
0.0107	20.3	.0000	1	Nate'd
0.0107	20.3	.0000	1	Nayarit
0.0107	20.3	.0000	1	Neapolitan's
0.0107	20.3	.0000	1	neckcurls
0.0107	20.3	.0000	1	neckerchiefs
0.0107	20.3	.0000	1	need'st
0.0107	20.3	.0000	1	needle's
0.0107	20.3	.0000	1	needlepoints
0.0107	20.3	.0000	1	neet
0.0107	20.3	.0000	1	Neilberry
0.0107	20.3	.0000	1	nephew's
0.0107	20.3	.0000	1	Neritos
0.0107	20.3	.0000	1	nesters
0.0107	20.3	.0000	1	never-rose
0.0107	20.3	.0000	1	Nevermore
0.0107	20.3	.0000	1	new-washed
0.0107	20.3	.0000	1	newes
0.0107	20.3	.0000	1	newness
0.0107	20.3	.0000	1	newsreel
0.0107	20.3	.0000	1	nice-smelling
0.0107	20.3	.0000	1	nieces
0.0107	20.3	.0000	1	Nielson
0.0107	20.3	.0000	1	Nightly
0.0107	20.3	.0000	1	Nilssons
0.0107	20.3	.0000	1	nimble-wittedness
0.0107	20.3	.0000	1	ninepins
0.0107	20.3	.0000	1	ninety-degree
0.0107	20.3	.0000	1	ninth-inning
0.0107	20.3	.0000	1	no-o-o-o-o
0.0107	20.3	.0000	1	nobleman's
THE PRECEDING WORD TYPE OCCUPIES RANK 76800				
0.0107	20.3	.0000	1	nonchalantly
0.0107	20.3	.0000	1	noncommittal
0.0107	20.3	.0000	1	nonplussed
0.0107	20.3	.0000	1	Noon
0.0107	20.3	.0000	1	Norfield
0.0107	20.3	.0000	1	Norwood
0.0107	20.3	.0000	1	nose-to-concrete
0.0107	20.3	.0000	1	now-familiar
0.0107	20.3	.0000	1	nowise
0.0107	20.3	.0000	1	nurse-midwives
0.0107	20.3	.0000	1	Nutley
0.0107	20.3	.0000	1	nuzzle
0.0107	20.3	.0000	1	O-U-T
0.0107	20.3	.0000	1	o'erstare
0.0107	20.3	.0000	1	Oars
0.0107	20.3	.0000	1	obligin'
0.0107	20.3	.0000	1	octopi
0.0107	20.3	.0000	1	oddments
0.0107	20.3	.0000	1	off-center
0.0107	20.3	.0000	1	off-handedly
0.0107	20.3	.0000	1	off-scene
0.0107	20.3	.0000	1	off-stage
0.0107	20.3	.0000	1	offa
0.0107	20.3	.0000	1	offend'st
0.0107	20.3	.0000	1	oft-repeated
0.0107	20.3	.0000	1	ofttimes
0.0107	20.3	.0000	1	ohhhhhh
0.0107	20.3	.0000	1	oil-cloth-covered
0.0107	20.3	.0000	1	oil-lamp
0.0107	20.3	.0000	1	oke
0.0107	20.3	.0000	1	Olegna
0.0107	20.3	.0000	1	Olympos
0.0107	20.3	.0000	1	Onandagos
0.0107	20.3	.0000	1	onct
0.0107	20.3	.0000	1	Oneidas
0.0107	20.3	.0000	1	onetime
0.0107	20.3	.0000	1	oop
0.0107	20.3	.0000	1	opes
0.0107	20.3	.0000	1	orange-crate
0.0107	20.3	.0000	1	orange-yellowy
0.0107	20.3	.0000	1	orating
0.0107	20.3	.0000	1	Orbitville
0.0107	20.3	.0000	1	organdie
0.0107	20.3	.0000	1	ornerier
0.0107	20.3	.0000	1	Orville's
0.0107	20.3	.0000	1	Osa's
0.0107	20.3	.0000	1	ostentation
0.0107	20.3	.0000	1	OTHERS
0.0107	20.3	.0000	1	Ou-dis-sun
0.0107	20.3	.0000	1	oul
0.0107	20.3	.0000	1	Oursler
0.0107	20.3	.0000	1	out-of-beat
0.0107	20.3	.0000	1	out-of-control
0.0107	20.3	.0000	1	out-of-focusness
0.0107	20.3	.0000	1	outbid
0.0107	20.3	.0000	1	outbrave
0.0107	20.3	.0000	1	outdoes
0.0107	20.3	.0000	1	outlaw's
0.0107	20.3	.0000	1	outsi
0.0107	20.3	.0000	1	Outsider
0.0107	20.3	.0000	1	outtrick
0.0107	20.3	.0000	1	over-clean
0.0107	20.3	.0000	1	overbear
0.0107	20.3	.0000	1	overcharged
0.0107	20.3	.0000	1	overcharging
0.0107	20.3	.0000	1	overclouded
0.0107	20.3	.0000	1	overgrow
0.0107	20.3	.0000	1	overpeer
0.0107	20.3	.0000	1	overpraise
0.0107	20.3	.0000	1	oversocks
0.0107	20.3	.0000	1	overthrows
0.0107	20.3	.0000	1	overtrusting
0.0107	20.3	.0000	1	ox-beef
0.0107	20.3	.0000	1	oxsters
0.0107	20.3	.0000	1	oyster-stew
0.0107	20.3	.0000	1	Pa'd
0.0107	20.3	.0000	1	page's
0.0107	20.3	.0000	1	Pagosa
0.0107	20.3	.0000	1	paid-for
0.0107	20.3	.0000	1	palls
0.0107	20.3	.0000	1	panatela
0.0107	20.3	.0000	1	panicstricken
0.0107	20.3	.0000	1	panoramic
0.0107	20.3	.0000	1	pantomimed
0.0107	20.3	.0000	1	paper-doily
0.0107	20.3	.0000	1	Papists
0.0107	20.3	.0000	1	parcheesi
0.0107	20.3	.0000	1	parchment-yellow
0.0107	20.3	.0000	1	pardner
0.0107	20.3	.0000	1	pardon-me's
0.0107	20.3	.0000	1	Pardoned
0.0107	20.3	.0000	1	paroquets
0.0107	20.3	.0000	1	Parrish
0.0107	20.3	.0000	1	parsons'
0.0107	20.3	.0000	1	passado
0.0107	20.3	.0000	1	pasuke
0.0107	20.3	.0000	1	pate
0.0107	20.3	.0000	1	patens
0.0107	20.3	.0000	1	pathos
0.0107	20.3	.0000	1	pathway's
THE PRECEDING WORD TYPE OCCUPIES RANK 76900				
0.0107	20.3	.0000	1	patrolmen
0.0107	20.3	.0000	1	Patron
0.0107	20.3	.0000	1	Pavel
0.0107	20.3	.0000	1	paymaster
0.0107	20.3	.0000	1	pearl's
0.0107	20.3	.0000	1	pearlers
0.0107	20.3	.0000	1	peasant's
0.0107	20.3	.0000	1	Peascod
0.0107	20.3	.0000	1	Pederek's
0.0107	20.3	.0000	1	peepers'
0.0107	20.3	.0000	1	peevish
0.0107	20.3	.0000	1	Penelope's
0.0107	20.3	.0000	1	PENNA-30
0.0107	20.3	.0000	1	penny-wide
0.0107	20.3	.0000	1	pennyworth
0.0107	20.3	.0000	1	Pepallistank
0.0107	20.3	.0000	1	perchance
0.0107	20.3	.0000	1	peremptory
0.0107	20.3	.0000	1	perforce

U	SFI	D	F	Word Type
0.0107	20.3	.0000	1	perjur'd
0.0107	20.3	.0000	1	perjured
0.0107	20.3	.0000	1	perpendicularly
0.0107	20.3	.0000	1	Persephone's
0.0107	20.3	.0000	1	persistency
0.0107	20.3	.0000	1	personification
0.0107	20.3	.0000	1	personifies
0.0107	20.3	.0000	1	pervaded
0.0107	20.3	.0000	1	Peshtank
0.0107	20.3	.0000	1	Phaistos
0.0107	20.3	.0000	1	Phoebus'
0.0107	20.3	.0000	1	phooey
0.0107	20.3	.0000	1	Physician
0.0107	20.3	.0000	1	physique
0.0107	20.3	.0000	1	piblokto
0.0107	20.3	.0000	1	pick-a-back
0.0107	20.3	.0000	1	picture's
0.0107	20.3	.0000	1	Piedra
0.0107	20.3	.0000	1	pig-trails
0.0107	20.3	.0000	1	pigheaded
0.0107	20.3	.0000	1	pigtailed
0.0107	20.3	.0000	1	pilferer
0.0107	20.3	.0000	1	pilotage
0.0107	20.3	.0000	1	pinwheel-shaped
0.0107	20.3	.0000	1	pipe's
0.0107	20.3	.0000	1	Pippa's
0.0107	20.3	.0000	1	Pirates'
0.0107	20.3	.0000	1	pitiless
0.0107	20.3	.0000	1	pitying
0.0107	20.3	.0000	1	Piwitak
0.0107	20.3	.0000	1	pizened
0.0107	20.3	.0000	1	plain-song
0.0107	20.3	.0000	1	plane-tree
0.0107	20.3	.0000	1	planesmen
0.0107	20.3	.0000	1	Plants
0.0107	20.3	.0000	1	Plantscheman
0.0107	20.3	.0000	1	plateglass
0.0107	20.3	.0000	1	platitude
0.0107	20.3	.0000	1	plats
0.0107	20.3	.0000	1	playfellow
0.0107	20.3	.0000	1	plip
0.0107	20.3	.0000	1	Plop
0.0107	20.3	.0000	1	ploughman
0.0107	20.3	.0000	1	Plutonian
0.0107	20.3	.0000	1	pneumothorax
0.0107	20.3	.0000	1	Pockhapockink
0.0107	20.3	.0000	1	poet-teacher
0.0107	20.3	.0000	1	Polites
0.0107	20.3	.0000	1	Polyktor
0.0107	20.3	.0000	1	pomander
0.0107	20.3	.0000	1	pompously
0.0107	20.3	.0000	1	poore
0.0107	20.3	.0000	1	porkeaters
0.0107	20.3	.0000	1	Porpoises'
0.0107	20.3	.0000	1	PortArthur
0.0107	20.3	.0000	1	postilions
0.0107	20.3	.0000	1	Potpan
0.0107	20.3	.0000	1	potroast
0.0107	20.3	.0000	1	prairieside
0.0107	20.3	.0000	1	Pramnian
0.0107	20.3	.0000	1	Pre
0.0107	20.3	.0000	1	Preacher's
0.0107	20.3	.0000	1	prearranged
0.0107	20.3	.0000	1	precepts
0.0107	20.3	.0000	1	precincts
0.0107	20.3	.0000	1	precipated
0.0107	20.3	.0000	1	prefixed
0.0107	20.3	.0000	1	preparest
0.0107	20.3	.0000	1	prereading
0.0107	20.3	.0000	1	presage
0.0107	20.3	.0000	1	pressure's
0.0107	20.3	.0000	1	Pretense
0.0107	20.3	.0000	1	pricksong
0.0107	20.3	.0000	1	Prig
0.0107	20.3	.0000	1	primroses
0.0107	20.3	.0000	1	printers'
0.0107	20.3	.0000	1	Priss
0.0107	20.3	.0000	1	Pritchard
0.0107	20.3	.0000	1	privates
0.0107	20.3	.0000	1	prizefighters
0.0107	20.3	.0000	1	procures

THE PRECEDING WORD TYPE OCCUPIES RANK 77000

U	SFI	D	F	Word Type
0.0107	20.3	.0000	1	profanity
0.0107	20.3	.0000	1	Prometheus'
0.0107	20.3	.0000	1	pronto
0.0107	20.3	.0000	1	Prop
0.0107	20.3	.0000	1	prorogue
0.0107	20.3	.0000	1	Provis
0.0107	20.3	.0000	1	provisioned
0.0107	20.3	.0000	1	prudently
0.0107	20.3	.0000	1	pugnus
0.0107	20.3	.0000	1	pulsed
0.0107	20.3	.0000	1	pulseless
0.0107	20.3	.0000	1	Pumpkin-eater
0.0107	20.3	.0000	1	punto
0.0107	20.3	.0000	1	Purdey's
0.0107	20.3	.0000	1	purled
0.0107	20.3	.0000	1	purple-tinted
0.0107	20.3	.0000	1	purpos'd
0.0107	20.3	.0000	1	pursing
0.0107	20.3	.0000	1	pushmi-pullyus
0.0107	20.3	.0000	1	Pylos
0.0107	20.3	.0000	1	quarter-blood
0.0107	20.3	.0000	1	quavered
0.0107	20.3	.0000	1	quavering
0.0107	20.3	.0000	1	question's
0.0107	20.3	.0000	1	quibbled
0.0107	20.3	.0000	1	quieting
0.0107	20.3	.0000	1	quinquina
0.0107	20.3	.0000	1	qvick
0.0107	20.3	.0000	1	r-right
0.0107	20.3	.0000	1	rabbity
0.0107	20.3	.0000	1	Rachel's
0.0107	20.3	.0000	1	racketing
0.0107	20.3	.0000	1	raffish
0.0107	20.3	.0000	1	rafted
0.0107	20.3	.0000	1	rag-bag
0.0107	20.3	.0000	1	raggedly
0.0107	20.3	.0000	1	rain-receptive
0.0107	20.3	.0000	1	rainbow's
0.0107	20.3	.0000	1	rainingest
0.0107	20.3	.0000	1	rambunctiousness
0.0107	20.3	.0000	1	ranch-house
0.0107	20.3	.0000	1	ranchhouse
0.0107	20.3	.0000	1	rangy
0.0107	20.3	.0000	1	Ransome
0.0107	20.3	.0000	1	raptured
0.0107	20.3	.0000	1	rapturous
0.0107	20.3	.0000	1	rasher
0.0107	20.3	.0000	1	rat-tat
0.0107	20.3	.0000	1	rattlesnake-skin
0.0107	20.3	.0000	1	readier
0.0107	20.3	.0000	1	reason's
0.0107	20.3	.0000	1	reasonableness
0.0107	20.3	.0000	1	rebukes
0.0107	20.3	.0000	1	recant
0.0107	20.3	.0000	1	reciter
0.0107	20.3	.0000	1	recites
0.0107	20.3	.0000	1	reck'ning
0.0107	20.3	.0000	1	recognise
0.0107	20.3	.0000	1	recoiled
0.0107	20.3	.0000	1	recommence
0.0107	20.3	.0000	1	recreations
0.0107	20.3	.0000	1	Rector
0.0107	20.3	.0000	1	red-coat
0.0107	20.3	.0000	1	red-lipped
0.0107	20.3	.0000	1	reddening
0.0107	20.3	.0000	1	redly
0.0107	20.3	.0000	1	redoubt
0.0107	20.3	.0000	1	redwings
0.0107	20.3	.0000	1	refinisher
0.0107	20.3	.0000	1	refueled
0.0107	20.3	.0000	1	regalia
0.0107	20.3	.0000	1	regimental
0.0107	20.3	.0000	1	rehash
0.0107	20.3	.0000	1	relegate
0.0107	20.3	.0000	1	relevancy
0.0107	20.3	.0000	1	relocation
0.0107	20.3	.0000	1	remarkin'
0.0107	20.3	.0000	1	remembrances
0.0107	20.3	.0000	1	remonstrating
0.0107	20.3	.0000	1	repassing
0.0107	20.3	.0000	1	repress
0.0107	20.3	.0000	1	requisition
0.0107	20.3	.0000	1	requite
0.0107	20.3	.0000	1	restoreth
0.0107	20.3	.0000	1	resurrect
0.0107	20.3	.0000	1	Retail
0.0107	20.3	.0000	1	retinue
0.0107	20.3	.0000	1	revels
0.0107	20.3	.0000	1	revenged
0.0107	20.3	.0000	1	reverberation
0.0107	20.3	.0000	1	reverenced
0.0107	20.3	.0000	1	reverso
0.0107	20.3	.0000	1	reverted
0.0107	20.3	.0000	1	revisit
0.0107	20.3	.0000	1	Reynard's
0.0107	20.3	.0000	1	rheumatiz
0.0107	20.3	.0000	1	Rialto
0.0107	20.3	.0000	1	RIBBY
0.0107	20.3	.0000	1	Riblov
0.0107	20.3	.0000	1	Rices

THE PRECEDING WORD TYPE OCCUPIES RANK 77100

U	SFI	D	F	Word Type
0.0107	20.3	.0000	1	richly-carved
0.0107	20.3	.0000	1	ridge-pole
0.0107	20.3	.0000	1	ridgetops
0.0107	20.3	.0000	1	Ridley
0.0107	20.3	.0000	1	Rieseberg
0.0107	20.3	.0000	1	Rigby's
0.0107	20.3	.0000	1	robberies
0.0107	20.3	.0000	1	robin's-egg
0.0107	20.3	.0000	1	roll-the-shoe-button
0.0107	20.3	.0000	1	rollrock
0.0107	20.3	.0000	1	roly
0.0107	20.3	.0000	1	root-hold
0.0107	20.3	.0000	1	rootingest
0.0107	20.3	.0000	1	ropes'
0.0107	20.3	.0000	1	Rosebud's
0.0107	20.3	.0000	1	Rosina
0.0107	20.3	.0000	1	Rossum
0.0107	20.3	.0000	1	Rossum's
0.0107	20.3	.0000	1	round-ups
0.0107	20.3	.0000	1	rounde
0.0107	20.3	.0000	1	Roylott
0.0107	20.3	.0000	1	Roylott's
0.0107	20.3	.0000	1	Roylotts
0.0107	20.3	.0000	1	roysterers
0.0107	20.3	.0000	1	rubicund
0.0107	20.3	.0000	1	RUFE
0.0107	20.3	.0000	1	ruffs
0.0107	20.3	.0000	1	ruinin'
0.0107	20.3	.0000	1	Ruler
0.0107	20.3	.0000	1	Rumbles
0.0107	20.3	.0000	1	rumpling
0.0107	20.3	.0000	1	run'st
0.0107	20.3	.0000	1	runagate
0.0107	20.3	.0000	1	Runkleman's
0.0107	20.3	.0000	1	runn
0.0107	20.3	.0000	1	runn'th
0.0107	20.3	.0000	1	runneth
0.0107	20.3	.0000	1	running-down
0.0107	20.3	.0000	1	Rychit
0.0107	20.3	.0000	1	Ryuho
0.0107	20.3	.0000	1	S-
0.0107	20.3	.0000	1	s'prise
0.0107	20.3	.0000	1	sa-a-ay
0.0107	20.3	.0000	1	sachet
0.0107	20.3	.0000	1	Saco
0.0107	20.3	.0000	1	Sad
0.0107	20.3	.0000	1	Sadler
0.0107	20.3	.0000	1	safe-cracker
0.0107	20.3	.0000	1	safes
0.0107	20.3	.0000	1	Safeway
0.0107	20.3	.0000	1	Sahib
0.0107	20.3	.0000	1	Sakes
0.0107	20.3	.0000	1	Salish
0.0107	20.3	.0000	1	Salishan
0.0107	20.3	.0000	1	Sallyann
0.0107	20.3	.0000	1	Saloon
0.0107	20.3	.0000	1	sam
0.0107	20.3	.0000	1	sanctorum
0.0107	20.3	.0000	1	sanctum
0.0107	20.3	.0000	1	sandaled
0.0107	20.3	.0000	1	sandworm
0.0107	20.3	.0000	1	Sankhicani
0.0107	20.3	.0000	1	Saosquahanaunks
0.0107	20.3	.0000	1	Sappleton
0.0107	20.3	.0000	1	sapsucker
0.0107	20.3	.0000	1	sardonic
0.0107	20.3	.0000	1	sassed
0.0107	20.3	.0000	1	Satch
0.0107	20.3	.0000	1	Satchell
0.0107	20.3	.0000	1	Satisfaction
0.0107	20.3	.0000	1	Sattisfield
0.0107	20.3	.0000	1	savin'
0.0107	20.3	.0000	1	savvy
0.0107	20.3	.0000	1	sawn
0.0107	20.3	.0000	1	Saxony's
0.0107	20.3	.0000	1	scabby-kneed
0.0107	20.3	.0000	1	scalesome
0.0107	20.3	.0000	1	scamperings
0.0107	20.3	.0000	1	scanted
0.0107	20.3	.0000	1	scape
0.0107	20.3	.0000	1	Scar
0.0107	20.3	.0000	1	scarified
0.0107	20.3	.0000	1	scenery's
0.0107	20.3	.0000	1	Schachachgokhos
0.0107	20.3	.0000	1	Schka'ak
0.0107	20.3	.0000	1	Schlapp
0.0107	20.3	.0000	1	schnell
0.0107	20.3	.0000	1	schoolbell
0.0107	20.3	.0000	1	schoolyard's
0.0107	20.3	.0000	1	Schuler
0.0107	20.3	.0000	1	Schwanammek
0.0107	20.3	.0000	1	schwannack
0.0107	20.3	.0000	1	scoreless
0.0107	20.3	.0000	1	scraggy
0.0107	20.3	.0000	1	Scratch's
0.0107	20.3	.0000	1	screech-owl's
0.0107	20.3	.0000	1	scrimmages
0.0107	20.3	.0000	1	scrip
0.0107	20.3	.0000	1	scruff
0.0107	20.3	.0000	1	scruples

THE PRECEDING WORD TYPE OCCUPIES RANK 77200

U	SFI	D	F	Word Type
0.0107	20.3	.0000	1	scrutinizes
0.0107	20.3	.0000	1	Sea-Nymphs
0.0107	20.3	.0000	1	sea-beasts
0.0107	20.3	.0000	1	sea-fog
0.0107	20.3	.0000	1	Sea-goddess
0.0107	20.3	.0000	1	sea-green
0.0107	20.3	.0000	1	sea-otter
0.0107	20.3	.0000	1	seabag
0.0107	20.3	.0000	1	seagulls'
0.0107	20.3	.0000	1	Seathl
0.0107	20.3	.0000	1	Seaton
0.0107	20.3	.0000	1	sech
0.0107	20.3	.0000	1	sed
0.0107	20.3	.0000	1	see'
0.0107	20.3	.0000	1	seedstitch
0.0107	20.3	.0000	1	seedtime
0.0107	20.3	.0000	1	seem'd
0.0107	20.3	.0000	1	seem'st
0.0107	20.3	.0000	1	segue
0.0107	20.3	.0000	1	sehe
0.0107	20.3	.0000	1	self-correction
0.0107	20.3	.0000	1	self-instruction
0.0107	20.3	.0000	1	semifantastic
0.0107	20.3	.0000	1	sentencing
0.0107	20.3	.0000	1	Seon
0.0107	20.3	.0000	1	Sergeant-Major
0.0107	20.3	.0000	1	Seribriakov
0.0107	20.3	.0000	1	serious-looking
0.0107	20.3	.0000	1	ses
0.0107	20.3	.0000	1	set-gun
0.0107	20.3	.0000	1	SETS
0.0107	20.3	.0000	1	Setsu's
0.0107	20.3	.0000	1	sevenscore
0.0107	20.3	.0000	1	seventy-odd
0.0107	20.3	.0000	1	sha'l
0.0107	20.3	.0000	1	shade-preserved
0.0107	20.3	.0000	1	shadow-papers
0.0107	20.3	.0000	1	Shakespearean
0.0107	20.3	.0000	1	Shalehaha
0.0107	20.3	.0000	1	Shammah
0.0107	20.3	.0000	1	sharp-faced
0.0107	20.3	.0000	1	Shave
0.0107	20.3	.0000	1	shelter-box
0.0107	20.3	.0000	1	shepherds'
0.0107	20.3	.0000	1	Sherwood's
0.0107	20.3	.0000	1	shies
0.0107	20.3	.0000	1	shimmy
0.0107	20.3	.0000	1	shindigs
0.0107	20.3	.0000	1	shinned
0.0107	20.3	.0000	1	shinnied
0.0107	20.3	.0000	1	Ship-Trap
0.0107	20.3	.0000	1	shipwrecks
0.0107	20.3	.0000	1	shirt-sleeves
0.0107	20.3	.0000	1	shiverings
0.0107	20.3	.0000	1	Shochoh
0.0107	20.3	.0000	1	shop-window
0.0107	20.3	.0000	1	Shortleg
0.0107	20.3	.0000	1	shouldst
0.0107	20.3	.0000	1	show'rs
0.0107	20.3	.0000	1	showering
0.0107	20.3	.0000	1	showoff
0.0107	20.3	.0000	1	shudderingly
0.0107	20.3	.0000	1	shut-ins
0.0107	20.3	.0000	1	Sibylla
0.0107	20.3	.0000	1	sick-bed
0.0107	20.3	.0000	1	side-wall
0.0107	20.3	.0000	1	signally
0.0107	20.3	.0000	1	Signior
0.0107	20.3	.0000	1	signiors
0.0107	20.3	.0000	1	sil
0.0107	20.3	.0000	1	silkiest
0.0107	20.3	.0000	1	SilverCity
0.0107	20.3	.0000	1	silver-haired
0.0107	20.3	.0000	1	silver-studded
0.0107	20.3	.0000	1	single-headed
0.0107	20.3	.0000	1	single-hooved
0.0107	20.3	.0000	1	single-motored
0.0107	20.3	.0000	1	single-shot
0.0107	20.3	.0000	1	single-soled
0.0107	20.3	.0000	1	sirrah
0.0107	20.3	.0000	1	Sitwell
0.0107	20.3	.0000	1	six-guns
0.0107	20.3	.0000	1	six-hundred
0.0107	20.3	.0000	1	six-letter
0.0107	20.3	.0000	1	skedaddlin'
0.0107	20.3	.0000	1	Skippy
0.0107	20.3	.0000	1	skirled
0.0107	20.3	.0000	1	skittered
0.0107	20.3	.0000	1	skittery
0.0107	20.3	.0000	1	Skyward
0.0107	20.3	.0000	1	slaine
0.0107	20.3	.0000	1	sland'red
0.0107	20.3	.0000	1	slanderous
0.0107	20.3	.0000	1	slaught'red
0.0107	20.3	.0000	1	slaveboy
0.0107	20.3	.0000	1	slavish
0.0107	20.3	.0000	1	Sleamish
0.0107	20.3	.0000	1	sleekly
0.0107	20.3	.0000	1	sleepwalker
0.0107	20.3	.0000	1	slick-talking

THE PRECEDING WORD TYPE OCCUPIES RANK 77300

U	SFI	D	F	Word Type
0.0107	20.3	.0000	1	slicked-up
0.0107	20.3	.0000	1	sliding's
0.0107	20.3	.0000	1	slinger
0.0107	20.3	.0000	1	sloth's
0.0107	20.3	.0000	1	slow-down
0.0107	20.3	.0000	1	slow-paced
0.0107	20.3	.0000	1	slow-rising
0.0107	20.3	.0000	1	slow-speaking
0.0107	20.3	.0000	1	Slue-Foot
0.0107	20.3	.0000	1	slugfests
0.0107	20.3	.0000	1	sluttish
0.0107	20.3	.0000	1	small-paned
0.0107	20.3	.0000	1	Smiggles
0.0107	20.3	.0000	1	smiths
0.0107	20.3	.0000	1	SMOKE
0.0107	20.3	.0000	1	smoke-curl
0.0107	20.3	.0000	1	smoke-infested
0.0107	20.3	.0000	1	smoke-like
0.0107	20.3	.0000	1	smoke-wreathed
0.0107	20.3	.0000	1	Smug
0.0107	20.3	.0000	1	snail-paced
0.0107	20.3	.0000	1	snaith
0.0107	20.3	.0000	1	snaring
0.0107	20.3	.0000	1	sneerified-like
0.0107	20.3	.0000	1	sniggering
0.0107	20.3	.0000	1	snipers
0.0107	20.3	.0000	1	sniveling
0.0107	20.3	.0000	1	SNOUT
0.0107	20.3	.0000	1	Snow-on-the-Mountain
0.0107	20.3	.0000	1	snowdraped
0.0107	20.3	.0000	1	snubbed
0.0107	20.3	.0000	1	snubbing
0.0107	20.3	.0000	1	snuffbox
0.0107	20.3	.0000	1	SNUG
0.0107	20.3	.0000	1	so'm
0.0107	20.3	.0000	1	socialist-hated
0.0107	20.3	.0000	1	socialite
0.0107	20.3	.0000	1	soft-like
0.0107	20.3	.0000	1	Soldiers'
0.0107	20.3	.0000	1	solemnize
0.0107	20.3	.0000	1	solicitor
0.0107	20.3	.0000	1	solicitously
0.0107	20.3	.0000	1	solid-board
0.0107	20.3	.0000	1	Solly
0.0107	20.3	.0000	1	Solyman
0.0107	20.3	.0000	1	somberly
0.0107	20.3	.0000	1	someding
0.0107	20.3	.0000	1	soon's
0.0107	20.3	.0000	1	sooth
0.0107	20.3	.0000	1	Sopel
0.0107	20.3	.0000	1	Sophy
0.0107	20.3	.0000	1	sort-out
0.0107	20.3	.0000	1	sound-minded
0.0107	20.3	.0000	1	Southcott
0.0107	20.3	.0000	1	Sowback
0.0107	20.3	.0000	1	spadeful
0.0107	20.3	.0000	1	spanks
0.0107	20.3	.0000	1	speak'st
0.0107	20.3	.0000	1	spear's
0.0107	20.3	.0000	1	speckles
0.0107	20.3	.0000	1	speed-mad
0.0107	20.3	.0000	1	spets
0.0107	20.3	.0000	1	spinners'
0.0107	20.3	.0000	1	spited
0.0107	20.3	.0000	1	splashless
0.0107	20.3	.0000	1	splice
0.0107	20.3	.0000	1	splot
0.0107	20.3	.0000	1	sportswoman
0.0107	20.3	.0000	1	sprinklings
0.0107	20.3	.0000	1	spunkier
0.0107	20.3	.0000	1	square-dance
0.0107	20.3	.0000	1	Squash
0.0107	20.3	.0000	1	squidging
0.0107	20.3	.0000	1	squiggle
0.0107	20.3	.0000	1	Stafford
0.0107	20.3	.0000	1	stagestruck
0.0107	20.3	.0000	1	stammer
0.0107	20.3	.0000	1	stand'st
0.0107	20.3	.0000	1	star-crossed
0.0107	20.3	.0000	1	Starveling
0.0107	20.3	.0000	1	STATE
0.0107	20.3	.0000	1	Stateroom
0.0107	20.3	.0000	1	staunch

U	SFI	D	F	Word Type
0.0107	20.3	.0000	1	staving
0.0107	20.3	.0000	1	stealers
0.0107	20.3	.0000	1	steel-blue
0.0107	20.3	.0000	1	steeled
0.0107	20.3	.0000	1	steep-roofed
0.0107	20.3	.0000	1	steeple-sliding's
0.0107	20.3	.0000	1	Stephens
0.0107	20.3	.0000	1	steppers
0.0107	20.3	.0000	1	stept
0.0107	20.3	.0000	1	sterilizer
0.0107	20.3	.0000	1	sterilizes
0.0107	20.3	.0000	1	sternest
0.0107	20.3	.0000	1	stick-up
0.0107	20.3	.0000	1	sties
0.0107	20.3	.0000	1	stiffest
0.0107	20.3	.0000	1	Stillson
0.0107	20.3	.0000	1	stingiest

THE PRECEDING WORD TYPE OCCUPIES RANK 77400

U	SFI	D	F	Word Type
0.0107	20.3	.0000	1	stipulate
0.0107	20.3	.0000	1	Stockholm's
0.0107	20.3	.0000	1	stockmen's
0.0107	20.3	.0000	1	stomper
0.0107	20.3	.0000	1	stone-blue
0.0107	20.3	.0000	1	stone-wall
0.0107	20.3	.0000	1	stonepipe
0.0107	20.3	.0000	1	stonily
0.0107	20.3	.0000	1	stony-eyed
0.0107	20.3	.0000	1	storyteller's
0.0107	20.3	.0000	1	straightaways
0.0107	20.3	.0000	1	STRANGWAYS'
0.0107	20.3	.0000	1	Strangways'
0.0107	20.3	.0000	1	STREET
0.0107	20.3	.0000	1	strewed
0.0107	20.3	.0000	1	strong-withered
0.0107	20.3	.0000	1	stronghold
0.0107	20.3	.0000	1	strutworks
0.0107	20.3	.0000	1	Stumpland
0.0107	20.3	.0000	1	sturdier
0.0107	20.3	.0000	1	Styx
0.0107	20.3	.0000	1	subornation
0.0107	20.3	.0000	1	Sudha
0.0107	20.3	.0000	1	sufferance
0.0107	20.3	.0000	1	Suggett
0.0107	20.3	.0000	1	sulled
0.0107	20.3	.0000	1	sun-and-wind
0.0107	20.3	.0000	1	sun-seeking
0.0107	20.3	.0000	1	sun-split
0.0107	20.3	.0000	1	sun-tan
0.0107	20.3	.0000	1	sunflower-crown
0.0107	20.3	.0000	1	Sunny's
0.0107	20.3	.0000	1	sunrays
0.0107	20.3	.0000	1	sunsheen
0.0107	20.3	.0000	1	sunslanting
0.0107	20.3	.0000	1	sunstruck
0.0107	20.3	.0000	1	sunward
0.0107	20.3	.0000	1	supernaturally
0.0107	20.3	.0000	1	surcease
0.0107	20.3	.0000	1	surety
0.0107	20.3	.0000	1	surface-wind
0.0107	20.3	.0000	1	susceptibilities
0.0107	20.3	.0000	1	suspiciousness
0.0107	20.3	.0000	1	susurrus
0.0107	20.3	.0000	1	Sven
0.0107	20.3	.0000	1	swaddled
0.0107	20.3	.0000	1	swan's
0.0107	20.3	.0000	1	sweet-sour
0.0107	20.3	.0000	1	Sweet's
0.0107	20.3	.0000	1	sweetish
0.0107	20.3	.0000	1	swimmin'
0.0107	20.3	.0000	1	swoon
0.0107	20.3	.0000	1	Syringa
0.0107	20.3	.0000	1	t'day
0.0107	20.3	.0000	1	Taco
0.0107	20.3	.0000	1	taco
0.0107	20.3	.0000	1	TACO
0.0107	20.3	.0000	1	tail-feather
0.0107	20.3	.0000	1	tail-light
0.0107	20.3	.0000	1	tailing
0.0107	20.3	.0000	1	talcumed
0.0107	20.3	.0000	1	talk'st
0.0107	20.3	.0000	1	tallies
0.0107	20.3	.0000	1	tameness
0.0107	20.3	.0000	1	Tangari
0.0107	20.3	.0000	1	tangibility
0.0107	20.3	.0000	1	tangled-up
0.0107	20.3	.0000	1	tarantula's
0.0107	20.3	.0000	1	tardiness
0.0107	20.3	.0000	1	tarred
0.0107	20.3	.0000	1	teary
0.0107	20.3	.0000	1	teashop
0.0107	20.3	.0000	1	tediousness
0.0107	20.3	.0000	1	tell-tale
0.0107	20.3	.0000	1	tempest-tost
0.0107	20.3	.0000	1	Templecombe
0.0107	20.3	.0000	1	ten-league
0.0107	20.3	.0000	1	ten-month
0.0107	20.3	.0000	1	tendril
0.0107	20.3	.0000	1	Teniers
0.0107	20.3	.0000	1	tenn
0.0107	20.3	.0000	1	tergiversation
0.0107	20.3	.0000	1	Tewkesbury
0.0107	20.3	.0000	1	thataway
0.0107	20.3	.0000	1	theatrically
0.0107	20.3	.0000	1	them's
0.0107	20.3	.0000	1	thick-growing
0.0107	20.3	.0000	1	thick-spread
0.0107	20.3	.0000	1	things'll
0.0107	20.3	.0000	1	THIRTYONE
0.0107	20.3	.0000	1	Thisbe
0.0107	20.3	.0000	1	THOU
0.0107	20.3	.0000	1	thousand-year-old
0.0107	20.3	.0000	1	three-act
0.0107	20.3	.0000	1	three-corner
0.0107	20.3	.0000	1	three-hours'
0.0107	20.3	.0000	1	three-hundred-mile
0.0107	20.3	.0000	1	three-mile-thick
0.0107	20.3	.0000	1	throstle
0.0107	20.3	.0000	1	throw-away

THE PRECEDING WORD TYPE OCCUPIES RANK 77500

U	SFI	D	F	Word Type
0.0107	20.3	.0000	1	thumper
0.0107	20.3	.0000	1	thunderin'
0.0107	20.3	.0000	1	ti-tum-tum-tum
0.0107	20.3	.0000	1	tiddlywinks
0.0107	20.3	.0000	1	tiewig
0.0107	20.3	.0000	1	tillers
0.0107	20.3	.0000	1	timeworn
0.0107	20.3	.0000	1	Timpie
0.0107	20.3	.0000	1	tinder-box
0.0107	20.3	.0000	1	tingles
0.0107	20.3	.0000	1	tithe
0.0107	20.3	.0000	1	toboggans
0.0107	20.3	.0000	1	todo
0.0107	20.3	.0000	1	Toes
0.0107	20.3	.0000	1	Tolan
0.0107	20.3	.0000	1	TOMMY
0.0107	20.3	.0000	1	tommy
0.0107	20.3	.0000	1	toneless
0.0107	20.3	.0000	1	tonelessly
0.0107	20.3	.0000	1	Tonquas
0.0107	20.3	.0000	1	toolroom
0.0107	20.3	.0000	1	tootingest
0.0107	20.3	.0000	1	top-hat
0.0107	20.3	.0000	1	top-rating
0.0107	20.3	.0000	1	torchbearers
0.0107	20.3	.0000	1	torturer
0.0107	20.3	.0000	1	Torwal's
0.0107	20.3	.0000	1	tough-minded
0.0107	20.3	.0000	1	tough-talking
0.0107	20.3	.0000	1	tourist-class
0.0107	20.3	.0000	1	toy-size
0.0107	20.3	.0000	1	traffickers
0.0107	20.3	.0000	1	trailer's
0.0107	20.3	.0000	1	tramway
0.0107	20.3	.0000	1	transacted
0.0107	20.3	.0000	1	transfigured
0.0107	20.3	.0000	1	Trapeze
0.0107	20.3	.0000	1	tree-trunks
0.0107	20.3	.0000	1	Tricksters
0.0107	20.3	.0000	1	trifled
0.0107	20.3	.0000	1	Trimble-toe
0.0107	20.3	.0000	1	trite
0.0107	20.3	.0000	1	trompin
0.0107	20.3	.0000	1	trompin'
0.0107	20.3	.0000	1	trounce
0.0107	20.3	.0000	1	trousers'
0.0107	20.3	.0000	1	trumped-up
0.0107	20.3	.0000	1	Tsarevna
0.0107	20.3	.0000	1	Tubal
0.0107	20.3	.0000	1	tucker
0.0107	20.3	.0000	1	tug-of-war
0.0107	20.3	.0000	1	tumbly-looking
0.0107	20.3	.0000	1	turkey-cock
0.0107	20.3	.0000	1	turn-off
0.0107	20.3	.0000	1	turn'd
0.0107	20.3	.0000	1	Turnham
0.0107	20.3	.0000	1	turnkey
0.0107	20.3	.0000	1	Turnpike
0.0107	20.3	.0000	1	Turns
0.0107	20.3	.0000	1	tusky
0.0107	20.3	.0000	1	tussocky
0.0107	20.3	.0000	1	TV-ese
0.0107	20.3	.0000	1	twelvemonth
0.0107	20.3	.0000	1	twenty-one-gun
0.0107	20.3	.0000	1	twenty-vun
0.0107	20.3	.0000	1	twentyseven-mile
0.0107	20.3	.0000	1	two-score
0.0107	20.3	.0000	1	two-three
0.0107	20.3	.0000	1	Tybalt's
0.0107	20.3	.0000	1	tyke
0.0107	20.3	.0000	1	Tyndal's
0.0107	20.3	.0000	1	ulster
0.0107	20.3	.0000	1	Ultimus
0.0107	20.3	.0000	1	umph
0.0107	20.3	.0000	1	umpteenth
0.0107	20.3	.0000	1	unacquainted
0.0107	20.3	.0000	1	unbecoming
0.0107	20.3	.0000	1	unbecomingly
0.0107	20.3	.0000	1	unbeliever
0.0107	20.3	.0000	1	unbuilt
0.0107	20.3	.0000	1	unceasingly
0.0107	20.3	.0000	1	unchangeable
0.0107	20.3	.0000	1	UNCLE
0.0107	20.3	.0000	1	unclimbed
0.0107	20.3	.0000	1	uncomplaining
0.0107	20.3	.0000	1	Under-the-Hill
0.0107	20.3	.0000	1	underhang
0.0107	20.3	.0000	1	underlay
0.0107	20.3	.0000	1	underscoring
0.0107	20.3	.0000	1	undervalued
0.0107	20.3	.0000	1	Underworld
0.0107	20.3	.0000	1	undeserving
0.0107	20.3	.0000	1	undistinguishable
0.0107	20.3	.0000	1	undramatic
0.0107	20.3	.0000	1	uneconomic
0.0107	20.3	.0000	1	unenlightened
0.0107	20.3	.0000	1	unenterprising
0.0107	20.3	.0000	1	unentertaining
0.0107	20.3	.0000	1	unfeathered
0.0107	20.3	.0000	1	unfoldment

THE PRECEDING WORD TYPE OCCUPIES RANK 77600

U	SFI	D	F	Word Type
0.0107	20.3	.0000	1	unforded
0.0107	20.3	.0000	1	unfunny
0.0107	20.3	.0000	1	ungenerous
0.0107	20.3	.0000	1	ungratefulness
0.0107	20.3	.0000	1	unhallowed
0.0107	20.3	.0000	1	unheedy
0.0107	20.3	.0000	1	unimpressed
0.0107	20.3	.0000	1	uninjured
0.0107	20.3	.0000	1	unleashes
0.0107	20.3	.0000	1	unlessoned
0.0107	20.3	.0000	1	unlifelike
0.0107	20.3	.0000	1	unmolested
0.0107	20.3	.0000	1	unnamable
0.0107	20.3	.0000	1	unnaturally
0.0107	20.3	.0000	1	unofficially
0.0107	20.3	.0000	1	unpeopled
0.0107	20.3	.0000	1	unpowdered
0.0107	20.3	.0000	1	unpracticed
0.0107	20.3	.0000	1	unprosperous
0.0107	20.3	.0000	1	unquestioningly
0.0107	20.3	.0000	1	unshaped
0.0107	20.3	.0000	1	unsolicited
0.0107	20.3	.0000	1	unstick
0.0107	20.3	.0000	1	unsubstantial
0.0107	20.3	.0000	1	untellable
0.0107	20.3	.0000	1	untill
0.0107	20.3	.0000	1	untrespassed
0.0107	20.3	.0000	1	untwist
0.0107	20.3	.0000	1	unwadded
0.0107	20.3	.0000	1	unwillingness
0.0107	20.3	.0000	1	unwitting
0.0107	20.3	.0000	1	unworthier
0.0107	20.3	.0000	1	up-and-downstage
0.0107	20.3	.0000	1	upbraided
0.0107	20.3	.0000	1	upholsterers'
0.0107	20.3	.0000	1	upraising
0.0107	20.3	.0000	1	usurer
0.0107	20.3	.0000	1	uttermost
0.0107	20.3	.0000	1	Uzbekistan
0.0107	20.3	.0000	1	v'ile
0.0107	20.3	.0000	1	vailing
0.0107	20.3	.0000	1	vait
0.0107	20.3	.0000	1	VanDenk
0.0107	20.3	.0000	1	VanRipper
0.0107	20.3	.0000	1	VanTassel's
0.0107	20.3	.0000	1	Vanderpool's
0.0107	20.3	.0000	1	Vaseline
0.0107	20.3	.0000	1	vasty
0.0107	20.3	.0000	1	vaulty
0.0107	20.3	.0000	1	vaunting
0.0107	20.3	.0000	1	veinous
0.0107	20.3	.0000	1	velvet-lined
0.0107	20.3	.0000	1	venge
0.0107	20.3	.0000	1	Vengeance
0.0107	20.3	.0000	1	Venusian
0.0107	20.3	.0000	1	vermillion
0.0107	20.3	.0000	1	vests
0.0107	20.3	.0000	1	vicariously
0.0107	20.3	.0000	1	Vicky
0.0107	20.3	.0000	1	Vilas
0.0107	20.3	.0000	1	Vilhelm
0.0107	20.3	.0000	1	vill
0.0107	20.3	.0000	1	villainously
0.0107	20.3	.0000	1	vin
0.0107	20.3	.0000	1	virtue's
0.0107	20.3	.0000	1	visitation
0.0107	20.3	.0000	1	visitin'
0.0107	20.3	.0000	1	vivere
0.0107	20.3	.0000	1	Vixen
0.0107	20.3	.0000	1	vizor
0.0107	20.3	.0000	1	Vlassovs
0.0107	20.3	.0000	1	vonFrankenstein
0.0107	20.3	.0000	1	vulgarity
0.0107	20.3	.0000	1	Vultures
0.0107	20.3	.0000	1	W'Tassone
0.0107	20.3	.0000	1	wa'n't
0.0107	20.3	.0000	1	wads
0.0107	20.3	.0000	1	wag's
0.0107	20.3	.0000	1	waistcoats
0.0107	20.3	.0000	1	wakening
0.0107	20.3	.0000	1	Waldhoning
0.0107	20.3	.0000	1	walkin'
0.0107	20.3	.0000	1	walking-shoe
0.0107	20.3	.0000	1	WallaWalla
0.0107	20.3	.0000	1	wallop
0.0107	20.3	.0000	1	Wallowa
0.0107	20.3	.0000	1	wallows
0.0107	20.3	.0000	1	want-wit
0.0107	20.3	.0000	1	wantin'
0.0107	20.3	.0000	1	warden's
0.0107	20.3	.0000	1	wat'ry
0.0107	20.3	.0000	1	watch's
0.0107	20.3	.0000	1	water-skaters
0.0107	20.3	.0000	1	water-worms
0.0107	20.3	.0000	1	watersplash
0.0107	20.3	.0000	1	Wave
0.0107	20.3	.0000	1	waves'
0.0107	20.3	.0000	1	wayfarer
0.0107	20.3	.0000	1	waylaid
0.0107	20.3	.0000	1	weaklings

THE PRECEDING WORD TYPE OCCUPIES RANK 77700

U	SFI	D	F	Word Type
0.0107	20.3	.0000	1	weal
0.0107	20.3	.0000	1	Wear
0.0107	20.3	.0000	1	weathers
0.0107	20.3	.0000	1	weaver's
0.0107	20.3	.0000	1	wedding-dress
0.0107	20.3	.0000	1	Wedge
0.0107	20.3	.0000	1	weds
0.0107	20.3	.0000	1	Weedemris's
0.0107	20.3	.0000	1	weep'st
0.0107	20.3	.0000	1	Welikan
0.0107	20.3	.0000	1	well-appareled
0.0107	20.3	.0000	1	well-based
0.0107	20.3	.0000	1	well-fashioned
0.0107	20.3	.0000	1	well-flowered
0.0107	20.3	.0000	1	well-liked
0.0107	20.3	.0000	1	well-named
0.0107	20.3	.0000	1	well-oiled
0.0107	20.3	.0000	1	well-trimmed
0.0107	20.3	.0000	1	well-turned
0.0107	20.3	.0000	1	Weller's
0.0107	20.3	.0000	1	wench's
0.0107	20.3	.0000	1	weraday
0.0107	20.3	.0000	1	Weser
0.0107	20.3	.0000	1	westering
0.0107	20.3	.0000	1	wether
0.0107	20.3	.0000	1	Whaling
0.0107	20.3	.0000	1	whereto
0.0107	20.3	.0000	1	whichway
0.0107	20.3	.0000	1	whims
0.0107	20.3	.0000	1	Whipsnade
0.0107	20.3	.0000	1	whispy
0.0107	20.3	.0000	1	white-blazed
0.0107	20.3	.0000	1	white-clothed
0.0107	20.3	.0000	1	white-oak
0.0107	20.3	.0000	1	white-streaked
0.0107	20.3	.0000	1	whitecock
0.0107	20.3	.0000	1	Whiterside
0.0107	20.3	.0000	1	who'd've
0.0107	20.3	.0000	1	who'da
0.0107	20.3	.0000	1	wholehearted
0.0107	20.3	.0000	1	whoo-haw
0.0107	20.3	.0000	1	whoo-ooo-wooo
0.0107	20.3	.0000	1	whore
0.0107	20.3	.0000	1	wicked-looking
0.0107	20.3	.0000	1	wields
0.0107	20.3	.0000	1	wild-goose
0.0107	20.3	.0000	1	wildy
0.0107	20.3	.0000	1	Wilse's
0.0107	20.3	.0000	1	wincing
0.0107	20.3	.0000	1	windmill's
0.0107	20.3	.0000	1	window-dresser's
0.0107	20.3	.0000	1	window's
0.0107	20.3	.0000	1	windpuff-bonnet
0.0107	20.3	.0000	1	wine-flask
0.0107	20.3	.0000	1	wing'd
0.0107	20.3	.0000	1	Winklers
0.0107	20.3	.0000	1	Winkles
0.0107	20.3	.0000	1	wishmaking
0.0107	20.3	.0000	1	witchdoctor's
0.0107	20.3	.0000	1	witness's
0.0107	20.3	.0000	1	wits'
0.0107	20.3	.0000	1	Wittmer
0.0107	20.3	.0000	1	woe-begone
0.0107	20.3	.0000	1	wolfishly
0.0107	20.3	.0000	1	wolvish
0.0107	20.3	.0000	1	wolvish-ravening
0.0107	20.3	.0000	1	WOMEN
0.0107	20.3	.0000	1	wonderful-looking
0.0107	20.3	.0000	1	wood-birds
0.0107	20.3	.0000	1	Woodlawns'
0.0107	20.3	.0000	1	woodman
0.0107	20.3	.0000	1	woos
0.0107	20.3	.0000	1	word-bringer
0.0107	20.3	.0000	1	worm-eaten
0.0107	20.3	.0000	1	worriment
0.0107	20.3	.0000	1	worthier
0.0107	20.3	.0000	1	wott
0.0107	20.3	.0000	1	Wouser
0.0107	20.3	.0000	1	wouye
0.0107	20.3	.0000	1	WQXR
0.0107	20.3	.0000	1	Wrath
0.0107	20.3	.0000	1	wrathfully
0.0107	20.3	.0000	1	Wren's
0.0107	20.3	.0000	1	wrestler's
0.0107	20.3	.0000	1	wrong'st
0.0107	20.3	.0000	1	Wyatt
0.0107	20.3	.0000	1	WYCHERLY
0.0107	20.3	.0000	1	y-you
0.0107	20.3	.0000	1	yammering
0.0107	20.3	.0000	1	Yap-yurrr
0.0107	20.3	.0000	1	yaws
0.0107	20.3	.0000	1	yayo
0.0107	20.3	.0000	1	Yealland
0.0107	20.3	.0000	1	Yedda
0.0107	20.3	.0000	1	yellow-bellied
0.0107	20.3	.0000	1	yellow-gray
0.0107	20.3	.0000	1	yellow-orangey
0.0107	20.3	.0000	1	Yengwe's
0.0107	20.3	.0000	1	yerself
0.0107	20.3	.0000	1	yessuh

THE PRECEDING WORD TYPE OCCUPIES RANK 77800

U	SFI	D	F	Word Type
0.0107	20.3	.0000	1	yesternight
0.0107	20.3	.0000	1	yip
0.0107	20.3	.0000	1	yokel
0.0107	20.3	.0000	1	youngs
0.0107	20.3	.0000	1	youngster's
0.0107	20.3	.0000	1	yourn
0.0107	20.3	.0000	1	zany
0.0107	20.3	.0000	1	zealously
0.0107	20.3	.0000	1	Zeus-bred
0.0107	20.3	.0000	1	Zeus'
0.0107	20.3	.0000	1	Zoos
0.0107	20.3	.0000	1	Zorab
0.0107	20.3	.0000	1	zun-zun-zun
0.0107	20.3	.0000	1	zun-zunned
0.0107	20.3	.0000	1	1499
0.0107	20.3	.0000	1	15-16
0.0107	20.3	.0000	1	1876-1941
0.0107	20.3	.0000	1	19-21
0.0107	20.3	.0000	1	22-caliber
0.0107	20.3	.0000	1	5-eyed
0.0107	20.3	.0000	1	644-ton
0.0107	20.3	.0000	1	6700-foot**
0.0107	20.3	.0000	1	7X-3824
0.0107	20.3	.0000	1	700-foot
0.0107	20.3	.0000	1	76th
0.0107	20.3	.0000	1	9W-7679
0.0107	20.3	.0000	1	9762
0.0105	20.2	.0000	1	(C2H4Cl)2S**
0.0105	20.2	.0000	1	$11-million
0.0105	20.2	.0000	1	$121
0.0105	20.2	.0000	1	$127
0.0105	20.2	.0000	1	$318
0.0105	20.2	.0000	1	$337
0.0105	20.2	.0000	1	$383
0.0105	20.2	.0000	1	$475
0.0105	20.2	.0000	1	$525
0.0105	20.2	.0000	1	$540
0.0105	20.2	.0000	1	$61
0.0105	20.2	.0000	1	$74
0.0105	20.2	.0000	1	-NO2
0.0105	20.2	.0000	1	-1016
0.0105	20.2	.0000	1	-1060
0.0105	20.2	.0000	1	-1099
0.0105	20.2	.0000	1	-1276
0.0105	20.2	.0000	1	-1300
0.0105	20.2	.0000	1	-1306

U	SFI	D	F	Word Type
0.0105	20.2	.0000	1	-1654
0.0105	20.2	.0000	1	-1741
0.0105	20.2	.0000	1	-1881
0.0105	20.2	.0000	1	-196
0.0105	20.2	.0000	1	-562
0.0105	20.2	.0000	1	-858
0.0105	20.2	.0000	1	'till
0.0105	20.2	.0000	1	'30s
0.0105	20.2	.0000	1	A-bomb
0.0105	20.2	.0000	1	A-bombs
0.0105	20.2	.0000	1	Aarau
0.0105	20.2	.0000	1	abdicating
0.0105	20.2	.0000	1	abdomen-wagging
0.0105	20.2	.0000	1	Abdullah's
0.0105	20.2	.0000	1	Aberdares
0.0105	20.2	.0000	1	Aberdeenshire
0.0105	20.2	.0000	1	aberrant
0.0105	20.2	.0000	1	aberrantly
0.0105	20.2	.0000	1	ability-to-pay
0.0105	20.2	.0000	1	abnormality
0.0105	20.2	.0000	1	abnormally
0.0105	20.2	.0000	1	abomination
0.0105	20.2	.0000	1	Abstract
0.0105	20.2	.0000	1	Abstraction
0.0105	20.2	.0000	1	abstractions
0.0105	20.2	.0000	1	abstractly
0.0105	20.2	.0000	1	abstractness
0.0105	20.2	.0000	1	abutments
0.0105	20.2	.0000	1	Academie
0.0105	20.2	.0000	1	Accepted
0.0105	20.2	.0000	1	Access
0.0105	20.2	.0000	1	accomplishes
0.0105	20.2	.0000	1	Accounts
0.0105	20.2	.0000	1	accrual
0.0105	20.2	.0000	1	acculturation
0.0105	20.2	.0000	1	Acculturation
0.0105	20.2	.0000	1	accumulator
0.0105	20.2	.0000	1	accuracies
0.0105	20.2	.0000	1	Acer
0.0105	20.2	.0000	1	Aceraceae
0.0105	20.2	.0000	1	aces
0.0105	20.2	.0000	1	acquisitions
0.0105	20.2	.0000	1	Acraea
0.0105	20.2	.0000	1	actinomycosis
0.0105	20.2	.0000	1	actinopterygians
0.0105	20.2	.0000	1	actually-used
0.0105	20.2	.0000	1	acutely
0.0105	20.2	.0000	1	adamanteus
0.0105	20.2	.0000	1	Aden's
0.0105	20.2	.0000	1	adherence
0.0105	20.2	.0000	1	Adige
0.0105	20.2	.0000	1	Adobe
0.0105	20.2	.0000	1	adopts
0.0105	20.2	.0000	1	Adriaen
THE PRECEDING WORD TYPE OCCUPIES RANK 77900				
0.0105	20.2	.0000	1	advantageously
0.0105	20.2	.0000	1	Aegina
0.0105	20.2	.0000	1	Aegir
0.0105	20.2	.0000	1	aerodynamically
0.0105	20.2	.0000	1	aeronauts
0.0105	20.2	.0000	1	Affair
0.0105	20.2	.0000	1	affectation
0.0105	20.2	.0000	1	affinities
0.0105	20.2	.0000	1	affirms
0.0105	20.2	.0000	1	affording
0.0105	20.2	.0000	1	AFL**
0.0105	20.2	.0000	1	Africana
0.0105	20.2	.0000	1	Afrika
0.0105	20.2	.0000	1	Aga
0.0105	20.2	.0000	1	again-great
0.0105	20.2	.0000	1	agar-agar
0.0105	20.2	.0000	1	age-long
0.0105	20.2	.0000	1	age's
0.0105	20.2	.0000	1	ageless
0.0105	20.2	.0000	1	aggravate
0.0105	20.2	.0000	1	aggregation
0.0105	20.2	.0000	1	agouti
0.0105	20.2	.0000	1	agoutis
0.0105	20.2	.0000	1	Agricola's
0.0105	20.2	.0000	1	agriculturists
0.0105	20.2	.0000	1	agronomy
0.0105	20.2	.0000	1	Ainsworth's
0.0105	20.2	.0000	1	air-cushion
0.0105	20.2	.0000	1	air-intake
0.0105	20.2	.0000	1	air-navigation
0.0105	20.2	.0000	1	aircraft's
0.0105	20.2	.0000	1	Ajmer
0.0105	20.2	.0000	1	Akasaka
0.0105	20.2	.0000	1	Akhenaton
0.0105	20.2	.0000	1	al-Janubiyah
0.0105	20.2	.0000	1	al-Yaman
0.0105	20.2	.0000	1	Alabian
0.0105	20.2	.0000	1	Albertus
0.0105	20.2	.0000	1	albumen
0.0105	20.2	.0000	1	Albuquerque
0.0105	20.2	.0000	1	Alcelaphus
0.0105	20.2	.0000	1	alces
0.0105	20.2	.0000	1	alchemists'
0.0105	20.2	.0000	1	Alcide
0.0105	20.2	.0000	1	Aldrich-Vreeland
0.0105	20.2	.0000	1	Alegre
0.0105	20.2	.0000	1	Aleksandrovich
0.0105	20.2	.0000	1	Alemanni
0.0105	20.2	.0000	1	Alexanders
0.0105	20.2	.0000	1	Alexandrians
0.0105	20.2	.0000	1	Ali's
0.0105	20.2	.0000	1	aligning
0.0105	20.2	.0000	1	alkalies
0.0105	20.2	.0000	1	alkalosis
0.0105	20.2	.0000	1	all-electric
0.0105	20.2	.0000	1	all-embracing
0.0105	20.2	.0000	1	all-too-ailing
0.0105	20.2	.0000	1	allaying
0.0105	20.2	.0000	1	allele
0.0105	20.2	.0000	1	alleles
0.0105	20.2	.0000	1	alleviation
0.0105	20.2	.0000	1	allies'
0.0105	20.2	.0000	1	Alloy
0.0105	20.2	.0000	1	alloy-surface
0.0105	20.2	.0000	1	alluvium
0.0105	20.2	.0000	1	Almon
0.0105	20.2	.0000	1	Am's
0.0105	20.2	.0000	1	ambivalent
0.0105	20.2	.0000	1	American-designed
0.0105	20.2	.0000	1	americana
0.0105	20.2	.0000	1	Americanist
0.0105	20.2	.0000	1	Amesbury
0.0105	20.2	.0000	1	amics
0.0105	20.2	.0000	1	amidships
0.0105	20.2	.0000	1	Amintore
0.0105	20.2	.0000	1	amoebalike
0.0105	20.2	.0000	1	Amphibia
0.0105	20.2	.0000	1	Amphibian
0.0105	20.2	.0000	1	Amphibians
0.0105	20.2	.0000	1	Amphibole
0.0105	20.2	.0000	1	Amsterdam's
0.0105	20.2	.0000	1	amyotrophic
0.0105	20.2	.0000	1	AN-FO
0.0105	20.2	.0000	1	anabolism
0.0105	20.2	.0000	1	anagram
0.0105	20.2	.0000	1	anarchism
0.0105	20.2	.0000	1	ancylostomiasis
0.0105	20.2	.0000	1	Andrija
0.0105	20.2	.0000	1	anesthesia
0.0105	20.2	.0000	1	anesthetize
0.0105	20.2	.0000	1	anglerfishes
0.0105	20.2	.0000	1	Anglicanism
0.0105	20.2	.0000	1	angstroms
0.0105	20.2	.0000	1	Anguis
0.0105	20.2	.0000	1	Anio
0.0105	20.2	.0000	1	anise
0.0105	20.2	.0000	1	AnnalenderPhysik
0.0105	20.2	.0000	1	Annals
0.0105	20.2	.0000	1	annihilate
0.0105	20.2	.0000	1	annihilating
THE PRECEDING WORD TYPE OCCUPIES RANK 78000				
0.0105	20.2	.0000	1	Anniversary
0.0105	20.2	.0000	1	annul
0.0105	20.2	.0000	1	Ansgar
0.0105	20.2	.0000	1	anti-Communist
0.0105	20.2	.0000	1	anti-Federalist
0.0105	20.2	.0000	1	Anti-Injunction
0.0105	20.2	.0000	1	anti-masque
0.0105	20.2	.0000	1	anti-war
0.0105	20.2	.0000	1	Anticleia
0.0105	20.2	.0000	1	anticlimactic
0.0105	20.2	.0000	1	anticlimax
0.0105	20.2	.0000	1	Antipater
0.0105	20.2	.0000	1	antipope
0.0105	20.2	.0000	1	Antiquaries
0.0105	20.2	.0000	1	Antiquities
0.0105	20.2	.0000	1	Antun
0.0105	20.2	.0000	1	Anxious
0.0105	20.2	.0000	1	APARTHEID
0.0105	20.2	.0000	1	apartment-type
0.0105	20.2	.0000	1	apartness
0.0105	20.2	.0000	1	Ape
0.0105	20.2	.0000	1	aphid-tenders
0.0105	20.2	.0000	1	APO
0.0105	20.2	.0000	1	Apo
0.0105	20.2	.0000	1	appanage
0.0105	20.2	.0000	1	apparitions
0.0105	20.2	.0000	1	appended
0.0105	20.2	.0000	1	applied-research
0.0105	20.2	.0000	1	appointees
0.0105	20.2	.0000	1	apportioning
0.0105	20.2	.0000	1	appraisals
0.0105	20.2	.0000	1	appropriating
0.0105	20.2	.0000	1	apteryx
0.0105	20.2	.0000	1	Aptonga
0.0105	20.2	.0000	1	Aquavit
0.0105	20.2	.0000	1	aqueous
0.0105	20.2	.0000	1	Arabshah
0.0105	20.2	.0000	1	Arapaima
0.0105	20.2	.0000	1	Araucana
0.0105	20.2	.0000	1	Araucania
0.0105	20.2	.0000	1	arbitrate
0.0105	20.2	.0000	1	Arbitration
0.0105	20.2	.0000	1	arbitrator
0.0105	20.2	.0000	1	arborealists
0.0105	20.2	.0000	1	Arboretum
0.0105	20.2	.0000	1	Arcangelo
0.0105	20.2	.0000	1	arch-rival
0.0105	20.2	.0000	1	Archbald
0.0105	20.2	.0000	1	architect-engineer
0.0105	20.2	.0000	1	Architects
0.0105	20.2	.0000	1	Architecture
0.0105	20.2	.0000	1	archpredator
0.0105	20.2	.0000	1	areal
0.0105	20.2	.0000	1	Argenteuil
0.0105	20.2	.0000	1	aridity
0.0105	20.2	.0000	1	Aristotelian
0.0105	20.2	.0000	1	Arithmetick
0.0105	20.2	.0000	1	Arius
0.0105	20.2	.0000	1	Arizona-Mexico
0.0105	20.2	.0000	1	Armagh
0.0105	20.2	.0000	1	Armenians
0.0105	20.2	.0000	1	Arminius'
0.0105	20.2	.0000	1	Armorial
0.0105	20.2	.0000	1	Arnoldus
0.0105	20.2	.0000	1	Arp
0.0105	20.2	.0000	1	Arpi
0.0105	20.2	.0000	1	arribadas
0.0105	20.2	.0000	1	Arrigo
0.0105	20.2	.0000	1	arrow-fire
0.0105	20.2	.0000	1	arrow-swift
0.0105	20.2	.0000	1	art-collecting
0.0105	20.2	.0000	1	art-work
0.0105	20.2	.0000	1	Artaphernes
0.0105	20.2	.0000	1	Artemis
0.0105	20.2	.0000	1	arteriole
0.0105	20.2	.0000	1	arterioles
0.0105	20.2	.0000	1	Artibonite
0.0105	20.2	.0000	1	artifact
0.0105	20.2	.0000	1	Artificial
0.0105	20.2	.0000	1	artisan-cultivator
0.0105	20.2	.0000	1	Artists
0.0105	20.2	.0000	1	Arundel
0.0105	20.2	.0000	1	Asahi
0.0105	20.2	.0000	1	Asbestos
0.0105	20.2	.0000	1	ascetic
0.0105	20.2	.0000	1	ash-Sha'biyah
0.0105	20.2	.0000	1	Ashcan
0.0105	20.2	.0000	1	Ashtead
0.0105	20.2	.0000	1	Asid
0.0105	20.2	.0000	1	Asoka
0.0105	20.2	.0000	1	Assassinations
0.0105	20.2	.0000	1	assemblages
0.0105	20.2	.0000	1	asserting
0.0105	20.2	.0000	1	assertion
0.0105	20.2	.0000	1	assessments
0.0105	20.2	.0000	1	assessors
0.0105	20.2	.0000	1	assimilating
0.0105	20.2	.0000	1	association's
0.0105	20.2	.0000	1	assortments
0.0105	20.2	.0000	1	astounds
THE PRECEDING WORD TYPE OCCUPIES RANK 78100				
0.0105	20.2	.0000	1	astrolabes
0.0105	20.2	.0000	1	astronautical
0.0105	20.2	.0000	1	Asyut
0.0105	20.2	.0000	1	Atkins
0.0105	20.2	.0000	1	Atlantis
0.0105	20.2	.0000	1	atomic-scale
0.0105	20.2	.0000	1	atomoi
0.0105	20.2	.0000	1	Aton
0.0105	20.2	.0000	1	attacker
0.0105	20.2	.0000	1	attars
0.0105	20.2	.0000	1	audio-visual
0.0105	20.2	.0000	1	Auditorium
0.0105	20.2	.0000	1	auditorium's
0.0105	20.2	.0000	1	augurs
0.0105	20.2	.0000	1	Augustinians
0.0105	20.2	.0000	1	Augustulus
0.0105	20.2	.0000	1	Austen
0.0105	20.2	.0000	1	Austrasia
0.0105	20.2	.0000	1	Austrasians
0.0105	20.2	.0000	1	Austrian-Hungarian
0.0105	20.2	.0000	1	authenticity
0.0105	20.2	.0000	1	authoritatively
0.0105	20.2	.0000	1	Authorized
0.0105	20.2	.0000	1	authorizes
0.0105	20.2	.0000	1	autics
0.0105	20.2	.0000	1	automa-
0.0105	20.2	.0000	1	automate
0.0105	20.2	.0000	1	automatization
0.0105	20.2	.0000	1	Autostrada
0.0105	20.2	.0000	1	averse
0.0105	20.2	.0000	1	Avgustincic
0.0105	20.2	.0000	1	aviculturists
0.0105	20.2	.0000	1	avowed
0.0105	20.2	.0000	1	Axes
0.0105	20.2	.0000	1	Axis-held
0.0105	20.2	.0000	1	Ayyubid
0.0105	20.2	.0000	1	azarae
0.0105	20.2	.0000	1	azimuth
0.0105	20.2	.0000	1	azimuths
0.0105	20.2	.0000	1	azote
0.0105	20.2	.0000	1	B-17
0.0105	20.2	.0000	1	B-25
0.0105	20.2	.0000	1	Babb
0.0105	20.2	.0000	1	Babington
0.0105	20.2	.0000	1	baboon's
0.0105	20.2	.0000	1	babyish
0.0105	20.2	.0000	1	Bacchus
0.0105	20.2	.0000	1	Bachman's
0.0105	20.2	.0000	1	back-to-the-wall
0.0105	20.2	.0000	1	backcountry
0.0105	20.2	.0000	1	backtracking
0.0105	20.2	.0000	1	Bacon's
0.0105	20.2	.0000	1	Bahawalpur
0.0105	20.2	.0000	1	Balanchine's
0.0105	20.2	.0000	1	balata
0.0105	20.2	.0000	1	Balder's
0.0105	20.2	.0000	1	Balkh
0.0105	20.2	.0000	1	Ballets
0.0105	20.2	.0000	1	ballistas
0.0105	20.2	.0000	1	balloon-tire
0.0105	20.2	.0000	1	Baluchistan
0.0105	20.2	.0000	1	Balzac's
0.0105	20.2	.0000	1	Bambara-Maninka
0.0105	20.2	.0000	1	Bampton
0.0105	20.2	.0000	1	bane
0.0105	20.2	.0000	1	banks'
0.0105	20.2	.0000	1	Bao
0.0105	20.2	.0000	1	baobab
0.0105	20.2	.0000	1	barbican
0.0105	20.2	.0000	1	barbtailed
0.0105	20.2	.0000	1	barge's
0.0105	20.2	.0000	1	Barnave
0.0105	20.2	.0000	1	baroness
0.0105	20.2	.0000	1	barrios
0.0105	20.2	.0000	1	Barro
0.0105	20.2	.0000	1	Barulas
0.0105	20.2	.0000	1	Barwalde
0.0105	20.2	.0000	1	basslike
0.0105	20.2	.0000	1	bat-eared
0.0105	20.2	.0000	1	batterylike
0.0105	20.2	.0000	1	bauble
0.0105	20.2	.0000	1	Baudelaire
0.0105	20.2	.0000	1	bay-breasted
0.0105	20.2	.0000	1	Bayliss
0.0105	20.2	.0000	1	bean-root
0.0105	20.2	.0000	1	bear-berry
0.0105	20.2	.0000	1	Bearers
0.0105	20.2	.0000	1	Beauchamps
0.0105	20.2	.0000	1	Bedarieux
0.0105	20.2	.0000	1	Bedouins
0.0105	20.2	.0000	1	beers
0.0105	20.2	.0000	1	beetle-browed
0.0105	20.2	.0000	1	beetling
0.0105	20.2	.0000	1	behaviorally
0.0105	20.2	.0000	1	beheadings
0.0105	20.2	.0000	1	belatedly
0.0105	20.2	.0000	1	Belgaum
0.0105	20.2	.0000	1	beltlike
0.0105	20.2	.0000	1	bembecids
0.0105	20.2	.0000	1	Bembex
THE PRECEDING WORD TYPE OCCUPIES RANK 78200				
0.0105	20.2	.0000	1	BEMS
0.0105	20.2	.0000	1	Benavente
0.0105	20.2	.0000	1	beneficiary
0.0105	20.2	.0000	1	Benet
0.0105	20.2	.0000	1	bent-kneed
0.0105	20.2	.0000	1	Bentham's
0.0105	20.2	.0000	1	benzene
0.0105	20.2	.0000	1	bequeath
0.0105	20.2	.0000	1	Berain
0.0105	20.2	.0000	1	beri-beri
0.0105	20.2	.0000	1	berrypickers
0.0105	20.2	.0000	1	Beslic
0.0105	20.2	.0000	1	best-informed
0.0105	20.2	.0000	1	best-prepared
0.0105	20.2	.0000	1	bestiary
0.0105	20.2	.0000	1	Betrothed
0.0105	20.2	.0000	1	bewilderingly
0.0105	20.2	.0000	1	bewitching
0.0105	20.2	.0000	1	bible
0.0105	20.2	.0000	1	bichir
0.0105	20.2	.0000	1	bichirs
0.0105	20.2	.0000	1	Bickell
0.0105	20.2	.0000	1	biennially
0.0105	20.2	.0000	1	biennials
0.0105	20.2	.0000	1	bighorn
0.0105	20.2	.0000	1	Bilskilnir
0.0105	20.2	.0000	1	bioastronautics
0.0105	20.2	.0000	1	bioengineer
0.0105	20.2	.0000	1	Biological
0.0105	20.2	.0000	1	biologically
0.0105	20.2	.0000	1	biome
0.0105	20.2	.0000	1	biomes
0.0105	20.2	.0000	1	biophysicists
0.0105	20.2	.0000	1	bird-borne
0.0105	20.2	.0000	1	bird-hunting
0.0105	20.2	.0000	1	birdbander
0.0105	20.2	.0000	1	birdlife
0.0105	20.2	.0000	1	Birth
0.0105	20.2	.0000	1	Birthplace
0.0105	20.2	.0000	1	bishoprics
0.0105	20.2	.0000	1	Bizerte
0.0105	20.2	.0000	1	black-necked
0.0105	20.2	.0000	1	bladders
0.0105	20.2	.0000	1	bladderwort's
0.0105	20.2	.0000	1	Bleek
0.0105	20.2	.0000	1	blenny
0.0105	20.2	.0000	1	blindfolds
0.0105	20.2	.0000	1	Blitzkrieg
0.0105	20.2	.0000	1	block-signal
0.0105	20.2	.0000	1	blood-group
0.0105	20.2	.0000	1	bloodless
0.0105	20.2	.0000	1	bloodlines
0.0105	20.2	.0000	1	Bloomfield's
0.0105	20.2	.0000	1	blowflies
0.0105	20.2	.0000	1	blowouts
0.0105	20.2	.0000	1	blue-domed
0.0105	20.2	.0000	1	blue-red
0.0105	20.2	.0000	1	bluefish
0.0105	20.2	.0000	1	bluish-green
0.0105	20.2	.0000	1	boas
0.0105	20.2	.0000	1	Boccaccio's
0.0105	20.2	.0000	1	body-nourishing
0.0105	20.2	.0000	1	Bogislav
0.0105	20.2	.0000	1	Bohol
0.0105	20.2	.0000	1	boids
0.0105	20.2	.0000	1	Boito
0.0105	20.2	.0000	1	bombard
0.0105	20.2	.0000	1	bombsight
0.0105	20.2	.0000	1	Bonapartists
0.0105	20.2	.0000	1	bone-chilling
0.0105	20.2	.0000	1	bone-dry
0.0105	20.2	.0000	1	book-loving
0.0105	20.2	.0000	1	Bookshelf
0.0105	20.2	.0000	1	Borba
0.0105	20.2	.0000	1	Bordes
0.0105	20.2	.0000	1	boreal
0.0105	20.2	.0000	1	borehole
0.0105	20.2	.0000	1	boreholes
0.0105	20.2	.0000	1	boresomely
0.0105	20.2	.0000	1	Bosanquet
0.0105	20.2	.0000	1	Bosnia-Hercegovina
0.0105	20.2	.0000	1	boss'
0.0105	20.2	.0000	1	Botanic
0.0105	20.2	.0000	1	Botanical
0.0105	20.2	.0000	1	bottomland
0.0105	20.2	.0000	1	Boudry
0.0105	20.2	.0000	1	Bouguereau
0.0105	20.2	.0000	1	Boulanger
0.0105	20.2	.0000	1	boulder's
0.0105	20.2	.0000	1	Boulton
0.0105	20.2	.0000	1	Bovary
0.0105	20.2	.0000	1	Bovidae
0.0105	20.2	.0000	1	bow-sprit
0.0105	20.2	.0000	1	Boxwood
0.0105	20.2	.0000	1	Boydell's
0.0105	20.2	.0000	1	brakemen
0.0105	20.2	.0000	1	Bravery
0.0105	20.2	.0000	1	brawny
0.0105	20.2	.0000	1	breakthroughs
0.0105	20.2	.0000	1	breccia
THE PRECEDING WORD TYPE OCCUPIES RANK 78300				
0.0105	20.2	.0000	1	breeder
0.0105	20.2	.0000	1	Breeding
0.0105	20.2	.0000	1	Brenner
0.0105	20.2	.0000	1	Breton-speaking
0.0105	20.2	.0000	1	Bretons
0.0105	20.2	.0000	1	Bretton
0.0105	20.2	.0000	1	brevetted
0.0105	20.2	.0000	1	Brevoortia
0.0105	20.2	.0000	1	Briand

U	SFI	D	F	Word Type
0.0105	20.2	.0000	1	Bridalveil
0.0105	20.2	.0000	1	Brieux
0.0105	20.2	.0000	1	brigand-warrior
0.0105	20.2	.0000	1	bright-winged
0.0105	20.2	.0000	1	brindle-colored
0.0105	20.2	.0000	1	brinks
0.0105	20.2	.0000	1	Brittany's
0.0105	20.2	.0000	1	broad-gauge
0.0105	20.2	.0000	1	broadhorn
0.0105	20.2	.0000	1	bromeliads
0.0105	20.2	.0000	1	bronchoscope
0.0105	20.2	.0000	1	Bronislaw
0.0105	20.2	.0000	1	Bronk
0.0105	20.2	.0000	1	brotherhoods
0.0105	20.2	.0000	1	browsers
0.0105	20.2	.0000	1	brushstroke
0.0105	20.2	.0000	1	brushwork
0.0105	20.2	.0000	1	budgereegahs
0.0105	20.2	.0000	1	budgerigar
0.0105	20.2	.0000	1	budworm
0.0105	20.2	.0000	1	buffaloe
0.0105	20.2	.0000	1	buffbreasted
0.0105	20.2	.0000	1	Buffon's
0.0105	20.2	.0000	1	Bufo
0.0105	20.2	.0000	1	Buford
0.0105	20.2	.0000	1	bug-eyed
0.0105	20.2	.0000	1	Bukidnon
0.0105	20.2	.0000	1	Bulan
0.0105	20.2	.0000	1	bulblike
0.0105	20.2	.0000	1	Bulgars
0.0105	20.2	.0000	1	bulkiest
0.0105	20.2	.0000	1	Buna
0.0105	20.2	.0000	1	Bundi
0.0105	20.2	.0000	1	Bundy
0.0105	20.2	.0000	1	Bungay
0.0105	20.2	.0000	1	burgomaster
0.0105	20.2	.0000	1	Burgundians
0.0105	20.2	.0000	1	burnsides
0.0105	20.2	.0000	1	bushmasters
0.0105	20.2	.0000	1	Busoni
0.0105	20.2	.0000	1	butting
0.0105	20.2	.0000	1	button-pushing
0.0105	20.2	.0000	1	Buxaceae
0.0105	20.2	.0000	1	Buxus
0.0105	20.2	.0000	1	bytownite
0.0105	20.2	.0000	1	C-OH
0.0105	20.2	.0000	1	C'lina
0.0105	20.2	.0000	1	CaF2
0.0105	20.2	.0000	1	caama
0.0105	20.2	.0000	1	Caballo
0.0105	20.2	.0000	1	Cabanel
0.0105	20.2	.0000	1	cabooses
0.0105	20.2	.0000	1	cactuslike
0.0105	20.2	.0000	1	caecilians
0.0105	20.2	.0000	1	Caedmon's
0.0105	20.2	.0000	1	caffra
0.0105	20.2	.0000	1	Cajamarca
0.0105	20.2	.0000	1	Cakste
0.0105	20.2	.0000	1	Calaveras
0.0105	20.2	.0000	1	calcic
0.0105	20.2	.0000	1	Californium
0.0105	20.2	.0000	1	Caltech's
0.0105	20.2	.0000	1	Calton
0.0105	20.2	.0000	1	Calvinistic
0.0105	20.2	.0000	1	Camargo
0.0105	20.2	.0000	1	Cambrai
0.0105	20.2	.0000	1	Cameroon
0.0105	20.2	.0000	1	Camillo
0.0105	20.2	.0000	1	camouflages
0.0105	20.2	.0000	1	Campaign
0.0105	20.2	.0000	1	Campania
0.0105	20.2	.0000	1	Canal's
0.0105	20.2	.0000	1	canalization
0.0105	20.2	.0000	1	cancerous
0.0105	20.2	.0000	1	Cancionero
0.0105	20.2	.0000	1	candiru
0.0105	20.2	.0000	1	Cane
0.0105	20.2	.0000	1	canebrakes
0.0105	20.2	.0000	1	Cannae
0.0105	20.2	.0000	1	Canons
0.0105	20.2	.0000	1	cantcher
0.0105	20.2	.0000	1	Canticles
0.0105	20.2	.0000	1	canvassed
0.0105	20.2	.0000	1	Capet
0.0105	20.2	.0000	1	capitalizes
0.0105	20.2	.0000	1	capitulation
0.0105	20.2	.0000	1	capping
0.0105	20.2	.0000	1	capriciousness
0.0105	20.2	.0000	1	Captiva
0.0105	20.2	.0000	1	Capture
0.0105	20.2	.0000	1	capybara

THE PRECEDING WORD TYPE OCCUPIES RANK 78400

U	SFI	D	F	Word Type
0.0105	20.2	.0000	1	capybaras
0.0105	20.2	.0000	1	Caravaggio
0.0105	20.2	.0000	1	Carbon
0.0105	20.2	.0000	1	carbonic-acid
0.0105	20.2	.0000	1	carbonized
0.0105	20.2	.0000	1	carbonol
0.0105	20.2	.0000	1	cardiovascular
0.0105	20.2	.0000	1	Cardorna
0.0105	20.2	.0000	1	care-free
0.0105	20.2	.0000	1	careyeros
0.0105	20.2	.0000	1	Carloman
0.0105	20.2	.0000	1	Carlyle's
0.0105	20.2	.0000	1	Carmina
0.0105	20.2	.0000	1	carnauba
0.0105	20.2	.0000	1	Carnot
0.0105	20.2	.0000	1	Carolingian
0.0105	20.2	.0000	1	Carraccis
0.0105	20.2	.0000	1	Carre
0.0105	20.2	.0000	1	Carthusian
0.0105	20.2	.0000	1	caryatid
0.0105	20.2	.0000	1	Casilinum
0.0105	20.2	.0000	1	casing-stones
0.0105	20.2	.0000	1	cassowaries
0.0105	20.2	.0000	1	castrum
0.0105	20.2	.0000	1	catabolism

U	SFI	D	F	Word Type
0.0105	20.2	.0000	1	cataclysmic
0.0105	20.2	.0000	1	Catapult
0.0105	20.2	.0000	1	cataracts
0.0105	20.2	.0000	1	Catcher
0.0105	20.2	.0000	1	catechism
0.0105	20.2	.0000	1	catheter's
0.0105	20.2	.0000	1	Catholepistemiad
0.0105	20.2	.0000	1	Catholican
0.0105	20.2	.0000	1	Catholicizing
0.0105	20.2	.0000	1	catolicos
0.0105	20.2	.0000	1	catus
0.0105	20.2	.0000	1	causal
0.0105	20.2	.0000	1	Cavalcanti
0.0105	20.2	.0000	1	cave-bear
0.0105	20.2	.0000	1	Cavitation
0.0105	20.2	.0000	1	Caxias
0.0105	20.2	.0000	1	Ceara
0.0105	20.2	.0000	1	Cedars
0.0105	20.2	.0000	1	Celestina
0.0105	20.2	.0000	1	Cellach
0.0105	20.2	.0000	1	Censorship
0.0105	20.2	.0000	1	censured
0.0105	20.2	.0000	1	centralization
0.0105	20.2	.0000	1	centres
0.0105	20.2	.0000	1	centrioles
0.0105	20.2	.0000	1	cerements
0.0105	20.2	.0000	1	ceremonially
0.0105	20.2	.0000	1	cesium
0.0105	20.2	.0000	1	chaffinch
0.0105	20.2	.0000	1	Chagatai
0.0105	20.2	.0000	1	Challoner
0.0105	20.2	.0000	1	Chalons-sur-Marne
0.0105	20.2	.0000	1	Chambal
0.0105	20.2	.0000	1	Chamonix
0.0105	20.2	.0000	1	Champion's
0.0105	20.2	.0000	1	chancy
0.0105	20.2	.0000	1	changeover
0.0105	20.2	.0000	1	Channing
0.0105	20.2	.0000	1	characin
0.0105	20.2	.0000	1	characins
0.0105	20.2	.0000	1	chariot's
0.0105	20.2	.0000	1	Charleston's
0.0105	20.2	.0000	1	charterers
0.0105	20.2	.0000	1	check-ups
0.0105	20.2	.0000	1	check-writing
0.0105	20.2	.0000	1	Cheselden
0.0105	20.2	.0000	1	chiaro
0.0105	20.2	.0000	1	chiaroscuro
0.0105	20.2	.0000	1	Chiba
0.0105	20.2	.0000	1	Chichen
0.0105	20.2	.0000	1	chickarees
0.0105	20.2	.0000	1	Chickasaws
0.0105	20.2	.0000	1	Chin
0.0105	20.2	.0000	1	Chinese-Japanese
0.0105	20.2	.0000	1	chive
0.0105	20.2	.0000	1	Chlodwig
0.0105	20.2	.0000	1	Choctaws
0.0105	20.2	.0000	1	chokecherry
0.0105	20.2	.0000	1	cholesterol
0.0105	20.2	.0000	1	chomping
0.0105	20.2	.0000	1	choosiness
0.0105	20.2	.0000	1	choreodrame
0.0105	20.2	.0000	1	chorister
0.0105	20.2	.0000	1	Christianized
0.0105	20.2	.0000	1	Christianizing
0.0105	20.2	.0000	1	Chrysostom
0.0105	20.2	.0000	1	cichlid
0.0105	20.2	.0000	1	Cichlidae
0.0105	20.2	.0000	1	cichlids
0.0105	20.2	.0000	1	Cid
0.0105	20.2	.0000	1	cinnamic
0.0105	20.2	.0000	1	CIO**
0.0105	20.2	.0000	1	circularly
0.0105	20.2	.0000	1	circulars
0.0105	20.2	.0000	1	circumvent

THE PRECEDING WORD TYPE OCCUPIES RANK 78500

U	SFI	D	F	Word Type
0.0105	20.2	.0000	1	cis
0.0105	20.2	.0000	1	Cithaeron
0.0105	20.2	.0000	1	Citizen
0.0105	20.2	.0000	1	Citizenship
0.0105	20.2	.0000	1	city-sized
0.0105	20.2	.0000	1	city-suburbs
0.0105	20.2	.0000	1	civitas
0.0105	20.2	.0000	1	clairvoyance
0.0105	20.2	.0000	1	clapboards
0.0105	20.2	.0000	1	Class-J
0.0105	20.2	.0000	1	classicists
0.0105	20.2	.0000	1	Claudian
0.0105	20.2	.0000	1	Clause
0.0105	20.2	.0000	1	clear-minded
0.0105	20.2	.0000	1	clefts
0.0105	20.2	.0000	1	cleric
0.0105	20.2	.0000	1	clerked
0.0105	20.2	.0000	1	Clerks
0.0105	20.2	.0000	1	Clermont-Ferrand
0.0105	20.2	.0000	1	clients'
0.0105	20.2	.0000	1	climatologists
0.0105	20.2	.0000	1	clingfish
0.0105	20.2	.0000	1	clock-wise
0.0105	20.2	.0000	1	cloisonne
0.0105	20.2	.0000	1	closable
0.0105	20.2	.0000	1	close-fitting
0.0105	20.2	.0000	1	close-grained
0.0105	20.2	.0000	1	closed-canopy
0.0105	20.2	.0000	1	Cloth
0.0105	20.2	.0000	1	Clouds
0.0105	20.2	.0000	1	cloverleafs
0.0105	20.2	.0000	1	clumsiest
0.0105	20.2	.0000	1	Cluniac
0.0105	20.2	.0000	1	Clupeiformes
0.0105	20.2	.0000	1	co-ordinated
0.0105	20.2	.0000	1	coadjutor
0.0105	20.2	.0000	1	coagulated
0.0105	20.2	.0000	1	coagulation
0.0105	20.2	.0000	1	coal-mine
0.0105	20.2	.0000	1	coalesced
0.0105	20.2	.0000	1	coamings

U	SFI	D	F	Word Type
0.0105	20.2	.0000	1	coaxial
0.0105	20.2	.0000	1	cobble-stones
0.0105	20.2	.0000	1	cobra-injected
0.0105	20.2	.0000	1	cocaine
0.0105	20.2	.0000	1	Cockcroft
0.0105	20.2	.0000	1	cockscomb
0.0105	20.2	.0000	1	codesigner
0.0105	20.2	.0000	1	coexistence
0.0105	20.2	.0000	1	coffee-house
0.0105	20.2	.0000	1	Cogniet
0.0105	20.2	.0000	1	Cohen's
0.0105	20.2	.0000	1	cohune
0.0105	20.2	.0000	1	Coimbra
0.0105	20.2	.0000	1	cold-bloodedness
0.0105	20.2	.0000	1	cold-hearted
0.0105	20.2	.0000	1	Colet
0.0105	20.2	.0000	1	Colin
0.0105	20.2	.0000	1	Collage
0.0105	20.2	.0000	1	collated
0.0105	20.2	.0000	1	collateral
0.0105	20.2	.0000	1	Collected
0.0105	20.2	.0000	1	Collection
0.0105	20.2	.0000	1	collectivized
0.0105	20.2	.0000	1	colloidal
0.0105	20.2	.0000	1	Colonus
0.0105	20.2	.0000	1	COLOR
0.0105	20.2	.0000	1	colourless
0.0105	20.2	.0000	1	combatted
0.0105	20.2	.0000	1	comique
0.0105	20.2	.0000	1	Comique
0.0105	20.2	.0000	1	Commedia
0.0105	20.2	.0000	1	commensurate
0.0105	20.2	.0000	1	Commission's
0.0105	20.2	.0000	1	commonly-rooted
0.0105	20.2	.0000	1	Commune
0.0105	20.2	.0000	1	Communist-dominated
0.0105	20.2	.0000	1	comparativist
0.0105	20.2	.0000	1	compartmentizer
0.0105	20.2	.0000	1	Compass
0.0105	20.2	.0000	1	competes
0.0105	20.2	.0000	1	complicates
0.0105	20.2	.0000	1	complicating
0.0105	20.2	.0000	1	Compostela
0.0105	20.2	.0000	1	Compton
0.0105	20.2	.0000	1	Comte
0.0105	20.2	.0000	1	conceivable
0.0105	20.2	.0000	1	conceiving
0.0105	20.2	.0000	1	Concerning
0.0105	20.2	.0000	1	Conchos
0.0105	20.2	.0000	1	conciseness
0.0105	20.2	.0000	1	Conclusions
0.0105	20.2	.0000	1	condominium
0.0105	20.2	.0000	1	Conduct
0.0105	20.2	.0000	1	confectioners
0.0105	20.2	.0000	1	Conferences
0.0105	20.2	.0000	1	confiscation
0.0105	20.2	.0000	1	Confraternity
0.0105	20.2	.0000	1	congeal
0.0105	20.2	.0000	1	congenially

THE PRECEDING WORD TYPE OCCUPIES RANK 78600

U	SFI	D	F	Word Type
0.0105	20.2	.0000	1	congregating
0.0105	20.2	.0000	1	Conies
0.0105	20.2	.0000	1	conjectures
0.0105	20.2	.0000	1	connoting
0.0105	20.2	.0000	1	consecrator
0.0105	20.2	.0000	1	Conservancy
0.0105	20.2	.0000	1	CONSERVATIVE
0.0105	20.2	.0000	1	conservatively
0.0105	20.2	.0000	1	Constantinos
0.0105	20.2	.0000	1	Constituent
0.0105	20.2	.0000	1	constituting
0.0105	20.2	.0000	1	constraints
0.0105	20.2	.0000	1	constricts
0.0105	20.2	.0000	1	constructivists
0.0105	20.2	.0000	1	Consultation
0.0105	20.2	.0000	1	Consumer
0.0105	20.2	.0000	1	continent-sized
0.0105	20.2	.0000	1	continentals
0.0105	20.2	.0000	1	continuations
0.0105	20.2	.0000	1	continuous-tone
0.0105	20.2	.0000	1	Contract
0.0105	20.2	.0000	1	Contracting
0.0105	20.2	.0000	1	contrariness
0.0105	20.2	.0000	1	contributor
0.0105	20.2	.0000	1	convertibility
0.0105	20.2	.0000	1	convoke
0.0105	20.2	.0000	1	convoking
0.0105	20.2	.0000	1	convoluted
0.0105	20.2	.0000	1	convolutions
0.0105	20.2	.0000	1	convoys
0.0105	20.2	.0000	1	Cooch's
0.0105	20.2	.0000	1	coolers
0.0105	20.2	.0000	1	cooters
0.0105	20.2	.0000	1	copal-burning
0.0105	20.2	.0000	1	Copenhagen's
0.0105	20.2	.0000	1	Coplas
0.0105	20.2	.0000	1	Coppelia
0.0105	20.2	.0000	1	Copts
0.0105	20.2	.0000	1	copulation
0.0105	20.2	.0000	1	copulatory
0.0105	20.2	.0000	1	coral-snake
0.0105	20.2	.0000	1	Coralli
0.0105	20.2	.0000	1	coralreef
0.0105	20.2	.0000	1	Corelli
0.0105	20.2	.0000	1	corkscrews
0.0105	20.2	.0000	1	Corliss
0.0105	20.2	.0000	1	corn-husking
0.0105	20.2	.0000	1	Corneille
0.0105	20.2	.0000	1	cornucopian
0.0105	20.2	.0000	1	Corporations
0.0105	20.2	.0000	1	corpuscular
0.0105	20.2	.0000	1	Correction
0.0105	20.2	.0000	1	correlates
0.0105	20.2	.0000	1	Correspondenz
0.0105	20.2	.0000	1	Corsite
0.0105	20.2	.0000	1	corsite
0.0105	20.2	.0000	1	cortical

U	SFI	D	F	Word Type
0.0105	20.2	.0000	1	Corumba
0.0105	20.2	.0000	1	Corunna
0.0105	20.2	.0000	1	costumed
0.0105	20.2	.0000	1	COT
0.0105	20.2	.0000	1	Cota
0.0105	20.2	.0000	1	COTA
0.0105	20.2	.0000	1	Cote
0.0105	20.2	.0000	1	Cotopaxi
0.0105	20.2	.0000	1	cotta
0.0105	20.2	.0000	1	cottonlike
0.0105	20.2	.0000	1	Coughlin
0.0105	20.2	.0000	1	Coulomb's
0.0105	20.2	.0000	1	counsel-less
0.0105	20.2	.0000	1	counteracting
0.0105	20.2	.0000	1	counterbalancing
0.0105	20.2	.0000	1	counterpoise
0.0105	20.2	.0000	1	counterpull
0.0105	20.2	.0000	1	Cournand
0.0105	20.2	.0000	1	cow-crazy
0.0105	20.2	.0000	1	cow-shaped
0.0105	20.2	.0000	1	cowries
0.0105	20.2	.0000	1	cradling
0.0105	20.2	.0000	1	craftmanship
0.0105	20.2	.0000	1	craig
0.0105	20.2	.0000	1	Craig's
0.0105	20.2	.0000	1	cramping
0.0105	20.2	.0000	1	cramplike
0.0105	20.2	.0000	1	Cranmer
0.0105	20.2	.0000	1	cratered
0.0105	20.2	.0000	1	Crawshaw's
0.0105	20.2	.0000	1	cream-thick
0.0105	20.2	.0000	1	creativeness
0.0105	20.2	.0000	1	creaturarum
0.0105	20.2	.0000	1	Creatures
0.0105	20.2	.0000	1	credence
0.0105	20.2	.0000	1	creditor
0.0105	20.2	.0000	1	Creole
0.0105	20.2	.0000	1	cretin
0.0105	20.2	.0000	1	criss-crossed
0.0105	20.2	.0000	1	Crisscross
0.0105	20.2	.0000	1	cristobalite
0.0105	20.2	.0000	1	criterion
0.0105	20.2	.0000	1	CroMagnon

THE PRECEDING WORD TYPE OCCUPIES RANK 78700

U	SFI	D	F	Word Type
0.0105	20.2	.0000	1	crocks
0.0105	20.2	.0000	1	crocus
0.0105	20.2	.0000	1	crofter
0.0105	20.2	.0000	1	Cronje
0.0105	20.2	.0000	1	cross-channel
0.0105	20.2	.0000	1	cross-referenced
0.0105	20.2	.0000	1	crossbills
0.0105	20.2	.0000	1	crossbreeding
0.0105	20.2	.0000	1	crossfire
0.0105	20.2	.0000	1	Crotalus
0.0105	20.2	.0000	1	crude-oil
0.0105	20.2	.0000	1	crudities
0.0105	20.2	.0000	1	crumblike
0.0105	20.2	.0000	1	crustacea
0.0105	20.2	.0000	1	cryogenicist
0.0105	20.2	.0000	1	cryologist
0.0105	20.2	.0000	1	cryptic
0.0105	20.2	.0000	1	crystallizes
0.0105	20.2	.0000	1	crystallizing
0.0105	20.2	.0000	1	Ctesibius
0.0105	20.2	.0000	1	cubical
0.0105	20.2	.0000	1	cubism
0.0105	20.2	.0000	1	Cugnot
0.0105	20.2	.0000	1	Cugnot's
0.0105	20.2	.0000	1	Culdee
0.0105	20.2	.0000	1	culled
0.0105	20.2	.0000	1	Culp's
0.0105	20.2	.0000	1	Cunha
0.0105	20.2	.0000	1	curriculums
0.0105	20.2	.0000	1	cut-stone
0.0105	20.2	.0000	1	cyan
0.0105	20.2	.0000	1	cycadeoids
0.0105	20.2	.0000	1	cycads
0.0105	20.2	.0000	1	cyclical
0.0105	20.2	.0000	1	cyclopropane
0.0105	20.2	.0000	1	cynic
0.0105	20.2	.0000	1	cypreth
0.0105	20.2	.0000	1	cyprome
0.0105	20.2	.0000	1	cytoplasm's
0.0105	20.2	.0000	1	C2H2**
0.0105	20.2	.0000	1	C2H4Cl2**
0.0105	20.2	.0000	1	C2H5
0.0105	20.2	.0000	1	C2H5OH
0.0105	20.2	.0000	1	C2H6
0.0105	20.2	.0000	1	d'Annunzio
0.0105	20.2	.0000	1	d'Armes
0.0105	20.2	.0000	1	d'action
0.0105	20.2	.0000	1	daggerlike
0.0105	20.2	.0000	1	Dahshur
0.0105	20.2	.0000	1	daks
0.0105	20.2	.0000	1	Damaged
0.0105	20.2	.0000	1	Damnable
0.0105	20.2	.0000	1	damselfly
0.0105	20.2	.0000	1	Danegeld
0.0105	20.2	.0000	1	Danish-Americans
0.0105	20.2	.0000	1	Darcy's
0.0105	20.2	.0000	1	Darien
0.0105	20.2	.0000	1	dart-hurling
0.0105	20.2	.0000	1	Dart's
0.0105	20.2	.0000	1	darters
0.0105	20.2	.0000	1	dashboards
0.0105	20.2	.0000	1	Datis
0.0105	20.2	.0000	1	Davidson
0.0105	20.2	.0000	1	Davies
0.0105	20.2	.0000	1	Davis'
0.0105	20.2	.0000	1	Davisson
0.0105	20.2	.0000	1	deAlvarado
0.0105	20.2	.0000	1	deBalboa
0.0105	20.2	.0000	1	deBalzac
0.0105	20.2	.0000	1	deBeauregard
0.0105	20.2	.0000	1	deBenserade
0.0105	20.2	.0000	1	deClavijo
0.0105	20.2	.0000	1	deCorbeil

U	SFI	D	F	Word Type
0.0105	20.2	.0000	1	deCordoba
0.0105	20.2	.0000	1	deCoulomb
0.0105	20.2	.0000	1	DeForest
0.0105	20.2	.0000	1	deFrederic
0.0105	20.2	.0000	1	deGasperi
0.0105	20.2	.0000	1	deGasperi's
0.0105	20.2	.0000	1	DeKay's
0.0105	20.2	.0000	1	deLaFontaine
0.0105	20.2	.0000	1	deLaplace
0.0105	20.2	.0000	1	deLegaspi
0.0105	20.2	.0000	1	deLisle
0.0105	20.2	.0000	1	deMendoza
0.0105	20.2	.0000	1	deMindanao
0.0105	20.2	.0000	1	deMonte
0.0105	20.2	.0000	1	deMontejo
0.0105	20.2	.0000	1	deMusique
0.0105	20.2	.0000	1	dePerthes
0.0105	20.2	.0000	1	deRojas
0.0105	20.2	.0000	1	deSaint-Exupery
0.0105	20.2	.0000	1	deSanMartin
0.0105	20.2	.0000	1	DeSaussure
0.0105	20.2	.0000	1	deUlua
0.0105	20.2	.0000	1	deUrsua
0.0105	20.2	.0000	1	deactivated
0.0105	20.2	.0000	1	dead-air
0.0105	20.2	.0000	1	debt-free
0.0105	20.2	.0000	1	debunked
THE PRECEDING WORD TYPE OCCUPIES RANK 78800				
0.0105	20.2	.0000	1	Debye
0.0105	20.2	.0000	1	decalogue
0.0105	20.2	.0000	1	Decatur
0.0105	20.2	.0000	1	Deccan
0.0105	20.2	.0000	1	deceased's
0.0105	20.2	.0000	1	decentralization
0.0105	20.2	.0000	1	decimate
0.0105	20.2	.0000	1	decimators
0.0105	20.2	.0000	1	Decmocratic-Republican
0.0105	20.2	.0000	1	decorates
0.0105	20.2	.0000	1	Decoration
0.0105	20.2	.0000	1	deductive
0.0105	20.2	.0000	1	deep-bodied
0.0105	20.2	.0000	1	deep-frozen
0.0105	20.2	.0000	1	deepsea
0.0105	20.2	.0000	1	defecates
0.0105	20.2	.0000	1	defecation
0.0105	20.2	.0000	1	defensible
0.0105	20.2	.0000	1	defoliation
0.0105	20.2	.0000	1	defrosters
0.0105	20.2	.0000	1	degenerative
0.0105	20.2	.0000	1	del-norte
0.0105	20.2	.0000	1	Delmar
0.0105	20.2	.0000	1	deltaic
0.0105	20.2	.0000	1	deltoids
0.0105	20.2	.0000	1	Democratic-Republican
0.0105	20.2	.0000	1	Dendrobates
0.0105	20.2	.0000	1	densest
0.0105	20.2	.0000	1	denticles
0.0105	20.2	.0000	1	dentures
0.0105	20.2	.0000	1	denudation
0.0105	20.2	.0000	1	departmental
0.0105	20.2	.0000	1	depletion
0.0105	20.2	.0000	1	depopulated
0.0105	20.2	.0000	1	depose
0.0105	20.2	.0000	1	depredations
0.0105	20.2	.0000	1	Derain
0.0105	20.2	.0000	1	Descamisados
0.0105	20.2	.0000	1	desecration
0.0105	20.2	.0000	1	Deserved
0.0105	20.2	.0000	1	desiccation
0.0105	20.2	.0000	1	Desiderius
0.0105	20.2	.0000	1	desoxyribonucleic
0.0105	20.2	.0000	1	despot
0.0105	20.2	.0000	1	despotic
0.0105	20.2	.0000	1	Dessalines
0.0105	20.2	.0000	1	Detached
0.0105	20.2	.0000	1	deteriorates
0.0105	20.2	.0000	1	determinant
0.0105	20.2	.0000	1	determinism
0.0105	20.2	.0000	1	deterred
0.0105	20.2	.0000	1	Detlev
0.0105	20.2	.0000	1	detonating
0.0105	20.2	.0000	1	Detrick
0.0105	20.2	.0000	1	Deum
0.0105	20.2	.0000	1	Deut
0.0105	20.2	.0000	1	dharma
0.0105	20.2	.0000	1	diCavour
0.0105	20.2	.0000	1	diTallano
0.0105	20.2	.0000	1	diagnosticians
0.0105	20.2	.0000	1	Dial
0.0105	20.2	.0000	1	dialectics
0.0105	20.2	.0000	1	dialectology
0.0105	20.2	.0000	1	Dialogues
0.0105	20.2	.0000	1	diamond-shaped
0.0105	20.2	.0000	1	diaries
0.0105	20.2	.0000	1	diarist
0.0105	20.2	.0000	1	diarium
0.0105	20.2	.0000	1	diatomic
0.0105	20.2	.0000	1	dichloride
0.0105	20.2	.0000	1	dichromate
0.0105	20.2	.0000	1	dicta
0.0105	20.2	.0000	1	Didelphidae
0.0105	20.2	.0000	1	die-casting
0.0105	20.2	.0000	1	Diet
0.0105	20.2	.0000	1	diffusionists
0.0105	20.2	.0000	1	dilettantes
0.0105	20.2	.0000	1	diminishes
0.0105	20.2	.0000	1	Dingwall
0.0105	20.2	.0000	1	diodes
0.0105	20.2	.0000	1	diplomas
0.0105	20.2	.0000	1	Diptera
0.0105	20.2	.0000	1	direct-dialing
0.0105	20.2	.0000	1	disability-insurance
0.0105	20.2	.0000	1	disarranged
0.0105	20.2	.0000	1	disconcertingly
0.0105	20.2	.0000	1	disconnects
0.0105	20.2	.0000	1	Discontinuity
0.0105	20.2	.0000	1	discounted
0.0105	20.2	.0000	1	Discourse
0.0105	20.2	.0000	1	discrepancy
0.0105	20.2	.0000	1	discriminating
0.0105	20.2	.0000	1	discriminatory
0.0105	20.2	.0000	1	disguising
0.0105	20.2	.0000	1	disinfectants
0.0105	20.2	.0000	1	disinterested
0.0105	20.2	.0000	1	dislocated
0.0105	20.2	.0000	1	dislodges
0.0105	20.2	.0000	1	dismember
0.0105	20.2	.0000	1	Disobedience
THE PRECEDING WORD TYPE OCCUPIES RANK 78900				
0.0105	20.2	.0000	1	disparagingly
0.0105	20.2	.0000	1	dispassionately
0.0105	20.2	.0000	1	disrupting
0.0105	20.2	.0000	1	disruptive
0.0105	20.2	.0000	1	dissatified
0.0105	20.2	.0000	1	dissects
0.0105	20.2	.0000	1	dissimilarities
0.0105	20.2	.0000	1	dissipates
0.0105	20.2	.0000	1	dissociate
0.0105	20.2	.0000	1	distensible
0.0105	20.2	.0000	1	districting
0.0105	20.2	.0000	1	diversify
0.0105	20.2	.0000	1	Divina
0.0105	20.2	.0000	1	Divinity
0.0105	20.2	.0000	1	divorcement
0.0105	20.2	.0000	1	doctor-to-be
0.0105	20.2	.0000	1	documenting
0.0105	20.2	.0000	1	Dodoma
0.0105	20.2	.0000	1	doers
0.0105	20.2	.0000	1	doke
0.0105	20.2	.0000	1	Doktor
0.0105	20.2	.0000	1	dollmaking
0.0105	20.2	.0000	1	Dolomites
0.0105	20.2	.0000	1	Dome
0.0105	20.2	.0000	1	dome-shelled
0.0105	20.2	.0000	1	Domenichino
0.0105	20.2	.0000	1	Dominicans
0.0105	20.2	.0000	1	domino
0.0105	20.2	.0000	1	Domitia
0.0105	20.2	.0000	1	Domitian's
0.0105	20.2	.0000	1	domus
0.0105	20.2	.0000	1	Donaldson's
0.0105	20.2	.0000	1	Donatello's
0.0105	20.2	.0000	1	Donatism
0.0105	20.2	.0000	1	Done
0.0105	20.2	.0000	1	Dongola
0.0105	20.2	.0000	1	Donne
0.0105	20.2	.0000	1	Dooley's
0.0105	20.2	.0000	1	Dositej
0.0105	20.2	.0000	1	double-acting
0.0105	20.2	.0000	1	double-bar
0.0105	20.2	.0000	1	double-crested
0.0105	20.2	.0000	1	doughy
0.0105	20.2	.0000	1	dowitchers
0.0105	20.2	.0000	1	downwards
0.0105	20.2	.0000	1	Doxiadis'
0.0105	20.2	.0000	1	dragline
0.0105	20.2	.0000	1	draglines
0.0105	20.2	.0000	1	Drapers'
0.0105	20.2	.0000	1	drawling
0.0105	20.2	.0000	1	Dreadful
0.0105	20.2	.0000	1	Dredges
0.0105	20.2	.0000	1	Drilling
0.0105	20.2	.0000	1	drizzling
0.0105	20.2	.0000	1	dropsy
0.0105	20.2	.0000	1	Drzic
0.0105	20.2	.0000	1	DuPage
0.0105	20.2	.0000	1	duPont
0.0105	20.2	.0000	1	dualism
0.0105	20.2	.0000	1	duality
0.0105	20.2	.0000	1	Dufay
0.0105	20.2	.0000	1	Dulawan
0.0105	20.2	.0000	1	Dumbbell
0.0105	20.2	.0000	1	Dunstaffnage
0.0105	20.2	.0000	1	duo-tones
0.0105	20.2	.0000	1	duotones
0.0105	20.2	.0000	1	duplication
0.0105	20.2	.0000	1	duplication-deficient
0.0105	20.2	.0000	1	duplications
0.0105	20.2	.0000	1	dux
0.0105	20.2	.0000	1	dwarfing
0.0105	20.2	.0000	1	dyings
0.0105	20.2	.0000	1	dysuria
0.0105	20.2	.0000	1	Eagle-Pass
0.0105	20.2	.0000	1	early-American
0.0105	20.2	.0000	1	earth-years
0.0105	20.2	.0000	1	easy-to-use
0.0105	20.2	.0000	1	echidna
0.0105	20.2	.0000	1	eddies
0.0105	20.2	.0000	1	Edenton
0.0105	20.2	.0000	1	Edgerton
0.0105	20.2	.0000	1	Edgeware
0.0105	20.2	.0000	1	editing
0.0105	20.2	.0000	1	Editions
0.0105	20.2	.0000	1	eerily
0.0105	20.2	.0000	1	EFFECT
0.0105	20.2	.0000	1	effusion
0.0105	20.2	.0000	1	Egbert
0.0105	20.2	.0000	1	egg-producing
0.0105	20.2	.0000	1	Egoist
0.0105	20.2	.0000	1	egotists
0.0105	20.2	.0000	1	egret
0.0105	20.2	.0000	1	ElAlamein
0.0105	20.2	.0000	1	ElDorado
0.0105	20.2	.0000	1	elasmobranchs
0.0105	20.2	.0000	1	elbow-rubbing
0.0105	20.2	.0000	1	elbowroom
0.0105	20.2	.0000	1	Electors
0.0105	20.2	.0000	1	electric-driven
0.0105	20.2	.0000	1	electric-shock
THE PRECEDING WORD TYPE OCCUPIES RANK 79000				
0.0105	20.2	.0000	1	Electromagnet
0.0105	20.2	.0000	1	electromotive
0.0105	20.2	.0000	1	electroplaxes
0.0105	20.2	.0000	1	electrostatic
0.0105	20.2	.0000	1	electrostatics
0.0105	20.2	.0000	1	Eleuthere
0.0105	20.2	.0000	1	elfin
0.0105	20.2	.0000	1	Elginbrod
0.0105	20.2	.0000	1	Elgon
0.0105	20.2	.0000	1	Elizur
0.0105	20.2	.0000	1	ellipsoidal
0.0105	20.2	.0000	1	elliptic
0.0105	20.2	.0000	1	elongate
0.0105	20.2	.0000	1	Elvey
0.0105	20.2	.0000	1	emaciation
0.0105	20.2	.0000	1	Emax**
0.0105	20.2	.0000	1	embassy
0.0105	20.2	.0000	1	embellishments
0.0105	20.2	.0000	1	embodying
0.0105	20.2	.0000	1	Embryophyta
0.0105	20.2	.0000	1	emigres
0.0105	20.2	.0000	1	eminences
0.0105	20.2	.0000	1	empowers
0.0105	20.2	.0000	1	empyema
0.0105	20.2	.0000	1	enameling
0.0105	20.2	.0000	1	enamelists
0.0105	20.2	.0000	1	encamp
0.0105	20.2	.0000	1	enchant
0.0105	20.2	.0000	1	encroachment
0.0105	20.2	.0000	1	endocrinology
0.0105	20.2	.0000	1	endorse
0.0105	20.2	.0000	1	endowing
0.0105	20.2	.0000	1	endures
0.0105	20.2	.0000	1	endwise
0.0105	20.2	.0000	1	enemas
0.0105	20.2	.0000	1	energy-laden
0.0105	20.2	.0000	1	enginemen
0.0105	20.2	.0000	1	English-style
0.0105	20.2	.0000	1	Engynes
0.0105	20.2	.0000	1	enhancement
0.0105	20.2	.0000	1	enlargements
0.0105	20.2	.0000	1	enlightening
0.0105	20.2	.0000	1	Enlightenment
0.0105	20.2	.0000	1	enormities
0.0105	20.2	.0000	1	enshrined
0.0105	20.2	.0000	1	enslavement
0.0105	20.2	.0000	1	enterpriser
0.0105	20.2	.0000	1	enthusiasts
0.0105	20.2	.0000	1	entraps
0.0105	20.2	.0000	1	envisaged
0.0105	20.2	.0000	1	envisions
0.0105	20.2	.0000	1	Ephraem
0.0105	20.2	.0000	1	epilepsy
0.0105	20.2	.0000	1	Episcopius
0.0105	20.2	.0000	1	epithalamium
0.0105	20.2	.0000	1	epitomize
0.0105	20.2	.0000	1	equally-spaced
0.0105	20.2	.0000	1	equate
0.0105	20.2	.0000	1	equitable
0.0105	20.2	.0000	1	eradicate
0.0105	20.2	.0000	1	Ercilla
0.0105	20.2	.0000	1	Erectheum
0.0105	20.2	.0000	1	erectness
0.0105	20.2	.0000	1	Erivan
0.0105	20.2	.0000	1	erring
0.0105	20.2	.0000	1	Erwin
0.0105	20.2	.0000	1	Essence
0.0105	20.2	.0000	1	ester
0.0105	20.2	.0000	1	estrangement
0.0105	20.2	.0000	1	etat
0.0105	20.2	.0000	1	etcher
0.0105	20.2	.0000	1	etches
0.0105	20.2	.0000	1	Eteocles
0.0105	20.2	.0000	1	Ethelred
0.0105	20.2	.0000	1	Ethelwulf
0.0105	20.2	.0000	1	ethers
0.0105	20.2	.0000	1	ethnographic
0.0105	20.2	.0000	1	Ethnological
0.0105	20.2	.0000	1	ethnologist
0.0105	20.2	.0000	1	Ethnology
0.0105	20.2	.0000	1	ethnology
0.0105	20.2	.0000	1	Ethylene
0.0105	20.2	.0000	1	Etruscan-Roman
0.0105	20.2	.0000	1	euchromatin
0.0105	20.2	.0000	1	Eumenides
0.0105	20.2	.0000	1	Eunotosaurus
0.0105	20.2	.0000	1	euphorbias
0.0105.	20.2	.0000	1	euthytonon
0.0105	20.2	.0000	1	evacuations
0.0105	20.2	.0000	1	evenly-placed
0.0105	20.2	.0000	1	ever-broader
0.0105	20.2	.0000	1	ever-cloudless
0.0105	20.2	.0000	1	ever-greater
0.0105	20.2	.0000	1	everlengthening
0.0105	20.2	.0000	1	everted
0.0105	20.2	.0000	1	evisceration
0.0105	20.2	.0000	1	evocative
0.0105	20.2	.0000	1	evolutional
0.0105	20.2	.0000	1	evolutionist
0.0105	20.2	.0000	1	exactitude
THE PRECEDING WORD TYPE OCCUPIES RANK 79100				
0.0105	20.2	.0000	1	examiner's
0.0105	20.2	.0000	1	excavator
0.0105	20.2	.0000	1	exchangeable
0.0105	20.2	.0000	1	excitation
0.0105	20.2	.0000	1	excommunicated
0.0105	20.2	.0000	1	excrescence
0.0105	20.2	.0000	1	excrescences
0.0105	20.2	.0000	1	excreting
0.0105	20.2	.0000	1	excretions
0.0105	20.2	.0000	1	excusable
0.0105	20.2	.0000	1	Exec
0.0105	20.2	.0000	1	exhibitionist
0.0105	20.2	.0000	1	exocrine
0.0105	20.2	.0000	1	exocrines
0.0105	20.2	.0000	1	expectancies
0.0105	20.2	.0000	1	expeditious
0.0105	20.2	.0000	1	Explosive
0.0105	20.2	.0000	1	expressionists
0.0105	20.2	.0000	1	expropriation
0.0105	20.2	.0000	1	exstrophy
0.0105	20.2	.0000	1	extrasensory
0.0105	20.2	.0000	1	extravagance
0.0105	20.2	.0000	1	extremist
0.0105	20.2	.0000	1	extrudes
0.0105	20.2	.0000	1	exudations
0.0105	20.2	.0000	1	eye-filling
0.0105	20.2	.0000	1	Fabius
0.0105	20.2	.0000	1	Faesulae
0.0105	20.2	.0000	1	fair-haired
0.0105	20.2	.0000	1	fair-sized
0.0105	20.2	.0000	1	fair-to-middling
0.0105	20.2	.0000	1	Falconer
0.0105	20.2	.0000	1	falconets
0.0105	20.2	.0000	1	fallacies
0.0105	20.2	.0000	1	Falmouth
0.0105	20.2	.0000	1	Falster
0.0105	20.2	.0000	1	family-operated
0.0105	20.2	.0000	1	Far-Traveler
0.0105	20.2	.0000	1	far-seeing
0.0105	20.2	.0000	1	farmer-mechanics
0.0105	20.2	.0000	1	farre
0.0105	20.2	.0000	1	Farrell
0.0105	20.2	.0000	1	Farrell's
0.0105	20.2	.0000	1	fasciculations
0.0105	20.2	.0000	1	fascinate
0.0105	20.2	.0000	1	Fascists
0.0105	20.2	.0000	1	fashionably
0.0105	20.2	.0000	1	faster-growing
0.0105	20.2	.0000	1	fathering
0.0105	20.2	.0000	1	fatigue-ridden
0.0105	20.2	.0000	1	Fatimid
0.0105	20.2	.0000	1	Faust-book
0.0105	20.2	.0000	1	Faust's
0.0105	20.2	.0000	1	Fausten
0.0105	20.2	.0000	1	Faversham
0.0105	20.2	.0000	1	Favre
0.0105	20.2	.0000	1	Fawcett's
0.0105	20.2	.0000	1	fawn-
0.0105	20.2	.0000	1	Fayette
0.0105	20.2	.0000	1	fear-provoking
0.0105	20.2	.0000	1	federal-state
0.0105	20.2	.0000	1	federations
0.0105	20.2	.0000	1	feigning
0.0105	20.2	.0000	1	Feldspar
0.0105	20.2	.0000	1	felling
0.0105	20.2	.0000	1	fellowmen
0.0105	20.2	.0000	1	fern-choked
0.0105	20.2	.0000	1	Fernandez
0.0105	20.2	.0000	1	Fernando
0.0105	20.2	.0000	1	ferromagnetic
0.0105	20.2	.0000	1	Ferruccio
0.0105	20.2	.0000	1	fetish
0.0105	20.2	.0000	1	Fettes
0.0105	20.2	.0000	1	Feudalism
0.0105	20.2	.0000	1	fewness
0.0105	20.2	.0000	1	fibres
0.0105	20.2	.0000	1	fibrillae
0.0105	20.2	.0000	1	field-glass
0.0105	20.2	.0000	1	Fielding's
0.0105	20.2	.0000	1	Fiers
0.0105	20.2	.0000	1	Fiesole
0.0105	20.2	.0000	1	Filling
0.0105	20.2	.0000	1	finger-stop
0.0105	20.2	.0000	1	fingernail-sized
0.0105	20.2	.0000	1	finlike
0.0105	20.2	.0000	1	Fiorello
0.0105	20.2	.0000	1	fire-belching
0.0105	20.2	.0000	1	fire-control
0.0105	20.2	.0000	1	fire-safe
0.0105	20.2	.0000	1	fireproofed
0.0105	20.2	.0000	1	firewoods
0.0105	20.2	.0000	1	first-amendment
0.0105	20.2	.0000	1	first-graders
0.0105	20.2	.0000	1	fish-lizards
0.0105	20.2	.0000	1	five-color
0.0105	20.2	.0000	1	five-quarter
0.0105	20.2	.0000	1	flach
0.0105	20.2	.0000	1	flag-raising
0.0105	20.2	.0000	1	flamethrowers
0.0105	20.2	.0000	1	Flatfish
THE PRECEDING WORD TYPE OCCUPIES RANK 79200				
0.0105	20.2	.0000	1	flatfish
0.0105	20.2	.0000	1	flattish
0.0105	20.2	.0000	1	flivvers
0.0105	20.2	.0000	1	floodlit
0.0105	20.2	.0000	1	florentia
0.0105	20.2	.0000	1	Florentia
0.0105	20.2	.0000	1	Flounder
0.0105	20.2	.0000	1	flour-milling
0.0105	20.2	.0000	1	flow-meter
0.0105	20.2	.0000	1	flow-rate
0.0105	20.2	.0000	1	Flowering
0.0105	20.2	.0000	1	flowerlike
0.0105	20.2	.0000	1	fluctuate
0.0105	20.2	.0000	1	fluctuated
0.0105	20.2	.0000	1	fluctuates
0.0105	20.2	.0000	1	flumes
0.0105	20.2	.0000	1	Fluorescent
0.0105	20.2	.0000	1	fluorescing
0.0105	20.2	.0000	1	fluoridating
0.0105	20.2	.0000	1	fluorine-containing
0.0105	20.2	.0000	1	fluorocarbons
0.0105	20.2	.0000	1	fluoroscope
0.0105	20.2	.0000	1	Fluoroscope
0.0105	20.2	.0000	1	fluoroscopes
0.0105	20.2	.0000	1	fluosilicate
0.0105	20.2	.0000	1	flyingfish
0.0105	20.2	.0000	1	Foa
0.0105	20.2	.0000	1	Foa's
0.0105	20.2	.0000	1	foiled
0.0105	20.2	.0000	1	folksong
0.0105	20.2	.0000	1	folksongs
0.0105	20.2	.0000	1	food-rich
0.0105	20.2	.0000	1	football-sized
0.0105	20.2	.0000	1	fora
0.0105	20.2	.0000	1	foragers
0.0105	20.2	.0000	1	forages

U	SFI	D	F	Word Type
0.0105	20.2	.0000	1	foramen
0.0105	20.2	.0000	1	fording
0.0105	20.2	.0000	1	Forebearance
0.0105	20.2	.0000	1	forebrain
0.0105	20.2	.0000	1	foregoes
0.0105	20.2	.0000	1	foreknowledge
0.0105	20.2	.0000	1	foremen
0.0105	20.2	.0000	1	forepart
0.0105	20.2	.0000	1	foresails
0.0105	20.2	.0000	1	forest-loving
0.0105	20.2	.0000	1	forgings
0.0105	20.2	.0000	1	Former
0.0105	20.2	.0000	1	Forteviot
0.0105	20.2	.0000	1	forwarders
0.0105	20.2	.0000	1	four-year-olds
0.0105	20.2	.0000	1	Fourneyron
0.0105	20.2	.0000	1	fowl's
0.0105	20.2	.0000	1	fowle
0.0105	20.2	.0000	1	Fox-Davies
0.0105	20.2	.0000	1	FPC
0.0105	20.2	.0000	1	FPO
0.0105	20.2	.0000	1	Fragment
0.0105	20.2	.0000	1	frailer
0.0105	20.2	.0000	1	Franc
0.0105	20.2	.0000	1	Franciscus
0.0105	20.2	.0000	1	francium
0.0105	20.2	.0000	1	Franck
0.0105	20.2	.0000	1	Franconia
0.0105	20.2	.0000	1	Frane
0.0105	20.2	.0000	1	Frankfurt-on-Oder
0.0105	20.2	.0000	1	Frans
0.0105	20.2	.0000	1	free-born
0.0105	20.2	.0000	1	free-lance
0.0105	20.2	.0000	1	free-swimming
0.0105	20.2	.0000	1	Freemasons
0.0105	20.2	.0000	1	FregatPullada
0.0105	20.2	.0000	1	freight-train
0.0105	20.2	.0000	1	Freons
0.0105	20.2	.0000	1	fricatives
0.0105	20.2	.0000	1	Frick
0.0105	20.2	.0000	1	Frietchie
0.0105	20.2	.0000	1	Frietchie's
0.0105	20.2	.0000	1	froglets
0.0105	20.2	.0000	1	fruit-eating
0.0105	20.2	.0000	1	fruitflies
0.0105	20.2	.0000	1	fruitfull
0.0105	20.2	.0000	1	fuel-eating
0.0105	20.2	.0000	1	full-color
0.0105	20.2	.0000	1	fully-developed
0.0105	20.2	.0000	1	functionalism
0.0105	20.2	.0000	1	fundamentalist
0.0105	20.2	.0000	1	fungous
0.0105	20.2	.0000	1	fungus-blighted
0.0105	20.2	.0000	1	funiculars
0.0105	20.2	.0000	1	Furman
0.0105	20.2	.0000	1	Furnace
0.0105	20.2	.0000	1	futa
0.0105	20.2	.0000	1	Gabriele
0.0105	20.2	.0000	1	gadgetry
0.0105	20.2	.0000	1	gagging
0.0105	20.2	.0000	1	Gaite
0.0105	20.2	.0000	1	gall-making
0.0105	20.2	.0000	1	gallery-going
0.0105	20.2	.0000	1	galleys

THE PRECEDING WORD TYPE OCCUPIES RANK 79300

U	SFI	D	F	Word Type
0.0105	20.2	.0000	1	galvanize
0.0105	20.2	.0000	1	Gambia's
0.0105	20.2	.0000	1	game-rich
0.0105	20.2	.0000	1	gap-jawed
0.0105	20.2	.0000	1	garishly
0.0105	20.2	.0000	1	garnering
0.0105	20.2	.0000	1	gatherer
0.0105	20.2	.0000	1	Gattamelata
0.0105	20.2	.0000	1	Gautier
0.0105	20.2	.0000	1	gazetteer
0.0105	20.2	.0000	1	GazzetedesBeaux-Arts
0.0105	20.2	.0000	1	geisha
0.0105	20.2	.0000	1	general-studies
0.0105	20.2	.0000	1	generalogy
0.0105	20.2	.0000	1	genet
0.0105	20.2	.0000	1	geneticist
0.0105	20.2	.0000	1	Gens
0.0105	20.2	.0000	1	geochemist
0.0105	20.2	.0000	1	geoduck's
0.0105	20.2	.0000	1	geomagnetic
0.0105	20.2	.0000	1	geometrizing
0.0105	20.2	.0000	1	Geometry
0.0105	20.2	.0000	1	Georgetown's
0.0105	20.2	.0000	1	Georgius
0.0105	20.2	.0000	1	Ger
0.0105	20.2	.0000	1	German's
0.0105	20.2	.0000	1	Germer
0.0105	20.2	.0000	1	Gernsback
0.0105	20.2	.0000	1	Gernsback's
0.0105	20.2	.0000	1	Gesner
0.0105	20.2	.0000	1	gestes
0.0105	20.2	.0000	1	Ghetto
0.0105	20.2	.0000	1	Ghiberti
0.0105	20.2	.0000	1	Ghiorso
0.0105	20.2	.0000	1	Giessen
0.0105	20.2	.0000	1	gigantism
0.0105	20.2	.0000	1	gill-breathing
0.0105	20.2	.0000	1	gill-like
0.0105	20.2	.0000	1	Gilles
0.0105	20.2	.0000	1	Gillmore
0.0105	20.2	.0000	1	gimcrack
0.0105	20.2	.0000	1	ginkgoes
0.0105	20.2	.0000	1	Ginsburg
0.0105	20.2	.0000	1	Gintings
0.0105	20.2	.0000	1	Girondists
0.0105	20.2	.0000	1	glaciers'
0.0105	20.2	.0000	1	glaciologists
0.0105	20.2	.0000	1	Glackens
0.0105	20.2	.0000	1	Gladsome
0.0105	20.2	.0000	1	glassblowing
0.0105	20.2	.0000	1	glassmaker
0.0105	20.2	.0000	1	glassmakers
0.0105	20.2	.0000	1	glassworkers
0.0105	20.2	.0000	1	gleemen
0.0105	20.2	.0000	1	glia
0.0105	20.2	.0000	1	Glidden
0.0105	20.2	.0000	1	globus
0.0105	20.2	.0000	1	Glockner
0.0105	20.2	.0000	1	Glomar
0.0105	20.2	.0000	1	glory-hole
0.0105	20.2	.0000	1	gluteal
0.0105	20.2	.0000	1	glyptodons
0.0105	20.2	.0000	1	gobies
0.0105	20.2	.0000	1	godparents
0.0105	20.2	.0000	1	gold-work
0.0105	20.2	.0000	1	goldenrods
0.0105	20.2	.0000	1	Goldsmith
0.0105	20.2	.0000	1	Golosov
0.0105	20.2	.0000	1	Gomarus
0.0105	20.2	.0000	1	Goncharov
0.0105	20.2	.0000	1	gondola-style
0.0105	20.2	.0000	1	googolplex
0.0105	20.2	.0000	1	goose-flesh
0.0105	20.2	.0000	1	Gospels
0.0105	20.2	.0000	1	Gospertie
0.0105	20.2	.0000	1	Goth
0.0105	20.2	.0000	1	Gotthold
0.0105	20.2	.0000	1	gouged-out
0.0105	20.2	.0000	1	government-sponsored
0.0105	20.2	.0000	1	governor-general
0.0105	20.2	.0000	1	Grabner
0.0105	20.2	.0000	1	Grafton
0.0105	20.2	.0000	1	Grandeur
0.0105	20.2	.0000	1	grass-tree
0.0105	20.2	.0000	1	gratings
0.0105	20.2	.0000	1	grave-stones
0.0105	20.2	.0000	1	graveside
0.0105	20.2	.0000	1	graylag
0.0105	20.2	.0000	1	Grays
0.0105	20.2	.0000	1	GreatBritian
0.0105	20.2	.0000	1	great-berried
0.0105	20.2	.0000	1	great-circle
0.0105	20.2	.0000	1	grebe
0.0105	20.2	.0000	1	Greely
0.0105	20.2	.0000	1	GreenBay
0.0105	20.2	.0000	1	green-blue
0.0105	20.2	.0000	1	green-gray
0.0105	20.2	.0000	1	green-tipped
0.0105	20.2	.0000	1	greenback
0.0105	20.2	.0000	1	Greeneville

THE PRECEDING WORD TYPE OCCUPIES RANK 79400

U	SFI	D	F	Word Type
0.0105	20.2	.0000	1	greenish-gray
0.0105	20.2	.0000	1	Gretchen
0.0105	20.2	.0000	1	greystone
0.0105	20.2	.0000	1	Gross
0.0105	20.2	.0000	1	Grosseteste
0.0105	20.2	.0000	1	Grotius
0.0105	20.2	.0000	1	ground-clinging
0.0105	20.2	.0000	1	guanay
0.0105	20.2	.0000	1	guardrail
0.0105	20.2	.0000	1	Guibert
0.0105	20.2	.0000	1	guideposts
0.0105	20.2	.0000	1	guilding
0.0105	20.2	.0000	1	Guinicelli
0.0105	20.2	.0000	1	gullying
0.0105	20.2	.0000	1	Gustavus's
0.0105	20.2	.0000	1	Gutta-Percha
0.0105	20.2	.0000	1	guttation
0.0105	20.2	.0000	1	gybing
0.0105	20.2	.0000	1	gymnocercus
0.0105	20.2	.0000	1	h/mc
0.0105	20.2	.0000	1	h/mv
0.0105	20.2	.0000	1	Habitat
0.0105	20.2	.0000	1	hackberry
0.0105	20.2	.0000	1	hackneyed
0.0105	20.2	.0000	1	Hadfield
0.0105	20.2	.0000	1	hair-coloring
0.0105	20.2	.0000	1	hairiness
0.0105	20.2	.0000	1	half-built
0.0105	20.2	.0000	1	half-century
0.0105	20.2	.0000	1	Halleck
0.0105	20.2	.0000	1	hallmarks
0.0105	20.2	.0000	1	halogens
0.0105	20.2	.0000	1	Halton
0.0105	20.2	.0000	1	Hamatreya
0.0105	20.2	.0000	1	Hamiltonians
0.0105	20.2	.0000	1	hand-blown
0.0105	20.2	.0000	1	hand-stuffed
0.0105	20.2	.0000	1	hand-sucking
0.0105	20.2	.0000	1	Hanibal
0.0105	20.2	.0000	1	Hankow
0.0105	20.2	.0000	1	Hannibal's
0.0105	20.2	.0000	1	Hara
0.0105	20.2	.0000	1	harassing
0.0105	20.2	.0000	1	harassments
0.0105	20.2	.0000	1	hard-coated
0.0105	20.2	.0000	1	hard-hat
0.0105	20.2	.0000	1	Harder
0.0105	20.2	.0000	1	Hares
0.0105	20.2	.0000	1	Harlowe
0.0105	20.2	.0000	1	harmlessness
0.0105	20.2	.0000	1	Haro
0.0105	20.2	.0000	1	Harte
0.0105	20.2	.0000	1	Harte's
0.0105	20.2	.0000	1	Hasdrubal
0.0105	20.2	.0000	1	hatchlings
0.0105	20.2	.0000	1	haulage
0.0105	20.2	.0000	1	Hazard
0.0105	20.2	.0000	1	he-man
0.0105	20.2	.0000	1	head-hunters
0.0105	20.2	.0000	1	headlamp
0.0105	20.2	.0000	1	heart-stopper
0.0105	20.2	.0000	1	heartburn
0.0105	20.2	.0000	1	hearthside
0.0105	20.2	.0000	1	heartwood
0.0105	20.2	.0000	1	Heating
0.0105	20.2	.0000	1	heavier-featured
0.0105	20.2	.0000	1	heavier-than-air
0.0105	20.2	.0000	1	heavily-fortified
0.0105	20.2	.0000	1	Heavy
0.0105	20.2	.0000	1	heavy-industry
0.0105	20.2	.0000	1	Heisenberg
0.0105	20.2	.0000	1	heliconiids
0.0105	20.2	.0000	1	Heliconius
0.0105	20.2	.0000	1	helicopter-landing
0.0105	20.2	.0000	1	helmet-like
0.0105	20.2	.0000	1	Helmont
0.0105	20.2	.0000	1	Helms
0.0105	20.2	.0000	1	Helsingor
0.0105	20.2	.0000	1	hemilaryngectomized
0.0105	20.2	.0000	1	hemipenis
0.0105	20.2	.0000	1	hemisphere's
0.0105	20.2	.0000	1	hemorrhage
0.0105	20.2	.0000	1	Heralds'
0.0105	20.2	.0000	1	Herault
0.0105	20.2	.0000	1	Herbart
0.0105	20.2	.0000	1	Herbart's
0.0105	20.2	.0000	1	Heriot-Watt
0.0105	20.2	.0000	1	Hermanns
0.0105	20.2	.0000	1	Hermansen
0.0105	20.2	.0000	1	hermits
0.0105	20.2	.0000	1	Hernan
0.0105	20.2	.0000	1	hernia
0.0105	20.2	.0000	1	herringbone
0.0105	20.2	.0000	1	Herstal
0.0105	20.2	.0000	1	Herzen's
0.0105	20.2	.0000	1	Hesse-Cassel
0.0105	20.2	.0000	1	HF
0.0105	20.2	.0000	1	hhd
0.0105	20.2	.0000	1	hibernicus
0.0105	20.2	.0000	1	Hibiya

THE PRECEDING WORD TYPE OCCUPIES RANK 79500

U	SFI	D	F	Word Type
0.0105	20.2	.0000	1	hideousness
0.0105	20.2	.0000	1	Hieron
0.0105	20.2	.0000	1	HighPoint
0.0105	20.2	.0000	1	high-efficiency
0.0105	20.2	.0000	1	high-mountain
0.0105	20.2	.0000	1	high-resistance
0.0105	20.2	.0000	1	high-technology
0.0105	20.2	.0000	1	high-test
0.0105	20.2	.0000	1	Highbury
0.0105	20.2	.0000	1	HighlandPark
0.0105	20.2	.0000	1	hill-city
0.0105	20.2	.0000	1	hind-gut
0.0105	20.2	.0000	1	Hindenburg
0.0105	20.2	.0000	1	Hindu's
0.0105	20.2	.0000	1	hinny
0.0105	20.2	.0000	1	Hippolyte
0.0105	20.2	.0000	1	Historia
0.0105	20.2	.0000	1	history's
0.0105	20.2	.0000	1	Hittin
0.0105	20.2	.0000	1	Hoder
0.0105	20.2	.0000	1	Hof
0.0105	20.2	.0000	1	hogshead
0.0105	20.2	.0000	1	Hohe
0.0105	20.2	.0000	1	Hoher
0.0105	20.2	.0000	1	holdfast
0.0105	20.2	.0000	1	Holdheim
0.0105	20.2	.0000	1	hollow-horned
0.0105	20.2	.0000	1	Holman
0.0105	20.2	.0000	1	Holnicote
0.0105	20.2	.0000	1	holostean
0.0105	20.2	.0000	1	home-disposal
0.0105	20.2	.0000	1	homelier
0.0105	20.2	.0000	1	honey-clear
0.0105	20.2	.0000	1	honeypots
0.0105	20.2	.0000	1	hooklets
0.0105	20.2	.0000	1	Horde
0.0105	20.2	.0000	1	hormon
0.0105	20.2	.0000	1	hormonal
0.0105	20.2	.0000	1	Hornet
0.0105	20.2	.0000	1	hornified
0.0105	20.2	.0000	1	Horror
0.0105	20.2	.0000	1	horror-struck
0.0105	20.2	.0000	1	horsedrawn
0.0105	20.2	.0000	1	horseradish
0.0105	20.2	.0000	1	Hosea
0.0105	20.2	.0000	1	Hoss
0.0105	20.2	.0000	1	hostage
0.0105	20.2	.0000	1	hotbox
0.0105	20.2	.0000	1	householder
0.0105	20.2	.0000	1	Huey
0.0105	20.2	.0000	1	Hugo's
0.0105	20.2	.0000	1	Huguenot
0.0105	20.2	.0000	1	Hulagu
0.0105	20.2	.0000	1	humanists
0.0105	20.2	.0000	1	humanization
0.0105	20.2	.0000	1	humanly
0.0105	20.2	.0000	1	humiliatingly
0.0105	20.2	.0000	1	Hun
0.0105	20.2	.0000	1	hungers
0.0105	20.2	.0000	1	hungriest
0.0105	20.2	.0000	1	hunters'
0.0105	20.2	.0000	1	Huntly
0.0105	20.2	.0000	1	Hussayn
0.0105	20.2	.0000	1	Hussein
0.0105	20.2	.0000	1	hustles
0.0105	20.2	.0000	1	Huxley's
0.0105	20.2	.0000	1	hv/c
0.0105	20.2	.0000	1	Hvar
0.0105	20.2	.0000	1	Hyderabad
0.0105	20.2	.0000	1	hydraulicking
0.0105	20.2	.0000	1	Hydrocarbon
0.0105	20.2	.0000	1	hydrogen-filled
0.0105	20.2	.0000	1	hydrophytes
0.0105	20.2	.0000	1	hydroxyl
0.0105	20.2	.0000	1	Hymen
0.0105	20.2	.0000	1	HYMETTUS
0.0105	20.2	.0000	1	HYMN
0.0105	20.2	.0000	1	hyperacidity
0.0105	20.2	.0000	1	hypertrophy
0.0105	20.2	.0000	1	hypochondriac
0.0105	20.2	.0000	1	hypodermic
0.0105	20.2	.0000	1	Hysteria
0.0105	20.2	.0000	1	H5
0.0105	20.2	.0000	1	I-S
0.0105	20.2	.0000	1	iambic
0.0105	20.2	.0000	1	ibises
0.0105	20.2	.0000	1	icebound
0.0105	20.2	.0000	1	ichthyological
0.0105	20.2	.0000	1	ichthyologist
0.0105	20.2	.0000	1	iciness
0.0105	20.2	.0000	1	iconoclast
0.0105	20.2	.0000	1	ida-maia
0.0105	20.2	.0000	1	idolatrous
0.0105	20.2	.0000	1	ieper
0.0105	20.2	.0000	1	Igorots
0.0105	20.2	.0000	1	III-A
0.0105	20.2	.0000	1	Ilion
0.0105	20.2	.0000	1	ill-fitted
0.0105	20.2	.0000	1	ill-treated
0.0105	20.2	.0000	1	Illana

THE PRECEDING WORD TYPE OCCUPIES RANK 79600

U	SFI	D	F	Word Type
0.0105	20.2	.0000	1	Illilouette
0.0105	20.2	.0000	1	illustrators
0.0105	20.2	.0000	1	imaginal
0.0105	20.2	.0000	1	imagists
0.0105	20.2	.0000	1	imbalances
0.0105	20.2	.0000	1	imbued
0.0105	20.2	.0000	1	Immanuel
0.0105	20.2	.0000	1	immersion
0.0105	20.2	.0000	1	imminence
0.0105	20.2	.0000	1	immutable
0.0105	20.2	.0000	1	impala
0.0105	20.2	.0000	1	impasto
0.0105	20.2	.0000	1	imperfection
0.0105	20.2	.0000	1	imperialist
0.0105	20.2	.0000	1	impersonator
0.0105	20.2	.0000	1	impinge
0.0105	20.2	.0000	1	imponderable
0.0105	20.2	.0000	1	impracticable
0.0105	20.2	.0000	1	impregnable
0.0105	20.2	.0000	1	inapplicable
0.0105	20.2	.0000	1	inauspicious
0.0105	20.2	.0000	1	Incan
0.0105	20.2	.0000	1	incertain
0.0105	20.2	.0000	1	incisions
0.0105	20.2	.0000	1	incited
0.0105	20.2	.0000	1	inclemencies
0.0105	20.2	.0000	1	inclined-type
0.0105	20.2	.0000	1	incombustible
0.0105	20.2	.0000	1	incommunicado
0.0105	20.2	.0000	1	incompressibility
0.0105	20.2	.0000	1	inconsistencies
0.0105	20.2	.0000	1	inconspicuously
0.0105	20.2	.0000	1	incrustations
0.0105	20.2	.0000	1	incubating
0.0105	20.2	.0000	1	incubations
0.0105	20.2	.0000	1	incurious
0.0105	20.2	.0000	1	indefatigably
0.0105	20.2	.0000	1	indexers
0.0105	20.2	.0000	1	indexing
0.0105	20.2	.0000	1	indignity
0.0105	20.2	.0000	1	indiscriminatingly
0.0105	20.2	.0000	1	indisposition
0.0105	20.2	.0000	1	Individual
0.0105	20.2	.0000	1	Indo-Pakistan
0.0105	20.2	.0000	1	indolence
0.0105	20.2	.0000	1	inducing
0.0105	20.2	.0000	1	indus
0.0105	20.2	.0000	1	industrializing
0.0105	20.2	.0000	1	inelastic
0.0105	20.2	.0000	1	ineradicable
0.0105	20.2	.0000	1	inexhaustible
0.0105	20.2	.0000	1	inextricable
0.0105	20.2	.0000	1	infection-free
0.0105	20.2	.0000	1	infestation
0.0105	20.2	.0000	1	infests
0.0105	20.2	.0000	1	Infielders
0.0105	20.2	.0000	1	infrastructure
0.0105	20.2	.0000	1	infringement
0.0105	20.2	.0000	1	ingeniators
0.0105	20.2	.0000	1	ingeniously
0.0105	20.2	.0000	1	ingested
0.0105	20.2	.0000	1	inhibitors
0.0105	20.2	.0000	1	inhumane
0.0105	20.2	.0000	1	inhumation
0.0105	20.2	.0000	1	Initiative
0.0105	20.2	.0000	1	initiator
0.0105	20.2	.0000	1	inmate
0.0105	20.2	.0000	1	Inner
0.0105	20.2	.0000	1	Inscribed
0.0105	20.2	.0000	1	insect-ridden
0.0105	20.2	.0000	1	insets
0.0105	20.2	.0000	1	insolvency
0.0105	20.2	.0000	1	insomniacs
0.0105	20.2	.0000	1	instability
0.0105	20.2	.0000	1	instigating
0.0105	20.2	.0000	1	instrument-maker
0.0105	20.2	.0000	1	instrument-makers
0.0105	20.2	.0000	1	Insulation
0.0105	20.2	.0000	1	intangibles
0.0105	20.2	.0000	1	Intellectual
0.0105	20.2	.0000	1	Inter-American
0.0105	20.2	.0000	1	inter-church
0.0105	20.2	.0000	1	intercellular
0.0105	20.2	.0000	1	Intercollegian
0.0105	20.2	.0000	1	intercommunication
0.0105	20.2	.0000	1	interconnecting
0.0105	20.2	.0000	1	Interest
0.0105	20.2	.0000	1	Interesting
0.0105	20.2	.0000	1	interfold
0.0105	20.2	.0000	1	interglacial
0.0105	20.2	.0000	1	intergrowths
0.0105	20.2	.0000	1	intermeshing
0.0105	20.2	.0000	1	intermingling
0.0105	20.2	.0000	1	intermolecular
0.0105	20.2	.0000	1	interneurons
0.0105	20.2	.0000	1	interrelation
0.0105	20.2	.0000	1	intertwining
0.0105	20.2	.0000	1	intravenous
0.0105	20.2	.0000	1	intruded
0.0105	20.2	.0000	1	intuitionism

U	SFI	D	F	Word Type
THE PRECEDING WORD TYPE OCCUPIES RANK 79700				
0.0105	20.2	.0000	1	Invaded
0.0105	20.2	.0000	1	Inventions
0.0105	20.2	.0000	1	Investiture
0.0105	20.2	.0000	1	invoices
0.0105	20.2	.0000	1	Iofan
0.0105	20.2	.0000	1	Ionia
0.0105	20.2	.0000	1	Ionian-Greek
0.0105	20.2	.0000	1	ionic
0.0105	20.2	.0000	1	ipse
0.0105	20.2	.0000	1	Irenee
0.0105	20.2	.0000	1	iridescence
0.0105	20.2	.0000	1	Irish-Italian
0.0105	20.2	.0000	1	irked
0.0105	20.2	.0000	1	iron-poor
0.0105	20.2	.0000	1	iron-tipped
0.0105	20.2	.0000	1	ironmonger
0.0105	20.2	.0000	1	irradiation
0.0105	20.2	.0000	1	irrevocable
0.0105	20.2	.0000	1	irruptive
0.0105	20.2	.0000	1	Isis
0.0105	20.2	.0000	1	Islamabad
0.0105	20.2	.0000	1	island-hopping
0.0105	20.2	.0000	1	Island's
0.0105	20.2	.0000	1	Ismailis
0.0105	20.2	.0000	1	Ismene
0.0105	20.2	.0000	1	isogonic
0.0105	20.2	.0000	1	isopropyl
0.0105	20.2	.0000	1	issuer
0.0105	20.2	.0000	1	istoriya
0.0105	20.2	.0000	1	Italian-born
0.0105	20.2	.0000	1	ithomiids
0.0105	20.2	.0000	1	Itza
0.0105	20.2	.0000	1	IUD
0.0105	20.2	.0000	1	IV-A
0.0105	20.2	.0000	1	jabiru
0.0105	20.2	.0000	1	jacanas
0.0105	20.2	.0000	1	jackals'
0.0105	20.2	.0000	1	jackknife-and-baling-wire
0.0105	20.2	.0000	1	Jacopone
0.0105	20.2	.0000	1	Jacquard
0.0105	20.2	.0000	1	Jagello
0.0105	20.2	.0000	1	Jagiello
0.0105	20.2	.0000	1	Jagiellonian
0.0105	20.2	.0000	1	jambiya
0.0105	20.2	.0000	1	JAMES
0.0105	20.2	.0000	1	Jas
0.0105	20.2	.0000	1	Jasomirgott
0.0105	20.2	.0000	1	jasper
0.0105	20.2	.0000	1	Jean-Philippe
0.0105	20.2	.0000	1	jelutong
0.0105	20.2	.0000	1	jerboas
0.0105	20.2	.0000	1	Jevric
0.0105	20.2	.0000	1	Jiro
0.0105	20.2	.0000	1	jist
0.0105	20.2	.0000	1	joke-telling
0.0105	20.2	.0000	1	Jord
0.0105	20.2	.0000	1	JOSEPH
0.0105	20.2	.0000	1	Joule
0.0105	20.2	.0000	1	Juchi
0.0105	20.2	.0000	1	Judges
0.0105	20.2	.0000	1	Judgment
0.0105	20.2	.0000	1	Jumhuriyah
0.0105	20.2	.0000	1	Justus
0.0105	20.2	.0000	1	juts
0.0105	20.2	.0000	1	Kabukiza
0.0105	20.2	.0000	1	Kabul
0.0105	20.2	.0000	1	Kaffir
0.0105	20.2	.0000	1	kaingin
0.0105	20.2	.0000	1	Kalgan
0.0105	20.2	.0000	1	Kalimantan
0.0105	20.2	.0000	1	Kamchatka
0.0105	20.2	.0000	1	Kant
0.0105	20.2	.0000	1	Kantrowitz
0.0105	20.2	.0000	1	Kaplan
0.0105	20.2	.0000	1	Kappa
0.0105	20.2	.0000	1	Kappas
0.0105	20.2	.0000	1	Karo
0.0105	20.2	.0000	1	Kashgar
0.0105	20.2	.0000	1	Katahdin
0.0105	20.2	.0000	1	Katmai
0.0105	20.2	.0000	1	Kazinga
0.0105	20.2	.0000	1	Kendeigh
0.0105	20.2	.0000	1	Khaghan
0.0105	20.2	.0000	1	Khairpar
0.0105	20.2	.0000	1	Khairpur
0.0105	20.2	.0000	1	Khalifa
0.0105	20.2	.0000	1	khan
0.0105	20.2	.0000	1	Khazar
0.0105	20.2	.0000	1	Khersonskaya
0.0105	20.2	.0000	1	KHITAN
0.0105	20.2	.0000	1	Khrushchev's
0.0105	20.2	.0000	1	Khyber
0.0105	20.2	.0000	1	Kidney
0.0105	20.2	.0000	1	kindreds
0.0105	20.2	.0000	1	king-maker
0.0105	20.2	.0000	1	kingfishers
0.0105	20.2	.0000	1	Kingstown
0.0105	20.2	.0000	1	Kingsville
0.0105	20.2	.0000	1	Kirov
0.0105	20.2	.0000	1	Kirtland's
THE PRECEDING WORD TYPE OCCUPIES RANK 79800				
0.0105	20.2	.0000	1	Kitai
0.0105	20.2	.0000	1	Kitchens
0.0105	20.2	.0000	1	Kitimat
0.0105	20.2	.0000	1	Kitts
0.0105	20.2	.0000	1	kiva
0.0105	20.2	.0000	1	kiwis
0.0105	20.2	.0000	1	Klondike
0.0105	20.2	.0000	1	klystron
0.0105	20.2	.0000	1	knighted
0.0105	20.2	.0000	1	Knjizevnost
0.0105	20.2	.0000	1	knob-kneed
0.0105	20.2	.0000	1	KNO3
0.0105	20.2	.0000	1	Koehler
0.0105	20.2	.0000	1	Kohara's
0.0105	20.2	.0000	1	Kohistan
0.0105	20.2	.0000	1	Koldewey
0.0105	20.2	.0000	1	Koodoesberg
0.0105	20.2	.0000	1	Koornheert
0.0105	20.2	.0000	1	Korps
0.0105	20.2	.0000	1	Kotah
0.0105	20.2	.0000	1	Kotri
0.0105	20.2	.0000	1	Koussevitzky
0.0105	20.2	.0000	1	Kqq'/r2**
0.0105	20.2	.0000	1	Krakatoa
0.0105	20.2	.0000	1	Krefeld
0.0105	20.2	.0000	1	Krsinic
0.0105	20.2	.0000	1	Krym
0.0105	20.2	.0000	1	Kshatriyas
0.0105	20.2	.0000	1	Kunsthistorisches
0.0105	20.2	.0000	1	Kuriles
0.0105	20.2	.0000	1	Kurland
0.0105	20.2	.0000	1	Kush
0.0105	20.2	.0000	1	Kutch
0.0105	20.2	.0000	1	l'Abbe
0.0105	20.2	.0000	1	L'Academie
0.0105	20.2	.0000	1	L'Ami
0.0105	20.2	.0000	1	LaFilleMalCardee
0.0105	20.2	.0000	1	lab's
0.0105	20.2	.0000	1	labella
0.0105	20.2	.0000	1	labor-management
0.0105	20.2	.0000	1	Labourer
0.0105	20.2	.0000	1	Lacandon
0.0105	20.2	.0000	1	lacemaking
0.0105	20.2	.0000	1	Lacerta
0.0105	20.2	.0000	1	lacertas
0.0105	20.2	.0000	1	lacquerware
0.0105	20.2	.0000	1	Lagrange
0.0105	20.2	.0000	1	Lair
0.0105	20.2	.0000	1	lairs
0.0105	20.2	.0000	1	LAKE
0.0105	20.2	.0000	1	Lakehurst
0.0105	20.2	.0000	1	Lamont-Doherty
0.0105	20.2	.0000	1	Lampedusa
0.0105	20.2	.0000	1	Lampedusa's
0.0105	20.2	.0000	1	Lanao
0.0105	20.2	.0000	1	lance-shaped
0.0105	20.2	.0000	1	land-based
0.0105	20.2	.0000	1	landlubber
0.0105	20.2	.0000	1	Langenaltheim
0.0105	20.2	.0000	1	Langerhans
0.0105	20.2	.0000	1	languidly
0.0105	20.2	.0000	1	Lanham
0.0105	20.2	.0000	1	lanthanide
0.0105	20.2	.0000	1	Laplace
0.0105	20.2	.0000	1	larders
0.0105	20.2	.0000	1	Larsh
0.0105	20.2	.0000	1	last-mentioned
0.0105	20.2	.0000	1	Lat
0.0105	20.2	.0000	1	lathes
0.0105	20.2	.0000	1	Latimer
0.0105	20.2	.0000	1	Latinized
0.0105	20.2	.0000	1	laudamus
0.0105	20.2	.0000	1	lauded
0.0105	20.2	.0000	1	Laudes
0.0105	20.2	.0000	1	Laudi
0.0105	20.2	.0000	1	Laurier
0.0105	20.2	.0000	1	lava-built
0.0105	20.2	.0000	1	laves
0.0105	20.2	.0000	1	lavished
0.0105	20.2	.0000	1	lavishing
0.0105	20.2	.0000	1	LAW
0.0105	20.2	.0000	1	laxatives
0.0105	20.2	.0000	1	layman's
0.0105	20.2	.0000	1	lead-bismuth
0.0105	20.2	.0000	1	leaf's
0.0105	20.2	.0000	1	leafhoppers
0.0105	20.2	.0000	1	leathernecks
0.0105	20.2	.0000	1	Lechfeld
0.0105	20.2	.0000	1	Leconte
0.0105	20.2	.0000	1	Lectureship
0.0105	20.2	.0000	1	leering
0.0105	20.2	.0000	1	Leesburg
0.0105	20.2	.0000	1	legalized
0.0105	20.2	.0000	1	Legaspi
0.0105	20.2	.0000	1	legation
0.0105	20.2	.0000	1	legend-like
0.0105	20.2	.0000	1	legislates
0.0105	20.2	.0000	1	Legislative
0.0105	20.2	.0000	1	Lehman
0.0105	20.2	.0000	1	Leitha
THE PRECEDING WORD TYPE OCCUPIES RANK 79900				
0.0105	20.2	.0000	1	Lelia
0.0105	20.2	.0000	1	lemming
0.0105	20.2	.0000	1	lemur-and
0.0105	20.2	.0000	1	Lemuria
0.0105	20.2	.0000	1	lemurlike
0.0105	20.2	.0000	1	Lenard's
0.0105	20.2	.0000	1	leng
0.0105	20.2	.0000	1	lens-shaped
0.0105	20.2	.0000	1	lento
0.0105	20.2	.0000	1	Leonide
0.0105	20.2	.0000	1	Leopardi's
0.0105	20.2	.0000	1	lepidopterist
0.0105	20.2	.0000	1	LesFauves
0.0105	20.2	.0000	1	less-charged
0.0105	20.2	.0000	1	less-than-carload
0.0105	20.2	.0000	1	Lessing
0.0105	20.2	.0000	1	letter-carrier
0.0105	20.2	.0000	1	letter-number
0.0105	20.2	.0000	1	leveling-off
0.0105	20.2	.0000	1	Leverkuhn
0.0105	20.2	.0000	1	Lewes
0.0105	20.2	.0000	1	Leyte
0.0105	20.2	.0000	1	Libby
0.0105	20.2	.0000	1	libel
0.0105	20.2	.0000	1	Liberal
0.0105	20.2	.0000	1	liberalist
0.0105	20.2	.0000	1	liberalizing
0.0105	20.2	.0000	1	librarianship
0.0105	20.2	.0000	1	librettists
0.0105	20.2	.0000	1	Liebig's
0.0105	20.2	.0000	1	Liechtenstein
0.0105	20.2	.0000	1	Lienz
0.0105	20.2	.0000	1	lieut
0.0105	20.2	.0000	1	life-or-death
0.0105	20.2	.0000	1	light-activated
0.0105	20.2	.0000	1	light-pink
0.0105	20.2	.0000	1	light-reacting
0.0105	20.2	.0000	1	light-requiring
0.0105	20.2	.0000	1	light-splashed
0.0105	20.2	.0000	1	light's
0.0105	20.2	.0000	1	lightweights
0.0105	20.2	.0000	1	Liguasan
0.0105	20.2	.0000	1	Ligurian
0.0105	20.2	.0000	1	Liliaceae
0.0105	20.2	.0000	1	Liman
0.0105	20.2	.0000	1	limiters
0.0105	20.2	.0000	1	Lindberg
0.0105	20.2	.0000	1	lined-up
0.0105	20.2	.0000	1	Lingala
0.0105	20.2	.0000	1	Linguistics
0.0105	20.2	.0000	1	liniments
0.0105	20.2	.0000	1	Lion-hearted
0.0105	20.2	.0000	1	liquefying
0.0105	20.2	.0000	1	liquidation
0.0105	20.2	.0000	1	little-seen
0.0105	20.2	.0000	1	live-born
0.0105	20.2	.0000	1	Livermore
0.0105	20.2	.0000	1	Lockean
0.0105	20.2	.0000	1	locomotive's
0.0105	20.2	.0000	1	lodes
0.0105	20.2	.0000	1	Loew
0.0105	20.2	.0000	1	Logic
0.0105	20.2	.0000	1	Logick
0.0105	20.2	.0000	1	logistics
0.0105	20.2	.0000	1	Lolland
0.0105	20.2	.0000	1	loners
0.0105	20.2	.0000	1	long-haul
0.0105	20.2	.0000	1	long-run
0.0105	20.2	.0000	1	long-running
0.0105	20.2	.0000	1	longjeray
0.0105	20.2	.0000	'	longstanding
0.0105	20.2	.0000	1	Lonigan
0.0105	20.2	.0000	1	Lorentz
0.0105	20.2	.0000	1	Lorient
0.0105	20.2	.0000	1	Lorrain
0.0105	20.2	.0000	1	Losses
0.0105	20.2	.0000	1	Lothair
0.0105	20.2	.0000	1	low-altitude
0.0105	20.2	.0000	1	low-paid
0.0105	20.2	.0000	1	low-resistance
0.0105	20.2	.0000	1	low-veld
0.0105	20.2	.0000	1	low-yield
0.0105	20.2	.0000	1	lower-grade
0.0105	20.2	.0000	1	Lowestoft
0.0105	20.2	.0000	1	loyalists
0.0105	20.2	.0000	1	Lubarda
0.0105	20.2	.0000	1	Lucic
0.0105	20.2	.0000	1	luckananee
0.0105	20.2	.0000	1	Lucretius
0.0105	20.2	.0000	1	Luks
0.0105	20.2	.0000	1	lumbar
0.0105	20.2	.0000	1	lumber-carrying
0.0105	20.2	.0000	1	luminaries
0.0105	20.2	.0000	1	Luminescence
0.0105	20.2	.0000	1	lynxes
0.0105	20.2	.0000	1	Lyra
0.0105	20.2	.0000	1	MacAlpin
0.0105	20.2	.0000	1	macaques
0.0105	20.2	.0000	1	Macdonald's
0.0105	20.2	.0000	1	Macquart
THE PRECEDING WORD TYPE OCCUPIES RANK 80000				
0.0105	20.2	.0000	1	Magdeburg's
0.0105	20.2	.0000	1	Magdeburgers
0.0105	20.2	.0000	1	magic-carpet
0.0105	20.2	.0000	1	Magister
0.0105	20.2	.0000	1	magnes
0.0105	20.2	.0000	1	Magnes
0.0105	20.2	.0000	1	Magnet
0.0105	20.2	.0000	1	magnetic-extraction
0.0105	20.2	.0000	1	magnetization
0.0105	20.2	.0000	1	magnetometer
0.0105	20.2	.0000	1	maidservant
0.0105	20.2	.0000	1	Maidservant
0.0105	20.2	.0000	1	Maidstone
0.0105	20.2	.0000	1	mailable
0.0105	20.2	.0000	1	maiming
0.0105	20.2	.0000	1	Mainichi
0.0105	20.2	.0000	1	mainlands
0.0105	20.2	.0000	1	majesty's
0.0105	20.2	.0000	1	Majorinus
0.0105	20.2	.0000	1	makers'
0.0105	20.2	.0000	1	Malays
0.0105	20.2	.0000	1	maleo
0.0105	20.2	.0000	1	maligayang
0.0105	20.2	.0000	1	Malinowski
0.0105	20.2	.0000	1	Mallarme's
0.0105	20.2	.0000	1	Mameluke
0.0105	20.2	.0000	1	man-dominated
0.0105	20.2	.0000	1	Manet
0.0105	20.2	.0000	1	manifestoes
0.0105	20.2	.0000	1	Mann's
0.0105	20.2	.0000	1	mannishness
0.0105	20.2	.0000	1	manservant
0.0105	20.2	.0000	1	mantids
0.0105	20.2	.0000	1	mantled
0.0105	20.2	.0000	1	Manufactures
0.0105	20.2	.0000	1	Manufacturing
0.0105	20.2	.0000	1	many-bladed
0.0105	20.2	.0000	1	many-faced
0.0105	20.2	.0000	1	many-year
0.0105	20.2	.0000	1	Manzoni's
0.0105	20.2	.0000	1	marabou
0.0105	20.2	.0000	1	Maranhao
0.0105	20.2	.0000	1	Marathi
0.0105	20.2	.0000	1	Marches
0.0105	20.2	.0000	1	mari
0.0105	20.2	.0000	1	Maringer
0.0105	20.2	.0000	1	Marino
0.0105	20.2	.0000	1	marinus
0.0105	20.2	.0000	1	Marismas
0.0105	20.2	.0000	1	Marko
0.0105	20.2	.0000	1	Markt
0.0105	20.2	.0000	1	Marlowe's
0.0105	20.2	.0000	1	Marmosa
0.0105	20.2	.0000	1	Maronite
0.0105	20.2	.0000	1	Martel
0.0105	20.2	.0000	1	Marulic
0.0105	20.2	.0000	1	Marye's
0.0105	20.2	.0000	1	Masjumi
0.0105	20.2	.0000	1	mass-produced-parts
0.0105	20.2	.0000	1	Massine's
0.0105	20.2	.0000	1	mastaba
0.0105	20.2	.0000	1	Matamoros
0.0105	20.2	.0000	1	materiel
0.0105	20.2	.0000	1	matter's
0.0105	20.2	.0000	1	Mauritshuis
0.0105	20.2	.0000	1	Maurya
0.0105	20.2	.0000	1	May-Day
0.0105	20.2	.0000	1	mayfly's
0.0105	20.2	.0000	1	Mayling
0.0105	20.2	.0000	1	Mayon
0.0105	20.2	.0000	1	mazes
0.0105	20.2	.0000	1	Mazuranic
0.0105	20.2	.0000	1	Mazzini
0.0105	20.2	.0000	1	McC
0.0105	20.2	.0000	1	McCulloch
0.0105	20.2	.0000	1	McGeorge
0.0105	20.2	.0000	1	meagerness
0.0105	20.2	.0000	1	mean-fowt
0.0105	20.2	.0000	1	meat-cleaver
0.0105	20.2	.0000	1	mecca
0.0105	20.2	.0000	1	Mechanick
0.0105	20.2	.0000	1	Medawar
0.0105	20.2	.0000	1	mediation
0.0105	20.2	.0000	1	medicine's
0.0105	20.2	.0000	1	Medicine's
0.0105	20.2	.0000	1	mediocrities
0.0105	20.2	.0000	1	medusa-like
0.0105	20.2	.0000	1	Meetings
0.0105	20.2	.0000	1	Megaceros
0.0105	20.2	.0000	1	megadeaths
0.0105	20.2	.0000	1	Megalithic
0.0105	20.2	.0000	1	Megalopolis
0.0105	20.2	.0000	1	Mei-ling
0.0105	20.2	.0000	1	Meiji
0.0105	20.2	.0000	1	Meinhof
0.0105	20.2	.0000	1	meiotic
0.0105	20.2	.0000	1	Meissen
0.0105	20.2	.0000	1	Mej
0.0105	20.2	.0000	1	melancholia
0.0105	20.2	.0000	1	Melnikov
THE PRECEDING WORD TYPE OCCUPIES RANK 80100				
0.0105	20.2	.0000	1	melopomene
0.0105	20.2	.0000	1	memberships
0.0105	20.2	.0000	1	membrane-lined
0.0105	20.2	.0000	1	mendicant
0.0105	20.2	.0000	1	Mendoza
0.0105	20.2	.0000	1	Mephistopheles
0.0105	20.2	.0000	1	Merchiston
0.0105	20.2	.0000	1	Merope
0.0105	20.2	.0000	1	Merovingian
0.0105	20.2	.0000	1	Merriam's
0.0105	20.2	.0000	1	Merrimack
0.0105	20.2	.0000	1	mesometeorology
0.0105	20.2	.0000	1	mesophyll
0.0105	20.2	.0000	1	mesosaur
0.0105	20.2	.0000	1	mesosaurs
0.0105	20.2	.0000	1	Mestrovic
0.0105	20.2	.0000	1	metal's
0.0105	20.2	.0000	1	metallurgical
0.0105	20.2	.0000	1	metallurgy
0.0105	20.2	.0000	1	metalmarks
0.0105	20.2	.0000	1	Metaphysics
0.0105	20.2	.0000	1	Methodism
0.0105	20.2	.0000	1	Metraux
0.0105	20.2	.0000	1	metre-making
0.0105	20.2	.0000	1	metres
0.0105	20.2	.0000	1	metrical
0.0105	20.2	.0000	1	metropolises
0.0105	20.2	.0000	1	MICHIGAN
0.0105	20.2	.0000	1	Michigan-Canadian
0.0105	20.2	.0000	1	Mickiewicz
0.0105	20.2	.0000	1	microbial
0.0105	20.2	.0000	1	microphotographs
0.0105	20.2	.0000	1	microworld
0.0105	20.2	.0000	1	mid-Europe
0.0105	20.2	.0000	1	mid-Victorian
0.0105	20.2	.0000	1	mid-continental
0.0105	20.2	.0000	1	mid-1400's
0.0105	20.2	.0000	1	mid-1600's
0.0105	20.2	.0000	1	mid-18th
0.0105	20.2	.0000	1	mid-1960's
0.0105	20.2	.0000	1	mid-1960s
0.0105	20.2	.0000	1	mid-20th
0.0105	20.2	.0000	1	Midcontinent
0.0105	20.2	.0000	1	middle-income
0.0105	20.2	.0000	1	midges
0.0105	20.2	.0000	1	Midianite
0.0105	20.2	.0000	1	Midsayap
0.0105	20.2	.0000	1	Miers
0.0105	20.2	.0000	1	migraine
0.0105	20.2	.0000	1	migrators
0.0105	20.2	.0000	1	mildness
0.0105	20.2	.0000	1	mile-round
0.0105	20.2	.0000	1	Mill's
0.0105	20.2	.0000	1	Millais'
0.0105	20.2	.0000	1	Milosavljevic
0.0105	20.2	.0000	1	Milutin
0.0105	20.2	.0000	1	mineral-processing
0.0105	20.2	.0000	1	mingaco
0.0105	20.2	.0000	1	Minnehaha
0.0105	20.2	.0000	1	miocene
0.0105	20.2	.0000	1	Miquelon
0.0105	20.2	.0000	1	Misanthrope
0.0105	20.2	.0000	1	misanthrope

U	SFI	D	F	Word Type
0.0105	20.2	.0000	1	mischiefmaker
0.0105	20.2	.0000	1	Miserables
0.0105	20.2	.0000	1	misrepresent
0.0105	20.2	.0000	1	mist-shrouded
0.0105	20.2	.0000	1	MIT'S**
0.0105	20.2	.0000	1	Mitchel
0.0105	20.2	.0000	1	Mithridatic
0.0105	20.2	.0000	1	mitzvah
0.0105	20.2	.0000	1	moa
0.0105	20.2	.0000	1	moats
0.0105	20.2	.0000	1	Modena
0.0105	20.2	.0000	1	Moewe
0.0105	20.2	.0000	1	molesters
0.0105	20.2	.0000	1	molluscs
0.0105	20.2	.0000	1	momenta
0.0105	20.2	.0000	1	monarch's
0.0105	20.2	.0000	1	monarchists
0.0105	20.2	.0000	1	Monetary
0.0105	20.2	.0000	1	monocotyledon
0.0105	20.2	.0000	1	monogamy
0.0105	20.2	.0000	1	monotheistic
0.0105	20.2	.0000	1	montmorillonite
0.0105	20.2	.0000	1	moodier
0.0105	20.2	.0000	1	moom
0.0105	20.2	.0000	1	moorhens
0.0105	20.2	.0000	1	mooselike
0.0105	20.2	.0000	1	Moralls
0.0105	20.2	.0000	1	morasses
0.0105	20.2	.0000	1	Mordvinov
0.0105	20.2	.0000	1	mortalities
0.0105	20.2	.0000	1	mos
0.0105	20.2	.0000	1	mother-inherited
0.0105	20.2	.0000	1	mother-substitute
0.0105	20.2	.0000	1	Mottley
0.0105	20.2	.0000	1	Moulins
0.0105	20.2	.0000	1	MountVernon
0.0105	20.2	.0000	1	mountainlike
THE PRECEDING WORD TYPE OCCUPIES RANK 80200				
0.0105	20.2	.0000	1	mountains'
0.0105	20.2	.0000	1	Mover
0.0105	20.2	.0000	1	mozo
0.0105	20.2	.0000	1	mudskippers
0.0105	20.2	.0000	1	multi-million-dollar
0.0105	20.2	.0000	1	multibillion-dollar
0.0105	20.2	.0000	1	multifamily
0.0105	20.2	.0000	1	multilaterally
0.0105	20.2	.0000	1	Munchen
0.0105	20.2	.0000	1	murexes
0.0105	20.2	.0000	1	muscle-powered
0.0105	20.2	.0000	1	musculoskeletal
0.0105	20.2	.0000	1	Museum's
0.0105	20.2	.0000	1	Museums
0.0105	20.2	.0000	1	Muskegon
0.0105	20.2	.0000	1	Musketeers
0.0105	20.2	.0000	1	mustards
0.0105	20.2	.0000	1	Mutsuhito
0.0105	20.2	.0000	1	MV
0.0105	20.2	.0000	1	mynahs
0.0105	20.2	.0000	1	Mysteries
0.0105	20.2	.0000	1	mythologies
0.0105	20.2	.0000	1	myxomatosis
0.0105	20.2	.0000	1	NaNO3
0.0105	20.2	.0000	1	NaOH
0.0105	20.2	.0000	1	nacre
0.0105	20.2	.0000	1	Nadia
0.0105	20.2	.0000	1	nail-biting
0.0105	20.2	.0000	1	Nama
0.0105	20.2	.0000	1	Names
0.0105	20.2	.0000	1	NAPOLEONITE
0.0105	20.2	.0000	1	Narcotics
0.0105	20.2	.0000	1	Nasution
0.0105	20.2	.0000	1	natrolite
0.0105	20.2	.0000	1	nautiloids
0.0105	20.2	.0000	1	nautilus
0.0105	20.2	.0000	1	Naziism
0.0105	20.2	.0000	1	Nearctic
0.0105	20.2	.0000	1	nebiim
0.0105	20.2	.0000	1	nebula's
0.0105	20.2	.0000	1	nebular
0.0105	20.2	.0000	1	necessitates
0.0105	20.2	.0000	1	necrosis
0.0105	20.2	.0000	1	nectaries
0.0105	20.2	.0000	1	Negras
0.0105	20.2	.0000	1	negundo
0.0105	20.2	.0000	1	nematocysts
0.0105	20.2	.0000	1	nematode
0.0105	20.2	.0000	1	Neo-Classicism
0.0105	20.2	.0000	1	neon-lighted
0.0105	20.2	.0000	1	nephrons
0.0105	20.2	.0000	1	Nerva
0.0105	20.2	.0000	1	nerve-frazzling
0.0105	20.2	.0000	1	nervous-system
0.0105	20.2	.0000	1	nest-mound
0.0105	20.2	.0000	1	nestmates
0.0105	20.2	.0000	1	Neuchatel
0.0105	20.2	.0000	1	Neuroses
0.0105	20.2	.0000	1	Neustria
0.0105	20.2	.0000	1	Neustrians
0.0105	20.2	.0000	1	Neutra
0.0105	20.2	.0000	1	neutralization
0.0105	20.2	.0000	1	NewAlbany
0.0105	20.2	.0000	1	NewBrunswick
0.0105	20.2	.0000	1	NewMexico-Texas-Mexico
0.0105	20.2	.0000	1	NewYear's
0.0105	20.2	.0000	1	New-Mexico
0.0105	20.2	.0000	1	Newell
0.0105	20.2	.0000	1	newsletters
0.0105	20.2	.0000	1	nh/(2p)**
0.0105	20.2	.0000	1	NH3
0.0105	20.2	.0000	1	NH4Cl
0.0105	20.2	.0000	1	Niagara's
0.0105	20.2	.0000	1	nicety
0.0105	20.2	.0000	1	night-blooming
0.0105	20.2	.0000	1	nightingales
0.0105	20.2	.0000	1	nightmarishly
0.0105	20.2	.0000	1	Nigrae
0.0105	20.2	.0000	1	nikau
0.0105	20.2	.0000	1	Nikos
0.0105	20.2	.0000	1	nips
0.0105	20.2	.0000	1	nitration
0.0105	20.2	.0000	1	nitrogen-poor
0.0105	20.2	.0000	1	nitroglycerin
0.0105	20.2	.0000	1	nitron
0.0105	20.2	.0000	1	Njegos
0.0105	20.2	.0000	1	NLF
0.0105	20.2	.0000	1	NLRB
0.0105	20.2	.0000	1	no-knock
0.0105	20.2	.0000	1	nobiliary
0.0105	20.2	.0000	1	noblesse
0.0105	20.2	.0000	1	node
0.0105	20.2	.0000	1	Nollet
0.0105	20.2	.0000	1	nominee's
0.0105	20.2	.0000	1	non-electrical
0.0105	20.2	.0000	1	non-fathers
0.0105	20.2	.0000	1	non-military
0.0105	20.2	.0000	1	non-moving
0.0105	20.2	.0000	1	nonaggression
0.0105	20.2	.0000	1	nonagricultural
THE PRECEDING WORD TYPE OCCUPIES RANK 80300				
0.0105	20.2	.0000	1	noncommercial
0.0105	20.2	.0000	1	nonconformity
0.0105	20.2	.0000	1	noncrystalline
0.0105	20.2	.0000	1	nondecorative
0.0105	20.2	.0000	1	nonelectrical
0.0105	20.2	.0000	1	nonembryonic
0.0105	20.2	.0000	1	nonengineers
0.0105	20.2	.0000	1	nonfamilial
0.0105	20.2	.0000	1	nonfunctional
0.0105	20.2	.0000	1	nongame
0.0105	20.2	.0000	1	nonhomologous
0.0105	20.2	.0000	1	nonmigratory
0.0105	20.2	.0000	1	nonmoving
0.0105	20.2	.0000	1	nonpetroleum
0.0105	20.2	.0000	1	nonpigmented
0.0105	20.2	.0000	1	nonpurulent
0.0105	20.2	.0000	1	nonreligious
0.0105	20.2	.0000	1	nonrepresentational
0.0105	20.2	.0000	1	nonscriptural
0.0105	20.2	.0000	1	nonsleeping
0.0105	20.2	.0000	1	nonsongbirds
0.0105	20.2	.0000	1	nonspecialized
0.0105	20.2	.0000	1	nonteaching
0.0105	20.2	.0000	1	nonuniform
0.0105	20.2	.0000	1	nonuniformity
0.0105	20.2	.0000	1	nonvolcanic
0.0105	20.2	.0000	1	nooses
0.0105	20.2	.0000	1	Nord
0.0105	20.2	.0000	1	north-eastern
0.0105	20.2	.0000	1	Northlands
0.0105	20.2	.0000	1	northward-flowing
0.0105	20.2	.0000	1	nost
0.0105	20.2	.0000	1	not-too-distant
0.0105	20.2	.0000	1	note-issuing
0.0105	20.2	.0000	1	notification
0.0105	20.2	.0000	1	notoriety
0.0105	20.2	.0000	1	Novara
0.0105	20.2	.0000	1	Novgorod
0.0105	20.2	.0000	1	Novi
0.0105	20.2	.0000	1	now-or-never
0.0105	20.2	.0000	1	NO2
0.0105	20.2	.0000	1	NO3
0.0105	20.2	.0000	1	nubs
0.0105	20.2	.0000	1	Nuevo
0.0105	20.2	.0000	1	Numeration
0.0105	20.2	.0000	1	numerously
0.0105	20.2	.0000	1	Nunez
0.0105	20.2	.0000	1	nurture
0.0105	20.2	.0000	1	nuthatches
0.0105	20.2	.0000	1	nutlets
0.0105	20.2	.0000	1	Nyasaland
0.0105	20.2	.0000	1	nymph's
0.0105	20.2	.0000	1	Nymphalidae
0.0105	20.2	.0000	1	oath's
0.0105	20.2	.0000	1	Oblast
0.0105	20.2	.0000	1	oblast
0.0105	20.2	.0000	1	obliterating
0.0105	20.2	.0000	1	obliterative
0.0105	20.2	.0000	1	Oblomov
0.0105	20.2	.0000	1	oblongata
0.0105	20.2	.0000	1	oblongifolia
0.0105	20.2	.0000	1	Obradovic
0.0105	20.2	.0000	1	Obras
0.0105	20.2	.0000	1	obscures
0.0105	20.2	.0000	1	obsesses
0.0105	20.2	.0000	1	obsessional
0.0105	20.2	.0000	1	obsessive-compulsive
0.0105	20.2	.0000	1	obstetrical
0.0105	20.2	.0000	1	obstructing
0.0105	20.2	.0000	1	Obyknovennaya
0.0105	20.2	.0000	1	Occupations
0.0105	20.2	.0000	1	ocellaris
0.0105	20.2	.0000	1	Odessa
0.0105	20.2	.0000	1	ODOACER
0.0105	20.2	.0000	1	ODOVACAR
0.0105	20.2	.0000	1	Oenothera
0.0105	20.2	.0000	1	Oersted's
0.0105	20.2	.0000	1	off-normal
0.0105	20.2	.0000	1	offensively
0.0105	20.2	.0000	1	Officials
0.0105	20.2	.0000	1	offsetting
0.0105	20.2	.0000	1	Ohmer
0.0105	20.2	.0000	1	oilseeds
0.0105	20.2	.0000	1	Okeford
0.0105	20.2	.0000	1	okey
0.0105	20.2	.0000	1	Okla
0.0105	20.2	.0000	1	old-man's
0.0105	20.2	.0000	1	olefins
0.0105	20.2	.0000	1	olive-drab
0.0105	20.2	.0000	1	olive-growing
0.0105	20.2	.0000	1	ologies
0.0105	20.2	.0000	1	Omdurman
0.0105	20.2	.0000	1	omissions
0.0105	20.2	.0000	1	omnivorous
0.0105	20.2	.0000	1	once-for-all
0.0105	20.2	.0000	1	one-in-a-million
0.0105	20.2	.0000	1	one-inch-wide
0.0105	20.2	.0000	1	one-up
0.0105	20.2	.0000	1	onesided
0.0105	20.2	.0000	1	oozy
THE PRECEDING WORD TYPE OCCUPIES RANK 80400				
0.0105	20.2	.0000	1	Opaiva
0.0105	20.2	.0000	1	opera-ballets
0.0105	20.2	.0000	1	operable
0.0105	20.2	.0000	1	Ophelia
0.0105	20.2	.0000	1	opinionated
0.0105	20.2	.0000	1	orbicular
0.0105	20.2	.0000	1	Orbis
0.0105	20.2	.0000	1	ore-bearing
0.0105	20.2	.0000	1	organism's
0.0105	20.2	.0000	1	organization's
0.0105	20.2	.0000	1	orient
0.0105	20.2	.0000	1	orienting
0.0105	20.2	.0000	1	originates
0.0105	20.2	.0000	1	orogeny
0.0105	20.2	.0000	1	Orosius
0.0105	20.2	.0000	1	ORTHODOX
0.0105	20.2	.0000	1	Ortler
0.0105	20.2	.0000	1	OsTimbiras
0.0105	20.2	.0000	1	oscillators
0.0105	20.2	.0000	1	ossuaries
0.0105	20.2	.0000	1	Ostarrichi
0.0105	20.2	.0000	1	osteitis
0.0105	20.2	.0000	1	Osteoglossidae
0.0105	20.2	.0000	1	ostracoderms
0.0105	20.2	.0000	1	ostrich-like
0.0105	20.2	.0000	1	ostrichlike
0.0105	20.2	.0000	1	Ostrogoths
0.0105	20.2	.0000	1	Othere
0.0105	20.2	.0000	1	Ottonians
0.0105	20.2	.0000	1	Oudewater
0.0105	20.2	.0000	1	out-dated
0.0105	20.2	.0000	1	out-of-town
0.0105	20.2	.0000	1	outdistance
0.0105	20.2	.0000	1	Outfielders
0.0105	20.2	.0000	1	outfitting
0.0105	20.2	.0000	1	outlay
0.0105	20.2	.0000	1	outproduced
0.0105	20.2	.0000	1	outweighed
0.0105	20.2	.0000	1	ovalbumin
0.0105	20.2	.0000	1	Over
0.0105	20.2	.0000	1	over-represented
0.0105	20.2	.0000	1	overactive
0.0105	20.2	.0000	1	overcharge
0.0105	20.2	.0000	1	overexposure
0.0105	20.2	.0000	1	overfishing
0.0105	20.2	.0000	1	overgrazing
0.0105	20.2	.0000	1	overgrowth
0.0105	20.2	.0000	1	overleapt
0.0105	20.2	.0000	1	overloads
0.0105	20.2	.0000	1	overlord
0.0105	20.2	.0000	1	overridden
0.0105	20.2	.0000	1	Overseas
0.0105	20.2	.0000	1	overspreading
0.0105	20.2	.0000	1	overstuffed
0.0105	20.2	.0000	1	overtaxed
0.0105	20.2	.0000	1	overthrust
0.0105	20.2	.0000	1	ovipositor
0.0105	20.2	.0000	1	ovoviviparous
0.0105	20.2	.0000	1	owner-operated
0.0105	20.2	.0000	1	oxidizing
0.0105	20.2	.0000	1	oxpecker
0.0105	20.2	.0000	1	oxygenated
0.0105	20.2	.0000	1	oxygenates
0.0105	20.2	.0000	1	P-shaped
0.0105	20.2	.0000	1	Paardeberg
0.0105	20.2	.0000	1	pablum
0.0105	20.2	.0000	1	pacas
0.0105	20.2	.0000	1	Paccard
0.0105	20.2	.0000	1	pacta
0.0105	20.2	.0000	1	paddlefish
0.0105	20.2	.0000	1	paeans
0.0105	20.2	.0000	1	Pakistanis
0.0105	20.2	.0000	1	Palamedes
0.0105	20.2	.0000	1	Palaquium
0.0105	20.2	.0000	1	palates
0.0105	20.2	.0000	1	Palatines
0.0105	20.2	.0000	1	Palavicini
0.0105	20.2	.0000	1	paleoanthropological
0.0105	20.2	.0000	1	paleoanthropology
0.0105	20.2	.0000	1	Paleontologists
0.0105	20.2	.0000	1	Palermo
0.0105	20.2	.0000	1	palintonon
0.0105	20.2	.0000	1	palm-fringed
0.0105	20.2	.0000	1	palm-like
0.0105	20.2	.0000	1	palm's
0.0105	20.2	.0000	1	palmate
0.0105	20.2	.0000	1	palmately
0.0105	20.2	.0000	1	Palmyra
0.0105	20.2	.0000	1	PaloAlto's
0.0105	20.2	.0000	1	pangolin
0.0105	20.2	.0000	1	Panini's
0.0105	20.2	.0000	1	pantheistic
0.0105	20.2	.0000	1	pantomime-ballets
0.0105	20.2	.0000	1	Panzer
0.0105	20.2	.0000	1	Papacy
0.0105	20.2	.0000	1	paper-devourers
0.0105	20.2	.0000	1	papery
0.0105	20.2	.0000	1	Papin
0.0105	20.2	.0000	1	Papineau
0.0105	20.2	.0000	1	Pappenheim
THE PRECEDING WORD TYPE OCCUPIES RANK 80500				
0.0105	20.2	.0000	1	Pappenheim's
0.0105	20.2	.0000	1	paralysed
0.0105	20.2	.0000	1	paranoia
0.0105	20.2	.0000	1	paranoid
0.0105	20.2	.0000	1	Paraphrase
0.0105	20.2	.0000	1	PARAPLEGIA
0.0105	20.2	.0000	1	Parapsychology
0.0105	20.2	.0000	1	PARAPSYCHOLOGY
0.0105	20.2	.0000	1	parasitized
0.0105	20.2	.0000	1	Parents
0.0105	20.2	.0000	1	Parisienne
0.0105	20.2	.0000	1	park's
0.0105	20.2	.0000	1	Parkes
0.0105	20.2	.0000	1	parklands
0.0105	20.2	.0000	1	Parkman
0.0105	20.2	.0000	1	parliamentarian
0.0105	20.2	.0000	1	parliaments
0.0105	20.2	.0000	1	Parma
0.0105	20.2	.0000	1	Parnassians
0.0105	20.2	.0000	1	Parnassus
0.0105	20.2	.0000	1	paroled
0.0105	20.2	.0000	1	Parr
0.0105	20.2	.0000	1	parsimonious
0.0105	20.2	.0000	1	partakes
0.0105	20.2	.0000	1	particle's
0.0105	20.2	.0000	1	Parties
0.0105	20.2	.0000	1	partly-finished
0.0105	20.2	.0000	1	party-hat
0.0105	20.2	.0000	1	Pas-de-Calais
0.0105	20.2	.0000	1	Pasig
0.0105	20.2	.0000	1	pasko
0.0105	20.2	.0000	1	pasqueflower
0.0105	20.2	.0000	1	pastes
0.0105	20.2	.0000	1	Patchogue
0.0105	20.2	.0000	1	patriarchs
0.0105	20.2	.0000	1	Patriotic
0.0105	20.2	.0000	1	Paulina
0.0105	20.2	.0000	1	pawns
0.0105	20.2	.0000	1	Payne-Aldrich
0.0105	20.2	.0000	1	Pb
0.0105	20.2	.0000	1	Pd
0.0105	20.2	.0000	1	Pea
0.0105	20.2	.0000	1	Peace-Loving
0.0105	20.2	.0000	1	peaceffully
0.0105	20.2	.0000	1	pearlfish
0.0105	20.2	.0000	1	Peck's
0.0105	20.2	.0000	1	Pecourt
0.0105	20.2	.0000	1	pectoral
0.0105	20.2	.0000	1	pectoralis
0.0105	20.2	.0000	1	Pedja
0.0105	20.2	.0000	1	Peenemunde
0.0105	20.2	.0000	1	peg-tops
0.0105	20.2	.0000	1	Peking's
0.0105	20.2	.0000	1	pelecypods
0.0105	20.2	.0000	1	Pelee
0.0105	20.2	.0000	1	Peloponnesian
0.0105	20.2	.0000	1	pelvises
0.0105	20.2	.0000	1	Pemberton
0.0105	20.2	.0000	1	penal
0.0105	20.2	.0000	1	pencil-thick
0.0105	20.2	.0000	1	Peninsular
0.0105	20.2	.0000	1	penis
0.0105	20.2	.0000	1	penlike
0.0105	20.2	.0000	1	Pennsylvania-born
0.0105	20.2	.0000	1	penny-pinching
0.0105	20.2	.0000	1	Pentateuch
0.0105	20.2	.0000	1	pentothal
0.0105	20.2	.0000	1	peoplehood
0.0105	20.2	.0000	1	Pepin's
0.0105	20.2	.0000	1	pepperation
0.0105	20.2	.0000	1	Percentage
0.0105	20.2	.0000	1	perchlike
0.0105	20.2	.0000	1	perennially
0.0105	20.2	.0000	1	perfume-making
0.0105	20.2	.0000	1	periostracum
0.0105	20.2	.0000	1	peripherally
0.0105	20.2	.0000	1	Perish
0.0105	20.2	.0000	1	Perons
0.0105	20.2	.0000	1	perpetuated
0.0105	20.2	.0000	1	perpetuator
0.0105	20.2	.0000	1	perplexes
0.0105	20.2	.0000	1	persecutor
0.0105	20.2	.0000	1	persevere
0.0105	20.2	.0000	1	Persian-speaking
0.0105	20.2	.0000	1	Perthshire
0.0105	20.2	.0000	1	perusal
0.0105	20.2	.0000	1	perversions
0.0105	20.2	.0000	1	perversity
0.0105	20.2	.0000	1	pervious
0.0105	20.2	.0000	1	Peten
0.0105	20.2	.0000	1	Peterborough
0.0105	20.2	.0000	1	petro-chemical
0.0105	20.2	.0000	1	petrographical
0.0105	20.2	.0000	1	Petrovic
0.0105	20.2	.0000	1	Peuple
0.0105	20.2	.0000	1	Peyrere
0.0105	20.2	.0000	1	PhD
0.0105	20.2	.0000	1	PhD's**
0.0105	20.2	.0000	1	Phalerum
0.0105	20.2	.0000	1	pharmacology
THE PRECEDING WORD TYPE OCCUPIES RANK 80600				
0.0105	20.2	.0000	1	pharoahs
0.0105	20.2	.0000	1	phasmids
0.0105	20.2	.0000	1	pheasant-like
0.0105	20.2	.0000	1	Phenomena
0.0105	20.2	.0000	1	phenotype
0.0105	20.2	.0000	1	Philbrook
0.0105	20.2	.0000	1	Philipp
0.0105	20.2	.0000	1	philistine
0.0105	20.2	.0000	1	Philistinism
0.0105	20.2	.0000	1	Philon
0.0105	20.2	.0000	1	Philon's
0.0105	20.2	.0000	1	philosopher's
0.0105	20.2	.0000	1	phlox
0.0105	20.2	.0000	1	Phoberomys
0.0105	20.2	.0000	1	phobia
0.0105	20.2	.0000	1	Phobia
0.0105	20.2	.0000	1	phonation
0.0105	20.2	.0000	1	phonemics
0.0105	20.2	.0000	1	phosphoglyceric
0.0105	20.2	.0000	1	Phosphorescence
0.0105	20.2	.0000	1	photoelectrons
0.0105	20.2	.0000	1	photojournalism
0.0105	20.2	.0000	1	photomaterials
0.0105	20.2	.0000	1	photomechanical
0.0105	20.2	.0000	1	photosensitive
0.0105	20.2	.0000	1	Phramid

U	SFI	D	F	Word Type
0.0105	20.2	.0000	1	Phyllobates
0.0105	20.2	.0000	1	Physalia
0.0105	20.2	.0000	1	physician-naturalists
0.0105	20.2	.0000	1	physicists'
0.0105	20.2	.0000	1	physiographically
0.0105	20.2	.0000	1	physiologists
0.0105	20.2	.0000	1	pianist's
0.0105	20.2	.0000	1	picayune
0.0105	20.2	.0000	1	Pictavia
0.0105	20.2	.0000	1	Picts
0.0105	20.2	.0000	1	picturesquely
0.0105	20.2	.0000	1	pied-billed
0.0105	20.2	.0000	1	Pieve
0.0105	20.2	.0000	1	pilchards
0.0105	20.2	.0000	1	pinnately
0.0105	20.2	.0000	1	pinpointing
0.0105	20.2	.0000	1	PinusCaribaea
0.0105	20.2	.0000	1	PinusPalustris
0.0105	20.2	.0000	1	pinwheel-like
0.0105	20.2	.0000	1	pinworms
0.0105	20.2	.0000	1	Pious
0.0105	20.2	.0000	1	Pirandello's
0.0105	20.2	.0000	1	Pisistratus
0.0105	20.2	.0000	1	piston-cylinder
0.0105	20.2	.0000	1	pitchforked
0.0105	20.2	.0000	1	Pittman
0.0105	20.2	.0000	1	placoderms
0.0105	20.2	.0000	1	Plagioclases
0.0105	20.2	.0000	1	planers
0.0105	20.2	.0000	1	planets'
0.0105	20.2	.0000	1	planktonic
0.0105	20.2	.0000	1	plant-feeding
0.0105	20.2	.0000	1	plantlike
0.0105	20.2	.0000	1	Plastics
0.0105	20.2	.0000	1	plastics-like
0.0105	20.2	.0000	1	plastron
0.0105	20.2	.0000	1	Plataeans
0.0105	20.2	.0000	1	Pleasantburg
0.0105	20.2	.0000	1	Pleasonton
0.0105	20.2	.0000	1	plebiscites
0.0105	20.2	.0000	1	pledging
0.0105	20.2	.0000	1	plenitude
0.0105	20.2	.0000	1	plenties
0.0105	20.2	.0000	1	plentifull
0.0105	20.2	.0000	1	plesiosaurs
0.0105	20.2	.0000	1	plexuses
0.0105	20.2	.0000	1	Pliocene
0.0105	20.2	.0000	1	pliocene
0.0105	20.2	.0000	1	plosives
0.0105	20.2	.0000	1	Plowman
0.0105	20.2	.0000	1	Plumbing
0.0105	20.2	.0000	1	plummet
0.0105	20.2	.0000	1	pneumatically
0.0105	20.2	.0000	1	Poem
0.0105	20.2	.0000	1	Poetical
0.0105	20.2	.0000	1	Politicks
0.0105	20.2	.0000	1	Politics
0.0105	20.2	.0000	1	Politika
0.0105	20.2	.0000	1	Politische
0.0105	20.2	.0000	1	pollination
0.0105	20.2	.0000	1	pollinators
0.0105	20.2	.0000	1	Polyglotta
0.0105	20.2	.0000	1	Polynices
0.0105	20.2	.0000	1	Pompeiian
0.0105	20.2	.0000	1	pond's
0.0105	20.2	.0000	1	ponderosity
0.0105	20.2	.0000	1	ponders
0.0105	20.2	.0000	1	Ponkapog
0.0105	20.2	.0000	1	Popple
0.0105	20.2	.0000	1	popularization
0.0105	20.2	.0000	1	porcupinefish
0.0105	20.2	.0000	1	porcupinefishes
0.0105	20.2	.0000	1	Position
0.0105	20.2	.0000	1	positron

THE PRECEDING WORD TYPE OCCUPIES RANK 80700

U	SFI	D	F	Word Type
0.0105	20.2	.0000	1	post-Homeric
0.0105	20.2	.0000	1	post-apostolic
0.0105	20.2	.0000	1	post-impressionist
0.0105	20.2	.0000	1	post-romantic
0.0105	20.2	.0000	1	postern
0.0105	20.2	.0000	1	posthole
0.0105	20.2	.0000	1	posthumas
0.0105	20.2	.0000	1	posthumes
0.0105	20.2	.0000	1	posthumous
0.0105	20.2	.0000	1	Posthumous
0.0105	20.2	.0000	1	posthumously
0.0105	20.2	.0000	1	postulating
0.0105	20.2	.0000	1	pothooks
0.0105	20.2	.0000	1	Potowomut
0.0105	20.2	.0000	1	poular
0.0105	20.2	.0000	1	Pouring
0.0105	20.2	.0000	1	powder-down
0.0105	20.2	.0000	1	Pozzuoli
0.0105	20.2	.0000	1	prairieland
0.0105	20.2	.0000	1	Praises
0.0105	20.2	.0000	1	pre-Communist
0.0105	20.2	.0000	1	pre-European
0.0105	20.2	.0000	1	pre-eminent
0.0105	20.2	.0000	1	pre-historic
0.0105	20.2	.0000	1	pre-man
0.0105	20.2	.0000	1	preaches
0.0105	20.2	.0000	1	preachments
0.0105	20.2	.0000	1	precisioned-machined
0.0105	20.2	.0000	1	preclude
0.0105	20.2	.0000	1	precognitive
0.0105	20.2	.0000	1	precursors
0.0105	20.2	.0000	1	predator's
0.0105	20.2	.0000	1	predicated
0.0105	20.2	.0000	1	predisposing
0.0105	20.2	.0000	1	predominately
0.0105	20.2	.0000	1	Predrag
0.0105	20.2	.0000	1	preengineering
0.0105	20.2	.0000	1	prehatched
0.0105	20.2	.0000	1	prehistorian
0.0105	20.2	.0000	1	prehuman
0.0105	20.2	.0000	1	premedical
0.0105	20.2	.0000	1	premiership
0.0105	20.2	.0000	1	premolar
0.0105	20.2	.0000	1	Prendergast
0.0105	20.2	.0000	1	Presern
0.0105	20.2	.0000	1	pressure-and-catalysis
0.0105	20.2	.0000	1	presupposes
0.0105	20.2	.0000	1	pretexts
0.0105	20.2	.0000	1	Prevost
0.0105	20.2	.0000	1	priest-teacher
0.0105	20.2	.0000	1	Primeiros
0.0105	20.2	.0000	1	primitiveness
0.0105	20.2	.0000	1	Primoz
0.0105	20.2	.0000	1	Primrose
0.0105	20.2	.0000	1	Prince-Bishop
0.0105	20.2	.0000	1	PRINTING
0.0105	20.2	.0000	1	printings
0.0105	20.2	.0000	1	prison-reform
0.0105	20.2	.0000	1	prizefight
0.0105	20.2	.0000	1	pro-democratic
0.0105	20.2	.0000	1	problematical
0.0105	20.2	.0000	1	process-color
0.0105	20.2	.0000	1	prodigiously
0.0105	20.2	.0000	1	profusely
0.0105	20.2	.0000	1	progenitor
0.0105	20.2	.0000	1	prognosticators
0.0105	20.2	.0000	1	prohibit
0.0105	20.2	.0000	1	proliferated
0.0105	20.2	.0000	1	promenades
0.0105	20.2	.0000	1	prominently
0.0105	20.2	.0000	1	promulgation
0.0105	20.2	.0000	1	pronged
0.0105	20.2	.0000	1	pronghorns
0.0105	20.2	.0000	1	propane
0.0105	20.2	.0000	1	propellent
0.0105	20.2	.0000	1	propensity
0.0105	20.2	.0000	1	property-owning
0.0105	20.2	.0000	1	prophet-leaders
0.0105	20.2	.0000	1	proportionality
0.0105	20.2	.0000	1	proportionately
0.0105	20.2	.0000	1	Propulsion
0.0105	20.2	.0000	1	proroguing
0.0105	20.2	.0000	1	proscribed
0.0105	20.2	.0000	1	prosecuting
0.0105	20.2	.0000	1	prosimian
0.0105	20.2	.0000	1	prosimians
0.0105	20.2	.0000	1	Prospects
0.0105	20.2	.0000	1	prostate
0.0105	20.2	.0000	1	prostatis
0.0105	20.2	.0000	1	protein-rich
0.0105	20.2	.0000	1	Protestantism
0.0105	20.2	.0000	1	Protests
0.0105	20.2	.0000	1	protistans
0.0105	20.2	.0000	1	Protococcus
0.0105	20.2	.0000	1	protrusion
0.0105	20.2	.0000	1	Proustian
0.0105	20.2	.0000	1	prowlers
0.0105	20.2	.0000	1	Pseudoalleles
0.0105	20.2	.0000	1	pseudoallelism
0.0105	20.2	.0000	1	pseudonym

THE PRECEDING WORD TYPE OCCUPIES RANK 80800

U	SFI	D	F	Word Type
0.0105	20.2	.0000	1	pseudopodia
0.0105	20.2	.0000	1	psychical
0.0105	20.2	.0000	1	psychogenic
0.0105	20.2	.0000	1	psychokinesis
0.0105	20.2	.0000	1	psychoneuroses
0.0105	20.2	.0000	1	Psychotherapy
0.0105	20.2	.0000	1	public-health
0.0105	20.2	.0000	1	Publication
0.0105	20.2	.0000	1	publicists
0.0105	20.2	.0000	1	puffers
0.0105	20.2	.0000	1	Pulangi
0.0105	20.2	.0000	1	pulvilli
0.0105	20.2	.0000	1	Pump
0.0105	20.2	.0000	1	Punishment
0.0105	20.2	.0000	1	pupal
0.0105	20.2	.0000	1	pupas
0.0105	20.2	.0000	1	pupation
0.0105	20.2	.0000	1	purchasers
0.0105	20.2	.0000	1	pursues
0.0105	20.2	.0000	1	push-button-controlled
0.0105	20.2	.0000	1	Pyramid's
0.0105	20.2	.0000	1	python's
0.0105	20.2	.0000	1	q's
0.0105	20.2	.0000	1	qat
0.0105	20.2	.0000	1	quadriceps
0.0105	20.2	.0000	1	quantized
0.0105	20.2	.0000	1	quasi-public
0.0105	20.2	.0000	1	queries
0.0105	20.2	.0000	1	queues
0.0105	20.2	.0000	1	quiescence
0.0105	20.2	.0000	1	quiescent
0.0105	20.2	.0000	1	Quinault
0.0105	20.2	.0000	1	Quintero
0.0105	20.2	.0000	1	Quivira
0.0105	20.2	.0000	1	Rabbinical
0.0105	20.2	.0000	1	Rabbis
0.0105	20.2	.0000	1	Rabelais
0.0105	20.2	.0000	1	Racial
0.0105	20.2	.0000	1	Racine
0.0105	20.2	.0000	1	Radar
0.0105	20.2	.0000	1	radar-wind
0.0105	20.2	.0000	1	Radcliffe-Brown
0.0105	20.2	.0000	1	Radcliffe's
0.0105	20.2	.0000	1	raddiator
0.0105	20.2	.0000	1	radially
0.0105	20.2	.0000	1	Radicals
0.0105	20.2	.0000	1	radome
0.0105	20.2	.0000	1	radomes
0.0105	20.2	.0000	1	Raeburn
0.0105	20.2	.0000	1	Raffaele
0.0105	20.2	.0000	1	Ragang
0.0105	20.2	.0000	1	railraods
0.0105	20.2	.0000	1	railway-signal
0.0105	20.2	.0000	1	Rajah
0.0105	20.2	.0000	1	Rameses
0.0105	20.2	.0000	1	rankness
0.0105	20.2	.0000	1	Rann
0.0105	20.2	.0000	1	raptorial
0.0105	20.2	.0000	1	rare-earth
0.0105	20.2	.0000	1	rarefaction
0.0105	20.2	.0000	1	rasps
0.0105	20.2	.0000	1	ratchets
0.0105	20.2	.0000	1	ratel
0.0105	20.2	.0000	1	rationalism
0.0105	20.2	.0000	1	ravished
0.0105	20.2	.0000	1	Rays
0.0105	20.2	.0000	1	razor-thin
0.0105	20.2	.0000	1	reabsorb
0.0105	20.2	.0000	1	real-estate
0.0105	20.2	.0000	1	reapportion
0.0105	20.2	.0000	1	rear-guard
0.0105	20.2	.0000	1	reassert
0.0105	20.2	.0000	1	reawakened
0.0105	20.2	.0000	1	Rebate
0.0105	20.2	.0000	1	rebates
0.0105	20.2	.0000	1	Rebild
0.0105	20.2	.0000	1	rebus
0.0105	20.2	.0000	1	receptionists
0.0105	20.2	.0000	1	reciprocate
0.0105	20.2	.0000	1	recirculate
0.0105	20.2	.0000	1	recirculates
0.0105	20.2	.0000	1	recluse
0.0105	20.2	.0000	1	recomment
0.0105	20.2	.0000	1	recondition
0.0105	20.2	.0000	1	reconnoitering
0.0105	20.2	.0000	1	reconquest
0.0105	20.2	.0000	1	reconsideration
0.0105	20.2	.0000	1	Reconstructionist
0.0105	20.2	.0000	1	reconstructions
0.0105	20.2	.0000	1	reconstructs
0.0105	20.2	.0000	1	record-buying
0.0105	20.2	.0000	1	Recruitment
0.0105	20.2	.0000	1	recrystallized
0.0105	20.2	.0000	1	rectified
0.0105	20.2	.0000	1	recuperated
0.0105	20.2	.0000	1	recurrently
0.0105	20.2	.0000	1	red-billed
0.0105	20.2	.0000	1	red-shouldered
0.0105	20.2	.0000	1	red-tailed
0.0105	20.2	.0000	1	redesign

THE PRECEDING WORD TYPE OCCUPIES RANK 80900

U	SFI	D	F	Word Type
0.0105	20.2	.0000	1	redirecting
0.0105	20.2	.0000	1	rediscovering
0.0105	20.2	.0000	1	redpolls
0.0105	20.2	.0000	1	Reedy
0.0105	20.2	.0000	1	reestablishment
0.0105	20.2	.0000	1	referenced
0.0105	20.2	.0000	1	Referendum
0.0105	20.2	.0000	1	Reflector
0.0105	20.2	.0000	1	reforestation
0.0105	20.2	.0000	1	REFORM
0.0105	20.2	.0000	1	Reformers
0.0105	20.2	.0000	1	refract
0.0105	20.2	.0000	1	refrigerants
0.0105	20.2	.0000	1	Refrigeration
0.0105	20.2	.0000	1	refutes
0.0105	20.2	.0000	1	regents
0.0105	20.2	.0000	1	regimen
0.0105	20.2	.0000	1	regurgitate
0.0105	20.2	.0000	1	rehabilitated
0.0105	20.2	.0000	1	rehashing
0.0105	20.2	.0000	1	Reign
0.0105	20.2	.0000	1	reinserted
0.0105	20.2	.0000	1	reinsertion
0.0105	20.2	.0000	1	reinterpreted
0.0105	20.2	.0000	1	rejections
0.0105	20.2	.0000	1	relativistic
0.0105	20.2	.0000	1	relearning
0.0105	20.2	.0000	1	relocating
0.0105	20.2	.0000	1	remade
0.0105	20.2	.0000	1	Remembrance
0.0105	20.2	.0000	1	renderings
0.0105	20.2	.0000	1	Reni
0.0105	20.2	.0000	1	reorganizing
0.0105	20.2	.0000	1	replenishes
0.0105	20.2	.0000	1	reprogram
0.0105	20.2	.0000	1	reptiles'
0.0105	20.2	.0000	1	Republika
0.0105	20.2	.0000	1	repurchases
0.0105	20.2	.0000	1	resale
0.0105	20.2	.0000	1	resets
0.0105	20.2	.0000	1	resettling
0.0105	20.2	.0000	1	Resistant
0.0105	20.2	.0000	1	resistible
0.0105	20.2	.0000	1	Rest
0.0105	20.2	.0000	1	restiveness
0.0105	20.2	.0000	1	Resumption
0.0105	20.2	.0000	1	retaken
0.0105	20.2	.0000	1	retest
0.0105	20.2	.0000	1	reticulate
0.0105	20.2	.0000	1	retrofire
0.0105	20.2	.0000	1	retromorphosis
0.0105	20.2	.0000	1	reunification
0.0105	20.2	.0000	1	revere
0.0105	20.2	.0000	1	revives
0.0105	20.2	.0000	1	revolutionist
0.0105	20.2	.0000	1	Revulgo
0.0105	20.2	.0000	1	Rey's
0.0105	20.2	.0000	1	reyes
0.0105	20.2	.0000	1	Rh
0.0105	20.2	.0000	1	Rh-negative
0.0105	20.2	.0000	1	Rh-positive
0.0105	20.2	.0000	1	rhea
0.0105	20.2	.0000	1	Rheims
0.0105	20.2	.0000	1	Rheims-Challoner
0.0105	20.2	.0000	1	Rheims-Douay
0.0105	20.2	.0000	1	Rheneia
0.0105	20.2	.0000	1	rhesus
0.0105	20.2	.0000	1	Rhetorick
0.0105	20.2	.0000	1	rhizome
0.0105	20.2	.0000	1	RhodeIsland's
0.0105	20.2	.0000	1	rhythm-keeper
0.0105	20.2	.0000	1	Ribe
0.0105	20.2	.0000	1	rice's
0.0105	20.2	.0000	1	ricewater
0.0105	20.2	.0000	1	ricocheting
0.0105	20.2	.0000	1	ridged
0.0105	20.2	.0000	1	ridleys
0.0105	20.2	.0000	1	right-thinking
0.0105	20.2	.0000	1	Rijksmuseum
0.0105	20.2	.0000	1	Ringstrasse
0.0105	20.2	.0000	1	RioGrande
0.0105	20.2	.0000	1	ripener
0.0105	20.2	.0000	1	Rivals
0.0105	20.2	.0000	1	river-craft
0.0105	20.2	.0000	1	riverbeds
0.0105	20.2	.0000	1	riverfront
0.0105	20.2	.0000	1	riverless
0.0105	20.2	.0000	1	Roach
0.0105	20.2	.0000	1	roadbeds
0.0105	20.2	.0000	1	Roash
0.0105	20.2	.0000	1	Robespierre
0.0105	20.2	.0000	1	Roby
0.0105	20.2	.0000	1	rock-fill
0.0105	20.2	.0000	1	rocketeers
0.0105	20.2	.0000	1	Rockhill
0.0105	20.2	.0000	1	Rockhurst
0.0105	20.2	.0000	1	rococo
0.0105	20.2	.0000	1	Roderick
0.0105	20.2	.0000	1	Rodrigo
0.0105	20.2	.0000	1	roll-call

THE PRECEDING WORD TYPE OCCUPIES RANK 81000

U	SFI	D	F	Word Type
0.0105	20.2	.0000	1	rollability
0.0105	20.2	.0000	1	Rolland
0.0105	20.2	.0000	1	Romagna
0.0105	20.2	.0000	1	Romain
0.0105	20.2	.0000	1	Romanized
0.0105	20.2	.0000	1	Romanovich
0.0105	20.2	.0000	1	romanticist
0.0105	20.2	.0000	1	romanticized
0.0105	20.2	.0000	1	Rookwood
0.0105	20.2	.0000	1	root-hair
0.0105	20.2	.0000	1	rootstock
0.0105	20.2	.0000	1	rootstocks
0.0105	20.2	.0000	1	ropy
0.0105	20.2	.0000	1	Rosin
0.0105	20.2	.0000	1	Rossetti
0.0105	20.2	.0000	1	rotational
0.0105	20.2	.0000	1	Rotenturmstrasse
0.0105	20.2	.0000	1	Rothschild
0.0105	20.2	.0000	1	rough-and-tumble
0.0105	20.2	.0000	1	roughs
0.0105	20.2	.0000	1	Rougon
0.0105	20.2	.0000	1	round-bottom
0.0105	20.2	.0000	1	Rousseauist
0.0105	20.2	.0000	1	roves
0.0105	20.2	.0000	1	royalist
0.0105	20.2	.0000	1	rubber-producing
0.0105	20.2	.0000	1	Rubens'
0.0105	20.2	.0000	1	rudiments
0.0105	20.2	.0000	1	rug's
0.0105	20.2	.0000	1	ruggedness
0.0105	20.2	.0000	1	ruminants
0.0105	20.2	.0000	1	Ruslan
0.0105	20.2	.0000	1	rust-colored
0.0105	20.2	.0000	1	ruthenium
0.0105	20.2	.0000	1	Ruwenzori's
0.0105	20.2	.0000	1	Ruy
0.0105	20.2	.0000	1	Ry
0.0105	20.2	.0000	1	Ryukyu
0.0105	20.2	.0000	1	S-shaped
0.0105	20.2	.0000	1	Sabellicus
0.0105	20.2	.0000	1	Sabi
0.0105	20.2	.0000	1	Sable
0.0105	20.2	.0000	1	SABRA
0.0105	20.2	.0000	1	SAC
0.0105	20.2	.0000	1	sacraments
0.0105	20.2	.0000	1	sacredly
0.0105	20.2	.0000	1	sacrificial
0.0105	20.2	.0000	1	Sadi
0.0105	20.2	.0000	1	Safawid
0.0105	20.2	.0000	1	Saginaw
0.0105	20.2	.0000	1	sago
0.0105	20.2	.0000	1	Saint-Leon
0.0105	20.2	.0000	1	saints'
0.0105	20.2	.0000	1	SALADIN
0.0105	20.2	.0000	1	Salah-al-Din
0.0105	20.2	.0000	1	SALAMANDER
0.0105	20.2	.0000	1	Salic
0.0105	20.2	.0000	1	saltmaking
0.0105	20.2	.0000	1	Salzburgers
0.0105	20.2	.0000	1	Salzgries
0.0105	20.2	.0000	1	sambuqs
0.0105	20.2	.0000	1	Samios
0.0105	20.2	.0000	1	Sampling
0.0105	20.2	.0000	1	SanMartin
0.0105	20.2	.0000	1	sanatana
0.0105	20.2	.0000	1	Sango
0.0105	20.2	.0000	1	Sanibel
0.0105	20.2	.0000	1	Santos-Dumont
0.0105	20.2	.0000	1	Saone
0.0105	20.2	.0000	1	sap-transporting
0.0105	20.2	.0000	1	Sapotaceae
0.0105	20.2	.0000	1	saran-plastic
0.0105	20.2	.0000	1	Sardou
0.0105	20.2	.0000	1	Saskia's
0.0105	20.2	.0000	1	Sassanian
0.0105	20.2	.0000	1	satirist
0.0105	20.2	.0000	1	satirizes
0.0105	20.2	.0000	1	Saunderstown
0.0105	20.2	.0000	1	Savery
0.0105	20.2	.0000	1	Scandal
0.0105	20.2	.0000	1	scavenged
0.0105	20.2	.0000	1	scavenging
0.0105	20.2	.0000	1	Schechter
0.0105	20.2	.0000	1	scheduling
0.0105	20.2	.0000	1	Scheele
0.0105	20.2	.0000	1	Schleswig-Holstein
0.0105	20.2	.0000	1	schooled
0.0105	20.2	.0000	1	Schrodinger
0.0105	20.2	.0000	1	scintillant
0.0105	20.2	.0000	1	scions

U	SFI	D	F	Word Type
0.0105	20.2	.0000	1	sclerosis
0.0105	20.2	.0000	1	SCOLECITE
0.0105	20.2	.0000	1	scolecite
0.0105	20.2	.0000	1	SCONE
0.0105	20.2	.0000	1	Scottish-born
0.0105	20.2	.0000	1	scourges
0.0105	20.2	.0000	1	scratched-up
0.0105	20.2	.0000	1	Scribe
0.0105	20.2	.0000	1	scrubs
0.0105	20.2	.0000	1	Sculpture

THE PRECEDING WORD TYPE OCCUPIES RANK 81100

U	SFI	D	F	Word Type
0.0105	20.2	.0000	1	scup
0.0105	20.2	.0000	1	scuro
0.0105	20.2	.0000	1	scythed
0.0105	20.2	.0000	1	Scyths
0.0105	20.2	.0000	1	sea-floor
0.0105	20.2	.0000	1	sea-turtle
0.0105	20.2	.0000	1	searobins
0.0105	20.2	.0000	1	sebaceous
0.0105	20.2	.0000	1	Sebastopol
0.0105	20.2	.0000	1	Secessionists
0.0105	20.2	.0000	1	secretary-stenographer
0.0105	20.2	.0000	1	secretin
0.0105	20.2	.0000	1	Secy
0.0105	20.2	.0000	1	sedatives
0.0105	20.2	.0000	1	seditious
0.0105	20.2	.0000	1	see'uh
0.0105	20.2	.0000	1	seed-pod
0.0105	20.2	.0000	1	Segonzac
0.0105	20.2	.0000	1	Segundos
0.0105	20.2	.0000	1	seizures
0.0105	20.2	.0000	1	Selection
0.0105	20.2	.0000	1	self-advancement
0.0105	20.2	.0000	1	self-awareness
0.0105	20.2	.0000	1	self-centeredness
0.0105	20.2	.0000	1	self-correcting
0.0105	20.2	.0000	1	self-deprecatory
0.0105	20.2	.0000	1	self-effacing
0.0105	20.2	.0000	1	self-effacingly
0.0105	20.2	.0000	1	self-forgetting
0.0105	20.2	.0000	1	self-limited
0.0105	20.2	.0000	1	self-medication
0.0105	20.2	.0000	1	self-repair
0.0105	20.2	.0000	1	self-stabilizing
0.0105	20.2	.0000	1	Seljuk
0.0105	20.2	.0000	1	semi-feudal
0.0105	20.2	.0000	1	semiannual
0.0105	20.2	.0000	1	semiaquatic
0.0105	20.2	.0000	1	semiconducting
0.0105	20.2	.0000	1	seminary
0.0105	20.2	.0000	1	seminomadic
0.0105	20.2	.0000	1	semiparasites
0.0105	20.2	.0000	1	semipermeable
0.0105	20.2	.0000	1	semiprocessed
0.0105	20.2	.0000	1	semiprofessional
0.0105	20.2	.0000	1	semirotary
0.0105	20.2	.0000	1	semita
0.0105	20.2	.0000	1	senates
0.0105	20.2	.0000	1	separateness
0.0105	20.2	.0000	1	separations
0.0105	20.2	.0000	1	Serafin
0.0105	20.2	.0000	1	Serbians
0.0105	20.2	.0000	1	serenaded
0.0105	20.2	.0000	1	serval
0.0105	20.2	.0000	1	servanda
0.0105	20.2	.0000	1	seuerall
0.0105	20.2	.0000	1	seven-foot
0.0105	20.2	.0000	1	seventeen-year
0.0105	20.2	.0000	1	Sewage
0.0105	20.2	.0000	1	sewing-machine
0.0105	20.2	.0000	1	Shafii
0.0105	20.2	.0000	1	shaftless
0.0105	20.2	.0000	1	shagbark
0.0105	20.2	.0000	1	Shah-i-Zind
0.0105	20.2	.0000	1	shamefacedly
0.0105	20.2	.0000	1	Shandy
0.0105	20.2	.0000	1	Shanter
0.0105	20.2	.0000	1	Sharecropper
0.0105	20.2	.0000	1	shark-infested
0.0105	20.2	.0000	1	sharklike
0.0105	20.2	.0000	1	sharp-clawed
0.0105	20.2	.0000	1	sharp-tailed
0.0105	20.2	.0000	1	sharp-toothed
0.0105	20.2	.0000	1	sharpshin
0.0105	20.2	.0000	1	shatterproof
0.0105	20.2	.0000	1	Shay
0.0105	20.2	.0000	1	sheep-stealing
0.0105	20.2	.0000	1	sheepherding
0.0105	20.2	.0000	1	shenanigans
0.0105	20.2	.0000	1	Shia
0.0105	20.2	.0000	1	shibboleth
0.0105	20.2	.0000	1	shimmies
0.0105	20.2	.0000	1	shiners
0.0105	20.2	.0000	1	Shinn
0.0105	20.2	.0000	1	Shinto
0.0105	20.2	.0000	1	shipmasts
0.0105	20.2	.0000	1	shipmates
0.0105	20.2	.0000	1	shirtless
0.0105	20.2	.0000	1	Sholes
0.0105	20.2	.0000	1	shoppers'
0.0105	20.2	.0000	1	shoptalk
0.0105	20.2	.0000	1	short-circuit
0.0105	20.2	.0000	1	short-necked
0.0105	20.2	.0000	1	short-tempered
0.0105	20.2	.0000	1	Shovels
0.0105	20.2	.0000	1	Show-Off
0.0105	20.2	.0000	1	shred
0.0105	20.2	.0000	1	shrike
0.0105	20.2	.0000	1	shrikes
0.0105	20.2	.0000	1	Shrine
0.0105	20.2	.0000	1	shrublike

THE PRECEDING WORD TYPE OCCUPIES RANK 81200

U	SFI	D	F	Word Type
0.0105	20.2	.0000	1	shuns
0.0105	20.2	.0000	1	shunts
0.0105	20.2	.0000	1	Shutt
0.0105	20.2	.0000	1	Si
0.0105	20.2	.0000	1	SiO2
0.0105	20.2	.0000	1	Sian
0.0105	20.2	.0000	1	Sibbald
0.0105	20.2	.0000	1	Siberians
0.0105	20.2	.0000	1	Sicilies
0.0105	20.2	.0000	1	sick-benefit
0.0105	20.2	.0000	1	Sickles
0.0105	20.2	.0000	1	Sickness
0.0105	20.2	.0000	1	side-wheelers
0.0105	20.2	.0000	1	siegecraft
0.0105	20.2	.0000	1	Sierra-Cascades
0.0105	20.2	.0000	1	Sif
0.0105	20.2	.0000	1	Sigel
0.0105	20.2	.0000	1	Sikkeland
0.0105	20.2	.0000	1	Silica
0.0105	20.2	.0000	1	silicic
0.0105	20.2	.0000	1	silicofluoride
0.0105	20.2	.0000	1	Silicon
0.0105	20.2	.0000	1	silky-haired
0.0105	20.2	.0000	1	silver-buckled
0.0105	20.2	.0000	1	silverwork
0.0105	20.2	.0000	1	Simbal
0.0105	20.2	.0000	1	Simbirsk
0.0105	20.2	.0000	1	simulates
0.0105	20.2	.0000	1	simulators
0.0105	20.2	.0000	1	simultaneity
0.0105	20.2	.0000	1	sine
0.0105	20.2	.0000	1	singes
0.0105	20.2	.0000	1	single-electron
0.0105	20.2	.0000	1	single-manned
0.0105	20.2	.0000	1	single-piece
0.0105	20.2	.0000	1	single-sail
0.0105	20.2	.0000	1	single-ship
0.0105	20.2	.0000	1	sinus
0.0105	20.2	.0000	1	sisters'
0.0105	20.2	.0000	1	Sisyphus
0.0105	20.2	.0000	1	sitter's
0.0105	20.2	.0000	1	Sittingbourne
0.0105	20.2	.0000	1	six-by-eight-inch
0.0105	20.2	.0000	1	sixpenny
0.0105	20.2	.0000	1	skeletally
0.0105	20.2	.0000	1	skeleton-key
0.0105	20.2	.0000	1	skullcaps
0.0105	20.2	.0000	1	skylarks
0.0105	20.2	.0000	1	Skylax
0.0105	20.2	.0000	1	Slang
0.0105	20.2	.0000	1	slayings
0.0105	20.2	.0000	1	Slayton
0.0105	20.2	.0000	1	sledgehammers
0.0105	20.2	.0000	1	sleekness
0.0105	20.2	.0000	1	sliderule
0.0105	20.2	.0000	1	slimness
0.0105	20.2	.0000	1	slipware
0.0105	20.2	.0000	1	Sloan's
0.0105	20.2	.0000	1	slotters
0.0105	20.2	.0000	1	slowly-moving
0.0105	20.2	.0000	1	sluices
0.0105	20.2	.0000	1	small-leafed
0.0105	20.2	.0000	1	smashers
0.0105	20.2	.0000	1	Smith-Hughes
0.0105	20.2	.0000	1	smog-free
0.0105	20.2	.0000	1	snake-free
0.0105	20.2	.0000	1	Snoqualmie
0.0105	20.2	.0000	1	snorkeling
0.0105	20.2	.0000	1	snow-choked
0.0105	20.2	.0000	1	snowfields
0.0105	20.2	.0000	1	snowslides
0.0105	20.2	.0000	1	snuffboxes
0.0105	20.2	.0000	1	soapweed
0.0105	20.2	.0000	1	Socinian
0.0105	20.2	.0000	1	sockeye
0.0105	20.2	.0000	1	Socotra
0.0105	20.2	.0000	1	sodium-aluminum
0.0105	20.2	.0000	1	soft-cushioned
0.0105	20.2	.0000	1	soft-shells
0.0105	20.2	.0000	1	soil-dwelling
0.0105	20.2	.0000	1	Solecki's
0.0105	20.2	.0000	1	solid-state
0.0105	20.2	.0000	1	somatic
0.0105	20.2	.0000	1	sometime-editor
0.0105	20.2	.0000	1	Sommerfeld
0.0105	20.2	.0000	1	songbird
0.0105	20.2	.0000	1	soothsayers
0.0105	20.2	.0000	1	soreness
0.0105	20.2	.0000	1	Soule
0.0105	20.2	.0000	1	SouthDakota's
0.0105	20.2	.0000	1	South-African
0.0105	20.2	.0000	1	Southend
0.0105	20.2	.0000	1	southward-flowing
0.0105	20.2	.0000	1	Soviet-trained
0.0105	20.2	.0000	1	spadelike
0.0105	20.2	.0000	1	Spaniel
0.0105	20.2	.0000	1	sparser
0.0105	20.2	.0000	1	spastic
0.0105	20.2	.0000	1	special-effects
0.0105	20.2	.0000	1	Specie

THE PRECEDING WORD TYPE OCCUPIES RANK 81300

U	SFI	D	F	Word Type
0.0105	20.2	.0000	1	specious
0.0105	20.2	.0000	1	speckle
0.0105	20.2	.0000	1	spectrograms
0.0105	20.2	.0000	1	speedsters
0.0105	20.2	.0000	1	sphere's
0.0105	20.2	.0000	1	spiderwort
0.0105	20.2	.0000	1	spike-toothed
0.0105	20.2	.0000	1	Spill
0.0105	20.2	.0000	1	Spiro
0.0105	20.2	.0000	1	split-letter
0.0105	20.2	.0000	1	Spohr
0.0105	20.2	.0000	1	spoliation
0.0105	20.2	.0000	1	sponsorship
0.0105	20.2	.0000	1	spoonbills
0.0105	20.2	.0000	1	sports-loving
0.0105	20.2	.0000	1	sprains
0.0105	20.2	.0000	1	spreadings
0.0105	20.2	.0000	1	spring-blooming
0.0105	20.2	.0000	1	spring-fed
0.0105	20.2	.0000	1	spring-like
0.0105	20.2	.0000	1	springhase
0.0105	20.2	.0000	1	sprit-sail
0.0105	20.2	.0000	1	spruced-up
0.0105	20.2	.0000	1	squabs
0.0105	20.2	.0000	1	squandering
0.0105	20.2	.0000	1	square-meter
0.0105	20.2	.0000	1	squaresails
0.0105	20.2	.0000	1	squib
0.0105	20.2	.0000	1	squiggling
0.0105	20.2	.0000	1	StAmbrose
0.0105	20.2	.0000	1	StBartholomew's
0.0105	20.2	.0000	1	StStephen's
0.0105	20.2	.0000	1	StVitus
0.0105	20.2	.0000	1	stably
0.0105	20.2	.0000	1	stagnating
0.0105	20.2	.0000	1	stand-in
0.0105	20.2	.0000	1	standardize
0.0105	20.2	.0000	1	stantibus
0.0105	20.2	.0000	1	Starling
0.0105	20.2	.0000	1	Starving
0.0105	20.2	.0000	1	state-supported
0.0105	20.2	.0000	1	states-general
0.0105	20.2	.0000	1	Statuary
0.0105	20.2	.0000	1	statutory
0.0105	20.2	.0000	1	stay-at-homes
0.0105	20.2	.0000	1	steadiest
0.0105	20.2	.0000	1	steam-propelled
0.0105	20.2	.0000	1	steam's
0.0105	20.2	.0000	1	steel-gray
0.0105	20.2	.0000	1	steepsided
0.0105	20.2	.0000	1	Stefano
0.0105	20.2	.0000	1	steinbok
0.0105	20.2	.0000	1	Steller's
0.0105	20.2	.0000	1	Stendhal
0.0105	20.2	.0000	1	stenography
0.0105	20.2	.0000	1	Stenopterygius
0.0105	20.2	.0000	1	stenotype
0.0105	20.2	.0000	1	Stephane
0.0105	20.2	.0000	1	Sterne
0.0105	20.2	.0000	1	Steuben
0.0105	20.2	.0000	1	Stewart's
0.0105	20.2	.0000	1	stewpan
0.0105	20.2	.0000	1	stigmas
0.0105	20.2	.0000	1	still-active
0.0105	20.2	.0000	1	still-molten
0.0105	20.2	.0000	1	stills
0.0105	20.2	.0000	1	stinkjims
0.0105	20.2	.0000	1	stipulations
0.0105	20.2	.0000	1	stirrings
0.0105	20.2	.0000	1	stock-
0.0105	20.2	.0000	1	stock-share
0.0105	20.2	.0000	1	stockroom
0.0105	20.2	.0000	1	stonemasonry
0.0105	20.2	.0000	1	stoppage
0.0105	20.2	.0000	1	storied
0.0105	20.2	.0000	1	Strachan
0.0105	20.2	.0000	1	straight-grained
0.0105	20.2	.0000	1	strainers
0.0105	20.2	.0000	1	straitened
0.0105	20.2	.0000	1	straplike
0.0105	20.2	.0000	1	streaky
0.0105	20.2	.0000	1	Strengthening
0.0105	20.2	.0000	1	streptococci
0.0105	20.2	.0000	1	stress-resistance
0.0105	20.2	.0000	1	Strikes
0.0105	20.2	.0000	1	string-propelled
0.0105	20.2	.0000	1	strip-mining
0.0105	20.2	.0000	1	strivings
0.0105	20.2	.0000	1	stroboscopic
0.0105	20.2	.0000	1	Stromboli
0.0105	20.2	.0000	1	Stromont
0.0105	20.2	.0000	1	strong-winged
0.0105	20.2	.0000	1	Structuralist
0.0105	20.2	.0000	1	Struve
0.0105	20.2	.0000	1	Studs
0.0105	20.2	.0000	1	sturgeons
0.0105	20.2	.0000	1	sub-kingdom
0.0105	20.2	.0000	1	Subarctic
0.0105	20.2	.0000	1	subbirds
0.0105	20.2	.0000	1	subcaste

THE PRECEDING WORD TYPE OCCUPIES RANK 81400

U	SFI	D	F	Word Type
0.0105	20.2	.0000	1	subcastes
0.0105	20.2	.0000	1	subclass
0.0105	20.2	.0000	1	subcommittees
0.0105	20.2	.0000	1	subcooling
0.0105	20.2	.0000	1	subgroups
0.0105	20.2	.0000	1	Subjection
0.0105	20.2	.0000	1	subjects'
0.0105	20.2	.0000	1	submarine-infested
0.0105	20.2	.0000	1	subsists
0.0105	20.2	.0000	1	subspecies
0.0105	20.2	.0000	1	subsystem
0.0105	20.2	.0000	1	subtleties
0.0105	20.2	.0000	1	successions
0.0105	20.2	.0000	1	succumbed
0.0105	20.2	.0000	1	succumbs
0.0105	20.2	.0000	1	Sudras
0.0105	20.2	.0000	1	suffocates
0.0105	20.2	.0000	1	suffruticosa
0.0105	20.2	.0000	1	Sukkur
0.0105	20.2	.0000	1	Sulawesi
0.0105	20.2	.0000	1	sulfadiazine
0.0105	20.2	.0000	1	Sulu
0.0105	20.2	.0000	1	sumo
0.0105	20.2	.0000	1	Sumual
0.0105	20.2	.0000	1	sun-diety
0.0105	20.2	.0000	1	sunfishes
0.0105	20.2	.0000	1	Sung
0.0105	20.2	.0000	1	sunlike
0.0105	20.2	.0000	1	Sunni
0.0105	20.2	.0000	1	Sunnite
0.0105	20.2	.0000	1	sunt
0.0105	20.2	.0000	1	superabundance
0.0105	20.2	.0000	1	supermachines
0.0105	20.2	.0000	1	supernaturalism
0.0105	20.2	.0000	1	superstition-ridden
0.0105	20.2	.0000	1	superswift
0.0105	20.2	.0000	1	supervisory
0.0105	20.2	.0000	1	suppuration
0.0105	20.2	.0000	1	supralaryngeal
0.0105	20.2	.0000	1	Supremacy
0.0105	20.2	.0000	1	surfeit
0.0105	20.2	.0000	1	surgeonfish
0.0105	20.2	.0000	1	Surgeons
0.0105	20.2	.0000	1	Surrealism
0.0105	20.2	.0000	1	Survival
0.0105	20.2	.0000	1	suzerainty
0.0105	20.2	.0000	1	svet
0.0105	20.2	.0000	1	Svibul
0.0105	20.2	.0000	1	swatting
0.0105	20.2	.0000	1	Swayne
0.0105	20.2	.0000	1	sweat-soaked
0.0105	20.2	.0000	1	swervings
0.0105	20.2	.0000	1	swindlers
0.0105	20.2	.0000	1	swinging-sector
0.0105	20.2	.0000	1	symmetrically
0.0105	20.2	.0000	1	synod
0.0105	20.2	.0000	1	synovial
0.0105	20.2	.0000	1	Syracusans
0.0105	20.2	.0000	1	syringe
0.0105	20.2	.0000	1	Taal
0.0105	20.2	.0000	1	tabulates
0.0105	20.2	.0000	1	tactile
0.0105	20.2	.0000	1	tagua
0.0105	20.2	.0000	1	tail-lashing
0.0105	20.2	.0000	1	Tajik
0.0105	20.2	.0000	1	Takeshi
0.0105	20.2	.0000	1	Talayan
0.0105	20.2	.0000	1	Talin
0.0105	20.2	.0000	1	Tambora
0.0105	20.2	.0000	1	Tamburlaine
0.0105	20.2	.0000	1	Tamerlane's
0.0105	20.2	.0000	1	tampering
0.0105	20.2	.0000	1	Tampico
0.0105	20.2	.0000	1	tanagers
0.0105	20.2	.0000	1	tandem
0.0105	20.2	.0000	1	tantamount
0.0105	20.2	.0000	1	tarbooshes
0.0105	20.2	.0000	1	Tarentum
0.0105	20.2	.0000	1	Tariffs
0.0105	20.2	.0000	1	Tarlton
0.0105	20.2	.0000	1	Tarlton's
0.0105	20.2	.0000	1	tarnishing
0.0105	20.2	.0000	1	tarsier-like
0.0105	20.2	.0000	1	tastier
0.0105	20.2	.0000	1	tastiest
0.0105	20.2	.0000	1	Tauern
0.0105	20.2	.0000	1	taxi-laden
0.0105	20.2	.0000	1	taxpaying
0.0105	20.2	.0000	1	Te
0.0105	20.2	.0000	1	teacher-training
0.0105	20.2	.0000	1	technologies
0.0105	20.2	.0000	1	technology-oriented
0.0105	20.2	.0000	1	teem
0.0105	20.2	.0000	1	Teflon
0.0105	20.2	.0000	1	Tekrit
0.0105	20.2	.0000	1	Telegonus
0.0105	20.2	.0000	1	telegraphs
0.0105	20.2	.0000	1	telemeter
0.0105	20.2	.0000	1	teleost
0.0105	20.2	.0000	1	telepathic

THE PRECEDING WORD TYPE OCCUPIES RANK 81500

U	SFI	D	F	Word Type
0.0105	20.2	.0000	1	telepathy
0.0105	20.2	.0000	1	Telephotography
0.0105	20.2	.0000	1	teleprinter
0.0105	20.2	.0000	1	telescoped
0.0105	20.2	.0000	1	teletypewriter
0.0105	20.2	.0000	1	television-receiving
0.0105	20.2	.0000	1	Telford
0.0105	20.2	.0000	1	tellurium
0.0105	20.2	.0000	1	telophase
0.0105	20.2	.0000	1	temensis
0.0105	20.2	.0000	1	temerity
0.0105	20.2	.0000	1	Temur
0.0105	20.2	.0000	1	ten-decimal-digit
0.0105	20.2	.0000	1	tenant-farming
0.0105	20.2	.0000	1	tenesmus
0.0105	20.2	.0000	1	tenet
0.0105	20.2	.0000	1	tentacled
0.0105	20.2	.0000	1	Terminal
0.0105	20.2	.0000	1	Terrarum
0.0105	20.2	.0000	1	terrestris
0.0105	20.2	.0000	1	terseness
0.0105	20.2	.0000	1	test-ban
0.0105	20.2	.0000	1	testy
0.0105	20.2	.0000	1	Texas-Mexican
0.0105	20.2	.0000	1	Textile
0.0105	20.2	.0000	1	textile-printing
0.0105	20.2	.0000	1	Thar
0.0105	20.2	.0000	1	Theatre-Lyrique
0.0105	20.2	.0000	1	Theatrum
0.0105	20.2	.0000	1	thenceforward
0.0105	20.2	.0000	1	Theological
0.0105	20.2	.0000	1	Theophile
0.0105	20.2	.0000	1	Theophrastus
0.0105	20.2	.0000	1	Theoria
0.0105	20.2	.0000	1	Theories
0.0105	20.2	.0000	1	theorize
0.0105	20.2	.0000	1	theorizings
0.0105	20.2	.0000	1	thermoelectrical
0.0105	20.2	.0000	1	Thermoelectricity
0.0105	20.2	.0000	1	thermosetting
0.0105	20.2	.0000	1	thermostatic
0.0105	20.2	.0000	1	thingumabobs
0.0105	20.2	.0000	1	thinke
0.0105	20.2	.0000	1	thirdly
0.0105	20.2	.0000	1	THOR
0.0105	20.2	.0000	1	Thore
0.0105	20.2	.0000	1	three-celled
0.0105	20.2	.0000	1	three-color
0.0105	20.2	.0000	1	three-score
0.0105	20.2	.0000	1	three-to-four-pound
0.0105	20.2	.0000	1	Threnody
0.0105	20.2	.0000	1	throes
0.0105	20.2	.0000	1	throughways

U	SFI	D	F	Word Type
0.0105	20.2	.0000	1	Thruway
0.0105	20.2	.0000	1	tic
0.0105	20.2	.0000	1	Tiefer
0.0105	20.2	.0000	1	Tientsin
0.0105	20.2	.0000	1	Tiepolo
0.0105	20.2	.0000	1	tile-roofed
0.0105	20.2	.0000	1	tilework
0.0105	20.2	.0000	1	tillable
0.0105	20.2	.0000	1	Tilly's
0.0105	20.2	.0000	1	timberline
0.0105	20.2	.0000	1	Timur-i-leng
0.0105	20.2	.0000	1	Timurid
0.0105	20.2	.0000	1	Tiverton
0.0105	20.2	.0000	1	Todi
0.0105	20.2	.0000	1	toilet-trained
0.0105	20.2	.0000	1	tolerates
0.0105	20.2	.0000	1	tollways
0.0105	20.2	.0000	1	tongue-wagging
0.0105	20.2	.0000	1	tongueless
0.0105	20.2	.0000	1	Took
0.0105	20.2	.0000	1	topgrade
0.0105	20.2	.0000	1	topical-plan
0.0105	20.2	.0000	1	TOPOGRAPHY
0.0105	20.2	.0000	1	Torbjorn
0.0105	20.2	.0000	1	Torch
0.0105	20.2	.0000	1	torn-up
0.0105	20.2	.0000	1	torso
0.0105	20.2	.0000	1	tossup
0.0105	20.2	.0000	1	ToursPoitiers
0.0105	20.2	.0000	1	towers'
0.0105	20.2	.0000	1	toxicity
0.0105	20.2	.0000	1	traceable
0.0105	20.2	.0000	1	tracheids
0.0105	20.2	.0000	1	trade-unions
0.0105	20.2	.0000	1	Trademark
0.0105	20.2	.0000	1	TRADEMARK
0.0105	20.2	.0000	1	traditor
0.0105	20.2	.0000	1	traditors
0.0105	20.2	.0000	1	trafficking
0.0105	20.2	.0000	1	Tragicall
0.0105	20.2	.0000	1	Trans-Canada
0.0105	20.2	.0000	1	Transcaucasia
0.0105	20.2	.0000	1	transcendental
0.0105	20.2	.0000	1	Transistor
0.0105	20.2	.0000	1	Translation
0.0105	20.2	.0000	1	translocated
0.0105	20.2	.0000	1	transpire

THE PRECEDING WORD TYPE OCCUPIES RANK 81600

U	SFI	D	F	Word Type
0.0105	20.2	.0000	1	transplantations
0.0105	20.2	.0000	1	transshipment
0.0105	20.2	.0000	1	transuranium
0.0105	20.2	.0000	1	traumas
0.0105	20.2	.0000	1	treacheries
0.0105	20.2	.0000	1	treasonable
0.0105	20.2	.0000	1	Treaties
0.0105	20.2	.0000	1	Treatises
0.0105	20.2	.0000	1	trefoil
0.0105	20.2	.0000	1	TrentinoAlto
0.0105	20.2	.0000	1	trephination
0.0105	20.2	.0000	1	trephined
0.0105	20.2	.0000	1	Trevithick
0.0105	20.2	.0000	1	trial-and-error
0.0105	20.2	.0000	1	triangular-shaped
0.0105	20.2	.0000	1	Triassic
0.0105	20.2	.0000	1	Tribunal
0.0105	20.2	.0000	1	Tridacna
0.0105	20.2	.0000	1	tridymite
0.0105	20.2	.0000	1	Trimble
0.0105	20.2	.0000	1	trinitrotoluene
0.0105	20.2	.0000	1	triple-moated
0.0105	20.2	.0000	1	Tristan
0.0105	20.2	.0000	1	triton
0.0105	20.2	.0000	1	troy
0.0105	20.2	.0000	1	Troyon
0.0105	20.2	.0000	1	trs
0.0105	20.2	.0000	1	Truce
0.0105	20.2	.0000	1	truly-spaced
0.0105	20.2	.0000	1	Trumpeter
0.0105	20.2	.0000	1	trumpetings
0.0105	20.2	.0000	1	trunk-like
0.0105	20.2	.0000	1	Truth-in-Lending
0.0105	20.2	.0000	1	tsar's
0.0105	20.2	.0000	1	Tsinghua
0.0105	20.2	.0000	1	Tsung-jen
0.0105	20.2	.0000	1	tuataras'
0.0105	20.2	.0000	1	tube-shaped
0.0105	20.2	.0000	1	tuco-tuco
0.0105	20.2	.0000	1	tucunare
0.0105	20.2	.0000	1	tufa
0.0105	20.2	.0000	1	Tului
0.0105	20.2	.0000	1	Tungusic
0.0105	20.2	.0000	1	tunnel-like
0.0105	20.2	.0000	1	Tupi
0.0105	20.2	.0000	1	turbaned
0.0105	20.2	.0000	1	turbid
0.0105	20.2	.0000	1	turbine-driven
0.0105	20.2	.0000	1	turbogenerators
0.0105	20.2	.0000	1	turboprop
0.0105	20.2	.0000	1	Turkic-speaking
0.0105	20.2	.0000	1	turkie
0.0105	20.2	.0000	1	turkies
0.0105	20.2	.0000	1	Turners
0.0105	20.2	.0000	1	turnstone
0.0105	20.2	.0000	1	Turnverein
0.0105	20.2	.0000	1	Turpin's
0.0105	20.2	.0000	1	turtle-shaped
0.0105	20.2	.0000	1	Tuxtla
0.0105	20.2	.0000	1	tweaked
0.0105	20.2	.0000	1	twice-a-day
0.0105	20.2	.0000	1	Twisted
0.0105	20.2	.0000	1	two-and-a-quarter-million
0.0105	20.2	.0000	1	two-carat
0.0105	20.2	.0000	1	two-pronged
0.0105	20.2	.0000	1	two-to-five
0.0105	20.2	.0000	1	Tylor
0.0105	20.2	.0000	1	type-wheel
0.0105	20.2	.0000	1	typecasting
0.0105	20.2	.0000	1	Types
0.0105	20.2	.0000	1	typewriterlike
0.0105	20.2	.0000	1	Tyrolese
0.0105	20.2	.0000	1	U-boat
0.0105	20.2	.0000	1	Udolpho
0.0105	20.2	.0000	1	Ueno
0.0105	20.2	.0000	1	Ulixes
0.0105	20.2	.0000	1	Ultimos
0.0105	20.2	.0000	1	ultra-high
0.0105	20.2	.0000	1	Ulyanovsk
0.0105	20.2	.0000	1	umbilicus
0.0105	20.2	.0000	1	Umbria
0.0105	20.2	.0000	1	Umjetnost
0.0105	20.2	.0000	1	unarguably
0.0105	20.2	.0000	1	unassailable
0.0105	20.2	.0000	1	unbend
0.0105	20.2	.0000	1	unbridged
0.0105	20.2	.0000	1	uncoil
0.0105	20.2	.0000	1	unconciousness
0.0105	20.2	.0000	1	unconditional
0.0105	20.2	.0000	1	unconditioned
0.0105	20.2	.0000	1	unconfirmed
0.0105	20.2	.0000	1	uncountable
0.0105	20.2	.0000	1	under-represented
0.0105	20.2	.0000	1	underbody
0.0105	20.2	.0000	1	underestimate
0.0105	20.2	.0000	1	underpaid
0.0105	20.2	.0000	1	underpasses
0.0105	20.2	.0000	1	undertakers
0.0105	20.2	.0000	1	underwriters
0.0105	20.2	.0000	1	undesirables

THE PRECEDING WORD TYPE OCCUPIES RANK 81700

U	SFI	D	F	Word Type
0.0105	20.2	.0000	1	unequalled
0.0105	20.2	.0000	1	unequivocally
0.0105	20.2	.0000	1	unfailing
0.0105	20.2	.0000	1	unfathomed
0.0105	20.2	.0000	1	unforgivably
0.0105	20.2	.0000	1	unfused
0.0105	20.2	.0000	1	unglazed
0.0105	20.2	.0000	1	ungripping
0.0105	20.2	.0000	1	ungulates
0.0105	20.2	.0000	1	unhelped
0.0105	20.2	.0000	1	unhindered
0.0105	20.2	.0000	1	unicorns
0.0105	20.2	.0000	1	unilateral
0.0105	20.2	.0000	1	unimagined
0.0105	20.2	.0000	1	unimprovable
0.0105	20.2	.0000	1	unintelligibility
0.0105	20.2	.0000	1	Unionists
0.0105	20.2	.0000	1	unleavened
0.0105	20.2	.0000	1	Unlicensed
0.0105	20.2	.0000	1	unmatched
0.0105	20.2	.0000	1	Unmoved
0.0105	20.2	.0000	1	unorganized
0.0105	20.2	.0000	1	unpalatable
0.0105	20.2	.0000	1	unpoliced
0.0105	20.2	.0000	1	unprecedentedly
0.0105	20.2	.0000	1	unprepossessing
0.0105	20.2	.0000	1	unquiet
0.0105	20.2	.0000	1	Unready
0.0105	20.2	.0000	1	unready
0.0105	20.2	.0000	1	unrevealing
0.0105	20.2	.0000	1	unruined
0.0105	20.2	.0000	1	unsaddled
0.0105	20.2	.0000	1	unsavoury
0.0105	20.2	.0000	1	unshielded
0.0105	20.2	.0000	1	unsuitability
0.0105	20.2	.0000	1	unsweetened
0.0105	20.2	.0000	1	untouchables
0.0105	20.2	.0000	1	unwatering
0.0105	20.2	.0000	1	unwittingly
0.0105	20.2	.0000	1	up-and-coming
0.0105	20.2	.0000	1	up-to-dateness
0.0105	20.2	.0000	1	upholds
0.0105	20.2	.0000	1	Uppsala
0.0105	20.2	.0000	1	uranium-graphite
0.0105	20.2	.0000	1	Uranus'
0.0105	20.2	.0000	1	Urban's
0.0105	20.2	.0000	1	ureteral
0.0105	20.2	.0000	1	urethers
0.0105	20.2	.0000	1	urethra
0.0105	20.2	.0000	1	Urey's
0.0105	20.2	.0000	1	uric
0.0105	20.2	.0000	1	Uriel
0.0105	20.2	.0000	1	Urinarum
0.0105	20.2	.0000	1	Urine
0.0105	20.2	.0000	1	uroscopy
0.0105	20.2	.0000	1	Urubamba
0.0105	20.2	.0000	1	Usnea
0.0105	20.2	.0000	1	usque
0.0105	20.2	.0000	1	utilitarians
0.0105	20.2	.0000	1	vacancies
0.0105	20.2	.0000	1	vacuum-seal
0.0105	20.2	.0000	1	vacuums
0.0105	20.2	.0000	1	vagus
0.0105	20.2	.0000	1	Vaisyas
0.0105	20.2	.0000	1	validly
0.0105	20.2	.0000	1	Valley's
0.0105	20.2	.0000	1	vanDelft
0.0105	20.2	.0000	1	VanDorn
0.0105	20.2	.0000	1	vanderMeer
0.0105	20.2	.0000	1	vang
0.0105	20.2	.0000	1	Vanolis
0.0105	20.2	.0000	1	vapor-tube
0.0105	20.2	.0000	1	vari-typers
0.0105	20.2	.0000	1	Varian's
0.0105	20.2	.0000	1	variants
0.0105	20.2	.0000	1	vascular
0.0105	20.2	.0000	1	vase-shaped
0.0105	20.2	.0000	1	vaster
0.0105	20.2	.0000	1	veal-calipee
0.0105	20.2	.0000	1	Vedras
0.0105	20.2	.0000	1	vegetarians
0.0105	20.2	.0000	1	vegetative
0.0105	20.2	.0000	1	velum
0.0105	20.2	.0000	1	Veneto-Illyrian
0.0105	20.2	.0000	1	venial
0.0105	20.2	.0000	1	venom-filled
0.0105	20.2	.0000	1	venomous
0.0105	20.2	.0000	1	ventilators
0.0105	20.2	.0000	1	ventricular
0.0105	20.2	.0000	1	venturer
0.0105	20.2	.0000	1	venule
0.0105	20.2	.0000	1	venules
0.0105	20.2	.0000	1	verifiable
0.0105	20.2	.0000	1	Vermeer's
0.0105	20.2	.0000	1	versification
0.0105	20.2	.0000	1	versified
0.0105	20.2	.0000	1	Versions
0.0105	20.2	.0000	1	very-high-frequency
0.0105	20.2	.0000	1	Vesnin
0.0105	20.2	.0000	1	vetch

THE PRECEDING WORD TYPE OCCUPIES RANK 81800

U	SFI	D	F	Word Type
0.0105	20.2	.0000	1	veterinarians
0.0105	20.2	.0000	1	vibration-free
0.0105	20.2	.0000	1	Vicar
0.0105	20.2	.0000	1	Vice-Presidents
0.0105	20.2	.0000	1	Vichy-French
0.0105	20.2	.0000	1	vicissitudes
0.0105	20.2	.0000	1	Victorien
0.0105	20.2	.0000	1	vie
0.0105	20.2	.0000	1	viejo
0.0105	20.2	.0000	1	Vienna's
0.0105	20.2	.0000	1	Viennis
0.0105	20.2	.0000	1	Vietminh
0.0105	20.2	.0000	1	viewer's
0.0105	20.2	.0000	1	Views
0.0105	20.2	.0000	1	Vigarini
0.0105	20.2	.0000	1	VII'S
0.0105	20.2	.0000	1	viking
0.0105	20.2	.0000	1	viral
0.0105	20.2	.0000	1	VIRGIL
0.0105	20.2	.0000	1	Virgins
0.0105	20.2	.0000	1	Virunga
0.0105	20.2	.0000	1	visas
0.0105	20.2	.0000	1	Visayas
0.0105	20.2	.0000	1	Vishinsky
0.0105	20.2	.0000	1	Visigoths
0.0105	20.2	.0000	1	visualizing
0.0105	20.2	.0000	1	Vitanuova
0.0105	20.2	.0000	1	vivipara
0.0105	20.2	.0000	1	viviparity
0.0105	20.2	.0000	1	viviparous
0.0105	20.2	.0000	1	viviparus
0.0105	20.2	.0000	1	vizcacha
0.0105	20.2	.0000	1	vizcachas
0.0105	20.2	.0000	1	Vlaminck
0.0105	20.2	.0000	1	voiding
0.0105	20.2	.0000	1	Voivodina
0.0105	20.2	.0000	1	Volcanoes
0.0105	20.2	.0000	1	volcanologist
0.0105	20.2	.0000	1	volcanologists
0.0105	20.2	.0000	1	vole
0.0105	20.2	.0000	1	voles
0.0105	20.2	.0000	1	vols
0.0105	20.2	.0000	1	vonFrisch
0.0105	20.2	.0000	1	vonGoethe
0.0105	20.2	.0000	1	vonGuericke
0.0105	20.2	.0000	1	vonLiebig
0.0105	20.2	.0000	1	vonder
0.0105	20.2	.0000	1	vonderOsten-Sacken
0.0105	20.2	.0000	1	vulcanizing
0.0105	20.2	.0000	1	Vyatka
0.0105	20.2	.0000	1	Waddill
0.0105	20.2	.0000	1	wags
0.0105	20.2	.0000	1	wainscoting
0.0105	20.2	.0000	1	wakefulness
0.0105	20.2	.0000	1	Walcheren
0.0105	20.2	.0000	1	walkie-talkies
0.0105	20.2	.0000	1	Wallenstein
0.0105	20.2	.0000	1	Walpole's
0.0105	20.2	.0000	1	wantonness
0.0105	20.2	.0000	1	Warlock
0.0105	20.2	.0000	1	warlords
0.0105	20.2	.0000	1	warm-bloodedness
0.0105	20.2	.0000	1	warranted
0.0105	20.2	.0000	1	warrior-ruler
0.0105	20.2	.0000	1	waste-disposal
0.0105	20.2	.0000	1	watchtowers
0.0105	20.2	.0000	1	Water-Jug
0.0105	20.2	.0000	1	water-cutting
0.0105	20.2	.0000	1	water-proof
0.0105	20.2	.0000	1	water-raising
0.0105	20.2	.0000	1	Waterford
0.0105	20.2	.0000	1	waterholes
0.0105	20.2	.0000	1	waterpowered
0.0105	20.2	.0000	1	Waterwheel
0.0105	20.2	.0000	1	Waveney
0.0105	20.2	.0000	1	wax-lined
0.0105	20.2	.0000	1	WCC
0.0105	20.2	.0000	1	wearer's
0.0105	20.2	.0000	1	weaverbirds
0.0105	20.2	.0000	1	Weber's
0.0105	20.2	.0000	1	well-aimed
0.0105	20.2	.0000	1	well-insulated
0.0105	20.2	.0000	1	well-marked
0.0105	20.2	.0000	1	well-scrubbed
0.0105	20.2	.0000	1	Wessex
0.0105	20.2	.0000	1	WestHartford
0.0105	20.2	.0000	1	Westernized
0.0105	20.2	.0000	1	westward-
0.0105	20.2	.0000	1	Weymouth
0.0105	20.2	.0000	1	wheat-shipping
0.0105	20.2	.0000	1	whimsey
0.0105	20.2	.0000	1	white-rumped
0.0105	20.2	.0000	1	white-throated
0.0105	20.2	.0000	1	wholsome
0.0105	20.2	.0000	1	whorls
0.0105	20.2	.0000	1	Wienne
0.0105	20.2	.0000	1	Wiesbaden
0.0105	20.2	.0000	1	Wilfrid
0.0105	20.2	.0000	1	Wilmarth
0.0105	20.2	.0000	1	wind-borne

THE PRECEDING WORD TYPE OCCUPIES RANK 81900

U	SFI	D	F	Word Type
0.0105	20.2	.0000	1	wind-pollinated
0.0105	20.2	.0000	1	wind-streamed
0.0105	20.2	.0000	1	wind-trained
0.0105	20.2	.0000	1	windlasses
0.0105	20.2	.0000	1	wing-fingers
0.0105	20.2	.0000	1	Winston-Salem
0.0105	20.2	.0000	1	wirephoto
0.0105	20.2	.0000	1	wistful-looking
0.0105	20.2	.0000	1	Withdrawal
0.0105	20.2	.0000	1	withered-looking
0.0105	20.2	.0000	1	Within
0.0105	20.2	.0000	1	wobbles
0.0105	20.2	.0000	1	Wohler
0.0105	20.2	.0000	1	Wolfenbuttel
0.0105	20.2	.0000	1	wolflike
0.0105	20.2	.0000	1	Wollaston
0.0105	20.2	.0000	1	Women's
0.0105	20.2	.0000	1	Wonders
0.0105	20.2	.0000	1	woodcarvers
0.0105	20.2	.0000	1	Woodville
0.0105	20.2	.0000	1	Woolwich
0.0105	20.2	.0000	1	word-abusers
0.0105	20.2	.0000	1	worlde
0.0105	20.2	.0000	1	worm-like
0.0105	20.2	.0000	1	Worship
0.0105	20.2	.0000	1	wound-healing
0.0105	20.2	.0000	1	wrack
0.0105	20.2	.0000	1	wrasse's
0.0105	20.2	.0000	1	wrasses
0.0105	20.2	.0000	1	wrings
0.0105	20.2	.0000	1	Wulfstan
0.0105	20.2	.0000	1	wurstmacher's
0.0105	20.2	.0000	1	Wurttemberg
0.0105	20.2	.0000	1	Wyville
0.0105	20.2	.0000	1	Xenopus
0.0105	20.2	.0000	1	Xenopus'
0.0105	20.2	.0000	1	XVI'S
0.0105	20.2	.0000	1	XVII
0.0105	20.2	.0000	1	Yahwism
0.0105	20.2	.0000	1	yams
0.0105	20.2	.0000	1	yardmaster
0.0105	20.2	.0000	1	yearbooks
0.0105	20.2	.0000	1	Yeardley
0.0105	20.2	.0000	1	Yeats
0.0105	20.2	.0000	1	yellow-dog
0.0105	20.2	.0000	1	yellowlegs
0.0105	20.2	.0000	1	yellowwood
0.0105	20.2	.0000	1	Yo-wipe
0.0105	20.2	.0000	1	yoking
0.0105	20.2	.0000	1	Yomiuri
0.0105	20.2	.0000	1	yrs
0.0105	20.2	.0000	1	Yuval
0.0105	20.2	.0000	1	YWCA'S
0.0105	20.2	.0000	1	Zafar
0.0105	20.2	.0000	1	Zalamea
0.0105	20.2	.0000	1	zeolite
0.0105	20.2	.0000	1	zeolites
0.0105	20.2	.0000	1	Zephaniah
0.0105	20.2	.0000	1	Zholtovski
0.0105	20.2	.0000	1	ziggurat
0.0105	20.2	.0000	1	Zionist
0.0105	20.2	.0000	1	Zipporah
0.0105	20.2	.0000	1	Zoarces
0.0105	20.2	.0000	1	zoogeographic
0.0105	20.2	.0000	1	zoogeographical
0.0105	20.2	.0000	1	zoogeographically
0.0105	20.2	.0000	1	zooplankton
0.0105	20.2	.0000	1	000-mile-per-hour
0.0105	20.2	.0000	1	000-year
0.0105	20.2	.0000	1	000-year-old
0.0105	20.2	.0000	1	007
0.0105	20.2	.0000	1	010
0.0105	20.2	.0000	1	02115
0.0105	20.2	.0000	1	029
0.0105	20.2	.0000	1	035
0.0105	20.2	.0000	1	039
0.0105	20.2	.0000	1	046
0.0105	20.2	.0000	1	049
0.0105	20.2	.0000	1	084
0.0105	20.2	.0000	1	086
0.0105	20.2	.0000	1	08647
0.0105	20.2	.0000	1	1/250
0.0105	20.2	.0000	1	1ntil
0.0105	20.2	.0000	1	10-bell
0.0105	20.2	.0000	1	10-inch-long
0.0105	20.2	.0000	1	10-8
0.0105	20.2	.0000	1	10/24ths
0.0105	20.2	.0000	1	10022
0.0105	20.2	.0000	1	10027
0.0105	20.2	.0000	1	1008
0.0105	20.2	.0000	1	101st
0.0105	20.2	.0000	1	1030
0.0105	20.2	.0000	1	1042
0.0105	20.2	.0000	1	1115
0.0105	20.2	.0000	1	1137
0.0105	20.2	.0000	1	1138-1193
0.0105	20.2	.0000	1	1164
0.0105	20.2	.0000	1	1171
0.0105	20.2	.0000	1	1181-1226
0.0105	20.2	.0000	1	1187

THE PRECEDING WORD TYPE OCCUPIES RANK 82000

U	SFI	D	F	Word Type
0.0105	20.2	.0000	1	1191
0.0105	20.2	.0000	1	1192
0.0105	20.2	.0000	1	12-member
0.0105	20.2	.0000	1	12-month
0.0105	20.2	.0000	1	12-23
0.0105	20.2	.0000	1	1220
0.0105	20.2	.0000	1	1221
0.0105	20.2	.0000	1	123-acre
0.0105	20.2	.0000	1	1235
0.0105	20.2	.0000	1	1238
0.0105	20.2	.0000	1	1264
0.0105	20.2	.0000	1	1265-1321
0.0105	20.2	.0000	1	1300's
0.0105	20.2	.0000	1	1304-1374
0.0105	20.2	.0000	1	1360's
0.0105	20.2	.0000	1	1361

U	SFI	D	F	Word Type
0.0105	20.2	.0000	1	1369
0.0105	20.2	.0000	1	1398
0.0105	20.2	.0000	1	1399
0.0105	20.2	.0000	1	14-carat
0.0105	20.2	.0000	1	14/24ths
0.0105	20.2	.0000	1	142-foot
0.0105	20.2	.0000	1	1420's
0.0105	20.2	.0000	1	1421
0.0105	20.2	.0000	1	1430's
0.0105	20.2	.0000	1	1446
0.0105	20.2	.0000	1	1457
0.0105	20.2	.0000	1	1460
0.0105	20.2	.0000	1	14621
0.0105	20.2	.0000	1	1465
0.0105	20.2	.0000	1	1468
0.0105	20.2	.0000	1	1471
0.0105	20.2	.0000	1	1478
0.0105	20.2	.0000	1	1485
0.0105	20.2	.0000	1	1490-1540
0.0105	20.2	.0000	1	1491-1547
0.0105	20.2	.0000	1	1495
0.0105	20.2	.0000	1	1497-98
0.0105	20.2	.0000	1	15-square-yard
0.0105	20.2	.0000	1	150-pound
0.0105	20.2	.0000	1	150-ton
0.0105	20.2	.0000	1	1509
0.0105	20.2	.0000	1	1512-1548
0.0105	20.2	.0000	1	1519-1559
0.0105	20.2	.0000	1	1519-21
0.0105	20.2	.0000	1	1526-27
0.0105	20.2	.0000	1	1527
0.0105	20.2	.0000	1	1530
0.0105	20.2	.0000	1	1536
0.0105	20.2	.0000	1	1560-1609
0.0105	20.2	.0000	1	1561
0.0105	20.2	.0000	1	1568-1644
0.0105	20.2	.0000	1	1569-1589
0.0105	20.2	.0000	1	1570
0.0105	20.2	.0000	1	1584
0.0105	20.2	.0000	1	1589
0.0105	20.2	.0000	1	1593
0.0105	20.2	.0000	1	16-mm
0.0105	20.2	.0000	1	1609-1610
0.0105	20.2	.0000	1	1618-1648
0.0105	20.2	.0000	1	1634-1693
0.0105	20.2	.0000	1	1636-1705
0.0105	20.2	.0000	1	1638
0.0105	20.2	.0000	1	1643-1715
0.0105	20.2	.0000	1	1653-1713
0.0105	20.2	.0000	1	1655-1729
0.0105	20.2	.0000	1	1656-1742
0.0105	20.2	.0000	1	1657
0.0105	20.2	.0000	1	1665
0.0105	20.2	.0000	1	1667
0.0105	20.2	.0000	1	1669
0.0105	20.2	.0000	1	1676
0.0105	20.2	.0000	1	1683-1764
0.0105	20.2	.0000	1	1684
0.0105	20.2	.0000	1	1686
0.0105	20.2	.0000	1	1688-1752
0.0105	20.2	.0000	1	1697
0.0105	20.2	.0000	1	1697-1763
0.0105	20.2	.0000	1	1698
0.0105	20.2	.0000	1	1698-1739
0.0105	20.2	.0000	1	170-foot
0.0105	20.2	.0000	1	1706-1739
0.0105	20.2	.0000	1	1706-1790
0.0105	20.2	.0000	1	1717-57
0.0105	20.2	.0000	1	1719
0.0105	20.2	.0000	1	1724-1806
0.0105	20.2	.0000	1	1726-1751
0.0105	20.2	.0000	1	1727
0.0105	20.2	.0000	1	1727-1753
0.0105	20.2	.0000	1	1727-1810
0.0105	20.2	.0000	1	1729
0.0105	20.2	.0000	1	1729-1808
0.0105	20.2	.0000	1	1731-1810
0.0105	20.2	.0000	1	1736-1801
0.0105	20.2	.0000	1	1740-1782
0.0105	20.2	.0000	1	1741-1787
0.0105	20.2	.0000	1	1742-86
0.0105	20.2	.0000	1	1743-1793
0.0105	20.2	.0000	1	1745-1829
0.0105	20.2	.0000	1	1747-1748
THE PRECEDING WORD TYPE OCCUPIES RANK 82100				
0.0105	20.2	.0000	1	1751
0.0105	20.2	.0000	1	1755-1806
0.0105	20.2	.0000	1	1755-1824
0.0105	20.2	.0000	1	1755-1828
0.0105	20.2	.0000	1	1758-1840
0.0105	20.2	.0000	1	1760-1767
0.0105	20.2	.0000	1	1760-1842
0.0105	20.2	.0000	1	1760's
0.0105	20.2	.0000	1	1773-1836
0.0105	20.2	.0000	1	1777-78
0.0105	20.2	.0000	1	1783-1842
0.0105	20.2	.0000	1	1785-
0.0105	20.2	.0000	1	1787-90
0.0105	20.2	.0000	1	1790-93
0.0105	20.2	.0000	1	1793-95
0.0105	20.2	.0000	1	1799-1850
0.0105	20.2	.0000	1	18-inch
0.0105	20.2	.0000	1	18-year-old
0.0105	20.2	.0000	1	18-20
0.0105	20.2	.0000	1	1800-1860
0.0105	20.2	.0000	1	1803-1869
0.0105	20.2	.0000	1	1804-1864
0.0105	20.2	.0000	1	1804-1876
0.0105	20.2	.0000	1	1804-85
0.0105	20.2	.0000	1	1805-1872
0.0105	20.2	.0000	1	1806-1873
0.0105	20.2	.0000	1	1807-1869
0.0105	20.2	.0000	1	1807-1882
0.0105	20.2	.0000	1	1809-1880
0.0105	20.2	.0000	1	1810-1861
0.0105	20.2	.0000	1	1811-1872
0.0105	20.2	.0000	1	1813-1890
0.0105	20.2	.0000	1	1814-24
0.0105	20.2	.0000	1	1817-1849
0.0105	20.2	.0000	1	1817-1862
0.0105	20.2	.0000	1	1818-1894
0.0105	20.2	.0000	1	1820-1878
0.0105	20.2	.0000	1	1821-1867
0.0105	20.2	.0000	1	1821-1880
0.0105	20.2	.0000	1	1823-1902
0.0105	20.2	.0000	1	1824-81
0.0105	20.2	.0000	1	1826-1827
0.0105	20.2	.0000	1	1827-75
0.0105	20.2	.0000	1	1828-1829
0.0105	20.2	.0000	1	1829-1896
0.0105	20.2	.0000	1	1830-1914
0.0105	20.2	.0000	1	1831-1849
0.0105	20.2	.0000	1	1832-1887
0.0105	20.2	.0000	1	1833-1884
0.0105	20.2	.0000	1	1833-1896
0.0105	20.2	.0000	1	1834-82
0.0105	20.2	.0000	1	1836-1882
0.0105	20.2	.0000	1	1836-1907
0.0105	20.2	.0000	1	1837-1920
0.0105	20.2	.0000	1	1837-38
0.0105	20.2	.0000	1	1840-1902
0.0105	20.2	.0000	1	1841-1915
0.0105	20.2	.0000	1	1841-1922
0.0105	20.2	.0000	1	1844-1896
0.0105	20.2	.0000	1	1846-1923
0.0105	20.2	.0000	1	1846-1924
0.0105	20.2	.0000	1	1848-1923
0.0105	20.2	.0000	1	1851-1929
0.0105	20.2	.0000	1	1852-54
0.0105	20.2	.0000	1	1853-1856
0.0105	20.2	.0000	1	1854-1891
0.0105	20.2	.0000	1	1855-1925
0.0105	20.2	.0000	1	1856-1925
0.0105	20.2	.0000	1	1856-1940
0.0105	20.2	.0000	1	1857-1911
0.0105	20.2	.0000	1	1859-1927
0.0105	20.2	.0000	1	1861-1865
0.0105	20.2	.0000	1	1861-71
0.0105	20.2	.0000	1	1864-70
0.0105	20.2	.0000	1	1868-1869
0.0105	20.2	.0000	1	1872-1926
0.0105	20.2	.0000	1	1874-1960
0.0105	20.2	.0000	1	1878-1950
0.0105	20.2	.0000	1	1879-1939
0.0105	20.2	.0000	1	1879-1955
0.0105	20.2	.0000	1	1880-1881
0.0105	20.2	.0000	1	1884-1939
0.0105	20.2	.0000	1	1884-1960
0.0105	20.2	.0000	1	1886-1961
0.0105	20.2	.0000	1	1887-
0.0105	20.2	.0000	1	1887-1949
0.0105	20.2	.0000	1	1888-1891
0.0105	20.2	.0000	1	1891-1895
0.0105	20.2	.0000	1	1892-
0.0105	20.2	.0000	1	1895-1967
0.0105	20.2	.0000	1	1896-1898
0.0105	20.2	.0000	1	1897-
0.0105	20.2	.0000	1	19-26
0.0105	20.2	.0000	1	19th-
0.0105	20.2	.0000	1	19th-century
0.0105	20.2	.0000	1	1906-
0.0105	20.2	.0000	1	1908-
0.0105	20.2	.0000	1	1910s
0.0105	20.2	.0000	1	1913-
0.0105	20.2	.0000	1	1915-1941
THE PRECEDING WORD TYPE OCCUPIES RANK 82200				
0.0105	20.2	.0000	1	1922-24
0.0105	20.2	.0000	1	1927-1961
0.0105	20.2	.0000	1	1929-
0.0105	20.2	.0000	1	1936-1938
0.0105	20.2	.0000	1	1938-1943
0.0105	20.2	.0000	1	1940-54
0.0105	20.2	.0000	1	198-199
0.0105	20.2	.0000	1	1980
0.0105	20.2	.0000	1	2H20
0.0105	20.2	.0000	1	20
0.0105	20.2	.0000	1	200-pound
0.0105	20.2	.0000	1	20014
0.0105	20.2	.0000	1	210-acre
0.0105	20.2	.0000	1	23-karat
0.0105	20.2	.0000	1	24-by-6-inch
0.0105	20.2	.0000	1	25-pounder
0.0105	20.2	.0000	1	250-million-pound
0.0105	20.2	.0000	1	274-237B
0.0105	20.2	.0000	1	3-man
0.0105	20.2	.0000	1	3-manned
0.0105	20.2	.0000	1	3-to-4-year
0.0105	20.2	.0000	1	3-way
0.0105	20.2	.0000	1	3-13
0.0105	20.2	.0000	1	3-17
0.0105	20.2	.0000	1	3d-century
0.0105	20.2	.0000	1	30's
0.0105	20.2	.0000	1	300-
0.0105	20.2	.0000	1	300-ton
0.0105	20.2	.0000	1	306-337
0.0105	20.2	.0000	1	32-year-old
0.0105	20.2	.0000	1	326B
0.0105	20.2	.0000	1	327BC
0.0105	20.2	.0000	1	33-foot
0.0105	20.2	.0000	1	344-foot
0.0105	20.2	.0000	1	365th
0.0105	20.2	.0000	1	37-foot
0.0105	20.2	.0000	1	37-year-old
0.0105	20.2	.0000	1	375-800
0.0105	20.2	.0000	1	4-20
0.0105	20.2	.0000	1	400-horsepower
0.0105	20.2	.0000	1	42-mile
0.0105	20.2	.0000	1	434-493
0.0105	20.2	.0000	1	46219
0.0105	20.2	.0000	1	466
0.0105	20.2	.0000	1	47-fold
0.0105	20.2	.0000	1	478
0.0105	20.2	.0000	1	499
0.0105	20.2	.0000	1	5-mile-long
0.0105	20.2	.0000	1	5th-century
0.0105	20.2	.0000	1	50-man
0.0105	20.2	.0000	1	50-pounders
0.0105	20.2	.0000	1	511
0.0105	20.2	.0000	1	529
0.0105	20.2	.0000	1	538
0.0105	20.2	.0000	1	539
0.0105	20.2	.0000	1	554
0.0105	20.2	.0000	1	574
0.0105	20.2	.0000	1	594-foot
0.0105	20.2	.0000	1	60-day
0.0105	20.2	.0000	1	600-odd
0.0105	20.2	.0000	1	612-foot
0.0105	20.2	.0000	1	620-foot
0.0105	20.2	.0000	1	657
0.0105	20.2	.0000	1	6720
0.0105	20.2	.0000	1	6853
0.0105	20.2	.0000	1	687-714
0.0105	20.2	.0000	1	688
0.0105	20.2	.0000	1	689
0.0105	20.2	.0000	1	6891
0.0105	20.2	.0000	1	69th
0.0105	20.2	.0000	1	693-foot
0.0105	20.2	.0000	1	700-square-mile
0.0105	20.2	.0000	1	700's
0.0105	20.2	.0000	1	709
0.0105	20.2	.0000	1	742-814
0.0105	20.2	.0000	1	7600
0.0105	20.2	.0000	1	771
0.0105	20.2	.0000	1	78%
0.0105	20.2	.0000	1	80-inch
0.0105	20.2	.0000	1	800-mile-thick
0.0105	20.2	.0000	1	806
0.0105	20.2	.0000	1	808
0.0105	20.2	.0000	1	826
0.0105	20.2	.0000	1	839
0.0105	20.2	.0000	1	852-foot
0.0105	20.2	.0000	1	860-mile
0.0105	20.2	.0000	1	881
0.0105	20.2	.0000	1	883
0.0105	20.2	.0000	1	90-foot-square
0.0105	20.2	.0000	1	90-footer
0.0105	20.2	.0000	1	90s
0.0105	20.2	.0000	1	903
0.0105	20.2	.0000	1	908
0.0105	20.2	.0000	1	909
0.0105	20.2	.0000	1	92d
0.0105	20.2	.0000	1	9200
0.0105	20.2	.0000	1	925
0.0105	20.2	.0000	1	930
0.0105	20.2	.0000	1	935
0.0105	20.2	.0000	1	939
THE PRECEDING WORD TYPE OCCUPIES RANK 82300				
0.0105	20.2	.0000	1	965
0.0105	20.2	.0000	1	995
0.0101	20.0	.0000	4	arris
0.0101	20.0	.0000	4	casehardening
0.0101	20.0	.0000	4	clamping
0.0101	20.0	.0000	4	cleats
0.0101	20.0	.0000	4	crosshatching
0.0101	20.0	.0000	4	diestock
0.0101	20.0	.0000	4	ductility
0.0101	20.0	.0000	4	farad
0.0101	20.0	.0000	4	hardenability
0.0101	20.0	.0000	4	high-carbon
0.0101	20.0	.0000	4	low-carbon
0.0101	20.0	.0000	4	machining
0.0101	20.0	.0000	4	magneto
0.0101	20.0	.0000	4	Ohm's
0.0101	20.0	.0000	4	peen
0.0101	20.0	.0000	4	picofarad
0.0101	20.0	.0000	4	resistivity
0.0101	20.0	.0000	4	right-side
0.0101	20.0	.0000	4	roundnose
0.0101	20.0	.0000	4	spokeshave
0.0101	20.0	.0000	4	spray-gun
0.0101	20.0	.0000	4	sprue
0.0101	20.0	.0000	4	10-2
0.0101	20.0	.0000	4	15-12
0.0097	19.8	.0000	3	Acrilan
0.0097	19.8	.0000	3	armholes
0.0097	19.8	.0000	3	blackheads
0.0097	19.8	.0000	3	broadcloth
0.0097	19.8	.0000	3	chives
0.0097	19.8	.0000	3	Cookbook
0.0097	19.8	.0000	3	disobeys
0.0097	19.8	.0000	3	dry-heat
0.0097	19.8	.0000	3	Everett's
0.0097	19.8	.0000	3	fruit-flavored
0.0097	19.8	.0000	3	fruitades
0.0097	19.8	.0000	3	garnishes
0.0097	19.8	.0000	3	granulated
0.0097	19.8	.0000	3	greys
0.0097	19.8	.0000	3	Homemakers
0.0097	19.8	.0000	3	interfaced
0.0097	19.8	.0000	3	interfacings
0.0097	19.8	.0000	3	lay-away
0.0097	19.8	.0000	3	minimum-care
0.0097	19.8	.0000	3	nutritive
0.0097	19.8	.0000	3	Roquefort
0.0097	19.8	.0000	3	sportswear
0.0097	19.8	.0000	3	stayline
0.0097	19.8	.0000	3	sweetpotatoes
0.0097	19.8	.0000	3	twill
0.0097	19.8	.0000	3	uncombed
0.0097	19.8	.0000	3	underpressing
0.0097	19.8	.0000	3	well-pressed
0.0097	19.8	.0000	3	winder
0.0092	19.7	.0000	5	3D
0.0089	19.5	.0000	4	bandwagons
0.0089	19.5	.0000	4	Bradbury
0.0089	19.5	.0000	4	restatement
0.0081	19.1	.0000	1	(s)incerely
0.0081	19.1	.0000	1	(y)ours
0.0081	19.1	.0000	1	-age
0.0081	19.1	.0000	1	-cation
0.0081	19.1	.0000	1	-cur
0.0081	19.1	.0000	1	-ella
0.0081	19.1	.0000	1	-eous
0.0081	19.1	.0000	1	-fle
0.0081	19.1	.0000	1	-ol
0.0081	19.1	.0000	1	-onym
0.0081	19.1	.0000	1	-onyma
0.0081	19.1	.0000	1	-ry
0.0081	19.1	.0000	1	-ty
0.0081	19.1	.0000	1	-ul
0.0081	19.1	.0000	1	-ure
0.0081	19.1	.0000	1	/-fel/**
0.0081	19.1	.0000	1	/au/**
0.0081	19.1	.0000	1	/aw/**
0.0081	19.1	.0000	1	/azh/
0.0081	19.1	.0000	1	/er/
0.0081	19.1	.0000	1	/et/**
0.0081	19.1	.0000	1	/shel/**
0.0081	19.1	.0000	1	/shes/**
0.0081	19.1	.0000	1	/tran(t)s-et-lant-ik/**
0.0081	19.1	.0000	1	/u
0.0081	19.1	.0000	1	/u/**
0.0081	19.1	.0000	1	/ud
0.0081	19.1	.0000	1	/ul/
0.0081	19.1	.0000	1	ity
0.0081	19.1	.0000	1	'coon's
0.0081	19.1	.0000	1	'most
0.0081	19.1	.0000	1	'nuff
0.0081	19.1	.0000	1	'simmon
0.0081	19.1	.0000	1	'49-ers
0.0081	19.1	.0000	1	'49ers
0.0081	19.1	.0000	1	ABA
0.0081	19.1	.0000	1	a-
0.0081	19.1	.0000	1	A-A-B
0.0081	19.1	.0000	1	A-B
0.0081	19.1	.0000	1	A-C-sharp-E
0.0081	19.1	.0000	1	A-J
THE PRECEDING WORD TYPE OCCUPIES RANK 82400				
0.0081	19.1	.0000	1	a-a-all
0.0081	19.1	.0000	1	a-banging
0.0081	19.1	.0000	1	a-blazin'
0.0081	19.1	.0000	1	a-chawin'
0.0081	19.1	.0000	1	a-clanging
0.0081	19.1	.0000	1	a-courtin's
0.0081	19.1	.0000	1	a-crying
0.0081	19.1	.0000	1	a-drooping
0.0081	19.1	.0000	1	a-drying
0.0081	19.1	.0000	1	a-e
0.0081	19.1	.0000	1	a-flirtin's
0.0081	19.1	.0000	1	a-floating
0.0081	19.1	.0000	1	a-flying
0.0081	19.1	.0000	1	a-gainst
0.0081	19.1	.0000	1	a-glow
0.0081	19.1	.0000	1	a-hanging
0.0081	19.1	.0000	1	a-hauling
0.0081	19.1	.0000	1	a-having
0.0081	19.1	.0000	1	a-hoeing
0.0081	19.1	.0000	1	a-holidaying
0.0081	19.1	.0000	1	a-io-la
0.0081	19.1	.0000	1	a-leaping
0.0081	19.1	.0000	1	a-leaving
0.0081	19.1	.0000	1	a-light
0.0081	19.1	.0000	1	a-marketing
0.0081	19.1	.0000	1	a-milking
0.0081	19.1	.0000	1	A-natural
0.0081	19.1	.0000	1	a-pitching
0.0081	19.1	.0000	1	a-puffing
0.0081	19.1	.0000	1	a-scratching
0.0081	19.1	.0000	1	a-scurrying
0.0081	19.1	.0000	1	a-selling
0.0081	19.1	.0000	1	a-shine
0.0081	19.1	.0000	1	a-sickalum
0.0081	19.1	.0000	1	a-sitting
0.0081	19.1	.0000	1	a-squealing
0.0081	19.1	.0000	1	a-takin'
0.0081	19.1	.0000	1	a-tingle
0.0081	19.1	.0000	1	a-twirling
0.0081	19.1	.0000	1	a-waitin'
0.0081	19.1	.0000	1	a-wand'ring
0.0081	19.1	.0000	1	a-wassailing
0.0081	19.1	.0000	1	a-whistling
0.0081	19.1	.0000	1	ABAB
0.0081	19.1	.0000	1	abandoner
0.0081	19.1	.0000	1	abbe
0.0081	19.1	.0000	1	Abednego
0.0081	19.1	.0000	1	Abroad
0.0081	19.1	.0000	1	absorb-achieve
0.0081	19.1	.0000	1	According
0.0081	19.1	.0000	1	Ach
0.0081	19.1	.0000	1	Across
0.0081	19.1	.0000	1	acrylic
0.0081	19.1	.0000	1	Adagissimo
0.0081	19.1	.0000	1	Adding
0.0081	19.1	.0000	1	addlegrams
0.0081	19.1	.0000	1	advisability
0.0081	19.1	.0000	1	Aenglisc
0.0081	19.1	.0000	1	Aetna
0.0081	19.1	.0000	1	African-American
0.0081	19.1	.0000	1	Afro-Cuban
0.0081	19.1	.0000	1	Afternoon
0.0081	19.1	.0000	1	Again
0.0081	19.1	.0000	1	Ago
0.0081	19.1	.0000	1	ahl-bay-neez
0.0081	19.1	.0000	1	airiness
0.0081	19.1	.0000	1	Albeniz
0.0081	19.1	.0000	1	Alberich
0.0081	19.1	.0000	1	alcorque
0.0081	19.1	.0000	1	Alder
0.0081	19.1	.0000	1	Alders
0.0081	19.1	.0000	1	ale-drinker
0.0081	19.1	.0000	1	alike-words
0.0081	19.1	.0000	1	aliveness
0.0081	19.1	.0000	1	Alle
0.0081	19.1	.0000	1	allelon
0.0081	19.1	.0000	1	alleluia
0.0081	19.1	.0000	1	Alouette
0.0081	19.1	.0000	1	alphabetized
0.0081	19.1	.0000	1	alphabetizing

U	SFI	D	F	Word Type
0.0081	19.1	.0000	1	Alrang
0.0081	19.1	.0000	1	als
0.0081	19.1	.0000	1	amare
0.0081	19.1	.0000	1	ambulant
0.0081	19.1	.0000	1	ame
0.0081	19.1	.0000	1	Amici
0.0081	19.1	.0000	1	amman
0.0081	19.1	.0000	1	Ammunition
0.0081	19.1	.0000	1	Amneris
0.0081	19.1	.0000	1	amnesty
0.0081	19.1	.0000	1	Amplitude
0.0081	19.1	.0000	1	amuses
0.0081	19.1	.0000	1	An'
0.0081	19.1	.0000	1	analytically
0.0081	19.1	.0000	1	Ancestry
0.0081	19.1	.0000	1	Anchorage's
0.0081	19.1	.0000	1	ancy
0.0081	19.1	.0000	1	Andalouse
0.0081	19.1	.0000	1	Anna's
0.0081	19.1	.0000	1	ant-

THE PRECEDING WORD TYPE OCCUPIES RANK 82500

U	SFI	D	F	Word Type
0.0081	19.1	.0000	1	Antes
0.0081	19.1	.0000	1	Antonyms
0.0081	19.1	.0000	1	antonyms-words
0.0081	19.1	.0000	1	ap
0.0081	19.1	.0000	1	appall
0.0081	19.1	.0000	1	apprehended
0.0081	19.1	.0000	1	Arabeske
0.0081	19.1	.0000	1	arabeske
0.0081	19.1	.0000	1	arcade
0.0081	19.1	.0000	1	ard
0.0081	19.1	.0000	1	arpeggio
0.0081	19.1	.0000	1	arpeggios
0.0081	19.1	.0000	1	Artistic
0.0081	19.1	.0000	1	Asar
0.0081	19.1	.0000	1	Ascalon
0.0081	19.1	.0000	1	aspectus
0.0081	19.1	.0000	1	asphalt's
0.0081	19.1	.0000	1	aspic
0.0081	19.1	.0000	1	aspirate
0.0081	19.1	.0000	1	assimilate
0.0081	19.1	.0000	1	astro
0.0081	19.1	.0000	1	at-tic
0.0081	19.1	.0000	1	atchitamon
0.0081	19.1	.0000	1	Atira
0.0081	19.1	.0000	1	Attorney-General
0.0081	19.1	.0000	1	Aubade
0.0081	19.1	.0000	1	aubade
0.0081	19.1	.0000	1	auditors
0.0081	19.1	.0000	1	aural
0.0081	19.1	.0000	1	aureus
0.0081	19.1	.0000	1	Aurora
0.0081	19.1	.0000	1	authored
0.0081	19.1	.0000	1	autobiographical**
0.0081	19.1	.0000	1	autoloading
0.0081	19.1	.0000	1	aviatress
0.0081	19.1	.0000	1	aviatrix
0.0081	19.1	.0000	1	avis
0.0081	19.1	.0000	1	avocation
0.0081	19.1	.0000	1	avoidance
0.0081	19.1	.0000	1	awa'
0.0081	19.1	.0000	1	Azul
0.0081	19.1	.0000	1	A1**
0.0081	19.1	.0000	1	A3d**
0.0081	19.1	.0000	1	A4ly**
0.0081	19.1	.0000	1	A7
0.0081	19.1	.0000	1	B-I-N-G-O
0.0081	19.1	.0000	1	B-line
0.0081	19.1	.0000	1	B'y
0.0081	19.1	.0000	1	Ba-o
0.0081	19.1	.0000	1	baas
0.0081	19.1	.0000	1	Babes
0.0081	19.1	.0000	1	baconburger
0.0081	19.1	.0000	1	Baffin's
0.0081	19.1	.0000	1	Bagpiper
0.0081	19.1	.0000	1	Bagpipes
0.0081	19.1	.0000	1	Baked
0.0081	19.1	.0000	1	Balalyka
0.0081	19.1	.0000	1	Balanchine
0.0081	19.1	.0000	1	Ballade
0.0081	19.1	.0000	1	Baller
0.0081	19.1	.0000	1	Ballet-Russe
0.0081	19.1	.0000	1	ballet-drama
0.0081	19.1	.0000	1	ballet's
0.0081	19.1	.0000	1	Ballroom
0.0081	19.1	.0000	1	ballrooms
0.0081	19.1	.0000	1	banjo-like
0.0081	19.1	.0000	1	Banshee
0.0081	19.1	.0000	1	bap
0.0081	19.1	.0000	1	Baptiste's
0.0081	19.1	.0000	1	bar-ley
0.0081	19.1	.0000	1	Bar-tock
0.0081	19.1	.0000	1	Barber's
0.0081	19.1	.0000	1	baritone-horn
0.0081	19.1	.0000	1	baritones
0.0081	19.1	.0000	1	barkers
0.0081	19.1	.0000	1	barn-raising
0.0081	19.1	.0000	1	Barnby
0.0081	19.1	.0000	1	Barrel
0.0081	19.1	.0000	1	Barrie's
0.0081	19.1	.0000	1	Bartica
0.0081	19.1	.0000	1	Bartok's
0.0081	19.1	.0000	1	bas
0.0081	19.1	.0000	1	bassoon's
0.0081	19.1	.0000	1	Bateau
0.0081	19.1	.0000	1	battin'
0.0081	19.1	.0000	1	Baum
0.0081	19.1	.0000	1	Bayreuth
0.0081	19.1	.0000	1	beaked
0.0081	19.1	.0000	1	Bearer
0.0081	19.1	.0000	1	beau-ti-ful
0.0081	19.1	.0000	1	beauty's
0.0081	19.1	.0000	1	Because
0.0081	19.1	.0000	1	Beckmesser's
0.0081	19.1	.0000	1	bedbug
0.0081	19.1	.0000	1	bede
0.0081	19.1	.0000	1	Bedrich
0.0081	19.1	.0000	1	bee-ee-ee
0.0081	19.1	.0000	1	Before
0.0081	19.1	.0000	1	beforehead
0.0081	19.1	.0000	1	begetteth

THE PRECEDING WORD TYPE OCCUPIES RANK 82600

U	SFI	D	F	Word Type
0.0081	19.1	.0000	1	Beggar-man
0.0081	19.1	.0000	1	begining
0.0081	19.1	.0000	1	belfries
0.0081	19.1	.0000	1	Believe
0.0081	19.1	.0000	1	Bellini's
0.0081	19.1	.0000	1	Benedictine
0.0081	19.1	.0000	1	benz
0.0081	19.1	.0000	1	Berg
0.0081	19.1	.0000	1	Berkshire
0.0081	19.1	.0000	1	Bernstein's
0.0081	19.1	.0000	1	bespoken
0.0081	19.1	.0000	1	Bess's
0.0081	19.1	.0000	1	better-organized
0.0081	19.1	.0000	1	BiSHvet
0.0081	19.1	.0000	1	bibble
0.0081	19.1	.0000	1	biddan
0.0081	19.1	.0000	1	Billing's
0.0081	19.1	.0000	1	Billion
0.0081	19.1	.0000	1	bird-catcher
0.0081	19.1	.0000	1	bird-feeding
0.0081	19.1	.0000	1	Bizet's
0.0081	19.1	.0000	1	black-brow'd
0.0081	19.1	.0000	1	Blair
0.0081	19.1	.0000	1	blaws
0.0081	19.1	.0000	1	Blitzen
0.0081	19.1	.0000	1	Bloch
0.0081	19.1	.0000	1	Blockflote
0.0081	19.1	.0000	1	Blue-Tail
0.0081	19.1	.0000	1	blue-wing
0.0081	19.1	.0000	1	Boating
0.0081	19.1	.0000	1	boatmen's
0.0081	19.1	.0000	1	Boatmen's
0.0081	19.1	.0000	1	Boccherini
0.0081	19.1	.0000	1	Bog
0.0081	19.1	.0000	1	Boheme
0.0081	19.1	.0000	1	Bohemia's
0.0081	19.1	.0000	1	Bohm
0.0081	19.1	.0000	1	bolero
0.0081	19.1	.0000	1	Bolton
0.0081	19.1	.0000	1	bones-O
0.0081	19.1	.0000	1	bonked
0.0081	19.1	.0000	1	boo-shy-lo-ree
0.0081	19.1	.0000	1	Boogie-Woogie
0.0081	19.1	.0000	1	boom–m–m
0.0081	19.1	.0000	1	Borodin's
0.0081	19.1	.0000	1	bossa
0.0081	19.1	.0000	1	Bottoms
0.0081	19.1	.0000	1	boughte
0.0081	19.1	.0000	1	bourdon
0.0081	19.1	.0000	1	bow-wow
0.0081	19.1	.0000	1	bowers
0.0081	19.1	.0000	1	boy-wonder
0.0081	19.1	.0000	1	Brahmin
0.0081	19.1	.0000	1	Bran
0.0081	19.1	.0000	1	Brandon
0.0081	19.1	.0000	1	Bravest
0.0081	19.1	.0000	1	brek'fast**
0.0081	19.1	.0000	1	Brennan
0.0081	19.1	.0000	1	Breve
0.0081	19.1	.0000	1	bringer
0.0081	19.1	.0000	1	Britannia
0.0081	19.1	.0000	1	Britten's
0.0081	19.1	.0000	1	brocades
0.0081	19.1	.0000	1	brokenheartedly
0.0081	19.1	.0000	1	Bruley
0.0081	19.1	.0000	1	Bryant's
0.0081	19.1	.0000	1	BuenaVista
0.0081	19.1	.0000	1	bueno
0.0081	19.1	.0000	1	buffa
0.0081	19.1	.0000	1	bulbous
0.0081	19.1	.0000	1	Bulfinch
0.0081	19.1	.0000	1	bullock's
0.0081	19.1	.0000	1	bummer
0.0081	19.1	.0000	1	bunny's
0.0081	19.1	.0000	1	Bunny's
0.0081	19.1	.0000	1	burger
0.0081	19.1	.0000	1	burn'd
0.0081	19.1	.0000	1	Busch-Reisinger
0.0081	19.1	.0000	1	Bushi
0.0081	19.1	.0000	1	Bushvelt
0.0081	19.1	.0000	1	busybody
0.0081	19.1	.0000	1	butane
0.0081	19.1	.0000	1	By
0.0081	19.1	.0000	1	byways
0.0081	19.1	.0000	1	cab-in
0.0081	19.1	.0000	1	cabacas
0.0081	19.1	.0000	1	cadenzas
0.0081	19.1	.0000	1	Caillet
0.0081	19.1	.0000	1	cakewalk
0.0081	19.1	.0000	1	Caldara
0.0081	19.1	.0000	1	Calicut
0.0081	19.1	.0000	1	call-and-response
0.0081	19.1	.0000	1	Calypso-style
0.0081	19.1	.0000	1	cam'
0.0081	19.1	.0000	1	Camayos
0.0081	19.1	.0000	1	canaller
0.0081	19.1	.0000	1	candelabrum
0.0081	19.1	.0000	1	candidate's
0.0081	19.1	.0000	1	candle-lighting
0.0081	19.1	.0000	1	Cannab'lic

THE PRECEDING WORD TYPE OCCUPIES RANK 82700

U	SFI	D	F	Word Type
0.0081	19.1	.0000	1	Canon
0.0081	19.1	.0000	1	canonic
0.0081	19.1	.0000	1	Cantalupo
0.0081	19.1	.0000	1	cantatas
0.0081	19.1	.0000	1	Canzonetta
0.0081	19.1	.0000	1	Caprice
0.0081	19.1	.0000	1	captivated
0.0081	19.1	.0000	1	carelesly
0.0081	19.1	.0000	1	carillons
0.0081	19.1	.0000	1	Carmen's
0.0081	19.1	.0000	1	carping
0.0081	19.1	.0000	1	carramba
0.0081	19.1	.0000	1	carroway
0.0081	19.1	.0000	1	Caruso's
0.0081	19.1	.0000	1	Cascabel
0.0081	19.1	.0000	1	caterpillar's
0.0081	19.1	.0000	1	cation
0.0081	19.1	.0000	1	catkin
0.0081	19.1	.0000	1	cats'
0.0081	19.1	.0000	1	cauld
0.0081	19.1	.0000	1	cawtion
0.0081	19.1	.0000	1	ceable
0.0081	19.1	.0000	1	Cecile
0.0081	19.1	.0000	1	Celebrate
0.0081	19.1	.0000	1	Celesta
0.0081	19.1	.0000	1	cen
0.0081	19.1	.0000	1	centrum
0.0081	19.1	.0000	1	century-old
0.0081	19.1	.0000	1	cept
0.0081	19.1	.0000	1	ceremonials
0.0081	19.1	.0000	1	Ceremony
0.0081	19.1	.0000	1	cerise
0.0081	19.1	.0000	1	cerulean
0.0081	19.1	.0000	1	Cervantes'
0.0081	19.1	.0000	1	Cesar
0.0081	19.1	.0000	1	cha-cha
0.0081	19.1	.0000	1	Chaffey
0.0081	19.1	.0000	1	Chameleon
0.0081	19.1	.0000	1	Chaminade
0.0081	19.1	.0000	1	changers
0.0081	19.1	.0000	1	chantey-man
0.0081	19.1	.0000	1	Char-ley
0.0081	19.1	.0000	1	Charge
0.0081	19.1	.0000	1	Charleton's
0.0081	19.1	.0000	1	Charming
0.0081	19.1	.0000	1	Chasse
0.0081	19.1	.0000	1	chastens
0.0081	19.1	.0000	1	chastised
0.0081	19.1	.0000	1	Che
0.0081	19.1	.0000	1	CHECK
0.0081	19.1	.0000	1	cheerly
0.0081	19.1	.0000	1	cheeseburger
0.0081	19.1	.0000	1	chek-r
0.0081	19.1	.0000	1	chek-rz
0.0081	19.1	.0000	1	cher
0.0081	19.1	.0000	1	chiliburger
0.0081	19.1	.0000	1	chinese
0.0081	19.1	.0000	1	chloros
0.0081	19.1	.0000	1	choc'late
0.0081	19.1	.0000	1	chocallo
0.0081	19.1	.0000	1	choreographers
0.0081	19.1	.0000	1	Christoph
0.0081	19.1	.0000	1	chromatically
0.0081	19.1	.0000	1	chuckle-head
0.0081	19.1	.0000	1	Chy-kof-skih
0.0081	19.1	.0000	1	cible
0.0081	19.1	.0000	1	cinches
0.0081	19.1	.0000	1	cion
0.0081	19.1	.0000	1	clang-a-clang-a-clang
0.0081	19.1	.0000	1	clap-snap
0.0081	19.1	.0000	1	Clarinet
0.0081	19.1	.0000	1	clarinet's
0.0081	19.1	.0000	1	clarinetist
0.0081	19.1	.0000	1	Classicism
0.0081	19.1	.0000	1	Clavier
0.0081	19.1	.0000	1	claymore
0.0081	19.1	.0000	1	clearly-written
0.0081	19.1	.0000	1	clipe
0.0081	19.1	.0000	1	clothier
0.0081	19.1	.0000	1	Clown's
0.0081	19.1	.0000	1	clude
0.0081	19.1	.0000	1	Cluett
0.0081	19.1	.0000	1	coachmen
0.0081	19.1	.0000	1	Coady's
0.0081	19.1	.0000	1	coalminer
0.0081	19.1	.0000	1	Coalminer's
0.0081	19.1	.0000	1	coat's
0.0081	19.1	.0000	1	cock-a-doo-dle-doo
0.0081	19.1	.0000	1	cock-a-doodle-do
0.0081	19.1	.0000	1	cocks'
0.0081	19.1	.0000	1	cocos
0.0081	19.1	.0000	1	Coh-dah-ee
0.0081	19.1	.0000	1	Cohans
0.0081	19.1	.0000	1	colleen
0.0081	19.1	.0000	1	colly
0.0081	19.1	.0000	1	color's
0.0081	19.1	.0000	1	Colossus
0.0081	19.1	.0000	1	com-mand
0.0081	19.1	.0000	1	com-pan-ion
0.0081	19.1	.0000	1	com-pan-y

THE PRECEDING WORD TYPE OCCUPIES RANK 82800

U	SFI	D	F	Word Type
0.0081	19.1	.0000	1	Come-All-Ye
0.0081	19.1	.0000	1	commodore's
0.0081	19.1	.0000	1	comparatives
0.0081	19.1	.0000	1	composers'
0.0081	19.1	.0000	1	composit
0.0081	19.1	.0000	1	con'tent**
0.0081	19.1	.0000	1	Conan
0.0081	19.1	.0000	1	concert-going
0.0081	19.1	.0000	1	concert-master
0.0081	19.1	.0000	1	concertmaster
0.0081	19.1	.0000	1	concerto-grosso
0.0081	19.1	.0000	1	Conductors
0.0081	19.1	.0000	1	conquer'd
0.0081	19.1	.0000	1	consomme
0.0081	19.1	.0000	1	consonance
0.0081	19.1	.0000	1	consonant-vowel
0.0081	19.1	.0000	1	consonare
0.0081	19.1	.0000	1	contempory
0.0081	19.1	.0000	1	content'**
0.0081	19.1	.0000	1	contrabass
0.0081	19.1	.0000	1	contras
0.0081	19.1	.0000	1	Contrasts
0.0081	19.1	.0000	1	Conversation
0.0081	19.1	.0000	1	Cookie's
0.0081	19.1	.0000	1	Coon
0.0081	19.1	.0000	1	copper's
0.0081	19.1	.0000	1	Cordovan
0.0081	19.1	.0000	1	corn-picking
0.0081	19.1	.0000	1	cornett
0.0081	19.1	.0000	1	cosmo
0.0081	19.1	.0000	1	costureras
0.0081	19.1	.0000	1	counter-tenor
0.0081	19.1	.0000	1	countermarching
0.0081	19.1	.0000	1	countermelodies
0.0081	19.1	.0000	1	countree
0.0081	19.1	.0000	1	Courbet
0.0081	19.1	.0000	1	court-martial
0.0081	19.1	.0000	1	cover'd
0.0081	19.1	.0000	1	Coverdale
0.0081	19.1	.0000	1	crabba
0.0081	19.1	.0000	1	cravin'
0.0081	19.1	.0000	1	creche
0.0081	19.1	.0000	1	crescendos
0.0081	19.1	.0000	1	Crested
0.0081	19.1	.0000	1	crew-ew-ew
0.0081	19.1	.0000	1	Critic
0.0081	19.1	.0000	1	crochet
0.0081	19.1	.0000	1	crossin'
0.0081	19.1	.0000	1	crosspoles
0.0081	19.1	.0000	1	Crouse
0.0081	19.1	.0000	1	crwth
0.0081	19.1	.0000	1	ct
0.0081	19.1	.0000	1	Culloden
0.0081	19.1	.0000	1	Culloden's
0.0081	19.1	.0000	1	Cyclopean
0.0081	19.1	.0000	1	cyning
0.0081	19.1	.0000	1	czardas
0.0081	19.1	.0000	1	C7-chord
0.0081	19.1	.0000	1	D-F-A
0.0081	19.1	.0000	1	D-major
0.0081	19.1	.0000	1	d'Arezzo
0.0081	19.1	.0000	1	daeges
0.0081	19.1	.0000	1	daeges-eage
0.0081	19.1	.0000	1	Dagata
0.0081	19.1	.0000	1	dailies
0.0081	19.1	.0000	1	Dalry
0.0081	19.1	.0000	1	damask
0.0081	19.1	.0000	1	dampers
0.0081	19.1	.0000	1	Damrosch
0.0081	19.1	.0000	1	Dancairo
0.0081	19.1	.0000	1	dance-drama
0.0081	19.1	.0000	1	dance-hall
0.0081	19.1	.0000	1	danceband
0.0081	19.1	.0000	1	dancelike
0.0081	19.1	.0000	1	dancer's
0.0081	19.1	.0000	1	dancers'
0.0081	19.1	.0000	1	dancy
0.0081	19.1	.0000	1	darkens
0.0081	19.1	.0000	1	darlin'
0.0081	19.1	.0000	1	darum
0.0081	19.1	.0000	1	Dawes
0.0081	19.1	.0000	1	dawn's
0.0081	19.1	.0000	1	daylong
0.0081	19.1	.0000	1	DeKoven's
0.0081	19.1	.0000	1	deMille
0.0081	19.1	.0000	1	DeSylva
0.0081	19.1	.0000	1	de-li-cious
0.0081	19.1	.0000	1	death's
0.0081	19.1	.0000	1	deathly
0.0081	19.1	.0000	1	debke
0.0081	19.1	.0000	1	Decca
0.0081	19.1	.0000	1	December's
0.0081	19.1	.0000	1	Deciso
0.0081	19.1	.0000	1	decrescendos
0.0081	19.1	.0000	1	Dedicated
0.0081	19.1	.0000	1	Dee-ah-geel-yehf
0.0081	19.1	.0000	1	deep-drenched
0.0081	19.1	.0000	1	deep-felt
0.0081	19.1	.0000	1	deep-pitched
0.0081	19.1	.0000	1	defection

THE PRECEDING WORD TYPE OCCUPIES RANK 82900

U	SFI	D	F	Word Type
0.0081	19.1	.0000	1	Defender
0.0081	19.1	.0000	1	Delibes
0.0081	19.1	.0000	1	Delilah's
0.0081	19.1	.0000	1	Deller
0.0081	19.1	.0000	1	Dello
0.0081	19.1	.0000	1	deplored
0.0081	19.1	.0000	1	deported
0.0081	19.1	.0000	1	deske
0.0081	19.1	.0000	1	Desmond
0.0081	19.1	.0000	1	desperadoes
0.0081	19.1	.0000	1	Dett
0.0081	19.1	.0000	1	deviates
0.0081	19.1	.0000	1	devotee
0.0081	19.1	.0000	1	devotional
0.0081	19.1	.0000	1	devotions
0.0081	19.1	.0000	1	Diaghilef
0.0081	19.1	.0000	1	diaphragms
0.0081	19.1	.0000	1	diatonic
0.0081	19.1	.0000	1	diedalum
0.0081	19.1	.0000	1	Dieu
0.0081	19.1	.0000	1	dif-
0.0081	19.1	.0000	1	diminuendo
0.0081	19.1	.0000	1	diminution
0.0081	19.1	.0000	1	DIRECTIONS
0.0081	19.1	.0000	1	dirge-like
0.0081	19.1	.0000	1	dis-cover
0.0081	19.1	.0000	1	disappearances
0.0081	19.1	.0000	1	dishonestly
0.0081	19.1	.0000	1	disirregardless
0.0081	19.1	.0000	1	dispels
0.0081	19.1	.0000	1	Dispute
0.0081	19.1	.0000	1	disseminated
0.0081	19.1	.0000	1	divertimentos
0.0081	19.1	.0000	1	divisi
0.0081	19.1	.0000	1	divot
0.0081	19.1	.0000	1	do-mi-sol
0.0081	19.1	.0000	1	do-si-do
0.0081	19.1	.0000	1	doctorlum
0.0081	19.1	.0000	1	dog-vane
0.0081	19.1	.0000	1	dom
0.0081	19.1	.0000	1	donare
0.0081	19.1	.0000	1	Doney
0.0081	19.1	.0000	1	donkey-engine

744 RANK LIST

U	SFI	D	F	Word Type
0.0081	19.1	.0000	1	doob-kee
0.0081	19.1	.0000	1	Douai
0.0081	19.1	.0000	1	Douay
0.0081	19.1	.0000	1	double-entry
0.0081	19.1	.0000	1	double-flute
0.0081	19.1	.0000	1	double-letter
0.0081	19.1	.0000	1	double-pointed
0.0081	19.1	.0000	1	douce
0.0081	19.1	.0000	1	Dowland
0.0081	19.1	.0000	1	down-O
0.0081	19.1	.0000	1	downward-moving
0.0081	19.1	.0000	1	Doyle
0.0081	19.1	.0000	1	Doyle's
0.0081	19.1	.0000	1	dramatizations
0.0081	19.1	.0000	1	dramatizes
0.0081	19.1	.0000	1	Dreadnaught
0.0081	19.1	.0000	1	drear
0.0081	19.1	.0000	1	Dromadaire
0.0081	19.1	.0000	1	drover
0.0081	19.1	.0000	1	drumstick
0.0081	19.1	.0000	1	duce
0.0081	19.1	.0000	1	ducere
0.0081	19.1	.0000	1	Duckling's
0.0081	19.1	.0000	1	Duggan
0.0081	19.1	.0000	1	dulband
0.0081	19.1	.0000	1	dulcimer
0.0081	19.1	.0000	1	dum
0.0081	19.1	.0000	1	Dummy's
0.0081	19.1	.0000	1	duo
0.0081	19.1	.0000	1	duodecem
0.0081	19.1	.0000	1	Dupre
0.0081	19.1	.0000	1	Durbach
0.0081	19.1	.0000	1	Dvorak's
0.0081	19.1	.0000	1	dw
0.0081	19.1	.0000	1	dwelleth
0.0081	19.1	.0000	1	e-natural
0.0081	19.1	.0000	1	eage
0.0081	19.1	.0000	1	eam
0.0081	19.1	.0000	1	EAR
0.0081	19.1	.0000	1	Earl's
0.0081	19.1	.0000	1	earpiece
0.0081	19.1	.0000	1	earth-writing-thing
0.0081	19.1	.0000	1	easily-copied
0.0081	19.1	.0000	1	easily-recognized
0.0081	19.1	.0000	1	Easter-hunt-and-party
0.0081	19.1	.0000	1	Easterner's
0.0081	19.1	.0000	1	eczema
0.0081	19.1	.0000	1	ed/**
0.0081	19.1	.0000	1	ed'esen**
0.0081	19.1	.0000	1	edits
0.0081	19.1	.0000	1	editus
0.0081	19.1	.0000	1	ee's
0.0081	19.1	.0000	1	eels'
0.0081	19.1	.0000	1	eerigi
0.0081	19.1	.0000	1	egz
0.0081	19.1	.0000	1	eight-armed
0.0081	19.1	.0000	1	eight-day

THE PRECEDING WORD TYPE OCCUPIES RANK 83000

U	SFI	D	F	Word Type
0.0081	19.1	.0000	1	eighteenth-
0.0081	19.1	.0000	1	eighth-note
0.0081	19.1	.0000	1	eighty-year-old
0.0081	19.1	.0000	1	Eine
0.0081	19.1	.0000	1	eistedd
0.0081	19.1	.0000	1	eisteddfod
0.0081	19.1	.0000	1	ekenama
0.0081	19.1	.0000	1	ekskus'**
0.0081	19.1	.0000	1	ekskuz'**
0.0081	19.1	.0000	1	Elector
0.0081	19.1	.0000	1	electrocution
0.0081	19.1	.0000	1	electronic-age
0.0081	19.1	.0000	1	electronically-used
0.0081	19.1	.0000	1	elektor
0.0081	19.1	.0000	1	elevate
0.0081	19.1	.0000	1	Elevator
0.0081	19.1	.0000	1	Elgar
0.0081	19.1	.0000	1	ella
0.0081	19.1	.0000	1	Ellsworth's
0.0081	19.1	.0000	1	elves'
0.0081	19.1	.0000	1	em
0.0081	19.1	.0000	1	Em'rald
0.0081	19.1	.0000	1	embouchure
0.0081	19.1	.0000	1	embued
0.0081	19.1	.0000	1	Emotions
0.0081	19.1	.0000	1	En
0.0081	19.1	.0000	1	en-
0.0081	19.1	.0000	1	ency
0.0081	19.1	.0000	1	Engla
0.0081	19.1	.0000	1	Englisc
0.0081	19.1	.0000	1	engraven
0.0081	19.1	.0000	1	Engulfed
0.0081	19.1	.0000	1	enharmonic
0.0081	19.1	.0000	1	ens
0.0081	19.1	.0000	1	enshrining
0.0081	19.1	.0000	1	enthrone
0.0081	19.1	.0000	1	enticing
0.0081	19.1	.0000	1	Equador
0.0081	19.1	.0000	1	equalization
0.0081	19.1	.0000	1	Erda
0.0081	19.1	.0000	1	erh-hu
0.0081	19.1	.0000	1	Erl
0.0081	19.1	.0000	1	Erl-King's
0.0081	19.1	.0000	1	Erlkonig
0.0081	19.1	.0000	1	ern
0.0081	19.1	.0000	1	ern**
0.0081	19.1	.0000	1	erth
0.0081	19.1	.0000	1	Escamillo's
0.0081	19.1	.0000	1	Esterhazy
0.0081	19.1	.0000	1	ethereally
0.0081	19.1	.0000	1	ethnomusicologists
0.0081	19.1	.0000	1	Eto
0.0081	19.1	.0000	1	etude
0.0081	19.1	.0000	1	Eulenspiegel
0.0081	19.1	.0000	1	Ev'ry
0.0081	19.1	.0000	1	ev'ryone
0.0081	19.1	.0000	1	ev'rything
0.0081	19.1	.0000	1	ev'rywhere
0.0081	19.1	.0000	1	evenness
0.0081	19.1	.0000	1	everchanging
0.0081	19.1	.0000	1	everwidening
0.0081	19.1	.0000	1	evict
0.0081	19.1	.0000	1	evolves
0.0081	19.1	.0000	1	Ewigen
0.0081	19.1	.0000	1	exigencies
0.0081	19.1	.0000	1	Exit
0.0081	19.1	.0000	1	exotic-sounding
0.0081	19.1	.0000	1	Experimenting
0.0081	19.1	.0000	1	expositions
0.0081	19.1	.0000	1	expound
0.0081	19.1	.0000	1	Exquise
0.0081	19.1	.0000	1	extention
0.0081	19.1	.0000	1	extraction
0.0081	19.1	.0000	1	extraordinary**
0.0081	19.1	.0000	1	exuberantly
0.0081	19.1	.0000	1	F-A
0.0081	19.1	.0000	1	factotum
0.0081	19.1	.0000	1	faeger
0.0081	19.1	.0000	1	fah-yah
0.0081	19.1	.0000	1	Falke
0.0081	19.1	.0000	1	Falling
0.0081	19.1	.0000	1	Fancy
0.0081	19.1	.0000	1	fant
0.0081	19.1	.0000	1	fantasia
0.0081	19.1	.0000	1	Fantasy
0.0081	19.1	.0000	1	far-fallen
0.0081	19.1	.0000	1	Fargo
0.0081	19.1	.0000	1	farm-er
0.0081	19.1	.0000	1	Fath'r
0.0081	19.1	.0000	1	faux-bourdon
0.0081	19.1	.0000	1	fauxbourdon
0.0081	19.1	.0000	1	fawn's
0.0081	19.1	.0000	1	FBS
0.0081	19.1	.0000	1	feeblest
0.0081	19.1	.0000	1	Feed
0.0081	19.1	.0000	1	Fella
0.0081	19.1	.0000	1	fellow-composer
0.0081	19.1	.0000	1	fellow-scientists
0.0081	19.1	.0000	1	felt-covered
0.0081	19.1	.0000	1	Feng

THE PRECEDING WORD TYPE OCCUPIES RANK 83100

U	SFI	D	F	Word Type
0.0081	19.1	.0000	1	Festivals
0.0081	19.1	.0000	1	fests
0.0081	19.1	.0000	1	fiddlin'
0.0081	19.1	.0000	1	Fidelio
0.0081	19.1	.0000	1	Fiesta
0.0081	19.1	.0000	1	figure-eight
0.0081	19.1	.0000	1	Filipino
0.0081	19.1	.0000	1	fingerboard
0.0081	19.1	.0000	1	fingerings
0.0081	19.1	.0000	1	fire-cracker
0.0081	19.1	.0000	1	Fireball
0.0081	19.1	.0000	1	first-movement
0.0081	19.1	.0000	1	first-space
0.0081	19.1	.0000	1	Fishing
0.0081	19.1	.0000	1	fists-full
0.0081	19.1	.0000	1	five-line
0.0081	19.1	.0000	1	five-seven
0.0081	19.1	.0000	1	flams
0.0081	19.1	.0000	1	flatters
0.0081	19.1	.0000	1	Flemmons
0.0081	19.1	.0000	1	Flentrop
0.0081	19.1	.0000	1	fleugel
0.0081	19.1	.0000	1	flex
0.0081	19.1	.0000	1	flinched
0.0081	19.1	.0000	1	Flipper-Flopper
0.0081	19.1	.0000	1	flirtatious
0.0081	19.1	.0000	1	floatin'
0.0081	19.1	.0000	1	Flock
0.0081	19.1	.0000	1	floe
0.0081	19.1	.0000	1	floorwalker
0.0081	19.1	.0000	1	Fludde
0.0081	19.1	.0000	1	fluent
0.0081	19.1	.0000	1	flunky
0.0081	19.1	.0000	1	flute-like
0.0081	19.1	.0000	1	flute's
0.0081	19.1	.0000	1	foeman's
0.0081	19.1	.0000	1	fol-de-rol
0.0081	19.1	.0000	1	folk-sing
0.0081	19.1	.0000	1	folk-singing
0.0081	19.1	.0000	1	folk-song
0.0081	19.1	.0000	1	folk-songs
0.0081	19.1	.0000	1	foller
0.0081	19.1	.0000	1	follis
0.0081	19.1	.0000	1	foot-weary
0.0081	19.1	.0000	1	footnote
0.0081	19.1	.0000	1	for'hed**
0.0081	19.1	.0000	1	for'id
0.0081	19.1	.0000	1	formalism
0.0081	19.1	.0000	1	Formica
0.0081	19.1	.0000	1	fortissimo
0.0081	19.1	.0000	1	forty-niner
0.0081	19.1	.0000	1	Forty-niners
0.0081	19.1	.0000	1	forty-sixth
0.0081	19.1	.0000	1	four-beat
0.0081	19.1	.0000	1	Four-in-Line
0.0081	19.1	.0000	1	four-minute
0.0081	19.1	.0000	1	four-octave
0.0081	19.1	.0000	1	four-step
0.0081	19.1	.0000	1	four-voice
0.0081	19.1	.0000	1	frac
0.0081	19.1	.0000	1	Frackenpohl
0.0081	19.1	.0000	1	Fragrant
0.0081	19.1	.0000	1	Franck's
0.0081	19.1	.0000	1	Frankincense
0.0081	19.1	.0000	1	Franko
0.0081	19.1	.0000	1	Frederica
0.0081	19.1	.0000	1	freeflowing
0.0081	19.1	.0000	1	Freischuetz
0.0081	19.1	.0000	1	Frequency
0.0081	19.1	.0000	1	fresche
0.0081	19.1	.0000	1	Friar's
0.0081	19.1	.0000	1	friend-like
0.0081	19.1	.0000	1	Friska
0.0081	19.1	.0000	1	frittering
0.0081	19.1	.0000	1	frivolously
0.0081	19.1	.0000	1	Frobel
0.0081	19.1	.0000	1	froggie
0.0081	19.1	.0000	1	frolicsome
0.0081	19.1	.0000	1	fuguing
0.0081	19.1	.0000	1	fumare
0.0081	19.1	.0000	1	fume
0.0081	19.1	.0000	1	Fundamentals
0.0081	19.1	.0000	1	Funeral
0.0081	19.1	.0000	1	fung
0.0081	19.1	.0000	1	fungo
0.0081	19.1	.0000	1	funmaking
0.0081	19.1	.0000	1	funny**
0.0081	19.1	.0000	1	funny-man
0.0081	19.1	.0000	1	Furnberg
0.0081	19.1	.0000	1	furor
0.0081	19.1	.0000	1	furthered
0.0081	19.1	.0000	1	Gabrielli
0.0081	19.1	.0000	1	gambols
0.0081	19.1	.0000	1	gamelans
0.0081	19.1	.0000	1	garten
0.0081	19.1	.0000	1	Gayane
0.0081	19.1	.0000	1	GBD
0.0081	19.1	.0000	1	gelata
0.0081	19.1	.0000	1	gelatina
0.0081	19.1	.0000	1	gelee

THE PRECEDING WORD TYPE OCCUPIES RANK 83200

U	SFI	D	F	Word Type
0.0081	19.1	.0000	1	gent
0.0081	19.1	.0000	1	gentiles
0.0081	19.1	.0000	1	geo-graph-y
0.0081	19.1	.0000	1	geous
0.0081	19.1	.0000	1	Gerakina
0.0081	19.1	.0000	1	German-speaking
0.0081	19.1	.0000	1	Germanys
0.0081	19.1	.0000	1	Gershwin's
0.0081	19.1	.0000	1	gerunds
0.0081	19.1	.0000	1	gess
0.0081	19.1	.0000	1	gesse
0.0081	19.1	.0000	1	gewgaw
0.0081	19.1	.0000	1	Giannini
0.0081	19.1	.0000	1	gie's
0.0081	19.1	.0000	1	gigue
0.0081	19.1	.0000	1	Gilmore's
0.0081	19.1	.0000	1	Gladness
0.0081	19.1	.0000	1	Gliere
0.0081	19.1	.0000	1	Gliere's
0.0081	19.1	.0000	1	Glinka
0.0081	19.1	.0000	1	gloomier
0.0081	19.1	.0000	1	gloomiest
0.0081	19.1	.0000	1	glorification
0.0081	19.1	.0000	1	gluvz
0.0081	19.1	.0000	1	gnome
0.0081	19.1	.0000	1	Gnomes
0.0081	19.1	.0000	1	godfather
0.0081	19.1	.0000	1	Goethe-Lieder
0.0081	19.1	.0000	1	Goldsworthy
0.0081	19.1	.0000	1	Goodbye
0.0081	19.1	.0000	1	Goodman's
0.0081	19.1	.0000	1	Got
0.0081	19.1	.0000	1	Goths
0.0081	19.1	.0000	1	Gotterdammerung
0.0081	19.1	.0000	1	Gottschalk's
0.0081	19.1	.0000	1	Gracieuse
0.0081	19.1	.0000	1	grah-nah-dohs
0.0081	19.1	.0000	1	gram-mar
0.0081	19.1	.0000	1	Gramophone
0.0081	19.1	.0000	1	Granados
0.0081	19.1	.0000	1	graper
0.0081	19.1	.0000	1	gravitated
0.0081	19.1	.0000	1	grazioso
0.0081	19.1	.0000	1	greggers
0.0081	19.1	.0000	1	Grenadiers
0.0081	19.1	.0000	1	Grg
0.0081	19.1	.0000	1	Griffes
0.0081	19.1	.0000	1	grinder's
0.0081	19.1	.0000	1	gringo
0.0081	19.1	.0000	1	griz-ze-ly
0.0081	19.1	.0000	1	Ground-Gopher's
0.0081	19.1	.0000	1	guiro
0.0081	19.1	.0000	1	gullible
0.0081	19.1	.0000	1	Gulliby
0.0081	19.1	.0000	1	gulyas
0.0081	19.1	.0000	1	Gunther
0.0081	19.1	.0000	1	Gustaf
0.0081	19.1	.0000	1	Gut
0.0081	19.1	.0000	1	Gynt's
0.0081	19.1	.0000	1	gypsy-like
0.0081	19.1	.0000	1	gz
0.0081	19.1	.0000	1	G7
0.0081	19.1	.0000	1	H'
0.0081	19.1	.0000	1	Habanera
0.0081	19.1	.0000	1	half-boot
0.0081	19.1	.0000	1	half-steps
0.0081	19.1	.0000	1	half-tones
0.0081	19.1	.0000	1	Hallelujahs
0.0081	19.1	.0000	1	Halowe'en
0.0081	19.1	.0000	1	Hamishah
0.0081	19.1	.0000	1	hammerin'
0.0081	19.1	.0000	1	hand-sewn
0.0081	19.1	.0000	1	handcart
0.0081	19.1	.0000	1	handier
0.0081	19.1	.0000	1	Handy
0.0081	19.1	.0000	1	Harbach
0.0081	19.1	.0000	1	hard-shelled
0.0081	19.1	.0000	1	hard-wood
0.0081	19.1	.0000	1	harp-like
0.0081	19.1	.0000	1	harp's
0.0081	19.1	.0000	1	harum
0.0081	19.1	.0000	1	hat's
0.0081	19.1	.0000	1	Hatikvah
0.0081	19.1	.0000	1	haud
0.0081	19.1	.0000	1	Hauschka
0.0081	19.1	.0000	1	hautboy
0.0081	19.1	.0000	1	hawse
0.0081	19.1	.0000	1	Haymaker's
0.0081	19.1	.0000	1	he-bear
0.0081	19.1	.0000	1	heal-all
0.0081	19.1	.0000	1	heav'nly
0.0081	19.1	.0000	1	Heav'nly
0.0081	19.1	.0000	1	heav'ns
0.0081	19.1	.0000	1	heaven-thoughts
0.0081	19.1	.0000	1	hee-haw
0.0081	19.1	.0000	1	heel-tapping
0.0081	19.1	.0000	1	heel-toe-step-step-step
0.0081	19.1	.0000	1	Heitor
0.0081	19.1	.0000	1	heli
0.0081	19.1	.0000	1	Hennig

THE PRECEDING WORD TYPE OCCUPIES RANK 83300

U	SFI	D	F	Word Type
0.0081	19.1	.0000	1	Hens
0.0081	19.1	.0000	1	herdsman's
0.0081	19.1	.0000	1	Herfordshire
0.0081	19.1	.0000	1	Heroic
0.0081	19.1	.0000	1	heroine's
0.0081	19.1	.0000	1	Hi-Fi
0.0081	19.1	.0000	1	hieland
0.0081	19.1	.0000	1	High-School
0.0081	19.1	.0000	1	hinched
0.0081	19.1	.0000	1	Hindemith's
0.0081	19.1	.0000	1	holiness
0.0081	19.1	.0000	1	Hollanders
0.0081	19.1	.0000	1	hollow-log
0.0081	19.1	.0000	1	hom
0.0081	19.1	.0000	1	home-built
0.0081	19.1	.0000	1	home-feeling
0.0081	19.1	.0000	1	homo-
0.0081	19.1	.0000	1	hooraying
0.0081	19.1	.0000	1	hop-skip-jumping
0.0081	19.1	.0000	1	Hopes
0.0081	19.1	.0000	1	hopital
0.0081	19.1	.0000	1	Hopkinson's
0.0081	19.1	.0000	1	hor
0.0081	19.1	.0000	1	Hora
0.0081	19.1	.0000	1	hora
0.0081	19.1	.0000	1	Hornpipe
0.0081	19.1	.0000	1	hornswoggle
0.0081	19.1	.0000	1	horsehairs
0.0081	19.1	.0000	1	Hospodi
0.0081	19.1	.0000	1	hot-cross
0.0081	19.1	.0000	1	households'
0.0081	19.1	.0000	1	houselights
0.0081	19.1	.0000	1	Hovhaness
0.0081	19.1	.0000	1	huehuetls
0.0081	19.1	.0000	1	Huey's
0.0081	19.1	.0000	1	humanistic
0.0081	19.1	.0000	1	humidor
0.0081	19.1	.0000	1	Humpty-Dumpty
0.0081	19.1	.0000	1	Hung
0.0081	19.1	.0000	1	huntsman's
0.0081	19.1	.0000	1	hus
0.0081	19.1	.0000	1	huskie
0.0081	19.1	.0000	1	Husky
0.0081	19.1	.0000	1	hwit
0.0081	19.1	.0000	1	hwiz
0.0081	19.1	.0000	1	hygienic
0.0081	19.1	.0000	1	hymn-like
0.0081	19.1	.0000	1	H2O
0.0081	19.1	.0000	1	i-n-g
0.0081	19.1	.0000	1	I'se
0.0081	19.1	.0000	1	ian
0.0081	19.1	.0000	1	IB
0.0081	19.1	.0000	1	Ibert
0.0081	19.1	.0000	1	Ibsen's
0.0081	19.1	.0000	1	ical
0.0081	19.1	.0000	1	id
0.0081	19.1	.0000	1	identically
0.0081	19.1	.0000	1	ideo-o-o
0.0081	19.1	.0000	1	idolize
0.0081	19.1	.0000	1	Idue
0.0081	19.1	.0000	1	igh
0.0081	19.1	.0000	1	ignoramus
0.0081	19.1	.0000	1	Igorot
0.0081	19.1	.0000	1	ilekt'**
0.0081	19.1	.0000	1	ill-favored
0.0081	19.1	.0000	1	im-
0.0081	19.1	.0000	1	immanent
0.0081	19.1	.0000	1	impalpable
0.0081	19.1	.0000	1	impersonation
0.0081	19.1	.0000	1	Impressionists
0.0081	19.1	.0000	1	improvision
0.0081	19.1	.0000	1	in'crease**
0.0081	19.1	.0000	1	inadequately
0.0081	19.1	.0000	1	inadvisable
0.0081	19.1	.0000	1	inartistic
0.0081	19.1	.0000	1	inattention
0.0081	19.1	.0000	1	increase'**
0.0081	19.1	.0000	1	Ind'ans
0.0081	19.1	.0000	1	Ines
0.0081	19.1	.0000	1	inkiness
0.0081	19.1	.0000	1	Innocent
0.0081	19.1	.0000	1	ins
0.0081	19.1	.0000	1	insecare
0.0081	19.1	.0000	1	interactive
0.0081	19.1	.0000	1	interj
0.0081	19.1	.0000	1	interpolated
0.0081	19.1	.0000	1	interpretative
0.0081	19.1	.0000	1	Invention
0.0081	19.1	.0000	1	invocation
0.0081	19.1	.0000	1	Invocation
0.0081	19.1	.0000	1	io-la
0.0081	19.1	.0000	1	io-li
0.0081	19.1	.0000	1	ior
0.0081	19.1	.0000	1	ipu
0.0081	19.1	.0000	1	ir-
0.0081	19.1	.0000	1	Irish-American
0.0081	19.1	.0000	1	irl
0.0081	19.1	.0000	1	ism
0.0081	19.1	.0000	1	IV-1
0.0081	19.1	.0000	1	J-i-n-g-o

THE PRECEDING WORD TYPE OCCUPIES RANK 83400

U	SFI	D	F	Word Type
0.0081	19.1	.0000	1	jack-o-lanterns
0.0081	19.1	.0000	1	Jackman's
0.0081	19.1	.0000	1	Janacek
0.0081	19.1	.0000	1	jay-bird
0.0081	19.1	.0000	1	jazzmen
0.0081	19.1	.0000	1	jellybean

U	SFI	D	F	Word Type
0.0081	19.1	.0000	1	Jemmy's
0.0081	19.1	.0000	1	jeopardize
0.0081	19.1	.0000	1	jesting
0.0081	19.1	.0000	1	jetliner
0.0081	19.1	.0000	1	Jevan
0.0081	19.1	.0000	1	jingle-jangle
0.0081	19.1	.0000	1	jiujitsu
0.0081	19.1	.0000	1	job's
0.0081	19.1	.0000	1	jobber's
0.0081	19.1	.0000	1	Joio
0.0081	19.1	.0000	1	jota
0.0081	19.1	.0000	1	Journeyman's
0.0081	19.1	.0000	1	jousted
0.0081	19.1	.0000	1	Joyeuse
0.0081	19.1	.0000	1	joyful'st
0.0081	19.1	.0000	1	Joyous
0.0081	19.1	.0000	1	Jubilee
0.0081	19.1	.0000	1	Juliet's
0.0081	19.1	.0000	1	June-bug
0.0081	19.1	.0000	1	jus
0.0081	19.1	.0000	1	kachina
0.0081	19.1	.0000	1	Kaleidoscope
0.0081	19.1	.0000	1	kamikaze
0.0081	19.1	.0000	1	Kammermusik
0.0081	19.1	.0000	1	Kapellmeister
0.0081	19.1	.0000	1	kar'ver**
0.0081	19.1	.0000	1	kas**
0.0081	19.1	.0000	1	Katharine
0.0081	19.1	.0000	1	ken-tah-ten
0.0081	19.1	.0000	1	Kennan
0.0081	19.1	.0000	1	kh
0.0081	19.1	.0000	1	Khah-tchah-too-ree-ahn
0.0081	19.1	.0000	1	Khatchaturian
0.0081	19.1	.0000	1	kiddies
0.0081	19.1	.0000	1	Kimio
0.0081	19.1	.0000	1	Kismet
0.0081	19.1	.0000	1	kloun
0.0081	19.1	.0000	1	kn
0.0081	19.1	.0000	1	Kodaly's
0.0081	19.1	.0000	1	Kopylow
0.0081	19.1	.0000	1	Koussevitsky
0.0081	19.1	.0000	1	kr
0.0081	19.1	.0000	1	Kreisler
0.0081	19.1	.0000	1	Krenek
0.0081	19.1	.0000	1	kro
0.0081	19.1	.0000	1	krol
0.0081	19.1	.0000	1	kul
0.0081	19.1	.0000	1	kum
0.0081	19.1	.0000	1	Kyrie
0.0081	19.1	.0000	1	la-ah
0.0081	19.1	.0000	1	Laconia
0.0081	19.1	.0000	1	Landler
0.0081	19.1	.0000	1	lang's
0.0081	19.1	.0000	1	laqueus
0.0081	19.1	.0000	1	larghetto
0.0081	19.1	.0000	1	largo
0.0081	19.1	.0000	1	Lassan
0.0081	19.1	.0000	1	Latin-Americans
0.0081	19.1	.0000	1	Latin-French
0.0081	19.1	.0000	1	laudas
0.0081	19.1	.0000	1	Laurence's
0.0081	19.1	.0000	1	lavanderas
0.0081	19.1	.0000	1	Layo
0.0081	19.1	.0000	1	Lazaroni
0.0081	19.1	.0000	1	leath-er
0.0081	19.1	.0000	1	left-right
0.0081	19.1	.0000	1	legalum
0.0081	19.1	.0000	1	Leghorn
0.0081	19.1	.0000	1	Lemuel
0.0081	19.1	.0000	1	Leonore
0.0081	19.1	.0000	1	Leron
0.0081	19.1	.0000	1	Liang
0.0081	19.1	.0000	1	Liberians
0.0081	19.1	.0000	1	librettos
0.0081	19.1	.0000	1	lide
0.0081	19.1	.0000	1	lieber
0.0081	19.1	.0000	1	lighte
0.0081	19.1	.0000	1	lightnin'
0.0081	19.1	.0000	1	likened
0.0081	19.1	.0000	1	Liking
0.0081	19.1	.0000	1	Lind's
0.0081	19.1	.0000	1	linin'
0.0081	19.1	.0000	1	Linstead
0.0081	19.1	.0000	1	liquid-filled
0.0081	19.1	.0000	1	lisle
0.0081	19.1	.0000	1	Lititz
0.0081	19.1	.0000	1	littera
0.0081	19.1	.0000	1	litterbug
0.0081	19.1	.0000	1	liturgies
0.0081	19.1	.0000	1	liturgy
0.0081	19.1	.0000	1	living's
0.0081	19.1	.0000	1	lks
0.0081	19.1	.0000	1	lm
0.0081	19.1	.0000	1	Locality
THE PRECEDING WORD TYPE OCCUPIES RANK 83500				
0.0081	19.1	.0000	1	Loeffler
0.0081	19.1	.0000	1	Loewe
0.0081	19.1	.0000	1	loftiness
0.0081	19.1	.0000	1	log-roller
0.0081	19.1	.0000	1	Lohengrin
0.0081	19.1	.0000	1	lon
0.0081	19.1	.0000	1	Long-Playing
0.0081	19.1	.0000	1	looking'
0.0081	19.1	.0000	1	looser
0.0081	19.1	.0000	1	lopes
0.0081	19.1	.0000	1	Loretta's
0.0081	19.1	.0000	1	Loud
0.0081	19.1	.0000	1	Love-Song
0.0081	19.1	.0000	1	lovesick
0.0081	19.1	.0000	1	low-heeled
0.0081	19.1	.0000	1	Lowd
0.0081	19.1	.0000	1	lower-pitched
0.0081	19.1	.0000	1	lowest-sounding
0.0081	19.1	.0000	1	lphbt
0.0081	19.1	.0000	1	Lucia's
0.0081	19.1	.0000	1	Lucien
0.0081	19.1	.0000	1	Luening
0.0081	19.1	.0000	1	lulling
0.0081	19.1	.0000	1	Lune
0.0081	19.1	.0000	1	lurks
0.0081	19.1	.0000	1	lusong
0.0081	19.1	.0000	1	luster-glossed
0.0081	19.1	.0000	1	lute-like
0.0081	19.1	.0000	1	luz
0.0081	19.1	.0000	1	Lvovsky
0.0081	19.1	.0000	1	lyceum
0.0081	19.1	.0000	1	Lyndol
0.0081	19.1	.0000	1	lyricist
0.0081	19.1	.0000	1	Lyrics
0.0081	19.1	.0000	1	Ma'oz
0.0081	19.1	.0000	1	machine's
0.0081	19.1	.0000	1	madly-moving
0.0081	19.1	.0000	1	maestoso
0.0081	19.1	.0000	1	Magnificat
0.0081	19.1	.0000	1	Mahon
0.0081	19.1	.0000	1	mahout
0.0081	19.1	.0000	1	maid's
0.0081	19.1	.0000	1	Maids
0.0081	19.1	.0000	1	maitre
0.0081	19.1	.0000	1	majorettes
0.0081	19.1	.0000	1	Maler
0.0081	19.1	.0000	1	Mambron
0.0081	19.1	.0000	1	manana
0.0081	19.1	.0000	1	mandarin
0.0081	19.1	.0000	1	Manitou
0.0081	19.1	.0000	1	mann
0.0081	19.1	.0000	1	mant
0.0081	19.1	.0000	1	manus
0.0081	19.1	.0000	1	many-a
0.0081	19.1	.0000	1	many-headed
0.0081	19.1	.0000	1	many-voiced
0.0081	19.1	.0000	1	Manzuoli
0.0081	19.1	.0000	1	mappa
0.0081	19.1	.0000	1	Marais
0.0081	19.1	.0000	1	march-like
0.0081	19.1	.0000	1	Marines'
0.0081	19.1	.0000	1	markhzan
0.0081	19.1	.0000	1	Marry
0.0081	19.1	.0000	1	Martinville
0.0081	19.1	.0000	1	Mastersinger's
0.0081	19.1	.0000	1	matchless
0.0081	19.1	.0000	1	Mathis
0.0081	19.1	.0000	1	matinee
0.0081	19.1	.0000	1	Matthison
0.0081	19.1	.0000	1	mb
0.0081	19.1	.0000	1	mbx
0.0081	19.1	.0000	1	McArthur
0.0081	19.1	.0000	1	McIntire
0.0081	19.1	.0000	1	McManus
0.0081	19.1	.0000	1	Mede
0.0081	19.1	.0000	1	mediate
0.0081	19.1	.0000	1	Meh-nah-tee
0.0081	19.1	.0000	1	mel
0.0081	19.1	.0000	1	Melchior
0.0081	19.1	.0000	1	mellophone
0.0081	19.1	.0000	1	Menorah
0.0081	19.1	.0000	1	Mercadante
0.0081	19.1	.0000	1	merchandising
0.0081	19.1	.0000	1	merges
0.0081	19.1	.0000	1	merle
0.0081	19.1	.0000	1	Merriam-Webster's
0.0081	19.1	.0000	1	Meshach
0.0081	19.1	.0000	1	Metaphor
0.0081	19.1	.0000	1	metre
0.0081	19.1	.0000	1	Michie
0.0081	19.1	.0000	1	Microgroove
0.0081	19.1	.0000	1	mid-eighth
0.0081	19.1	.0000	1	middles
0.0081	19.1	.0000	1	Mikrokosmos
0.0081	19.1	.0000	1	milepost
0.0081	19.1	.0000	1	miles'
0.0081	19.1	.0000	1	Milhaud
0.0081	19.1	.0000	1	militare
0.0081	19.1	.0000	1	millin'
0.0081	19.1	.0000	1	minor-modal
THE PRECEDING WORD TYPE OCCUPIES RANK 83600				
0.0081	19.1	.0000	1	Minorca
0.0081	19.1	.0000	1	minstrel-show
0.0081	19.1	.0000	1	Mintie
0.0081	19.1	.0000	1	Minute
0.0081	19.1	.0000	1	minute1**
0.0081	19.1	.0000	1	minutus
0.0081	19.1	.0000	1	mistempered
0.0081	19.1	.0000	1	mixolydian
0.0081	19.1	.0000	1	mizzle
0.0081	19.1	.0000	1	Modiste
0.0081	19.1	.0000	1	modulating
0.0081	19.1	.0000	1	modulations
0.0081	19.1	.0000	1	molto
0.0081	19.1	.0000	1	monarchies
0.0081	19.1	.0000	1	monkey-baby's
0.0081	19.1	.0000	1	monkeyish
0.0081	19.1	.0000	1	monodic
0.0081	19.1	.0000	1	monody
0.0081	19.1	.0000	1	Monteverdi's
0.0081	19.1	.0000	1	Moods
0.0081	19.1	.0000	1	moon-silvered
0.0081	19.1	.0000	1	moonstruck
0.0081	19.1	.0000	1	moony
0.0081	19.1	.0000	1	Morales
0.0081	19.1	.0000	1	more's
0.0081	19.1	.0000	1	Moreen
0.0081	19.1	.0000	1	Morelia
0.0081	19.1	.0000	1	Morley
0.0081	19.1	.0000	1	Morn
0.0081	19.1	.0000	1	mort
0.0081	19.1	.0000	1	most-loved
0.0081	19.1	.0000	1	motel**
0.0081	19.1	.0000	1	motio
0.0081	19.1	.0000	1	Motive
0.0081	19.1	.0000	1	motus
0.0081	19.1	.0000	1	Mousehawk's
0.0081	19.1	.0000	1	mouthpieces
0.0081	19.1	.0000	1	mundi
0.0081	19.1	.0000	1	munth
0.0081	19.1	.0000	1	Musette
0.0081	19.1	.0000	1	musicales
0.0081	19.1	.0000	1	Musicianship
0.0081	19.1	.0000	1	Mussorgsky's
0.0081	19.1	.0000	1	musters
0.0081	19.1	.0000	1	muv'e**
0.0081	19.1	.0000	1	mykes
0.0081	19.1	.0000	1	myna
0.0081	19.1	.0000	1	Nachtmusik
0.0081	19.1	.0000	1	Nacimiento
0.0081	19.1	.0000	1	nae
0.0081	19.1	.0000	1	naiads
0.0081	19.1	.0000	1	nakuba
0.0081	19.1	.0000	1	narrating
0.0081	19.1	.0000	1	narrow-necked
0.0081	19.1	.0000	1	Nassau-Weilburg
0.0081	19.1	.0000	1	Nativity
0.0081	19.1	.0000	1	naturalize
0.0081	19.1	.0000	1	ne-brath-ka
0.0081	19.1	.0000	1	Nebuchadnezzar's
0.0081	19.1	.0000	1	neck's
0.0081	19.1	.0000	1	neglectful
0.0081	19.1	.0000	1	neighb'ring
0.0081	19.1	.0000	1	nekename
0.0081	19.1	.0000	1	neoclassical
0.0081	19.1	.0000	1	nes
0.0081	19.1	.0000	1	neumes
0.0081	19.1	.0000	1	neuralgia
0.0081	19.1	.0000	1	Niblock
0.0081	19.1	.0000	1	Nickname
0.0081	19.1	.0000	1	nightcaps
0.0081	19.1	.0000	1	Nijinsky
0.0081	19.1	.0000	1	Nimes
0.0081	19.1	.0000	1	nine-tail
0.0081	19.1	.0000	1	Nineties
0.0081	19.1	.0000	1	ninth-century
0.0081	19.1	.0000	1	Nobby
0.0081	19.1	.0000	1	nobleness
0.0081	19.1	.0000	1	nocturne
0.0081	19.1	.0000	1	nominees
0.0081	19.1	.0000	1	non-pentatonic
0.0081	19.1	.0000	1	non-spelling
0.0081	19.1	.0000	1	noncitizens
0.0081	19.1	.0000	1	None
0.0081	19.1	.0000	1	nonliturgical
0.0081	19.1	.0000	1	nonmusician
0.0081	19.1	.0000	1	nonper
0.0081	19.1	.0000	1	noontide's
0.0081	19.1	.0000	1	Norma
0.0081	19.1	.0000	1	Norseman's
0.0081	19.1	.0000	1	Northerner
0.0081	19.1	.0000	1	Northland's
0.0081	19.1	.0000	1	Norwegians'
0.0081	19.1	.0000	1	Notation
0.0081	19.1	.0000	1	note-reading
0.0081	19.1	.0000	1	Nots
0.0081	19.1	.0000	1	noun-forming
0.0081	19.1	.0000	1	novel**
0.0081	19.1	.0000	1	November's
0.0081	19.1	.0000	1	Noye's
0.0081	19.1	.0000	1	ns
THE PRECEDING WORD TYPE OCCUPIES RANK 83700				
0.0081	19.1	.0000	1	nub
0.0081	19.1	.0000	1	num-ber
0.0081	19.1	.0000	1	nurses'
0.0081	19.1	.0000	1	nym
0.0081	19.1	.0000	1	Nyu
0.0081	19.1	.0000	1	Nyu's
0.0081	19.1	.0000	1	o-ending
0.0081	19.1	.0000	1	O-lulu
0.0081	19.1	.0000	1	o'wakin'
0.0081	19.1	.0000	1	ob
0.0081	19.1	.0000	1	obcur
0.0081	19.1	.0000	1	Oberndorf
0.0081	19.1	.0000	1	objectionably
0.0081	19.1	.0000	1	oboist
0.0081	19.1	.0000	1	oc-
0.0081	19.1	.0000	1	occasioned
0.0081	19.1	.0000	1	Occasions
0.0081	19.1	.0000	1	oclock
0.0081	19.1	.0000	1	Octet
0.0081	19.1	.0000	1	ode
0.0081	19.1	.0000	1	oe
0.0081	19.1	.0000	1	off-beat
0.0081	19.1	.0000	1	off'ring
0.0081	19.1	.0000	1	offbeats
0.0081	19.1	.0000	1	Oil's
0.0081	19.1	.0000	1	ol
0.0081	19.1	.0000	1	Oleana
0.0081	19.1	.0000	1	ombrella
0.0081	19.1	.0000	1	Omnipotent
0.0081	19.1	.0000	1	on-ly
0.0081	19.1	.0000	1	on'ist**
0.0081	19.1	.0000	1	one-of-a-kind
0.0081	19.1	.0000	1	one-space
0.0081	19.1	.0000	1	one-voiced
0.0081	19.1	.0000	1	Onegin
0.0081	19.1	.0000	1	oom-pa
0.0081	19.1	.0000	1	oom-pah
0.0081	19.1	.0000	1	oom-pah-pah
0.0081	19.1	.0000	1	oops
0.0081	19.1	.0000	1	Opferlied
0.0081	19.1	.0000	1	Orah
0.0081	19.1	.0000	1	Oranges
0.0081	19.1	.0000	1	ordaining
0.0081	19.1	.0000	1	ordinals
0.0081	19.1	.0000	1	organ-man
0.0081	19.1	.0000	1	Oriental-sounding
0.0081	19.1	.0000	1	orig/i/nal
0.0081	19.1	.0000	1	Orm
0.0081	19.1	.0000	1	Orrego-Salas
0.0081	19.1	.0000	1	orse
0.0081	19.1	.0000	1	ort
0.0081	19.1	.0000	1	Orth
0.0081	19.1	.0000	1	os
0.0081	19.1	.0000	1	Osiris
0.0081	19.1	.0000	1	ots
0.0081	19.1	.0000	1	Ottorino
0.0081	19.1	.0000	1	ou's
0.0081	19.1	.0000	1	out-ring
0.0081	19.1	.0000	1	Outdoors
0.0081	19.1	.0000	1	outpourings
0.0081	19.1	.0000	1	Outside
0.0081	19.1	.0000	1	overdoing
0.0081	19.1	.0000	1	Overture-Fantasie
0.0081	19.1	.0000	1	Paderewski
0.0081	19.1	.0000	1	Pairs
0.0081	19.1	.0000	1	Paisley
0.0081	19.1	.0000	1	Pajama
0.0081	19.1	.0000	1	Palomita
0.0081	19.1	.0000	1	paly
0.0081	19.1	.0000	1	Pamina
0.0081	19.1	.0000	1	Pandora's
0.0081	19.1	.0000	1	panpipe
0.0081	19.1	.0000	1	Panpipes
0.0081	19.1	.0000	1	Papageno
0.0081	19.1	.0000	1	papaya
0.0081	19.1	.0000	1	parare
0.0081	19.1	.0000	1	pard-ner
0.0081	19.1	.0000	1	Parlour
0.0081	19.1	.0000	1	Parnassian
0.0081	19.1	.0000	1	Paroo
0.0081	19.1	.0000	1	part-ner
0.0081	19.1	.0000	1	Parts
0.0081	19.1	.0000	1	passar
0.0081	19.1	.0000	1	passenger's
0.0081	19.1	.0000	1	passus
0.0081	19.1	.0000	1	passuum
0.0081	19.1	.0000	1	pastorals
0.0081	19.1	.0000	1	pastus
0.0081	19.1	.0000	1	pat-a-pat-a
0.0081	19.1	.0000	1	pat-a-pat-a-pan
0.0081	19.1	.0000	1	patere
0.0081	19.1	.0000	1	Pathetic
0.0081	19.1	.0000	1	patting-stamping
0.0081	19.1	.0000	1	Peale
0.0081	19.1	.0000	1	Peas
0.0081	19.1	.0000	1	pedis
0.0081	19.1	.0000	1	Peerce
0.0081	19.1	.0000	1	pelere
0.0081	19.1	.0000	1	Pennies
0.0081	19.1	.0000	1	penta
THE PRECEDING WORD TYPE OCCUPIES RANK 83800				
0.0081	19.1	.0000	1	Penurious
0.0081	19.1	.0000	1	per'fect**
0.0081	19.1	.0000	1	perad'**
0.0081	19.1	.0000	1	Percussion
0.0081	19.1	.0000	1	perfect'**
0.0081	19.1	.0000	1	Performers
0.0081	19.1	.0000	1	Periods
0.0081	19.1	.0000	1	perish-ed
0.0081	19.1	.0000	1	Perla
0.0081	19.1	.0000	1	Pernambuco
0.0081	19.1	.0000	1	persecute
0.0081	19.1	.0000	1	personable
0.0081	19.1	.0000	1	peruke
0.0081	19.1	.0000	1	peskily
0.0081	19.1	.0000	1	pez
0.0081	19.1	.0000	1	Phile
0.0081	19.1	.0000	1	phon
0.0081	19.1	.0000	1	phonic
0.0081	19.1	.0000	1	phono
0.0081	19.1	.0000	1	pianissimo
0.0081	19.1	.0000	1	pianist-composer
0.0081	19.1	.0000	1	Picardie
0.0081	19.1	.0000	1	piccolo's
0.0081	19.1	.0000	1	pictogram
0.0081	19.1	.0000	1	pictography
0.0081	19.1	.0000	1	picture-like
0.0081	19.1	.0000	1	pid
0.0081	19.1	.0000	1	Pierrette
0.0081	19.1	.0000	1	Pierrot
0.0081	19.1	.0000	1	Piglet
0.0081	19.1	.0000	1	pike-poles
0.0081	19.1	.0000	1	Pins
0.0081	19.1	.0000	1	pipelayer
0.0081	19.1	.0000	1	pirated
0.0081	19.1	.0000	1	pit-sih-kah-toh
0.0081	19.1	.0000	1	plaguey
0.0081	19.1	.0000	1	plaguy
0.0081	19.1	.0000	1	Planquette
0.0081	19.1	.0000	1	play-song
0.0081	19.1	.0000	1	Playing
0.0081	19.1	.0000	1	playings
0.0081	19.1	.0000	1	pleads
0.0081	19.1	.0000	1	pleasurability
0.0081	19.1	.0000	1	ploughboy's
0.0081	19.1	.0000	1	plowin'
0.0081	19.1	.0000	1	plsnt
0.0081	19.1	.0000	1	plugger
0.0081	19.1	.0000	1	pneu-mo-ni-a
0.0081	19.1	.0000	1	pneuma
0.0081	19.1	.0000	1	pneumograph
0.0081	19.1	.0000	1	pneumon
0.0081	19.1	.0000	1	pocketful
0.0081	19.1	.0000	1	podium
0.0081	19.1	.0000	1	pokers
0.0081	19.1	.0000	1	polar**
0.0081	19.1	.0000	1	pole-holders
0.0081	19.1	.0000	1	Polina's
0.0081	19.1	.0000	1	polka-dotted
0.0081	19.1	.0000	1	polkas
0.0081	19.1	.0000	1	Pollyanna
0.0081	19.1	.0000	1	Polonaise
0.0081	19.1	.0000	1	Polovtzian
0.0081	19.1	.0000	1	polyester
0.0081	19.1	.0000	1	polyharmony
0.0081	19.1	.0000	1	polyphonically
0.0081	19.1	.0000	1	polyphony
0.0081	19.1	.0000	1	polytonality
0.0081	19.1	.0000	1	pome
0.0081	19.1	.0000	1	Pomilui
0.0081	19.1	.0000	1	poo-ee-lee

U	SFI	D	F	Word Type
0.0081	19.1	.0000	1	Poo-poo
0.0081	19.1	.0000	1	poofreader
0.0081	19.1	.0000	1	poolside
0.0081	19.1	.0000	1	poom
0.0081	19.1	.0000	1	popularize
0.0081	19.1	.0000	1	Porridge
0.0081	19.1	.0000	1	portaged
0.0081	19.1	.0000	1	Posada
0.0081	19.1	.0000	1	Potato
0.0081	19.1	.0000	1	Poulenc
0.0081	19.1	.0000	1	Poverty's
0.0081	19.1	.0000	1	Powerful
0.0081	19.1	.0000	1	prances
0.0081	19.1	.0000	1	Praties
0.0081	19.1	.0000	1	pray'rs
0.0081	19.1	.0000	1	pre-recorded
0.0081	19.1	.0000	1	preamplifier
0.0081	19.1	.0000	1	preciseness
0.0081	19.1	.0000	1	prefixing
0.0081	19.1	.0000	1	Preis
0.0081	19.1	.0000	1	pres'ent**
0.0081	19.1	.0000	1	present'**
0.0081	19.1	.0000	1	preservationist
0.0081	19.1	.0000	1	pretekt'**
0.0081	19.1	.0000	1	Pretender
0.0081	19.1	.0000	1	primitive-sounding
0.0081	19.1	.0000	1	Privy
0.0081	19.1	.0000	1	prods
0.0081	19.1	.0000	1	productively
0.0081	19.1	.0000	1	professors'
THE PRECEDING WORD TYPE OCCUPIES RANK 83900				
0.0081	19.1	.0000	1	prog'ress**
0.0081	19.1	.0000	1	progress'**
0.0081	19.1	.0000	1	Proh-koh-fee-ehf
0.0081	19.1	.0000	1	proj'ect**
0.0081	19.1	.0000	1	project'**
0.0081	19.1	.0000	1	Prokofieff
0.0081	19.1	.0000	1	prologue
0.0081	19.1	.0000	1	Prologue
0.0081	19.1	.0000	1	PRONOUNCE
0.0081	19.1	.0000	1	pronunication
0.0081	19.1	.0000	1	ps
0.0081	19.1	.0000	1	psalm-tunes
0.0081	19.1	.0000	1	Psalter
0.0081	19.1	.0000	1	psaltery
0.0081	19.1	.0000	1	ptomaine
0.0081	19.1	.0000	1	pudding-string
0.0081	19.1	.0000	1	puilis
0.0081	19.1	.0000	1	pum
0.0081	19.1	.0000	1	punters
0.0081	19.1	.0000	1	puppet-clown
0.0081	19.1	.0000	1	pureta
0.0081	19.1	.0000	1	purple-blue
0.0081	19.1	.0000	1	Purse
0.0081	19.1	.0000	1	putzes
0.0081	19.1	.0000	1	py
0.0081	19.1	.0000	1	Pyle's
0.0081	19.1	.0000	1	pyr
0.0081	19.1	.0000	1	q-z
0.0081	19.1	.0000	1	Quail's
0.0081	19.1	.0000	1	quarter-note
0.0081	19.1	.0000	1	quarterly
0.0081	19.1	.0000	1	quatre
0.0081	19.1	.0000	1	question-answer
0.0081	19.1	.0000	1	Quinten
0.0081	19.1	.0000	1	Quintet
0.0081	19.1	.0000	1	Quipu
0.0081	19.1	.0000	1	quy
0.0081	19.1	.0000	1	R-i-n-g-o
0.0081	19.1	.0000	1	Rachmaninoff's
0.0081	19.1	.0000	1	racoon
0.0081	19.1	.0000	1	radio-phonographs
0.0081	19.1	.0000	1	Raeder
0.0081	19.1	.0000	1	raftsmen
0.0081	19.1	.0000	1	Raftsmen
0.0081	19.1	.0000	1	Ragshag
0.0081	19.1	.0000	1	Ragtime
0.0081	19.1	.0000	1	ragtime-blues
0.0081	19.1	.0000	1	Rah-coh-tsee
0.0081	19.1	.0000	1	Rahck-mah-nee-nawf
0.0081	19.1	.0000	1	railroad's
0.0081	19.1	.0000	1	rain-bringers
0.0081	19.1	.0000	1	Rainy
0.0081	19.1	.0000	1	rambunctious
0.0081	19.1	.0000	1	rancho
0.0081	19.1	.0000	1	rancour
0.0081	19.1	.0000	1	rasgueado
0.0081	19.1	.0000	1	rath-er
0.0081	19.1	.0000	1	rathskeller
0.0081	19.1	.0000	1	Rattlin'
0.0081	19.1	.0000	1	rauschpfeife
0.0081	19.1	.0000	1	Ravens
0.0081	19.1	.0000	1	re-animated
0.0081	19.1	.0000	1	re-appear
0.0081	19.1	.0000	1	re-arrange
0.0081	19.1	.0000	1	re-examine
0.0081	19.1	.0000	1	re-write
0.0081	19.1	.0000	1	reach'd
0.0081	19.1	.0000	1	reappearance
0.0081	19.1	.0000	1	rebab
0.0081	19.1	.0000	1	rec'ord**
0.0081	19.1	.0000	1	recitare
0.0081	19.1	.0000	1	record'**
0.0081	19.1	.0000	1	recurs
0.0081	19.1	.0000	1	red-wing
0.0081	19.1	.0000	1	Redding
0.0081	19.1	.0000	1	Reel
0.0081	19.1	.0000	1	reenters
0.0081	19.1	.0000	1	Regimental
0.0081	19.1	.0000	1	regrettable
0.0081	19.1	.0000	1	Remendado
0.0081	19.1	.0000	1	remits
0.0081	19.1	.0000	1	remittance
0.0081	19.1	.0000	1	remitting
0.0081	19.1	.0000	1	remorseful
0.0081	19.1	.0000	1	renditions
0.0081	19.1	.0000	1	reoccurrence
0.0081	19.1	.0000	1	repetions
0.0081	19.1	.0000	1	reprieved
0.0081	19.1	.0000	1	rerecord
0.0081	19.1	.0000	1	resonators
0.0081	19.1	.0000	1	Resound
0.0081	19.1	.0000	1	respells
0.0081	19.1	.0000	1	rev'rently
0.0081	19.1	.0000	1	Rhapsodies
0.0081	19.1	.0000	1	Rheinhold
0.0081	19.1	.0000	1	rheum
0.0081	19.1	.0000	1	rheuma
0.0081	19.1	.0000	1	rheumy
0.0081	19.1	.0000	1	Rhinegold
0.0081	19.1	.0000	1	RIAA
THE PRECEDING WORD TYPE OCCUPIES RANK 84000				
0.0081	19.1	.0000	1	riddle-ma-ree
0.0081	19.1	.0000	1	Riegger
0.0081	19.1	.0000	1	Rienzi
0.0081	19.1	.0000	1	Rig-A-Jig-Jig
0.0081	19.1	.0000	1	ripplin'
0.0081	19.1	.0000	1	rist
0.0081	19.1	.0000	1	Rival
0.0081	19.1	.0000	1	river-boatmen
0.0081	19.1	.0000	1	river-snow
0.0081	19.1	.0000	1	riverboatman
0.0081	19.1	.0000	1	road-
0.0081	19.1	.0000	1	Rochlitz
0.0081	19.1	.0000	1	Rock-a
0.0081	19.1	.0000	1	Roh-see-nee
0.0081	19.1	.0000	1	Roll-off
0.0081	19.1	.0000	1	Romance
0.0081	19.1	.0000	1	Rondeau
0.0081	19.1	.0000	1	Rosamunde
0.0081	19.1	.0000	1	Rosenkavalier
0.0081	19.1	.0000	1	rote
0.0081	19.1	.0000	1	Roumania
0.0081	19.1	.0000	1	Roundup
0.0081	19.1	.0000	1	rove
0.0081	19.1	.0000	1	rovin'
0.0081	19.1	.0000	1	roving's
0.0081	19.1	.0000	1	Roxane
0.0081	19.1	.0000	1	rub-ber
0.0081	19.1	.0000	1	Rubbly
0.0081	19.1	.0000	1	ruehmen
0.0081	19.1	.0000	1	Sabre
0.0081	19.1	.0000	1	Saens
0.0081	19.1	.0000	1	Sagwa
0.0081	19.1	.0000	1	sail'd
0.0081	19.1	.0000	1	Sailor's
0.0081	19.1	.0000	1	SaintNicholas
0.0081	19.1	.0000	1	Sainte
0.0081	19.1	.0000	1	sairly
0.0081	19.1	.0000	1	Samoan
0.0081	19.1	.0000	1	saner
0.0081	19.1	.0000	1	sanest
0.0081	19.1	.0000	1	Sapete
0.0081	19.1	.0000	1	Saro
0.0081	19.1	.0000	1	sarpent
0.0081	19.1	.0000	1	Satan's
0.0081	19.1	.0000	1	Satie
0.0081	19.1	.0000	1	Sauria
0.0081	19.1	.0000	1	sauterne
0.0081	19.1	.0000	1	Sauternes
0.0081	19.1	.0000	1	Savior's
0.0081	19.1	.0000	1	scala
0.0081	19.1	.0000	1	scale-step
0.0081	19.1	.0000	1	scale-tones
0.0081	19.1	.0000	1	scalewise
0.0081	19.1	.0000	1	scallions
0.0081	19.1	.0000	1	scandere
0.0081	19.1	.0000	1	scareder
0.0081	19.1	.0000	1	scarum
0.0081	19.1	.0000	1	Scat
0.0081	19.1	.0000	1	schalmei
0.0081	19.1	.0000	1	Schelomo
0.0081	19.1	.0000	1	scherzos
0.0081	19.1	.0000	1	Schoenberg
0.0081	19.1	.0000	1	scholasticism
0.0081	19.1	.0000	1	school-band
0.0081	19.1	.0000	1	Schuman's
0.0081	19.1	.0000	1	Schumanns
0.0081	19.1	.0000	1	Schwanda
0.0081	19.1	.0000	1	Schwarzkopf
0.0081	19.1	.0000	1	schwas
0.0081	19.1	.0000	1	sci
0.0081	19.1	.0000	1	scientist-philosopher
0.0081	19.1	.0000	1	Scores
0.0081	19.1	.0000	1	scowly
0.0081	19.1	.0000	1	scriba
0.0081	19.1	.0000	1	Scrubs
0.0081	19.1	.0000	1	scssrs
0.0081	19.1	.0000	1	sculpting
0.0081	19.1	.0000	1	scuppernongs
0.0081	19.1	.0000	1	seal-oil
0.0081	19.1	.0000	1	seamstresses
0.0081	19.1	.0000	1	seashores
0.0081	19.1	.0000	1	seaways
0.0081	19.1	.0000	1	seclude
0.0081	19.1	.0000	1	second-line
0.0081	19.1	.0000	1	seedy
0.0081	19.1	.0000	1	segl
0.0081	19.1	.0000	1	segonku
0.0081	19.1	.0000	1	selectively
0.0081	19.1	.0000	1	self-A14**
0.0081	19.1	.0000	1	self-loading
0.0081	19.1	.0000	1	self-movable
0.0081	19.1	.0000	1	selfishly
0.0081	19.1	.0000	1	selinon
0.0081	19.1	.0000	1	semivowels
0.0081	19.1	.0000	1	sents
0.0081	19.1	.0000	1	seolc
0.0081	19.1	.0000	1	September's
0.0081	19.1	.0000	1	serenades
0.0081	19.1	.0000	1	Serene
0.0081	19.1	.0000	1	servire
THE PRECEDING WORD TYPE OCCUPIES RANK 84100				
0.0081	19.1	.0000	1	servus
0.0081	19.1	.0000	1	Sessions
0.0081	19.1	.0000	1	Sets
0.0081	19.1	.0000	1	seven-eleven
0.0081	19.1	.0000	1	seven-note
0.0081	19.1	.0000	1	Shakespearian
0.0081	19.1	.0000	1	Shaking
0.0081	19.1	.0000	1	shamisen
0.0081	19.1	.0000	1	shammash
0.0081	19.1	.0000	1	shamrock
0.0081	19.1	.0000	1	shanteyman's
0.0081	19.1	.0000	1	shanty-men
0.0081	19.1	.0000	1	shaped-note
0.0081	19.1	.0000	1	sharping
0.0081	19.1	.0000	1	Shaw-stah-koh-vitch
0.0081	19.1	.0000	1	she-bang
0.0081	19.1	.0000	1	sheap
0.0081	19.1	.0000	1	Shearing
0.0081	19.1	.0000	1	sheepherder's
0.0081	19.1	.0000	1	shen**
0.0081	19.1	.0000	1	shill's
0.0081	19.1	.0000	1	Shines
0.0081	19.1	.0000	1	shion
0.0081	19.1	.0000	1	shirttails
0.0081	19.1	.0000	1	shofar
0.0081	19.1	.0000	1	short-long
0.0081	19.1	.0000	1	shovin'
0.0081	19.1	.0000	1	showman's
0.0081	19.1	.0000	1	shr
0.0081	19.1	.0000	1	Shvet
0.0081	19.1	.0000	1	Sibelius'
0.0081	19.1	.0000	1	side-shows
0.0081	19.1	.0000	1	Siegmeister
0.0081	19.1	.0000	1	sight-sing
0.0081	19.1	.0000	1	silekt'**
0.0081	19.1	.0000	1	Silhouette
0.0081	19.1	.0000	1	Simile
0.0081	19.1	.0000	1	Simoneaux
0.0081	19.1	.0000	1	simonize
0.0081	19.1	.0000	1	sinfonia
0.0081	19.1	.0000	1	singable
0.0081	19.1	.0000	1	singe
0.0081	19.1	.0000	1	singers'
0.0081	19.1	.0000	1	singing-school
0.0081	19.1	.0000	1	single-footer
0.0081	19.1	.0000	1	single-note
0.0081	19.1	.0000	1	single-reed
0.0081	19.1	.0000	1	Sings
0.0081	19.1	.0000	1	six-note
0.0081	19.1	.0000	1	six-syllable
0.0081	19.1	.0000	1	six-ton
0.0081	19.1	.0000	1	Skating
0.0081	19.1	.0000	1	skedaddle
0.0081	19.1	.0000	1	skeleton-like
0.0081	19.1	.0000	1	skeletons'
0.0081	19.1	.0000	1	skinflint
0.0081	19.1	.0000	1	skoal
0.0081	19.1	.0000	1	skor
0.0081	19.1	.0000	1	skull-and-bones
0.0081	19.1	.0000	1	skylark
0.0081	19.1	.0000	1	Slav
0.0081	19.1	.0000	1	sleepin'
0.0081	19.1	.0000	1	sleepyhead
0.0081	19.1	.0000	1	Sleigh
0.0081	19.1	.0000	1	slick-tongued
0.0081	19.1	.0000	1	slightingly
0.0081	19.1	.0000	1	Slippers
0.0081	19.1	.0000	1	sluggards
0.0081	19.1	.0000	1	slurring
0.0081	19.1	.0000	1	snap-clap-pat-stamp
0.0081	19.1	.0000	1	snap-clap-stamp
0.0081	19.1	.0000	1	snapping-clapping
0.0081	19.1	.0000	1	snapping-clapping-thigh
0.0081	19.1	.0000	1	snaw
0.0081	19.1	.0000	1	snow-sea's
0.0081	19.1	.0000	1	snow-wreaths
0.0081	19.1	.0000	1	snowbank
0.0081	19.1	.0000	1	snowhouse
0.0081	19.1	.0000	1	so-ber
0.0081	19.1	.0000	1	socc
0.0081	19.1	.0000	1	sod-buster
0.0081	19.1	.0000	1	soft-loud
0.0081	19.1	.0000	1	Soldier's
0.0081	19.1	.0000	1	Soliloquy
0.0081	19.1	.0000	1	soliloquy
0.0081	19.1	.0000	1	solon
0.0081	19.1	.0000	1	song-chants
0.0081	19.1	.0000	1	song-theme
0.0081	19.1	.0000	1	songwriter
0.0081	19.1	.0000	1	sopsorghum
0.0081	19.1	.0000	1	Sou'
0.0081	19.1	.0000	1	sou'wester
0.0081	19.1	.0000	1	soul-stirring
0.0081	19.1	.0000	1	soulful
0.0081	19.1	.0000	1	sound-
0.0081	19.1	.0000	1	sound-alike
0.0081	19.1	.0000	1	Southerly
0.0081	19.1	.0000	1	Spangled
0.0081	19.1	.0000	1	spanky
0.0081	19.1	.0000	1	sparely
THE PRECEDING WORD TYPE OCCUPIES RANK 84200				
0.0081	19.1	.0000	1	spartan
0.0081	19.1	.0000	1	spelling-pattern
0.0081	19.1	.0000	1	spicere
0.0081	19.1	.0000	1	spicky
0.0081	19.1	.0000	1	Spillville
0.0081	19.1	.0000	1	spinets
0.0081	19.1	.0000	1	Spinoza
0.0081	19.1	.0000	1	Spirituals
0.0081	19.1	.0000	1	Spoken
0.0081	19.1	.0000	1	squiddin'
0.0081	19.1	.0000	1	ssion
0.0081	19.1	.0000	1	stain'd
0.0081	19.1	.0000	1	stalemate
0.0081	19.1	.0000	1	stamp-clap
0.0081	19.1	.0000	1	standardization
0.0081	19.1	.0000	1	startin'
0.0081	19.1	.0000	1	starvin'
0.0081	19.1	.0000	1	stat
0.0081	19.1	.0000	1	stately-flowing
0.0081	19.1	.0000	1	staunchest
0.0081	19.1	.0000	1	steady-beat
0.0081	19.1	.0000	1	Steens
0.0081	19.1	.0000	1	Steffe
0.0081	19.1	.0000	1	stem-down
0.0081	19.1	.0000	1	stem-up
0.0081	19.1	.0000	1	stenographer
0.0081	19.1	.0000	1	Stentor
0.0081	19.1	.0000	1	stentorian
0.0081	19.1	.0000	1	step-and-a-half
0.0081	19.1	.0000	1	step-bends
0.0081	19.1	.0000	1	step-pictures
0.0081	19.1	.0000	1	stepsisters
0.0081	19.1	.0000	1	Stille
0.0081	19.1	.0000	1	stilt
0.0081	19.1	.0000	1	stoic
0.0081	19.1	.0000	1	stoke
0.0081	19.1	.0000	1	stoneworker
0.0081	19.1	.0000	1	straight-tubed
0.0081	19.1	.0000	1	Straus
0.0081	19.1	.0000	1	streptos
0.0081	19.1	.0000	1	Strings
0.0081	19.1	.0000	1	strip-ed
0.0081	19.1	.0000	1	strongly-accented
0.0081	19.1	.0000	1	strum-a-strum-a-strum
0.0081	19.1	.0000	1	stutter
0.0081	19.1	.0000	1	Styles
0.0081	19.1	.0000	1	stylistically
0.0081	19.1	.0000	1	sub-dominate
0.0081	19.1	.0000	1	subject-predicate-object
0.0081	19.1	.0000	1	subjective
0.0081	19.1	.0000	1	suck'd
0.0081	19.1	.0000	1	Suffixes
0.0081	19.1	.0000	1	sug-
0.0081	19.1	.0000	1	Sugar-Plum
0.0081	19.1	.0000	1	Summertime
0.0081	19.1	.0000	1	sunder
0.0081	19.1	.0000	1	sup-
0.0081	19.1	.0000	1	supper**
0.0081	19.1	.0000	1	sur
0.0081	19.1	.0000	1	surge's
0.0081	19.1	.0000	1	suronder
0.0081	19.1	.0000	1	Susquehan-i-a
0.0081	19.1	.0000	1	Susyanna
0.0081	19.1	.0000	1	swallow-tail
0.0081	19.1	.0000	1	Swan's
0.0081	19.1	.0000	1	sweethearts
0.0081	19.1	.0000	1	Swell
0.0081	19.1	.0000	1	swift-slapping
0.0081	19.1	.0000	1	swigglenit
0.0081	19.1	.0000	1	swimsuits
0.0081	19.1	.0000	1	syllabize
0.0081	19.1	.0000	1	Symphonies
0.0081	19.1	.0000	1	syncopate
0.0081	19.1	.0000	1	Syne
0.0081	19.1	.0000	1	Synthesizer
0.0081	19.1	.0000	1	Szigeti
0.0081	19.1	.0000	1	T'Lagunna
0.0081	19.1	.0000	1	ta-ta-ta-ta-taa
0.0081	19.1	.0000	1	taai
0.0081	19.1	.0000	1	tab-let
0.0081	19.1	.0000	1	tableau
0.0081	19.1	.0000	1	tam-tams
0.0081	19.1	.0000	1	tamale
0.0081	19.1	.0000	1	tamber
0.0081	19.1	.0000	1	tambo
0.0081	19.1	.0000	1	Tambourin
0.0081	19.1	.0000	1	Tamino
0.0081	19.1	.0000	1	tampers
0.0081	19.1	.0000	1	Tamping
0.0081	19.1	.0000	1	Tanglewood
0.0081	19.1	.0000	1	Tanko
0.0081	19.1	.0000	1	Tape
0.0081	19.1	.0000	1	tape-recorder
0.0081	19.1	.0000	1	tarantella
0.0081	19.1	.0000	1	taxare
0.0081	19.1	.0000	1	Tayluer
0.0081	19.1	.0000	1	teacher-dictated
0.0081	19.1	.0000	1	teacher-friend
0.0081	19.1	.0000	1	teasingly
0.0081	19.1	.0000	1	tect
THE PRECEDING WORD TYPE OCCUPIES RANK 84300				
0.0081	19.1	.0000	1	tectus
0.0081	19.1	.0000	1	tegere
0.0081	19.1	.0000	1	Tekel
0.0081	19.1	.0000	1	ten-note
0.0081	19.1	.0000	1	ten-penny
0.0081	19.1	.0000	1	tendere
0.0081	19.1	.0000	1	tenors
0.0081	19.1	.0000	1	tens**
0.0081	19.1	.0000	1	tenuto
0.0081	19.1	.0000	1	Terra
0.0081	19.1	.0000	1	terra-cotta
0.0081	19.1	.0000	1	th'unbroken
0.0081	19.1	.0000	1	Thebom
0.0081	19.1	.0000	1	Thelma's
0.0081	19.1	.0000	1	thematic
0.0081	19.1	.0000	1	theme-and-variations
0.0081	19.1	.0000	1	therefor
0.0081	19.1	.0000	1	thesauruses
0.0081	19.1	.0000	1	thirtieth
0.0081	19.1	.0000	1	this-worldliness
0.0081	19.1	.0000	1	Thorndike-Barnhart
0.0081	19.1	.0000	1	Three-Cornered
0.0081	19.1	.0000	1	three-letters
0.0081	19.1	.0000	1	three-space
0.0081	19.1	.0000	1	thrum
0.0081	19.1	.0000	1	Thumbelina
0.0081	19.1	.0000	1	thund'ring
0.0081	19.1	.0000	1	thunder's
0.0081	19.1	.0000	1	Thunderer
0.0081	19.1	.0000	1	Tibbo
0.0081	19.1	.0000	1	Tierce
0.0081	19.1	.0000	1	tikling
0.0081	19.1	.0000	1	Tikling

U	SFI	D	F	Word Type
0.0081	19.1	.0000	1	tilde
0.0081	19.1	.0000	1	Till's
0.0081	19.1	.0000	1	timber-workers
0.0081	19.1	.0000	1	timbrels
0.0081	19.1	.0000	1	Timbres
0.0081	19.1	.0000	1	Timbucktoo
0.0081	19.1	.0000	1	ting-a-ling-a-ling
0.0081	19.1	.0000	1	tinga
0.0081	19.1	.0000	1	Tirilita
0.0081	19.1	.0000	1	tis
0.0081	19.1	.0000	1	titan
0.0081	19.1	.0000	1	tocar
0.0081	19.1	.0000	1	Told
0.0081	19.1	.0000	1	tonalities
0.0081	19.1	.0000	1	tonare
0.0081	19.1	.0000	1	tone-the
0.0081	19.1	.0000	1	tonelle
0.0081	19.1	.0000	1	tongue-twister
0.0081	19.1	.0000	1	Tonkurst
0.0081	19.1	.0000	1	toolechest
0.0081	19.1	.0000	1	top-o
0.0081	19.1	.0000	1	top-sail
0.0081	19.1	.0000	1	topses
0.0081	19.1	.0000	1	tor
0.0081	19.1	.0000	1	tord
0.0081	19.1	.0000	1	toreadors
0.0081	19.1	.0000	1	torsos
0.0081	19.1	.0000	1	Tosca
0.0081	19.1	.0000	1	Toyland
0.0081	19.1	.0000	1	tra-la-la-la
0.0081	19.1	.0000	1	trade-name
0.0081	19.1	.0000	1	traffic's
0.0081	19.1	.0000	1	trail-O
0.0081	19.1	.0000	1	trainees
0.0081	19.1	.0000	1	tram
0.0081	19.1	.0000	1	transcriptions
0.0081	19.1	.0000	1	transfigures
0.0081	19.1	.0000	1	transposition
0.0081	19.1	.0000	1	Trara
0.0081	19.1	.0000	1	trashy
0.0081	19.1	.0000	1	Traveled
0.0081	19.1	.0000	1	Travelstead's
0.0081	19.1	.0000	1	trck
0.0081	19.1	.0000	1	tree-e-e-e-t
0.0081	19.1	.0000	1	treh-pahk
0.0081	19.1	.0000	1	trepak
0.0081	19.1	.0000	1	tricking
0.0081	19.1	.0000	1	tricolor
0.0081	19.1	.0000	1	trigraph
0.0081	19.1	.0000	1	trios
0.0081	19.1	.0000	1	Triste
0.0081	19.1	.0000	1	troppo
0.0081	19.1	.0000	1	trouble-some
0.0081	19.1	.0000	1	trousseau
0.0081	19.1	.0000	1	trouvere
0.0081	19.1	.0000	1	truix
0.0081	19.1	.0000	1	Trunk
0.0081	19.1	.0000	1	Tsur
0.0081	19.1	.0000	1	tuch
0.0081	19.1	.0000	1	Tuileries
0.0081	19.1	.0000	1	Tulle
0.0081	19.1	.0000	1	tulle
0.0081	19.1	.0000	1	Tum
0.0081	19.1	.0000	1	tummy-aches
0.0081	19.1	.0000	1	Tura
0.0081	19.1	.0000	1	Turnover
0.0081	19.1	.0000	1	turtledoves

THE PRECEDING WORD TYPE OCCUPIES RANK 84400

U	SFI	D	F	Word Type
0.0081	19.1	.0000	1	twelve-bar
0.0081	19.1	.0000	1	twen-ty
0.0081	19.1	.0000	1	twen-ty-three
0.0081	19.1	.0000	1	twent-ty-one
0.0081	19.1	.0000	1	Twenty-Four
0.0081	19.1	.0000	1	Twenty-Third
0.0081	19.1	.0000	1	twenty-penny
0.0081	19.1	.0000	1	Twenty-second
0.0081	19.1	.0000	1	Two-Part
0.0081	19.1	.0000	1	two-months
0.0081	19.1	.0000	1	two-stringed
0.0081	19.1	.0000	1	two-syllables
0.0081	19.1	.0000	1	two-vowel
0.0081	19.1	.0000	1	Tycoon
0.0081	19.1	.0000	1	Typewriter
0.0081	19.1	.0000	1	Tyr
0.0081	19.1	.0000	1	Ubdugs
0.0081	19.1	.0000	1	ud
0.0081	19.1	.0000	1	ue
0.0081	19.1	.0000	1	ui
0.0081	19.1	.0000	1	uilla
0.0081	19.1	.0000	1	Ukrania
0.0081	19.1	.0000	1	ul
0.0081	19.1	.0000	1	ump
0.0081	19.1	.0000	1	unA2ed**
0.0081	19.1	.0000	1	un-known
0.0081	19.1	.0000	1	una
0.0081	19.1	.0000	1	unaltered
0.0081	19.1	.0000	1	unbidden
0.0081	19.1	.0000	1	uncrushed
0.0081	19.1	.0000	1	unda
0.0081	19.1	.0000	1	undersong
0.0081	19.1	.0000	1	undimmed
0.0081	19.1	.0000	1	Undimmed
0.0081	19.1	.0000	1	uni
0.0081	19.1	.0000	1	uninked
0.0081	19.1	.0000	1	uninspired
0.0081	19.1	.0000	1	unkindliness
0.0081	19.1	.0000	1	unmixed
0.0081	19.1	.0000	1	unrolls
0.0081	19.1	.0000	1	unromantic
0.0081	19.1	.0000	1	unstaged
0.0081	19.1	.0000	1	unstinting
0.0081	19.1	.0000	1	unsyncopated
0.0081	19.1	.0000	1	untaught
0.0081	19.1	.0000	1	untwisted
0.0081	19.1	.0000	1	up-beat
0.0081	19.1	.0000	1	Upharsin
0.0081	19.1	.0000	1	upon't
0.0081	19.1	.0000	1	upper-grade
0.0081	19.1	.0000	1	urb
0.0081	19.1	.0000	1	useable
0.0081	19.1	.0000	1	ush
0.0081	19.1	.0000	1	ute
0.0081	19.1	.0000	1	v's
0.0081	19.1	.0000	1	vacation's
0.0081	19.1	.0000	1	vagabonds
0.0081	19.1	.0000	1	vagrant's
0.0081	19.1	.0000	1	Valabre
0.0081	19.1	.0000	1	Valen
0.0081	19.1	.0000	1	valkyries
0.0081	19.1	.0000	1	Vardell
0.0081	19.1	.0000	1	Variety
0.0081	19.1	.0000	1	Vayr-dee
0.0081	19.1	.0000	1	VCC
0.0081	19.1	.0000	1	Vechernitsi
0.0081	19.1	.0000	1	veni-
0.0081	19.1	.0000	1	venier
0.0081	19.1	.0000	1	verbally
0.0081	19.1	.0000	1	verbum
0.0081	19.1	.0000	1	VHMF
0.0081	19.1	.0000	1	vict'ry
0.0081	19.1	.0000	1	Victrola
0.0081	19.1	.0000	1	Vidalitas
0.0081	19.1	.0000	1	Villa-Lopos
0.0081	19.1	.0000	1	villanus
0.0081	19.1	.0000	1	vincere
0.0081	19.1	.0000	1	Vinyl
0.0081	19.1	.0000	1	violin-piano
0.0081	19.1	.0000	1	Violins
0.0081	19.1	.0000	1	violists
0.0081	19.1	.0000	1	violoncellos
0.0081	19.1	.0000	1	viols
0.0081	19.1	.0000	1	Virtues
0.0081	19.1	.0000	1	viser
0.0081	19.1	.0000	1	vito
0.0081	19.1	.0000	1	Vlast
0.0081	19.1	.0000	1	vocalis
0.0081	19.1	.0000	1	Vocalise
0.0081	19.1	.0000	1	Voi
0.0081	19.1	.0000	1	volar
0.0081	19.1	.0000	1	vonBulow
0.0081	19.1	.0000	1	VonBulow's
0.0081	19.1	.0000	1	vonEisenstein
0.0081	19.1	.0000	1	VonTilzer
0.0081	19.1	.0000	1	vonWeber
0.0081	19.1	.0000	1	vordt
0.0081	19.1	.0000	1	vowel-consonant-consonant
0.0081	19.1	.0000	1	vowel-consonant-final
0.0081	19.1	.0000	1	vowel-vowel

THE PRECEDING WORD TYPE OCCUPIES RANK 84500

U	SFI	D	F	Word Type
0.0081	19.1	.0000	1	vowel-y
0.0081	19.1	.0000	1	voyageurs'
0.0081	19.1	.0000	1	vulcanize
0.0081	19.1	.0000	1	VVC
0.0081	19.1	.0000	1	Vysehrad
0.0081	19.1	.0000	1	waddle-dee-dee
0.0081	19.1	.0000	1	wafted
0.0081	19.1	.0000	1	wahka
0.0081	19.1	.0000	1	Walkure
0.0081	19.1	.0000	1	Wan
0.0081	19.1	.0000	1	Wandering
0.0081	19.1	.0000	1	Want
0.0081	19.1	.0000	1	washerwomen
0.0081	19.1	.0000	1	waspish
0.0081	19.1	.0000	1	wassail
0.0081	19.1	.0000	1	wate
0.0081	19.1	.0000	1	way-hay
0.0081	19.1	.0000	1	Wayfaring
0.0081	19.1	.0000	1	wayte-pipes
0.0081	19.1	.0000	1	Webern's
0.0081	19.1	.0000	1	wee-le-wahl
0.0081	19.1	.0000	1	Weinberger
0.0081	19.1	.0000	1	Weinzierl
0.0081	19.1	.0000	1	welkin
0.0081	19.1	.0000	1	well-established
0.0081	19.1	.0000	1	well-modulated
0.0081	19.1	.0000	1	well-read
0.0081	19.1	.0000	1	Well-tempered
0.0081	19.1	.0000	1	wen
0.0081	19.1	.0000	1	wep-i-ed
0.0081	19.1	.0000	1	wharfs
0.0081	19.1	.0000	1	white-wing
0.0081	19.1	.0000	1	whole-tones
0.0081	19.1	.0000	1	Whom
0.0081	19.1	.0000	1	wide-range
0.0081	19.1	.0000	1	wide-spread
0.0081	19.1	.0000	1	widely-spread
0.0081	19.1	.0000	1	wielewaal
0.0081	19.1	.0000	1	Wien
0.0081	19.1	.0000	1	wienerwurst
0.0081	19.1	.0000	1	Winds
0.0081	19.1	.0000	1	WING
0.0081	19.1	.0000	1	Winnemucca
0.0081	19.1	.0000	1	Winter's
0.0081	19.1	.0000	1	Wodehouse
0.0081	19.1	.0000	1	Woden
0.0081	19.1	.0000	1	wood-cutter's
0.0081	19.1	.0000	1	word-maker
0.0081	19.1	.0000	1	word-rhythms
0.0081	19.1	.0000	1	word-structure
0.0081	19.1	.0000	1	wordmakers
0.0081	19.1	.0000	1	work-study
0.0081	19.1	.0000	1	world-end
0.0081	19.1	.0000	1	Wormwood
0.0081	19.1	.0000	1	worning
0.0081	19.1	.0000	1	Wotan
0.0081	19.1	.0000	1	Wotan's
0.0081	19.1	.0000	1	WRITE
0.0081	19.1	.0000	1	Wshngtn
0.0081	19.1	.0000	1	wurgen
0.0081	19.1	.0000	1	WWJ
0.0081	19.1	.0000	1	Wycliffe
0.0081	19.1	.0000	1	Wycliffe's
0.0081	19.1	.0000	1	Wykeham
0.0081	19.1	.0000	1	Xeres
0.0081	19.1	.0000	1	Xochipilli
0.0081	19.1	.0000	1	xylophone-like
0.0081	19.1	.0000	1	Yang
0.0081	19.1	.0000	1	yawny
0.0081	19.1	.0000	1	yellow-wing
0.0081	19.1	.0000	1	yew
0.0081	19.1	.0000	1	Yodel
0.0081	19.1	.0000	1	yodelling
0.0081	19.1	.0000	1	Youmans
0.0081	19.1	.0000	1	yuletide
0.0081	19.1	.0000	1	Zaandam
0.0081	19.1	.0000	1	zapatero
0.0081	19.1	.0000	1	Zeno
0.0081	19.1	.0000	1	zeroes
0.0081	19.1	.0000	1	zhen
0.0081	19.1	.0000	1	zither-like
0.0081	19.1	.0000	1	1-77
0.0081	19.1	.0000	1	1d
0.0081	19.1	.0000	1	111-127
0.0081	19.1	.0000	1	113-127
0.0081	19.1	.0000	1	1176
0.0081	19.1	.0000	1	12-bar
0.0081	19.1	.0000	1	121b
0.0081	19.1	.0000	1	124-126
0.0081	19.1	.0000	1	1300-1500
0.0081	19.1	.0000	1	1320
0.0081	19.1	.0000	1	136-157
0.0081	19.1	.0000	1	1400-1600
0.0081	19.1	.0000	1	1430
0.0081	19.1	.0000	1	150-year
0.0081	19.1	.0000	1	1507
0.0081	19.1	.0000	1	1535
0.0081	19.1	.0000	1	1555-1612
0.0081	19.1	.0000	1	1556
0.0081	19.1	.0000	1	1575

THE PRECEDING WORD TYPE OCCUPIES RANK 84600

U	SFI	D	F	Word Type
0.0081	19.1	.0000	1	1628
0.0081	19.1	.0000	1	1658-1695
0.0081	19.1	.0000	1	1685-1759
0.0081	19.1	.0000	1	1709
0.0081	19.1	.0000	1	1732-1809
0.0081	19.1	.0000	1	1741
0.0081	19.1	.0000	1	1782-1852
0.0081	19.1	.0000	1	1786-1826
0.0081	19.1	.0000	1	1797-1828
0.0081	19.1	.0000	1	18-25
0.0081	19.1	.0000	1	1809-1847
0.0081	19.1	.0000	1	1810-1849
0.0081	19.1	.0000	1	1811-1886
0.0081	19.1	.0000	1	1815-1892
0.0081	19.1	.0000	1	1817-1823
0.0081	19.1	.0000	1	1824-1884
0.0081	19.1	.0000	1	1833-1897
0.0081	19.1	.0000	1	1838-1875
0.0081	19.1	.0000	1	1853-1890
0.0081	19.1	.0000	1	1854-1932
0.0081	19.1	.0000	1	1858-1924
0.0081	19.1	.0000	1	1862-1918
0.0081	19.1	.0000	1	1864-1949
0.0081	19.1	.0000	1	1870-1948
0.0081	19.1	.0000	1	1874-1951
0.0081	19.1	.0000	1	1874-1954
0.0081	19.1	.0000	1	1882-
0.0081	19.1	.0000	1	1898-1937
0.0081	19.1	.0000	1	2-27
0.0081	19.1	.0000	1	22-23-24
0.0081	19.1	.0000	1	26-29
0.0081	19.1	.0000	1	2650
0.0081	19.1	.0000	1	27-34
0.0081	19.1	.0000	1	28-29-30
0.0081	19.1	.0000	1	31-32-33
0.0081	19.1	.0000	1	31-35
0.0081	19.1	.0000	1	32-measure
0.0081	19.1	.0000	1	40-41
0.0081	19.1	.0000	1	49'ers
0.0081	19.1	.0000	1	55th
0.0081	19.1	.0000	1	6a
0.0081	19.1	.0000	1	6080
0.0081	19.1	.0000	1	66-68
0.0081	19.1	.0000	1	7-D
0.0081	19.1	.0000	1	76-77
0.0081	19.1	.0000	1	800-1150
0.0081	19.1	.0000	1	82-89
0.0081	19.1	.0000	1	827-869
0.0081	19.1	.0000	1	88th
0.0081	19.1	.0000	1	90th
0.0081	19.1	.0000	1	91a
0.0076	18.8	.0000	3	acid-core
0.0076	18.8	.0000	3	amps
0.0076	18.8	.0000	3	bimetal-strip
0.0076	18.8	.0000	3	disassembly
0.0076	18.8	.0000	3	dry-sand
0.0076	18.8	.0000	3	E/I
0.0076	18.8	.0000	3	E/R
0.0076	18.8	.0000	3	F-1
0.0076	18.8	.0000	3	footings
0.0076	18.8	.0000	3	Gothics
0.0076	18.8	.0000	3	headsaw
0.0076	18.8	.0000	3	heat-treating
0.0076	18.8	.0000	3	hertz
0.0076	18.8	.0000	3	kilohertz
0.0076	18.8	.0000	3	knurled
0.0076	18.8	.0000	3	knurling
0.0076	18.8	.0000	3	lofting
0.0076	18.8	.0000	3	malleability
0.0076	18.8	.0000	3	microfarad
0.0076	18.8	.0000	3	moldable
0.0076	18.8	.0000	3	nicks
0.0076	18.8	.0000	3	one-view
0.0076	18.8	.0000	3	ratchet
0.0076	18.8	.0000	3	readjust
0.0076	18.8	.0000	3	roughing
0.0076	18.8	.0000	3	round-head
0.0076	18.8	.0000	3	R1
0.0076	18.8	.0000	3	R2
0.0076	18.8	.0000	3	skive
0.0076	18.8	.0000	3	slurry
0.0076	18.8	.0000	3	stretchout
0.0076	18.8	.0000	3	superheterodyne
0.0076	18.8	.0000	3	templates
0.0076	18.8	.0000	3	Testers
0.0076	18.8	.0000	3	thumbnail
0.0076	18.8	.0000	3	tinned
0.0076	18.8	.0000	3	Tools
0.0076	18.8	.0000	3	0-1
0.0076	18.8	.0000	3	1153
0.0076	18.8	.0000	3	16-4
0.0076	18.8	.0000	3	20-19
0.0076	18.8	.0000	3	27-12
0.0076	18.8	.0000	3	27-13
0.0076	18.8	.0000	3	27-15
0.0076	18.8	.0000	3	27-16
0.0076	18.8	.0000	3	27-8
0.0076	18.8	.0000	3	48-1
0.0076	18.8	.0000	3	663
0.0074	18.7	.0000	4	one-point

THE PRECEDING WORD TYPE OCCUPIES RANK 84700

U	SFI	D	F	Word Type
0.0074	18.7	.0000	4	plasticine
0.0074	18.7	.0000	4	stitchery
0.0074	18.7	.0000	4	two-point
0.0067	18.3	.0000	3	Blair's
0.0067	18.3	.0000	3	Boarding-House
0.0067	18.3	.0000	3	Langewiesche
0.0067	18.3	.0000	3	loveth
0.0067	18.3	.0000	3	new-sawn
0.0067	18.3	.0000	3	quandary
0.0067	18.3	.0000	3	rhetorical
0.0067	18.3	.0000	3	ten-horse
0.0067	18.3	.0000	3	trodden
0.0064	18.1	.0000	2	Areas
0.0064	18.1	.0000	2	batiste
0.0064	18.1	.0000	2	BLT
0.0064	18.1	.0000	2	braising
0.0064	18.1	.0000	2	buttering
0.0064	18.1	.0000	2	casseroles
0.0064	18.1	.0000	2	centerpieces
0.0064	18.1	.0000	2	charge-account
0.0064	18.1	.0000	2	colorfast
0.0064	18.1	.0000	2	corded
0.0064	18.1	.0000	2	Cracker
0.0064	18.1	.0000	2	crease-resistant
0.0064	18.1	.0000	2	crispness
0.0064	18.1	.0000	2	custards
0.0064	18.1	.0000	2	deep-yellow
0.0064	18.1	.0000	2	Dressing
0.0064	18.1	.0000	2	dressmaker's
0.0064	18.1	.0000	2	Dynel
0.0064	18.1	.0000	2	easy-to-eat
0.0064	18.1	.0000	2	endive
0.0064	18.1	.0000	2	endosperm
0.0064	18.1	.0000	2	fabric-to-fabric
0.0064	18.1	.0000	2	fashion-right
0.0064	18.1	.0000	2	footrest
0.0064	18.1	.0000	2	gabardine
0.0064	18.1	.0000	2	goiter
0.0064	18.1	.0000	2	grainline
0.0064	18.1	.0000	2	gristle
0.0064	18.1	.0000	2	grosgrain
0.0064	18.1	.0000	2	guide-sheet
0.0064	18.1	.0000	2	inactivity
0.0064	18.1	.0000	2	indigestion
0.0064	18.1	.0000	2	interlining
0.0064	18.1	.0000	2	keying
0.0064	18.1	.0000	2	laundered
0.0064	18.1	.0000	2	less-tender
0.0064	18.1	.0000	2	living-area
0.0064	18.1	.0000	2	long-staple
0.0064	18.1	.0000	2	lunch-box
0.0064	18.1	.0000	2	machine-baste
0.0064	18.1	.0000	2	MERINGUE
0.0064	18.1	.0000	2	moist-heat
0.0064	18.1	.0000	2	moistureproof
0.0064	18.1	.0000	2	neck-and-opening
0.0064	18.1	.0000	2	nonwoven
0.0064	18.1	.0000	2	nutritionists
0.0064	18.1	.0000	2	one-crust
0.0064	18.1	.0000	2	one-cup
0.0064	18.1	.0000	2	orangeade
0.0064	18.1	.0000	2	outer-edge
0.0064	18.1	.0000	2	over-cooked
0.0064	18.1	.0000	2	preshrinking
0.0064	18.1	.0000	2	puckering
0.0064	18.1	.0000	2	ravel
0.0064	18.1	.0000	2	readymade
0.0064	18.1	.0000	2	rustproof
0.0064	18.1	.0000	2	salt-and-peppers
0.0064	18.1	.0000	2	scalded
0.0064	18.1	.0000	2	self-fabric
0.0064	18.1	.0000	2	self-knowledge
0.0064	18.1	.0000	2	set-in
0.0064	18.1	.0000	2	sleazy
0.0064	18.1	.0000	2	slip-stitch
0.0064	18.1	.0000	2	spooned
0.0064	18.1	.0000	2	spreader
0.0064	18.1	.0000	2	staystitch-plus
0.0064	18.1	.0000	2	staystitched
0.0064	18.1	.0000	2	stewing
0.0064	18.1	.0000	2	strong-flavored
0.0064	18.1	.0000	2	style-right
0.0064	18.1	.0000	2	timbales
0.0064	18.1	.0000	2	top-stitch
0.0064	18.1	.0000	2	undercollar
0.0064	18.1	.0000	2	undercuff
0.0064	18.1	.0000	2	underfold
0.0064	18.1	.0000	2	underlap
0.0064	18.1	.0000	2	underpress
0.0064	18.1	.0000	2	understitch
0.0064	18.1	.0000	2	unripened
0.0064	18.1	.0000	2	Vicara
0.0064	18.1	.0000	2	vinegars
0.0064	18.1	.0000	2	voile
0.0064	18.1	.0000	2	wardrobes
0.0064	18.1	.0000	2	water-repellent
0.0064	18.1	.0000	2	well-fitting

U	SFI	D	F	Word Type
0.0064	18.1	.0000	2	with-grain
0.0064	18.1	.0000	2	14-16-17
0.0064	18.1	.0000	2	156-157
				THE PRECEDING WORD TYPE OCCUPIES RANK 84800
0.0064	18.1	.0000	2	299
0.0064	18.1	.0000	2	408
0.0064	18.1	.0000	2	45%
0.0055	17.4	.0000	3	all-over
0.0055	17.4	.0000	3	Bomar
0.0055	17.4	.0000	3	converging
0.0055	17.4	.0000	3	Cubists
0.0055	17.4	.0000	3	gouache
0.0055	17.4	.0000	3	Jabberwock
0.0055	17.4	.0000	3	Medusae
0.0055	17.4	.0000	3	woodcut
0.0050	17.0	.0000	2	A-A
0.0050	17.0	.0000	2	annealed
0.0050	17.0	.0000	2	backsaw
0.0050	17.0	.0000	2	black-iron
0.0050	17.0	.0000	2	Bolt
0.0050	17.0	.0000	2	bookend
0.0050	17.0	.0000	2	bunsen
0.0050	17.0	.0000	2	burred
0.0050	17.0	.0000	2	carburizing
0.0050	17.0	.0000	2	Caring
0.0050	17.0	.0000	2	chamfered
0.0050	17.0	.0000	2	Coarse
0.0050	17.0	.0000	2	collotype
0.0050	17.0	.0000	2	coremaker
0.0050	17.0	.0000	2	crimping
0.0050	17.0	.0000	2	crosscutting
0.0050	17.0	.0000	2	cutting-plane
0.0050	17.0	.0000	2	dado-head
0.0050	17.0	.0000	2	deg
0.0050	17.0	.0000	2	drawknife
0.0050	17.0	.0000	2	edge-to-edge
0.0050	17.0	.0000	2	Ein**
0.0050	17.0	.0000	2	Eout**
0.0050	17.0	.0000	2	etchings
0.0050	17.0	.0000	2	Foerstner
0.0050	17.0	.0000	2	fusibility
0.0050	17.0	.0000	2	gages
0.0050	17.0	.0000	2	green-sand
0.0050	17.0	.0000	2	half-round
0.0050	17.0	.0000	2	Hd
0.0050	17.0	.0000	2	heat-treatment
0.0050	17.0	.0000	2	heavy-in
0.0050	17.0	.0000	2	inductance
0.0050	17.0	.0000	2	J-2
0.0050	17.0	.0000	2	Lg
0.0050	17.0	.0000	2	mechanic's
0.0050	17.0	.0000	2	medium-hard
0.0050	17.0	.0000	2	medium-soft
0.0050	17.0	.0000	2	micromicrofarad
0.0050	17.0	.0000	2	Nos
0.0050	17.0	.0000	2	one-millionth
0.0050	17.0	.0000	2	oxyacetylene
0.0050	17.0	.0000	2	peening
0.0050	17.0	.0000	2	pictorially
0.0050	17.0	.0000	2	planishing
0.0050	17.0	.0000	2	plat
0.0050	17.0	.0000	2	presswork
0.0050	17.0	.0000	2	R/N
0.0050	17.0	.0000	2	rapid-traverse
0.0050	17.0	.0000	2	right-cut
0.0050	17.0	.0000	2	rosin-core
0.0050	17.0	.0000	2	router
0.0050	17.0	.0000	2	rubber-covered
0.0050	17.0	.0000	2	sanders
0.0050	17.0	.0000	2	scribing
0.0050	17.0	.0000	2	Secs
0.0050	17.0	.0000	2	sectioned
0.0050	17.0	.0000	2	semiskilled
0.0050	17.0	.0000	2	setscrew
0.0050	17.0	.0000	2	Sharpening
0.0050	17.0	.0000	2	skived
0.0050	17.0	.0000	2	slip-roll
0.0050	17.0	.0000	2	squarenose
0.0050	17.0	.0000	2	stretch-out
0.0050	17.0	.0000	2	superimposing
0.0050	17.0	.0000	2	sweat-soldered
0.0050	17.0	.0000	2	table-clamp
0.0050	17.0	.0000	2	tenons
0.0050	17.0	.0000	2	Tester
0.0050	17.0	.0000	2	Tests
0.0050	17.0	.0000	2	thermocouple
0.0050	17.0	.0000	2	tongue-and-groove
0.0050	17.0	.0000	2	treaters
0.0050	17.0	.0000	2	triangulation
0.0050	17.0	.0000	2	upholstering
0.0050	17.0	.0000	2	veiner
0.0050	17.0	.0000	2	video
0.0050	17.0	.0000	2	voltmeter
0.0050	17.0	.0000	2	wattage
0.0050	17.0	.0000	2	weldability
0.0050	17.0	.0000	2	whipstitch
0.0050	17.0	.0000	2	10-1
0.0050	17.0	.0000	2	10-10
0.0050	17.0	.0000	2	10-15
0.0050	17.0	.0000	2	10-16
0.0050	17.0	.0000	2	10-17c
0.0050	17.0	.0000	2	10-18
0.0050	17.0	.0000	2	10d
0.0050	17.0	.0000	2	1157
				THE PRECEDING WORD TYPE OCCUPIES RANK 84900
0.0050	17.0	.0000	2	13-10a
0.0050	17.0	.0000	2	15-10
0.0050	17.0	.0000	2	16-13a
0.0050	17.0	.0000	2	17-2
0.0050	17.0	.0000	2	17-3
0.0050	17.0	.0000	2	20-2
0.0050	17.0	.0000	2	20-3
0.0050	17.0	.0000	2	25-12
0.0050	17.0	.0000	2	27-1
0.0050	17.0	.0000	2	27-10
0.0050	17.0	.0000	2	27-14
0.0050	17.0	.0000	2	28-1
0.0050	17.0	.0000	2	33-4B
0.0050	17.0	.0000	2	4-13
0.0050	17.0	.0000	2	4-14
0.0050	17.0	.0000	2	48-2
0.0050	17.0	.0000	2	50-1
0.0050	17.0	.0000	2	6-10
0.0050	17.0	.0000	2	6-32
0.0050	17.0	.0000	2	659
0.0050	17.0	.0000	2	662
0.0050	17.0	.0000	2	71-1
0.0045	16.5	.0000	2	Bumble
0.0045	16.5	.0000	2	cookout
0.0045	16.5	.0000	2	crossways
0.0045	16.5	.0000	2	culturist
0.0045	16.5	.0000	2	curbstone
0.0045	16.5	.0000	2	Dottie
0.0045	16.5	.0000	2	Evans's
0.0045	16.5	.0000	2	gold-leafed
0.0045	16.5	.0000	2	high-strung
0.0045	16.5	.0000	2	Irving's
0.0045	16.5	.0000	2	j's
0.0045	16.5	.0000	2	Keep-Off-the-Grass
0.0045	16.5	.0000	2	Marston
0.0045	16.5	.0000	2	monster's
0.0045	16.5	.0000	2	naaah
0.0045	16.5	.0000	2	Salmagundi
0.0045	16.5	.0000	2	sluicing
0.0045	16.5	.0000	2	supersaturated
0.0037	15.7	.0000	2	allover
0.0037	15.7	.0000	2	Banning
0.0037	15.7	.0000	2	Bayeux
0.0037	15.7	.0000	2	Beanery
0.0037	15.7	.0000	2	Bror
0.0037	15.7	.0000	2	Chardin
0.0037	15.7	.0000	2	Chardin's
0.0037	15.7	.0000	2	Cubists'
0.0037	15.7	.0000	2	cut-and-paste
0.0037	15.7	.0000	2	eared
0.0037	15.7	.0000	2	eclectic
0.0037	15.7	.0000	2	Fearing
0.0037	15.7	.0000	2	Gogh's
0.0037	15.7	.0000	2	grater
0.0037	15.7	.0000	2	heightens
0.0037	15.7	.0000	2	hierogylph
0.0037	15.7	.0000	2	Inky
0.0037	15.7	.0000	2	Karnak
0.0037	15.7	.0000	2	Klee's
0.0037	15.7	.0000	2	Leonardo's
0.0037	15.7	.0000	2	Magritte
0.0037	15.7	.0000	2	Maillol
0.0037	15.7	.0000	2	marbleizing
0.0037	15.7	.0000	2	monoprinting
0.0037	15.7	.0000	2	monoprints
0.0037	15.7	.0000	2	Nolde
0.0037	15.7	.0000	2	peoplish
0.0037	15.7	.0000	2	Post-Impressionist
0.0037	15.7	.0000	2	pre-Greek
0.0037	15.7	.0000	2	Raoul
0.0037	15.7	.0000	2	scratchboard
0.0037	15.7	.0000	2	serapes
0.0037	15.7	.0000	2	Tobey's
0.0037	15.7	.0000	2	Toulouse-Lautrec
0.0037	15.7	.0000	2	tri-level
0.0037	15.7	.0000	2	Utter
0.0037	15.7	.0000	2	vorpal
0.0037	15.7	.0000	2	Vuillard
0.0037	15.7	.0000	2	Workers'
0.0037	15.7	.0000	2	Zorach
0.0032	15.1	.0000	1	A-line
0.0032	15.1	.0000	1	acetates
0.0032	15.1	.0000	1	acidify
0.0032	15.1	.0000	1	Agilon
0.0032	15.1	.0000	1	ahing
0.0032	15.1	.0000	1	allergies
0.0032	15.1	.0000	1	allergy
0.0032	15.1	.0000	1	alpaca
0.0032	15.1	.0000	1	anxieties
0.0032	15.1	.0000	1	Appetizers
0.0032	15.1	.0000	1	appliques
0.0032	15.1	.0000	1	Applying
0.0032	15.1	.0000	1	Arnel
0.0032	15.1	.0000	1	baby-sitters
0.0032	15.1	.0000	1	back-to-school
0.0032	15.1	.0000	1	Ban-Lon
0.0032	15.1	.0000	1	barbecued
0.0032	15.1	.0000	1	basic-type
0.0032	15.1	.0000	1	bateau
0.0032	15.1	.0000	1	bathrobes
				THE PRECEDING WORD TYPE OCCUPIES RANK 85000
0.0032	15.1	.0000	1	becomingness
0.0032	15.1	.0000	1	bent-handled
0.0032	15.1	.0000	1	bias-binding
0.0032	15.1	.0000	1	blouse-and-skirt
0.0032	15.1	.0000	1	bloused
0.0032	15.1	.0000	1	blue-purple
0.0032	15.1	.0000	1	blue-violet
0.0032	15.1	.0000	1	Bobbin
0.0032	15.1	.0000	1	bodkin
0.0032	15.1	.0000	1	bogey
0.0032	15.1	.0000	1	bothersome
0.0032	15.1	.0000	1	bras
0.0032	15.1	.0000	1	bread-crumb
0.0032	15.1	.0000	1	breadboard
0.0032	15.1	.0000	1	Brie
0.0032	15.1	.0000	1	brine-cured
0.0032	15.1	.0000	1	Broil
0.0032	15.1	.0000	1	budgetmaking
0.0032	15.1	.0000	1	bulkiness
0.0032	15.1	.0000	1	burping
0.0032	15.1	.0000	1	Cake
0.0032	15.1	.0000	1	calcium-poor
0.0032	15.1	.0000	1	canned-heat
0.0032	15.1	.0000	1	caramelizes
0.0032	15.1	.0000	1	carotene
0.0032	15.1	.0000	1	cashmere
0.0032	15.1	.0000	1	center-front
0.0032	15.1	.0000	1	Cerealia
0.0032	15.1	.0000	1	chapping
0.0032	15.1	.0000	1	Chemistry
0.0032	15.1	.0000	1	chignon
0.0032	15.1	.0000	1	clarification
0.0032	15.1	.0000	1	clean-finish
0.0032	15.1	.0000	1	cliques
0.0032	15.1	.0000	1	closures
0.0032	15.1	.0000	1	Clothing
0.0032	15.1	.0000	1	color-fast
0.0032	15.1	.0000	1	Consider
0.0032	15.1	.0000	1	convalescing
0.0032	15.1	.0000	1	Cooked
0.0032	15.1	.0000	1	correlating
0.0032	15.1	.0000	1	cotton-blend
0.0032	15.1	.0000	1	cotton-percale
0.0032	15.1	.0000	1	cotton-twill
0.0032	15.1	.0000	1	cream-style
0.0032	15.1	.0000	1	creamy/white
0.0032	15.1	.0000	1	crepes
0.0032	15.1	.0000	1	crewel
0.0032	15.1	.0000	1	crimp
0.0032	15.1	.0000	1	crocking
0.0032	15.1	.0000	1	Crotch
0.0032	15.1	.0000	1	Crust
0.0032	15.1	.0000	1	cupids
0.0032	15.1	.0000	1	curdling
0.0032	15.1	.0000	1	curealls
0.0032	15.1	.0000	1	curtaining
0.0032	15.1	.0000	1	cut-marshmallows
0.0032	15.1	.0000	1	Cutting
0.0032	15.1	.0000	1	Dacron-wool
0.0032	15.1	.0000	1	Dacrons
0.0032	15.1	.0000	1	darns
0.0032	15.1	.0000	1	dated-looking
0.0032	15.1	.0000	1	decorators
0.0032	15.1	.0000	1	Desserts
0.0032	15.1	.0000	1	detracts
0.0032	15.1	.0000	1	diced
0.0032	15.1	.0000	1	dirndl
0.0032	15.1	.0000	1	disastrously
0.0032	15.1	.0000	1	discerning
0.0032	15.1	.0000	1	displeasing
0.0032	15.1	.0000	1	disposable
0.0032	15.1	.0000	1	disproportionately
0.0032	15.1	.0000	1	divided-collar
0.0032	15.1	.0000	1	dole
0.0032	15.1	.0000	1	don't's
0.0032	15.1	.0000	1	draping
0.0032	15.1	.0000	1	dried-fruit
0.0032	15.1	.0000	1	durable-press
0.0032	15.1	.0000	1	Dynel-acetate-viscose
0.0032	15.1	.0000	1	eartips
0.0032	15.1	.0000	1	ease-stitch
0.0032	15.1	.0000	1	easy-to-grasp
0.0032	15.1	.0000	1	easy-to-handle
0.0032	15.1	.0000	1	economy-minded
0.0032	15.1	.0000	1	edge-stitch
0.0032	15.1	.0000	1	egg-and-milk
0.0032	15.1	.0000	1	egg-milk
0.0032	15.1	.0000	1	elasticized
0.0032	15.1	.0000	1	Emmenthaler
0.0032	15.1	.0000	1	emulsion
0.0032	15.1	.0000	1	ESSENTIAL
0.0032	15.1	.0000	1	Estimate
0.0032	15.1	.0000	1	extenders
0.0032	15.1	.0000	1	feta
0.0032	15.1	.0000	1	Fitted
0.0032	15.1	.0000	1	flaked
0.0032	15.1	.0000	1	Flap
0.0032	15.1	.0000	1	flat-edged
0.0032	15.1	.0000	1	flatware
0.0032	15.1	.0000	1	flours
				THE PRECEDING WORD TYPE OCCUPIES RANK 85100
0.0032	15.1	.0000	1	flower-shaped
0.0032	15.1	.0000	1	flowerets
0.0032	15.1	.0000	1	fluffy-to-moist
0.0032	15.1	.0000	1	Fluflon
0.0032	15.1	.0000	1	fluorescents
0.0032	15.1	.0000	1	food-budget
0.0032	15.1	.0000	1	food-buying
0.0032	15.1	.0000	1	food-preparation
0.0032	15.1	.0000	1	food's
0.0032	15.1	.0000	1	FOODS
0.0032	15.1	.0000	1	fortifying
0.0032	15.1	.0000	1	fourteen-day
0.0032	15.1	.0000	1	front-bodice
0.0032	15.1	.0000	1	fruitade
0.0032	15.1	.0000	1	frypan
0.0032	15.1	.0000	1	full-bodied
0.0032	15.1	.0000	1	Gelatin
0.0032	15.1	.0000	1	gelatinize
0.0032	15.1	.0000	1	girdles
0.0032	15.1	.0000	1	gjetost
0.0032	15.1	.0000	1	glibly
0.0032	15.1	.0000	1	good-quality
0.0032	15.1	.0000	1	Gouda
0.0032	15.1	.0000	1	gradings
0.0032	15.1	.0000	1	grainlines
0.0032	15.1	.0000	1	grandma's
0.0032	15.1	.0000	1	grapefruits
0.0032	15.1	.0000	1	gravies
0.0032	15.1	.0000	1	griddlecakes
0.0032	15.1	.0000	1	Gruyere
0.0032	15.1	.0000	1	Guests
0.0032	15.1	.0000	1	guests'
0.0032	15.1	.0000	1	Gustavson
0.0032	15.1	.0000	1	half-bang
0.0032	15.1	.0000	1	half-pound
0.0032	15.1	.0000	1	half-truths
0.0032	15.1	.0000	1	hand-printed
0.0032	15.1	.0000	1	hand-sew
0.0032	15.1	.0000	1	hand-stitching
0.0032	15.1	.0000	1	hangings
0.0032	15.1	.0000	1	hard-crusted
0.0032	15.1	.0000	1	heat-sensitive
0.0032	15.1	.0000	1	heirloom
0.0032	15.1	.0000	1	Helanca
0.0032	15.1	.0000	1	Hemmed
0.0032	15.1	.0000	1	high-yoked
0.0032	15.1	.0000	1	hip-length
0.0032	15.1	.0000	1	hoagy
0.0032	15.1	.0000	1	homogenization
0.0032	15.1	.0000	1	hook-and-eye
0.0032	15.1	.0000	1	hook-and-ladder
0.0032	15.1	.0000	1	hopsacking
0.0032	15.1	.0000	1	housecoats
0.0032	15.1	.0000	1	housekeeper's
0.0032	15.1	.0000	1	imparts
0.0032	15.1	.0000	1	Influence
0.0032	15.1	.0000	1	insomnia
0.0032	15.1	.0000	1	interlinings
0.0032	15.1	.0000	1	invalid's
0.0032	15.1	.0000	1	iodized
0.0032	15.1	.0000	1	irks
0.0032	15.1	.0000	1	irritate
0.0032	15.1	.0000	1	itemized
0.0032	15.1	.0000	1	itemizes
0.0032	15.1	.0000	1	jellied
0.0032	15.1	.0000	1	kerchief
0.0032	15.1	.0000	1	KIND
0.0032	15.1	.0000	1	kinsfolk
0.0032	15.1	.0000	1	laminates
0.0032	15.1	.0000	1	lamination
0.0032	15.1	.0000	1	larding
0.0032	15.1	.0000	1	launders
0.0032	15.1	.0000	1	left-off
0.0032	15.1	.0000	1	lengthening-shortening
0.0032	15.1	.0000	1	lifter
0.0032	15.1	.0000	1	living-dining
0.0032	15.1	.0000	1	Logan's
0.0032	15.1	.0000	1	Logans
0.0032	15.1	.0000	1	long-leg
0.0032	15.1	.0000	1	long-pronged
0.0032	15.1	.0000	1	lower-priced
0.0032	15.1	.0000	1	LOYALTY
0.0032	15.1	.0000	1	luncheons
0.0032	15.1	.0000	1	Lunches
0.0032	15.1	.0000	1	machine-stitched
0.0032	15.1	.0000	1	machine-worked
0.0032	15.1	.0000	1	malformed
0.0032	15.1	.0000	1	malts
0.0032	15.1	.0000	1	manipulative
0.0032	15.1	.0000	1	margarines
0.0032	15.1	.0000	1	marring
0.0032	15.1	.0000	1	maturities
0.0032	15.1	.0000	1	measurement-line
0.0032	15.1	.0000	1	mediumweight
0.0032	15.1	.0000	1	melba
0.0032	15.1	.0000	1	Meringue
0.0032	15.1	.0000	1	mild-flavored
0.0032	15.1	.0000	1	mild-fruit
0.0032	15.1	.0000	1	mildew-resistant
0.0032	15.1	.0000	1	Milium
				THE PRECEDING WORD TYPE OCCUPIES RANK 85200
0.0032	15.1	.0000	1	milk-and-egg
0.0032	15.1	.0000	1	misdeed
0.0032	15.1	.0000	1	mishandling
0.0032	15.1	.0000	1	mix-matches
0.0032	15.1	.0000	1	moderate-priced
0.0032	15.1	.0000	1	moisture-proof
0.0032	15.1	.0000	1	Mold
0.0032	15.1	.0000	1	moth-resistant
0.0032	15.1	.0000	1	mozzarella
0.0032	15.1	.0000	1	Muenster
0.0032	15.1	.0000	1	Muffins
0.0032	15.1	.0000	1	multi-purpose
0.0032	15.1	.0000	1	multifilament
0.0032	15.1	.0000	1	mysost
0.0032	15.1	.0000	1	Nationality
0.0032	15.1	.0000	1	natural-fiber
0.0032	15.1	.0000	1	natural-looking
0.0032	15.1	.0000	1	necessitate
0.0032	15.1	.0000	1	neck-and-armhole
0.0032	15.1	.0000	1	neck-and-sleeve
0.0032	15.1	.0000	1	neck-opening
0.0032	15.1	.0000	1	neckedge
0.0032	15.1	.0000	1	Neckline
0.0032	15.1	.0000	1	no-sift
0.0032	15.1	.0000	1	non-fat
0.0032	15.1	.0000	1	non-woven
0.0032	15.1	.0000	1	nonirritating
0.0032	15.1	.0000	1	nonslippery
0.0032	15.1	.0000	1	nonstretch
0.0032	15.1	.0000	1	nth
0.0032	15.1	.0000	1	Nursing
0.0032	15.1	.0000	1	NUTRIENTS
0.0032	15.1	.0000	1	Nutrition
0.0032	15.1	.0000	1	nutritionally
0.0032	15.1	.0000	1	nutritionist
0.0032	15.1	.0000	1	nylon-cotton
0.0032	15.1	.0000	1	oblongs
0.0032	15.1	.0000	1	obviates
0.0032	15.1	.0000	1	off-hand
0.0032	15.1	.0000	1	often-asked
0.0032	15.1	.0000	1	ohing
0.0032	15.1	.0000	1	oil-plugged
0.0032	15.1	.0000	1	one-and-a-half
0.0032	15.1	.0000	1	one-dish
0.0032	15.1	.0000	1	one-half-inch
0.0032	15.1	.0000	1	one-hundred-and-eight
0.0032	15.1	.0000	1	one-wall
0.0032	15.1	.0000	1	oolong
0.0032	15.1	.0000	1	open-mesh
0.0032	15.1	.0000	1	orange-pekoe
0.0032	15.1	.0000	1	Orlons
0.0032	15.1	.0000	1	out-of-season
0.0032	15.1	.0000	1	outlast
0.0032	15.1	.0000	1	OUTSIDE
0.0032	15.1	.0000	1	over-cooking
0.0032	15.1	.0000	1	overbeat
0.0032	15.1	.0000	1	overblouses
0.0032	15.1	.0000	1	overcasting
0.0032	15.1	.0000	1	overcook
0.0032	15.1	.0000	1	overemphasizing

U	SFI	D	F	Word Type
0.0032	15.1	.0000	1	overfill
0.0032	15.1	.0000	1	overmix
0.0032	15.1	.0000	1	overmixed
0.0032	15.1	.0000	1	overstays
0.0032	15.1	.0000	1	overstitch
0.0032	15.1	.0000	1	overwhelms
0.0032	15.1	.0000	1	overwhip
0.0032	15.1	.0000	1	Paese
0.0032	15.1	.0000	1	pageboy
0.0032	15.1	.0000	1	pan-broiling
0.0032	15.1	.0000	1	pan-fried
0.0032	15.1	.0000	1	pan-frying
0.0032	15.1	.0000	1	pastel-colored
0.0032	15.1	.0000	1	pastry-lined
0.0032	15.1	.0000	1	patching
0.0032	15.1	.0000	1	permanents
0.0032	15.1	.0000	1	Petroni
0.0032	15.1	.0000	1	pin-
0.0032	15.1	.0000	1	pincushions
0.0032	15.1	.0000	1	pleasingly
0.0032	15.1	.0000	1	pliability
0.0032	15.1	.0000	1	po'boy
0.0032	15.1	.0000	1	pocket's
0.0032	15.1	.0000	1	poly-unsaturated
0.0032	15.1	.0000	1	pompadours
0.0032	15.1	.0000	1	poor-boy
0.0032	15.1	.0000	1	poplin
0.0032	15.1	.0000	1	pot-roasting
0.0032	15.1	.0000	1	powder-like
0.0032	15.1	.0000	1	practicality
0.0032	15.1	.0000	1	practice-plan
0.0032	15.1	.0000	1	prattling
0.0032	15.1	.0000	1	pre-cooked
0.0032	15.1	.0000	1	pre-shrink
0.0032	15.1	.0000	1	precooked
0.0032	15.1	.0000	1	preheat
0.0032	15.1	.0000	1	press-on
0.0032	15.1	.0000	1	presser-bar
0.0032	15.1	.0000	1	primost
0.0032	15.1	.0000	1	prohibitions
THE PRECEDING WORD TYPE OCCUPIES RANK 85300				
0.0032	15.1	.0000	1	provolone
0.0032	15.1	.0000	1	puckers
0.0032	15.1	.0000	1	pumpkin-egg
0.0032	15.1	.0000	1	purls
0.0032	15.1	.0000	1	quick-change
0.0032	15.1	.0000	1	ramie
0.0032	15.1	.0000	1	Rating
0.0032	15.1	.0000	1	raveling
0.0032	15.1	.0000	1	ravels
0.0032	15.1	.0000	1	Rayon
0.0032	15.1	.0000	1	red-violet
0.0032	15.1	.0000	1	red-wine
0.0032	15.1	.0000	1	redecorate
0.0032	15.1	.0000	1	redirect
0.0032	15.1	.0000	1	redirection
0.0032	15.1	.0000	1	redo
0.0032	15.1	.0000	1	refold
0.0032	15.1	.0000	1	refrigerate
0.0032	15.1	.0000	1	refrozen
0.0032	15.1	.0000	1	rejuvenating
0.0032	15.1	.0000	1	reliquefied
0.0032	15.1	.0000	1	remedying
0.0032	15.1	.0000	1	reprimand
0.0032	15.1	.0000	1	resift
0.0032	15.1	.0000	1	RESPECT
0.0032	15.1	.0000	1	respinning
0.0032	15.1	.0000	1	respun
0.0032	15.1	.0000	1	rewhipped
0.0032	15.1	.0000	1	ribbonlike
0.0032	15.1	.0000	1	rickrack
0.0032	15.1	.0000	1	ricotta
0.0032	15.1	.0000	1	role-playing
0.0032	15.1	.0000	1	romaine
0.0032	15.1	.0000	1	rose-red
0.0032	15.1	.0000	1	round-bowled
0.0032	15.1	.0000	1	ruffler
0.0032	15.1	.0000	1	runny
0.0032	15.1	.0000	1	Saaba
0.0032	15.1	.0000	1	sailcloth
0.0032	15.1	.0000	1	Salad
0.0032	15.1	.0000	1	salad-maker
0.0032	15.1	.0000	1	salami
0.0032	15.1	.0000	1	salesperson
0.0032	15.1	.0000	1	saltines
0.0032	15.1	.0000	1	Sanforizing
0.0032	15.1	.0000	1	sateen
0.0032	15.1	.0000	1	Sauce
0.0032	15.1	.0000	1	saute
0.0032	15.1	.0000	1	sauteed
0.0032	15.1	.0000	1	scald
0.0032	15.1	.0000	1	Science's
0.0032	15.1	.0000	1	scrumptious
0.0032	15.1	.0000	1	seamless
0.0032	15.1	.0000	1	seamlines
0.0032	15.1	.0000	1	see-through
0.0032	15.1	.0000	1	self-improvement
0.0032	15.1	.0000	1	self-interfacing
0.0032	15.1	.0000	1	self-regard
0.0032	15.1	.0000	1	semifermented
0.0032	15.1	.0000	1	semiripened
0.0032	15.1	.0000	1	serious-minded
0.0032	15.1	.0000	1	Sewing
0.0032	15.1	.0000	1	shape-holding
0.0032	15.1	.0000	1	shirring
0.0032	15.1	.0000	1	shirting
0.0032	15.1	.0000	1	Side-Seam
0.0032	15.1	.0000	1	side-seam
0.0032	15.1	.0000	1	sifter
0.0032	15.1	.0000	1	Sirup
0.0032	15.1	.0000	1	sixty-inch
0.0032	15.1	.0000	1	skin-deep
0.0032	15.1	.0000	1	sleeve-or-armhole
0.0032	15.1	.0000	1	sleevecap
0.0032	15.1	.0000	1	slip-stitches
0.0032	15.1	.0000	1	slipstitch
0.0032	15.1	.0000	1	slot-seam

U	SFI	D	F	Word Type
0.0032	15.1	.0000	1	smallness
0.0032	15.1	.0000	1	smocked
0.0032	15.1	.0000	1	soil-
0.0032	15.1	.0000	1	spandex
0.0032	15.1	.0000	1	spotlessly
0.0032	15.1	.0000	1	spun-bonded
0.0032	15.1	.0000	1	Spunized
0.0032	15.1	.0000	1	Stagecrafter's
0.0032	15.1	.0000	1	stay-stitching
0.0032	15.1	.0000	1	staylines
0.0032	15.1	.0000	1	Stilton
0.0032	15.1	.0000	1	Stirred
0.0032	15.1	.0000	1	stocking-covered
0.0032	15.1	.0000	1	stretchability
0.0032	15.1	.0000	1	Substitute
0.0032	15.1	.0000	1	suitability
0.0032	15.1	.0000	1	Superloft
0.0032	15.1	.0000	1	sweet-flavored
0.0032	15.1	.0000	1	Tack
0.0032	15.1	.0000	1	taffetas
0.0032	15.1	.0000	1	tart-fruit
0.0032	15.1	.0000	1	Taslan
0.0032	15.1	.0000	1	teen-ager's
0.0032	15.1	.0000	1	tenderizer
THE PRECEDING WORD TYPE OCCUPIES RANK 85400				
0.0032	15.1	.0000	1	Textralized
0.0032	15.1	.0000	1	texturized
0.0032	15.1	.0000	1	theine
0.0032	15.1	.0000	1	Thigh
0.0032	15.1	.0000	1	three-months'
0.0032	15.1	.0000	1	three-ply
0.0032	15.1	.0000	1	timbale
0.0032	15.1	.0000	1	tomboyish
0.0032	15.1	.0000	1	top-stitched
0.0032	15.1	.0000	1	top-stitching
0.0032	15.1	.0000	1	Topping
0.0032	15.1	.0000	1	topstitching
0.0032	15.1	.0000	1	trichinosis
0.0032	15.1	.0000	1	tricot
0.0032	15.1	.0000	1	tricots
0.0032	15.1	.0000	1	tuck-in
0.0032	15.1	.0000	1	turn-under
0.0032	15.1	.0000	1	twill-weave
0.0032	15.1	.0000	1	two-crust
0.0032	15.1	.0000	1	two-ply
0.0032	15.1	.0000	1	two-strip
0.0032	15.1	.0000	1	two-wall
0.0032	15.1	.0000	1	unbuttered
0.0032	15.1	.0000	1	uncompromisingly
0.0032	15.1	.0000	1	under-stitching
0.0032	15.1	.0000	1	underclothing
0.0032	15.1	.0000	1	underfolds
0.0032	15.1	.0000	1	undergarments
0.0032	15.1	.0000	1	UNDERSTANDING
0.0032	15.1	.0000	1	undivided
0.0032	15.1	.0000	1	unfermented
0.0032	15.1	.0000	1	unflavored
0.0032	15.1	.0000	1	ungreased
0.0032	15.1	.0000	1	unnotched
0.0032	15.1	.0000	1	unpin
0.0032	15.1	.0000	1	untoasted
0.0032	15.1	.0000	1	Upside-Down
0.0032	15.1	.0000	1	V-neck
0.0032	15.1	.0000	1	Vegetable
0.0032	15.1	.0000	1	Vegetable-Fruit
0.0032	15.1	.0000	1	Vitamin
0.0032	15.1	.0000	1	Vitamins
0.0032	15.1	.0000	1	waistlines
0.0032	15.1	.0000	1	wales
0.0032	15.1	.0000	1	wash-and-wear
0.0032	15.1	.0000	1	washcloths
0.0032	15.1	.0000	1	water-displacement
0.0032	15.1	.0000	1	wearings
0.0032	15.1	.0000	1	weiners
0.0032	15.1	.0000	1	well-nourished
0.0032	15.1	.0000	1	well-prepared
0.0032	15.1	.0000	1	well-shaped
0.0032	15.1	.0000	1	WHEN
0.0032	15.1	.0000	1	whiny
0.0032	15.1	.0000	1	Whipped
0.0032	15.1	.0000	1	white-shirt-tie-jacket
0.0032	15.1	.0000	1	white-wine
0.0032	15.1	.0000	1	whiteheads
0.0032	15.1	.0000	1	WHOM
0.0032	15.1	.0000	1	Width
0.0032	15.1	.0000	1	wilts
0.0032	15.1	.0000	1	winders
0.0032	15.1	.0000	1	wool-Vicara-nylon
0.0032	15.1	.0000	1	wool-nylon
0.0032	15.1	.0000	1	workbaskets
0.0032	15.1	.0000	1	worktables
0.0032	15.1	.0000	1	wrinkle-resistance
0.0032	15.1	.0000	1	Y-Teens
0.0032	15.1	.0000	1	1/0
0.0032	15.1	.0000	1	1/4-cup
0.0032	15.1	.0000	1	110-111
0.0032	15.1	.0000	1	221-222
0.0032	15.1	.0000	1	282-283
0.0032	15.1	.0000	1	29-6
0.0032	15.1	.0000	1	3-inch-deep
0.0032	15.1	.0000	1	334
0.0032	15.1	.0000	1	4-strips**
0.0032	15.1	.0000	1	4/0
0.0032	15.1	.0000	1	446
0.0032	15.1	.0000	1	48-52
0.0032	15.1	.0000	1	63%
0.0032	15.1	.0000	1	7-
0.0032	15.1	.0000	1	8-inch-square
0.0025	14.0	.0000	1	acid-type
0.0025	14.0	.0000	1	adjusters
0.0025	14.0	.0000	1	Aldalox
0.0025	14.0	.0000	1	alkalis
0.0025	14.0	.0000	1	Aloxite
0.0025	14.0	.0000	1	Alundum
0.0025	14.0	.0000	1	ammeter
0.0025	14.0	.0000	1	anneal
0.0025	14.0	.0000	1	Applied

U	SFI	D	F	Word Type
0.0025	14.0	.0000	1	art-object
0.0025	14.0	.0000	1	B-B
0.0025	14.0	.0000	1	backings
0.0025	14.0	.0000	1	bakelite
0.0025	14.0	.0000	1	ball-type
0.0025	14.0	.0000	1	band-iron
0.0025	14.0	.0000	1	bar-tap
0.0025	14.0	.0000	1	beakhorn
THE PRECEDING WORD TYPE OCCUPIES RANK 85500				
0.0025	14.0	.0000	1	Beam
0.0025	14.0	.0000	1	Bearing
0.0025	14.0	.0000	1	bevel-edged
0.0025	14.0	.0000	1	beveling
0.0025	14.0	.0000	1	bichromate
0.0025	14.0	.0000	1	billfold
0.0025	14.0	.0000	1	bindery
0.0025	14.0	.0000	1	blocking-in
0.0025	14.0	.0000	1	blonded
0.0025	14.0	.0000	1	blowhorn
0.0025	14.0	.0000	1	blued
0.0025	14.0	.0000	1	blunger
0.0025	14.0	.0000	1	blungering
0.0025	14.0	.0000	1	bookbinders
0.0025	14.0	.0000	1	bookends
0.0025	14.0	.0000	1	bookracks
0.0025	14.0	.0000	1	boot-strap
0.0025	14.0	.0000	1	Braddock-Rowe
0.0025	14.0	.0000	1	breadraising
0.0025	14.0	.0000	1	broken-out
0.0025	14.0	.0000	1	bullchain
0.0025	14.0	.0000	1	burring
0.0025	14.0	.0000	1	B3
0.0025	14.0	.0000	1	capacitive
0.0025	14.0	.0000	1	capscrews
0.0025	14.0	.0000	1	carbon-paper
0.0025	14.0	.0000	1	cast-metal
0.0025	14.0	.0000	1	center-punch
0.0025	14.0	.0000	1	centerless
0.0025	14.0	.0000	1	chamfering
0.0025	14.0	.0000	1	chisel's
0.0025	14.0	.0000	1	clearances
0.0025	14.0	.0000	1	cloverleaf
0.0025	14.0	.0000	1	clutters
0.0025	14.0	.0000	1	cold-metal
0.0025	14.0	.0000	1	cold-rolled
0.0025	14.0	.0000	1	cold-type
0.0025	14.0	.0000	1	colloid
0.0025	14.0	.0000	1	compositors
0.0025	14.0	.0000	1	Connections
0.0025	14.0	.0000	1	constant-level
0.0025	14.0	.0000	1	Copperplate
0.0025	14.0	.0000	1	core-type
0.0025	14.0	.0000	1	coretype
0.0025	14.0	.0000	1	corrosion-resisting
0.0025	14.0	.0000	1	crankpin
0.0025	14.0	.0000	1	cresent
0.0025	14.0	.0000	1	cross-grained
0.0025	14.0	.0000	1	cross-hatching
0.0025	14.0	.0000	1	cross-peen
0.0025	14.0	.0000	1	crossgrain
0.0025	14.0	.0000	1	Crystolon
0.0025	14.0	.0000	1	cyanide
0.0025	14.0	.0000	1	cyaniding
0.0025	14.0	.0000	1	cylinder-head
0.0025	14.0	.0000	1	cylindrically
0.0025	14.0	.0000	1	Dado
0.0025	14.0	.0000	1	Dams
0.0025	14.0	.0000	1	deadcenter
0.0025	14.0	.0000	1	debark
0.0025	14.0	.0000	1	decals
0.0025	14.0	.0000	1	decharged
0.0025	14.0	.0000	1	deform
0.0025	14.0	.0000	1	dehumidifiers
0.0025	14.0	.0000	1	detailing
0.0025	14.0	.0000	1	detector-mixer
0.0025	14.0	.0000	1	diamond-cone
0.0025	14.0	.0000	1	diamond-faced
0.0025	14.0	.0000	1	diemakers
0.0025	14.0	.0000	1	dimensioned
0.0025	14.0	.0000	1	direct-current
0.0025	14.0	.0000	1	disassembled
0.0025	14.0	.0000	1	disassembling
0.0025	14.0	.0000	1	discordant
0.0025	14.0	.0000	1	distortions
0.0025	14.0	.0000	1	double-ground
0.0025	14.0	.0000	1	double-hung
0.0025	14.0	.0000	1	double-seaming
0.0025	14.0	.0000	1	double-strength
0.0025	14.0	.0000	1	Drafting
0.0025	14.0	.0000	1	driers
0.0025	14.0	.0000	1	dry-writing
0.0025	14.0	.0000	1	durably
0.0025	14.0	.0000	1	Durite
0.0025	14.0	.0000	1	earth-parking
0.0025	14.0	.0000	1	electric-arc
0.0025	14.0	.0000	1	electric-heating
0.0025	14.0	.0000	1	electrocharged
0.0025	14.0	.0000	1	electrotyping
0.0025	14.0	.0000	1	Emeri
0.0025	14.0	.0000	1	enameled
0.0025	14.0	.0000	1	Engineering
0.0025	14.0	.0000	1	engraver
0.0025	14.0	.0000	1	Eout
0.0025	14.0	.0000	1	escutcheon
0.0025	14.0	.0000	1	extrusion-type
0.0025	14.0	.0000	1	face-planing
0.0025	14.0	.0000	1	Fahnestock
0.0025	14.0	.0000	1	faired
0.0025	14.0	.0000	1	ferrous
THE PRECEDING WORD TYPE OCCUPIES RANK 85600				
0.0025	14.0	.0000	1	ferrous-metal
0.0025	14.0	.0000	1	fid
0.0025	14.0	.0000	1	fillister
0.0025	14.0	.0000	1	Film-o-type
0.0025	14.0	.0000	1	fine-mesh
0.0025	14.0	.0000	1	fineness
0.0025	14.0	.0000	1	fire-fighting

U	SFI	D	F	Word Type
0.0025	14.0	.0000	1	fire-resistant
0.0025	14.0	.0000	1	flange
0.0025	14.0	.0000	1	flanged
0.0025	14.0	.0000	1	flat-head
0.0025	14.0	.0000	1	flat-surface
0.0025	14.0	.0000	1	flathead
0.0025	14.0	.0000	1	fluxes
0.0025	14.0	.0000	1	forcefulness
0.0025	14.0	.0000	1	Format
0.0025	14.0	.0000	1	forming-press
0.0025	14.0	.0000	1	Fotosetter
0.0025	14.0	.0000	1	foundrymen
0.0025	14.0	.0000	1	frustum
0.0025	14.0	.0000	1	full-thread
0.0025	14.0	.0000	1	gas-welding
0.0025	14.0	.0000	1	gaskets
0.0025	14.0	.0000	1	general-purpose
0.0025	14.0	.0000	1	Graaff
0.0025	14.0	.0000	1	gradation
0.0025	14.0	.0000	1	graduations
0.0025	14.0	.0000	1	Gudea
0.0025	14.0	.0000	1	halfround
0.0025	14.0	.0000	1	hand-hammering
0.0025	14.0	.0000	1	hand-screw
0.0025	14.0	.0000	1	hand-tool
0.0025	14.0	.0000	1	hard-soldered
0.0025	14.0	.0000	1	hard-to-get-to
0.0025	14.0	.0000	1	hardened-steel
0.0025	14.0	.0000	1	hasps
0.0025	14.0	.0000	1	HB
0.0025	14.0	.0000	1	headrig
0.0025	14.0	.0000	1	heat-treat
0.0025	14.0	.0000	1	heat-treated
0.0025	14.0	.0000	1	heterodyning
0.0025	14.0	.0000	1	hex
0.0025	14.0	.0000	1	Hex
0.0025	14.0	.0000	1	hexagonal-shaped
0.0025	14.0	.0000	1	hexagons
0.0025	14.0	.0000	1	high-gloss
0.0025	14.0	.0000	1	hole-machining
0.0025	14.0	.0000	1	house-wiring
0.0025	14.0	.0000	1	household-use
0.0025	14.0	.0000	1	Hultgren
0.0025	14.0	.0000	1	hultgren
0.0025	14.0	.0000	1	i-f
0.0025	14.0	.0000	1	incised
0.0025	14.0	.0000	1	inductor
0.0025	14.0	.0000	1	ingenius
0.0025	14.0	.0000	1	intaglio
0.0025	14.0	.0000	1	intermediate-frequency
0.0025	14.0	.0000	1	IR
0.0025	14.0	.0000	1	irregular-grained
0.0025	14.0	.0000	1	jig-boring
0.0025	14.0	.0000	1	Joining
0.0025	14.0	.0000	1	kerfs
0.0025	14.0	.0000	1	knurl
0.0025	14.0	.0000	1	layover
0.0025	14.0	.0000	1	lead-alloy-coated
0.0025	14.0	.0000	1	lead-coated
0.0025	14.0	.0000	1	left-handers
0.0025	14.0	.0000	1	legibility
0.0025	14.0	.0000	1	Lenz's
0.0025	14.0	.0000	1	Lettering
0.0025	14.0	.0000	1	LH2
0.0025	14.0	.0000	1	light-dark
0.0025	14.0	.0000	1	light-faced
0.0025	14.0	.0000	1	light-sensitized
0.0025	14.0	.0000	1	liquid-salt
0.0025	14.0	.0000	1	lithoink
0.0025	14.0	.0000	1	lockup
0.0025	14.0	.0000	1	lodestones
0.0025	14.0	.0000	1	looseness
0.0025	14.0	.0000	1	low-temperature
0.0025	14.0	.0000	1	LOX
0.0025	14.0	.0000	1	machinability
0.0025	14.0	.0000	1	machine-built
0.0025	14.0	.0000	1	machinists
0.0025	14.0	.0000	1	machinists'
0.0025	14.0	.0000	1	make-ready
0.0025	14.0	.0000	1	mandrel
0.0025	14.0	.0000	1	Manufactured
0.0025	14.0	.0000	1	Materials
0.0025	14.0	.0000	1	medium-carbon
0.0025	14.0	.0000	1	metal-cutting
0.0025	14.0	.0000	1	metal-foil
0.0025	14.0	.0000	1	metalworker's
0.0025	14.0	.0000	1	metalworkers
0.0025	14.0	.0000	1	microstructural
0.0025	14.0	.0000	1	milo
0.0025	14.0	.0000	1	modules
0.0025	14.0	.0000	1	moisture-
0.0025	14.0	.0000	1	molder
0.0025	14.0	.0000	1	molder's
THE PRECEDING WORD TYPE OCCUPIES RANK 85700				
0.0025	14.0	.0000	1	mouldings
0.0025	14.0	.0000	1	moving-coil
0.0025	14.0	.0000	1	multi-story
0.0025	14.0	.0000	1	multimeters
0.0025	14.0	.0000	1	multitooth
0.0025	14.0	.0000	1	Mylar
0.0025	14.0	.0000	1	needle-case
0.0025	14.0	.0000	1	nicking
0.0025	14.0	.0000	1	non-magnetic
0.0025	14.0	.0000	1	non-metallic
0.0025	14.0	.0000	1	nondevelopable
0.0025	14.0	.0000	1	nonmarring
0.0025	14.0	.0000	1	Np**
0.0025	14.0	.0000	1	Nprimary/Nsecondary**
0.0025	14.0	.0000	1	Ns**
0.0025	14.0	.0000	1	one-lane
0.0025	14.0	.0000	1	open-mouth
0.0025	14.0	.0000	1	orthographic
0.0025	14.0	.0000	1	overdisplay
0.0025	14.0	.0000	1	overtighten
0.0025	14.0	.0000	1	parallel-line
0.0025	14.0	.0000	1	parkways
0.0025	14.0	.0000	1	part-assembly

U	SFI	D	F	Word Type
0.0025	14.0	.0000	1	paste-up
0.0025	14.0	.0000	1	peened
0.0025	14.0	.0000	1	penetrator
0.0025	14.0	.0000	1	pentagrid
0.0025	14.0	.0000	1	perforating
0.0025	14.0	.0000	1	permanent-magnet
0.0025	14.0	.0000	1	photofilm
0.0025	14.0	.0000	1	photogelatin
0.0025	14.0	.0000	1	plane-iron
0.0025	14.0	.0000	1	planer-type
0.0025	14.0	.0000	1	planographic
0.0025	14.0	.0000	1	plasterboard
0.0025	14.0	.0000	1	platemakers
0.0025	14.0	.0000	1	platemaking
0.0025	14.0	.0000	1	play-by-play
0.0025	14.0	.0000	1	polymetals
0.0025	14.0	.0000	1	pop-up-type
0.0025	14.0	.0000	1	preheats
0.0025	14.0	.0000	1	presensitized
0.0025	14.0	.0000	1	press-like
0.0025	14.0	.0000	1	pressman
0.0025	14.0	.0000	1	prick-punch
0.0025	14.0	.0000	1	pritchel
0.0025	14.0	.0000	1	Processes
0.0025	14.0	.0000	1	proportionate
0.0025	14.0	.0000	1	Pulsa-Jet
0.0025	14.0	.0000	1	quadrangular
0.0025	14.0	.0000	1	quads
0.0025	14.0	.0000	1	rabbet-and-dado
0.0025	14.0	.0000	1	rabbeting
0.0025	14.0	.0000	1	radial-line
0.0025	14.0	.0000	1	rattail
0.0025	14.0	.0000	1	re-drawn
0.0025	14.0	.0000	1	reactance
0.0025	14.0	.0000	1	reamed
0.0025	14.0	.0000	1	reaming
0.0025	14.0	.0000	1	reapply
0.0025	14.0	.0000	1	recessed
0.0025	14.0	.0000	1	reclose
0.0025	14.0	.0000	1	recomended
0.0025	14.0	.0000	1	reddish-colored
0.0025	14.0	.0000	1	retainer
0.0025	14.0	.0000	1	RH
0.0025	14.0	.0000	1	ripsaw
0.0025	14.0	.0000	1	Rockwell-C
0.0025	14.0	.0000	1	rosin-
0.0025	14.0	.0000	1	rosin-type
0.0025	14.0	.0000	1	round-split
0.0025	14.0	.0000	1	saddle-clamp
0.0025	14.0	.0000	1	sand-like
0.0025	14.0	.0000	1	sand-resin
0.0025	14.0	.0000	1	saw-table
0.0025	14.0	.0000	1	saw's
0.0025	14.0	.0000	1	sawyer
0.0025	14.0	.0000	1	Scraping
0.0025	14.0	.0000	1	scribed
0.0025	14.0	.0000	1	scriber
0.0025	14.0	.0000	1	seam-welding
0.0025	14.0	.0000	1	seamer
0.0025	14.0	.0000	1	sectional-view
0.0025	14.0	.0000	1	segma
0.0025	14.0	.0000	1	semi-finished
0.0025	14.0	.0000	1	semi-gloss
0.0025	14.0	.0000	1	semigloss
0.0025	14.0	.0000	1	sharp-edged
0.0025	14.0	.0000	1	sharpenings
0.0025	14.0	.0000	1	sheetmetal
0.0025	14.0	.0000	1	shell-type
0.0025	14.0	.0000	1	shim
0.0025	14.0	.0000	1	short-blade
0.0025	14.0	.0000	1	shorted
0.0025	14.0	.0000	1	showcard
0.0025	14.0	.0000	1	side-facing
0.0025	14.0	.0000	1	single-point
0.0025	14.0	.0000	1	single-story
0.0025	14.0	.0000	1	Size
0.0025	14.0	.0000	1	skiving

THE PRECEDING WORD TYPE OCCUPIES RANK 85800

U	SFI	D	F	Word Type
0.0025	14.0	.0000	1	slotter
0.0025	14.0	.0000	1	slotting
0.0025	14.0	.0000	1	sloyd
0.0025	14.0	.0000	1	smooth-textured
0.0025	14.0	.0000	1	Smoothing
0.0025	14.0	.0000	1	soft-soldered
0.0025	14.0	.0000	1	soft-soldering
0.0025	14.0	.0000	1	Soldering
0.0025	14.0	.0000	1	solenoid
0.0025	14.0	.0000	1	speed-change
0.0025	14.0	.0000	1	Speedball
0.0025	14.0	.0000	1	spindle-reverse
0.0025	14.0	.0000	1	spindle-reversing
0.0025	14.0	.0000	1	spring-driven
0.0025	14.0	.0000	1	Static
0.0025	14.0	.0000	1	steel-rolling
0.0025	14.0	.0000	1	step-down
0.0025	14.0	.0000	1	step-up
0.0025	14.0	.0000	1	stonemasons
0.0025	14.0	.0000	1	straight-peen
0.0025	14.0	.0000	1	stretch-outs
0.0025	14.0	.0000	1	structural-steel
0.0025	14.0	.0000	1	sturdiness
0.0025	14.0	.0000	1	subassemblies
0.0025	14.0	.0000	1	surform
0.0025	14.0	.0000	1	S2S
0.0025	14.0	.0000	1	S3
0.0025	14.0	.0000	1	S4
0.0025	14.0	.0000	1	T-square
0.0025	14.0	.0000	1	T-tap
0.0025	14.0	.0000	1	table-feed
0.0025	14.0	.0000	1	tacky
0.0025	14.0	.0000	1	Tang
0.0025	14.0	.0000	1	tangency
0.0025	14.0	.0000	1	tap's
0.0025	14.0	.0000	1	template
0.0025	14.0	.0000	1	thermocouples
0.0025	14.0	.0000	1	Thermostat
0.0025	14.0	.0000	1	thonging
0.0025	14.0	.0000	1	thread-diameter
0.0025	14.0	.0000	1	Three-M-Ite
0.0025	14.0	.0000	1	three-view
0.0025	14.0	.0000	1	thumbnails
0.0025	14.0	.0000	1	tinning
0.0025	14.0	.0000	1	titanate
0.0025	14.0	.0000	1	TL
0.0025	14.0	.0000	1	Tone
0.0025	14.0	.0000	1	tool-
0.0025	14.0	.0000	1	tool-and-die
0.0025	14.0	.0000	1	tool-steel
0.0025	14.0	.0000	1	tracings
0.0025	14.0	.0000	1	Tri-M-Ite
0.0025	14.0	.0000	1	troubleshooting
0.0025	14.0	.0000	1	truing
0.0025	14.0	.0000	1	truncated
0.0025	14.0	.0000	1	turbopumps
0.0025	14.0	.0000	1	two-coil
0.0025	14.0	.0000	1	typography
0.0025	14.0	.0000	1	u-shape
0.0025	14.0	.0000	1	unbent
0.0025	14.0	.0000	1	undersize
0.0025	14.0	.0000	1	Unified
0.0025	14.0	.0000	1	unscrewing
0.0025	14.0	.0000	1	unwieldy
0.0025	14.0	.0000	1	upstore
0.0025	14.0	.0000	1	V-belt
0.0025	14.0	.0000	1	V-block
0.0025	14.0	.0000	1	vacuum-tube
0.0025	14.0	.0000	1	Varityper
0.0025	14.0	.0000	1	VAXY
0.0025	14.0	.0000	1	vee
0.0025	14.0	.0000	1	ventilate
0.0025	14.0	.0000	1	venturi
0.0025	14.0	.0000	1	visibiility
0.0025	14.0	.0000	1	volcanic-force
0.0025	14.0	.0000	1	Voltage
0.0025	14.0	.0000	1	vulcanite
0.0025	14.0	.0000	1	welders
0.0025	14.0	.0000	1	whetting
0.0025	14.0	.0000	1	wide-angle
0.0025	14.0	.0000	1	wood-products
0.0025	14.0	.0000	1	work-up
0.0025	14.0	.0000	1	workmanlike
0.0025	14.0	.0000	1	Xerographic
0.0025	14.0	.0000	1	Y14
0.0025	14.0	.0000	1	0-1-2
0.0025	14.0	.0000	1	0-3
0.0025	14.0	.0000	1	0-3-4
0.0025	14.0	.0000	1	0-4
0.0025	14.0	.0000	1	0-4-1
0.0025	14.0	.0000	1	00025
0.0025	14.0	.0000	1	097
0.0025	14.0	.0000	1	1-to
0.0025	14.0	.0000	1	1-1a
0.0025	14.0	.0000	1	1-1b
0.0025	14.0	.0000	1	1-1957
0.0025	14.0	.0000	1	1-2a
0.0025	14.0	.0000	1	1-2b
0.0025	14.0	.0000	1	1-2c
0.0025	14.0	.0000	1	1-3a

THE PRECEDING WORD TYPE OCCUPIES RANK 85900

U	SFI	D	F	Word Type
0.0025	14.0	.0000	1	1-3b
0.0025	14.0	.0000	1	1-3c
0.0025	14.0	.0000	1	1-3d
0.0025	14.0	.0000	1	1-3e
0.0025	14.0	.0000	1	1/10th
0.0025	14.0	.0000	1	1/2-foot-long
0.0025	14.0	.0000	1	1/2-13
0.0025	14.0	.0000	1	1/40
0.0025	14.0	.0000	1	10-story-high
0.0025	14.0	.0000	1	10-14
0.0025	14.0	.0000	1	10-17a
0.0025	14.0	.0000	1	10-17b
0.0025	14.0	.0000	1	10-18b
0.0025	14.0	.0000	1	10-19a
0.0025	14.0	.0000	1	10-5
0.0025	14.0	.0000	1	100/Eout
0.0025	14.0	.0000	1	100/2
0.0025	14.0	.0000	1	100000/200
0.0025	14.0	.0000	1	1037
0.0025	14.0	.0000	1	1053
0.0025	14.0	.0000	1	1054
0.0025	14.0	.0000	1	11-1
0.0025	14.0	.0000	1	11-2
0.0025	14.0	.0000	1	11-3
0.0025	14.0	.0000	1	11-4
0.0025	14.0	.0000	1	110-4A
0.0025	14.0	.0000	1	110-5
0.0025	14.0	.0000	1	110-6
0.0025	14.0	.0000	1	1141
0.0025	14.0	.0000	1	1142
0.0025	14.0	.0000	1	1143
0.0025	14.0	.0000	1	1145
0.0025	14.0	.0000	1	1156
0.0025	14.0	.0000	1	1158
0.0025	14.0	.0000	1	1159
0.0025	14.0	.0000	1	1166-1168
0.0025	14.0	.0000	1	12-10
0.0025	14.0	.0000	1	12-11
0.0025	14.0	.0000	1	12-5
0.0025	14.0	.0000	1	12-9
0.0025	14.0	.0000	1	1279
0.0025	14.0	.0000	1	13NC
0.0025	14.0	.0000	1	13-10b
0.0025	14.0	.0000	1	13-11a
0.0025	14.0	.0000	1	13-9
0.0025	14.0	.0000	1	138-foot
0.0025	14.0	.0000	1	1397
0.0025	14.0	.0000	1	14-day
0.0025	14.0	.0000	1	14-3
0.0025	14.0	.0000	1	1494
0.0025	14.0	.0000	1	15-21
0.0025	14.0	.0000	1	15-3
0.0025	14.0	.0000	1	15-4
0.0025	14.0	.0000	1	15-9
0.0025	14.0	.0000	1	152-8
0.0025	14.0	.0000	1	153-1
0.0025	14.0	.0000	1	153-2
0.0025	14.0	.0000	1	153-3
0.0025	14.0	.0000	1	153-4
0.0025	14.0	.0000	1	154-1
0.0025	14.0	.0000	1	154-2
0.0025	14.0	.0000	1	16-1
0.0025	14.0	.0000	1	16-13b
0.0025	14.0	.0000	1	16-13c
0.0025	14.0	.0000	1	16-13d
0.0025	14.0	.0000	1	16-2
0.0025	14.0	.0000	1	16-5
0.0025	14.0	.0000	1	17-1
0.0025	14.0	.0000	1	17-4
0.0025	14.0	.0000	1	17-5
0.0025	14.0	.0000	1	17-7
0.0025	14.0	.0000	1	18-4
0.0025	14.0	.0000	1	18-5
0.0025	14.0	.0000	1	19-2
0.0025	14.0	.0000	1	19-3
0.0025	14.0	.0000	1	2-16
0.0025	14.0	.0000	1	2-49
0.0025	14.0	.0000	1	2-50
0.0025	14.0	.0000	1	2-9
0.0025	14.0	.0000	1	20-1
0.0025	14.0	.0000	1	20-18
0.0025	14.0	.0000	1	20d
0.0025	14.0	.0000	1	200/1000
0.0025	14.0	.0000	1	200/2
0.0025	14.0	.0000	1	204-207
0.0025	14.0	.0000	1	22-7a
0.0025	14.0	.0000	1	22-7b
0.0025	14.0	.0000	1	22-8
0.0025	14.0	.0000	1	25-10
0.0025	14.0	.0000	1	25-11
0.0025	14.0	.0000	1	25-13
0.0025	14.0	.0000	1	25-14
0.0025	14.0	.0000	1	25-15
0.0025	14.0	.0000	1	25-16
0.0025	14.0	.0000	1	26-3a
0.0025	14.0	.0000	1	26-3b
0.0025	14.0	.0000	1	26-3c
0.0025	14.0	.0000	1	26-3d
0.0025	14.0	.0000	1	27-11
0.0025	14.0	.0000	1	27-4

THE PRECEDING WORD TYPE OCCUPIES RANK 86000

U	SFI	D	F	Word Type
0.0025	14.0	.0000	1	27-6
0.0025	14.0	.0000	1	27-7
0.0025	14.0	.0000	1	27-9
0.0025	14.0	.0000	1	28-2
0.0025	14.0	.0000	1	28-3
0.0025	14.0	.0000	1	28-4
0.0025	14.0	.0000	1	29-1
0.0025	14.0	.0000	1	29-10C
0.0025	14.0	.0000	1	29-12
0.0025	14.0	.0000	1	29-13
0.0025	14.0	.0000	1	3-11
0.0025	14.0	.0000	1	30-or
0.0025	14.0	.0000	1	30-story
0.0025	14.0	.0000	1	30-1
0.0025	14.0	.0000	1	30-2
0.0025	14.0	.0000	1	30-3
0.0025	14.0	.0000	1	30-4
0.0025	14.0	.0000	1	30-5
0.0025	14.0	.0000	1	30-6
0.0025	14.0	.0000	1	30-7
0.0025	14.0	.0000	1	3000-kg
0.0025	14.0	.0000	1	30418
0.0025	14.0	.0000	1	30418a
0.0025	14.0	.0000	1	31-1a
0.0025	14.0	.0000	1	31-1b
0.0025	14.0	.0000	1	32nds
0.0025	14.0	.0000	1	320-288
0.0025	14.0	.0000	1	35-10
0.0025	14.0	.0000	1	35-11
0.0025	14.0	.0000	1	35-6
0.0025	14.0	.0000	1	35-7
0.0025	14.0	.0000	1	35-8
0.0025	14.0	.0000	1	35-9
0.0025	14.0	.0000	1	36-line
0.0025	14.0	.0000	1	362-foot
0.0025	14.0	.0000	1	4-12
0.0025	14.0	.0000	1	4-15
0.0025	14.0	.0000	1	4-28
0.0025	14.0	.0000	1	4-29
0.0025	14.0	.0000	1	4-30
0.0025	14.0	.0000	1	4-31
0.0025	14.0	.0000	1	4-32
0.0025	14.0	.0000	1	4-60
0.0025	14.0	.0000	1	4-61
0.0025	14.0	.0000	1	4-62
0.0025	14.0	.0000	1	4-63
0.0025	14.0	.0000	1	4-93
0.0025	14.0	.0000	1	4-94
0.0025	14.0	.0000	1	4-95
0.0025	14.0	.0000	1	4-96
0.0025	14.0	.0000	1	4-97
0.0025	14.0	.0000	1	40d
0.0025	14.0	.0000	1	414
0.0025	14.0	.0000	1	45-1
0.0025	14.0	.0000	1	45-2B
0.0025	14.0	.0000	1	45-5
0.0025	14.0	.0000	1	46-2
0.0025	14.0	.0000	1	46-3
0.0025	14.0	.0000	1	47th
0.0025	14.0	.0000	1	473
0.0025	14.0	.0000	1	48-3
0.0025	14.0	.0000	1	48-4
0.0025	14.0	.0000	1	48-5
0.0025	14.0	.0000	1	48-6
0.0025	14.0	.0000	1	48-7
0.0025	14.0	.0000	1	5-1
0.0025	14.0	.0000	1	5-28
0.0025	14.0	.0000	1	5-29
0.0025	14.0	.0000	1	5-3a
0.0025	14.0	.0000	1	5-3b
0.0025	14.0	.0000	1	5-3c
0.0025	14.0	.0000	1	5-30
0.0025	14.0	.0000	1	5-31
0.0025	14.0	.0000	1	5-32
0.0025	14.0	.0000	1	5-33
0.0025	14.0	.0000	1	5-35
0.0025	14.0	.0000	1	5/32
0.0025	14.0	.0000	1	5/34
0.0025	14.0	.0000	1	50/50
0.0025	14.0	.0000	1	54-2
0.0025	14.0	.0000	1	548
0.0025	14.0	.0000	1	552
0.0025	14.0	.0000	1	553-557
0.0025	14.0	.0000	1	558-568
0.0025	14.0	.0000	1	58-11
0.0025	14.0	.0000	1	58-12
0.0025	14.0	.0000	1	58-13
0.0025	14.0	.0000	1	58-14
0.0025	14.0	.0000	1	58-15
0.0025	14.0	.0000	1	58-16
0.0025	14.0	.0000	1	58-17
0.0025	14.0	.0000	1	58-18
0.0025	14.0	.0000	1	58-19
0.0025	14.0	.0000	1	58-20
0.0025	14.0	.0000	1	58-6
0.0025	14.0	.0000	1	58-7
0.0025	14.0	.0000	1	58-8
0.0025	14.0	.0000	1	596
0.0025	14.0	.0000	1	6-
0.0025	14.0	.0000	1	6-million

THE PRECEDING WORD TYPE OCCUPIES RANK 86100

U	SFI	D	F	Word Type
0.0025	14.0	.0000	1	6-11
0.0025	14.0	.0000	1	6-11a
0.0025	14.0	.0000	1	6-11b
0.0025	14.0	.0000	1	6-11c
0.0025	14.0	.0000	1	6-11d
0.0025	14.0	.0000	1	6-22
0.0025	14.0	.0000	1	6-23
0.0025	14.0	.0000	1	6-24
0.0025	14.0	.0000	1	6-6
0.0025	14.0	.0000	1	6/32
0.0025	14.0	.0000	1	61-10
0.0025	14.0	.0000	1	61-11
0.0025	14.0	.0000	1	61-12
0.0025	14.0	.0000	1	61-13
0.0025	14.0	.0000	1	61-14
0.0025	14.0	.0000	1	61-9
0.0025	14.0	.0000	1	658
0.0025	14.0	.0000	1	66-1B
0.0025	14.0	.0000	1	66-2
0.0025	14.0	.0000	1	66-3
0.0025	14.0	.0000	1	66-4
0.0025	14.0	.0000	1	6600
0.0025	14.0	.0000	1	664
0.0025	14.0	.0000	1	665
0.0025	14.0	.0000	1	67-1
0.0025	14.0	.0000	1	67-2A
0.0025	14.0	.0000	1	67-3
0.0025	14.0	.0000	1	67-4
0.0025	14.0	.0000	1	67-5
0.0025	14.0	.0000	1	67-6
0.0025	14.0	.0000	1	67-7
0.0025	14.0	.0000	1	68-1
0.0025	14.0	.0000	1	7-12
0.0025	14.0	.0000	1	7-13
0.0025	14.0	.0000	1	7-14
0.0025	14.0	.0000	1	70-1
0.0025	14.0	.0000	1	73-2
0.0025	14.0	.0000	1	75-1
0.0025	14.0	.0000	1	796
0.0025	14.0	.0000	1	811
0.0025	14.0	.0000	1	82-degree
0.0025	14.0	.0000	1	822-824
0.0025	14.0	.0000	1	85Hoover
0.0025	14.0	.0000	1	855
0.0025	14.0	.0000	1	858
0.0025	14.0	.0000	1	86-1
0.0025	14.0	.0000	1	86-2
0.0025	14.0	.0000	1	9-31
0.0025	14.0	.0000	1	9-32
0.0025	14.0	.0000	1	9-33
0.0025	14.0	.0000	1	9-34
0.0025	14.0	.0000	1	9/64
0.0025	14.0	.0000	1	90-degree
0.0025	14.0	.0000	1	926
0.0025	14.0	.0000	1	976
0.0025	14.0	.0000	1	977
0.0025	14.0	.0000	1	979
0.0022	13.5	.0000	1	abraded
0.0022	13.5	.0000	1	actor's
0.0022	13.5	.0000	1	Addison's
0.0022	13.5	.0000	1	admonition
0.0022	13.5	.0000	1	Altenbergian
0.0022	13.5	.0000	1	anti-gun
0.0022	13.5	.0000	1	anti-hunting
0.0022	13.5	.0000	1	apparels
0.0022	13.5	.0000	1	assiduity
0.0022	13.5	.0000	1	assiduous
0.0022	13.5	.0000	1	Association's
0.0022	13.5	.0000	1	Audrey's
0.0022	13.5	.0000	1	autumn-tired
0.0022	13.5	.0000	1	B-58
0.0022	13.5	.0000	1	balky
0.0022	13.5	.0000	1	ballfield
0.0022	13.5	.0000	1	Bang-All
0.0022	13.5	.0000	1	Bazaar
0.0022	13.5	.0000	1	berated
0.0022	13.5	.0000	1	Bijou
0.0022	13.5	.0000	1	black-and-tan
0.0022	13.5	.0000	1	black-stump
0.0022	13.5	.0000	1	Blackie
0.0022	13.5	.0000	1	blacking
0.0022	13.5	.0000	1	blood-swollen
0.0022	13.5	.0000	1	blurs
0.0022	13.5	.0000	1	Bowers'
0.0022	13.5	.0000	1	Bracebridge
0.0022	13.5	.0000	1	broadness
0.0022	13.5	.0000	1	brown-painted

U	SFI	D	F	Word Type
0.0022	13.5	.0000	1	bushmeat
0.0022	13.5	.0000	1	caddies
0.0022	13.5	.0000	1	calliope
0.0022	13.5	.0000	1	camatutpeg
0.0022	13.5	.0000	1	camatutpegged
0.0022	13.5	.0000	1	camp-stools
0.0022	13.5	.0000	1	Carpenter's
0.0022	13.5	.0000	1	Casualty
0.0022	13.5	.0000	1	Cather
0.0022	13.5	.0000	1	cause-and-effect
0.0022	13.5	.0000	1	Cheaper
0.0022	13.5	.0000	1	checklist
0.0022	13.5	.0000	1	clapboarding
THE PRECEDING WORD TYPE OCCUPIES RANK 86200				
0.0022	13.5	.0000	1	clopping
0.0022	13.5	.0000	1	close-growing
0.0022	13.5	.0000	1	coastwise
0.0022	13.5	.0000	1	cock-a-doodle
0.0022	13.5	.0000	1	coffee-room
0.0022	13.5	.0000	1	combustible
0.0022	13.5	.0000	1	compound-complex
0.0022	13.5	.0000	1	comprehensible
0.0022	13.5	.0000	1	confuses
0.0022	13.5	.0000	1	conjointly
0.0022	13.5	.0000	1	coquette
0.0022	13.5	.0000	1	Cosmos
0.0022	13.5	.0000	1	Cousteau's
0.0022	13.5	.0000	1	Crayon
0.0022	13.5	.0000	1	crost
0.0022	13.5	.0000	1	crudeness
0.0022	13.5	.0000	1	Cummins
0.0022	13.5	.0000	1	customers'
0.0022	13.5	.0000	1	daisy's
0.0022	13.5	.0000	1	Daphnia
0.0022	13.5	.0000	1	Day's
0.0022	13.5	.0000	1	Dell's
0.0022	13.5	.0000	1	deluded
0.0022	13.5	.0000	1	dem
0.0022	13.5	.0000	1	dexterously
0.0022	13.5	.0000	1	diffidently
0.0022	13.5	.0000	1	disabuse
0.0022	13.5	.0000	1	disquietude
0.0022	13.5	.0000	1	doted
0.0022	13.5	.0000	1	down-hearted
0.0022	13.5	.0000	1	downhearted
0.0022	13.5	.0000	1	Dozen
0.0022	13.5	.0000	1	Easterners
0.0022	13.5	.0000	1	ejaculations
0.0022	13.5	.0000	1	emanate
0.0022	13.5	.0000	1	Engle
0.0022	13.5	.0000	1	enlighten
0.0022	13.5	.0000	1	eveners
0.0022	13.5	.0000	1	Excellent
0.0022	13.5	.0000	1	exemplify
0.0022	13.5	.0000	1	extinguish
0.0022	13.5	.0000	1	extrapolating
0.0022	13.5	.0000	1	flippant
0.0022	13.5	.0000	1	florid-faced
0.0022	13.5	.0000	1	forestaysail
0.0022	13.5	.0000	1	four-ply
0.0022	13.5	.0000	1	fruitfulness
0.0022	13.5	.0000	1	Gallegher
0.0022	13.5	.0000	1	Geary
0.0022	13.5	.0000	1	Gent
0.0022	13.5	.0000	1	giants'
0.0022	13.5	.0000	1	glassily
0.0022	13.5	.0000	1	glassy-eyed
0.0022	13.5	.0000	1	glow'd
0.0022	13.5	.0000	1	grass-grown
0.0022	13.5	.0000	1	great-great-grandmother
0.0022	13.5	.0000	1	gregarious
0.0022	13.5	.0000	1	grilles
0.0022	13.5	.0000	1	gudgeon
0.0022	13.5	.0000	1	Guggenheim's
0.0022	13.5	.0000	1	gunshot
0.0022	13.5	.0000	1	Hance's
0.0022	13.5	.0000	1	hand-crank
0.0022	13.5	.0000	1	hardest-earned
0.0022	13.5	.0000	1	hardest-to-beat
0.0022	13.5	.0000	1	hat-securer
0.0022	13.5	.0000	1	Having
0.0022	13.5	.0000	1	Hesperus
0.0022	13.5	.0000	1	hi-ho
0.0022	13.5	.0000	1	hick'ry
0.0022	13.5	.0000	1	Hillock
0.0022	13.5	.0000	1	Hinckley
0.0022	13.5	.0000	1	homered
0.0022	13.5	.0000	1	horehound
0.0022	13.5	.0000	1	horrorstricken
0.0022	13.5	.0000	1	house-painter
0.0022	13.5	.0000	1	huddles
0.0022	13.5	.0000	1	immersing
0.0022	13.5	.0000	1	imperishable
0.0022	13.5	.0000	1	Ina
0.0022	13.5	.0000	1	Ingersoll
0.0022	13.5	.0000	1	insuperable
0.0022	13.5	.0000	1	irksome
0.0022	13.5	.0000	1	ironbarred
0.0022	13.5	.0000	1	Kathie
0.0022	13.5	.0000	1	keelboatman's
0.0022	13.5	.0000	1	keelboatmen
0.0022	13.5	.0000	1	Keys
0.0022	13.5	.0000	1	kindheartedness
0.0022	13.5	.0000	1	Kuching
0.0022	13.5	.0000	1	la-di-da
0.0022	13.5	.0000	1	Lalley
0.0022	13.5	.0000	1	lengthier
0.0022	13.5	.0000	1	lichee
0.0022	13.5	.0000	1	linsey-woolsey
0.0022	13.5	.0000	1	long-anticipated
0.0022	13.5	.0000	1	long-projected
0.0022	13.5	.0000	1	looters
0.0022	13.5	.0000	1	loudest-talking
0.0022	13.5	.0000	1	lupins
THE PRECEDING WORD TYPE OCCUPIES RANK 86300				
0.0022	13.5	.0000	1	lutefisk
0.0022	13.5	.0000	1	Malaga
0.0022	13.5	.0000	1	Marketbasket
0.0022	13.5	.0000	1	mashie
0.0022	13.5	.0000	1	milk-jug
0.0022	13.5	.0000	1	Minimum
0.0022	13.5	.0000	1	model-makers'
0.0022	13.5	.0000	1	Models
0.0022	13.5	.0000	1	Modjeska's
0.0022	13.5	.0000	1	mollified
0.0022	13.5	.0000	1	mollify
0.0022	13.5	.0000	1	Moonmen
0.0022	13.5	.0000	1	nettle
0.0022	13.5	.0000	1	niggerhead
0.0022	13.5	.0000	1	nippers
0.0022	13.5	.0000	1	non-voting
0.0022	13.5	.0000	1	nonfirearms
0.0022	13.5	.0000	1	Norvay
0.0022	13.5	.0000	1	Norvegian
0.0022	13.5	.0000	1	NRA
0.0022	13.5	.0000	1	O'Farrell
0.0022	13.5	.0000	1	offsprings'
0.0022	13.5	.0000	1	out-roar
0.0022	13.5	.0000	1	overhears
0.0022	13.5	.0000	1	owlet
0.0022	13.5	.0000	1	palmed
0.0022	13.5	.0000	1	parade's
0.0022	13.5	.0000	1	pattens
0.0022	13.5	.0000	1	penalize
0.0022	13.5	.0000	1	penholder
0.0022	13.5	.0000	1	Pepe's
0.0022	13.5	.0000	1	perfecter
0.0022	13.5	.0000	1	peripatetic
0.0022	13.5	.0000	1	Phrases
0.0022	13.5	.0000	1	piccalilli
0.0022	13.5	.0000	1	pidgin
0.0022	13.5	.0000	1	pink-and-white
0.0022	13.5	.0000	1	Playground
0.0022	13.5	.0000	1	policy-holders
0.0022	13.5	.0000	1	Pontoosuc
0.0022	13.5	.0000	1	prattles
0.0022	13.5	.0000	1	presumption
0.0022	13.5	.0000	1	provokingly
0.0022	13.5	.0000	1	psalmody
0.0022	13.5	.0000	1	racehorse
0.0022	13.5	.0000	1	raspy
0.0022	13.5	.0000	1	rebuilds
0.0022	13.5	.0000	1	recuperates
0.0022	13.5	.0000	1	Registrar's
0.0022	13.5	.0000	1	relegated
0.0022	13.5	.0000	1	reprimanded
0.0022	13.5	.0000	1	restates
0.0022	13.5	.0000	1	retraces
0.0022	13.5	.0000	1	ring'd
0.0022	13.5	.0000	1	riotously
0.0022	13.5	.0000	1	Rip's
0.0022	13.5	.0000	1	romping
0.0022	13.5	.0000	1	rosy-cheeked
0.0022	13.5	.0000	1	rubber-heeled
0.0022	13.5	.0000	1	rust-brown
0.0022	13.5	.0000	1	Saardam
0.0022	13.5	.0000	1	SanFranciscan
0.0022	13.5	.0000	1	sandpaper-like
0.0022	13.5	.0000	1	Satisfactory
0.0022	13.5	.0000	1	saturate
0.0022	13.5	.0000	1	scrapping
0.0022	13.5	.0000	1	scrutinizing
0.0022	13.5	.0000	1	seagull
0.0022	13.5	.0000	1	self-adjustment
0.0022	13.5	.0000	1	self-inflicted
0.0022	13.5	.0000	1	semiannually
0.0022	13.5	.0000	1	sentence's
0.0022	13.5	.0000	1	seventy-sixth
0.0022	13.5	.0000	1	shingling
0.0022	13.5	.0000	1	Shooting
0.0022	13.5	.0000	1	shopkeepers'
0.0022	13.5	.0000	1	shovelful
0.0022	13.5	.0000	1	sidehill
0.0022	13.5	.0000	1	Sketch
0.0022	13.5	.0000	1	Sketchbook
0.0022	13.5	.0000	1	soliciting
0.0022	13.5	.0000	1	southard
0.0022	13.5	.0000	1	spinnaker
0.0022	13.5	.0000	1	sportsman-hunter
0.0022	13.5	.0000	1	STANFORD
0.0022	13.5	.0000	1	Steffens
0.0022	13.5	.0000	1	Stegner's
0.0022	13.5	.0000	1	Steinbeck's
0.0022	13.5	.0000	1	stomacher
0.0022	13.5	.0000	1	storm-swelled
0.0022	13.5	.0000	1	strap-iron
0.0022	13.5	.0000	1	sunbeam
0.0022	13.5	.0000	1	surgeon-dentist
0.0022	13.5	.0000	1	swiftest-moving
0.0022	13.5	.0000	1	tableaus
0.0022	13.5	.0000	1	taloned
0.0022	13.5	.0000	1	Tartar's
0.0022	13.5	.0000	1	thankfully
0.0022	13.5	.0000	1	therewith
0.0022	13.5	.0000	1	thoughtlessness
THE PRECEDING WORD TYPE OCCUPIES RANK 86400				
0.0022	13.5	.0000	1	three-sentence
0.0022	13.5	.0000	1	tickly
0.0022	13.5	.0000	1	trespassers
0.0022	13.5	.0000	1	tweeter
0.0022	13.5	.0000	1	unaccepting
0.0022	13.5	.0000	1	unattended
0.0022	13.5	.0000	1	Uniform
0.0022	13.5	.0000	1	unintentional
0.0022	13.5	.0000	1	UnitedStages
0.0022	13.5	.0000	1	UNIVERSITY
0.0022	13.5	.0000	1	unveil'd
0.0022	13.5	.0000	1	verb-adverb
0.0022	13.5	.0000	1	watchmaker
0.0022	13.5	.0000	1	watchmaker's
0.0022	13.5	.0000	1	well-earned
0.0022	13.5	.0000	1	well-focused
0.0022	13.5	.0000	1	wellbuilt
0.0022	13.5	.0000	1	whisps
0.0022	13.5	.0000	1	whittles
0.0022	13.5	.0000	1	Wolfeboro
0.0022	13.5	.0000	1	wonderworld
0.0022	13.5	.0000	1	wood-carved
0.0022	13.5	.0000	1	woofer
0.0022	13.5	.0000	1	110-12
0.0022	13.5	.0000	1	15
0.0022	13.5	.0000	1	23-24
0.0022	13.5	.0000	1	29-30
0.0022	13.5	.0000	1	300-500
0.0022	13.5	.0000	1	32-33
0.0022	13.5	.0000	1	89-90
0.0018	12.7	.0000	1	abstractionism
0.0018	12.7	.0000	1	acquirement
0.0018	12.7	.0000	1	after-life
0.0018	12.7	.0000	1	after-the-storm
0.0018	12.7	.0000	1	Anger
0.0018	12.7	.0000	1	Apples
0.0018	12.7	.0000	1	applique
0.0018	12.7	.0000	1	Archaic
0.0018	12.7	.0000	1	architects'
0.0018	12.7	.0000	1	Ariel
0.0018	12.7	.0000	1	Armitage's
0.0018	12.7	.0000	1	Arp's
0.0018	12.7	.0000	1	artistically
0.0018	12.7	.0000	1	Bandersnatch
0.0018	12.7	.0000	1	Baptistry
0.0018	12.7	.0000	1	Bar-Tal
0.0018	12.7	.0000	1	Baranoff
0.0018	12.7	.0000	1	basilica
0.0018	12.7	.0000	1	bequeaths
0.0018	12.7	.0000	1	birdbaths
0.0018	12.7	.0000	1	bisons
0.0018	12.7	.0000	1	blockiness
0.0018	12.7	.0000	1	blurriness
0.0018	12.7	.0000	1	body-like
0.0018	12.7	.0000	1	Brants
0.0018	12.7	.0000	1	Braque's
0.0018	12.7	.0000	1	brinish
0.0018	12.7	.0000	1	brushstrokes
0.0018	12.7	.0000	1	buffeted
0.0018	12.7	.0000	1	Callay
0.0018	12.7	.0000	1	Callister
0.0018	12.7	.0000	1	Callooh
0.0018	12.7	.0000	1	candy-filled
0.0018	12.7	.0000	1	cannoneers
0.0018	12.7	.0000	1	carding
0.0018	12.7	.0000	1	Caveman
0.0018	12.7	.0000	1	Chagall
0.0018	12.7	.0000	1	Chaldeans
0.0018	12.7	.0000	1	Classicists
0.0018	12.7	.0000	1	cliffside
0.0018	12.7	.0000	1	Coals
0.0018	12.7	.0000	1	Cock's
0.0018	12.7	.0000	1	colander
0.0018	12.7	.0000	1	CONCEPTUAL
0.0018	12.7	.0000	1	Corbusier
0.0018	12.7	.0000	1	Coreen
0.0018	12.7	.0000	1	Cosimo
0.0018	12.7	.0000	1	craftsmen's
0.0018	12.7	.0000	1	cubists
0.0018	12.7	.0000	1	cumming's
0.0018	12.7	.0000	1	cummings
0.0018	12.7	.0000	1	custodian
0.0018	12.7	.0000	1	dairyman
0.0018	12.7	.0000	1	darker-blue
0.0018	12.7	.0000	1	Daumier's
0.0018	12.7	.0000	1	davenport
0.0018	12.7	.0000	1	Deauville
0.0018	12.7	.0000	1	dependability
0.0018	12.7	.0000	1	Deposition
0.0018	12.7	.0000	1	depressor
0.0018	12.7	.0000	1	dimly-lit
0.0018	12.7	.0000	1	dream-perfect
0.0018	12.7	.0000	1	Echoes
0.0018	12.7	.0000	1	Edouard
0.0018	12.7	.0000	1	Eggplants
0.0018	12.7	.0000	1	Elie
0.0018	12.7	.0000	1	epic-loving
0.0018	12.7	.0000	1	Escher
0.0018	12.7	.0000	1	Expectancy
0.0018	12.7	.0000	1	Expressionist
THE PRECEDING WORD TYPE OCCUPIES RANK 86500				
0.0018	12.7	.0000	1	Expressionists
0.0018	12.7	.0000	1	eye-spacing
0.0018	12.7	.0000	1	family-style
0.0018	12.7	.0000	1	fan-like
0.0018	12.7	.0000	1	Fauves
0.0018	12.7	.0000	1	Feininger
0.0018	12.7	.0000	1	Fetes
0.0018	12.7	.0000	1	fetishes
0.0018	12.7	.0000	1	Filippino
0.0018	12.7	.0000	1	fixative
0.0018	12.7	.0000	1	foils
0.0018	12.7	.0000	1	frabjous
0.0018	12.7	.0000	1	Fragonard's
0.0018	12.7	.0000	1	Fraternity
0.0018	12.7	.0000	1	fresco
0.0018	12.7	.0000	1	Freund
0.0018	12.7	.0000	1	Frienze
0.0018	12.7	.0000	1	frieze
0.0018	12.7	.0000	1	frivolities
0.0018	12.7	.0000	1	frumious
0.0018	12.7	.0000	1	fur-like
0.0018	12.7	.0000	1	galumphing
0.0018	12.7	.0000	1	Gathering
0.0018	12.7	.0000	1	Gauguin's
0.0018	12.7	.0000	1	Gericault
0.0018	12.7	.0000	1	Giacometti
0.0018	12.7	.0000	1	Giacometti's
0.0018	12.7	.0000	1	gold-enameled
0.0018	12.7	.0000	1	Goya
0.0018	12.7	.0000	1	GrandCanyonSuite
0.0018	12.7	.0000	1	Greco's
0.0018	12.7	.0000	1	Guadalajara
0.0018	12.7	.0000	1	handprint
0.0018	12.7	.0000	1	Harmens
0.0018	12.7	.0000	1	Harmenszoon
0.0018	12.7	.0000	1	harsh-sounding
0.0018	12.7	.0000	1	Hatshepsut
0.0018	12.7	.0000	1	Heaving
0.0018	12.7	.0000	1	highrise
0.0018	12.7	.0000	1	Hillmer
0.0018	12.7	.0000	1	Hofmann's
0.0018	12.7	.0000	1	IDEA
0.0018	12.7	.0000	1	idealization
0.0018	12.7	.0000	1	IDEAS
0.0018	12.7	.0000	1	ignominious
0.0018	12.7	.0000	1	Impressionists'
0.0018	12.7	.0000	1	inflate
0.0018	12.7	.0000	1	Ingres
0.0018	12.7	.0000	1	Jalisco
0.0018	12.7	.0000	1	Jean-Baptiste
0.0018	12.7	.0000	1	Jean-Francois
0.0018	12.7	.0000	1	Jour
0.0018	12.7	.0000	1	Jubjub
0.0018	12.7	.0000	1	junior-high-school
0.0018	12.7	.0000	1	juxtapose
0.0018	12.7	.0000	1	Kandinsky
0.0018	12.7	.0000	1	Kauffer
0.0018	12.7	.0000	1	Keelmen
0.0018	12.7	.0000	1	Kienholz
0.0018	12.7	.0000	1	Kienholz's
0.0018	12.7	.0000	1	Kites
0.0018	12.7	.0000	1	Klee
0.0018	12.7	.0000	1	L'Avion
0.0018	12.7	.0000	1	labo
0.0018	12.7	.0000	1	lace-like
0.0018	12.7	.0000	1	later-day
0.0018	12.7	.0000	1	Leger
0.0018	12.7	.0000	1	Lehmbruck
0.0018	12.7	.0000	1	Lindner
0.0018	12.7	.0000	1	Lippi
0.0018	12.7	.0000	1	LOOKING
0.0018	12.7	.0000	1	low-life
0.0018	12.7	.0000	1	Lyonel
0.0018	12.7	.0000	1	Madonna's
0.0018	12.7	.0000	1	Maillol's
0.0018	12.7	.0000	1	mangers
0.0018	12.7	.0000	1	manila
0.0018	12.7	.0000	1	manxome
0.0018	12.7	.0000	1	Marin's
0.0018	12.7	.0000	1	Masons'
0.0018	12.7	.0000	1	Maurits
0.0018	12.7	.0000	1	McKnight
0.0018	12.7	.0000	1	medium-
0.0018	12.7	.0000	1	Mies
0.0018	12.7	.0000	1	Minos
0.0018	12.7	.0000	1	Minos'
0.0018	12.7	.0000	1	Minotaur
0.0018	12.7	.0000	1	Mondrian's
0.0018	12.7	.0000	1	Nadelman
0.0018	12.7	.0000	1	near-vertical
0.0018	12.7	.0000	1	Neo-Classical
0.0018	12.7	.0000	1	Neo-Stoic
0.0018	12.7	.0000	1	Nervi's
0.0018	12.7	.0000	1	NEW
0.0018	12.7	.0000	1	nib
0.0018	12.7	.0000	1	nocturnes
0.0018	12.7	.0000	1	nonabsorbent
0.0018	12.7	.0000	1	Nuages
0.0018	12.7	.0000	1	organ-grinder
0.0018	12.7	.0000	1	organ-grinder's
THE PRECEDING WORD TYPE OCCUPIES RANK 86600				
0.0018	12.7	.0000	1	Osgood's
0.0018	12.7	.0000	1	outdistances
0.0018	12.7	.0000	1	outerspace
0.0018	12.7	.0000	1	overdressed
0.0018	12.7	.0000	1	paint's
0.0018	12.7	.0000	1	Pascin
0.0018	12.7	.0000	1	pen's
0.0018	12.7	.0000	1	pharaoh-god
0.0018	12.7	.0000	1	Philosopher
0.0018	12.7	.0000	1	pink-robbed
0.0018	12.7	.0000	1	plasterer's
0.0018	12.7	.0000	1	pointillism
0.0018	12.7	.0000	1	pointless
0.0018	12.7	.0000	1	Pollaiuolo
0.0018	12.7	.0000	1	Popeye
0.0018	12.7	.0000	1	Post-Impressionists
0.0018	12.7	.0000	1	pre-Hellenic
0.0018	12.7	.0000	1	pressing-down
0.0018	12.7	.0000	1	prides
0.0018	12.7	.0000	1	PRIMARY
0.0018	12.7	.0000	1	printmaker
0.0018	12.7	.0000	1	projectile-hurling
0.0018	12.7	.0000	1	propaganda-style
0.0018	12.7	.0000	1	Pullock
0.0018	12.7	.0000	1	Puppet
0.0018	12.7	.0000	1	quickdrying
0.0018	12.7	.0000	1	re-making
0.0018	12.7	.0000	1	rebozo
0.0018	12.7	.0000	1	Reclining
0.0018	12.7	.0000	1	recreate
0.0018	12.7	.0000	1	Returning
0.0018	12.7	.0000	1	reunions
0.0018	12.7	.0000	1	Rijn
0.0018	12.7	.0000	1	Rohe
0.0018	12.7	.0000	1	Rosselli
0.0018	12.7	.0000	1	roughen
0.0018	12.7	.0000	1	round-nib
0.0018	12.7	.0000	1	row-type
0.0018	12.7	.0000	1	Samothrace
0.0018	12.7	.0000	1	Savoie
0.0018	12.7	.0000	1	Seeganna
0.0018	12.7	.0000	1	SEEING
0.0018	12.7	.0000	1	Self-Destroying
0.0018	12.7	.0000	1	Seurat
0.0018	12.7	.0000	1	Shahn
0.0018	12.7	.0000	1	Shattuck
0.0018	12.7	.0000	1	shimmers
0.0018	12.7	.0000	1	shut-in
0.0018	12.7	.0000	1	Sirenes
0.0018	12.7	.0000	1	sixth-century

U	SFI	D	F	Word Type
0.0018	12.7	.0000	1	sketchily
0.0018	12.7	.0000	1	small-size
0.0018	12.7	.0000	1	smaller-appearing
0.0018	12.7	.0000	1	snicker-snack
0.0018	12.7	.0000	1	Sortie
0.0018	12.7	.0000	1	stabile
0.0018	12.7	.0000	1	stabiles
0.0018	12.7	.0000	1	Stained
0.0018	12.7	.0000	1	Stoic
0.0018	12.7	.0000	1	Stoneworkers'
0.0018	12.7	.0000	1	stylize
0.0018	12.7	.0000	1	Sunflowers
0.0018	12.7	.0000	1	super-beings
0.0018	12.7	.0000	1	teacups
0.0018	12.7	.0000	1	ten-
0.0018	12.7	.0000	1	tenseness
0.0018	12.7	.0000	1	textural
0.0018	12.7	.0000	1	three-and-one-half
0.0018	12.7	.0000	1	three-dimensions
0.0018	12.7	.0000	1	Tinguely's
0.0018	12.7	.0000	1	top-side
0.0018	12.7	.0000	1	torn-paper
0.0018	12.7	.0000	1	trivialities
0.0018	12.7	.0000	1	Tugendhut
0.0018	12.7	.0000	1	tulgey
0.0018	12.7	.0000	1	Tumtum
0.0018	12.7	.0000	1	uffish
0.0018	12.7	.0000	1	unflinchingly
0.0018	12.7	.0000	1	unsegregated
0.0018	12.7	.0000	1	upsweep
0.0018	12.7	.0000	1	Utrillo
0.0018	12.7	.0000	1	VanGogh
0.0018	12.7	.0000	1	VanGogh's
0.0018	12.7	.0000	1	Vasari
0.0018	12.7	.0000	1	vaseline
0.0018	12.7	.0000	1	Venard
0.0018	12.7	.0000	1	Vinci's
0.0018	12.7	.0000	1	VISUAL
0.0018	12.7	.0000	1	visually
0.0018	12.7	.0000	1	votive
0.0018	12.7	.0000	1	Wassily
0.0018	12.7	.0000	1	wax-crayon
0.0018	12.7	.0000	1	Wedding
0.0018	12.7	.0000	1	Weeping
0.0018	12.7	.0000	1	well-designed
0.0018	12.7	.0000	1	what-if
0.0018	12.7	.0000	1	whiffling
0.0018	12.7	.0000	1	womans's
0.0018	12.7	.0000	1	WOODY
0.0018	12.7	.0000	1	Wylie's

THE PRECEDING WORD TYPE OCCUPIES RANK 86700

U	SFI	D	F	Word Type
0.0018	12.7	.0000	1	Yachts
0.0018	12.7	.0000	1	yellow-ochre
0.0018	12.7	.0000	1	zebra's
0.0018	12.7	.0000	1	zigzags
0.0018	12.7	.0000	1	1515
0.0018	12.7	.0000	1	1684-1721
0.0018	12.7	.0000	1	1699-1779
0.0018	12.7	.0000	1	1703-1770
0.0018	12.7	.0000	1	1748-1825
0.0018	12.7	.0000	1	1780-1867
0.0018	12.7	.0000	1	1791-1824
0.0018	12.7	.0000	1	1796-1875
0.0018	12.7	.0000	1	1798-1863
0.0018	12.7	.0000	1	1812-1867
0.0018	12.7	.0000	1	1814-1874
0.0018	12.7	.0000	1	1840-1917
0.0018	12.7	.0000	1	1861-1944
0.0018	12.7	.0000	1	1881-1919
0.0018	12.7	.0000	1	3d
0.0018	12.7	.0000	1	54-55
0.0018	12.7	.0000	1	54-59
0.0005	07.3	.0000	3	Baptism
0.0004	05.5	.0000	2	JESUS
0.0004	05.5	.0000	2	LORD
0.0004	05.5	.0000	2	Parable
0.0004	05.5	.0000	2	Person
0.0004	05.5	.0000	2	Pharisees
0.0004	05.5	.0000	2	SAYS
0.0004	05.5	.0000	2	Sower
0.0002	02.5	.0000	1	anointed
0.0002	02.5	.0000	1	Apostles
0.0002	02.5	.0000	1	Granddaughter
0.0002	02.5	.0000	1	Incarnation
0.0002	02.5	.0000	1	Levi's
0.0002	02.5	.0000	1	prayer-songs
0.0002	02.5	.0000	1	publicans
0.0002	02.5	.0000	1	sacrament
0.0002	02.5	.0000	1	sanctified
0.0002	02.5	.0000	1	Sinless
0.0002	02.5	.0000	1	trespasses

Guide to the Frequency Distributions

The following pages contain frequency distributions for the total AHI Corpus, for each grade level, and for each subject category.

The frequency distributions were produced in the course of analyzing the data in terms of the log-normal model of word-frequency distribution described on pages xxi–xxviii.

Note that these frequency distributions are ordered from low frequency to high frequency. Each line of the frequency distributions contains the following information:

1. Rank(s) for the type or types with a given occurrence frequency. That is, when more than one type has a given occurrence frequency, a range of ranks is given. Rank is defined as the number that is assigned to a type if the types are ordered and numbered (1, 2, 3, . . .) from the type of highest frequency down to the types of lowest frequency.

2. The occurrence frequency. For the frequency distribution of the total Corpus, this has the same meaning as F in the Alphabetical and Rank Lists. For the frequency distribution of a particular division (grade or subject) of the Corpus, it has the same meaning as the frequency of the type in that division. It is the number of times that the type (or types) is (are) found in the total Corpus or division thereof. The first line of each frequency distribution refers to an occurrence frequency of 1; the last line contains the occurrence frequency for the word type of highest frequency.

3. SFI, the Standard Frequency Index. In these frequency distributions, SFI is used only as a convenient scale on which to report word probabilities, and only in that sense does it have the same meaning as the SFI values shown in the Alphabetical List and the Rank List. It is not adjusted for D. It is related to word probability, π, by the formula $\mathrm{SFI} = 10(\log_{10}\pi + 10)$ or $\pi = 10^{[.1(\mathrm{SFI}) - 10]}$. Thus, for $\mathrm{SFI} = 90$, $\pi = .1$; for $\mathrm{SFI} = 80$, $\pi = .01$, etc. The SFI given here is actually the value corresponding to the probability for the "upper bound" of the interval, i.e., at $(f + \frac{1}{2})$, where $f =$ the occurrence frequency. This is done to reflect the fact that the types in a given interval may be regarded as having probabilities ranging from $(f - .5)/N$ to $(f + .5)/N$, where N is the total number of tokens in the sample.

4. F, the number of types with the specified occurrence frequency. (Note that this is not the same F that is listed for given word types in the Alphabetical and Rank lists.) This F can be thought of as a frequency of frequencies.

5. Tokens. The number of tokens accounted for by these types. The number of tokens is the occurrence frequency multiplied by F (the number of types).

6. Cumulative tokens. This is the cumulated sum of the tokens in successive lines of the frequency distribution up to and including the given line. It is the number of tokens in the sample accounted for by all types with a given occurrence frequency or less. The value in the last line of the distribution is the total number of tokens in the sample.

7. Cumulative proportion of tokens. This is equal to the cumulative tokens divided by N.

8. Y, the normal deviate corresponding to the cumulative proportion of tokens. When the cumulative proportion is .5, the normal deviate is 0.0. The normal deviate is the number of standard deviations below $(-)$ or above $(+)$ the mean of a normal distribution up to which the frequency distribution contains a given proportional area (the total area of the normal distribution being set equal to 1). The normal deviate for

the last line of the frequency distribution is indicated as "+INF," that is, positive infinity, since the cumulative area at this point is 1.0000.

9. Cumulative types. This is the cumulative sum of the column headed "F" and hence of the number of types up to and including a given interval of the frequency distribution. The value in the last line gives the total number of types in the sample.

10. Cumulative proportion of types. This is the number of cumulative types divided by n, where n is the total number of types in the sample.

11. Z, the normal deviate corresponding to the cumulative proportion of types.

The normal-deviate values are useful in making plots of the distributions on lognormal coordinates, as explained on pages xxiv–xxv.

These frequency distributions can be used to obtain the rank of a given word type in the total AHI Corpus or a given section of it. Find the F or the category frequency in the Alphabetical List and look up this number in the column of the frequency distribution headed "Occ. F." Read off the rank or range of ranks.

These frequency distributions can also be used to determine what proportion of the sample is accounted for by the first X words in word frequency. Find X in the column headed "Rank" and read off the cumulative proportion in the *immediately preceding line*. Then subtract this number from 1.0000. For example, in the frequency distribution for the total Corpus, it can be found that the first 50 types account for $(1-.5954)$ or .4046 of the tokens.

Rank	Occ. F	SFI	F	Tokens	Cum. Tokens	Cum. P Tokens	Y	Cum. Types	Cum. P Types	Z
51663-86741	1	34.7	35079	35079	35079	0.0069	-2.46	35079	0.404411	-0.24
39748-51662	2	36.9	11915	23830	58909	0.0116	-2.27	46994	0.541774	0.10
33456-39747	3	38.4	6292	18876	77785	0.0153	-2.16	53286	0.614312	0.29
29280-33455	4	39.5	4176	16704	94489	0.0186	-2.08	57462	0.662455	0.42
26305-29279	5	40.3	2975	14875	109364	0.0215	-2.02	60437	0.696752	0.52
24035-26304	6	41.1	2270	13620	122984	0.0242	-1.97	62707	0.722922	0.59
22107-24034	7	41.7	1928	13496	136480	0.0268	-1.93	64635	0.745149	0.66
20573-22106	8	42.2	1534	12272	148752	0.0292	-1.89	66169	0.762834	0.72
19276-20572	9	42.7	1297	11673	160425	0.0315	-1.86	67466	0.777787	0.76
18182-19275	10	43.1	1094	10940	171365	0.0337	-1.83	68560	0.790399	0.81
17197-18181	11	43.5	985	10835	182200	0.0358	-1.80	69545	0.801755	0.85
16316-17196	12	43.9	881	10572	192772	0.0379	-1.78	70426	0.811911	0.88
15563-16315	13	44.2	753	9789	202561	0.0398	-1.75	71179	0.820592	0.92
14917-15562	14	44.5	646	9044	211605	0.0416	-1.73	71825	0.828040	0.95
14337-14916	15	44.8	580	8700	220305	0.0433	-1.71	72405	0.834726	0.97
13804-14336	16	45.1	533	8528	228833	0.0450	-1.70	72938	0.840871	1.00
13294-13803	17	45.4	510	8670	237503	0.0467	-1.68	73448	0.846751	1.02
12855-13293	18	45.6	439	7902	245405	0.0482	-1.66	73887	0.851812	1.04
12449-12854	19	45.8	406	7714	253119	0.0497	-1.65	74293	0.856492	1.06
12056-12448	20	46.1	393	7860	260979	0.0513	-1.63	74686	0.861023	1.08
11691-12055	21	46.3	365	7665	268644	0.0528	-1.62	75051	0.865231	1.10
11336-11690	22	46.5	355	7810	276454	0.0543	-1.60	75406	0.869324	1.12
11028-11335	23	46.6	308	7084	283538	0.0557	-1.59	75714	0.872874	1.14
10748-11027	24	46.8	280	6720	290258	0.0570	-1.58	75994	0.876102	1.16
10458-10747	25	47.0	290	7250	297508	0.0585	-1.57	76284	0.879446	1.17
10212-10457	26	47.2	246	6396	303904	0.0597	-1.56	76530	0.882282	1.19
9973-10211	27	47.3	239	6453	310357	0.0610	-1.55	76769	0.885037	1.20
9760- 9972	28	47.5	213	5964	316321	0.0622	-1.54	76982	0.887493	1.21
9551- 9759	29	47.6	209	6061	322382	0.0634	-1.53	77191	0.889902	1.23
9355- 9550	30	47.8	196	5880	328262	0.0645	-1.52	77387	0.892162	1.24
9170- 9354	31	47.9	185	5735	333997	0.0656	-1.51	77572	0.894295	1.25
8975- 9169	32	48.1	195	6240	340237	0.0669	-1.50	77767	0.896543	1.26
8795- 8974	33	48.2	180	5940	346177	0.0680	-1.49	77947	0.898618	1.27
8632- 8794	34	48.3	163	5542	351719	0.0691	-1.48	78110	0.900497	1.28
8473- 8631	35	48.4	159	5565	357284	0.0702	-1.47	78269	0.902330	1.29
8339- 8472	36	48.6	134	4824	362108	0.0712	-1.47	78403	0.903875	1.30
8185- 8338	37	48.7	154	5698	367806	0.0723	-1.46	78557	0.905650	1.31
8049- 8184	38	48.8	136	5168	372974	0.0733	-1.45	78693	0.907218	1.32
7925- 8048	39	48.9	124	4836	377810	0.0742	-1.44	78817	0.908648	1.33
7775- 7924	40	49.0	150	6000	383810	0.0754	-1.44	78967	0.910377	1.34
7661- 7774	41	49.1	114	4674	388484	0.0763	-1.43	79081	0.911691	1.35
7528- 7660	42	49.2	133	5586	394070	0.0774	-1.42	79214	0.913224	1.36
7404- 7527	43	49.3	124	5332	399402	0.0785	-1.42	79338	0.914654	1.37
7276- 7403	44	49.4	128	5632	405034	0.0796	-1.41	79466	0.916130	1.38
7172- 7275	45	49.5	104	4680	409714	0.0805	-1.40	79570	0.917329	1.39
7087- 7171	46	49.6	85	3910	413624	0.0813	-1.40	79655	0.918308	1.39
6992- 7086	47	49.7	95	4465	418089	0.0822	-1.39	79750	0.919404	1.40
6898- 6991	48	49.8	94	4512	422601	0.0830	-1.38	79844	0.920487	1.41
6798- 6897	49	49.9	100	4900	427501	0.0840	-1.38	79944	0.921640	1.42
6711- 6797	50	50.0	87	4350	431851	0.0849	-1.37	80031	0.922643	1.42
6618- 6710	51	50.1	93	4743	436594	0.0858	-1.37	80124	0.923715	1.43
6532- 6617	52	50.1	86	4472	441066	0.0867	-1.36	80210	0.924707	1.44
6443- 6531	53	50.2	89	4717	445783	0.0876	-1.36	80299	0.925733	1.44
6364- 6442	54	50.3	79	4266	450049	0.0884	-1.35	80378	0.926644	1.45
6275- 6363	55	50.4	89	4895	454944	0.0894	-1.34	80467	0.927670	1.46
6205- 6274	56	50.5	70	3920	458864	0.0902	-1.34	80537	0.928477	1.46
6117- 6204	57	50.5	88	5016	463880	0.0912	-1.33	80625	0.929491	1.47
6049- 6116	58	50.6	68	3944	467824	0.0919	-1.33	80693	0.930275	1.48
5969- 6048	59	50.7	80	4720	472544	0.0929	-1.32	80773	0.931197	1.48
5905- 5968	60	50.8	64	3840	476384	0.0936	-1.32	80837	0.931935	1.49
5837- 5904	61	50.8	68	4148	480532	0.0944	-1.31	80905	0.932719	1.50
5774- 5836	62	50.9	63	3906	484438	0.0952	-1.31	80968	0.933446	1.50
5708- 5773	63	51.0	66	4158	488596	0.0960	-1.30	81034	0.934206	1.51
5657- 5707	64	51.0	51	3264	491860	0.0967	-1.30	81085	0.934794	1.51
5612- 5656	65	51.1	45	2925	494785	0.0972	-1.30	81130	0.935313	1.52
5549- 5611	66	51.2	63	4158	498943	0.0980	-1.29	81193	0.936039	1.52
5489- 5548	67	51.2	60	4020	502963	0.0988	-1.29	81253	0.936731	1.53
5434- 5488	68	51.3	55	3740	506703	0.0996	-1.28	81308	0.937365	1.53
5371- 5433	69	51.4	63	4347	511050	0.1004	-1.28	81371	0.938092	1.54
5309- 5370	70	51.4	62	4340	515390	0.1013	-1.27	81433	0.938806	1.54
5250- 5308	71	51.5	59	4189	519579	0.1021	-1.27	81492	0.939487	1.55
5206- 5249	72	51.5	44	3168	522747	0.1027	-1.27	81536	0.939994	1.55
5141- 5205	73	51.6	65	4745	527492	0.1037	-1.26	81601	0.940743	1.56
5093- 5140	74	51.7	48	3552	531044	0.1044	-1.26	81649	0.941296	1.56
5048- 5092	75	51.7	45	3375	534419	0.1050	-1.25	81694	0.941815	1.57
5007- 5047	76	51.8	41	3116	537535	0.1056	-1.25	81735	0.942288	1.57
4957- 5006	77	51.8	50	3850	541385	0.1064	-1.25	81785	0.942864	1.58
4923- 4956	78	51.9	34	2652	544037	0.1069	-1.24	81819	0.943256	1.58
4880- 4922	79	51.9	43	3397	547434	0.1076	-1.24	81862	0.943752	1.59
4836- 4879	80	52.0	44	3520	550954	0.1083	-1.24	81906	0.944259	1.59
4788- 4835	81	52.0	48	3888	554842	0.1090	-1.23	81954	0.944813	1.60
4756- 4787	82	52.1	32	2624	557466	0.1095	-1.23	81986	0.945182	1.60
4712- 4755	83	52.2	44	3652	561118	0.1103	-1.23	82030	0.945689	1.60
4675- 4711	84	52.2	37	3108	564226	0.1109	-1.22	82067	0.946115	1.61
4628- 4674	85	52.3	47	3995	568221	0.1117	-1.22	82114	0.946657	1.61
4587- 4627	86	52.3	41	3526	571747	0.1124	-1.21	82155	0.947130	1.62
4543- 4586	87	52.4	44	3828	575575	0.1131	-1.21	82199	0.947637	1.62
4507- 4542	88	52.4	36	3168	578743	0.1137	-1.21	82235	0.948052	1.63
4470- 4506	89	52.5	37	3293	582036	0.1144	-1.20	82272	0.948479	1.63
4437- 4469	90	52.5	33	2970	585006	0.1150	-1.20	82305	0.948859	1.63
4412- 4436	91	52.5	25	2275	587281	0.1154	-1.20	82330	0.949147	1.64
4373- 4411	92	52.6	39	3588	590869	0.1161	-1.19	82369	0.949597	1.64
4334- 4372	93	52.6	39	3627	594496	0.1168	-1.19	82408	0.950047	1.65
4296- 4333	94	52.7	38	3572	598068	0.1175	-1.19	82446	0.950485	1.65
4263- 4295	95	52.7	33	3135	601203	0.1181	-1.18	82479	0.950865	1.65
4232- 4262	96	52.8	31	2976	604179	0.1187	-1.18	82510	0.951223	1.66
4203- 4231	97	52.8	29	2813	606992	0.1193	-1.18	82539	0.951557	1.66
4174- 4202	98	52.9	29	2842	609834	0.1198	-1.18	82568	0.951891	1.66
4146- 4173	99	52.9	28	2772	612606	0.1204	-1.17	82596	0.952214	1.67
4118- 4145	100	53.0	28	2800	615406	0.1209	-1.17	82624	0.952537	1.67
4096- 4117	101	53.0	22	2222	617628	0.1214	-1.17	82646	0.952790	1.67
4065- 4095	102	53.0	31	3162	620790	0.1220	-1.17	82677	0.953148	1.68
4036- 4064	103	53.1	29	2987	623777	0.1226	-1.16	82706	0.953482	1.68
4001- 4035	104	53.1	35	3640	627417	0.1233	-1.16	82741	0.953886	1.68
3978- 4000	105	53.2	23	2415	629832	0.1238	-1.16	82764	0.954151	1.69
3954- 3977	106	53.2	24	2544	632376	0.1243	-1.15	82788	0.954428	1.69
3927- 3953	107	53.2	27	2889	635265	0.1248	-1.15	82815	0.954739	1.69
3900- 3926	108	53.3	27	2916	638181	0.1254	-1.15	82842	0.955050	1.70
3872- 3899	109	53.3	28	3052	641233	0.1260	-1.15	82870	0.955373	1.70
3848- 3871	110	53.4	24	2640	643873	0.1265	-1.14	82894	0.955650	1.70
3828- 3847	111	53.4	20	2220	646093	0.1270	-1.14	82914	0.955880	1.70
3807- 3827	112	53.4	21	2352	648445	0.1274	-1.14	82935	0.956122	1.71
3786- 3806	113	53.5	21	2373	650818	0.1279	-1.14	82956	0.956364	1.71
3766- 3785	114	53.5	20	2280	653098	0.1283	-1.13	82976	0.956595	1.71
3743- 3765	115	53.6	23	2645	655743	0.1289	-1.13	82999	0.956860	1.72
3723- 3742	116	53.6	20	2320	658063	0.1293	-1.13	83019	0.957091	1.72

Rank	Occ. F	SFI	F	Tokens	Cum. Tokens	Cum. P Tokens	Y	Cum. Types	Cum. P Types	Z
3693- 3722	117	53.6	30	3510	661573	0.1300	-1.13	83049	0.957437	1.72
3669- 3692	118	53.7	24	2832	664405	0.1306	-1.12	83073	0.957713	1.72
3649- 3668	119	53.7	20	2380	666785	0.1310	-1.12	83093	0.957944	1.73
3633- 3648	120	53.7	16	1920	668705	0.1314	-1.12	83109	0.958128	1.73
3610- 3632	121	53.8	23	2783	671488	0.1320	-1.12	83132	0.958393	1.73
3594- 3609	122	53.8	16	1952	673440	0.1323	-1.12	83148	0.958578	1.73
3569- 3593	123	53.9	25	3075	676515	0.1329	-1.11	83173	0.958866	1.74
3549- 3568	124	53.9	20	2480	678995	0.1334	-1.11	83193	0.959097	1.74
3527- 3548	125	53.9	22	2750	681745	0.1340	-1.11	83215	0.959350	1.74
3502- 3526	126	54.0	25	3150	684895	0.1346	-1.10	83240	0.959638	1.75
3481- 3501	127	54.0	21	2667	687562	0.1351	-1.10	83261	0.959881	1.75
3461- 3480	128	54.0	20	2560	690122	0.1356	-1.10	83281	0.960111	1.75
3445- 3460	129	54.1	16	2064	692186	0.1360	-1.10	83297	0.960296	1.75
3423- 3444	130	54.1	22	2860	695046	0.1366	-1.10	83319	0.960549	1.76
3405- 3422	131	54.1	18	2358	697404	0.1370	-1.09	83337	0.960757	1.76
3378- 3404	132	54.2	27	3564	700968	0.1377	-1.09	83364	0.961068	1.76
3363- 3377	133	54.2	15	1995	702963	0.1381	-1.09	83379	0.961241	1.77
3341- 3362	134	54.2	22	2948	705911	0.1387	-1.09	83401	0.961495	1.77
3328- 3340	135	54.3	13	1755	707666	0.1391	-1.08	83414	0.961644	1.77
3307- 3327	136	54.3	21	2856	710522	0.1396	-1.08	83435	0.961887	1.77
3289- 3306	137	54.3	18	2466	712988	0.1401	-1.08	83453	0.962094	1.78
3274- 3288	138	54.3	15	2070	715058	0.1405	-1.08	83468	0.962267	1.78
3250- 3273	139	54.4	24	3336	718394	0.1412	-1.08	83492	0.962544	1.78
3226- 3249	140	54.4	24	3360	721754	0.1418	-1.07	83516	0.962820	1.78
3213- 3225	141	54.4	13	1833	723587	0.1422	-1.07	83529	0.962970	1.79
3201- 3212	142	54.5	12	1704	725291	0.1425	-1.07	83541	0.963109	1.79
3178- 3200	143	54.5	23	3289	728580	0.1432	-1.07	83564	0.963374	1.79
3167- 3177	144	54.5	11	1584	730164	0.1435	-1.06	83575	0.963500	1.79
3150- 3166	145	54.6	17	2465	732629	0.1440	-1.06	83592	0.963696	1.80
3130- 3149	146	54.6	20	2920	735549	0.1445	-1.06	83612	0.963927	1.80
3109- 3129	147	54.6	21	3087	738636	0.1452	-1.06	83633	0.964169	1.80
3098- 3108	148	54.7	11	1628	740264	0.1455	-1.06	83644	0.964296	1.80
3081- 3097	149	54.7	17	2533	742797	0.1460	-1.05	83661	0.964492	1.81
3065- 3080	150	54.7	16	2400	745197	0.1464	-1.05	83677	0.964676	1.81
3047- 3064	151	54.7	18	2718	747915	0.1470	-1.05	83695	0.964884	1.81
3027- 3046	152	54.8	20	3040	750955	0.1476	-1.05	83715	0.965115	1.81
3010- 3026	153	54.8	17	2601	753556	0.1481	-1.04	83732	0.965311	1.82
2998- 3009	154	54.8	12	1848	755404	0.1484	-1.04	83744	0.965449	1.82
2983- 2997	155	54.9	15	2325	757729	0.1489	-1.04	83759	0.965622	1.82
2969- 2982	156	54.9	14	2184	759913	0.1493	-1.04	83773	0.965783	1.82
2945- 2968	157	54.9	24	3768	763681	0.1501	-1.04	83797	0.966060	1.83
2934- 2944	158	54.9	11	1738	765419	0.1504	-1.03	83808	0.966187	1.83
2916- 2933	159	55.0	18	2862	768281	0.1510	-1.03	83826	0.966394	1.83
2904- 2915	160	55.0	12	1920	770201	0.1514	-1.03	83838	0.966533	1.83
2890- 2903	161	55.0	14	2254	772455	0.1518	-1.03	83852	0.966694	1.83
2873- 2889	162	55.0	17	2754	775209	0.1523	-1.03	83869	0.966890	1.84
2868- 2872	163	55.1	5	815	776024	0.1525	-1.03	83874	0.966948	1.84
2849- 2867	164	55.1	19	3116	779140	0.1531	-1.02	83893	0.967167	1.84
2839- 2848	165	55.1	10	1650	780790	0.1534	-1.02	83903	0.967282	1.84
2824- 2838	166	55.1	15	2490	783280	0.1539	-1.02	83918	0.967455	1.84
2807- 2823	167	55.2	17	2839	786119	0.1545	-1.02	83935	0.967651	1.85
2794- 2806	168	55.2	13	2184	788303	0.1549	-1.02	83948	0.967801	1.85
2783- 2793	169	55.2	11	1859	790162	0.1553	-1.01	83959	0.967927	1.85
2769- 2782	170	55.3	14	2380	792542	0.1557	-1.01	83973	0.968089	1.85
2756- 2768	171	55.3	13	2223	794765	0.1562	-1.01	83986	0.968239	1.86
2744- 2755	172	55.3	12	2064	796829	0.1566	-1.01	83998	0.968377	1.86
2730- 2743	173	55.3	14	2422	799251	0.1571	-1.01	84012	0.968539	1.86
2718- 2729	174	55.4	12	2088	801339	0.1575	-1.00	84024	0.968677	1.86
2703- 2717	175	55.4	15	2625	803964	0.1580	-1.00	84039	0.968850	1.86
2693- 2702	176	55.4	10	1760	805724	0.1583	-1.00	84049	0.968965	1.87
2689- 2692	177	55.4	4	708	806432	0.1585	-1.00	84053	0.969011	1.87
2678- 2688	178	55.5	11	1958	808390	0.1589	-1.00	84064	0.969138	1.87
2664- 2677	179	55.5	14	2506	810896	0.1594	-1.00	84078	0.969299	1.87
2652- 2663	180	55.5	12	2160	813056	0.1598	-1.00	84090	0.969438	1.87
2640- 2651	181	55.5	12	2172	815228	0.1602	-0.99	84102	0.969576	1.87
2625- 2639	182	55.5	15	2730	817958	0.1607	-0.99	84117	0.969749	1.88
2615- 2624	183	55.6	10	1830	819788	0.1611	-0.99	84127	0.969864	1.88
2599- 2614	184	55.6	16	2944	822732	0.1617	-0.99	84143	0.970049	1.88
2589- 2598	185	55.6	10	1850	824582	0.1620	-0.99	84153	0.970164	1.88
2581- 2588	186	55.6	8	1488	826070	0.1623	-0.98	84161	0.970256	1.88
2575- 2580	187	55.7	6	1122	827192	0.1626	-0.98	84167	0.970325	1.89
2565- 2574	188	55.7	10	1880	829072	0.1629	-0.98	84177	0.970441	1.89
2551- 2564	189	55.7	14	2646	831718	0.1634	-0.98	84191	0.970602	1.89
2544- 2550	190	55.7	7	1330	833048	0.1637	-0.98	84198	0.970683	1.89
2530- 2543	191	55.8	14	2674	835722	0.1642	-0.98	84212	0.970844	1.89
2523- 2529	192	55.8	7	1344	837066	0.1645	-0.98	84219	0.970925	1.89
2512- 2522	193	55.8	11	2123	839189	0.1649	-0.97	84230	0.971052	1.90
2496- 2511	194	55.8	16	3104	842293	0.1655	-0.97	84246	0.971236	1.90
2488- 2495	195	55.8	8	1560	843853	0.1658	-0.97	84254	0.971328	1.90
2477- 2487	196	55.9	11	2156	846009	0.1663	-0.97	84265	0.971455	1.90
2468- 2476	197	55.9	9	1773	847782	0.1666	-0.97	84274	0.971559	1.90
2449- 2467	198	55.9	19	3762	851544	0.1673	-0.96	84293	0.971778	1.91
2440- 2448	199	55.9	9	1791	853335	0.1677	-0.96	84302	0.971882	1.91
2430- 2439	200	56.0	10	2000	855335	0.1681	-0.96	84312	0.971997	1.91
2421- 2429	201	56.0	9	1809	857144	0.1684	-0.96	84321	0.972101	1.91
2410- 2420	202	56.0	11	2222	859366	0.1689	-0.96	84332	0.972228	1.91
2403- 2409	203	56.0	7	1421	860787	0.1692	-0.96	84339	0.972308	1.92
2389- 2402	204	56.0	14	2856	863643	0.1697	-0.96	84353	0.972470	1.92
2382- 2388	205	56.1	7	1435	865078	0.1700	-0.95	84360	0.972550	1.92
2371- 2381	206	56.1	11	2266	867344	0.1704	-0.95	84371	0.972677	1.92
2361- 2370	207	56.1	10	2070	869414	0.1709	-0.95	84381	0.972793	1.92
2355- 2360	208	56.1	6	1248	870662	0.1711	-0.95	84387	0.972862	1.92
2341- 2354	209	56.1	14	2926	873588	0.1717	-0.95	84401	0.973023	1.93
2333- 2340	210	56.2	8	1680	875268	0.1720	-0.95	84409	0.973115	1.93
2327- 2332	211	56.2	6	1266	876534	0.1723	-0.95	84415	0.973185	1.93
2319- 2326	212	56.2	8	1696	878230	0.1726	-0.94	84423	0.973277	1.93
2310- 2318	213	56.2	9	1917	880147	0.1730	-0.94	84432	0.973381	1.93
2301- 2309	214	56.2	9	1926	882073	0.1733	-0.94	84441	0.973484	1.93
2291- 2300	215	56.3	10	2150	884223	0.1738	-0.94	84451	0.973600	1.94
2280- 2290	216	56.3	11	2376	886599	0.1742	-0.94	84462	0.973726	1.94
2273- 2279	217	56.3	7	1519	888118	0.1745	-0.94	84469	0.973807	1.94
2268- 2272	218	56.3	5	1090	889208	0.1747	-0.94	84474	0.973865	1.94
2260- 2267	219	56.3	8	1752	890960	0.1751	-0.93	84482	0.973957	1.94
2255- 2259	220	56.4	5	1100	892060	0.1753	-0.93	84487	0.974015	1.94
2246- 2254	221	56.4	9	1989	894049	0.1757	-0.93	84496	0.974118	1.95
2239- 2245	222	56.4	7	1554	895603	0.1760	-0.93	84503	0.974199	1.95
2230- 2238	223	56.4	9	2007	897610	0.1764	-0.93	84512	0.974303	1.95
2224- 2229	224	56.4	6	1344	898954	0.1767	-0.93	84518	0.974372	1.95
2212- 2223	225	56.5	12	2700	901654	0.1772	-0.93	84530	0.974510	1.95
2203- 2211	226	56.5	9	2034	903688	0.1776	-0.92	84539	0.974614	1.95
2193- 2202	227	56.5	10	2270	905958	0.1780	-0.92	84549	0.974729	1.96
2186- 2192	228	56.5	7	1596	907554	0.1783	-0.92	84556	0.974810	1.96
2178- 2185	229	56.5	8	1832	909386	0.1787	-0.92	84564	0.974902	1.96
2170- 2177	230	56.6	8	1840	911226	0.1791	-0.92	84572	0.974994	1.96
2162- 2169	231	56.6	8	1848	913074	0.1794	-0.92	84580	0.975087	1.96
2156- 2161	232	56.6	6	1392	914466	0.1797	-0.92	84586	0.975156	1.96

Rank	Occ. F	SFI	F	Tokens	Cum. Tokens	Cum. P Tokens	Y	Cum. Types	Cum. P Types	Z
2147- 2155	233	56.6	9	2097	916563	0.1801	-0.91	84595	0.975260	1.96
2140- 2146	234	56.6	7	1638	918201	0.1804	-0.91	84602	0.975340	1.97
2134- 2139	235	56.7	6	1410	919611	0.1807	-0.91	84608	0.975410	1.97
2125- 2133	236	56.7	9	2124	921735	0.1811	-0.91	84617	0.975513	1.97
2121- 2124	237	56.7	4	948	922683	0.1813	-0.91	84621	0.975559	1.97
2114- 2120	238	56.7	7	1666	924349	0.1816	-0.91	84628	0.975640	1.97
2108- 2113	239	56.7	6	1434	925783	0.1819	-0.91	84634	0.975709	1.97
2097- 2107	240	56.7	11	2640	928423	0.1824	-0.91	84645	0.975836	1.97
2088- 2096	241	56.8	9	2169	930592	0.1829	-0.90	84654	0.975940	1.98
2077- 2087	242	56.8	11	2662	933254	0.1834	-0.90	84665	0.976067	1.98
2068- 2076	243	56.8	9	2187	935441	0.1838	-0.90	84674	0.976170	1.98
2058- 2067	244	56.8	10	2440	937881	0.1843	-0.90	84684	0.976286	1.98
2053- 2057	245	56.8	5	1225	939106	0.1845	-0.90	84689	0.976343	1.98
2045- 2052	246	56.9	8	1968	941074	0.1849	-0.90	84697	0.976436	1.99
2034- 2044	247	56.9	11	2717	943791	0.1855	-0.89	84708	0.976562	1.99
2024- 2033	248	56.9	10	2480	946271	0.1860	-0.89	84718	0.976678	1.99
2014- 2023	249	56.9	10	2490	948761	0.1864	-0.89	84728	0.976793	1.99
2010- 2013	250	56.9	4	1000	949761	0.1866	-0.89	84732	0.976839	1.99
2004- 2009	251	56.9	6	1506	951267	0.1869	-0.89	84738	0.976908	1.99
1996- 2003	252	57.0	8	2016	953283	0.1873	-0.89	84746	0.977000	2.00
1987- 1995	253	57.0	9	2277	955560	0.1878	-0.89	84755	0.977104	2.00
1981- 1986	254	57.0	6	1524	957084	0.1881	-0.88	84761	0.977173	2.00
1973- 1980	255	57.0	8	2040	959124	0.1885	-0.88	84769	0.977266	2.00
1965- 1972	256	57.0	8	2048	961172	0.1889	-0.88	84777	0.977358	2.00
1952- 1964	257	57.0	13	3341	964513	0.1895	-0.88	84790	0.977508	2.00
1946- 1951	258	57.1	6	1548	966061	0.1898	-0.88	84796	0.977577	2.01
1937- 1945	259	57.1	9	2331	968392	0.1903	-0.88	84805	0.977681	2.01
1931- 1936	260	57.1	6	1560	969952	0.1906	-0.88	84811	0.977750	2.01
1929- 1930	261	57.1	2	522	970474	0.1907	-0.88	84813	0.977773	2.01
1923- 1928	262	57.1	6	1572	972046	0.1910	-0.87	84819	0.977842	2.01
1916- 1922	263	57.1	7	1841	973887	0.1914	-0.87	84826	0.977923	2.01
1909- 1915	264	57.2	7	1848	975735	0.1917	-0.87	84833	0.978003	2.01
1904- 1908	265	57.2	5	1325	977060	0.1920	-0.87	84838	0.978061	2.02
1899- 1903	266	57.2	5	1330	978390	0.1923	-0.87	84843	0.978119	2.02
1893- 1898	267	57.2	6	1602	979992	0.1926	-0.87	84849	0.978188	2.02
1892	268	57.2	1	268	980260	0.1926	-0.87	84850	0.978199	2.02
1889- 1891	269	57.2	3	807	981067	0.1928	-0.87	84853	0.978234	2.02
1883- 1888	270	57.3	6	1620	982687	0.1931	-0.87	84859	0.978303	2.02
1877- 1882	271	57.3	6	1626	984313	0.1934	-0.87	84865	0.978372	2.02
1875- 1876	272	57.3	2	544	984857	0.1935	-0.86	84867	0.978395	2.02
1872- 1874	273	57.3	3	819	985676	0.1937	-0.86	84870	0.978430	2.02
1868- 1871	274	57.3	4	1096	986772	0.1939	-0.86	84874	0.978476	2.02
1859- 1867	275	57.3	9	2475	989247	0.1944	-0.86	84883	0.978580	2.03
1854- 1858	276	57.4	5	1380	990627	0.1947	-0.86	84888	0.978638	2.03
1851- 1853	277	57.4	3	831	991458	0.1948	-0.86	84891	0.978672	2.03
1840- 1850	278	57.4	11	3058	994516	0.1954	-0.86	84902	0.978799	2.03
1834- 1839	279	57.4	6	1674	996190	0.1958	-0.86	84908	0.978868	2.03
1830- 1833	280	57.4	4	1120	997310	0.1960	-0.86	84912	0.978914	2.03
1824- 1829	281	57.4	6	1686	998996	0.1963	-0.85	84918	0.978983	2.03
1819- 1823	282	57.4	5	1410	1000406	0.1966	-0.85	84923	0.979041	2.03
1810- 1818	283	57.5	9	2547	1002953	0.1971	-0.85	84932	0.979145	2.04
1801- 1809	284	57.5	9	2556	1005509	0.1976	-0.85	84941	0.979249	2.04
1799- 1800	285	57.5	2	570	1006079	0.1977	-0.85	84943	0.979272	2.04
1794- 1798	286	57.5	5	1430	1007509	0.1980	-0.85	84948	0.979329	2.04
1790- 1793	287	57.5	4	1148	1008657	0.1982	-0.85	84952	0.979375	2.04
1786- 1789	288	57.5	4	1152	1009809	0.1984	-0.85	84956	0.979421	2.04
1784- 1785	289	57.6	2	578	1010387	0.1986	-0.85	84958	0.979445	2.04
1780- 1783	290	57.6	4	1160	1011547	0.1988	-0.85	84962	0.979491	2.04
1775- 1779	291	57.6	5	1455	1013002	0.1991	-0.84	84967	0.979548	2.04
1768- 1774	292	57.6	7	2044	1015046	0.1995	-0.84	84974	0.979629	2.05
1764- 1767	293	57.6	4	1172	1016218	0.1997	-0.84	84978	0.979675	2.05
1757- 1763	294	57.6	7	2058	1018276	0.2001	-0.84	84985	0.979756	2.05
1755- 1756	295	57.6	2	590	1018866	0.2002	-0.84	84987	0.979779	2.05
1753- 1754	296	57.7	2	592	1019458	0.2003	-0.84	84989	0.979802	2.05
1750- 1752	297	57.7	3	891	1020349	0.2005	-0.84	84992	0.979837	2.05
1744- 1749	298	57.7	6	1788	1022137	0.2009	-0.84	84998	0.979906	2.05
1742- 1743	299	57.7	2	598	1022735	0.2010	-0.84	85000	0.979929	2.05
1737- 1741	300	57.7	5	1500	1024235	0.2013	-0.84	85005	0.979986	2.05
1732- 1736	301	57.7	5	1505	1025740	0.2016	-0.84	85010	0.980044	2.05
1729- 1731	302	57.7	3	906	1026646	0.2017	-0.84	85013	0.980079	2.06
1723- 1728	303	57.8	6	1818	1028464	0.2021	-0.83	85019	0.980148	2.06
1719- 1722	304	57.8	4	1216	1029680	0.2023	-0.83	85023	0.980194	2.06
1712- 1718	305	57.8	7	2135	1031815	0.2028	-0.83	85030	0.980275	2.06
1709- 1711	306	57.8	3	918	1032733	0.2029	-0.83	85033	0.980309	2.06
1703- 1708	307	57.8	6	1842	1034575	0.2033	-0.83	85039	0.980378	2.06
1696- 1702	308	57.8	7	2156	1036731	0.2037	-0.83	85046	0.980459	2.06
1694- 1695	309	57.8	2	618	1037349	0.2039	-0.83	85048	0.980482	2.06
1691- 1693	310	57.9	3	930	1038279	0.2040	-0.83	85051	0.980517	2.06
1690	311	57.9	1	311	1038590	0.2041	-0.83	85052	0.980528	2.06
1684- 1689	312	57.9	6	1872	1040462	0.2045	-0.83	85058	0.980597	2.07
1682- 1683	313	57.9	2	626	1041088	0.2046	-0.83	85060	0.980620	2.07
1675- 1681	314	57.9	7	2198	1043286	0.2050	-0.82	85067	0.980701	2.07
1671- 1674	315	57.9	4	1260	1044546	0.2053	-0.82	85071	0.980747	2.07
1668- 1670	316	57.9	3	948	1045494	0.2055	-0.82	85074	0.980782	2.07
1662- 1667	317	58.0	6	1902	1047396	0.2058	-0.82	85080	0.980851	2.07
1657- 1661	318	58.0	5	1590	1048986	0.2061	-0.82	85085	0.980909	2.07
1652- 1656	319	58.0	5	1595	1050581	0.2065	-0.82	85090	0.980966	2.07
1647- 1651	320	58.0	5	1600	1052181	0.2068	-0.82	85095	0.981024	2.08
1642- 1646	321	58.0	5	1605	1053786	0.2071	-0.82	85100	0.981082	2.08
1639- 1641	322	58.0	3	966	1054752	0.2073	-0.82	85103	0.981116	2.08
1636- 1638	323	58.0	3	969	1055721	0.2075	-0.82	85106	0.981151	2.08
1630- 1635	324	58.0	6	1944	1057665	0.2078	-0.81	85112	0.981220	2.08
1624- 1629	325	58.1	6	1950	1059615	0.2082	-0.81	85118	0.981289	2.08
1622- 1623	326	58.1	2	652	1060267	0.2084	-0.81	85120	0.981312	2.08
1615- 1621	327	58.1	7	2289	1062556	0.2088	-0.81	85127	0.981393	2.08
1611- 1614	328	58.1	4	1312	1063868	0.2091	-0.81	85131	0.981439	2.08
1608- 1610	329	58.1	3	987	1064855	0.2093	-0.81	85134	0.981474	2.09
1602- 1607	330	58.1	6	1980	1066835	0.2096	-0.81	85140	0.981543	2.09
1594- 1601	331	58.1	8	2648	1069483	0.2102	-0.81	85148	0.981635	2.09
1589- 1593	332	58.2	5	1660	1071143	0.2105	-0.80	85153	0.981693	2.09
1587- 1588	333	58.2	2	666	1071809	0.2106	-0.80	85155	0.981716	2.09
1583- 1586	334	58.2	4	1336	1073145	0.2109	-0.80	85159	0.981762	2.09
1577- 1582	335	58.2	6	2010	1075155	0.2113	-0.80	85165	0.981831	2.09
1575- 1576	336	58.2	2	672	1075827	0.2114	-0.80	85167	0.981854	2.09
1567- 1574	337	58.2	8	2696	1078523	0.2119	-0.80	85175	0.981946	2.10
1563- 1566	338	58.2	4	1352	1079875	0.2122	-0.80	85179	0.981992	2.10
1556- 1562	339	58.2	7	2373	1082248	0.2127	-0.80	85186	0.982073	2.10
1551- 1555	340	58.3	5	1700	1083948	0.2130	-0.80	85191	0.982131	2.10
1547- 1550	341	58.3	4	1364	1085312	0.2133	-0.80	85195	0.982177	2.10
1543- 1546	342	58.3	4	1368	1086680	0.2135	-0.79	85199	0.982223	2.10
1536- 1542	343	58.3	7	2401	1089081	0.2140	-0.79	85206	0.982304	2.10
1528- 1535	344	58.3	8	2752	1091833	0.2146	-0.79	85214	0.982396	2.11
1523- 1527	345	58.3	5	1725	1093558	0.2149	-0.79	85219	0.982453	2.11
1515- 1522	346	58.3	8	2768	1096326	0.2154	-0.79	85227	0.982546	2.11
1508- 1514	347	58.3	7	2429	1098755	0.2159	-0.79	85234	0.982626	2.11
1505- 1507	348	58.4	3	1044	1099799	0.2161	-0.79	85237	0.982661	2.11

Rank	Occ. F	SFI	F	Tokens	Cum. Tokens	Cum. P Tokens	Y	Cum. Types	Cum. P Types	Z
1501- 1504	349	58.4	4	1396	1101195	0.2164	-0.78	85241	0.982707	2.11
1498- 1500	350	58.4	3	1050	1102245	0.2166	-0.78	85244	0.982742	2.11
1496- 1497	351	58.4	2	702	1102947	0.2167	-0.78	85246	0.982765	2.11
1493- 1495	352	58.4	3	1056	1104003	0.2170	-0.78	85249	0.982799	2.12
1490- 1492	353	58.4	3	1059	1105062	0.2172	-0.78	85252	0.982834	2.12
1485- 1489	354	58.4	5	1770	1106832	0.2175	-0.78	85257	0.982892	2.12
1483- 1484	355	58.4	2	710	1107542	0.2176	-0.78	85259	0.982915	2.12
1478- 1482	356	58.5	5	1780	1109322	0.2180	-0.78	85264	0.982972	2.12
1474- 1477	357	58.5	4	1428	1110750	0.2183	-0.78	85268	0.983018	2.12
1471- 1473	358	58.5	3	1074	1111824	0.2185	-0.78	85271	0.983053	2.12
1467- 1470	359	58.5	4	1436	1113260	0.2188	-0.78	85275	0.983099	2.12
1461- 1466	360	58.5	6	2160	1115420	0.2192	-0.77	85281	0.983168	2.12
1455- 1460	361	58.5	6	2166	1117586	0.2196	-0.77	85287	0.983237	2.13
1452- 1454	362	58.5	3	1086	1118672	0.2198	-0.77	85290	0.983272	2.13
1450- 1451	363	58.5	2	726	1119398	0.2200	-0.77	85292	0.983295	2.13
1443- 1449	364	58.6	7	2548	1121946	0.2205	-0.77	85299	0.983376	2.13
1442	365	58.6	1	365	1122311	0.2205	-0.77	85300	0.983387	2.13
1437- 1441	367	58.6	5	1835	1124146	0.2209	-0.77	85305	0.983445	2.13
1435- 1436	368	58.6	2	736	1124882	0.2211	-0.77	85307	0.983468	2.13
1433- 1434	369	58.6	2	738	1125620	0.2212	-0.77	85309	0.983491	2.13
1427- 1432	370	58.6	6	2220	1127840	0.2216	-0.77	85315	0.983560	2.13
1422- 1426	371	58.6	5	1855	1129695	0.2220	-0.77	85320	0.983618	2.13
1421	372	58.6	1	372	1130067	0.2221	-0.77	85321	0.983629	2.14
1419- 1420	373	58.7	2	746	1130813	0.2222	-0.76	85323	0.983652	2.14
1417- 1418	374	58.7	2	748	1131561	0.2224	-0.76	85325	0.983676	2.14
1415- 1416	375	58.7	2	750	1132311	0.2225	-0.76	85327	0.983699	2.14
1411- 1414	376	58.7	4	1504	1133815	0.2228	-0.76	85331	0.983745	2.14
1409- 1410	377	58.7	2	754	1134569	0.2230	-0.76	85333	0.983768	2.14
1403- 1408	378	58.7	6	2268	1136837	0.2234	-0.76	85339	0.983837	2.14
1396- 1402	379	58.7	7	2653	1139490	0.2239	-0.76	85346	0.983918	2.14
1394- 1395	380	58.7	2	760	1140250	0.2241	-0.76	85348	0.983941	2.14
1391- 1393	381	58.7	3	1143	1141393	0.2243	-0.76	85351	0.983975	2.14
1389- 1390	383	58.8	2	766	1142159	0.2244	-0.76	85353	0.983998	2.14
1388	384	58.8	1	384	1142543	0.2245	-0.76	85354	0.984010	2.14
1386- 1387	385	58.8	2	770	1143313	0.2247	-0.76	85356	0.984033	2.15
1381- 1385	386	58.8	5	1930	1145243	0.2251	-0.76	85361	0.984091	2.15
1378- 1380	387	58.8	3	1161	1146404	0.2253	-0.75	85364	0.984125	2.15
1376- 1377	389	58.8	2	778	1147182	0.2254	-0.75	85366	0.984148	2.15
1372- 1375	390	58.9	4	1560	1148742	0.2257	-0.75	85370	0.984194	2.15
1368- 1371	391	58.9	4	1564	1150306	0.2261	-0.75	85374	0.984240	2.15
1365- 1367	392	58.9	3	1176	1151482	0.2263	-0.75	85377	0.984275	2.15
1360- 1364	393	58.9	5	1965	1153447	0.2267	-0.75	85382	0.984333	2.15
1358- 1359	394	58.9	2	788	1154235	0.2268	-0.75	85384	0.984356	2.15
1356- 1357	395	58.9	2	790	1155025	0.2270	-0.75	85386	0.984379	2.15
1351- 1355	396	58.9	5	1980	1157005	0.2274	-0.75	85391	0.984436	2.16
1349- 1350	397	58.9	2	794	1157799	0.2275	-0.75	85393	0.984459	2.16
1346- 1348	398	58.9	3	1194	1158993	0.2278	-0.75	85396	0.984494	2.16
1340- 1345	399	58.9	6	2394	1161387	0.2282	-0.74	85402	0.984563	2.16
1339	400	59.0	1	400	1161787	0.2283	-0.74	85403	0.984575	2.16
1336- 1338	401	59.0	3	1203	1162990	0.2285	-0.74	85406	0.984609	2.16
1333- 1335	402	59.0	3	1206	1164196	0.2288	-0.74	85409	0.984644	2.16
1326- 1332	403	59.0	7	2821	1167017	0.2293	-0.74	85416	0.984725	2.16
1323- 1325	404	59.0	3	1212	1168229	0.2296	-0.74	85419	0.984759	2.16
1319- 1322	406	59.0	4	1624	1169853	0.2299	-0.74	85423	0.984805	2.16
1316- 1318	407	59.0	3	1221	1171074	0.2301	-0.74	85426	0.984840	2.17
1313- 1315	409	59.1	3	1227	1172301	0.2304	-0.74	85429	0.984874	2.17
1308- 1312	410	59.1	5	2050	1174351	0.2308	-0.74	85434	0.984932	2.17
1302- 1307	411	59.1	6	2466	1176817	0.2313	-0.73	85440	0.985001	2.17
1297- 1301	412	59.1	5	2060	1178877	0.2317	-0.73	85445	0.985059	2.17
1292- 1296	413	59.1	5	2065	1180942	0.2321	-0.73	85450	0.985117	2.17
1287- 1291	414	59.1	5	2070	1183012	0.2325	-0.73	85455	0.985174	2.17
1286	415	59.1	1	415	1183427	0.2326	-0.73	85456	0.985186	2.18
1283- 1285	416	59.1	3	1248	1184675	0.2328	-0.73	85459	0.985220	2.18
1282	417	59.1	1	417	1185092	0.2329	-0.73	85460	0.985232	2.18
1278- 1281	418	59.2	4	1672	1186764	0.2332	-0.73	85464	0.985278	2.18
1274- 1277	419	59.2	4	1676	1188440	0.2335	-0.73	85468	0.985324	2.18
1270- 1273	420	59.2	4	1680	1190120	0.2339	-0.73	85472	0.985370	2.18
1267- 1269	421	59.2	3	1263	1191383	0.2341	-0.73	85475	0.985405	2.18
1264- 1266	422	59.2	3	1266	1192649	0.2344	-0.72	85478	0.985439	2.18
1262- 1263	423	59.2	2	846	1193495	0.2345	-0.72	85480	0.985462	2.18
1259- 1261	424	59.2	3	1272	1194767	0.2348	-0.72	85483	0.985497	2.18
1256- 1258	425	59.2	3	1275	1196042	0.2350	-0.72	85486	0.985532	2.18
1255	426	59.2	1	426	1196468	0.2351	-0.72	85487	0.985543	2.18
1253- 1254	427	59.2	2	854	1197322	0.2353	-0.72	85489	0.985566	2.19
1250- 1252	428	59.3	3	1284	1198606	0.2355	-0.72	85492	0.985601	2.19
1248- 1249	429	59.3	2	858	1199464	0.2357	-0.72	85494	0.985624	2.19
1245- 1247	430	59.3	3	1290	1200754	0.2360	-0.72	85497	0.985658	2.19
1244	431	59.3	1	431	1201185	0.2360	-0.72	85498	0.985670	2.19
1239- 1243	432	59.3	5	2160	1203345	0.2365	-0.72	85503	0.985728	2.19
1237- 1238	433	59.3	2	866	1204211	0.2366	-0.72	85505	0.985751	2.19
1236	435	59.3	1	435	1204646	0.2367	-0.72	85506	0.985762	2.19
1235	436	59.3	1	436	1205082	0.2368	-0.72	85507	0.985774	2.19
1232- 1234	437	59.3	3	1311	1206393	0.2371	-0.72	85510	0.985808	2.19
1231	438	59.4	1	438	1206831	0.2372	-0.72	85511	0.985820	2.19
1229- 1230	439	59.4	2	878	1207709	0.2373	-0.71	85513	0.985843	2.19
1226- 1228	440	59.4	3	1320	1209029	0.2376	-0.71	85516	0.985877	2.19
1224- 1225	442	59.4	2	884	1209913	0.2378	-0.71	85518	0.985901	2.19
1220- 1223	443	59.4	4	1772	1211685	0.2381	-0.71	85522	0.985947	2.20
1217- 1219	444	59.4	3	1332	1213017	0.2384	-0.71	85525	0.985981	2.20
1214- 1216	445	59.4	3	1335	1214352	0.2386	-0.71	85528	0.986016	2.20
1212- 1213	446	59.4	2	892	1215244	0.2388	-0.71	85530	0.986039	2.20
1208- 1211	447	59.4	4	1788	1217032	0.2392	-0.71	85534	0.986085	2.20
1207	449	59.5	1	449	1217481	0.2393	-0.71	85535	0.986097	2.20
1206	450	59.5	1	450	1217931	0.2393	-0.71	85536	0.986108	2.20
1203- 1205	451	59.5	3	1353	1219284	0.2396	-0.71	85539	0.986143	2.20
1202	452	59.5	1	452	1219736	0.2397	-0.71	85540	0.986154	2.20
1201	453	59.5	1	453	1220189	0.2398	-0.71	85541	0.986166	2.20
1200	454	59.5	1	454	1220643	0.2399	-0.71	85542	0.986177	2.20
1198- 1199	455	59.5	2	910	1221553	0.2401	-0.71	85544	0.986200	2.20
1197	456	59.5	1	456	1222009	0.2401	-0.71	85545	0.986212	2.20
1193- 1196	457	59.5	4	1828	1223837	0.2405	-0.70	85549	0.986258	2.20
1191- 1192	458	59.5	2	916	1224753	0.2407	-0.70	85551	0.986281	2.21
1188- 1190	459	59.6	3	1377	1226130	0.2410	-0.70	85554	0.986316	2.21
1184- 1187	460	59.6	4	1840	1227970	0.2413	-0.70	85558	0.986362	2.21
1177- 1183	461	59.6	7	3227	1231197	0.2419	-0.70	85565	0.986442	2.21
1173- 1176	462	59.6	4	1848	1233045	0.2423	-0.70	85569	0.986488	2.21
1172	463	59.6	1	463	1233508	0.2424	-0.70	85570	0.986500	2.21
1171	464	59.6	1	464	1233972	0.2425	-0.70	85571	0.986512	2.21
1168- 1170	465	59.6	3	1395	1235367	0.2428	-0.70	85574	0.986546	2.21
1167	467	59.6	1	467	1235834	0.2429	-0.70	85575	0.986558	2.21
1165- 1166	468	59.6	2	936	1236770	0.2430	-0.70	85577	0.986581	2.21
1159- 1164	469	59.7	6	2814	1239584	0.2436	-0.69	85583	0.986650	2.22
1158	470	59.7	1	470	1240054	0.2437	-0.69	85584	0.986661	2.22
1156- 1157	471	59.7	2	942	1240996	0.2439	-0.69	85586	0.986684	2.22
1151- 1155	473	59.7	5	2365	1243361	0.2443	-0.69	85591	0.986742	2.22
1149- 1150	474	59.7	2	948	1244309	0.2445	-0.69	85593	0.986765	2.22

Rank	Occ. F	SFI	F	Tokens	Cum. Tokens	Cum. P Tokens	Y	Cum. Types	Cum. P Types	Z
1147- 1148	475	59.7	2	950	1245259	0.2447	-0.69	85595	0.986788	2.22
1143- 1146	476	59.7	4	1904	1247163	0.2451	-0.69	85599	0.986834	2.22
1141- 1142	477	59.7	2	954	1248117	0.2453	-0.69	85601	0.986857	2.22
1138- 1140	478	59.7	3	1434	1249551	0.2456	-0.69	85604	0.986892	2.22
1136- 1137	479	59.7	2	958	1250509	0.2457	-0.69	85606	0.986915	2.22
1132- 1135	480	59.8	4	1920	1252429	0.2461	-0.69	85610	0.986961	2.23
1131	481	59.8	1	481	1252910	0.2462	-0.69	85611	0.986973	2.23
1128- 1130	482	59.8	3	1446	1254356	0.2465	-0.69	85614	0.987007	2.23
1125- 1127	483	59.8	3	1449	1255805	0.2468	-0.68	85617	0.987042	2.23
1123- 1124	484	59.8	2	968	1256773	0.2470	-0.68	85619	0.987065	2.23
1118- 1122	485	59.8	5	2425	1259198	0.2474	-0.68	85624	0.987123	2.23
1116- 1117	486	59.8	2	972	1260170	0.2476	-0.68	85626	0.987146	2.23
1114- 1115	487	59.8	2	974	1261144	0.2478	-0.68	85628	0.987169	2.23
1113	488	59.8	1	488	1261632	0.2479	-0.68	85629	0.987180	2.23
1110- 1112	489	59.8	3	1467	1263099	0.2482	-0.68	85632	0.987215	2.23
1109	490	59.8	1	490	1263589	0.2483	-0.68	85633	0.987226	2.23
1107- 1108	491	59.8	2	982	1264571	0.2485	-0.68	85635	0.987249	2.23
1106	492	59.9	1	492	1265063	0.2486	-0.68	85636	0.987261	2.23
1105	493	59.9	1	493	1265556	0.2487	-0.68	85637	0.987272	2.23
1102- 1104	495	59.9	3	1485	1267041	0.2490	-0.68	85640	0.987307	2.24
1099- 1101	497	59.9	3	1491	1268532	0.2493	-0.68	85643	0.987342	2.24
1098	498	59.9	1	498	1269030	0.2494	-0.68	85644	0.987353	2.24
1096- 1097	499	59.9	2	998	1270028	0.2496	-0.68	85646	0.987376	2.24
1095	500	59.9	1	500	1270528	0.2497	-0.68	85647	0.987388	2.24
1092- 1094	501	59.9	3	1503	1272031	0.2500	-0.67	85650	0.987422	2.24
1089- 1091	502	59.9	3	1506	1273537	0.2503	-0.67	85653	0.987457	2.24
1087- 1088	504	60.0	2	1008	1274545	0.2505	-0.67	85655	0.987480	2.24
1085- 1086	505	60.0	2	1010	1275555	0.2507	-0.67	85657	0.987503	2.24
1082- 1084	507	60.0	3	1521	1277076	0.2510	-0.67	85660	0.987538	2.24
1081	508	60.0	1	508	1277584	0.2511	-0.67	85661	0.987549	2.24
1080	509	60.0	1	509	1278093	0.2512	-0.67	85662	0.987561	2.24
1077- 1079	510	60.0	3	1530	1279623	0.2515	-0.67	85665	0.987595	2.24
1076	511	60.0	1	511	1280134	0.2516	-0.67	85666	0.987607	2.24
1073- 1075	512	60.0	3	1536	1281670	0.2519	-0.67	85669	0.987641	2.25
1072	514	60.0	1	514	1282184	0.2520	-0.67	85670	0.987653	2.25
1070- 1071	515	60.1	2	1030	1283214	0.2522	-0.67	85672	0.987676	2.25
1067- 1069	516	60.1	3	1548	1284762	0.2525	-0.67	85675	0.987711	2.25
1065- 1066	517	60.1	2	1034	1285796	0.2527	-0.67	85677	0.987734	2.25
1062- 1064	518	60.1	3	1554	1287350	0.2530	-0.67	85680	0.987768	2.25
1060- 1061	519	60.1	2	1038	1288388	0.2532	-0.66	85682	0.987791	2.25
1056- 1059	520	60.1	4	2080	1290468	0.2536	-0.66	85686	0.987837	2.25
1055	521	60.1	1	521	1290989	0.2537	-0.66	85687	0.987849	2.25
1054	522	60.1	1	522	1291511	0.2538	-0.66	85688	0.987860	2.25
1052- 1053	523	60.1	2	1046	1292557	0.2540	-0.66	85690	0.987883	2.25
1049- 1051	524	60.1	3	1572	1294129	0.2543	-0.66	85693	0.987918	2.25
1047- 1048	526	60.1	2	1052	1295181	0.2545	-0.66	85695	0.987941	2.26
1046	527	60.2	1	527	1295708	0.2546	-0.66	85696	0.987953	2.26
1045	529	60.2	1	529	1296237	0.2547	-0.66	85697	0.987964	2.26
1044	530	60.2	1	530	1296767	0.2548	-0.66	85698	0.987976	2.26
1040- 1043	531	60.2	4	2124	1298891	0.2552	-0.66	85702	0.988022	2.26
1037- 1039	532	60.2	3	1596	1300487	0.2556	-0.66	85705	0.988056	2.26
1034- 1036	533	60.2	3	1599	1302086	0.2559	-0.66	85708	0.988091	2.26
1032- 1033	534	60.2	2	1068	1303154	0.2561	-0.66	85710	0.988114	2.26
1030- 1031	535	60.2	2	1070	1304224	0.2563	-0.65	85712	0.988137	2.26
1027- 1029	536	60.2	3	1608	1305832	0.2566	-0.65	85715	0.988172	2.26
1026	537	60.2	1	537	1306369	0.2567	-0.65	85716	0.988183	2.26
1024- 1025	538	60.2	2	1076	1307445	0.2569	-0.65	85718	0.988206	2.26
1022- 1023	539	60.3	2	1078	1308523	0.2571	-0.65	85720	0.988229	2.26
1016- 1021	540	60.3	6	3240	1311763	0.2578	-0.65	85726	0.988298	2.27
1015	541	60.3	1	541	1312304	0.2579	-0.65	85727	0.988310	2.27
1013- 1014	543	60.3	2	1086	1313390	0.2581	-0.65	85729	0.988333	2.27
1009- 1012	544	60.3	4	2176	1315566	0.2585	-0.65	85733	0.988379	2.27
1007- 1008	545	60.3	2	1090	1316656	0.2587	-0.65	85735	0.988402	2.27
1006	548	60.3	1	548	1317204	0.2588	-0.65	85736	0.988414	2.27
1004- 1005	549	60.3	2	1098	1318302	0.2591	-0.65	85738	0.988437	2.27
1003	552	60.4	1	552	1318854	0.2592	-0.65	85739	0.988448	2.27
1001- 1002	554	60.4	2	1108	1319962	0.2594	-0.65	85741	0.988471	2.27
998- 1000	555	60.4	3	1665	1321627	0.2597	-0.64	85744	0.988506	2.27
995- 997	556	60.4	3	1668	1323295	0.2600	-0.64	85747	0.988541	2.27
990- 994	557	60.4	5	2785	1326080	0.2606	-0.64	85752	0.988598	2.28
988- 989	558	60.4	2	1116	1327196	0.2608	-0.64	85754	0.988621	2.28
985- 987	560	60.4	3	1680	1328876	0.2611	-0.64	85757	0.988656	2.28
983- 984	561	60.4	2	1122	1329998	0.2614	-0.64	85759	0.988679	2.28
982	562	60.4	1	562	1330560	0.2615	-0.64	85760	0.988690	2.28
981	563	60.4	1	563	1331123	0.2616	-0.64	85761	0.988702	2.28
978- 980	565	60.5	3	1695	1332818	0.2619	-0.64	85764	0.988737	2.28
977	567	60.5	1	567	1333385	0.2620	-0.64	85765	0.988748	2.28
974- 976	568	60.5	3	1704	1335089	0.2624	-0.64	85768	0.988783	2.28
972- 973	572	60.5	2	1144	1336233	0.2626	-0.64	85770	0.988806	2.28
970- 971	573	60.5	2	1146	1337379	0.2628	-0.63	85772	0.988829	2.28
968- 969	574	60.5	2	1148	1338527	0.2630	-0.63	85774	0.988852	2.29
966- 967	575	60.5	2	1150	1339677	0.2633	-0.63	85776	0.988875	2.29
965	579	60.6	1	579	1340256	0.2634	-0.63	85777	0.988886	2.29
964	580	60.6	1	580	1340836	0.2635	-0.63	85778	0.988898	2.29
963	581	60.6	1	581	1341417	0.2636	-0.63	85779	0.988909	2.29
962	582	60.6	1	582	1341999	0.2637	-0.63	85780	0.988921	2.29
959- 961	583	60.6	3	1749	1343748	0.2641	-0.63	85783	0.988956	2.29
957- 958	584	60.6	2	1168	1344916	0.2643	-0.63	85785	0.988979	2.29
956	585	60.6	1	585	1345501	0.2644	-0.63	85786	0.988990	2.29
953- 955	586	60.6	3	1758	1347259	0.2648	-0.63	85789	0.989025	2.29
952	587	60.6	1	587	1347846	0.2649	-0.63	85790	0.989036	2.29
951	589	60.6	1	589	1348435	0.2650	-0.63	85791	0.989048	2.29
948- 950	590	60.6	3	1770	1350205	0.2653	-0.63	85794	0.989082	2.29
946- 947	591	60.7	2	1182	1351387	0.2656	-0.63	85796	0.989105	2.29
943- 945	592	60.7	3	1776	1353163	0.2659	-0.63	85799	0.989140	2.30
941- 942	593	60.7	2	1186	1354349	0.2661	-0.62	85801	0.989163	2.30
938- 940	594	60.7	3	1782	1356131	0.2665	-0.62	85804	0.989198	2.30
936- 937	595	60.7	2	1190	1357321	0.2667	-0.62	85806	0.989221	2.30
933- 935	597	60.7	3	1791	1359112	0.2671	-0.62	85809	0.989255	2.30
931- 932	598	60.7	2	1196	1360308	0.2673	-0.62	85811	0.989278	2.30
930	599	60.7	1	599	1360907	0.2674	-0.62	85812	0.989290	2.30
925- 929	600	60.7	5	3000	1363907	0.2680	-0.62	85817	0.989348	2.30
923- 924	601	60.7	2	1202	1365109	0.2683	-0.62	85819	0.989371	2.30
919- 922	602	60.7	4	2408	1367517	0.2687	-0.62	85823	0.989417	2.30
918	603	60.7	1	603	1368120	0.2689	-0.62	85824	0.989428	2.31
915- 917	604	60.7	3	1812	1369932	0.2692	-0.62	85827	0.989463	2.31
914	606	60.8	1	606	1370538	0.2693	-0.61	85828	0.989474	2.31
912- 913	607	60.8	2	1214	1371752	0.2696	-0.61	85830	0.989497	2.31
911	608	60.8	1	608	1372360	0.2697	-0.61	85831	0.989509	2.31
908- 910	610	60.8	3	1830	1374190	0.2700	-0.61	85834	0.989544	2.31
906- 907	611	60.8	2	1222	1375412	0.2703	-0.61	85836	0.989567	2.31
905	612	60.8	1	612	1376024	0.2704	-0.61	85837	0.989578	2.31
904	613	60.8	1	613	1376637	0.2705	-0.61	85838	0.989590	2.31
902- 903	615	60.8	2	1230	1377867	0.2708	-0.61	85840	0.989613	2.31
901	616	60.8	1	616	1378483	0.2709	-0.61	85841	0.989624	2.31
897- 900	617	60.8	4	2468	1380951	0.2714	-0.61	85845	0.989670	2.31
896	618	60.8	1	618	1381569	0.2715	-0.61	85846	0.989682	2.31
893- 895	619	60.9	3	1857	1383426	0.2719	-0.61	85849	0.989716	2.32
888- 892	620	60.9	5	3100	1386526	0.2725	-0.61	85854	0.989774	2.32
886- 887	624	60.9	2	1248	1387774	0.2727	-0.60	85856	0.989797	2.32
884- 885	625	60.9	2	1250	1389024	0.2730	-0.60	85858	0.989820	2.32
880- 883	626	60.9	4	2504	1391528	0.2735	-0.60	85862	0.989866	2.32
879	627	60.9	1	627	1392155	0.2736	-0.60	85863	0.989878	2.32
878	630	60.9	1	630	1392785	0.2737	-0.60	85864	0.989889	2.32
877	633	61.0	1	633	1393418	0.2738	-0.60	85865	0.989901	2.32
876	634	61.0	1	634	1394052	0.2739	-0.60	85866	0.989912	2.32
874- 875	636	61.0	2	1272	1395324	0.2742	-0.60	85868	0.989936	2.32
872- 873	637	61.0	2	1274	1396598	0.2744	-0.60	85870	0.989959	2.32
869- 871	638	61.0	3	1914	1398512	0.2748	-0.60	85873	0.989993	2.33
867- 868	639	61.0	2	1278	1399790	0.2751	-0.60	85875	0.990016	2.33
866	640	61.0	1	640	1400430	0.2752	-0.60	85876	0.990028	2.33
865	641	61.0	1	641	1401071	0.2753	-0.60	85877	0.990039	2.33
863- 864	642	61.0	2	1284	1402355	0.2756	-0.60	85879	0.990062	2.33
862	643	61.0	1	643	1402998	0.2757	-0.60	85880	0.990074	2.33
861	645	61.0	1	645	1403643	0.2758	-0.60	85881	0.990085	2.33
859- 860	646	61.0	2	1292	1404935	0.2761	-0.59	85883	0.990108	2.33
858	647	61.0	1	647	1405582	0.2762	-0.59	85884	0.990120	2.33
856- 857	648	61.1	2	1296	1406878	0.2765	-0.59	85886	0.990143	2.33
855	650	61.1	1	650	1407528	0.2766	-0.59	85887	0.990155	2.33
850- 854	651	61.1	5	3255	1410783	0.2772	-0.59	85892	0.990212	2.33
849	652	61.1	1	652	1411435	0.2774	-0.59	85893	0.990224	2.33
848	653	61.1	1	653	1412088	0.2775	-0.59	85894	0.990235	2.34
847	654	61.1	1	654	1412742	0.2776	-0.59	85895	0.990247	2.34
844- 846	656	61.1	3	1968	1414710	0.2780	-0.59	85898	0.990281	2.34
840- 843	658	61.1	4	2632	1417342	0.2785	-0.59	85902	0.990327	2.34
839	659	61.1	1	659	1418001	0.2787	-0.59	85903	0.990339	2.34
838	660	61.1	1	660	1418661	0.2788	-0.59	85904	0.990351	2.34
837	661	61.1	1	661	1419322	0.2789	-0.59	85905	0.990362	2.34
834- 836	662	61.1	3	1986	1421308	0.2793	-0.58	85908	0.990397	2.34
832- 833	663	61.2	2	1326	1422634	0.2796	-0.58	85910	0.990420	2.34
830- 831	667	61.2	2	1334	1423968	0.2798	-0.58	85912	0.990443	2.34
829	669	61.2	1	669	1424637	0.2800	-0.58	85913	0.990454	2.34
828	672	61.2	1	672	1425309	0.2801	-0.58	85914	0.990466	2.34
826- 827	673	61.2	2	1346	1426655	0.2804	-0.58	85916	0.990489	2.35
825	674	61.2	1	674	1427329	0.2805	-0.58	85917	0.990500	2.35
824	675	61.2	1	675	1428004	0.2806	-0.58	85918	0.990512	2.35
821- 823	677	61.2	3	2031	1430035	0.2810	-0.58	85921	0.990547	2.35
820	678	61.2	1	678	1430713	0.2812	-0.58	85922	0.990558	2.35
817- 819	679	61.3	3	2037	1432750	0.2816	-0.58	85925	0.990593	2.35
816	680	61.3	1	680	1433430	0.2817	-0.58	85926	0.990604	2.35
815	681	61.3	1	681	1434111	0.2818	-0.58	85927	0.990616	2.35
814	683	61.3	1	683	1434794	0.2820	-0.58	85928	0.990627	2.35
813	684	61.3	1	684	1435478	0.2821	-0.58	85929	0.990639	2.35
812	685	61.3	1	685	1436163	0.2822	-0.58	85930	0.990650	2.35
810- 811	687	61.3	2	1374	1437537	0.2825	-0.58	85932	0.990673	2.35
808- 809	688	61.3	2	1376	1438913	0.2828	-0.57	85934	0.990696	2.35
805- 807	689	61.3	3	2067	1440980	0.2832	-0.57	85937	0.990731	2.35
804	693	61.3	1	693	1441673	0.2833	-0.57	85938	0.990743	2.35
803	694	61.4	1	694	1442367	0.2834	-0.57	85939	0.990754	2.36
799- 802	695	61.4	4	2780	1445147	0.2840	-0.57	85943	0.990800	2.36
798	696	61.4	1	696	1445843	0.2841	-0.57	85944	0.990812	2.36
795- 797	701	61.4	3	2103	1447946	0.2845	-0.57	85947	0.990846	2.36
793- 794	702	61.4	2	1404	1449350	0.2848	-0.57	85949	0.990869	2.36
791- 792	705	61.4	2	1410	1450760	0.2851	-0.57	85951	0.990892	2.36
789- 790	706	61.4	2	1412	1452172	0.2854	-0.57	85953	0.990915	2.36
787- 788	707	61.4	2	1414	1453586	0.2856	-0.57	85955	0.990938	2.36
786	708	61.4	1	708	1454294	0.2858	-0.57	85956	0.990950	2.36
785	709	61.4	1	709	1455003	0.2859	-0.57	85957	0.990962	2.36
783- 784	710	61.4	2	1420	1456423	0.2862	-0.56	85959	0.990985	2.36
782	711	61.5	1	711	1457134	0.2863	-0.56	85960	0.990996	2.37
781	712	61.5	1	712	1457846	0.2865	-0.56	85961	0.991008	2.37
779- 780	713	61.5	2	1426	1459272	0.2868	-0.56	85963	0.991031	2.37
778	716	61.5	1	716	1459988	0.2869	-0.56	85964	0.991042	2.37
775- 777	717	61.5	3	2151	1462139	0.2873	-0.56	85967	0.991077	2.37
774	718	61.5	1	718	1462857	0.2875	-0.56	85968	0.991088	2.37
773	719	61.5	1	719	1463576	0.2876	-0.56	85969	0.991100	2.37
772	720	61.5	1	720	1464296	0.2878	-0.56	85970	0.991111	2.37
771	721	61.5	1	721	1465017	0.2879	-0.56	85971	0.991123	2.37
770	723	61.5	1	723	1465740	0.2880	-0.56	85972	0.991135	2.37
769	724	61.5	1	724	1466464	0.2882	-0.56	85973	0.991146	2.37
767- 768	725	61.5	2	1450	1467914	0.2885	-0.56	85975	0.991169	2.37
766	726	61.5	1	726	1468640	0.2886	-0.56	85976	0.991181	2.37
765	727	61.6	1	727	1469367	0.2887	-0.56	85977	0.991192	2.37
764	728	61.6	1	728	1470095	0.2889	-0.56	85978	0.991204	2.37
762- 763	730	61.6	2	1460	1471555	0.2892	-0.56	85980	0.991227	2.38
758- 761	731	61.6	4	2924	1474479	0.2898	-0.55	85984	0.991273	2.38
757	732	61.6	1	732	1475211	0.2899	-0.55	85985	0.991284	2.38
755- 756	734	61.6	2	1468	1476679	0.2902	-0.55	85987	0.991307	2.38
754	735	61.6	1	735	1477414	0.2903	-0.55	85988	0.991319	2.38
753	736	61.6	1	736	1478150	0.2905	-0.55	85989	0.991331	2.38
752	737	61.6	1	737	1478887	0.2906	-0.55	85990	0.991342	2.38
751	739	61.6	1	739	1479626	0.2908	-0.55	85991	0.991354	2.38
750	740	61.6	1	740	1480366	0.2909	-0.55	85992	0.991365	2.38
749	741	61.6	1	741	1481107	0.2911	-0.55	85993	0.991377	2.38
747- 748	742	61.6	2	1484	1482591	0.2913	-0.55	85995	0.991400	2.38
746	744	61.7	1	744	1483335	0.2915	-0.55	85996	0.991411	2.38
744- 745	747	61.7	2	1494	1484829	0.2918	-0.55	85998	0.991434	2.38
743	748	61.7	1	748	1485577	0.2919	-0.55	85999	0.991446	2.38
742	749	61.7	1	749	1486326	0.2921	-0.55	86000	0.991457	2.38
739- 741	750	61.7	3	2250	1488576	0.2925	-0.55	86003	0.991492	2.39
736- 738	751	61.7	3	2253	1490829	0.2930	-0.54	86006	0.991526	2.39
735	753	61.7	1	753	1491582	0.2931	-0.54	86007	0.991538	2.39
734	755	61.7	1	755	1492337	0.2933	-0.54	86008	0.991550	2.39
731- 733	756	61.7	3	2268	1494605	0.2937	-0.54	86011	0.991584	2.39
730	760	61.7	1	760	1495365	0.2939	-0.54	86012	0.991596	2.39
728- 729	761	61.8	2	1522	1496887	0.2942	-0.54	86014	0.991619	2.39
727	762	61.8	1	762	1497649	0.2943	-0.54	86015	0.991630	2.39
725- 726	766	61.8	2	1532	1499181	0.2946	-0.54	86017	0.991653	2.39
724	767	61.8	1	767	1499948	0.2948	-0.54	86018	0.991665	2.39
723	768	61.8	1	768	1500716	0.2949	-0.54	86019	0.991676	2.39
722	769	61.8	1	769	1501485	0.2951	-0.54	86020	0.991688	2.39
720- 721	770	61.8	2	1540	1503025	0.2954	-0.54	86022	0.991711	2.40
719	771	61.8	1	771	1503796	0.2955	-0.54	86023	0.991722	2.40
718	774	61.8	1	774	1504570	0.2957	-0.54	86024	0.991734	2.40
716- 717	776	61.8	2	1552	1506122	0.2960	-0.54	86026	0.991757	2.40
715	777	61.8	1	777	1506899	0.2961	-0.54	86027	0.991769	2.40
712- 714	779	61.9	3	2337	1509236	0.2966	-0.53	86030	0.991803	2.40
711	782	61.9	1	782	1510018	0.2967	-0.53	86031	0.991815	2.40
708- 710	785	61.9	3	2355	1512373	0.2972	-0.53	86034	0.991849	2.40
706- 707	790	61.9	2	1580	1513953	0.2975	-0.53	86036	0.991872	2.40
705	792	61.9	1	792	1514745	0.2977	-0.53	86037	0.991884	2.40
703- 704	793	61.9	2	1586	1516331	0.2980	-0.53	86039	0.991907	2.40

Rank		Occ. F	SFI	F	Tokens	Cum. Tokens	Cum. P Tokens	Y	Cum. Types	Cum. P Types	Z
	702	795	61.9	1	795	1517126	0.2981	−0.53	86040	0.991918	2.41
699–	701	797	62.0	3	2391	1519517	0.2986	−0.53	86043	0.991953	2.41
	698	799	62.0	1	799	1520316	0.2988	−0.53	86044	0.991965	2.41
	697	800	62.0	1	800	1521116	0.2989	−0.53	86045	0.991976	2.41
	696	802	62.0	1	802	1521918	0.2991	−0.53	86046	0.991988	2.41
	695	804	62.0	1	804	1522722	0.2992	−0.53	86047	0.991999	2.41
	694	805	62.0	1	805	1523527	0.2994	−0.53	86048	0.992011	2.41
	693	808	62.0	1	808	1524335	0.2996	−0.53	86049	0.992022	2.41
	692	810	62.0	1	810	1525145	0.2997	−0.53	86050	0.992034	2.41
690–	691	811	62.0	2	1622	1526767	0.3000	−0.52	86052	0.992057	2.41
688–	689	812	62.0	2	1624	1528391	0.3003	−0.52	86054	0.992080	2.41
	687	813	62.0	1	813	1529204	0.3005	−0.52	86055	0.992091	2.41
685–	686	814	62.0	2	1628	1530832	0.3008	−0.52	86057	0.992114	2.41
681–	684	817	62.1	4	3268	1534100	0.3015	−0.52	86061	0.992161	2.42
	680	819	62.1	1	819	1534919	0.3016	−0.52	86062	0.992172	2.42
	679	820	62.1	1	820	1535739	0.3018	−0.52	86063	0.992184	2.42
	678	824	62.1	1	824	1536563	0.3020	−0.52	86064	0.992195	2.42
676–	677	825	62.1	2	1650	1538213	0.3023	−0.52	86066	0.992218	2.42
	675	827	62.1	1	827	1539040	0.3024	−0.52	86067	0.992230	2.42
	674	828	62.1	1	828	1539868	0.3026	−0.52	86068	0.992241	2.42
	673	831	62.1	1	831	1540699	0.3028	−0.52	86069	0.992253	2.42
	672	833	62.1	1	833	1541532	0.3029	−0.52	86070	0.992264	2.42
670–	671	834	62.1	2	1668	1543200	0.3033	−0.52	86072	0.992287	2.42
668–	669	835	62.2	2	1670	1544870	0.3036	−0.51	86074	0.992310	2.42
666–	667	836	62.2	2	1672	1546542	0.3039	−0.51	86076	0.992333	2.42
	665	837	62.2	1	837	1547379	0.3041	−0.51	86077	0.992345	2.42
663–	664	838	62.2	2	1676	1549055	0.3044	−0.51	86079	0.992368	2.43
	662	839	62.2	1	839	1549894	0.3046	−0.51	86080	0.992380	2.43
	661	840	62.2	1	840	1550734	0.3047	−0.51	86081	0.992391	2.43
659–	660	841	62.2	2	1682	1552416	0.3051	−0.51	86083	0.992414	2.43
	658	843	62.2	1	843	1553259	0.3052	−0.51	86084	0.992426	2.43
656–	657	844	62.2	2	1688	1554947	0.3056	−0.51	86086	0.992449	2.43
654–	655	846	62.2	2	1692	1556639	0.3059	−0.51	86088	0.992472	2.43
	653	847	62.2	1	847	1557486	0.3061	−0.51	86089	0.992483	2.43
	652	848	62.2	1	848	1558334	0.3062	−0.51	86090	0.992495	2.43
650–	651	849	62.2	2	1698	1560032	0.3066	−0.51	86092	0.992518	2.43
	649	850	62.2	1	850	1560882	0.3067	−0.51	86093	0.992529	2.43
	648	851	62.2	1	851	1561733	0.3069	−0.50	86094	0.992541	2.43
	647	852	62.2	1	852	1562585	0.3071	−0.50	86095	0.992553	2.43
	646	853	62.2	1	853	1563438	0.3072	−0.50	86096	0.992564	2.44
	645	855	62.3	1	855	1564293	0.3074	−0.50	86097	0.992576	2.44
642–	644	857	62.3	3	2571	1566864	0.3079	−0.50	86100	0.992610	2.44
	641	858	62.3	1	858	1567722	0.3081	−0.50	86101	0.992622	2.44
638–	640	859	62.3	3	2577	1570299	0.3086	−0.50	86104	0.992656	2.44
	637	860	62.3	1	860	1571159	0.3088	−0.50	86105	0.992668	2.44
	636	861	62.3	1	861	1572020	0.3089	−0.50	86106	0.992679	2.44
634–	635	863	62.3	2	1726	1573746	0.3093	−0.50	86108	0.992702	2.44
	633	867	62.3	1	867	1574613	0.3094	−0.50	86109	0.992714	2.44
	632	871	62.3	1	871	1575484	0.3096	−0.50	86110	0.992725	2.44
630–	631	872	62.3	2	1744	1577228	0.3099	−0.50	86112	0.992748	2.44
	629	874	62.4	1	874	1578102	0.3101	−0.50	86113	0.992760	2.45
	628	877	62.4	1	877	1578979	0.3103	−0.50	86114	0.992772	2.45
	627	878	62.4	1	878	1579857	0.3105	−0.49	86115	0.992783	2.45
	626	879	62.4	1	879	1580736	0.3106	−0.49	86116	0.992795	2.45
	625	880	62.4	1	880	1581616	0.3108	−0.49	86117	0.992806	2.45
623–	624	881	62.4	2	1762	1583378	0.3112	−0.49	86119	0.992829	2.45
	622	882	62.4	1	882	1584260	0.3113	−0.49	86120	0.992841	2.45
	621	885	62.4	1	885	1585145	0.3115	−0.49	86121	0.992852	2.45
617–	620	886	62.4	4	3544	1588689	0.3122	−0.49	86125	0.992898	2.45
	616	887	62.4	1	887	1589576	0.3124	−0.49	86126	0.992910	2.45
	615	891	62.4	1	891	1590467	0.3125	−0.49	86127	0.992921	2.45
	614	892	62.4	1	892	1591359	0.3127	−0.49	86128	0.992933	2.45
	613	894	62.4	1	894	1592253	0.3129	−0.49	86129	0.992944	2.45
611–	612	895	62.5	2	1790	1594043	0.3133	−0.49	86131	0.992968	2.46
608–	610	900	62.5	3	2700	1596743	0.3138	−0.49	86134	0.993002	2.46
606–	607	902	62.5	2	1804	1598547	0.3141	−0.48	86136	0.993025	2.46
	605	904	62.5	1	904	1599451	0.3143	−0.48	86137	0.993037	2.46
	604	906	62.5	1	906	1600357	0.3145	−0.48	86138	0.993048	2.46
602–	603	908	62.5	2	1816	1602173	0.3148	−0.48	86140	0.993071	2.46
	601	909	62.5	1	909	1603082	0.3150	−0.48	86141	0.993083	2.46
599–	600	910	62.5	2	1820	1604902	0.3154	−0.48	86143	0.993106	2.46
	598	911	62.5	1	911	1605813	0.3156	−0.48	86144	0.993117	2.46
596–	597	913	62.5	2	1826	1607639	0.3159	−0.48	86146	0.993140	2.46
	595	914	62.5	1	914	1608553	0.3161	−0.48	86147	0.993152	2.47
	594	915	62.6	1	915	1609468	0.3163	−0.48	86148	0.993164	2.47
	593	917	62.6	1	917	1610385	0.3165	−0.48	86149	0.993175	2.47
	592	919	62.6	1	919	1611304	0.3166	−0.48	86150	0.993187	2.47
	591	921	62.6	1	921	1612225	0.3168	−0.48	86151	0.993198	2.47
	590	923	62.6	1	923	1613148	0.3170	−0.48	86152	0.993210	2.47
588–	589	925	62.6	2	1850	1614998	0.3174	−0.48	86154	0.993233	2.47
586–	587	926	62.6	2	1852	1616850	0.3177	−0.47	86156	0.993256	2.47
	585	927	62.6	1	927	1617777	0.3179	−0.47	86157	0.993267	2.47
	584	928	62.6	1	928	1618705	0.3181	−0.47	86158	0.993279	2.47
	583	929	62.6	1	929	1619634	0.3183	−0.47	86159	0.993290	2.47
581–	582	930	62.6	2	1860	1621494	0.3186	−0.47	86161	0.993313	2.47
579–	580	933	62.6	2	1866	1623360	0.3190	−0.47	86163	0.993336	2.47
	578	934	62.6	1	934	1624294	0.3192	−0.47	86164	0.993348	2.48
	577	935	62.6	1	935	1625229	0.3194	−0.47	86165	0.993360	2.48
	576	937	62.7	1	937	1626166	0.3196	−0.47	86166	0.993371	2.48
	575	938	62.7	1	938	1627104	0.3197	−0.47	86167	0.993383	2.48
	574	939	62.7	1	939	1628043	0.3199	−0.47	86168	0.993394	2.48
572–	573	940	62.7	2	1880	1629923	0.3203	−0.47	86170	0.993417	2.48
569–	571	945	62.7	3	2835	1632758	0.3209	−0.47	86173	0.993452	2.48
	568	946	62.7	1	946	1633704	0.3210	−0.46	86174	0.993463	2.48
	567	948	62.7	1	948	1634652	0.3212	−0.46	86175	0.993475	2.48
	566	949	62.7	1	949	1635601	0.3214	−0.46	86176	0.993486	2.48
	565	950	62.7	1	950	1636551	0.3216	−0.46	86177	0.993498	2.48
	564	951	62.7	1	951	1637502	0.3218	−0.46	86178	0.993509	2.48
	563	953	62.7	1	953	1638455	0.3220	−0.46	86179	0.993521	2.48
	562	955	62.7	1	955	1639410	0.3222	−0.46	86180	0.993532	2.49
	561	956	62.7	1	956	1640366	0.3224	−0.46	86181	0.993544	2.49
559–	560	962	62.8	2	1924	1642290	0.3227	−0.46	86183	0.993567	2.49
	558	964	62.8	1	964	1643254	0.3229	−0.46	86184	0.993579	2.49
	557	965	62.8	1	965	1644219	0.3231	−0.46	86185	0.993590	2.49
	556	967	62.8	1	967	1645186	0.3233	−0.46	86186	0.993602	2.49
	555	968	62.8	1	968	1646154	0.3235	−0.46	86187	0.993613	2.49
	554	969	62.8	1	969	1647123	0.3237	−0.46	86188	0.993625	2.49
	553	972	62.8	1	972	1648095	0.3239	−0.46	86189	0.993636	2.49
	552	974	62.8	1	974	1649069	0.3241	−0.46	86190	0.993648	2.49
550–	551	976	62.8	2	1952	1651021	0.3244	−0.46	86192	0.993671	2.49
	549	978	62.8	1	978	1651999	0.3246	−0.45	86193	0.993682	2.49
	548	980	62.8	1	980	1652979	0.3248	−0.45	86194	0.993694	2.49
	547	983	62.9	1	983	1653962	0.3250	−0.45	86195	0.993705	2.50
545–	546	984	62.9	2	1968	1655930	0.3254	−0.45	86197	0.993728	2.50
542–	544	990	62.9	3	2970	1658900	0.3260	−0.45	86200	0.993763	2.50
	541	992	62.9	1	992	1659892	0.3262	−0.45	86201	0.993775	2.50
538–	540	993	62.9	3	2979	1662871	0.3268	−0.45	86204	0.993809	2.50
	537	994	62.9	1	994	1663865	0.3270	−0.45	86205	0.993821	2.50
	536	995	62.9	1	995	1664860	0.3272	−0.45	86206	0.993832	2.50
	535	996	62.9	1	996	1665856	0.3274	−0.45	86207	0.993844	2.50
	534	998	62.9	1	998	1666854	0.3276	−0.45	86208	0.993855	2.50
532–	533	1002	62.9	2	2004	1668858	0.3280	−0.45	86210	0.993878	2.51
	531	1003	62.9	1	1003	1669861	0.3281	−0.45	86211	0.993890	2.51
	530	1004	63.0	1	1004	1670865	0.3283	−0.44	86212	0.993901	2.51
526–	529	1005	63.0	4	4020	1674885	0.3291	−0.44	86216	0.993947	2.51
	525	1008	63.0	1	1008	1675893	0.3293	−0.44	86217	0.993959	2.51
	524	1014	63.0	1	1014	1676907	0.3295	−0.44	86218	0.993971	2.51
	523	1015	63.0	1	1015	1677922	0.3297	−0.44	86219	0.993982	2.51
521–	522	1016	63.0	2	2032	1679954	0.3301	−0.44	86221	0.994005	2.51
	520	1021	63.0	1	1021	1680975	0.3303	−0.44	86222	0.994017	2.51
	519	1022	63.0	1	1022	1681997	0.3305	−0.44	86223	0.994028	2.51
	518	1024	63.0	1	1024	1683021	0.3307	−0.44	86224	0.994040	2.51
	517	1026	63.0	1	1026	1684047	0.3309	−0.44	86225	0.994051	2.52
	516	1030	63.1	1	1030	1685077	0.3311	−0.44	86226	0.994063	2.52
514–	515	1032	63.1	2	2064	1687141	0.3315	−0.44	86228	0.994086	2.52
	513	1033	63.1	1	1033	1688174	0.3317	−0.44	86229	0.994097	2.52
	512	1041	63.1	1	1041	1689215	0.3320	−0.43	86230	0.994109	2.52
510–	511	1043	63.1	2	2086	1691301	0.3324	−0.43	86232	0.994132	2.52
508–	509	1044	63.1	2	2088	1693389	0.3328	−0.43	86234	0.994155	2.52
506–	507	1046	63.1	2	2092	1695481	0.3332	−0.43	86236	0.994178	2.52
504–	505	1048	63.1	2	2096	1697577	0.3336	−0.43	86238	0.994201	2.52
	503	1049	63.1	1	1049	1698626	0.3338	−0.43	86239	0.994213	2.52
501–	502	1051	63.2	2	2102	1700728	0.3342	−0.43	86241	0.994236	2.53
	500	1052	63.2	1	1052	1701780	0.3344	−0.43	86242	0.994247	2.53
498–	499	1056	63.2	2	2112	1703892	0.3348	−0.43	86244	0.994270	2.53
495–	497	1057	63.2	3	3171	1707063	0.3355	−0.42	86247	0.994305	2.53
	494	1060	63.2	1	1060	1708123	0.3357	−0.42	86248	0.994316	2.53
492–	493	1061	63.2	2	2122	1710245	0.3361	−0.42	86250	0.994339	2.53
	491	1062	63.2	1	1062	1711307	0.3363	−0.42	86251	0.994351	2.53
	490	1063	63.2	1	1063	1712370	0.3365	−0.42	86252	0.994362	2.53
	489	1065	63.2	1	1065	1713435	0.3367	−0.42	86253	0.994374	2.53
	488	1071	63.2	1	1071	1714506	0.3369	−0.42	86254	0.994386	2.54
	487	1072	63.2	1	1072	1715578	0.3371	−0.42	86255	0.994397	2.54
	486	1075	63.3	1	1075	1716653	0.3373	−0.42	86256	0.994409	2.54
	485	1076	63.3	1	1076	1717729	0.3376	−0.42	86257	0.994420	2.54
483–	484	1077	63.3	2	2154	1719883	0.3380	−0.42	86259	0.994443	2.54
	482	1079	63.3	1	1079	1720962	0.3382	−0.42	86260	0.994455	2.54
479–	481	1081	63.3	3	3243	1724205	0.3388	−0.42	86263	0.994489	2.54
	478	1084	63.3	1	1084	1725289	0.3390	−0.42	86264	0.994501	2.54
	477	1087	63.3	1	1087	1726376	0.3393	−0.41	86265	0.994512	2.54
	476	1092	63.3	1	1092	1727468	0.3395	−0.41	86266	0.994524	2.54
474–	475	1095	63.3	2	2190	1729658	0.3399	−0.41	86268	0.994547	2.55
	473	1106	63.4	1	1106	1730764	0.3401	−0.41	86269	0.994559	2.55
	472	1107	63.4	1	1107	1731871	0.3403	−0.41	86270	0.994570	2.55
470–	471	1109	63.4	2	2218	1734089	0.3408	−0.41	86272	0.994593	2.55
	469	1110	63.4	1	1110	1735199	0.3410	−0.41	86273	0.994605	2.55
	468	1112	63.4	1	1112	1736311	0.3412	−0.41	86274	0.994616	2.55
	467	1115	63.4	1	1115	1737426	0.3414	−0.41	86275	0.994628	2.55
	466	1117	63.4	1	1117	1738543	0.3416	−0.41	86276	0.994639	2.55
	465	1122	63.4	1	1122	1739665	0.3419	−0.41	86277	0.994651	2.55
463–	464	1123	63.4	2	2246	1741911	0.3423	−0.41	86279	0.994674	2.55
460–	462	1131	63.5	3	3393	1745304	0.3430	−0.40	86282	0.994708	2.56
	459	1132	63.5	1	1132	1746436	0.3432	−0.40	86283	0.994720	2.56
	458	1133	63.5	1	1133	1747569	0.3434	−0.40	86284	0.994731	2.56
	457	1134	63.5	1	1134	1748703	0.3436	−0.40	86285	0.994743	2.56
	456	1135	63.5	1	1135	1749838	0.3439	−0.40	86286	0.994754	2.56
	455	1138	63.5	1	1138	1750976	0.3441	−0.40	86287	0.994766	2.56
	454	1140	63.5	1	1140	1752116	0.3443	−0.40	86288	0.994778	2.56
	453	1141	63.5	1	1141	1753257	0.3445	−0.40	86289	0.994789	2.56
	452	1144	63.5	1	1144	1754401	0.3448	−0.40	86290	0.994801	2.56
	451	1145	63.5	1	1145	1755546	0.3450	−0.40	86291	0.994812	2.56
	450	1148	63.5	1	1148	1756694	0.3452	−0.40	86292	0.994824	2.56
	449	1168	63.6	1	1168	1757862	0.3454	−0.40	86293	0.994835	2.56
	448	1170	63.6	1	1170	1759032	0.3457	−0.40	86294	0.994847	2.57
	447	1171	63.6	1	1171	1760203	0.3459	−0.40	86295	0.994858	2.57
	446	1173	63.6	1	1173	1761376	0.3461	−0.40	86296	0.994870	2.57
	445	1174	63.6	1	1174	1762550	0.3464	−0.40	86297	0.994881	2.57
	444	1180	63.7	1	1180	1763730	0.3466	−0.39	86298	0.994893	2.57
	443	1183	63.7	1	1183	1764913	0.3468	−0.39	86299	0.994904	2.57
	442	1184	63.7	1	1184	1766097	0.3471	−0.39	86300	0.994916	2.57
	441	1187	63.7	1	1187	1767284	0.3473	−0.39	86301	0.994927	2.57
	440	1190	63.7	1	1190	1768474	0.3475	−0.39	86302	0.994939	2.57
438–	439	1192	63.7	2	2384	1770858	0.3480	−0.39	86304	0.994962	2.57
	437	1196	63.7	1	1196	1772054	0.3482	−0.39	86305	0.994974	2.57
435–	436	1198	63.7	2	2396	1774450	0.3487	−0.39	86307	0.994997	2.58
	434	1203	63.7	1	1203	1775653	0.3489	−0.39	86308	0.995008	2.58
	433	1207	63.8	1	1207	1776860	0.3492	−0.39	86309	0.995020	2.58
	432	1211	63.8	1	1211	1778071	0.3494	−0.39	86310	0.995031	2.58
	431	1214	63.8	1	1214	1779285	0.3497	−0.39	86311	0.995043	2.58
	430	1216	63.8	1	1216	1780501	0.3499	−0.39	86312	0.995054	2.58
	429	1217	63.8	1	1217	1781718	0.3501	−0.38	86313	0.995066	2.58
	428	1219	63.8	1	1219	1782937	0.3504	−0.38	86314	0.995077	2.58
	427	1223	63.8	1	1223	1784160	0.3506	−0.38	86315	0.995089	2.58
	426	1225	63.8	1	1225	1785385	0.3509	−0.38	86316	0.995100	2.58
	425	1227	63.8	1	1227	1786612	0.3511	−0.38	86317	0.995112	2.58
	424	1229	63.8	1	1229	1787841	0.3513	−0.38	86318	0.995123	2.58
	423	1231	63.8	1	1231	1789072	0.3516	−0.38	86319	0.995135	2.59
	422	1233	63.8	1	1233	1790305	0.3518	−0.38	86320	0.995146	2.59
	421	1235	63.9	1	1235	1791540	0.3521	−0.38	86321	0.995158	2.59
	420	1240	63.9	1	1240	1792780	0.3523	−0.38	86322	0.995170	2.59
	419	1249	63.9	1	1249	1794029	0.3526	−0.38	86323	0.995181	2.59
	418	1260	63.9	1	1260	1795289	0.3528	−0.38	86324	0.995193	2.59
	417	1263	63.9	1	1263	1796552	0.3530	−0.38	86325	0.995204	2.59
	416	1266	64.0	1	1266	1797818	0.3533	−0.38	86326	0.995216	2.59
	415	1274	64.0	1	1274	1799092	0.3535	−0.38	86327	0.995227	2.59
	414	1275	64.0	1	1275	1800367	0.3538	−0.38	86328	0.995239	2.59
	413	1279	64.0	1	1279	1801646	0.3540	−0.37	86329	0.995250	2.59
	412	1280	64.0	1	1280	1802926	0.3543	−0.37	86330	0.995262	2.59
410–	411	1281	64.0	2	2562	1805488	0.3548	−0.37	86332	0.995285	2.60
	409	1283	64.0	1	1283	1806771	0.3551	−0.37	86333	0.995296	2.60
	408	1286	64.0	1	1286	1808057	0.3553	−0.37	86334	0.995308	2.60
	407	1288	64.0	1	1288	1809345	0.3556	−0.37	86335	0.995319	2.60
	406	1289	64.0	1	1289	1810634	0.3558	−0.37	86336	0.995331	2.60
	405	1294	64.1	1	1294	1811928	0.3561	−0.37	86337	0.995342	2.60
	404	1303	64.1	1	1303	1813231	0.3563	−0.37	86338	0.995354	2.60
	403	1304	64.1	1	1304	1814535	0.3566	−0.37	86339	0.995366	2.60
	402	1308	64.1	1	1308	1815843	0.3568	−0.37	86340	0.995377	2.60
	401	1311	64.1	1	1311	1817154	0.3571	−0.37	86341	0.995389	2.60
	400	1317	64.1	1	1317	1818471	0.3574	−0.37	86342	0.995400	2.60
	399	1321	64.1	1	1321	1819792	0.3576	−0.36	86343	0.995412	2.61
	398	1325	64.2	1	1325	1821117	0.3579	−0.36	86344	0.995423	2.61
	397	1331	64.2	1	1331	1822448	0.3581	−0.36	86345	0.995435	2.61

Rank	Occ. F	SFI	F	Tokens	Cum. Tokens	Cum. P Tokens	Y	Cum. Types	Cum. P Types	Z
396	1336	64.2	1	1336	1823784	0.3584	−0.36	86346	0.995446	2.61
395	1337	64.2	1	1337	1825121	0.3587	−0.36	86347	0.995458	2.61
394	1339	64.2	1	1339	1826460	0.3589	−0.36	86348	0.995469	2.61
393	1345	64.2	1	1345	1827805	0.3592	−0.36	86349	0.995481	2.61
392	1347	64.2	1	1347	1829152	0.3595	−0.36	86350	0.995492	2.61
391	1352	64.2	1	1352	1830504	0.3597	−0.36	86351	0.995504	2.61
389– 390	1357	64.3	2	2714	1833218	0.3603	−0.36	86353	0.995527	2.61
388	1366	64.3	1	1366	1834584	0.3605	−0.36	86354	0.995538	2.61
387	1370	64.3	1	1370	1835954	0.3608	−0.36	86355	0.995550	2.62
386	1371	64.3	1	1371	1837325	0.3611	−0.36	86356	0.995561	2.62
385	1372	64.3	1	1372	1838697	0.3613	−0.35	86357	0.995573	2.62
383– 384	1374	64.3	2	2748	1841445	0.3619	−0.35	86359	0.995596	2.62
381– 382	1376	64.3	2	2752	1844197	0.3624	−0.35	86361	0.995619	2.62
380	1380	64.3	1	1380	1845577	0.3627	−0.35	86362	0.995631	2.62
378– 379	1387	64.4	2	2774	1848351	0.3632	−0.35	86364	0.995654	2.62
377	1397	64.4	1	1397	1849748	0.3635	−0.35	86365	0.995665	2.62
376	1398	64.4	1	1398	1851146	0.3638	−0.35	86366	0.995677	2.63
375	1401	64.4	1	1401	1852547	0.3640	−0.35	86367	0.995688	2.63
374	1403	64.4	1	1403	1853950	0.3643	−0.35	86368	0.995700	2.63
373	1408	64.4	1	1408	1855358	0.3646	−0.35	86369	0.995711	2.63
372	1409	64.4	1	1409	1856767	0.3649	−0.35	86370	0.995723	2.63
371	1414	64.4	1	1414	1858181	0.3652	−0.34	86371	0.995734	2.63
370	1416	64.4	1	1416	1859597	0.3654	−0.34	86372	0.995746	2.63
369	1418	64.5	1	1418	1861015	0.3657	−0.34	86373	0.995757	2.63
368	1420	64.5	1	1420	1862435	0.3660	−0.34	86374	0.995769	2.63
367	1421	64.5	1	1421	1863856	0.3663	−0.34	86375	0.995781	2.63
366	1423	64.5	1	1423	1865279	0.3666	−0.34	86376	0.995792	2.63
365	1438	64.5	1	1438	1866717	0.3668	−0.34	86377	0.995804	2.64
364	1439	64.5	1	1439	1868156	0.3671	−0.34	86378	0.995815	2.64
363	1445	64.5	1	1445	1869601	0.3674	−0.34	86379	0.995827	2.64
362	1453	64.6	1	1453	1871054	0.3677	−0.34	86380	0.995838	2.64
361	1469	64.6	1	1469	1872523	0.3680	−0.34	86381	0.995850	2.64
360	1473	64.6	1	1473	1873996	0.3683	−0.34	86382	0.995861	2.64
359	1484	64.6	1	1484	1875480	0.3686	−0.34	86383	0.995873	2.64
358	1489	64.7	1	1489	1876969	0.3688	−0.33	86384	0.995884	2.64
357	1490	64.7	1	1490	1878459	0.3691	−0.33	86385	0.995896	2.64
356	1499	64.7	1	1499	1879958	0.3694	−0.33	86386	0.995907	2.64
355	1501	64.7	1	1501	1881459	0.3697	−0.33	86387	0.995919	2.65
354	1502	64.7	1	1502	1882961	0.3700	−0.33	86388	0.995930	2.65
353	1507	64.7	1	1507	1884468	0.3703	−0.33	86389	0.995942	2.65
352	1511	64.7	1	1511	1885979	0.3706	−0.33	86390	0.995953	2.65
351	1513	64.7	1	1513	1887492	0.3709	−0.33	86391	0.995965	2.65
350	1514	64.7	1	1514	1889006	0.3712	−0.33	86392	0.995977	2.65
349	1525	64.8	1	1525	1890531	0.3715	−0.33	86393	0.995988	2.65
347– 348	1534	64.8	2	3068	1893599	0.3721	−0.33	86395	0.996011	2.65
346	1535	64.8	1	1535	1895134	0.3724	−0.33	86396	0.996023	2.65
345	1545	64.8	1	1545	1896679	0.3727	−0.32	86397	0.996034	2.65
344	1556	64.9	1	1556	1898235	0.3730	−0.32	86398	0.996046	2.66
343	1557	64.9	1	1557	1899792	0.3733	−0.32	86399	0.996057	2.66
342	1564	64.9	1	1564	1901356	0.3736	−0.32	86400	0.996069	2.66
341	1566	64.9	1	1566	1902922	0.3739	−0.32	86401	0.996080	2.66
340	1570	64.9	1	1570	1904492	0.3743	−0.32	86402	0.996092	2.66
339	1574	64.9	1	1574	1906066	0.3746	−0.32	86403	0.996103	2.66
338	1575	64.9	1	1575	1907641	0.3749	−0.32	86404	0.996115	2.66
337	1577	64.9	1	1577	1909218	0.3752	−0.32	86405	0.996126	2.66
336	1592	65.0	1	1592	1910810	0.3755	−0.32	86406	0.996138	2.66
335	1599	65.0	1	1599	1912409	0.3758	−0.32	86407	0.996149	2.66
334	1604	65.0	1	1604	1914013	0.3761	−0.32	86408	0.996161	2.67
333	1606	65.0	1	1606	1915619	0.3764	−0.31	86409	0.996172	2.67
332	1616	65.0	1	1616	1917235	0.3768	−0.31	86410	0.996184	2.67
331	1619	65.0	1	1619	1918854	0.3771	−0.31	86411	0.996196	2.67
330	1623	65.0	1	1623	1920477	0.3774	−0.31	86412	0.996207	2.67
329	1629	65.1	1	1629	1922106	0.3777	−0.31	86413	0.996219	2.67
328	1637	65.1	1	1637	1923743	0.3780	−0.31	86414	0.996230	2.67
326– 327	1645	65.1	2	3290	1927033	0.3787	−0.31	86416	0.996253	2.67
325	1654	65.1	1	1654	1928687	0.3790	−0.31	86417	0.996265	2.68
324	1661	65.1	1	1661	1930348	0.3793	−0.31	86418	0.996276	2.68
323	1663	65.1	1	1663	1932011	0.3797	−0.31	86419	0.996288	2.68
322	1674	65.2	1	1674	1933685	0.3800	−0.31	86420	0.996299	2.68
321	1690	65.2	1	1690	1935375	0.3803	−0.30	86421	0.996311	2.68
320	1694	65.2	1	1694	1937069	0.3807	−0.30	86422	0.996322	2.68
319	1696	65.2	1	1696	1938765	0.3810	−0.30	86423	0.996334	2.68
318	1711	65.3	1	1711	1940476	0.3813	−0.30	86424	0.996345	2.68
317	1712	65.3	1	1712	1942188	0.3817	−0.30	86425	0.996357	2.68
316	1715	65.3	1	1715	1943903	0.3820	−0.30	86426	0.996368	2.68
315	1725	65.3	1	1725	1945628	0.3823	−0.30	86427	0.996380	2.69
314	1736	65.3	1	1736	1947364	0.3827	−0.30	86428	0.996392	2.69
313	1738	65.3	1	1738	1949102	0.3830	−0.30	86429	0.996403	2.69
312	1741	65.3	1	1741	1950843	0.3834	−0.30	86430	0.996415	2.69
311	1748	65.4	1	1748	1952591	0.3837	−0.30	86431	0.996426	2.69
310	1752	65.4	1	1752	1954343	0.3841	−0.29	86432	0.996438	2.69
309	1755	65.4	1	1755	1956098	0.3844	−0.29	86433	0.996449	2.69
308	1757	65.4	1	1757	1957855	0.3847	−0.29	86434	0.996461	2.69
307	1768	65.4	1	1768	1959623	0.3851	−0.29	86435	0.996472	2.69
306	1781	65.4	1	1781	1961404	0.3854	−0.29	86436	0.996484	2.70
305	1783	65.4	1	1783	1963187	0.3858	−0.29	86437	0.996495	2.70
304	1785	65.5	1	1785	1964972	0.3861	−0.29	86438	0.996507	2.70
303	1789	65.5	1	1789	1966761	0.3865	−0.29	86439	0.996518	2.70
302	1798	65.5	1	1798	1968559	0.3868	−0.29	86440	0.996530	2.70
300– 301	1801	65.5	2	3602	1972161	0.3876	−0.29	86442	0.996553	2.70
299	1804	65.5	1	1804	1973965	0.3879	−0.28	86443	0.996564	2.70
298	1812	65.5	1	1812	1975777	0.3883	−0.28	86444	0.996576	2.70
297	1825	65.5	1	1825	1977602	0.3886	−0.28	86445	0.996588	2.71
296	1828	65.6	1	1828	1979430	0.3890	−0.28	86446	0.996599	2.71
295	1836	65.6	1	1836	1981266	0.3893	−0.28	86447	0.996611	2.71
294	1843	65.6	1	1843	1983109	0.3897	−0.28	86448	0.996622	2.71
293	1848	65.6	1	1848	1984957	0.3901	−0.28	86449	0.996634	2.71
292	1854	65.6	1	1854	1986811	0.3904	−0.28	86450	0.996645	2.71
291	1884	65.7	1	1884	1988695	0.3908	−0.28	86451	0.996657	2.71
289– 290	1886	65.7	2	3772	1992467	0.3915	−0.28	86453	0.996680	2.71
288	1899	65.7	1	1899	1994366	0.3919	−0.27	86454	0.996691	2.72
287	1903	65.7	1	1903	1996269	0.3923	−0.27	86455	0.996703	2.72
286	1904	65.7	1	1904	1998173	0.3927	−0.27	86456	0.996714	2.72
285	1911	65.7	1	1911	2000084	0.3930	−0.27	86457	0.996726	2.72
284	1914	65.8	1	1914	2001998	0.3934	−0.27	86458	0.996737	2.72
283	1920	65.8	1	1920	2003918	0.3938	−0.27	86459	0.996749	2.72
282	1923	65.8	1	1923	2005841	0.3942	−0.27	86460	0.996760	2.72
281	1924	65.8	1	1924	2007765	0.3946	−0.27	86461	0.996772	2.72
280	1939	65.8	1	1939	2009704	0.3949	−0.27	86462	0.996783	2.72
279	1942	65.8	1	1942	2011646	0.3953	−0.27	86463	0.996795	2.73
278	1956	65.8	1	1956	2013602	0.3957	−0.26	86464	0.996807	2.73
277	1958	65.9	1	1958	2015560	0.3961	−0.26	86465	0.996818	2.73
276	1962	65.9	1	1962	2017522	0.3965	−0.26	86466	0.996830	2.73
275	1977	65.9	1	1977	2019499	0.3969	−0.26	86467	0.996841	2.73
274	1980	65.9	1	1980	2021479	0.3972	−0.26	86468	0.996853	2.73
273	1985	65.9	1	1985	2023464	0.3976	−0.26	86469	0.996864	2.73

Rank	Occ. F	SFI	F	Tokens	Cum. Tokens	Cum. P Tokens	Y	Cum. Types	Cum. P Types	Z
272	1988	65.9	1	1988	2025452	0.3980	−0.26	86470	0.996876	2.73
271	2002	65.9	1	2002	2027454	0.3984	−0.26	86471	0.996887	2.74
270	2003	66.0	1	2003	2029457	0.3988	−0.26	86472	0.996899	2.74
269	2016	66.0	1	2016	2031473	0.3992	−0.26	86473	0.996910	2.74
268	2028	66.0	1	2028	2033501	0.3996	−0.25	86474	0.996922	2.74
267	2036	66.0	1	2036	2035537	0.4000	−0.25	86475	0.996933	2.74
266	2041	66.0	1	2041	2037578	0.4004	−0.25	86476	0.996945	2.74
265	2044	66.0	1	2044	2039622	0.4008	−0.25	86477	0.996956	2.74
264	2051	66.1	1	2051	2041673	0.4012	−0.25	86478	0.996968	2.74
263	2059	66.1	1	2059	2043732	0.4016	−0.25	86479	0.996979	2.75
262	2085	66.1	1	2085	2045817	0.4020	−0.25	86480	0.996991	2.75
261	2092	66.1	1	2092	2047909	0.4024	−0.25	86481	0.997003	2.75
260	2094	66.1	1	2094	2050003	0.4029	−0.25	86482	0.997014	2.75
259	2100	66.2	1	2100	2052103	0.4033	−0.24	86483	0.997026	2.75
258	2113	66.2	1	2113	2054216	0.4037	−0.24	86484	0.997037	2.75
257	2129	66.2	1	2129	2056345	0.4041	−0.24	86485	0.997049	2.75
256	2146	66.3	1	2146	2058491	0.4045	−0.24	86486	0.997060	2.75
255	2154	66.3	1	2154	2060645	0.4049	−0.24	86487	0.997072	2.76
254	2155	66.3	1	2155	2062800	0.4054	−0.24	86488	0.997083	2.76
253	2176	66.3	1	2176	2064976	0.4058	−0.24	86489	0.997095	2.76
252	2178	66.3	1	2178	2067154	0.4062	−0.24	86490	0.997106	2.76
250– 251	2237	66.4	2	4474	2071628	0.4071	−0.24	86492	0.997129	2.76
249	2245	66.4	1	2245	2073873	0.4075	−0.23	86493	0.997141	2.76
248	2250	66.5	1	2250	2076123	0.4080	−0.23	86494	0.997152	2.76
247	2262	66.5	1	2262	2078385	0.4084	−0.23	86495	0.997164	2.77
246	2277	66.5	1	2277	2080662	0.4089	−0.23	86496	0.997175	2.77
245	2278	66.5	1	2278	2082940	0.4093	−0.23	86497	0.997187	2.77
244	2281	66.5	1	2281	2085221	0.4098	−0.23	86498	0.997199	2.77
243	2298	66.5	1	2298	2087519	0.4102	−0.23	86499	0.997210	2.77
242	2303	66.6	1	2303	2089822	0.4107	−0.23	86500	0.997222	2.77
241	2307	66.6	1	2307	2092129	0.4111	−0.22	86501	0.997233	2.77
240	2316	66.6	1	2316	2094445	0.4116	−0.22	86502	0.997245	2.78
239	2324	66.6	1	2324	2096769	0.4120	−0.22	86503	0.997256	2.78
238	2331	66.6	1	2331	2099100	0.4125	−0.22	86504	0.997268	2.78
237	2343	66.6	1	2343	2101443	0.4130	−0.22	86505	0.997279	2.78
235– 236	2357	66.7	2	4714	2106157	0.4139	−0.22	86507	0.997302	2.78
234	2363	66.7	1	2363	2108520	0.4144	−0.22	86508	0.997314	2.78
233	2372	66.7	1	2372	2110892	0.4148	−0.22	86509	0.997325	2.79
232	2376	66.7	1	2376	2113268	0.4153	−0.21	86510	0.997337	2.79
231	2392	66.7	1	2392	2115660	0.4158	−0.21	86511	0.997348	2.79
230	2431	66.8	1	2431	2118091	0.4162	−0.21	86512	0.997360	2.79
229	2435	66.8	1	2435	2120526	0.4167	−0.21	86513	0.997371	2.79
228	2487	66.9	1	2487	2123013	0.4172	−0.21	86514	0.997383	2.79
227	2490	66.9	1	2490	2125503	0.4177	−0.21	86515	0.997395	2.79
226	2491	66.9	1	2491	2127994	0.4182	−0.21	86516	0.997406	2.80
225	2500	66.9	1	2500	2130494	0.4187	−0.21	86517	0.997418	2.80
224	2509	66.9	1	2509	2133003	0.4192	−0.20	86518	0.997429	2.80
223	2529	67.0	1	2529	2135532	0.4197	−0.20	86519	0.997441	2.80
222	2532	67.0	1	2532	2138064	0.4202	−0.20	86520	0.997452	2.80
221	2545	67.0	1	2545	2140609	0.4207	−0.20	86521	0.997464	2.80
220	2575	67.0	1	2575	2143184	0.4212	−0.20	86522	0.997475	2.80
219	2581	67.1	1	2581	2145765	0.4217	−0.20	86523	0.997487	2.81
218	2582	67.1	1	2582	2148347	0.4222	−0.20	86524	0.997498	2.81
217	2588	67.1	1	2588	2150935	0.4227	−0.20	86525	0.997510	2.81
216	2596	67.1	1	2596	2153531	0.4232	−0.19	86526	0.997521	2.81
215	2599	67.1	1	2599	2156130	0.4237	−0.19	86527	0.997533	2.81
213– 214	2611	67.1	2	5222	2161352	0.4247	−0.19	86529	0.997556	2.81
212	2612	67.1	1	2612	2163964	0.4252	−0.19	86530	0.997567	2.82
211	2625	67.1	1	2625	2166589	0.4258	−0.19	86531	0.997579	2.82
210	2626	67.1	1	2626	2169215	0.4263	−0.19	86532	0.997590	2.82
209	2629	67.1	1	2629	2171844	0.4268	−0.18	86533	0.997602	2.82
208	2638	67.1	1	2638	2174482	0.4273	−0.18	86534	0.997614	2.82
207	2646	67.2	1	2646	2177128	0.4278	−0.18	86535	0.997625	2.82
206	2647	67.2	1	2647	2179775	0.4284	−0.18	86536	0.997637	2.83
205	2655	67.2	1	2655	2182430	0.4289	−0.18	86537	0.997648	2.83
204	2657	67.2	1	2657	2185087	0.4294	−0.18	86538	0.997660	2.83
203	2680	67.2	1	2680	2187767	0.4299	−0.18	86539	0.997671	2.83
202	2685	67.2	1	2685	2190452	0.4305	−0.18	86540	0.997683	2.83
201	2690	67.2	1	2690	2193142	0.4310	−0.17	86541	0.997694	2.83
200	2705	67.3	1	2705	2195847	0.4315	−0.17	86542	0.997706	2.83
199	2720	67.3	1	2720	2198567	0.4320	−0.17	86543	0.997717	2.84
198	2727	67.3	1	2727	2201294	0.4326	−0.17	86544	0.997729	2.84
197	2734	67.3	1	2734	2204028	0.4331	−0.17	86545	0.997740	2.84
196	2761	67.3	1	2761	2206789	0.4337	−0.17	86546	0.997752	2.84
195	2777	67.4	1	2777	2209566	0.4342	−0.17	86547	0.997763	2.84
194	2799	67.4	1	2799	2212365	0.4348	−0.16	86548	0.997775	2.84
193	2801	67.4	1	2801	2215166	0.4353	−0.16	86549	0.997786	2.85
192	2824	67.4	1	2824	2217990	0.4359	−0.16	86550	0.997798	2.85
191	2831	67.5	1	2831	2220821	0.4364	−0.16	86551	0.997810	2.85
190	2832	67.5	1	2832	2223653	0.4370	−0.16	86552	0.997821	2.85
188– 189	2835	67.5	2	5670	2229323	0.4381	−0.16	86554	0.997844	2.85
187	2837	67.5	1	2837	2232160	0.4386	−0.15	86555	0.997856	2.86
186	2881	67.5	1	2881	2235041	0.4392	−0.15	86556	0.997867	2.86
185	2885	67.5	1	2885	2237926	0.4398	−0.15	86557	0.997879	2.86
184	2900	67.6	1	2900	2240826	0.4404	−0.15	86558	0.997890	2.86
183	2924	67.6	1	2924	2243750	0.4409	−0.15	86559	0.997902	2.86
182	2953	67.6	1	2953	2246703	0.4415	−0.15	86560	0.997913	2.86
181	2961	67.6	1	2961	2249664	0.4421	−0.15	86561	0.997925	2.87
180	2987	67.7	1	2987	2252651	0.4427	−0.14	86562	0.997936	2.87
179	3006	67.7	1	3006	2255657	0.4433	−0.14	86563	0.997948	2.87
177– 178	3030	67.7	2	6060	2261717	0.4445	−0.14	86565	0.997971	2.87
176	3057	67.8	1	3057	2264774	0.4451	−0.14	86566	0.997982	2.88
175	3115	67.9	1	3115	2267889	0.4457	−0.14	86567	0.997994	2.88
174	3122	67.9	1	3122	2271011	0.4463	−0.14	86568	0.998006	2.88
173	3197	68.0	1	3197	2274208	0.4469	−0.13	86569	0.998017	2.88
172	3222	68.0	1	3222	2277430	0.4475	−0.13	86570	0.998029	2.88
171	3276	68.1	1	3276	2280706	0.4482	−0.13	86571	0.998040	2.88
170	3293	68.1	1	3293	2283999	0.4488	−0.13	86572	0.998052	2.89
169	3308	68.1	1	3308	2287307	0.4495	−0.13	86573	0.998063	2.89
168	3324	68.2	1	3324	2290631	0.4501	−0.13	86574	0.998075	2.89
167	3362	68.2	1	3362	2293993	0.4508	−0.12	86575	0.998086	2.89
166	3366	68.2	1	3366	2297359	0.4515	−0.12	86576	0.998098	2.89
165	3398	68.2	1	3398	2300757	0.4521	−0.12	86577	0.998109	2.90
164	3421	68.3	1	3421	2304178	0.4528	−0.12	86578	0.998121	2.90
163	3470	68.3	1	3470	2307648	0.4535	−0.12	86579	0.998132	2.90
162	3476	68.3	1	3476	2311124	0.4542	−0.12	86580	0.998144	2.90
161	3555	68.4	1	3555	2314679	0.4549	−0.11	86581	0.998155	2.90
160	3572	68.5	1	3572	2318251	0.4556	−0.11	86582	0.998167	2.91
159	3673	68.6	1	3673	2321924	0.4563	−0.11	86583	0.998178	2.91
158	3715	68.6	1	3715	2325639	0.4570	−0.11	86584	0.998190	2.91
157	3748	68.7	1	3748	2329387	0.4578	−0.11	86585	0.998201	2.91
156	3766	68.7	1	3766	2333153	0.4585	−0.10	86586	0.998213	2.91
155	3814	68.7	1	3814	2336967	0.4592	−0.10	86587	0.998225	2.92
154	3855	68.8	1	3855	2340822	0.4600	−0.10	86588	0.998236	2.92
153	3873	68.8	1	3873	2344695	0.4608	−0.10	86589	0.998248	2.92
152	3875	68.8	1	3875	2348570	0.4615	−0.10	86590	0.998259	2.92

Rank	Occ. F	SFI	F	Tokens	Cum. Tokens	Cum. P Tokens	Y	Cum. Types	Cum. P Types	Z
151	3892	68.8	1	3892	2352462	0.4623	−0.09	86591	0.998271	2.92
150	3894	68.8	1	3894	2356356	0.4631	−0.09	86592	0.998282	2.93
149	3916	68.9	1	3916	2360272	0.4638	−0.09	86593	0.998294	2.93
148	3926	68.9	1	3926	2364198	0.4646	−0.09	86594	0.998305	2.93
147	3929	68.9	1	3929	2368127	0.4654	−0.09	86595	0.998317	2.93
146	3942	68.9	1	3942	2372069	0.4661	−0.08	86596	0.998328	2.93
145	3966	68.9	1	3966	2376035	0.4669	−0.08	86597	0.998340	2.94
144	4067	69.0	1	4067	2380102	0.4677	−0.08	86598	0.998351	2.94
143	4070	69.0	1	4070	2384172	0.4685	−0.08	86599	0.998363	2.94
142	4089	69.1	1	4089	2388261	0.4693	−0.08	86600	0.998374	2.94
141	4132	69.1	1	4132	2392393	0.4701	−0.07	86601	0.998386	2.95
140	4147	69.1	1	4147	2396540	0.4710	−0.07	86602	0.998397	2.95
139	4184	69.2	1	4184	2400724	0.4718	−0.07	86603	0.998409	2.95
138	4207	69.2	1	4207	2404931	0.4726	−0.07	86604	0.998421	2.95
137	4223	69.2	1	4223	2409154	0.4734	−0.07	86605	0.998432	2.95
136	4225	69.2	1	4225	2413379	0.4743	−0.06	86606	0.998444	2.96
135	4240	69.2	1	4240	2417619	0.4751	−0.06	86607	0.998455	2.96
134	4255	69.2	1	4255	2421874	0.4759	−0.06	86608	0.998467	2.96
133	4285	69.3	1	4285	2426159	0.4768	−0.06	86609	0.998478	2.96
132	4307	69.3	1	4307	2430466	0.4776	−0.06	86610	0.998490	2.97
131	4358	69.3	1	4358	2434824	0.4785	−0.05	86611	0.998501	2.97
130	4377	69.3	1	4377	2439201	0.4793	−0.05	86612	0.998513	2.97
129	4408	69.4	1	4408	2443609	0.4802	−0.05	86613	0.998524	2.97
128	4413	69.4	1	4413	2448022	0.4811	−0.05	86614	0.998536	2.98
127	4632	69.6	1	4632	2452654	0.4820	−0.05	86615	0.998547	2.98
126	4647	69.6	1	4647	2457301	0.4829	−0.04	86616	0.998559	2.98
125	4667	69.6	1	4667	2461968	0.4838	−0.04	86617	0.998570	2.98
124	4676	69.6	1	4676	2466644	0.4847	−0.04	86618	0.998582	2.98
123	4746	69.7	1	4746	2471390	0.4857	−0.04	86619	0.998594	2.99
122	4815	69.8	1	4815	2476205	0.4866	−0.03	86620	0.998605	2.99
121	4914	69.8	1	4914	2481119	0.4876	−0.03	86621	0.998617	2.99
120	4933	69.9	1	4933	2486052	0.4885	−0.03	86622	0.998628	3.00
119	5019	69.9	1	5019	2491071	0.4895	−0.03	86623	0.998640	3.00
118	5022	69.9	1	5022	2496093	0.4905	−0.02	86624	0.998651	3.00
117	5023	69.9	1	5023	2501116	0.4915	−0.02	86625	0.998663	3.00
116	5071	70.0	1	5071	2506187	0.4925	−0.02	86626	0.998674	3.01
115	5275	70.2	1	5275	2511462	0.4935	−0.02	86627	0.998686	3.01
114	5343	70.2	1	5343	2516805	0.4946	−0.01	86628	0.998697	3.01
113	5386	70.2	1	5386	2522191	0.4956	−0.01	86629	0.998709	3.01
112	5388	70.2	1	5388	2527579	0.4967	−0.01	86630	0.998720	3.02
111	5442	70.3	1	5442	2533021	0.4978	−0.01	86631	0.998732	3.02
110	5448	70.3	1	5448	2538469	0.4988	−0.00	86632	0.998743	3.02
109	5486	70.3	1	5486	2543955	0.4999	−0.00	86633	0.998755	3.02
108	5607	70.4	1	5607	2549562	0.5010	0.00	86634	0.998766	3.03
107	5611	70.4	1	5611	2555173	0.5021	0.01	86635	0.998778	3.03
106	5655	70.5	1	5655	2560828	0.5032	0.01	86636	0.998789	3.03
105	5700	70.5	1	5700	2566528	0.5044	0.01	86637	0.998801	3.04
104	5777	70.6	1	5777	2572305	0.5055	0.01	86638	0.998813	3.04
103	5785	70.6	1	5785	2578090	0.5066	0.02	86639	0.998824	3.04
102	5789	70.6	1	5789	2583879	0.5078	0.02	86640	0.998836	3.04
101	5858	70.6	1	5858	2589737	0.5089	0.02	86641	0.998847	3.05
100	5862	70.6	1	5862	2595599	0.5101	0.03	86642	0.998859	3.05
99	5915	70.7	1	5915	2601514	0.5112	0.03	86643	0.998870	3.05
98	5997	70.7	1	5997	2607541	0.5124	0.03	86644	0.998882	3.06
97	6059	70.8	1	6059	2613570	0.5136	0.03	86645	0.998893	3.06
96	6180	70.8	1	6180	2619750	0.5148	0.04	86646	0.998905	3.06
95	6204	70.9	1	6204	2625954	0.5160	0.04	86647	0.998916	3.07
94	6220	70.9	1	6220	2632174	0.5173	0.04	86648	0.998928	3.07
93	6583	71.1	1	6583	2638757	0.5186	0.05	86649	0.998939	3.07
92	6612	71.1	1	6612	2645369	0.5198	0.05	86650	0.998951	3.08
91	6635	71.2	1	6635	2652004	0.5212	0.05	86651	0.998962	3.08
90	6882	71.3	1	6882	2658886	0.5225	0.06	86652	0.998974	3.08
89	6916	71.3	1	6916	2665802	0.5239	0.06	86653	0.998985	3.09
88	7009	71.4	1	7009	2672811	0.5252	0.06	86654	0.998997	3.09
87	7073	71.4	1	7073	2679884	0.5266	0.07	86655	0.999009	3.09
86	7169	71.5	1	7169	2687053	0.5280	0.07	86656	0.999020	3.10
85	7194	71.5	1	7194	2694247	0.5295	0.07	86657	0.999032	3.10
84	7206	71.5	1	7206	2701453	0.5309	0.08	86658	0.999043	3.10
83	7457	71.7	1	7457	2708910	0.5323	0.08	86659	0.999055	3.11
82	7512	71.7	1	7512	2716422	0.5338	0.08	86660	0.999066	3.11
81	7532	71.7	1	7532	2723954	0.5353	0.09	86661	0.999078	3.11
80	7576	71.7	1	7576	2731530	0.5368	0.09	86662	0.999089	3.12
79	7645	71.8	1	7645	2739175	0.5383	0.10	86663	0.999101	3.12
78	7655	71.8	1	7655	2746830	0.5398	0.10	86664	0.999112	3.13
77	7898	71.9	1	7898	2754728	0.5413	0.10	86665	0.999124	3.13
76	7982	72.0	1	7982	2762710	0.5429	0.11	86666	0.999135	3.13
75	7989	72.0	1	7989	2770699	0.5445	0.11	86667	0.999147	3.14
74	8333	72.1	1	8333	2779032	0.5461	0.12	86668	0.999158	3.14
73	8441	72.2	1	8441	2787473	0.5478	0.12	86669	0.999170	3.15
72	8483	72.2	1	8483	2795956	0.5494	0.12	86670	0.999181	3.15
71	8518	72.2	1	8518	2804474	0.5511	0.13	86671	0.999193	3.15
70	8585	72.3	1	8585	2813059	0.5528	0.13	86672	0.999205	3.16
69	9696	72.8	1	9696	2822755	0.5547	0.14	86673	0.999216	3.16
68	9846	72.9	1	9846	2832601	0.5566	0.14	86674	0.999228	3.17
67	9992	72.9	1	9992	2842593	0.5586	0.15	86675	0.999239	3.17
66	10085	73.0	1	10085	2852678	0.5606	0.15	86676	0.999251	3.17
65	10369	73.1	1	10369	2863047	0.5626	0.16	86677	0.999262	3.18
64	10620	73.2	1	10620	2873667	0.5647	0.16	86678	0.999274	3.18
63	10703	73.2	1	10703	2884370	0.5668	0.17	86679	0.999285	3.19
62	10729	73.2	1	10729	2895099	0.5689	0.17	86680	0.999297	3.19
61	11188	73.4	1	11188	2906287	0.5711	0.18	86681	0.999308	3.20
60	11215	73.4	1	11215	2917502	0.5733	0.18	86682	0.999320	3.20
59	11375	73.5	1	11375	2928877	0.5756	0.19	86683	0.999331	3.21
58	11534	73.6	1	11534	2940411	0.5778	0.20	86684	0.999343	3.21
57	11543	73.6	1	11543	2951954	0.5801	0.20	86685	0.999354	3.22
56	11611	73.6	1	11611	2963565	0.5824	0.21	86686	0.999366	3.22
55	11997	73.7	1	11997	2975562	0.5847	0.21	86687	0.999377	3.23
54	12022	73.7	1	12022	2987584	0.5871	0.22	86688	0.999389	3.23
53	12158	73.8	1	12158	2999742	0.5895	0.23	86689	0.999400	3.24
52	12252	73.8	1	12252	3011994	0.5919	0.23	86690	0.999412	3.24
51	12496	73.9	1	12496	3024490	0.5944	0.24	86691	0.999424	3.25
50	12646	74.0	1	12646	3037136	0.5968	0.25	86692	0.999435	3.26
49	12695	74.0	1	12695	3049831	0.5993	0.25	86693	0.999447	3.26
48	12776	74.0	1	12776	3062607	0.6018	0.26	86694	0.999458	3.27
47	12907	74.0	1	12907	3075514	0.6044	0.26	86695	0.999470	3.27
46	13258	74.2	1	13258	3088772	0.6070	0.27	86696	0.999481	3.28
45	13303	74.2	1	13303	3102075	0.6096	0.28	86697	0.999493	3.29
44	13653	74.3	1	13653	3115728	0.6123	0.29	86698	0.999504	3.29
43	14016	74.4	1	14016	3129744	0.6150	0.29	86699	0.999516	3.30
42	14290	74.5	1	14290	3144034	0.6178	0.30	86700	0.999527	3.31
41	14696	74.6	1	14696	3158730	0.6207	0.31	86701	0.999539	3.31
40	15194	74.8	1	15194	3173924	0.6237	0.32	86702	0.999550	3.32
39	15247	74.8	1	15247	3189171	0.6267	0.32	86703	0.999562	3.33
38	15309	74.8	1	15309	3204480	0.6297	0.33	86704	0.999573	3.33
37	15311	74.8	1	15311	3219791	0.6327	0.34	86705	0.999585	3.34
36	15886	74.9	1	15886	3235677	0.6359	0.35	86706	0.999596	3.35
35	16452	75.1	1	16452	3252129	0.6391	0.36	86707	0.999608	3.36
34	16997	75.2	1	16997	3269126	0.6424	0.36	86708	0.999620	3.37
33	17031	75.2	1	17031	3286157	0.6458	0.37	86709	0.999631	3.38
32	17709	75.4	1	17709	3303866	0.6493	0.38	86710	0.999643	3.38
31	18645	75.6	1	18645	3322511	0.6529	0.39	86711	0.999654	3.39
30	19196	75.8	1	19196	3341707	0.6567	0.40	86712	0.999666	3.40
29	19976	75.9	1	19976	3361683	0.6606	0.41	86713	0.999677	3.41
28	20189	76.0	1	20189	3381872	0.6646	0.43	86714	0.999689	3.42
27	20511	76.1	1	20511	3402383	0.6686	0.44	86715	0.999700	3.43
26	21283	76.2	1	21283	3423666	0.6728	0.45	86716	0.999712	3.44
25	22337	76.4	1	22337	3446003	0.6772	0.46	86717	0.999723	3.45
24	22799	76.5	1	22799	3468802	0.6817	0.47	86718	0.999735	3.46
23	23301	76.6	1	23301	3492103	0.6862	0.49	86719	0.999746	3.48
22	23746	76.7	1	23746	3515849	0.6909	0.50	86720	0.999758	3.49
21	23975	76.7	1	23975	3539824	0.6956	0.51	86721	0.999769	3.50
20	25932	77.1	1	25932	3565756	0.7007	0.53	86722	0.999781	3.52
19	27620	77.3	1	27620	3593376	0.7061	0.54	86723	0.999792	3.53
18	29268	77.6	1	29268	3622644	0.7119	0.56	86724	0.999804	3.55
17	30455	77.8	1	30455	3653099	0.7179	0.58	86725	0.999816	3.56
16	32208	78.0	1	32208	3685307	0.7242	0.60	86726	0.999827	3.58
15	35454	78.4	1	35454	3720761	0.7312	0.62	86727	0.999839	3.60
14	36482	78.6	1	36482	3757243	0.7383	0.64	86728	0.999850	3.62
13	39322	78.9	1	39322	3796565	0.7461	0.66	86729	0.999862	3.64
12	40934	79.1	1	40934	3837499	0.7541	0.69	86730	0.999873	3.66
11	46249	79.6	1	46249	3883748	0.7632	0.72	86731	0.999885	3.68
10	47284	79.7	1	47284	3931032	0.7725	0.75	86732	0.999896	3.71
9	47443	79.7	1	47443	3978475	0.7818	0.78	86733	0.999908	3.74
8	50957	80.0	1	50957	4029432	0.7918	0.81	86734	0.999919	3.77
7	60852	80.8	1	60852	4090284	0.8038	0.86	86735	0.999931	3.81
6	99108	82.9	1	99108	4189392	0.8233	0.93	86736	0.999942	3.86
5	121347	83.8	1	121347	4310739	0.8471	1.02	86737	0.999954	3.91
4	124959	83.9	1	124959	4435698	0.8717	1.13	86738	0.999965	3.98
3	133899	84.2	1	133899	4569597	0.8980	1.27	86739	0.999977	4.07
2	146001	84.6	1	146001	4715598	0.9267	1.45	86740	0.999988	4.23
1	373123	88.7	1	373123	5088721	1.0000	+INF.	86741	1.000000	+INF.

Rank	Occ. F	SFI	F	Tokens	Cum. Tokens	Cum. P Tokens	Y	Cum. Types	Cum. P Types	Z
14515-23477	1	42.5	8963	8963	8963	0.0107	-2.30	8963	0.381778	-0.30
11351-14514	2	44.7	3164	6328	15291	0.0182	-2.09	12127	0.516548	0.04
9501-11350	3	46.2	1850	5550	20841	0.0248	-1.96	13977	0.595349	0.24
8269-9500	4	47.3	1232	4928	25769	0.0306	-1.87	15209	0.647825	0.38
7355-8268	5	48.2	914	4570	30339	0.0361	-1.80	16123	0.686757	0.49
6614-7354	6	48.9	741	4446	34785	0.0414	-1.74	16864	0.718320	0.58
6051-6613	7	49.5	563	3941	38726	0.0461	-1.68	17427	0.742301	0.65
5609-6050	8	50.0	442	3536	42262	0.0503	-1.64	17869	0.761128	0.71
5235-5608	9	50.5	374	3366	45628	0.0543	-1.60	18243	0.777058	0.76
4926-5234	10	51.0	309	3090	48718	0.0579	-1.57	18552	0.790220	0.81
4627-4925	11	51.4	299	3289	52007	0.0618	-1.54	18851	0.802956	0.85
4353-4626	12	51.7	274	3288	55295	0.0658	-1.51	19125	0.814627	0.90
4131-4352	13	52.1	222	2886	58181	0.0692	-1.48	19347	0.824083	0.93
3933-4130	14	52.4	198	2772	60953	0.0725	-1.46	19545	0.832517	0.96
3774-3932	15	52.7	159	2385	63338	0.0753	-1.44	19704	0.839289	0.99
3619-3773	16	52.9	155	2480	65818	0.0783	-1.42	19859	0.845892	1.02
3481-3618	17	53.2	138	2346	68164	0.0811	-1.40	19997	0.851770	1.04
3356-3480	18	53.4	125	2250	70414	0.0837	-1.38	20122	0.857094	1.07
3243-3355	19	53.7	113	2147	72561	0.0863	-1.36	20235	0.861907	1.09
3127-3242	20	53.9	116	2320	74881	0.0891	-1.35	20351	0.866848	1.11
3044-3126	21	54.1	83	1743	76624	0.0911	-1.33	20434	0.870384	1.13
2950-3043	22	54.3	94	2068	78692	0.0936	-1.32	20528	0.874388	1.15
2853-2949	23	54.5	97	2231	80923	0.0962	-1.30	20625	0.878519	1.17
2753-2852	24	54.6	100	2400	83323	0.0991	-1.29	20725	0.882779	1.19
2678-2752	25	54.8	75	1875	85198	0.1013	-1.27	20800	0.885973	1.21
2608-2677	26	55.0	70	1820	87018	0.1035	-1.26	20870	0.888955	1.22
2544-2607	27	55.1	64	1728	88746	0.1055	-1.25	20934	0.891681	1.24
2487-2543	28	55.3	57	1596	90342	0.1074	-1.24	20991	0.894109	1.25
2425-2486	29	55.5	62	1798	92140	0.1096	-1.23	21053	0.896750	1.26
2375-2424	30	55.6	50	1500	93640	0.1114	-1.22	21103	0.898880	1.28
2320-2374	31	55.7	55	1705	95345	0.1134	-1.21	21158	0.901222	1.29
2273-2319	32	55.9	47	1504	96849	0.1152	-1.20	21205	0.903224	1.30
2222-2272	33	56.0	51	1683	98532	0.1172	-1.19	21256	0.905397	1.31
2178-2221	34	56.1	44	1496	100028	0.1190	-1.18	21300	0.907271	1.32
2137-2177	35	56.3	41	1435	101463	0.1207	-1.17	21341	0.909017	1.33
2089-2136	36	56.4	48	1728	103191	0.1227	-1.16	21389	0.911062	1.35
2057-2088	37	56.5	32	1184	104375	0.1241	-1.15	21421	0.912425	1.36
2019-2056	38	56.6	38	1444	105819	0.1258	-1.15	21459	0.914043	1.37
1982-2018	39	56.7	37	1443	107262	0.1276	-1.14	21496	0.915619	1.38
1944-1981	40	56.8	38	1520	108782	0.1294	-1.13	21534	0.917238	1.39
1908-1943	41	56.9	36	1476	110258	0.1311	-1.12	21570	0.918772	1.40
1875-1907	42	57.0	33	1386	111644	0.1328	-1.11	21603	0.920177	1.41
1854-1874	43	57.1	21	903	112547	0.1338	-1.11	21624	0.921072	1.41
1825-1853	44	57.2	29	1276	113823	0.1354	-1.10	21653	0.922307	1.42
1786-1824	45	57.3	39	1755	115578	0.1375	-1.09	21692	0.923968	1.43
1760-1785	46	57.4	26	1196	116774	0.1389	-1.09	21718	0.925076	1.44
1739-1759	47	57.5	21	987	117761	0.1400	-1.08	21739	0.925970	1.45
1718-1738	48	57.6	21	1008	118769	0.1412	-1.07	21760	0.926865	1.45
1688-1717	49	57.7	30	1470	120239	0.1430	-1.07	21790	0.928142	1.46
1663-1687	50	57.8	25	1250	121489	0.1445	-1.06	21815	0.929207	1.47
1637-1662	51	57.9	26	1326	122815	0.1461	-1.05	21841	0.930315	1.48
1619-1636	52	58.0	18	936	123751	0.1472	-1.05	21859	0.931081	1.48
1604-1618	53	58.0	15	795	124546	0.1481	-1.04	21874	0.931720	1.49
1583-1603	54	58.1	21	1134	125680	0.1495	-1.04	21895	0.932615	1.50
1562-1582	55	58.2	21	1155	126835	0.1508	-1.03	21916	0.933509	1.50
1545-1561	56	58.3	17	952	127787	0.1520	-1.03	21933	0.934233	1.51
1522-1544	57	58.3	23	1311	129098	0.1535	-1.02	21956	0.935213	1.52
1498-1521	58	58.4	24	1392	130490	0.1552	-1.01	21980	0.936235	1.52
1483-1497	59	58.5	15	885	131375	0.1562	-1.01	21995	0.936874	1.53
1458-1482	60	58.6	25	1500	132875	0.1580	-1.00	22020	0.937939	1.54
1437-1457	61	58.6	21	1281	134156	0.1595	-1.00	22041	0.938834	1.55
1413-1436	62	58.7	24	1488	135644	0.1613	-0.99	22065	0.939856	1.55
1392-1412	63	58.8	21	1323	136967	0.1629	-0.98	22086	0.940750	1.56
1364-1391	64	58.8	28	1792	138759	0.1650	-0.97	22114	0.941943	1.57
1347-1363	65	58.9	17	1105	139864	0.1663	-0.97	22131	0.942667	1.58
1328-1346	66	59.0	19	1254	141118	0.1678	-0.96	22150	0.943477	1.58
1314-1327	67	59.0	14	938	142056	0.1689	-0.96	22164	0.944073	1.59
1293-1313	68	59.1	21	1428	143484	0.1706	-0.95	22185	0.944967	1.60
1284-1292	69	59.2	9	621	144105	0.1714	-0.95	22194	0.945351	1.60
1276-1283	70	59.2	8	560	144665	0.1720	-0.95	22202	0.945692	1.60
1262-1275	71	59.3	14	994	145659	0.1732	-0.94	22216	0.946288	1.61
1253-1261	72	59.4	9	648	146307	0.1740	-0.94	22225	0.946671	1.61
1238-1252	73	59.4	15	1095	147402	0.1753	-0.93	22240	0.947310	1.62
1225-1237	74	59.5	13	962	148364	0.1764	-0.93	22253	0.947864	1.62
1216-1224	75	59.5	9	675	149039	0.1772	-0.93	22262	0.948247	1.63
1202-1215	76	59.6	14	1064	150103	0.1785	-0.92	22276	0.948844	1.63
1186-1201	77	59.6	16	1232	151335	0.1800	-0.92	22292	0.949525	1.64
1172-1185	78	59.7	14	1092	152427	0.1813	-0.91	22306	0.950121	1.65
1164-1171	79	59.8	8	632	153059	0.1820	-0.91	22314	0.950462	1.65
1149-1163	80	59.8	15	1200	154259	0.1835	-0.90	22329	0.951101	1.66
1139-1148	81	59.9	10	810	155069	0.1844	-0.90	22339	0.951527	1.66
1129-1138	82	59.9	10	820	155889	0.1854	-0.90	22349	0.951953	1.66
1119-1128	83	60.0	10	830	156719	0.1864	-0.89	22359	0.952379	1.67
1107-1118	84	60.0	12	1008	157727	0.1876	-0.89	22371	0.952890	1.67
1093-1106	85	60.1	14	1190	158917	0.1890	-0.88	22385	0.953486	1.68
1083-1092	86	60.1	10	860	159777	0.1900	-0.88	22395	0.953912	1.68
1071-1082	87	60.2	12	1044	160821	0.1913	-0.87	22407	0.954423	1.69
1064-1070	88	60.2	7	616	161437	0.1920	-0.87	22414	0.954722	1.69
1058-1063	89	60.3	6	534	161971	0.1926	-0.87	22420	0.954977	1.70
1047-1057	90	60.3	11	990	162961	0.1938	-0.86	22431	0.955446	1.70
1036-1046	91	60.4	11	1001	163962	0.1950	-0.86	22442	0.955914	1.71
1027-1035	92	60.4	9	828	164790	0.1960	-0.86	22451	0.956298	1.71
1016-1026	93	60.5	11	1023	165813	0.1972	-0.85	22462	0.956766	1.71
1001-1015	94	60.5	15	1410	167223	0.1989	-0.85	22477	0.957405	1.72
990-1000	95	60.6	11	1045	168268	0.2001	-0.84	22488	0.957874	1.73
981-989	96	60.6	9	864	169132	0.2011	-0.84	22497	0.958257	1.73
977-980	97	60.6	4	388	169520	0.2016	-0.84	22501	0.958427	1.73
972-976	98	60.7	5	490	170010	0.2022	-0.83	22506	0.958640	1.74
963-971	99	60.7	9	891	170901	0.2032	-0.83	22515	0.959024	1.74
956-962	100	60.8	7	700	171601	0.2041	-0.83	22522	0.959322	1.74
947-955	101	60.8	9	909	172510	0.2052	-0.82	22531	0.959705	1.75
941-946	102	60.9	6	612	173122	0.2059	-0.82	22537	0.959961	1.75
933-940	103	60.9	8	824	173946	0.2069	-0.82	22545	0.960302	1.75
928-932	104	60.9	5	520	174466	0.2075	-0.82	22550	0.960515	1.76
923-927	105	61.0	5	525	174991	0.2081	-0.81	22555	0.960728	1.76
916-922	106	61.0	7	742	175733	0.2090	-0.81	22562	0.961026	1.76
906-915	107	61.1	10	1070	176803	0.2103	-0.81	22572	0.961452	1.77
897-905	108	61.1	9	972	177775	0.2114	-0.80	22581	0.961835	1.77
889-896	109	61.1	8	872	178647	0.2125	-0.80	22589	0.962176	1.78
878-888	110	61.2	11	1210	179857	0.2139	-0.79	22600	0.962644	1.78
872-877	111	61.2	6	666	180523	0.2147	-0.79	22606	0.962900	1.79
868-871	112	61.3	4	448	180971	0.2152	-0.79	22610	0.963070	1.79
861-867	113	61.3	7	791	181762	0.2162	-0.79	22617	0.963368	1.79
854-860	114	61.3	7	798	182560	0.2171	-0.78	22624	0.963667	1.79
848-853	115	61.4	6	690	183250	0.2179	-0.78	22630	0.963922	1.80
842-847	116	61.4	6	696	183946	0.2188	-0.78	22636	0.964178	1.80
836-841	117	61.5	6	702	184648	0.2196	-0.77	22642	0.964433	1.80
829-835	118	61.5	7	826	185474	0.2206	-0.77	22649	0.964731	1.81
822-828	119	61.5	7	833	186307	0.2216	-0.77	22656	0.965030	1.81
813-821	120	61.6	9	1080	187387	0.2229	-0.76	22665	0.965413	1.82
810-812	121	61.6	3	363	187750	0.2233	-0.76	22668	0.965541	1.82
805-809	122	61.6	5	610	188360	0.2240	-0.76	22673	0.965754	1.82
798-804	123	61.7	7	861	189221	0.2250	-0.76	22680	0.966052	1.83
791-797	124	61.7	7	868	190089	0.2261	-0.75	22687	0.966350	1.83
786-790	125	61.7	5	625	190714	0.2268	-0.75	22692	0.966563	1.83
784-785	126	61.8	2	252	190966	0.2271	-0.75	22694	0.966648	1.83
777-783	127	61.8	7	889	191855	0.2282	-0.74	22701	0.966946	1.84
774-776	128	61.8	3	384	192239	0.2286	-0.74	22704	0.967074	1.84
771-773	129	61.9	3	387	192626	0.2291	-0.74	22707	0.967202	1.84
766-770	130	61.9	5	650	193276	0.2299	-0.74	22712	0.967415	1.84
762-765	131	61.9	4	524	193800	0.2305	-0.74	22716	0.967585	1.85
754-761	132	62.0	8	1056	194856	0.2317	-0.73	22724	0.967926	1.85
742-753	133	62.0	12	1596	196452	0.2336	-0.73	22736	0.968437	1.86
741	134	62.0	1	134	196586	0.2338	-0.73	22737	0.968480	1.86
735-740	135	62.1	6	810	197396	0.2348	-0.72	22743	0.968735	1.86
729-734	136	62.1	6	816	198212	0.2357	-0.72	22749	0.968991	1.87
726-728	137	62.1	3	411	198623	0.2362	-0.72	22752	0.969119	1.87
721-725	138	62.2	5	690	199313	0.2370	-0.72	22757	0.969332	1.87
718-720	139	62.2	3	417	199730	0.2375	-0.71	22760	0.969459	1.87
710-717	140	62.2	8	1120	200850	0.2389	-0.71	22768	0.969800	1.88
707-709	141	62.3	3	423	201273	0.2394	-0.71	22771	0.969928	1.88
702-706	142	62.3	5	710	201983	0.2402	-0.71	22776	0.970141	1.88
699-701	143	62.3	3	429	202412	0.2407	-0.70	22779	0.970269	1.88
694-698	144	62.4	5	720	203132	0.2416	-0.70	22784	0.970482	1.89
687-693	145	62.4	7	1015	204147	0.2428	-0.70	22791	0.970780	1.89
679-686	146	62.4	8	1168	205315	0.2442	-0.69	22799	0.971121	1.90
673-678	147	62.4	6	882	206197	0.2452	-0.69	22805	0.971376	1.90
672	148	62.5	1	148	206345	0.2454	-0.69	22806	0.971419	1.90
666-671	149	62.5	6	894	207239	0.2465	-0.69	22812	0.971674	1.91
659-665	150	62.5	7	1050	208289	0.2477	-0.68	22819	0.971973	1.91
656-658	152	62.6	3	456	208745	0.2483	-0.68	22822	0.972100	1.91
652-655	153	62.6	4	612	209357	0.2490	-0.68	22826	0.972271	1.92
647-651	154	62.6	5	770	210127	0.2499	-0.67	22831	0.972484	1.92
644-646	155	62.7	3	465	210592	0.2504	-0.67	22834	0.972611	1.92
643	156	62.7	1	156	210748	0.2506	-0.67	22835	0.972654	1.92
642	157	62.7	1	157	210905	0.2508	-0.67	22836	0.972697	1.92
639-641	158	62.8	3	474	211379	0.2514	-0.67	22839	0.972824	1.92
636-638	159	62.8	3	477	211856	0.2520	-0.67	22842	0.972952	1.93
634-635	160	62.8	2	320	212176	0.2523	-0.67	22844	0.973037	1.93
632-633	161	62.8	2	322	212498	0.2527	-0.67	22846	0.973123	1.93
627-631	162	62.9	5	810	213308	0.2537	-0.66	22851	0.973336	1.93
620-626	163	62.9	7	1141	214449	0.2550	-0.66	22858	0.973634	1.94
618-619	164	62.9	2	328	214777	0.2554	-0.66	22860	0.973719	1.94
613-617	165	62.9	5	825	215602	0.2564	-0.65	22865	0.973932	1.94
611-612	166	63.0	2	332	215934	0.2568	-0.65	22867	0.974017	1.94
607-610	167	63.0	4	668	216602	0.2576	-0.65	22871	0.974187	1.95
603-606	168	63.0	4	672	217274	0.2584	-0.65	22875	0.974358	1.95
599-602	169	63.0	4	676	217950	0.2592	-0.65	22879	0.974528	1.95
594-598	170	63.1	5	850	218800	0.2602	-0.64	22884	0.974741	1.96
589-593	171	63.1	5	855	219655	0.2612	-0.64	22889	0.974954	1.96
586-588	172	63.1	3	516	220171	0.2618	-0.64	22892	0.975082	1.96
580-585	173	63.1	6	1038	221209	0.2631	-0.63	22898	0.975338	1.97
577-579	174	63.2	3	522	221731	0.2637	-0.63	22901	0.975465	1.97
573-576	175	63.2	4	700	222431	0.2645	-0.63	22905	0.975636	1.97
571-572	176	63.2	2	352	222783	0.2649	-0.63	22907	0.975721	1.97
569-570	177	63.2	2	354	223137	0.2654	-0.63	22909	0.975806	1.97
563-568	178	63.3	6	1068	224205	0.2666	-0.62	22915	0.976062	1.98
562	179	63.3	1	179	224384	0.2669	-0.62	22916	0.976104	1.98
560-561	180	63.3	2	360	224744	0.2673	-0.62	22918	0.976189	1.98
558-559	181	63.3	2	362	225106	0.2677	-0.62	22920	0.976275	1.98
552-557	182	63.4	6	1092	226198	0.2690	-0.62	22926	0.976530	1.99
548-551	183	63.4	4	732	226930	0.2699	-0.61	22930	0.976701	1.99
544-547	184	63.4	4	736	227666	0.2708	-0.61	22934	0.976871	1.99
543	185	63.4	1	185	227851	0.2710	-0.61	22935	0.976914	1.99
540-542	186	63.5	3	558	228409	0.2716	-0.61	22938	0.977041	2.00
538-539	187	63.5	2	374	228783	0.2721	-0.61	22940	0.977127	2.00
535-537	188	63.5	3	564	229347	0.2728	-0.60	22943	0.977254	2.00
530-534	189	63.5	5	945	230292	0.2739	-0.60	22948	0.977467	2.00
528-529	191	63.6	2	382	230674	0.2743	-0.60	22950	0.977552	2.01
527	192	63.6	1	192	230866	0.2746	-0.60	22951	0.977595	2.01
524-526	193	63.6	3	579	231445	0.2752	-0.60	22954	0.977723	2.01
520-523	194	63.6	4	776	232221	0.2762	-0.59	22958	0.977893	2.01
518-519	195	63.7	2	390	232611	0.2766	-0.59	22960	0.977978	2.01
516-517	197	63.7	2	394	233005	0.2771	-0.59	22962	0.978064	2.02
512-515	198	63.7	4	792	233797	0.2780	-0.59	22966	0.978234	2.02
511	199	63.8	1	199	233996	0.2783	-0.59	22967	0.978277	2.02
510	200	63.8	1	200	234196	0.2785	-0.59	22968	0.978319	2.02
504-509	201	63.8	6	1206	235402	0.2800	-0.58	22974	0.978575	2.03
501-503	202	63.8	3	606	236008	0.2807	-0.58	22977	0.978703	2.03
499-500	203	63.8	2	406	236414	0.2812	-0.58	22979	0.978788	2.03
498	204	63.9	1	204	236618	0.2814	-0.58	22980	0.978830	2.03
494-497	205	63.9	4	820	237438	0.2824	-0.58	22984	0.979001	2.03
491-493	206	63.9	3	618	238056	0.2831	-0.57	22987	0.979128	2.04
490	207	63.9	1	207	238263	0.2834	-0.57	22988	0.979171	2.04
486-489	208	63.9	4	832	239095	0.2843	-0.57	22992	0.979341	2.04
485	209	64.0	1	209	239304	0.2846	-0.57	22993	0.979384	2.04
482-484	210	64.0	3	630	239934	0.2853	-0.57	22996	0.979512	2.04
479-481	211	64.0	3	633	240567	0.2861	-0.56	22999	0.979640	2.05
477-478	212	64.0	2	424	240991	0.2866	-0.56	23001	0.979725	2.05
475-476	213	64.0	2	426	241417	0.2871	-0.56	23003	0.979810	2.05
474	214	64.1	1	214	241631	0.2874	-0.56	23004	0.979853	2.05
473	215	64.1	1	215	241846	0.2876	-0.56	23005	0.979895	2.05
470-472	216	64.1	3	648	242494	0.2884	-0.56	23008	0.980023	2.05
468-469	217	64.1	2	434	242928	0.2889	-0.56	23010	0.980108	2.06
467	218	64.1	1	218	243146	0.2892	-0.56	23011	0.980151	2.06
465-466	221	64.2	2	442	243588	0.2897	-0.55	23013	0.980236	2.06
460-464	222	64.2	5	1110	244698	0.2910	-0.55	23018	0.980449	2.06
458-459	223	64.2	2	446	245144	0.2915	-0.55	23020	0.980534	2.06
456-457	224	64.3	2	448	245592	0.2921	-0.55	23022	0.980619	2.07
454-455	226	64.3	2	452	246044	0.2926	-0.55	23024	0.980704	2.07
448-453	227	64.3	6	1362	247406	0.2942	-0.54	23030	0.980960	2.07
446-447	228	64.3	2	456	247862	0.2948	-0.54	23032	0.981045	2.08
445	229	64.4	1	229	248091	0.2950	-0.54	23033	0.981088	2.08
443-444	230	64.4	2	460	248551	0.2956	-0.54	23035	0.981173	2.08
439-442	232	64.4	4	928	249479	0.2967	-0.53	23039	0.981343	2.08
438	233	64.4	1	233	249712	0.2970	-0.53	23040	0.981386	2.08
435-437	234	64.5	3	702	250414	0.2978	-0.53	23043	0.981514	2.09
432-434	235	64.5	3	705	251119	0.2986	-0.53	23046	0.981642	2.09
430-431	236	64.5	2	472	251591	0.2992	-0.53	23048	0.981727	2.09
429	237	64.5	1	237	251828	0.2995	-0.53	23049	0.981769	2.09
428	238	64.5	1	238	252066	0.2998	-0.53	23050	0.981812	2.09
427	239	64.5	1	239	252305	0.3001	-0.52	23051	0.981855	2.09

Rank	Occ. F	SFI	F	Tokens	Cum. Tokens	Cum. P Tokens	Y	Cum. Types	Cum. P Types	Z
424– 426	240	64.6	3	720	253025	0.3009	−0.52	23054	0.981982	2.10
423	241	64.6	1	241	253266	0.3012	−0.52	23055	0.982025	2.10
422	242	64.6	1	242	253508	0.3015	−0.52	23056	0.982068	2.10
421	243	64.6	1	243	253751	0.3018	−0.52	23057	0.982110	2.10
419– 420	245	64.7	2	490	254241	0.3024	−0.52	23059	0.982195	2.10
416– 418	246	64.7	3	738	254979	0.3032	−0.52	23062	0.982323	2.10
414– 415	248	64.7	2	496	255475	0.3038	−0.51	23064	0.982408	2.11
412– 413	249	64.7	2	498	255973	0.3044	−0.51	23066	0.982493	2.11
411	250	64.7	1	250	256223	0.3047	−0.51	23067	0.982536	2.11
409– 410	251	64.8	2	502	256725	0.3053	−0.51	23069	0.982621	2.11
407– 408	252	64.8	2	504	257229	0.3059	−0.51	23071	0.982706	2.11
405– 406	253	64.8	2	506	257735	0.3065	−0.51	23073	0.982792	2.12
404	254	64.8	1	254	257989	0.3068	−0.50	23074	0.982834	2.12
400– 403	258	64.9	4	1032	259021	0.3080	−0.50	23078	0.983005	2.12
397– 399	259	64.9	3	777	259798	0.3090	−0.50	23081	0.983132	2.12
396	261	64.9	1	261	260059	0.3093	−0.50	23082	0.983175	2.12
395	263	65.0	1	263	260322	0.3096	−0.50	23083	0.983218	2.13
393– 394	264	65.0	2	528	260850	0.3102	−0.50	23085	0.983303	2.13
392	265	65.0	1	265	261115	0.3105	−0.49	23086	0.983345	2.13
390– 391	266	65.0	2	532	261647	0.3112	−0.49	23088	0.983431	2.13
387– 389	268	65.0	3	804	262451	0.3121	−0.49	23091	0.983558	2.13
385– 386	269	65.1	2	538	262989	0.3128	−0.49	23093	0.983644	2.14
382– 384	270	65.1	3	810	263799	0.3137	−0.49	23096	0.983771	2.14
380– 381	274	65.1	2	548	264347	0.3144	−0.48	23098	0.983856	2.14
376– 379	276	65.2	4	1104	265451	0.3157	−0.48	23102	0.984027	2.15
374– 375	277	65.2	2	554	266005	0.3163	−0.48	23104	0.984112	2.15
373	278	65.2	1	278	266283	0.3167	−0.48	23105	0.984155	2.15
372	279	65.2	1	279	266562	0.3170	−0.48	23106	0.984197	2.15
368– 371	280	65.2	4	1120	267682	0.3183	−0.47	23110	0.984368	2.15
367	281	65.2	1	281	267963	0.3187	−0.47	23111	0.984410	2.15
365– 366	282	65.3	2	564	268527	0.3193	−0.47	23113	0.984495	2.16
364	283	65.3	1	283	268810	0.3197	−0.47	23114	0.984538	2.16
362– 363	284	65.3	2	568	269378	0.3204	−0.47	23116	0.984623	2.16
360– 361	285	65.3	2	570	269948	0.3210	−0.46	23118	0.984708	2.16
358– 359	286	65.3	2	572	270520	0.3217	−0.46	23120	0.984794	2.16
357	287	65.3	1	287	270807	0.3221	−0.46	23121	0.984836	2.17
354– 356	288	65.4	3	864	271671	0.3231	−0.46	23124	0.984964	2.17
353	289	65.4	1	289	271960	0.3234	−0.46	23125	0.985007	2.17
350– 352	293	65.4	3	879	272839	0.3245	−0.46	23128	0.985134	2.17
347– 349	294	65.4	3	882	273721	0.3255	−0.45	23131	0.985262	2.18
345– 346	297	65.5	2	594	274315	0.3262	−0.45	23133	0.985347	2.18
344	299	65.5	1	299	274614	0.3266	−0.45	23134	0.985390	2.18
343	300	65.5	1	300	274914	0.3269	−0.45	23135	0.985433	2.18
342	301	65.5	1	301	275215	0.3273	−0.45	23136	0.985475	2.18
339– 341	302	65.6	3	906	276121	0.3284	−0.44	23139	0.985603	2.19
338	303	65.6	1	303	276424	0.3287	−0.44	23140	0.985645	2.19
337	304	65.6	1	304	276728	0.3291	−0.44	23141	0.985688	2.19
336	305	65.6	1	305	277033	0.3295	−0.44	23142	0.985731	2.19
333– 335	307	65.6	3	921	277954	0.3306	−0.44	23145	0.985858	2.19
332	308	65.6	1	308	278262	0.3309	−0.44	23146	0.985901	2.19
331	309	65.7	1	309	278571	0.3313	−0.44	23147	0.985944	2.20
330	310	65.7	1	310	278881	0.3317	−0.44	23148	0.985986	2.20
328– 329	312	65.7	2	624	279505	0.3324	−0.43	23150	0.986071	2.20
327	313	65.7	1	313	279818	0.3328	−0.43	23151	0.986114	2.20
326	314	65.7	1	314	280132	0.3332	−0.43	23152	0.986157	2.20
325	315	65.7	1	315	280447	0.3335	−0.43	23153	0.986199	2.20
324	319	65.8	1	319	280766	0.3339	−0.43	23154	0.986242	2.20
323	320	65.8	1	320	281086	0.3343	−0.43	23155	0.986284	2.21
321– 322	321	65.8	2	642	281728	0.3350	−0.43	23157	0.986370	2.21
320	322	65.8	1	322	282050	0.3354	−0.42	23158	0.986412	2.21
319	324	65.9	1	324	282374	0.3358	−0.42	23159	0.986455	2.21
317– 318	331	66.0	2	662	283036	0.3366	−0.42	23161	0.986540	2.21
316	333	66.0	1	333	283369	0.3370	−0.42	23162	0.986583	2.21
315	334	66.0	1	334	283703	0.3374	−0.42	23163	0.986625	2.22
314	335	66.0	1	335	284038	0.3378	−0.42	23164	0.986668	2.22
313	336	66.0	1	336	284374	0.3382	−0.42	23165	0.986710	2.22
312	337	66.0	1	337	284711	0.3386	−0.42	23166	0.986753	2.22
311	340	66.1	1	340	285051	0.3390	−0.42	23167	0.986796	2.22
310	341	66.1	1	341	285392	0.3394	−0.41	23168	0.986838	2.22
309	344	66.1	1	344	285736	0.3398	−0.41	23169	0.986881	2.22
308	345	66.1	1	345	286081	0.3402	−0.41	23170	0.986923	2.22
307	346	66.1	1	346	286427	0.3406	−0.41	23171	0.986966	2.23
304– 306	347	66.2	3	1041	287468	0.3419	−0.41	23174	0.987094	2.23
303	353	66.2	1	353	287821	0.3423	−0.41	23175	0.987136	2.23
301– 302	354	66.2	2	708	288529	0.3431	−0.40	23177	0.987221	2.23
300	355	66.3	1	355	288884	0.3436	−0.40	23178	0.987264	2.23
299	357	66.3	1	357	289241	0.3440	−0.40	23179	0.987307	2.24
297– 298	361	66.3	2	722	289963	0.3448	−0.40	23181	0.987392	2.24
294– 296	362	66.3	3	1086	291049	0.3461	−0.40	23184	0.987520	2.24
291– 293	366	66.4	3	1098	292147	0.3474	−0.39	23187	0.987647	2.25
290	367	66.4	1	367	292514	0.3479	−0.39	23188	0.987690	2.25
289	368	66.4	1	368	292882	0.3483	−0.39	23189	0.987733	2.25
287– 288	370	66.4	2	740	293622	0.3492	−0.39	23191	0.987818	2.25
286	371	66.5	1	371	293993	0.3496	−0.39	23192	0.987860	2.25
283– 285	372	66.5	3	1116	295109	0.3510	−0.38	23195	0.987988	2.26
282	374	66.5	1	374	295483	0.3514	−0.38	23196	0.988031	2.26
279– 281	375	66.5	3	1125	296608	0.3527	−0.38	23199	0.988159	2.26
278	378	66.5	1	378	296986	0.3532	−0.38	23200	0.988201	2.26
276– 277	379	66.5	2	758	297744	0.3541	−0.37	23202	0.988286	2.27
274– 275	380	66.6	2	760	298504	0.3550	−0.37	23204	0.988372	2.27
273	384	66.6	1	384	298888	0.3555	−0.37	23205	0.988414	2.27
272	386	66.6	1	386	299274	0.3559	−0.37	23206	0.988457	2.27
270– 271	388	66.6	2	776	300050	0.3568	−0.37	23208	0.988542	2.27
269	390	66.7	1	390	300440	0.3573	−0.37	23209	0.988585	2.28
268	394	66.7	1	394	300834	0.3578	−0.36	23210	0.988627	2.28
266– 267	396	66.7	2	792	301626	0.3587	−0.36	23212	0.988712	2.28
265	397	66.7	1	397	302023	0.3592	−0.36	23213	0.988755	2.28
263– 264	398	66.8	2	796	302819	0.3601	−0.36	23215	0.988840	2.28
262	399	66.8	1	399	303218	0.3606	−0.36	23216	0.988883	2.29
261	400	66.8	1	400	303618	0.3611	−0.36	23217	0.988925	2.29
259– 260	402	66.8	2	804	304422	0.3620	−0.35	23219	0.989011	2.29
257– 258	403	66.8	2	806	305228	0.3630	−0.35	23221	0.989096	2.29
256	406	66.8	1	406	305634	0.3635	−0.35	23222	0.989138	2.30
255	407	66.9	1	407	306041	0.3640	−0.35	23223	0.989181	2.30
254	409	66.9	1	409	306450	0.3644	−0.35	23224	0.989223	2.30
252– 253	411	66.9	2	822	307272	0.3654	−0.34	23226	0.989309	2.30
250– 251	412	66.9	2	824	308096	0.3664	−0.34	23228	0.989394	2.30
249	418	67.0	1	418	308514	0.3669	−0.34	23229	0.989436	2.31
247– 248	422	67.0	2	844	309358	0.3679	−0.34	23231	0.989522	2.31
246	424	67.0	1	424	309782	0.3684	−0.34	23232	0.989564	2.31
245	425	67.0	1	425	310207	0.3689	−0.33	23233	0.989607	2.31
243– 244	426	67.1	2	852	311059	0.3699	−0.33	23235	0.989692	2.31
242	429	67.1	1	429	311488	0.3704	−0.33	23236	0.989735	2.32
240– 241	430	67.1	2	860	312348	0.3715	−0.33	23238	0.989820	2.32
239	431	67.1	1	431	312779	0.3720	−0.33	23239	0.989862	2.32
237– 238	433	67.1	2	866	313645	0.3730	−0.32	23241	0.989948	2.32

Rank	Occ. F	SFI	F	Tokens	Cum. Tokens	Cum. P Tokens	Y	Cum. Types	Cum. P Types	Z
235– 236	435	67.1	2	870	314515	0.3740	−0.32	23243	0.990033	2.33
234	436	67.2	1	436	314951	0.3746	−0.32	23244	0.990075	2.33
233	445	67.2	1	445	315396	0.3751	−0.32	23245	0.990118	2.33
232	446	67.3	1	446	315842	0.3756	−0.32	23246	0.990161	2.33
231	447	67.3	1	447	316289	0.3762	−0.32	23247	0.990203	2.33
229– 230	448	67.3	2	896	317185	0.3772	−0.31	23249	0.990288	2.34
228	451	67.3	1	451	317636	0.3778	−0.31	23250	0.990331	2.34
227	455	67.3	1	455	318091	0.3783	−0.31	23251	0.990374	2.34
226	457	67.4	1	457	318548	0.3788	−0.31	23252	0.990416	2.34
225	460	67.4	1	460	319008	0.3794	−0.31	23253	0.990459	2.34
224	465	67.4	1	465	319473	0.3799	−0.31	23254	0.990501	2.35
223	471	67.5	1	471	319944	0.3805	−0.30	23255	0.990544	2.35
222	472	67.5	1	472	320416	0.3811	−0.30	23256	0.990587	2.35
221	473	67.5	1	473	320889	0.3816	−0.30	23257	0.990629	2.35
220	484	67.6	1	484	321373	0.3822	−0.30	23258	0.990672	2.35
219	487	67.6	1	487	321860	0.3828	−0.30	23259	0.990714	2.35
218	488	67.6	1	488	322348	0.3834	−0.30	23260	0.990757	2.36
217	492	67.7	1	492	322840	0.3839	−0.30	23261	0.990799	2.36
216	494	67.7	1	494	323334	0.3845	−0.29	23262	0.990842	2.36
215	497	67.7	1	497	323831	0.3851	−0.29	23263	0.990885	2.36
214	499	67.7	1	499	324330	0.3857	−0.29	23264	0.990927	2.36
213	501	67.8	1	501	324831	0.3863	−0.29	23265	0.990970	2.36
212	505	67.8	1	505	325336	0.3869	−0.29	23266	0.991012	2.37
211	506	67.8	1	506	325842	0.3875	−0.29	23267	0.991055	2.37
209– 210	511	67.8	2	1022	326864	0.3887	−0.28	23269	0.991140	2.37
208	514	67.9	1	514	327378	0.3893	−0.28	23270	0.991183	2.37
207	520	67.9	1	520	327898	0.3900	−0.28	23271	0.991225	2.37
206	521	67.9	1	521	328419	0.3906	−0.28	23272	0.991268	2.38
204– 205	525	68.0	2	1050	329469	0.3918	−0.27	23274	0.991353	2.38
202– 203	529	68.0	2	1058	330527	0.3931	−0.27	23276	0.991438	2.38
201	532	68.0	1	532	331059	0.3937	−0.27	23277	0.991481	2.39
200	536	68.0	1	536	331595	0.3944	−0.27	23278	0.991524	2.39
199	537	68.1	1	537	332132	0.3950	−0.27	23279	0.991566	2.39
198	538	68.1	1	538	332670	0.3956	−0.26	23280	0.991609	2.39
197	544	68.1	1	544	333214	0.3963	−0.26	23281	0.991651	2.39
196	545	68.1	1	545	333759	0.3969	−0.26	23282	0.991694	2.40
195	557	68.2	1	557	334316	0.3976	−0.26	23283	0.991737	2.40
193– 194	568	68.3	2	1136	335452	0.3989	−0.26	23285	0.991822	2.40
192	569	68.3	1	569	336021	0.3996	−0.25	23286	0.991864	2.40
191	570	68.3	1	570	336591	0.4003	−0.25	23287	0.991907	2.40
190	574	68.3	1	574	337165	0.4010	−0.25	23288	0.991950	2.41
189	575	68.4	1	575	337740	0.4017	−0.25	23289	0.991992	2.41
188	578	68.4	1	578	338318	0.4023	−0.25	23290	0.992035	2.41
187	581	68.4	1	581	338899	0.4030	−0.25	23291	0.992077	2.41
185– 186	582	68.4	2	1164	340063	0.4044	−0.24	23293	0.992163	2.42
184	591	68.5	1	591	340654	0.4051	−0.24	23294	0.992205	2.42
183	595	68.5	1	595	341249	0.4058	−0.24	23295	0.992248	2.42
182	597	68.5	1	597	341846	0.4065	−0.24	23296	0.992290	2.42
181	602	68.6	1	602	342448	0.4073	−0.23	23297	0.992333	2.42
180	604	68.6	1	604	343052	0.4080	−0.23	23298	0.992375	2.43
177– 179	610	68.6	3	1830	344882	0.4102	−0.23	23301	0.992503	2.43
176	615	68.6	1	615	345497	0.4109	−0.23	23302	0.992546	2.43
175	617	68.7	1	617	346114	0.4116	−0.22	23303	0.992588	2.44
173– 174	622	68.7	2	1244	347358	0.4131	−0.22	23305	0.992674	2.44
172	627	68.7	1	627	347985	0.4138	−0.22	23306	0.992716	2.44
170– 171	629	68.7	2	1258	349243	0.4153	−0.21	23308	0.992801	2.45
169	631	68.8	1	631	349874	0.4161	−0.21	23309	0.992844	2.45
168	634	68.8	1	634	350508	0.4168	−0.21	23310	0.992887	2.45
167	635	68.8	1	635	351143	0.4176	−0.21	23311	0.992929	2.45
166	636	68.8	1	636	351779	0.4184	−0.21	23312	0.992972	2.46
165	641	68.8	1	641	352420	0.4191	−0.20	23313	0.993014	2.46
164	663	69.0	1	663	353083	0.4199	−0.20	23314	0.993057	2.46
163	672	69.0	1	672	353755	0.4207	−0.20	23315	0.993100	2.46
162	685	69.1	1	685	354440	0.4215	−0.20	23316	0.993142	2.46
161	689	69.1	1	689	355129	0.4223	−0.20	23317	0.993185	2.47
160	695	69.2	1	695	355824	0.4232	−0.19	23318	0.993227	2.47
159	711	69.3	1	711	356535	0.4240	−0.19	23319	0.993270	2.47
158	714	69.3	1	714	357249	0.4249	−0.19	23320	0.993313	2.47
157	718	69.3	1	718	357967	0.4257	−0.19	23321	0.993355	2.48
156	731	69.4	1	731	358698	0.4266	−0.19	23322	0.993398	2.48
155	734	69.4	1	734	359432	0.4275	−0.18	23323	0.993440	2.48
154	739	69.4	1	739	360171	0.4283	−0.18	23324	0.993483	2.48
153	752	69.5	1	752	360923	0.4292	−0.18	23325	0.993526	2.49
152	758	69.6	1	758	361681	0.4301	−0.18	23326	0.993568	2.49
151	759	69.6	1	759	362440	0.4310	−0.17	23327	0.993611	2.49
150	760	69.6	1	760	363200	0.4319	−0.17	23328	0.993653	2.49
149	762	69.6	1	762	363962	0.4328	−0.17	23329	0.993696	2.49
146– 148	772	69.6	3	2316	366278	0.4356	−0.16	23332	0.993824	2.50
145	781	69.7	1	781	367059	0.4365	−0.16	23333	0.993866	2.50
144	785	69.7	1	785	367844	0.4375	−0.16	23334	0.993909	2.51
143	786	69.7	1	786	368630	0.4384	−0.16	23335	0.993951	2.51
142	790	69.7	1	790	369420	0.4393	−0.15	23336	0.993994	2.51
141	793	69.7	1	793	370213	0.4403	−0.15	23337	0.994037	2.51
140	810	69.8	1	810	371023	0.4412	−0.15	23338	0.994079	2.52
139	827	69.9	1	827	371850	0.4422	−0.15	23339	0.994122	2.52
138	830	69.9	1	830	372680	0.4432	−0.14	23340	0.994164	2.52
137	834	70.0	1	834	373514	0.4442	−0.14	23341	0.994207	2.52
136	844	70.0	1	844	374358	0.4452	−0.14	23342	0.994250	2.53
135	847	70.0	1	847	375205	0.4462	−0.14	23343	0.994292	2.53
133– 134	858	70.1	2	1716	376921	0.4483	−0.13	23345	0.994377	2.53
132	865	70.1	1	865	377786	0.4493	−0.13	23346	0.994420	2.54
131	881	70.2	1	881	378667	0.4503	−0.12	23347	0.994463	2.54
130	896	70.3	1	896	379563	0.4514	−0.12	23348	0.994505	2.54
129	900	70.3	1	900	380463	0.4525	−0.12	23349	0.994548	2.55
128	901	70.3	1	901	381364	0.4535	−0.12	23350	0.994590	2.55
127	904	70.3	1	904	382268	0.4546	−0.11	23351	0.994633	2.55
126	914	70.4	1	914	383182	0.4557	−0.11	23352	0.994676	2.55
125	938	70.5	1	938	384120	0.4568	−0.11	23353	0.994718	2.56
124	957	70.6	1	957	385077	0.4580	−0.11	23354	0.994761	2.56
123	960	70.6	1	960	386037	0.4591	−0.10	23355	0.994803	2.56
122	965	70.6	1	965	387002	0.4602	−0.10	23356	0.994846	2.57
121	978	70.7	1	978	387980	0.4614	−0.10	23357	0.994889	2.57
120	986	70.7	1	986	388966	0.4626	−0.09	23358	0.994931	2.57
119	991	70.7	1	991	389957	0.4638	−0.09	23359	0.994974	2.57
118	1008	70.8	1	1008	390965	0.4650	−0.09	23360	0.995016	2.58
117	1047	71.0	1	1047	392012	0.4662	−0.08	23361	0.995059	2.58
116	1056	71.0	1	1056	393068	0.4675	−0.08	23362	0.995102	2.58
115	1058	71.0	1	1058	394126	0.4687	−0.08	23363	0.995144	2.59
114	1064	71.0	1	1064	395190	0.4700	−0.08	23364	0.995187	2.59
113	1067	71.0	1	1067	396257	0.4713	−0.07	23365	0.995229	2.59
112	1079	71.1	1	1079	397336	0.4725	−0.07	23366	0.995272	2.60
111	1085	71.1	1	1085	398421	0.4738	−0.07	23367	0.995315	2.60
110	1099	71.2	1	1099	399520	0.4751	−0.06	23368	0.995357	2.60
109	1106	71.2	1	1106	400626	0.4764	−0.06	23369	0.995400	2.60
108	1112	71.2	1	1112	401738	0.4778	−0.06	23370	0.995442	2.61
107	1115	71.2	1	1115	402853	0.4791	−0.05	23371	0.995485	2.61

Rank	Occ. F	SFI	F	Tokens	Cum. Tokens	Cum. P Tokens	Y	Cum. Types	Cum. P Types	Z
106	1119	71.2	1	1119	403972	0.4804	-0.05	23372	0.995528	2.61
105	1153	71.4	1	1153	405125	0.4818	-0.05	23373	0.995570	2.62
104	1159	71.4	1	1159	406284	0.4832	-0.04	23374	0.995613	2.62
103	1162	71.4	1	1162	407446	0.4846	-0.04	23375	0.995655	2.62
102	1179	71.5	1	1179	408625	0.4860	-0.04	23376	0.995698	2.63
101	1206	71.6	1	1206	409831	0.4874	-0.03	23377	0.995740	2.63
100	1207	71.6	1	1207	411038	0.4888	-0.03	23378	0.995783	2.63
98– 99	1210	71.6	2	2420	413458	0.4917	-0.02	23380	0.995868	2.64
97	1231	71.7	1	1231	414689	0.4932	-0.02	23381	0.995911	2.64
96	1241	71.7	1	1241	415930	0.4947	-0.01	23382	0.995953	2.65
95	1256	71.7	1	1256	417186	0.4961	-0.01	23383	0.995996	2.65
94	1270	71.8	1	1270	418456	0.4977	-0.01	23384	0.996039	2.66
93	1278	71.8	1	1278	419734	0.4992	-0.00	23385	0.996081	2.66
92	1279	71.8	1	1279	421013	0.5007	0.00	23386	0.996124	2.66
90– 91	1297	71.9	2	2594	423607	0.5038	0.01	23388	0.996209	2.67
89	1314	71.9	1	1314	424921	0.5053	0.01	23389	0.996252	2.67
88	1315	71.9	1	1315	426236	0.5069	0.02	23390	0.996294	2.68
87	1334	72.0	1	1334	427570	0.5085	0.02	23391	0.996337	2.68
86	1363	72.1	1	1363	428933	0.5101	0.03	23392	0.996379	2.69
85	1400	72.2	1	1400	430333	0.5118	0.03	23393	0.996422	2.69
84	1465	72.4	1	1465	431798	0.5135	0.03	23394	0.996465	2.69
83	1477	72.4	1	1477	433275	0.5153	0.04	23395	0.996507	2.70
82	1485	72.5	1	1485	434760	0.5170	0.04	23396	0.996550	2.70
81	1489	72.5	1	1489	436249	0.5188	0.05	23397	0.996592	2.71
80	1517	72.6	1	1517	437766	0.5206	0.05	23398	0.996635	2.71
79	1518	72.6	1	1518	439284	0.5224	0.06	23399	0.996678	2.71
78	1554	72.7	1	1554	440838	0.5243	0.06	23400	0.996720	2.72
77	1580	72.7	1	1580	442418	0.5262	0.07	23401	0.996763	2.72
76	1631	72.9	1	1631	444049	0.5281	0.07	23402	0.996805	2.73
75	1682	73.0	1	1682	445731	0.5301	0.08	23403	0.996848	2.73
74	1700	73.1	1	1700	447431	0.5321	0.08	23404	0.996891	2.74
73	1704	73.1	1	1704	449135	0.5341	0.09	23405	0.996933	2.74
72	1744	73.2	1	1744	450879	0.5362	0.09	23406	0.996976	2.75
71	1760	73.2	1	1760	452639	0.5383	0.10	23407	0.997018	2.75
70	1762	73.2	1	1762	454401	0.5404	0.10	23408	0.997061	2.75
69	1773	73.2	1	1773	456174	0.5425	0.11	23409	0.997104	2.76
68	1791	73.3	1	1791	457965	0.5446	0.11	23410	0.997146	2.76
67	1809	73.3	1	1809	459774	0.5468	0.12	23411	0.997189	2.77
66	1854	73.4	1	1854	461628	0.5490	0.12	23412	0.997231	2.77
65	1867	73.5	1	1867	463495	0.5512	0.13	23413	0.997274	2.78
64	1874	73.5	1	1874	465369	0.5534	0.13	23414	0.997316	2.78
63	1909	73.6	1	1909	467278	0.5557	0.14	23415	0.997359	2.79
62	1953	73.7	1	1953	469231	0.5580	0.15	23416	0.997402	2.79
61	1979	73.7	1	1979	471210	0.5604	0.15	23417	0.997444	2.80
60	1981	73.7	1	1981	473191	0.5627	0.16	23418	0.997487	2.81
58– 59	1996	73.8	2	3992	477183	0.5675	0.17	23420	0.997572	2.82
57	2110	74.0	1	2110	479293	0.5700	0.18	23421	0.997615	2.82
56	2121	74.0	1	2121	481414	0.5725	0.18	23422	0.997657	2.83
55	2168	74.1	1	2168	483582	0.5751	0.19	23423	0.997700	2.83
54	2206	74.2	1	2206	485788	0.5777	0.20	23424	0.997742	2.84
53	2265	74.3	1	2265	488053	0.5804	0.20	23425	0.997785	2.85
52	2317	74.4	1	2317	490370	0.5832	0.21	23426	0.997828	2.85

Rank	Occ. F	SFI	F	Tokens	Cum. Tokens	Cum. P Tokens	Y	Cum. Types	Cum. P Types	Z
51	2401	74.6	1	2401	492771	0.5860	0.22	23427	0.997870	2.86
50	2406	74.6	1	2406	495177	0.5889	0.22	23428	0.997913	2.86
49	2507	74.7	1	2507	497684	0.5919	0.23	23429	0.997955	2.87
48	2570	74.9	1	2570	500254	0.5949	0.24	23430	0.997998	2.88
47	2583	74.9	1	2583	502837	0.5980	0.25	23431	0.998041	2.88
46	2619	74.9	1	2619	505456	0.6011	0.26	23432	0.998083	2.89
45	2679	75.0	1	2679	508135	0.6043	0.26	23433	0.998126	2.90
44	2702	75.1	1	2702	510837	0.6075	0.27	23434	0.998168	2.91
43	2715	75.1	1	2715	513552	0.6107	0.28	23435	0.998211	2.91
42	2758	75.2	1	2758	516310	0.6140	0.29	23436	0.998254	2.92
41	2796	75.2	1	2796	519106	0.6174	0.30	23437	0.998296	2.93
40	2939	75.4	1	2939	522045	0.6208	0.31	23438	0.998339	2.94
39	2958	75.5	1	2958	525003	0.6244	0.32	23439	0.998381	2.94
38	2967	75.5	1	2967	527970	0.6279	0.33	23440	0.998424	2.95
37	3043	75.6	1	3043	531013	0.6315	0.34	23441	0.998467	2.96
36	3122	75.7	1	3122	534135	0.6352	0.35	23442	0.998509	2.97
35	3260	75.9	1	3260	537395	0.6391	0.36	23443	0.998552	2.98
34	3279	75.9	1	3279	540674	0.6430	0.37	23444	0.998594	2.99
33	3323	76.0	1	3323	543997	0.6470	0.38	23445	0.998637	3.00
32	3328	76.0	1	3328	547325	0.6509	0.39	23446	0.998680	3.01
31	3331	76.1	1	3331	550656	0.6549	0.40	23447	0.998722	3.02
30	3394	76.1	1	3394	554050	0.6589	0.41	23448	0.998765	3.03
29	3482	76.2	1	3482	557532	0.6631	0.42	23449	0.998807	3.04
28	3493	76.2	1	3493	561025	0.6672	0.43	23450	0.998850	3.05
27	3596	76.3	1	3596	564621	0.6715	0.44	23451	0.998892	3.06
26	3687	76.4	1	3687	568308	0.6759	0.46	23452	0.998935	3.07
25	3735	76.5	1	3735	572043	0.6803	0.47	23453	0.998978	3.08
24	3763	76.5	1	3763	575806	0.6848	0.48	23454	0.999020	3.10
23	4060	76.8	1	4060	579866	0.6896	0.49	23455	0.999063	3.11
22	4221	77.0	1	4221	584087	0.6946	0.51	23456	0.999105	3.12
21	4415	77.2	1	4415	588502	0.6999	0.52	23457	0.999148	3.14
20	4451	77.2	1	4451	592953	0.7052	0.54	23458	0.999191	3.15
19	4750	77.5	1	4750	597703	0.7108	0.56	23459	0.999233	3.17
18	4826	77.6	1	4826	602529	0.7166	0.57	23460	0.999276	3.18
17	5080	77.8	1	5080	607609	0.7226	0.59	23461	0.999318	3.20
16	6018	78.5	1	6018	613627	0.7298	0.61	23462	0.999361	3.22
15	6056	78.6	1	6056	619683	0.7370	0.63	23463	0.999404	3.24
14	6107	78.6	1	6107	625790	0.7442	0.66	23464	0.999446	3.26
13	6349	78.8	1	6349	632139	0.7518	0.68	23465	0.999489	3.28
12	6962	79.2	1	6962	639101	0.7601	0.71	23466	0.999531	3.31
11	7336	79.4	1	7336	646437	0.7688	0.73	23467	0.999574	3.34
10	9135	80.4	1	9135	655572	0.7796	0.77	23468	0.999617	3.36
9	9206	80.4	1	9206	664778	0.7906	0.81	23469	0.999659	3.40
8	10121	80.8	1	10121	674899	0.8026	0.85	23470	0.999702	3.43
7	10778	81.1	1	10778	685677	0.8155	0.90	23471	0.999744	3.47
6	14636	82.4	1	14636	700313	0.8329	0.97	23472	0.999787	3.52
5	18241	83.4	1	18241	718554	0.8545	1.06	23473	0.999830	3.58
4	20392	83.8	1	20392	738946	0.8788	1.17	23474	0.999872	3.66
3	20509	83.9	1	20509	759455	0.9032	1.30	23475	0.999915	3.76
2	20742	83.9	1	20742	780197	0.9279	1.46	23476	0.999957	3.93
1	60660	88.6	1	60660	840857	1.0000	+INF.	23477	1.000000	+INF.

Rank	Occ. F	SFI	F	Tokens	Cum. Tokens	Cum. P Tokens	Y	Cum. Types	Cum. P Types	Z
15563-25324	1	42.9	9762	9762	9762	0.0126	-2.24	9762	0.385484	-0.29
11971-15562	2	45.1	3592	7184	16946	0.0218	-2.02	13354	0.527326	0.07
9906-11970	3	46.5	2065	6195	23141	0.0298	-1.88	15419	0.608869	0.28
8555- 9905	4	47.6	1351	5404	28545	0.0368	-1.79	16770	0.662218	0.42
7600- 8554	5	48.5	955	4775	33320	0.0429	-1.72	17725	0.699929	0.52
6908- 7599	6	49.2	692	4152	37472	0.0483	-1.66	18417	0.727255	0.60
6267- 6907	7	49.8	641	4487	41959	0.0540	-1.61	19058	0.752567	0.68
5791- 6266	8	50.4	476	3808	45767	0.0589	-1.56	19534	0.771363	0.74
5375- 5790	9	50.9	416	3744	49511	0.0638	-1.52	19950	0.787790	0.80
5069- 5374	10	51.3	306	3060	52571	0.0677	-1.49	20256	0.799874	0.84
4757- 5068	11	51.7	312	3432	56003	0.0721	-1.46	20568	0.812194	0.89
4501- 4756	12	52.1	256	3072	59075	0.0761	-1.43	20824	0.822303	0.92
4293- 4500	13	52.4	208	2704	61779	0.0796	-1.41	21032	0.830516	0.96
4076- 4292	14	52.7	217	3038	64817	0.0835	-1.38	21249	0.839085	0.99
3866- 4075	15	53.0	210	3150	67967	0.0875	-1.36	21459	0.847378	1.03
3695- 3865	16	53.3	171	2736	70703	0.0910	-1.33	21630	0.854130	1.05
3547- 3694	17	53.5	148	2516	73219	0.0943	-1.31	21778	0.859975	1.08
3423- 3546	18	53.8	124	2232	75451	0.0972	-1.30	21902	0.864871	1.10
3299- 3422	19	54.0	124	2356	77807	0.1002	-1.28	22026	0.869768	1.13
3198- 3298	20	54.2	101	2020	79827	0.1028	-1.27	22127	0.873756	1.14
3079- 3197	21	54.4	119	2499	82326	0.1060	-1.25	22246	0.878455	1.17
2980- 3078	22	54.6	99	2178	84504	0.1088	-1.23	22345	0.882365	1.19
2876- 2979	23	54.8	104	2392	86896	0.1119	-1.22	22449	0.886471	1.21
2796- 2875	24	55.0	80	1920	88816	0.1144	-1.20	22529	0.889630	1.22
2707- 2795	25	55.2	89	2225	91041	0.1172	-1.19	22618	0.893145	1.24
2624- 2706	26	55.3	83	2158	93199	0.1200	-1.17	22701	0.896422	1.26
2557- 2623	27	55.5	67	1809	95008	0.1223	-1.16	22768	0.899068	1.28
2480- 2556	28	55.6	77	2156	97164	0.1251	-1.15	22845	0.902109	1.29
2432- 2479	29	55.8	48	1392	98556	0.1269	-1.14	22893	0.904004	1.30
2381- 2431	30	55.9	51	1530	100086	0.1289	-1.13	22944	0.906018	1.32
2336- 2380	31	56.1	45	1395	101481	0.1307	-1.12	22989	0.907795	1.33
2292- 2335	32	56.2	44	1408	102889	0.1325	-1.11	23033	0.909532	1.34
2244- 2291	33	56.3	48	1584	104473	0.1345	-1.11	23081	0.911428	1.35
2194- 2243	34	56.5	50	1700	106173	0.1367	-1.10	23131	0.913402	1.36
2145- 2193	35	56.6	49	1715	107888	0.1389	-1.09	23180	0.915337	1.37
2093- 2144	36	56.7	52	1872	109760	0.1413	-1.07	23232	0.917391	1.39
2039- 2092	37	56.8	54	1998	111758	0.1439	-1.06	23286	0.919523	1.40
1995- 2038	38	57.0	44	1672	113430	0.1461	-1.05	23330	0.921260	1.41
1956- 1994	39	57.1	39	1521	114951	0.1480	-1.04	23369	0.922800	1.42
1923- 1955	40	57.2	33	1320	116271	0.1497	-1.04	23402	0.924104	1.43
1887- 1922	41	57.3	36	1476	117747	0.1516	-1.03	23438	0.925525	1.44
1856- 1886	42	57.4	31	1302	119049	0.1533	-1.02	23469	0.926749	1.45
1826- 1855	43	57.5	30	1290	120339	0.1550	-1.02	23499	0.927934	1.46
1787- 1825	44	57.6	39	1716	122055	0.1572	-1.01	23538	0.929474	1.47
1764- 1786	45	57.7	23	1035	123090	0.1585	-1.00	23561	0.930382	1.48
1737- 1763	46	57.8	27	1242	124332	0.1601	-0.99	23588	0.931448	1.49
1709- 1736	47	57.9	28	1316	125648	0.1618	-0.99	23616	0.932554	1.50
1680- 1708	48	58.0	29	1392	127040	0.1636	-0.98	23645	0.933699	1.50
1662- 1679	49	58.0	18	882	127922	0.1647	-0.98	23663	0.934410	1.51
1634- 1661	50	58.1	28	1400	129322	0.1665	-0.97	23691	0.935516	1.52
1609- 1633	51	58.2	25	1275	130597	0.1682	-0.96	23716	0.936503	1.53
1577- 1608	52	58.3	32	1664	132261	0.1703	-0.95	23748	0.937766	1.54
1554- 1576	53	58.4	23	1219	133480	0.1719	-0.95	23771	0.938675	1.54
1535- 1553	54	58.5	19	1026	134506	0.1732	-0.94	23790	0.939425	1.55
1506- 1534	55	58.5	29	1595	136101	0.1753	-0.93	23819	0.940570	1.56
1492- 1505	56	58.6	14	784	136885	0.1763	-0.93	23833	0.941123	1.56
1472- 1491	57	58.7	20	1140	138025	0.1777	-0.92	23853	0.941913	1.57
1450- 1471	58	58.8	22	1276	139301	0.1794	-0.92	23875	0.942782	1.58
1431- 1449	59	58.8	19	1121	140422	0.1808	-0.91	23894	0.943532	1.59
1410- 1430	60	58.9	21	1260	141682	0.1825	-0.91	23915	0.944361	1.59
1392- 1409	61	59.0	18	1098	142780	0.1839	-0.90	23933	0.945072	1.60
1377- 1391	62	59.1	15	930	143710	0.1851	-0.90	23948	0.945664	1.60
1350- 1376	63	59.1	27	1701	145411	0.1873	-0.89	23975	0.946730	1.61
1336- 1349	64	59.2	14	896	146307	0.1884	-0.88	23989	0.947283	1.62
1318- 1335	65	59.3	18	1170	147477	0.1899	-0.88	24007	0.947994	1.63
1306- 1317	66	59.3	12	792	148269	0.1909	-0.87	24019	0.948468	1.63
1292- 1305	67	59.4	14	938	149207	0.1921	-0.87	24033	0.949021	1.64
1270- 1291	68	59.5	22	1496	150703	0.1941	-0.86	24055	0.949889	1.64
1253- 1269	69	59.5	17	1173	151876	0.1956	-0.86	24072	0.950561	1.65
1242- 1252	70	59.6	11	770	152646	0.1966	-0.85	24083	0.950995	1.65
1232- 1241	71	59.6	10	710	153356	0.1975	-0.85	24093	0.951390	1.66
1215- 1231	72	59.7	17	1224	154580	0.1991	-0.84	24110	0.952061	1.67
1191- 1214	73	59.8	24	1752	156332	0.2013	-0.84	24134	0.953009	1.67
1179- 1190	74	59.8	12	888	157220	0.2025	-0.83	24146	0.953483	1.68
1168- 1178	75	59.9	11	825	158045	0.2035	-0.83	24157	0.953917	1.68
1155- 1167	76	59.9	13	988	159033	0.2048	-0.82	24170	0.954431	1.69
1139- 1154	77	60.0	16	1232	160265	0.2064	-0.82	24186	0.955062	1.70
1125- 1138	78	60.0	14	1092	161357	0.2078	-0.81	24200	0.955615	1.70
1117- 1124	79	60.1	8	632	161989	0.2086	-0.81	24208	0.955931	1.71
1103- 1116	80	60.2	14	1120	163109	0.2100	-0.81	24222	0.956484	1.71
1097- 1102	81	60.2	6	486	163595	0.2107	-0.80	24228	0.956721	1.71
1081- 1096	82	60.3	16	1312	164907	0.2124	-0.80	24244	0.957353	1.72
1071- 1080	83	60.3	10	830	165737	0.2134	-0.79	24254	0.957748	1.73
1054- 1070	84	60.4	17	1428	167165	0.2153	-0.79	24271	0.958419	1.73
1041- 1053	85	60.4	13	1105	168270	0.2167	-0.78	24284	0.958932	1.74
1029- 1040	86	60.5	12	1032	169302	0.2180	-0.78	24296	0.959406	1.74
1019- 1028	87	60.5	10	870	170172	0.2191	-0.78	24306	0.959801	1.75
1005- 1018	88	60.6	14	1232	171404	0.2207	-0.77	24320	0.960354	1.75
995- 1004	89	60.6	10	890	172294	0.2219	-0.77	24330	0.960749	1.76
986- 994	90	60.7	9	810	173104	0.2229	-0.76	24339	0.961104	1.76
977- 985	91	60.7	9	819	173923	0.2240	-0.76	24348	0.961459	1.77
962- 976	92	60.8	15	1380	175303	0.2257	-0.75	24363	0.962052	1.78
953- 961	93	60.8	9	837	176140	0.2268	-0.75	24372	0.962407	1.78
943- 952	94	60.9	10	940	177080	0.2280	-0.75	24382	0.962802	1.78
932- 942	95	60.9	11	1045	178125	0.2294	-0.74	24393	0.963236	1.79
921- 931	96	60.9	11	1056	179181	0.2307	-0.74	24404	0.963671	1.79
912- 920	97	61.0	9	873	180054	0.2319	-0.73	24413	0.964026	1.80
896- 911	98	61.0	16	1568	181622	0.2339	-0.73	24429	0.964658	1.81
891- 895	99	61.1	5	495	182117	0.2345	-0.72	24434	0.964855	1.81
884- 890	100	61.1	7	700	182817	0.2354	-0.72	24441	0.965132	1.81
873- 883	101	61.2	11	1111	183928	0.2369	-0.72	24452	0.965566	1.82
872	102	61.2	1	102	184030	0.2370	-0.72	24453	0.965606	1.82
856- 871	103	61.2	16	1648	185678	0.2391	-0.71	24469	0.966238	1.83
851- 855	104	61.3	5	520	186198	0.2398	-0.71	24474	0.966435	1.83
840- 850	105	61.3	11	1155	187353	0.2413	-0.70	24485	0.966869	1.84
831- 839	106	61.4	9	954	188307	0.2425	-0.70	24494	0.967225	1.84
824- 830	107	61.4	7	749	189056	0.2435	-0.70	24501	0.967501	1.85
821- 823	108	61.5	3	324	189380	0.2439	-0.69	24504	0.967620	1.85
811- 820	109	61.5	10	1090	190470	0.2453	-0.69	24514	0.968014	1.85
805- 810	110	61.5	6	660	191130	0.2461	-0.69	24520	0.968251	1.86
800- 804	111	61.6	5	555	191685	0.2468	-0.68	24525	0.968449	1.86
791- 799	112	61.6	9	1008	192693	0.2481	-0.68	24534	0.968804	1.86
789- 790	113	61.6	2	226	192919	0.2484	-0.68	24536	0.968883	1.86
783- 788	114	61.7	6	684	193603	0.2493	-0.68	24542	0.969120	1.87
776- 782	115	61.7	7	805	194408	0.2504	-0.67	24549	0.969397	1.87
768- 775	116	61.8	8	928	195336	0.2515	-0.67	24557	0.969712	1.88
763- 767	117	61.8	5	585	195921	0.2523	-0.67	24562	0.969910	1.88
757- 762	118	61.8	6	708	196629	0.2532	-0.66	24568	0.970147	1.88
752- 756	119	61.9	5	595	197224	0.2540	-0.66	24573	0.970344	1.89
748- 751	120	61.9	4	480	197704	0.2546	-0.66	24577	0.970502	1.89
740- 747	121	61.9	8	968	198672	0.2558	-0.66	24585	0.970818	1.89
734- 739	122	62.0	6	732	199404	0.2568	-0.65	24591	0.971055	1.90
730- 733	123	62.0	4	492	199896	0.2574	-0.65	24595	0.971213	1.90
726- 729	124	62.1	4	496	200392	0.2581	-0.65	24599	0.971371	1.90
724- 725	125	62.1	2	250	200642	0.2584	-0.65	24601	0.971450	1.90
716- 723	126	62.1	8	1008	201650	0.2597	-0.64	24609	0.971766	1.91
712- 715	127	62.2	4	508	202158	0.2603	-0.64	24613	0.971924	1.91
707- 711	128	62.2	5	640	202798	0.2612	-0.64	24618	0.972121	1.91
704- 706	129	62.2	3	387	203185	0.2617	-0.64	24621	0.972240	1.91
699- 703	130	62.3	5	650	203835	0.2625	-0.64	24626	0.972437	1.92
690- 698	131	62.3	9	1179	205014	0.2640	-0.63	24635	0.972793	1.92
686- 689	132	62.3	4	528	205542	0.2647	-0.63	24639	0.972951	1.93
682- 685	133	62.4	4	532	206074	0.2654	-0.63	24643	0.973108	1.93
679- 681	134	62.4	3	402	206476	0.2659	-0.63	24646	0.973227	1.93
674- 678	135	62.4	5	675	207151	0.2668	-0.62	24651	0.973424	1.93
669- 673	136	62.4	5	680	207831	0.2676	-0.62	24656	0.973622	1.94
664- 668	137	62.5	5	685	208516	0.2685	-0.62	24661	0.973819	1.94
657- 663	138	62.5	7	966	209482	0.2698	-0.61	24668	0.974096	1.94
656	139	62.5	1	139	209621	0.2699	-0.61	24669	0.974135	1.95
650- 655	140	62.6	6	840	210461	0.2710	-0.61	24675	0.974372	1.95
644- 649	141	62.6	6	846	211307	0.2721	-0.61	24681	0.974609	1.95
638- 643	142	62.6	6	852	212159	0.2732	-0.60	24687	0.974846	1.96
634- 637	143	62.7	4	572	212731	0.2739	-0.60	24691	0.975004	1.96
632- 633	144	62.7	2	288	213019	0.2743	-0.60	24693	0.975083	1.96
628- 631	145	62.7	4	580	213599	0.2751	-0.60	24697	0.975241	1.96
626- 627	146	62.8	2	292	213891	0.2754	-0.60	24699	0.975320	1.97
620- 625	147	62.8	6	882	214773	0.2766	-0.59	24705	0.975557	1.97
615- 619	148	62.8	5	740	215513	0.2775	-0.59	24710	0.975754	1.97
611- 614	149	62.8	4	596	216109	0.2783	-0.59	24714	0.975912	1.98
607- 610	150	62.9	4	600	216709	0.2791	-0.59	24718	0.976070	1.98
601- 606	151	62.9	6	906	217615	0.2802	-0.58	24724	0.976307	1.98
593- 600	152	62.9	8	1216	218831	0.2818	-0.58	24732	0.976623	1.99
590- 592	153	63.0	3	459	219290	0.2824	-0.58	24735	0.976741	1.99
586- 589	154	63.0	4	616	219906	0.2832	-0.57	24739	0.976899	1.99
581- 585	155	63.0	5	775	220681	0.2842	-0.57	24744	0.977097	2.00
576- 580	156	63.0	5	780	221461	0.2852	-0.57	24749	0.977294	2.00
571- 575	157	63.1	5	785	222246	0.2862	-0.56	24754	0.977492	2.00
569- 570	158	63.1	2	316	222562	0.2866	-0.56	24756	0.977571	2.01
568	159	63.1	1	159	222721	0.2868	-0.56	24757	0.977610	2.01
565- 567	160	63.2	3	480	223201	0.2874	-0.56	24760	0.977729	2.01
558- 564	161	63.2	7	1127	224328	0.2889	-0.56	24767	0.978005	2.01
555- 557	162	63.2	3	486	224814	0.2895	-0.55	24770	0.978123	2.02
552- 554	163	63.2	3	489	225303	0.2901	-0.55	24773	0.978242	2.02
548- 551	164	63.3	4	656	225959	0.2910	-0.55	24777	0.978400	2.02
540- 547	165	63.3	8	1320	227279	0.2927	-0.55	24785	0.978716	2.03
535- 539	166	63.3	5	830	228109	0.2938	-0.54	24790	0.978913	2.03
530- 534	167	63.3	5	835	228944	0.2948	-0.54	24795	0.979111	2.04
528- 529	168	63.4	2	336	229280	0.2953	-0.54	24797	0.979190	2.04
526- 527	169	63.4	2	338	229618	0.2957	-0.54	24799	0.979269	2.04
524- 525	170	63.4	2	340	229958	0.2961	-0.54	24801	0.979348	2.04
521- 523	171	63.4	3	513	230471	0.2968	-0.53	24804	0.979466	2.04
518- 520	172	63.5	3	516	230987	0.2975	-0.53	24807	0.979585	2.05
517	173	63.5	1	173	231160	0.2977	-0.53	24808	0.979624	2.05
514- 516	174	63.5	3	522	231682	0.2984	-0.53	24811	0.979743	2.05
513	175	63.5	1	175	231857	0.2986	-0.53	24812	0.979782	2.05
512	176	63.6	1	176	232033	0.2988	-0.53	24813	0.979822	2.05
510- 511	177	63.6	2	354	232387	0.2993	-0.53	24815	0.979900	2.05
507- 509	178	63.6	3	534	232921	0.2999	-0.52	24818	0.980019	2.05
501- 506	179	63.6	6	1074	233995	0.3013	-0.52	24824	0.980256	2.06
498- 500	180	63.7	3	540	234535	0.3020	-0.52	24827	0.980374	2.06
496- 497	181	63.7	2	362	234897	0.3025	-0.52	24829	0.980453	2.06
493- 495	182	63.7	3	546	235443	0.3032	-0.52	24832	0.980572	2.07
492	183	63.7	1	183	235626	0.3034	-0.51	24833	0.980611	2.07
489- 491	184	63.8	3	552	236178	0.3041	-0.51	24836	0.980730	2.07
487- 488	185	63.8	2	370	236548	0.3046	-0.51	24838	0.980809	2.07
484- 486	186	63.8	3	558	237106	0.3053	-0.51	24841	0.980927	2.07
480- 483	187	63.8	4	748	237854	0.3063	-0.51	24845	0.981085	2.08
476- 479	188	63.9	4	752	238606	0.3073	-0.50	24849	0.981243	2.08
474- 475	190	63.9	2	380	238986	0.3078	-0.50	24851	0.981322	2.08
471- 473	191	63.9	3	573	239559	0.3085	-0.50	24854	0.981440	2.08
468- 470	192	63.9	3	576	240135	0.3092	-0.50	24857	0.981559	2.09
464- 467	193	64.0	4	772	240907	0.3102	-0.50	24861	0.981717	2.09
461- 463	194	64.0	3	582	241489	0.3110	-0.49	24864	0.981835	2.09
460	195	64.0	1	195	241684	0.3112	-0.49	24865	0.981875	2.09
459	196	64.0	1	196	241880	0.3115	-0.49	24866	0.981914	2.09
458	197	64.1	1	197	242077	0.3117	-0.49	24867	0.981954	2.10
456- 457	198	64.1	2	396	242473	0.3122	-0.49	24869	0.982033	2.10
453- 455	199	64.1	3	597	243070	0.3130	-0.49	24872	0.982151	2.10
452	200	64.1	1	200	243270	0.3133	-0.49	24873	0.982191	2.10
451	202	64.2	1	202	243472	0.3135	-0.49	24874	0.982230	2.10
450	203	64.2	1	203	243675	0.3138	-0.49	24875	0.982270	2.10
447- 449	204	64.2	3	612	244287	0.3146	-0.48	24878	0.982388	2.11
443- 446	205	64.2	4	820	245107	0.3156	-0.48	24882	0.982546	2.11
441- 442	206	64.2	2	412	245519	0.3162	-0.48	24884	0.982625	2.11
439- 440	207	64.3	2	414	245933	0.3167	-0.48	24886	0.982704	2.11
437- 438	208	64.3	2	416	246349	0.3172	-0.48	24888	0.982783	2.11
436	209	64.3	1	209	246558	0.3175	-0.47	24889	0.982823	2.12
435	210	64.3	1	210	246768	0.3178	-0.47	24890	0.982862	2.12
431- 434	211	64.4	4	844	247612	0.3189	-0.47	24894	0.983020	2.12
428- 430	212	64.4	3	636	248248	0.3197	-0.47	24897	0.983139	2.12
427	213	64.4	1	213	248461	0.3200	-0.47	24898	0.983178	2.12
425- 426	214	64.4	2	428	248889	0.3205	-0.47	24900	0.983257	2.13
423- 424	215	64.4	2	430	249319	0.3211	-0.46	24902	0.983336	2.13
422	216	64.5	1	216	249535	0.3213	-0.46	24903	0.983375	2.13
420- 421	217	64.5	2	434	249969	0.3219	-0.46	24905	0.983454	2.13
417- 419	219	64.5	3	657	250626	0.3227	-0.46	24908	0.983573	2.13
415- 416	220	64.5	2	440	251066	0.3233	-0.46	24910	0.983652	2.14
411- 414	222	64.6	4	888	251954	0.3245	-0.46	24914	0.983810	2.14
407- 410	223	64.6	4	892	252846	0.3256	-0.45	24918	0.983968	2.14
405- 406	224	64.6	2	448	253294	0.3262	-0.45	24920	0.984047	2.15
403- 404	225	64.6	2	450	253744	0.3268	-0.45	24922	0.984126	2.15
401- 402	226	64.6	2	452	254196	0.3273	-0.45	24924	0.984205	2.15
400	227	64.7	1	227	254423	0.3276	-0.45	24925	0.984244	2.15
396- 399	229	64.7	4	916	255339	0.3288	-0.44	24929	0.984402	2.15
394- 395	230	64.7	2	460	255799	0.3294	-0.44	24931	0.984481	2.16
393	231	64.7	1	231	256030	0.3297	-0.44	24932	0.984521	2.16
392	233	64.8	1	233	256263	0.3300	-0.44	24933	0.984560	2.16
391	234	64.8	1	234	256497	0.3303	-0.44	24934	0.984600	2.16
390	235	64.8	1	235	256732	0.3306	-0.44	24935	0.984639	2.16
389	236	64.8	1	236	256968	0.3309	-0.44	24936	0.984679	2.16
388	237	64.9	1	237	257205	0.3312	-0.44	24937	0.984718	2.16
387	238	64.9	1	238	257443	0.3315	-0.44	24938	0.984757	2.16

Rank		Occ. F	SFI	F	Tokens	Cum. Tokens	Cum. P Tokens	Y	Cum. Types	Cum. P Types	Z
	386	239	64.9	1	239	257682	0.3318	-0.43	24939	0.984797	2.16
383-	385	240	64.9	3	720	258402	0.3328	-0.43	24942	0.984915	2.17
	382	241	64.9	1	241	258643	0.3331	-0.43	24943	0.984955	2.17
378-	381	242	64.9	4	968	259611	0.3343	-0.43	24947	0.985113	2.17
	377	243	65.0	1	243	259854	0.3346	-0.43	24948	0.985152	2.17
375-	376	245	65.0	2	490	260344	0.3353	-0.43	24950	0.985231	2.18
	374	247	65.0	1	247	260591	0.3356	-0.42	24951	0.985271	2.18
372-	373	248	65.1	2	496	261087	0.3362	-0.42	24953	0.985350	2.18
	371	249	65.1	1	249	261336	0.3365	-0.42	24954	0.985389	2.18
	370	250	65.1	1	250	261586	0.3369	-0.42	24955	0.985429	2.18
	369	251	65.1	1	251	261837	0.3372	-0.42	24956	0.985468	2.18
366-	368	252	65.1	3	756	262593	0.3382	-0.42	24959	0.985587	2.19
363-	365	253	65.1	3	759	263352	0.3391	-0.41	24962	0.985705	2.19
361-	362	254	65.2	2	508	263860	0.3398	-0.41	24964	0.985784	2.19
	360	256	65.2	1	256	264116	0.3401	-0.41	24965	0.985824	2.19
358-	359	257	65.2	2	514	264630	0.3408	-0.41	24967	0.985903	2.19
356-	357	258	65.2	2	516	265146	0.3414	-0.41	24969	0.985982	2.20
	355	259	65.2	1	259	265405	0.3418	-0.41	24970	0.986021	2.20
353-	354	261	65.3	2	522	265927	0.3425	-0.41	24972	0.986100	2.20
	352	262	65.3	1	262	266189	0.3428	-0.40	24973	0.986140	2.20
349-	351	266	65.4	3	798	266987	0.3438	-0.40	24976	0.986258	2.20
347-	348	267	65.4	2	534	267521	0.3445	-0.40	24978	0.986337	2.21
	346	268	65.4	1	268	267789	0.3448	-0.40	24979	0.986377	2.21
343-	345	269	65.4	3	807	268596	0.3459	-0.40	24982	0.986495	2.21
	342	270	65.4	1	270	268866	0.3462	-0.40	24983	0.986534	2.21
	341	271	65.4	1	271	269137	0.3466	-0.39	24984	0.986574	2.21
	340	272	65.5	1	272	269409	0.3469	-0.39	24985	0.986613	2.21
337-	339	274	65.5	3	822	270231	0.3480	-0.39	24988	0.986732	2.22
	336	275	65.5	1	275	270506	0.3483	-0.39	24989	0.986771	2.22
334-	335	276	65.5	2	552	271058	0.3491	-0.39	24991	0.986850	2.22
	333	277	65.5	1	277	271335	0.3494	-0.39	24992	0.986890	2.22
	332	279	65.6	1	279	271614	0.3498	-0.39	24993	0.986929	2.22
330-	331	280	65.6	2	560	272174	0.3505	-0.38	24995	0.987008	2.23
	329	282	65.6	1	282	272456	0.3509	-0.38	24996	0.987048	2.23
	328	283	65.6	1	283	272739	0.3512	-0.38	24997	0.987087	2.23
326-	327	284	65.6	2	568	273307	0.3520	-0.38	24999	0.987166	2.23
324-	325	285	65.7	2	570	273877	0.3527	-0.38	25001	0.987245	2.23
	323	286	65.7	1	286	274163	0.3531	-0.38	25002	0.987285	2.23
	322	288	65.7	1	288	274451	0.3534	-0.38	25003	0.987324	2.24
	321	289	65.7	1	289	274740	0.3538	-0.38	25004	0.987364	2.24
318-	320	291	65.7	3	873	275613	0.3549	-0.37	25007	0.987482	2.24
315-	317	292	65.8	3	876	276489	0.3561	-0.37	25010	0.987601	2.24
	314	293	65.8	1	293	276782	0.3564	-0.37	25011	0.987640	2.25
312-	313	294	65.8	2	588	277370	0.3572	-0.37	25013	0.987719	2.25
309-	311	301	65.9	3	903	278273	0.3584	-0.36	25016	0.987838	2.25
	308	303	65.9	1	303	278576	0.3587	-0.36	25017	0.987877	2.25
305-	307	304	65.9	3	912	279488	0.3599	-0.36	25020	0.987996	2.26
	304	305	65.9	1	305	279793	0.3603	-0.36	25021	0.988035	2.26
	303	308	66.0	1	308	280101	0.3607	-0.36	25022	0.988075	2.26
	302	313	66.1	1	313	280414	0.3611	-0.36	25023	0.988114	2.26
	301	316	66.1	1	316	280730	0.3615	-0.35	25024	0.988154	2.26
	300	317	66.1	1	317	281047	0.3619	-0.35	25025	0.988193	2.26
298-	299	319	66.1	2	638	281685	0.3627	-0.35	25027	0.988272	2.27
	297	320	66.2	1	320	282005	0.3632	-0.35	25028	0.988311	2.27
	296	321	66.2	1	321	282326	0.3636	-0.35	25029	0.988351	2.27
	295	322	66.2	1	322	282648	0.3640	-0.35	25030	0.988390	2.27
	294	323	66.2	1	323	282971	0.3644	-0.35	25031	0.988430	2.27
292-	293	324	66.2	2	648	283619	0.3652	-0.34	25033	0.988509	2.27
289-	291	326	66.2	3	978	284597	0.3665	-0.34	25036	0.988627	2.28
287-	288	328	66.3	2	656	285253	0.3673	-0.34	25038	0.988706	2.28
	286	330	66.3	1	330	285583	0.3678	-0.34	25039	0.988746	2.28
	285	332	66.3	1	332	285915	0.3682	-0.34	25040	0.988785	2.28
	284	333	66.3	1	333	286248	0.3686	-0.34	25041	0.988825	2.28
	283	334	66.3	1	334	286582	0.3691	-0.33	25042	0.988864	2.29
280-	282	335	66.4	3	1005	287587	0.3703	-0.33	25045	0.988983	2.29
278-	279	336	66.4	2	672	288259	0.3712	-0.33	25047	0.989062	2.29
	277	337	66.4	1	337	288596	0.3716	-0.33	25048	0.989101	2.29
	276	338	66.4	1	338	288934	0.3721	-0.33	25049	0.989141	2.30
	275	346	66.5	1	346	289280	0.3725	-0.33	25050	0.989180	2.30
272-	274	348	66.5	3	1044	290324	0.3739	-0.32	25053	0.989299	2.30
270-	271	349	66.5	2	698	291022	0.3748	-0.32	25055	0.989378	2.30
268-	269	350	66.5	2	700	291722	0.3757	-0.32	25057	0.989457	2.31
	267	351	66.6	1	351	292073	0.3761	-0.32	25058	0.989496	2.31
	266	352	66.6	1	352	292425	0.3766	-0.31	25059	0.989536	2.31
264-	265	354	66.6	2	708	293133	0.3775	-0.31	25061	0.989615	2.31
	263	356	66.6	1	356	293489	0.3779	-0.31	25062	0.989654	2.31
261-	262	359	66.7	2	718	294207	0.3789	-0.31	25064	0.989733	2.32
	260	362	66.7	1	362	294569	0.3793	-0.31	25065	0.989772	2.32
	259	363	66.7	1	363	294932	0.3798	-0.31	25066	0.989812	2.32
	258	364	66.7	1	364	295296	0.3803	-0.30	25067	0.989851	2.32
	257	370	66.8	1	370	295666	0.3807	-0.30	25068	0.989891	2.32
	256	371	66.8	1	371	296037	0.3812	-0.30	25069	0.989930	2.32
	255	374	66.8	1	374	296411	0.3817	-0.30	25070	0.989970	2.33
	254	375	66.8	1	375	296786	0.3822	-0.30	25071	0.990009	2.33
	253	376	66.9	1	376	297162	0.3827	-0.30	25072	0.990049	2.33
	252	377	66.9	1	377	297539	0.3832	-0.30	25073	0.990088	2.33
	251	378	66.9	1	378	297917	0.3836	-0.30	25074	0.990128	2.33
248-	250	379	66.9	3	1137	299054	0.3851	-0.29	25077	0.990246	2.34
	247	380	66.9	1	380	299434	0.3856	-0.29	25078	0.990286	2.34
244-	246	381	66.9	3	1143	300577	0.3871	-0.29	25081	0.990404	2.34
	243	382	66.9	1	382	300959	0.3876	-0.29	25082	0.990444	2.34
241-	242	387	67.0	2	774	301733	0.3886	-0.28	25084	0.990523	2.35
	240	388	67.0	1	388	302121	0.3891	-0.28	25085	0.990562	2.35
	239	390	67.0	1	390	302511	0.3896	-0.28	25086	0.990602	2.35
	238	391	67.0	1	391	302902	0.3901	-0.28	25087	0.990641	2.35
	237	392	67.0	1	392	303294	0.3906	-0.28	25088	0.990681	2.35
	236	397	67.1	1	397	303691	0.3911	-0.28	25089	0.990720	2.35
	235	400	67.1	1	400	304091	0.3916	-0.28	25090	0.990760	2.36
233-	234	401	67.1	2	802	304893	0.3926	-0.27	25092	0.990839	2.36
	232	404	67.2	1	404	305297	0.3932	-0.27	25093	0.990878	2.36
	231	408	67.2	1	408	305705	0.3937	-0.27	25094	0.990918	2.36
	230	410	67.2	1	410	306115	0.3942	-0.27	25095	0.990957	2.36
228-	229	413	67.3	2	826	306941	0.3953	-0.27	25097	0.991036	2.37
226-	227	414	67.3	2	828	307769	0.3963	-0.26	25099	0.991115	2.37
	225	416	67.3	1	416	308185	0.3969	-0.26	25100	0.991155	2.37
221-	224	418	67.3	4	1672	309857	0.3990	-0.26	25104	0.991313	2.38
	220	421	67.3	1	421	310278	0.3996	-0.25	25105	0.991352	2.38
	219	423	67.4	1	423	310701	0.4001	-0.25	25106	0.991392	2.38
217-	218	424	67.4	2	848	311549	0.4012	-0.25	25108	0.991471	2.39
	216	426	67.4	1	426	311975	0.4018	-0.25	25109	0.991510	2.39
214-	215	428	67.4	2	856	312831	0.4029	-0.25	25111	0.991589	2.39
	213	432	67.5	1	432	313263	0.4034	-0.24	25112	0.991628	2.39
	212	436	67.5	1	436	313699	0.4040	-0.24	25113	0.991668	2.39
	211	441	67.5	1	441	314140	0.4045	-0.24	25114	0.991707	2.40
	210	442	67.6	1	442	314582	0.4051	-0.24	25115	0.991747	2.40
	209	448	67.6	1	448	315030	0.4057	-0.24	25116	0.991786	2.40
	208	452	67.7	1	452	315482	0.4063	-0.24	25117	0.991826	2.40
206-	207	457	67.7	2	914	316396	0.4074	-0.23	25119	0.991905	2.40
	205	459	67.7	1	459	316855	0.4080	-0.23	25120	0.991944	2.41
203-	204	466	67.8	2	932	317787	0.4092	-0.23	25122	0.992023	2.41
	202	467	67.8	1	467	318254	0.4098	-0.23	25123	0.992063	2.41
	201	473	67.9	1	473	318727	0.4104	-0.23	25124	0.992102	2.41
	200	474	67.9	1	474	319201	0.4111	-0.22	25125	0.992142	2.42
	199	479	67.9	1	479	319680	0.4117	-0.22	25126	0.992181	2.42
	198	481	67.9	1	481	320161	0.4123	-0.22	25127	0.992221	2.42
	197	482	67.9	1	482	320643	0.4129	-0.22	25128	0.992260	2.42
	196	486	68.0	1	486	321129	0.4135	-0.22	25129	0.992300	2.42
194-	195	487	68.0	2	974	322103	0.4148	-0.22	25131	0.992379	2.43
	193	490	68.0	1	490	322593	0.4154	-0.21	25132	0.992418	2.43
	192	491	68.0	1	491	323084	0.4161	-0.21	25133	0.992458	2.43
	191	493	68.0	1	493	323577	0.4167	-0.21	25134	0.992497	2.43
	190	504	68.1	1	504	324081	0.4173	-0.21	25135	0.992537	2.43
	189	506	68.1	1	506	324587	0.4180	-0.21	25136	0.992576	2.44
	188	516	68.2	1	516	325103	0.4187	-0.21	25137	0.992616	2.44
	187	519	68.3	1	519	325622	0.4193	-0.20	25138	0.992655	2.44
	186	520	68.3	1	520	326142	0.4200	-0.20	25139	0.992695	2.44
	185	525	68.3	1	525	326667	0.4207	-0.20	25140	0.992734	2.44
	184	528	68.3	1	528	327195	0.4214	-0.20	25141	0.992774	2.45
	183	534	68.4	1	534	327729	0.4220	-0.20	25142	0.992813	2.45
	182	535	68.4	1	535	328264	0.4227	-0.19	25143	0.992853	2.45
	181	538	68.4	1	538	328802	0.4234	-0.19	25144	0.992892	2.45
	180	541	68.4	1	541	329343	0.4241	-0.19	25145	0.992932	2.45
	179	543	68.5	1	543	329886	0.4248	-0.19	25146	0.992971	2.46
	178	546	68.5	1	546	330432	0.4255	-0.19	25147	0.993011	2.46
	177	548	68.5	1	548	330980	0.4262	-0.19	25148	0.993050	2.46
175-	176	549	68.5	2	1098	332078	0.4276	-0.18	25150	0.993129	2.46
173-	174	553	68.5	2	1106	333184	0.4291	-0.18	25152	0.993208	2.47
	172	554	68.5	1	554	333738	0.4298	-0.18	25153	0.993248	2.47
	171	555	68.5	1	555	334293	0.4305	-0.18	25154	0.993287	2.47
	170	566	68.6	1	566	334859	0.4312	-0.17	25155	0.993326	2.47
	169	568	68.6	1	568	335427	0.4320	-0.17	25156	0.993366	2.48
	168	575	68.7	1	575	336002	0.4327	-0.17	25157	0.993405	2.48
	167	578	68.7	1	578	336580	0.4334	-0.17	25158	0.993445	2.48
	166	579	68.7	1	579	337159	0.4342	-0.17	25159	0.993484	2.48
	165	580	68.7	1	580	337739	0.4349	-0.16	25160	0.993524	2.49
	164	582	68.8	1	582	338321	0.4357	-0.16	25161	0.993563	2.49
	163	591	68.8	1	591	338912	0.4364	-0.16	25162	0.993603	2.49
	162	596	68.9	1	596	339508	0.4372	-0.16	25163	0.993642	2.49
	161	605	68.9	1	605	340113	0.4380	-0.16	25164	0.993682	2.49
	160	622	69.0	1	622	340735	0.4388	-0.15	25165	0.993721	2.50
	159	624	69.1	1	624	341359	0.4396	-0.15	25166	0.993761	2.50
	158	629	69.1	1	629	341988	0.4404	-0.15	25167	0.993800	2.50
	157	649	69.2	1	649	342637	0.4412	-0.15	25168	0.993840	2.50
	156	655	69.3	1	655	343292	0.4421	-0.15	25169	0.993879	2.51
	155	657	69.3	1	657	343949	0.4429	-0.14	25170	0.993919	2.51
	154	658	69.3	1	658	344607	0.4438	-0.14	25171	0.993958	2.51
	153	665	69.3	1	665	345272	0.4446	-0.14	25172	0.993998	2.51
	152	669	69.4	1	669	345941	0.4455	-0.14	25173	0.994037	2.51
	151	670	69.4	1	670	346611	0.4464	-0.13	25174	0.994077	2.52
	150	680	69.4	1	680	347291	0.4472	-0.13	25175	0.994116	2.52
	149	681	69.4	1	681	347972	0.4481	-0.13	25176	0.994156	2.52
	148	683	69.4	1	683	348655	0.4490	-0.13	25177	0.994195	2.52
	147	685	69.5	1	685	349340	0.4499	-0.13	25178	0.994235	2.53
	146	689	69.5	1	689	350029	0.4508	-0.12	25179	0.994274	2.53
	145	695	69.5	1	695	350724	0.4517	-0.12	25180	0.994314	2.53
	144	700	69.6	1	700	351424	0.4526	-0.12	25181	0.994353	2.53
	143	703	69.6	1	703	352127	0.4535	-0.12	25182	0.994393	2.54
	142	714	69.6	1	714	352841	0.4544	-0.11	25183	0.994432	2.54
	141	715	69.6	1	715	353556	0.4553	-0.11	25184	0.994472	2.54
	140	716	69.7	1	716	354272	0.4562	-0.11	25185	0.994511	2.54
	139	717	69.7	1	717	354989	0.4571	-0.11	25186	0.994551	2.55
	138	718	69.7	1	718	355707	0.4581	-0.11	25187	0.994590	2.55
	137	723	69.7	1	723	356430	0.4590	-0.10	25188	0.994630	2.55
	136	725	69.7	1	725	357155	0.4599	-0.10	25189	0.994669	2.55
	135	730	69.7	1	730	357885	0.4609	-0.10	25190	0.994709	2.56
	134	746	69.8	1	746	358631	0.4618	-0.10	25191	0.994748	2.56
	133	752	69.9	1	752	359383	0.4628	-0.09	25192	0.994788	2.56
	132	762	69.9	1	762	360145	0.4638	-0.09	25193	0.994827	2.56
	131	765	69.9	1	765	360910	0.4648	-0.09	25194	0.994866	2.57
	130	772	70.0	1	772	361682	0.4658	-0.09	25195	0.994906	2.57
	129	773	70.0	1	773	362455	0.4668	-0.08	25196	0.994945	2.57
	128	775	70.0	1	775	363230	0.4678	-0.08	25197	0.994985	2.57
	127	783	70.0	1	783	364013	0.4688	-0.08	25198	0.995024	2.58
	126	785	70.0	1	785	364798	0.4698	-0.08	25199	0.995064	2.58
	125	789	70.1	1	789	365587	0.4708	-0.07	25200	0.995103	2.58
123-	124	795	70.1	2	1590	367177	0.4728	-0.07	25202	0.995182	2.59
	122	805	70.2	1	805	367982	0.4739	-0.07	25203	0.995222	2.59
	121	808	70.2	1	808	368790	0.4749	-0.06	25204	0.995261	2.59
	120	812	70.2	1	812	369602	0.4760	-0.06	25205	0.995301	2.60
	119	830	70.3	1	830	370432	0.4770	-0.06	25206	0.995340	2.60
	118	844	70.4	1	844	371276	0.4781	-0.05	25207	0.995380	2.60
	117	845	70.4	1	845	372121	0.4792	-0.05	25208	0.995419	2.61
	116	850	70.4	1	850	372971	0.4803	-0.05	25209	0.995459	2.61
	115	890	70.6	1	890	373861	0.4814	-0.05	25210	0.995498	2.61
	114	893	70.6	1	893	374754	0.4826	-0.04	25211	0.995538	2.61
	113	895	70.6	1	895	375649	0.4837	-0.04	25212	0.995577	2.62
	112	897	70.6	1	897	376546	0.4849	-0.04	25213	0.995617	2.62
	111	901	70.6	1	901	377447	0.4861	-0.03	25214	0.995656	2.62
	110	902	70.7	1	902	378349	0.4872	-0.03	25215	0.995696	2.63
	109	906	70.7	1	906	379255	0.4884	-0.03	25216	0.995735	2.63
	108	930	70.8	1	930	380185	0.4896	-0.03	25217	0.995775	2.63
	107	942	70.8	1	942	381127	0.4908	-0.02	25218	0.995814	2.64
	106	954	70.9	1	954	382081	0.4920	-0.02	25219	0.995854	2.64
	105	955	70.9	1	955	383036	0.4933	-0.02	25220	0.995893	2.64
	104	957	70.9	1	957	383993	0.4945	-0.01	25221	0.995933	2.65
	103	969	71.0	1	969	384962	0.4957	-0.01	25222	0.995972	2.65
	102	977	71.0	1	977	385939	0.4970	-0.01	25223	0.996012	2.65
	101	1005	71.1	1	1005	386944	0.4983	-0.00	25224	0.996051	2.66
	100	1016	71.2	1	1016	387960	0.4996	-0.00	25225	0.996091	2.66
	99	1021	71.2	1	1021	388981	0.5009	0.00	25226	0.996130	2.66
	98	1026	71.2	1	1026	390007	0.5022	0.01	25227	0.996170	2.67
	97	1035	71.2	1	1035	391042	0.5036	0.01	25228	0.996209	2.67
	96	1049	71.3	1	1049	392091	0.5049	0.01	25229	0.996249	2.67
	95	1074	71.4	1	1074	393165	0.5063	0.02	25230	0.996288	2.68
	94	1093	71.5	1	1093	394258	0.5077	0.02	25231	0.996328	2.68
	93	1107	71.5	1	1107	395365	0.5091	0.02	25232	0.996367	2.68
	92	1123	71.6	1	1123	396488	0.5106	0.03	25233	0.996407	2.69
	91	1125	71.6	1	1125	397613	0.5120	0.03	25234	0.996446	2.69
	90	1128	71.6	1	1128	398741	0.5135	0.03	25235	0.996486	2.70
	89	1131	71.6	1	1131	399872	0.5149	0.04	25236	0.996525	2.70
	88	1134	71.6	1	1134	401006	0.5164	0.04	25237	0.996565	2.70
	87	1137	71.7	1	1137	402143	0.5179	0.04	25238	0.996604	2.71

Rank	Occ. F	SFI	F	Tokens	Cum. Tokens	Cum. P Tokens	Y	Cum. Types	Cum. P Types	Z
86	1141	71.7	1	1141	403284	0.5193	0.05	25239	0.996643	2.71
85	1153	71.7	1	1153	404437	0.5208	0.05	25240	0.996683	2.71
84	1201	71.9	1	1201	405638	0.5224	0.06	25241	0.996722	2.72
83	1209	71.9	1	1209	406847	0.5239	0.06	25242	0.996762	2.72
82	1211	71.9	1	1211	408058	0.5255	0.06	25243	0.996801	2.73
81	1264	72.1	1	1264	409322	0.5271	0.07	25244	0.996841	2.73
80	1269	72.1	1	1269	410591	0.5287	0.07	25245	0.996880	2.73
79	1276	72.2	1	1276	411867	0.5304	0.08	25246	0.996920	2.74
78	1309	72.3	1	1309	413176	0.5321	0.08	25247	0.996959	2.74
77	1312	72.3	1	1312	414488	0.5338	0.08	25248	0.996999	2.75
76	1331	72.3	1	1331	415819	0.5355	0.09	25249	0.997038	2.75
75	1344	72.4	1	1344	417163	0.5372	0.09	25250	0.997078	2.76
74	1357	72.4	1	1357	418520	0.5390	0.10	25251	0.997117	2.76
73	1372	72.5	1	1372	419892	0.5407	0.10	25252	0.997157	2.77
72	1393	72.5	1	1393	421285	0.5425	0.11	25253	0.997196	2.77
71	1400	72.6	1	1400	422685	0.5443	0.11	25254	0.997236	2.77
70	1464	72.8	1	1464	424149	0.5462	0.12	25255	0.997275	2.78
69	1534	73.0	1	1534	425683	0.5482	0.12	25256	0.997315	2.78
68	1591	73.1	1	1591	427274	0.5502	0.13	25257	0.997354	2.79
67	1605	73.2	1	1605	428879	0.5523	0.13	25258	0.997394	2.79
66	1625	73.2	1	1625	430504	0.5544	0.14	25259	0.997433	2.80
65	1667	73.3	1	1667	432171	0.5565	0.14	25260	0.997473	2.80
64	1725	73.5	1	1725	433896	0.5588	0.15	25261	0.997512	2.81
62– 63	1730	73.5	2	3460	437356	0.5632	0.16	25263	0.997591	2.82
61	1763	73.6	1	1763	439119	0.5655	0.16	25264	0.997631	2.82
60	1839	73.7	1	1839	440958	0.5679	0.17	25265	0.997670	2.83
59	1857	73.8	1	1857	442815	0.5702	0.18	25266	0.997710	2.84
58	1874	73.8	1	1874	444689	0.5727	0.18	25267	0.997749	2.84
57	1913	73.9	1	1913	446602	0.5751	0.19	25268	0.997789	2.85
56	1923	73.9	1	1923	448525	0.5776	0.20	25269	0.997828	2.85
55	1956	74.0	1	1956	450481	0.5801	0.20	25270	0.997868	2.86
54	1957	74.0	1	1957	452438	0.5826	0.21	25271	0.997907	2.86
53	2016	74.1	1	2016	454454	0.5852	0.22	25272	0.997947	2.87
52	2023	74.2	1	2023	456477	0.5878	0.22	25273	0.997986	2.88
51	2043	74.2	1	2043	458520	0.5905	0.23	25274	0.998026	2.88
50	2049	74.2	1	2049	460569	0.5931	0.24	25275	0.998065	2.89
49	2117	74.4	1	2117	462686	0.5958	0.24	25276	0.998105	2.90
48	2135	74.4	1	2135	464821	0.5986	0.25	25277	0.998144	2.90
47	2167	74.5	1	2167	466988	0.6014	0.26	25278	0.998183	2.91
46	2230	74.6	1	2230	469218	0.6042	0.26	25279	0.998223	2.92
45	2271	74.7	1	2271	471489	0.6072	0.27	25280	0.998262	2.92
44	2304	74.7	1	2304	473793	0.6101	0.28	25281	0.998302	2.93
43	2316	74.7	1	2316	476109	0.6131	0.29	25282	0.998341	2.94
42	2500	75.1	1	2500	478609	0.6163	0.30	25283	0.998381	2.94
41	2516	75.1	1	2516	481125	0.6196	0.30	25284	0.998420	2.95
40	2560	75.2	1	2560	483685	0.6229	0.31	25285	0.998460	2.96
39	2611	75.3	1	2611	486296	0.6262	0.32	25286	0.998499	2.97
38	2612	75.3	1	2612	488908	0.6296	0.33	25287	0.998539	2.98
37	2655	75.3	1	2655	491563	0.6330	0.34	25288	0.998578	2.98
36	2669	75.4	1	2669	494232	0.6365	0.35	25289	0.998618	2.99
35	2710	75.4	1	2710	496942	0.6399	0.36	25290	0.998657	3.00
34	2758	75.5	1	2758	499700	0.6435	0.37	25291	0.998697	3.01
33	2774	75.5	1	2774	502474	0.6471	0.38	25292	0.998736	3.02
32	2778	75.5	1	2778	505252	0.6506	0.39	25293	0.998776	3.03
31	2781	75.5	1	2781	508033	0.6542	0.40	25294	0.998815	3.04
30	2940	75.8	1	2940	510973	0.6580	0.41	25295	0.998855	3.05
29	2990	75.9	1	2990	513963	0.6619	0.42	25296	0.998894	3.06
28	3260	76.2	1	3260	517223	0.6661	0.43	25297	0.998934	3.07
27	3370	76.4	1	3370	520593	0.6704	0.44	25298	0.998973	3.08
26	3387	76.4	1	3387	523980	0.6748	0.45	25299	0.999013	3.09
25	3440	76.5	1	3440	527420	0.6792	0.47	25300	0.999052	3.11
24	3455	76.5	1	3455	530875	0.6836	0.48	25301	0.999092	3.12
23	3509	76.6	1	3509	534384	0.6882	0.49	25302	0.999131	3.13
22	3651	76.7	1	3651	538035	0.6929	0.50	25303	0.999171	3.15
21	3988	77.1	1	3988	542023	0.6980	0.52	25304	0.999210	3.16
20	4130	77.3	1	4130	546153	0.7033	0.53	25305	0.999250	3.17
19	4301	77.4	1	4301	550454	0.7089	0.55	25306	0.999289	3.19
18	4387	77.5	1	4387	554841	0.7145	0.57	25307	0.999329	3.21
17	4871	78.0	1	4871	559712	0.7208	0.59	25308	0.999368	3.22
16	4924	78.0	1	4924	564636	0.7271	0.60	25309	0.999408	3.24
15	5279	78.3	1	5279	569915	0.7339	0.62	25310	0.999447	3.26
14	5796	78.7	1	5796	575711	0.7414	0.65	25311	0.999487	3.28
13	6211	79.0	1	6211	581922	0.7494	0.67	25312	0.999526	3.31
12	7019	79.6	1	7019	588941	0.7584	0.70	25313	0.999566	3.33
11	7242	79.7	1	7242	596183	0.7677	0.73	25314	0.999605	3.36
10	7453	79.8	1	7453	603636	0.7773	0.76	25315	0.999645	3.39
9	8304	80.3	1	8304	611940	0.7880	0.80	25316	0.999684	3.42
8	9166	80.7	1	9166	621106	0.7998	0.84	25317	0.999724	3.45
7	9518	80.9	1	9518	630624	0.8121	0.89	25318	0.999763	3.50
6	13995	82.6	1	13995	644619	0.8301	0.95	25319	0.999803	3.54
5	18408	83.7	1	18408	663027	0.8538	1.05	25320	0.999842	3.60
4	18458	83.8	1	18458	681485	0.8776	1.16	25321	0.999882	3.68
3	18760	83.8	1	18760	700245	0.9018	1.29	25322	0.999921	3.78
2	19280	83.9	1	19280	719525	0.9266	1.45	25323	0.999960	3.95
1	57013	88.7	1	57013	776538	1.0000	+INF.	25324	1.000000	+INF.

Rank	Occ. F	SFI	F Tokens	Cum. Tokens	Cum. P Tokens	Y	Cum. Types	Cum. P Types	Z
16617-28488	1	43.7	11872	11872	0.0187	-2.08	11872	0.416737	-0.21
12503-16616	2	46.0	4114	8228	20100	0.0317	-1.86	15986	0.561149	0.15
10226-12502	3	47.4	2277	6831	26931	0.0425	-1.72	18263	0.641077	0.36
8732-10225	4	48.5	1494	5976	32907	0.0519	-1.63	19757	0.693520	0.51
7715- 8731	5	49.4	1017	5085	37992	0.0599	-1.56	20774	0.729219	0.61
6893- 7714	6	50.1	822	4932	42924	0.0677	-1.49	21596	0.758074	0.70
6221- 6892	7	50.7	672	4704	47628	0.0751	-1.44	22268	0.781662	0.78
5660- 6220	8	51.3	561	4488	52116	0.0822	-1.39	22829	0.801355	0.85
5206- 5659	9	51.8	454	4086	56202	0.0886	-1.35	23283	0.817291	0.91
4842- 5205	10	52.2	364	3640	59842	0.0943	-1.31	23647	0.830069	0.95
4571- 4841	11	52.6	271	2981	62823	0.0990	-1.29	23918	0.839582	0.99
4299- 4570	12	52.9	272	3264	66087	0.1042	-1.26	24190	0.849129	1.03
4068- 4298	13	53.3	231	3003	69090	0.1089	-1.23	24421	0.857238	1.07
3862- 4067	14	53.6	206	2884	71974	0.1135	-1.21	24627	0.864469	1.10
3665- 3861	15	53.9	197	2955	74929	0.1181	-1.18	24824	0.871384	1.13
3491- 3664	16	54.2	174	2784	77713	0.1225	-1.16	24998	0.877492	1.16
3338- 3490	17	54.4	153	2601	80314	0.1266	-1.14	25151	0.882863	1.19
3200- 3337	18	54.6	138	2484	82798	0.1305	-1.12	25289	0.887707	1.21
3083- 3199	19	54.9	117	2223	85021	0.1340	-1.11	25406	0.891814	1.24
2965- 3082	20	55.1	118	2360	87381	0.1378	-1.09	25524	0.895956	1.26
2859- 2964	21	55.3	106	2226	89607	0.1413	-1.07	25630	0.899677	1.28
2749- 2858	22	55.5	110	2420	92027	0.1451	-1.06	25740	0.903538	1.30
2648- 2748	23	55.7	101	2323	94350	0.1488	-1.04	25841	0.907084	1.32
2574- 2647	24	55.9	74	1776	96126	0.1516	-1.03	25915	0.909681	1.34
2500- 2573	25	56.0	74	1850	97976	0.1545	-1.02	25989	0.912279	1.35
2425- 2499	26	56.2	75	1950	99926	0.1575	-1.00	26064	0.914912	1.37
2358- 2424	27	56.4	67	1809	101735	0.1604	-0.99	26131	0.917263	1.39
2296- 2357	28	56.5	62	1736	103471	0.1631	-0.98	26193	0.919440	1.40
2233- 2295	29	56.7	63	1827	105298	0.1660	-0.97	26256	0.921651	1.42
2163- 2232	30	56.8	70	2100	107398	0.1693	-0.96	26326	0.924108	1.43
2098- 2162	31	57.0	65	2015	109413	0.1725	-0.94	26391	0.926390	1.45
2047- 2097	32	57.1	51	1632	111045	0.1751	-0.93	26442	0.928180	1.46
1996- 2046	33	57.2	51	1683	112728	0.1777	-0.92	26493	0.929971	1.48
1930- 1995	34	57.4	66	2244	114972	0.1813	-0.91	26559	0.932287	1.49
1877- 1929	35	57.5	53	1855	116827	0.1842	-0.90	26612	0.934148	1.51
1823- 1876	36	57.6	54	1944	118771	0.1873	-0.89	26666	0.936043	1.52
1789- 1822	37	57.7	34	1258	120029	0.1892	-0.88	26700	0.937237	1.53
1760- 1788	38	57.8	29	1102	121131	0.1910	-0.87	26729	0.938255	1.54
1720- 1759	39	57.9	40	1560	122691	0.1934	-0.87	26769	0.939659	1.55
1683- 1719	40	58.1	37	1480	124171	0.1958	-0.86	26806	0.940958	1.56
1648- 1682	41	58.2	35	1435	125606	0.1980	-0.85	26841	0.942186	1.57
1624- 1647	42	58.3	24	1008	126614	0.1996	-0.84	26865	0.943029	1.58
1593- 1623	43	58.4	31	1333	127947	0.2017	-0.84	26896	0.944117	1.59
1558- 1592	44	58.5	35	1540	129487	0.2041	-0.83	26931	0.945345	1.60
1520- 1557	45	58.6	38	1710	131197	0.2068	-0.82	26969	0.946679	1.61
1491- 1519	46	58.7	29	1334	132531	0.2089	-0.81	26998	0.947697	1.62
1466- 1490	47	58.7	25	1175	133706	0.2108	-0.80	27023	0.948575	1.63
1436- 1465	48	58.8	30	1440	135146	0.2131	-0.80	27053	0.949628	1.64
1414- 1435	49	58.9	22	1078	136224	0.2148	-0.79	27075	0.950400	1.65
1392- 1413	50	59.0	22	1100	137324	0.2165	-0.78	27097	0.951172	1.66
1370- 1391	51	59.1	22	1122	138446	0.2183	-0.78	27119	0.951945	1.66
1346- 1369	52	59.2	24	1248	139694	0.2202	-0.77	27143	0.952787	1.67
1321- 1345	53	59.3	25	1325	141019	0.2223	-0.76	27168	0.953665	1.68
1299- 1320	54	59.3	22	1188	142207	0.2242	-0.76	27190	0.954437	1.69
1280- 1298	55	59.4	19	1045	143252	0.2258	-0.75	27209	0.955104	1.70
1257- 1279	56	59.5	23	1288	144540	0.2279	-0.75	27232	0.955911	1.71
1233- 1256	57	59.6	24	1368	145908	0.2300	-0.74	27256	0.956754	1.71
1210- 1232	58	59.6	23	1334	147242	0.2321	-0.73	27279	0.957561	1.72
1194- 1209	59	59.7	16	944	148186	0.2336	-0.73	27295	0.958123	1.73
1185- 1193	60	59.8	9	540	148726	0.2345	-0.72	27304	0.958439	1.73
1164- 1184	61	59.9	21	1281	150007	0.2365	-0.72	27325	0.959176	1.74
1151- 1163	62	59.9	13	806	150813	0.2378	-0.71	27338	0.959632	1.75
1136- 1150	63	60.0	15	945	151758	0.2393	-0.71	27353	0.960159	1.75
1125- 1135	64	60.1	11	704	152462	0.2404	-0.71	27364	0.960545	1.76
1107- 1124	65	60.1	18	1170	153632	0.2422	-0.70	27382	0.961177	1.76
1088- 1106	66	60.2	19	1254	154886	0.2442	-0.69	27401	0.961844	1.77
1069- 1087	67	60.3	19	1273	156159	0.2462	-0.69	27420	0.962511	1.78
1060- 1068	68	60.3	9	612	156771	0.2472	-0.68	27429	0.962826	1.78
1048- 1059	69	60.4	12	828	157599	0.2485	-0.68	27441	0.963248	1.79
1033- 1047	70	60.5	15	1050	158649	0.2501	-0.67	27456	0.963774	1.80
1019- 1032	71	60.5	14	994	159643	0.2517	-0.67	27470	0.964266	1.80
998- 1018	72	60.6	21	1512	161155	0.2541	-0.66	27491	0.965003	1.81
982- 997	73	60.6	16	1168	162323	0.2559	-0.66	27507	0.965564	1.82
967- 981	74	60.7	15	1110	163433	0.2577	-0.65	27522	0.966091	1.83
959- 966	75	60.8	8	600	164033	0.2586	-0.65	27530	0.966372	1.83
945- 958	76	60.8	14	1064	165097	0.2603	-0.64	27544	0.966863	1.84
933- 944	77	60.9	12	924	166021	0.2617	-0.64	27556	0.967284	1.84
919- 932	78	60.9	14	1092	167113	0.2635	-0.63	27570	0.967776	1.85
912- 918	79	61.0	7	553	167666	0.2643	-0.63	27577	0.968022	1.85
903- 911	80	61.0	9	720	168386	0.2655	-0.63	27586	0.968338	1.86
889- 902	81	61.1	14	1134	169520	0.2673	-0.62	27600	0.968829	1.86
880- 888	82	61.1	9	738	170258	0.2684	-0.62	27609	0.969145	1.87
867- 879	83	61.2	13	1079	171337	0.2701	-0.61	27622	0.969601	1.87
857- 866	84	61.2	10	840	172177	0.2715	-0.61	27632	0.969952	1.88
843- 856	85	61.3	14	1190	173367	0.2733	-0.60	27646	0.970444	1.89
832- 842	86	61.3	11	946	174313	0.2748	-0.60	27657	0.970830	1.89
826- 831	87	61.4	6	522	174835	0.2756	-0.60	27663	0.971040	1.90
817- 825	88	61.4	9	792	175627	0.2769	-0.59	27672	0.971356	1.90
809- 816	89	61.5	8	712	176339	0.2780	-0.59	27680	0.971637	1.91
806- 808	90	61.5	3	270	176609	0.2784	-0.59	27683	0.971742	1.91
796- 805	91	61.6	10	910	177519	0.2799	-0.58	27693	0.972093	1.91
792- 795	92	61.6	4	368	177887	0.2805	-0.58	27697	0.972234	1.91
786- 791	93	61.7	6	558	178445	0.2813	-0.58	27703	0.972445	1.92
781- 785	94	61.7	5	470	178915	0.2821	-0.58	27708	0.972620	1.92
772- 780	95	61.8	9	855	179770	0.2834	-0.57	27717	0.972936	1.93
767- 771	96	61.8	5	480	180250	0.2842	-0.57	27722	0.973111	1.93
760- 766	97	61.9	7	679	180929	0.2852	-0.57	27729	0.973357	1.93
752- 759	98	61.9	8	784	181713	0.2865	-0.56	27737	0.973638	1.94
745- 751	99	62.0	7	693	182406	0.2876	-0.56	27744	0.973884	1.94
735- 744	100	62.0	10	1000	183406	0.2892	-0.56	27754	0.974235	1.95
726- 734	101	62.0	9	909	184315	0.2906	-0.55	27763	0.974551	1.95
722- 725	102	62.1	4	408	184723	0.2912	-0.55	27767	0.974691	1.95
714- 721	103	62.1	8	824	185547	0.2925	-0.55	27775	0.974972	1.96
706- 713	104	62.2	8	832	186379	0.2938	-0.54	27783	0.975253	1.96
703- 705	105	62.2	3	315	186694	0.2943	-0.54	27786	0.975358	1.97
693- 702	106	62.3	10	1060	187754	0.2960	-0.54	27796	0.975709	1.97
683- 692	107	62.3	10	1070	188824	0.2977	-0.53	27806	0.976060	1.98
674- 682	108	62.3	9	972	189796	0.2992	-0.53	27815	0.976376	1.98
666- 673	109	62.4	8	872	190668	0.3006	-0.52	27823	0.976657	1.99
660- 665	110	62.4	6	660	191328	0.3016	-0.52	27829	0.976867	1.99
653- 659	111	62.4	7	777	192105	0.3029	-0.52	27836	0.977113	2.00
644- 652	112	62.5	9	1008	193113	0.3045	-0.51	27845	0.977429	2.00
639- 643	113	62.5	5	565	193678	0.3053	-0.51	27850	0.977605	2.01
633- 638	114	62.6	6	684	194362	0.3064	-0.51	27856	0.977815	2.01
631- 632	115	62.6	2	230	194592	0.3068	-0.50	27858	0.977885	2.01
628- 630	116	62.6	3	348	194940	0.3073	-0.50	27861	0.977991	2.01
621- 627	117	62.7	7	819	195759	0.3086	-0.50	27868	0.978236	2.02
614- 620	118	62.7	7	826	196585	0.3099	-0.50	27875	0.978482	2.02
608- 613	119	62.8	6	714	197299	0.3111	-0.49	27881	0.978693	2.03
601- 607	120	62.8	7	840	198139	0.3124	-0.49	27888	0.978938	2.03
600	121	62.8	1	121	198260	0.3126	-0.49	27889	0.978974	2.03
595- 599	122	62.9	5	610	198870	0.3135	-0.49	27894	0.979149	2.04
588- 594	123	62.9	7	861	199731	0.3149	-0.48	27901	0.979395	2.04
586- 587	124	62.9	2	248	199979	0.3153	-0.48	27903	0.979465	2.04
577- 585	125	63.0	9	1125	201104	0.3171	-0.48	27912	0.979781	2.05
573- 576	126	63.0	4	504	201608	0.3179	-0.47	27916	0.979921	2.05
571- 572	127	63.0	2	254	201862	0.3183	-0.47	27918	0.979992	2.05
561- 570	128	63.1	10	1280	203142	0.3203	-0.47	27928	0.980343	2.06
554- 560	129	63.1	7	903	204045	0.3217	-0.46	27935	0.980588	2.07
546- 553	130	63.1	8	1040	205085	0.3233	-0.46	27943	0.980869	2.07
542- 545	131	63.2	4	524	205609	0.3242	-0.46	27947	0.981010	2.08
534- 541	132	63.2	8	1056	206665	0.3258	-0.45	27955	0.981290	2.08
530- 533	133	63.2	4	532	207197	0.3267	-0.45	27959	0.981431	2.08
528- 529	134	63.3	2	268	207465	0.3271	-0.45	27961	0.981501	2.09
527	135	63.3	1	135	207600	0.3273	-0.45	27962	0.981536	2.09
523- 526	136	63.3	4	544	208144	0.3282	-0.45	27966	0.981676	2.09
518- 522	137	63.4	5	685	208829	0.3292	-0.44	27971	0.981852	2.09
516- 517	138	63.4	2	276	209105	0.3297	-0.44	27973	0.981922	2.10
514- 515	139	63.4	2	278	209383	0.3301	-0.44	27975	0.981992	2.10
506- 513	140	63.5	8	1120	210503	0.3319	-0.43	27983	0.982273	2.10
502- 505	141	63.5	4	564	211067	0.3328	-0.43	27987	0.982414	2.11
498- 501	142	63.5	4	568	211635	0.3337	-0.43	27991	0.982554	2.11
491- 497	143	63.5	7	1001	212636	0.3352	-0.43	27998	0.982800	2.12
485- 490	144	63.6	6	864	213500	0.3366	-0.42	28004	0.983010	2.12
480- 484	145	63.6	5	725	214225	0.3377	-0.42	28009	0.983186	2.12
475- 479	146	63.6	5	730	214955	0.3389	-0.42	28014	0.983361	2.13
472- 474	147	63.7	3	441	215396	0.3396	-0.41	28017	0.983467	2.13
468- 471	148	63.7	4	592	215988	0.3405	-0.41	28021	0.983607	2.13
465- 467	149	63.7	3	447	216435	0.3412	-0.41	28024	0.983712	2.14
461- 464	150	63.8	4	600	217035	0.3422	-0.41	28028	0.983853	2.14
456- 460	151	63.8	5	755	217790	0.3434	-0.40	28033	0.984028	2.15
452- 455	152	63.8	4	608	218398	0.3443	-0.40	28037	0.984169	2.15
449- 451	153	63.8	3	459	218857	0.3450	-0.40	28040	0.984274	2.15
446- 448	154	63.9	3	462	219319	0.3458	-0.40	28043	0.984379	2.15
442- 445	155	63.9	4	620	219939	0.3468	-0.39	28047	0.984520	2.16
438- 441	156	63.9	4	624	220563	0.3477	-0.39	28051	0.984660	2.16
436- 437	157	63.9	2	314	220877	0.3482	-0.39	28053	0.984730	2.16
431- 435	158	64.0	5	790	221667	0.3495	-0.39	28058	0.984906	2.17
426- 430	159	64.0	5	795	222462	0.3507	-0.38	28063	0.985081	2.17
422- 425	160	64.0	4	640	223102	0.3517	-0.38	28067	0.985222	2.18
421	161	64.1	1	161	223263	0.3520	-0.38	28068	0.985257	2.18
420	162	64.1	1	162	223425	0.3522	-0.38	28069	0.985292	2.18
416- 419	163	64.1	4	652	224077	0.3533	-0.38	28073	0.985432	2.18
412- 415	164	64.1	4	656	224733	0.3543	-0.37	28077	0.985573	2.19
410- 411	165	64.2	2	330	225063	0.3548	-0.37	28079	0.985643	2.19
406- 409	166	64.2	4	664	225727	0.3559	-0.37	28083	0.985783	2.19
405	167	64.2	1	167	225894	0.3561	-0.37	28084	0.985819	2.19
400- 404	168	64.2	5	840	226734	0.3575	-0.37	28089	0.985994	2.20
396- 399	169	64.3	4	676	227410	0.3585	-0.36	28093	0.986134	2.20
394- 395	170	64.3	2	340	227750	0.3591	-0.36	28095	0.986205	2.20
391- 393	171	64.3	3	513	228263	0.3599	-0.36	28098	0.986310	2.21
389- 390	172	64.3	2	344	228607	0.3604	-0.36	28100	0.986380	2.21
386- 388	173	64.4	3	519	229126	0.3612	-0.36	28103	0.986485	2.21
381- 385	175	64.4	5	875	230001	0.3626	-0.35	28108	0.986661	2.22
378- 380	176	64.4	3	528	230529	0.3634	-0.35	28111	0.986766	2.22
377	178	64.5	1	178	230707	0.3637	-0.35	28112	0.986801	2.22
374- 376	179	64.5	3	537	231244	0.3646	-0.35	28115	0.986907	2.22
373	180	64.5	1	180	231424	0.3649	-0.35	28116	0.986942	2.22
371- 372	181	64.6	2	362	231786	0.3654	-0.34	28118	0.987012	2.23
369- 370	182	64.6	2	364	232150	0.3660	-0.34	28120	0.987082	2.23
366- 368	183	64.6	3	549	232699	0.3669	-0.34	28123	0.987188	2.23
364- 365	185	64.7	2	370	233069	0.3675	-0.34	28125	0.987258	2.23
363	186	64.7	1	186	233255	0.3677	-0.34	28126	0.987293	2.24
360- 362	187	64.7	3	561	233816	0.3686	-0.34	28129	0.987398	2.24
359	188	64.7	1	188	234004	0.3689	-0.33	28130	0.987433	2.24
358	189	64.8	1	189	234193	0.3692	-0.33	28131	0.987468	2.24
355- 357	190	64.8	3	570	234763	0.3701	-0.33	28134	0.987574	2.24
351- 354	192	64.8	4	768	235531	0.3713	-0.33	28138	0.987714	2.25
347- 350	193	64.8	4	772	236303	0.3726	-0.33	28142	0.987854	2.25
344- 346	194	64.9	3	582	236885	0.3735	-0.32	28145	0.987960	2.26
341- 343	196	64.9	3	588	237473	0.3744	-0.32	28148	0.988065	2.26
340	197	64.9	1	197	237670	0.3747	-0.32	28149	0.988100	2.26
338- 339	198	65.0	2	396	238066	0.3753	-0.32	28151	0.988170	2.26
337	199	65.0	1	199	238265	0.3756	-0.32	28152	0.988206	2.26
336	200	65.0	1	200	238465	0.3760	-0.32	28153	0.988241	2.26
334- 335	203	65.1	2	406	238871	0.3766	-0.31	28155	0.988311	2.27
333	204	65.1	1	204	239075	0.3769	-0.31	28156	0.988346	2.27
332	205	65.1	1	205	239280	0.3772	-0.31	28157	0.988381	2.27
326- 331	206	65.1	6	1236	240516	0.3792	-0.31	28163	0.988592	2.28
325	207	65.1	1	207	240723	0.3795	-0.31	28164	0.988627	2.28
323- 324	209	65.2	2	418	241141	0.3802	-0.31	28166	0.988697	2.28
319- 322	210	65.2	4	840	241981	0.3815	-0.30	28170	0.988837	2.28
314- 318	213	65.3	5	1065	243046	0.3832	-0.30	28175	0.989013	2.29
312- 313	214	65.3	2	428	243474	0.3839	-0.30	28177	0.989083	2.29
311	215	65.3	1	215	243689	0.3842	-0.29	28178	0.989118	2.29
310	218	65.4	1	218	243907	0.3845	-0.29	28179	0.989153	2.30
309	219	65.4	1	219	244126	0.3849	-0.29	28180	0.989188	2.30
308	221	65.4	1	221	244347	0.3852	-0.29	28181	0.989223	2.30
307	223	65.5	1	223	244570	0.3856	-0.29	28182	0.989259	2.30
306	224	65.5	1	224	244794	0.3859	-0.29	28183	0.989294	2.30
305	225	65.5	1	225	245019	0.3863	-0.29	28184	0.989329	2.30
302- 304	229	65.6	3	687	245706	0.3874	-0.29	28187	0.989434	2.31
301	230	65.6	1	230	245936	0.3877	-0.29	28188	0.989469	2.31
300	231	65.6	1	231	246167	0.3881	-0.28	28189	0.989504	2.31
298- 299	232	65.6	2	464	246631	0.3888	-0.28	28191	0.989575	2.31
296- 297	233	65.7	2	466	247097	0.3896	-0.28	28193	0.989645	2.31
295	234	65.7	1	234	247331	0.3899	-0.28	28194	0.989680	2.31
294	236	65.7	1	236	247567	0.3903	-0.28	28195	0.989715	2.32
290- 293	239	65.8	4	956	248523	0.3918	-0.27	28199	0.989855	2.32
288- 289	242	65.8	2	484	249007	0.3926	-0.27	28201	0.989926	2.32
287	244	65.9	1	244	249251	0.3930	-0.27	28202	0.989961	2.32
286	245	65.9	1	245	249496	0.3934	-0.27	28203	0.989996	2.33
283- 285	247	65.9	3	741	250237	0.3945	-0.27	28206	0.990101	2.33
282	248	65.9	1	248	250485	0.3949	-0.27	28207	0.990136	2.33
281	250	66.0	1	250	250735	0.3953	-0.27	28208	0.990171	2.33
280	251	66.0	1	251	250986	0.3957	-0.26	28209	0.990206	2.33
279	252	66.0	1	252	251238	0.3961	-0.26	28210	0.990241	2.34
278	254	66.0	1	254	251492	0.3965	-0.26	28211	0.990277	2.34
277	255	66.1	1	255	251747	0.3969	-0.26	28212	0.990312	2.34
275- 276	258	66.1	2	516	252263	0.3977	-0.26	28214	0.990382	2.34
273- 274	259	66.1	2	518	252781	0.3985	-0.26	28216	0.990452	2.34
271- 272	260	66.1	2	520	253301	0.3994	-0.26	28218	0.990522	2.35

Rank	Occ. F	SFI	F	Tokens	Cum. Tokens	Cum. P Tokens	Y	Cum. Types	Cum. P Types	Z
268– 270	261	66.2	3	783	254084	0.4006	−0.25	28221	0.990628	2.35
267	262	66.2	1	262	254346	0.4010	−0.25	28222	0.990663	2.35
265– 266	264	66.2	2	528	254874	0.4018	−0.25	28224	0.990733	2.35
264	266	66.2	1	266	255140	0.4022	−0.25	28225	0.990768	2.36
263	267	66.3	1	267	255407	0.4027	−0.25	28226	0.990803	2.36
262	268	66.3	1	268	255675	0.4031	−0.25	28227	0.990838	2.36
261	270	66.3	1	270	255945	0.4035	−0.24	28228	0.990873	2.36
259– 260	271	66.3	2	542	256487	0.4044	−0.24	28230	0.990944	2.36
256– 258	272	66.3	3	816	257303	0.4057	−0.24	28233	0.991049	2.37
255	273	66.3	1	273	257576	0.4061	−0.24	28234	0.991084	2.37
254	275	66.4	1	275	257851	0.4065	−0.24	28235	0.991119	2.37
252– 253	276	66.4	2	552	258403	0.4074	−0.23	28237	0.991189	2.37
251	277	66.4	1	277	258680	0.4078	−0.23	28238	0.991224	2.37
250	278	66.4	1	278	258958	0.4083	−0.23	28239	0.991259	2.38
249	280	66.5	1	280	259238	0.4087	−0.23	28240	0.991295	2.38
248	281	66.5	1	281	259519	0.4092	−0.23	28241	0.991330	2.38
244– 247	283	66.5	4	1132	260651	0.4109	−0.23	28245	0.991470	2.39
242– 243	285	66.5	2	570	261221	0.4118	−0.22	28247	0.991540	2.39
239– 241	287	66.6	3	861	262082	0.4132	−0.22	28250	0.991646	2.39
237– 238	289	66.6	2	578	262660	0.4141	−0.22	28252	0.991716	2.40
233– 236	290	66.6	4	1160	263820	0.4159	−0.21	28256	0.991856	2.40
232	291	66.6	1	291	264111	0.4164	−0.21	28257	0.991891	2.40
231	293	66.7	1	293	264404	0.4169	−0.21	28258	0.991926	2.41
230	295	66.7	1	295	264699	0.4173	−0.21	28259	0.991961	2.41
229	297	66.7	1	297	264996	0.4178	−0.21	28260	0.991997	2.41
227– 228	298	66.7	2	596	265592	0.4187	−0.21	28262	0.992067	2.41
226	301	66.8	1	301	265893	0.4192	−0.20	28263	0.992102	2.41
224– 225	302	66.8	2	604	266497	0.4202	−0.20	28265	0.992172	2.42
223	303	66.8	1	303	266800	0.4206	−0.20	28266	0.992207	2.42
222	304	66.8	1	304	267104	0.4211	−0.20	28267	0.992242	2.42
221	305	66.8	1	305	267409	0.4216	−0.20	28268	0.992277	2.42
220	306	66.8	1	306	267715	0.4221	−0.20	28269	0.992313	2.42
219	307	66.9	1	307	268022	0.4226	−0.20	28270	0.992348	2.43
218	310	66.9	1	310	268332	0.4230	−0.19	28271	0.992383	2.43
217	311	66.9	1	311	268643	0.4235	−0.19	28272	0.992418	2.43
216	313	66.9	1	313	268956	0.4240	−0.19	28273	0.992453	2.43
215	314	67.0	1	314	269270	0.4245	−0.19	28274	0.992488	2.43
214	316	67.0	1	316	269586	0.4250	−0.19	28275	0.992523	2.43
213	319	67.0	1	319	269905	0.4255	−0.19	28276	0.992558	2.44
212	320	67.0	1	320	270225	0.4260	−0.19	28277	0.992593	2.44
211	322	67.1	1	322	270547	0.4265	−0.19	28278	0.992628	2.44
209– 210	323	67.1	2	646	271193	0.4276	−0.18	28280	0.992699	2.44
208	324	67.1	1	324	271517	0.4281	−0.18	28281	0.992734	2.44
207	327	67.1	1	327	271844	0.4286	−0.18	28282	0.992769	2.45
206	329	67.2	1	329	272173	0.4291	−0.18	28283	0.992804	2.45
204– 205	332	67.2	2	664	272837	0.4302	−0.18	28285	0.992874	2.45
203	334	67.2	1	334	273171	0.4307	−0.17	28286	0.992909	2.45
202	336	67.2	1	336	273507	0.4312	−0.17	28287	0.992944	2.45
201	337	67.3	1	337	273844	0.4317	−0.17	28288	0.992979	2.46
199– 200	340	67.3	2	680	274524	0.4328	−0.17	28290	0.993050	2.46
196– 198	341	67.3	3	1023	275547	0.4344	−0.17	28293	0.993155	2.47
195	343	67.3	1	343	275890	0.4350	−0.16	28294	0.993190	2.47
194	346	67.4	1	346	276236	0.4355	−0.16	28295	0.993225	2.47
193	353	67.5	1	353	276589	0.4361	−0.16	28296	0.993260	2.47
191– 192	360	67.5	2	720	277309	0.4372	−0.16	28298	0.993330	2.47
190	361	67.6	1	361	277670	0.4378	−0.16	28299	0.993366	2.48
188– 189	363	67.6	2	726	278396	0.4389	−0.15	28301	0.993436	2.48
187	364	67.6	1	364	278760	0.4395	−0.15	28302	0.993471	2.48
186	370	67.7	1	370	279130	0.4401	−0.15	28303	0.993506	2.48
185	371	67.7	1	371	279501	0.4407	−0.15	28304	0.993541	2.49
184	372	67.7	1	372	279873	0.4412	−0.15	28305	0.993576	2.49
182– 183	374	67.7	2	748	280621	0.4424	−0.14	28307	0.993646	2.49
181	375	67.7	1	375	280996	0.4430	−0.14	28308	0.993682	2.49
180	377	67.7	1	377	281373	0.4436	−0.14	28309	0.993717	2.50
179	378	67.8	1	378	281751	0.4442	−0.14	28310	0.993752	2.50
178	380	67.8	1	380	282131	0.4448	−0.14	28311	0.993787	2.50
177	381	67.8	1	381	282512	0.4454	−0.14	28312	0.993822	2.50
176	386	67.8	1	386	282898	0.4460	−0.14	28313	0.993857	2.50
175	394	67.9	1	394	283292	0.4466	−0.13	28314	0.993892	2.51
174	396	68.0	1	396	283688	0.4473	−0.13	28315	0.993927	2.51
172– 173	398	68.0	2	796	284484	0.4485	−0.13	28317	0.993997	2.51
171	402	68.0	1	402	284886	0.4491	−0.13	28318	0.994033	2.51
170	403	68.0	1	403	285289	0.4498	−0.13	28319	0.994068	2.52
169	405	68.1	1	405	285694	0.4504	−0.12	28320	0.994103	2.52
168	408	68.1	1	408	286102	0.4511	−0.12	28321	0.994138	2.52
167	410	68.1	1	410	286512	0.4517	−0.12	28322	0.994173	2.52
166	423	68.2	1	423	286935	0.4524	−0.12	28323	0.994208	2.52
165	434	68.4	1	434	287369	0.4531	−0.12	28324	0.994243	2.53
164	436	68.4	1	436	287805	0.4537	−0.12	28325	0.994278	2.53
163	441	68.4	1	441	288246	0.4544	−0.11	28326	0.994313	2.53
162	445	68.5	1	445	288691	0.4551	−0.11	28327	0.994348	2.53
160– 161	452	68.5	2	904	289595	0.4566	−0.11	28329	0.994419	2.54
158– 159	454	68.6	2	908	290503	0.4580	−0.11	28331	0.994489	2.54
157	458	68.6	1	458	290961	0.4587	−0.10	28332	0.994524	2.54
156	460	68.6	1	460	291421	0.4594	−0.10	28333	0.994559	2.55
155	462	68.6	1	462	291883	0.4602	−0.10	28334	0.994594	2.55
154	463	68.6	1	463	292346	0.4609	−0.10	28335	0.994629	2.55
153	468	68.7	1	468	292814	0.4616	−0.10	28336	0.994664	2.55
152	469	68.7	1	469	293283	0.4624	−0.09	28337	0.994699	2.56
151	470	68.7	1	470	293753	0.4631	−0.09	28338	0.994735	2.56
150	477	68.8	1	477	294230	0.4639	−0.09	28339	0.994770	2.56
149	478	68.8	1	478	294708	0.4646	−0.09	28340	0.994805	2.56
148	480	68.8	1	480	295188	0.4654	−0.09	28341	0.994840	2.56
147	483	68.8	1	483	295671	0.4661	−0.08	28342	0.994875	2.57
146	488	68.9	1	488	296159	0.4669	−0.08	28343	0.994910	2.57
145	489	68.9	1	489	296648	0.4677	−0.08	28344	0.994945	2.57
144	498	69.0	1	498	297146	0.4685	−0.08	28345	0.994980	2.57
143	499	69.0	1	499	297645	0.4693	−0.08	28346	0.995015	2.58
142	513	69.1	1	513	298158	0.4701	−0.08	28347	0.995050	2.58
141	516	69.1	1	516	298674	0.4709	−0.07	28348	0.995086	2.58
138– 140	517	69.1	3	1551	300225	0.4733	−0.07	28351	0.995191	2.59
136– 137	523	69.2	2	1046	301271	0.4750	−0.06	28353	0.995261	2.59
135	534	69.3	1	534	301805	0.4758	−0.06	28354	0.995296	2.60
133– 134	536	69.3	2	1072	302877	0.4775	−0.06	28356	0.995366	2.60
132	539	69.3	1	539	303416	0.4784	−0.05	28357	0.995402	2.60
131	542	69.3	1	542	303958	0.4792	−0.05	28358	0.995437	2.61
129– 130	543	69.3	2	1086	305044	0.4809	−0.05	28360	0.995507	2.61
128	544	69.3	1	544	305588	0.4818	−0.05	28361	0.995542	2.62
127	551	69.4	1	551	306139	0.4827	−0.04	28362	0.995577	2.62
126	553	69.4	1	553	306692	0.4835	−0.04	28363	0.995612	2.62
125	554	69.4	1	554	307246	0.4844	−0.04	28364	0.995647	2.62
124	564	69.5	1	564	307810	0.4853	−0.04	28365	0.995682	2.63
123	565	69.5	1	565	308375	0.4862	−0.03	28366	0.995717	2.63
122	566	69.5	1	566	308941	0.4871	−0.03	28367	0.995753	2.63
121	569	69.5	1	569	309510	0.4880	−0.03	28368	0.995788	2.63
120	574	69.6	1	574	310084	0.4889	−0.03	28369	0.995823	2.64
119	578	69.6	1	578	310662	0.4898	−0.03	28370	0.995858	2.64
118	579	69.6	1	579	311241	0.4907	−0.02	28371	0.995893	2.64
117	584	69.6	1	584	311825	0.4916	−0.02	28372	0.995928	2.65
116	601	69.8	1	601	312426	0.4926	−0.02	28373	0.995963	2.65
115	615	69.9	1	615	313041	0.4935	−0.02	28374	0.995998	2.65
114	618	69.9	1	618	313659	0.4945	−0.01	28375	0.996033	2.65
113	621	69.9	1	621	314280	0.4955	−0.01	28376	0.996068	2.66
112	625	69.9	1	625	314905	0.4965	−0.01	28377	0.996104	2.66
111	631	70.0	1	631	315536	0.4975	−0.01	28378	0.996139	2.66
110	646	70.1	1	646	316182	0.4985	−0.00	28379	0.996174	2.67
109	655	70.1	1	655	316837	0.4995	−0.00	28380	0.996209	2.67
108	664	70.2	1	664	317501	0.5006	0.00	28381	0.996244	2.67
107	668	70.2	1	668	318169	0.5016	0.00	28382	0.996279	2.68
106	672	70.3	1	672	318841	0.5027	0.01	28383	0.996314	2.68
105	676	70.3	1	676	319517	0.5037	0.01	28384	0.996349	2.68
103– 104	680	70.3	2	1360	320877	0.5059	0.01	28386	0.996419	2.69
102	709	70.5	1	709	321586	0.5070	0.02	28387	0.996455	2.69
101	713	70.5	1	713	322299	0.5081	0.02	28388	0.996490	2.70
100	716	70.5	1	716	323015	0.5093	0.02	28389	0.996525	2.70
99	717	70.5	1	717	323732	0.5104	0.03	28390	0.996560	2.70
98	759	70.8	1	759	324491	0.5116	0.03	28391	0.996595	2.71
97	776	70.9	1	776	325267	0.5128	0.03	28392	0.996630	2.71
96	785	70.9	1	785	326052	0.5140	0.04	28393	0.996665	2.71
95	798	71.0	1	798	326850	0.5153	0.04	28394	0.996700	2.72
94	802	71.0	1	802	327652	0.5166	0.04	28395	0.996735	2.72
93	812	71.1	1	812	328464	0.5179	0.04	28396	0.996771	2.72
92	819	71.1	1	819	329283	0.5191	0.05	28397	0.996806	2.73
91	825	71.1	1	825	330108	0.5204	0.05	28398	0.996841	2.73
90	828	71.2	1	828	330936	0.5217	0.05	28399	0.996876	2.73
89	829	71.2	1	829	331765	0.5231	0.06	28400	0.996911	2.74
88	887	71.5	1	887	332652	0.5245	0.06	28401	0.996946	2.74
87	888	71.5	1	888	333540	0.5259	0.06	28402	0.996981	2.75
86	889	71.5	1	889	334429	0.5273	0.07	28403	0.997016	2.75
85	899	71.5	1	899	335328	0.5287	0.07	28404	0.997051	2.75
84	926	71.6	1	926	336254	0.5301	0.08	28405	0.997086	2.76
83	934	71.7	1	934	337188	0.5316	0.08	28406	0.997122	2.76
82	953	71.8	1	953	338141	0.5331	0.08	28407	0.997157	2.77
81	959	71.8	1	959	339100	0.5346	0.09	28408	0.997192	2.77
80	974	71.9	1	974	340074	0.5362	0.09	28409	0.997227	2.77
79	976	71.9	1	976	341050	0.5377	0.09	28410	0.997262	2.78
78	985	71.9	1	985	342035	0.5392	0.10	28411	0.997297	2.78
77	992	71.9	1	992	343027	0.5408	0.10	28412	0.997332	2.79
76	993	71.9	1	993	344020	0.5424	0.11	28413	0.997367	2.79
75	1058	72.2	1	1058	345078	0.5440	0.11	28414	0.997402	2.79
74	1066	72.3	1	1066	346144	0.5457	0.11	28415	0.997437	2.80
73	1069	72.3	1	1069	347213	0.5474	0.12	28416	0.997473	2.80
72	1084	72.3	1	1084	348297	0.5491	0.12	28417	0.997508	2.81
71	1112	72.4	1	1112	349409	0.5509	0.13	28418	0.997543	2.81
70	1125	72.5	1	1125	350534	0.5526	0.13	28419	0.997578	2.82
69	1158	72.6	1	1158	351692	0.5545	0.14	28420	0.997613	2.82
68	1187	72.7	1	1187	352879	0.5563	0.14	28421	0.997648	2.83
67	1198	72.8	1	1198	354077	0.5582	0.15	28422	0.997683	2.83
66	1252	73.0	1	1252	355329	0.5602	0.15	28423	0.997718	2.84
65	1261	73.0	1	1261	356590	0.5622	0.16	28424	0.997753	2.84
64	1327	73.2	1	1327	357917	0.5643	0.16	28425	0.997788	2.85
63	1330	73.2	1	1330	359247	0.5664	0.17	28426	0.997824	2.85
62	1335	73.2	1	1335	360582	0.5685	0.17	28427	0.997859	2.86
61	1365	73.3	1	1365	361947	0.5706	0.18	28428	0.997894	2.86
60	1399	73.4	1	1399	363346	0.5728	0.18	28429	0.997929	2.87
59	1411	73.5	1	1411	364757	0.5751	0.19	28430	0.997964	2.87
58	1447	73.6	1	1447	366204	0.5774	0.20	28431	0.997999	2.88
56– 57	1464	73.6	2	2928	369132	0.5820	0.21	28433	0.998069	2.89
55	1489	73.7	1	1489	370621	0.5843	0.21	28434	0.998104	2.90
54	1520	73.8	1	1520	372141	0.5867	0.22	28435	0.998140	2.90
53	1523	73.8	1	1523	373664	0.5891	0.23	28436	0.998175	2.91
52	1563	73.9	1	1563	375227	0.5916	0.23	28437	0.998210	2.91
51	1639	74.1	1	1639	376866	0.5942	0.24	28438	0.998245	2.92
50	1651	74.2	1	1651	378517	0.5968	0.24	28439	0.998280	2.93
49	1674	74.2	1	1674	380191	0.5994	0.25	28440	0.998315	2.93
48	1677	74.2	1	1677	381868	0.6020	0.26	28441	0.998350	2.94
47	1685	74.2	1	1685	383553	0.6047	0.27	28442	0.998385	2.95
45– 46	1701	74.3	2	3402	386955	0.6101	0.28	28444	0.998455	2.96
44	1729	74.4	1	1729	388684	0.6128	0.29	28445	0.998491	2.97
43	1762	74.4	1	1762	390446	0.6156	0.29	28446	0.998526	2.97
42	1852	74.7	1	1852	392298	0.6185	0.30	28447	0.998561	2.98
41	1861	74.7	1	1861	394159	0.6214	0.31	28448	0.998596	2.99
40	1889	74.7	1	1889	396048	0.6244	0.32	28449	0.998631	3.00
39	1891	74.7	1	1891	397939	0.6274	0.32	28450	0.998666	3.00
38	1897	74.8	1	1897	399836	0.6304	0.33	28451	0.998701	3.01
37	1911	74.8	1	1911	401747	0.6334	0.34	28452	0.998736	3.02
36	2004	75.0	1	2004	403751	0.6365	0.35	28453	0.998771	3.03
35	2005	75.0	1	2005	405756	0.6397	0.36	28454	0.998806	3.04
34	2033	75.1	1	2033	407789	0.6429	0.37	28455	0.998842	3.05
33	2045	75.1	1	2045	409834	0.6461	0.37	28456	0.998877	3.06
32	2176	75.4	1	2176	412010	0.6496	0.38	28457	0.998912	3.07
31	2239	75.5	1	2239	414249	0.6531	0.39	28458	0.998947	3.07
30	2328	75.6	1	2328	416577	0.6568	0.40	28459	0.998982	3.08
29	2431	75.8	1	2431	419008	0.6606	0.41	28460	0.999017	3.10
28	2473	75.9	1	2473	421481	0.6645	0.42	28461	0.999052	3.11
27	2500	76.0	1	2500	423981	0.6684	0.44	28462	0.999087	3.12
26	2516	76.0	1	2516	426497	0.6724	0.45	28463	0.999122	3.13
25	2531	76.0	1	2531	429028	0.6764	0.46	28464	0.999157	3.14
24	2688	76.3	1	2688	431716	0.6806	0.47	28465	0.999193	3.15
23	2737	76.4	1	2737	434453	0.6850	0.48	28466	0.999228	3.17
22	2833	76.5	1	2833	437286	0.6894	0.49	28467	0.999263	3.18
21	2900	76.6	1	2900	440186	0.6940	0.51	28468	0.999298	3.19
20	3127	76.9	1	3127	443313	0.6989	0.52	28469	0.999333	3.21
19	3269	77.1	1	3269	446582	0.7041	0.54	28470	0.999368	3.22
18	3422	77.3	1	3422	450004	0.7095	0.55	28471	0.999403	3.24
17	3629	77.6	1	3629	453633	0.7152	0.57	28472	0.999438	3.26
16	3914	77.9	1	3914	457547	0.7214	0.59	28473	0.999473	3.28
15	4582	78.6	1	4582	462129	0.7286	0.61	28474	0.999509	3.30
14	4690	78.7	1	4690	466819	0.7360	0.63	28475	0.999544	3.32
13	4760	78.8	1	4760	471579	0.7435	0.65	28476	0.999579	3.34
12	5002	79.0	1	5002	476581	0.7514	0.68	28477	0.999614	3.36
11	5248	79.2	1	5248	481829	0.7596	0.71	28478	0.999649	3.39
10	5682	79.5	1	5682	487511	0.7686	0.73	28479	0.999684	3.42
9	5897	79.7	1	5897	493408	0.7779	0.77	28480	0.999719	3.45
8	6227	79.9	1	6227	499635	0.7877	0.80	28481	0.999754	3.49
7	7716	80.9	1	7716	507351	0.7999	0.84	28482	0.999789	3.53
6	12971	83.1	1	12971	520322	0.8203	0.92	28483	0.999824	3.57
5	14518	83.6	1	14518	534840	0.8432	1.01	28484	0.999860	3.63
4	15103	83.8	1	15103	549943	0.8670	1.11	28485	0.999895	3.71
3	16755	84.2	1	16755	566698	0.8934	1.25	28486	0.999930	3.81
2	18861	84.7	1	18861	585559	0.9232	1.43	28487	0.999965	3.98
1	48724	88.9	1	48724	634283	1.0000	+INF.	28488	1.000000	+INF.

Rank	Occ. F	SFI	F	Tokens	Cum. Tokens	Cum. P Tokens	Y	Cum. Types	Cum. P Types	Z
17512-29736	1	43.5	12225	12225	12225	0.0183	-2.09	12225	0.411118	-0.22
13066-17511	2	45.7	4446	8892	21117	0.0316	-1.86	16671	0.560634	0.15
10662-13065	3	47.2	2404	7212	28329	0.0424	-1.72	19075	0.641478	0.36
9104-10661	4	48.3	1558	6232	34561	0.0517	-1.63	20633	0.693873	0.51
7969- 9103	5	49.2	1135	5675	40236	0.0602	-1.55	21768	0.732042	0.62
7151- 7968	6	49.9	818	4908	45144	0.0676	-1.49	22586	0.759551	0.70
6485- 7150	7	50.5	666	4662	49806	0.0746	-1.44	23252	0.781948	0.78
5899- 6484	8	51.0	586	4688	54494	0.0816	-1.39	23838	0.801655	0.85
5428- 5898	9	51.5	471	4239	58733	0.0879	-1.35	24309	0.817494	0.91
5066- 5427	10	52.0	362	3620	62353	0.0934	-1.32	24671	0.829668	0.95
4724- 5065	11	52.4	342	3762	66115	0.0990	-1.29	25013	0.841169	1.00
4442- 4723	12	52.7	282	3384	69499	0.1041	-1.26	25295	0.850652	1.04
4176- 4441	13	53.1	266	3458	72957	0.1092	-1.23	25561	0.859598	1.08
3976- 4175	14	53.4	200	2800	75757	0.1134	-1.21	25761	0.866324	1.11
3787- 3975	15	53.7	189	2835	78592	0.1177	-1.19	25950	0.872680	1.14
3615- 3786	16	53.9	172	2752	81344	0.1218	-1.17	26122	0.878464	1.17
3457- 3614	17	54.2	158	2686	84030	0.1258	-1.15	26280	0.883777	1.19
3303- 3456	18	54.4	154	2772	86802	0.1300	-1.13	26434	0.888956	1.22
3159- 3302	19	54.7	144	2736	89538	0.1341	-1.11	26578	0.893799	1.25
3034- 3158	20	54.9	125	2500	92038	0.1378	-1.09	26703	0.898002	1.27
2921- 3033	21	55.1	113	2373	94411	0.1414	-1.07	26816	0.901802	1.29
2809- 2920	22	55.3	112	2464	96875	0.1450	-1.06	26928	0.905569	1.31
2716- 2808	23	55.5	93	2139	99014	0.1482	-1.04	27021	0.908696	1.33
2626- 2715	24	55.6	90	2160	101174	0.1515	-1.03	27111	0.911723	1.35
2555- 2625	25	55.8	71	1775	102949	0.1541	-1.02	27182	0.914111	1.37
2473- 2554	26	56.0	82	2132	105081	0.1573	-1.01	27264	0.916868	1.38
2394- 2472	27	56.1	79	2133	107214	0.1605	-0.99	27343	0.919525	1.40
2323- 2393	28	56.3	71	1988	109202	0.1635	-0.98	27414	0.921913	1.42
2268- 2322	29	56.5	55	1595	110797	0.1659	-0.97	27469	0.923762	1.43
2211- 2267	30	56.6	57	1710	112507	0.1684	-0.96	27526	0.925679	1.44
2138- 2210	31	56.7	73	2263	114770	0.1718	-0.95	27599	0.928134	1.46
2071- 2137	32	56.9	67	2144	116914	0.1750	-0.93	27666	0.930387	1.48
2015- 2070	33	57.0	56	1848	118762	0.1778	-0.92	27722	0.932271	1.49
1959- 2014	34	57.1	56	1904	120666	0.1807	-0.91	27778	0.934154	1.51
1928- 1958	35	57.3	31	1085	121751	0.1823	-0.91	27809	0.935196	1.52
1892- 1927	36	57.4	36	1296	123047	0.1842	-0.90	27845	0.936407	1.53
1840- 1891	37	57.5	52	1924	124971	0.1871	-0.89	27897	0.938156	1.54
1794- 1839	38	57.6	46	1748	126719	0.1897	-0.88	27943	0.939703	1.55
1758- 1793	39	57.7	36	1404	128123	0.1918	-0.87	27979	0.940913	1.56
1724- 1757	40	57.8	34	1360	129483	0.1939	-0.86	28013	0.942057	1.57
1691- 1723	41	57.9	33	1353	130836	0.1959	-0.86	28046	0.943166	1.58
1665- 1690	42	58.0	26	1092	131928	0.1975	-0.85	28072	0.944041	1.59
1629- 1664	43	58.1	36	1548	133476	0.1998	-0.84	28108	0.945252	1.60
1593- 1628	44	58.2	36	1584	135060	0.2022	-0.83	28144	0.946462	1.61
1566- 1592	45	58.3	27	1215	136275	0.2040	-0.83	28171	0.947370	1.62
1543- 1565	46	58.4	23	1058	137333	0.2056	-0.82	28194	0.948144	1.63
1514- 1542	47	58.5	29	1363	138696	0.2077	-0.81	28223	0.949119	1.64
1485- 1513	48	58.6	29	1392	140088	0.2097	-0.81	28252	0.950094	1.65
1460- 1484	49	58.7	25	1225	141313	0.2116	-0.80	28277	0.950935	1.65
1436- 1459	50	58.8	24	1200	142513	0.2134	-0.79	28301	0.951742	1.66
1401- 1435	51	58.9	35	1785	144298	0.2160	-0.79	28336	0.952919	1.67
1376- 1400	52	59.0	25	1300	145598	0.2180	-0.78	28361	0.953760	1.68
1360- 1375	53	59.0	16	848	146446	0.2193	-0.77	28377	0.954298	1.69
1331- 1359	54	59.1	29	1566	148012	0.2216	-0.77	28406	0.955273	1.70
1315- 1330	55	59.2	16	880	148892	0.2229	-0.76	28422	0.955811	1.70
1296- 1314	56	59.3	19	1064	149956	0.2245	-0.76	28441	0.956450	1.71
1277- 1295	57	59.3	19	1083	151039	0.2261	-0.75	28460	0.957089	1.72
1261- 1276	58	59.4	16	928	151967	0.2275	-0.75	28476	0.957627	1.72
1240- 1260	59	59.5	21	1239	153206	0.2294	-0.74	28497	0.958333	1.73
1216- 1239	60	59.6	24	1440	154646	0.2315	-0.73	28521	0.959140	1.74
1197- 1215	61	59.6	19	1159	155805	0.2333	-0.73	28540	0.959779	1.75
1176- 1196	62	59.7	21	1302	157107	0.2352	-0.72	28561	0.960486	1.76
1160- 1175	63	59.8	16	1008	158115	0.2367	-0.72	28577	0.961024	1.76
1140- 1159	64	59.8	20	1280	159395	0.2387	-0.71	28597	0.961696	1.77
1124- 1139	65	59.9	16	1040	160435	0.2402	-0.71	28613	0.962234	1.78
1107- 1123	66	60.0	17	1122	161557	0.2419	-0.70	28630	0.962806	1.78
1097- 1106	67	60.0	10	670	162227	0.2429	-0.70	28640	0.963142	1.79
1083- 1096	68	60.1	14	952	163179	0.2443	-0.69	28654	0.963613	1.79
1064- 1082	69	60.2	19	1311	164490	0.2463	-0.69	28673	0.964252	1.80
1051- 1063	70	60.2	13	910	165400	0.2476	-0.68	28686	0.964689	1.81
1035- 1050	71	60.3	16	1136	166536	0.2493	-0.68	28702	0.965227	1.81
1022- 1034	72	60.4	13	936	167472	0.2507	-0.67	28715	0.965665	1.82
1009- 1021	73	60.4	13	949	168421	0.2522	-0.67	28728	0.966102	1.83
992- 1008	74	60.5	17	1258	169679	0.2541	-0.66	28745	0.966673	1.83
978- 991	75	60.5	14	1050	170729	0.2556	-0.66	28759	0.967144	1.84
960- 977	76	60.6	18	1368	172097	0.2577	-0.65	28777	0.967749	1.85
945- 959	77	60.6	15	1155	173252	0.2594	-0.65	28792	0.968254	1.86
933- 944	78	60.7	12	936	174188	0.2608	-0.64	28804	0.968657	1.86
925- 932	79	60.8	8	632	174820	0.2617	-0.64	28812	0.968927	1.87
917- 924	80	60.8	8	640	175460	0.2627	-0.64	28820	0.969196	1.87
907- 916	81	60.9	10	810	176270	0.2639	-0.63	28830	0.969532	1.87
896- 906	82	60.9	11	902	177172	0.2653	-0.63	28841	0.969902	1.88
880- 895	83	61.0	16	1328	178500	0.2673	-0.62	28857	0.970440	1.89
864- 879	84	61.0	16	1344	179844	0.2693	-0.62	28873	0.970978	1.90
855- 863	85	61.1	9	765	180609	0.2704	-0.61	28882	0.971281	1.90
848- 854	86	61.1	7	602	181211	0.2713	-0.61	28889	0.971516	1.90
839- 847	87	61.2	9	783	181994	0.2725	-0.61	28898	0.971819	1.91
825- 838	88	61.2	14	1232	183226	0.2743	-0.60	28912	0.972289	1.92
819- 824	89	61.3	6	534	183760	0.2751	-0.60	28918	0.972491	1.92
809- 818	90	61.3	10	900	184660	0.2765	-0.59	28928	0.972827	1.92
800- 808	91	61.4	9	819	185479	0.2777	-0.59	28937	0.973130	1.93
794- 799	92	61.4	6	552	186031	0.2785	-0.59	28943	0.973332	1.93
787- 793	93	61.5	7	651	186682	0.2795	-0.58	28950	0.973567	1.94
782- 786	94	61.5	5	470	187152	0.2802	-0.58	28955	0.973736	1.94
776- 781	95	61.6	6	570	187722	0.2811	-0.58	28961	0.973937	1.94
766- 775	96	61.6	10	960	188682	0.2825	-0.58	28971	0.974274	1.95
755- 765	97	61.6	11	1067	189749	0.2841	-0.57	28982	0.974644	1.95
749- 754	98	61.7	6	588	190337	0.2850	-0.57	28988	0.974845	1.96
744- 748	99	61.7	5	495	190832	0.2857	-0.57	28993	0.975013	1.96
740- 743	100	61.8	4	400	191232	0.2863	-0.56	28997	0.975148	1.96
734- 739	101	61.8	6	606	191838	0.2872	-0.56	29003	0.975350	1.97
725- 733	102	61.9	9	918	192756	0.2886	-0.56	29012	0.975652	1.97
711- 724	103	61.9	14	1442	194198	0.2908	-0.55	29026	0.976123	1.98
704- 710	104	61.9	7	728	194926	0.2919	-0.55	29033	0.976359	1.98
697- 703	105	62.0	7	735	195661	0.2930	-0.54	29040	0.976594	1.99
692- 696	106	62.0	5	530	196191	0.2937	-0.54	29045	0.976762	1.99
687- 691	107	62.1	5	535	196726	0.2945	-0.54	29050	0.976930	1.99
682- 686	108	62.1	5	540	197266	0.2954	-0.54	29055	0.977098	2.00
671- 681	109	62.1	11	1199	198465	0.2971	-0.53	29066	0.977468	2.00
668- 670	110	62.2	3	330	198795	0.2976	-0.53	29069	0.977569	2.01
659- 667	111	62.2	9	999	199794	0.2991	-0.53	29078	0.977872	2.01
651- 658	112	62.3	8	896	200690	0.3005	-0.52	29086	0.978141	2.02
646- 650	113	62.3	5	565	201255	0.3013	-0.52	29091	0.978309	2.02
639- 645	114	62.3	7	798	202053	0.3025	-0.52	29098	0.978544	2.02
633- 638	115	62.4	6	690	202743	0.3036	-0.51	29104	0.978746	2.03
627- 632	116	62.4	6	696	203439	0.3046	-0.51	29110	0.978948	2.03
620- 626	117	62.5	7	819	204258	0.3058	-0.51	29117	0.979183	2.04
614- 619	118	62.5	6	708	204966	0.3069	-0.50	29123	0.979385	2.04
609- 613	119	62.5	5	595	205561	0.3078	-0.50	29128	0.979553	2.04
605- 608	120	62.6	4	480	206041	0.3085	-0.50	29132	0.979687	2.05
601- 604	121	62.6	4	484	206525	0.3092	-0.50	29136	0.979822	2.05
594- 600	122	62.6	7	854	207379	0.3105	-0.49	29143	0.980058	2.05
593	123	62.7	1	123	207502	0.3107	-0.49	29144	0.980091	2.06
586- 592	124	62.7	7	868	208370	0.3120	-0.49	29151	0.980327	2.06
575- 585	125	62.7	11	1375	209745	0.3140	-0.48	29162	0.980697	2.07
568- 574	126	62.8	7	882	210627	0.3154	-0.48	29169	0.980932	2.07
562- 567	127	62.8	6	762	211389	0.3165	-0.48	29175	0.981134	2.08
555- 561	128	62.8	7	896	212285	0.3178	-0.47	29182	0.981369	2.08
549- 554	129	62.9	6	774	213059	0.3190	-0.47	29188	0.981571	2.09
544- 548	130	62.9	5	650	213709	0.3200	-0.47	29193	0.981739	2.09
542- 543	131	62.9	2	262	213971	0.3204	-0.47	29195	0.981807	2.09
537- 541	132	63.0	5	660	214631	0.3214	-0.46	29200	0.981975	2.10
532- 536	133	63.0	5	665	215296	0.3223	-0.46	29205	0.982143	2.10
529- 531	134	63.0	3	402	215698	0.3230	-0.46	29208	0.982244	2.10
523- 528	135	63.1	6	810	216508	0.3242	-0.46	29214	0.982445	2.11
520- 522	136	63.1	3	408	216916	0.3248	-0.45	29217	0.982546	2.11
516- 519	137	63.1	4	548	217464	0.3256	-0.45	29221	0.982681	2.11
510- 515	138	63.2	6	828	218292	0.3268	-0.45	29227	0.982883	2.12
507- 509	139	63.2	3	417	218709	0.3275	-0.45	29230	0.982984	2.12
501- 506	140	63.2	6	840	219549	0.3287	-0.44	29236	0.983185	2.12
497- 500	141	63.3	4	564	220113	0.3296	-0.44	29240	0.983320	2.13
492- 496	142	63.3	5	710	220823	0.3306	-0.44	29245	0.983488	2.13
488- 491	143	63.3	4	572	221395	0.3315	-0.44	29249	0.983622	2.14
483- 487	144	63.4	5	720	222115	0.3326	-0.43	29254	0.983791	2.14
479- 482	145	63.4	4	580	222695	0.3334	-0.43	29258	0.983925	2.14
476- 478	146	63.4	3	438	223133	0.3341	-0.43	29261	0.984026	2.15
470- 475	147	63.4	6	882	224015	0.3354	-0.43	29267	0.984228	2.15
469	148	63.5	1	148	224163	0.3356	-0.42	29268	0.984261	2.15
468	149	63.5	1	149	224312	0.3358	-0.42	29269	0.984295	2.15
466- 467	150	63.5	2	300	224612	0.3363	-0.42	29271	0.984362	2.15
463- 465	151	63.6	3	453	225065	0.3370	-0.42	29274	0.984463	2.16
458- 462	152	63.6	5	760	225825	0.3381	-0.42	29279	0.984631	2.16
455- 457	153	63.6	3	459	226284	0.3388	-0.42	29282	0.984732	2.16
453- 454	154	63.6	2	308	226592	0.3393	-0.41	29284	0.984800	2.16
451- 452	155	63.7	2	310	226902	0.3397	-0.41	29286	0.984867	2.17
450	156	63.7	1	156	227058	0.3400	-0.41	29287	0.984900	2.17
448- 449	157	63.7	2	314	227372	0.3404	-0.41	29289	0.984968	2.17
444- 447	158	63.8	4	632	228004	0.3414	-0.41	29293	0.985102	2.17
441- 443	159	63.8	3	477	228481	0.3421	-0.41	29296	0.985203	2.18
439- 440	160	63.8	2	320	228801	0.3426	-0.41	29298	0.985270	2.18
437- 438	161	63.8	2	322	229123	0.3431	-0.40	29300	0.985338	2.18
433- 436	162	63.9	4	648	229771	0.3440	-0.40	29304	0.985472	2.18
430- 432	164	63.9	3	492	230263	0.3448	-0.40	29307	0.985573	2.19
429	165	63.9	1	165	230428	0.3450	-0.40	29308	0.985607	2.19
427- 428	166	64.0	2	332	230760	0.3455	-0.40	29310	0.985674	2.19
426	167	64.0	1	167	230927	0.3458	-0.40	29311	0.985708	2.19
423- 425	168	64.0	3	504	231431	0.3465	-0.39	29314	0.985808	2.19
420- 422	169	64.0	3	507	231938	0.3473	-0.39	29317	0.985909	2.19
418- 419	170	64.1	2	340	232278	0.3478	-0.39	29319	0.985977	2.20
414- 417	172	64.1	4	688	232966	0.3488	-0.39	29323	0.986111	2.20
410- 413	173	64.1	4	692	233658	0.3498	-0.39	29327	0.986246	2.20
406- 409	174	64.2	4	696	234354	0.3509	-0.38	29331	0.986380	2.21
404- 405	175	64.2	2	350	234704	0.3514	-0.38	29333	0.986447	2.21
398- 403	176	64.2	6	1056	235760	0.3530	-0.38	29339	0.986649	2.22
394- 397	177	64.2	4	708	236468	0.3540	-0.37	29343	0.986784	2.22
389- 393	178	64.3	5	890	237358	0.3554	-0.37	29348	0.986952	2.22
387- 388	179	64.3	2	358	237716	0.3559	-0.37	29350	0.987019	2.23
385- 386	180	64.3	2	360	238076	0.3565	-0.37	29352	0.987086	2.23
384	181	64.3	1	181	238257	0.3567	-0.37	29353	0.987120	2.23
382- 383	183	64.4	2	366	238623	0.3573	-0.37	29355	0.987187	2.23
380- 381	184	64.4	2	368	238991	0.3578	-0.36	29357	0.987255	2.23
379	185	64.4	1	185	239176	0.3581	-0.36	29358	0.987288	2.23
378	186	64.5	1	186	239362	0.3584	-0.36	29359	0.987322	2.24
377	187	64.5	1	187	239549	0.3587	-0.36	29360	0.987355	2.24
376	188	64.5	1	188	239737	0.3589	-0.36	29361	0.987389	2.24
375	189	64.5	1	189	239926	0.3592	-0.36	29362	0.987423	2.24
373- 374	190	64.6	2	380	240306	0.3598	-0.36	29364	0.987490	2.24
371- 372	192	64.6	2	384	240690	0.3604	-0.36	29366	0.987557	2.24
370	193	64.6	1	193	240883	0.3607	-0.36	29367	0.987591	2.24
369	194	64.6	1	194	241077	0.3609	-0.36	29368	0.987624	2.25
366- 368	195	64.7	3	585	241662	0.3618	-0.35	29371	0.987725	2.25
365	196	64.7	1	196	241858	0.3621	-0.35	29372	0.987759	2.25
364	197	64.7	1	197	242055	0.3624	-0.35	29373	0.987793	2.25
363	198	64.7	1	198	242253	0.3627	-0.35	29374	0.987826	2.25
361- 362	199	64.8	2	398	242651	0.3633	-0.35	29376	0.987893	2.25
358- 360	200	64.8	3	600	243251	0.3642	-0.35	29379	0.987994	2.26
357	201	64.8	1	201	243452	0.3645	-0.35	29380	0.988028	2.26
353- 356	202	64.8	4	808	244260	0.3657	-0.34	29384	0.988162	2.26
352	203	64.8	1	203	244463	0.3660	-0.34	29385	0.988196	2.26
350- 351	204	64.9	2	408	244871	0.3666	-0.34	29387	0.988263	2.27
347- 349	205	64.9	3	615	245486	0.3676	-0.34	29390	0.988364	2.27
346	206	64.9	1	206	245692	0.3679	-0.34	29391	0.988398	2.27
343- 345	207	64.9	3	621	246313	0.3688	-0.34	29394	0.988499	2.27
340- 342	209	65.0	3	627	246940	0.3697	-0.33	29397	0.988600	2.28
339	210	65.0	1	210	247150	0.3700	-0.33	29398	0.988633	2.28
338	211	65.0	1	211	247361	0.3704	-0.33	29399	0.988667	2.28
337	212	65.0	1	212	247573	0.3707	-0.33	29400	0.988701	2.28
335- 336	214	65.1	2	428	248001	0.3713	-0.33	29402	0.988768	2.28
334	215	65.1	1	215	248216	0.3716	-0.33	29403	0.988801	2.28
333	216	65.1	1	216	248432	0.3720	-0.33	29404	0.988835	2.28
332	219	65.2	1	219	248651	0.3723	-0.33	29405	0.988869	2.29
331	220	65.2	1	220	248871	0.3726	-0.32	29406	0.988902	2.29
329- 330	221	65.2	2	442	249313	0.3733	-0.32	29408	0.988970	2.29
328	223	65.2	1	223	249536	0.3736	-0.32	29409	0.989003	2.29
326- 327	224	65.3	2	448	249984	0.3743	-0.32	29411	0.989070	2.29
325	225	65.3	1	225	250209	0.3746	-0.32	29412	0.989104	2.29
323- 324	226	65.3	2	452	250661	0.3753	-0.32	29414	0.989171	2.30
322	228	65.3	1	228	250889	0.3756	-0.32	29415	0.989205	2.30
319- 321	230	65.4	3	690	251579	0.3767	-0.31	29418	0.989306	2.30
315- 318	232	65.4	4	928	252507	0.3781	-0.31	29422	0.989440	2.31
314	233	65.4	1	233	252740	0.3784	-0.31	29423	0.989474	2.31
312- 313	234	65.5	2	468	253208	0.3791	-0.31	29425	0.989541	2.31
310- 311	235	65.5	2	470	253678	0.3798	-0.31	29427	0.989609	2.31
307- 309	237	65.5	3	711	254389	0.3809	-0.30	29430	0.989709	2.32
306	238	65.5	1	238	254627	0.3812	-0.30	29431	0.989743	2.32
305	239	65.5	1	239	254866	0.3816	-0.30	29432	0.989777	2.32
304	240	65.6	1	240	255106	0.3820	-0.30	29433	0.989810	2.32
301- 303	242	65.6	3	726	255832	0.3830	-0.30	29436	0.989911	2.32
295- 300	245	65.7	6	1470	257302	0.3852	-0.29	29442	0.990113	2.33
294	246	65.7	1	246	257548	0.3856	-0.29	29443	0.990147	2.33
293	247	65.7	1	247	257795	0.3860	-0.29	29444	0.990180	2.33
292	248	65.7	1	248	258043	0.3864	-0.29	29445	0.990214	2.33

Rank	Occ. F	SFI	F	Tokens	Cum. Tokens	Cum. P Tokens	Y	Cum. Types	Cum. P Types	Z
291	250	65.7	1	250	258293	0.3867	-0.29	29446	0.990247	2.34
289–290	251	65.8	2	502	258795	0.3875	-0.29	29448	0.990315	2.34
286–288	252	65.8	3	756	259551	0.3886	-0.28	29451	0.990416	2.34
285	254	65.8	1	254	259805	0.3890	-0.28	29452	0.990449	2.34
284	255	65.8	1	255	260060	0.3894	-0.28	29453	0.990483	2.34
283	256	65.8	1	256	260316	0.3898	-0.28	29454	0.990517	2.35
282	257	65.9	1	257	260573	0.3901	-0.28	29455	0.990550	2.35
281	259	65.9	1	259	260832	0.3905	-0.28	29456	0.990584	2.35
280	260	65.9	1	260	261092	0.3909	-0.28	29457	0.990617	2.35
279	262	65.9	1	262	261354	0.3913	-0.28	29458	0.990651	2.35
278	264	66.0	1	264	261618	0.3917	-0.27	29459	0.990685	2.35
277	266	66.0	1	266	261884	0.3921	-0.27	29460	0.990718	2.35
276	267	66.0	1	267	262151	0.3925	-0.27	29461	0.990752	2.36
274–275	270	66.1	2	540	262691	0.3933	-0.27	29463	0.990819	2.36
273	272	66.1	1	272	262963	0.3937	-0.27	29464	0.990853	2.36
271–272	277	66.2	2	554	263517	0.3945	-0.27	29466	0.990920	2.36
270	278	66.2	1	278	263795	0.3950	-0.27	29467	0.990954	2.36
269	279	66.2	1	279	264074	0.3954	-0.27	29468	0.990987	2.37
266–268	280	66.2	3	840	264914	0.3966	-0.26	29471	0.991088	2.37
263–265	281	66.2	3	843	265757	0.3979	-0.26	29474	0.991189	2.37
259–262	282	66.3	4	1128	266885	0.3996	-0.25	29478	0.991324	2.38
258	283	66.3	1	283	267168	0.4000	-0.25	29479	0.991357	2.38
257	284	66.3	1	284	267452	0.4004	-0.25	29480	0.991391	2.38
254–256	285	66.3	3	855	268307	0.4017	-0.25	29483	0.991492	2.39
253	287	66.3	1	287	268594	0.4021	-0.25	29484	0.991525	2.39
251–252	288	66.4	2	576	269170	0.4030	-0.25	29486	0.991593	2.39
249–250	289	66.4	2	578	269748	0.4039	-0.24	29488	0.991660	2.39
247–248	291	66.4	2	582	270330	0.4047	-0.24	29490	0.991727	2.40
246	292	66.4	1	292	270622	0.4052	-0.24	29491	0.991761	2.40
245	293	66.4	1	293	270915	0.4056	-0.24	29492	0.991794	2.40
244	295	66.5	1	295	271210	0.4061	-0.24	29493	0.991828	2.40
243	296	66.5	1	296	271506	0.4065	-0.24	29494	0.991862	2.40
242	297	66.5	1	297	271803	0.4070	-0.24	29495	0.991895	2.40
241	298	66.5	1	298	272101	0.4074	-0.23	29496	0.991929	2.41
240	300	66.5	1	300	272401	0.4078	-0.23	29497	0.991963	2.41
239	302	66.6	1	302	272703	0.4083	-0.23	29498	0.991996	2.41
237–238	303	66.6	2	606	273309	0.4092	-0.23	29500	0.992063	2.41
236	308	66.6	1	308	273617	0.4097	-0.23	29501	0.992097	2.41
235	313	66.7	1	313	273930	0.4101	-0.23	29502	0.992131	2.41
234	317	66.8	1	317	274247	0.4106	-0.23	29503	0.992164	2.42
232–233	318	66.8	2	636	274883	0.4116	-0.22	29505	0.992232	2.42
230–231	319	66.8	2	638	275521	0.4125	-0.22	29507	0.992299	2.42
226–229	321	66.8	4	1284	276805	0.4144	-0.22	29511	0.992433	2.43
225	322	66.8	1	322	277127	0.4149	-0.21	29512	0.992467	2.43
224	324	66.9	1	324	277451	0.4154	-0.21	29513	0.992501	2.43
223	325	66.9	1	325	277776	0.4159	-0.21	29514	0.992534	2.43
221–222	326	66.9	2	652	278428	0.4169	-0.21	29516	0.992602	2.44
220	328	66.9	1	328	278756	0.4174	-0.21	29517	0.992635	2.44
218–219	329	66.9	2	658	279414	0.4183	-0.21	29519	0.992702	2.44
216–217	330	66.9	2	660	280074	0.4193	-0.20	29521	0.992770	2.45
215	333	67.0	1	333	280407	0.4198	-0.20	29522	0.992803	2.45
214	335	67.0	1	335	280742	0.4203	-0.20	29523	0.992837	2.45
213	337	67.0	1	337	281079	0.4208	-0.20	29524	0.992871	2.45
212	340	67.1	1	340	281419	0.4214	-0.20	29525	0.992904	2.45
211	343	67.1	1	343	281762	0.4219	-0.20	29526	0.992938	2.45
210	344	67.1	1	344	282106	0.4224	-0.20	29527	0.992971	2.46
209	345	67.1	1	345	282451	0.4229	-0.19	29528	0.993005	2.46
207–208	346	67.1	2	692	283143	0.4239	-0.19	29530	0.993072	2.46
205–206	347	67.2	2	694	283837	0.4250	-0.19	29532	0.993140	2.46
204	348	67.2	1	348	284185	0.4255	-0.19	29533	0.993173	2.47
203	351	67.2	1	351	284536	0.4260	-0.19	29534	0.993207	2.47
202	352	67.2	1	352	284888	0.4265	-0.19	29535	0.993240	2.47
201	359	67.3	1	359	285247	0.4271	-0.18	29536	0.993274	2.47
199–200	361	67.3	2	722	285969	0.4282	-0.18	29538	0.993341	2.48
198	363	67.4	1	363	286332	0.4287	-0.18	29539	0.993375	2.48
197	364	67.4	1	364	286696	0.4293	-0.18	29540	0.993409	2.48
196	366	67.4	1	366	287062	0.4298	-0.18	29541	0.993442	2.48
194–195	367	67.4	2	734	287796	0.4309	-0.17	29543	0.993510	2.48
193	370	67.4	1	370	288166	0.4315	-0.17	29544	0.993543	2.49
192	371	67.5	1	371	288537	0.4320	-0.17	29545	0.993577	2.49
191	373	67.5	1	373	288910	0.4326	-0.17	29546	0.993610	2.49
189–190	374	67.5	2	748	289658	0.4337	-0.17	29548	0.993678	2.49
187–188	375	67.5	2	750	290408	0.4348	-0.16	29550	0.993745	2.50
186	377	67.5	1	377	290785	0.4354	-0.16	29551	0.993779	2.50
185	379	67.5	1	379	291164	0.4359	-0.16	29552	0.993812	2.50
184	387	67.6	1	387	291551	0.4365	-0.16	29553	0.993846	2.50
182–183	390	67.7	2	780	292331	0.4377	-0.16	29555	0.993913	2.51
181	396	67.7	1	396	292727	0.4383	-0.16	29556	0.993947	2.51
180	397	67.7	1	397	293124	0.4389	-0.15	29557	0.993980	2.51
178–179	398	67.8	2	796	293920	0.4401	-0.15	29559	0.994048	2.51
177	404	67.8	1	404	294324	0.4407	-0.15	29560	0.994081	2.52
176	405	67.8	1	405	294729	0.4413	-0.15	29561	0.994115	2.52
175	407	67.9	1	407	295136	0.4419	-0.15	29562	0.994148	2.52
174	408	67.9	1	408	295544	0.4425	-0.14	29563	0.994182	2.52
172–173	410	67.9	2	820	296364	0.4437	-0.14	29565	0.994249	2.53
171	415	67.9	1	415	296779	0.4443	-0.14	29566	0.994283	2.53
170	422	68.0	1	422	297201	0.4450	-0.14	29567	0.994317	2.53
169	423	68.0	1	423	297624	0.4456	-0.14	29568	0.994350	2.53
168	426	68.1	1	426	298050	0.4463	-0.14	29569	0.994384	2.54
167	431	68.1	1	431	298481	0.4469	-0.13	29570	0.994417	2.54
166	434	68.1	1	434	298915	0.4475	-0.13	29571	0.994451	2.54
165	459	68.4	1	459	299374	0.4482	-0.13	29572	0.994485	2.54
164	461	68.4	1	461	299835	0.4489	-0.13	29573	0.994518	2.54
163	464	68.4	1	464	300299	0.4496	-0.13	29574	0.994552	2.55
162	467	68.5	1	467	300766	0.4503	-0.12	29575	0.994586	2.55
161	471	68.5	1	471	301237	0.4510	-0.12	29576	0.994619	2.55
160	479	68.6	1	479	301716	0.4517	-0.12	29577	0.994653	2.55
159	480	68.6	1	480	302196	0.4525	-0.12	29578	0.994687	2.55
158	484	68.6	1	484	302680	0.4532	-0.12	29579	0.994720	2.56
157	486	68.6	1	486	303166	0.4539	-0.12	29580	0.994754	2.56
155–156	491	68.7	2	982	304148	0.4554	-0.11	29582	0.994821	2.56
154	492	68.7	1	492	304640	0.4561	-0.11	29583	0.994855	2.57
153	502	68.8	1	502	305142	0.4569	-0.11	29584	0.994888	2.57
152	503	68.8	1	503	305645	0.4576	-0.11	29585	0.994922	2.57
151	504	68.8	1	504	306149	0.4584	-0.10	29586	0.994956	2.57
150	505	68.8	1	505	306654	0.4591	-0.10	29587	0.994989	2.58
149	507	68.8	1	507	307161	0.4599	-0.10	29588	0.995023	2.58
148	519	68.9	1	519	307680	0.4607	-0.10	29589	0.995056	2.58
147	520	68.9	1	520	308200	0.4614	-0.10	29590	0.995090	2.58
146	521	68.9	1	521	308721	0.4622	-0.09	29591	0.995124	2.58
145	522	68.9	1	522	309243	0.4630	-0.09	29592	0.995157	2.59
144	523	68.9	1	523	309766	0.4638	-0.09	29593	0.995191	2.59
143	528	69.0	1	528	310294	0.4646	-0.09	29594	0.995225	2.59
141–142	529	69.0	2	1058	311352	0.4662	-0.08	29596	0.995292	2.60
140	539	69.1	1	539	311891	0.4670	-0.08	29597	0.995326	2.60
139	540	69.1	1	540	312431	0.4678	-0.08	29598	0.995359	2.60
137–138	542	69.1	2	1084	313515	0.4694	-0.08	29600	0.995426	2.61
136	549	69.2	1	549	314064	0.4702	-0.07	29601	0.995460	2.61
134–135	558	69.2	2	1116	315180	0.4719	-0.07	29603	0.995527	2.61
133	563	69.3	1	563	315743	0.4727	-0.07	29604	0.995561	2.62
132	569	69.3	1	569	316312	0.4736	-0.07	29605	0.995595	2.62
131	576	69.4	1	576	316888	0.4745	-0.06	29606	0.995628	2.62
130	579	69.4	1	579	317467	0.4753	-0.06	29607	0.995662	2.62
129	588	69.5	1	588	318055	0.4762	-0.06	29608	0.995695	2.63
128	596	69.5	1	596	318651	0.4771	-0.06	29609	0.995729	2.63
127	597	69.5	1	597	319248	0.4780	-0.06	29610	0.995763	2.63
126	606	69.6	1	606	319854	0.4789	-0.05	29611	0.995796	2.64
125	614	69.6	1	614	320468	0.4798	-0.05	29612	0.995830	2.64
124	615	69.6	1	615	321083	0.4807	-0.05	29613	0.995864	2.64
122–123	618	69.7	2	1236	322319	0.4826	-0.04	29615	0.995931	2.65
121	622	69.7	1	622	322941	0.4835	-0.04	29616	0.995964	2.65
120	623	69.7	1	623	323564	0.4845	-0.04	29617	0.995998	2.65
119	630	69.7	1	630	324194	0.4854	-0.04	29618	0.996032	2.65
118	640	69.8	1	640	324834	0.4864	-0.03	29619	0.996065	2.66
117	652	69.9	1	652	325486	0.4873	-0.03	29620	0.996099	2.66
116	659	69.9	1	659	326145	0.4883	-0.03	29621	0.996133	2.66
115	664	70.0	1	664	326809	0.4893	-0.03	29622	0.996166	2.67
114	684	70.1	1	684	327493	0.4903	-0.02	29623	0.996200	2.67
113	685	70.1	1	685	328178	0.4914	-0.02	29624	0.996233	2.67
112	696	70.2	1	696	328874	0.4924	-0.02	29625	0.996267	2.68
111	723	70.3	1	723	329597	0.4935	-0.02	29626	0.996301	2.68
109–110	731	70.4	2	1462	331059	0.4957	-0.01	29628	0.996368	2.68
108	735	70.4	1	735	331794	0.4968	-0.01	29629	0.996402	2.69
106–107	741	70.5	2	1482	333276	0.4990	-0.00	29631	0.996469	2.69
105	759	70.6	1	759	334035	0.5001	0.00	29632	0.996503	2.70
104	775	70.6	1	775	334810	0.5013	0.00	29633	0.996536	2.70
102–103	776	70.7	2	1552	336362	0.5036	0.01	29635	0.996603	2.71
101	777	70.7	1	777	337139	0.5048	0.01	29636	0.996637	2.71
99–100	780	70.7	2	1560	338699	0.5071	0.02	29638	0.996704	2.72
98	787	70.7	1	787	339486	0.5083	0.02	29639	0.996738	2.72
97	801	70.8	1	801	340287	0.5095	0.02	29640	0.996772	2.72
96	830	70.9	1	830	341117	0.5107	0.03	29641	0.996805	2.73
95	833	71.0	1	833	341950	0.5120	0.03	29642	0.996839	2.73
94	848	71.0	1	848	342798	0.5133	0.03	29643	0.996872	2.73
93	851	71.1	1	851	343649	0.5145	0.04	29644	0.996906	2.74
92	866	71.1	1	866	344515	0.5158	0.04	29645	0.996940	2.74
91	880	71.2	1	880	345395	0.5171	0.04	29646	0.996973	2.74
90	889	71.2	1	889	346284	0.5185	0.05	29647	0.997007	2.75
89	898	71.3	1	898	347182	0.5198	0.05	29648	0.997041	2.75
88	901	71.3	1	901	348083	0.5212	0.05	29649	0.997074	2.76
87	909	71.3	1	909	348992	0.5225	0.06	29650	0.997108	2.76
86	940	71.5	1	940	349932	0.5239	0.06	29651	0.997141	2.76
85	943	71.5	1	943	350875	0.5253	0.06	29652	0.997175	2.77
84	974	71.6	1	974	351849	0.5268	0.07	29653	0.997209	2.77
83	985	71.7	1	985	352834	0.5283	0.07	29654	0.997242	2.78
82	1016	71.8	1	1016	353850	0.5298	0.07	29655	0.997276	2.78
81	1017	71.8	1	1017	354867	0.5313	0.08	29656	0.997310	2.78
80	1038	71.9	1	1038	355905	0.5329	0.08	29657	0.997343	2.79
79	1053	72.0	1	1053	356958	0.5345	0.09	29658	0.997377	2.79
78	1076	72.1	1	1076	358034	0.5361	0.09	29659	0.997411	2.80
76–77	1082	72.1	2	2164	360198	0.5393	0.10	29661	0.997478	2.80
75	1084	72.1	1	1084	361282	0.5409	0.10	29662	0.997511	2.81
74	1096	72.2	1	1096	362378	0.5426	0.11	29663	0.997545	2.81
73	1110	72.2	1	1110	363488	0.5442	0.11	29664	0.997579	2.82
72	1144	72.3	1	1144	364632	0.5459	0.12	29665	0.997612	2.82
71	1149	72.4	1	1149	365781	0.5477	0.12	29666	0.997646	2.83
70	1185	72.5	1	1185	366966	0.5494	0.12	29667	0.997680	2.83
69	1226	72.6	1	1226	368192	0.5513	0.13	29668	0.997713	2.84
68	1233	72.7	1	1233	369425	0.5531	0.13	29669	0.997747	2.84
67	1302	72.9	1	1302	370727	0.5551	0.14	29670	0.997780	2.85
66	1383	73.2	1	1383	372110	0.5571	0.14	29671	0.997814	2.85
65	1400	73.2	1	1400	373510	0.5592	0.15	29672	0.997848	2.85
64	1402	73.2	1	1402	374912	0.5613	0.15	29673	0.997881	2.86
63	1419	73.3	1	1419	376331	0.5635	0.16	29674	0.997915	2.87
62	1473	73.4	1	1473	377804	0.5657	0.17	29675	0.997949	2.87
61	1481	73.5	1	1481	379285	0.5679	0.17	29676	0.997982	2.88
59–60	1493	73.5	2	2986	382271	0.5724	0.18	29678	0.998049	2.89
58	1497	73.5	1	1497	383768	0.5746	0.19	29679	0.998083	2.89
57	1508	73.5	1	1508	385276	0.5769	0.19	29680	0.998117	2.90
56	1521	73.6	1	1521	386797	0.5791	0.20	29681	0.998150	2.90
55	1545	73.6	1	1545	388342	0.5814	0.21	29682	0.998184	2.91
54	1557	73.7	1	1557	389899	0.5838	0.21	29683	0.998218	2.91
53	1575	73.7	1	1575	391474	0.5861	0.22	29684	0.998251	2.92
52	1610	73.8	1	1610	393084	0.5885	0.22	29685	0.998285	2.93
51	1641	73.9	1	1641	394725	0.5910	0.23	29686	0.998318	2.93
50	1660	74.0	1	1660	396385	0.5935	0.24	29687	0.998352	2.94
49	1665	74.0	1	1665	398050	0.5960	0.24	29688	0.998386	2.95
48	1691	74.0	1	1691	399741	0.5985	0.25	29689	0.998419	2.95
47	1710	74.1	1	1710	401451	0.6011	0.26	29690	0.998453	2.96
46	1717	74.1	1	1717	403168	0.6036	0.26	29691	0.998487	2.97
45	1757	74.2	1	1757	404925	0.6063	0.27	29692	0.998520	2.97
44	1848	74.4	1	1848	406773	0.6090	0.28	29693	0.998554	2.98
43	1849	74.4	1	1849	408622	0.6118	0.28	29694	0.998588	2.99
42	1855	74.4	1	1855	410477	0.6146	0.29	29695	0.998621	2.99
41	1857	74.4	1	1857	412334	0.6174	0.30	29696	0.998655	3.00
40	1876	74.5	1	1876	414210	0.6202	0.31	29697	0.998688	3.01
39	1946	74.6	1	1946	416156	0.6231	0.31	29698	0.998722	3.02
38	2043	74.9	1	2043	418199	0.6261	0.32	29699	0.998756	3.02
37	2044	74.9	1	2044	420243	0.6292	0.33	29700	0.998789	3.03
36	2057	74.9	1	2057	422300	0.6323	0.34	29701	0.998823	3.04
35	2088	75.0	1	2088	424388	0.6354	0.35	29702	0.998857	3.05
34	2197	75.2	1	2197	426585	0.6387	0.35	29703	0.998890	3.06
33	2198	75.2	1	2198	428783	0.6420	0.36	29704	0.998924	3.07
32	2313	75.4	1	2313	431096	0.6455	0.37	29705	0.998957	3.08
31	2533	75.8	1	2533	433629	0.6492	0.38	29706	0.998991	3.09
30	2544	75.8	1	2544	436173	0.6531	0.39	29707	0.999025	3.10
29	2570	75.9	1	2570	438743	0.6569	0.40	29708	0.999058	3.11
28	2648	76.0	1	2648	441391	0.6609	0.41	29709	0.999092	3.12
27	2708	76.1	1	2708	444099	0.6649	0.43	29710	0.999126	3.13
26	2854	76.3	1	2854	446953	0.6692	0.44	29711	0.999159	3.14
25	2950	76.5	1	2950	449903	0.6736	0.45	29712	0.999193	3.15
24	3020	76.6	1	3020	452923	0.6781	0.46	29713	0.999227	3.17
23	3185	76.8	1	3185	456108	0.6829	0.48	29714	0.999260	3.18
22	3198	76.8	1	3198	459306	0.6877	0.49	29715	0.999294	3.19
21	3262	76.9	1	3262	462568	0.6926	0.50	29716	0.999327	3.21
20	3648	77.4	1	3648	466216	0.6980	0.52	29717	0.999361	3.22
19	3846	77.6	1	3846	470062	0.7038	0.54	29718	0.999395	3.24
18	3886	77.6	1	3886	473948	0.7096	0.55	29719	0.999428	3.25
17	3944	77.7	1	3944	477892	0.7155	0.57	29720	0.999462	3.27
16	4471	78.3	1	4471	482363	0.7222	0.59	29721	0.999496	3.29
15	4805	78.6	1	4805	487168	0.7294	0.61	29722	0.999529	3.31
14	4852	78.6	1	4852	492020	0.7367	0.63	29723	0.999563	3.33

Rank	Occ. F	SFI	F	Tokens	Cum. Tokens	Cum. P Tokens	Y	Cum. Types	Cum. P Types	Z	Rank	Occ. F	SFI	F	Tokens	Cum. Tokens	Cum. P Tokens	Y	Cum. Types	Cum. P Types	Z
13	5184	78.9	1	5184	497204	0.7444	0.66	29724	0.999596	3.35	6	13202	83.0	1	13202	548937	0.8219	0.92	29731	0.999832	3.59
12	5504	79.2	1	5504	502708	0.7527	0.68	29725	0.999630	3.37	5	15353	83.6	1	15353	564290	0.8449	1.01	29732	0.999865	3.64
11	5809	79.4	1	5809	508517	0.7614	0.71	29726	0.999664	3.40	4	16148	83.8	1	16148	580438	0.8691	1.12	29733	0.999899	3.72
10	6315	79.8	1	6315	514832	0.7708	0.74	29727	0.999697	3.43	3	17715	84.2	1	17715	598153	0.8956	1.26	29734	0.999933	3.82
9	6385	79.8	1	6385	521217	0.7804	0.77	29728	0.999731	3.46	2	19534	84.7	1	19534	617687	0.9248	1.44	29735	0.999966	3.99
8	6440	79.8	1	6440	527657	0.7900	0.81	29729	0.999765	3.50	1	50209	88.8	1	50209	667896	1.0000	+INF.	29736	1.000000	+INF.
7	8078	80.8	1	8078	535735	0.8021	0.85	29730	0.999798	3.54											

Rank	Occ. F	SFI	F	Tokens	Cum. Tokens	Cum. P Tokens	Y	Cum. Types	Cum. P Types	Z
24169-42180	1	42.0	18012	18012	18012	0.0188	-2.08	18012	0.427027	-0.18
17940-24168	2	44.2	6229	12458	30470	0.0318	-1.85	24241	0.574704	0.19
14608-17939	3	45.6	3332	9996	40466	0.0423	-1.72	27573	0.653698	0.40
12457-14607	4	46.7	2151	8604	49070	0.0513	-1.63	29724	0.704694	0.54
10873-12456	5	47.6	1584	7920	56990	0.0595	-1.56	31308	0.742247	0.65
9694-10872	6	48.3	1179	7074	64064	0.0669	-1.50	32487	0.770199	0.74
8742-9693	7	48.9	952	6664	70728	0.0739	-1.45	33439	0.792769	0.82
7992-8741	8	49.5	750	6000	76728	0.0801	-1.40	34189	0.810550	0.88
7369-7991	9	50.0	623	5607	82335	0.0860	-1.37	34812	0.825320	0.94
6868-7368	10	50.4	501	5010	87345	0.0912	-1.33	35313	0.837198	0.98
6415-6867	11	50.8	453	4983	92328	0.0964	-1.30	35766	0.847937	1.03
6040-6414	12	51.2	375	4500	96828	0.1011	-1.28	36141	0.856828	1.07
5708-6039	13	51.5	332	4316	101144	0.1057	-1.25	36473	0.864699	1.10
5446-5707	14	51.8	262	3668	104812	0.1095	-1.23	36735	0.870910	1.13
5172-5445	15	52.1	274	4110	108922	0.1138	-1.21	37009	0.877406	1.16
4947-5171	16	52.4	225	3600	112522	0.1175	-1.19	37234	0.882741	1.19
4742-4946	17	52.6	205	3485	116007	0.1212	-1.17	37439	0.887601	1.21
4543-4741	18	52.9	199	3582	119589	0.1249	-1.15	37638	0.892319	1.24
4342-4542	19	53.1	201	3819	123408	0.1289	-1.13	37839	0.897084	1.27
4191-4341	20	53.3	151	3020	126428	0.1321	-1.12	37990	0.900664	1.29
4026-4190	21	53.5	165	3465	129893	0.1357	-1.10	38155	0.904576	1.31
3878-4025	22	53.7	148	3256	133149	0.1391	-1.08	38303	0.908084	1.33
3740-3877	23	53.9	138	3174	136323	0.1424	-1.07	38441	0.911356	1.35
3619-3739	24	54.1	121	2904	139227	0.1454	-1.06	38562	0.914225	1.37
3500-3618	25	54.3	119	2975	142202	0.1485	-1.04	38681	0.917046	1.39
3407-3499	26	54.4	93	2418	144620	0.1511	-1.03	38774	0.919251	1.40
3305-3406	27	54.6	102	2754	147374	0.1539	-1.02	38876	0.921669	1.42
3203-3304	28	54.7	102	2856	150230	0.1569	-1.01	38978	0.924087	1.43
3124-3202	29	54.9	79	2291	152521	0.1593	-1.00	39057	0.925960	1.45
3056-3123	30	55.0	68	2040	154561	0.1615	-0.99	39125	0.927572	1.46
2969-3055	31	55.2	87	2697	157258	0.1643	-0.98	39212	0.929635	1.47
2894-2968	32	55.3	75	2400	159658	0.1668	-0.97	39287	0.931413	1.49
2813-2893	33	55.4	81	2673	162331	0.1696	-0.96	39368	0.933333	1.50
2744-2812	34	55.6	69	2346	164677	0.1720	-0.95	39437	0.934969	1.51
2685-2743	35	55.7	59	2065	166742	0.1742	-0.94	39496	0.936368	1.52
2605-2684	36	55.8	80	2880	169622	0.1772	-0.93	39576	0.938265	1.54
2547-2604	37	55.9	58	2146	171768	0.1794	-0.92	39634	0.939640	1.55
2494-2546	38	56.0	53	2014	173782	0.1815	-0.91	39687	0.940896	1.56
2439-2493	39	56.2	55	2145	175927	0.1838	-0.90	39742	0.942200	1.57
2391-2438	40	56.3	48	1920	177847	0.1858	-0.89	39790	0.943338	1.58
2345-2390	41	56.4	46	1886	179733	0.1877	-0.89	39836	0.944429	1.59
2291-2344	42	56.5	54	2268	182001	0.1901	-0.88	39890	0.945709	1.60
2242-2290	43	56.6	49	2107	184108	0.1923	-0.87	39939	0.946871	1.62
2203-2241	44	56.7	39	1716	185824	0.1941	-0.86	39978	0.947795	1.62
2162-2202	45	56.8	41	1845	187669	0.1960	-0.86	40019	0.948767	1.63
2119-2161	46	56.9	43	1978	189647	0.1981	-0.85	40062	0.949787	1.64
2071-2118	47	57.0	48	2256	191903	0.2005	-0.84	40110	0.950925	1.65
2039-2070	48	57.0	32	1536	193439	0.2021	-0.83	40142	0.951683	1.66
1999-2038	49	57.1	40	1960	195399	0.2041	-0.83	40182	0.952632	1.67
1971-1998	50	57.2	28	1400	196799	0.2056	-0.82	40210	0.953295	1.68
1929-1970	51	57.3	42	2142	198941	0.2078	-0.81	40252	0.954291	1.69
1900-1928	52	57.4	29	1508	200449	0.2094	-0.81	40281	0.954979	1.70
1875-1899	53	57.5	25	1325	201774	0.2108	-0.80	40306	0.955571	1.70
1846-1874	54	57.6	29	1566	203340	0.2124	-0.80	40335	0.956259	1.71
1814-1845	55	57.6	32	1760	205100	0.2142	-0.79	40367	0.957018	1.72
1786-1813	56	57.7	28	1568	206668	0.2159	-0.79	40395	0.957681	1.72
1755-1785	57	57.8	31	1767	208435	0.2177	-0.78	40426	0.958416	1.73
1726-1754	58	57.9	29	1682	210117	0.2195	-0.77	40455	0.959104	1.74
1702-1725	59	57.9	24	1416	211533	0.2210	-0.77	40479	0.959673	1.75
1681-1701	60	58.0	21	1260	212793	0.2223	-0.76	40500	0.960171	1.75
1652-1680	61	58.1	29	1769	214562	0.2241	-0.76	40529	0.960858	1.76
1621-1651	62	58.1	31	1922	216484	0.2261	-0.75	40560	0.961593	1.77
1593-1620	63	58.2	28	1764	218248	0.2280	-0.75	40588	0.962257	1.78
1567-1592	64	58.3	26	1664	219912	0.2297	-0.74	40614	0.962873	1.79
1541-1566	65	58.4	26	1690	221602	0.2315	-0.73	40640	0.963490	1.79
1525-1540	66	58.4	16	1056	222658	0.2326	-0.73	40656	0.963869	1.80
1508-1524	67	58.5	17	1139	223797	0.2338	-0.73	40673	0.964272	1.80
1484-1507	68	58.5	24	1632	225429	0.2355	-0.72	40697	0.964841	1.81
1468-1483	69	58.6	16	1104	226533	0.2366	-0.72	40713	0.965220	1.81
1451-1467	70	58.7	17	1190	227723	0.2379	-0.71	40730	0.965623	1.82
1432-1450	71	58.7	19	1349	229072	0.2393	-0.71	40749	0.966074	1.83
1409-1431	72	58.8	23	1656	230728	0.2410	-0.70	40772	0.966619	1.83
1390-1408	73	58.9	19	1387	232115	0.2425	-0.70	40791	0.967070	1.84
1374-1389	74	58.9	16	1184	233299	0.2437	-0.69	40807	0.967449	1.84
1364-1373	75	59.0	10	750	234049	0.2445	-0.69	40817	0.967686	1.85
1346-1363	76	59.0	18	1368	235417	0.2459	-0.69	40835	0.968113	1.85
1336-1345	77	59.1	10	770	236187	0.2467	-0.68	40845	0.968350	1.86
1318-1335	78	59.1	18	1404	237591	0.2482	-0.68	40863	0.968777	1.86
1291-1317	79	59.2	27	2133	239724	0.2504	-0.67	40890	0.969417	1.87
1271-1290	80	59.2	20	1600	241324	0.2521	-0.67	40910	0.969891	1.88
1256-1270	81	59.3	15	1215	242539	0.2533	-0.66	40925	0.970247	1.88
1243-1255	82	59.4	13	1066	243605	0.2545	-0.66	40938	0.970555	1.89
1230-1242	83	59.4	13	1079	244684	0.2556	-0.66	40951	0.970863	1.89
1216-1229	84	59.5	14	1176	245860	0.2568	-0.65	40965	0.971195	1.90
1204-1215	85	59.5	12	1020	246880	0.2579	-0.65	40977	0.971479	1.90
1196-1203	86	59.6	8	688	247568	0.2586	-0.65	40985	0.971669	1.91
1182-1195	87	59.6	14	1218	248786	0.2599	-0.64	40999	0.972001	1.91
1168-1181	88	59.7	14	1232	250018	0.2612	-0.64	41013	0.972333	1.92
1149-1167	89	59.7	19	1691	251709	0.2629	-0.63	41032	0.972783	1.92
1134-1148	90	59.8	15	1350	253059	0.2643	-0.63	41047	0.973139	1.93
1119-1133	91	59.8	15	1365	254424	0.2658	-0.63	41062	0.973495	1.93
1110-1118	92	59.9	9	828	255252	0.2666	-0.62	41071	0.973708	1.94
1103-1109	93	59.9	7	651	255903	0.2673	-0.62	41078	0.973874	1.94
1093-1102	94	59.9	10	940	256843	0.2683	-0.62	41088	0.974111	1.94
1082-1092	95	60.0	11	1045	257888	0.2694	-0.61	41099	0.974372	1.95
1063-1081	96	60.0	19	1824	259712	0.2713	-0.61	41118	0.974822	1.96
1054-1062	97	60.1	9	873	260585	0.2722	-0.61	41127	0.975036	1.96
1047-1053	98	60.1	7	686	261271	0.2729	-0.60	41134	0.975201	1.96
1037-1046	99	60.2	10	990	262261	0.2740	-0.60	41144	0.975439	1.97
1027-1036	100	60.2	10	1000	263261	0.2750	-0.60	41154	0.975676	1.97
1013-1026	101	60.3	14	1414	264675	0.2765	-0.59	41168	0.976008	1.98
1002-1012	102	60.3	11	1122	265797	0.2776	-0.59	41179	0.976268	1.98
993-1001	103	60.3	9	927	266724	0.2786	-0.59	41188	0.976482	1.99
976-992	104	60.4	17	1768	268492	0.2805	-0.58	41205	0.976885	1.99
969-975	105	60.4	7	735	269227	0.2812	-0.58	41212	0.977051	2.00
962-968	106	60.5	7	742	269969	0.2820	-0.58	41219	0.977217	2.00
956-961	107	60.5	6	642	270611	0.2827	-0.57	41225	0.977359	2.00
947-955	108	60.5	9	972	271583	0.2837	-0.57	41234	0.977572	2.01
937-946	109	60.6	10	1090	272673	0.2848	-0.57	41244	0.977809	2.01
931-936	110	60.6	6	660	273333	0.2855	-0.57	41250	0.977952	2.01
924-930	111	60.7	7	777	274110	0.2863	-0.56	41257	0.978118	2.02
917-923	112	60.7	7	784	274894	0.2871	-0.56	41264	0.978284	2.02
903-916	113	60.7	14	1582	276476	0.2888	-0.56	41278	0.978615	2.03
893-902	114	60.8	10	1140	277616	0.2900	-0.55	41288	0.978853	2.03
889-892	115	60.8	4	460	278076	0.2905	-0.55	41292	0.978947	2.03
885-888	116	60.9	4	464	278540	0.2910	-0.55	41296	0.979042	2.03

Rank	Occ. F	SFI	F	Tokens	Cum. Tokens	Cum. P Tokens	Y	Cum. Types	Cum. P Types	Z
877-884	117	60.9	8	936	279476	0.2919	-0.55	41304	0.979232	2.04
868-876	118	60.9	9	1062	280538	0.2930	-0.54	41313	0.979445	2.04
860-867	119	61.0	8	952	281490	0.2940	-0.54	41321	0.979635	2.05
852-859	120	61.0	8	960	282450	0.2950	-0.54	41329	0.979825	2.05
844-851	121	61.0	8	968	283418	0.2961	-0.54	41337	0.980014	2.05
840-843	122	61.1	4	488	283906	0.2966	-0.53	41341	0.980109	2.06
828-839	123	61.1	12	1476	285382	0.2981	-0.53	41353	0.980394	2.06
820-827	124	61.1	8	992	286374	0.2991	-0.53	41361	0.980583	2.07
815-819	125	61.2	5	625	286999	0.2998	-0.52	41366	0.980702	2.07
805-814	126	61.2	10	1260	288259	0.3011	-0.52	41376	0.980939	2.07
798-804	127	61.2	7	889	289148	0.3020	-0.52	41383	0.981105	2.08
791-797	128	61.3	7	896	290044	0.3030	-0.52	41390	0.981271	2.08
782-790	129	61.3	9	1161	291205	0.3042	-0.51	41399	0.981484	2.09
778-781	130	61.3	4	520	291725	0.3047	-0.51	41403	0.981579	2.09
770-777	131	61.4	8	1048	292773	0.3058	-0.51	41411	0.981769	2.09
763-769	132	61.4	7	924	293697	0.3068	-0.50	41418	0.981935	2.10
757-762	133	61.4	6	798	294495	0.3076	-0.50	41424	0.982077	2.10
753-756	134	61.5	4	536	295031	0.3082	-0.50	41428	0.982172	2.10
747-752	135	61.5	6	810	295841	0.3090	-0.50	41434	0.982314	2.10
739-746	136	61.5	8	1088	296929	0.3102	-0.50	41442	0.982504	2.11
731-738	137	61.6	8	1096	298025	0.3113	-0.49	41450	0.982693	2.11
725-730	138	61.6	6	828	298853	0.3122	-0.49	41456	0.982835	2.12
721-724	139	61.6	4	556	299409	0.3128	-0.49	41460	0.982930	2.12
713-720	140	61.7	8	1120	300529	0.3139	-0.48	41468	0.983120	2.12
710-712	141	61.7	3	423	300952	0.3144	-0.48	41471	0.983191	2.12
705-709	142	61.7	5	710	301662	0.3151	-0.48	41476	0.983310	2.13
699-704	143	61.8	6	858	302520	0.3160	-0.48	41482	0.983452	2.13
692-698	144	61.8	7	1008	303528	0.3171	-0.48	41489	0.983618	2.13
687-691	145	61.8	5	725	304253	0.3178	-0.47	41494	0.983736	2.14
680-686	146	61.8	7	1022	305275	0.3189	-0.47	41501	0.983902	2.14
674-679	147	61.9	6	882	306157	0.3198	-0.47	41507	0.984045	2.15
667-673	148	61.9	7	1036	307193	0.3209	-0.47	41514	0.984210	2.15
658-666	149	61.9	9	1341	308534	0.3223	-0.46	41523	0.984424	2.16
653-657	150	62.0	5	750	309284	0.3231	-0.46	41528	0.984542	2.16
646-652	151	62.0	7	1057	310341	0.3242	-0.46	41535	0.984708	2.16
639-645	152	62.0	7	1064	311405	0.3253	-0.45	41542	0.984874	2.17
635-638	153	62.1	4	612	312017	0.3259	-0.45	41546	0.984969	2.17
627-634	154	62.1	8	1232	313249	0.3272	-0.45	41554	0.985159	2.17
626	155	62.1	1	155	313404	0.3274	-0.45	41555	0.985183	2.17
623-625	156	62.1	3	468	313872	0.3279	-0.45	41558	0.985254	2.18
613-622	157	62.2	10	1570	315442	0.3295	-0.44	41568	0.985491	2.18
612	158	62.2	1	158	315600	0.3297	-0.44	41569	0.985514	2.18
609-611	159	62.2	3	477	316077	0.3302	-0.44	41572	0.985586	2.19
602-608	160	62.2	7	1120	317197	0.3313	-0.44	41579	0.985752	2.19
598-601	161	62.3	4	644	317841	0.3320	-0.43	41583	0.985846	2.19
595-597	162	62.3	3	486	318327	0.3325	-0.43	41586	0.985917	2.19
591-594	163	62.3	4	652	318979	0.3332	-0.43	41590	0.986012	2.20
585-590	164	62.4	6	984	319963	0.3342	-0.43	41596	0.986155	2.20
579-584	165	62.4	6	990	320953	0.3353	-0.43	41602	0.986297	2.21
576-578	166	62.4	3	498	321451	0.3358	-0.42	41605	0.986368	2.21
575	167	62.4	1	167	321618	0.3360	-0.42	41606	0.986392	2.21
574	168	62.5	1	168	321786	0.3361	-0.42	41607	0.986415	2.21
572-573	169	62.5	2	338	322124	0.3365	-0.42	41609	0.986463	2.21
570-571	171	62.5	2	342	322466	0.3368	-0.42	41611	0.986510	2.21
564-569	172	62.6	6	1032	323498	0.3379	-0.42	41617	0.986652	2.22
561-563	173	62.6	3	519	324017	0.3385	-0.42	41620	0.986724	2.22
555-560	174	62.6	6	1044	325061	0.3396	-0.41	41626	0.986866	2.22
554	175	62.6	1	175	325236	0.3397	-0.41	41627	0.986889	2.22
549-553	176	62.7	5	880	326116	0.3407	-0.41	41632	0.987008	2.23
543-548	177	62.7	6	1062	327178	0.3418	-0.41	41638	0.987150	2.23
542	178	62.7	1	178	327356	0.3419	-0.41	41639	0.987174	2.23
536-541	179	62.7	6	1074	328430	0.3431	-0.40	41645	0.987316	2.24
533-535	180	62.8	3	540	328970	0.3436	-0.40	41648	0.987387	2.24
531-532	181	62.8	2	362	329332	0.3440	-0.40	41650	0.987435	2.24
529-530	182	62.8	2	364	329696	0.3444	-0.40	41652	0.987482	2.24
527-528	183	62.8	2	366	330062	0.3448	-0.40	41654	0.987530	2.24
523-526	184	62.8	4	736	330798	0.3455	-0.40	41658	0.987624	2.25
518-522	185	62.9	5	925	331723	0.3465	-0.39	41663	0.987743	2.25
514-517	186	62.9	4	744	332467	0.3473	-0.39	41667	0.987838	2.25
509-513	187	62.9	5	935	333402	0.3483	-0.39	41672	0.987956	2.26
505-508	188	62.9	4	752	334154	0.3490	-0.39	41676	0.988051	2.26
503-504	189	63.0	2	378	334532	0.3494	-0.39	41678	0.988099	2.26
499-502	190	63.0	4	760	335292	0.3502	-0.38	41682	0.988193	2.26
497-498	191	63.0	2	382	335674	0.3506	-0.38	41684	0.988241	2.26
496	192	63.0	1	192	335866	0.3508	-0.38	41685	0.988265	2.27
495	193	63.1	1	193	336059	0.3510	-0.38	41686	0.988288	2.27
493-494	194	63.1	2	388	336447	0.3514	-0.38	41688	0.988336	2.27
490-492	195	63.1	3	585	337032	0.3521	-0.38	41691	0.988407	2.27
489	197	63.1	1	197	337229	0.3523	-0.38	41692	0.988431	2.27
488	198	63.2	1	198	337427	0.3525	-0.38	41693	0.988454	2.27
487	200	63.2	1	200	337627	0.3527	-0.38	41694	0.988478	2.27
483-486	201	63.2	4	804	338431	0.3535	-0.38	41698	0.988573	2.28
480-482	202	63.3	3	606	339037	0.3541	-0.37	41701	0.988644	2.28
477-479	203	63.3	3	609	339646	0.3548	-0.37	41704	0.988715	2.28
473-476	204	63.3	4	816	340462	0.3556	-0.37	41708	0.988810	2.28
470-472	205	63.3	3	615	341077	0.3563	-0.37	41711	0.988881	2.29
466-469	206	63.3	4	824	341901	0.3571	-0.37	41715	0.988976	2.29
463-465	207	63.4	3	621	342522	0.3578	-0.36	41718	0.989047	2.29
458-462	208	63.4	5	1040	343562	0.3589	-0.36	41723	0.989165	2.30
457	209	63.4	1	209	343771	0.3591	-0.36	41724	0.989189	2.30
455-456	210	63.4	2	420	344191	0.3595	-0.36	41726	0.989237	2.30
452-454	211	63.4	3	633	344824	0.3602	-0.36	41729	0.989308	2.30
451	212	63.5	1	212	345036	0.3604	-0.36	41730	0.989331	2.30
449-450	213	63.5	2	426	345462	0.3609	-0.36	41732	0.989379	2.30
445-448	214	63.5	4	856	346318	0.3618	-0.35	41736	0.989474	2.31
443-444	215	63.5	2	430	346748	0.3622	-0.35	41738	0.989521	2.31
441-442	216	63.5	2	432	347180	0.3627	-0.35	41740	0.989568	2.31
440	217	63.6	1	217	347397	0.3629	-0.35	41741	0.989592	2.31
437-439	218	63.6	3	654	348051	0.3636	-0.35	41744	0.989663	2.31
434-436	219	63.6	3	657	348708	0.3643	-0.35	41747	0.989734	2.32
433	220	63.6	1	220	348928	0.3645	-0.35	41748	0.989758	2.32
432	221	63.6	1	221	349149	0.3647	-0.35	41749	0.989782	2.32
430-431	223	63.7	2	446	349595	0.3652	-0.34	41751	0.989829	2.32
426-429	224	63.7	4	896	350491	0.3661	-0.34	41755	0.989924	2.32
422-425	226	63.7	4	904	351395	0.3671	-0.34	41759	0.990019	2.33
421	227	63.8	1	227	351622	0.3673	-0.34	41760	0.990043	2.33
420	228	63.8	1	228	351850	0.3675	-0.34	41761	0.990066	2.33
416-419	229	63.8	4	916	352766	0.3685	-0.34	41765	0.990161	2.33
415	231	63.8	1	231	352997	0.3687	-0.34	41766	0.990185	2.33
411-414	232	63.9	4	928	353925	0.3697	-0.33	41770	0.990280	2.34
410	233	63.9	1	233	354158	0.3699	-0.33	41771	0.990303	2.34
408-409	234	63.9	2	468	354626	0.3704	-0.33	41773	0.990351	2.34
405-407	235	63.9	3	705	355331	0.3712	-0.33	41776	0.990422	2.34
404	236	63.9	1	236	355567	0.3714	-0.33	41777	0.990446	2.34
400-403	237	63.9	4	948	356515	0.3724	-0.33	41781	0.990541	2.35
399	238	64.0	1	238	356753	0.3727	-0.32	41782	0.990564	2.35

Rank	Occ. F	SFI	F	Tokens	Cum. Tokens	Cum. P Tokens	Y	Cum. Types	Cum. P Types	Z
398	239	64.0	1	239	356992	0.3729	-0.32	41783	0.990588	2.35
396–397	240	64.0	2	480	357472	0.3734	-0.32	41785	0.990635	2.35
393–395	243	64.1	3	729	358201	0.3742	-0.32	41788	0.990706	2.35
392	245	64.1	1	245	358446	0.3744	-0.32	41789	0.990730	2.35
389–391	246	64.1	3	738	359184	0.3752	-0.32	41792	0.990801	2.36
388	247	64.1	1	247	359431	0.3755	-0.32	41793	0.990825	2.36
386–387	249	64.2	2	498	359929	0.3760	-0.32	41795	0.990872	2.36
383–385	252	64.2	3	756	360685	0.3768	-0.31	41798	0.990944	2.36
379–382	253	64.2	4	1012	361697	0.3778	-0.31	41802	0.991038	2.37
377–378	255	64.3	2	510	362207	0.3784	-0.31	41804	0.991086	2.37
374–376	256	64.3	3	768	362975	0.3792	-0.31	41807	0.991157	2.37
373	257	64.3	1	257	363232	0.3794	-0.31	41808	0.991181	2.37
371–372	258	64.3	2	516	363748	0.3800	-0.31	41810	0.991228	2.38
370	259	64.3	1	259	364007	0.3802	-0.30	41811	0.991252	2.38
369	260	64.3	1	260	364267	0.3805	-0.30	41812	0.991275	2.38
367–368	261	64.4	2	522	364789	0.3810	-0.30	41814	0.991323	2.38
364–366	262	64.4	3	786	365575	0.3819	-0.30	41817	0.991394	2.38
363	263	64.4	1	263	365838	0.3821	-0.30	41818	0.991418	2.38
362	264	64.4	1	264	366102	0.3824	-0.30	41819	0.991441	2.38
361	267	64.5	1	267	366369	0.3827	-0.30	41820	0.991465	2.39
358–360	268	64.5	3	804	367173	0.3835	-0.30	41823	0.991536	2.39
356–357	269	64.5	2	538	367711	0.3841	-0.29	41825	0.991584	2.39
354–355	270	64.5	2	540	368251	0.3847	-0.29	41827	0.991631	2.39
353	271	64.5	1	271	368522	0.3849	-0.29	41828	0.991655	2.39
352	272	64.5	1	272	368794	0.3852	-0.29	41829	0.991678	2.39
349–351	273	64.6	3	819	369613	0.3861	-0.29	41832	0.991750	2.40
348	274	64.6	1	274	369887	0.3864	-0.29	41833	0.991773	2.40
347	277	64.6	1	277	370164	0.3867	-0.29	41834	0.991797	2.40
346	278	64.6	1	278	370442	0.3870	-0.29	41835	0.991821	2.40
345	281	64.7	1	281	370723	0.3872	-0.29	41836	0.991844	2.40
344	283	64.7	1	283	371006	0.3875	-0.29	41837	0.991868	2.40
343	285	64.7	1	285	371291	0.3878	-0.28	41838	0.991892	2.40
342	286	64.8	1	286	371577	0.3881	-0.28	41839	0.991916	2.41
338–341	289	64.8	4	1156	372733	0.3893	-0.28	41843	0.992010	2.41
334–337	290	64.8	4	1160	373893	0.3906	-0.28	41847	0.992105	2.41
333	291	64.8	1	291	374184	0.3909	-0.28	41848	0.992129	2.41
332	292	64.9	1	292	374476	0.3912	-0.28	41849	0.992153	2.42
330–331	293	64.9	2	586	375062	0.3918	-0.27	41851	0.992200	2.42
329	295	64.9	1	295	375357	0.3921	-0.27	41852	0.992224	2.42
328	296	64.9	1	296	375653	0.3924	-0.27	41853	0.992247	2.42
327	297	64.9	1	297	375950	0.3927	-0.27	41854	0.992271	2.42
326	298	64.9	1	298	376248	0.3930	-0.27	41855	0.992295	2.42
325	299	65.0	1	299	376547	0.3933	-0.27	41856	0.992319	2.42
324	301	65.0	1	301	376848	0.3936	-0.27	41857	0.992342	2.42
323	302	65.0	1	302	377150	0.3940	-0.27	41858	0.992366	2.43
322	303	65.0	1	303	377453	0.3943	-0.27	41859	0.992390	2.43
319–321	306	65.1	3	918	378371	0.3952	-0.27	41862	0.992461	2.43
318	307	65.1	1	307	378678	0.3956	-0.26	41863	0.992485	2.43
317	309	65.1	1	309	378987	0.3959	-0.26	41864	0.992508	2.43
316	311	65.1	1	311	379298	0.3962	-0.26	41865	0.992532	2.43
314–315	312	65.1	2	624	379922	0.3969	-0.26	41867	0.992579	2.44
313	313	65.2	1	313	380235	0.3972	-0.26	41868	0.992603	2.44
312	315	65.2	1	315	380550	0.3975	-0.26	41869	0.992627	2.44
311	316	65.2	1	316	380866	0.3978	-0.26	41870	0.992651	2.44
310	317	65.2	1	317	381183	0.3982	-0.26	41871	0.992674	2.44
309	319	65.2	1	319	381502	0.3985	-0.26	41872	0.992698	2.44
307–308	321	65.3	2	642	382144	0.3992	-0.26	41874	0.992745	2.44
306	322	65.3	1	322	382466	0.3995	-0.25	41875	0.992769	2.45
303–305	324	65.3	3	972	383438	0.4005	-0.25	41878	0.992840	2.45
301–302	326	65.3	2	652	384090	0.4012	-0.25	41880	0.992888	2.45
300	327	65.3	1	327	384417	0.4016	-0.25	41881	0.992911	2.45
297–299	329	65.4	3	987	385404	0.4026	-0.25	41884	0.992982	2.46
296	330	65.4	1	330	385734	0.4029	-0.25	41885	0.993006	2.46
295	332	65.4	1	332	386066	0.4033	-0.24	41886	0.993030	2.46
294	334	65.4	1	334	386400	0.4036	-0.24	41887	0.993054	2.46
293	335	65.4	1	335	386735	0.4040	-0.24	41888	0.993077	2.46
291–292	336	65.5	2	672	387407	0.4047	-0.24	41890	0.993125	2.46
290	337	65.5	1	337	387744	0.4050	-0.24	41891	0.993148	2.46
289	339	65.5	1	339	388083	0.4054	-0.24	41892	0.993172	2.47
288	342	65.5	1	342	388425	0.4057	-0.24	41893	0.993196	2.47
286–287	343	65.5	2	686	389111	0.4065	-0.24	41895	0.993243	2.47
285	345	65.6	1	345	389456	0.4068	-0.24	41896	0.993267	2.47
283–284	346	65.6	2	692	390148	0.4075	-0.23	41898	0.993314	2.47
282	348	65.6	1	348	390496	0.4079	-0.23	41899	0.993338	2.47
281	350	65.6	1	350	390846	0.4083	-0.23	41900	0.993362	2.48
279–280	355	65.7	2	710	391556	0.4090	-0.23	41902	0.993409	2.48
278	258	65.7	1	358	391914	0.4094	-0.23	41903	0.993433	2.48
277	359	65.7	1	359	392273	0.4098	-0.23	41904	0.993457	2.48
276	360	65.8	1	360	392633	0.4101	-0.23	41905	0.993480	2.48
275	361	65.8	1	361	392994	0.4105	-0.23	41906	0.993504	2.48
273–274	362	65.8	2	724	393718	0.4113	-0.22	41908	0.993551	2.49
272	363	65.8	1	363	394081	0.4116	-0.22	41909	0.993575	2.49
268–271	365	65.8	4	1460	395541	0.4132	-0.22	41913	0.993670	2.49
267	366	65.8	1	366	395907	0.4136	-0.22	41914	0.993694	2.49
266	368	65.9	1	368	396275	0.4139	-0.22	41915	0.993717	2.50
265	371	65.9	1	371	396646	0.4143	-0.22	41916	0.993741	2.50
264	375	65.9	1	375	397021	0.4147	-0.22	41917	0.993765	2.50
263	377	66.0	1	377	397398	0.4151	-0.21	41918	0.993788	2.50
262	378	66.0	1	378	397776	0.4155	-0.21	41919	0.993812	2.50
261	380	66.0	1	380	398156	0.4159	-0.21	41920	0.993836	2.50
259–260	383	66.0	2	766	398922	0.4167	-0.21	41922	0.993883	2.51
258	384	66.0	1	384	399306	0.4171	-0.21	41923	0.993907	2.51
255–257	385	66.0	3	1155	400461	0.4183	-0.21	41926	0.993978	2.51
253–254	386	66.1	2	772	401233	0.4191	-0.20	41928	0.994026	2.51
252	389	66.1	1	389	401622	0.4195	-0.20	41929	0.994049	2.52
250–251	392	66.1	2	784	402406	0.4203	-0.20	41931	0.994097	2.52
249	395	66.2	1	395	402801	0.4208	-0.20	41932	0.994120	2.52
248	397	66.2	1	397	403198	0.4212	-0.20	41933	0.994144	2.52
247	398	66.2	1	398	403596	0.4216	-0.20	41934	0.994168	2.52
246	400	66.2	1	400	403996	0.4220	-0.20	41935	0.994192	2.52
245	401	66.2	1	401	404397	0.4224	-0.20	41936	0.994215	2.53
244	404	66.3	1	404	404801	0.4228	-0.19	41937	0.994239	2.53
243	405	66.3	1	405	405206	0.4233	-0.19	41938	0.994263	2.53
242	406	66.3	1	406	405612	0.4237	-0.19	41939	0.994286	2.53
241	407	66.3	1	407	406019	0.4241	-0.19	41940	0.994310	2.53
240	412	66.3	1	412	406431	0.4245	-0.19	41941	0.994334	2.53
239	413	66.4	1	413	406844	0.4250	-0.19	41942	0.994357	2.53
238	418	66.4	1	418	407262	0.4254	-0.19	41943	0.994381	2.54
237	419	66.4	1	419	407681	0.4259	-0.19	41944	0.994405	2.54
236	420	66.4	1	420	408101	0.4263	-0.19	41945	0.994429	2.54
232–235	422	66.4	4	1688	409789	0.4281	-0.18	41949	0.994523	2.54
230–231	424	66.5	2	848	410637	0.4289	-0.18	41951	0.994571	2.55
229	425	66.5	1	425	411062	0.4294	-0.18	41952	0.994595	2.55
227–228	426	66.5	2	852	411914	0.4303	-0.18	41954	0.994642	2.55
226	427	66.5	1	427	412341	0.4307	-0.17	41955	0.994666	2.55
225	429	66.5	1	429	412770	0.4312	-0.17	41956	0.994689	2.55
224	433	66.6	1	433	413203	0.4316	-0.17	41957	0.994713	2.56
223	434	66.6	1	434	413637	0.4321	-0.17	41958	0.994737	2.56
221–222	441	66.6	2	882	414519	0.4330	-0.17	41960	0.994784	2.56
218–220	443	66.7	3	1329	415848	0.4344	-0.17	41963	0.994855	2.57
217	450	66.7	1	450	416298	0.4349	-0.16	41964	0.994879	2.57
216	452	66.7	1	452	416750	0.4353	-0.16	41965	0.994903	2.57
215	453	66.8	1	453	417203	0.4358	-0.16	41966	0.994926	2.57
214	457	66.8	1	457	417660	0.4363	-0.16	41967	0.994950	2.57
212–213	458	66.8	2	916	418576	0.4372	-0.16	41969	0.994998	2.58
211	459	66.8	1	459	419035	0.4377	-0.16	41970	0.995021	2.58
210	466	66.9	1	466	419501	0.4382	-0.16	41971	0.995045	2.58
209	467	66.9	1	467	419968	0.4387	-0.15	41972	0.995069	2.58
208	471	66.9	1	471	420439	0.4392	-0.15	41973	0.995092	2.58
207	472	66.9	1	472	420911	0.4397	-0.15	41974	0.995116	2.58
205–206	481	67.0	2	962	421873	0.4407	-0.15	41976	0.995164	2.59
204	482	67.0	1	482	422355	0.4412	-0.15	41977	0.995187	2.59
203	484	67.0	1	484	422839	0.4417	-0.15	41978	0.995211	2.59
202	485	67.1	1	485	423324	0.4422	-0.15	41979	0.995235	2.59
201	489	67.1	1	489	423813	0.4427	-0.14	41980	0.995258	2.59
200	498	67.2	1	498	424311	0.4432	-0.14	41981	0.995282	2.60
199	499	67.2	1	499	424810	0.4437	-0.14	41982	0.995306	2.60
198	500	67.2	1	500	425310	0.4443	-0.14	41983	0.995329	2.60
197	502	67.2	1	502	425812	0.4448	-0.14	41984	0.995353	2.60
196	505	67.2	1	505	426317	0.4453	-0.14	41985	0.995377	2.60
195	507	67.2	1	507	426824	0.4458	-0.14	41986	0.995401	2.60
194	510	67.3	1	510	427334	0.4464	-0.13	41987	0.995424	2.61
193	511	67.3	1	511	427845	0.4469	-0.13	41988	0.995448	2.61
192	512	67.3	1	512	428357	0.4475	-0.13	41989	0.995472	2.61
191	513	67.3	1	513	428870	0.4480	-0.13	41990	0.995495	2.61
190	516	67.3	1	516	429386	0.4485	-0.13	41991	0.995519	2.61
189	517	67.3	1	517	429903	0.4491	-0.13	41992	0.995543	2.62
187–188	520	67.4	2	1040	430943	0.4502	-0.13	41994	0.995590	2.62
186	521	67.4	1	521	431464	0.4507	-0.12	41995	0.995614	2.62
185	523	67.4	1	523	431987	0.4512	-0.12	41996	0.995638	2.62
184	526	67.4	1	526	432513	0.4518	-0.12	41997	0.995661	2.62
183	528	67.4	1	528	433041	0.4523	-0.12	41998	0.995685	2.63
182	530	67.4	1	530	433571	0.4529	-0.12	41999	0.995709	2.63
181	533	67.5	1	533	434104	0.4535	-0.12	42000	0.995733	2.63
179–180	534	67.5	2	1068	435172	0.4546	-0.11	42002	0.995780	2.63
178	537	67.5	1	537	435709	0.4551	-0.11	42003	0.995804	2.64
177	541	67.5	1	541	436250	0.4557	-0.11	42004	0.995827	2.64
176	543	67.5	1	543	436793	0.4563	-0.11	42005	0.995851	2.64
175	553	67.6	1	553	437346	0.4568	-0.11	42006	0.995875	2.64
174	554	67.6	1	554	437900	0.4574	-0.11	42007	0.995898	2.64
173	557	67.7	1	557	438457	0.4580	-0.11	42008	0.995922	2.65
172	563	67.7	1	563	439020	0.4586	-0.10	42009	0.995946	2.65
171	570	67.8	1	570	439590	0.4592	-0.10	42010	0.995970	2.65
170	572	67.8	1	572	440162	0.4598	-0.10	42011	0.995993	2.65
169	576	67.8	1	576	440738	0.4604	-0.10	42012	0.996017	2.65
168	578	67.8	1	578	441316	0.4610	-0.10	42013	0.996041	2.66
167	584	67.9	1	584	441900	0.4616	-0.10	42014	0.996064	2.66
166	587	67.9	1	587	442487	0.4622	-0.09	42015	0.996088	2.66
164–165	590	67.9	2	1180	443667	0.4634	-0.09	42017	0.996136	2.66
163	600	68.0	1	600	444267	0.4641	-0.09	42018	0.996159	2.67
162	601	68.0	1	601	444868	0.4647	-0.09	42019	0.996183	2.67
161	602	68.0	1	602	445470	0.4653	-0.09	42020	0.996207	2.67
160	605	68.0	1	605	446075	0.4660	-0.09	42021	0.996230	2.67
159	608	68.0	1	608	446683	0.4666	-0.08	42022	0.996254	2.67
158	609	68.0	1	609	447292	0.4672	-0.08	42023	0.996278	2.68
157	629	68.2	1	629	447921	0.4679	-0.08	42024	0.996302	2.68
156	640	68.3	1	640	448561	0.4686	-0.08	42025	0.996325	2.68
155	648	68.3	1	648	449209	0.4692	-0.08	42026	0.996349	2.68
153–154	649	68.3	2	1298	450507	0.4706	-0.07	42028	0.996396	2.69
151–152	650	68.3	2	1300	451807	0.4719	-0.07	42030	0.996444	2.69
150	654	68.3	1	654	452461	0.4726	-0.07	42031	0.996467	2.69
149	657	68.4	1	657	453118	0.4733	-0.07	42032	0.996491	2.70
148	693	68.6	1	693	453811	0.4740	-0.07	42033	0.996515	2.70
147	694	68.6	1	694	454505	0.4748	-0.06	42034	0.996539	2.70
146	698	68.6	1	698	455203	0.4755	-0.06	42035	0.996562	2.70
145	703	68.7	1	703	455906	0.4762	-0.06	42036	0.996586	2.71
144	709	68.7	1	709	456615	0.4770	-0.06	42037	0.996610	2.71
142–143	711	68.7	2	1422	458037	0.4785	-0.05	42039	0.996657	2.71
140–141	713	68.7	2	1426	459463	0.4799	-0.05	42041	0.996705	2.72
139	721	68.8	1	721	460184	0.4807	-0.05	42042	0.996728	2.72
138	725	68.8	1	725	460909	0.4815	-0.05	42043	0.996752	2.72
137	739	68.9	1	739	461648	0.4822	-0.04	42044	0.996776	2.72
136	752	69.0	1	752	462400	0.4830	-0.04	42045	0.996799	2.73
135	757	69.0	1	757	463157	0.4838	-0.04	42046	0.996823	2.73
134	770	69.1	1	770	463927	0.4846	-0.04	42047	0.996847	2.73
133	783	69.1	1	783	464710	0.4854	-0.04	42048	0.996871	2.73
131–132	784	69.1	2	1568	466278	0.4871	-0.03	42050	0.996918	2.74
130	789	69.2	1	789	467067	0.4879	-0.03	42051	0.996942	2.74
129	801	69.2	1	801	467868	0.4887	-0.03	42052	0.996965	2.74
128	804	69.2	1	804	468672	0.4896	-0.03	42053	0.996989	2.75
127	806	69.3	1	806	469478	0.4904	-0.02	42054	0.997013	2.75
125–126	807	69.3	2	1614	471092	0.4921	-0.02	42056	0.997060	2.75
124	808	69.3	1	808	471900	0.4929	-0.02	42057	0.997084	2.76
123	813	69.3	1	813	472713	0.4938	-0.02	42058	0.997108	2.76
122	815	69.3	1	815	473528	0.4946	-0.01	42059	0.997131	2.76
121	817	69.3	1	817	474345	0.4955	-0.01	42060	0.997155	2.77
120	840	69.4	1	840	475185	0.4964	-0.01	42061	0.997179	2.77
119	865	69.6	1	865	476050	0.4973	-0.01	42062	0.997202	2.77
118	886	69.7	1	886	476936	0.4982	-0.00	42063	0.997226	2.77
117	892	69.7	1	892	477828	0.4991	-0.00	42064	0.997250	2.78
116	893	69.7	1	893	478721	0.5001	0.00	42065	0.997274	2.78
115	899	69.7	1	899	479620	0.5010	0.00	42066	0.997297	2.78
114	907	69.8	1	907	480527	0.5019	0.00	42067	0.997321	2.78
113	923	69.8	1	923	481450	0.5029	0.01	42068	0.997345	2.79
112	929	69.9	1	929	482379	0.5039	0.01	42069	0.997368	2.79
111	938	69.9	1	938	483317	0.5049	0.01	42070	0.997392	2.79
110	947	70.0	1	947	484264	0.5058	0.01	42071	0.997416	2.80
109	950	70.0	1	950	485214	0.5068	0.02	42072	0.997440	2.80
108	951	70.0	1	951	486165	0.5078	0.02	42073	0.997463	2.80
107	953	70.0	1	953	487118	0.5088	0.02	42074	0.997487	2.81
106	962	70.0	1	962	488080	0.5098	0.02	42075	0.997511	2.81
105	993	70.2	1	993	489073	0.5109	0.03	42076	0.997534	2.81
103–104	995	70.2	2	1990	491063	0.5130	0.03	42078	0.997582	2.82
102	1033	70.3	1	1033	492096	0.5140	0.04	42079	0.997605	2.82
101	1038	70.4	1	1038	493134	0.5151	0.04	42080	0.997629	2.82
100	1040	70.4	1	1040	494174	0.5162	0.04	42081	0.997653	2.83
98–99	1065	70.5	2	2130	496304	0.5184	0.05	42083	0.997700	2.83
97	1078	70.5	1	1078	497382	0.5196	0.05	42084	0.997724	2.84
96	1088	70.6	1	1088	498470	0.5207	0.05	42085	0.997748	2.84
95	1092	70.6	1	1092	499562	0.5218	0.05	42086	0.997771	2.84
94	1096	70.6	1	1096	500658	0.5230	0.06	42087	0.997795	2.85
93	1099	70.6	1	1099	501757	0.5241	0.06	42088	0.997819	2.85

Rank	Occ. F	SFI	F	Tokens	Cum. Tokens	Cum. P Tokens	Y	Cum. Types	Cum. P Types	Z
92	1139	70.8	1	1139	502896	0.5253	0.06	42089	0.997843	2.85
91	1145	70.8	1	1145	504041	0.5265	0.07	42090	0.997866	2.86
90	1166	70.9	1	1166	505207	0.5277	0.07	42091	0.997890	2.86
89	1177	70.9	1	1177	506384	0.5290	0.07	42092	0.997914	2.86
88	1188	70.9	1	1188	507572	0.5302	0.08	42093	0.997937	2.87
87	1216	71.0	1	1216	508788	0.5315	0.08	42094	0.997961	2.87
86	1233	71.1	1	1233	510021	0.5328	0.08	42095	0.997985	2.88
85	1243	71.1	1	1243	511264	0.5341	0.09	42096	0.998008	2.88
84	1247	71.1	1	1247	512511	0.5354	0.09	42097	0.998032	2.88
83	1269	71.2	1	1269	513780	0.5367	0.09	42098	0.998056	2.89
82	1274	71.2	1	1274	515054	0.5380	0.10	42099	0.998080	2.89
81	1276	71.2	1	1276	516330	0.5393	0.10	42100	0.998103	2.89
80	1317	71.4	1	1317	517647	0.5407	0.10	42101	0.998127	2.90
79	1344	71.5	1	1344	518991	0.5421	0.11	42102	0.998151	2.90
78	1367	71.5	1	1367	520358	0.5436	0.11	42103	0.998174	2.91
77	1371	71.6	1	1371	521729	0.5450	0.11	42104	0.998198	2.91
76	1473	71.9	1	1473	523202	0.5465	0.12	42105	0.998222	2.92
75	1526	72.0	1	1526	524728	0.5481	0.12	42106	0.998246	2.92
74	1544	72.1	1	1544	526272	0.5497	0.12	42107	0.998269	2.92
73	1566	72.1	1	1566	527838	0.5514	0.13	42108	0.998293	2.93
72	1600	72.2	1	1600	529438	0.5530	0.13	42109	0.998317	2.93
71	1671	72.4	1	1671	531109	0.5548	0.14	42110	0.998340	2.94
70	1692	72.5	1	1692	532801	0.5566	0.14	42111	0.998364	2.94
69	1724	72.6	1	1724	534525	0.5584	0.15	42112	0.998388	2.95
68	1727	72.6	1	1727	536252	0.5602	0.15	42113	0.998412	2.95
67	1731	72.6	1	1731	537983	0.5620	0.16	42114	0.998435	2.95
66	1776	72.7	1	1776	539759	0.5638	0.16	42115	0.998459	2.96
65	1848	72.9	1	1848	541607	0.5657	0.17	42116	0.998483	2.96
64	1867	72.9	1	1867	543474	0.5677	0.17	42117	0.998506	2.97
63	1911	73.0	1	1911	545385	0.5697	0.17	42118	0.998530	2.97
62	1936	73.1	1	1936	547321	0.5717	0.18	42119	0.998554	2.98
61	1972	73.1	1	1972	549293	0.5738	0.18	42120	0.998577	2.98
60	1995	73.2	1	1995	551288	0.5759	0.19	42121	0.998601	2.99
59	2007	73.2	1	2007	553295	0.5780	0.20	42122	0.998625	2.99
58	2022	73.2	1	2022	555317	0.5801	0.20	42123	0.998649	3.00
57	2054	73.3	1	2054	557371	0.5822	0.21	42124	0.998672	3.01
56	2056	73.3	1	2056	559427	0.5844	0.21	42125	0.998696	3.01
55	2060	73.3	1	2060	561487	0.5865	0.22	42126	0.998720	3.02
54	2081	73.4	1	2081	563568	0.5887	0.22	42127	0.998743	3.02
53	2084	73.4	1	2084	565652	0.5909	0.23	42128	0.998767	3.03
52	2090	73.4	1	2090	567742	0.5930	0.24	42129	0.998791	3.03
51	2113	73.4	1	2113	569855	0.5953	0.24	42130	0.998815	3.04
50	2182	73.6	1	2182	572037	0.5975	0.25	42131	0.998838	3.05
49	2184	73.6	1	2184	574221	0.5998	0.25	42132	0.998862	3.05
48	2224	73.7	1	2224	576445	0.6021	0.26	42133	0.998886	3.06
47	2226	73.7	1	2226	578671	0.6045	0.26	42134	0.998909	3.06
46	2300	73.8	1	2300	580971	0.6069	0.27	42135	0.998933	3.07
45	2325	73.9	1	2325	583296	0.6093	0.28	42136	0.998957	3.08
44	2332	73.9	1	2332	585628	0.6117	0.28	42137	0.998981	3.08
43	2434	74.1	1	2434	588062	0.6143	0.29	42138	0.999004	3.09
42	2436	74.1	1	2436	590498	0.6168	0.30	42139	0.999028	3.10
41	2537	74.2	1	2537	593035	0.6195	0.30	42140	0.999052	3.11
40	2604	74.3	1	2604	595639	0.6222	0.31	42141	0.999075	3.11
39	2727	74.5	1	2727	598366	0.6250	0.32	42142	0.999099	3.12
38	2826	74.7	1	2826	601192	0.6280	0.33	42143	0.999123	3.13
37	2904	74.8	1	2904	604096	0.6310	0.33	42144	0.999146	3.14
36	2905	74.8	1	2905	607001	0.6341	0.34	42145	0.999170	3.15
35	2919	74.8	1	2919	609920	0.6371	0.35	42146	0.999194	3.15
34	3023	75.0	1	3023	612943	0.6403	0.36	42147	0.999218	3.16
33	3069	75.1	1	3069	616012	0.6435	0.37	42148	0.999241	3.17
32	3198	75.2	1	3198	619210	0.6468	0.38	42149	0.999265	3.18
31	3424	75.5	1	3424	622634	0.6504	0.39	42150	0.999289	3.20
30	3650	75.8	1	3650	626284	0.6542	0.40	42151	0.999312	3.21
29	3840	76.0	1	3840	630124	0.6582	0.41	42152	0.999336	3.22
28	3913	76.1	1	3913	634037	0.6623	0.42	42153	0.999360	3.23
27	4061	76.3	1	4061	638098	0.6665	0.43	42154	0.999384	3.23
26	4272	76.5	1	4272	642370	0.6710	0.44	42155	0.999407	3.24
25	4285	76.5	1	4285	646655	0.6755	0.46	42156	0.999431	3.25
24	4332	76.6	1	4332	650987	0.6800	0.47	42157	0.999455	3.27
23	4355	76.6	1	4355	655342	0.6846	0.48	42158	0.999478	3.28
22	4531	76.8	1	4531	659873	0.6893	0.49	42159	0.999502	3.29
21	4567	76.8	1	4567	664440	0.6941	0.51	42160	0.999526	3.31
20	4657	76.9	1	4657	669097	0.6989	0.52	42161	0.999550	3.32
19	5007	77.2	1	5007	674104	0.7042	0.54	42162	0.999573	3.33
18	6122	78.1	1	6122	680226	0.7105	0.55	42163	0.999597	3.35
17	6141	78.1	1	6141	686367	0.7170	0.57	42164	0.999621	3.37
16	6532	78.3	1	6532	692899	0.7238	0.59	42165	0.999644	3.39
15	6614	78.4	1	6614	699513	0.7307	0.61	42166	0.999668	3.40
14	6648	78.4	1	6648	706161	0.7376	0.64	42167	0.999692	3.42
13	7526	79.0	1	7526	713687	0.7455	0.66	42168	0.999715	3.45
12	7720	79.1	1	7720	721407	0.7536	0.69	42169	0.999739	3.47
11	8355	79.4	1	8355	729762	0.7623	0.71	42170	0.999763	3.49
10	8506	79.5	1	8506	738268	0.7712	0.74	42171	0.999787	3.52
9	8715	79.6	1	8715	746983	0.7803	0.77	42172	0.999810	3.55
8	9070	79.8	1	9070	756053	0.7898	0.81	42173	0.999834	3.59
7	10782	80.5	1	10782	766835	0.8010	0.85	42174	0.999858	3.63
6	18926	83.0	1	18926	785761	0.8208	0.92	42175	0.999881	3.68
5	22488	83.7	1	22488	808249	0.8443	1.01	42176	0.999905	3.73
4	23836	84.0	1	23836	832085	0.8692	1.12	42177	0.999929	3.80
3	26967	84.5	1	26967	859052	0.8973	1.27	42178	0.999953	3.90
2	29402	84.9	1	29402	888454	0.9281	1.46	42179	0.999976	4.07
1	68874	88.6	1	68874	957328	1.0000	+INF.	42180	1.000000	+INF.

Rank	Occ. F	SFI	F	Tokens	Cum. Tokens	Cum. P Tokens	Y	Cum. Types	Cum. P Types	Z
18287-32709	1	44.0	14423	14423	14423	0.0240	-1.98	14423	0.440949	-0.15
13430-18286	2	46.2	4857	9714	24137	0.0402	-1.75	19280	0.589440	0.23
10864-13429	3	47.7	2566	7698	31835	0.0530	-1.62	21846	0.667890	0.43
9150-10863	4	48.7	1714	6856	38691	0.0644	-1.52	23560	0.720291	0.58
7995-9149	5	49.6	1155	5775	44466	0.0741	-1.45	24715	0.755602	0.69
7098-7994	6	50.3	897	5382	49848	0.0830	-1.39	25612	0.783026	0.78
6402-7097	7	51.0	696	4872	54720	0.0911	-1.33	26308	0.804305	0.86
5831-6401	8	51.5	571	4568	59288	0.0987	-1.29	26879	0.821762	0.92
5388-5830	9	52.0	443	3987	63275	0.1054	-1.25	27322	0.835305	0.98
5015-5387	10	52.4	373	3730	67005	0.1116	-1.22	27695	0.846709	1.02
4670-5014	11	52.8	345	3795	70800	0.1179	-1.19	28040	0.857256	1.07
4382-4669	12	53.2	288	3456	74256	0.1237	-1.16	28328	0.866061	1.11
4112-4381	13	53.5	270	3510	77766	0.1295	-1.13	28598	0.874316	1.15
3896-4111	14	53.8	216	3024	80790	0.1345	-1.11	28814	0.880920	1.18
3699-3895	15	54.1	197	2955	83745	0.1395	-1.08	29011	0.886942	1.21
3511-3698	16	54.4	188	3008	86753	0.1445	-1.06	29199	0.892690	1.24
3335-3510	17	54.6	176	2992	89745	0.1495	-1.04	29375	0.898071	1.27
3187-3334	18	54.9	148	2664	92409	0.1539	-1.02	29523	0.902596	1.30
3045-3186	19	55.1	142	2698	95107	0.1584	-1.00	29665	0.906937	1.32
2927-3044	20	55.3	118	2360	97467	0.1623	-0.98	29783	0.910544	1.34
2810-2926	21	55.5	117	2457	99924	0.1664	-0.97	29900	0.914121	1.37
2704-2809	22	55.7	106	2332	102256	0.1703	-0.95	30006	0.917362	1.39
2626-2703	23	55.9	78	1794	104050	0.1733	-0.94	30084	0.919747	1.40
2535-2625	24	56.1	91	2184	106234	0.1769	-0.93	30175	0.922529	1.42
2445-2534	25	56.3	90	2250	108484	0.1807	-0.91	30265	0.925280	1.44
2370-2444	26	56.4	75	1950	110434	0.1839	-0.90	30340	0.927573	1.46
2295-2369	27	56.6	75	2025	112459	0.1873	-0.89	30415	0.929866	1.47
2232-2294	28	56.8	63	1764	114223	0.1902	-0.88	30478	0.931792	1.49
2187-2231	29	56.9	45	1305	115528	0.1924	-0.87	30523	0.933168	1.50
2126-2186	30	57.1	61	1830	117358	0.1954	-0.86	30584	0.935033	1.51
2076-2125	31	57.2	50	1550	118908	0.1980	-0.85	30634	0.936562	1.53
2014-2075	32	57.3	62	1984	120892	0.2013	-0.84	30696	0.938457	1.54
1934-2013	33	57.5	80	2640	123532	0.2057	-0.82	30776	0.940903	1.56
1890-1933	34	57.6	44	1496	125028	0.2082	-0.81	30820	0.942248	1.57
1846-1889	35	57.7	44	1540	126568	0.2108	-0.80	30864	0.943594	1.59
1781-1845	36	57.8	65	2340	128908	0.2147	-0.79	30929	0.945581	1.60
1735-1780	37	58.0	46	1702	130610	0.2175	-0.78	30975	0.946987	1.62
1704-1734	38	58.1	31	1178	131788	0.2195	-0.77	31006	0.947935	1.63
1668-1703	39	58.2	36	1404	133192	0.2218	-0.77	31042	0.949035	1.64
1625-1667	40	58.3	43	1720	134912	0.2247	-0.76	31085	0.950350	1.65
1583-1624	41	58.4	42	1722	136634	0.2275	-0.75	31127	0.951634	1.66
1538-1582	42	58.5	45	1890	138524	0.2307	-0.74	31172	0.953010	1.67
1499-1537	43	58.6	39	1677	140201	0.2335	-0.73	31211	0.954202	1.69
1469-1498	44	58.7	30	1320	141521	0.2357	-0.72	31241	0.955119	1.70
1436-1468	45	58.8	33	1485	143006	0.2382	-0.71	31274	0.956128	1.71
1405-1435	46	58.9	31	1426	144432	0.2405	-0.70	31305	0.957076	1.72
1379-1404	47	59.0	26	1222	145654	0.2426	-0.70	31331	0.957871	1.73
1356-1378	48	59.1	23	1104	146758	0.2444	-0.69	31354	0.958574	1.73
1334-1355	49	59.2	22	1078	147836	0.2462	-0.69	31376	0.959247	1.74
1315-1333	50	59.2	19	950	148786	0.2478	-0.68	31395	0.959828	1.75
1292-1314	51	59.3	23	1173	149959	0.2497	-0.68	31418	0.960531	1.76
1270-1291	52	59.4	22	1144	151103	0.2516	-0.67	31440	0.961203	1.76
1234-1269	53	59.5	36	1908	153011	0.2548	-0.66	31476	0.962304	1.78
1208-1233	54	59.6	26	1404	154415	0.2572	-0.65	31502	0.963099	1.79
1191-1207	55	59.7	17	935	155350	0.2587	-0.65	31519	0.963619	1.79
1173-1190	56	59.7	18	1008	156358	0.2604	-0.64	31537	0.964169	1.80
1149-1172	57	59.8	24	1368	157726	0.2627	-0.64	31561	0.964903	1.81
1134-1148	58	59.9	15	870	158596	0.2641	-0.63	31576	0.965361	1.82
1122-1133	59	60.0	12	708	159304	0.2653	-0.63	31588	0.965728	1.82
1107-1121	60	60.0	15	900	160204	0.2668	-0.62	31603	0.966187	1.83
1090-1106	61	60.1	17	1037	161241	0.2685	-0.62	31620	0.966706	1.83
1076-1089	62	60.2	14	868	162109	0.2700	-0.61	31634	0.967134	1.84
1059-1075	63	60.2	17	1071	163180	0.2718	-0.61	31651	0.967654	1.85
1047-1058	64	60.3	12	768	163948	0.2730	-0.60	31663	0.968021	1.85
1028-1046	65	60.4	19	1235	165183	0.2751	-0.60	31682	0.968602	1.86
1018-1027	66	60.4	10	660	165843	0.2762	-0.59	31692	0.968908	1.86
997-1017	67	60.5	21	1407	167250	0.2785	-0.59	31713	0.969550	1.87
982-996	68	60.6	15	1020	168270	0.2802	-0.58	31728	0.970008	1.88
967-981	69	60.6	15	1035	169305	0.2820	-0.58	31743	0.970467	1.89
956-966	70	60.7	11	770	170075	0.2832	-0.57	31754	0.970803	1.89
941-955	71	60.8	15	1065	171140	0.2850	-0.57	31769	0.971262	1.90
924-940	72	60.8	17	1224	172364	0.2871	-0.56	31786	0.971781	1.91
910-923	73	60.9	14	1022	173386	0.2888	-0.56	31800	0.972209	1.91
895-909	74	60.9	15	1110	174496	0.2906	-0.55	31815	0.972668	1.92
885-894	75	61.0	10	750	175246	0.2919	-0.55	31825	0.972974	1.93
878-884	76	61.1	7	532	175778	0.2927	-0.55	31832	0.973188	1.93
867-877	77	61.1	11	847	176625	0.2942	-0.54	31843	0.973524	1.94
859-866	78	61.2	8	624	177249	0.2952	-0.54	31851	0.973769	1.94
846-858	79	61.2	13	1027	178276	0.2969	-0.53	31864	0.974166	1.95
839-845	80	61.3	7	560	178836	0.2978	-0.53	31871	0.974380	1.95
829-838	81	61.3	10	810	179646	0.2992	-0.53	31881	0.974686	1.95
814-828	82	61.4	15	1230	180876	0.3012	-0.52	31896	0.975144	1.96
800-813	83	61.4	14	1162	182038	0.3032	-0.52	31910	0.975572	1.97
793-799	84	61.5	7	588	182626	0.3041	-0.51	31917	0.975786	1.97
785-792	85	61.5	8	680	183306	0.3053	-0.51	31925	0.976031	1.98
781-784	86	61.6	4	344	183650	0.3059	-0.51	31929	0.976153	1.98
772-780	87	61.6	9	783	184433	0.3072	-0.50	31938	0.976428	1.99
762-771	88	61.7	10	880	185313	0.3086	-0.50	31948	0.976734	1.99
747-761	89	61.7	15	1335	186648	0.3108	-0.49	31963	0.977193	2.00
734-746	90	61.8	13	1170	187818	0.3128	-0.49	31976	0.977590	2.01
727-733	91	61.8	7	637	188455	0.3139	-0.48	31983	0.977804	2.01
719-726	92	61.9	8	736	189191	0.3151	-0.48	31991	0.978049	2.02
708-718	93	61.9	11	1023	190214	0.3168	-0.48	32002	0.978385	2.02
702-707	94	62.0	6	564	190778	0.3177	-0.47	32008	0.978569	2.03
691-701	95	62.0	11	1045	191823	0.3195	-0.47	32019	0.978905	2.03
686-690	96	62.1	5	480	192303	0.3203	-0.47	32024	0.979058	2.03
679-685	97	62.1	7	679	192982	0.3214	-0.46	32031	0.979272	2.04
672-678	98	62.1	7	686	193668	0.3225	-0.46	32038	0.979486	2.04
665-671	99	62.2	7	693	194361	0.3237	-0.46	32045	0.979700	2.05
654-664	100	62.2	11	1100	195461	0.3255	-0.45	32056	0.980036	2.05
648-653	101	62.3	6	606	196067	0.3265	-0.45	32062	0.980219	2.06
642-647	102	62.3	6	612	196679	0.3275	-0.45	32068	0.980403	2.06
631-641	103	62.4	11	1133	197812	0.3294	-0.44	32079	0.980739	2.07
624-630	104	62.4	7	728	198540	0.3306	-0.44	32086	0.980953	2.07
615-623	105	62.4	9	945	199485	0.3322	-0.43	32095	0.981228	2.08
610-614	106	62.5	5	530	200015	0.3331	-0.43	32100	0.981381	2.08
604-609	107	62.5	6	642	200657	0.3342	-0.43	32106	0.981565	2.09
600-603	108	62.6	4	432	201089	0.3349	-0.43	32110	0.981687	2.09
593-599	109	62.6	7	763	201852	0.3362	-0.42	32117	0.981901	2.09
583-592	110	62.6	10	1100	202952	0.3380	-0.42	32127	0.982207	2.10
575-582	111	62.7	8	888	203840	0.3395	-0.41	32135	0.982451	2.11
567-574	112	62.7	8	896	204736	0.3410	-0.41	32143	0.982696	2.11
558-566	113	62.8	9	1017	205753	0.3427	-0.41	32152	0.982971	2.12
551-557	114	62.8	7	798	206551	0.3440	-0.40	32159	0.983185	2.12
547-550	115	62.8	4	460	207011	0.3448	-0.40	32163	0.983307	2.13
540-546	116	62.9	7	812	207823	0.3461	-0.40	32170	0.983521	2.13

Rank	Occ. F	SFI	F	Tokens	Cum. Tokens	Cum. P Tokens	Y	Cum. Types	Cum. P Types	Z
532-539	117	62.9	8	936	208759	0.3477	-0.39	32178	0.983766	2.14
525-531	118	63.0	7	826	209585	0.3490	-0.39	32185	0.983980	2.14
518-524	119	63.0	7	833	210418	0.3504	-0.38	32192	0.984194	2.15
513-517	120	63.0	5	600	211018	0.3514	-0.38	32197	0.984347	2.15
506-512	121	63.1	7	847	211865	0.3528	-0.38	32204	0.984561	2.16
502-505	122	63.1	4	488	212353	0.3537	-0.38	32208	0.984683	2.16
500-501	123	63.1	2	246	212599	0.3541	-0.37	32210	0.984744	2.16
497-499	124	63.2	3	372	212971	0.3547	-0.37	32213	0.984836	2.17
491-496	125	63.2	6	750	213721	0.3559	-0.37	32219	0.985019	2.17
485-490	126	63.2	6	756	214477	0.3572	-0.37	32225	0.985203	2.18
483-484	127	63.3	2	254	214731	0.3576	-0.36	32227	0.985264	2.18
476-482	128	63.3	7	896	215627	0.3591	-0.36	32234	0.985478	2.18
473-475	129	63.3	3	387	216014	0.3597	-0.36	32237	0.985570	2.19
467-472	130	63.4	6	780	216794	0.3610	-0.36	32243	0.985753	2.19
462-466	131	63.4	5	655	217449	0.3621	-0.35	32248	0.985906	2.19
460-461	132	63.4	2	264	217713	0.3626	-0.35	32250	0.985967	2.20
458-459	133	63.5	2	266	217979	0.3630	-0.35	32252	0.986028	2.20
451-457	134	63.5	7	938	218917	0.3646	-0.35	32259	0.986242	2.20
446-450	135	63.5	5	675	219592	0.3657	-0.34	32264	0.986395	2.21
442-445	136	63.6	4	544	220136	0.3666	-0.34	32268	0.986517	2.21
437-441	138	63.6	5	690	220826	0.3678	-0.34	32273	0.986670	2.22
432-436	139	63.7	5	695	221521	0.3689	-0.33	32278	0.986823	2.22
430-431	140	63.7	2	280	221801	0.3694	-0.33	32280	0.986884	2.22
422-429	141	63.7	8	1128	222929	0.3713	-0.33	32288	0.987129	2.23
421	142	63.8	1	142	223071	0.3715	-0.33	32289	0.987159	2.23
418-420	143	63.8	3	429	223500	0.3722	-0.33	32292	0.987251	2.23
416-417	144	63.8	2	288	223788	0.3727	-0.32	32294	0.987312	2.24
412-415	145	63.8	4	580	224368	0.3737	-0.32	32298	0.987435	2.24
410-411	146	63.9	2	292	224660	0.3741	-0.32	32300	0.987496	2.24
407-409	147	63.9	3	441	225101	0.3749	-0.32	32303	0.987588	2.24
403-406	148	63.9	4	592	225693	0.3759	-0.32	32307	0.987710	2.25
399-402	149	64.0	4	596	226289	0.3769	-0.31	32311	0.987832	2.25
398	150	64.0	1	150	226439	0.3771	-0.31	32312	0.987863	2.25
397	151	64.0	1	151	226590	0.3774	-0.31	32313	0.987893	2.25
395-396	152	64.0	2	304	226894	0.3779	-0.31	32315	0.987954	2.26
393-394	153	64.1	2	306	227200	0.3784	-0.31	32317	0.988015	2.26
390-392	154	64.1	3	462	227662	0.3791	-0.31	32320	0.988107	2.26
388-389	155	64.1	2	310	227972	0.3797	-0.31	32322	0.988168	2.26
381-387	156	64.2	7	1092	229064	0.3815	-0.30	32329	0.988382	2.27
378-380	157	64.2	3	471	229535	0.3823	-0.30	32332	0.988474	2.27
377	158	64.2	1	158	229693	0.3825	-0.30	32333	0.988505	2.27
376	159	64.2	1	159	229852	0.3828	-0.30	32334	0.988535	2.27
371-375	160	64.3	5	800	230652	0.3841	-0.29	32339	0.988688	2.28
368-370	161	64.3	3	483	231135	0.3849	-0.29	32342	0.988780	2.28
365-367	162	64.3	3	486	231621	0.3857	-0.29	32345	0.988872	2.29
364	163	64.4	1	163	231784	0.3860	-0.29	32346	0.988902	2.29
363	164	64.4	1	164	231948	0.3863	-0.29	32347	0.988933	2.29
361-362	165	64.4	2	330	232278	0.3868	-0.29	32349	0.988994	2.29
360	167	64.5	1	167	232445	0.3871	-0.29	32350	0.989024	2.29
356-359	168	64.5	4	672	233117	0.3882	-0.28	32354	0.989147	2.30
351-355	169	64.5	5	845	233962	0.3896	-0.28	32359	0.989300	2.30
350	170	64.5	1	170	234132	0.3899	-0.28	32360	0.989330	2.30
349	171	64.6	1	171	234303	0.3902	-0.28	32361	0.989361	2.30
347-348	172	64.6	2	344	234647	0.3908	-0.28	32363	0.989422	2.31
344-346	173	64.6	3	519	235166	0.3916	-0.28	32366	0.989514	2.31
343	174	64.6	1	174	235340	0.3919	-0.27	32367	0.989544	2.31
342	175	64.7	1	175	235515	0.3922	-0.27	32368	0.989575	2.31
338-341	176	64.7	4	704	236219	0.3934	-0.27	32372	0.989697	2.32
336-337	177	64.7	2	354	236573	0.3940	-0.27	32374	0.989758	2.32
334-335	178	64.7	2	356	236929	0.3946	-0.27	32376	0.989819	2.32
333	179	64.8	1	179	237108	0.3949	-0.27	32377	0.989850	2.32
330-332	182	64.8	3	546	237654	0.3958	-0.26	32380	0.989942	2.32
326-329	183	64.9	4	732	238386	0.3970	-0.26	32384	0.990064	2.33
325	185	64.9	1	185	238571	0.3973	-0.26	32385	0.990094	2.33
322-324	187	64.9	3	561	239132	0.3982	-0.26	32388	0.990186	2.33
319-321	188	65.0	3	564	239696	0.3992	-0.26	32391	0.990278	2.34
318	189	65.0	1	189	239885	0.3995	-0.25	32392	0.990308	2.34
313-317	190	65.0	5	950	240835	0.4011	-0.25	32397	0.990461	2.34
312	191	65.0	1	191	241026	0.4014	-0.25	32398	0.990492	2.35
311	192	65.1	1	192	241218	0.4017	-0.25	32399	0.990522	2.35
309-310	193	65.1	2	386	241604	0.4024	-0.25	32401	0.990584	2.35
307-308	196	65.1	2	392	241996	0.4030	-0.25	32403	0.990645	2.35
305-306	197	65.2	2	394	242390	0.4037	-0.24	32405	0.990706	2.35
303-304	199	65.2	2	398	242788	0.4043	-0.24	32407	0.990767	2.36
300-302	200	65.2	3	600	243388	0.4053	-0.24	32410	0.990859	2.36
296-299	202	65.3	4	808	244196	0.4067	-0.24	32414	0.990981	2.36
294-295	203	65.3	2	406	244602	0.4074	-0.23	32416	0.991042	2.37
293	204	65.3	1	204	244806	0.4077	-0.23	32417	0.991073	2.37
292	205	65.3	1	205	245011	0.4080	-0.23	32418	0.991103	2.37
289-291	206	65.4	3	618	245629	0.4091	-0.23	32421	0.991195	2.37
286-288	207	65.4	3	621	246250	0.4101	-0.23	32424	0.991287	2.38
281-285	208	65.4	5	1040	247290	0.4118	-0.22	32429	0.991440	2.38
280	210	65.4	1	210	247500	0.4122	-0.22	32430	0.991470	2.39
278-279	211	65.5	2	422	247922	0.4129	-0.22	32432	0.991531	2.39
276-277	212	65.5	2	424	248346	0.4136	-0.22	32434	0.991593	2.39
274-275	216	65.6	2	432	248778	0.4143	-0.22	32436	0.991654	2.39
273	217	65.6	1	217	248995	0.4147	-0.22	32437	0.991684	2.39
271-272	218	65.6	2	436	249431	0.4154	-0.21	32439	0.991745	2.40
268-270	219	65.6	3	657	250088	0.4165	-0.21	32442	0.991837	2.40
266-267	220	65.6	2	440	250528	0.4172	-0.21	32444	0.991898	2.40
264-265	223	65.7	2	446	250974	0.4180	-0.21	32446	0.991959	2.41
263	224	65.7	1	224	251198	0.4183	-0.21	32447	0.991990	2.41
261-262	225	65.7	2	450	251648	0.4191	-0.20	32449	0.992051	2.41
260	226	65.8	1	226	251874	0.4195	-0.20	32450	0.992082	2.41
259	228	65.8	1	228	252102	0.4199	-0.20	32451	0.992112	2.41
257-258	229	65.8	2	458	252560	0.4206	-0.20	32453	0.992173	2.42
256	230	65.8	1	230	252790	0.4210	-0.20	32454	0.992204	2.42
254-255	237	66.0	2	474	253264	0.4218	-0.20	32456	0.992265	2.42
253	238	66.0	1	238	253502	0.4222	-0.20	32457	0.992296	2.42
252	239	66.0	1	239	253741	0.4226	-0.20	32458	0.992326	2.42
250-251	241	66.0	2	482	254223	0.4234	-0.19	32460	0.992387	2.43
249	242	66.1	1	242	254465	0.4238	-0.19	32461	0.992418	2.43
248	243	66.1	1	243	254708	0.4242	-0.19	32462	0.992449	2.43
246-247	244	66.1	2	488	255196	0.4250	-0.19	32464	0.992510	2.43
245	245	66.1	1	245	255441	0.4254	-0.19	32465	0.992540	2.43
244	246	66.1	1	246	255687	0.4258	-0.19	32466	0.992571	2.44
243	250	66.2	1	250	255937	0.4262	-0.19	32467	0.992601	2.44
242	251	66.2	1	251	256188	0.4267	-0.18	32468	0.992632	2.44
241	252	66.2	1	252	256440	0.4271	-0.18	32469	0.992663	2.44
240	253	66.3	1	253	256693	0.4275	-0.18	32470	0.992693	2.44
239	259	66.4	1	259	256952	0.4279	-0.18	32471	0.992724	2.44
238	260	66.4	1	260	257212	0.4284	-0.18	32472	0.992754	2.44
236-237	261	66.4	2	522	257734	0.4292	-0.18	32474	0.992815	2.45
235	262	66.4	1	262	257996	0.4297	-0.18	32475	0.992846	2.45
233-234	263	66.4	2	526	258522	0.4305	-0.17	32477	0.992907	2.45
230-232	264	66.4	3	792	259314	0.4319	-0.17	32480	0.992999	2.46

Rank	Occ. F	SFI	F	Tokens	Cum. Tokens	Cum. P Tokens	Y	Cum. Types	Cum. P Types	Z
229	265	66.5	1	265	259579	0.4323	-0.17	32481	0.993029	2.46
227- 228	266	66.5	2	532	260111	0.4332	-0.17	32483	0.993091	2.46
225- 226	269	66.5	2	538	260649	0.4341	-0.17	32485	0.993152	2.47
224	270	66.5	1	270	260919	0.4345	-0.16	32486	0.993182	2.47
223	273	66.6	1	273	261192	0.4350	-0.16	32487	0.993213	2.47
220- 222	274	66.6	3	822	262014	0.4364	-0.16	32490	0.993305	2.47
218- 219	276	66.6	2	552	262566	0.4373	-0.16	32492	0.993366	2.48
217	277	66.6	1	277	262843	0.4377	-0.16	32493	0.993396	2.48
215- 216	279	66.7	2	558	263401	0.4387	-0.15	32495	0.993457	2.48
213- 214	285	66.8	2	570	263971	0.4396	-0.15	32497	0.993519	2.48
212	286	66.8	1	286	264257	0.4401	-0.15	32498	0.993549	2.49
211	288	66.8	1	288	264545	0.4406	-0.15	32499	0.993580	2.49
210	289	66.8	1	289	264834	0.4411	-0.15	32500	0.993610	2.49
209	291	66.9	1	291	265125	0.4415	-0.15	32501	0.993641	2.49
207- 208	292	66.9	2	584	265709	0.4425	-0.14	32503	0.993702	2.49
206	293	66.9	1	293	266002	0.4430	-0.14	32504	0.993733	2.50
204- 205	294	66.9	2	588	266590	0.4440	-0.14	32506	0.993794	2.50
202- 203	295	66.9	2	590	267180	0.4450	-0.14	32508	0.993855	2.50
201	298	67.0	1	298	267478	0.4455	-0.14	32509	0.993885	2.51
200	300	67.0	1	300	267778	0.4460	-0.14	32510	0.993916	2.51
199	303	67.0	1	303	268081	0.4465	-0.13	32511	0.993947	2.51
197- 198	305	67.1	2	610	268691	0.4475	-0.13	32513	0.994008	2.51
196	308	67.1	1	308	268999	0.4480	-0.13	32514	0.994038	2.51
195	311	67.1	1	311	269310	0.4485	-0.13	32515	0.994069	2.52
193- 194	313	67.2	2	626	269936	0.4496	-0.13	32517	0.994130	2.52
192	317	67.2	1	317	270253	0.4501	-0.13	32518	0.994161	2.52
191	320	67.3	1	320	270573	0.4506	-0.12	32519	0.994191	2.52
190	323	67.3	1	323	270896	0.4511	-0.12	32520	0.994222	2.53
189	325	67.3	1	325	271221	0.4517	-0.12	32521	0.994252	2.53
188	327	67.4	1	327	271548	0.4522	-0.12	32522	0.994283	2.53
187	329	67.4	1	329	271877	0.4528	-0.12	32523	0.994313	2.53
184- 186	332	67.4	3	996	272873	0.4544	-0.11	32526	0.994405	2.54
183	334	67.5	1	334	273207	0.4550	-0.11	32527	0.994436	2.54
182	338	67.5	1	338	273545	0.4556	-0.11	32528	0.994466	2.54
181	339	67.5	1	339	273884	0.4561	-0.11	32529	0.994497	2.54
180	341	67.5	1	341	274225	0.4567	-0.11	32530	0.994527	2.54
179	344	67.6	1	344	274569	0.4573	-0.11	32531	0.994558	2.55
178	345	67.6	1	345	274914	0.4578	-0.11	32532	0.994589	2.55
177	348	67.6	1	348	275262	0.4584	-0.10	32533	0.994619	2.55
176	350	67.7	1	350	275612	0.4590	-0.10	32534	0.994650	2.55
173- 175	352	67.7	3	1056	276668	0.4608	-0.10	32537	0.994741	2.56
171- 172	354	67.7	2	708	277376	0.4619	-0.10	32539	0.994803	2.56
170	355	67.7	1	355	277731	0.4625	-0.09	32540	0.994833	2.56
169	358	67.8	1	358	278089	0.4631	-0.09	32541	0.994864	2.57
167- 168	361	67.8	2	722	278811	0.4643	-0.09	32543	0.994925	2.57
166	363	67.8	1	363	279174	0.4649	-0.09	32544	0.994955	2.57
165	366	67.9	1	366	279540	0.4655	-0.09	32545	0.994986	2.57
164	367	67.9	1	367	279907	0.4662	-0.08	32546	0.995017	2.58
163	372	67.9	1	372	280279	0.4668	-0.08	32547	0.995047	2.58
161- 162	378	68.0	2	756	281035	0.4680	-0.08	32549	0.995108	2.58
160	384	68.1	1	384	281419	0.4687	-0.08	32550	0.995139	2.59
159	385	68.1	1	385	281804	0.4693	-0.08	32551	0.995170	2.59
158	386	68.1	1	386	282190	0.4700	-0.08	32552	0.995200	2.59
157	396	68.2	1	396	282586	0.4706	-0.07	32553	0.995231	2.59
156	397	68.2	1	397	282983	0.4713	-0.07	32554	0.995261	2.59
154- 155	401	68.3	2	802	283785	0.4726	-0.07	32556	0.995322	2.60
153	405	68.3	1	405	284190	0.4733	-0.07	32557	0.995353	2.60
152	410	68.3	1	410	284600	0.4740	-0.07	32558	0.995384	2.60
151	418	68.4	1	418	285018	0.4747	-0.06	32559	0.995414	2.61
150	425	68.5	1	425	285443	0.4754	-0.06	32560	0.995445	2.61
149	434	68.6	1	434	285877	0.4761	-0.06	32561	0.995475	2.61
148	436	68.6	1	436	286313	0.4768	-0.06	32562	0.995506	2.61
147	440	68.7	1	440	286753	0.4776	-0.06	32563	0.995536	2.61
146	441	68.7	1	441	287194	0.4783	-0.05	32564	0.995567	2.62
145	443	68.7	1	443	287637	0.4790	-0.05	32565	0.995598	2.62
144	444	68.7	1	444	288081	0.4798	-0.05	32566	0.995628	2.62
143	446	68.7	1	446	288527	0.4805	-0.05	32567	0.995659	2.62
142	449	68.7	1	449	288976	0.4813	-0.05	32568	0.995689	2.63
141	450	68.8	1	450	289426	0.4820	-0.05	32569	0.995720	2.63
140	455	68.8	1	455	289881	0.4828	-0.04	32570	0.995750	2.63
139	460	68.8	1	460	290341	0.4835	-0.04	32571	0.995781	2.63
137- 138	461	68.9	2	922	291263	0.4851	-0.04	32573	0.995842	2.64
136	462	68.9	1	462	291725	0.4858	-0.04	32574	0.995873	2.64
135	469	68.9	1	469	292194	0.4866	-0.03	32575	0.995903	2.64
134	470	68.9	1	470	292664	0.4874	-0.03	32576	0.995934	2.65
133	476	69.0	1	476	293140	0.4882	-0.03	32577	0.995964	2.65
131- 132	484	69.1	2	968	294108	0.4898	-0.03	32579	0.996026	2.65
130	485	69.1	1	485	294593	0.4906	-0.02	32580	0.996056	2.66
129	487	69.1	1	487	295080	0.4914	-0.02	32581	0.996087	2.66
128	488	69.1	1	488	295568	0.4922	-0.02	32582	0.996117	2.66
127	496	69.2	1	496	296064	0.4931	-0.02	32583	0.996148	2.66
125- 126	499	69.2	2	998	297062	0.4947	-0.01	32585	0.996209	2.67
124	514	69.3	1	514	297576	0.4956	-0.01	32586	0.996240	2.67
123	515	69.3	1	515	298091	0.4964	-0.01	32587	0.996270	2.68
122	521	69.4	1	521	298612	0.4973	-0.01	32588	0.996301	2.68
121	522	69.4	1	522	299134	0.4982	-0.00	32589	0.996331	2.68
120	525	69.4	1	525	299659	0.4991	-0.00	32590	0.996362	2.68
117- 119	531	69.5	3	1593	301252	0.5017	0.00	32593	0.996454	2.69
116	538	69.5	1	538	301790	0.5026	0.01	32594	0.996484	2.70
115	557	69.7	1	557	302347	0.5035	0.01	32595	0.996515	2.70
114	558	69.7	1	558	302905	0.5045	0.01	32596	0.996545	2.70
113	566	69.7	1	566	303471	0.5054	0.01	32597	0.996576	2.70
112	572	69.8	1	572	304043	0.5064	0.02	32598	0.996606	2.71
111	573	69.8	1	573	304616	0.5073	0.02	32599	0.996637	2.71
110	574	69.8	1	574	305190	0.5083	0.02	32600	0.996668	2.71
109	587	69.9	1	587	305777	0.5092	0.02	32601	0.996698	2.72
107- 108	600	70.0	2	1200	306977	0.5112	0.03	32603	0.996759	2.72
106	602	70.0	1	602	307579	0.5122	0.03	32604	0.996790	2.73
105	608	70.1	1	608	308187	0.5133	0.03	32605	0.996820	2.73
104	609	70.1	1	609	308796	0.5143	0.04	32606	0.996851	2.73
103	611	70.1	1	611	309407	0.5153	0.04	32607	0.996882	2.74
102	617	70.1	1	617	310024	0.5163	0.04	32608	0.996912	2.74
101	642	70.3	1	642	310666	0.5174	0.04	32609	0.996943	2.74
100	646	70.3	1	646	311312	0.5185	0.05	32610	0.996973	2.74
99	661	70.4	1	661	311973	0.5196	0.05	32611	0.997004	2.75
98	666	70.5	1	666	312639	0.5207	0.05	32612	0.997034	2.75
97	674	70.5	1	674	313313	0.5218	0.05	32613	0.997065	2.75
96	679	70.5	1	679	313992	0.5229	0.06	32614	0.997096	2.76
95	688	70.6	1	688	314680	0.5241	0.06	32615	0.997126	2.76
94	690	70.6	1	690	315370	0.5252	0.06	32616	0.997157	2.77
93	699	70.7	1	699	316069	0.5264	0.07	32617	0.997187	2.77
92	701	70.7	1	701	316770	0.5275	0.07	32618	0.997218	2.77
91	710	70.7	1	710	317480	0.5287	0.07	32619	0.997248	2.78
90	721	70.8	1	721	318201	0.5299	0.08	32620	0.997279	2.78
89	739	70.9	1	739	318940	0.5312	0.08	32621	0.997310	2.78
88	744	70.9	1	744	319684	0.5324	0.08	32622	0.997340	2.79
87	758	71.0	1	758	320442	0.5337	0.08	32623	0.997371	2.79
86	761	71.0	1	761	321203	0.5349	0.09	32624	0.997401	2.79
85	764	71.0	1	764	321967	0.5362	0.09	32625	0.997432	2.80
84	772	71.1	1	772	322739	0.5375	0.09	32626	0.997462	2.80
83	775	71.1	1	775	323514	0.5388	0.10	32627	0.997493	2.81
82	818	71.3	1	818	324332	0.5401	0.10	32628	0.997524	2.81
81	824	71.4	1	824	325156	0.5415	0.10	32629	0.997554	2.81
80	835	71.4	1	835	325991	0.5429	0.11	32630	0.997585	2.82
79	842	71.5	1	842	326833	0.5443	0.11	32631	0.997615	2.82
78	860	71.6	1	860	327693	0.5457	0.11	32632	0.997646	2.83
77	899	71.8	1	899	328592	0.5472	0.12	32633	0.997676	2.83
76	908	71.8	1	908	329500	0.5487	0.12	32634	0.997707	2.83
75	922	71.9	1	922	330422	0.5503	0.13	32635	0.997738	2.84
74	928	71.9	1	928	331350	0.5518	0.13	32636	0.997768	2.84
73	931	71.9	1	931	332281	0.5534	0.13	32637	0.997799	2.85
72	955	72.0	1	955	333236	0.5550	0.14	32638	0.997829	2.85
71	956	72.0	1	956	334192	0.5566	0.14	32639	0.997860	2.86
70	961	72.0	1	961	335153	0.5582	0.15	32640	0.997890	2.86
69	964	72.1	1	964	336117	0.5598	0.15	32641	0.997921	2.87
68	972	72.1	1	972	337089	0.5614	0.15	32642	0.997952	2.87
67	975	72.1	1	975	338064	0.5630	0.16	32643	0.997982	2.88
66	984	72.1	1	984	339048	0.5646	0.16	32644	0.998013	2.88
65	991	72.2	1	991	340039	0.5663	0.17	32645	0.998043	2.89
64	1066	72.5	1	1066	341105	0.5681	0.17	32646	0.998074	2.89
63	1084	72.6	1	1084	342189	0.5699	0.18	32647	0.998104	2.90
62	1085	72.6	1	1085	343274	0.5717	0.18	32648	0.998135	2.90
61	1114	72.7	1	1114	344388	0.5735	0.19	32649	0.998166	2.91
60	1151	72.8	1	1151	345539	0.5755	0.19	32650	0.998196	2.91
58- 59	1167	72.9	2	2334	347873	0.5793	0.20	32652	0.998257	2.92
57	1203	73.0	1	1203	349076	0.5814	0.21	32653	0.998288	2.93
56	1211	73.0	1	1211	350287	0.5834	0.21	32654	0.998318	2.93
55	1230	73.1	1	1230	351517	0.5854	0.22	32655	0.998349	2.94
54	1232	73.1	1	1232	352749	0.5875	0.22	32656	0.998380	2.94
53	1242	73.1	1	1242	353991	0.5895	0.23	32657	0.998410	2.95
52	1272	73.3	1	1272	355263	0.5917	0.23	32658	0.998441	2.96
51	1283	73.3	1	1283	356546	0.5938	0.24	32659	0.998471	2.96
50	1290	73.3	1	1290	357836	0.5959	0.24	32660	0.998502	2.97
49	1298	73.3	1	1298	359134	0.5981	0.25	32661	0.998532	2.97
48	1323	73.4	1	1323	360457	0.6003	0.25	32662	0.998563	2.98
47	1347	73.5	1	1347	361804	0.6025	0.26	32663	0.998594	2.99
46	1351	73.5	1	1351	363155	0.6048	0.27	32664	0.998624	2.99
45	1371	73.6	1	1371	364526	0.6071	0.27	32665	0.998655	3.00
44	1382	73.6	1	1382	365908	0.6094	0.28	32666	0.998685	3.01
43	1463	73.9	1	1463	367371	0.6118	0.28	32667	0.998716	3.02
42	1497	74.0	1	1497	368868	0.6143	0.29	32668	0.998747	3.02
41	1581	74.2	1	1581	370449	0.6169	0.30	32669	0.998777	3.03
40	1606	74.3	1	1606	372055	0.6196	0.30	32670	0.998808	3.04
39	1651	74.4	1	1651	373706	0.6224	0.31	32671	0.998838	3.05
38	1741	74.6	1	1741	375447	0.6253	0.32	32672	0.998869	3.05
37	1826	74.8	1	1826	377273	0.6283	0.33	32673	0.998899	3.06
36	1912	75.0	1	1912	379185	0.6315	0.34	32674	0.998930	3.07
35	1946	75.1	1	1946	381131	0.6347	0.34	32675	0.998960	3.08
34	2092	75.4	1	2092	383223	0.6382	0.35	32676	0.998991	3.09
33	2096	75.4	1	2096	385319	0.6417	0.36	32677	0.999022	3.10
32	2137	75.5	1	2137	387456	0.6453	0.37	32678	0.999052	3.11
31	2167	75.6	1	2167	389623	0.6489	0.38	32679	0.999083	3.12
30	2257	75.8	1	2257	391880	0.6526	0.39	32680	0.999113	3.13
29	2263	75.8	1	2263	394143	0.6564	0.40	32681	0.999144	3.14
28	2321	75.9	1	2321	396464	0.6603	0.41	32682	0.999175	3.15
27	2374	76.0	1	2374	398838	0.6642	0.42	32683	0.999205	3.16
26	2447	76.1	1	2447	401285	0.6683	0.44	32684	0.999236	3.17
25	2515	76.2	1	2515	403800	0.6725	0.45	32685	0.999266	3.18
24	2610	76.4	1	2610	406410	0.6768	0.46	32686	0.999297	3.19
23	2615	76.4	1	2615	409025	0.6812	0.47	32687	0.999327	3.21
22	2822	76.7	1	2822	411847	0.6859	0.48	32688	0.999358	3.22
21	2981	77.0	1	2981	414828	0.6909	0.50	32689	0.999389	3.23
20	3040	77.0	1	3040	417868	0.6959	0.51	32690	0.999419	3.25
19	3188	77.3	1	3188	421056	0.7012	0.53	32691	0.999450	3.26
18	3211	77.3	1	3211	424267	0.7066	0.54	32692	0.999480	3.28
17	3592	77.8	1	3592	427859	0.7126	0.56	32693	0.999511	3.30
16	3852	78.1	1	3852	431711	0.7190	0.58	32694	0.999541	3.31
15	3901	78.1	1	3901	435612	0.7255	0.60	32695	0.999572	3.33
14	4254	78.5	1	4254	439866	0.7326	0.62	32696	0.999602	3.35
13	4418	78.7	1	4418	444284	0.7399	0.64	32697	0.999633	3.38
12	4759	79.0	1	4759	449043	0.7478	0.67	32698	0.999664	3.40
11	4819	79.0	1	4819	453862	0.7559	0.69	32699	0.999694	3.43
10	5001	79.2	1	5001	458863	0.7642	0.72	32700	0.999725	3.45
9	5109	79.3	1	5109	463972	0.7727	0.75	32701	0.999755	3.49
8	5809	79.9	1	5809	469781	0.7824	0.78	32702	0.999786	3.52
7	7276	80.8	1	7276	477057	0.7945	0.82	32703	0.999817	3.56
6	12579	83.2	1	12579	489636	0.8154	0.90	32704	0.999847	3.61
5	14623	83.9	1	14623	504259	0.8398	0.99	32705	0.999878	3.67
4	15135	84.0	1	15135	519394	0.8650	1.10	32706	0.999908	3.74
3	16687	84.4	1	16687	536081	0.8928	1.24	32707	0.999939	3.84
2	20095	85.2	1	20095	556176	0.9263	1.45	32708	0.999969	4.01
1	44281	88.7	1	44281	600457	1.0000	+INF.	32709	1.000000	+INF.

Rank	Occ. F	SFI	F	Tokens	Cum. Tokens	Cum. P Tokens	Y	Cum. Types	Cum. P Types	Z
16840–30693	1	44.9	13854	13854	13854	0.0283	−1.91	13854	0.451373	−0.12
12204–16839	2	47.1	4636	9272	23126	0.0472	−1.67	18490	0.602417	0.26
9758–12203	3	48.5	2446	7338	30464	0.0622	−1.54	20936	0.682110	0.47
8256– 9757	4	49.6	1502	6008	36472	0.0745	−1.44	22438	0.731046	0.62
7093– 8255	5	50.5	1163	5815	42287	0.0864	−1.36	23601	0.768938	0.74
6302– 7092	6	51.2	791	4746	47033	0.0961	−1.30	24392	0.794709	0.82
5735– 6301	7	51.9	567	3969	51002	0.1042	−1.26	24959	0.813182	0.89
5223– 5734	8	52.4	512	4096	55098	0.1126	−1.21	25471	0.829863	0.95
4814– 5222	9	52.9	409	3681	58779	0.1201	−1.17	25880	0.843189	1.01
4437– 4813	10	53.3	377	3770	62549	0.1278	−1.14	26257	0.855472	1.06
4121– 4436	11	53.7	316	3476	66025	0.1349	−1.10	26573	0.865767	1.11
3843– 4120	12	54.1	278	3336	69361	0.1417	−1.07	26851	0.874825	1.15
3615– 3842	13	54.4	228	2964	72325	0.1477	−1.05	27079	0.882253	1.19
3420– 3614	14	54.7	195	2730	75055	0.1533	−1.02	27274	0.888606	1.22
3248– 3419	15	55.0	172	2580	77635	0.1586	−1.00	27446	0.894210	1.25
3077– 3247	16	55.3	171	2736	80371	0.1642	−0.98	27617	0.899782	1.28
2922– 3076	17	55.5	155	2635	83006	0.1696	−0.96	27772	0.904832	1.31
2789– 2921	18	55.8	133	2394	85400	0.1745	−0.94	27905	0.909165	1.34
2665– 2788	19	56.0	124	2356	87756	0.1793	−0.92	28029	0.913205	1.36
2537– 2664	20	56.2	128	2560	90316	0.1845	−0.90	28157	0.917375	1.39
2454– 2536	21	56.4	83	1743	92059	0.1881	−0.89	28240	0.920079	1.41
2375– 2453	22	56.6	79	1738	93797	0.1916	−0.87	28319	0.922653	1.42
2277– 2374	23	56.8	98	2254	96051	0.1962	−0.86	28417	0.925846	1.45
2186– 2276	24	57.0	91	2184	98235	0.2007	−0.84	28508	0.928811	1.47
2106– 2185	25	57.2	80	2000	100235	0.2048	−0.82	28588	0.931418	1.49
2025– 2105	26	57.3	81	2106	102341	0.2091	−0.81	28669	0.934057	1.51
1958– 2024	27	57.5	67	1809	104150	0.2128	−0.80	28736	0.936239	1.52
1887– 1957	28	57.7	71	1988	106138	0.2168	−0.78	28807	0.938553	1.54
1846– 1886	29	57.8	41	1189	107327	0.2192	−0.77	28848	0.939889	1.55
1787– 1845	30	57.9	59	1770	109097	0.2229	−0.76	28907	0.941811	1.57
1717– 1786	31	58.1	70	2170	111267	0.2273	−0.75	28977	0.944091	1.59
1654– 1716	32	58.2	63	2016	113283	0.2314	−0.73	29040	0.946144	1.61
1605– 1653	33	58.4	49	1617	114900	0.2347	−0.72	29089	0.947740	1.62
1567– 1604	34	58.5	38	1292	116192	0.2374	−0.71	29127	0.948979	1.64
1534– 1566	35	58.6	33	1155	117347	0.2397	−0.71	29160	0.950054	1.65
1484– 1533	36	58.7	50	1800	119147	0.2434	−0.70	29210	0.951683	1.66
1449– 1483	37	58.8	35	1295	120442	0.2460	−0.69	29245	0.952823	1.67
1420– 1448	38	59.0	29	1102	121544	0.2483	−0.68	29274	0.953768	1.68
1382– 1419	39	59.1	38	1482	123026	0.2513	−0.67	29312	0.955006	1.70
1349– 1381	40	59.2	33	1320	124346	0.2540	−0.66	29345	0.956081	1.71
1324– 1348	41	59.3	25	1025	125371	0.2561	−0.66	29370	0.956896	1.72
1285– 1323	42	59.4	39	1638	127009	0.2595	−0.65	29409	0.958166	1.73
1251– 1284	43	59.5	34	1462	128471	0.2624	−0.64	29443	0.959274	1.74
1225– 1250	44	59.6	26	1144	129615	0.2648	−0.63	29469	0.960121	1.75
1201– 1224	45	59.7	24	1080	130695	0.2670	−0.62	29493	0.960903	1.76
1180– 1200	46	59.8	21	966	131661	0.2690	−0.62	29514	0.961587	1.77
1154– 1179	47	59.9	26	1222	132883	0.2715	−0.61	29540	0.962434	1.78
1129– 1153	48	60.0	25	1200	134083	0.2739	−0.60	29565	0.963249	1.79
1113– 1128	49	60.0	16	784	134867	0.2755	−0.60	29581	0.963770	1.80
1090– 1112	50	60.1	23	1150	136017	0.2779	−0.59	29604	0.964520	1.81
1068– 1089	51	60.2	22	1122	137139	0.2801	−0.58	29626	0.965236	1.81
1047– 1067	52	60.3	21	1092	138231	0.2824	−0.58	29647	0.965921	1.82
1025– 1046	53	60.4	22	1166	139397	0.2848	−0.57	29669	0.966637	1.83
1007– 1024	54	60.5	18	972	140369	0.2867	−0.56	29687	0.967224	1.84
988– 1006	55	60.5	19	1045	141414	0.2889	−0.56	29706	0.967843	1.85
968– 987	56	60.6	20	1120	142534	0.2912	−0.55	29726	0.968494	1.86
956– 967	57	60.7	12	684	143218	0.2926	−0.55	29738	0.968885	1.86
935– 955	58	60.8	21	1218	144436	0.2951	−0.54	29759	0.969570	1.87
912– 934	59	60.8	23	1357	145793	0.2978	−0.53	29782	0.970319	1.89
898– 911	60	60.9	14	840	146633	0.2995	−0.53	29796	0.970775	1.89
893– 897	61	61.0	5	305	146938	0.3002	−0.52	29801	0.970938	1.89
871– 892	62	61.1	22	1364	148302	0.3029	−0.52	29823	0.971655	1.91
851– 870	63	61.1	20	1260	149562	0.3055	−0.51	29843	0.972306	1.92
837– 850	64	61.2	14	896	150458	0.3074	−0.50	29857	0.972762	1.92
820– 836	65	61.3	17	1105	151563	0.3096	−0.50	29874	0.973316	1.93
809– 819	66	61.3	11	726	152289	0.3111	−0.49	29885	0.973675	1.94
798– 808	67	61.4	11	737	153026	0.3126	−0.49	29896	0.974033	1.94
786– 797	68	61.5	12	816	153842	0.3143	−0.48	29908	0.974424	1.95
771– 785	69	61.5	15	1035	154877	0.3164	−0.48	29923	0.974913	1.96
763– 770	70	61.6	8	560	155437	0.3175	−0.47	29931	0.975173	1.96
748– 762	71	61.6	15	1065	156502	0.3197	−0.47	29946	0.975662	1.97
736– 747	72	61.7	12	864	157366	0.3215	−0.46	29958	0.976053	1.98
724– 735	73	61.8	12	876	158242	0.3233	−0.46	29970	0.976444	1.99
713– 723	74	61.8	11	814	159056	0.3249	−0.45	29981	0.976803	1.99
700– 712	75	61.9	13	975	160031	0.3269	−0.45	29994	0.977226	2.00
695– 699	76	61.9	5	380	160411	0.3277	−0.45	29999	0.977389	2.00
684– 694	77	62.0	11	847	161258	0.3294	−0.44	30010	0.977747	2.01
675– 683	78	62.1	9	702	161960	0.3308	−0.44	30019	0.978041	2.01
667– 674	79	62.1	8	632	162592	0.3321	−0.43	30027	0.978301	2.02
661– 666	80	62.2	6	480	163072	0.3331	−0.43	30033	0.978497	2.02
655– 660	81	62.2	6	486	163558	0.3341	−0.43	30039	0.978692	2.03
647– 654	82	62.3	8	656	164214	0.3355	−0.42	30047	0.978953	2.03
636– 646	83	62.3	11	913	165127	0.3373	−0.42	30058	0.979311	2.04
628– 635	84	62.4	8	672	165799	0.3387	−0.42	30066	0.979572	2.04
620– 627	85	62.4	8	680	166479	0.3401	−0.41	30074	0.979833	2.05
615– 619	86	62.5	5	430	166909	0.3410	−0.41	30079	0.979995	2.05
605– 614	87	62.5	10	870	167779	0.3427	−0.41	30089	0.980321	2.06
600– 604	88	62.6	5	440	168219	0.3436	−0.40	30094	0.980484	2.06
593– 599	89	62.6	7	623	168842	0.3449	−0.40	30101	0.980712	2.07
583– 592	90	62.7	10	900	169742	0.3467	−0.39	30111	0.981038	2.08
575– 582	91	62.7	8	728	170470	0.3482	−0.39	30119	0.981299	2.08
569– 574	92	62.8	6	552	171022	0.3494	−0.39	30125	0.981494	2.09
568	93	62.8	1	93	171115	0.3496	−0.39	30126	0.981527	2.09
564– 567	94	62.9	4	376	171491	0.3503	−0.38	30130	0.981657	2.09
557– 563	95	62.9	7	665	172156	0.3517	−0.38	30137	0.981885	2.09
554– 556	96	62.9	3	288	172444	0.3523	−0.38	30140	0.981983	2.10
545– 553	97	63.0	9	873	173317	0.3540	−0.37	30149	0.982276	2.10
540– 544	98	63.0	5	490	173807	0.3551	−0.37	30154	0.982439	2.11
531– 539	99	63.1	9	891	174698	0.3569	−0.37	30163	0.982732	2.11
521– 530	100	63.1	10	1000	175698	0.3589	−0.36	30173	0.983058	2.12
517– 520	101	63.2	4	404	176102	0.3597	−0.36	30177	0.983188	2.12
513– 516	102	63.2	4	408	176510	0.3606	−0.36	30181	0.983319	2.13
510– 512	103	63.3	3	309	176819	0.3612	−0.36	30184	0.983416	2.13
499– 509	104	63.3	11	1144	177963	0.3635	−0.35	30195	0.983775	2.14
493– 498	105	63.3	6	630	178593	0.3648	−0.35	30201	0.983970	2.14
488– 492	106	63.4	5	530	179123	0.3659	−0.34	30206	0.984133	2.15
483– 487	107	63.4	5	535	179658	0.3670	−0.34	30211	0.984296	2.15
480– 482	108	63.5	3	324	179982	0.3677	−0.34	30214	0.984394	2.15
478– 479	109	63.5	2	218	180200	0.3681	−0.34	30216	0.984459	2.16
471– 477	110	63.5	7	770	180970	0.3697	−0.33	30223	0.984687	2.16
458– 470	111	63.6	13	1443	182413	0.3726	−0.32	30236	0.985111	2.17
453– 457	112	63.6	5	560	182973	0.3738	−0.32	30241	0.985273	2.18
449– 452	113	63.7	4	452	183425	0.3747	−0.32	30245	0.985404	2.18
444– 448	114	63.7	5	570	183995	0.3759	−0.32	30250	0.985567	2.19
439– 443	115	63.7	5	575	184570	0.3770	−0.31	30255	0.985730	2.19
435– 438	116	63.8	4	464	185034	0.3780	−0.31	30259	0.985860	2.19
430– 434	117	63.8	5	585	185619	0.3792	−0.31	30264	0.986023	2.20
426– 429	118	63.8	4	472	186091	0.3801	−0.31	30268	0.986153	2.20
423– 425	119	63.9	3	357	186448	0.3809	−0.30	30271	0.986251	2.20
419– 422	120	63.9	4	480	186928	0.3819	−0.30	30275	0.986381	2.21
413– 418	121	63.9	6	726	187654	0.3833	−0.30	30281	0.986577	2.21
408– 412	122	64.0	5	610	188264	0.3846	−0.29	30286	0.986740	2.22
403– 407	123	64.0	5	615	188879	0.3858	−0.29	30291	0.986903	2.22
397– 402	124	64.1	6	744	189623	0.3874	−0.29	30297	0.987098	2.23
394– 396	125	64.1	3	375	189998	0.3881	−0.28	30300	0.987196	2.23
390– 393	126	64.1	4	504	190502	0.3892	−0.28	30304	0.987326	2.24
388– 389	128	64.2	2	256	190758	0.3897	−0.28	30306	0.987391	2.24
385– 387	129	64.2	3	387	191145	0.3905	−0.28	30309	0.987489	2.24
381– 384	130	64.3	4	520	191665	0.3915	−0.28	30313	0.987619	2.25
376– 380	131	64.3	5	655	192320	0.3929	−0.27	30318	0.987782	2.25
370– 375	132	64.3	6	792	193112	0.3945	−0.27	30324	0.987978	2.26
368– 369	133	64.4	2	266	193378	0.3950	−0.27	30326	0.988043	2.26
364– 367	134	64.4	4	536	193914	0.3961	−0.26	30330	0.988173	2.26
361– 363	135	64.4	3	405	194319	0.3970	−0.26	30333	0.988271	2.27
357– 360	136	64.5	4	544	194863	0.3981	−0.26	30337	0.988401	2.27
355– 356	137	64.5	2	274	195137	0.3986	−0.26	30339	0.988466	2.27
353– 354	138	64.5	2	276	195413	0.3992	−0.26	30341	0.988532	2.27
352	139	64.5	1	139	195552	0.3995	−0.25	30342	0.988564	2.28
351	140	64.6	1	140	195692	0.3998	−0.25	30343	0.988597	2.28
348– 350	141	64.6	3	423	196115	0.4006	−0.25	30346	0.988694	2.28
346– 347	142	64.6	2	284	196399	0.4012	−0.25	30348	0.988760	2.28
344– 345	143	64.7	2	286	196685	0.4018	−0.25	30350	0.988825	2.28
342– 343	144	64.7	2	288	196973	0.4024	−0.25	30352	0.988890	2.29
340– 341	145	64.7	2	290	197263	0.4030	−0.25	30354	0.988955	2.29
337– 339	146	64.8	3	438	197701	0.4039	−0.24	30357	0.989053	2.29
333– 336	147	64.8	4	588	198289	0.4051	−0.24	30361	0.989183	2.30
330– 332	148	64.8	3	444	198733	0.4060	−0.24	30364	0.989281	2.30
329	149	64.8	1	149	198882	0.4063	−0.24	30365	0.989313	2.30
326– 328	150	64.9	3	450	199332	0.4072	−0.23	30368	0.989411	2.30
323– 325	151	64.9	3	453	199785	0.4081	−0.23	30371	0.989509	2.31
321– 322	152	64.9	2	304	200089	0.4087	−0.23	30373	0.989574	2.31
315– 320	153	65.0	6	918	201007	0.4106	−0.23	30379	0.989770	2.32
313– 314	154	65.0	2	308	201315	0.4112	−0.22	30381	0.989835	2.32
312	155	65.0	1	155	201470	0.4116	−0.22	30382	0.989867	2.32
311	156	65.0	1	156	201626	0.4119	−0.22	30383	0.989900	2.32
310	157	65.1	1	157	201783	0.4122	−0.22	30384	0.989933	2.32
308– 309	158	65.1	2	316	202099	0.4128	−0.22	30386	0.989998	2.33
307	159	65.1	1	159	202258	0.4132	−0.22	30387	0.990030	2.33
303– 306	160	65.2	4	640	202898	0.4145	−0.22	30391	0.990161	2.33
302	161	65.2	1	161	203059	0.4148	−0.22	30392	0.990193	2.33
301	162	65.2	1	162	203221	0.4151	−0.21	30393	0.990226	2.33
300	163	65.2	1	163	203384	0.4155	−0.21	30394	0.990258	2.34
294– 299	164	65.3	6	984	204368	0.4175	−0.21	30400	0.990454	2.34
293	165	65.3	1	165	204533	0.4178	−0.21	30401	0.990486	2.34
290– 292	167	65.3	3	501	205034	0.4188	−0.20	30404	0.990584	2.35
285– 289	168	65.4	5	840	205874	0.4206	−0.20	30409	0.990747	2.36
284	169	65.4	1	169	206043	0.4209	−0.20	30410	0.990780	2.36
283	170	65.4	1	170	206213	0.4212	−0.20	30411	0.990812	2.36
281– 282	171	65.4	2	342	206555	0.4219	−0.20	30413	0.990877	2.36
277– 280	172	65.5	4	688	207243	0.4234	−0.19	30417	0.991008	2.37
276	173	65.5	1	173	207416	0.4237	−0.19	30418	0.991040	2.37
273– 275	174	65.5	3	522	207938	0.4248	−0.19	30421	0.991138	2.37
270– 272	175	65.5	3	525	208463	0.4258	−0.19	30424	0.991236	2.38
268– 269	176	65.6	2	352	208815	0.4266	−0.19	30426	0.991301	2.38
266– 267	177	65.6	2	354	209169	0.4273	−0.18	30428	0.991366	2.38
265	178	65.6	1	178	209347	0.4277	−0.18	30429	0.991399	2.38
263– 264	179	65.6	2	358	209705	0.4284	−0.18	30431	0.991464	2.39
262	182	65.7	1	182	209887	0.4288	−0.18	30432	0.991496	2.39
259– 261	184	65.8	3	552	210439	0.4299	−0.18	30435	0.991594	2.39
257– 258	185	65.8	2	370	210809	0.4306	−0.17	30437	0.991659	2.39
256	186	65.8	1	186	210995	0.4310	−0.17	30438	0.991692	2.40
255	187	65.8	1	187	211182	0.4314	−0.17	30439	0.991724	2.40
254	189	65.9	1	189	211371	0.4318	−0.17	30440	0.991757	2.40
251– 253	191	65.9	3	573	211944	0.4330	−0.17	30443	0.991855	2.40
249– 250	192	65.9	2	384	212328	0.4337	−0.17	30445	0.991920	2.41
248	194	66.0	1	194	212522	0.4341	−0.17	30446	0.991953	2.41
247	195	66.0	1	195	212717	0.4345	−0.16	30447	0.991985	2.41
246	196	66.0	1	196	212913	0.4349	−0.16	30448	0.992018	2.41
244– 245	198	66.1	2	396	213309	0.4357	−0.16	30450	0.992083	2.41
243	199	66.1	1	199	213508	0.4362	−0.16	30451	0.992115	2.41
241– 242	203	66.2	2	406	213914	0.4370	−0.16	30453	0.992181	2.42
239– 240	205	66.2	2	410	214324	0.4378	−0.16	30455	0.992246	2.42
238	206	66.3	1	206	214530	0.4382	−0.16	30456	0.992278	2.42
235– 237	208	66.3	3	624	215154	0.4395	−0.15	30459	0.992376	2.43
232– 234	209	66.3	3	627	215781	0.4408	−0.15	30462	0.992474	2.43
231	211	66.4	1	211	215992	0.4412	−0.15	30463	0.992506	2.43
227– 230	212	66.4	4	848	216840	0.4430	−0.14	30467	0.992637	2.44
226	213	66.4	1	213	217053	0.4434	−0.14	30468	0.992669	2.44
223– 225	215	66.4	3	645	217698	0.4447	−0.14	30471	0.992767	2.45
221– 222	217	66.5	2	434	218132	0.4456	−0.14	30473	0.992832	2.45
217– 220	219	66.5	4	876	219008	0.4474	−0.13	30477	0.992963	2.46
216	221	66.6	1	221	219229	0.4478	−0.13	30478	0.992995	2.46
215	222	66.6	1	222	219451	0.4483	−0.13	30479	0.993028	2.46
214	225	66.6	1	225	219676	0.4488	−0.13	30480	0.993060	2.46
213	226	66.7	1	226	219902	0.4492	−0.13	30481	0.993093	2.46
211– 212	228	66.7	2	456	220358	0.4501	−0.13	30483	0.993158	2.47
210	229	66.7	1	229	220587	0.4506	−0.12	30484	0.993191	2.47
209	234	66.8	1	234	220821	0.4511	−0.12	30485	0.993223	2.47
207– 208	235	66.8	2	470	221291	0.4521	−0.12	30487	0.993288	2.47
205– 206	236	66.8	2	472	221763	0.4530	−0.12	30489	0.993353	2.48
204	239	66.9	1	239	222002	0.4535	−0.12	30490	0.993386	2.48
203	242	66.9	1	242	222244	0.4540	−0.12	30491	0.993419	2.48
202	243	67.0	1	243	222487	0.4545	−0.11	30492	0.993451	2.48
198– 201	244	67.0	4	976	223463	0.4565	−0.11	30496	0.993582	2.49
197	245	67.0	1	245	223708	0.4570	−0.11	30497	0.993614	2.49
194– 196	246	67.0	3	738	224446	0.4585	−0.10	30500	0.993712	2.50
193	248	67.1	1	248	224694	0.4590	−0.10	30501	0.993744	2.50
192	250	67.1	1	250	224944	0.4595	−0.10	30502	0.993777	2.50
191	253	67.1	1	253	225197	0.4600	−0.10	30503	0.993810	2.50
187– 190	254	67.2	4	1016	226213	0.4621	−0.10	30507	0.993940	2.51
185– 186	255	67.2	2	510	226723	0.4631	−0.09	30509	0.994005	2.51
183– 184	256	67.2	2	512	227235	0.4642	−0.09	30511	0.994070	2.52
182	258	67.2	1	258	227493	0.4647	−0.09	30512	0.994103	2.52
181	260	67.3	1	260	227753	0.4653	−0.09	30513	0.994135	2.52
180	261	67.3	1	261	228014	0.4658	−0.09	30514	0.994168	2.52
179	262	67.3	1	262	228276	0.4663	−0.08	30515	0.994201	2.52
178	268	67.4	1	268	228544	0.4669	−0.08	30516	0.994233	2.53
177	269	67.4	1	269	228813	0.4674	−0.08	30517	0.994266	2.53
176	272	67.5	1	272	229085	0.4680	−0.08	30518	0.994298	2.53
175	273	67.5	1	273	229358	0.4685	−0.08	30519	0.994331	2.53
174	279	67.6	1	279	229637	0.4691	−0.08	30520	0.994363	2.53
173	280	67.6	1	280	229917	0.4697	−0.08	30521	0.994396	2.54

Rank	Occ. F	SFI	F	Tokens	Cum. Tokens	Cum. P Tokens	Y	Cum. Types	Cum. P Types	Z
171– 172	281	67.6	2	562	230479	0.4708	-0.07	30523	0.994461	2.54
169– 170	283	67.6	2	566	231045	0.4720	-0.07	30525	0.994526	2.54
168	284	67.6	1	284	231329	0.4726	-0.07	30526	0.994559	2.55
166– 167	286	67.7	2	572	231901	0.4737	-0.07	30528	0.994624	2.55
165	289	67.7	1	289	232190	0.4743	-0.06	30529	0.994657	2.55
164	291	67.7	1	291	232481	0.4749	-0.06	30530	0.994689	2.55
163	292	67.8	1	292	232773	0.4755	-0.06	30531	0.994722	2.56
162	294	67.8	1	294	233067	0.4761	-0.06	30532	0.994754	2.56
159– 161	296	67.8	3	888	233955	0.4779	-0.06	30535	0.994852	2.57
158	298	67.9	1	298	234253	0.4785	-0.05	30536	0.994885	2.57
157	300	67.9	1	300	234553	0.4791	-0.05	30537	0.994917	2.57
156	303	67.9	1	303	234856	0.4798	-0.05	30538	0.994950	2.57
155	304	67.9	1	304	235160	0.4804	-0.05	30539	0.994983	2.57
154	307	68.0	1	307	235467	0.4810	-0.05	30540	0.995015	2.58
153	309	68.0	1	309	235776	0.4816	-0.05	30541	0.995048	2.58
152	314	68.1	1	314	236090	0.4823	-0.04	30542	0.995080	2.58
151	315	68.1	1	315	236405	0.4829	-0.04	30543	0.995113	2.58
150	317	68.1	1	317	236722	0.4836	-0.04	30544	0.995145	2.59
149	319	68.1	1	319	237041	0.4842	-0.04	30545	0.995178	2.59
148	323	68.2	1	323	237364	0.4849	-0.04	30546	0.995211	2.59
146– 147	325	68.2	2	650	238014	0.4862	-0.03	30548	0.995276	2.60
145	326	68.2	1	326	238340	0.4869	-0.03	30549	0.995308	2.60
143– 144	329	68.3	2	658	238998	0.4882	-0.03	30551	0.995373	2.60
142	334	68.3	1	334	239332	0.4889	-0.03	30552	0.995406	2.60
140– 141	335	68.4	2	670	240002	0.4903	-0.02	30554	0.995471	2.61
139	338	68.4	1	338	240340	0.4910	-0.02	30555	0.995504	2.61
137– 138	344	68.5	2	688	241028	0.4924	-0.02	30557	0.995569	2.62
136	350	68.5	1	350	241378	0.4931	-0.02	30558	0.995602	2.62
135	353	68.6	1	353	241731	0.4938	-0.02	30559	0.995634	2.62
134	359	68.7	1	359	242090	0.4945	-0.01	30560	0.995667	2.62
133	363	68.7	1	363	242453	0.4953	-0.01	30561	0.995699	2.63
132	366	68.7	1	366	242819	0.4960	-0.01	30562	0.995732	2.63
131	368	68.8	1	368	243187	0.4968	-0.01	30563	0.995764	2.63
130	374	68.8	1	374	243561	0.4975	-0.01	30564	0.995797	2.64
129	377	68.9	1	377	243938	0.4983	-0.00	30565	0.995830	2.64
128	379	68.9	1	379	244317	0.4991	-0.00	30566	0.995862	2.64
127	382	68.9	1	382	244699	0.4999	-0.00	30567	0.995895	2.64
126	386	69.0	1	386	245085	0.5007	0.00	30568	0.995927	2.65
125	391	69.0	1	391	245476	0.5015	0.00	30569	0.995960	2.65
124	393	69.1	1	393	245869	0.5023	0.01	30570	0.995993	2.65
123	396	69.1	1	396	246265	0.5031	0.01	30571	0.996025	2.65
122	399	69.1	1	399	246664	0.5039	0.01	30572	0.996058	2.66
120– 121	412	69.3	2	824	247488	0.5056	0.01	30574	0.996123	2.66
119	419	69.3	1	419	247907	0.5064	0.02	30575	0.996155	2.67
117– 118	425	69.4	2	850	248757	0.5082	0.02	30577	0.996221	2.67
116	431	69.5	1	431	249188	0.5090	0.02	30578	0.996253	2.67
115	432	69.5	1	432	249620	0.5099	0.02	30579	0.996286	2.68
113– 114	434	69.5	2	868	250488	0.5117	0.03	30581	0.996351	2.68
112	435	69.5	1	435	250923	0.5126	0.03	30582	0.996383	2.69
111	440	69.5	1	440	251363	0.5135	0.03	30583	0.996416	2.69
110	444	69.6	1	444	251807	0.5144	0.04	30584	0.996449	2.69
109	455	69.7	1	455	252262	0.5153	0.04	30585	0.996481	2.70
108	458	69.7	1	458	252720	0.5163	0.04	30586	0.996514	2.70
107	459	69.7	1	459	253179	0.5172	0.04	30587	0.996546	2.70
106	460	69.7	1	460	253639	0.5181	0.05	30588	0.996579	2.70
105	462	69.8	1	462	254101	0.5191	0.05	30589	0.996612	2.71
104	464	69.8	1	464	254565	0.5200	0.05	30590	0.996644	2.71
103	467	69.8	1	467	255032	0.5210	0.05	30591	0.996677	2.71
102	468	69.8	1	468	255500	0.5219	0.06	30592	0.996709	2.72
101	473	69.9	1	473	255973	0.5229	0.06	30593	0.996742	2.72
100	482	69.9	1	482	256455	0.5239	0.06	30594	0.996774	2.72
99	496	70.1	1	496	256951	0.5249	0.06	30595	0.996807	2.73
98	497	70.1	1	497	257448	0.5259	0.06	30596	0.996840	2.73
97	510	70.2	1	510	257958	0.5270	0.07	30597	0.996872	2.73
96	519	70.3	1	519	258477	0.5280	0.07	30598	0.996905	2.74
95	528	70.3	1	528	259005	0.5291	0.07	30599	0.996937	2.74
94	532	70.4	1	532	259537	0.5302	0.08	30600	0.996970	2.74
93	545	70.5	1	545	260082	0.5313	0.08	30601	0.997003	2.75
92	549	70.5	1	549	260631	0.5324	0.08	30602	0.997035	2.75
91	554	70.5	1	554	261185	0.5335	0.08	30603	0.997068	2.76
89– 90	568	70.6	2	1136	262321	0.5359	0.09	30605	0.997133	2.76
88	569	70.7	1	569	262890	0.5370	0.09	30606	0.997165	2.77
87	586	70.8	1	586	263476	0.5382	0.10	30607	0.997198	2.77
86	608	70.9	1	608	264084	0.5395	0.10	30608	0.997231	2.77
85	613	71.0	1	613	264697	0.5407	0.10	30609	0.997263	2.78
84	641	71.2	1	641	265338	0.5420	0.11	30610	0.997296	2.78
83	655	71.3	1	655	265993	0.5434	0.11	30611	0.997328	2.79
82	665	71.3	1	665	266658	0.5447	0.11	30612	0.997361	2.79
80– 81	666	71.3	2	1332	267990	0.5474	0.12	30614	0.997426	2.80
79	668	71.4	1	668	268658	0.5488	0.12	30615	0.997459	2.80
78	671	71.4	1	671	269329	0.5502	0.13	30616	0.997491	2.81
76– 77	676	71.4	2	1352	270681	0.5529	0.13	30618	0.997556	2.81
75	716	71.7	1	716	271397	0.5544	0.14	30619	0.997589	2.82
74	738	71.8	1	738	272135	0.5559	0.14	30620	0.997622	2.82
73	746	71.8	1	746	272881	0.5574	0.14	30621	0.997654	2.83
72	776	72.0	1	776	273657	0.5590	0.15	30622	0.997687	2.83
71	777	72.0	1	777	274434	0.5606	0.15	30623	0.997719	2.84
70	782	72.0	1	782	275216	0.5622	0.16	30624	0.997752	2.84
69	783	72.0	1	783	275999	0.5638	0.16	30625	0.997784	2.85
68	786	72.1	1	786	276785	0.5654	0.16	30626	0.997817	2.85
67	807	72.2	1	807	277592	0.5671	0.17	30627	0.997850	2.86
66	812	72.2	1	812	278404	0.5687	0.17	30628	0.997882	2.86
65	830	72.3	1	830	279234	0.5704	0.18	30629	0.997915	2.86
64	844	72.4	1	844	280078	0.5721	0.18	30630	0.997947	2.87
63	846	72.4	1	846	280924	0.5739	0.19	30631	0.997980	2.88
62	853	72.4	1	853	281777	0.5756	0.19	30632	0.998013	2.88
61	855	72.4	1	855	282632	0.5774	0.20	30633	0.998045	2.89
60	888	72.6	1	888	283520	0.5792	0.20	30634	0.998078	2.89
59	894	72.6	1	894	284414	0.5810	0.20	30635	0.998110	2.90
58	907	72.7	1	907	285321	0.5829	0.21	30636	0.998143	2.90
57	912	72.7	1	912	286233	0.5847	0.21	30637	0.998175	2.91
56	925	72.8	1	925	287158	0.5866	0.22	30638	0.998208	2.91
55	940	72.8	1	940	288098	0.5885	0.22	30639	0.998241	2.92
54	947	72.9	1	947	289045	0.5905	0.23	30640	0.998273	2.92
53	952	72.9	1	952	289997	0.5924	0.23	30641	0.998306	2.93
52	956	72.9	1	956	290953	0.5944	0.24	30642	0.998338	2.94
51	986	73.0	1	986	291939	0.5964	0.24	30643	0.998371	2.94
50	1007	73.1	1	1007	292946	0.5984	0.25	30644	0.998403	2.95
49	1008	73.1	1	1008	293954	0.6005	0.25	30645	0.998436	2.95
48	1009	73.1	1	1009	294963	0.6025	0.26	30646	0.998469	2.96
47	1076	73.4	1	1076	296039	0.6047	0.27	30647	0.998501	2.97
46	1100	73.5	1	1100	297139	0.6070	0.27	30648	0.998534	2.97
45	1101	73.5	1	1101	298240	0.6092	0.28	30649	0.998566	2.98
44	1134	73.7	1	1134	299374	0.6116	0.28	30650	0.998599	2.99
43	1166	73.8	1	1166	300540	0.6139	0.29	30651	0.998632	3.00
42	1173	73.8	1	1173	301713	0.6163	0.30	30652	0.998664	3.00
41	1203	73.9	1	1203	302916	0.6188	0.30	30653	0.998697	3.01
40	1243	74.0	1	1243	304159	0.6213	0.31	30654	0.998729	3.02
39	1261	74.1	1	1261	305420	0.6239	0.32	30655	0.998762	3.03
38	1320	74.3	1	1320	306740	0.6266	0.32	30656	0.998794	3.03
37	1374	74.5	1	1374	308114	0.6294	0.33	30657	0.998827	3.04
36	1392	74.5	1	1392	309506	0.6323	0.34	30658	0.998860	3.05
35	1421	74.6	1	1421	310927	0.6352	0.35	30659	0.998892	3.06
34	1454	74.7	1	1454	312381	0.6381	0.35	30660	0.998925	3.07
33	1684	75.4	1	1684	314065	0.6416	0.36	30661	0.998957	3.08
32	1690	75.4	1	1690	315755	0.6450	0.37	30662	0.998990	3.09
31	1708	75.4	1	1708	317463	0.6485	0.38	30663	0.999023	3.10
30	1730	75.5	1	1730	319193	0.6520	0.39	30664	0.999055	3.11
29	1794	75.6	1	1794	320987	0.6557	0.40	30665	0.999088	3.12
28	1896	75.9	1	1896	322883	0.6596	0.41	30666	0.999120	3.13
27	1945	76.0	1	1945	324828	0.6636	0.42	30667	0.999153	3.14
26	2053	76.2	1	2053	326881	0.6677	0.43	30668	0.999185	3.15
25	2068	76.3	1	2068	328949	0.6720	0.45	30669	0.999218	3.16
24	2076	76.3	1	2076	331025	0.6762	0.46	30670	0.999251	3.17
23	2310	76.7	1	2310	333335	0.6809	0.47	30671	0.999283	3.19
22	2347	76.8	1	2347	335682	0.6857	0.48	30672	0.999316	3.20
21	2503	77.1	1	2503	338185	0.6908	0.50	30673	0.999348	3.22
20	2660	77.4	1	2660	340845	0.6963	0.51	30674	0.999381	3.23
19	2863	77.7	1	2863	343708	0.7021	0.53	30675	0.999413	3.25
18	2953	77.8	1	2953	346661	0.7082	0.55	30676	0.999446	3.26
17	2955	77.8	1	2955	349616	0.7142	0.57	30677	0.999479	3.28
16	3040	77.9	1	3040	352656	0.7204	0.58	30678	0.999511	3.30
15	3119	78.0	1	3119	355775	0.7268	0.60	30679	0.999544	3.32
14	3122	78.0	1	3122	358897	0.7332	0.62	30680	0.999576	3.34
13	3699	78.8	1	3699	362596	0.7407	0.65	30681	0.999609	3.36
12	3714	78.8	1	3714	366310	0.7483	0.67	30682	0.999642	3.38
11	3887	79.0	1	3887	370197	0.7562	0.69	30683	0.999674	3.41
10	4027	79.2	1	4027	374224	0.7645	0.72	30684	0.999707	3.44
9	4162	79.3	1	4162	378386	0.7730	0.75	30685	0.999739	3.47
8	4765	79.9	1	4765	383151	0.7827	0.78	30686	0.999772	3.51
7	7026	81.6	1	7026	390177	0.7970	0.83	30687	0.999804	3.55
6	10302	83.2	1	10302	400479	0.8181	0.91	30688	0.999837	3.59
5	11705	83.8	1	11705	412184	0.8420	1.00	30689	0.999870	3.65
4	12320	84.0	1	12320	424504	0.8672	1.11	30690	0.999902	3.72
3	13219	84.3	1	13219	437723	0.8942	1.25	30691	0.999935	3.83
2	17042	85.4	1	17042	454765	0.9290	1.47	30692	0.999967	3.99
1	34762	88.5	1	34762	489527	1.0000	+INF.	30693	1.000000	+INF.

Rank	Occ. F	SFI	F	Tokens	Cum. Tokens	Cum. P Tokens	Y	Cum. Types	Cum. P Types	Z
7762-15985	1	50.9	8224	8224	8224	0.0675	-1.49	8224	0.514482	0.04
5168-7761	2	53.1	2594	5188	13412	0.1100	-1.23	10818	0.676759	0.46
3887-5167	3	54.6	1281	3843	17255	0.1416	-1.07	12099	0.756897	0.70
3080-3886	4	55.7	807	3228	20483	0.1681	-0.96	12906	0.807382	0.87
2563-3079	5	56.5	517	2585	23068	0.1893	-0.88	13423	0.839725	0.99
2170-2562	6	57.3	393	2358	25426	0.2086	-0.81	13816	0.864310	1.10
1910-2169	7	57.9	260	1820	27246	0.2235	-0.76	14076	0.880576	1.18
1666-1909	8	58.4	244	1952	29198	0.2396	-0.71	14320	0.895840	1.26
1485-1665	9	58.9	181	1629	30827	0.2529	-0.67	14501	0.907163	1.32
1326-1484	10	59.4	159	1590	32417	0.2660	-0.63	14660	0.917110	1.39
1210-1325	11	59.7	116	1276	33693	0.2764	-0.59	14776	0.924367	1.44
1090-1209	12	60.1	120	1440	35133	0.2883	-0.56	14896	0.931874	1.49
1005-1089	13	60.4	85	1105	36238	0.2973	-0.53	14981	0.937191	1.53
928-1004	14	60.8	77	1078	37316	0.3062	-0.51	15058	0.942008	1.57
871-927	15	61.0	57	855	38171	0.3132	-0.49	15115	0.945574	1.60
809-870	16	61.3	62	992	39163	0.3213	-0.46	15177	0.949453	1.64
759-808	17	61.6	50	850	40013	0.3283	-0.44	15227	0.952581	1.67
711-758	18	61.8	48	864	40877	0.3354	-0.43	15275	0.955583	1.70
674-710	19	62.0	37	703	41580	0.3412	-0.41	15312	0.957898	1.73
633-673	20	62.3	41	820	42400	0.3479	-0.39	15353	0.960463	1.76
599-632	21	62.5	34	714	43114	0.3537	-0.38	15387	0.962590	1.78
572-598	22	62.7	27	594	43708	0.3586	-0.36	15414	0.964279	1.80
545-571	23	62.9	27	621	44329	0.3637	-0.35	15441	0.965968	1.82
523-544	24	63.0	22	528	44857	0.3680	-0.34	15463	0.967344	1.84
489-522	25	63.2	34	850	45707	0.3750	-0.32	15497	0.969471	1.87
469-488	26	63.4	20	520	46227	0.3793	-0.31	15517	0.970722	1.89
439-468	27	63.5	30	810	47037	0.3859	-0.29	15547	0.972599	1.92
421-438	28	63.7	18	504	47541	0.3901	-0.28	15565	0.973725	1.94
409-420	29	63.8	12	348	47889	0.3929	-0.27	15577	0.974476	1.95
394-408	30	64.0	15	450	48339	0.3966	-0.26	15592	0.975414	1.97
381-393	31	64.1	13	403	48742	0.3999	-0.25	15605	0.976228	1.98
369-380	32	64.3	12	384	49126	0.4031	-0.25	15617	0.976978	1.99
355-368	33	64.4	14	462	49588	0.4069	-0.24	15631	0.977854	2.01
347-354	34	64.5	8	272	49860	0.4091	-0.23	15639	0.978355	2.02
334-346	35	64.6	13	455	50315	0.4128	-0.22	15652	0.979168	2.04
325-333	36	64.8	9	324	50639	0.4155	-0.21	15661	0.979731	2.05
314-324	37	64.9	11	407	51046	0.4188	-0.20	15672	0.980419	2.06
307-313	38	65.0	7	266	51312	0.4210	-0.20	15679	0.980857	2.07
301-306	39	65.1	6	234	51546	0.4229	-0.19	15685	0.981232	2.08
293-300	40	65.2	8	320	51866	0.4255	-0.19	15693	0.981733	2.09
285-292	41	65.3	8	328	52194	0.4282	-0.18	15701	0.982233	2.10
280-284	42	65.4	5	210	52404	0.4300	-0.18	15706	0.982546	2.11
272-279	43	65.5	8	344	52748	0.4328	-0.17	15714	0.983047	2.12
264-271	44	65.6	8	352	53100	0.4357	-0.16	15722	0.983547	2.13
255-263	45	65.7	9	405	53505	0.4390	-0.15	15731	0.984110	2.15
252-254	46	65.8	3	138	53643	0.4401	-0.15	15734	0.984298	2.15
243-251	47	65.9	9	423	54066	0.4436	-0.14	15743	0.984861	2.17
237-242	48	66.0	6	288	54354	0.4460	-0.14	15749	0.985236	2.18
234-236	49	66.1	3	147	54501	0.4472	-0.13	15752	0.985424	2.18
229-233	50	66.2	5	250	54751	0.4492	-0.13	15757	0.985737	2.19
224-228	51	66.3	5	255	55006	0.4513	-0.12	15762	0.986049	2.20
222-223	52	66.3	2	104	55110	0.4522	-0.12	15764	0.986175	2.20
219-221	53	66.4	3	159	55269	0.4535	-0.12	15767	0.986362	2.21
214-218	54	66.5	5	270	55539	0.4557	-0.11	15772	0.986675	2.22
212-213	55	66.6	2	110	55649	0.4566	-0.11	15774	0.986800	2.22
207-211	56	66.7	5	280	55929	0.4589	-0.10	15779	0.987113	2.23
205-206	57	66.7	2	114	56043	0.4598	-0.10	15781	0.987238	2.23
202-204	58	66.8	3	174	56217	0.4612	-0.10	15784	0.987426	2.24
201	59	66.9	1	59	56276	0.4617	-0.10	15785	0.987488	2.24
199-200	60	67.0	2	120	56396	0.4627	-0.09	15787	0.987613	2.24
196-198	61	67.0	3	183	56579	0.4642	-0.09	15790	0.987801	2.25
194-195	62	67.1	2	124	56703	0.4652	-0.09	15792	0.987926	2.25
190-193	63	67.2	4	252	56955	0.4673	-0.08	15796	0.988176	2.26
189	64	67.2	1	64	57019	0.4678	-0.08	15797	0.988239	2.26
185-188	65	67.3	4	260	57279	0.4700	-0.08	15801	0.988489	2.27
180-184	67	67.4	5	335	57614	0.4727	-0.07	15806	0.988802	2.28
175-179	68	67.5	5	340	57954	0.4755	-0.06	15811	0.989115	2.29
174	69	67.6	1	69	58023	0.4761	-0.06	15812	0.989177	2.30
170-173	70	67.6	4	280	58303	0.4784	-0.05	15816	0.989428	2.31
166-169	71	67.7	4	284	58587	0.4807	-0.05	15820	0.989678	2.31
165	72	67.7	1	72	58659	0.4813	-0.05	15821	0.989740	2.32
160-164	73	67.8	5	365	59024	0.4843	-0.04	15826	0.990053	2.33
159	74	67.9	1	74	59098	0.4849	-0.04	15827	0.990116	2.33
157-158	75	67.9	2	150	59248	0.4861	-0.03	15829	0.990241	2.34
154-156	76	68.0	3	228	59476	0.4880	-0.03	15832	0.990429	2.34
152-153	77	68.0	2	154	59630	0.4893	-0.03	15834	0.990554	2.35
151	78	68.1	1	78	59708	0.4899	-0.03	15835	0.990616	2.35
147-150	79	68.1	4	316	60024	0.4925	-0.02	15839	0.990866	2.36
146	81	68.3	1	81	60105	0.4931	-0.02	15840	0.990929	2.36
144-145	82	68.3	2	164	60269	0.4945	-0.01	15842	0.991054	2.37
142-143	83	68.4	2	166	60435	0.4959	-0.01	15844	0.991179	2.37
141	84	68.4	1	84	60519	0.4965	-0.01	15845	0.991242	2.38
140	85	68.5	1	85	60604	0.4972	-0.01	15846	0.991304	2.38
137-139	86	68.5	3	258	60862	0.4994	-0.00	15849	0.991492	2.39
136	87	68.6	1	87	60949	0.5001	0.00	15850	0.991555	2.39
135	88	68.6	1	88	61037	0.5008	0.00	15851	0.991617	2.39
134	89	68.7	1	89	61126	0.5015	0.00	15852	0.991680	2.39
132-133	91	68.8	2	182	61308	0.5030	0.01	15854	0.991805	2.40
131	92	68.8	1	92	61400	0.5038	0.01	15855	0.991867	2.40
129-130	93	68.8	2	186	61586	0.5053	0.01	15857	0.991992	2.41
128	94	68.9	1	94	61680	0.5061	0.02	15858	0.992055	2.41
124-127	95	68.9	4	380	62060	0.5092	0.02	15862	0.992305	2.42
122-123	96	69.0	2	192	62252	0.5108	0.03	15864	0.992430	2.43
121	97	69.0	1	97	62349	0.5116	0.03	15865	0.992493	2.43
119-120	100	69.2	2	200	62549	0.5132	0.03	15867	0.992618	2.44
118	103	69.3	1	103	62652	0.5140	0.04	15868	0.992681	2.44
117	105	69.4	1	105	62757	0.5149	0.04	15869	0.992743	2.44
113-116	106	69.4	4	424	63181	0.5184	0.05	15873	0.992993	2.46
110-112	107	69.5	3	321	63502	0.5210	0.05	15876	0.993181	2.47
109	108	69.5	1	108	63610	0.5219	0.05	15877	0.993244	2.47
107-108	109	69.5	2	218	63828	0.5237	0.06	15879	0.993369	2.48
106	113	69.7	1	113	63941	0.5246	0.06	15880	0.993431	2.48
105	114	69.7	1	114	64055	0.5256	0.06	15881	0.993494	2.48
104	116	69.8	1	116	64171	0.5265	0.07	15882	0.993556	2.49
103	118	69.9	1	118	64289	0.5275	0.07	15883	0.993619	2.49
102	119	69.9	1	119	64408	0.5285	0.07	15884	0.993682	2.49
101	120	70.0	1	120	64528	0.5294	0.07	15885	0.993744	2.50
99-100	121	70.0	2	242	64770	0.5314	0.08	15887	0.993869	2.50
98	126	70.2	1	126	64896	0.5325	0.08	15888	0.993932	2.51
96-97	127	70.2	2	254	65150	0.5345	0.09	15890	0.994057	2.52
94-95	128	70.2	2	256	65406	0.5366	0.09	15892	0.994182	2.52
93	130	70.3	1	130	65536	0.5377	0.09	15893	0.994245	2.53
92	131	70.3	1	131	65667	0.5388	0.10	15894	0.994307	2.53
91	133	70.4	1	133	65800	0.5399	0.10	15895	0.994370	2.53
89-90	134	70.4	2	268	66068	0.5421	0.11	15897	0.994495	2.54
88	135	70.5	1	135	66203	0.5432	0.11	15898	0.994557	2.55
87	139	70.6	1	139	66342	0.5443	0.11	15899	0.994620	2.55
85-86	142	70.7	2	284	66626	0.5467	0.12	15901	0.994745	2.56
84	143	70.7	1	143	66769	0.5478	0.12	15902	0.994808	2.56
82-83	146	70.8	2	292	67061	0.5502	0.13	15904	0.994933	2.57
81	147	70.8	1	147	67208	0.5514	0.13	15905	0.994995	2.58
80	154	71.0	1	154	67362	0.5527	0.13	15906	0.995058	2.58
79	163	71.3	1	163	67525	0.5540	0.14	15907	0.995120	2.58
78	164	71.3	1	164	67689	0.5554	0.14	15908	0.995183	2.59
75-77	166	71.4	3	498	68187	0.5595	0.15	15911	0.995371	2.60
73-74	168	71.4	2	336	68523	0.5622	0.16	15913	0.995496	2.61
72	171	71.5	1	171	68694	0.5636	0.16	15914	0.995558	2.62
71	172	71.5	1	172	68866	0.5650	0.16	15915	0.995621	2.62
70	177	71.6	1	177	69043	0.5665	0.17	15916	0.995683	2.63
69	178	71.7	1	178	69221	0.5679	0.17	15917	0.995746	2.63
68	183	71.8	1	183	69404	0.5694	0.17	15918	0.995809	2.64
67	188	71.9	1	188	69592	0.5710	0.18	15919	0.995871	2.64
66	195	72.1	1	195	69787	0.5726	0.18	15920	0.995934	2.65
65	198	72.1	1	198	69985	0.5742	0.19	15921	0.995996	2.65
64	200	72.2	1	200	70185	0.5759	0.19	15922	0.996059	2.66
63	201	72.2	1	201	70386	0.5775	0.20	15923	0.996121	2.66
62	209	72.4	1	209	70595	0.5792	0.20	15924	0.996184	2.67
61	210	72.4	1	210	70805	0.5809	0.20	15925	0.996246	2.67
60	219	72.6	1	219	71024	0.5827	0.21	15926	0.996309	2.68
59	220	72.6	1	220	71244	0.5845	0.21	15927	0.996372	2.68
58	229	72.7	1	229	71473	0.5864	0.22	15928	0.996434	2.69
57	234	72.8	1	234	71707	0.5883	0.22	15929	0.996497	2.70
56	235	72.9	1	235	71942	0.5903	0.23	15930	0.996559	2.70
54-55	250	73.1	2	500	72442	0.5944	0.24	15932	0.996684	2.71
53	253	73.2	1	253	72695	0.5964	0.24	15933	0.996747	2.72
52	255	73.2	1	255	72950	0.5985	0.25	15934	0.996809	2.73
51	258	73.3	1	258	73208	0.6007	0.26	15935	0.996872	2.73
50	259	73.3	1	259	73467	0.6028	0.26	15936	0.996935	2.74
49	262	73.3	1	262	73729	0.6049	0.27	15937	0.996997	2.75
47-48	263	73.3	2	526	74255	0.6092	0.28	15939	0.997122	2.76
46	264	73.4	1	264	74519	0.6114	0.28	15940	0.997185	2.77
45	265	73.4	1	265	74784	0.6136	0.29	15941	0.997247	2.78
44	278	73.6	1	278	75062	0.6159	0.29	15942	0.997310	2.78
43	282	73.7	1	282	75344	0.6182	0.30	15943	0.997373	2.79
42	290	73.8	1	290	75634	0.6206	0.31	15944	0.997435	2.80
41	304	74.0	1	304	75938	0.6231	0.31	15945	0.997498	2.81
40	317	74.2	1	317	76255	0.6257	0.32	15946	0.997560	2.81
39	326	74.3	1	326	76581	0.6283	0.33	15947	0.997623	2.82
38	330	74.3	1	330	76911	0.6310	0.33	15948	0.997685	2.83
37	345	74.5	1	345	77256	0.6339	0.34	15949	0.997748	2.84
36	346	74.5	1	346	77602	0.6367	0.35	15950	0.997810	2.85
35	371	74.8	1	371	77973	0.6398	0.36	15951	0.997873	2.86
34	387	75.0	1	387	78360	0.6429	0.37	15952	0.997936	2.87
33	397	75.1	1	397	78757	0.6462	0.38	15953	0.997998	2.88
32	407	75.2	1	407	79164	0.6495	0.38	15954	0.998061	2.89
31	431	75.5	1	431	79595	0.6531	0.39	15955	0.998123	2.90
30	438	75.6	1	438	80033	0.6567	0.40	15956	0.998186	2.91
29	446	75.6	1	446	80479	0.6603	0.41	15957	0.998248	2.92
28	479	75.9	1	479	80958	0.6642	0.42	15958	0.998311	2.93
27	499	76.1	1	499	81457	0.6683	0.44	15959	0.998373	2.94
26	504	76.2	1	504	81961	0.6725	0.45	15960	0.998436	2.95
25	528	76.4	1	528	82489	0.6768	0.46	15961	0.998499	2.97
24	533	76.4	1	533	83022	0.6812	0.47	15962	0.998561	2.98
23	571	76.7	1	571	83593	0.6859	0.48	15963	0.998624	2.99
22	580	76.8	1	580	84173	0.6906	0.50	15964	0.998686	3.01
21	608	77.0	1	608	84781	0.6956	0.51	15965	0.998749	3.02
20	617	77.0	1	617	85398	0.7007	0.53	15966	0.998811	3.04
19	620	77.1	1	620	86018	0.7058	0.54	15967	0.998874	3.05
18	627	77.1	1	627	86645	0.7109	0.56	15968	0.998936	3.07
17	655	77.3	1	655	87300	0.7163	0.57	15969	0.998999	3.09
16	743	77.9	1	743	88043	0.7224	0.59	15970	0.999062	3.11
15	792	78.1	1	792	88835	0.7289	0.61	15971	0.999124	3.13
14	816	78.3	1	816	89651	0.7356	0.63	15972	0.999187	3.15
12-13	817	78.3	2	1634	91285	0.7490	0.67	15974	0.999312	3.20
11	852	78.4	1	852	92137	0.7560	0.69	15975	0.999374	3.23
10	968	79.0	1	968	93105	0.7639	0.72	15976	0.999437	3.26
9	1057	79.4	1	1057	94162	0.7726	0.75	15977	0.999499	3.29
8	1162	79.8	1	1162	95324	0.7821	0.78	15978	0.999562	3.33
7	1549	81.0	1	1549	96873	0.7948	0.82	15979	0.999625	3.37
6	2497	83.1	1	2497	99370	0.8153	0.90	15980	0.999687	3.42
5	2871	83.7	1	2871	102241	0.8389	0.99	15981	0.999750	3.48
4	3217	84.2	1	3217	105458	0.8653	1.10	15982	0.999812	3.56
3	3404	84.5	1	3404	108862	0.8932	1.24	15983	0.999875	3.66
2	4418	85.6	1	4418	113280	0.9294	1.47	15984	0.999937	3.84
1	8600	88.5	1	8600	121880	1.0000	+INF.	15985	1.000000	+INF.

Rank	Occ. F	SFI	F	Tokens	Cum. Tokens	Cum. P Tokens	Y	Cum. Types	Cum. P Types	Z
20585-33296	1	41.0	12712	12712	12712	0.0107	-2.30	12712	0.381788	-0.30
15866-20584	2	43.2	4719	9438	22150	0.0187	-2.08	17431	0.523516	0.06
13183-15865	3	44.7	2683	8049	30199	0.0255	-1.95	20114	0.604097	0.26
11408-13182	4	45.8	1775	7100	37299	0.0315	-1.86	21889	0.657406	0.41
10065-11407	5	46.7	1343	6715	44014	0.0372	-1.78	23232	0.697741	0.52
9111-10064	6	47.4	954	5724	49738	0.0420	-1.73	24186	0.726394	0.60
8287- 9110	7	48.0	824	5768	55506	0.0469	-1.68	25010	0.751141	0.68
7617- 8286	8	48.6	670	5360	60866	0.0515	-1.63	25680	0.771264	0.74
7099- 7616	9	49.0	518	4662	65528	0.0554	-1.59	26198	0.786821	0.80
6631- 7098	10	49.5	468	4680	70208	0.0593	-1.56	26666	0.800877	0.84
6241- 6630	11	49.9	390	4290	74498	0.0630	-1.53	27056	0.812590	0.89
5894- 6240	12	50.2	347	4164	78662	0.0665	-1.50	27403	0.823012	0.93
5600- 5893	13	50.6	294	3822	82484	0.0697	-1.48	27697	0.831842	0.96
5306- 5599	14	50.9	294	4116	86600	0.0732	-1.45	27991	0.840672	1.00
5071- 5305	15	51.2	235	3525	90125	0.0762	-1.43	28226	0.847729	1.03
4875- 5070	16	51.4	196	3136	93261	0.0788	-1.41	28422	0.853616	1.05
4676- 4874	17	51.7	199	3383	96644	0.0817	-1.39	28621	0.859593	1.08
4483- 4675	18	51.9	193	3474	100118	0.0846	-1.37	28814	0.865389	1.10
4317- 4482	19	52.2	166	3154	103272	0.0873	-1.36	28980	0.870375	1.13
4168- 4316	20	52.4	149	2980	106252	0.0898	-1.34	29129	0.874850	1.15
4005- 4167	21	52.6	163	3423	109675	0.0927	-1.32	29292	0.879745	1.17
3864- 4004	22	52.8	141	3102	112777	0.0953	-1.31	29433	0.883980	1.20
3732- 3863	23	53.0	132	3036	115813	0.0979	-1.29	29565	0.887944	1.22
3618- 3731	24	53.2	114	2736	118549	0.1002	-1.28	29679	0.891368	1.23
3520- 3617	25	53.3	98	2450	120999	0.1023	-1.27	29777	0.894312	1.25
3419- 3519	26	53.5	101	2626	123625	0.1045	-1.26	29878	0.897345	1.27
3325- 3418	27	53.7	94	2538	126163	0.1066	-1.24	29972	0.900168	1.28
3247- 3324	28	53.8	78	2184	128347	0.1085	-1.23	30050	0.902511	1.30
3147- 3246	29	54.0	100	2900	131247	0.1109	-1.22	30150	0.905514	1.31
3058- 3146	30	54.1	89	2670	133917	0.1132	-1.21	30239	0.908187	1.33
2983- 3057	31	54.3	75	2325	136242	0.1152	-1.20	30314	0.910440	1.34
2907- 2982	32	54.4	76	2432	138674	0.1172	-1.19	30390	0.912722	1.36
2835- 2906	33	54.5	72	2376	141050	0.1192	-1.18	30462	0.914885	1.37
2772- 2834	34	54.6	63	2142	143192	0.1210	-1.17	30525	0.916777	1.38
2704- 2771	35	54.8	68	2380	145572	0.1231	-1.16	30593	0.918819	1.40
2647- 2703	36	54.9	57	2052	147624	0.1248	-1.15	30650	0.920531	1.41
2590- 2646	37	55.0	57	2109	149733	0.1266	-1.14	30707	0.922243	1.42
2539- 2589	38	55.1	51	1938	151671	0.1282	-1.13	30758	0.923775	1.43
2496- 2538	39	55.2	43	1677	153348	0.1296	-1.13	30801	0.925066	1.44
2449- 2495	40	55.3	47	1880	155228	0.1312	-1.12	30848	0.926478	1.45
2399- 2448	41	55.5	50	2050	157278	0.1330	-1.11	30898	0.927979	1.46
2356- 2398	42	55.6	43	1806	159084	0.1345	-1.11	30941	0.929271	1.47
2315- 2355	43	55.7	41	1763	160847	0.1360	-1.10	30982	0.930502	1.48
2263- 2314	44	55.8	52	2288	163135	0.1379	-1.09	31034	0.932064	1.49
2227- 2262	45	55.9	36	1620	164755	0.1393	-1.08	31070	0.933145	1.50
2199- 2226	46	55.9	28	1288	166043	0.1404	-1.08	31098	0.933986	1.51
2165- 2198	47	56.0	34	1598	167641	0.1417	-1.07	31132	0.935007	1.51
2128- 2164	48	56.1	37	1776	169417	0.1432	-1.07	31169	0.936118	1.52
2101- 2127	49	56.2	27	1323	170740	0.1443	-1.06	31196	0.936929	1.53
2073- 2100	50	56.3	28	1400	172140	0.1455	-1.06	31224	0.937770	1.54
2036- 2072	51	56.4	37	1887	174027	0.1471	-1.05	31261	0.938882	1.55
2006- 2035	52	56.5	30	1560	175587	0.1484	-1.04	31291	0.939783	1.55
1978- 2005	53	56.6	28	1484	177071	0.1497	-1.04	31319	0.940623	1.56
1953- 1977	54	56.6	25	1350	178421	0.1508	-1.03	31344	0.941374	1.57
1902- 1952	55	56.7	51	2805	181226	0.1532	-1.02	31395	0.942906	1.58
1880- 1901	56	56.8	22	1232	182458	0.1542	-1.02	31417	0.943567	1.59
1851- 1879	57	56.9	29	1653	184111	0.1556	-1.01	31446	0.944438	1.59
1825- 1850	58	56.9	26	1508	185619	0.1569	-1.01	31472	0.945219	1.60
1808- 1824	59	57.0	17	1003	186622	0.1578	-1.00	31489	0.945729	1.60
1787- 1807	60	57.1	21	1260	187882	0.1588	-1.00	31510	0.946360	1.61
1769- 1786	61	57.2	18	1098	188980	0.1598	-1.00	31528	0.946900	1.62
1740- 1768	62	57.2	29	1798	190778	0.1613	-0.99	31557	0.947771	1.62
1717- 1739	63	57.3	23	1449	192227	0.1625	-0.98	31580	0.948462	1.63
1702- 1716	64	57.4	15	960	193187	0.1633	-0.98	31595	0.948913	1.63
1681- 1701	65	57.4	21	1365	194552	0.1645	-0.98	31616	0.949543	1.64
1654- 1680	66	57.5	27	1782	196334	0.1660	-0.97	31643	0.950354	1.65
1634- 1653	67	57.6	20	1340	197674	0.1671	-0.97	31663	0.950955	1.65
1612- 1633	68	57.6	22	1496	199170	0.1684	-0.96	31685	0.951616	1.66
1594- 1611	69	57.7	18	1242	200412	0.1694	-0.96	31703	0.952156	1.67
1577- 1593	70	57.8	17	1190	201602	0.1704	-0.95	31720	0.952667	1.67
1555- 1576	71	57.8	22	1562	203164	0.1717	-0.95	31742	0.953328	1.68
1540- 1554	72	57.9	15	1080	204244	0.1727	-0.94	31757	0.953778	1.68
1515- 1539	73	57.9	25	1825	206069	0.1742	-0.94	31782	0.954529	1.69
1502- 1514	74	58.0	13	962	207031	0.1750	-0.93	31795	0.954919	1.69
1483- 1501	75	58.0	19	1425	208456	0.1762	-0.93	31814	0.955490	1.70
1463- 1482	76	58.1	20	1520	209976	0.1775	-0.92	31834	0.956091	1.71
1449- 1462	77	58.2	14	1078	211054	0.1784	-0.92	31848	0.956511	1.71
1438- 1448	78	58.2	11	858	211912	0.1791	-0.92	31859	0.956842	1.72
1427- 1437	79	58.3	11	869	212781	0.1799	-0.92	31870	0.957172	1.72
1410- 1426	80	58.3	17	1360	214141	0.1810	-0.91	31887	0.957683	1.73
1400- 1409	81	58.4	10	810	214951	0.1817	-0.91	31897	0.957983	1.73
1386- 1399	82	58.4	14	1148	216099	0.1827	-0.91	31911	0.958403	1.73
1375- 1385	83	58.5	11	913	217012	0.1834	-0.90	31922	0.958734	1.74
1361- 1374	84	58.5	14	1176	218188	0.1844	-0.90	31936	0.959154	1.74
1350- 1360	85	58.6	11	935	219123	0.1852	-0.90	31947	0.959485	1.74
1341- 1349	86	58.6	9	774	219897	0.1859	-0.89	31956	0.959755	1.75
1333- 1340	87	58.7	8	696	220593	0.1865	-0.89	31964	0.959995	1.75
1321- 1332	88	58.7	12	1056	221649	0.1874	-0.89	31976	0.960356	1.75
1305- 1320	89	58.8	16	1424	223073	0.1886	-0.88	31992	0.960836	1.76
1296- 1304	90	58.8	9	810	223883	0.1893	-0.88	32001	0.961106	1.76
1284- 1295	91	58.9	12	1092	224975	0.1902	-0.88	32013	0.961467	1.77
1278- 1283	92	58.9	6	552	225527	0.1906	-0.88	32019	0.961647	1.77
1262- 1277	93	59.0	16	1488	227015	0.1919	-0.87	32035	0.962128	1.78
1252- 1261	94	59.0	10	940	227955	0.1927	-0.87	32045	0.962428	1.78
1244- 1251	95	59.1	8	760	228715	0.1933	-0.87	32053	0.962668	1.78
1234- 1243	96	59.1	10	960	229675	0.1942	-0.86	32063	0.962968	1.79
1218- 1233	97	59.2	16	1552	231227	0.1955	-0.86	32079	0.963449	1.79
1212- 1217	98	59.2	6	588	231815	0.1960	-0.86	32085	0.963629	1.79
1203- 1211	99	59.2	9	891	232706	0.1967	-0.85	32094	0.963900	1.80
1193- 1202	100	59.3	10	1000	233706	0.1976	-0.85	32104	0.964200	1.80
1185- 1192	101	59.3	8	808	234514	0.1982	-0.85	32112	0.964440	1.80
1178- 1184	102	59.4	7	714	235228	0.1988	-0.85	32119	0.964650	1.81
1167- 1177	103	59.4	11	1133	236361	0.1998	-0.84	32130	0.964981	1.81
1158- 1166	104	59.5	9	936	237297	0.2006	-0.84	32139	0.965251	1.82
1150- 1157	105	59.5	8	840	238137	0.2013	-0.84	32147	0.965491	1.82
1140- 1149	106	59.5	10	1060	239197	0.2022	-0.83	32157	0.965792	1.82
1136- 1139	107	59.6	4	428	239625	0.2026	-0.83	32161	0.965912	1.82
1126- 1135	108	59.6	10	1080	240705	0.2035	-0.83	32171	0.966212	1.83
1114- 1125	109	59.7	12	1308	242013	0.2046	-0.83	32183	0.966573	1.83
1104- 1113	110	59.7	10	1100	243113	0.2055	-0.82	32193	0.966873	1.84
1094- 1103	111	59.7	10	1110	244223	0.2064	-0.82	32203	0.967173	1.84
1085- 1093	112	59.8	9	1008	245231	0.2073	-0.82	32212	0.967444	1.84
1077- 1084	113	59.8	8	904	246135	0.2081	-0.81	32220	0.967684	1.85
1068- 1076	114	59.9	9	1026	247161	0.2089	-0.81	32229	0.967954	1.85
1062- 1067	115	59.9	6	690	247851	0.2095	-0.81	32235	0.968134	1.85
1054- 1061	116	59.9	8	928	248779	0.2103	-0.81	32243	0.968375	1.86
1044- 1053	117	60.0	10	1170	249949	0.2113	-0.80	32253	0.968675	1.86
1037- 1043	118	60.0	7	826	250775	0.2120	-0.80	32260	0.968885	1.86
1031- 1036	119	60.0	6	714	251489	0.2126	-0.80	32266	0.969065	1.87
1019- 1030	120	60.1	12	1440	252929	0.2138	-0.79	32278	0.969426	1.87
1010- 1018	121	60.1	9	1089	254018	0.2147	-0.79	32287	0.969696	1.88
1007- 1009	122	60.2	3	366	254384	0.2150	-0.79	32290	0.969786	1.88
1001- 1006	123	60.2	6	738	255122	0.2157	-0.79	32296	0.969966	1.88
992- 1000	124	60.2	9	1116	256238	0.2166	-0.78	32305	0.970237	1.88
989- 991	125	60.3	3	375	256613	0.2169	-0.78	32308	0.970327	1.89
984- 988	126	60.3	5	630	257243	0.2175	-0.78	32313	0.970477	1.89
976- 983	127	60.3	8	1016	258259	0.2183	-0.78	32321	0.970717	1.89
971- 975	128	60.4	5	640	258899	0.2189	-0.78	32326	0.970867	1.89
965- 970	129	60.4	6	774	259673	0.2195	-0.77	32332	0.971048	1.90
959- 964	130	60.4	6	780	260453	0.2202	-0.77	32338	0.971228	1.90
948- 958	131	60.5	11	1441	261894	0.2214	-0.77	32349	0.971558	1.90
941- 947	132	60.5	7	924	262818	0.2222	-0.76	32356	0.971768	1.91
933- 940	133	60.5	8	1064	263882	0.2231	-0.76	32364	0.972009	1.91
926- 932	134	60.6	7	938	264820	0.2239	-0.76	32371	0.972219	1.91
923- 925	135	60.6	3	405	265225	0.2242	-0.76	32374	0.972309	1.92
918- 922	136	60.6	5	680	265905	0.2248	-0.76	32379	0.972459	1.92
910- 917	137	60.7	8	1096	267001	0.2257	-0.75	32387	0.972699	1.92
901- 909	138	60.7	9	1242	268243	0.2268	-0.75	32396	0.972970	1.93
895- 900	139	60.7	6	834	269077	0.2275	-0.75	32402	0.973150	1.93
891- 894	140	60.7	4	560	269637	0.2279	-0.75	32406	0.973270	1.93
887- 890	141	60.8	4	564	270201	0.2284	-0.74	32410	0.973390	1.93
883- 886	142	60.8	4	568	270769	0.2289	-0.74	32414	0.973510	1.94
876- 882	143	60.8	7	1001	271770	0.2297	-0.74	32421	0.973721	1.94
870- 875	144	60.9	6	864	272634	0.2305	-0.74	32427	0.973901	1.94
868- 869	145	60.9	2	290	272924	0.2307	-0.74	32429	0.973961	1.94
860- 867	146	60.9	8	1168	274092	0.2317	-0.73	32437	0.974201	1.95
851- 859	147	61.0	9	1323	275415	0.2328	-0.73	32446	0.974471	1.95
842- 850	148	61.0	9	1332	276747	0.2339	-0.73	32455	0.974742	1.96
836- 841	149	61.0	6	894	277641	0.2347	-0.72	32461	0.974922	1.96
833- 835	150	61.0	3	450	278091	0.2351	-0.72	32464	0.975012	1.96
828- 832	151	61.1	5	755	278846	0.2357	-0.72	32469	0.975162	1.96
821- 827	152	61.1	7	1064	279910	0.2366	-0.72	32476	0.975372	1.97
820	153	61.1	1	153	280063	0.2367	-0.72	32477	0.975402	1.97
818- 819	154	61.2	2	308	280371	0.2370	-0.72	32479	0.975462	1.97
812- 817	155	61.2	6	930	281301	0.2378	-0.71	32485	0.975643	1.97
809- 811	156	61.2	3	468	281769	0.2382	-0.71	32488	0.975733	1.97
805- 808	157	61.2	4	628	282397	0.2387	-0.71	32492	0.975853	1.97
799- 804	158	61.3	6	948	283345	0.2395	-0.71	32498	0.976033	1.98
793- 798	159	61.3	6	954	284299	0.2403	-0.71	32504	0.976213	1.98
788- 792	160	61.3	5	800	285099	0.2410	-0.70	32509	0.976363	1.98
784- 787	161	61.4	4	644	285743	0.2415	-0.70	32513	0.976484	1.99
781- 783	162	61.4	3	486	286229	0.2420	-0.70	32516	0.976574	1.99
776- 780	163	61.4	5	815	287044	0.2426	-0.70	32521	0.976724	1.99
774- 775	164	61.4	2	328	287372	0.2429	-0.70	32523	0.976784	1.99
771- 773	165	61.5	3	495	287867	0.2433	-0.70	32526	0.976874	1.99
768- 770	166	61.5	3	498	288365	0.2438	-0.69	32529	0.976964	1.99
765- 767	167	61.5	3	501	288866	0.2442	-0.69	32532	0.977054	2.00
761- 764	168	61.5	4	672	289538	0.2448	-0.69	32536	0.977174	2.00
758- 760	170	61.6	3	510	290048	0.2452	-0.69	32539	0.977265	2.00
753- 757	171	61.6	5	855	290903	0.2459	-0.69	32544	0.977415	2.00
752	172	61.6	1	172	291075	0.2461	-0.69	32545	0.977445	2.00
748- 751	173	61.7	4	692	291767	0.2466	-0.69	32549	0.977565	2.01
743- 747	174	61.7	5	870	292637	0.2474	-0.68	32554	0.977715	2.01
740- 742	175	61.7	3	525	293162	0.2478	-0.68	32557	0.977805	2.01
737- 739	176	61.7	3	528	293690	0.2483	-0.68	32560	0.977895	2.01
734- 736	177	61.8	3	531	294221	0.2487	-0.68	32563	0.977985	2.01
733	178	61.8	1	178	294399	0.2489	-0.68	32564	0.978015	2.01
728- 732	179	61.8	5	895	295294	0.2496	-0.68	32569	0.978166	2.02
721- 727	180	61.8	7	1260	296554	0.2507	-0.67	32576	0.978376	2.02
718- 720	181	61.9	3	543	297097	0.2511	-0.67	32579	0.978466	2.02
717	183	61.9	1	183	297280	0.2513	-0.67	32580	0.978496	2.02
712- 716	184	61.9	5	920	298200	0.2521	-0.67	32585	0.978646	2.03
707- 711	185	62.0	5	925	299125	0.2529	-0.67	32590	0.978796	2.03
704- 706	186	62.0	3	558	299683	0.2533	-0.66	32593	0.978886	2.03
701- 703	187	62.0	3	561	300244	0.2538	-0.66	32596	0.978976	2.03
697- 700	188	62.0	4	752	300996	0.2544	-0.66	32600	0.979097	2.04
692- 696	189	62.0	5	945	301941	0.2552	-0.66	32605	0.979247	2.04
691	190	62.1	1	190	302131	0.2554	-0.66	32606	0.979277	2.04
689- 690	191	62.1	2	382	302513	0.2557	-0.66	32608	0.979337	2.04
682- 688	192	62.1	7	1344	303857	0.2569	-0.65	32615	0.979547	2.04
680- 681	193	62.1	2	386	304243	0.2572	-0.65	32617	0.979607	2.05
676- 679	194	62.2	4	776	305019	0.2578	-0.65	32621	0.979727	2.05
672- 675	195	62.2	4	780	305799	0.2585	-0.65	32625	0.979847	2.05
668- 671	196	62.2	4	784	306583	0.2592	-0.65	32629	0.979968	2.05
662- 667	197	62.2	6	1182	307765	0.2602	-0.64	32635	0.980148	2.06
661	198	62.2	1	198	307963	0.2603	-0.64	32636	0.980178	2.06
658- 660	199	62.3	3	597	308560	0.2608	-0.64	32639	0.980268	2.06
656- 657	200	62.3	2	400	308960	0.2612	-0.64	32641	0.980328	2.06
651- 655	201	62.3	5	1005	309965	0.2620	-0.64	32646	0.980478	2.06
649- 650	202	62.3	2	404	310369	0.2624	-0.64	32648	0.980538	2.06
646- 648	203	62.4	3	609	310978	0.2629	-0.63	32651	0.980628	2.07
645	204	62.4	1	204	311182	0.2631	-0.63	32652	0.980658	2.07
644	205	62.4	1	205	311387	0.2632	-0.63	32653	0.980688	2.07
640- 643	206	62.4	4	824	312211	0.2639	-0.63	32657	0.980808	2.07
638- 639	207	62.4	2	414	312625	0.2643	-0.63	32659	0.980869	2.07
634- 637	208	62.5	4	832	313457	0.2650	-0.63	32663	0.980989	2.07
631- 633	209	62.5	3	627	314084	0.2655	-0.63	32666	0.981079	2.08
628- 630	210	62.5	3	630	314714	0.2660	-0.62	32669	0.981169	2.08
623- 627	211	62.5	5	1055	315769	0.2669	-0.62	32674	0.981319	2.08
620- 622	212	62.5	3	636	316405	0.2675	-0.62	32677	0.981409	2.08
618- 619	213	62.6	2	426	316831	0.2678	-0.62	32679	0.981469	2.09
616- 617	214	62.6	2	428	317259	0.2682	-0.62	32681	0.981529	2.09
610- 615	215	62.6	6	1290	318549	0.2693	-0.61	32687	0.981709	2.09
609	217	62.6	1	217	318766	0.2695	-0.61	32688	0.981740	2.09
605- 608	218	62.7	4	872	319638	0.2702	-0.61	32692	0.981860	2.09
604	219	62.7	1	219	319857	0.2704	-0.61	32693	0.981890	2.09
600- 603	220	62.7	4	880	320737	0.2711	-0.61	32697	0.982010	2.10
599	221	62.7	1	221	320958	0.2713	-0.61	32698	0.982040	2.10
597- 598	222	62.7	2	444	321402	0.2717	-0.61	32700	0.982100	2.10
595- 596	223	62.8	2	446	321848	0.2721	-0.61	32702	0.982160	2.10
589- 594	224	62.8	6	1344	323192	0.2732	-0.60	32708	0.982340	2.10
588	225	62.8	1	225	323417	0.2734	-0.60	32709	0.982370	2.11
586- 587	226	62.8	2	452	323869	0.2738	-0.60	32711	0.982430	2.11
584- 585	227	62.8	2	454	324323	0.2742	-0.60	32713	0.982490	2.11
581- 583	228	62.9	3	684	325007	0.2747	-0.60	32716	0.982580	2.11
578- 580	229	62.9	3	687	325694	0.2753	-0.60	32719	0.982671	2.11
574- 577	230	62.9	4	920	326614	0.2761	-0.59	32723	0.982791	2.12
572- 573	232	62.9	2	464	327078	0.2765	-0.59	32725	0.982851	2.12
570- 571	233	63.0	2	466	327544	0.2769	-0.59	32727	0.982911	2.12
566- 569	235	63.0	4	940	328484	0.2777	-0.59	32731	0.983031	2.12
565	237	63.0	1	237	328721	0.2779	-0.59	32732	0.983061	2.12
563- 564	238	63.0	2	476	329197	0.2783	-0.59	32734	0.983121	2.12

Rank	Occ. F	SFI	F	Tokens	Cum. Tokens	Cum. P Tokens	Y	Cum. Types	Cum. P Types	Z
560– 562	240	63.1	3	720	329917	0.2789	-0.59	32737	0.983211	2.13
559	241	63.1	1	241	330158	0.2791	-0.59	32738	0.983241	2.13
556– 558	242	63.1	3	726	330884	0.2797	-0.58	32741	0.983331	2.13
555	244	63.2	1	244	331128	0.2799	-0.58	32742	0.983361	2.13
554	245	63.2	1	245	331373	0.2801	-0.58	32743	0.983391	2.13
553	248	63.2	1	248	331621	0.2803	-0.58	32744	0.983421	2.13
550– 552	249	63.2	3	747	332368	0.2810	-0.58	32747	0.983512	2.13
549	250	63.3	1	250	332618	0.2812	-0.58	32748	0.983542	2.13
543– 548	251	63.3	6	1506	334124	0.2824	-0.58	32754	0.983722	2.14
542	252	63.3	1	252	334376	0.2827	-0.57	32755	0.983752	2.14
541	253	63.3	1	253	334629	0.2829	-0.57	32756	0.983782	2.14
537– 540	254	63.3	4	1016	335645	0.2837	-0.57	32760	0.983902	2.14
533– 536	255	63.3	4	1020	336665	0.2846	-0.57	32764	0.984022	2.14
532	256	63.4	1	256	336921	0.2848	-0.57	32765	0.984052	2.15
531	257	63.4	1	257	337178	0.2850	-0.57	32766	0.984082	2.15
527– 530	258	63.4	4	1032	338210	0.2859	-0.57	32770	0.984202	2.15
524– 526	259	63.4	3	777	338987	0.2866	-0.56	32773	0.984292	2.15
522– 523	260	63.4	2	520	339507	0.2870	-0.56	32775	0.984352	2.15
520– 521	261	63.4	2	522	340029	0.2874	-0.56	32777	0.984412	2.15
518– 519	262	63.5	2	524	340553	0.2879	-0.56	32779	0.984473	2.16
516– 517	263	63.5	2	526	341079	0.2883	-0.56	32781	0.984533	2.16
513– 515	265	63.5	3	795	341874	0.2890	-0.56	32784	0.984623	2.16
511– 512	266	63.5	2	532	342406	0.2894	-0.56	32786	0.984683	2.16
510	267	63.5	1	267	342673	0.2897	-0.55	32787	0.984713	2.16
508– 509	268	63.6	2	536	343209	0.2901	-0.55	32789	0.984773	2.16
506– 507	269	63.6	2	538	343747	0.2906	-0.55	32791	0.984833	2.17
504– 505	270	63.6	2	540	344287	0.2910	-0.55	32793	0.984893	2.17
503	271	63.6	1	271	344558	0.2913	-0.55	32794	0.984923	2.17
501– 502	272	63.6	2	544	345102	0.2917	-0.55	32796	0.984983	2.17
497– 500	273	63.6	4	1092	346194	0.2926	-0.55	32800	0.985103	2.17
495– 496	275	63.7	2	550	346744	0.2931	-0.54	32802	0.985163	2.17
491– 494	276	63.7	4	1104	347848	0.2940	-0.54	32806	0.985283	2.18
488– 490	277	63.7	3	831	348679	0.2947	-0.54	32809	0.985374	2.18
487	278	63.7	1	278	348957	0.2950	-0.54	32810	0.985404	2.18
483– 486	280	63.7	4	1120	350077	0.2959	-0.54	32814	0.985524	2.18
479– 482	282	63.8	4	1128	351205	0.2969	-0.53	32818	0.985644	2.19
477– 478	283	63.8	2	566	351771	0.2974	-0.53	32820	0.985704	2.19
476	284	63.8	1	284	352055	0.2976	-0.53	32821	0.985734	2.19
475	285	63.8	1	285	352340	0.2978	-0.53	32822	0.985764	2.19
471– 474	286	63.8	4	1144	353484	0.2988	-0.53	32826	0.985884	2.19
469– 470	287	63.9	2	574	354058	0.2993	-0.53	32828	0.985944	2.20
467– 468	288	63.9	2	576	354634	0.2998	-0.53	32830	0.986004	2.20
464– 466	289	63.9	3	867	355501	0.3005	-0.52	32833	0.986094	2.20
462– 463	290	63.9	2	580	356081	0.3010	-0.52	32835	0.986154	2.20
461	291	63.9	1	291	356372	0.3013	-0.52	32836	0.986184	2.20
459– 460	292	63.9	2	584	356956	0.3017	-0.52	32838	0.986245	2.20
458	293	63.9	1	293	357249	0.3020	-0.52	32839	0.986275	2.21
455– 457	294	64.0	3	882	358131	0.3027	-0.52	32842	0.986365	2.21
454	296	64.0	1	296	358427	0.3030	-0.52	32843	0.986395	2.21
451– 453	298	64.0	3	894	359321	0.3037	-0.51	32846	0.986485	2.21
450	299	64.0	1	299	359620	0.3040	-0.51	32847	0.986515	2.21
448– 449	301	64.1	2	602	360222	0.3045	-0.51	32849	0.986575	2.21
446– 447	302	64.1	2	604	360826	0.3050	-0.51	32851	0.986635	2.22
445	303	64.1	1	303	361129	0.3053	-0.51	32852	0.986665	2.22
439– 444	304	64.1	6	1824	362953	0.3068	-0.50	32858	0.986845	2.22
438	305	64.1	1	305	363258	0.3071	-0.50	32859	0.986875	2.22
437	306	64.1	1	306	363564	0.3073	-0.50	32860	0.986905	2.22
436	308	64.2	1	308	363872	0.3076	-0.50	32861	0.986935	2.22
435	309	64.2	1	309	364181	0.3079	-0.50	32862	0.986965	2.23
433– 434	310	64.2	2	620	364801	0.3084	-0.50	32864	0.987025	2.23
431– 432	311	64.2	2	622	365423	0.3089	-0.50	32866	0.987086	2.23
430	312	64.2	1	312	365735	0.3092	-0.50	32867	0.987116	2.23
429	313	64.2	1	313	366048	0.3094	-0.50	32868	0.987146	2.23
427– 428	314	64.2	2	628	366676	0.3100	-0.50	32870	0.987206	2.23
424– 426	315	64.3	3	945	367621	0.3108	-0.49	32873	0.987296	2.24
423	317	64.3	1	317	367938	0.3110	-0.49	32874	0.987326	2.24
421– 422	318	64.3	2	636	368574	0.3116	-0.49	32876	0.987386	2.24
419– 420	319	64.3	2	638	369212	0.3121	-0.49	32878	0.987446	2.24
417– 418	320	64.3	2	640	369852	0.3126	-0.49	32880	0.987506	2.24
416	322	64.4	1	322	370174	0.3129	-0.49	32881	0.987536	2.24
414– 415	323	64.4	2	646	370820	0.3135	-0.49	32883	0.987596	2.24
410– 413	324	64.4	4	1296	372116	0.3146	-0.48	32887	0.987716	2.25
405– 409	325	64.4	5	1625	373741	0.3159	-0.48	32892	0.987866	2.25
403– 404	326	64.4	2	652	374393	0.3165	-0.48	32894	0.987926	2.25
402	327	64.4	1	327	374720	0.3168	-0.48	32895	0.987956	2.26
401	328	64.4	1	328	375048	0.3170	-0.48	32896	0.987987	2.26
398– 400	329	64.4	3	987	376035	0.3179	-0.47	32899	0.988077	2.26
397	331	64.5	1	331	376366	0.3182	-0.47	32900	0.988107	2.26
396	333	64.5	1	333	376699	0.3184	-0.47	32901	0.988137	2.26
394– 395	334	64.5	2	668	377367	0.3190	-0.47	32903	0.988197	2.26
392– 393	335	64.5	2	670	378037	0.3196	-0.47	32905	0.988257	2.27
391	337	64.6	1	337	378374	0.3199	-0.47	32906	0.988287	2.27
389– 390	338	64.6	2	676	379050	0.3204	-0.47	32908	0.988347	2.27
386– 388	342	64.6	3	1026	380076	0.3213	-0.46	32911	0.988437	2.27
384– 385	345	64.7	2	690	380766	0.3219	-0.46	32913	0.988497	2.27
383	346	64.7	1	346	381112	0.3222	-0.46	32914	0.988527	2.27
382	347	64.7	1	347	381459	0.3225	-0.46	32915	0.988557	2.28
381	348	64.7	1	348	381807	0.3228	-0.46	32916	0.988587	2.28
379– 380	349	64.7	2	698	382505	0.3233	-0.46	32918	0.988647	2.28
378	350	64.7	1	350	382855	0.3236	-0.46	32919	0.988677	2.28
377	353	64.8	1	353	383208	0.3239	-0.46	32920	0.988707	2.28
375– 376	354	64.8	2	708	383916	0.3245	-0.46	32922	0.988767	2.28
372– 374	355	64.8	3	1065	384981	0.3254	-0.45	32925	0.988858	2.29
371	359	64.8	1	359	385340	0.3257	-0.45	32926	0.988888	2.29
370	360	64.8	1	360	385700	0.3260	-0.45	32927	0.988918	2.29
368– 369	362	64.9	2	724	386424	0.3267	-0.45	32929	0.988978	2.29
367	366	64.9	1	366	386790	0.3270	-0.45	32930	0.989008	2.29
366	368	64.9	1	368	387158	0.3273	-0.45	32931	0.989038	2.29
364– 365	377	65.0	2	754	387912	0.3279	-0.45	32933	0.989098	2.29
362– 363	380	65.1	2	760	388672	0.3286	-0.44	32935	0.989158	2.30
360– 361	383	65.1	2	766	389438	0.3292	-0.44	32937	0.989218	2.30
359	384	65.1	1	384	389822	0.3295	-0.44	32938	0.989248	2.30
358	385	65.1	1	385	390207	0.3299	-0.44	32939	0.989278	2.30
357	387	65.2	1	387	390594	0.3302	-0.44	32940	0.989308	2.30
356	388	65.2	1	388	390982	0.3305	-0.44	32941	0.989338	2.30
354– 355	389	65.2	2	778	391760	0.3312	-0.44	32943	0.989398	2.30
353	391	65.2	1	391	392151	0.3315	-0.44	32944	0.989428	2.31
351– 352	392	65.2	2	784	392935	0.3322	-0.43	32946	0.989488	2.31
350	393	65.2	1	393	393328	0.3325	-0.43	32947	0.989518	2.31
349	395	65.2	1	395	393723	0.3328	-0.43	32948	0.989548	2.31
344– 348	397	65.3	5	1985	395708	0.3345	-0.43	32953	0.989698	2.32
341– 343	399	65.3	3	1197	396905	0.3355	-0.42	32956	0.989789	2.32
339– 340	400	65.3	2	800	397705	0.3362	-0.42	32958	0.989849	2.32
337– 338	406	65.4	2	812	398517	0.3369	-0.42	32960	0.989909	2.32
336	407	65.4	1	407	398924	0.3372	-0.42	32961	0.989939	2.32
335	411	65.4	1	411	399335	0.3376	-0.42	32962	0.989969	2.33
334	413	65.4	1	413	399748	0.3379	-0.42	32963	0.989999	2.33
333	414	65.4	1	414	400162	0.3383	-0.42	32964	0.990029	2.33
332	419	65.5	1	419	400581	0.3386	-0.42	32965	0.990059	2.33
330– 331	420	65.5	2	840	401421	0.3393	-0.41	32967	0.990119	2.33
325– 329	421	65.5	5	2105	403526	0.3411	-0.41	32972	0.990269	2.34
324	422	65.5	1	422	403948	0.3415	-0.41	32973	0.990299	2.34
322– 323	424	65.5	2	848	404796	0.3422	-0.41	32975	0.990359	2.34
321	425	65.6	1	425	405221	0.3425	-0.41	32976	0.990389	2.34
320	427	65.6	1	427	405648	0.3429	-0.40	32977	0.990419	2.34
319	430	65.6	1	430	406078	0.3433	-0.40	32978	0.990449	2.34
318	431	65.6	1	431	406509	0.3436	-0.40	32979	0.990479	2.34
317	432	65.6	1	432	406941	0.3440	-0.40	32980	0.990509	2.35
316	433	65.6	1	433	407374	0.3444	-0.40	32981	0.990539	2.35
315	434	65.7	1	434	407808	0.3447	-0.40	32982	0.990569	2.35
313– 314	435	65.7	2	870	408678	0.3455	-0.40	32984	0.990629	2.35
312	436	65.7	1	436	409114	0.3458	-0.40	32985	0.990660	2.35
311	437	65.7	1	437	409551	0.3462	-0.40	32986	0.990690	2.35
310	439	65.7	1	439	409990	0.3466	-0.39	32987	0.990720	2.35
309	441	65.7	1	441	410431	0.3469	-0.39	32988	0.990750	2.36
308	442	65.7	1	442	410873	0.3473	-0.39	32989	0.990780	2.36
307	444	65.7	1	444	411317	0.3477	-0.39	32990	0.990810	2.36
306	445	65.8	1	445	411762	0.3481	-0.39	32991	0.990840	2.36
305	449	65.8	1	449	412211	0.3485	-0.39	32992	0.990870	2.36
304	451	65.8	1	451	412662	0.3488	-0.39	32993	0.990900	2.36
303	454	65.8	1	454	413116	0.3492	-0.39	32994	0.990930	2.36
302	457	65.9	1	457	413573	0.3496	-0.39	32995	0.990960	2.36
301	461	65.9	1	461	414034	0.3500	-0.39	32996	0.990990	2.37
300	463	65.9	1	463	414497	0.3504	-0.38	32997	0.991020	2.37
299	464	65.9	1	464	414961	0.3508	-0.38	32998	0.991050	2.37
297– 298	465	65.9	2	930	415891	0.3516	-0.38	33000	0.991110	2.37
296	466	66.0	1	466	416357	0.3520	-0.38	33001	0.991140	2.37
295	467	66.0	1	467	416824	0.3524	-0.38	33002	0.991170	2.37
294	468	66.0	1	468	417292	0.3527	-0.38	33003	0.991200	2.37
293	473	66.0	1	473	417765	0.3531	-0.38	33004	0.991230	2.38
292	474	66.0	1	474	418239	0.3535	-0.38	33005	0.991260	2.38
291	475	66.0	1	475	418714	0.3540	-0.37	33006	0.991290	2.38
289– 290	476	66.1	2	952	419666	0.3548	-0.37	33008	0.991350	2.38
288	477	66.1	1	477	420143	0.3552	-0.37	33009	0.991380	2.38
286– 287	478	66.1	2	956	421099	0.3560	-0.37	33011	0.991440	2.38
285	481	66.1	1	481	421580	0.3564	-0.37	33012	0.991470	2.39
284	485	66.1	1	485	422065	0.3568	-0.37	33013	0.991500	2.39
283	488	66.2	1	488	422553	0.3572	-0.37	33014	0.991530	2.39
282	491	66.2	1	491	423044	0.3576	-0.36	33015	0.991561	2.39
281	494	66.2	1	494	423538	0.3580	-0.36	33016	0.991591	2.39
280	499	66.3	1	499	424037	0.3585	-0.36	33017	0.991621	2.39
279	504	66.3	1	504	424541	0.3589	-0.36	33018	0.991651	2.39
278	509	66.3	1	509	425050	0.3593	-0.36	33019	0.991681	2.39
277	511	66.4	1	511	425561	0.3597	-0.36	33020	0.991711	2.40
276	512	66.4	1	512	426073	0.3602	-0.36	33021	0.991741	2.40
275	515	66.4	1	515	426588	0.3606	-0.36	33022	0.991771	2.40
274	516	66.4	1	516	427104	0.3610	-0.36	33023	0.991801	2.40
273	520	66.4	1	520	427624	0.3615	-0.35	33024	0.991831	2.40
272	523	66.5	1	523	428147	0.3619	-0.35	33025	0.991861	2.40
271	524	66.5	1	524	428671	0.3624	-0.35	33026	0.991891	2.40
270	525	66.5	1	525	429196	0.3628	-0.35	33027	0.991921	2.41
268– 269	527	66.5	2	1054	430250	0.3637	-0.35	33029	0.991981	2.41
267	529	66.5	1	529	430779	0.3642	-0.35	33030	0.992011	2.41
266	531	66.5	1	531	431310	0.3646	-0.35	33031	0.992041	2.41
265	536	66.6	1	536	431846	0.3651	-0.34	33032	0.992071	2.41
264	537	66.6	1	537	432383	0.3655	-0.34	33033	0.992101	2.41
262– 263	539	66.6	2	1078	433461	0.3664	-0.34	33035	0.992161	2.42
261	544	66.6	1	544	434005	0.3669	-0.34	33036	0.992191	2.42
260	545	66.6	1	545	434550	0.3673	-0.34	33037	0.992221	2.42
258– 259	546	66.6	2	1092	435642	0.3683	-0.34	33039	0.992281	2.42
257	548	66.7	1	548	436190	0.3687	-0.34	33040	0.992311	2.42
256	554	66.7	1	554	436744	0.3692	-0.33	33041	0.992341	2.42
255	556	66.7	1	556	437300	0.3697	-0.33	33042	0.992371	2.43
254	557	66.7	1	557	437857	0.3701	-0.33	33043	0.992401	2.43
253	562	66.8	1	562	438419	0.3706	-0.33	33044	0.992432	2.43
252	563	66.8	1	563	438982	0.3711	-0.33	33045	0.992462	2.43
251	565	66.8	1	565	439547	0.3716	-0.33	33046	0.992492	2.43
250	567	66.8	1	567	440114	0.3720	-0.33	33047	0.992522	2.43
249	568	66.8	1	568	440682	0.3725	-0.33	33048	0.992552	2.43
248	574	66.9	1	574	441256	0.3730	-0.32	33049	0.992582	2.44
247	577	66.9	1	577	441833	0.3735	-0.32	33050	0.992612	2.44
245– 246	580	66.9	2	1160	442993	0.3745	-0.32	33052	0.992672	2.44
244	581	66.9	1	581	443574	0.3750	-0.32	33053	0.992702	2.44
243	583	66.9	1	583	444157	0.3755	-0.32	33054	0.992732	2.44
242	591	67.0	1	591	444748	0.3760	-0.32	33055	0.992762	2.45
241	594	67.0	1	594	445342	0.3765	-0.31	33056	0.992792	2.45
240	596	67.0	1	596	445938	0.3770	-0.31	33057	0.992822	2.45
239	597	67.0	1	597	446535	0.3775	-0.31	33058	0.992852	2.45
238	598	67.0	1	598	447133	0.3780	-0.31	33059	0.992882	2.45
237	601	67.1	1	601	447734	0.3785	-0.31	33060	0.992912	2.45
236	606	67.1	1	606	448340	0.3790	-0.31	33061	0.992942	2.45
235	607	67.1	1	607	448947	0.3795	-0.31	33062	0.992972	2.46
234	614	67.2	1	614	449561	0.3800	-0.31	33063	0.993002	2.46
233	617	67.2	1	617	450178	0.3805	-0.30	33064	0.993032	2.46
231– 232	618	67.2	2	1236	451414	0.3816	-0.30	33066	0.993092	2.46
230	622	67.2	1	622	452036	0.3821	-0.30	33067	0.993122	2.46
229	626	67.2	1	626	452662	0.3826	-0.30	33068	0.993152	2.47
228	630	67.3	1	630	453292	0.3832	-0.30	33069	0.993182	2.47
227	632	67.3	1	632	453924	0.3837	-0.30	33070	0.993212	2.47
226	633	67.3	1	633	454557	0.3843	-0.29	33071	0.993242	2.47
224– 225	635	67.3	2	1270	455827	0.3853	-0.29	33073	0.993302	2.47
223	637	67.3	1	637	456464	0.3859	-0.29	33074	0.993333	2.47
222	640	67.3	1	640	457104	0.3864	-0.29	33075	0.993363	2.48
221	645	67.4	1	645	457749	0.3869	-0.29	33076	0.993393	2.48
220	652	67.4	1	652	458401	0.3875	-0.29	33077	0.993423	2.48
219	657	67.4	1	657	459058	0.3881	-0.28	33078	0.993453	2.48
217– 218	659	67.5	2	1318	460376	0.3892	-0.28	33080	0.993513	2.48
215– 216	661	67.5	2	1322	461698	0.3903	-0.28	33082	0.993573	2.49
214	669	67.5	1	669	462367	0.3909	-0.28	33083	0.993603	2.49
213	671	67.5	1	671	463038	0.3914	-0.28	33084	0.993633	2.49
212	675	67.6	1	675	463713	0.3920	-0.27	33085	0.993663	2.49
211	680	67.6	1	680	464393	0.3926	-0.27	33086	0.993693	2.49
208– 210	682	67.6	3	2046	466439	0.3943	-0.27	33089	0.993783	2.50
207	683	67.6	1	683	467122	0.3949	-0.27	33090	0.993813	2.50
205– 206	701	67.7	2	1402	468524	0.3961	-0.26	33092	0.993873	2.50
204	720	67.8	1	720	469244	0.3967	-0.26	33093	0.993903	2.51
203	721	67.9	1	721	469965	0.3973	-0.26	33094	0.993933	2.51
201– 202	723	67.9	2	1446	471411	0.3985	-0.26	33096	0.993999	2.51
200	725	67.9	1	725	472136	0.3991	-0.26	33097	0.994023	2.51
199	735	67.9	1	735	472871	0.3997	-0.25	33098	0.994053	2.52
198	744	68.0	1	744	473615	0.4004	-0.25	33099	0.994083	2.52
197	747	68.0	1	747	474362	0.4010	-0.25	33100	0.994113	2.52

Rank		Occ. F	SFI	F	Tokens	Cum. Tokens	Cum. P Tokens	Y	Cum. Types	Cum. P Types	Z
	196	748	68.0	1	748	475110	0.4016	−0.25	33101	0.994143	2.52
	195	752	68.0	1	752	475862	0.4023	−0.25	33102	0.994173	2.52
	194	757	68.1	1	757	476619	0.4029	−0.25	33103	0.994204	2.52
	193	762	68.1	1	762	477381	0.4035	−0.24	33104	0.994233	2.53
	192	763	68.1	1	763	478144	0.4042	−0.24	33105	0.994264	2.53
	191	764	68.1	1	764	478908	0.4048	−0.24	33106	0.994294	2.53
	190	779	68.2	1	779	479687	0.4055	−0.24	33107	0.994324	2.53
	189	786	68.2	1	786	480473	0.4062	−0.24	33108	0.994354	2.53
187–	188	791	68.3	2	1582	482055	0.4075	−0.23	33110	0.994414	2.54
	186	797	68.3	1	797	482852	0.4082	−0.23	33111	0.994444	2.54
	185	811	68.4	1	811	483663	0.4089	−0.23	33112	0.994474	2.54
	184	817	68.4	1	817	484480	0.4095	−0.23	33113	0.994504	2.54
	183	821	68.4	1	821	485301	0.4102	−0.23	33114	0.994534	2.54
	182	827	68.4	1	827	486128	0.4109	−0.23	33115	0.994564	2.55
	181	835	68.5	1	835	486963	0.4116	−0.22	33116	0.994594	2.55
	180	837	68.5	1	837	487800	0.4124	−0.22	33117	0.994624	2.55
	179	843	68.5	1	843	488643	0.4131	−0.22	33118	0.994654	2.55
	178	844	68.5	1	844	489487	0.4138	−0.22	33119	0.994684	2.55
	177	877	68.7	1	877	490364	0.4145	−0.22	33120	0.994714	2.56
	176	878	68.7	1	878	491242	0.4153	−0.21	33121	0.994744	2.56
	175	879	68.7	1	879	492121	0.4160	−0.21	33122	0.994774	2.56
	174	881	68.7	1	881	493002	0.4167	−0.21	33123	0.994804	2.56
	173	884	68.7	1	884	493886	0.4175	−0.21	33124	0.994834	2.56
	172	885	68.7	1	885	494771	0.4182	−0.21	33125	0.994864	2.57
	171	889	68.8	1	889	495660	0.4190	−0.20	33126	0.994894	2.57
	170	890	68.8	1	890	496550	0.4197	−0.20	33127	0.994924	2.57
	169	895	68.8	1	895	497445	0.4205	−0.20	33128	0.994954	2.57
	168	896	68.8	1	896	498341	0.4213	−0.20	33129	0.994984	2.57
	167	909	68.9	1	909	499250	0.4220	−0.20	33130	0.995014	2.58
	166	914	68.9	1	914	500164	0.4228	−0.19	33131	0.995044	2.58
	165	917	68.9	1	917	501081	0.4236	−0.19	33132	0.995074	2.58
163–	164	929	69.0	2	1858	502939	0.4251	−0.19	33134	0.995135	2.59
	162	932	69.0	1	932	503871	0.4259	−0.19	33135	0.995165	2.59
160–	161	940	69.0	2	1880	505751	0.4275	−0.18	33137	0.995225	2.59
	159	944	69.0	1	944	506695	0.4283	−0.18	33138	0.995255	2.59
	158	945	69.0	1	945	507640	0.4291	−0.18	33139	0.995285	2.60
	157	955	69.1	1	955	508595	0.4299	−0.18	33140	0.995315	2.60
	156	964	69.1	1	964	509559	0.4307	−0.17	33141	0.995345	2.60
	155	971	69.1	1	971	510530	0.4316	−0.17	33142	0.995375	2.60
153–	154	975	69.2	2	1950	512480	0.4332	−0.17	33144	0.995435	2.61
	152	977	69.2	1	977	513457	0.4340	−0.17	33145	0.995465	2.61
	151	983	69.2	1	983	514440	0.4349	−0.16	33146	0.995495	2.61
	150	996	69.3	1	996	515436	0.4357	−0.16	33147	0.995525	2.61
	149	1002	69.3	1	1002	516438	0.4366	−0.16	33148	0.995555	2.62
	148	1024	69.4	1	1024	517462	0.4374	−0.16	33149	0.995585	2.62
	147	1032	69.4	1	1032	518494	0.4383	−0.16	33150	0.995615	2.62
	146	1033	69.4	1	1033	519527	0.4392	−0.15	33151	0.995645	2.62
	145	1034	69.4	1	1034	520561	0.4400	−0.15	33152	0.995675	2.63
	144	1035	69.4	1	1035	521596	0.4409	−0.15	33153	0.995705	2.63
142–	143	1064	69.5	2	2128	523724	0.4427	−0.14	33155	0.995765	2.63
	141	1068	69.6	1	1068	524792	0.4436	−0.14	33156	0.995795	2.64
	140	1071	69.6	1	1071	525863	0.4445	−0.14	33157	0.995825	2.64
	139	1072	69.6	1	1072	526935	0.4454	−0.14	33158	0.995855	2.64
	138	1080	69.6	1	1080	528015	0.4463	−0.13	33159	0.995885	2.64
	137	1124	69.8	1	1124	529139	0.4473	−0.13	33160	0.995915	2.64
	136	1137	69.8	1	1137	530276	0.4483	−0.13	33161	0.995945	2.65
	135	1138	69.8	1	1138	531414	0.4492	−0.13	33162	0.995975	2.65
	134	1141	69.8	1	1141	532555	0.4502	−0.13	33163	0.996005	2.65
	133	1146	69.9	1	1146	533701	0.4512	−0.12	33164	0.996036	2.66
	132	1159	69.9	1	1159	534860	0.4521	−0.12	33165	0.996066	2.66
	131	1163	69.9	1	1163	536023	0.4531	−0.12	33166	0.996096	2.66
	130	1175	70.0	1	1175	537198	0.4541	−0.12	33167	0.996126	2.66
128–	129	1200	70.1	2	2400	539598	0.4561	−0.11	33169	0.996186	2.67
	127	1203	70.1	1	1203	540801	0.4572	−0.11	33170	0.996216	2.67
	126	1214	70.1	1	1214	542015	0.4582	−0.11	33171	0.996246	2.67
	125	1241	70.2	1	1241	543256	0.4592	−0.10	33172	0.996276	2.68
	124	1263	70.3	1	1263	544519	0.4603	−0.10	33173	0.996306	2.68
	123	1267	70.3	1	1267	545786	0.4614	−0.10	33174	0.996336	2.68
	122	1271	70.3	1	1271	547057	0.4624	−0.09	33175	0.996366	2.68
	121	1293	70.4	1	1293	548350	0.4635	−0.09	33176	0.996396	2.69
	120	1306	70.4	1	1306	549656	0.4646	−0.09	33177	0.996426	2.69
	119	1326	70.5	1	1326	550982	0.4658	−0.09	33178	0.996456	2.69
117–	118	1351	70.6	2	2702	553684	0.4680	−0.08	33180	0.996516	2.70
	116	1352	70.6	1	1352	555036	0.4692	−0.08	33181	0.996546	2.70
	115	1382	70.7	1	1382	556418	0.4704	−0.07	33182	0.996576	2.70
	114	1384	70.7	1	1384	557802	0.4715	−0.07	33183	0.996606	2.71
	113	1400	70.7	1	1400	559202	0.4727	−0.07	33184	0.996636	2.71
	112	1426	70.8	1	1426	560628	0.4739	−0.07	33185	0.996666	2.71
	111	1436	70.8	1	1436	562064	0.4751	−0.06	33186	0.996696	2.72
	110	1440	70.9	1	1440	563504	0.4763	−0.06	33187	0.996726	2.72
	109	1469	70.9	1	1469	564973	0.4776	−0.06	33188	0.996756	2.72
	108	1475	71.0	1	1475	566448	0.4788	−0.05	33189	0.996786	2.73
	107	1501	71.0	1	1501	567949	0.4801	−0.05	33190	0.996816	2.73
	106	1518	71.1	1	1518	569467	0.4814	−0.05	33191	0.996846	2.73
	105	1532	71.1	1	1532	570999	0.4827	−0.04	33192	0.996876	2.73
	104	1551	71.2	1	1551	572550	0.4840	−0.04	33193	0.996907	2.74
	103	1555	71.2	1	1555	574105	0.4853	−0.04	33194	0.996937	2.74
	102	1558	71.2	1	1558	575663	0.4866	−0.03	33195	0.996967	2.74
	101	1569	71.2	1	1569	577232	0.4880	−0.03	33196	0.996997	2.75
	100	1581	71.3	1	1581	578813	0.4893	−0.03	33197	0.997027	2.75
	99	1588	71.3	1	1588	580401	0.4906	−0.02	33198	0.997057	2.75
	98	1592	71.3	1	1592	581993	0.4920	−0.02	33199	0.997087	2.76
	97	1600	71.3	1	1600	583593	0.4933	−0.02	33200	0.997117	2.76
	96	1601	71.3	1	1601	585194	0.4947	−0.01	33201	0.997147	2.76
	95	1609	71.3	1	1609	586803	0.4960	−0.01	33202	0.997177	2.77
	94	1615	71.4	1	1615	588418	0.4974	−0.01	33203	0.997207	2.77
	93	1642	71.4	1	1642	590060	0.4988	−0.00	33204	0.997237	2.77
	92	1654	71.5	1	1654	591714	0.5002	0.00	33205	0.997267	2.78
	91	1675	71.5	1	1675	593389	0.5016	0.00	33206	0.997297	2.78
	90	1689	71.5	1	1689	595078	0.5030	0.01	33207	0.997327	2.79
	89	1690	71.6	1	1690	596768	0.5045	0.01	33208	0.997357	2.79
	88	1747	71.7	1	1747	598515	0.5059	0.01	33209	0.997387	2.79
	87	1749	71.7	1	1749	600264	0.5074	0.02	33210	0.997417	2.80
	86	1773	71.8	1	1773	602037	0.5089	0.02	33211	0.997447	2.80
	85	1812	71.9	1	1812	603849	0.5105	0.03	33212	0.997477	2.80
	84	1854	72.0	1	1854	605703	0.5120	0.03	33213	0.997507	2.81
	83	1857	72.0	1	1857	607560	0.5136	0.03	33214	0.997537	2.81
	82	1883	72.0	1	1883	609443	0.5152	0.04	33215	0.997567	2.82
	81	1920	72.1	1	1920	611363	0.5168	0.04	33216	0.997597	2.82
79–	80	1938	72.1	2	3876	615239	0.5201	0.05	33218	0.997657	2.83
	78	1958	72.2	1	1958	617197	0.5217	0.05	33219	0.997687	2.83
	77	1959	72.2	1	1959	619156	0.5234	0.06	33220	0.997717	2.84
	76	2016	72.3	1	2016	621172	0.5251	0.06	33221	0.997747	2.84
	75	2047	72.4	1	2047	623219	0.5268	0.07	33222	0.997777	2.84
	74	2069	72.4	1	2069	625288	0.5286	0.07	33223	0.997808	2.85
	73	2080	72.5	1	2080	627368	0.5303	0.08	33224	0.997838	2.85
	72	2105	72.5	1	2105	629473	0.5321	0.08	33225	0.997868	2.86
	71	2234	72.8	1	2234	631707	0.5340	0.09	33226	0.997898	2.86
	70	2243	72.8	1	2243	633950	0.5359	0.09	33227	0.997928	2.87
	69	2260	72.8	1	2260	636210	0.5378	0.09	33228	0.997958	2.87
	68	2262	72.8	1	2262	638472	0.5397	0.10	33229	0.997988	2.88
	67	2270	72.8	1	2270	640742	0.5416	0.10	33230	0.998018	2.88
	66	2271	72.8	1	2271	643013	0.5436	0.11	33231	0.998048	2.89
	65	2333	73.0	1	2333	645346	0.5455	0.11	33232	0.998078	2.89
	64	2355	73.0	1	2355	647701	0.5475	0.12	33233	0.998108	2.90
	63	2398	73.1	1	2398	650099	0.5495	0.12	33234	0.998138	2.90
	62	2479	73.2	1	2479	652578	0.5516	0.13	33235	0.998168	2.91
	61	2538	73.3	1	2538	655116	0.5538	0.14	33236	0.998198	2.91
	60	2594	73.4	1	2594	657710	0.5560	0.14	33237	0.998228	2.92
	59	2640	73.5	1	2640	660350	0.5582	0.15	33238	0.998258	2.92
	58	2641	73.5	1	2641	662991	0.5604	0.15	33239	0.998288	2.93
	57	2690	73.6	1	2690	665681	0.5627	0.16	33240	0.998318	2.93
	56	2750	73.7	1	2750	668431	0.5650	0.16	33241	0.998348	2.94
	55	2758	73.7	1	2758	671189	0.5674	0.17	33242	0.998378	2.94
	54	2879	73.9	1	2879	674068	0.5698	0.18	33243	0.998408	2.95
	53	2961	74.0	1	2961	677029	0.5723	0.18	33244	0.998438	2.96
	52	2974	74.0	1	2974	680003	0.5748	0.19	33245	0.998468	2.96
	51	2995	74.0	1	2995	682998	0.5774	0.20	33246	0.998498	2.97
	50	3077	74.2	1	3077	686075	0.5800	0.20	33247	0.998528	2.97
	49	3100	74.2	1	3100	689175	0.5826	0.21	33248	0.998558	2.98
	48	3107	74.2	1	3107	692282	0.5852	0.22	33249	0.998588	2.99
	47	3140	74.2	1	3140	695422	0.5879	0.22	33250	0.998618	2.99
	46	3275	74.4	1	3275	698697	0.5906	0.23	33251	0.998648	3.00
	45	3288	74.4	1	3288	701985	0.5934	0.24	33252	0.998679	3.01
	44	3443	74.6	1	3443	705428	0.5963	0.24	33253	0.998709	3.01
	43	3592	74.8	1	3592	709020	0.5994	0.25	33254	0.998739	3.02
	42	3633	74.9	1	3633	712653	0.6024	0.26	33255	0.998769	3.03
	41	3835	75.1	1	3835	716488	0.6057	0.27	33256	0.998799	3.04
	40	4098	75.4	1	4098	720586	0.6091	0.28	33257	0.998829	3.04
	39	4189	75.5	1	4189	724775	0.6127	0.29	33258	0.998859	3.05
	38	4254	75.6	1	4254	729029	0.6163	0.30	33259	0.998889	3.06
	37	4393	75.7	1	4393	733422	0.6200	0.31	33260	0.998919	3.07
	36	4470	75.8	1	4470	737892	0.6238	0.32	33261	0.998949	3.08
	35	4484	75.8	1	4484	742376	0.6276	0.33	33262	0.998979	3.08
	34	4488	75.8	1	4488	746864	0.6313	0.34	33263	0.999009	3.09
	33	4523	75.8	1	4523	751387	0.6352	0.35	33264	0.999039	3.10
	32	4721	76.0	1	4721	756108	0.6392	0.36	33265	0.999069	3.11
	31	4800	76.1	1	4800	760908	0.6432	0.37	33266	0.999099	3.12
	30	4834	76.1	1	4834	765742	0.6473	0.38	33267	0.999129	3.13
	29	4836	76.1	1	4836	770578	0.6514	0.39	33268	0.999159	3.14
	28	4921	76.2	1	4921	775499	0.6556	0.40	33269	0.999189	3.15
	27	4954	76.2	1	4954	780453	0.6597	0.41	33270	0.999219	3.16
	26	4991	76.3	1	4991	785444	0.6640	0.42	33271	0.999249	3.17
	25	5144	76.4	1	5144	790588	0.6683	0.44	33272	0.999279	3.19
	24	5917	77.0	1	5917	796505	0.6733	0.45	33273	0.999309	3.20
	23	6175	77.2	1	6175	802680	0.6785	0.46	33274	0.999339	3.21
	22	7003	77.7	1	7003	809683	0.6844	0.48	33275	0.999369	3.22
	21	7051	77.8	1	7051	816734	0.6904	0.50	33276	0.999399	3.24
	20	7058	77.8	1	7058	823792	0.6964	0.51	33277	0.999429	3.25
	19	7511	78.0	1	7511	831303	0.7027	0.53	33278	0.999459	3.27
	18	7540	78.0	1	7540	838843	0.7091	0.55	33279	0.999489	3.28
	17	8013	78.3	1	8013	846856	0.7159	0.57	33280	0.999519	3.30
	16	8611	78.6	1	8611	855467	0.7232	0.59	33281	0.999549	3.32
	15	8804	78.7	1	8804	864271	0.7306	0.61	33282	0.999579	3.34
	14	8996	78.8	1	8996	873267	0.7382	0.64	33283	0.999610	3.36
	13	10718	79.6	1	10718	883985	0.7473	0.67	33284	0.999640	3.38
	12	10901	79.6	1	10901	894886	0.7565	0.70	33285	0.999670	3.41
	11	11772	80.0	1	11772	906658	0.7664	0.73	33286	0.999700	3.43
	10	11777	80.0	1	11777	918435	0.7764	0.76	33287	0.999730	3.46
	9	13361	80.5	1	13361	931796	0.7877	0.80	33288	0.999760	3.49
	8	15374	81.1	1	15374	947170	0.8007	0.84	33289	0.999790	3.53
	7	18511	81.9	1	18511	965681	0.8163	0.90	33290	0.999820	3.57
	6	19114	82.1	1	19114	984795	0.8325	0.96	33291	0.999850	3.61
	5	24365	83.1	1	24365	1009160	0.8531	1.05	33292	0.999880	3.67
	4	28905	83.9	1	28905	1038065	0.8775	1.16	33293	0.999910	3.75
	3	31302	84.2	1	31302	1069367	0.9040	1.30	33294	0.999940	3.85
	2	31329	84.2	1	31329	1100696	0.9305	1.48	33295	0.999970	4.01
	1	82275	88.4	1	82275	1182971	1.0000	+INF.	33296	1.000000	+INF.

Rank	Occ. F	SFI	F	Tokens	Cum. Tokens	Cum. P Tokens	Y	Cum. Types	Cum. P Types	Z
8725-16183	1	47.2	7459	7459	7459	0.0263	-1.94	7459	0.460916	-0.10
6197-8724	2	49.5	2528	5056	12515	0.0442	-1.70	9987	0.617129	0.30
4961-6196	3	50.9	1236	3708	16223	0.0573	-1.58	11223	0.693506	0.51
4161-4960	4	52.0	800	3200	19423	0.0685	-1.49	12023	0.742940	0.65
3624-4160	5	52.9	537	2685	22108	0.0780	-1.42	12560	0.776123	0.76
3233-3623	6	53.6	391	2346	24454	0.0863	-1.36	12951	0.800284	0.84
2918-3232	7	54.2	315	2205	26659	0.0941	-1.32	13266	0.819749	0.91
2656-2917	8	54.8	262	2096	28755	0.1015	-1.27	13528	0.835939	0.98
2439-2655	9	55.3	217	1953	30708	0.1084	-1.24	13745	0.849348	1.03
2272-2438	10	55.7	167	1670	32378	0.1143	-1.20	13912	0.859668	1.08
2118-2271	11	56.1	154	1694	34072	0.1202	-1.17	14066	0.869184	1.12
1970-2117	12	56.4	148	1776	35848	0.1265	-1.14	14214	0.878329	1.17
1846-1969	13	56.8	124	1612	37460	0.1322	-1.12	14338	0.885991	1.21
1767-1845	14	57.1	79	1106	38566	0.1361	-1.10	14417	0.890873	1.23
1667-1766	15	57.4	100	1500	40066	0.1414	-1.07	14517	0.897052	1.26
1583-1666	16	57.7	84	1344	41410	0.1461	-1.05	14601	0.902243	1.29
1502-1582	17	57.9	81	1377	42787	0.1510	-1.03	14682	0.907248	1.32
1431-1501	18	58.1	71	1278	44065	0.1555	-1.01	14753	0.911636	1.35
1382-1430	19	58.4	49	931	44996	0.1588	-1.00	14802	0.914663	1.37
1342-1381	20	58.6	40	800	45796	0.1616	-0.99	14842	0.917135	1.39
1289-1341	21	58.8	53	1113	46909	0.1655	-0.97	14895	0.920410	1.41
1233-1288	22	59.0	56	1232	48141	0.1699	-0.95	14951	0.923871	1.43
1203-1232	23	59.2	30	690	48831	0.1723	-0.95	14981	0.925725	1.44
1164-1202	24	59.4	39	936	49767	0.1756	-0.93	15020	0.928134	1.46
1133-1163	25	59.5	31	775	50542	0.1784	-0.92	15051	0.930050	1.48
1092-1132	26	59.7	41	1066	51608	0.1821	-0.91	15092	0.932584	1.50
1064-1091	27	59.9	28	756	52364	0.1848	-0.90	15120	0.934314	1.51
1032-1063	28	60.0	32	896	53260	0.1880	-0.89	15152	0.936291	1.52
1005-1031	29	60.2	27	783	54043	0.1907	-0.88	15179	0.937960	1.54
976-1004	30	60.3	29	870	54913	0.1938	-0.86	15208	0.939752	1.55
959-975	31	60.5	17	527	55440	0.1956	-0.86	15225	0.940802	1.56
931-958	32	60.6	28	896	56336	0.1988	-0.85	15253	0.942532	1.58
911-930	33	60.7	20	660	56996	0.2011	-0.84	15273	0.943768	1.59
893-910	34	60.9	18	612	57608	0.2033	-0.83	15291	0.944880	1.60
875-892	35	61.0	18	630	58238	0.2055	-0.82	15309	0.945993	1.61
851-874	36	61.1	24	864	59102	0.2086	-0.81	15333	0.947476	1.62
837-850	37	61.2	14	518	59620	0.2104	-0.81	15347	0.948341	1.63
818-836	38	61.3	19	722	60342	0.2129	-0.80	15366	0.949515	1.64
793-817	39	61.4	25	975	61317	0.2164	-0.78	15391	0.951060	1.66
776-792	40	61.6	17	680	61997	0.2188	-0.78	15408	0.952110	1.67
753-775	41	61.7	23	943	62940	0.2221	-0.77	15431	0.953531	1.68
735-752	42	61.8	18	756	63696	0.2248	-0.76	15449	0.954644	1.69
713-734	43	61.9	22	946	64642	0.2281	-0.75	15471	0.956003	1.71
699-712	44	62.0	14	616	65258	0.2303	-0.74	15485	0.956868	1.72
683-698	45	62.1	16	720	65978	0.2328	-0.73	15501	0.957857	1.73
670-682	46	62.2	13	598	66576	0.2349	-0.72	15514	0.958660	1.74
650-669	47	62.2	20	940	67516	0.2383	-0.71	15534	0.959896	1.75
635-649	48	62.3	15	720	68236	0.2408	-0.70	15549	0.960823	1.76
629-634	49	62.4	6	294	68530	0.2418	-0.70	15555	0.961194	1.76
620-628	50	62.5	9	450	68980	0.2434	-0.70	15564	0.961750	1.77
601-619	51	62.6	19	969	69949	0.2468	-0.68	15583	0.962924	1.79
585-600	52	62.7	16	832	70781	0.2498	-0.68	15599	0.963913	1.80
569-584	53	62.8	16	848	71629	0.2528	-0.67	15615	0.964901	1.81
559-568	54	62.8	10	540	72169	0.2547	-0.66	15625	0.965519	1.82
549-558	55	62.9	10	550	72719	0.2566	-0.65	15635	0.966137	1.83
548	56	63.0	1	56	72775	0.2568	-0.65	15636	0.966199	1.83
539-547	57	63.1	9	513	73288	0.2586	-0.65	15645	0.966755	1.84
529-538	58	63.1	10	580	73868	0.2607	-0.64	15655	0.967373	1.84
522-528	59	63.2	7	413	74281	0.2621	-0.64	15662	0.967806	1.85
515-521	60	63.3	7	420	74701	0.2636	-0.63	15669	0.968238	1.86
505-514	61	63.4	10	610	75311	0.2658	-0.63	15679	0.968856	1.86
494-504	62	63.4	11	682	75993	0.2682	-0.62	15690	0.969536	1.87
491-493	63	63.5	3	189	76182	0.2688	-0.62	15693	0.969721	1.88
487-490	64	63.6	4	256	76438	0.2697	-0.61	15697	0.969968	1.88
480-486	65	63.6	7	455	76893	0.2714	-0.61	15704	0.970401	1.89
471-479	66	63.7	9	594	77487	0.2735	-0.60	15713	0.970957	1.90
466-470	67	63.8	5	335	77822	0.2746	-0.60	15718	0.971266	1.90
458-465	68	63.8	8	544	78366	0.2766	-0.59	15726	0.971760	1.91
453-457	69	63.9	5	345	78711	0.2778	-0.59	15731	0.972069	1.91
447-452	70	64.0	6	420	79131	0.2793	-0.59	15737	0.972440	1.92
441-446	71	64.0	6	426	79557	0.2808	-0.58	15743	0.972811	1.92
438-440	72	64.1	3	216	79773	0.2815	-0.58	15746	0.972996	1.93
434-437	73	64.1	4	292	80065	0.2825	-0.58	15750	0.973243	1.93
426-433	74	64.2	8	592	80657	0.2846	-0.57	15758	0.973738	1.94
422-425	75	64.3	4	300	80957	0.2857	-0.57	15762	0.973985	1.94
418-421	76	64.3	4	304	81261	0.2868	-0.56	15766	0.974232	1.95
414-417	77	64.4	4	308	81569	0.2879	-0.56	15770	0.974479	1.95
407-413	78	64.4	7	546	82115	0.2898	-0.55	15777	0.974912	1.96
402-406	79	64.5	5	395	82510	0.2912	-0.55	15782	0.975221	1.96
397-401	80	64.5	5	400	82910	0.2926	-0.55	15787	0.975530	1.97
394-396	82	64.6	3	246	83156	0.2935	-0.54	15790	0.975715	1.97
391-393	83	64.7	3	249	83405	0.2943	-0.54	15793	0.975901	1.98
386-390	84	64.7	5	420	83825	0.2958	-0.54	15798	0.976210	1.98
383-385	85	64.8	3	255	84080	0.2967	-0.53	15801	0.976395	1.98
379-382	86	64.8	4	344	84424	0.2979	-0.53	15805	0.976642	1.99
377-378	87	64.9	2	174	84598	0.2985	-0.53	15807	0.976766	1.99
369-376	88	64.9	8	704	85302	0.3010	-0.52	15815	0.977260	2.00
365-368	89	65.0	4	356	85658	0.3023	-0.52	15819	0.977507	2.00
362-364	90	65.0	3	270	85928	0.3032	-0.52	15822	0.977693	2.01
359-361	91	65.1	3	273	86201	0.3042	-0.51	15825	0.977878	2.01
358	92	65.1	1	92	86293	0.3045	-0.51	15826	0.977940	2.01
354-357	94	65.2	4	376	86669	0.3059	-0.51	15830	0.978187	2.02
351-353	96	65.3	3	288	86957	0.3069	-0.50	15833	0.978372	2.02
350	97	65.4	1	97	87054	0.3072	-0.50	15834	0.978434	2.02
349	98	65.4	1	98	87152	0.3076	-0.50	15835	0.978496	2.02
342-348	99	65.5	7	693	87845	0.3100	-0.50	15842	0.978928	2.03
340-341	100	65.5	2	200	88045	0.3107	-0.49	15844	0.979052	2.03
336-339	101	65.5	4	404	88449	0.3121	-0.49	15848	0.979299	2.04
334-335	102	65.6	2	204	88653	0.3129	-0.49	15850	0.979423	2.04
332-333	103	65.6	2	206	88859	0.3136	-0.49	15852	0.979546	2.04
330-331	104	65.7	2	208	89067	0.3143	-0.48	15854	0.979670	2.05
327-329	105	65.7	3	315	89382	0.3154	-0.48	15857	0.979855	2.05
324-326	106	65.7	3	318	89700	0.3166	-0.48	15860	0.980041	2.05
318-323	108	65.8	6	648	90348	0.3188	-0.47	15866	0.980412	2.06
316-317	109	65.9	2	218	90566	0.3196	-0.47	15868	0.980535	2.06
315	110	65.9	1	110	90676	0.3200	-0.47	15869	0.980597	2.07
314	111	65.9	1	111	90787	0.3204	-0.47	15870	0.980659	2.07
313	112	66.0	1	112	90899	0.3208	-0.47	15871	0.980720	2.07
311-312	113	66.0	2	226	91125	0.3216	-0.46	15873	0.980844	2.07
310	115	66.1	1	115	91240	0.3220	-0.46	15874	0.980906	2.07
308-309	116	66.1	2	232	91472	0.3228	-0.46	15876	0.981029	2.08
307	117	66.2	1	117	91589	0.3232	-0.46	15877	0.981091	2.08
305-306	118	66.2	2	236	91825	0.3240	-0.46	15879	0.981215	2.08
300-304	119	66.3	5	595	92420	0.3261	-0.45	15884	0.981524	2.09
298-299	120	66.3	2	240	92660	0.3270	-0.45	15886	0.981647	2.09
295-297	122	66.4	3	366	93026	0.3283	-0.44	15889	0.981833	2.09
293-294	123	66.4	2	246	93272	0.3292	-0.44	15891	0.981956	2.10
290-292	124	66.4	3	372	93644	0.3305	-0.44	15894	0.982142	2.10
287-289	125	66.5	3	375	94019	0.3318	-0.43	15897	0.982327	2.10
284-286	126	66.5	3	378	94397	0.3331	-0.43	15900	0.982512	2.11
282-283	127	66.5	2	254	94651	0.3340	-0.43	15902	0.982636	2.11
278-281	128	66.6	4	512	95163	0.3358	-0.42	15906	0.982883	2.12
276-277	129	66.6	2	258	95421	0.3367	-0.42	15908	0.983007	2.12
274-275	130	66.6	2	260	95681	0.3377	-0.42	15910	0.983130	2.12
272-273	131	66.7	2	262	95943	0.3386	-0.42	15912	0.983254	2.13
269-271	132	66.7	3	396	96339	0.3400	-0.41	15915	0.983439	2.13
268	133	66.7	1	133	96472	0.3404	-0.41	15916	0.983501	2.13
266-267	134	66.8	2	268	96740	0.3414	-0.41	15918	0.983625	2.14
262-265	135	66.8	4	540	97280	0.3433	-0.40	15922	0.983872	2.14
257-261	136	66.8	5	680	97960	0.3457	-0.40	15927	0.984181	2.15
255-256	137	66.9	2	274	98234	0.3467	-0.39	15929	0.984304	2.15
252-254	138	66.9	3	414	98648	0.3481	-0.39	15932	0.984490	2.16
250-251	139	66.9	2	278	98926	0.3491	-0.39	15934	0.984613	2.16
248-249	141	67.0	2	282	99208	0.3501	-0.39	15936	0.984737	2.16
245-247	143	67.0	3	429	99637	0.3516	-0.38	15939	0.984922	2.17
243-244	144	67.1	2	288	99925	0.3526	-0.38	15941	0.985046	2.17
242	145	67.1	1	145	100070	0.3531	-0.38	15942	0.985108	2.17
241	146	67.1	1	146	100216	0.3537	-0.38	15943	0.985170	2.17
240	147	67.2	1	147	100363	0.3542	-0.37	15944	0.985231	2.18
239	148	67.2	1	148	100511	0.3547	-0.37	15945	0.985293	2.18
237-238	149	67.2	2	298	100809	0.3558	-0.37	15947	0.985417	2.18
234-236	150	67.3	3	450	101259	0.3573	-0.37	15950	0.985602	2.19
233	152	67.3	1	152	101411	0.3579	-0.36	15951	0.985664	2.19
232	153	67.3	1	153	101564	0.3584	-0.36	15952	0.985726	2.19
231	155	67.4	1	155	101719	0.3590	-0.36	15953	0.985788	2.19
230	156	67.4	1	156	101875	0.3595	-0.36	15954	0.985849	2.19
229	157	67.4	1	157	102032	0.3601	-0.36	15955	0.985911	2.19
226-228	161	67.6	3	483	102515	0.3618	-0.35	15958	0.986097	2.20
225	162	67.6	1	162	102677	0.3623	-0.35	15959	0.986158	2.20
223-224	163	67.6	2	326	103003	0.3635	-0.35	15961	0.986282	2.21
220-222	164	67.6	3	492	103495	0.3652	-0.34	15964	0.986467	2.21
218-219	165	67.7	2	330	103825	0.3664	-0.34	15966	0.986591	2.21
217	166	67.7	1	166	103991	0.3670	-0.34	15967	0.986653	2.22
215-216	167	67.7	2	334	104325	0.3682	-0.34	15969	0.986776	2.22
214	168	67.7	1	168	104493	0.3688	-0.34	15970	0.986838	2.22
211-213	170	67.8	3	510	105003	0.3706	-0.33	15973	0.987023	2.23
209-210	175	67.9	2	350	105353	0.3718	-0.33	15975	0.987147	2.23
208	177	68.0	1	177	105530	0.3724	-0.33	15976	0.987209	2.23
206-207	178	68.0	2	356	105886	0.3737	-0.32	15978	0.987332	2.24
205	179	68.0	1	179	106065	0.3743	-0.32	15979	0.987394	2.24
204	180	68.0	1	180	106245	0.3749	-0.32	15980	0.987456	2.24
203	181	68.1	1	181	106426	0.3756	-0.32	15981	0.987518	2.24
202	182	68.1	1	182	106608	0.3762	-0.32	15982	0.987580	2.24
201	184	68.1	1	184	106792	0.3769	-0.31	15983	0.987641	2.25
199-200	188	68.2	2	376	107168	0.3782	-0.31	15985	0.987765	2.25
198	191	68.3	1	191	107359	0.3789	-0.31	15986	0.987827	2.25
197	192	68.3	1	192	107551	0.3795	-0.31	15987	0.987889	2.25
196	193	68.3	1	193	107744	0.3802	-0.30	15988	0.987950	2.26
195	194	68.4	1	194	107938	0.3809	-0.30	15989	0.988012	2.26
193-194	195	68.4	2	390	108328	0.3823	-0.30	15991	0.988136	2.26
192	196	68.4	1	196	108524	0.3830	-0.30	15992	0.988197	2.26
191	198	68.5	1	198	108722	0.3837	-0.30	15993	0.988259	2.27
190	199	68.5	1	199	108921	0.3844	-0.29	15994	0.988321	2.27
189	200	68.5	1	200	109121	0.3851	-0.29	15995	0.988383	2.27
188	201	68.5	1	201	109322	0.3858	-0.29	15996	0.988445	2.27
187	202	68.5	1	202	109524	0.3865	-0.29	15997	0.988506	2.27
186	203	68.6	1	203	109727	0.3872	-0.29	15998	0.988568	2.28
185	205	68.6	1	205	109932	0.3879	-0.28	15999	0.988630	2.28
184	206	68.6	1	206	110138	0.3887	-0.28	16000	0.988692	2.28
183	208	68.7	1	208	110346	0.3894	-0.28	16001	0.988754	2.28
182	211	68.7	1	211	110557	0.3902	-0.28	16002	0.988815	2.28
177-181	212	68.8	5	1060	111617	0.3939	-0.27	16007	0.989124	2.29
176	213	68.8	1	213	111830	0.3946	-0.27	16008	0.989186	2.30
173-175	215	68.8	3	645	112475	0.3969	-0.26	16011	0.989372	2.30
172	217	68.9	1	217	112692	0.3977	-0.26	16012	0.989433	2.31
169-171	218	68.9	3	654	113346	0.4000	-0.25	16015	0.989619	2.31
168	219	68.9	1	219	113565	0.4008	-0.25	16016	0.989681	2.31
167	221	68.9	1	221	113786	0.4015	-0.25	16017	0.989742	2.32
166	224	69.0	1	224	114010	0.4023	-0.25	16018	0.989804	2.32
165	227	69.0	1	227	114237	0.4031	-0.25	16019	0.989866	2.32
164	228	69.1	1	228	114465	0.4039	-0.24	16020	0.989928	2.32
163	231	69.1	1	231	114696	0.4048	-0.24	16021	0.989989	2.33
162	234	69.2	1	234	114930	0.4056	-0.24	16022	0.990051	2.33
161	236	69.2	1	236	115166	0.4064	-0.24	16023	0.990113	2.33
160	237	69.2	1	237	115403	0.4073	-0.23	16024	0.990175	2.33
159	238	69.3	1	238	115641	0.4081	-0.23	16025	0.990237	2.34
158	239	69.3	1	239	115880	0.4089	-0.23	16026	0.990298	2.34
156-157	241	69.3	2	482	116362	0.4106	-0.23	16028	0.990422	2.34
155	243	69.3	1	243	116605	0.4115	-0.22	16029	0.990484	2.34
154	245	69.4	1	245	116850	0.4124	-0.22	16030	0.990546	2.35
152-153	247	69.4	2	494	117344	0.4141	-0.22	16032	0.990669	2.35
151	250	69.5	1	250	117594	0.4150	-0.21	16033	0.990731	2.35
150	256	69.6	1	256	117850	0.4159	-0.21	16034	0.990793	2.36
149	258	69.6	1	258	118108	0.4168	-0.21	16035	0.990855	2.36
148	259	69.6	1	259	118367	0.4177	-0.21	16036	0.990916	2.36
147	263	69.7	1	263	118630	0.4186	-0.21	16037	0.990978	2.36
145-146	267	69.7	2	534	119164	0.4205	-0.20	16039	0.991102	2.37
143-144	272	69.8	2	544	119708	0.4224	-0.20	16041	0.991225	2.37
142	274	69.9	1	274	119982	0.4234	-0.19	16042	0.991287	2.38
141	275	69.9	1	275	120257	0.4244	-0.19	16043	0.991349	2.38
140	280	70.0	1	280	120537	0.4254	-0.19	16044	0.991411	2.38
139	281	70.0	1	281	120818	0.4264	-0.19	16045	0.991472	2.39
138	284	70.0	1	284	121102	0.4274	-0.18	16046	0.991534	2.39
137	285	70.0	1	285	121387	0.4284	-0.18	16047	0.991596	2.39
136	286	70.0	1	286	121673	0.4294	-0.18	16048	0.991658	2.39
135	288	70.1	1	288	121961	0.4304	-0.18	16049	0.991720	2.40
133-134	290	70.1	2	580	122541	0.4324	-0.17	16051	0.991843	2.40
132	292	70.1	1	292	122833	0.4335	-0.17	16052	0.991905	2.40
131	293	70.2	1	293	123126	0.4345	-0.16	16053	0.991967	2.41
130	296	70.2	1	296	123422	0.4356	-0.16	16054	0.992029	2.41
129	297	70.2	1	297	123719	0.4366	-0.16	16055	0.992090	2.41
128	300	70.3	1	300	124019	0.4377	-0.16	16056	0.992152	2.42
127	302	70.3	1	302	124321	0.4387	-0.15	16057	0.992214	2.42
125-126	303	70.3	2	606	124927	0.4409	-0.15	16059	0.992338	2.42
124	304	70.3	1	304	125231	0.4419	-0.15	16060	0.992399	2.43
123	310	70.4	1	310	125541	0.4430	-0.14	16061	0.992461	2.43
122	314	70.5	1	314	125855	0.4441	-0.14	16062	0.992523	2.43
121	315	70.5	1	315	126170	0.4453	-0.14	16063	0.992585	2.44
120	330	70.7	1	330	126500	0.4464	-0.13	16064	0.992647	2.44
119	332	70.7	1	332	126832	0.4476	-0.13	16065	0.992708	2.44
118	333	70.7	1	333	127165	0.4488	-0.13	16066	0.992770	2.45
117	340	70.8	1	340	127505	0.4500	-0.13	16067	0.992832	2.45

Rank	Occ. F	SFI	F	Tokens	Cum. Tokens	Cum. P Tokens	Y	Cum. Types	Cum. P Types	Z
116	347	70.9	1	347	127852	0.4512	-0.12	16068	0.992894	2.45
115	352	70.9	1	352	128204	0.4524	-0.12	16069	0.992956	2.45
114	354	71.0	1	354	128558	0.4537	-0.12	16070	0.993017	2.46
112–113	356	71.0	2	712	129270	0.4562	-0.11	16072	0.993141	2.46
111	358	71.0	1	358	129628	0.4575	-0.11	16073	0.993203	2.47
110	359	71.0	1	359	129987	0.4587	-0.10	16074	0.993264	2.47
109	369	71.2	1	369	130356	0.4600	-0.10	16075	0.993326	2.47
108	377	71.2	1	377	130733	0.4614	-0.10	16076	0.993388	2.48
107	379	71.3	1	379	131112	0.4627	-0.09	16077	0.993450	2.48
106	383	71.3	1	383	131495	0.4640	-0.09	16078	0.993512	2.48
103–105	384	71.3	3	1152	132647	0.4681	-0.08	16081	0.993697	2.49
102	396	71.5	1	396	133043	0.4695	-0.08	16082	0.993759	2.50
101	397	71.5	1	397	133440	0.4709	-0.07	16083	0.993821	2.50
100	400	71.5	1	400	133840	0.4723	-0.07	16084	0.993882	2.51
98–99	405	71.6	2	810	134650	0.4752	-0.06	16086	0.994006	2.51
96–97	406	71.6	2	812	135462	0.4780	-0.06	16088	0.994130	2.52
94–95	411	71.6	2	822	136284	0.4809	-0.05	16090	0.994253	2.53
93	412	71.6	1	412	136696	0.4824	-0.04	16091	0.994315	2.53
91–92	414	71.7	2	828	137524	0.4853	-0.04	16093	0.994439	2.54
90	417	71.7	1	417	137941	0.4868	-0.03	16094	0.994500	2.54
89	422	71.7	1	422	138363	0.4883	-0.03	16095	0.994562	2.55
88	425	71.8	1	425	138788	0.4898	-0.03	16096	0.994624	2.55
87	429	71.8	1	429	139217	0.4913	-0.02	16097	0.994686	2.55
86	433	71.8	1	433	139650	0.4928	-0.02	16098	0.994748	2.56
85	435	71.9	1	435	140085	0.4944	-0.01	16099	0.994809	2.56
83–84	446	72.0	2	892	140977	0.4975	-0.01	16101	0.994933	2.57
82	454	72.1	1	454	141431	0.4991	-0.00	16102	0.994995	2.58
81	459	72.1	1	459	141890	0.5007	0.00	16103	0.995057	2.58
80	466	72.2	1	466	142356	0.5024	0.01	16104	0.995118	2.58
79	475	72.2	1	475	142831	0.5040	0.01	16105	0.995180	2.59
78	487	72.4	1	487	143318	0.5058	0.01	16106	0.995242	2.59
77	498	72.5	1	498	143816	0.5075	0.02	16107	0.995304	2.60
76	503	72.5	1	503	144319	0.5093	0.02	16108	0.995366	2.60
75	528	72.7	1	528	144847	0.5112	0.03	16109	0.995427	2.61
74	532	72.7	1	532	145379	0.5130	0.03	16110	0.995489	2.61
73	555	72.9	1	555	145934	0.5150	0.04	16111	0.995551	2.62
72	558	72.9	1	558	146492	0.5170	0.04	16112	0.995613	2.62
71	561	73.0	1	561	147053	0.5189	0.05	16113	0.995674	2.63
70	565	73.0	1	565	147618	0.5209	0.05	16114	0.995736	2.63
68–69	569	73.0	2	1138	148756	0.5250	0.06	16116	0.995860	2.64
67	583	73.1	1	583	149339	0.5270	0.07	16117	0.995922	2.65
66	597	73.2	1	597	149936	0.5291	0.07	16118	0.995983	2.65
65	598	73.2	1	598	150534	0.5312	0.08	16119	0.996045	2.66
64	604	73.3	1	604	151138	0.5334	0.08	16120	0.996107	2.66
63	608	73.3	1	608	151746	0.5355	0.09	16121	0.996169	2.67
62	621	73.4	1	621	152367	0.5377	0.09	16122	0.996231	2.67
61	622	73.4	1	622	152989	0.5399	0.10	16123	0.996292	2.68
59–60	623	73.4	2	1246	154235	0.5443	0.11	16125	0.996416	2.69
58	654	73.6	1	654	154889	0.5466	0.12	16126	0.996478	2.69
57	682	73.8	1	682	155571	0.5490	0.12	16127	0.996540	2.70
56	704	74.0	1	704	156275	0.5515	0.13	16128	0.996601	2.71
55	727	74.1	1	727	157002	0.5541	0.14	16129	0.996663	2.71
54	740	74.2	1	740	157742	0.5567	0.14	16130	0.996725	2.72
53	742	74.2	1	742	158484	0.5593	0.15	16131	0.996787	2.73
52	755	74.3	1	755	159239	0.5620	0.16	16132	0.996849	2.73
51	767	74.3	1	767	160006	0.5647	0.16	16133	0.996910	2.74
50	778	74.4	1	778	160784	0.5674	0.17	16134	0.996972	2.74
49	932	75.2	1	932	161716	0.5707	0.18	16135	0.997034	2.75
48	939	75.2	1	939	162655	0.5740	0.19	16136	0.997096	2.76
47	940	75.2	1	940	163595	0.5773	0.20	16137	0.997157	2.77
46	945	75.2	1	945	164540	0.5807	0.20	16138	0.997219	2.77
45	966	75.3	1	966	165506	0.5841	0.21	16139	0.997281	2.78
44	967	75.3	1	967	166473	0.5875	0.22	16140	0.997343	2.79
43	1003	75.5	1	1003	167476	0.5910	0.23	16141	0.997405	2.79
42	1014	75.5	1	1014	168490	0.5946	0.24	16142	0.997466	2.80
41	1027	75.6	1	1027	169517	0.5982	0.25	16143	0.997528	2.81
40	1052	75.7	1	1052	170569	0.6019	0.26	16144	0.997590	2.82
39	1053	75.7	1	1053	171622	0.6057	0.27	16145	0.997652	2.83
38	1064	75.7	1	1064	172686	0.6094	0.28	16146	0.997714	2.84
37	1085	75.8	1	1085	173771	0.6132	0.29	16147	0.997775	2.84
36	1116	76.0	1	1116	174887	0.6172	0.30	16148	0.997837	2.85
35	1118	76.0	1	1118	176005	0.6211	0.31	16149	0.997899	2.86
34	1124	76.0	1	1124	177129	0.6251	0.32	16150	0.997961	2.87
33	1210	76.3	1	1210	178339	0.6294	0.33	16151	0.998023	2.88
31–32	1215	76.3	2	2430	180769	0.6379	0.35	16153	0.998146	2.90
30	1226	76.4	1	1226	181995	0.6423	0.36	16154	0.998208	2.91
29	1268	76.5	1	1268	183263	0.6467	0.38	16155	0.998270	2.92
28	1271	76.5	1	1271	184534	0.6512	0.39	16156	0.998332	2.93
27	1272	76.5	1	1272	185806	0.6557	0.40	16157	0.998393	2.95
25–26	1281	76.6	2	2562	188368	0.6647	0.43	16159	0.998517	2.97
24	1409	77.0	1	1409	189777	0.6697	0.44	16160	0.998579	2.98
23	1476	77.2	1	1476	191253	0.6749	0.45	16161	0.998641	3.00
22	1502	77.2	1	1502	192755	0.6802	0.47	16162	0.998702	3.01
20–21	1607	77.5	2	3214	195969	0.6916	0.50	16164	0.998826	3.04
19	1674	77.7	1	1674	197643	0.6975	0.52	16165	0.998888	3.06
18	1675	77.7	1	1675	199318	0.7034	0.53	16166	0.998949	3.08
17	1766	77.9	1	1766	201084	0.7096	0.55	16167	0.999011	3.09
16	1882	78.2	1	1882	202966	0.7163	0.57	16168	0.999073	3.11
14–15	1930	78.3	2	3860	206826	0.7299	0.61	16170	0.999197	3.15
13	2069	78.6	1	2069	208895	0.7372	0.63	16171	0.999258	3.18
12	2150	78.8	1	2150	211045	0.7448	0.66	16172	0.999320	3.20
11	2301	79.1	1	2301	213346	0.7529	0.68	16173	0.999382	3.23
10	2803	80.0	1	2803	216149	0.7628	0.72	16174	0.999444	3.26
9	2975	80.2	1	2975	219124	0.7733	0.75	16175	0.999506	3.29
8	4501	82.0	1	4501	223625	0.7892	0.80	16176	0.999567	3.33
7	5168	82.6	1	5168	228793	0.8074	0.87	16177	0.999629	3.37
6	5909	83.2	1	5909	234702	0.8283	0.95	16178	0.999691	3.42
5	6346	83.5	1	6346	241048	0.8507	1.04	16179	0.999753	3.48
4	6437	83.6	1	6437	247485	0.8734	1.14	16180	0.999815	3.56
3	7466	84.2	1	7466	254951	0.8997	1.28	16181	0.999876	3.67
2	8106	84.6	1	8106	263057	0.9283	1.46	16182	0.999938	3.84
1	20310	88.6	1	20310	283367	1.0000	+INF.	16183	1.000000	+INF.

Rank	Occ. F	SFI	F	Tokens	Cum. Tokens	Cum. P Tokens	Y	Cum. Types	Cum. P Types	Z
3650– 7423	1	54.1	3774	3774	3774	0.0653	−1.51	3774	0.508420	0.02
2405– 3649	2	56.4	1245	2490	6264	0.1084	−1.23	5019	0.676142	0.46
1844– 2404	3	57.8	561	1683	7947	0.1375	−1.09	5580	0.751718	0.68
1506– 1843	4	58.9	338	1352	9299	0.1609	−0.99	5918	0.797252	0.83
1254– 1505	5	59.8	252	1260	10559	0.1828	−0.90	6170	0.831200	0.96
1089– 1253	6	60.5	165	990	11549	0.1999	−0.84	6335	0.853428	1.05
955– 1088	7	61.1	134	938	12487	0.2161	−0.79	6469	0.871481	1.13
858– 954	8	61.7	97	776	13263	0.2296	−0.74	6566	0.884548	1.20
766– 857	9	62.2	92	828	14091	0.2439	−0.69	6658	0.896942	1.26
701– 765	10	62.6	65	650	14741	0.2551	−0.66	6723	0.905698	1.31
635– 700	11	63.0	66	726	15467	0.2677	−0.62	6789	0.914590	1.37
591– 634	12	63.4	44	528	15995	0.2768	−0.59	6833	0.920517	1.41
558– 590	13	63.7	33	429	16424	0.2843	−0.57	6866	0.924963	1.44
509– 557	14	64.0	49	686	17110	0.2961	−0.54	6915	0.931564	1.49
470– 508	15	64.3	39	585	17695	0.3063	−0.51	6954	0.936818	1.53
445– 469	16	64.6	25	400	18095	0.3132	−0.49	6979	0.940186	1.56
412– 444	17	64.8	33	561	18656	0.3229	−0.46	7012	0.944632	1.59
388– 411	18	65.1	24	432	19088	0.3304	−0.44	7036	0.947865	1.62
369– 387	19	65.3	19	361	19449	0.3366	−0.42	7055	0.950424	1.65
350– 368	20	65.5	19	380	19829	0.3432	−0.40	7074	0.952984	1.67
329– 349	21	65.7	21	441	20270	0.3508	−0.38	7095	0.955813	1.70
318– 328	22	65.9	11	242	20512	0.3550	−0.37	7106	0.957295	1.72
309– 317	23	66.1	9	207	20719	0.3586	−0.36	7115	0.958507	1.73
290– 308	24	66.3	19	456	21175	0.3665	−0.34	7134	0.961067	1.76
281– 289	25	66.4	9	225	21400	0.3704	−0.33	7143	0.962279	1.78
269– 280	26	66.6	12	312	21712	0.3758	−0.32	7155	0.963896	1.80
257– 268	27	66.8	12	324	22036	0.3814	−0.30	7167	0.965513	1.82
249– 256	28	66.9	8	224	22260	0.3853	−0.29	7175	0.966590	1.83
236– 248	29	67.1	13	377	22637	0.3918	−0.27	7188	0.968342	1.86
227– 235	30	67.2	9	270	22907	0.3965	−0.26	7197	0.969554	1.87
222– 226	31	67.4	5	155	23062	0.3992	−0.26	7202	0.970228	1.88
217– 221	32	67.5	5	160	23222	0.4019	−0.25	7207	0.970901	1.89
211– 216	33	67.6	6	198	23420	0.4054	−0.24	7213	0.971710	1.91
205– 210	34	67.8	6	204	23624	0.4089	−0.23	7219	0.972518	1.92
197– 204	35	67.9	8	280	23904	0.4137	−0.22	7227	0.973596	1.94
188– 196	36	68.0	9	324	24228	0.4193	−0.20	7236	0.974808	1.96
184– 187	37	68.1	4	148	24376	0.4219	−0.20	7240	0.975347	1.97
180– 183	38	68.2	4	152	24528	0.4245	−0.19	7244	0.975886	1.98
178– 179	39	68.3	2	78	24606	0.4259	−0.19	7246	0.976155	1.98
173– 177	40	68.5	5	200	24806	0.4293	−0.18	7251	0.976829	1.99
167– 172	41	68.6	6	246	25052	0.4336	−0.17	7257	0.977637	2.01
162– 166	42	68.7	5	210	25262	0.4372	−0.16	7262	0.978311	2.02
160– 161	43	68.8	2	86	25348	0.4387	−0.15	7264	0.978580	2.03
158– 159	44	68.9	2	88	25436	0.4403	−0.15	7266	0.978849	2.03
155– 157	45	69.0	3	135	25571	0.4426	−0.14	7269	0.979254	2.04
149– 154	46	69.1	6	276	25847	0.4474	−0.13	7275	0.980062	2.06
145– 148	47	69.1	4	188	26035	0.4506	−0.12	7279	0.980601	2.07
144	48	69.2	1	48	26083	0.4515	−0.12	7280	0.980736	2.07
140– 143	49	69.3	4	196	26279	0.4548	−0.11	7284	0.981274	2.08
136– 139	50	69.4	4	200	26479	0.4583	−0.10	7288	0.981813	2.09
134– 135	51	69.5	2	102	26581	0.4601	−0.10	7290	0.982083	2.10
131– 133	52	69.6	3	156	26737	0.4628	−0.09	7293	0.982487	2.11
130	53	69.7	1	53	26790	0.4637	−0.09	7294	0.982622	2.11
126– 129	54	69.7	4	216	27006	0.4674	−0.08	7298	0.983160	2.12
124– 125	55	69.8	2	110	27116	0.4693	−0.08	7300	0.983430	2.13
120– 123	56	69.9	4	224	27340	0.4732	−0.07	7304	0.983969	2.14
117– 119	58	70.1	3	174	27514	0.4762	−0.06	7307	0.984373	2.15
115– 116	60	70.2	2	120	27634	0.4783	−0.05	7309	0.984642	2.16
111– 114	61	70.3	4	244	27878	0.4825	−0.04	7313	0.985181	2.17
110	64	70.5	1	64	27942	0.4836	−0.04	7314	0.985316	2.18
109	65	70.5	1	65	28007	0.4848	−0.04	7315	0.985451	2.18
108	66	70.6	1	66	28073	0.4859	−0.04	7316	0.985585	2.19
107	67	70.7	1	67	28140	0.4871	−0.03	7317	0.985720	2.19
105– 106	68	70.7	2	136	28276	0.4894	−0.03	7319	0.985989	2.20
103– 104	69	70.8	2	138	28414	0.4918	−0.02	7321	0.986259	2.20
102	70	70.9	1	70	28484	0.4930	−0.02	7322	0.986394	2.21
100– 101	71	70.9	2	142	28626	0.4955	−0.01	7324	0.986663	2.22
99	72	71.0	1	72	28698	0.4967	−0.01	7325	0.986798	2.22
98	74	71.1	1	74	28772	0.4980	−0.01	7326	0.986932	2.22
96– 97	75	71.2	2	150	28922	0.5006	0.00	7328	0.987202	2.23
94– 95	76	71.2	2	152	29074	0.5032	0.01	7330	0.987471	2.24
93	77	71.3	1	77	29151	0.5046	0.01	7331	0.987606	2.24
92	79	71.4	1	79	29230	0.5059	0.01	7332	0.987741	2.25
91	80	71.4	1	80	29310	0.5073	0.02	7333	0.987876	2.25
88– 90	82	71.5	3	246	29556	0.5116	0.03	7336	0.988280	2.27
85– 87	83	71.6	3	249	29805	0.5159	0.04	7339	0.988684	2.28
84	88	71.9	1	88	29893	0.5174	0.04	7340	0.988819	2.28
82– 83	89	71.9	2	178	30071	0.5205	0.05	7342	0.989088	2.29
81	91	72.0	1	91	30162	0.5221	0.06	7343	0.989223	2.30
78– 80	92	72.0	3	276	30438	0.5268	0.07	7346	0.989627	2.31
77	93	72.1	1	93	30531	0.5284	0.07	7347	0.989762	2.32
76	94	72.1	1	94	30625	0.5301	0.08	7348	0.989896	2.32
75	96	72.2	1	96	30721	0.5317	0.08	7349	0.990031	2.33
74	99	72.4	1	99	30820	0.5334	0.08	7350	0.990166	2.33
73	100	72.4	1	100	30920	0.5352	0.09	7351	0.990300	2.34
72	102	72.5	1	102	31022	0.5369	0.09	7352	0.990435	2.34
71	104	72.6	1	104	31126	0.5387	0.10	7353	0.990570	2.35
69– 70	105	72.6	2	210	31336	0.5424	0.11	7355	0.990839	2.36
68	106	72.7	1	106	31442	0.5442	0.11	7356	0.990974	2.36
66– 67	107	72.7	2	214	31656	0.5479	0.12	7358	0.991243	2.38
65	108	72.7	1	108	31764	0.5498	0.13	7359	0.991378	2.38
64	110	72.8	1	110	31874	0.5517	0.13	7360	0.991513	2.39
63	111	72.9	1	111	31985	0.5536	0.13	7361	0.991648	2.39
62	113	72.9	1	113	32098	0.5556	0.14	7362	0.991782	2.40
61	115	73.0	1	115	32213	0.5575	0.14	7363	0.991917	2.41
60	120	73.2	1	120	32333	0.5596	0.15	7364	0.992052	2.41
58– 59	121	73.2	2	242	32575	0.5638	0.16	7366	0.992321	2.42
57	123	73.3	1	123	32698	0.5659	0.17	7367	0.992456	2.43
55– 56	125	73.4	2	250	32948	0.5703	0.18	7369	0.992725	2.44
53– 54	126	73.4	2	252	33200	0.5746	0.19	7371	0.992995	2.46
52	129	73.5	1	129	33329	0.5769	0.19	7372	0.993129	2.46
51	130	73.5	1	130	33459	0.5791	0.20	7373	0.993264	2.47
50	131	73.6	1	131	33590	0.5814	0.21	7374	0.993399	2.48
49	137	73.8	1	137	33727	0.5838	0.21	7375	0.993534	2.49
48	143	74.0	1	143	33870	0.5862	0.22	7376	0.993668	2.49
47	149	74.1	1	149	34019	0.5888	0.22	7377	0.993803	2.50
46	150	74.2	1	150	34169	0.5914	0.23	7378	0.993938	2.51
45	153	74.2	1	153	34322	0.5941	0.24	7379	0.994072	2.52
44	156	74.3	1	156	34478	0.5968	0.24	7380	0.994207	2.52
43	158	74.4	1	158	34636	0.5995	0.25	7381	0.994342	2.53
42	162	74.5	1	162	34798	0.6023	0.26	7382	0.994477	2.54
41	164	74.5	1	164	34962	0.6051	0.27	7383	0.994611	2.55
40	167	74.6	1	167	35129	0.6080	0.27	7384	0.994746	2.56
39	173	74.8	1	173	35302	0.6110	0.28	7385	0.994881	2.57
38	177	74.9	1	177	35479	0.6141	0.29	7386	0.995015	2.58
37	183	75.0	1	183	35662	0.6172	0.30	7387	0.995150	2.59
36	185	75.1	1	185	35847	0.6204	0.31	7388	0.995285	2.60
35	189	75.2	1	189	36036	0.6237	0.32	7389	0.995420	2.61
34	197	75.3	1	197	36233	0.6271	0.32	7390	0.995554	2.62
33	204	75.5	1	204	36437	0.6307	0.33	7391	0.995689	2.63
32	212	75.7	1	212	36649	0.6343	0.34	7392	0.995824	2.64
31	221	75.8	1	221	36870	0.6382	0.35	7393	0.995959	2.65
29– 30	230	76.0	2	460	37330	0.6461	0.37	7395	0.996228	2.67
28	236	76.1	1	236	37566	0.6502	0.39	7396	0.996363	2.68
27	240	76.2	1	240	37806	0.6544	0.40	7397	0.996497	2.70
26	243	76.2	1	243	38049	0.6586	0.41	7398	0.996632	2.71
25	255	76.5	1	255	38304	0.6630	0.42	7399	0.996767	2.72
24	259	76.5	1	259	38563	0.6675	0.43	7400	0.996902	2.74
23	266	76.6	1	266	38829	0.6721	0.45	7401	0.997036	2.75
22	283	76.9	1	283	39112	0.6770	0.46	7402	0.997171	2.77
21	300	77.2	1	300	39412	0.6822	0.47	7403	0.997306	2.78
20	326	77.5	1	326	39738	0.6878	0.49	7404	0.997440	2.80
19	349	77.8	1	349	40087	0.6938	0.51	7405	0.997575	2.82
18	358	77.9	1	358	40445	0.7000	0.52	7406	0.997710	2.84
17	363	78.0	1	363	40808	0.7063	0.54	7407	0.997845	2.85
16	370	78.1	1	370	41178	0.7127	0.56	7408	0.997979	2.87
15	380	78.2	1	380	41558	0.7193	0.58	7409	0.998114	2.90
14	387	78.3	1	387	41945	0.7260	0.60	7410	0.998249	2.92
13	396	78.4	1	396	42341	0.7328	0.62	7411	0.998383	2.94
12	403	78.4	1	403	42744	0.7398	0.64	7412	0.998518	2.97
11	427	78.7	1	427	43171	0.7472	0.67	7413	0.998653	3.00
10	456	79.0	1	456	43627	0.7551	0.69	7414	0.998788	3.03
9	545	79.8	1	545	44172	0.7645	0.72	7415	0.998922	3.07
8	738	81.1	1	738	44910	0.7773	0.76	7416	0.999057	3.11
7	815	81.5	1	815	45725	0.7914	0.81	7417	0.999192	3.15
6	1116	82.9	1	1116	46841	0.8107	0.88	7418	0.999326	3.21
5	1241	83.3	1	1241	48082	0.8322	0.96	7419	0.999461	3.27
4	1471	84.1	1	1471	49553	0.8577	1.07	7420	0.999596	3.35
3	1682	84.6	1	1682	51235	0.8868	1.21	7421	0.999731	3.46
2	1944	85.3	1	1944	53179	0.9204	1.41	7422	0.999865	3.64
1	4597	89.0	1	4597	57776	1.0000	+INF.	7423	1.000000	+INF.

Rank	Occ. F	SFI	F	Tokens	Cum. Tokens	Cum. P Tokens	Y	Cum. Types	Cum. P Types	Z
10800-19987	1	47.3	9188	9188	9188	0.0331	-1.84	9188	0.459699	-0.10
7650-10799	2	49.5	3150	6300	15488	0.0557	-1.59	12338	0.617301	0.30
5977- 7649	3	51.0	1673	5019	20507	0.0738	-1.45	14011	0.701006	0.53
4997- 5976	4	52.1	980	3920	24427	0.0879	-1.35	14991	0.750037	0.67
4222- 4996	5	53.0	775	3875	28302	0.1018	-1.27	15766	0.788813	0.80
3702- 4221	6	53.7	520	3120	31422	0.1131	-1.21	16286	0.814830	0.90
3284- 3701	7	54.3	418	2926	34348	0.1236	-1.16	16704	0.835743	0.98
2920- 3283	8	54.9	364	2912	37260	0.1341	-1.11	17068	0.853955	1.05
2643- 2919	9	55.3	277	2493	39753	0.1430	-1.07	17345	0.867814	1.12
2409- 2642	10	55.8	234	2340	42093	0.1515	-1.03	17579	0.879522	1.17
2205- 2408	11	56.2	204	2244	44337	0.1595	-1.00	17783	0.889728	1.23
2050- 2204	12	56.5	155	1860	46197	0.1662	-0.97	17938	0.897483	1.27
1927- 2049	13	56.9	123	1599	47796	0.1720	-0.95	18061	0.903637	1.30
1804- 1926	14	57.2	123	1722	49518	0.1782	-0.92	18184	0.909791	1.34
1688- 1803	15	57.5	116	1740	51258	0.1844	-0.90	18300	0.915595	1.38
1585- 1687	16	57.7	103	1648	52906	0.1904	-0.88	18403	0.920748	1.41
1516- 1584	17	58.0	69	1173	54079	0.1946	-0.86	18472	0.924201	1.43
1451- 1515	18	58.2	65	1170	55249	0.1988	-0.85	18537	0.927453	1.46
1393- 1450	19	58.5	58	1102	56351	0.2028	-0.83	18595	0.930355	1.48
1333- 1392	20	58.7	60	1200	57551	0.2071	-0.82	18655	0.933357	1.50
1269- 1332	21	58.9	64	1344	58895	0.2119	-0.80	18719	0.936559	1.53
1221- 1268	22	59.1	48	1056	59951	0.2157	-0.79	18767	0.938960	1.55
1173- 1220	23	59.3	48	1104	61055	0.2197	-0.77	18815	0.941362	1.57
1130- 1172	24	59.5	43	1032	62087	0.2234	-0.76	18858	0.943513	1.58
1087- 1129	25	59.6	43	1075	63162	0.2273	-0.75	18901	0.945665	1.60
1050- 1086	26	59.8	37	962	64124	0.2307	-0.74	18938	0.947516	1.62
1032- 1049	27	60.0	18	486	64610	0.2325	-0.73	18956	0.948416	1.63
998- 1031	28	60.1	34	952	65562	0.2359	-0.72	18990	0.950118	1.65
976- 997	29	60.3	22	638	66200	0.2382	-0.71	19012	0.951218	1.66
936- 975	30	60.4	40	1200	67400	0.2425	-0.70	19052	0.953220	1.68
909- 935	31	60.5	27	837	68237	0.2455	-0.69	19079	0.954570	1.69
888- 908	32	60.7	21	672	68909	0.2480	-0.68	19100	0.955621	1.70
867- 887	33	60.8	21	693	69602	0.2505	-0.67	19121	0.956672	1.71
842- 866	34	60.9	25	850	70452	0.2535	-0.66	19146	0.957923	1.73
824- 841	35	61.1	18	630	71082	0.2558	-0.66	19164	0.958823	1.74
799- 823	36	61.2	25	900	71982	0.2590	-0.65	19189	0.960074	1.75
777- 798	37	61.3	22	814	72796	0.2619	-0.64	19211	0.961175	1.76
756- 776	38	61.4	21	798	73594	0.2648	-0.63	19232	0.962225	1.78
743- 755	39	61.5	13	507	74101	0.2666	-0.62	19245	0.962876	1.79
723- 742	40	61.6	20	800	74901	0.2695	-0.61	19265	0.963876	1.80
705- 722	41	61.7	18	738	75639	0.2722	-0.61	19283	0.964777	1.81
689- 704	42	61.8	16	672	76311	0.2746	-0.60	19299	0.965578	1.82
672- 688	43	61.9	17	731	77042	0.2772	-0.59	19316	0.966428	1.83
652- 671	44	62.0	20	880	77922	0.2804	-0.58	19336	0.967429	1.84
636- 651	45	62.1	16	720	78642	0.2830	-0.57	19352	0.968229	1.86
624- 635	46	62.2	12	552	79194	0.2850	-0.57	19364	0.968830	1.86
611- 623	47	62.3	13	611	79805	0.2872	-0.56	19377	0.969480	1.87
597- 610	48	62.4	14	672	80477	0.2896	-0.55	19391	0.970181	1.88
582- 596	49	62.5	15	735	81212	0.2922	-0.55	19406	0.970931	1.89
578- 581	50	62.6	4	200	81412	0.2929	-0.54	19410	0.971131	1.90
569- 577	51	62.7	9	459	81871	0.2946	-0.54	19419	0.971582	1.90
550- 568	52	62.8	19	988	82859	0.2982	-0.53	19438	0.972532	1.92
540- 549	53	62.8	10	530	83389	0.3001	-0.52	19448	0.973032	1.93
530- 539	54	62.9	10	540	83929	0.3020	-0.52	19458	0.973533	1.94
519- 529	55	63.0	11	605	84534	0.3042	-0.51	19469	0.974083	1.94
514- 518	56	63.1	5	280	84814	0.3052	-0.51	19474	0.974333	1.95
505- 513	57	63.2	9	513	85327	0.3070	-0.50	19483	0.974784	1.96
496- 504	58	63.2	9	522	85849	0.3089	-0.50	19492	0.975234	1.96
488- 495	59	63.3	8	472	86321	0.3106	-0.49	19500	0.975634	1.97
480- 487	60	63.4	8	480	86801	0.3123	-0.49	19508	0.976034	1.98
476- 479	61	63.4	4	244	87045	0.3132	-0.49	19512	0.976234	1.98
464- 475	62	63.5	12	744	87789	0.3159	-0.48	19524	0.976835	1.99
454- 463	63	63.6	10	630	88419	0.3182	-0.47	19534	0.977335	2.00
442- 453	64	63.7	12	768	89187	0.3209	-0.47	19546	0.977936	2.01
437- 441	65	63.7	5	325	89512	0.3221	-0.46	19551	0.978186	2.02
435- 436	66	63.8	2	132	89644	0.3226	-0.46	19553	0.978286	2.02
425- 434	67	63.9	10	670	90314	0.3250	-0.45	19563	0.978786	2.03
419- 424	68	63.9	6	408	90722	0.3264	-0.45	19569	0.979086	2.04
406- 418	69	64.0	13	897	91619	0.3297	-0.44	19582	0.979737	2.05
400- 405	70	64.0	6	420	92039	0.3312	-0.44	19588	0.980037	2.05
395- 399	71	64.1	5	355	92394	0.3325	-0.43	19593	0.980287	2.06
387- 394	72	64.2	8	576	92970	0.3345	-0.43	19601	0.980687	2.07
383- 386	73	64.2	4	292	93262	0.3356	-0.42	19605	0.980888	2.07
378- 382	74	64.3	5	370	93632	0.3369	-0.42	19610	0.981138	2.08
374- 377	75	64.3	4	300	93932	0.3380	-0.42	19614	0.981338	2.08
371- 373	76	64.4	3	228	94160	0.3388	-0.42	19617	0.981488	2.09
368- 370	77	64.5	3	231	94391	0.3396	-0.41	19620	0.981638	2.09
365- 367	78	64.5	3	234	94625	0.3405	-0.41	19623	0.981788	2.09
362- 364	79	64.6	3	237	94862	0.3413	-0.41	19626	0.981938	2.10
353- 361	80	64.6	9	720	95582	0.3439	-0.40	19635	0.982388	2.11
351- 352	81	64.7	2	162	95744	0.3445	-0.40	19637	0.982489	2.11
347- 350	82	64.7	4	328	96072	0.3457	-0.40	19641	0.982689	2.11
342- 346	83	64.8	5	415	96487	0.3472	-0.39	19646	0.982939	2.12
332- 341	84	64.8	10	840	97327	0.3502	-0.38	19656	0.983439	2.13
331	85	64.9	1	85	97412	0.3505	-0.38	19657	0.983489	2.13
327- 330	86	64.9	4	344	97756	0.3518	-0.38	19661	0.983689	2.14
323- 326	88	65.0	4	352	98108	0.3530	-0.38	19665	0.983890	2.14
322	89	65.1	1	89	98197	0.3533	-0.38	19666	0.983940	2.14
320- 321	90	65.1	2	180	98377	0.3540	-0.37	19668	0.984040	2.15
318- 319	91	65.2	2	182	98559	0.3546	-0.37	19670	0.984140	2.15
316- 317	92	65.2	2	184	98743	0.3553	-0.37	19672	0.984240	2.15
312- 315	93	65.3	4	372	99115	0.3566	-0.37	19676	0.984440	2.16
309- 311	94	65.3	3	282	99397	0.3577	-0.36	19679	0.984590	2.16
305- 308	95	65.4	4	380	99777	0.3590	-0.36	19683	0.984790	2.16
303- 304	96	65.4	2	192	99969	0.3597	-0.36	19685	0.984890	2.17
301- 302	97	65.5	2	194	100163	0.3604	-0.36	19687	0.984990	2.17
300	99	65.5	1	99	100262	0.3608	-0.36	19688	0.985040	2.17
298- 299	100	65.6	2	200	100462	0.3615	-0.35	19690	0.985140	2.17
295- 297	101	65.6	3	303	100765	0.3626	-0.35	19693	0.985290	2.18
294	102	65.7	1	102	100867	0.3630	-0.35	19694	0.985340	2.18
291- 293	103	65.7	3	309	101176	0.3641	-0.35	19697	0.985491	2.18
290	104	65.8	1	104	101280	0.3644	-0.35	19698	0.985541	2.18
285- 289	105	65.8	5	525	101805	0.3663	-0.34	19703	0.985791	2.19
284	106	65.8	1	106	101911	0.3667	-0.34	19704	0.985841	2.19
282- 283	107	65.9	2	214	102125	0.3675	-0.34	19706	0.985941	2.20
278- 281	108	65.9	4	432	102557	0.3690	-0.33	19710	0.986141	2.20
276- 277	109	66.0	2	218	102775	0.3698	-0.33	19712	0.986241	2.20
275	111	66.0	1	111	102886	0.3702	-0.33	19713	0.986291	2.21
272- 274	112	66.1	3	336	103222	0.3714	-0.33	19716	0.986441	2.21
270- 271	113	66.1	2	226	103448	0.3722	-0.33	19718	0.986541	2.21
269	114	66.1	1	114	103562	0.3726	-0.32	19719	0.986591	2.21
268	115	66.2	1	115	103677	0.3731	-0.32	19720	0.986641	2.22
267	116	66.2	1	116	103793	0.3735	-0.32	19721	0.986691	2.22
263- 266	117	66.3	4	468	104261	0.3752	-0.32	19725	0.986891	2.22
261- 262	118	66.3	2	236	104497	0.3760	-0.32	19727	0.986992	2.23
260	119	66.3	1	119	104616	0.3764	-0.31	19728	0.987042	2.23
258- 259	120	66.4	2	240	104856	0.3773	-0.31	19730	0.987142	2.23
257	121	66.4	1	121	104977	0.3777	-0.31	19731	0.987192	2.23
256	123	66.5	1	123	105100	0.3782	-0.31	19732	0.987242	2.23
255	124	66.5	1	124	105224	0.3786	-0.31	19733	0.987292	2.24
251- 254	125	66.5	4	500	105724	0.3804	-0.30	19737	0.987492	2.24
247- 250	126	66.6	4	504	106228	0.3822	-0.30	19741	0.987692	2.25
244- 246	127	66.6	3	381	106609	0.3836	-0.30	19744	0.987842	2.25
243	128	66.7	1	128	106737	0.3841	-0.29	19745	0.987892	2.25
241- 242	129	66.7	2	258	106995	0.3850	-0.29	19747	0.987992	2.26
240	130	66.7	1	130	107125	0.3855	-0.29	19748	0.988042	2.26
239	131	66.8	1	131	107256	0.3859	-0.29	19749	0.988092	2.26
235- 238	132	66.8	4	528	107784	0.3878	-0.28	19753	0.988292	2.27
233- 234	133	66.8	2	266	108050	0.3888	-0.28	19755	0.988392	2.27
232	134	66.8	1	134	108184	0.3893	-0.28	19756	0.988442	2.27
229- 231	135	66.9	3	405	108589	0.3907	-0.28	19759	0.988593	2.28
228	137	66.9	1	137	108726	0.3912	-0.28	19760	0.988643	2.28
227	138	67.0	1	138	108864	0.3917	-0.27	19761	0.988693	2.28
225- 226	139	67.0	2	278	109142	0.3927	-0.27	19763	0.988793	2.28
223- 224	143	67.1	2	286	109428	0.3938	-0.27	19765	0.988893	2.29
220- 222	144	67.2	3	432	109860	0.3953	-0.27	19768	0.989043	2.29
218- 219	145	67.2	2	290	110150	0.3964	-0.26	19770	0.989143	2.30
216- 217	147	67.2	2	294	110444	0.3974	-0.26	19772	0.989243	2.30
213- 215	148	67.3	3	444	110888	0.3990	-0.26	19775	0.989393	2.30
211- 212	149	67.3	2	298	111186	0.4001	-0.25	19777	0.989493	2.31
210	151	67.4	1	151	111337	0.4006	-0.25	19778	0.989543	2.31
209	152	67.4	1	152	111489	0.4012	-0.25	19779	0.989593	2.31
203- 208	153	67.4	6	918	112407	0.4045	-0.24	19785	0.989893	2.32
202	157	67.5	1	157	112564	0.4050	-0.24	19786	0.989943	2.32
201	158	67.6	1	158	112722	0.4056	-0.24	19787	0.989993	2.33
199- 200	160	67.6	2	320	113042	0.4068	-0.24	19789	0.990094	2.33
197- 198	162	67.7	2	324	113366	0.4079	-0.23	19791	0.990194	2.33
196	163	67.7	1	163	113529	0.4085	-0.23	19792	0.990244	2.34
193- 195	168	67.8	3	504	114033	0.4103	-0.23	19795	0.990394	2.34
190- 192	169	67.9	3	507	114540	0.4122	-0.22	19798	0.990544	2.35
189	174	68.0	1	174	114714	0.4128	-0.22	19799	0.990594	2.35
188	175	68.0	1	175	114889	0.4134	-0.22	19800	0.990644	2.35
187	176	68.0	1	176	115065	0.4140	-0.22	19801	0.990694	2.35
184- 186	178	68.1	3	534	115599	0.4160	-0.21	19804	0.990844	2.36
183	179	68.1	1	179	115778	0.4166	-0.21	19805	0.990894	2.36
182	182	68.2	1	182	115960	0.4173	-0.21	19806	0.990944	2.36
181	184	68.2	1	184	116144	0.4179	-0.21	19807	0.990994	2.37
180	186	68.3	1	186	116330	0.4186	-0.21	19808	0.991044	2.37
178- 179	187	68.3	2	374	116704	0.4199	-0.20	19810	0.991144	2.37
177	188	68.3	1	188	116892	0.4206	-0.20	19811	0.991194	2.37
174- 176	189	68.3	3	567	117459	0.4227	-0.20	19814	0.991344	2.38
172- 173	191	68.4	2	382	117841	0.4240	-0.19	19816	0.991444	2.38
170- 171	192	68.4	2	384	118225	0.4254	-0.19	19818	0.991544	2.39
169	193	68.4	1	193	118418	0.4261	-0.19	19819	0.991594	2.39
168	196	68.5	1	196	118614	0.4268	-0.18	19820	0.991645	2.39
167	197	68.5	1	197	118811	0.4275	-0.18	19821	0.991695	2.40
165- 166	198	68.5	2	396	119207	0.4289	-0.18	19823	0.991795	2.40
163- 164	199	68.6	2	398	119605	0.4304	-0.18	19825	0.991895	2.40
162	200	68.6	1	200	119805	0.4311	-0.17	19826	0.991945	2.41
161	201	68.6	1	201	120006	0.4318	-0.17	19827	0.991995	2.41
159- 160	204	68.7	2	408	120414	0.4333	-0.17	19829	0.992095	2.41
158	207	68.7	1	207	120621	0.4340	-0.17	19830	0.992145	2.42
157	208	68.8	1	208	120829	0.4348	-0.16	19831	0.992195	2.42
156	212	68.8	1	212	121041	0.4355	-0.16	19832	0.992245	2.42
155	213	68.9	1	213	121254	0.4363	-0.16	19833	0.992295	2.42
153- 154	214	68.9	2	428	121682	0.4379	-0.16	19835	0.992395	2.43
152	215	68.9	1	215	121897	0.4386	-0.15	19836	0.992445	2.43
151	216	68.9	1	216	122113	0.4394	-0.15	19837	0.992495	2.43
150	219	69.0	1	219	122332	0.4402	-0.15	19838	0.992545	2.43
148- 149	220	69.0	2	440	122772	0.4418	-0.15	19840	0.992645	2.44
146- 147	224	69.1	2	448	123220	0.4434	-0.14	19842	0.992745	2.44
145	226	69.1	1	226	123446	0.4442	-0.14	19843	0.992795	2.45
144	230	69.2	1	230	123676	0.4450	-0.14	19844	0.992845	2.45
143	231	69.2	1	231	123907	0.4459	-0.14	19845	0.992895	2.45
141- 142	233	69.2	2	466	124373	0.4475	-0.13	19847	0.992995	2.46
140	236	69.3	1	236	124609	0.4484	-0.13	19848	0.993045	2.46
138- 139	239	69.4	2	478	125087	0.4501	-0.13	19850	0.993146	2.46
137	240	69.4	1	240	125327	0.4510	-0.12	19851	0.993196	2.47
136	241	69.4	1	241	125568	0.4518	-0.12	19852	0.993246	2.47
134- 135	243	69.4	2	486	126054	0.4536	-0.12	19854	0.993346	2.48
133	246	69.5	1	246	126300	0.4545	-0.11	19855	0.993396	2.48
132	248	69.5	1	248	126548	0.4554	-0.11	19856	0.993446	2.48
131	255	69.6	1	255	126803	0.4563	-0.11	19857	0.993496	2.48
130	256	69.7	1	256	127059	0.4572	-0.11	19858	0.993546	2.49
129	262	69.8	1	262	127321	0.4581	-0.11	19859	0.993596	2.49
128	263	69.8	1	263	127584	0.4591	-0.10	19860	0.993646	2.49
127	267	69.8	1	267	127851	0.4600	-0.10	19861	0.993696	2.49
126	269	69.9	1	269	128120	0.4610	-0.10	19862	0.993746	2.50
125	281	70.1	1	281	128401	0.4620	-0.10	19863	0.993796	2.50
124	282	70.1	1	282	128683	0.4630	-0.09	19864	0.993846	2.50
123	283	70.1	1	283	128966	0.4641	-0.09	19865	0.993896	2.51
122	285	70.1	1	285	129251	0.4651	-0.09	19866	0.993946	2.51
121	291	70.2	1	291	129542	0.4661	-0.08	19867	0.993996	2.51
120	294	70.3	1	294	129836	0.4672	-0.08	19868	0.994046	2.51
118- 119	295	70.3	2	590	130426	0.4693	-0.08	19870	0.994146	2.52
117	296	70.3	1	296	130722	0.4704	-0.07	19871	0.994196	2.52
116	299	70.3	1	299	131021	0.4715	-0.07	19872	0.994246	2.53
115	300	70.3	1	300	131321	0.4725	-0.07	19873	0.994296	2.53
114	301	70.4	1	301	131622	0.4736	-0.07	19874	0.994346	2.53
112- 113	302	70.4	2	604	132226	0.4758	-0.06	19876	0.994446	2.54
111	304	70.4	1	304	132530	0.4769	-0.06	19877	0.994496	2.54
110	305	70.4	1	305	132835	0.4780	-0.06	19878	0.994546	2.55
108- 109	312	70.5	2	624	133459	0.4802	-0.05	19880	0.994646	2.55
107	318	70.6	1	318	133777	0.4814	-0.05	19881	0.994696	2.56
105- 106	321	70.6	2	642	134419	0.4837	-0.04	19883	0.994797	2.56
104	323	70.7	1	323	134742	0.4848	-0.04	19884	0.994847	2.57
103	325	70.7	1	325	135067	0.4860	-0.04	19885	0.994897	2.57
101- 102	328	70.7	2	656	135723	0.4884	-0.03	19887	0.994997	2.58
100	329	70.7	1	329	136052	0.4896	-0.03	19888	0.995047	2.58
99	333	70.8	1	333	136385	0.4908	-0.02	19889	0.995097	2.58
96- 98	336	70.8	3	1008	137393	0.4944	-0.01	19892	0.995247	2.59
95	338	70.9	1	338	137731	0.4956	-0.01	19893	0.995297	2.60
94	341	70.9	1	341	138072	0.4968	-0.01	19894	0.995347	2.60
93	342	70.9	1	342	138414	0.4981	-0.00	19895	0.995397	2.60
92	355	71.1	1	355	138769	0.4993	-0.00	19896	0.995447	2.61
91	359	71.1	1	359	139128	0.5006	0.00	19897	0.995497	2.61
90	363	71.2	1	363	139491	0.5019	0.00	19898	0.995547	2.62
89	365	71.2	1	365	139856	0.5032	0.01	19899	0.995597	2.62
88	370	71.2	1	370	140226	0.5046	0.01	19900	0.995647	2.62
86- 87	371	71.3	2	742	140968	0.5072	0.02	19902	0.995747	2.63
85	374	71.3	1	374	141342	0.5086	0.02	19903	0.995797	2.64
84	377	71.3	1	377	141719	0.5100	0.02	19904	0.995847	2.64

Rank	Occ. F	SFI	F	Tokens	Cum. Tokens	Cum. P Tokens	Y	Cum. Types	Cum. P Types	Z
83	381	71.4	1	381	142100	0.5113	0.03	19905	0.995897	2.64
82	386	71.4	1	386	142486	0.5127	0.03	19906	0.995947	2.65
81	394	71.5	1	394	142880	0.5141	0.04	19907	0.995997	2.65
80	396	71.5	1	396	143276	0.5156	0.04	19908	0.996047	2.66
79	410	71.7	1	410	143686	0.5170	0.04	19909	0.996097	2.66
78	415	71.7	1	415	144101	0.5185	0.05	19910	0.996147	2.66
77	420	71.8	1	420	144521	0.5200	0.05	19911	0.996198	2.67
76	423	71.8	1	423	144944	0.5216	0.05	19912	0.996248	2.67
75	425	71.8	1	425	145369	0.5231	0.06	19913	0.996298	2.68
74	453	72.1	1	453	145822	0.5247	0.06	19914	0.996348	2.68
73	467	72.3	1	467	146289	0.5264	0.07	19915	0.996398	2.69
72	473	72.3	1	473	146762	0.5281	0.07	19916	0.996448	2.69
70– 71	479	72.4	2	958	147720	0.5315	0.08	19918	0.996548	2.70
69	481	72.4	1	481	148201	0.5333	0.08	19919	0.996598	2.71
68	501	72.6	1	501	148702	0.5351	0.09	19920	0.996648	2.71
67	517	72.7	1	517	149219	0.5369	0.09	19921	0.996698	2.72
66	528	72.8	1	528	149747	0.5388	0.10	19922	0.996748	2.72
65	548	73.0	1	548	150295	0.5408	0.10	19923	0.996798	2.73
64	575	73.2	1	575	150870	0.5429	0.11	19924	0.996848	2.73
63	600	73.3	1	600	151470	0.5450	0.11	19925	0.996898	2.74
62	609	73.4	1	609	152079	0.5472	0.12	19926	0.996948	2.74
61	613	73.4	1	613	152692	0.5494	0.12	19927	0.996998	2.75
60	629	73.6	1	629	153321	0.5517	0.13	19928	0.997048	2.75
59	631	73.6	1	631	153952	0.5540	0.14	19929	0.997098	2.76
58	638	73.6	1	638	154590	0.5563	0.14	19930	0.997148	2.76
57	651	73.7	1	651	155241	0.5586	0.15	19931	0.997198	2.77
56	663	73.8	1	663	155904	0.5610	0.15	19932	0.997248	2.78
55	671	73.8	1	671	156575	0.5634	0.16	19933	0.997298	2.78
54	721	74.1	1	721	157296	0.5660	0.17	19934	0.997348	2.79
53	722	74.1	1	722	158018	0.5686	0.17	19935	0.997398	2.79
52	726	74.2	1	726	158744	0.5712	0.18	19936	0.997448	2.80
51	736	74.2	1	736	159480	0.5739	0.19	19937	0.997498	2.81
50	764	74.4	1	764	160244	0.5766	0.19	19938	0.997548	2.81
48– 49	767	74.4	2	1534	161778	0.5821	0.21	19940	0.997648	2.83
47	787	74.5	1	787	162565	0.5850	0.21	19941	0.997698	2.83
46	802	74.6	1	802	163367	0.5878	0.22	19942	0.997748	2.84
45	823	74.7	1	823	164190	0.5908	0.23	19943	0.997799	2.85
44	839	74.8	1	839	165029	0.5938	0.24	19944	0.997849	2.86
43	923	75.2	1	923	165952	0.5971	0.25	19945	0.997899	2.86
42	950	75.3	1	950	166902	0.6006	0.25	19946	0.997949	2.87
41	953	75.4	1	953	167855	0.6040	0.26	19947	0.997999	2.88
40	958	75.4	1	958	168813	0.6074	0.27	19948	0.998049	2.89
39	960	75.4	1	960	169773	0.6109	0.28	19949	0.998099	2.89
38	990	75.5	1	990	170763	0.6145	0.29	19950	0.998149	2.90
37	1008	75.6	1	1008	171771	0.6181	0.30	19951	0.998199	2.91
36	1013	75.6	1	1013	172784	0.6217	0.31	19952	0.998249	2.92
35	1027	75.7	1	1027	173811	0.6254	0.32	19953	0.998299	2.93
34	1028	75.7	1	1028	174839	0.6291	0.33	19954	0.998349	2.94
33	1101	76.0	1	1101	175940	0.6331	0.34	19955	0.998399	2.95
32	1110	76.0	1	1110	177050	0.6371	0.35	19956	0.998449	2.96
31	1143	76.1	1	1143	178193	0.6412	0.36	19957	0.998499	2.97
30	1185	76.3	1	1185	179378	0.6455	0.37	19958	0.998549	2.98
29	1203	76.4	1	1203	180581	0.6498	0.38	19959	0.998599	2.99
28	1229	76.5	1	1229	181810	0.6542	0.40	19960	0.998649	3.00
27	1247	76.5	1	1247	183057	0.6587	0.41	19961	0.998699	3.01
26	1254	76.5	1	1254	184311	0.6632	0.42	19962	0.998749	3.02
25	1272	76.6	1	1272	185583	0.6678	0.43	19963	0.998799	3.04
24	1357	76.9	1	1357	186940	0.6727	0.45	19964	0.998849	3.05
23	1425	77.1	1	1425	188365	0.6778	0.46	19965	0.998899	3.06
22	1532	77.4	1	1532	189897	0.6833	0.48	19966	0.998949	3.08
21	1583	77.6	1	1583	191480	0.6890	0.49	19967	0.998999	3.09
20	1600	77.6	1	1600	193080	0.6948	0.51	19968	0.999049	3.11
19	1678	77.8	1	1678	194758	0.7008	0.53	19969	0.999099	3.12
18	1779	78.1	1	1779	196537	0.7072	0.55	19970	0.999149	3.14
17	1791	78.1	1	1791	198328	0.7136	0.56	19971	0.999199	3.16
16	1937	78.4	1	1937	200265	0.7206	0.58	19972	0.999249	3.17
15	1944	78.4	1	1944	202209	0.7276	0.61	19973	0.999300	3.19
14	1945	78.5	1	1945	204154	0.7346	0.63	19974	0.999350	3.22
13	2657	79.8	1	2657	206811	0.7442	0.66	19975	0.999400	3.24
12	2956	80.3	1	2956	209767	0.7548	0.69	19976	0.999450	3.26
11	3056	80.4	1	3056	212823	0.7658	0.73	19977	0.999500	3.29
10	3205	80.6	1	3205	216028	0.7773	0.76	19978	0.999550	3.32
9	3272	80.7	1	3272	219300	0.7891	0.80	19979	0.999600	3.35
8	3362	80.8	1	3362	222662	0.8012	0.85	19980	0.999650	3.39
7	4451	82.0	1	4451	227113	0.8172	0.90	19981	0.999700	3.43
6	4724	82.3	1	4724	231837	0.8342	0.97	19982	0.999750	3.48
5	6309	83.6	1	6309	238146	0.8569	1.07	19983	0.999800	3.54
4	6511	83.7	1	6511	244657	0.8804	1.18	19984	0.999850	3.62
3	6769	83.9	1	6769	251426	0.9047	1.31	19985	0.999900	3.72
2	9142	85.2	1	9142	260568	0.9376	1.54	19986	0.999950	3.89
1	17339	88.0	1	17339	277907	1.0000	+INF.	19987	1.000000	+INF.

Rank	Occ. F	SFI	F	Tokens	Cum. Tokens	Cum. P Tokens	Y	Cum. Types	Cum. P Types	Z
6725-10781	1	45.9	4057	4057	4057	0.0105	-2.31	4057	0.376310	-0.32
5075-6724	2	48.1	1650	3300	7357	0.0190	-2.08	5707	0.529357	0.07
4237-5074	3	49.6	838	2514	9871	0.0255	-1.95	6545	0.607087	0.27
3669-4236	4	50.6	568	2272	12143	0.0313	-1.86	7113	0.659772	0.41
3249-3668	5	51.5	420	2100	14243	0.0367	-1.79	7533	0.698729	0.52
2946-3248	6	52.2	303	1818	16061	0.0414	-1.73	7836	0.726834	0.60
2697-2945	7	52.9	249	1743	17804	0.0459	-1.69	8085	0.749930	0.67
2522-2696	8	53.4	175	1400	19204	0.0495	-1.65	8260	0.766163	0.73
2349-2521	9	53.9	173	1557	20761	0.0536	-1.61	8433	0.782209	0.78
2220-2348	10	54.3	129	1290	22051	0.0569	-1.58	8562	0.794175	0.82
2097-2219	11	54.7	123	1353	23404	0.0604	-1.55	8685	0.805584	0.86
1982-2096	12	55.1	115	1380	24784	0.0639	-1.52	8800	0.816251	0.90
1904-1981	13	55.4	78	1014	25798	0.0666	-1.50	8878	0.823486	0.93
1826-1903	14	55.7	78	1092	26890	0.0694	-1.48	8956	0.830721	0.96
1751-1825	15	56.0	75	1125	28015	0.0723	-1.46	9031	0.837677	0.98
1689-1750	16	56.3	62	992	29007	0.0748	-1.44	9093	0.843428	1.01
1626-1688	17	56.5	63	1071	30078	0.0776	-1.42	9156	0.849272	1.03
1570-1625	18	56.8	56	1008	31086	0.0802	-1.40	9212	0.854466	1.06
1513-1569	19	57.0	57	1083	32169	0.0830	-1.39	9269	0.859753	1.08
1482-1512	20	57.2	31	620	32789	0.0846	-1.37	9300	0.862629	1.09
1437-1481	21	57.4	45	945	33734	0.0870	-1.36	9345	0.866803	1.11
1394-1436	22	57.6	43	946	34680	0.0895	-1.34	9388	0.870791	1.13
1359-1393	23	57.8	35	805	35485	0.0915	-1.33	9423	0.874038	1.15
1331-1358	24	58.0	28	672	36157	0.0933	-1.32	9451	0.876635	1.16
1308-1330	25	58.2	23	575	36732	0.0948	-1.31	9474	0.878768	1.17
1279-1307	26	58.3	29	754	37486	0.0967	-1.30	9503	0.881458	1.18
1251-1278	27	58.5	28	756	38242	0.0987	-1.29	9531	0.884055	1.20
1229-1250	28	58.7	22	616	38858	0.1002	-1.28	9553	0.886096	1.21
1198-1228	29	58.8	31	899	39757	0.1026	-1.27	9584	0.888971	1.22
1168-1197	30	59.0	30	900	40657	0.1049	-1.25	9614	0.891754	1.24
1139-1167	31	59.1	29	899	41556	0.1072	-1.24	9643	0.894444	1.25
1116-1138	32	59.2	23	736	42292	0.1091	-1.23	9666	0.896577	1.26
1099-1115	33	59.4	17	561	42853	0.1106	-1.22	9683	0.898154	1.27
1079-1098	34	59.5	20	680	43533	0.1123	-1.21	9703	0.900009	1.28
1057-1078	35	59.6	22	770	44303	0.1143	-1.20	9725	0.902050	1.29
1031-1056	36	59.7	26	936	45239	0.1167	-1.19	9751	0.904462	1.31
1014-1030	37	59.9	17	629	45868	0.1183	-1.18	9768	0.906038	1.32
998-1013	38	60.0	16	608	46476	0.1199	-1.18	9784	0.907522	1.33
980-997	39	60.1	18	702	47178	0.1217	-1.17	9802	0.909192	1.34
964-979	40	60.2	16	640	47818	0.1234	-1.16	9818	0.910676	1.34
947-963	41	60.3	17	697	48515	0.1252	-1.15	9835	0.912253	1.35
931-946	42	60.4	16	672	49187	0.1269	-1.14	9851	0.913737	1.36
916-930	43	60.5	15	645	49832	0.1286	-1.13	9866	0.915128	1.37
901-915	44	60.6	15	660	50492	0.1303	-1.13	9881	0.916520	1.38
889-900	45	60.7	12	540	51032	0.1317	-1.12	9893	0.917633	1.39
876-888	46	60.8	13	598	51630	0.1332	-1.11	9906	0.918839	1.40
868-875	47	60.9	8	376	52006	0.1342	-1.11	9914	0.919581	1.40
853-867	48	61.0	15	720	52726	0.1360	-1.10	9929	0.920972	1.41
836-852	49	61.1	17	833	53559	0.1382	-1.09	9946	0.922549	1.42
829-835	50	61.1	7	350	53909	0.1391	-1.08	9953	0.923198	1.43
816-828	51	61.2	13	663	54572	0.1408	-1.08	9966	0.924404	1.44
807-815	52	61.3	9	468	55040	0.1420	-1.07	9975	0.925239	1.44
799-806	53	61.4	8	424	55464	0.1431	-1.07	9983	0.925981	1.45
792-798	54	61.5	7	378	55842	0.1441	-1.06	9990	0.926630	1.45
781-791	55	61.6	11	605	56447	0.1456	-1.06	10001	0.927650	1.46
772-780	56	61.6	9	504	56951	0.1469	-1.05	10010	0.928485	1.46
763-771	57	61.7	9	513	57464	0.1482	-1.04	10019	0.929320	1.47
758-762	58	61.8	5	290	57754	0.1490	-1.04	10024	0.929784	1.47
751-757	59	61.9	7	413	58167	0.1501	-1.04	10031	0.930433	1.48
742-750	60	61.9	9	540	58707	0.1515	-1.03	10040	0.931268	1.49
736-741	61	62.0	6	366	59073	0.1524	-1.03	10046	0.931825	1.49
724-735	62	62.1	12	744	59817	0.1543	-1.02	10058	0.932938	1.50
717-723	63	62.1	7	441	60258	0.1555	-1.01	10065	0.933587	1.50
708-716	64	62.2	9	576	60834	0.1569	-1.01	10074	0.934422	1.51
697-707	65	62.3	11	715	61549	0.1588	-1.00	10085	0.935442	1.52
694-696	66	62.3	3	198	61747	0.1593	-1.00	10088	0.935720	1.52
685-693	67	62.4	9	603	62350	0.1609	-0.99	10097	0.936555	1.53
679-684	68	62.5	6	408	62758	0.1619	-0.99	10103	0.937112	1.53
672-678	69	62.5	7	483	63241	0.1632	-0.98	10110	0.937761	1.54
664-671	70	62.6	8	560	63801	0.1646	-0.98	10118	0.938503	1.54
657-663	71	62.7	7	497	64298	0.1659	-0.97	10125	0.939152	1.55
647-656	72	62.7	10	720	65018	0.1677	-0.96	10135	0.940080	1.56
642-646	73	62.8	5	365	65383	0.1687	-0.96	10140	0.940544	1.56
630-641	74	62.8	12	888	66271	0.1710	-0.95	10152	0.941657	1.57
620-629	75	62.9	10	750	67021	0.1729	-0.94	10162	0.942584	1.58
610-619	76	63.0	10	760	67781	0.1749	-0.94	10172	0.943512	1.58
606-609	77	63.0	4	308	68089	0.1757	-0.93	10176	0.943883	1.59
595-605	78	63.1	11	858	68947	0.1779	-0.92	10187	0.944903	1.60
587-594	79	63.1	8	632	69579	0.1795	-0.92	10195	0.945645	1.60
584-586	80	63.2	3	240	69819	0.1801	-0.91	10198	0.945923	1.61
576-583	81	63.2	8	648	70467	0.1818	-0.91	10206	0.946665	1.61
574-575	82	63.3	2	164	70631	0.1822	-0.91	10208	0.946851	1.62
571-573	83	63.3	3	249	70880	0.1829	-0.90	10211	0.947129	1.62
568-570	84	63.4	3	252	71132	0.1835	-0.90	10214	0.947407	1.62
562-567	85	63.4	6	510	71642	0.1848	-0.90	10220	0.947964	1.63
557-561	86	63.5	5	430	72072	0.1859	-0.89	10225	0.948428	1.63
554-556	87	63.5	3	261	72333	0.1866	-0.89	10228	0.948706	1.63
548-553	88	63.6	6	528	72861	0.1880	-0.89	10234	0.949263	1.64
543-547	89	63.6	5	445	73306	0.1891	-0.88	10239	0.949726	1.64
541-542	90	63.7	2	180	73486	0.1896	-0.88	10241	0.949912	1.64
540	91	63.7	1	91	73577	0.1898	-0.88	10242	0.950005	1.64
534-539	92	63.8	6	552	74129	0.1912	-0.87	10248	0.950561	1.65
527-533	93	63.8	7	651	74780	0.1929	-0.87	10255	0.951210	1.66
520-526	94	63.9	7	658	75438	0.1946	-0.86	10262	0.951860	1.66
515-519	95	63.9	5	475	75913	0.1958	-0.86	10267	0.952323	1.67
512-514	96	64.0	3	288	76201	0.1966	-0.85	10270	0.952602	1.67
509-511	97	64.0	3	291	76492	0.1973	-0.85	10273	0.952880	1.67
503-508	98	64.1	6	588	77080	0.1989	-0.85	10279	0.953437	1.68
499-502	99	64.1	4	396	77476	0.1999	-0.84	10283	0.953808	1.68
495-498	100	64.1	4	400	77876	0.2009	-0.84	10287	0.954179	1.69
485-494	101	64.2	10	1010	78886	0.2035	-0.83	10297	0.955106	1.70
483-484	102	64.2	2	204	79090	0.2040	-0.83	10299	0.955292	1.70
480-482	103	64.3	3	309	79399	0.2048	-0.82	10302	0.955570	1.70
479	104	64.3	1	104	79503	0.2051	-0.82	10303	0.955663	1.70
475-478	105	64.3	4	420	79923	0.2062	-0.82	10307	0.956034	1.71
467-474	106	64.4	8	848	80771	0.2084	-0.81	10315	0.956776	1.71
465-466	107	64.4	2	214	80985	0.2089	-0.81	10317	0.956961	1.72
462-464	108	64.5	3	324	81309	0.2098	-0.81	10320	0.957240	1.72
457-461	109	64.5	5	545	81854	0.2112	-0.80	10325	0.957703	1.72
452-456	110	64.5	5	550	82404	0.2126	-0.80	10330	0.958167	1.73
451	111	64.6	1	111	82515	0.2129	-0.80	10331	0.958260	1.73
449-450	112	64.6	2	224	82739	0.2135	-0.79	10333	0.958445	1.73
441-448	113	64.7	8	904	83643	0.2158	-0.79	10341	0.959187	1.74
438-440	114	64.7	3	342	83985	0.2167	-0.78	10344	0.959466	1.74
437	115	64.7	1	115	84100	0.2170	-0.78	10345	0.959558	1.75
433-436	116	64.8	4	464	84564	0.2182	-0.78	10349	0.959929	1.75
429-432	117	64.8	4	468	85032	0.2194	-0.77	10353	0.960301	1.75
424-428	118	64.9	5	590	85622	0.2209	-0.77	10358	0.960764	1.76
422-423	119	64.9	2	238	85860	0.2215	-0.77	10360	0.960950	1.76
420-421	120	64.9	2	240	86100	0.2221	-0.77	10362	0.961135	1.76
416-419	121	65.0	4	484	86584	0.2234	-0.76	10366	0.961506	1.77
413-415	123	65.0	3	369	86953	0.2243	-0.76	10369	0.961785	1.77
411-412	124	65.1	2	248	87201	0.2250	-0.76	10371	0.961970	1.77
408-410	125	65.1	3	375	87576	0.2259	-0.75	10374	0.962248	1.78
407	128	65.2	1	128	87704	0.2263	-0.75	10375	0.962341	1.78
404-406	129	65.2	3	387	88091	0.2273	-0.75	10378	0.962619	1.78
398-403	131	65.3	6	786	88877	0.2293	-0.74	10384	0.963176	1.79
395-397	132	65.3	3	396	89273	0.2303	-0.74	10387	0.963454	1.79
394	133	65.4	1	133	89406	0.2307	-0.74	10388	0.963547	1.79
392-393	135	65.4	2	270	89676	0.2314	-0.73	10390	0.963732	1.80
390-391	136	65.5	2	272	89948	0.2321	-0.73	10392	0.963918	1.80
386-389	137	65.5	4	548	90496	0.2335	-0.73	10396	0.964289	1.80
385	138	65.5	1	138	90634	0.2338	-0.73	10397	0.964382	1.80
384	139	65.6	1	139	90773	0.2342	-0.73	10398	0.964474	1.81
382-383	140	65.6	2	280	91053	0.2349	-0.72	10400	0.964660	1.81
380-381	141	65.6	2	282	91335	0.2356	-0.72	10402	0.964846	1.81
377-379	142	65.7	3	426	91761	0.2367	-0.72	10405	0.965124	1.81
376	143	65.7	1	143	91904	0.2371	-0.72	10406	0.965217	1.81
371-375	144	65.7	5	720	92624	0.2390	-0.71	10411	0.965680	1.82
368-370	146	65.8	3	438	93062	0.2401	-0.71	10414	0.965959	1.82
367	147	65.8	1	147	93209	0.2405	-0.70	10415	0.966051	1.83
366	148	65.8	1	148	93357	0.2408	-0.70	10416	0.966144	1.83
365	150	65.9	1	150	93507	0.2412	-0.70	10417	0.966237	1.83
363-364	151	65.9	2	302	93809	0.2420	-0.70	10419	0.966422	1.83
360-362	152	65.9	3	456	94265	0.2432	-0.70	10422	0.966701	1.83
359	153	66.0	1	153	94418	0.2436	-0.69	10423	0.966793	1.84
356-358	154	66.0	3	462	94880	0.2448	-0.69	10426	0.967072	1.84
354-355	155	66.0	2	310	95190	0.2456	-0.69	10428	0.967257	1.84
350-353	156	66.1	4	624	95814	0.2472	-0.68	10432	0.967628	1.85
347-349	157	66.1	3	471	96285	0.2484	-0.68	10435	0.967906	1.85
346	158	66.1	1	158	96443	0.2488	-0.68	10436	0.967999	1.85
344-345	160	66.2	2	320	96763	0.2496	-0.68	10438	0.968185	1.85
342-343	161	66.2	2	322	97085	0.2505	-0.67	10440	0.968370	1.86
340-341	164	66.3	2	328	97413	0.2513	-0.67	10442	0.968556	1.86
339	165	66.3	1	165	97578	0.2517	-0.67	10443	0.968648	1.86
335-338	166	66.3	4	664	98242	0.2534	-0.66	10447	0.969020	1.87
334	167	66.4	1	167	98409	0.2539	-0.66	10448	0.969112	1.87
333	168	66.4	1	168	98577	0.2543	-0.66	10449	0.969205	1.87
332	169	66.4	1	169	98746	0.2548	-0.66	10450	0.969298	1.87
331	170	66.4	1	170	98916	0.2552	-0.66	10451	0.969391	1.87
330	171	66.5	1	171	99087	0.2556	-0.66	10452	0.969483	1.87
327-329	174	66.5	3	522	99609	0.2570	-0.65	10455	0.969762	1.88
325-326	175	66.6	2	350	99959	0.2579	-0.65	10457	0.969947	1.88
323-324	176	66.6	2	352	100311	0.2588	-0.65	10459	0.970133	1.88
322	177	66.6	1	177	100488	0.2592	-0.65	10460	0.970225	1.88
321	178	66.6	1	178	100666	0.2597	-0.64	10461	0.970318	1.89
320	179	66.7	1	179	100845	0.2602	-0.64	10462	0.970411	1.89
318-319	181	66.7	2	362	101207	0.2611	-0.64	10464	0.970596	1.89
317	182	66.7	1	182	101389	0.2616	-0.64	10465	0.970689	1.89
315-316	183	66.8	2	366	101755	0.2625	-0.64	10467	0.970875	1.89
314	184	66.8	1	184	101939	0.2630	-0.63	10468	0.970967	1.90
311-313	186	66.8	3	558	102497	0.2644	-0.63	10471	0.971246	1.90
309-310	187	66.8	2	374	102871	0.2654	-0.63	10473	0.971431	1.90
308	188	66.9	1	188	103059	0.2659	-0.63	10474	0.971524	1.90
307	189	66.9	1	189	103248	0.2664	-0.62	10475	0.971617	1.91
303-306	190	66.9	4	760	104008	0.2683	-0.62	10479	0.971988	1.91
301-302	191	66.9	2	382	104390	0.2693	-0.61	10481	0.972173	1.91
300	193	67.0	1	193	104583	0.2698	-0.61	10482	0.972266	1.92
296-299	194	67.0	4	776	105359	0.2718	-0.61	10486	0.972637	1.92
294-295	195	67.0	2	390	105749	0.2728	-0.60	10488	0.972823	1.92
293	197	67.1	1	197	105946	0.2733	-0.60	10489	0.972915	1.93
291-292	201	67.2	2	402	106348	0.2744	-0.60	10491	0.973101	1.93
289-290	202	67.2	2	404	106752	0.2754	-0.60	10493	0.973286	1.93
288	205	67.2	1	205	106957	0.2759	-0.59	10494	0.973379	1.93
286-287	208	67.3	2	416	107373	0.2770	-0.59	10496	0.973565	1.94
285	209	67.3	1	209	107582	0.2775	-0.59	10497	0.973657	1.94
283-284	210	67.3	2	420	108002	0.2786	-0.59	10499	0.973843	1.94
282	213	67.4	1	213	108215	0.2792	-0.59	10500	0.973936	1.94
281	214	67.4	1	214	108429	0.2797	-0.58	10501	0.974028	1.94
277-280	215	67.5	4	860	109289	0.2819	-0.58	10505	0.974399	1.95
275-276	216	67.5	2	432	109721	0.2831	-0.57	10507	0.974585	1.95
274	217	67.5	1	217	109938	0.2836	-0.57	10508	0.974678	1.95
273	218	67.5	1	218	110156	0.2842	-0.57	10509	0.974770	1.96
272	219	67.5	1	219	110375	0.2848	-0.57	10510	0.974863	1.96
270-271	221	67.6	2	442	110817	0.2859	-0.57	10512	0.975049	1.96
268-269	223	67.6	2	446	111263	0.2870	-0.56	10514	0.975234	1.96
266-267	224	67.6	2	448	111711	0.2882	-0.56	10516	0.975420	1.97
264-265	225	67.6	2	450	112161	0.2894	-0.56	10518	0.975605	1.97
263	229	67.7	1	229	112390	0.2899	-0.55	10519	0.975698	1.97
261-262	231	67.8	2	462	112852	0.2911	-0.55	10521	0.975883	1.98
260	232	67.8	1	232	113084	0.2917	-0.55	10522	0.975976	1.98
259	233	67.8	1	233	113317	0.2923	-0.55	10523	0.976069	1.98
258	235	67.8	1	235	113552	0.2929	-0.54	10524	0.976162	1.98
257	236	67.9	1	236	113788	0.2936	-0.54	10525	0.976254	1.98
256	237	67.9	1	237	114025	0.2942	-0.54	10526	0.976347	1.98
253-255	240	67.9	3	720	114745	0.2960	-0.54	10529	0.976626	1.99
252	242	68.0	1	242	114987	0.2966	-0.53	10530	0.976718	1.99
251	243	68.0	1	243	115230	0.2973	-0.53	10531	0.976811	1.99
250	244	68.0	1	244	115474	0.2979	-0.53	10532	0.976904	1.99
248-249	245	68.0	2	490	115964	0.2992	-0.53	10534	0.977089	2.00
245-247	247	68.1	3	741	116705	0.3011	-0.52	10537	0.977368	2.00
244	249	68.1	1	249	116954	0.3017	-0.52	10538	0.977460	2.00
243	250	68.1	1	250	117204	0.3024	-0.52	10539	0.977553	2.01
242	251	68.1	1	251	117455	0.3030	-0.52	10540	0.977646	2.01
240-241	255	68.2	2	510	117965	0.3043	-0.51	10542	0.977831	2.01
236-239	259	68.3	4	1036	119001	0.3070	-0.50	10546	0.978202	2.02
235	260	68.3	1	260	119261	0.3077	-0.50	10547	0.978295	2.02
232-234	261	68.3	3	783	120044	0.3097	-0.50	10550	0.978573	2.03
230-231	262	68.3	2	524	120568	0.3110	-0.49	10552	0.978759	2.03
229	263	68.3	1	263	120831	0.3117	-0.49	10553	0.978852	2.03
228	267	68.4	1	267	121098	0.3124	-0.49	10554	0.978944	2.03
227	271	68.5	1	271	121369	0.3131	-0.49	10555	0.979037	2.03
226	273	68.5	1	273	121642	0.3138	-0.49	10556	0.979130	2.04
224-225	274	68.5	2	548	122190	0.3152	-0.48	10558	0.979315	2.04
223	275	68.5	1	275	122465	0.3159	-0.48	10559	0.979408	2.04
222	277	68.5	1	277	122742	0.3167	-0.48	10560	0.979501	2.04
221	278	68.6	1	278	123020	0.3174	-0.48	10561	0.979594	2.05
220	280	68.6	1	280	123300	0.3181	-0.47	10562	0.979686	2.05
219	281	68.6	1	281	123581	0.3188	-0.47	10563	0.979779	2.05
218	283	68.6	1	283	123864	0.3196	-0.47	10564	0.979872	2.05
217	284	68.7	1	284	124148	0.3203	-0.47	10565	0.979965	2.05
216	285	68.7	1	285	124433	0.3210	-0.46	10566	0.980057	2.05

Rank		Occ. F	SFI	F	Tokens	Cum. Tokens	Cum. P Tokens	Y	Cum. Types	Cum. P Types	Z
214-	215	286	68.7	2	572	125005	0.3225	-0.46	10568	0.980243	2.06
	213	287	68.7	1	287	125292	0.3232	-0.46	10569	0.980336	2.06
	212	289	68.7	1	289	125581	0.3240	-0.46	10570	0.980429	2.06
210-	211	293	68.8	2	586	126167	0.3255	-0.45	10572	0.980614	2.07
208-	209	297	68.9	2	594	126761	0.3270	-0.45	10574	0.980799	2.07
	207	298	68.9	1	298	127059	0.3278	-0.45	10575	0.980892	2.07
205-	206	299	68.9	2	598	127657	0.3293	-0.44	10577	0.981078	2.08
	204	301	68.9	1	301	127958	0.3301	-0.44	10578	0.981171	2.08
202-	203	302	68.9	2	604	128562	0.3317	-0.44	10580	0.981356	2.08
200-	201	303	68.9	2	606	129168	0.3332	-0.43	10582	0.981542	2.09
198-	199	304	69.0	2	608	129776	0.3348	-0.43	10584	0.981727	2.09
	197	306	69.0	1	306	130082	0.3356	-0.42	10585	0.981820	2.09
195-	196	307	69.0	2	614	130696	0.3372	-0.42	10587	0.982005	2.10
	194	308	69.0	1	308	131004	0.3380	-0.42	10588	0.982098	2.10
	193	309	69.0	1	309	131313	0.3388	-0.42	10589	0.982191	2.10
190-	192	313	69.1	3	939	132252	0.3412	-0.41	10592	0.982469	2.11
	189	314	69.1	1	314	132566	0.3420	-0.41	10593	0.982562	2.11
187-	188	316	69.1	2	632	133198	0.3436	-0.40	10595	0.982747	2.11
185-	186	318	69.1	2	636	133834	0.3453	-0.40	10597	0.982933	2.12
	184	320	69.2	1	320	134154	0.3461	-0.40	10598	0.983026	2.12
	183	321	69.2	1	321	134475	0.3469	-0.39	10599	0.983118	2.12
181-	182	324	69.2	2	648	135123	0.3486	-0.39	10601	0.983304	2.13
	180	325	69.2	1	325	135448	0.3494	-0.39	10602	0.983397	2.13
	179	326	69.3	1	326	135774	0.3503	-0.38	10603	0.983489	2.13
	178	329	69.3	1	329	136103	0.3511	-0.38	10604	0.983582	2.13
	177	331	69.3	1	331	136434	0.3520	-0.38	10605	0.983675	2.14
175-	176	332	69.3	2	664	137098	0.3537	-0.38	10607	0.983860	2.14
	174	334	69.4	1	334	137432	0.3546	-0.37	10608	0.983953	2.14
	173	335	69.4	1	335	137767	0.3554	-0.37	10609	0.984046	2.15
	172	342	69.5	1	342	138109	0.3563	-0.37	10610	0.984139	2.15
169-	171	344	69.5	3	1032	139141	0.3590	-0.36	10613	0.984417	2.15
	168	347	69.5	1	347	139488	0.3599	-0.36	10614	0.984510	2.16
166-	167	349	69.6	2	698	140186	0.3617	-0.35	10616	0.984695	2.16
	165	351	69.6	1	351	140537	0.3626	-0.35	10617	0.984788	2.16
163-	164	352	69.6	2	704	141241	0.3644	-0.35	10619	0.984974	2.17
161-	162	353	69.6	2	706	141947	0.3662	-0.34	10621	0.985159	2.17
159-	160	367	69.8	2	734	142681	0.3681	-0.34	10623	0.985345	2.18
157-	158	373	69.8	2	746	143427	0.3700	-0.33	10625	0.985530	2.18
155-	156	376	69.9	2	752	144179	0.3720	-0.33	10627	0.985716	2.19
	154	382	69.9	1	382	144561	0.3729	-0.32	10628	0.985808	2.19
	153	384	70.0	1	384	144945	0.3739	-0.32	10629	0.985901	2.19
	152	385	70.0	1	385	145330	0.3749	-0.32	10630	0.985994	2.20
	151	390	70.0	1	390	145720	0.3759	-0.32	10631	0.986087	2.20
	150	401	70.2	1	401	146121	0.3770	-0.31	10632	0.986179	2.20
	149	403	70.2	1	403	146524	0.3780	-0.31	10633	0.986272	2.20
	148	406	70.2	1	406	146930	0.3791	-0.31	10634	0.986365	2.21
146-	147	407	70.2	2	814	147744	0.3812	-0.30	10636	0.986550	2.21
	145	410	70.2	1	410	148154	0.3822	-0.30	10637	0.986643	2.22
	144	414	70.3	1	414	148568	0.3833	-0.30	10638	0.986736	2.22
	143	418	70.3	1	418	148986	0.3844	-0.29	10639	0.986829	2.22
141-	142	422	70.4	2	844	149830	0.3865	-0.29	10641	0.987014	2.23
139-	140	423	70.4	2	846	150676	0.3887	-0.28	10643	0.987200	2.23
	138	426	70.4	1	426	151102	0.3898	-0.28	10644	0.987292	2.24
	137	434	70.5	1	434	151536	0.3909	-0.28	10645	0.987385	2.24
	136	438	70.5	1	438	151974	0.3921	-0.27	10646	0.987478	2.24
134-	135	443	70.6	2	886	152860	0.3944	-0.27	10648	0.987663	2.25
132-	133	444	70.6	2	888	153748	0.3966	-0.26	10650	0.987849	2.25
130-	131	445	70.6	2	890	154638	0.3989	-0.26	10652	0.988034	2.26
	129	452	70.7	1	452	155090	0.4001	-0.25	10653	0.988127	2.26
	128	457	70.7	1	457	155547	0.4013	-0.25	10654	0.988220	2.26
	127	465	70.8	1	465	156012	0.4025	-0.25	10655	0.988313	2.27
	126	468	70.8	1	468	156480	0.4037	-0.24	10656	0.988406	2.27
	125	472	70.9	1	472	156952	0.4049	-0.24	10657	0.988498	2.27
	124	473	70.9	1	473	157425	0.4061	-0.24	10658	0.988591	2.28
122-	123	475	70.9	2	950	158375	0.4086	-0.23	10660	0.988777	2.28
	121	478	70.9	1	478	158853	0.4098	-0.23	10661	0.988869	2.29
	120	479	70.9	1	479	159332	0.4111	-0.22	10662	0.988962	2.29
	119	483	71.0	1	483	159815	0.4123	-0.22	10663	0.989055	2.29
	118	494	71.1	1	494	160309	0.4136	-0.22	10664	0.989148	2.30
	117	497	71.1	1	497	160806	0.4149	-0.22	10665	0.989240	2.30
	116	502	71.1	1	502	161308	0.4162	-0.21	10666	0.989333	2.30
	115	503	71.1	1	503	161811	0.4174	-0.21	10667	0.989426	2.31
	114	504	71.1	1	504	162315	0.4187	-0.21	10668	0.989519	2.31
	113	520	71.3	1	520	162835	0.4201	-0.20	10669	0.989611	2.31
	112	529	71.4	1	529	163364	0.4215	-0.20	10670	0.989704	2.32
	111	530	71.4	1	530	163894	0.4228	-0.19	10671	0.989797	2.32
109-	110	533	71.4	2	1066	164960	0.4256	-0.19	10673	0.989982	2.33
107-	108	545	71.5	2	1090	166050	0.4284	-0.18	10675	0.990168	2.33
	106	546	71.5	1	546	166596	0.4298	-0.18	10676	0.990261	2.34
	105	563	71.6	1	563	167159	0.4312	-0.17	10677	0.990353	2.34
	104	571	71.7	1	571	167730	0.4327	-0.17	10678	0.990446	2.34
	103	573	71.7	1	573	168303	0.4342	-0.17	10679	0.990539	2.35
	102	577	71.7	1	577	168880	0.4357	-0.16	10680	0.990632	2.35
	101	585	71.8	1	585	169465	0.4372	-0.16	10681	0.990724	2.35
	100	587	71.8	1	587	170052	0.4387	-0.15	10682	0.990817	2.36
	99	589	71.8	1	589	170641	0.4402	-0.15	10683	0.990910	2.36
	98	592	71.8	1	592	171233	0.4418	-0.15	10684	0.991003	2.37
	97	602	71.9	1	602	171835	0.4433	-0.14	10685	0.991095	2.37
	96	607	72.0	1	607	172442	0.4449	-0.14	10686	0.991188	2.37
94-	95	609	72.0	2	1218	173660	0.4480	-0.13	10688	0.991374	2.38
	93	616	72.0	1	616	174276	0.4496	-0.13	10689	0.991466	2.39
	92	620	72.0	1	620	174896	0.4512	-0.12	10690	0.991559	2.39
	91	644	72.2	1	644	175540	0.4529	-0.12	10691	0.991652	2.39
	90	653	72.3	1	653	176193	0.4546	-0.11	10692	0.991745	2.40
	89	657	72.3	1	657	176850	0.4562	-0.11	10693	0.991837	2.40
	88	662	72.3	1	662	177512	0.4580	-0.11	10694	0.991930	2.41
	87	665	72.3	1	665	178177	0.4597	-0.10	10695	0.992023	2.41
	86	683	72.5	1	683	178860	0.4614	-0.10	10696	0.992116	2.41
	85	684	72.5	1	684	179544	0.4632	-0.09	10697	0.992208	2.42
83-	84	685	72.5	2	1370	180914	0.4667	-0.08	10699	0.992394	2.43
	82	696	72.5	1	696	181610	0.4685	-0.08	10700	0.992487	2.43
80-	81	704	72.6	2	1408	183018	0.4722	-0.07	10702	0.992672	2.44
	79	707	72.6	1	707	183725	0.4740	-0.07	10703	0.992765	2.45
	78	714	72.7	1	714	184439	0.4758	-0.06	10704	0.992858	2.45
	77	716	72.7	1	716	185155	0.4777	-0.06	10705	0.992951	2.45
	76	719	72.7	1	719	185874	0.4795	-0.05	10706	0.993043	2.46
	75	731	72.8	1	731	186605	0.4814	-0.05	10707	0.993136	2.46
	74	752	72.9	1	752	187357	0.4834	-0.04	10708	0.993229	2.47
	73	757	72.9	1	757	188114	0.4853	-0.04	10709	0.993322	2.47
	72	762	72.9	1	762	188876	0.4873	-0.03	10710	0.993414	2.48
70-	71	763	72.9	2	1526	190402	0.4912	-0.02	10712	0.993600	2.49
	69	772	73.0	1	772	191174	0.4932	-0.02	10713	0.993693	2.49
	68	779	73.0	1	779	191953	0.4952	-0.01	10714	0.993785	2.50
	67	785	73.1	1	785	192738	0.4972	-0.01	10715	0.993878	2.51
	66	847	73.4	1	847	193585	0.4994	-0.00	10716	0.993971	2.51
	65	865	73.5	1	865	194450	0.5017	0.00	10717	0.994064	2.52
	64	870	73.5	1	870	195320	0.5039	0.01	10718	0.994156	2.52
	63	876	73.5	1	876	196196	0.5062	0.02	10719	0.994249	2.53
	62	878	73.6	1	878	197074	0.5084	0.02	10720	0.994342	2.53
	61	904	73.7	1	904	197978	0.5108	0.03	10721	0.994435	2.54
	60	912	73.7	1	912	198890	0.5131	0.03	10722	0.994527	2.54
	59	924	73.8	1	924	199814	0.5155	0.04	10723	0.994620	2.55
	58	955	73.9	1	955	200769	0.5180	0.05	10724	0.994713	2.56
	57	971	74.0	1	971	201740	0.5205	0.05	10725	0.994806	2.56
	56	976	74.0	1	976	202716	0.5230	0.06	10726	0.994898	2.57
	55	997	74.1	1	997	203713	0.5255	0.06	10727	0.994991	2.58
	54	1047	74.3	1	1047	204760	0.5283	0.07	10728	0.995084	2.58
	53	1066	74.4	1	1066	205826	0.5310	0.08	10729	0.995177	2.59
	52	1081	74.5	1	1081	206907	0.5338	0.08	10730	0.995269	2.59
	51	1097	74.5	1	1097	208004	0.5366	0.09	10731	0.995362	2.60
	50	1103	74.5	1	1103	209107	0.5395	0.10	10732	0.995455	2.61
	49	1174	74.8	1	1174	210281	0.5425	0.11	10733	0.995548	2.62
	48	1185	74.9	1	1185	211466	0.5456	0.11	10734	0.995640	2.62
	47	1199	74.9	1	1199	212665	0.5486	0.12	10735	0.995733	2.63
	46	1224	75.0	1	1224	213889	0.5518	0.13	10736	0.995826	2.64
	45	1239	75.0	1	1239	215128	0.5550	0.14	10737	0.995919	2.65
	44	1281	75.2	1	1281	216409	0.5583	0.15	10738	0.996011	2.65
	43	1321	75.3	1	1321	217730	0.5617	0.16	10739	0.996104	2.66
	42	1355	75.4	1	1355	219085	0.5652	0.16	10740	0.996197	2.67
	41	1361	75.5	1	1361	220446	0.5687	0.17	10741	0.996290	2.68
	40	1368	75.5	1	1368	221814	0.5722	0.18	10742	0.996382	2.69
	39	1473	75.8	1	1473	223287	0.5760	0.19	10743	0.996475	2.69
	38	1500	75.9	1	1500	224787	0.5799	0.20	10744	0.996568	2.70
	37	1501	75.9	1	1501	226288	0.5838	0.21	10745	0.996661	2.71
	36	1518	75.9	1	1518	227806	0.5877	0.22	10746	0.996754	2.72
	35	1582	76.1	1	1582	229388	0.5918	0.23	10747	0.996846	2.73
	34	1668	76.3	1	1668	231056	0.5961	0.24	10748	0.996939	2.74
	33	1679	76.4	1	1679	232735	0.6004	0.25	10749	0.997032	2.75
	32	1702	76.4	1	1702	234437	0.6048	0.27	10750	0.997125	2.76
	31	1766	76.6	1	1766	236203	0.6094	0.28	10751	0.997217	2.77
	30	1805	76.7	1	1805	238008	0.6140	0.29	10752	0.997310	2.78
	29	1810	76.7	1	1810	239818	0.6187	0.30	10753	0.997403	2.79
	28	1883	76.9	1	1883	241701	0.6236	0.31	10754	0.997496	2.81
	27	1885	76.9	1	1885	243586	0.6284	0.33	10755	0.997588	2.82
	26	1922	77.0	1	1922	245508	0.6334	0.34	10756	0.997681	2.83
	25	1941	77.0	1	1941	247449	0.6384	0.35	10757	0.997774	2.84
	24	1961	77.0	1	1961	249410	0.6434	0.37	10758	0.997867	2.86
	23	2054	77.2	1	2054	251464	0.6487	0.38	10759	0.997959	2.87
	22	2060	77.3	1	2060	253524	0.6541	0.40	10760	0.998052	2.89
	21	2155	77.5	1	2155	255679	0.6596	0.41	10761	0.998145	2.90
	20	2183	77.5	1	2183	257862	0.6652	0.43	10762	0.998238	2.92
	19	2265	77.7	1	2265	260127	0.6711	0.44	10763	0.998330	2.93
	18	2278	77.7	1	2278	262405	0.6770	0.46	10764	0.998423	2.95
	17	2645	78.3	1	2645	265050	0.6838	0.48	10765	0.998516	2.97
	16	2658	78.4	1	2658	267708	0.6906	0.50	10766	0.998609	2.99
	15	2702	78.4	1	2702	270410	0.6976	0.52	10767	0.998701	3.01
	14	3191	79.2	1	3191	273601	0.7059	0.54	10768	0.998794	3.03
	13	3967	80.1	1	3967	277568	0.7161	0.57	10769	0.998887	3.06
	12	4075	80.2	1	4075	281643	0.7266	0.60	10770	0.998980	3.08
	11	4081	80.2	1	4081	285724	0.7371	0.63	10771	0.999072	3.11
	10	4210	80.4	1	4210	289934	0.7480	0.67	10772	0.999165	3.14
	9	4215	80.4	1	4215	294149	0.7589	0.70	10773	0.999258	3.18
	8	4254	80.4	1	4254	298403	0.7698	0.74	10774	0.999351	3.22
	7	7343	82.8	1	7343	305746	0.7888	0.80	10775	0.999443	3.26
	6	7589	82.9	1	7589	313335	0.8084	0.87	10776	0.999536	3.31
	5	8068	83.2	1	8068	321403	0.8292	0.95	10777	0.999629	3.37
	4	9158	83.7	1	9158	330561	0.8528	1.05	10778	0.999722	3.45
	3	10090	84.2	1	10090	340651	0.8788	1.17	10779	0.999814	3.56
	2	14747	85.8	1	14747	355398	0.9169	1.38	10780	0.999907	3.74
	1	32221	89.2	1	32221	387619	1.0000	+INF.	10781	1.000000	+INF.

Rank	Occ. F	SFI	F	Tokens	Cum. Tokens	Cum. P Tokens	Y	Cum. Types	Cum. P Types	Z
12635-21043	1	44.7	8409	8409	8409	0.0167	-2.13	8409	0.399610	-0.25
9619-12634	2	47.0	3016	6032	14441	0.0287	-1.90	11425	0.542936	0.11
7992- 9618	3	48.4	1627	4881	19322	0.0384	-1.77	13052	0.620254	0.31
6843- 7991	4	49.5	1149	4596	23918	0.0475	-1.67	14201	0.674856	0.45
5981- 6842	5	50.4	862	4310	28228	0.0561	-1.59	15063	0.715820	0.57
5387- 5980	6	51.1	594	3564	31792	0.0631	-1.53	15657	0.744048	0.66
4896- 5386	7	51.7	491	3437	35229	0.0700	-1.48	16148	0.767381	0.73
4478- 4895	8	52.3	418	3344	38573	0.0766	-1.43	16566	0.787245	0.80
4142- 4477	9	52.8	336	3024	41597	0.0826	-1.39	16902	0.803212	0.85
3871- 4141	10	53.2	271	2710	44307	0.0880	-1.35	17173	0.816091	0.90
3658- 3870	11	53.6	213	2343	46650	0.0926	-1.32	17386	0.826213	0.94
3451- 3657	12	53.9	207	2484	49134	0.0976	-1.30	17593	0.836050	0.98
3254- 3450	13	54.3	197	2561	51695	0.1026	-1.27	17790	0.845412	1.02
3072- 3253	14	54.6	182	2548	54243	0.1077	-1.24	17972	0.854061	1.05
2951- 3071	15	54.9	121	1815	56058	0.1113	-1.22	18093	0.859811	1.08
2799- 2950	16	55.2	152	2432	58490	0.1161	-1.19	18245	0.867034	1.11
2680- 2798	17	55.4	119	2023	60513	0.1202	-1.17	18364	0.872689	1.14
2598- 2679	18	55.7	82	1476	61989	0.1231	-1.16	18446	0.876586	1.16
2492- 2597	19	55.9	106	2014	64003	0.1271	-1.14	18552	0.881623	1.18
2395- 2491	20	56.1	97	1940	65943	0.1309	-1.12	18649	0.886233	1.21
2315- 2394	21	56.3	80	1680	67623	0.1343	-1.11	18729	0.890035	1.23
2230- 2314	22	56.5	85	1870	69493	0.1380	-1.09	18814	0.894074	1.25
2163- 2229	23	56.7	67	1541	71034	0.1410	-1.08	18881	0.897258	1.27
2079- 2162	24	56.9	84	2016	73050	0.1450	-1.06	18965	0.901250	1.29
2018- 2078	25	57.0	61	1525	74575	0.1481	-1.04	19026	0.904149	1.31
1953- 2017	26	57.2	65	1690	76265	0.1514	-1.03	19091	0.907238	1.32
1881- 1952	27	57.4	72	1944	78209	0.1553	-1.01	19163	0.910659	1.34
1832- 1880	28	57.5	49	1372	79581	0.1580	-1.00	19212	0.912988	1.36
1782- 1831	29	57.7	50	1450	81031	0.1609	-0.99	19262	0.915364	1.37
1736- 1781	30	57.8	46	1380	82411	0.1636	-0.98	19308	0.917550	1.39
1687- 1735	31	58.0	49	1519	83930	0.1667	-0.97	19357	0.919878	1.40
1645- 1686	32	58.1	42	1344	85274	0.1693	-0.96	19399	0.921874	1.42
1597- 1644	33	58.2	48	1584	86858	0.1725	-0.94	19447	0.924155	1.43
1562- 1596	34	58.4	35	1190	88048	0.1748	-0.94	19482	0.925819	1.45
1528- 1561	35	58.5	34	1190	89238	0.1772	-0.93	19516	0.927434	1.46
1489- 1527	36	58.6	39	1404	90642	0.1800	-0.92	19555	0.929288	1.47
1457- 1488	37	58.7	32	1184	91826	0.1823	-0.91	19587	0.930808	1.48
1429- 1456	38	58.8	28	1064	92890	0.1844	-0.90	19615	0.932139	1.49
1392- 1428	39	58.9	37	1443	94333	0.1873	-0.89	19652	0.933897	1.51
1367- 1391	40	59.1	25	1000	95333	0.1893	-0.88	19677	0.935085	1.51
1342- 1366	41	59.2	25	1025	96358	0.1913	-0.87	19702	0.936273	1.52
1315- 1341	42	59.3	27	1134	97492	0.1936	-0.86	19729	0.937556	1.53
1291- 1314	43	59.4	24	1032	98524	0.1956	-0.86	19753	0.938697	1.54
1267- 1290	44	59.5	24	1056	99580	0.1977	-0.85	19777	0.939837	1.55
1244- 1266	45	59.6	23	1035	100615	0.1998	-0.84	19800	0.940930	1.56
1229- 1243	46	59.7	15	690	101305	0.2012	-0.84	19815	0.941643	1.57
1213- 1228	47	59.7	16	752	102057	0.2026	-0.83	19831	0.942404	1.58
1189- 1212	48	59.8	24	1152	103209	0.2049	-0.82	19855	0.943544	1.59
1171- 1188	49	59.9	18	882	104091	0.2067	-0.82	19873	0.944400	1.59
1152- 1170	50	60.0	19	950	105041	0.2086	-0.81	19892	0.945302	1.60
1135- 1151	51	60.1	17	867	105908	0.2103	-0.81	19909	0.946110	1.61
1116- 1134	52	60.2	19	988	106896	0.2123	-0.80	19928	0.947013	1.62
1098- 1115	53	60.3	18	954	107850	0.2141	-0.79	19946	0.947869	1.62
1079- 1097	54	60.3	19	1026	108876	0.2162	-0.79	19965	0.948772	1.63
1061- 1078	55	60.4	18	990	109866	0.2182	-0.78	19983	0.949627	1.64
1052- 1060	56	60.5	9	504	110370	0.2192	-0.78	19992	0.950055	1.65
1033- 1051	57	60.6	19	1083	111453	0.2213	-0.77	20011	0.950958	1.65
1015- 1032	58	60.7	18	1044	112497	0.2234	-0.76	20029	0.951813	1.66
990- 1014	59	60.7	25	1475	113972	0.2263	-0.75	20054	0.953001	1.67
977- 989	60	60.8	13	780	114752	0.2279	-0.75	20067	0.953619	1.68
965- 976	61	60.9	12	732	115484	0.2293	-0.74	20079	0.954189	1.69
942- 964	62	60.9	23	1426	116910	0.2321	-0.73	20102	0.955282	1.70
931- 941	63	61.0	11	693	117603	0.2335	-0.73	20113	0.955805	1.70
916- 930	64	61.1	15	960	118563	0.2354	-0.72	20128	0.956518	1.71
905- 915	65	61.1	11	715	119278	0.2368	-0.72	20139	0.957040	1.72
888- 904	66	61.2	17	1122	120400	0.2391	-0.71	20156	0.957848	1.73
876- 887	67	61.3	12	804	121204	0.2407	-0.70	20168	0.958418	1.73
869- 875	68	61.3	7	476	121680	0.2416	-0.70	20175	0.958751	1.74
854- 868	69	61.4	15	1035	122715	0.2437	-0.69	20190	0.959464	1.74
842- 853	70	61.5	12	840	123555	0.2453	-0.69	20202	0.960034	1.75
835- 841	71	61.5	7	497	124052	0.2463	-0.69	20209	0.960367	1.75
823- 834	72	61.6	12	864	124916	0.2480	-0.68	20221	0.960937	1.76
814- 822	73	61.6	9	657	125573	0.2493	-0.68	20230	0.961365	1.77
805- 813	74	61.7	9	666	126239	0.2507	-0.67	20239	0.961792	1.77
798- 804	75	61.8	7	525	126764	0.2517	-0.67	20246	0.962125	1.78
792- 797	76	61.8	6	456	127220	0.2526	-0.67	20252	0.962410	1.78
786- 791	77	61.9	6	462	127682	0.2535	-0.66	20258	0.962695	1.78
782- 785	78	61.9	4	312	127994	0.2541	-0.66	20262	0.962885	1.79
775- 781	79	62.0	7	553	128547	0.2552	-0.66	20269	0.963218	1.79
769- 774	80	62.0	6	480	129027	0.2562	-0.66	20275	0.963503	1.79
763- 768	81	62.1	6	486	129513	0.2572	-0.65	20281	0.963788	1.80
751- 762	82	62.1	12	984	130497	0.2591	-0.65	20293	0.964359	1.80
743- 750	83	62.2	8	664	131161	0.2604	-0.64	20301	0.964739	1.81
733- 742	84	62.2	10	840	132001	0.2621	-0.64	20311	0.965214	1.81
727- 732	85	62.3	6	510	132511	0.2631	-0.63	20317	0.965499	1.82
721- 726	86	62.3	6	516	133027	0.2641	-0.63	20323	0.965784	1.82
716- 720	87	62.4	5	435	133462	0.2650	-0.63	20328	0.966022	1.83
710- 715	88	62.4	6	528	133990	0.2661	-0.62	20334	0.966307	1.83
700- 709	89	62.5	10	890	134880	0.2678	-0.62	20344	0.966782	1.84
696- 699	90	62.5	4	360	135240	0.2685	-0.62	20348	0.966972	1.84
687- 695	91	62.6	9	819	136059	0.2702	-0.61	20357	0.967400	1.84
679- 686	92	62.6	8	736	136795	0.2716	-0.61	20365	0.967780	1.85
668- 678	93	62.7	11	1023	137818	0.2737	-0.60	20376	0.968303	1.86
661- 667	94	62.7	7	658	138476	0.2750	-0.60	20383	0.968636	1.86
654- 660	95	62.8	7	665	139141	0.2763	-0.59	20390	0.968968	1.87
643- 653	96	62.8	11	1056	140197	0.2784	-0.59	20401	0.969491	1.87
632- 642	97	62.9	11	1067	141264	0.2805	-0.58	20412	0.970014	1.88
625- 631	98	62.9	7	686	141950	0.2819	-0.58	20419	0.970346	1.89
620- 624	99	63.0	5	495	142445	0.2828	-0.57	20424	0.970584	1.89
613- 619	100	63.0	7	700	143145	0.2842	-0.57	20431	0.970917	1.89
608- 612	101	63.0	5	505	143650	0.2852	-0.57	20436	0.971154	1.90
600- 607	102	63.1	8	816	144466	0.2869	-0.56	20444	0.971534	1.90
593- 599	103	63.1	7	721	145187	0.2883	-0.56	20451	0.971867	1.91
588- 592	104	63.2	5	520	145707	0.2893	-0.56	20456	0.972105	1.91
583- 587	105	63.2	5	525	146232	0.2904	-0.55	20461	0.972342	1.92
576- 582	106	63.3	7	742	146974	0.2918	-0.55	20468	0.972675	1.92
570- 575	107	63.3	6	642	147616	0.2931	-0.54	20474	0.972960	1.93
566- 569	108	63.3	4	432	148048	0.2940	-0.54	20478	0.973150	1.93
563- 565	109	63.4	3	327	148375	0.2946	-0.54	20481	0.973293	1.93
556- 562	110	63.4	7	770	149145	0.2961	-0.54	20488	0.973625	1.94
552- 555	111	63.5	4	444	149589	0.2970	-0.53	20492	0.973816	1.94
548- 551	112	63.5	4	448	150037	0.2979	-0.53	20496	0.974006	1.94
543- 547	113	63.5	5	565	150602	0.2990	-0.53	20501	0.974243	1.95
538- 542	114	63.6	5	570	151172	0.3002	-0.52	20506	0.974481	1.95
536- 537	115	63.6	2	230	151402	0.3006	-0.52	20508	0.974576	1.95
527- 535	116	63.6	9	1044	152446	0.3027	-0.52	20517	0.975004	1.96
522- 526	117	63.7	5	585	153031	0.3039	-0.51	20522	0.975241	1.96
519- 521	118	63.7	3	354	153385	0.3046	-0.51	20525	0.975384	1.97
515- 518	119	63.8	4	476	153861	0.3055	-0.51	20529	0.975574	1.97
507- 514	120	63.8	8	960	154821	0.3074	-0.50	20537	0.975954	1.98
505- 506	121	63.8	2	242	155063	0.3079	-0.50	20539	0.976049	1.98
502- 504	122	63.9	3	366	155429	0.3086	-0.50	20542	0.976192	1.98
497- 501	123	63.9	5	615	156044	0.3098	-0.50	20547	0.976429	1.99
491- 496	124	63.9	6	744	156788	0.3113	-0.49	20553	0.976714	1.99
486- 490	125	64.0	5	625	157413	0.3126	-0.49	20558	0.976952	1.99
484- 485	126	64.0	2	252	157665	0.3131	-0.49	20560	0.977047	2.00
480- 483	127	64.0	4	508	158173	0.3141	-0.48	20564	0.977237	2.00
476- 479	128	64.1	4	512	158685	0.3151	-0.48	20568	0.977427	2.00
474- 475	129	64.1	2	258	158943	0.3156	-0.48	20570	0.977522	2.01
471- 473	130	64.1	3	390	159333	0.3164	-0.48	20573	0.977665	2.01
466- 470	131	64.2	5	655	159988	0.3177	-0.47	20578	0.977902	2.01
465	133	64.2	1	133	160121	0.3179	-0.47	20579	0.977950	2.01
461- 464	134	64.3	4	536	160657	0.3190	-0.47	20583	0.978140	2.02
456- 460	135	64.3	5	675	161332	0.3203	-0.47	20588	0.978378	2.02
451- 455	136	64.3	5	680	162012	0.3217	-0.46	20593	0.978615	2.03
449- 450	137	64.4	2	274	162286	0.3222	-0.46	20595	0.978710	2.03
447- 448	139	64.4	2	278	162564	0.3228	-0.46	20597	0.978805	2.03
446	140	64.5	1	140	162704	0.3231	-0.46	20598	0.978853	2.03
443- 445	141	64.5	3	423	163127	0.3239	-0.46	20601	0.978995	2.03
440- 442	142	64.5	3	426	163553	0.3248	-0.45	20604	0.979138	2.04
438- 439	143	64.5	2	286	163839	0.3253	-0.45	20606	0.979233	2.04
434- 437	144	64.6	4	576	164415	0.3265	-0.45	20610	0.979423	2.04
428- 433	145	64.6	6	870	165285	0.3282	-0.44	20616	0.979708	2.05
424- 427	146	64.6	4	584	165869	0.3294	-0.44	20620	0.979898	2.05
421- 423	147	64.7	3	441	166310	0.3302	-0.44	20623	0.980041	2.05
417- 420	148	64.7	4	592	166902	0.3314	-0.44	20627	0.980231	2.06
414- 416	149	64.7	3	447	167349	0.3323	-0.43	20630	0.980374	2.06
413	151	64.8	1	151	167500	0.3326	-0.43	20631	0.980421	2.06
412	152	64.8	1	152	167652	0.3329	-0.43	20632	0.980469	2.06
410- 411	153	64.8	2	306	167958	0.3335	-0.43	20634	0.980564	2.07
408- 409	154	64.9	2	308	168266	0.3341	-0.43	20636	0.980659	2.07
407	155	64.9	1	155	168421	0.3344	-0.43	20637	0.980706	2.07
406	156	64.9	1	156	168577	0.3347	-0.43	20638	0.980754	2.07
405	157	65.0	1	157	168734	0.3350	-0.43	20639	0.980801	2.07
404	158	65.0	1	158	168892	0.3354	-0.43	20640	0.980849	2.07
401- 403	160	65.0	3	480	169372	0.3363	-0.42	20643	0.980991	2.07
398- 400	161	65.1	3	483	169855	0.3373	-0.42	20646	0.981134	2.08
397	162	65.1	1	162	170017	0.3376	-0.42	20647	0.981181	2.08
393- 396	163	65.1	4	652	170669	0.3389	-0.42	20651	0.981371	2.08
389- 392	164	65.1	4	656	171325	0.3402	-0.41	20655	0.981562	2.09
382- 388	165	65.2	7	1155	172480	0.3425	-0.41	20662	0.981894	2.09
381	166	65.2	1	166	172646	0.3428	-0.40	20663	0.981942	2.10
380	167	65.2	1	167	172813	0.3431	-0.40	20664	0.981989	2.10
378- 379	168	65.2	2	336	173149	0.3438	-0.40	20666	0.982084	2.10
376- 377	169	65.3	2	338	173487	0.3445	-0.40	20668	0.982179	2.10
373- 375	170	65.3	3	510	173997	0.3455	-0.40	20671	0.982322	2.10
372	172	65.3	1	172	174169	0.3458	-0.40	20672	0.982369	2.11
365- 371	173	65.4	7	1211	175380	0.3482	-0.39	20679	0.982702	2.11
362- 364	174	65.4	3	522	175902	0.3493	-0.39	20682	0.982845	2.12
358- 361	175	65.4	4	700	176602	0.3507	-0.38	20686	0.983035	2.12
354- 357	176	65.4	4	704	177306	0.3521	-0.38	20690	0.983225	2.13
353	177	65.5	1	177	177483	0.3524	-0.38	20691	0.983272	2.13
351- 352	178	65.5	2	356	177839	0.3531	-0.38	20693	0.983367	2.13
350	179	65.5	1	179	178018	0.3535	-0.38	20694	0.983415	2.13
348- 349	180	65.5	2	360	178378	0.3542	-0.37	20696	0.983510	2.13
344- 347	182	65.6	4	728	179106	0.3556	-0.37	20700	0.983700	2.14
343	183	65.6	1	183	179289	0.3560	-0.37	20701	0.983748	2.14
342	184	65.6	1	184	179473	0.3564	-0.37	20702	0.983795	2.14
340- 341	185	65.7	2	370	179843	0.3571	-0.37	20704	0.983890	2.14
337- 339	186	65.7	3	558	180401	0.3582	-0.36	20707	0.984033	2.15
335- 336	187	65.7	2	374	180775	0.3590	-0.36	20709	0.984128	2.15
332- 334	188	65.7	3	564	181339	0.3601	-0.36	20712	0.984270	2.15
330- 331	189	65.8	2	378	181717	0.3608	-0.36	20714	0.984365	2.15
327- 329	190	65.8	3	570	182287	0.3620	-0.35	20717	0.984508	2.16
325- 326	191	65.8	2	382	182669	0.3627	-0.35	20719	0.984603	2.16
320- 324	192	65.8	5	960	183629	0.3646	-0.35	20724	0.984841	2.17
318- 319	193	65.8	2	386	184015	0.3654	-0.34	20726	0.984936	2.17
316- 317	194	65.9	2	388	184403	0.3662	-0.34	20728	0.985031	2.17
314- 315	197	65.9	2	394	184797	0.3669	-0.34	20730	0.985126	2.17
312- 313	198	66.0	2	396	185193	0.3677	-0.34	20732	0.985221	2.18
311	199	66.0	1	199	185392	0.3681	-0.34	20733	0.985268	2.18
310	200	66.0	1	200	185592	0.3685	-0.34	20734	0.985316	2.18
305- 309	201	66.0	5	1005	186597	0.3705	-0.33	20739	0.985553	2.18
304	202	66.0	1	202	186799	0.3709	-0.33	20740	0.985601	2.19
301- 303	203	66.1	3	609	187408	0.3721	-0.33	20743	0.985743	2.19
299- 300	204	66.1	2	408	187816	0.3729	-0.32	20745	0.985838	2.19
297- 298	208	66.2	2	416	188232	0.3738	-0.32	20747	0.985934	2.20
296	209	66.2	1	209	188441	0.3742	-0.32	20748	0.985981	2.20
295	210	66.2	1	210	188651	0.3746	-0.32	20749	0.986029	2.20
294	211	66.2	1	211	188862	0.3750	-0.32	20750	0.986076	2.20
292- 293	212	66.3	2	424	189286	0.3759	-0.32	20752	0.986171	2.20
290- 291	213	66.3	2	426	189712	0.3767	-0.31	20754	0.986266	2.20
289	214	66.3	1	214	189926	0.3771	-0.31	20755	0.986314	2.21
288	215	66.3	1	215	190141	0.3775	-0.31	20756	0.986361	2.21
284- 287	217	66.4	4	868	191009	0.3793	-0.31	20760	0.986551	2.21
283	218	66.4	1	218	191227	0.3797	-0.31	20761	0.986599	2.21
282	219	66.4	1	219	191446	0.3801	-0.31	20762	0.986646	2.22
281	220	66.4	1	220	191666	0.3806	-0.30	20763	0.986694	2.22
280	222	66.5	1	222	191888	0.3810	-0.30	20764	0.986741	2.22
277- 279	223	66.5	3	669	192557	0.3823	-0.30	20767	0.986884	2.22
276	224	66.5	1	224	192781	0.3828	-0.30	20768	0.986932	2.22
274- 275	225	66.5	2	450	193231	0.3837	-0.30	20770	0.987027	2.23
273	226	66.5	1	226	193457	0.3841	-0.29	20771	0.987074	2.23
272	229	66.6	1	229	193686	0.3846	-0.29	20772	0.987122	2.23
270- 271	231	66.6	2	462	194148	0.3855	-0.29	20774	0.987217	2.23
269	232	66.6	1	232	194380	0.3860	-0.29	20775	0.987264	2.23
268	233	66.7	1	233	194613	0.3864	-0.29	20776	0.987312	2.24
267	234	66.7	1	234	194847	0.3869	-0.29	20777	0.987359	2.24
265- 266	235	66.7	2	470	195317	0.3878	-0.28	20779	0.987454	2.24
262- 264	241	66.8	3	723	196040	0.3893	-0.28	20782	0.987597	2.24
260- 261	242	66.8	2	484	196524	0.3902	-0.28	20784	0.987692	2.25
259	243	66.8	1	243	196767	0.3907	-0.28	20785	0.987739	2.25
258	244	66.9	1	244	197011	0.3912	-0.28	20786	0.987787	2.25
256- 257	245	66.9	2	490	197501	0.3922	-0.27	20788	0.987882	2.25
254- 255	246	66.9	2	492	197993	0.3931	-0.27	20790	0.987977	2.26
253	247	66.9	1	247	198240	0.3936	-0.27	20791	0.988024	2.26
252	252	67.0	1	252	198492	0.3941	-0.27	20792	0.988072	2.26
250- 251	254	67.0	2	508	199000	0.3951	-0.27	20794	0.988167	2.26
248- 249	255	67.1	2	510	199510	0.3962	-0.26	20796	0.988262	2.27
247	256	67.1	1	256	199766	0.3967	-0.26	20797	0.988310	2.27
245- 246	257	67.1	2	514	200280	0.3977	-0.26	20799	0.988405	2.27
242- 244	259	67.1	3	777	201057	0.3992	-0.26	20802	0.988547	2.28

Rank	Occ. F	SFI	F	Tokens	Cum. Tokens	Cum. P Tokens	Y	Cum. Types	Cum. P Types	Z
241	260	67.1	1	260	201317	0.3997	-0.25	20803	0.988595	2.28
240	262	67.2	1	262	201579	0.4003	-0.25	20804	0.988642	2.28
239	263	67.2	1	263	201842	0.4008	-0.25	20805	0.988690	2.28
237- 238	264	67.2	2	528	202370	0.4018	-0.25	20807	0.988785	2.28
236	265	67.2	1	265	202635	0.4024	-0.25	20808	0.988832	2.28
235	267	67.3	1	267	202902	0.4029	-0.25	20809	0.988880	2.29
234	268	67.3	1	268	203170	0.4034	-0.24	20810	0.988927	2.29
233	270	67.3	1	270	203440	0.4040	-0.24	20811	0.988975	2.29
231- 232	271	67.3	2	542	203982	0.4050	-0.24	20813	0.989070	2.29
229- 230	273	67.3	2	546	204528	0.4061	-0.24	20815	0.989165	2.30
228	274	67.4	1	274	204802	0.4067	-0.24	20816	0.989213	2.30
227	275	67.4	1	275	205077	0.4072	-0.23	20817	0.989260	2.30
225- 226	276	67.4	2	552	205629	0.4083	-0.23	20819	0.989355	2.30
224	277	67.4	1	277	205906	0.4089	-0.23	20820	0.989403	2.30
222- 223	278	67.4	2	556	206462	0.4100	-0.23	20822	0.989498	2.31
221	279	67.4	1	279	206741	0.4105	-0.23	20823	0.989545	2.31
220	280	67.5	1	280	207021	0.4111	-0.22	20824	0.989593	2.31
219	281	67.5	1	281	207302	0.4116	-0.22	20825	0.989640	2.31
217- 218	282	67.5	2	564	207866	0.4127	-0.22	20827	0.989735	2.32
215- 216	284	67.5	2	568	208434	0.4139	-0.22	20829	0.989830	2.32
213- 214	285	67.5	2	570	209004	0.4150	-0.21	20831	0.989925	2.32
212	288	67.6	1	288	209292	0.4156	-0.21	20832	0.989973	2.33
211	290	67.6	1	290	209582	0.4162	-0.21	20833	0.990020	2.33
210	291	67.6	1	291	209873	0.4167	-0.21	20834	0.990068	2.33
209	294	67.7	1	294	210167	0.4173	-0.21	20835	0.990115	2.33
208	295	67.7	1	295	210462	0.4179	-0.21	20836	0.990163	2.33
207	296	67.7	1	296	210758	0.4185	-0.21	20837	0.990210	2.33
206	298	67.7	1	298	211056	0.4191	-0.20	20838	0.990258	2.34
204- 205	299	67.7	2	598	211654	0.4203	-0.20	20840	0.990353	2.34
202- 203	300	67.8	2	600	212254	0.4215	-0.20	20842	0.990448	2.34
201	302	67.8	1	302	212556	0.4221	-0.20	20843	0.990496	2.35
200	305	67.8	1	305	212861	0.4227	-0.20	20844	0.990543	2.35
199	308	67.9	1	308	213169	0.4233	-0.19	20845	0.990591	2.35
198	309	67.9	1	309	213478	0.4239	-0.19	20846	0.990638	2.35
197	311	67.9	1	311	213789	0.4245	-0.19	20847	0.990686	2.35
196	312	67.9	1	312	214101	0.4251	-0.19	20848	0.990733	2.35
194- 195	315	68.0	2	630	214731	0.4264	-0.19	20850	0.990828	2.36
193	317	68.0	1	317	215048	0.4270	-0.18	20851	0.990876	2.36
190- 192	318	68.0	3	954	216002	0.4289	-0.18	20854	0.991018	2.37
188- 189	324	68.1	2	648	216650	0.4302	-0.18	20856	0.991113	2.37
187	326	68.1	1	326	216976	0.4308	-0.17	20857	0.991161	2.37
186	328	68.1	1	328	217304	0.4315	-0.17	20858	0.991208	2.37
185	329	68.2	1	329	217633	0.4321	-0.17	20859	0.991256	2.38
184	330	68.2	1	330	217963	0.4328	-0.17	20860	0.991304	2.38
183	334	68.2	1	334	218297	0.4335	-0.17	20861	0.991351	2.38
182	335	68.2	1	335	218632	0.4341	-0.17	20862	0.991399	2.38
180- 181	336	68.2	2	672	219304	0.4355	-0.16	20864	0.991494	2.39
179	349	68.4	1	349	219653	0.4361	-0.16	20865	0.991541	2.39
178	350	68.4	1	350	220003	0.4368	-0.16	20866	0.991589	2.39
177	354	68.5	1	354	220357	0.4375	-0.16	20867	0.991636	2.39
175- 176	356	68.5	2	712	221069	0.4390	-0.15	20869	0.991731	2.40
174	357	68.5	1	357	221426	0.4397	-0.15	20870	0.991779	2.40
173	358	68.5	1	358	221784	0.4404	-0.15	20871	0.991826	2.40
172	360	68.5	1	360	222144	0.4411	-0.15	20872	0.991874	2.40
169- 171	361	68.6	3	1083	223227	0.4432	-0.14	20875	0.992016	2.41
167- 168	362	68.6	2	724	223951	0.4447	-0.14	20877	0.992111	2.41
166	366	68.6	1	366	224317	0.4454	-0.14	20878	0.992159	2.42
165	367	68.6	1	367	224684	0.4461	-0.14	20879	0.992206	2.42
164	368	68.6	1	368	225052	0.4469	-0.13	20880	0.992254	2.42
163	372	68.7	1	372	225424	0.4476	-0.13	20881	0.992301	2.42
162	374	68.7	1	374	225798	0.4483	-0.13	20882	0.992349	2.43
161	376	68.7	1	376	226174	0.4491	-0.13	20883	0.992396	2.43
159- 160	380	68.8	2	760	226934	0.4506	-0.12	20885	0.992492	2.43
158	381	68.8	1	381	227315	0.4514	-0.12	20886	0.992539	2.43
157	383	68.8	1	383	227698	0.4521	-0.12	20887	0.992587	2.44
156	385	68.8	1	385	228083	0.4529	-0.12	20888	0.992634	2.44
154- 155	388	68.9	2	776	228859	0.4544	-0.11	20890	0.992729	2.44
153	390	68.9	1	390	229249	0.4552	-0.11	20891	0.992777	2.45
151- 152	395	69.0	2	790	230039	0.4568	-0.11	20893	0.992872	2.45
150	397	69.0	1	397	230436	0.4576	-0.11	20894	0.992919	2.45
149	399	69.0	1	399	230835	0.4584	-0.10	20895	0.992967	2.46
148	401	69.0	1	401	231236	0.4591	-0.10	20896	0.993014	2.46
147	402	69.0	1	402	231638	0.4599	-0.10	20897	0.993062	2.46
146	405	69.1	1	405	232043	0.4608	-0.10	20898	0.993109	2.46
145	408	69.1	1	408	232451	0.4616	-0.10	20899	0.993157	2.47
144	409	69.1	1	409	232860	0.4624	-0.09	20900	0.993204	2.47
143	411	69.1	1	411	233271	0.4632	-0.09	20901	0.993252	2.47
142	418	69.2	1	418	233689	0.4640	-0.09	20902	0.993299	2.47
141	427	69.3	1	427	234116	0.4649	-0.09	20903	0.993347	2.48
140	433	69.3	1	433	234549	0.4657	-0.09	20904	0.993394	2.48
139	442	69.4	1	442	234991	0.4666	-0.08	20905	0.993442	2.48
138	444	69.5	1	444	235435	0.4675	-0.08	20906	0.993490	2.48
137	445	69.5	1	445	235880	0.4684	-0.08	20907	0.993537	2.49
135- 136	447	69.5	2	894	236774	0.4701	-0.07	20909	0.993632	2.49
134	448	69.5	1	448	237222	0.4710	-0.07	20910	0.993680	2.49
132- 133	453	69.5	2	906	238128	0.4728	-0.07	20912	0.993775	2.50
131	455	69.6	1	455	238583	0.4737	-0.07	20913	0.993822	2.50
130	457	69.6	1	457	239040	0.4746	-0.06	20914	0.993870	2.50
129	458	69.6	1	458	239498	0.4756	-0.06	20915	0.993917	2.51
127- 128	459	69.6	2	918	240416	0.4774	-0.06	20917	0.994012	2.51
126	460	69.6	1	460	240876	0.4783	-0.05	20918	0.994060	2.52
125	463	69.6	1	463	241339	0.4792	-0.05	20919	0.994107	2.52
124	465	69.7	1	465	241804	0.4801	-0.05	20920	0.994155	2.52
123	466	69.7	1	466	242270	0.4811	-0.05	20921	0.994202	2.52
122	467	69.7	1	467	242737	0.4820	-0.05	20922	0.994250	2.53
121	469	69.7	1	469	243206	0.4829	-0.04	20923	0.994297	2.53
120	471	69.7	1	471	243677	0.4839	-0.04	20924	0.994345	2.53
119	472	69.7	1	472	244149	0.4848	-0.04	20925	0.994392	2.54
117- 118	476	69.8	2	952	245101	0.4867	-0.03	20927	0.994487	2.54
116	494	69.9	1	494	245595	0.4877	-0.03	20928	0.994535	2.54
115	503	70.0	1	503	246098	0.4887	-0.03	20929	0.994582	2.55
114	519	70.1	1	519	246617	0.4897	-0.03	20930	0.994630	2.55
113	522	70.2	1	522	247139	0.4907	-0.02	20931	0.994678	2.55
112	546	70.4	1	546	247685	0.4918	-0.02	20932	0.994725	2.56
111	554	70.4	1	554	248239	0.4929	-0.02	20933	0.994773	2.56
110	556	70.4	1	556	248795	0.4940	-0.02	20934	0.994820	2.56
109	559	70.5	1	559	249354	0.4951	-0.01	20935	0.994868	2.57
108	578	70.6	1	578	249932	0.4963	-0.01	20936	0.994915	2.57
107	587	70.7	1	587	250519	0.4974	-0.01	20937	0.994963	2.57
106	595	70.7	1	595	251114	0.4986	-0.00	20938	0.995010	2.58
105	609	70.8	1	609	251723	0.4998	-0.00	20939	0.995058	2.58
104	612	70.9	1	612	252335	0.5010	0.00	20940	0.995105	2.58
103	613	70.9	1	613	252948	0.5023	0.01	20941	0.995153	2.59
102	621	70.9	1	621	253569	0.5035	0.01	20942	0.995200	2.59
101	626	70.9	1	626	254195	0.5047	0.01	20943	0.995248	2.59
100	630	71.0	1	630	254825	0.5060	0.02	20944	0.995295	2.60
99	637	71.0	1	637	255462	0.5073	0.02	20945	0.995343	2.60
98	638	71.0	1	638	256100	0.5085	0.02	20946	0.995390	2.60
97	644	71.1	1	644	256744	0.5098	0.02	20947	0.995438	2.61
96	649	71.1	1	649	257393	0.5111	0.03	20948	0.995485	2.61
95	656	71.2	1	656	258049	0.5124	0.03	20949	0.995533	2.61
94	661	71.2	1	661	258710	0.5137	0.03	20950	0.995580	2.62
93	662	71.2	1	662	259372	0.5150	0.04	20951	0.995628	2.62
92	665	71.2	1	665	260037	0.5163	0.04	20952	0.995676	2.63
91	669	71.2	1	669	260706	0.5177	0.04	20953	0.995723	2.63
90	670	71.2	1	670	261376	0.5190	0.05	20954	0.995771	2.63
89	671	71.2	1	671	262047	0.5203	0.05	20955	0.995818	2.64
88	685	71.3	1	685	262732	0.5217	0.05	20956	0.995866	2.64
87	690	71.4	1	690	263422	0.5231	0.06	20957	0.995913	2.64
86	734	71.6	1	734	264156	0.5245	0.06	20958	0.995961	2.65
85	737	71.7	1	737	264893	0.5260	0.07	20959	0.996008	2.65
84	746	71.7	1	746	265639	0.5275	0.07	20960	0.996056	2.66
83	757	71.8	1	757	266396	0.5290	0.07	20961	0.996103	2.66
82	760	71.8	1	760	267156	0.5305	0.08	20962	0.996151	2.67
81	770	71.8	1	770	267926	0.5320	0.08	20963	0.996198	2.67
80	772	71.9	1	772	268698	0.5335	0.08	20964	0.996246	2.67
79	776	71.9	1	776	269474	0.5351	0.09	20965	0.996293	2.68
77- 78	778	71.9	2	1556	271030	0.5382	0.10	20967	0.996388	2.69
76	783	71.9	1	783	271813	0.5397	0.10	20968	0.996436	2.69
75	785	71.9	1	785	272598	0.5413	0.10	20969	0.996483	2.70
74	795	72.0	1	795	273393	0.5429	0.11	20970	0.996531	2.70
73	799	72.0	1	799	274192	0.5444	0.11	20971	0.996578	2.70
72	801	72.0	1	801	274993	0.5460	0.12	20972	0.996626	2.71
71	807	72.1	1	807	275800	0.5476	0.12	20973	0.996673	2.71
70	827	72.2	1	827	276627	0.5493	0.12	20974	0.996721	2.72
69	838	72.2	1	838	277465	0.5509	0.13	20975	0.996768	2.72
68	846	72.3	1	846	278311	0.5526	0.13	20976	0.996816	2.73
67	856	72.3	1	856	279167	0.5543	0.14	20977	0.996864	2.73
66	862	72.3	1	862	280029	0.5560	0.14	20978	0.996911	2.74
65	863	72.3	1	863	280892	0.5577	0.15	20979	0.996959	2.74
64	896	72.5	1	896	281788	0.5595	0.15	20980	0.997006	2.75
63	910	72.6	1	910	282698	0.5613	0.15	20981	0.997054	2.75
62	914	72.6	1	914	283612	0.5631	0.16	20982	0.997101	2.76
61	929	72.7	1	929	284541	0.5650	0.16	20983	0.997149	2.76
60	939	72.7	1	939	285480	0.5669	0.17	20984	0.997196	2.77
58- 59	952	72.8	2	1904	287384	0.5706	0.18	20986	0.997291	2.78
57	960	72.8	1	960	288344	0.5725	0.18	20987	0.997339	2.79
56	965	72.8	1	965	289309	0.5745	0.19	20988	0.997386	2.79
55	1002	73.0	1	1002	290311	0.5764	0.19	20989	0.997434	2.80
54	1039	73.1	1	1039	291350	0.5785	0.20	20990	0.997481	2.80
53	1042	73.2	1	1042	292392	0.5806	0.20	20991	0.997529	2.81
52	1060	73.2	1	1060	293452	0.5827	0.21	20992	0.997576	2.82
51	1115	73.5	1	1115	294567	0.5849	0.21	20993	0.997624	2.82
50	1135	73.5	1	1135	295702	0.5872	0.22	20994	0.997671	2.83
49	1185	73.7	1	1185	296887	0.5895	0.23	20995	0.997719	2.84
48	1247	73.9	1	1247	298134	0.5920	0.23	20996	0.997766	2.84
47	1248	73.9	1	1248	299382	0.5945	0.24	20997	0.997814	2.85
46	1259	74.0	1	1259	300641	0.5970	0.25	20998	0.997862	2.86
45	1288	74.1	1	1288	301929	0.5995	0.25	20999	0.997909	2.86
44	1331	74.2	1	1331	303260	0.6022	0.26	21000	0.997957	2.87
43	1333	74.2	1	1333	304593	0.6048	0.27	21001	0.998004	2.88
42	1405	74.5	1	1405	305998	0.6076	0.27	21002	0.998052	2.89
41	1433	74.5	1	1433	307431	0.6104	0.28	21003	0.998099	2.89
40	1438	74.6	1	1438	308869	0.6133	0.29	21004	0.998147	2.90
39	1532	74.8	1	1532	310401	0.6163	0.30	21005	0.998194	2.91
38	1587	75.0	1	1587	311988	0.6195	0.30	21006	0.998242	2.92
37	1668	75.2	1	1668	313656	0.6228	0.31	21007	0.998289	2.93
36	1686	75.2	1	1686	315342	0.6262	0.32	21008	0.998337	2.94
35	1728	75.4	1	1728	317070	0.6296	0.33	21009	0.998384	2.94
34	1745	75.4	1	1745	318815	0.6330	0.34	21010	0.998432	2.95
33	1747	75.4	1	1747	320562	0.6365	0.35	21011	0.998479	2.96
32	1806	75.5	1	1806	322368	0.6401	0.36	21012	0.998527	2.97
31	1850	75.7	1	1850	324218	0.6438	0.37	21013	0.998574	2.98
30	1851	75.7	1	1851	326069	0.6475	0.38	21014	0.998622	2.99
29	1934	75.8	1	1934	328003	0.6513	0.39	21015	0.998669	3.00
28	1994	76.0	1	1994	329997	0.6552	0.40	21016	0.998717	3.02
27	1996	76.0	1	1996	331993	0.6592	0.41	21017	0.998764	3.03
26	2141	76.3	1	2141	334134	0.6635	0.42	21018	0.998812	3.04
25	2205	76.4	1	2205	336339	0.6678	0.43	21019	0.998859	3.05
24	2268	76.5	1	2268	338607	0.6723	0.45	21020	0.998907	3.06
23	2282	76.6	1	2282	340889	0.6769	0.46	21021	0.998954	3.08
22	2330	76.7	1	2330	343219	0.6815	0.47	21022	0.999002	3.09
21	2553	77.1	1	2553	345772	0.6866	0.49	21023	0.999050	3.11
20	2591	77.1	1	2591	348363	0.6917	0.50	21024	0.999097	3.12
19	2606	77.1	1	2606	350969	0.6969	0.52	21025	0.999145	3.14
18	2703	77.3	1	2703	353672	0.7023	0.53	21026	0.999192	3.15
17	2737	77.4	1	2737	356409	0.7077	0.55	21027	0.999240	3.17
16	3023	77.8	1	3023	359432	0.7137	0.56	21028	0.999287	3.19
15	3142	78.0	1	3142	362574	0.7199	0.58	21029	0.999335	3.21
14	3750	78.7	1	3750	366324	0.7274	0.60	21030	0.999382	3.23
13	3754	78.7	1	3754	370078	0.7348	0.63	21031	0.999430	3.25
12	3825	78.8	1	3825	373903	0.7424	0.65	21032	0.999477	3.28
11	3960	79.0	1	3960	377863	0.7503	0.68	21033	0.999525	3.30
10	4099	79.1	1	4099	381962	0.7584	0.70	21034	0.999572	3.33
9	4188	79.2	1	4188	386150	0.7667	0.73	21035	0.999620	3.37
8	4715	79.7	1	4715	390865	0.7761	0.76	21036	0.999667	3.40
7	6528	81.1	1	6528	397393	0.7891	0.80	21037	0.999715	3.45
6	9826	82.9	1	9826	407219	0.8086	0.87	21038	0.999762	3.49
5	12184	83.8	1	12184	419403	0.8328	0.97	21039	0.999810	3.55
4	12274	83.9	1	12274	431677	0.8571	1.07	21040	0.999857	3.63
3	13798	84.4	1	13798	445475	0.8845	1.20	21041	0.999905	3.73
2	17840	85.5	1	17840	463315	0.9200	1.40	21042	0.999952	3.90
1	40305	89.0	1	40305	503620	1.0000	+INF.	21043	1.000000	+INF.

Rank	Occ. F	SFI	F	Tokens	Cum. Tokens	Cum. P Tokens	Y	Cum. Types	Cum. P Types	Z
4845- 8845	1	48.5	4001	4001	4001	0.0190	-2.07	4001	0.452346	-0.12
3544- 4844	2	50.8	1301	2602	6603	0.0314	-1.86	5302	0.599435	0.25
2838- 3543	3	52.2	706	2118	8721	0.0415	-1.73	6008	0.679254	0.47
2352- 2837	4	53.3	486	1944	10665	0.0507	-1.64	6494	0.734200	0.63
2038- 2351	5	54.2	314	1570	12235	0.0582	-1.57	6808	0.769700	0.74
1820- 2037	6	54.9	218	1308	13543	0.0644	-1.52	7026	0.794347	0.82
1635- 1819	7	55.5	185	1295	14838	0.0706	-1.47	7211	0.815263	0.90
1493- 1634	8	56.1	142	1136	15974	0.0760	-1.43	7353	0.831317	0.96
1374- 1492	9	56.6	119	1071	17045	0.0811	-1.40	7472	0.844771	1.01
1286- 1373	10	57.0	88	880	17925	0.0853	-1.37	7560	0.854720	1.06
1216- 1285	11	57.4	70	770	18695	0.0890	-1.35	7630	0.862634	1.09
1146- 1215	12	57.7	70	840	19535	0.0930	-1.32	7700	0.870548	1.13
1086- 1145	13	58.1	60	780	20315	0.0967	-1.30	7760	0.877332	1.16
1028- 1085	14	58.4	58	812	21127	0.1005	-1.28	7818	0.883889	1.19
973- 1027	15	58.7	55	825	21952	0.1045	-1.26	7873	0.890107	1.23
927- 972	16	58.9	46	736	22688	0.1080	-1.24	7919	0.895308	1.26
891- 926	17	59.2	36	612	23300	0.1109	-1.22	7955	0.899378	1.28
854- 890	18	59.4	37	666	23966	0.1140	-1.21	7992	0.903561	1.30
825- 853	19	59.7	29	551	24517	0.1167	-1.19	8021	0.906840	1.32
788- 824	20	59.9	37	740	25257	0.1202	-1.17	8058	0.911023	1.35
755- 787	21	60.1	33	693	25950	0.1235	-1.16	8091	0.914754	1.37
736- 754	22	60.3	19	418	26368	0.1255	-1.15	8110	0.916902	1.38
713- 735	23	60.5	23	529	26897	0.1280	-1.14	8133	0.919502	1.40
682- 712	24	60.7	31	744	27641	0.1315	-1.12	8164	0.923007	1.43
668- 681	25	60.8	14	350	27991	0.1332	-1.11	8178	0.924590	1.44
651- 667	26	61.0	17	442	28433	0.1353	-1.10	8195	0.926512	1.45
637- 650	27	61.2	14	378	28811	0.1371	-1.09	8209	0.928095	1.46
623- 636	28	61.3	14	392	29203	0.1390	-1.09	8223	0.929678	1.47
611- 622	29	61.5	12	348	29551	0.1406	-1.08	8235	0.931034	1.48
600- 610	30	61.6	11	330	29881	0.1422	-1.07	8246	0.932278	1.49
589- 599	31	61.8	11	341	30222	0.1438	-1.06	8257	0.933522	1.50
580- 588	32	61.9	9	288	30510	0.1452	-1.06	8266	0.934539	1.51
566- 579	33	62.0	14	462	30972	0.1474	-1.05	8280	0.936122	1.52
557- 565	34	62.2	9	306	31278	0.1488	-1.04	8289	0.937140	1.53
546- 556	35	62.3	11	385	31663	0.1507	-1.03	8300	0.938383	1.54
538- 545	36	62.4	8	288	31951	0.1520	-1.03	8308	0.939288	1.55
528- 537	37	62.5	10	370	32321	0.1538	-1.02	8318	0.940418	1.56
522- 527	38	62.6	6	228	32549	0.1549	-1.02	8324	0.941097	1.56
517- 521	39	62.7	5	195	32744	0.1558	-1.01	8329	0.941662	1.57
509- 516	40	62.8	8	320	33064	0.1573	-1.01	8337	0.942566	1.58
500- 508	41	63.0	9	369	33433	0.1591	-1.00	8346	0.943584	1.59
493- 499	42	63.1	7	294	33727	0.1605	-0.99	8353	0.944375	1.59
486- 492	43	63.2	7	301	34028	0.1619	-0.99	8360	0.945167	1.60
478- 485	44	63.3	8	352	34380	0.1636	-0.98	8368	0.946071	1.61
469- 477	45	63.4	9	405	34785	0.1655	-0.97	8377	0.947089	1.62
466- 468	46	63.4	3	138	34923	0.1662	-0.97	8380	0.947428	1.62
462- 465	47	63.5	4	188	35111	0.1671	-0.97	8384	0.947880	1.62
459- 461	48	63.6	3	144	35255	0.1678	-0.96	8387	0.948219	1.63
456- 458	49	63.7	3	147	35402	0.1685	-0.96	8390	0.948558	1.63
448- 455	50	63.8	8	400	35802	0.1704	-0.95	8398	0.949463	1.64
442- 447	51	63.9	6	306	36108	0.1718	-0.95	8404	0.950141	1.65
436- 441	52	64.0	6	312	36420	0.1733	-0.94	8410	0.950820	1.65
429- 435	53	64.1	7	371	36791	0.1751	-0.93	8417	0.951611	1.66
424- 428	54	64.1	5	270	37061	0.1763	-0.93	8422	0.952176	1.67
415- 423	55	64.2	9	495	37556	0.1787	-0.92	8431	0.953194	1.68
407- 414	56	64.3	8	448	38004	0.1808	-0.91	8439	0.954098	1.69
402- 406	57	64.4	5	285	38289	0.1822	-0.91	8444	0.954664	1.69
396- 401	58	64.4	6	348	38637	0.1838	-0.90	8450	0.955342	1.70
392- 395	59	64.5	4	236	38873	0.1850	-0.90	8454	0.955794	1.70
390- 391	60	64.6	2	120	38993	0.1855	-0.89	8456	0.956020	1.71
386- 389	61	64.7	4	244	39237	0.1867	-0.89	8460	0.956473	1.71
379- 385	62	64.7	7	434	39671	0.1888	-0.88	8467	0.957264	1.72
376- 378	63	64.8	3	189	39860	0.1897	-0.88	8470	0.957603	1.72
373- 375	64	64.9	3	192	40052	0.1906	-0.88	8473	0.957942	1.73
372	65	64.9	1	65	40117	0.1909	-0.87	8474	0.958055	1.73
370- 371	66	65.0	2	132	40249	0.1915	-0.87	8476	0.958281	1.73
368- 369	67	65.1	2	134	40383	0.1922	-0.87	8478	0.958508	1.73
365- 367	68	65.1	3	204	40587	0.1931	-0.87	8481	0.958847	1.74
361- 364	69	65.2	4	276	40863	0.1944	-0.86	8485	0.959299	1.74
357- 360	70	65.3	4	280	41143	0.1958	-0.86	8489	0.959751	1.75
352- 356	71	65.3	5	355	41498	0.1975	-0.85	8494	0.960317	1.75
349- 351	72	65.4	3	216	41714	0.1985	-0.85	8497	0.960656	1.76
344- 348	73	65.4	5	365	42079	0.2002	-0.84	8502	0.961221	1.77
339- 343	74	65.5	5	370	42449	0.2020	-0.83	8507	0.961786	1.77
336- 338	75	65.6	3	225	42674	0.2031	-0.83	8510	0.962125	1.78
333- 335	76	65.6	3	228	42902	0.2041	-0.83	8513	0.962465	1.78
331- 332	77	65.7	2	154	43056	0.2049	-0.82	8515	0.962691	1.78
328- 330	78	65.7	3	234	43290	0.2060	-0.82	8518	0.963030	1.79
326- 327	79	65.8	2	158	43448	0.2067	-0.82	8520	0.963256	1.79
324- 325	81	65.9	2	162	43610	0.2075	-0.82	8522	0.963482	1.79
320- 323	82	65.9	4	328	43938	0.2091	-0.81	8526	0.963934	1.80
318- 319	83	66.0	2	166	44104	0.2099	-0.81	8528	0.964161	1.80
315- 317	84	66.0	3	252	44356	0.2111	-0.80	8531	0.964500	1.81
313- 314	85	66.1	2	170	44526	0.2119	-0.80	8533	0.964726	1.81
312	86	66.1	1	86	44612	0.2123	-0.80	8534	0.964839	1.81
310- 311	87	66.2	2	174	44786	0.2131	-0.80	8536	0.965065	1.81
306- 309	88	66.2	4	352	45138	0.2148	-0.79	8540	0.965517	1.82
304- 305	89	66.3	2	178	45316	0.2156	-0.79	8542	0.965743	1.82
303	91	66.4	1	91	45407	0.2161	-0.79	8543	0.965856	1.82
300- 302	92	66.4	3	276	45683	0.2174	-0.78	8546	0.966196	1.83
299	93	66.5	1	93	45776	0.2178	-0.78	8547	0.966309	1.83
298	94	66.5	1	94	45870	0.2183	-0.78	8548	0.966422	1.83
297	95	66.6	1	95	45965	0.2187	-0.78	8549	0.966535	1.83
296	96	66.6	1	96	46061	0.2192	-0.77	8550	0.966648	1.83
292- 295	99	66.8	4	396	46457	0.2211	-0.77	8554	0.967100	1.84
287- 291	100	66.8	5	500	46957	0.2234	-0.76	8559	0.967665	1.85
286	101	66.8	1	101	47058	0.2239	-0.76	8560	0.967778	1.85
283- 285	102	66.9	3	306	47364	0.2254	-0.75	8563	0.968118	1.85
282	103	66.9	1	103	47467	0.2259	-0.75	8564	0.968231	1.86
280- 281	104	67.0	2	208	47675	0.2269	-0.75	8566	0.968457	1.86
279	105	67.0	1	105	47780	0.2274	-0.75	8567	0.968570	1.86
278	106	67.0	1	106	47886	0.2279	-0.75	8568	0.968683	1.86
273- 277	107	67.1	5	535	48421	0.2304	-0.74	8573	0.969248	1.87
271- 272	108	67.1	2	216	48637	0.2314	-0.73	8575	0.969474	1.87
270	109	67.2	1	109	48746	0.2320	-0.73	8576	0.969587	1.87
269	110	67.2	1	110	48856	0.2325	-0.73	8577	0.969700	1.88
267- 268	111	67.2	2	222	49078	0.2335	-0.73	8579	0.969926	1.88
265- 266	112	67.3	2	224	49302	0.2346	-0.72	8581	0.970153	1.88
262- 264	115	67.4	3	345	49647	0.2362	-0.72	8584	0.970492	1.89
260- 261	118	67.5	2	236	49883	0.2374	-0.71	8586	0.970718	1.89
258- 259	120	67.6	2	240	50123	0.2385	-0.71	8588	0.970944	1.89
256- 257	121	67.6	2	242	50365	0.2397	-0.71	8590	0.971170	1.90
255	122	67.7	1	122	50487	0.2402	-0.71	8591	0.971283	1.90
253- 254	123	67.7	2	246	50733	0.2414	-0.70	8593	0.971509	1.90
249- 252	124	67.7	4	496	51229	0.2438	-0.69	8597	0.971962	1.91
247- 248	126	67.8	2	252	51481	0.2450	-0.69	8599	0.972188	1.91
244- 246	127	67.8	3	381	51862	0.2468	-0.68	8602	0.972527	1.92
243	128	67.9	1	128	51990	0.2474	-0.68	8603	0.972640	1.92
240- 242	129	67.9	3	387	52377	0.2492	-0.68	8606	0.972979	1.93
239	130	67.9	1	130	52507	0.2498	-0.67	8607	0.973092	1.93
238	133	68.0	1	133	52640	0.2505	-0.67	8608	0.973205	1.93
233- 237	135	68.1	5	675	53315	0.2537	-0.66	8613	0.973770	1.94
232	136	68.1	1	136	53451	0.2543	-0.66	8614	0.973884	1.94
230- 231	137	68.2	2	274	53725	0.2556	-0.66	8616	0.974110	1.94
225- 229	138	68.2	5	690	54415	0.2589	-0.65	8621	0.974675	1.95
223- 224	140	68.3	2	280	54695	0.2603	-0.64	8623	0.974901	1.96
222	142	68.3	1	142	54837	0.2609	-0.64	8624	0.975014	1.96
221	143	68.3	1	143	54980	0.2616	-0.64	8625	0.975127	1.96
219- 220	144	68.4	2	288	55268	0.2630	-0.63	8627	0.975353	1.97
218	145	68.4	1	145	55413	0.2637	-0.63	8628	0.975466	1.97
216- 217	146	68.4	2	292	55705	0.2651	-0.63	8630	0.975692	1.97
215	148	68.5	1	148	55853	0.2658	-0.63	8631	0.975806	1.97
211- 214	149	68.5	4	596	56449	0.2686	-0.62	8635	0.976258	1.98
210	150	68.5	1	150	56599	0.2693	-0.61	8636	0.976371	1.98
209	151	68.6	1	151	56750	0.2700	-0.61	8637	0.976484	1.99
208	152	68.6	1	152	56902	0.2708	-0.61	8638	0.976597	1.99
207	154	68.7	1	154	57056	0.2715	-0.61	8639	0.976710	1.99
204- 206	155	68.7	3	465	57521	0.2737	-0.60	8642	0.977049	2.00
203	156	68.7	1	156	57677	0.2744	-0.60	8643	0.977162	2.00
201- 202	157	68.7	2	314	57991	0.2759	-0.59	8645	0.977388	2.00
200	159	68.8	1	159	58150	0.2767	-0.59	8646	0.977501	2.00
198- 199	160	68.8	2	320	58470	0.2782	-0.59	8648	0.977727	2.01
196- 197	162	68.9	2	324	58794•	0.2798	-0.58	8650	0.977954	2.01
195	163	68.9	1	163	58957	0.2805	-0.58	8651	0.978067	2.02
194	165	69.0	1	165	59122	0.2813	-0.58	8652	0.978180	2.02
192- 193	167	69.0	2	334	59456	0.2829	-0.57	8654	0.978406	2.02
188- 191	169	69.1	4	676	60132	0.2861	-0.56	8658	0.978858	2.03
186- 187	171	69.1	2	342	60474	0.2878	-0.56	8660	0.979084	2.04
185	173	69.2	1	173	60647	0.2886	-0.56	8661	0.979197	2.04
183- 184	174	69.2	2	348	60995	0.2902	-0.55	8663	0.979423	2.04
182	177	69.3	1	177	61172	0.2911	-0.55	8664	0.979536	2.04
180- 181	178	69.3	2	356	61528	0.2928	-0.55	8666	0.979763	2.05
179	179	69.3	1	179	61707	0.2936	-0.54	8667	0.979876	2.05
178	180	69.3	1	180	61887	0.2945	-0.54	8668	0.979989	2.05
176- 177	182	69.4	2	364	62251	0.2962	-0.54	8670	0.980215	2.06
175	183	69.4	1	183	62434	0.2971	-0.53	8671	0.980328	2.06
174	185	69.5	1	185	62619	0.2980	-0.53	8672	0.980441	2.06
173	186	69.5	1	186	62805	0.2988	-0.53	8673	0.980554	2.07
171- 172	188	69.5	2	376	63181	0.3006	-0.52	8675	0.980780	2.07
170	189	69.6	1	189	63370	0.3015	-0.52	8676	0.980893	2.07
166- 169	190	69.6	4	760	64130	0.3052	-0.51	8680	0.981345	2.08
165	191	69.6	1	191	64321	0.3061	-0.51	8681	0.981458	2.08
164	192	69.6	1	192	64513	0.3070	-0.50	8682	0.981571	2.09
162- 163	193	69.6	2	386	64899	0.3088	-0.50	8684	0.981798	2.09
161	194	69.7	1	194	65093	0.3097	-0.50	8685	0.981911	2.09
160	195	69.7	1	195	65288	0.3107	-0.49	8686	0.982024	2.10
159	196	69.7	1	196	65484	0.3116	-0.49	8687	0.982137	2.10
157- 158	197	69.7	2	394	65878	0.3135	-0.49	8689	0.982363	2.11
156	198	69.8	1	198	66076	0.3144	-0.48	8690	0.982476	2.11
154- 155	199	69.8	2	398	66474	0.3163	-0.48	8692	0.982702	2.11
152- 153	203	69.9	2	406	66880	0.3182	-0.47	8694	0.982928	2.12
151	206	69.9	1	206	67086	0.3192	-0.47	8695	0.983041	2.12
150	207	69.9	1	207	67293	0.3202	-0.47	8696	0.983154	2.12
149	208	70.0	1	208	67501	0.3212	-0.46	8697	0.983267	2.13
148	210	70.0	1	210	67711	0.3222	-0.46	8698	0.983380	2.13
147	211	70.0	1	211	67922	0.3232	-0.46	8699	0.983493	2.13
146	216	70.1	1	216	68138	0.3242	-0.46	8700	0.983607	2.13
145	217	70.1	1	217	68355	0.3253	-0.45	8701	0.983720	2.14
144	222	70.2	1	222	68577	0.3263	-0.45	8702	0.983833	2.14
143	224	70.3	1	224	68801	0.3274	-0.45	8703	0.983946	2.14
141- 142	225	70.3	2	450	69251	0.3295	-0.44	8705	0.984172	2.15
140	228	70.4	1	228	69479	0.3306	-0.44	8706	0.984285	2.15
139	229	70.4	1	229	69708	0.3317	-0.44	8707	0.984398	2.15
138	230	70.4	1	230	69938	0.3328	-0.43	8708	0.984511	2.16
137	233	70.5	1	233	70171	0.3339	-0.43	8709	0.984624	2.16
136	234	70.5	1	234	70405	0.3350	-0.43	8710	0.984737	2.16
135	235	70.5	1	235	70640	0.3361	-0.42	8711	0.984850	2.17
133- 134	236	70.5	2	472	71112	0.3384	-0.42	8713	0.985076	2.17
132	240	70.6	1	240	71352	0.3395	-0.41	8714	0.985189	2.18
131	241	70.6	1	241	71593	0.3407	-0.41	8715	0.985302	2.18
130	243	70.6	1	243	71836	0.3418	-0.41	8716	0.985415	2.18
129	245	70.7	1	245	72081	0.3430	-0.40	8717	0.985529	2.18
128	249	70.7	1	249	72330	0.3442	-0.40	8718	0.985642	2.19
127	250	70.8	1	250	72580	0.3454	-0.40	8719	0.985755	2.19
126	252	70.8	1	252	72832	0.3466	-0.39	8720	0.985868	2.19
125	253	70.8	1	253	73085	0.3478	-0.39	8721	0.985981	2.20
124	255	70.8	1	255	73340	0.3490	-0.39	8722	0.986094	2.20
122- 123	258	70.9	2	516	73856	0.3514	-0.38	8724	0.986320	2.21
121	259	70.9	1	259	74115	0.3527	-0.38	8725	0.986433	2.21
120	260	70.9	1	260	74375	0.3539	-0.37	8726	0.986546	2.21
119	261	70.9	1	261	74636	0.3551	-0.37	8727	0.986659	2.22
117- 118	266	71.0	2	532	75168	0.3577	-0.36	8729	0.986885	2.22
116	267	71.0	1	267	75435	0.3589	-0.36	8730	0.986998	2.23
115	269	71.1	1	269	75704	0.3602	-0.36	8731	0.987111	2.23
114	272	71.1	1	272	75976	0.3615	-0.35	8732	0.987224	2.23
113	273	71.1	1	273	76249	0.3628	-0.35	8733	0.987337	2.24
112	274	71.2	1	274	76523	0.3641	-0.35	8734	0.987450	2.24
111	276	71.2	1	276	76799	0.3654	-0.34	8735	0.987564	2.24
110	284	71.3	1	284	77083	0.3668	-0.34	8736	0.987677	2.25
109	293	71.5	1	293	77376	0.3682	-0.34	8737	0.987790	2.25
108	296	71.5	1	296	77672	0.3696	-0.33	8738	0.987903	2.25
106- 107	297	71.5	2	594	78266	0.3724	-0.33	8740	0.988129	2.26
105	305	71.6	1	305	78571	0.3739	-0.32	8741	0.988242	2.26
104	307	71.7	1	307	78878	0.3753	-0.32	8742	0.988355	2.27
103	308	71.7	1	308	79186	0.3768	-0.31	8743	0.988468	2.27
102	309	71.7	1	309	79495	0.3783	-0.31	8744	0.988581	2.28
101	310	71.7	1	310	79805	0.3797	-0.31	8745	0.988694	2.28
100	315	71.8	1	315	80120	0.3812	-0.30	8746	0.988807	2.28
98- 99	319	71.8	2	638	80758	0.3843	-0.29	8748	0.989033	2.29
97	321	71.8	1	321	81079	0.3858	-0.29	8749	0.989146	2.30
96	324	71.9	1	324	81403	0.3873	-0.29	8750	0.989259	2.30
95	328	71.9	1	328	81731	0.3889	-0.28	8751	0.989372	2.30
93- 94	329	72.0	2	658	82389	0.3920	-0.27	8753	0.989599	2.31
92	342	72.1	1	342	82731	0.3937	-0.27	8754	0.989712	2.32
91	343	72.1	1	343	83074	0.3953	-0.27	8755	0.989825	2.32
90	348	72.2	1	348	83422	0.3970	-0.26	8756	0.989938	2.32
89	351	72.2	1	351	83773	0.3986	-0.26	8757	0.990051	2.33
87- 88	354	72.3	2	708	84481	0.4020	-0.25	8759	0.990277	2.34
86	367	72.4	1	367	84848	0.4037	-0.24	8760	0.990390	2.34
85	368	72.4	1	368	85216	0.4055	-0.24	8761	0.990503	2.35
84	372	72.5	1	372	85588	0.4073	-0.23	8762	0.990616	2.35
83	381	72.6	1	381	85969	0.4091	-0.23	8763	0.990729	2.35

Grp	Rank	Occ. F	SFI	F	Tokens	Cum. Tokens	Cum. P Tokens	Y	Cum. Types	Cum. P Types	Z
	82	388	72.7	1	388	86357	0.4109	-0.23	8764	0.990842	2.36
80-	81	400	72.8	2	800	87157	0.4147	-0.22	8766	0.991068	2.37
	79	402	72.8	1	402	87559	0.4166	-0.21	8767	0.991181	2.37
77-	78	406	72.9	2	812	88371	0.4205	-0.20	8769	0.991408	2.38
75-	76	417	73.0	2	834	89205	0.4245	-0.19	8771	0.991634	2.39
	74	420	73.0	1	420	89625	0.4265	-0.19	8772	0.991747	2.40
	73	422	73.0	1	422	90047	0.4285	-0.18	8773	0.991860	2.40
	72	428	73.1	1	428	90475	0.4305	-0.18	8774	0.991973	2.41
	71	446	73.3	1	446	90921	0.4326	-0.17	8775	0.992086	2.41
	70	453	73.3	1	453	91374	0.4348	-0.16	8776	0.992199	2.42
	69	456	73.4	1	456	91830	0.4370	-0.16	8777	0.992312	2.42
	68	478	73.6	1	478	92308	0.4392	-0.15	8778	0.992425	2.43
	67	485	73.6	1	485	92793	0.4415	-0.15	8779	0.992538	2.43
	66	503	73.8	1	503	93296	0.4439	-0.14	8780	0.992651	2.44
	65	505	73.8	1	505	93801	0.4463	-0.13	8781	0.992764	2.45
	64	513	73.9	1	513	94314	0.4488	-0.13	8782	0.992877	2.45
	63	514	73.9	1	514	94828	0.4512	-0.12	8783	0.992990	2.46
	62	523	74.0	1	523	95351	0.4537	-0.12	8784	0.993103	2.46
	61	536	74.1	1	536	95887	0.4563	-0.11	8785	0.993216	2.47
	60	546	74.2	1	546	96433	0.4589	-0.10	8786	0.993330	2.47
	59	548	74.2	1	548	96981	0.4615	-0.10	8787	0.993443	2.48
	58	549	74.2	1	549	97530	0.4641	-0.09	8788	0.993556	2.49
	57	567	74.3	1	567	98097	0.4668	-0.08	8789	0.993669	2.49
	56	580	74.4	1	580	98677	0.4695	-0.08	8790	0.993782	2.50
	55	585	74.4	1	585	99262	0.4723	-0.07	8791	0.993895	2.51
	54	590	74.5	1	590	99852	0.4751	-0.06	8792	0.994008	2.51
	53	593	74.5	1	593	100445	0.4780	-0.06	8793	0.994121	2.52
	52	594	74.5	1	594	101039	0.4808	-0.05	8794	0.994234	2.53
	51	606	74.6	1	606	101645	0.4837	-0.04	8795	0.994347	2.53
	50	614	74.7	1	614	102259	0.4866	-0.03	8796	0.994460	2.54
	49	625	74.7	1	625	102884	0.4896	-0.03	8797	0.994573	2.55
	48	636	74.8	1	636	103520	0.4926	-0.02	8798	0.994686	2.55
	47	646	74.9	1	646	104166	0.4957	-0.01	8799	0.994799	2.56
	46	647	74.9	1	647	104813	0.4987	-0.00	8800	0.994912	2.57
	45	665	75.0	1	665	105478	0.5019	0.00	8801	0.995025	2.58
	44	671	75.0	1	671	106149	0.5051	0.01	8802	0.995138	2.59
	43	679	75.1	1	679	106828	0.5083	0.02	8803	0.995252	2.59
	42	727	75.4	1	727	107555	0.5118	0.03	8804	0.995365	2.60
	41	743	75.5	1	743	108298	0.5153	0.04	8805	0.995478	2.61
38-	40	767	75.6	1	767	109065	0.5190	0.05	8806	0.995591	2.62
	39	785	75.7	2	1570	110635	0.5264	0.07	8808	0.995817	2.64
	37	807	75.8	1	807	111442	0.5303	0.08	8809	0.995930	2.65
	36	843	76.0	1	843	112285	0.5343	0.09	8810	0.996043	2.66
34-	35	845	76.0	2	1690	113975	0.5423	0.11	8812	0.996269	2.68
	33	922	76.4	1	922	114897	0.5467	0.12	8813	0.996382	2.69
	32	925	76.4	1	925	115822	0.5511	0.13	8814	0.996495	2.70
	31	992	76.7	1	992	116814	0.5558	0.14	8815	0.996608	2.71
	30	994	76.8	1	994	117808	0.5606	0.15	8816	0.996721	2.72
	29	1026	76.9	1	1026	118834	0.5655	0.16	8817	0.996834	2.73
	28	1037	76.9	1	1037	119871	0.5704	0.18	8818	0.996947	2.74
	27	1051	77.0	1	1051	120922	0.5754	0.19	8819	0.997060	2.75
	26	1110	77.2	1	1110	122032	0.5807	0.20	8820	0.997173	2.77
	25	1113	77.2	1	1113	123145	0.5860	0.22	8821	0.997287	2.78
	24	1175	77.5	1	1175	124320	0.5916	0.23	8822	0.997400	2.79
	23	1254	77.8	1	1254	125574	0.5975	0.25	8823	0.997513	2.81
	22	1278	77.8	1	1278	126852	0.6036	0.26	8824	0.997626	2.82
	21	1370	78.1	1	1370	128222	0.6101	0.28	8825	0.997739	2.84
	20	1584	78.8	1	1584	129806	0.6177	0.30	8826	0.997852	2.86
	19	1598	78.8	1	1598	131404	0.6253	0.32	8827	0.997965	2.87
	18	1616	78.9	1	1616	133020	0.6330	0.34	8828	0.998078	2.89
	17	1680	79.0	1	1680	134700	0.6409	0.36	8829	0.998191	2.91
	16	1702	79.1	1	1702	136402	0.6490	0.38	8830	0.998304	2.93
	15	1807	79.3	1	1807	138209	0.6576	0.41	8831	0.998417	2.95
	14	2296	80.4	1	2296	140505	0.6686	0.44	8832	0.998530	2.97
	13	2414	80.7	1	2414	142919	0.6801	0.47	8833	0.998643	3.00
	12	2706	81.1	1	2706	145625	0.6929	0.50	8834	0.998756	3.02
	11	2722	81.1	1	2722	148347	0.7059	0.54	8835	0.998869	3.05
	10	3575	82.3	1	3575	151922	0.7229	0.59	8836	0.998982	3.09
	9	3782	82.6	1	3782	155704	0.7409	0.65	8837	0.999095	3.12
	8	4320	83.1	1	4320	160024	0.7614	0.71	8838	0.999209	3.16
	7	4339	83.1	1	4339	164363	0.7821	0.78	8839	0.999322	3.20
	6	4618	83.4	1	4618	168981	0.8041	0.86	8840	0.999435	3.26
	5	4745	83.5	1	4745	173726	0.8266	0.94	8841	0.999548	3.32
	4	5344	84.1	1	5344	179070	0.8521	1.05	8842	0.999661	3.40
	3	5923	84.5	1	5923	184993	0.8803	1.18	8843	0.999774	3.51
	2	6680	85.0	1	6680	191673	0.9120	1.35	8844	0.999887	3.69
	1	18484	89.4	1	18484	210157	1.0000	+INF.	8845	1.000000	+INF.

Rank	Occ. F	SFI	F	Tokens	Cum. Tokens	Cum. P Tokens	Y	Cum. Types	Cum. P Types	Z
11093-18076	1	44.7	6984	6984	6984	0.0137	-2.21	6984	0.386369	-0.29
8519-11092	2	46.9	2574	5148	12132	0.0238	-1.98	9558	0.528767	0.07
7129- 8518	3	48.4	1390	4170	16302	0.0319	-1.85	10948	0.605665	0.27
6204- 7128	4	49.5	925	3700	20002	0.0392	-1.76	11873	0.656838	0.40
5555- 6203	5	50.3	649	3245	23247	0.0455	-1.69	12522	0.692742	0.50
5037- 5554	6	51.0	518	3108	26355	0.0516	-1.63	13040	0.721399	0.59
4601- 5036	7	51.7	436	3052	29407	0.0576	-1.58	13476	0.745519	0.66
4234- 4600	8	52.2	367	2936	32343	0.0633	-1.53	13843	0.765822	0.73
3963- 4233	9	52.7	271	2439	34782	0.0681	-1.49	14114	0.780814	0.77
3727- 3962	10	53.1	236	2360	37142	0.0727	-1.46	14350	0.793870	0.82
3524- 3726	11	53.5	203	2233	39375	0.0771	-1.42	14553	0.805101	0.86
3309- 3523	12	53.9	215	2580	41955	0.0822	-1.39	14768	0.816995	0.90
3131- 3308	13	54.2	178	2314	44269	0.0867	-1.36	14946	0.826842	0.94
3001- 3130	14	54.5	130	1820	46089	0.0903	-1.34	15076	0.834034	0.97
2863- 3000	15	54.8	138	2070	48159	0.0943	-1.31	15214	0.841668	1.00
2733- 2862	16	55.1	130	2080	50239	0.0984	-1.29	15344	0.848860	1.03
2635- 2732	17	55.3	98	1666	51905	0.1017	-1.27	15442	0.854282	1.05
2540- 2634	18	55.6	95	1710	53615	0.1050	-1.25	15537	0.859537	1.08
2426- 2539	19	55.8	114	2166	55781	0.1093	-1.23	15651	0.865844	1.11
2349- 2425	20	56.0	77	1540	57321	0.1123	-1.21	15728	0.870104	1.13
2253- 2348	21	56.2	96	2016	59337	0.1162	-1.19	15824	0.875415	1.15
2182- 2252	22	56.4	71	1562	60899	0.1193	-1.18	15895	0.879343	1.17
2119- 2181	23	56.6	63	1449	62348	0.1221	-1.16	15958	0.882828	1.19
2049- 2118	24	56.8	70	1680	64028	0.1254	-1.15	16028	0.886701	1.21
1997- 2048	25	57.0	52	1300	65328	0.1280	-1.14	16080	0.889577	1.22
1946- 1996	26	57.2	51	1326	66654	0.1305	-1.12	16131	0.892399	1.24
1891- 1945	27	57.3	55	1485	68139	0.1335	-1.11	16186	0.895441	1.26
1834- 1890	28	57.5	57	1596	69735	0.1366	-1.10	16243	0.898595	1.27
1775- 1833	29	57.6	59	1711	71446	0.1399	-1.08	16302	0.901859	1.29
1732- 1774	30	57.8	43	1290	72736	0.1425	-1.07	16345	0.904238	1.31
1693- 1731	31	57.9	39	1209	73945	0.1448	-1.06	16384	0.906395	1.32
1647- 1692	32	58.0	46	1472	75417	0.1477	-1.05	16430	0.908940	1.33
1608- 1646	33	58.2	39	1287	76704	0.1502	-1.04	16469	0.911098	1.35
1581- 1607	34	58.3	27	918	77622	0.1520	-1.03	16496	0.912591	1.36
1546- 1580	35	58.4	35	1225	78847	0.1544	-1.02	16531	0.914528	1.37
1507- 1545	36	58.5	39	1404	80251	0.1572	-1.01	16570	0.916685	1.38
1482- 1506	37	58.7	25	925	81176	0.1590	-1.00	16595	0.918068	1.39
1460- 1481	38	58.8	22	836	82012	0.1606	-0.99	16617	0.919285	1.40
1437- 1459	39	58.9	23	897	82909	0.1624	-0.98	16640	0.920558	1.41
1406- 1436	40	59.0	31	1240	84149	0.1648	-0.97	16671	0.922273	1.42
1377- 1405	41	59.1	29	1189	85338	0.1671	-0.97	16700	0.923877	1.43
1351- 1376	42	59.2	26	1092	86430	0.1693	-0.96	16726	0.925315	1.44
1319- 1350	43	59.3	32	1376	87806	0.1720	-0.95	16758	0.927086	1.45
1300- 1318	44	59.4	19	836	88642	0.1736	-0.94	16777	0.928137	1.46
1281- 1299	45	59.5	19	855	89497	0.1753	-0.93	16796	0.929188	1.47
1257- 1280	46	59.6	24	1104	90601	0.1775	-0.93	16820	0.930516	1.48
1234- 1256	47	59.7	23	1081	91682	0.1796	-0.92	16843	0.931788	1.49
1214- 1233	48	59.8	20	960	92642	0.1814	-0.91	16863	0.932894	1.50
1189- 1213	49	59.9	25	1225	93867	0.1838	-0.90	16888	0.934277	1.51
1159- 1188	50	60.0	30	1500	95367	0.1868	-0.89	16918	0.935937	1.52
1142- 1158	51	60.0	17	867	96234	0.1885	-0.88	16935	0.936878	1.53
1115- 1141	52	60.1	27	1404	97638	0.1912	-0.87	16962	0.938371	1.54
1095- 1114	53	60.2	20	1060	98698	0.1933	-0.87	16982	0.939478	1.55
1078- 1094	54	60.3	17	918	99616	0.1951	-0.86	16999	0.940418	1.56
1061- 1077	55	60.4	17	935	100551	0.1969	-0.85	17016	0.941359	1.57
1042- 1060	56	60.4	19	1064	101615	0.1990	-0.85	17035	0.942410	1.58
1022- 1041	57	60.5	20	1140	102755	0.2013	-0.84	17055	0.943516	1.58
1007- 1021	58	60.6	15	870	103625	0.2030	-0.83	17070	0.944346	1.59
998- 1006	59	60.7	9	531	104156	0.2040	-0.83	17079	0.944844	1.60
985- 997	60	60.7	13	780	104936	0.2055	-0.82	17092	0.945563	1.60
971- 984	61	60.8	14	854	105790	0.2072	-0.82	17106	0.946338	1.61
954- 970	62	60.9	17	1054	106844	0.2093	-0.81	17123	0.947278	1.62
936- 953	63	60.9	18	1134	107978	0.2115	-0.80	17141	0.948274	1.63
927- 935	64	61.0	9	576	108554	0.2126	-0.80	17150	0.948772	1.63
913- 926	65	61.1	14	910	109464	0.2144	-0.79	17164	0.949546	1.64
893- 912	66	61.1	20	1320	110784	0.2170	-0.78	17184	0.950653	1.65
876- 892	67	61.2	17	1139	111923	0.2192	-0.77	17201	0.951593	1.66
867- 875	68	61.3	9	612	112535	0.2204	-0.77	17210	0.952091	1.67
856- 866	69	61.3	11	759	113294	0.2219	-0.77	17221	0.952700	1.67
838- 855	70	61.4	18	1260	114554	0.2244	-0.76	17239	0.953695	1.68
826- 837	71	61.5	12	852	115406	0.2260	-0.75	17251	0.954359	1.69
817- 825	72	61.5	9	648	116054	0.2273	-0.75	17260	0.954857	1.69
811- 816	73	61.6	6	438	116492	0.2282	-0.74	17266	0.955189	1.70
804- 810	74	61.6	7	518	117010	0.2292	-0.74	17273	0.955576	1.70
792- 803	75	61.7	12	900	117910	0.2309	-0.74	17285	0.956240	1.71
783- 791	76	61.8	9	684	118594	0.2323	-0.73	17294	0.956738	1.71
772- 782	77	61.8	11	847	119441	0.2339	-0.73	17305	0.957347	1.72
767- 771	78	61.9	5	390	119831	0.2347	-0.72	17310	0.957623	1.72
762- 766	79	61.9	5	395	120226	0.2355	-0.72	17315	0.957900	1.73
754- 761	80	62.0	8	640	120866	0.2367	-0.72	17323	0.958343	1.73
750- 753	81	62.0	4	324	121190	0.2374	-0.71	17327	0.958564	1.73
739- 749	82	62.1	11	902	122092	0.2391	-0.71	17338	0.959172	1.74
723- 738	83	62.1	16	1328	123420	0.2417	-0.70	17354	0.960057	1.75
716- 722	84	62.2	7	588	124008	0.2429	-0.70	17361	0.960445	1.76
706- 715	85	62.2	10	850	124858	0.2445	-0.69	17371	0.960998	1.76
697- 705	86	62.3	9	774	125632	0.2461	-0.69	17380	0.961496	1.77
696	87	62.3	1	87	125719	0.2462	-0.69	17381	0.961551	1.77
690- 695	88	62.4	6	528	126247	0.2473	-0.68	17387	0.961883	1.77
683- 689	89	62.4	7	623	126870	0.2485	-0.68	17394	0.962270	1.78
674- 682	90	62.5	9	810	127680	0.2501	-0.67	17403	0.962768	1.78
667- 673	91	62.5	7	637	128317	0.2513	-0.67	17410	0.963156	1.79
662- 666	92	62.6	5	460	128777	0.2522	-0.67	17415	0.963432	1.79
649- 661	93	62.6	13	1209	129986	0.2546	-0.66	17428	0.964151	1.80
643- 648	94	62.7	6	564	130550	0.2557	-0.66	17434	0.964483	1.81
638- 642	95	62.7	5	475	131025	0.2566	-0.65	17439	0.964760	1.81
633- 637	96	62.8	5	480	131505	0.2576	-0.65	17444	0.965037	1.81
624- 632	97	62.8	9	873	132378	0.2593	-0.65	17453	0.965534	1.82
617- 623	98	62.9	7	686	133064	0.2606	-0.64	17460	0.965922	1.82
612- 616	99	62.9	5	495	133559	0.2616	-0.64	17465	0.966198	1.83
606- 611	100	62.9	6	600	134159	0.2628	-0.63	17471	0.966530	1.83
602- 605	101	63.0	4	404	134563	0.2636	-0.63	17475	0.966751	1.84
598- 601	102	63.0	4	408	134971	0.2644	-0.63	17479	0.966973	1.84
594- 597	103	63.1	4	412	135383	0.2652	-0.63	17483	0.967194	1.84
587- 593	104	63.1	7	728	136111	0.2666	-0.62	17490	0.967581	1.85
584- 586	105	63.2	3	315	136426	0.2672	-0.62	17493	0.967747	1.85
577- 583	106	63.2	7	742	137168	0.2687	-0.62	17500	0.968135	1.85
568- 576	107	63.2	9	963	138131	0.2705	-0.61	17509	0.968632	1.86
565- 567	108	63.3	3	324	138455	0.2712	-0.61	17512	0.968798	1.86
557- 564	109	63.3	8	872	139327	0.2729	-0.60	17520	0.969241	1.87
552- 556	110	63.4	5	550	139877	0.2740	-0.60	17525	0.969518	1.87
549- 551	111	63.4	3	333	140210	0.2746	-0.60	17528	0.969684	1.88
543- 548	112	63.4	6	672	140882	0.2759	-0.59	17534	0.970015	1.88
535- 542	113	63.5	8	904	141786	0.2777	-0.59	17542	0.970458	1.89
532- 534	114	63.5	3	342	142128	0.2784	-0.59	17545	0.970624	1.89
528- 531	115	63.5	4	460	142588	0.2793	-0.59	17549	0.970845	1.89
524- 527	116	63.6	4	464	143052	0.2802	-0.58	17553	0.971067	1.90

Rank	Occ. F	SFI	F	Tokens	Cum. Tokens	Cum. P Tokens	Y	Cum. Types	Cum. P Types	Z
519- 523	117	63.6	5	585	143637	0.2813	-0.58	17558	0.971343	1.90
512- 518	118	63.7	7	826	144463	0.2829	-0.57	17565	0.971730	1.91
508- 511	119	63.7	4	476	144939	0.2839	-0.57	17569	0.971952	1.91
502- 507	120	63.7	6	720	145659	0.2853	-0.57	17575	0.972284	1.92
499- 501	121	63.8	3	363	146022	0.2860	-0.57	17578	0.972450	1.92
495- 498	122	63.8	4	488	146510	0.2870	-0.56	17582	0.972671	1.92
489- 494	123	63.8	6	738	147248	0.2884	-0.56	17588	0.973003	1.93
485- 488	124	63.9	4	496	147744	0.2894	-0.56	17592	0.973224	1.93
480- 484	125	63.9	5	625	148369	0.2906	-0.55	17597	0.973501	1.93
477- 479	126	63.9	3	378	148747	0.2913	-0.55	17600	0.973667	1.94
474- 476	127	64.0	3	381	149128	0.2921	-0.55	17603	0.973833	1.94
472- 473	128	64.0	2	256	149384	0.2926	-0.55	17605	0.973943	1.94
471	129	64.0	1	129	149513	0.2928	-0.55	17606	0.973999	1.94
469- 470	130	64.1	2	260	149773	0.2933	-0.54	17608	0.974109	1.94
468	131	64.1	1	131	149904	0.2936	-0.54	17609	0.974165	1.95
467	132	64.1	1	132	150036	0.2939	-0.54	17610	0.974220	1.95
462- 466	133	64.2	5	665	150701	0.2952	-0.54	17615	0.974497	1.95
460- 461	134	64.2	2	268	150969	0.2957	-0.54	17617	0.974607	1.95
453- 459	135	64.2	7	945	151914	0.2975	-0.53	17624	0.974994	1.96
450- 452	136	64.3	3	408	152322	0.2983	-0.53	17627	0.975160	1.96
448- 449	137	64.3	2	274	152596	0.2989	-0.53	17629	0.975271	1.96
444- 447	139	64.4	4	556	153152	0.3000	-0.52	17633	0.975492	1.97
440- 443	140	64.4	4	560	153712	0.3011	-0.52	17637	0.975714	1.97
437- 439	141	64.4	3	423	154135	0.3019	-0.52	17640	0.975880	1.98
433- 436	142	64.5	4	568	154703	0.3030	-0.52	17644	0.976101	1.98
428- 432	143	64.5	5	715	155418	0.3044	-0.51	17649	0.976377	1.98
425- 427	144	64.5	3	432	155850	0.3052	-0.51	17652	0.976543	1.99
423- 424	145	64.5	2	290	156140	0.3058	-0.51	17654	0.976654	1.99
421- 422	146	64.6	2	292	156432	0.3064	-0.51	17656	0.976765	1.99
415- 420	147	64.6	6	882	157314	0.3081	-0.50	17662	0.977097	2.00
412- 414	148	64.6	3	444	157758	0.3090	-0.50	17665	0.977263	2.00
409- 411	149	64.7	3	447	158205	0.3099	-0.50	17668	0.977429	2.00
407- 408	150	64.7	2	300	158505	0.3104	-0.49	17670	0.977539	2.01
405- 406	151	64.7	2	302	158807	0.3110	-0.49	17672	0.977650	2.01
403- 404	152	64.8	2	304	159111	0.3116	-0.49	17674	0.977761	2.01
400- 402	153	64.8	3	459	159570	0.3125	-0.49	17677	0.977926	2.01
398- 399	154	64.8	2	308	159878	0.3131	-0.49	17679	0.978037	2.01
396- 397	155	64.8	2	310	160188	0.3137	-0.49	17681	0.978148	2.02
395	156	64.9	1	156	160344	0.3140	-0.48	17682	0.978203	2.02
392- 394	158	64.9	3	474	160818	0.3150	-0.48	17685	0.978369	2.02
389- 391	159	64.9	3	477	161295	0.3159	-0.48	17688	0.978535	2.02
387- 388	161	65.0	2	322	161617	0.3165	-0.48	17690	0.978646	2.03
383- 386	162	65.0	4	648	162265	0.3178	-0.47	17694	0.978867	2.03
382	164	65.1	1	164	162429	0.3181	-0.47	17695	0.978922	2.03
378- 381	165	65.1	4	660	163089	0.3194	-0.47	17699	0.979144	2.04
375- 377	166	65.1	3	498	163587	0.3204	-0.47	17702	0.979310	2.04
372- 374	167	65.2	3	501	164088	0.3214	-0.46	17705	0.979475	2.04
367- 371	168	65.2	5	840	164928	0.3230	-0.46	17710	0.979752	2.05
363- 366	169	65.2	4	676	165604	0.3244	-0.46	17714	0.979973	2.05
361- 362	170	65.2	2	340	165944	0.3250	-0.45	17716	0.980084	2.06
357- 360	171	65.3	4	684	166628	0.3264	-0.45	17720	0.980305	2.06
356	172	65.3	1	172	166800	0.3267	-0.45	17721	0.980361	2.06
352- 355	173	65.3	4	692	167492	0.3280	-0.45	17725	0.980582	2.07
349- 351	174	65.3	3	522	168014	0.3291	-0.44	17728	0.980748	2.07
348	175	65.4	1	175	168189	0.3294	-0.44	17729	0.980803	2.07
347	176	65.4	1	176	168365	0.3298	-0.44	17730	0.980859	2.07
342- 346	178	65.4	5	890	169255	0.3315	-0.44	17735	0.981135	2.08
341	179	65.5	1	179	169434	0.3319	-0.43	17736	0.981191	2.08
339- 340	180	65.5	2	360	169794	0.3326	-0.43	17738	0.981301	2.08
336- 338	181	65.5	3	543	170337	0.3336	-0.43	17741	0.981467	2.09
335	182	65.5	1	182	170519	0.3340	-0.43	17742	0.981522	2.09
328- 334	183	65.6	7	1281	171800	0.3365	-0.42	17749	0.981910	2.09
327	184	65.6	1	184	171984	0.3368	-0.42	17750	0.981965	2.10
325- 326	186	65.6	2	372	172356	0.3376	-0.42	17752	0.982076	2.10
324	187	65.6	1	187	172543	0.3379	-0.42	17753	0.982131	2.10
322- 323	188	65.7	2	376	172919	0.3387	-0.42	17755	0.982242	2.10
320- 321	190	65.7	2	380	173299	0.3394	-0.41	17757	0.982352	2.10
318- 319	191	65.7	2	382	173681	0.3402	-0.41	17759	0.982463	2.11
317	192	65.8	1	192	173873	0.3405	-0.41	17760	0.982518	2.11
314- 316	193	65.8	3	579	174452	0.3417	-0.41	17763	0.982684	2.11
313	195	65.8	1	195	174647	0.3421	-0.41	17764	0.982740	2.11
311- 312	196	65.9	2	392	175039	0.3428	-0.40	17766	0.982850	2.12
310	199	65.9	1	199	175238	0.3432	-0.40	17767	0.982906	2.12
307- 309	201	66.0	3	603	175841	0.3444	-0.40	17770	0.983071	2.12
303- 306	202	66.0	4	808	176649	0.3460	-0.40	17774	0.983293	2.13
301- 302	203	66.0	2	406	177055	0.3468	-0.39	17776	0.983403	2.13
300	205	66.0	1	205	177260	0.3472	-0.39	17777	0.983459	2.13
299	206	66.1	1	206	177466	0.3476	-0.39	17778	0.983514	2.13
298	207	66.1	1	207	177673	0.3480	-0.39	17779	0.983569	2.13
297	209	66.1	1	209	177882	0.3484	-0.39	17780	0.983625	2.14
296	211	66.2	1	211	178093	0.3488	-0.39	17781	0.983680	2.14
295	212	66.2	1	212	178305	0.3492	-0.39	17782	0.983735	2.14
293- 294	213	66.2	2	426	178731	0.3501	-0.39	17784	0.983846	2.14
291- 292	214	66.2	2	428	179159	0.3509	-0.38	17786	0.983957	2.14
290	216	66.3	1	216	179375	0.3513	-0.38	17787	0.984012	2.14
289	217	66.3	1	217	179592	0.3517	-0.38	17788	0.984067	2.15
288	219	66.3	1	219	179811	0.3522	-0.38	17789	0.984123	2.15
285- 287	220	66.4	3	660	180471	0.3535	-0.38	17792	0.984289	2.15
282- 284	221	66.4	3	663	181134	0.3548	-0.37	17795	0.984455	2.16
281	222	66.4	1	222	181356	0.3552	-0.37	17796	0.984510	2.16
280	225	66.5	1	225	181581	0.3556	-0.37	17797	0.984565	2.16
279	226	66.5	1	226	181807	0.3561	-0.37	17798	0.984620	2.16
278	227	66.5	1	227	182034	0.3565	-0.37	17799	0.984676	2.16
276- 277	228	66.5	2	456	182490	0.3574	-0.37	17801	0.984786	2.16
275	229	66.5	1	229	182719	0.3579	-0.36	17802	0.984842	2.17
272- 274	231	66.6	3	693	183412	0.3592	-0.36	17805	0.985008	2.17
270- 271	232	66.6	2	464	183876	0.3601	-0.36	17807	0.985118	2.17
269	237	66.7	1	237	184113	0.3606	-0.36	17808	0.985174	2.17
267- 268	239	66.7	2	478	184591	0.3615	-0.35	17810	0.985284	2.18
266	240	66.7	1	240	184831	0.3620	-0.35	17811	0.985340	2.18
265	242	66.8	1	242	185073	0.3625	-0.35	17812	0.985395	2.18
264	243	66.8	1	243	185316	0.3630	-0.35	17813	0.985450	2.18
263	244	66.8	1	244	185560	0.3634	-0.35	17814	0.985506	2.18
262	245	66.8	1	245	185805	0.3639	-0.35	17815	0.985561	2.19
259- 261	246	66.8	3	738	186543	0.3654	-0.34	17818	0.985727	2.19
258	247	66.9	1	247	186790	0.3658	-0.34	17819	0.985782	2.19
255- 257	248	66.9	3	744	187534	0.3673	-0.34	17822	0.985948	2.20
254	250	66.9	1	250	187784	0.3678	-0.34	17823	0.986004	2.20
253	251	66.9	1	251	188035	0.3683	-0.34	17824	0.986059	2.20
249- 252	253	67.0	4	1012	189047	0.3703	-0.33	17828	0.986280	2.21
246- 248	256	67.0	3	768	189815	0.3718	-0.33	17831	0.986446	2.21
245	258	67.0	1	258	190073	0.3723	-0.33	17832	0.986501	2.21
244	259	67.1	1	259	190332	0.3728	-0.32	17833	0.986557	2.21
243	260	67.1	1	260	190592	0.3733	-0.32	17834	0.986612	2.21
241- 242	261	67.1	2	522	191114	0.3743	-0.32	17836	0.986723	2.22
239- 240	262	67.1	2	524	191638	0.3753	-0.32	17838	0.986833	2.22

Rank		Occ. F	SFI	F	Tokens	Cum. Tokens	Cum. P Tokens	Y	Cum. Types	Cum. P Types	Z
237-	238	263	67.1	2	526	192164	0.3764	-0.32	17840	0.986944	2.22
234-	236	264	67.1	3	792	192956	0.3779	-0.31	17843	0.987110	2.23
232-	233	266	67.2	2	532	193488	0.3790	-0.31	17845	0.987221	2.23
230-	231	268	67.2	2	536	194024	0.3800	-0.31	17847	0.987331	2.24
	229	269	67.2	1	269	194293	0.3805	-0.30	17848	0.987387	2.24
	228	271	67.3	1	271	194564	0.3811	-0.30	17849	0.987442	2.24
	227	272	67.3	1	272	194836	0.3816	-0.30	17850	0.987497	2.24
	226	273	67.3	1	273	195109	0.3821	-0.30	17851	0.987553	2.24
	225	274	67.3	1	274	195383	0.3827	-0.30	17852	0.987608	2.24
223-	224	275	67.3	2	550	195933	0.3838	-0.30	17854	0.987718	2.25
	222	277	67.4	1	277	196210	0.3843	-0.29	17855	0.987774	2.25
	221	278	67.4	1	278	196488	0.3848	-0.29	17856	0.987829	2.25
	220	280	67.4	1	280	196768	0.3854	-0.29	17857	0.987884	2.25
	219	283	67.4	1	283	197051	0.3859	-0.29	17858	0.987940	2.26
	218	284	67.5	1	284	197335	0.3865	-0.29	17859	0.987995	2.26
216-	217	285	67.5	2	570	197905	0.3876	-0.29	17861	0.988106	2.26
	215	286	67.5	1	286	198191	0.3882	-0.28	17862	0.988161	2.26
213-	214	288	67.5	2	576	198767	0.3893	-0.28	17864	0.988272	2.27
211-	212	289	67.5	2	578	199345	0.3904	-0.28	17866	0.988382	2.27
	210	290	67.6	1	290	199635	0.3910	-0.28	17867	0.988438	2.27
	209	291	67.6	1	291	199926	0.3916	-0.28	17868	0.988493	2.27
207-	208	292	67.6	2	584	200510	0.3927	-0.27	17870	0.988604	2.28
	206	293	67.6	1	293	200803	0.3933	-0.27	17871	0.988659	2.28
	205	296	67.6	1	296	201099	0.3939	-0.27	17872	0.988714	2.28
	204	297	67.7	1	297	201396	0.3945	-0.27	17873	0.988770	2.28
	203	298	67.7	1	298	201694	0.3950	-0.27	17874	0.988825	2.28
	202	299	67.7	1	299	201993	0.3956	-0.26	17875	0.988880	2.29
	201	300	67.7	1	300	202293	0.3962	-0.26	17876	0.988936	2.29
199-	200	301	67.7	2	602	202895	0.3974	-0.26	17878	0.989046	2.29
	198	302	67.7	1	302	203197	0.3980	-0.26	17879	0.989102	2.29
196-	197	304	67.8	2	608	203805	0.3992	-0.26	17881	0.989212	2.30
	195	305	67.8	1	305	204110	0.3998	-0.25	17882	0.989268	2.30
	194	306	67.8	1	306	204416	0.4004	-0.25	17883	0.989323	2.30
	193	307	67.8	1	307	204723	0.4010	-0.25	17884	0.989378	2.30
191-	192	311	67.9	2	622	205345	0.4022	-0.25	17886	0.989489	2.31
189-	190	312	67.9	2	624	205969	0.4034	-0.24	17888	0.989599	2.31
	188	315	67.9	1	315	206284	0.4040	-0.24	17889	0.989655	2.31
	187	317	67.9	1	317	206601	0.4046	-0.24	17890	0.989710	2.32
	186	321	68.0	1	321	206922	0.4053	-0.24	17891	0.989765	2.32
184-	185	322	68.0	2	644	207566	0.4065	-0.24	17893	0.989876	2.32
182-	183	326	68.1	2	652	208218	0.4078	-0.23	17895	0.989987	2.33
179-	181	327	68.1	3	981	209199	0.4097	-0.23	17898	0.990153	2.33
	178	329	68.1	1	329	209528	0.4104	-0.23	17899	0.990208	2.33
	177	330	68.1	1	330	209858	0.4110	-0.22	17900	0.990263	2.34
	176	333	68.2	1	333	210191	0.4117	-0.22	17901	0.990319	2.34
	175	336	68.2	1	336	210527	0.4123	-0.22	17902	0.990374	2.34
	174	340	68.2	1	340	210867	0.4130	-0.22	17903	0.990429	2.34
	173	343	68.3	1	343	211210	0.4137	-0.22	17904	0.990485	2.34
	172	352	68.4	1	352	211562	0.4144	-0.22	17905	0.990540	2.35
	171	356	68.4	1	356	211918	0.4151	-0.21	17906	0.990595	2.35
	170	358	68.5	1	358	212276	0.4158	-0.21	17907	0.990651	2.35
	169	361	68.5	1	361	212637	0.4165	-0.21	17908	0.990706	2.35
	168	363	68.5	1	363	213000	0.4172	-0.21	17909	0.990761	2.36
	167	365	68.5	1	365	213365	0.4179	-0.21	17910	0.990817	2.36
	166	369	68.6	1	369	213734	0.4186	-0.21	17911	0.990872	2.36
	165	372	68.6	1	372	214106	0.4193	-0.20	17912	0.990927	2.36
	164	374	68.7	1	374	214480	0.4201	-0.20	17913	0.990982	2.36
	163	380	68.7	1	380	214860	0.4208	-0.20	17914	0.991038	2.37
	162	385	68.8	1	385	215245	0.4216	-0.20	17915	0.991093	2.37
	161	390	68.8	1	390	215635	0.4223	-0.20	17916	0.991148	2.37
	160	393	68.9	1	393	216028	0.4231	-0.19	17917	0.991204	2.37
158-	159	398	68.9	2	796	216824	0.4247	-0.19	17919	0.991314	2.38
	157	399	68.9	1	399	217223	0.4255	-0.19	17920	0.991370	2.38
	156	401	69.0	1	401	217624	0.4262	-0.19	17921	0.991425	2.38
	155	402	69.0	1	402	218026	0.4270	-0.18	17922	0.991480	2.39
153-	154	404	69.0	2	808	218834	0.4286	-0.18	17924	0.991591	2.39
	152	405	69.0	1	405	219239	0.4294	-0.18	17925	0.991646	2.39
	151	409	69.0	1	409	219648	0.4302	-0.18	17926	0.991702	2.40
	150	411	69.1	1	411	220059	0.4310	-0.17	17927	0.991757	2.40
	149	413	69.1	1	413	220472	0.4318	-0.17	17928	0.991812	2.40
	148	414	69.1	1	414	220886	0.4326	-0.17	17929	0.991868	2.40
	147	415	69.1	1	415	221301	0.4334	-0.17	17930	0.991923	2.41
	146	416	69.1	1	416	221717	0.4343	-0.17	17931	0.991978	2.41
	145	417	69.1	1	417	222134	0.4351	-0.16	17932	0.992034	2.41
	144	424	69.2	1	424	222558	0.4359	-0.16	17933	0.992089	2.41
	143	428	69.2	1	428	222986	0.4367	-0.16	17934	0.992144	2.42
141-	142	439	69.3	2	878	223864	0.4385	-0.15	17936	0.992255	2.42
	140	444	69.4	1	444	224308	0.4393	-0.15	17937	0.992310	2.42
	139	445	69.4	1	445	224753	0.4402	-0.15	17938	0.992366	2.43
	138	447	69.4	1	447	225200	0.4411	-0.15	17939	0.992421	2.43
136-	137	452	69.5	2	904	226104	0.4428	-0.14	17941	0.992531	2.43
	135	455	69.5	1	455	226559	0.4437	-0.14	17942	0.992587	2.44
	134	459	69.5	1	459	227018	0.4446	-0.14	17943	0.992642	2.44
	133	462	69.6	1	462	227480	0.4455	-0.14	17944	0.992697	2.44
	132	464	69.6	1	464	227944	0.4464	-0.13	17945	0.992753	2.44
	131	467	69.6	1	467	228411	0.4474	-0.13	17946	0.992808	2.45
	130	470	69.6	1	470	228881	0.4483	-0.13	17947	0.992863	2.45
	129	473	69.7	1	473	229354	0.4492	-0.13	17948	0.992919	2.45
	128	482	69.8	1	482	229836	0.4502	-0.13	17949	0.992974	2.46
	127	485	69.8	1	485	230321	0.4511	-0.12	17950	0.993029	2.46
	126	493	69.9	1	493	230814	0.4521	-0.12	17951	0.993085	2.46
	125	500	69.9	1	500	231314	0.4531	-0.12	17952	0.993140	2.46
	124	518	70.1	1	518	231832	0.4541	-0.12	17953	0.993195	2.47
	123	525	70.1	1	525	232357	0.4551	-0.11	17954	0.993251	2.47
	122	529	70.2	1	529	232886	0.4561	-0.11	17955	0.993306	2.47
120-	121	533	70.2	2	1066	233952	0.4582	-0.10	17957	0.993417	2.48
	119	536	70.2	1	536	234488	0.4593	-0.10	17958	0.993472	2.48
	118	541	70.3	1	541	235029	0.4603	-0.10	17959	0.993527	2.49
116-	117	545	70.3	2	1090	236119	0.4625	-0.09	17961	0.993638	2.49
	115	547	70.3	1	547	236666	0.4635	-0.09	17962	0.993693	2.49
	114	549	70.3	1	549	237215	0.4646	-0.09	17963	0.993749	2.50
	113	550	70.3	1	550	237765	0.4657	-0.09	17964	0.993804	2.50
	112	555	70.4	1	555	238320	0.4668	-0.08	17965	0.993859	2.50
	111	562	70.4	1	562	238882	0.4679	-0.08	17966	0.993915	2.51
	110	571	70.5	1	571	239453	0.4690	-0.08	17967	0.993970	2.51
	109	574	70.5	1	574	240027	0.4701	-0.07	17968	0.994025	2.51
	108	576	70.5	1	576	240603	0.4712	-0.07	17969	0.994081	2.52
	107	579	70.5	1	579	241182	0.4724	-0.07	17970	0.994136	2.52
	106	582	70.6	1	582	241764	0.4735	-0.07	17971	0.994191	2.52
	105	588	70.6	1	588	242352	0.4747	-0.06	17972	0.994246	2.53
	104	589	70.6	1	589	242941	0.4758	-0.06	17973	0.994302	2.53
	103	602	70.7	1	602	243543	0.4770	-0.06	17974	0.994357	2.53
	102	604	70.7	1	604	244147	0.4782	-0.05	17975	0.994412	2.54
	101	606	70.7	1	606	244753	0.4794	-0.05	17976	0.994468	2.54
	100	612	70.8	1	612	245365	0.4806	-0.05	17977	0.994523	2.54
	99	624	70.9	1	624	245989	0.4818	-0.05	17978	0.994578	2.55
	98	625	70.9	1	625	246614	0.4830	-0.04	17979	0.994634	2.55
	97	631	70.9	1	631	247245	0.4843	-0.04	17980	0.994689	2.55
95-	96	638	71.0	2	1276	248521	0.4868	-0.03	17982	0.994800	2.56
	94	651	71.1	1	651	249172	0.4880	-0.03	17983	0.994855	2.57
	93	694	71.3	1	694	249866	0.4894	-0.03	17984	0.994910	2.57
	92	703	71.4	1	703	250569	0.4908	-0.02	17985	0.994966	2.57
	91	711	71.4	1	711	251280	0.4922	-0.02	17986	0.995021	2.58
	90	713	71.5	1	713	251993	0.4936	-0.02	17987	0.995076	2.58
	89	717	71.5	1	717	252710	0.4950	-0.01	17988	0.995132	2.59
	88	725	71.5	1	725	253435	0.4964	-0.01	17989	0.995187	2.59
	87	728	71.5	1	728	254163	0.4978	-0.01	17990	0.995242	2.59
	86	738	71.6	1	738	254901	0.4992	-0.00	17991	0.995298	2.60
	85	753	71.7	1	753	255654	0.5007	0.00	17992	0.995353	2.60
	84	773	71.8	1	773	256427	0.5022	0.01	17993	0.995408	2.61
	83	777	71.8	1	777	257204	0.5038	0.01	17994	0.995464	2.61
	82	787	71.9	1	787	257991	0.5053	0.01	17995	0.995519	2.61
	81	793	71.9	1	793	258784	0.5069	0.02	17996	0.995574	2.62
	80	804	72.0	1	804	259588	0.5084	0.02	17997	0.995630	2.62
	79	810	72.0	1	810	260398	0.5100	0.03	17998	0.995685	2.63
	78	818	72.0	1	818	261216	0.5116	0.03	17999	0.995740	2.63
	77	842	72.2	1	842	262058	0.5133	0.03	18000	0.995795	2.64
	76	864	72.3	1	864	262922	0.5150	0.04	18001	0.995851	2.64
	75	886	72.4	1	886	263808	0.5167	0.04	18002	0.995906	2.64
	74	887	72.4	1	887	264695	0.5184	0.05	18003	0.995961	2.65
	73	890	72.4	1	890	265585	0.5202	0.05	18004	0.996017	2.65
	72	902	72.5	1	902	266487	0.5219	0.06	18005	0.996072	2.66
	71	903	72.5	1	903	267390	0.5237	0.06	18006	0.996127	2.66
	70	909	72.5	1	909	268299	0.5255	0.06	18007	0.996183	2.67
	69	915	72.5	1	915	269214	0.5273	0.07	18008	0.996238	2.67
	68	918	72.6	1	918	270132	0.5291	0.07	18009	0.996293	2.68
	67	922	72.6	1	922	271054	0.5309	0.08	18010	0.996349	2.68
	66	951	72.7	1	951	272005	0.5327	0.08	18011	0.996404	2.69
	65	978	72.8	1	978	272983	0.5347	0.09	18012	0.996459	2.69
63-	64	990	72.9	2	1980	274963	0.5385	0.10	18014	0.996570	2.70
	62	1055	73.2	1	1055	276018	0.5406	0.10	18015	0.996625	2.71
	61	1059	73.2	1	1059	277077	0.5427	0.11	18016	0.996681	2.71
	60	1116	73.4	1	1116	278193	0.5449	0.11	18017	0.996736	2.72
	59	1122	73.4	1	1122	279315	0.5471	0.12	18018	0.996791	2.73
	58	1123	73.4	1	1123	280438	0.5493	0.12	18019	0.996847	2.73
	57	1133	73.5	1	1133	281571	0.5515	0.13	18020	0.996902	2.74
	56	1194	73.7	1	1194	282765	0.5538	0.14	18021	0.996957	2.74
	55	1205	73.7	1	1205	283970	0.5562	0.14	18022	0.997013	2.75
	54	1219	73.8	1	1219	285189	0.5586	0.15	18023	0.997068	2.76
	53	1224	73.8	1	1224	286413	0.5610	0.15	18024	0.997123	2.76
	52	1228	73.8	1	1228	287641	0.5634	0.16	18025	0.997179	2.77
	51	1281	74.0	1	1281	288922	0.5659	0.17	18026	0.997234	2.77
	50	1296	74.0	1	1296	290218	0.5684	0.17	18027	0.997289	2.78
	49	1297	74.1	1	1297	291515	0.5710	0.18	18028	0.997344	2.79
	48	1333	74.2	1	1333	292848	0.5736	0.19	18029	0.997400	2.79
	47	1338	74.2	1	1338	294186	0.5762	0.19	18030	0.997455	2.80
	46	1341	74.2	1	1341	295527	0.5788	0.20	18031	0.997510	2.81
	45	1431	74.5	1	1431	296958	0.5816	0.21	18032	0.997566	2.82
	44	1501	74.7	1	1501	298459	0.5846	0.21	18033	0.997621	2.82
	43	1517	74.7	1	1517	299976	0.5875	0.22	18034	0.997676	2.83
	42	1535	74.8	1	1535	301511	0.5905	0.23	18035	0.997732	2.84
	41	1539	74.8	1	1539	303050	0.5936	0.24	18036	0.997787	2.85
	40	1550	74.8	1	1550	304600	0.5966	0.24	18037	0.997842	2.85
	39	1551	74.8	1	1551	306151	0.5996	0.25	18038	0.997898	2.86
	38	1574	74.9	1	1574	307725	0.6027	0.26	18039	0.997953	2.87
	37	1652	75.1	1	1652	309377	0.6059	0.27	18040	0.998008	2.88
	36	1658	75.1	1	1658	311035	0.6092	0.28	18041	0.998064	2.89
	35	1691	75.2	1	1691	312726	0.6125	0.29	18042	0.998119	2.90
	34	1719	75.3	1	1719	314445	0.6159	0.29	18043	0.998174	2.91
	33	1798	75.5	1	1798	316243	0.6194	0.30	18044	0.998230	2.92
	32	1910	75.7	1	1910	318153	0.6231	0.31	18045	0.998285	2.93
	31	1926	75.8	1	1926	320079	0.6269	0.32	18046	0.998340	2.94
	30	1967	75.9	1	1967	322046	0.6308	0.33	18047	0.998396	2.95
	29	1980	75.9	1	1980	324026	0.6346	0.34	18048	0.998451	2.96
	28	2052	76.0	1	2052	326078	0.6387	0.35	18049	0.998506	2.97
	27	2074	76.1	1	2074	328152	0.6427	0.37	18050	0.998562	2.98
	26	2086	76.1	1	2086	330238	0.6468	0.38	18051	0.998617	2.99
	25	2175	76.3	1	2175	332413	0.6511	0.39	18052	0.998672	3.01
	24	2439	76.8	1	2439	334852	0.6558	0.40	18053	0.998728	3.02
	23	2604	77.1	1	2604	337456	0.6609	0.42	18054	0.998783	3.03
	22	2764	77.3	1	2764	340220	0.6664	0.43	18055	0.998838	3.05
	21	2815	77.4	1	2815	343035	0.6719	0.45	18056	0.998894	3.06
	20	2836	77.4	1	2836	345871	0.6774	0.46	18057	0.998949	3.08
	19	2888	77.5	1	2888	348759	0.6831	0.48	18058	0.999004	3.09
	18	2918	77.6	1	2918	351677	0.6888	0.49	18059	0.999059	3.11
	17	3030	77.7	1	3030	354707	0.6947	0.51	18060	0.999115	3.13
	16	3102	77.8	1	3102	357809	0.7008	0.53	18061	0.999170	3.15
	15	3114	77.9	1	3114	360923	0.7069	0.54	18062	0.999225	3.17
	14	3281	78.1	1	3281	364204	0.7133	0.56	18063	0.999281	3.19
	13	3411	78.2	1	3411	367615	0.7200	0.58	18064	0.999336	3.21
	12	3551	78.4	1	3551	371166	0.7270	0.60	18065	0.999391	3.23
	11	5227	80.1	1	5227	376393	0.7372	0.63	18066	0.999447	3.26
	10	5877	80.6	1	5877	382270	0.7487	0.67	18067	0.999502	3.29
	9	6526	81.1	1	6526	388796	0.7615	0.71	18068	0.999557	3.32
	8	7632	81.7	1	7632	396428	0.7764	0.76	18069	0.999613	3.36
	7	9361	82.6	1	9361	405789	0.7948	0.82	18070	0.999668	3.40
	6	10510	83.1	1	10510	416299	0.8154	0.90	18071	0.999723	3.45
	5	10588	83.2	1	10588	426887	0.8361	0.98	18072	0.999779	3.51
	4	10752	83.2	1	10752	437639	0.8572	1.07	18073	0.999834	3.59
	3	13914	84.4	1	13914	451553	0.8844	1.20	18074	0.999889	3.69
	2	18793	85.7	1	18793	470346	0.9212	1.41	18075	0.999945	3.87
	1	40224	89.0	1	40224	510570	1.0000	+INF.	18076	1.000000	+INF.

Rank	Occ. F	SFI	F	Tokens	Cum. Tokens	Cum. P Tokens	Y	Cum. Types	Cum. P Types	Z
7675-13850	1	48.6	6176	6176	6176	0.0295	-1.89	6176	0.445921	-0.14
5540-7674	2	50.8	2135	4270	10446	0.0499	-1.65	8311	0.600072	0.25
4393-5539	3	52.2	1147	3441	13887	0.0663	-1.50	9458	0.682888	0.48
3658-4392	4	53.3	735	2940	16827	0.0804	-1.40	10193	0.735957	0.63
3179-3657	5	54.2	479	2395	19222	0.0918	-1.33	10672	0.770541	0.74
2809-3178	6	54.9	370	2220	21442	0.1024	-1.27	11042	0.797256	0.83
2498-2808	7	55.5	311	2177	23619	0.1128	-1.21	11353	0.819711	0.91
2257-2497	8	56.1	241	1928	25547	0.1220	-1.16	11594	0.837112	0.98
2052-2256	9	56.6	205	1845	27392	0.1308	-1.12	11799	0.851913	1.04
1873-2051	10	57.0	179	1790	29182	0.1394	-1.08	11978	0.864838	1.10
1740-1872	11	57.4	133	1463	30645	0.1464	-1.05	12111	0.874440	1.15
1623-1739	12	57.8	117	1404	32049	0.1531	-1.02	12228	0.882888	1.19
1526-1622	13	58.1	97	1261	33310	0.1591	-1.00	12325	0.889892	1.23
1444-1525	14	58.4	82	1148	34458	0.1646	-0.98	12407	0.895812	1.26
1363-1443	15	58.7	81	1215	35673	0.1704	-0.95	12488	0.901661	1.29
1290-1362	16	59.0	73	1168	36841	0.1760	-0.93	12561	0.906931	1.32
1230-1289	17	59.2	60	1020	37861	0.1808	-0.91	12621	0.911264	1.35
1170-1229	18	59.5	60	1080	38941	0.1860	-0.89	12681	0.915596	1.38
1123-1169	19	59.7	47	893	39834	0.1903	-0.88	12728	0.918989	1.40
1085-1122	20	59.9	38	760	40594	0.1939	-0.86	12766	0.921733	1.42
1043-1084	21	60.1	42	882	41476	0.1981	-0.85	12808	0.924765	1.44
1001-1042	22	60.3	42	924	42400	0.2025	-0.83	12850	0.927798	1.46
968-1000	23	60.5	33	759	43159	0.2061	-0.82	12883	0.930180	1.48
925-967	24	60.7	43	1032	44191	0.2111	-0.80	12926	0.933285	1.50
896-924	25	60.9	29	725	44916	0.2145	-0.79	12955	0.935379	1.52
865-895	26	61.0	31	806	45722	0.2184	-0.78	12986	0.937617	1.54
831-864	27	61.2	34	918	46640	0.2228	-0.76	13020	0.940072	1.56
806-830	28	61.3	25	700	47340	0.2261	-0.75	13045	0.941877	1.57
778-805	29	61.5	28	812	48152	0.2300	-0.74	13073	0.943899	1.59
757-777	30	61.6	21	630	48782	0.2330	-0.73	13094	0.945415	1.60
738-756	31	61.8	19	589	49371	0.2358	-0.72	13113	0.946787	1.61
719-737	32	61.9	19	608	49979	0.2387	-0.71	13132	0.948159	1.63
701-718	33	62.0	18	594	50573	0.2416	-0.70	13150	0.949458	1.64
687-700	34	62.2	14	476	51049	0.2438	-0.69	13164	0.950469	1.65
661-686	35	62.3	26	910	51959	0.2482	-0.68	13190	0.952347	1.67
641-660	36	62.4	20	720	52679	0.2516	-0.67	13210	0.953791	1.68
629-640	37	62.5	12	444	53123	0.2537	-0.66	13222	0.954657	1.69
607-628	38	62.6	22	836	53959	0.2577	-0.65	13244	0.956245	1.71
594-606	39	62.8	13	507	54466	0.2601	-0.64	13257	0.957184	1.72
583-593	40	62.9	11	440	54906	0.2623	-0.64	13268	0.957978	1.73
573-582	41	63.0	10	410	55316	0.2642	-0.63	13278	0.958700	1.74
568-572	42	63.1	5	210	55526	0.2652	-0.63	13283	0.959061	1.74
558-567	43	63.2	10	430	55956	0.2673	-0.62	13293	0.959783	1.75
550-557	44	63.3	8	352	56308	0.2689	-0.62	13301	0.960361	1.75
539-549	45	63.4	11	495	56803	0.2713	-0.61	13312	0.961155	1.76
529-538	46	63.5	10	460	57263	0.2735	-0.60	13322	0.961877	1.77
521-528	47	63.6	8	376	57639	0.2753	-0.60	13330	0.962455	1.78
515-520	48	63.6	6	288	57927	0.2767	-0.59	13336	0.962888	1.79
502-514	49	63.7	13	637	58564	0.2797	-0.58	13349	0.963827	1.80
497-501	50	63.8	5	250	58814	0.2809	-0.58	13354	0.964188	1.80
487-496	51	63.9	10	510	59324	0.2834	-0.57	13364	0.964910	1.81
484-486	52	64.0	3	156	59480	0.2841	-0.57	13367	0.965126	1.81
476-483	53	64.1	8	424	59904	0.2861	-0.56	13375	0.965704	1.82
467-475	54	64.2	9	486	60390	0.2884	-0.56	13384	0.966354	1.83
458-466	55	64.2	9	495	60885	0.2908	-0.55	13393	0.967004	1.84
454-457	56	64.3	4	224	61109	0.2919	-0.55	13397	0.967292	1.84
449-453	57	64.4	5	285	61394	0.2932	-0.54	13402	0.967653	1.85
442-448	58	64.5	7	406	61800	0.2952	-0.54	13409	0.968159	1.85
438-441	59	64.5	4	236	62036	0.2963	-0.54	13413	0.968448	1.86
429-437	60	64.6	9	540	62576	0.2989	-0.53	13422	0.969097	1.87
421-428	61	64.7	8	488	63064	0.3012	-0.52	13430	0.969675	1.88
416-420	62	64.7	5	310	63374	0.3027	-0.52	13435	0.970036	1.88
406-415	63	64.8	10	630	64004	0.3057	-0.51	13445	0.970758	1.89
402-405	64	64.9	4	256	64260	0.3069	-0.50	13449	0.971047	1.90
392-401	65	65.0	10	650	64910	0.3100	-0.50	13459	0.971769	1.91
388-391	66	65.0	4	264	65174	0.3113	-0.49	13463	0.972058	1.91
382-387	67	65.1	6	402	65576	0.3132	-0.49	13469	0.972491	1.92
376-381	68	65.1	6	408	65984	0.3152	-0.48	13475	0.972924	1.93
371-375	69	65.2	5	345	66329	0.3168	-0.48	13480	0.973285	1.93
369-370	70	65.3	2	140	66469	0.3175	-0.47	13482	0.973430	1.93
363-368	71	65.3	6	426	66895	0.3195	-0.47	13488	0.973863	1.94
357-362	72	65.4	6	432	67327	0.3216	-0.46	13494	0.974296	1.95
351-356	73	65.5	6	438	67765	0.3237	-0.46	13500	0.974729	1.96
346-350	74	65.5	5	370	68135	0.3254	-0.45	13505	0.975090	1.96
343-345	75	65.6	3	225	68360	0.3265	-0.45	13508	0.975307	1.97
341-342	76	65.6	2	152	68512	0.3272	-0.45	13510	0.975451	1.97
337-340	77	65.7	4	308	68820	0.3287	-0.44	13514	0.975740	1.97
335-336	78	65.7	2	156	68976	0.3295	-0.44	13516	0.975884	1.98
331-334	79	65.8	4	316	69292	0.3310	-0.44	13520	0.976173	1.98
328-330	80	65.8	3	240	69532	0.3321	-0.43	13523	0.976390	1.98
326-327	81	65.9	2	162	69694	0.3329	-0.43	13525	0.976534	1.99
323-325	82	66.0	3	246	69940	0.3341	-0.43	13528	0.976751	1.99
321-322	83	66.0	2	166	70106	0.3349	-0.43	13530	0.976895	1.99
319-320	84	66.1	2	168	70274	0.3357	-0.42	13532	0.977040	2.00
317-318	85	66.1	2	170	70444	0.3365	-0.42	13534	0.977184	2.00
314-316	86	66.2	3	258	70702	0.3377	-0.42	13537	0.977401	2.00
311-313	87	66.2	3	261	70963	0.3389	-0.42	13540	0.977617	2.01
310	88	66.3	1	88	71051	0.3394	-0.41	13541	0.977690	2.01
304-309	89	66.3	6	534	71585	0.3419	-0.41	13547	0.978123	2.02
297-303	90	66.4	7	630	72215	0.3449	-0.40	13554	0.978628	2.03
296	91	66.4	1	91	72306	0.3454	-0.40	13555	0.978700	2.03
295	92	66.5	1	92	72398	0.3458	-0.40	13556	0.978773	2.03
293-294	93	66.5	2	186	72584	0.3467	-0.39	13558	0.978917	2.03
292	94	66.5	1	94	72678	0.3471	-0.39	13559	0.978989	2.03
289-291	95	66.6	3	285	72963	0.3485	-0.39	13562	0.979206	2.04
285-288	96	66.6	4	384	73347	0.3503	-0.38	13566	0.979495	2.04
282-284	97	66.7	3	291	73638	0.3517	-0.38	13569	0.979711	2.05
276-281	98	66.7	6	588	74226	0.3545	-0.37	13575	0.980144	2.06
274-275	99	66.8	2	198	74424	0.3555	-0.37	13577	0.980289	2.06
269-273	100	66.8	5	500	74924	0.3579	-0.36	13582	0.980650	2.07
266-268	101	66.9	3	303	75227	0.3593	-0.36	13585	0.980866	2.07
264-265	102	66.9	2	204	75431	0.3603	-0.36	13587	0.981011	2.08
263	103	66.9	1	103	75534	0.3608	-0.36	13588	0.981083	2.08
261-262	105	67.0	2	210	75744	0.3618	-0.35	13590	0.981227	2.08
260	106	67.1	1	106	75850	0.3623	-0.35	13591	0.981300	2.08
259	107	67.1	1	107	75957	0.3628	-0.35	13592	0.981372	2.08
257-258	108	67.1	2	216	76173	0.3638	-0.35	13594	0.981516	2.09
255-256	109	67.2	2	218	76391	0.3649	-0.35	13596	0.981661	2.09
254	110	67.2	1	110	76501	0.3654	-0.34	13597	0.981733	2.09
250-253	111	67.3	4	444	76945	0.3675	-0.34	13601	0.982022	2.10
249	112	67.3	1	112	77057	0.3681	-0.34	13602	0.982094	2.10
242-248	113	67.3	7	791	77848	0.3718	-0.33	13609	0.982599	2.11
241	115	67.4	1	115	77963	0.3724	-0.33	13610	0.982671	2.11
239-240	116	67.5	2	232	78195	0.3735	-0.32	13612	0.982816	2.12
236-238	117	67.5	3	351	78546	0.3752	-0.32	13615	0.983032	2.12
234-235	118	67.5	2	236	78782	0.3763	-0.32	13617	0.983177	2.12
233	119	67.6	1	119	78901	0.3769	-0.31	13618	0.983249	2.13
231-232	123	67.7	2	246	79147	0.3780	-0.31	13620	0.983393	2.13
226-230	125	67.8	5	625	79772	0.3810	-0.30	13625	0.983754	2.14
224-225	126	67.8	2	252	80024	0.3822	-0.30	13627	0.983899	2.14
222-223	129	67.9	2	258	80282	0.3835	-0.30	13629	0.984043	2.15
221	130	67.9	1	130	80412	0.3841	-0.29	13630	0.984115	2.15
218-220	132	68.0	3	396	80808	0.3860	-0.29	13633	0.984332	2.15
217	133	68.0	1	133	80941	0.3866	-0.29	13634	0.984404	2.15
215-216	134	68.1	2	268	81209	0.3879	-0.28	13636	0.984549	2.16
211-214	135	68.1	4	540	81749	0.3905	-0.28	13640	0.984838	2.17
209-210	136	68.1	2	272	82021	0.3918	-0.27	13642	0.984982	2.17
207-208	137	68.2	2	274	82295	0.3931	-0.27	13644	0.985126	2.17
205-206	138	68.2	2	276	82571	0.3944	-0.27	13646	0.985271	2.18
202-204	143	68.4	3	429	83000	0.3964	-0.26	13649	0.985487	2.18
200-201	144	68.4	2	288	83288	0.3978	-0.26	13651	0.985632	2.19
199	145	68.4	1	145	83433	0.3985	-0.26	13652	0.985704	2.19
198	146	68.4	1	146	83579	0.3992	-0.26	13653	0.985776	2.19
196-197	147	68.5	2	294	83873	0.4006	-0.25	13655	0.985921	2.20
192-195	148	68.5	4	592	84465	0.4034	-0.24	13659	0.986209	2.20
190-191	149	68.5	2	298	84763	0.4049	-0.24	13661	0.986354	2.21
188-189	150	68.6	2	300	85063	0.4063	-0.24	13663	0.986498	2.21
187	151	68.6	1	151	85214	0.4070	-0.24	13664	0.986570	2.21
186	152	68.6	1	152	85366	0.4077	-0.23	13665	0.986643	2.22
184-185	153	68.7	2	306	85672	0.4092	-0.23	13667	0.986787	2.22
182-183	154	68.7	2	308	85980	0.4107	-0.23	13669	0.986931	2.22
181	155	68.7	1	155	86135	0.4114	-0.22	13670	0.987004	2.23
180	156	68.7	1	156	86291	0.4122	-0.22	13671	0.987076	2.23
179	157	68.8	1	157	86448	0.4129	-0.22	13672	0.987148	2.23
178	158	68.8	1	158	86606	0.4137	-0.22	13673	0.987220	2.23
177	160	68.8	1	160	86766	0.4144	-0.22	13674	0.987292	2.24
176	161	68.9	1	161	86927	0.4152	-0.21	13675	0.987365	2.24
175	162	68.9	1	162	87089	0.4160	-0.21	13676	0.987437	2.24
173-174	163	68.9	2	326	87415	0.4175	-0.21	13678	0.987581	2.24
172	164	69.0	1	164	87579	0.4183	-0.21	13679	0.987653	2.25
171	165	69.0	1	165	87744	0.4191	-0.20	13680	0.987726	2.25
170	168	69.1	1	168	87912	0.4199	-0.20	13681	0.987798	2.25
169	169	69.1	1	169	88081	0.4207	-0.20	13682	0.987870	2.25
166-168	170	69.1	3	510	88591	0.4231	-0.19	13685	0.988087	2.26
165	171	69.1	1	171	88762	0.4240	-0.19	13686	0.988159	2.26
163-164	172	69.2	2	344	89106	0.4256	-0.19	13688	0.988303	2.27
160-162	174	69.2	3	522	89628	0.4281	-0.18	13691	0.988520	2.27
159	175	69.2	1	175	89803	0.4289	-0.18	13692	0.988592	2.28
157-158	178	69.3	2	356	90159	0.4306	-0.17	13694	0.988736	2.28
155-156	181	69.4	2	362	90521	0.4324	-0.17	13696	0.988881	2.29
154	182	69.4	1	182	90703	0.4332	-0.17	13697	0.988953	2.29
153	183	69.4	1	183	90886	0.4341	-0.17	13698	0.989025	2.29
151-152	184	69.5	2	368	91254	0.4359	-0.16	13700	0.989170	2.30
149-150	185	69.5	2	370	91624	0.4376	-0.16	13702	0.989314	2.30
148	186	69.5	1	186	91810	0.4385	-0.15	13703	0.989386	2.30
146-147	188	69.5	2	376	92186	0.4403	-0.15	13705	0.989531	2.31
145	189	69.6	1	189	92375	0.4412	-0.15	13706	0.989603	2.31
144	190	69.6	1	190	92565	0.4421	-0.15	13707	0.989675	2.31
142-143	192	69.6	2	384	92949	0.4440	-0.14	13709	0.989819	2.32
141	193	69.7	1	193	93142	0.4449	-0.14	13710	0.989892	2.32
140	194	69.7	1	194	93336	0.4458	-0.14	13711	0.989964	2.32
139	195	69.7	1	195	93531	0.4467	-0.13	13712	0.990036	2.33
138	196	69.7	1	196	93727	0.4477	-0.13	13713	0.990108	2.33
137	198	69.8	1	198	93925	0.4486	-0.13	13714	0.990180	2.33
136	201	69.8	1	201	94126	0.4496	-0.13	13715	0.990253	2.34
133-135	202	69.9	3	606	94732	0.4525	-0.12	13718	0.990469	2.34
132	205	69.9	1	205	94937	0.4535	-0.12	13719	0.990541	2.35
131	207	70.0	1	207	95144	0.4544	-0.11	13720	0.990614	2.35
130	208	70.0	1	208	95352	0.4554	-0.11	13721	0.990686	2.35
129	209	70.0	1	209	95561	0.4564	-0.11	13722	0.990758	2.36
127-128	210	70.0	2	420	95981	0.4584	-0.10	13724	0.990902	2.36
125-126	211	70.0	2	422	96403	0.4605	-0.10	13726	0.991047	2.37
123-124	212	70.1	2	424	96827	0.4625	-0.09	13728	0.991191	2.37
121-122	214	70.1	2	428	97255	0.4645	-0.09	13730	0.991336	2.38
120	215	70.1	1	215	97470	0.4656	-0.09	13731	0.991408	2.38
119	217	70.2	1	217	97687	0.4666	-0.08	13732	0.991480	2.39
116-118	223	70.3	3	669	98356	0.4698	-0.08	13735	0.991697	2.40
114-115	225	70.3	2	450	98806	0.4719	-0.07	13737	0.991841	2.40
112-113	226	70.3	2	452	99258	0.4741	-0.06	13739	0.991986	2.41
111	229	70.4	1	229	99487	0.4752	-0.06	13740	0.992058	2.41
110	230	70.4	1	230	99717	0.4763	-0.06	13741	0.992130	2.41
107-109	238	70.6	3	714	100431	0.4797	-0.05	13744	0.992347	2.43
106	241	70.6	1	241	100672	0.4808	-0.05	13745	0.992419	2.43
105	244	70.7	1	244	100916	0.4820	-0.05	13746	0.992491	2.43
104	246	70.7	1	246	101162	0.4832	-0.04	13747	0.992563	2.44
102-103	248	70.7	2	496	101658	0.4856	-0.04	13749	0.992708	2.44
101	251	70.8	1	251	101909	0.4868	-0.03	13750	0.992780	2.45
100	255	70.9	1	255	102164	0.4880	-0.03	13751	0.992852	2.45
99	265	71.0	1	265	102429	0.4892	-0.03	13752	0.992924	2.45
98	272	71.1	1	272	102701	0.4905	-0.02	13753	0.992996	2.46
97	274	71.2	1	274	102975	0.4918	-0.02	13754	0.993069	2.46
96	275	71.2	1	275	103250	0.4932	-0.02	13755	0.993141	2.46
94-95	276	71.2	2	552	103802	0.4958	-0.01	13757	0.993285	2.47
93	288	71.4	1	288	104090	0.4972	-0.01	13758	0.993357	2.48
92	293	71.5	1	293	104383	0.4986	-0.00	13759	0.993430	2.48
91	294	71.5	1	294	104677	0.5000	-0.00	13760	0.993502	2.48
90	296	71.5	1	296	104973	0.5014	0.00	13761	0.993574	2.49
89	297	71.5	1	297	105270	0.5028	0.01	13762	0.993646	2.49
88	298	71.5	1	298	105568	0.5042	0.01	13763	0.993718	2.50
87	299	71.6	1	299	105867	0.5057	0.01	13764	0.993791	2.50
86	301	71.6	1	301	106168	0.5071	0.02	13765	0.993863	2.50
85	308	71.7	1	308	106476	0.5086	0.02	13766	0.993935	2.51
84	315	71.8	1	315	106791	0.5101	0.03	13767	0.994007	2.51
83	317	71.8	1	317	107108	0.5116	0.03	13768	0.994079	2.52
82	321	71.9	1	321	107429	0.5131	0.03	13769	0.994152	2.52
81	322	71.9	1	322	107751	0.5147	0.04	13770	0.994224	2.53
80	324	71.9	1	324	108075	0.5162	0.04	13771	0.994296	2.53
79	325	71.9	1	325	108400	0.5178	0.04	13772	0.994368	2.53
78	327	71.9	1	327	108727	0.5193	0.05	13773	0.994440	2.54
77	338	72.1	1	338	109065	0.5209	0.05	13774	0.994513	2.54
76	340	72.1	1	340	109405	0.5226	0.06	13775	0.994585	2.55
75	342	72.1	1	342	109747	0.5242	0.06	13776	0.994657	2.55
74	344	72.2	1	344	110091	0.5258	0.06	13777	0.994729	2.56
73	347	72.2	1	347	110438	0.5275	0.07	13778	0.994801	2.56
72	354	72.3	1	354	110792	0.5292	0.07	13779	0.994874	2.57
71	359	72.3	1	359	111151	0.5309	0.08	13780	0.994946	2.57
70	360	72.4	1	360	111511	0.5326	0.08	13781	0.995018	2.58
69	361	72.4	1	361	111872	0.5343	0.09	13782	0.995090	2.58
68	379	72.6	1	379	112251	0.5362	0.09	13783	0.995162	2.59
67	382	72.6	1	382	112633	0.5380	0.10	13784	0.995235	2.59
66	395	72.8	1	395	113028	0.5399	0.10	13785	0.995307	2.60
65	397	72.8	1	397	113425	0.5418	0.10	13786	0.995379	2.60

Rank		Occ. F	SFI	F	Tokens	Cum. Tokens	Cum. P Tokens	Y	Cum. Types	Cum. P Types	Z
62-	64	400	72.8	1	400	113825	0.5437	0.11	13787	0.995451	2.61
	63	401	72.8	2	802	114627	0.5475	0.12	13789	0.995596	2.62
	61	402	72.8	1	402	115029	0.5494	0.12	13790	0.995668	2.63
	60	403	72.8	1	403	115432	0.5513	0.13	13791	0.995740	2.63
	59	433	73.2	1	433	115865	0.5534	0.13	13792	0.995812	2.64
	58	434	73.2	1	434	116299	0.5555	0.14	13793	0.995884	2.64
	57	437	73.2	1	437	116736	0.5576	0.14	13794	0.995957	2.65
55-	56	448	73.3	2	896	117632	0.5619	0.16	13796	0.996101	2.66
	54	450	73.3	1	450	118082	0.5640	0.16	13797	0.996173	2.67
	53	455	73.4	1	455	118537	0.5662	0.17	13798	0.996245	2.67
	52	473	73.5	1	473	119010	0.5684	0.17	13799	0.996318	2.68
	51	474	73.6	1	474	119484	0.5707	0.18	13800	0.996390	2.69
	50	482	73.6	1	482	119966	0.5730	0.18	13801	0.996462	2.69
	49	498	73.8	1	498	120464	0.5754	0.19	13802	0.996534	2.70
	48	502	73.8	1	502	120966	0.5778	0.20	13803	0.996606	2.71
	47	504	73.8	1	504	121470	0.5802	0.20	13804	0.996679	2.71
	46	521	74.0	1	521	121991	0.5827	0.21	13805	0.996751	2.72
	45	536	74.1	1	536	122527	0.5852	0.22	13806	0.996823	2.73
	44	554	74.2	1	554	123081	0.5879	0.22	13807	0.996895	2.74
	43	562	74.3	1	562	123643	0.5906	0.23	13808	0.996967	2.74
	42	566	74.3	1	566	124209	0.5933	0.24	13809	0.997040	2.75
	41	589	74.5	1	589	124798	0.5961	0.24	13810	0.997112	2.76
	40	591	74.5	1	591	125389	0.5989	0.25	13811	0.997184	2.77
	39	599	74.6	1	599	125988	0.6018	0.26	13812	0.997256	2.78
	38	603	74.6	1	603	126591	0.6046	0.27	13813	0.997329	2.79
	37	607	74.6	1	607	127198	0.6075	0.27	13814	0.997401	2.79
	36	666	75.0	1	666	127864	0.6107	0.28	13815	0.997473	2.80
	35	701	75.3	1	701	128565	0.6141	0.29	13816	0.997545	2.81
	34	702	75.3	1	702	129267	0.6174	0.30	13817	0.997617	2.82
	33	714	75.3	1	714	129981	0.6208	0.31	13818	0.997689	2.83
	32	719	75.4	1	719	130700	0.6243	0.32	13819	0.997762	2.84

Rank	Occ. F	SFI	F	Tokens	Cum. Tokens	Cum. P Tokens	Y	Cum. Types	Cum. P Types	Z
31	731	75.4	1	731	131431	0.6278	0.33	13820	0.997834	2.85
30	735	75.5	1	735	132166	0.6313	0.34	13821	0.997906	2.86
29	749	75.5	1	749	132915	0.6349	0.34	13822	0.997978	2.87
28	751	75.6	1	751	133666	0.6384	0.35	13823	0.998051	2.89
27	864	76.2	1	864	134530	0.6426	0.37	13824	0.998123	2.90
26	873	76.2	1	873	135403	0.6467	0.38	13825	0.998195	2.91
25	887	76.3	1	887	136290	0.6510	0.39	13826	0.998267	2.92
24	932	76.5	1	932	137222	0.6554	0.40	13827	0.998339	2.94
23	939	76.5	1	939	138161	0.6599	0.41	13828	0.998412	2.95
22	947	76.6	1	947	139108	0.6644	0.42	13829	0.998484	2.96
21	1076	77.1	1	1076	140184	0.6696	0.44	13830	0.998556	2.98
20	1118	77.3	1	1118	141302	0.6749	0.45	13831	0.998628	3.00
19	1171	77.5	1	1171	142473	0.6805	0.47	13832	0.998700	3.01
18	1220	77.7	1	1220	143693	0.6863	0.49	13833	0.998773	3.03
17	1385	78.2	1	1385	145078	0.6929	0.50	13834	0.998845	3.05
16	1430	78.3	1	1430	146508	0.6998	0.52	13835	0.998917	3.07
15	1471	78.5	1	1471	147979	0.7068	0.54	13836	0.998989	3.09
14	1556	78.7	1	1556	149535	0.7142	0.57	13837	0.999061	3.11
13	1566	78.7	1	1566	151101	0.7217	0.59	13838	0.999134	3.13
12	1611	78.9	1	1611	152712	0.7294	0.61	13839	0.999206	3.16
11	1618	78.9	1	1618	154330	0.7371	0.63	13840	0.999278	3.19
10	1808	79.4	1	1808	156138	0.7458	0.66	13841	0.999350	3.22
9	1903	79.6	1	1903	158041	0.7549	0.69	13842	0.999422	3.25
8	2532	80.8	1	2532	160573	0.7670	0.73	13843	0.999495	3.29
7	3219	81.9	1	3219	163792	0.7823	0.78	13844	0.999567	3.33
6	4609	83.4	1	4609	168401	0.8043	0.86	13845	0.999639	3.38
5	4631	83.4	1	4631	173032	0.8265	0.94	13846	0.999711	3.44
4	5232	84.0	1	5232	178264	0.8515	1.04	13847	0.999783	3.52
3	5902	84.5	1	5902	184166	0.8796	1.17	13848	0.999856	3.63
2	7220	85.4	1	7220	191386	0.9141	1.37	13849	0.999928	3.80
1	17978	89.3	1	17978	209364	1.0000	+INF.	13850	1.000000	+INF.

Rank	Occ. F	SFI	F	Tokens	Cum. Tokens	Cum. P Tokens	Y	Cum. Types	Cum. P Types	Z
2617- 5231	1	55.0	2615	2615	2615	0.0546	-1.60	2615	0.499904	-0.00
1772- 2616	2	57.2	845	1690	4305	0.0899	-1.34	3460	0.661441	0.42
1360- 1771	3	58.6	412	1236	5541	0.1157	-1.20	3872	0.740203	0.64
1119- 1359	4	59.7	241	964	6505	0.1358	-1.10	4113	0.786274	0.79
961- 1118	5	60.6	158	790	7295	0.1523	-1.03	4271	0.816479	0.90
823- 960	6	61.3	138	828	8123	0.1696	-0.96	4409	0.842860	1.01
734- 822	7	61.9	89	623	8746	0.1826	-0.91	4498	0.859874	1.08
653- 733	8	62.5	81	648	9394	0.1962	-0.86	4579	0.875358	1.15
588- 652	9	63.0	65	585	9979	0.2084	-0.81	4644	0.887784	1.21
553- 587	10	63.4	35	350	10329	0.2157	-0.79	4679	0.894475	1.25
516- 552	11	63.8	37	407	10736	0.2242	-0.76	4716	0.901548	1.29
486- 515	12	64.2	30	360	11096	0.2317	-0.73	4746	0.907283	1.32
462- 485	13	64.5	24	312	11408	0.2382	-0.71	4770	0.911871	1.35
427- 461	14	64.8	35	490	11898	0.2485	-0.68	4805	0.918562	1.40
410- 426	15	65.1	17	255	12153	0.2538	-0.66	4822	0.921812	1.42
383- 409	16	65.4	27	432	12585	0.2628	-0.63	4849	0.926974	1.45
357- 382	17	65.6	26	442	13027	0.2720	-0.61	4875	0.931944	1.49
343- 356	18	65.9	14	252	13279	0.2773	-0.59	4889	0.934620	1.51
330- 342	19	66.1	13	247	13526	0.2825	-0.58	4902	0.937106	1.53
313- 329	20	66.3	17	340	13866	0.2896	-0.55	4919	0.940356	1.56
298- 312	21	66.5	15	315	14181	0.2961	-0.54	4934	0.943223	1.58
289- 297	22	66.7	9	198	14379	0.3003	-0.52	4943	0.944944	1.60
276- 288	23	66.9	13	299	14678	0.3065	-0.51	4956	0.947429	1.62
267- 275	24	67.1	9	216	14894	0.3110	-0.49	4965	0.949149	1.64
254- 266	25	67.3	13	325	15219	0.3178	-0.47	4978	0.951634	1.66
244- 253	26	67.4	10	260	15479	0.3232	-0.46	4988	0.953546	1.68
235- 243	27	67.6	9	243	15722	0.3283	-0.44	4997	0.955267	1.70
230- 234	28	67.7	5	140	15862	0.3312	-0.44	5002	0.956222	1.71
227- 229	29	67.9	3	87	15949	0.3331	-0.43	5005	0.956796	1.71
219- 226	30	68.0	8	240	16189	0.3381	-0.42	5013	0.958325	1.73
212- 218	31	68.2	7	217	16406	0.3426	-0.41	5020	0.959664	1.75
207- 211	32	68.3	5	160	16566	0.3459	-0.40	5025	0.960619	1.76
203- 206	33	68.4	4	132	16698	0.3487	-0.39	5029	0.961384	1.77
199- 202	34	68.6	4	136	16834	0.3515	-0.38	5033	0.962149	1.78
195- 198	35	68.7	4	140	16974	0.3545	-0.37	5037	0.962913	1.79
189- 194	36	68.8	6	216	17190	0.3590	-0.36	5043	0.964060	1.80
185- 188	37	68.9	4	148	17338	0.3621	-0.35	5047	0.964825	1.81
181- 184	38	69.1	4	152	17490	0.3652	-0.34	5051	0.965590	1.82
178- 180	39	69.2	3	117	17607	0.3677	-0.34	5054	0.966163	1.83
171- 177	40	69.3	7	280	17887	0.3735	-0.32	5061	0.967501	1.85
167- 170	41	69.4	4	164	18051	0.3769	-0.31	5065	0.968266	1.86
164- 166	42	69.5	3	126	18177	0.3796	-0.31	5068	0.968840	1.86
159- 163	43	69.6	5	215	18392	0.3841	-0.29	5073	0.969795	1.88
156- 158	44	69.7	3	132	18524	0.3868	-0.29	5076	0.970369	1.89
152- 155	45	69.8	4	180	18704	0.3906	-0.28	5080	0.971134	1.90
144- 151	46	69.9	8	368	19072	0.3983	-0.26	5088	0.972663	1.92
142- 143	47	70.0	2	94	19166	0.4002	-0.25	5090	0.973045	1.93
138- 141	48	70.1	4	192	19358	0.4042	-0.24	5094	0.973810	1.94
135- 137	49	70.1	3	147	19505	0.4073	-0.23	5097	0.974383	1.95
132- 134	50	70.2	3	150	19655	0.4104	-0.23	5100	0.974957	1.96
129- 131	51	70.3	3	153	19808	0.4136	-0.22	5103	0.975530	1.97
126- 128	52	70.4	3	156	19964	0.4169	-0.21	5106	0.976104	1.98
123- 125	53	70.5	3	159	20123	0.4202	-0.20	5109	0.976677	1.99
122	54	70.6	1	54	20177	0.4213	-0.20	5110	0.976869	1.99
117- 121	55	70.6	5	275	20452	0.4271	-0.18	5115	0.977824	2.01
115- 116	56	70.7	2	112	20564	0.4294	-0.18	5117	0.978207	2.02
114	57	70.8	1	57	20621	0.4306	-0.17	5118	0.978398	2.02
112- 113	58	70.9	2	116	20737	0.4330	-0.17	5120	0.978780	2.03
111	60	71.0	1	60	20797	0.4343	-0.17	5121	0.978971	2.03
108- 110	61	71.1	3	183	20980	0.4381	-0.16	5124	0.979545	2.04
107	62	71.2	1	62	21042	0.4394	-0.15	5125	0.979736	2.05
105- 106	63	71.2	2	126	21168	0.4420	-0.15	5127	0.980119	2.06
102- 104	64	71.3	3	192	21360	0.4461	-0.14	5130	0.980692	2.07
100- 101	65	71.4	2	130	21490	0.4488	-0.13	5132	0.981074	2.08
99	66	71.4	1	66	21556	0.4501	-0.13	5133	0.981265	2.08
98	67	71.5	1	67	21623	0.4515	-0.12	5134	0.981457	2.08
96- 97	68	71.6	2	136	21759	0.4544	-0.11	5136	0.981839	2.09
95	69	71.6	1	69	21828	0.4558	-0.11	5137	0.982030	2.10
94	70	71.7	1	70	21898	0.4573	-0.11	5138	0.982221	2.10
93	71	71.7	1	71	21969	0.4588	-0.10	5139	0.982413	2.11
92	72	71.8	1	72	22041	0.4603	-0.10	5140	0.982604	2.11
90- 91	73	71.9	2	146	22187	0.4633	-0.09	5142	0.982986	2.12
88- 89	78	72.1	2	156	22343	0.4666	-0.08	5144	0.983368	2.13
87	79	72.2	1	79	22422	0.4682	-0.08	5145	0.983559	2.13
86	81	72.3	1	81	22503	0.4699	-0.08	5146	0.983751	2.14
84- 85	83	72.4	2	166	22669	0.4734	-0.07	5148	0.984133	2.15
81- 83	85	72.5	3	255	22924	0.4787	-0.05	5151	0.984707	2.16
80	88	72.7	1	88	23012	0.4805	-0.05	5152	0.984898	2.17
79	92	72.9	1	92	23104	0.4825	-0.04	5153	0.985089	2.17
78	96	73.0	1	96	23200	0.4845	-0.04	5154	0.985280	2.18
77	97	73.1	1	97	23297	0.4865	-0.03	5155	0.985471	2.18
76	98	73.1	1	98	23395	0.4885	-0.03	5156	0.985662	2.19
75	102	73.3	1	102	23497	0.4907	-0.02	5157	0.985854	2.19
74	103	73.3	1	103	23600	0.4928	-0.02	5158	0.986045	2.20
72- 73	108	73.6	2	216	23816	0.4973	-0.01	5160	0.986427	2.21
71	110	73.6	1	110	23926	0.4996	-0.00	5161	0.986618	2.21
70	112	73.7	1	112	24038	0.5020	0.00	5162	0.986809	2.22
69	114	73.8	1	114	24152	0.5044	0.01	5163	0.987001	2.23
68	115	73.8	1	115	24267	0.5068	0.02	5164	0.987192	2.23
67	116	73.9	1	116	24383	0.5092	0.02	5165	0.987383	2.24
66	117	73.9	1	117	24500	0.5116	0.03	5166	0.987574	2.24
64- 65	118	73.9	2	236	24736	0.5165	0.04	5168	0.987956	2.26
63	123	74.1	1	123	24859	0.5191	0.05	5169	0.988148	2.26
62	126	74.2	1	126	24985	0.5217	0.05	5170	0.988339	2.27
61	131	74.4	1	131	25116	0.5245	0.06	5171	0.988530	2.27
60	132	74.4	1	132	25248	0.5272	0.07	5172	0.988721	2.28
59	133	74.5	1	133	25381	0.5300	0.08	5173	0.988912	2.29
57- 58	137	74.6	2	274	25655	0.5357	0.09	5175	0.989295	2.30
56	139	74.6	1	139	25794	0.5386	0.10	5176	0.989486	2.31
55	144	74.8	1	144	25938	0.5417	0.10	5177	0.989677	2.31
54	145	74.8	1	145	26083	0.5447	0.11	5178	0.989868	2.32
53	146	74.9	1	146	26229	0.5477	0.12	5179	0.990059	2.33
52	149	74.9	1	149	26378	0.5508	0.13	5180	0.990250	2.34
51	150	75.0	1	150	26528	0.5540	0.14	5181	0.990442	2.34
50	152	75.0	1	152	26680	0.5571	0.14	5182	0.990633	2.35
49	156	75.1	1	156	26836	0.5604	0.15	5183	0.990824	2.36
47- 48	158	75.2	2	316	27152	0.5670	0.17	5185	0.991206	2.37
46	160	75.3	1	160	27312	0.5703	0.18	5186	0.991397	2.38
45	161	75.3	1	161	27473	0.5737	0.19	5187	0.991589	2.39
44	163	75.3	1	163	27636	0.5771	0.19	5188	0.991780	2.40
43	164	75.4	1	164	27800	0.5805	0.20	5189	0.991971	2.41
41- 42	168	75.5	2	336	28136	0.5875	0.22	5191	0.992353	2.43
40	170	75.5	1	170	28306	0.5911	0.23	5192	0.992544	2.43
38- 39	179	75.7	2	358	28664	0.5986	0.25	5194	0.992927	2.45
37	181	75.8	1	181	28845	0.6024	0.26	5195	0.993118	2.46
36	182	75.8	1	182	29027	0.6062	0.27	5196	0.993309	2.47
35	183	75.8	1	183	29210	0.6100	0.28	5197	0.993500	2.48
34	186	75.9	1	186	29396	0.6139	0.29	5198	0.993691	2.49
33	192	76.0	1	192	29588	0.6179	0.30	5199	0.993883	2.51
32	197	76.2	1	197	29785	0.6220	0.31	5200	0.994074	2.52
31	204	76.3	1	204	29989	0.6262	0.32	5201	0.994265	2.53
30	205	76.3	1	205	30194	0.6305	0.33	5202	0.994456	2.54
29	208	76.4	1	208	30402	0.6349	0.34	5203	0.994647	2.55
28	214	76.5	1	214	30616	0.6393	0.36	5204	0.994838	2.56
27	219	76.6	1	219	30835	0.6439	0.37	5205	0.995030	2.58
26	223	76.7	1	223	31058	0.6486	0.38	5206	0.995221	2.59
25	227	76.8	1	227	31285	0.6533	0.39	5207	0.995412	2.61
24	228	76.8	1	228	31513	0.6581	0.41	5208	0.995603	2.62
23	234	76.9	1	234	31747	0.6630	0.42	5209	0.995794	2.64
22	252	77.2	1	252	31999	0.6682	0.44	5210	0.995985	2.65
21	276	77.6	1	276	32275	0.6740	0.45	5211	0.996177	2.67
20	312	78.1	1	312	32587	0.6805	0.47	5212	0.996368	2.68
19	313	78.2	1	313	32900	0.6870	0.49	5213	0.996559	2.70
18	351	78.7	1	351	33251	0.6944	0.51	5214	0.996750	2.72
17	357	78.7	1	357	33608	0.7018	0.53	5215	0.996941	2.74
16	361	78.8	1	361	33969	0.7094	0.55	5216	0.997132	2.76
15	376	79.0	1	376	34345	0.7172	0.57	5217	0.997324	2.79
14	396	79.2	1	396	34741	0.7255	0.60	5218	0.997515	2.81
13	401	79.2	1	401	35142	0.7339	0.62	5219	0.997706	2.83
12	402	79.2	1	402	35544	0.7422	0.65	5220	0.997897	2.86
11	407	79.3	1	407	35951	0.7507	0.68	5221	0.998088	2.89
10	410	79.3	1	410	36361	0.7593	0.70	5222	0.998279	2.93
9	475	80.0	1	475	36836	0.7692	0.74	5223	0.998471	2.96
8	504	80.2	1	504	37340	0.7798	0.77	5224	0.998662	3.00
7	906	82.8	1	906	38246	0.7987	0.84	5225	0.998853	3.05
6	1036	83.4	1	1036	39282	0.8203	0.92	5226	0.999044	3.10
5	1112	83.7	1	1112	40394	0.8435	1.01	5227	0.999235	3.17
4	1259	84.2	1	1259	41653	0.8698	1.13	5228	0.999426	3.25
3	1422	84.7	1	1422	43075	0.8995	1.28	5229	0.999618	3.37
2	1749	85.6	1	1749	44824	0.9360	1.52	5230	0.999809	3.55
1	3063	88.1	1	3063	47887	1.0000	+INF.	5231	1.000000	+INF.

Rank	Occ. F	SFI	F	Tokens	Cum. Tokens	Cum. P Tokens	Y	Cum. Types	Cum. P Types	Z
64	400	72.8	1	400	113825	0.5437	0.11	13787	0.995451	2.61
62– 63	401	72.8	2	802	114627	0.5475	0.12	13789	0.995596	2.62
61	402	72.8	1	402	115029	0.5494	0.12	13790	0.995668	2.63
60	403	72.8	1	403	115432	0.5513	0.13	13791	0.995740	2.63
59	433	73.2	1	433	115865	0.5534	0.13	13792	0.995812	2.64
58	434	73.2	1	434	116299	0.5555	0.14	13793	0.995884	2.64
57	437	73.2	1	437	116736	0.5576	0.14	13794	0.995957	2.65
55– 56	448	73.3	2	896	117632	0.5619	0.16	13796	0.996101	2.66
54	450	73.3	1	450	118082	0.5640	0.16	13797	0.996173	2.67
53	455	73.4	1	455	118537	0.5662	0.17	13798	0.996245	2.67
52	473	73.5	1	473	119010	0.5684	0.17	13799	0.996318	2.68
51	474	73.6	1	474	119484	0.5707	0.18	13800	0.996390	2.69
50	482	73.6	1	482	119966	0.5730	0.18	13801	0.996462	2.69
49	498	73.8	1	498	120464	0.5754	0.19	13802	0.996534	2.70
48	502	73.8	1	502	120966	0.5778	0.20	13803	0.996606	2.71
47	504	73.8	1	504	121470	0.5802	0.20	13804	0.996679	2.71
46	521	74.0	1	521	121991	0.5827	0.21	13805	0.996751	2.72
45	536	74.1	1	536	122527	0.5852	0.22	13806	0.996823	2.73
44	554	74.2	1	554	123081	0.5879	0.22	13807	0.996895	2.74
43	562	74.3	1	562	123643	0.5906	0.23	13808	0.996967	2.74
42	566	74.3	1	566	124209	0.5933	0.24	13809	0.997040	2.75
41	589	74.5	1	589	124798	0.5961	0.24	13810	0.997112	2.76
40	591	74.5	1	591	125389	0.5989	0.25	13811	0.997184	2.77
39	599	74.6	1	599	125988	0.6018	0.26	13812	0.997256	2.78
38	603	74.6	1	603	126591	0.6046	0.27	13813	0.997329	2.79
37	607	74.6	1	607	127198	0.6075	0.27	13814	0.997401	2.79
36	666	75.0	1	666	127864	0.6107	0.28	13815	0.997473	2.80
35	701	75.3	1	701	128565	0.6141	0.29	13816	0.997545	2.81
34	702	75.3	1	702	129267	0.6174	0.30	13817	0.997617	2.82
33	714	75.3	1	714	129981	0.6208	0.31	13818	0.997689	2.83
32	719	75.4	1	719	130700	0.6243	0.32	13819	0.997762	2.84
31	731	75.4	1	731	131431	0.6278	0.33	13820	0.997834	2.85
30	735	75.5	1	735	132166	0.6313	0.34	13821	0.997906	2.86
29	749	75.5	1	749	132915	0.6349	0.34	13822	0.997978	2.87
28	751	75.6	1	751	133666	0.6384	0.35	13823	0.998051	2.89
27	864	76.2	1	864	134530	0.6426	0.37	13824	0.998123	2.90
26	873	76.2	1	873	135403	0.6467	0.38	13825	0.998195	2.91
25	887	76.3	1	887	136290	0.6510	0.39	13826	0.998267	2.92
24	932	76.5	1	932	137222	0.6554	0.40	13827	0.998339	2.94
23	939	76.5	1	939	138161	0.6599	0.41	13828	0.998412	2.95
22	947	76.6	1	947	139108	0.6644	0.42	13829	0.998484	2.96
21	1076	77.1	1	1076	140184	0.6696	0.44	13830	0.998556	2.98
20	1118	77.3	1	1118	141302	0.6749	0.45	13831	0.998628	3.00
19	1171	77.5	1	1171	142473	0.6805	0.47	13832	0.998700	3.01
18	1220	77.7	1	1220	143693	0.6863	0.49	13833	0.998773	3.03
17	1385	78.2	1	1385	145078	0.6929	0.50	13834	0.998845	3.05
16	1430	78.3	1	1430	146508	0.6998	0.52	13835	0.998917	3.07
15	1471	78.5	1	1471	147979	0.7068	0.54	13836	0.998989	3.09
14	1556	78.7	1	1556	149535	0.7142	0.57	13837	0.999061	3.11
13	1566	78.7	1	1566	151101	0.7217	0.59	13838	0.999134	3.13
12	1611	78.9	1	1611	152712	0.7294	0.61	13839	0.999206	3.16
11	1618	78.9	1	1618	154330	0.7371	0.63	13840	0.999278	3.19
10	1808	79.4	1	1808	156138	0.7458	0.66	13841	0.999350	3.22
9	1903	79.6	1	1903	158041	0.7549	0.69	13842	0.999422	3.25
8	2532	80.8	1	2532	160573	0.7670	0.73	13843	0.999495	3.29
7	3219	81.9	1	3219	163792	0.7823	0.78	13844	0.999567	3.33
6	4609	83.4	1	4609	168401	0.8043	0.86	13845	0.999639	3.38
5	4631	83.4	1	4631	173032	0.8265	0.94	13846	0.999711	3.44
4	5232	84.0	1	5232	178264	0.8515	1.04	13847	0.999783	3.52
3	5902	84.5	1	5902	184166	0.8796	1.17	13848	0.999856	3.63
2	7220	85.4	1	7220	191386	0.9141	1.37	13849	0.999928	3.80
1	17978	89.3	1	17978	209364	1.0000	+INF.	13850	1.000000	+INF.

Rank	Occ. F	SFI	F	Tokens	Cum. Tokens	Cum. P Tokens	Y	Cum. Types	Cum. P Types	Z
2617– 5231	1	55.0	2615	2615	2615	0.0546	-1.60	2615	0.499904	-0.00
1772– 2616	2	57.2	845	1690	4305	0.0899	-1.34	3460	0.661441	0.42
1360– 1771	3	58.6	412	1236	5541	0.1157	-1.20	3872	0.740203	0.64
1119– 1359	4	59.7	241	964	6505	0.1358	-1.10	4113	0.786274	0.79
961– 1118	5	60.6	158	790	7295	0.1523	-1.03	4271	0.816479	0.90
823– 960	6	61.3	138	828	8123	0.1696	-0.96	4409	0.842860	1.01
734– 822	7	61.9	89	623	8746	0.1826	-0.91	4498	0.859874	1.08
653– 733	8	62.5	81	648	9394	0.1962	-0.86	4579	0.875358	1.15
588– 652	9	63.0	65	585	9979	0.2084	-0.81	4644	0.887784	1.21
553– 587	10	63.4	35	350	10329	0.2157	-0.79	4679	0.894475	1.25
516– 552	11	63.8	37	407	10736	0.2242	-0.76	4716	0.901548	1.29
486– 515	12	64.2	30	360	11096	0.2317	-0.73	4746	0.907283	1.32
462– 485	13	64.5	24	312	11408	0.2382	-0.71	4770	0.911871	1.35
427– 461	14	64.8	35	490	11898	0.2485	-0.68	4805	0.918562	1.40
410– 426	15	65.1	17	255	12153	0.2538	-0.66	4822	0.921812	1.42
383– 409	16	65.4	27	432	12585	0.2628	-0.63	4849	0.926974	1.45
357– 382	17	65.6	26	442	13027	0.2720	-0.61	4875	0.931944	1.49
343– 356	18	65.9	14	252	13279	0.2773	-0.59	4889	0.934620	1.51
330– 342	19	66.1	13	247	13526	0.2825	-0.58	4902	0.937106	1.53
313– 329	20	66.3	17	340	13866	0.2896	-0.55	4919	0.940356	1.56
298– 312	21	66.5	15	315	14181	0.2961	-0.54	4934	0.943223	1.58
289– 297	22	66.7	9	198	14379	0.3003	-0.52	4943	0.944944	1.60
276– 288	23	66.9	13	299	14678	0.3065	-0.51	4956	0.947429	1.62
267– 275	24	67.1	9	216	14894	0.3110	-0.49	4965	0.949149	1.64
254– 266	25	67.3	13	325	15219	0.3178	-0.47	4978	0.951634	1.66
244– 253	26	67.4	10	260	15479	0.3232	-0.46	4988	0.953546	1.68
235– 243	27	67.6	9	243	15722	0.3283	-0.44	4997	0.955267	1.70
230– 234	28	67.7	5	140	15862	0.3312	-0.44	5002	0.956222	1.71
227– 229	29	67.9	3	87	15949	0.3331	-0.43	5005	0.956796	1.71
219– 226	30	68.0	8	240	16189	0.3381	-0.42	5013	0.958325	1.73
212– 218	31	68.2	7	217	16406	0.3426	-0.41	5020	0.959664	1.75
207– 211	32	68.3	5	160	16566	0.3459	-0.40	5025	0.960619	1.76
203– 206	33	68.4	4	132	16698	0.3487	-0.39	5029	0.961384	1.77
199– 202	34	68.6	4	136	16834	0.3515	-0.38	5033	0.962149	1.78
195– 198	35	68.7	4	140	16974	0.3545	-0.37	5037	0.962913	1.79
189– 194	36	68.8	6	216	17190	0.3590	-0.36	5043	0.964060	1.80
185– 188	37	68.9	4	148	17338	0.3621	-0.35	5047	0.964825	1.81
181– 184	38	69.1	4	152	17490	0.3652	-0.34	5051	0.965590	1.82
178– 180	39	69.2	3	117	17607	0.3677	-0.34	5054	0.966163	1.83
171– 177	40	69.3	7	280	17887	0.3735	-0.32	5061	0.967501	1.85
167– 170	41	69.4	4	164	18051	0.3769	-0.31	5065	0.968266	1.86
164– 166	42	69.5	3	126	18177	0.3796	-0.31	5068	0.968840	1.86
159– 163	43	69.6	5	215	18392	0.3841	-0.29	5073	0.969795	1.88
156– 158	44	69.7	3	132	18524	0.3868	-0.29	5076	0.970369	1.89
152– 155	45	69.8	4	180	18704	0.3906	-0.28	5080	0.971134	1.90
144– 151	46	69.9	8	368	19072	0.3983	-0.26	5088	0.972663	1.92
142– 143	47	70.0	2	94	19166	0.4002	-0.25	5090	0.973045	1.93
138– 141	48	70.1	4	192	19358	0.4042	-0.24	5094	0.973810	1.94
135– 137	49	70.1	3	147	19505	0.4073	-0.23	5097	0.974383	1.95
132– 134	50	70.2	3	150	19655	0.4104	-0.23	5100	0.974957	1.96
129– 131	51	70.3	3	153	19808	0.4136	-0.22	5103	0.975530	1.97
126– 128	52	70.4	3	156	19964	0.4169	-0.21	5106	0.976104	1.98
123– 125	53	70.5	3	159	20123	0.4202	-0.20	5109	0.976677	1.99
122	54	70.6	1	54	20177	0.4213	-0.20	5110	0.976869	1.99
117– 121	55	70.6	5	275	20452	0.4271	-0.18	5115	0.977824	2.01
115– 116	56	70.7	2	112	20564	0.4294	-0.18	5117	0.978207	2.02
114	57	70.8	1	57	20621	0.4306	-0.17	5118	0.978398	2.02
112– 113	58	70.9	2	116	20737	0.4330	-0.17	5120	0.978780	2.03
111	60	71.0	1	60	20797	0.4343	-0.17	5121	0.978971	2.03
108– 110	61	71.1	3	183	20980	0.4381	-0.16	5124	0.979545	2.04
107	62	71.2	1	62	21042	0.4394	-0.15	5125	0.979736	2.05
105– 106	63	71.2	2	126	21168	0.4420	-0.15	5127	0.980119	2.06
102– 104	64	71.3	3	192	21360	0.4461	-0.14	5130	0.980692	2.07
100– 101	65	71.4	2	130	21490	0.4488	-0.13	5132	0.981074	2.08
99	66	71.4	1	66	21556	0.4501	-0.13	5133	0.981265	2.08
98	67	71.5	1	67	21623	0.4515	-0.12	5134	0.981457	2.08
96– 97	68	71.6	2	136	21759	0.4544	-0.11	5136	0.981839	2.09
95	69	71.6	1	69	21828	0.4558	-0.11	5137	0.982030	2.10
94	70	71.7	1	70	21898	0.4573	-0.11	5138	0.982221	2.10
93	71	71.7	1	71	21969	0.4588	-0.10	5139	0.982413	2.11
92	72	71.8	1	72	22041	0.4603	-0.10	5140	0.982604	2.11
90– 91	73	71.9	2	146	22187	0.4633	-0.09	5142	0.982986	2.12
88– 89	78	72.1	2	156	22343	0.4666	-0.08	5144	0.983368	2.13
87	79	72.2	1	79	22422	0.4682	-0.08	5145	0.983559	2.13
86	81	72.3	1	81	22503	0.4699	-0.08	5146	0.983751	2.14
84– 85	83	72.4	2	166	22669	0.4734	-0.07	5148	0.984133	2.15

Rank	Occ. F	SFI	F	Tokens	Cum. Tokens	Cum. P Tokens	Y	Cum. Types	Cum. P Types	Z
81– 83	85	72.5	3	255	22924	0.4787	-0.05	5151	0.984707	2.16
80	88	72.7	1	88	23012	0.4805	-0.05	5152	0.984898	2.17
79	92	72.9	1	92	23104	0.4825	-0.04	5153	0.985089	2.17
78	96	73.0	1	96	23200	0.4845	-0.04	5154	0.985280	2.18
77	97	73.1	1	97	23297	0.4865	-0.03	5155	0.985471	2.18
76	98	73.1	1	98	23395	0.4885	-0.03	5156	0.985662	2.19
75	102	73.3	1	102	23497	0.4907	-0.02	5157	0.985854	2.19
74	103	73.3	1	103	23600	0.4928	-0.02	5158	0.986045	2.20
72– 73	108	73.6	2	216	23816	0.4973	-0.01	5160	0.986427	2.21
71	110	73.6	1	110	23926	0.4996	-0.00	5161	0.986618	2.21
70	112	73.7	1	112	24038	0.5020	0.00	5162	0.986809	2.22
69	114	73.8	1	114	24152	0.5044	0.01	5163	0.987001	2.23
68	115	73.8	1	115	24267	0.5068	0.02	5164	0.987192	2.23
67	116	73.9	1	116	24383	0.5092	0.02	5165	0.987383	2.24
66	117	73.9	1	117	24500	0.5116	0.03	5166	0.987574	2.24
64– 65	118	73.9	2	236	24736	0.5165	0.04	5168	0.987956	2.26
63	123	74.1	1	123	24859	0.5191	0.05	5169	0.988148	2.26
62	126	74.2	1	126	24985	0.5217	0.05	5170	0.988339	2.27
61	131	74.4	1	131	25116	0.5245	0.06	5171	0.988530	2.27
60	132	74.4	1	132	25248	0.5272	0.07	5172	0.988721	2.28
59	133	74.5	1	133	25381	0.5300	0.08	5173	0.988912	2.29
57– 58	137	74.6	2	274	25655	0.5357	0.09	5175	0.989295	2.30
56	139	74.6	1	139	25794	0.5386	0.10	5176	0.989486	2.31
55	144	74.8	1	144	25938	0.5417	0.10	5177	0.989677	2.31
54	145	74.8	1	145	26083	0.5447	0.11	5178	0.989868	2.32
53	146	74.9	1	146	26229	0.5477	0.12	5179	0.990059	2.33
52	149	74.9	1	149	26378	0.5508	0.13	5180	0.990250	2.34
51	150	75.0	1	150	26528	0.5540	0.14	5181	0.990442	2.34
50	152	75.0	1	152	26680	0.5571	0.14	5182	0.990633	2.35
49	156	75.1	1	156	26836	0.5604	0.15	5183	0.990824	2.36
47– 48	158	75.2	2	316	27152	0.5670	0.17	5185	0.991206	2.37
46	160	75.3	1	160	27312	0.5703	0.18	5186	0.991397	2.38
45	161	75.3	1	161	27473	0.5737	0.19	5187	0.991589	2.39
44	163	75.3	1	163	27636	0.5771	0.19	5188	0.991780	2.40
43	164	75.4	1	164	27800	0.5805	0.20	5189	0.991971	2.41
41– 42	168	75.5	2	336	28136	0.5875	0.22	5191	0.992353	2.43
40	170	75.5	1	170	28306	0.5911	0.23	5192	0.992544	2.43
38– 39	179	75.7	2	358	28664	0.5986	0.25	5194	0.992927	2.45
37	181	75.8	1	181	28845	0.6024	0.26	5195	0.993118	2.46
36	182	75.8	1	182	29027	0.6062	0.27	5196	0.993309	2.47
35	183	75.8	1	183	29210	0.6100	0.28	5197	0.993500	2.48
34	186	75.9	1	186	29396	0.6139	0.29	5198	0.993691	2.49
33	192	76.0	1	192	29588	0.6179	0.30	5199	0.993883	2.51
32	197	76.2	1	197	29785	0.6220	0.31	5200	0.994074	2.52
31	204	76.3	1	204	29989	0.6262	0.32	5201	0.994265	2.53
30	205	76.3	1	205	30194	0.6305	0.33	5202	0.994456	2.54
29	208	76.4	1	208	30402	0.6349	0.34	5203	0.994647	2.55
28	214	76.5	1	214	30616	0.6393	0.36	5204	0.994838	2.56
27	219	76.6	1	219	30835	0.6439	0.37	5205	0.995030	2.58
26	223	76.7	1	223	31058	0.6486	0.38	5206	0.995221	2.59
25	227	76.8	1	227	31285	0.6533	0.39	5207	0.995412	2.61
24	228	76.8	1	228	31513	0.6581	0.41	5208	0.995603	2.62
23	234	76.9	1	234	31747	0.6630	0.42	5209	0.995794	2.64
22	252	77.2	1	252	31999	0.6682	0.44	5210	0.995985	2.65
21	276	77.6	1	276	32275	0.6740	0.45	5211	0.996177	2.67
20	312	78.1	1	312	32587	0.6805	0.47	5212	0.996368	2.68
19	313	78.2	1	313	32900	0.6870	0.49	5213	0.996559	2.70
18	351	78.7	1	351	33251	0.6944	0.51	5214	0.996750	2.72
17	357	78.7	1	357	33608	0.7018	0.53	5215	0.996941	2.74
16	361	78.8	1	361	33969	0.7094	0.55	5216	0.997132	2.76
15	376	79.0	1	376	34345	0.7172	0.57	5217	0.997324	2.79
14	396	79.2	1	396	34741	0.7255	0.60	5218	0.997515	2.81
13	401	79.2	1	401	35142	0.7339	0.62	5219	0.997706	2.83
12	402	79.2	1	402	35544	0.7422	0.65	5220	0.997897	2.86
11	407	79.3	1	407	35951	0.7507	0.68	5221	0.998088	2.89
10	410	79.3	1	410	36361	0.7593	0.70	5222	0.998279	2.93
9	475	80.0	1	475	36836	0.7692	0.74	5223	0.998471	2.96
8	504	80.2	1	504	37340	0.7798	0.77	5224	0.998662	3.00
7	906	82.8	1	906	38246	0.7987	0.84	5225	0.998853	3.05
6	1036	83.4	1	1036	39282	0.8203	0.92	5226	0.999044	3.10
5	1112	83.7	1	1112	40394	0.8435	1.01	5227	0.999235	3.17
4	1259	84.2	1	1259	41653	0.8698	1.13	5228	0.999426	3.25
3	1422	84.7	1	1422	43075	0.8995	1.28	5229	0.999618	3.37
2	1749	85.6	1	1749	44824	0.9360	1.52	5230	0.999809	3.55
1	3063	88.1	1	3063	47887	1.0000	+INF.	5231	1.000000	+INF.

Rank	Occ. F	SFI	F	Tokens	Cum. Tokens	Cum. P Tokens	Y	Cum. Types	Cum. P Types	Z
4103– 7152	1	52.5	3050	3050	3050	0.0366	−1.79	3050	0.426454	−0.19
3000– 4102	2	54.8	1103	2206	5256	0.0630	−1.53	4153	0.580677	0.20
2419– 2999	3	56.2	581	1743	6999	0.0839	−1.38	4734	0.661913	0.42
2015– 2418	4	57.3	404	1616	8615	0.1033	−1.26	5138	0.718400	0.58
1756– 2014	5	58.2	259	1295	9910	0.1188	−1.18	5397	0.754614	0.69
1573– 1755	6	58.9	183	1098	11008	0.1320	−1.12	5580	0.780201	0.77
1409– 1572	7	59.5	164	1148	12156	0.1458	−1.05	5744	0.803132	0.85
1273– 1408	8	60.1	136	1088	13244	0.1588	−1.00	5880	0.822148	0.92
1173– 1272	9	60.6	100	900	14144	0.1696	−0.96	5980	0.836130	0.98
1051– 1172	10	61.0	122	1220	15364	0.1842	−0.90	6102	0.853188	1.05
977– 1050	11	61.4	74	814	16178	0.1940	−0.86	6176	0.863535	1.10
906– 976	12	61.8	71	852	17030	0.2042	−0.83	6247	0.873462	1.14
850– 905	13	62.1	56	728	17758	0.2130	−0.80	6303	0.881292	1.18
799– 849	14	62.4	51	714	18472	0.2215	−0.77	6354	0.888423	1.22
762– 798	15	62.7	37	555	19027	0.2282	−0.74	6391	0.893596	1.25
722– 761	16	63.0	40	640	19667	0.2359	−0.72	6431	0.899189	1.28
670– 721	17	63.2	52	884	20551	0.2465	−0.69	6483	0.906460	1.32
633– 669	18	63.5	37	666	21217	0.2544	−0.66	6520	0.911633	1.35
607– 632	19	63.7	26	494	21711	0.2604	−0.64	6546	0.915268	1.37
587– 606	20	63.9	20	400	22111	0.2652	−0.63	6566	0.918065	1.39
564– 586	21	64.1	23	483	22594	0.2710	−0.61	6589	0.921281	1.41
536– 563	22	64.3	28	616	23210	0.2783	−0.59	6617	0.925196	1.44
519– 535	23	64.5	17	391	23601	0.2830	−0.57	6634	0.927573	1.46
495– 518	24	64.7	24	576	24177	0.2899	−0.55	6658	0.930928	1.48
472– 494	25	64.9	23	575	24752	0.2968	−0.53	6681	0.934144	1.51
451– 471	26	65.0	21	546	25298	0.3034	−0.51	6702	0.937081	1.53
428– 450	27	65.2	23	621	25919	0.3108	−0.49	6725	0.940296	1.56
412– 427	28	65.3	16	448	26367	0.3162	−0.48	6741	0.942534	1.58
405– 411	29	65.5	7	203	26570	0.3186	−0.47	6748	0.943512	1.58
389– 404	30	65.6	16	480	27050	0.3244	−0.46	6764	0.945749	1.60
371– 388	31	65.8	18	558	27608	0.3311	−0.44	6782	0.948266	1.63
361– 370	32	65.9	10	320	27928	0.3349	−0.43	6792	0.949664	1.64
352– 360	33	66.0	9	297	28225	0.3385	−0.42	6801	0.950923	1.65
335– 351	34	66.2	17	578	28803	0.3454	−0.40	6818	0.953300	1.68
325– 334	35	66.3	10	350	29153	0.3496	−0.39	6828	0.954698	1.69
314– 324	36	66.4	11	396	29549	0.3544	−0.37	6839	0.956236	1.71
311– 313	37	66.5	3	111	29660	0.3557	−0.37	6842	0.956655	1.71
304– 310	38	66.6	7	266	29926	0.3589	−0.36	6849	0.957634	1.72
301– 303	39	66.8	3	117	30043	0.3603	−0.36	6852	0.958054	1.73
290– 300	40	66.9	11	440	30483	0.3656	−0.34	6863	0.959592	1.75
282– 289	41	67.0	8	328	30811	0.3695	−0.33	6871	0.960710	1.76
276– 281	42	67.1	6	252	31063	0.3725	−0.33	6877	0.961549	1.77
263– 275	43	67.2	13	559	31622	0.3792	−0.31	6890	0.963367	1.79
255– 262	44	67.3	8	352	31974	0.3834	−0.30	6898	0.964485	1.81
247– 254	45	67.4	8	360	32334	0.3878	−0.29	6906	0.965604	1.82
240– 246	46	67.5	7	322	32656	0.3916	−0.28	6913	0.966583	1.83
238– 239	47	67.6	2	94	32750	0.3927	−0.27	6915	0.966862	1.84
232– 237	48	67.6	6	288	33038	0.3962	−0.26	6921	0.967701	1.85
224– 231	49	67.7	8	392	33430	0.4009	−0.25	6929	0.968820	1.86
221– 223	50	67.8	3	150	33580	0.4027	−0.25	6932	0.969239	1.87
213– 220	51	67.9	8	408	33988	0.4076	−0.23	6940	0.970358	1.89
210– 212	52	68.0	3	156	34144	0.4095	−0.23	6943	0.970777	1.89
204– 209	53	68.1	6	318	34462	0.4133	−0.22	6949	0.971616	1.91
198– 203	54	68.2	6	324	34786	0.4172	−0.21	6955	0.972455	1.92
194– 197	55	68.2	4	220	35006	0.4198	−0.20	6959	0.973015	1.93
190– 193	56	68.3	4	224	35230	0.4225	−0.20	6963	0.973574	1.94
185– 189	57	68.4	5	285	35515	0.4259	−0.19	6968	0.974273	1.95
179– 184	58	68.5	6	348	35863	0.4301	−0.18	6974	0.975112	1.96
177– 178	59	68.5	2	118	35981	0.4315	−0.17	6976	0.975391	1.97
175– 176	60	68.6	2	120	36101	0.4329	−0.17	6978	0.975671	1.97
172– 174	61	68.7	3	183	36284	0.4351	−0.16	6981	0.976091	1.98
170– 171	62	68.7	2	124	36408	0.4366	−0.16	6983	0.976370	1.98
168– 169	63	68.8	2	126	36534	0.4381	−0.16	6985	0.976650	1.99
164– 167	64	68.9	4	256	36790	0.4412	−0.15	6989	0.977209	2.00
161– 163	65	69.0	3	195	36985	0.4435	−0.14	6992	0.977629	2.01
159– 160	66	69.0	2	132	37117	0.4451	−0.14	6994	0.977908	2.01
157– 158	67	69.1	2	134	37251	0.4467	−0.13	6996	0.978188	2.02
155– 156	68	69.1	2	136	37387	0.4484	−0.13	6998	0.978468	2.02
153– 154	69	69.2	2	138	37525	0.4500	−0.13	7000	0.978747	2.03
150– 152	70	69.3	3	210	37735	0.4525	−0.12	7003	0.979167	2.04
148– 149	71	69.3	2	142	37877	0.4542	−0.11	7005	0.979446	2.04
146– 147	72	69.4	2	144	38021	0.4560	−0.11	7007	0.979726	2.05
144– 145	73	69.5	2	146	38167	0.4577	−0.11	7009	0.980006	2.05
143	74	69.5	1	74	38241	0.4586	−0.10	7010	0.980145	2.06
139– 142	75	69.6	4	300	38541	0.4622	−0.09	7014	0.980705	2.07
138	76	69.6	1	76	38617	0.4631	−0.09	7015	0.980844	2.07
136– 137	77	69.7	2	154	38771	0.4650	−0.09	7017	0.981124	2.08
133– 135	78	69.7	3	234	39005	0.4678	−0.08	7020	0.981544	2.09
132	79	69.8	1	79	39084	0.4687	−0.08	7021	0.981683	2.09
130– 131	80	69.8	2	160	39244	0.4706	−0.07	7023	0.981963	2.10
128– 129	81	69.9	2	162	39406	0.4726	−0.07	7025	0.982243	2.10
127	83	70.0	1	83	39489	0.4736	−0.07	7026	0.982383	2.11
124– 126	84	70.1	3	252	39741	0.4766	−0.06	7029	0.982802	2.12
121– 123	85	70.1	3	255	39996	0.4796	−0.05	7032	0.983221	2.13
119– 120	86	70.2	2	172	40168	0.4817	−0.05	7034	0.983501	2.13
117– 118	87	70.2	2	174	40342	0.4838	−0.04	7036	0.983781	2.14
113– 116	88	70.3	4	352	40694	0.4880	−0.03	7040	0.984340	2.15
111– 112	90	70.4	2	180	40874	0.4902	−0.02	7042	0.984620	2.16

Rank	Occ. F	SFI	F	Tokens	Cum. Tokens	Cum. P Tokens	Y	Cum. Types	Cum. P Types	Z
108– 110	91	70.4	3	273	41147	0.4934	−0.02	7045	0.985039	2.17
107	92	70.5	1	92	41239	0.4945	−0.01	7046	0.985179	2.17
105– 106	93	70.5	2	186	41425	0.4968	−0.01	7048	0.985459	2.18
102– 104	94	70.5	3	282	41707	0.5002	0.00	7051	0.985878	2.19
100– 101	95	70.6	2	190	41897	0.5024	0.01	7053	0.986158	2.20
96– 99	96	70.6	4	384	42281	0.5070	0.02	7057	0.986717	2.22
91– 95	97	70.7	5	485	42766	0.5129	0.03	7062	0.987416	2.24
89– 90	99	70.8	2	198	42964	0.5152	0.04	7064	0.987696	2.25
87– 88	102	70.9	2	204	43168	0.5177	0.04	7066	0.987975	2.26
86	105	71.0	1	105	43273	0.5189	0.05	7067	0.988115	2.26
85	107	71.1	1	107	43380	0.5202	0.05	7068	0.988255	2.27
83– 84	108	71.1	2	216	43596	0.5228	0.06	7070	0.988535	2.27
82	109	71.2	1	109	43705	0.5241	0.06	7071	0.988674	2.28
81	112	71.3	1	112	43817	0.5255	0.06	7072	0.988814	2.28
80	113	71.3	1	113	43930	0.5268	0.07	7073	0.988954	2.29
79	114	71.4	1	114	44044	0.5282	0.07	7074	0.989094	2.29
78	115	71.4	1	115	44159	0.5296	0.07	7075	0.989234	2.30
77	117	71.5	1	117	44276	0.5310	0.08	7076	0.989374	2.30
76	118	71.5	1	118	44394	0.5324	0.08	7077	0.989513	2.31
75	120	71.6	1	120	44514	0.5338	0.08	7078	0.989653	2.31
73– 74	123	71.7	2	246	44760	0.5368	0.09	7080	0.989933	2.32
71– 72	124	71.7	2	248	45008	0.5397	0.10	7082	0.990213	2.33
70	128	71.9	1	128	45136	0.5413	0.10	7083	0.990352	2.34
68– 69	130	71.9	2	260	45396	0.5444	0.11	7085	0.990632	2.35
67	131	72.0	1	131	45527	0.5460	0.12	7086	0.990772	2.36
66	132	72.0	1	132	45659	0.5476	0.12	7087	0.990912	2.36
65	133	72.0	1	133	45792	0.5492	0.12	7088	0.991051	2.37
64	134	72.1	1	134	45926	0.5508	0.13	7089	0.991191	2.37
63	136	72.1	1	136	46062	0.5524	0.13	7090	0.991331	2.38
62	137	72.2	1	137	46199	0.5540	0.14	7091	0.991471	2.39
60– 61	141	72.3	2	282	46481	0.5574	0.14	7093	0.991751	2.40
58– 59	142	72.3	2	284	46765	0.5608	0.15	7095	0.992030	2.41
56– 57	150	72.6	2	300	47065	0.5644	0.16	7097	0.992310	2.42
55	151	72.6	1	151	47216	0.5662	0.17	7098	0.992450	2.43
54	152	72.6	1	152	47368	0.5681	0.17	7099	0.992589	2.44
53	155	72.7	1	155	47523	0.5699	0.18	7100	0.992729	2.44
52	157	72.8	1	157	47680	0.5718	0.18	7101	0.992869	2.45
51	166	73.0	1	166	47846	0.5738	0.19	7102	0.993009	2.46
50	172	73.2	1	172	48018	0.5758	0.19	7103	0.993149	2.46
49	174	73.2	1	174	48192	0.5779	0.20	7104	0.993289	2.47
48	180	73.4	1	180	48372	0.5801	0.20	7105	0.993428	2.48
47	183	73.4	1	183	48555	0.5823	0.21	7106	0.993568	2.49
46	184	73.4	1	184	48739	0.5845	0.21	7107	0.993708	2.50
45	185	73.5	1	185	48924	0.5867	0.22	7108	0.993848	2.50
44	186	73.5	1	186	49110	0.5889	0.22	7109	0.993988	2.51
43	194	73.7	1	194	49304	0.5913	0.23	7110	0.994128	2.52
42	196	73.7	1	196	49500	0.5936	0.24	7111	0.994267	2.53
41	202	73.9	1	202	49702	0.5960	0.24	7112	0.994407	2.54
40	203	73.9	1	203	49905	0.5985	0.25	7113	0.994547	2.55
39	208	74.0	1	208	50113	0.6010	0.26	7114	0.994687	2.55
38	216	74.1	1	216	50329	0.6036	0.26	7115	0.994827	2.56
37	225	74.3	1	225	50554	0.6063	0.27	7116	0.994966	2.57
36	229	74.4	1	229	50783	0.6090	0.28	7117	0.995106	2.58
34– 35	231	74.4	2	462	51245	0.6145	0.29	7119	0.995386	2.60
33	235	74.5	1	235	51480	0.6174	0.30	7120	0.995526	2.61
32	272	75.1	1	272	51752	0.6206	0.31	7121	0.995665	2.62
31	277	75.2	1	277	52029	0.6239	0.32	7122	0.995805	2.64
30	286	75.4	1	286	52315	0.6274	0.32	7123	0.995945	2.65
29	290	75.4	1	290	52605	0.6309	0.33	7124	0.996085	2.66
28	314	75.8	1	314	52919	0.6346	0.34	7125	0.996225	2.67
27	327	75.9	1	327	53246	0.6385	0.35	7126	0.996365	2.68
26	342	76.1	1	342	53588	0.6426	0.37	7127	0.996504	2.70
25	356	76.3	1	356	53944	0.6469	0.38	7128	0.996644	2.71
24	358	76.3	1	358	54302	0.6512	0.39	7129	0.996784	2.72
23	372	76.5	1	372	54674	0.6557	0.40	7130	0.996924	2.74
22	374	76.5	1	374	55048	0.6602	0.41	7131	0.997064	2.75
21	411	76.9	1	411	55459	0.6651	0.43	7132	0.997204	2.77
20	430	77.1	1	430	55889	0.6702	0.44	7133	0.997343	2.79
19	488	77.7	1	488	56377	0.6761	0.46	7134	0.997483	2.80
18	596	78.5	1	596	56973	0.6832	0.48	7135	0.997623	2.82
17	629	78.8	1	629	57602	0.6908	0.50	7136	0.997763	2.84
16	632	78.8	1	632	58234	0.6984	0.52	7137	0.997903	2.86
15	673	79.1	1	673	58907	0.7064	0.54	7138	0.998042	2.88
14	717	79.3	1	717	59624	0.7150	0.57	7139	0.998182	2.91
13	839	80.0	1	839	60463	0.7251	0.60	7140	0.998322	2.93
12	964	80.6	1	964	61427	0.7366	0.63	7141	0.998462	2.96
11	984	80.7	1	984	62411	0.7484	0.67	7142	0.998602	2.99
10	1018	80.9	1	1018	63429	0.7607	0.71	7143	0.998742	3.02
9	1119	81.3	1	1119	64548	0.7741	0.75	7144	0.998881	3.06
8	1214	81.6	1	1214	65762	0.7886	0.80	7145	0.999021	3.10
7	1477	82.5	1	1477	67239	0.8063	0.86	7146	0.999161	3.14
6	1612	82.9	1	1612	68851	0.8257	0.94	7147	0.999301	3.19
5	2252	84.3	1	2252	71103	0.8527	1.05	7148	0.999441	3.26
4	2260	84.3	1	2260	73363	0.8798	1.17	7149	0.999581	3.34
3	2416	84.6	1	2416	75779	0.9088	1.33	7150	0.999720	3.45
2	2693	85.1	1	2693	78472	0.9411	1.56	7151	0.999860	3.63
1	4915	87.7	1	4915	83387	1.0000	+INF.	7152	1.000000	+INF.

Rank	Occ. F	SFI	F	Tokens	Cum. Tokens	Cum. P Tokens	Y	Cum. Types	Cum. P Types	Z
3460– 6272	1	53.6	2813	2813	2813	0.0430	−1.72	2813	0.448501	−0.13
2521– 3459	2	55.8	939	1878	4691	0.0718	−1.46	3752	0.598214	0.25
2000– 2520	3	57.3	521	1563	6254	0.0957	−1.31	4273	0.681282	0.47
1657– 1999	4	58.4	343	1372	7626	0.1167	−1.19	4616	0.735969	0.63
1421– 1656	5	59.2	236	1180	8806	0.1347	−1.10	4852	0.773597	0.75
1242– 1420	6	60.0	179	1074	9880	0.1511	−1.03	5031	0.802136	0.85
1111– 1241	7	60.6	131	917	10797	0.1652	−0.97	5162	0.823023	0.93
1007– 1110	8	61.1	104	832	11629	0.1779	−0.92	5266	0.839605	0.99
916– 1006	9	61.6	91	819	12448	0.1904	−0.88	5357	0.854114	1.05
839– 915	10	62.1	77	770	13218	0.2022	−0.83	5434	0.866390	1.11
780– 838	11	62.5	59	649	13867	0.2121	−0.80	5493	0.875797	1.15
718– 779	12	62.8	62	744	14611	0.2235	−0.76	5555	0.885682	1.20
673– 717	13	63.1	45	585	15196	0.2324	−0.73	5600	0.892857	1.24
633– 672	14	63.5	40	560	15756	0.2410	−0.70	5640	0.899235	1.28
591– 632	15	63.7	42	630	16386	0.2506	−0.67	5682	0.905931	1.32
556– 590	16	64.0	35	560	16946	0.2592	−0.65	5717	0.911511	1.35
524– 555	17	64.3	32	544	17490	0.2675	−0.62	5749	0.916614	1.38
501– 523	18	64.5	23	414	17904	0.2739	−0.60	5772	0.920281	1.41
473– 500	19	64.7	28	532	18436	0.2820	−0.58	5800	0.924745	1.44
448– 472	20	65.0	25	500	18936	0.2897	−0.55	5825	0.928731	1.47
433– 447	21	65.2	15	315	19251	0.2945	−0.54	5840	0.931122	1.48
418– 432	22	65.4	15	330	19581	0.2995	−0.53	5855	0.933514	1.50
397– 417	23	65.6	21	483	20064	0.3069	−0.50	5876	0.936862	1.53
377– 396	24	65.7	20	480	20544	0.3142	−0.48	5896	0.940051	1.56
359– 376	25	65.9	18	450	20994	0.3211	−0.46	5914	0.942921	1.58
344– 358	26	66.1	15	390	21384	0.3271	−0.45	5929	0.945313	1.60
330– 343	27	66.2	14	378	21762	0.3329	−0.43	5943	0.947545	1.62
315– 329	28	66.4	15	420	22182	0.3393	−0.41	5958	0.949936	1.64
308– 314	29	66.5	7	203	22385	0.3424	−0.41	5965	0.951052	1.66
296– 307	30	66.7	12	360	22745	0.3479	−0.39	5977	0.952966	1.67
285– 295	31	66.8	11	341	23086	0.3531	−0.38	5988	0.954719	1.69
275– 284	32	67.0	10	320	23406	0.3580	−0.36	5998	0.956314	1.71
262– 274	33	67.1	13	429	23835	0.3646	−0.35	6011	0.958386	1.73
255– 261	34	67.2	7	238	24073	0.3682	−0.34	6018	0.959503	1.74
251– 254	35	67.3	4	140	24213	0.3704	−0.33	6022	0.960140	1.75
244– 250	36	67.5	7	252	24465	0.3742	−0.32	6029	0.961256	1.77
236– 243	37	67.6	8	296	24761	0.3788	−0.31	6037	0.962532	1.78
229– 235	38	67.7	7	266	25027	0.3828	−0.30	6044	0.963648	1.79
225– 228	39	67.8	4	156	25183	0.3852	−0.29	6048	0.964286	1.80
218– 224	40	67.9	7	280	25463	0.3895	−0.28	6055	0.965402	1.82
210– 217	41	68.0	8	328	25791	0.3945	−0.27	6063	0.966677	1.83
205– 209	42	68.1	5	210	26001	0.3977	−0.26	6068	0.967474	1.84
201– 204	43	68.2	4	172	26173	0.4004	−0.25	6072	0.968112	1.85
198– 200	44	68.3	3	132	26305	0.4024	−0.25	6075	0.968591	1.86
194– 197	45	68.4	4	180	26485	0.4051	−0.24	6079	0.969228	1.87
185– 193	46	68.5	9	414	26899	0.4115	−0.22	6088	0.970663	1.89
178– 184	47	68.6	7	329	27228	0.4165	−0.21	6095	0.971779	1.91
175– 177	48	68.7	3	144	27372	0.4187	−0.21	6098	0.972258	1.92
172– 174	49	68.8	3	147	27519	0.4209	−0.20	6101	0.972736	1.92
165– 171	50	68.9	7	350	27869	0.4263	−0.19	6108	0.973852	1.94
163– 164	51	69.0	2	102	27971	0.4279	−0.18	6110	0.974171	1.95
159– 162	52	69.0	4	208	28179	0.4310	−0.17	6114	0.974809	1.96
151– 158	53	69.1	8	424	28603	0.4375	−0.16	6122	0.976084	1.98
146– 150	54	69.2	5	270	28873	0.4417	−0.15	6127	0.976881	1.99
142– 145	55	69.3	4	220	29093	0.4450	−0.14	6131	0.977519	2.01
140– 141	56	69.4	2	112	29205	0.4467	−0.13	6133	0.977838	2.01
136– 139	58	69.5	4	232	29437	0.4503	−0.12	6137	0.978476	2.02
134– 135	59	69.6	2	118	29555	0.4521	−0.12	6139	0.978795	2.03
133	60	69.7	1	60	29615	0.4530	−0.12	6140	0.978954	2.03
130– 132	62	69.8	3	186	29801	0.4558	−0.11	6143	0.979432	2.04
128– 129	63	69.9	2	126	29927	0.4578	−0.11	6145	0.979751	2.05
127	64	69.9	1	64	29991	0.4588	−0.10	6146	0.979911	2.05
124– 126	65	70.0	3	195	30186	0.4617	−0.10	6149	0.980389	2.06
121– 123	66	70.1	3	198	30384	0.4648	−0.09	6152	0.980867	2.07
119– 120	67	70.1	2	134	30518	0.4668	−0.08	6154	0.981186	2.08
115– 118	68	70.2	4	272	30790	0.4710	−0.07	6158	0.981824	2.09
111– 114	69	70.3	4	276	31066	0.4752	−0.06	6162	0.982462	2.11
108– 110	70	70.3	3	210	31276	0.4784	−0.05	6165	0.982940	2.12
107	71	70.4	1	71	31347	0.4795	−0.05	6166	0.983099	2.12
105– 106	73	70.5	2	146	31493	0.4817	−0.05	6168	0.983418	2.13
104	74	70.6	1	74	31567	0.4829	−0.04	6169	0.983578	2.13
103	75	70.6	1	75	31642	0.4840	−0.04	6170	0.983737	2.14
100– 102	76	70.7	3	228	31870	0.4875	−0.03	6173	0.984216	2.15
98– 99	77	70.7	2	154	32024	0.4899	−0.03	6175	0.984534	2.16
96– 97	78	70.8	2	156	32180	0.4922	−0.02	6177	0.984853	2.17
93– 95	79	70.8	3	237	32417	0.4959	−0.01	6180	0.985332	2.18
92	81	71.0	1	81	32498	0.4971	−0.01	6181	0.985491	2.18
90– 91	82	71.0	2	164	32662	0.4996	−0.00	6183	0.985810	2.19
87– 89	83	71.1	3	249	32911	0.5034	0.01	6186	0.986288	2.21
84– 86	84	71.1	3	252	33163	0.5073	0.02	6189	0.986767	2.22
82– 83	85	71.2	2	170	33333	0.5099	0.02	6191	0.987085	2.23
81	89	71.4	1	89	33422	0.5112	0.03	6192	0.987245	2.23
80	92	71.5	1	92	33514	0.5126	0.03	6193	0.987404	2.24
78– 79	95	71.6	2	190	33704	0.5155	0.04	6195	0.987723	2.25
77	97	71.7	1	97	33801	0.5170	0.04	6196	0.987883	2.25
76	98	71.8	1	98	33899	0.5185	0.05	6197	0.988042	2.26
74– 75	100	71.9	2	200	34099	0.5216	0.05	6199	0.988361	2.27
71– 73	101	71.9	3	303	34402	0.5262	0.07	6202	0.988839	2.28
70	102	72.0	1	102	34504	0.5278	0.07	6203	0.988999	2.29
68– 69	103	72.0	2	206	34710	0.5309	0.08	6205	0.989318	2.30
67	105	72.1	1	105	34815	0.5325	0.08	6206	0.989477	2.31
65– 66	106	72.1	2	212	35027	0.5358	0.09	6208	0.989796	2.32
62– 64	107	72.2	3	321	35348	0.5407	0.10	6211	0.990274	2.34
61	109	72.2	1	109	35457	0.5424	0.11	6212	0.990434	2.34
59– 60	110	72.3	2	220	35677	0.5457	0.11	6214	0.990753	2.36
58	111	72.3	1	111	35788	0.5474	0.12	6215	0.990912	2.36
56– 57	112	72.4	2	224	36012	0.5509	0.13	6217	0.991231	2.38
54– 55	114	72.4	2	228	36240	0.5543	0.14	6219	0.991550	2.39
53	115	72.5	1	115	36355	0.5561	0.14	6220	0.991709	2.40
52	117	72.5	1	117	36472	0.5579	0.15	6221	0.991869	2.40
51	127	72.9	1	127	36599	0.5598	0.15	6222	0.992028	2.41
50	137	73.2	1	137	36736	0.5619	0.16	6223	0.992188	2.42
49	142	73.4	1	142	36878	0.5641	0.16	6224	0.992347	2.43
48	143	73.4	1	143	37021	0.5663	0.17	6225	0.992506	2.43
47	144	73.4	1	144	37165	0.5685	0.17	6226	0.992666	2.44
46	145	73.5	1	145	37310	0.5707	0.18	6227	0.992825	2.45
45	147	73.5	1	147	37457	0.5730	0.18	6228	0.992985	2.46
44	149	73.6	1	149	37606	0.5752	0.19	6229	0.993144	2.46
43	150	73.6	1	150	37756	0.5775	0.20	6230	0.993304	2.47
42	152	73.7	1	152	37908	0.5799	0.20	6231	0.993463	2.48
40– 41	156	73.8	2	312	38220	0.5846	0.21	6233	0.993782	2.50
39	161	73.9	1	161	38381	0.5871	0.22	6234	0.993941	2.51
38	162	74.0	1	162	38543	0.5896	0.23	6235	0.994101	2.52
37	168	74.1	1	168	38711	0.5921	0.23	6236	0.994260	2.53
36	170	74.2	1	170	38881	0.5947	0.24	6237	0.994420	2.54
35	175	74.3	1	175	39056	0.5974	0.25	6238	0.994579	2.55
34	185	74.5	1	185	39241	0.6002	0.25	6239	0.994739	2.56
33	188	74.6	1	188	39429	0.6031	0.26	6240	0.994898	2.57
32	192	74.7	1	192	39621	0.6061	0.27	6241	0.995057	2.58
31	194	74.7	1	194	39815	0.6090	0.28	6242	0.995217	2.59
30	195	74.8	1	195	40010	0.6120	0.28	6243	0.995376	2.60
29	209	75.1	1	209	40219	0.6152	0.29	6244	0.995536	2.61
28	228	75.4	1	228	40447	0.6187	0.30	6245	0.995695	2.63
27	240	75.7	1	240	40687	0.6224	0.31	6246	0.995855	2.64
26	248	75.8	1	248	40935	0.6262	0.32	6247	0.996014	2.65
25	250	75.8	1	250	41185	0.6300	0.33	6248	0.996173	2.67
24	265	76.1	1	265	41450	0.6340	0.34	6249	0.996333	2.68
23	266	76.1	1	266	41716	0.6381	0.35	6250	0.996492	2.70
22	282	76.4	1	282	41998	0.6424	0.36	6251	0.996652	2.71
21	333	77.1	1	333	42331	0.6475	0.38	6252	0.996811	2.73
20	358	77.4	1	358	42689	0.6530	0.39	6253	0.996971	2.74
19	370	77.5	1	370	43059	0.6586	0.41	6254	0.997130	2.76
18	372	77.6	1	372	43431	0.6643	0.42	6255	0.997290	2.78
17	399	77.9	1	399	43830	0.6704	0.44	6256	0.997449	2.80
16	403	77.9	1	403	44233	0.6766	0.46	6257	0.997608	2.82
15	506	78.9	1	506	44739	0.6843	0.48	6258	0.997768	2.84
14	515	79.0	1	515	45254	0.6922	0.50	6259	0.997927	2.87
13	529	79.1	1	529	45783	0.7003	0.53	6260	0.998087	2.89
12	599	79.6	1	599	46382	0.7095	0.55	6261	0.998246	2.92
11	662	80.1	1	662	47044	0.7196	0.58	6262	0.998406	2.95
10	682	80.2	1	682	47726	0.7300	0.61	6263	0.998565	2.98
9	728	80.5	1	728	48454	0.7412	0.65	6264	0.998724	3.02
8	818	81.0	1	818	49272	0.7537	0.69	6265	0.998884	3.06
7	1364	83.2	1	1364	50636	0.7745	0.75	6266	0.999043	3.10
6	1530	83.7	1	1530	52166	0.7980	0.83	6267	0.999203	3.16
5	1646	84.0	1	1646	53812	0.8231	0.93	6268	0.999362	3.22
4	1762	84.3	1	1762	55574	0.8501	1.04	6269	0.999522	3.30
3	1973	84.8	1	1973	57547	0.8803	1.18	6270	0.999681	3.42
2	2148	85.2	1	2148	59695	0.9131	1.36	6271	0.999841	3.60
1	5680	89.4	1	5680	65375	1.0000	+INF.	6272	1.000000	+INF.

Rank	Occ. F	SFI	F	Tokens	Cum. Tokens	Cum. P Tokens	Y	Cum. Types	Cum. P Types	Z
4103- 7152	1	52.5	3050	3050	3050	0.0366	-1.79	3050	0.426454	-0.19
3000- 4102	2	54.8	1103	2206	5256	0.0630	-1.53	4153	0.580677	0.20
2419- 2999	3	56.2	581	1743	6999	0.0839	-1.38	4734	0.661913	0.42
2015- 2418	4	57.3	404	1616	8615	0.1033	-1.26	5138	0.718400	0.58
1756- 2014	5	58.2	259	1295	9910	0.1188	-1.18	5397	0.754614	0.69
1573- 1755	6	58.9	183	1098	11008	0.1320	-1.12	5580	0.780201	0.77
1409- 1572	7	59.5	164	1148	12156	0.1458	-1.05	5744	0.803132	0.85
1273- 1408	8	60.1	136	1088	13244	0.1588	-1.00	5880	0.822148	0.92
1173- 1272	9	60.6	100	900	14144	0.1696	-0.96	5980	0.836130	0.98
1051- 1172	10	61.0	122	1220	15364	0.1842	-0.90	6102	0.853188	1.05
977- 1050	11	61.4	74	814	16178	0.1940	-0.86	6176	0.863535	1.10
906- 976	12	61.8	71	852	17030	0.2042	-0.83	6247	0.873462	1.14
850- 905	13	62.1	56	728	17758	0.2130	-0.80	6303	0.881292	1.18
799- 849	14	62.4	51	714	18472	0.2215	-0.77	6354	0.888423	1.22
762- 798	15	62.7	37	555	19027	0.2282	-0.74	6391	0.893596	1.25
722- 761	16	63.0	40	640	19667	0.2359	-0.72	6431	0.899189	1.28
670- 721	17	63.2	52	884	20551	0.2465	-0.69	6483	0.906460	1.32
633- 669	18	63.5	37	666	21217	0.2544	-0.66	6520	0.911633	1.35
607- 632	19	63.7	26	494	21711	0.2604	-0.64	6546	0.915268	1.37
587- 606	20	63.9	20	400	22111	0.2652	-0.63	6566	0.918065	1.39
564- 586	21	64.1	23	483	22594	0.2710	-0.61	6589	0.921281	1.41
536- 563	22	64.3	28	616	23210	0.2783	-0.59	6617	0.925196	1.44
519- 535	23	64.5	17	391	23601	0.2830	-0.57	6634	0.927573	1.46
495- 518	24	64.7	24	576	24177	0.2899	-0.55	6658	0.930928	1.48
472- 494	25	64.9	23	575	24752	0.2968	-0.53	6681	0.934144	1.51
451- 471	26	65.0	21	546	25298	0.3034	-0.51	6702	0.937081	1.53
428- 450	27	65.2	23	621	25919	0.3108	-0.49	6725	0.940296	1.56
412- 427	28	65.3	16	448	26367	0.3162	-0.48	6741	0.942534	1.58
405- 411	29	65.5	7	203	26570	0.3186	-0.47	6748	0.943512	1.58
389- 404	30	65.6	16	480	27050	0.3244	-0.46	6764	0.945749	1.60
371- 388	31	65.8	18	558	27608	0.3311	-0.44	6782	0.948266	1.63
361- 370	32	65.9	10	320	27928	0.3349	-0.43	6792	0.949664	1.64
352- 360	33	66.0	9	297	28225	0.3385	-0.42	6801	0.950923	1.65
335- 351	34	66.2	17	578	28803	0.3454	-0.40	6818	0.953300	1.68
325- 334	35	66.3	10	350	29153	0.3496	-0.39	6828	0.954698	1.69
314- 324	36	66.4	11	396	29549	0.3544	-0.37	6839	0.956236	1.71
311- 313	37	66.5	3	111	29660	0.3557	-0.37	6842	0.956655	1.71
304- 310	38	66.6	7	266	29926	0.3589	-0.36	6849	0.957634	1.72
301- 303	39	66.8	3	117	30043	0.3603	-0.36	6852	0.958054	1.73
290- 300	40	66.9	11	440	30483	0.3656	-0.34	6863	0.959592	1.75
282- 289	41	67.0	8	328	30811	0.3695	-0.33	6871	0.960710	1.76
276- 281	42	67.1	6	252	31063	0.3725	-0.33	6877	0.961549	1.77
263- 275	43	67.2	13	559	31622	0.3792	-0.31	6890	0.963367	1.79
255- 262	44	67.3	8	352	31974	0.3834	-0.30	6898	0.964485	1.81
247- 254	45	67.4	8	360	32334	0.3878	-0.29	6906	0.965604	1.82
240- 246	46	67.5	7	322	32656	0.3916	-0.28	6913	0.966583	1.83
238- 239	47	67.6	2	94	32750	0.3927	-0.27	6915	0.966862	1.84
232- 237	48	67.6	6	288	33038	0.3962	-0.26	6921	0.967701	1.85
224- 231	49	67.7	8	392	33430	0.4009	-0.25	6929	0.968820	1.86
221- 223	50	67.8	3	150	33580	0.4027	-0.25	6932	0.969239	1.87
213- 220	51	67.9	8	408	33988	0.4076	-0.23	6940	0.970358	1.89
210- 212	52	68.0	3	156	34144	0.4095	-0.23	6943	0.970777	1.89
204- 209	53	68.1	6	318	34462	0.4133	-0.22	6949	0.971616	1.91
198- 203	54	68.2	6	324	34786	0.4172	-0.21	6955	0.972455	1.92
194- 197	55	68.2	4	220	35006	0.4198	-0.20	6959	0.973015	1.93
190- 193	56	68.3	4	224	35230	0.4225	-0.20	6963	0.973574	1.94
185- 189	57	68.4	5	285	35515	0.4259	-0.19	6968	0.974273	1.95
179- 184	58	68.5	6	348	35863	0.4301	-0.18	6974	0.975112	1.96
177- 178	59	68.5	2	118	35981	0.4315	-0.17	6976	0.975391	1.97
175- 176	60	68.6	2	120	36101	0.4329	-0.17	6978	0.975671	1.97
172- 174	61	68.7	3	183	36284	0.4351	-0.16	6981	0.976091	1.98
170- 171	62	68.7	2	124	36408	0.4366	-0.16	6983	0.976370	1.98
168- 169	63	68.8	2	126	36534	0.4381	-0.16	6985	0.976650	1.99
164- 167	64	68.9	4	256	36790	0.4412	-0.15	6989	0.977209	2.00
161- 163	65	69.0	3	195	36985	0.4435	-0.14	6992	0.977629	2.01
159- 160	66	69.0	2	132	37117	0.4451	-0.14	6994	0.977908	2.01
157- 158	67	69.1	2	134	37251	0.4467	-0.13	6996	0.978188	2.02
155- 156	68	69.1	2	136	37387	0.4484	-0.13	6998	0.978468	2.02
153- 154	69	69.2	2	138	37525	0.4500	-0.13	7000	0.978747	2.03
150- 152	70	69.3	3	210	37735	0.4525	-0.12	7003	0.979167	2.04
148- 149	71	69.3	2	142	37877	0.4542	-0.11	7005	0.979446	2.04
146- 147	72	69.4	2	144	38021	0.4560	-0.11	7007	0.979726	2.05
144- 145	73	69.5	2	146	38167	0.4577	-0.11	7009	0.980006	2.05
143	74	69.5	1	74	38241	0.4586	-0.10	7010	0.980145	2.06
139- 142	75	69.6	4	300	38541	0.4622	-0.09	7014	0.980705	2.07
138	76	69.6	1	76	38617	0.4631	-0.09	7015	0.980844	2.07
136- 137	77	69.7	2	154	38771	0.4650	-0.09	7017	0.981124	2.08
133- 135	78	69.7	3	234	39005	0.4678	-0.08	7020	0.981544	2.09
132	79	69.8	1	79	39084	0.4687	-0.08	7021	0.981683	2.09
130- 131	80	69.8	2	160	39244	0.4706	-0.07	7023	0.981963	2.10
128- 129	81	69.9	2	162	39406	0.4726	-0.07	7025	0.982243	2.10
127	83	70.0	1	83	39489	0.4736	-0.07	7026	0.982383	2.11
124- 126	84	70.1	3	252	39741	0.4766	-0.06	7029	0.982802	2.12
121- 123	85	70.1	3	255	39996	0.4796	-0.05	7032	0.983221	2.13
119- 120	86	70.2	2	172	40168	0.4817	-0.05	7034	0.983501	2.13
117- 118	87	70.2	2	174	40342	0.4838	-0.04	7036	0.983781	2.14
113- 116	88	70.3	4	352	40694	0.4880	-0.03	7040	0.984340	2.15
111- 112	90	70.4	2	180	40874	0.4902	-0.02	7042	0.984620	2.16
108- 110	91	70.4	3	273	41147	0.4934	-0.02	7045	0.985039	2.17
107	92	70.5	1	92	41239	0.4945	-0.01	7046	0.985179	2.17
105- 106	93	70.5	2	186	41425	0.4968	-0.01	7048	0.985459	2.18
102- 104	94	70.5	3	282	41707	0.5002	0.00	7051	0.985878	2.19
100- 101	95	70.6	2	190	41897	0.5024	0.01	7053	0.986158	2.20
96- 99	96	70.6	4	384	42281	0.5070	0.02	7057	0.986717	2.22
91- 95	97	70.7	5	485	42766	0.5129	0.03	7062	0.987416	2.24
89- 90	99	70.8	2	198	42964	0.5152	0.04	7064	0.987696	2.25
87- 88	102	70.9	2	204	43168	0.5177	0.04	7066	0.987975	2.26
86	105	71.0	1	105	43273	0.5189	0.05	7067	0.988115	2.26
85	107	71.1	1	107	43380	0.5202	0.05	7068	0.988255	2.27
83- 84	108	71.1	2	216	43596	0.5228	0.06	7070	0.988535	2.27
82	109	71.2	1	109	43705	0.5241	0.06	7071	0.988674	2.28
81	112	71.3	1	112	43817	0.5255	0.06	7072	0.988814	2.28
80	113	71.3	1	113	43930	0.5268	0.07	7073	0.988954	2.29
79	114	71.4	1	114	44044	0.5282	0.07	7074	0.989094	2.29
78	115	71.4	1	115	44159	0.5296	0.07	7075	0.989234	2.30
77	117	71.5	1	117	44276	0.5310	0.08	7076	0.989374	2.30
76	118	71.5	1	118	44394	0.5324	0.08	7077	0.989513	2.31
75	120	71.6	1	120	44514	0.5338	0.08	7078	0.989653	2.31
73- 74	123	71.7	2	246	44760	0.5368	0.09	7080	0.989933	2.32
71- 72	124	71.7	2	248	45008	0.5397	0.10	7082	0.990213	2.33
70	128	71.9	1	128	45136	0.5413	0.10	7083	0.990352	2.34
68- 69	130	71.9	2	260	45396	0.5444	0.11	7085	0.990632	2.35
67	131	72.0	1	131	45527	0.5460	0.12	7086	0.990772	2.36
66	132	72.0	1	132	45659	0.5476	0.12	7087	0.990912	2.36
65	133	72.0	1	133	45792	0.5492	0.12	7088	0.991051	2.37
64	134	72.1	1	134	45926	0.5508	0.13	7089	0.991191	2.37
63	136	72.1	1	136	46062	0.5524	0.13	7090	0.991331	2.38
62	137	72.2	1	137	46199	0.5540	0.14	7091	0.991471	2.39
60- 61	141	72.3	2	282	46481	0.5574	0.14	7093	0.991751	2.40
58- 59	142	72.3	2	284	46765	0.5608	0.15	7095	0.992030	2.41
56- 57	150	72.6	2	300	47065	0.5644	0.16	7097	0.992310	2.42
55	151	72.6	1	151	47216	0.5662	0.17	7098	0.992450	2.43
54	152	72.6	1	152	47368	0.5681	0.17	7099	0.992589	2.44
53	155	72.7	1	155	47523	0.5699	0.18	7100	0.992729	2.44
52	157	72.8	1	157	47680	0.5718	0.18	7101	0.992869	2.45
51	166	73.0	1	166	47846	0.5738	0.19	7102	0.993009	2.46
50	172	73.2	1	172	48018	0.5758	0.19	7103	0.993149	2.46
49	174	73.2	1	174	48192	0.5779	0.20	7104	0.993289	2.47
48	180	73.4	1	180	48372	0.5801	0.20	7105	0.993428	2.48
47	183	73.4	1	183	48555	0.5823	0.21	7106	0.993568	2.49
46	184	73.4	1	184	48739	0.5845	0.21	7107	0.993708	2.50
45	185	73.5	1	185	48924	0.5867	0.22	7108	0.993848	2.50
44	186	73.5	1	186	49110	0.5889	0.22	7109	0.993988	2.51
43	194	73.7	1	194	49304	0.5913	0.23	7110	0.994128	2.52
42	196	73.7	1	196	49500	0.5936	0.24	7111	0.994267	2.53
41	202	73.9	1	202	49702	0.5960	0.24	7112	0.994407	2.54
40	203	73.9	1	203	49905	0.5985	0.25	7113	0.994547	2.55
39	208	74.0	1	208	50113	0.6010	0.26	7114	0.994687	2.55
38	216	74.1	1	216	50329	0.6036	0.26	7115	0.994827	2.56
37	225	74.3	1	225	50554	0.6063	0.27	7116	0.994966	2.57
36	229	74.4	1	229	50783	0.6090	0.28	7117	0.995106	2.58
34- 35	231	74.4	2	462	51245	0.6145	0.29	7119	0.995386	2.60
33	235	74.5	1	235	51480	0.6174	0.30	7120	0.995526	2.61
32	272	75.1	1	272	51752	0.6206	0.31	7121	0.995665	2.62
31	277	75.2	1	277	52029	0.6239	0.32	7122	0.995805	2.64
30	286	75.4	1	286	52315	0.6274	0.32	7123	0.995945	2.65
29	290	75.4	1	290	52605	0.6309	0.33	7124	0.996085	2.66
28	314	75.8	1	314	52919	0.6346	0.34	7125	0.996225	2.67
27	327	75.9	1	327	53246	0.6385	0.35	7126	0.996365	2.68
26	342	76.1	1	342	53588	0.6426	0.37	7127	0.996504	2.70
25	356	76.3	1	356	53944	0.6469	0.38	7128	0.996644	2.71
24	358	76.3	1	358	54302	0.6512	0.39	7129	0.996784	2.72
23	372	76.5	1	372	54674	0.6557	0.40	7130	0.996924	2.74
22	374	76.5	1	374	55048	0.6602	0.41	7131	0.997064	2.75
21	411	76.9	1	411	55459	0.6651	0.43	7132	0.997204	2.77
20	430	77.1	1	430	55889	0.6702	0.44	7133	0.997343	2.79
19	488	77.7	1	488	56377	0.6761	0.46	7134	0.997483	2.80
18	596	78.5	1	596	56973	0.6832	0.48	7135	0.997623	2.82
17	629	78.8	1	629	57602	0.6908	0.50	7136	0.997763	2.84
16	632	78.8	1	632	58234	0.6984	0.52	7137	0.997903	2.86
15	673	79.1	1	673	58907	0.7064	0.54	7138	0.998042	2.88
14	717	79.3	1	717	59624	0.7150	0.57	7139	0.998182	2.91
13	839	80.0	1	839	60463	0.7251	0.60	7140	0.998322	2.93
12	964	80.6	1	964	61427	0.7366	0.63	7141	0.998462	2.96
11	984	80.7	1	984	62411	0.7484	0.67	7142	0.998602	2.99
10	1018	80.9	1	1018	63429	0.7607	0.71	7143	0.998742	3.02
9	1119	81.3	1	1119	64548	0.7741	0.75	7144	0.998881	3.06
8	1214	81.6	1	1214	65762	0.7886	0.80	7145	0.999021	3.10
7	1477	82.5	1	1477	67239	0.8063	0.86	7146	0.999161	3.14
6	1612	82.9	1	1612	68851	0.8257	0.94	7147	0.999301	3.19
5	2252	84.3	1	2252	71103	0.8527	1.05	7148	0.999441	3.26
4	2260	84.3	1	2260	73363	0.8798	1.17	7149	0.999581	3.34
3	2416	84.6	1	2416	75779	0.9088	1.33	7150	0.999720	3.45
2	2693	85.1	1	2693	78472	0.9411	1.56	7151	0.999860	3.63
1	4915	87.7	1	4915	83387	1.0000	+INF.	7152	1.000000	+INF.

Rank	Occ. F	SFI	F	Tokens	Cum. Tokens	Cum. P Tokens	Y	Cum. Types	Cum. P Types	Z
3460-6272	1	53.6	2813	2813	2813	0.0430	-1.72	2813	0.448501	-0.13
2521-3459	2	55.8	939	1878	4691	0.0718	-1.46	3752	0.598214	0.25
2000-2520	3	57.3	521	1563	6254	0.0957	-1.31	4273	0.681282	0.47
1657-1999	4	58.4	343	1372	7626	0.1167	-1.19	4616	0.735969	0.63
1421-1656	5	59.2	236	1180	8806	0.1347	-1.10	4852	0.773597	0.75
1242-1420	6	60.0	179	1074	9880	0.1511	-1.03	5031	0.802136	0.85
1111-1241	7	60.6	131	917	10797	0.1652	-0.97	5162	0.823023	0.93
1007-1110	8	61.1	104	832	11629	0.1779	-0.92	5266	0.839605	0.99
916-1006	9	61.6	91	819	12448	0.1904	-0.88	5357	0.854114	1.05
839-915	10	62.1	77	770	13218	0.2022	-0.83	5434	0.866390	1.11
780-838	11	62.5	59	649	13867	0.2121	-0.80	5493	0.875797	1.15
718-779	12	62.8	62	744	14611	0.2235	-0.76	5555	0.885682	1.20
673-717	13	63.1	45	585	15196	0.2324	-0.73	5600	0.892857	1.24
633-672	14	63.5	40	560	15756	0.2410	-0.70	5640	0.899235	1.28
591-632	15	63.7	42	630	16386	0.2506	-0.67	5682	0.905931	1.32
556-590	16	64.0	35	560	16946	0.2592	-0.65	5717	0.911511	1.35
524-555	17	64.3	32	544	17490	0.2675	-0.62	5749	0.916614	1.38
501-523	18	64.5	23	414	17904	0.2739	-0.60	5772	0.920281	1.41
473-500	19	64.7	28	532	18436	0.2820	-0.58	5800	0.924745	1.44
448-472	20	65.0	25	500	18936	0.2897	-0.55	5825	0.928731	1.47
433-447	21	65.2	15	315	19251	0.2945	-0.54	5840	0.931122	1.48
418-432	22	65.4	15	330	19581	0.2995	-0.53	5855	0.933514	1.50
397-417	23	65.6	21	483	20064	0.3069	-0.50	5876	0.936862	1.53
377-396	24	65.7	20	480	20544	0.3142	-0.48	5896	0.940051	1.56
359-376	25	65.9	18	450	20994	0.3211	-0.46	5914	0.942921	1.58
344-358	26	66.1	15	390	21384	0.3271	-0.45	5929	0.945313	1.60
330-343	27	66.2	14	378	21762	0.3329	-0.43	5943	0.947545	1.62
315-329	28	66.4	15	420	22182	0.3393	-0.41	5958	0.949936	1.64
308-314	29	66.5	7	203	22385	0.3424	-0.41	5965	0.951052	1.66
296-307	30	66.7	12	360	22745	0.3479	-0.39	5977	0.952966	1.67
285-295	31	66.8	11	341	23086	0.3531	-0.38	5988	0.954719	1.69
275-284	32	67.0	10	320	23406	0.3580	-0.36	5998	0.956314	1.71
262-274	33	67.1	13	429	23835	0.3646	-0.35	6011	0.958386	1.73
255-261	34	67.2	7	238	24073	0.3682	-0.34	6018	0.959503	1.74
251-254	35	67.3	4	140	24213	0.3704	-0.33	6022	0.960140	1.75
244-250	36	67.5	7	252	24465	0.3742	-0.32	6029	0.961256	1.77
236-243	37	67.6	8	296	24761	0.3788	-0.31	6037	0.962532	1.78
229-235	38	67.7	7	266	25027	0.3828	-0.30	6044	0.963648	1.79
225-228	39	67.8	4	156	25183	0.3852	-0.29	6048	0.964286	1.80
218-224	40	67.9	7	280	25463	0.3895	-0.28	6055	0.965402	1.82
210-217	41	68.0	8	328	25791	0.3945	-0.27	6063	0.966677	1.83
205-209	42	68.1	5	210	26001	0.3977	-0.26	6068	0.967474	1.84
201-204	43	68.2	4	172	26173	0.4004	-0.25	6072	0.968112	1.85
198-200	44	68.3	3	132	26305	0.4024	-0.25	6075	0.968591	1.86
194-197	45	68.4	4	180	26485	0.4051	-0.24	6079	0.969228	1.87
185-193	46	68.5	9	414	26899	0.4115	-0.22	6088	0.970663	1.89
178-184	47	68.6	7	329	27228	0.4165	-0.21	6095	0.971779	1.91
175-177	48	68.7	3	144	27372	0.4187	-0.21	6098	0.972258	1.92
172-174	49	68.8	3	147	27519	0.4209	-0.20	6101	0.972736	1.92
165-171	50	68.9	7	350	27869	0.4263	-0.19	6108	0.973852	1.94
163-164	51	69.0	2	102	27971	0.4279	-0.18	6110	0.974171	1.95
159-162	52	69.0	4	208	28179	0.4310	-0.17	6114	0.974809	1.96
151-158	53	69.1	8	424	28603	0.4375	-0.16	6122	0.976084	1.98
146-150	54	69.2	5	270	28873	0.4417	-0.15	6127	0.976881	1.99
142-145	55	69.3	4	220	29093	0.4450	-0.14	6131	0.977519	2.01
140-141	56	69.4	2	112	29205	0.4467	-0.13	6133	0.977838	2.01
136-139	58	69.5	4	232	29437	0.4503	-0.12	6137	0.978476	2.02
134-135	59	69.6	2	118	29555	0.4521	-0.12	6139	0.978795	2.03
133	60	69.7	1	60	29615	0.4530	-0.12	6140	0.978954	2.03
130-132	62	69.8	3	186	29801	0.4558	-0.11	6143	0.979432	2.04
128-129	63	69.9	2	126	29927	0.4578	-0.11	6145	0.979751	2.05
127	64	69.9	1	64	29991	0.4588	-0.10	6146	0.979911	2.05
124-126	65	70.0	3	195	30186	0.4617	-0.10	6149	0.980389	2.06
121-123	66	70.1	3	198	30384	0.4648	-0.09	6152	0.980867	2.07
119-120	67	70.1	2	134	30518	0.4668	-0.08	6154	0.981186	2.08
115-118	68	70.2	4	272	30790	0.4710	-0.07	6158	0.981824	2.09
111-114	69	70.3	4	276	31066	0.4752	-0.06	6162	0.982462	2.11
108-110	70	70.3	3	210	31276	0.4784	-0.05	6165	0.982940	2.12
107	71	70.4	1	71	31347	0.4795	-0.05	6166	0.983099	2.12
105-106	73	70.5	2	146	31493	0.4817	-0.05	6168	0.983418	2.13
104	74	70.6	1	74	31567	0.4829	-0.04	6169	0.983578	2.13
103	75	70.6	1	75	31642	0.4840	-0.04	6170	0.983737	2.14
100-102	76	70.7	3	228	31870	0.4875	-0.03	6173	0.984216	2.15
98-99	77	70.7	2	154	32024	0.4899	-0.03	6175	0.984534	2.16
96-97	78	70.8	2	156	32180	0.4922	-0.02	6177	0.984853	2.17
93-95	79	70.8	3	237	32417	0.4959	-0.01	6180	0.985332	2.18
92	81	71.0	1	81	32498	0.4971	-0.01	6181	0.985491	2.18
90-91	82	71.0	2	164	32662	0.4996	-0.00	6183	0.985810	2.19
87-89	83	71.1	3	249	32911	0.5034	0.01	6186	0.986288	2.21
84-86	84	71.1	3	252	33163	0.5073	0.02	6189	0.986767	2.22
82-83	85	71.2	2	170	33333	0.5099	0.02	6191	0.987085	2.23
81	89	71.4	1	89	33422	0.5112	0.03	6192	0.987245	2.23
80	92	71.5	1	92	33514	0.5126	0.03	6193	0.987404	2.24
78-79	95	71.6	2	190	33704	0.5155	0.04	6195	0.987723	2.25
77	97	71.7	1	97	33801	0.5170	0.04	6196	0.987883	2.25
76	98	71.8	1	98	33899	0.5185	0.05	6197	0.988042	2.26
74-75	100	71.9	2	200	34099	0.5216	0.05	6199	0.988361	2.27
71-73	101	71.9	3	303	34402	0.5262	0.07	6202	0.988839	2.28
70	102	72.0	1	102	34504	0.5278	0.07	6203	0.988999	2.29
68-69	103	72.0	2	206	34710	0.5309	0.08	6205	0.989318	2.30
67	105	72.1	1	105	34815	0.5325	0.08	6206	0.989477	2.31
65-66	106	72.1	2	212	35027	0.5358	0.09	6208	0.989796	2.32
62-64	107	72.2	3	321	35348	0.5407	0.10	6211	0.990274	2.34
61	109	72.2	1	109	35457	0.5424	0.11	6212	0.990434	2.34
59-60	110	72.3	2	220	35677	0.5457	0.11	6214	0.990753	2.36
58	111	72.3	1	111	35788	0.5474	0.12	6215	0.990912	2.36
56-57	112	72.4	2	224	36012	0.5509	0.13	6217	0.991231	2.38
54-55	114	72.4	2	228	36240	0.5543	0.14	6219	0.991550	2.39
53	115	72.5	1	115	36355	0.5561	0.14	6220	0.991709	2.40
52	117	72.5	1	117	36472	0.5579	0.15	6221	0.991869	2.40
51	127	72.9	1	127	36599	0.5598	0.15	6222	0.992028	2.41
50	137	73.2	1	137	36736	0.5619	0.16	6223	0.992188	2.42
49	142	73.4	1	142	36878	0.5641	0.16	6224	0.992347	2.43
48	143	73.4	1	143	37021	0.5663	0.17	6225	0.992506	2.43
47	144	73.4	1	144	37165	0.5685	0.17	6226	0.992666	2.44
46	145	73.5	1	145	37310	0.5707	0.18	6227	0.992825	2.45
45	147	73.5	1	147	37457	0.5730	0.18	6228	0.992985	2.46
44	149	73.6	1	149	37606	0.5752	0.19	6229	0.993144	2.46
43	150	73.6	1	150	37756	0.5775	0.20	6230	0.993304	2.47
42	152	73.7	1	152	37908	0.5799	0.20	6231	0.993463	2.48
40-41	156	73.8	2	312	38220	0.5846	0.21	6233	0.993782	2.50
39	161	73.9	1	161	38381	0.5871	0.22	6234	0.993941	2.51
38	162	74.0	1	162	38543	0.5896	0.23	6235	0.994101	2.52
37	168	74.1	1	168	38711	0.5921	0.23	6236	0.994260	2.53
36	170	74.2	1	170	38881	0.5947	0.24	6237	0.994420	2.54
35	175	74.3	1	175	39056	0.5974	0.25	6238	0.994579	2.55
34	185	74.5	1	185	39241	0.6002	0.25	6239	0.994739	2.56
33	188	74.6	1	188	39429	0.6031	0.26	6240	0.994898	2.57
32	192	74.7	1	192	39621	0.6061	0.27	6241	0.995057	2.58
31	194	74.7	1	194	39815	0.6090	0.28	6242	0.995217	2.59
30	195	74.8	1	195	40010	0.6120	0.28	6243	0.995376	2.60
29	209	75.1	1	209	40219	0.6152	0.29	6244	0.995536	2.61
28	228	75.4	1	228	40447	0.6187	0.30	6245	0.995695	2.63
27	240	75.7	1	240	40687	0.6224	0.31	6246	0.995855	2.64
26	248	75.8	1	248	40935	0.6262	0.32	6247	0.996014	2.65
25	250	75.8	1	250	41185	0.6300	0.33	6248	0.996173	2.67
24	265	76.1	1	265	41450	0.6340	0.34	6249	0.996333	2.68
23	266	76.1	1	266	41716	0.6381	0.35	6250	0.996492	2.70
22	282	76.4	1	282	41998	0.6424	0.36	6251	0.996652	2.71
21	333	77.1	1	333	42331	0.6475	0.38	6252	0.996811	2.73
20	358	77.4	1	358	42689	0.6530	0.39	6253	0.996971	2.74
19	370	77.5	1	370	43059	0.6586	0.41	6254	0.997130	2.76
18	372	77.6	1	372	43431	0.6643	0.42	6255	0.997290	2.78
17	399	77.9	1	399	43830	0.6704	0.44	6256	0.997449	2.80
16	403	77.9	1	403	44233	0.6766	0.46	6257	0.997608	2.82
15	506	78.9	1	506	44739	0.6843	0.48	6258	0.997768	2.84
14	515	79.0	1	515	45254	0.6922	0.50	6259	0.997927	2.87
13	529	79.1	1	529	45783	0.7003	0.53	6260	0.998087	2.89
12	599	79.6	1	599	46382	0.7095	0.55	6261	0.998246	2.92
11	662	80.1	1	662	47044	0.7196	0.58	6262	0.998406	2.95
10	682	80.2	1	682	47726	0.7300	0.61	6263	0.998565	2.98
9	728	80.5	1	728	48454	0.7412	0.65	6264	0.998724	3.02
8	818	81.0	1	818	49272	0.7537	0.69	6265	0.998884	3.06
7	1364	83.2	1	1364	50636	0.7745	0.75	6266	0.999043	3.10
6	1530	83.7	1	1530	52166	0.7980	0.83	6267	0.999203	3.16
5	1646	84.0	1	1646	53812	0.8231	0.93	6268	0.999362	3.22
4	1762	84.3	1	1762	55574	0.8501	1.04	6269	0.999522	3.30
3	1973	84.8	1	1973	57547	0.8803	1.18	6270	0.999681	3.42
2	2148	85.2	1	2148	59695	0.9131	1.36	6271	0.999841	3.60
1	5680	89.4	1	5680	65375	1.0000	+INF.	6272	1.000000	+INF.

Rank	Occ. F	SFI	F	Tokens	Cum. Tokens	Cum. P Tokens	Y	Cum. Types	Cum. P Types	Z
10139-18415	1	46.9	8277	8277	8277	0.0273	-1.92	8277	0.449471	-0.13
7319-10138	2	49.2	2820	5640	13917	0.0458	-1.69	11097	0.602607	0.26
5748-7318	3	50.6	1571	4713	18630	0.0614	-1.54	12668	0.687917	0.49
4800-5747	4	51.7	948	3792	22422	0.0739	-1.45	13616	0.739397	0.64
4116-4799	5	52.6	684	3420	25842	0.0851	-1.37	14300	0.776541	0.76
3599-4115	6	53.3	517	3102	28944	0.0953	-1.31	14817	0.804616	0.86
3188-3598	7	53.9	411	2877	31821	0.1048	-1.25	15228	0.826935	0.94
2913-3187	8	54.5	275	2200	34021	0.1121	-1.22	15503	0.841868	1.00
2665-2912	9	55.0	248	2232	36253	0.1194	-1.18	15751	0.855335	1.06
2463-2664	10	55.4	202	2020	38273	0.1261	-1.15	15953	0.866305	1.11
2282-2462	11	55.8	181	1991	40264	0.1326	-1.11	16134	0.876134	1.16
2149-2281	12	56.1	133	1596	41860	0.1379	-1.09	16267	0.883356	1.19
2015-2148	13	56.5	134	1742	43602	0.1436	-1.06	16401	0.890633	1.23
1877-2014	14	56.8	138	1932	45534	0.1500	-1.04	16539	0.898126	1.27
1770-1876	15	57.1	107	1605	47139	0.1553	-1.01	16646	0.903937	1.30
1676-1769	16	57.4	94	1504	48643	0.1602	-0.99	16740	0.909042	1.33
1609-1675	17	57.6	67	1139	49782	0.1640	-0.98	16807	0.912680	1.36
1531-1608	18	57.8	78	1404	51186	0.1686	-0.96	16885	0.916916	1.38
1475-1530	19	58.1	56	1064	52250	0.1721	-0.95	16941	0.919957	1.40
1427-1474	20	58.3	48	960	53210	0.1753	-0.93	16989	0.922563	1.42
1372-1426	21	58.5	55	1155	54365	0.1791	-0.92	17044	0.925550	1.44
1315-1371	22	58.7	57	1254	55619	0.1832	-0.90	17101	0.928645	1.47
1271-1314	23	58.9	44	1012	56631	0.1865	-0.89	17145	0.931034	1.48
1228-1270	24	59.1	43	1032	57663	0.1899	-0.88	17188	0.933370	1.50
1187-1227	25	59.2	41	1025	58688	0.1933	-0.87	17229	0.935596	1.52
1156-1186	26	59.4	31	806	59494	0.1960	-0.86	17260	0.937279	1.53
1120-1155	27	59.6	36	972	60466	0.1992	-0.84	17296	0.939234	1.55
1091-1119	28	59.7	29	812	61278	0.2018	-0.84	17325	0.940809	1.56
1049-1090	29	59.9	42	1218	62496	0.2058	-0.82	17367	0.943090	1.58
1020-1048	30	60.0	29	870	63366	0.2087	-0.81	17396	0.944665	1.60
986-1019	31	60.2	34	1054	64420	0.2122	-0.80	17430	0.946511	1.61
962-985	32	60.3	24	768	65188	0.2147	-0.79	17454	0.947814	1.62
939-961	33	60.4	23	759	65947	0.2172	-0.78	17477	0.949063	1.64
916-938	34	60.6	23	782	66729	0.2198	-0.77	17500	0.950312	1.65
892-915	35	60.7	24	840	67569	0.2226	-0.76	17524	0.951616	1.66
871-891	36	60.8	21	756	68325	0.2250	-0.76	17545	0.952756	1.67
863-870	37	60.9	8	296	68621	0.2260	-0.75	17553	0.953190	1.68
840-862	38	61.0	23	874	69495	0.2289	-0.74	17576	0.954439	1.69
828-839	39	61.0	12	468	69963	0.2304	-0.74	17588	0.955091	1.70
807-827	40	61.3	21	840	70803	0.2332	-0.73	17609	0.956231	1.71
787-806	41	61.4	20	820	71623	0.2359	-0.72	17629	0.957317	1.72
768-786	42	61.5	19	798	72421	0.2385	-0.71	17648	0.958349	1.73
750-767	43	61.6	18	774	73195	0.2411	-0.70	17666	0.959327	1.74
738-749	44	61.7	12	528	73723	0.2428	-0.70	17678	0.959978	1.75
726-737	45	61.8	12	540	74263	0.2446	-0.69	17690	0.960630	1.76
708-725	46	61.9	18	828	75091	0.2473	-0.68	17708	0.961607	1.77
700-707	47	61.9	8	376	75467	0.2486	-0.68	17716	0.962042	1.77
693-699	48	62.0	7	336	75803	0.2497	-0.68	17723	0.962422	1.78
676-692	49	62.1	17	833	76636	0.2524	-0.67	17740	0.963345	1.79
659-675	50	62.2	17	850	77486	0.2552	-0.66	17757	0.964268	1.80
646-658	51	62.3	13	663	78149	0.2574	-0.65	17770	0.964974	1.81
635-645	52	62.4	11	572	78721	0.2593	-0.65	17781	0.965572	1.82
630-634	53	62.5	5	265	78986	0.2602	-0.64	17786	0.965843	1.82
620-629	54	62.5	10	540	79526	0.2619	-0.64	17796	0.966386	1.83
607-619	55	62.6	13	715	80241	0.2643	-0.63	17809	0.967092	1.84
597-606	56	62.7	10	560	80801	0.2661	-0.62	17819	0.967635	1.85
579-596	57	62.8	18	1026	81827	0.2695	-0.61	17837	0.968612	1.86
572-578	58	62.8	7	406	82233	0.2709	-0.61	17844	0.968993	1.87
563-571	59	62.9	9	531	82764	0.2726	-0.60	17853	0.969481	1.87
557-562	60	63.0	6	360	83124	0.2738	-0.60	17859	0.969807	1.88
549-556	61	63.1	8	488	83612	0.2754	-0.60	17867	0.970242	1.88
545-548	62	63.1	4	248	83860	0.2762	-0.59	17871	0.970459	1.89
533-544	63	63.2	12	756	84616	0.2787	-0.59	17883	0.971110	1.90
527-532	64	63.3	6	384	85000	0.2800	-0.58	17889	0.971436	1.90
518-526	65	63.3	9	585	85585	0.2819	-0.58	17898	0.971925	1.91
509-517	66	63.4	9	594	86179	0.2839	-0.57	17907	0.972414	1.92
503-508	67	63.5	6	402	86581	0.2852	-0.57	17913	0.972740	1.92
497-502	68	63.5	6	408	86989	0.2865	-0.56	17919	0.973065	1.93
488-496	69	63.6	9	621	87610	0.2886	-0.56	17928	0.973554	1.94
478-487	70	63.7	10	700	88310	0.2909	-0.55	17938	0.974097	1.94
472-477	71	63.7	6	426	88736	0.2923	-0.55	17944	0.974423	1.95
468-471	72	63.8	4	288	89024	0.2932	-0.54	17948	0.974640	1.95
457-467	73	63.8	11	803	89827	0.2959	-0.54	17959	0.975238	1.96
454-456	74	63.9	3	222	90049	0.2966	-0.53	17962	0.975400	1.97
449-453	75	64.0	5	375	90424	0.2978	-0.53	17967	0.975672	1.97
443-448	76	64.0	6	456	90880	0.2993	-0.53	17973	0.975998	1.98
437-442	77	64.1	6	462	91342	0.3009	-0.52	17979	0.976324	1.98
430-436	78	64.1	7	546	91888	0.3027	-0.52	17986	0.976704	1.99
426-429	79	64.2	4	316	92204	0.3037	-0.51	17990	0.976921	1.99
421-425	80	64.2	5	400	92604	0.3050	-0.51	17995	0.977192	2.00
415-420	81	64.3	6	486	93090	0.3066	-0.51	18001	0.977518	2.00
410-414	82	64.3	5	410	93500	0.3080	-0.50	18006	0.977790	2.01
403-409	83	64.4	7	581	94081	0.3099	-0.50	18013	0.978170	2.02
397-402	84	64.4	6	504	94585	0.3115	-0.49	18019	0.978496	2.02
395-396	85	64.5	2	170	94755	0.3121	-0.49	18021	0.978604	2.03
392-394	86	64.5	3	258	95013	0.3130	-0.49	18024	0.978767	2.03
389-391	87	64.6	3	261	95274	0.3138	-0.49	18027	0.978930	2.03
387-388	88	64.6	2	176	95450	0.3144	-0.48	18029	0.979039	2.03
382-386	89	64.7	5	445	95895	0.3159	-0.48	18034	0.979310	2.04
379-381	90	64.7	3	270	96165	0.3167	-0.48	18037	0.979473	2.04
376-378	91	64.8	3	273	96438	0.3176	-0.47	18040	0.979636	2.05
375	92	64.8	1	92	96530	0.3179	-0.47	18041	0.979690	2.05
372-374	93	64.9	3	279	96809	0.3189	-0.47	18044	0.979853	2.05
367-371	94	64.9	5	470	97279	0.3204	-0.47	18049	0.980125	2.06
360-366	95	65.0	7	665	97944	0.3226	-0.46	18056	0.980505	2.06
357-359	96	65.0	3	288	98232	0.3236	-0.46	18059	0.980668	2.07
352-356	97	65.1	5	485	98717	0.3252	-0.45	18064	0.980939	2.07
349-351	98	65.1	3	294	99011	0.3261	-0.45	18067	0.981102	2.08
343-348	99	65.2	6	594	99605	0.3281	-0.45	18073	0.981428	2.08
341-342	100	65.2	2	200	99805	0.3287	-0.44	18075	0.981537	2.09
340	101	65.2	1	101	99906	0.3291	-0.44	18076	0.981591	2.09
333-339	102	65.3	7	714	100620	0.3314	-0.44	18083	0.981971	2.10
332	103	65.3	1	103	100723	0.3318	-0.44	18084	0.982026	2.10
328-331	104	65.4	4	416	101139	0.3331	-0.43	18088	0.982243	2.10
325-327	105	65.4	3	315	101454	0.3342	-0.43	18091	0.982406	2.11
322-324	106	65.5	3	318	101772	0.3352	-0.43	18094	0.982569	2.11
321	107	65.5	1	107	101879	0.3356	-0.42	18095	0.982623	2.11
319-320	108	65.5	2	216	102095	0.3363	-0.42	18097	0.982731	2.11
315-318	109	65.6	4	436	102531	0.3377	-0.42	18101	0.982949	2.12
312-314	110	65.6	3	330	102861	0.3388	-0.42	18104	0.983112	2.12
310-311	111	65.6	2	222	103083	0.3395	-0.41	18106	0.983220	2.13
308-309	112	65.7	2	224	103307	0.3403	-0.41	18108	0.983329	2.13
305-307	113	65.7	3	339	103646	0.3414	-0.41	18111	0.983492	2.13
303-304	115	65.8	2	230	103876	0.3421	-0.41	18113	0.983600	2.13
299-302	116	65.8	4	464	104340	0.3437	-0.40	18117	0.983818	2.14
296-298	117	65.9	3	351	104691	0.3448	-0.40	18120	0.983980	2.14
292-295	118	65.9	4	472	105163	0.3464	-0.40	18124	0.984198	2.15
288-291	120	66.0	4	480	105643	0.3480	-0.39	18128	0.984415	2.15
287	122	66.1	1	122	105765	0.3484	-0.39	18129	0.984469	2.16
285-286	123	66.1	2	246	106011	0.3492	-0.39	18131	0.984578	2.16
283-284	124	66.1	2	248	106259	0.3500	-0.39	18133	0.984686	2.16
275-282	125	66.2	8	1000	107259	0.3533	-0.38	18141	0.985121	2.17
274	127	66.2	1	127	107386	0.3537	-0.38	18142	0.985175	2.17
270-273	128	66.3	4	512	107898	0.3554	-0.37	18146	0.985392	2.18
269	130	66.3	1	130	108028	0.3558	-0.37	18147	0.985447	2.18
267-268	131	66.4	2	262	108290	0.3567	-0.37	18149	0.985555	2.18
266	132	66.4	1	132	108422	0.3571	-0.37	18150	0.985610	2.19
264-265	133	66.4	2	266	108688	0.3580	-0.36	18152	0.985718	2.19
262-263	134	66.5	2	268	108956	0.3589	-0.36	18154	0.985827	2.19
261	135	66.5	1	135	109091	0.3593	-0.36	18155	0.985881	2.19
258-260	136	66.5	3	408	109499	0.3607	-0.36	18158	0.986044	2.20
257	137	66.6	1	137	109636	0.3611	-0.36	18159	0.986098	2.20
256	138	66.6	1	138	109774	0.3616	-0.35	18160	0.986153	2.20
255	139	66.6	1	139	109913	0.3620	-0.35	18161	0.986207	2.20
253-254	140	66.7	2	280	110193	0.3630	-0.35	18163	0.986315	2.21
252	141	66.7	1	141	110334	0.3634	-0.35	18164	0.986370	2.21
251	142	66.7	1	142	110476	0.3639	-0.35	18165	0.986424	2.21
249-250	143	66.7	2	286	110762	0.3648	-0.35	18167	0.986533	2.21
246-248	144	66.8	3	432	111194	0.3662	-0.34	18170	0.986696	2.22
244-245	145	66.8	2	290	111484	0.3672	-0.34	18172	0.986804	2.22
242-243	146	66.8	2	292	111776	0.3682	-0.34	18174	0.986913	2.22
241	147	66.9	1	147	111923	0.3686	-0.34	18175	0.986967	2.23
239-240	148	66.9	2	296	112219	0.3696	-0.33	18177	0.987076	2.23
238	150	67.0	1	150	112369	0.3701	-0.33	18178	0.987130	2.23
237	152	67.0	1	152	112521	0.3706	-0.33	18179	0.987184	2.23
234-236	153	67.0	3	459	112980	0.3721	-0.33	18182	0.987347	2.24
233	156	67.1	1	156	113136	0.3726	-0.32	18183	0.987402	2.24
231-232	158	67.2	2	316	113452	0.3737	-0.32	18185	0.987510	2.24
230	159	67.2	1	159	113611	0.3742	-0.32	18186	0.987564	2.24
228-229	161	67.3	2	322	113933	0.3753	-0.32	18188	0.987673	2.25
226-227	162	67.3	2	324	114257	0.3763	-0.32	18190	0.987782	2.25
225	163	67.3	1	163	114420	0.3769	-0.31	18191	0.987836	2.25
224	164	67.3	1	164	114584	0.3774	-0.31	18192	0.987890	2.25
223	165	67.4	1	165	114749	0.3780	-0.31	18193	0.987945	2.26
220-222	168	67.4	3	504	115253	0.3796	-0.31	18196	0.988108	2.26
217-219	169	67.5	3	507	115760	0.3813	-0.30	18199	0.988270	2.27
216	170	67.5	1	170	115930	0.3818	-0.30	18200	0.988325	2.27
214-215	171	67.5	2	342	116272	0.3830	-0.30	18202	0.988433	2.27
213	173	67.6	1	173	116445	0.3835	-0.30	18203	0.988488	2.27
212	174	67.6	1	174	116619	0.3841	-0.29	18204	0.988542	2.27
206-211	175	67.6	6	1050	117669	0.3876	-0.29	18210	0.988868	2.29
204-205	177	67.7	2	354	118023	0.3887	-0.28	18212	0.988976	2.29
203	180	67.7	1	180	118203	0.3893	-0.28	18213	0.989031	2.29
201-202	182	67.8	2	364	118567	0.3905	-0.28	18215	0.989139	2.30
198-200	183	67.8	3	549	119116	0.3923	-0.27	18218	0.989302	2.30
196-197	185	67.9	2	370	119486	0.3936	-0.27	18220	0.989411	2.30
194-195	187	67.9	2	374	119860	0.3948	-0.27	18222	0.989519	2.31
192-193	190	68.0	2	380	120240	0.3960	-0.26	18224	0.989628	2.31
191	192	68.0	1	192	120432	0.3967	-0.26	18225	0.989682	2.31
190	193	68.0	1	193	120625	0.3973	-0.26	18226	0.989737	2.32
189	194	68.1	1	194	120819	0.3980	-0.26	18227	0.989791	2.32
186-188	195	68.1	3	585	121404	0.3999	-0.25	18230	0.989954	2.32
184-185	196	68.1	2	392	121796	0.4012	-0.25	18232	0.990062	2.33
183	197	68.1	1	197	121993	0.4018	-0.25	18233	0.990117	2.33
181-182	198	68.2	2	396	122389	0.4031	-0.25	18235	0.990225	2.33
180	199	68.2	1	199	122588	0.4038	-0.24	18236	0.990280	2.34
179	200	68.2	1	200	122788	0.4044	-0.24	18237	0.990334	2.34
178	201	68.2	1	201	122989	0.4051	-0.24	18238	0.990388	2.34
177	203	68.3	1	203	123192	0.4058	-0.24	18239	0.990443	2.34
175-176	206	68.3	2	412	123604	0.4071	-0.23	18241	0.990551	2.35
174	208	68.4	1	208	123812	0.4078	-0.23	18242	0.990605	2.35
173	209	68.4	1	209	124021	0.4085	-0.23	18243	0.990660	2.35
172	212	68.5	1	212	124233	0.4092	-0.23	18244	0.990714	2.35
171	216	68.5	1	216	124449	0.4099	-0.23	18245	0.990768	2.36
170	217	68.6	1	217	124666	0.4106	-0.23	18246	0.990823	2.36
167-169	219	68.6	3	657	125323	0.4128	-0.22	18249	0.990986	2.37
166	221	68.6	1	221	125544	0.4135	-0.22	18250	0.991040	2.37
165	222	68.7	1	222	125766	0.4142	-0.22	18251	0.991094	2.37
164	223	68.7	1	223	125989	0.4150	-0.21	18252	0.991148	2.37
163	225	68.7	1	225	126214	0.4157	-0.21	18253	0.991203	2.37
162	226	68.7	1	226	126440	0.4165	-0.21	18254	0.991257	2.38
161	231	68.8	1	231	126671	0.4172	-0.21	18255	0.991311	2.38
160	232	68.8	1	232	126903	0.4180	-0.21	18256	0.991366	2.38
159	233	68.9	1	233	127136	0.4188	-0.21	18257	0.991420	2.38
158	235	68.9	1	235	127371	0.4195	-0.20	18258	0.991474	2.39
155-157	238	69.0	3	714	128085	0.4219	-0.20	18261	0.991637	2.39
153-154	240	69.0	2	480	128565	0.4235	-0.19	18263	0.991746	2.40
151-152	243	69.0	2	486	129051	0.4251	-0.19	18265	0.991854	2.40
150	244	69.1	1	244	129295	0.4259	-0.19	18266	0.991909	2.40
149	246	69.1	1	246	129541	0.4267	-0.18	18267	0.991963	2.41
148	247	69.1	1	247	129788	0.4275	-0.18	18268	0.992017	2.41
147	251	69.2	1	251	130039	0.4283	-0.18	18269	0.992072	2.41
146	253	69.2	1	253	130292	0.4292	-0.18	18270	0.992126	2.41
144-145	255	69.3	2	510	130802	0.4308	-0.17	18272	0.992235	2.42
143	256	69.3	1	256	131058	0.4317	-0.17	18273	0.992289	2.42
141-142	258	69.3	2	516	131574	0.4334	-0.17	18275	0.992397	2.43
140	260	69.3	1	260	131834	0.4342	-0.17	18276	0.992452	2.43
139	263	69.4	1	263	132097	0.4351	-0.16	18277	0.992506	2.43
138	265	69.4	1	265	132362	0.4360	-0.16	18278	0.992560	2.44
137	270	69.5	1	270	132632	0.4369	-0.16	18279	0.992615	2.44
136	272	69.5	1	272	132904	0.4378	-0.16	18280	0.992669	2.44
135	278	69.6	1	278	133182	0.4387	-0.15	18281	0.992723	2.44
134	286	69.7	1	286	133468	0.4396	-0.15	18282	0.992778	2.45
133	290	69.8	1	290	133758	0.4406	-0.15	18283	0.992832	2.45
131-132	293	69.9	2	586	134344	0.4425	-0.14	18285	0.992940	2.45
130	294	69.9	1	294	134638	0.4435	-0.14	18286	0.992995	2.46
129	296	69.9	1	296	134934	0.4444	-0.14	18287	0.993049	2.46
128	297	69.9	1	297	135231	0.4454	-0.14	18288	0.993103	2.46
127	299	69.9	1	299	135530	0.4464	-0.13	18289	0.993158	2.47
126	303	70.0	1	303	135833	0.4474	-0.13	18290	0.993212	2.47
124-125	306	70.0	2	612	136445	0.4494	-0.13	18292	0.993321	2.47
123	311	70.1	1	311	136756	0.4504	-0.12	18293	0.993375	2.48
122	313	70.1	1	313	137069	0.4515	-0.12	18294	0.993429	2.48
121	321	70.2	1	321	137390	0.4525	-0.12	18295	0.993484	2.48
120	322	70.3	1	322	137712	0.4536	-0.12	18296	0.993538	2.49
119	331	70.4	1	331	138043	0.4547	-0.11	18297	0.993592	2.49
118	340	70.5	1	340	138383	0.4558	-0.11	18298	0.993646	2.49
117	342	70.5	1	342	138725	0.4569	-0.11	18299	0.993701	2.49
116	343	70.5	1	343	139068	0.4581	-0.11	18300	0.993755	2.50
115	344	70.5	1	344	139412	0.4592	-0.10	18301	0.993809	2.50
114	346	70.6	1	346	139758	0.4603	-0.10	18302	0.993864	2.50
113	350	70.6	1	350	140108	0.4615	-0.10	18303	0.993918	2.51

Rank		Occ. F	SFI	F	Tokens	Cum. Tokens	Cum. P Tokens	Y	Cum. Types	Cum. P Types	Z
	112	358	70.7	1	358	140466	0.4627	−0.09	18304	0.993972	2.51
110–	111	360	70.7	2	720	141186	0.4650	−0.09	18306	0.994081	2.52
	109	365	70.8	1	365	141551	0.4662	−0.08	18307	0.994135	2.52
	108	371	70.9	1	371	141922	0.4675	−0.08	18308	0.994190	2.52
	107	373	70.9	1	373	142295	0.4687	−0.08	18309	0.994244	2.53
	106	378	71.0	1	378	142673	0.4699	−0.08	18310	0.994298	2.53
	105	384	71.0	1	384	143057	0.4712	−0.07	18311	0.994352	2.53
	104	388	71.1	1	388	143445	0.4725	−0.07	18312	0.994407	2.54
	103	389	71.1	1	389	143834	0.4738	−0.07	18313	0.994461	2.54
101–	102	394	71.1	2	788	144622	0.4764	−0.06	18315	0.994570	2.55
	100	398	71.2	1	398	145020	0.4777	−0.06	18316	0.994624	2.55
98–	99	401	71.2	2	802	145822	0.4803	−0.05	18318	0.994732	2.56
	97	403	71.2	1	403	146225	0.4816	−0.05	18319	0.994787	2.56
95–	96	410	71.3	2	820	147045	0.4843	−0.04	18321	0.994895	2.57
	94	414	71.4	1	414	147459	0.4857	−0.04	18322	0.994950	2.57
92–	93	424	71.5	2	848	148307	0.4885	−0.03	18324	0.995058	2.58
	91	430	71.5	1	430	148737	0.4899	−0.03	18325	0.995113	2.58
	90	433	71.5	1	433	149170	0.4913	−0.02	18326	0.995167	2.59
	89	435	71.6	1	435	149605	0.4928	−0.02	18327	0.995221	2.59
	88	438	71.6	1	438	150043	0.4942	−0.01	18328	0.995276	2.60
	87	439	71.6	1	439	150482	0.4957	−0.01	18329	0.995330	2.60
	86	440	71.6	1	440	150922	0.4971	−0.01	18330	0.995384	2.60
84–	85	453	71.7	2	906	151828	0.5001	0.00	18332	0.995493	2.61
	83	454	71.8	1	454	152282	0.5016	0.00	18333	0.995547	2.62
	82	457	71.8	1	457	152739	0.5031	0.01	18334	0.995601	2.62
	81	465	71.9	1	465	153204	0.5046	0.01	18335	0.995656	2.62
	80	480	72.0	1	480	153684	0.5062	0.02	18336	0.995710	2.63
78–	79	502	72.2	2	1004	154688	0.5095	0.02	18338	0.995819	2.64
	77	505	72.2	1	505	155193	0.5112	0.03	18339	0.995873	2.64
	76	508	72.2	1	508	155701	0.5128	0.03	18340	0.995927	2.65
	75	520	72.3	1	520	156221	0.5146	0.04	18341	0.995982	2.65
	74	521	72.3	1	521	156742	0.5163	0.04	18342	0.996036	2.66
	73	546	72.6	1	546	157288	0.5181	0.05	18343	0.996090	2.66
	72	547	72.6	1	547	157835	0.5199	0.05	18344	0.996144	2.66
	71	552	72.6	1	552	158387	0.5217	0.05	18345	0.996199	2.67
	70	560	72.7	1	560	158947	0.5235	0.06	18346	0.996253	2.67
	69	565	72.7	1	565	159512	0.5254	0.06	18347	0.996307	2.68
	68	572	72.8	1	572	160084	0.5273	0.07	18348	0.996362	2.68
	67	583	72.8	1	583	160667	0.5292	0.07	18349	0.996416	2.69
	66	589	72.9	1	589	161256	0.5311	0.08	18350	0.996470	2.69
	65	602	73.0	1	602	161858	0.5331	0.08	18351	0.996525	2.70
	64	603	73.0	1	603	162461	0.5351	0.09	18352	0.996579	2.70
	63	642	73.3	1	642	163103	0.5372	0.09	18353	0.996633	2.71
	62	643	73.3	1	643	163746	0.5393	0.10	18354	0.996687	2.72
	61	655	73.3	1	655	164401	0.5415	0.10	18355	0.996742	2.72
	60	672	73.5	1	672	165073	0.5437	0.11	18356	0.996796	2.73
	59	678	73.5	1	678	165751	0.5459	0.12	18357	0.996850	2.73
	58	701	73.6	1	701	166452	0.5483	0.12	18358	0.996905	2.74
	57	724	73.8	1	724	167176	0.5506	0.13	18359	0.996959	2.74
	56	732	73.8	1	732	167908	0.5531	0.13	18360	0.997013	2.75
	55	733	73.8	1	733	168641	0.5555	0.14	18361	0.997068	2.76
	54	734	73.8	1	734	169375	0.5579	0.15	18362	0.997122	2.76
	53	739	73.9	1	739	170114	0.5603	0.15	18363	0.997176	2.77
	52	776	74.1	1	776	170890	0.5629	0.16	18364	0.997230	2.77
	51	781	74.1	1	781	171671	0.5654	0.16	18365	0.997285	2.78
	50	793	74.2	1	793	172464	0.5681	0.17	18366	0.997339	2.79
	49	840	74.4	1	840	173304	0.5708	0.18	18367	0.997393	2.79
	48	843	74.4	1	843	174147	0.5736	0.19	18368	0.997448	2.80
	47	845	74.4	1	845	174992	0.5764	0.19	18369	0.997502	2.81
	46	883	74.6	1	883	175875	0.5793	0.20	18370	0.997556	2.81
	45	887	74.7	1	887	176762	0.5822	0.21	18371	0.997611	2.82
	44	908	74.8	1	908	177670	0.5852	0.22	18372	0.997665	2.83
	43	922	74.8	1	922	178592	0.5882	0.22	18373	0.997719	2.84
	42	954	75.0	1	954	179546	0.5914	0.23	18374	0.997774	2.84
	41	1010	75.2	1	1010	180556	0.5947	0.24	18375	0.997828	2.85
	40	1012	75.2	1	1012	181568	0.5980	0.25	18376	0.997882	2.86
	39	1027	75.3	1	1027	182595	0.6014	0.26	18377	0.997936	2.87
	38	1035	75.3	1	1035	183630	0.6048	0.27	18378	0.997991	2.88
	37	1038	75.3	1	1038	184668	0.6083	0.27	18379	0.998045	2.89
	36	1065	75.5	1	1065	185733	0.6118	0.28	18380	0.998099	2.89
	35	1072	75.5	1	1072	186805	0.6153	0.29	18381	0.998154	2.90
	34	1100	75.6	1	1100	187905	0.6189	0.30	18382	0.998208	2.91
	33	1111	75.6	1	1111	189016	0.6226	0.31	18383	0.998262	2.92
	32	1173	75.9	1	1173	190189	0.6264	0.32	18384	0.998317	2.93
	31	1236	76.1	1	1236	191425	0.6305	0.33	18385	0.998371	2.94
	30	1289	76.3	1	1289	192714	0.6348	0.34	18386	0.998425	2.95
	29	1322	76.4	1	1322	194036	0.6391	0.36	18387	0.998479	2.96
	28	1355	76.5	1	1355	195391	0.6436	0.37	18388	0.998534	2.97
	27	1440	76.8	1	1440	196831	0.6483	0.38	18389	0.998588	2.99
	26	1502	76.9	1	1502	198333	0.6533	0.39	18390	0.998642	3.00
	25	1645	77.3	1	1645	199978	0.6587	0.41	18391	0.998697	3.01
	24	1857	77.9	1	1857	201835	0.6648	0.43	18392	0.998751	3.02
	23	1860	77.9	1	1860	203695	0.6709	0.44	18393	0.998805	3.04
	22	1907	78.0	1	1907	205602	0.6772	0.46	18394	0.998860	3.05
	21	1925	78.0	1	1925	207527	0.6835	0.48	18395	0.998914	3.07
	20	1936	78.0	1	1936	209463	0.6899	0.50	18396	0.998968	3.08
	19	2144	78.5	1	2144	211607	0.6970	0.52	18397	0.999022	3.10
	18	2238	78.7	1	2238	213845	0.7044	0.54	18398	0.999077	3.11
	17	2289	78.8	1	2289	216134	0.7119	0.56	18399	0.999131	3.13
	16	2294	78.8	1	2294	218428	0.7195	0.58	18400	0.999185	3.15
	15	2434	79.0	1	2434	220862	0.7275	0.61	18401	0.999240	3.17
	14	2546	79.2	1	2546	223408	0.7359	0.63	18402	0.999294	3.19
	13	2661	79.4	1	2661	226069	0.7446	0.66	18403	0.999348	3.22
	12	3037	80.0	1	3037	229106	0.7546	0.69	18404	0.999403	3.24
	11	3514	80.6	1	3514	232620	0.7662	0.73	18405	0.999457	3.27
	10	3618	80.8	1	3618	236238	0.7781	0.77	18406	0.999511	3.30
	9	3656	80.8	1	3656	239894	0.7902	0.81	18407	0.999566	3.33
	8	4081	81.3	1	4081	243975	0.8036	0.85	18408	0.999620	3.37
	7	4533	81.7	1	4533	248508	0.8185	0.91	18409	0.999674	3.41
	6	5479	82.6	1	5479	253987	0.8366	0.98	18410	0.999728	3.46
	5	6021	83.0	1	6021	260008	0.8564	1.06	18411	0.999783	3.52
	4	6739	83.5	1	6739	266747	0.8786	1.17	18412	0.999837	3.59
	3	7829	84.1	1	7829	274576	0.9044	1.31	18413	0.999891	3.70
	2	10332	85.3	1	10332	284908	0.9384	1.54	18414	0.999946	3.87
	1	18695	87.9	1	18695	303603	1.0000	+INF.	18415	1.000000	+INF.

Rank	Occ. F	SFI	F	Tokens	Cum. Tokens	Cum. P Tokens	Y	Cum. Types	Cum. P Types	Z
13014-23737	1	46.0	10724	10724	10724	0.0286	-1.90	10724	0.451784	-0.12
9429-13013	2	48.2	3585	7170	17894	0.0477	-1.67	14309	0.602814	0.26
7452-9428	3	49.7	1977	5931	23825	0.0636	-1.53	16286	0.686102	0.48
6261-7451	4	50.8	1191	4764	28589	0.0763	-1.43	17477	0.736277	0.63
5385-6260	5	51.7	876	4380	32969	0.0879	-1.35	18353	0.773181	0.75
4741-5384	6	52.4	644	3864	36833	0.0983	-1.29	18997	0.800312	0.84
4270-4740	7	53.0	471	3297	40130	0.1070	-1.24	19468	0.820154	0.92
3876-4269	8	53.6	394	3152	43282	0.1155	-1.20	19862	0.836753	0.98
3532-3875	9	54.0	344	3096	46378	0.1237	-1.16	20206	0.851245	1.04
3268-3531	10	54.5	264	2640	49018	0.1308	-1.12	20470	0.862367	1.09
3057-3267	11	54.9	211	2321	51339	0.1369	-1.09	20681	0.871256	1.13
2849-3056	12	55.2	208	2496	53835	0.1436	-1.06	20889	0.880019	1.18
2670-2848	13	55.6	179	2327	56162	0.1498	-1.04	21068	0.887559	1.21
2520-2669	14	55.9	150	2100	58262	0.1554	-1.01	21218	0.893879	1.25
2392-2519	15	56.2	128	1920	60182	0.1605	-0.99	21346	0.899271	1.28
2267-2391	16	56.4	125	2000	62182	0.1659	-0.97	21471	0.904537	1.31
2164-2266	17	56.7	103	1751	63933	0.1705	-0.95	21574	0.908876	1.33
2048-2163	18	56.9	116	2088	66021	0.1761	-0.93	21690	0.913763	1.36
1954-2047	19	57.2	94	1786	67807	0.1809	-0.91	21784	0.917723	1.39
1863-1953	20	57.4	91	1820	69627	0.1857	-0.89	21875	0.921557	1.42
1783-1862	21	57.6	80	1680	71307	0.1902	-0.88	21955	0.924927	1.44
1701-1782	22	57.8	82	1804	73111	0.1950	-0.86	22037	0.928382	1.46
1645-1700	23	58.0	56	1288	74399	0.1985	-0.85	22093	0.930741	1.48
1582-1644	24	58.2	63	1512	75911	0.2025	-0.83	22156	0.933395	1.50
1531-1581	25	58.3	51	1275	77186	0.2059	-0.82	22207	0.935544	1.52
1475-1530	26	58.5	56	1456	78642	0.2098	-0.81	22263	0.937903	1.54
1424-1474	27	58.7	51	1377	80019	0.2134	-0.79	22314	0.940051	1.56
1381-1423	28	58.8	43	1204	81223	0.2167	-0.78	22357	0.941863	1.57
1344-1380	29	59.0	37	1073	82296	0.2195	-0.77	22394	0.943422	1.58
1308-1343	30	59.1	36	1080	83376	0.2224	-0.76	22430	0.944938	1.60
1269-1307	31	59.2	39	1209	84585	0.2256	-0.75	22469	0.946581	1.61
1232-1268	32	59.4	37	1184	85769	0.2288	-0.74	22506	0.948140	1.63
1201-1231	33	59.5	31	1023	86792	0.2315	-0.73	22537	0.949446	1.64
1173-1200	34	59.6	28	952	87744	0.2341	-0.73	22565	0.950626	1.65
1146-1172	35	59.8	27	945	88689	0.2366	-0.72	22592	0.951763	1.66
1128-1145	36	59.9	18	648	89337	0.2383	-0.71	22610	0.952521	1.67
1101-1127	37	60.0	27	999	90336	0.2410	-0.70	22637	0.953659	1.68
1073-1100	38	60.1	28	1064	91400	0.2438	-0.69	22665	0.954838	1.69
1055-1072	39	60.2	18	702	92102	0.2457	-0.69	22683	0.955597	1.70
1035-1054	40	60.3	20	800	92902	0.2478	-0.68	22703	0.956439	1.71
1008-1034	41	60.4	27	1107	94009	0.2508	-0.67	22730	0.957577	1.72
984-1007	42	60.5	24	1008	95017	0.2535	-0.66	22754	0.958588	1.73
965-983	43	60.6	19	817	95834	0.2556	-0.66	22773	0.959388	1.74
950-964	44	60.7	15	660	96494	0.2574	-0.65	22788	0.960020	1.75
933-949	45	60.8	17	765	97259	0.2594	-0.65	22805	0.960736	1.76
915-932	46	60.9	18	828	98087	0.2616	-0.64	22823	0.961495	1.77
895-914	47	61.0	20	940	99027	0.2642	-0.63	22843	0.962337	1.78
882-894	48	61.1	13	624	99651	0.2658	-0.63	22856	0.962885	1.79
861-881	49	61.2	21	1029	100680	0.2686	-0.62	22877	0.963770	1.80
842-860	50	61.3	19	950	101630	0.2711	-0.61	22896	0.964570	1.81
821-841	51	61.4	21	1071	102701	0.2740	-0.60	22917	0.965455	1.82
806-820	52	61.5	15	780	103481	0.2760	-0.59	22932	0.966087	1.83
782-805	53	61.5	24	1272	104753	0.2794	-0.58	22956	0.967098	1.84
768-781	54	61.6	14	756	105509	0.2814	-0.58	22970	0.967688	1.85
757-767	55	61.7	11	605	106114	0.2831	-0.57	22981	0.968151	1.85
748-756	56	61.8	9	504	106618	0.2844	-0.57	22990	0.968530	1.86
731-747	57	61.9	17	969	107587	0.2870	-0.56	23007	0.969246	1.87
719-730	58	61.9	12	696	108283	0.2888	-0.56	23019	0.969752	1.88
704-718	59	62.0	15	885	109168	0.2912	-0.55	23034	0.970384	1.89
693-703	60	62.1	11	660	109828	0.2930	-0.54	23045	0.970847	1.89
679-692	61	62.1	14	854	110682	0.2952	-0.54	23059	0.971437	1.90
671-678	62	62.2	8	496	111178	0.2966	-0.53	23067	0.971774	1.91
662-670	63	62.3	9	567	111745	0.2981	-0.53	23076	0.972153	1.91
653-661	64	62.4	9	576	112321	0.2996	-0.53	23085	0.972532	1.92
640-652	65	62.4	13	845	113166	0.3019	-0.52	23098	0.973080	1.93
631-639	66	62.5	9	594	113760	0.3035	-0.51	23107	0.973459	1.93
624-630	67	62.6	7	469	114229	0.3047	-0.51	23114	0.973754	1.94
615-623	68	62.6	9	612	114841	0.3063	-0.51	23123	0.974133	1.95
607-614	69	62.7	8	552	115393	0.3078	-0.50	23131	0.974470	1.95
596-606	70	62.7	11	770	116163	0.3099	-0.50	23142	0.974934	1.96
583-595	71	62.8	13	923	117086	0.3123	-0.49	23155	0.975481	1.97
570-582	72	62.9	13	936	118022	0.3148	-0.48	23168	0.976029	1.98
564-569	73	62.9	6	438	118460	0.3160	-0.48	23174	0.976282	1.98
556-563	74	63.0	8	592	119052	0.3176	-0.47	23182	0.976619	1.99
545-555	75	63.0	11	825	119877	0.3198	-0.47	23193	0.977082	2.00
528-544	76	63.1	17	1292	121169	0.3232	-0.46	23210	0.977798	2.01
520-527	77	63.2	8	616	121785	0.3249	-0.45	23218	0.978135	2.02
510-519	78	63.2	10	780	122565	0.3269	-0.45	23228	0.978557	2.02
504-509	79	63.3	6	474	123039	0.3282	-0.44	23234	0.978809	2.03
496-503	80	63.3	8	640	123679	0.3299	-0.44	23242	0.979146	2.04
493-495	81	63.4	3	243	123922	0.3306	-0.44	23245	0.979273	2.04
486-492	82	63.4	7	574	124496	0.3321	-0.43	23252	0.979568	2.04
482-485	83	63.5	4	332	124828	0.3330	-0.43	23256	0.979736	2.05
479-481	84	63.5	3	252	125080	0.3336	-0.43	23259	0.979863	2.05
471-478	85	63.6	8	680	125760	0.3355	-0.42	23267	0.980200	2.06
466-470	86	63.6	5	430	126190	0.3366	-0.42	23272	0.980410	2.06
459-465	87	63.7	7	609	126799	0.3382	-0.42	23279	0.980705	2.07
454-458	88	63.7	5	440	127239	0.3394	-0.41	23284	0.980916	2.07
449-453	89	63.8	5	445	127684	0.3406	-0.41	23289	0.981126	2.08
448	90	63.8	1	90	127774	0.3408	-0.41	23290	0.981169	2.08
447	91	63.9	1	91	127865	0.3411	-0.41	23291	0.981211	2.08
443-446	92	63.9	4	368	128233	0.3421	-0.41	23295	0.981379	2.08
436-442	93	64.0	7	651	128884	0.3438	-0.40	23302	0.981674	2.09
430-435	94	64.0	6	564	129448	0.3453	-0.40	23308	0.981927	2.10
425-429	95	64.1	5	475	129923	0.3466	-0.39	23313	0.982138	2.10
423-424	96	64.1	2	192	130115	0.3471	-0.39	23315	0.982222	2.10
419-422	97	64.2	4	388	130503	0.3481	-0.39	23319	0.982390	2.11
416-418	98	64.2	3	294	130797	0.3489	-0.39	23322	0.982517	2.11
410-415	99	64.2	6	594	131391	0.3505	-0.38	23328	0.982769	2.11
407-409	100	64.3	3	300	131691	0.3513	-0.38	23331	0.982896	2.12
406	101	64.3	1	101	131792	0.3516	-0.38	23332	0.982938	2.12
403-405	102	64.4	3	306	132098	0.3524	-0.38	23335	0.983064	2.12
397-402	103	64.4	6	618	132716	0.3540	-0.37	23341	0.983317	2.13
394-396	104	64.5	3	312	133028	0.3549	-0.37	23344	0.983444	2.13
388-393	105	64.5	6	630	133658	0.3565	-0.37	23350	0.983696	2.14
385-387	106	64.5	3	318	133976	0.3574	-0.37	23353	0.983823	2.14
383-384	107	64.6	2	214	134190	0.3579	-0.36	23355	0.983907	2.14
378-382	108	64.6	5	540	134730	0.3594	-0.36	23360	0.984118	2.15
375-377	109	64.7	3	327	135057	0.3603	-0.36	23363	0.984244	2.15
369-374	110	64.7	6	660	135717	0.3620	-0.35	23369	0.984497	2.16
363-368	111	64.7	6	666	136383	0.3638	-0.35	23375	0.984749	2.16
361-362	112	64.8	2	224	136607	0.3644	-0.35	23377	0.984834	2.17
359-360	113	64.8	2	226	136833	0.3650	-0.35	23379	0.984918	2.17
352-358	114	64.8	7	798	137631	0.3671	-0.34	23386	0.985213	2.18
348-351	115	64.9	4	460	138091	0.3684	-0.34	23390	0.985381	2.18
346-347	116	64.9	2	232	138323	0.3690	-0.33	23392	0.985466	2.18
343-345	117	65.0	3	351	138674	0.3699	-0.33	23395	0.985592	2.19
340-342	118	65.0	3	354	139028	0.3709	-0.33	23398	0.985718	2.19
337-339	119	65.0	3	357	139385	0.3718	-0.33	23401	0.985845	2.19
335-336	120	65.1	2	240	139625	0.3724	-0.33	23403	0.985929	2.20
332-334	122	65.1	3	366	139991	0.3734	-0.32	23406	0.986055	2.20
329-331	123	65.2	3	369	140360	0.3744	-0.32	23409	0.986182	2.20
327-328	125	65.2	2	250	140610	0.3751	-0.32	23411	0.986266	2.20
322-326	126	65.3	5	630	141240	0.3768	-0.31	23416	0.986477	2.21
318-321	127	65.3	4	508	141748	0.3781	-0.31	23420	0.986645	2.22
313-317	128	65.4	5	640	142388	0.3798	-0.31	23425	0.986856	2.22
311-312	130	65.4	2	260	142648	0.3805	-0.30	23427	0.986940	2.22
309-310	131	65.5	2	262	142910	0.3812	-0.30	23429	0.987024	2.23
305-308	132	65.5	4	528	143438	0.3826	-0.30	23433	0.987193	2.23
303-304	133	65.5	2	266	143704	0.3833	-0.30	23435	0.987277	2.23
302	134	65.5	1	134	143838	0.3837	-0.30	23436	0.987319	2.24
298-301	135	65.6	4	540	144378	0.3851	-0.29	23440	0.987488	2.24
295-297	136	65.6	3	408	144786	0.3862	-0.29	23443	0.987614	2.24
294	137	65.6	1	137	144923	0.3866	-0.29	23444	0.987656	2.25
291-293	138	65.7	3	414	145337	0.3877	-0.29	23447	0.987783	2.25
289-290	140	65.7	2	280	145617	0.3884	-0.28	23449	0.987867	2.25
286-288	142	65.8	3	426	146043	0.3896	-0.28	23452	0.987993	2.26
285	143	65.8	1	143	146186	0.3899	-0.28	23453	0.988036	2.26
280-284	144	65.9	5	720	146906	0.3919	-0.27	23458	0.988246	2.27
279	145	65.9	1	145	147051	0.3923	-0.27	23459	0.988288	2.27
278	146	65.9	1	146	147197	0.3926	-0.27	23460	0.988330	2.27
276-277	148	66.0	2	296	147493	0.3934	-0.27	23462	0.988415	2.27
273-275	149	66.0	3	447	147940	0.3946	-0.27	23465	0.988541	2.27
272	150	66.0	1	150	148090	0.3950	-0.27	23466	0.988583	2.28
270-271	151	66.1	2	302	148392	0.3958	-0.26	23468	0.988667	2.28
269	152	66.1	1	152	148544	0.3962	-0.26	23469	0.988710	2.28
267-268	154	66.2	2	308	148852	0.3971	-0.26	23471	0.988794	2.28
265-266	157	66.2	2	314	149166	0.3979	-0.26	23473	0.988878	2.29
263-264	158	66.3	2	316	149482	0.3987	-0.26	23475	0.988962	2.29
262	159	66.3	1	159	149641	0.3992	-0.26	23476	0.989004	2.29
259-261	160	66.3	3	480	150121	0.4004	-0.25	23479	0.989131	2.29
258	162	66.4	1	162	150283	0.4009	-0.25	23480	0.989173	2.30
257	164	66.4	1	164	150447	0.4013	-0.25	23481	0.989215	2.30
256	166	66.5	1	166	150613	0.4018	-0.25	23482	0.989257	2.30
254-255	167	66.5	2	334	150947	0.4026	-0.25	23484	0.989341	2.30
253	168	66.5	1	168	151115	0.4031	-0.25	23485	0.989384	2.30
252	169	66.6	1	169	151284	0.4035	-0.24	23486	0.989426	2.31
250-251	170	66.6	2	340	151624	0.4045	-0.24	23488	0.989510	2.31
249	171	66.6	1	171	151795	0.4049	-0.24	23489	0.989552	2.31
247-248	172	66.6	2	344	152139	0.4058	-0.24	23491	0.989636	2.31
246	173	66.7	1	173	152312	0.4063	-0.24	23492	0.989679	2.31
244-245	175	66.7	2	350	152662	0.4072	-0.23	23494	0.989763	2.32
243	176	66.7	1	176	152838	0.4077	-0.23	23495	0.989805	2.32
237-242	177	66.8	6	1062	153900	0.4105	-0.23	23501	0.990058	2.33
233-236	178	66.8	4	712	154612	0.4124	-0.22	23505	0.990226	2.33
232	181	66.8	1	181	154793	0.4129	-0.22	23506	0.990268	2.34
230-231	183	66.9	2	366	155159	0.4139	-0.22	23508	0.990353	2.34
229	186	67.0	1	186	155345	0.4144	-0.22	23509	0.990395	2.34
228	188	67.0	1	188	155533	0.4149	-0.22	23510	0.990437	2.34
226-227	190	67.1	2	380	155913	0.4159	-0.21	23512	0.990521	2.35
224-225	191	67.1	2	382	156295	0.4169	-0.21	23514	0.990605	2.35
222-223	192	67.1	2	384	156679	0.4179	-0.21	23516	0.990690	2.35
221	193	67.1	1	193	156872	0.4185	-0.21	23517	0.990732	2.35
220	195	67.2	1	195	157067	0.4190	-0.20	23518	0.990774	2.36
218-219	199	67.3	2	398	157465	0.4200	-0.20	23520	0.990858	2.36
217	200	67.3	1	200	157665	0.4206	-0.20	23521	0.990900	2.36
216	201	67.3	1	201	157866	0.4211	-0.20	23522	0.990942	2.36
215	202	67.3	1	202	158068	0.4216	-0.20	23523	0.990984	2.36
214	203	67.3	1	203	158271	0.4222	-0.20	23524	0.991027	2.37
212-213	204	67.4	2	408	158679	0.4233	-0.19	23526	0.991111	2.37
210-211	205	67.4	2	410	159089	0.4244	-0.19	23528	0.991195	2.37
208-209	206	67.4	2	412	159501	0.4255	-0.19	23530	0.991279	2.38
204-207	207	67.4	4	828	160329	0.4277	-0.18	23534	0.991448	2.38
203	210	67.5	1	210	160539	0.4282	-0.18	23535	0.991490	2.39
201-202	211	67.5	2	422	160961	0.4294	-0.18	23537	0.991574	2.39
199-200	212	67.5	2	424	161385	0.4305	-0.18	23539	0.991659	2.39
198	214	67.6	1	214	161599	0.4311	-0.17	23540	0.991701	2.40
197	215	67.6	1	215	161814	0.4316	-0.17	23541	0.991743	2.40
195-196	216	67.6	2	432	162246	0.4328	-0.17	23543	0.991827	2.40
192-194	217	67.6	3	651	162897	0.4345	-0.16	23546	0.991953	2.41
191	218	67.7	1	218	163115	0.4351	-0.16	23547	0.991996	2.41
190	220	67.7	1	220	163335	0.4357	-0.16	23548	0.992038	2.41
189	221	67.7	1	221	163556	0.4363	-0.16	23549	0.992080	2.41
187-188	222	67.7	2	444	164000	0.4375	-0.16	23551	0.992164	2.42
186	225	67.8	1	225	164225	0.4381	-0.16	23552	0.992206	2.42
184-185	226	67.8	2	452	164677	0.4393	-0.15	23554	0.992290	2.42
181-183	227	67.8	3	681	165358	0.4411	-0.15	23557	0.992417	2.43
178-180	228	67.8	3	684	166042	0.4429	-0.14	23560	0.992543	2.43
176-177	230	67.9	2	460	166502	0.4441	-0.14	23562	0.992628	2.44
175	233	67.9	1	233	166735	0.4448	-0.14	23563	0.992670	2.44
174	235	68.0	1	235	166970	0.4454	-0.14	23564	0.992712	2.44
173	237	68.0	1	237	167207	0.4460	-0.14	23565	0.992754	2.44
172	242	68.1	1	242	167449	0.4467	-0.13	23566	0.992796	2.45
170-171	244	68.1	2	488	167937	0.4480	-0.13	23568	0.992880	2.45
168-169	245	68.2	2	490	168427	0.4493	-0.13	23570	0.992965	2.46
167	247	68.2	1	247	168674	0.4499	-0.13	23571	0.993007	2.46
166	248	68.2	1	248	168922	0.4506	-0.12	23572	0.993049	2.46
165	249	68.2	1	249	169171	0.4513	-0.12	23573	0.993091	2.46
164	253	68.3	1	253	169424	0.4519	-0.12	23574	0.993133	2.46
161-163	255	68.3	3	765	170189	0.4540	-0.12	23577	0.993259	2.47
159-160	259	68.4	2	518	170707	0.4554	-0.11	23579	0.993344	2.48
157-158	261	68.4	2	522	171229	0.4568	-0.11	23581	0.993428	2.48
156	265	68.5	1	265	171494	0.4575	-0.11	23582	0.993470	2.48
154-155	268	68.6	2	536	172030	0.4589	-0.10	23584	0.993554	2.49
153	271	68.6	1	271	172301	0.4596	-0.10	23585	0.993596	2.49
152	274	68.6	1	274	172575	0.4603	-0.10	23586	0.993639	2.49
151	278	68.7	1	278	172853	0.4611	-0.10	23587	0.993681	2.49
150	281	68.8	1	281	173134	0.4618	-0.10	23588	0.993723	2.50
149	286	68.8	1	286	173420	0.4626	-0.09	23589	0.993765	2.50
147-148	290	68.9	2	580	174000	0.4641	-0.09	23591	0.993849	2.50
146	292	68.9	1	292	174292	0.4649	-0.09	23592	0.993891	2.51
145	298	69.0	1	298	174590	0.4657	-0.09	23593	0.993933	2.51
144	301	69.1	1	301	174891	0.4665	-0.08	23594	0.993976	2.51
142-143	303	69.1	2	606	175497	0.4681	-0.08	23596	0.994060	2.52
140-141	309	69.2	2	618	176115	0.4698	-0.08	23598	0.994144	2.52
139	310	69.2	1	310	176425	0.4706	-0.07	23599	0.994186	2.52
138	311	69.2	1	311	176736	0.4714	-0.07	23600	0.994228	2.53
137	317	69.3	1	317	177053	0.4723	-0.07	23601	0.994271	2.53
135-136	318	69.3	2	636	177689	0.4740	-0.07	23603	0.994355	2.53
134	320	69.3	1	320	178009	0.4748	-0.06	23604	0.994397	2.54
132-133	324	69.4	2	648	178657	0.4766	-0.06	23606	0.994481	2.54
131	326	69.4	1	326	178983	0.4774	-0.06	23607	0.994523	2.54

Rank		Occ. F	SFI	F	Tokens	Cum. Tokens	Cum. P Tokens	Y	Cum. Types	Cum. P Types	Z
128–	130	331	69.5	1	331	179314	0.4783	-0.05	23608	0.994565	2.55
	129	334	69.5	2	668	179982	0.4801	-0.05	23610	0.994650	2.55
	127	336	69.5	1	336	180318	0.4810	-0.05	23611	0.994692	2.56
	126	339	69.6	1	339	180657	0.4819	-0.05	23612	0.994734	2.56
	125	343	69.6	1	343	181000	0.4828	-0.04	23613	0.994776	2.56
	124	349	69.7	1	349	181349	0.4837	-0.04	23614	0.994818	2.56
	123	351	69.7	1	351	181700	0.4847	-0.04	23615	0.994860	2.57
	122	353	69.7	1	353	182053	0.4856	-0.04	23616	0.994902	2.57
	121	363	69.9	1	363	182416	0.4866	-0.03	23617	0.994945	2.57
	120	370	69.9	1	370	182786	0.4876	-0.03	23618	0.994987	2.57
	119	372	70.0	1	372	183158	0.4886	-0.03	23619	0.995029	2.58
	118	373	70.0	1	373	183531	0.4896	-0.03	23620	0.995071	2.58
	117	380	70.1	1	380	183911	0.4906	-0.02	23621	0.995113	2.58
	116	382	70.1	1	382	184293	0.4916	-0.02	23622	0.995155	2.59
	115	390	70.2	1	390	184683	0.4926	-0.02	23623	0.995197	2.59
113–	114	391	70.2	2	782	185465	0.4947	-0.01	23625	0.995282	2.60
	112	400	70.3	1	400	185865	0.4958	-0.01	23626	0.995324	2.60
	111	403	70.3	1	403	186268	0.4969	-0.01	23627	0.995366	2.60
	110	419	70.5	1	419	186687	0.4980	-0.01	23628	0.995408	2.61
	109	421	70.5	1	421	187108	0.4991	-0.00	23629	0.995450	2.61
	108	422	70.5	1	422	187530	0.5002	0.00	23630	0.995492	2.61
	107	426	70.6	1	426	187956	0.5014	0.01	23631	0.995534	2.61
	106	427	70.6	1	427	188383	0.5025	0.01	23632	0.995577	2.62
	105	429	70.6	1	429	188812	0.5037	0.01	23633	0.995619	2.62
	104	434	70.6	1	434	189246	0.5048	0.01	23634	0.995661	2.62
	103	436	70.7	1	436	189682	0.5060	0.01	23635	0.995703	2.63
	102	439	70.7	1	439	190121	0.5071	0.02	23636	0.995745	2.63
	101	452	70.8	1	452	190573	0.5084	0.02	23637	0.995787	2.63
	100	454	70.8	1	454	191027	0.5096	0.02	23638	0.995829	2.64
	99	460	70.9	1	460	191487	0.5108	0.03	23639	0.995871	2.64
97–	98	461	70.9	2	922	192409	0.5132	0.03	23641	0.995956	2.65
	96	463	70.9	1	463	192872	0.5145	0.04	23642	0.995998	2.65
	95	476	71.0	1	476	193348	0.5158	0.04	23643	0.996040	2.66
	94	481	71.1	1	481	193829	0.5170	0.04	23644	0.996082	2.66
	93	484	71.1	1	484	194313	0.5183	0.05	23645	0.996124	2.66
	92	487	71.1	1	487	194800	0.5196	0.05	23646	0.996166	2.67
	91	502	71.3	1	502	195302	0.5210	0.05	23647	0.996208	2.67
	90	512	71.4	1	512	195814	0.5223	0.06	23648	0.996251	2.67
	89	519	71.4	1	519	196333	0.5237	0.06	23649	0.996293	2.68
	88	520	71.4	1	520	196853	0.5251	0.06	23650	0.996335	2.68
	87	524	71.5	1	524	197377	0.5265	0.07	23651	0.996377	2.69
	86	537	71.6	1	537	197914	0.5279	0.07	23652	0.996419	2.69
	85	539	71.6	1	539	198453	0.5294	0.07	23653	0.996461	2.69
	84	543	71.6	1	543	198996	0.5308	0.08	23654	0.996503	2.70
	83	548	71.7	1	548	199544	0.5323	0.08	23655	0.996545	2.70
	82	562	71.8	1	562	200106	0.5338	0.08	23656	0.996588	2.71
	81	570	71.8	1	570	200676	0.5353	0.09	23657	0.996630	2.71
79–	80	579	71.9	2	1158	201834	0.5384	0.10	23659	0.996714	2.72
	78	582	71.9	1	582	202416	0.5399	0.10	23660	0.996756	2.72
	77	593	72.0	1	593	203009	0.5415	0.10	23661	0.996798	2.73
	76	599	72.0	1	599	203608	0.5431	0.11	23662	0.996840	2.73
	75	603	72.1	1	603	204211	0.5447	0.11	23663	0.996882	2.73
	74	604	72.1	1	604	204815	0.5463	0.12	23664	0.996925	2.74
72–	73	611	72.1	2	1222	206037	0.5496	0.12	23666	0.997009	2.75
	71	613	72.1	1	613	206650	0.5512	0.13	23667	0.997051	2.75
	70	628	72.2	1	628	207278	0.5529	0.13	23668	0.997093	2.76
	69	641	72.3	1	641	207919	0.5546	0.14	23669	0.997135	2.76
	68	643	72.3	1	643	208562	0.5563	0.14	23670	0.997177	2.77
	67	670	72.5	1	670	209232	0.5581	0.15	23671	0.997220	2.77
	66	671	72.5	1	671	209903	0.5599	0.15	23672	0.997262	2.78
	65	686	72.6	1	686	210589	0.5617	0.16	23673	0.997304	2.78
	64	692	72.7	1	692	211281	0.5636	0.16	23674	0.997346	2.79

Rank		Occ. F	SFI	F	Tokens	Cum. Tokens	Cum. P Tokens	Y	Cum. Types	Cum. P Types	Z
	63	723	72.9	1	723	212004	0.5655	0.16	23675	0.997388	2.79
	62	736	72.9	1	736	212740	0.5675	0.17	23676	0.997430	2.80
60–	61	740	73.0	2	1480	214220	0.5714	0.18	23678	0.997514	2.81
	59	770	73.1	1	770	214990	0.5735	0.19	23679	0.997557	2.81
	58	774	73.2	1	774	215764	0.5755	0.19	23680	0.997599	2.82
	57	775	73.2	1	775	216539	0.5776	0.20	23681	0.997641	2.83
	56	799	73.3	1	799	217338	0.5797	0.20	23682	0.997683	2.83
	55	810	73.3	1	810	218148	0.5819	0.21	23683	0.997725	2.84
	54	828	73.4	1	828	218976	0.5841	0.21	23684	0.997767	2.84
	53	841	73.5	1	841	219817	0.5864	0.22	23685	0.997809	2.85
	52	844	73.5	1	844	220661	0.5886	0.22	23686	0.997851	2.86
	51	846	73.5	1	846	221507	0.5909	0.23	23687	0.997894	2.86
	50	885	73.7	1	885	222392	0.5932	0.24	23688	0.997936	2.86
	49	887	73.7	1	887	223279	0.5956	0.24	23689	0.997978	2.87
	48	891	73.8	1	891	224170	0.5980	0.25	23690	0.998020	2.88
	47	893	73.8	1	893	225063	0.6004	0.25	23691	0.998062	2.89
	46	963	74.1	1	963	226026	0.6029	0.26	23692	0.998104	2.90
	45	1066	74.5	1	1066	227092	0.6058	0.27	23693	0.998146	2.90
	44	1105	74.7	1	1105	228197	0.6087	0.28	23694	0.998188	2.91
	43	1122	74.8	1	1122	229319	0.6117	0.28	23695	0.998231	2.92
	42	1137	74.8	1	1137	230456	0.6147	0.29	23696	0.998273	2.92
	41	1222	75.1	1	1222	231678	0.6180	0.30	23697	0.998315	2.93
	40	1231	75.2	1	1231	232909	0.6213	0.31	23698	0.998357	2.94
	39	1232	75.2	1	1232	234141	0.6246	0.32	23699	0.998399	2.95
	38	1249	75.2	1	1249	235390	0.6279	0.33	23700	0.998441	2.96
	37	1250	75.2	1	1250	236640	0.6312	0.34	23701	0.998483	2.96
	36	1349	75.6	1	1349	237989	0.6348	0.34	23702	0.998526	2.97
	35	1393	75.7	1	1393	239382	0.6385	0.35	23703	0.998568	2.98
	34	1410	75.8	1	1410	240792	0.6423	0.36	23704	0.998610	2.99
	33	1414	75.8	1	1414	242206	0.6461	0.37	23705	0.998652	3.00
	32	1428	75.8	1	1428	243634	0.6499	0.39	23706	0.998694	3.01
	31	1432	75.8	1	1432	245066	0.6537	0.40	23707	0.998736	3.02
	30	1437	75.8	1	1437	246503	0.6575	0.41	23708	0.998778	3.03
	29	1457	75.9	1	1457	247960	0.6614	0.42	23709	0.998820	3.04
	28	1532	76.1	1	1532	249492	0.6655	0.43	23710	0.998863	3.05
	27	1536	76.1	1	1536	251028	0.6696	0.44	23711	0.998905	3.06
	26	1573	76.2	1	1573	252601	0.6738	0.45	23712	0.998947	3.07
	25	1774	76.8	1	1774	254375	0.6785	0.46	23713	0.998989	3.09
	24	1830	76.9	1	1830	256205	0.6834	0.48	23714	0.999031	3.10
	23	1863	77.0	1	1863	258068	0.6884	0.49	23715	0.999073	3.11
	22	1909	77.1	1	1909	259977	0.6935	0.51	23716	0.999115	3.13
	21	1968	77.2	1	1968	261945	0.6987	0.52	23717	0.999157	3.14
	20	2008	77.3	1	2008	263963	0.7041	0.54	23718	0.999200	3.16
	19	2255	77.8	1	2255	266208	0.7101	0.55	23719	0.999242	3.17
	18	2289	77.9	1	2289	268497	0.7162	0.57	23720	0.999284	3.19
	17	2374	78.0	1	2374	270871	0.7225	0.59	23721	0.999326	3.21
	16	2647	78.5	1	2647	273518	0.7296	0.61	23722	0.999368	3.22
	15	2671	78.5	1	2671	276189	0.7367	0.63	23723	0.999410	3.24
	14	2800	78.7	1	2800	278989	0.7442	0.66	23724	0.999452	3.26
	13	2876	78.8	1	2876	281865	0.7519	0.68	23725	0.999494	3.29
	12	2946	79.0	1	2946	284811	0.7597	0.71	23726	0.999537	3.31
	11	3078	79.1	1	3078	287889	0.7679	0.73	23727	0.999579	3.34
	10	3149	79.2	1	3149	291038	0.7763	0.76	23728	0.999621	3.37
	9	3936	80.2	1	3936	294974	0.7868	0.80	23729	0.999663	3.40
	8	4276	80.6	1	4276	299250	0.7982	0.84	23730	0.999705	3.44
	7	4781	81.1	1	4781	304031	0.8110	0.88	23731	0.999747	3.48
	6	6344	82.3	1	6344	310375	0.8279	0.95	23732	0.999789	3.53
	5	8967	83.8	1	8967	319342	0.8518	1.04	23733	0.999831	3.58
	4	9793	84.2	1	9793	329135	0.8780	1.16	23734	0.999874	3.66
	3	9876	84.2	1	9876	339011	0.9043	1.31	23735	0.999916	3.76
	2	10699	84.6	1	10699	349710	0.9328	1.50	23736	0.999958	3.93
	1	25175	88.3	1	25175	374885	1.0000	+INF.	23737	1.000000	+INF.

Rank	Occ. F	SFI	F	Tokens	Cum. Tokens	Cum. P Tokens	Y	Cum. Types	Cum. P Types	Z
13252-25545	1	47.4	12294	12294	12294	0.0454	-1.69	12294	0.481268	-0.05
9316-13251	2	49.6	3936	7872	20166	0.0744	-1.44	16230	0.635349	0.35
7320- 9315	3	51.1	1996	5988	26154	0.0965	-1.30	18226	0.713486	0.56
6024- 7319	4	52.2	1296	5184	31338	0.1156	-1.20	19522	0.764220	0.72
5090- 6023	5	53.1	934	4670	36008	0.1329	-1.11	20456	0.800783	0.84
4528- 5089	6	53.8	562	3372	39380	0.1453	-1.06	21018	0.822783	0.93
4032- 4527	7	54.4	496	3472	42852	0.1581	-1.00	21514	0.842200	1.00
3603- 4031	8	55.0	429	3432	46284	0.1708	-0.95	21943	0.858994	1.08
3291- 3602	9	55.4	312	2808	49092	0.1811	-0.91	22255	0.871208	1.13
3005- 3290	10	55.9	286	2860	51952	0.1917	-0.87	22541	0.882404	1.19
2751- 3004	11	56.3	254	2794	54746	0.2020	-0.83	22795	0.892347	1.24
2549- 2750	12	56.6	202	2424	57170	0.2109	-0.80	22997	0.900254	1.28
2353- 2548	13	57.0	196	2548	59718	0.2203	-0.77	23193	0.907927	1.33
2170- 2352	14	57.3	183	2562	62280	0.2298	-0.74	23376	0.915091	1.37
2038- 2169	15	57.6	132	1980	64260	0.2371	-0.72	23508	0.920258	1.41
1910- 2037	16	57.8	128	2048	66308	0.2446	-0.69	23636	0.925269	1.44
1799- 1909	17	58.1	111	1887	68195	0.2516	-0.67	23747	0.929614	1.47
1692- 1798	18	58.3	107	1926	70121	0.2587	-0.65	23854	0.933803	1.50
1604- 1691	19	58.6	88	1672	71793	0.2649	-0.63	23942	0.937248	1.53
1529- 1603	20	58.8	75	1500	73293	0.2704	-0.61	24017	0.940184	1.56
1450- 1528	21	59.0	79	1659	74952	0.2765	-0.59	24096	0.943277	1.58
1388- 1449	22	59.2	62	1364	76316	0.2816	-0.58	24158	0.945704	1.60
1327- 1387	23	59.4	61	1403	77719	0.2867	-0.56	24219	0.948092	1.63
1280- 1326	24	59.6	47	1128	78847	0.2909	-0.55	24266	0.949931	1.64
1217- 1279	25	59.7	63	1575	80422	0.2967	-0.53	24329	0.952398	1.67
1170- 1216	26	59.9	47	1222	81644	0.3012	-0.52	24376	0.954238	1.69
1114- 1169	27	60.1	56	1512	83156	0.3068	-0.50	24432	0.956430	1.71
1075- 1113	28	60.2	39	1092	84248	0.3108	-0.49	24471	0.957956	1.73
1040- 1074	29	60.4	35	1015	85263	0.3146	-0.48	24506	0.959327	1.74
998- 1039	30	60.5	42	1260	86523	0.3192	-0.47	24548	0.960971	1.76
969- 997	31	60.7	29	899	87422	0.3225	-0.46	24577	0.962106	1.78
939- 968	32	60.8	30	960	88382	0.3261	-0.45	24607	0.963280	1.79
906- 938	33	60.9	33	1089	89471	0.3301	-0.44	24640	0.964572	1.81
881- 905	34	61.0	25	850	90321	0.3332	-0.43	24665	0.965551	1.82
852- 880	35	61.2	29	1015	91336	0.3370	-0.42	24694	0.966686	1.83
831- 851	36	61.3	21	756	92092	0.3398	-0.41	24715	0.967508	1.85
806- 830	37	61.4	25	925	93017	0.3432	-0.40	24740	0.968487	1.86
783- 805	38	61.5	23	874	93891	0.3464	-0.40	24763	0.969387	1.87
757- 782	39	61.6	26	1014	94905	0.3502	-0.38	24789	0.970405	1.89
733- 756	40	61.7	24	960	95865	0.3537	-0.38	24813	0.971345	1.90
715- 732	41	61.9	18	738	96603	0.3564	-0.37	24831	0.972049	1.91
694- 714	42	62.0	21	882	97485	0.3597	-0.36	24852	0.972871	1.92
671- 693	43	62.1	23	989	98474	0.3633	-0.35	24875	0.973772	1.94
663- 670	44	62.2	8	352	98826	0.3646	-0.35	24883	0.974085	1.94
646- 662	45	62.2	17	765	99591	0.3674	-0.34	24900	0.974750	1.96
623- 645	46	62.3	23	1058	100649	0.3713	-0.33	24923	0.975651	1.97
609- 622	47	62.4	14	658	101307	0.3738	-0.32	24937	0.976199	1.98
598- 608	48	62.5	11	528	101835	0.3757	-0.32	24948	0.976629	1.99
575- 597	49	62.6	23	1127	102962	0.3799	-0.31	24971	0.977530	2.01
565- 574	50	62.7	10	500	103462	0.3817	-0.30	24981	0.977921	2.01
551- 564	51	62.8	14	714	104176	0.3844	-0.29	24995	0.978469	2.02
537- 550	52	62.9	14	728	104904	0.3870	-0.29	25009	0.979017	2.03
525- 536	53	63.0	12	636	105540	0.3894	-0.28	25021	0.979487	2.04
514- 524	54	63.0	11	594	106134	0.3916	-0.28	25032	0.979918	2.05
502- 513	55	63.1	12	660	106794	0.3940	-0.27	25044	0.980388	2.06
490- 501	56	63.2	12	672	107466	0.3965	-0.26	25056	0.980857	2.07
478- 489	57	63.3	12	684	108150	0.3990	-0.26	25068	0.981327	2.08
469- 477	58	63.3	9	522	108672	0.4009	-0.25	25077	0.981679	2.09
462- 468	59	63.4	7	413	109085	0.4025	-0.25	25084	0.981953	2.10
454- 461	60	63.5	8	480	109565	0.4042	-0.24	25092	0.982267	2.10
446- 453	61	63.6	8	488	110053	0.4060	-0.24	25100	0.982580	2.11
437- 445	62	63.6	9	558	110611	0.4081	-0.23	25109	0.982932	2.12
425- 436	63	63.7	12	756	111367	0.4109	-0.23	25121	0.983402	2.13
414- 424	64	63.8	11	704	112071	0.4135	-0.22	25132	0.983832	2.14
409- 413	65	63.8	5	325	112396	0.4147	-0.22	25137	0.984028	2.15
401- 408	66	63.9	8	528	112924	0.4166	-0.21	25145	0.984341	2.15
391- 400	67	64.0	10	670	113594	0.4191	-0.20	25155	0.984733	2.16
383- 390	68	64.0	8	544	114138	0.4211	-0.20	25163	0.985046	2.17
375- 382	69	64.1	8	552	114690	0.4231	-0.19	25171	0.985359	2.18
369- 374	70	64.2	6	420	115110	0.4247	-0.19	25177	0.985594	2.19
363- 368	71	64.2	6	426	115536	0.4263	-0.19	25183	0.985829	2.19
356- 362	72	64.3	7	504	116040	0.4281	-0.18	25190	0.986103	2.20
352- 355	73	64.3	4	292	116332	0.4292	-0.18	25194	0.986260	2.20
346- 351	74	64.4	6	444	116776	0.4308	-0.17	25200	0.986494	2.21
343- 345	75	64.4	3	225	117001	0.4317	-0.17	25203	0.986612	2.21
336- 342	76	64.5	7	532	117533	0.4336	-0.17	25210	0.986886	2.22
325- 335	77	64.6	11	847	118380	0.4368	-0.16	25221	0.987316	2.24
318- 324	78	64.6	7	546	118926	0.4388	-0.15	25228	0.987590	2.24
311- 317	79	64.7	7	553	119479	0.4408	-0.15	25235	0.987864	2.25
307- 310	80	64.7	4	320	119799	0.4420	-0.15	25239	0.988021	2.26
303- 306	81	64.8	4	324	120123	0.4432	-0.14	25243	0.988178	2.26
296- 302	82	64.8	7	574	120697	0.4453	-0.14	25250	0.988452	2.27
292- 295	83	64.9	4	332	121029	0.4465	-0.13	25254	0.988608	2.28
287- 291	84	64.9	5	420	121449	0.4481	-0.13	25259	0.988804	2.28
285- 286	85	65.0	2	170	121619	0.4487	-0.13	25261	0.988882	2.29
282- 284	86	65.0	3	258	121877	0.4497	-0.13	25264	0.989000	2.29
277- 281	87	65.1	5	435	122312	0.4513	-0.12	25269	0.989196	2.30
269- 276	89	65.2	8	712	123024	0.4539	-0.12	25277	0.989509	2.31
268	90	65.2	1	90	123114	0.4542	-0.11	25278	0.989548	2.31
263- 267	91	65.3	5	455	123569	0.4559	-0.11	25283	0.989744	2.32
262	92	65.3	1	92	123661	0.4562	-0.11	25284	0.989783	2.32
258- 261	93	65.4	4	372	124033	0.4576	-0.11	25288	0.989939	2.32
256- 257	94	65.4	2	188	124221	0.4583	-0.10	25290	0.990018	2.33
254- 255	95	65.5	2	190	124411	0.4590	-0.10	25292	0.990096	2.33
253	96	65.5	1	96	124507	0.4594	-0.10	25293	0.990135	2.33
251- 252	97	65.6	2	194	124701	0.4601	-0.10	25295	0.990213	2.33
244- 250	98	65.6	7	686	125387	0.4626	-0.09	25302	0.990487	2.35
242- 243	99	65.6	2	198	125585	0.4633	-0.09	25304	0.990566	2.35
241	100	65.7	1	100	125685	0.4637	-0.09	25305	0.990605	2.35
240	101	65.7	1	101	125786	0.4641	-0.09	25306	0.990644	2.35
237- 239	102	65.8	3	306	126092	0.4652	-0.09	25309	0.990761	2.36
235- 236	103	65.8	2	206	126298	0.4660	-0.09	25311	0.990840	2.36
233- 234	104	65.9	2	208	126506	0.4667	-0.08	25313	0.990918	2.36
230- 232	105	65.9	3	315	126821	0.4679	-0.08	25316	0.991035	2.37
228- 229	106	65.9	2	212	127033	0.4687	-0.08	25318	0.991114	2.37
227	107	66.0	1	107	127140	0.4691	-0.08	25319	0.991153	2.37
225- 226	108	66.0	2	216	127356	0.4699	-0.08	25321	0.991231	2.38
223- 224	109	66.1	2	218	127574	0.4707	-0.07	25323	0.991309	2.38
221- 222	110	66.1	2	220	127794	0.4715	-0.07	25325	0.991388	2.38
214- 220	111	66.1	7	777	128571	0.4744	-0.06	25332	0.991662	2.39
213	112	66.2	1	112	128683	0.4748	-0.06	25333	0.991701	2.40
211- 212	113	66.2	2	226	128909	0.4756	-0.06	25335	0.991779	2.40
209- 210	114	66.3	2	228	129137	0.4764	-0.06	25337	0.991857	2.40
207- 208	115	66.3	2	230	129367	0.4773	-0.06	25339	0.991936	2.41
204- 206	117	66.4	3	351	129718	0.4786	-0.05	25342	0.992053	2.41
203	118	66.4	1	118	129836	0.4790	-0.05	25343	0.992092	2.41
199- 202	119	66.4	4	476	130312	0.4808	-0.05	25347	0.992249	2.42
197- 198	121	66.5	2	242	130554	0.4817	-0.05	25349	0.992327	2.42
195- 196	122	66.6	2	244	130798	0.4826	-0.04	25351	0.992406	2.43
194	123	66.6	1	123	130921	0.4830	-0.04	25352	0.992445	2.43
192- 193	124	66.6	2	248	131169	0.4839	-0.04	25354	0.992523	2.43
189- 191	126	66.7	3	378	131547	0.4853	-0.04	25357	0.992640	2.44
188	128	66.8	1	128	131675	0.4858	-0.04	25358	0.992680	2.44
186- 187	129	66.8	2	258	131933	0.4868	-0.03	25360	0.992758	2.45
184- 185	130	66.8	2	260	132193	0.4877	-0.03	25362	0.992836	2.45
182- 183	131	66.9	2	262	132455	0.4887	-0.03	25364	0.992914	2.45
180- 181	132	66.9	2	264	132719	0.4897	-0.03	25366	0.992993	2.46
178- 179	136	67.0	2	272	132991	0.4907	-0.02	25368	0.993071	2.46
175- 177	137	67.1	3	411	133402	0.4922	-0.02	25371	0.993188	2.47
174	138	67.1	1	138	133540	0.4927	-0.02	25372	0.993228	2.47
172- 173	139	67.1	2	278	133818	0.4937	-0.02	25374	0.993306	2.47
171	140	67.1	1	140	133958	0.4942	-0.01	25375	0.993345	2.48
169- 170	141	67.2	2	282	134240	0.4953	-0.01	25377	0.993423	2.48
168	145	67.3	1	145	134385	0.4958	-0.01	25378	0.993463	2.48
167	146	67.3	1	146	134531	0.4964	-0.01	25379	0.993502	2.48
166	148	67.4	1	148	134679	0.4969	-0.01	25380	0.993541	2.49
165	149	67.4	1	149	134828	0.4974	-0.01	25381	0.993580	2.49
163- 164	150	67.4	2	300	135128	0.4986	-0.00	25383	0.993658	2.49
161- 162	152	67.5	2	304	135432	0.4997	-0.00	25385	0.993737	2.50
159- 160	153	67.5	2	306	135738	0.5008	0.00	25387	0.993815	2.50
156- 158	154	67.6	3	462	136200	0.5025	0.01	25390	0.993932	2.51
155	155	67.6	1	155	136355	0.5031	0.01	25391	0.993971	2.51
153- 154	157	67.6	2	314	136669	0.5042	0.01	25393	0.994050	2.52
152	159	67.7	1	159	136828	0.5048	0.01	25394	0.994089	2.52
151	160	67.7	1	160	136988	0.5054	0.01	25395	0.994128	2.52
149- 150	161	67.8	2	322	137310	0.5066	0.02	25397	0.994206	2.52
148	162	67.8	1	162	137472	0.5072	0.02	25398	0.994245	2.53
146- 147	163	67.8	2	326	137798	0.5084	0.02	25400	0.994324	2.53
144- 145	164	67.8	2	328	138126	0.5096	0.02	25402	0.994402	2.54
142- 143	165	67.9	2	330	138456	0.5108	0.03	25404	0.994480	2.54
140- 141	167	67.9	2	334	138790	0.5121	0.03	25406	0.994559	2.55
139	169	68.0	1	169	138959	0.5127	0.03	25407	0.994598	2.55
137- 138	170	68.0	2	340	139299	0.5139	0.03	25409	0.994676	2.55
136	171	68.0	1	171	139470	0.5146	0.04	25410	0.994715	2.56
133- 135	172	68.0	3	516	139986	0.5165	0.04	25413	0.994833	2.56
132	173	68.1	1	173	140159	0.5171	0.04	25414	0.994872	2.57
131	177	68.2	1	177	140336	0.5178	0.04	25415	0.994911	2.57
129- 130	179	68.2	2	358	140694	0.5191	0.05	25417	0.994989	2.58
128	180	68.2	1	180	140874	0.5198	0.05	25418	0.995028	2.58
127	181	68.3	1	181	141055	0.5204	0.05	25419	0.995067	2.58
124- 126	182	68.3	3	546	141601	0.5224	0.06	25422	0.995185	2.59
123	185	68.4	1	185	141786	0.5231	0.06	25423	0.995224	2.59
121- 122	186	68.4	2	372	142158	0.5245	0.06	25425	0.995302	2.60
120	189	68.4	1	189	142347	0.5252	0.06	25426	0.995342	2.60
119	190	68.5	1	190	142537	0.5259	0.06	25427	0.995381	2.60
118	194	68.6	1	194	142731	0.5266	0.07	25428	0.995420	2.61
117	195	68.6	1	195	142926	0.5273	0.07	25429	0.995459	2.61
115- 116	196	68.6	2	392	143318	0.5288	0.07	25431	0.995537	2.61
114	197	68.6	1	197	143515	0.5295	0.07	25432	0.995576	2.62
113	198	68.6	1	198	143713	0.5302	0.08	25433	0.995616	2.62
112	199	68.7	1	199	143912	0.5310	0.08	25434	0.995655	2.62
111	202	68.7	1	202	144114	0.5317	0.08	25435	0.995694	2.63
110	204	68.8	1	204	144318	0.5325	0.08	25436	0.995733	2.63
109	205	68.8	1	205	144523	0.5332	0.08	25437	0.995772	2.63
107- 108	206	68.8	2	412	144935	0.5347	0.09	25439	0.995850	2.64
106	207	68.8	1	207	145142	0.5355	0.09	25440	0.995890	2.64
105	208	68.9	1	208	145350	0.5363	0.09	25441	0.995929	2.65
103- 104	209	68.9	2	418	145768	0.5378	0.09	25443	0.996007	2.65
102	210	68.9	1	210	145978	0.5386	0.10	25444	0.996046	2.66
99- 101	211	68.9	3	633	146611	0.5409	0.10	25447	0.996164	2.67
98	212	68.9	1	212	146823	0.5417	0.10	25448	0.996203	2.67
97	214	69.0	1	214	147037	0.5425	0.11	25449	0.996242	2.67
96	217	69.0	1	217	147254	0.5433	0.11	25450	0.996281	2.68
95	219	69.1	1	219	147473	0.5441	0.11	25451	0.996320	2.68
94	228	69.3	1	228	147701	0.5449	0.11	25452	0.996359	2.68
93	230	69.3	1	230	147931	0.5458	0.12	25453	0.996399	2.69
91- 92	244	69.6	2	488	148419	0.5476	0.12	25455	0.996477	2.69
90	254	69.7	1	254	148673	0.5485	0.12	25456	0.996516	2.70
89	257	69.8	1	257	148930	0.5495	0.12	25457	0.996555	2.70
88	258	69.8	1	258	149188	0.5504	0.13	25458	0.996594	2.71
87	259	69.8	1	259	149447	0.5514	0.13	25459	0.996633	2.71
86	260	69.8	1	260	149707	0.5523	0.13	25460	0.996673	2.71
85	263	69.9	1	263	149970	0.5533	0.13	25461	0.996712	2.72
84	269	70.0	1	269	150239	0.5543	0.14	25462	0.996751	2.72
83	271	70.0	1	271	150510	0.5553	0.14	25463	0.996790	2.73
81- 82	279	70.1	2	558	151068	0.5574	0.14	25465	0.996868	2.73
80	281	70.2	1	281	151349	0.5584	0.15	25466	0.996907	2.74
79	282	70.2	1	282	151631	0.5594	0.15	25467	0.996947	2.74
78	284	70.2	1	284	151915	0.5605	0.15	25468	0.996986	2.75
77	285	70.2	1	285	152200	0.5615	0.15	25469	0.997025	2.75
76	288	70.3	1	288	152488	0.5626	0.16	25470	0.997064	2.75
73- 75	291	70.3	3	873	153361	0.5658	0.17	25473	0.997181	2.77
72	292	70.3	1	292	153653	0.5669	0.17	25474	0.997221	2.77
71	295	70.4	1	295	153948	0.5680	0.17	25475	0.997260	2.78
70	301	70.5	1	301	154249	0.5691	0.17	25476	0.997299	2.78
68- 69	309	70.6	2	618	154867	0.5714	0.18	25478	0.997377	2.79
67	310	70.6	1	310	155177	0.5725	0.18	25479	0.997416	2.80
66	335	70.9	1	335	155512	0.5738	0.19	25480	0.997455	2.80
64- 65	339	71.0	2	678	156190	0.5763	0.19	25482	0.997534	2.81
63	341	71.0	1	341	156531	0.5775	0.20	25483	0.997573	2.82
62	347	71.1	1	347	156878	0.5788	0.20	25484	0.997612	2.82
61	368	71.3	1	368	157246	0.5802	0.20	25485	0.997651	2.83
60	370	71.4	1	370	157616	0.5815	0.21	25486	0.997690	2.83
59	374	71.4	1	374	157990	0.5829	0.21	25487	0.997729	2.84
58	380	71.5	1	380	158370	0.5843	0.21	25488	0.997769	2.84
57	384	71.5	1	384	158754	0.5857	0.22	25489	0.997808	2.85
56	406	71.8	1	406	159160	0.5872	0.22	25490	0.997847	2.85
55	415	71.9	1	415	159575	0.5888	0.22	25491	0.997886	2.86
54	423	71.9	1	423	159998	0.5903	0.23	25492	0.997925	2.87
53	448	72.2	1	448	160446	0.5920	0.23	25493	0.997964	2.87
52	459	72.3	1	459	160905	0.5937	0.24	25494	0.998003	2.88
51	482	72.5	1	482	161387	0.5954	0.24	25495	0.998043	2.88
50	491	72.6	1	491	161878	0.5972	0.25	25496	0.998082	2.89
49	498	72.6	1	498	162376	0.5991	0.25	25497	0.998121	2.90
48	500	72.7	1	500	162876	0.6009	0.26	25498	0.998160	2.90
47	538	73.0	1	538	163414	0.6029	0.26	25499	0.998199	2.91
46	539	73.0	1	539	163953	0.6049	0.27	25500	0.998238	2.92
45	548	73.1	1	548	164501	0.6069	0.27	25501	0.998278	2.92
44	562	73.2	1	562	165063	0.6090	0.28	25502	0.998317	2.93
43	564	73.2	1	564	165627	0.6111	0.28	25503	0.998356	2.94
42	569	73.2	1	569	166196	0.6132	0.29	25504	0.998395	2.95
41	614	73.6	1	614	166810	0.6154	0.29	25505	0.998434	2.95

Rank	Occ. F	SFI	F	Tokens	Cum. Tokens	Cum. P Tokens	Y	Cum. Types	Cum. P Types	Z
40	641	73.7	1	641	167451	0.6178	0.30	25506	0.998473	2.96
39	669	73.9	1	669	168120	0.6203	0.31	25507	0.998512	2.97
38	676	74.0	1	676	168796	0.6228	0.31	25508	0.998552	2.98
37	678	74.0	1	678	169474	0.6253	0.32	25509	0.998591	2.99
36	746	74.4	1	746	170220	0.6280	0.33	25510	0.998630	3.00
35	767	74.5	1	767	170987	0.6309	0.33	25511	0.998669	3.00
34	771	74.5	1	771	171758	0.6337	0.34	25512	0.998708	3.01
33	811	74.8	1	811	172569	0.6367	0.35	25513	0.998747	3.02
32	831	74.9	1	831	173400	0.6398	0.36	25514	0.998786	3.03
31	836	74.9	1	836	174236	0.6428	0.37	25515	0.998826	3.04
30	910	75.3	1	910	175146	0.6462	0.38	25516	0.998865	3.05
29	918	75.3	1	918	176064	0.6496	0.38	25517	0.998904	3.06
28	1013	75.7	1	1013	177077	0.6533	0.39	25518	0.998943	3.07
27	1033	75.8	1	1033	178110	0.6571	0.40	25519	0.998982	3.08
26	1041	75.8	1	1041	179151	0.6610	0.42	25520	0.999021	3.10
25	1061	75.9	1	1061	180212	0.6649	0.43	25521	0.999060	3.11
24	1071	76.0	1	1071	181283	0.6688	0.44	25522	0.999100	3.12
23	1074	76.0	1	1074	182357	0.6728	0.45	25523	0.999139	3.13
22	1128	76.2	1	1128	183485	0.6770	0.46	25524	0.999178	3.15
21	1129	76.2	1	1129	184614	0.6811	0.47	25525	0.999217	3.16
20	1169	76.3	1	1169	185783	0.6854	0.48	25526	0.999256	3.18
19	1216	76.5	1	1216	186999	0.6899	0.50	25527	0.999295	3.19
18	1437	77.2	1	1437	188436	0.6952	0.51	25528	0.999334	3.21
17	1497	77.4	1	1497	189933	0.7008	0.53	25529	0.999374	3.23
16	1550	77.6	1	1550	191483	0.7065	0.54	25530	0.999413	3.25
15	1575	77.6	1	1575	193058	0.7123	0.56	25531	0.999452	3.26
14	1756	78.1	1	1756	194814	0.7188	0.58	25532	0.999491	3.29
13	1942	78.6	1	1942	196756	0.7259	0.60	25533	0.999530	3.31
12	1968	78.6	1	1968	198724	0.7332	0.62	25534	0.999569	3.33
11	2024	78.7	1	2024	200748	0.7407	0.65	25535	0.999609	3.36
9–10	2173	79.0	2	4346	205094	0.7567	0.70	25537	0.999687	3.42
8	2213	79.1	1	2213	207307	0.7649	0.72	25538	0.999726	3.46
7	3576	81.2	1	3576	210883	0.7781	0.77	25539	0.999765	3.50
6	5718	83.2	1	5718	216601	0.7991	0.84	25540	0.999804	3.55
5	5902	83.4	1	5902	222503	0.8209	0.92	25541	0.999843	3.60
4	6768	84.0	1	6768	229271	0.8459	1.02	25542	0.999883	3.68
3	8453	84.9	1	8453	237724	0.8771	1.16	25543	0.999922	3.78
2	11934	86.4	1	11934	249658	0.9211	1.41	25544	0.999961	3.95
1	21382	89.0	1	21382	271040	1.0000	+INF.	25545	1.000000	+INF.

Rank	Occ. F	SFI	F	Tokens	Cum. Tokens	Cum. P Tokens	Y	Cum. Types	Cum. P Types	Z
15091-29296	1	46.8	14206	14206	14206	0.0451	-1.69	14206	0.484913	-0.04
10511-15090	2	49.0	4580	9160	23366	0.0743	-1.44	18786	0.641248	0.36
8130-10510	3	50.5	2381	7143	30509	0.0970	-1.30	21167	0.722522	0.59
6652-8129	4	51.6	1478	5912	36421	0.1158	-1.20	22645	0.772972	0.75
5638-6651	5	52.4	1014	5070	41491	0.1319	-1.12	23659	0.807585	0.87
4923-5637	6	53.2	715	4290	45781	0.1455	-1.06	24374	0.831991	0.96
4342-4922	7	53.8	581	4067	49848	0.1584	-1.00	24955	0.851823	1.04
3896-4341	8	54.3	446	3568	53416	0.1698	-0.96	25401	0.867047	1.11
3497-3895	9	54.8	399	3591	57007	0.1812	-0.91	25800	0.880666	1.18
3183-3496	10	55.2	314	3140	60147	0.1912	-0.87	26114	0.891384	1.23
2916-3182	11	55.6	267	2937	63084	0.2005	-0.84	26381	0.900498	1.28
2711-2915	12	56.0	205	2460	65544	0.2083	-0.81	26586	0.907496	1.33
2505-2710	13	56.3	206	2678	68222	0.2168	-0.78	26792	0.914528	1.37
2343-2504	14	56.6	162	2268	70490	0.2240	-0.76	26954	0.920057	1.41
2207-2342	15	56.9	136	2040	72530	0.2305	-0.74	27090	0.924700	1.44
2091-2206	16	57.2	116	1856	74386	0.2364	-0.72	27206	0.928659	1.47
1990-2090	17	57.5	101	1717	76103	0.2419	-0.70	27307	0.932107	1.49
1882-1989	18	57.7	108	1944	78047	0.2480	-0.68	27415	0.935793	1.52
1784-1881	19	57.9	98	1862	79909	0.2540	-0.66	27513	0.939138	1.55
1694-1783	20	58.1	90	1800	81709	0.2597	-0.64	27603	0.942210	1.57
1618-1693	21	58.3	76	1596	83305	0.2648	-0.63	27679	0.944805	1.60
1537-1617	22	58.5	81	1782	85087	0.2704	-0.61	27760	0.947570	1.62
1464-1536	23	58.7	73	1679	86766	0.2758	-0.60	27833	0.950061	1.65
1397-1463	24	58.9	67	1608	88374	0.2809	-0.58	27900	0.952348	1.67
1353-1396	25	59.1	44	1100	89474	0.2844	-0.57	27944	0.953850	1.68
1300-1352	26	59.3	53	1378	90852	0.2887	-0.56	27997	0.955659	1.70
1244-1299	27	59.4	56	1512	92364	0.2936	-0.54	28053	0.957571	1.72
1195-1243	28	59.6	49	1372	93736	0.2979	-0.53	28102	0.959244	1.74
1156-1194	29	59.7	39	1131	94867	0.3015	-0.52	28141	0.960575	1.76
1111-1155	30	59.9	45	1350	96217	0.3058	-0.51	28186	0.962111	1.78
1071-1110	31	60.0	40	1240	97457	0.3097	-0.50	28226	0.963476	1.79
1024-1070	32	60.1	47	1504	98961	0.3145	-0.48	28273	0.965080	1.81
996-1023	33	60.3	28	924	99885	0.3175	-0.47	28301	0.966036	1.83
971-995	34	60.4	25	850	100735	0.3202	-0.47	28326	0.966890	1.84
937-970	35	60.5	34	1190	101925	0.3239	-0.46	28360	0.968050	1.85
908-936	36	60.6	29	1044	102969	0.3273	-0.45	28389	0.969040	1.87
875-907	37	60.8	33	1221	104190	0.3311	-0.44	28422	0.970167	1.88
853-874	38	60.9	22	836	105026	0.3338	-0.43	28444	0.970918	1.89
829-852	39	61.0	24	936	105962	0.3368	-0.42	28468	0.971737	1.91
797-828	40	61.1	32	1280	107242	0.3408	-0.41	28500	0.972829	1.92
779-796	41	61.2	18	738	107980	0.3432	-0.40	28518	0.973443	1.93
754-778	42	61.3	25	1050	109030	0.3465	-0.39	28543	0.974297	1.95
740-753	43	61.4	14	602	109632	0.3484	-0.39	28557	0.974775	1.96
721-739	44	61.5	19	836	110468	0.3511	-0.38	28576	0.975423	1.97
710-720	45	61.6	11	495	110963	0.3527	-0.38	28587	0.975799	1.97
693-709	46	61.7	17	782	111745	0.3551	-0.37	28604	0.976379	1.98
673-692	47	61.8	20	940	112685	0.3581	-0.36	28624	0.977062	2.00
659-672	48	61.9	14	672	113357	0.3603	-0.36	28638	0.977540	2.01
640-658	49	62.0	19	931	114288	0.3632	-0.35	28657	0.978188	2.02
630-639	50	62.1	10	500	114788	0.3648	-0.35	28667	0.978529	2.02
620-629	51	62.1	10	510	115298	0.3664	-0.34	28677	0.978871	2.03
603-619	52	62.2	17	884	116182	0.3693	-0.33	28694	0.979451	2.04
591-602	53	62.3	12	636	116818	0.3713	-0.33	28706	0.979861	2.05
578-590	54	62.4	13	702	117520	0.3735	-0.32	28719	0.980304	2.06
568-577	55	62.5	10	550	118070	0.3753	-0.32	28729	0.980646	2.07
558-567	56	62.5	10	560	118630	0.3770	-0.31	28739	0.980987	2.07
548-557	57	62.6	10	570	119200	0.3788	-0.31	28749	0.981328	2.08
535-547	58	62.7	13	754	119954	0.3812	-0.30	28762	0.981772	2.09
526-534	59	62.8	9	531	120485	0.3829	-0.30	28771	0.982079	2.10
514-525	60	62.8	12	720	121205	0.3852	-0.29	28783	0.982489	2.11
498-513	61	62.9	16	976	122181	0.3883	-0.28	28799	0.983035	2.12
491-497	62	63.0	7	434	122615	0.3897	-0.28	28806	0.983274	2.13
479-490	63	63.0	12	756	123371	0.3921	-0.27	28818	0.983684	2.14
473-478	64	63.1	6	384	123755	0.3933	-0.27	28824	0.983889	2.14
467-472	65	63.2	6	390	124145	0.3946	-0.27	28830	0.984093	2.15
458-466	66	63.3	9	594	124739	0.3964	-0.26	28839	0.984401	2.15
443-457	67	63.3	15	1005	125744	0.3996	-0.25	28854	0.984913	2.17
438-442	68	63.4	5	340	126084	0.4007	-0.25	28859	0.985083	2.17
430-437	69	63.4	8	552	126636	0.4025	-0.25	28867	0.985356	2.18
425-429	70	63.5	5	350	126986	0.4036	-0.24	28872	0.985527	2.18
418-424	71	63.6	7	497	127483	0.4052	-0.24	28879	0.985766	2.19
411-417	72	63.6	7	504	127987	0.4068	-0.24	28886	0.986005	2.20
403-410	73	63.7	8	584	128571	0.4086	-0.23	28894	0.986278	2.21
400-402	74	63.7	3	222	128793	0.4093	-0.23	28897	0.986380	2.21
393-399	75	63.8	7	525	129318	0.4110	-0.22	28904	0.986619	2.21
391-392	76	63.9	2	152	129470	0.4115	-0.22	28906	0.986688	2.22
384-390	77	63.9	7	539	130009	0.4132	-0.22	28913	0.986926	2.22
381-383	78	64.0	3	234	130243	0.4139	-0.22	28916	0.987029	2.23
379-380	79	64.0	2	158	130401	0.4144	-0.22	28918	0.987097	2.23
376-378	80	64.1	3	240	130641	0.4152	-0.21	28921	0.987200	2.23
374-375	81	64.1	2	162	130803	0.4157	-0.21	28923	0.987268	2.23
369-373	82	64.2	5	410	131213	0.4170	-0.21	28928	0.987438	2.24
364-368	83	64.2	5	415	131628	0.4183	-0.21	28933	0.987609	2.24
358-363	84	64.3	6	504	132132	0.4199	-0.20	28939	0.987814	2.25
354-357	85	64.3	4	340	132472	0.4210	-0.20	28943	0.987951	2.26
346-353	86	64.4	8	688	133160	0.4232	-0.19	28951	0.988224	2.26
339-345	87	64.4	7	609	133769	0.4251	-0.19	28958	0.988463	2.27
338	88	64.5	1	88	133857	0.4254	-0.19	28959	0.988497	2.27
331-337	89	64.5	7	623	134480	0.4274	-0.18	28966	0.988736	2.28
330	90	64.6	1	90	134570	0.4277	-0.18	28967	0.988770	2.28
329	91	64.6	1	91	134661	0.4280	-0.18	28968	0.988804	2.28
327-328	92	64.7	2	184	134845	0.4286	-0.18	28970	0.988872	2.29
322-326	93	64.7	5	465	135310	0.4300	-0.18	28975	0.989043	2.29
316-321	94	64.8	6	564	135874	0.4318	-0.17	28981	0.989248	2.30
309-315	95	64.8	7	665	136539	0.4339	-0.17	28988	0.989487	2.31
308	96	64.9	1	96	136635	0.4343	-0.17	28989	0.989521	2.31
305-307	97	64.9	3	291	136926	0.4352	-0.16	28992	0.989623	2.31
300-304	98	65.0	5	490	137416	0.4367	-0.16	28997	0.989794	2.32
298-299	99	65.0	2	198	137614	0.4374	-0.16	28999	0.989862	2.32
297	100	65.0	1	100	137714	0.4377	-0.16	29000	0.989896	2.32
292-296	101	65.1	5	505	138219	0.4393	-0.15	29005	0.990067	2.33
290-291	102	65.1	2	204	138423	0.4399	-0.15	29007	0.990135	2.33
287-289	103	65.2	3	309	138732	0.4409	-0.15	29010	0.990238	2.34
286	104	65.2	1	104	138836	0.4412	-0.15	29011	0.990272	2.34
284-285	105	65.3	2	210	139046	0.4419	-0.15	29013	0.990340	2.34
282-283	106	65.3	2	212	139258	0.4426	-0.14	29015	0.990408	2.34
280-281	107	65.3	2	214	139472	0.4433	-0.14	29017	0.990476	2.34
279	108	65.4	1	108	139580	0.4436	-0.14	29018	0.990511	2.35
275-278	109	65.4	4	436	140016	0.4450	-0.14	29022	0.990647	2.35
272-274	110	65.5	3	330	140346	0.4460	-0.14	29025	0.990750	2.36
268-271	111	65.5	4	444	140790	0.4475	-0.13	29029	0.990886	2.36
263-267	112	65.5	5	560	141350	0.4492	-0.13	29034	0.991057	2.37
259-262	113	65.6	4	452	141802	0.4507	-0.12	29038	0.991193	2.37
256-258	114	65.6	3	342	142144	0.4518	-0.12	29041	0.991296	2.38
253-255	116	65.7	3	348	142492	0.4529	-0.12	29044	0.991398	2.38
250-252	117	65.7	3	351	142843	0.4540	-0.12	29047	0.991500	2.39
247-249	118	65.8	3	354	143197	0.4551	-0.11	29050	0.991603	2.39
244-246	119	65.8	3	357	143554	0.4562	-0.11	29053	0.991705	2.40
242-243	120	65.8	2	240	143794	0.4570	-0.11	29055	0.991774	2.40
241	121	65.9	1	121	143915	0.4574	-0.11	29056	0.991808	2.40
240	122	65.9	1	122	144037	0.4578	-0.11	29057	0.991842	2.40
237-239	123	65.9	3	369	144406	0.4590	-0.10	29060	0.991944	2.41
236	124	66.0	1	124	144530	0.4593	-0.10	29061	0.991978	2.41
234-235	125	66.0	2	250	144780	0.4601	-0.10	29063	0.992047	2.41
231-233	126	66.0	3	378	145158	0.4613	-0.10	29066	0.992149	2.42
230	127	66.1	1	127	145285	0.4617	-0.10	29067	0.992183	2.42
227-229	128	66.1	3	384	145669	0.4630	-0.09	29070	0.992286	2.42
223-226	129	66.1	4	516	146185	0.4646	-0.09	29074	0.992422	2.43
220-222	130	66.2	3	390	146575	0.4658	-0.09	29077	0.992525	2.43
219	131	66.2	1	131	146706	0.4663	-0.08	29078	0.992559	2.44
218	132	66.2	1	132	146838	0.4667	-0.08	29079	0.992593	2.44
217	135	66.3	1	135	146973	0.4671	-0.08	29080	0.992627	2.44
216	136	66.4	1	136	147109	0.4675	-0.08	29081	0.992661	2.44
215	137	66.4	1	137	147246	0.4680	-0.08	29082	0.992695	2.44
214	139	66.5	1	139	147385	0.4684	-0.08	29083	0.992729	2.44
212-213	140	66.5	2	280	147665	0.4693	-0.08	29085	0.992798	2.45
211	143	66.6	1	143	147808	0.4698	-0.08	29086	0.992832	2.45
209-210	144	66.6	2	288	148096	0.4707	-0.07	29088	0.992900	2.45
207-208	146	66.7	2	292	148388	0.4716	-0.07	29090	0.992968	2.46
205-206	150	66.8	2	300	148688	0.4726	-0.07	29092	0.993037	2.46
204	151	66.8	1	151	148839	0.4730	-0.07	29093	0.993071	2.46
203	153	66.9	1	153	148992	0.4735	-0.07	29094	0.993105	2.46
202	154	66.9	1	154	149146	0.4740	-0.07	29095	0.993139	2.46
201	156	67.0	1	156	149302	0.4745	-0.06	29096	0.993173	2.47
200	157	67.0	1	157	149459	0.4750	-0.06	29097	0.993207	2.47
199	158	67.0	1	158	149617	0.4755	-0.06	29098	0.993241	2.47
198	159	67.0	1	159	149776	0.4760	-0.06	29099	0.993276	2.47
196-197	162	67.1	2	324	150100	0.4770	-0.06	29101	0.993344	2.48
193-195	163	67.2	3	489	150589	0.4786	-0.05	29104	0.993446	2.48
192	165	67.2	1	165	150754	0.4791	-0.05	29105	0.993480	2.48
190-191	166	67.2	2	332	151086	0.4802	-0.05	29107	0.993549	2.49
186-189	167	67.3	4	668	151754	0.4823	-0.04	29111	0.993685	2.49
184-185	168	67.3	2	336	152090	0.4834	-0.04	29113	0.993753	2.50
183	170	67.3	1	170	152260	0.4839	-0.04	29114	0.993788	2.50
182	171	67.4	1	171	152431	0.4845	-0.04	29115	0.993822	2.50
181	172	67.4	1	172	152603	0.4850	-0.04	29116	0.993856	2.50
178-180	173	67.4	3	519	153122	0.4867	-0.03	29119	0.993958	2.51
176-177	174	67.4	2	348	153470	0.4878	-0.03	29121	0.994026	2.51
174-175	176	67.5	2	352	153822	0.4889	-0.03	29123	0.994095	2.52
172-173	177	67.5	2	354	154176	0.4900	-0.03	29125	0.994163	2.52
170-171	178	67.5	2	356	154532	0.4911	-0.02	29127	0.994231	2.53
169	179	67.6	1	179	154711	0.4917	-0.02	29128	0.994265	2.53
167-168	181	67.6	2	362	155073	0.4929	-0.02	29130	0.994334	2.53
165-166	184	67.7	2	368	155441	0.4940	-0.01	29132	0.994402	2.54
164	185	67.7	1	185	155626	0.4946	-0.01	29133	0.994436	2.54
162-163	186	67.7	2	372	155998	0.4958	-0.01	29135	0.994504	2.54
160-161	187	67.8	2	374	156372	0.4970	-0.01	29137	0.994573	2.55
159	188	67.8	1	188	156560	0.4976	-0.01	29138	0.994607	2.55
157-158	190	67.8	2	380	156940	0.4988	-0.00	29140	0.994675	2.55
156	191	67.8	1	191	157131	0.4994	-0.00	29141	0.994709	2.56
155	192	67.9	1	192	157323	0.5000	0.00	29142	0.994743	2.56
153-154	194	67.9	2	388	157711	0.5012	0.00	29144	0.994812	2.56
150-152	197	68.0	3	591	158302	0.5031	0.01	29147	0.994914	2.57
147-149	199	68.0	3	597	158899	0.5050	0.01	29150	0.995016	2.58
146	200	68.0	1	200	159099	0.5056	0.01	29151	0.995050	2.58
144-145	202	68.1	2	404	159503	0.5069	0.02	29153	0.995119	2.58
142-143	208	68.2	2	416	159919	0.5083	0.02	29155	0.995187	2.59
141	209	68.2	1	209	160128	0.5089	0.02	29156	0.995221	2.59
140	210	68.3	1	210	160338	0.5096	0.02	29157	0.995255	2.59
139	219	68.4	1	219	160557	0.5103	0.03	29158	0.995289	2.60
138	220	68.5	1	220	160777	0.5110	0.03	29159	0.995324	2.60
136-137	222	68.5	2	444	161221	0.5124	0.03	29161	0.995392	2.60
135	223	68.5	1	223	161444	0.5131	0.03	29162	0.995426	2.61
134	226	68.6	1	226	161670	0.5138	0.03	29163	0.995460	2.61
133	227	68.6	1	227	161897	0.5145	0.04	29164	0.995494	2.61
132	228	68.6	1	228	162125	0.5153	0.04	29165	0.995528	2.61
131	229	68.6	1	229	162354	0.5160	0.04	29166	0.995562	2.62
130	231	68.7	1	231	162585	0.5167	0.04	29167	0.995597	2.62
128-129	234	68.7	2	468	163053	0.5182	0.05	29169	0.995665	2.62
127	237	68.8	1	237	163290	0.5190	0.05	29170	0.995699	2.63
126	240	68.8	1	240	163530	0.5197	0.05	29171	0.995733	2.63
125	242	68.9	1	242	163772	0.5205	0.05	29172	0.995767	2.63
123-124	250	69.0	2	500	164272	0.5221	0.06	29174	0.995836	2.64
122	257	69.1	1	257	164529	0.5229	0.06	29175	0.995870	2.64
121	261	69.2	1	261	164790	0.5237	0.06	29176	0.995904	2.64
120	262	69.2	1	262	165052	0.5246	0.06	29177	0.995938	2.65
119	263	69.2	1	263	165315	0.5254	0.06	29178	0.995972	2.65
118	266	69.3	1	266	165581	0.5263	0.07	29179	0.996006	2.65
117	269	69.3	1	269	165850	0.5271	0.07	29180	0.996040	2.66
116	270	69.3	1	270	166120	0.5280	0.07	29181	0.996074	2.66
115	273	69.4	1	273	166393	0.5288	0.07	29182	0.996109	2.66
113-114	279	69.5	2	558	166951	0.5306	0.08	29184	0.996177	2.67
112	282	69.5	1	282	167233	0.5315	0.08	29185	0.996211	2.67
111	284	69.6	1	284	167517	0.5324	0.08	29186	0.996245	2.67
110	286	69.6	1	286	167803	0.5333	0.08	29187	0.996279	2.68
108-109	290	69.7	2	580	168383	0.5352	0.09	29189	0.996348	2.68
107	296	69.7	1	296	168679	0.5361	0.09	29190	0.996382	2.69
106	298	69.8	1	298	168977	0.5370	0.09	29191	0.996416	2.69
105	300	69.8	1	300	169277	0.5380	0.10	29192	0.996450	2.69
104	304	69.9	1	304	169581	0.5390	0.10	29193	0.996484	2.70
103	306	69.9	1	306	169887	0.5399	0.10	29194	0.996518	2.70
102	311	70.0	1	311	170198	0.5409	0.10	29195	0.996552	2.70
101	314	70.0	1	314	170512	0.5419	0.11	29196	0.996587	2.71
100	316	70.0	1	316	170828	0.5429	0.11	29197	0.996621	2.71
99	324	70.1	1	324	171152	0.5440	0.11	29198	0.996655	2.71
97-98	325	70.1	2	650	171802	0.5460	0.12	29200	0.996723	2.72
96	330	70.2	1	330	172132	0.5471	0.12	29201	0.996757	2.72
94-95	331	70.2	2	662	172794	0.5492	0.12	29203	0.996825	2.73
92-93	340	70.3	2	680	173474	0.5513	0.13	29205	0.996894	2.74
91	347	70.4	1	347	173821	0.5524	0.13	29206	0.996928	2.74
90	362	70.6	1	362	174183	0.5536	0.13	29207	0.996962	2.74
89	372	70.7	1	372	174555	0.5548	0.14	29208	0.996996	2.75
88	384	70.9	1	384	174939	0.5560	0.14	29209	0.997030	2.75
87	385	70.9	1	385	175324	0.5572	0.14	29210	0.997064	2.75
85-86	390	70.9	2	780	176104	0.5597	0.15	29212	0.997133	2.76
84	391	70.9	1	391	176495	0.5609	0.15	29213	0.997167	2.77
83	407	71.1	1	407	176902	0.5622	0.16	29214	0.997201	2.77
82	409	71.1	1	409	177311	0.5635	0.16	29215	0.997235	2.77
80-81	433	71.4	2	866	178177	0.5663	0.17	29217	0.997303	2.78
79	441	71.5	1	441	178618	0.5677	0.17	29218	0.997338	2.79
78	454	71.6	1	454	179072	0.5691	0.17	29219	0.997372	2.79
77	467	71.7	1	467	179539	0.5706	0.18	29220	0.997406	2.80

Rank	Occ. F	SFI	F	Tokens	Cum. Tokens	Cum. P Tokens	Y	Cum. Types	Cum. P Types	Z
	76	468 71.7	1	468	180007	0.5721	0.18	29221	0.997440	2.80
	75	471 71.8	1	471	180478	0.5736	0.19	29222	0.997474	2.80
	74	472 71.8	1	472	180950	0.5751	0.19	29223	0.997508	2.81
72-	73	474 71.8	2	948	181898	0.5781	0.20	29225	0.997576	2.82
	71	475 71.8	1	475	182373	0.5796	0.20	29226	0.997611	2.82
	70	486 71.9	1	486	182859	0.5812	0.20	29227	0.997645	2.83
	69	499 72.0	1	499	183358	0.5827	0.21	29228	0.997679	2.83
	68	511 72.1	1	511	183869	0.5844	0.21	29229	0.997713	2.84
	67	523 72.2	1	523	184392	0.5860	0.22	29230	0.997747	2.84
	66	525 72.2	1	525	184917	0.5877	0.22	29231	0.997781	2.85
	65	539 72.3	1	539	185456	0.5894	0.23	29232	0.997815	2.85
	64	543 72.4	1	543	185999	0.5911	0.23	29233	0.997850	2.86
	63	544 72.4	1	544	186543	0.5929	0.23	29234	0.997884	2.86
	62	554 72.5	1	554	187097	0.5946	0.24	29235	0.997918	2.87
	61	564 72.5	1	564	187661	0.5964	0.24	29236	0.997952	2.87
	60	566 72.6	1	566	188227	0.5982	0.25	29237	0.997986	2.88
	59	578 72.6	1	578	188805	0.6001	0.25	29238	0.998020	2.88
	58	588 72.7	1	588	189393	0.6019	0.26	29239	0.998054	2.89
	57	599 72.8	1	599	189992	0.6038	0.26	29240	0.998088	2.89
	56	600 72.8	1	600	190592	0.6057	0.27	29241	0.998123	2.90
54-	55	607 72.9	2	1214	191806	0.6096	0.28	29243	0.998191	2.91
	53	627 73.0	1	627	192433	0.6116	0.28	29244	0.998225	2.92
	52	651 73.2	1	651	193084	0.6137	0.29	29245	0.998259	2.92
	51	662 73.2	1	662	193746	0.6158	0.29	29246	0.998293	2.93
	50	666 73.3	1	666	194412	0.6179	0.30	29247	0.998327	2.93
	49	669 73.3	1	669	195081	0.6200	0.31	29248	0.998362	2.94
	48	672 73.3	1	672	195753	0.6221	0.31	29249	0.998396	2.95
	47	687 73.4	1	687	196440	0.6243	0.32	29250	0.998430	2.95
	46	697 73.5	1	697	197137	0.6265	0.32	29251	0.998464	2.96
	45	721 73.6	1	721	197858	0.6288	0.33	29252	0.998498	2.97
	44	742 73.7	1	742	198600	0.6312	0.34	29253	0.998532	2.97
42-	43	748 73.8	2	1496	200096	0.6359	0.35	29255	0.998600	2.99
	41	756 73.8	1	756	200852	0.6383	0.35	29256	0.998635	3.00
	40	824 74.2	1	824	201676	0.6410	0.36	29257	0.998669	3.00
	39	849 74.3	1	849	202525	0.6437	0.37	29258	0.998703	3.01
	38	878 74.5	1	878	203403	0.6465	0.38	29259	0.998737	3.02
	37	898 74.6	1	898	204301	0.6493	0.38	29260	0.998771	3.03
36	916 74.6	1	916	205217	0.6522	0.39	29261	0.998805	3.04	
35	929 74.7	1	929	206146	0.6552	0.40	29262	0.998839	3.05	
34	956 74.8	1	956	207102	0.6582	0.41	29263	0.998874	3.05	
33	998 75.0	1	998	208100	0.6614	0.42	29264	0.998908	3.06	
32	1035 75.2	1	1035	209135	0.6647	0.43	29265	0.998942	3.07	
31	1043 75.2	1	1043	210178	0.6680	0.43	29266	0.998976	3.08	
30	1093 75.4	1	1093	211271	0.6715	0.44	29267	0.999010	3.09	
29	1147 75.6	1	1147	212418	0.6751	0.45	29268	0.999044	3.10	
28	1162 75.7	1	1162	213580	0.6788	0.46	29269	0.999078	3.11	
27	1213 75.9	1	1213	214793	0.6827	0.48	29270	0.999112	3.13	
26	1255 76.0	1	1255	216048	0.6866	0.49	29271	0.999147	3.14	
25	1328 76.3	1	1328	217376	0.6909	0.50	29272	0.999181	3.15	
24	1392 76.5	1	1392	218768	0.6953	0.51	29273	0.999215	3.16	
23	1482 76.7	1	1482	220250	0.7000	0.52	29274	0.999249	3.17	
22	1501 76.8	1	1501	221751	0.7048	0.54	29275	0.999283	3.19	
21	1521 76.8	1	1521	223272	0.7096	0.55	29276	0.999317	3.20	
20	1568 77.0	1	1568	224840	0.7146	0.57	29277	0.999351	3.22	
19	1667 77.2	1	1667	226507	0.7199	0.58	29278	0.999386	3.23	
18	1701 77.3	1	1701	228208	0.7253	0.60	29279	0.999420	3.25	
17	1861 77.7	1	1861	230069	0.7312	0.62	29280	0.999454	3.27	
16	2017 78.1	1	2017	232086	0.7376	0.64	29281	0.999488	3.28	
15	2055 78.1	1	2055	234141	0.7441	0.66	29282	0.999522	3.30	
14	2253 78.6	1	2253	236394	0.7513	0.68	29283	0.999556	3.32	
13	2366 78.8	1	2366	238760	0.7588	0.70	29284	0.999590	3.35	
12	2476 79.0	1	2476	241236	0.7667	0.73	29285	0.999624	3.37	
11	2549 79.1	1	2549	243785	0.7748	0.75	29286	0.999659	3.40	
10	2606 79.2	1	2606	246391	0.7831	0.78	29287	0.999693	3.43	
9	2628 79.2	1	2628	249019	0.7914	0.81	29288	0.999727	3.46	
8	2887 79.6	1	2887	251906	0.8006	0.84	29289	0.999761	3.49	
7	3086 79.9	1	3086	254992	0.8104	0.88	29290	0.999795	3.53	
6	5892 82.7	1	5892	260884	0.8291	0.95	29291	0.999829	3.58	
5	7833 84.0	1	7833	268717	0.8540	1.05	29292	0.999863	3.64	
4	8262 84.2	1	8262	276979	0.8803	1.18	29293	0.999898	3.71	
3	8623 84.4	1	8623	285602	0.9077	1.33	29294	0.999932	3.81	
2	8855 84.5	1	8855	294457	0.9358	1.52	29295	0.999966	3.98	
1	20186 88.1	1	20186	314643	1.0000	+INF.	29296	1.000000	+INF.	

Rank	Occ. F		SFI	F	Tokens	Cum. Tokens	Cum. P Tokens	Y	Cum. Types	Cum. P Types	Z
436-	863	1	65.1	428	428	428	0.0931	-1.32	428	0.495944	-0.01
302-	435	2	67.4	134	268	696	0.1515	-1.03	562	0.651217	0.39
227-	301	3	68.8	75	225	921	0.2004	-0.84	637	0.738123	0.64
184-	226	4	69.9	43	172	1093	0.2379	-0.71	680	0.787949	0.80
141-	183	5	70.8	43	215	1308	0.2847	-0.57	723	0.837775	0.99
119-	140	6	71.5	22	132	1440	0.3134	-0.49	745	0.863268	1.10
107-	118	7	72.1	12	84	1524	0.3317	-0.44	757	0.877173	1.16
101-	106	8	72.7	6	48	1572	0.3421	-0.41	763	0.884125	1.20
94-	100	9	73.2	7	63	1635	0.3558	-0.37	770	0.892236	1.24
84-	93	10	73.6	10	100	1735	0.3776	-0.31	780	0.903824	1.30
77-	83	11	74.0	7	77	1812	0.3943	-0.27	787	0.911935	1.35
70-	76	12	74.3	7	84	1896	0.4126	-0.22	794	0.920046	1.41
64-	69	13	74.7	6	78	1974	0.4296	-0.18	800	0.926999	1.45
61-	63	14	75.0	3	42	2016	0.4387	-0.15	803	0.930475	1.48
58-	60	15	75.3	3	45	2061	0.4485	-0.13	806	0.933951	1.51
	57	16	75.6	1	16	2077	0.4520	-0.12	807	0.935110	1.51
51-	56	17	75.8	6	102	2179	0.4742	-0.06	813	0.942063	1.57
48-	50	18	76.0	3	54	2233	0.4860	-0.04	816	0.945539	1.60
42-	47	19	76.3	6	114	2347	0.5108	0.03	822	0.952491	1.67
39-	41	20	76.5	3	60	2407	0.5238	0.06	825	0.955968	1.71
	38	21	76.7	1	21	2428	0.5284	0.07	826	0.957126	1.72
35-	37	22	76.9	3	66	2494	0.5428	0.11	829	0.960603	1.76
32-	34	23	77.1	3	69	2563	0.5578	0.15	832	0.964079	1.80
30-	31	24	77.3	2	48	2611	0.5682	0.17	834	0.966396	1.83
	29	25	77.4	1	25	2636	0.5737	0.19	835	0.967555	1.85
	28	26	77.6	1	26	2662	0.5793	0.20	836	0.968714	1.86
	27	28	77.9	1	28	2690	0.5854	0.22	837	0.969873	1.88
	26	29	78.1	1	29	2719	0.5917	0.23	838	0.971031	1.90
24-	25	31	78.4	2	62	2781	0.6052	0.27	840	0.973349	1.93
	23	34	78.8	1	34	2815	0.6126	0.29	841	0.974508	1.95
	22	35	78.9	1	35	2850	0.6202	0.31	842	0.975666	1.97
	21	37	79.1	1	37	2887	0.6283	0.33	843	0.976825	1.99
	20	38	79.2	1	38	2925	0.6366	0.35	844	0.977984	2.01
18-	19	39	79.3	2	78	3003	0.6535	0.39	846	0.980301	2.06
16-	17	40	79.5	2	80	3083	0.6709	0.44	848	0.982619	2.11
	15	41	79.6	1	41	3124	0.6799	0.47	849	0.983777	2.14
	14	45	80.0	1	45	3169	0.6897	0.49	850	0.984936	2.17
	13	46	80.1	1	46	3215	0.6997	0.52	851	0.986095	2.20
11-	12	60	81.2	2	120	3335	0.7258	0.60	853	0.988412	2.27
	10	66	81.6	1	66	3401	0.7402	0.64	854	0.989571	2.31
	9	69	81.8	1	69	3470	0.7552	0.69	855	0.990730	2.35
	8	74	82.1	1	74	3544	0.7713	0.74	856	0.991889	2.40
	7	76	82.2	1	76	3620	0.7878	0.80	857	0.993047	2.46
	6	78	82.3	1	78	3698	0.8048	0.86	858	0.994206	2.52
	5	86	82.7	1	86	3784	0.8235	0.93	859	0.995365	2.60
	4	126	84.4	1	126	3910	0.8509	1.04	860	0.996524	2.70
	3	172	85.7	1	172	4082	0.8884	1.22	861	0.997682	2.83
	2	219	86.8	1	219	4301	0.9360	1.52	862	0.998841	3.05
	1	294	88.1	1	294	4595	1.0000	+INF.	863	1.000000	+INF.

Guide to the
Frequency Distribution Graphs

These graphs depict the obtained token and type distributions for the total AHI Corpus and for the grade and subject samples. They also show lines for the theoretical distributions from which the obtained distributions may be presumed to have been drawn and for the sample distributions expected on the basis of the lognormal model.

The construction of these graphs, and their interpretation, is explained on pages xxiv–xxviii.

The obtained distributions are plotted with the symbols Z and Y; in each graph, the upper set of points (Z) is for the obtained type distribution, while the lower set of points (Y) is for the obtained token distribution. Because of the large number of points in the middle of the distributions, only selected points are plotted. Points for the corresponding expected distributions are connected by lines.

The base line for each graph is marked in terms of SFI, used as a scale for measuring word probabilities. The ordinate is marked in terms of normal-deviate values. See the Guide to the Frequency Distributions (pages 753–754) for explanations of these measures.

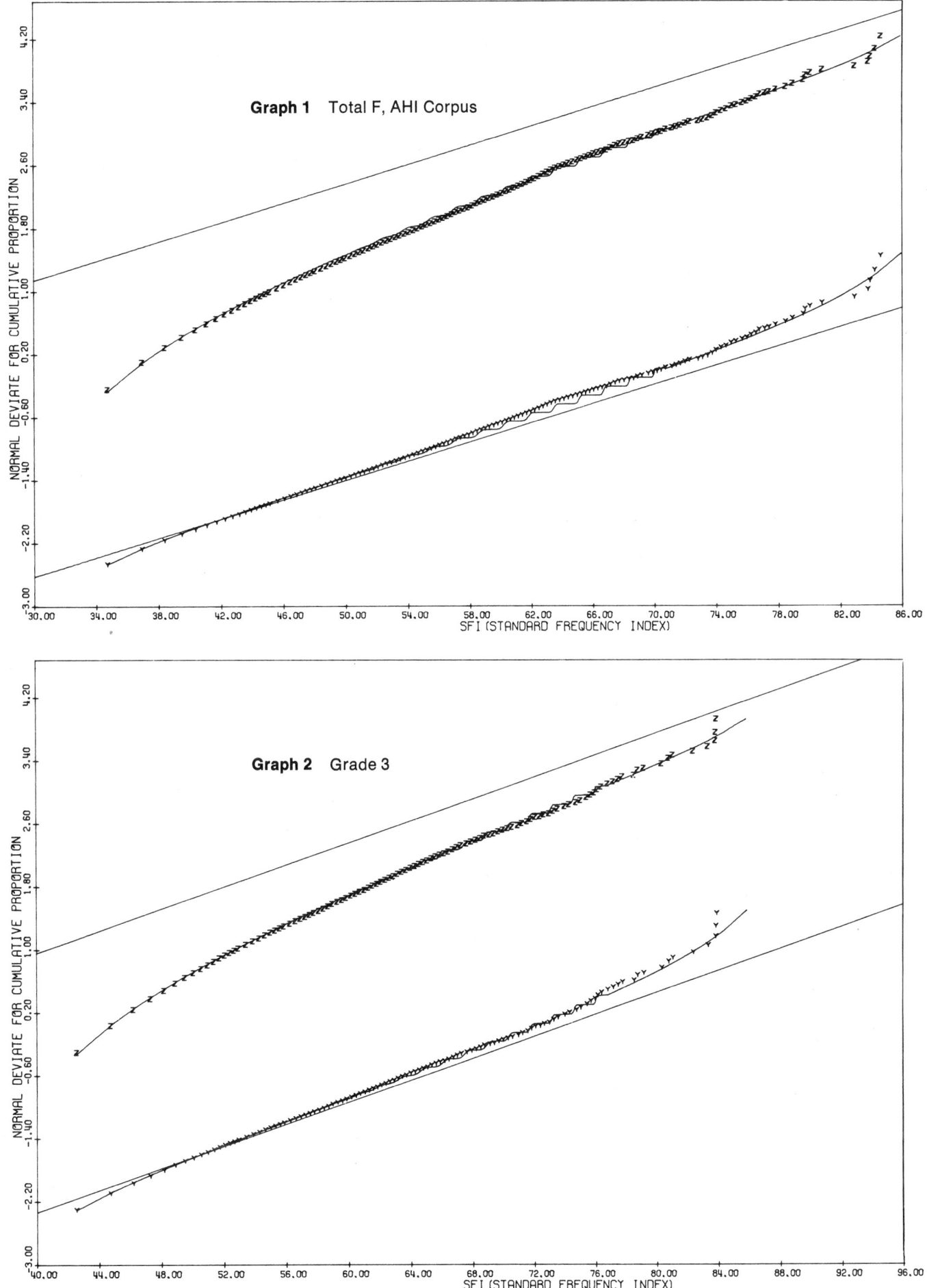

Graph 1 Total F, AHI Corpus

Graph 2 Grade 3

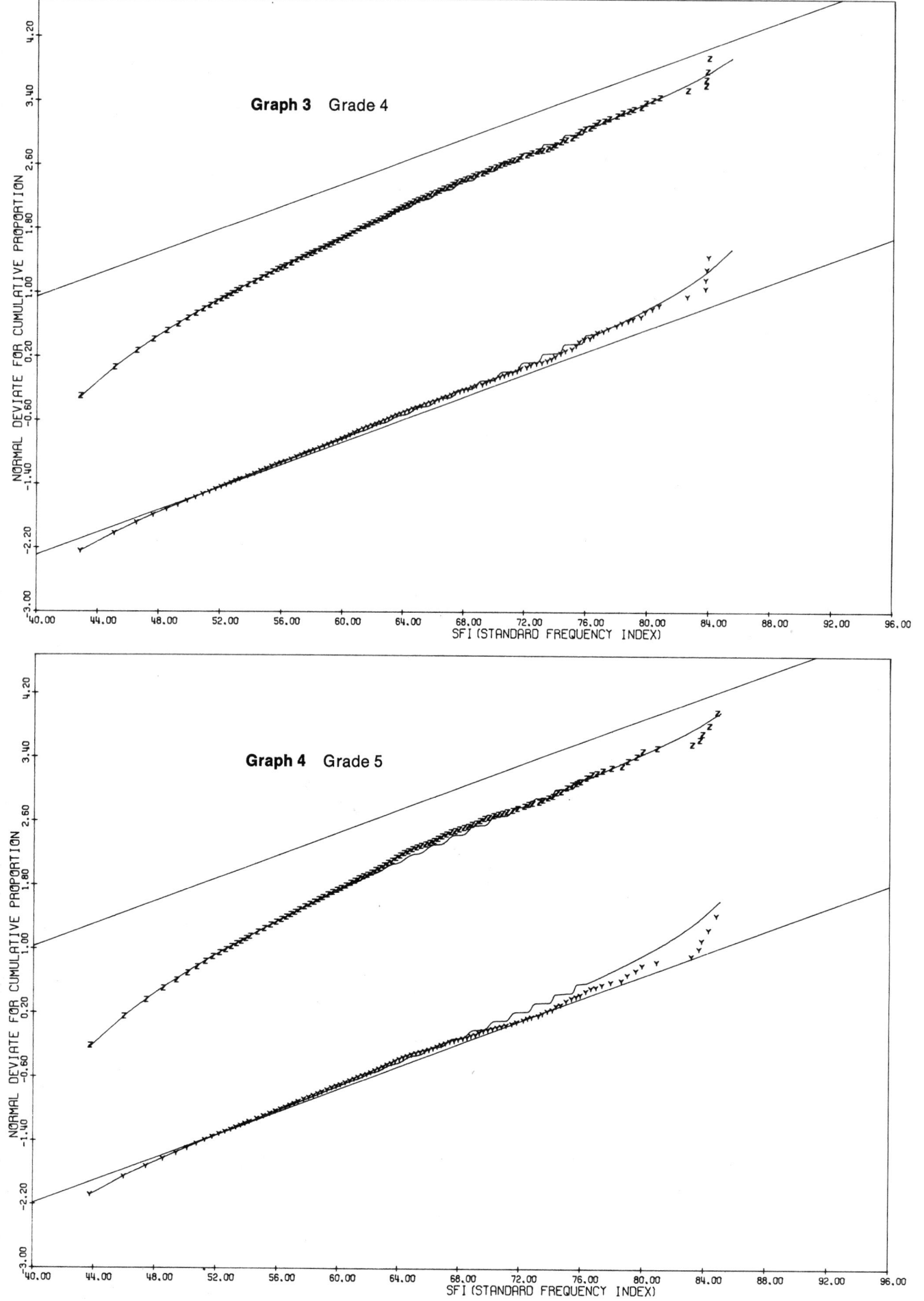

814

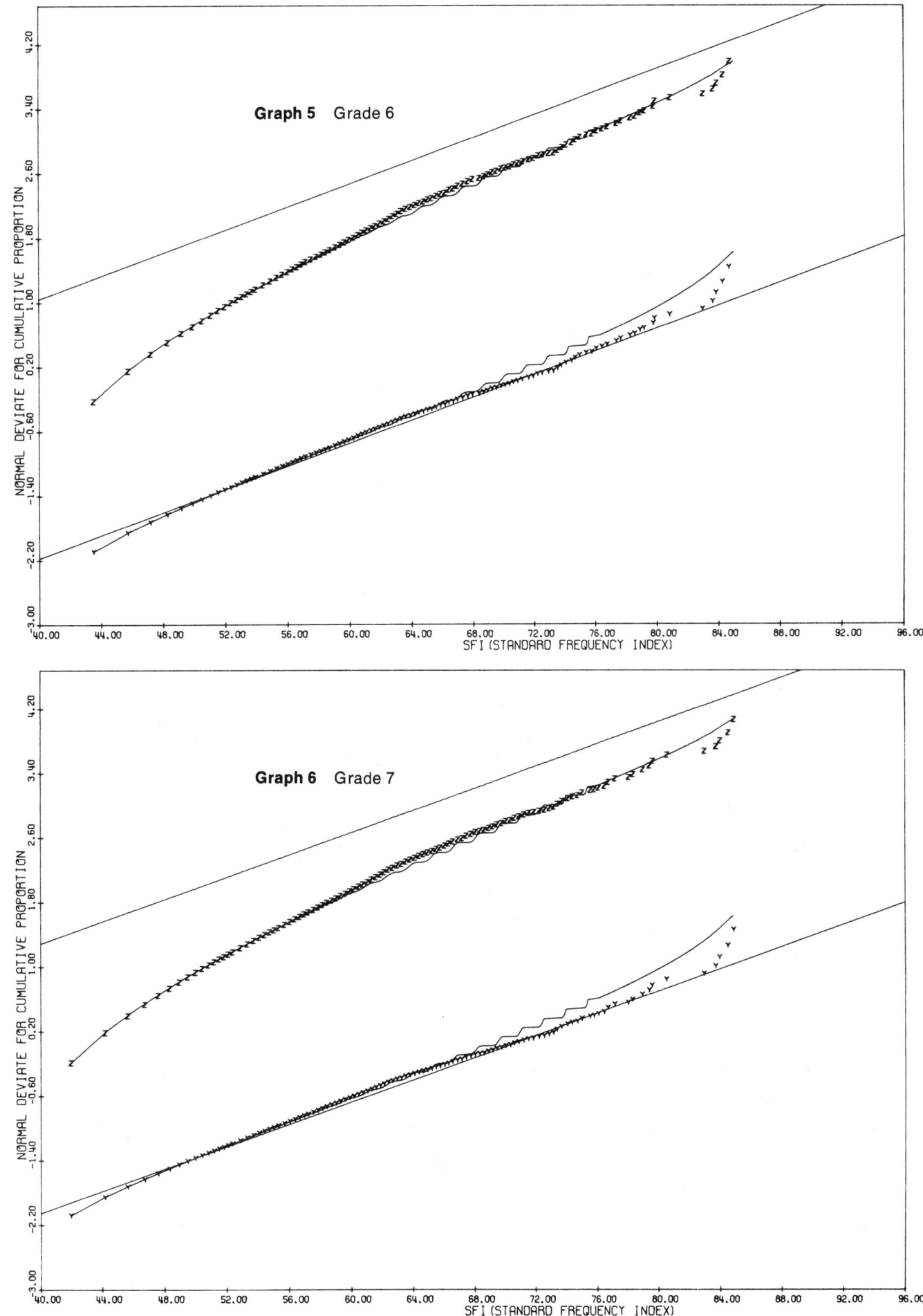

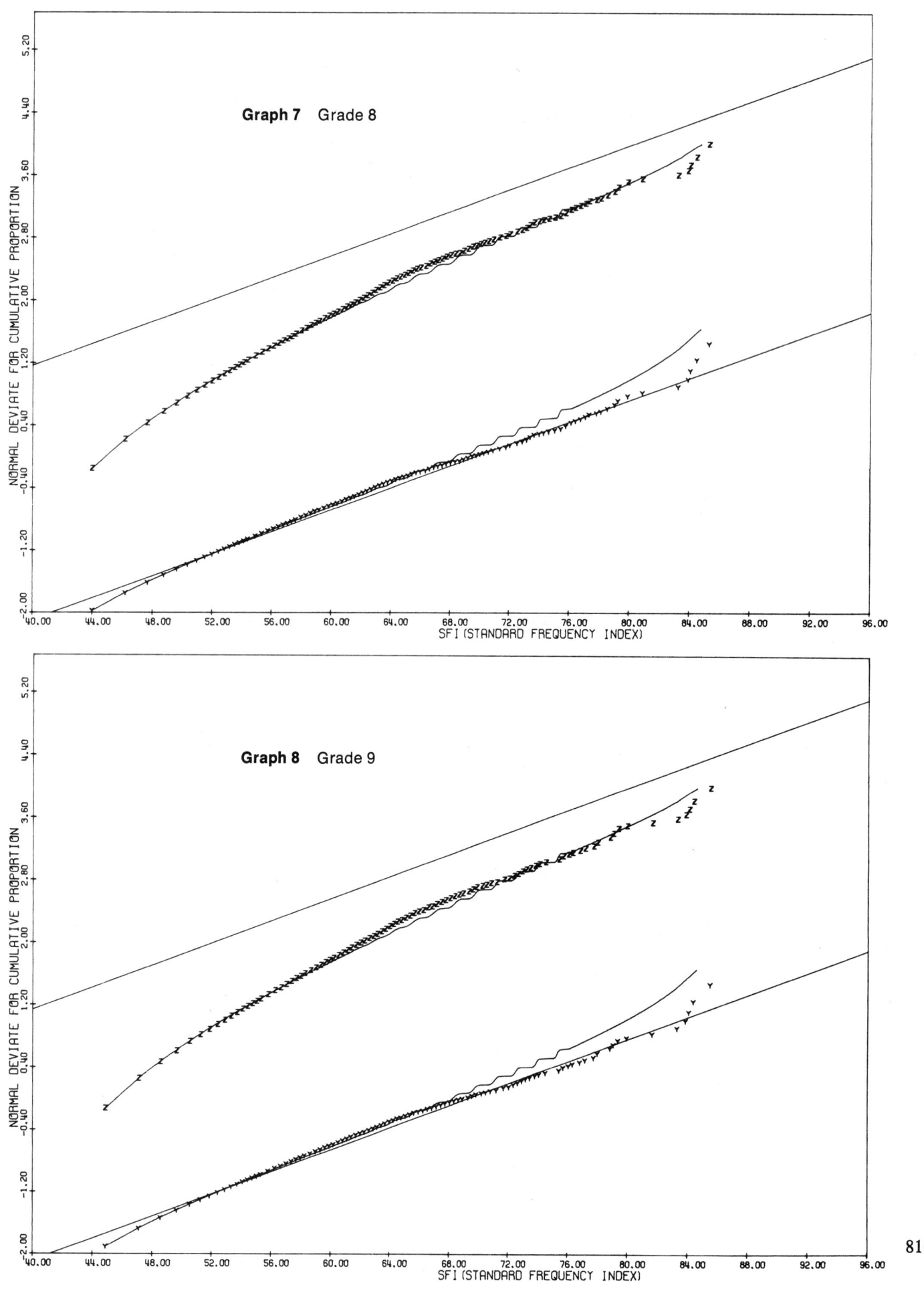

Graph 7   Grade 8

Graph 8   Grade 9

816

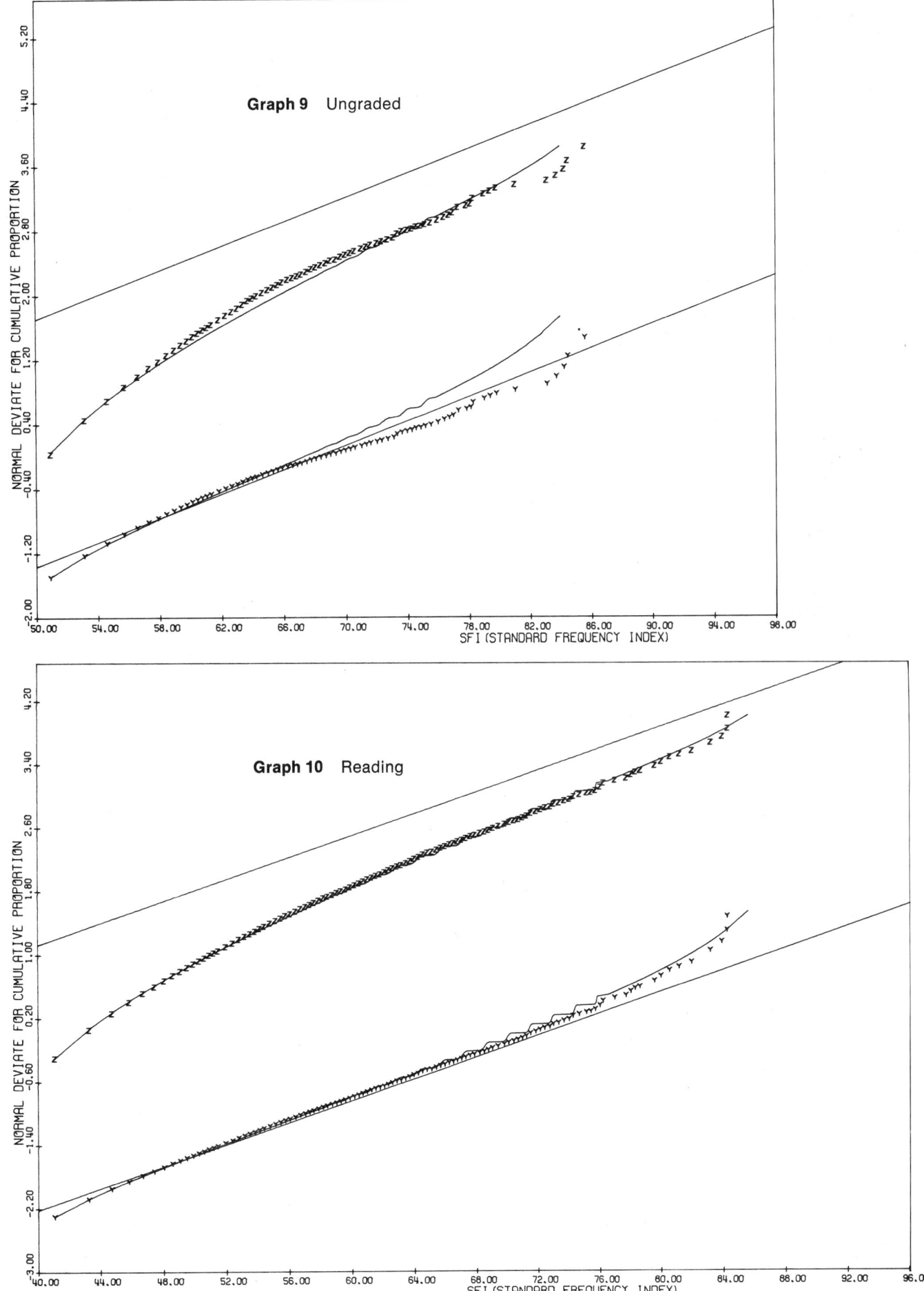

Graph 9 Ungraded

NORMAL DEVIATE FOR CUMULATIVE PROPORTION

SFI (STANDARD FREQUENCY INDEX)

Graph 10 Reading

NORMAL DEVIATE FOR CUMULATIVE PROPORTION

SFI (STANDARD FREQUENCY INDEX)

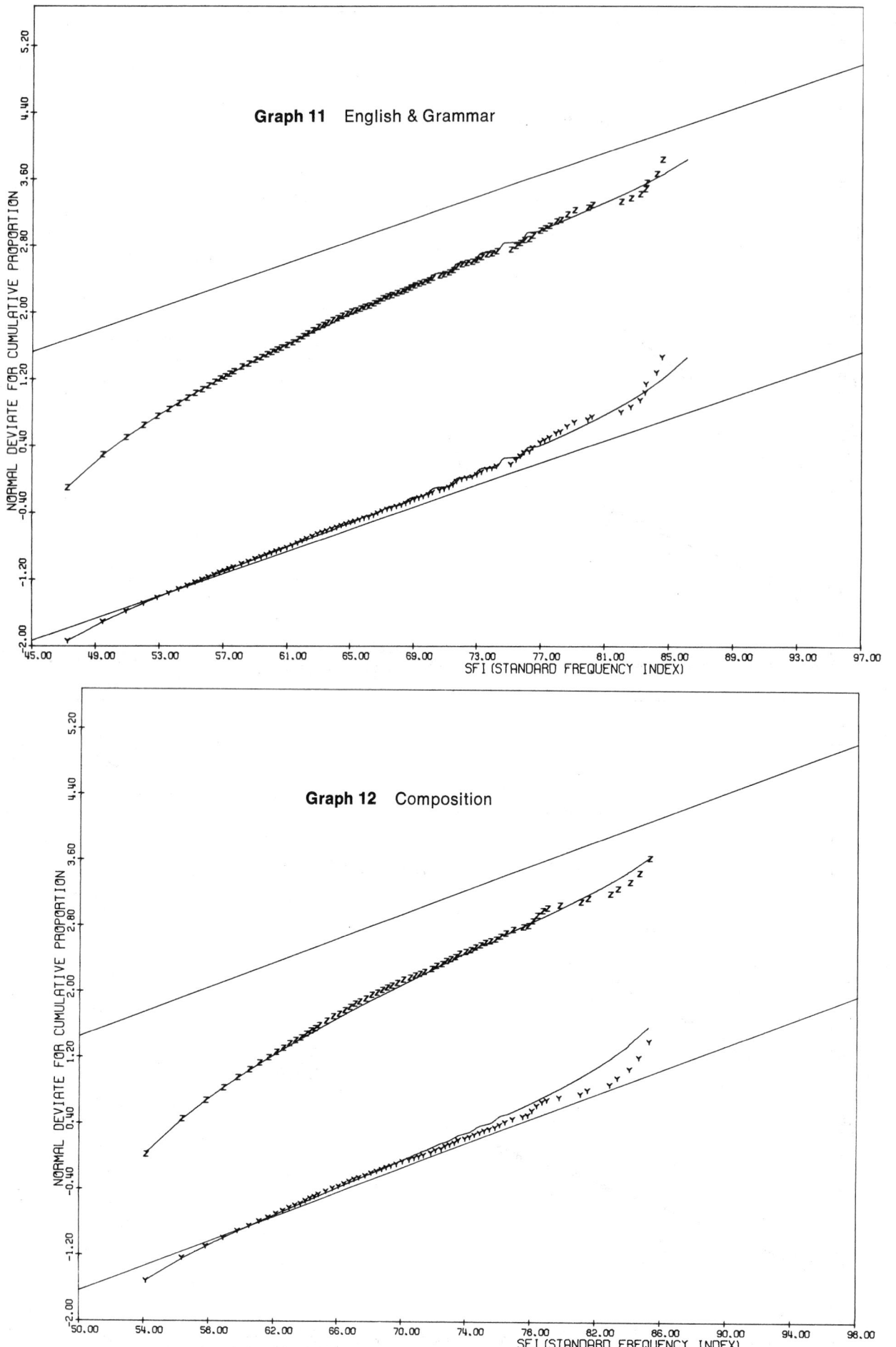

Graph 11 English & Grammar

Graph 12 Composition

818

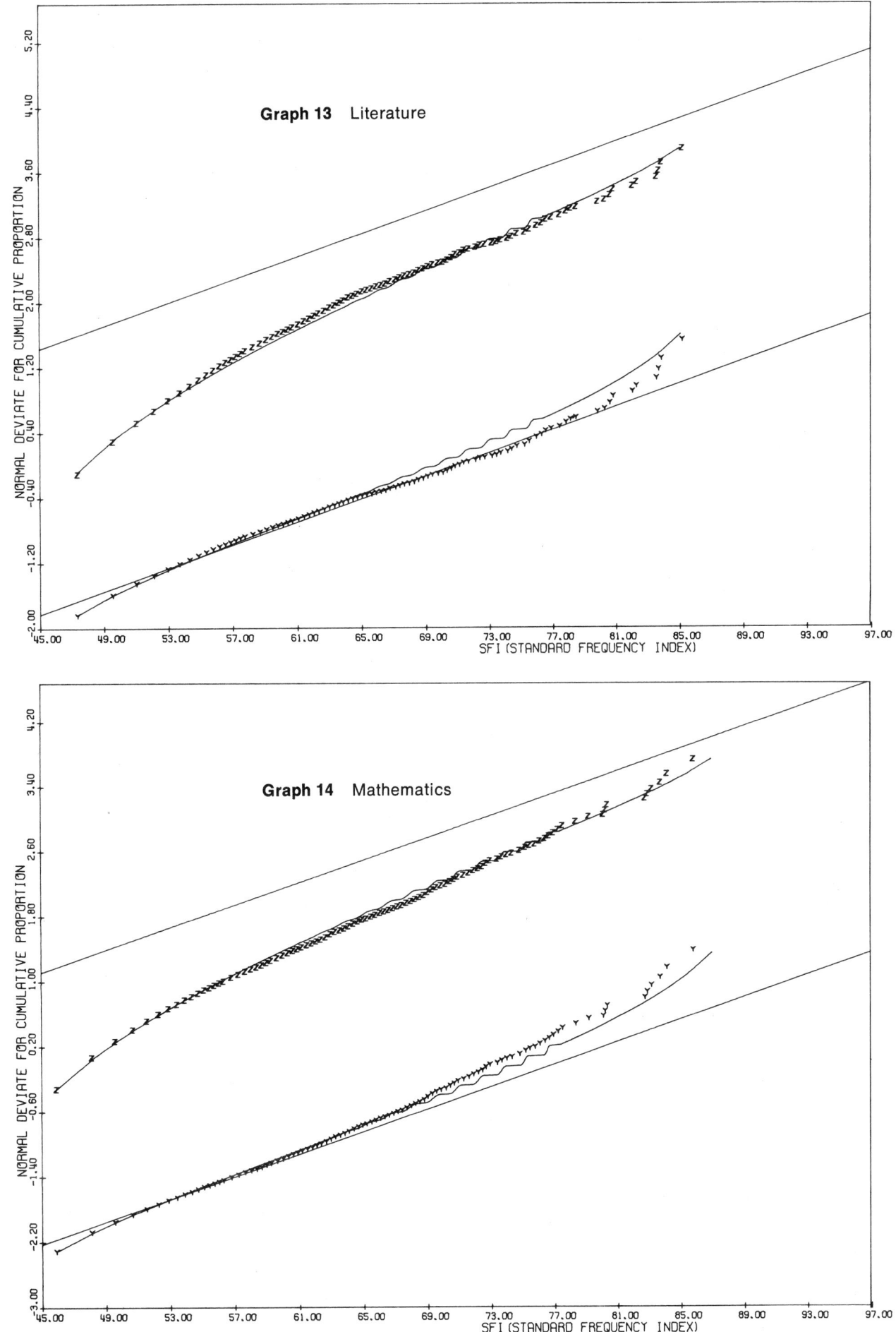

819

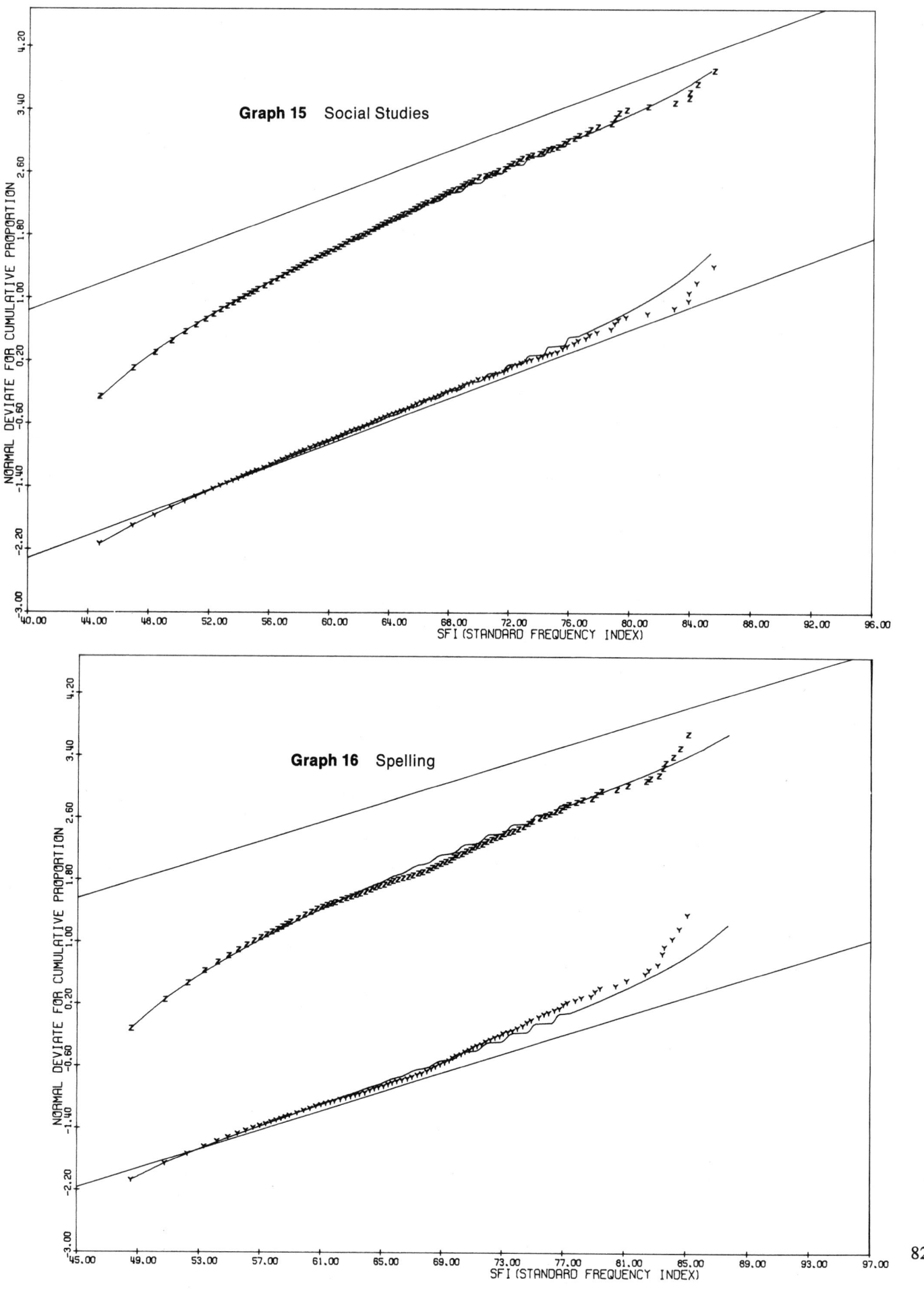

820

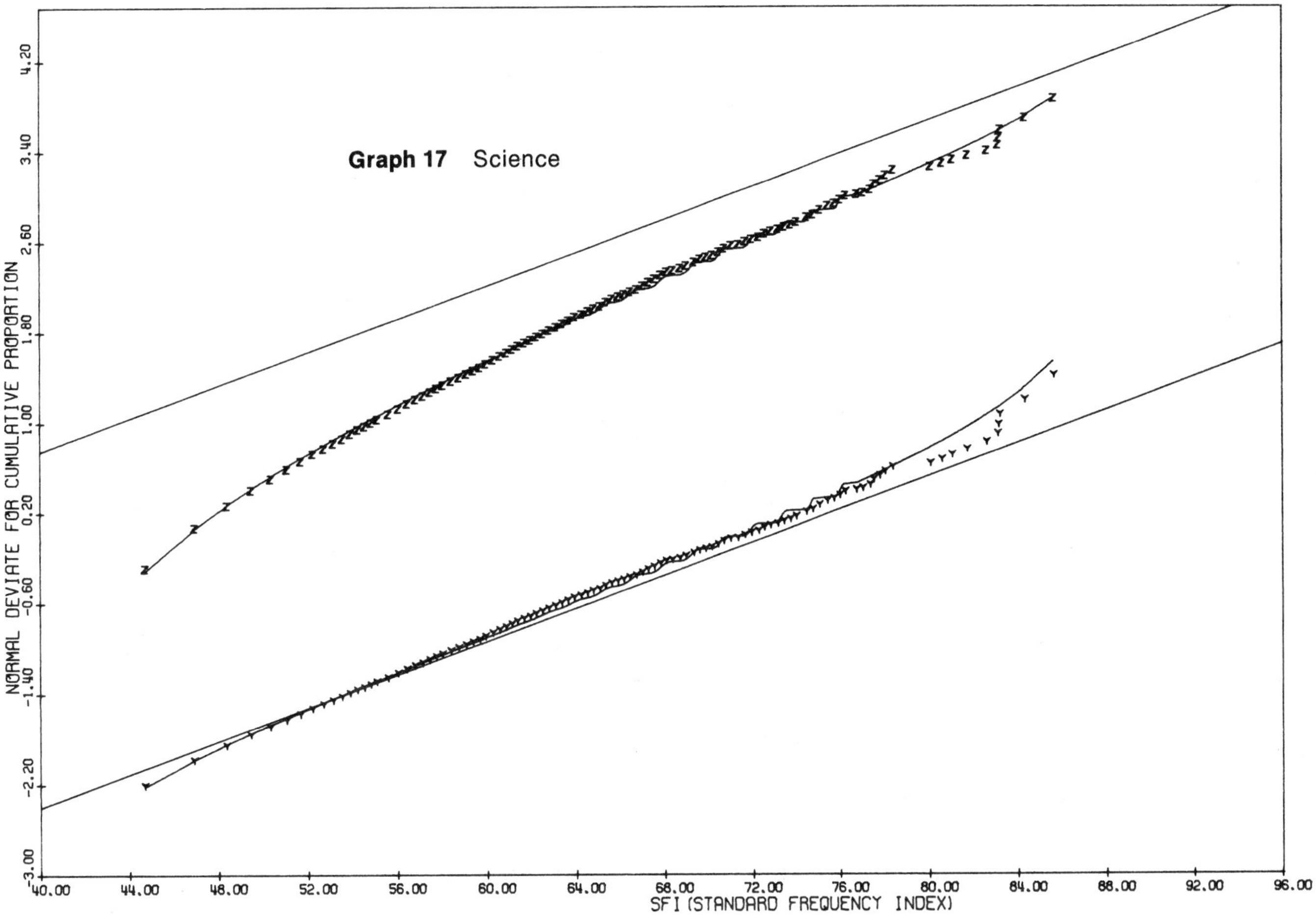

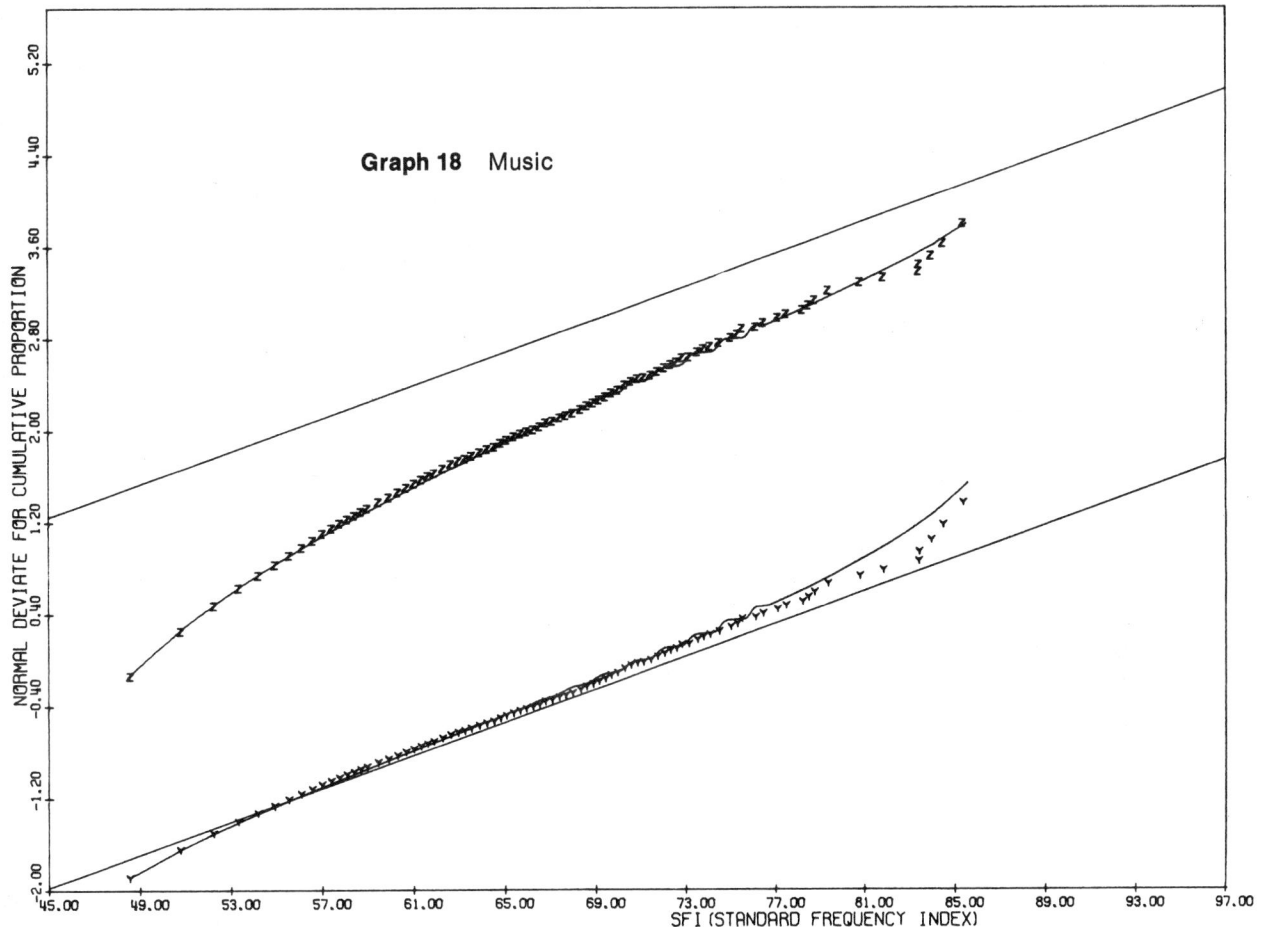

Graph 17 Science

Graph 18 Music

821

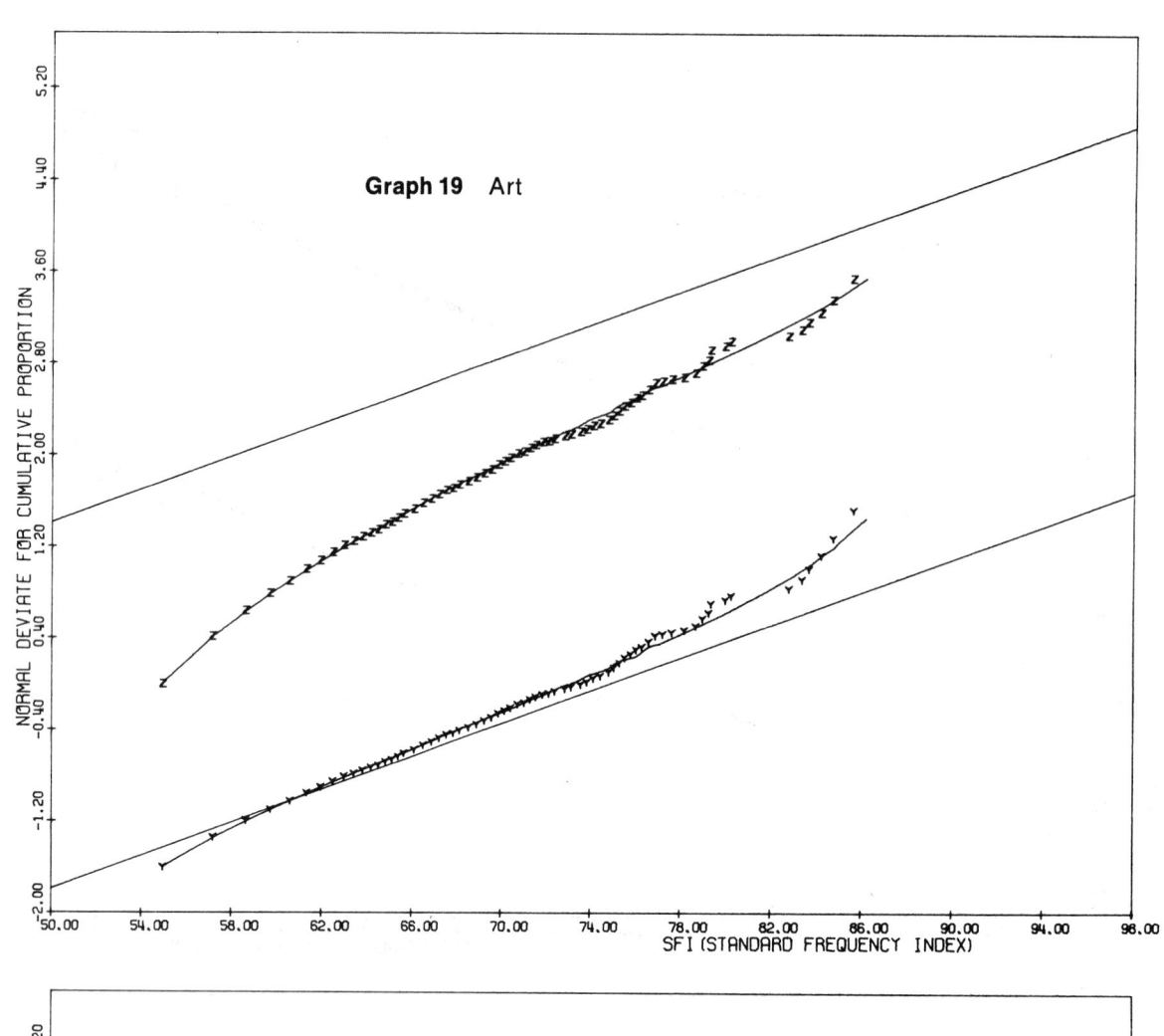

Graph 19   Art

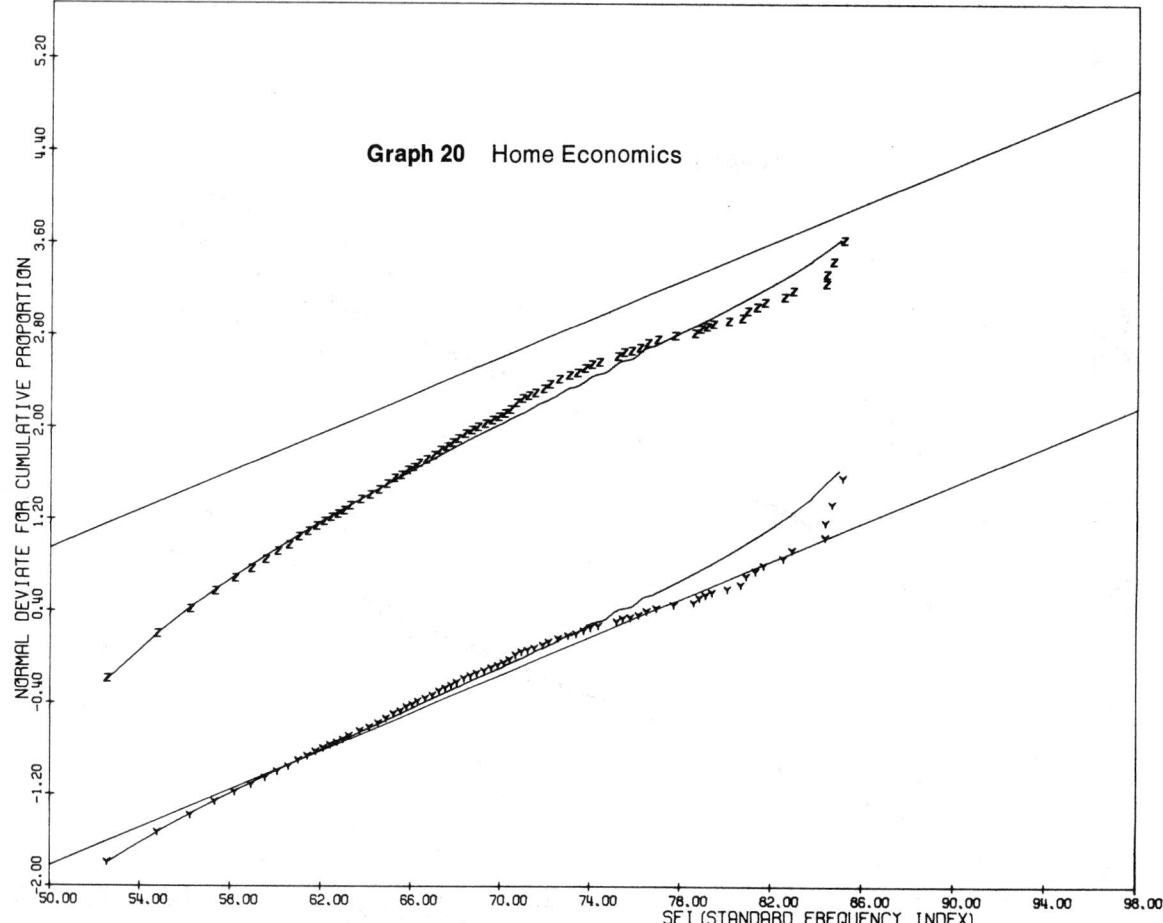

Graph 20   Home Economics

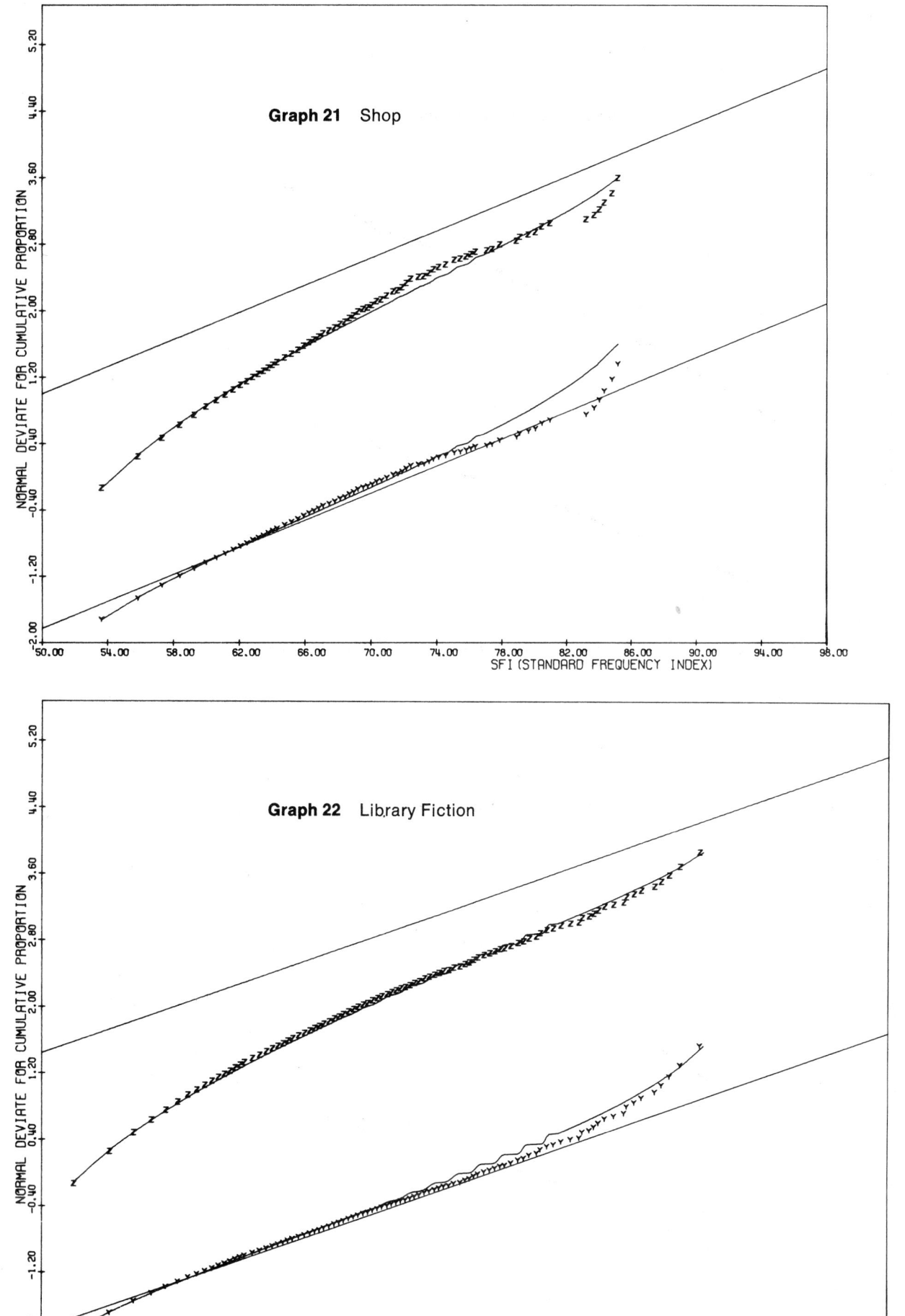

Graph 21 Shop

NORMAL DEVIATE FOR CUMULATIVE PROPORTION

SFI (STANDARD FREQUENCY INDEX)

Graph 22 Library Fiction

NORMAL DEVIATE FOR CUMULATIVE PROPORTION

SFI (STANDARD FREQUENCY INDEX)

823

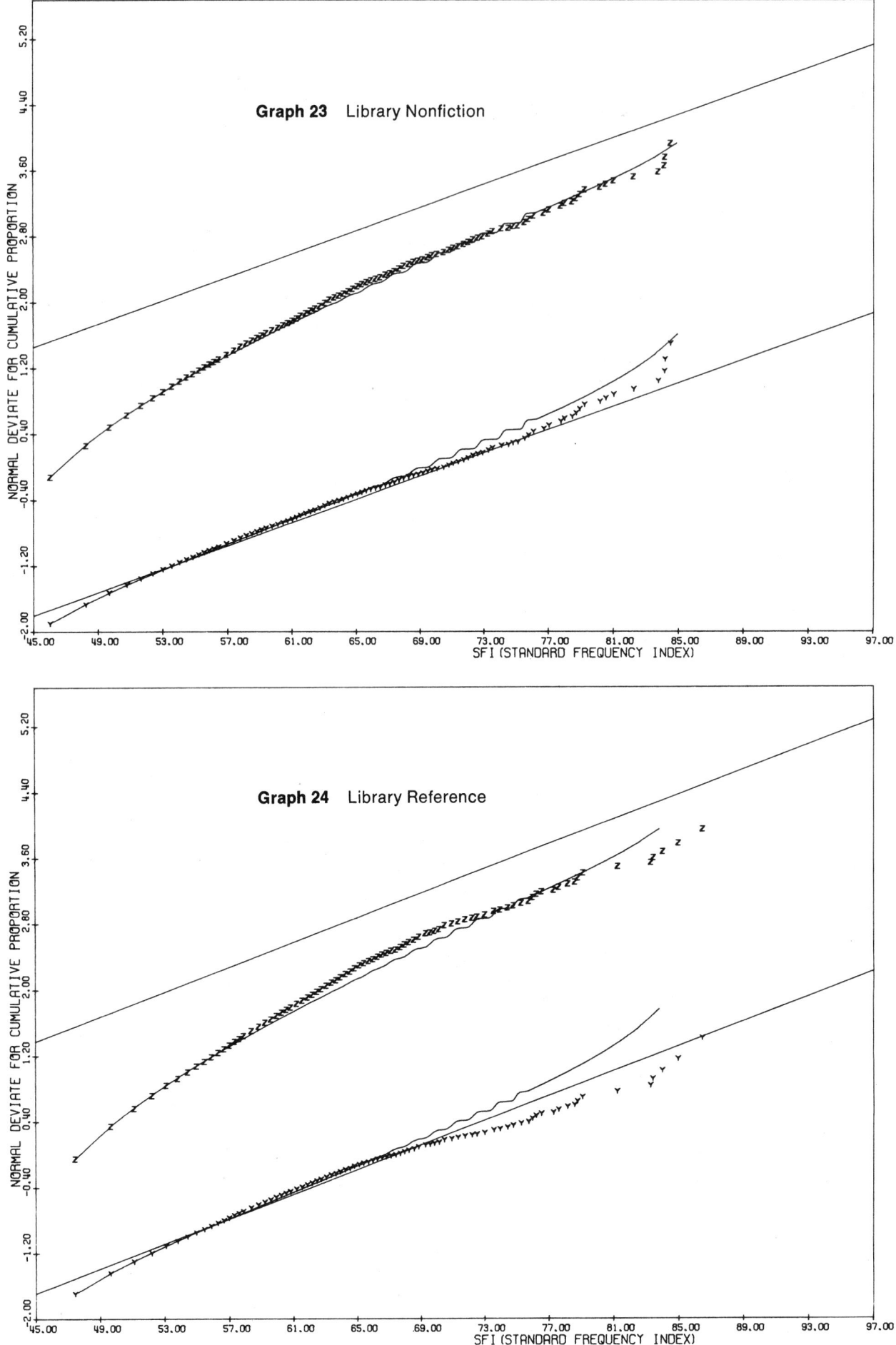

Graph 23 Library Nonfiction

Graph 24 Library Reference

824

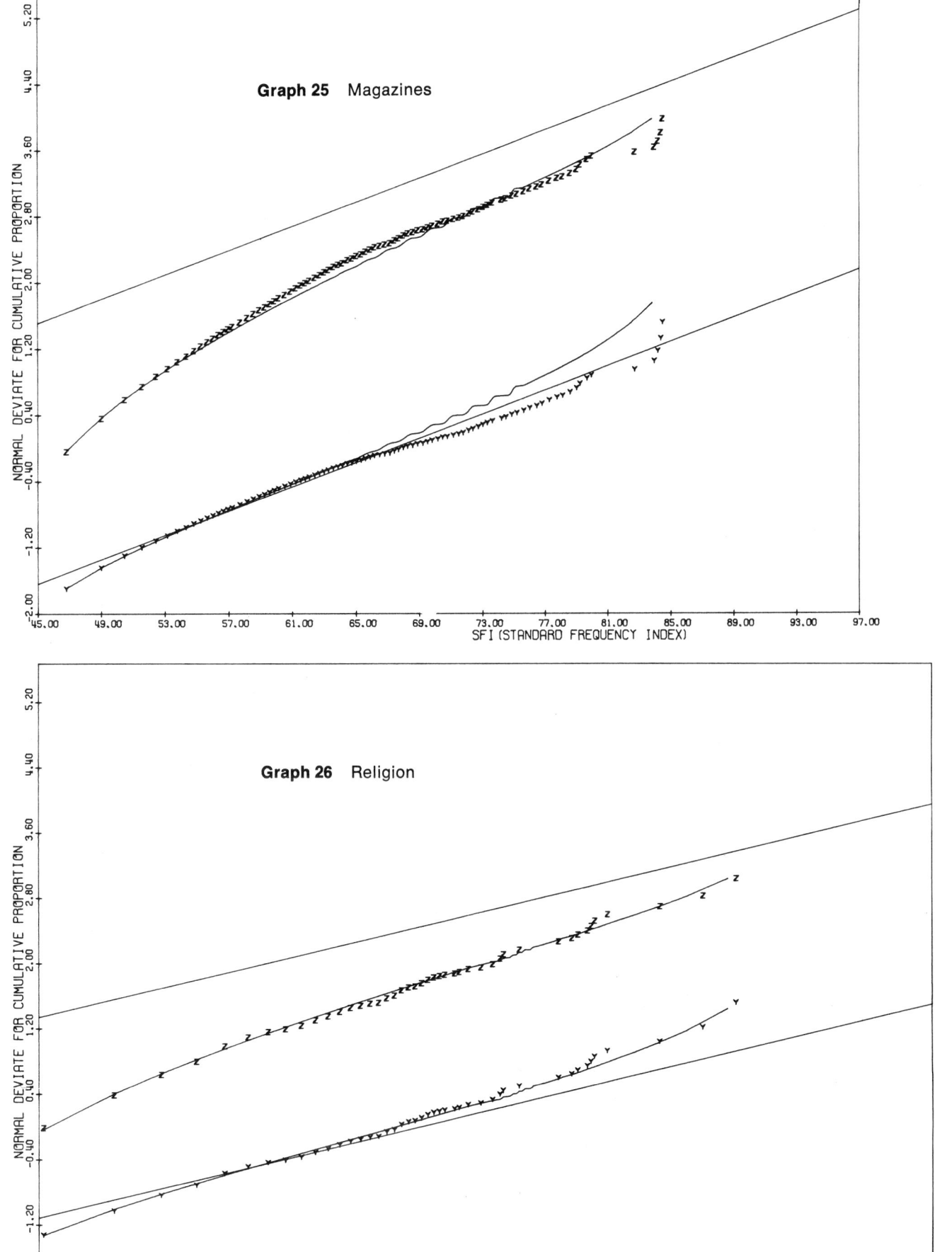

Graph 25   Magazines

Graph 26   Religion

825

Appendix A. Survey Respondents

The respondents are listed here in the groups covered by the survey—public, Roman Catholic, and independent schools. Within each group, the organization is alphabetical by state and then by city. As explained in the introductory material on the survey, the exceptionally strong response from Roman Catholic schools relative to public schools made it necessary to exclude from analysis some of the Roman Catholic questionnaires. The exclusions are indicated by asterisks.

Public School Systems

W. O. Briscoe
Assistant Superintendent
Gadsden City Schools
Gadsden, Alabama

Dr. Luther Charles Sprayberry
Superintendent of Education
Tuscaloosa County Board of
   Education
Tuscaloosa, Alabama

Dr. Carlisle H. Kramer
Superintendent
Anchorage Borough School District
Anchorage, Alaska

Dr. George N. Smith
Superintendent
Mesa Public Schools
Mesa, Arizona

Floyd W. Parsons
Superintendent of Schools
Little Rock Public Schools
Little Rock, Arkansas

Miss Madeline Warren
Director of Library Services
Alum Rock Union Elementary School
   District
San Jose, California

Miss Mabel M. Bumgardner
Coordinator, Instructional Materials
   Services
Cupertino Union School District
Cupertino, California

Mrs. Marion K. Wood
Coordinator, School Library Services
Fullerton Elementary
Fullerton, California

John J. Mamola
Principal, Fremont Elementary School
Sacramento City Unified School
   District
Sacramento, California

Dr. Robert A. Bennett
Specialist—Language Arts
San Diego City Schools
San Diego, California

Charles F. Kenney
Superintendent of Schools
Santa Ana Unified and Junior College
   Districts
Santa Ana, California

Dr. Clifford S. Thyberg
Superintendent of Schools
West Covina Unified School District
West Covina, California

Jerry E. Reed
Supervisor of English
Denver Public Schools
Denver, Colorado

P. L. Schmelzer
Assistant Superintendent
Poudre School District
Fort Collins, Colorado

Milton Van Vlack
Project Consultant for Curriculum
   Materials
Hartford Public Schools
Hartford, Connecticut

Mrs. Ettyce H. Moore
Executive Assistant to the Deputy
   Superintendent
Washington D. C. Public Schools
Washington, D. C.

Pledger V. Sullivan
Assistant Superintendent of Adminis-
   tration
Okaloosa County School System
Crestview, Florida

Mrs. Eunice H. Sims
Coordinator of English
Atlanta Public School System
Atlanta, Georgia

Snell A. Mills, Jr.
Assistant Director of Instruction for Instructional Materials and Equipment
DeKalb County School System
Decatur, Georgia

Robert A. Burns
Director of Elementary Education
Boise Public Schools
Boise, Idaho

Kent Paulson
Elementary Math and Science Consultant
Elkhart Community Schools
Elkhart, Indiana

William W. Lyon
Director of Instruction
Muncie Community Schools
Muncie, Indiana

Mrs. Nina L. Davis
Technical Assistant to the Superintendent
Wichita Public Schools
Wichita, Kansas

Simeon W. Marcotte
Elementary Supervisor
Acadia Parish School Board
Crowley, Louisiana

Robert J. Boudreaux
Supervisor
St. Mary Parish School Board
Franklin, Louisiana

Dr. Rodney E. Wells
Superintendent of Schools
Portland Public Schools
Portland, Maine

Dr. John L. Carnochan, Jr.
Superintendent of Schools
Board of Education of Frederick County
Frederick, Maryland

Edward J. Moran
Director of Secondary Instruction
Framingham School Department
Framingham, Massachusetts

James Fitzgerald
Superintendent of Schools
Waltham School System
Waltham, Massachusetts

Neil Van Dis
Director, Elementary Education
Battle Creek Public Schools
Battle Creek, Michigan

Dr. James D. Berry
Director, Instructional Services
Detroit Public Schools
Detroit, Michigan

Mrs. Lois DeMaagd
Administrative Assistant
Grand Rapids Public School System
Grand Rapids, Michigan

Mrs. Norma E. Hahn
Secretary to Assistant Superintendent
Muskegon Public Schools
Muskegon, Michigan

Raymond La Frey
Coordinator of Language Arts
Wayne Community School District
Wayne, Michigan

Hugh Schoephoerster
Coordinator of Elementary Curriculum
Anoka-Hennepin Independent School District 11
Anoka, Minnesota

Dr. Robert W. Ash
Administrative Assistant
White Bear Lake Area Public Schools
White Bear Lake, Minnesota

R. B. Layton
Assistant Superintendent of Curriculum and Communications
Jackson Public Schools
Jackson, Mississippi

Glen Bailey
Director of Elementary Education
Independence Public Schools
Independence, Missouri

Dr. Earl G. Herminghaus
Director, Division of Curriculum Services
St. Louis Public Schools
St. Louis, Missouri

Mrs. Evelyn Montgomery
Assistant Director of Curriculum
Omaha Public Schools
Omaha, Nebraska

Harvey N. Dondero
Associate Superintendent, Communications Division
Clark County School District
Las Vegas, Nevada

Gabriel H. Reuben
Superintendent of Schools
Willingboro Township Schools
Willingboro, New Jersey

Michael W. White
Director of Instruction
Albuquerque Public Schools
Albuquerque, New Mexico

John C. O'Hagan
Supervisor of English and Reading
Albany Public Schools
Albany, New York

Dr. Charles E. Davis
Superintendent
Elmira Enlarged City District
Elmira, New York

Miss Ruth Meares
Supervisor
Columbus County School System
Whiteville, North Carolina

Charles H. Chewning, Sr.
Superintendent
Durham County School System
Durham, North Carolina

Kenneth Sherwood
Curriculum Project Coordinator
Grand Forks Public Schools
Grand Forks, North Dakota

Francis S. Martines
Coordinator for Curriculum
Cleveland Public Schools
Cleveland, Ohio

Mrs. Katie Von Thaer
Supervisor of Primary Education
Warren City Schools
Warren, Ohio

Jacob M. Horst
Supervisor of English
Allentown School District
Allentown, Pennsylvania

Dr. Edwin Hasson
Director of Elementary Education
Butler Area School District
Butler, Pennsylvania

Mrs. Kathleen M. Rihs
Pittsburgh Public Schools
Pittsburgh, Pennsylvania

Dr. Thomas K. Barratt
Superintendent
Warren County School District
Warren, Pennsylvania

Domenic R. DiLuglio
Superintendent
Warwick School Department
Warwick, Rhode Island

Dr. Billie D. Holladay
Director of Elementary Education
Charleston County Schools
Charleston, South Carolina

Evelyn S. Irwin
Reading Consultant
Greenwood School District #50
Greenwood, South Carolina

Dr. Claud E. Kitchens
Assistant Superintendent
Richland County District #1, Columbia Public Schools
Columbia, South Carolina

Marshall G. Howell
Supervisor, Text Books
Hamilton County, Tennessee Board of
    Education
Chattanooga, Tennessee

Raymond J. Free
Director of Curriculum
Galena Park Independent School
    District
Galena Park, Texas

Dr. Richard D. Slatter
Associate Deputy Superintendent,
    Curriculum, Educational Research,
    & Program Development
Houston Independent School District
Houston, Texas

Miss Frances Wilson
Administrative Secretary to the Super-
    intendent
Lubbock Public Schools
Lubbock, Texas

G. B. Wadzeck
Superintendent of Schools
San Angelo Independent School
    District
San Angelo, Texas

L. D. Adams
Superintendent
Richmond Public Schools
Richmond, Virginia

Dr. Lester L. Cummins
Assistant Superintendent – Instruction
Federal Way Public Schools
Federal Way, Washington

Mrs. Jean R. Kennelly
Director of Libraries
Yakima Public Schools
Yakima, Washington

Sherman C. Trail
Assistant Superintendent
Raleigh County School System
Beckley, West Virginia

Olin C. Nutter
Superintendent
Cabell County Board of Education
Huntington, West Virginia

Roland Olenchek
Administrative Assistant
Milwaukee Public Schools
Milwaukee, Wisconsin

Miss Myrtle L. Nyberg
Elementary Consultant
    and
Mrs. Alice Maronn
English Language Arts and Social
    Studies Consultant
Joint City School District #1
West Allis, Wisconsin

Maurice F. Griffith
Superintendent of Schools
Casper-Midwest Schools
Casper, Wyoming

Roman Catholic Schools

Sister Mark
English Teacher
St. Mary's School*
Kodiak, Alaska

Sister Jean Ann Wilburn, S.C.
Diocesan Elementary Consultant
Dioceses of Phoenix & Tucson*
Tucson, Arizona

Sister Suzanne, D.C.
Primary Coordinator
Our Lady of Talpa School
Los Angeles, California

Sister Catherine Regan, C.S.J.
Supervisor
Archdiocese of Hartford
West Hartford, Connecticut

Sister M. Eamon O'Neil
Assistant Superintendent
Diocese of Wilmington
Wilmington, Delaware

Sister M. Madeline, R.S.M.
Director of Elementary Education
Catholic Archdiocese of Atlanta*
Atlanta, Georgia

Sister Nadine Schafer
Elementary Schools Consultant
Catholic Diocese of Honolulu
Honolulu, Hawaii

Sister M. Gertrude Wemhoff, O.S.B.
Community Supervisor
Diocese of Boise*
Cottonwood, Idaho

Sister M. Lois
Curriculum Director
Chicago Archdiocese
Chicago, Illinois

Sister Ramona Lunsford, O.S.F.
Supervisor
Archdiocese of Indianapolis*
Indianapolis, Indiana

Sister Elizabeth Clare, O.P.
Diocesan Elementary Supervisor
Diocese of Des Moines
Des Moines, Iowa

Rev. Charles W. Regan
Superintendent of Catholic Schools
Diocese of Wichita*
Wichita, Kansas

Sister Rose Speckner, O.P.
Assistant Superintendent of Schools
Catholic School System,
Archdiocese of Louisville*
Louisville, Kentucky

Sister Claire Germaine Henritzy, C.S.J.
Supervisor
Catholic Schools of the Diocese of
    Baton Rouge*
Baton Rouge, Louisiana

Sister Mary Dolorine Moran
Teacher-Librarian
Catholic School System, Archdiocese
    of Baltimore*
Baltimore, Maryland

Sister M. Iona Taylor
Language Arts Consultant
Catholic Schools of Detroit*
Detroit, Michigan

Sister Victoria Houle, C.S.J.
Director of Elementary Education
Archdiocese of St. Paul and Minne-
    apolis*
St. Paul, Minnesota

Sister Mary Louise Reinke, O.S.F.
Reading Consultant
Mississippi Catholic Schools*
Jackson, Mississippi

Sister Mary Patricius
Coordinator of Elementary Education
St. Thomas More School System
Omaha, Nebraska

Rev. George C. Wolf
Principal
Bishop Manogue High School*
Reno, Nevada

Sister Barbara Connell, S.C.
Supervisor of Schools
Sisters of Charity, So. Province
West Orange, New Jersey

Rev. Gregg D. Petri, O.F.M.
Diocesan Director of Education
Diocese of Gallup
Gallup, New Mexico

Dr. John H. Kleffner
Superintendent of Catholic Schools
Diocese of Oklahoma City & Tulsa
Oklahoma City, Oklahoma

Sister Margaret Evans, O.P.
Superintendent of Schools
Diocese of Galveston-Houston
Houston, Texas

Sister Aurea Goulet, C.S.C.
School Supervisor
Diocese of Burlington*
Rutland, Vermont

Sister Elaine McCarren, S.C.N.
Director of Elementary Education
Department of Education
Diocese of Richmond*
Richmond, Virginia

Sister Irma Sherman
Curriculum Coordinator
Archdiocese of Seattle*
Seattle, Washington

Monsignor James A. Hartman
Superintendent of Schools
Diocese of Cheyenne*
Cheyenne, Wyoming

Independent Schools

Frederick A. DiazGranados
Headmaster, Lower School
Ojai Valley School
Ojai, California

Dr. Kenneth Veronda
Director
Southwestern Academy
San Marino, California

Kenneth L. Harris
Headmaster
Miami Country Day and Resident School
Miami, Florida

Harry D. McLachlin
Instructor
Fay School
Southboro, Massachusetts

Miss Judith Todd
Educational Secretary
McLaren School
Esopus, New York

A. Michael DeSisto
Lake Grove School
Lake Grove, New York

Mrs. Evelyn Koon
Principal
Dallas Academy
Dallas, Texas

Marjorie F. Graham
Principal
Radford School for Girls
El Paso, Texas

Appendix B. The Sampling Texts

These are the sources from which the Intermediate Corpus was drawn. The dates given are the copyright dates for the editions sampled. In the acquisition of the sampling texts, the edition most frequently specified by the survey respondents was sought, but it was often necessary to accept the most recent edition available – up to the November 1969 date of survey. In a few cases, a 1970 copyright was accepted. The titles are listed here by subject and grade and then alphabetically by title. For information on the sampling procedure itself, see pages xv–xviii. A summary of the number of titles and samples falling in different grades and subjects is given in Table A-3 on pages xvi and xvii.

Reading, Grade 3

G. McCracken *et al., Basic Reading 3-1* (J. B. Lippincott Company, Philadelphia, 1964).

A. Harris and M. Clark, *Better Than Gold* (The Macmillan Company, New York, 1965).

E. A. Betts and C. M. Welch, *Beyond Treasure Valley* (American Book Company, Cincinnati, 1965).

I. S. Black *et al., City Sidewalks* (The Macmillan Company, New York, 1966).

P. McKee *et al., Climbing Higher* (Houghton Mifflin Company, Boston, 1966).

D. H. Russell *et al., Finding New Neighbors – 100 Edition* (Ginn and Company, Boston, 1966).

D. H. Russell *et al., Friends Far and Near* (Ginn and Company, Boston, 1966).

B. H. VanRoekel and M. Kluwe, *From Bicycles to Boomerangs* (Harper & Row, Publishers, New York, 1966).

M. O'Donnell, *From Faraway Places* (Harper & Row, Publishers, New York, 1966).

P. McKee *et al., Looking Ahead* (Houghton Mifflin Company, Boston, 1966).

H. M. Robinson *et al., More Roads to Follow* (Scott, Foresman and Company, Glenview, 1965).

B. Feldner and L. Schafer, *More Than Words* (The Macmillan Company, New York, 1966).

H. M. Robinson *et al., Roads to Follow* (Scott, Foresman and Company, Glenview, 1964).

H. M. Robinson *et al., Speeding Away* (Scott, Foresman and Company, Glenview, 1968).

H. M. Robinson *et al., Splendid Journey* (Scott, Foresman and Company, Glenview, 1968).

Reading, Grade 4

E. A. Betts and C. M. Welch, *American Adventures* (American Book Company, Cincinnati, 1965).

G. McCracken and C. Walcutt, *Basic Reading* (J. B. Lippincott Company, Philadelphia, 1965).

W. D. Sheldon, *Believe and Make-Believe* (Allyn and Bacon, Boston, 1968).

J. C. Coleman *et al., Danger Below* (Field Educational Publications, San Francisco, 1967).

M. O'Donnell, *Engine Whistles* (Row, Peterson and Company, Evanston, 1957).

J. Coleman *et al., Frogmen In Action* (Harr Wagner Publishing Company, San Francisco, 1967).

M. O'Donnell and J. L. Cooper, *From Codes to Captains* (Harper & Row, Publishers, New York, 1963).

831

P. McKee *et al., High Roads* (Houghton Mifflin Company, Boston, 1966).

M. Gartler, *The Magic Word* (The Macmillan Company, New York, 1966).

H. M. Robinson *et al., Open Highways, Book 4* (Scott, Foresman and Company, Glenview, 1965).

D. H. Russell *et al., Roads to Everywhere – 100 Edition* (Ginn and Company, Boston, 1966).

Sister M. Sheila, P.B.V.M., and Sister M. M. Michael, O.P., *This is Our Land* (Ginn and Company, Boston, 1965).

E. L. Evertts & B. H. VanRoekel, *Trade Winds* (Harper & Row, Publishers, New York, 1966).

H. M. Robinson *et al., Ventures* (Scott, Foresman and Company, Glenview, 1965).

H. M. Robinson *et al., Wide Horizons, Book 4* (Scott, Foresman and Company, Glenview, 1965).

Reading, Grade 5

A. J. Harris *et al., Bold Journeys* (The Macmillan Company, New York, 1966).

E. L. Evertts and B. H. VanRoekel, *Crossroads* (Harper & Row, Publishers, New York, 1966).

H. M. Robinson *et al., Open Highways, Book 5* (Scott, Foresman and Company, Glenview, 1966).

D. H. Russell *et al., Trails to Treasure* (Ginn and Company, Boston, 1966).

H. M. Robinson *et al., Vistas* (Scott, Foresman and Company, Glenview, 1965).

Reading, Grade 6

P. McKee *et al., Bright Peaks* (Houghton Mifflin Company, Boston, 1966).

H. M. Robinson *et al., Cavalcades* (Scott, Foresman and Company, Glenview, 1965).

A. J. Harris *et al., Into New Worlds* (The Macmillan Company, New York, 1966).

H. M. Robinson *et al., Open Highways, Book 6* (Scott, Foresman and Company, Glenview, 1966).

E. L. Evertts and B. VanRoekel, *Seven Seas* (Harper & Row, Publishers, New York, 1966).

H. M. Robinson *et al., Wide Horizons, Book 6* (Scott, Foresman and Company, Glenview, 1965).

D. H. Russell *et al., Wings to Adventure* (Ginn and Company, Boston, 1966).

Reading, Grade 7

J. C. Gainsburg, *Advanced Skills in Reading, Book 1* (The Macmillan Company, New York, 1967).

A. Jewett *et al., Adventure Bound* (Houghton Mifflin Company, Boston, 1965).

N. B. Smith, *Be A Better Reader, Book 1* (Prentice-Hall, Englewood Cliffs, 1969).

N. B. Smith, *Be A Better Reader – Foundations A* (Prentice-Hall, Englewood Cliffs, 1968).

N. B. Smith, *Be A Better Reader – Foundations B* (Prentice-Hall, Englewood Cliffs, 1968).

M. B. Smiley *et al., Coping* (The Macmillan Company, New York, 1966).

H. M. Robinson *et al., Dimensions* (Scott, Foresman and Company, Glenview, 1967).

M. A. Gunn *et al., Discovery Through Reading – 100 Edition* (Ginn and Company, Boston, 1967).

M. B. Smiley *et al., A Family is a Way of Feeling* (The Macmillan Company, New York, 1966).

H. L. Herber, *Learning Your Language/One* (Follett Educational Corporation, Chicago, 1969).

H. M. Robinson *et al., Open Highways, Book 7* (Scott, Foresman and Company, Glenview, 1967).

J. F. Kennedy, *Profiles In Courage* (Harper & Row, Publishers, New York, 1964).

H. Bamman *et al., Riddler* (Field Educational Publications, San Francisco, 1967).

M. B. Smiley *et al., Stories in Song and Verse* (The Macmillan Company, New York, 1966).

H. G. Felsen, *Street Rod* (Random House, New York, 1953).

R. E. Shafer and A. S. McDonald, *Success in Reading, Book 1* (Silver Burdett Company, Morristown, 1967).

J. B. McDowell *et al., Wide, Wide World – Cathedral Edition* (Scott, Foresman and Company, Glenview, 1966).

M. B. Smiley *et al., Who Am I?* (The Macmillan Company, New York, 1966).

H. Bamman and R. Whitehead, *Wheels* (Harr Wagner Publishing Company, San Francisco, 1967).

Reading, Grade 8

E. M. Pumphrey and I. M. Kincheloe, *Adventures Ahead* (Harcourt, Brace & World, New York, 1962).

J. B. McDowell *et al., All Around America – Cathedral Edition* (Scott, Foresman and Company, Glenview, 1966).

H. Bamman *et al., Bearcat* (Field Educational Publications, San Francisco, 1967).

H. M. Robinson *et al., Challenges* (Scott, Foresman and Company, Glenview, 1967).

M. A. Gunn *et al., Exploration Through Reading* (Ginn and Company, Boston, 1967).

A. Jewett *et al., Journeys Into America* (Houghton Mifflin Company, Boston, 1965).

H. M. Robinson *et al., Open Highways, Book 8* (Scott, Foresman and Company, Glenview, 1967).

A. M. Caughran and L. H. Mountain, *Reading, Book 1* (American Book Company, Cincinnati, 1965).

H. Bamman and R. Whitehead, *Smashup* (Field Educational Publications, San Francisco, 1967).

Reading, Grade 9

J. C. Gainsburg, *Advanced Skills in Reading, Book 3* (The Macmillan Company, New York, 1964).

J. C. Bushman *et al., Scope/Reading 1* (Harper & Row, Publishers, New York, 1967).

Reading Supplementary, Grade 3

M. Goodwin, *Alonzo and the Army of Ants* (Harper & Row, Publishers, New York, 1966).

M. DeJong, *The Big Goose and the Little White Duck* (Harper & Row, Publishers, New York, 1938).

M. Lewiton, *Candita's Choice* (Harper & Row, Publishers, New York, 1959).

N. S. Carlson, *Carnival In Paris* (Harper & Row, Publishers, New York, 1962).

S. Hoff, *Danny and the Dinosaur* (Harper & Row, Publishers, New York, 1958).

M. Calhoun, *Depend on Katie John* (Harper & Row, Publishers, New York, 1961).

J. A. Overberg and C. C. Peardon, *A Discovery Book — Better Than Gold* (The Macmillan Company, New York, 1970).

H. G. Shane and K. B. Hester, *Doorways to Adventure* (Laidlaw Brothers, River Forest, 1966).

M. Lewiton, *Faces Looking Up* (Harper & Row, Publishers, New York, 1960).

N. B. Smith *et al., Fun All Around* (The Bobbs-Merrill Company, Indianapolis, 1960).

C. Bonsall, *It's Mine!* (Harper & Row, Publishers, New York, 1964).

P. Parish, *Let's Be Indians* (Harper & Row, Publishers, New York, 1962).

E. H. Minarik, *Little Bear's Friend* (Harper & Row, Publishers, New York, 1960).

C. R. Stone and A. E. Burton, *New Practice Readers, Book A* (Webster Division, McGraw-Hill Book Company, New York, 1960).

C. C. Grover and D. G. Anderson, *New Practice Readers, Book B* (Webster Division, McGraw-Hill Book Company, New York, 1960).

M. DeJong, *Nobody Plays With a Cabbage* (Harper & Row, Publishers, New York, 1962).

U. W. Leavell *et al., Open Roads* (American Book Company, Cincinnati, 1961).

C. D. Buchanan, *Programmed Reading for Adults, Book 5* (Webster Division, McGraw-Hill Book Company, New York, 1968).

C. D. Buchanan, *Programmed Reading for Adults, Book 6* (Webster Division, McGraw-Hill Book Company, New York, 1966).

C. D. Buchanan, *Programmed Reading for Adults, Book 7* (Webster Division, McGraw-Hill Book Company, New York, 1967).

C. D. Buchanan, *Programmed Reading for Adults, Book 8* (Webster Division, McGraw-Hill Book Company, New York, 1967).

New Reading Skill Builder, Level 3, Parts 1 and 2 (Reader's Digest Services, Pleasantville, 1966).

G. Selden, *Oscar Lobster's Fair Exchange* (Harper & Row, Publishers, New York, 1966).

F. Phleger, *Red Tag Comes Back* (Harper & Row, Publishers, New York, 1961).

E. C. Neville, *The Seventeenth Street Gang* (Harper & Row, Publishers, New York, 1966).

C. Greene, *Soldiers and Sailors — What Do They Do?* (Harper & Row, Publishers, New York, 1963).

B. Martin, Jr., *Sounds of the Storyteller* (Holt, Rinehart and Winston, New York, 1966).

D. H. Parker and G. Scannell, *SRA Reading Laboratory Ia* (Science Research Associates, Chicago, 1961).

D. H. Parker and G. Scannell, *SRA Reading Laboratory Ib* (Science Research Associates, Chicago, 1961).

D. H. Parker and G. Scannell, *SRA Reading Laboratory Ic* (Science Research Associates, Chicago, 1961).

F. W. DeLancey and W. J. Iverson, *Story Carnival* (L. W. Singer Company, New York, 1965).

H. M. Robinson *et al., Think-and-Do, Book 3, Part 1 — Roads to Follow* (Scott, Foresman and Company, Glenview, 1965).

H. M. Robinson *et al., Think-and-Do, Book 3, Part 2 — More Roads to Follow* (Scott, Foresman and Company, Glenview, 1965).

W. E. Young *et al., Uncle Funny Bunny* (Charles E. Merrill Publishing Co., Columbus, 1961).

R. M. Pearl, *The Wonder World of Metals* (Harper & Row, Publishers, New York, 1966).

P. Wilson, *Workbook for From Faraway Places* (Harper & Row, Publishers, New York, 1969).

Reading Supplementary, Grade 4

S. Taylor, *All-Of-A-Kind Family* (Dell Publishing Company, New York, 1951).

M. Embry, *The Bluenosed Witch* (Holiday House, New York, 1956).

D. H. Russell *et al., Down Story Roads* (Ginn and Company, Boston, 1968).

A. Brenner, *A Hero By Mistake* (William R. Scott, New York, 1953).

C. Hoff, *Johnny Texas* (Follett Publishing Company, Chicago, 1950).

H. G. Shane *et al., Magic and Laughter* (Laidlaw Brothers, River Forest, 1964).

C. R. Stone, *New Practice Readers, Book C* (Webster Division, McGraw-Hill Book Company, New York, 1962).

New Reading Skill Builder, Level 4, Parts 1 and 2 (Reader's Digest Services, Pleasantville, 1967).

U. W. Leavell *et al., Paths to Follow* (American Book Company, Cincinnati, 1964).

P. A. Witty and A. M. Freeland, *Peacock Lane* (D. C. Heath and Company, Lexington, 1964).

B. Martin, Jr., *Sounds of Mystery* (Holt, Rinehart and Winston, New York, 1967).

D. H. Parker, *SRA Reading Laboratory IIa* (Science Research Associates, Chicago, 1969).

H. M. Robinson *et al., Think-and-Do, Book 4 — Open Highways* (Scott, Foresman and Company, Glenview, 1965).

H. M. Robinson *et al., Think-and-Do, Book 4 — Ventures* (Scott, Foresman and Company, Glenview, 1965).

J. C. Coleman *et al., Whale Hunt* (Harr Wagner Publishing Company, San Francisco, 1967).

Reading Supplementary, Grade 5

D. H. Russell *et al., Along Story Trails* (Ginn and Company, Boston, 1968).

U. W. Leavell *et al., Frontiers to Explore* (American Book Company, Cincinnati, 1964).

J. Rambeau and N. Rambeau, *The Mystery of the Midnight Visitor* (Harr Wagner Publishing Company, San Francisco, 1962).

C. R. Stone and C. C. Grover, *New Practice Readers, Book D* (Webster Division, McGraw-Hill Book Company, New York, 1962).

C. R. Stone *et al., New Practice Readers, Book E* (Webster Division, McGraw-Hill Book Company, New York, 1962).

New Reading Skill Builder, Level 5, Parts 1 and 2 (Reader's Digest Services, Pleasantville, *Part 1* 1967 and *Part 2* 1968).

P. A. Witty and A. M. Freeland, *Silver Web* (D. C. Heath and Company, Lexington, 1964).

B. Martin, Jr., *Sounds of a Young Hunter* (Holt, Rinehart and Winston, New York, 1967).

D. H. Parker, *SRA Reading Laboratory IIb* (Science Research Associates, Chicago, 1960).

H. M. Robinson *et al., Think-and-Do, Book 5 — Open Highways* (Scott, Foresman and Company, Glenview, 1966).

H. M. Robinson *et al., Think-and-Do, Book 5 — Vistas* (Scott, Foresman and Company, Glenview, 1965).

W. E. Young *et al., Tom Trott* (Charles E. Merrill Publishing Co., Columbus, 1961).

H. G. Shane *et al., Words With Wings* (Laidlaw Brothers, River Forest, 1964).

Reading Supplementary, Grade 6

A. Feagles, *Casey, The Utterly Impossible Horse* (Young Scott Books, New York, 1960).

H. G. Shane and K. B. Hester, *Courage and Adventure* (Laidlaw Brothers, River Forest, 1964).

J. Grimm and W. Grimm, *Fairy Tales* (The World Publishing Company, Cleveland, 1947).

R. Field, *Hitty: Her First Hundred Years* (The Macmillan Company, New York, 1957).

New Reading Skill Builder, Level 6, Parts 1 and 2 (Reader's Digest Services, Pleasantville, 1968).

D. H. Russell *et al., On Story Wings* (Ginn and Company, Boston, 1968).

W. E. Young *et al., Pat the Pilot* (Charles E. Merrill Publishing Co., Columbus, 1961).

J. M. Barrie, *Peter Pan* (Grosset & Dunlap, New York, 1911).

C. Brink, *The Pink Motel* (The Macmillan Company, New York, 1959).

K. Grahame, *The Reluctant Dragon* (Holiday House, New York, 1966).

B. Martin, Jr., *Sounds of a Distant Drum* (Holt, Rinehart and Winston, New York, 1967).

D. H. Parker, *SRA Reading Laboratory IIc* (Science Research Associates, Chicago, 1960).

G. L. Bond *et al., Stories to Remember* (Lyons and Carnahan, Chicago, 1962).

H. M. Robinson *et al., Think-and-Do, Book 6 — Cavalcades* (Scott, Foresman and Company, Glenview, 1965).

H. M. Robinson *et al., Think-and-Do, Book 6 — Open Highways* (Scott, Foresman and Company, Glenview, 1966).

P. A. Witty and A. M. Freeland, *Treasure Gold* (D. C. Heath and Company, Lexington, 1968).

Le Grand, *When the Mississippi Was Wild* (Abingdon Press, Nashville, 1952).

U. W. Leavell *et al., Widening Horizons* (American Book Company, Cincinnati, 1964).

Reading Supplementary, Grade 7

Advanced Reading Skill Builder, Books 1 and 2 (Reader's Digest Services, Pleasantville, 1958).

D. Gates, *Blue Willow* (The Viking Press, New York, 1968).

C. C. Grover *et al., New Practice Readers, Book F* (Webster Division, McGraw-Hill Book Company, New York, 1962).

C. C. Grover and D. G. Anderson, *New Practice Readers, Book G* (Webster Division, McGraw-Hill Book Company, New York, 1961).

Read (American Education Publications, Columbus: nine issues selected from January 1 through November 15, 1969).

H. M. Robinson *et al., Skillbook 7 — Open Highways* (Scott, Foresman and Company, Glenview, 1968).

D. H. Parker, *SRA Reading Laboratory IIIa* (Science Research Associates, Chicago, 1957).

Reading Supplementary, Grade 8

Advanced Reading Skill Builder, Books 3 and 4 (Reader's Digest Services, Pleasantville, 1958).

W. S. Gray *et al., Basic Reading Skills for Junior High School Use* (Scott, Foresman and Company, Glenview, 1957).

C. Fadiman *et al., Five American Adventures* (Harcourt, Brace & World, New York, 1963).

J. R. Squire and B. L. Squire, *Greek Myths and Legends* (The Macmillan Company, New York, 1967).

Reading Supplementary, Grade 9

J. H. Coleman and A. Jungeblut, *Reading For Meaning 9* (J. B. Lippincott Company, Philadelphia, 1965).

D. H. Parker *et al., SRA Reading Laboratory IVa* (Science Research Associates, Chicago, 1959).

Reading Supplementary, Ungraded

W. A. McCall and L. M. Crabbs, *McCall-Crabbs Standard Test Lessons in Reading, Book C* (Teachers College Press, Columbia University, New York, 1961).

English & Grammar, Grade 3

H. Shane *et al., English 3* (Laidlaw Brothers, River Forest, 1967).

H. C. Reid and H. W. Crane, *Ginn Elementary English 3* (Ginn and Company, Boston, 1970).

D. Conlin *et al., Our Language Today 3* (American Book Company, Cincinnati, 1967).

P. Roberts, *The Roberts English Series, Book 3* (Harcourt, Brace & World, New York, 1966).

English & Grammar, Grade 4

B. R. Tabachnick and D. W. Andersen, *Ginn Elementary English 4* (Ginn and Company, Boston, 1967).

T. Pollock *et al., The Macmillan English Series 4* (The Macmillan Company, New York, 1967).

D. Conlin and A. Lefcourt, *Our Language Today 4* (American Book Company, Cincinnati, 1967).

P. Roberts, *The Roberts English Series, Book 4* (Harcourt, Brace & World, New York, 1966).

English & Grammar, Grade 5

J. C. Maxwell, *Ginn Elementary English 5* (Ginn and Company, Boston, 1967).

T. Pollock *et al., The Macmillan English Series 5* (The Macmillan Company, New York, 1967).

D. Conlin and H. Fillmer, *Our Language Today 5* (American Book Company, Cincinnati, 1967).

P. Roberts, *The Roberts English Series, Book 5* (Harcourt, Brace & World, New York, 1966).

English & Grammar, Grade 6

H. Shane *et al., English 6* (Laidlaw Brothers, River Forest, 1967).

T. Pollock *et al., The Macmillan English Series 6* (The Macmillan Company, New York, 1967).

D. Conlin and N. Thompson, *Our Language Today 6* (American Book Company, Cincinnati, 1967).

P. Roberts, *The Roberts English Series 6* (Harcourt, Brace & World, New York, 1966).

English & Grammar, Grade 7

N. Postman *et al., Discovering Your Language* (Holt, Rinehart and Winston, New York, 1967).

J. E. Warriner *et al., English Grammar and Composition 7* (Harcourt, Brace & World, New York, 1965).

D. M. Wolfe *et al., Enjoying English 7* (L. W. Singer Company, New York, 1966).

M. A. Dawson *et al., Language for Daily Use 7* (Harcourt, Brace & World, New York, 1965).

T. Pollock and R. Rounds, *The Macmillan English Series 7* (The Macmillan Company, New York, 1967).

H. I. Christ, *Modern English in Action 7* (D. C. Heath and Company, Lexington, 1968).

W. Harsh *et al., New Approaches to Language and Composition, Book 7* (Laidlaw Brothers, River Forest, 1969).

D. A. Conlin *et al., Our Language Today 7* (American Book Company, Cincinnati, 1966).

P. Roberts, *The Roberts English Series 7* (Harcourt, Brace & World, New York, 1967).

English & Grammar, Grade 8

J. E. Warriner *et al., English Grammar and Composition 8* (Harcourt, Brace & World, New York, 1965).

H. I. Christ and J. Carlin, *Modern English in Action 8* (D. C. Heath and Company, Lexington, 1968).

W. Harsh *et al., New Approaches to Language and Composition, Book 8* (Laidlaw Brothers, River Forest, 1969).

D. Conlin *et al., Our Language Today 8* (American Book Company, Cincinnati, 1966).

P. Roberts, *The Roberts English Series 8* (Harcourt, Brace & World, New York, 1967).

N. Postman & H. C. Damon, *The Uses of Language* (Holt, Rinehart and Winston, New York, 1967).

English & Grammar, Grade 9

G. Papashvily and H. Papashvily, *Anything Can Happen* (Harper & Row, Publishers, New York, 1945).

J. E. Warriner *et al., English Grammar and Composition 9* (Harcourt, Brace & World, New York, 1965).

J. E. Warriner *et al., English Workshop 9* (Harcourt, Brace & World, New York, 1970).

D. M. Wolfe *et al., Enjoying English 9* (L. W. Singer Company, New York, 1966).

R. K. Corbin *et al., Guide to Modern English* (Scott, Foresman and Company, Glenview, 1965).

J. C. Bushman *et al., Language In Your Life 3* (Harper & Row, Publishers, New York, 1968).

T. Pollock *et al., The Macmillan English Series 9* (The Macmillan Company, New York, 1964).

W. Stegner *et al., Modern Composition, Book 3* (Holt, Rinehart and Winston, New York, 1969). *Note:* This text should have been sampled in Composition, Grade 9, rather than English & Grammar, Grade 9; clerical error.

D. A. Conlin and G. R. Herman, *Modern Grammar and Composition 1* (American Book Company, Cincinnati, 1967).

H. I. Christ, *Modern English in Action 9* (D. C. Heath and Company, Lexington, 1968).

M. John *et al., The New Building Better English 9* (Harper & Row, Publishers, New York, 1965).

P. Roberts, *The Roberts English Series 9* (Harcourt, Brace & World, New York, 1969).

English & Grammar, Ungraded

C. E. Funk, *Horsefeathers and Other Curious Words* (Harper & Row, Publishers, New York, 1958).

M. S. Ernst, *Words. English Roots and How They Grow* (Alfred A. Knopf, New York, 1954).

I. Asimov, *Words from History* (Houghton Mifflin Company, Boston, 1968).

Composition, Grade 3

J. H. Treanor, *English Composition 3* (The Macmillan Company, New York, 1966).

Composition, Grade 4

J. H. Treanor, *English Composition 4* (The Macmillan Company, New York, 1964).

R. M. Townsend, *Imaginary Line Handwriting, Book 4* (Steck-Vaughn Company, Austin, 1966).

Composition, Grade 5

J. H. Treanor, *English Composition 5* (The Macmillan Company, New York, 1964).

Composition, Grade 6

J. H. Treanor, *English Composition 6* (The Macmillan Company, New York, 1966).

Composition, Grade 7

D. J. Nunan, *Composition: Models and Exercises, Book 7* (Harcourt, Brace & World, New York, 1965).

J. H. Treanor, *English Composition 7* (The Macmillan Company, New York, 1964).

Composition, Grade 8

D. J. Nunan, *Composition: Models and Exercises, Book 8* (Harcourt, Brace & World, New York, 1965).

H. T. Fillmer *et al., Composition Through Literature B* (American Book Company, Cincinnati, 1967).

Composition, Grade 9

D. A. Wilbur, *Composition: Models and Exercises, Book 9* (Harcourt, Brace & World, New York, 1966).

K. M. Blickhahn *et al., Writing: Unit-Lessons in Composition, Book 1, Level C* (Ginn and Company, Boston, 1964).

D. P. Brown *et al., Writing: Unit-Lessons in Composition, Book 2, Level A* (Ginn and Company, Boston, 1964).

Literature, Grade 3

P. A. Witty and A. M. Freeland, *Meadow Green* (D. C. Heath and Company, Lexington, 1968).

Literature, Grade 4

E. Johnson *et al., Anthology of Children's Literature* (Houghton Mifflin Company, Boston, 1959).

L. Jacobs *et al., Magic Carpet* (Charles E. Merrill Publishing Co., Columbus, 1966).

M. Early *et al., Much Majesty* (Harcourt, Brace & World, New York, 1968).

Literature, Grade 5

E. M. Johnson and L. B. Jacobs, *Enchanted Isles* (Charles E. Merrill Publishing Co., Columbus, 1960).

Literature, Grade 6

E. M. Johnson and L. B. Jacobs, *Adventure Lands* (Charles E. Merrill Publishing Co., Columbus, 1960).

Literature, Grade 7

E. C. O'Daly *et al., Adventures for Readers, Book 1* (Harcourt, Brace & World, New York, 1968).

I. M. Kincheloe and E. M. Pumphrey, *Adventures for You* (Harcourt, Brace & World, New York, 1962).

C. Richter, *The Light in the Forest* (Alfred A. Knopf, New York, 1966).

J. Steinbeck, *The Pearl* (Bantam Books, New York, 1947).

R. Picozzi, *Plays to Enjoy* (The Macmillan Company, New York, 1970).

D. Pettit, *Poems to Enjoy* (The Macmillan Company, New York, 1970).

R. C. Pooley *et al., Projection in Literature* (Scott, Foresman and Company, Glenview, 1967).

N. H. Naas and M. H. Lewittes, *Readings to Enjoy* (The Macmillan Company, New York, 1970).

N. Hoopes, *Stories to Enjoy* (The Macmillan Company, New York, 1970).

M. B. Smiley *et al., A Western Sampler* (The Macmillan Company, New York, 1967).

Literature, Grade 8

E. W. Nieman and E. C. O'Daly, *Adventures for Readers, Book 2—Laureate Edition* (Harcourt, Brace & World, New York, 1963).

R. C. Pooley *et al., Counterpoint in Literature* (Scott, Foresman and Company, Glenview, 1967).

E. G. Stull, *Larger Than Life* (Holt, Rinehart and Winston, New York, 1968).

H. B. Maloney, *Plays to Remember* (The Macmillan Company, New York, 1970).

D. Pettit, *Poems to Remember* (The Macmillan Company, New York, 1970).

S. Schlakman, *Readings to Remember* (The Macmillan Company, New York, 1970).

S. Crane, *The Red Badge of Courage* (Grosset and Dunlap, New York, 1925).

S. Schlakman, *Stories to Remember* (The Macmillan Company, New York, 1970).

Literature, Grade 9

E. K. Clark and H. Potell, *Adventures for Today* (Harcourt, Brace & World, New York, 1962).

F. X. Connolly *et al., Adventures in Reading—Classic Edition* (Harcourt, Brace & World, New York, 1968).

M. W. Barrows, *Currents in Drama* (The Macmillan Company, New York, 1968).

V. Alwin, *Currents in Fiction* (The Macmillan Company, New York, 1968).

J. E. Bush, *Currents in Nonfiction* (The Macmillan Company, New York, 1968).

R. Corbin, *Currents in Poetry* (The Macmillan Company, New York, 1968).

W. E. Barrett, *The Lilies of the Field* (Doubleday & Company, Garden City, 1962).

William Shakespeare, *The Merchant of Venice* (New American Library, New York, 1965).

W. J. Halliburton and M. E. Pelkonen, *New Worlds of Literature* (Harcourt, Brace & World, New York, 1966).

Homer, *The Odyssey* (W. W. Norton & Company, New York, 1967).

R. C. Pooley *et al., Outlooks through Literature* (Scott, Foresman and Company, Glenview, 1968).

William Shakespeare, *Romeo and Juliet* (New American Library, New York, 1964).

Charles Dickens, *A Tale of Two Cities* (Lancer Books, New York, 1968).

H. Lee, *To Kill A Mockingbird* (J. B. Lippincott Company, Philadelphia, 1960).

M. E. Chase *et al., Values in Literature* (Houghton Mifflin Company, Boston, 1968).

R. C. Pooley *et al., Vanguard* (Scott, Foresman and Company, Glenview, 1961).

Literature, Ungraded

A. Jewett *et al., Literature for Life* (Houghton Mifflin Company, Boston, 1958).

Mathematics, Grade 3

E. Deans *et al., Developing Mathematics* (American Book Company, Cincinnati, 1968).

E. D. Nichols *et al., Elementary Mathematics Patterns and Structure 3* (Holt, Rinehart and Winston, New York, 1968).

R. E. Eicholz and P. G. O'Daffer, *Elementary School Mathematics, Book 3* (Addison-Wesley Publishing Company, Reading, 1968).

R. L. Morton *et al., Modern Arithmetic Through Discovery 3* (Silver Burdett Company, Morristown, 1964).

E. R. Duncan *et al., Modern School Mathematics, Structure and Use, Book 3* (Houghton Mifflin Company, Boston, 1970).

Mathematics, Grade 4

E. D. Nichols *et al., Elementary Mathematics Patterns and Structure 4* (Holt, Rinehart and Winston, New York, 1968).

R. E. Eicholz and P. G. O'Daffer, *Elementary School Mathematics, Book 4* (Addison-Wesley Publishing Company, Reading, 1968).

Greater Cleveland Mathematics Program 4 (Science Research Associates, Chicago, 1965).

E. R. Duncan *et al.*, *Modern School Mathematics, Structure and Use, Book 4* (Houghton Mifflin Company, Boston, 1970).

Mathematics, Grade 5

E. D. Nichols *et al.*, *Elementary Mathematics Patterns and Structure 5* (Holt, Rinehart and Winston, New York, 1968).

R. E. Eicholz and P. G. O'Daffer, *Elementary School Mathematics, Book 5* (Addison-Wesley Publishing Company, Reading, 1968).

Greater Cleveland Mathematics Program 5 (Science Research Associates, Chicago, 1965).

R. L. Morton *et al.*, *Modern Arithmetic Through Discovery 5* (Silver Burdett Company, Morristown, 1963).

E. R. Duncan *et al.*, *Modern School Mathematics, Structure and Use, Book 5* (Houghton Mifflin Company, Boston, 1970).

Mathematics, Grade 6

E. D. Nichols *et al.*, *Elementary Mathematics Patterns and Structure 6* (Holt, Rinehart and Winston, New York, 1968).

R. E. Eicholz and P. G. O'Daffer, *Elementary School Mathematics, Book 6* (Addison-Wesley Publishing Company, Reading, 1968).

R. L. Morton *et al.*, *Modern Arithmetic Through Discovery 6* (Silver Burdett Company, Morristown, 1963).

E. R. Duncan *et al.*, *Modern School Mathematics, Structure and Use, Book 6* (Houghton Mifflin Company, Boston, 1970).

Mathematics, Grade 7

R. E. Eicholz *et al.*, *Basic Modern Mathematics, First Course* (Addison-Wesley Publishing Company, Reading, 1965).

M. Keedy *et al.*, *Exploring Modern Mathematics, Book 1* (Holt, Rinehart and Winston, New York, 1963).

E. T. McSwain *et al.*, *Mathematics 7* (Laidlaw Brothers, River Forest, 1963).

M. F. Rosskopf *et al.*, *Modern Mathematics Through Discovery, Book 1* (Silver Burdett Company, Morristown, 1964).

M. Dolciani *et al.*, *Modern School Mathematics, Structure and Method 7* (Houghton Mifflin Company, Boston, 1967).

R. E. Eicholz *et al.*, *School Mathematics I* (Addison-Wesley Publishing Company, Reading, 1967).

E. Deans *et al.*, *Structuring Mathematics* (American Book Company, Cincinnati, 1966).

Mathematics, Grade 8

R. E. Eicholz *et al.*, *Basic Modern Mathematics, Second Course* (Addison-Wesley Publishing Company, Reading, 1965).

M. L. Keedy *et al.*, *Exploring Modern Mathematics, Book 2* (Holt, Rinehart and Winston, New York, 1968).

E. Deans *et al.*, *Extending Mathematics* (American Book Company, Cincinnati, 1966).

E. T. McSwain *et al.*, *Mathematics 8* (Laidlaw Brothers, River Forest, 1963).

M. Dolciani *et al.*, *Modern School Mathematics, Structure and Method 8* (Houghton Mifflin Company, Boston, 1967).

R. E. Eicholz *et al.*, *School Mathematics II* (Addison-Wesley Publishing Company, Reading, 1967).

Mathematics, Grade 9

M. Dolciani *et al.*, *Modern Algebra, Structure and Method, Book 1* (Houghton Mifflin Company, Boston, 1965).

K. E. Brown *et al.*, *General Mathematics, Book 1* (Laidlaw Brothers, River Forest, 1968).

R. E. Eicholz *et al.*, *Modern General Mathematics* (Addison-Wesley Publishing Company, Reading, 1965).

K. C. Skeen and E. H. Whitmore, *Modern Mathematics, Book 1, Number Systems — Structure* (L. W. Singer Company, New York, 1966).

M. Dolciani *et al.*, *Modern School Mathematics, Algebra I* (Houghton Mifflin Company, Boston, 1967).

E. D. Nichols, *Pre-Algebra Mathematics* (Holt, Rinehart and Winston, New York, 1965).

Mathematics Supplementary, Grade 3

N. J. Lennes and L. R. Traver, *The Lennes Essentials of Arithmetic 3* (Laidlaw Brothers, River Forest, 1964).

E. Deans *et al.*, *Modern Mathematics Laboratory 3* (American Book Company, Cincinnati, 1968).

R. W. Wirtz *et al.*, *Math Workshop, Level C* (Encyclopaedia Britannica Press, Chicago, 1965).

M. F. Willerding, *Workbook: Elementary Mathematics Patterns and Structure 3* (Holt, Rinehart and Winston, New York, 1966).

E. R. Duncan *et al.*, *Workbook to Accompany Modern School Mathematics, Structure and Use, Book 3* (Houghton Mifflin Company, Boston, 1967).

Mathematics Supplementary, Grade 4

R. E. Eicholz *et al.*, *Elementary School Mathematics, Getting Ready 4* (Addison-Wesley Publishing Company, Reading, 1968).

N. J. Lennes and L. R. Traver, *The Lennes Essentials of Arithmetic 4* (Laidlaw Brothers, River Forest, 1964).

M. F. Willerding, *Workbook: Elementary Mathematics Patterns and Structure 4* (Holt, Rinehart and Winston, New York, 1966).

E. R. Duncan *et al., Workbook to Accompany Modern School Mathematics, Structure and Use, Book 4* (Houghton Mifflin Company, Boston, 1967).

Mathematics Supplementary, Grade 5

R. E. Eicholz *et al., Elementary School Mathematics, Getting Ready 5* (Addison-Wesley Publishing Company, Reading, 1968).

R. W. Wirtz *et al., Math Workshop, Level E* (Encyclopaedia Britannica Press, Chicago, 1967).

E. R. Duncan *et al., Workbook to Accompany Modern School Mathematics, Structure and Use, Book 5* (Houghton Mifflin Company, Boston, 1967).

Mathematics Supplementary, Grade 6

C. Proctor and P. Johnson, *Computational Skills Development Kit* (Science Research Associates, Chicago, 1965).

R. E. Eicholz *et al., Elementary School Mathematics, Getting Ready 6* (Addison-Wesley Publishing Company, Reading, 1968).

M. D. Sullivan, *Programmed Math, Book 7, Decimals* (Webster Division, McGraw-Hill Book Company, New York, 1968).

E. R. Duncan *et al., Workbook to Accompany Modern School Mathematics, Structure and Use, Book 6* (Houghton Mifflin Company, Boston, 1967).

Mathematics Supplementary, Grade 7

C. F. Brumfiel *et al., Arithmetic Concepts and Skills* (Addison-Wesley Publishing Company, Reading, 1963).

C. W. Nelson, *Exploring Modern Mathematics, Book 1, Programmed Supplement* (Holt, Rinehart and Winston, New York, 1968).

E. Deans *et al., Modern Mathematics Laboratory 7* (American Book Company, Cincinnati, 1968).

P. O. Redgrave, *Programmed Practice for Modern School Mathematics, Book 7* (Houghton Mifflin Company, Boston, 1967).

Mathematics Supplementary, Grade 8

W. H. Glenn and D. A. Johnson, *Computing Devices* (Webster Publishing Company, St. Louis, 1961).

C. W. Nelson, *Exploring Modern Mathematics, Book 2, Programmed Supplement* (Holt, Rinehart and Winston, New York, 1968).

C. F. Brumfiel *et al., Introduction to Mathematics* (Addison-Wesley Publishing Company, Reading, 1961).

D. A. Johnson and W. H. Glenn, *Invitation to Mathematics* (Webster Publishing Company, St. Louis, 1960).

M. C. Herrick, *Modern Mathematics for Achievement, Books 3-8* (Houghton Mifflin Company, Boston, 1966).

M. C. Herrick *et al., Modern Mathematics for Achievement, Second Course, Books 3-8* (Houghton Mifflin Company, Boston, 1967).

P. O. Redgrave, *Programmed Practice for Modern School Mathematics, Book 8* (Houghton Mifflin Company, Boston, 1967).

D. A. Johnson and W. H. Glenn, *Topology, The Rubber-Sheet Geometry* (Webster Division, McGraw-Hill Book Company, New York, 1960).

Mathematics Supplementary, Grade 9

F. M. Morgan and J. Zartman, *Geometry – Plane, Solid and Coordinate* (Houghton Mifflin Company, Boston, 1968).

W. W. Hart *et al., Mathematics in Daily Use* (D. C. Heath and Company, Lexington, 1966).

P. Redgrave and J. Roberge, *Programmed Practice for Modern Algebra, Structure and Method, Book 1* (Houghton Mifflin Company, Boston, 1963).

Mathematics Supplementary, Ungraded

M. Seltzer, *Bases and Numerals, An Introduction to Numeration* (The Macmillan Company, New York, 1963).

F. Wohlfort and A. Sheridan, *Supplementary Experiences in Arithmetic* (Holt, Rinehart and Winston, New York, 1965).

Social Studies, Grade 3

P. R. Hanna *et al., In City, Town, and Country* (Scott, Foresman and Company, Glenview, 1965).

K. D. Wann *et al., Learning About Our Country* (Allyn and Bacon, Boston, 1967).

P. Cutright *et al., Living in America Today and Yesterday* (The Macmillan Company, New York, 1969).

L. Senesh, *Our Working World, Cities at Work* (Science Research Associates, Chicago, 1967).

V. P. Weaver, *People Use the Earth* (Silver Burdett Company, Morristown, 1966).

C. W. Sorensen, *Ways of Our Land* (Silver Burdett Company, Morristown, 1965).

A. McIntire and W. Hill, *Working Together* (Follett Publishing Company, Chicago, 1965).

Social Studies, Grade 4

D. Goetz, *At Home Around the World* (Ginn and Company, Boston, 1968).

H. H. Gross *et al., Exploring Regions Near and Far* (Follett Educational Corporation, Chicago, 1969).

P. R. Hanna *et al., In All Our States* (Scott, Foresman and Company, Glenview, 1965).

H. D. Drummond, *A Journey Through Many Lands* (Allyn and Bacon, Boston, 1964).

K. S. Cooper *et al., Learning to Look at our World* (Silver Burdett Company, Morristown, 1967).

P. Cutright *et al., Living in Our Country and Other Lands* (The Macmillan Company, New York, 1966).

C. W. Sorensen *et al., Our Big World* (Silver Burdett Company, Morristown, 1968).

F. M. King *et al., Regions and Social Needs* (Laidlaw Brothers, River Forest, 1968).

D. M. Fraser and H. F. Yeager, *Under Freedom's Banner* (American Book Company, Cincinnati, 1964).

Social Studies, Grade 5

K. S. Cooper *et al., The Changing New World, North and South America* (Silver Burdett Company, Morristown, 1969).

K. S. Cooper *et al., The Changing New World, United States and Canada* (Silver Burdett Company, Morristown, 1964).

H. H. Gross *et al., Exploring Regions of the Western Hemisphere* (Follett Publishing Company, Chicago, 1966).

O. S. Hamer *et al., Exploring the New World* (Follett Publishing Company, Chicago, 1965).

H. D. Drummond, *Journeys Through the Americas* (Allyn and Bacon, Boston, 1969).

P. Cutright *et al., Living in the Americas* (The Macmillan Company, New York, 1966).

W. Havighurst, *Midwest and Great Plains* (The Fideler Company, Grand Rapids, 1967).

J. E. Jennings and M. H. Smith, *The South* (The Fideler Company, Grand Rapids, 1968).

C. L. Ver Steeg, *The Story of Our Country* (Harper & Row, Publishers, New York, 1965).

M. E. Mason and W. H. Cartwright, *Trail Blazers of American History* (Ginn and Company, Boston, 1966).

K. T. Whittemore *et al., United States, Canada, and Latin America* (Ginn and Company, Boston, 1966).

C. Samford *et al., You and the United States* (Benefic Press, Westchester, 1966).

G. S. Brown *et al., Your Country and Mine, Our American Neighbors* (Ginn and Company, Boston, 1969).

Social Studies, Grade 6

K. S. Cooper *et al., The Changing Old World* (Silver Burdett Company, Morristown, 1969).

H. D. Drummond, *The Eastern Hemisphere* (Allyn and Bacon, Boston, 1969).

R. M. Glendinning *et al., Eurasia, Africa and Australia* (Ginn and Company, Boston, 1966).

W. H. Gray *et al., Exploring American Neighbors* (Follett Publishing Company, Chicago, 1967).

O. S. Hamer *et al., Exploring the Old World* (Follett Publishing Company, Chicago, 1965).

R. A. Harper *et al., Learning About Latin America* (Silver Burdett Company, Morristown, 1964).

P. Cutright *et al., Living in the Old World* (The Macmillan Company, New York, 1969).

H. H. Barrows *et al., Old World Lands* (Silver Burdett Company, Morristown, 1964).

C. W. Sorensen *et al., A World View* (Silver Burdett Company, Morristown, 1964).

G. Dawson *et al., Your World and Mine, Neighbors in the Air Age* (Ginn and Company, Boston, 1965).

Social Studies, Grade 7

R. M. Glendinning, *Eurasia* (Ginn and Company, Boston, 1969).

N. Carls *et al., Knowing Our Neighbors in the Eastern Hemisphere* (Holt, Rinehart and Winston, New York, 1968).

M. Uttley *et al., Latin America, Africa, and Australia* (Ginn and Company, Boston, 1969).

P. Cutright *et al., Living as World Neighbors* (The Macmillan Company, New York, 1969).

E. R. Kolevzon and J. A. Heine, *Our World and Its Peoples* (Allyn and Bacon, Boston, 1968).

G. P. Morrill *et al., Southeast Asia* (American Education Publications, Columbus, 1966).

Sister Marion S.C.H. *et al., Southern Neighbors* (W. H. Sadlier, New York, 1960).

R. W. Steen and F. Donecker, *Texas, Our Heritage* (Steck-Vaughn Company, Austin, 1962).

L. De Vorsey and J. A. Hodgkins, *Western Europe, Eastern Europe* (W. H. Sadlier, New York, 1969).

H. D. Drummond, *The Western Hemisphere* (Allyn and Bacon, Boston, 1965).

R. M. Glendinning *et al., Your Country and the World* (Ginn and Company, Boston, 1966).

Social Studies, Grade 8

J. R. Reich and E. L. Biller, *Building the American Nation* (Harcourt, Brace & World, New York, 1968).

S. H. Bronz *et al., The Challenge of America* (Holt, Rinehart and Winston, New York, 1968).

H. Kublin, *China* (Houghton Mifflin Company, Boston, 1968).

R. E. Gross and V. Devereaux, *Civics In Action* (Field Educational Publications, San Francisco, 1966).

A. O. Kownslar and D. B. Frizzle, *Discovering American History* (Holt, Rinehart and Winston, New York, 1967).

M. Schwartz and J. O'Connor, *Exploring American History* (Globe Book Company, New York, 1968).

W. L. Katz, *Eyewitness: The Negro in American History* (Pitman Publishing Corporation, New York, 1967).

H. F. Graff, *The Free and the Brave* (Rand McNally & Company, Chicago, 1967).

R. Liebman and G. Young, *The Growth of America* (Prentice-Hall, Englewood Cliffs, 1964).

H. H. Eibling *et al., History of Our United States* (Laidlaw Brothers, River Forest, 1969).

F. R. Pitts, *Japan* (The Fideler Company, Grand Rapids, 1966).

J. W. Caughey *et al., Land of the Free* (Benziger Brothers, New York, 1965).

N. Carls *et al., Our United States in a World of Neighbors* (Holt, Rinehart and Winston, New York, 1964).

H. H. Eibling *et al., The Story of America* (Laidlaw Brothers, River Forest, 1965).

M. B. Casner *et al., Story of the American Nation* (Harcourt, Brace & World, New York, 1967).

H. B. Wilder *et al., This is America's Story* (Houghton Mifflin Company, Boston, 1966).

D. Sharkey and I. G. Williams, *You and Your Government* (W. H. Sadlier, New York, 1967).

Social Studies, Grade 9

W. H. Hartley and W. S. Vincent, *American Civics* (Harcourt, Brace & World, New York, 1970).

J. H. McCrocklin, *Building Citizenship* (Allyn and Bacon, Boston, 1966).

N. I. Clark *et al., Civics for Americans* (The Macmillan Company, New York, 1965).

S. E. Dimond and E. F. Pflieger, *Civics for Citizens* (J. B. Lippincott Company, Philadelphia, 1965).

M. Schwartz and J. O'Connor, *Exploring a Changing World* (Globe Book Company, New York, 1966).

A. G. Mazour and J. M. Peoples, *Men and Nations* (Harcourt, Brace & World, New York, 1968).

S. Israel *et al., World Geography Today* (Holt, Rinehart and Winston, New York, 1966).

C. F. Kohn and D. W. Drummond, *The World Today, Its Patterns and Cultures* (Webster Division, McGraw-Hill Book Company, New York, 1966).

H. F. Smith *et al., Your Life as a Citizen* (Ginn and Company, Boston, 1965).

Social Studies Supplementary, Grade 3

J. R. Bochert and J. McGuigan, *Around the Home* (Rand McNally & Company, Chicago, 1961).

A. Martucci, *The Earth: Maps and Globes* (Noble and Noble, New York, 1965).

Know Your World (American Education Publications, Columbus: five issues selected from September 10 through October 8, 1969).

My First World Atlas (Hammond Incorporated, Maplewood, 1969).

C. W. Hunnicutt and J. D. Grambs, *Your Community and Mine* (L. W. Singer Company, New York, 1966).

Social Studies Supplementary, Grade 4

C. Fielstra and H. Fielstra, *Africa, With Focus on Nigeria* (Franklin Publications, Pasadena, 1963).

H. Bauer, *California Mission Days* (Doubleday & Company, New York, 1951).

Classroom Atlas (Rand McNally & Company, Chicago, 1969).

D. Hackler, *How Charts and Drawings Help Us* (Benefic Press, Westchester, 1965).

L. S. Minugh and N. K. Cory, *Japan* (Franklin Publications, Pasadena, 1963).

R. Naslund and C. M. Brown, *Map and Globe Skills* (Science Research Associates, Chicago, 1964).

Scholastic News Explorer (Scholastic Magazines, New York: six issues selected from January 17 through May 9, 1969).

Social Studies Supplementary, Grade 5

S. R. Tompkins, *Alaska* (The Fideler Company, Grand Rapids, 1968).

E. Fergusson, *Hawaii* (The Fideler Company, Grand Rapids, 1967).

J. W. Maynard and D. T. Peck, *Map Skills For Today's Geography* (American Education Publications, Columbus, 1965).

H. H. Eibling *et al., Our Country's Story* (Laidlaw Brothers, River Forest, 1961).

Scholastic NewsTime (Scholastic Magazines, New York: eight issues selected from January 31 through May 9, 1969).

Social Studies Supplementary, Grade 6

E. L. Greenblatt and M. L. Greenblatt, *Ancient Peoples of Mexico* (Franklin Publications, Pasadena, 1962).

P. F. Ross, *Mexico* (The Fideler Company, Grand Rapids, 1970).

E. Lindop *et al., Understanding Latin America* (Ginn and Company, Boston, 1966).

Social Studies Supplementary, Grade 7

W. D. Allen, *Africa* (The Fideler Company, Grand Rapids, 1968).

Junior Review (Scholastic Magazines, New York: six issues selected from September 15 through October 20, 1969).

H. H. Eibling, *Our Beginnings in the Old World* (Laidlaw Brothers, River Forest, 1962).

M. Gartler *et al., Understanding Egypt* (Laidlaw Brothers, River Forest, 1965).

M. Gartler *et al., Understanding Ethiopia* (Laidlaw Brothers, River Forest, 1965).

M. Gartler *et al., Understanding Greece* (Laidlaw Brothers, River Forest, 1964).

M. Gartler *et al., Understanding Israel* (Laidlaw Brothers, River Forest, 1965).

M. Gartler *et al., Understanding Turkey* (Laidlaw Brothers, River Forest, 1965).

Social Studies Supplementary, Grade 8

B. A. Weisberger, *The Age of Steel and Steam* (Time, Inc., New York, 1964).

W. E. Leuchtenburg, *The Great Age of Change* (Time, Inc., New York, 1964).

T. Kroeber, *Ishi, Last of His Tribe* (Parnassus Press, Berkeley, 1964).

I. Starr *et al., Living American Documents* (Harcourt, Brace & World, New York, 1961).

R. B. Morris *et al., The Making of a Nation* (Time, Inc., New York, 1963).

R. B. Morris *et al., The New World* (Time, Inc., New York, 1963).

E. Ritter *et al., Our Oriental Americans* (McGraw-Hill Book Company, New York, 1965).

M. L. Coit *et al., The Sweep Westward* (Time, Inc., New York, 1963).

T. H. Williams *et al., The Union Restored* (Time, Inc., New York, 1963).

T. H. Williams *et al., The Union Sundered* (Time, Inc., New York, 1963).

E. R. May *et al., War, Boom and Bust* (Time, Inc., New York, 1964).

Social Studies Supplementary, Grade 9

R. W. Logan and I. S. Cohen, *The American Negro* (Houghton Mifflin Company, Boston, 1967).

American Observer (Scholastic Magazines, New York: four issues selected from September 15 through October 6, 1969).

T. W. Wallbank and A. Schrier, *Living World History* (Scott, Foresman and Company, Glenview, 1964).

R. E. Gross and F. MacGraw, *Man's World, A Physical Geography* (Scholastic Book Services, New York, 1966).

D. W. Oliver and F. M. Newmann, *Taking A Stand* (American Education Publications, Columbus, 1967).

Social Studies Supplementary, Ungraded

R. A. Nashlund and C. M. Brown, *Map & Globe Skills MG II* (Science Research Associates, Chicago, 1964).

Spelling, Grade 3

W. Kottmeyer and A. Claus, *Basic Goals in Spelling, Sequence A, Book 3* (Webster Division, McGraw-Hill Book Company, New York, 1968).

D. C. Rogers *et al., My Word Book 3* (Lyons and Carnahan, Chicago, 1966).

N. Bremer and G. Long, *Skills in Spelling, Book 3* (McCormick-Mathers Publishing Company, New York, 1967).

R. Madden *et al., Sound and Sense in Spelling 3* (Harcourt, Brace & World, New York, 1968).

Spelling, Grade 4

W. Kottmeyer and A. Claus, *Basic Goals in Spelling, Sequence B, Book 4* (Webster Division, McGraw-Hill Book Company, New York, 1968).

D. C. Rogers *et al., My Word Book 4* (Lyons and Carnahan, Chicago, 1966).

R. Madden *et al., Sound and Sense in Spelling 4* (Harcourt, Brace & World, New York, 1968).

R. E. McHale *et al., Spelling 4* (Laidlaw Brothers, River Forest, 1967).

Spelling, Grade 5

W. Kottmeyer and A. Claus, *Basic Goals in Spelling, Sequence B, Book 5* (Webster Division, McGraw-Hill Book Company, New York, 1968).

D. C. Rogers *et al., My Word Book 5* (Lyons and Carnahan, Chicago, 1966).

R. Madden *et al., Sound and Sense in Spelling 5* (Harcourt, Brace & World, New York, 1968).

R. E. McHale *et al., Spelling 5* (Laidlaw Brothers, River Forest, 1967).

Spelling, Grade 6

W. Kottmeyer and A. Claus, *Basic Goals in Spelling, Sequence B, Book 6* (Webster Division, McGraw-Hill Book Company, New York, 1968).

D. C. Rogers *et al., My Word Book 6* (Lyons and Carnahan, Chicago, 1966).

R. Madden *et al., Sound and Sense In Spelling 6* (Harcourt, Brace & World, New York, 1968).

R. E. McHale *et al., Spelling 6* (Laidlaw Brothers, River Forest, 1967).

Spelling, Grade 7

W. Kottmeyer and A. Claus, *Basic Goals in Spelling, Sequence C, Book 7* (Webster Division, McGraw-Hill Book Company, New York, 1968).

N. Bremer and P. Prouse, *Skills in Spelling, Book 7* (McCormick-Mathers Publishing Company, New York, 1967).

R. Madden *et al., Sound and Sense in Spelling 7* (Harcourt, Brace & World, New York, 1968).

R. E. McHale *et al., Spelling 7* (Laidlaw Brothers, River Forest, 1967).

Spelling, Grade 8

W. Kottmeyer and A. Claus, *Basic Goals in Spelling, Sequence C, Book 8* (Webster Division, McGraw-Hill Book Company, New York, 1968).

M. Botel *et al., 1620 Power Words* (Follett Publishing Company, Chicago, 1966).

N. Bremer and P. Prouse, *Skills in Spelling, Book 8* (McCormick-Mathers Publishing Company, New York, 1967).

Spelling, Grade 9

D. H. Patton *et al., Common Words* (Charles E. Merrill Publishing Co., Columbus, 1970).

Spelling Supplementary, Grade 3

D. H. Patton and E. M. Johnson, *Language Mastery Speller 3* (Charles E. Merrill Publishing Co., Columbus, 1968).

Spelling Supplementary, Grade 4

D. H. Patton and E. M. Johnson, *Language Mastery Speller 4* (Charles E. Merrill Publishing Co., Columbus, 1968).

Spelling Supplementary, Grade 5

D. H. Patton and E. M. Johnson, *Language Mastery Speller 5* (Charles E. Merrill Publishing Co., Columbus, 1968).

Spelling Supplementary, Grade 6

D. H. Patton and E. M. Johnson, *Language Mastery Speller 6* (Charles E. Merrill Publishing Co., Columbus, 1968).

Spelling Supplementary, Grade 7

M. Monroe *et al., Spelling Our Language, Book 7* (Scott, Foresman and Company, Glenview, 1969).

Spelling Supplementary, Grade 9

A. M. Works, *A Vocabulary Builder, Book 4* (Educators Publishing Service, Cambridge, 1964).

Science, Grade 3

P. F. Brandwein *et al., Concepts in Science 3* (Harcourt, Brace & World, New York, 1966).

O. E. Byrd *et al., Health 3* (Laidlaw Brothers, River Forest, 1966).

W. J. Jacobson *et al., Learning in Science* (American Book Company, Cincinnati, 1965).

H. A. Smith *et al., Science 3* (Laidlaw Brothers, River Forest, 1966).

H. Schneider and N. Schneider, *Science Far and Near 3* (D. C. Heath and Company, Lexington, 1968).

J. D. Barnard *et al., Science for Tomorrow's World 3* (The Macmillan Company, New York, 1966).

J. G. Navarra and J. Zafforoni, *Today's Basic Science 3: The Scientist Experiments* (Harper & Row, Publishers, New York, 1967).

Science, Grade 4

P. F. Brandwein *et al., Concepts in Science 4* (Harcourt, Brace & World, New York, 1966).

O. E. Byrd *et al., Health 4* (Laidlaw Brothers, River Forest, 1966).

H. A. Smith *et al., Science 4* (Laidlaw Brothers, River Forest, 1966).

H. Schneider and N. Schneider, *Science in Your Life 4* (D. C. Heath and Company, Lexington, 1968).

J. G. Navarra and J. Zafforoni, *Today's Basic Science 4: The Scientist and His Method* (Harper & Row, Publishers, New York, 1967).

Science, Grade 5

P. F. Brandwein *et al., Concepts in Science 5* (Harcourt, Brace & World, New York, 1966).

O. E. Byrd *et al., Health 5* (Laidlaw Brothers, River Forest, 1966).

W. J. Jacobson *et al., Inquiring Into Science* (American Book Company, Cincinnati, 1968).

J. D. Barnard *et al., Science for Tomorrow's World 5* (The Macmillan Company, New York, 1966).

H. Schneider and N. Schneider, *Science in Our World 5* (D. C. Heath and Company, Lexington, 1968).

J. G. Navarra and J. Zafforoni, *Today's Basic Science 5: The Scientist and His Hypotheses* (Harper & Row, Publishers, New York, 1967).

Science, Grade 6

P. F. Brandwein *et al., Concepts in Science 6* (Harcourt, Brace & World, New York, 1966).

O. E. Byrd *et al., Health 6* (Laidlaw Brothers, River Forest, 1966).

W. J. Jacobson *et al.*, *Investigating in Science* (American Book Company, Cincinnati, 1968).

H. Schneider and N. Schneider, *Science for Today and Tomorrow 6* (D. C. Heath and Company, Lexington, 1968).

J. G. Navarra and J. Zafforoni, *Today's Basic Science 6: The Scientist and Tomorrow* (Harper & Row, Publishers, New York, 1967).

Science, Grade 7

W. A. Thurber and R. E. Kilburn, *Exploring Life Science* (Allyn and Bacon, Boston, 1966).

W. W. Bauer *et al.*, *Health for All, Book 7* (Scott, Foresman and Company, Glenview, 1965).

J. G. Navarra *et al.*, *Life and the Molecule, The Biological Sciences* (Harper & Row, Publishers, New York, 1966).

P. F. Brandwein *et al.*, *Life, Its Forms and Changes* (Harcourt, Brace & World, New York, 1968).

S. S. Blanc *et al.*, *Modern Science 1* (Holt, Rinehart and Winston, New York, 1963).

J. G. Navarra *et al.*, *Today's Basic Science 7: The Molecule and the Biosphere* (Harper & Row, Publishers, New York, 1965).

P. F. Brandwein *et al.*, *The World of Living Things* (Harcourt, Brace and World, New York, 1964).

Science, Grade 8

H. D. MacCracken *et al.*, *Earth Science* (L. W. Singer Company, New York, 1968).

W. A. Thurber and R. E. Kilburn, *Exploring Earth Science* (Allyn and Bacon, Boston, 1965).

W. W. Bauer *et al.*, *Health for All, Book 8* (Scott, Foresman and Company, Glenview, 1965).

W. B. Herron and N. P. Palmer, *Matter, Life and Energy* (Lyons and Carnahan, Chicago, 1965).

S. S. Blanc *et al.*, *Modern Science 2* (Holt, Rinehart and Winston, New York, 1963).

J. G. Navarra and J. Garone, *Today's Basic Science 8: The Atom and the Earth* (Harper & Row, Publishers, New York, 1965).

P. F. Brandwein *et al.*, *The World of Matter-Energy* (Harcourt, Brace & World, New York, 1964).

Science, Grade 9

S. N. Namowitz and D. B. Stone, *Earth Science, The World We Live In* (American Book Company, Cincinnati, 1969).

Introductory Physical Science (Prentice-Hall, Englewood Cliffs, 1967).

Investigating the Earth (Houghton Mifflin Company, Boston, 1967).

W. Ramsey and R. Burckley, *Modern Earth Science* (Holt, Rinehart and Winston, New York, 1965).

J. Otto and A. Towle, *Modern Biology* (Holt, Rinehart and Winston, New York, 1965).

W. O. Brooks *et al.*, *Modern Physical Science* (Holt, Rinehart and Winston, New York, 1966).

Science Supplementary, Grade 3

W. J. Jacobson *et al.*, *The Air Around You* (American Book Company, Cincinnati, 1968).

C. A. Schoenknecht, *Ants* (Follett Publishing Company, Chicago, 1961).

I. B. Wasson, *Birds* (Follett Publishing Company, Chicago, 1963).

W. J. Jacobson *et al.*, *Living Things on the Earth* (American Book Company, Cincinnati, 1965).

E. Victor, *Magnets* (Follett Publishing Company, Chicago, 1962).

D. Wood, *Plants with Seeds* (Follett Publishing Company, Chicago, 1963).

E. K. Meeks, *Snakes* (Follett Publishing Company, Chicago, 1962).

M. Tellander, *Space* (Follett Publishing Company, Chicago, 1960).

W. J. Jacobson *et al.*, *The Sun, Seasons and Climate* (American Book Company, Cincinnati, 1968).

Science Supplementary, Grade 4

P. Brandwein *et al.*, *Concepts in Science 4* (Harcourt, Brace & World, New York, 1968).

W. J. Jacobson *et al.*, *Exploring the Solar System* (American Book Company, Cincinnati, 1968).

B. B. Strasser, *Molecules in Motion* (Franklin Publications, Pasadena, 1967).

D. MacLean, *The Sea: A New Frontier* (Franklin Publications, Pasadena, 1967).

C. Lavaroni, *The Wonders of Water* (Franklin Publications, Pasadena, 1967).

Science Supplementary, Grade 5

B. M. Parker, *The Air About Us* (Row, Peterson and Company, Evanston, 1958).

B. M. Parker, *Gravity* (Row, Peterson and Company, Evanston, 1959).

B. M. Parker, *Water* (Harper & Row, Publishers, New York, 1958).

B. M. Parker and M. Downing, *You as a Machine* (Row, Peterson and Company, Evanston, 1958).

Science Supplementary, Grade 6

B. M. Parker and T. Park, *Animal Travels* (Row, Peterson and Company, Evanston, 1951).

B. M. Parker, *Animals We Know* (Row, Peterson and Company, Evanston, 1957).

B. M. Parker, *Clouds, Rain and Snow* (Harper & Row, Publishers, New York, 1957).

B. M. Parker, *Dependent Plants* (Row, Peterson and Company, Evanston, 1957).

B. M. Parker, *Electricity* (Row, Peterson and Company, Evanston, 1959).

B. M. Parker, *Flowers, Fruits, Seeds* (Row, Peterson and Company, Evanston, 1958).

W. J. Jacobson *et al., Insects and Senses* (American Book Company, Cincinnati, 1965).

B. M. Parker, *Living Things* (Row, Peterson and Company, Evanston, 1958).

B. M. Parker, *Machines* (Harper & Row, Publishers, New York, 1959).

B. M. Parker, *Plant and Animal Partnerships* (Row, Peterson and Company, Evanston, 1958).

B. M. Parker, *Saving Our Wildlife* (Row, Peterson and Company, Evanston, 1959).

B. M. Parker, *The Scientist and His Tools* (Harper & Row, Publishers, New York, 1959).

B. M. Parker, *Sound* (Row, Peterson and Company, Evanston, 1957).

B. M. Parker, *Spiders* (Row, Peterson and Company, Evanston, 1958).

B. M. Parker, *Toads and Frogs* (Harper & Row, Publishers, New York, 1959).

Science Supplementary, Grade 7

B. M. Parker and I. Podendorf, *Animal World* (Harper & Row, Publishers, New York, 1958).

B. M. Parker, *Ask the Weatherman* (Harper & Row, Publishers, New York, 1958).

Current Science (American Education Publications, Columbus: seven issues selected from October 8 through November 19, 1969).

R. Lapp *et al., Matter* (Time, Inc., New York, 1968).

D. Bergamini *et al., The Universe* (Time, Inc., New York, 1969).

P. D. Thompson *et al., Weather* (Time, Inc., New York, 1968).

Science Supplementary, Grade 8

S. N. Namowitz, *Activities in Earth Science* (American Book Company, Cincinnati, 1969).

B. M. Parker and R. Buchsbaum, *Balance in Nature* (Harper & Row, Publishers, New York, 1958).

B. M. Parker and M. Downing, *How We Are Built* (Harper & Row, Publishers, New York, 1959).

J. Gross and S. Kopilow, *Substances Around Us Change* (Follett Educational Corporation, Chicago, 1969).

Science Supplementary, Grade 9

J. Otto *et al., Modern Health* (Holt, Rinehart and Winston, New York, 1967).

Sportsmanlike Driving (McGraw-Hill Book Company, New York, 1961).

Science Supplementary, Ungraded

B. Dibner, *Alessandro Volta and the Electric Battery* (Franklin Watts, New York, 1964).

G. C. Wood, *Biology Experiments for High School Students* (American Cancer Society, New York, 1964).

A. Morgan, *The Boys' First Book of Radio and Electronics* (Charles Scribner's Sons, New York, 1954).

D. N. Ahnstrom, *The Complete Book of Helicopters* (The World Publishing Company, Cleveland, 1968).

W. M. Reed, *The Earth for Sam* (Harcourt, Brace & World, New York, 1960).

A. Defant, *Ebb and Flow, The Tides of Earth, Air, and Water* (The University of Michigan Press, Ann Arbor, 1958).

R. A. Dodge, *Elements of Biology* (Allyn and Bacon, Boston, 1964).

F. M. Branley, *Experiments in Sky Watching* (Thomas Y. Crowell Company, New York, 1967).

N. F. Beeler and F. M. Branley, *Experiments with Light* (Thomas Y. Crowell Company, New York, 1957).

F. H. Pough, *A Field Guide to Rocks and Minerals* (Houghton Mifflin Company, Boston, 1960).

W. Honegger *et al., Genetics: Heredity, Environment and Personality* (Dell Publishing Company, New York, 1962).

J. Texereau, *How to Make a Telescope* (Doubleday & Company, New York, 1963).

I. Asimov, *The Human Body* (Houghton Mifflin Company, Boston, 1963).

I. Asimov, *Inside the Atom* (Abelard-Schuman, Ltd., New York, 1966).

I. Asimov, *The Kingdom of the Sun* (Abelard-Schuman, Ltd., New York, 1963).

J. D. Witherspoon and R. H. Witherspoon, *The Living Laboratory, 200 Experiments for Amateur Biologists* (Doubleday & Company, New York, 1960).

P. De Kruif, *Microbe Hunters* (Harcourt, Brace & World, New York, 1953).

J. Sinkankas, *Mineralogy for Amateurs* (Van Nostrand-Reinhold, New York, 1964).

C. M. Christensen, *The Molds and Man* (University of Minnesota Press, Minneapolis, 1965).

G. Gamow, *The Moon* (Abelard-Schuman, Ltd., New York, 1959).

D. Alter *et al., Pictorial Astronomy* (Thomas Y. Crowell Company, New York, 1969).

C. B. Colby, *Soil Savers* (Coward-McCann, New York, 1957).

C. J. Hylander, *The World of Plant Life* (The Macmillan Company, New York, 1956).

Music, Grade 3

B. Landeck *et al., Making Music Your Own 3* (Silver Burdett Company, Morristown, 1968).

R. C. Berg *et al., Music For Young Americans, Exploring Music 3* (American Book Company, Cincinnati, 1966).

J. L. Mursell *et al., Music Now and Long Ago, Book 3* (Silver Burdett Company, Morristown, 1956).

L. B. Pitts *et al., Singing and Rhyming* (Ginn and Company, Boston, 1959).

W. R. Sur *et al., This is Music, Book 3* (Allyn and Bacon, Boston, 1967).

Music, Grade 4

E. Boardman and B. Landis, *Exploring Music, Book 4* (Holt, Rinehart and Winston, New York, 1966).

B. Landeck *et al., Making Music Your Own, Book 4* (Silver Burdett Company, Morristown, 1968).

W. Sur *et al., This is Music, Book 4* (Allyn and Bacon, Boston, 1967).

Music, Grade 5

E. Boardman and B. Landis, *Exploring Music, Book 5* (Holt, Rinehart and Winston, New York, 1966).

H. C. Youngberg *et al., Making Music Your Own* (Silver Burdett Company, Morristown, 1965).

W. Sur *et al., This is Music, Book 5* (Allyn and Bacon, Boston, 1967).

Music, Grade 6

E. Boardman and B. Landis, *Exploring Music, Book 6* (Holt, Rinehart and Winston, New York, 1966).

H. C. Youngberg, *Making Music Your Own 6* (Silver Burdett Company, Morristown, 1968).

W. Sur *et al., This is Music, Book 6* (Allyn and Bacon, Boston, 1967).

Music, Grade 7

C. Leonhard *et al., Discovering Music Together, Book 7* (Follett Publishing Company, Chicago, 1966).

H. R. Wilson *et al., Growing With Music, Book 7* (Prentice-Hall, Englewood Cliffs, 1966).

L. Eisman *et al., Making Music Your Own, Book 7* (Silver Burdett Company, Morristown, 1968).

R. C. Berg, *Music For Young Americans, Book 7* (American Book Company, New York, 1963).

I. Cooper *et al., Music In Our Life* (Silver Burdett Company, Morristown, 1967).

W. Sur *et al., This is Music, Book 7* (Allyn and Bacon, Boston, 1968).

Music, Grade 8

C. Leonhard *et al., Discovering Music Together, Book 8* (Follett Publishing Company, Chicago, 1966).

H. R. Wilson *et al., Growing With Music 8* (Prentice-Hall, Englewood Cliffs, 1966).

L. Eisman *et al., Making Music Your Own, Book 8* (Silver Burdett Company, Morristown, 1968).

R. C. Berg *et al., Music for Young Americans, Book 8* (American Book Company, New York, 1963).

I. Cooper *et al., Music In Our Times* (Silver Burdett Company, Morristown, 1967).

W. Sur *et al., This Is Music, Book 8* (Allyn and Bacon, Boston, 1968).

Music, Grade 9

H. R. Wilson, *Choral Musicianship Series, Book 1* (Silver Burdett Company, Morristown, 1955).

H. R. Wilson, *Choral Musicianship Series, Book 2* (Silver Burdett Company, Morristown, 1957).

L. B. Pitts *et al., Music Makers* (Ginn and Company, Boston, 1967).

E. Serposs and I. Singleton, *Music in Our Heritage* (Silver Burdett Company, Morristown, 1962).

Music, Ungraded

M. Wold and E. Cykler, *Music and Art in the Western World* (William C. Brown Company, Dubuque, 1967).

Art, Grade 3

B. Jefferson, *My World of Art, Book 3* (Allyn and Bacon, Boston, 1963).

K. Fearing *et al., Our Expanding Vision—Art . . . A Way to See 3* (W. S. Benson and Company, Austin, 1960).

F. Kysar *et al., Young Artists, Book 3* (Charles E. Merrill Publishing Company, Columbus, 1959).

Art, Grade 4

B. Jefferson and B. McGeary, *My World of Art, Book 4* (Allyn and Bacon, Boston, 1964).

K. Fearing *et al., Our Expanding Vision—Art . . . Discovering Your Way 4* (W. S. Benson and Company, Austin, 1960).

F. Kysar *et al., Young Artists, Book 4* (Charles E. Merrill Publishing Company, Columbus, 1959).

Art, Grade 5

C. E. Stafford and I. E. Johnson, *Art for You, Book 5* (Laidlaw Brothers, River Forest, 1960).

B. Jefferson and B. Fredette, *My World of Art, Book 5* (Allyn and Bacon, Boston, 1964).

Art, Grade 6

B. Jefferson and C. McGeary, *My World of Art, Book 6* (Allyn and Bacon, Boston, 1964).

F. Kysar *et al., Young Artists, Book 6* (Charles E. Merrill Publishing Company, Columbus, 1959).

Art, Grade 7

K. Fearing *et al., The Creative Eye, Vol. 1* (W. S. Benson and Company, Austin, 1969).

K. Fearing *et al., Our Expanding Vision—Art . . . You and the World 7* (W. S. Benson and Company, Austin, 1960).

F. Kysar *et al., Young Artists, Book 7* (Charles E. Merrill Publishing Company, Columbus, 1959).

Art, Grade 8

C. Heyne *et al., Art for Young America* (Chas. A. Bennett Company, Peoria, 1967).

J. M. Morman, *Art: Of Wonder & a World* (Art Education, New York, 1967).

Art, Grade 9

O. L. Riley, *Your Art Heritage* (McGraw-Hill Book Company, New York, 1952).

Home Economics, Grade 7

H. Fleck *et al., Exploring Home and Family Living* (Prentice-Hall, New York, 1965).

E. G. Jones and H. A. Burnham, *Junior Homemaking* (J. B. Lippincott Company, Philadelphia, 1958).

Simplicity Sewing Book (Simplicity Pattern Company, New York, 1969).

M. A. Duffie, *So—You Are Ready To Cook* (Burgess Publishing Company, Minneapolis, 1964).

F. M. Reiff, *Steps in Home Living* (Chas. A. Bennett Company, Peoria, 1966).

D. S. Lewis *et al., Tomorrow's Homemaker* (The Macmillan Company, New York, 1960).

N. Clayton, *Young Living* (Chas. A. Bennett Company, Peoria, 1970).

F. L. Harris and R. T. Withers, *Your Foods Book* (D. C. Heath and Company, Lexington, 1966).

Home Economics, Grade 8

E. Todd and F. Roberts, *Clothes for Teens* (D. C. Heath and Company, Lexington, 1969).

L. B. Pollard *et al., Experiences in Homemaking* (Ginn and Company, Boston, 1968).

H. M. Hatcher and M. E. Andrews, *Guide for Today's Home Living* (D. C. Heath and Company, Lexington, 1966).

M. S. Barclay and F. Champion, *Teen Guide To Homemaking* (Webster Division, McGraw-Hill Book Company, New York, 1961).

Home Economics, Grade 9

L. B. Pollard, *Experiences with Clothing* (Ginn and Company, Boston, 1968).

L. B. Pollard, *Experiences with Foods* (Ginn and Company, Boston, 1968).

M. Sturm *et al., Guide to Modern Clothing* (McGraw-Hill Book Company, New York, 1968).

B. Carson and M. C. Ramee, *How You Plan and Prepare Meals* (McGraw-Hill Book Company, New York, 1968).

K. McDermott and F. Nicholas, *Homemaking for Teenagers* (Chas. A. Bennett Company, Peoria, 1966).

C. Greer and E. Gibbs, *Your Home and You* (Allyn and Bacon, Boston, 1965).

Shop, Grade 7

S. L. Coover, *Drawing and Blueprint Reading* (McGraw-Hill Book Company, New York, 1966).

L. B. Smith and M. E. Maddox, *Elements of American Industry* (McKnight and McKnight Publishing Company, New York, 1966).

H. T. Glenn, *Exploring Power Mechanics* (Chas. A. Bennett Company, Peoria, 1967).

E. H. Curry *et al., General Industrial Arts* (D. Van Nostrand Company, New York, 1967).

C. H. Groneman and J. L. Feirer, *General Shop* (McGraw-Hill Book Company, New York, 1963).

V. C. Frylung and A. J. La Berge, *General Shop Woodworking* (McKnight and McKnight Publishing Company, New York, 1965).

C. H. Groneman, *General Woodworking* (McGraw-Hill Book Company, New York, 1964).

Shop, Grade 8

H. H. Gerrish, *Electricity* (The Goodheart-Willcox Company, Homewood, 1968).

J. L. Feirer, *I. A. Bench Woodwork* (Chas. A. Bennett Company, Peoria, 1965).

T. G. Boyd, *Metalworking* (The Goodheart-Willcox Company, Homewood, 1968).

P. Buban and M. Schmitt, *Understanding Electricity and Electronics* (McGraw-Hill Book Company, New York, 1969).

Shop, Grade 9

H. C. Spencer and J. T. Dygdon, *Basic Technical Drawing* (The Macmillan Company, New York, 1968).

J. L. Feirer, *Drawing and Planning for Industrial Arts* (Chas. A. Bennett Company, Peoria, 1963).

J. L. Feirer, *General Metals* (McGraw-Hill Book Company, New York, 1967).

J. L. Feirer, *Industrial Arts Woodworking* (Chas. A. Bennett Company, Peoria, 1965).

T. E. French and C. L. Svensen, *Mechanical Drawing* (Webster Division, McGraw-Hill Book Company, New York, 1966).

O. A. Ludwig and W. J. McCarthy, *Metalwork, Technology and Practice* (McKnight and McKnight Publishing Company, New York, 1969).

C. W. Hague, *Printing and Allied Graphic Arts* (The Bruce Publishing Company, New York, 1957).

Library Fiction, Grade 3

R. P. Holden, *All About Famous Scientific Expeditions* (Random House, New York, 1955). *Note:* This text should have been sampled in Library Nonfiction, Grade 3, rather than Library Fiction, Grade 3; clerical error.

W. Du Bois, *The Alligator Case* (Harper & Row, Publishers, New York, 1965).

C. Haywood, *Back to School with Betsy* (Harcourt, Brace & World, New York, 1943).

C. Haywood, *Betsy and the Circus* (William Morrow and Company, New York, 1954).

L. Ward, *The Biggest Bear* (Houghton Mifflin Company, Boston, 1952).

C. Haywood, *B is for Betsy* (Harcourt, Brace & World, New York, 1967).

G. C. Warner, *The Boxcar Children* (Albert Whitman and Company, Chicago, 1950).

E. G. Speare, *The Bronze Bow* (Houghton Mifflin Company, Boston, 1961).

E. S. McCall, *The Buttons and Mr. Pete* (Benefic Press, Westchester, 1961).

E. S. McCall, *The Buttons and the Little League* (Benefic Press, Westchester, 1961).

E. S. McCall, *The Buttons at the Farm* (Benefic Press, Westchester, 1961).

E. S. McCall, *The Buttons at the Soap Box Derby* (Benefic Press, Westchester, 1961).

E. W. Chandler, *Cowboy Sam and Sally* (Benefic Press, Westchester, 1964).

E. W. Chandler, *Cowboy Sam and the Airplane* (Benefic Press, Westchester, 1964).

E. W. Chandler, *Cowboy Sam and the Fair* (Benefic Press, Westchester, 1961).

E. W. Chandler, *Cowboy Sam and the Indians* (Benefic Press, Westchester, 1962).

E. W. Chandler, *Cowboy Sam and the Rodeo* (Benefic Press, Westchester, 1959).

E. W. Chandler, *Cowboy Sam and the Rustlers* (Benefic Press, Westchester, 1959).

H. A. Rey, *Curious George* (Houghton Mifflin Company, Boston, 1941).

C. Haywood, *Eddie and his Big Deals* (William Morrow and Company, New York, 1955).

C. Haywood, *Eddie's Green Thumb* (William Morrow and Company, New York, 1964).

B. Cleary, *Ellen Tebbits* (William Morrow and Company, New York, 1951).

N. S. Carlson, *The Empty Schoolhouse* (Harper & Row, Publishers, New York, 1965).

C. Bishop and K. Wiese, *The Five Chinese Brothers* (Coward-McCann, New York, 1938).

Dr. Seuss, *The 500 Hats of Bartholomew Cubbins* (The Vanguard Press, New York, 1938).

L. Lenski, *Judy's Journey* (J. B. Lippincott Company, Philadelphia, 1947).

L. Bemelmans, *Madeline's Rescue* (The Viking Press, New York, 1953).

B. Cleary, *Otis Spofford* (William Morrow and Company, New York, 1953).

A. Lindgren, *Pippi Longstocking* (The Viking Press, New York, 1950).

B. Cleary, *Ramona the Pest* (William Morrow and Company, New York, 1968).

R. Lawson, *Rabbit Hill* (The Viking Press, New York, 1944).

E. Enright, *Thimble Summer* (Holt, Rinehart and Winston, New York, 1966).

N. Agle and E. Wilson, *Three Boys and a Lighthouse* (Charles Scribner's Sons, New York, 1951).

Library Fiction, Grade 4

R. Lawson, *Ben and Me* (Little, Brown and Company, Boston, 1939).

E. B. White, *Charlotte's Web* (Dell Publishing Company, New York, 1952).

J. Williams and R. Abrashkin, *Danny Dunn and the Voice From Space* (McGraw-Hill Book Company, New York, 1967).

M. S. Stolz, *A Dog on Barkham Street* (Harper & Row, Publishers, New York, 1960).

W. Morey, *Gentle Ben* (E. P. Dutton and Company, New York, 1965).

B. Cleary, *Henry Huggins* (William Morrow and Company, New York, 1950).

R. Kipling, *Just So Stories* (Doubleday & Company, New York, 1912).

C. Haywood, *Little Eddie* (William Morrow and Company, New York, 1947).

W. D. Edmonds, *The Matchlock Gun* (Dodd, Mead and Company, New York, 1941).

R. Atwater and F. Atwater, *Mr. Popper's Penguins* (Little, Brown and Company, Boston, 1938).

W. James, *Smoky, the Cowhorse* (Charles Scribner's Sons, New York, 1929).

H. Lofting, *The Story of Doctor Dolittle* (J. B. Lippincott Company, Philadelphia, 1948).

E. H. Sechrist, *13 Ghostly Yarns* (Macrae Smith Company, Philadelphia, 1963).

N. S. Carlson, *The Talking Cat and other Stories of French Canada* (Harper & Row, Publishers, New York, 1952).

N. S. Carlson, *The Tomahawk Family* (Harper and Brothers, New York, 1960).

H. Lofting, *The Voyages of Doctor Dolittle* (J. B. Lippincott Company, Philadelphia, 1950).

Library Fiction, Grade 5

L. Carroll, *Alice's Adventures in Wonderland & Through The Looking Glass* (The Macmillan Company, New York, 1963).

E. Yates, *Amos Fortune, Free Man* (E. P. Dutton and Company, New York, 1950).

A. Lang, *Arabian Nights* (Childrens Press, Chicago, 1968).

M. Norton, *The Borrowers* (Harcourt, Brace & World, New York, 1953).

M. Stolz, *The Bully of Barkham Street* (Harper & Row, Publishers, New York, 1963).

R. McCloskey, *Homer Price* (The Viking Press, New York, 1943).

L. I. Wilder, *The Little House in the Big Woods* (Harper & Row, Publishers, New York, 1953).

L. I. Wilder, *Little House on the Prairie* (Harper & Row, Publishers, New York, 1935).

P. L. Travers, *Mary Poppins* (Harcourt, Brace & World, New York, 1962).

M. Henry, *Misty of Chincoteague* (Rand McNally & Company, Chicago, 1947).

L. Lenski, *Strawberry Girl* (J. B. Lippincott Company, Philadelphia, 1945).

M. DeJong, *The Wheel on the School* (Harper & Row, Publishers, New York, 1954).

Library Fiction, Grade 6

C. Collodi, *Adventures of Pinocchio* (Grosset & Dunlap, New York, 1946).

C. R. Brink, *Caddie Woodlawn* (The Macmillan Company, New York, 1935).

A. Sperry, *Call It Courage* (The Macmillan Company, New York, 1940).

A. C. de Angeli, *The Door in the Wall* (Doubleday & Company, New York, 1968).

S. O'Dell, *Island of the Blue Dolphins* (Houghton Mifflin Company, Boston, 1960).

M. Henry, *King of the Wind* (Rand McNally & Company, Chicago, 1948).

D. Defoe, *Robinson Crusoe* (The Macmillan Company, New York, 1962).

R. Sawyer, *Roller Skates* (The Viking Press, New York, 1936).

Library Fiction, Grade 7

M. Twain, *The Adventures of Huckleberry Finn* (Franklin Watts, New York, 1955).

M. Twain, *The Adventures of Tom Sawyer* (Grosset & Dunlap, New York, 1946).

J. Verne, *Around the World in 80 Days* (J. M. Dent and Sons, Ltd., London, 1968).

J. Kjelgaard, *Big Red* (Scholastic Book Services, New York, 1957).

A. Sewell, *Black Beauty* (Random House, New York, 1949).

W. Farley, *The Black Stallion* (Random House, New York, 1941).

B. Cleary, *Fifteen* (William Morrow and Company, New York, 1956).

H. Felsen, *Hot Rod* (E. P. Dutton and Company, New York, 1950).

S. Burnford, *The Incredible Journey* (Little, Brown and Company, Boston, 1961).

J. F. Cooper, *The Last of the Mohicans* (The World Publishing Company, Cleveland, 1957).

L. M. Alcott, *Little Women* (The Macmillan Company, New York, 1962).

E. Bagnold, *National Velvet* (William Morrow and Company, New York, 1949).

F. Gipson, *Old Yeller* (Harper & Row, Publishers, New York, 1956).

M. Twain, *The Prince and the Pauper* (The World Publishing Company, Cleveland, 1948).

R. L. Stevenson, *Treasure Island* (Dodd, Mead and Company, New York, 1956).

J. Verne, *20,000 Leagues Under the Sea* (Grosset & Dunlap, New York).

J. F. Carson, *The 23rd Street Crusaders* (Farrar, Straus and Giroux, New York, 1958).

J. London, *White Fang* (Lancer Books, New York, 1968).

M. K. Rawlings, *The Yearling* (Charles Scribner's Sons, New York, 1967).

Library Fiction, Grade 8

I. Hunt, *Across Five Aprils* (Follett Publishing Company, Chicago, 1964).

J. London, *The Call of the Wild* (Childrens Press, Chicago, 1968).

E. Forbes, *Johnny Tremain* (Houghton Mifflin Company, Boston, 1943).

K. Forbes, *Mama's Bank Account* (Harcourt, Brace & World, New York, 1943).

J. Steinbeck, *The Red Pony* (The Viking Press, New York, 1938).

Library Fiction, Grade 9

G. Orwell, *Animal Farm* (Harcourt, Brace & World, New York, 1954).

F. Bonham, *Durango Street* (E. P. Dutton and Company, New York, 1965).

E. Hemingway, *The Old Man and the Sea* (Charles Scribner's Sons, New York, 1952).

M. M. Craig, *Now That I'm Sixteen* (Thomas Y. Crowell Company, New York, 1959).

M. Wojciechowska, *Tuned Out* (Harper & Row, Publishers, New York, 1968).

Library Fiction, Ungraded

A. Dalgliesh, *Adam and the Golden Cock* (Charles Scribner's Sons, New York, 1959).

R. Dahl, *Charlie and the Chocolate Factory* (Alfred A. Knopf, New York, 1964).

B. R. Brinley, *The Mad Scientists' Club* (Macrae Smith Company, Philadelphia, 1965).

Library Nonfiction, Grade 3

C. Coombs, *Aerospace Pilot* (William Morrow and Company, New York, 1964).

M. Henry, *All About Horses* (Random House, New York, 1962).

A. Dalgliesh, *America Travels* (The Macmillan Company, New York, 1961).

P. Lathrop, *Animals of the Bible* (J. B. Lippincott Company, Philadelphia, 1937).

C. Birch, *Chinese Myths and Fantasies* (Henry Z. Walck, New York, 1961).

G. W. Johnson, *The Congress* (William Morrow and Company, New York, 1963).

A. Ford, *Davy Crockett* (G. P. Putnam's Sons, New York, 1961).

L. Pringle, *Dinosaurs and their World* (Harcourt, Brace & World, New York, 1968).

D. McCord, *Every Time I Climb a Tree* (Little, Brown and Company, Boston, 1967).

H. S. Commager, *The First Book of American History* (Franklin Watts, New York, 1957).

M. Williamson, *The First Book of Birds* (Franklin Watts, New York, 1951).

A. Ransome, *The Fool of the World and the Flying Ship* (Farrar, Straus and Giroux, New York, 1968).

R. Robinson, *Greatest World Series Thrillers* (Random House, New York, 1965).

I. Shapiro, *Heroes in American Folklore* (Julian Messner, New York, 1962).

D. Wood, *Hills and Harbors—The Middle Atlantic States* (Childrens Press, Chicago, 1962).

C. Fenton and D. Pallas, *Insects and Their World* (John Day Company, New York, 1956).

R. C. Andrews, *In the Days of the Dinosaurs* (Random House, New York, 1959).

V. Bartlett and J. Caldwell, *Let's Visit Italy* (John Day Company, New York, 1968).

S. H. Adams, *The Pony Express* (Random House, New York, 1950).

A. McGovern, *Runaway Slave—The Story of Harriet Tubman* (The Four Winds Press, New York, 1968).

M. Gardner, *Science Puzzlers* (Scholastic Book Services, New York, 1960).

D. Wood, *Sea and Sunshine—The South Atlantic States* (Childrens Press, Chicago, 1962).

E. Lindemann, *Some Animals are Very Small* (Crowell-Collier Press, New York, 1968).

K. Carter, *Ships and Seaports* (Childrens Press, Chicago, 1963).

A. Goldin, *Straight Hair, Curly Hair* (Thomas Y. Crowell, New York, 1966).

M. H. Arbuthnot, *Time for Poetry* (Scott, Foresman and Company, Glenview, 1959).

J. W. Purcell, *The True Book of African Animals* (Childrens Press, Chicago, 1954).

M. Friskey, *The True Book of Air Around Us* (Childrens Press, Chicago, 1953).

J. Lewellen, *The True Book of Airports and Airplanes* (Childrens Press, Chicago, 1956).

I. Podendorf, *The True Book of Animal Babies* (Childrens Press, Chicago, 1955).

P. Erickson, *The True Book of Animals of Small Pond* (Childrens Press, Chicago, 1953).

N. Carlisle and M. Carlisle, *The True Book of Automobiles* (Childrens Press, Chicago, 1965).

N. Carlisle and M. Carlisle, *The True Book of Bridges* (Childrens Press, Chicago, 1965).

P. B. Carona, *The True Book of Chemistry* (Childrens Press, Chicago, 1962).

M. Harmer, *The True Book of the Circus* (Childrens Press, Chicago, 1955).

R. Gates, *The True Book of Conservation* (Childrens Press, Chicago, 1959).

E. Posell, *The True Book of Deserts* (Childrens Press, Chicago, 1958).

M. L. Clark, *The True Book of Dinosaurs* (Childrens Press, Chicago, 1955).

I. Podendorf, *The True Book of Energy* (Childrens Press, Chicago, 1963).

J. Lewellen, *The True Book of Farm Animals* (Childrens Press, Chicago, 1954).

P. Witty, *The True Book of Freedom and our U.S. Family* (Childrens Press, Chicago, 1956).

O. V. Haynes, *The True Book of Health* (Childrens Press, Chicago, 1954).

J. W. Purcell, *The True Book of Holidays and Special Days* (Childrens Press, Chicago, 1955).

J. Lewellen, *The True Book of Honeybees* (Childrens Press, Chicago, 1953).

I. Podendorf, *The True Book of Insects* (Childrens Press, Chicago, 1954).

I. Podendorf, *The True Book of Jungles* (Childrens Press, Chicago, 1959).

J. Lewellen, *The True Book of Knights* (Childrens Press, Chicago, 1956).

I. Podendorf, *The True Book of Magnets & Electricity* (Childrens Press, Chicago, 1961).

B. Elkin, *The True Book of Money* (Childrens Press, Chicago, 1960).

J. Lewellen, *The True Book of Moon, Sun & Stars* (Childrens Press, Chicago, 1954).

K. Carter, *The True Book of Oceans* (Childrens Press, Chicago, 1958).

I. Podendorf, *The True Book of Pets* (Childrens Press, Chicago, 1954).

I. Podendorf, *The True Book of Plant Experiments* (Childrens Press, Chicago, 1960).

I. Podendorf, *The True Book of Seasons* (Childrens Press, Chicago, 1955).

I. Podendorf, *The True Book of Space* (Childrens Press, Chicago, 1965).

I. Podendorf, *The True Book of Spiders* (Childrens Press, Chicago, 1962).

J. Leavitt, *The True Book of Tools for Building* (Childrens Press, Chicago, 1955).

E. Posell, *The True Book of Transportation* (Childrens Press, Chicago, 1957).

I. Podendorf, *The True Book of Trees* (Childrens Press, Chicago, 1954).

I. Podendorf, *The True Book of Weather Experiments* (Childrens Press, Chicago, 1961).

E. Posell, *The True Book of Whales* (Childrens Press, Chicago, 1963).

M. Elting, *We are the Government* (Doubleday & Company, New York, 1967).

Library Nonfiction, Grade 4

M. E. Ward, *Adlai Stevenson, Young Ambassador* (The Bobbs-Merrill Company, Indianapolis, 1967).

M. Henry, *Album of Horses* (Rand McNally & Company, Chicago, 1951).

E. Wilson, *Annie Oakley, Little Sure Shot* (The Bobbs-Merrill Company, Indianapolis, 1962).

G. Van Riper, Jr., *Babe Ruth, Baseball Boy* (The Bobbs-Merrill Company, Indianapolis, 1959).

A. Weil, *Betsy Ross, Girl of Old Philadelphia* (The Bobbs-Merrill Company, Indianapolis, 1961).

B. Crocker, *Betty Crocker's New Boys and Girls Cookbook* (Golden Press, New York, 1965).

I. Parin d'Aulaire and E. Parin d'Aulaire, *Buffalo Bill* (Doubleday & Company, New York, 1952).

L. Dobler, *Cyrus McCormick, Farm Boy* (The Bobbs-Merrill Company, Indianapolis, 1961).

B. Smith, *Dan Webster, Union Boy* (The Bobbs-Merrill Company, Indianapolis, 1962).

H. S. Zim, *Dinosaurs* (William Morrow and Company, New York, 1954).

E. P. Myers, *Edward Bok, Young Editor* (The Bobbs-Merrill Company, Indianapolis, 1967).

J. L. Henry, *Elizabeth Blackwell, Girl Doctor* (The Bobbs-Merrill Company, Indianapolis, 1961).

A. Stevenson, *George Custer, Boy of Action* (The Bobbs-Merrill Company, Indianapolis, 1963).

E. P. Myers, *George Pullman, Young Sleeping Car Builder* (The Bobbs-Merrill Company, Indianapolis, 1963).

K. E. Wilkie, *George Rogers Clark, Boy of the Old Northwest* (The Bobbs-Merrill Company, Indianapolis, 1960).

A. Stevenson, *Israel Putnam, Fearless Boy* (The Bobbs-Merrill Company, Indianapolis, 1959).

M. B. Mitchell, *James Whitcomb Riley, Hoosier Boy* (The Bobbs-Merrill Company, Indianapolis, 1962).

O. W. Burt, *Jed Smith, Young Western Explorer* (The Bobbs-Merrill Company, Indianapolis, 1963).

G. Van Riper, Jr., *Jim Thorpe, Indian Athlete* (The Bobbs-Merrill Company, Indianapolis, 1961).

D. J. Snow, *John Paul Jones, Salt-Water Boy* (The Bobbs-Merrill Company, Indianapolis, 1962).

A. Weil, *John Philip Sousa, Marching Boy* (The Bobbs-Merrill Company, Indianapolis, 1959).

T. F. Barton, *John Smith, Jamestown Boy* (The Bobbs-Merrill Company, Indianapolis, 1966).

O. W. Burt, *John Wanamaker, Boy Merchant* (The Bobbs-Merrill Company, Indianapolis, 1962).

M. E. Schaaf, *Lew Wallace, Boy Writer* (The Bobbs-Merrill Company, Indianapolis, 1961).

C. B. Burnett, *Lucretia Mott, Girl of Old Nantucket* (The Bobbs-Merrill Company, Indianapolis, 1963).

G. H. Melin, *Maria Mitchell, Girl Astronomer* (The Bobbs-Merrill Company, Indianapolis, 1960).

J. B. Wagoner, *Martha Washington, Girl of Old Virginia* (The Bobbs-Merrill Company, Indianapolis, 1959).

K. E. Wilkie, *Mary Todd Lincoln, Girl of the Bluegrass* (The Bobbs-Merrill Company, Indianapolis, 1960).

A. Stevenson, *Nancy Hanks, Kentucky Girl* (The Bobbs-Merrill Company, Indianapolis, 1962).

F. W. Seymour, *Pocahontas, Brave Girl* (The Bobbs-Merrill Company, Indianapolis, 1961).

H. Peckham *Pontiac, Young Ottawa Leader* (The Bobbs-Merrill Company, Indianapolis, 1963).

A. Stevenson, *P. T. Barnum, Circus Boy* (The Bobbs-Merrill Company, Indianapolis, 1964).

O. W. Burt, *The Ringling Brothers, Circus Boys* (The Bobbs-Merrill Company, Indianapolis, 1962).

R. B. Jackson, *Road Race Round the World—New York to Paris, 1908* (Henry Z. Walck, New York, 1965).

J. L. Latham, *Sam Houston, Hero of Texas* (Garrard Publishing Company, Champaign, 1965).

D. J. Snow, *Samuel Morse, Inquisitive Boy* (The Bobbs-Merrill Company, Indianapolis, 1960).

I. Asimov, *Satellites in Outer Space* (Random House, New York, 1960).

K. E. Wilkie, *Simon Kenton, Young Trail Blazer* (The Bobbs-Merrill Company, Indianapolis, 1960).

H. B. Higgins, *Stephen Foster, Boy Minstrel* (The Bobbs-Merrill Company, Indianapolis, 1963).

L. A. Hickok, *The Story of Helen Keller* (Grosset & Dunlap, New York, 1958).

E. W. Parks, *Teddy Roosevelt, All-Round Boy* (The Bobbs-Merrill Company, Indianapolis, 1961).

R. Lawson, *They Were Strong and Good* (The Viking Press, New York, 1940).

A. Stevenson, *Virginia Dare, Mystery Girl* (The Bobbs-Merrill Company, Indianapolis, 1959).

H. B. Higgins, *Walter Reed, Boy Who Wanted to Know* (The Bobbs-Merrill Company, Indianapolis, 1961).

B. Smith, *William Bradford, Pilgrim Boy* (The Bobbs-Merrill Company, Indianapolis, 1963).

M. E. Mason, *William Penn, Friendly Boy* (The Bobbs-Merrill Company, Indianapolis, 1962).

G. Van Riper, Jr., *Will Rogers, Young Cowboy* (The Bobbs-Merrill Company, Indianapolis, 1962).

H. A. Monsell, *Woodrow Wilson, Boy President* (The Bobbs-Merrill Company, Indianapolis, 1959).

E. P. Myers, *F. W. Woolworth, Five and Ten Boy* (The Bobbs-Merrill Company, Indianapolis, 1962).

Library Nonfiction, Grade 5

R. C. Andrews, *All About Dinosaurs* (Random House, New York, 1953).

C. MacInnes *et al., Australia and New Zealand* (Time, Inc., New York, 1966).

L. Fessler, *China* (Time, Inc., New York, 1963).

G. MacEoin, *Colombia and Venezuela and the Guianas* (Time, Inc., New York, 1965).

J. Daugherty, *Daniel Boone* (The Viking Press, New York, 1939).

C. B. Colby, *Fighting Gear of World War II* (Coward-McCann, New York, 1961).

L. Untermeyer, *The Golden Treasure of Poetry* (Golden Press, New York, 1959).

J. McCarthy *et al., Ireland* (Time, Inc., New York, 1964).

R. St. John, *Israel* (Time, Inc., New York, 1968).

H. Kubly, *Italy* (Time, Inc., New York, 1968).

E. Rachlis *et al., The Low Countries* (Time, Inc., New York, 1968).

H. Innes *et al., Scandinavia* (Time, Inc., New York, 1963).

T. Hopkinson *et al., South Africa* (Time, Inc., New York, 1969).

H. Thomas *et al., Spain* (Time, Inc., New York, 1966).

H. Kubly *et al., Switzerland* (Time, Inc., New York, 1964).

R. Coughlan *et al., Tropical Africa* (Time, Inc., New York, 1966).

D. Stewart *et al., Turkey* (Time, Inc., New York, 1969).

P. O'Donovan *et al., The United States* (Time, Inc., New York, 1968).

Library Nonfiction, Grade 6

T. Bulfinch, *The Age of Fable* (New American Library, New York, 1962).

A. T. White, *All About Rocks and Minerals* (Random House, New York, 1955).

D. Dietz, *All About Satellites and Space Ships* (Random House, New York, 1958).

J. L. Latham, *Carry on, Mr. Bowditch* (Houghton Mifflin Company, Boston, 1955).

F. G. Menke, *The Encyclopedia of Sports* (A. S. Barnes and Company, Cranbury, 1969).

M. Bauer and E. Peyser, *How Music Grew* (G. P. Putnam's Sons, New York, 1939).

C. Meigs, *Invincible Louisa* (Little, Brown and Company, Boston, 1968).

M. Gardner, *Perplexing Puzzles and Tantalizing Teasers* (Simon and Schuster, New York, 1969).

F. N. Chrystie, *Pets* (Little, Brown and Company, Boston, 1964).

J. M. Rosenburg, *The Story of Baseball* (Random House, New York, 1968).

Library Nonfiction, Grade 7

J. Drachler, *African Heritage* (Crowell-Collier Publishing Company, New York, 1963).

C. L. Ripper, *Bats* (William Morrow and Company, New York, 1954).

J. Adamson, *Born Free* (Pantheon Books, New York, 1960).

J. L. Feirer, *Cabinetmaking and Millwork* (Chas. A. Bennett Company, Peoria, 1967).

F. Gilbreth, Jr., *et al.*, *Cheaper by the Dozen* (Thomas Y. Crowell Company, New York, 1963).

E. Tunis, *Colonial Living* (The World Publishing Company, Cleveland, 1957).

F. N. Magill, *Cyclopedia of Literary Characters* (Harper & Row, Publishers, New York, 1963).

T. A. Dooley, *Dr. Tom Dooley, My Story* (Ariel Books, New York, 1962).

E. L. Post, *The Emily Post Book of Etiquette for Young People* (Funk and Wagnalls Company, New York, 1967).

J. R. Lindbeck and I. Lathrop, *General Industry* (Chas. A. Bennett Company, Peoria, 1969).

K. Shippen and A. Seidlova, *The Heritage of Music* (The Viking Press, New York, 1963).

H. L. Masin, *How to Star in Basketball* (The Four Winds Press, New York, 1966).

R. Tregaskis, *John F. Kennedy and PT-109* (Random House, New York, 1962).

A. E. Chase, *Looking at Art* (Thomas Y. Crowell Company, New York, 1966).

W. Shirer, *The Rise and Fall of Adolf Hitler* (Random House, New York, 1961).

E. Yates, *Someday You'll Write* (E. P. Dutton and Company, New York, 1962).

V. Bailard and H. C. McKown, *So You Were Elected!* (McGraw-Hill Book Company, New York, 1966).

J. Dunaway *et al.*, *Sports Illustrated Book of Track and Field Running Events* (J. B. Lippincott Company, Philadelphia, 1968).

F. Kuhn, *The Story of the Secret Service* (Random House, New York, 1957).

J. Lester, *To Be A Slave* (The Dial Press, New York, 1968).

J. Auslander and F. E. Hill, *The Winged Horse Anthology* (Doubleday & Company, New York, 1929).

L. Hogben, *The Wonderful World of Mathematics* (Doubleday & Company, New York, 1968).

M. Y. Sachs *et al.*, *Worldmark Encyclopedia of the Nations* (Harper & Row, Publishers, New York, 1967), Vols. 2–5.

Library Nonfiction, Grade 8

A. Frank, *Anne Frank: The Diary of a Young Girl* (Pocket Books, New York, 1967).

B. W. Carlson, *The Junior Party Book* (Abingdon Press, Nashville, 1948).

T. Heyerdahl, *Kon-Tiki* (Pocket Books, New York, 1950).

H. Keller, *The Story of My Life* (Doubleday & Company, New York, 1954).

Library Nonfiction, Grade 9

J. H. Griffin, *Black Like Me* (Houghton Mifflin Company, Boston, 1961).

J. Gunther, *Death Be Not Proud* (Harper & Row, Publishers, New York, 1949).

J. Irwin and M. Rosenberger, *Modern Speech* (Holt, Rinehart and Winston, New York, 1966).

T. A. Dooley, *The Night They Burned the Mountain* (Farrar, Straus and Giroux, New York, 1960).

W. Lord, *A Night to Remember* (Holt, Rinehart and Winston, New York, 1955).

S. Jackson, *The Witchcraft of Salem Village* (Random House, New York, 1956).

Library Nonfiction, Ungraded

A. Jonas, *Archimedes and His Wonderful Discoveries* (Prentice-Hall, New York, 1963).

B. Grant, *The Boy Scout Encyclopedia* (Rand McNally & Company, Chicago, 1965).

E. Curie, *Madame Curie, RLS 24* (Houghton Mifflin Company, Boston, 1963).

D. C. Cooke, *Racing Cars That Made History* (G. P. Putnam's Sons, New York, 1960).

R. Graves *et al., New Larousse Encyclopedia of Mythology* (G. P. Putnam's Sons, New York, 1959).

Library General Reference, Grade 3

Childcraft (Field Enterprises Educational Corporation, Chicago, 1954), Vols. 3–5, 7, 9, 11, 13, 15.

D. A. Bennett and J. W. Watson, *The New Golden Encyclopedia* (Golden Press, New York, 1964).

M. Gartler *et al., Understanding Argentina* (Laidlaw Brothers, River Forest, 1964).

M. Gartler *et al., Understanding Denmark* (Laidlaw Brothers, River Forest, 1964).

M. Gartler *et al., Understanding France* (Laidlaw Brothers, River Forest, 1965).

M. Gartler *et al., Understanding Italy* (Laidlaw Brothers, River Forest, 1965).

M. Gartler *et al., Understanding the Philippines* (Laidlaw Brothers, River Forest, 1963).

Library General Reference, Grade 4

Britannica Junior Encyclopaedia (Encyclopaedia Britannica, Chicago, 1969), Vols. 2–15.

Hammond Medallion World Atlas (Hammond, Maplewood, 1966).

The New Book of Knowledge (Grolier, New York, 1967), Vols. 1, 3–10, 13, 14, 16, 18–20.

Library General Reference, Grade 5

Compton's Pictured Encyclopedia and Fact-Index (F. E. Compton Company, Chicago, 1968), Vols. 1, 3, 5, 9, 11, 13, 15, 17, 19, 21, 23, 24.

The World Book Encyclopedia (Field Enterprises Educational Corporation, Chicago, 1970), Vols. 1–20.

Library General Reference, Grade 6

H. J. Challand *et al., Young People's Science Encyclopedia* (Childrens Press, Chicago, 1964), Vols. 1–5, 7–15, 17–19.

Library General Reference, Grade 7

R. T. Peterson *et al., The Birds* (Time, Inc., New York, 1968).

F. C. Howell *et al., Early Man* (Time, Inc., New York, 1965).

A. Beiser *et al., The Earth* (Time, Inc., New York, 1963).

M. Wilson *et al., Energy* (Time, Inc., New York, 1963).

F. D. Ommanney *et al., The Fishes* (Time, Inc., New York, 1964).

P. Farb *et al., The Insects* (Time, Inc., New York, 1962).

A. Carr *et al., The Land and Wildlife of Africa* (Time, Inc., New York, 1964).

P. Farb *et al., The Land and Wildlife of North America* (Time, Inc., New York, 1966).

N. Bates *et al., The Land and Wildlife of South America* (Time, Inc., New York, 1964).

The Lincoln Library of Essential Information (Frontier Press, Memphis, 1959).

R. O'Brien *et al., Machines* (Time, Inc., New York, 1968).

R. Carrington *et al., The Mammals* (Time, Inc., New York, 1963).

B. S. Cayne, *Merit Students Encyclopedia* (Crowell-Collier Educational Corporation, New York, 1967), Vols. 2, 4, 6, 8, 10, 12, 14, 16, 18, 20.

L. J. Milne and M. Milne, *The Mountains* (Time, Inc., New York, 1969).

F. W. Wents, *The Plants* (Time, Inc., New York, 1963).

A. Carr *et al., The Reptiles* (Time, Inc., New York, 1963).

L. Engel *et al., The Sea* (Time, Inc., New York, 1969).

L. H. Long, *The World Almanac and Book of Facts — 1969 Edition* (Newspaper Enterprise Association, New York, 1968).

Library General Reference, Grade 8

W. D. Halsey *et al., Collier's Encyclopedia* (Crowell-Collier Publishing Company, New York, 1964), Vols. 1, 2, 4, 6, 8, 10, 12, 14, 16, 18, 20, 22, 23.

The Encyclopedia Americana (Americana Corporation, New York, 1964), Vols. 1–25, 27, 28.

Library General Reference, Grade 9

A. E. Nourse *et al., The Body* (Time, Inc., New York, 1964).

Encyclopaedia Britannica (Encyclopaedia Britannica, Chicago, 1962), Vols. 2–8, 10–12, 14, 16, 18, 20, 22, 23.

G. A. Cornish *et al., Encyclopedia International* (Grolier, New York, 1963), Vols. 1–3, 5–12, 14–18.

C. C. Furnas *et al., The Engineer* (Time, Inc., New York, 1966).

H. Margenau *et al., The Scientist* (Time, Inc., New York, 1964).

Library General Reference, Ungraded

E. C. Munro, *The Encyclopedia of Art* (Golden Press, New York, 1961).

McGraw-Hill Encyclopedia of Science and Technology (McGraw-Hill Book Company, New York, 1960), Vols. 4, 8, 12.

Magazines, Grade 3

Humpty Dumpty's Magazine for Little Children (Parents' Magazine Enterprises, New York: nine issues selected from January through November, 1969).

Jack and Jill (Perfect Film and Chemical Corporation, Philadelphia: eleven issues selected from January through November, 1969).

My Weekly Reader 3 (American Education Publications, Columbus: sixteen issues selected from April 9 through November 19, 1969).

Magazines, Grade 4

The Golden Magazine (Golden Press, New York: eleven issues selected from January through November, 1969).

Highlights for Children (Highlights for Children, Inc., Columbus: six issues selected from February through November, 1969).

My Weekly Reader 4 (American Education Publications, Columbus: nineteen issues selected from March 26 through November 19, 1969).

Magazines, Grade 5

American Girl (Girl Scouts of the U.S.A., New York: eleven issues selected from January through November, 1969).

Magazines, Grade 6

Boy's Life (Boy Scouts of America, New Brunswick: eleven issues selected from January through November, 1969).

Junior Scholastic (Scholastic Magazines, New York: sixteen issues selected from September 15, 1969, through February 2, 1970).

National Geographic (National Geographic Society, Washington, D. C.: eleven issues selected from January through November, 1969).

Magazines, Grade 7

American Heritage (American Heritage Publishing Co., New York: five issues selected from February through October, 1969).

Hot Rod (Petersen Publishing Company, Los Angeles: eight issues selected from January through September, 1969).

Life (Time, Inc., New York: seventeen issues selected from January 24 through November 7, 1969).

Natural History (The American Museum of Natural History, New York: nine issues selected from January through November, 1969).

Outdoor Life (Popular Science Publishing Co., New York: eleven issues selected from January through November, 1969).

Popular Mechanics (The Hearst Corporation, New York: eleven issues selected from January through November, 1969).

Popular Science (Popular Science Publishing Co., New York: ten issues selected from January through October, 1969).

Reader's Digest (The Reader's Digest Association, Pleasantville: eleven issues selected from January through November, 1969).

Seventeen (Triangle Publications, Philadelphia: eleven issues selected from January through November, 1969).

Sport (MacFadden-Bartell Corporation, New York: eleven issues selected from January through November, 1969).

Magazines, Grade 8

Newsweek (Newsweek, Inc., New York: thirty-five issues selected from February 3 through November 17, 1969).

Sports Illustrated (Time, Inc., New York: ten issues selected from September 15 through November 24, 1969).

Magazines, Grade 9

Look (Cowles Communications, New York: twenty-three issues selected from January 7 through November 18, 1969).

Time (Time, Inc., New York: twenty-four issues selected from January 17 through November 28, 1969).

U. S. News & World Report (U. S. News & World Report, Washington, D. C.: twenty-four issues selected from January 6 through November 24, 1969).

Magazines, Ungraded

American Home (Downe Publishing, New York: six issues selected from April through November, 1969).

The American West (The American West Publishing Company, Palo Alto: five issues selected from January through September, 1969).

Arizona Highways (The Arizona Highway Department, Phoenix: six issues selected from April through November, 1969).

Arts and Activities (Publishers' Development Corporation, Skokie: six issues selected from February, 1969, through June, 1970).

Audubon (National Audubon Society, New York: six issues selected from January through November, 1969).

Children's Digest (Parents' Magazine Enterprises, New York: six issues selected from April through November, 1969).

Farm Journal (Farm Journal, Inc., Philadelphia: six issues selected from April through November, 1969).

House & Garden (The Condé Nast Publications, New York: six issues selected from April through November, 1969).

Ideals (Ideals Publishing Co., Milwaukee: five issues selected from January through November, 1969).

McCall's (McCall Publishing Company, New York: six issues selected from April through November, 1969).

The New York Times Book Review (The New York Times, New York: six issues selected from April 27 through November 16, 1969).

Science Digest (The Hearst Corporation, New York: six issues selected from March through November, 1969).

Science & Mechanics (Davis Publications, New York: six issues selected from February through October, 1969).

Sports Afield (The Hearst Corporation, New York: six issues selected from March through November, 1969).

Travel (Travel Magazine, Floral Park: six issues selected from April through November, 1969).

Vogue (The Condé Nast Publications, New York: six issues selected from March 1 through June, 1969).

Young Miss (Parents' Magazine Enterprises, New York: six issues selected from March through November, 1969).

Religion, Grade 3

Sister M. Johnice, I.H.M., and Sister M. Elizabeth, I.H.M., *Children of the Kingdom* (Allyn and Bacon, Boston, 1966).

Sister M. Elizabeth, I.H.M., and Sister M. Johnice, I.H.M., *The Lord Jesus Says, Book 3* (Allyn and Bacon, Boston, 1965).

Religion, Grade 4

Sister M. V. Pfeiffer, O.S.U., and Sister M. G. Carroll, O.S.U., *Love the Lord, Grade 4* (W. H. Sadlier, New York, 1969).